W9-CJN-297

THE WORLD OF LEARNING

1980-81

THE WORLD OF LEARNING 1980-81

31st Edition

VOLUME ONE

1. INTERNATIONAL

2. AFGHANISTAN-QATAR

Martins Publishing Group Martins Publishing Group Martins Publishing Group Martins Publishing Group
Publishing Group Martins Publishing Group Martins Publishing Group Martins Publishing Group Martins
Martins Publishing Group Martins Publishing Group Martins Publishing Group Martins Publishing Group
Publishing Group Martins Publishing Group Martins Publishing Group Martins Publishing Group Martins

EUROPA PUBLICATIONS LIMITED

Martins Publishing Group Martins Publishing Group Martins Publishing Group Martins Publishing Group
Publishing Group Martins Publishing Group Martins Publishing Group Martins Publishing Group Martins
Martins Publishing Group Martins Publishing Group Martins Publishing Group Martins Publishing Group
Publishing Group Martins Publishing Group Martins Publishing Group Martins Publishing Group Martins
Martins Publishing Group Martins Publishing Group Martins Publishing Group Martins Publishing Group
Publishing Group Martins Publishing Group Martins Publishing Group Martins Publishing Group Martins

EUROPA PUBLICATIONS LIMITED 18 BEDFORD SQUARE LONDON WC1B 3JN

Library of Congress Catalog Card Number 47–30172

JAPAN
Maruzen Co. **Ltd., Tokyo**

INDIA
UBS Publishers' Distributors Pvt. Ltd., P.O.B. 1882, 5 Ansari Road, Daryaganj, Delhi 6

AUSTRALIA AND NEW ZEALAND
James Bennett (Collaroy) Pty. Ltd., Collaroy, N.S.W., Australia

British Library Cataloguing in Publication Data
The World of Learning 1980–81: thirty-first edition
1. Learned institutions and societies—Directories
060 AS2

ISBN 0–905118–52–9
ISSN 0084–2117

Printed and bound in England by
Staples Printers Rochester Limited
at The Stanhope Press.

FOREWORD

The 31st edition of The World of Learning contains new material throughout the book, notably in the chapters for Albania, China, Japan and Turkey. About 40 new universities are listed, including the new "open" universities in Costa Rica and Thailand.

In co-operation with IFLA we invite all institutions in the book to indicate by the sign † those of their periodical publications which are available for exchange. We ask readers who are interested in the exchange of publications to communicate directly with the institution concerned, and not with us.

We have once again tried to ensure that we include the latest possible information concerning entries in The World of Learning. Every year a folder containing the previous year's proof is sent to each entry; continuous research in the world press and educational journals, as well as contact with official sources all over the world, supplements this method of revision. We welcome information and suggestions from users of the book, concerning either existing entries or possible new material.

We are always grateful to those individuals and organizations who help us to bring our information up to date with their prompt replies. We particularly emphasize the necessity for revised entries to be returned to us without delay, since important material may otherwise be held over until a later edition. Only by maintaining a strict timetable can the regular production of such a large work as The World of Learning be assured.

November 1980

CONTENTS
VOLUME ONE

CONTENTS

An INDEX OF INSTITUTIONS appears at the end of Volume Two.

ABBREVIATIONS

A.A. .. Associate in Arts
A.A.S.A. .. Associate of Australian Society of Accountants
A.A.U.Q. .. Associate in Accountancy, University of Queensland
A.B. .. Bachelor of Arts
A.B.S.M. .. Associate of the Bendigo School of Mines
A.C.A. .. Associate of the Institute of Chartered Accountants
Acad. .. Academy; Academician
A.C.I.I. .. Associate of the Chartered Insurance Institute
A.C.I.S. .. Associate of the Chartered Institute of Secretaries
A.C.T. .. Australian Capital Territory
Admin. .. Administrative, Administration
Agr. de D. .. Agrégé de Droit
Agr. de M. .. Agrégé de Médecine
Agr. de Sc. .. Agrégé de Science
Agr. des L. .. Agrégé des Lettres
A.I.A. .. Associate of the Institute of Actuaries; American Institute of Architects
A.I.B. .. Associate of the Institute of Bankers
A.I.C.E. .. Associate of the Institution of Civil Engineers
A.I.C.E.A. .. Association of Industrial and Commercial Executive Accountants
A.I.Ch.E. .. American Institute of Chemical Engineers
A.I.C.T.A. .. Associate of the Imperial College of Tropical Agriculture
A.I.I.S. .. Associate of the Irish Institute of Secretaries
A.I.L. .. Associate of the Institute of Linguists
A.I.M. .. Associate of the Institution of Metallurgists
A.I.M.T.A. .. Associate of the Institute of Municipal Treasurers and Accountants
A.Inst.C.E. Associate of the Institution of Civil Engineers
A.K.C. .. Associate of King's College (London)
A.L.A. .. Associate of the Library Association
Ala. .. Alabama
A.L.S. .. Associate of the Linnaean Society
A.M. .. Master of Arts
A.M.A. .. Associate of the Museums Association
A.M.I.C.E. .. Associate Member of the Institution of Civil Engineers
A.M.I.E.E. .. Associate Member of the Institution of Electrical Engineers
A.M.I.E.R.E. Associate Member of the Institute of Electronic and Radio Engineers
A.M.I.Mech.E. Associate Member of the Institution of Mechanical Engineers
A.M.I.Struct.E. Associate Member of the Institution of Structural Engineers
A.M.T.P.I. Associate of Town Planning Institute
A.O. .. Order of Australia
A.P. .. Andhra Pradesh
Apdo. .. Apartado (Post Office Box)
A.R.A. .. Associate of the Royal Academy
A.R.A.M. .. Associate of the Royal Academy of Music
A.R.C.A. .. Associate of the Royal College of Art
A.R.C.M. .. Associate of the Royal College of Music
A.R.C.O. .. Associate of the Royal College of Organists
A.R.C.S. .. Associate of the Royal College of Science
A.R.E. .. Associate of the Royal Society of Painter Etchers
A.R.I.B.A. .. Associate of the Royal Institute of British Architects
A.R.I.C.S. .. Associate of the Royal Institution of Chartered Surveyors
Ariz. .. Arizona
Ark. .. Arkansas
A.R.P.S. .. Associate of the Royal Photographic Society
A.R.S.A. .. Associate of the Royal Scottish Academy; Associate of the Royal Society of Arts
A.R.W.S. .. Associate of the Royal Society of Painters in Water Colours
A.S.C.E. .. American Society of Civil Engineers
A.S.M.E. .. American Society of Mechanical Engineers
Asscn. .. Association
Assoc. .. Associate
Asst. .. Assistant
A.S.T.C. .. Associate of the Sydney Technical College
Atty. .. Attorney
A.T.I. .. Associate of the Textile Institute
Avv. .. Avvocato (Italian)

B.A. .. Bachelor of Arts
B.Agr. .. Bachelor of Agriculture
B.A.(Ed.) .. Bachelor of Arts in Education
B.A.O. .. Bachelor of Obstetrics
Bar.-at-Law Barrister-at-Law
B.Arch. .. Bachelor of Architecture
B.A.S. .. Bachelor in Agricultural Science
B.A.Sc. .. Bachelor of Applied Science
B.B.A. .. Bachelor of Business Administration
B.C.E. .. Bachelor of Civil Engineering
B.Ch.,B.Chir. Bachelor of Surgery
B.Chem.E. .. Bachelor of Chemical Engineering
B.C.L. .. Bachelor of Civil Law; Bachelor of Canon Law
B.Com(m). .. Bachelor of Commerce
B.C.S. (and B.Com.Sc.) Bachelor of Commercial Sciences
B.D. .. Bachelor of Divinity
B.D.S. .. Bachelor of Dental Surgery
B.E. .. Bachelor of Engineering; Bachelor of Education
B.Ec. .. Bachelor of Economics
B.Ed. .. Bachelor of Education
B.E.E. .. Bachelor of Electrical Engineering
B.Eng. .. Bachelor of Engineering
B.Eng.A. .. Bachelor of Agricultural Engineering
B.E.Sc. .. Bachelor of Engineering Science
B.F.A. .. Bachelor of Fine Arts
B.F(or). .. Bachelor of Forestry
B.I.D. .. Bachelor of Industrial Design
B.Lit(t). .. Bachelor of Letters
B.LL. .. Bachelor of Laws
B.L.S. .. Bachelor of Library Science
Blvd. .. Boulevard
B.M. .. Bachelor of Medicine
B.M.A. .. British Medical Association
B.M.E. .. Bachelor of Mining Engineering
B.Mus. .. Bachelor of Music
B.N. .. Bachelor of Nursing

B.Paed. (or Pd.) .. Bachelor of Pedagogy
B.P.E. .. Bachelor of Physical Education
B.Phar. .. Baccalauréat en Pharmacie
B.Pharm. .. Bachelor of Pharmacy
B.Phil. .. Bachelor of Philosophy
Br. .. .. Branch
Bro. .. Brother
B.S... .. Bachelor of Science; Bachelor of Surgery
B.S.A. .. Bachelor of Scientific Agriculture
B.Sc. .. Bachelor of Science
B.Sc.Agr. .. Bachelor of Science in Agriculture
B.Sc.C.E. .. Bachelor of Science in Civil Engineering
B.S.C. .. Bachelor of Science in Commerce
B.Sc.Com. .. Bachelor of Commercial Science
B.Sc.(Econ.) Bachelor of Science in Economics
B.Sc.(Eng.) Bachelor of Science in Engineering
B.Sc.F. .. Bachelor of Science in Forestry
B.S. in H.E. Bachelor of Science in Home Economics
B.Sc.(M.E.) Bachelor of Science in Mechanical Engineering
B.Sc.Met. .. Bachelor of Science in Metallurgy
B.Sc.Pharm. Bachelor of Science in Pharmacy
B.S.D. .. Bachelor of Didactic Science; Bachelor of Science in Dentistry
Bt. .. .. Baronet
B.Theol. .. Bachelor of Theology

c. .. .. circa (approximately)
C.A. .. Chartered Accountant
CAE .. College of Advanced Education
Calif. .. California
Cantab. .. Of Cambridge University
C.B. .. Companion of the Order of the Bath
C.B.E. .. Commander of the Order of the British Empire
C.C... .. Companion of the Order of Canada
C.Chem. .. Chartered Chemist
C.E. .. Civil Engineer
CEA .. Commissariat à l'Energie Atomique
C.Eng. .. Chartered Engineer
C.G.A. .. Certified General Accountant
C.G.I.A. .. City and Guilds Insignia Award
C.H. .. Companion of Honour
Chair. .. Chairman
Ch.B. .. Bachelor of Surgery
Ch.M. .. Master of Surgery
C.I.E. .. Companion of the Order of the Indian Empire
C.I.E.E. .. Companion of the Institution of Electrical Engineers
C.J. .. Compagnie de Jésus
C.M. .. Master in Surgery
C.M.G. .. Companion of the Order of St. Michael and St. George
C.N.A.A. .. Council for National Academic Awards
CNRS .. Centre National de la Recherche Scientifique
Co. .. .. Company; County
Colo. .. Colorado
Cmdr. .. Commander
Comm. .. Commission
Commr. .. Commissioner
Comp. T.I... Companion of the Textile Institute
Conf. .. Conference
Conn. .. Connecticut
Corpn. .. Corporation
Corresp. .. Correspondent, Corresponding
C.P.A. .. Certified Public Accountant; Chartered Patent Agent
C.P.H. .. Certificate of Public Health
Cr. .. Contador
C.S.I. .. Companion of the Order of the Star of India
CSIRO .. Commonwealth Scientific and Industrial Research Organization
C.S.S.F. .. Confédération des Sociétés Scientifiques Françaises
C.St.J. .. Commander of the Order of St. John of Jerusalem
Cttee. .. Committee
C.V.O. .. Commander of the Royal Victorian Order

D.Agr. .. Doctor of Agriculture
D.Arch. .. Doctor of Architecture
D.B. .. Bachelor of Divinity
D.B.A. .. Doctor of Business Administration
D.B.E. .. Dame Commander of the Order of the British Empire
D.C. .. District of Columbia
D.C.L. .. Doctor of Civil Law
D.C.M. .. Distinguished Conduct Medal
D.Cn.L. .. Doctor of Canon Law
D.C.S. .. Doctor of Commercial Science
D.C.T. .. Doctor of Christian Theology
D.D. .. Doctor of Divinity
D.D.C. .. Doctorat en droit canonique
D. de l'U. .. Docteur de l'Université
D.D.S. .. Doctor of Dental Surgery
D.Econ. .. Doctor of Economics
D.Ed. .. Doctor of Education
Del... .. Delegate, delegation; Delaware
D. en D. .. Docteur en Droit
D.Eng. .. Doctor of Engineering
Dept. .. Department
D. ès L. .. Docteur ès lettres
D. ès Sc. .. Docteur ès sciences
D.F. .. Doctor of Forestry; Distrito Federal
D.F.A. .. Doctor of Fine Arts
D.F.C. .. Distinguished Flying Cross
D.H.L. .. Doctor of Hebrew Literature
D.Hy. .. Doctor of Hygiene
Dir. .. Director
D. Iur. Utr. Doctor of both Civil and Canon Law
Div. .. Division
D.L. .. Doctor of Laws
D.Lett. .. Doctorat ès lettres
D.Lit(t). .. Doctor of Letters; Doctor of Literature
D.Litt.S. .. Doctor of Sacred Letters
D.L.S. .. Doctor of Library Science
D.M. .. Doctor of Medicine
D.M.A. .. Doctor of Musical Arts
D.Math.Sc. Doctor of Mathematical Science
D.Math.Stats. Doctor of Mathematical Statistics
D.M.D. .. Doctor of Medical Dentistry
D.Met. .. Doctor of Metallurgy
D.Mus. .. Doctor of Music
D.Oph. .. Doctor of Ophthalmology
Dott. .. Dottore (Italian)
Dott.L. .. Dottore in Lettere
D.Paed. .. Doctor of Paediatrics
D.Phil. .. Doctor of Philosophy
D.Phil.Nat. Doctor of Natural Philosophy
Dr. Ing. .. Doctor of Engineering
Dr. Jur. .. Doctor of Laws
Dr. Med. .. Doctor of Medicine
Dr.Med.Dent. Doctor of Dentistry
Dr.Med.Vet. Doctor of Veterinary Medicine
Dr. Oec. .. Doctor of Commerce
Dr. Phar. .. Doctor of Pharmacy
Dr.rer.Hort. Doctor of Horticulture
Dr.rer.Nat... Doctor of Natural Science
Dr.rer.Pol. Doctor of Political Science
Dr. Theol. .. Doctor of Theology
Drs... .. Doctorandus (term used in The Netherlands to denote a doctor's degree)
D.S.A. .. Doctor of Scientific Agriculture
D.S.C. .. Distinguished Service Cross
D.Sc. .. Doctor of Science

D.Sc.A. .. Doctor of Applied Science
D.Sc.Agr. .. Doctor of Science in Agriculture
D.Sc.Pol. .. Doctor of Political Sciences
D.Soc.Sc. .. Doctor of Social Sciences
D.S.I.R. .. Department of Scientific and Industrial Research
D.S.M. .. Distinguished Service Medal
D.S.O. .. Distinguished Service Order
D.S.T. .. Doctor of Sacred Theology
D.S.W. .. Doctor of Social Work
D.Tech. .. Doctor in Technology
D.Theol. .. Doctor of Theology
D.T.M.&H. .. Diploma in Tropical Medicine and Hygiene
D.U.(P.) .. Docteur de l'Université (de Paris)
D.V.M. .. Doctor of Veterinary Medicine
D.V.S. (Sc.) Doctor of Veterinary Science

ECOSOC .. Economic and Social Council (UN)
ECSC .. European Coal and Steel Community
EEC .. European Economic Community
ESCAP .. Economic and Social Commission for Asia and the Pacific
E.D. .. Doctor of Engineering (U.S.A.)
Ed.B. .. Bachelor of Education
Ed.D. .. Doctor of Education
Edn. .. Edition
Ed.M. .. Master of Education
E.E. .. Doctor of Electrical Engineering
Est... .. Established
E.T.H. .. Eidgenössische Technische Hochschule
Exec. .. Executive

f. .. founded
F.A.A. .. Fellow of the Australian Academy of Science
F.A.A.A.S... Fellow of the American Association for the Advancement of Science
F.A.C.C.A... Fellow of the Association of Certified and Corporate Accountants
F.A.C.D. .. Fellow of the American College of Dentistry
F.A.C.D.S... Fellow of the Australian College of Dental Surgeons
F.A.C.M.A. Fellow of the Australian College of Medical Administrators
F.A.C.P. .. Fellow of American College of Physicians
F.A.C.S. .. Fellow of the American College of Surgeons
F.A.H.A. .. Fellow of the Australian Academy of the Humanities
F.A.I. .. Fellow of the Chartered Auctioneers' and Estate Agents' Institute
F.A.I.A. .. Fellow of the American Institute of Architects
F.A.I.A.S... Fellow of the Australian Institute of Agricultural Sciences
F.A.I.M. .. Fellow of the Australian Institute of Management
F.A.I.P. .. Fellow of the Australian Institute of Physics
FAO .. Food and Agriculture Organization
F.A.S.A. .. Fellow of the Australian Society of Arts
F.A.S.E. .. Fellow of the Antiquarian Society, Edinburgh
F.A.S.S.A... Fellow of the Academy of the Social Sciences in Australia
F.B.A. .. Fellow of the British Academy
F.B.A.A. .. Fellow of the British Association of Accountants and Auditors
F.B.I.M. .. Fellow of the British Institute of Management
F.B.Ps.S. .. Fellow of the British Psychological Society
F.C.A. .. Fellow of the Institute of Chartered Accountants
F.C.I.C. .. Fellow of the Chemical Institute of Canada
F.C.I.I. .. Fellow of the Chartered Insurance Institute
F.C.I.S. .. Fellow of the Chartered Institute of Secretaries
F.C.I.T. .. Fellow of the Chartered Institute of Transport
F.C.R.A. .. Fellow of the College of Radiologists of Australasia
F.C.T. .. Federal Capital Territory
F.C.W.A. .. Fellow of the Chartered Institute of Cost and Works Accountants
F.D.S.R.C.S. Fellow of the Royal College of Surgeons in Dental Surgery
F.E. .. Fuels Engineer
Fed. .. Federation, Federal
F.E.I.S. .. Fellow of the Educational Institute of Scotland
F.F.A.R.C.S. Fellow of the Faculty of Anaesthetics, Royal College of Surgeons
F.F.D.R.C.S.I. Fellow of the Faculty of Dentistry, Royal College of Surgeons in Ireland
F.F.R. .. Fellow of the Faculty of Radiologists
F.G.A. .. Fellow of the Gemmological Association
F.G.S. .. Fellow of the Geological Society
F.I.A. .. Fellow of the Institute of Actuaries
F.I.A.L. .. Fellow of the International Institute of Arts and Letters
F.I.B. .. Fellow of the Institute of Bankers
F.I.Biol. .. Fellow of the Institute of Biology
F.I.C.D. .. Fellow of the Institute of Canadian Dentists
F.I.C.E.A... Fellow of Industrial and Commercial Executive Accountants
F.I.C.S. .. Fellow of the International College of Surgeons
F.I.E.Aust. Fellow of the Institute of Engineers of Australia
F.I.E.R.E. .. Fellow of the Institution of Electronic and Radio Engineers
F.I.I.S. .. Fellow of the Irish Institute of Secretaries
F.I.L. .. Fellow of the Institute of Linguists
Fil. Dr. .. Doctor of Philology
F.I.Inf.Sc. .. Fellow of the Institute of Information Scientists
F.I.M. .. Fellow of the Institution of Metallurgists
F.I.Mech.E. Fellow of the Institution of Mechanical Engineers
F.I.Min.E... Fellow of the Institution of Mining Engineers
F.I.M.L.T... Fellow of the Institute of Medical Laboratory Technology
F.Inst.E. .. Fellow of the Institute of Energy
F.Inst.P. .. Fellow of the Institute of Physics
F.Inst.Pet... Fellow of the Institute of Petroleum
F.I.R.E. .. Fellow of the Institution of Radio Engineers
F.I.R.E.E. .. Fellow of the Institution of Radio and Electronics Engineers (Australia)
F.J.I. .. Fellow of the Institute of Journalists
F.K.C. .. Fellow of King's College (London)
Fla. .. Florida
F.L.A. .. Fellow of the Library Association
F.L.A.A. .. Fellow of the Library Association of Australia
F.L.S. .. Fellow of the Linnaean Society
F.M.A. .. Fellow of the Museums Association
F.N.A. .. Fellow of the National Academy of Sciences (India)
F.N.Z.I.C. .. Fellow of the New Zealand Institute of Chemists
F.Ph.S. .. Fellow of the Philosophical Society of England
F.Phys.S. .. Fellow of the Physical Society
F.P.R.I. .. Fellow of the Plastics and Rubber Institute

F.R.A.C.I. .. Fellow of the Royal Australian Chemical Institute
F.R.A.C.P... Fellow of the Royal Australasian College of Physicians
F.R.A.C.S... Fellow of the Royal Australasian College of Surgeons
F.R.Ae.S. .. Fellow of the Royal Aeronautical Society
F.R.A.H.S. Fellow of the Royal Australian Historical Society
F.R.A.I. .. Fellow of the Royal Anthropological Institute
F.R.A.I.A... Fellow of the Royal Australian Institute of Architects
F.R.A.I.C. .. Fellow of the Architectural Institute of Canada
F.R.A.M. .. Fellow of the Royal Academy of Music
F.R.A.S. .. Fellow of the Royal Astronomical Society; Fellow of the Royal Asiatic Society
F.R.B.S. .. Fellow of the Royal Society of British Sculptors
F.R.C.M. .. Fellow of the Royal College of Music
F.R.C.O. .. Fellow of the Royal College of Organists
F.R.C.O.G... Fellow of the Royal College of Obstetricians and Gynaecologists
F.R.C.P.A. Fellow of the Royal College of Pathologists of Australia
F.R.C.P.(C.) Fellow of the Royal College of Physicians of Canada
F.R.C.P.ED. Fellow of the Royal College of Physicians of Edinburgh
F.R.C.P.I. .. Fellow of the Royal College of Physicians of Ireland
F.R.C.S.(C.) Fellow of the Royal College of Surgeons of Canada
F.R.C.S.ED. Fellow of the Royal College of Surgeons of Edinburgh
F.R.C.V.S. .. Fellow of the Royal College of Veterinary Surgeons
F.R.E.S. .. Fellow of the Royal Entomological Society of London
F.R.Econ.S. Fellow of the Royal Economic Society
F.R.G.S. .. Fellow of the Royal Geographical Society
F.R.Hist.S. Fellow of the Royal Historical Society
F.R.Hort.S. Fellow of the Royal Horticultural Society
F.R.I.B.A... Fellow of the Royal Institute of British Architects
F.R.I.C.S. .. Fellow of the Royal Institution of Chartered Surveyors
F.R.I.Z. .. Fellow of the Royal Institute of Zoologists
F.R.Met.Soc. Fellow of the Royal Meteorological Society
F.R.P.S. Fellow of the Royal Photographic Society
F.R.S. .. Fellow of the Royal Society
F.R.S.A. .. Fellow of the Royal Society of Arts
F.R.San.I. .. Fellow of the Royal Sanitary Institute
F.R.S.C. .. Fellow of the Royal Society of Canada; Fellow of the Royal Society of Chemistry
F.R.S.E. .. Fellow of the Royal Society of Edinburgh
F.R.S.G.S... Fellow of the Royal Scottish Geographical Society
F.R.S.H. .. Fellow of the Royal Society of Health
F.R.S.L. .. Fellow of the Royal Society of Literature
F.R.S.S. .. Fellow of the Royal Statistical Society
F.R.S.S.Af. Fellow of the Royal Society of South Africa
F.R.S.T.M... Fellow of the Royal Society of Tropical Medicine and Hygiene
F.S.A. .. Fellow of the Society of Antiquaries
F.S.A.(Scot.) Fellow of the Society of Antiquaries of Scotland
F.S.A.L.A... Fellow of the South African Library Association
F.S.B.E. .. Fellow of the Society for British Entomology
F.S.S. .. Fellow of the Statistical Society

F.T.C.D. .. Fellow of Trinity College, Dublin
F.T.C.L. .. Fellow of Trinity College of Music, London
F.T.I. .. Fellow of the Textile Institute
F.Z.S. .. Fellow of the Zoological Society

Ga. .. .. Georgia
G.B.E. .. Knight (or Dame) Grand Cross of the Order of the British Empire
G.C.B. .. Knight Grand Cross of the Order of the Bath
G.C.I.E. .. Knight Grand Commander of the Indian Empire
G.C.M.G. .. Knight Grand Cross of the Order of St. Michael and St. George
G.C.S.I. .. Knight Grand Commander of the Star of India
G.C.V.O. .. Knight Grand Cross of the Royal Victorian Order
Gen. .. General
Gov. .. Governor
Govt. .. Government

h.c. .. .. honoris causa
H.Q. .. Headquarters
H.E. .. His Eminence; His Excellency
H.M. .. His (or Her) Majesty
H.M.S.O. .. His (or Her) Majesty's Stationery Office
H.N.D. .. Higher National Diploma
Hon. .. Honourable; Honorary

Ia. .. .. Iowa
IAEA .. International Atomic Energy Agency
IAU .. International Astronomical Union
IBE.. .. International Bureau of Education
I.C.E. .. Institute of Civil Engineers
ICPHS .. International Council for Philosophy and Humanistic Studies
I.C.S. .. Indian Civil Service
ICSU .. International Council of Scientific Unions
Ida... .. Idaho
IFAN .. Institut Fondamental d'Afrique Noire
IFLA .. International Federation of Library Associations and Institutions
IGU .. International Geographical Union
Ill. .. .. Illinois
ILO.. .. International Labour Organization
IMS .. India Medical Service
IMU .. International Mathematical Union
Inc. .. .. Incorporated
Ind. .. .. Indiana; Independent
I.N.R.A. .. Institut National de la Recherche Agronomique
Int. .. .. International
ISME .. International Society for Music Education
I.S.O. .. Companion of the Imperial Service Order
IUB .. International Union of Biochemistry
IUBS .. International Union of Biological Sciences
IUCr .. International Union of Crystallography
IUGG .. International Union of Geodesy and Geophysics
IUGS .. International Union of Geological Sciences
IUHPS .. International Union of the History and Philosophy of Science
IUIS .. International Union of Immunological Societies
IUNS .. International Union of Nutritional Sciences
IUPAB .. International Union of Pure and Applied Biophysics
IUPAC .. International Union of Pure and Applied Chemistry
IUPAP .. International Union of Pure and Applied Physics
IUPHAR .. International Union of Pharmacology
IUPS .. International Union of Physiological Sciences

IUTAM .. International Union of Theoretical and Applied Mechanics

J.C.B. .. Juris Canonici Bachelor (Bachelor of Canon Law)
J.C.D. .. Juris Canonici Doctor (Doctor of Canon Law)
J.C.L. .. Juris Canonici Lector (Reader of Canon Law)
J.D. .. Doctor of Jurisprudence
J.P. .. Justice of the Peace
Jl. .. Jalan (Indonesia, Malaysia)
J.S.D. .. Doctor of Juristic Science
J.U.D(r). .. Juris utriusque Doctor (Doctor of both Civil and Canon Law)
Ju.D. .. Doctor of Law

Kan. .. Kansas
K.B.E. .. Knight Commander of the Order of the British Empire
K.C.B. .. Knight Commander of the Order of the Bath
K.C.I.E. .. Knight Commander of the Order of the Indian Empire
K.C.M.G. .. Knight Commander of the Order of St. Michael and St. George
K.C.S.I. .. Knight Commander of the Star of India
K.C.V.O. .. Knight Commander of the Royal Victorian Order
K.G. .. Knight of the Order of the Garter
K.P. .. Knight of the Order of St. Patrick
K.St.J. .. Knight of the Order of St. John of Jerusalem
K.T. .. Knight of the Order of the Thistle
Kt. .. .. Knight
Ky. .. .. Kentucky

La. .. .. Louisiana
L.C.L. .. Licentiate of Canon Law
L.D.S. .. Licentiate in Dental Surgery
L. ès L. .. Licencié ès lettres
L. ès Sc. .. Licencié ès sciences
L.H.D. .. Literarum Humaniorum Doctor (Doctor of Letters)
Lic. Droit et Sc. Pol. .. Licencié en Droit et Sciences Politiques
Lic.Med. .. Licentiate in Medicine
L.I.M. .. Licentiate of the Institution of Metallurgists
Litt.D. .. Doctor of Letters
LL.B. .. Bachelor of Laws
LL.D. .. Doctor of Laws
L.Lett. .. Licentiate of Letters
LL.L. .. Licentiate of Laws
LL.M. .. Master of Laws
L.M. .. Licentiate of Medicine or Midwifery
L.M.S. .. Licentiate in Medicine and Surgery
L.M.S.S.A. .. Licentiate in Medicine and Surgery of the Society of Apothecaries
L.Mus. .. Licentiate in Music
L.Ph. .. Licentiate of Philosophy
L.R.C.P. .. Licentiate of the Royal College of Physicians
L.R.C.S. .. Licentiate of the Royal College of Surgeons
L.R.P.S. .. Licentiate of the Royal Photographic Society
L.S. .. .. Library Science
L.S.A. .. Licentiate of Science in Agriculture
L.S.T. .. Licentiate in Sacred Theology
Lt. .. .. Lieutenant
L.Th. .. Licentiate or Master of Theology

M.A. .. Master of Arts
M.A.C.E. .. Member of the Australian College of Education
M.A.C.V.S. .. Member of the Australian College of Veterinary Surgeons
M.Agr. .. Master of Agriculture
M.A.L.S. .. Master of Arts in Library Science
Man. Manager, Managing; Manitoba
M.A.O. .. Master of Obstetrics
M.Arch. .. Master in Architecture
M.A.Sc. .. Master of Applied Science
M.A.S.C.E. .. Member of the Australian Society of Civil Engineers
Mass. Massachusetts
M.B. .. Bachelor of Medicine
M.B.A. .. Master of Business Administration
M.B.E. .. Member of the Order of the British Empire
M.B.I.M. .. Member of the British Institute of Management
M.C. .. Military Cross
M.C.D. .. Master of Civic Design
M.C.E. .. Master of Civil Engineering
M.Ch. .. Master of Surgery
M.Ch.D. .. Master of Dental Surgery
M.Ch.E. .. Master of Chemical Engineering
M.C.I.T. .. Member of the Chartered Institute of Transport
M.C.L. .. Master of Civil Law
M.Com(m). .. Master of Commerce
M.C.P. .. Master of City Planning
M.C.S. .. Master of Commercial Science
Md. .. Maryland
M.D. .. Doctor of Medicine
M.D.S. .. Master of Dental Surgery
M.E. .. Mechanical Engineer; Master of Education; Master of Engineering; Military Engineer; Mining Engineer
Me. .. Maine
M.Econ. .. Master of Economics
M.Ed. .. Master of Education
M.E.E. .. Master of Electrical Engineering
M.E.I.C. .. Member of the Engineering Institute of Canada
Mem(s). .. Member(s)
M.Aus.I.M.M. Member of the Australasian Institute of Mining and Metallurgy
M.Eng. .. Master of Engineering
M.F. .. Master of Forestry
M.F.A. .. Master of Fine Arts
Mgr. .. Monseigneur; Monsignor; Magister (Master's degree)
M.H.A. .. Member of the House of Assembly
M.H.R. .. Member of the House of Representatives
M.I.Biol. .. Member of the Institute of Biology
M.I.C.E. .. Member of the Institution of Civil Engineers
M.I.Chem.E. Member of the Institution of Chemical Engineers
Mich. .. Michigan
M.I.E.A. .. Member of the Institution of Engineers of Australia
M.I.E.E. .. Member of the Institution of Electrical Engineers
M.I.E.R.E. .. Member of the Institution of Electronic and Radio Engineers
M.I.L. .. Member of the Institute of Linguists
Mil. .. .. Military
M.I.Mar.E. .. Member of the Institute of Marine Engineers
M.I.Mech.E. Member of the Institution of Mechanical Engineers
M.I.Min.E. .. Member of the Institution of Mining Engineers
M.I.M.M. .. Member of the Institution of Mining and Metallurgy
Minn. .. Minnesota
Miss. .. Mississippi
M.I.P.E. .. Member of the Institution of Production Engineers

M.I.P.M. .. Member of the Institute of Personnel Management
M.I.Struct.E. Member of the Institution of Structural Engineers
M.I.T. .. Massachusetts Institute of Technology
M.I.W.E. .. Member of the Institute of Water Engineers
M.L. .. Master of Laws
M.L.A. .. Member of the Legislative Assembly; Master of Landscape Architecture
M.L.C. .. Member of the Legislative Council
M.Litt. .. Master of Letters
M.L.S. .. Master of Library Science
M.M.S.A. .. Master of Midwifery of the Society of Apothecaries
M.Mus. .. Master of Music
Mo. .. .. Missouri
Mont. .. Montana
M.P. .. Member of Parliament
M.P.H. .. Master of Public Health
M.Ph. .. Master of Philosophy
M.R.A.I.C. Member of the Royal Architectural Institute of Canada
M.R.A.S. .. Member of the Royal Asiatic Society
M.R.C.Path. Member of the Royal College of Pathologists
M.R.C.P.ED. Member of the Royal College of Physicians of Edinburgh
M.R.C.S.ED. Member of the Royal College of Surgeons of Edinburgh
M.R.C.V.S.. . Member of the Royal College of Veterinary Surgeons
M.R.I. .. Member of the Royal Institution
M.R.I.A. .. Member of the Royal Irish Academy
M.R.S.A. .. Member of the Royal Society of Arts
M.R.S.A.E. Member of Royal Society of Agricultural Engineers
M.R.C.S. .. Member of the Royal Society of Chemistry
M.R.S.L. .. Member of the Royal Society of Literature; Member of the Order of the Republic of Sierra Leone
M.S. .. Master of Science; Master of Surgery
M.S.A. .. Master of Scientific Agriculture
M.Sc. .. Master of Science
M.Sc.A. .. Master of Applied Science
M.Sc.Agr. .. Master of Science in Agriculture
M.Sc.(Chem. Tech.) .. Master of Science in Chemical Technology
M.Sc.D. .. Master of Science in Dentistry
M.Sc.F. .. Master of Science in Forestry
M.Sc.(Med.) Master of Science in Medicine
M.Sc.N. .. Master of Science in Nursing
M.Sc.Tech. .. Master of Science in Technology
M.S.D. .. Doctor of Medieval Studies
M.S.L. .. Licentiate of Medieval Studies
M.S.P. .. Master of Science in Pharmacy
M.Soc.Sc. .. Master of Social Science
M.S.W. .. Master of Social Work
M.Th. .. Master of Theology
M.T.P.I. .. Member of the Town Planning Institute
Mus.Bac. or B. Bachelor of Music
Mus.Doc. or D. Doctor of Music
Mus.M. .. Master of Music
M.V.O. .. Member of the Royal Victorian Order
M.V.Sc. .. Master of Veterinary Science

NASA .. National Aeronautics and Space Administration
N.B. .. New Brunswick
N.C. .. North Carolina
N.D. .. North Dakota
N.D.D. .. National Diploma in Dairying
Neb. .. Nebraska
Nev. .. Nevada
N.H. .. New Hampshire
N.J. .. New Jersey
N.M. .. New Mexico
N.S. .. Nova Scotia
N.S.W. .. New South Wales
N.U.I. .. National University of Ireland
N.Y. .. New York
N.Z. .. New Zealand

O. .. .. Ohio
OAS .. Organization of American States
O.B.E. .. Officer of the Order of the British Empire
OECD .. Organization for Economic Co-operation and Development
O.F.M. .. Order of Friars Minor
O.F.S. .. Orange Free State
Okla. .. Oklahoma
O.M. .. Member of the Order of Merit
O.M.I. .. Oblate of Mary Immaculate
On. .. .. Onorevole (Italian)
O.N.D. .. Ordinary National Diploma
Ont. .. Ontario
O.P. .. Order of Preachers (Dominicans)
Ore. .. .. Oregon
ORSTOM .. Office de la Recherche Scientifique et Technique Outre-Mer
O.S.B. .. Order of St. Benedict
O. St. J. .. Officer of (the Order of) St. John of Jerusalem
OStR. .. Oberstudienrat
Oxon. .. Of Oxford University

Pa. .. .. Pennsylvania
P.C. .. .. Privy Councillor
Pd.B. .. Bachelor of Pedagogy
Pd.D. .. Doctor of Pedagogy
Pd.M. .. Master of Pedagogy
P.E. .. Petroleum Engineer
P.E.I. .. Prince Edward Island
P.E.N. .. Poets, Playwrights, Essayists, Editors and Novelists (Club)
Ph.B. .. Bachelor of Philosophy
Ph.D. .. Doctor of Philosophy
Ph.G. .. Graduate in Pharmacy
Ph.L. .. Licentiate in Philosophy
Ph.M. .. Master of Philosophy
P.M.B. .. Private Mail Bag
P.O.B. .. Post Office Box
P.Q. .. Province of Quebec
P.R.A. .. President of the Royal Academy
Pres. .. President
P.R.I. .. President of the Royal Institute of Painters in Water Colours
P.R.I.B.A. .. President of the Royal Institute of British Architects
Prof. .. Professor
P.R.S. .. President of the Royal Society
P.R.S.A. .. President of the Royal Scottish Academy
Publ(s). .. Publication(s)

Q.C. .. Queen's Counsel
q.v. .. .. quod vide (which see)

R.A. .. Royal Academy; Royal Academician
R.A.C.P. .. Royal Australasian College of Physicians
R.A.C.S. .. Royal Australasian College of Surgeons
R.A.F. .. Royal Air Force
R.A.M. .. Royal Academy of Music
R.A.S. .. Royal Astronomical (or Asiatic) Society
R.B.A. .. Royal Society of British Artists
R.C.A. .. Member of the Royal Cambrian Academy; Member of the Royal Canadian Academy
R.C.M. .. Royal College of Music
R.C.S. .. Royal College of Surgeons
Rep. .. Representative; Represented
retd. .. retired

ABBREVIATIONS

Rev. .. Reverend
R.G.S. .. Royal Geographical Society
R.Hist.S. .. Royal Historical Society
R.I... .. Rhode Island; Royal Institute of Painters in Water Colours; Royal Institution
R.I.A. .. Royal Irish Academy; Registered Industrial and Cost Accountant
R.I.B.A. .. Royal Institute of British Architects
R.I.C.S. .. Royal Institution of Chartered Surveyors
R.M.P.A. .. Royal Medico-Psychological Association
R.N. .. Royal Navy
R.O.I. .. Royal Institute of Oil Painters
R.P. .. Member of the Royal Society of Portrait Painters
R.S.A. .. Royal Scottish Academy; Royal Society of Arts
R.S.C. .. Royal Society of Canada
R.S.F.S.R. Russian Soviet Federative Socialist Republic
R.S.W. .. Royal Scottish Society of Painters in Water Colours
Rt. Hon. .. Right Honourable
Rt. Rev. .. Right Reverend
R.W.S. .. Royal Society of Painters in Water Colours

S.A... .. South Africa(n)
S.C... .. South Carolina; Senior Counsel (Republic of Ireland)
Sc.B. .. Bachelor of Science
Sc.D. .. Doctor of Science
S.C.D. .. Doctor of Commercial Science
S.Dak. .. South Dakota
S.D.I. .. Selective Dissemination of Information
Sec. .. .. Secretary
S.J. .. .. Society of Jesus
S.J.D. .. Doctor of Juristic Science
S.M. .. Master of Science
S.R.R .. Socialist Republic of Romania
S.S.R. .. Soviet Socialist Republic
S.T.B. .. Bachelor of Sacred Theology
S.T.D. .. Doctor of Sacred Theology
S.Th.L. .. Sacrae Theologiae Lector (Reader or Professor of Sacred Theology)
S.T.M. .. Master of Sacred Theology
Supt. .. Superintendent

T.D. .. (Territorial) Efficiency Decoration; Tealta Dáil (Member of the Dail)
Tenn. .. Tennessee
Tex. .. Texas
Th.A. .. Associate in Theology
Th.B. .. Bachelor of Theology
Th.D. .. Doctor of Theology
Th.M. .. Master of Theology

U.G.C. .. University Grants Committee
U.K. .. United Kingdom
UN .. .. United Nations
UNDP .. United Nations Development Programme
UNESCO .. United Nations Educational, Scientific and Cultural Organization
UNICEF .. United Nations International Children's Emergency Fund
Univ. .. University
UNRWA .. United Nations Relief and Works Agency
U.P. .. Uttar Pradesh (United Provinces)
URSI .. Union Radio-Scientifique Internationale
U.S.A. .. United States of America
U.S.S.R. .. Union of Soviet Socialist Republics

Va. .. .. Virginia
V.C. .. Victoria Cross
Vols. .. Volumes
Vt. .. .. Vermont

W.A. .. Western Australia
Wash. .. Washington (State)
W.E.A. .. Workers' Educational Association
Wis. .. Wisconsin
W. Va. .. West Virginia
Wyo. .. Wyoming

† .. .. indicates a periodical title available for exchange

INTERNATIONAL

CONTENTS

UNESCO

UNITED NATIONS EDUCATIONAL, SCIENTIFIC AND CULTURAL ORGANIZATION

7 place de Fontenoy, 75700 Paris

Telephone: 577-16-10

Established in 1946 "for the purpose of advancing through the educational, scientific and cultural relations of the peoples of the world, the objectives of international peace and the common welfare of mankind".

FUNCTIONS

UNESCO's activities, which take three main forms as outlined below, are funded through a regular budget provided by member states and also through other sources, particularly the UNDP.

International Intellectual Co-operation

UNESCO assists the interchange of experience, knowledge and ideas through a world network of specialists. Apart from the work of its professional staff, UNESCO co-operates regularly with the national associations and international federations of scientists, artists, writers and educators, some of which it helped to establish.

UNESCO convenes conferences and meetings, and co-ordinates international scientific efforts; it helps to standardize procedures of documentation and provides clearing house services; it offers fellowships; and it publishes a wide range of specialized works, including source books and works of reference.

UNESCO promotes various international agreements, including the International Copyright Convention, which member states are invited to accept.

Operational Assistance

UNESCO has established missions which advise governments, particularly in the developing member countries, in the planning of projects; and it appoints experts to assist in carrying them out. The projects are concerned with the teaching of functional literacy to workers in development undertakings; teacher training; establishing of libraries and documentation centres; provision of training for journalists, radio, television and film workers; improvement of scientific and technical education; training of planners in cultural development; and the international exchange of persons and information.

Promotion of Peace

UNESCO organizes various research efforts on racial problems, and is particularly concerned with prevention of discrimination in education, and improving access for women to education. It has commissioned studies on various aspects of human rights and, through the associated schools which take part in its youth programme, has promoted activities to increase knowledge of international problems and improve mutual understanding.

MEMBER STATES

(*August* 1980)

Afghanistan
Albania
Algeria
Angola
Argentina
Australia
Austria
Bahrain
Bangladesh
Barbados
Belgium
Benin
Bolivia
Botswana
Brazil
Bulgaria
Burma
Burundi
Byelorussian S.S.R.
Cambodia
Cameroon
Canada
Cape Verde
Central African Republic
Chad
Chile
China, People's Republic
Colombia
Comoros
Congo People's Republic
Costa Rica
Cuba
Cyprus
Czechoslovakia
Denmark
Dominican Republic
Ecuador
Egypt
El Salvador
Ethiopia
Finland
France
Gabon
Gambia
German Democratic Republic
Germany, Federal Republic
Ghana
Greece
Grenada
Guatemala
Guinea
Guinea-Bissau
Guyana
Haiti
Honduras
Hungary
Iceland
India
Indonesia
Iran
Iraq
Ireland
Israel
Italy
Ivory Coast
Jamaica
Japan
Jordan
Kenya
Korea, Democratic People's Republic
Korea, Republic
Kuwait
Laos
Lebanon
Lesotho
Liberia
Libya
Luxembourg
Madagascar
Malawi
Malaysia
Mali
Malta
Mauritania
Mauritius
Mexico
Monaco
Mongolian People's Republic
Morocco
Mozambique
Namibia
Nepal
Netherlands
New Zealand
Nicaragua
Niger
Nigeria
Norway
Oman
Pakistan
Panama
Papua New Guinea
Paraguay
Peru
Philippines
Poland
Portugal
Qatar
Romania
Rwanda
St. Lucia
San Marino
São Tomé and Príncipe
Saudi Arabia
Senegal
Seychelles
Sierra Leone
Singapore
Somalia
Spain
Sri Lanka
Sudan
Surinam
Swaziland
Sweden
Switzerland
Syrian Arab Republic
Tanzania
Thailand
Togo
Trinidad and Tobago
Tunisia
Turkey
Uganda
Ukrainian S.S.R.
U.S.S.R.
United Arab Emirates
United Kingdom
United States of America
Upper Volta
Uruguay
Venezuela
Viet-Nam
Yemen Arab Republic
Yemen, People's Democratic Republic
Yugoslavia
Zaire
Zambia

Associate Member: British Eastern Caribbean Group

ORGANIZATION

GENERAL CONFERENCE

The supreme governing body of the Organization. Meets in ordinary session once in two years and is composed of representatives of the member states. Twenty-first session: Belgrade, 1980.

President: NAPOLÉON LEBLANC (Canada).

EXECUTIVE BOARD

Consists of 45 members. Prepares the programme to be submitted to the Conference and supervises its execution. Meets twice or sometimes three times a year.

Chairman: CHAMS ELDINE EL-WAKIL (Egypt).

SECRETARIAT

Director-General: AMADOU MAHTAR M'BOW (Senegal).

Deputy Director-General: FEDERICO MAYOR (Spain).

The Director-General has an international staff of 3,600 civil servants. Of the professional staff (specialists in various disciplines and administrators), about two-thirds are away from headquarters on technical assistance missions to member states.

Assistant Directors-General:

Administration: G. V. RAO (India).

Programme Support: G. V. RAO (acting).

Education: SIOMA TANGUIANE (U.S.S.R.).

Natural Sciences and their Application to Development: ABDUL-RAZZAK KADDOURA (Syria).

Social Sciences and their Applications: RODOLFO STAVENHAGEN (Mexico).

Culture and Communication: MAKAMINAN MAKAGIANSAR (Indonesia).

Co-operation for Development and External Relations: DRAGOLJUB NAJMAN (Yugoslavia).

Studies and Programming: JEAN KNAPP (France).

CO-OPERATING BODIES

National Commissions and Co-operating Bodies have been set up in most member states. These help to integrate work within the member states and the work of UNESCO.

REGIONAL OFFICES

LIAISON OFFICES

Office for Liaison with United Nations: Room 2401, UN Headquarters, New York, N.Y. 10017, U.S.A.

UNESCO Liaison Office in Geneva: Bureau Bocage 4, Palais des Nations, CH-1211 Geneva, Switzerland.

UNESCO Liaison Office in Washington: 918 16th St., N.W., Suite 201, Washington, D.C. 20006, U.S.A.

UNESCO Liaison Office for Ethiopia and with the Economic Commission for Africa (ECA) and the Organization of African Unity (OAU): P.O.B. 1177, Addis Ababa, Ethiopia.

UNESCO Liaison Office for the International Campaign for Venice: Palazzo Reale, Piazza San Marco 63, 30124 Venice, Italy.

UNESCO Education Offices

Regional Office for Education in Latin America and the Caribbean: P.O.B. 3187, Santiago, Chile.

Regional Office for Education in Asia and Oceania: P.O.B. 1425, Bangkok 11, Thailand.

Regional Office for Education in Africa: B.P. 3311, Dakar, Senegal.

Regional Office for Education in the Arab States: B.P. 5244, Ave. de la Cité Sportive, Beirut, Lebanon.

Regional Centre for Higher Education in Latin America and the Caribbean: Apdo. postal 62090, Edif. "Asovincar", Avda. los Chorros/Cruce, Calle Acueducto, Altos de Sebucan, Caracas 106, Venezuela.

UNESCO Science Offices

Regional Office for Science and Technology for Africa: P.O.B. 30592, Nairobi, Kenya.

Regional Office for Science and Technology for Latin America and the Caribbean: 1320 Bulevar Artigas, Apartado de Correos 859, Montevideo, Uruguay.

Regional Office for Science and Technology for the Arab States: 8 Abdel Rahman Fahmy St., Garden City, Cairo, Egypt.

Regional Office for Science and Technology for South and Central Asia: UNESCO House, 17 Jor Bagh, New Delhi 110003, India.

Regional Office for Science and Technology for Southeast Asia: UN Building (2nd Floor), Jl. Thamrin 14, Tromol Pos 273/JKT, Jakarta, Indonesia.

UNESCO Culture Offices

Regional Office for Culture in Latin America and the Caribbean: Calzada 551, esq. a D Vedado, Apdo. 4158, Havana, Cuba.

Regional Office for Culture and Book Development in Asia: 44/J/6 Razi Rd., P.E.C.H.S., Karachi 2904, Pakistan.

REGIONAL CENTRES

UNESCO Education Centres

Arab States Regional Centre for Functional Literacy in Rural Areas (ASFEC): Sirs-El-Layan, Menoufia, Egypt.

Regional Centre for Adult Education and Functional Literacy for Latin America: Patzcuaro, Michoacan, Mexico.

European Centre for Higher Education (CEPES): 39 rue Stirbei, Voda, Bucharest, Romania.

UNESCO Culture and Communication Centre

UNESCO Latin American Book Development Centre: Carrera 7A, No. 6-90, Piso 2, Apdo. Aéreo 17438, Bogotá, Colombia.

ACTIVITIES

About 200 issues of periodicals and 100 new publications are produced annually, and about 100 meetings and conferences and 30 seminars are held; close relations are maintained with 400 non-governmental organizations, some carrying out projects for UNESCO programmes.

Education. This sector receives roughly a third of the combined budgetary allocation for UNESCO's programmes (*see* budget, below); it spends on educational projects about half of the allocation for all UNESCO's programmes, on behalf of other sources, largely the UNDP.

UNESCO has an overall policy of regarding education as a lifelong process. Therefore one implication is the increasing priority given to pre-primary education as well as to adult education. The accent is now being placed on a global approach in which literacy training for adults is associated with the general introduction of primary education (known in many countries as basic education).

UNESCO continues to attach the fullest importance to the implementation of the right to education and its democratization, international understanding, co-operation and peace, as well as respect for human rights and fundamental freedoms, the struggle against discrimination in all its forms and the establishment of a new international economic order.

With regard to general scientific and technological education, UNESCO intensifies action designed to increase national capacities in science and technology education and to improve the quality of that education. Activities concerning the status of women and participation by women in development will be intensified. The reflexion on the future development of education will be continued. The main trends such as the connection between education and productive work and the linking of formal and non-formal education are expected to play a major role in the development of education systems for a long time to come.

Each year expert missions are sent to member states to advise on all matters concerning education. They also help with programmes for training abroad, and UNESCO provides study fellowships; in these forms of assistance priority is given to the rural regions of developing member countries.

Sciences. A network of regional offices spreads the application of science and technology in the developing member states.

Comprehensive and interdisciplinary missions are organized to assist developing countries in preparing strategies for the application of science and technology to socio-economic and cultural development, and identifying a series of operational projects which could be undertaken for implementation by UNESCO with the support of funding agencies such as UNDP.

The Science Sector promotes research and advanced training in all the major disciplines of basic science as well as in fundamental areas of technology, including in particular informatics and new energy sources. International and regional institutes are supported and a major subvention as well as numerous contracts are granted to the world's scientific community. Postgraduate training courses, training seminars and fellowships are available to assist young scientists from developing countries.

A programme focuses on the impact of science and technology on society and a quarterly journal, *Impact*, is published on this subject. Major intergovernmental scientific co-operation programmes are carried out on natural resources and environmental sciences. A quarterly journal, *Nature and Resources*, is published on this subject.

Under the Man and Biosphere (MAB) Programme scientific research and training is aimed at providing the scientific knowledge and trained personnel needed to manage natural resources of ecosystems in a rational and sustained manner. Under MAB, networks of integrated pilot projects for research, monitoring, demonstration and training are set up and an international network of biosphere reserves is established (177 such reserves have been established so far in 45 countries).

The International Hydrological Programme aims at developing a scientific basis for the rational management of water resources, both as regards quantity and quality. National Committees for this programme exist in 93 countries.

The Intergovernmental Oceanographic Commission, established in 1961, carries out global and regional investigations of the oceans and maintains ocean services with the concerted action of member states. Working in collaboration with the Commission, the UNESCO Division of Marine Sciences facilitates the transfer of knowledge and technology and assists countries to strengthen their capabilities in marine research and education, particularly through projects financed by extra-budgetary sources.

Culture and Communication

Culture. An established programme investigates cultures of Africa, Latin America and the Caribbean, the Arab world, Asia, Europe and Oceania. A group of experts is working on an eight-volume *General History of Africa*. A *History of the Civilizations of Central Asia* is now in preparation and a *General History of Latin America* and a *General History of the Caribbean* will also be undertaken. A ten-year plan for the systemic study of African oral traditions and the promotion of African languages is being implemented. Similar plans have also been launched in Asia and Oceania. International studies are carried out to shed light on the many and varied correlations existing between different cultures and on the points at which cultures converge and blend.

Within the programme of cultural development UNESCO's activity is centred on the promotion of cultural policies aiming at the enlargement of participation in cultural life, the democratization of culture as well as on the study of the cultural dimension of development. This involves also the training of specialists in cultural development, arts administration and cultural animation.

UNESCO also has a programme for the preservation and presentation of the cultural heritage. This includes publications and the preparation of international recommendations and conventions as well as a series of operational projects and international campaigns. Among the latter are the successful transfer of the Abu Simbel and Philae temples in Egypt (completed in 1980); the safeguarding of the city of Venice (Italy) and its surroundings; Moenjodaro (Pakistan); Borobudur (Indonesia); Fez (Morocco); and Sukhothai (Thailand).

Communication. UNESCO is playing a leading role in the establishment of a new world information and communication order. For this purpose UNESCO set up an International Commission for the Study of Communication Problems and published its report in 1980.

The Organization assists member states and professional organizations in developing: (a) free flow of information, (b) communication research, and (c) communication policies. Its communication documentation centre serves as a clearing house for communication research.

In 1978 UNESCO's General Conference adopted a Declaration on Fundamental Principles Concerning the Contribution of the Mass Media to Strengthening Peace and International Understanding, to the Promotion of Human Rights and to Countering Racialism, Apartheid and Incitement to War.

UNESCO also assists member states in the planning and development of their communication systems and the training of personnel, both under its regular programme and through the use of extra-budgetary resources.

In April 1980 UNESCO convened an Intergovernmental Conference for Co-operation on Activities, Needs and Programmes for Communication Development which proposed the establishment within the framework of UNESCO of an International Programme for the Development of Communication. This proposal was to be examined by the next session of UNESCO's General Conference in September–October 1980.

UNESCO operates a programme aimed at stimulating the production and reading of books. Within this programme an international committee of publishers, authors, librarians and booksellers has been set up.

To widen the knowledge of works of art, UNESCO publishes catalogues of reproductions of paintings and produces travelling exhibitions of reproductions of works of art. In another programme, translations of representative literary works written in the less widely known languages are published.

Social Sciences and their Applications. Since 1976 the programme has expanded so as to ensure world-wide development of the social sciences by:(a) strengthening national and regional institutions, with contributions to the African Centre for the Co-ordination of Social Science Research and Documentation for Africa South-of-the-Sahara (CERDAS), Kinshasa, Zaire; to the Centre for Social Science Research and Documentation for the Arab Region (ARCSS), Cairo, Egypt; and to the Association of Asian Social Science Councils, Seoul, Republic of Korea; UNESCO is also the executing agency for UNDP regional projects in co-operation with the Latin American Faculty of Social Sciences (FLACSO) and the Latin American

Social Science Council (CLACSO); (b) the conceptual development of the social sciences; (c) training; (d) exchange and diffusion of information; and (e) co-operation with International Non-Governmental Organizations such as the International Social Science Council and the International Committee for Social Science Documentation and Information.

Those activities concerning Human Rights and Peace include three major projects: (a) definition of human rights norms and action and study of socio-economic and cultural conditions for the promotion of human rights; (b) development of human rights teaching; (c) peace research, concentrating on obstacles to disarmament.

The programme on the application of social sciences to mankind's development problems, relates to environmental and population issues (with, for instance, annual subventions planned until 1983 to the International Union of Architects, and United Nations Fund for Population Activities), and lays stress on the study of the socio-cultural bases to the establishment of a new international economic order. Activities relating to development planning concern the elaboration and use in member states of methods and instruments of social analysis, social planning and evaluation of social action programmes.

Undertakings related to women in society correspond to the three objectives set for the UN Decade for Women: promotion of equality, their participation in development and their contribution to peace. Youth operational projects are well under way in co-operation with member states, with UNDP-financing to Indonesia, Madagascar and the Seychelles totalling $341,687 in 1978–81, and financial assistance to some 16 International Non-Governmental Youth Organizations.

An important feature of the programme is that activities appertaining to philosophy are associated with all its major aspects. Under contract to the International Council for Philosophy and the Humanities, support is given to its publication *Diogene*.

Bureau of Studies and Programming

General Information Programme: Information Systems and Services.

This is an intergovernmental programme concerned with the development and promotion of information systems and services in the fields of scientific and technological information, documentation, libraries and archives at the national, regional and international levels. Its activities, including those directed to the development of UNISIST, fall into the following themes:

(i) promotion of the formulation of information policies and plans; (ii) promotion and dissemination of methods, norms and standards for information handling; (iii) contribution to the development of information infrastructures; (iv) contribution to the development of specialized information systems; (v) promotion of the training and education of information specialists and users.

Since the Intergovernmental Conference on Scientific and Technological Information for Development (UNISIST

UNESCO BUDGET

(all sources of funds)

	1979–1980 U.S. $	1981–1983 (proposed) U.S. $
General Policy and Direction:		
General Conference	4,282,000	3,441,000
Executive Board	4,661,000	5,870,000
Directorate	825,000	1,457,000
Services of the Director-General	8,430,700	17,039,000
Participation in the joint machinery of the United Nations system	691,000	994,000
Programme Operations and Services:		
Education	155,646,100	277,391,800
Natural Sciences and their Application to Development	71,578,000	198,840,000
Social Sciences and their Applications	22,568,500	40,948,500
Culture and Communication	43,725,000	78,651,000
Copyright, Information Systems and Services, Statistics	14,442,000	29,094,200
Programme Supporting Services	23,624,100	46,325,600
Co-operation for Development and External Relations	21,497,200	33,622,200
General Administrative Services	24,013,600	46,900,000
Conference, Language and Document Services	18,201,100	39,842,600
Common Services	21,638,700	41,962,000
Appropriation Reserve	13,004,000	46,408,000
Capital Expenditure	6,229,000	8,700,000
Currency Fluctuation	26,116,000	79,937,000
Reserve for Draft Resolution	—	1,000,000
TOTAL	481,173,000	998,423,900

II) and the United Nations Conference on Science and Technology for Development (UNCSTD), held in 1979, the General Information Programme has decided to attach particular importance to socio-economic information and to the special needs of developing countries. Its programme will increasingly favour a user-oriented approach, and specifically, those users taking part in the development process; the programme will endeavour to facilitate the member states' choice, use, and adaptation of advanced information and communication technology.

PUBLICATIONS

UNESCO Courier: monthly illustrated journal devoted to the general interests of UNESCO; English, French, German, Spanish, Russian, Italian, Arabic, Japanese, Hindi, Tamil, Hebrew, Portuguese, Dutch, Turkish, Persian, Urdu, Catalan, Malaysian, Korean, Kiswahili, Croato-Serb, Serbo-Croat, Macedonian, Slovene, Chinese, Bulgarian and Finnish.

UNESCO Journal of Information Science, Librarianship and Archives Administration: quarterly, containing information of use to libraries, scientific research institutes, etc.; English, French, Spanish, Russian, and Arabic.

Copyright Bulletin: quarterly review of special studies and documentation on the legislation in different countries, and on UNESCO's work on behalf of the harmonization of the various copyright laws; trilingual (English-French-Spanish).

Museum: quarterly international review of museographical techniques intended for museum specialists; English, French and Spanish.

Impact of Science on Society: quarterly reports on science as a major force for social change. Describes and predicts the consequences of scientific development for the individual, for nations and for mankind as a whole; English, French and Spanish.

International Social Science Journal: quarterly journal providing a forum for professional debate on important topics of timely significance by international panels of scholars; English, French and Spanish.

Prospects: quarterly review aimed at giving decision-makers, administrators and planners in education in UNESCO member states an opportunity to exchange experiences; also intended to serve specialists in curricula and teaching methods, directors of innovatory institutions, and young people preparing for careers in education; English, French and Spanish.

Cultures: quarterly, exploring the concept and definition of the word culture, its development and the influence of cross-cultural contacts; English, French and Spanish.

INTERNATIONAL INSTITUTE FOR EDUCATIONAL PLANNING—IIEP

7-9 rue Eugène Delacroix, 75016 Paris, France

Established by UNESCO in 1963 to serve as a world centre for advanced training and research in educational planning. Its purpose is to help all member states of UNESCO in their social and economic development efforts, by enlarging the fund of knowledge about educational planning and the supply of competent experts in this field.

Legally and administratively a part of UNESCO, the Institute enjoys intellectual autonomy, and its policies and programme are controlled by its own Governing Board, under special statutes voted by the General Conference of UNESCO.

Chairman of Governing Board: Prof. TORSTEN HUSÉN (Sweden).

Director: MICHEL DEBEAUVAIS.

Publications include *IIEP Bulletin* (quarterly) and a *Brochure* setting out the role and activities of the institute. A catalogue of publications, listing over 400 titles, is available on request.

Budget: $2,896,000.

INTERNATIONAL BUREAU OF EDUCATION—IBE

Palais Wilson, 1211 Geneva 14, Switzerland

Founded in 1925, the IBE became an intergovernmental organization in July 1929 and was incorporated into UNESCO in January 1969.

COUNCIL

The Council of the IBE is composed of representatives of 24 member states designated by the General Conference of UNESCO. These are: Bulgaria, Central African Empire, Colombia, Congo, Cuba, France, India, Japan, Jordan, Liberia, Libya, Malaysia, Mexico, Morocco, Spain, Sri Lanka, Sweden, Switzerland, Tanzania, Togo, Uganda, U.S.S.R., U.S.A., Venezuela.

Director: J. B. CHANDLER (U.S.A.).

FUNCTIONS

International Conference on Education. 38th session, 1981: on the interaction between education and productive work.

International Education Library: 60,000 volumes; some 800 journals received regularly.

International educational reporting service: provides information on educational innovations.

International Exhibition on Education.

BUDGET

Financed from the budget of UNESCO.

PUBLICATIONS

Studies and Surveys in Comparative Education, series.

Experiments and Innovations in Education, series.

Educational Documentation and Information, quarterly bulletin.

Co-operative Educational Abstracting Service, periodical issues of abstracts of educational policy documents and *Country Education Profiles*.

Innovation, newsletter, every two months alternating with bibliographical *Awareness List*.

IBEDOC information, quarterly newsletter on educational documentation.

UNITED NATIONS UNIVERSITY

Toho Seimei Building,
15-1, Shibuya 2-chome, Shibuya-ku, Tokyo 150, Japan

The University is sponsored jointly by UN and UNESCO. It is an autonomous institution within the UN framework, guaranteed academic freedom by a charter approved by the General Assembly in 1973. Work began in September 1975, financed from an Endowment Fund and operational funds to which 30 countries have contributed. The University is not traditional in the sense of having students or awarding degrees, but works through 18 networks of collaborating institutions and individuals in over 60 countries. Initially, the University's research, advanced training and knowledge dissemination activities are concentrated in the areas of hunger, human and social development, and use and management of natural resources.

Rector: SOEDJATMOKO.

Chairman of Council: Dr. INES WESLEY-TANASKOVIC.

INTERNATIONAL COUNCIL OF SCIENTIFIC UNIONS

International Council of Scientific Unions (*Conseil international des unions scientifiques*): 51 blvd. de Montmorency, 75016 Paris, France.

The ICSU was founded in 1931, succeeding the International Research Council founded in 1919, to co-ordinate international efforts in the different branches of science and its applications; to initiate the formation of international associations or unions deemed to be useful to the progress of science; to enter into relations with the governments of the countries adhering to the Council in order to promote investigations falling within the competence of the Council. Adhering organizations represent 68 countries and 18 international unions. In December 1946 an agreement was signed between UNESCO and the ICSU recognizing the latter as the co-ordinating and representative body of international scientific unions.

Pres. Prof. C. DE JAGER; Vice-Pres. Prof. D. A. BEKOE; Sec.-Gen. Sir JOHN KENDREW; Treas. Prof. T. F. MALONE; Exec. Sec. F. W. G. BAKER. Publs. *ICSU Year Book*†, *ICSU Newsletter*†.

Committee

UNION REPRESENTATIVES:

IAU	Prof. P. WAYMAN
IUGG	Prof. G. D. GARLAND
URSI	Prof. W. N. CHRISTIANSEN
IUPAC	Prof. G. SMETS
IUPAP	Prof. L. SOSNOWSKI
IGU	Prof. W. MANSHARD
IUBS	Prof. E. DE ROBERTIS
IUHPS	Dr. E. FORBES
IUCr	Prof. A. MAGNELI
IUTAM	Prof. D. C. DRUCKER
IMU	Prof. L. CARLESON
IUB	Dr. W. J. WHELAN
IUPS	Prof. A. G. B. KOVACH
IUGS	Prof. R. TRUMPY
IUPAB	Prof. R. KEYNES
IUNS	Dr. D. HOLLINGSWORTH
IUPHAR	Prof. P. G. WASER
IUIS	Prof. J. H. HUMPHREY

NATIONAL REPRESENTATIVES:

Prof. G. L. ADA	(Australia)
Prof. A. DVORETZKY	(Israel)
Prof. G. D. GARLAND	(Canada)
Prof. A. GUINIER	(France)
Prof. O. HITTMAIR	(Austria)
Prof. I. MALECKI	(Poland)
Dr. M. MOKHTAR	(Egypt)
Prof. M. NICOLET	(Belgium)
Prof. J. SAHADE	(Argentina)
Prof. G. K. SKRYABIN	(U.S.S.R.)
Dr. M. G. P. STOKER	(U.K.)
Prof. K. THURAU	(Fed. Repub. of Germany)
Prof. I. WATANABE	(Japan)

UNIONS FEDERATED TO THE ICSU

International Astronomical Union (*Union astronomique internationale*): 61 ave. de l'Observatoire, 75014 Paris, France; f. 1919. Object: to facilitate co-operation between the astronomers of various countries and to further the study of astronomy in all its branches; 49 affiliated countries, *c.* 3,800 individual members.

Pres. Prof. M. K. V. BAPPU (India); Gen. Sec. Prof. P. A. WAYMAN (Ireland). Publs. *Transactions of the International Astronomical Union and Symposia organized by the International Astronomical Union.*

International Geographical Union (IGU) (*Union géographique internationale*): f. 1923. Objects: To encourage the study of problems relating to geography, to promote and co-ordinate research requiring international co-operation, and to organize international congresses and commissions; 85 mem. countries.

Pres. Prof. MICHAEL WISE (U.K.); Sec.-Treas. Prof. WALTHER MANSHARD, Geographisches Institut, Werderring 4, D-7800 Freiburg, Fed. Repub. of Germany.

International Mathematical Union: Collège de France, 11 pl. M. Berthelot, 75231 Paris Cedex 05, France; f. 1952 by a convention of delegates of national committees representing 22 countries which met in New York. Objects: To promote international co-operation in mathematics; to support and assist the International

Congress of Mathematicians and other international scientific meetings or conferences; to encourage and support other international mathematical activities considered likely to contribute to the development of mathematical science—pure, applied, or educational; 47 mem. countries; 2 commissions: Int. Comm. on Mathematical Instruction, Comm. for Development and Exchange.

Pres. Prof. L. CARLESON; Vice-Pres. Prof. M. NAGATA, J. V. PROKHOROV; Sec.-Gen. Prof. J. L. LIONS.

International Union of Biochemistry (*Union internationale de biochimie*): c/o Dept. of Biochemistry, University of Miami, School of Medicine, P.O.B. 016129, Miami, Florida 33101, U.S.A.; f. 1955. Objects: (*a*) to encourage the continuance of a series of International Congresses of Biochemistry, (*b*) to promote international co-ordination of research, discussion and publication, (*c*) to organize a permanent co-operation between the societies representing biochemistry in the adherent countries, and (*d*) to contribute to the advancement of biochemistry in all its international aspects. Forty-three adhering bodies, two assoc. adhering bodies.

Pres. Prof. H. G. WOOD (U.S.A.); Treas. Dr. W. F. J. CUTHBERTSON (U.K.); Sec.-Gen. Prof. WILLIAM J. WHELAN (U.S.A.).

International Union of Biological Sciences (*Union internationale des sciences biologiques*): 51 blvd. de Montmorency, 75016 Paris, France; f. 1919. Object: The promotion of international co-operation in biology. Forty-nine countries are represented.

Pres. Prof. E. DE ROBERTIS (Argentina); Sec.-Gen. Prof. E. S. AYENSU (Ghana/U.S.A.).

International Union of Crystallography (*Union internationale de cristallographie*): f. 1947. Objects: To promote international co-operation in crystallography; to contribute to the advancement of crystallography in all its aspects, including related topics concerning the non-crystalline states; to facilitate international standardization of methods, of units, of nomenclature and of symbols used in crystallography; and to form a focus for the relations of crystallography to other sciences; 30 member countries; 13 Commissions.

Pres. Prof. N. KATO (Japan); Gen. Sec. and Treas. Prof. S. E. RASMUSSEN (Denmark); Exec. Sec. Dr. J. N. KING, 5 Abbey Square, Chester, CH1 2HU, England. Publs. *Acta Crystallographica*, Section A every 2 months), Section B (monthly), *Journal of Applied Crystallography* (every 2 months), *Structure Reports* (2 vols. a year), *International Tables for X-Ray Crystallography*, *World Directory of Crystallographers*, *Index of Crystallographic Supplies*, Bibliographies, etc.

International Union of Geodesy and Geophysics (*Union géodésique et géophysique internationale*): Observatoire Royal, Ave. Circulaire, Brussels, Belgium; f. 1919. Objects: to promote the study of problems relating to the form and physics of the earth; to initiate, facilitate and co-ordinate research into those problems of geodesy and geophysics which require international co-operation; to provide for discussion, comparison and publication. The Union is a federation of 7 associations representing Geodesy, Seismology and Physics of the Earth's Interior, Physical Sciences of the Ocean, Volcanology and Chemistry of the Earth's Interior, Hydrological Sciences, Meteorology and Atmospheric Physics, Geomagnetism and Aeronomy, which meet at the General Assemblies of the Union. In addition, there are Joint Committees of the various associations either among themselves or with other unions. The Union organizes scientific meetings and also sponsors various permanent services, the object of which is to collect, analyse and publish geophysical data; 78 mem. countries.

Pres. G. D. GARLAND (Canada); Vice-Pres. N. SHEBALIN (U.S.S.R.); Sec. Gen. P. MELCHIOR (Belgium). Publs. *IUGG Chronicle* (every 2 months), *IUGG Monographs* (irregular), *Proceedings of Assemblies;* in addition each member association has its own series of publications.

International Union of Geological Sciences (*Union Internationale des sciences géologiques*): 601 Booth St., Room 177, Ottawa, Ontario, Canada K1A OE8; f. 1961 as an offspring of the International Geological Congress; mems. from 86 countries.

Pres. Prof. R. TRÜMPY (Switzerland); Vice-Pres. E. ALTINLI (Turkey), J. E. CUDJOE (Ghana), J. EFTEKHAR-NEZHAD (Iran), GY. GRASSELLY (Hungary), P. F. HOWARD (Australia), V. V. MENNER (U.S.S.R.), G. P. SALAS (Mexico), T. TATSUMI (Japan); Treas. J. REINEMUND (U.S.A.); Sec.-Gen. Dr. W. W. HUTCHISON (Canada). Publs. *Episodes, Geological Newsmagazine* (quarterly), Reviews or Annotated bibliographies on geological topics of current interest (irregular).

International Union of Immunological Societies (IUIS) (*Union Internationale des Sociétés d'Immunologie*): c/o Prof. J. B. Natvig, Institute of Immunology and Rheumatology, Rikshospitalet, The National Hospital, F. Qvams gate 1, Oslo 1, Norway; f. 1969; *c.* 13,000 mems.

Pres. Dr. M. SELA (Israel); Sec.-Gen. Prof. J. NATVIG (Norway).

International Union of Nutritional Sciences (IUNS) (*Union Internationale des Sciences de la Nutrition*): c/o Prof. J. C. Somogyi, Rüschlikon, Switzerland; f. 1946; to study the science of nutrition and its applications. Mems. from 43 countries.

Pres. Prof. P. ROINE (Finland); Vice-Pres. Prof. C. DEN HARTOG (Netherlands), Prof. J. MASEK (Czechoslovakia); Sec.-Gen. Prof. J. C. SOMOGYI (Switzerland); Treas. Dr. J. A. B. SMITH (Scotland).

International Union of Pharmacology (IUPHAR) (*Union Internationale de Pharmacologie*): c/o Prof. F. Gross, Dept. of Pharmacology, University of Heidelberg, Im Neuenheimer Feld 366, 6900 Heidelberg, Federal Republic of Germany; f. 1959 as section of Int. Union of Physiological Sciences, independent 1963; promotes international co-ordination of research, discussion, symposia, and publication in the field of pharmacology; co-operates with WHO in matters concerning drugs and drug research, and with related international unions; three-yearly international congresses; 45 national and regional mem. socs.

Pres. P. G. WASER (Switzerland); Sec.-Gen. F. GROSS (Fed. Repub. of Germany).

International Union of Physiological Sciences: c/o Prof. A. G. B. KOVÁCH, Exp. Research Dept., Semmelweis Medical University, Üllői-ut 78/A, 1082 Budapest, Hungary; f. 1953 to encourage the advancement of physiological sciences; to facilitate the dissemination of knowledge in the field of physiology; to promote the International Congresses of Physiology and such other meetings as may be useful for the advancement of physiological sciences; 51 mem. countries. Next Congress Sydney, 1983.

Pres. Prof. E. NEIL (U.K.); Sec. Prof. A. G. B. KOVÁCH (Hungary); Treas. Prof. J. M. BROOKHART (U.S.A.). Publs. *Newsletter* (annually), *World Directory of Physiologists* (every 3 years).

International Union of Pure and Applied Biophysics: Institute of Molecular Biology and Biophysics, ETH-Hönggerberg, CH-8093 Zurich, Switzerland; f. 1961. Aims: to organize international co-operation in biophysics and promote communication between biophysics and allied subjects, to encourage national co-operation between biophysical societies, and to contribute to the advancement of biophysical knowledge. Mems.: national bodies in 36 countries.

Pres. S. Ebashi (Japan); Sec.-Gen. K. Wüthrich (Switzerland). Publs. *Quarterly Reviews of Biophysics.*

International Union of Pure and Applied Chemistry—IUPAC (*Union internationale de chimie pure et appliquée*): Bank Court Chambers, 2-3 Pound Way, Cowley Centre, Oxford, OX4 3YF, England; f. 1919; Objects: to promote continuing co-operation among the chemists of the member countries; to study topics of international importance which require regulation, standardization or codification; to co-operate with other international organizations which deal with topics of a chemical nature; to contribute to the advancement of pure and applied chemistry in all its aspects; 42 member countries.

Pres. Prof. H. Zollinger (Switzerland); Sec.-Gen. Prof. G. Ourisson (France); Hon. Treas. Dr. W. Graulich (Fed. Rep. of Germany). Publs. *Pure and Applied Chemistry* (12 a year), *Chemistry International* (6 a year).

International Union of Pure and Applied Physics (*Union internationale de physique pure et appliquée*): f. 1922; Object: to promote and encourage international co-operation in physics. Thirty-nine countries are affiliated; 17 international commissions.

Pres. Prof. L. Sosnowski; Sec.-Gen. Prof. Larkin Kerwin, Univ. Laval, Quebec, G1K 7P4, Canada. Publ. *IUPAP News Bulletin* (5 or 6 a year).

International Union of Radio Science (*Union radio-scientifique internationale*): 81 rue de Nieuwenhove, 1180 Brussels; f. 1919. Objects: to develop scientific studies connected with radio science and especially (*a*) to promote and organize research necessitating international co-operation, and to facilitate the discussion and publication of the results of this research, (*b*) to facilitate the establishment of common radio measurement techniques and standards and (*c*) to stimulate and co-ordinate studies of the scientific aspects of telecommunications using electromagnetic waves. There are 36 national committees.

Pres. W. N. Christiansen (Australia); Sec.-Gen. J. Van Bladel (Belgium). Publs. *Proceedings of General Assemblies of the URSI*, *Information Bulletin* (quarterly), *Review of Radio Science.*

International Union of the History and Philosophy of Science: f. 1954 to promote research into the history and philosophy of science, to organize international congresses, and to co-operate with the other members of ICSU. Two divisions:

Division of the History of Science: Dept. of History, University of Edinburgh, Edinburgh, Scotland; Pres. Prof. A. T. Grigorian (U.S.S.R.); Sec. Prof. E. G. Forbes (U.K.).

Division of Logic, Methodology and Philosophy of Science: Queen's College, Oxford, U.K.; Pres. Prof. J. Łos (Poland); Sec. L. J. Cohen (U.K.).

International Union of Theoretical and Applied Mechanics (*Union internationale du mécanique théorique et appliquée*): c/o Chalmers University of Technology, S-41296 Gothenburg, Sweden; f. 1947; to form a link between persons and organizations engaged in scientific work (theoretical or experimental) in mechanics or in related sciences; to organize international meetings for subjects falling within this field; and to engage in other activities meant to promote the development of mechanics as a science; 33 mem. countries. The Union is directed by its General Assembly, which is composed of representatives of the organizations adhering and affiliated to the Union and of elected members.

Pres. Prof. F. I. Niordson (Denmark); Vice-Pres. Prof. H. Gortler (Fed. Rep. of Germany); Sec. Prof. J. Hult (Sweden).

Committees

Tasks which fall within the sphere of activities of two or more Unions have been undertaken by the following Scientific or Special Committees set up by the ICSU:

Committee on Data for Science and Technology (CODATA): f. 1966 by ICSU to improve the quality, reliability and accessibility of scientific data, including not only quantitative information on the properties and behaviour of matter, but also other experimental and observational data.

Pres. Prof. Masao Kotani (Japan); Secretariat: Phyllis Glaeser, 51 blvd. de Montmorency, 75016 Paris, France. Publs. *CODATA Newsletter*† (2 a year), *CODATA Bulletin*† (irregular), *International Compendium of Numerical Data Projects, International Conference Proceedings.*

Committee on Science and Technology for the Developing Countries (COSTED): f. 1966 (reconstituted 1972) for the encouragement of science and technology in developing countries, the organization of meetings, seminars and symposia related to science teaching and natural resources, and the identification of problems of relevance to developing countries. Mems.: 30 national mems., 23 corresponding and 9 individuals.

Pres. Prof. Y. Nayudamma (India); Sec. Dr. S. Radhakrishna, Dept. of Physics, Indian Institute of Technology, Madras 600036, India.

Committee on Space Research (COSPAR): 51 blvd. de Montmorency, 75016 Paris, France; f. 1958 to continue and foster, after the end of IGY, international co-operation in all sciences that make use of the new research tools of rockets, satellites and balloons.

Pres. Prof. J. F. Denisse (France); Vice-Pres. Acad. R. Z. Sagdeev (U.S.S.R.), Prof. L. E. Peterson (U.S.A.); Sec. Z. Niemirowicz. Publs. *COSPAR Information Bulletin, International Reference Atmosphere Tables, COSPAR Transactions Series, COSPAR Technique Manual Series, Proceedings of COSPAR Meetings.*

Committee on the Teaching of Science (CTS): f. 1961 as *Commission on Science Teaching*, superseded in 1969. Aims to promote activities related to science teaching at school and university level; 24 mems., including reps. from 15 unions federated to ICSU.

Chair. Prof. C. A. Taylor; Sec. J. L. Lewis, Malvern College, Malvern, Worcs., U.K. Publ. *Newsletter.*

ICSU-UATI Coordinating Committee on Water Research: 51 blvd. de Montmorency, 75016 Paris, France; f. 1964 as Scientific Cttee. on Water Research (COWAR,) name changed 1977; to consider the problem of international water resources in all its aspects, and to act as adviser on behalf of ICSU to UNESCO and other international bodies on problems pertaining to the International Hydrological Programme.

Pres. Prof. J. C. I. Dooge (Ireland); Sec. Prof. E. Plate (Fed. Rep. of Germany).

Scientific Committee on Antarctic Research (SCAR): f. 1958 after the close of the International Geophysical Year to continue the promotion of international co-operation in scientific research in the Antarctic. Mems.: 14 countries.

Pres. Prof. G. A. Knox; Vice-Pres. G. R. Laclavere; Sec. Dr. G. A. Avsiuk; Exec. Sec. G. E. Hemmen, Scott Polar Research Institute, Cambridge, CB2 1ER, England. Publ. *SCAR Bulletin* (3 times a year).

Scientific Committee on Oceanic Research (SCOR): f. 1957 to further international scientific activity in all branches of oceanic research; scientific advisory body to UNESCO and to Intergovernmental Oceanographic Commission. Mems.: Nominated Mems. by Nat. Cttees.

for Oceanic Research; Rep. Mems. of Affiliated Organizations; Invited Mems. by the Exec. Cttee.

Pres. Dr. K. N. FEDOROV (U.S.S.R.); Sec. Prof. H. CHARNOCK, Dept. of Oceanography, University of Southampton, Southampton, England. Publ. *SCOR Proceedings* (irregular).

Scientific Committee on Problems of the Environment (SCOPE): 51 blvd. de Montmorency, 75016 Paris, France; Pres. Prof. G. F. WHITE (U.S.A.).

SERVICES AND INTER-UNION COMMISSIONS

ICSU Abstracting Board: f. 1952 to organize and promote internationally the exchange and dissemination of information by secondary processing services in science and technology and to deal with matters related thereto. Member Countries: Belgium, France, South Africa, U.K., U.S.A. Member Unions: Int. Astronomical Union, Int. Union of Biological Sciences, Int. Union of Crystallography, Int. Union of Geological Sciences, Int. Union of Pure and Applied Chemistry, Int. Union of Pure and Applied Physics. Member Services: American Geological Institute, American Institute of Physics, Astronomy and Astro-physics Abstracts, British Library, Bulletin Signalétique-Bibliographie des Sciences de la Terre, Biosis, Cancernet-Sabir, Centre de Documentation des Industries Utilisatrices de Produits Agricoles, Chemical Abstracts Service, Chemie Information und Dokumentation/Berlin, Engineering Index Inc., ESRIN, Excerpta Medica, Instituto de Información y Documentación en Ciencia y Tecnologia, Informascience, INIS (IAEA), Inspec, Institute for Scientific Information, Japan Information Centre of Science and Technology, Physikalische Berichte, Psychological Abstracts, Referativnyi Zhurnal, U.K. Chemical Information Service, U.S. Dept. of Energy, U.S. National Library of Medicine, U.S. National Technical Information Service, Zentralblatt für Mathematik, Zoological Record.

Pres. Dr. M. DAY (U.S.A.); Secretariat: Miss MARTHE ORFUS, 51 blvd. de Montmorency, 75016 Paris, France. Publs. Lists, Reports, proceedings of meetings.

Federation of Astronomical and Geophysical Services (FAGS): f. 1956; federates the following Permanent Services: International Time Bureau, International Polar Motion Service, Permanent Service of Geomagnetic Indices, International Gravimetric Bureau, Quarterly Bulletin of Solar Activity, International Centre on Earth Tides, International Ursigram and World Days Service, Permanent Service on Mean Sea-Level, Permanent Service on the Fluctuation of Glaciers.

Pres. Dr. H. ENSLIN (Germany); Sec. Dr. C. BOUCHER, Institut Géographique National, Service de Géodésie, Nivellement et Métrologie, 2 ave. Pasteur, 94160 St.-Mandé, France.

Publs. *Quarterly Bulletin of Solar Activity, Tables of Geomagnetic Indices, Bulletin Mensuel du Bureau Central International de Séismologie, Bulletin Horaire*, etc.

Inter-Union Commission on Frequency Allocations for Radio Astronomy and Space Science (IUCAF): f. 1960 under auspices of URSI with representatives of URSI, IAU and COSPAR, to study the requirements for frequency bands and radio frequency protection for research in the fields of radio astronomy and space science, to make their requirements known to the appropriate frequency-allocation authorities.

Sec. Dr. F. HORNER, 10 Clarence Drive, Egham, Surrey TW20 0NL, England.

Inter-Union Commission on Radio Meteorology (IUCRM): f. 1959 by IUGG and URSI, to further the study of those aspects of meteorology and oceanography which affect the propagation of electromagnetic waves and the application of radio techniques to meteorology.

Pres. Dr. S. WICKERTS; Sec. Dr. J. C. KAIMAL, NOAA/WPL, Boulder, Colo. 80302, U.S.A.

Inter-Union Commission on Spectroscopy (IUCS): Chair. Prof. A. R. H. COLE, University of Western Australia, Nedlands, W A. 6009.

Inter-Union Commission on Solar and Terrestrial Physics (IUCSTP): *Ad hoc* committee founded in 1966 to co-ordinate symposia and programmes in the field of solar-terrestrial physics; 28 mems.

Pres. Dr. H. FRIEDMAN (U.S.A.); Secretariat: Dr. E. R. DYER, IUCSTP Office, National Academy of Sciences, 2101 Constitution Ave., Washington D.C. 20418, U.S.A. Publ. *STP Notes*.

INTERNATIONAL COUNCIL FOR PHILOSOPHY AND HUMANISTIC STUDIES

International Council for Philosophy and Humanistic Studies (ICPHS) (*Conseil international de la philosophie et des sciences humaines*): Secretariat: Maison de l'UNESCO, 1 rue Miollis, 75732 Paris Cedex 15, France; f. 1949 under the auspices of UNESCO to encourage respect for cultural autonomy by the comparative study of civilization, to contribute towards international understanding through a better knowledge of man, to develop international co-operation in philosophy, humanistic and kindred studies, to encourage the setting up of international organizations, to promote the dissemination of information in these fields, to sponsor works of learning, etc. The Council is composed of 13 international non-governmental organizations listed below. These organizations represent 130 countries. In 1951 an agreement was signed between UNESCO and ICPHS recognizing the latter as the co-ordinating and representative body of organizations in the field of philosophy and humanistic studies.

Pres. STANLEY C. ASTON (U.K.); Vice-Pres. J. BIALOSTOCKI (Poland), M. C. S. DISKUL (Thailand), A. KAGAME (Rwanda), J. M. KITAGAWA (U.S.A.), GRACIELA DE LA LAMA (Mexico), A. MERCIER (Switzerland); Sec.-Gen. JEAN D'ORMESSON (France); Treas. S. J. DE LAET (Belgium). Publs. *Bulletin of Information*† (biennially), *Diogenes* (quarterly).

UNIONS FEDERATED TO THE ICPHS

International Academic Union (*Union académique internationale*): Palais des Académies, 1 rue Ducale, Brussels, Belgium; f. 1919. Object: to promote international co-operation through collective research in philology, archaeology, history and political and social sciences. Affiliated countries: Australia, Austria, Belgium, Canada, China, Czechoslovakia, Denmark, Finland, France, Fed. Repub. of Germany, German Democratic Repub., Ghana, Greece, Hungary, India, Iran, Ireland, Israel, Italy, Japan, Repub. of Korea, Mexico, The Netherlands, Norway, Poland, Romania, Spain, Sweden, Switzerland, Turkey, U.K., U.S.A. and Yugoslavia.

Pres. M. CAGIANO DE AZEVEDO (Italy); Vice-Pres. E. CONDURACHI, T. YAMAMOTO; Admin. Sec. M. LEROY (Belgium). Publs. Dictionaries of International Law and Medieval Latin, *Monumenta Musicae Byzantinae*, Historical Documents concerning Japan, *Corpus Vasorum Antiquorum, Corpus Philosophorum, Corpus Vitrearum, Dictionnaire Pâli, Corpus des Troubadours*, etc.

International Association for the History of Religions (*Association internationale pour l'histoire des religions*): f. 1950 by the 7th International Congress for the Study of the History of Religions. Object: to promote the study of the history of religions through the international collaboration of all scholars whose research has a bearing on the subject, to organize congresses and to stimulate the production of works. Twenty member countries.

Pres. M. SIMON (France); Sec.-Gen. Prof. Z. WERBLOWSKY, Hebrew University of Jerusalem, Jerusalem, Israel.

International Committee of Historical Sciences (*Comité international des sciences historiques*): Union Bank of Switzerland, Lausanne, Switzerland; f. 1926; int. congresses since 1900 to work for the advancement of historical sciences by means of international coordination. Mems. in 50 countries. General assembly every two or three years.

Sec.-Gen. MICHEL FRANÇOIS (France), 270 Boulevard Raspail, 75014 Paris. Publs. Congress Reports, *Bulletin d'Information* (1953–80), *Bibliographie Internationale des Sciences Historiques* (1929–39, 1946–78), *World List of Historical Periodicals and Bibliographies, Bibliographie des travaux parus en Mélanges*, Vol. I, 1885–1939, Vol. II Supplement 1940–50, *Bibliographie de la Réforme, Histoire des Assemblées d'Etat, Répertoire des sources de l'Histoire des Mouvements Sociaux, Guia de las Personas que cultivan la Historia de America, Repertorium der diplomatischen Vertreter aller Länder, Excerpta Historica Nordica, Bibliographie internationale de l'Humanisme et de la Renaissance, Elenchus fontium historiae urbanae, Bibliographie internationale de l'histoire des Universités, de l'histoire des villes, Guide international d'histoire urbaine, Bibliographie de l'histoire des routes maritimes*, etc.

International Committee on the History of Art (*Comité international d'histoire de l'art*): Institut d'Art et d'Archéologie, 3 rue Michelet, 75006 Paris, France; f. 1930 by the 12th International Congress on the History of Art. Object: collaboration in the scientific study of the history of art. Mems. in 28 countries. International congress every five years; international symposium every two years.

Pres. Prof. GIULIO-CARLO ARGAN (Italy); Sec.-Gen. Prof. JACQUES THUILLIER (France); Treas. and Admin. Sec. Prof. ALFRED A. SCHMID (Switzerland). Publs. *Bulletin du CIHA, Corpus international des vitraux du Moyen Age, Répertoire d'Art et d'Archéologie* (quarterly).

International Congress of Africanists (*Congrès International des Africanistes*): f. 1900. Object: to develop international co-operation in the field of African Studies through periodic meetings and publications, to organize and promote research on an international basis and to serve as a body which shall encourage Africans to have a growing consciousness of their membership of the human race and to express themselves in all fields of human endeavour. The third Congress was held in 1972 at Addis Ababa, Ethiopia.

Pres. Mgr. T. TSHIBANGU-TSHISHIKU (Zaïre); Sec.-Gen. V. Y. MUDIMBE, Université Nationale du Zaïre, B.P. 1944, Lubumbashi, Zaire. Publ. *Proceedings of the Third International Congress of Africanists* (in English and French).

International Federation of Modern Languages and Literatures (*Fédération internationale des langues et littératures modernes*): Université de Provence, Centre d'Aix, 29 ave. Robert Schuman, 13100 Aix-en-Provence, France; f. 1928 as the International Committee on Modern Literary History; changed to its present form in 1951. Objects: to establish permanent contact between historians of literature, to develop or perfect facilities for their work and to promote the study of the history of modern literature. Nineteen member associations, with members in 92 countries. Congress every three years.

Pres. GEORGE WINCHESTER STONE (U.S.A.); Sec.-Gen. ANDRÉ M. ROUSSEAU (France). Publs. *Répertoire Chronologique des littératures modernes, Acts of the Triennial Congresses.*

International Federation of Philosophical Societies (*Fédération internationale des sociétés de philosophie—FISP*): f. 1948 under the auspices of UNESCO. Object: to encourage international co-operation in the field of philosophy, and to promote congresses, symposia and publications; 84 mem. societies from 40 countries and 15 international mem. societies.

Pres. A. DIEMER (Fed. Repub. of Germany); Sec.-Gen. ANDRÉ MERCIER, Universität Bern, Institut für exakte Wissenschaften, 3012 Bern, Sidlersstrasse 5, Switzerland; Publs. Under the auspices of FISP: *Proceedings of the International Congresses of Philosophy, An International Bibliography of Philosophy, Chroniques de Philosophie, Philosophers on their own work*, etc.

International Federation of the Societies of Classical Studies (*Fédération internationale des associations d'études classiques*): c/o Prof. F. Paschoud, 26 rue de Vermont, 1202 Geneva, Switzerland; f. 1948 under the auspices of UNESCO. Objects: to encourage research concerning the ancient civilizations of Greece and Rome; to group the main national associations so engaged; to ensure collaboration with relevant international organizations. Mems.: 58 societies in 34 countries; affiliated bodies include the International Society for Classical Bibliography, International Society for Classical Archaeology, International Society for Byzantine Studies, International Association for Latin Epigraphy, International Association of Papyrologists, Unione internazionale degli Istituti di Archeologia, Storia e Storia dell' Arte in Roma, Société d'histoire des droits de l'antiquité, Comité international des Etudes mycéniennes, Association internationale des Etudes patristiques, etc.

Pres. Prof. W. SCHMID (Fed. Repub. of Germany); Sec. Prof. F. PASCHOUD (Switzerland). Publs. *L'Année Philologique, Thesaurus linguae Latinae* and other reference works.

International Musicological Society (*Société internationale de musicologie*): f. 1927. Object: to promote musicological research, to encourage study in this field and to co-ordinate the work of musicologists throughout the world. Forty member countries.

Pres. LUDWIG FINSCHER (Fed. Repub. of Germany); Sec.-Gen. RUDOLF HÄUSLER, Case postale 1561, CH 4001 Basle, Switzerland. Publs. An International Repertory of Musical Sources, *Acta Musicologica, Documenta Musicologica, Catalogus Musicus, RILM, RIDIM.*

International Permanent Committee of Linguists (*Comité international permanent des linguistes*): f. 1928. Object: to work for the advancement of linguistics throughout the world and to encourage international co-operation in this field. Thirty-nine member countries.

Pres. Prof. R. H. ROBINS (U.K.); Sec.-Gen. Prof. E. M. UHLENBECK, Stationsplein 10, Leiden, The Netherlands. Publ. *Linguistic Bibliography* (annually).

International Union of Anthropological and Ethnological Sciences: see under ISSC.

International Union for Oriental and Asian Studies (*Union internationale des études orientales et asiatiques*): f. 1951 as the International Union of Orientalists under the auspices of UNESCO, name changed 1973. Object: to promote contacts between orientalists throughout the world, and to organize congresses, research and publications. Twenty-six member countries.

Pres. R. N. DANDEKAR; Sec.-Gen. L. BAZIN, 77 quai du Port-au-Fouarre, 94100 Saint-Maur, France. Publs. four oriental bibliographies, *Philologiae Turcicae Fundamenta, Materialien zum Sumerischen Lexickon, Sanskrit Dictionary, Corpus Inscriptionum Iranicarum, Linguistic Atlas of Iran, Matériels des parlers iraniens, Bibliographie Egyptologique*, etc.

International Union of Prehistoric and Protohistoric Sciences (*Union internationale des sciences préhistoriques et protohistoriques*): f. 1931. Object: to promote congresses and scientific work in the fields of Pre- and Protohistory. Eighty-eight member countries.

Pres. L. BALOUT (France); Sec.-Gen. O. KLINDT-JENSEN, Moesgaard, Højbjerg, Denmark. Publs. *Inventaria archaeologica, Archaeologia urbium*, etc.

INTERNATIONAL SOCIAL SCIENCE COUNCIL

International Social Science Council—ISSC (*Conseil International des Sciences Sociales — CISS*): Maison de l'UNESCO, 1 rue Miollis, 75015 Paris, France; f. 1952. Aims: the advancement of the social sciences throughout the world and their application to the major problems of the world; the spread of co-operation at an international level between specialists in the social sciences. ISSC has Standing Committees for: comparative research, problems of the environment, conceptual and terminological analysis (COCTA, est. in co-operation with IPSA and ISA), and Commissions on: world models, urban networks, world-social science development. It also has two permanent exterior bodies, the European Co-ordination Centre for Research and Documentation in the Social Sciences, in Vienna, f. 1963 (Pres. of Board of Dirs. A. SCHAFF) and the International Centre for Intergroup Relations, in Paris, f. 1965 in collaboration with the Ecole Pratique des Hautes Etudes, Paris (Dir. O. KLINEBERG).

Pres. A. SUMMERFIELD (U.K.); Vice-Pres. L. P. VIDYARTHI (India), V. A. VINOGRADOV (U.S.S.R.); Sec.-Gen. S. FRIEDMAN. Publs. *Social Science Information/Information sur les Sciences Sociales* (6 a year), *Newsletter* (3 a year).

ASSOCIATIONS FEDERATED TO THE ISSC

International Association of Legal Sciences (*Association internationale des sciences juridiques*): c/o ISSC, Unesco, 1 rue Miollis, 75015 Paris, France; f. 1950 to promote the mutual knowledge and understanding of nations and the increase of learning by encouraging throughout the world the study of foreign legal systems and the use of the comparative method in legal science. Governed by a President and an executive bureau of ten members known as the International Committee of Comparative Law. National committees in 46 countries.

Pres. V. O. REINIKAINEN (Finland); Vice-Pres. J. G. FLEMING (U.S.A.), M. CAPPELLETI (Italy); Sec.-Gen. S. FRIEDMAN (France); Dir. of Scientific Research Prof. H. KÖTZ (Fed. Repub. of Germany).

International Economic Association (*Association internationale des sciences économiques*): 4 rue de Chevreuse, 75006 Paris, France; f. 1949 to promote international collaboration for the advancement of economic knowledge and develop personal contacts between economists, and to encourage provision of means for the dissemination of economic knowledge. Member associations in 49 countries.

Pres. Prof. S. TSURU (Japan); Vice-Pres. F. MODIGLIANI (U.S.A.); Sec.-Gen. Prof. L. FAUVEL (France); Treas. Prof. H. GIERSCH (Fed. Repub. of Germany).

International Federation of Social Science Organizations (*Fédération internationale des organisations de science sociale*): c/o Dr. E. B. Andersen, Forskning Sekretariatet, Holmens Kanal 7, Copenhagen, Denmark; f. 1979 to succeed the Conference of National Social Science Councils and Analogous Bodies (f. 1975) to further the exchange of information, experience and ideas among its member organizations, to contribute to the more effective organization of research and teaching and to institution-building in the social sciences, and to facilitate co-operation and enlist mutual assistance in the planning and evaluation of programmes of major importance to members. 40 members.

Pres. G. ABAD (Ecuador); Sec. Gen. E. B. ANDERSEN (Denmark). Publs. *Newsletter, Directory of Social Science Councils and Analogous Bodies*.

International Geographical Union: see under ICSU.

International Institute of Administrative Sciences (*Institut international des sciences administratives*): 25 rue de la Charité, 1040 Brussels, Belgium; f. 1930; Objects: comparative examination of administrative experience in the various countries; research and programmes for improving administrative law and practices and for technical assistance. Mems.: 50 mem. states, 35 National Sections, corporate and individual members; library of 8,000 vols.; consultative status with UN and UNESCO; international congresses; special programme for schools and institutes of public administration; working groups on informatics and administration; working group on public works; working group on integrated budgeting systems; standing committees on law and science of public administration, administrative structures and management, personnel administration, planning and forecasting, public enterprise.

Pres. LAUREANO LÓPEZ RODÓ (Spain); Dir.-Gen. GUY BRAIBANT (France); Treas. CHARLES WATHOUR (Belgium). Publs. *International Review of Administrative Sciences* (quarterly), reports, readers, bibliographies.

International Law Association: 3 Paper Buildings, The Temple, London, E.C.4, England; f. 1873. Objects; study and advancement of international law, public and private; the promotion of international understanding and goodwill. 44 regional branches, *c.* 5,000 mems., 13 scientific cttees.

Pres. Prof. E. SYQUIA (Philippines); Chair. Exec. Council Lord WILBERFORCE, C.M.G., O.B.E.; Sec.-Gen. JOHN B. S. EDWARDS. Publs. Reports of biennial conferences.

International Peace Research Association (*Association Internationale de recherche pour la paix*): c/o Dr. Y. Sakamoto, Faculty of Law, Univ. of Tokyo, Bunkyo-ku, Tokyo 113, Japan; f. 1964, to encourage the development of interdisciplinary research into the conditions of peace and the causes of war; mems.: individuals (240 in 35 countries), research institutes (56 in 25 countries), national asscns. (6).

Sec.-Gen. Y. SAKAMOTO (Japan). Publs. *IPRA Newsletter, Conference Proceedings, Handbook on Peace Education.*

International Political Science Association (IPSA) (*Association Internationale de Science Politique*): c/o University of Ottawa, Ottawa, KIN 6N5, Canada; f. 1949; encourages national associations throughout the world, undertakes research and documentation, holds yearly round-table conferences and triennial congresses. Mems.: national asscns. in 36 countries, 91 associates, 690 individuals.

Pres. C. MENDES (Brazil); Sec.-Gen. J. E. TRENT (Canada). Publs. *Newsletter, International Political Science Abstracts* (bi-monthly), *International Bibliography of Political Science.*

International Sociological Association (*Association internationale de sociologie*): P.O.B. 719, Station "A", Montreal, Quebec, H3C 2V2, Canada; f. 1949; aims to promote sociological research, to develop personal contacts among the sociologists of all countries and to ensure the exchange of sociological information. To attain its aims the ISA has established 42 research committees on a wide variety of sociological topics; holds World Congresses every four years.

Pres. ULF HIMMELSTRAND (Sweden); Exec. Sec. M. RAFIE (Canada), K. JONASSOHN (Canada). Publs. *Current Sociology/Sociologie Contemporaine*† (3 a year), *World Congresses Transactions, Sage Studies in International Sociology, ISA Bulletin.*

International Union of Psychological Science (*Union internationale de psychologie scientifique*): f. 1951 at the thirteenth International Congress of Psychology (the first of which took place in 1889); congresses are held every four years. Membership: 40 national societies.

Pres. F. KLIX (German Democratic Repub.); Vice-Pres. M. ROZENSWEIG (U.S.A.), T. TOMASZEWSKI (Poland); Sec.-Gen. WAYNE H. HOLTZMAN, Hogg Foundation for Mental Health, University of Texas, Austin, Texas 78712, U.S.A.

International Union of Anthropological and Ethnological Sciences (*Union internationale des sciences anthropologiques et ethnologiques*): f. 1948 under the auspices of UNESCO. Object: to foster research and co-operation among anthropological and ethnological institutions. Mems.: 4 int. organizations, national and int. organizations in 59 countries. Also federated to ICPHS.

Pres. Prof. C. S. BELSHAW (Canada); Sec.-Gen. Dr. E. SUNDERLAND, Dept. of Anthropology, University of Durham, Durham DH1 3TG, England.

International Union for the Scientific Study of Population (*Union internationale pour l'étude scientifique de la population*): rue Forgeur 5, B-4000 Liège, Belgium; f. 1928, reconstituted 1947; to advance the progress of quantitative and qualitative demography as a science. Mems.: *c.* 1,380 scientists in 103 countries.

Pres. A. J. COALE (U.S.A.); Sec.-Gen. and Treas. M. LIVI-BACCI (Italy); Exec. Sec. B. REMICHE (Belgium). Publs. *Proceedings of the International Population Conference, Mexico City, 1977, IUSSP Newsletter, IUSSP Papers,* etc.

World Association for Public Opinion Research (*Association mondiale pour l'étude de l'opinion publique*): c/o Institut für Demoskopie Allensbach, 7753 Allensmach am Bodensee, Fed. Repub. of Germany; f. 1947 to establish and promote contacts between persons in the field of survey research on opinions, attitudes and behaviour of people in the various countries of the world; to further the use of objective, scientific survey research in national and international affairs. Mems.: 486 individuals in 26 countries.

Pres. E. NOELLE-NEUMANN (Fed. Rep. of Germany); Treas. P. H. VAN WESTENDORP (Netherlands).

World Federation for Mental Health (*Fédération mondiale pour la Santé Mentale*): 2255 Wesbrook Crescent, University of British Columbia, Vancouver, B.C. V6T 2A1, Canada; f. 1948. Objects: to promote among all people and nations the highest possible standard of mental health in the broadest biological, medical, educational, and social aspects; to work with ECOSOC, UNESCO, the World Health Organization, and other agencies of the United Nations, in so far as they promote mental health; to help other voluntary associations in the improvement of mental health services; and to further the establishment of better human relations.

Pres. GOWAN T. GUEST (Canada); Exec. Dir. R. L. BEISER (Canada). Publs. *Bulletin* (quarterly), *Annual Report.*

AUTONOMOUS CENTRES OF ISSC

European Co-ordination Centre for Research and Documentation in Social Sciences (*Centre Européen de Coordination de Recherche et de Documentation en Sciences Sociales*): Grünangergasse 2, A-1010 Vienna, Austria; f. 1963. Aims: to facilitate contacts and exchanges among researchers in the social sciences from the various European countries, having different socio-economic structures and political systems, the proposal and co-ordination of comparative multi-disciplinary research carried out by various competent research bodies—principally European but also from outside Europe. Administered by a Board of Directors and a Permanent Secretariat.

Pres. A. SCHAFF (Poland); Vice-Pres. H. FRIIS (Denmark); Dir. S. C. MILLS (U.K.). Publ. *Vienna Centre Newsletter.*

International Center for Intergroup Relations (*Centre international d'études des relations entre groupes ethniques*): 54 blvd. Raspail, 75270 Paris Cedex 06, France; f. 1965 jointly with the *Ecole des Hautes Etudes en Sciences Sociales.* It carries out surveys on intergroup relations on an international scale and on a cross-cultural basis.

Dir. O. KLINEBERG (U.S.A.).

INTERNATIONAL ASSOCIATION OF UNIVERSITIES—IAU

1 rue Miollis, 75732 Paris Cedex 15, France

Founded 1950 to promote practical academic co-operation and to assist university institutions throughout the world. Members: 717 universities and institutions of higher learning in 118 countries; 8 associate members (international university organizations).

ORGANIZATION

GENERAL CONFERENCE

Composed of the full and associate members and meets at least every five years. Discusses topics of special importance for the future of university education, determines general policy and elects the President and members of the Administrative Board.

MEETINGS	
Nice	1950
Istanbul	1955
Mexico City	1960
Tokyo	1965
Montreal	1970
Moscow	1975
Seventh General Conference: Manila,	1980

ADMINISTRATIVE BOARD

Composed of the President and eighteen other members. Meets annually. Gives effect to decisions of the General Conference and directs the work of the secretariat.

President (1975–80): ROGER GAUDRY, fmr. Rector, University of Montreal, Canada.

Vice-President (1975–80): K. L. SHRIMALI, fmr. Vice-Chancellor, Banaras Hindu University, India.

SECRETARIAT

The permanent secretariat of the Association, the International Universities Bureau, is responsible for the execution of its working programme and the administration of its affairs.

Secretary-General: D. J. AITKEN (U.K.).

PRINCIPAL ACTIVITIES

Documentation and Information: The secretariat is a source of information on higher education throughout the world. Its reference library of published and unpublished material in many languages is probably unique of its kind. An extensive network of contacts with national and international bodies, academic and governmental, facilitates the international exchange of information.

Research and Studies: These activities are most closely related to the themes of the General Conferences in an attempt to contribute in an international setting to the classification and resolution of major problems of higher educational policy. Since 1960 special efforts in this field have been concentrated in the Joint UNESCO-IAU Research Programme in Higher Education. In 1970 a new series of international seminars was inaugurated to promote the study of selected problems connected with the role of universities in the modern world.

Publications Programme: A quarterly Bulletin provides a chronicle of university affairs in all parts of the world. A series of reference works published at regular intervals gives detailed information about university institutions and organizations concerned with higher education. Special reports and issues in the series of "Papers" of the Association are devoted to select research themes and studies.

BUDGET

Annual expenditure amounts to approximately $510,000 excluding expenditure from special grants for the Joint UNESCO-IAU research programme.

SELECTED PUBLICATIONS

Bulletin of the International Association of Universities (English and French; quarterly).

International Handbook of Universities (English; every three years—8th edition, 1980).

World List of Universities, Other Institutions of Higher Education and University Organizations (English and French; every two years—14th edition, 1979).

The Social Responsibility of the University in Asian Countries (English and French editions).

Differing Types of Higher Education (English and French editions).

Higher Education and Development in South East Asia (English and French editions, published jointly with UNESCO).

New Methods of Teaching and Learning (English and French editions, published jointly with UNESCO).

Lifelong Education and University Resources (English and French editions, published jointly with UNESCO).

The Role of the University in Developing Countries: Its Responsibility toward the Natural and Cultural Environment (English and French editions).

OTHER INTERNATIONAL ORGANIZATIONS

AGRICULTURE

Food and Agriculture Organization of the United Nations (*Organisation des Nations Unies pour l'Alimentation et l'Agriculture*): Via delle Terme di Caracalla, Rome, Italy; f. 1945; Objects: to raise level of nutrition and living standards, improve production and distribution of food and agricultural products (including forestry and fishing), and better the conditions of rural populations. Its functions include the collection, collation and dissemination of information in its fields of interest, the encouragement and servicing of international consultation and the provision of technical advisers to help countries plan their economic development and eliminate impediments to it. Its wide-ranging field programme reaches into 128 countries, with over 2,800 projects; $222 million was invested in field activities during 1979. Main components of this total were $129 million from the UN Development Programme, $77 million from various trust funds expended on behalf of governments and other agencies, and $16 million under the Technical Co-operation Programme financed from FAO's own budget of $278,740,000 for the two years 1980–81. FAO is also playing an active role in mobilizing capital for agricultural development through its co-operative programmes with financing institutions. In 1978, FAO's Investment Centre sent out 214 missions to help 72 developing countries draw up investment projects, and 42 projects prepared with the Centre's help resulted in total investments of $3,800 million. Of the total amount of $13,000 of projects formulated by the Investment Centre and approved by financing institutions since 1965, nearly half was approved since 1977. With over 6,300 employees, FAO is the largest UN specialized agency. About 70 per cent of the nearly 4,000 professional staff members are at work in the field projects. A recent decentralization programme is strengthening FAO's work at the country level and includes the opening of offices in 60 developing countries. The FAO David Lubin Library holds 10,000 vols. and 10,000 periodicals.

Dir.-Gen. EDOUARD SAOUMA (Lebanon). Publs. *The State of Food and Agriculture* (annually), *Unasylva, World Animal Review* (quarterly), *Bulletin of Agricultural Economics and Statistics, FAO Documentation Current Bibliography* (monthly), *Plant Protection Bulletin, Ceres* (every 2 months), Yearbooks of Trade and Production in Agriculture, Forestry and Fisheries, and *c.* 1,000 specialized technical studies.

Commonwealth Agricultural Bureaux: Farnham House, Farnham Royal, Slough, Berks., SL2 3BN; f. in 1929 by agreement among the Governments of the British Commonwealth to act as effective clearing-houses for the interchange of information of value to research workers in agricultural sciences and forestry; each Bureau is an information service for scientists throughout the world; there are in all 14 separate centres (*see* below) under the control of the Exec. Council; Chair. R. B. RYANGA (Kenya); Exec. Dir. N. G. JONES.

Commonwealth Institute of Entomology: 56 Queen's Gate, British Museum (Natural History), Cromwell Road, London, SW7 5JR; f. 1913 for the collection, co-ordination, and dissemination of all information bearing upon injurious and useful insects and other arthropods; undertakes identifications; Dir. N. C. PANT, M.SC.AGR., PH.D. Publs. *Bulletin of Entomological Research* (quarterly), *Review of Applied Entomology Series A-Agriculture, Series B-Medical and Veterinary* (monthly), *Distribution Maps of Pests* (18 yearly).

Commonwealth Mycological Institute: Ferry Lane, Kew, Richmond, Surrey, TW9 3AF; f. 1920 for the collection and dissemination of information on the fungal, bacterial, virus, physiological and soil disorders of plants and on all deleterious fungi of economic importance; undertakes identifications; Dir. A. JOHNSTON, B.SC., A.I.C.T.A., F.I.BIOL. Publs. *Review of Plant Pathology* (monthly), *Distribution Maps of Plant Diseases* (3 each month), *Index of Fungi* (twice a year), *Review of Medical and Veterinary Mycology* (quarterly), *Commonwealth Phytopathological News* (bi-monthly), *Mycological Papers* (irregular), *Phytopathological Papers* (irregular), *Descriptions of Pathogenic Fungi and Bacteria* (quarterly), *Bibliography of Systematic Mycology* (bi-annual).

Commonwealth Institute of Biological Control: Gordon Street, Curepe, Trinidad, West Indies; f. 1927 as the Farham House Laboratory of the Imperial Institute of Entomology; transferred to Canada 1940 and to Trinidad 1962; its purpose is the biological control of injurious insects and noxious weeds, and the collection and distribution throughout the Commonwealth of beneficial organisms with which to attack the pests; Dir. F. D. BENNETT, PH.D. Publs. *A Catalogue of the Parasites and Predators of Insect Pests, Technical Bulletin of Biological Control, Technical Communications.*

Commonwealth Institute of Helminthology: The White House, 103 St. Peter's St., St. Albans, Herts. AL1 3EW; f. 1929; collates world research literature on helminth parasites of animals and on nematode (eelworm) parasites of plants, with reference particularly to those of economic importance; Dir. P. S. GOOCH, B.SC. (acting). Publs. *Helminthological Abstracts: Series A—Animal and Human Helminthology* (monthly); *Series B—Plant Nematology* (quarterly), *Protozoological Abstracts* (monthly).

Commonwealth Bureau of Agricultural Economics: Dartington House, Little Clarendon St., Oxford, OX1 2HH; f. 1966 to abstract the world's literature on agricultural policy; agricultural products; supply, demand and prices; marketing and distribution of agricultural products; international trade; finance and credit; economics of production; co-operative and collective arrangements; education, training and advisory services; rural sociology; research methods and techniques; Dir. J. O. JONES, M.A. Publs. *World Agricultural Economics and Rural Sociology Abstracts* (monthly), *Rural Development Abstracts, Rural Extension Education and Training Abstracts, Recreation and Tourism Abstracts* (quarterly).

Commonwealth Bureau of Animal Breeding and Genetics: The King's Buildings, West Mains Road, Edinburgh, EH9 3JX; f. 1929 for the collection and abstracting of the world's literature on the breeding and the genetics of animals, and for the dissemination of this information throughout the world; Dir. J. D. TURTON, B.SC. M.R.C.V.S., D.T.V.M. Publ. *Animal Breeding Abstracts, Poultry Abstracts* (monthly).

Commonwealth Bureau of Animal Health: Central Veterinary Laboratory, New Haw, Weybridge, Surrey, KT15 3NB; f. 1929; provides world-wide information service in veterinary science and closely related subjects; Dir. R. MACK, M.R.C.V.S. Publs. *Index Veterinarius, The Veterinary Bulletin* (monthly), *Small Animal Abstracts, Pig News and Information* (quarterly), *Animal Disease and Occurrence* (2 a year).

Commonwealth Bureau of Dairy Science and Technology: Shinfield, Reading, Berks., RG2 9BB; f. 1938 for the collection, collation, and distribution of scientific and technological information on dairy husbandry, milk and milk products, and the economics, physiology, microbiology, chemistry and physics of dairying for the benefit of research workers, teachers, advisory officers, etc.; Dir. E. J. MANN, N.D.D., C.D.D. Publ. *Dairy Science Abstracts* (monthly).

Commonwealth Forestry Bureau: at Commonwealth Forestry Institute, South Parks Rd., Oxford, OX1 3RD; f. 1938 for the collection and abstracting of the world's literature on forestry, forest products and their utilization, and for the dissemination of this information throughout the world; Dir. W. FINLAYSON, B.SC. Publs. *Forestry Abstracts, Forest Products Abstracts* (monthly), *Card Title Service* (weekly).

Commonwealth Bureau of Horticulture and Plantation Crops: East Malling Research Station, near Maidstone, Kent, ME19 6BJ; f. 1929 as a clearing-house of information on investigations into problems affecting horticulture and plantation crops throughout the world; Dir. D. J. O'D. BOURKE, M.A., F.L.S. (acting). Publs. *Horticultural Abstracts, Ornamental Horticulture, Cotton and Tropical Fibres Abstracts, Sorghum and Millets Abstracts, Tropical Oil Seeds Abstracts* (monthly).

Commonwealth Bureau of Nutrition: Rowett Research Institute, Bucksburn, Aberdeen. AB2 9SB; f. 1929 to collect and abstract the world's literature in the field of human and animal nutrition, and to disseminate this information throughout the world; Dir. A. A. WOODHAM, PH.D., F.R.I.C. Publ. *Nutrition Abstracts and Reviews:* Series A—*Human and Experimental* (monthly), Series B—*Livestock Feeds and Feeding* (monthly).

Commonwealth Bureau of Pastures and Field Crops: Hurley, nr. Maidenhead, Berks., SL6 5LR; f. 1929; publishes abstracts compiled from the world's scientific literature on grasses and grasslands, herbage plants, rangelands and annual field crops, and produces annotated bibliographies on selected subjects within its scope; Dir. P. J. BOYLE, M.A. Publs. *Herbage Abstracts, Field Crop Abstracts, Crop Physiology Abstracts, Potato Abstracts, Rice Abstracts, Seed Abstracts, Soyabean Abstracts* (all monthly), and occasional publications.

Commonwealth Bureau of Plant Breeding and Genetics: Department of Applied Biology, Downing St., Cambridge, CB2 3DX; f. 1929 to abstract and review current literature on the breeding and genetics of plants of economic importance and relevant publications in allied fields, such as plant pathology, applied statistics, and other sciences, and to maintain an information service on these subjects; Dir. Miss O. HOLBECK, B.SC. (acting). Publs. *Plant Breeding Abstracts, Arid Lands Abstracts* (monthly), *Triticale Abstracts, Maize Quality Protein Abstracts* (quarterly).

Commonwealth Bureau of Soils: Rothamsted Experimental Station, Harpenden, Herts., AL5 2JQ; f. 1929 for the collection and dissemination of information from the world scientific literature on all aspects of soils, the use of fertilizers, and the relationship between plants and soils, particularly plant nutrition; Dir. B. BUTTERS, M.SC., DIP.AGR., D.T.A., D.I.C., A.R.C.S. Publs. *Irrigation and Drainage Abstracts, Soils and Fertilizers* (monthly), series of Annotated Bibliographies (continuous), series of Technical Communications (occasional).

Dairy Society International (DSI) (*Société internationale laitière*): 3008 McKinley St., N.W., Washington, D.C. 20015, U.S.A.; f. 1946 to foster the extension of dairy and dairy industrial enterprise internationally through an interchange and dissemination of scientific, technological, economic, dietary and other relevant information and through a bringing together of persons and entities devoted thereto; organizer and sponsor of the first World Congress for Milk Utilisation.

Pres. JAMES E. CLICK (U.S.A.); Vice-Pres. MITSUGI SATO (Japan); Man. Dir. GEORGE W. WEIGOLD (U.S.A.); Sec. GORDON T. JEFFERS (U.S.A.). Publs. *DSI Report to Members, DSI Bulletin* (both approx. quarterly), *Market Frontier News, Dairy Situation Review* (6 times a year), and booklets on dairying in English and Spanish.

European Confederation of Agriculture (*Confédération Européenne de l'Agriculture*): C.p. 87, 5200 Brugg, Aargau, Switzerland; f. 1889 as International Confederation of Agriculture, re-formed in 1948 as European Confederation of Agriculture; represents the interests of European agriculture in the international field; 421 ordinary and 31 assoc. mems. from 19 countries.

Pres. Senator J. F. G. SCHLINGEMANN (Netherlands); Gen. Sec. Dr. M. COLLAUD (Switzerland). Publs. *Bulletin d'Information CEA, Rapport sur le marché international du lait et des produits laitiers* (quarterly); publs. on current technical, economic, social and cultural problems affecting European Agriculture, Annual Report on the General Assembly: *10 années Confédération Européenne de l'Agriculture, 25 années de travail en commun pour l'agriculture européenne.*

Inter-American Institute of Agricultural Sciences (*Instituto Interamericano de Ciencias Agrícolas*): Apdo. 10281, San José, Costa Rica; f. 1942; a specialized agency of the Organization of American States (OAS) to which Canada and Guyana also belong. Promotes economic and social development through graduate teaching, research, technical co-operation and communications. Maintains 4 regional offices in Guatemala, Dominican Repub., Peru and Uruguay; research centre at Turrialba, Costa Rica; also an Inter-American Center for Documentation and Agricultural Information (Turrialba); library of 60,000 vols. and 2,500 periodicals.

Dir. Dr. JOSÉ EMILIO GONÇALVES ARAUJO (Brazil). Publs. *Turrialba* (quarterly), *Desarrollo Rural en Las Américas* (3 a year), *Boletín Bibliográfico Agrícola* (quarterly); also bibliographies, technical bulletins, teaching materials, manuals and texts.

International Association of Agricultural Economists (*Conférence internationale des économistes agricoles*): 1211 West 22nd St., Oak Brook, Illinois 60521, U.S.A.; f. 1929 to foster the application of the science of agricultural economics in the improvement of the economic and social conditions of rural people and their associated communities; to advance knowledge of agricultural processes and the economic organization of agriculture; and to facilitate communication and exchange of information among those concerned with rural welfare throughout the world. Mems.: 2,000 from 86 countries.

Pres. D. K. BRITTON (U.K.); Vice-Pres. Admin. VICTOR I. NAZARENKO (U.S.S.R.); Vice-Pres. Programme

GLENN JOHNSON (U.S.A.); Gen. Sec. and Treas. R. J. HILDRETH (U.S.A.). Publs. *Proceedings of Conferences.*

International Association of Horticultural Producers (*Association Internationale des Producteurs de l'Horticulture*): Bezuidenhoutseweg 153, P.O.B. 361, 2502 BE, The Hague, Netherlands; f. 1948 to represent through its professional member organizations the common interests of commercial horticultural producers by means of frequent meetings, regular publications, press notices, resolutions and addresses to governments and international authorities. Mems.: Austria, Belgium, Canada, Czechoslovakia, Denmark, Finland, France, Fed. Repub. of Germany, Ireland, Israel, Italy, Luxembourg, Netherlands, Norway, Spain, Sweden, Switzerland, U.K.

Pres. R. MATHIS; Gen. Sec. Dr. N. LUITSE. Publs numerous.

International Centre for Advanced Mediterranean Agronomic Studies: Secretariat: 11 rue Newton, 75116 Paris; f. 1962. Objectives: to provide a supplementary technical, economic and social education for graduates of the higher schools and faculties of agriculture in Mediterranean countries at a postgraduate level; to examine the international problems posed by rural development and regional planning; to develop methods of investigation in ecological topics; to contribute to the development of a spirit of international co-operation among future agronomists and economists in Mediterranean countries. Scholarships may be granted by the governing body. Mems.: France, Greece, Italy, Portugal, Spain, Turkey, Yugoslavia.

Sec.-Gen. RAYMOND LIGNON. Publ. *Options Méditerranéennes* (every 2 months).

The Centre comprises three institutes:

The Mediterranean Agronomic Institute of Bari: courses on irrigation and drainage, soil conservation; Dir. ROBERTO GUICCIARDINI, Valenzano, Bari, P.O.B. 70100, Italy.

The Mediterranean Agronomic Institute of Montpellier: courses on rural and regional development; documentation on Mediterranean area; Dir. LOUIS MALASSIS, 3191 Route de Mende, 34011 Montpellier Cedex, France.

The Mediterranean Agronomic Institute of Zaragoza: courses on zootechnics, hortofruticulture and rural environment; Dir. MUT CATALA, Apdo. 202, Zaragoza, Spain.

International Commission of Agricultural Engineering (*Commission Internationale du Génie Rural—CIGR*): 17–21 rue de Javel, 75015 Paris, France; f. 1930. Objects: application of soil and water sciences to agricultural engineering; conservation, irrigation, land improvement and reclamation; rural construction and equipment; agricultural machinery; distribution of electricity in rural areas and its application in the general energy context; and the scientific organization of agricultural work. Mem. associations from 26 countries, individual mems. in 7 countries.

Pres. T. W. EDMINSTER (U.S.A.); Sec.-Gen. M. CARLIER (France).

International Commission for Food Industries (*Commission internationale des industries agricoles et alimentaires*): 35 rue du Général Foy, 75008 Paris, France; f. 1934. Objects: to develop international co-operation in promoting agricultural and food industries; to assemble scientific, technical and economic documentation for these industries through the Centre de Documentation des Industries Utilisatrices de Produits Agricoles (CDIUPA); to organize periodical international congresses and annual study sessions for agricultural and food industries; 35 initial mem. states.

Pres. Prof. JANOS HOLLO (Hungary); Sec.-Gen. GUY DARDENNE (France). Publs. *Food and Agriculture Industries Journal*, Proceedings of Congresses and Symposia, Calendar (2 a year).

International Committee on Veterinary Anatomical Nomenclature (ICVAN) (*Internationale Veterinär-Anatomische Nomenklatur-Kommission—IVANK*): Linke Bahngasse 11, Vienna 1030, Austria; f. 1957; 52 mems.

Pres. Prof. Dr. Dr. OSKAR SCHALLER (Austria); Vice-Pres. Prof. Dr. ROBERT E. HABEL (U.S.A.). Publ. Reports.

International Confederation of Technical Agricultural Engineers (*Confédération internationale des ingénieurs agronomes*): Beethovenstrasse 24, 8002 Zürich, Switzerland; f. 1930. Objects: to promote and develop relations between agricultural technicians of different countries for the purpose of mutual protection and assistance and for the co-ordination of their efforts in matters of mutual concern and in agricultural questions. Forty countries are represented in the Federation.

Pres. Prof. FRANCO ANGELINI (Italy); Vice-Pres. HELFRIED FABIAN (Germany); Gen. Sec. Prof. MINOS KYPRIADIS (Greece).

International Dairy Federation (*Fédération internationale de laiterie*): Square Vergote 41, 1040 Brussels, Belgium; f. 1903 to link all dairy associations in order to encourage the solution of scientific, technical and economic problems affecting the dairy industry. Mems.: national committees in 32 countries.

Pres. K. SAVAGE (Canada); Sec.-Gen. P. F. J. STAAL (Netherlands). Publs. *Annual Bulletin*†, *IDF News*, etc.

International Federation of Agricultural Producers: 1 rue d'Hauteville, 75010 Paris, France; f. 1946. Objects: to represent, in the international field, the interests of agricultural producers, by laying the co-ordinated views of the national member organizations before any appropriate international body; to exchange information and ideas and help develop understanding of world problems and their effects upon agricultural producers; to encourage efficiency of production, processing, and marketing of agricultural products. Farmers' organizations of 46 countries are represented in the Federation.

Pres. Sir. HENRY PLUMB (U.K.); Sec.-Gen. M. P. CRACKNELL. Publs. *IFAP News*† (monthly), *World Agriculture*† (quarterly), General Conference Reports, *Farming for Development*† (quarterly).

International Institute of Tropical Agriculture: Oyo Rd., P.M.B. 5320, Ibadan, Nigeria; f. 1967; funds provided by the Ford Foundation, Rockefeller Foundation, World Bank (IBRD), Canada, U.S., Iran, Netherlands, Nigeria, U.K., Belgium, Federal Germany, UNEP; four main research programmes: farming systems, grain legume improvement, cereal improvement, and root and tuber improvement; training programme for researchers in tropical agriculture; library of 15,000 vols.

Dir.-Gen. ERMOND H. HARTMANS. Publs. *Annual Report*, *IITA Letter* (3 a year), *Technical Bulletins*†, *IITA Reprints*†.

International Organization for Biological Control of Noxious Animals and Plants (IOBC) (*Organisation internationale de lutte biologique contre les ennemis des cultures—O.I.L.B.*): Dept. of Entomology of the Swiss Federal Institute of Technology (E.T.H.), E.T.H.-Zentrum, 8092 Zürich, Switzerland; f. 1955 to promote and co-ordinate research on biological and integrated control of pests and weeds. Mems.: public or private from 51 countries. Comprises regional sections based on biogeographical zones.

Pres. Prof. K. S. HAGEN (U.S.A.); Sec.-Gen. Dr. G. MATHYS (France). Publs. *Entomophaga* (4 times a year) and Newsletters.

International Seed Testing Association (*Association Internationale d'Essais de Semences*): Reckenholz, P.O.B. 412, CH-8046 Zürich, Switzerland; f. 1924. Aims: to promote uniformity in the testing and judgment of seeds, through research and by organizing triennial congresses and periodical training courses. Mems.: 60 countries.

Pres. A. WOLD (Norway); Hon. Sec.-Treas. Dr. C. ANSELME (France). Publs. *Seed Science and Technology* (quarterly), *ISTA News Bulletin* (quarterly).

International Society of Soil Science (*Association internationale de la science du sol*): c/o International Soil Museum, P.O.B. 353, Wageningen 6700 AJ, The Netherlands; f. 1924 to promote soil science and its applications. Mems.: 6,200 individuals and 51 associations in 118 countries engaged in the study of soil science.

Pres. Dr. J. S. KANWAR (India); Sec.-Gen. Dr. W. G. SOMBROEK. Publ. *Bulletin* (2 a year).

International Standing Committee of the Congress on Physiology and Pathology of Animal Reproduction and of Artificial Insemination (*Comité permanent international du congrès de physiologie et pathologie de la reproduction animale et la fécondation artificielle*): Royal Veterinary College, Boltons Park, Hawkshead Rd., Potters Bar, Herts., U.K.; f. 1948; an international standing committee was appointed after the first congress in Milan in 1948; Ninth International Congress Madrid 1980.

Pres. Prof. N. O. RASBECH (Denmark); Sec.-Gen. Prof. J. A. LAING (U.K.).

International Union of Forestry Research Organisations (*Union internationale des instituts de recherches forestières*): Secretariat: A-1131 Vienna, Austria; f. 1892. Object: international co-operation in the various branches of forestry research and related fields. Membership: *c.* 500 organizations in 90 countries, including forestry faculties, experimental stations, research institutes, etc.

Pres. Prof. WALTER LIESE (Fed. Repub. of Germany); Vice-Pres. Prof. T. SATOO (Japan); Sec. OTMAR BEIN (Austria). Publs. *Annual Report*, Congress Proceedings, *IUFRO News* (quarterly), scientific papers.

International Veterinary Association for Animal Production (*Association Internationale Vétérinaire de Production Animale*): c/o Sociedad Veterinaria de Zootecnía, Facultad de Veterinaria, Ciudad Univ., Madrid 3, Spain; f. 1951; mem. of World Veterinary Asscn.; zootechnical science, animal husbandry, ethology, animal behaviour, animal genetics and nutrition, economics, animal production; 1,400 mems.

Pres. of Exec. Cttee. Prof. A. DE VUYST (Belgium); Vice-Pres. Prof. Dr. T. BONADONNA (Italy), Prof. Dr. R. FERRANDO (France), Prof. Dr. A. VAZ (Portugal); Sec.-Gen. Prof. Dr. CARLOS LUIS DE CUENCA (Spain). Publs. *Proceedings of the World Congresses on Animal Feeding, Proceedings of the First World Congress on Genetics applied to Livestock Production, Proceedings of the First World Congress on Ethology applied to Zootechnics, Proceedings of the 9th International Congress on Animal Reproduction and Artificial Insemination, Zootechnia*† (quarterly).

World Association for Animal Production: Corso Trieste 67, 00198 Rome, Italy; f. 1965; organizes a conference every 5 years; regional discussions. Mems.: 13 societies (national and regional).

Pres. Prof. Dr. Y. NISHIKAWA; Sec.-Gen. Dr. K. KÁLLAY. Publ. *News Items*† (2 a year).

ARTS

African Cultural Institute (*Institut Culturel Africain*): 14 ave. du Président Lamine Guèye, Dakar, Senegal; f. 1971; scientific and cultural development, and African policies. Mems: 17 African states.

Dir.-Gen. BASILE KOSSOU. Publ. *ICA-Information*† (quarterly).

Association for Commonwealth Literature and Language Studies: Dept. of English, University of Guelph, Guelph, Ont. N1G 2W1, Canada; f. 1965 as an independent organization; encourages study in Commonwealth literatures and languages, including comparative studies, the relationship between literatures in English and indigenous literatures and languages, new kinds of English and use of mass media; holds triennial conferences and regional meetings; organizes visits and exchanges; collects source material and publishes creative, critical, historical and bibliographical material; 850 mems.

Chair. Prof. G. D. KILLAM; Vice-Chair. Prof. LESLIE MONKMAN, Prof. CECIL ABRAHAMS. Publ. *Bulletin*†.

Commonwealth Association of Museums: Science Museum, South Kensington, London, SW7 2DD, England; f. 1974; aims to maintain and strengthen links between members of the museum profession; encourages and assists members to obtain additional training and to attend appropriate conferences, seminars; collaborates with national and regional museum associations; national, institutional and individual mems. in 27 countries; General Assembly every three years.

Sec. J. C. ROBINSON (acting). Publ. *Newsletter*† (occasional).

Europa Nostra: 86 Vincent Square, London, SW1P 2PG, U.K.; f. 1963; European federation of associations for the protection of Europe's cultural and natural heritage; has produced a film and has a photographic and slide service; the Historic Towns Forum (800 mems.) provides links between historic towns of Europe; *c.* 2,000 mem. organizations.

Pres. Rt. Hon. The Lord DUNCAN-SANDYS; Dir. Miss F. SMITH.

European Cultural Foundation (*Fondation Européenne de la Culture*): Jan van Goyenkade 5, Amsterdam 1007 HN, Netherlands; f. 1954 to promote and encourage cultural and educational activities and scientific studies of mutual interest to European countries. A number of European national committees are active on behalf of the Foundation. The following institutes have been created to study the areas covered by Plan Europe 2000: Institute for Education, Paris; Institute for European Environmental Policy, Bonn; Institute for Intercontinental Co-operation, Madrid; European Centre for Political Studies, London; European Centre for Work and Society, Utrecht; European Co-operation Fund, Brussels.

Pres. Dr. Y. SCHOLTEN; Gen. Sec. R. GEORIS. Publs. *Annual Report, Newsletter.*

European Society of Culture (*Société Européenne de Culture*): San Marco 2516, 30124 Venice, Italy; f. 1950 to unite artists, poets, scientists, philosophers and others through mutual interests and friendship in order to safeguard and improve the conditions required for creative activity. Mems.: 2,000. Library of 5,000 vols.

Pres. ADRIANO BUZZATI-TRAVERSO (Italy); Vice-Pres. STANISLAO CESCHI (Italy), GERHARD FUNKE (Fed. Repub. of Germany), ALFRED KASTLER (France), JOHN ROBERT NELSON (U.S.A.), BORIS POLEVOÏ (U.S.S.R.); International Sec. MICHELLE CAMPAGNOLO-BOUVIER (Italy). Publ. *Comprendre* (annually).

Inter-American Association of Writers (*Asociación Inter-americana de Escritores*): Casilla de Correo 4852, Bazurco 3296, Dto. A, Buenos Aires, Argentina; f. 1942 to promote Latin American Literature.

Pres. SEBASTIAN V. DATZIRA COPELLO; Sec. MARIA E. PARDO M. DE GOMIS. Publs. *Hoja Informativa, Biblioteca Interamericana.*

International Amateur Theatre Association—Organization for Understanding and Education through Theatre: Herengracht 166-168, Amsterdam, Netherlands; f. 1952; members in 35 states; composed of national centres; organizes international conferences, colloquia, seminars, workshops, festivals including world festival of amateur theatre (every 4 years).

Pres. ART COLE (U.S.A.); Sec. LAJOS MATE (Hungary); Sec.-Gen. JOHN YTTEBORG. Publs. *Bulletin, AITA/IATA.*

International Association of Art (*Association internationale des arts plastiques*): UNESCO House, 1 rue Miollis, 75015 Paris, France; f. 1954; 73 national committees.

Sec.-Gen. DUNBAR MARSHALL-MALAGOLA (U.K.).

International Association of Art Critics (*Association Internationale des Critiques d'Art*): 11 rue Berryer, 75008 Paris; f. 1949 to promote international co-operation in the world of plastic arts (painting, sculpture, graphic arts, architecture); consultative status with UNESCO; 2,000 individuals and 46 National Sections.

Pres. ALEXANDRE CIRICI (Spain); Sec.-Gen. RAOUL-JEAN MOULIN (France). Publs. Reports of General Assemblies, *AICARC-Bulletin.*

International Association of Literary Critics (*Association Internationale des Critiques Littéraires*): 38 rue du Faubourg-St.-Jacques, 75014 Paris, France; f. 1969; UNESCO consultative status B; organizes congresses, etc.

Pres. ROBERT ANDRÉ. Publ. *Bulletin* (2 a year).

International Association of Museums of Arms and Military History—IAMAM (*Association internationale des musées d'armes et d'histoire militaire*): The National Army Museum, Royal Hospital Rd., London, SW3 4TH, U.K.; f. 1957; organization to establish contact between museums and other scientific institutions with collections of arms and armour, military equipment, uniforms, etc., which may be visited by the public; to promote the study of relevant groups of objects; triennial conferences. Mems.: 236 institutions in 48 countries.

Pres. ZDZISLAW ZYGULSKI, Jr. (Poland); Sec.-Gen. WILLIAM REID (U.K.). Publs. *Repertory of Museums of Arms and Military History, Glossarium Armorum: Arma Defensiva, Triennial Reports.*

International Centre for Ancient and Modern Tapestry (*Centre International de la Tapisserie Ancienne et Moderne*): 4 av. Villamont, 1005 Lausanne, Switzerland; f. 1961; sponsors a biennial international exhibition of contemporary tapestries in Lausanne and subsequently shown in other countries.

Pres. JEAN-PASCAL DELAMURAZ; Sec.-Gen. CLAUDE RITSCHARD. Publ. biennial exhibition brochure.

International Centre for the Study of the Preservation and Restoration of Cultural Property: Via di San Michele 13, 00153 Rome; f. 1959; intergovernmental institution; UNESCO Class A; assembles documentation and disseminates knowledge by way of publications and meetings; co-ordinates research, organizes training of specialists and short courses; offers technical advice; financed by 66 member countries. Library of 12,000 vols.

Dir. Dr. BERNARD FEILDEN; Deputy Dir. Dr. GIORGIO TORRACA. Publs. *Newsletter* (annually), *Index of Conservation Training* (with UNESCO, every 2 years).

International Centre of Films for Children and Young People—Cinema and Television (*Centre International du Film pour l'Enfance et la Jeunesse—Cinéma et Télévision*): 111 rue Notre Dame des Champs, 75006 Paris, France; f. 1957; a clearing-house of information about entertainment films (cinema and television) for children all over the world; 35 full mems. (National Centres), 27 assoc. mems.

Chair. HENRY GEDDES (U.K.); Sec.-Gen. LUCIEN GALANDRIN. Publ. *News from ICFCYP: Nouvelles du CIFEJ* (quarterly).

International Comparative Literature Association (*Association internationale de littérature comparée*): Institut de littératures modernes comparées, 17 rue de la Sorbonne, Paris 5e, France; f. 1954 to work for the development of the comparative study of literature. Member societies and individuals in 50 countries. Mems. in Europe: 800.

Pres. ROLAND MORTIER (Belgium); Secs.-Gen. DOUWE W. FOKKEMA, 31 Ramstraat, Utrecht, The Netherlands, FREDERICK GARBER, S.U.N.Y., Binghampton, N.Y. 13901, U.S.A.

International Council of Graphic Design Associations (ICOGRADA): Warren House, St. Paul's Cray Rd., Chislehurst, Kent, U.K.; f. 1963. Objects: to raise the standards of graphic designs and professional practice and the professional status of graphic designers; to collect and exchange information relating to graphic design; to organize exhibitions and congresses and to issue reports and surveys. Mems.: 28 professional associations from 20 countries and one international organization.

Pres. F. LJØRRING; Sec.-Gen. PETER KNEEBONE. Publ. *Icographic.*

International Council on Monuments and Sites (ICOMOS) (*Conseil international des monuments et des sites*): 75 rue du Temple, 75003 Paris, France; f. 1965. Objects: to promote the study and preservation of monuments and sites; to arouse and cultivate the interest of the authorities and people of every country in their monuments and sites and in their cultural heritage; to involve those public authorities, departments, institutions and individuals interested in the preservation and study of monuments and sites; Documentation Centre on preservation and restoration of monuments and sites. Mems.: *c.* 2,500, and 59 national cttees.

Pres. Prof. RAYMOND M. LEMAIRE (Belgium); Sec.-Gen. Dr. ERNEST A. CONNALLY (U.S.A.). Publs. *Monumentum* (2 a year), *Proceedings of Symposia, Bulletin* (annually), *Newsletter* (quarterly).

International Council of Museums (ICOM): Maison de l'UNESCO, 1 rue Miollis, 75732 Paris, France; f. 1946. A professional organization, open to all members of the museum profession, set up to provide an appropriate organization to further international co-operation among museums, and to be the co-ordinating and representative international body furthering museum interests. In 65 countries belonging to ICOM a National Committee on International Co-operation among Museums has been organized, each as widely representative as possible of museum interests. The chairmen of these national committees form the Advisory Committee of ICOM. There are twenty international committees and five international affiliated associations on specialized subjects. Mems.: 7,000 individual and institutional members from 119 countries.

Pres. H. LANDAIS (France); Vice-Pres. V. SOUSLOV (U.S.S.R.), P. PERROT (U.S.A.); Sec.-Gen. LUIS MONREAL. Publs. *ICOM News* (quarterly), *International museological bibliography* (annually).

International Federation for Theatre Research (*Fédération internationale pour la recherche théâtrale*): c/o Prof. T. LAWRENSON, Lancaster University, England; f. 1955 by 21 countries at the International Conference on Theatre History, London; founded Istituto Internazionale per la Ricerca Teatrale, Casa Goldoni, Venice; annual international course in theatre history.

Chair. Prof. ROLF ROHMER (German Democratic Repub.); Secs.-Gen. Mlle ROSE MARIE MOUDOUÈS (France), Prof. T. LAWRENSON (U.K.). Publs. *Theatre Research International*† (English and French, 3 a year) and occasional transactions.

International Film and Television Council (International Council for Film and Television and all other Audiovisual Media of Communication) (*Conseil International du Cinéma et de la Télévision et de tout autre Moyen Audiovisuel de Communication*): 1 rue Miollis, 75732 Paris Cedex 15, France; f. 1959 under auspices of UNESCO; seeks to provide a link of information and joint action between member-organizations, and to assist them in the international work they do in films and television. Mems.: 36 international associations and federations and 12 associates.

Pres. Prof. ENRICO FULCHIGNONI. Publ. *Newsletter* (monthly in English, French and Arabic).

International Institute for Conservation of Historic and Artistic Works (*Institut International pour la Conservation des Objets d'Art et d'Histoire*): 6 Buckingham St., London, WC2N 6BA, England; f. 1950. Aims: to provide a permanent organization for co-ordinating and improving the knowledge, methods and working standards needed to protect and preserve precious materials of all kinds. Gives information on research into all processes connected with conservation, both scientific and technical, and on the development of those processes. Mems.: 2,500 individual, 350 institutional mems.

Pres. H. KORTAN; Sec.-Gen. N. S. BROMMELLE; Treas. S. G. REES-JONES. Publs. *Studies in Conservation* (quarterly), *Art and Archaeology Technical Abstracts* (2 a year), *IIC Bulletin* (every 2 months), Reprints and/or proceedings of triennial international congresses.

International Literary and Artistic Association (*Association littéraire et artistique internationale*): Cercle de la Librairie, 117 blvd. St. Germain, 75006 Paris, France; f. 1878 at Congress of Paris, presided over by Victor Hugo. Objects: The protection of the rights and interests of writers and artists of all lands; extension of copyright conventions, etc. The Association has national groups in Belgium, Denmark, the German Federal Republic, Greece, Italy, Monaco, the Netherlands, Norway, Portugal, Sweden, Switzerland and Turkey and members in Brazil, Luxembourg, Japan, Argentina, New Zealand, U.K., U.S.A.

Pres. MARCEL BOUTET; Perm. Sec. M. FRANÇON.

International Robert Musil Society (*Internationale Robert-Musil-Gesellschaft*): 6600 Saarbrucken 11, St. Johanner Stadtwald, Fed. Repub. of Germany; f. 1974 under the patronage of Bruno Kreisky (Austria), to promote international co-operation in research and publications on Musil and editions of his writings. 55 founder mems. from 25 countries.

Pres. Prof. Dr. MARIE-LOUISE ROTH (France); Vice-Pres. Prof. Dr. ERNST SCHÖNWIESE (Austria), Dr. HANS ZELLER (Switzerland); Sec.-Gen. Prof. Dr. ULRICH KARTHAUS, ANNETTE DAIGGER (Fed. Repub. of Germany). Publ. *Musil-Forum*†.

International Theatre Institute (*Institut international du théâtre*): UNESCO, 1 rue Miollis, Paris 15e, France; f. 1948 to facilitate cultural exchanges and international understanding in the domain of the theatre; conferences, publications. Mems.: 58 member nations.

Pres. JANUSZ WARMINSKI (Poland); Sec.-Gen. JEAN DARCANTE. Publ. *International Theatre Information* (quarterly).

International Union for the Protection of Literary and Artistic Works (*Union internationale pour la protection des oeuvres littéraires et artistiques*): 34 Chemin des Colombettes, 1211 Geneva 20, Switzerland; f. 1886. Library of 18,000 vols. Mems.: governments of 71 countries.

Dir.-Gen. Dr. ARPAD BOGSCH (U.S.A.). Publs. *Le Droit d'Auteur* (monthly), *Copyright* (monthly), *Noticias de la OMPI* (quarterly in Spanish).

International Union of Amateur Cinema (*Union internationale du cinéma d'amateurs*): f. 1937 to encourage development of art, techniques and critical judgment among amateurs, to facilitate contacts between national associations and to promote the exchange of films. Mems.: national federations in 32 countries.

Sec. Gen. Mme D. PLAETENS, 57 Ave. Gambetta, 7100 La Louvière, Belgium.

International Union of Architects (*Union internationale des architectes*): 51 rue Raynouard, 75016 Paris, France; f. 1948. Mems. in 81 countries; 13th Congress Mexico 1978.

Pres. LOUIS DEMOLL (U.S.A.); Gen. Sec. MICHEL LANTHONIE (France). Publ. *Bulletin d'information*† (monthly).

Organization for Museums, Monuments and Sites of Africa (*Organisation pour les Musées, les Monuments et les Sites d'Afrique*): P.O.B. 3343, Accra, Ghana; f. 1975; aims to foster the collection, study and conservation of the natural and cultural heritage of Africa; co-operation between member countries through seminars, workshops, conferences, etc., exchange of personnel, developing training facilities, and drawing up legislative and administrative measures. Mems. from 22 countries.

Pres. Dr. J. M. ESSOMBA (Cameroon); Sec.-Gen. K. A. MYLES (Ghana).

P.E.N., International (*A World Association of Writers*): 7 Dilke St., London, S.W.3; f. 1921 by Mrs. Dawson Scott under the presidency of John Galsworthy to promote co-operation between writers all over the world in the interests of literature, freedom of expression and international goodwill. 79 autonomous centres throughout the world, with total membership about 8,000.

International Pres. PER WÄSTBERG (Sweden); Gen. Sec. PETER ELSTOB. Publs. *Bulletin of Selected Books* (in English and French, with the assistance of UNESCO), various regional bulletins, etc.

Society of African Culture: 18 rue des Ecoles, Paris 5e, France; f. 1956 to create unity and friendship among African scholars for the encouragement of their own cultures and the development of a universal culture. Mems.: from 22 countries.

Pres. Dr. ERIC WILLIAMS; Sec.-Gen. ALIOUNE DIOP. Publ. *Présence Africaine* (quarterly).

World Academy of Art and Sciences, *see* under International—Science.

World Crafts Council: 22 West 55th St., New York, N.Y. 10019, U.S.A.; f. 1964 to promote the interests of crafts and craftsmen throughout the world. Mems.: from 86 countries.

Pres. The Lord REILLY; Sec.-Gen. AKE H. HULDT. Publs. *World Crafts Directory*, *Bulletin* (*c.* 3 a year).

BIBLIOGRAPHY

Centre International de Documentation Concernant les Expressions Plastiques (CIDEP): Fondation Singer-Polignac; f. 1963; collection of books, drawings, films and slides relating to the psychopathology of expression in the plastic arts.

Dir. Dr. C. WIART, Clinique des Maladies mentales et de l'Encéphale, 100 rue de la Santé, Paris 14e, France.

Commonwealth Library Association: P.O.B. 534, Kingston 10, Jamaica, West Indies; f. 1972; to improve libraries in the Commonwealth; to forge and maintain professional links between librarians; to support and encourage library associations; to promote the status and education of librarians and the reciprocal recognition of qualifications; to initiate research projects; 50 national assons., 160 affiliated mems.

Pres. Dr. PAUL XUEREB, LL.B.; Sec. Mrs. C. P. FRAY. Publ. *COMLA Newsletter* (quarterly).

International Association for the Development of Documentation, Libraries and Archives in Africa: B.P. 375, Dakar, Senegal; f. 1957 to promote planning and organization of archives, libraries, documentation centres and museums in all African countries.

Pres. BERNARD DADIE (Ivory Coast); Sec. ZACHEUS S. ALI (Nigeria).

International Association for Mass Communication Research (*Association internationale des études et recherches sur l'information*): c/o Prof. J. D. HALLORAN, Centre for Mass Communication Research, Univ. of Leicester, 104 Regent Rd., Leicester, LE1 7LT, U.K.; f. 1957 to disseminate information on teaching and research in mass media; to encourage research; to provide a forum for the exchange of information; to bring about improvements in communication practice, policy and research; and to encourage the improvement of training for journalism. Mem. organizations and individuals in 62 countries.

Pres. Prof. JAMES D. HALLORAN (U.K.); Sec.-Gen. EMIL DUSISKA (German Democratic Republic).

International Association of Agricultural Librarians and Documentalists—IAALD (*Association Internationale des Bibliothécaires et Documentalistes Agricoles*): Library, Ministry of Agriculture, Fisheries and Food, Central Veterinary Laboratory, New Haw, Weybridge, Surrey, KT15 3NB, U.K.; f. 1955; Objects: to promote, internationally and nationally, agricultural library science and documentation, as well as the professional interests of agricultural librarians and documentalists. The Association has 520 mems., representing 60 countries, and is affiliated to the International Federation of Library Associations and to the Fédération Internationale de Documentation.

Pres. PH. ARIES (France); Sec.-Treas. D. E. GRAY (U.K.). Publs. *Quarterly Bulletin*, *Current Agricultural Serials* (2 vols.), *Primer for Agricultural Libraries*.

International Association of Bibliophiles (*Association Internationale de Bibliophilie*): c/o Bibliothèque Nationale, 58 rue de Richelieu, 75084 Paris Cedex 02, France; f. 1963 to form a meeting point for bibliophiles from different countries, to organize conferences; international congress every 2 years. Mems.: 400.

Pres. FREDERICK B. ADAMS (U.S.A.); Sec.-Gen. ANTOINE CORON (France). Publ. *Le Bulletin du Bibliophile*.

International Association of Documentalists and Information Officers—IAD: 74 rue des Saints-Pères, 75007 Paris, France; f. 1962 to serve the professional interests of documentalists and to work on the problems of documentation at an international level. Mems.: approx. 700.

Gen. Sec. Dr. JACQUES SAMAIN. Publ. *Monthly News* (mems. only).

International Association of Law Libraries—IALL (*Association internationale des bibliothèques de droit*): Law Library, Vanderbilt University, Nashville, Tennessee, U.S.A.; f. 1958 to offer worldwide co-operation in the development of law libraries and the collection of legal documentation. Mems.: over 500 in nearly 60 countries.

Pres. Prof. IGOR I. KAVASS (U.S.A.); 1st Vice-Pres. Dr. KLAUS MENZINGER (Fed. Repub. of Germany); 2nd Vice-Pres. Dr. IVAN SIPKOV (U.S.A.); Sec. ADOLPH SPRUDZS (U.S.A.); Treas. Prof. ARNO LIIVAK (U.S.A.). Publs. *International Journal of Law Libraries* (6 a year).

International Association of Metropolitan City Libraries (INTAMEL): Hamburger Öffentliche Bücherhallen, Gertrudenkirchof 9, 2000 Hamburg 1, Fed. Repub. of Germany; f. 1967 to encourage international co-operation between large city libraries, and in particular the exchange of books, exhibitions, staff and information and participation in the work of the International Federation of Library Associations.

Pres. J. EYSSEN (Fed. Repub. of Germany); Sec.-Treas. F. ANDRAE (Fed. Repub. of Germany).

International Association of Music Libraries (*Association internationale des bibliothèques musicales*): c/o Musikaliska akademiens bibliotek, Nybrokajen 11, (S-)111 48 Stockholm, Sweden; f. 1951 to facilitate co-operation between music libraries and information centres, compile music bibliographies, and to promote the professional. training of music librarians and documentalists Mems: national branches in 18 countries.

Pres. BRIAN REDFERN (U.K.); Sec.-Gen. ANDERS LÖNN (Sweden). Publ. *Fontes artis musicae* (every 3 months).

International Association of Technological University Libraries—IATUL (*Association internationale des bibliothèques d'universités polytechniques*): c/o Bibliotheek Technische Hogeschool Twente, Campus Drienerlo, P.O.B. 217, 7500 AE Enschede, Netherlands; f. 1955 to promote co-operation between member libraries and conduct research on library problems. Mems.: 98 university libraries in 32 countries.

Pres. Dr. G. A. HAMEL (Netherlands). Publ. *IATUL Proceedings*.

International Audio-Visual Technical Centre (*Centre Technique Audio-Visuel International*): Foundation-Lamoriniérestraat 236, 2000 Antwerp; f. 1960 to promote audio-visual media, at the service of educational, cultural, economical, professional and social activities; reference library of more than 30,000 books and documents; BNLX Film Catalogue; workshops, Institute for Multi-Media Education, Institute for Permanent Learning. Board of Directors composed of 52 members, representing 18 countries.

International Pres. LOUIS MAJOR; First Pres. JOHN MADDISON (U.K.); Pres. J. FOURMOY (Belgium); Vice-Pres. Dr. P. KING (U.S.A.), Dr. H. SCHALLER (Germany); Sec.-Gen. Ir. A. J. SALESSE-LAVERGNE (France); Man. Dir. K. SIMONS (Belgium). Publs. *Bibliographical References*†, *Studies and Reports*†, News-Letter, AV-Agenda, functional film cards†, occasional papers†.

International Board on Books for Young People (IBBY): Leonhardsgraben 38A, Ch-4051 Basel, Switzerland; f. 1953 to support and unify those forces in all countries connected with children's book work; to encourage the distribution of good children's books; to promote the scientific investigation into problems of juvenile books; to organize educational aid for developing countries; to organize International Children's Book Day and a biennial international congress; to present the Hans Christian Andersen Medal every two years to a living author and illustrator whose work is an outstanding contribution to juvenile literature. Mems.: National Sections in 44 countries and individuals.

Pres. KNUD-EIGIL HAUBERG-TYCHSEN (Denmark); Sec. Mrs. LEENA MAISSEN (Switzerland). Publs. *Bookbird* (quarterly), *20 Years of IBBY, Congress Reports 1972–78, International Guide to Sources of Information about Children's Literature.*

International Bureau of Fiscal Documentation: Muiderpoort, P.O.B. 20237, Sarphatistraat 124, 1000 HE Amsterdam, Netherlands; an independent organization, f. 1938 to supply information on fiscal law and its application; specialized library on international taxation.

Pres. Dr. K. V. ANTAL; Managing Dir. Prof. J. VAN HOORN, Jr. Publs. *Bulletin for International Fiscal Documentation*† (monthly in English and French), *European Taxation* (monthly review of European tax law and problems). Loose Leaf services: *Supplementary Service to European Taxation, Taxation of Patent Royalties, Dividends, Interest, in Europe, The Taxation of Companies in Europe, The Taxation of Private Investment Income, Value Added Taxation in Europe, Tax Treaty Guides, Corporate Taxation in Latin America, African Tax Systems, Taxes and Investment in the Middle East, Taxes and Investment in Asia and the Pacific, Tax News Service*†; Range of surveys, books and monographs.

International Committee for Social Science Documentation (*Comité international pour la documentation des sciences sociales*): 17 rue d'Assas, 75006 Paris, France; f. 1950 to collect and disseminate information on documentation services in social sciences, help improve documentation, advise societies on problems of documentation and to draw up rules likely to improve the presentation of all documents. Members from international associations specializing in social sciences or in documentation, and from other specialized fields.

Pres. GYÖRGY RÓZSA (Hungary); Sec.-Gen. JEAN MEYRIAT (France). Publs. *International Political Science Abstracts* (quarterly), *International Social Science Bibliographies* (annual, four series), and occasional bibliographies, directories and reports.

International Council of Theological Library Associations (Conseil International des Associations de Bibliothèques de Theologie): 5000 Köln 1, Gereonstr. 2–4, Fed. Repub. of Germany; f. 1961.

Pres. HERMAN MORLION; Sec. Dr. J. A. CERVELLÓ-MARGALEF.

International Council on Archives (*Conseil international des archives*): 60 rue des Francs-Bourgeois, 75003 Paris, France; f. 1948. Mems.: 734 from 121 countries.

Pres. Dr. OSCAR GAUYE (Switzerland); Gen. Secs. Dr. CARLOS WYFFELS (Belgium), Dr. WILFRED SMITH (Canada); Exec. Sec. Dr. CHARLES KECSKEMETI (France). Publs. *Archivum*† (annual), *ADPA/Archives and Automation* (irregular), *Bulletin of the ICA* (2 a year), and various regional bulletins.

International Federation for Documentation (*Fédération internationale de documentation*): P.O.B. 30115, 2500 GC, The Hague, Netherlands; f. 1895 to promote, through international co-operation, research in and development of documentation, which includes organization, storage, retrieval, dissemination and evaluation of information in the fields of science, technology, social sciences, arts and humanities; 70 national mems., 2 international mems., 270 affiliates in 62 countries. Cttees. for: Universal Decimal Classification; Classification research; Research on the theoretical basis of information; Education and training; Terminology of information and documentation; Linguistics in documentation; Information for industry; Patent Information and Documentation; Social Sciences Documentation; Broad System of Ordering (BSO).

Pres. H. ARNTZ; Sec.-Gen. K. R. BROWN. Publs. *FID News Bulletin*† (monthly), *R & D Projects in Documentation and Librarianship* (every 2 months), *International Forum on Information and Documentation* (quarterly), *FID Directory, FID Publications List, Annual Report, Extensions and Corrections to the UDC* (annually), Proceedings of Congresses and Seminars, UDC editions in several languages, Studies on Information Science, Manuals, Bibliographies and Directories.

International Federation of Film Archives (*Fédération internationale des archives du film*): Coudenberg 70, 1000 Brussels, Belgium; f. 1938 to encourage the creation of archives in all countries for the collection and conservation of the film heritage of each land; to facilitate co-operation and exchanges between these film archives; to promote public interest in the art of the cinema; to aid research in this field and to compile new documentation; conducts research; publishes manuals, etc.; holds annual congresses. Mems.: 47 countries.

Pres. WOLFGANG KLAUE (German Democratic Repub.); Sec.-Gen. ROBERT DAUDELIN (Canada).

International Federation of Library Associations and Institutions—IFLA (*Fédération internationale des associations de bibliothécaires et des bibliothèques*): Netherlands Congress Building, Churchillplein 10, P.O.B. 82128, 2508 EC, The Hague, Netherlands; f. 1927. Object: to promote international library co-operation in all fields of library activity, and to provide a representative body in matters of international interest. Mems.: 160 Associations in 110 countries, also Institutional Mems. and Affiliates.

Pres. Mrs. E. GRANHEIM (Norway); Sec.-Gen. Miss M. WIJNSTROOM (Netherlands). Publs. *IFLA Journal* (quarterly), *IFLA Annual, IFLA Directory* (every 2 years).

International Institute for Children's Literature and Reading Research (*Institut International de Littérature pour Enfants et de Recherches sur la Lecture*): 1040 Vienna, Mayrhofgasse 6, Austria; f. 1965 as an international documentation and advisory centre of juvenile literature; promotes international research and maintains specialized library; arranges conferences and exhibitions; compiles recommendation lists. Mems.: individual and group members in 26 countries.

Dir. Dr. RICHARD BAMBERGER (Austria). Publs. *Bookbird*† (quarterly, in co-operation with the International Board on Books for Young People), *Jugend und Buch*† (quarterly), *Schriften zur Jugendlektüre* (occasional).

International Scientific Film Library (*Cinémathèque Scientifique Internationale*): 31 rue Vautier, B-1040 Brussels, Belgium; f. 1961; created under the patronage of the International Scientific Film Association and the Belgian Ministry of National Education and Culture; to preserve the most outstanding scientific and technical films and also to promote the knowledge, study, widest possible dissemination and the rationalization of the production of scientific films. Mems.: 49.

Dir.-Curator P. BORMANS (Belgium). Publs. Catalogue of Films Deposited, *The Pioneers of the Scientific Cinema* (series).

International Translations Centre (formerly European Translations Centre): Doelenstraat 101, 2611 NS Delft, The Netherlands; f. 1960; an international clearing-house for translations made by industries and scientific institutes in the field of science and technology; deals mainly with translations from Slav, Chinese and Japanese languages into a Western language; edits *World Trans-index* (monthly), *Journals in Translation* (irregular), *Five-Year Cumulations of World Index of Scientific Translations*; provides information free of charge and copies of translations at cost of reproduction and a small handling fee. The Centre is managed by a Board composed of representatives of 12 countries.

Pres. Mrs. N. de Mamantoff (France); Dir. D. van Bergeijk.

International Youth Library (*Internationale Jugendbibliothek*): Kaulbachstr. 11A, 8 Munich 22, Fed. Repub. of Germany; f. 1948 as an associated project of UNESCO. Objects: to encourage the reading interest of children and young people all over the world; to promote international co-operation and understanding through mutual exchange in the field of children's literature; to provide information and advice to students, teachers, publishers, etc.; to organize exhibitions. Maintains a library of 350,000 vols.

Pres. of the Library Board Wolfgang Vogelsgesang; Dir. Walter Scherf. Publs. Catalogues of various exhibitions, *The Best of the Best*†.

Ligue des Bibliothèques Européennes de Recherche (LIBER): c/o Riksbibliotektjenesten, P.O. 2439 Solli, Oslo 2, Norway; f. 1971 to establish close collaboration between the general research libraries of Europe, and national university libraries in particular; and to help in finding practical ways of improving the quality of the services these libraries provide. Mems.: 166.

Pres. Gerhard Munthe. Publ *LIBER Bulletin* (2 a year).

ECONOMICS, POLITICAL SCIENCE AND SOCIOLOGY

International Labour Organisation (ILO): 4 Route des Morillons, CH 1211 Geneva 22, Switzerland; f. 1919, became Specialized Agency of UN in 1946; aims to build a code of international labour law and practice, is concerned with the safety, health and social security of workers and provides technical experts where needed by member countries; sets out to improve labour conditions, raise living standards and promote productive employment in all countries. Mems.: 144 countries.

Dir.-Gen. Francis Blanchard (France). Publs. *International Labour Review, Official Bulletin, Legislative Series, Bulletin of Labour Statistics, Year Book of Labour Statistics, Social and Labour Bulletin, International Labour Documentation*, studies and reports.

Two organizations set up by ILO are referred to below: the International Institute for Labour Studies, and the ILO International Centre for Advanced Technical and Vocational Training.

African Training and Research Centre in Administration for Development (*Centre Africain de Formation et de Recherche Administratives pour le Développement—CAFRAD*): 19 rue Abou Alla El Maari, B.P. 310, Tangier, Morocco; f. 1964 by agreement between Morocco and UNESCO; training of African senior civil servants; research into administrative problems in Africa, documentation of results, and the provision of a consultation service for governments and organizations in Africa; holds frequent seminars. Mems.: Algeria, Botswana, Burundi, Cameroon, Central African Empire, Chad, Egypt, Gabon, Gambia, Ghana, Guinea-Bissau, Ivory Coast, Kenya, Liberia, Libya, Mauritania, Mauritius, Morocco, Niger, Nigeria, Senegal, Sierra Leone, Somalia, Sudan, Swaziland, Tanzania, Togo, Tunisia, Uganda, Upper Volta, Zaire, Zambia; a UNDP project since 1971.

Pres. Mohamed Birouk; Dir.-Gen. Joseph E. Kariuki. Publs. *African Administrative Studies*† (2 a year), *CAFRAD News* (2 a year, English, French and Arabic), *African Administrative Abstracts* (quarterly, also in French), *Information Bulletin* (8 a year, also in French).

Association of International Accountants Ltd. (by guarantee): Turvey Abbey, Turvey, Bedfordshire, England; f. 1928; provides an international organization for qualified accountants in all parts of the world, and safeguards their professional status; examinations are conducted throughout the world; 18,000 mems. and students.

Chair. J. R. A. Turnbull, F.A.I.A.; Sec.-Gen. L. de Quidt, F.C.I.S., F.A.I.A. Publ. *The International Accountant* (quarterly).

Atlantic Institute for International Affairs (*Institut Atlantique des Affaires Internationales*): 120 rue de Longchamp, 75116 Paris, France; f. 1961; private international organization to conduct non-governmental research and encourage discussion of all problems common to the industrialized countries in their relations with one another and with other parts of the world. Library of 4,000 vols. and *c.* 29,000 clippings. Mems. from 18 countries.

Dir.-Gen. Martin J. Hillenbrand (U.S.A.). Publ. *The Atlantic Papers*† (4 a year).

Econometric Society: Dept. of Economics, Northwestern University, Evanston, Ill. 60201, U.S.A.; f. 1930 to promote studies aimed at unification of the theoretical-quantitative and the empirical-quantitative approach to economic problems; 6,000 mems.

Treas. Robert J. Gordon; Sec. Julie P. Gordon (U.S.A.). Publ. *Econometrica* (6 a year).

European Centre for Population Studies (*Centre européen d'etudes de population*): Pauwenlaan 17, 2566 TA The Hague, Netherlands; f. 1953 to conduct research and provide information on European population problems. Mems.: demographers and other population scientists from 24 European countries.

Pres. Dr. E. Hofsten (Sweden); Sec.-Gen. and Treas. Dr. G. Beyer (Netherlands). Publs. *European Demographic Information Bulletin* (quarterly), *European Demographic Monographs* (series).

Hansard Society for Parliamentary Government: 16 Gower St., London, WC1E 6DP, U.K.; f. 1944, present title adopted 1956. Aims to promote parliamentary government in all parts of the world; conducts research work, and educational work in schools. Mems in 72 countries.

Sec. Maxine Vlieland. Publ. *Parliamentary Affairs* (quarterly).

Institute for International Sociological Research: P.O.B. 100705, 5000 Cologne 1, Fed. Repub. of Germany; f. 1964; diplomatic and international affairs, social and political sciences, moral and behavioural sciences, arts and literature; 132 Life Fellows, 44 Assoc. Fellows; 14 research centres.

Pres., Chair. Exec. Cttee. and Dir.-Gen. Consul Dr. Edward S. Ellenberg. Publs. *Diplomatic Observer* (monthly), *Newsletter, Bulletin* (quarterly), *Annual Report*, etc.

Affiliated institutes:

Academy of Diplomacy and International Affairs (ADIA) (*Académie Diplomatique et des Affaires internationales*): f. 1972; 120 Life Fellows (elected) and unlimited mems.; Pres. Consul Dr. EDWARD S. ELLENBERG.

International Academy of Social and Moral Sciences, Arts and Letters (IASMAL) (*Académie Internationale des Sciences Sociales et Morales, des Arts et des Lettres*): f. 1972; 160 Life Fellows and unlimited mems.; Pres. Consul Dr. EDWARD S. ELLENBERG.

International Academy of Political Science and Constitutional History (*Académie Internationale de science politique et d'histoire constitutionelle*): c/o Prof. G. S. LANGROD, 88 blvd. Péreire, Paris 17e; f. 1936; scientific studies of constitutional and parliamentary history; full and associate members (total 75) from 39 countries.

Pres. Prof. M. PRÉLOT (France); Sec.-Gen. Prof. G. S. LANGROD (France). Publ. *Politique*.

International African Institute (IAI) (*Institut africain international*): 38 King St., London, WC2E 8JR, U.K.; f. 1926; information centre on African social sciences, cultures and languages; conducts research programmes, holds seminars and conferences. Mems.: 1,750 in 83 countries.

Chair. Prof. J. F. ADE AJAYI. Publs. *Africa, African Languages* and numerous monographs.

International Association Futuribles: 55 rue de Varennes, 75007 Paris, France; f. 1967 as International Committee of Futuribles; aims to provide a link, information clearing-house, research facilities and point of contact between the groups in various countries engaged on studies of the future; research on specific problems in the fields of development, environment, energy, growth, welfare programmes, etc.; library and documentation system: 90,000 entries. Board of Dirs.: 25 mems. from 14 countries.

Pres. PHILIPPE DE SEYNES (U.S.A.); Sec.-Gen. and Exec. Dir. HUGUES DE JOUVENEL (France). Publs. *Futuribles* (monthly), *Futur-Informations* (monthly), *Futuribles Newsletter* (quarterly).

International Association of Schools of Social Work: Freytaggasse 32, 1210 Vienna, Austria; f. 1929 to provide international leadership and encourage high standards in social work education. Mems.: 494 schools of social work in 68 countries and 22 associations of schools.

Pres. ROBIN H. JONES (U.K.); Sec.-Gen. MARGUERITE MATHIEU (Canada). Publs. *International Social Work* (quarterly), *Directory of Members, IASSW News*.

International Centre for Advanced Technical and Vocational Training (*Centre international de perfectionnement professionnel et technique*): 201 via Ventimiglia, 10127 Turin, Italy; f. 1965 by International Labour Organisation to offer advanced training facilities for managers, training and trade union officials, and technical specialists from all over the world but primarily from developing countries; the majority of courses are organized at the specific request of a sponsoring body.

Dir. A. ABOUGHANEM (France).

International Commission for the History of Representative and Parliamentary Institutions (*Commission internationale pour l'histoire des assemblées d'états*): Arts Bldg., University of Sussex, Falmer, Brighton, BN1 9QN, England; f. 1936 to encourage research on the origin and history of representative and parliamentary institutions. Mems.: individuals in 31 countries.

Pres. A. MARONGIU (Italy); Sec. Miss V. CROMWELL (U.K.). Publ. *Reports*.

International Council on Social Welfare (*Conseil international de l'action sociale*): f. 1928 to provide an international forum for the discussion of social work and related issues. Mems.: 68 committees and 24 international organizations.

Pres. LUCIEN MEHL (France); Sec.-Gen. INGRID GELINEK, Berggasse 9, 1090 Vienna, Austria. Publs. *Conference Bulletin, International Social Work* (quarterly), *International Newsletter* (quarterly), *Proceedings of International Conferences on Social Welfare* (biennial), Regional Newsletters.

International Federation of Business and Professional Women (*Fédération Internationale des Femmes de Carrières Libérales et Commerciales*): 54 Bloomsbury St., London, WC1B 3QU, England; f. 1930. Objects: to promote the interests of business and professional women, and in particular to bring their specialized knowledge and skills to play a more effective part in the world government organizations. Mems.: over 300,000.

Gen. Sec. Mrs. BEATRICE KYLE. Publ. *Widening Horizons* (4 a year).

International Fiscal Association: c/o Erasmus Univ., P.O.B. 1738, 3000 DR Rotterdam, Netherlands; f. 1938, Statutes renewed November 1969. Aims: to study and advance international and comparative law with regard to public finance and especially international and comparative fiscal law and the financial and economic aspects of taxation. Mems.: approx. 5,500 in more than 80 countries, national branches in 29 countries.

Pres. A. G. DAVIES (U.K.); Sec.-Gen. Prof. Dr. J. H. CHRISTIAANSE (Netherlands). Publs. *Cahiers de Droit Fiscal International* (Studies on International Fiscal Law), *Yearbook of the International Fiscal Association*.

International Gypsy Committee (*Komitia Lumiati Romani*): Résidence les Fougères, Bât. D5, 77210 Avon, France; f. 1954; is working towards cultural and political unity of the 12,000,000 Romanies throughout the world; makes known difficulties and social needs through the Council of Europe, UNESCO and other international agencies.

Pres. VANKO ROUDA; Sec.-Gen. LEULEA ROUDA. Publs. *Romano Drom* (every 2 months), *La Voix Mondiale Tzigane* (quarterly), *O Nevo Drom* (monthly).

International Institute for Labour Studies: C.P. 6, CH-1211 Geneva 22, Switzerland; f. 1960 by ILO; aim to promote better understanding and objective study in all countries of policy issues relating to labour; current programmes: courses for persons in government, management, trade unions and research who influence labour policy; assistance for the development of national centres for labour studies; promoting research on and discussion of developing countries, including the holding of symposia. Activities are organized under three technical sectors: Economic Change and Social Policy, Dynamics of Industrial Relations Systems Quality of Working Life and Social Perspectives.

Chair. of the Board FRANCIS BLANCHARD (Dir.-Gen., ILO); Dir. ALBERT TÉVOÉDJRÈ. Publs. *Labour and Society*†, Research Series, Public Lecture Series.

International Institute for Ligurian Studies (*Istituto Internazionale di Studi Liguri*): Museo Bicknell 39, *bis* Via Romana, Bordighera, Italy; f. 1947 to conduct research on ancient monuments and regional traditions in the north-west arc of the Mediterranean. Library of 60,000 vols. Members in France, Italy, Spain, Switzerland.

Pres. MARTIN ALMAGRO (Spain); Vice-Pres. COSIMO COSTA (Italy), PAUL-ALBERT FEVRIER (France); Dir. FRANCISCA PALLARÉS (Italy).

International Institute for Sociology (*Institut International de Sociologie—IIS*): Palais Wilson, C.P. 7, 1211 Geneva

14, Switzerland; f. 1893 to further the study of sociology. Mems.: 300 representing 45 countries.

Pres. F. GOVAERTS (Belgium). Publ. *Revue de l'Institut International de Sociologie.*

International Institute of Philosophy—IIP (*Institut international de philosophie—IIP*): 8 rue Jean-Calvin, 75005 Paris, France; f. 1937. Aims: to link philosophers and to establish collaboration between them. Mems.: 110 in 37 countries.

Pres. P. RICOEUR (France); Sec.-Gen. YVON BELAVAL (France). Publs. *Bibliographie de la Philosophie* (quarterly), *Philosophy and World Community*, *Philosophy in the Mid-Century* (4 vols.), *Contemporary Philosophy* (4 vols.), Proceedings of annual meetings.

International Numismatic Commission (*Commission internationale de numismatique*): Oslo University Coin Collection, Frederiksgate 2, Oslo 1, Norway; f. 1936 to facilitate co-operation between scholars in the sphere of numismatics. Mems.: national organizations in 26 countries.

Pres. R. A. G. CARSON (U.K.); Sec. K. SKAARE (Norway).

International Peace Academy: 777 United Nations Plaza, New York, N.Y. 10017, U.S.A.; f. 1971 to develop training and education programmes for professionals in the skills required for settlement of international disputes; an autonomous and strictly non-political institution.

Pres. Maj.-Gen. (retd.) INDAR JIT RIKHYE (India); Exec. Vice-Pres. JOHN MROZ. Publs. *IPA News Notes* (2 a year), *IPA Reports* (irregular), *Coping with Conflict* (annually), special reports and studies.

International Society for Community Development: 345 East 46th St., New York, N.Y. 10017, U.S.A.; f. 1962 to advance the understanding and application of community development principles and practices. Mems.: 500.

Pres. GLEN LEET. Publs. Journals and Newsletter.

International Society for Ethnology and Folklore (SIEF): f. 1964 to establish and maintain collaboration between specialists in folklore and ethnology; organizes commissions, symposia, congresses, etc.; affiliated to Int. Union of Anthropological and Ethnological Sciences and ICPHS; close links with International Folk Music Council and International Council of Museums. Mems.: 504.

Pres. Prof. MIHAI POP (Romania), Inst. of Ethnology, Str. Nikos Beloiannis 25, Bucharest, Romania; Vice-Pres. Prof. J. CUISENIER, Prof. K. C. PEETERS and R. M. DORSON. Publ. *Bulletin d'Informations SIEF* (annual).

International Society for the Study of Medieval Philosophy (*Société Internationale pour l'Etude de la Philosophie Médiévale—SIEPM*): c/o Institut supérieur de Philosophie, Collège Thomas More (SH3), Chemin d'Aristote 1, 1348 Louvain-la-Neuve, Belgium; f. 1958 to promote the study of medieval thought and the collaboration between individuals and institutions concerned in this field; organizes international congresses every five years, the next to be held at Cracow in 1982. Mems in 46 countries.

Pres. WOLFGANG KLUXEN (Fed. Rep. of Germany); Vice-Pres. Z. KUKSEWICZ (Poland), J. MURDOCH (U.S.A.), G. VERBEKE (Belgium); Sec. CHRISTIAN WENIN (Belgium). Publ. *Bulletin de Philosophie Médiévale* (annually).

International Society of Social Defence (*Société internationale de défense sociale*): f. 1945, present title adopted 1949. Aims: to combat crime, to protect society and to prevent citizens from being tempted to commit criminal actions. Mems.: Legal experts, doctors and sociologists in 35 countries.

Pres. MARC ANCEL (France); Sec.-Gen. A. BERIA DI ARGENTINE (Italy), c/o Centro Nazionale di Prevenzione e Difesa Sociale, Piazza Castello 3, 20121 Milan; Treas. YVONNE MARX (France). Publ. *Cahiers de défense sociale* (*Bulletin de la Société internationale de défense sociale*) (annually).

Inter-Parliamentary Union: Place du Petit-Saconnex, 1209 Geneva, Switzerland; f. 1889 to promote personal contacts among the members of the world's Parliaments and unite them in common action for international peace and co-operation; studies political, economic, social, juridical, cultural and environmental problems of international significance; organizes conferences; maintains regular contact with UN Specialized Agencies; maintains library and International Centre for Parliamentary Documentation. World membership: 90 Parliamentary Groups.

Pres. of Inter-Parliamentary Council RAFAEL CALDERA (Venezuela); Sec.-Gen. PIO-CARLO TERENZIO (Italy). Publs. *Inter-Parliamentary Bulletin*†, *Constitutional and Parliamentary Information*, *Chronicle of Parliamentary Elections and Developments*, *Parliaments of the World—A Reference Compendium.*

Organisation for Economic Co-operation and Development—OECD: 2 rue André-Pascal, 75016 Paris; f. 1961; under the responsibility of three Committees (Scientific and Technological Policy, Education, Manpower and Social Affairs), and of two Directorates (Scientific Affairs; Social Affairs, Manpower and Education), OECD is concerned with the impact of science, technology, education and the changing pattern of employment structures on the balance of economic and social development of its 24 member countries and with the implications of technological development for the environment as well as with the broader aspects of policy to meet new social objectives; it aims at being informative, promotional and catalytic through surveys of the current situation, identification of tentative policies and the establishment of a statistical and methodological base in support of government decision making; serves as an international clearing-house for exchanges of information and provides a forum where experts and policy makers can discuss common issues and benefit from mutual co-operation. Special programmes include the Programme for Educational Building and the Centre for Educational Research and Innovation. Another project is now being conducted: Institutional Management in Higher Education (IMHE).

Sec.-Gen. EMILE VAN LENNEP (Netherlands).

Pan-African Institute for Development (*Institut Pan-Africain pour le Développement*): 3 rue de Varembé, C.P. 38, 1211 Geneva, Switzerland; f. 1965 for the training of African Development staff; 60 professional staff; regional insts. in Cameroon, Upper Volta, Zambia.

Sec.-Gen. J. YANNEY EWUSIE.

Society for International Development (*Société Internationale pour le Développement*): Palazzo Civiltà del Lavoro, 00144 Rome, Italy; f. 1957 to provide a forum for the exchange of ideas, fact, and experience among all persons professionally concerned with the vital problems of economic and social development in modernizing societies. Mems.: 6,000 from 1,000 organizations in 134 countries.

Pres. JAMES P. GRANT; Sec.-Gen. PONNA WIGNARAJA. Publs. *International Development Review*†, *Compass* (quarterly).

Stockholm International Peace Research Institute: Sveavägen 166, 113 46 Stockholm, Sweden; f. 1966 for research into problems of peace and conflict with particular attention to the problems of disarmament and arms regulation. About 50 mems., half of whom are research workers.

Dir. FRANK BARNABY (U.K.); Chair. ROLF BJÖRNERSTEDT. Publs. *SIPRI Yearbook, Monographs.*

Statistical Institute for Asia and the Pacific: Economic Co-operation Centre Bldg. Annex, 42 Honmura-cho, Ichigaya Shinjuku-ku, Tokyo 162, Japan; f. 1970s independent institute to train professional statisticians for government service, research and related activitie; as recommended by Resolution 75 (XXIII) of ESCAP, for mem. and assoc. mem. countries; three courses a year: General (6 months) and two Advanced (6 weeks each); also "country courses" given at a country's request to deal with a specific subject. Mems.: 30 Fellows (General course), 15 Fellows (per Advanced course). Library of 4,000 vols.

Project Man. and Dir. J. G. MILLER. Publs. *Newsletter* (irregular), occasional papers.

United Nations Institute for Training and Research—UNITAR (*Institut des Nations Unies pour la formation et la recherche*): 801 United Nations Plaza, New York, N.Y. 10017, U.S.A.; f. 1965 as an autonomous body within the framework of the United Nations; it aims, by training and research, to enhance the effectiveness of the United Nations in achieving the major objectives of the Organization, in particular the maintenance of peace and security and the promotion of economic and social development; it conducts seminars for diplomats and others who work with the UN system and carries out training, either at UN headquarters or in the field, which has special relevance for developing countries; it conducts research into problems of concern to the UN system.

Exec. Dir. Dr. DAVIDSON S. H. W. NICOL (Sierra Leone). Publs. over 50 titles in English and some in French, Spanish and Russian; *Unitar News* and *Nouvelles de l'Unitar* (several times a year).

Vienna Institute for Development (*Wiener Institut für Entwicklungsfragen*): A-1010 Vienna, Kärntner Str. 25, Austria; f. 1964 to disseminate information on problems and achievements of developing countries by all possible means in order to convince the public of industrialized nations of the necessity to increase development aid and to strengthen international co-operation; research programmes. Mems. from 20 countries.

Pres. BRUNO KREISKY (Austria); Vice-Pres. AHMED BEN SALAH (Tunisia), WILLY BRANDT (Fed. Repub. of Germany), B. K. NEHRU (India), B. R. SEN (India); Dir. ARNE HASELBACH (Austria).

World Council of Management (*Conseil Mondial de Management*): c/o NIVE, Nederlandse Vereniging voor Management, Van Alkemadelaan 700, 2019 The Hague, Netherlands; f. 1926, present name 1976; promotes scientific and professional management; research, education, training, development and practice; mem. organizations in 40 countries.

World Society for Ekistics: c/o Athens Center of Ekistics, 24 Strat. Syndesmou St., Athens 136, Greece; f. 1965; aims to promote the development of knowledge and ideas concerning human settlements by research and through publications, conferences, scholarships, etc.; to encourage the development and expansion of education in ekistics; to educate public opinion concerning ekistics; to recognize the benefits and necessity of an interdisciplinary approach to the needs of human settlements, and to promote and emphasize such an approach. Mems.: 283.

Pres. T. A. LAMBO; Sec.-Gen.-Treas. PANAYIS PSOMOPOULOS.

EDUCATION

African and Malagasy Council on Higher Education (*Conseil africain et malgache de l'enseignement supérieur—CAMES*): B.P. 134, Ouagadougou, Upper Volta; f. 1968 to ensure co-ordination between member states in the fields of higher education and research. Mems.: governments of French-speaking African countries and Malagasy.

Sec.-Gen. Prof. JOSEPH KI ZERBO (Upper Volta).

Association des Universités Partiellement ou Entièrement de Langue Française (AUPELF): Université de Montréal, B.P. 6128, Montreal H3C 3J7, Canada; f. 1961; aims: documentation, co-ordination, co-operation, exchange; 123 mems., 16 assoc. mems. (A), 324 assoc. mems. (B).

Pres. PAUL LACOSTE (Canada); Vice-Pres. Mme ROSE EHOLIÉ (Ivory Coast), MICHEL GUILLOU (France), ANDRÉ JAUMOTTE (Belgium); Sec.-Gen. MAURICE-ETIENNE BEUTLER. Publs. *Revue de l'Aupelf*† (2 a year), *Répertoire des Cours d'été*† (annually), *Idées*† (irregular), *universités*† (quarterly).

Association for the European University Community (*Association pour la Communauté Européenne Universitaire*): 2 rue Mérimée, 75116 Paris Cedex, France; f. 1965 to promote co-operation among universities, exchanges between students and staff; mutual recognition of diplomas; study sessions and seminars on Europe; language courses; specialized bibliography of publications on Europe.

Dir. JEAN-CLAUDE MASCLET. Publ. *Nouvelles Universitaires Européennes/European University News* (6 a year).

Association of African Universities (*Association des Universités Africaines*): P.O.B. 5744, Accra-North, Ghana; f. 1967 to promote exchanges, contacts and co-operation between university institutions in Africa, to study and make known educational and related needs in Africa and co-ordinate means whereby these needs may be met. Mems.: 70 university institutions.

Pres. Prof. A. G. JOHNSON (Togo); Vice-Pres. Prof. J. F. ADE AJAYI (Nigeria); Sec.-Gen. Prof. LEVY MAKANY (Congo); Publs. *List of Staff Vacancies in African Universities* (monthly), *Newsletter* ((quarterly).

Association of Arab Universities: Scientific Computation Centre, Tharwat St., Orman P.O., Giza, Egypt; f. 1964 to consolidate co-operation between Arab universities and institutions of higher education. Mems.: 52 universities.

Sec.-Gen. Dr. MURSI AHMED. Publs. *Bulletin* (2 a year), *Directory of Arab Universities, Directory of Teaching Staff of Arab Universities, Proceedings of Seminars.*

Association of Caribbean Universities and Research Institutes: P.O.B. 11532, Caparra Heights Station, San Juan, Puerto Rico 00922; f. 1968 to foster contact and collaboration between member universities and institutes; conferences, meetings, seminars, etc.; circulation of information through newsletters, bulletins; facilitates co-operation and the pooling of resources in research; encourages exchange of staff and students. Mems.: 50.

Sec.-Gen. Dr. THOMAS MATHEWS. Publ. *Caribbean Educational Bulletin* (quarterly).

Association of Commonwealth Universities: John Foster House, 36 Gordon Square, London WC1H 0PF, England; f. 1913; organizes quinquennial congresses of Commonwealth universities, conferences of executive heads of Commonwealth universities (twice every 5 years) and other smaller meetings, acts as a liaison office and general information centre, provides an advisory service for the filling of university staff teaching vacancies overseas, and administers the Third World Academic Exchanges Programme, the T.H.E.S. Third World Academic Exchange Fellowship and the Commonwealth Foundation/C.I.D.A. Administrative Travelling Fellowship Scheme; it also provides secretariats for the Commonwealth Scholarship Commission in the United Kingdom, for the Marshall Aid Commemoration Commission, and for the Kennedy Memorial Trust; library of 12,000 vols. Mems.: 228 universities and university colleges.

Chair. Dr. C. R. MITRA; Sec. Gen. A. CHRISTODOULOU. Publs. *Commonwealth Universities Yearbook, Schedule of Postgraduate Courses in United Kingdom Universities, Compendium of University Entrance Requirements for First Degree Courses in the United Kingdom, List of University Institutions in the Commonwealth* (all annually), *Register of Research Strengths of Universities in the Developing Countries of the Commonwealth, Awards for Commonwealth University Academic Staff, Scholarships Guide for Commonwealth Postgraduate Students, Grants for Study Visits by University Administrators and Librarians, Financial Aid for First Degree Study at Commonwealth Universities, Higher Education in the United Kingdom: A Handbook for Students from Overseas* (in conjunction with British Council) (all every 2 years), *ACU Bulletin of Current Documentation* (5 a year), *Acumen* (4 or 5 a year), *Reports of Proceedings of Congresses of the Universities of the Commonwealth* (quinquennial).

Association of Institutes for European Studies (*Association des instituts d'études européennes*): Centre Européen de la Culture, 122 rue de Lausanne, Geneva, Switzerland; f. 1951 to co-ordinate activities of member institutes in teaching and research, exchange information, provide a centre for documentation. Thirty-two member institutes in nine countries.

Pres. Prof. E. CEREXHE (Belgium); Sec.-Gen. DUSAN SIDJANSKI. Publs. *Annuaire, Nouvelles de l'AIEE, Bulletin.*

Association of International Colleges and Universities: 27 place de l'Université, 13625 Aix-en-Provence, France; f. 1971 to promote co-operation among independent institutions; 12 mem. univs. and colleges.

Pres. Dr. JOHN S. BAILEY; Sec.-Gen. Dr. HERBERT MAZA.

Association of Southeast Asian Institutions of Higher Learning: f. 1956 to promote the economic, cultural and social welfare of the people of Southeast Asia by means of educational co-operation and research programmes; to foster the cultivation of a sense of regional identity and interdependence and to co-operate with other regional and international organizations; serves as a clearing-house for information, provides opportunities for discussion and recognizes distinctive academic achievements. Mems.: 50 university institutions.

Exec. Sec. Prof. PRACHOOM CHOMCHAI, Ratasastra Building, Chulalongkorn University, Henri Dunant Rd., Bangkok 5, Thailand. Publ. *Newsletter.*

Centre for Educational Research and Innovation: c/o OECD, 2 rue André-Pascal, 75016 Paris, France; f. 1968 to support the efforts of member countries, to encourage experiments in educational innovation and stimulate co-operation in research and development work on educational problems; projects under way deal with relations between education and society, development and exchange of innovations in the teaching/learning process, and strengthening national and international arrangements for educational innovations.

Dir. JAMES GASS. Publ. *Innovation in Education* (3 a year).

Comparative Education Society in Europe (*Association d'éducation comparée en Europe*): 51 rue de la Concorde, 1050 Brussels, Belgium; f. 1961 to promote teaching and research in comparative and international education; the Society organizes conferences and promotes literature. Mems.: in 37 countries.

Pres. Prof. D. KALLEN (France); Vice-Pres. Prof. P. FURTER (Switzerland), Prof. W. MITTER (Fed. Repub. of Germany); Sec.-Treas. Prof. H. VAN DAELE (Belgium). Publs. *Proceedings, Newsletter* (quarterly).

Confederation of the Universities of Central America (*Confederación Universitaria Centroamericana*): Apdo. 37, Ciudad Universitaria, San José, Costa Rica, C.A.; f. 1948 to plan the regional integration of higher education in Central America and to maintain the autonomous structure of the member universities. Mems.: Univ. of S. Carlos, Guatemala, Univ. of El Salvador, Univ. of Costa Rica, National Univ., Costa Rica, National Autonomous Univ. of Honduras, National Autonomous Univ. of Nicaragua, Univ. of Panama.

Pres. Dr. MARIANO FIALLOS OYANGUREN (Nicaragua); Sec. Gen. Lic. GUILLERMO MOLINA CHOCANO. Publs. *Estudios sociales Centroamericanos*† (3 a year), *Revista Centroamericana de Ciencias de la Salud* (3 a year), *Boletín Informativo* (quarterly).

Council for Cultural Co-operation: Council of Europe, ave. de l'Europe, 67006 Strasbourg-Cedex, France; f. 1962 to draw up and implement the educational and cultural programme of the Council of Europe; current projects include: new content and methods of education of the 14-18 age group; reform and development of tertiary education; development of adult education; new approaches to the teaching of modern languages; implementation of cultural development policies; cultural role of mass media; a project for a computerized European Documentation and Information System for Education (EUDISED) and activities in the fields of cultural enrichment, the management of cultural affairs, and Sport for All. A Higher Education Scholarship Scheme, an educational documentation centre, a residential European Youth Centre and a European Youth Foundation have been created. Mems.: 22 states.

Publs. Series *Education in Europe:* many titles; *Annual Report CCC*†; specialized studies, catalogues and handbooks; Review *Education and Culture*† (3 times a year); *News Letter/Faits Nouveaux* (4-6 a year); *EUDISED R & D Bulletin* (4 a year).

European Association of Teachers (*Association européenne des enseignants—AEDE*): 122 rue de Lausanne, Geneva, Switzerland; f. 1956 to develop among teachers an understanding of the problems of European unification and to harmonize contents and methods of teaching; national sections established in the Federal Republic of Germany, Austria, Belgium, Denmark, Luxembourg, Italy, Switzerland, France, Greece and Great Britain.

Pres. J.-C. KECH (Belgium); Sec.-Gen. Prof. S. MOSER (Switzerland). Publs. two European and eight national reviews.

European Bureau of Adult Education (*Bureau européen de l'éducation populaire*): Nieuweweg 4, P.O.B. 367, 3800 AJ Amersfoort, Netherlands; f. 1953 to encourage co-operation between adult education organizations on questions of methods, materials, and exchange of individuals; arranges study sessions and tours. Members in 16 European countries and associate members in America and Australia.

Pres. H. DOLFF (Fed. Repub. of Germany); Dir. W. BAX. Publs. *Notes and Studies, Directory, Newsletter.*

European Foundation for Management Development (EFMD): Place Stéphanie 20, 1050 Brussels, Belgium; f. 1971 (incorporating the European Association of Management Training Centres and the International University Contact for Management Education); to help improve the quality of management development within the economic, social and cultural context of Europe and in harmony with its overall needs; to promote dialogue between organizations, groups and individuals engaged in management development; to provide information on developments in management sciences. Mems.: 120 institutions, 6 international affiliates, 9 associates, 350 individuals.

Dir.-Gen. JEAN-FRANÇOIS PONCET. Publs. *International Management Development (IMD)* (bi-monthly), *Documentation on Books* (monthly), *Management International Review* (monthly).

Fédération Internationale des Professeurs de Français (*International Federation of Teachers of French*): 1 ave. Léon Journault, 92310 Sèvres, France; f. 1969 to group together and assist teachers of French as a first or second language throughout the world. Mems.: 60 national associations representing about 35,000 teachers, and some individual mems. 5th Congress July 1981, Rio de Janeiro, Brazil.

Pres. JÜRGEN OLBERT (Fed. Repub. of Germany); Sec.-Gen. MAY COLLET (France). Publs. *Bulletin* (2 a year), *Une Lettre de la FIPF* (quarterly).

Ibero-American Bureau of Education (*Oficina de Educación Iberoamericana*): Ciudad Universitaria, Madrid 3, Spain; f. 1949; an intergovernmental organization for educational, scientific, and technological co-operation in the Ibero-American countries; provides information and documentation on development of education; encourages cultural and educational exchange; organizes training courses; Congress (ministerial level) meets every 3 years. Mems.: govts. of 17 countries.

Sec.-Gen. GUILLERMO LOHMANN VILLENA. Publs. *Plana*† (monthly bulletin), *Impacto*† (quarterly, Spanish edition of Unesco's *Impact*), *Indices de Revistas de Bibliotecología* (quarterly).

Institute of Education: Fondation Européenne de la Culture, Université Dauphine, 1 place du Maréchal de Lattre de Tassigny, 75116 Paris, France; f. 1975 by the European Cultural Foundation, the European Commission, the International Council for Educational Development; it is an integral part of the Foundation but has academic autonomy; its main purpose is the study of specific policy issues in post-compulsory and higher education; research programmes and seminars undertaken for the three founding bodies, the Council of Europe, European governments, and other foundations, universities, or regional and local bodies.

Chair. Prof. ASA BRIGGS; Dir. Dr. LADISLAV CERYCH. Publs. *European Journal of Education* (quarterly in English), reports, etc.

Inter-American Council for Education, Science and Culture: General Secretariat of the Organization of American States, Washington, D.C. 20006, U.S.A.; f. 1970 as an organ of the OAS, replacing the Inter-American Cultural Council. Aims: to promote friendly relations and mutual understanding among the American people through educational, scientific and cultural co-operation and exchange; to help prepare the inhabitants of member states to contribute fully to their progress; to stimulate intellectual and artistic expression and help protect, preserve and increase the cultural heritage; to recommend procedures for intensifying the integration of the countries' efforts and periodically to evaluate these efforts. Mems.: the 25 mems. of OAS.

Exec. Sec. EDUARDO GONZÁLEZ REYES (Venezuela).

International Association for Educational and Vocational Guidance (*Association Internationale d'Orientation Scolaire et Professionnelle—AIOSP*): Postfach der BA, 8500 Nuremberg, Fed. Rep. of Germany; f. 1951 to contribute to the development of vocational guidance and promote contact between persons associated with it. Mems.: 40,000 from 40 countries.

Pres. Dr. E. DONALD SUPER (U.S.A.); Sec.-Gen. J. SCHAEFER (Fed. Rep. of Germany). Publ *Bulletin-AIOSP.*

International Association for Educational and Vocational Information (*Association internationale d'information scolaire universitaire et professionnelle*): 20 rue de l'Estrapade, 75005 Paris, France; f. 1956 to facilitate co-operation between national organizations concerned with supplying information to university and college students and secondary pupils and their parents, to compare methods and act as an international documentation centre, and to encourage the establishment of other national organizations. Mems.: national organizations in 30 countries.

Pres. C. VIMONT (France); Vice-Pres. Dr. LEVERKUS (Germany), M. KAWKA (Poland), M. AMARA (Tunisia), E. LAMA (Italy); Sec.-Gen. L. TODOROV (France). Publ. *Informations universitaires et professionnelles internationales* (quarterly).

International Association for the Exchange of Students for Technical Experience (IAESTE): Odos Patission 42, Athens, Greece; f. 1948 to organize exchange of students for on-the-job training. Mems.: 44 national committees and 3 co-operating institutions.

Gen. Sec. GEORGE ANEMOYANNIS. Publ. *Annual Report*†.

International Association of Dental Students: c/o Dr. John E. Seear, the Medical Protection Society Ltd., 50 Hallam St., London W1N 6DE, U.K.; f. 1951 to promote international contact between dental students, to advance and stimulate their interest in the science and art of dentistry, to promote exchanges and international congresses; Annual Congress and General Assembly August 1981, Alexandria, Egypt. Mems.: 100,000 students in 23 countries.

Pres. WOJCIECH CZEWOJA-KOWALSKI (U.K.); Sec. Gen. Dr. STEFAN EDGREN (Sweden). Publs. *IADS Newsletter* (quarterly), *Exchange Guide, Information Guide.*

International Association of Students in Economics and Commercial Sciences (*Association Internationale des Etudiants en Sciences Economiques et Commerciales—AIESEC*): Ave. A. Buyl 123, 1050 Brussels, Belgium; f. 1949 to promote international understanding through management training schemes, seminars, conferences, study tours and educational seminar traineeship programmes. Mems.: 340 universities in 58 countries.

Sec.-Gen. JOAN WILSON. Publs. *Compendium, Annual Report, Link Letter*† (quarterly), *Seminar Reports*, and sundry national committee publications.

International Association of University Professors and Lecturers: 6 rue de la République, 94160 Saint Mandé, France; f. 1944; statutes ratified 1947. Object: the development of academic fraternity amongst university teachers and research workers; the protection of independence and freedom of teaching and research; the furtherance of the interests of all university teachers; and the consideration of academic problems. Mems.: 186,000 in 35 countries.

Hon. Sec. Prof. F. MAURO. Publs. *Communication, The Recruitment and Training of University Teachers.*

International Baccalaureate Office (IBO): Palais Wilson, 1211 Geneva 14, Switzerland; f. as International Schools Examination Syndicate 1964, as IBO 1967. Aims: the planning of curricula and an international university entrance examination, the International Baccalaureate, acceptable to universities throughout the world. The first full Baccalaureate examination was held in 1970 and recognition has been obtained to date from many of the major universities in Europe, U.S.A., Middle East and Australia. An international Examining Board has been constituted, and more than 140 schools are participating.

Chair. of Council: JOHN GOORMAGHTIGH (Belgium); Dir. GÉRARD RENAUD (France).

International Bureau of Education (*Bureau international d'éducation*): (*see* chapter on UNESCO).

International Centre for Agricultural Education (CIEA) (*Internationales Studienzentrum für landwirtschaftliches Bildungswesen*): Federal Office for Agriculture, CH-3003 Berne, Switzerland; f. 1958; organizes international courses on vocational education and teaching in agriculture every two years; 12th course, July 1980.

Pres. Dr. W. THOMANN (Switzerland); Dir. J.-P. CHAVAN (Switzerland).

International Coordinating Committee for the Presentation of Science and the Development of Out-of-school Scientific Activities (ICC): 125 rue de Veeweyde, 1070 Brussels, Belgium; f. 1962 to co-ordinate and promote on an international level out-of-school scientific activities in co-operation with other international organizations; non-governmental, UNESCO consultative status 1967. Mems.: in 31 countries, associate mems. and correspondents in 108 countries.

Pres. Dr. ZAGAR (Yugoslavia); Sec.-Gen. R. OTTHIERS (Belgium). Publs. *Out-of-School Scientific and Technical Education*† (English, French), *ICC Bulletin*†.

International Council for Adult Education: 29 Prince Arthur Ave., Toronto, Canada M5R 1B2; f. 1973 to provide a network for international communication and information exchange; to encourage and stimulate the role of adult education in development; to strengthen research, training and organization of adult education, especially in developing countries. Mems.: 55 representatives of national and regional organizations, also liaison and reciprocal mems.

Pres. ROBERT GARDNER; Sec.-Gen. B. L. HALL. Publ. *Convergence*† (quarterly).

International Federation of Catholic Universities (*Fédération Internationale des Universités Catholiques—FIUC*): Secretariat: 77 *bis* rue de Grenelle, Paris 7e, France; f. 1949 to ensure a strong bond of mutual assistance among all Catholic universities in the search for truth to help to solve problems of growth and development, and to co-operate with other international organizations; 147 mems. in 34 countries.

Pres. Rev. HERVÉ CARRIER (Italy); Sec.-Gen. E. BONE (Catholic Univ., Louvain). Publs. *Annuarium Catholicarum Universitatum Foederationis, Catholicarum Institutorum de Studiis Superioribus Catalogues, Supplementa Annuari et Catalogi, Documenta, Educational Planning, Monographs.*

International Federation of "Ecole Moderne" Movements (*Fédération internationale des mouvements d'école moderne*): 42 Grande Rue, 92310 Sèvres, France; f. 1957 to bring into contact associations devoted to the improvement of school organization and to work for the adoption of techniques advocated by C. Freinet; conducts courses for teachers, promotes interschool exchanges of correspondence and magazines. Mems.: associations of teachers in 38 countries.

Pres. ROGER UEBERSCHLAG (France); Sec. RENÉ LINARES (France). Publs. *L'Educateur* (two a month), *Bibliothèque de Travail, Bibliothèque de Travail Junior, Bibliothèque de Travail Sonore, Bibliothèque de l'Ecole Moderne, Art Enfantin, Lien Fimem* (quarterly), *Multilettre* (monthly), etc.

International Federation of Organisations for School Correspondence and Exchange (*Fédération internationale des organisations de correspondance et d'échanges scolaires—FIOCES*): 29 rue d'Ulm, 75230 Paris Cedex 05, France; f. 1929. Aims: to contribute to the knowledge of foreign languages and civilisations and to bring together young people of all nations by furthering international scholastic exchanges including: international scholastic correspondence, individual and group visits to foreign countries, individual accommodation with families, placements in international holiday camps, etc. Mems.: comprises 72 national bureaux of scholastic correspondence and exchange in 32 countries.

Pres. JAMES PLATT (U.K.); Sec.-Gen. JOSEPH MAJAULT (France); Exec. Sec. ANDRÉE ELMARY (France). Publ. *Bulletin* (annually).

International Federation of University Women (*Fédération internationale des femmes diplômées des universités*): 37 Quai Wilson, 1201 Geneva, Switzerland; f. 1919. Object: to promote understanding and friendship between university women irrespective of race, nationality, religion or political opinions, to encourage international co-operation, to further the development of education, to represent university women in international organizations, to encourage the full application of their knowledge and skills to the problems which arise at all levels of public life and to encourage their participation in the solving of these problems; sponsors regional seminars; consultative status with the appropriate intergovernmental organizations; administers fellowships and study grants; provides assistance for university women in need; undertakes studies dealing with the status of women. Affiliates 55 national associations with 236,000 mems.

Pres. Dame DAPHNE PURVES (N.Z.); Exec. Sec. ALICE PAQUIER. Publs. *Newsletter*† (annual), *Communiqué* (2 a year, limited circulation), *Triennial Report.*

International Federation of Workers' Educational Associations: ÖGB, Postfach 155, Vienna, Austria; f. 1947 to promote co-operation between national bodies concerned with workers' education, through clearing-house services, exchange of information, publications, conferences, summer schools, etc.

Pres. IVAR LEVERAAS (Norway); Gen. Sec. KARL HUMMEL (Austria).

International Institute for Adult Literacy Methods: P.O.B. 1555, Teheran, Iran; f. 1968 by UNESCO and the Government of Iran; carries out comparative studies of the methods, media and techniques used in literacy programmes; maintains documentation service and library on literacy; arranges seminars.

Dir Dr. JOHN W. RYAN. Publs. *Literacy Review* (3 a year), *Awareness List* (3 a year, in co-operation with UNESCO), *Literacy in Development* (monograph series in English, Spanish and Arabic).

International Institute for Educational Planning: (*see* chapter on UNESCO).

International League for Child and Adult Education (*Ligue Internationale de l'Enseignement, de l'Education et de la Culture Populaire*): 3 rue Récamier, 75341 Paris Cedex 07, France; f. 1947; to further the ideal of public education untrammelled by moral, intellectual, racial or political obstacles. Mems. over 4 million from 25 countries.

Pres. Prof. ARNOULD CLAUSSE (Belgium); Sec.-Gen. ALBERT JENGER (France).

International Phonetic Association (IPA): University College, Gower St., London, WC1E 6BT, U.K.; f. 1886 to promote the scientific study of phonetics and its applications. Mems.: 800.

Pres. (vacant); Sec. Dr. J. C. WELLS (U.K.); Treas. Prof. A. C. GIMSON (U.K.). Publ. *Journal of the International Phonetic Association* (twice yearly).

International Schools Association (ISA): Palais Wilson 35, 1211 Geneva 14, Switzerland; f. 1951 to co-ordinate work in International Schools and promote their development; merged in 1968 with the Conference of Internationally-minded Schools (CIS) and now counts in its membership a number of selected national schools; member schools maintain the highest standards and accept pupils of all nationalities, irrespective of sex, race and creed; ISA carries out curriculum research; convenes annual Conferences on problems of curriculum and educational reform; has consultative status with UNESCO and ECOSOC. Mems.: 75 schools throughout the world.

Chair. Dr. PAUL SCHEID. Publs. *Educational Bulletin*† and *Magazine*† (5 a year).

International Society for Business Education (*Société internationale pour l'enseignement commercial*): 1052 Le Mont sur Lausanne, Switzerland; f. 1901 to organize international courses and congresses on business education. Mems.: national organizations and individuals in 16 countries.

Pres. BO LJUNGMAN (Sweden); Dir. Prof. FELIX SCHMID (Switzerland). Publ. *International Review for Business Education.*

International Society for Education through Art—INSEA (*Société Internationale pour l'Education Artistique*): c/o 106 rue du Point du Jour, 92100 Boulogne, France; f. 1951 to unite art teachers throughout the world, to exchange information and co-ordinate research into art education. A Category "B" Society of UNESCO, being the non-governmental world organization for the study of art education, international congresses, exhibitions and other activities. Approximately 1,000 members.

World Pres. Mme. AIMÉE HUMBERT (France). Publ. *Education through Art* (annual).

International Union of Students (*Union internationale des étudiants*): P.O.B. 58, 17th November St., 11001 Prague 01, Czechoslovakia; f. 1946 by World Student Congress in Prague. Objects: to defend the rights and interests of students, to strive for peace, national independence, academic freedom and democratic education and to unite the student movement in furtherance of these objectives. Activities include conferences, meetings, solidarity campaigns, relief projects, award of scholarships, travel and exchange, sports events, cultural projects, publicity and other activities in the furtherance of the Union's aims. Nationally representative student organizations of 103 countries are members.

Pres. MIROSLAV ŠTĚPÁN (Czechoslovakia); Gen. Sec. FATHI EL-FADL (Sudan). Publs. *World Student News, News Service, African Bulletin, Arab Bulletin, Asian Bulletin, Chile Bulletin, DE—Bulletin, European Bulletin* (monthly), *Latin America Bulletin* (monthly), *Young Cinema and Theatre, Democratisation of Education, Sport Bulletin* (quarterly).

International University Exchange Fund: P.O.B. 108, 1211 Geneva 24, Switzerland; Regional Offices: P.O.B. 50334, Lusaka, Zambia; Apdo. 381, San Pedro Montes de Oca, San José, Costa Rica; London Office: International Development Centre, Parnell House, 25 Wilton Rd., London, SW1V 1JS; f. 1961 as an international non-governmental organization assisting refugees, primarily from Africa and Latin America, in the field of education and educational placement. Co-operates in development and other projects in Africa and Latin America. There were 2,500 scholarships awarded in 1979.

Dir. HASSIM SOUMARÉ (acting). Publs. reports on political situation in Southern Africa and Latin America.

International Young Christian Workers (*Jeunesse ouvrière chrétienne internationale*): 26 rue Juste Lipse, 1040 Brussels, Belgium; f. 1925 to give social, economic and educational aid to the young worker; holds international councils. Mems.: national organizations in 85 countries.

Pres. JOSE LUIS VELEZ (Puerto Rico).

International Youth and Student Movement for the United Nations (ISMUN) (*Mouvement international des jeunes et des étudiants pour les Nations Unies*): c/o Palais des Nations, 1211 Geneva 10, Switzerland; f. 1949; works with young people and students for the aims and ideals of the United Nations: holds seminars, undertakes research, lobbying on human rights, social and economic development, disarmament, environment, and UN operation with specific reference to the role of young people. Mems.: associations in 45 countries.

Sec.-Gen. RICARDO DOMINICE. Publs. *Square Deal Analysis and Action* (every 2 months), *Square Deal Reference Documents* (list updated annually), *Newsletter* (monthly), Reports of seminars, conferences, etc.

Latin American Institute for Educational Communication (*Instituto Latinoamericano de la Comunicación Educativa*): Apdo. Postal 94-328, Mexico 10, D.F., Mexico; f. 1956; supported by UNESCO and the Mexican Government to provide leadership in educational communication and instructional technology to Latin America; regional co-operation in research, experimentation, production and distribution of AV materials; training in educational technology at the Center for Training and Advanced Studies on Educational Communication; Center of AV Documentation for Latin America (CEDAL); specific technical assistance at mems.' request.

Dir-Gen. Dr. JOSÉ M. ALVAREZ MANILLA. Publ. *Síntesis Informativa*† (every 2 months).

Montessori International Association (*Association Montessori Internationale*): Koninginneweg 131, 1075 CN Amsterdam, Holland; f. 1929; to propagate the ideals and educational methods of Dr. Maria Montessori and to spread knowledge on child development without racial, religious or political prejudice. Branches in 13 countries. Activities: organizing training courses for teachers in 12 countries, and international congresses connected with education, creation of new training centres and new national Montessori Associations; organizing international study conferences.

Pres. Dr. J. A. LAUWERIJS; Dir.-Gen. MARIO M. MONTESSORI; Organizing Sec. Mrs. H. VAN SON; Treas. H. STEENBERGH. Publs. *Communications* (3 or 4 a year), Congress Report, etc.

Organisation of the Catholic Universities of Latin America (*Organización de Universidades Católicas de América Latina—ODUCAL*): f. 1953; aims to assist the cultural development of Latin America and to promote the activities of Catholic higher education in the region;

mems.: 34 Catholic universities in Argentina, Brazil, Colombia, Cuba, Ecuador, Mexico, Peru, Puerto Rico, and Venezuela.

Pres. Mgr. Dr. OCTAVIO N. DERISI; Sec.-Gen. Dr. EDUARDO MIRAS, Pontifical Catholic University of Buenos Aires, Juncal 1912, Buenos Aires, Argentina.

Pax Romana: B.P. 1062, 1701 Fribourg, Switzerland; f. 1921; two branches from 1947: the student branch—*International Movement of Catholic Students* (60 national federations); the graduate branch—*International Catholic Movement for Intellectual and Cultural Affairs* (60 national federations and 5 international professional federations).

Sec.-Gen. (IMCS) ZOZIMO LEE; Sec.-Gen. (ICMICA) ERIC SOTTAS. Publs. *Convergence* (English and French, 4 a year), and national and professional federation publications.

Regional Centre for Adult Education and Functional Literacy for Latin America (*Centro Regional de Alfabetización Funcional en las Zonas Rurales de América Latina*): Pátzcuaro, Michoacán, Mexico; f. 1951 under the auspices of UNESCO; runs courses on fundamental and vocational education and is closely linked with development programmes for Latin America. Library of *c.* 55,000 vols. Dir. ADALBERTO VELÁZQUEZ S. Publs. *Boletín Informativo*† (monthly), *Indice de Información*† (every 2 months), *Educacion y Adultos*† (quarterly).

Southeast Asian Ministers of Education Organization (SEAMEO): c/o SEAMES, Darakarn Bldg., 920 Sukhumvit Rd., Bangkok 11, Thailand; f. 1965. Objects: to promote co-operation among the Southeast Asian nations through co-operative projects and programmes in education, science and culture; 7 regional centres/projects. Mems.: Indonesia, Kampuchea, Laos, Malaysia, Philippines, Singapore, Thailand and Viet-Nam. Associate Mems.: Australia, France, New Zealand.

Pres. H.E. Dr. ONOFRE D. CORPUZ (Philippines); Dir. Dr. ADUL WICHIENCHARDEN. Publs. reports of conferences and seminars, annual reports, quarterly periodical, technical publications.

Standing Conference of Rectors, Presidents and Vice-Chancellors of the European Universities (CRE) (*Conférence permanente des recteurs, présidents et vice-chanceliers des universités européennes—CRE*): 10 rue du Conseil Général, 1211 Geneva 4, Switzerland; f. 1959 to achieve and develop co-operation between the executive heads of all European Universities and between their teachers, research workers and students. Organizes General Assemblies every 5 years of all European universities, and conferences twice each year; clearing house for information. Mems.: 360 universities in 23 European countries.

Pres. Prof. Dr. GERRIT VOSSERS (Netherlands); Sec.-Gen. ANDRIS BARBLAN (Switzerland). Publ. *CRE Information* (quarterly).

Standing Conference on University Problems: c/o Council of Europe, F-67006 Strasbourg-Cedex, France; f. 1968 under the Council for Cultural Co-operation, set up within the Council of Europe by the signatories of the European Cultural Convention, to promote co-operation among European countries in the field of higher education and research and to propose activities for the CCC annual programme. Mems.: representatives of institutions of tertiary education and senior government officials from the twenty-two countries signatories of the European Cultural Convention.

Chair. P. SABOURIN (France); Sec. J. P. MASSUE.

Unesco European Centre for Higher Education (*Centre européen pour l'enseignement supérieur—CEPES*): 39 str. Stirbei Voda, 70732 Bucharest, Romania; f. 1972; documentation, information and statistics, European network of liaison officers, thematic activities for European co-operation in higher education.

Dir. AUDUN ØFJORD. Publ. *Higher Education in Europe* (every 3 months in English, French, Russian).

Unesco Institute for Education (*Institut de l'Unesco pour l'Education/Unesco-Institut für Pädagogik*): 58 Feldbrunnenstr., 2 Hamburg 13, Federal Republic of Germany; f. 1952 as an autonomous international research organization jointly sponsored by UNESCO and the Government of the Federal Republic of Germany; its main concern is the content and quality of education, and its main activities are research, diffusion, promotion and documentation.

Dir. R. DAVE (India). Publs. *International Review of Education* (quarterly), series on International Studies in Education, Educational Research and Practice, Monographs, Advances in Lifelong Education, Bibliographical Lists on Lifelong Education (3 a year), *Lifelong Education* (3 a year).

Union of the Universities of Latin America (*Unión de Universidades de América Latina*): **Secretariat: Apdo.** 70232, Ciudad Universitaria, México 20, D.F., Mexico; f. 1949 to link the Latin American universities and contribute to the cultural integration of the regional nations; organizes General Assemblies and Conferences; permanent statistical work; Center of University Information and Documentation. Mems.: 114 universities in 20 countries.

Pres. Dr. FERNANDO HINESTROSA (Colombia); Sec.-Gen. Dr. PEDRO ROJAS (Mexico). Publs. *Universidades* (review) (quarterly), *Gaceta UDUAL* (monthly), *Censo Universitario Latinoamericano* (every 2 years).

World Association for Educational Research (*Association Mondiale des Sciences de l'Education*): f. 1953, present title adopted 1977. Aims: to encourage research in educational sciences by organizing congresses, issuing publications, the exchange of information, etc. Individual members in 49 countries.

Pres. Prof. M.-L. VAN HERREWEGHE (Belgium); Secretariat: Henri Dunantlaan 1, B-9000 Ghent, Belgium. Publ. *Communicationes*† (2 a year).

World Confederation of Organisations of the Teaching Profession: WCOTP, 5 Avenue du Moulin, 1110 Morges (Vaud), Switzerland; f. 1952. Purposes: to foster a conception of education directed toward the promotion of international understanding and good will; to improve teaching methods, educational organization and the training of teachers to equip them better to serve the interests of youth; to defend the rights and the material and moral interests of the teaching profession; to promote closer relationships between teachers in different countries. Membership: 116 national teachers' associations in 76 countries.

Sec.-Gen. JOHN M. THOMPSON (U.K.). Publs. *Annual Report* (in English, French and Spanish), *Echo* (quarterly newsletter in English, French, Spanish, Japanese, Korean, Chinese, German and Greek).

International Council on Health, Physical Education and Recreation: 1201 Sixteenth St., N.W., Washington, D.C. 20036, U.S.A.; f. 1958 by the World Confederation of Organisations of the Teaching Profession to encourage the development of programmes in health, physical education and recreation throughout the world.

World Education Fellowship: 33 Kinnaird Ave., London, W4 3SH, U.K.; f. 1921 to promote the exchange and practice of progressive educational ideas in all parts of the world; sections and groups in 22 countries.

Pres. Dr. MADHURI SHAH; Sec. Mrs. R. CROMMELIN. Publ. *The New Era* (incorporating *World Studies Bulletin* and *Ideas*) (6 issues per annum).

World Student Christian Federation (WSCF) (*Fédération Universelle des Associations Chrétiennes d'Etudiants—FUACE*): Centre John Knox, 27 chemin des Crêts-de-Pregny, 1218 Grand Saconnex (GE), Switzerland; f. 1895; an ecumencial student, university and secondary school organization with participants from all major Christian confessions; related groups in 100 countries.

Chair. BEREKET YEBIO (Ethiopia); Gen. Sec. Dr. EMIDIO CAMPI (Italy). Publs. *WSCF Books*, *WSCF Dossier* (occasional), *WSCF Journal* (quarterly).

World Union of Jewish Students: 247 Gray's Inn Rd., London WC1X 8QZ, England; f. 1924 to act as an umbrella organization for national student bodies and to act in educational and political matters where possible in co-operation with non-Jewish student organizations, International Young Non-Governmental Organizations, etc.; organizes Project Areivim, a service programme for Diaspora communities; divided into six regions; organizes Congress every three years. Mems.: 34 national unions representing over 17,000 students.

Chair. ANETA JOSEFOWICZ; Sec.-Gen. IRVING WALLACH. Publs. *OLAM*† (quarterly), *ELUL*† (every 2 months) and others in English, French, Spanish and Hebrew.

World University Service: 260 High Rd., London, N15, England; f. 1920 to provide mutual assistance from pooled resources of the world university community to meet the urgent needs and problems facing universities and university students in various parts of the world. Its programme includes a Research Action Unit to investigate and evaluate socio-political issues, projects to combat prejudice and discrimination, Social Action and Community Development projects, and a limited number of emergency and university welfare programmes. Mems.: 65 National Committees.

Chair. Prof. W. FOX-DECENT; Gen. Sec. (vacant). Publs. *WUS Action* (quarterly), *Annual Report*, Reports on Conference, Seminars and Research.

ENGINEERING AND TECHNOLOGY

Union of International Engineering Organizations (UIEO) (*Union des associations techniques internationales*): 112 blvd. Haussmann, 75008 Paris, France; f. 1951. Activities: The co-ordination of international congresses planned by member organizations, collaboration with UNESCO, the publication of technical bibliographies and of technical dictionaries in several languages. Membership: 19 international organizations.

Chair. H. J. SCHOEMAKER (Netherlands); Sec.-Gen. R. PÉLISSIER (France).

MEMBER ORGANIZATIONS

Fédération Internationale de la Précontrainte (*International Organisation for the development of concrete, prestressing and related materials and techniques*): Wexham Springs, Slough SL3 6PL, England; f. 1952; aims to promote Groups for the advancement of prestressing and related development in all countries, to act as a link between Associations, Committees and Federation Groups on all aspects of prestressing, to exchange opinions on scientific and technical problems, in particular by the organization of international congresses and symposia, and to promote research and development work; 43 mem. countries.

Pres. Prof. R. LACROIX (France); Sec.-Gen. B. W. SHACKLOCK (U.K.). Publs. *Proceedings of Congresses and Symposia*, technical reports, guides to good practice, recommendations.

International Association for Bridge and Structural Engineering (*Association Internationale des Ponts et Charpentes*): Secretariat: AIPC-IVBH-IABSE, ETH-Hönggerberg, CH-8093 Zürich, Switzerland; f. 1929. Aims: international co-operation among scientists, engineers and manufacturers; interchange of knowledge, ideas and the results of research work in the sphere of bridge and structural engineering in general, whether in steel, concrete or another material. Mems.: 3,050 from 72 countries.

Pres. Prof. BRUNO THUERLIMANN; Exec. Dir. ALAIN GOLAY. Publs. *IABSE Periodica* (*Surveys*, *Journal*, *Proceedings*, *Structures*, *Bulletin*; 4 a year), Reports of Symposia and Congresses (3 a year).

International Association for Hydraulic Research (*Association Internationale de Recherches Hydrauliques*): P.O. Box 177, 2600 MH Delft, Netherlands; f. 1935; 2,300 individual mems., 270 corporate mems.

Sec. J. E. PRINS (Netherlands). Publs. *Journal* (quarterly, in English or French, and a summary in either language), *Directory of Hydraulic Research Institutes and Laboratories* (every 5 or 6 years), *Proceedings of Biennial Congresses*.

International Commission on Irrigation and Drainage (*Commission internationale des irrigations et du drainage*): 48 Nyaya Marg, Chanakyapuri, New Delhi 110 021, India; f. 1950. Mems.: 76 countries.

Pres. R. DARVES-BORNOZ (France); Sec.-Gen. K. K. FRAMJI (India).

International Commission on Large Dams (*Commission internationale des grands barrages*): 151 blvd. Haussmann, 75008 Paris, France; f. 1925. Mems.: 71 countries.

Sec.-Gen. J. COTILLON.

International Committee of Foundry Technical Associations (*Comité International des Associations Techniques de Fonderie*): Walchestrasse 27, Case Postale 2815, CH-8023 Zurich, Switzerland; f. 1927 to bring together mem. associations in the technical field and promote their joint action in matters of common interest; annual congress; next congresses, Oct. 1981, Varna (Bulgaria), April 1982, Chicago (U.S.A.). Mems.: 33 national associations.

Pres. T. R. WILTSE (U.S.A.); Sec.-Gen. Dr. J. GERSTER (Switzerland).

International Conference on Large High Voltage Electric Systems (*Conférence Internationale des Grands Réseaux Electriques à Haute Tension*): 112 blvd. Haussmann, 75008 Paris, France; f. 1921; electrical aspects of electricity generation, sub-stations and transformer stations, high voltage electrical lines, interconnection of systems and their operation and protection. Mems.: 3,000.

Pres. R. GUCK; Sec.-Gen. R. PÉLISSIER (France). Publ. *Electra* (every 2 months).

International Federation of Automatic Control (IFAC) (*Fédération Internationale de l'Automatique*): IFAC Secretariat, Schlossplatz 12, A-2361, Laxenburg, Austria; f. 1957 to promote the science and technology of control in the broadest sense in all systems, e.g. engineering, physical, biological, social and economical, in both theory and application. Mems.: 40 national member organizations.

Pres. Prof. Y. SAWARAGI (Japan); Vice-Pres. Prof. T. VÁMOS (Hungary), Prof. M. THOMA (Fed. Repub. of Germany); Hon. Sec. F. MARGULIES (Austria). Publs.

IFAC Journal Automatica (mainly selected papers of IFAC-sponsored symposia; bi-monthly), *IFAC Newsletter.*

International Federation of Surveyors (*Fédération internationale des géomètres*): Fliederweg 11, CH-3600 Thun, Switzerland; f. 1878. Activities: nine technical commissions in three groups: Professional Organization and Activities; Surveys and Mapping; Land Administration; 50 national associations are affiliated.

Pres. Prof. Dr. H. MATTHIAS (Switzerland); Sec.-Gen. H. R. DÜTSCHLER (Switzerland). Publs. Reports of Congresses and bulletins.

International Gas Union (*Union Internationale de l'Industrie du Gaz*): 62 rue de Courcelles, 75008 Paris, France; f. 1931. Mems.: 36.

Sec.-Gen. B. GOUDAL.

International Institute of Welding (*Institut international de la soudure*): 54 Prince's Gate, Exhibition Rd., London SW7 2PG, U.K.; f. 1948. Mems.: 55 societies in 38 countries.

Pres. Dr. U. GIRARDI (Italy); Sec.-Gen. P. D. BOYD (U.K.). Publ. *Welding in the World* (bi-monthly).

International Institution for Production Engineering Research (*Collège international pour l'étude scientifique des techniques de production mécanique—CIRP*): 19 rue Blanche, 75009 Paris, France; f. 1950. Aims to promote by scientific research the study of mechanical processing of all solid materials including checks on efficiency and quality of work. Mems.: 137, and 69 correspondents in 26 countries.

Founder Pres. Prof. A. PORTEVIN (France); Pres. Prof. J. PEKLENIK (Yugoslavia); Sec.-Gen. Prof. F. LE MAITRE (France). Publs. *Annals* (annual), *Dictionary of Production Engineering.*

International Society for Soil Mechanics and Foundation Engineering (*Société internationale de mécanique des sols et de travaux de fondations*): Dept. of Civil Engineering, Kings College, Strand, London WC2R 2LS, U.K.; f. 1936; 52 national mem. societies, *c.* 11,000 individual mems.

Pres. Prof. M. FUKUOKA (Japan); Sec. J. K. T. L. NASH (U.K.). Publs. *Conference Proceedings, Geotechnical Abstracts* (monthly).

International Union for Electroheat (*Union Internationale d'Electrothermie*): 79 rue de Micromesnil, 75008 Paris, France; f. 1953, present title adopted 1957. Mems.: national committees in 20 countries and assoc. mems. in other countries.

Pres. E. TIBERGHIEN (Belgium); Gen. Delegate C. BARBAZANGES (France).

International Union of Public Transport (*Union Internationale des Transports Publics*): 19 Avenue de l'Uruguay, 1050 Brussels, Belgium; f. 1885 to study all problems related to the operation of public transportation; library of 10,000 vols. Mems.: 1,400.

Pres. Dr. Ing. F. PAMPEL (Fed. Repub. of Germany); Sec.-Gen. A. J. JACOBS (Belgium). Publs. *Review, Biblio-Index* (quarterly), *Reports* (every 2 years).

International Union of Testing and Research Laboratories on Materials and Structures—RILEM (*Réunion Internationale des Laboratoires d'Essais et de Recherches sur les Matériaux et les Constructions*): 12 rue Brancion, Paris 15e, France; f. 1947. Mems.: 720.

Pres. Prof. T. ERISMANN (Switzerland). Publ. *Materials and Structures—Research and Testing* (bi-monthly).

Permanent International Association of Navigation Congresses (*Association Internationale Permanente des Congrès de Navigation*): Résidence Palace, Quartier Jordaens, 155 rue de la Loi, 1040 Brussels, Belgium; f. 1885 to promote inland and ocean navigation by fostering and encouraging progress in the design, construction, improvement, maintenance and operation of inland and maritime waterways, ports and of coastal areas for the benefit of mankind. Mems.: 2,060 individual mems., 600 corporate mems.

Sec.-Gen. H. VANDERVELDEN (Belgium). Publs. *PIANC Bulletin*† (3 a year), *Papers of Congresses, Account of Proceedings of Congresses* (every 4 years), *Technical dictionary.*

Permanent International Association of Road Congresses (*Association Internationale Permanente des Congrès de la Route*): 43 ave. du Président Wilson, 75116 Paris, France; f. 1909 to help to promote a world network of roads; 1,640 mems.

Pres. M. MILNE (U.K.); Sec.-Gen. M. HUET. Publs. *Bulletin, Dictionnaires Techniques Routiers, Rapports.*

World Energy Conference, The: Central Office, 34 St. James's St., London, SW1A 1HD, U.K.; f. in 1924 in Great Britain, upon the initiative of the late D. N. Dunlop, to form a link between various branches of power and fuel technology. It maintains a liaison between national experts (engineers, administrators, scientists and economists) throughout the world. There are now 76 National Committees. Conferences are held every three years. The International Executive Council meets every year. Last conference Munich, Sept. 1980; theme: "Energy for our world".

Pres. A. G. MUTDOGAN (Turkey); Chair. of Int. Exec. Council Dr. S. O. HULTIN (Finland); Sec.-Gen. E. RUTTLEY. Publs. *Transactions of Conferences, W.E.C. Survey of Energy Resources* (every 6 years, new edition 1980), *Technical Data on Fuel* (new edition, S.I. Units, 1976), *Technical Study Committee Reports, Directory of Energy Information Centres,* Conservation Commission Reports, etc.

OTHER ORGANIZATIONS

European Organisation for Civil Aviation Electronics—EUROCAE: (*Organisation Européenne pour l'Equipement Electronique de l'Aviation Civile*): 11 rue Hamelin, 75783 Paris Cedex 16, France; f. 1963; the organization studies and advises on problems related to the application of electronics and electronic equipment to aviation and prepares minimum performance specifications which administrations in Europe may use for approving equipment; 56 mems.

Pres. J. PAGNARD; Sec.-Gen. T. J. McWIGGAN.

International Association on Water Pollution Research: f. 1965 to encourage international communication, cooperative effort, and a maximum exchange of information on water quality management; to sponsor regular international meetings; to provide a scientific medium for the publication of research reports and to shorten the time-lag between development of research and its application. Mems.: 25 national, 230 associates, 1,000 individuals.

Pres. BERTIL HAWERMAN (Sweden); Sec.-Treas. R. FAIRALL, Chichester House, 278 High Holborn, London, WC1V 7HE, England. Publs. *Water Research* (monthly), proceedings of biennial international conferences and *Progress in Water Technology* (every two months).

International Cargo Handling Co-ordination Association (ICHCA): Abford House, 15 Wilton Rd., London, SW1V 1LX, England; f. 1952. Aims to foster economy and efficiency in the movement of goods from origin to destination. Mems.: over 1,800 in more than 90 countries.

Pres. Dr. J. E. JANSSON (Finland); Sec.-Gen. PATRICK FINLAY. Publs. *Cargo Systems* (monthly), *Cargo Handling Abstracts* (quarterly), various technical publications.

International Commission on Glass (ICG) (*Commission internationale du verre—CIV*): c/o J. Götz, Vysoka Skola Chem.-Technol. Katedra Technologie Silikatu, Suchbatarova 1905, 166 28 Prague 6, Czechoslovakia; f. 1933 in Venice to encourage co-operative effort in glass technology and to facilitate the exchange of information on the art, science and technology of glass. Mems.: national societies, institutes or individuals in 20 countries.

Hon. Pres. B. LONG (France); Pres. P. GILARD (Belgium); Hon. Treas. P. LE CLERC (France); Hon. Sec. J. GÖTZ (Czechoslovakia). Publs. *Bibliography of Glass Literature, Dictionary of Glass Making* (in six languages), etc.

International Commission on Illumination (*Commission internationale de l'éclairage*): 52 blvd. Malesherbes, 75008 Paris, France; f. 1900 as International Commission on Photometry, reorganized as C.I.E. 1913. Objects: to provide an international forum for all matters relating to the science and art of illumination; to promote by all appropriate means the study of such matters; to provide for the interchange of information between the different countries; to agree upon and to publish international recommendations. Mems.: 29 affiliated National Illumination Committees.

Exec. Sec. P. LEMAIGRE-VOREAUX. Publs. *Comptes Rendus* of quadrennial plenary sessions, *International Lighting Vocabulary* in French, English, German and Russian, containing 530 terms with definitions, *International recommendations for colours of light signals, lighting of roads for motorized traffic and tunnel lighting*, technical committee reports, etc.

International Council for Building Research, Studies and Documentation (CIB) (*Conseil international du bâtiment pour la recherche, l'étude et la documentation*): 704 Weena, P.O.B. 20704, 3001 JA Rotterdam, Netherlands; f. 1953 to, encourage and facilitate co-operation in building research, studies and documentation in all aspects.

Pres. S. E. LUNDBY (Norway); Sec.-Gen. J. R. JANSSENS (Belgium). Publs. *Building Research and Practice* (bimonthly), *Directory of Building Research and Development Organizations*, CIB Congress books (every 3 years), etc.

International Electrotechnical Commission (*Commission Electrotechnique Internationale*): 1–3 rue de Varembé, 1211 Geneva 20, Switzerland; f. 1906 to promote international co-operation in the electrotechnical industry; has originated a multilanguage vocabulary with more than 100,000 terms; originated the "International System" (S.I.) of units of measurement; established world-wide standards for electrical equipment and installations; 42 national cttees.

Pres. W. A. MCADAMS (U.S.A.); Gen. Sec. C. J. STANFORD (U.K.).

International Federation for Housing and Planning (*Fédération internationale pour l'habitation, l'urbanisme et l'aménagement des territoires*): Wassenaarseweg 43, 2596 CG The Hague, Netherlands; f. 1913 to promote throughout the world the study and practice of housing and regional, town and country planning, to secure higher standards of housing, the improvement of towns and cities and a better distribution of the population.

Pres. Ir. TH. QUENÉ (Netherlands); Sec.-Gen. JON H. LÉONS (Netherlands). Publs. *News Sheet* (7 a year), Congress and Seminar Reports, and occasional special publications.

International Federation of Operational Research Societies: IMSOR, Bldg. 349, Tech. Univ. of Denmark, 2800 Lyngby; f. 1959. Aims: the development of operational research as a unified science and its advancement in all nations of the world. Mems.: 31 national societies with *c.* 24,000 mems., and 6 kindred societies.

Pres. Prof. ROGER H. COLLCUTT (U.K.); Chair. External Affairs Cttee. Dr. DAVID B. HERTZ (U.S.A.); Sec. Mrs. HELLE WELLING. Publs. *International Abstracts in Operations Research, Proceedings of International Conferences on OR* (triennial).

International Federation of Societies of Automobile Engineers (FISITA) (*Fédération internationale des sociétés d'ingénieurs des techniques de l'automobile*): 3 ave. du Président Wilson, F75116 Paris, France; f. 1947 to promote the exchange of information between member societies, ensure standardization of techniques and terms, to conduct research on technical and managerial problems and generally to encourage the technical development of mechanical transport. Member organizations in 18 countries.

Pres. DIARMUID DOWNS; Sec.-Gen. E. P. DAVIES.

International Institute of Refrigeration (*Institut International du Froid*): 177 blvd. Malesherbes, 75017 Paris, France; intergovernmental organization created June 21st, 1920. Object: the study of all technical, scientific, economic and industrial questions concerning refrigeration. Study and research are undertaken, under the direction of a Scientific Council, by International Commissions, the number and duties of which are decided by the General Conference. Mems.: 55 countries.

Dir. M. ANQUEZ (France). Publs. *Bulletin de l'IIF* (in French and English), *Proceedings of Meetings of Scientific and Technical Commissions, International Journal of Refrigeration* and basic publications.

International Iron and Steel Institute (IISI) (*Institut international du fer et de l'acier*): Ave. Hamoir 12/14, B-1180 Brussels, Belgium; f. 1967. Objects: to promote the welfare and interests of the world's steel industries; to undertake research in all aspects of steel industries; to serve as a forum for exchange of knowledge and discussion of problems relating to steel industries; to collect, disseminate and maintain statistics and information; to serve as a liaison body between international and national steel organizations. Members in 42 countries.

Chair. D. SPETHMANN (Fed. Rep. of Germany); Vice-Chair. EISHIRO SAITO (Japan), FREDERICK G. JAICKS (U.S.A.); Sec.-Gen. LENHARD J. HOLSCHUH. Publs. *Conference Proceedings, Statistical and Economic Reports, Technical Surveys, Bulletins, World Steel in Figures 1980.*

International Organization for Standardization (*Organisation internationale de normalisation*): 1 rue de Varembé, C.P. 56, 1211 Geneva 20, Switzerland; f. 1947 to promote the development of standards in the world with a view to facilitating the international exchange of goods and services, and to developing mutual co-operation in the spheres of intellectual, scientific, technological and economic activity. Mems.: 87.

Pres. HENRI DURAND (France); Vice-Pres. RALPH L. HENNESSY (Canada); Sec.-Gen. O. STUREN. Publs. *ISO International Standards, ISO Memento* (annual), *ISO Catalogue* (annual), *ISO Bulletin* (monthly), *ISO Annual Review.*

International Society for Photogrammetry (*Société internationale de Photogrammétrie*): U.S. Geological Survey 516, Reston, Va. 22092, U.S.A.; f. 1910; research and information on the application of aerial and space photography and remote sensing to resource inventory, exploration and mapping. 66 member countries.

Pres. Dr. F. J. DOYLE (U.S.A.); Sec.-Gen. Dr. G. KONECNY (Fed. Repub. of Germany). Publs. *International Archives of Photogrammetry* (biennially), *Photogrammetria* (every 2 months).

LAW

The Hague Conference on Private International Law (*Conférence de La Haye de droit international privé*): Javastraat 2c, The Hague, Netherlands; f. 1893 to work for the unification of the rules of private international law. Mems.: governments of Argentina, Australia, Austria, Belgium, Canada, Czechoslovakia, Denmark, Egypt, Finland, France, Fed. Repub. of Germany, Greece, Ireland, Israel, Italy, Japan, Luxembourg, Netherlands, Norway, Portugal, Spain, Surinam, Sweden, Switzerland, Turkey, U.K., U.S.A., Venezuela, Yugoslavia.

Sec.-Gen. Dr. Georges A. L. Droz. Publs. *Actes and Documents* relating to each Session; various printed and mimeographed documents.

Institute of International Law (*Institut de droit international*): 52 ave. Atlantique, Bte. 10, 1150 Brussels, Belgium; f. 1873. Objects: To promote the development of international law by endeavouring to formulate general principles in accordance with civilized ethical standards, and by giving assistance to genuine attempts at the gradual and progressive codification of international law. Mems. limited to 60 members and 72 associates from all over the world.

Sec.-Gen. Prof. Paul de Visscher (Belgium). Publs. *Annuaire de l'Institut de Droit international*, 58 vols., *Tableau général des Résolutions (1873–1956)*.

Inter-American Bar Association: Suite 315, 1730 K Street, N.W., Washington, D.C. 20006, U.S.A.; f. 1940; mems.: bar associations and individual lawyers in 21 countries.

Sec.-Gen. John O. Dahlgren (U.S.A.). Publs. *Newsletter* (quarterly), *Conference Proceedings*.

Intergovernmental Copyright Committee: Copyright Division, Unesco, place de Fontenoy, 75700 Paris, France. Objects: to study the problems concerning the application and operation of the Universal Copyright Convention and to make provision for the periodic revisions of this Convention. Mems.: Algeria, Australia, Brazil, Costa Rica, France, Federal Republic of Germany, Ghana, India, Israel, Italy, Japan, Mexico, Netherlands, Senegal, Sweden, Tunisia, U.K., U.S.A., U.S.S.R. and Yugoslavia.

Chair. Ndéné Ndiaye (Senegal).

International Association for Penal Law (*Association internationale de droit pénal*): Faculté de Droit, 12 place du Panthéon, Paris 5e, France; f. 1924. Objects: To promote co-operation between those who, in different countries, are engaged in the study or practice of criminal law, to study crime, its causes and its cure, and to further the theoretical and practical development of international penal law; 800 mems.

Pres. H. H. Jescheck; Gen. Sec. M. Ch. Bassiouni. Publ. *Revue Internationale de Droit Pénal* (2 a year).

International Association for Philosophy of Law and Social Philosophy: 25 ave. des Hametons, 1170 Brussels, Belgium; f. 1909 for scientific research in philosophy of law and social philosophy at an international level; holds congresses and conferences. Mems.: over 2,000.

Sec.-Gen. Dr. H. Hubien. Publ. *Archiv für Rechts- und Sozial-philosophie* (quarterly).

International Association of Democratic Lawyers (IADL) (*Association internationale des Juristes Démocrates*): 49 avenue Jupiter, 1190 Brussels, Belgium; f. 1946; aims to facilitate contacts and exchanges of view between lawyers and lawyers' associations and to foster understanding and goodwill; to work together to achieve the aims of the Charter of the United Nations. Mems. from 65 countries; in consultative status with U.N. Economic and Social Council and with UNESCO.

Pres. Joë Nordmann (France); Sec.-Gen. Gerhard Stuby (Fed. Repub. of Germany); Publs. *Revue de Droit Contemporain* (twice a year; also published in English), *Bulletins*.

International Bar Association: Byron House, 7/9 St. James's St., London, SW1A 1EE, U.K.; f. 1947. Membership comprises 80 national bar associations of 54 countries and 6,000 individual lawyers.

Pres. E. Neil McKelvey (Canada); Sec.-Gen. John P. Bracken (U.S.A.); Treas. Dr. Harald Foglar-Deinhardtstein (Austria); Exec. Dir. Madeleine May. Publs. *International Bar News*, *International Legal Practitioner* (2 a year), *International Business Lawyer* (11 a year).

International Commission of Jurists (*Commission internationale de juristes*): P.O.B. 120, 109 route de Chêne, 1224 Chêne-Bougeries/Geneva, Switzerland; f. 1952 to promote and strengthen the Rule of Law in all its practical manifestations—institutions, legislation, procedures, etc.—and to defend it through the mobilization of world legal opinion in cases of general and systematic violation of, or serious threat to, such principles of justice.

Pres. Kéba M'Baye (Senegal); Sec.-Gen. Niall MacDermot (U.K.). Publs. Special reports, *The Review* (2 a year), *ICJ Newsletter* (quarterly), *Bulletin of the Centre for the Independence of Judges and Lawyers* (2 a year).

International Confederation of Societies of Authors and Composers (*Confédération internationale des sociétés d'auteurs et compositeurs*): 11 rue Keppler, 75116 Paris, France; f. 1926 to ensure more effective protection of the rights of authors and composers, to improve legislation on literary and artistic rights, and to organize research on problems concerning the rights of authors; participates in preparatory work for inter-governmental conferences on authors' rights. Member societies in 51 countries.

Pres. Stanley Adams (U.S.A.); Sec.-Gen. Jean-Alexis Ziegler. Publ. *Interauteurs*.

International Federation for European Law—FIDE: Drève des Renards 6, 1180 Brussels, Belgium; f. 1961 to advance studies on European law among members of the European Community by co-ordinating activities of member societies and by organizing regular colloquies on topical problems of European law. Mems.: 9 national associations.

Pres. Prof. O. Lando; Sec. H. Rasmussen.

International Institute for the Unification of Private Law (UNIDROIT) (*Institut international pour l'unification du droit privé*): via Panisperna 28, 00184 Rome, Italy; f. 1926 to undertake studies in comparative law, to prepare for the establishment of uniform legislation, to prepare drafts of international agreements on private law and to organize conferences and publish works on such subjects. Drafts of uniform laws on a number of subjects have either been submitted to diplomatic conferences of adoption or presented to the UN, the Council of Europe and the Intergovernmental Maritime Consultative Organization; meetings of organizations concerned with the unification of law; international congresses on private law; library of 210,000 vols. Mems.: governments of 49 countries.

Pres. Mario Matteucci (Italy); Sec.-Gen. Riccardo Monaco (Italy). Publs. *Uniform Law Review* (2 a year), *Digest of Legal Activities of International Organizations*, *News Bulletin* (quarterly), etc.

International Institute of Space Law (IISL) (*Institut International de Droit de l'Espace*): 250, rue Saint-Jacques, Paris 5e, France; f. 1960 at the XI Congress of the International Astronautical Federation; holds meetings, makes studies on juridical and sociological aspects of astronautics; publishes reports; makes awards; holds an annual Colloquium. Mems.: 400 individuals elected for life.

Pres. Mme. DIEDERICKS-VERSCHOOR (Netherlands); Vice-Pres. E. GALLOWAY (U.S.A.), G. P. ZHUKOV (U.S.S.R.); Sec. E. FASAN (Austria). Publs. *Proceedings of Colloquia, Annual Bibliography of Space Law and Related Matters, Reports on Teaching of Space Law, Proceedings of Symposia on Teaching.*

International Juridical Institute (*Institut juridique international*): Permanent Office for the Supply of Int. Legal Information, 6 Oranjestraat, The Hague, Netherlands; f. 1918. Object: To supply information in connection with any matter of international interest, not being of a secret nature, respecting international, municipal and foreign law and the application thereof.

Governing Board: Chair. W. L. HAARDT; Sec. J. VAN RIJN VAN ALKEMADE; Dir. C. D. VAN BOESCHOTEN, LL.D.

International Maritime Committee (*Comité maritime international*): 17 Borzestraat, B-2000 Antwerp, Belgium; f. 1897 to contribute to the unification of maritime and commercial law, maritime customs, usages and practices; promotes the establishment of national associations of maritime law and co-operates with other international associations or organizations having the same object; work includes drafting of conventions on collisions at sea, salvage and assistance at sea, limitation of shipowners' liability, maritime mortgages, etc. Mems.: national associations in 34 countries.

Pres. FRANCESCO BERLINGIERI (Italy); Secs.-Gen. (Executive) JAN RAMBERG, (Administrative and Treas.) HENRI VOET. Publs. *CMI News Letter, Year Book.*

International Union of Lawyers (*Union internationale des Avocats*): 82 ave. F. D. Roosevelt, 1050 Brussels, Belgium; f. 1927 to promote the independence and freedom of lawyers, and defend their ethical and material interests on an international level; to contribute to the development of international order based on law. Mems.: 84 (group), 1,500 (corresponding).

Pres. HAROLD H. HEALY, Jr. (U.S.A.); Secs.-Gen. FRANÇOIS MARTIN (France), MARIO SCAMONI (Italy), ANTONIO PLASENCIA (Spain), FRANS KELLERHALS (Switzerland); Treas. LUCIEN JANSON (Belgium). Publ. *Bulletin* (quarterly).

World Peace Through Law Center—WPTLC: Suite 800, 1000 Connecticut Ave. N.W., Washington, D.C. 20036, U.S.A.; f. 1963 to promote the continued development of international law and legal maintenance of world order; biennial world conferences, World Law Day, demonstration trials, research and action programmes and publications have contributed to the growth of law and legal institutions by focusing on matters of international concern. Mems.: lawyers, jurists and legal scholars in over 140 countries.

Pres. CHARLES S. RHYNE (U.S.A.); Vice-Pres. ALPHONSE BONI (Africa), LUIS M. BOFFI-BOGGERO (The Americas), R. JETHMALANI (Asia and Australasia), CARLO FORNARIO (Europe); Sec.-Gen. WILLIAM S. THOMPSON (U.S.A.); Exec. Dir. MARGARETHA M. HENNEBERRY (U.S.A.). Publs. *World Jurist, World Legal Directory, World Law Review*, research reports and pamphlet series, etc.

Affiliated bodies:

World Association of Judges—WAJ: f. 1966; to mobilize judicial leaders on important transnational legal issues and to improve the administration of justice.

World Pres. Hon. Dr. T. O. ELIAS (ICJ); Sec. Hon. SANSERN KRAICHITTI (Thailand); Treas. Hon. V. R. KRISHNA IYER (India); Exec. Sec. MARGARETHA M. HENNEBERRY (U.S.A.).

World Association of Lawyers—WAL: f. 1975; to develop transnational law and improve lawyers' expertise in related areas; over 70 committees studying the development of international law.

Exec. Sec. MARGARETHA M. HENNEBERRY (U.S.A.).

World Association of Law Professors—WALP: f. 1975; to focus the attention of legal scholars and teachers on transnational legal issues, and improve scholarship and education in international legal matters, including training, practice, administration of justice, human rights, the environment and co-ordination of legal systems.

Co-Chair. ATLE GRAHL-MADSEN (Norway), JOHN N. HAZARD (U.S.A.); Exec. Sec. MARGARETHA M. HENNEBERRY (U.S.A.).

World Association of Law Students—WALS: f. 1976; to focus the attention of law students on transnational legal issues, and foster world-wide communication and co-operation among law students and student organizations interested in international legal matters.

Pres. RUFUS RODRIGUEZ (Philippines); Exec. Sec. MARGARETHA M. HENNEBERRY (U.S.A.).

MEDICINE AND PUBLIC HEALTH

World Health Organization (*Organisation mondiale de la Santé*): avenue Appia, 1211 Geneva 27, Switzerland; f. 1948. WHO, a specialized agency of the United Nations, is an inter-governmental agency charged under the terms of its constitution "to act as the directing and co-ordinating authority on international health work". WHO has proclaimed the goal of "Health for all by the year 2000"—i.e. the attainment of a level of health that permits a socially and economically productive life. WHO carries out a variety of programmes including: research promotion and development through a network of collaborating national laboratories; development of national health services; family health; mental health; prevention and control of communicable diseases; promotion of environmental health; development of health manpower suited to particular needs; quality control of prophylactic, diagnostic and therapeutic substances and development of policies to enable third world countries to meet their needs for pharmaceuticals. In May 1980 it was announced that the global campaign against smallpox had succeeded in eradicating the disease. 155 mem. states and 1 associate; budget for 1980–81 U.S. $427,290,000; library of 100,000 vols., 3,200 periodicals and 2,000 other serials.

Dir.-Gen. Dr. HALFDAN MAHLER (Denmark). Publs. *Bulletin*† (WHO scientific papers and surveys, every 2 months), *Chronicle*† (monthly), *International Digest of Health Legislation*†, *World Health Statistics Report*† (quarterly), *World Health Statistics Annual*, *Weekly Epidemiological Record*, *Monograph Series*, *Public Health Papers*, *Technical Report Series*, *Official Records*. *WHO Offset Publication* (irregular), *World Health*† (monthly magazine intended for the general public).

Council for International Organisations of Medical Sciences (CIOMS) (*Conseil des organisations internationales des sciences médicales*): Secretariat: c/o WHO, avenue Appia, 1211 Geneva 27, Switzerland; f. 1949. Object: to facilitate and co-ordinate the activities of its members, to act as a co-ordinating centre between them and the national institutions, to maintain collaboration with the UN, to promote international activities in the field of medical sciences, to serve the scientific interests of the international biomedical community; 43 international associations, national academic and research councils in 25 countries, 23 associate mems.

Pres. Dr. M. BELCHIOR (Brazil); Exec. Sec. Dr. Z. BANKOWSKI (Poland). Publs. *Calendar of International and Regional Congresses* (annual), *Proceedings of Symposia*, *International Nomenclature of Diseases*.

INTERNATIONAL MEMBERS OF CIOMS

International Academy of Legal and Social Medicine (*Académie internationale de médecine légale et de médecine sociale*): c/o Prof. B. VOLARIĆ, Ul. Narodnog ustanka 9A, Rijeka, Yugoslavia; f. 1938. Holds an international Congress and General Assembly every three years.

Pres. Prof. MILČINSKI; Vice-Pres. Prof. GROMOV, Prof. RAEKALLIO, Prof. SPANN; Sec.-Gen. Prof. VOLARIĆ; Treas. Dr. ANDRE (Belgium).

International Association for the Prevention of Blindness (*Association internationale de prophylaxie de la cécité*): c/o 3885 Round Top Drive, Honolulu, Hawaii 96813, U.S.A.; f. 1927. Object: To study through international investigation the causes which may result in blindness or impaired vision, to encourage and promote measures calculated to eliminate such causes, and to disseminate knowledge on all matters pertaining to the use and care of the eyes.

Pres. Sir JOHN WILSON (U.K.); Gen. Sec. Dr. W. J. HOLMES (U.S.A.). Publ. *Journal of Social Ophthalmology* (2 a year).

International Association of Allergology (*Association Internationale d'Allergologie*): 1390 Sherbrooke St. West, Montreal H3G 1K2, Quebec, Canada; f. 1945. Object: to further work in the educational, research and practical medical aspects of allergy diseases. Membership: 39 national societies.

Pres. Dr. E. MATHOV (Argentina); Sec.-Gen. Dr. L. HENDERSON (U.S.A.).

International Association of Gerontology (IAG): Weizmann Institute of Science, P.O.B. 26, Rehovot, Israel; f. 1950 to promote contacts between people interested in the study of gerontology and to organize meetings and congresses. Mems.: 39 national societies and groups in 34 countries.

Pres. Prof. DAVID DANON (Israel); Sec. Dr. S. J. LEIBOVICH (Israel).

International Cardiovascular Society (*Société Internationale Cardiovasculaire*): 6 Beacon St., Boston, Mass. 02108, U.S.A.; f. 1950 to stimulate research and to exchange ideas on an international basis at biennial conferences. Mems.: 2,000.

Sec.-Gen. Dr. JOHN OCHSNER (U.S.A.). Publ. *Journal of Cardiovascular Surgery* (6 a year).

International College of Surgeons, The (*Le Collège International de Chirurgiens*): 1516 Lake Shore Drive, Chicago, Ill. 60610, U.S.A.; f. Geneva 1935, inc. Washington 1940. Organized as a world-wide institution for the advancement of the art and science of surgery, and to create a common bond among the surgeons of all nations and promote the highest standards of surgery; *c.* 14,000 mems.

Pres. Prof. CLAUDE ROMIEU (France); Int. Sec.-Gen. Dr. LUIS GRAÑA (U.S.A.). Publ. *International Surgery*.

International Dental Federation (*Fédération Dentaire Internationale*): f. 1900.

Exec. Dir. Dr. J. E. AHLBERG, 64 Wimpole St., London, W1M 8AL, U.K. Publ. *International Dental Journal and News Letter* (quarterly).

International Diabetes Federation (*Fédération internationale du diabète*): 10 Queen Anne St., London W1M 0BD, England; f. 1949. The objectives of the IDF are to further the acquisition and dissemination of useful and accurate information regarding Diabetes Mellitus, and to undertake such activities as will improve the physical and socio-economic welfare of persons afflicted with the disorder. Member associations in 55 countries.

Pres. Prof. A. E. RENOLD (Switzerland); Sec.-Gen. Dr. JAMES G. L. JACKSON (U.K.); Treas. Prof. E. F. PFEIFFER (Fed. Repub. of Germany). Publ. *IDF Bulletin* (3 a year).

International Epidemiological Association (*Association Internationale d'Epidémiologie*): c/o Dr. A. I. ADAMS, Health Commission of New South Wales, P.O.B. 2626, Sydney, N.S.W. 2001, Australia; f. 1954.

Chair. Dr. JAN KOSTRZEWSKI. Publ. *International Journal of Epidemiology* (quarterly).

International Federation for Medical and Biological Engineering (*Fédération Internationale d'Electronique Médicale et des Techniques Biologiques*): f. 1959 to promote international co-operation and communication among societies interested in life and engineering sciences. Member societies in 21 countries.

Pres. Prof. M. SAITO (Japan); Sec.-Gen. Dr. J. A. HOPPS, National Research Council of Canada, Room 164, Bldg. M-50, Ottawa, Ont. K1A 0R8, Canada. Publs. *Medical and Biological Engineering* (bi-monthly), *Proceedings of International Conference on Medical and Biological Engineering* (every 3 years).

International Federation of Ophthalmological Societies (*Fédération Internationale des Sociétés d'Ophtalmologie*): f. 1953; organizes the international congresses of ophthalmology; 60 national societies are affiliated.

Pres. Dr. JULES FRANÇOIS (Belgium); Sec. Prof. A. DEUTMAN, Dept. of Ophthalmology, University of Nijmegen, Philips van Leijdenlaan 15, Nijmegen, The Netherlands; Treas. Dr. STREIFF (Switzerland). Publ. *Acta*.

International Federation of Oto-Rhino-Laryngological Societies (*Fédération Internationale des sociétés oto-rhino-laryngologiques*): P.O.B. 19-136, México, DF, Mexico; f. 1965. Aims: to promote scientific and clinical research into oto-rhino-laryngology. Mems.: from 55 countries. Last congress: Argentina, 1977.

Pres. Dr. J. M. TATO (Argentina); Exec. Dir. Dr. FRANCISCO HERNÁNDEZ OROZCO (Mexico).

International Federation of Physical Medicine and Rehabilitation: f. 1952; international congresses every four years; next congress: Stockholm, May 1980; 38 national mem. societies.

Hon. Sec. Dr. A. P. M. VAN GESTEL, "Zonhove", Nieuwstraat, SON NB, Netherlands.

International Federation of Societies for Electroencephalography and Clinical Neurophysiology (*Fédération Internationale des Sociétés d'Electro-encéphalographie et de Neurophysiologie Clinique*): f. 1949. Object: to attain the highest level of knowledge in the field of electro-encephalography and clinical neuro-physiology in all the countries of the world; 41 mem. organizations (nat. societies).

Pres. Dr. R. NAQUET (France); Sec. Dr. R. J. ELLINGSON, Nebraska Psychiatric Institute, 602 South 44th Ave., Omaha, Neb. 68105, U.S.A. Publ. *Electroencephalography and Clinical Neurophysiology* (monthly).

International Federation of Surgical Colleges (*Fédération Internationale des Collèges de Chirurgie*): Secretariat: Royal College of Surgeons of Edinburgh, Nicolson St., Edinburgh, Scotland; f. Stockholm 1958. Object: The improvement and maintenance of the standards of surgery throughout the world, by establishment and maintenance of co-operation and interchange of medical and surgical information; encouragement of high standards of education, training and research in surgery and its allied sciences; provision of surgery, surgical training and surgical hospitals of high standard to countries of the world requesting aid. Membership: 45 national colleges or societies and 126 associates.

Pres. J. E. RHOADS (U.S.A.); Hon. Pres. Sir HARRY PLATT (U.K.); Vice-Pres. J. A. ROSS (U.K.), Prof. F. LINDER (Fed. Repub. of Germany); Sec. JOHN COOK (U.K.); Treas. Prof. W. P. LONGMIRE, Jr. (U.S.A.). Publs. *News Bulletin*.

International League Against Epilepsy (*Ligue internationale contre l'épilepsie*): c/o Sec.-Gen., Room 114, National Institutes of Health, Bethesda, Md. 20205, U.S.A.; f. 1909 to collect and disseminate information concerning epilepsy, to promote treatment of epileptic patients and to foster co-operation with other international institutions in similar fields. Mems.: national organizations (branches) and individuals in 25 countries.

Pres. DAVID D. DALY (U.S.A.); Sec.-Gen. J. KIFFIN PENRY (U.S.A.). Publ. *Epilepsia* (quarterly).

International League Against Rheumatism (*Ligue internationale contre le Rhumatisme*): f. 1928. Objects: To promote international co-operation for the study and control of rheumatic diseases; to encourage the foundation of national leagues against rheumatism; to organize regular international congresses and to act as a connecting link between national leagues and international organizations.

Pres. R. G. ROBINSON (Australia); Exec. Sec. H. STULZ, P.O.B. 145, 4011 Basel, Switzerland. Publs. *R: Bulletin de la Ligue Internationale contre le Rhumatisme*, *Annals of the Rheumatic Diseases* (in England), *Revue de Rhumatisme* (in France), *Rheumatismo* (in Italy) and *Arthritis and Rheumatism* (U.S.A.), etc.

International Leprosy Association (*Société internationale contre la lèpre*): 16 Bridgefield Rd., Sutton, Surrey, England; f. 1931 to promote international co-operation in work on leprosy.

Pres. M. F. LECHAT; Sec. Dr. S. G. BROWNE (U.K.). Publ. *International Journal of Leprosy and Other Mycobacterial Diseases*† (quarterly).

International Pediatric Association (*Association Internationale de Pédiatrie*): Château de Longchamp, Bois de Boulogne, 75016 Paris, France; f. 1912.

Pres. Dr. P. ROYER (France); Exec. Dir. Dr. I. DOGRAMACI (Turkey); Sec.-Treas. Dr. E. ROSSI (Switzerland).

International Society of Art and Psychopathology (*Société Internationale de Psychopathologie de l'Expression*): Centre Hospitalier St. Anne, 100 rue de la Santé, 75014 Paris; f. 1959 to bring together the various specialists interested in the problems of expression and artistic activities in connection with psychiatric, sociological and psychological research, as well as in the use of methods applied in fields other than that of mental illness. Mems.: 625.

Pres. Prof. VOLMAT (France); Sec.-Gen. Dr. C. WIART (France); Treas. Mme L. R. SCHWOB (France). Publ. *Confinia Psychiatrica* (quarterly).

International Society of Audiology (*Société Internationale d'Audiologie*): f. 1952 to advance the study of audiology and protect human hearing; 300 individual mems.

Sec.-Gen. Prof. R. HINCHCLIFFE, 330 Gray's Inn Rd., London, WC1X 8EE, England. Publs. Congress Reports, *Audiology, the Journal of Auditory Communication* (bi-monthly).

International Society of Blood Transfusion (*Société Internationale de Transfusion Sanguine*): 53 blvd. Diderot, 75012 Paris, France; f. 1938. Mems.: about 800 in 64 countries.

Pres. B. P. L. MOORE (Canada); Sec.-Gen. C. SALMON (France). Publ. *Vox Sanguinis*.

International Society of Criminology (*Société internationale de criminologie*): 4 rue de Mondovi, Paris 1e, France; f. 1934. Object: to promote the development of the sciences in their application to the criminal phenomenon; 1,200 mems.

Pres. DENIS SZABO (Canada); Gen. Sec. JACQUES VERIN (France).

International Society and Federation of Cardiology: C.P. 117, 1211 Geneva 12, Switzerland; f. 1978; inc. Int. Cardiology Federation and Int. Society of Cardiology; aims to promote the study, prevention and relief of cardiovascular diseases through scientific and public education programmes and exchange of materials between its affiliated societies and foundations and with other agencies having related interests; organizes world congresses every four years; next congress: 1982, Moscow, U.S.S.R.

Pres. Dr. HENRY NEUFELD (Israel); Sec. Dr. JORGE SONÍ (Mexico).

International Society of Geographical Pathology (ISGP) (*Société internationale de pathologie géographique*): University Hospital, Zürich, Switzerland; f. 1931 to study the relations which may exist between diseases and the geographical environments in which they occur. Mems.: national and regional committees in 42 countries.

Sec.-Gen. Prof. J. R. RUTTNER (Switzerland). Publ. Transactions of the Conferences (every 3 years).

International Society of the History of Medicine (*Société internationale d'histoire de la médecine*): f. 1921. Object: To study all questions relating to the history of biological and medical sciences.

Sec.-Gen. Dr. LOUIS DULIEU, 22 rue François Villeneuve, 34000 Montpellier, France.

International Society of Internal Medicine (*Federation of the National Societies of Internal Medicine*): f. 1948. Object: to encourage research and education in internal medicine; to sponsor the International Congress of Internal Medicine every other year. Mems.: 29 national societies, 3,000 individuals from 54 countries.

Pres. Dr. DAVID HUGHES (U.K.); Sec. Dr. P. C. FREI, Dépt. de Médecine, Centre Hospitalier Universitaire Vaudois, 1011 Lausanne, Switzerland.

International Society of Lymphology: Stefanienstrasse 8, 7800 Freiburg, Fed. Repub. of Germany; f. 1966 to further progress in lymphology and allied subjects; organizes international working groups, co-operates with other national and international organizations; international congresses and postgraduate courses. Mems.: 400.

Pres. H. A. DUMONT (U.S.A.); Sec.-Gen. H. WEISSLEDER (Fed. Repub. of Germany). Publs. *Lymphology* (quarterly), *Progress in Lymphology I and II*, congress proceedings.

International Society of Orthopaedic Surgery and Traumatology (*Société internationale de chirurgie orthopédique et de traumatologie*): 43 rue des Champs-Elysées, Brussels, Belgium; f. 1929. Objects: To contribute to the progress of science by the study of questions pertaining to orthopaedic surgery and traumatology. Congresses are convened every three years. 75 member countries, 2,550 members.

Pres. K. T. DHOLAKIA (India); Sec.-Gen. ROBERT DE MARNEFFE (Belgium). Publ. *International Orthopaedics.*

International Union Against Cancer (*Union internationale contre le cancer*): 3 rue du Conseil Général, 1205 Geneva, Switzerland; f. 1933; a non-governmental voluntary organization devoted solely to promoting on an international level the campaign against cancer in its research, therapeutic and preventive aspects. Mems.: 200 organizations in 78 countries.

Pres. Prof. U. VERONESI; Sec.-Gen. Dr. G. P. MURPHY (U.S.A.). Publs. *UICC Bulletin* (quarterly), *International Journal of Cancer* (monthly), *UICC Monographs, UICC Technical Reports.*

International Union against Tuberculosis (*Union internationale contre la tuberculose*): 3 rue Georges Ville, 75116 Paris, France; f. 1920. Object: to co-ordinate the efforts of anti-tuberculosis associations, to promote programmes and research in tuberculosis control, chest diseases and community health, to co-operate in these respects with the World Health Organization, to promote international and regional conferences on the above subjects, to collect and disseminate relevant information, to assist in developing country programmes in co-operation with national associations. Mems.: associations in 101 countries; 3,600 individual mems. and 5,000 promotion mems.

Pres. Prof. A GYSELEN; Chair. of Exec. Cttee. Dr. H. COUDREAU; Exec. Dir. Dr. A. ROUILLON; Hon. Treas. JEAN-PIERRE MALLET. Publs. *Bulletin*† (including conference proceedings).

International Union against Venereal Diseases and Treponematoses (*Union internationale contre le péril vénérien et les tréponématoses*): Institut A. Fournier, 25 blvd. Saint-Jacques, Paris 14e, France; f. 1923. Mems. in 48 countries; has consultative status with WHO.

Pres. Dr. R. D. CATTERALL; Sec.-Gen. Prof. A. LUGER.

International Union for Health Education (*Union internationale d'Education pour la Santé*): 9 rue Newton, 75116 Paris, France; f. 1951. Mems.: organizations in 24 countries, groups and individuals in 80 countries.

Pres. A. MACKIE (U.K.); Sec.-Gen. Dr. E. BERTHET (France). Publ. *International Journal of Health Education* (quarterly, in a three-language edition in English, French and German).

International Union of Angiology (*Union Internationale d'Angéiologie*): f. 1955. Mems.: 19 national societies

Pres. Prof. REINIS; Sec.-Gen. Prof. TESI, 11 via Bonifacio Lupi, Florence, Italy. Publ. *Angéiologie* (8 a year).

International Union of Therapeutics (*Union Internationale de Thérapeutique*): C.H.U. St. Antoine, 27 rue Chaligny, Paris 12e, France; f. 1934; 560 mems. from 22 countries.

Gen. Sec. Prof. J. DRY.

Medical Women's International Association (*Association Internationale des Femmes Médecins*): f. 1919 to facilitate contacts between medical women and to encourage their co-operation in matters connected with international health problems. MWIA Congresses and General Assemblies every two years. Mems.: national associations in 37 countries and individuals.

Pres. Dr. BERYL CORNER (U.K.); Hon. Sec. Dr. M. KYRLE, c/o MWIA Secretariat, Weihburggasse 10–12, A-1010 Vienna, Austria.

Permanent International Committee of Congresses of Comparative Pathology (*Comité International Permanent des Congrès de Pathologie Comparée*): c/o 4 rue Théodule-Ribot, Paris 17e, France; f. 1912 to study social maladies of man, animals, and plants. Mems.: national committees.

Pres. Prof. R. TRUHAUT (France); Sec. L. GROLLET (France). Publ. *Revue de Pathologie comparée et de Médecine Expérimentale.*

World Association of Societies of Anatomic and Clinical Pathology: f. 1947, formerly International Society of Clinical Pathology; Objects: to initiate permanent co-operation between the national associations of pathology; to assist their scientific and technical action and to promote the development of pathology in every aspect. Membership: 35 national associations.

Pres. Prof. H. A. SISSONS (U.K.); Hon. Sec. Prof. A. C. RITCHIE, Banting Inst., 100 College St., Toronto, Ont. M5G 1L5, Canada. Publ. *Newsletter* (quarterly).

World Federation of Neurology (*Fédération Mondiale de Neurologie*): f. 1957.

Pres. Prof. SIGVALD REFSUM; Sec.-Treas.-Gen. PALLE JUUL-JENSEN, Kommunehospitalet, Aarhus, Denmark. Publs. *Journal of the Neurological Sciences, Acta Neuropathologica, Journal für Hirnforschung, Journal de Génétique Humaine.*

World Federation of Societies of Anaesthesiologists— WFSA (*Federación Mundial de Sociedades de Anestesiólogos/Weltverband der Anaesthesisten-Gesellschaften*): c/o Dept. of Anesthesiology RN-10, University of Washington, Seattle, WA. 98195, U.S.A.; f. 1955. Aims: to make available the highest standards of anaesthesia to all peoples of the world; Mems.: Societies in 70 countries and 2 associate mem. countries; 47,000 individual mems.

Pres. Prof. QUINTIN J. GOMEZ (Philippines); Sec. Prof. J. J. BONICA (U.S.A.); Treas. Prof. CARLOS RIVAS (Venezuela).

World Medical Association (*Association Médicale Mondiale*): 1841 Broadway, New York, N.Y. 10023; f. September 1947. Objects: To serve humanity by endeavouring to achieve the highest international standards in medical education, medical science, medical art and medical ethics, and health care for all people. The Unit of membership is the national medical association. The Association has established relations with the World Health Organization, UNESCO, and other international bodies. H.Q., Ferney-Voltaire, France; six regional secretaries. Mems.: 62 national medical associations.

Sec.-Gen. Dr. A. WYNEN (Belgium) (acting); Treas. Dr. HORST BOURMER (Fed. Repub. of Germany). Publs. *World Medical Journal, International News Items.*

World Organisation of Gastroenterology (*Organisation mondiale de gastro-entérologie—OMGE*): Dept. of Gastroenterology, Hospital de San Pablo, Barcelona 25, Spain; f. 1935 to conduct research and contribute to the progress generally of the study of gastroenterology. Mem. societies and groups in 56 countries.

Pres. Dr. JOEL VALENCIA PARPARCEN (Venezuela); Sec.-Gen. Dr. FRANCISCO VILLARDELL (Spain). Publ. *Bulletin* (annual).

World Psychiatric Association (*Association Mondiale de Psychiatrie*): Psych. Universitätsklinik, 74–76 Währinger Gürtel, 1090 Vienna, Austria; f. 1961 at the 3rd World Congress of Psychiatry in Montreal. Aims: the exchange, in all languages, of information concerning the problems of mental illness; the strengthening of relationships between psychiatrists in all countries; the establishment of working relations with WHO, UNESCO and other international organizations; the organization of World Psychiatric Congresses and of regional and inter-regional scientific meetings. Mems.: 76 national societies totalling 66,000 individual psychiatrists.

Pres. Prof. P. PICHOT; Vice-Pres. Dr. S. H. FRAZIER; Sec.-Gen. Prof. PETER BERNER; Treas. Prof. K. KRYSPIN-EXNER.

ASSOCIATE MEMBERS OF CIOMS

International Association of Microbiological Societies (IAMS) (*Association internationale des sociétés de microbiologie*): CNRS/LCB, 31 chemin Joseph Aiguier, 13274 Marseille Cedex 2, France; f. 1930. Mems.: 68 national societies.

Pres. Prof. H. P. R. SEELIGER (Fed. Repub. of Germany); Sec.-Gen. Prof. J. C. SENEZ (France); Treas. Prof. S. GLOVER (U.K.). Publs. *International Journal of Systematic Bacteriology* (quarterly), *Intervirology* (monthly), *Journal of Biological Standardization* (quarterly).

International Committee of Military Medicine and Pharmacy (*Comité international de médecine et de pharmacie militaires*): Hôpital Militaire, Liège, Belgium; f. 1921. Object: to promote world co-operation on questions of military medicine and to foster its international and humanitarian character. It also administers the *International Military Medical Record Office* (Office International de Documentation de Médecine Militaire), f. 1930; Eighty-nine countries are represented on the Committee.

Pres. Gen. Méd. A. ICOCHEA DE VIVANCO (Peru); Sec.-Gen. Col. Méd. J. MATHIEU (Belgium). Publ. *Revue Internationale des Services de Santé des Armées*† (monthly).

International Congress on Tropical Medicine and Malaria (*Congrès International de Médecine Tropicale et de Paludisme*): Secretariat: c/o Dr. E. C. Garcia, Institute of Public Health, P.O.B. EA-460, Manila, Philippines; Congresses are held quinquennially, the last in Manila in November 1980.

Pres. Prof. B. D. CABRERA; Sec.-Gen. Dr. E. C. GARCIA.

Rehabilitation International—International Society for Rehabilitation of the Disabled (*Société Internationale pour la Réadaptation des Handicapés*): 432 Park Ave. South, New York, N.Y. 10016, U.S.A.; f. 1922; member organizations in 61 countries.

Pres. KENNETH T. JENKINS (Australia); Sec.-Gen. NORMAN ACTON (U.S.A.). Publ. *International Rehabilitation Review*† (quarterly, in English and Japanese), *International Journal of Rehabilitation Research* (quarterly in English, French or German with summaries in English, French, German and Spanish).

World Veterinary Association (*Association Mondiale Vétérinaire*): 70 route du Pont Butin, Petit-Lancy/Ge, Switzerland; f. 1863; mem. organizations in 65 countries, 14 assoc. mems.

Pres. Prof. Dr. R. VUILLAUME; Sec.-Treas. Dr. M. LEUENBERGER. Publs. *News Items* (2 a year), *1975 World Catalogue of Veterinary Films and Films of Veterinary Interest, News Letters* (5 a year).

Association for Medical Education in Europe: c/o University Dept. of Psychiatry, Royal Edinburgh Hospital, Morningside Park, Edinburgh, EH10 5HF, Scotland; f. 1972 to promote and integrate the study of medical education in the countries of Europe. Mems.: all Asscns. for Medical Education in European countries having such associations.

Pres. Prof. H. J. WALTON; Sec. Dr. S. RÖSSNER.

Collegium Internationale Allergologicum: P.O.B. 273, CH-4002 Basle, Switzerland; f. 1954; an international group for the study of scientific and clinical problems in allergy and related branches of medicine and immunology. The Collegium aims to promote the humble spirit of scientific enquiry, friendly co-operation, good fellowship and professional relationships in the field of allergy. Mems.: 182 from 27 countries.

Pres. G. B. WEST; Hon. Sec. A. DE WECK; Sec.-Treas. P. DUKOR. Publ. *International Archives of Allergy and Applied Immunology*.

International Agency for Research on Cancer (*Centre International de Recherche sur le Cancer*): 150 cours Albert Thomas, 69372 Lyon Cedex 2, France; f. 1965 as an Agency of the World Health Organization; to promote international collaboration in cancer research; 11 mem. countries; library of 2,800 vols., 280 journals; annual budget 29 million francs.

Dir. Dr. J. HIGGINSON. Publ. *Annual Report*†.

International Association for Child and Adolescent Psychiatry and Allied Professions (*Association internationale de psychiatrie de l'enfant et de l'adolescent et de professions affiliées*): Maudsley Hospital, Denmark Hill, London SE5 8AZ, England; f. 1948 to promote the study, treatment, care and prevention of mental disorders and deficiencies of children, adolescents and their families by promoting research and practice through collaboration with allied professions. Mems.: national associations and individual membership in 33 countries.

Pres. LIONEL HERSOV (U.K.); Sec.-Gen. RICHARD LANDSOWN (U.K.); Treas. NORMAN LOURIE (U.S.A.). Publs. Yearbooks, newsletter (annually).

International Association for the Study of the Liver: Unité de Recherches de Physiopathologie Hépatique, Hôpital Beaujon, 92118 Clichy Cedex, France; f. 1958 for the informal exchange of scientific data on the liver. Mems. 379.

Pres. KUNIO OKUDA (Japan); Sec. JEAN-PIERRE BENHAMOU (France).

International Association of Agricultural Medicine and Rural Health (*Association Internationale de Médecine Agricole*): f. 1961 to study the problems of medicine in agriculture in all countries and to prevent the pestilences caused by the conditions of work in agriculture. Mems.: *c.* 350.

Pres. Prof. PAVEL MACUCH (Czechoslovakia); Sec.-Gen. Prof. TOSHIKAZU WAKATSUKI, Saku Central Hospital, 197 Usuda-machi, Minamisaku-Gun, Nagano 384–03, Japan.

International Association of Applied Psychology (*Association internationale de psychologie appliquée*): 47 rue César Franck, 4000-Liège, Belgium; f. 1920, present title adopted in 1955. Aims: to establish contacts between those carrying out scientific work on applied psychology, to promote research and the adoption of measures contributing to this work. Members: 2,687 in 87 countries.

Pres. Dr. E. A. FLEISHMAN (U.S.A.); Vice-Pres. Prof. C. LEVY-LEBOYER (France); Sec.-Gen. and Treas. Prof. R. PIRET (Belgium). Publ. *International Review of Applied Psychology* (quarterly).

International Association of Asthmology (*Association Internationale d'Asthmologie—INTERASMA*): Dpto. de Alergologia, Clinica Universitaria, Apdo. 192, Pamplona, Spain; f. 1954 to advance medical knowledge of bronchial asthma and allied disorders; *c.* 1,000 mems. in 51 countries.

Pres. Prof. L. JÄGER (German Democratic Rep.); Sec.-Gen. Prof. A. OEHLING (Spain). Publ. *Allergologia et Immunopathologia* (every 2 months).

International Association of Oral Surgeons: 36 Skindergade, 1159 Copenhagen K, Denmark; f. 1963 to advance the science and art of Oral Surgery; 1,350 mems.

Pres. Prof. W. A. M. van der Kwast (Netherlands); Sec.-Gen. Dr. Jørgen Rud (Denmark). Publ. *International Journal of Oral Surgery* (bi-monthly).

International Brain Research Organization (IBRO): f. 1960 to assist all branches of neuroscience; 1,600 mems.

Chair. Prof. Masao Ito (Japan); Sec.-Gen. Dr. M. A. B. Brazier, UCLA Medical Center, Los Angeles, Calif. 90024, U.S.A. Publs. *IBRO News, Neuroscience* (every 2 months), IBRO Monograph Series.

International Cell Research Organisation (*Organisation Internationale de Recherche sur la Cellule*): c/o UNESCO, Place de Fontenoy, Paris 7e, France; f. 1962 to create, encourage and promote co-operation between scientists of different disciplines throughout the world for the advancement of fundamental knowledge of the cell, normal and abnormal; organizes international training courses and exchange of scientists, etc.; 400 mems.

Chair. Prof. J. W. M. La Riviere (Netherlands); Vice-Chair. Dr. D. Mazia (U.S.A.); Treas. Dr. J. Harel (France).

International Center of Information on Antibiotics: 32 Blvd. de la Constitution, Liège, Belgium; f. 1961 to gather information on antibiotics and strains producing them; to establish contact with discoverers of antibiotics with a view to obtaining samples and filing information; to establish contact with the curators of culture collections, and with research workers in order to avoid duplication of investigations and confusion in the scientific literature; to spread information by means of a bulletin. 1,000 corresponding members.

Dir. Prof. M. Welsch; Senior Scientist in Charge Dr. L. Delcambe. Publ. *Information Bulletin* (irregular).

International Council of Nurses: 37 rue de Vermont, P.O.B. 42, 1211 Geneva 20, Switzerland; f. 1899; federation of national nurses' asscns. in 89 countries.

Pres. Olive Anstey (Australia); Exec. Dir. Winifred Logan. Publ. *International Nursing Review.*

International Cystic Fibrosis Association: 202 East 44th St., New York, N.Y. 10017, U.S.A.; f. 1964 to disseminate current information on cystic fibrosis in those areas of the world where the disease occurs and to stimulate participation of scientific and medical researchers to the end that the disease will be resolved. Conducts annual medical symposia. Mems.: 23 national organizations.

Pres. George N. Barrie, Jr. (U.S.A.); Chair. Scientific/Medical Advisory Committee Prof. Ettore Rossi (Switzerland).

International Federation of Anatomists (*Fédération internationale des associations d'anatomistes*): 45 rue des Sts. Pères, 75270 Paris Cedex 06, France; f. 1903. Mems.: 30 national associations. Library of 6,600 vols.

Sec.-Gen. Prof. A. Delmas. Publ. *Publication du Congrès International* (every 5 years).

International Federation of Gynaecology and Obstetrics (*Fédération internationale de gynécologie et d'obstétrique—FIGO*): f. 1954; assists and contributes to research in gynaecology and obstetrics; aims to facilitate the exchange of information and perfect methods of teaching; organizes international congresses. Membership: national societies in 83 countries.

Pres. Dr. Keith P. Russell (U.S.A.); Sec.-Gen. Dr. J. S. Tomkinson, 27 Sussex Place, Regent's Park, London, NW1 4RG, U.K. Publ. *Journal.*

International Federation of Multiple Sclerosis Societies: Stubenring 6/4/9A, 1010 Vienna, Austria; f. 1967 to co-ordinate and further the work of national multiple sclerosis organizations throughout the world, to stimulate and encourage scientific research in this and related neurological diseases, to collect and disseminate information and to provide counsel and active help in furthering the development of voluntary national multiple sclerosis organizations.

Pres. James D. Wolfensohn; Sec.-Gen. Sidney L. O'Donoghue. Publ. *MS Newsletter* (quarterly in English, French, German).

International Federation of Physical Education (*Fédération Internationale d'Education Physique—FIEP*): 65240 Arreau, France; f. 1923. Aims at national physical education; organizes international congresses and courses. Mems. in 90 countries.

Pres. Dr. P.E. P. Seurin; Sec.-Gen. J. C. Andrews. Publ. *FIEP Bulletin* (quarterly in English, French, Spanish, Portuguese).

International Federation of Thermalism and Climatism (*Fédération internationale du thermalisme et du climatisme—FITEC*): Postfach 142, 7310 Bad Ragaz, Switzerland; f. 1947. Aims: promoting international collaboration in technical, economic and medical problems of thermalism and climatism. Mems.: 26 full mem. countries.

Chair. Dr. G. Ebrard; Gen. Sec. Dr. U. Lisowsky. Publ. *Bulletin d'information FITEC.*

International Hospital Federation (*Fédération internationale des hôpitaux*): 126 Albert St., London, NW1 7NX, England; f. 1947; an independent organization supported by subscribing mems. in *c.* 90 countries; aims to promote improvements in the planning of hospitals and health services through international conferences, study tours, training courses, information services, publications and research and development projects; mems.: national hospital and health service organizations, governmental and non-governmental, individuals from disciplines and occupations concerned with health services and professional, commercial and industrial firms working in the health service field.

Pres. Dr. F. Kohler (Switzerland); Treas. Sir Reginald Wilson (U.K.); Dir.-Gen. M. C. Hardie (U.K.). Publ. *World Hospitals* (quarterly; English with French and Spanish supplements).

International League of Societies for the Mentally Handicapped (*Ligue internationale des associations d'aide aux handicapés mentaux*): 13 rue Forestière, 1050 Brussels, Belgium; f. 1960 to promote the interests of the mentally handicapped without regard to nationality, race or creed; furthers co-operation between national bodies, organizes congresses and symposia. Consultative status with UNESCO, official relations with WHO, ILO and ECOSOC. Mems.: 82 mem. socs. in 63 countries.

Pres. Prof. Gunnar Dybwad (U.S.A.); Sec.-Gen. J. Gemaehling (France). Publs. Proceedings of Conferences, Symposia etc., brochures and pamphlets.

International Medical Alliance (*Alliance Médicale Internationale—A.M.I.*): 48 Ave. Kléber, 75116 Paris; f. 1962 to develop knowledge of acupuncture and natural medicines in the world; mem. societies in 62 countries; monthly meetings and research work.

Pres. Dr. de Tymowski; Sec. Dr. Fievet. Publ. *International Service for Acupuncture* (quarterly).

International Optometric and Optical League: 65 Brook St., London, W1Y 2DT; f. 1927. Aims to co-ordinate efforts to provide a good standard of ophthalmic optical (optometric) care throughout the world; in pursuance of this object the League is active in providing a forum for exchange of ideas between different countries; a large part of its work is concerned with optometric education, and advice upon standards of qualification. The League also interests itself in legislation in relation to optometry throughout the world. Mems.: 27 countries.

Pres. G. A. WHEATCROFT (U.K.); Sec. P. A. SMITH (U.K.). Publs. *Reports, Interoptics, Optometric Syllabus and Teaching Guide*, etc.

International Organization Against Trachoma (*Organisation internationale contre le trachome*): f. 1923 for the research and study of trachomatous conjunctivitis and ophthalmological tropical and sub-tropical diseases.

Pres. Prof. GABRIEL COSCAS, C.H.U. Créteil, 94000 Créteil, France; Sec.-Gen. (vacant). Publ. *Revue du Trachome*† (quarterly).

International Psycho-Analytical Association: 829 Park Ave., Baltimore, Md. 21201, U.S.A.; f. 1908 to hold meetings to define and promulgate the theory and teaching of psychoanalysis, to act as a forum for scientific discussions, to control and regulate training and to contribute to the interdisciplinary area which is common to the behavioural sciences. Mems.: 4,500.

Pres. EDWARD D. JOSEPH (U.S.A.); Sec. FRANCIS MCLAUGHLIN (U.S.A.). Publs. *IPA Bulletin, President's Newsletter, Monograph.*

International Scientific Council for Trypanosomiasis Research and Control (*Conseil scientifique international de recherches sur les trypanosomiases et leur contrôle*): Secretariat: OAU/STRC, Ports Authority Building, Marina P.M.B. 2359, Lagos, Nigeria; f. 1949. Objects: To review the work on tsetse and trypanosomiasis problems carried out by the organizations and workers concerned in laboratories and in the field; to stimulate further research and discussion and to promote co-ordination between research workers and organizations in the different countries in Africa, and to provide a regular opportunity for the discussion of particular problems and for the exposition of new experiments and discoveries.

International Society for Clinical Electrophysiology of Vision (*Société Internationale d'Electrorétinographie Clinique*): 180 Schiedamsevest, Rotterdam 1, Netherlands; f. 1958; 300 mems. Publs. *Bibliographic Service and Newsletter, Proceedings of Symposium* (annually).

International Society for Clinical and Experimental Hypnosis (ISCEH): Psychiatric Clinic, Charles University, Pha 2, Ke Karlova 11, Prague 2, Czechoslovakia; f. 1958 as an affiliate of the World Federation of Mental Health; to stimulate and improve professional research, discussion and publications pertinent to the scientific study of hypnosis; to encourage co-operative relations among scientific disciplines with regard to the study and application of hypnosis; to bring together persons using hypnosis and set up standards for professional training and adequacy. Affiliated to the World Federation of Mental Health.

Pres. Dr. MARTIN T. ORNE (Unit for Experimental Psychiatry, University of Pennsylvania, 111 North Forty-Ninth St., Philadelphia, Pa. 19139, U.S.A.

International Society for Research on Civilization Diseases and Vital Substances (*Société Internationale pour la Recherche sur les Maladies de Civilisation et les Substances Vitales*): Bemeroder Strasse 61, 3 Hannover-Kirchrode, Federal Republic of Germany; f. 1954; research into causes of civilization diseases and damages and responsibilities of human society; research in improvement of foodstuffs by ensuring retention of their natural properties; combat use of chemical products, prohibit harmful additives; organizes annual International Convention on Civilization Diseases, Vital Substances, Nutrition, Living conditions, Disharmony in the Environment. 1,100 mems. in 80 countries.

Pres. Dr. med. ST. KLEIN; First Acting Pres. Dr. med. MAX ODENS. Publs. *Recherche sur l'Environnement* (6 vols. annually, in three languages), *Protectio Vitae* (6 per year).

International Society of Cybernetic Medicine (*Société internationale de médecine cybernétique—SIMC*): 348 Via Roma, 80134 Naples, Italy; f. 1958; aims to promote international co-operation in the use of cybernetic methods in the biological and medical sciences; organizes congresses; individual and collective members in various countries.

Pres. Prof. A. MASTURZO (Italy); Sec. Dr. P. BATTARRA (Italy). Publ. *Cybernetic Medicine* (quarterly).

International Society of Haematology (*Société Internationale d'Hématologie*): f. 1946. Objects: To promote and foster the exchange and diffusion of information and ideas relating to blood and blood-forming tissues throughout the world; to provide a forum for discussion of haematologic problems on an international scale and to encourage scientific investigation of these problems; to promote the advancement of haematology and its recognition as a branch of the biological sciences; to attempt to standardize on an international scale haematological methods and nomenclature; to promote a better understanding of the scientific basic principles of haematology among practitioners of haematology and physicians in general, and to foster better understanding and a greater interest in clinical haematologic problems among scientific investigators in the field of haematology.

Sec.-Gen. (Inter-American Division) Dr. L. SÁNCHEZ MEDAL, Apdo. postal 41–711, México 10, DF, México; (European and African Division) Prof. J. W. STEWART, School of Pathology, Middlesex Hospital Medical School, Riding House St., London W1P 7LD, England; (Asian-Pacific Division) Dr. A. LOVRIC, Red Cross Blood Transfusion Service, 153 Clarence St., Sydney, N.S.W. 2000, Australia.

International Society of Radiology (*Société Internationale de Radiologie*): f. 1953. Objects: to develop and advance medical radiology by giving radiologists in different countries an opportunity of personally submitting their experiences, exchanging and discussing their ideas, and forming personal bonds with their colleagues; there are four permanent International Commissions: (*a*) on Radiological Protection, (*b*) on Radiation Units and Measurements, (*c*) on Presentation of Results (Cancer), (*d*) on Radiological Education and Information; these Commissions meet during each Congress, held at four-yearly intervals.

Pres. Prof. N. C. CAMINHA (Brazil); Vice-Pres. Prof. L. JEANMART (Belgium); Hon. Sec.-Treas. Dr. W. A. FUCHS, Dept. of Diagnostic Radiology, University Hospital, Inselspital, Berne, Switzerland.

International Society of Surgery (*Société internationale de chirurgie*): 43 rue des Champs-Elysées, 1050 Brussels, Belgium; f. 1902; organizes congresses; 3,300 mems.

Sec.-Gen. Prof. J. VAN GEERTRUYDEN; Treas. Dr. J. P. VANHOVE. Publ. *World Journal of Surgery* (every 2 months).

International Union of Railway Medical Services (*Union Internationale des Services Médicaux des Chemins de Fer*): 85 rue de France, 1070 Brussels, Belgium; f. 1948.

Pres. Dr. E. ETZ (Austria).

Pan-American Medical Association (PAMA): 745 Fifth Ave., New York, N.Y. 10022, U.S.A.; f. 1925. Objects: to interchange medical knowledge and research among countries of the western hemisphere; to strengthen, through the medical profession, bonds of friendship among peoples of the western hemisphere; to hold Inter-American congresses; to send seminars to various

American countries; to grant postgraduate scholarships to doctors of western hemisphere nations. A charter has been granted for the establishment of the Pan-American Post Graduate Medical School in New York. Next Inter-American Congress, New Orleans, March 1982. Mems.: 15,000 doctors in 24 countries.

Dir.-Gen. JOSEPH J. ELLER, M.D.

Permanent Commission and International Association on Occupational Health (*Commission Permanente et Association Internationale pour la Médecine du Travail*): Quality House, Chancery Lane, London, WC2A 1HP, U.K.; f. 1906 to organize international meetings, to study new facts in the field of industrial medicine, to draw the attention of authorities to the results of study and investigation in industrial medicine, and to organize meetings on national or international problems of industrial medicine. Membership: 720 representatives from 56 countries.

Pres. Prof. ENRICO C. VIGLIANI (Italy); Gen. Sec. and Treas. Dr. ROBERT MURRAY (U.K.).

World Association of Veterinary Microbiologists, Immunologists and Specialists in Infectious Diseases (*Association Mondiale des Vétérinaires Microbiologistes, Immunologistes et Spécialistes des Maladies Infectieuses*): Ecole Nationale Vétérinaire d'Alfort, 7 ave. du Général de Gaulle, 94704 Maisons-Alfort Cedex, France; f. 1967 to facilitate international contacts in the field of veterinary microbiologists, immunologists and specialists in infectious diseases.

Pres. Prof. CH. PILET (France).

World Confederation for Physical Therapy: 16/19 Eastcastle St., London W1N 7PA, England; f. 1951 to encourage improved standards of physical therapy in training and practice; to promote exchange of information between nations; to assist the development of informed public opinion regarding physical therapy; to co-operate with appropriate agencies of UN and national and international organizations; members in 41 countries, and in 1 provisionally approved.

Pres. EUGENE MICHELS; Sec.-Gen. Miss E. M. MCKAY (U.K.). Publ. *Proceedings of Congresses.*

World Federation of Neurosurgical Societies (*Fédération Mondiale des Sociétés de Neurochirurgie*): Pr. Bernhardlaan 60, Oegstgeest, Netherlands; f. 1957 to facilitate the exchange of knowledge and to encourage research. 48 mem. societies and affiliated organizations.

Pres. Dr. CHARLES G. DRAKE; Sec. Prof. Dr. W. LUYENDIJK.

MUSIC

International Music Council—IMC (*Conseil international de la musique*): UNESCO, 1 rue Miollis, 75732 Paris Cedex 15, France; f. 1949 under the auspices of UNESCO to foster the exchange of musicians, music (written and recorded), and information; to support contemporary composers and young professional musicians; to foster appreciation of music by the public. Mems.: 18 international non-governmental organizations, 60 national committees, 17 individual mems.

Pres. JOHN PETER LEE ROBERTS (Canada); Sec.-Gen. DIMITER CHRISTOFF (Bulgaria); Exec. Sec. JACK BORNOFF (U.K.). Publ. *The World of Music* (quarterly).

MEMBERS OF IMC

European Association of Music Festivals (*Association européenne des festivals de musique*): Centre Européen de la Culture, 122 rue de Lausanne, Geneva, Switzerland; f. 1951. Aims to maintain high artistic standards in festivals, widen the field of operation, organize joint propaganda and publicity. Mems.: 38 festivals in Austria, Belgium, Czechoslovakia, Finland, France, Fed. Repub. of Germany, Great Britain, Greece, Hungary, Israel, Italy, Japan, Netherlands, Norway, Poland, Spain, Switzerland, Turkey, Yugoslavia.

Pres. DENIS DE ROUGEMONT (Switzerland); Artistic Counsellor FRANZ WALTER. Publs. *Festivals, Season* (annually).

Federation of International Music Competitions (*Fédération des Concours Internationaux de Musique*): 12 rue de l'Hôtel de Ville, 1204 Geneva, Switzerland; f. 1957; co-ordinates the activities of members and maintains links between them, arranges the calendar of competitions, helps competition-winners to get to know each other; 59 member organizations.

Pres. PIERRE COLOMBO; Sec.-Gen. Mme. ALINE VERNET. Publ. annual programme of competitions.

International Federation of Musicians (*Fédération internationale des musiciens*): Hofackerstrasse 7, 8032 Zürich, Switzerland; f. 1948, to promote and protect the interests of musicians in affiliated unions and to institute protective measures to safeguard musicians against the abuse of their performances; promotes the international exchange of musicians; makes agreements with other international organizations in the interest of member unions and of the profession. Mems. 34 unions totalling 112,771 members in 32 countries.

Pres. JOHN MORTON (U.K.); Gen. Sec. RUDOLF LEUZINGER (Switzerland).

International Federation of Youth and Music (*Fédération internationale des jeunesses musicales*): Palais des Beaux-Arts, 10 rue Royale, 1000 Brussels, Belgium; f. 1945 to promote the development of musical appreciation among young people, to encourage the creation of new societies and to ensure co-operation between national societies. Member organizations in 35 countries.

Sec.-Gen. HADELIN DONNET (Belgium). Publ. *Rapport Annuel de l'Assemblée Générale.*

International Folk Music Council (*Conseil internationalde la musique populaire*): Department of Music, Queen's University, Kingston, Ontario, Canada; f. 1947 to further the preservation, study and practice of the folk music (including dance) of all countries; biennial conferences. 1,050 mems.

Pres. POUL ROVSING OLSEN (Denmark); Sec.-Gen. Prof. GRAHAM GEORGE (Canada). Publs. *Yearbook, Bulletin* (twice yearly).

International Institute for Comparative Music Studies and Documentation (*Internationales Institut für Vergleichende Musikstudien und Dokumentation*): Winklerstrasse 20, 1000 Berlin 33, Fed. Repub. of Germany; f. 1963; an undertaking of the City of Berlin to study practical means of integrating the non-occidental musical cultures into world culture and of helping the preservation of authentic traditional music; the Institute works in close co-operation with the International Music Council and UNESCO. Annual Festival of Traditional Music. Mems. from 20 countries.

Dir. IVAN VANDOR; Gen.-Sec. MICHAEL JENNE. Publs. *Unesco Anthology of the Orient, Unesco Anthology of African Music, Musical Sources, Musical Atlas* (record series), *The World of Music* (quarterly), in association with the International Music Council and UNESCO.

International Institute for Audio-Visual Communication and Cultural Development—MEDIACULT (formerly International Institute for Music, Dance and Theatre):

A-1030 Vienna, Metternichgasse 12, Austria; f. 1969; studies, seminars, TV workshops.

Pres. ROBERT WANGERMÉE; Gen. Sec. WILFRIED SCHEIB; Dir. KURT BLAUKOPF. Publs. *Progress Reports, Newsletters, Research Documents.*

International Music Centre (*Internationales Musikzentrum—IMZ*): 1030 Vienna, Lothringerstr. 20, Austria; f. 1961 for the promotion and dissemination of music through the technical media (film, television, radio, gramophone); co-operates with other international organizations such as EBU, OIRT; organizes congresses, seminars and screenings on music in the audio-visual media; organizes competitions to strengthen relations between composers, interpreters and technicians, with particular emphasis on the promotion of the young generation; exhibitions of scores, manuscripts, records and books. Mems.: 48 Broadcasting Organizations, 19 Associates.

Pres. L. NADELMANN (Switzerland); Gen. Sec. Prof. W. SCHEIB (Austria); Exec. Sec. Dr. Y. O. WINTERSTEIN. Publs. *IMZ Reports, UNESCO Catalogue, IMZ Bulletin* (regular information in English, French and German).

International Musicological Society (*Société internationale de musicologie*): *see under* International Council for Philosophy and Humanistic Studies.

International Society for Contemporary Music (*Société internationale pour la musique contemporaine*): c/o Studio de Musique Contemporaine, 7 blvd. Jaques-Dalcroze, CH-1204 Geneva, Switzerland; f. 1922 to promote the development of contemporary music and to organize annual World Music Days. Member organizations in 30 countries.

Pres. JACQUES GUYONNET (Switzerland); Sec.-Gen. RUDOLF HEINEMANN (Fed. Repub. of Germany); Treas. PAUL WIEGMANS (Netherlands).

International Society for Music Education: f. 1953 to stimulate music education as a part of general education and community life; organizes international conferences and seminars; co-operates with other international music organizations; acts as an advisory body to UNESCO; co-operates with organizations representing other fields of education; 15th International Conference in Bristol, England, July 1982.

Pres. NAOHIRO FUKUI (Japan); Sec.-Gen. JOHN RITCHIE, The School of Music, The University of Canterbury, Christchurch 1, New Zealand. Publs. *ISME Year Book, Reports of ISME Conferences and Seminars.*

SCIENCE

Association for the Taxonomic Study of Tropical African Flora (*Association pour l'Etude Taxonomique de la Flore d'Afrique Tropicale—AETFAT*): Botanical Research Institute, Dept. of Agriculture and Fisheries, Private Bag X101, Pretoria 0001, South Africa; f. 1950. Mems.: approx. 600 from 69 countries.

Pres. Prof. J. P. M. BRENAN (U.K.); Sec.-Gen. Dr. B. DE WINTER (South Africa). Publs. *AETFAT Bulletin, AETFAT Index* (both annually), *Proceedings.*

Association of Information Dissemination Centers: c/o Secretariat, P.O.B. 8105, Athens, Georgia 30601, U.S.A.; f. 1968; independent organization with 150 centres representing industry, government and academia in the U.S.A., Canada, Europe, Israel, Japan, India, South Africa and Australia; to promote applied technology of information storage and retrieval, and research and development for more efficient use of data bases.

Pres. D. U. WILDE; Sec. K. DURKIN. Publ. *Newsletter* (quarterly).

Biometric Society, The (BS) (*Société internationale de biométrie*): Dept. of Statistics, Colorado State University, Fort Collins, Colo. 80523, U.S.A.; f. 1947; an international society for the advancement of quantitative biological science through the development of quantitative theories and the application, development and dissemination of effective mathematical and statistical techniques; the Society has 11 regional organizations and 10 national groups, is affiliated with the International Statistical Institute and the World Health Organization, and constitutes the Section of Biometry of the International Union of Biological Sciences. Mems.: over 5,000 in more than 70 different countries.

Pres. Dr. J. A. NELDER (U.K.); Sec. Prof. J. S. WILLIAMS (U.S.A.); Treas. Dr. L. A. NELSON (U.S.A.); Vice-Pres. Dr. H. L. LEROY (Switzerland). Publ. *Biometrics* (quarterly).

Charles Darwin Foundation for the Galapagos Isles (*Fundación Charles Darwin para las Islas Galápagos*): Greensted Hall, Ongar, Essex CM5 9LD, England; f. 1959 to organize and maintain the Charles Darwin Research Station in the Galapagos Islands and to advise the Government of Ecuador on scientific research and conservation in the archipelago.

Pres. Dr. PETER KRAMER (Fed. Repub. of Germany); Vice-Pres. C. BONIFAZ J. (Ecuador); Sec.-Gen. G. T. CORLEY SMITH (U.K.); Secs. for the Americas Dr. THOMAS SIMKIN (U.S.A.), Dr. D. CHALLINOR (U.S.A.). Publ. *Noticias de Galápagos* (2 a year).

Circum-Pacific Council for Energy and Mineral Resources: c/o Office of International Geology, MS 52, U.S. Geological Survey, 345 Middlefield Rd., Menlo Park, Calif. 94025, U.S.A.; f. 1974 at the first Circum-Pacific Energy and Mineral Resources Conference, with the co-operation of 46 international geoscience organizations; sponsors conferences, meetings, research; supports and operates regional projects, including the Circum-Pacific Map Project, and international training schools.

Chair. MICHEL T. HALBOUTY (U.S.A.).

Commonwealth Geographical Bureau: Dept. of Geography, School of Oriental and African Studies, Malet St., London, WC1E 7H8, England; f. 1968; encourages the development of geographical research and study, particularly in developing Commonwealth countries, through assistance to the profession; regional seminars, assistance for study visits; a board of management represents four regions: Asia, Africa, Americas, Australasia.

Dir. Prof. R. W. STEEL (U.K.). Publ. *Newsletter* (irreg.).

Euratom (*European Atomic Energy Community*): 200 rue de la Loi, Brussels, Belgium. Based on a formal treaty signed in Rome in March 1957, at the same time as the treaty establishing the EEC. It aims to integrate the programmes of member states for the peaceful uses of atomic energy; since 1967 combined with the ECSC and EEC.

Pres. of Commission of the European Communities ROY JENKINS (U.K.).

European Association for the Exchange of Technical Literature in the Field of Metallurgy (*Association Européenne pour l'Echange de la Littérature Technique dans le Domaine de la Sidérurgie*): P.O.B. 443, Luxembourg; f. 1959 to promote translation and exchange of technical literature in metallurgy especially from the U.S.S.R.

and the Far East for the benefit of industry, research institutes, etc. in the European Community. Mem. institutes in 6 countries.

Pres. G. BAUHOFF (Fed. Repub. of Germany); Vice-Pres. L. LACASSE (Belgium). Publs. Lists of translations (monthly), bibliographical index-cards.

European Institute of Environmental Cybernetics: Athens 513, Greece; f. 1970 to bring together scientists and scholars with cross-sectional background and research interests and to conduct multi-disciplinary educational and research activities studying the interactions between man and his environment (natural and technical).

Publs. reports†.

European Molecular Biology Organization (EMBO) (*Organisation européenne de biologie moléculaire*): 6900 Heidelberg 1, Postfach 1022-40, Federal Republic of Germany; f. 1964. Objects: to promote collaboration in the field of molecular biology; to award fellowships for training and research. Mems. approximately 460.

Chair. Prof. R. MONIER (France); Deputy Chair. Sir HANS KORNBERG (U.K.); Sec.-Gen. Prof. N. O. KJELDGAARD (Denmark); Exec. Sec. Dr. J. TOOZE.

European Organization for Nuclear Research (CERN) (*Organisation européenne pour la recherche nucléaire*): 1211 Geneva 23, Switzerland; established in 1954 at the instigation of UNESCO. A co-operative organization of the governments of Austria, Belgium, Denmark, France, Federal Republic of Germany, Greece, Italy, The Netherlands, Norway, Sweden, Switzerland and United Kingdom for the purpose of carrying out and co-ordinating research on fundamental particles. CERN is the largest European laboratory for high energy physics, equipped with three proton accelerators: a synchrocyclotron of 600 MeV, a synchrotron of 28 GeV and a synchrotron of 400 GeV. Intersecting storage rings have been built for colliding beam physics alongside the synchrotron of 28 GeV, and a project to collide beams of protons and antiprotons inside the 400 GeV synchrotron and the intersecting storage rings is scheduled for completion in 1981.

Pres. of the Council Prof. J. TEILLAC (France); Dir.-Gen. Dr. HERWIG SCHOPPER (Fed. Rep. of Germany). Publs. *Annual Report* (in English and French), *CERN Courier* (monthly in English and French), scientific and technical reports, etc.

European Science Foundation: 1 quai Lezay-Marnésia, 67000 Strasbourg, France; f. 1974 to advance co-operation in basic research; to promote mobility of research workers; to assist the free flow of information and ideas; to facilitate co-operation in the use of existing facilities, in assessing and executing appropriate projects of major importance, and in the provision of expensive specialized services. Mems.: 47 organizations from 18 countries.

Pres. HUBERT CURIEN (France); Sec.-Gen. J. GOORMAGHTIGH (Belgium). Publs. *Annual Report* (in English and French), *Synchrotron Radiation Newsletter* (quarterly).

European Southern Observatory (*Organisation européenne pour des recherches astronomiques dans l'hémisphère austral*): Karl Schwarzchild Str. 2, 8046 Garching b. München, Federal Republic of Germany; f. 1962; aims: astronomical research in the southern hemisphere, construction and operation of an international observatory in Chile (*see* under Chile), fostering European co-operation in astronomy; mems.: govts. of Belgium, Denmark, Fed. Germany, France, The Netherlands, Sweden.

Dir.-Gen. Prof. Dr. L. WOLTJER. Publs. *Annual Report*, *The Messenger* (quarterly), reports.

European Space Agency: 8–10 rue Mario Nikis, 75738 Paris, Cedex 15, France; f. 1964 as European Space Research Organization, name changed 1975 after merger with European Space Vehicle Launcher Development Organization; to provide for, and to promote, collaboration among European states in space research and technology and their space applications exclusively for peaceful purposes; provides scientific agencies of the member countries with the necessary technical facilities for the carrying out of space experiments, ranging from the study of the near terrestrial environment to that of steliar astronomy. Also responsible for a European programme of application satellite projects, including telecommunications, air-traffic control and meteorology; responsible for Spacelab and Ariane Launcher. Maintains the following establishments: European Space Research and Technology Centre (ESTEC) Noordwijk, Netherlands; European Space Operations Centre (ESOC), Darmstadt, Fed. Repub. of Germany; Information Retrieval Service (IRS), Frascati, Italy. Mems.: Belgium, Denmark, France, Fed. Repub. of Germany, Ireland, Italy, Netherlands, Spain, Sweden, Switzerland and U.K.; Austria, Canada and Norway enjoy observer status.

Dir.-Gen. ERIK QUISTGAARD (Denmark). Publs. *Annual General Report*†, *Bulletin*†, *Reports*†, *Notes*†, *Memoranda*.

Foundation for International Scientific Co-ordination (*Fondation "Pour la Science", Centre international de Synthèse*): 12 rue Colbert, Paris 2e, France; f. 1924.

Founder HENRI BERR; Dir. JACQUES ROGER (France). Publs. *Revue de Synthèse*, *Revue d'Histoire des Sciences et de leurs applications*, *Semaines de Synthèse*, *L'Evolution de l'Humanité*.

Institute of Mathematical Statistics: 3401 Investment Blvd. 6, Hayward, Calif. 94545, U.S.A.; f. 1935; 3,150 mems.

Pres. G. E. P. BOX; Exec. Sec. MARTIN FOX. Publs. *Annals of Probability*, *Annals of Statistics* (6 a year).

Intergovernmental Bureau for Informatics (IBI) (*Bureau Intergouvernemental pour l'Informatique*): C.P. 10253, Viale della Civiltà del Lavoro 23, 00144, Rome, Italy; f. 1961 by international treaty to promote the development, application and exchange of experience and techniques in the study of informatics; to collect, analyse and disseminate knowledge in informatics; to assist and advise the governments of member countries and other international organizations, and provide the member states with studies and general programmes acquired or achieved by the IBI or one of its members; General Assembly meets every two years. Mems.: Algeria, Argentina, Bolivia, Brazil, Cameroon, Chile, Congo, Cuba, Ecuador, France, Gabon, Ghana, Haiti, Iran, Iraq, Israel, Italy, Ivory Coast, Jordan, Lebanon, Madagascar, Mexico, Morocco, Nigeria, Senegal, Spain, Swaziland, Tunisia, Zaire.

Dir. Prof. F. A. BERNASCONI. Publ. quarterly newsletter†.

Intergovernmental Oceanographic Commission (IOC) (*Commission Océanographique Intergouvernementale*): c/o UNESCO, place de Fontenoy, 75700 Paris, France; f. 1960 to promote scientific investigation with a view to learning more about the nature and resources of the oceans, through the concerted action of its members. Mems.: 103 governments.

Chair. Dr. A. AYALA-CASTANARES (Mexico); Sec. D. P. D. SCOTT. Publs. *Summary Reports of Sessions* (every 2 years), *IOC Technical Series* (several a year).

International Academy of Astronautics (IAA) (*Académie Internationale d'Astronautique*): 250 rue Saint-Jacques, 75005 Paris, France; f. 1960 at the XI Congress of the

International Astronautical Federation; holds scientific meetings and makes scientific studies and reports, awards and prizes, including the annual Daniel and Florence Guggenheim International Astronautics Award of $1,000; maintains several Committees including the Manned Research on Celestial Bodies (MARECEBO), History of Rockets and Astronautics, Space Relativity, Space Rescue and Safety Studies, Man-in-Space Studies, Gas Dynamics of Explosions and Reactive Systems, Communication with Extra-Terrestrial Intelligence (CETI), Energy and Space and Scientific-Legal Liaison Committees. Mems.: 545 in 31 countries.

Pres. C. S. DRAPER (U.S.A.); Vice-Pres. H. A. BJURSTEDT (Sweden), E. A. BRUN (France), L. G. NAPOLITANO (Italy), A. MIKHAILOV (U.S.S.R.). Publs. *Acta Astronautica* (12 issues a year), *Proceedings of Symposia, Astronautical Multilingual Dictionary, The International Academy of Astronautics—The First Decade* (brochure).

International Association for Biological Oceanography: c/o Institut für Meereskunde an der Universität Kiel, Düsternbrookerweg 20, 23 Kiel, Fed. Repub. of Germany; f. 1966 to promote the study of the biology of the sea.

Pres. TIMOTHY R. PARSONS (Canada); Sec. JOHN COSFLOW (U.S.A.).

International Association for Cybernetics (*Association internationale de cybernétique*): Palais des Expositions, Place André Rijckmans, Namur, Belgium; f. 1957 to ensure liaison between research workers engaged in various sectors of cybernetics, to promote the development of the science and of its applications and to disseminate information about it. Mems.: organizations, institutes, associations, industrial firms and individuals in 35 countries.

Pres. Prof. GEORGES R. BOULANGER (Belgium); Man. Administrator J. LEMAIRE (Belgium). Publs. *Cybernetica* (quarterly), *Proceedings of the International Congresses on Cybernetics, Cybernetics—Work in Progress* (series).

International Association for Mathematics and Computers in Simulation (*Association internationale pour les mathématiques et Calculateurs en simulation*; formerly International Association for Analogue Computation): c/o E.R.M., Electricité, 30 ave. de la Renaissance, 1040 Brussels, Belgium; f. 1955 to further the study of general methods for modelling and computer simulation of dynamic systems. Mems. 47 assoc. mems., 300 full mems.

Pres. R. VICHNEVETSKY (U.S.A.); Sec.-Gen. PAUL VAN REMOORTERE (Belgium); Treas. MARC ACHEROY (Belgium). Publs. *Proceedings, Newsletter* (quarterly).

International Association for Plant Physiology (IAPP): Rothamsted Experimental Station, Harpenden, Herts. AL5 2JQ, England; f. 1955 to promote the development of plant physiology at the international level through international congresses and symposia and by the publication of plant physiology matters and the promotion of co-operation between national and international associations and scientific journals. Mems.: national societies of plant physiology and related international groups.

Pres. Prof. A QUISPEL; Gen. Sec. Prof. C. P. WHITTINGHAM.

International Association for Plant Taxonomy (*Association internationale pour la taxonomie végétale*): Bureau for Plant Taxonomy and Nomenclature, Room 1904, Tweede Transitorium, Uithof, 3584 CS Utrecht, Netherlands; f. 1950 to promote the development of plant taxonomy and encourage contacts between people and institutes interested in this work. Mems. Institutes and individuals in 83 countries.

Pres. A. TAKHTAJAN (U.S.S.R.); Sec.-Gen. F. A. STAFLEU (Netherlands). Publs. *Taxon* (4 a year), *Regnum vegetable* (4 a year).

International Association for the Physical Sciences of the Ocean (IAPSO) (*Association internationale des Sciences physiques de l'Océan*): LaFond Oceanic Consultants, P.O.B. 7325, San Diego, Calif. 92107, U.S.A.; f. 1919 to promote the study of scientific problems relating to the Oceans, chiefly in so far as such study may be carried out by the aid of mathematics, physics and chemistry; to initiate, facilitate and co-ordinate research; to provide for discussion, comparison and publication. Mems.: 71 member states.

Pres. Prof. DEVENDRA LAL; Sec.-Gen. Dr. E. C. LA FOND (U.S.A.). Publs. *Publications Scientifiques* (irregularly), *Procès-Verbaux* (every 2–4 years).

International Association of Geodesy (*Association internationale de géodésie—AIG*): 39 ter rue Gay Lussac, 75005 Paris, France; f. 1922 to promote the study of all scientific problems of geodesy and encourage geodetic research; to promote and co-ordinate international co-operation in this field; to publish results. Mems.: national committees in 61 countries.

Pres. Prof. H. MORITZ (Austria); Sec. Ing. Gen. M. LOUIS (France). Publs. *Bulletin géodésique, Travaux de l'AIG, Bibliographie géodésique internationale, Publications spéciales.*

International Association of Geomagnetism and Aeronomy—IAGA (*Association internationale de géomagnétisme et d'aéronomie—AIGA*): f. 1919. Aims.: the study of magnetism and aeronomy of the earth and other bodies of the solar system and of the interplanetary medium and its interaction with these bodies. Mems.: the countries which adhere to the International Union of Geodesy and Geophysics are eligible as members.

Pres. K. D. COLE (Australia); Vice-Pres. A. J. DESSLER (U.S.A.), M. GADSDEN (U.K.); Sec.-Gen. N. FUKUSHIMA, Geophysics Research Laboratory, University of Tokyo, Tokyo 113, Japan. Publs. *Transactions of the General Assemblies* (every 4 years), *Transactions of the Scientific Assemblies* (every 4 years between the General Assemblies), *IAGA Bulletins* (irregular), *IAGA News* (annually).

International Association of Meteorology and Atmospheric Physics (IAMAP) (*Association Internationale de Météorologie et de Physique de l'Atmosphère*): c/o National Center for Atmospheric Research, P.O.B. 3000, Boulder, Colo. 80307, U.S.A.; f. 1919 to organize research symposia and co-ordinate research in atmospheric science fields; an Association of the International Union of Geodesy and Geophysics.

Pres. Dr. C. JUNGE (Fed. Repub. of Germany); Sec. S. RUTTENBERG (U.S.A.). Publs. *IAMAP News Bulletin* (irregular), *IAMAP Assembly Proceedings*† (every 2 years).

International Association of Sedimentologists (*Association Internationale de Sédimentologie*): c/o Dr. C. MONTY, Centre d'Analyses Paléoecol. et Sed., Lab. de Paléontologie Animale, Université de Liège, 7 place du 20 Août, 4000 Liège, Belgium; f. 1952; 1,400 mems.

Pres. Prof. K. J. HSÜ (Switzerland); Sec.-Gen. Dr. C. MONTY (Belgium); Treas. Dr. S. D. NIO (Netherlands). Publs. *Sedimentology, Newsletter* (6 a year), special publications.

International Association of Theoretical and Applied Limnology (*Association internationale de Limnologie Théorique et Appliquée*): W. K. Kellogg Biological Station, Michigan State University, Hickory Corners, Mich. 49060, U.S.A., f. 1922; 2,900 mems. Twenty-first Congress: Kyoto, Japan, August 1980.

Pres. S. A. FEDOTOV (U.S.S.R.); Gen. Sec. and Treas. Prof. ROBERT G. WETZEL (U.S.A.). Publs. *Verhandlungen, Mitteilungen.*

International Association of Volcanology and Chemistry of the Earth's Interior (IAVCEI) (*Association Internationale de Volcanologie et de Chimie de l' Intérieur de la Terre*): c/o Dept. of Geology, University Park, Nottingham NG7 2RD, England; f. 1919 to promote scientific investigation and discussion in volcanology and in those aspects of petrology and geochemistry relating to the composition of the interior of the Earth.

Pres. R. W. DECKER (U.S.A.); Sec. P. E. BAKER (U.K.). Publs. *Bulletin Volcanologique, Catalogue of the Active Volcanoes of the World including Solfatara Fields, Newsletter, Volcanic Data Sheets.*

International Association of Wood Anatomists (*Association Internationale des Anatomistes du Bois*): c/o Rijksherbarium, Leiden, Netherlands; f. 1931 for the purpose of study, documentation and exchange of information on the anatomy of wood; 350 mems. in 46 countries.

Exec. Sec. Dr. P. BAAS. Publ. *IAWA Bulletin.*

International Astronautical Federation (IAF) (*Fédération Internationale d'Astronautique*): 250 rue Saint Jacques, 75005 Paris, France; f. 1950; Constitution adopted at the XII Congress in Washington 1961; to foster the development of astronautics for peaceful purposes at national and international levels. The 28th Congress was held in Prague in 1977. The IAF created the International Academy of Astronautics (IAA), the International Institute of Space Law (IISL) (for information on these bodies, *see* elsewhere in this chapter), and committees on Bio-astronautics, Education, Application Satellites, Lighter-than-Air Systems, Space Energy and Power, Student Activities and Supervised Youth Rocket Experiments. Annual student awards. Mems.: 58 national astronautical societies in 36 countries.

Pres. M. BARRÈRE (France); Vice-Pres. T. P. ANDJELIĆ (Yugoslavia), A. JAUMOTTE (Belgium), L. I. SEDOV (U.S.S.R.), R. PEŠEK (Czechoslovakia), S. SAITO (Japan); Exec. Sec. H. VAN GELDER. Publs. *Proceedings* of Annual Congresses, *Symposia* and Working Group Reports.

International Atomic Energy Agency (IAEA): Vienna International Centre, P.O.B. 100, A-1400 Vienna, Austria. The Statute of the Agency was unanimously approved by 80 nations meeting at the UN headquarters in New York on October 26th, 1956. Mems.: 110 states. The Board of Governors, consisting of 34 members designated or elected on a technological and regional basis, carries out the functions of the Agency. Aims: the contribution of atomic energy to peace, health and prosperity throughout the world; to provide materials, services, equipment and facilities; to foster the exchange of scientific and technical information on peaceful uses of atomic energy; to encourage the exchange and training of scientists and experts in the field of atomic energy; to establish health and safety standards and to prepare a comprehensive set of safety codes and guides covering all aspects of building and operating nuclear power plants; to establish safeguards against the military use of any materials and equipment provided through the Agency and to apply these safeguards in accordance with the Treaty on the Non-Proliferation of Nuclear Weapons; joint library (with UNIDO and other UN organizations) of 46,000 vols., 400,000 reports, 2,600 periodicals; micro-card clearing-house. The International Nuclear Information System (INIS) provides world-wide coverage of literature on all aspects of peaceful uses of nuclear energy; it has become the first fully decentralized computer-based nuclear science abstracting service. The IAEA Energy and Economic Data Bank provides information on the world's energy situation and related economic parameters, based on data obtained from member states.

Dir.-Gen. Dr. SIGVARD EKLUND (Sweden); Scientific Advisory Committee: C. CASTRO MADERO (Argentina), F. CULLER (U.S.A.), I. DOSTROVSKY (Israel), M. A. N. EL GUEBEILY (Egypt), B. GOLDSCHMIDT (France), L. GUTIÉRREZ-JODRA (Spain), W. HAEFELE (Fed. Rep. of Germany), J. JENNEKENS (Canada), MALU WA KALENGA (Zaire), W. C. MARSHALL (U.K.), J. MINCZEWSKI (Poland), W. MURATA (Japan), H. N. SETHNA (India), I. URSU (Romania), A. A. VASILIEV (U.S.S.R.). Publs. *Nuclear Fusion* (every 2 months), *Atomic Energy Review, IAEA Bulletin* (quarterly).

International Botanical Congress (*Congrès International de Botanique*): 13th Congress, August 1981, University of Sydney, N.S.W. 2006, Australia; sponsored by the Australian Academy of Science; f. 1864 to inform botanists of recent progress in plant sciences; programme divided into sections: nomenclature; molecular, metabolic, cellular and structural, developmental, environmental, community, genetic, systematic and evolutionary, bryological, fungal, marine and fresh water, historical and applied botany.

Pres. and Chair. of Organizing Cttee. R. N. ROBERTSON; Exec. Sec. W. J. CRAM.

International Bureau of Weights and Measures (*Bureau International des Poids et Mesures*): Pavillon de Breteuil, 92310 Sèvres, France; f. 1875 for the preservation of standards of the International System of Units (SI) and world-wide unification of the units of measurement; determination of national standards; precision measurements in Physics. 45 member states.

Pres. J. V. DUNWORTH (U.K.); Vice-Pres. P. HONTI (Hungary), D. KIND (Fed. Repub. of Germany); Sec. J. DE BOER (Netherlands); Dir. PIERRE GIACOMO (France). Publs. *Procès-Verbaux* (annually), *Sessions des Sept Comités Consultatifs auprès du Comité International* (every few years for each committee), *Comptes Rendus des Conférences Générales* (every 4 years), *Recueil de Travaux* (every few years).

International Centre for Theoretical Physics: P.O.B. 586, Trieste 34100, Italy; f. 1964; sponsored by the International Atomic Energy Agency and UNESCO; work in high-energy physics, condensed matter physics, plasma physics, atomic physics, nuclear physics, applicable mathematics, physics of the earth, atmosphere and oceans; library of 17,000 vols.

Dir. ABDUS SALAM (Pakistan); Admin. A. M. HAMENDE (Belgium).

International Commission for Optics (*Commission Internationale d'Optique*): c/o Dept. of Applied Physics, Delft University of Technology, Lorentzweg 1, 2628 CJ Delft, Netherlands; f. 1948 to contribute on an international basis to the progress of theoretical and instrumental optics and its application, through conferences, colloquia, summer schools, etc., and to promote international agreement on nomenclature, specifications, etc. 24 member countries.

Pres. Prof. A. LOHMANN (Fed. Repub. of Germany); Sec.-Gen. Prof. H. J. FRANKENA (Netherlands).

International Commission for the Scientific Exploration of the Mediterranean Sea (*Commission Internationale pour l'Exploration Scientifique de la Mer Méditerranée*): 16 blvd. de Suisse, Monte Carlo, Monaco; f. 1919 for scientific exploration of the Mediterranean Sea, the study of physical and chemical oceanography, marine geology and geophysics, marine pollution, microbiology, biochemistry, plankton, benthos, lagoons, marine radioactivity, marine vertebrates, island biology, underwater exploration; 17 mem. countries.

Pres. H. R. H. The Prince RAINIER OF MONACO; Sec.-Gen. Cdt. J. Y. COUSTEAU (France). Publs. *Rapports et Procès-Verbaux*.

International Commission on Zoological Nomenclature (*Commission internationale de nomenclature zoologique*): c/o British Museum (Natural History), Cromwell Rd., London, SW7 5BD; f. 1895; the Commission, formerly a standing organ of the International Congresses, now reports to the Division of Zoology of IUBS; the Commission has judicial powers to determine all matters relating to the interpretation of the *International Code of Zoological Nomenclature* and also plenary powers to suspend the operation of the *Code* where strict application would lead to confusion and instability of nomenclature; the Commission is responsible also for maintaining and developing the *Official Lists of Names in Zoology* and the *Official Indexes of Names in Zoology*.

Pres. C. W. SABROSKY (U.S.A.); Sec. R. V. MELVILLE (U.K.). Publs. *Bulletin of Zoological Nomenclature, Opinions and Declarations rendered by the International Commission on Zoological Nomenclature*, etc.

International Council for Bird Preservation: 219c Huntingdon Rd., Cambridge CB3 0DL, England; f. 1922; determines status of bird species throughout the world and compiles data on all endangered species; identifies conservation problems and priorities; promotes, initiates and co-ordinates conservation projects and international conventions; stimulates international action for the prevention of the pollution of the sea by oil and other toxic substances; national sections in 65 countries.

Pres. Prof. S. DILLON RIPLEY (U.S.A.); Vice-Pres. Dr. Y. YAMASHINA (Japan), Prof. K. CURRY-LINDAHL (Sweden); Dir. Dr. CHRISTOPH IMBODEN (U.K.). Publs. *Bulletin, ICBP Newsletter*.

International Council for the Exploration of the Sea (ICES) (*Conseil International pour l'Exploration de la Mer—CIEM*): Palægade 2–4, DK 1261, Copenhagen K, Denmark; f. 1902 to promote and encourage research and investigations for the study of the sea, particularly those related to the living resources thereof. Area of interest: The Atlantic Ocean and its adjacent sea, and primarily the North Atlantic. Library of 12,000 vols., 1,100 journals. Mems.: Governments of 18 countries.

Sec.-Gen HANS TAMBS-LYCHE. Publs. *Journal du Conseil Rapports et Procès-Verbaux, Bulletin Statistique, ICES Oceanographic Data Lists and Inventories, Annales Biologiques, Cooperative Research Reports, Fiches d'Identification du Zooplancton*, etc.

International Federation for Cell Biology (*Fédération Internationale de Biologie Cellulaire*).

Pres. Dr. D. MAZIA; Sec.-Gen. Dr. L. M. FRANKS, Imperial Cancer Research Fund, Lincoln's Inn Fields, London, W.C.2, U.K.

International Federation of Societies for Electron Microscopy (*Féd. Internationale des Sociétés de Microscopie Electronique*): c/o 284 Hearst Mining Bldg., University of California, Berkeley, Calif., U.S.A.; f. 1955. Mems.: representative organizations of 26 countries.

Pres. Prof. J. LE POOLE (Netherlands); Sec. Prof. GARETH THOMAS (U.S.A.).

International Food Information Service: Editorial Office, Lane End House, Shinfield, Reading, RG2 9BB, England; f. 1968 by the Institut für Dokumentationswesen (Frankfurt), the Institute of Food Technologists (Chicago) and the Commonwealth Agricultural Bureaux for the collection and dissemination of scientific and technological information on foods and their processing.

Man. Dirs. E. J. MANN, N.D.D., C.D.D., U. SCHÜTZSACK. Publ. *Food Science & Technology Abstracts* (monthly).

International Foundation of the High-Altitude Research Stations, Jungfraujoch and Gornergrat (*Fondation internationale des stations scientifiques du Jungfraujoch et du Gornergrat*): 5 Sidlerstrasse, 3012 Berne, Switzerland; f. 1931.

Pres. Prof. H. DEBRUNNER.

International Geological Congress (*Congrès géologique international*): 77-79 rue Claude Bernard, 75005 Paris, France; f. 1878 to contribute to the advancement of investigations relating to the study of the Earth and other planets, considered from the theoretical and practical points of view; the congress is held every four years (26th Congress, Paris, July 1980).

Pres. Org. Cttee. J. AUBOUIN; Sec.-Gen. PAUL SANGNIER (France). Publs. *Extended Abstracts, General Proceedings*.

The International Glaciological Society: Cambridge, CB2 1ER, England; f. 1936 to stimulate interest in and encourage research into the scientific and technical problems of snow and ice in all countries. Mems.: 1,050.

Pres. Dr. L. W. GOLD (Canada); Vice-Pres. Dr. C. R. BENTLEY (U.S.A.), Dr. O. ORHEIM (Norway), Dr. C. SWITHINBANK (U.K.; Sec.-Gen. Mrs. H. RICHARDSON. Publs. *Journal of Glaciology* (quarterly), *Ice* (News Bulletin—3 year).

International Hydrographic Organization (*Organisation hydrographique internationale*): ave. Président J. F. Kennedy, Monte Carlo; f. 1921. Objects: To establish a close and permanent association among the hydrographic offices of its members; to co-ordinate the hydrographic work of these offices in order to render navigation easier and safer; to obtain uniformity in charts and hydrographic documents; to encourage the adoption of the best methods of conducting hydrographic surveys and improvement in the theory and practice of hydrography; to encourage surveying in those areas where accurate charts are lacking; to encourage co-ordination of hydrographic surveys with relevant oceanographic activities and to provide for co-operation between the IHO and international organizations in the field of oceanography; to extend and facilitate the application of oceanographic knowledge for the benefit of navigators. Library of 750 vols., 100 periodicals and collection of charts published by member states. Forty-seven member states.

Pres. Rear-Adm. G. S. RITCHIE (U.K.); Dirs. Rear-Adm D. C. KAPOOR (India), Capt. J. E. AYRES (U.S.A.). Publs. *The International Hydrographic Review* (twice yearly), *International Hydrographic Bulletin* (monthly), *Yearbook*, special publications on various technical subjects, all in English and French, *General Bathymetric Chart of the Oceans* (in 24 sheets).

International Institute for Applied Systems Analysis: 2361 Laxenburg, Austria; f. 1972 on the initiative of the U.S.A. and the U.S.S.R.; conducts and supports collaborative and individual research in relation to problems of modern societies arising from scientific and technological development, and undertakes its own studies into both methodological and applied research in the fields of energy systems, food and agriculture, resources and environment, population dynamics, systems analysis, cybernetics, operations research, and management techniques. Mems.: organizations from 17 countries.

Chair. Prof. J. M. GVISHIANI (U.S.S.R.); Dir. Dr. R. E. LEVIEN (U.S.A.); Sec. Dr. A. BELOZELOV (U.S.S.R.). Publs. research reports and conference proceedings.

International Institute of Seismology and Earthquake Engineering: c/o J. Kazuo Minami, Building Research Institute, Ministry of Construction, 3-chome Hyakunincho, Shinjuku-ku, Tokyo, Japan; f. 1962. Object: To carry out training and research works on seismology and earthquake engineering for the purpose of fostering these research activities in the developing countries, and to undertake survey, research, guidance and analysis of information on earthquakes and their related matters. Mems.: *c.* 25.

Pres. Dr. E. ROSENBLUTH, Instituto de Ingenieria, Ciudad Universitaria, Mexico 20, D.F. Publs. *Bulletin of IISEE*† (annual), *Individual Study Report*† (annual), *Progress Report*† (annual), *Year Book*†, *Lecture Note*† (occasional).

International Mineralogical Association: f. 1958 to further international co-operation in the science of mineralogy. Mems.: national societies in many countries.

Sec. Dr. CHRISTEL TENNYSON, Institut für Mineralogie, Berlin-Charlottenburg, Hardenbergstr. 35, Fed. Repub. of Germany. Publs. *World Directories* (Mineralogists; Mineral Collections).

International Organisation of Legal Metrology (*Organisation internationale de métrologie légale*): 11 rue Turgot, Paris 9e, France; f. 1955 to serve as documentation and information centre on methods of verifying and checking measurements, to study ways of harmonization and to determine the general principles of legal metrology. Mems.: governments of 43 countries.

Pres. A. J. VAN MALE (Netherlands); Dir. B. ATHANÉ. Publs. *Bulletin* (quarterly), *International Recommendations*.

International Ornithological Congress (*Congrès International Ornithologique*): c/o R. Nöhring, Zoologischer Garten, Hardenbergplatz 8, 1 Berlin 30, Fed. Repub. of Germany; f. 1884.

Pres. Prof. D. S. FARNER (U.S.A.); Sec.-Gen. R. NÖHRING (Fed. Repub. of Germany).

International Palaeontological Association (formerly the International Palaeontological Union): Geolog.-Paläontolog. Inst., Universität Göttingen, Fed. Repub. of Germany; f. 1933 following the meeting of the International Geological Congress. Affiliated to the Int. Union of Geological Sciences and the Int. Union of Biological Sciences. Meets every four years at International Geological Congress. Mems.: national organizations, research groups and ordinary members.

Pres. Prof. C. TEICHERT (U.S.A.); Sec.-Gen. Prof. O. H. WALLISER (Fed. Repub. of Germany).

International Polar Motion Service (*Service international du Mouvement Polaire*): replaced in 1962 the International Latitude Service, founded in 1899. Object: To make observations in the latitude and time stations all over the world for the study of all problems relating to the polar motion. Central Bureau of the Service collects astronomical observations, determines motion and distributes data and results obtained.

Dir. Dr. S. YUMI, Central Bureau of the IPMS, International Latitude Observatory of Mizusawa, Iwateke 023, Japan. Publs. *Monthly Notes, Annual Reports*.

International Primatological Society: c/o Dr. Allan M. Schrier, Psychology Dept., Brown University, Providence, R.I. 02912, U.S.A.; f. 1964 to promote primatological science in all fields. Mems.: about 750.

Pres. Dr. W. A. MASON (U.S.A.); Sec.-Gen. Dr. ALLAN M. SCHRIER (U.S.A.). Publs. *Proceedings of meetings* (every 2 years), *International Journal of Primatology*.

International Society for Human and Animal Mycology (ISHAM) (*Société Internationale de Mycologie Humaine et Animale*): c/o Prof. W. LOEFFLER; Gen. Sec., Gellertstr. 11A, 4052 Basel, Switzerland; f. 1954 to pursue the study of fungi pathogenic for man and animals; 754 mems. from 67 countries.

Pres. Prof. G. SEGRETAIN; Gen. Sec. Dr. W. LOEFFLER (Switzerland). Publs. *Sabouraudia* (annually in 4 parts), *ISHAM Mycoses Newsletter* (2 a year).

International Society for Tropical Ecology: c/o Botany Dept., Banaras Hindu University, Varanasi 5, India; f. 1960 to promote and develop the science of ecology in the tropics in the service of man; to publish a journal to aid ecologists in the tropics in communication of their findings; and to hold symposia from time to time to summarize the state of knowledge in particular or general fields of tropical ecology. Mems.: 450.

Pres. Prof. F. B. GOLLEY; Sec. K. C. MISRA. Publ. *Tropical Ecology* (twice a year).

International Society for Vegetation Science (*Association Internationale de Phytosociologie*): c/o Prof. Dr. Drs. h.c. REINHOLD TÜXEN, 3260 Rinteln I, Ortsteil Todenmann, Fed. Repub. of Germany; f. 1937; aims for the development and unification of phytosociology; 620 mems.

Pres. Prof. Dr. Dr. h.c. J. LEBRUN (Belgium); Sec. Prof. Drs. h.c. REINHOLD TÜXEN. Publ. *Phytocoenologia*.

International Society of Biometeorology: f. 1956. Aims: to unite all biometeorologists working in the fields of Agriculture, Botanical, Cosmic, Entomological, Forest, Human, Veterinarian, Zoological and other branches of Biometeorology. Mems.: 450 individuals, nationals of 50 countries.

Pres. Prof. Dr. H. LIETH; Sec. Dr. B. PRIMAULT (Switzerland), Witikonerstrasse 446, 8053 Zurich, Switzerland. Publ. *International Journal of Biometeorology*.

International Society of Development Biologists: Dept. of Biological Sciences, Dartmouth College, Hanover, N.H. 03755, U.S.A.; f. 1911 as *International Institute of Embryology*; aims to promote the study of developmental biology and to promote international co-operation among the investigators in this field; the Society is the Developmental Biology Section of the International Union of Biological Sciences (*q.v.*). Mems.: 900.

Pres. Prof. A. MOSCONA (U.S.A.); Int. Sec. Prof. N. LE DOUARIN (France); Sec.-Treas. Prof. M. SPIEGEL (U.S.A.).

International Society of Electrochemistry (ISE) (*Société Internationale d'Electrochimie*): Ecole Polytechnique Fédérale de Lausanne, Département des Matériaux, 34 chemin de Bellerive, CH-1007 Lausanne, Switzerland; f. 1949 to promote the free exchange of information in Electrochemistry between all member countries; 740 mems.; 35 countries.

Pres. Prof. P. GALLONE (Italy); Sec.-Gen. Prof. D. LANDOLT (Switzerland). Publ. *Electrochimica Acta* (monthly).

International Speleological Congresses (*Congrès Internationaux de Spéléologie*: f. 1958; over 200 individuals; Sec.-Gen. Dr. H. TRIMMEL, Bundesdenkmalamt, Hofburg, Säulenstiege, 2 stock, 1010 Vienna, Austria.

International Statistical Institute (*Institut international de statistique*): Prinses Beatrixlaan 428, 2270 AZ Voorburg, Netherlands; f. 1885; the International Statistical Institute is an autonomous society devoted to the development and improvement of statistical methods and their application throughout the world; 7 hon. mems., 1,100 ordinary mems., 150 *ex-officio* mems., 28 corporate mems., 32 affiliated organizations; administers statistical education centre in Calcutta in co-operation with UNESCO; conducts the World Fertility Survey in collaboration with the UN and the International Union for the Scientific Study of Population.

Pres. E. MALINVAUD (France); Sec.-Treas./Dir. Permanent Office E. LUNENBERG. Publs. *International Statistical Review* (3 a year), *Bulletin* (proceedings of biennial sessions), *Statistical Theory and Methods Abstracts* (quarterly), *Dictionary of Statistical Terms*, *International Statistical Information* (3 a year), *Directory of Statistical Societies*, *Directory of National Statistical Agencies*.

International Tables of Selected Constants (*Tables Internationales de Constantes Sélectionnées*): Université P. et M. Curie (Paris VI), Faculté des Sciences, Tour 13, 4 place Jussieu, 75230 Paris Cedex 05, France; f. 1909. Object: to publish all the constants and numerical data concerning the pure and applied physico-chemical sciences.

Pres. Prof. G. AMAT (France); Dir. S. BOURCIER (France). Publs. 19 Tables since 1947.

International Time Bureau (*Bureau international de l'heure*): 61 ave. de l'Observatoire, 75014 Paris, France; f. 1912 to act as a centre for all astronomical or physical determinations of time. Membership: 64 observatories and laboratories.

Dir. Dr. B. GUINOT (Astronomer, Paris Observatory). Publs. *Circul. A, B/C, D, Annual Report.*

International Union for Conservation of Nature and Natural Resources (*Union Internationale pour la Conservation de la Nature et de ses Ressources*): 1110 Morges, Switzerland; f. 1948 to promote international co-operation in scientific research and in applying ecological concepts for conservation of nature and natural resources; to ensure the perpetuation of biological diversity and genetic resources of wild animals and plants in their natural environment; to disseminate information, ecological guidelines and techniques of conservation in preserving wildlife habitats and other natural landscape features for their ethical, aesthetic, scientific, educational and economic values; to facilitate the understanding of ecological principles and biological productivity for the long-term economic and social welfare of mankind. Mems.: 28 international organizations, governments of 51 countries, 342 government agencies and national organizations in 103 countries, 11 affiliates.

Pres. Prof. MOHAMED EL-KASSAS (Egypt); Dir.-Gen. Dr. DAVID MUNRO (Canada). Publs. *Bulletin* (monthly), *Annual Report, United Nations List of National Parks and Equivalent Reserves.*

International Union for Quaternary Research (INQUA): f. 1928; Field of activities: geology, geography, prehistory, palaeontology, palynology, pedology.

Pres. Exec. Comm. Prof. JANE M. SOONS, Dept. of Geography, University of Canterbury, Christchurch, New Zealand; Sec.-Treas. Prof. R. PAEPE, Vrije Universiteit Brussel, Kwartairgeologie, Pleinlaan 2, 1050 Brussels, Belgium. Publs. *Proceedings* of Congresses.

International Union for the Study of Social Insects (*Union Internationale pour l'Etude des Insectes Sociaux*): c/o P. E. Howse, Dept. of Zoology, Univ. of Southampton, Southampton, U.K.; f. 1951. Mems.: over 500 individuals from 24 countries.

Pres. Prof. C. D. MICHENER; Sec.-Gen. Dr. P. E. HOWSE. Publs. *Insectes sociaux, Congress Proceedings*, etc.

International Waterfowl Research Bureau (*Bureau International de Recherches sur les Oiseaux d'Eau*): Slimbridge, Glos. GL2 7BX, England; f. 1954 to promote and co-ordinate research on and conservation of waterfowl; 32 mem. countries.

Dir. Prof. G. V. T. MATTHEWS. Publs. *Bulletin*† (every 6 months) and special volumes†.

Joint Institute for Nuclear Research: Head Post Office, P.O. Box 79, Moscow, U.S.S.R.; f. 1956 to further collaboration in nuclear research between the member countries, and find more possibilities for peaceful use of atomic energy; maintains six laboratories of the Joint Institute: The laboratories of Nuclear Problems, High Energies, Theoretical Physics, Neutron Physics, Nuclear Reactions, and Computing and Automation. Mems.: 11 countries.

Dir. N. N. BOGOLUBOV (U.S.S.R.).

OECD Nuclear Energy Agency (NEA): 38 blvd. Suchet, Paris 16e, France (formerly European Nuclear Energy Agency (ENEA), f. 1958, name changed 1972); assesses the future role of nuclear energy as a contributor to economic progress, and encourages co-operation between governments towards its optimum development; encourages harmonization of governments' regulatory policies and practices in the nuclear field and co-operation on health and safety, radioactive waste management and nuclear third party liability and insurance; prepares forecasts of uranium resources, production and demand, and of developments in the nuclear fuel cycle; establishes and operates common services, with particular reference to scientific information in the nuclear field; sponsors research and development undertakings jointly organized and operated by OECD countries; contributes to improved public understanding by publication of authoritative and impartial analyses and assessments on relevant questions. Operates, in collaboration with IAEA and FAO, an international project on irradiation preservation of foodstuffs, based in Germany; operates the Halden (Norway) experimental reactor and the European Company for the Chemical Processing of Irradiated Fuels (EUROCHEMIC) at Mol (Belgium); maintains NEA Data Bank for compilation and exchange of computer programmes and nuclear data (Saclay, France). Mems.: 23 countries.

Dir.-Gen. I. G. K. WILLIAMS. Publ. *Annual Report*†.

Pacific Science Association (*Association Scientifique du Pacifique*): P.O.B. 17801, Honolulu, Hawaii 96817, U.S.A.; f. 1920 to co-operate in the study of scientific problems relating to the Pacific region; sponsors congresses and inter-congresses. Mems.: scientists and scientific institutions interested in the Pacific.

Pres. Dr. J. A. R. MILES (New Zealand); Sec. BRENDA BISHOP (New Zealand). Publs. *Information Bulletin*†, *Congress Proceedings.*

Pan-American Institute of Geography and History (*Instituto Panamericano de Geografía e Historia*): Ex-Arzobispado 29, Mexico 18, D.F., Mexico; f. 1929; membership: the nations of the Organization of American States except Barbados, Jamaica, Trinidad and Tobago; for the stimulation and co-ordination of cartographic, geographic, historical, geophysical and related work in the Western hemisphere; library of 60,000 vols. and 24,000 maps; periodicals collection of 54,000 vols.

Sec.-Gen. Ing. JOSE A. SÁENZ G. (Panama). Publs. *Revista de Historia de América, Boletín de Antropología Americana, Revista Geográfica, Revista Cartográfica, Folklore Americano, Revista Geofisica, Boletin Aereo.*

Permanent Committee of the International Congress of Entomology (*Comité permanent du congrès international d'entomologie*): f. 1910 to act as a link between periodic congresses and to arrange the venue for each congress; the committee is also the entomology section of the International Union of Biological Sciences.

Pres. Dr. J. C. M. CARVALHO (Brazil); Sec. Dr. L. A. MOUND, c/o British Museum (Natural History), Cromwell Rd., London, S.W.7. Publ. *Proceedings* (after each Congress).

Permanent International Committee for Genetics Congresses (*Comité permanent des congrès internationaux de génétique*) (The Genetics Section of the IUBS): Biological Laboratory, The University, Kyoto, Japan; 18 mem. countries.

Pres. Prof. Dr. S. J. Geerts (Netherlands); Sec.-Gen. Prof. R. Riley, Plant Breeding Institute, Maris Lane, Trumpington, Cambridge CB2 2LQ, England.

World Academy of Art and Sciences: f. 1960; a forum for discussion of important topics by distinguished scientists; to act as an objective advisory body; 317 mems. (Fellows) in 43 countries.

Pres. Walter Isard (U.S.A.); Vice-Pres. Julian Aleksandrowicz (Poland), George E. G. Catlin (U.K.), Sir John C. Eccles (Australia), Ivan Malek (Czechoslovakia), Guiseppe Medici (Italy), Carl-Goran Heden (Sweden), Albert-Györgyi (U.S.A.), Morris L. West (Australia); Sec.-Gen. John McHale, Center for Integrative Studies, 5th Floor, New Library Wing, University of Houston, Texas 77004, U.S.A. Publs. *WAAS Newsletter* (3 or 4 a year), Conference Reports, Occasional Papers.

World Meteorological Organization (*Organisation Météorologique Mondiale*): Secretariat: Case postale 5, CH-1211 Geneva 20, Switzerland; f. 1951. Objects: World-wide co-operation in making meteorological and hydrometeorological observations and in standardizing their publication, promotion of rapid weather information services, application of meteorology to human activities, encouragement of research and training in meteorology. Mems.: 147 states and five territories maintaining their own meteorological or hydrometeorological services. Constituent bodies: Congress, Executive Committee, six regional associations, eight technical commissions.

Pres. R. L. Kintanar (Philippines); Sec.-Gen. A. C. Wiin Nielsen (Denmark). Publs. Reports of meetings of constituent bodies, Regulations, Technical Manuals and Notes, *International Cloud Atlas*, *WMO Bulletin* (quarterly).

World Organisation of General Systems and Cybernetics: c/o Dr. J. Rose, College of Technology, Blackburn, BB2 1LH, England; f. 1969 to act as clearing-house for all societies concerned with cybernetics, systems and allied subjects, to aim for the recognition of cybernetics as a bona fide science and to maintain liaison with other international bodies. Mems.: national and international organizations in 42 countries; 25 hon. fellows.

Dir.-Gen. Dr. J. Rose (U.K.). Publs. *International Journal of Cybernetics and Systems "Kybernetes"* (quarterly), *Computers in Medicine*, congress proceedings, *Abstracts of Papers*, monographs (every 3 years).

AFGHANISTAN

Population 15,540,000

LEARNED SOCIETIES AND RESEARCH INSTITUTES

Afghanistan Academy of Sciences: Kabul; f. 1979; research in various fields of science, technology, humanities and culture; Pres. Dr. Gul Mohammad Noorzai.

Institutes

Institute of Social Sciences: philosophy, economics, history, archaeology; Pres. Dr. Hakim Helali; publs. *Afghanistan* (quarterly in English, French and German), *Ariana* (quarterly in Pashto and Dari).

Institute of Natural Sciences: botany, zoology, geology and chemistry, seismology, computer centre, plants museum and botanical garden.

Institute of Languages and Literature: linguistics, literature and folklore; study of Pashto and Dari languages, and Afghanistan dialects; publs. *Kabul Magazine*, *Zayray Weekly*.

Central Library.

Central Archives.

Encyclopedia: work on dictionaries translating from and into Pashto.

International Centre for Pashto Studies: research, compilation and translation; publ. *Pashto Quarterly*.

Asia Foundation: P.O.B. 257, Kabul; f. 1955; assists local institutions and organizations concerned with educational and socio-economic development; Representative Joel W. Scarborough.

British Institute of Afghan Studies: P.O.B. 3052, Kabul; f. 1972; supported and controlled by the Society for Afghan Studies, c/o British Academy, Piccadilly, London, W.1; research centre for British scholars working in the fields of archaeology, history, culture, languages, geography, and related subjects; Dir. R. H. Pinder-Wilson; publs. *Annual Report*†, *Afghan Studies* (annually).

Cercle Culturel Français: Shahr-iNau, Kabul.

Department of Mines and Geology: Ministry of Mines and Industries, Kabul; f. 1918; geological and mineralogical research and exploitation; library of 5,000 vols.; Pres. S. H. Mirzad; Gen. Dir. of Mines A. A. Akefie; Gen. Dir. of Geology A. S. Salah; publ. *Bulletin of Geology of Afghanistan*.

Goethe Institut: P.O.B. 191, Kabul; f. 1966; German language and culture; library of 4,500 vols.; Dir. Jens Uwe Braun.

Institute of Cartography: Ministry of Mines and Industries, Kabul; Pres. Eng. Muzaffarud Din Yaqubi.

Institute of Public Health: Ansari Wat, Kabul; f. 1962; Functions: public health training and research; Government reference laboratory; study of indigenous diseases; compilation and publication of statistical data and analysis; Dir. Dr. S. M. Sadique; publs. *Afghan Journal of Public Health* (2 per month), books and pamphlets.

LIBRARIES

Library of the National Bank: Ibn Sina Wat, Kabul.

Library of the Press and Information Department: Sanaii Wat, Kabul; f. 1931; 28,000 vols. and 800 MSS. in Persian, Arabic and Pashtu languages; Dir. Mohammed Sarwar Rona.

Ministry of Education Library: Kabul.

Public Library: Charaii-i-Malik Asghar, Kabul; f. 1920; attached to the Ministry of Information and Culture; 60,000 vols., 433 MSS., 30 current periodicals; research library; Dir. Mohamad Omar Seddiqui.

University Library: Kabul; 120,000 vols.; Librarian Mohamad Ibrahim Studah.

Women's Welfare Society Library: Kabul.

MUSEUMS

Bamian Museum: Bamian.

Ghazni Museum: Ghazni.

Herat Museum: Herat.

Kabul Museum: Darul Aman, Kabul; f. 1922; archaeological collections of the prehistoric, Greco-Roman, Buddhic and Islamic periods; Kushan art; coin collections; ethnographical collections; Dir. A. A. Motamedi. (Closed temporarily).

Kandahar Museum: Kandahar.

Maimana Museum: Maimana.

Mazar-i-Sharif Museum: Mazar-i-Sharif.

UNIVERSITIES

KABUL POHANTOON
(Kabul University)
KABUL

Telephone: 42546.

Founded 1932.

Languages of instruction: Dari (Persian), Pashtu, English; Academic year: March to January.

President: ABDUL SA'IDI.

Vice-President for Academic Affairs: Prof. ABDUL S. AZIMI.

Vice-President for Student Affairs: Dr. MOHAMAD ANWAR SULTAN.

Vice-President for Administration: Dr. ZAMIN ALI.

Registrar: Dr. ASSADULLAH HABIB.

Librarian: MOHAMAD IBRAHIM STUDAH.

Number of teachers: 1,115.

Number of students: 9,865.

Publications: *Adab*, *Wazhma* (both literature monthly), *Huqooq* (law and political science), *Afghan Medical Journal*, *Elm-wa-Fun* (art), *Shariaat* (Islamic law), *Science*, all quarterly, *Geography* (annual).

DEANS:

Faculty of Medicine: Prof. KHAIR MOHD. ARSALA.

Faculty of Pharmacy: Dr. FAZLE A. EHRARI.

Faculty of Veterinary Medicine: Dr. FAQIR MOHAMMAD ZAMARAY.

Faculty of Law and Political Science: Dr. MOHAMMAD WALI YOSOFI.

Faculty of Science: Dr. MOHAMMAD RASUL.

Faculty of Letters: Prof. MIR HUSSAIN SHAH.

Faculty of Economics: Dr. SAID ABDULLAH KAZEM.

Faculty of Agriculture: Dr. M. HASHEM.

Faculty of Engineering: Dr. ZAR JAN BAHA.

Faculty of Islamic Law: Dr. ABDOL JALIL.

Polytechnic Institute: Dr. FAQIR MOHAMMAD YAQUBI.

Nangarhar Medical College: Dr SHAIRZAD YAQUBI.

University Hospitals: Dr. A. G. MOTAWAKIL.

UNIVERSITY OF NANGRAHAR
JALALABAD

Founded 1962 from Medical Faculty of Kabul University.

State control; Academic year: September to June; Language of instruction: Pashto.

Chancellor: Dr. AMINI GULZAR.

Registrar: M. NASRULLAH.

Librarian: M. SHEKIB.

Number of teachers: 90.

Number of students; 2,350.

Publication: *Scientific Journal.*

DEANS:

Faculty of Medicine: A. K. FAQOOR.

Faculty of Education: G. STANAH.

Faculty of Agriculture: M. N. HABIBI.

Faculty of Engineering: M. MOHENSIE.

PROFESSORS AND HEADS OF DEPARTMENT:

AFZAL, M., Anaesthesia
AHMADIE, A. S., Paediatrics
AHMEDZI, A. S., Internal Medicine
ALAYAR, M. A., Forensic Medicine
AQA, M., Pharmacology
DANISHWAR, F. H., Obstetrics and Gynaecology
DOST, M., Microbiology
EHSAN, A. R., Surgery
FAQOOR, A. K., Chemistry
GHAZUNFARI, M. A., Ophthalmology
GHULAM, S., Radiology
HABIBURAHMAN, Anatomy
MOTI-ZADEH, S., Neuropsychiatry
MUNGLE, M. A., Preventive Medicine
NUMAN, S., Cardiology and Physiology
PRAW, S. M., Biology
SAYEDAH, Mrs., Biochemistry
SHEKIB, M. A., Mathematics and Physics
SHINWARIE, M. N., Internal Medicine
SHOKOOR, S. A., Ear, Nose and Throat
SIDDIQUI, M. S., Pathology
SIDDIQUI, Mrs., Psychology
SINGH, P., Dermatology

COLLEGES

Afghan Institute of Technology: Kabul; f. 1951; secondary level technical school; Departments of Aviation, Automotive-Diesel, Machine Tools, Building Construction, Civil and Electrical-Electronics Technology; 450 students; 50 staff; library of 6,000 vols.; Dir. GHULAM SAKHI.

Institute of Arabic and Religious Study: Kabul.

Other centres include: the Najmul-Madares, Nangrahar; the Jamé and Fakhrul Madares, Herat; the Asadia Madrasa, Mazar-i-Sharif; the Takharistan Madrasa, Kunduz; the Zahir Shahi Madrasa, Maimana.

Institute of Industrial Management: Kabul; f. 1962; open to graduates of the School of Commerce; *c.* 30 teachers, 330 students; 4-year degree course; Pres. Dr. AZIMI.

Kabul Art School: Bibi Mahro, nr. Kabul; music, painting and sculpture courses.

School of Agriculture: Kabul; f. 1924.

School of Commerce: Kabul; f. 1943; banking, commercial law, economics, business administration, finance.

School of Mechanics: Kabul; for apprentice trainees.

ALBANIA

Population 2,620,000

ACADEMY

ACADEMY OF SCIENCES

TIRANA

Founded 1972.

President: ALEKS BUDA.
Vice-Presidents: KOLË POPA, PETRIT RADOVICKA.
Scientific Secretary: LUAN OMARI.

MEMBERS:

BUDA, ALEKS (History, mem. of Presidium).
BEKTESHI, SELAUDIN (Medicine).
ÇABEJ, EQEREM (Linguistics, mem. of Presidium).
ÇAMI, FOTO (Philosophy, mem. of Presidium).
DEDJA, BEDRI (Pedagogics, Psychology).
DOMI, MAHIR (Linguistics).
HOXHA, FEJZI (Medicine).
KËLLICI, ZIJA (Mechanical Engineering).
KOSTALLARI, ANDROKLI (Linguistics, mem. of Presidium).
KUMBARO, HAJREDIN (Metallurgy).
KUNESHKA, SOTIR (Physics).
MARA, HEKURAN (Economics).
OMARI, LUAN (Jurisprudence, mem. of Presidium).
PAPARISTO, KOLË (Botany).
PËRMETI, MENTOR (Genetics and Plant Selection, mem. of Presidium).
POLLO, STEFANAQ (History, mem. of Presidium).
POPA, KOLË (Chemistry, mem. of Presidium).
RADOVICKA, PETRIT (Hydraulic Engineering, mem. of Presidium).
SHUTERIQI, DHIMITËR (Literature).

CORRESPONDING MEMBERS:

DAJA, BESIM (Architecture).
KAKARIQI, ZEF (Veterinary Science).
PILIKA, PETRAQ (Mathematics).
PREZA, BAJRAM (Medicine).
XHOLI, ZIJA (Philosophy).

ATTACHED RESEARCH INSTITUTES:

Instituti i Gjuhësisë dhe i Letërsisë (*Institute of Lniguistics and Literature*): Tirana; f. 1974; Dir. ANDROKLI KOSTALLARI; publs. *Studia Albanica*† (quarterly, in French), *Studime Filologjike*† (Study of Philology, every 2 months).

Instituti i Historisë (*Institute of History*): Tirana; f. 1947; Dir. STEFANAQ POLLO; publ. *Studime Historike*† (Study of History, every 2 months).

Instituti i Kulturës Popullore (*Institute of National Culture*): Tirana; f. 1947; Dir. ALFRED UCI; publ. *Etnografia Shqiptare*† (Albanian Ethnography, irregular).

Instituti i Studimeve Ekonomike (*Institute of Economic Studies*): Tirana; f. 1969; Dir. HASAN BANJA; publ. *Probleme Ekonomike*† (Economic Problems, monthly).

Qendra e Kërkimeve Arkeologjike (*Centre for Archaeological Research*): Tirana; f. 1948 as Archaeological Museum; Dir. ALEKSANDRA MANO; publ. *Iliria*† (Illyria, irregular).

Instituti Hidrometeorologjik (*Institute of Hydrometeorology*): Tirana; f. 1949; Dir. JAVER ÇOBANI; publs. *Buletini Hidrometeorologjik*† (Bulletin of Hydrometeorology, monthly, annually), *Punime meteorologjike dhe hidrologjike*† (Meteorological and Hydrological Studies, irregular).

Instituti i Fizikës Bërthamore (*Institute of Nuclear Physics*): Tirana; f. 1971; Dir. SKËNDER KOJA.

Qendra e Matematikës Llogaritëse (*Centre of Computer Mathematics*): Tirana; f. 1971; Dir. KRISTIAN BUKUROSHI.

Qendra e Kërkimeve Biologjike (*Centre of Biological Research*): Tirana; f, 1978; Dir. TEKI TARTARI.

Qendra Sizmologjike (*Seismological Centre*): Tirana; f. 1972; Dir. EDUARD SULSTAROVA; publ. *Buletini Sizmologjik*† (Seismological Bulletin, in Albanian and English).

Laboratori i Kërkimeve Hidraulike (*Laboratory of Hydraulic Research*): Tirana; f. 1972; Dir. PANDI STRATOBËRDHA.

Biblioteka Shkencore (*Scientific Library*): Tirana; f. 1972; 150,000 vols; Dir. AFËRDITA BUDO.

LEARNED SOCIETIES

Bashkimi i Gazetarëve të Shqipërisë (*Association of Journalists of Albania*): Tirana; Pres. AGIM POPA; publ. *Tribuna e Gazetarit* (Journalists' Tribune).

Komiteti Shqiptar për Marrëdhënie Kulturore me botën e jashtme (*Albanian Committee for Cultural Relations Abroad*): Tirana; Pres. JAVER MALO.

Lidhja e Shkrimtarëve dhe e Artistëve të Shqipërisë (*League of Artists and Writers of Albania*): Tirana; f. 1957; Pres. DRITËRO AGOLLI; publ. *Nëntori* (monthly Review), *Drita* (weekly journal).

RESEARCH INSTITUTES

Instituti i Studimeve Marksiste-leniniste pranë KQ të PPSH (*Institute of Marxist-Leninist Studies at the Central Committee of the Labour Party of Albania*): Tirana; f. 1956; Dir. NEXHMIJE HOXHA; publ. *Përmbledhje Studimesh* (Collections of Studies, irregular).

Instituti i Gjeologjisë, Naftës dhe Gazit (*Institute of Geology, Oil and Gas*): Fier; f. 1956; Dir. PETRAQ XHAÇKA; publ. *Nafta dhe Gazi* (Oil and Gas, every 2 months).

Instituti i Studimeve dhe Projektimeve të Gjeologjisë dhe Minierave (*Institute for Studies and Designs of Geology and Mines*): Tirana; f. 1962; Dir. BASHKIM LLESHI; publ. *Përmbledhje Studimesh* (Collections of Studies, irregular, with Faculty of Geology and Mines of University).

Instituti i Studimeve dhe Projektimeve Teknologjike Minerare (*Institute for Studies and Technological and Mineral Designs*): Tirana; f. 1962; Dir. ROLAND AVRAMI.

Instituti i Studimeve dhe Projektimeve Mekanike (*Institute for Mechanical Studies and Designs*): Tirana; f. 1970; Dir. LLAZAR XHAJANKA.

Instituti i Kërkimeve Bujqësore (*Institute of Agricultural Research*): Lushnje; f. 1947; Dir. MENTOR PËRMETI; publ. *Mbrojtja e bimëve* (Plant Protection, quarterly).
Stations attached to Institute:
Stacioni i misrit dhe i orizit (corn, rice); Shkodër.
Stacioni i perimeve dhe i patates (vegetables, potatoes); Tirana.
Stacioni i foragjereve (animal fodder); Krujë.
Stacioni i panxhar sheqerit (sugarbeet); Korçë.
Stacioni i duhanit (tobacco); Cërrik.
Stacioni i mbrojtjes së bimëve (plant protection); Durrës.

Instituti i Kërkimeve të Blegtorisë (*Institute of Veterinary Research*): Tirana; f. 1928; Dir. SOTIR PASKO; publ. *Zooteknika dhe Veterinaria* (Zootechnics and Veterinary quarterly).

Stations attached to the Institute:

Stacioni i zooteknikës (zootechnics); Shkodër.
Stacioni i bagëtive të imta (sheep); Korçë.
Stacioni i bletës dhe i krimbit mendafshit (bees, silkworms); Krabë, Tiranë.

Instituti i Studimit të Tokave (*Institute of Soil Studies*): Tirana; f. 1969; Dir. LEFTER VESHO; publ. *Toka Bujqësore* (Farm Land, quarterly).

Instituti i Studimeve dhe i Projektimeve të Veprave të Kullimit dhe Ujitjes (*Institute of Irrigation and Drainage Studies and Designs*): Tirana; f. 1970; Dir. DHIMITËR VOGLI.

Stacioni i frutikulturës (*Fruit Growing Station*): Vlorë; f. 1971; Dir. EJUP METAJ.

Stacioni i mekanizimit të bujqësisë (*Agricultural Mechanization Station*): Tirana; f. 1971.

Stacioni i pyjeve dhe i kulturave etero-vajore (*Forestry and Oil-bearing Plants Station*): Tirana; f. 1979; publ. *Ekonomia pyjore* (Forestry Economics, quarterly).

Instituti i Studimeve dhe Projektimeve të urbanistikës dhe të Arkitekturës (ISP Nr. 1) (*Institute of Urban Planning and Architectural Studies and Design*): Tirana; f. 1966; Dir. SOKRAT MOSKO.

Instituti i Studimeve dhe i Projektimeve të Rrugëve të Hekurudhave (ISP Nr. 2) (*Institute of Road and Railway Studies and Design*): Tirana; f. 1966; Dir. MITAT DEMIRI.

Instituti i Studimeve dhe i Projektimeve të Hidrocentraleve (ISP Nr. 3) (*Institute of Hydropowerstation Studies and Design*): Tirana; f. 1966; Dir. PANDI ÇEZMAXHIU.

Instituti i Studimeve dhe i Projektimeve të Veprave Industriale (*Institute of Industrial Project Studies and Design*); Tirana; f. 1966.

Instituti i Studimeve dhe i Teknologjisë në Ndërtim (ISTN Nr. 5) (*Institute of Building Technology Studies*): Tirana; f. 1966.

Ndërmarrja e studimeve inxhiniero-gjeologjike e gjeodezike (*Centre of Geological and Engineering Studies*): Tirana; f. 1966; Dir. ANESTI LUBONJA.

Instituti i Studimeve Pedagogjike (*Institute of Pedagogical Studies*): Tirana; f. 1970; Dir. SOTIR TEMO; publs. *Revista Pedagogjike*† (Pedagogical Journal, quarterly), Bulletins (on school mathematics, physics, chemistry, language, etc., irregular.)

Instituti i Monumenteve të Kulturës (*Institute of Cultural Monuments*): Tirana; f. 1965; Dir. SOTIR KOSTA; publ. *Monumentet*† (Monuments, 2 a year).

Instituti i Mjekësisë Popullore (*Institute of Folk Medicine*): Tirana; f. 1974; Dir. PETRIT KOKALARI; publ. *Përmbledhje Studimesh* (Collections of Studies, irregular).

Instituti i Higjenës, Epidemiologjisë dhe i prodhimeve imunobiologjike (*Institute of Hygiene, Epidemiology and Immunobiological Products*): Tirana; f. 1969; Dir. TAHIR CENKO; publ. *Buletini i Institutit të Higjenës dhe Epidemiologjisë*† (Bulletin of Hygiene and Epidemiology, 2 a year).

Instituti i Kërkimeve Kimiko-Teknologjike të Industrisë së Lehtë dhe Ushqimore (*Institute of Chemical and Technological Research of Food and Light Industry*): Tirana; f. 1962; Dir. LILJANA BOJAXHIU; publ. *Përmbledhje Studimesh* (Collections of Studies, irregular).

Stacioni i Studimeve dhe i Kërkimeve të Peshkimit (*Fisheries Research*): Durrës; f. 1960; Dir. ARQILE DOKO.

LIBRARIES

National Library: Tirana; f. 1922; 792,000 vols.; Dir. MARIKA VOGLI; publs. *National Bibliography* (monthly), and others.

Durrës Public Library: f. 1945; 132,000 vols.

Elbasan Public Library: f. 1934; 284,000 vols.

Gjirokastër Public Library: 90,000 vols.

Korça Public Library: f. 1938; 139,000 vols.

Shkoder Public Library: Shkoder; f. 1935; 192,000 vols.

There are libraries in other towns, and attached to most of the above Research Institutes.

MUSEUMS

Tirana

Albanian Folk Culture Museum: attached to the Institute of National Culture; exhibits include agricultural tools of all periods, stock-breeding equipment, interiors and exteriors, household objects, textiles and customs, local crafts and ceramics up to the present day.

Fine Arts Gallery: Dir. DHIMITRAQ TREBICKA.

Lenin-Stalin Museum: f. 1954.

Museum of Archaeology and Ethnography: f. 1948; attached to the Centre of Archaeological Research of the Academy of Sciences; exhibits of the palaeolithic, neolithic and bronze ages; objects of the Illyrian culture, the iron age, and the Greek and Roman periods of colonization; Albanian exhibits from ancient times to the middle ages.

Museum of the Struggle for National Liberation: f. 1949; exhibits trace the history of the Albanian people from the struggles against the Ottomans to the present day; Dir. BALLKIZE HAXHIHYSENI.

Natural Science Museum: attached to the University of Tirana; exhibits relating to zoology, botany, geology and mineralogy.

Party Museum: house where the Labour Party of Albania was founded.

Youth Museum: house where the organization of young communists was founded.

Berat

Architecture Museum.

District Historical Museum.

Ethnographic Museum.

Durrës

Archaeological Museum.

Ethnographic Museum.

Museum of the Struggle for National Liberation.

Elbasan

K. Kristoforidhi House-Museum: the birth-place of the patriot and linguist (1825–1895).

Museum of the Struggle for National Liberation.

Q. Stafa House-Museum: the birth-place of the national hero (1921–1942).

Fier

Archaeological Museum: exhibits include archaeological items from the former town of Apollonia.

District Historical Museum.

Gjirokastër

Ethnographic Museum.

Museum of the Struggle for National Liberation.

National Renaissance Museum.

Korçë

Fine Arts Gallery.

V. Mio House-Museum: house where the painter worked.

Museum of Albanian Medieval Art.

Museum of Education.

Museum of the Struggle for National Liberation.

National Renaissance Museum.

Përmet

District Historical Museum.

Frashëri Brothers Museum: the birth-place of the brothers Frashëri, Abdyl (1839–92), Naim (1846–1900), Sami (1850–1904).

Shkodër

Atheism Museum.

District Historical Museum.

Luigi Gurakuqi House-Museum: house where the patriot lived (1879–1925).

Migjeni House-Museum: where the writer Migjeni (1911–38) lived.

Vaso Pascha House-Museum: house where the patriot lived (1820–92).

Vlorë

District Historical Museum.

Independence Museum.

Hysni Kapo House-Museum: Terbaç; Kapo (1915–79) was a member of the Politburo and a Secretary of the Central Committee of the Albanian Party of Labour.

Nushi Brothers Museum: Vuno.

UNIVERSITY

UNIVERSITETI TIRANËS
(University of Tirana)

TIRANA

Founded 1957.

Rector: Prof. PETRIT RADOVICKA.

Vice-Rectors: Doc. SHPRESA ZENELAJ, Prof. BESIM DAJA, HASAN MUÇOSTEPA.

Library Director: ZIHNI RESO.

Library of 500,000 vols.

Number of teachers: 881.

Number of students: 16,000.

Publications: *Buletini i Shkencave Natyrore*† (Natural Sciences, quarterly), *Buletini i Shkencave Teknike*† (Technical Sciences, quarterly), *Buletini i Shkencave Mjekësore*† (Medicine, quarterly), *Përmbledhje studimesh*† (collection of studies, quarterly, with Institutes of Geological Research.

DEANS:

Faculty of Natural Science: Prof. OSMAN KRAJA.

Faculty of Engineering: Sc. Dr. Doc. FEHMI SHEHU.

Faculty of Medicine: Doc. CIRIL PISTOLI.

Faculty of History and Philology: Doc. VITORE BALLVORA.

Faculty of Political and Juridical Sciences: Prof. ZIJA XHOLI.

Faculty of Economics: Prof. DEKO RUSI.

Faculty of Geology and Mining: Prof. ESHREF PUMO.

HIGHER INSTITUTES

Instituti i Lartë Bujqësor (*Institute of Agriculture*): Kamzë, Tirana; f. 1951; library of 70,000 vols.

Rector: LUFTER XHUVELI.

Vice-Rector: SYRJA HYSI.

Librarian: MIRDASH KALO.

Library of 93,000 vols.

Publication: *Buletini i Shkencave Bujqësore*† (Bulletin of Agricultural Sciences, quarterly).

DEANS:

Faculty of Agriculture: Doc. SKËNDER XHIKU.

Faculty of Veterinary Science: Doc. VASIL TAGARI.

Faculty of Forestry: AGRON REKA.

Faculty of Agricultural Economics: NEVRUZ MALINDI.

Instituti i Lartë Bujqësor Korçë (*Higher Agricultural Institute*): f. 1971; library of 12,000 vols.; Dir. KRISTAQ KOTONIKA.

Instituti i Lartë i Arteve, Tiranë (*Fine Arts Higher Institute*); f. 1959; library of 20,000 vols.; Dir. IBRAHIM MADHI.

Instituti i Kulturës Fizike "Vojo Kushi" Tiranë (*"Vojo Kushi" Institute of Physical Culture*): f. 1958; library of 25,000 vols.; Dir. FLUTURA ÇELKUPA; publ. *Buletini i Kulturës Fizike e Sporteve* (Bulletin of Physical Culture and Sports, monthly).

Instituti i Lartë Pedagogjik, Shkodër (*Higher Pedagogical Institute*): f. 1957; library of 77,000 vols.; Dir. DHORA LLOJA; publ. *Buletin shkencor* (Scientific Bulletin, 2 a year).

Instituti i Lartë Pedagogjik "Aleksandër Xhuvani" Elbasan (*Higher Pedagogical Institute "A. Xhuvani"*): f. 1971; library of 17,500 vols.; Dir. VASIL KAMANI.

Instituti i Lartë Pedagogjik Gjirokastër (*Higher Pedagogical Institute*); f. 1971; library of 11,100 vols.; Dir. VASIL BILUSHI.

ALGERIA

Population 18,515,000

LEARNED SOCIETIES

Association Africaine de Cartographie: Inc. B.P. 69, Hussein-Dey, Algiers; f. 1975 to encourage the development of cartography, organize conferences and other meetings, promote establishment of training institutions; two centres, one in Kenya for cartographic services and one in Nigeria for training; mems.: principal cartographic services of 27 African countries, assoc. membership is open to professional institutions and groups; Chair. HENRY GADEGBEKU STEPAHN (Ghana); Sec. Gen. MOHAMED BOUALGA (Algeria).

British Council: 6 ave. Souidani Boudjemàa, Algiers; library of 20,600 vols. and 60 periodicals; Rep. W. E. N. KENSDALE.

El-Djazairia El-Mossilia: 1 rue de la Poudrière, Algiers; f. 1930; cultural society, particularly concerned with Arab classical music; 452 mems.; Pres. ALI BENMERABET; Sec.-Gen. ABDELKADER RAHAL.

Goethe Institut: Centre Culturel Allemand, 165 chemin Sfinjda, Algiers; f. 1963; Dir. GEORG BECKER.

Istituto Italiano di Cultura: 7 rue Hamami, Algiers; f. 1964; library of 3,500 vols.; Dir. Prof. DOMENICO GHIO.

Section de Diffusion Scientifique et Technique du Centre Culturel Français d'Alger: 7 rue du Capitaine Médecin Kassani Issad, Algiers; distributes scientific, technical, medical and industrial information; library of 18,000 vols. and 350 periodicals; Dir. NICOLE NATALIS; publ. bibliographical bulletin.

Services Culturels et de Coopération: 25 chemin Abdelkader-Gaddouche, Hydra, Algiers; attached to the French Embassy; co-operates with the Algerian Government in educational, cultural and technical matters; Dir. GABRIEL BEIS.

Société Archéologique du Département de Constantine: Musée Gustave Mercier, Constantine; f. 1852; 250 mems.; library of 10,000 vols.; Pres. Dr. BAGHLI (acting); publ. *Recueil des Notices et Mémoires.*

Société Historique Algérienne: c/o Faculté des Lettres, University of Algiers; f. 1963; 600 mems.; publ. *Revue d'Histoire et Civilisation du Maghreb.*

Union des Ecrivains Algériens (*Algerian Writers' Union*): 12 rue Ali Boumendjel, Algiers; f. 1963; 60 mems.; awards an annual literary prize of 10,000 dinars for creative writing.

RESEARCH INSTITUTES

Centre National de Recherches et Expérimentations Forestières (CNREF): B.P. 63, El Mouradia, Algiers; f. 1911; library of 2,500 vols.; Dir. A. ZERHOUNI; publs. *Les Annales du CNREF, Notes Techniques Forestières.*

Centre National de Recherches Historiques: Présidence du Conseil, Algiers; f. 1974; Dir. M. TOUILI.

Direction des Mines et de la Géologie, Sous-Direction de la Géologie: Immeuble Le Colisée, Rue Ahmed Bey, Algiers; f. 1883, re-named 1980; research, publications, maps; library of 50,000 vols., periodicals, maps and aerial photographs; Dir. RACHID OUAHMED; publs. *Bulletin, Notices Explicatives des Cartes Géologiques, Cartes Géologiques.*

Institut de Bibliothéconomie et des Sciences Documentaires: University of Algiers; f. 1975.

Institut National d'Hygiène et de Sécurité: 10 rue Mohamed Belouizdad, Place du 1er mai, Algiers; f. 1972; studies and research in the fields of hygiene and safety at work; 22 staff; library of 4,000 vols., 380 periodicals; Dir. Gen. CHÉRIF SOUAMI; publ. *Revue Algérienne de Prévention*† (quarterly).

Institut National de Cartographie: 123 rue de Tripoli, B.P. 69, Hussein-Dey, Algiers; f. 1967; national cartography and surveying centre; cartography, hydrography and remote sensing; under trusteeship of Ministry of Defence; 500 staff; Dir. MOHAMED BOUALGA; publs. maps† (100 to 150 a year).

Institut National de la Recherche Agronomique: Jardin d'Essais du Hamma, B.P. 15, El Annasser, Algiers; Dir. M. HAMADI; publs. *Revue de la Recherche Agronomique*†, *Bulletin d'Agronomie Saharienne*†.

Institut Pasteur d'Algérie: rue du Dr. Laveran, Algiers; f. 1910; research and higher studies in microbiology, parasitology and immunology; preparation of vaccines and sera in conjunction with the health services of Algeria; 425 staff; the library contains 46,570 vols., 500 periodicals; Dir. Prof. M. BENHASSINE; publ. *Archives de l'Institut Pasteur d'Algérie*† (annual).

Organisme National de la Recherche Scientifique: 27 rue Si Arezki Abri, Hydra, Algiers; main executive body for government policy; Dir. S. DJEBAILI. Research centres:

Centre de Recherches Anthropologiques, Préhistoriques et Ethnographiques (CRAPE): 3 blvd. Franklin Roosevelt, Algiers; f. 1957; Dir. M. BELKAID.

Centre National de Recherches sur les Zones Arides (CNRZA): Béni-Abbès, Belchar; Dir. Mme. N. BOUNAGA (acting).

Centre de Recherches Océanographiques et des Pêches (CROP): Jetée Nord, Amirauté, Algiers; Dir. RACHID SEMROUD.

Centre de Recherches sur les Ressources Biologiques Terrestres (CRBT): 2 rue Didouche Mourad, Algiers; Dir. SALAH DJEBAILI.

Centre des Sciences et de la Technologie Nucléaires (CSTN): B.P. 1147, blvd. Frantz Fanon, Algiers; Dir. ABDELOUAHAB BENNINI.

Centre National de Recherches et d'Application des Géosciences (CRAG): 2 rue Didouche Mourad, Algiers; Dir. N. E. KAZI-TANI.

Centre Universitaire de Recherches, d'Etudes et de Réalisations (CURER): Université de Constantine, Route de Aïn El Bey, Constantine; Dir. L. FELLAH.

Centre d'Informations Scientifiques et Techniques et de Transferts Technologiques (CISTTT): B.P. 315, blvd. Frantz Fanon, Algiers; Dir. SID-AHMED LARIBI.

Centre de Recherches en Economie Appliquées (CREA): 20 rue Mustapha Khallef, El Biar, Algiers; Dir. ABDELATIF BENACHENHOU.

Centre de Recherches en Architecture et Urbanisme (CRAU): B.P. 2, El-Harrach, Algiers; Dir. AMEZIANE IKENE.

Centre National d'Etudes et de Recherches pour l'Aménagement du Territoire (CNERAT): 2 rue Professor Vincent, Algiers; Dir. MESSAOUD TAIEB.

Centre d'Etudes et de Recherches Agronomiques (CERAG): El-Harrach, Algiers; Dir. M. KHOURI (acting).

Centre de Coordination des Etudes et des Recherches sur les Infrastructures, les Equipements du Ministère de l'Enseignement Supérieur et de la Recherche Scientifique: 1 rue Bachir Attar, Algiers; Dir. A. GUEDIRI.

Station d'Energie Solaire: Obsrevatoire de Bouzaréah, Algiers; Dir. M. BOUHADEF.

Observatoire Astronomique: Bouzaréah, Algiers; Dir. M. GUEZLOUN.

LIBRARIES AND ARCHIVES

Algiers

Archives Nationales: Palais du Gouvernement, Esplanade d'Afrique.

Bibliothèque Nationale: 1 ave. Frantz Fanon; f. 1835; more than 950,000 vols., including important collections on Africa and the Maghreb; Dir. MAHMOUD-AGHA BOUAYED; publs. *Bibliographie de l'Algérie*† (2 a year), *Publications*†, several collections in Arabic and French†.

Bibliothèque Universitaire: 2 rue Didouche Mourad; f. 1880; 600,000 vols.; Librarian Mlle ZOULIKHA BEKADDOUR.

Constantine

Bibliothèque Municipale: Hôtel de Ville; f. 1895; 25,000 vols.

Oran

Bibliothèque Aubert.

MUSEUMS

Algiers

Direction des Musées de l'Archéologie et des Monuments et Sites Historiques: 56 ave. Souidani Boudjemaà, Algiers; f. 1901 as Service des Antiquités; general administration of museums, restoration, conservation and archaeological excavations; 96 staff; library of 6,493 vols., 100 periodicals; Dir. MOUNIR BOUCHENAKI; publ. *Bulletin d'Archéologie Algérienne* (annually).

Musée de la Révolution 1954-62: items relating to contemporary history.

Musée du Mont Riant: collections from several countries.

Musée National de Préhistoire et d'Ethnographie du Bardo (*Pre-history and Ethnographic Museum*): 3 rue Franklin Roosevelt; f. 1928; Dir. F. Z. MATAOUI.

Musée National des Antiquités: Parc de la Liberté; f. 1897; exhibits include Algerian antiquities and Islamic art; Cur. MOHAMMED TEMMAM; publs. *Le Musée Stéphane Gsell, L'Art Musulman.*

Musée National des Beaux Arts d'Alger (*National Museum of Algiers*): Jardin d'Essai; f. 1930; exhibits include paintings, drawings, etchings, bronzes, reliefs; specialized History of Art library of 8,000 vols.; Dir. AHMED BAGHLI.

Constantine

Musée de Cirta: blvd. de la République; f. 1853; archaeological exhibits, art and research; 10 mems.; library of 20,000 vols.; Dir. AHMED GUEDDOUDA; publ. *Recueil et Mémoires de la Société Archéologique de Constantine*†.

El Biar

Musée National du Moudjahid: items relating to the contemporary history of Algeria 1954–62.

Oran

Musée Municipal: Blvd. Zabana; prehistory, Roman and Punic archaeology, ethnography, zoology, geology, botany, sculpture and painting; Dir. and Curator R. MASSON.

Musée de Tlemcen: place d'Alger; exhibits of Islamic art

Sétif

Musée de Sétif: Roman antiquities; Curator TAYEB HAFIANE.

Skikda

Musée de Skikda: Punic and Roman antiquities; modern art.

UNIVERSITIES

UNIVERSITÉ D'ALGER

2 RUE DIDOUCHE MOURAD, ALGIERS

Telephone: 64 69 70

Founded 1879 (reorganized 1909)

Languages of instruction: Arabic and French; State control; Academic year: October to June.

Rector: R. TOURI.

Number of teachers: 1,530.
Number of students: 17,086.

UNIVERSITY INSTITUTES:

Institut de Bibliothéconomie: f. 1974.

Institut des Sciences Médicales: 18 ave. Pasteur, Algiers; Dir. MOHAMED ABDELMOUMENE.

Institut de Droit, des Sciences Politiques et Administratives: Ben-Aknoun; f. 1885; 150 teachers, 4,000 students; library of 30,000 vols., 350 periodicals; Dir. NOUREDDINE TERKI; publ. *Revue algérienne des sciences juridiques, économiques et politiques*†.

Institut des Sciences Economiques: 2 rue Didouche Mourad, Algiers; Dir. ABDELLATIF BENACHENHOU.

Faculté des Lettres et Sciences Humaines: 2 rue Didouche Mourad, Algiers; Dir. DRISS CHABOU.

Faculté des Sciences: Dir. DAHO ALLAB.

Centre de Préparation à l'Enseignement Supérieur.

UNIVERSITÉ DES SCIENCES ET DE LA TECHNOLOGIE D'ALGER

B.P. 9, DAR-EL-BEIDA, ALGIERS

Telephone: 76-44-98.

Founded 1974.

Languages of instruction: Arabic, French; Academic year: September to June (2 semesters).

Rector: BENALI BENZAGHOU.
Vice-Rectors: AREZKI AMOKRANE, OTMAN DAMERDJI.
Secretary-General: BENAMAR FKHIKHER.

Number of teachers: 908.
Number of students: 8,477.

DIRECTORS:

Institute of Biology: CHAREF ZIDANE.
Institute of Chemistry: YOUCEF YOUSFI.
Institute of Mathematics: MOHAMED DJEDOUR.
Institute of Physics: HAMOUD LADJOUZE.
Institute of Earth Sciences: MOHAMED TEFIANI.
Institute of Electronics: ABDEL-HAMID ADANE.
National Polytechnic School: ABDELAZIZ OUABDESSELAM.

UNIVERSITÉ DE CONSTANTINE

ROUTE DE AIN EL-BEY, CONSTANTINE

Founded 1969.

Languages of instruction: Arabic and French.

Rector: (vacant).

Librarian: MAHMOUD SARI.
Secretary: CHELIHI BRAHIQ.

Library of 100,000 vols.
Number of teachers: 1,023.
Number of students: 8,340.

Institutes of Law and Administration, Arabic, Social Sciences, Psychology, Biology, Medicine, Architecture and Building, Physics, Chemistry, Mathematics, Earth Sciences, Economics, Foreign Languages; also a pre-University Centre and Audio-Visual department.

UNIVERSITÉ D'ORAN

B.P. 1524, ES-SENIA, ORAN
Telephone: 38-50-75.
Telex: 22-993 UNIREX ORAN.
Founded 1965.

Languages of instruction: Arabic and French; Academic year: September to July (2 semesters).

Rector: TALAHIT BAKHLOUF.
Vice-Rector for Postgraduate Studies and International Relations: M. BENNAI.
Secretary-General: A. LANASRI.
Librarian: KAMEL BENABDERRAHMANE.

Number of teachers: 1,000.
Number of students: 9,000.

Publications: *Cahier de Géographie de l'Ouest Algérien*, *Cahier du Centre de Documentation des Sciences Humaines*.

DIRECTORS:

Institute of Medicine: M. BENNAI.
Institute of Economics: D. BELDJILLALI.
Institute of Law and Administration: M. N. MAHIEDDIN.
Institute of Modern Languages: A. EL KEBIR.
Institute of Exact Sciences: F. BENHABIB.
Institute of Social Sciences: Mme CHEKAT.
Institute of Biology and Earth Sciences: Mme F. Z. EL ZEBIR.
Institute of Arabic Literature and Culture: A. MORTAD.

UNIVERSITÉ DES SCIENCES ET DE LA TECHNOLOGIE D'ORAN

ORAN
Founded 1975.

UNIVERSITÉ DE SÉTIF

SÉTIF
Founded 1978.
Telephone: 90-36-40.
Telex: 86077 UNSET DZ.

Rector: MUSTAPHA BOUKARI.
Registrar: R. OURAMTANE.
Librarian: C. CHIDEKH.

Number of teachers: 142.
Number of students: 1,375.

DIRECTORS:

Institute of Biology: M. KAABECHE.
Institute of Exact Sciences: M. HANNACHI.
Institute of Architecture: F. HARBOUCHE.
Institute of Precision Optics and Mechanics: M. SASSOUI.
Institute of Economics: S. BOUGHACHICHE.
Institute of Foreign Languages: A. RACHI.
Centre for Language Study: F. MALKI.

UNIVERSITY CENTRES

Université de Annaba: f. 1975; institute of mining and metallurgy; Dir. M. ARAB.

Centre Universitaire de Tlemcen: f. 1974; 11 teachers, 201 students; Dir. M. ALLAL.

Centre Universitaire de Tizi-Ouzou: f. 1975.

Centre Universitaire de Batna.

Centre Universitaire de Tiaret.

Centre Universitaire de Recherches, d'Etudes et de Réalisation à Constantine: Dir. A. BERERHI.

COLLEGES

Conservatoire Municipal de Musique et de Déclamation: 5 rue d'Igli, Oran; f. 1932; courses in music, dancing and dramatic art; 20 teachers, 500 students; Dir. GILLES ACHACHE.

Conservatoire de Musique et de Déclamation: 2 blvd. Ché Guévara, Algiers; f. 1920; library contains 6,800 vols.; 82 teachers, 2,300 students; Dir.-Gen. BACHETARZI MOHIEDDINE; Sec.-Gen. KADDOUR GUECHOUD.

Ecole Nationale des Beaux-Arts: Parc Zizyab, Algiers; 300 students; attached to the Ministry of Information and Culture; library of 6,000 vols.; Dir. BACHIR YELLES.

Ecole Nationale de la Marine Marchande: rue d'Angkor, Algiers.

Ecole Nationale Polytechnique: ave. Pasteur, El-Harrach, Algiers 10; f. 1962; attached to the University of Algiers; courses in civil engineering, electro-technics, telecommunications, chemical engineering and petro-chemistry, mechanical engineering, applied mathematics and econometrics, mining; library of 15,000 vols.; 99 teachers, 214 students; Dir. A. OUABDESSELAM.

Ecole Nationale Vétérinaire: El-Harrach, Algiers; 350 students; Dir. A. RAHAL.

Ecole Polytechnique d'Architecture et d'Urbanisme: B.P.2, El Harrach; f. 1970; attached to the University of Algiers; 91 staff, 409 students; library of 2,120 vols., 362 periodicals; Dir. M. MOKDAD.

Ecole Supérieure de Commerce d'Alger: Rampe F. Chasseriau, Algiers; f. 1900, attached to the University of Algiers 1966; 34 teachers, 485 students.

Ecole Supérieure d'Interprétariat: 8 rue Hamani, Algiers; f. 1964; attached to the University of Algiers; library of 2,200 vols.; 35 teachers, 191 students; Dir. A. DJEDOU; publ. *Echaab-Amal*.

Institut de Géographie: 3 rue du Professeur Vincent, Telemly, Algiers; 29 teachers, 244 students; Dir. M. MAHROUR.

Institut des Hydrocarbures: Boumerdes.

Institut Hydrométéorologique de Formation et de Recherche (IHFR): Gambetta, Oran; f. 1968; 250 students; library of 10,000 vols.; Dir. M. S. BOULAHYA; publ. *Les Cahiers de la Météorologie*† (irregular).

Institut National Agronomique: El Harrach, Algiers; f. 1966; 271 teachers, 850 students; library of 44,000 vols. and 850 periodicals; Dir. MOHAMMED SALAH KHOURI; Dir. of Studies MAHMOUD BEKKOUCHE; publ. *Annales*† (quarterly).

Institut d'Optique: Es-Senia, Oran; 19 students; Dir. A. LAZREG.

Institut de Psychologie Appliquée: 2 rue Didouche Mourad, Algiers; 222 students; Dir. M. HAMMICHE.

Institut des Sciences Politiques et de l'Information: B.P. Alger 493, 37 rue Larbi Ben M'Hidi, Algiers; f. 1976 as result of merger between Ecole Supérieure de Journalisme and Institut d'Etudes Politiques; attached to the University of Algiers; 30 teachers, 950 students; Dir. S. CHIKH.

Institut des Techniques de Planification: Complexes des Instituts de Technologie, Chemin de la Touche, Hydra, Algiers.

Institut des Télécommunications: Es-Senia, Oran; f. 1971.

ANGOLA

Population 6,761,000

LEARNED SOCIETIES AND RESEARCH INSTITUTES

Centro de Investigação Cientifica Algodeira (*Cotton Scientific Research Centre*): Instituto do Algodão de Angola, Estação Experimental de Onga-Zanga, Catete; fibre technology laboratory, agricultural machinery station, crop irrigation station (Bombagem); library; Dir. Eng. Agr. JOAQUIM RODRIGUES PEREIRA.

Centro Nacional de Documentação e Investigação Histórica (*National Centre of Historical Documentation and Research*): Rua Neves Ferreira 49/54, Luanda, C.P. 1267-C; f. 1933 as Arquivo Histórico de Angola, integrated with the Biblioteca Histórica de Museu de Angola in 1976, inaugurated as Centre de Documentação Histórica in 1977, present title 1980; archive of material on the history of Angola; 12,000 vols., 3,200 periodicals; Dir. MANUEL ANTÓNIO SEBASTIÃO.

Direcção Provincial dos Serviços de Geologia e Minas de Angola: C.P. 1260-C, Luanda; f. 1914; 506 mems.; Geology, Geological Mapping and Exploration of Mineral Deposits; library of 40,000 vols.; Dir. J. TRIGO MIRA; publs. *Boletim, Memória, Carta Geológica de Angola.*

Instituto de Investigação Agronómica de Angola (*Agricultural Research Institute of Angola*): C.P. 406, Huambo; f. 1962; research is conducted in soils and chemistry, agronomy, forestry and agricultural biology; agrarian documentation centre; 46 scientific staff; publs. *Série Técnica, Série Cientifica.*

Instituto de Investigação Medica de Angola (*Angola Medical Research Institute*): Luanda; f. 1955.

Instituto de Investigação Veterinária (*Institute for Veterinary Research*): C.P. 7, Huambo; f. 1965; 62 mems.; library of 6,141 vols.; Dir. Dr. J. M. S. DUARTE; publs. *Relatorio Anual*†, *Acta Veterinaria-separatas*† (annually).

Instituto Nacional de Hidrometeorologia e Geofisica: Rua Diogo Cão 20, C.P. 1288-C, Luanda; f. 1879 as Observatory; library of 10,000 vols.; Dir. JOAQUIM A. XAVIER (acting); publs. *Boletim geomagnético, Tabelas sismico preliminar* (monthly), *Observações Meteorológicas de Superfície, Observaçõs Meteorológicas de Altitude, Tabelas Astronómicas* (annually), *Anuário Geomagnetico, Anuário do Observatorio.*

LIBRARIES

Biblioteca Municipal: Caixa Postal 1227, Luanda; 14,600 vols.; Librarian ALBERTO SERRA JÚNIOR.

Biblioteca Nacional de Angola: Caixa Postal 2915, Luanda; 26,000 vols.; Dir. DOMINGOS VAN-DÚNEM.

Arquivo Histórico de Angola: *see* Museu de Angola.

MUSEUMS

Museu de Angola: C.P. 1267C, Luanda; f. 1938; art, history, zoology, ethnography; Dir. HENRIQUE ABRANCHES; publ. *Boletim do I.I.C.A.*

Museu de Congo: C.P. 11, Carmona; f. 1965; ethnography; Curator VIRGÍLIO PEREIRA.

Museu do Dundo: Dundo, Luanda; Ethnography, Anthropology, Zoology, Geology, Pre-history and History of Luanda; library of 8,000 vols.; Dir. of Biological Research Dr. A. DE BARROS MACHADO; publ. *Publicações Culturais da Companhia de Diamantes de Angola.*

Museu Regional da Huila: C.P. 445, Lubango; f. 1956; ethnology; Delegate SAMUEL AÇO.

UNIVERSITY

UNIVERSIDADE DE ANGOLA

C.P. 815, AV. 4 DE FEVEREIRO 7–2° ANDAR, LUANDA

Telephone: Luanda 70792.

Founded 1963.

State control; Academic year: April to February.

Rector: ANTÓNIO AGOSTINHO NETO.
Vice-Rector: JOÃO GARCIA BIRES.
Registrar: ALBERTO LUÍS GOMES.
Librarian: ANTÓNIO CERQUEIRA FERRAZ CORREIA.

Number of teachers: 293.
Number of students: 3,146.

Faculties of engineering, medicine, sciences, economics, agriculture (Huambo) and education (Lubango).

COLLEGE

Instituto de Educação e Serviço Social de Angola (*Angola Institute of Education and Social Service*): Antigo Aeroporto Emilio de Carvalho, C.P. 18071, Luanda; f. 1962; 42 teachers, 345 students; library of 3,054 vols.; Dir. MARIA CANDIDA SANTOS LOPES.

ARGENTINA

Population 26,729,000

ACADEMIES

Buenos Aires

Academia Argentina de Letras (*Argentine Academy of Letters*): Sánchez de Bustamante 2663, Buenos Aires 1425; f. 1931; 17 mems., 37 corresp. mems.; Pres. ANGEL J. BATTISTESSA; Vice-Pres. FERMÍN ESTRELLA GUTIÉRREZ; Sec. JUAN CARLOS GHIANO; Treas. JORGE VOCOS LESCANO; publs. *Boletín* (quarterly), *Serie de Clásicos Argentinos, Serie de Estudios Académicos, Serie de Discursos Académicos, Serie de Acuerdos acerca del Idioma, Boletín.*

MEMBERS:

LUIS ALFONSO
JORGE LUIS BORGES
MANUEL MUJICA LÁINEZ
EDUARDO MALLEA
OSVALDO LOUDET
RICARDO E. MOLINARI
BERNARDO GONZÁLEZ ARRILLI
RAÚL M. CASTAGNINO
BERNARDO CANAL FEIJÓO
EDUARDO GONZÁLEZ LANUZA
OCTAVIO N. DERISI
CARLOS VILLAFUERTE
FEDERICO PELTZER
ENRIQUE ANDERSON IMBERT
LUIS FEDERICO LELOIR
CARLOS ALBERTO RONCHI MARCH
ELÍAS CARPENA

Academia Nacional de Agronomía y Veterinaria (*Academy of Agronomy and Veterinary Science*): Arenales 1678; f. 1909; 35 mems.; Pres. Dr. ANTONIO PIRES; Sec.-Gen. Dr. ENRIQUE GARCIA MATA.

Academia Nacional de Bellas Artes (*National Academy of Fine Arts*): Sánchez de Bustamante 2663; f. 1936; 28 mems., 20 Argentinian and 36 foreign correspondents; Pres. Arq. ALFREDO C. CASARES; Vice-Pres. Dr. BONIFACIO DEL CARRIL; Sec.-Gen. JORGE D'URBANO; Pro-Sec. ARY BRIZZI; Treas. Arq. CLORINDO TESTA; publs. *Monografías de Artistas Argentinos, Serie Estudios, Cuaderno Especial: "Escenas del Campo Argentino" 1885–1900, Documentos de Arte Argentino, Documentos de Arte Colonial Sudamericano, Anuario.*

MEMBERS:

BADII, LIBERO
BARRAGAN, LUIS
BERNI, ANTONIO
BRAUN MENÉNDEZ, RICARDO
BUSTILLO, ALEJANDRO
BUTLER, HORACIO
CAAMAÑO, ROBERTO
CALUSIO, FERRUCCIO
CASTRO, WASHINGTON
ERIZE, JEANNETTE ARATA
GIMÉNEZ, ALBERTO EMILIO
GINASTERA, ALBERTO
IOMMI, ENIO
LABOURDETTE, JUAN CARLOS
LÓPEZ ANAYA, FERNANDO
MOTA, CARLOS DE LA
MUJICA LAÍNEZ, MANUEL
PRESAS, LEOPOLDO
REBUFFO, VÍCTOR
RIBERA, ADOLFO LUIS
RODRIGUEZ, ERNESTO B.
RUSSO, RAÚL
SACRISTE, EDUARDO
SCHENONE, HÉCTOR H.
SOLDI, RAÚL
TORRALLARDONA, CARLOS A.
URIBE, BASILIO M.
WILLIAMS, AMANCIO

Academia Nacional de Ciencias de Buenos Aires (*National Academy of Sciences of Buenos Aires*): Junin 1278; f. 1937; 29 mems.; Pres. Ing. Dr. MANUEL F. CASTELLO; Sec. Dr. PEDRO A. MAISSA.

Academia Nacional de Ciencias Exactas, Físicas y Naturales (*National Academy of Exact, Physical and Natural Sciences*): Avda. Alvear 1711, 1014 Buenos Aires; f. 1874; 30 mems.; Pres. Dr. LUÍS A. SANTALÓ; Secs. Dr. HORACIO CAMACHO, Ing. ORESTE MORETTO; publs. *Anales*†, *Revista Darwiniana*†, *Memoria.*

Academia Nacional de Derecho y Ciencias Sociales (*National Academy of Law and Social Sciences*): Avda. Presidente Figueroa Alcorta 2263; f. 1874; 25 mems.; Pres. AUGUSTIN MATIAZZO; Secs. Dr. A. G. PADILLA, L. MORENO; publ. *Anales.*

Academia Nacional de Geografía (*National Academy of Geography*): San Martín 336; f. 1956; all brs. of geography; 30 mems.; Pres. Ing. LORENZO DAGNINO PASTORE; Sec.-Gen. ERNESTO REGUERA SIERRA; publ. *Anales.*

Academia Nacional de la Historia (*National Academy of History*): Balcarce 139; 36 mems., 223 foreign corresp. mems.; Pres. Dr. ENRIQUE M. BARBA; Sec. Rear-Admiral LAURIO H. DESTÉFANI; publs. *Boletín*†, *Investigaciones y Ensayos*†, papers and theses.

Academia Nacional de Medicina (*National Academy of Medicine*): Las Heras 3092, 1425 Buenos Aires; f. 1822; 35 mems.; library of 50,000 vols.; Pres. Dr. HORACIO RODRIGUEZ CASTELLS; Sec.-Gen. Dr. DIEGO ZAVALETA; Dir. of Library Dr. FLORENCIO ETCHEVERRY BONEO; publ. *Boletín*† (2 a year).

Córdoba

Academia Nacional de Ciencias y Artes de Córdoba (*National Academy of Córdoba*): Avda. Vélez Sarsfield 229, Casilla Correo 36; f. 1869; 35 mems.; Pres. Dr. TELASCO GARCÍA CASTELLANOS; Sec. Dr. ALFREDO COCUCCI; publs. *Actas, Boletín, Miscelánea.*

Academia Nacional de Derecho y Ciencias Sociales (Córdoba) (*National Academy of Law and Social Sciences*) (*Córdoba*): Avda. Colón 93; f. 1941; 24 mems.; Pres. Dr. ALFREDO POVIÑA; Sec. Dr. JOSÉ A. BUTELER; publ. *Anales.*

LEARNED SOCIETIES

AGRICULTURE AND VETERINARY SCIENCE

Asociación Argentina de la Ciencia del Suelo (*Argentine Assn. of Soil Science*): Calle Cerviño 3101, Buenos Aires; f. 1958; 460 mems.; Pres. OSCAR J. GUEDES; Sec. Dr. DINO A. CAPPANNINI.

Sociedad Rural Argentina (*Agricultural Science Society*): Florida 460, 1005 Buenos Aires; f. 1886; 12,000 mems.; library: *see* libraries; Pres. Dr. JUAN A. PIRÁN.

ARCHITECTURE AND TOWN PLANNING

Sociedad Central de Arquitectos (*Architects' Association*): Montevideo 938, 1019 Buenos Aires; f. 1886; 7,000 mems.; library of 4,000 vols.; Pres. Arq. FRANCISCO J. GARCÍA VÁZQUEZ; Sec. Arq. RODOLFO HASSE; publ. *Boletín Informativo* (every 2 months).

THE ARTS

Fondo Nacional de las Artes (*National Arts Foundation*): Alsina 673, 1087 Buenos Aires; f. 1958 to promote and support the arts: library of 3,600 vols., gramophone records, slides; Librarian ARLETTE I. LÉVY; publs. *Informativo* (monthly), *Anuario del Teatro Argentino*, *Catálogo del Cine Argentino*, *Bibliografía Argentina de Artes y Letras* (quarterly).

BIBLIOGRAPHY, LIBRARY SCIENCE AND MUSEOLOGY

Asociación Archivistica Argentina (*Argentine Archivists' Association*): Leandro N. Alem 250, C.P. 1003, Buenos Aires; f. 1968; brings together organizations and private individuals interested in historical or administrative archives; to promote study, professional training and research in this field; 160 mems.; Pres. PABLO A. MERCADO; Sec.-Gen. Dr. AUGUSTO FERNÁNDEZ PINTO; publ. *Boletín*.

Asociación Argentina de Bibliotecas y Centros de Información Científicos y Técnicos (*Argentine Association of Scientific and Technical Libraries and Information Centres*): Santa Fé 1145, Buenos Aires; f. 1937; 84 mems.; Pres. ABILIO BASSETS; Tech. Sec. ERNESTO G. GIETZ; publ. *Union Catalogue of Scientific and Technical Publications*.

Asociación Bernardino Rivadavia—Biblioteca Popular: Avda. Colón 31, 8000 Bahía Blanca; f. 1882; library of 110,000 vols.; Pres. Ing. JOSÉ MARÍA ARANGO; Sec. Prof. RAÚL OSCAR GOUARNALUSSE; publ. *Boletín Informativo*.

Asociación de Bibliotecarios Graduados de la República Argentina (ABGRA) (*Association of Argentine Librarians*): C. C. 68, Suc. 1, 1401 Buenos Aires; f. 1953; 700 mems.; affiliated to IFLA; Pres. NILO SIDERO; Sec. E. S. IRIONDO; publs. *Boletín Informativo*†, *Memoria Anual*†, *Documentos Ocasionales*†, *Reuniones Nacionales de Bibliotecarios* (*Actas*, *Documentos de Base*)†.

Comisión Nacional de Museos y de Monumentos y Lugares Históricos (*Nat. Comm. for Museums and Historic Monuments and Sites*): Avda. de Mayo 556, Buenos Aires; f. 1938 to supervise museums and protect the national historical heritage; specialized library; Pres. JULIO C. GANCEDO; Gen. Sec. J. C. PALACIOS; publ. *Boletín*.

Comisión Protectora de Bibliotecas Populares (*Comm. for the Protection of Public Libraries*): Callao 1540, Buenos Aires; f. 1870; Pres. Dr. RÓMULO AMADEO; Sec. CÉSAR MARTINO; publ. *Boletín*.

ECONOMICS, LAW AND POLITICS

Academia de Ciencias Económicas (*Academy of Economic Sciences*): Avda. Alvear 1790, Buenos Aires; f. 1914; 35 mems.; library of 13,000 vols.; Pres. Dr. JOSÉ HERIBERTO MARTÍNEZ; Sec. Dr. JOSÉ S. ORÍA; publs. *Anales* and special editions.

Colegio de Abogados de Buenos Aires (*Buenos Aires Bar Association*): Montevideo 640, Buenos Aires; f. 1913; 1,400 mems.; library of 80,000 vols.; law and social sciences; Pres. ALBERTO ROBRERO ALBARRACÍN; Sec. Dr. C. E. PODESTA; publs. *Revista* and *Boletín*.

Colegio de Graduados en Ciencias Económicas (*Economics Graduates Association*): Viamonte 1582, Buenos Aires; f. 1891; cultural activities and safeguarding profession; library of 18,200 vols.; Pres. JORGE LUIS DIEGUEZ; Sec. ALFREDO CARLOS IANUCCI; publs. *Revista de Ciencias Económicas*, *Boletín Informativo*.

Sociedad Argentina de Criminología (*Argentine Criminology Society*): Libertad No. 555, Buenos Aires; f. 1933; attached to the Instituto de Criminología.

HISTORY, GEOGRAPHY, ARCHAEOLOGY

Asociación Paleontológica Argentina (*Argentine Association of Palaeontology*): Maipú 645, 1° piso, Buenos Aires; f. 1955; promotes all aspects of palaeontology and biostratigraphy, particularly of Argentina and South America; 400 mems.; Pres. ALBERTO C. RICCARDI; Sec. MIGUEL MANCEÑIDO; publ. *Ameghiniana* (quarterly).

Instituto Bonaerense de Numismática y Antigüedades (*Buenos Aires Inst. of Numismatics and Antiquities*): San Martín 336, Buenos Aires; f. 1872; 50 mems., 20 corresponding in Argentina, 37 abroad; Pres. HUMBERTO F. BURZIO; publs. *Boletín* and related works.

Junta de Historia Eclesiástica Argentina (*Council of Argentine Ecclesiastical History*): Reconquista 269, Buenos Aires; f. 1942; 50 mems., 64 corresp. mems. in Argentina, 6 abroad; Pres. R.P. RUBÉN GONZÁLEZ, O.P.; Sec. R. P. JOSÉ BRUNET, O. DE M.; publ. *Revista Archivum* (annually), *Boletín*.

Sociedad Argentina de Estudios Geográficos (*Argentine Society of Geographical Studies*): Avenida Santa Fé 1145, piso 4°, 1059 Buenos Aires; f. 1922; 4,000 mems.; library of 8,000 vols.; Pres. Prof. F. A. DAUS; Sec. Lic. JUAN ROCATAGLIATTA; publs. *Anales*, *Boletín*, *Geografía de la República Argentina*, *Serie Especial*.

INTERNATIONAL CULTURAL INSTITUTES

Alianza Francesa: Córdoba 946, 1054 Buenos Aires; f. 1893; 1,500 mems., 11,000 students; there are 140 brs. in Argentina with *c.* 35,000 students; library of 50,000 vols. on France and French literature; Dir. DANIEL LEFORT.

Asociación Dante Alighieri: Tucumán 1646—Olazábal 2417 y Rivadavia 6460, Buenos Aires; f. 1896; Italian cultural organization; 2,800 mems.; 66 teachers and 6,208 students; Pres. Dr. DIONISIO PETRIELLA; Sec. Ing. R. GIACOMPOL.

British Council: M. T. de Alvear 590, 4°, Buenos Aires; Representative A. A. EDMONDSON; co-operates with: **Asociaciones:** Bahiense de Cultura Inglesa, Bahia Blanca; Argentina de Cultura Británica, Córdoba; Argentina de Cultura Inglesa, Punta Alta; Rosarina de Cultura Inglesa, Rosario; Argentina de Cultura Inglesa, Santa Fé; Argentina de Cultura Inglesa, Buenos Aires; Asociación de Cultura Inglesa, Corrientes; also at Mar del Plata, Río Cuarto and Salta, Neuquen, Parana, Pergamino, Santiago del Estero, Venado Tuerto, Villa Ocampo; **Institutos:** Cultural Argentino-Británico, La Plata; Cultural Anglo-Argentino, Mendoza; Argentino de Cultura Británica, Quilmes; Cultural Anglo-Argentino, Tucumán; Cultural Argentino-Británico, Mercedes, San Luis; Instituto Chaqueño de Cultura Inglesa, Resistencia.

Institución Cultural Argentino-Germana (*Argentine-German Cultural Institute*): J. E. Uriburu 1222, Buenos Aires; f. 1960; Dir. Dr. J. SCHMIDT.

Instituto Cultural Argentino Norte-Americano (I.C.A.N.A.) (*Argentine-North American Cultural Institute*): Maipú 686, Buenos Aires; f. 1927; 500 mems.; library of 8,500 vols. on all aspects of American life and culture; Pres. Ing. LUIS FIORE; Sec. Dr. A. BRAUN.

Instituto Cuyano de Cultura Alemana (Goethe-Institut) (*German Cultural Institute of Cuyo*): Lavalle 417, Mendoza.

Istituto Italiano di Cultura (*Italian Cultural Institute*): M. T. de Alvear 1119, 3°, Buenos Aires; Dir. Prof. BRUNO LONDERO.

LANGUAGE AND LITERATURE

Academia Porteña del Lunfardo (*Academy of Argentine Slang*): Lavalle 1537, 9° C., 1048 Buenos Aires; f. 1962; 28 mems., 14 corresp. mems.; Pres. JOSÉ BARCIA; publs.

Diccionario de porteñismos y lunfardismos, Boletín, Memoria, Acta, Estatuto, Acuerdos, Comunicaciones.

Instituto de Literatura (*Institute of Literature*): Calle 47 No. 625, La Plata; f. 1968; ordinary and corresponding mems.; Dir. ARTURO CAMBOURS; publs. *Investigaciones, Boletín.*

P.E.N. Club Argentino (Centro Internacional de la Asociación P.E.N.) (*International P.E.N. Centre*): Rivadavia 4060, Buenos Aires; f. 1930; 100 mems.; monthly meeting and discussions; Pres. (vacant); publ. *Boletín.*

Sociedad Argentina de Estudios Linguisticos (*Argentine Soc. of Linguistic Research*): 11 de Septiembre 2262, Buenos Aires; f. 1935; Pres. DELFINA MOLINA Y VEDIA DE BASTIANINI; publ. *Por Nuestro Idioma.*

Sociedad General de Autores de la Argentina (Argentores) (*Argentine Society of Authors*): J. A. Pacheco de Melo 1820, Buenos Aires; f. 1910; 2,450 mems.; library of 58,000 vols.; Pres. EDMUNDO GUIBOURG; Sec. CÉSAR TIEMPO; publs. *Boletín Social* (quarterly), *Argentores* (monthly).

MEDICINE

Academia Argentina de Cirugía (Argentine Academy of Surgery): Avda. Santa Fé 1171, 1059 Buenos Aires; f. 1911; Pres. Dr. ALBERTTO E. LAURENCE; Sec. Gen. Dr. WOLFGANG G. LANGE.

Asociación Argentina de Biología y Medicina Nuclear (*Argentine Association for Biology and Nuclear Medicine*): Avda. Santa Fé 1145, Buenos Aires; f. 1963; 190 mems.; Pres. Dr. ANTONIO CODEVILLA; Sec. Dr. OSVALDO J. DEGROSSI.

Asociación Argentina de Farmacia y Bioquímica Industrial (*Argentine Industrial Biochemistry and Pharmacy Asscn.*): Avda. del Libertador General San Martin 7774, 1429 Buenos Aires; f. 1952; 1,200 mems.; library of 12,500 vols.; Pres. Dr. JOSÉ ALBERTO GOÍN; Sec. Dr. RAÚL REVILLA; publs. *Revista,*† *Boletín Informativo*† (monthly).

Asociación Farmacéutica y Bioquímica Argentina (*Pharmaceutical and Bio-chemical Association of Argentina*): Bartolomé Mitré 2041, Buenos Aires; library of 8,000 vols.

Asociación Médica Argentina (*Argentine Medical Association*): Santa Fé 1171, Buenos Aires; f. 1891; library of 30,000 vols.; Pres. Dr. EDUARDO L. CAPDEHOURAT.

Asociación Odontológica Argentina (*Dentists' Association of Argentina*): Junín 959, Buenos Aires; f. 1896; 5,500 mems.; library of 16,000 vols.; post-graduate school for dentists; Pres. Dr. JUAN R. CASTRO; Sec. Dr. CARLOS MAZARIEGOS; publ. *Revista.*

Federación Argentina de Asociaciones de Anestesiología: Terrero 411, Buenos Aires; f. 1945; 700 mems.; Pres. Dr. JACOBO SHOCRON; Sec. ARNOLD POLISENA; publs. *Revista Argentina de Anestesiología, Boletín Informativo.*

Federación del Patronato del Enfermo de Lepra de la República Argentina (*Federation of Argentine Asscns. for Aid to Lepers*): Beruti 2373/77, Buenos Aires; f. 1930, name changed 1973; to prevent and cure leprosy, carry out scientific research and health education and to support dispensaries; 20 affiliated cttees.; library: *see* Libraries; Pres. AMELIA BALDRICH DE SUSTAITA SEEBER; Sec.-Gen. Col. GUIDO ANTONINO MONTI; publ. *Temas de Leprologia* (quarterly).

Liga Argentina contra la Tuberculosis (*Argentine Anti-Tuberculosis League*): Santa Fé 4292, Buenos Aires; f. 1901; library of 140 series of periodicals; Pres. HORACIO RODRIGUEZ CASTELLS; Sec.-Gen. JULIO C. BLASKLEY; publs. *Revista Argentina de Tuberculosis y Enfermedades Pulmonares* (scientific), *La Doble Cruz* (popular).

Sociedad Argentina de Anatomia Normal y Patológica (*Argentine Society of Normal and Pathological Anatomy*): Santa Fé 1171, Buenos Aires; f. 1933; studies in pathology, histology, anatomy; 200 mems.; Pres. Dr. GRATO E. BUR; Sec. Dr. BORIS ELSNER; publ. *Archivos.*

Sociedad Argentina de Ciencias Neurológicas, Psiquiátricas y Neuroquirúrgicas (*Argentine Neurological, Neurosurgical and Psychiatric Society*): Santa Fé 1171, Buenos Aires; affiliated to Asociación Médica Argentina; f. 1920; 400 mems.; library of 35,000 vols.; Pres. Prof. Dr. DIEGO BRAGE; Sec. Prof. Dr. CARLOS MÁRQUEZ; publ. *Revista* (monthly).

Sociedad Argentina de Cirujanos (*Argentine Society of Surgeons*): Santa Fé 1171, Buenos Aires; f. 1939; Pres. Dr. N. E. BARRANTES; Sec. H. MONACO.

Sociedad Argentina de Dermatologia (*Argentine Society of Dermatology*): Santa Fé 1171, Buenos Aires; f. 1934; 140 mems.; Pres. Dr. DAVID GRINSPAN; Sec.-Gen. Dr. ANA R. DE KAMINSKY.

Sociedad Argentina de Endocrinologia y Metabolismo (*Argentine Society of Endocrinology and Metabolism*): Santa Fé 1171, Buenos Aires; f. 1944; 234 mems.; Pres. Dr. I. DE FORTEZA; Sec. Dr. R. S. CALANDRA.

Sociedad Argentina de Farmacologia y Terapéutica (*Argentine Society of Pharmacology and Therapeutics*): Santa Fé 1171, Buenos Aires; f. 1929; 100 mems.; Pres. Prof. Dr. MANUEL LITTER; Sec. Prof. Dr. ADOLFO ZUTEL.

Sociedad Argentina de Ciencias Fisiológicas (*Argentine Society of Physiological Sciences*): Obligado 2490, 1428 Buenos Aires; f. 1953; to promote research; symposia and congresses; 150 mems.; Pres. Prof. V. G. FOGLIA.

Sociedad Argentina de Gastroenterologia (*Argentine Society of Gastroenterology*): Santa Fé 1171, Buenos Aires; f. 1927; 900 mems.; Pres. Dr. ERMAN E. CROSETTI; Sec.-Gen. Dr. LEONARDO PINCHUK; publ. *Acta Gastroenterológica Latinoamericana.*

Sociedad Argentina de Gerontología y Geriatría (*Argentine Society of Gerontology and Geriatrics*): Santa Fé 1171, Buenos Aires; f. 1950; studies medical and social problems of old age; 160 mems.; Pres. Prof. Dr. FEDERICO PÉRGOLA; Sec. Dr. ROBERTO NÉSTOR TURSI.

Sociedad Argentina de Hematologia (*Argentine Society of Haematology*): Avda. Angel Gallardo 899, 1405 Buenos Aires; f. 1948; 350 mems.; Pres. Dr. GUILLERMO CARLOS VILASECA; Sec. Dr. EDUARDO DIBAR.

Sociedad Argentina de Investigación Clinica (*Argentine Society of Clinical Research*): Instituto de Investigaciones Médicas, U.B.A. Donato Alvarez 3150, 1427 Buenos Aires; f. 1960; Pres. Dr. VICTOR NAHMOD; Sec. Dr. RICARDO J. M. PUY; publ. *Medicina.*

Sociedad Argentina de Leprologia (*Argentine Society of Leprology*): Casilla de Correos 2899, Buenos Aires; f. 1954; organizes national and international meetings of doctors dealing with leprosy; Sec. J. C. GATTI; publ. *Leprología* (2 or 3 a year).

Sociedad Argentina de Micología (*Argentine Society of Mycology*): Ituzaingó 1066, 5000 Córdoba; f. 1961; 210 mems.; library; Pres. Prof. Dr. MANUEL SALAS MANTILLA; Sec. Prof. Dr. RODOLFO NÓBILE; publ. *Revista* (3 a year).

Sociedad Argentina de Oftalmología (*Argentine Ophthalmological Society*): Santa Fé 1171, Buenos Aires; f. 1920; 600 mems.; Pres. ALBERTO C. CREMONA; Sec. CIPRIANO D'ALESSANDRE; publ. *Archivos de Oftalmologia de Buenos Aires* (monthly).

Sociedad Argentina de Ortopedia y Traumatología (*Argentine Orthopaedic and Traumatology Society*): Marcelo T. de Alvear 1947, P.B. "A", 1122 Buenos Aires; f. 1936; 1,000 mems.; Pres. Prof. Dr. ALFREDO KOHN TEBNER;

Sec. Dr. Arturo Otaño Sahores; publ. *Boletín* (monthly).

Sociedad Argentina de Pediatría (*Argentine Paediatric Society*): Coronel Díaz 1971, Buenos Aires; f. 1911; 4,600 mems.; library of 2,000 vols.; Pres. Prof. Dr. Jorge Nocetti Fasolino; Sec. Dr. Narciso A. Ferrero; publ. *Archivos Argentinos de Pediatría* (every 2 months).

Sociedad de Cirugía de Buenos Aires (*Buenos Aires Surgical Society*): Santa Fé 1171, Buenos Aires; Pres. Ivan Goñi Moreno; Sec.-Gen. Guillermo I. Belleville.

Sociedad de Medicina Legal y Toxicología (*Society of Forensic Medicine and Toxicology*): Sarmiento 1271, Buenos Aires; f. 1929; 110 mems.; Pres. Dr. José Belbey; Sec. Dr. Alfredo G. Ferrer Zanchi; publ. *Archivos de Medicina Legal.*

Sociedad de Psicología Médica, Psicoanálisis y Medicina Psico-somática (*Society of Medical Psychology, Psychoanalysis and Psychosomatic Medicine*): Santa Fé 1171, Buenos Aires; f. 1940; Pres. Dr. C. M. Aslan; Sec. Dr. E. Kalma.

Natural Sciences

General

Asociación Argentina de Ciencias Naturales (*Argentine Association of Natural Sciences*): Avda. Angel Gallardo 470, 1405 Buenos Aires; f. 1912; 450 mems.; Pres. Raúl A. Ringuelet; Sec. Carmen de la Serna; publ. *Physis.*

Asociación Argentina para el Progreso de las Ciencias (*Association for the Advancement of Science*): Pacheco de Melo 1826, Buenos Aires; Pres. Dr. Alberto C. Taquini; Sec. Dr. Alejandro C. Paladini; publ. *Ciencia e Investigación.*

Sociedad Científica Argentina (*Argentine Scientific Society*): Avenida Santa Fé 1145, Buenos Aires; f. 1872; library of 78,294 vols.; 1,324 mems.; affiliations in Santa Fé, La Plata, Mendoza, San Juan; Pres. Eduardo Pouspeña; publ. *Anales*†.

Biological Sciences

Asociación Argentina de Ecología (*Argentine Association of Ecology*): Dpto. de Biología, Facultad de Ciencias, Universidad de Buenos Aires, Pabellón 2 Nuñez, Buenos Aires; f. 1972; 300 mems.; Pres. Dr. Ricardo Lutti; publ. *Ecology*†.

Sociedad Argentina de Biología (*Argentine Biological Society*): Obligado 2490, 1428 Buenos Aires; f. 1920; 180 mems.; Pres. Dr. Virgilio G. Foglia; Sec. Dr. Mirta Cattáneo de Peralta Ramos; publ. *Revista*† (2 a year).

Sociedad Argentina de Fisiología Vegetal (*Argentine Society of Plant Physiology*): Castelar, Buenos Aires; f. 1958; 140 mems.; Pres. Ing. Agr. Enrique M. Sívori.

Sociedad Entomológica Argentina (*Argentine Entomological Society*): Calle Maipú 267, Buenos Aires; f. 1925; publ. *Revista.*

Mathematical Sciences

Unión Matemática Argentina (*Argentine Mathematical Union*): Casilla 3588, 1000 Buenos Aires; f. 1936; Pres. Prof. Orlando Villamayor; Sec. Prof. Carlos G. D. Gregorio; publ. *Revista*†.

Physical Sciences

Asociación Argentina Amigos de la Astronomía (*Argentine Association for the Friends of Astronomy*): Avda. Patricias Argentinas 550, Buenos Aires; f. 1929; library of 4,000 vols.; 1,000 mems.; own observatory; Pres. Dr. F. P. Huberman; publ. *Revista Astronómica.*

Asociación Argentina de Astronomía: Observatorio Astronómico, 1900 La Plata; f. 1958; 120 mems.; Pres. Raúl Colomb; Sec. Hugu Levato; publ. *Boletín* (annual).

Asociación Argentina de Geofísicos y Geodestas (*Argentine Association of Geophysics and Geodetics*): Rivadavia 1917, Buenos Aires; f. 1959; Pres. Capt. Dr. Luis M. de la Canal; Sec. Agr. Rubén Rodriguez; publs. reports of scientific meetings, *Geoacta*† (2 a year), *Boletín* (3 a year).

Asociación Física Argentina (*Argentine Physics Association*): Casilla de Correo 5, Villa Elisa, Buenos Aires; f. 1944; Pres. Ernesto E. Galloni; Sec. Dr. Carlos Bollini; publ. *Revista.*

Asociación Geológica Argentina: Maipú 645, 1° piso, Buenos Aires; f. 1945; 1,900 mems.; publ. *Revista.*

Asociación Química Argentina (*Argentine Chemical Association*): Sánchez de Bustamante 1749, Buenos Aires; f. 1912; 5,000 mems.; library of 10,000 vols., 500 periodicals; Pres. Dr. Mario A. Crivelli; Sec. Dr. César Roitman; publs. *Anales de la Asociación Química Argentina, Industria y Química.*

Sociedad Argentina de Minería y Geología (*Argentine Society of Mining and Geology*): Avda. Sarmiento 2265, Castelar (F.N.D.S.), Provincia Buenos Aires; f. 1929; 160 mems.; Pres. Erwin Kittl; publ. *Revista Minera.*

Philosophy and Psychology

Sociedad Argentina de Psicología (*Buenos Aires Psychological Society*): Callao 1159, Buenos Aires; f. 1930; Pres. Juan Cuatrecasas.

Religion, Sociology and Anthropology

Asociación Latino-Americana de Sociología (A.L.A.S.) (*Latin-American Sociological Association*): Trejo 241, Córdoba; f. 1950; Pres. Prof. Alfredo Poviña; Sec.-Gen. Prof. Odorico Pires Pinto.

Sociedad Argentina de Antropología (*Argentine Anthropological Society*): Moreno 350, 1091 Buenos Aires; f. 1936; 250 mems.; Pres. C. Gradin; Sec. A. Cardich; publ. *Relaciones* (annually).

Technology

Asociación Argentina del Frío (*Argentine Refrigeration Association*): Cerrito 512, Buenos Aires; library.

Asociación Electrotécnica Argentina (*Argentine Electrotechnical Association*): Posadas 1659, 1112 Buenos Aires; f. 1913 to promote electrotechnics and standards for electrical equipment; 930 mems.; library of 1,553 vols.; Pres. Ernesto H. Rodil; publ. *Revista Electrotechnica*†.

Centro Argentino de Ingenieros (*Argentine Centre of Engineering*): Cerrito 1250, Buenos Aires; f. 1895; approx. 6,200 mems.; library of 18,000 vols. on engineering; Pres. Ing. Alberto R. Constantini; publs. *La Ingeniería* (quarterly), *Boletín* (monthly).

Federación Lanera Argentina (*Argentine Wool Federation*): Avda. Paseo Colón 823, 1063 Buenos Aires; f. 1929; aims to encourage all aspects of wool trade, from breeding to sales; 110 mems.; Pres. Manfred Hinsch; Sec. Pedro Lamblot; publs. *Boletín de Informaciones Laneras* (daily), *Monthly Statistics and Report*†.

RESEARCH INSTITUTES

(*see* also under Universities)

GENERAL

Instituto Torcuato di Tella: 11 de Septiembre 2139, 1428 Buenos Aires; f. 1958 to promote scientific research and artistic creativity to the benefit of the community on a national and international scale; administers research centres and higher education institutions; grants scholarships and fellowships; arranges conferences, courses, lectures; library of 40,000 vols.; Pres. ROBERTO CORTÉS CONDE; Dir. JAVIER VILLANUEVA; publs. annual report and research results.

AGRICULTURE AND VETERINARY SCIENCE

Centro de Investigaciones de Recursos Naturales (*Natural Resources Research Centre*): Castelar, Provincia de Buenos Aires; f. 1944, re-organized 1970; part of INTA (*see* below); research in soil conservation, fertility, pedology, botany, forestry, agronomical meteorology; library of 10,000 vols.; 91 research workers; Dir. F. ALBANI; publs. *Publicaciones Técnicas* (series), *Flora de la República Argentina, IDIA, Suplemento Forestal.*

Chacra Experimental de Barrow: C.C. 216, 7500 Tres Arroyos; f. 1923; provincial Ministry of Agriculture research station; pedigree stockbreeding; cereal genetics; library of 15,000 vols.; Dir. H. L. CARBAJO; publs. *Carpeta de Información Técnica*†, *Publicaciones Técnicas* (series)† (irregular).

Estación Experimental Agro-Industrial (*Agro-Industrial Experimental Research Station*): Obispo Colombres, C.C. 71, San Miguel de Tucumán; f. 1909; "Alfredo Guzmán" library; Dir. Ing. Agr. JOSÉ PLOPER; publs. *Revista Industrial y Agrícola de Tucumán* (quarterly), *Boletín, Circular Miscelánea* (irregular).

Estación Experimental Agropecuaria de Salta (I.N.T.A.) (*Salta Agricultural Experimental Research Station*): C.P. 228, Salta; f. 1960; under the Secretary of State for Agriculture; library of 1,500 vols., 174 periodicals; Dir. Ing. Agr. FRANCISCO HECTOR TELLECHEA.

Estación Experimental Agropecuaria Mendoza (*Mendoza Agricultural Experimental Research Station*): C.C. 3, Luján de Cuyo, Mendoc; f. 1958; attached to INTA (*see* below); Dir. Ing. Agr. JOSÉ VEGA.

Estación Experimental Regional Agropecuaria (*Regional Agricultural Experimental Station*): C.C. 31, 2700 Pergamino; f. 1912; attached to INTA (*see* below); library of 40,000 vols.; agricultural research; cultivates wheat, corn, flax, sunflower and forage plants; animal husbandry and breeding; agricultural extension service; statistics, economics and sociology departments; Dir. Ing. Agr. ALEJO W. P. R. VON DER PAHLEN; publs. some 40 technical publications annually in series, *Informe Técnico, Boletín de Divulgación Técnica.*

Instituto Agrario Argentino de Cultura Rural (*Agricultural Inst.*): Perú 277, Buenos Aires; f. 1937; library of 2,000 vols.; Dir. Dr. CORNELIO J. VIERA; Sec. Sta. MARÍA LUIS RIVAS; Technical Sec. EURIFUE ALFREDO VIVANA; publs. *Reseñas Argentinas, Reseñas, Comunicados.*

Instituto de Microbiología e Industrias Agropecuarias (I.N.T.A.) (*Agriculture and Microbiology Institute*): Villa Udaondo, Castelar, Provincia de Buenos Aires; f. 1944; Dir. Ing. Agr. ENRIQUE SCHIEL; publs. various reviews.

Instituto de Suelos y Agrotecnía (*Institute of Soils and Agricultural Technology*): Cerviño 3101, Buenos Aires; f. 1944; research in soil fertility, erosion studies; 30 mems.; library of 3,200 vols.; Dir. Ing. Agr. JORGE I. BELLATI; publs. *Técnicas Apartados de Artículos Tiradas Internas.*

Instituto Nacional de Tecnología Agropecuaria—INTA (*National Institute of Farming Technology*): Rivadavia 1439, 1033 Buenos Aires; f. 1956; to improve and extend agricultural and livestock technology and raise the standard of living of the rural population; numerous corporate mems.; National Dir. Ing. Agr. JORGE A. DEL AGUILA; Sec. LUIS ESPINOSA; publs. *Revista IDIA, Revista de Investigaciones Agropecuarias, Colección Científica, Colección Agropecuaria.*

Instituto Nacional de Vitivinicultura (*National Vine Growing and Wine Producing Institute*): San Martín 430, 5500 Mendoza; f. 1959; controls standards of wine production and promotes research in viticulture; library of 6,718 vols., 1,400 journals; Pres. Cnel. JUAN ESTEBAN VACCA; Dirs. LUIS PEDRO RICO, MARIO DOMINGO RODRIGUEZ.

ARCHITECTURE AND TOWN PLANNING

Centro de Estudios Urbanos y Regionales (CEUR) (*Centre for Urban and Regional Studies*): Bartolomé Mitre 2212, 1039 Buenos Aires; f. 1977; research advisory services and training in urban and regional development with particular reference to Argentina and Latin America; Dir. OSCAR YUJNOVSKY.

Instituto de Planeamiento Regional y Urbano (IPRU) (*Regional and Urban Planning Institute*): Calle México 625, 5 piso, Buenos Aires; f. 1952; research into problems of development of cities and regions in Latin America; Dirs. JOSÉ M. F. PASTOR, JOSÉ BONILLA; publs. *Plan, Cuadernos de IPRU.*

THE ARTS

Instituto Nacional de Estudios del Teatro (*National Institute for the Study of the Theatre*): Av. Córdoba 1199, 1055 Buenos Aires; f. 1936; library of 10,000 vols. on theatre, cinema, dance, folklore; also national theatre museum and archives; Dir. NESTOR SUAREZ ABOY; publ. *Boletín Informativo de Teatro*† (monthly).

BIBLIOGRAPHY AND LIBRARY SCIENCE

Instituto de Bibliografía del Ministerio de Educación de la Provincia de Buenos Aires (*Bibliographical Institute*): Calle 47 No. 510, 6° piso, La Plata; Dir. MARIA DEL CARMEN CRESPI DE BUSTOS; publs. *Bibliografía Argentina de Historia, Boletín de Información Bibliográfica.*

Centro de Documentación Bibliotecológica (*Centre for Library Science Documentation*): Universidad Nacional del Sur, Avda. Alem 1253, Bahía Blanca; f. 1962; all aspects of teaching and research in library science; library of 1,700 vols., 240 periodicals; Dir. Lic. ATILIO PERALTA; publs. *Bibliografía Bibliotecológica Argentina, Quien es Quien en la Bibliotecología Argentina, Guía de las Bibliotecas Universitarias Argentinas, Documentación Bibliotecológica, Indices de Revistas de Bibliotecología.*

ECONOMICS, LAW AND POLITICS

Centro de Estudios Económicos Sociales (*Socio-Economic Studies Centre*): Libertad 1050, Buenos Aires.

Centro de Investigaciones Económicas (*Economic Research Centre*): Instituto Torcuato Di Tella, 11 de Septiembre 2139, 1428 Buenos Aires; f. 1960; 10 researchers; library of 40,000 vols.; Dir. ANA M. MARTIRENA-MANTEL; publs. *Documentos de Trabajo, Cuadernos.*

Instituto Americano de Investigaciones Económicas, Jurídicas y Sociales (*American Institute of Economic, Juridical and Social Research*): Maipú 286, Buenos Aires; f. 1946; Pres. FRANCISCO A. RIZZUTO; Sec. Cnel. LUIS A. LEONI HOUSSAY.

Instituto de Desarrollo Económico y Social (*Institute of Economic and Social Development*): Güemes 3950, Buenos Aires; f. 1960; 800 mems.; library of 8,000 vols.; research, study, analysis, discussion of historical, social, economic, political and cultural problems of Latin America; Dir. ADOLFO CANITROT; Sec. MANUEL MORA Y ARAUJO; publs. *Desarrollo Económico, Revista de Ciencias Sociales* (quarterly).

Instituto Nacional de Estadística y Censos (*National Institute of Statistics and Censuses*): Hipólito Yrigoyen 250-12° piso, Buenos Aires; f. 1856; library of 18,000 vols.; Dir. CARLOS NORIEGA; publs. *Boletín de Estadística*† (quarterly), *Comercio Exterior Argentino*†, *Anuario Estadistico de la Republica Argentina*† (annually), censuses, information series.

Instituto para la Integración de América Latina (*Institute for Latin American Integration*): Cerrito 264, 2° piso, Casilla 39, Suc. 1, Buenos Aires; f. 1965 under auspices of Interamerican Development Bank to investigate all aspects of integration and train personnel; 30 mems.; documentation service of 40,000 documents, 10,000 books and 900 periodicals; Dir. Dr. EDUARDO R. CONESA; publs. *Integración Latinoamericana*† (monthly).

EDUCATION

Centro Internacional de Estudios Pedagógicos de Buenos Aires (*Buenos Aires International Education Centre*): Maipú 939, 1° piso, Buenos Aires.

Centro Nacional de Documentación e Información Educativa (*Centre for Educational Documentation and Information*): Ministerio de Cultura y Educación, Pizzurno 935, 4°, Buenos Aires; f. 1960; library of 16,000 vols.; Dir. FLORENCIA GUEVARA DE VATTEONE; publs. *Informaciones y Documentos* (quarterly), *Boletín Bibliográfico* (quarterly), series.

HISTORY, GEOGRAPHY, ARCHAEOLOGY

Departamento de Estudios Históricos Navales (*Department of Naval History Studies*): Comando en Jefe de la Armada, Avda. Com. Py y Corbeta Uruguay, Buenos Aires; f. 1957; naval history; specialized library; studio for the official Maritime Painter; Dir. Rear-Admiral LAURIO H. DESTEFANI; large number of publications, also paintings and medals.

Instituto Antártico Argentino (*Argentine Antarctic Institute*): Cerrito 1248, Buenos Aires; f. 1951; library of 10,000 vols. and over 1,000 charts, and scientific collection; maintains Estación Científica Almirante Brown at Paradise Harbour, Antarctica; Dir.-Gen. (vacant); Chief of Scientific Dept. RENÉ H. DALLINGER; publs. series *Publicaciones, Contribuciones* (irregular), *Boletín* (2 a year), *Boletín del S.C.A.R.* (3 a year, Spanish edn. of *S.C.A.R. Bulletin*).

Instituto de Estudios Americanos (*American Studies Institute*): México 524, Buenos Aires; Dir. MIGUEL ALFREDO OLIVERA.

Instituto Geográfico Militar (*Military Geographical Institute*): Avda. Cabildo 301, 1426 Buenos Aires; f. 1879; topographic survey of Argentina; library of 45,000 vols., 80,000 maps and plans; Dir. Cnel. LUIS JORGE BORRELLI; publs. *Anuario*; technical and scientific works.

LANGUAGE AND LITERATURE

Instituto de Filología Experimental (*Experimental Philology Institute*): Casilla 5571, 1000 Buenos Aires; f. 1949; library of 6,000 vols.; Dir. ENRIQUE R. DEL VALLE; publs. *Diccionario del turf, Lunfardología, etc.*

MEDICINE

Fundación Cossio: Las Heras 2393, Buenos Aires; f. 1957; medical foundation engaged in research, study and meetings, mainly in connection with cardiology and immunology.

Instituto de Biología y Medicina Experimental (*Institute of Biology and Experimental Medicine*): Obligado 2490, 1428 Buenos Aires; f. 1944; library of 15,000 vols.; Dir. Dr. VIRGILIO G. FOGLIA; publ. *Memoria* (annually).

Instituto de Hematología, Instituto Nacional de la Salud (*Institute of Haematology, National Health Institute*): Martinez de Hoz y Marconi, Haedo, Provincia de Buenos Aires; f. 1958; Dir. Prof. Dr. LUIS DELFER PODESTA.

Instituto de Investigaciones Médicas (*Institute of Medical Research*): Boul. Wilde 761, Rosario; f. 1948; Dir. Dr. SOL L. RABASA.

Instituto Nacional de Microbiología (*National Microbiological Institute*): Avda. Vélez Sarsfield 563, Buenos Aires; f. 1916; Dir. Dr. ANTONIO MANUEL VILCHES.

Servicio de Endocrinología y Metabolismo: Martínez de Hoz y Marconi, Villa Sarmiento, Buenos Aires; f. 1969; Dir. Prof. Dr. FELIPE A. DE LA BALZE.

NATURAL SCIENCES

General

Comisión de Investigaciones Científicas de la Provincia de Buenos Aires (*Buenos Aires Scientific Research Commission*): Calle 526 entre 10 y 11, 1900 La Plata; f. 1956; study of exact sciences, biology, earth sciences, technology; Pres. Dr. JUAN J. GAGLIARDINO; publs. *Informes*†, *Monografías*†, *Relatorios de Reuniones Científicas*†.

Consejo Nacional de Investigaciones Científicas y Técnicas (*National Council of Scientific and Technical Research*): Rivadavia 1917, 1033 Buenos Aires; f. 1958 to promote and undertake scientific and technical research, mainly through its 75 research institutes; maintains several scientific services; Pres. Dr. FERMÍN GARCÍA MARCOS; Exec. Sec. JOSÉ A. MONTERROSA; publ. *Informaciones*.

Fundación Miguel Lillo: Miguel Lillo 251, San Miguel de Tucumán; f. 1931; scientific research in natural history; library of 110,000 vols.; Dir. Dr. JOSÉ ANTONIO HAEDO ROSSI; publs. *Genera et Species Plantarum Argentinarum, Genera et Species Animalium Argentinorum, Lilloa, Acta Zoologica Lilloana, Acta Geologica Lilloana, Opera Lilloana, Miscelánea.*

- **Instituto de Botánica** (*Botanical Institute*): Dir. Dra MARTHA MARIA GRASSI.
- **Instituto de Geología** (*Geological Institute*): Dir. Geol. HUGO PEÑA.
- **Instituto de Zoología** (*Zoological Institute*): Lic. JUANA ROSA BENNAZAR DE HERRERA.
- **Museo de Historia Natural** (*Natural History Museum*): botanical, geological and zoological collections.

Biological Sciences

Centro de Investigaciones Bella Vista (*Bella Vista Research Centre*): José Manuel Estrada 66, Bella Vista, Corrientes; f. 1954; fish systematics, ecology and biology; library of 2,000 vols.; Dir. Lic. NÉSTOR RUBÉN IRIART; publ. *Estadística pesquera Argentina* (annually).

Centro de Investigación de Biología Marina (*Marine Biology Research Centre*): C.C. No. 157, 1650 San Martín, Buenos Aires; f. 1960; 36 mems.; library of 3,500 vols.; Dir. Dr. OSCAR KÜHNEMANN; publs. *Contribuciones Científicas*†, *Contribuciones Técnicas*†.

Estación Hidrobiológica (*Hydrobiology Station*): 7631 Quequén, Provincia de Buenos Aires; f. 1928; attached to Argentine Museum of Natural Sciences "B. Rivadavia"; concerned especially with marine hydrobiology, microplankton, fish, parasites, brackish water biology, etc.; Dir. Prof. ENRIQUE BALECH; publ. *Trabajos de la Estación Hidrobiológica* (irregular).

Instituto de Botánica "C. Spegazzini" (*Botanical Institute*): Calle 53, No. 477, 1900 La Plata, Buenos Aires; f. 1930; mycological collections from Argentina and all South America; studies on Mycology: Ascomycetes, Basidiomycetes, Uredinales and Hyphomycetes; affiliated to the Museo de la Plata; Dir. Prof. IRMA J. GAMUNDÍ DE AMOS; publs. contributions to reviews.

Instituto de Botánica "Darwinion" (*Botanical Institute*): Lavardén 200, San Isidro; f. 1911; attached to the Academia Nacional de Ciencias Exactas, Físicas y Naturales (*q.v.*); library of 70,000 vols., 650 periodicals; works dating from 16th century, including *Flora Brasiliensis* by Martius and Eichler, Linnaeus's works, collections of botanical journals, etc., herbarium of about 600,000 specimens, especially South American; Dir. Dr. ANGEL L. CABRERA; publs. *Revista Darwiniana* (2 a year), *Taxonomic Research of Argentine Flora*.

Instituto Municipal de Botánica Jardín Botánico "Carlos Thays" (*Botanical Gardens*): Santa Fé 3951, Buenos Aires; f. 1898; taxonomy of wild and cultivated plants; botanical museum; library of 1,000 vols. and 7,000 periodicals; Dir. ANTONIO AMADO GARCÍA; publs. *Index Seminum*†, *Revista del Instituto de Botánica*†.

Instituto Nacional de Investigación y Desarrollo Pesquero (*National Institute for Fisheries Research and Development*): Casilla 175, 7600 Mar del Plata; f. 1977; marine biology and ecology, fisheries technology, statistics and biology, microplankton, fish, parasites, brackish water economics, etc.; 200 mems.; library of 1,810 vols., 750 periodicals; Dir. Dr. ALBERTO O. CASELLAS; publs. *Contribuciones*†, *Revista*†, *Memoria Annual*†.

Instituto Nacional de Limnología (*Limnology Institute*): José Macía 1933/43, Santo Tomé, Provincia de Santa Fé; f. 1962; hydrological, biological and ecological research, including fishery biology; Dir. Prof. CLARICE T. PIGNALBERI DE HASSAN; publ. *Comunicaciones*.

Physical Sciences

Comisión Nacional de Energía Atómica (*National Atomic Energy Commission*): Avda. del Libertador 8250, 1429 Buenos Aires; Government agency; f. 1950 to promote and undertake scientific and industrial research and applications of nuclear transmutations and reactions; research centres in Buenos Aires, Constituyentes, Ezeiza and Bariloche; library: *see* Libraries; Pres. Vice-Admiral Dr. CARLOS CASTRO MADERO; publ. *Informes*.

Comisión Nacional de Investigaciones Espaciales (CNIE) (*National Commission for Space Research*): Avda. Pedro Zanni 250, 1104 Buenos Aires; f. 1960; responsible for research into the peaceful use of space; research carried out in co-operation with national and foreign organizations in space technology, solar and wind energy, remote sensing, atmospheric physics, etc.; 400 staff; library of 15,000 vols.; Pres. Brig. MIGUEL SÁNCHEZ PEÑA; Dir. V. ALBERTO LINDOW; publ. *Informe Argentino de Actividades COSPAR* (annually).

Centro Espacial Vicente Lopez: Avda. del Libertador 1513, Vicente Lopez; remote sensing.

Centro Espacial San Miguel—Observatorio Nacional de Física Cósmica: Avda. Mitre 3100, 1663 San Miguel; f. 1935; aerospace research, remote sensing, hail control, non-conventional energy, geophysics, atmospheric electricity, applied mathematics, meteorology, geology, solar physics; library of 65,000 vols.

Observatorio Astronómico: Laprida 854, Córdoba; f. 1871; attached to the University of Córdoba; Dir. Dr. C. R. FOURCADE; publ. *Resultados*.

Servicio Geológico Nacional (*National Geological Service*): Santa Fé 1548, Buenos Aires; attached to the State Sec. of Mining of Ministry of Economy; Dir. EDGARDO MENOYO; publs. *Mapa geológico-económico de la República Argentina* (scale 1:200,000), *Mapa hidrogeológico de la República Argentina*, *Estadística Minera de la República Argentina*, etc.

Servicio Meteorológico Nacional (*National Meteorological Service*): 25 de Mayo 658, Buenos Aires; f. 1872; library of 40,000 vols.; Dir. Com. JOSÉ EUGENIO ECHEVESTE; publs. *Contribuciones Estadísticas y Anales Climatológicos*, *Anales hidrológicos*, *Anales Geomagnéticos*, *Carta del Tiempo* (daily weather report), *Anales Sismológicos*, *Boletín Fenológico*, *Atlas Climático de la República Argentina*, etc.

Religion, Sociology and Anthropology

Departamento de Estudios Etnográficos y Coloniales (*Department of Ethnographical and Colonial Studies*): Calle 25 de Mayo 1470, 3000 Santa Fé; f. 1940; Hon. Dir. Dr. AGUSTÍN ZAPATA GOLLAN.

Instituto de Sociología (*Institute of Sociology*): José Hernández 2200, 3°A Buenos Aires; f. 1955; 250 mems.; library of 25,000 vols.; Dir. Dr. FERNANDO N. CUEVILLAS; publ. *Revista*.

Instituto de Sociología Aplicada (*Institute of Applied Sociology*): Casilla 5703 Correo Central, Buenos Aires; f. 1960; research institution concerned with the practical and theoretical application of sociology; Dir. ROBERTO ORTIGUEIRA.

Instituto Nacional de Antropología (*National Institute of Anthropology*): Calle 3 de Febrero 1370/78, Buenos Aires; f. 1943 as Instituto Nacional de la Tradición; attached to the Ministry of Culture and Education; anthropology, archaeology, folklore; 32 mems.; library of 20,000 vols.; Dir. Prof. JULIÁN CÁCERES FREYRE; Tech. Dir. Prof. SUSANA CHERTUDI; publ. *Cuadernos*.

Technology

Instituto Argentino de Racionalización de Materiales (IARM) (*Argentine Standards Institute*): Chile 1192, Buenos Aires; f. 1935; 1,650 mems.; library of 440,874 standards; Dir.-Gen. Ing. BEATRIZ GHIRELLI DE CIABURRI; Tech. Dir. Dra. ANGÉLICA DARÓ DE HUGHES; publs. *Dinámica IRAM* (monthly), *Normas IRAM*, *Catálogo General de Normas IRAM* (biennial), *IRAM Technología y Gestión* (quarterly).

Instituto de Investigación Aeronáutica y Espacial (I.I.A.E.) (*Aeronautics and Space Research Institute*): Guarnición Aérea, Avda. Fuerza Aérea Km. 5½, Córdoba; f. 1961; research, standardization, collaboration; library of 15,000 technical books, 220 dictionaries, 375 periodicals, also standards and reports; Dir. Com. UBALDO ALFONSO DÍAZ.

Instituto de Mecánica Aplicada y Estructuras (*Institute of Applied and Structural Mechanics*): Avda. Pellegrini 250, Rosario; f. 1962; experimental stress, analysis, models and structures, concrete soils and roads; library of 1,000 vols.; Dir. Ing. CARLOS LUIS TORREGIANI; publs. irregular.

Instituto Nacional de Tecnología Industrial (**I.N.T.I.**) (*National Institute of Industrial Technology*): Avda. Leandro N. Alem 1067, 1001 Buenos Aires; f. 1957; library of 20,000 vols., 3,000 magazines and 15,000 standards; Pres. Ing. JOSÉ ALCIDES RODRÍGUEZ; publ. *Boletín técnico* (irregular).

LIBRARIES AND ARCHIVES

Dirección de Bibliotecas Municipales (*Public Libraries Administration*): Calle Talcahuano 1261, Buenos Aires; f. 1928; comprises 24 Public Municipal Libraries in Buenos Aires with an aggregate of 350,000 vols.; Dir. Dr. J. R. LASCANO.

Buenos Aires

Archivo General de la Música Nacional (*National Music Archives*): Casilla 72, Sucursal 6; Dir. Dr. E. E. FEBBRARO.

Archivo General de la Nación (*National Archives*): Leandro N. Alem 246; f. 1821; 200,000 vols.; Dir. Dr. CÉSAR A. GARCÍA BELSUNCE; publ. *Revista* (annually).

Biblioteca Argentina para Ciegos (*Argentine Library for the Blind*): Lezica 3909; f. 1924; 13,598 vols. in Braille; Dir. MARIA PASCUAL DE MAONE; publs. *Burbujas, Hacia La Luz* (every 2 months).

Biblioteca Central de la Armada (*Central Library of the Navy*): Edificio "Libertad", Calle Comodoro Py y Corbeta Uruguay; bibliographical and reference material; administers a large number of smaller libraries run by the naval services; 70,000 vols.; publ. *Boletín Bibliográfico.*

Biblioteca Central de la Universidad del Salvador "Padre Guillermo Furlong, S.J.": Hipólito Yrigoyen 2447; f. 1956; 50,000 vols.; Dir. Prof. HÉCTOR FIOTTO; publs. *Anales, Stromata*† (weekly), *Boletín Bibliográfico.*

Biblioteca de la Comisión Nacional de Energía Atómica (*Library of the Atomic Energy Commission*): Avda. del Libertador 8250; f. 1950; 23,200 vols., 222,300 micro-cards and microfilms, reports on foreign atomic energy commissions; Librarian ELSA GUTIÉRREZ.

Biblioteca de la Sociedad Rural Argentina (*Library of Agricultural Sciences*): Florida 460, 1005 Buenos Aires; f. 1866; agricultural and veterinary science; 47,500 vols.; Dir. FERNANDO MENÉNDEZ BEHETY; publs. *Anales de la Sociedad Rural Argentina* (quarterly), *Boletín* (monthly), *Memoria* (annual).

Biblioteca de Leprología "Dr. Enrique P. Fidanza" (*Leprosy Library*): Federación del Patronato del Enfermo de Lepra de la República Argentina, Beruti 2373/77; f. 1930; 4,000 vols.; 35,000 cards in its catalogues; important sections on dermatology and tropical medicine; lending microfilms and slides service, museum of histopathology of skin; publ. *Temas de Leprología.*

Biblioteca del Banco Central de la República Argentina (*Central Bank Library*): Reconquista 266; f. 1935; 110,000 vols.; Dir. HORACIO POGLIANI; publ. *Boletín* (bi-monthly).

Biblioteca del Bibliotecario (*The Librarian's Library*): Callao 1540; f. 1944; 1,100 vols.; is a section of the Comisión Protectora de Bibliotecas Populares; Dir. RUBY A. ESCANDE.

Biblioteca del Ministerio de Economía (*Library of the Ministry of Economy*): H. Irigoyen 250; f. 1893; 55,000 vols.; economics, law and finance; Librarian CARLOS M. RODRÍGUEZ IBÁÑEZ.

Biblioteca del Ministerio de Relaciones Exteriores (*Ministry of Foreign Affairs Library*): Arenales 761; 50,000 vols.; Dir. HORACIO R. PIÑEYRO.

Biblioteca del Servicio Geológico Nacional (*Library of National Geological Service*): Santa Fé 1548, 3° piso; f. 1905; Dir. JOAQUIN SENABRE; 150,000 vols., 45,000 pamphlets, 15,000 maps; publs. *Boletín, Anales,* technical reports, statistics, maps, etc.

Biblioteca Nacional (*National Library*): México 564; f. 1810; 1,600,000 vols., 46,177 MSS.; Dir. JOSÉ EDMUNDO CLEMENTE; publs. *La Biblioteca, Bibliografía Nacional Argentina.*

Biblioteca Nacional de Aeronáutica (*Aeronautics Library*): Paraguay 748, Casilla de Correo 3389; 45,000 vols.; Chief Librarian MARÍA JULIA FERNÁNDEZ.

Biblioteca Nacional de Educación (*Education Library*): Rodríguez Peña 935; 105,000 vols.; f. 1870; Dir. Dr. NICOLÁS AUGUSTO RIVERO.

Biblioteca Nacional de Maestros (*National Library for Teachers*): Pizzurno 935; 100,000 vols.; general reference and education.

Biblioteca Nacional Militar (*National Military Library*) Charcas 745; f. 1940; 66,000 vols.; Librarian MARÍA ELOISA GUIRALDES.

Biblioteca Pública de Arte (*Public Art Library*): Avda. Libertador General San Martín 1473; f. 1910; 30,000 vols. on visual arts; part of the Museo Nacional de Bellas Artes; Dir. Sra. RAQUEL EDELMAN.

Biblioteca Pública del Colegio de Escribanos (*Library of the College of Notaries*): Callao 1542; f. 1886; 25,000 vols., law and social science; publs. *Boletín Informativo, Revista del Notariado.*

Biblioteca Tornquist: Ernesto Tornquist & Cía. Ltda., Bartolomé Mitre 559; f. 1916; 55,000 vols.; economic and social sciences; Dir JUAN JOSE GALLI.

Bibliotecas de la Universidad de Buenos Aires: Azcuénaga 280; Faculty of Law and Social Sciences 320,000 vols.; Faculty of Economics 195,000 vols.; Faculty of Exact and Natural Sciences 153,000 vols.; Faculty of Architecture and Town Planning 40,000 vols.; Faculty of Philosophy and Letters 310,000 vols.; Faculty of Engineering 105,000 vols.; Faculty of Medicine 660,000 vols.; Faculty of Agriculture and Veterinary Medicine 140,000 vols.; Faculty of Dentistry 32,000 vols.; Faculty of Pharmacy and Biochemistry 25,000 vols.; Nat. College of Buenos Aires 85,000 vols.; Library Science Institute 15,000 vols.

Centro de Documentación Internacional (*International Documentation Centre*): Avda. Eduardo Madero 235, 6° piso; f. 1959; 60,000 vols. specializing in publications of United Nations, Organization of American States, etc.; Dir. MARÍA MATILDE GUIGOU; publ. *Bibliographical Bulletin.*

Bahia Blanca

Biblioteca Central de la Universidad Nacional del Sur: Avda. Alem 1253; f. 1948; 85,000 vols., 1,000 periodicals; Dir. Lic. ATILIO PERALTA; publs. *Documentación Bibliotecológica, Ultimas Adquisiciones.*

Córdoba

Biblioteca de la Universidad Católica de Córdoba (*Library of Córdoba Catholic University*): Trejo 323, 5000 Córdoba; f. 1956; 80,500 vols.; Dir. Dra. ROSA HOFMANN DE BLANCO; publ. *Acta Scientifica* (irregular).

Biblioteca Mayor de la Universidad Nacional de Córdoba (*Library of Córdoba National University*): Calle Obispo Trejo y Sanabria 242, Casilla de Correo 63; f. 1614, reorganized 1818; 135,000 vols., including 3,650 periodicals and pre-1860 newspapers; 6 incunabula, rare editions from the library of the Jesuit founders of Colegio Máximo, also books from the Universidad de San Carlos; Centro de Documentación, containing 8,000 reference works; partial depository for UN publs.; Dir. JOAQUÍN GARCÍA; publs. irregular.

La Plata

Biblioteca del Ministerio de Gobierno de la Provincia de Buenos Aires (*Library of the Buenos Aires Province Ministry of the Interior*): Casa de Gobierno; 20,000 vols.; law, politics and economics.

Biblioteca de la Legislatura (*Law Library*): Casilla de Correo 101; 40,000 vols.; law, politics, and general reference; Dir. FACUNDO N. QUIROGA.

Biblioteca de la Universidad Nacional de la Plata (*Central Library of La Plata National University*): Plaza Rocha No. 137; f. 1884; *c.* 450,000 vols.; 12 incunabula, collection of South American newspapers relating to the Independence movement; rare translations of Cervantes; collection of some 17,000 vols. on South American history and geography and first travels in South America; documentation centre; Dir. Sra. HAYDÉE CERVANTES DE ARTOLA.

Mendoza

Biblioteca Central de la Universidad Nacional de Cuyo: Casilla Correo 420, Centro Universitario; f. 1939; 120,000 vols.; Dir. Prof. H. P. DE CHOCHOLOUS; publs. *Boletín Bibliográfico*†, *Cuadernos de la Biblioteca*† (both irregular).

Centro de Información Educativa (*Centre of Educational Information*): Centro Universitario; Dir. BORIS DUPLANCIC.

Biblioteca Pública General San Martín: Remedios Escalada de San Martín 1843; f. 1822; 100,000 vols.; Dir. SAMUEL MUÑOZ; publs. *Versión* (annually), *Boletín Bibliográfico.*

Pergamino, Buenos Aires

Biblioteca Pública Municipal "Dr. Joaquín Menéndez": San Martín 838; f. 1901; 58,000 vols.; Librarian ALICIA D. PARODI.

Rosario

Biblioteca Argentina "Dr. Juan Alvarez" de la Municipalidad de Rosario: Pasaje Dr. Juan Alvarez 1550; f. 1909; 118,926 vols.; works of the 16th to 20th centuries; Dir. ALDO FUENTES; Librarian RICARDO N. OTTONE.

Biblioteca Pública "Estanislao S. Zeballos": Bv. Oroño 1261; f. 1905; 20 mems.; 98,000 vols. specializing in economics, accountancy, business studies and statistics; Dir. OSCAR MATÍAS LÓPEZ; publs. *Aportes Bibliográficos*†, *Boletín de obras*†, *Síntesis de Publicaciones Periódicas*†.

San Miguel, Buenos Aires

Biblioteca de las Facultades de Filosofía y Teología S.I.: Av. Mitre 3226; f. 1931; central deposit library; 120,000 vols.; 700 periodicals received; Librarian Prof. GERARDO LOSADA; publ. *Stromata/Ciencia y Fe*†.

Tucumán

Biblioteca Central de la Universidad Nacional de Tucumán: Lamadrid 817, Casilla de Correo 167; f. 1917; 100,000 vols.; Dir. MARÍA ROSA DEL V. ANDREOZZI; publs. *Serie Ciencia de la Documentación*†, *Boletín Bibliográfico*†, *Colección del Sesquicentenario de la Independencia Argentina*†.

MUSEUMS

Buenos Aires

Museo Argentino de Ciencias Naturales "Bernardino Rivadavia", Instituto Nacional de Investigación de las Ciencias Naturales (*Argentine Museum of Natural Sciences*): Avenida Angel Gallardo 470, 1405 Buenos Aires; f. 1823; zoological, botanical and geological departments; 2,000,000 exhibits; library of 500,000 vols.; Dir. Lic. JOSÉ MARÍA GALLARDO; publs. *Comunicaciones*† and reviews on: Botanical Sciences, Geological Sciences, Zoological Sciences, Hydrobiology, Palaeontology, Entomology, Parasitology and Ecology; also pamphlets.

Museo de Armas de la Nación (*Arms Museum*): Santa Fé 750; f. 1904; library of 1,000 vols.; Curators M. S. ROMERO, D. RODRÍGUEZ, ALICIA ALVÁREZ.

Museo de Arte Moderno (*Museum of Modern Art*): Teatro General San Martín, Corrientes 1530; f. 1956; library of 2,000 vols.; permanent collection of Latin American paintings, especially Argentine, and contemporary schools; exhibitions, lectures, international conferences on contemporary music; Dir. GUILLERMO WHITELOW.

Museo de Bellas Artes de la Boca (*Fine Arts Museum*): Pedro Mendoza 1835; painting, sculpture, engravings, and maritime museum.

Museo de la Dirección Nacional del Antártico (*Museum of the Antarctic*): Angel Gallardo 470; departments of oceanography, geophysics, ionospherics, glaciology, microbiology, geology, palaeontology and biology; Dir. R. N. PANZARINI.

Museo de la Policia Federal Argentina (*Federal Police Museum*): San Martín 353, 7° y 8° pisos; f. 1899; history of the Police and criminal exhibits; Dir. A. E. RODRÍGUEZ.

Museo de Mineralogía y Geología (*Mineralogical and Geological Museum*): Perú 562; f. 1904; collection of minerals and rocks.

Museo Etnográfico "Juan B. Ambrosetti" (*Juan B. Ambrosetti Ethnographical Museum*): Moreno 350; attached to the Faculty of Philosophy and Letters of the University of Buenos Aires; f. 1904; library of 50,000 vols.; 150,000 exhibits; collections include: archaeological, relating to South America, in particular Argentina and Peru, and elsewhere; ethnographical, relating to the Americas, Africa, Asia, Oceania; anthropological, particularly relating to Argentina; Dir. Dr. JUAN A. VELLARD; publ. *Runa.*

Museo Histórico Nacional (*National History Museum*): Defensa 1600; f. 1889; library of 13,247 vols.; collections illustrating the revolution, national development, military history and heroes of the Independence; Dir. CARLOS O. BÓ.

Museo Histórico Sarmiento (*Sarmiento History Museum*): Cuba 2079; f. 1938; library of 13,000 vols.; Dir. Prof. ERNESTO LICEDA.

Museo Mitre (*Mitre Museum*): San Martín 336; f. 1907; preserves the household of Gen. Bartolomé Mitre; library of 66,621 vols. on American history, geography and ethnology; archive of 80,000 historical documents; Dir. Dr. JORGE CARLOS MITRE.

Museo Municipal "Brigadier-General Cornelio de Saavedra": Republiquetas 6309; f. 1942; furniture, paintings, clothing, jewellery, books, documents, arms, coins from 1800 onwards; Dir. CARLOS MARÍA GELLY Y OBES.

Museo Municipal de Arte Español "Enrique Larreta" (*Municipal Museum of Spanish Art*): Juramento 2291 y Obligado 2139; f. 1962; 13th-16th-century wood carvings, gilt objects and painted panels, paintings of Spanish School of 16th and 17th centuries, tapestries, furniture; small library; Dir. ISABEL PADILLA Y DE BORBÓN.

Museo Municipal de Arte Hispanoamericano "Isaac Fernández Blanco" (*Isaac Fernández Blanco Museum of Spanish-American Art*): Suipacha 1422; f. 1947; library of 2,500 vols.; art and decoration of Hispanic period, showing Spanish and South American origins; Curator GUIOMAR V. P. O. DE URGELL.

Museo Municipal de Numismática y Medallística (*Municipal Museum of Numismatics and Medals*): Banco Central, Calle Reconquista 258; Dir. Dr. JOSÉ MARÍA GONZÁLES CONDE.

Museo Nacional de Aeronáutica (*National Museum of Aeronautics*): Aeroparque de la Ciudad de Buenos Aires; f. 1962; Dir. Brig. EDMUNDO HUGO CIVATI BERNASCONI.

Museo Nacional de Arte Decorativo (*National Museum of Decorative Art*): Avda. del Libertador 1902; f. 1937; furniture, sculptures, tapestries, European and S. American works; presents lectures and concerts; Dir. Dr. FEDERICO ALDAO.

Museo Nacional de Arte Oriental (*National Museum of Oriental Art*): c/o Avda. del Libertador 1902, 1° piso; f. 1966; permanent and temporary exhibitions, audio-visual collections; specialized library; Curator Lic. ORLANDA YOKOHAMA DE FERNÁNDEZ.

Museo Nacional de Bellas Artes (*Nat. Museum of Fine Arts*): Avda. Libertador Gen. San Martín 1473; f. 1895; modern representative Argentine, American, European art, also classical; library of 35,000 vols.; Dir. SAMUEL F. OLIVER.

Museo Naval de la Nación: Paseo Victorica 630, Tigre; f. 1892; naval history, model ships, paintings, documents, medals; Dir. Capt. ENRIQUE GONZÁLEZ LONZIEME.

Museo Popular Juan N. Madero: Constitución 622, San Fernando; f. 1873; library of 70,000 vols.; history and general reference library aiming to supplement primary and secondary education; Pres. CARLOS DICHIARA.

Museo Social Argentino (*Argentine Museum of Sociology*): Av. Corrientes 1723; f. 1911; library of 50,000 vols.; Pres. Dr. GUILLERMO GARBARINI ISLAS; publ. *Boletín del Museo Social Argentino* (quarterly).

Córdoba

Museo Botánico (*Botanical Museum*): Universidad Nacional de Córdoba, Casilla de Correo 495; f. 1870; library of 8,000 vols.; Dir. Ing. Agr. ARMANDO T. HUNZIKER.

Museo Provincial de Bellas Artes "Emilio A. Caraffa" (*Provincial Museum of Fine Arts*): Avda. Hipólito Irigoyen 651; f. 1916; provincial art centre, including art library and archives; Argentine and foreign paintings, sculptures, drawings and engravings; temporary exhibitions, courses, visits and conferences; Dir. CARLOS MATÍAS FUNES.

Museo Provincial de Ciencias Naturales "Bartolomé Mitre" de Córdoba (*Córdoba Provincial Museum of Natural Sciences*): Avda. Hipólito Irigoyen 115, 5000 Córdoba; f. 1919, under the auspices of the Dirección de Historia, Letras y Ciencias of the province of Córdoba; geology, zoology and botany; organizes conferences and educational programmes; library of 3,400 vols. and periodicals; Dir. Dr. JUAN JOSÉ MURRA.

Corrientes

Museo Colonial, Histórico y de Bellas Artes (*Colonial, Historical and Fine Arts Museum*): Calle 9 de Julio No. 1044; f. 1929; pictorial and period exhibits relating to the Province; Dir. JUANA S. C. DE CASTILLO ODENA.

La Plata

Museo de La Plata (*La Plata Museum*): Paseo del Bosque; f. 1884; anthropological, archaeological, botanical, geological, mineralogical exhibits; contains comprehensive palaeontological collection, including Patagonian mammalia; library of 180,000 vols.; Dir. Dr. LUIS DE SANTIS; publs. *Anales, Revista, Notas, Theses.*

Luján

Museo Colonial e Histórico "Enrique Udaondo" (*"Enrique Udaondo" Colonial and Historical Museum*): Casilla de Correo 96; f. 1923; archaeology, history, furniture, silver, applied arts; library of 26,000 vols.; Dir. Prof. JUAN JOSÉ LOBO.

Museo de Transportes (*Transport Museum*): Avda. Nuestra Señora de Luján—25 de Mayo y Lezica y Torrezuri; f. 1942; history of Argentine transport from pre-Conquest times to present day.

Museo del Automóvil: Calles 25 de Mayo Avda. Nuestra Señora de Luján; contains vintage car collection.

Museo del Hombre Argentino: Frente Parque Ameghino entre Lavalle y 25 de Mayo.

Mendoza

Museo de Ciencias Naturales y Antropológicas "Juan Cornelio Moyano": Plaza Independencia; f. 1911; 60,000 exhibits; palaeontology, anthropology, archaeology, geology, folklore, etc.; unique specimens; specialized library of American and Argentine history; 18,000 vols.; rare editions; Dir. Prof. KETTY BÖHM DE SAURINA; publ. *Revista de Historia Natural.*

Paraná, Entre Ríos

Museo de Ciencias Naturales y Antropológicas de Entre Ríos: Av. Rivadavia 462, 3100; f. 1917; industry, anthropology, natural sciences; library contains 32,411 vols.; Dir. Prof. OLGA JORDAN DE BELTRAN; publ. research works.

Museo Histórico de Entre Ríos "Martiniano Leguizamón" (*Historical Museum*): Plaza Alvear; f. 1948; library of 19,000 vols.; history, folklore, numismatics; library specializing in regional, Argentine and American history; archives collection; Dir. SEGUNDO LUIS GIANELLO.

Rosario

Museo Histórico Provincial de Rosario "Dr. Julio Marc" (*Provincial History Museum*): Parque Independencia; f. 1939; local and national history collections; Hon. Dir. JORGE MARTÍNEZ DÍAZ.

Museo Municipal de Arte Decorativo "Firma y Odilo Estevez" (*Municipal Decorative Arts Museum*): Santa Fé 748; f. 1968; paintings by Goya, El Greco, David Boucher, Van Dyck, Ribera, etc.; antique glass, ivories, ceramics, 16th–18th-century furniture, silver, etc.; Curator P. A. SINOPOLI.

Museo Municipal de Bellas Artes "Juan B. Castagnino" (*Municipal Fine Arts Museum*): Parque Independencia; f. 1937; includes works by El Greco, Goya, Titian, José de Ribera, Valdes Leal; complete collection of Argentine art from 19th century to present; library of 3,000 vols. and 5,000 catalogues of works of art; Dir. HORACIO E. CORREAS.

San Carlos de Bariloche

Museo de la Patagonia "Perito Dr. Francisco P. Moreno": f. 1939; political history of Patagonia, ethnology, natural sciences; Dir. ALBERTO F. ANZIANO; publ. *Anales*.

Santa Fé

Museo de Bellas Artes "Rosa Galisteo de Rodriguez" (*Provincial Museum of Fine Arts*): 4 de Enero 1510; f. 1922; library of 30,200 vols.; collection of contemporary Argentine and modern art; organizes lectures, concerts, exhibitions; Dir. Sra. NYDIA PEREYRA SALVA DE IMPINI.

Museo Histórico Provincial de Santa Fé (*Provincial Museum of History*): San Martín 1480; f. 1943; Dir. RICARDO PASSEGGI CULLEN.

Museo Provincial de Ciencias Naturales "Florentino Ameghino": Moreno No. 2557, 3000; f. 1914; natural science museum; library of 6,000 vols.; Dir. Lic. CARLOS A. VIRASORO; publs. *Anales*†, *Comunicaciones*† (irregular).

Santiago del Estero

Museo Provincial de Arqueologia "Wagner": Calle Avellaneda; contains more than 135,000 archaeological findings of the Chaco-Santiagueno culture and findings of later cultures; ceramics, musical instruments and ceremonial objects; named after two French scholars, Emile and Duncan Wagner, who discovered most of the findings early this century; Dir. Miss OLIMPIA L. RIGHETTI.

Tandil

Museo Municipal de Bellas Artes de Tandil (*Municipal Museum of Fine Arts*): Chacabuco 357; f. 1920; paintings of Classical, Impressionist, Cubist and Modern Schools; small library; Dir. E. VALOR.

UNIVERSITIES

There are three main categories of Universities in Argentina: National (or Federal), which are supported by the Federal Budget; Provincial (or State), supported by the Provincial Budgets, and Private Universities, created and supported entirely by private initiative, but authorized to function by the Ministry of Education.

NATIONAL UNIVERSITIES

UNIVERSIDAD DE BUENOS AIRES

CALLE VIAMONTE 444/430,
BUENOS AIRES
Telephone 32-5854.

Founded 1821.

Rector: Dr. LUIS CARLOS CABRAL.

Vice-Rector: Dr. ALBERTO VICENTE DONNES.

Administrative Secretary: RAÚL DANIEL GRIGUOLI.

University Relations Secretary: CARLOS OSCAR FERNANDO BIANCHI.

Academic Secretary: Dr. ROBERTO ENRIQUE LUQUI.

Number of teachers: 3,440.

Number of students: 187,000.

Library: *see* under Libraries.

Publications: *Revista*†, *Boletin*† (quarterly), *Serie Publicaciones*†. The faculties publish their own periodicals.

DEANS:

Faculty of Law and Social Sciences (Avda. Pte. Figueroa Alcorte 2263): Dr. LUCAS JAIME LENNON.

Faculty of Economic Sciences (Córdoba 2122): Dr. JOSÉ PENA.

Faculty of Exact and Natural Sciences (Ciudad Universitaria—Núñez): Dr. CÉSAR ANSELMO TREJO.

Faculty of Architecture and Town Planning (Ciudad Universitaria—Núñez): Arq. HECTOR MARIO CORBACHO.

Faculty of Philosophy and Letters (25 de Mayo 217, 1°); Dr. ARTURO BERENGUER CARISOMO.

Faculty of Engineering (Paseo Colón 850): Ing. AUGUSTO LUIS BACQUÉ.

Faculty of Medicine (Paraguay 2155): Dr. ALBERTO VICENTE DONNES.

Faculty of Agriculture (Avda. San Martín 4453): Ing. ICHIRO MIZUNO.

Faculty of Dentistry (M. T. de Alvear 2142): Dr. GABINO FERNANDO GARCÍA.

Faculty of Pharmacy and Biochemistry (Junín 954): Prof. Dr. MARIO ALEJANDRO COPELLO.

Faculty of Veterinary Sciences (Avda. San Martín 4453): Dr. ALEJANDRO MURTAGH.

SELECTED AFFILIATED INSTITUTES:

Escuela Superior de Comercio "Carlos Pellegrini": Marcelo T. de Alvear 1851; f. 1890; incorporated in the University of Buenos Aires 1912; offers six-year course in commercial education.

Rector: Prof. ALVARO CARTELLI.

Colegio Nacional de Buenos Aires: Bolívar 263, Buenos Aires.

Rector: Prof. EDUARDO ANIBAL RÓMULO MANIGLIA.

Centro de Investigaciones Médicas (*Medical Research Centre*): General Donato Alvarez 3000, Buenos Aires.

Director: Dr. ALFREDO LANARI.

Instituto Bibliotecológico (*Library Science Institute*): Azcuénaga 280, Buenos Aires; f. 1943; co-ordinating office for University libraries; specialized library of 150,000 vols.

Director: HANS GUILLERMO GRAVENHORST.

UNIVERSIDAD NACIONAL DE CATAMARCA

REPÚBLICA 350,
5000 CATAMARCA
Telephone 24099, 24774.

Founded 1972.

Academic year: February to December.

Rector: Prof. JOSÉ LUQUE.

Vice-Rector: Lic. HUGO DEL CALZ MOYA.

Administrative Secretary: Dra. MARÍA A. CATTARUZZA DE CASAS.

Librarian: MARÍA EMILIA MARTÍNEZ.

Number of teachers: 304.

Number of students: 1,666.

Publication: *Aportes*†.

DEANS:

Department of Agricultural Sciences: Ing. Agr. GUILLERMO OSCAR MARTIN.

Department of Economics: Lic. HUGO DEL CALZ MOYA.

Department of Education: Prof. RAMÓN RUBÉN CASTILLO.

Department of Health Sciences: Lic. MARTA LEONOR SIPOWICZ.

Department of Technology: Agr. GREGORIO SEGUNDO PERDIGUERO.

PROFESSORS:

Department of Agricultural Sciences:

ANDRADA, ALBERTO BRUNO, Genetics
DA SILVA GAIBASSO, HUGO, Edaphology
DEGIORGI DE MAGLIOLA, LINA, Agricultural Microbiology
IRIARTE, ADOLFO ANTONIO, Physics
MALANO, HECTOR MIGUEL, Irrigation and Drainage
MARTIN, GUILLERMO OSCAR, Phytology
ZAIN EL DIN, JUAN CARLOS, Analytical Chemistry

Department of Economics:

BOYALLISN, ELÍAS, Professional Practice
FLORES, NELLY AZUCENA, Civil and Commercial Law
MARTIN CASTILLA, FRANCISCO, Statistics
MONTEVERDE, ENRIQUE D., Common Law
MOYA, HUGO DEL CALZ, Costing and Accounting
NAZARENO, HÉCTOR WALLIH, Public Finance
NOVILLO CORVALAN, SOFANOR, Social and Economic Theory
PESSINI MIEREZ, JUAN RAMÓN, Social and Economic Theory, Employment Legislation and Personnel Administration
TOLOZA, DANIEL EDUARDO, Accountancy and Administration

Department of Education:

BOSCH DE BLAMEY, MATILDE, Teaching Practice
GONZALEZ, OSCAR VALENTÍN, History
MARTINEZ, SAMUEL DEL PILAR, Genetics, Health Education, Histology and Embryology
PAIS, FEDERICO EMILIANO, Spanish, Spanish and Latin-American Philology
PERALTA GARCIA, ANÍBAL, Theory of Education and Sociology
PEREZ FUENTES, GERARDO, History
ROMERO, RAMONA IRMA, History of Education
SANTAMARIA DE LUQUE, NORA, English and Use of Language Laboratory
VARELA DALLA LASTA, LUIS, History and Political History

Department of Health Sciences:

FIGUEROA, DINA AURORA, Paediatric and Obstetric Nursing
GUIDETTI, BLANCA SUSANA, Medical and Surgical Nursing
LAVENA, ROBERTO FRANCISCO, Biophysics, Medical and Surgical Nursing, Physics, Basic Nursing
RODRIGUEZ, MARGARITA, Basic Nursing, Nutrition and Pharmacology
SIPOWICZ, MARTA LEONOR, History of Nursing, General Health

Department of Technology:

ABDALA, EDGARDO FREDDY, Technical Drawing and Geometry
ESPINOSA, JUAN ALBERTO, Mining Technology
FARFAN, HÉCTOR HUGO, Mineral Processing
HAAR, VÍCTOR HANSJÜRGEN, Topography, Photogrammetry and Interpretation
IMPERATORI, ORLANDO MARIO, Physics
JIMENEZ, FERNANDO FÉLIX, Mathematical Analysis, Computing and Mining Mechanics
LEHDER, FRANK ULRICO, Agrology
MAGLIOLA MUNDET, HORACIO, Mineral Geology
MATEOS, BENEDICTO MARCOS, Mining Techniques
MEDINA, VÍCTOR SEBASTIÁN, Town Planning
MICHAUD, CARLOS RUBÉN, General and Applied Hydraulics
NAVARRO GARCIA, LUIS F., Geology, Geomorphology
TOSELLI, GUSTAVO ADOLFO, Petrology and Mineralogy

UNIVERSIDAD NACIONAL DEL CENTRO DE LA PROVINCIA DE BUENOS AIRES

GRAL. PINTO 399, 7000 TANDIL
Telephone: 2-2062, 2063.

Founded 1975.

Academic year: February to December.

Rector: Dr. RAÚL CEFERINO ROQUE CRUZ.
Vice-Rector: Dr. ERNESTO EDUARDO BORGA.
Academic Secretary: Lic. DANIEL HUGO XODO.
Administrative Secretary: Cr. ROBERTO TASSARA.
Library Director: Prof. ZULEMA GRANDINETTI DE CAGLIOLO.

Number of teachers: 675.
Number of students: 2,345.
Publication: *Revista, Temas.*

DEANS:

Faculty of Agronomy: Dr. RAÚL SARNO.
Faculty of Economics: Cr. CARLOS A. LORENZO.
Faculty of Sciences: Lic. ROBERTO LUIS MOROSO.
Faculty of Humanities: Dr. ERNESTO EDUARDO BORGA.
Faculty of Engineering: Ing. JULIO A. FERRARO.
Faculty of Veterinary Science: Med. Vet. OSVALDO DE LA CANAL.

UNIVERSIDAD NACIONAL DEL COMAHUE

BUENOS AIRES 1400, NEUQUÉN
Telephone: 3718.

Founded 1971; comprises the Universidad Provincial del Neuquén and the Institutos de Profesorado of Río Negro.

Academic year: February to December.

Rector: Ing. JORGE CÉSAR LAURENT.
Academic Secretary: Ing. ALDO ANGEL BASTIANCIG.
Administrative Secretary: RUBÉN NÉSTOR SOSA (acting).
Librarian: Prof. MARTHA I. B. DE TOUCEDA.

Number of teachers: 698.
Number of students: 2,950.

DEANS:

Faculty of Social Sciences: DORA EDELMAN DE LERNER.
Faculty of Education: Lic. JORGE JOSÉ CHACTOURA.
Faculty of Agriculture: Ing. Agr. AEROS GWILYM JENKINS.
Faculty of Economics and Administration: EDGARDO ALBERTO PHIELIPP.
Faculty of Humanities: Cr. CÉSAR ALBERTO BOTTARO (acting).
Faculty of Engineering: Ing. MARIO EVER MORÁN.
Faculty of Tourism: Cr. CÉSAR ALBERTO BOTTARO.

DIRECTORS:

Higher School of Biology: Ing. JULIO ERNESTO ARROYO.
Higher School of Languages: Prof. MÓNICA VÁSQUEZ DE MURA.

Regional centres in Bariloche and Viedma.

UNIVERSIDAD NACIONAL DE CÓRDOBA

CALLE OBISPO TREJO Y SANABRIA 242, CÓRDOBA
Telephone: 47382.

Founded 1613; charter received from Phillip III of Spain 1622; fully established by Pope Urban VIII 1634; nationalised 1856.

Academic year: March to November.

Rector: Dr. JORGE ANDRES CLARIA OLMEDO.
Secretary-General: **Dr. JOSÉ MARÍA ESCALERA.**
Administrative Director: RODOLFO BAZAN.
Librarian: **Lic. JOAQUÍN GARCÍA.**

Number of teachers: 4,967.
Number of students: 43,463.
Library: *see* Libraries.
Publications: *Revista*† and various faculty publs.

DEANS:

Faculty of Law and Social Sciences: Dr. FRANCISCO QUINTANA FERREYRA.
Faculty of Medicine: Dr. ENRIQUE PEDRO AZNAREZ.
Faculty of Exact, Physical and Natural Sciences: Ing. ITALO PETTITI.
Faculty of Economics: Dr. REINALDO ANTONIO COLOME.
Faculty of Philosophy and Humanities: Dr. ALFREDO POVIÑA.
Faculty of Architecture and Town Planning: Arq. LUIS ARNALDO VALLE.
Faculty of Dentistry: Dr. ENRIQUE FERNANDEZ BODERAU.
Faculty of Chemical Sciences: Dr. ALEJANDRO MARTIN.

DIRECTORS:

School of Information Science: Dr. FRANCISCO PEREYRA.
School of Social Service: Lic. EDGARDO JUAN GENER.

Higher School of Languages: Prof. PIO ANNONE.
Institute of Agronomy: Ing. ENRIQUE JULIO RODRIGUEZ.
Institute of Mathematics, Astronomy and Physics: Ing. JUAN A. TIRAO.

UNIVERSIDAD NACIONAL DE CUYO

CENTRO UNIVERSITARIO, PARQUE GENERAL SAN MARTÍN, MENDOZA
Telephone: 217219.
Founded 1939.
Academic year: March to November.

Rector: Prof. Dr. PEDRO SANTOS MARTINEZ.
Secretary-General: Dr. GUILLERMO ALFREDO POSE.
Director-General of Administration: **Cont. Nac. LAUREANO GORRIZ.**
Librarian: **Prof. HEBE PAULIELLO DE CHOCHOLOUS.**

Library: *see* Libraries.
Number of teachers: 844.
Number of students: 7,579.

DEANS:

Faculty of Agriculture: Ing. Agr. ADOLFO RAMÓN MALLEA.
Faculty of Economics: Cont. JOSÉ JORGE MASELLI.
Faculty of Medicine: Dr. JULIO ENRIQUE CANTON.
Faculty of Political and Social Sciences: Lic. DENNIS F. CARDOZO BIRITOS.
Faculty of Engineering: Ing. MARIO A. BARRERA.
Faculty of Philosophy and Letters: Prof. LUIS BRUNO CAMPOY.

FULL PROFESSORS:

Faculty of Agriculture:
ALMELA PONS, GUILLERMO RAFAEL, Vegetal Therapeutics
AVELLANEDA, MANUEL OSCAR, Agricultural Chemistry
BAJUK, MARCOS, Specialized Agriculture
BOCKLET, MÁXIMO FEDERICO, Agrarian Industries
CANALI, FÁNORE, Mathematics
CHERUBINI, CARLOS, Agricultural Botany.
CONTARDI, HÉCTOR GERÓNIMO, Parks and Gardens
HERNANDEZ, LUIS HORACIO, Accountancy and Rural Administration
KLINGNER, ALFREDO EMILIO, Phytopathology
LOTTI, ALBERTO, Genetics
MACOLA, GUIDO SEBASTIÁN, Animal Biology
MAVRICH, ERNESTO GABINO, Statistics and Biometry
MELIS, FRANCISCO MELIS, Mechanics and Agricultural Machinery
MELIS, LUIS ORLANDO, Horticulture and Floriculture
MILONE, JORGE OSVALDO, General and Inorganic Chemistry
NIJENSOHN, LEÓN, Soil Science
PEPA, IRENE ALICIA, Drawing and Technical Photography
RIGONE DE PRITZ, MARIA JOSEFA, Agricultural and Industrial Microbiology
ROSELL, PEDRO FEDERICO, Organic and Biological Chemistry
TACCHINI, JORGE, Economics and Rural Legislation
VEGA, ROBERTO, Oenology
WELKERLING DE TACCHINI, EMMA MARÍA LUISA, Fruticulture
ZULUAGA, PEDRO ANDRÉS, Viticulture

Faculty of Economics:
CABEZA, ENRIQUE, Mathematics
CABEZAS, PEDRO G., Mathematics
CLARAMUNT, ANA M., Economics
FERRA, COLOMA, Economics
FORNERO, LUIS A., Statistics
INCHAUSPE, OSVALDO, Economic Resources
LINARES B., VIDAL, Economic History
MARÍN, ENRIQUE, Economics
MARTÍNEZ, JORGE, Economics and Banking Techniques
MORA, JOSÉ A., Economic Resources and Industrial Relations
NAVARRO VILCHES, FRANCISCO, Fundamentals of Economics
PALMADA, RECLUS, Economic Systems and Policy
PIACENTINI, ZULEMA T. DE, Agricultural Economics
RIZZO, MANGLIO B. L., Administration
VEGA, JUAN A., Finance
VERNIER, SERGIO, Tax Techniques

Faculty of Medicine:
BINIA, ALBERTO, Physiopathology
BURGOS, MARIO H., Histology and Embryology
CICCARELLI, ALBERTO S., Microbiology
GIMÉNEZ, DOMINGO, Microbiology
MARSANO, O. L., Biochemistry
PONCE ZUMINO, AMIRA Z., Physiology

Faculty of Political and Social Sciences:
CALDERÓN BOUCHET, RUBÉN, History of Political Thought
LEIVA HITA, FRANCISCO, Macroeconomics
MOLINA CABRERA, O. C., Economics
REY TUDELA, A., Economic and Financial Policy
SARAVI, MARIO GUILLERMO, History of Argentina
TRIVIÑO, LUIS, Social Anthropology
ZULETA ALVAREZ, ENRIQUE, History of Political Thought

Faculty of Philosophy and Letters:
ACEVEDO, EDBERTO O., American History
BERTONI, HUMBERTO, Latin Language and Culture
BRUGIAPAGLIA DE GREGORI, TERESA, Linguistics
BUJALDÓN, AURELIO, Latin Language and Culture
CAMPOY, LUIS BRUNO, Rural and Urban Sociology
CAPITANELLI, RICARDO, Geomorphology
CHACON, LUIS, Child and Adolescent Psychology.
CICCHITTI, VICENTE, Greek Language and Culture
COMADRÁN, JORGE, Argentine History
DOMINGUEZ DE ALVAREZ, MARÍA DEL PINO, History of Argentina
GIUSSO, RUBÉN OSCAR, General Linguistics
GRANERO, E. I., Greek Language and Literature
HUALDE DE PEREZ GUILOUH, M., Introduction to History
LUCERO, D. M., Spanish Literature
LUCERO, T. M., Modern History
MARTÍNEZ, PEDRO S., Argentine History
NALLIM, CARLOS O., Spanish Literature
NOUSSAN LETTRY, LUIS, History of Modern Philosophy
OSTUNI, JOSEFINA, Introduction to Geography
PANNOCCHIA, S. A., Geography of Anglo-Saxon America
PRO, DIEGO F., History of Argentine Philosophy
PUCEIRO DE ZULETA, EMILIA, Spanish Literature
RUIZ DÍAZ, ADOLFO, Introduction to Literature
RUIZ SÁNCHEZ, FRANCISCO, Education
SACCHERO, P., Anthropology
SARTOR, MARIO, Italian
SCARAMELLA, DORA, Greek Language and Literature
SCHOBINGER, JUAN, Prehistoric Archaeology
SORIA, CLAUDIO, Latin Language and Literature
SOSA, GERÓNIMO, Biogeography
SOUTO DE TAPHANEL, MARÍA TERESA, French
VELASCO, MATILDE, Argentine Regional Geography
ZAMORANO, MARIANO, Urban Geography

UNIVERSIDAD NACIONAL DE JUJUY

GORRITI 237,
4600 SAN SALVADOR DE JUJUY
Telephone: 23933.
Founded 1972.

Rector: Dr. SALVADOR COSENTINI.
Administrative Director: Cont. HUGO HORACIO MENDEZ.
Librarian: MARÍA E. CENTENO DE MARTÍNEZ.

Library of 18,000 vols.
Number of teachers: 253.
Number of students: 996.

DEANS:

Faculty of Economics: Cont. OMAR BLANCO.
Faculty of Engineering: Ing. ITALO PALANCA.
Faculty of Agriculture: Ing. Agr. NÉSTOR ALCOBA.

DIRECTORS:

Institute of Physics and Mathematics: Ing. ENRIQUE HAMITY.
Institute of Chemistry: Lic. AUGUSTO VRACKEN.
Institute of Geology: Dr. RAÚL CHOMNALES.

UNIVERSIDAD NACIONAL DE LA PAMPA

9 DE JULIO 149, 6300 SANTA ROSA, LA PAMPA
Telephone: 3109.
Founded 1958.
Academic year: April to November.

Rector: Prof. VICENTE MARÍA MARQUINA.
Registrar: JUAN JOSÉ COSTA.
Librarian: ROBERTO COUTURE DE TROISMONTS.

Number of professors: 522.
Number of students: 1,614.

DEANS:

Faculty of Economics: Dr. ALFREDO CARMEN ROBERTO.
Faculty of Human Sciences: Prof. JOSÉ RUFINO VILLARREAL.
Faculty of Exact and Natural Sciences: RICARDO JOSÉ TELLERIARTE.
Faculty of Agronomy: HÉCTOR FRANCISCO LORDA.
Faculty of Veterinary Science: Dr. RAÚL ANTONIO ALVAREZ.

UNIVERSIDAD NACIONAL DE LA PLATA

CALLE 7 No. 776,
LA PLATA
Telephone: 2-5501.
Founded 1884.

Rector: Dr. GUILLERMO G. GALLO.
Secretary-General: Cr. ELIO RUBÉN LLANOS.
Secretary, Administration: Cr. HÉCTOR ANTONIO GENORO.
Academic Secretary: Dr. WALTER GERARDO AGUIRRE.

Library: *see* Libraries.
Number of teachers: 1,209.
Number of students: *c.* 22,000.
Publication: *Revista de la Universidad.*

DEANS:

Faculty of Architecture: Arq. HILARI BANGO.
Faculty of Agriculture: Ing. Agr. MILÁN JORGE DIMITRI.
Faculty of Economic Sciences: Cr. ENRIQUE PEDRO SPADARI.
Faculty of Engineering: Ing. ROBERTO DIEGO COTTA.
Faculty of Exact Sciences: Dr. JESÚS SIMÓN WILFREDO CARROZZA.
Faculty of Humanities and Education: Prof. OMAR ARGERAMI.
Faculty of Juridical and Social Sciences: Dr. ALFREDO E. VES LOSADA.
Faculty of Medical Sciences: Dr. MANUEL SERGIO GARCIA MUTTO.
Faculty of Natural Sciences: Dr. CARLOS ALBERTO CINGOLANI.
Faculty of Veterinary Sciences: Dr. JOSÉ HUGO FERNANDEZ DE LIGER.
Faculty of Dentistry: Dr. TOMÁS FUCINI.
Faculty of Fine Arts: Lic. JORGE IVÁN LOPEZ ANAYA.

SELECTED AFFILIATED SCHOOLS AND INSTITUTES:

Colegio Nacional (*National College*): Dir. Prof. HORACIO PICCO.
Escuela Graduada "Joaquín V. González" (*Graduate School "Joaquín V. González"*): Dir. Prof. BEATRÍZ ARREGUI Y OLAECHEA.
Escuela de Periodismo (*School of Journalism*): Dir. Lic. DANIEL A. PABON.
Escuela Práctica de Agricultura y Ganadería "María Cruz y Manuel L. Inchausti" (*School of Agriculture and Stockbreeding*): Dir. Dr. ALFREDO SQUADRONE.
Instituto Superior del Observatorio Astronómico (*Astronomical Observatory*): Dir. Ing. JOSÉ MATEO.
Departamento de Cinematografía (*Dept. of Cinematography*): Dir. JUAN PABLO MANDARANO.

UNIVERSIDAD NACIONAL DEL LITORAL
(National University of the Littoral)

BOULEVAR PELLEGRINI 2750,
3000 SANTA FÉ
Telephone: 34461.
Founded 1919.

Academic year: March to December.
Rector: Dr. JORGE D. MALDONADO.
Vice-Rector: Cont. REALDO V. C. CHIANALINO.
Secretary-General: JORGE A. RAMÍREZ.
Administrative Director: Dr. MARCELLO A. CHEMES.

Number of teachers: 700.
Number of students: 8,591.
Publications: *Universidad*† (3 a year); works relating to the different Faculties and Institutes.

DEANS:

Faculty of Law and Social Sciences: Dr. ANTEO ENRIQUE RAMELLA.
Faculty of Chemical Engineering: Ing. Qco. AGUSTÍN CARPIO.
Faculty of Economics: Cont. REALDO V. CHIANALINO.
Faculty of Biochemistry and Biology: ROBERTO O. CASABIANCA (acting).
Faculty of Agronomy and Veterinary Science: Ing. Agr. CARLOS CÉSAR JOSÉ ORDANO.

DIRECTORS:

School of Teacher Training: Prof. MARIA DE LOS M. J. ROSAS DE DENNER.
Higher School of Hygiene: Dr. VALERIO J. CAFFER.
School of Agriculture and Veterinary Science: Dra. G. HILDA HERMOSI DE FOLADOR.
School of Agriculture, Stockbreeding and Farming: Ing. OLEGARIO A. TEJEDOR.
Institute of Technological Development in the Chemical Industry (INTEC): Dr. ALBERTO E. CASSANO.
Polytechnic Institute: Ing. EDUARDO ROSAS PUYA.
School of Food Science: JOSÉ F. PIVIDORI.
Higher Institute of Music: HÉCTOR ARIEL NARDI.
Institute of Food Technology: Ing. HECTOR C. FABRE.
Department of General and Applied Hydrology: Ing. JORGE E. RAMONEDA.
Department of Languages: Prof. NILDA B. ORMAECHEA.
Department of Philosophy: Dr. RAFAEL VIRASORO.

UNIVERSIDAD NACIONAL DE MAR DEL PLATA

JUAN BAUTISTA ALBERDI
No. 2695, 7600 MAR DEL PLATA,
PROVINCIA DE BUENOS AIRES
Telephone: 3-6658, 6659.
Founded 1961.

Academic year: March to December.
Rector: Dr. JOSÉ ANGEL ALVAREZ.
Vice-Rector: Ing. RICARDO CASANOVA.
Administrative Director: PAULINO GONZALEZ.
Secretary General: Cont. JOSÉ MANUEL MARTÍNEZ.
Academic Secretary: Lic. CARLOS ERNESTO GUTIERREZ.
Librarian: Prof. HORACIO ZABALA.

Number of teachers: 1,600.
Number of students: 5,500.
Publications: *Revista de Letras* (3 a year).

DEANS:

Faculty of Architecture and Planning: Arq. ALEJANDRO VILAR CASTEX.
Faculty of Economics and Social Sciences: Dr. MANUEL HERRADA.
Faculty of Economics: Cont. JUAN CARLOS GARCÍA PRIETO.
Faculty of Engineering: Ing. RICARDO CASANOVA.
Faculty of Humanities: Lic. CARLOS ERNESTO GUTIERREZ.
Faculty of Exact, Natural and Biological Sciences: Ing. ADOLFO DI MARCO.
Faculty of Agriculture: Ing. Agr. SIMÓN SANTOS.
Faculty of Law: Dr. PEDRO NÉSTOR CAZEAUX.
School of Occupational Therapy: T. O. MARTA ELVIRA SUTER.
School of Health Sciences: Dr. LUIS ANTONIO DE LA TORRE.
Institute for Marine Research: Capt. ALEJANDRO GIUNTINI.
Institute of Physical Education and Sport: Prof. RAÚL OSVALDO VERNE.
Institute of Methodology and Philosophy of Science: Dr. HECTOR JORGE PADRÓN.

UNIVERSIDAD NACIONAL DEL NORDESTE
(National University of the North-East)

25 DE MAYO No. 868,
CORRIENTES
Telephone: 25060, 23050, 25064, 23043.
Founded 1957.

Academic year: March to December.
Rector: Ing. JORGE ATLÁNTICO RODRIGUEZ.
Secretary-General for Academic Affairs: Prof. HÉCTOR ENRIQUE TAMBURINI.
Secretary-General, Administration: Ing. JUAN FEDERICO VEGLIA.

Librarian: ITALO JUAN METTINI.

Number of teachers: 2,332.

Number of students: 25,000.

Publications: *Revista Nordeste, Cuadernos Serie Agro, Serie Medicina, Serie Planeamiento, Revista de la Facultad de Derecho, Bomplandia y Veterinaria.*

DEANS:

Faculty of Engineering: Ing. MARIO BRUNO NATALINI.
Faculty of Architecture and Town Planning: Arq. OSCAR J. M. VERGES.
Faculty of Economic Sciences: Dr. ANTONIO C. BESIL.
Faculty of Humanities: Prof. LUIS ISE.
Faculty of Dentistry: Dr. MAURICIO OPEN.
Faculty of Medicine: Dr. LUIS A. MALGOR.
Faculty of Agricultural Sciences: Ing. Agr. HUGO W. MALDONADO.
Faculty of Veterinary Sciences: Dr. EDMUNDO H. RESOAGLI.
Faculty of Law, Social Sciences and Politics: Dr. JORGE I. GARCÍA.
Faculty of Sciences and Surveying: Agrim. Nac. FELIPE LUIS ZIBELMAN.
Faculty of Agricultural Engineering: Ing. EDUARDO F. KAENEL.
Faculty of Natural Resources: C.P.N. JOSÉ A. GAIT.

UNIVERSIDAD NACIONAL DE LA PATAGONIA SAN JUAN BOSCO

C.C.786, CORREO CENTRAL, 9000 COMODORO RIVADAVIA, CHUBUT

Telephone: 3396.

Founded 1980 by merger of Universidad de la Patagonia San Juan Bosco and Universidad Nacional de la Patagonia.

Academic year: February to December.

Rector: Lic. NORBERTO SORRENTINO, O.P.
Academic Secretary: Dr. JORGE IGNACIO AGUERO BOHM.
Administrative Secretary: Cont. LUIS DOMINGO STEFANELLI.

Number of teachers: 240.

Number of students: 1,049.

Faculties of sciences, economics and social sciences (in Trelew), arts and education (in Río Gallegos); dept. of oceanography (in Trelew); schools of social work, art and design, nursing, forestry (in Esquel).

UNIVERSIDAD NACIONAL DE RÍO CUARTO

CAMPUS UNIVERSITARIO, ENLACE 8 Y KM. 603, RÍO CUARTO

Founded 1962, reorganized 1971.

Academic year: March to November.

Faculties of agriculture, engineering, economics, education, humanities, nursing, veterinary medicine.

UNIVERSIDAD NACIONAL DE ROSARIO

CÓRDOBA 1814, ROSARIO

Telephone: 49492.

Founded 1968.

Academic year: April to October.

Rector: Dr. HUMBERTO A. RICCOMI.
Secretary, Academic Affairs: Lic. ENZO B. LURASCHI.
Secretary, Administration: Dr. MARCELO T. RODRÍGUEZ.
Secretary for Economics and Finance: Cont. JUAN ANGEL ARRIGHI.
Secretary for Student Affairs: Dr. ALFREDO LUIS BORGHI.

Number of teachers: 3,542.

Number of students: 28,891.

DEANS:

Faculty of Economic Sciences: Dr. MIGUEL A. CHIARPENELLO.
Faculty of Medical Sciences: Dr. VÍCTOR AUGUSTÍN FRIGIERI.
Faculty of Humanities and Arts: Lic. NANCY DI PIERO DE WARR.
Faculty of Law: VIRGILIO SANCHEZ ALMEYRA.
Faculty of Agricultural Sciences: Ing. Agr. ENRIQUE HÉCTOR PERALTA.
Faculty of Odontology: Dr. JUAN CARLOS SCAPINI.
Faculty of Biochemical Sciences: Dr. FRANCISCO ROBERTO SETA.
Faculty of Architecture: Arq. J. HUGO CAGGIANO.
Faculty of Pure Sciences and Engineering: Ing. RAFAEL L. GALLI.
Faculty of Political Science and International Relations: Dr. EDUARDO SUTTER SCHNEIDER.
Faculty of Veterinary Sciences: Dr. LUIS NECHI.

UNIVERSIDAD NACIONAL DE SALTA

BUENOS AIRES 177, 4400 SALTA

Telephone: 14252.

Founded 1972.

Rector: Dr. AGUSTÍN C. GONZÁLEZ DEL PINO.
Administrative Secretary: Lic. VÍCTOR VAN CAUWLAERT.

Library of 25,228 vols., 27,130 periodicals.

Number of teachers: 716.

Number of students: 3,830.

DIRECTORS:

Department of Humanities: Dr. OSCAR OÑATIVIA.
Department of Health Sciences: Dr. CECILIO MORÓN JIMÉNEZ.
Department of Technological Sciences: Ing. RICARDO JOSÉ BORLA.
Department of Economics: C.P.N. HÉCTOR MARIO CAMPASTRO.
Department of Natural Sciences: Ing. Agr. MLADEN TONCOVICH.
Department of Exact Sciences: Lic. ROQUE RIGGIO.

ATTACHED INSTITUTE:

Consejo de Investigación (Research Council): Pres. Ing. PÉREZ FELIPOFF.

UNIVERSIDAD NACIONAL DE SANTIAGO DEL ESTERO

AVDA. BELGRANO (S.) 1912, 4000 SANTIAGO DEL ESTERO

Telephone: 1955/5727.

Founded 1973.

Rector: Dr. ARIÉL ALVAREZ VALDES.
Registrar: Dr. PEDRO NASSER.
Librarian: Prof. NÉSTOR URTUBEY.

Library of 20,000 vols.

Number of teachers: 400.

Number of students: 1,700.

DIRECTORS:

Department of Basic Sciences: Ing. MARIO MEDINA.
Department of Social Sciences: Dr. GUIDO P. FREDIANI.
Department of Infra-structural Engineering: Ing. GABRIEL MIGUEL RAED.
Department of Natural Resources: Ing. JOSÉ ANTONIO LÓPEZ.

ATTACHED INSTITUTE:

Centro Educativo Rural (Rural Education Centre): Dir. Ing. LEOPOLDO FLORES.

UNIVERSIDAD NACIONAL DEL SUR

(National University of the South)

AVENIDA COLÓN 80, 8000 BAHÍA BLANCA

Telephone: 24986.

Founded 1956.

Academic year: February to December.

Rector: Lic. RICARDO E. BARA.
Academic General Secretary: Lic. CARLOS A. ROBLEDO.
Scientific and Technological General Secretary: Dr. RAMÓN A. ROSELL.
Technical Administrative General Secretary: Cr. ROBERTO MENGHINI.
Librarian: Lic. ATILIO PERALTA.

Library: *see* Libraries.

Number of teachers: 460.

Number of students: 4,515.

DIRECTORS:

Department of Agriculture: Ing. Agr. OSVALDO FERNANDEZ.
Department of Economics: Cont. WALTER OMAR ESPÓSITO.
Department of Exact Sciences: Dr. LEOPOLDO M. ANTONELLI.
Department of Natural Sciences: Dr. RICARDO BOLAND.
Department of Social Sciences: Dr. ANTONIO CAMARERO BENITO.
Department of Engineering: Ing. OSCAR A. ANDRÉS.
Argentine Institute of Oceanography: Lic. LEONCIO MONTESARCHIO.

Institute of Biochemical Research: Dr. Nicolás G. Bazán.
Institute of Mathematics: Dra. María Inés Platzeck.
Chemical Engineering Pilot Plant: Ing. Esteban Brignole.

UNIVERSIDAD NACIONAL DE TUCUMÁN
(National University of Tucumán)

AYACUCHO 491, 4000 SAN MIGUEL DE TUCUMÁN

Telephone: 17123.

Founded 1914.

Academic year: April to December.

Rector: Dr. Carlos Raúl Landa.
Secretary, Administration: Luis Alberto Terán.
Secretary, Academic Affairs: Dr. Aída Pesce de Ruíz Holgado.

Library: *see* Libraries.
Number of teachers: *c.* 2,367.
Number of students: *c.* 17,723.

Publications: *Memoria Annual*†, faculty reviews, etc.†

Deans:

Faculty of Exact Sciences and Technology: Ing. Pablo E. de la Vega.
Faculty of Agriculture and Animal Husbandry: Ing. Edmundo A. Zerrizuela.
Faculty of Philosophy and Letters: Prof. Teodoro Ricardo Ricci.
Faculty of Architecture and Town Planning: Arq. Alberto Raúl Nicolini.
Faculty of Biochemistry, Chemistry and Pharmacy: Ing. Danley Arturo Callieri.
Faculty of Economics: Dr. Raúl Pedro Mentz.
Faculty of Medicine: Dr. Gerardo Palacios.
Faculty of Dentistry: Dr. Raúl Díaz.
Faculty of Law and Social Sciences: Dr. Adolfo Eusebio Colombres.
Faculty of Natural Sciences: Lic. Zlatko Tomsic.

UNIVERSIDAD TECNOLÓGICA NACIONAL

25 DE MAYO 564, BUENOS AIRES

Telephone: 41-0071.

Founded 1959.

State controlled; Academic year: April to November.

Rector: Ing. José Fermín Colina.

Number of students: 34,000.

Publication: *Boletín Informativo.*

Courses (mainly evening) in Construction, Electrical and Electronic Engineering, Chemistry, Metallurgy, Mechanics, Nautical Engineering, Textiles. Regional branches in 10 cities.

ESCUELA DE INGENIERÍA AERONÁUTICA

GUARNICIÓN AÉREA, 5103 CÓRDOBA

Telephone: 63958.

Founded 1947.

Academic year: February to November.

Director: Com. Nestor Edmundo Fernandez.

Library of 1,750 vols.
Number of students: 33.

Three-year courses for military personnel and civilians.

PRIVATE UNIVERSITIES

UNIVERSIDAD DEL ACONCAGUA

CATAMARCA 147, 5500 MENDOZA

Telephone: 24-1257.

Founded 1968.

Academic year: April to October.

Rector: Lic. José Enrique Montecino.
Secretary-General: Oscar David Cerutti.
Librarian: Profa. Josefina Delamarre de Monserrat.

Number of teachers: 251.
Number of students: 884.

Deans:

Faculty of Social Sciences and Administration: Alberto Cyrlen Zabala.
Faculty of Economics and Commerce: Rolando Galli Rey.
Faculty of Psychology: Dr. Adelmo Pesce.
School of Phono-audiology: Dr. Osvaldo S. Caballero.

UNIVERSIDAD ARGENTINA DE LA EMPRESA
(Argentine University of Business Studies)

LIBERTAD 1340, BUENOS AIRES

Telephone: 44-0476.

Founded 1962.

Academic year: March to December.

Rector: Dr. Natalio Schvarzer.
Vice-Rector: Dr. Alfredo Camperchioli.
Academic Secretary: Dr. Norberto E. Fraga.
Administrative Secretary: Dr. Armando S. Carlsson.
Librarian: Rodolfo Löhe.

Library of 13,213 vols.
Number of teachers: 800.
Number of students: 6,500.

Publications: *Informe, Bancar, Energia.*

Deans and Directors:

Pre-university Studies: Dra. María Cristina Serrano.
Faculty of Economic Sciences: Lic. Alfredo Gutierrez Girault.
Faculty of Administrative Science: Dr. Alvaro J. Marí-Arriaga.
Faculty of Law and Social Sciences: Dr. Fernando Mascheroni.
Faculty of Engineering: Ing. Jorge H. Meier.
Faculty of Agricultural Sciences: Ing. Agr. Enrique A. Iglesias.
Institute of Research in Economics and Finance: Dr. José A. Martelliti.
Centre for Energy Studies: Ing. Tomás Erdelyi.
University Extension Courses: Dr. Angel Daniel Vergara del Carril.

UNIVERSIDAD ARGENTINA "JOHN F. KENNEDY"

CALLE BARTOLOMÉ MITRE 1407, BUENOS AIRES

Telephone: 45-4338.

Founded 1961.

President: Dr. Miguel Herrera Figueroa.
Registrar: Pedro R. David.
Librarian: Dr. Esteban Tahy.

Library of 50,000 vols.
Number of teachers: 200.
Number of students: 2,000.

Schools of Arts and Science, Business Administration, Demography and Tourism, Dramatic Art, Education, Graduate Studies, Journalism, Political Science, Public Relations, Psychology, Sociology.

UNIVERSIDAD DE BELGRANO

FEDERICO LACROZE 1959, BUENOS AIRES

Telephone: 772-4014/18.

Founded 1964.

Academic year: March to November.

Rector: Dr. Avelino José Porto.
Vice-Rector: Alberto Adolfo Campos.
Secretary-General for Academic Affairs: Eustaquio Castro.
Secretary-General for Economics and Finance: Jorge Félix Massucco.
Secretary-General for Institutions: Roberto Russell.
Librarian: Daniel Augusto Filipini.

Library of 22,000 vols.
Number of teachers: 1,300.
Number of students: 8,800.

Publications: *Vigencia*† (monthly), *La Situación Internacional* (monthly).

Deans:

Faculty of Humanities: Dr. Alberto Bravo Larraburu.
Faculty of Economics: Dr. José Aromando.
Faculty of Law and Social Sciences: Dr. Felipe Mario Liporace.
Faculty of Architecture: Arq. Jorge Ricardo Rosa.

Faculty of Technology: Dr. HORACIO BOSCH.
Faculty of Graduate Studies: Prof. ALDO JORGE PEREZ.

DIRECTORS:

Institute of Sociology and History: HÉCTOR RUBÉN ZORRILLA.
Institute of Psychology: HÉCTOR FERNÁNDEZ ALVAREZ.
Institute of Architectural Planning: MABEL FERNÁNDEZ.
Institute of Public Law: MARIO JUSTO LÓPEZ.
Institute of Private Law: MARIO ALBERTO MOLMENTI.
Institute of International Studies: MARCELO MONTSERRAT.
Institute of Strategic Studies: JOSÉ TEÓFILO GOYRET.
Institute of Technological Research: JOSÉ SCHLEIN.
Institute of Economic and Financial Research: HUGO BREME.
Institute of Management and Accounting Research: DIONISIO LOPEZ CASCANTE.

UNIVERSIDAD CATÓLICA ARGENTINA "SANTA MARÍA DE LOS BUENOS AIRES"

JUNCAL 1912, BUENOS AIRES
Telephone: 44-1035.
Founded 1958.

Academic year: March to November.

Rector: Mgr. Dr. OCTAVIO NICOLÁS DERISI.
Vice-Rectors: Mgr. GUILLERMO PEDRO BLANCO, Dr. FRANCISCO VALSECCHI.
Academic Secretary: Pbro. Dr. EDUARDO MIRÁS.
Administrative Secretary: Prof. SECUNDINO N. GARCÍA.

Number of teachers: 2,900.
Number of students: 11,000.

Publications: *Anuario, Universitas, El Derecho, Sapientia* (quarterly).

DEANS:

Faculty of Philosophy and Letters: Mgr. GUILLERMO P. BLANCO.
Faculty of Law and Political Science: Dr. SANTIAGO DE ESTRADA.
Faculty of Economic and Social Sciences: MANUEL GONZÁLEZ ABAD.
Faculty of Theology: Mgr. Lic. CARMELO GIAQUINTA.
Faculty of Physical Sciences, Mathematics and Engineering: Ing. ARTURO BIGNOLI.
Faculty of Humanities and Education (Mendoza): Prof. ANA DEL CARMEN PIOVERA.
Faculty of Arts and Music: Mtro. ROBERTO CAAMAÑO.
Faculty of Agriculture: Ing. Agr. EMILIO J. COMPTE.
Faculty of Economics (Mendoza): Prof. FRANCISCO ENRIQUE GAVACI.
Faculty of Social Sciences (Rosario): Dr. BERNARDO DAVID DIEZ.
Faculty of Chemistry (Rosario): Ing. NÉLIDA RUIZ DE FITTIPALDI.

DIRECTORS:

Institute of Culture: Dr. BENITO RAFFO MAGNASCO.
Institute of Health Sciences: Dr. LUIS BUSTOS FERNÁNDEZ.
Institute of University Extension: Dr. MIGUEL ANGEL IRIBARNE.
Institute of Pre-University Studies: Prof. JORGE FLORIAN OLIVER.

UNIVERSIDAD DEL MUSEO SOCIAL ARGENTINO
(University of the Argentine Museum of Sociology)

CORRIENTES 1723, BUENOS AIRES
Founded 1961.

Rector: Prof. Dr. GUILLERMO GARBARINI ISLAS.

Faculties of sociology, journalism, humanities, politics, law and economics, and information studies.

UNIVERSIDAD DEL SALVADOR
(University of the Saviour)

ALBERTI 158, BUENOS AIRES
Telephone: 47-3619, 1692.
Founded 1959.

Private University of the Society of Jesus; Language of instruction: Spanish; Academic year: January to December.

Rector: Lic. FRANCISCO JOSÉ PIÑÓN.
Academic Vice-Rector: Profa. MARÍA MERCEDES M. TERREN.
Vice-Rector (Economics): Dr. ENRIQUE A. BETTA.
Vice-Rector (Research and Extension): Lic. EDUARDO SUAREZ.
Vice-Rector (Training): R. P. VÍCTOR MARANGONI.
Secretary-General: Lic. JORGE JOSÉ ARMAS.
Librarian: Prof. HÉCTOR D. FIOTTO.

Library: *see* under Libraries.
Number of teachers: 1,002.
Number of students: 4,350.

Publications: *Anales, Signos Universitarios, Atenea.*

DEANS:

Faculty of Juridical Sciences: Dr. RICARDO LEVENNE.
Faculty of Philosophy: Dr. CARLOS CULLEN.
Faculty of History and Letters: Dra. LIDIA ALFARO DE LANZONE.
Faculty of Medicine: Dr. LUIS GONZALEZ MONTANER.
Faculty of Psychology: Lic. MABEL ALLERAND.
Faculty of Social Sciences: Lic. JOSÉ ALBERTO BONIFACIO.
Faculty of Theology: Dr. MIGUEL A. FIORITO, S.J.
Faculty of Psychopedagogy: Prof. HÉCTOR DANIEL FIOTTO.
Faculty of Educational Sciences and Social Communication: Prof. MERCEDES TERRÉN.
Faculty of Specialized Engineering: Ing. AQUILINO LOPEZ DIEZ.
Faculty of Human Relations: Ing. AQUILINO LOPEZ DIEZ.

UNIVERSIDAD CATÓLICA DE CÓRDOBA

OBISPO TREJO 323, CÓRDOBA
Telephone: 38389.
Founded 1956.

Academic year: March to November.

Chancellor: Mgr. RAÚL PRIMATESTA, Cardinal Archbishop of Córdoba.
Vice-Chancellor: R.P. ANDRÉS M. SWINNEN, S.J.
Rector: R.P. JORGE A. FOURCADE, S.J.
Vice-Rector for Development: R. P. JEAN SONET.
Academic Vice-Rector: Ing. CARLOS DIAMANTI.
Vice-Rector for Education: R.P. JOSÉ ALVAREZ.
Vice-Rector for Economy: Cont. NÉSTOR GIRAUDO.
Academic Secretary: Lic. JUAN SARDO.
Librarian: Sra. ROSA HOFFMAN DE BLANCO.

Library: *see* Libraries.
Number of teachers: 700.
Number of students: 4,100.

DEANS:

Faculty of Architecture: Arq. B. VILLASUSO.
Faculty of Agriculture: Ing. Agr. OSCAR EDUARDO MELO.
Faculty of Economics and Administration: Cont. ROBERTO FRANCISCO CONTRERAS.
Faculty of Law and Social Sciences: Dr. JORGE I. FRAGA.
Faculty of Philosophy and Humanities: Lic. LUISA S. DE CERVANTES.
Faculty of Engineering: Ing. ALEJANDRO D. MAROCHI.
Faculty of Medicine: Dr. ALFREDO RODRIGUEZ.
Faculty of Chemical Sciences: Dr. JUAN G. DURIGNEUX.
Faculty of Political Sciences and International Relations: Dr. ALFREDO MOONEY.

UNIVERSIDAD CATÓLICA DE CUYO
(Catholic University of Cuyo)

AVDA. IGNACIO DE LA ROZA 1516 OESTE, 5400 RIVADAVIA, SAN JUAN
Telephone: 30291.
Founded 1953.

Language of instruction: Spanish; Academic year: April to March.

Chancellor: (vacant).

Rector: Mgr. Dr. FRANCISCO MANFREDI.

Vice-Rector (Academic): Dr. PABLO H. OLIVARES.

Vice-Rector (Administrative): Dr. ANTONIO O. JUAREZ.

Number of teachers: 310.
Number of students: 1,100.

Publications: *Cuadernos, Boletin Anual.*

DEANS:

Faculty of Law and Social Sciences: Dr. EMILIO OSCAR DANERI.

Faculty of Economic Sciences: ANTONIO ORLANDO JUAREZ.

Faculty of Philosophy and Humanities: Dr. JESÚS MUÑOZ, S.J.

Faculty of Nutrition Sciences: PEDRO LOHN.

University School of Nursing: Prof. IRMA G. PANTANO.

UNIVERSIDAD CATÓLICA DE LA PLATA

(Catholic University of La Plata)

CALLE 13 No. 1227, LA PLATA
Telephone: 021-41291.
Founded 1968.

Rector: Dr. OSVALDO MAMMONI.

Faculties of law, sociology, architecture, statistics and economics.

UNIVERSIDAD NOTARIAL ARGENTINA

(Argentine University for Lawyers)

CALLE 51 No. 435, 1900 LA PLATA
Telephone: La Plata 2-9283.
Founded 1965.

Academic year: March to June, August to November.

Rector: Dr. TOMÁS DIEGO BERNARD.

Vice-Rector: Dr. SALVADOR ROQUE PERROTTA.

Secretary-General: Dr. NORBERTO BENSEÑOR.

Librarian: ANA MARÍA LOCKART SIARRA.

Number of teachers: *c.* 55.
Number of students: *c.* 3,326.

Publications: *Cuadernos Notariales, Ediciones U.N.A.*

UNIVERSIDAD DE MENDOZA

DIAGONAL DAG HAMMARSKJÖLD 750,
5500 MENDOZA
Telephone: 247017.
Founded 1960.

Language of instruction: Spanish; Academic year: March to November.

Rector: Ing. SALVADOR PULIAFITO.

Vice-Rector: Dr. HECTOR CORVALÁN LIMA.

Administrative Officer: Mrs. AMÉRICA A. DE UMANSKY.

Number of teachers: 229.
Number of students: 1,932.

Publication: *Idearium*†.

DEANS:

Faculty of Law and Social Sciences: Dr. HECTOR CORVALÁN LIMA.

Faculty of Architecture and Town Planning: Arq. RICARDO BEKERMAN.

Faculty of Electronics and Electrical Engineering: Ing. CELESTE D'INCA.

UNIVERSIDAD "JUAN AGUSTÍN MAZA"

SALTA 1690-URQUIZA 350,
5500 MENDOZA
Telephone: 251998.
Founded 1960.

Language of instruction: Spanish; Private control; Academic year: April to March.

Rector: Ing. ROBERTO M. DE ROSSETTI.

Vice-Rector: Farm. JUAN FACUNDO CIVIT.

Secretary-General: Prof. ROLANDO ALBERTO LUCERO.

Librarian: HUGO ARMANDO COLL.

Number of teachers: 260.
Number of students: 875.

Publication: *Anuario de la Universidad "Juan Agustín Maza".*

DEANS:

Faculty of Engineering: Ing. JUAN CARLOS ZAPORTA.

Faculty of Pharmacy and Biochemistry: Farm. ANTONIO ANDRÉS GUYÓN.

Faculty of Physical Mathematical Sciences: Prof. JOSEFINA BERTA COSENTINO.

Technological Faculty of Oenology and Fruit Growing and Horticulture: Pbro. Enól. FRANCISCO OREGLIA.

Faculty of Journalism: Lic. TERESITA SALLENAVE DE SAGUI.

School of Nutrition: ANA B. YANELLI DE ARANITI.

UNIVERSIDAD DE MORÓN

CABILDO 134, MORÓN,
PROVINCIA DE BUENOS AIRES
Telephone: 629-2404/6127/6064.
Founded 1960.

Rector: Dr. EDMUNDO F. SAVASTANO.

Vice-Rector: Ing. SATURNINO S. ROCCHI.

Academic Secretary: Dr. ERNESTO O. PERALTA.

Administrative Secretary: Cont. JOSÉ ECHECHIQUÍA.

Library Director: LILIANA ELSA FICHTER.

Number of teachers: 1,350.
Number of students: 11,800.

Publications: *Revista de la Universidad*† (2 a year), *Periódico* (monthly).

DEANS AND DIRECTORS:

Faculty of Law and Social Sciences: Dr. ALBRANÉ H. MALCERVELLI.

Faculty of Engineering: Ing. CELESTINO MARCELINO ARCE.

Faculty of Exact, Chemical and Natural Sciences: Ing. ARIEL FELDSTEIN.

Faculty of Philosophy and Letters: Dra. DINA VICTORIA PICOTTI DE CAMARA.

Faculty of Agronomy: Ing. Agr. SATURNINO S. ROCCHI.

Faculty of Economics: Dr. ALFREDO J. BÓZZOLA.

Faculty of Architecture: Arq. ALVARO S. DE LA TORRE.

Higher Institute of Technology: Dr. PABLO F. M. ENNIS.

Higher Institute of Tourism: Prof. GUILLERMO MIERSCH.

Diocesan School of Social Service: Mons. GERARDO T. FARREL.

UNIVERSIDAD DEL NORTE SANTO TOMÁS DE AQUINO

C.P. 32,
SAN MIGUEL DE TUCUMÁN
Telephone: 27543.
Founded 1965.

Academic year: April to November.

Chancellor: Mgr. BLAS VICTORIO CONRERO, Archbishop of Tucumán.

Rector: R.P. Fr. Dr. ANÍBAL ERNESTO FÓSBERY, O.P.

Vice-Rector: R.P. Fr. Dr. LUIS SANTIAGO FERRO, O.P.

Secretary-General: Dr. OSCAR CARLOS D'AGOSTINO.

Director of the Library: HUGO ANTONIO BARBER.

Number of teachers: 235.
Number of students: 1,115.

DEANS:

Faculty of Humanities: Prof. MARY DEL VALLE YOSHIDA.

Faculty of Law and Social Sciences: Dr. ALBERTO GALLO CAINZO.

Faculty of Economics and Administration: Cont. ALFONSO MARCILLA.

Faculty of Industrial Engineering: Agr. CARLOS CÉSAR SALMORAIGHI.

Faculty of Business Administration: Dr. CARLOS FERMIN AGUILAR.

University Centre in Concepción: Ing. EDMUNDO NOÉ GRAMAJO.

UNIVERSIDAD DE LA PATAGONIA "SAN JUAN BOSCO"

GENERAL MOSCONI, COMODORO RIVADAVIA, PROVINCIA DEL CHUBUT
Telephone: 4248.
Founded 1961.
Academic year: April to December.

Chancellor: Dr. ARGIMIRO DANIEL MOURE.
Rector: Dr. LINO MARCOS BUDIÑO.
Registrar: Dr. PEDRO LUIS RONCHINO.
Librarian: Dr. MANUEL JESUS MOLINA.

Number of teachers: 114.
Number of students: 710.
Publication: *Anales.*

DEANS:

School of Sciences: Ing. SANTIAGO LUIS COSTA.
School of Humanities: Dr. OSVALDO FRANCELLA.

UNIVERSIDAD CATÓLICA DE SALTA
(Catholic University of Salta)

CIUDAD UNIVERSITARIA, CASTAÑARES, SALTA
Telephone: 19000.
Founded 1967.

Rector: Rev. GEORGE W. HAAS, S.J.
Secretary-General: Contador JOSÉ SAN FILIPPO.
Librarian: CONSUELO SCHUMANN.

Library of 18,000 vols.
Number of teachers: 90.

DEANS:

Faculty of Arts and Sciences: Lic. RODOLFO LEMOS MORGAN.
Faculty of Economics and Administration: Cont. GUSTAVO E. WIERNA.
Faculty of Engineering: Ing. EUGENIO MARTÍNEZ.
School of Social Service: Lic. CÉSAR LIZARDO SÁNCHEZ.
School of Law: Dr. CARLOS M. CORNEJO COSTAS.

UNIVERSIDAD CATÓLICA DE SANTA FÉ
(Catholic University of Santa Fé)

ECHAGÜE 7151, 3000 SANTA FÉ
Telephone: 63030.
Founded 1959.
Academic year: February to December.

Rector: Dr. LEO W. HILLAR PUXEDDU.
Vice-Rector: Dra. MABEL F. DE ARTEAGA MOSCA.
Secretary (Co-ordination and General Relations): Prof. MARIA DELFINA BARREIRO.
Librarian: Sra. NORA E. DE SALTO.

Number of teachers: 300.
Number of students: 1,782

DEANS:

Faculty of Law: Dr. CESAR REY LEYES.
Faculty of Economic Sciences: Cont. PEDRO BUCHARA.
Faculty of Education: Dra. MABEL F. DE ARTEAGA MOSCA.
Faculty of Philosophy: Pbro. ERNESTO LEYENDECKER.
Faculty of History: Dr. LEO W. HILLAR PUXEDDU.
Faculty of Letters: Prof. NIDIA BURIASSO.
Faculty of Architecture: (vacant).
Faculty of Soil Science: Lic. RODOLFO CALAMANTE.

UNIVERSIDAD CATÓLICA DE SANTIAGO DEL ESTERO

LIBERTAD 321, 4200 SANTIAGO DEL ESTERO
Telephone: 3820, 1579.
Founded 1960.

Rector: Mgr. Lic. LUCIANO BERETTA.
Administrative Director: Cont. CARLOS ALLONES.
Librarian: MIRTA VIZGARRA DE CASTRO.

Number of teachers: 219.
Number of students: 1,515.

DEANS:

Faculty of Politics, Social Sciences and Law: Dr. PEDRO MAXIMILIANO ARNEDO.
Faculty of Economics: Cont. LUIS RICARDO SUÁREZ.
Faculty of Education: Profa. MARÍA DEL VALLE SGOIFO.

DIRECTORS:

Department of Philosophy and Theology: R. P. CÉSAR ACOSTA.
Department of Applied Mathematics: Ing. GRACIELA BARCHINI DE GIMENEZ.

COLLEGES

Centro de Altos Estudios en Ciencias Exactas (*Centre of Advanced Studies in Exact Sciences*): Solis 550, Buenos Aires; f. 1968; private; Rector Dr. HORACIO E. BOSCH.

Escuela Argentina de Periodismo (*Argentine School of Journalism*): 1425-Santa Fé 4320, Buenos Aires; f. 1953 to train university students of journalism and professional journalists; "Mariano Moreno" library of over 1,500 vols.; Rector CARLOS JESÚS ABREGÚ; publ. *Periodismo.*

Escuela de Ciencias de la Administración (*School of Business Administration*): Perú Bernardo Irigoyen Concordia, Entre Rios; f. 1970.

Escuela Nacional de Educación Técnica: No. 1, Ruta Nacional No. 22, Plaza Huincul, Neuquén; f. 1953; 467 students; Dir. Ing. ARMANDO PARIS.

Escuela Nacional de Educación Técnica: No. 4, Lacarra 535, Buenos Aires.

Facultad de Ciencias Aplicadas a la Industria (*College of Applied Industrial Sciences*): Cnte. Salas 227, San Rafael, Mendoza; f. 1961; petrochemical and mineralurgical engineering and food technology; library of 1,580 vols.; Dir. JULIO A. MENDEZ.

Instituto Superior de Ciencias: General Paz 1010, Río Cuarto, Córdoba; f. 1959; 132 staff, 650 students; library of 4,550 vols.; Rector Prof. HÉCTOR S. TENAGLIA; Sec. ISIDRO A. CORDERO.

Instituto Superior de Ciencias Económicas de Jujuy (*Jujuy Higher Institute of Economic Sciences*): Otero 369, San Salvador de Jujuy; 35 mems.; Rector Dra. HILDA ELENA FERNÁNDEZ.

Instituto Superior del Hogar Agrícola "Ing. Agr. Dr. Tomás Amadeo" (*Higher Institute of Domestic Agriculture*): Casilla 59, 6550 Bolívar, Provincia de Buenos Aires; f. 1948; courses in agriculture and horticulture; 10 teachers, 80 students; Dir. Dra. AMELIA YUÑO.

Instituto Técnico Superior "Otto Krause": Paseo Colón 450, Buenos Aires.

Instituto Tecnológico de Buenos Aires: Avda. Emilio Madero 351/99, Buenos Aires; f. 1960; private; 140 teachers, 300 students; Rector Vice-Adml. CARLOS ALBERTO GARZONI.

SCHOOLS OF ART AND MUSIC

Buenos Aires

Conservatorio Municipal de Música "Manuel de Falla": Corrientes 1530, Teatro municipal; 1,500 mems.; Dir. AUGUSTO B. RATTENBACH.

Conservatorio Nacional de Música "Carlos López Buchardo" (*National Conservatoire of Music*): Callao 1521; f. 1924; library of 1,000 vols. and 12,000 musical scores; Rector MARÍA MAGDALENA GARCÍA ROBSON DE MOREIRA.

Escuela Nacional de Arte Dramático (*National School of Drama*): French 3614; f. 1924; 100 students; library of 1,900 vols.; Rector CAMILO DA PASANO; Sec. ESTER LÍA SOLOETA.

Escuela Nacional de Bellas Artes "Manuel Belgrano": Cerrito 1350; f. 1904; courses in fine and applied arts, history of art, psychology and pedagogics; 160 teachers, 1,000 students; library of 1,600 vols.; Dir. MARÍA L. SAN MARTIN.

Escuela Nacional de Bellas Artes "Prilidiano Pueyrredón": Las Heras 1749; f. 1905; Depts. of painting, engraving and sculpture; 373 students; library of 5,700 vols.; Dir. JORGE E. LEZAMA.

Escuela Superior de Bellas Artes "Ernesto de la Cárcova": Avda. Costanera Sur Esq. Brasil; f. 1923; painting, sculpture, engraving and décors; museum of tracings; 156 staff; library of 4,500 vols.; Rector Prof. JORGE E. LEZAMA.

AUSTRALIA

Population 14,248,500

ACADEMIES

AUSTRALIAN ACADEMY OF SCIENCE

P.O.B. 783, CANBERRA CITY, A.C.T. 2601.

Founded and incorporated by Royal Charter in 1954 to promote, declare and disseminate scientific knowledge; to establish and maintain standards of scientific endeavour and achievement in the natural sciences in Australia; and to recognize outstanding contributions to the advancement of science. The Academy took over the functions of the Australian National Research Council in 1955.

COUNCIL

President: Dr. L. T. EVANS, A.O., D.SC., F.R.S.

Treasurer: Dr. N. K. BOARDMAN, SC.D., F.R.S.

Secretary (Physical Sciences): Prof. N. H. FLETCHER, D.SC.

Secretary (Biological Sciences): Prof. R. PORTER, D.M., D.SC.

Foreign Secretary: Prof. G. L. ADA, D.SC.

Members: Prof. B. D. O. ANDERSON, PH.D., F.R.S.; Prof. A. R. H. COLE, D.PHIL.; Dr. H. J. FRITH, D.SC.AGR.; Prof. D. H. GREEN, PH.D.; Prof. M. HOLMAN, D.SC.; Prof. P. I. KORNER, M.D.; Prof. A. J. PITTARD, D.SC.; Prof. R. B. POTTS, D.SC.; Prof. J. M. SWAN, D.SC.; Prof. H. R. WALLACE, D.SC.

Executive Secretary: H. A. W. SOUTHON, M.A.

Publications: *Year Book, Records, Science and Industry Forum Reports, Reports, Conference Proceedings.*

FELLOWS:

ADA, GORDON LESLIE, D.SC.
ALBERT, ADRIEN, D.SC.
ANDERSON, BRIAN DAVID OUTRAM, PH.D.
ANDERSON, JOHN ROBERT, PH.D.
ANDERSON, JOHN STUART, PH.D., F.R.S.
ANDREWARTHA, HERBERT GEORGE, D.SC.
ANGYAL, STEPHEN JOHN, O.B.E., D.SC.

BADGER, Sir GEOFFREY MALCOLM, D.SC.
BARKER, JOHN ADAIR, D.SC.
BARNES, ERIC STEPHEN, PH.D.
BAXTER, Sir (JOHN) PHILIP, K.B.E., C.M.G., PH.D.
BAXTER, RODNEY JAMES, PH.D.
BAYLISS, Sir NOEL STANLEY, C.B.E., PH.D.
BECKWITH, ATHELSTAN LAURENCE JOHNSON, D.PHIL.
BENNETT, MARTIN ARTHUR, D.SC.
BIRCH, ARTHUR JOHN, PH.D., F.R.S.
BIRCH, LOUIS CHARLES, D.SC.
BISHOP, PETER ORLEBAR, M.B., B.S., D.SC.
BLANDEN, R. V., PH.D.
BLATT, JOHN MARKUS, PH.D.
BOARDMAN, NORMAN KEITH, SC.D., F.R.S.
BOAS, WALTER, DR.ING.
BOWEN, EDWARD GEORGE, C.B.E., PH.D.
BOYDEN, STEPHEN VICKERS, PH.D.
BROWN, ROBERT HANBURY, D.SC., F.R.S.
BROWN, RONALD DRAYTON, PH.D.
BUCHDAHL, HANS ADOLPH, D.SC.
BURNET, Sir (FRANK) MACFARLANE, O.M., K.B.E., M.D., F.R.S., Nobel Laureate
BURNSTOCK, GEOFFREY, D.SC.
BUTLER, STUART THOMAS, D.SC.

CATCHESIDE, DAVID GUTHRIE, D.SC., F.R.S.
CAVILL, GEORGE WILLIAM KENNETH, D.SC.
CHRISTIANSEN, WILBUR NORMAN, D.SC.
CLAREBROUGH, LEO MICHAEL, D.SC.
COLE, ANDREW REGINALD HOWARD, PH.D.
COMPSTON, WILLIAM, PH.D.
COOMBS, HERBERT COLE, PH.D.
COSTIN, ALEC BAILEE, D.SC.AGR.
COURTICE, FREDERICK COLIN, D.SC.
COWLEY, JOHN MAXWELL, D.SC.
CRAGG, BRIAN GASTOW, PH.D.
CRAIG, DAVID PARKER, D.SC., F.R.S.
CROMPTON, R. W., PH.D.
CURTIS, DAVID RODERICK, PH.D., F.R.S.

DAVIES, LOUIS WALTER, D.PHIL.
DAVIS, EDWARD HUGHESDON, B.SC.
DAY, MAXWELL FRANK COOPER, D.PHIL.
DENTON, D. A., M.B.B.S.
DICK, ALEXANDER THOMAS, O.B.E., D.SC.
DONALD, COLIN MALCOLM, C.B.E., D.SC.AGR.

ECCLES, Sir JOHN (CAREW), Kt., D.PHIL., F.R.S., Nobel Laureate
ELLIOTT, WILLIAM HERDMAN ,PH.D.
ELLIS, GRAEME READE ANTHONY, PH.D.
EMMENS, CLIFFORD WALTER, D.SC.
EVANS, LLOYD THOMAS, D.SC., F.R.S.

FAZEKAS DE ST. GROTH, STEPHEN NICHOLAS EMERY EGON M.D.
FENNER, FRANK JOHN, C.M.G., M.B.E., M.D., F.R.S.
FLETCHER, NEVILLE HORNER, D.SC.
FORREST, Sir JAMES ALEXANDER, Kt.
FRANKEL, Sir OTTO (HERZBERG), Kt., D.SC., F.R.S.
FRASER, ALEX STEWART, PH.D.
FRASER, ROBERT DONALD BRUCE, D.SC.

GAGE, PETER WILLIAM, PH.D.
GANI, JOSEPH MARK, D.SC.
GASCOIGNE, SIDNEY CHARLES BARTHOLOMEW, PH.D.
GIBSON, FRANK WILLIAM ERNEST, D.PHIL., F.R.S.
GIOVANELLI, RONALD GORDON, D.SC.
GLAESSNER, MARTIN FRITZ, D.SC.
GREEN, DAVID HEADLEY, PH.D.
GREEN, HERBERT SYDNEY, D.SC.
GUNNING, B. E. S., D.SC.

HALES, ANTON L., PH.D.
HALPERN, BERTHOLD, PH.D.
HAMANN, SEFTON DAVIDSON, PH.D.
HANNAN, EDWARD JAMES, PH.D.
HAYES, WILLIAM, SC.D., F.R.S.
HEAD, ALAN KENNETH, D.SC.
HEYDE, CHRISTOPHER CHARLES, D.SC.
HILL, DOROTHY, C.B.E., D.SC., F.R.S.
HILLS, EDWIN SHERBON, D.SC., F.R.S.
HOLDEN, GEORGE, K.B.E., D.PHIL.
HOLLOWAY, B. W., D.SC.
HOLMAN, MOLLIE ELIZABETH, D.SC.
HORRIDGE, GEORGE ADRIAN, PH.D., F.R.S.
HURLEY, ANDREW CROWTHER, PH.D.
HURST, CHARLES ANGAS, PH.D.
HUSH, NOEL SYDNEY, D.SC.
HUXLEY, Sir LEONARD
HYDE, BRUCE GODFREY, D.SC.

JORDAN, DENIS OSWALD, D.SC.

KELLY, GREGORY MAXWELL, PH.D.
KERR, ALLEN, PH.D.
KEY, KENNETH HEDLEY LEWIS, D.SC.
KORNER, PAUL IVAN, M.D.

LAMPARD, DOUGLAS GEOFFREY, PH.D.
LANCASTER, HENRY OLIVER, M.D., D.SC.
LANCE, JAMES WALDO, M.D.
LAW, PHILLIP GARTH, C.B.E., D.APP.SC.
LE COUTEUR, KENNETH JAMES, PH.D.
LE FEVRE, RAYMOND JAMES WOOD, D.SC., F.R.S.
LEVICK, WILLIAM RUSSELL, M.SC.

Linnane, Anthony William, ph.d., f.r.s.
Lyons, Lawrence Ernest, d.sc.

McIntyre, Archibald Keverall, d.sc.
Macfarlane, Walter Victor, m.d.
Mahler, Kurt, d.sc., f.r.s.
Mahony, John Joseph, ph.d.
Main, Albert Russell, ph.d.
Mark, Richard Freeman.
Martin, Sir Leslie (Harold), Kt., c.b.e., ph.d., f.r.s.
Martin, Raymond Leslie, sc.d.
Mathieson, Alexander McLeod, d.sc.
McLennan, Sir Ian (Munro), g.c.m.g., k.b.e., b.e.e.
Metcalf, Donald, m.d.
Meyer, Richard Ernst, dr.sc.techn.
Michael, James Henry, ph.d.
Miller, Jacques Francis Albert Pierre, d.sc., f.r.s.
Mills, Bernard Yarnton, d.sc.eng., f.r.s.
Minnett, Harry Clive, o.b.e., b.e.
Moodie, Alexander Forbes, b.sc.
Moran, Patrick Alfred Pierce, d.sc., f.r.s.
Morris, Bede, d.phil.
Morrison, James Douglas, d.sc.

Neumann, Bernhard Hermann, d.sc., f.r.s.
Newton, John Oswald, d.sc.
Ninham, Barry William, ph.d.
Norrish, Keith, ph.d.
Nossal, Sir Gustav (Joseph Victor), c.b.e., ph.d.

Ogston, Alexander George, d.phil., f.r.s.
Oliphant, Sir Mark (Laurence Elwin), k.b.e. k.st.j., d.sc., f.r.s.
Öpik, Armin Alexander, d.phil.nat.
Osmond, Charles Barry, ph.d.

Paltridge, Garth William, d.sc.
Parker, A. J., ph.d.
Pate, John Stewart, d.sc.
Paterson, Mervyn Silas, sc.d.
Peacock, William James, ph.d.
Philip, John Robert, d.sc., f.r.s.
Piddington, John Hobart, ph.d.
Pitman, Edwin James George, m.a., d.sc.
Pittard, Alfred James, d.sc.
Porter, Robert, d.m., d.sc.
Potts, Renfrey Burnard, d.sc.
Prescott, James Arthur, c.b.e., d.sc., f.r.s.
Price, Sir James Robert, k.b.e., d.sc.
Priestley, Charles Henry Brian, sc.d., f.r.s.

Quirk, James Patrick, d.sc.

Rees, Albert Lloyd George, c.b.e., d.sc.
Rendel, James Meadows, ph.d.
Ringwood, Alfred Edward, ph.d., f.r.s.
Robertson, Sir Rutherford Ness, Kt., c.m.g., d.sc., f.r.s.
Robinson, Brian John, ph.d.
Robinson, Derek William, d.phil.
Roderick, Jack William, ph.d.
Rogers, George Ernest, ph.d.
Rogers, William Percy, d.sc.
Room, Thomas Gerald, sc.d., f.r.s.
Ross, Ian Gordon, ph.d.

Sanders, John Veysey, ph.d.
Sargeson, Alan McLeod, ph.d.
Sharman, Geoffrey Bruce, d.sc.
Shoppee, Charles William, d.sc., f.r.s.
Slatyer, Ralph Owen, d.sc.(agric.), f.r.s.
Smith-White, Spencer, d.sc.agr.
Solomon, David Henry, d.sc.
Sprent, John Frederick Adrian, d.sc.
Stacey, F. D., d.sc.
Stanton, Richard Limon, ph.d.
Stokes, Robert Harold, d.sc.
Street, Robert, d.sc.
Sunderland, Sir Sydney, Kt., c.m.g., m.d., d.sc.
Swan, John Melvin, d.sc.
Swinbank, William Christopher, d.sc.
Szekeres, George, d.sc.

Tanner, R. I., ph.d.
Taylor, Stuart Ross, d.sc.
Thompson, Arthur Melville, b.sc.
Titterton, Sir Ernest (William), Kt., c.m.g., ph.d.
Trikojus ,Victor Martin, c.b.e., d.sc.
Trudinger, Neil Sydney, ph.d.
Turner, Arthur William, o.b.e., d.sc., d.v.sc.
Turner, John Stewart, ph.d.

Underwood, Eric John, c.b.e., ph.d., f.r.s.

Wall, Gordon Elliott, ph.d.
Wallace, Henry Robert, d.sc.
Walsh, Sir Alan, d.sc., f.r.s.
Walsh, Robert John, o.b.e., f.r.a.c.p.
Wardrop, Alan Buchanan, d.sc.
Waring, Horace, d.sc.
Wark, Sir Ian (William), Kt., c.m.g., c.b.e., d.sc.
Waterhouse, Douglas Frew, c.m.g., d.sc., f.r.s.
Watson, Irvine Armstrong, c.b.e., ph.d.
Watson-Munro, Charles Norman, o.b.e., d.sc.
Weiss, Donald Eric, o.b.e., d.sc.
Wharton, Ronald Harry, ph.d.
Whelan, Robert Ford, m.d., d.sc.
White, Sir Frederick (William George), k.b.e., ph.d., f.r.s.
White, Guy Kendall, d.phil.
White, Michael James Denham, d.sc., f.r.s.
Wild, John Paul, c.b.e., sc.d., f.r.s.
Williams, William Thomas, d.sc.
Wittrick, William Henry, sc.d.
Womersley, Hugh Bryan Spencer, d.sc.
Woolley, Sir Richard (van der Riet), Kt., o.b.e., ph.d., f.r.s.
Worner, Howard Knox, c.b.e., d.sc.

AUSTRALIAN ACADEMY OF THE HUMANITIES

G.P.O. BOX 93, CANBERRA, A.C.T. 2600

Founded and incorporated by Royal Charter in 1969 for the advancement of scholarship and of interest in an understanding of the Humanities, that is to say, in Language, Literature, History, Philosophy and the Fine Arts.

Council

President: Prof. Wang Gungwu, ph.d.

Secretary: Prof. E. Kamenka, ph.d.

Treasurer: Prof. R. W. V. Elliott, m.a.

Editor: Prof. G. A. Wilkes, d.phil.

Members: I. P. Barko, R. A. Bauman, C. I. E. Donaldson, J. P. Hardy, A. H. Johns, O. M. Roe.

Publications: *Proceedings, Monographs, Occasional Papers.*

Fellows

Anderson, Gordon Athel, d.mus.
Armstrong, David Malet, ph.d.
Auchmuty, James Johnston, c.b.e., ph.d., m.r.i.a., f.r.hist.s., f.i.a.l.
‡Aurousseau, Marcel, m.c., d.litt., f.r.g.s.
‡Bailey, Sir Harold Walter, Kt., d.litt., f.b.a.
Bauman, Richard Alexander, ph.d.
Barko, Ivan Peter, lic.phil. & lett., d.u.
Barnard, Noel, ph.d.
Basham, Arthur Llewellyn, d.lit., f.r.a.s., f.s.a.
Benn, Stanley Isaac, b.sc.(econ.), f.a.s.s.a.
‡Bissell, Claude Thomas, d.litt., ll.d, f.r.s., (can.).
Blainey, Geoffrey Norman, m.a., f.a.s.s.a.
Bolton, Geoffrey Curgenven, d.phil., f.r.hist.s., f.a.s.s.a.
Bowman, John, d.phil., f.r.a.s.
Brissenden, Robert Francis, ph.d.
‡Brown, Philip Lawrence, b.a.
Brown, Robert, ph.d., f.a.s.s.a.
Burke, Sir Joseph Terence, k.b.e., m.a., f.a.s.s.a.

Cambitoglou, Alexander ,d.phil.
Campbell, Keith Kennedy, b.phil.
‡Capell, Arthur, ph.d.
Chambers, Leigh Ross, d.de l'u.
Chisholm, Alan Rowland, o.b.e., officier de la légion d'honneur, cavaliere dell' ordine al merito, b.a.
‡Christesen, Clement, o.b.e., d.litt.
Clark, Charles manning Hope, m.a., f.a.s.s.a.
Clarke, Graeme Wilber, m.a.
Coe, Richard Nelson, ph.d.
Collinson, Patrick, ph.d., f.r.hist.s.
Colmer, John Anthony, ph.d.
‡Coombs, Herbert Cole, d.litt., ll.d., f.a.a.
‡Cowen, Sir Zelman, a.k., g.c.m.g., g.c.v.o., k.st.j., q.c.
Crawford, Raymond Maxwell, c.b.e., m.a.
Crowley, Francis Keble, ph.d.
Culican, William, m.a.

DE BRAY, REGINALD GEORGE ARTHUR, PH.D.
DE JONG, JAN WILLEM, DR.PHIL
DE RACHEWILTZ, IGOR, PH.D.
DONALDSON, CHARLES IAN EDWARD, M.A.

EDWARDS, WILLIAM ALLAN, M.A.
ELLIOTT, BRIAN ROBINSON, D.LITT., D.U.
ELLIOTT, RALPH WARREN VICTOR, M.A.
ELLIS, BRIAN DAVID, B.PHIL.

FARRELL, RALPH BARSTOW, DAS GROSSE VERDIENSTKREUZ DES VERDIENSTORDENS DER BUNDESREPUBLIK DEUTSCHLAND, DR.PHIL.
FENNELL, TREVOR GARTH, D. DE L'U.
FITZGERALD, CHARLES PATRICK, LITT.D., F.A.S.S.A.
FITZPATRICK, KATHLEEN ELIZABETH, M.A., F.A.C.E.
FORSYTH, ELLIOTT CHRISTOPHER, D.DE L'U., F.A.C.E.
FRENCH, ALFRED, M.A.
FRODSHAM, JOHN DAVID, PH.D.

GASKING, DOUGLAS AIDAN TRIST, M.A.
GELLIE, GEORGE HENRY, M.A.
GODDARD, LEONARD, M.A.
GOLDBERG, SAMUEL LOUIS, B.LITT.
GOLLAN, ROBIN ALLENBY, PH.D.
GOLSON, JACK, M.A.
GREENWOOD, GORDON, PH.D., F.A.S.S.A.

HALLAM, HERBERT ENOCH, PH.D., F.R.HIST.S.
HALLIDAY, MICHAEL ANGUS KIRKWOOD, PH.D.
HANCOCK, Sir (WILLIAM) KEITH, K.B.E., CAVALIERE UFFICIALE DELL' ORDINE AL MERITO, D.LITT., F.B.A.
HARDY, JOHN PHILIPS, M.A.
‡HASLUCK, Sir PAUL (MEERNAA CAEDWALLA), G.C.M.G., G.C.V.O., K.ST.J., M.A.
HERCUS, LUISE A., PH.D.
HO, PENG YOKE, PH.D., D.SC., F.INST.P.
HOFF, URSULA, O.B.E., D.LITT., F.M.A.
HOPE, ALEX DERWENT, O.B.E., LITT.D.
HORNE, COLIN JAMES, M.LITT., A.M.

INGLIS, KENNETH STANLEY, D.PHIL., F.A.S.S.A.

‡JEFFARES, ALEXANDER NORMAN, D.PHIL., F.R.S.L., F.R.S.A.
JOHNS, ANTHONY HEARLE, PH.D.

KAMENKA, EUGENE, PH.D., F.A.S.S.A.
KELLER, ERNEST, PH.D.
KIRSOP, WALLACE, D. DE L'U.
KRAMER, LEONIE JUDITH, D.PHIL., M.A.C.E.

LA NAUZE, JOHN ANDREW, LITT.D., F.A.S.S.A.
LAWLER, JAMES RONALD, D. DE L'U.
LAYCOCK, DONALD CLARENCE, PH.D.
LIU, TS'UN-YAN, D.LIT., F.R.A.S.
LOW, DONALD ANTHONY, D.PHIL., F.A.S.S.A.

MCAULEY, JAMES PHILLIP, M.A.
MCBRYDE, ISABEL, PH.D., F.R.A.I., F.S.A.
MCCLOSKEY, HENRY JOHN, PH.D.
MCCREDIE, ANDREW DALGARNO, M.A., D.PHIL.
MACDONAGH, OLIVER ORMOND GERARD, PH.D.
‡MCMANNERS, JOHN, OFFICER OF THE ORDER OF KING GEORGE OF THE HELLENES, M.A., F.R.HIST.S.
MARES, FRANCIS HUGH, M.A.
MARSH, DERICK RUPERT CLEMENT, PH.D.
MILGATE, WESLEY, M.A.
MITCHELL, ALEXANDER GEORGE, PH.D., C.B.E.
MONRO, DAVID HECTOR, M.A., F.A.S.S.A.
MOWATT, DAVID GUTHRIE, PH.D.
MULVANEY, DEREK JOHN, PH.D., F.S.A.
‡MYER, KENNETH BAILLIEU, D.S.C., F.A.S.S.A.

NERLICH, GRAHAM CHARLES, D.PHIL.

O'FARRELL, PATRICK JAMES, PH.D.
OLIVER, HAROLD JAMES, M.A.
OSBORN, ERIC FRANCIS, PH.D.

PARTRIDGE, PERCY HERBERT, M.A., F.A.S.S.A.
PASSMORE, JOHN ARTHUR, M.A., F.A.S.S.A.
PATRICK, ALISON, PH.D.
POYNTER, JOHN RIDDOCH, PH.D., F.A.S.S.A.

RITCHIE, WILLIAM, PH.D.
RIZVI, SAIYID ATHAR ABBAS, D.LITT.
ROBINSON, JUDITH OGILVIE, D. DE L'U., D. ÈS L.
ROE, OWEN MICHAEL, PH.D.
ROSE, ROBERT BARRIE, M.A.
ROUTLEY, RICHARD, M.A.
RUDÉ, GEORGE FREDERICK ELLIOT, D.LITT., F.R.HIST.S.
RUSSELL, GEORGE HARRISON, PH.D.
RYCKMANS, PIERRA, PH.D.

SAMUEL, RICHARD HERBERT, DAS GROSSE VERDIENSTKREUZ DES VERDIENSTORDENS DER BUNDESREPUBLIK DEUTSCHLAND, DR. PHIL., F.A.C.E.
SCHULZ, GERHARD ERNST OTTO, DR.PHIL.
SERLE, ALAN GEOFFREY, D.PHIL., F.A.S.S.A.
SHAW, ALAN GEORGE LEWERS, M.A., F.A.S.S.A.
SHIPP, GEORGE PELHAM, D.LITT.
SINCLAIR, KEITH VAL, LITT.D., F.S.A.
SMART, JOHN JAMIESON CARSWELL, B.PHIL.
SMIT, JACOB, OFFICER IN THE ORDER OF ORANGE NASSAU, D.LITT.
SMITH, BERNARD WILLIAM, PH.D., F.S.A.
SMITH, FRANCIS BARRYMORE, PH.D.
SPATE, OSKAR HERMAN KHRISTIAN, PH.D., F.A.S.S.A.
STEPHENS, ANTHONY RENWICK, PH.D.
STOUT, ALAN KER, M.A., F.A.S.S.A.
STOVE, DAVID CHARLES, B.A.
STRETTON, HUGH, M.A., F.A.S.S.A.
‡SUSSEX, RONALD THOMAS, M.A., D.LITT.

TAUMAN, LEON, D.ÈS L.
TOMORY, PETER, M.A.
TRENDALL, ARTHUR DALE, C.M.G., K.C.S.G., COMMENDATORE DELL' ORDINE AL MERITO, D.LITT., F.S.A., F.B.A.
TRIEBEL, LOUIS AUGUSTUS, D.LITT.
TUNLEY, DAVID EVATT, D.LITT.
TURNER, GEORGE WILLIAM, M.A.

WANG, GUNGWU, PH.D.
WARD, JOHN MANNING, M.A., LL.B., F.A.S.S.A., F.R.A.H.S.
WEAVER, PAUL RICHARD CARY, PH.D.
WEST, FRANCIS JAMES, PH.D., F.R.HIST.S.
‡WHITE, Sir HAROLD (LESLIE), Kt., C.B.E., M.A., F.L.A.A., F.A.S.S.A.
WILKES, GERALD ALFRED, D.PHIL.
WILLIS, JAMES, PH.D.
WILSON, TREVOR GORDON, D.PHIL., F.R.HIST.S.
WRIGHT, JUDITH ARUNDELL, D.LITT.
WURM, STEPHEN ADOLPHE, DR.PHIL., F.A.S.S.A.

YOUNGSON, ALEXANDER JOHN, D.LITT., F.A.S.S.A.

‡ Hon. Fellow.

ACADEMY OF THE SOCIAL SCIENCES IN AUSTRALIA

NATIONAL LIBRARY BUILDING,
CANBERRA, A.C.T. 2600

Founded in 1952 as the Social Science Research Council of Australia, name changed 1971. Its functions are the promotion of research and teaching in the Social Sciences, to assist in the publication of research, to provide advisory services, and to maintain contacts with international organizations of social scientists.

EXECUTIVE COMMITTEE

President: Prof. A. G. L. SHAW.

Director: Emer. Prof. W. D. BORRIE.

Treasurer: Prof. J. D. B. MILLER.

Members: Prof. D. A. AITKIN, Prof. H. C. BROOKFIELD, Prof. N. T. FEATHER, Prof. FAY GALE, Prof. F. H. G. GRUEN, Dr. J. P. KEEVES, Prof. P. LAWRENCE.

Publications: *Annual Report*, sponsored research.

FELLOWS

AITKIN, D. A.
ALEXANDER, F.
ANDREWS, J.
APPLEYARD, R. T.
ARGY, V. E.
ARNDT, H. W.
BARNES, J. A.
BEDDIE, B. D.
BENN, S. I.
BERNDT, R. M.
BLAINEY, G. N.
BOLTON, G. C.
BORRIE, W. D.
BOURKE, P.
BOWEN, I.
BOXER, A. H.
BRENNAN, T.
BROOKFIELD, H. C.
BROOM, L.
BROWN, P. R.
BROWN, R. G.
BROWN, R. R.
BULL, H. N.
BURNS, A. L.
BURTON, H.
CALDWELL, J. C.
CAMERON, B. D.
CAMPBELL, E.
CAMPBELL, K. O.
CAPELL, A.
CHAMBERS, R. J.
CHAMPION, R. A.
CLARK, C. G.
CLARK, C. M. H.
COCHRANE, D.
CONNELL, W. F.

Coombs, H. C.
Corden, W. M.
Cowen, Sir Zelman
Crawford, Sir John
Crittenden, B. S.
Davies, A. F.
Davis, S. R.
Day, R. H.
Derham, Sir David
Dillon, J. L.
Dunn, S. S.
Edwards, H. R.
Feather, N. T.
Fisk, E. K.
Fitzgerald, C. P.
Ford, H. A. J.
Gale, Fay
Gates, R. C.
Geddes, W. R.
Gibb, C. A.
Glow, P. H.
Goldberg, L.
Goodnow, J.
Grant, J. McB.
Greenwood, G.
Gregory, R. G.
Gruen, F. H. G.
Hancock, K. J.
Harcourt, G. C.
Harper, N. D.
Hasluck, Sir Paul
Henderson, R. F.
Hiatt, L. R.
Hogbin, I.
Howard, C.
Hughes, C. A.
Inglis, K. S.
Isaac, J. E.
Jarrett, F. G.
Jayawardena, C.
Jones, F. L.
Kakwani, N. C.
Kamenka, E.
Karmel, P. H.
Keats, J. A.
Keesing, R. M.
Keeves, J. P.
La Nauze, J. A.
Lawrence, P.
Lawton, G. H.
Legge, J. D.
Lloyd, P. J.
Logan, M. I.
Loveday, P.
Lovibond, S. H.
Low, D. A.
McBriar, A. M.
MacDonagh, O. O. G. M.
McGee, T. G.
Mackie, J. A. C.
Mann, L.
Martin, A. W.
Mathews, R. L.
Mayer, H.
Melville, Sir Leslie
Miller, J. D. B.
Monro, D. H.
Munn, N. L.
Musgrave, P. W.
Myer, K.
Neale, R. G.
Neutze, G. M.
Nevile, J. W.
Oeser, O. A.
O'Neil, W. M.
O'Neill, R. J.
Over, R.
Parker, R. S.
Partridge, P. H.
Passmore, J. A.
Perkins, J. O. N.
Pitchford, J. D.
Pollard, A. H.
Pollard, J. H.
Powell, A. A. L.
Poynter, J. R.
Prescott, J. R. V.
Prest, W.
Price, C. A.
Rawson, D. W.
Reay, Marie
Rigby, T. H.
Ross, J.
Rowley, C. D.
Russell, R. W.
Ruzicka, L. T.
Ryan, K. W.
Sackville, R.
Sawer, G.
Scott, P.
Scott, W. A.
Selleck, R. J. W.
Serle, A. G.
Shatwell, K. O.
Shaw, A. G. L.
Sheehan, P. W.
Simkin, G. G. F.
Sinclair, W. A.
Smith, R. H. T.
Smolicz, J. J.
Snape, R. H.
Spann, R. N.
Spate, O. H. K.
Spearritt, D.
Stanner, W. E. H.
Stoljar, S. J.
Stone, J. O.
Stone, Julius
Stout, A. K.
Stretton, H.
Sutcliffe, J. P.
Taft, R.
Turner, L. C. F.
Turnovsky, S. J.
Vickers, D.
Walker, K. F.
Wallace, R. H.
Waller, P. L.
Ward, J. M.
Ward, R. G.
Welford, A. T.
White, Sir Harold
Williams, Sir Bruce
Wilson, Sir Roland
Wright, F. K.
Wurm, S.
Youngson, A. J.
Zubrzycki, J.

AUSTRALIAN ACADEMY OF TECHNOLOGICAL SCIENCES

191 ROYAL PARADE, PARKVILLE, VIC. 3052

Founded in 1976 to promote the application of scientific knowledge to practical purposes and to provide a forum for discussion and advice to government and the community in relation to the application of scientific knowledge; to initiate and sponsor multi-disciplinary studies; to encourage research and education in technological sciences; to provide an incentive for the pursuit of technological sciences; to develop an effective liaison with other Australian Academies; to collaborate with professional institutes and other learned societies and education institutions; to establish and maintain relations between the Academy and overseas bodies having the same objectives as the Academy.

Council

President: Sir Ian McLennan, K.C.M.G., K.B.E., F.A.A.

Vice-Presidents: Dr. K. T. H. Farrer, O.B.E., Sir David Zeidler, C.B.E.

Hon. Secretary: Dr. H. K. Worner, C.B.E., F.A.A.

Hon. Treasurer: Sir John Holland.

Members: Prof. G. A. Bird, Dr. B. D. Booth, Dr. L. W. Davies, A.O., F.A.A., Dr. R. G. Downes, C.B., Dr. R. A. Durie, Dr. J. L. Farrands, J. E. Kolm, Dr. Nancy F. Millis, M.B.E., Prof. D. E. Tribe, O.B.E., Dr. D. E. Weiss, O.B.E., F.A.A.

Executive Officer: Miss B. E. Jacka, A.M., M.B.E.

Publications: *Annual Report, Handbook, Symposia Series* (Resources of Australia), *Innovation in Australian Technology.*

Royal Fellow

H.R.H. The Prince Philip, Duke of Edinburgh, K.G., K.T., G.B.E., O.M., F.R.S., F.A.A.

Honorary Fellows

Oliphant, Sir Mark, A.C., K.B.E., M.A., PH.D., F.A.A., F.R.S.
Butement, Dr. W. A. S., C.B.E., D.SC.
Cowen, Sir Zelman, A.K., G.C.M.G., K.ST.J., Q.C., F.A.S.S.A.

Fellows:

Alder, K. F., M.SC.
Allen, J. A., M.SC., PH.D.

Badger, Sir Geoffrey, A.O., PH.D., D.SC., F.A.A.
Barton, Sir Charles, O.B.E., E.D., B.E.
Baxter, Sir Philip, K.B.E., C.M.G., PH.D., F.A.A.
Billings, A. R., PH.D.
Bird, G. A., M.E., PH.D.
Blackwood, Sir Robert, M.C.E., B.E.E.
Bolto, B. A., PH.D.
Booth, B. D., PH.D.
Bowen, B. K., B.SC.
Bradshaw, A. V., B.SC., A.R.S.M.
Brett, P. R., B.SC.
Butcher, A. Dunbavin, C.M.G., M.SC.

Callcott, T. G., D.APP.SC.
Callinan, Sir Bernard, C.B.E., D.S.O., M.C., B.C.E.
Chaikin, M., O.B.E., PH.D., DIP.ENG.
Christian, C. S., C.M.G., M.S.
Christian, J. H. B., PH.D.
Clark, Sir Lindesay, A.C., K.B.E., C.M.G., M.C., B.SC., M.M.E.
Clements, F. W., O.B.E., M.D., B.S., D.T.M., D.P.H.
Connolly, Sir Willis, C.B.E., B.E.E., B.COMM.
Coombes, L. P., C.B.E., D.F.C., B.SC.ENG.
Cuming, M. A., C.M.G., B.SC., D.I.C.
Cumming, R. W., A.M., M.E.
Curtis, J. H., B.SC., B.E., B.A.

Davies, L. W., A.O., D.PHIL., F.A.A.
Dewar, R. A., M.SC.
Dick, Miss M. I. B., M.SC.
Downes, R. G., C.B., D.AGR.SC.
Dun, R. B. M., PH.D.
Durie, R. A., PH.D., D.SC., D.I.C.

Espie, Sir Frank, O.B.E., B.E., F.S.A.S.M.

Farrands, J. L., PH.D., D.I.C.
Farrer, K. T. H., O.B.E., D.SC., M.A.
Ferguson, K. A., PH.D.
Fink, P. T., C.B.E., B.E.
Fisher, Sir George, C.M.G., B.E.(MIN.).
Fleming, I. B., O.B.E., M.SC.
Foots, Sir James, B.M.E.
Ford, D. L., A.S.T.C., M.SC., PH.D.
Fraser, A. McD., PH.D., D.I.C.
Fraser, R. D. L., I.S.O.
Frith, H. J., A.O., D.SC.AGR., F.A.A.

George, D. W., A.O., PH.D.
Gibbs, W. J., O.B.E., M.SC., S.M.

GILMOUR, A. J., PH.D.
GLADSTONES, J. S., PH.D.
GREEN, Maj.-Gen. K. D., O.B.E., E.D., B.C.E.

HALLSWORTH, E. G., PH.D., D.SC.
HAMER, A. W., B.SC., M.A.
HENRY, R. W., C.B.E., B.SC.
HENZELL, E. F., D.PHIL.
HEPBURN, J. A.
HIGGINS, H. G., D.APP.SC.
HOLLAND, Sir JOHN, B.C.E.
HUNT, K. H., M.A., M.MECH.E.

JOUBERT, P. N., B.E.

KARBOWIAK, A. E., PH.D., D.SC.(ENG.)
KELSALL, D. F., M.A., PH.D.
KIRKWOOD, J. B., A.S.T.C.
KNIGHT, Sir ALLAN, C.M.G., M.E., B.SC., B.COMM.
KOLM, J. E., ING.CHEM.

LANSDOWN, R. B., C.B.E., B.EC.
LAW, P. G., A.O., C.B.E., M.SC.
LAZENBY, A., M.SC., PH.D., M.A.
LIPSON, M., PH.D.
LONERAGAN, J. F., PH.D.
LYNCH, A. J., PH.D., D.SC.

MACKAY, B. H., B.SC.
MADIGAN, R. T., O.B.E., M.E., LL.B., F.S.A.S.M.
MATHESON, Sir LOUIS, K.B.E., C.M.G., M.SC., PH.D.
MCCRACKEN, K. G., PH.D., D.SC.
MCCUTCHEON, Sir OSBORN.
MCLENNAN, Sir IAN, K.C.M.G., K.B.E., F.A.A., B.E.E.
MESSERLE, H. K., M.ENG.SC., PH.D., D.SC.
MILLINGTON, R. J., M.SC., PH.D.
MILLIS, NANCY F., M.B.E., M.AGR.SC., PH.D.
MINNETT, K. C., O.B.E., F.A.A., B.SC., B.E.
MORLEY, F. H. W., PH.D.
MORSE, R. N., A.O., B.SC., B.E.
MUNCEY, R. W. R., M.E.E., D.APP.SC.
MURRAY, K. E., D.SC.
MYERS, R. H., C.B.E., M.SC., PH.D.

NEWNHAM, I. E., M.B.E., M.SC.
NIXON, J. C., PH.D.

OLLEY, JUNE N., PH.D., D.SC.

PARBO, Sir ARVI, B.E.
PEARSON, A. J., M.SC.
PERRY, R. A., M.SC.
PICKERING, R. W., M.SC., PH.D., D.I.C.
POLMEAR, I. J., M.SC., D.ENG.
POSSINGHAM, J. V., M.SC., D.PHIL., D.SC.

PRICE, D. G., B.E.
PRYOR, L. D., D.SC.

RALPH, B. J. F., PH.D.
RANKINE, B. C., M.SC., D.SC.(AG.).
RICHARDS, P. N., M.E., D.APP.SC.
RIGBY, G. A., M.SC., PH.D.
RODERICK, J. W., M.A., M.SC., PH.D., F.A.A.
ROSSITER, R. C., D.SC.(AGRIC.).
RUDD, E. A., B.SC., A.M.

SCHAETZEL, S. S., B.SC., D.I.C.
SCOTT, W. J., D.SC.
SEIDLER, H., O.B.E., M.ARCH.
SOLOMON, D. H., A.S.T.C., PH.D., D.SC., F.A.A.
SOMERSET, Sir HENRY, C.B.E., M.SC.
STERN, L., DIPL.AERO.ENG.
STRATH, J. A. W., B.SC., M.A.

TANNER, R. I., M.S., PH.D., F.A.A.
TAYLOR, D. S., PH.D.
TAYLOR, G. H., M.SC., D.SC., DR.RER.NAT.
TEGART, W. J. MCG., M.SC., PH.D.
TRACEY, M. V., A.O., M.A.
TRIBE, D. E., O.B.E., PH.D., D.AGR.SC.
TURNER, HELEN NEWTON, O.B.E., D.SC.

UNDERWOOD, E. J., A.O., C.B.E., PH.D., D.SC.AGR., F.A.A., F.R.S.

VERNON, Sir JAMES, A.C., C.B.E., PH.D.
VICKERY, J. R., O.B.E., M.SC., PH.D.
VINCENT, J. M., D.SC.(AG.).

WALLS, G. W., D.SC.
WARD, R. G., M.A., PH.D.
WARK, Sir IAN, C.M.G., C.B.E., PH.D., D.SC., F.A.A.
WARRELL, E. G., M.C.E.
WATSON, I. A., C.B.E., PH.D., F.A.A.
WATT, J. S., M.SC.
WEICKHARDT, L. E., C.B.E., M.SC.
WEISS, D. E., O.B.E., D.SC., F.A.A.
WHITTON, W. I., M.SC., PH.D.
WILD, J. P., C.B.E., M.A., SC.D., F.R.S., F.A.A.
WILLIAMS, L. S., D.PHIL.
WILLS, H. A., O.B.E., B.E.
WILSON, A. R. W., M.SC., PH.D.
WILTSHIRE, Sir FREDERICK, C.B.E., B.A.
WINSTON, D., C.B.E., A.M.
WOODALL, R., M.SC.
WOODS, M. W., O.B.E., D.PHIL.
WORNER, H. K., C.B.E., D.SC., F.A.A.
WORNER, H. W., D.SC.

ZEIDLER, Sir DAVID, C.B.E., M.SC.

LEARNED SOCIETIES

AGRICULTURE AND VETERINARY SCIENCE

Australian Agricultural Council: Commonwealth Dept. of Primary Industry, Canberra, A.C.T.; f. 1934 to provide means for regular consultation between individual States and Commonwealth in respect of agricultural production and marketing (excluding forestry and fisheries), to promote the welfare and standards of Australian agricultural industries and to foster the adoption of national policies in regard to these industries; 9 mems. comprising the 6 State Ministers for Agriculture and the Government Ministers for Commonwealth and the Northern Territory; Chair. the Commonwealth Minister for Primary Industry, the Hon. P. J. NIXON, M.P.; Sec. W. D. SALTER.

Standing Committee on Agriculture: f. 1927; associated as an advisory body with the Australian Agricultural Council; additional functions are the co-ordination of agricultural research and of quarantine measures relating to pests and diseases of plants and animals; 13 mems. comprising the 6 State Directors of Agriculture and heads of Australian Government Departments with a direct or indirect interest in Agriculture; Sec. W. D. SALTER.

There is also a Standing Committee on Soil Conservation associated with the Council.

Australian Society of Dairy Technology Incorporated: Dairy Industry House, 576 St. Kilda Rd., Melbourne, Vic. 3004; f. 1946; divisions in each State and 13 sections in country areas; 1,200 mems.; Pres. G. G. SMITH; Sec. R. A. WILSON; publ. *The Australian Journal of Dairy Technology*† (quarterly).

Australian Veterinary Association: 134–136 Hampden Rd., Artarmon, N.S.W.; f. 1921; professional association; 2,600 mems.; Pres. W. J. PEARSON; Exec. Dir. W. F. BASSAM; publ. *Australian Veterinary Journal* (monthly), *AVA Newsletter* (fortnightly), *Australian Advances in Veterinary Science, Annual Conference Papers.*

ARCHITECTURE AND TOWN PLANNING

Australian Council of National Trusts: 14 Martin Place, Sydney, N.S.W. 2000; f. 1965; Federal Council of the State National Trusts established for the conservation of lands and buildings of beauty or of national, historic, scientific, architectural or cultural interest and aboriginal relics and wildlife; Sec. R. N. WALKER; publs. *Historic Buildings of Australia, Conservation and Restoration of Buildings* (series).

Australian Institute of Quantity Surveyors: P.O.B. 534, Crows Nest, N.S.W. 2065; f. 1971; 1,050 mems.; Federal

Pres. G. F. WARD; Hon. Federal Sec. J. SILVERSMITH; publ. *The Building Economist* (quarterly).

Royal Australian Institute of Architects: 2A Mugga Way, Red Hill, A.C.T. 2603; inc. 1930; 6,000 mems.; Exec. Dir. D. C. R. BAILEY; Sec. J. H. NELSON; publ. *Architecture Australia* (every 2 months).

THE ARTS

Arts Council of Australia: Suite 605, 6th Floor, Phoenix House, 32 Bridge St., Sydney, N.S.W. 2000; f. 1946; approx. 20,000 mems.; takes professional drama, music, opera, ballet and art exhibitions to schools and country towns; arranges weekend and vacation schools in the arts, festivals; autonomous divisions in all States; Federal Pres. Sen. DAVID HAMER, D.S.C.; Federal Admin. JENNY BOTT.

Australasian and Pacific Society for Eighteenth-Century Studies: c/o Humanities Research Centre, Australian National University, P.O.B. 4, Canberra, A.C.T. 2600; f. 1970; one of the sponsoring bodies of the Nichol Smith Seminars; *c.* 80 mems.; Pres. Emer. Prof. C. J. HORNE; Sec. Dr. J. C. EADE.

Australian and New Zealand Association for Medieval and Renaissance Studies: c/o Humanities Research Centre, Australian National University, P.O.B. 4, Canberra, A.C.T. 2600; f. 1968; runs conferences every 18 months; *c.* 150 mems.; Editor Dr. J. C. EADE; publ. *Parergon*.

Australian Elizabethan Theatre Trust, The: 153 Dowling St., Potts Point, N.S.W. 2011; f. 1954 to promote drama, opera, ballet and other theatre art in Australia; acts as service org. for Int. Theatre Inst.; 5,500 mems.; Patron Her Majesty the Queen; Pres. Sir JAMES DARLING; Chair. Sir IAN POTTER; Gen. Man. JEFFRY JOYNTON-SMITH; publ. *The Australian Theatre Year Book*.

Contemporary Art Society of Australia: P.O.B. 3271, G.P.O. Sydney, N.S.W. 2001 (Federal Executive); also in Melbourne, Perth, Hobart and Adelaide; f. 1939 in Melbourne.

Musicological Society of Australia: c/o Union Box 300, University of New South Wales, P.O.B. 1, Kensington, N.S.W. 2033; f. 1963; the study of music as an art and science, especially Australasian and Oceanic music; *c.* 250 mems.; Pres. MARGARET KARTOMI; Sec. CAROL WILLIAMS; publ. *Musicology* (irregular), *Newsletter* (2 a year).

Royal Art Society of New South Wales: 25-27 Walker St., North Sydney 2060, N.S.W.; f. 1880; for the promotion of traditional Australian art in the community; 525 mems.; Pres. Sir ERIK LANGKER, K.S.J., O.B.E.; Hon. Sec. JUNE GOSS; publ. *News Sheet* (monthly).

Royal Queensland Art Society: Box 1602, G.P.O., Brisbane, Qld. 4001; f. 1886; 780 mems.; Pres. H. RICHARDSON; Sec. L. HERITAGE.

Royal South Australian Society of Arts: Institute Bldg., North Terrace, Adelaide, S.A.; f. 1856; 1,250 mems.; Pres. ELIZABETH MANLEY; Hon. Sec. JOHN WOODROFFE; publ. *Kalori* (quarterly).

Victorian Artists' Society: 430 Albert St., East Melbourne, Vic. 3002; f. 1870; 1,000 mems.; five exhibitions annually; Pres. EDWARD HEFFERNAN; Sec. THELMA VOWELL; publs. *V.A.S. News Letter*, *Annual Report*, *Gallery on Eastern Hill*.

BIBLIOGRAPHY, MUSEOLOGY AND LIBRARY SCIENCE

Bibliographical Society of Australia and New Zealand: c/o Sec. Trevor Mills, State Library of Victoria, Melbourne, Vic. 3000; f. 1969 to promote research in bibliography; 140 individual and 60 institutional mems.; Pres. Dr. H. H. R. LOVE; publs. *Bulletin* (2 a year), *Broadsheet* (3 or 4 a year), *Occasional Publications*.

Library Association of Australia: Science Centre, 35 Clarence St., Sydney, N.S.W. 2000; f. 1937; 8,500 mems.; Pres. W. D. RICHARDSON; Exec. Dir. G. R. BOWER; publs. *Australian Library Journal* (quarterly), *Incite* (fortnightly).

Museums Association of Australia: c/o Hon. Sec. JOHN WADE, Museum of Applied Arts and Sciences, 659 Harris St., Sydney, N.S.W. 2007; f. 1937 to promote and improve museums and to further advances in museum education, conservation and research; 600 individual and 50 institutional mems.; Pres. Prof. BARRIE REYNOLDS, M.SC., D.PHIL.; publs. *Kalori* (2 a year), *Kalori Quarterly Newsletter*.

ECONOMICS, LAW AND POLITICS

Australasian Political Studies Association: Politics Dept., Flinders University, Bedford Park, S.A. 5042; Pres. Prof. D. AITKIN; Hon. Sec. R. DEANGELIS; publs. *Politics* (2 a year), monographs.

Australian Bar Association: Owen Dixon Chambers, 205 William St., Melbourne; 1962 to advance the interests of barristers; to maintain and strengthen the position of the Bar, maintaining its independence and the rule of law; to maintain and improve standards of instruction and training of barristers; *c.* 1,800 mems.; Pres. H. C. BERKELEY, Q.C.; Sec. D. M. BRENNAN.

Australian Institute of Credit Management: f. 1967 to provide a national and professional organization for credit managers and those engaged in the control of credit; holds conferences, discussions; maintains educational programmes at CAEs; *c.* 2,500 mems.; divisions in all States; Pres. K. D. PEARS; Registrar V. G. PULFORD, c/o Ley, Pulford & Co., 37 Swanston St., Melbourne, Vic. 3000; publ. *Credit Review* (every 2 months).

Australian Institute of International Affairs: Box E 181, Post Office, Canberra, A.C.T. 2600; f. 1932; 2,660 mems.; brs. in all States; Pres. Rt. Hon. Sir GARFIELD BARWICK; Dir. RALPH L. HARRY; publ. *The Australian Outlook* (3 a year).

Australian Institute of Management: Suite 6, 476 St. Kilda Rd., Melbourne 3004; f. 1941; professional management association; information and training services; 13,000 professional mems., 3,700 company mems.; brs. in all states; Dir. National Centre R. B. DENNISTON.

Australian Institute of Political Science: 2nd Floor, 32 Market St., Sydney, N.S.W. 2000; Chair. Dr. T. CONLON; publ. *The Australian Quarterly*.

Committee for Economic Development of Australia: 3rd Floor, 186 Exhibition St., Melbourne, Vic. 3000; f. 1960 to develop discussion, research and interdisciplinary communication in the interests of the development of the national economy and the future of Australia; 450 Trustees; Pres. D. H. MERRY; Dir. P. GREY.

Commonwealth Institute of Valuers: 119 York St., Sydney; f. 1926; professional and examining body; 5,000 mems.; Pres. H. O. THOMAS; Registrar JOAN MARSTON; publ. *The Valuer* (quarterly).

Economic Society of Australia and New Zealand: University of Melbourne, Parkville, Vic. 3052; 3,500 mems.; branches in each State capital and also in Auckland, Christchurch; Pres. Prof. G. C. HARCOURT; Hon. Sec. R. H. SCOTT; publ. *The Economic Record*.

Institute of Public Affairs: 289 Flinders Lane, Melbourne, Vic. 3000; f. 1943; non-profit educational organization to study economic and industrial problems and to advance the cause of free enterprise in Australia;

supported by over 500 organizations and 1,500 individuals; Pres. Sir WILFRED BROOKES; Dir. ROGER NEAVE; publs. *I.P.A. Review* (quarterly), *I.P.A. Facts* (every 2 months).

Law Council of Australia: 160 Queen St., Melbourne, 3000; f. 1933; 11 constituent bodies representing 16,000 mems.; Pres. P. R. CRANSWICK; Sec.-Gen. R. HOWELL; publs. *Australian Law News* (quarterly), *Australian Legal Directory* (annually).

Law Society of New South Wales: 170 Phillip St., Sydney; f. 1884; 6,500 mems.; library of 13,000 vols.; Pres. A. J. MITCHELL; Sec. R. A. KEARSLEY; publ. *Law Society Journal* (11 a year).

EDUCATION

Australian Association of Adult Education: P.O.B. 1346, Canberra City, A.C.T. 2601; f. 1961; acts as a national clearing house, document and abstracting centre for Unesco; co-ordinates and encourages continuing education at national level; publishes educational books; liaises with and advises governments and their departments; holds national and international conferences, etc.; 500 mems., also corporate mems.; library of 1,000 vols.; Chair. B. BRENNAN; Sec. D. S. ROBERTSON; publs. *Australian Journal of Adult Education* (3 a year), *Newsletter* (every 2 months).

Australian College of Education: 916 Swanston St., Carlton, Vic. 3053; f. 1959; an association of educators from every field of education throughout Australia; encourages professional advancement of its members and the national development of education; chapters in each state and territory; conducts national and chapter conferences, surveys and studies, etc.; 5,500 mems.; Registrar T. H. TIMPSON; publs. *Unicorn*†, *Bulletin* (quarterly), report of annual conference, chapter newsletters, etc.

Australian Conference of Principals of Colleges of Advanced Education: Churchill House, 218 Northbourne Ave., Braddon, A.C.T. 2601; f. 1975; studies problems of CAEs; formulates policies, conducts research and provides information; represents members in liaison with government, educational bodies and the community; Chair. G. W. MUIR; Sec. J. R. SCUTT; publs. *Newsletter*, reference documents, information statements.

Australian Research Grants Committee: Dept. of Science, P.O.B. 449, Woden, A.C.T. 2606; f. 1965 for the allocation of research grants which stimulate high-level research in the physical sciences, biological sciences, chemical sciences, earth sciences, applied sciences, social sciences and the humanities by individuals or research teams; 18 mems.; Chair. Prof. I. G. Ross, F.A.A.; Sec. K. E. CREECH; publs. annual reports.

Australian Vice-Chancellors' Committee: P.O.B. 1142, Canberra City, A.C.T. 2601; f. 1920; takes counsel on matters of mutual concern to Australian Universities; 19 mems.; Chair. Prof. D. W. GEORGE, A.O. (Vice-Chancellor, Univ. of Newcastle); Sec. F. S. HAMBLY, B.EC.; publs. *Occasional Papers, Chairman's Report* (irregular), *Report on Australian-Asian Universities Co-operation Scheme* (annually), *Information Summaries* (irregular), *Vacancy Lists*.

Council of Adult Education: 256 Flinders St., Melbourne, Vic. 3000; f. 1947; statutory body which plans, provides and supervises adult education in Victoria; 25 mems.; library of 60,000 vols.; Chair. F. J. KENDALL; Dir. A. R. DELVES; publs. *Courses for Adults, Directory* (annually), *Syllabus of Classes* (quarterly), *Group Affairs* (every 2 months), *Annual Report*.

Victoria Institute of Colleges: Invergowrie, 21 Coppin Grove, Hawthorn, Vic. 3122; f. 1965; planning and co-ordination of educational development in the 13 affiliated Colleges of Advanced Education in Victoria; awards degrees for approved courses of study; Exec. Vice-Pres. H. J. HALSTEAD, B.A., A.F.I.M.A., F.A.C.E., M.A.C.S.; Registrar Mrs. E. C. DALE. (*See* also under Colleges.)

HISTORY, GEOGRAPHY AND ARCHAEOLOGY

Australian Institute of Cartographers: G.P.O. Box H592, Perth, W.A. 6001; f. 1953; holds bi-annual conferences; 1,370 mems.; Pres. R. G. ROBERTS; Sec. A. G. YOUNG; publ. *Cartography* (2 a year).

Australian Numismatic Society: incorporating the Numismatic Society of N.S.W.: Box R4 Royal Exchange, Sydney, N.S.W. 2000; f. 1913; 400 mems.; Pres. O. C. FLEMING; Sec. T. E. HANLEY; publs. *Report* (monthly), *Year Book*.

Geographical Society of New South Wales: Truscott Primary School, Truscott St., North Ryde, N.S.W. 2113; f. 1927; 1,300 mems.; Hon. Sec. R. CARDEW; publ. *The Australian Geographer*.

Institute of Australian Geographers: Dept. of Geography, Univ. of Newcastle, N.S.W. 2308; f. 1958; acts as a discussion forum, publishes research, and promotes the advancement of Australian geography internationally; 290 mems.; Pres. Prof. J. WARD; Hon. Sec. R. LOUGHRAN; publ. *Australian Geographical Studies* (2 a year).

Royal Australian Historical Society: History House, 133 Macquarie St., Sydney; f. 1901; 2,600 mems.; Gen. Sec. W. O. C. ROBERTS; Editors: Dr. H. KING, Assoc. Prof. B. H. FLETCHER; publ. *Journal*.

Royal Geographical Society of Australasia, Queensland, Inc.: Gregory Court, 370 George St., Brisbane, Qld. 4000; f. 1885; 300 mems.; Pres. T. C. THYNNE; Sec. J. H. GRIFFITHS; Editor R. S. DICK; publ. *Queensland Geographical Journal, Sphere Magazine*.

Royal Historical Society of Queensland: G.P.O. Box 1811, Brisbane, Qld. 4001; f. 1913; 600 mems., library; research; historical documents preserved and filed; historical museum; Pres. Commdr. NORMAN S. PIXLEY; Sec. Mrs. N. SEFFRIN; publs. *Bulletin* (monthly), *Journal* (annually).

Royal Historical Society of Victoria: 459 Collins St., Melbourne, Vic. 3000; f. 1909; research; collection of historical material; exhibitions; 1,100 mems.; library of 3,000 vols.; MSS., photographs, paintings and prints; Pres. Lt.-Col. H. C. LEE-ARCHER; Dir. H. N. WARREN; publs. *Victorian Historical Journal* (quarterly), *Newsletter* (monthly).

Royal Western Australian Historical Society: Stirling House, 49 Broadway, Nedlands, W.A. 6009; f. 1926; 1,500 mems.; Pres. Sir FRANCIS BURT; Sec. Mrs. C. MACKLIN; publs. *Early Days* (annually), *Newsletter* (monthly).

Society of Australian Genealogists: Richmond Villa, 120 Kent St., Sydney, N.S.W. 2000; f. 1932; 1,600 mems.; Pres. K. A. JOHNSON; Hon. Sec. Miss J. WATSON; publ. *Descent*.

INTERNATIONAL CULTURAL ORGANIZATIONS

Alliance Française de Canberra: 66 McCaughey St., Turner, A.C.T. 2601; f. 1945 to promote French language and culture; organizes French courses, lectures, film-shows, social events; brs. in all major towns; *c.* 500 mems.; library of 800 vols.; Pres. Dr. H. LOOFS; Dir. S. PRECA; publ. *Chantecler*.

British Council: Edgecliff Centre, 203–233 New South Head Rd., Edgecliff, Sydney, N.S.W. 2027; f. 1947; Rep. A. MACKENZIE SMITH, O.B.E., M.C.

Istituto Italiano di Cultura (*Italian Cultural Institute*): Elm Tree House, 233 Domain Rd., South Yarra, Melbourne, Vic. 3141; f. 1961; *c.* 600 mems.; library of 6,300 vols.; Dir. Prof. ANDREA TOSSI; publ. *Quaderni.*

U.S. International Communication Agency (American Center): National Press Club Bldg., 16 National Circuit, Barton, A.C.T. 2600.

LANGUAGE AND LITERATURE

English Association—Sydney Branch: 62 Victoria Ave., Chatswood, N.S.W. 2067; f. 1923; 120 mems.; Pres. S. E. LEE, B.A.; Hon. Sec. M. M. LEE; publ. *Southerly* (quarterly).

Fellowship of Australian Writers: Box 3448, G.P.O., Sydney, N.S.W. 2001; f. 1928; 3,500 national mems.; brs. in all states; Pres. JOHN WRIGHT; Sec. KATE WRIGHT; publ. *Bulletin* (every 2 months).

International P.E.N. (Sydney Centre): P.O.B. 997 G.P.O., Sydney, N.S.W. 2001; f. 1931; 100 mems.; Pres. STEPHEN KELEN; Sec. FRANK TRIST; publ. *Newsletter* (2 a year).

MEDICINE

Australasian College of Dermatologists: 271 Bridge Rd., Glebe, N.S.W. 2037; f. 1966: 235 mems.: Pres. Dr. M. T. HAVYATT; Sec. Dr. R. P. ARMATI; publ. *The Australasian Journal of Dermatology* (3 a year).

Australian Association of Neurologists: Division of Neurology, Prince Henry Hospital, Little Bay, N.S.W. 2036; f. 1950 to bring together clinical neurologists and scientific workers in the field of the nervous system and its diseases by such means as meetings, provision of special facilities and assistance in any publications on these matters; 207 mems.; Pres. Prof. J. W. LANCE; Hon. Sec. Dr. M. ANTHONY; publ. *Clinical and Experimental Neurology* (annually).

Australian Dental Association: 116 Pacific Highway, North Sydney, N.S.W. 2060; f. 1928; 5,000 mems.; Federal Pres. W. DONALD HEFFRON, B.D.S., F.I.C.D.; Federal Sec. COLIN HART WALL, B.D.S., F.I.C.D.; publ. *Australian Dental Journal.*

Australian Institute of Anatomy, The: Canberra City, A.C.T. 2601; f. 1931; administered by the Community Health Branch of the Australian Dept. of Health; Officer-in-Charge C. A. NETTLE.

Australian Optometrical Association: 204 Drummond St., Carlton, Vic. 3053; publ. *Australian Journal of Optometry.*

Australian Physiological and Pharmacological Society: f. 1960 for the advancement of sciences of Physiology and Pharmacology; 416 mems.; National Sec. Dr. S. R. O'DONNELL, Dept. Physiology and Pharmacology, Univ. of Queensland, Brisbane, Qld. 4067; publ. *Proceedings* (2 a year).

Australian Physiotherapy Association (N.S.W.): G.P.O. Box 4135, Sydney, N.S.W. 2001; f. 1905; provides postgraduate courses; 1,300 mems.; library of 250 vols.; Pres. DOREEN M. MOORE; Exec. Dir. ELIZABETH RICH; publ. *N.S.W. Physiotherapy Bulletin* (monthly).

College of Nursing, Australia: 2–6 Arthur St., Melbourne, Vic. 3004; aims to promote improvements in nursing practice through education and research; grants Fellowships to graduates of approved courses; Hon. Dir. Miss P. V. SLATER, O.B.E., M.A., B.SC.

Postgraduate Medical Foundation: University of Sydney, P.O.B. H111, Australia Square, N.S.W. 2000; f. 1958 to co-operate with the Postgraduate Committee in Medicine within the Coppleson Postgraduate Medical Institute and the Faculty of Medicine within the University of Sydney, in the furtherance of postgraduate education and research in medicine; Pres. Sir ROBERT CRICHTON-BROWN, C.B.E., T.D.

Royal Australasian College of Dental Surgeons: 229 Macquarie St., Sydney, N.S.W. 2000; f. 1965; holds scientific meetings and administers examinations; 750 Fellows; Pres. W. O. READ; Hon. Sec. G. WING; publ. *Annals.*

Royal Australasian College of Physicians: 145 Macquarie St., Sydney, N.S.W.; f. 1938; 18 Hon. Fellows, 3,191 Fellows; Pres. Dr. A. KERR GRANT (S.A.); Hon. Sec. Dr. R. J. MULHEARN (N.S.W.); publ. *Australian and New Zealand Journal of Medicine.*

Royal Australasian College of Radiologists, The: 37 Lower Fort St., Millers Point, N.S.W. 2000; 1,000 mems.; Hon. Sec. Dr. W. A. SORBY; publ. *Australasian Radiology.*

Royal Australasian College of Surgeons: Spring St., Melbourne, Vic. 3000; Sec. R. A. CHAPMAN; publ. *Australian and New Zealand Journal of Surgery* (6 a year).

Royal Australian College of Ophthalmologists: 27 Commonwealth St., Sydney, N.S.W. 2010; f. 1969 (formerly Ophthalmological Society of Australia); 500 mems.; Pres. Dr. G. W. HARLEY; Hon. Sec. Dr. MICHAEL STEINER; publ. *Australian Journal of Ophthalmology*† (4 a year).

Royal College of Pathologists of Australasia: 82 Windmill St., Sydney, N.S.W. 2000; f. 1956; 883 Fellows; Pres. Prof. E. S. FINCKH; Hon. Sec. Dr. R. A. OSBORN; publ. *Pathology*†.

NATURAL SCIENCES

General

Australian and New Zealand Association for the Advancement of Science (ANZAAS): Challis House, Martin Place, Sydney, N.S.W. 2001; f. 1886; 3,000 mems.; Divisions in all Australian States, New Zealand and Papua New Guinea; Exec. Officer P. LEVER-NAYLOR; publ. *Search*† (10 a year).

Australian Conservation Foundation: 672B Glenferrie Rd., Hawthorn, Vic. 3122; f. 1965; conservation of the resources of land, air and water of the Commonwealth and its territories at national level; 8,300 mems.; library of 3,500 vols.; Pres. M. WILCOX, Q.C.; Dir. Dr. GEOFF MOSLEY; publs. *Newsletter, Habitat Australia,* occasional publs.

Royal Society of New South Wales: 35 Clarence St., Sydney, N.S.W. 2000; f. 1821; 390 mems., 50 assoc. mems.; Pres. G. S. GIBBONS; Sec. L. A. DRAKE; library of 400,000 vols.; publs. *Journal* and *Proceedings.*

Royal Society of Queensland: P.O.B. 50, St. Lucia, Qld. 4067; f. 1884; 350 mems.; library of 75,000 vols.; Pres. Prof. B. RIGSBY; Sec. Dr. R. T. WILLIAMS; publ. *Proceedings*† (annually).

Royal Society of South Australia Inc.: State Library Bldg., North Terrace, Adelaide; f. 1853; 300 mems.; publ. *Transactions*†.

Royal Society of Tasmania: G.P.O. Box 1166M, Hobart, Tas. 7001; f. 1843; 500 mems.; library of 38,000 vols; Pres. H.E. THE GOVERNOR; Hon. Sec. D. R. GREGG, M.SC.; publ. *Papers and Proceedings*†.

Royal Society of Victoria: 9 Victoria St., Melbourne, Vic. 3000; f. 1854; 640 mems.; Pres. Prof. L. L. STUBBS; Hon. Sec. T. A. DARRAGH; publ. *Proceedings.*

Royal Society of Western Australia: Western Australian Museum, Perth; f. 1913; study of botany, zoology, geology and anthropology; 276 mems.; Pres. Dr. J. R.

de Laeter; Secs. P. Bridgewater, A. Petch; publ. *Journal*† (quarterly).

Biological Sciences

Australian Entomological Society: c/o Plant Research Institute, Swan St., Burnley, Vic. 3121; f. 1965; 573 mems., 8 assocs., 4 affiliated societies; Pres. Dr. C. N. Smithers; Sec. Dr. P. Williams; publs. *News Bulletin, Journal* (quarterly), occasional publs.

Australian Society for Fish Biology: c/o N.S.W. State Fisheries, 211 Kent St., Sydney 2000; f. 1971 to promote the study of fish and fisheries in Australia and provide a communications medium for Australian fish workers; 320 mems.; Pres. G. R. Allen; Sec. G. W. Henry; publ. *Newsletter* (2 a year).

Australian Society for Limnology: f. 1961; 370 mems.; Pres. P. S. Lake; Sec.-Treas. I. C. Campbell, Water Studies Centre, Caulfield Inst. of Technology, Caulfield East, Vic. 3145; publs. *Newsletter* (quarterly), *Special Publications* (approx. annually).

Australian Society for Microbiology: Clunies Ross House, 191 Royal Parade, Parkville, Vic. 3052; f. 1959; 378 mems.; Pres. Dr. N. F. Millis; Hon. Sec. Dr. V. A. Stanisich; publ. *News* (6 a year).

Australian Society for Parasitology: McMaster Lab. CSIRO, Private Bag 1, P.O., Glebe, N.S.W. 2037, f. 1964; 250 mems., 10 Fellows; Pres. Dr. A.D. Donald; Hon. Sec. Dr. P. J. Waller; publ. *International Journal of Parasitology*.

Ecological Society of Australia Inc.: P.O.B. 1564, Canberra, A.C.T. 2601; f. 1960 to promote the scientific study of plants and animals in relation to their environment, and publication of the results of research; to facilitate the exchange of ideas amongst ecologists; to promote the application of ecological principles to the development, utilization and conservation of Australian natural resources; to advise government and other agencies; to foster the reservation of natural areas for scientific and recreational purposes; 560 mems.; Pres. Dr. G. Scott; Sec. Dr. P. Ladiges; publs. *Proceedings, Bulletin, Australian Journal of Ecology, Memoirs*.

Entomological Society of New South Wales: Box 22, Five Dock, Sydney, N.S.W. 2046; f. 1952; 170 mems.; Pres. J. M. E. Anderson; Hon. Sec. D. R. J. Smith; publ. *General and Applied Entomology*.

Entomological Society of Queensland: Entomology Dept., University of Queensland, St. Lucia, Brisbane, Qld. 4067; independent; f. 1923; 343 mems.; Pres. R. Wylie; Sec. E. Dahms; publ. *News Bulletin*† (10 a year).

Field Naturalists Club of Victoria: National Herbarium, Domain, South Yarra, Vic. 3141; f. 1880; study of natural history and conservation of environment; 1,000 mems.; Pres. Dr. Brian Smith; publs. *The Victorian Naturalist* (every 2 months), etc.

Linnean Society of New South Wales: Science Centre, 35–43 Clarence St., Sydney; f. 1874; study and promotion of research in the natural sciences; 302 mems.; 20,000 vols. in library; Hon. Sec. Mrs. B. J. Stoddard; publ. *Proceedings*†.

Malacological Society of Australia: c/o Western Australian Museum, Francis St., Perth 6000; f. 1955; *c.* 600 mems.; Pres. Dr. F. E. Wells; Sec. L. M. Joll; publs. *Australian Shell News* (quarterly), *Journal* (annually).

Royal Australasian Ornithologists Union: 21 Gladstone St., Moonee Ponds, Vic. 3039; f. 1901; 2,000 mems.; Pres. Dr. H. N. B. Wettenhall; Sec. S. J. Cowling; publs. *Newsletter* (quarterly), *Emu*† (quarterly), *Atlas Newsletter* (quarterly).

Royal Zoological Society of New South Wales: Taronga Zoo, Mosman, N.S.W. 2088; f. 1879; 2,500 mems.; Pres. Dr. G. Grigg; Sec. Mrs. M. Wray; publs. *Australian Zoologist, Koolewong*.

Royal Zoological Society of South Australia: Frome Rd., Adelaide, S.A.; f. 1878; maintains public Zoological Gardens; 563 mems.; Pres. C. C. Burfield; Dir. Dr. C. C. Mueller; publ. *Report*.

Wildlife Preservation Society of Australia: P.O.B. 3428, G.P.O., Sydney; f. 1909; 700 mems.; Pres. Vincent Serventy; Hon. Sec. Jill Thompson; publs. *Australian Wildlife* (annually), *Newsletter* (quarterly).

Zoological Board of Victoria: P.O.B. 74, Parkville, Vic.; est. 1937 as successor to Royal Zoological and Acclimatisation Society of Victoria (f. 1861); responsible for the management of the Royal Melbourne Zoological Gardens, Sir Colin Mackenzie Fauna Park and Werribee Zoological Park; 11 mems.; Chair. A. Dunbavin Butcher; Dir. J. H. Sullivan.

Mathematics

Australian Mathematical Society: Dept. of Mathematics, Univ. of Western Australia, Nedlands, W.A. 6009; f. 1956; 710 mems.; Pres. Dr. D. G. Hurley; Sec. Dr. J. Gani; publs. *Journal* (Series A and B), *Bulletin, Gazette*.

Statistical Society of Australia: c/o Statistics Dept., Australian National Univ., P.O.B. 4, Canberra, A.C.T. 2600; f. 1959; 657 mems.; Pres. Dr. C. C. Heyde; Hon. Sec.-Treas. Dr. D. J. Daley; publ. *The Australian Journal of Statistics*†, *Newsletter* (4 a year).

Physical Sciences

Astronomical Society of Australia: c/o Astronomy Dept., Sydney University, N.S.W. 2006; f. 1966; 250 mems.; Pres. Prof. D. S. Mathewson; Secs. Dr. L. R. Allen, Dr. M. S. Bessel; Editor Dr. R. X. McGee; publ. *Proceedings* (annually).

Astronomical Society of South Australia (Inc): G.P.O. Box 199, Adelaide 5001; f. 1892; 250 mems.; library of 200 vols.; Pres. W. Bradfield; Sec. R. C. Dawson; publs. *The Bulletin* (monthly), *Astronomical Data* (annually).

Astronomical Society of Tasmania: G.P.O. Box 154-B, Hobart; f. 1930; 50 mems.; Sec. M. George.

Astronomical Society of Victoria: Box 1059J, G.P.O. Melbourne, Vic. 3001; f. 1922; amateur astronomy; 500 mems.; library of over 1,000 vols.; publs. *The Journal* (bi-monthly), *Yearbook*.

Astronomical Society of Western Australia: Box S 1460, G.P.O., Perth, W.A. 6001; f. 1950; 125 mems.; Pres. F. Ward; Sec. A. Murray, M.A., B.SC.; publ. *Journal*† (monthly).

Australian Biochemical Society: c/o Dr. H. C. Robinson, Dept. of Biochemistry, Monash University, Clayton, Vic. 3168; f. 1955; 1,250 mems.; Pres. F. Gibson; publ. *Proceedings* (annual).

Australian Institute of Physics: Science House Pty. Ltd., 35 Clarence St., Sydney, N.S.W. 2000; f. 1963; 1,770 mems.; Pres. Prof. H. C. Bolton; Hon. Sec. Dr. J. R. Bird; publ. *The Australian Physicist* (monthly).

Geological Society of Australia: Challis House, 10 Martin Place., Sydney, N.S.W. 2000; f. 1953; 2,800 mems.; Pres. Dr. C. D. Branch; Sec. B. C. Youngs; publ. *Journal* (2 a year).

Royal Australian Chemical Institute: 191 Royal Parade, Parkville, Vic. 3052; f. 1917, inc. by Royal Charter 1932; it is both the qualifying body for professional chemists and a learned society which aims to promote the science and practice of chemistry in all its branches;

6,800 mems.; Hon. Gen. Sec. M. J. Jordan; Exec. Sec. P. W. Woodhouse; publ. *Chemistry in Australia*† (monthly).

Philosophy and Psychology

Australasian Association of Philosophy: Dept. of Philosophy, La Trobe University, Melbourne; f. 1923; 400 mems.; brs. throughout Australia and New Zealand; Pres. K. K. Campbell; Sec. Aubrey Townsend; publ. *Australasian Journal of Philosophy*† (quarterly).

The Australian Psychological Society: National Science Centre, 191 Royal Parade, Parkville, Vic. 3052; f. 1966; 2,700 mems.; to advance scientific study and professional practice of psychology and enhance contribution of psychology to promotion of public welfare; Pres. Prof. R. C. King; Exec. Officer Dr. F. D. Kiellerup; Gen. Sec. Mrs. E. P. Muir; library (in process of formation); publs. *Australian Journal of Psychology, Australian Psychologist, Bulletin.*

Religion, Sociology and Anthropology

Anthropological Society of New South Wales: c/o Australian Museum, 6-8 College St., Sydney; f. 1928; 125 mems.; Pres. F. P. Dickson; Hon. Sec. Dr. J. R. Specht; publ. *Mankind* (2 a year).

Sociological Association of Australia and New Zealand: c/o Dept. of Sociology, Univ. of Wollongong, Wollongong, N.S.W. 2500; f. 1963; aims to promote development of sociology in Australia and New Zealand; 800 mems.; Pres. Assoc. Prof. C. V. Baldock; Sec. K. Salleh; publ. *The Australian and New Zealand Journal of Sociology* (3 per year).

Technology

Australasian Institute of Metals, The: 191 Royal Parade, Parkville 3052; inc. 1946; branches at Adelaide, Brisbane, Melbourne, Newcastle, Perth, Port Kembla, Sydney, Christchurch (N.Z.) and Auckland (N.Z.); 2,800 mems.; Hon. Fed. Sec. G. G. Brown; Exec. Dir. R. R. Green; publs. *Metals Forum* (quarterly), *Definitions of Metallurgical Terms, Handbook, Metals Australasia* (monthly).

Australasian Institute of Mining and Metallurgy, The: Clunies Ross House, 191 Royal Parade, Parkville, Vic. 3052; f. 1893; incorporated by Royal Charter 1955; 6,400 mems.; Pres. R. T. Madigan, O.B.E.; Chief Exec. Officer W. E. Vance; publs. *Proceedings, Monthly Bulletin, Conference Series* and *Symposia "S" Series* and Monographs.

Australian Institute of Food Science and Technology: 14 Brisbane Rd., Castle Hill, N.S.W. 2154; Pres. Prof. R. A. Edwards, F.A.I.F.S.T.; Hon. Gen. Sec. Dr. M. K. Shaw, F.A.I.F.S.T.

Chartered Institute of Transport, Australian Council: c/o Sec. H. J. Lawrence, 3/10 Anderson St., Templestowe, Vic. 3106. *See* main entry under U.K.

Institution of Engineers, Australia: 11 National Circuit, Barton, A.C.T.; f. 1919, Royal Charter 1938; brs. in each state and 5 constituent colleges; 32,000 mems.; Pres. Prof. L. A. Endersbee, M.E., F.I.E.AUST.; Sec. E. D. Storr, B.E., M.ENG.SC., F.I.E.AUST.; publs. *Engineers Australia* (25 a year), *Civil Engineering Transactions, Electrical Engineering Transactions, Mechanical Engineering Transactions, Chemical Engineering in Australia, General Engineering Transactions.*

Constituent Colleges:

College of Chemical Engineers: f. 1975.
College of Civil Engineers: f. 1975.
College of Electrical Engineers: f. 1975.
College of Mechanical Engineers: f. 1975.
General College of Engineering: f. 1975.

Institution of Radio and Electronics Engineers Australia: Science Centre, 35–43 Clarence St., Sydney, N.S.W. 2000; f. 1932, Royal Charter 1967; divisions in each State, A.C.T. and Singapore Chapter; *c.* 3,000 mems.; Pres. E. J. Wilkinson; Gen. Sec. Heather Harriman; publs. *Monitor* (monthly), *Proceedings of the I.R.E.E.* (quarterly).

Royal Aeronautical Society (Australian Division): Clunies Ross House, 191 Royal Parade, Parkville, Vic. 3052; f. 1927; Pres. F. W. Austin, F.R.AE.S.; Hon. Sec. B. A. J. Scoles, F.R.AE.S.

Society of Automotive Engineers—Australasia: 191 Royal Parade, Parkville, Vic. 3052; f. 1927; 2,700 mems.; Pres. J. E. Whitesell; Exec. Dir. L. M. Trounce; publs. *SAE—News* (monthly), *SAE—Australasia*† (every 2 months), *Recommended Practices*†.

RESEARCH INSTITUTES

(*See* also under Universities)

Agriculture and Veterinary Science

Australian Institute of Agricultural Science: 191 Royal Parade, Parkville, Vic. 3052; f. 1935; 3,000 mems.; publs. *Journal, A Manual of Australian Agriculture.*

Commonwealth Forestry and Timber Bureau: Dept. of Primary Industry, Canberra, A.C.T.; f. 1925; economic and policy research; Dir.-Gen. A. G. Hanson.

Soil Conservation Service of N.S.W.: Box R201, Royal Exchange Post Office, Pitt St., Sydney, N.S.W. 2000; f. 1939; conservation of soil resources and mitigation of soil erosion; 213 officers; Comm. G. H. Knowles, B.SC.; publ. *Journal* (quarterly).

Architecture and Town Planning

Metropolitan Research Trust: P.O.B. 597, Canberra City, A.C.T. 2601; f. 1968 to promote and sponsor applied research on urban land issues, the dissemination and application of findings; current programme is devoted to urban land economics, policy and management; Chair. P. F. Harrison; Research Dir. R. W. Archer.

Education

Australian Council for Educational Research Ltd., The: Frederick St., Hawthorn, Vic. 3122; f. 1930; 16 mems. of whom 6 are elected by State Institutes for Educational Research; Pres. Emer. Prof. P. H. Karmel; Dir. Dr. J. P. Keeves; publs. *Australian Journal of Education* (3 a year), *Australian Education Index* (quarterly), *Australian Education Review* (irregular), *Newsletter* (irregular), occasional Research Series and papers.

History

Tasmanian Historical Research Association: f. 1951; 500 mems.; Pres. Prof. Michael Roe; Sec. Mrs. E. A. McLeod, P.O.B. 441, Sandy Bay, Tas. 7005; publ. *Papers and Proceedings* (quarterly).

Medicine

Australian Radiation Laboratory (Australian Department of Health): Lower Plenty Rd., Yallambie, Vic. 3085; f. 1929; research, development and scientific services in relation to the public health aspects of ionizing radiations and of microwave, laser and ultraviolet radiations, environmental radiation, mining and milling of radioactive ores, radiation dosimetry and quality assurance of radiopharmaceuticals; library of 3,000 vols.; Dir. Dr. K. H. LOKAN.

Baker Medical Research Institute: Commercial Rd., Prahran, Vic. 3181; f. 1926; basic and clinical research on cardiovascular disease and hypertension; affiliated to Monash University, Alfred Hospital, and including the Alfred Hospital Clinical Research Unit (f. 1949); 70 mems.; library of 15,000 vols.; Chair. J. C. HABERSBERGER, B.COMM.; Dir. P. I. KORNER, M.D., M.SC., F.R.A.C.P., F.A.A.; publs. *Annual Report*, *Research.*

Commonwealth Serum Laboratories Commission: Parkville, Vic. 3052; f. 1916 for research, production and marketing of biologicals; 1,100 mems.; Burnet Library of 5,000 vols.; Dir. Dr. N. J. MCCARTHY, M.A., M.B.B.S., M.ADMIN., F.R.A.C.G.P., F.A.C.M.A.; publs. Medical, Veterinary, Diagnostic and Cell Culture Handbooks (every 2–3 years), *Annual Report of Activities.*

Institute of Dental Research, The: United Dental Hospital, 2 Chalmers St., Sydney, N.S.W.; f. 1946; for research into biological problems relating to dental health; library of 2,500 vols.; Dir. Prof. K. W. KNOX, M.SC., PH.D.; publ. *Biennial Report.*

Institute of Medical and Veterinary Science: Frome Rd., Adelaide; est. 1938 for purpose of research into diseases of human beings and animals, and to provide a diagnostic pathology service for the Royal Adelaide Hospital and for the State through 12 regional laboratories; teaching is provided for the Univ. of Adelaide Medical School; 870 staff; Chair. A. G. MCGREGOR, M.A., LL.B.; Dir. JAMES A. BONNIN, M.D., B.S., F.R.C.P.A., F.R.A.C.P.; publ. *Annual Report*†.

Institute of Mental Health Research and Postgraduate Training: 35 Poplar Rd., Parkville, Vic. 3052; f. 1955 with responsibility to the Mental Health Division, Health Commission of Victoria to study and develop aspects of prevention of mental illness and mental retardation, to carry out research in the field of social and biological psychiatry and to promote community understanding of mental health problems; library of *c.* 37,000 vols.; Dir. Dr. JOHN M. G. GRIGOR; publ. *Statistical Bulletin* (annually).

Kolling Institute of Medical Research: Royal North Shore Hospital of Sydney, St. Leonards, N.S.W. 2065; f. 1930, reorganized 1974; research in immunology, oncology and experimental pathology; 27 full-time and visiting staff; Dir. Dr. D. S. NELSON; publ. *Biennial Report.*

National Health and Medical Research Council: P.O.B. 100, Woden, A.C.T. 2606; f. 1936 to inquire into, advise and make recommendations to the Australian and State Governments on public health legislation and administration and on any other matters relating to health, medical and dental care and medical research; 27 mems.; Chair. Dr. GWYN HOWELLS (Dir.-Gen. of Health); Sec. Dr. K. W. EDMONDSON; publs. *Session Reports* (2 a year), *Medical Research Report* (annually), special publications.

Queensland Institute of Medical Research: Bramston Terrace, Brisbane, Qld. 4006; f. 1947; research into medical problems important in the Australian and Asian Pacific region; current areas are tropical medicine, virology, oncology, cell biology, molecular biology; 60 professional staff; library of 14,327 vols.; Chair. of Council P. G. LIVINGSTONE (Dir.-Gen. of Health and Medical Services); Dir. C. KIDSON; Librarian Mrs. CORAL TILLETT; publ. *Annual Report*†.

Walter and Eliza Hall Institute of Medical Research: Royal Melbourne Hospital, P.O. Victoria 3050; f. 1916; Dir. Prof. Sir GUSTAV NOSSAL; publ. *Annual Report.*

SCIENCES

General

Commonwealth Scientific and Industrial Research Organization (CSIRO): Canberra, A.C.T. (P.O.B. 225, Dickson, A.C.T. 2602); library: *see* Libraries.

Chairman: J. P. WILD, C.B.E., M.A., SC.D., F.T.S., F.A.A., F.R.S.

Secretary: L. G. WILSON, M.SC.

First Assistant Secretary (*Science Liaison*): P. F. BUTLER.

Chairmen of State Committees:

K. E. GIBSON, B.SC. (Queensland), L. C. BRODIE-HALL, C.M.G., A.W.A.S.M. (Western Australia), J. E. HARRIS, B.E. (South Australia), Prof. P. SCOTT, F.A.S.S.A. (Tasmania), J. E. KOLM, M.SC. (Victoria), A. BODEN, B.SC., F.R.A.C.I. (New South Wales).

Overseas Liaison Officers:

Minister (*Scientific*), *London:* R. M. MOORE, A.O., D.SC.AGR.

Counsellor (*Scientific*), *Tokyo:* T. D. GRACE, PH.D.

Counsellor (*Scientific*), *Washington:* J. H. WHITTEM, B.V.SC.

Counsellor (*Scientific*), *Moscow:* J. G. DOWNES, B.SC.

Directors:

Institute of Animal and Food Sciences: K. A. FERGUSON, PH.D.

Institute of Biological Resources: M. V. TRACEY, M.A.

Institute of Earth Resources: I. E. NEWNHAM, M.B.E., M.SC.

Institute of Industrial Technology: H. W. WORNER, D.SC.

Institute of Physical Sciences: J. R. PHILIP, D.SC.

Bureau of Scientific Services: S. LATTIMORE, B.SC.

Planning and Advisory Unit: D. E. WEISS, O.B.E., D.SC.

Chiefs of Divisions:

Animal Health, Melbourne: A. K. LASCELLES, M.V.SC., PH.D., F.A.C.V.SC.

Animal Production, Sydney: T. W. SCOTT, PH.D.

Applied Geomechanics, Melbourne: D. F. KELSALL, M.A., PH.D.

Applied Organic Chemistry, Melbourne: D. H. SOLOMON, PH.D., D.SC., F.A.A., F.T.S.

Applied Physics, Sydney: W. R. BLEVIN, D.SC. (acting).

Atmospheric Physics, Melbourne: G. B. TUCKER, PH.D.

Building Research, Melbourne: F. A. BLAKEY, PH.D.

Chemical Physics, Melbourne: L. T. CHADDERTON, PH.D., D.SC.

Chemical Technology, Melbourne: H. G. HIGGINS, B.SC.

Cloud Physics, Sydney: J. WARNER, B.SC., B.E.

Computing Research, Canberra: P. J. CLARINGBOLD, PH.D., F.S.S., F.A.C.S.

Entomology, Canberra: D. F. WATERHOUSE, C.M.G., D.SC., F.A.A., F.R.S.

Environmental Mechanics, Canberra: D. SMILES, PH.D.

Fisheries and Oceanography, Sydney: D. J. ROCHFORD, B.SC.

Food Research, Sydney: J. H. B. CHRISTIAN, PH.D.

Forest Research, Canberra: M. F. C. DAY, A.O., PH.D., F.A.A.

Horticultural Research, Adelaide: J. V. POSSINGHAM, M.SC., D.PHIL., PH.D.

Human Nutrition, Adelaide: B. S. HETZEL, M.D., F.R.C.P., F.R.A.C.P.
Irrigation Research, Griffith, N.S.W.: P. E. KRIEDEMANN, PH.D.
Land Resources Management, Perth: R. A. PERRY, M.SC.
Land Use Research, Canberra: R. J. MILLINGTON, M.SC., PH.D.
Materials Science, Melbourne: J. R. ANDERSON, PH.D., SC.D., F.A.A..
Mathematics and Statistics, Canberra: J. M. GANI, PH.D., D.I.C., D.SC., F.A.A.
Mechanical Engineering, Melbourne: B. RAWLINGS, M.ENG.SC., PH.D., C.ENG., F.I.C.E.
Mineral Chemistry, Melbourne: D. F. A. KOCH, M.SC., PH.D.
Mineral Engineering, Melbourne: D. F. KELSALL, M.A., PH.D.
Mineral Physics, Sydney: K. G. MCCRACKEN, D.SC., PH.D.
Mineralogy, Perth: A. J GASKIN, M.SC.
Plant Industry, Canberra: W. J. PEACOCK, PH.D., F.A.A.
Process Technology, Sydney: A. V. BRADSHAW, B.SC.
Protein Chemistry, Melbourne: W. G. CREWTHER, D.SC.
Radiophysics, Sydney: H. C. MINNETT, O.B.E., B.SC., B.E., F.A.A.
Soils, Adelaide: A. E. MARTIN, D.AGR.SC.
Textile Industry, Geelong, Victoria: D. S. TAYLOR, PH.D.
Textile Physics, Sydney: A. R. HALY, D.SC.
Tropical Crops and Pastures, Brisbane: E. F. HENZELL, D.PHIL.
Wildlife Research, Canberra: H. J. FRITH, D.SC.AGR., F.A.A., F.T.S.

Officers-in-Charge of Units:
Australian Numerical Meteorology Research Centre: Melbourne; D. J. GAUNTLETT, PH.D.
Centre for Animal Research and Development, Indonesia: R. H. WHARTON, M.SC., PH.D., F.A.A.
Centre for International Research Co-operation, Canberra: A. F. GURNETT-SMITH, B.AGR.SC.
Central Information Library and Editorial Section, Canberra; P. J. JUDGE, M.A.
Commercial Group, Canberra; P. A. GRANT.
Science Communication Unit, Canberra: (vacant).
Fuel Geoscience, Sydney: G. H. TAYLOR, D.SC., DR.RER.NAT.
Molecular and Cellular Biology, Sydney: G. W. GRIGG, PH.D.
Wheat Research, Sydney: E. E. BOND, M.B.E., A.R.M.T.C., F.R.A.C.I.

Australian National Radio Astronomy Observatory: Parkes, N.S.W.; f. 1961; research in radio astronomy, principally with 210-ft. radio telescope; operated by CSIRO Division of Radiophysics, P.O.B. 76, Epping, N.S.W. 2121; Chief of Division H. C. MINNETT, O.B.E., B.SC., B.E., F.A.A.

Culgoora Solar Observatory: Culgoora, near Narrabri, N.S.W.; f. 1967; solar research on both optical and radio wavelengths; optical section operated by CSIRO Division of Applied Physics (*see* above); radio section operated by CSIRO Division of Radiophysics (*see* above).

Publications: *Australian Journal of: Agricultural Research*† (every 2 months), *Botany*† (every 2 months), *Biological Sciences*† (every 2 months), *Chemistry*† (monthly), *Experimental Agriculture and Animal Husbandry*† (every 2 months), *Forest Research*† (quarterly), *Marine and Freshwater Research*† (every 2 months), *Physics*† (every 2 months), *Plant Physiology*† (every 2 months), *Soil Research*† (3 a year), *Zoology*† (quarterly), *Australian Wildlife Research*† (3 a year), *CSIRO Industrial Research News*† (every 2 months), *ECOS-CSIRO Environmental Research*†, *Rural Research* (quarterly), *Australian Science Index*, *CSIRO Index* (monthly), *Brunonia* (irregular), *The Mathematical Scientist* (2 a year), *Food Research Quarterly*.

Biological Sciences

Australian Institute of Marine Science: P.M.B. 3, Townsville, Qld. 4810; f. 1972; carries out research in marine science emphasizing tropics; 84 staff; vessel fleet; library of 1,000 vols.; Dir. Dr. J. S. BUNT; Sec. R. MCCULLOUGH; publs. *Annual Report*†, monographs, technical reports, etc.

National Biological Standards Laboratories: P.O.B. 462, Canberra, A.C.T. 2601; f. 1958 to ensure that therapeutic goods used for medical treatment are safe and effective; library of 14,000 vols. and 3,000 microfiche; Dir. LEIGH F. DODSON, M.B., B.S., DIP.CLIN.PATH., D.PHIL.

Royal Botanic Gardens and National Herbarium of New South Wales: Sydney, N.S.W. 2000; f. 1816; 28-hectare living plant collection and herbarium of 1,000,000 specimens; library of 16,000 items; Mt. Tomah Annexe for temperate plant collections; specialization in research on Australian native plants; Dir. L. A. S. JOHNSON, D.SC.; publs. *Telopea*, *Flora of New South Wales*.

Royal Botanic Gardens and National Herbarium of Victoria: Birdwood Ave., S. Yarra, Vic.; f. 1846; 94-acre plant collection and Herbarium of 2,000,000 specimens; library of 28,500 vols.; Cranbourne annex for Research Institute for growing display and study of native Australian plants; Dir. and Govt. Botanist D. M. CHURCHILL, M.A., PH.D.; publs. *Guide*, *Muelleria*.

Mathematics

Australian Bureau of Statistics: Canberra, A.C.T.; f. 1906; Australian Statistician R. J. CAMERON; library of 47,000 vols.; publs. *Yearbook Australia*, *Pocket Yearbook of Australian Statistics*, and some 1,050 other titles listed in *Catalogue of ABS Publications*.

Physical Sciences

Australian Atomic Energy Commission Research Establishment: Private Mail Bag, Sutherland, N.S.W. 2232; f. 1955; production and application of radioisotopes; research on effects and applications of radiation, uranium processing including environmental aspects and waste treatment, science and technology of nuclear reactors; library is principal Australian library for atomic energy; Dir. Emer. Prof. S. T. BUTLER, M.SC., PH.D., D.SC., F.A.I.P., F.A.A.; publs. *Annual Report*†, scientific reports and papers.

Bureau of Mineral Resources, Geology and Geophysics: Constitution Ave., Parkes, A.C.T., P.O.B. 378, Canberra City, A.C.T. 2601; f. 1946 to obtain geological and geophysical information for development of mineral resources; engineering and urban geology; hydrogeology; geophysical observatories; mineral and petroleum economics; advisory and documentation services; professional staff: 300; library of 19,000 vols., 6,000 serials; Dir. L. W. WILLIAMS (acting); publs. include *Bulletins*†, *Reports*†, *Petroleum Search Subsidy Act Publications*†, *Australian Mineral Industry Reviews*† (annually and quarterly), *BMR Journal of Australian Geology and Geophysics*, *Yearbook*, many geological and geophysical maps.

Commonwealth of Australia Bureau of Meteorology: G.P.O. Box 1289K, Melbourne, Vic. 3001; f. 1908; regional offices in Perth, Adelaide, Brisbane, Sydney, Hobart,

Darwin, Canberra and Melbourne; Dir. Dr. J. W. Zillman; publs. daily weather bulletins and charts, monthly, seasonal and annual rainfall maps and statistical summaries, publications on special subjects, climatological reviews, *Australian Meteorological Magazine*†. *Meteorological Studies*†.

Geological Survey of New South Wales: Dept. of Mineral Resources, Sydney; f. 1874; research and advice in the geosciences, inc. compilation of standard series geological and metallogenic maps; 68 professional staff; Dir. Dr. N. M. Markham; publs. *Quarterly Notes*†, *Geological Memoirs*†, *Palaeontological Memoirs*†, *Ethnological Memoirs*, *Bulletins*†, *Records*†, *Mineral Resources*†, *Technical Reports*, *Mineral Industry*†, *Geological Survey Reports*, *Geological Maps*†, etc.

Geological Survey of Queensland: Dept. of Mines, Mineral House, 41 George St., Brisbane, Qld. 4000; f. 1868; engineering geology, economic geology, regional mapping, urban and environmental geology, petroleum geology, geophysics, palaeontology, palynology, coal section, computer and information services; 147 staff; library of 3,800 vols.; Chief Geologist R. J. Allen; publs. *Publications*†, *Records*, *Reports*†, *Maps*, Queensland Mines Dept. *Annual Report*†, *Queensland Government Mining Journal*†.

Geological Survey of Western Australia: Mineral House, 66 Adelaide Terrace, Perth, W.A. 6000; f. 1896; 100 mems.; library of 70,000 vols.; Dir. A. F. Trendall; publs. *Bulletin*, *Annual Progress Report*, *Mineral Resources Bulletin*, *Explanatory Notes* (1 : 250,000 maps), *Report Series*.

Government Observatory: Sydney; f. 1856; Govt. Astronomer W. H. Robertson; publs. *Astrographic Catalogue* (Sydney section), *Sydney Observatory Papers*.

Mount Stromlo and Siding Spring Observatories: Private Bag, Woden P.O., A.C.T. 2606; f. 1924 as Commonwealth Observatory; research in astrophysics, inc. all phases of galactic and extra-galactic astronomy; transferred to Australian National University 1956; library of 12,000 vols.; Dir. D. S. Mathewson.

Perth Observatory: Bickley, W.A. 6076; f. 1896; positional astronomy, photometry and planet observations; library of 6,000 vols.; Govt. Astronomer Dr. I. Nikoloff; publ. *Communications*† (irregular).

Riverview College Observatory: Lane Cove, N.S.W. 2066; f. 1908; world-wide standard seismograph network station 1962; Dir. Lawrence Drake, s.j.

South Australian Department of Mines and Energy: Box 151, P.O. Eastwood, S.A. 5063; f. 1892; Geological Survey of South Australia; resources, mining, energy and engineering services directorates; *c.* 280 staff, incl. geophysicists, paleontologists, geologists and mining engineers; library of 25,000 vols.; Dir.-Gen. B. P. Webb; publs. *Annual Report*†, *Geological Survey Bulletin*†, *Mineral Resources Review*† (2 a year), *Geological Survey*, *Reports of Investigations*†, *Quarterly Geological Notes*, *Mineral Industry Quarterly*, geological maps†.

Tasmanian Geological Survey: c/o Department of Mines, G.P.O. Box 124B, Hobart 7001; f. 1860; library of 2,100 monographs and 529 serials; Chief Geologist I. B. Jennings; publs. *Geological Survey Bulletins*†, *Geological Survey Papers*, *Technical Reports*, *Geological Survey Maps*†, *Explanatory Reports*†.

Religion, Sociology and Anthropology

Australian Institute of Aboriginal Studies: P.O.B. 553, Canberra City, A.C.T. 2601; f. 1961; statutory body since 1964; provides funds, promotes research and publishes books on all aspects of Aboriginal studies, traditional and contemporary; library of 20,000 vols.; resource centre of 12,000 sound tapes, 400 films, 60,000 colour slides, 66,000 photographic prints; Principal Dr. P. J. Ucko; publs. *Australian Aboriginal Studies*, *Bibliographies*, *Manuals*, *Newsletter*† (2 a year), *Regional and Research Studies*, records of Aboriginal music.

Australian Institute of Archaeology: 174 Collins St., Melbourne, Vic. 3000; f. 1946 to investigate all discoveries and results which the Institute or any other organization shall publish, calculated to have bearing upon the authenticity, historicity, accuracy and inspiration of the Holy Scriptures; teaching programmes and exhibitions on the ancient Near East and/or Biblical archaeology; library and museum (Ancient Times House, 116 Little Bourke St., Melbourne) with a collection of pottery and other artifacts of Biblical lands and of Cypriot pottery; Pres. J. A. Thompson, m.a., m.sc., ph.d.; Dir. Rev. G. G. Garner, b.a., b.d.; publ. *Buried History* (quarterly).

Technology

Australian Mineral Development Laboratories, The: Flemington St., Frewville, South Australia 5063; f. 1960; Contract Research and Technical Consulting organization providing services in Mineral Engineering, Chemical Metallurgy, Analytical Chemistry, Materials Technology, Mineralogy and Petrology, Operations Research, Computer Services and Project Development; 224 staff; Chair. of Council Russell J. Burge; Man. Dir. Norton Jackson; publ. *Annual Report*.

Australian Road Research Board: 500 Burwood Highway, Vermont South, Melbourne, Vic. 3131; f. 1960; research related to the design, planning, construction, maintenance and use of roads; library of *c.* 30,000 vols. and journals; Exec. Dir. M. G. Lay, m.eng.sc., ph.d., f.i.e.aust., m.a.s.c.e.; Sec. R. J. Membrey, a.a.s.a., a.c.i.s.; publs. *Australian Road Research Journal* (quarterly), *Proceedings of Biennial Conference*, *ARR Research Reports*, *Australian Road Index*.

Australian Wool Corporation: "Wool House", 369 Royal Parade, Parkville, Vic. 3052; f. 1936; wool promotion, marketing research, testing and research, statistical and technical services; fibre marketing; Chair. D. J. Asimus; Chief Gen. Man. Dr. A. J. Farnworth; publs. *Annual Report*, etc.

Department of Defence: Defence Science and Technology Organisation:

Advanced Engineering Laboratory: P.O.B. 2151, G.P.O., Adelaide, S.A. 5001; f. 1949; engineering design, development of mechanical, electrical and electronic equipment for Defence Force; test facilities, standards, engineering support for other DSTO laboratories; Chief Supt. E. B. Davis; publs. *Annual Report*, scientific and technical reports.

Aeronautical Research Laboratories: P.O.B. 4331, G.P.O., Melbourne, Vic. 3001; f. 1939; research and development in aeronautics, particularly aerodynamics, materials, propulsion (gas turbines) and structures; Chief Supt. J. M. Evans (acting); publs. *Annual Report*, technical reports and notes.

Armed Forces Food Science Establishment: P.O.B. 147, Scottsdale, Tas. 7254; f. 1959; research and development of calorific and nutritive requirements of Defence Force; conduct of trials to ensure satisfactory storage life under all conditions, the acceptability of rations and the effectiveness of personnel using rations; analytical, bacteriological and physiological research equipment and food processing facilities; Dir. and Defence Food Science Adviser Dr. R. J. Richards; publs. *Annual Report*, scientific and technical reports.

Central Studies Establishment: Campbell Park Offices, Canberra, A.C.T.; f. 1969; operational research and systems analysis for defence applications; Supt. P. W. BOWE; Chief Defence Scientist Prof. P. T. FINK; publs. *Annual Report*, scientific reports.

Engineering Development Establishment: Private Bag No. 12, P.O., Ascot Vale, Vic. 3032; f. 1943; Trials and Proving Wing at Monegeetta, Vic.; engineering design and redesign of materiel; evaluation of prototypes and existing defence equipment; data bank for test standards for Defence Force equipment; Head J. C. WISDOM; publs. *Annual Report*, technical reports.

Electronics Research Laboratory: P.O.B. 2151, G.P.O., Adelaide, S.A. 5001; f. 1949; analytical studies applying mathematical modelling techniques for Defence Force; research and development in radio, electronics, radar, infra-red applications, optics, electro-optics, electronic warfare, surveillance and navigation; Chief Supt. M. S. KIRKPATRICK; publs. *Annual Report*, scientific and technical reports.

Joint Tropical Trials Research Establishment: P.O.B. 838, Innisfail, Qld. 4860; f. 1962; joint UK/Australian research and investigation into the mechanisms of degradation of materials and equipment, measurement and classification of tropical environments; facilities and equipment for trials and evaluation of materiel in hot/dry and hot/wet conditions for Defence Force; Officer-in-charge L. J. LLOYD; publs. various papers.

Materials Research Laboratories: P.O.B. 50, Ascot Vale, Vic. 3032; f. 1917; research and development in organic and physical chemistry, physics, metallurgy, explosive materials and ballistics; protection of personnel and equipment; provision of analysis and testing facilities; Chief Supt. Dr. H. L. WAIN; publs. *Annual Report*, scientific and technical reports.

Royal Australian Navy Research Laboratory: P.O.B. 706, Darlinghurst, N.S.W. 2010; f. 1956; research into underwater acoustics, oceanography, sonar, mining and mine countermeasures; research and analysis of maritime exercises; Supt. Dr. W. F. HUNTER; publs. scientific and technical reports.

Trials Resources Laboratory: P.O.B. 2151, G.P.O., Adelaide, S.A. 5001; f. 1949; maintenance and operation of the Woomera Range including the organization of Woomera trials; analysis of trials data; research and development of measurement techniques and data analysis; Supt. E. C. MONTGOMERY; publs. *Annual Report*, scientific and technical reports.

Weapons Systems Research Laboratory: P.O.B. 2151, G.P.O., Adelaide, S.A. 5001; f. 1949; research and development in propulsion, marine physics, weapons systems and aeroballistics applied to the fields of combustion and efficiency of propellants, underwater surveillance techniques, missile and guided weapons development; upper atmosphere research; Chief Supt. J. W. CROMPTON; publs. *Annual Report*, scientific and technical reports.

LIBRARIES AND ARCHIVES

AUSTRALIAN CAPITAL TERRITORY

Australian Archives: P.O.B. 34, Dickson, A.C.T. 2602, Archival Authority of the Commonwealth Government since 1961; responsible for the evaluation, analysis and preservation of records; compiles Commonwealth Register of Record Series and provides an Information Bureau on all aspects of records and archives administration; undertakes the administration of access policies and offers user and extension services for government departments and the public; permanent holdings of national archives include documents, maps, plans, films, photographs, records and paintings currently estimated to be in excess of 10 million items; these date from 1827 and are derived from a variety of sources including Commonwealth Territories and persons associated with the Commonwealth; regional offices in State capitals; Dir.-Gen. Prof. R. G. NEALE; Dir. Dr. K. PENNY; publ. *Inventories* (irregular).

Australian National University Library: Canberra, A.C.T.; f. 1948; 1,025,000 vols.; R. G. Menzies Building (social sciences and Asian studies collections) 431,000 vols., J. B. Chifley Building (humanities and undergraduate collections) 315,000 vols., Science libraries 213,000 vols., Law Library 66,000 vols.; Librarian (vacant).

Australian Patent, Trade Marks and Designs Office Library: Scarborough House, Phillip, P.O.B. 200, Woden, A.C.T. 2606; f. 1904; library of 16,500 vols., 375 periodicals; Australian and foreign patent specifications, science and technology and industrial property; Librarian Miss H. N. MCGREGOR.

Department of Education Library: P.O.B. 826, Woden, A.C.T. 2606; f. 1945 as Commonwealth Office of Education Library; educational research, comparative education, primary and secondary education, teacher training, educational psychology, general language teaching, child migrant education, technical and further education; OECD and UNESCO materials; 20,000 vols.; Sec. K. N. JONES, C.B.E.; Librarian G. R. PACKARD; publs. *Education News*, *Hemisphere* (every 2 months), *UNESCO News* (2 a month), *English: a New Language*, *OECD Activities in Education* (irregular).

National Library of Australia: Canberra, A.C.T.; f. 1902; reference and research library. One section provides lending services for residents of the Australian Capital Territory; copyright deposit library for Australian publications; central documentary and educational film library; important holdings of Australiana, including Petherick, Ferguson and Nan Kivell collections and Mathews Ornithological collection and of English literature, American history and publications in Asian languages: 1,625,000 vols., 83,000 current serial titles, 820,000 maps and aerial photographs, 27,400 pictures and prints, 191,000 photographs, 134,000 reels of microfilm, 18,153,000 metres of moving picture films; Dir.-Gen. Dr. G. CHANDLER; publs. *Annual Report of the Council*, *Australian Books, a select list* (annually), *Australian Films*, *Australian Government Publications* (annually), *Australian Maps* (quarterly and annually), *Australian National Bibliography* (weekly, monthly and annually), *Australian Public Affairs Information Service* (monthly and annually), *Catalogue of 16-mm. Films*, *Current Australian Serials* (annually), *Guide to Collections of Manuscripts Relating to Australia*, *Historical Records of Australia*, *Serials in Australian Libraries, social sciences and humanities*, *Newspapers in Australian Libraries: a union list*, *Index Atlas to Maps in Series in the Map Collection* (Part 1 *Australia*, Part 2 *New Guinea*), various monographic publications.

NEW SOUTH WALES

Archives Office of New South Wales: 2 Globe St., The Rocks, Sydney 2000; f. 1961; Principal Archivist D. J. CROSS, B.A., A.L.A.A. (acting).

Auchmuty Library, University of Newcastle: N.S.W. 2308; f. 1965; 450,000 vols.; Librarian E. FLOWERS, M.A., A.L.A.A.

City of Sydney Public Library: Central Library, Q.V. Bldg., 473 George St., Sydney, N.S.W. 2000; f. 1909; 5 brs.; 290,000 vols.; City Librarian SARAH WALTERS; publs. *Annual Report, A Select List of Music Scores.*

High Court of Australia Library: Parkes, A.C.T. 2600; f. 1903; private library of the Justices of the Court and barristers appearing before it; 90,000 vols in Canberra; Librarian W. FORD.

Library of the University of New England: Armidale, N.S.W. 2351; f. 1954; 455,000 vols.; Librarian S. W. RICHARDSON, B.SC.(EDUC.), M.LIB.SC., A.L.A.A.

Newcastle Region Public Library: Cultural Centre, Newcastle, N.; f. 1948; reference and lending services 357,235 vols.; Dir. C. E. SMITH, B.A., F.L.A.A.; publs. *Newcastle Morning Herald Index* (from 1861, annual), *Monographs* (irregular), *Archival Inventories* (irregular).

Parliamentary Library of New South Wales: Parliament House, Sydney, N.S.W. 2000; over 140,000 vols.; Chief Officer R. L. COPE, M.A., PH.D., F.L.A.A.; publs. *Annual Report, Reference Monographs.*

State Library of New South Wales: Macquarie St., Sydney 2000; f. 1826; State copyright privileges; 1,457,324 vols.; includes Mitchell and Dixson Libraries, Galleries of Australiana and of historical pictures of Australasia and the Pacific; State Librarian R. F. DOUST, B.A., M.LIB., F.L.A.A.

University of New South Wales Libraries: Kensington, Sydney, N.S.W. 2033; f. 1949; 1 million vols. at Kensington and other centres; Librarian A. HORTON.

University of Sydney Library: University, Sydney, N.S.W. 2006; f. 1852; 2,281,013 vols.; Librarian HARRISON BRYAN.

QUEENSLAND

Queensland Parliamentary Library: Parliament House, George St., Brisbane, Qld. 4000; f. 1860; information service to members of State Legislature; statistics, economics, politics, law and education; over 100,000 vols.; Librarian R. J. N. BANNENBERG; publs. *Index to Articles from Periodicals Currently Received*† (quarterly), *Queensland Parliamentary Handbook*† (every 3 years), *Comparative Legislation Bulletin*† (2 a year).

State Library of Queensland: William St., Brisbane; f. 1896; 607,474 items; the state reference library, non-lending except through its extension services, includes John Oxley Library of Queenslandiana; has library deposit privileges; State Librarian S. L. RYAN; publs. *Queensland Government Publications*† (quarterly), *Selected Serial Resources*† (quarterly), *Directory of State and Public Library Service in Queensland*†, *Public Libraries in Queensland: Statistical Bulletin*† (annually).

Supreme Court Library: George St., Brisbane; f. 1862; 55,000 vols.; Librarian R. J. THOMSON, B.A., A.L.A.A.; publ. *Information Bulletin*†.

University of Queensland Library: St. Lucia, Brisbane 4067; f. 1911; 1,188,968 vols.; 38,900 microform reels, 169,000 microfiches; 24,500 A/V items; Librarian F. D. O. FIELDING, M.A., A.L.A., F.L.A.A.

SOUTH AUSTRALIA

Flinders University Library: Bedford Park, S.A. 5042; f. 1963; 420,000 vols.; University Librarian N. STOCKDALE, B.A.

Library of the South Australian Institute of Technology: David Murray Library, North Terrace, Adelaide; The Levels Campus Library, Pooraka; Whyalla Campus Library, Whyalla; f. 1889, reorganized 1955; 160,000 vols.; Librarian C. R. TAYLOR, B.SC., A.L.A.A.

Library of the University of Adelaide: Adelaide, S.A. 5001; f. 1876; 1,050,000 vols.; Librarian I. D. RAYMOND, M.A., M.S.

State Library of South Australia: (formerly Public Library of South Australia), North Terrace, Adelaide; f. 1884; State copyright privileges; reference, lending and bibliographical services; 949,000 vols.; State Librarian R. K. OLDING, B.EC., F.L.A.A.; publs. *South Australiana*† (twice yearly), *Pinpointer*† (two-monthly), *Index to Australian Book Reviews*† (quarterly), *Annual Report*†.

TASMANIA

State Library of Tasmania: Murray St., Hobart; f. 1944; 1,150,000 vols., 5,200 documentary films, 150,000 records and cassettes; special collections; State Librarian W. L. BROWN; publs. *Annual Report, Bibliographies, Guide to Public Records,* etc.

University of Tasmania Library: Hobart; f. 1889; 408,500 vols.; special collection on Quakerism; Librarian J. E. SCRIVENER, B.A., A.L.A., A.L.A.A.; publs. *Union List of Higher Degree Theses in Australian Libraries, Annual Report.*

VICTORIA

Central Catholic Library: 343 Elizabeth St., Melbourne; f. 1923; theology, sociology, church history, liturgy; 35,000 vols.; Dir. JOHN A. PHILLIPS, S.J., S.T.L.

Commonwealth Scientific and Industrial Research Organization Libraries: 314 Albert St., East Melbourne, Vic. 3002; the system covers over 70 Divisional and field station collections; maintains a union catalogue of holdings and indexes to the Organization's research work; Chief Librarian P. H. DAWE, B.A., A.L.A.A.; publs. *Accessions List, Scientific Serials in Australian Libraries, SSAL Supplement.*

La Trobe University Library: Bundoora, Vic. 3083; f. 1964; 450,000 vols.; special emphasis on Latin America; Chief Librarian D. H. BORCHARDT, M.A., A.L.A., F.L.A.A.; publs. *News*† (quarterly), *Annual Report*†, *Library Publications*† (series).

Monash University Library: Clayton, Vic.; f. 1961; 1,030,000 vols.; Librarian T. B. SOUTHWELL, B.A., A.L.A.A.

Parliament Library: Parliament House, Spring St., Melbourne, Vic. 3002; f. 1851; 150,000 vols.; social sciences, parliamentary papers, debates, statutes; Librarian Miss J. MCGOVERN, B.A., A.L.A.A.

Public Record Office of Victoria: 19th Floor, 44th Level, Nauru House, 80 Collins St., Melbourne, Vic. 3000; f. 1973; 80,000 linear ft. of public records; Keeper H. W. NUNN, B.A.

State Library of Victoria: 328 Swanston St., Melbourne, Vic. 3000; f. 1853; the state general reference library and legal depository; 1,032,430 vols.; special collections include La Trobe (Australiana) art, music and performing arts, Anderson Chess Collection; Principal Librarian MARGERY C. RAMSAY; publ. *La Trobe Library Journal*† (2 a year).

University of Melbourne Library: Parkville, Vic. 3052; f. 1855; 869,697 vols.; Librarian W. D. RICHARDSON. B.A., A.L.A.A., F.L.A.

WESTERN AUSTRALIA

Library of the University of Western Australia: Nedlands, W.A. 6009; f. 1913; 700,000 vols.; Librarian ARTHUR ELLIS.

Library Service of Western Australia: 102 Beaufort St., Perth, W.A., 6000; Reference Division: f. 1887; State Reference Library (inc. Central Music Library) and State Archives 323,015 vols.; 2,938m. archives, 19,776 scores, 11,053 serial titles, 28 m. microfiche, 16,919 reels microfilm, also photographs, maps, cassettes, etc.; copyright privilege; Lending Division: f. 1954; operates via 181 public libraries; 1,299,535 vols., 2,292 cassettes, 286 reels microfilm; State Film Centre: 160 James St., Perth; film lending collection of *c.* 5,000 titles; State Librarian ROBERT SHARMAN, B.A., F.L.A.A.

MUSEUMS AND ART GALLERIES

A.C.T.

Australian War Memorial: P.O.B. 345, Canberra City, A.C.T. 2601; f. 1917; national war memorial museum and art gallery illustrating and recording aspects of all wars in which the Armed Forces of Australia have been engaged; 64 dioramas, 11,000 works of art, 40,000 relics, library of 80,000 vols., 500,000 photographs, 4 million metres of cine film, and repository of Australian Operational records; administered by a Board of Trustees; Dir. N. J. FLANAGAN; publs. official histories of Australia at war.

NEW SOUTH WALES

Art Gallery of New South Wales: Domain, Sydney; f. 1874; representative collection of Australian art, Aboriginal and Melanesian art; collections of British 18th-20th-century art; European painting and sculpture (15th-20th century); Asian art, particularly Chinese and Japanese ceramics; Australian, British and European prints and drawings; Dir. EDMUND CAPON; publs. *Exhibition Catalogues*, etc.

Australian Museum: 6–8 College St., Sydney 2000; f. 1827; natural history, anthropology, palaeontology, mineralogy; Dir. D. J. G. GRIFFIN, PH.D.; library of 66,000 vols.; publs. *Records*†, *Memoirs*†, *Australian Natural History* (quarterly magazine) and other monographs.

Geological and Mining Museum: 36 George St., Sydney 2000; f. 1876; displays on Mining, Geology, Minerals, Ores, Fossils; Curator R. G. HIRST.

Macleay Museum: Univ. of Sydney, Sydney; Collection started 1790, given to University 1888; zoology, ethnology, Chinese ceramics and 19th-century scientific instruments; history and technology; Dir. Dr. P. J. STANBURY.

Museum of Applied Arts and Sciences: Harris St., Ultimo, Sydney 2007; f. 1880; administered by Board of 7 Trustees; ceramics, glassware, Asian arts, textiles, costume, musical instruments, horology, arms and armour, numismatics, engineering, transport, planetarium; library of 12,000 vols.; Dir. L. G. SHARP, D.PHIL.; publs. bulletins, guides, leaflets, *Annual Report*†, etc.

Nicholson Museum of Antiquities: Univ. of Sydney, Sydney; f. 1860; collection of Egyptian, Near Eastern Cypriot, European, Greek and Roman antiquities; Curator Prof. A. CAMBITOGLOU, M.A., PH.D., D.PHIL., F.A.H.A., F.S.A., F.ATHENS ARCH. SOC.

J. L. Shellshear Museum of Comparative Anatomy and Physical Anthropology: Dept. of Anatomy, Univ. of Sydney; f. 1958; comparative racial series of human skulls, skeletons, brains, and marsupials; Curator Prof. of Anatomy.

War Memorial Gallery of Fine Arts: University of Sydney, Sydney; f. 1959 to further interest in and knowledge of the fine arts; frequent loan exhibitions of pictures and objects.

J. T. Wilson Museum of Human Anatomy: Dept. of Anatomy, Univ. of Sydney; f. 1886; includes 1,000 dissected parts and cross sections of the human body; Curator Prof. Dept. of Anatomy.

QUEENSLAND

Queensland Art Gallery: (temporary address) M.I.M. Bldg., 160 Ann St., Brisbane 4000; f. 1895; paintings, drawings, prints, sculpture, ceramics and decorative arts covering broadly history of Australian art; British and European paintings, prints, drawings and sculpture; Dir. RAOUL MELLISH.

Queensland Herbarium: Meiers Rd., Indooroopilly, 4068 (formerly Botanic Museum and Herbarium, f. 1889); studies of flora and mapping of vegetation of Queensland, plant ecology, weeds, poisonous plants and economic botany; 500,000 specimens; library of 10,000 vols.; Dir. R. W. JOHNSON; publ. *Austrobaileya*†.

Queensland Museum: Gregory Terrace, Fortitude Valley, 4006; f. 1871; library of 70,000 vols.; zoology, geology, history, ethnology, technology; Dir. A. BARTHOLOMAI, PH.D.; publ. *Memoirs*†.

SOUTH AUSTRALIA

Art Gallery of South Australia, The: North Terrace, Adelaide, S.A. 5000; f. 1881; comprehensive collection of Australian works of art, British and European painting, prints, drawings and sculpture 16th–20th centuries, English and European furniture, silver and glass; English, European and South East Asian ceramics and antiquities; arms, armour, coins and medals; early S. Australian pictures, relics and stamps (housed in S. Australian Historical Museum); education services and country travelling exhibition; Dir. DAVID THOMAS; publs. *Bulletin* (annual), *Annual Report*†, exhibition catalogues†.

South Australian Museum: North Terrace, Adelaide, S.A. 5000; f. 1856; historical, anthropological, archaeological, geological, meteoritic and zoological material mainly from Southern and Central Australia, Papua New Guinea and the Pacific; the Australian ethnological collection is outstanding, and, for South and Central districts, the best in existence; world's largest collection of tektites; materials conservation; education and advisory services; library of *c.* 35,000 vols.; Dir. JOHN K. LING, PH.D.; publ. *Records*†.

TASMANIA

Queen Victoria Museum and Art Gallery: Wellington St., Launceston; f. 1891; library of 7,000 vols.; collections comprise pure and applied art, Tasmanian history, Tasmanian and general anthropology, Tasmanian botany, geology, palaeontology and zoology; Dir. C. B. TASSELL, B.SC.; publs. *Records*†, *Annual Report.*

Tasmanian Museum and Art Gallery: 5 Argyle St., Hobart 7001 (G.P.O. Box No. 1164-M); f. 1843; art, natural and human history, applied science, with emphasis on Tasmania and Australia as a whole; important collections relating to Tasmanian Aborigines; a branch museum (West Coast Pioneers' Memorial Museum) dealing in particular with mining, at Zeehan; Dir. D. R. GREGG, M.SC.; publs. handbooks†, exhibition catalogues†, *Annual Report*†.

VICTORIA

National Gallery of Victoria: 180 St. Kilda Rd., Melbourne; f. 1859; Old Masters and depts. of Prints and Drawings, Modern European Art, Australian Art, Decorative Art, Asian Art, Antiquities, Photography, Tribal Art; library of 20,000 vols., and slides; Dir. ERIC B. ROWLISON, B.A.; Sec. R. P. NOLAN, B.COM., A.A.S.A.; publs. *Art Bulletin of Victoria*†, catalogues†.

National Museum of Victoria: 285-321 Russell St., Melbourne, Vic. 3000; f. 1854; zoology, geology, palaeontology, mineralogy, petrology and anthropology; library of 47,000 vols.; Dir. Dr. BARRY R. WILSON; publ. *Memoirs*† (annually).

Science Museum of Victoria: 304–328 Swanston St., Melbourne 3000; f. 1870; history of science, applied science; displays and reserve collections in agriculture, astronomy, arms and armour, economic geology, electricity and electronics, engineering, horology, numismatics and transport; observatory, H. V. McKay Planetarium, joint Science Museum and Wireless Inst. of Australia (Victorian Division), Amateur Radio Station, VK3AOM, Environment Protection Authority Air Monitoring Station; education service; library of 8,500 vols.; Dir. F. J. E. KENDALL, B.AGR.SC.; publs. *Report of Activities* (annually), information sheets.

WESTERN AUSTRALIA

Art Gallery of Western Australia, The: 47 James St., Perth; f. 1895; British, European and Australian paintings, prints, drawings, sculpture, craft items, comprehensive tribal art collection from Africa through to South East Asia and Australian Aboriginal; Dir. W. F. ELLIS; publs. *Annual Report, Bulletin, Perth Survey of Drawing*, major exhibition illustrated catalogues and posters.

Western Australian Museum, The: Francis St., Perth; f. 1891; Natural Science Division: zoology, palaeontology, meteoritics; Human Studies Division: anthropology, archaeology, regional history and technology, and maritime archaeology; Professional Services Division: material conservation, displays, publs., library and education; aboriginal sites; branches: Western Australian Maritime Museum, Fremantle Museum, Albany Residency Museum; 196 staff; library 6,000 vols., 280 journals; Dir. J. L. BANNISTER; publs. *Records*†, *Special Publications*†, *Annual Report*†, *Information Series*.

UNIVERSITIES

THE UNIVERSITY OF ADELAIDE

ADELAIDE, S.A. 5001

Telephone: 2234333.

Telegraphic Address: UNIVAD.

Founded 1874.

Opened 1876.

Autonomous institution established by Act of Parliament.

Academic year: March to December.

Chancellor: Hon. J. J. BRAY, LL.D.

Vice-Chancellor: Prof. D. R. STRANKS, M.SC., PH.D.

Deputy Vice-Chancellors: Prof. E. S. BARNES, PH.D., F.A.A., Prof. K. A. PROVINS, M.A., PH.D.

Registrar: F. J. O'NEILL, B.SC.

Librarian: I. D. RAYMOND, M.A., M.S., A.L.A.A.

Number of full-time teachers: 654, including 69 professors.

Number of students: 9,034.

Publications: *Australian Journal of Experimental Biology and Medical Science*† (bi-monthly), *The Joseph Fisher Lecture in Commerce*; *Reports of Summer Schools*; *Adelaide Law Review*† (annual); *Australian Economic Papers* (every 6 months); *Southern Review* (every 6 months).

DEANS:

Faculty of Agricultural Science: C. J. DRISCOLL, PH.D., D.SC.

Faculty of Architecture and Planning: D. A. L. SAUNDERS, M.ARCH., F.R.A.I.A.

Faculty of Arts: F. H. MARES, M.A., F.A.H.A.

Faculty of Dentistry: J. C. THONARD, PH.D., F.R.C.PATH.

Faculty of Economics: D. T. HEALEY, M.A.

Faculty of Engineering: R. E. LUXTON, PH.D.

Faculty of Law: M. J. DETMOLD, LL.B.

Faculty of Mathematical Sciences: E. O. TUCK, PH.D.

Faculty of Medicine: D. ROWLEY, M.D., PH.D.

Faculty of Music: M. J. FOX, M.MUS., A.R.C.M.

Faculty of Science: J. R. PRESCOTT, PH.D., D.PHIL.

CHAIRMEN OF BOARDS OF STUDIES:

Aboriginal: T. BROWN, D.D.SC., F.R.A.C.D.S.

Environmental: H. STRETTON, M.A., F.A.H.A., F.A.S.S.A.

Research: A. M. SNOSWELL, PH.D.

PROFESSORS:

BECKWITH, A. L. J., D.PHIL., F.A.A., Organic Chemistry
BENNETT, J. H., M.A., PH.D., Genetics
BOGNER, R. E., PH.D., M.E., Electrical Engineering.
BOYD, D. M., B.SC., Geophysics
BROWN, T., D.D.SC., F.R.A.C.D.S., Restorative Dentistry
BROWNING, T. O., PH.D., Entomology
BRUCE, M. I., PH.D., Physical Chemistry
CASTLES, A. C., J.D., Law
COGHLAN, B. L. D., PH.D., German
COLMER, J. A., M.A., PH.D., F.A.H.A., English Language and Literature
COX, L. W., M.B., CH.B., F.R.C.S., F.R.A.C.S., F.AUST.C.O.G., Obstetrics and Gynaecology
DAVIES, J. C., B.A., D. DE L'U., French
DE LA LANDE, I. S., M.SC., PH.D., Pharmacology
DRISCOLL, C. J., PH.D., D.SC., Agronomy
ELLIOTT, W. H., M.A., PH.D., F.A.A., Biochemistry
ELMSLIE, R. G., M.D., F.R.A.C.S., Surgery
GALE, F. G., PH.D., F.A.S.S.A., Geography
GALLIVER, D., M.A., A.R.C.M., Music
GLOW, P.H., PH.D., F.A.S.S.A., Psychology
GOUGH, A. G., D.PHIL., History
GREEN, H. S., PH.D., D.SC., F.A.A., Mathematical Physics
HARCOURT, G. C., M.COM., PH.D., F.A.S.S.A., Economics
HENDERSON, M. S., M.EC., PH.D., Commerce
HIRST, F., M.SC., PH.D., F.INST.P., F.A.I.P., Computing Science
HURST, C. A., PH.D., F.A.A., Mathematical Physics
JACKA, F. J., PH.D., *Director*, Mawson Institute for Antarctic Research
JAMES, A. T., M.SC., PH.D., Mathematical Statistics
JARRETT, F. G., PH.D., F.A.S.S.A., Economics
JOHN, I. D., M.A., PH.D., Psychology
JORDAN, D. O., D.SC., PH.D., F.R.I.C., F.A.A., Physical Chemistry
KAPFERER, B., PH.D., Anthropology
LUCKE, H. K., DR.JUR., M.C.J., Law
LUDBROOK, J., CH.M., M.D., F.R.C.S., F.R.A.C.S., Surgery
LUXTON, R. E., PH.D., Mechanical Engineering
MCCREDIE, A. D., M.A., D.PHIL., F.A.H.A., Music
MCFARLANE, B. J., M.EC., Politics
MANWELL, C., M.S., PH.D., F.A.A.A.S., Zoology
MARJORIBANKS, K., B.SC., M.ED., PH.D., Education
MARTIN, P. G., PH.D., Botany
MAXWELL, G. M., M.D., M.R.C.P., F.R.A.C.P., Paediatrics
MILLER, D. R., PH.D., Materials Science
MORAN, W., PH.D., Pure Mathematics
MURRELL, T. G. C., D.T.M. & H., M.D., M.R.A.C.G.P., Community Medicine
NERLICH, G. C., M.A., F.A.H.A., Philosophy
NICHOLAS, D. J. D., M.A., PH.D., D,SC., Agricultural Biochemistry and Soil Science.
PALEG, L. G., D.SC., PH.D., Plant Physiology
PILOWSKY, I., M.D., D.P.M., F.R.A.N.Z.C.P., F.R.C.PSYCH., F.R.A.C.P., Psychiatry
POSWILLO, D. E., D.D.S., D.SC., F.D.S.R.C.S., F.R.A.C.D.S., F.I.BIOL., Oral Pathology and Oral Surgery
POTTS, R. B., D.PHIL., D.SC., F.A.A., Applied Mathematics
PRIEDKALNS, J., PH.D., M.A., Anatomy
PRESCOTT, J. R., PH.D., D.PHIL., Physics
QUIRK, J. P., PH.D., D.SC., F.A.I.A.S., F.R.A.C.I., F.A.A., Director Waite Agricultural Research Institute
ROBERTSON, J. S., D.PHIL., F.R.A.C.P., M.C.P.A., Pathology
ROGERS, G. E., M.SC., PH.D., F.A.A., Biochemistry
ROGERS, W. P., M.SC., D.SC., F.A.A., Parasitology
ROWLEY, D., M.D., PH.D, Microbiology and Immunology
RUTLAND, R. W. R., PH.D., F.G.S., Geology
SAUNDERS, D. A. L., M.ARCH., F.R.A.I.A., Architecture
SHEARMAN, D. J. C., PH.D., F.R.C.P.ED., Medicine
TAIT, R. W. F., PH.D., Chemical Engineering
THONARD, J. C., PH.D., F.R.C.PATH., Oral Biology
TREVASKIS, J. R., M.A., Classics
TUCK, E. O., PH.D., Applied Mathematics
VEALE, J. L., M.B., CH.B., F.R.A.C.P., Human Physiology and Pharmacology
VERNON-ROBERTS, B., M.D., PH.D., M.R.C.PATH., Pathology
WALLACE, H. R., PH.D., D.SC., F.A.A., Plant Pathology

WANGEL, A. G., M.D., D.PHIL., M.R.C.P., F.R.A.C.P., Medicine
WARBURTON, J. W., M.A., *Director*, Continuing Education
WARNER, R. F., M.E., PH.D., Civil Engineering
WELFORD, A. T., M.A., SC.D., F.A.S.S.A., Psychology
WILLIAMS, W. D., PH.D., D.SC., Zoology
WILSON, T. G., M.A., D.PHIL., F.A.H.A., History
WOMERSLEY, H. B. S., D.SC., F.A.A., Botany
YPMA, P. J. M., M.SC., PH.D., Economic Geology

ATTACHED RESEARCH INSTITUTES:

Mawson Institute for Antarctic Research: f. 1959; research and postgraduate teaching; principal field is upper atmosphere physics; collections include the library, MSS and specimens of Antarctic explorer Sir Douglas Mawson; Dir. Dr. F. JACKA.

Waite Agricultural Research Institute: Private Bag No. 1, Glen Osmond, S.A. 5064; f. 1924; Dir. Prof. J. P. QUIRK; Sec. O. G. JONES; publ. *Biennial Report*.

AFFILIATED RESIDENTIAL COLLEGES:

St. Mark's College Inc.: North Adelaide; f. 1924; number of students: 135.
Master: P. G. EDWARDS, D.PHIL.

St. Ann's College Inc.: North Adelaide; f. 1939; number of students: 130.
Principal: Dr. V. C. KENNY.

Aquinas College Inc.: North Adelaide; f. 1947; number of students: 103.
Rector: Rev. Father I. HOWELLS, S.J., PH.D.

Lincoln College Inc.: North Adelaide; f. 1951; number of students: 184.
Master: J. W. WHITEHEAD, B.D., PH.D.

Kathleen Lumley College Inc.: North Adelaide; f. 1967; number of students (postgraduate): 60.
Master: J. H. COATES, PH.D.

ASSOCIATED INSTITUTE AND COLLEGE:

S.A. Institute of Technology: *see* under Colleges of Advanced Education.

Roseworthy Agricultural College: *see* under Colleges of Advanced Education.

THE AUSTRALIAN NATIONAL UNIVERSITY

P.O.B. 4, CANBERRA, A.C.T. 2600

Founded 1946.

Telephone: Canberra 495111.
Telegraphic Address: Natuniv, Canberra.

Undergraduate students were accepted for the first time in 1960, when the Canberra University College (f. 1929) became part of the University.

Academic year: March to December.

Chancellor: Sir JOHN CRAWFORD, A.C., C.B.E., M.EC., F.A.I.A.S., F.A.S.S.A.
Pro-Chancellor: The Hon. Mr. Justice BLACKBURN, O.B.E., B.A., B.C.L.
Vice-Chancellor: Prof. D. A. LOW, M.A., D.PHIL., F.A.H.A., F.A.S.S.A.
Deputy Vice-Chancellor: Prof. I. G. ROSS, M.SC., PH.D., F.R.A.C.I., F.A.A.
Registrar: G. E. DICKER, B.A.
Secretary: W. R. WILLIAMS, B.SC.
Librarian: (vacant).
Library: See under Libraries.

Publications†: *University Calendar, Annual Report, Faculty Handbook, ANU Reporter, Degree Courses Booklets.*

Institute of Advanced Studies‡: *Chairman of the Board:* Prof. R. G. WARD, M.A., PH.D., F.A.S.S.A.

Number of academic staff: 556, including 66 professors.

Number of postgraduate students: 388.

‡ Including University Centres.

DIRECTORS AND SCHOOLS:

Research School of Biological Sciences: *Director:* Prof. B. JOHN, PH.D., D.SC., F.I.BIOL.

PROFESSORS:

CARR, D. J., PH.D., F.I.BIOL., Developmental Biology
GUNNING, B. E. S., PH.D., D.SC., F.A.A., F.R.S., Developmental Biology
HORRIDGE, G. A., M.A., PH.D., SC.D., F.A.A., F.R.S., Neurobiology
MARK, R. F., M.MED.SCI., M.B.CH.B., C.E.S., DR. 3E CYCLE, F.A.A., Behavioural Biology
OSMOND, C. B., M.SC., PH.D., F.A.A., Environmental Biology
PATEMAN, J. A., M.A., PH.D., F.R.S., Genetics

Research School of Chemistry: *Dean:* Prof. D. P. CRAIG, M.SC., PH.D., D.SC., F.R.I.C., F.R.A.C.I., F.A.A., F.R.S.

PROFESSORS:

BIRCH, A. J., C.M.G., M.SC., D.PHIL., F.R.I.C., F.R.A.C.I., F.A.A., F.R.S., Organic Chemistry
CRAIG, D. P., M.SC., PH.D., D.SC., F.R.I.C., F.R.A.C.I., F.A.A., F.R.S., Physical and Theoretical Chemistry
HYDE, B. G., PH.D., D.SC., F.R.A.C.I., F.R.I.C., F.I.P., F.A.A., Inorganic Chemistry
SARGESON, A. M., PH.D., F.R.A.C.I., F.A.A., Inorganic Chemistry

Research School of Earth Sciences: *Director:* Prof. A. E. RINGWOOD, M.SC., PH.D., F.A.A., F.R.S.

PROFESSORS:

GUSTAFSON, L. B., M.S., PH.D., Economic Geology
LAMBECK, K., D.PHIL., D.SC., Geophysics
RINGWOOD, A.E., M.SC, PH.D., F.A.A., F.R.S., Geochemistry
TURNER, J. S., M.SC., PH.D., F.I.P., F.R.MET.S., F.A.A., Geophysical Fluid Dynamics

John Curtin School of Medical Research: *Director:* Prof. R. PORTER, D.SC., M.A., B.CH., D.M., F.A.A.

PROFESSORS:

ADA, G. L., D.SC., F.A.A., Microbiology
BISHOP, P. O., M.B., B.S., D.SC., F.A.A., F.R.S., Physiology
CURTIS, D. R., M.B., B.S., PH.D., F.A.A., F.R.S., Pharmacology
GIBSON, F. W. E., D.PHIL., D.SC., F.A.A., F.R.S., Biochemistry
MORRIS, B., D.PHIL., F.A.A., Immunology
NICHOL, L. W., PH.D., D.SC., F.R.A.C.I., Physical Biochemistry

Research School of Pacific Studies: *Director:* (vacant).

PROFESSORS:

ARNDT, H. W., M.A., B.LITT., F.A.S.S.A., Economics
CORDEN, W. M., M.COM., M.A., PH.D., F.A.S.S.A., Economics
DAWS, G. A., M.A., PH.D., Pacific and South-East Asian History
FREEMAN, J. D., PH.D., F.A.S.S.A., Anthropology
GOLSON, J., M.A., F.A.H.A., Prehistory
KEESING, R. M., A.M., PH.D., F.A.S.S.A., Anthropology
LOW, D. A., M.A., D.PHIL., F.A.H.A., F.A.S.S.A., South Asian History
MACKIE, J. A. C., M.A., F.A.S.S.A., Political and Social Change
MILLER, J. D. B., M.EC., M.A., F.A.S.S.A., International Relations
WALKER, D., M.A., PH.D., Biogeography and Geomorphology
WANG GUNGWU, M.A., PH.D., F.A.H.A., Far Eastern History
WARD, R. G., M.A., PH.D., F.A.S.S.A., Human Geography
WURM, S. A., DR.PHIL., F.A.S.S.A., F.A.H.A., Linguistics

Research School of Physical Sciences: *Director:* Prof. J. H. CARVER, PH.D., SC.D., F.A.I.P.

PROFESSORS:

CARVER, J. H., PH.D., SC.D., F.A.I.P., Ultraviolet Physics
EDWARDS, R. E., PH.D., Mathematics
GASCOIGNE, S. C. B., M.SC., PH.D., F.A.A., Astronomy
KANEFF, S., PH.D., F.I.E.AUST., Engineering Physics
LE COUTEUR, K. J., M.A., PH.D., F.A.A., Theoretical Physics
MATHEWSON, D. S., PH.D., Astronomy
NEWTON, J. O., M.A., PH.D., D.SC., F.A.A., Nuclear Physics
NINHAM, B. W., M.SC., PH.D., F.A.A., Applied Mathematics
RUNCIMAN, W. A., D.SC., F.I.P., F.A.I.P., F.G.A., Solid State Physics
SNYDER, A. W., PH.D., D.SC., Applied Mathematics
TITTERTON, Sir ERNEST W., C.M.G., M.SC., PH.D., F.R.S.A., F.A.A., Nuclear Physics

Research School of Social Sciences: *Director:* Prof. G. M. NEUTZE, M.AGR.SC., D.PHIL., F.A.S.S.A.

PROFESSORS:

AITKIN, D. A., M.A., PH.D., F.A.S.S.A., Political Science
BUTLIN, N. G., B.EC., F.A.S.S.A., Economic History
CALDWELL, J. C., PH.D., F.A.S.S.A., Demography
GRUEN, F. H. G., M.S.(AG.EC.), A.M., F.A.S.S.A., Economics
HANNAN, E. J., PH.D., F.A.A., Statistics
INGLIS, K. S., M.A., D.PHIL., F.A.H.A., F.A.S.S.A., History
JONES, F. L., PH.D., F.A.S.S.A., Sociology
KAMENKA, E., PH.D., F.A.S.S.A., F.A.H.A., History of Ideas.
MACDONAGH, O. O. G., M.A., PH.D., F.R.HIST.S., F.A.S.S.A., F.A.H.A., History

MORAN, P. A. P., M.A., SC.D., D.SC., F.A.A., F.R.S., Statistics
SMART, J. J. C., M.A., B.PHIL., F.A.H.A., Philosophy
STOLJAR, S. J., PH.D., LL.D., F.A.S.S.A., Law
SWAN, T. W., B.EC., Economics

The Faculties: *Chairman of the Board:* Prof. D. J. WHALAN, LL.M., PH.D.

Number of academic staff: 405, including 41 professors.

Number of postgraduate students: 708.

Number of undergraduate students: 5,028.

DEANS:

Faculty of Arts: Dr. W. S. RAMSON, M.A., PH.D.

PROFESSORS:

DIXON, R. M. W., M.A., PH.D., Linguistics
FORGE, J. A. W., M.A., Anthropology
GOLLAN, R. A., M.A., PH.D., F.A.H.A., Australian History
HARDY, J. P., M.A., D.PHIL., F.A.H.A., English
HERBST, P., M.A., Philosophy
JOHNSON, R. St.C., M.A., Classics
KUHN, H., DR.PHIL., Germanic Languages
MOLONY, J. N., S.T.L., M.A., PH.D., History
MULVANEY, D. J., M.A., PH.D., F.A.H.A., F.S.A., Prehistory
RICHARDSON, J. L., B.A., Political Science
SCALES, D. P., D.DE L'U., French
WILLIAMS, C. M., D.PHIL., History
ZUBRZYCKI, J., C.B.E., M.SC.(ECON.), F.A.S.S.A., Sociology

Faculty of Asian Studies: Dr. R. R. C. DE CRESPIGNY, PH.D.

PROFESSORS:

ALFONSO, A., A.M., LIC.PHIL., D.PHIL., Japanese
DE JONG, J. W., DR.PHIL., F.A.H.A., South Asian and Buddhist Studies
JOHNS, A. H., PH.D., F.A.H.A., Indonesian Languages and Literatures
LIU TS'UN-YAN, PH.D., D.LIT., DIP.ED., F.A.H.A., Chinese

Faculty of Economics: Prof. A. D. BARTON, PH.D., F.A.S.A.

PROFESSORS:

BARTON, A. D., PH.D., F.A.S.A., Accounting
HEATHCOTE, C. R., M.A., PH.D., Mathematical Statistics
MATHEWS, R. L., C.B.E., B.COM., F.A.S.S.A., Centre for Research on Federal Financial Relations
PITCHFORD, J. D., M.COM., PH.D., F.A.S.S.A., Economics
TERRELL, R. D., PH.D., Econometrics
TURNOVSKY, S. J., M.A., PH.D., F.A.S.S.A., Economics

Faculty of Law: Prof. A. D. HAMBLY, LL.M.

PROFESSORS:

GREIG, D. W., LL.D., M.A., Law
HAMBLY, A. D., LL.M., Law
WHALAN, D. J., LL.M., PH.D., Law
ZINES, L. R., LL.M., Robert Garran Professor of Law

Faculty of Science: Dr. K. S. W. CAMPBELL, PH.D.

PROFESSORS:

BACHELARD, E. P., M.F., PH.D., Forestry
BARNETT, S. A., M.A., Zoology
BRENT, R. P., PH.D., Computer Science
BROWN, A., M.A., PH.D., F.R.A.S., Applied Mathematics
BROWN, D. A., M.SC., PH.D., F.G.S., F.G.S.A., Geology
BUCHDAHL, H. A., D.SC., F.A.A., Theoretical Physics
GRIFFIN, D. M., M.A., PH.D., SC.D., F.R.S.A., Forestry
HINDS, S., PH.D., Physics
ROSS, I. G., M.SC., PH.D., F.R.A.C.I., F.A.A., Physical Chemistry
SCOTT, W. A., M.S., PH.D., F.A.PS.S., F.A.S.S.A., Psychology
TRUDINGER, N. S., M.S., PH.D., F.A.A., Pure Mathematics
WARREN WILSON, J., M.A., D.PHIL., D.SC., F.I.BIOL., Botany
WARRENER, R. N., PH.D., F.R.A.C.I., Organic Chemistry
WILLIAMS, J. F., M.SC., PH.D., F.R.A.C.I., Biochemistry

UNIVERSITY CENTRES:

Centre for Continuing Education: Dir. C. DUKE, M.A., PH.D.

Centre for Foreign Politics (Western Europe): Dir. A. L. BURNS, M.A., F.A.S.S.A.

Centre for Resources and Environmental Studies: Dir. Prof. G. H. TAYLOR, DR.RER.NAT., D.SC.

Computer Services Centre: Dir. R. R. LANDFORD, B.COM.

Humanities Research Centre: Dir. Prof. C. I. E. DONALDSON, M.A., F.A.H.A.

Instructional Resources Unit: Dir. C. A. CLARK, B.D., TH.L.

NHMRC Social Psychiatry Unit: Dir. A. S. HENDERSON, M.D., CH.B., F.R.A.C.P., M.R.C.P.

North Australia Research Unit: Dir. F. H. BAUER, M.A., PH.D.

Office for Research in Academic Methods: Head A. H. MILLER, B.SC., B.A.

Survey Research Centre: Dir. R. G. JONES, M.SC. (acting).

DEAKIN UNIVERSITY

GEELONG, VICTORIA 3217
Telephone: (052) 47 1111.

Founded 1974.

Academic year: March to November (two semesters).

Chancellor: P. N. THWAITES, O.B.E., M.A., B.ED.

Vice-Chancellor and Principal: Prof. F. R. JEVONS, M.A., PH.D., D.SC.

Vice-Principal: K. D. STEWART, B.EC., F.A.S.A., F.A.C.I.A., F.C.I.S.A.

Registrar: A. L. PRITCHARD, B.SC., B.ED.

Dean of Educational Services: J. E. GOUGH, M.A., D.C.P., M.ED.ADMIN., M.A.PS.S., M.A.C.E., A.A.I.M.

Chief Librarian: Miss M. A. CAMERON, B.A., A.L.A.A.

Number of teachers: *c.* 250.

Number of full-time students: *c.* 3,000.

Publications: *Multi-volume Calendar* containing Annual Report, Handbook, Information for Students, A Guide to Off-Campus Studies, Statistics†.

FOUNDATION DEANS:

School of Education: J. G. WALLACE, M.A., M.ED., PH.D.

School of Engineering and Architecture: R. A. WILLIAMS, PH.D., A.S.T.C., M.I.E.AUST., C.ENG., M.I.PROD.E.

School of Humanities: M. J. CHARLESWORTH, M.A., PH.D.

School of Management: D. G. LETHBRIDGE, M.SC., M.B.I.M.

School of Sciences: M. H. BRIGGS, M.SC., PH.D., D.SC., F.R.I.C., F.I.BIOL., M.R.C.PATH.

School of Social Sciences: F. J. WEST, PH.D., F.R.HIST.S., F.A.H.A.

PROFESSORS:

BATE, W., M.A., Australian Studies
BOND, A. M., PH.D., D.SC., Chemistry
BORLAND, K., B.ARCH., F.R.A.I.A., Architecture
BRIGGS, M. H., M.SC., PH.D., D.SC., F.R.I.C., F.I.BIOL., M.R.C.PATH., Human Biology
CHARLESWORTH, M. J., M.A., PH.D., Philosophy
GARNER, B. J., PH.D., Computing
LETHBRIDGE, D. G. M.SC., M.B.I.M., Management
REID, I. W., M.A., PH.D., Literature
WAHLQVIST, M.L., B.MED.SC., M.B., B.S., M.D., Human Biology
WALLACE, J. G., M.A., M.ED., PH.D., Education
WEST, F. J., PH.D., F.R.HIST.S., F.A.H.A., History and Government
WILLIAMS, R. A., PH.D., A.S.T.C., M.I.E. AUST., C.ENG., M.I.PROD.E., Engineering

FLINDERS UNIVERSITY OF SOUTH AUSTRALIA

BEDFORD PARK, SOUTH AUSTRALIA 5042
Telephone: 275-3911.
Telegraphic Address: Flinduniv, Adelaide.

Founded 1966; previously established in 1963 as the University of Adelaide at Bedford Park.

Academic year: March to November (3 terms).

Chancellor: The Hon. Sir CHARLES BRIGHT, K.B.E., B.A., LL.B.

Vice-Chancellor: Prof. K. J. HANCOCK, PH.D., F.A.S.S.A.

Registrar: H. J. BUCHAN, B.SC.

Librarian: N. STOCKDALE, B.A.

Library: *see* Libraries.

Number of teachers: 318 full-time, including 52 professors.

Number of students: 3,850.

Publications: *Calendar* (annual), *Annual Report, Australian Economic Papers* (with University of Adelaide, twice-yearly), *Australian Bulletin of Labour* (quarterly), *Information* (annually).

CHAIRMEN OF SCHOOLS:
Humanities: Prof. E. D. LEMIRE.
Social Sciences: Dr. J. D. E. PLANT.
Physical Sciences: Dr. B. G. BAKER.
Biological Sciences: Prof. E. M. MARTIN.
Mathematical Sciences: Prof. G. I. GAUDRY.
Medicine: Prof. G. J. FRAENKEL.
Earth Sciences: Prof. G. W. LENNON.
Education: R. J. PADDICK.

PROFESSORS:
ABRAHAMSON, B., M.SC., S.M., PH.D., Mathematics
ANDERSON, J., M.ED., PH.D., Education
BENNESS, G. T., M.B.B.S., F.R.A.C.R., Medicine
BERRY, M. N., M.D., D.PHIL., F.R.C.P.A., Clinical Biochemistry
BEVAN, D. J. M., M.SC. PH.D., D.I.C., Chemistry
BIRKETT, D. J., B.SC., M.B.B.S., D.PHIL., M.R.A.C.P., Clinical Pharmacology
BLANDY, R. J., M.A., PH.D., Economics
BLEVIN, H. A., M.SC., PH.D., Physics
BOURKE, P. F., PH.D., F.A.S.S.A., American Studies
BRENNAN, M. H., PH.D., Physics
BROOK, D., PH.D., Visual Arts
BROWN, R. G., DIP.SOC.STUD., M.S.S., PH.D., F.A.S.S.A., Social Administration
CHALMERS, J. P., M.B.B.S., PH.D., F.R.A.C.P., Medicine
CLARK, A. M., M.SC., PH.D., Biology
CLARK-LEWIS, J. W., B.PHARM., D.SC., PH.D., Chemistry
COMIN, G. A. A., D.L., Italian
COSTER, D. J., M.B.B.S., F.R.S.C., F.R.A.C.S., Ophthalmology
COUSINS, M. J., M.B., B.S., F.F.A.R.A.C.S., F.F.A.R.C.S., Anaesthetics
DARROCH, J. N., M.A., DIP.STATS., PH.D., Mathematics
FEATHER, N. T., M.A., PH.D., F.A.S.S.A., Psychology
FRAENKEL, G. J., B.M., M.CH., F.R.C.S., F.R.A.C.S., F.A.C.S., Medicine
GARRAD, K., M.A., PH.D., Spanish
GAUDRY, G. I., PH.D., Mathematics
GEFFEN, L. B., M.SC., D.PHIL., F.R.A.C.P., Human Biology
HOLMES, J. W., M.SC., Earth Sciences
HOPE, A. B., PH.D., Biology
JONES, W. R., M.D., B.S., PH.D., F.R.C.O.G., Obstetrics and Gynaecology
KALUCY, R. S., M.B.B.S., F.R.A.C.P., M.A.N.Z.C.P., M.R.C.PSYCH., Psychiatry
KLUVANEK, I., C.SC., Applied Mathematics
KNEEBONE, C. M., M.B.B.S., M.SC., F.R.A.C.P., Paediatrics
LAURIE, I. S., M.A., PH.D., French
LE MIRE, E. D., M.A., PH.D., English
LENNON, G. W., M.A., Earth Sciences
MANN, L., M.A., PH.D., F.A.S.S.A., Psychology
MARTIN, E. M., M.SC., PH.D., Biology
MCCARTHY, I. E., PH.D., Physics
MCCASKILL, M., M.A., PH.D., Geography
MEDLIN, B. H., M.A., B.PHIL., Philosophy
MOORE, R. J., M.A., PH.D., History
MURRAY, A. W., PH.D., Biology
POWER, C. N., PH.D., Education
RADFORD, A. J., M.B., B.S., S.M.HYG., F.R.A.C.P., M.R.C.P., F.R.C.P.E., M.F.C.M., D.T.M. & H., Primary Care and Community Medicine
RICHARDS, E. S., PH.D., History
ROGERS, A. W., M.B., M.A., D.SC., PH.D., Human Morphology
SCHWERDTFEGER, P., M.SC., PH.D., Earth Sciences
SINCLAIR, W. A., M.COM., D.PHIL., F.A.S.S.A., Economic History
SMITH, D. S., D.PHYS.MED., M.R.C.P., F.R.C.P.(E.), Rehabilitation
SZELENYI, I., C.SC., Sociology
VON DER BORCH, C. C., PH.D., Earth Sciences
WATTS, J. MCK., M.B., B.S., F.R.A.C.S., Surgery
WEIGOLD, E., PH.D., Physics
WHITEHEAD, R., CH.B., M.D., F.R.C.PATH., Pathology

ATTACHED INSTITUTES:

Centre for Research in The New Literatures in English: Dir. Dr. S. C. HARREX.

Centre for Applied Social and Survey Research: Dir. Dr. R. J. STIMSON.

Centre for Neuroscience: Sec. Prof. L. B. GEFFEN.

Flinders University Cancer Research Unit: Dir. Prof. L. B. GEFFEN.

Flinders Institute for Atmospheric and Marine Sciences: Dir. Prof. P. SCHWERDTFEGER.

National Institute of Labour Studies: Dir. Prof. R. J. BLANDY.

Institute for Energy Studies: Dir. Dr. E. L. MURRAY.

Institute for Australasian Geodynamics: Dir. Dr. F. H. CHAMALAUN.

Institute for Atomic Studies: Dir. Dr. P. J. O. TEUBNER.

GRIFFITH UNIVERSITY

NATHAN, QUEENSLAND 4111
Telephone: Brisbane 275-7111.

Founded 1971.

State control; Academic year: February to November.

Undergraduate courses began in March 1975. The university is organized in Schools and is committed to interdisciplinary studies.

Chancellor: Sir THEODOR BRAY, C.B.E.
Vice-Chancellor: Emer. Prof. F. J. WILLETT, D.S.C., M.A., M.B.A.
Registrar: J. TOPLEY, B.ED.
Librarian: S. B. PAGE, B.A.

Number of teachers: 173.

Number of students: 1,793.

Publication: *University Handbook* (annually).

CHAIRMEN OF SCHOOLS:
School of Australian Environmental Studies: D. W. CONNELL, M.SC., PH.D.
School of Humanities: L. CANTRELL, M.A.
School of Modern Asian Studies: Prof. C. P. MACKERRAS, M.LITT., PH.D.
School of Science: D. M. DODDRELL, PH.D., D.SC.

FOUNDATION PROFESSORS:
BROWNLEA, A. A., M.A., PH.D., School of Australian Environmental Studies
CATON, H. P., M.A., PH.D., School of Humanities
FIELD, A. A., M.A., PH.D., School of Humanities
GUTHRIE, R. D., PH.D., D.SC., School of Science
HO, P. Y., M.SC., PH.D., D.SC., School of Modern Asian Studies
MASTERS, C. J., D.SC., PH.D., School of Science
PARLANGE, J.-Y., PH.D., School of Australian Environmental Studies
PRESLEY, C. F., B.A., B.LITT., School of Humanities
ROSE, C. W., PH.D., School of Australian Environmental Studies
SEGALL, R. L., PH.D., F.A.I.P., F.I.P., School of Science

JAMES COOK UNIVERSITY OF NORTH QUEENSLAND

TOWNSVILLE,
QUEENSLAND 4811
Telephone: Townsville 81-4111.

Founded 1970.

Academic year: March to November.

Chancellor: Hon. Mr. Justice JOSEPH PATRICK GEORGE KNEIPP, LL.B.
Deputy Chancellor: H. T. PRIESTLEY, B.E., F.I.E.E., F.I.E.AUST., F.A.I.M.
Vice-Chancellor: K. J. C. BACK, M.SC., PH.D.
Deputy Vice-Chancellor: D. H. TROLLOPE, M.SC., PH.D., D.ENG., F.I.E. AUST., F.A.S.C.E.
Registrar: K. N. P. CHESTER, B.COM., A.A.U.Q.
Librarian: C. J. HUNT, B.A., M.LITT., A.L.A.

Number of teachers: 210 full-time, including 19 professors.

Number of students: 1,896.

Publications: *Calendar*, *Student Handbook*, *Annual Report*, *Research and Publications Report*, *Tropical Veterinary Science Handbook*, *Tropical Marine Biology Handbook*, *Enrolment Information Booklet* (all annually).

DEANS:
Faculty of Arts: P. P. COURTENAY, PH.D., F.R.G.S.
Faculty of Commerce and Economics: S. J. ROGERS, B.SC.(ECON).
Faculty of Education: E. SCOTT, B.A., PH.D., M.A.PS.S., F.A.C.E.
Faculty of Engineering: B. S. BEST, PH.D., M.I.E.AUST.
Faculty of Science: P. J. STEPHENSON, PH.D., D.I.C.

PROFESSORS:
ARLETT P. L., PH.D., C.ENG., F.I.E.E., M.I.MECH.E., M.I.E.E.E., Electrical and Electronic Engineering
BURDON-JONES, C., PH.D., F.INST.BIOL., Marine Biology
CAMPBELL, R. S. F., PH.D., M.R.C.V.S., F.R.C.PATH., F.A.C.V.SC., Tropical Veterinary Science
DALTON, B. J., M.A., D.PHIL., History
GRIFFITHS, D. J., PH.D., Botany
HARRIS, C. P., M.ECON., PH.D., F.I.I.S.E., A.A.U.Q., A.A.S.A., A.B.I.A., Economics
HESELTINE, H. P., M.A., PH.D., English
KEARNEY, G. E., PH.D., F.A.PS.S., F.B.PS.S., Behavioural Sciences

LACY, W. C., M.S., PH.D., Geology
OLIVER, J., PH.D., F.R.G.S., F.R.MET.SC., Geography
RENNIE, B. C., M.A., PH.D., Mathematics
REYNOLDS, B. G., M.A., M.SC., D.PHIL., A.M.A., Material Culture
RICHARDS, G. N., PH.D., D.SC., F.R.I.C., F.R.A.C.I., Chemistry
ROGERS, S.J., B.SC.(ECON.), Commerce
SCOTT, E., PH.D., M.A.PS.S., F.A.C.E. Education
STARK, K. P., PH.D., M.I.E.AUST., Systems Engineering
SUSSEX, R. T., M.A., LL.B., D. DE L'U., French
TROLLOPE, D. H., M.SC., PH.D., D.ENG., F.I.E.AUST., F.A.S.C.E., Civil Engineering
WARD, J. F., D.I.C., PH.D., F.I.E.E., F.A.I.P., F.R.S.A., M.I.E.AUST., Physics

LA TROBE UNIVERSITY

BUNDOORA, VICTORIA 3083

Telephone: 478-3122.

Founded 1964.

Chancellor: The Hon. Mr. Justice R. A. SMITHERS, LL.B.

Vice-Chancellor: Prof. J. F. SCOTT, M.A.

Registrar: D. D. NEILSON, B.EC.

Chief Librarian: D. H. BORCHARDT, M.A., DIP.N.Z.LIB.SCH., A.L.A., F.L.A.A.

Number of teachers: 505.

Number of students: 8,709.

DEANS:

School of Agriculture: P. R. CARNEGIE, PH.D.

School of Behavioural Sciences: K. T. NG, PH.D.

School of Biological Sciences: I. W. B. THORNTON, PH.D.

School of Economics: F. G. DAVIDSON, M.A.

School of Education: M. N. LOVEGROVE, M.A., PH.D.

School of Humanities: R. J. PINKERTON, B.A., B.PHIL.

School of Physical Sciences: K. D. COLE, D.SC.

School of Social Sciences: J. M. FITZGERALD, PH.D., LL.M.

PROFESSORS:

BISNO, H., M.S.W., A.C.S.W., Social Work
BLACKSHIELD, A. R., LL.M., Legal Studies
BURLEY, S.P., PH.D., M.A.I.P., Econometrics
CARNEGIE, P. R., PH.D., Agriculture
CLARK, A. W., M.A., PH.D., Sociology
COLE, K. D., M.SC., D.SC., F.A.I.P., F.INST.P., Physics
CRITTENDEN, B., M.A., PH.D., Education
DAVIDSON, F. G., M.A., Economics
DAVIES, D. ELWYN, PH.D., F.INST.P., F.A.I.P., Physics
DIXON, P. B., A.M., PH.D., Economics
ELIEZER, C. J., M.A., PH.D., M.SC., D.SC., BAR.-AT-LAW, F.I.M.A., Applied Mathematics
ELLIS, B. D., B.SC., B.A., B.PHIL., F.A.H.A., Philosophy
FORSYTH, E. C., B.A., D.U., F.A.H.A., F.A.C.E., French
FRASER, S.E., M.A.(ED.), M.A., ED.D., PH.D., Education
FREEBAIRN, J. W., M.AG.EC., PH.D., Agricultural Economics
GOLDMAN, R. J., M.A., PH.D., F.B.PS.S., Education
GREGORY, J., M.A., PH.D., History
HUMBLE, L. K., Music
JONES, E. L., M.A., D.PHIL., Economics
JOYCE, R. B., B.A., LL.B., M.LITT., History
MCCLOSKEY, H. J., M.A., PH.D., LITT.D., F.A.H.A., Philosophy
MAGEE, R. J., M.SC., PH.D., D.SC., F.I.C.I., F.R.A.C.I., F.R.I.C., F.R.S.H., Inorganic and Analytical Chemistry
MARITZ, J. S., D.SC., Mathematical Statistics
MARTIN, R. M., M.A., PH.D., Politics
MOND, B., M.A., PH.D., Pure Mathematics
MORRISON, J. D., PH.D., D.SC., F.R.A.C.I., F.A.A., Physical Chemistry
OVER, R., PH.D., Psychology
PARSONS, P. A., SC.D., PH.D., Genetics and Human Variation
RYDON, J., PH.D., Politics
SALMOND, J. A., M.A., PH.D., American History
SINGER, G., M.A., PH.D., F.A.PS.S., Psychology
STONE, PH.D., Biochemistry
THOMPSON, R. W., M.A., Spanish
THORNTON, I. W. B., PH.D., F.L.S., F.R.E.S., Zoology
TOMORY, P. A., M.A., F.A.H.A., Art History
TOPSOM, R. D., M.SC., PH.D., F.R.I.C., F.R.A.C.I., F.N.Z.I.C., Organic Chemistry
VAN STEVENINCK, R. F. M., M.A., PH.D., Agriculture
VELIZ, C., PH.D., Sociology
WAID, J. S., PH.D., D.PHIL., M.I.BIOL., M.A.S.M., Microbiology
WARDROP, A. B., M.SC., PH.D., D.SC., F.A.A., Botany
WHITE, A. J. R., PH.D., Geology
WILD, R. A., PH.D., Sociology
WOLFSOHN, H. A., B.A., Politics

MACQUARIE UNIVERSITY

NORTH RYDE, N.S.W. 2113

Telephone: Sydney 888-8000.

Founded 1964 (opened 1967).

Chancellor: Emer. Prof. P. H. PARTRIDGE, A.C., M.A., F.A.H.A., F.A.S.S.A.

Deputy Chancellor: His Hon. Judge J. F. LINCOLN.

Vice-Chancellor: Emeritus Prof. E. C. WEBB, M.A., PH.D., F.R.A.C.I.

Deputy Vice-Chancellors: Emeritus Prof. B. E. MANSFIELD, M.A., Emeritus Prof. G. A. BARCLAY, PH.D., F.R.A.C.I.

Registrar: A. J. T. FORD, M.C., B.EC., A.A.S.A.

Librarian: E. H. WILKINSON, M.A.

Number of teachers: *c.* 570 (including 42 professors).

Number of students: *c.* 10,500.

Publication: *Calendar* (annual).

HEADS OF SCHOOLS:

School of Behavioural Sciences: Prof. I. K. WATERHOUSE, M.A., PH.D., F.B.PS.S., F.A.PS.S.

School of Biological Sciences: Assoc. Prof. D. W. COOPER, PH.D.

School of Chemistry: Prof. B. F. GRAY, M.SC., PH.D., D.SC.

School of Earth Sciences: Prof. J. L. DAVIES, M.A., PH.D.

School of Economic and Financial Studies: Prof. N. T. DRANE, B.EC., A.M.

School of Education: Prof. P. J. FOSTER, PH.D.

School of English and Linguistics: Assoc. Prof. E. M. LIGGINS, M.A. PH.D.

School of History, Philosophy and Politics: Asoc. Prof. B. H. HARRIS, M. A., PH.D.

School of Law: J. R. PEDEN, LL.M., S.J.D.

School of Mathematics and Physics: Prof. R. E. AITCHISON, M.SC.

School of Modern Languages: Prof. K. J. GOESCH, B.A., DIP.ED., DE D. L'U.

Centre for Environmental Studies: Prof. F. H. TALBOT, M.SC., PH.D.

PROFESSORS:

AITCHISON, R. E. M.SC., Electronics
AITKIN, D. A., M.A., PH.D., Politics
ARGY, V. E., B.A., B.EC., Economics
CHONG, F., M.A., M.SC., PH.D., Mathematics
CONNELL, R. W., PH.D., Sociology
DAVIES, J. L., M.A., PH.D., Geography
DELBRIDGE, A., M.A., Linguistics
DEUTSCHER, M. J., B.A., B.PHIL., Philosophy
DRANE, N. T., B.EC., A.M., Economics
FOSTER, P. J., PH.D., Education
GIBBS, A. M., M.A., B.LITT., English
GOESCH, K. J., D. DE L'U., French
GOODNOW, J. J., PH.D., Psychology
GRAY, B. F., M.SC., PH.D., D.SC., Chemistry
HAMMER, A. G., M.A., Psychology
HOSTETLER, B. A., M.A., PH.D., Geology
HOWARD, P. F., B.SC., A.M., PH.D., Geology
JAYAWARDENA, C., B.A., PH.D., Anthropology
JOHNSTON, E. M., M.A., PH.D., F.R.H.S., History
JUDGE, E. A., M.A., History
MASON, P., PH.D., D.SC., F.INST.P., Physics
MCGLASHAN, L. R. P., DIP.ED., DR.PHIL., German
MCKERN, R. B., B.E., D.B.A., M.I.C.E., Management
MCNEIL, D. R., M.SC., PH.D., Statistics
MERCER, F. V., PH.D., Biology
MILTHORPE, F. L., M.SC.AGR., D.SC., D.I.C., Biology
PEDEN, J. R., LL.M., S.J.D., Law
PHILP, H. W. S., M.A., A.M., PH.D., F.A.C.E., F.B.PS.S., F.A.PS.S., Education
PIPER, H. W., M.A., D.LITT., English
POLLARD, J. H., PH.D., F.I.A., F.S.S., Economic Statistics
ROSE, A. J., M.A., Geography
SHARMAN, G. B., B.SC., D.SC., Biology
TALBOT, F. H., M.SC., PH.D., Environmental Studies
THROSBY, C. D., M.SC.AGR., PH.D., Economics
VAN DER POORTEN, A. J., PH.D., M.B.A., Mathematics
VOZOFF, K., M.SC., PH.D., Geophysics
WARD, J., PH.D., Special Education
WARD, J. C., M.A., D.PHIL., F.R.S., Physics
WATERHOUSE, I. K., M.A., PH.D., F.B.PS.S., F.A.PS.S., Psychology
WATERSON, D. B., M.A., PH.D., History

UNIVERSITY OF MELBOURNE

PARKVILLE, VICTORIA 3052

Telephone: 345-1844.

Founded 1853.

Chancellor: Prof. Emer. R. D. WRIGHT, M.B., M.S., D.SC., F.R.A.C.P.

Deputy Chancellors: Rt. Hon. Sir NINIAN STEPHEN, K.B.E., LL.B., Dr. M. BLACKWOOD, M.B.E., PH.D., M.SC.
Vice-Chancellor and Principal: Prof. Sir DAVID DERHAM, K.B.E., C.M.G., M.B.E., B.A., LL.M.
Deputy Vice-Chancellor: Prof. P. W. WHITTON, PH.D., M.E.(C.ENG.), D.I.C., F.I.E.AUST.
Deputy Vice-Chancellor (Research): Prof. J. R. POYNTER, M.A., PH.D., F.A.S.S.A., F.A.H.A.
Vice-Principal: R. D. MARGINSON, B.COM., DIP. PUB. ADMIN.
Registrar: J. B. POTTER, E.D., F.R.M.T.C., F.I.R.E.E.
Librarian: W. D. RICHARDSON, B.A., F.L.A., A.L.A.A.

Number of teachers: 1,209, including 112 professors.

Number of students: 16,214.

Publications: *Calendar, Faculty Handbooks, Research Report, Annual Report* (annually), *Gazette* (quarterly), *The Melbourne Graduate Newsletter* (monthly), *Staff News* (monthly).

DEANS:

Faculty of Agriculture and Forestry: J. H. CHINNER, B.SC., F.I.W.SC., F.I.F.A.
Faculty of Architecture, Building and Town and Regional Planning: Prof. A. RODGER, B.SC., B.ARCH., R.I.B.A., A.R.I.A.S., F.R.A.I.A.
Faculty of Arts: E. A. HUCK, M.A.
Faculty of Dental Science: Prof. P. C. READE, M.D.S., PH.D., M.D.SC., F.D.S.R.C.S., M.R.C.PATH.
Faculty of Economics and Commerce: Prof. L. R. WEBB, PH.D.
Faculty of Education: Prof. K. C. LEE DOW, B.SC., B.ED., A.R.A.C.I.
Faculty of Engineering: Prof. L. K. STEVENS, PH.D., M.I.C.E., M.I.E.A.
Faculty of Law: Prof. C. HOWARD, PH.D., LL.D.
Faculty of Medicine: Prof. D. G. PENINGTON, M.A., D.M., B.CH., F.R.C.P., F.R.A.C.P., F.R.C.P.A.
Faculty of Music: M. COOKE, M.MUS., M.A.C.E.
Faculty of Science: Prof. C. A. RAMM, M.SC., PH.D., F.INST.P., F.A.I.P.
Faculty of Veterinary Science: Prof. K. V. F. JUBB, M.SC., PH.D., M.V.SC., F.A.C.V.SC.

PROFESSORS:

ADAMS, K. M., M.SC., DR.TECH.SC., S.M.I.E.E.E., Electronics and Communication
ANDERSON, J. H., M.SC., PH.D., Electrical Engineering
ATTWOOD, H. D., M.D., CH.B., F.R.A.C.P., F.R.C.P.A., F.R.C.PATH., Pathology
AUSTIN, A. G., M.C., M.ED., Education
BEISCHER, N. A., M.D., B.S., M.G.O., F.R.A.C.S., F.R.C.S.(ED.), F.R.C.O.G., F.A.G.O., Obstetrics and Gynaecology
BENNETT, R. C., M.B., M.S., F.R.C.S., F.R.A.C.S., Surgery
BESWICK, D. G., M.A., PH.D., M.A.PS.S., M.A.C.E., Study of Higher Education
BLAINEY, G. N., A.O., M.A., History
BLOOD, D. C., M.V.SC., F.A.C.V.SC., Veterinary Medicine
BOLOTIN, H., M.S., PH.D., F.A.I.P., F.A.P.S., Physics
BREARLEY, M. N., M.SC., M.A., PH.D., Mathematics, R.A.A.F. Academy
BRIMER, M., M.A., F.R.C.O., L.R.S.M., L.R.A.M., A.R.C.M., U.P.L.M., A.D.C.M., Music
BROOKFIELD, H. C., PH.D., Geography
BROWN, J. B., M.SC., PH.D., D.SC., Obstetrics and Gynaecology
BUCKLEY, V. T., M.A., English
CAMERON, D. W., M.SC., M.A., SC.D., PH.D., F.R.A.C.I., Organic Chemistry
CAMPBELL, G. D., PH.D., Zoology
CHAMBERS, T. C., M.SC., PH.D., Botany
CHEEK, D. B., M.D., B.S., D.SC., Paediatrics
CHRISTIE, G. S., M.D., B.S., F.R.A.C.S., F.R.A.C.P., F.R.C.P.A., F.R.C.PATH., Pathology
CLARK, G. M., M.B., M.S., PH.D., F.R.C.S., F.R.C.S.(ED.), F.R.A.C.S., Otolaryngology
CLARK, S. D., PH.D., Law
CLARKE, G. W., M.A., LITT.D., F.A.H.A., Classical Studies
CLUNIE, G. J. A., M.B. CH.M., F.R.C.S.(E.), F.R.C.S., F.R.A.C.S., Surgery
COLE, B.L., PH.D., L.O.SC., Optometry
CROCK, G. W., M.B., B.S., F.R.C.S., F.R.A.C.S., F.R.A.C.P., Ophthalmology
DANKS, D. M., M.D., B.S., F.R.A.C.P., Paediatrics
DARIAN-SMITH, I., B.S., M.D., Physiology
DAVIES, A. F., M.A., Political Science
DAVIES, B. M., B.CH., M.D., D.C.H., D.P.M., F.R.C.P., F.R.A.C.P., F.A.N.Z.C.P., M.R.C. PSYCH., Psychiatry
DAY, A. J., D.SC., M.D., D.PHIL., Physiology
DENING, G. M., M.A., PH.D., History
DENNISON, P. J., M.A., D.PHIL., PH.D., F.R.C.O., Music
DENTON, D. A., M.S., B.S., Experimental Physiology and Medicine
DOWNING, C. G. E., D.SC., F.I.E.C., F.A.S.A.E., F.C.S.A.E., F.A.I.C., M.A.E.S.A., F.I.E.A., Agricultural Engineering
DOYLE, A. E., M.D., B.S., F.R.C.P., F.R.A.C.P., Medicine
DUCKWORTH, C. R., M.A., PH.D., French
EVANS, J. B., B.SC., B.M.E., M.AUST.I.M.M., M.C.I.M.M., P.ENG., Mining and Metallurgy
FELPERIN, H., M.A., PH.D., English
FORD, H. A. J., LL.M., S.J.D., Commercial Law
GELLIE, G. H., M.A., F.A.H.A., Classical Studies
GODDARD, L., B.PHIL., M.A., Philosophy
HAMMOND, S. B., PH.D., F.A.PS.S., Psychology
HARDY, K. J., M.B., B.S., F.R.A.C.S., F.A.C.S., Surgery
HARE, W. S. C., M.D., B.S., D.D.R., F.R.A.C.P., F.R.C.R., F.R.A.C.R., D.D.U., Radiology
HEALY, T. W., M.SC., PH.D., A.R.A.C.I., Physical Chemistry
HENDERSON, R. F., C.M.G., M.A., PH.D., M.COM., Applied Economic Research
HIRD, F. J. R., PH.D., M.AGR.SC., D.SC., Biochemistry
HOME, R. W., PH.D., History and Philosophy of Science
HOWARD, C., LL.M., LL.D., PH.D., Law
JOUBERT, P. N., M.E., A.F.R.AE.S., M.I.E. AUST., Mechanical Engineering
JUBB, K. V. F., M.V.SC., M.SC., PH.D., F.A.C.V.SC., Veterinary Pathology
KINCAID-SMITH, PRISCILLA S., C.B.E., B.SC., B.CH., M.D., D.C.P., F.R.C.P., F.R.A.C.P., Medicine
KNOX, R. B., PH.D., Botany
KUNE, G. A., M.B., B.S., F.R.C.S., F.R.A.C.S., F.A.C.S., Surgery
LANHAM, D. J., LL.B., B.C.L., Law
LAWSON, J. D., M.E., PH.D., M.A.S.C.E., F.I.E.AUST., Civil Engineering
LEACH, S. J., PH.D., D.SC., Biochemistry
LEDGAR, F. W., M.A., PH.D., M.T.R.P., F.R.T.P.I., F.R.A.P.I., Town and Regional Planning
LEE DOW, K. C., B.SC., B.ED., A.R.A.C.I., Education
LLOYD, A. G., B.EC., M.AGR.SC., Agricultural Economics
LOUIS, W. J., M.D., B.S., F.R.A.C.P., Clinical Pharmacology and Therapeutics
LOVELL, R. R. H., A.O., M.D., B.S., M.SC., F.R.C.P., F.R.A.C.P., M.R.C.S., Medicine
LOVERING, J. F., M.SC., PH.D., Geology
LUNTZ, H., B.A., LL.B., B.C.L., Law
MCCORMICK, C. A., B.A., Italian
MCKELLAR, B. H. J., PH.D., F.INST.P., F.A.P.S., Theoretical Physics
MANION, M., PH.D., Fine Arts
MARTIN, T. J., M.D., B.S., F.R.C.A.P., Medicine
MILLER, C. F., M.S., PH.D., Mathematics
NICOL, R. E. G., M.B.A., PH.D., F.A.S.A., Accounting
NOSSAL, Sir GUSTAV, K.B.E., M.B., B.S., B.SC.(MED.), PH.D., F.R.A.C.P., F.R.C.P.A., F.A.C.M.A., F.A.A., Medical Biology
O'DONNELL, T. A., PH.D., D.SC., F.R.A.C.I., Inorganic Chemistry
OPAT, G. I., M.SC., PH.D., F.A.I.P., Experimental Physics
PENINGTON, D. G., M.A., D.M., B.CH., F.R.C.P., F.R.A.C.P., F.R.C.P.A., Medicine
PEPPERELL, R. J., M.D., M.B., B.S., M.G.O., F.R.A.C.P., M.R.C.O.G., F.A.G.O., Obstetrics and Gynaecology
PERKINS, J. O. N., M.A., PH.D., M.COM., Economics
PITTARD, A. J., PH.D., D.SC., DIP.PHARM., F.A.A., Microbiology
POOLE, P. C., PH.D., F.B.C.S., M.A.C.S., Computer Science
POWELL, A., PH.D., F.A.S.S.A., Economic Research
POWER, J. M., A.M., PH.D., F.I.M.A., Political Science
PRINSLEY, D. M., M.D., B.S., F.R.C.P.(ED.), F.R.A.C.P., F.R.S.H., Gerontology and Geriatric Medicine
RAMM, C. A., M.SC., PH.D., F.INST.P., F.A.I.P., Dean of Science
RAND, M. J., PH.D., M.SC., Pharmacology
RAY, I. J., M.B., B.S., PH.D., Anatomy
READE, P. C., M.D.S., PH.D., M.D.SC., F.D.S.R.C.S., M.R.C.PATH., Dental Medicine and Surgery
RODGER, A., B.SC., B.ARCH., R.I.B.A., A.R.A.I.S., F.R.A.I.A., Architecture
ROSE, P. J. B., PH.D., Commerce and Business Administration
ROSENBLAT, S., M.SC., PH.D., F.I.M.A., Mathematics
RUSSELL, G. H., M.A., PH.D., English Language and Literature
RYAN, G. B., M.D., B.S., PH.D., F.R.C.P.A., F.R.A.C.P., Anatomy
SCHEDVIN, B., PH.D., Economic History
SCHREIBER, G. H., DR.MED., Biochemistry (Medical)
SCHULZ, G. E., DR.PHIL., F.A.H.A., Germanic Studies
SCRIVENER, J. C., M.E.(CIV.), PH.D., D.I.C., F.N.Z.I.E., Building
SEDDON, G., M.SC., PH.D., Environmental Studies
SIEMON, S. R., M.APP.SC., M.E., C.ENG., F.I.CHEM.E., A.M.A.I.CH.E., F.R.A.C.I., F.N.Z.I.C., F.I.E.AUST., M.INST.F., Chemical Engineering
SIMON, H. F., M.A., Oriental Studies
SIMON, L., PH.D., Mathematics
SOPER, C. S., B.COM., Economics
SPICER, B. M., PH.D., D.SC., F.INST.P., F.A.I.P., Physics

STANLEY, G. V., PH.D., A.B.PS.S., F.A.PS.S.S., Psychology
START, K. B., M.ED., PH.D., A.B.P.S., M.A.PS.S., Education
STEVENS, L. K., PH.D., M.ENG.SC., M.I.C.E., F.I.E.AUST., Civil Engineering
STOREY, E., D.D.SC., PH.D., Child Dental Health
STUBBS, L. L., D.AGR.SC., F.A.I.A.S., Plant Pathology
SUSSEX, R. D., M.A., PH.D., Russian
THOMPSON, C. J., PH.D., F.I.M.A., Mathematics
TRIBE, D. E., O.B.E., PH.D., D.AG.SC., F.T.S., F.A.I.A.S., Animal Nutrition
TULLOH, N. MCC., D.AGR.SC., PH.D., F.A.I.A.S., Agriculture and Forestry
WATERSON, J. G., B.D.S., B.SC.DENT., PH.D., F.R.A.C.D.S., Conservative Dentistry
WEARING, A. J., M.A., PH.D., M.B.PS.S., M.A.PS.S., Psychology
WEBB, L. R., PH.D., Economics
WEBSTER, R. W., M.B., B.S., F.R.A.C.G.P., F.R.A.C.P., Community Health
WHITE, D. O., M.D., M.SC., PH.D., F.R.C.P.A., Microbiology
WHITTEN, M., PH.D., Genetics
WILLIAMS, E. J., D.SC., F.I.M.S., M.I.S.I., Statistics
WILLIAMS, R. A., M.SC.(ECON), PH.D., Econometrics
WRIGHT, F. K., B.MET.E., B.COM., F.A.S.A. Accounting

AFFILIATED COLLEGES:

Trinity College.
Ormond College.
Queen's College.
St. Hilda's College.
St. Mary's College.
Newman College.
University College.
Janet Clarke Hall.
Whitley College.
Ridley College.
Graduate House.

MONASH UNIVERSITY

WELLINGTON ROAD,
CLAYTON, VICTORIA 3168

Telephone: Melbourne (03) 541-0811.
Telegraphic Address: Monashuni, Melbourne.
Telex: AA 32691.

Founded 1958 (opened 1961).

Chancellor: The Hon. Sir RICHARD MOULTON EGGLESTON, Q.C., LL.B.
Deputy Chancellor: The Hon. JOSEPH EZRA ISAAC, PH.D., F.A.S.S.A.
Vice-Chancellor: R. L. MARTIN, PH.D., SC.D. D.SC., F.R.A.C.I., F.R.I.C., F.A.A.
Deputy Vice-Chancellor: W. A. G. SCOTT, B.A., B.LITT.
Pro-Vice-Chancellor: B. O. WEST, PH.D., F.R.A.C.I.
Comptroller: L. W. CANDY, A.A.S.A.
Registrar: J. D. BUTCHART, O.B.E., B.EC., B.A.
Librarian: T. B. SOUTHWELL, B.A.

Number of teachers: 986 (873 full-time).

Number of students: 13,983.

Publications: *Calendar, Faculty Handbooks, University Council Report, Research Report, University Brochure* (annual); *Monash Reporter* (monthly); *Monash Review* (quarterly), *Sound* (weekly).

DEANS:

Faculty of Arts: J. D. LEGGE, M.A., D.PHIL., F.A.S.S.A.
Faculty of Economics and Politics: D. COCHRANE, C.B.E., PH.D., F.A.S.S.A.
Faculty of Education: P. W. MUSGRAVE, M.A., PH.D., F.A.S.S.A.
Faculty of Engineering: L. A. ENDERS, M.E., F.I.E.AUST., F.A.S.C.E., M.AUST.-I.M.M.
Faculty of Law: R. BAXT, LL.M.
Faculty of Medicine: G. C. SCHOFIELD, M.D., CH.B., D.PHIL., F.R.A.C.P., F.R.A.C.M.A.
Faculty of Science: J. M. SWAN, D.SC., PH.D., F.R.A.C.I., F.A.A.

PROFESSORS:

ALLAN, D. E., M.A., BAR-AT-LAW, Law
BODI, L., PH.D., German
BOLTON, H. C., PH.D., F.A.I.P., Theoretical Physics
BORNSTEIN, J., D.SC., M.D., F.R.A.C.P. Biochemistry
BOSS, P., M.A., Social Work
BOURA, A. L. A., PH.D., D.SC., F.I.BIOL., Pharmacology
BRADLEY, D., M.A., English
BROWN, R. D., M.SC., PH.D., F.R.A.C.I., F.A.A., Chemistry
BRUNT, MAUREEN D., PH.D., Economics
BURGER, H. G., M.D., B.S., F.R.A.C.P., Medicine
CAMPBELL, ENID M., LL.B., B.EC., PH.D., Law
CANNY, M. J. P., M.A., PH.D., Botany
CARSON, N. E., M.B., B.S., F.R.A.C.P., F.R.A.C.G.P., Community Practice
CLARK, A. C. L., M.D., B.S., F.R.A.C.P., Paediatrics
CLARKE, W. C., M.A., PH.D., Geography
COLLINS, A. K., M.ED., PH.D., DIP.ED., M.A.PS.S., Administration
CRISP, J. D. C., M.E., C.ENG., F.I.E.AUST., F.I.MECH.E., F.S.A.S.M., Engineering Dynamics
CROSSLEY, J. N., M.A., D.PHIL., Pure Mathematics
CULLEN, J. M., M.A., D.PHIL., Zoology
DAVIS, S. R., LL.B., PH.D., F.A.S.S.A., Politics
DAY, R. H., PH.D., F.B.PS.S., F.A.PS.S., F.A.S.S.A., Psychology
DE KRETSER, D. M., M.B., B.S., M.D., F.R.A.C.P., Anatomy
ELLINGER, E. P., M.JUR., D.PHIL., Law
EMY, H. V., PH.D., Politics
EWENS, W. J., M.A., PH.D., Mathematical Statistics
FAINE, S., B.MED.SC., M.D., CH.B., D.PHIL., F.R.C.P.A., F.A.A.M., M.A.S.M., Microbiology
FENSHAM, P. J., M.SC., PH.D., F.R.A.C.I., Education
FINCH, P. D., B.A., Mathematical Statistics
FIRKIN, B. G., M.B., B.S., B.SC.(MED.), F.R.A.C.P., F.R.C.P.A., Medicine
FITZROY, P. T., M.S.I.E., PH.D., Administration
GARAGNON, J. R., M. ÈS. L., AGR. DE L'UNI., French
GARLICK, H. W., M.D., B.S., F.R.C.P., F.R.A.C.P., Medicine
GILES, D. E. A., PH.D., Econometrics
HAMMARSTRÖM, U. G. E., FIL.DR., Linguistics
HASTINGS, N. A. J., M.A., PH.D., Operations Research
HEAD, J. G., B.EC., B.PHIL., Economics
HENRY, A. S., M.A., PH.D., Classical Studies
HOBBS, B. E., PH.D., Geology
HOLLOWAY, B. W., PH.D., D.SC., Genetics
HOLMAN, MOLLIE E., D.PHIL., D.SC., F.A.A., Physiology
HUGHES, Sir EDWARD, C.B.E., M.D., M.S., F.R.C.S., F.A.C.S., F.R.A.C.S., Surgery
HUNT, K. H., M.A., M.MECH.E., F.I.E.AUST., F.I.MECH.E., F.T.S., M.A.S.M.E., Mechanism
IRONSIDE, W., M.D., CH.B., D.P.M., F.R.C.PSYCH., F.R.A.C.P., F.A.N.Z.C.P., Psychological Medicine
JACKSON, F. C., PH.D., Philosophy
JACKSON, W. R., PH.D., D.SC., F.R.A.C.I., Organic Chemistry
JOHNSTON, C. I., M.B., B.S., F.R.A.C.P., Medicine
JONES, T. A., M.A., L.MUS., Music
KEIGHTLEY, R. G., PH.D., Spanish
KEMP, D. A., PH.D., Politics
KORNER, P. I., M.D., M.SC.,F.A.A.,F.R.A.C.P., Medicine
LAMPARD, D. G., M.SC., PH.D., C.ENG., F.I.E.E., F.I.E.E.E., F.I.R.E.E.AUST., F.A.A, F.I.E.AUST., F.A.I.P., Electrical Engineering
LAURENSON, E. M., PH.D., F.I.E.AUST., Civil Engineering
LINNANE, A. W., D.SC., PH.D., F.R.S., F.A.A., Biochemistry
LOGAN, M. I., PH.D., F.A.S.S.A., Geography
LOWTHER, D. A., PH.D., Biochemistry
MCBRIAR, A. M., B.A., D.PHIL., F.A.S.S.A., History
MCCARTY, J. W., PH.D., Economic History
MCCAUGHEY, A. P., B.A., Visual Arts
MARSHALL, V. C., M.B.B.S., F.R.A.C.S., F.A.C.S., Surgery
MARVAN, J., PH.D., Russian
MELBOURNE, W. H., PH.D., D.I.C., M.I.E.AUST., M.R.AE.S., Fluid Mechanics
MILLER, J. B., M.A., PH.D., Pure Mathematics
MORTON, B. R., M.SC., PH.D., Applied Mathematics
MURRAY, N. W., PH.D., F.I.E.AUST., M.I.C.E., M.I.STRUCT.E., Structural Engineering
NAIRN, R. C., M.D., CH.B., PH.D., F.R.C.PATH.,F.R.A.C.P.,F.R.C.P.A.,F.R.S.E., Pathology
NEALE, MARIE D., O.B.E., M.A., PH.D., F.B.PS.S., F.A.PS.S., Education
NEUSTUPNY, J. V., PROM.FIL., PH.D., C.SC., Japanese
OFFICER, R. R., M.AG.EC., M.B.A., PH.D., Accounting and Finance
OPIT, L. J., M.B., B.S., B.SC., F.R.C.S., F.R.A.C.S., Social and Preventive Medicine
PARISH, R. M., PH.D., Economics
PEIRSON, C. G., M.EC., A.A.S.A., Accounting and Finance
POLMEAR, I. J., M.SC., D.ENG., F.I.M., F.I.E.AUST., Materials Engineering
PORTER, M. G., M.A., PH.D., Director, Centre of Policy Studies
POTTER, O. E., PH.D., D.SC., F.I.CHEM.E., M.A.I.CH.E., A.R.A.C.I., Chemical Engineering
PRESTON, G. B., M.A., D.PHIL., Pure Mathematics
PRIESTLEY, C.H.B., A.O., M.A., SC.D., F.R.S., F.A.A., F.INST.P., Meteorology

Rachinger, W. A., m.sc., ph.d., f.a.i.p., Experimental Physics
Ricklefs, M. C., ph.d., History
Scott, W. H., ph.d., Anthropology and Sociology
Selleck, R. J. W., ph.d., f.a.s.s.a., Education
Shaw, A. G. L., m.a., f.a.s.s.a., f.a.h.a., History
Singer, P., m.a., b.phil., Philosophy
Skinner, C., ph.d., dip.o.a.s., f.r.a.s., Indonesian and Malay
Smith, T. F., ph.d., Physics
Snape, R. H., ph.d., f.a.s.s.a., Economics
Swift, M. G., ph.d., Anthropology and Sociology
Taft, R., m.a., ph.d., f.a.ps.s., f.a.s.s.a., Education
Tisher, R. P. m.sc., ph.d., Education
Van der Borght, R. F. E., lic.sc.math., dr.ès sc., Applied Mathematics
Wallace, C. S., ph.d., Computer Science
Waller, P. L., ll.b., b.c.l., f.a.s.s.a., Law
Warren, J. W., m.a., ph.d., Zoology
Weeramantry, C. G., ll.d., Law
West, B. O., ph.d., f.r.a.c.i., Inorganic Chemistry
Westfold, K. C., b.sc., m.a., d.phil., Astronomy
Whyte, Jean, a.m., f.l.a.a., Librarianship
Wood, E. C., m.b., b.s., f.r.c.s., f.r.c.o.g., f.a.g.o., Obstetrics and Gynaecology

Affiliated Institutes:

Baker Medical Research Institute: *see* under Research Institutes.

National Museum of Victoria: *see* under Museums.

Leo Cussen Institute for Continuing Education.

Mannix College.

MURDOCH UNIVERSITY

MURDOCH, W.A. 6150

Telephone: 09-3322211.

Founded 1973; postgraduate courses began 1974; undergraduate courses began 1975.

State control; Academic year: March to November.

Chancellor: The Hon. Sir Ronald Wilson, k.b.e., c.m.g.

Vice-Chancellor: Dr. F. M. G. Willson, m.a., d.phil.

Deputy Vice-Chancellor: Prof. A. McB. Kerr, ph.d.

Secretary: D. D. Dunn, ll.b., b.a.

Librarian: W. G. Buick, m.a.

Number of teachers: 178.

Number of students: 201 postgraduate, 2,278 undergraduate.

Publications: *Handbook and Calendar, Annual Report, Murdoch News* (monthly).

Deans:

School of Education: Prof. B. McGaw.
School of Environmental and Life Sciences: Prof. D. C. O'Connor.
School of Human Communication: Dr. Horst Ruthrof, ph.d.
School of Mathematical and Physical Sciences: Prof. A. P. Robertson.
School of Social Inquiry: Prof. R. D. Savage.
School of Veterinary Studies: Prof. M. E. Nairn.

Professors:

School of Education:
Hill, B. V., m.a., ph.d., Education
McGaw, B., m.ed., ph.d., Education

School of Environmental and Life Sciences:
Dilworth, M. J., ph.d., Biology
Loneragan, J. F., ph.d., Biological Sciences
O'Connor, D. C., m.sc., ph.d., Environmental Studies
Potter, I. C., ph.d., Animal Biology

School of Human Communication:
Frodsham, J. D., m.a., ph.d., f.a.h.a., Literature

School of Mathematical and Physical Sciences:
Mainsbridge, B., ph.d., Physics
Parker, A. J., ph.d., Chemistry
Robertson, A. P., m.a., ph.d., f.i.m.a., Mathematics

School of Social Enquiry:
Bolton, G. C., m.a., d.phil., f.r.hist.s., f.a.h.a., History
Kerr, A. McB., m.a., ph.d., Economics
Raser, J. R., m.a., ph.d., Social Inquiry
Savage, R. D., ph.d., d.sc., f.b.ps.s., Psychology

School of Veterinary Studies:
Clark, W. T., ph.d., f.r.c.v.s., Small Animal Medicine and Surgery
Howell, J. McC., ph.d., d.v.sc., Pathology
Nairn, M. E., m.sc., ph.d., Clinical Pathology
Swan, R. A., ph.d., m.p.v.m., Veterinary Clinical Studies
Wales, R. G., ph.d., d.v.sc., Physiology

Directors:

Educational Services and Teaching Resources Unit: Dr. R. I. McDonald.

External Studies Unit: P. de C. Guiton, m.a.

Institute of Environmental Science: Prof. D. O'Connor.

Institute for Social Programme Evaluation: Dr. R. Stratton.

UNIVERSITY OF NEW ENGLAND

ARMIDALE, N.S.W. 2351

Telephone: Armidale (067) 72-2911.

Founded 1954.

Academic year: March to November (2 semesters).

Chancellor and Chairman of the Council: The Rt. Hon. Sir Frank Kitto, k.b.e., b.a., ll.b.

Deputy Chancellor: R. C. Robertson-Cunninghame, d.phil.

Vice-Chancellor: Prof. R. C. Gates, a.o., b.com., m.a., f.a.ss.a

Pro-Vice-Chancellor: Prof. J. L. Dillon, ph.d., f.a.ss.a.

Registrar: T. C. Lamble, b.a.

Academic Secretary: D. C. Williams, b.ec., a.a.s.a.(sen.).

Librarian: S. W. Richardson, b.sc., m.lib.sc., a.l.a.a.

Library: *see under* Libraries.

Number of teachers: 447, including 41 professors.

Number of students: 8,461.

Publications: *Calendar, Annual Report, Study Guide, Postgraduate Handbook* (annually), *Student Services, Information for Overseas Students,* etc.

Deans:

Faculty of Arts: W. G. Maddox, m.a., m.sc.

Faculty of Science: J. W. Ducker, ph.d., f.r.i.c.

Faculty of Rural Science: M. K. Hill, m.agr.sc., ph.d.

Faculty of Economic Studies: J. R. Anderson, m.sc.agr., ph.d.

Faculty of Education: W. B. Olphert, m.a.

Faculty of Resource Management: S. J. Perrens, m.eng.sci., ph.d., a.n.c.a.e., m.i.e. (aust.), f.i.agric.e.

Professors:

Anderson, G. A., d.mus., f.a.h.a., Music
Arasaratnam, S., ph.d., History
Barker, J. S. F., ph.d., Animal Science
Bishop, J. H., m.a., Classics and Ancient History
Burr, E. J., m.sc., ph.d., Computing Science
Burton, J. R., b.e., f.i.e.(aust.), Resource Engineering
Cumming, A., m.a., ph.d., m.a.c.e., f.r.hist.s., Education
Dillon, J. L., ph.d., f.a.s.s.a., Agricultural Economics and Business Management
Drake, P., ph.d., a.a.s.a., Economics
Elkin, P. K., b.a., b.litt., d.phil., English
Evans, J. V., d.sc., m.r.c.v.s., Physiology
Falconer, I. R., ph.d., d.sc., c.chem., f.r.i.c., f.i.biol., Biochemistry and Nutrition
Fitzgerald, D., m.a., ph.d., Behavioural Studies in Education
Fletcher, N. H., m.a., ph.d., d.sc., f.a.a., f.inst.p., f.a.i.p., m.a.a.s., Physics
Franklin, R. L., m.a., ll.m., ph.d., Philosophy
Gregson, R. A. M., ph.d., f.b.ps.s., f.n.z.ps.s., f.s.s., Psychology
Guise, J. W. B., m.a., ph.d., Economic Statistics
Hainsworth, J. D., m.a., English
Haydon, S. C., m.a., ph.d., f.inst.p., f.a.i.p., Physics
Jones, G. C., m.a., d.u., Romance Languages
Lea, D. A. M., ph.d., Geography
Leng, R. A., ph.d., d.rur.sc., Biochemistry and Nutrition
McClymont, G. L., a.o., ph.d., f.a.i.a.s., Biochemistry and Nutrition
McWilliam, J. R., m.f., ph.d., Agronomy and Soil Science
Marson, E. L., b.a., ph.d., German
Meredith, G. G., m.com., ph.d., a.a.u.q., f.a.s.a., Accounting and Financial Management
Milburn, J. A., ph.d., Botany
Morris, G. R., ph.d., Mathematics
Musgrave, W. F., m.sc.agr., ph.d., Agricultural Economics and Business Management
Nalson, J. S., m.sc., ph.d., Sociology

NEALE, R. S., B.SC.(ECON)., M.A., Economic History
O'FARRELL, A. F., B.SC., A.R.C.S., F.R.E.S., F.I.BIOL., Zoology
OLLIER, C. D., D.SC., F.G.S., F.R.G.S., Geography
RIGGS, N. V., PH.D., F.R.A.C.I., Organic Chemistry
SMITH, R. C. T., M.A., D.PHIL., Mathematics
STANTON, R. L., M.SC., PH.D., F.A.A., Geology
STIMSON, V. R., D.SC., Physical and Inorganic Chemistry
TATZ, C. M., M.A., PH.D., Politics
TREADGOLD, M. L., PH.D., Economics
WALTON, J. H., M.A., Education (Curriculum Studies)
WILKINSON, J. F. G., D.SC., PH.D., F.M.S.A., Geology

ATTACHED RESEARCH INSTITUTES:

Agricultural Business Research Institute: Dir. P. A. RICKARDS, B.AG.SC.

Financial Management Research Centre: Dir. Prof. G. G. MEREDITH, F.A.S.A., M.COM., PH.D., A.A.U.Q.

Commonwealth Council for Educational Administration: Dir. H. T. B. HARRIS, B.A.

Animal Genetics and Breeding Unit: Dir. K. HAMMOND, PH.D.

Australian Rural Adjustment Unit: Dir. Prof. W. F. MUSGRAVE, M.SC.AGR., PH.D.

Institute for Higher Education: Dir. R. McCAIG, PH.D.

THE UNIVERSITY OF NEW SOUTH WALES

POST OFFICE BOX 1,
KENSINGTON, N.S.W. 2033
Telephone: 663-0351.

Founded 1948.

Incorporated by Act of Parliament 1968.

Chancellor: The Hon. Mr. Justice SAMUELS, Q.C., M.A., F.I.E.AUST.

Deputy Chancellor: Dr. F. M. MATHEWS, B.E., F.S.T.C.

Vice-Chancellor and Principal: Prof. RUPERT H. MYERS, C.B.E., M.SC., PH.D., F.I.M., F.A.I.M., F.R.A.C.I., F.T.S., M.AUST.I.M.M.

Pro-Vice Chancellors: RAYMUND M. GOLDING, PH.D., F.N.Z.I.C., F.INST.P., F.R.A.C.I.; JOHN B. THORNTON, B.A., B.SC.; REX E. VOWELS, A.O., M.E., S.M.I.E.E.E., C.ENG., F.I.E.AUST., M.I.E.E.

Registrar: I. R. WAY, M.B.A., F.I.E.AUST.

Librarian: ALLAN R. HORTON, B.A., F.L.A.A.

Number of teachers: 1,234.

Number of students: 17,780.

Publications: *Calendar* (annual), *Faculty Handbooks, Annual Report of Council, Research and Publications Report* (annual), *Uniken, Approach to Physical Sciences, Australian Journal of Management, Ratcliffe Memorial Lectures.*

DEANS:

Faculty of Science: V. T. BUCHWALD.
Faculty of Architecture: Prof. G. E. ROBERTS.
Faculty of Engineering: Prof. H. R. VALLENTINE.
Faculty of Applied Science: Prof. M. CHAIKIN.
Faculty of Arts: Prof. F. J. CROWLEY.
Faculty of Commerce: Prof. A. S. CARRINGTON.
Faculty of Medicine: Prof. R. J. WALSH.
Faculty of Biological Sciences: Prof. E. O. P. THOMPSON.
Faculty of Military Studies: Prof. G. V. H. WILSON.
Faculty of Law: Prof. R. G. NETTHEIM.

PROFESSORS:

ALLEN, M. W., PH.D., Computer Science
ANDERSON, D. J., PH.D., Botany
ANGUS-LEPPAN, P. V., PH.D., Surveying
BAKER, L., M.A., S.R.N., S.R.M.N., Social Work
BALL, R. J., PH.D., Australian Graduate School of Management
BEARMAN, R. J., PH.D., Chemistry, Military Studies
BEAVIS, F. C., M.A., PH.D., Applied Geology
BEDDIE, B. D., PH.D., Government, Military Studies
BENNETT, G., PH.D., Operations Research
BEVERIDGE, J., A.O., M.B., B.S., Paediatrics
BLACKET, R. B., M.D., B.S., Medicine
BLATT, J. M., PH.D., Applied Mathematics
BLUNDEN, W. R., B.SC., B.E., Traffic Engineering
BOWLES, J. S., M.SC., Physical Metallurgy (Research Professor)
BROOKES, C. H. P., M.ENG.SC., D.PHIL., Information Systems
BROWN, G., M.A., PH.D., Pure Mathematics
BROWN, L. B., M.A., PH.D., Psychology
BRYANT, R. A. A., M.E., Mechanical Engineering—Nuffield Research Professor
BUCHWALD, V. T., M.SC., PH.D., Applied Mathematics
BURNS, J., M.SC., PH.D., Mathematics, Military Studies
CAREY, H. M., M.B., B.S., M.SC., Obstetrics and Gynaecology
CARRINGTON, A. S., M.COM., Accountancy
CAVILL, G. W. K., M.SC., PH.D., D.SC., Organic Chemistry
CHAIKIN, M., O.B.E., PH.D., Textile Technology
CHAPMAN, T. G., PH.D., Engineering, Military Studies
CHAUSSIVERT, J. S. J., M. ÈS L., French
CHESTERMAN, M., LL.M., Law
CIZOVA, TATJANA, DIP.SLAV. STUDIES, Russian
COOPER, G. N., M.SC., PH.D., Medical Microbiology
COOPER, M., PH.D., Education
COX, K. R., M.B., M.S., M.A., Centre for Medical Education, Research and Development
CROWLEY, F. K., M.A., PH.D., D.PHIL., History
DANIELS, E. C., M.ARCH., Architecture
DAVIES, L. W., A.O., D.PHIL., Electrical Engineering (Solid State Electronics)
DAVIS, J., M.B.A., A.M., Australian Graduate School of Management
DAWSON, T. J., PH.D., Zoology
DRINKWATER, D. J., M.A., PH.D., Education
DUGGINS, R. K., PH.D., Mechanical Engineering, Military Studies
DUNPHY, D. C., M.ED., PH.D., Behavioural Science
EDWARDS, R. A. N., PH.D., Food Technology
ENCEL, S., M.A., PH.D., Sociology
EVANS, F. J., B.SC., B.E., Electrical Engineering
FELL, C. J. D., PH.D., C.ENG., M.I.CHEM.E., Chemical Engineering and Industrial Chemistry
FEUGHELMAN, M., D.SC., Textile Physics
FINK, P. T., C.B.E., B.E., C.ENG., Mechanical Engineering
FISHER, M. R., PH.D., Australian Graduate School of Management
FORREST, R. B., D.GEOL.SCI., Surveying
FOWLER, R. T., PH.D., D.SC.ENG., C.ENG., Chemical Engineering and Industrial Chemistry
FREELAND, J. M., D.F.C., M.ARCH., D.LITT., Architecture
GAGE, P. W., PH.D., D.SC., Physiology and Pharmacology
GARNER, B. J., M.A., PH.D., Geography
GLOVER, W. E., M.D., B.CH., B.A.O., Physiology
GOLDING, R. M., M.SC., PH.D., Theoretical and Physical Chemistry
GOLDSMID, H. J., PH.D., D.SC., Experimental Physics
GOVETT, G. J. S., PH.D., D.I.C., F.I.M.M., Applied Geology
GREEN, H. E., M.E., PH.D., Electrical Engineering, Military Studies
HALL, R. F., M.A., PH.D., General Studies
HAMBLIN, C. L., M.A., PH.D., Philosophy
HARDING, D. E., B.A., LL.M., Law
HASKELL, J. C., M.ARCH., Architecture
HASOFER, A. M., PH.D., Statistics
HEWSON, J., PH.D., Economics
HICKIE, J. B., M.B., B.S., Medicine
HORA, H., DR.RER.NAT., Theoretical Physics
HUCKSTEP, R. L., C.M.G., M.A., M.D., Traumatic and Orthopaedic Surgery
HUKINS, A. A., M.SC., PH.D., Science Education
JOHNSON, R., M.A., Spanish
KAKWANI, N. C., M.A., PH.D., Statistics
KARBOWIAK, A. E., D.SC., C.ENG., Electrical Engineering—Communications
KASPER, W. E., DR.RER.POL., Military Studies (Economics)
KEMP, M. C., M.A., PH.D., Economics (Research Professor)
KILOH, L. G., M.D., B.SC., Psychiatry
KING, P. T., M.SC., PH.D., Political Science
LANCE, J. W., C.B.E., M.D., B.S., Neurology
LAWRENCE, R. J., M.A., PH.D., Social Work
LAYTON, R. A., M.EC., Marketing
LEDERER, J., M.SC., A.S.T.C., Optometry
LEE, I. K., M.ENG.SC., PH.D., Civil Engineering
LIVINGSTONE, S. E., PH.D., D.SC., Inorganic Chemistry
LLOYD DAVIES, H., PH.D., Pastoral Sciences
LOVIBOND, S. H., M.A., PH.D., Psychology
LYKKE, A. W. J., M.D., B.S., F.R.C.P.A., M.R.C.PATH., Pathology
MA, R. A., B.COM., M.B.A., Accountancy
MABBUTT, J. A., M.A., Geography
MARTIN, B. K., M.A., M.LITT., English
McCALLUM, D. M., M.A., Political Science
McMANUS, M., PH.D., Economics
MARSHALL, K. C., M.S., PH.D., Microbiology
MILBORROW, B. V., PH.D., D.SC., Biochemistry
MILFULL, J. R., PH.D., German Studies
MITCHELL, R. M., B.MED.SC., M.B.CHM., Surgery
MUIR, H., B.MET.E., SC.D., Physical Metallurgy
MURNAGHAN, G. F., M.D., CH.M., Surgery
NETTHEIM, R. G., A.M., L.L.B., Law
NEVILE, J. W., M.A., PH.D., Economics
NILAND, J. R., M.COM., PH.D., Economics

O'FARRELL, P. J., M.A., PH.D., History
OLIVER, H. J., M.A., English
OLSSON, R. C., M.B.A., PH.D., Finance
O'SULLIVAN, W. J., PH.D., Medical Biochemistry
OXLEY, P. L. B., PH.D., C.ENG., Production Engineering
PALMER, G. R., M.EC., PH.D., Health Administration
PITNEY, W. R., M.D., B.S., Medicine
REES, N. W., PH.D., Electrical Engineering
RIMMER, W. G., M.A., PH.D., A.M., Economic History
ROBERTS, G. E., B.ARCH., M.C.D., Architecture
ROBINSON, D., M.A., D.PHIL., Pure Mathematics
RONAYNE, J., M.A., PH.D., History and Philosophy of Science
ROST, F. W. D., M.B., B.S., PH.D., Anatomy
ROXBOROUGH, F. F., PH.D., C.ENG., Mining Engineering
RYAN, J. L., PH.D., Accountancy
SACKVILLE, R., LL.M., Law
SHANNON, J. S., PH.D., D.SC., Chemistry
SHEARER, I. A., LL.M., S.J.D., Law
SINNETT, P., M.D., B.S., Community Medicine
SMYTHE, L. E., M.SC., PH.D., Analytical Chemistry
STRINGER, J., M.A., Australian Graduate School of Management
SVENSSON, N. L., M.MECH.E., PH.D., C.ENG., Mechanical Engineering
TAYLOR, K. N. R., PH.D., Experimental Physics
THOM, B. G., PH.D., Geography, Military Studies
THOMAS, H., M.B.A., PH.D., Australian Graduate School of Management
THOMPSON, E. O. P., M.SC., PH.D., SC.D., Biochemistry
THOMPSON, J. J., PH.D., Nuclear Engineering
THORNTON, J. B., B.A., B.SC., History and Philosophy of Science
TOAKLEY, A. R., B.A., M.ENG.SC., PH.D., Building
TRACY, G. D., M.B., B.S., Surgery
TRIMM, D. L., PH.D., D.I.C., Chemical Engineering and Industrial Chemistry
VALLENTINE, H. R., M.S., Civil Engineering
VOWELS, R. E., A.O., M.E., C.ENG., Electrical Engineering
WADE, D. N., M.B., B.S., D.PHIL., Clinical Pharmacology
WALKER, R., PH.D., A.C.A., Accountancy
WALSH, R. J., A.O., O.B.E., M.B.B.S., Human Genetics
WARREN, B. A., M.B.B.S., D.PHIL., F.R.C.P.A., F.R.C.PATH., Pathology
WEBSTER, I. W., M.D.B.S., Community Medicine
WEINSTOCK, M., M.SC., Librarianship
WESTERMAN, H. L., M.E., Town Planning
WHITMORE, H., LL.B., S.J.D., Law
WICKEN, A. J., M.A., PH.D., Australian Graduate School of Management
WILENSKI, P., M.B.B.S., M.A., M.P.A., Australian Graduate School of Management
WILSON, G. V. H., M.SC., PH.D., D.SC., Physics, Military Studies
WOODHEAD, R. W., M.E., Civil Engineering
YERBURY, D., PH.D., Australian Graduate School of Management

ASSOCIATE COLLEGE:

W. S. and L. B. Robinson University College: Wentworth Rd., Broken Hill, N.S.W. 2880; f. 1959.

Director: Prof. J. E. ANDERSEN, PH.D.

Number of teachers: 16.

Number of students: 126.

HEADS OF DEPARTMENT:

Mining and Mineral Sciences: L. J. THOMAS, PH.D.

Science: J. E. ANDERSEN, PH.D.

ASSOCIATED INSTITUTE:

Australian Graduate School of Management: *see* under Colleges.

UNIVERSITY OF NEWCASTLE

NEWCASTLE, N.S.W. 2308

Telephone: 68-0401.

Telex: NEWUN 28194.

Founded 1965.

State control; Academic year: March to November (3 terms).

Chancellor: Sir BEDE CALLAGHAN, C.B.E., F.A.I.M., F.B.I.A.

Vice-Chancellor and Principal: Prof. D. W. GEORGE, A.O., PH.D., F.T.S., F.I.E.E., F.I.MECH.E., F.I.E.AUST., F.A.I.P.

Vice-Principal and Deputy Vice-Chancellor: Prof. A. D. TWEEDIE, M.A.

Deputy Vice-Chancellor: Prof. L. N. SHORT, M.SC., D.PHIL., F.A.C.E., F.R.S.A.

Secretary: P. D. ALEXANDER, B.A.

Librarian: E. FLOWERS, M.A., A.L.A.A.

Library: *see* under Libraries.

Number of teachers: 356.

Number of students: 4,302.

Publications: *Calendar, Annual Report, Financial Statements* (annual), *A Bibliographical Record of the University* (every 3 years), *Gazette, University News.*

DEANS:

Faculty of Architecture: Prof. E. C. PARKER.

Faculty of Arts: Prof. R. G. TANNER.

Faculty of Economics and Commerce: Prof. K. E. LINDGREN.

Faculty of Education: Prof. R. S. LAURA.

Faculty of Engineering: Prof. A. W. ROBERTS.

Faculty of Mathematics: Prof. R. G. KEATS.

Faculty of Medicine: Prof. D. C. MADDISON.

Faculty of Science: Prof. B. BOETTCHER.

PROFESSORS:

Faculty of Architecture:
PARKER, E. C., A.S.T.C., F.R.A.I.A., Architecture

Faculty of Arts:
BURROWS, J. F., M.A., PH.D., English
CARTER, M. P., PH.D., Sociology
CATTELL, N. R., M.A., PH.D., Linguistics
CRANFIELD, G. A., PH.D., Modern History
DUTTON, K. R., M.A., D.U., M.A.C.E., French
FROST, D. L., M.A., PH.D., English
HOOKER, C. A., PH.D., Philosophy
JORDAN, R. J., M.A., PH.D., Drama
MOWATT, D. G., PH.D., F.A.H.A., German
ROBINSON, K. W., M.A., Geography
TANNER, R. G., M.A., Latin
TWEEDIE, A. D., M.A., Geography

Faculty of Economics and Commerce:
JAGER, M. O., B.COM., F.A.S.A., Commerce
JOHNS, B. L., M.A., Economics
LINDGREN, K. E., M.A., PH.D., Legal Studies
SHARPE, I. G., M.A., PH.D., Economics
TISDELL, C. A., PH.D., Economics
WILLIAMS, A. J., PH.D., A.F.A.I.M., A.A.S.A., M.A.C.E., M.A.I.E.A., Commerce
WINSEN, J. K., M.COM., M.A., PH.D., A.A.S.A., Commerce

Faculty of Education:
BIGGS, J. B., PH.D., Education
LAURA, R. S., M.DIV., M.A., D.PHIL., Education
SHORT, L. N., M.SC., D.PHIL., F.A.C.E., F.R.S.A., Education

Faculty of Engineering:
ANDERSON, B. D. O., PH.D., F.A.A., F.I.E.E.E., F.I.E.AUST., M.S.I.A.M., Electrical Engineering
ANTONIA, R. A., M.ENG.SC., PH.D., Mechanical Engineering
GEORGE, D. W., A.O., PH.D., F.T.S., F.I.E.E., F.I.MECH.E., F.I.E.AUST., F.A.I.P., Engineering
HALL, E. O., M.SC., PH.D., M.AUS.I.M.M., Metallurgy
HENDERSON, F. M., M.SC., M.I.C.E., M.A.S.C.E., F.I.E.AUST., M.N.Z.I.E., Civil Engineering
JAMESON, G. J. PH.D., A.S.T.C., Chemical Engineering
MOORE, J. B., M.ENG.SC., PH.D., S.M.I.E.E.E., Electrical Engineering
ROBERTS, A. W., PH.D., A.S.T.C., F.I.E.AUST., M.I.MECH.E., Industrial Engineering

Faculty of Mathematics:
KEATS, R. G., PH.D., F.I.M.A., F.A.S.A., Mathematics
ROBINSON, R. W., M.A., PH.D., Mathematics

Faculty of Medicine:
CLANCY, R. L., B.SC.(MED)., M.B., B.S., PH.D., F.R.A.C.P. F.R.A.C.P.(C), Pathology
CLARKE, R. M., M.A., M.B., B.CHIR., PH.D., M.D., Anatomy
KELLERMAN, G. M., M.B., B.S., M.SC., F.A.A.C.B., F.R.A.C.P., Medical Biochemistry
LEEDER, S. R., B.SC.(MED)., M.B., B.S., PH.D., F.R.A.C.P., M.F.C.M., Community Medicine
MORGAN, T. O., B.SC., M.B., B.S., M.D., F.R.A.C.P., Medicine
MADDISON, D. C., M.B., B.S., D.P.M., F.R.A.C.P., F.A.N.Z.C.P., Medicine
RAPHAEL, B., M.B., B.S., M.D., D.P.M. (R.A.N.Z.C.P.), F.R.A.N.Z.P., M.R.C. (PSYCH.), Psychiatry
ROBINSON, J. S., D.R.C.O.G., M.R.C.O.G., Reproductive Medicine
SMITH, A. J., M.A., D.M., B.CHIR., F.R.C.P., Clinical Pharmacology
WHITE, S. W., M.B., B.S., M.D., Human Physiology

Faculty of Science:
BOETTCHER, B., PH.D., Biological Sciences
KEATS, J. A., A.M., PH.D., F.B.PS.S., F.A.PS.S., F.A.S.S.A., Psychology
KING, M. G., PH.D., F.A.PS.S., M.A.P.S.S., Psychology
MACDONALD, R. J., PH.D., Physics
PICKERING, W. F. J., PH.D., D.SC., A.S.T.C., F.R.A.C.I., Chemistry

UNIVERSITY OF QUEENSLAND

ST. LUCIA, BRISBANE, QUEENSLAND 4067

Telephone: Brisbane 07-377111.

Telegraphic Address: Brisbane University.

Founded 1909.

Academic year: February to November (two semesters)

Chancellor: The Hon. Sir WALTER CAMPBELL, LL.B., M.A.

Deputy Chancellor: Sir LIONEL McCRAY, F.A.S.A., A.C.I.S., F.A.I.M.

Vice-Chancellor: Prof. BRIAN WILSON.

Deputy Vice-Chancellor (Academic): Prof. G. N. DAVIES, D.D.S., F.A.C.D., F.D.S.R.C.S.

Deputy Vice-Chancellor (Fabric and Finance): J. E. RITCHIE, B.COM., F.A.I.M.

Registrar: S. A. RAYNER, M.A., M.ED., ED.D.

Librarian: F. D. O. FIELDING, M.A., A.L.A., F.L.A.A.

Library: *see* Libraries.

Number of teachers: 1,164 full-time, including 103 professors.

Number of students: 18,517.

Publications: *University Calendar*†, *Higher Degree Handbook*†, *Undergraduate Degree Handbook, Statistics, University of Queensland Papers*†, *Know Your University, University News, Inaugural Lectures, Vice-Chancellor's Report.*

DEANS:

Faculty of Agricultural Science: S. A. WARING, PH.D.

Faculty of Architecture: H. S. MURISON, M.ARCH., A.R.I.B.A., F.R.A.I.A.

Faculty of Arts: R. A. SECKOLD, M.A., D.U.

Faculty of Commerce and Economics: H. M. KOLSEN, PH.D.

Faculty of Dentistry: K. F. ADKINS, M D.SC., PH.D., M.R.C.PATH.

Faculty of Education: B. W. CARSS, M.S., PH.D., M.A.C.S.

Faculty of Engineering: D. J. NICKLIN, PH.D., F.I.CHEM.E.

Faculty of Law: R. N. BARBER, LL.M., M.A.

Faculty of Medicine: R. L. DOHERTY, M.D., M.P.H., F.R.C.P.A., F.R.A.C.P.

Faculty of Music: P. K. BRACANIN, M.A., PH.D., A.MUS.

Faculty of Science: R. J. LADD, PH.D., M.R.C.V.S.

Faculty of Social Work: F. PAVLIN, M.SOC.WK., M.A.PS.S.

Faculty of Veterinary Science: T. J. HEATH, PH.D., M.R.C.V.S., M.A.C.V.S.

PROFESSORS:

ACKROYD, JOYCE I., PH.D., DIP.ED., Japanese Language and Literature
BADDELEY, H., M.B., B.S., D.M.R.D., F.F.R., Radiology
BASS, L., DR.PHIL., M.A., F.I.P., Mathematics
BASSETT, G. W., M.A., DIP.ED., PH.D., F.A.C.E., Education
BOYCE, P. J., M.A., PH.D., Political Science
BRITTEN, E. J., M.SC., PH.D., F.A.A.A.S., Agriculture
BULLOCK, K. J., PH.D., Mechanical Engineering
BURNETT, W., M.B., CH.M., F.R.C.S., F.R.F.P.S., F.R.A.C.S., Surgery
CAMPBELL, W. J., M.A., DIP.ED., PH.D., DIP.A.I.E., M.A.PS.S., Education
CHAMBERLAIN, EDNA R., M.A., A.I.H.A., Social Work
CHRISTA, B., M.A., PH.D., Russian
DARE, J. G., PH.D., PH.C., F.P.S., F.S.H.P., M.P.S., Pharmacy
DAVIS, C. S., D.F.C., M.SC., PH.D., Mathematics
DOWLING, D. F., D.V.SC., PH.D., M.R.C.V.S., Animal Husbandry
EADIE, M. J., M.D., PH.D., F.R.A.C.P., Neurology and Neuropharmacology
EDWARDS, P. D., PH.D., M.A., English
EMMERSON, B. T., B.S., M.D., F.R.A.C.P., Medicine
ENGLISH, P. B., M.V.SC., PH.D., M.R.C.V.S., M.A.C.V.SC., Veterinary Clinical Studies
EVANS, G. T., PH.D., Education
FRANCIS, J., C.B.E., D.SC., F.R.C.V.S., F.A.C.V.SC., F.R.S.M., Veterinary Preventive Medicine
GLOVER, T. D., M.A., D.SC., PH.D., Veterinary Science
GOODMAN, F. O., PH.D., D.SC., Theoretical Physics
GOODWIN, K. L., M.A., D.PHIL., English
GREENWOOD, G., M.A., PH.D., F.A.SS.A., History
GUNN, M. W., M.SC., PH.D., F.I.R.E.E., F.I.E.AUST., Electrical Engineering
HAMILTON, K. G., M.A., PH.D., English Language and Literature
HAWKER, R. W., M.D., B.S., PH.D., F.R.A.C.P., F.R.A.C.S., Physiology
HOLBOROW, L. C., PH.D., Philosophy
HOLMES, J. H., M.A., PH.D., Geography
KEEBLE, L. B., M.C., M.A., F.R.I.C.S., P.P.R.T.P.I., F.R.A.P.I., Regional and Town Planning
KERR, J. F. R., B.SC., M.B.B.S., PH.D., M.R.C.P., M.R.A.C.P., F.R.C.P.A., M.R.C. PATH., Pathology
KETTLE, D. S., D.SC., F.R.E.S., F.I.BIOL., Entomology
KOLSEN, H. M., PH.D., Economics
KRUGER, B. J., D.D.S., D.D.SC., PH.D., Oral Biology
LAMBERTON, D. McL., D.PHIL., Economics
LAVERTY, J. R., PH.D., External Studies
LEOPOLD, K., M.A., PH.D., German
LIPTON, S., M.SC., F.B.C.S., Statistics and Probability
LYONS, L. E., M.SC., PH.D., D.SC., F.A.A., F.R.A.C.I., Physical Chemistry
McBRIDE, G., PH.D., Ethology
McELWAIN, D. W., E.D., M.A., PH.D., F.B.PS.S., F.A.PS.S., Psychology
MACKAY, E. V., M.B., B.S., D.G.O., F.R.C.O.G., F.R.C.S.ED., F.R.A.C.S., Obstetrics and Gynaecology
MILNS, R. D., M.A., Classics and Ancient History
MOLYNEUX, G. S., PH.D., F.D.S.R.C.S., M.A.C.E., Anatomy
NICKLIN, D. J., PH.D., F.I.CHEM.E., Chemical Engineering
NICKSON, N. J., D.MUS., A.R.C.M., Music
O'CONNOR, C., PH.D., M.A.SC.E., M.I.E.AUST., Civil Engineering
O'REGAN, R. S., B.A., LL.M., Law
PARNELL, T. M., B.SC., B.E., PH.D., M.I.P.P.S., M.A.I.P., M.I.A., M.I.E.E.E., Engineering
PARSONS, R. W., D.PHIL., F.S.A.S.M., F.INST P., F.A.I.P., Experimental Physics
PETER, H. W., M.A., PH.D., F.A.I.M., Business Administration
PILLOW, A. F., PH.D., F.I.M.A., Applied Mathematics
PLOWMAN, R. A., PH.D., D.SC., A.S.T.C., F.R.A.C.I., Inorganic Chemistry
POUND, A. W., M.B, B.S., M.R.C.P.A., Pathology
POWELL, L. W., M.B.B.S., M.R.A.C.P., Medicine
POWELL, R. N., M.SC., PH.D., Dentistry
RENDLE-SHORT, T. J., M.A., M.D., F.R.A.C.P., F.R.C.P., D.C.H., Child Health
REX, M. A. E., M.A., PH.D., Veterinary Surgery
RIGSBY, B. J., PH.D., Anthropology
ROSE, G. A., PH.D., F.A.C.S., M.I.E.E.E., M.A.C.M., Computer Science
RYAN, J. G. P., B.SC., M.B.B.S., Community Practice
RYAN, K. W., LL.B., PH.D., Law
SAINI, B. S., PH.D., F.R.I.B.A., F.R.A.I.A.. Architecture
SARGENT, G. E. G., A.R.C.S., B.SC., M.I.M.M., F.G.S., M.AUST.I.S.M.M., F.R.A.S., Economic Geology
SCOTT, K. J., M.SC.AGR., PH.D., Biochemistry
SCOTT, R. D., PH.D., Public Administration
SHEEHAN, P. W., PH.D., Psychology
SIMPSON-MORGAN, M. W., PH.D., Animal Husbandry
SINGHAL, D. P., M.A., PH.D., D.LITT., F.R.A.S., F.R.HIST.S., History
SKERMAN, V. B. D., D.SC., Q.D.A., F.W.A.A.S., Microbiology
SPECHT, R. L., M.SC., PH.D., Botany
SPENCER, M. C., M.A., D.PHIL., French
SPRENT, J. F. A., D.SC., PH.D., F.R.C.V.S., F.A.A., F.A.C.V.SC., Parasitology
STACEY, F. D., PH.D., D.SC., F.A.I.P., Applied Physics
STALKER, R. J., PH.D., M.SC.ENG., Mechanical Engineering
STEPHENS, R. R., B.DS., L.D.S.R.C.S., L.R.C.P., M.R.C.S., F.F.D.R.C.S.I., Restorative Dentistry
STEPHENSON, W., M.B.E., PH.D., D.SC., F.A.C.E., Zoology
SUTHERLAND, M. D., M.SC., D.SC., F.R.A.C.I., Chemistry
SUTTON, K. C. T., LL.M., PH.D., Law
TARLO, H., LL.B., M.A., Law
THOMIS, M., M.A., PH.D., History
THOMSON, J. M., D.SC., Zoology
THORBURN, G. D., B.SC., M.B., B.S., M.D., M.R.A.C.P., Physiology
TYRER, J. W. H., B.S., M.D., F.R.C.P., F.R.A.C.P., F.R.C.P.ED., Medicine
VYBORNY, R., R.N.DR., C.SC., Mathematics
WATERHOUSE, J. B., M.SC., PH.D., Palaeontology and Stratigraphy
WATSON, D. J., M.A., PH.D., Accounting
WATTS, BETTY H., O.B.E., PH.D., F.A.C.E., Special Education
WESTERN, J. S., M.A., PH.D., M.A.PS.S., Sociology
WHITEHEAD, J. D., M.A., PH.D., Physics
WHITLOCK, F. A., M.A., M.D., F.A.N.Z.C.P., D.P.M., M.R.C.P., Psychiatry
WHITMORE, R. L., PH.D., D.SC., F.I.MIN.E., M.I.M.M., M.AUS.I.M.M., F.I.P., F.I.F., Mining and Metallurgy
WILSON, A. F., D.SC., F.M.S.A., F.G.A.A., M.AUS.I.M.M., F.G.S., Geology and Mineralogy
WILSON, G. L., D.PHIL., Agriculture
ZERNER, B., M.SC., PH.D., F.R.A.C.I., Biochemistry

AFFILIATED RESIDENTIAL COLLEGES:

Emmanuel College: Principal Prof. R. A. BUSCH, CH.ST.J., E.D., M.A., B.D., M.R.E.

St. John's College: Warden Rev. Dr. P. F. CARNLEY, B.A., PH.D., TH.L.

King's College: Master Rev. Dr. I. H. GRIMMETT, M.A., B.D., TH.D.

The Women's College: Principal Mrs. J. BELL, M.A.

St. Leo's College: Rector Rev. C. V. HURLEY, S.J., B.A., B.ED., M.A.C.E.

Duchesne College: Principal Sister MARY LEAHY, R.S.C.J., B.A.

Union College: Warden Dr. H. W. Bradbury, M.A., B.SC., M.B., B.S.

Cromwell College: Principal Rev. Dr. H. C. KROHN, M.A., ED.D.

International House: Warden I. M. B. CRIBB, B.A., B.ED., M.A.C.E.

Grace College: Principal Mrs. E. PATTERSON, B.A., B.ED., M.A.C.E.

ATTACHED RESEARCH INSTITUTES:

Fred and Eleanor Schonell Educational Research Centre: Hood St., St. Lucia, Queensland 4067; Dir. Prof. B. H. WATTS, O.B.E., PH.D., F.A.C.E.

Julius Kruttschnitt Mineral Research Centre: Isles Rd., Indooroopilly, Queensland 4068; Dir. Dr. A. J. LYNCH, D.SC., PH.D., A.S.T.C., M.AUS.I.M.M.

Tertiary Education Institute: University of Queensland, St. Lucia, Queensland 4067; Dir. Prof. E. ROE, M.A., PH.D.

THE UNIVERSITY OF SYDNEY

N.S.W. 2006

Telephone: 692-1122.

Telegraphic Address: Univsyd, Sydney.

Telex: 20056.

Founded 1850.

Private control; Academic year: February to December.

Chancellor: Sir HERMANN BLACK, M.EC., F.C.I.S.

Deputy Chancellor: The Hon. Mr. Justice D. M. SELBY, E.D., B.A., LL.B.

Vice-Chancellor and Principal: Prof. Sir BRUCE WILLIAMS, K.B.E., M.A., M.A.(ECON.), F.A.S.S.A.

Deputy Vice-Chancellors: Prof. M. G. TAYLOR, M.D., B.S., PH.D., D.SC., F.R.A.C.P., Prof. J. M. WARD, ,M.A., LL.B., F.A.H.A., F.A.S.S.A., F.R.A.H.S.

Assistant Vice-Chancellor and Registrar: K. W. KNIGHT, PH.D., M.EC., A.L.A.A.

Library: *see under* Libraries.

Number of teachers: *c.* 1,250.

Number of students 17,960.

Publications: *Calendar*, *Research Report*, *Annual Report*, Faculty Handbooks, Examination Papers (annually), *Postgraduate Study in the University of Sydney* (irregularly), *Department of Adult Education Syllabus* (annually), *The University of Sydney News* (weekly during term), *The Gazette* (half-yearly), *Current Affairs Bulletin* (monthly), *Oceania* (quarterly), *Archaeology and Physical Anthropology in Oceania* (3 a year), *Oceania Linguistics Monographs* (irregularly), *Bulletin of the Postgraduate Committee in Medicine* (monthly), *Sydney Law Review* (annually), *Review of Indonesian and Malayan Affairs* (2 a year), *Kronolog* (Computer Centre, several a year), *Focus* (Careers and Appts. Service, 3 a year), *Abacus* (2 a year), *Aust. Economic History Review* (2 a year), *Journal of the Oriental Society of Australia* (annually), *Dental Outlook* (quarterly), *Acta Structorum* (annually), *University of Sydney Archives Record* (3 a year).

DEANS:

Faculty of Agriculture: L. N. BALAAM, M.SC.

Faculty of Architecture: R. N. JOHNSON, A.O., B.ARCH., F.R.I.B.A., L.F.R.A.I.A.

Faculty of Arts: P. M. LAHY, PH.D.

Faculty of Dentistry: N. D. MARTIN, M.D.S., F.A.C.D., F.I.C.D., F.A.P.H.A., F.R.A.C.D.S., A.I.A.O.P.

Faculty of Economics: S. SALSBURY, A.M., PH.D.

Faculty of Engineering: P. B. JONES, M.ENG.SC., PH.D., F.I.S.AUST.

Faculty of Law: J. G. MACINOLTY, LL.M.

Faculty of Medicine: R. S. GYE, B.SC.(MED.), M.B., B.S., M.A., D.PHIL., F.R.A.C.S., F.R.C.S.

Faculty of Science: J. R. SIMONS, PH.D., M.SC.

Faculty of Veterinary Science: J. R. EGERTON, B.V.SC., M.A.C.V.SC., M.A.S.M.

PROFESSORS:

ANDERSON, D. T., PH.D., D.SC., Biology
ANDERSON, R. A., PH.D., M.P.S., Pharmaceutics
ANDREWS, G. A., M.B., B.S., F.R.C.P., F.A.C.M.A., Community and Geriatric Medicine
ANNISON, E. F., PH.D., D.SC., F.R.I.C., Animal Husbandry
ARMSTRONG, D. M., PH.D., F.A.H.A., Philosophy
BALL, S., PH.D., Education
BARKO, I., LIC.PHIL.L., D.U., F.A.H.A., French
BASTEN, A., M.B., B.S., D.PHIL., M.R.C.P., F.R.C.P.A., F.R.A.C.P., Immunology
BENNETT, J. M., PH.D., Computer Science
BEUMONT, P. J. V., M.SC., M.B., CH.B., M.PHIL., D.P.M., M.R.C.P.ED., F.R.C. PSYCH., M.R.A.N.Z.C.P., R.C.P. & S., Psychiatry
BILGER, R. W., D.PHIL., M.I.E.AUST., Mechanical Engineering
BILLSON, F. A., M.B.B.S., D.O., F.R.C.S.ED., F.R.C.S., F.R.A.C.S., F.A.C.S., F.R.A.C.O., Ophthalmology and Eye Health
BIRCH, L. C., D.SC., F.A.A., Biology
BIRD, G. A., PH.D., M.E., A.F.A.I.A.A., Aeronautical Engineering
BLACK, R. H., E.D., M.D., B.S., DIP.ANTH., D.T.M. & H., F.R.A.C.P., Tropical Medicine
BLUNT, M. J., M.B., B.S., PH.D., Anatomy
BRENNAN, T., M.A., Social Administration
BRIDGES-WEBB, C., M.B., B.S., M.D., F.R.A.C.G.P., Community Medicine
BROWN, R. H., D.SC., D.I.C., M.I.E.E., F.R.S., F.R.A.S., F.A.A., Physics, Astronomy
BUCHANAN, N., PH.D., M.R.C.S., L.R.C.P., F.C.P.(S.A.), Paediatrics
BURKE, W., PH.D., Physiology
BUTTERFIELD, R. M., PH.D., D.V.SC., F.A.C.V.SC., Veterinary Anatomy
CAMBITOGLOU, A., D.PHIL., PH.D., M.A., F.S.A., F.A.H.A., Archaeology
CAMERON, D. A., M.D.S., PH.D., Pathology
CAMPBELL, K. O., M.P.A., A.M., PH.D., F.A.S.S.A., Agricultural Economics
CAMPBELL-ALLEN, D., M.A., M.R.AE.S., F.I.E.AUST., Civil Engineering (Concrete Technology)
CASTALDI, P. A., M.D., B.S., F.R.A.C.P., F.R.C.P.A., Medicine
CHAMBERS, R. J., D.SC.ECON., F.A.S.A., A.C.I.S., Accounting
CHAMPION, R. A., M.A., F.A.PS.S., F.A.S.S.A., Psychology
CLELAND, K. W., M.B., B.S., Histology and Embryology
COLLIS-GEORGE, N., PH.D., M.SC., Soil Science
CORINA, J. G., M.A., D.PHIL., Industrial Relations
COWAN, H. J., D.ENG., PH.D., M.SC., F.A.S.C.E., F.I.E.AUST., F.I.STRUCT.E., Architectural Science
DALY, M. T., B.A., PH.D., Geography
DAVIDSON, L. A. G., M.D. F.R.C.P., F.R.C.P.ED., F.R.A.C.P., Environmental Health
DAVIS, A. R., M.A., Oriental Studies
DAVIS, E. H., B.SC.(ENG.), F.I.E.AUST., Civil Engineering (Soil Mechanics)
DEVERALL, B. J., PH.D., D.I.C., Plant Pathology
DOMICELJ, S., B.ARCH., M.R.A.P.I., M.R.T.P.I., Town and Country Planning
DUNSTON, A. J., M.A., Latin
EBIED, R. Y., B.A., F.R.A.S., Semitic Studies
EDWARDS, M. J., M.V.SC., PH.D., M.R.C.V.S., M.A.C.V.SC., Veterinary Clinical Studies
EGERTON, J. R., B.V.SC., M.A.C.V.SC., M.A.S.M., Veterinary Medicine
FINCKH, E. S., M.D., B.S., F.R.C.P.A., F.R.C.PATH., F.R.A.C.P., Pathology
FREEMAN, H. C., M.SC., PH.D., F.R.A.C.I., Inorganic Chemistry
GALLAGHER, C. H., PH.D., D.V.SC., F.A.C.V.SC., F.R.C.PATH., Veterinary Pathology
GEDDES, W. R., M.A., PH.D., Anthropology
GYE, R. S., M.A., D.PHIL., B.SC.(MED.), M.B., B.S., F.R.A.C.S., F.R.C.S., Medicine
HALLIDAY, M. A. K., M.A., PH.D., Linguistics
HENNESSY, J. B., D.PHIL., F.S.A., Archaeology
HEYDON, J. D., B.C.L., M.A., Law
HOGAN, W. P., M.A., PH.D., Economics
HUDSON, C. N., M.B., M.CHIR., F.R.C.S., F.R.C.O.G., Obstetrics and Gynaecology
HUSH, N. S., D.SC., M.SC., F.A.A., F.R.A.C.I., Theoretical Chemistry
JACOBS, M. G., M.A., History
JENKINS, A. E., M.ENG.SC., PH.D., F.I.M., M.AUST.I.M.M., M.R.A.C.I., M.I.A.M., Materials and Mining Engineering
JOHNSON, D. H. N., M.A., LL.B., International Law
JOHNSON, R. N., B.ARCH., F.R.I.B.A., L.F.R.A.I.A., Architecture
JOHNSTON, G. A. R., PH.D., Pharmacology
JOLLY, M., M.D.S., D.D.SC., F.R.A.C.D.S., Oral Medicine and Oral Surgery
JOSEPH, D., M.B., B.S., F.F.A.R.C.S., F.F.A.R.A.C.S., Anaesthetics
KELLY, D. T., M.B., F.R.A.C.P., F.A.C.C., Cardiology
KELLY, G. M., PH.D., F.A.A., Pure Mathematics
KERR, C. B., D.PHIL., M.B., B.S., F.R.A.C.P., M.F.C.M., Preventive and Social Medicine

KLINEBERG, I. J., PH.D., M.D.S., Prosthetic Dentistry
KNOX, K. W., M.SC., PH.D., Oral Biology
KRAMER, L. J., O.B.E., D.PHIL., F.A.H.A., M.A.C.E., Australian Literature
KUCHEL, P. W., PH.D., Biochemistry
LANE, P. H., S.J.D., L.L.M., LL.D., Law
LANGFORD-SMITH, T., M.SC., PH.D., Geography
LANGLANDS, A. O., B.SC., M.B., CH.B., D.M.R.T., F.R.C.R., Radiotherapy
LATTER, B. D. H., PH.D., Biology (Genetics)
LAWRENCE, J. R., M.B., B.S., F.R.A.C.P., Medicine
LAWRENCE, P., M.A., PH.D., Anthropology
LESTER, K. S., PH.D., D.D.SC., F.R.A.C.D.S., Dentistry
LEY, P., PH.D., Psychology
LITTLE, J. M., M.D., M.S., F.R.A.C.S., Surgery
LYELL, J. S., M.D.S., F.A.C.D., F.R.A.C.D.S., Operative Dentistry
MCCUSKER, C. B. A., D.SC., M.R.I.A., High Energy Nuclear Physics
MCGOVERN, V. J., M.D., CH.B., F.R.A.C.P., F.R.C.P.A., F.R.C.PATH., Pathology
MCLEOD, J. G., M.B., B.S., B.SC.(MED.), D.PHIL., F.R.C.P., F.R.A.C.P., Medicine
MARTIN, N. D., M.D.S., F.A.C.D., F.I.C.D., F.A.P.H.A., F.R.A.C.D.S., A.I.A.O.P., Preventive Dentistry
MAY, J., M.B., B.S., F.R.A.C.S., Surgery
MAYER, H., M.A., Political Theory
MELROSE, D. B., D.PHIL., Physics
MESSEL, H., PH.D., Physics
MESSERLE, H. K., D.SC., PH.D., M.ENG.SC., S.M.I.E.E.E., F.I.E.E., F.I.E.AUST., F.A.I.P., F.I.R.E.E., Electrical Engineering
MILLS, B. Y., A.C., D.SC.ENG., F.R.S., F.A.A., Physics, Astrophysics
MILLS, G., M.A., Economics
MILTON, G. W., M.B., B.S., F.R.C.S., F.R.A.C.S., Surgery
MOORE, W. J., PH.D., F.R.A.C.I., Physical Chemistry
MORISON, W. L., D.PHIL., Law
MULLINS, M. G. C., PH.D., Horticulture
NORMAN, M. J. T., PH.D., Agronomy
PARSONS, R. W., B.A., LL.B., Law
PHEILS, M. T., M.A., M.B., M.CHIR., L.R.C.P., F.R.C.S., F.R.A.C.S., F.A.C.S., Surgery
PHILIP, G. M., D.SC., PH.D., F.G.S., M.A.I.M.M., Geology
PIPER, D. W., M.D., B.S., F.R.C.P., F.R.A.C.P., Medicine
PITMAN, M. G., M.A., PH.D., Biology (Plant Physiology)
PLATT, P., M.A., B.MUS., B.LITT., Music
PRINCE, R. G. H., PH.D., F.I.CHEM.E., F.I.E.AUST., Chemical Engineering
RANKIN, J. G. D'A., M.B.B.S., F.R.A.C.P., F.R.C.P.CAN., Medicine
REDDICK, J. A. C. H., M.A., D.PHIL., German
REES, S. J., PH.D., Social Work
REEVE, T. S., C.B.E., M.B., B.S., F.A.C.S., F.R.A.C.S., Surgery
RITCHIE, W., M.A., PH.D., F.A.H.A., Greek
RIZZO, G. L., D.LITT., Italian
ROBINSON, T. J., M.SC.AGRIC., PH.D., SC.D., Animal Husbandry
ROGERS, H. L., M.A., Early English Literature and Language
RUTHERFORD, R. S. G., M.A., Economic Statistics
SALSBURY, S., M., A.M., PH.D., Economic History
SCHREUDER, D. M., D.PHIL., History
SENETA, E., M.SC., PH.D., Mathematical Statistics
SHARPE, E. J., M.A., TEOL.D., Religious Studies
SHAW, J., PH.D., F.R.A.C.P., Clinical Pharmacology
SHEARMAN, R. P., M.D., B.S., D.G.O., F.R.C.O.G., Obstetrics and Gynaecology
SHEIL, A. G. R., B.SC., M.A., M.B.B.S., F.R.C.S., F.R.A.C.S., Surgery
SPANN, R. N., M.A., Government and Public Administration
SPATE, V. M., M.A., PH.D., Contemporary Art
SPEARRITT, D., M.A., M.ED., ED.D., Education
STAPLETON, T., M.A., B.M., B.CH., D.M., D.C.H., F.R.C.P., F.R.A.C.P., Child Health
STERNHELL, S., PH.D., D.SC., F.R.A.C.I., Organic Chemistry
SUTCLIFFE, J. P., M.A., PH.D., F.A.S.S.A., Psychology
TANNER, R. I., M.S., PH.D., M.I.MECH.E., M.A.S.M.E., M.A.I.CH.E., F.T.S., Mechanical Engineering
TATTERSALL, M. H. N., M.A., M.D., M.SC., M.R.C.P., F.R.S.M., Cancer Research
TAY, A. E.-S., PH.D., Jurisprudence
TAYLOR, M. G., M.D., PH.D., F.R.A.C.P., Physiology
TAYLOR, T. K. F., D.PHIL., M.B., B.S., F.R.C.S., F.R.C.S.E., F.R.A.C.S., Orthopaedics and Traumatic Surgery
TCHAN, Y.-T., D. ES SC., ING.AGR., Microbiology
THOMSON, J. A., M.SC., M.AGR.SC., PH.D., Biology
TITCHEN, D. A., M.A., PH.D., Veterinary Physiology
TRAHAIR, N. S., M.ENG.SC., PH.D., Civil Engineering
TRUSWELL, A. S., M.D., CH.B., M.R.C.P., Human Nutrition
TURNER, J. F., PH.D., M.SC., F.R.A.C.I., Agricultural Chemistry
TURNEY, C., M.E.D., PH.D., Education
TURTLE, J. R., M.D., B.S., F.R.A.C.P., Medicine
WAKE, R. G., PH.D., M.SC., Biochemistry
WALL, G. E., PH.D., F.A.A., Pure Mathematics
WARD, J. M., M.A., LL.B., F.A.H.A., F.A.S.S.A., F.R.A.H.S., History
WATSON, T. R., PH.D., M.SC., A.R.A.C.I., Pharmaceutical Chemistry
WATSON-MUNRO, C. N., O.B.E., D.SC., M.I.E.E., F.INST.P., F.A.A., Plasma Physics
WEBBER, G. P., M.SC., M.T.C.P., F.R.A.I.A., A.R.I.B.A., Architecture
WELLS, M. C., M.COM., PH.D., A.C.A.N.Z., A.A.S.A., Accounting
WILKES, G. A., D.PHIL., M.A., DIP.ED., F.A.H.A., English Literature
WILSON, P. R., M.SC., PH.D., F.R.A.S., Applied Mathematics
WOODMAN, R. A., LL.M., Law
WORSLEY, P. J., D.LITT., Indonesian and Malayan Studies
YOUNG, J. A., M.D., D.SC., F.R.A.C.P., Physiology

ATTACHED INSTITUTES:

Commonwealth Institute of Health: incorporating (1930) Australian Institute of Tropical Medicine, Townsville, Queensland, and (1980) School of Public Health and Tropical Medicine; library of 30,000 vols.; Principal L. A. G. DAVIDSON, M.D., F.R.C.P., F.R.C.P.E., F.R.A.C.P.

Institute of Child Health: Royal Alexandria Hospital for Children; Dir. Prof. T. STAPLETON.

Institute for Dental Research: United Dental Hospital of Sydney; Dir. Prof. K. W. KNOX.

Sydney Cancer Therapy Unit/Ludwig Institute for Cancer Research: Dir. Prof. M. H. N. TATTERSALL.

Westmead Centre: Westmead, N.S.W. 2145; f. 1978; university teaching hospital and research centre; clinical depts. of medicine, surgery, obstetrics and gynaecology, paediatrics, community health and geriatrics; clinical chairs in pathology, radiotherapy and psychiatry; library of 50,000 vols.; 40 staff; Gen. Supt. Dr. B. J. AMOS.

UNIVERSITY OF TASMANIA

252 C, GPO HOBART, TASMANIA 7001

Telephone: Hobart 230561.

Founded 1890.

Chancellor: Sir JOHN CAMERON, C.B.E., M.A.
Vice-Chancellor: Prof. Emer. D. E. CARO, O.B.E., M.SC., PH.D., F.I.P., F.A.I.P.
Registrar: K. R. SKINNER, B.A.
Librarian: J. E. SCRIVENER, B.A., A.L.A., A.L.A.A.
Bursar: G. T. BRIGGS, B.COM.

Library: *see under* Libraries.

Number of teachers: 303.

Number of students: 3,517.

Publications: *Calendar, Faculty Handbooks, Law Review, Research Report* (annually), and various occasional publications.

DEANS:

Faculty of Agricultural Science: J. J. YATES, PH.D.
Faculty of Arts: Prof. I. H. SMITH, B.A., D.U.
Faculty of Economics and Commerce: Prof. P. E. M. STANDISH, PH.D., A.C.A.
Faculty of Education: Prof. K. F. COLLIS, PH.D., M.A.PS.S., M.A.C.E.
Faculty of Engineering: Prof. C. H. MILLER, D.PHIL., F.I.E.AUST., F.I.R.E.E. AUST., F.I.E.E.
Faculty of Law: J. B. BLACKWOOD, LL.B.
Faculty of Medicine: Prof. A. F. COBBOLD, PH.D.
Faculty of Science: E. R. GUILER, A.M., PH.D., F.Z.S.

PROFESSORS AND HEADS OF DEPARTMENTS:

Faculty of Agricultural Science:
WADE, G. C., M.AGR.SC., D.SC., F.A.I.A.S.

Faculty of Arts:
CARDNO, J. A., M.A., F.B.PS.S., F.A.PS.S., F.A.P.A., Psychology
COLMAN, E. A. M., M.A., PH.D., English
CROOK, R. K. N., A.M., PH.D., Sociology
GELBER, H. G., M.A., PH.D., Political Science
JOSKE, W. D., M.A., PH.D., Philosophy
KRUUP, K., DR. MED., M. A. PS. S., M.I.A.A.PS., Psychology
LEVETT, J. A., B.A., A.L.A.A., School of Librarianship (Dir.)
ROE, O. M., M.A., PH.D., F.A.H.A., History
ROSE, R. B., M.A., F.A.H.A., History

SMITH, I. H., B.A., D.U., French
TISCH, J. H., DR.PHIL., German
WEAVER, P. R. C., M.A., PH.D., F.A.H.A., Classics

Faculty of Economics and Commerce:
GRANT, J. McB., M.EC., F.A.S.S.A., Applied Economics
STANDISH, P. E. M., PH.D., A.C.A., Accounting
TAPLIN, J. H. E., M.AG.EC., PH.D., Transport Economics

Centre for Education:
COLLIS, K. F., M.ED., PH.D., M.A.PS.S., M.A.C.E., Educational Studies
HUGHES, P. W., M.SC., Teacher Education

Faculty of Engineering:
MILLER, C. H., D.PHIL., B.E., F.I.E.AUST., F.I.R.E.E.AUST., F.I.E.E., Electrical Engineering
OLIVER, A. R., M.E., F.S.A.S.M., F.I.E. AUST., Civil and Mechanical Engineering
ZWART, P. R., B.SC., I.T.C., M.I.S.AUST., School of Surveying (Dir.)

Faculty of Law:
BATES, F. A., LL.M., Law
DUNBAR, N. C. H., LL.M., J.S.D.

Faculty of Medicine:
BOYD, G. W., M.D., B.S., PH.D., F.R.A.C.P.
CORREY, J. F., M.B.B.S., F.R.C.O.G., F.A.G.O., F.R.A.C.S., F.AUST.C.O.G., Obstetrics and Gynaecology
COBBOLD, A. F., PH.D., Physiology
HOLDSWORTH, E. S., PH.D., D.SC., F.R.I.C., Biochemistry
KAY, D. W. K., B.CH., M.A., D.M., D.P.M., F.R.C.P., F.R.C.PSYCH., M.R.A.N.C.P., Psychiatry
LEWIS, I. C., CH.B., M.D., F.R.C.P., F.R.A.C.P., D.P.H., D.C.H., F.A.C.E., Child Health
LICKISS, J. N., B.SC.MED., M.D., F.R.A.C.P., F.R.C.P., Community Health
POLACK, A. E., M.PHARM., PH.D., School of Pharmacy (Dir.)
RODDA, R. A., CH.B., M.D., F.R.C.PATH., F.R.C.P.A., Pathology
SHEPHERD, J. J., M.D., CH.B., F.R.C.S., F.R.A.C.S., Surgery
WENDELL-SMITH, C. P., M.B.B.S., PH.D., D.OBST., R.C.O.G., F.A.C.E., Anatomy

Faculty of Science:
BLOOM, H., D.SC., PH.D., D.I.C., F.N.Z.I.C., F.R.A.C.I., Chemistry
DELBOURGO, R., PH.D., D.SC., F.A.I.P., A.R.C.S., Physics
ELLIOTT, D., M.SC., M.S.E., PH.D., Applied Mathematics
ELLIS, G. R. A., PH.D., D.SC., F.A.A. F.A.I.P., F.R.A.S., Physics
GREEN, D. H., M.SC., PH.D., F.A.A., Geology
JACKSON, W. D., B.SC., PH.D., Botany
JOHNSON, B., B.SC.AGR., PH.D., Zoology
LIDL, R., DR.PHIL., Pure Mathematics
SALE, A. H. J., PH.D., D.T.S., M.A.C.M., M.B.C.S., M.A.C.S., Information Science
SCOTT, P., O.B.E., M.SC.(ECON.), PH.D., F.A.S.S.A., Geography

Centre for Environmental Studies:
JONES, R., PH.D. (Director)

Conservatorium of Music:
SEDIVKA, J., F.T.C.L. (Dir.)

School of Art:
PARR, G.

Higher Education and Research Advisory Centre:
STANTON, H. E., M.A., PH.D. (Director)

UNIVERSITY OF WESTERN AUSTRALIA

NEDLANDS,
WESTERN AUSTRALIA 6009
Telephone: 380-3838.

Founded 1911.

Chancellor: The Hon. Sir LAWRENCE JACKSON, K.C.M.G., LL.B., F.A.C.E.

Pro-Chancellor: D. H. AITKEN, I.S.O., B.E., F.I.E.AUST., F.C.I.T., F.A.I.M.

Vice-Chancellor: Prof. R. STREET, PH.D., D.SC., F.I.P., F.A.I.P., F.A.A.

Deputy Vice-Chancellor: Prof. G. S. REID, PH.D.

Registrar: (vacant).

Vice-Principal: R. ANGELONI, O.B.E., M.A.

Librarian: A. ELLIS, F.L.A., A.L.A.A.

Number of teachers: 610.
Number of students: 9,787.

Publications: *Calendar, Faculty Handbooks, University News, Annual Report, Report on Research, Research Review.*

DEANS:

Faculty of Agriculture: Dr. N. A. GOODCHILD.
Faculty of Architecture: P. J. GRIGG.
Faculty of Arts: Prof. H. E. HALLAM.
Faculty of Dental Science: Dr. A. J. LEWIS.
Faculty of Economics and Commerce: D. W. G. TRELOAR.
Faculty of Education: Dr. F. COULTER.
Faculty of Engineering: Dr. J. MILLS.
Faculty of Law: Assoc. Prof. A. F. DICKEY.
Faculty of Medicine: Prof. R. A. JOSKE.
Faculty of Science: Dr. B. E. BALME.

PROFESSORS:

ALLBROOK, D. B., M.B., B.S., PH.D., Anatomy
ALLEN-WILLIAMS, D. J. F., M.A., PH.D., F.I.E.A., F.I.MECH.E., M.I.C.E., M.I.E.E., Mechanical Engineering
APPLEYARD, R. T., M.A., PH.D., F.A.S.S.A., Economic History
BEILIN, L. J., M.D., M.A., F.R.C.P., F.R.A.C.P., Medicine
BERNDT, R. M., M.A., PH.D., F.A.S.S.A., F.R.A.I., F.F.A.A.A., Anthropology
BILLINGS, A. R., PH.D., F.I.E.E., S.M.I.E.E.E., F.I.E.AUST., Electrical Engineering
BLAKERS, A. L., M.A., PH.D., Mathematics
BLOOMFIELD, J., M.SC., PH.D., Physical Education
BOAK, C. D., M.A., PH.D., French Studies
BOWDEN, R. J., M.A., PH.D., Applied Economics
BOYLE, A. J. F., PH.D., F.INST.P., F.A.I.P., Physics
BRADSHAW, S. D., PH.D., Zoology
BROWN, P. R., PH.D., A.A.S.A., A.S.I.A., Finance
BROWN, R. H., S.M., F.I.E.AUST., M.I.MECH.E., M.I.PROD.E., Mechanical Engineering
BUCKINGHAM, M. J., PH.D., F.A.I.P., Theoretical Physics
CALLAWAY, F. A., C.M.G., O.B.E., MUS.B., A.R.C.M., F.R.A.M., F.T.C.L., F.A.C.E., Music
CATCHPOLE, B. N., M.D., CH.M., M.D., F.R.C.S., F.R.A.C.S., Surgery
CLYDE, D. H., PH.D., F.I.E.AUST., Civil Engineering
COLE, A. R. H., D.PHIL., F.A.A., F.R.A.C.I., Physical Chemistry
CONSTABLE, I. J., M.B., B.S., F.R.C.S.ED., M.R.A.C.O., F.R.A.C.S., Ophthalmology
CURNOW, D. H., PH.D., F.R.A.C.I., F.A.A.C.B., F.R.C.P.A., Clinical Biochemistry
EDWARDS, E. J., B.L., LL.B., S.J.D., Law
FIGGIS, B. N., M.SC., PH.D., D.SC., F.R.A.C.I., Inorganic Chemistry
GERMAN, G. A., M.B., CH.B., F.A.N.Z.C.P., F.R.C.P.ED., F.R.C.PSYCH., D.P.M., Psychiatry
GRAVE, S. A., M.A., PH.D., Philosophy
HALLAM, H. E., M.A., PH.D., F.R.HIST.S., F.A.H.A., Medieval History
HARRIS, P. G., M.SC., PH.D., F.G.S., F.I.M.M., Geology
HUGO-BRUNT, M., M.C.D., M.ARCH., F.R.A.I.A., F.R.I.B.A., M.R.A.P.I., F.R.T.P.I., M.R.A.I.C., M.T.P.I.C., M.I.A., A.I.P., Architecture
HUMPAGE, W. D., PH.D., F.I.E.E., F.I.E.AUST., Electrical Engineering
IMBERGER, J., M.ENG.SC., PH.D., Civil Engineering
JAYASURIYA, D. L., PH.D., A.B.PS.S., Social Work
JEFFERIES, P. R., M.SC., PH.D., Organic Chemistry
JONES, M. E., M.A., English
JORY, E. J., PH.D., Classics and Ancient History
JOSKE, R. A., M.D., PH.D., F.R.A.C.P., M.R.C.P., Medicine
KAKULAS, B. A., A.O., M.B., B.S., M.D., F.R.A.C.P., F.R.C.P.A., F.R.C.PATH., Neuropathology
KAMIEN, M., M.D., D.PM., D.C.H., M.R.C.P., F.R.A.C.P., F.R.A.C.G.P., General Practice
LEWIS, A. J., D.D.SC., D.D.S., F.R.A.C.D.S., F.I.C.D., Restorative Dentistry
LINDSAY, J. M., M.A., PH.D., German
LONGTON, P. A., M.A., F.R.A.I., F.O.R., Marketing
LOURENS, R. M. C., M.COM., PH.D., A.C.A., A.C.M.A., A.C.I.S., C.A.(S.A.), F.A.I.M., Accounting
MACDONALD, W. B., M.D., F.R.A.C.P., Child Health
MAHONY, J. J., PH.D., F.I.M.A., F.A.A., Mathematics
MAIN, A. R., PH.D., F.A.A., Zoology
MARSH, D. R. C., PH.D., F.A.H.A., English
MARTIN, J. D., M.D., F.R.C.O.G., F.AUST.-C.O.G., Obstetrics and Gynaecology
MOIR, R. J., D.SC.(AGRIC.), F.A.I.A.S., F.A.S.A.P., F.A.C.VET.SC., Animal Science and Production
MORGAN, E. H., M.B., B.S., PH.D., D.SC., Physiology
MORKEL, A. T., M.SC., M.B.L., D.SC., Management
NADE, S. M. L., B.SC., M.D., F.R.C.S., M.R.C.P., Orthopaedic Surgery
OLIVER, I. T., D.SC., PH.D., Biochemistry
PARKER, C. A., PH.D., Soil Science and Plant Nutrition
PATE, J. S., PH.D., D.SC., Botany
PATERSON, J. W., B.SC., M.B., B.S., M.R.C.P., A.K.C., F.R.C.P., M.R.A.C.P., Clinical Pharmacology
PAYNE, D. J., LL.B., M.A., Law
POSNER, A. M., PH.D., SC.D., Soil Science and Plant Nutrition
PRIEST, T. A., M.ED., F.A.C.E., Education
REEVES, P. D., M.A., PH.D., Modern History
ROHL, J. S., PH.D., F.B.C.S., Computer Science
ROSS, J., PH.D., F.A.S.S.A., F.A.P.S.S., Psychology

SANSOM, B., PH.D., Anthropology
SCOTT, J. A., M.A., Italian
SILBERSTEIN, J. P. O., PH.D., Mathematics
SIMMONDS, W. J., B.SC., M.B., B.S., D.PHIL., F.R.A.C.P., Physiology
SPEED, T. P., PH.D., F.R.A.C.P., Mathematics
STANLEY, N. F., D.SC., F.R.C.P.A., M.A.S.M., Microbiology
STERN, W. R., M.SC.AGR., PH.D., Agronomy
SUTHERLAND, K. J. G., M.D.SC., M.B., B.S., L.D.S., F.D.S.R.C.S., F.D.S.R.C.S.ED., F.R.A.C.D.S., F.I.C.D., F.A.C.D., Dental Science
TANNOCK, P. D., M.ED., PH.D., Education
TAYLOR, R. R., M.B., B.S., F.R.A.C.P., Cardiology
TUNLEY, D. E., M.MUS., D.LITT., D.S.C.M., L.T.C.L., F.A.H.A., Music
WALTERS, M. N.-I., M.D., F.R.A.C.P., F.R.C.P.A., F.R.C.PATH., Pathology
WEBB, M. J., M.A., F.R.G.S., M.I.B.G., Geography
WILLIAMS, J. F., PH.D., F.INST.P., Physics
WILLIS, J. A., PH.D., F.A.H.A., Classics and Ancient History
YATES, J. A., PH.D., F.A.PS.S., Psychology

UNIVERSITY OF WOLLONGONG

P.O.B. 1144, WOLLONGONG, N.S.W. 2500
Telephone: 29-7311.
Telex: 29022.

Founded 1975 (previously a College of the University of New South Wales).

State control; Academic year: March to November (two sessions).

Chancellor: The Hon. Mr. Justice ROBERT MARSDEN HOPE, C.M.G., LL.B.

Vice-Chancellor: Emer. Prof. L. M. BIRT, PH.D., D.PHIL.

Deputy Vice-Chancellor: Prof. A. M. CLARKE, PH.D.

Registrar: R. F. STEWART, B.COM.

Academic Registrar: B. C. MOLDRICH, B.A.

Librarian: J. C. HAZELL, B.A., A.L.A.A.

Number of teachers: 190.
Number of students: 2,871.

Publications: *Calendar*†, *Annual Report*, *The University of Wollongong Campus News*, Information Booklets and Brochures†.

PROFESSORS:

Faculty of Science:
BROWN, A. D., Biology
COOK, A. C., Geology
FISHER, P., Physics
HALPERN, B., Chemistry

Faculty of Social Sciences:
BLAKEY, K. A., Economics
HILL, S. C. ,Sociology
KING, R. C., Education
RYAN, J. B., Accountancy
WILSON, M. G. A., Geography

Faculty of Engineering:
BRINSON, G., Metallurgy
MARSHALL, S. A., Mechanical Engineering
SMITH, B. H., Electrical Engineering

Faculty of Humanities:
CHIPMAN, J. L. C., Philosophy
DUNCAN, R., History
JOHNSTON, R., History and Philosophy of Science
LEAL, R. B., European Languages
SOUTHALL, R. G. T., English

Faculty of Mathematics:
BLAKE, J. R., Mathematics
REINFELDS, J., Computing Science

COLLEGES OF ADVANCED EDUCATION

There are about 80 Colleges of Advanced Education which provide vocational courses at university level. A selection is given below but for reasons of space we omit those specializing in teacher training.

A.C.T.

Canberra College of Advanced Education: P.O.B. 1, Belconnen, A.C.T. 2616; f. 1967; 245 teachers (full-time), 5,300 students; library of 338,000 vols.; Principal Dr. S. S. RICHARDSON, C.B.E., M.A., LL.D.; Registrar R. L. JORY, PH.D.; Librarian V. CRITTENDEN, B.A., B.L.S., M.SC., A.L.A.A.; publs. *Handbook*†, *Annual Report*†, *College News* (quarterly), *College Diary* (fortnightly).

HEADS OF SCHOOLS:
Administrative Studies: R. L. WETTENHALL, M.A., PH.D.
Applied Science: C. E. WALLINGTON, M.SC.
Education: P. W. HUGHES, M.SC.
Environmental Design: R. K. H. JOHNSON, B.ARCH., F.R.A.I.A., M.R.A.P.I., A.A.I.L.A., A.R.I.B.A., F.R.T.I.P.
Information Sciences: D. L. OVERHEU, PH.D.
Liberal Studies: W. F. MANDLE, M.A.

Canberra School of Music: William Herbert Place, Canberra City, A.C.T. 2601; f. 1965; 4-year degree course, also part-time studies; library of 4,000 vols., 13,000 scores and sheet music, 4,500 sound recordings, 150 serial titles; 18 teachers, 50 full-time and 250 part-time students; Dir. E. V. LLEWELLYN, C.B.E.; Sec. D. R. CORNWELL; publ. *Handbook* (annual).

NEW SOUTH WALES

Cumberland College of Health Sciences: P.O.B. 170, Lidcombe, N.S.W. 2141; f. 1973; courses in medical record administration, nursing, orthoptics, occupational therapy, physiotherapy, speech therapy and rehabilitation counselling; 1,400 students; library of 27,000 vols.; Principal J. O. MILLER, M.ED., ED.D.; Registrar R. WOODHAM.

Hawkesbury Agricultural College: Richmond, N.S.W. 2753; f. 1891; degree and diploma courses in agriculture, food technology, home economics, horticulture, food control, animal production, environmental health and valuation; post-graduate diploma courses in agriculture, family and consumer science; food sciences, extension; 80 teachers, 1,100 students; library of 50,000 vols.; Principal Dr. F. G. SWAIN; Sec. J. W. PIRIE; publ. *Calendar* (annually).

Mitchell College of Advanced Education: Bathurst, N.S.W. 1795; f. 1970; degree and diploma courses in teacher education, business and administrative studies, liberal and applied arts; 190 staff, 3,658 students; Principal E. A. B. PHILLIPS; Registrar D. A. STACE; publs. *Handbook*†, *Annual Report*, *Prospectus*, *Semester Journal*.

National Institute of Dramatic Art at the University of New South Wales: P.O.B. 1, Kensington, N.S.W. 2033; f. 1958; courses in acting, technical production, design and direction; Dir. J. R. CLARK; publ. *Handbook*.

New South Wales Institute of Technology: Box 123, Broadway, N.S.W. 2007; f. 1965; 315 teachers, 8,000 students; library of 212,000 vols.; Chancellor The Hon. Mr. Justice J. H. WOOTTEN, B.A., LL.B.; Pres. R. L. WERNER, M.SC., PH.D., A.S.T.C., F.R.A.C.I.; Registrar J. W. MCMILLAN, M.ENG.SC., M.A., M.A.C.E.; publs. *Calendar*, *Prospectus*†, *Research Report*, *Undergraduate Studies Booklets* (annually).

DEANS:
Faculty of Architecture and Building: D. J. O. FERRY, PH.D., F.R.I.C.S., F.I.Q.S., A.A.I.Q.S.
Faculty of Business Studies: B. L. HUNT, M.B.A., PH.D., F.A.I.M.
Faculty of Engineering: P. J. PARR, M.SC., PH.D.
Faculty of Humanities and Social Sciences: A. G. HAMMER, M.A.
Faculty of Law: G. W. BARTHOLOMEW, B.SC., LL.M.
Faculty of Mathematical and Computing Sciences: V. X. GLEDHILL, PH.D.
Faculty of Science: N. C. STEPHENSON, M.SC., PH.D., D.SC., F.R.A.C.I.

New South Wales State Conservatorium of Music: Macquarie St., Sydney, N.S.W. 2000; f. 1916; brs. at Newcastle and Wollongong; comprises High School and Schools of Education, Opera, Music Theatre, Composition Studies, Practical Studies and Extension Studies; conducts master classes, workshops, seminars, concert and opera seasons; 185 staff; 507 students (1,800 part-time); library of 5,000 vols., 5,000 recordings, 60,000 music MSS.; Dir. REX HOBCROFT; Registrar KEVIN WILLIAMS; Librarian MARGARET CALDWELL.

Newcastle College of Advanced Education: P.O.B. 84, Waratah, N.S.W. 2298; f. 1949 as Teachers College, now being developed as multi-vocational college; 208 teachers, 2,700 students; library of 86,000 vols.; Principal Dr. EDWARD RICHARDSON, PH.D.

Orange Agricultural College: P.O.B. 883, Orange, N.S.W. 2800; f. 1973; assoc. diploma courses in farm management, farm secretarial studies and environmental control; Principal R. J. NAPIER.

School of Art and Design (Dept. of Technical and Further Education): Forbes St., Darlinghurst, N.S.W. 2010; courses at 9 Sydney metropolitan colleges and more than 45 country colleges in N.S.W.; Head DON MITCHELL, A.S.T.C.

Riverina College of Advanced Education: P.O.B. 588, Wagga Wagga, N.S.W. 2650; f. 1972; courses in computing, education, applied sciences, creative arts, business studies, liberal studies, agriculture, library and information science, medical and laboratory technology, nursing, radiography, taxation law, clinical science; library of 114,000 vols., 1,900 periodicals; Principal Dr. C. D. BLAKE.

VICTORIA

Ballarat College of Advanced Education: Ballarat; f. 1976 by merger of the tertiary division of the Ballarat School of Mines and Industries and the State College of Victoria at Ballarat; courses (first and higher degree and diploma) in various branches of applied sciences, education, engineering, business studies, social sciences and humanities, art and librarianship; affiliated to the Victoria Institute of Colleges (*q.v.*); library of 95,000 vols.; 160 full-time teachers, 1,257 full-time and 472 part-time students; Principal E. J. BARKER, B.MECH.E., M.I.MECH.E., M.A.C.E.

Bendigo College of Advanced Education: P.O.B. 199, Bendigo, Vic. 3550; courses in applied sciences, art, business studies, engineering, humanities, computer science and teacher education; 1,700 students; library of 100,000 vols.; affiliated to the Victoria Institute of Colleges (*q.v.*); Dir. Dr. M. H. MCKAY.

Burnley Horticultural College: Swan St., Burnley, Vic. 3121; Principal B. G. PELL.

Caulfield Institute of Technology: 900 Dandenong Rd., P.O.B. 197, Caulfield East Vic. 3145; affiliated with the Victoria Institute of Colleges (*q.v.*); 295 staff, 4,863 students; library of 84,412 monographs, 2,339 periodicals; Dir. R. W. CUMMING, A.M., M.E., C.ENG., F.H.F.S.; Sec. M. W. BLANK, B.SC., A.A.S.A., M.A.C.E.; publs. *Handbook*, *Annual Report.*

HEADS OF SCHOOLS:

Applied Science: E. W. HEMINGWAY, PH.D., D.I.C., M.SC., C.ENG., F.I.E.AUST., A.F.R.AE.S., F.I.MECH.E.

David Syme Business School: J. O. MILLER, A.O., M.ED. ADMIN., F.A.S.A.

Engineering: T. BROWNLEE, B.SC.(ELEC. ENG.), M.E.E., C.ENG., M.I.E.E., F.I.E. AUST.

General Studies: H. W. FAREY, F.R.M.I.T., DIP. TEXTILE DESIGN, T.T.T.C., F.R.S.A. (acting).

Dookie Agricultural College: Vic. 3647; f. 1886; agriculture and food production, horticulture; Principal I. S. MCMILLAN; Registrar D. E. KERLIN.

Footscray Institute of Technology: Ballarat Rd. and Nicholson St., Footscray, Vic. 3011; degree and diploma courses in various branches of applied science, business, engineering, social science; affiliated to the Victoria Institute of Colleges (*q.v.*); 2,100 students; library of 70,000 vols.; Dir. D. R. MILLS; Registrar J. MCDONALD.

Gippsland Institute of Advanced Education: Switchback Rd., Churchill, Vic. 3842; f. 1968; affiliated to the Victoria Institute of Colleges (*q.v.*); library of 55,000 vols. and 8,500 periodicals; Dir. M. W. HOPPER, B.A., B.SC., M.A.C.E.; Librarian C. W. TOLLEY, M.A., A.N.Z.L.A.; Academic Registrar J. W. MAYNARD, M.R.I.P.A.; publs. *Annual Handbook*†, *External Studies Booklet*†.

DEANS OF SCHOOLS:

Business and Social Sciences: K. W. HINCE, B.COM.

Arts and Education: (vacant).

Engineering and Applied Science: N. W. TERRILL, M.SC., T.T.T.C., A.R.A.C.I., F.A.I.E.

Longerenong Agricultural College: Dooen, Via Horsham, Vic. 3401; f. 1889; diploma and certificate courses in agriculture; Principal J. F. LONSDALE; Registrar R. B. GOODCHILD.

Prahran College of Advanced Education: 142 High St., Prahran, Vic. 3181; tertiary, technical and further education courses in art and design, business, general studies, applied social sciences, furniture studies; affiliated to the Victoria Institute of Colleges (*q.v.*); 470 staff, 3,606 students; library of 45,000 vols.; Dir. Dr. C. CAMPBELL; Registrar L. T. CULLEN; publ. *Handbook* (annual).

Preston Institute of Technology: Plenty Rd., Bundoora, Vic. 3083; courses in art and design, business, applied science (chemistry), engineering, nursing, recreation, social work and physical education; affiliated to the Victoria Institute of Colleges (*q.v.*); Principal Dr. J. B. RITCHIE; Registrar A. WESSON.

Royal Melbourne Institute of Technology: 124 La Trobe St., Melbourne, Vic. 3000; f. 1887; RMIT Advanced College affiliated to the Victoria Institute of Colleges (*q.v.*); Emily McPherson College was amalgamated with RMIT in 1979; library of 253,764 vols.; 1,043 teachers (499 part-time), 11,117 students (6,019 part-time); Dir. Dr. B. W. SMITH; Registrar J. A. MCINDOE; publs. *Handbook*†, *Annual Report*†, *Research Report*†, *Guide to Courses* (annually).

DEANS:

Faculty of Applied Science: F. C. JAMES, M.SC., F.M.T.C., F.R.A.C.I.

Faculty of Architecture and Building: G. C. GUNN, A.R.A.I.A.

Faculty of Art: C. BARRIE, A.M.T.C., A.I.D.I.A., F.R.S.A.

Faculty of Business: N. V. ANTHONY, M.B.A., F.A.S.A.

Faculty of Engineering: D. G. BEANLAND, M.SC., PH.D., F.I.E.AUST., F.I.R.E.E.(AUST.).

Faculty of Humanities and Social Sciences: (vacant).

Graduate School of Management: K. H. F. FARGHER, E.D., M.B.A., PH.D., F.A.I.EX.

Victorian School of Forestry: Creswick, Vic. 3363; f. 1910; Principal J. G. EDGAR.

Swinburne Institute of Technology: P.O.B. 218, Hawthorn, Vic. 3122; 5,119 students; library of 166,000 vols.; Dir. Dr. W. R. LONGWORTH, M.SC., PH.D., C.CHEM., F.R.I.C., F.R.A.C.I., F.A.C.E.; Registrar G. L. WILLIAMSON, B.SC., F.R.I.P.A.; publs. *Handbook*†, *Course Brochures*†.

DEANS:

Faculty of Applied Science: P. F. NELSON, D.APP.SC., F.R.A.C.I.

Faculty of Art: I. MCNEILAGE, T.T.T.C.

Faculty of Arts: C. K. MCDONALD, B.SC., B.ED., M.A., M.A.C.E.

Faculty of Business: M. H. HUNTER, B.COM., M.ADMIN., F.A.S.A.

Faculty of Engineering: L. M. GILLAN, PH.D., M.ENG.SC., A.S.M.B., A.A.I.P., M.A.I.M.E., M.A.I.A.A.

Victorian College of Pharmacy: 381 Royal Parade, Parkville, Vic. 3052; f. 1881; affiliated to the Victoria Institute of Colleges (*q.v.*); 400 students; library of 12,500 vols.; Dean G. N. VAUGHAN; Registrar

R. BURNET; publs. *College Handbook*†, *College Course Book*† (annually).

Victorian College of the Arts: 234 St. Kilda Rd., Melbourne, Vic. 3004; f. 1972; inc. fmr. National Gallery of Victoria Art School; degree, diploma and graduate diploma courses in fine art, music, dance and drama, and assoc. diploma course in opera; Dir. LENTON PARR, A.M.

Warrnambool Institute of Advanced Education: P.O.B. 423, Warrnambool, Vic. 3280; degree course in applied science (with aquatic science emphasis), business (accounting), social science and education (primary teaching) and fine art, diploma courses in same fields except business; graduate diplomas in accounting and municipal engineering; external studies; affiliated to the Victoria Institute of Colleges (*q.v.*); Principal DAVID ROACH; Business Man. RAY LUMSDEN; publ. *Handbook*† (annually).

QUEENSLAND

Capricornia Institute of Advanced Education: Rockhampton, Qld 4700; f. 1967; diploma, degree and postgraduate courses in applied sciences, arts, business, education and engineering; library of 86,000 vols.; 169 teachers, 2,300 students; Dir. Dr. A. S. APPLETON; Registrar B. L. BARTLEY; publs. *Handbook, Prospectus, Annual Report.*

CHAIRMEN OF SCHOOLS:

Administrative and General Studies: D. SADLER.

Education: R. BEEVERS.

Engineering: F. SCHRODER.

Science: J. SMITH.

Darling Downs Institute of Advanced Education: Darling Heights, Toowoomba, Qld. 4350; f. 1967; courses in applied sciences, engineering, business studies, creative arts, music, behavioural science, humanities and education; library of 115,000 vols.; 220 teachers, 4,800 (including external) students; Dir. L. J. BARKER; Registrar B. J. CAMERON; publs. *Handbook, Calendar* (annually).

HEADS OF SCHOOLS:

IMISON, K., Education.

LEDWIDGE, T. J., Engineering.

MCCORMACK, F. G., Business Studies.

MCNALLY, P. T., Arts.

ROBERTS, B., Applied Science.

Queensland Agricultural College: Lawes, Queensland 4343; courses in food technology, hospitality management, horticulture, rural management, poultry technology and rural technology; Dir. Dr. T. M. MORRISON.

Queensland Conservatorium of Music: Gardens Point, George St., Brisbane, Qld. 4000; f. 1957; 75 teachers, 637 students; library of 4,470 vols., 4,637 recordings, 14,000 scores and 96 periodicals; Dir. R. WALES, M.A., L.C.S.M., L.T.C.L.

Queensland Institute of Technology, Brisbane: Gardens Point, Brisbane, Qld. 4000; courses at masters, degree and assoc. diploma level in professional areas in applied science, health science, engineering, law, architecture, librarianship, building and business studies; library of 108,313 monographs, 4,436 serial titles 54,282 A.V. items; Dir. Dr. A. M. FRASER (to March 1981); Registrar B. S. WATERS; publs. *Q.I.T. Newsletter, Admission Procedures Booklet*, handbooks.

SOUTH AUSTRALIA

Roseworthy Agricultural College: Roseworthy, S.A. 5371; f. 1885; courses in agriculture, oenology, natural resources, farm management, horse husbandry; Dir. Dr. D. B. WILLIAMS; publ. *Calendar* (annually), *Annual Report.*

South Australian Institute of Technology: North Terrace, Adelaide, S.A.; f. 1889; 945 staff, 6,018 students; library: *see* Libraries; Dir. E. W. MILLS, PH.D., F.R.I.C., F.R.A.C.I.; publs. *Prospectus, Register of Research Projects* (annual).

PROFESSORS:

ATKINS, K. J., PH.D., Civil Engineering

CHRISTIE, B. J. F., PH.D., Pharmacy

CULVER, R. V., PH.D., D.I.C., A.S.A.S.M., C.ENG., Chemical Technology

LEE, D. H., M.SC., Mathematics

NORTHCOTE, R. S., M.SC., PH.D., Computer Studies

SMYTH, R. W., PH.D., Mechanical Engineering

South Australian Institute of Technology—Whyalla Campus: Nicolson Ave., Whyalla Norrie, S.A. 5608; f. 1965; courses in accountancy, chemistry, mechanical engineering, electrical engineering, metallurgy, medical technology, pharmacy and social work; Principal A. C. J. JOHNSON.

Torrens College of Advanced Education: Holbrooks Rd., Underdale, S.A. 5032; f. 1972; art, applied science, performing arts.

WESTERN AUSTRALIA

Western Australian Institute of Technology: Hayman Rd., South Bentley, W.A. 6102; f. 1967; 650 teachers, 11,497 students; library of 237,000 vols.; Dir. D. W. WATTS, PH.D.; publs. *Calendar, Annual Report, School Handbooks, The Reporter*† (fortnightly), *Gazette*† (quarterly).

DEANS:

School of Applied Science: J. R. DE LAETER, PH.D.

School of Business and Administration: K. HALL, PH.D.

School of Engineering and Surveying: A. H. NASH, M.ED., PH.D.

School of Health Sciences: M. LIVERIS, PH.D.

School of Mining and Mineral Technology (inc. *W.A. School of Mines*): I. O. JONES, PH.D.

School of Social Sciences: N. F. DUFTY, M.A., M.ED., PH.D.

School of Teacher Education: L. L. FOSTER, M.ED., PH.D.

School of The Arts and Design: D. J. G. HOLROYDE, M.A.

TASMANIA

Tasmanian College of Advanced Education: Newnham Campus, P.O.B. 1214, Launceston, Tas. 7250; Mt. Nelson Campus, P.O.B. 1415P, Hobart, Tas. 7001; f. 1968; courses in applied science, art, business administration, music, teacher education, environmental design, librarianship, social work, legal practice, general studies, technology; 233 teachers, 2,827 students; library: Mt. Nelson 124,000 vols., Newnham 60,000 vols.; Principal Dr. C. A. O'FLAHERTY; Registrar T. R. RODGERS.

HEADS OF DIVISIONS:

BACK, R. D., Administrative Studies

BLEST, D. C., M.SC., PH.D., General Studies

HAWARD, G. G., B.A., D.U.P., Teacher Education (Newnham)

MALE, D. J., M.A., B.E., Science and Technology

MCNEILL, B. H., B.A., Environmental Design

MILLER, D. L., B.A., Education Services

PARR, G., Art (Mt. Nelson)

RADVANSKY, J. G., Teacher Education (Mt. Nelson)

SEDIVKA, J. B., Conservatorium of Music

TANTON, R., Art (Newnham)

COLLEGES

Australian Administrative Staff College: Kunyung Rd., Mt. Eliza, Vic. 3930; f. 1955; residential courses for senior managers, administrators and younger executives; library of 6,400 vols.; Chief Exec. and Principal Emer. Prof. W. G. WALKER, PH.D., T.C., F.A.C.E., F.C.C.E.A.; Registrar P. W. OSBORN, B.SC., F.R.A.C.I., F.INST.D.; Librarian RUTH DOIG, A.L.A., A.L.A.A.; publ. *Annual College Journal.*

Australian Graduate School of Management: P.O.B. 1, Kensington, N.S.W.

2033; f. 1975; postgraduate M.B.A./M.P.A. and Ph.D. courses, residential courses for executives; 25 faculty mems.; library of 14,000 vols.; attached to University of N.S.W.; Dir. Prof. J. G. DAVIS, M.B.A., A.M.; publ. *Australian Journal of Management.*

Australian School of Nuclear Technology: Lucas Heights, via Sutherland, N.S.W. 2232; f. 1964; a co-operative enterprise of the University of N.S.W. and the Australian Atomic Energy Commission; courses in production and use of radio-isotopes, radionuclides in medicine and radiation protection; Principal D. A. NEWMARCH, B.SC., B.A., M.R.INST.PHIL.

AUSTRIA

Population 7,505,700

ACADEMY

Österreichische Akademie der Wissenschaften (*Austrian Academy of Sciences*): 1010 Vienna, Dr. Ignaz Seipel-Platz 2; Telephone: 52-15-86; f. 1847.

President: Prof. Dr. DDr. h.c. HERBERT HUNGER.

Vice-President: Prof. Dipl.-Ing. Dr. ERWIN PLÖCKINGER.

General Secretary: Prof. Dr. Dr. h.c. LEOPOLD SCHMETTERER.

Secretary: Prof. Dr. MANFRED MAYRHOFER.

Library: *see under* Libraries.

111 mems., 354 corresponding mems., 24 honorary mems.

Publs. ***Almanach, Anzeiger math.-nat. Klasse, Anzeiger phil.-hist. Klasse, Sitzungsberichte math.-nat. Klasse Abt. I, II, Sitzungsberichte phil.-hist. Klasse, Denkschriften der Gesamtakademie, Denkschriften math.-nat. Klasse, Denkschriften phil.-hist. Klasse, Monatshefte für Chemie***; various committee reports.

Section for Mathematics and Natural Sciences:

AUERSWALD, WILHELM.
BREITINGER, EMIL.
BURKARD, OTTO.
DEUTSCH, ERWIN.
EHRENDORFER, FRIEDRICH.
FERRARI D'OCCHIEPPO, KONRADIN.
FINK, JULIUS.
FRANZ, HERBERT.
GUTMANN, VIKTOR.
HAUPT, HERMANN.
HAYEK, ERICH.
HEINRICH, GERHARD.
HERITSCH, HAYMO.
HITTMAIR, OTTO.
HLAWKA, EDMUND.
HORNYKIEWICZ, OLEH.
KARLIK, BERTA.
KINZL, HANS.
KLAUDY, PETER.
KNOLL, FRITZ.
KOMAREK, KURT.
KÖNIG, HERBERT W.
KONZETT, HERIBERT.
KRAMES, JOSEF.
KRATKY, OTTO.
KRAUPP, OTTO.
KÜHNELT, WILHELM.
LARCHER, WALTER.
LINTNER, KARL.
LIST, HANS.
MAYRHOFER-KRAMMEL, OTTO.
METZ, KARL.
NOWOTNY, HANS.
ORTNER, GUSTAV.
PARKUS, HEINZ.
PASCHKE, FRITZ.
PETRASCHECK, WALTHER E.
PISCHINGER, ANTON.
PLÖCKINGER, ERWIN.
POROD, GÜNTHER.
PÖTZL, HANS.
RINNER, KARL.
SCHEDLING, JOHANN.
SCHMETTERER, LEOPOLD.
SCHMID, ERICH.
SEITELBERGER, FRANZ.
STEINHAUSER, FERDINAND.
STETTER, GEORG.
STROTZKA, HANS.
THIRRING, WALTER.
TRENKLER, HERBERT.
TUPPY, HANS.
VIETORIS, LEOPOLD.
WEINZIERL, PETER.
WUNDERLICH, WALTER.
ZAPFE, HELMUTH.
ZEMANN, JOSEF.

Section for Philosophy and Historical Sciences:

ANTONIOLLI, WALTER.
APPELT, HEINRICH.
ARNBERGER, ERIK.
BALTL, HERMANN.
BOBEK, HANS.
BRUCKMANN, GERHART.
DEMELIUS, HEINRICH.
DEMUS, OTTO.
FICHTENAU, HEINRICH.
FOLTINEK, HERBERT.
GÖBL, ROBERT.
GRASBERGER, FRANZ.
GRASS, NIKOLAUS.
HAMANN, GÜNTHER.
HAMM, JOSEF.
HANSLIK, RUDOLF.
HEINTEL, ERICH.
HÖFLER, OTTO.
HUNGER, HERBERT.
HUTER, FRANZ.
KASER, MAX.
KINDERMANN, HEINZ.
KIRSTEN, ERNST.
KOZIOL, HERBERT.
KRAUS, WALTHER.
LECHNER, KARL.
LESKY, ALBIN.
LUTZ, HEINRICH.
MAYRHOFER, MANFRED.
NOLL, RUDOLF.
OGRIS, WERNER.
PÄCHT, OTTO.
PITTIONI, RICHARD.
POSCH, FRITZ.
REICHARDT, ROBERT.
REIFFENSTEIN, INGO.
SCHACHERMEYR, FRITZ.
SCHMIDT, LEOPOLD.
SCHWABL, HANS.
SCHWIND, FRITZ.
SEDLMAYR, HANS.
SEIDLER, HERBERT.
SELB, WALTER.
STOLL, GEROLD.
VEROSTA, STEPHAN.
VETTERS, HERMANN.
WANDRUSZKA, ADAM.
WANDRUSZKA, MARIO.
WEBER, WILHELM.
WELZIG, WERNER.
WIESFLECKER, HERMANN.
WILBURG, WALTER.
WOLFRAM, RICHARD.
WYTRZENS, GÜNTHER.
ZÖLLNER, ERICH.

COMMISSIONS OF THE ACADEMY

Österreichisches Biographisches Lexicon (*Comm. for Austrian Biographical Encyclopaedia*): Chair. Prof. Dr. ZÖLLNER.

Kommission für Raumforschung (*Comm. for Environmental Research*): Chair. Prof. Dr. BOBEK.

Kommission für Hochalpine Forschungen (*Comm. for Alpine Research*): Chair. Prof. Dr. STEINHAUSER.

Kommission für Schallforschung (*Comm. for Sound Research*): Chair. Prof. Dr. GRAF.

Kommission für die Herausgabe eines Catalogus Faunae Austriae (*Comm. for Publication of a Catalogue of Austrian Fauna*): Chair. Prof. Dr. KÜHNELT.

Kommission für Ökologie und SCOPE (*Comm. for Ecology and SCOPE*): Chair. Prof. Dr. W. KÜHNELT.

Historische Kommission (*Historical Comm.*): Chair. Prof. Dr. FICHTENAU.

Kommission für Europarecht (*Comm. for European Law*): Chair. Prof. Dr. SCHWIND.

Iranische Kommission (*Comm. for Iran*): Chair. Prof. Dr. MAYRHOFER.

Kommission für die Archäologische Erforschung Kleinasiens (*Comm. for Archaeological Research of Asia Minor*): Chair. Prof. Dr. SCHACHERMEYR.

Kirchenväter Kommission (*Patristics Comm.*): Chair. Prof. Dr. HANSLIK.

Kommission für Schrift- und Buchwesen des Mittelalters (*Comm. for Scripts and Books of the Middle Ages*): Chair. Prof. Dr. HUNGER.

Kommission zur Erforschung des Römischen Limes im Gebiete von Ober- und Niederösterreich (*Comm. for Roman Boundaries Research in Upper and Lower Austria*): Chair. Prof. Dr. VETTERS.

Kommission für Mykenische Forschung (*Comm. for Research in Mycenae*): Chair. Prof. Dr. SCHACHERMEYR.

Kommission für Linguistik und Kommunikationsforschung (*Comm. for Linguistics and Communication Research*): Chair. Prof. Dr. MARIO WANDRUSZKA.

Kommission für Altgermanistik (*Comm. for Old German*): Chair. Prof. Dr. HÖFLER.

Phonogramm-Archivs-Kommission (*Phonogram Archives Comm.*): Chair. Prof. Dr. KÜHNELT.

Kommission für Mundartkunde und Namenforschung (*Comm. for the Study of Dialects and Names*): Chair. Prof. Dr. REIFFENSTEIN.

Kommission für das Corpus Vasorum Antiquorum (*Comm. for the Corpus Vasorum Antiquorum*): Chair. Frau Prof. Dr. KENNER.

Kommission für das Corpus Signorum Imperii Romani (*Comm. for the Corpus Signorum Imperii Romani*): Chair. Frau Prof. Dr. KENNER.

Dr. Friedrich Tessmann-Sammlung: Chair. Prof. Dr. HUTER.

Kommission für Musikforschung (*Comm. for Music Research*): Chair. Dir. Dr. GRASBERGER.

Kommission für Byzantinistik (*Comm. for Byzantine Studies*): Chair. Prof. Dr. HUNGER.

Kommission für Geschichte Österreichs (*Comm. for Austrian History*): Chair. Prof. Dr. A. WANDRUSZKA.

Kommission für Wirtschafts-, Sozial- und Stadtgeschichte (*Comm. for Economic, Social and Municipal History*): Chair. Prof. Dr. HOFFMANN.

Kommission für Theatergeschichte Österreichs (*Comm. for the History of the Austrian Theatre*): Chair. Prof. Dr. KINDERMANN.

Kommission für die Tabula Imperii Byzantini: Chair. Prof Dr. HUNGER.

Kommission für Frühchristliche und Ostchristliche Kunst (*Comm. for Early and East Christian Art*): Chair. Prof. Dr. DEMUS.

Kommission für die Geschichte der österr.-ungar. Monarchie (*Comm. for Austro-Hungarian History*): Chair. Prof. Dr. A. WANDRUSZKA.

Numismatische Kommission (*Numismatical Comm.*): Chair. Prof. Dr. GÖBL.

Kommission für den Volkskundeatlas in Österreich (*Comm. for the Folklore Atlas in Austria*): Chair. Prof. Dr. R. WOLFRAM.

Ausgrabungen in Ephesos (*Excavations in Ephesus*): Chair. Prof. Dr. VETTERS.

Kommission für das Corpus der Kleinasiatischen Mosaiken (*Comm. for the Corpus of the Mosaics of Asia Minor*): Chair. Prof. Dr. VETTERS.

Kommission für das Lexicon Iconographicum Mythologiae Classicae—LIMC (*Comm. for the Iconographical Dictionary of Classical Mythology*): Chair. Prof. Dr. VETTERS.

Rechtschreibungskommission (*Comm. for Orthography Research*): Chair. Prof. Dr. SEIDLER.

Kommission für Menschenrechte (*Comm. for Human Rights*): Chair. Prof. Dr. ERMACORA.

INSTITUTES ATTACHED TO THE ACADEMY

Institut für Vergleichende Verhaltensforschung (*Institute of Comparative Behaviour Research*): A-1160 Vienna, Savoyenstrasse 1A; and A-7082 Donnerskirchen, Bergstrasse 10; Dir. Prof. O. KOENIG.

Institut für Umweltwissenschaften und Naturschutz (*Inst. of Environmental Sciences and Conservation*): A-8010 Graz. Heinrichstr. 5/3; and A-1010 Vienna, Messepalast, Stiege 14; Dir. Prof. Dr. FRANZ WOLKINGER.

Institut für Radiumforschung und Kernphysik (*Institute of Radium Research and Nuclear Physics*): A-1090 Vienna, Boltzmanngasse 3; Dir. Prof. Dr. HERBERT VONACH.

Institut für Limnologie (*Institute of Limnology*): A-1090 Vienna, Berggasse 18/13; and A-3293 Lunz am See, Lunzamt 54; Dir. Prof. Dr. HEINZ LÖFFLER.

Institut für Hochenergiephysik (*Institute of High Energy Physics*): A-1050 Vienna, Nikolsdorfergasse 18; Dir. Doz. Dr. W. MAJEROTTO.

Institut für Molekularbiologie (*Institute of Molecular Biology*): A-5020 Salzburg, Billrothstr. 11; Dir. Dr. J. V. SMALL.

Institut für Informationsverarbeitung (*Institute of Information Processing*): A-1010 Vienna, Fleischmarkt 20; Dir. Prof. Dr. E. HLAWKA.

Institut für Hirnforschung (*Institute of Brain Research*): A-1090 Vienna, Schwarzspanierstrasse 17; Dir. Prof. Dr. F. SEITELBERGER.

Institut für Mittelalterliche Realienkunde Österreichs (*Institute of Exact Sciences of Medieval Austria*): A-3500 Krems an der Donau, Körnermarkt 13; Dir. Prof. Dr. H. KÜHNEL.

Institut für Kartographie (*Institute of Cartography*): A-1010 Vienna, Universitätsstrasse 7; Dir. Prof. Dr. E. ARNBERGER.

Erich-Schmid-Institut für Festkörperphysik (*Solid State Physics Institute*): A-8700 Leoben, Jahnstr. 12; Dir. Prof. Dr. H. P. STÜWE.

Institut für Weltraumforschung (*Space Research Institute*): A-8010 Graz, Halbärthgasse 1; Dir. Prof. Dr. O. BURKARD.

Institut für Sozio-Ökonomische Entwicklungsforschung (*Institute of Sociological-Economic Development Research*): A-1010 Vienna, Fleischmarkt 20; Dir. Prof. Dr. ROBERT REICHARDT.

Institut für Röntgenfeinstrukturforschung (*Institute of X-Ray Research*): 8010 Graz, Steyrergasse 17; Dir. Prof. Dr. OTTO KRATKY.

Institut für Publikumsforschung (*Institute of Public Research*): A-1010 Vienna, Hanuschgasse 3; Dir. Prof. Dr. MARGRET DIETRICH.

Institut für Gegenwartsvolkskunde (*Institute of Contemporary Folklore Research*): Volkskundemuseum, 1080 Vienna, Laudongasse 15-19; Dir. Dr. KLAUS BEITL.

Institut für Demographie (*Institute of Demography*): A-1033 Vienna, Hintere Zollamstr. 4; Dir. Prof. Dr. LOTHAR BOSSE.

LEARNED SOCIETIES

AGRICULTURE AND VETERINARY SCIENCE

Österreichische Gesellschaft der Tierärzte (*Austrian Society of Veterinary Surgeons*): 1030 Vienna, Linke Bahngasse 11; f. 1919; *c.* 550 mems.; Pres. Dr. W. KROCZA; Vice-Pres. Dr. A. WEGSCHEIDER; publ. *Wiener Tierärztliche Monatsschrift* (monthly).

ARCHITECTURE AND TOWN PLANNING

Österreichischer Ingenieur- und Architektenverein (*Assn. of Austrian Engineers and Architects*): A-1010 Vienna, Eschenbachgasse 9; f. 1848; *c.* 7,000 mems.; library of 31,000 vols.; Pres. KARL RABUS, DIPL.ING.; Gen. Sec. FRIEDRICH SMOLA, DIPL.ING.; publs. *Österreichische Ingenieur-Zeitschrift* (monthly).

Zentralvereinigung der Architekten Österreichs (*Central Assn. of Austrian Architects*): Vienna I, Salvatorgasse 10; f. 1907; cultural assn.; *c.* 700 mems.; Pres. Prof. EUGEN WÖRLE; Sec. MARGARETE NIMMRICHTER.

THE ARTS

Arbeitsgemeinschaft für Kunst und Wissenschaft (*League of Associations for Art and Science*): A-1090 Vienna, Maria Theresien-Strasse 11; f. 1953; cultural politics for arts, science and education; 250,000 mems.; Pres. Prof. Dr. ROBERT REICHARDT; Gen. Sec. DDDr. KARL RÖSSEL-MAJDAN.

Bundesdenkmalamt (*Federal Monuments Office*): Vienna I, Hofburg; f. 1850; protection and restoration of historical, artistic and cultural monuments; has control of excavations and art export; 124 mems.; library of 11,500 vols.; Pres. Min. Rat. Dr. ERWIN THALHAMMER; publs. include periodicals and year book.

Franz Lehár-Gesellschaft (*Franz Lehár Society*): Vienna VI, Theobaldgasse 16; f. 1949; Pres. Dr. jur. JOSEF GUHSWALD.

Gesellschaft der Musikfreunde in Wien (*Society of Friends of Music in Vienna*): A-1010 Vienna, Bösendorferstrasse 12; f. 1812; 6,020 mems.; choir of 400 mems.; library: *see* Libraries; collection of music, MSS., instruments, etc.; Pres. Prof. Dr. HORST HASCHEK; Gen. Sec. Prof. ALBERT MOSER.

Johann Strauss-Gesellschaft (*Johann Strauss Society*): 1030 Vienna, Lothringerstr. 20; f. 1936; Pres. BRUNO MAREK; publ. *Mitteilungen* (3 a year).

Kunsthistorische Gesellschaft (*Art History Society*): Vienna I, Universitätsstrasse Nr. 7; f. 1956; 153 mems.; Dir. Prof. Dr. G. SCHMIDT.

Künstlerhaus (Gesellschaft bildender Künstler Wiens) (*Vienna Artists Asscn.*): Vienna I, Karlsplatz 5; f. 1861; 336 mems.; Pres. Prof. HANS MAYR.

Österreichische Gesellschaft für Christliche Kunst (*Austrian Society for Christian Art*): 1010 Vienna I, Stephansplatz 3; f. 1909, refounded 1952; 133 mems.; reports, discussions and exhibitions; Pres. Prof. ALFRED CREPAZ.

Österreichische Gesellschaft für Filmwissenschaft, Kommunikations- und Medien Forschung (*Austrian Society for Film Sciences, Research on Communications and Media*): Vienna 1010, Rauhensteingasse 5; f. 1952; encouragement of scientific research for film and television; 196 mems.; Pres. Prof. Dr. HEINZ KINDERMANN; Gen. Sec. Prof. Dr. LUDWIG GESEK; publs. *Filmkunst* (quarterly) and *Mitteilungen* (8–10 a year).

Österreichische Gesellschaft für Kommunikationsfragen (*Austrian Society for Communication*): 1010 Vienna, Bankgasse 8; aims to improve and encourage co-operation between communication researchers and communication practitioners (journalists, media workers); Sec. Gen. Dr. ROMAN HUMMEL; publ. *Medien-Journal* (quarterly).

Österreichische Gesellschaft für Musik (*Austrian Music Society*): A-1010 Vienna I, Hanuschgasse 3; f. 1964; information service, lectures, exhibitions; library of 1,000 vols. mainly on contemporary music, and records; Gen. Sec. Prof. Dr. H. GOERTZ; publs. *Beiträge* (annually) and others.

Österreichische Gesellschaft für Volkslied- und Volkstanzpflege (Volksgesang-Verein Wien) (*Austrian Society for the Fostering of Folk Song and Dance*): 1070 Vienna VII, Kirchengasse 41; f. 1889; Dir. Prof. GEORG KOTEK; publ. *Proceedings* (quarterly).

Österreichischer Komponistenbund (*Association of Austrian Composers*): A-1030 Vienna, Baumannstrasse 8-10; f. 1913; promotes the interests and works of Austrian composers and encourages contact between them and the public; 380 mems.; Pres. Prof. K. RAPF; Sec. B. SCHOLLUM; publ. *Mitteilungsblatt* (7 a year).

Österreichischer Richard Wagner-Verband (*Austrian Richard Wagner Association*): A-1050 Vienna, P.O.B. 116; f. 1909; 95 mems.; Pres. FRANZ EUGEN DOSTAL; Sec. Dr. EDITH ARLT.

Wiener Beethoven Gesellschaft (*Vienna Beethoven Society*): A-1190 Vienna, Heiligenstadt, Probusgasse 6; f. 1954; 550 mems.; Pres. Prof. Dr. ALBERT MITRINGER; publ. *Mitteilungsblatt der W.G.B.* (quarterly).

Wiener Konzerthausgesellschaft (*Vienna Concert Hall Society*): A-1030 Vienna, Lothringerstrasse 20; f. 1913; 3,000 mems.; Pres. Ing. Dr. h.c. MANFRED MAUTNER MARKHOF; Gen. Sec. Dr. HANS LANDESMANN.

Wiener Männergesang-Verein (*Vienna Men's Choral Society*): Vienna I, Bösendorferstrasse 12; f. 1843; 273 mems.; Pres. Ing. KURT STEPAN; Conductor Prof. Dr. FRANZ XAVER MEYER; publ. *Mitteilungen* (irregular).

Wiener Philharmoniker, Die (*Vienna Philharmonic Society*): 1010 Vienna I, Bösendorferstrasse 12; f. 1842; 140 mems.; Pres. Prof. ALFRED ALTENBURGER; Sec. Prof. PAUL FÜRST.

Wiener Secession (*Vienna Secessionist Group*): Vienna I, Friedrichstrasse 12; f. 1897 for the promotion of art exhibitions in its own hall and abroad, cultural exchange; 150 mems.; Pres. H. J. PAINITZ; publs. numerous catalogues.

BIBLIOGRAPHY, LIBRARY SCIENCE AND MUSEOLOGY

Oberösterreichischer Musealverein—Gesellschaft für Landeskunde (*Museums Association of Upper Austria*): Linz, Landstr., Ursulinenhof; f. 1833; 1,200 mems.; Chair. Dr. KURT HOLTER; publs. *Jahrbuch*†, *Beiträge zur Landeskunde von Oberösterreich*†, *Schriftenreihe*.

Österreichische Gesellschaft für Dokumentation und Information (*Austrian Society for Documentation and Information*): Hohenstaufengasse 3, A-1014 Vienna; f. 1951; 150 mems.; Pres. R. BAYER, DIPL.ING.; publ. *ÖGDI-Mitteilungen*† (3 a year).

Österreichisches Institut für Bibliographie (*Austrian Institute of Bibliography*): Vienna I, Rathausplatz 4; f. 1949; Dir. Dr. OSKAR LANGER.

Vereinigung Österreichischer Bibliothekare (*Austrian Librarians Association*): 1014 Vienna, Josefsplatz 1; f. 1946; 750 mems.; Pres. Dr. F. KROLLER; publs. *Biblos, Mitteilungen* (quarterly).

ECONOMICS, LAW AND POLITICS

Nationalökonomische Gesellschaft (*Austrian Economic Association*): A-1010 Vienna, Institut für Wirtschaftswissenschaften der Universität Wien, Dr. Karl Lueger Ring 1; f. 1917; *c.* 100 mems.; Chair. Prof. Dr. WILHELM WEBER; Vice-Chair. Prof. DDr. ADOLF NUSSBAUMER; Sec.-Gen. Prof. Dr. GEORG WINCKLER.

Österreichische Gesellschaft für Aussenpolitik und Internationale Beziehungen (*Austrian Society for Foreign Policy and International Relations*): A-1010 Vienna, Josefsplatz 6; f. 1958; lectures, discussions; 500 mems.; library of 3,000 vols., 100 periodicals; Pres. Dr. G. FÜRSTENBERG; Sec.-Gen. Dr. MARIO MARQUET; publ. *Österreichische Zeitschrift für Aussenpolitik* (quarterly).

Österreichische Gesellschaft für Kirchenrecht (*Austrian Society for Ecclesiastical Law*): Vienna I, Dr. Karl Lueger-Ring 1; f. 1949.

Österreichische Gesellschaft für Wirtschaftspolitik (*Austrian Association for Economic Policy*): Vienna XIX, Franz Klein-Gasse 1/48; f. 1947; Pres. Dr. R. KERSCHAGL.

Österreichische Gesellschaft für Statistik und Informatik (*Austrian Society for Statistics and Information Science*): 1014 Vienna I, Neue Hofburg, Heldenplatz, P.O.B. 148; f. 1951 to promote theoretical and applied statistics; 497 mems.; Pres. Prof. Dr. L. BOSSE, Prof. Dr. L. SCHMETTERER; publ. *Mitteilungsblatt* (quarterly).

Wiener Juristische Gesellschaft (*Vienna Legal Asscn.*): 1010 Vienna, Stephansplatz 8A; f. 1867; 600 mems.; Pres. Dr. FRANZ SCHNEIDER; Hon. Sec. ALFRED KOBZINA.

EDUCATION

Österreichische Rektorenkonferenz (*Conference of Rectors*): 1010 Vienna, Schottengasse 1; to consult on post-secondary education, co-ordinate activities of all Austrian universities, and to discuss and initiate reforms in higher education; Pres. Prof. MANFRIED WELAN, Rector of the Agricultural University of Vienna; Sec.-Gen. Dr. F. EBERHARD.

Verband der Akademikerinnen Österreichs (*Austrian Branch of the International Federation of University Women*): A-1010 Vienna I, Reitschulgasse 2; f. 1922 to promote scientific and professional advancement of university graduates, to foster relations with IFUW branches; 850 mems.; Pres. Hofrat Dr. ADELHEID SCHIMAK; Sec. Mag.art. ANGELIKA PLANK; publ. *VVO-Mitteilungen*.

HISTORY, GEOGRAPHY AND ARCHAEOLOGY

Geschichtsverein für Kärnten (*Historical Asscn. of Carinthia*): Klagenfurt, Museumgasse 2; f. 1844; 1,439 mems.; Dir. Prof. Dr. GOTBERT MORO; publs. *Carinthia I* (annually), *Archiv für Vaterland, Kärntner Heimatatlas, Sonderschriften*, etc.

Heraldisch-Genealogische Gesellschaft "Adler" ("*Eagle" Heraldic and Genealogical Society*): 1010 Vienna, Haarhof 4A; f. 1870; 600 mems.; library of 36,000 vols.; Pres. Prof. Dr. HANNS JÄGER-SUNSTENAU; Sec.-Gen. Dr. Baron ANDREAS CORNARO; publs. *Jahrbuch, Zeitschrift*† (quarterly).

Historische Landeskommission für Steiermark (*Styrian Historical Land Commission*): 8010 Graz, Hamerlinggasse 3/II; f. 1892; 30 mems.; Pres. Prof. KURT JUNGWIRTH; Sec. Univ. Prof. Dr. OTHMAR PICKL; publs. *Forschungen zur geschichtlichen Landeskunde der Steiermark, Veröffentlichungen, Quellen zur geschichtlichen Landeskunde der Steiermark*.

Historischer Verein für Steiermark (*Styrian Historical Asscn.*): 8010 Graz, Hamerlinggasse 3; f. 1850; 1,400 mems.; Chair. Dr. FRITZ POSCH; Sec. HEDWIG SCHMITZER; publs. *Zeitschrift*†, *Beiträge zur Erforschung Steierischer Geschichtsquellen*†, *Blätter für Heimatkunde*†.

Kommission für neuere Geschichte Österreichs (*Commission for Modern Austrian History*): 1010 Vienna, Institut für Geschichte, Universität; f. 1900; 18 mems.; Chair. Prof. Dr. ERICH ZÖLLNER.

Orientalische Gesellschaft (*Oriental Society*): A-1010 Vienna I, Universitätsstrasse 7/V; f. 1952; Pres. Prof. Dr. ANDREAS TIETZE.

Österreichische Byzantinische Gesellschaft (*Austrian Byzantine Society*): 1010 Vienna, Postgasse 7-9; f. 1946; 150 mems.; Pres. Prof. Dr. HERBERT HUNGER.

Österreichische Geographische Gesellschaft (*Austrian Geographical Society*): A-1071 Vienna, Karl Schweighofergasse 3; f. 1856; 1,500 mems.; Pres. Prof. Dr. E. WINKLER; library: *see* Libraries; publ. *Mitteilungen* (2 a year).

Österreichische Gesellschaft für Archäologie: A-1010 Vienna, Hofburg, Säulenstiege; f. 1972; archaeology, epigraphy, numismatics; 190 mems.; Pres. Dr. HANNS-JÖRG UBL; publ. *Römisches Österreich* (annually).

Österreichische Numismatische Gesellschaft (*Austrian Numismatic Society*): A-1010 Vienna, Burgring 5; f. 1870; Pres. Dr. HERBERT WENZEL; publs. *Numismatische Zeitschrift, Mitteilungen*.

Verband Österreichischer Geschichtsvereine (*Union of Austrian Historical Asscns.*): Postamt 1015 Vienna, Postfach 263; f. 1949; 85 mem. societies; Man. Vice-Pres. Dr. BERNHARD KOCH; Gen. Sec. Dr. FELIX CZEIKE; publ. *Veröffentlichungen*.

Verein für Geschichte der Stadt Wien (*Association for the History of the City of Vienna*): 1082 Vienna, Wiener Stadt- und Landesarchiv, Rathaus; f. 1853; 1,250 mems.; Chair. Dr. ERWIN M. AUER; Sec. Dr. FELIX CZEIKE; publs. *Wiener Geschichtsblätter*†, *Jahrbuch*†, *Forschungen und Beiträge zur Wiener Stadtgeschichte, Geschichte der Stadt Wien* (2nd series).

INTERNATIONAL CULTURAL INSTITUTES

Afro-Asiatisches Institut in Wien (*Afro-Asian Institute in Vienna*): A-1090 Vienna, Türkenstrasse 3; f. 1959; cultural and other exchange between Austria and African and Asian countries, lectures, economic and social research, seminars; library of *c.* 1,000 vols.; Pres. Bishop Dr. A. WAGNER; Gen. Sec. G. BITTNER; publ. *Treffpunkte*† (quarterly).

Amerika-Haus Wien: A-1010 Vienna, Friedrich Schmidtplatz 2; f. 1946; library of 10,000 vols., 240 periodicals.

British Council: A-1010 Vienna, Schenkenstr. 4; f. 1946; library (*see* Libraries); Rep. J. G. MILLS.

Institut Français: Vienna I, Lobkowitzplatz 2; f. 1946; language courses, lectures, exhibitions, concerts; 40,000 vols. in library; Dir. MARC CANO; Gen. Sec. JEAN-ROLAND MELLINGER; brs. in Innsbruck, Graz, Salzburg, Linz.

Istituto Italiano di Cultura: Vienna 1030, Ungargasse 43; Dir. Prof. R. TONELLI.

Österreich-Institut (*Austrian Institute*): Vienna I, Judenplatz 11; f. 1945; Gen. Dir. Dr. M. SCHANTL.

Österreichisch-Ungarische Vereinigung zur Pflege kultureller Beziehungen (*Austro-Hungarian Asscn. for Cultural Interests*): Vienna II, Hollandstrasse 4; f. 1950; 1,000 mems.; exhibitions, concerts, lectures; Pres. Prof. Dr. FRITZ WEBER; Dir. DDr. PETER HAESELER; publ. *Neues aus Ungarn* (quarterly).

Österreichisches College (*Austrian College*): 1010 Vienna, Reichsratsstr. 17/III; f. 1945; independent; congress centre: Alpbach/Tyrol; international congresses: Alpbach European Forum (multidisciplinary, held each August), Dialogue Congresses (on the relations between Western Europe and other cultural and economic regions, held each June), Vienna European Forum (organizes various events throughout the year in co-operation with the international Club Alpbach for European Culture); Pres. Prof OTTO MOLDEN; publs. *Proceedings of the Alpbach European Forum, Proceedings of the Dialogue Congresses* (annually).

LANGUAGE AND LITERATURE

Arbeitsgemeinschaft der Altphilologen Österreichs (*Austrian Philology Asscn.*): A-1030 Vienna, 3 Ungargasse 39/6a; f. 1921; 936 mems.; Chair. Dr. HANS MALICSEK; Sec. Dr. THEOPHIL TROMBALLA.

Eranos Vindobonensis: A-1010 Vienna, Institut für Klass. Philologie, Universität; f. 1885; philological society; 150 mems.; Sec. Dr. J. DIVJAK.

Gesellschaft für Klassische Philologie in Innsbruck (*Classical Philological Society of Innsbruck*): Innsbruck, Neue Universität, Institut für Klassische Philologie, Innrain 52; f. 1958; 200 mems.; Dir. (vacant); publ. *Acta philologica Aenipotana*.

Österreichische Exlibris-Gesellschaft (ÖEG) (*Austrian Bookplate-collectors' Society*): A-1090 Vienna, Turkenstrasse 17/4; f. 1903; 500 mems.; Chair. Prof. Dr. GUSTAV DICHLER; publs. *Jahrbuch, Mitteilungen*, books.

Österreichische Gesellschaft für Literatur (*Austrian Literary Society*): A-1010 Vienna, Herrengasse 5; f. 1961; Pres. Dr. W. KRAUS.

Österreichischer PEN-Club (*Austrian PEN Club*): Concordia Haus, Bankgasse 8, Vienna I; f. 1922; Pres. A. LERNET-HOLENIA; Sec. Mrs. DOROTHEA ZEEMAN.

Wiener Goethe-Verein (*Vienna Goethe Association*): A-1010 Vienna, Reitschulgasse 2; f. 1878; lectures, poetry readings; 300 mems.; *c.* 2,000 books; Pres. Prof. Dr. CONRAD H. LESTER; Vice-Pres. Prof. Dr. HERBERT ZEMAN; publ. *Jahrbuch*.

Wiener Sprachgesellschaft (*Vienna Language Society*): 1010 Vienna, Universität Institut für Sprachwissenschaft; f. 1947; 200 mems.; Pres. Prof. Dr. W. V. DRESSLER; Sec. Dr. O. E. PFEIFFER; publ. *Die Sprache* (annually).

MEDICINE

Ärztegesellschaft Innsbruck (*Medical Society of Innsbruck*): Innsbruck, Medizinische Fakultät der Universität; f. 1894; 900 mems.; library of 5,600 vols.; Pres. Prof. Dr. G. NIEBAUER; Sec. Prof. Dr. J. ZELGER; publs. *Wiener Klinische Wochenschrift, Münchener Medizinische Wochenschrift*.

Gesellschaft der Ärzte (*Vienna Society of Physicians*): A-1090 Vienna 9, Frankgasse 8; f. 1837; 1,278 mems.; 200,000 vols. and 25,900 monographs in library; Pres. Prof. Dr. O. NOVOTNY; Secs. Prof. W. HOLCZABEK, Prof. E. ZWEYMÜLLER; publ. *Wiener Klinische Wochenschrift*†.

Gesellschaft der Chirurgen in Wien (*Society of Surgeons*): Vienna IX, Allgemeines Krankenhaus, Alserstrasse 4; f. 1935; 141 mems.; Dirs. Prof. Dr. PAUL FUCHSIG and Prof. Dr. JOHANN NAURATIL.

Internationale Paracelsus-Gesellschaft: A-5020 Salzburg, Faberstr. 16; f. 1950; 315 mems., 27 mem. asscns.; Pres. Prof. Dr. K. GOLDAMMER; Gen. Sec. Prof. Dr. Dr. h.c. S. DOMANDL; publs. *Salzburger Beiträge zur Paracelsusforschung, Parcelsus-Briefe*.

Österreichische Ärztegesellschaft für Psychotherapie (*Austrian Medical Society of Psychotherapy*): A-1090 Vienna, Mariannengasse 10; f. 1950; Pres. Prof. V. E. FRANKL.

Österreichische Dermatologische Gesellschaft (*Dermatological Society*): A-1090 Vienna, Alserstr. 4, Allgemeines Krankenhaus; Pres. Prof. Dr. G. NIEBAUER; Hon. Pres. Prof. Dr. G. RIEHL; Sec. Prof. Dr. H. EBNER.

Österreichische Gesellschaft für Anästhesiologie, Reanimation und Intensivtherapie (*Austrian Society for the Study of Anaesthesia and Intensive Therapy*): 1090 Vienna, Spitalgasse 23; f. 1951; 430 mems.; Pres. Dr. W. LIST; Sec. Dr. J. NEUMARK; publ. *Der Anaesthesist*.

Österreichische Gesellschaft für Arbeitsmedizin (*Austrian Society for Industrial Medicine*): A-1090 Vienna, Schwarzspanierstr. 17; f. 1954; 250 mems.; Pres. Prof. Dr. V. LACHNIT; Sec. Dr. CH. FRIEBERGER.

Österreichische Gesellschaft für Balneologie und medizinische Klimatologie (*Austrian Society for Balneology and Medical Climatology*): Physiological Section of Paracelsus Institute, A-4540 Bad Hall; Pres. Prof. Dr. H. HELLAUER.

Österreichische Gesellschaft für Chirurgie (*Austrian Society for Surgery*): 1090 Vienna 9, Alserstr. 4; f. 1958; 450 mems.; Dir. Prim. Dr. WAYAND.

Österreichische Gesellschaft für Elektroencephalographie und klinische Neurophysiologie (*Austrian EEG-Society*): 1090 Vienna, Universitätsnervenklinik, Spitalgasse 23; f. 1953; 64 mems.; library of 600 vols.; Pres. Prof. Dr. H. LECHNER, Prof. Dr. E. DEISENHAMMER, Prof. Dr. K. PATEISKY; Secs. Prof. Dr. E. SCHERZER and Dr. S. ENGE; publ. *Wiener Zeitschrift für Nervenheilkunde* (quarterly).

Österreichische Gesellschaft für Geriatrie (*Austrian Society for Geriatrics*): Vienna XIV, Hütteldorfer Strasse 188; f. 1955; experimental gerontology, geriatric clinic, geriatric sociology; 200 mems.; library of 2,000 vols.; Pres. Prof. Dr. W. DOBERAUER; Sec. Prof. Dr. P. KÖNIGSTEIN; publs. *Scriptum Geriatricum* (yearly)†, *Aktuelle Gerontologie* (monthly).

Österreichische Gesellschaft für Hals-Nasen-Ohrenheilkunde, Kopf und Halschirurgie (*Austrian Society of ENT Science, Head and Neck Surgery*): A-1090 Vienna, Alserstr. 4; f. 1892; 270 mems.; Pres. Dr. KARL KRUMPHOLZ; publ. *Zeitschrift Laryngologie*.

Österreichische Gesellschaft für Innere Medizin (*Austrian Society for Internal Medicine*): A-1097 Vienna, Garnisongasse 13, Allgemeines Krankenhaus; f. 1886; 400 mems.; Dirs. Prof. Dr. K. FELLINGER, Prof. Dr. E. DEUTSCH, Prof. Dr. H. BRAUNSTEINER, Prof. Dr. H. GOTSCH; publ. *Wiener Zeitschrift für Innere Medizin*.

Österreichische Gesellschaft für Kinderheilkunde (*Austrian Society for Paediatrics*): A-5016 Salzburg, Postfach 11; f. 1962; 631 mems.; Pres. Dr. W. WALDMANN; Sec. Dr. O. STÖLLINGER; publ. *Pädiatrie und Pädologie* (4 a year).

Österreichische Gesellschaft für Urologie (*Austrian Society for Urology*): 1090 Vienna IX, Alserstr. 4 (Urologie Universitätsklinik); 257 mems.; Pres. Prof. Dr. G. HUBMER.

Österreichische Gesellschaft zum Studium der Sterilität und Fertilität (*Austrian Society for the Study of Sterility and Fertility*): 1097 Vienna, Universitäts Frauenklinik, Spitalgasse 23; Pres. Prof. Dr. O. DAPUNT; Sec. Doz. Dr. W. H. F. SCHNEIDER.

Österreichische Ophthalmologische Gesellschaft (*Austrian Ophthalmological Society*): A-1090 Vienna, Spitalgasse 2; f. 1955; 360 mems.; library of 2,100 vols.; Pres. Dr. Prof. Dr. E. KUTSCHERA; Sec. Dr. P. DROBEC; publ. *Sitzungsbericht*† (annually).

Österreichische Röntgengesellschaft—Gesellschaft für Medizinische Radiologie und Nuklearmedizin (*Austrian Radiography Society*): A-1090 Vienna, Mariannengasse 10; f. 1946; 321 mems.; Pres. Prof. Dr. H. H. ELLEGAST.

Wiener Medizinische Akademie für Ärztliche Fortbildung (*Vienna Medical Academy for Further Medical Education*): 1090 Vienna, Alserstrasse 4; f. 1896; Pres. Prof. Dr. O. MAYRHOFER; Sec. Dr. H. PIETSCHMANN.

Wiener Verein für Psychiatrie und Neurologie (*Vienna Society for Psychiatry and Neurology*): A-1090 Vienna, Lazarettgasse 14, Psychiatrische und Neurologische Universitätskliniken; f. 1868; Pres. Univ.-Doz. Dr. W. SOLMS; Secs. Univ.-Doz. Dr. E. SLUGA, Dr. H. SCHANDA.

NATURAL SCIENCES

General

Naturwissenschaftlicher Verein für Kärnten (*Carinthian Asscn. of Natural Sciences*): A-9020 Klagenfurt, Museumgasse 2; f. 1848; 1,300 mems.; Pres. Dr. HANS SAMPL; publs. *Carinthia II* (annually with special issues), *Der Karinthin* (Mineralogy, Geology).

Verband der Wissenschaftlichen Gesellschaften Österreichs (*Asscn. of Austrian Scientific Organizations*): 1070 Vienna VII, Lindengasse 37; f. 1949 to expand the development of scientific activity; 278 mems.; publs. *Österreichische Hochschulzeitung* (monthly), *Aus Österreichs Wissenschaft, Dissertationen der Universitäten Wien, Bodenkultur Wien, Technischen Universität Wien, Linz, Salzburg, Wirtschaftsuniversität Wien, Gesamtverzeichnis österreichischer Dissertationen*, etc.

Biological Sciences

Österreichische Mykologische (pilzkundliche) Gesellschaft (*Austrian Mycological Society*); A-1030 Vienna, Rennweg 14; f. 1919; 200 mems.; Pres. Prof. Dr. M. MOSER.

Wiener Entomologische Gesellschaft (*Entomological Society of Vienna*): 1010 Vienna I, Rathausstrasse 11; f. 1916; 350 mems.; Man. HANS REISSER; publ. *Zeitschrift*.

Zoologisch-Botanische Gesellschaft in Wien (*Zoological-Botanical Society*): 1010 Vienna, Burgring 7, Naturhistorisches Museum; f. 1851; sections for botany, zoology, entomology, ornithology and development of biological instruction; 540 mems.; library of 10,000 vols.; Pres. Prof. Dr. KARL HÖFLER; Gen. Sec. Prof. Dr. ENGELBERT BANCHER; publs. *Verhandlungen, Abhandlungen, Koleopterologische Rundschau*.

Mathematics

Mathematisch-Physikalische Gesellschaft in Innsbruck (*Mathematics and Physics Society of Innsbruck*): A-6020 Innsbruck, Innrain 52; f. 1936; 120 mems.; Chair. Prof. Dr. LEOPOLD VIETORIS.

Österreichische Mathematische Gesellschaft (*Austrian Mathematical Society*): 1040 Vienna, Technische Universität, Gusshausstr. 27; f. 1904; 850 mems.; Pres. Prof. Dr. PETER GRUBER; publ. *International Mathematical News* (3 a year).

Physical Sciences

Astronomischer Verein (*Astronomical Asscn.*): A-1238 Vienna, Hasenwartgasse 32; f. 1924; 1,500 mems.; Pres. JOHANN ALBRECHT; Sec. HERMANN MUCKE; publs. *Der Sternenbote*†, *Österreichischer Himmelskalender.*

Chemisch-Physikalische Gesellschaft in Wien (*Vienna Chemico-Physical Society*): Strudlhofgasse 4, A-1090 Vienna; f. 1869; 260 mems.; Dir. Prof. W. KUMMER; Sec. Dr. H. POSCH.

Österreichische Biochemische Gesellschaft (*Austrian Biochemical Society*): A-1235 Vienna, c/o Sandoz Forschungs-Inst. GmbH, Brunnerstr. 59; f. 1952; 420 mems.; Pres. Prof. Dr. E. WINTERSBERGER; Sec. Doz. Dr. G. HÖGENAUER.

Österreichische Geologische Gesellschaft (*Austrian Geological Society*): A-1030 Vienna, Geologische Bundesanstalt, Rasumofskygasse 23; f. 1907; 500 mems.; Dir. Prof. Dr. H. W. FLÜGEL; publ. *Mitteilungen.*

Österreichische Gesellschaft für Erdölwissenschaften (*Austrian Society for Petroleum Sciences*): A-1031 Vienna, Erdbergstr. 72; f. 1960; to promote petroleum sciences, grants university scholarships; 490 mems.; Pres. Prof. Dipl. Ing. Dr. LEO MACKOWSKI; Sec. Dr. P. MESSINGER; publs. *Erdöl Erdgas Zeitschrift*, scientific papers.

Österreichische Gesellschaft für Klinische Chemie (*Austrian Society of Clinical Chemistry*): A-1090 Vienna, Währingerstr. 10; f. 1968; 424 mems.; Pres. Dr. H. J. GIBITZ; Sec. Dr. W. HOHENWALLNER.

Österreichische Gesellschaft für Meteorologie (*Austrian Meteorological Society*): A-1190 Vienna, Hohe Warte 38; f. 1865; to promote meteorological research by financial aid and organization of lectures; 210 mems.; Pres. Prof. Dr. FRIEDICH LAUSCHER; Sec. Dr. J. WILLFARTH; publ. *Wetter und Leben* (quarterly).

Österreichische Gesellschaft für Mikrochemie und Analytische Chemie (*Austrian Society for Micro- and Analytical Chemistry*): Graz, Universitätsplatz 2; f. 1948; 250 mems.; Dir. Prof. Dr. MARIA KUHNERT-BRANDSTÄTTER; Sec. Prof. Dr. ROBERT KELLNER.

Österreichische Physikalische Gesellschaft (*Austrian Physical Society*): 1082 Vienna, Lenaugasse 10; f. 1950; 660 mems.; Pres. Prof. Dr. H. HEINRICH; Exec. Sec. Dr. W. MAJEROTTO.

Verein Österreichischer Chemiker (*Association of Austrian Chemists*): A-1010 Vienna, Eschenbachgasse 9; f. 1897; lectures, conferences, awards grants to students; 1,650 mems., 700 mems. in attached societies; Pres. Dr. J. HARMS; Gen. Sec. Prof. Dr. H. SCHINDLBAUER; publs. *Österreichische Chemie Zeitschrift*, *Monatshefte für Chemie* (in conjunction with the Austrian Academy of Sciences).

PHILOSOPHY AND PSYCHOLOGY

Berufsverband Österreichischer Psychologen (*Professional Federation of Austrian Psychologists*): A-1010 Vienna, Liebiggasse 5; f. 1953; 700 mems.; Dirs. Dr. E. HOFER, Dr. K. HÖFNER, Dr. R. ZUCHA.

Gesellschaft für Ethische Kultur (*Society for Ethical Culture*): Vienna III, Zaunergasse Nr. 12; f. 1894; Dir. R. FREY.

Gesellschaft für Jugendkriminologie und Psychogogik (*Society for Juvenile Criminology and Psycho-Pedagogics*): Vienna XII, Schönbrunner Strasse 291; f. 1956; Dir. Prof. Dr. F. STUMPFL.

Österreichische Gesellschaft für Parapsychologie (*Austrian Society for Parapsychology*): A-1040 Vienna, Gusshausstrasse 27; f. 1927; 400 mems.; small library; Pres. Prof. Dr. HELLMUT HOFMANN; Gen. Sec. Dr. KÄTHE HAUN.

Österreichische Gesellschaft für Psychologie (*Austrian Psychology Association*): Vienna VI, Linke Wienzeile 118; f. 1946; Dir. Dr. M. PIPEREK.

Philosophische Gesellschaft Wien (*Philosophical Society of Vienna*): 1010 Vienna, Universitätsstrasse 7/11/11; f. 1954; 100 mems.; Dir. Prof. Dr. ERICH HEINTEL.

Sigmund Freud-Gesellschaft (*Sigmund Freud Society*): A-1090 Vienna, Berggasse 19; f. 1968; history and application of psychoanalysis; 1,085 mems.; library of 15,000 vols.; archives; Sigmund Freud museum; Pres. Dr. H. LEUPOLD-LÖWENTHAL; Vice-Pres. DDr. ELLA LINGENS; publ. *Sigmund Freud House Bulletin*† (2 a year).

Wiener Psychoanalytische Vereinigung (*Vienna Psychoanalytical Assn.*): A-1010 Vienna, Doblhoffgasse 9; f. 1908, closed during the war, re-opened 1946; 36 mems.; library of 10,000 vols., museum; Pres. Dr. H. LEUPOLD-LOEWENTHAL; Vice-Pres. Dr. A. BECKER; Sec. Dr. W. SOLMS-ROEDELHEIM.

RELIGION, SOCIOLOGY AND ANTHROPOLOGY

Anthropologische Gesellschaft in Wien (*Vienna Anthropological Society*): A-1014 Vienna I, Burgring 7, Postfach 417; f. 1870; 335 mems.; Pres. Prof. Dr. WALTER HIRSCHBERG; Sec. Dr. FRITZ ECKART BARTH; publs. *Mitteilungen*†, *Anthropologische Forschungen*, *Ethnologische Forschungen*, *Prähistorische Forschungen*, *Volkskundliche Veröffentlichungen*, *Völkerkundliche Veröffentlichungen.*

Evangelische Akademie in Wien (*Evangelical Academy in Vienna*): A-1096 Vienna, Schwarzspanierstr. 13, Postfach 15; f. 1955; Dir. ULRICH TRINKS.

Gesellschaft für die Geschichte des Protestantismus in Österreich (*Society for History of Protestantism in Austria*): 1180 Vienna, Severin-Schreiber-Gasse 3; f. 1879; 251 mems.; Chair. Prof. Dr. PETER F. BARTON; publ. *Jahrbuch*†.

Österreichische Ethnologische Gesellschaft (*Austrian Ethnological Society*): A-1014 Vienna, Museum für Völkerkunde, Neue Hofburg; f. 1957; 221 mems.; Pres. Prof. Dr. A. SLAWIK; Sec. Oberrat Dr. HANNS PETER; publ. *Wiener Völkerkundliche Mitteilungen* (annually).

Österreichische Gesellschaft für Soziologie (*Austrian Sociological Society*): Postfach 114, A-1037 Vienna; f. 1950; Pres. P. KELLERMANN; Sec. R. BURGER; publ. *Österreichische Zeitschrift für Soziologie* (quarterly).

Sozialwissenschaftliche Arbeitsgemeinschaft (*Social Science Study Association*): Vienna I, Freyung 6/6/III/8; Dir. Dr. A. PRALSOCH.

Verein für Landeskunde von Niederösterreich und Wien (*Asscn. for regional studies of Lower Austria and Vienna*): 1014 Vienna I, Herrengasse 11; f. 1864; 1,500 mems.; Pres. Hofrat Dr. O. F. WINTER; Gen. Sec. Hofrat Univ.-Doz. Dr. H. FEIGL; *Unsere Heimat*†, *Jahrbuch für Landeskunde von Niederösterreich*†, *Forschungen zur Landeskunde von Niederösterreich*†.

Verein für Volkskunde (*Ethnographical Asscn.*): A-1080 Vienna, Laudongasse 15/19; f. 1894; 700 mems.; Pres. Prof. Dr. LEOPOLD SCHMIDT; Sec. Dr. KLAUS BEITL; publs. *Österreichische Zeitschrift für Volkskunde*†, *Volkskunde in Österreich*†, *Österreichische Volkskundliche Bibliographie*, also special publs.

Wiener Katholische Akademie (*Vienna Catholic Academy*): A-1010 Vienna I, Freyung 6; f. 1945; seminars and lectures for catholic academies, scientific work-groups, publications; 230 mems.; Pres. Bischof Dr. J. WEINBACHER; Gen. Sec. Dr. KLAUS PORSTNER; publ. *Religion-Wissenschaft-Kultur*† (annually).

TECHNOLOGY

Österreichisches Bauzentrum (*Austrian Building Centre*): 1090 Vienna, Palais Liechtenstein; f. 1957; 1,800 mems.; Pres. HUBERT HRASTNIK; publs. *Bauforum* (6 a year), *Baukatalog* (annually).

Österreichisches Institut für Formgebung (*Austrian Institute for Design*): 1030 Vienna, Salesianergasse 1; f. 1958; 130 mems.; promotion of ideas and results of, and expert advice on industrial design; Pres. Prof. Dipl. Ing. KARL MANG.

Österreichischer Verein für Vermessungswesen und Photogrammetrie (*Austrian Asscn. for Surveying and Photogrammetry*): A-1082 Vienna, Friedrich Schmidt-Platz 3; f. 1903; 600 mems.; Pres. Dipl.-Ing. FRIEDRICH HRBEK; publ. *Österreichische Zeitschrift für Vermessungswesen und Photogrammetrie*†.

RESEARCH INSTITUTES

(*see* also under Universities)

AGRICULTURE AND VETERINARY SCIENCE

Agrarwirtschaftliches Institut des Bundesministeriums für Land- und Forstwirtschaft (*Institute of Agricultural Economics*): 1133 Vienna 13, Schweizertalstrasse 36; f. 1960; applied research and documentation in the field of agricultural economics, agricultural policies, rural sociology, regional planning studies and related subjects; library of 21,000 vols. and 540 periodicals; Dir. HANS ALFONS; publs. *Monatsberichte*† (monthly), *Schrifttum* (2 a month), *Schriftenreihe*† (irregular), *Informationen über internationale Preise* (weekly).

Bundesanstalt für veterinärmedizinische Untersuchungen (*Federal Institute for Veterinary Research*): A-4021 Linz, Kudlichstrasse 27; f. 1947; Dir. Dr. KALUSCH ADOLF OTTO.

Bundesversuchsanstalt für Alpenländische Landwirtschaft, Gumpenstein (*Federal Test Establishment for Alpine Agriculture in Gumpenstein*): 8952 Irdning, Steiermark; f. 1947; research into Alpine economics, with emphasis on agriculture; library of 4,000 vols.; Dir. Dr. ANTON BRUCKNER; publs. *Versuchsergebnisse, Forschungsberichte und Tagungsberichte der Referate für Grünland, Getreidebau, Hackfrucht, Tierzucht, Landtechnik, Landwirtschafliches Bauwesen, Betriebswirtschaft.*

Forstliche Bundesversuchsanstalt (*Federal Forest Research Station*): A-1131 Vienna, Schönbrunn-Tirolergarten; f. 1874; library of 23,500 vols.; Dir. HANS EGGER; publs. *Mitteilungen, Angewandte Pflanzensoziologie* (irregular), *Informationsdienst* (monthly).

Landesanstalt für Pflanzenzucht und Samenprüfung (*National Establishment for Plant Cultivation and Seed Testing*): A-6074 Rinn, Tirol; f. 1939; Dirs. Dr. E. MAYR, Dipl. Ing. L. KÖCK.

Landwirtschaftlich-Chemische Bundesversuchsanstalt Wien (*Federal Institute for Agricultural Chemistry in Vienna*): A-1020 Vienna, Trunnerstrasse 1; f. 1869; chemistry of soils and foodstuffs, plant and animal nutrition, certification and analysis of wines, spirits and fruit juices; 100 mems.; library of 7,000 vols.; Dir. Prof. Dipl. Ing. Dr. W. BECK; publ. *Versuchsberichte.*

ARCHITECTURE AND TOWN PLANNING

Österreichische Gesellschaft für Raumforschung und Raumplanung (*Austrian Society for Regional Research and Regional Planning*): A-1040 Vienna, Karlsplatz 13; f. 1954; 1,000 mems.; Pres. DDr. ALOIS LUGGER; Chair. Prof. Dr. RUDOLF WURZER; library of 2,000 vols.; publs. *Berichte zur Raumforschung und Raumplanung*† (two-monthly), *Schriftenreihe zur Raumforschung und Raumplanung* (irregular).

Österreichisches Institut für Raumplanung (*Austrian Institute for Regional and Urban Planning*): A-1011 Vienna I, Franz Josefs Kai 27; f. 1957; 42 mems.; library of *c.* 15,000 vols.; Dir. Dr. M. SCRUBERER; publ. *Mitteilungen* (every 2 months).

THE ARTS

Gesellschaft für Vergleichende Kunstforschung (*Society of Comparative Art Research*): 1010 Vienna, Stephansplatz 4; f. 1932; 500 mems.; Chair. Prof. Dr. RUPERT FEUCHTMÜLLER; publs. *Kunstwissenschaftliche Jahresgabe*†, *Mitteilungen*†.

Institut für Österreichische Kunstforschung (*Institute of Austrian Art Research*): 1010 Vienna, Hofburg, Schweizerhof, Säulenstiege; affiliated to the Bundesdenkmalamt (*see under* Learned Societies); f. 1911; research and documentation of works of art in Austria; 10 mems.; library of 15,000 vols.; Chief Officer Doz. Dr. EVA FRODL-KRAFT; publs. *Österreichische Zeitschrift für Kunst und Denkmalpflege* (2 a year), *Wiener Jahrbuch für Kunstgeschichte* (annually), *Studien zur österreichischen Kunstgeschichte, Studien zu Denkmalpflege und Denkmalschutz* (irregular), etc.

Wiener Gesellschaft für Theaterforschung (*Viennese Society for Theatre Research*): 1010 Vienna, Hofburg, Batthyanystiege; f. 1944; 200 mems.; Pres. Prof. Dr. MARGRET DIETRICH; Gen. Sec. Dr. OTTO G. SCHINDLER; publ. *Jahrbuch.*

BIBLIOGRAPHY, LIBRARY SCIENCE AND MUSEOLOGY

Österreichisches Institut für Bibliotheksforschung (*Austrian Institute for Library Research*): 1014 Vienna, Josefplatz 1; f. 1966; Pres. DDr. J. STUMMVOLL; Sec. Dr. J. MAYERHÖFER; publ. *Biblos.*

ECONOMICS, LAW AND POLITICS

Diplomatische Akademie Wien (*Diplomatic Academy of Vienna*): 1040 Vienna, Favoritenstr. 15; f. 18th century as Orientalische Akademie, then Konsularakademie, present title 1964; admits 20–25 postgraduates including foreign students annually; languages of instruction German, English and French; studies in languages, history, politics, economics, law; preparation for careers in diplomacy, international organizations, business, banking administration; Dir. Amb. Dr. H. PFUSTERSCHMID-HARDTENSTEIN; publ. *Jahrbuch* (with English summaries).

Institut für angewandte Sozial- und Wirtschaftsforschung (*Institute for Applied Social and Economic Research*): 1010 Vienna I, Renngasse 12; f. 1961; Dir. Univ.-Prof. Dr. Dr. K. WENGER.

Institut für Höhere Studien und Wissenschaftliche Forschung Wien (*Vienna Institute for Advanced Studies and Scientific Research*): A-1060 Vienna VI, Stumpergasse 56; f. 1963; postgraduate training and research in economics, industrial administration and operations research, sociology and political science, mathematical methods and computer applications to the social sciences; Dirs. Prof. Dr. ANATOL RAPOPORT, Dr. ERHARD FÜRST; publs. *IHS—Journal, Empirical Economics, International Journal of Game Theory.*

Institut für Politische Wissenschaft (*Institute for Political Science*): A-5020 Salzburg, Mönchsberg 2A; 7 mems.; library of 14,000 vols.; Dir. Prof. Dr. FRANZ MARTIN SCHMÖLZ.

Institut für Sozialpolitik und Sozialreform (*Institute for Social Politics and Social Reform*): 1010 Vienna, Ebendorferstr. 6/IV; f. 1953; Pres. Dr. JOSEF TAUS; publ. *Gesellschaft und Politik*†.

Österreichische Forschungsstiftung für Entwicklungshilfe (*Austrian Foundation for Development Research*): A-1090 Vienna, Türkenstrasse 3/III; f. 1967; research, documentation and information on development aid, developing countries and international development, particularly relating to Austria; library of 10,000 vols.;

Pres. Dr. A. Wagner; Dir. Dr. Hermann Krobath; publs. *Internationale Entwicklung*† (quarterly), *Entwicklungsforschung und Entwicklungspolitik*† (research monographs), *Handbook of Austrian Development Aid.*

Österreichische Gesellschaft für langfristige Entwicklungsforschung (Zukunftsforschung) (*Austrian Society for Long-term Development Research*): Institut für Sozio-ökonomische Entwicklungs-forschung, Fleischmarkt 20-22, A-1010 Vienna; f. 1973; to arouse public interest in a systematic analysis of long-term trends; to conduct and promote courses and lectures in futurology research; to provide a basis for an exchange of information on long-term research in science, politics and economy, and to co-operate on a national and international level in questions of long-term development research; 80 mems.; Pres. Prof. Gerhart Bruckmann; Gen. Sec. Dr. Peter Fleissner.

Österreichisches Forschungsinstitut für Wirtschaft und Politik (*Austrian Research Institute for Economics and Politics*): Salzburg, Sigmund Haffner-Gasse 16; f. 1945.

Österreichisches Institut für Entwicklungshilfe und technische Zusammenarbeit mit den Entwicklungsländern (*Austrian Institute for Development Aid and Technical Co-operation with the Developing Countries*): 1010 Vienna, Grillparzerstr. 14; f. 1963; projects for training of young people; Pres. Dr. Franz-Josef Mayer-Gunthof, Erich Hofstetter, m.p.

Österreichisches Institut für Wirtschaftsforschung (*Austrian Institute for Economic Research*): A-1103 Vienna, Postfach 91; f. 1926; Dir. Prof. Hans Seidel; publs. *Monatsberichte*† (monthly), *Empirica*† (2 a year).

Österreichisches Meinungs- und Marktforschungsinstitut (*Austrian Public Opinion and Market Research Institute*): 1030 Vienna, Streichergasse 3; Dir. Dr. F. Karmasin.

Österreichisches Ost- und Südosteuropa-Institut (*Austrian Institute of East and South-East European Studies*): 1010 Vienna, Josefsplatz 6; f. 1958; departments of geography, history, Eastern economics, international relations, Eastern academy (Institute of Learning); library of 13,000 vols., 1,400 (700 current) periodicals and documents; Dir. Prof. Dr. R. Plaschka; publs. *Österreichische Osthefte*† (quarterly), *Presseschau Ostwirtschaft*† (monthly).

Österreichisches Statistiches Zentralamt (*Austrian Central Statistical Office*): A-1014 Vienna, Heldenplatz, Neue Burg; f. 1863; library of 120,800 vols.; Pres. Prof. Dr. Lothar Bosse; publs. *Statistisches Handbuch für die Republik Österreich* (yearly), *Statistische Nachrichten* (monthly).

Wirtschaftsförderungsinstitut der Bundeskammer der gewerblichen Wirtschaft (*Institute for Economic Development of the Austrian Federal Chamber of Commerce*): 1010 Vienna, Hoher Markt 3, f. 1946; 251,000 mem. firms; adult education, management and vocational training, public relations for Austrian economy, consulting service, trade fairs; Man. Dir. Dr. Franz Kirchmair; publs. bulletins and brochures.

History, Geography and Archaeology

Österreichische Arbeitsgemeinschaft für Ur- und Frühgeschichte (*Austrian Study Association for Pre- and Early History*): 1070 Vienna, Universitätsstr. 7/II/1; f. 1950; *c.* 450 mems.; Dir. Dr. G. Langmann; publ. *Mitteilungen*† (2 a year).

Medicine

Bundesstaatliche Anstalt für experimentellpharmakologische und balneologische Untersuchungen (*Federal State Establishment for Experimental Pharmacological and Balneological Research*): 1090 Vienna, Währinger Strasse 13A; f. 1948; Dir. Dr. Ing. Eichler.

Österreichische Gesellschaft für Sexualforschung (*Austrian Society for Sexual Research*): Vienna XVIII, Währinger Strasse 79; f. 1954; Pres. Dr. A. Werkgartner.

Serotherapeutisches Institut Wien (*Sero-Therapeutic Institute Vienna*): Vienna X, Triester Strasse 50; f. 1894.

Natural Sciences

General

Fonds zur Förderung der wissenschaftlichen Forschung (*Austrian Scientific Research Fund*): 1090 Vienna, Garnisongasse 7/20; f. 1968; all Austrian universities with their faculties and the Austrian Academy of Science are mems.; with the Austrian Industrial Research Fund, it forms *Österreichischer Forschungsrat* (Austrian Research Council), co-ordinating scientific, applied and industrial research and development and advising the Federal and State governments on scientific matters; Pres. Prof. Dr. Hans Tuppy, Prof. Dr. Fritz Paschke, Prof. Dr. Ingo Reiffenstein; Sec. Gen. Dr. Raoul F. Kneucker.

Institut für Wissenschaft und Kunst (*Institute for Science and Art*): 1090 Vienna, Berggasse 17 and 1070 Vienna, Museumstr. 5; f. 1946; 500 mems.; research, lectures, etc.; Pres. Prof. Dr. A. Gisel; publ. *Mitteilungen.*

Institut für Wissenschaftstheorie (*Institute for the Theory of Science*): Internationales Forschungszentrum, A-5020 Salzburg, Mönchsberg 2; f. 1961; library of 7,000 vols.; Dir. Univ.-Prof. Dr. Paul Weingartner; publ. *Forschungsgespräche* (irregular).

Biological Sciences

Biologische Station Neusiedler See (*Biological Station Neusiedler See*): Amt d. Burgenl. Landesregierung, Abt. XII/3N, A-7142 Illmitz; f. 1949; Dir. Dr. F. Sauerzopf.

Botanisches Institut und Botanischer Garten (*Botanical Institute and Garden*): 1030 Vienna III, Rennweg 14; f. 1754 (Garden) and 1844 (Institute); *c.* 70 mems.; *c.* 50,000 vols. in library; Dir. Prof. Dr. Friedrich Ehrendorfer; publ. *Plant Systematics and Evolution* (quarterly).

Institut für angewandte Pflanzensoziologie (*Institute for Applied Sociology of Plants*): 9020 Klagenfurt, St. Georgen, Sandhof; f. 1928; Dir. Prof. E. Aichinger.

Physical Sciences

Atominstitut der Österreichischen Universitäten (*Atomic Institute of the Austrian Universities*): Vienna II, Schüttelstrasse 115; f. 1958; 60 mems.; training of advanced students and basic research; depts. of electron- and X-ray physics, health physics, nuclear physics and technology, neutron- and solid state physics, radio chemistry; Dirs. Prof. Dr. Gernot Eder, Prof. Dr. Helmut Rauch.

Bundesanstalt für Wasserhaushalt von Karstgebieten (*Federal Survey of the Hydrology of Karst-areas*): 1010 Vienna, Herrengasse 8; f. 1929; library of 540 vols.; study of practical problems of karst-areas, especially karst-hydrology; Dir. Dr. F. Bauer; publ. *Beiträge zur Alpinen Karstforschung* (irregular).

Geologische Bundesanstalt (*Geological Survey of Austria*): 1031 Vienna, Rasumofskygasse 23; f. 1849; 78 mems.; library of 200,000 vols.; Dir. Dr. F. Ronner; publs. *Verhandlungen*†, *Jahrbuch*†, *Abhandlungen*†, geological maps.

Hydrographisches Zentralbüro (*Central Hydrographical Office*): Vienna III, Marxergasse 2; f. 1893; library of 12,000 vols.; Sec. H. Schimpf; publs. *Hydrographisches Jahrbuch von Österreich* (annually), *Beiträge zur Hydrographie Österreichs* (irregular).

Institut für Astronomie der Universität Innsbruck: 6020 Innsbruck, Universitätsstr. 4; f. 1904; photometry, astrometry, radioastronomy; library of 4,598 vols.; Dir. Univ. Prof. Dr. J. PFLEIDERER; publ. *Mitteilungen* (irregular).

Institut für Astronomie der Universität Wien (*Vienna University Observatory*): Türkenschanzstr. 17; f. 1755; joined with L. Figl Observatory for Astrophysics; 16 mems.; galactic astronomy; library of 15,000 vols.; publs. *Mitteilungen*†, *Annalen*†.

L. Figl Observatorium für Astrophysik: A-1180 Vienna, Türkenschanzstr. 17; St. Corona at Schöpfl (Vienna forest); f. 1969.

Ludwig Boltzmann Institut für Festkörperphysik (*Ludwig Boltzmann Institute for Solid State Physics*): A-1060 Vienna VI, Kopernikusgasse 15; f. 1965; investigation of semiconductors and quasi-one-dimensional organic metals; Dir. Prof. Dr. KARLHEINZ SEEGER.

Österreichische Gesellschaft für Weltraumforschung (*Austrian Society for Space Research*): Innsbruck, Postfach 67; f. 1952; Pres. Prof. Dr. F. HECHT.

Österreichische Kommission für Internationale Erdmessung (*Austrian Commission for International Geodesy*): A-1040 Vienna, Gusshausstrasse 27–29; f. 1863; 20 mems.; Pres. Dr. Dr.-Ing. E.h. KARL RINNER; Sec. Prof. Dr. KURT BRETTERBAUER.

Sonnenobservatorium Kanzelhöhe der Universität Graz (*Kanzelhöhe Solar Observatory*): A-9520 Sattendorf; f. 1943; small library; Dir. Prof. Dr. H. HAUPT; publ. *Mitteilungen* (irregular).

Sternwarte Kremsmünster (*Kremsmünster Observatory*): A-4550 Kremsmünster; f. 1748; meteorological observations (synoptic and climatic), seismic, atmospheric electricity; library of *c.* 2,000 vols.; Dir. Dr. P. ANSGAR RABENALT.

Wiener Volkssternwarte—Kuffner Sternwarte (*Vienna Public Observatory—Kuffner Observatory*): A-1160 Vienna, Johann Staud-Strasse 10; f. 1886; astrophotography, astrospectroscopy, library of 1,770 vols.; Dir. Prof. W. JASCHEK.

Zentralanstalt für Meteorologie und Geodynamik (*Central Institute for Meteorology and Geodynamics*): A-1190 Vienna, Hohe Warte 38; f. 1851; 130 mems.; library of 80,000 vols.; Dir. Prof. Dr. HEINZ REUTER; publs. yearbooks† and bulletins†.

PHILOSOPHY AND PSYCHOLOGY

Psychotechnisches Institut Wien (*Psychotechnical Institute, Vienna*): A-1190 Vienna, Vegagasse 4; f. 1926; training of supervisors of all levels; library of 4,000 vols.; Dir. Hofrat Dr. GUIDO HACKL; publ. *Mensch und Arbeit*†.

RELIGION, SOCIOLOGY AND ANTHROPOLOGY

Institut für Kirchliche Sozialforschung (*Institute of Socio-Religious Research*): Vienna I, Grillparzerstr. 5; Dir. Dr. H. BOGENSBERGER.

Institut für Kirchliche Zeitgeschichte (*Institute of Contemporary Ecclesiastical History*): Salzburg, Mönchsberg 2A; f. 1961; 5 mems.; Dir. Prof. Dr. E. WEINZIERL; publs. *Hirtenbriefe aus Deutschland, Österreich und der Schweiz* (yearly) and studies.

Institut für Religionswissenschaft und Theologie (*Institute of Religious Knowledge and Theology*): Salzburg, Mönchsberg 2A; f. 1961; 4 mems.; library of 8,500 vols. and prints; Dir. Prof. DDr. LUDGER BERNHARD; publs. ***Salzburger Patristische Studien, Aevum Christianum*** and *Kairos.*

Österreichische Arbeitsgemeinschaft für Kunde des Slawentums und Osteuropas (*Austrian Study Association for Knowledge of Slav Territories and Eastern Europe*): Vienna I, Liebiggasse 5/I; f. 1951; Dir. Prof. Dr. G. HÜTTL-WORTH.

TECHNOLOGY

Bundesanstalt für Wasserbauversuche und hydrometrische Prüfung (*Federal Experimental Establishment for Hydraulics and Hydrometry*): 1090 Vienna, Severingasse 7; f. 1913; 12 mems.; Dir. G. PLATZER.

Forschungsinstitut für Technikgeschichte am Technischen Museum für Industrie und Gewerbe in Wien (*Research Institute for the History of Technology in Vienna*): A-1140 Vienna, Mariahilfer Strasse 212; f. 1931; Dir. Dipl. Ing. R. NIEDERHUEMER.

Institut für Arbeits- und Baubetriebswissenschaft (*Institute for Work and Building Management Science*): Vienna IX, Fürstengasse 1; f. 1946; 200 mems.; Dir. Dr. G. DRESSEL.

Institut für Gewerbeforschung (*Institute for Small Business Research*): 1180 Vienna, Türkenschanzstrasse 18; f. 1954; library of 2,000 vols.; Pres. Prof. Dr. E. HRUSCHKA; Dir. Dr. E. FROEHLICH; publ. *IfG-Mitteilungen*† (2 a year).

Österreichische Studiengesellschaft für Kybernetik (*Austrian Society for Cybernetic Studies*): A-1010 Vienna I, Schottengasse 3; f. 1970; theoretical and applied research in cybernetics and computer science; training courses and scientific meetings; offers special services to business and official administrations; organizes European Meeting on Cybernetics and Systems Research (2 a year); 32 ord., 326 corresp. mems.; Pres. Prof. Dr. ROBERT TRAPPL; publs. *Systems and Cybernetics*† (quarterly), *Reports*† (irregular).

Österreichisches Faserforschungsinstitut (*Austrian Fibre Research Institute*): A-1050 Vienna, Spengergasse 20; f. 1951; Pres. Dipl. Ing. F. ADENSAMER; Dir. Prof. Dr. W. LEBENSAFT.

Österreichisches Forschungszentrum Seibersdorf G.m.b.H. (**ÖFZ**) (*Austrian Research Centre, Seibersdorf*): A-1082 Vienna, Lenaugasse 10; f. 1956, name changed 1980; the ÖFZ is a limited company of which the capital is shared by the Austrian Government (51 per cent), State industries (26 per cent) and private enterprises (23 per cent); operates the Seibersdorf Research Centre with the 12-MW Swimming Pool Tank Type Reactor "Astra", and the Departments of Physics, Electronics, Chemistry, Metallurgy, Health Physics, Reactor Safety, Isotope Application, Biology and Agriculture; 500 employees; library of over 13,000 vols.; Technical-Scientific Dir. Prof. Dr. FRANZ JEGLITSCH; Admin. Commercial Dir. Dkfm. WOLFGANG BADERLE; publs. Reports of the various departments.

Österreichisches Giesserei-Institut (*Austrian Foundry Institute*): A-8700 Leoben, Parkstr. 21; f. 1952; 135 mems.; research and development; Man. and Tech. Dir. Dipl.-Ing. Dr. mont. ROLAND HUMMER; publ. *Giesserei Rundschau*†.

Österreichisches Holzforschungsinstitut der Österreichischen Gesellschaft für Holzforschung (*Austrian Wood Research Institute of the Austrian Wood Research Society*): A-1030 Vienna, Arsenal, Franz Grillstr. 7; f. 1947; 500 mems.; 10,000 vols.; Dirs. Techn. Rat Prof. Dr. techn. h.c. HERBERT NEUSSER, Dipl. Ing. HUBERT POSCH, Dipl.-Ing. REINHOLD BAYER; publs. *Holzforschung und Holzverwertung* (6 a year), *Schrifttumskarteidienst der ÖGH* (twice monthly).

Österreichisches Institut für Bauforschung (*Austrian Institute for Building Research*): A-1190 Vienna, An den langen Lüssen 1; f. 1959; Chief Officers Dipl. Ing. Dr. MICHAEL WACHBERGER, Ing. GÜNTER SPIELMANN; publ. *ib-Nachrichten* (quarterly).

Österreichisches Institut für technische Forschung und Entwicklung (*Austrian Institute for Technical Research and Development*): Vienna XIX, Muthgasse 64A; f. 1946; Dir. Dr. K. KUSCHEL.

Österreichisches Normungsinstitut (ON) (*Austrian Standards Institute*): A-1021 Vienna II, Postfach 130, Leopoldsgasse 4; f. 1920; government-supervised private institute for standardization in all fields; 4,500 mems.; library of 510 vols. and 85 periodicals; Pres. Prof. DDr. OSCAR VAS; Man. Dir. Ing. JOSEF MAURER; Chief Librarian HELMUT FELBER; publ. *ÖNORM*† (10 a year).

Physikalisch-technische Versuchsanstalt für Wärme- und Schalltechnik am Technologischen Gewerbemuseum (*Physical-technical Institute for Research on Heat and Noise Technology at the Technological Industrial Museum*): A-1090 Vienna, Währinger Strasse 59; f. 1925; Dir. Dr. JUDITH LANG.

Zentrum für Elektronenmikroskopie (*Centre for Electron Microscopy*): 8010 Graz, Steyrergasse 17; f. 1959; Pres. Dr. F. NIEDERL; Dir. Dr. F. GRASENICK.

LIBRARIES AND ARCHIVES

ARCHIVES

Vienna

Archiv der Universität Wien (*University of Vienna Archives*): Vienna I, Postgasse 9; f. 1708; records dating back to fourteenth century; Archivist Prof. Dr. FRANZ GALL.

Archiv des Stiftes Schotten (*Schotten Foundation Archives*): Vienna I, Freyung 6; f. 1155; archives of the Benedictine monastery; Archivist Prof. P. CÖLESTIN RAPF.

Diözesanarchiv Wien (*Vienna Diocesan Archives*): 1010 Vienna, Wollzeile 2, erzbisch. Palais; f. 1936; *c.* 30,000 vols., 4,000 documents and files; Dir. Dr. ANNEMARIE FENZL; publ. *Beiträge* (6 a year).

Niederösterreichisches Landesarchiv (*Lower Austrian Provincial Archives*): Vienna I, Herrengasse 11; f. 16th century; 25,000 vols.; Reporter Dr. JOHANNES GRUENDLER; Chief Archivist FRANZ STUNDNER.

Österreichisches Staatsarchiv (*Austrian State Archives*): 1010 Vienna I, Minoritenplatz I; f. 1945; library of State Archives; 490,000 vols.; Domestic, Court and State Archives; General Administrative Archives; Finance and Treasury Archives; War Archives; Transport Archives; Gen. Dir. Dr. RUDOLF NECK; publ. *Mitteilungen*.

Wiener Stadt- und Landesarchiv (*Municipal Archives*): A-1082 Vienna, Felderstrasse 1, Rathaus; records from 13th century; Dir. Prof. Dr. FELIX CZEIKE.

Zentralarchiv des Deutschen Ordens: A-1010 Vienna, Singerstrasse 7; f. 1852; *c.* 6,500 vols.; Archivist Dr. BERNHARD DEMEL.

Provinces

Burgenländisches Landesarchiv (*Burgenland Provincial Archives*): 7001 Eisenstadt, Freiheitsplatz 1, Landhaus; f. 1921; Dir. Dr. AUGUST ERNST.

Kärntner Landesarchiv (*Carinthian Provincial Archives*): 9020 Klagenfurt, Landhaus; f. 1904; Archivists Dr. WILHELM NEUMANN, Dr. ALFRED OGRIS, Dr. EVELYNE ANTONITSCH.

Landesarchiv Salzburg (*Salzburg Provincial Archives*): 5010 Salzburg, Michael-Pacher-Strasse 40; f. 1945; 15,000 vols. in library; Dir. Dr. FRANZ PAGITZ.

Oberösterreichisches Landesarchiv (*Upper Austrian Provincial Archives*): Linz, Anzengruberstrasse 19; f. 1896; library of 42,000 vols.; Dir. Dr. ALOIS ZAUNER.

Steiermärkisches Landesarchiv (*Styrian Provincial Archives*): Graz, Bürgergasse 2A; f. 1811; Dir. Dr. GERHARD PFERSCHY; publs. *Mitteilungen*† (yearly), *Veröffentlichungen* (irregular).

Stiftsarchiv des Zisterzienserstiftes (*Cistercian Foundation Archives*): Heilingenkreuz bei Baden; archives dating from the founding of the monastery in A.D. 1133; Archivist P. HERMANN WATZL.

Tiroler Landesarchiv (*Tyrolese Provincial Archives*): A-6010 Innsbruck, Herrengasse 1; and Maria-Theresienstrasse 43 (Landhaus); f. 13th century, records from 11th century; Dir. Prof. Dr. FRIDOLIN DÖRRER; publs. *Tiroler Geschichtsquellen*†, *Ortschroniken*† (irregular).

Vorarlberger Landesarchiv (*Vorarlberg Provincial Archives*): A-6901 Bregenz, Kirchstr. 28; f. 1898; Dir. DDr. KARL HEINZ BURMEISTER.

LIBRARIES

Vienna

Administrative Bibliothek und Österreichische Rechtsdokumentation im Bundeskanzleramt (*Administrative Library and Law Documentation of the Chancellery*): A-1010 Vienna, Herrengasse 23; f. 1849; 420,000 vols. on jurisprudence, politics, economics, statutes, etc.: Dir. Dr. O. SIMMLER.

Bibliothek der Akademie der Bildenden Künste (*Library of the Academy of Fine Arts*): Vienna I, Schillerplatz 3: f. 1773; 62,758 vols. on art and history of art; Dir. Hofrat Dr. ALBERT MASSICZEK; publs. catalogues of exhibitions†.

Bibliothek der Akademie der Wissenschaften (*Library of the Academy of Sciences*): A-1010 Vienna, Ignaz Seipel-Platz 2; f. 1847; 300,000 vols.; Dir. BEATE AMSTÄDTER.

Bibliothek der Generaldirektion der Österreichischen Bundesbahnen (*General Administration Library of the Austrian Federal Railways*): Vienna II, Praterstern 3; f. 1896; 105,000 vols., 315 maps; Librarian Dr. Ing. M. SCHOBER.

Bibliothek der Hochschule für Bodenkultur (*Library of the State University of Agriculture and Forestry*): Vienna XIX, Peter-Jordan-Str. 82; f. 1872; 129,000 vols.; Librarian Dr. WILLIBALD OGIELLO.

Bibliothek der Hochschule für Musik und darstellende Kunst in Wien (*Library of the University for Music and Dramatic Art*): A-1037 Vienna, Lothringerstr. 18; f. 1909; 79,000 vols., 2,400 gramophone records, 852 sound tapes; Bruno Walter Archive; Dir. Dr. WOLFGANG PERNAUER.

Bibliothek der Kammer der gewerblichen Wirtschaft für Wien (*Vienna Chamber of Commerce Library*): A-1010 Vienna, Stubenring 8-10; f. 1849; 155,381 vols.; Dir. MAX PHILIPPI.

Bibliothek der Mechitaristenkongregation: 1070 Vienna, Mechitaristengasse 4; f. 1773; philology; 200,000 vols.; 2,500 Armenian MSS.; all current Armenian newspapers and periodicals; Dir. P. AUGUSTIN SZEKOULIAN; publ. *Handes Amsorya* (quarterly).

Bibliothek der Österreichischen Geographischen Gesellschaft (*Library of the Austrian Geographical Society*): A-1071 Vienna, Karl Schweighofergasse 3; f. 1856; 21,000 vols.; Librarian Prof. Dr. ERICH WOLDAN.

Bibliothek der Technischen Universität (*Library of the Technical University*): 1040 Vienna, Karlsplatz 13; f. 1815; 646,696 vols.; Dir. Dr. JOSEF WAWROSCH.

Bibliothek der Veterinärmedizinischen Universität Wien (*Library of the Veterinary University*): 1030 Vienna, Linke Bahngasse 11; f. 1767; 55,000 vols.; Dir. Dr. WALTER GIROLLA.

Bibliothek der Wirtschaftsuniversität (*Library of the University of Economics*): 1190 Vienna Franz Klein-Gasse 1; f. 1898; 207,000 vols.; Dir. Dr. F. BISCHOF.

Bibliothek des Bundesministeriums für Finanzen (*Library of the Ministry of Finance*): A-1015 Vienna, Himmelpfortgasse 4; f. 1810; administration, finance, economics, law; 205,000 vols.; Librarian JOHANN HEGEDÜS.

Bibliothek des Bundesministeriums für Land- u. Forstwirtschaft (*Library of the Ministry of Agriculture and Forestry*): A-1010 Vienna, Stubenring 1; f. 1868; 100,000 vols.; Librarian Dr. CHRISTIANA WOLFF.

Bibliothek der Bundesministerien für soziale Verwaltung und für Gesundheit und Umweltschutz (*Library of the Federal Ministries of Social Administration and of Health and Environmental Protection*): Stubenring I, A-1010 Vienna; f. 1917; 100,000 vols.; Dir. Dr. HANS WAGNER.

Bibliothek des Bundesministeriums für Unterricht und Kunst (*Library of the Ministry of Education and the Arts*): A-1014 Vienna, Minoritenplatz 5; f. 1849; 310,000 vols.; collection on the history of Austrian science and pedagogy since 1848; collection of all state approved school books since 1848 and of annual secondary school programmes; administrative library of the Ministry of Science and Research, documentation on research policy; Dir. Mag. G. SILVESTRI; publs. *Verzeichnis des Bücherzuwachses*† (monthly), *Forschungspolitische Dokumentation*† (quarterly).

Bibliothek des Instituts für Österreichische Geschichtsforschung (*Library of the Institute of Austrian Historical Research*): A-1010 Vienna, Dr. Karl Lueger Ring I; f. 1854; 50,000 vols.; Librarian Doz. Dr. OSKAR PAUSCH; publ. *Verzeichnis der Zeitschriften des Instituts.*

Bibliothek des Kriegsarchivs Wien (*Library of the War Archives Dept. of the Austrian State Archives*): Vienna VII, Stiftgasse 2; f. 1776; military history and science; 395,250 vols.; Librarian Dr. EDITH WOHLGEMUTH.

Bibliothek des Österreichischen Statistischen Zentralamtes (*Library of the Austrian Central Office of Statistics*): Postfach 41, A-1014 Vienna; f. 1829; *c.* 123,300 vols.; Librarian Dr. ALFRED DOHNAL.

British Council Library: A-1010 Vienna, Schenkenstr. 4; f. 1946; 28,566 vols.; 129 periodicals; Librarian Mrs. S. J. MILLS, M.A., A.L.A.

Bücherei des Österreichischen Patentamtes (*Library of the Austrian Patents Office*): A-1014 Vienna, Kohlmarkt 8-10; f. 1899; 226,000 vols.; Dir. Dr. HERMES MASSIMO; publs. *Österreichisches Patentblatt*†, *Österreichischer Markenanzeiger*†, *Patentschriften.*

Bundesstaatliche Paedagogische Bibliothek beim Landesschulrat für Niederösterreich (*Library of the Lower Austrian Education Authority*): A-1014 Vienna, Herrengasse 23; f. 1923; 150,000 vols.; Dir. Dr. GERTRUDE MIKSCH.

Fakultätsbibliothek für Rechtswissenschaften (*Legal Studies Library*): Vienna I, Universität, Dr. Karl Luegerring 1; f. 1922; 166,000 vols., 1,050 periodicals; Dir. MARIANNE METZ.

Niederösterreichische Landesbibliothek (*Lower Austrian Provincial Library*): Vienna I, Teinfaltstrasse 8; f. 1813; 103,542 vols.; Dir. Dr. EDUARD RONGE.

Österreichische Nationalbibliothek (*Austrian National Library*): Vienna I, Josefsplatz; f. in 16th century; 2,510,000 vols.; Gen. Dir. Dr. JOSEF ZESSNER-SPITZENBERG; the library consists of nine collections and technical departments including the *Institut für Restaurierung* for the restoration of books.

Printed Books Collection: includes 2,510,000 vols., 15,500 periodicals, etc.

Manuscript Collection: includes 37,000 MSS., 7,884 incunabula, 200,000 autographs, etc.

Music Collection: includes 45,000 music MSS., 93,000 vols. of printed music, etc.

Map Collection: includes 215,300 maps, 210,000 geographical-topographical pictures, 137 globes, etc.

Papyri Collection: includes approx. 100,000 papyri, etc.

Portrait Collection and Picture Archive: includes approx. 643,000 portraits (drawings and photographs), 750,000 photographic negatives, etc.

Theatre Collection: 1,242,800 items including drama texts, autographs, costume and stage designs, prints, photographs, stage models, cinema collection.

Publs. *Ausstellungskatakaloge*†, *Jahresberichte*† (annually), *Museion, Corpus Papyrorum Raineri*†, *Mitteilungen aus der Papyrussammlung*†, *Palatina-Nachrichten, Biblosschriften*† (irreg.).

Parlamentsbibliothek (*Library of Parliament*): A-1017 Vienna, Dr. Karl Renner Ring 3; f. 1869; 220,000 vols.; Dir. Dr. THEODOR STOEHR.

Sammlungen der Gesellschaft der Musikfreunde in Wien (*Archives and Library of the Society of Friends of Music in Vienna*): 1010 Vienna, Bösendorferstrasse 12; f. 1812; 15,500 vols.; 60,000 scores; original, first and early editions; music autographs, historical instruments, letters, portraits, etc.; Dir. Dr. OTTO BIBA.

Sozialwissenschaftliche Studienbibliothek der Kammer für Arbeiter und Angestellte für Wien (*Social Sciences Library of the Chamber of Workers of Vienna*): 1040 Vienna, Prinz Eugenstr. 20-22; 175,162 vols., 972 periodicals; Dir. Dr. MARIA BIEBL.

Städtische Büchereien der Gemeinde Wien (*Municipal Libraries of Vienna*): 1080 Vienna, Skodagasse 20; 53 brs.; 1 central library, 2 travelling libraries; Dir. Dr. HEINZ RIEDER.

Universitätsbibliothek Wien (*Vienna University Library*): Vienna I, Dr. Karl Lueger Ring 1; f. 1365, restored 1777; 1,895,813 vols. (main library), and 2,215,000 vols. (departments); Dir. Hofrat Dr. F. RENNHOFER.

Wiener Stadt- und Landesbibliothek (*Vienna City and Provincial Library*): Vienna I, Rathaus; f. 1856; 310,000 vols., 205,000 MSS., 60,000 musical items, 15,000 MSS. musical items; Dir. Hofrat Mag. Dr. FRANZ PATZER.

Zentralbibliothek der Physikalischen Institute der Universität Wien (*Central Library of the Physics Institutes of Vienna University*): Boltzmanngasse 5, 1090 Vienna; f. 1946; 103,000 vols., 2,316 periodicals, 390,000 atomic energy reports, 165,000 reprints; Dir. Dr. WOLFGANG KERBER.

Zentralbibliothek im Justizpalast (*Central Library of the Palace of Justice*): Vienna I, Museumstrasse 12; f. 1823; 70,000 vols.; Dir. Mag. RICHARD PITZINGER.

Zentrale Verwaltungsbibliothek für Wirtschaft und Technik (*Central Library for Economics and Technology*): Bundesministerium für Handel, Gewerbe u. Industrie und Bundesministerium für Bauten und Technik, 1011 Vienna I, Stubenring 1; f. 1850; library of 125,574 vols.; Dir. Dr. ELFRIEDE DREXLER.

Provinces

Bibliothek der Benediktinerabtei (*Library of the Benedictine Abbey*): Admont; f. 1074; 145,000 vols., 1,103 MSS., 900 incunabula; Dir. Dr. P. ADALBERT KRAUSE.

Bibliothek der Benediktinerabtei (*Library of the Benedictine Abbey*): A-8732 Seckau; f. 1883; 160,000 vols.; Dir. Dr. P. BENNO ROTH.

Bibliothek der Benediktiner-Erzabtei St. Peter (*Library of the Benedictine Abbey of St. Peter*): Salzburg, St. Peter-Bezirk 1; f. 700; 120,000 vols., 1,300 MSS., 923 incunabula; Dir. Dr. KARL HERMANN.

Bibliothek des Augustiner-Chorherrenstiftes (*Library of the Augustine Canonical Foundation*): Klosterneuburg, Stiftsplatz 1; f. *c.* 1100; 180,000 vols., 1,250 MSS., 836 incunabula; Dir. DDr. FLORIDUS RÖHRIG.

Bibliothek des Augustiner-Chorherrenstiftes (*Library of the Augustine Canonical Foundation*): A-4490 St. Florian; f. 1071; 135,000 vols., 885 MSS., 800 incunabula; Dir. Prof. DDr. KARL REHBERGER.

Bibliothek des Benediktinerklosters Melk in Niederösterreich (*Library of the Melk Benedictine Monastery in Lower Austria*): Stift Melk, A-3390 Austria; 80,000 vols. mostly dating from before the nineteenth century, 1,800 codices and 750 incunabula; Librarian Fr. SEVERIN NOWAK.

Bibliothek des Oberösterreichischen Landesmuseums (*Library of the Upper Austrian Provincial Museum*): Linz/Donau, Museumstrasse 14; f. 1836; 80,000 vols.; Librarian Dr. ALFRED MARKS.

Bundesstaatliche Studien-Bibliothek (*Federal Public Library*): Klagenfurt, Kaufmanngasse 11; f. 1775; 400,000 vols., 261 MSS., 255 incunabula; Dir. Dr. ERNST BENISCHKE.

Bundesstaatliche Studien-Bibliothek (*Federal Public Library*): A-4020 Linz, Schillerplatz 2; f. 1774; 210,000 vols.; Dir. Dr. FRANZ WILFLINGSEDER.

Burgenländische Landesbibliothek (*Burgenland Provincial Library*): 7001 Eisenstadt, Freiheitsplatz 1, Landhaus; f. 1922; 20,000 vols.

Steiermärkische Landesbibliothek (*Styrian Provincial Library*): Graz, Kalchberggasse 2; f. 1811; 500,000 vols.; Dir. Dr. H. HEGENBARTH.

Universitätsbibliothek der Montanuniversität (*Library of the Mining and Metallurgical University*): A-8700 Leoben, Franz-Josef-Strasse 18; f. 1850; 87,953 vols.; Librarian PETER SIKA.

Universitätsbibliothek der Technischen Universität Graz (*Technical University Library*): A-8010 Graz, Technikerstrasse 4; f. 1875; 120,000 vols.; Dir. Dr. K. F. STOCK.

Universitätsbibliothek Graz (*University Library, Graz*): Graz, Universitätsplatz 3; f. 1586; 950,000 vols.; Dir. Dr. FRANZ KROLLER; publs. *Jahresbericht*†, *Fachliche Benützungsanleitungen*†, *Bibliographische Informationen*†, *Schriftenreihe EDV-Projekt 1*†, *Grazer Zeitschriften-Verzeichnis*†.

Universitätsbibliothek Innsbruck (*University Library, Innsbruck*): Innrain 50; f. 1746; 800,000 vols., 1,100 MSS., 2,000 incunabula; Dir. Dr. OSWALD STRANZINGER.

Universitätsbibliothek Salzburg (*Salzburg University Library*): Salzburg, Universitätsplatz 1; f. 1623; 300,000 vols., 1,100 MSS., 1,400 incunabula; Dir. Dr. KARL FORSTNER.

Vorarlberger Landesbibliothek (*Vorarlberg Provincial Library*): 6901 Bregenz, Kirchstr. 28; f. 1977; 90,000 vols.; Dir. Dr. EBERHARD TIEFENTHALER.

MUSEUMS AND ART GALLERIES

Vienna

Bundesmobilienverwaltung (*National Furniture Collection*): Pres. Dr. HERBERT BUCHSBAUM.

1. *Bundessammlung alter Stilmöbel:* Vienna VII, Mariahilferstrasse 88; f. 1780; a collection illustrating different periods of Austrian furniture.
2. *Schausammlung der ehemaligen Hoftafel-und Silberkammer:* Vienna I, Hofburg; a collection of tableware and silver formerly belonging to the Imperial household.

Erzbischöfliches Dom- und Diözesanmuseum (*Archiepiscopal Cathedral and Diocesan Museum*): Vienna I, Rotenturmstr. 2; f. 1933; ecclesiastical art; Dir. Prof. Dr. RUDOLF BACHLEITNER; Curator DDr. JAKOB WEINBACHER.

Galerie Graf Czernin (*Count Czernin Art Gallery*): Vienna VIII, Friedrich Schmidt Platz 4; f. 1800; paintings; Dir. Count EUGEN CZERNIN; Curator Dr. KARL TRAUTTMANSDORFF.

Gemäldegalerie der Akademie der Bildenden Künste (*Academy of Fine Arts Gallery*): Vienna I, Schillerplatz 3; f. 1822; 14th-20th-century paintings; Curator Dr. HERIBERT HUTTER.

Graphische Sammlung Albertina (*Albertina Graphic Art Collection*): Vienna I, Augustinerstrasse 1; f. 1769; 44,000 drawings; sketch-books and miniatures; over one million prints; collection of posters; 40,000 vols. in reference library; Dir. Hofrat Prof. Dr. WALTER KOSCHATZKY.

Heeresgeschichtliches Museum (*Military History Museum*): Vienna III, Arsenal; f. 1891; exhibits dating from Thirty Years War to First World War—objects include swords, Turkish weapons, artillery armour, uniforms, flags, paintings and sketches; library of about 30,000 vols.; Dir. Dr. JOH-CHRISTOPH ALLMAYER-BECK.

Historisches Museum der Stadt Wien (*Historical Museum of the City of Vienna*): Vienna IV, Karlsplatz; f. 1888; local relics of prehistoric, Roman and medieval times; ceramics, plastics, tombstones; topographic and cultural history of Vienna from 1500 to the present; glass-paintings, paintings by Viennese artists and portraits of Viennese personalities; Dir. Hofrat Dr. ROBERT WAISSENBERGER.

Associated Museums include:

Adalbert Stifter-Museum: Vienna I, Mölkerbastei 8; contains a large part of the paintings of the writer Adalbert Stifter.

Beethoven-Wohnung: Vienna I, Molkerbastel 8 (Pasqualati-Haus): Beethoven relics housed in one of his lodgings.

Beethoven-Wohnung: Vienna XIX, Döblinger Haupstr. 92 (Eroica-Haus); f. 1970; here Beethoven worked on his third symphony.

Beethoven-Wohnung: Vienna XIX, Probusgasse 6; f. 1970; here Beethoven lived while writing his "Heiligenstadttestament".

Haydn-Museum: Vienna VI, Haydngasse 19; f. 1904; portraits, MSS. and other relics in the house where Haydn lived and died.

Hermesvilla: Vienna XIII, Lainzer Tiergarten; former summer residence of the Empress Elisabeth.

Mozart-Wohnung: Vienna I, Domgasse 5; Mozart's home from 1784 to 1787.

Pratermuseum: Vienna II, Planetarium; f. 1964.

Römische Baureste Am Hof: Vienna I, Am Hof 9; f. 1957; ruins of a Roman canal.

Römische Ruinen unter dem Hohen Markt: Vienna I, Hohen Markt 3; f. 1950; ruins of Roman soldiers' houses.

Schubert-Museum: Vienna IX, Nussdorferstrasse 54; f. 1912; Schubert's birthplace; portraits, MSS. and other relics.

Schubert Sterbezimmer: Vienna IV, Kettenbrückengasse 6; room where Schubert died.

Johann Strauss-Wohnung: Vienna II, Praterstr. 54; f. 1976; Strauss's home from 1863 to 1870; paintings, furniture and instruments.

Uhrenmuseum (*Clock Museum*): Vienna I, Schulhof 2; f. 1917; includes historic wheelclocks.

Virgilkapelle: Vienna I, Stephansplatz, U-Bahn-Station; chapel and collection of historic Viennese ceramics.

Otto Wagner Pavillon: Vienna IV, Karlsplatz.

Josefinum: A-1090 Vienna IX, Währinger Strasse 25; f. by the Emperor Joseph II in 1785 as a college for military surgeons; contains University Institutes for Pharmacognosy and the History of Medicine; library of *c.* 50,000 historical medical books, an 18th-century wax anatomical collection and a collection of pictures; Dir. Prof. Dr. ERNA LESKY.

Kunsthistorisches Museum (*Museum of Fine Arts*): A-1010 Vienna, Burgring 5; f. 1891 from Hapsburg Imperial collections; library of 85,000 vols.; Chief Dir. and Dir. of Picture Gallery Dr. FRIDERIKE KLAUNER; Curator of Egyptian Collection Dr. HELMÜTH SATZINGER; Dir. of Antiquities Dr. WOLFGANG OBERLEITNER; Curator of State Carriages, Historical Costumes, Library and Reproduction Dept. Dr. GEORG KUGLER; Curator of Plastics and Handicrafts Dr. MANFRED LEITHE-JASPER; Dir. of Armour Dr. ORTWIN GAMBER; Curator of Musical Instruments Dr. KURT WEGERER; Dir. of Numismatics Dr. BERNARD KOCH; Curator of the Educational Dept. Dr. GUDRUN ROTTER.

Associated Collections include:

Weltliche und Geistliche Schatzkammer (*Collection of Secular and Ecclesiastical Treasures*): A-1010 Vienna, Hofburg, Schweizerhof, Säulenstiege; insignia and personal relics of Holy Roman Empire and Hapsburg dynasty; ecclesiastical collection of the Hapsburgs; church furniture, relics, vestments, etc., from 10th to 19th centuries; Curator Dr. MANFRED LEITHE-JASPER.

Wagenburg (*Carriage Collection*): A-1130 Vienna, Schloss Schönbrunn; state carriages of the Hapsburg dynasty; Dir. GEORG KUGLER.

Kupferstichkabinett der Akademie der bildenden Künste (*Graphic Art Collection of the Academy of Fine Arts*): Vienna I, Schillerplatz 3; f. 1773; 28,800 drawings, 29,297 prints, 21,032 photographs; library (*see* above); Dir. Dr. ALBERT MASSICZEK.

Museum des 20. Jahrhunderts (*Museum of the 20th Century*): Vienna III, Schweizergarten; f. 1962; works by Munch, Bonnard, Nolde, Kandinsky, Klee, Beckmann, Ernst, Kokoschka, Léger, Matisse, Moore, Laurens, Wotruba. etc.; Dir. Dr. GERHARD LUECKER.

Museum für Völkerkunde (*Ethnological Museum*): 1014 Vienna, Neue Burg, Ringstrassentrakt; f. 1876, reorganized 1928; library of about 90,000 vols.; Dir. Univ. Prof. Dr. HANS MANNDORFF; publs. *Archiv für Völkerkunde* (annual), *Veröffentlichungen zum Archiv für Völkerkunde*.

Naturhistorisches Museum (*Natural History Museum*): A-1014 Vienna I, Burgring 7; f. 1748 by Emperor Franz I, present building opened 1889; mineralogical collection, geology, palaeontology, zoology, botany, anthropology, prehistory; library of *c.* 300,000 books; First Dir. Hofrat Dr. OLIVER E. PAGET; publ. *Annalen*.

Niederösterreichisches Landes-Museum (*Provincial Museum of Lower Austria*): 1014 Vienna I, Herrengasse 9; f. 1912; sections: natural history, historical (art, pottery and domestic utensils from medieval times), art, folklore; library of 3,000 vols.; Dir. Prof. Dr. JOHANNES GRÜNDLER; publ. *Kulturberichte aus Niederösterreich*.

Österreichische Galerie (*Austrian Gallery*): Oberes and Unteres Belvedere, 1030 Vienna III, Prinz Eugenstrasse 27; Dir. Dr. HANS AURENHAMMER; publ. *Mitteilungen*; the Gallery has the following three sections:

Museum mittelalterlicher Österreichischer Kunst (*Museum of Austrian Art of the Middle Ages*): Orangerie des Belvedere, Vienna III, Rennweg 6A; f. 1953; collection of Austrian medieval paintings and sculptures, especially 14th to 16th century.

Österreichisches Barockmuseum (*Austrian Baroque Museum*): Unteres Belvedere, Vienna III, Rennweg 6A; f. 1923, re-org. 1975; Austrian Baroque art (paintings and sculptures).

Österreichische Galerie des XIX. und XX. Jahrhunderts (*Austrian Gallery of the XIX and XX Centuries*): Oberes Belvedere, Vienna III, Prinz Eugenstrasse 27; f. 1924 and 1929; collection of 19th and 20th century Austrian paintings and sculptures.

Österreichisches Gesellschafts- und Wirtschafts-Museum (*Austrian Museum of Sociology and Economics*): Vienna 5, Vogelsanggasse 36; f. 1925; collection of archives, maps, photographs, etc.; guest school; Dir. JOSEF DOCEKAL; publ. *Blick in die Österreichische Wirtschaft* (annually).

Österreichisches Museum für Angewandte Kunst(*Austrian Museum of Applied Art*): A-1010 Vienna, Stubenring 5; f. 1864; applied arts from Roman to modern times; library of 100,000 vols., 250,000 prints, 267 periodicals; Dir. DDr. HERHART EGGER; publ. *Alte und moderne Kunst* (twice monthly).

Österreichisches Museum für Volkskunde (*Austrian Museum of Folk Life and Folk Art*): A-1080 Vienna, Laudongasse 15/19; f. 1895; Dir. Dr. KLAUS BEITL; publs. *Veröffentlichungen* (18 vols.), *Raabse Märchen-Reihe* (6 vols.), catalogues†.

Sammlung Religiöse Volkskunst (*Collection of Popular Religious Art*): Vienna I, Johannesgasse 8 (Ursulinenkloster); f. 1965.

Aussenstelle Schlossmuseum Gobelsburg: 3551 Gobelsburg bei Langenlois; f. 1966; ceramics, furniture, glass, housed in castle.

Ethnographisches Museum Schloss Kittsee: A-2421 Kittsee, Burgenland; f. 1974; folk art and folk life of countries in the east and south-east of Europe; housed in castle.

Schönbrunn Palast und Park (*Schönbrunn Palace and Park*): Vienna XIII; former Imperial summer residence built between 1695 and 1700, and altered between 1743 and 1749; panelled rooms and galleries, furniture, and tapestries; baroque and botanical gardens; Europe's oldest zoological garden built in 1752, with original baroque centre, modern enclosures and one of Central Europe's biggest aquariums.

Technisches Museum für Industrie und Gewerbe in Wien mit Österreichisches Eisenbahn-museum und Post- und Telegraphen-museum (*Trade and Industrial Museum of Technology in Vienna, with Austrian Railway Museum and Post and Telegraph Museum*): A-1140 Vienna, Mariahilferstr. 212; f. 1907, opened 1918; has 30 depts. covering all branches of technical science and technology; research section opened in 1931; library of 40,000 vols.; Dir. Dipl. Ing. R. NIEDERHUEMER; publ. *Blätter für Technikgeschichte*† (annual).

Provinces

Botanischer Garten des Landes Kärnten (*Botanical Garden of Carinthia*): 9020 Klagenfurt, Kinkstrasse 6; f. 1865; cultivation of central and southern Alpine flora; school and adult education in nature preservation; cytological research; library of *c.* 200 vols.; Dirs. Dr. GERFRIED H. LEUTE, FRANZ ZEITLER.

Burgenländisches Landesmuseum (*Burgenland Provincial Museum*): 7000 Eisenstadt, Museumgasse 1-5; f. 1926; geology, history of art, archaeology, botany, zoology, ethnology; 25,000 vols.; Dir. Dr. A. J. OHRENBERGER; publ. *Wissenschaftlichen Arbeiten aus dem Burgenland*, catalogues.

Graphisches Kabinett Stift Göttweig (*Museum of Graphic Art of the Göttweig Foundation*): A-3511 Stift Göttweig, Post Furth; 21,000 items from the 16th century to the present day; library of *c.* 65,000 vols. (history, law, theology, history of art, sciences); 2,750 archives (1054–1900); Dir. Dr. GREGOR MARTIN LECHNER, O.S.B.; publ. catalogue to accompany annual exhibitions†.

Haus der Natur (*Natural History Museum*): Salzburg, Museumplatz 5; f 1924; 80 sections (zoology, botany, anthropology, hygiene, geology, palaeontology, biology); Dir. Prof. DDr. EDUARD PAUL TRATZ.

Hofburg (*Imperial Palace*): Innsbruck, Rennweg 1; imperial collection, including Giant's Hall and House Chapel; Dir. Dipl. Ing. F. PAMMER.

Krahnletz Museum: A-3730 Eggenburg, Krahnletzplatz; collection started in 1866; museum erected in 1901; 24 sections; geology, palaeontology, prehistory, ethnology; Pres. Dr. H. REINHART; Curator WERNER VASICEK; publ. *Katalogreihe des Krahnletz-Museums.*

Kunsthistorische Sammlungen (*Collections of Historical Art*): 6020 Innsbruck, Schloss Ambras; f. 1580; contains collections of armour, furniture, pictures and sculpture; Curator Dr. ELISABETH SCHEICHER.

Landesmuseum für Kärnten (*Provincial Museum of Carinthia*): A-9010 Klagenfurt, Museumgasse 2; f. 1844; divided into: (1) History; (2) Pre-historic, Roman and Early Christian antiquities; (3) History of Arts; (4) Natural History; (5) Numismatics; (6) Folk Arts and Crafts; special Alpine museum of models, panoramas and maps; Dir. Dr. G. PICCOTTINI; library of 80,000 vols.; Librarian Dr. J. HÖCK; publs. *Carinthia I* (history and folklore), *Carinthia II* (science), *Archiv für Vaterländische Geschichte und Topographie, Kärntner Museumsschriften, Buchreihe, Kärntner Heimatleben.*

Mozart Museum: Salzburg, Getreidegasse 9; birthplace of Wolfgang Amadeus Mozart; converted in 1880 into a museum containing souvenirs of the composer.

Mozarteum: 5020 Salzburg, Schwarzstrasse 26; f. 1914 by the international "Stiftung Mozarteum" and comprising an academy of music, concert rooms, a library of MSS., books and other Mozart memorabilia. (*See* also under Colleges.)

Museum Carnuntinum: Bad Deutsch Altenburg; f. 1904; Curator Dr. EDUARD VORBECK.

Museum für Ur- und Fruhgeschichte (*Museum for Prehistory*): 2262 Stillfried/March, Niederösterreich; f. 1914; archaeological and palaeontological finds from the Stillfried district; Dir. GERHARD ANTL; publ. *Museumsnachrichten* (3–4 a year).

Neue Galerie der Stadt Linz—Wolfgang Gurlitt Museum: 4040 Linz, Lentia 2000, Blütenstr.; f. 1947; museum and art gallery containing paintings and drawings of 19th and 20th centuries; library of art books including 8,000 catalogues; exhibitions of contemporary art; Dir. PETER BAUM.

Oberösterreichisches Landesmuseum (*Regional Museum for Upper Austria*): Linz, Museumstr. 14 and Tummelplatz 10 (Linzer Schloss); f. 1833; library of 90,000 vols.; Dir. Dr. HERMANN KOHI; publ. *Forschungen in Lauriacum.*

Salzburger Museum Carolino-Augusteum: A-5010 Salzburg, Museumsplatz 6, Postfach 525; f. 1834; Roman remains, prehistoric exhibits, art, coins, musical instruments, costumes, peasants' art; library of 60,000 vols. and archives; Dir. Dr. A. ROHRMOSER; publ. *Jahresschrift* (from 1955); Attached museums:

Burgmuseum (*Castle Museum*): Hohensalzburg; f. 1952; armoury, exhibits relating to judicature, furniture.

Spielzeugmuseum (*Museum of Toys*): Burgerspital; f. 1978.

Volkskundemuseum (*Museum of Folklore*): situated in park of Hellbrunn castle near Salzburg (Monatsschlösschen); f. 1924; rustic costumes and furniture, peasants' art.

Salzburger Residenz-Galerie: Salzburg, Residenzplatz 1; f. 1923; contains European paintings, 16th–20th centuries; Dir. Dr. FRANZ NAROBE.

Schloss Hellbrunn (*Hellbrunn Castle*): Salzburg; built 1613–19 and f. as museum by the municipality 1922; contains murals, furniture, folklore and period dwellings, German Baroque garden with mechanical water devices, deer park and open-air theatre.

Schlossmuseum Gobelsburg Österreichische Volkskunst (*Gobelsburg Castle Museum of Austrian Folk Art*): A-3551 bei Krems, Lower Austria; f. 1966; under direction of the *Österreichisches Museum für Volkskunde*; permanent exhibition of Austrian majolica and folk art, etc.; Dir. Pater BERTRAND BAUMANN.

Steiermärkisches Landesmuseum Joanneum (*Provincial Museum of Styria*): A-8010 Graz, Raubergasse 10/1; f. 1811; Dir. Dr. FRIEDRICH WAIDACHER; departments:

Abteilung für Geologie, Paläontologie und Bergbau (*Dept. of Geology, Palaeontology and Mining*): A-8010 Graz, Raubergasse 10; geological collection on history of mining in Styria; Chair. Univ.-Doz. Dr. WALTER GRÄF.

Abteilung für Mineralogie (*Dept. of Mineralogy*): A-8010 Graz, Raubergasse 10; Chair. Dr. ADOLF ALKER.

Abteilung für Botanik (*Botany Dept.*): 8010 Graz, Raubergasse 10; Chair. Dr. DETLEF ERNET.

Abteilung für Zoologie (*Zoology Dept.*): 8010 Graz, Raubergasse 10; Chair. Dr. ERICH KREISSL.

Abteilung für Vor- und Frühgeschichte und Münzensammlung (*Dept. of Pre- and Early History and Coin Collection*): A-8020 Graz, Eggenberger Allee 90; Chair. Dr. ERICH HUDECZEK.

Abteilung für Kunstgewerbe (*Applied Art Dept.*): A-8010 Graz, Neutorgasse 45; f. 1890; furniture, old carriages, period living-rooms; gold, silver and ironwork, ceramics and applied art, pictures and engravings; Chair. Dr. GERTRUD SMOLA.

Landeszeughaus (*Provincial Arsenal*): A-8010 Graz, Herrengasse 10; built 1642; collection of weapons, armour, cannon and firearms of the 16th and 17th centuries; Chair. Dr. PETER KRENN.

Alte Galerie (*Old Gallery*): A-8010 Graz, Neutorgasse 45; painting and sculpture of the Gothic Renaissance and the Baroque period up to 1800; also drawings and engravings of 15th-18th centuries; Chair. Dr. KURT WOISETSCHLÄGER.

Neue Galerie (*New Gallery*): A-8010 Graz, Sackstrasse 16; painting, drawing and sculpture of 19th and 20th centuries; Chair. Prof. DDr. WILFRIED SKREINER.

Steierisches Volkskundemuseum (*Styrian Museum of Folklore*): A-8010 Graz, Paulustorgasse 13; peasant houses and costume, development of agricultural implements, etc.; Chair. Dr. SEPP WALTER.

Jagdmuseum (*Hunting Museum*): A-8020 Graz, Eggenberger Allee 90; history of hunting in Austria; Chair. PHILIPP MERAN.

Schloss Eggenberg (*Eggenberg Castle*): A-8020 Graz, Eggenberger Allee 90; built in 1625; Chair. FRIEDRICH KRYZA-GERSCH.

Landschaftsmuseum Schloss Trautenfels (*Trautenfels Museum*): A-8951 Trautenfels im Ennstal; Chair. Dr. VOLKER HÄNSEL.

Bild- und Tonarchiv (*Picture and Sound Archives*): 8010 Graz, Sackstrasse 17; Chair. Dr. ARMGARD SCHIFFER.

Aussenstelle Stainz (*Stainz branch*): 8510 Stainz (Schloss); Styrian ethnographic collections; Chair. Dr. MARIA KUNDEGRABER.

Tiroler Landes-Museum Ferdinandeum (*Tyrolese Provincial Museum*): Innsbruck, Museumstr. 15; f. 1823; ancient and early history, art, coins, medals, etc.; 100,000 vols. in library; Dir. Dr. ERICH EGG; publ. *Museum Report*† (annually).

Tiroler Landeskundliches Museum: Innsbruck, Zeughausgasse; f. 1973; mineralogy, mining, manufacture, mapping, hunting, musical, technical, vehicles, locomotives, military; Pres. Prof. Dr. JOSEF LADURNER; Dir. Dr. ERICH EGG.

Tiroler Volkskunstmuseum (*Tyrolese Popular Art Museum*): A-6020 Innsbruck, Universitätsstrasse 2; f. 1888 and 1929; peasant interiors, costumes, domestic utensils, Tyrolese religious and secular peasant craft; Pres. Dr. FRITZ PRIOR; Dir. Dr. HANS GSCHNITZER.

Vorarlberger Landesmuseum (*Vorarlberg Provincial Museum*): Bregenz, Kornmarkt; f. 1857; collections showing the archaeology, art and folklore of the region; Dir. Univ. Prof. Dr. ELMAR VONBANK; publs. *Jahrbuch*†, *Schriften*.

UNIVERSITIES

(Following the University Organization Bill, implemented in 1973, all institutions of higher education now have university status.)

UNIVERSITÄT GRAZ
(Graz University)

8010 GRAZ,
UNIVERSITÄTSPLATZ 3

Telephone: 31-5-81.

Founded 1586.

State control; Academic year: October to September (two terms).

Rector: Dr. FRIEDRICH HAUSMANN.
Pro-Rector: Dr. KURT FREISITZER.
Chief Administrative Officer: HR.Dr. A. FETSCH.
Librarian: HR.Dr. F. KROLLER.

Library: *see under* Libraries.
Number of teachers: 1,245.
Number of students: 17,176.

DEANS:

Faculty of Catholic Theology: DDr. P. ASVELD.
Faculty of Law: Dr. G. WESENER.
Faculty of Business Administration and Economics: Dkfm. Dr. H.-P. LIEBMANN.
Faculty of Medicine: Dr. H. LECHNER.
Faculty of Liberal Arts: Dr. R. FLOTZINGER.
Faculty of Science: Dr. L. REICH.

PROFESSORS:

Faculty of Catholic Theology:

AMON, K., Ecclesiastical History
ASVELD, P., Philosophy and Fundamental Theology
BAUER, J., Oecumenical Theology
BRUCH, R., Moral Theology
GASTGEBER, K., Pastoral Theology
GRUBER, W., Dogmatics
HARNONCOURT, P., Liturgy
KOLB, A., Philosophy
KORHERR, E., Catechetics
MARBÖCK, J., Old Testament
SCHEDL, P. C., Bible Knowledge
SCHWENDENWEIN, H., Canon Law
ZEHRER, F., New Testament
ZSIFKOVITS, V., Christian Sociology

Faculty of Law:

BALTL, H., History of German and Austrian Law
BRÜNNER, CH., Public Law
FENYVES, A., Civil Law
FUNK, B. CH., Public Law
GINTHER, K., International Law
JELINEK, W., Civil Procedure, Private International Law, Agricultural Law
KRÄNZLEIN, A., Roman Law
KREJCI, H., Civil Law
MANTL, W., Political Science and Constitutional Law
NOVAK, R., Austrian Administrative Law
RUPPE, H. G., Financial Law
SCHICK, P., Criminal Law and Criminology
SCHILCHER, B., Private Law
SCHNIZER, H., Church Law
SCHWARZ, W., Labour Law
SEILER, R., Criminal Law and Criminology
STEININGER, V., Civil Law
SUTTER, B., European and Comparative History of Law
WEINBERGER, O., Philosophy of Law
WESENER, G., Roman Law
WÜNSCH, H., Commercial Law

Faculty of Business Administration and Economics:

ACHAM, K., Sociology
BEINSEN, L., Political Economy
EGGER, A., Management
FREISITZER, K., Sociology
HÜLSMANN, J., Statistics, Econometry and Operations Research
KRAUS, H., Organization and Industrial Data Processing
LECHNER, K., Industrial Economics
LIEBMANN, H. P., Marketing
MANDL, G., Business, Methodology of Economics
SCHLEICHER, ST., Political Economy
SCHÖPFER, G., Economic and Social History
SEIDL, C., Finance and Public Economy
SWOBODA, P., Industrial Economics
TICHY, G., Political Economy

Faculty of Medicine:

BURGHARDT, E., Midwifery and Gynaecology
BURKL, W., Histology and Embryology
HADORN, B., Paediatrics
HEPPNER, H., Neurosurgery
HOFMANN, H., Ophthalmology
HOLASEK, A., Physiological Chemistry
KENNER, T., Physiology
KLINGENBERG, H., Functional Pathology
KÖLE, H., Dental Medicine
KRAFT-KINZ, J., Surgery
KRESBACH, H., Venereal and Skin Diseases
LECHNER, H., Psychiatry and Neurology
LEMBECK, F., Pharmacology
LIST, W., Anaesthesiology
MARESCH, W., Forensic Medicine
MESSERKLINGER, W., Oto-Rhino-Laryngology
MÖSE, J., Hygiene
RATZENHOFER, M., Pathological Anatomy
ROSENKRANZ, W., Medical Biology and Human Genetics
SAILER, S., Internal Medicine
SAUER, H., Paediatric Surgery
THIEL, W., Anatomy
TRITTHART, H., Medical Physics
VOGLER, E., Radiology

Faculty of Liberal Arts:

BERNHARD, G., Physical Training
BLÖSCHL, L., Pedagogics
DENISON, N., General and Applied Linguistics
DIEZ, E., Archaeology of Art
DÖNT, E., Classical Philology
FILL, A., English Philology
FLOTZINGER, R., Music
FRANZ, G., History of Art
FREUNDLICH, R., Philosophy
HAFNER, S., Slavonic Philology
HALLER, R., Research Foundation
HAUPTMANN, F., South-East European History
HAUSMANN, F., Medieval History
HIMMEL, H., German Philology
HUTTERER, CL., German Philology
JAKSCHE, H., Slavonic Philology
KRACHER, A., German Philology
KREMERS, D., Romance Philology
LIND, G. R., Romance Philology
MITTELBERGER, H., Translation, Interpretation and Comparative Philology
MOSER, O., Folklore
PEPER, J., American Studies
PICKL, O., Economic and Social History
RIEHLE, W., English Philology
SEEL, H., Pedagogics
SIMON, H., Romance Philology
STANZEL, F., English Philology
TOPITSCH, E., Philosophy
WALTER-KLINGENSTEIN, G., Modern History
WEILER, J. Pre-History
WIESFLECKER, H., Austrian History

Faculty of Science:

BAUMANN, K., Theoretical Physics
FIEBER, H., Mathematics
FLOR, P., Mathematics
FLÜGEL, H., Geology and Palaeontology
HÄRTEL, O., Plant Anatomy and Physiology
HAUPT, H., Astronomy
HERAN, H., Zoology
HERITSCH, H., Mineralogy and Petrography
HUBER, H., Psychology
JANOSCHEK, R., Theoretical Chemistry
KAPPEL, F. Mathematics
KARTNIG, TH., Pharmacognosy
KUKOVETZ, W., Pharmacology and Toxicology

LEITNER, W., Geography
MITTENECKER, E., Psychology
MITTER, H., Physics
NACHBAUR, E., Inorganic and Analytical Chemistry
PASCHINGER, H., Geography
POELT, J., Botany
POROD, G., Experimental Physics
REICH, L., Mathematics
SCHAUENSTEIN, E., Biochemistry
SCHURZ, J., Physical Chemistry
SCHUSTER, R., Zoology
ZIGEUNER, G., Pharmaceutical Chemistry

LEOPOLD-FRANZENS UNIVERSITÄT INNSBRUCK (Innsbruck University)

6020 INNSBRUCK, UNIVERSITÄTSSTRASSE 2-6, and INNRAIN 52

Telephone: 33601.

Founded 1669.

Rector: Prof. Dr. HERBERT BRAUNSTEINER.
Pro-Rector: Prof. Dr. FRANZ FLIRI.
Chief Administrative Officer: Mag. ALBERT PITTRACHER.
Librarian: Dr. OSWALD STRANZINGER.

Library: *see* Libraries.

Number of teachers: *c.* 360.
Number of students: 13,000.

Publications: *Nachrichtenblatt, Vorlesungsverzeichnis.*

DEANS:

Faculty of Theology: Prof. Dr. H. B. MEYER.
Faculty of Law: Prof. Dr. P. PERNTHALER.
Faculty of Social and Economic Science: Prof. Dr. CH. SMEKAL.
Faculty of Medicine: Prof. Dr. K. KRYSPIN-EXNER.
Faculty of Arts: Prof. Dr. A. MASSER.
Faculty of Science: Prof. Dr. W. WIESER.
Faculty of Construction Engineering and Architecture: Prof. Arch. Dipl.-Ing. R. HENSCHKER.

PROFESSORS:

Faculty of Theology:
CORETH, E., Christian Philosophy
DARLAP, A., Church History
GAMPER, A., Old Testament Theology
KEHL, N., New Testament Studies
KERN, W., Fundamental Theology
MEYER, H. B., Liturgy
MUCK, O., Christian Philosophy
MÜHLSTEIGER, J., Church Law
RICHTER, V., Christian Philosophy
ROTTER, H., Moral Theology
SBANDI, P., Pastoral Psychology
SCHWAGER, R., Dogmatics
STENGER, H., Pastoral Psychology
STOCK, K., Biblical Theology
VASS, G., Dogmatics

Faculty of Law:
BERTEL, C., Austrian Penal Law and Criminology
EBERT, K., History of German Law and Economy
FAISTENBERGER, C., Austrian Civil Law
GRASS, N., German Law
HORAK, F., Roman Law
KIPP, H. G., Common Law and Philosophy of Law
KLECATSKY, H., Political Science and Austrian Constitutional Law, Administration Theory and Law
LEISCHING, P., Church Law
MAYRHOFER, H., Civil Law
NOWAKOWSKI, F., Austrian Penal Law and Criminology
PERNTHALER, P., Constitutional and Administrative Law
RABER, F., Roman Law
REICHERT-FACILIDES, F., Foreign Law and Austrian Private Law
ROTH, G. H. Commercial Law
SCHNORR, G., Industrial and Social Law
SPRUNG, R., Austrian Civil Court Procedure
WIMMER, N., Austrian Constitutional Law

Faculty of Social and Economic Science:
ANDREAE, C.-A., Political Economy
BRATSCHITSCH, R., Industrial Economics
HINTERHUBER, H., Industrial Economics
HOLUB, H. W., Political Economy
KAUFER, E., National Economy
LEXA, H., Industrial Economics
MARINELL, G., Statistics
MARZEN, W., Industrial Economics
MOREL, J., Sociology
PELINKA, A., Political Science
SMEKAL, C., Financial Science
SOCHER, K., Political Economy

Faculty of Medicine:
AMBACH, W., Medical Physics
BAUER, R., Orthopaedics
BENGER, J., Hygiene
BERGER, H., Paediatrics
BODNER, E., Surgery
BRAUNSTEINER, H., Internal Medicine
DAPUNT, O., Gynaecology and Obstetrics
DEETJEN, P., Physiology
GAUSCH, K., Dental Medicine
GERSTENBRAND, F., Neurology
GRUNICKE, H., Medical Chemistry
GSCHNITZER, F., Surgery
HAID, B., Anaesthetics
HEINZ, K., Ophthalmology
HENN, R., Forensic Medicine
KONZETT, H., Pharmacology and Toxicology
KRYSPIN-EXNER, K., Psychiatry
MARBERGER, H., Urinology
OLBRICH, E., Biostatistics
PIRKER, E., Radiology
PLATZER, WERNER, Anatomy
PROPST, A., Pathological Anatomy
RICCABONA, G., Nuclear Medicine
RUSSE, O., Accident Surgery
SACHSENMAIER, W., Biochemistry
SCHLORHAUFER, W., Audiology and Phoniatrics
SCHMIDT, W., Histology and Embryology
SCHRÖCKSNADEL, H., Medical Biology
SPOENDLIN, H., Otolaryngology
WICK, G., General and Experimental Pathology
WILFLINGSEDER, P., Plastic and Restorative Surgery
WINKLER, H., Biochemical Pharmacology
WOLFF, K., Skin and Venereal Diseases

Faculty of Arts:
DOPPLER, A., History of Austrian Literature
FETZ, F., Physical Education
FREY, G., Philosophy and Epistemology
HAGENEDER, O., Medieval History
HAMPL, F., Ancient History
HÄNDEL, P., Classical Philology
ILG, K., Folklore
KONSTANTINOVIC, Z., Comparative Literature
KROMER, K., Prehistory and Early History
KRÖMER, W., Romance Philology
KÜHNELT, H. H., English Language and Literature
MASSER, A., Old German Literature
MEID, W., Comparative Linguistics
MUTH, R., Classical Philology and Archaeology
NEUTSCH, B., Classical Archaeology
OBERHUBER, K., Oriental Languages and Cultures
PLANGG, G., Romance Philology
RAINER, J., Austrian History
RÖD, W., Philosophy
SALMEN, W., Music
SCHEER, B., Modern English and American Literature
SCHELESNIKER, H., Slavonic Studies
STRNAD, A., Modern History
THURNHER, E., Modern German Language and Literature
WEISS, R., Pedagogics

Faculty of Science:
ALBRECHT, R., Numerical Mathematics
BOBLETER, O., Radio-chemistry
BOLLE, J. H., Meteorology and Geophysics
CAP, F., Theoretical Physics
ENGELBRECHT, A., Inorganic and Analytical Chemistry
FLIRI, F., Geography
GORNIK, E., Physics
GRUBER, J., Physical Chemistry
HOHENLOHE-ÖHRINGEN, K., Organic and Pharmaceutical Chemistry
JANETSCHEK, H., Zoology
KLEBELSBERG, D., Psychology
KLÖTZER, W., Organic and Pharmaceutical Chemistry
KOHLER, I., Psychology
KOLB, J., Experimental Physics
KUHNERT, MARIA, Pharmacognosy
LARCHER, W., Botany
LEIDLMAIR, ADOLF, Geography
LIEDL, R., Mathematics
LOOS, O., Mathematics
MOSER, MEINHARD, Microbiology
OBERST, U., Mathematics
PFLEIDERER, J., Astronomy
PICHLER, H., Theoretical Meteorology
PITSCHMAN, H., Systematic and Geographical Botany
ROTHLEITNER, J., Theoretical Physics
SCHWARZHANS, K. E., Inorganic and Analytical Chemistry
SCHWEIGER, M., Biochemistry
WIESER, W., Zoological Physiology

Faculty of Construction Engineering and Architecture:
BARTH, O., Architectural Design
BLÜMEL, O., Chemistry and Technology of Building Materials
BRANDSTAETTER, F., Physics
CICHOCKI, F., Steel and Wood Construction
DAUM, J., Construction Engineering
EMBACHER, W., Surveying
HEIGL, F., Town Planning
HELMBERG, G., Mathematics
HENSCHKER, R. Construction Engineering
INGERLE, K., Domestic and Industrial Sanitation
KOPP, E., Railway Construction and Transport System
KREMSER, H., Mathematics
LESSMANN, H., Building Planning and Estimating
MAJER, J., Mechanics II
MOSER, K., Construction Statistics

RUDELSTORFER, K., Road Construction and Traffic Planning
SCHOBER, W., Foundation Engineering
SEEBER, G., Hydraulics
TSCHUPIK, J., Geometry
WEINLICH, R., Construction and Design of Tall Buildings
WICKE, M., Reinforced Concrete Construction

AFFILIATED INSTITUTE:

Alpine Forschungsstelle der Universität Innsbruck in Obergurgl (*Alpine Research Department of the University of Innsbruck in Obergurgl*): A-6020 Innsbruck, Universitätsstr. 4; f. 1951.

UNIVERSITÄT FÜR BILDUNGSWISSENSCHAFTEN KLAGENFURT

A 9020 KLAGENFURT,
UNIVERSITÄTSSTRASSE 65
Telephone: 04222/23-7-30.
Founded 1970.
Academic year: October to February, March to June.

Rector: Prof. Dr. GÜNTHER HÖDL.
Vice-Rector: Prof. Dr. JOSEF KLINGLER.
Chief Administrative Officer: ADOLF RANNACHER.
Librarian: Dr. ERNST BENISCHKE.

Number of teachers: 46.
Number of students: *c.* 1,500.
Publication: *Verzeichnis der Lehrveranstaltungen und Personalstand* (catalogue, 2 a year).

PROFESSORS:

ARNOLD, UWE, Philosophy
ASPETSBERGER, FRIEDBERT, German Philology
BACKÉ, BRUNO, Geography
BERGER, ALBERT, German Philology
BODENHÖFER, HANS-JOACHIM, Development Economics
BRANDSTETTER, ALOIS, German Philology
DÖRFLER, WILLIBALD, Mathematics
FISCHER, ROLAND, Mathematics
HEINTEL, PETER, Philosophy and Group Dynamics
HÖDL, GÜNTHER, Medieval History and Studies Related to History
KELLERMANN, PAUL, Development Sociology
KLINGER, JOSEF, Educational Theory
KUNA, FRANZ MATTHÄUS, English and American Studies
LÖSCHENKOHL, ERICH, Psychology and Developmental Psychology
MAYERTHALER, WILHELM, General and Applied Philology
MELEZINEK, ADOLF, Teaching Methods
MÜLLER, WINIFRIED, Mathematics
NEMSER, WILLIAM, English and American Studies
NEUHÄUSER, RUDOLF, Slavic Studies
NEWEKLOWSKY, GERHARD, Slavic Studies
POHL, HEINZ-DIETER, General Philology
POSCH, PETER, Curriculum Studies
RUMPLER, HELMUT, Modern and Austrian History
SCHAUSBERGER, NORBERT, Modern Austrian History
SCHÖLER, WALTER, Education
SCHULZ-BUSCHHAUS, ULRICH, Romance Studies
SEGER, MARTIN, Geography
STETTNER, HARO, Mathematics
TROTSENBURG, EDMUND ADOLF VAN, Education
VERNAY, HENRI, Romance Studies and General and Applied Philology
VÖLKL, FRANZ, Educational Psychology

UNIVERSITÄT SALZBURG
(Salzburg University)

5020 SALZBURG,
RESIDENZPLATZ 1
Telephone: 44-5-11

Founded 1622; closed 1810; College 1810–50, independent faculty of Catholic Theology 1850–1962; reconstituted 1962.

State control; Academic year: October to end of June.

Rector: Prof. DDr. WOLFGANG BEILNER.
Pro-Rector: Prof. Dr. WILHELM J. REVERS.
Director: Dr. RAIMUND SPRUZINA.
Librarian: Dr. KARL FORSTNER.

Library: *see under* Libraries.
Number of teachers: *c.* 750.
Number of students: *c.* 7,900.
Publications: *Year Book*†, *University Prospectuses*†.

DEANS:

Faculty of Catholic Theology: Prof. Dr. FRANZ SCHMÖLZ.
Faculty of Law: Prof. Dr. HEINZ SCHÄFFER.
Faculty of Arts: Prof. Dr. MICHAEL SCHMOLKE.
Faculty of Natural Science: Prof. Dr. PETER ZINTERHOF.

PROFESSORS:

Faculty of Catholic Theology:
BEILNER, W., New Testament Studies
BERNHARD, L., Ecumenical Theology
FÜGLISTER, N., Old Testament Studies
GRIESL, G., Pastoral Theology
HERMANN, F., Ecclesiastical History
HOLBÖCK, F., Dogmatics
KÖHLER, W., Christian Philosophy and Psychology
LÄPPLE, A., Catechetics and Religious Education
NEIDL, W., Christian Philosophy
NIKOLASCH, F., Liturgy
PAUS, A., Epistemology and Religious Studies
REHRL, S., Moral Theology
SCHMÖLZ, F., Political Theory

Faculty of Law:
BUSCHMANN, A., German Legal History, German Private and Civil Law
EVERS, H.-U., Public Law
FLORETTA. H., Labour and Social Law
HAGEN, J., Sociology of Law
HARRER, G., Forensic Psychiatry
HONSELL, H., Roman Law and Civil Law
KOJA, F., Public Law
KOPPENSTEINER, H.-G., Civil, Commercial and Economic Law
KYRER, A., Economics
MATSCHER, F., Law of Civil Procedure
MAYER-MALY, T., German and Austrian Civil Law and Roman Law
MIEHSLER, H., International Law and Foreign Public Law
MIGSCH, E., Civil Law
OSTHEIM, R., Commercial Law and Civil Law
POTOTSCHNIG, F., Canon Law
PÜTZ-NEUHAUSER, G., Economics
RINGHOFER, K., Public Law
SCHÄFFER, H., Public Law
SCHWIMANN, M., International Civil Law
TAMMELO, I., Austrian Constitutional Law and Legal Philosophy
TRIFFTERER, O., Austrian and International Criminal Law
WALDSTEIN W., Roman Law
WÖLKART, N., Forensic Medicine
ZIPF, H., Criminal Law

Faculty of Arts:
BAEHR, R., Romance Languages
CROLL, G., Musicology
DALFEN, J., Classical Philosophy
DRACHMAN, G., Linguistics
FAUPEL, K., Politics
FELLNER, F., Modern History
FUHRMANN, F., History of Austrian Art
GÖNNER, R., Pedagogics
HASLINGER, A., History of Austrian Literature
KOLLER, H., Medieval History
MAYER, G., Slavic Languages
MESSERER, G., History of Art, Medieval and Modern
MORSCHER, E., Philosophy
MÜLLER, U., Old German Literature
NIEDERMANN, E., Physical Training
PANAGL, O., Linguistics
PFLIGERSDORFFER, G., Classical Philology
RASSEM, M., Sociology
REIFFENSTEIN, I., German Language and Literature
SCHMIDINGER, H., Medieval History
SCHMOLKE, M., Journalism and Communications
STÜRZL, E., English Language and Literature
TRUCHLAR, L., English and American Philology
VÖLKL, K., Ancient History
WAGNER, H., Austrian History
WALTER, H., Archaeology
WANDRUSZKA, M., Romance Philology
WEINGARTNER, P., Philosophy
WEISS, W., German Language and Literature
WYSOCKI, J., Economic and Social History
ZAIC, F., English Language and Literature.

Faculty of Natural Sciences:
ADAM, H., Zoology
CZIHAK, G., Biology
FLORIAN, A., Mathematics
FRASL, G., Geology
GERL, P., Mathematics
HEUBERGER, H., Geography
KIERMAYER, O., Botany
POHL, E., Physics
REVERS, W., Psychology
RIEDL, H., Geography
ROTH, E., Psychology
SCHWEIGER, F., Mathematics
STRACK, H. -B., Biochemistry
WAGNER, H., Botany
WERNER, H., Science Teaching
ZINTERHOF, P., Mathematics

UNIVERSITÄT WIEN
(Vienna University)

1010 VIENNA,
DR. KARL LUEGER-RING 1
Telephone: 0222-43-00.
Founded 1365.

Rector: Prof. Dr. WINFRIED PLATZGUMMER.

Pro-Rector: Prof. Dr. RICHARD PLASCHKA.

Administrative Officer: Dipl. Ing. Dr. F. SKACEL.

Librarian: Hofrat Dr. F. RENNHOFER.

Archivist: Prof. Dr. F. GALL.

Library: *see under* Libraries.

Number of teachers: 2,406.

Number of students: 43,078.

DEANS:

Faculty of Catholic Theology: Prof. Dr. G. GRESHAKE.

Faculty of Protestant Theology: Prof. Dr. K. LÜTHI.

Faculty of Law and Political Science: Prof. DDr. R. HOKE.

Faculty of Social Sciences and Economics: Prof. Dr. DDr. W. WEBER.

Faculty of Medicine: Prof. Dr. W. AUERSWALD.

Faculty of Philosophy: Prof. Dr. L. PROKOP.

Faculty of Humanities: Prof. Dr. H. SCHWABEL.

Faculty of Natural Sciences: Prof. Dr. K. LINTNER.

PROFESSORS:

Faculty of Catholic Theology:

DORDETT, A., Canon Law
EMMINGHAUS, J., Sacramental Theology and Liturgy
GRESHAKE, G., Dogmatics
HÖRMANN, K., Moral Theology
KORNFELD, W., Old Testament and Biblical-Oriental Languages
KREMER, J., New Testament
LANGER, W., Religious Education
LENZENWEGER, J., Ecclesiastical History
MÜLLER, J., Religious Education
REIKERSDORFER, J., Fundamental Theology.
SCHULTE, R., O.S.B., Dogmatics
SUTTNER, E., Patrology and Eastern Churches
VORBICHLER, P. A., Divinity
WEILER, R., Ethics and Social Sciences
WUCHERER, K. A., Christian Philosophy and Mysticism

Faculty of Protestant Theology:

DANTINE, W., Systematic Theology
LÜTHI, K., Systematic Theology
NIEDERWIMMER, K., New Testament
RADDATZ, A., Ecclesiastical History, Christian Archaeology and Sacred Art
SAUER, G., Old Testament and Biblical Archaeology
SCHMIDT-LAUBER, H. CH., Practical Theology
STEIN, A., Canon Law

Faculty of Law and Political Science:

BURGSTALLER, M., Criminal Law and Criminology
BYDLINSKI, F., Civil Law
ERMACORA, F., Theory of the State and Austrian Constitutional Law, Administration and Austrian Administration Law
FASCHING, H. W., Civil Procedure
FROTZ, G., Commercial Law, Negotiable Instruments Law
HAUSMANINGER, H., Roman Law
HOKE, R., German Law, Austrian Constitutional and Administrative Law
KOZIOL, H., Civil Law
KRALIK, W., Civil Procedure
LEITMAIER, C., Canon Law
MELICHAR, E., Theory of the State and Austrian Constitutional Law, Administration and Austrian Administration Law
OGRIS, W., German Law and Austrian Constitutional and Administrative History
ÖHLINGER, T., Civil Law
PLATZGUMMER, W., Criminal Law
SCHÖNHERR, F., Commercial Law and Negotiable Instruments Law
SCHWIND, F. Civil Law and International Private Law
SELB, W., Roman Law and History of Ancient Law
STOLL, G., Austrian Financial Law
TOMANDL, T., Labour Law and Social Law
VEROSTA, S., International Law, Philosophy of Law
WALTER, R., Public Law
WELSER, R., Civil Law
WENGER, K., Public Law
WINKLER, G., Austrian State Law
ZEMANEK, K., International Law and Organizations

Faculty of Social Sciences and Economics:

BRUCKMANN, G., Statistics
GERLICH, P., Political Science
LOITLSBERGER, E., Business Administration
NUSSBAUMER, A., Economics (Economic Theory and Economic Policy)
OROSEL, G., Economics
REICHARDT, R., Sociology and Social Philosophy
ROSENMAYR, L., Social Philosophy and Sociology
SCHMETTERER, L., Statistics
STREISSLER, E., Economics, Econometrics and Economic History
VINEK, G., Statistics
WEBER, W., Political Economy and Finance
WINCKLER, G., Economics

Faculty of Medicine:

AUERSWALD, W., Physiology
BECKER, H. J., Biology
BERNER, E. P., Psychiatry
BURIAN, K., Oto-rhino-laryngology
CHIARI, K., Orthopaedics
DEUTSCH-KEMPNY, E., Internal Medicine
FERNER, H., Anatomy
FLAMM, H., Hygiene
FRITSCH, A., Surgery
GABL, F., Clinical Chemistry and Laboratory Diagnosis
GEYER, G., Internal Medicine
GISEL, A., Applied Anatomy
GITSCH, E., Gynaecology and Obstetrics
GRABNER, G., Medical Computer Science
HAIDER, M., Environmental Hygiene
HOLCZABEK, W., Corrective Medicine
HOLZNER, J. J., Pathological Anatomy
HORNYKIEWICZ, O., Biochemical Pharmacology
HRUBY, K., Ophthalmology
JANISCH, H., Gynaecology and Obstetrics
JANTSCH, H., Physical Medicine
KAINDL, F., Cardiology
KAISER, E., Medical Chemistry
KÄRCHER, K. H., Radiology
KERESZTESI, K., Dental Medicine
KOOS, W., Neurosurgery
KRAUPP, O., Pharmacology
KRAUSE, W., Topographic Anatomy
KUNZ, C., Virology
LACHNIT, V., Occupational Medicine
LINDNER, A., General and Experimental Pathology
MAYRHOFER-KRAMMEL, O., Anaesthesiology
NAVRATIL, J., Surgery
NIEBAUER, G., Dermatology
NOVOTNY, O., Oto-rhino-laryngology
PETSCHE, H., Neurophysiology
PSENNER, L., Diagnostic Radiology
REISNER, H., Clinical Neurology
RUMMELHARDT, J., Urology
SCHEDLING, J., Medical Physics
SCHWARZACHER, H. G., Histology and Embryology
SEITELBERGER, F., Neurology
SLEZAK, H., Ophthalmology
SPÄNGLER, H., Accident Surgery
SPEISER, P., Blood Group Serology
SPIEL, W., Child and Juvenile Neuropsychiatry
SPITZY, K. H., Chemotherapy
STEFFEN, C., Immunology
STOCKINGER, L., Micromorphology and Electron Microscopy
STROTZKA, H., Psychology
STUMPF, C., Neuropharmacology
TAPPEINER, J., Dermatology and Syphilology
TRAPPL, R., Medical Cybernetics
TROJAN, E., Accident Surgery
TUPPY, H., Biochemistry
WEWALKA, F., Gastroenterology and Hepatology
WIEDERMANN, G., Specific Prophylaxis and Tropical Medicine
WINTERSBERGER, E., Medical Chemistry
WOHLZOGEN, F. X., Medical Statistics
WUNDERER, S., Maxillary Surgery
ZWEYMÜLLER, E., Paediatrics

Faculty of Philosophy:

ARNBERGER, E., Geography with special regard to cartography
BENEDIKT, M., Philosophy
BODZENTA, E., Sociology
DIETRICH, M., Theatre Arts
DOSTAL, W., Ethnology
FINK, J., Geography
FISCHER, G., Psychological Methodology and Mathematical Psychology
GUTTMANN, G., Experimental and Applied Psychology
HEINTEL, E., Philosophy
HEITGER, M., Theoretical Pedagogy
LICHTENBERGER, E., Geography
MADER, J., Philosophy (with special regard to its history)
OESER, E., Philosophy (Theory of Science—Exact Science)
OLECHOWSKI, R., Pedagogics
PAUPIÉ, K., Journalism
PROKOP, L., Physiology of Physical Education
ROLLET, B., Educational Psychology
SCHNEIDER, H., Philosophy of Politics and Ideological Criticism
SOBOTKA, R., Physical Education
STIGLBAUER, K., Geography
TROGER, E., Regional and General Geography
ULMER, K., Philosophy
WOLF, K., Pedagogics
ZDARZIL, H., Adult and Extra-Mura Education

Faculty of Humanities:

AMBROS, A. A., Arabic and Islamic Studies
APPELT, H., Medieval History and complimentary subjects to the study of history
ARNOLD, D., Egyptian Studies
BAUER, G., English and American Language and Literature

BIRKHAN, H., Old and Middle High German Language and Literature
DOBESCH, G., Roman History, Antiquities and Epigraphy
DRESSLER, W., General and Applied Linguistics
FELGENHAUER, F., Pre-History of Man
FICHTENAU, H., Medieval History and complimentary subjects to the study of history
FILLITZ, H., Art History
FOLTINEK, H., English and American Language and Literature
FÖDERMAYR, F.,Comparative Musicology
FRIESINGER, H., Prehistory
GAAL, K., Ethnology
GÖBL, R., Ancient Numismatics and Pre-Mohammedan History of the Middle East
HAMANN, G., Modern History
HEINZ, G., Art History
HINTERHÄAUSER, H., Romance Philology with special regard to Hispanic Studies
HIRSCH, H., Old Semitic Philology and Oriental Archaeology
HUNGER, H., Byzantine Studies
HÜTTL-FOLTER, G., Russian Studies
KANDUTH, E., Romance Philology
KATAČIĆ, R., Slavic Philology
KENNER, H., Classical Archaeology
KIRSTEN, E., Greek History, Classical Studies and Epigraphy
KNITTLER, H., Economic and Social History
KORNINGER, S., English Language and Literature
LADSTÄTTER, O., Sinology
LEITSCH, W., East European History
LINHART, S., Japanese Studies
LUTZ, H., Modern History
MARES, F. W., Slavic Philology
MAYRHOFER, M., General and Indo-European Linguistics
MITTERAUER, M., Social History
MUKAROUSKY, H., African Studies
OBERHAMMER, G., Indology
PLASCHKA, R., East European History with special regard to Western and Eastern Slavs
POLLAK, W., Romance Philology
PRIMMER, A., Classical Philology
REDEI, K., Finno-Ugric studies
RÖMER, F., Classical Philology
SCHMIDT, G., History of Medieval and Modern Art
SCHUBERT, K., Judaic Studies
SCHWABL, H., Classical Philology
SOLTA, G. R., Indo-European Linguistics
STEINKELLNER, E., Buddhism and Tibetology
STOURZH, G., Modern History
TIETZE, A., Turkish and Islamic Studies
VETTERS, H., Classical Archaeology
WAGNER, R., History of Austrian Art
WANDRUSZKA, A., Austrian History
WEINZIERL, E., Modern History
WELZIG, W., History of Modern German Literature
WESSELY, O., Musicology
WIESINGER, P., German Language and Early German Literature
WOLFRAM, H., Medieval History and complimentary subjects to the study of history
WYTRZENS, G., Slavic Philology
ZACHARASIEWICZ, W., English and American Language and Literature
ZEMAN, H., Modern German Literature
ZÖLLNER, E., Austrian History with special regard to modern times and other auxiliary sciences

Faculty of Natural Sciences:

BARTL, A., Theoretical Physics
BRODA, E., Applied Physical Chemistry and Radiochemistry
BURIAN, K., Plant Anatomy and Physiology
CEHAK, K., General Meteorology
CHRISTIAN, C., Logistics
CIGLER, J., Mathematics
EHRENDORFER, F., Botany
EXNER, C. Geology
GETOFF, N., Radiation Chemistry and Photochemistry
GROSZER, S., Mathematics
GUTDEUTSCH, R., Geophysics
HEISTRACHER, P., Pharmacodynamics and Toxicology
HEJTMANEK, J., Mathematics
HIGATSBERGER, J., Experimental Physics
HLAWKA, E., Mathematics
HOFFMANN-OSTENHOF, O., Biochemistry
HUBER, J. F., Analytical Chemistry
JENTZSCH, K., Pharmacognosy
KAINZ, G., Special Analytical Chemistry
KINZEL, H., Chemical Plant Physiology
KLAUS, W., Paleobotany and Palynology
KOMAREK, K., Inorganic Chemistry
KRATZL, K., General and Organic Chemistry with special regard to Biology
LINTNER, K., Physics
LÖFFLER, H., Zoology (Limnology)
NECKEL, A., Physical Chemistry
OLAJ, O., Chemical Physics
PAPP, A., Micropaleontology
PIETSCHMANN, H., Theoretical Physics
PREINING, O., Experimental Physics
REITER, H., Mathematics
REUTER, H., Theoretical Meteorology
RICHTER, W., Mineralogy and Petrography
RIEDL, R. Zoology (Biology of Marine Animals)
SCHALLER, F., Zoology
SCHINDLER, H., Plant Anatomy and Physiology
SCHLÖGL, K., Organic Chemistry
SCHÖCK, G., Physics
SCHÖNFELD, T., Special Inorganic Chemistry
SCHUSTER, P., Theoretical Organic Chemistry
SEEGER, I., Applied Physics
SEXL, R., Theoretical Physics
SIGMUND, K., Mathematics
STANGLER, F., Experimental Physics (Low-Temperature Physics)
STICKLER, R., Physical Chemistry
THENIUS, E., Paleontology and Paleobiology
THIRRING, W., Theoretical Physics
TOLLMANN, A., Geology
VOGEL, ST., Systematic Botany
VONACH, H., Physics with special regard to radium research and nuclear physics
WARHANEK, H., Experimental Physics
WEINZIERL, P., Physics
WENDELBERGER, G., Plant Sociology and Vegetation
WOESS, E., Botany (Cytology and Genetics)
ZBIRAL, E., Food Chemistry and Organic Chemistry
ZAPFE, H., Paleontology
ZEMANN, J., Mineralogy

TECHNISCHE UNIVERSITÄT GRAZ
(Graz Technical University)

8010 GRAZ,
RECHBAUERSTRASSE 12
Telephone: 0316/77-5-11.
Founded 1811.

Rector: Prof. Arch. Dipl. Ing. WERNER HOLLOMEY.

Pro-Rector: Prof. Dr. LUDWIG BREITENHUBER.

Chief Administrative Officer: H. P. PAULA.

Librarian: Dr. K. F. STOCK.

Library: *see* Libraries.
Number of teachers: 490.
Number of students: 4,600.

DEANS:

Faculty of Architecture: Prof. Dipl. Ing. Dr. techn. HARALD EGGER.
Faculty of Constructional Engineering: Prof. Dipl. Ing. Dr. techn. FRITZ BAUER.
Faculty of Mechanical Engineering: Prof. Dipl. Ing. Dr. techn. RUDOLPH PISCHINGER.
Faculty of Electrical Engineering: Prof. Dipl. Ing. Dr. techn. ALFRED LESCHANZ.
Faculty of Natural Sciences: Prof. Dr. phil. FRIEDRICH PALTAUF.

PROFESSORS:

AICHHOLZER, G., Electrical Engineering
BAUER, F., Ferro-concrete Construction
BAUER, K., Haulage and Machine Design
BAUER, K. W., Mathematics
BERGMANN, H., Hydromechanics, Hydraulics and Hydrology
BRANDL, H., Soil and Rock Engineering
BREITENHUBER, L., Nuclear Physics
BREITLING, P., Building and Town Planning
DIETER, U., Mathematical Statistics
DIMITRIOU, S., History of Art
DOMIATY, R., Mathematics III
EGGER, H., Elevations and Planes
FLORIAN, H., Applied Mathematics
FRITZSCHE, W., High Frequency Technique and Electronics
GILLI, P. V., Steam Engines
GINELLI, A., Construction and Design
GRETLER, W., Theory of Mechanical Engineering
HABERFELLNER, R., Management
HAHN, W., Mathematics
HENGGE, E., Inorganic Chemistry
HOKE, G., Design
HÖLLER, H., Technical Petrography and Mineralogy
HOLLOMEY, W., Building and Design
HUBENY, K., Geodesy
HUMMEL, K., Organic Chemistry
JÄGER, H., Experimental Physics
JERICHA, H., Thermal Turbo-machinery
JUD, W., Machine Principles
KLEMENT, P., Building Statics
KLOSE, J., Interior Decorations and Design
KLUGAR, K., Transport Technology
KÖSTENBERGER, H., Roadbuilding and Road Transport
KORDESCH, K. V., Inorganic Chemical Technology
LAFFERTY, R., Biochemical Technology
LEDINEGG, E., Theoretical Physics
LESCHANZ, A., High-voltage techniques
MAURER, H., Information Processing
MEISSL, P., Mathematics and Numerical Geodesy
MORITZ, H., Geodesy
MOSER, F., Methodology
MUCKENHUBER, R., Construction and Operation of Electrical Systems
NEMECEK, E., Hydraulics, Agricultural and Industrial Water Construction
PALTAUF, F., Biochemistry

PISCHINGER, R., Thermodynamics
POVSE, T., Study of Raw Materials and Welding Technology
REISCHL, F., Constructional Engineering
RESINGER, F., Timberwork and Elevation
RICHTER, K., Electrical Engineering
RIEDLER, W., Information Methodology and Wave Propagation
RINNER, K., Geodesy
SCHNEIDER, G., Control Techniques
SCHUY, S., Electro- and Biomedical Technology
SIMMLER, H., Water Supply and Structural Water Construction
STARK, H., Pulp, Paper and Fibre Technology
STAUDINGER, G., Instrument constructino and Mechanical Techniques
TORKAR, K., Physical Chemistry
VEIT, W., Industrial Management
VOGLER, H., Geometry
WEIDMANN, H., Organic Chemistry
WEISS, H., Electrical Engineering
WOHINZ, J., Industrial Management
WOHLHART, K., Theory of machines
ZIEGLER, G., Hydraulics

TECHNISCHE UNIVERSITÄT WIEN
(Vienna Technical University)

1040 VIENNA, KARLSPLATZ 13
Telephone: 65 76 41.
Founded 1815.

State control; Academic year: October to June (two terms).

Rector: Prof. Dr. phil. WILFRIED NÖBAUER.
Pro-Rector: Prof. Dr. phil. OTTO HITTMAIR.
Chief Administrative Officer: Dr. JOSEF SCHWABL.
Librarian: Dr. JOSEF WAWROSCH.

Library: *see under* Libraries.
Number of teachers: 1,275.
Number of students: *c.* 8,403.
Publications: *Informationen, Schriftenreihe, Vorlesungs- und Personalverzeichnis, Mitteilungsblatt.*

DEANS:

Faculty of Regional Planning and Architecture: Prof. Dipl. Ing. Arch. ROBERT KRIER.
Faculty of Civil Engineering: Prof. Dr. WALTER KEMMERLING.
Faculty of Mechanical Engineering: Prof. Dr. HERBERT KAZDA.
Faculty of Electrical Engineering: Prof. Dr. HERBERT STIMMER.
Faculty of Natural Sciences: Prof. Dr. ALFRED SCHMIDT.

UNIVERSITÄT FÜR BODENKULTUR WIEN
(Agricultural University)

1180 VIENNA,
GREGOR MENDELSTRASSE 33
Telephone: 34-25-00.
Founded 1872.
State control.

Rector: Prof. Dr. jur. MANFRIED WELAN.
Pro-Rector: Prof. Dipl. Ing. Dr. RUDOLF FRAUENDORFER.
Registrar: Dr. iur. FRIEDRICH WEISS.
Librarian: Dr. phil. WILLIBALD OGIELLO.

Library: *see* Libraries.
Number of teachers: 281, including 56 professors.
Number of students: 2,500.
Publications: *Die Bodenkultur, Centralblatt für das gesamte Forstwesen* (quarterly), *BOKU—Informationen* (2 a year).

JOHANNES KEPLER UNIVERSITÄT LINZ

4045 LINZ-AUHOF
Telephone: 07222-31381.
Founded as College 1966, present name 1975.

State control; Academic year: October to June.

Rector: Prof. Dr. PETER OBERNDORFER.
Pro-Rector: Prof. Dr. RUDOLF WOHLGENANNT.
Administrative Director: Dr. iur. O. KÖCKINGER.
Librarian: Dr. phil. ROBERT REHBERGER.

Library: 72,500 vols.
Number of teachers: 248.
Number of students: 3,842.

DEANS:

Faculty of Law: Prof. Dr. HANS-ERNST FOLZ.
Faculty of Social and Economic Studies: Prof. Dr. L. J. HEINRICH.
Faculty of Applied and Natural Science: Prof. Dr. BRUNO BUCHBERGER.

WIRTSCHAFTSUNIVERSITÄT WIEN
(Vienna University of Commerce)

A-1190 VIENNA,
FRANZ KLEIN-GASSE 1
Telephone: 34-75-44.
Founded 1898.

Rector: Prof. Dr. ALOIS BRUSATTI.
Pro-Rector: Prof. Dr. WILFRIED SCHNEIDER.
Registrar: Dr. H. D. LIBOWITZKY.
Librarian: Dr. F. BISCHOF.

Library: *see* Libraries.
Number of teachers: 262.
Number of students: 8,800.

PROFESSORS:

BERNECKER, P., Tourist Trade
BRUSATTI, A., History
BURGHARDT, A., Sociology
CLEMENT, W., Political Economy and Finance
DERFLINGER, G., Statistics
DORALT, P., Law
EDER, A., Pedagogics
ESCHENBACH, R., Business Management
FALLER, P., Transport
GRÜN, O., Business Management
HANNAK, K., Law
HASCHKA, H., English Language
HOFMANN, M., Business Management
HÖLZL, J., Technology
HRUSCHKA, E., Business Training
JONASCH, F., Business Management
KOREN, S., Political Economy and Finance
KORINEK, Public Law
LAGER, A., Financial Law
MATIS, H., History
NOWAK, A., Social Law
PETER, H., Romance Philology
PICHLER, H., Political Economy
PURCELL, H. D., English Language
RILL, H., Public Law
ROPPERT, J., Statistics
SCHNEIDER, W., Pedagogics
SCHÖPF, A., Political Economy and Finance
SCHWEIGER G., Advertising and Market Research
SEICHT, G., Business Management
SINNHUBER, K., Geography
STÖHR, W., Space-planning
STREMITZER, H., Business Management
TAGWERKER, H., Political Economy
THEUER, G., Business Management
TOPRITZHOFER, E., Operations Research
WEIS, E., Romance Philology
WINKLER, E., Geography

MONTANUNIVERSITÄT LEOBEN
(University of Mining and Metallurgy)

A-8700 LEOBEN,
KAISER FRANZ-JOSEF STR. 18
Telephone: 03842 25-55.
Founded 1840.

Languages of instruction: German and English.

Rector: Prof. Dr. HEIN-PETER STÜWE.
Pro-Rector: Prof. Dr. ALBERT OBERHOFER.
Librarian: PETER SIKA.

Library: *see* Libraries.
Number of students: *c.* 1,000.

PROFESSORS:

BARGMANN, H. W., Mechanics
BAUER, G., Physics
CZIKEL, J., Foundry Technology
FEDER, G., Sublevel Construction
FETTWEIS, G., Mining Engineering
FISCHMEISTER, H., Physical Metallurgy and Material Testing
GAHLEITNER, A., Electrical Engineering
GAMSJÄGER, H., Physical Chemistry
GRIMMER, K., Materials Handling
HEINEMANN, Z., Reservoir Engineering
HIEBLER, H., Ferrous Metallurgy
HOLZER, H., Geology and Mineral Resources
IMRICH, W., Applied Mathematics
KNAPPE, W., Plastics Processing
KOPPELMANN, J., Chemical and Physical Technology of Plastics
LORBACH, M., Petroleum Engineering
OBERHOFER, A. F., Economy, Industrial Management and Industrial Engineering
RAJAKOVICS, G., Mechanical Engineering
SCHMIDT, W. J., Prospecting and Mineral Economics
SCHNITZER, F., Mathematics
SCHWENZFEIER, W., Deformation Processing and Steel Mill Machineries
SPICKERNAGEL, H., Mine Surveying, Subsidence Problems
STACHEL, H., Applied Geometry
STEINER, H., Mineral Processing
STUMPFL, E., Mineralogy and Petrology
STÜWE, H., Physical Metallurgy
TROJER, F., Refractory Materials, Ceramics, Glass and Cement

Ussar, M. B., Heat Technology, Furnaces and Energy
Weber, F., Geophysics
Zitter, H., General and Analytical Chemistry

VETERINÄRMEDIZINISCHE UNIVERSITÄT WIEN
(Veterinary University)

A-1030 VIENNA,
LINKE BAHNGASSE 11
Telephone: 735581.
Founded 1767.

Rector: Prof. Dr. Dr. h.c. Hermann Willinger.
Pro-Rector: Dr. Dr. Oskar Schaller.
Administrative Director: Dr. Herbert Maska.

Library: *see* Libraries.
Teaching staff: 135.
Number of students: 1,400.

Publication: *Wiener Tierärztliche Monatschrift.*

Professors:

Arbeiter, K., Obstetrics, Gynaecology and Clinical Endocrinology
Brandl, E., Milk Hygiene and Technology
Bürki, F., Virology
Eisenmenger, E., Surgery and Ophthalmology
Glawischnig, E., Internal Medicine and Contagious Diseases
Grünberg, W., Fish Pathology, Laboratory Animal Research
Jaksch, W., Internal Medicine and Contagious Diseases
Keck, G., Medical Physics
Kment, A., Physiology
Knezevic, P., Veterinary Orthopaedics
Köhler, H., Pathology and Forensic Medicine
Leibetseder, J., Animal Nutrition
Lipp, W., Histology and Embryology
Onderscheka, K., Wildlife Management Research
Pobisch, R., Radiology
Prändl, O., Meat Hygiene and Nutrition
Schaller, O., Systematic and Topographical Anatomy
Schleger, W., Animal Husbandry and Genetics
Supperer, R., Parasitology and General Zoology
Weiser, M., Medical Chemistry
Willinger, H., Bacteriology and Animal Hygiene

AKADEMIE DER BILDENDEN KÜNSTE
(Academy of Fine Arts)

1010 VIENNA, SCHILLERPLATZ 3
Founded 1692.

Rector: Prof. Dr. Franz Mairinger.
Pro-Rector: Prof. Maximilian Melcher.

Library: *see* Libraries.
Number of teachers: 90.
Number of students: 560.

HOCHSCHULE FÜR ANGEWANDTE KUNST IN WIEN
(University of Applied Art in Vienna)

A-1011 VIENNA, STUBENRING 3
Founded 1868.

Rector: Prof. Oswald Oberhuber.
Vice-Rector: Prof. Dr. Manfred Wagner.
Registrar: Mag. iur. Dr. Heinz Adamek.
Librarian: Dr. Rosa Maria Steinbauer.

Library of 25,000 vols.
Number of teachers: 160.
Number of students: 800.

Publications: *Berichte*† (quarterly), *Studienführer*†, *Prospect*† (annually).

Deans:

Department of Architecture: Prof. Mag. arch. Wilhelm Holzbauer.
Department of Interior Design and Planning: Prof. Mag. arch. Hans Hollein.
Department of Painting and Graphic Arts: Prof. Wolfgang Hutter.
Department of Plastic Arts: Prof. Dipl.-Ing. Arch. Carl Auböck.
Department of Theatre Arts, Textiles and Design: Prof. Margarethe Soulek-Rader.
Department of General Art: Prof. Adolf Frohner.

HOCHSCHULE FÜR KÜNSTLERISCHE UND INDUSTRIELLE GESTALTUNG
(Academy of Industrial and Art Design)

4020 LINZ, HAUPTPLATZ 8
Founded 1947, present status 1973.

Rector: Prof. Helmuth Gsöllpointner.
Vice-Rector: Prof. Hannes Haybäck.
Registrar: Othmar Köckinger.

Library of 7,000 vols.
Number of teachers: 95.
Number of students: 400.

HOCHSCHULE FÜR MUSIK UND DARSTELLENDE KUNST
(University of Music and Dramatic Art)

A-1037 VIENNA III,
LOTHRINGERSTRASSE 18
Telephone: 56-16-85.

Founded 1817 as "Conservatorium der Gesellschaft der Musikfreunde", nationalized 1909.

Rector: Prof. Dr. Helmut Schwarz.
Vice-Rector: Prof. Dr. Gottfried Scholz.
Registrar: Erich Tischberger.
Librarian: Dr. Wolfgang Pernauer.

Number of teachers: 383.
Number of students: 2,559.

Deans:

Department of Theory, Composition and Orchestral Conducting: Prof. Thomas C. David.
Department of Keyboard Instruments: Prof. Hans Graf.
Department of String Instruments: Prof. Tobias Kühne.
Department of Wind and Percussion: Prof. Friedrich Gabler.
Department of Music Education: Prof. Hans M. Kneihs.
Department of Church Music: Prof. Dr. Hans Haselböck.
Department of Voice and Operatic Art: (vacant).
Department of Drama and Production: Prof. Walter Hoesslin.
Department of Film and Television: Prof. Hannelore Götzinger.

Affiliated Institutes:

Institut für Volksmusikforschung: Dir. Prof. Walter Deutsch.
Institut für Musiksoziologie und musikpädagogische Forschung: Dir. Prof. Kurt Blaukopf.
Institut für Atem- und Stimmerziehung: Dir. Prof. Margarete Sparber.
Institut für Österreichische Dramaturgie: Dir. Prof. Dr. Kurt Becsi.
Institut für harmonikale Grundlagenforschung: Dir. Prof. Dr. Rudolf Haase.
Institut für Elektroakustik: Dir. Prof. Roman Haubenstock-Ramati.
Institut für Organalogische Forschung und Dokumentation: Dir. Prof. Dr. Rudolf Scholz.
Institut für Wiener Klangstil: Dir. Prof. Dr. Eduard Melkus.
Institut für kirchenmusikalische Volksbildung: Dir. Prof. Dr. Hans Haselböck.
Institut für Musikanalytik: Dir. Prof. Dr. Gottfried Scholz.
Institut für kulturelles Management, künstlerische Betriebsführung und Öffentlichkeitsarbeit: Dir. Hofrat Prof. Dr. Ernst Haeusserman.

HOCHSCHULE FÜR MUSIK UND DARSTELLENDE KUNST IN GRAZ
(University of Music and Dramatic Art in Graz)

A-8010 GRAZ,
LEONHARDSTRASSE 15,
P.O.B. 208
Telephone: 32-0-53/54.
Founded 1963.

State control; language of instruction: German; Academic year: October to June.

Rector: Prof. Dr. OTTO KOLLERITSCH.
Vice-Rector: Prof. Dr. LEO WITOSZYNSKYJ.
Registrar: Frau ANNA MARIA MAIER.

Number of teachers: 80.
Number of students: 900.

DIRECTORS:

Department of Theory and Composition: Prof. A. DOBROWOLSKI.
Department of Keyboard Instruments: Prof. R. SCHWENZER.
Department of String Instruments: Prof. J. CHRONOPOULOS.
Department of Wind and Percussion Instruments: Prof. F. WALDSTÄDTER.
Department of Pedagogy: Prof. Dr. F. KORČAK.
Department of Church Music: Dr. J. TRUMMER.
Department of Singing, Choirleading and Drama: Prof. P. BAUMGARTEN.
Department of Jazz: Prof. Dr. H. NEUWIRTH.

HOCHSCHULE FÜR MUSIK UND DARSTELLENDE KUNST "MOZARTEUM" IN SALZBURG
("Mozarteum" University of Music and Dramatic Art in Salzburg)

5020 SALZBURG,
MIRABELLPLATZ 1

Founded 1914.

Rector: Prof. FRANZ RICHTER-HERF.
Vice-Rector: Prof. JOSEF F. DOPPELBAUER.

Number of teachers: 210.
Number of students: 1,830.

(*See* also Museums.)

COLLEGES OF TECHNOLOGY

Höhere Technische Bundeslehranstalt für Waffentechnik, Werkzeug- und Vorrichtungsbau (*Federal College for Weapons and Tools Construction*): 9170 Ferlach; f. 1877; 45 teachers, 540 students; Dir. Ing. V. LANDERL.

Höhere Technische Bundeslehranstalt (*Federal College of Technology*): 8018 Graz, Ortweinplatz 1; f. 1876; construction engineering, crafts, arts and design; 126 teachers, 1,050 students; Dir. Dipl. Ing. Dr. HORST ALTENBURGER.

Höhere Technische Bundeslehr- und Versuchsanstalt (*Federal College of Technology*): 8051 Graz; f. 1919; mechanical, electrical, communication and production engineering; 132 teachers; 1,353 students; Dir. Dipl.-Ing. Dr.techn. RAIMUND KLEIN.

Höhere Technische Bundeslehr- und Versuchanstalt (*Federal College of Technology*): 6020 Innsbruck, Anichstrasse 26–28; f. 1877; communication, mechanical and electrical engineering; 140 teachers; 1,100 students; Dir. Dipl.-Ing. HERBERT PADINGER.

Höhere Bundeslehr- und Versuchsanstalt für Wein- und Obstbau (*Federal College of Viticulture and Pomology*): A-3400 Klosterneuburg, Wienerstrasse 74; f. 1860; 25 teachers, 150 students; library of 30,000 vols.; Dir. Dr. F. PRILLINGER; publ. *Mitteilungen-Klosterneuburg*†.

Höhere Technische Bundeslehranstalt (*Federal College of Technology*): 3500 Krems, Alauntalstrasse 29; f. 1942; underground and surface engineering, technical drawing; 90 teachers, 800 students; Dir. Hofrat Dipl.-Ing. HEINRICH WERNER.

Berg- und Huttenschule Leoben (*Mining and Foundry Engineering College*): 8700 Leoben, Max-Tendler-Strasse 3; f. 1865; trains mine-inspectors and foundry engineers; 35 teachers, 115 students; Dir. Prof. RUDOLF DOBROWSKY.

Höhere Technische Bundeslehranstalt Salzburg (*Federal College of Technology*): 5010 Salzburg, Rudolfskai 42; f. 1876; civil, electrical, mechanical and textile engineering; *c.* 150 teachers, *c.* 1,000 students; Dir. Mag. arch. HERMANN REHRL.

Höhere Technische Bundeslehranstalt Steyr (*Federal College of Technology*): 4400 Steyr, Schlüsselhofgasse 63; f. 1874; mechanical, motor vehicle and communication engineering and electronics; 104 teachers, 1,053 students; Dir. Dipl.-Ing. WILHELM JURKOWSKI.

Höhere Bundeslehr- und Versuchsanstalt für Textilindustrie (*Federal College of Textile Technology*): 1050 Vienna, Spengergasse 20; f. 1758; 100 teachers, 600 students; Dir. Dipl.-Ing. H. WIEHART.

Höhere Graphische Bundes-Lehr- und Versuchsanstalt (*Federal Technical College of Graphic Arts*): A-1140 Vienna, Leyserstr. 6; f. 1888 by H.M. Emperor Franz Joseph I; photography, commercial art, reproduction and printing processes; library of 25,000 vols.; 92 teachers, 446 students; Dir. Prof. Dr. WILHELM MUTSCHLECHNER.

Höhere Bundeslehr- und Versuchsanstalt, Technologisches Gewerbemuseum (*Federal College of Technology*): A-1090 Vienna, Währingerstrasse 59; f. 1879; experimental and test laboratories authorized to grant public certificates; *c.* 250 teachers, *c.* 1,800 students; Dir. Dipl.-Ing. Dr. WALTER BRANDSTETTER; publ. *Jahresbericht* (annual report).

Höhere Technische Bundeslehr- und Versuchsanstalt Wien (*Federal College of Technology*): A-1015 Vienna, Schellinggasse 13; f. 1846; teachers 320, students 2,500; Pres. PAUL RIEDL; publ. *Jahresbericht*†.

Höhere Technische Bundeslehr- und Versuchsanstalt (*Federal College of Technology*): 3340 Waidhofen an der Ybbs, Postfach 87; f. 1890; electrical, mechanical and production engineering; 72 teachers, 732 students; Dir. Dipl.-Ing. JOHANN DULLNIG.

SCHOOLS OF ART AND MUSIC

Kärntner Landeskonservatorium (*Carinthian Conservatory of Music*): A-9020 Klagenfurt, Miesstalerstrasse 8; f. 1931; 44 teachers, 788 students; library of 22,088 vols.; Dir. Dr. WALTER LANGER; publ. *Jahresbericht* (annual report).

Konservatorium der Stadt Innsbruck (*Innsbruck Municipal Conservatory*): A-6020 Innsbruck, Museumstrasse 17a; f. 1818; 132 teachers, 2,500 students; library of 28,000 vols. and musical notes; Dir. Dr. BRUNO WIND.

Konservatorium der Stadt Wien (*Vienna Municipal Conservatory*): 1010 Vienna, Johannesgasse 4A; f. 1938; consists of Konservatorium (teaching staff 108; students 1,272), affiliated to it are 17 Musikschulen (teaching staff 226; students 3,076) and the Kindersingschule (teaching staff 29; students 3,676); Principal Prof. JOSEF M. MÜLLER.

BAHAMAS

Population 225,000

LEARNED SOCIETIES

Bahamas Historical Society: P.O.B. N1715, Nassau; f. 1959; 375 mems.; Pres. Dr. PAUL ALBURY; Corresp. Sec. Dr. PAUL POAD; publ. *Journal* (annually).

Bahamas National Trust: P.O.B. ES6029, Nassau.

LIBRARIES AND ARCHIVES

John Harvard Lending Library: P.O.B. F40, Freeport, Grand Bahama; f. 1966; an all-volunteer adult lending library; *c.* 30,000 vols.; Head Volunteer Mrs. BARBARA BEISER.

Nassau Public Library: P.O.B. N3210, Nassau; f. 1837; *c.* 50,000 vols. including 1,000 vols. of Bahamiana; museum attached.

Public Records Office: P.O.B. N3913, Nassau; Archivist Mrs. GAIL SAUNDERS; publ. *Guide to Records of the Bahamas.*

Ranfurly Out Island Library: P.O.B. N8350, Nassau.

MUSEUM

Bahamia Museum: P.O.B. N1510, Nassau.

COLLEGES

University of the West Indies Extra-Mural Department: P.O.B. N1184, Nassau; f. 1965; adult education; Representative Mrs. G. HAMILTON, B.A.

College of the Bahamas: P.O.B. N4912, Nassau; f. 1974; junior community college on two campuses; gives associate degrees in arts, science, business administration, secretarial studies; teacher training; adult education; affiliated to University of West Indies, Florida International University and University of Miami for further degree courses; 150 staff, 3,000 students; library of 40,000 vols.; Principal Dr. JACOB BYNOE; Vice-Principal KEVA BETHEL; Registrar ROGER BROWN.

BAHRAIN

Population 340,000

LEARNED SOCIETIES

Bahrain Historical and Archaeological Society: P.O.B. 5087; f. 1958, re-activated 1970 for the Third International Conference on Asian Archaeology, held in Bahrain; organizes film shows, lectures, discussions and visits to archaeological sites in Bahrain and neighbouring countries; 252 mems.; Pres. Dr. ABDUL LATIF KANOO; Sec. Mrs. JEAN HIRST; publ. *Dilmun* (2 a year).

Bahrain Society of Engineers: P.O.B. 835, Manama; f. 1972; 155 mems.; Pres. HASSAN FAKHRO; Sec. HUSSAIN TADAYON; publ. *Al-Mohandes* (2 a year).

Bahrain Writers and Literators Association: P.O.B. 1010, Manama; f. 1969 to promote the literary movement in Bahrain; publishes members' writings; holds cultural seminars and lectures; 35 mems.; library of *c.* 500 vols.; Pres. ALAWI AL HASHIMI; Sec. IBRAHIM ABDULLAH GHULOOM.

British Council: P.O.B. 452, Al Mathaf Square, Manama; f. 1957; library of 11,552 vols., 45 periodicals; Rep. H. B. BENDING.

MUSEUM

Bahrain Museum: P.O.B. 43, Manama; f. 1970; archaeological research; collections of remains and artefacts from the Middle Stone Age to the 7th century A.D.; graphic presentation of principal Sumerian legends relating to Dilmun; ethnographical section; Dir. SHAIKHA HAYA AL KHALIFA.

COLLEGES

Gulf Technical College: Isa Town; f. 1968; depts. of engineering, business administration, building and civil engineering, English; library of 12,000 vols.; 60 teachers; 538 full-time, 152 part-time, 620 evening students; Principal D. J. LONGMAN.

UNIVERSITY COLLEGE OF ARTS, SCIENCE AND EDUCATION

P.O.B. 1082

Telephone: 682748.

Founded 1979.

Rector: WILLIAM A. STUART, M.A., ED.D.
Director of Administration: J. HALWACHI, B.SC.
Co-ordinator of Academic Affairs: D. J. DANIELS, PH.D.
Librarian: R. N. ABDULLA.

Library of 15,000 vols.
Number of teachers: 50.
Number of students: 185.

CHAIRMEN OF DEPARTMENTS:

Biology: M. A. HASHEM, M.SC., DR.RER.NAT.
Chemistry: G. L. DUNCAN, PH.D.
Education: I. K. SHEHAB, PH.D.
Mathematics: M. S. ARORA, M.A., PH.D.
Physics: S. TORNKVIST, M.SC., PH.D.
Psychology: H. EL-ABD, M.A., PH.D.
Arabic and Islamic Affairs: A. L. M. AL-MAHMOUD, M.A.
English: H. DHAIF, M.A., PH.D.
Humanities: A. SABT, PH.D.
Communication: H. ARRASJID, M.A.ED., M.ED., ED.D.

BANGLADESH

Population 86,643,000

LEARNED SOCIETIES AND RESEARCH INSTITUTES

Alliance Française de Chittagong: P.O.B. 342, Jamshedya House, 123 K.B. Fazlul Quador Rd., Chittagong; f. 1965 to promote French language and culture and establish cultural exchange with Bangladesh; 150 mems.; 80-100 students; library of 1,500 vols. in French; Pres. Dr. M. S. QURESHI; Dir. of Studies GÉRARD DUPUY.

Animal Husbandry Research Institute: Comilla; f. 1947; 69 staff; preparation of sera and vaccine; Deputy Dir. M. ABDUL QUADER, D.V.M.S., P.G.

Asia Foundation, The: G.P.O. Box 666, Dacca; f. 1955; one of 12 branches of the main organization in the U.S.A. (*q.v.*); to assist local institutions and organizations concerned with educational and socio-economic development; Rep. J. M. DILLARD.

Bangla Academy: Burdwan House, Dacca 2; f. 1972 as amalgamation of former Bengali Academy and Central Board for Development of Bengali; promotion of culture and development of the Bengali language and literature; to produce and translate in Bangla scientific works, reference books, dictionaries, etc. and to promote research into the Bangla language; library of 102,000 vols.; Dir.-Gen. Dr. ASHRAF H. SIDDIQI; Sec. ABDUS SATTAR KHAN; publs. *Research Journal, Science Journal* (quarterly, in Bangla), *Journal* (2 a year, in English), *Uttaradhikar* (literary, monthly), *Dhan Shaliker Desh* (juvenile, monthly).

Bangladesh Council of Scientific and Industrial Research: Mirpur Rd., Dhanmondi, Dacca 5; f. 1955; Chair. Prof. N. A. KHAN; Sec. Dr. A. K. M. AHSANULLAH; publs. *Bangladesh Journal of Scientific and Industrial Research, News Letter, Bijnaner Joyjattra, Purogami Bijnan.*

BCSIR Laboratories, Dacca. Ten divisions: Food Technology and Applied Nutrition; Natural Products; Glass and Ceramics; Fibre and Polymer; Fuel Technology; Leather Technology; Physical Instrumentation; Analytical; Industrial Physics; Pilot Plant and Process Development; Dir. Dr. ALIM BISWAS.

BCSIR Laboratories, Chittagong. Five divisions: Chemistry, Botany, Pharmacology, Microbiology, Workshop; Dir. Dr. M. MANZUR-E-KHUDA.

BCSIR Laboratories, Rajshahi. Four divisions: Lac Research; Oils, Fats and Waxes; Fibres; Fruit Processing and Preservation; Dir. Dr. MIR AMJAD ALI. (*See also* BANSDOC, below.)

Bangladesh Economic Association: c/o Economics Dept., Dacca University, Dacca; f. 1958 to promote economic research; Pres. Dr. MAZHARUL HUQ; Sec. Dr. S. R. BOSE.

Bangladesh Institute of Development Studies: Adamjee Court, Motijheel Commercial Area, Dacca 2; f. 1957; basic research on development; training in socio-economic development and demography; population study centre; library of 51,436 books and reports, 881 periodicals, 18,000 micro-fiches and 90 reels of microfilms of Indian Census reports; Chair. Dr. MONOWAR HOSSAIN (acting); publs. *Bangladesh Development Studies*† (quarterly), Research Monograph Series, Research Report Series†, BIDS Library Bibliography Series, BIDS Library Documentation Series.

Bangladesh Jute Research Institute: Tejgaon, Dacca; f. 1951 for agricultural and technological research on jute; Dirs. Dr. Q. A. AHMED, M.SC., PH.D. (Agriculture), Dr. M. KASEM ALI, M.AG., M.S., PH.D. (Seed Production), Dr. M. MANZUR-I-KHUDA, M.SC., D.I.C., PH.D. (Technology).

Bangladesh National Scientific and Technical Documentation Centre (BANSDOC): Science Laboratories, Dhanmondi, Dacca 5; f. 1963 to collect and disseminate information on all branches of science and technology; services include document procurement, bibliography compilation, translation, scientific slides, scientific contacts, bibliographies for symposia; Officer-in-Charge AHSAN A. BISWAS.

British Council: P.O.B. 161, 5 Fuller Rd., Ramna, Dacca 2; library (*see* Libraries); Rep. V. G. BENNETT.

German Cultural Institute: House Kalpana, 7 Green Rd., P.O.B. 108, Dhanmondi R/A, Dacca 5; f. 1961; 350 mems.; library of 4,890 vols.; Dir. M. M. SHEIKH.

International Centre for Diarrhoeal Disease Research, Bangladesh: G.P.O. Box 128, Dacca 2; f. 1960 as Pakistan-SEATO Cholera Research Laboratory, 1974 Cholera Research Laboratory, present name 1978, endorsed by an international meeting in Geneva representing 26 countries, multilateral and non-governmental organizations; non-profit centre for research, education and training; 743 staff; library of 12,057 vols.; Dir. WILLIAM B. GREENOUGH III; publs. *Annual Report*†, *Working Papers*†, *Scientific Reports*†, *Monographs*†, *Monthly Newsletter*†.

Library Association of Bangladesh: c/o Library, Bangladesh Univ. of Engineering and Technology, Dacca 2; f. 1956; Pres. M. SHAHABUDDIN; Sec. ABU BAKR SIDDIQUE; publ. *The Eastern Librarian* (3 a year).

Malaria Institute: Mahakhali, Tejgaon, Dacca 5; f. 1947; library of 2,700 vols.; training in malariology for medical graduates and malaria eradication personnel (professional and non-professional); entomological, protozoological and malariometric surveys, biological testing of insecticides; therapeutic and suppressive trials on anti-malaria drugs; Dir. (vacant).

Society of Arts, Literature and Welfare: Society Park, Chittagong; f. 1948 for the advancement of art, literature, education, culture and welfare through literary and musical conferences, debates, etc.; over 500 mems. and 1,000 associates; management vested in a General Council, which elects a working committee; Gen. Sec. MUSHARREF HUSSAIN.

Varendra Research Museum: Rajshahi; f. 1910; under control of University of Rajshahi since 1964; objects: investigation and encouragement of history, archaeology, anthropology, literature and art; collection and preservation of archaeological and other relics, ancient MSS., etc., and publication of original works on these subjects; library of about 10,000 vols.; 7,570 items in museum, including 4,500 ancient MSS.; Dir. Dr. M. RAHMAN, M.A., PH.D., F.R.A.S.; publ. *Journal*† (annually).

LIBRARIES AND ARCHIVES

American Cultural Center Library: 525 Road No. 8, Dhanmondi, R. A., Dacca 5; 8,000 vols., 154 periodicals; br. in Chittagong.

British Council Libraries: P.O.B. 161, Dacca; f. 1953; 48,475 vols., 212 periodicals; Librarian K. G. SPEARS, B.SC.; Chittagong: Laldighi (South); f. 1959; 14,972 vols., 61 periodicals; Rajshahi: Malopara, P.O.B. 9; f. 1960; 18,092 vols., 55 periodicals.

Central Public Library: Shahbagh, Dacca 2; 75,000 vols., 98 periodicals; Librarian A. M. MOTAHAR ALI KHAN.

Chittagong Public Library: P.O.B. 771, Chittagong; f. 1963; 23,309 vols., 135 periodicals; Librarian A. K. M ABDUL MANNAN.

Dacca University Library: Dacca 2; f. 1921; 318,000 vols. and over 20,000 MSS.; Librarian M. A. AZIZ, PH.D. (acting).

Directorate of Archives and Libraries: 106 Central Rd., Dacca 5; f. 1971; controlling office for the National Archives and National Library, and co-ordinating centre for Archives and Libraries at national level; National Library of 16,000 vols. mostly acquired under Copyright Deposit Law; Dir. Dr. K. M. KARIM; publs. *Annual Report of the National Archives*†, *Bangladesh National Bibliography* (annually), *Article Index* (quarterly).

University of Rajshahi Library: Rajshahi; f. 1955; 163,210 vols., 800 journals; Librarian A. RAZZAQUE, M.A., F.L.A.

MUSEUMS

Balda Museum: Dacca; f. 1927; art and archaeology; Superintendent MUHAMMAD HANNAN.

Dacca Museum: P.O.B. 355, Ramna, Dacca; f. 1913; library of 14,000 vols.; art and archaeology of Bengal; Dir. ENAMUL HAQUE, M.A., D.PHIL., A.M.A.; publs. *Bangladesh Lalitkala, Annual Report, Catalogues, Buddhist and Brahmanical Iconography, Coins and Chronology of Independent Sultans of Bengal, Treasures in Dacca Museum* series.

Varendra Research Museum: *see under* Research Institutes.

UNIVERSITIES

BANGLADESH AGRICULTURAL UNIVERSITY

P.O. AGRICULTURAL UNIVERSITY, MYMENSINGH
Telephone: PBX 2191.

Founded 1961.

Autonomous control; Languages of instruction: English and Bengali; Academic year: July to June.

Chancellor: PRIME MINISTER OF THE PEOPLE'S REPUBLIC OF BANGLADESH.

Vice-Chancellor: M. U. AHMED CHOWDHURY, M.R.C.V.S.

Registrar: M. M. RAHMAN, M.A., LL.B.

Librarian: A. K. M. ABDUN NUR, M.A., DIP.LIB.SC.

Number of teachers: 361.
Number of students: 3,011.

Publications: *Bangladesh Journal of Agricultural Science*†, *Bangladesh Journal of Animal Science*†, *Bangladesh Journal of Horticulture*† (2 a year), *Bangladesh Journal of Veterinary Science*† (quarterly).

DEANS:

Faculty of Agriculture: Prof. M. A. WADUD MIAN, PH.D.

Faculty of Animal Husbandry: Prof. M. SHAFIUR RAHMAN, PH.D.

Faculty of Veterinary Science: Prof. SHAIKH HEFEZUDDIN, PH.D.

Faculty of Agricultural Economics and Rural Sociology: Prof. M. A. ALI, M.A., PH.D.

Faculty of Agricultural Engineering and Technology: Prof. M. R. BISWAS, M.ENG., PH.D.

Faculty of Fisheries: Prof. A. K. M. A. HAQUE, M.SC., PH.D.

PROFESSORS:

Veterinary Science:

CHOWDHURY, T. I. M. F., PH.D., Microbiology and Hygiene
SHAIKH, H., M.S., PH.D., Parasitology

Agriculture:

AHMED, M., M.SC., M.S., PH.D., Entomology
BHUIYAN, Z. H., M.SC., M.S.A., PH.D., Soil Science
CHOUDHURY, A. R., PH.D., Genetics and Plant Breeding
CHOUDHURY, S. H., M.SC., D.I.C., PH.D., Crop Botany
HAQUE, A., M.SC., PH.D., Crop Botany
HUSAIN, A., M.AG., M.S., PH.D., Horticulture
HUSSAIN, M., PH.D., Biochemistry
MAHBOOB, S. G., M.AG., PH.D., Agricultural Extension and Teacher Training
MIAN, M. A. W., M.SC., PH.D., Plant Pathology
MUHSI, A. A. A., PH.D., Crop Botany
SHAMSUDDIN, A. M., PH.D., Agronomy

Animal Husbandry:

LATIF, M. A., M.SC., PH.D., Poultry Science
RAHIM, Q. M. F., M.S., PH.D., Animal Breeding and Genetics
RAHMAN, M. S., PH.D., Dairy Science

Agricultural Engineering and Technology:

BISWAS, M. R., M.ENG., PH.D., Irrigation and Water Management
HUSSAIN, A. A. MAINUL, PH.D., Farm Power and Machinery

Agricultural Economics and Rural Sociology:

ALI, M. A., M.A., PH.D., Agricultural Statistics
HUSSAIN, A. M. M., M.A., PH.D., Co-operation and Marketing

Fisheries:

HAQUE, A. K. M. A., M.SC., PH.D., Fisheries Biology and Limnology

DIRECTORS:

Graduate Training Institute: Dr. ABDUL HALIM.

Agricultural University Extension Project: Dr. ANWARUL KARIM.

BANGLADESH UNIVERSITY OF ENGINEERING AND TECHNOLOGY

RAMNA, DACCA
Telephone: 280016, 242332.

Founded 1962.

Language of instruction: English; Academic year: January to December.

Vice-Chancellor: Prof. WAHIDUDDIN AHMAD, PH.D., M.I.E.

Registrar: K. M. ZAHIRUDDIN, M.SC.

Comptroller: A. H. CHOWDHURY, M.A.

Librarian: M. SHAHABUDDIN, M.SC., M.A.

Library of 72,500 vols.
Number of teachers: 275.
Number of students: 2,238.

Publications: *Annual Report, University Calendar.*

DEANS:

Faculty of Architecture and Planning: Prof. M. A. MUKTADIR, PH.D.

Faculty of Engineering: Prof. NOORUDDIN AHMED, PH.D.

Faculty of Civil Engineering: Prof. SAHRAB UDDIN AHMED, PH.D.

PROFESSORS:

AFZAL, S. A., M.SC., D.I.C., PH.D., Mathematics
AHMED, N., M.SC., PH.D., Chemical Engineering
AHMED, S., M.S., PH.D., Electrical Engineering
AHMED, S. U., M.SC., PH.D., Civil Engineering
ALI, M. M., M.ARCH., Architecture
AZIM, M. A., B.SC., DR.ING., Mechanical Engineering
CHOWDHURY, J. R., M.SC., PH.D., Civil Engineering
EUSUFZAI, S. H. K., M.S., PH.D., Civil Engineering

Habib, A., m.s., ph.d., Civil Engineering
Hamidur Rahman Khan, A. K. M., Dir., Institute of Flood Control and Drainage Research
Hannan, A., m.s., ph.d., Water Resources Engineering
Huq, A. F. M. A., m.eng., ph.d., Mechanical Engineering
Huq, A. M. A., m.sc., ph.d., Mechanical Engineering
Huq, A. M. Z., m.sc., m.s., ph.d., Electrical Engineering
Hussain, A., m.s., ph.d., Mechanical Engineering
Ibrahim, M., ph.d., Metallurgical Engineering
Islam, O., m.s., ph.d., Mechanical Engineering
Khan, M. H., m.s., ph.d., Mechanical Engineering
Mahdi, S., m.s., ph.d., Electrical Engineering
Mahmud, I., m.sc., ph.d., Chemical Engineering
Muktadir, M. A., ph.d., Architecture
Patwari, A. M., m.s., m.a., ph.d., Electrical Engineering
Rashid, M. A., m.s., ph.d., Civil Engineering
Shahjahan, M., m.s., ph.d., Water Resources Engineering
Zaman, M. J., ph.d., Chemical Engineering

UNIVERSITY OF CHITTAGONG

UNIVERSITY POST OFFICE, CHITTAGONG

Telephone: PBX 210131/210134.

Founded 1966.

Languages of instruction: Bengali and English; Academic year: July to June.

Vice-Chancellor: Prof. Abdul Karim, m.a., ph.d.

Registrar: Muhammad Khalilur Rahman, m.a.

Librarian: Shamsul Alam, m.a., m.s.l.s.

Library of 76,172 vols.

Number of teachers: 309.

Number of students: 24,612 (29,439 in affiliated colleges).

Deans:

Faculty of Arts: Prof. A. M. Serajuddin.
Faculty of Commerce: Prof. S. Shamsuzzoha.
Faculty of Education: Prof. M. N. Islam.
Faculty of Engineering: M. A. Bari.
Faculty of Law: R. Rahman.
Faculty of Medicine: (vacant).
Faculty of Science: Prof. A. K. S. Ahmed.
Faculty of Social Sciences: Prof. R. I. Chowdhury.

Professors:

Ahmed, A. K. S., Chemistry
Ahmed, E. U., Physics
Ali, M., English
Anisuzzaman, A. T. M., Bengali
Anisuzzaman, M., Political Science
Bhuiyan, A. L., Marine Biology
Chowdhury, R. I., Political Science
Ghafur, M. A., Arabic and Persian
Hossain, M. F., Mathematics
Khan, M. A. A., Botany
Khan, M. A. I., Accounting
Khan, M. U. A., Islamic History and Culture
Rahman, M., History
Sarajuddin, A. M., History
Shamsuzzoha, S., Management
Yunus, M., Economics

There are 64 affiliated colleges.

Attached Institute:

Institute of Forestry: f. 1977; Dir. Dr. M. B. Zaman.

UNIVERSITY OF DACCA

RAMNA, DACCA

Telephone: 255379.

Founded 1921.

Language of instruction: English; Academic year: July to June (three terms.)

Chancellor: President of the People's Republic of Bangladesh.

Vice-Chancellor: Prof. F. H. Chowdhury.

Registrar: Nuruddin Ahmed, b.a.

Librarian: M. K. Ali, m.a., ed.d., c.s.c. (acting).

Library: *see* Libraries.

Number of teaching staff: 850.

Number of students: 72,763 (including affiliated and constituent colleges).

Publications: *Calendar, Annual Report, Dacca University Studies* (2 a year).

Deans:

Faculty of Arts: Dr. A. Sharif, m.a., ph.d.
Faculty of Commerce: Dr. M. Habibullah, m.b.a., m.com., ph.d.
Faculty of Science: Dr. A. K. M. Siddiq, m.sc., ph.d.
Faculty of Law: Lutful Kabir, ph.d.
Faculty of Medicine: Masharul Imam, m.b.b.s., m.sc.
Faculty of Education: Mrs. Maliha Khatun, m.a.
Faculty of Education Extension and Research: A. K. M. Obaidullah, m.sc., b.ed., ph.d.
Faculty of Fine Arts: Dr. A. Sharif, m.a., ph.d. (acting).
Faculty of Social Sciences: A. K. M. Nazmul Karim, m.a., ph.d.
Faculty of Biological Sciences: Dr. Aminul Islam, m.sc., ph.d.
Faculty of Post-graduate Medical Sciences and Research: N. Islam, m.b.b.s., t.d.d., f.r.c.p.ed.

Professors:

Afsaruddin, M., m.a., Sociology
Ahmad, I., m.sc., ph.d., Soil Science
Ahmad, M., m.a., ph.d., Institute of Business Administration
Ahmadullah, A. K., m.s.w., m.sc., Institute of Social Welfare and Research
Ahmed, A. F. S., m.a., ph.d., History
Ahmed, K., m.sc., ph.d., Biochemistry
Ahmed, M., m.sc., ph.d., Chemistry
Ali, M. R., m.a., ph.d., Psychology
Ameen, M., m.sd., ph.d., Zoology
Aziz, M. A., m.a., m.s.s., ph.d., International Relations
Begum, Mrs. Q. Nessa, m.sc., ph.d., Physics
Chowdhury, A. F. S. I., m.a., ph.d., English
Chowdhury, A. M., ph.d., History
Chowdhury, A. M., ph.d., Physics
Chowdhury, K., m.a., English
Fakruzzaman, M., ph.d., Psychology
Farouk, A., m.a., ph.d., Marketing
Fatta, Q. A., ph.d., Botany
Gupta, H. S., ph.d., Physics
Habibullah, M., m.com., ph.d., Accounting
Haider, S. Z., m.sc., ph.d., Chemistry
Haque, M. S., m.a., ed.d., Institute of Education and Research
Haque, S. M. A., m.sc., ph.d., Mathematics
Hoque, M. M., m.sc., ph.d., Chemistry
Hossain, K. M. Z., m.sc., Zoology
Hossain, K. T., m.a., ph.d., Economics
Hossain, M., m.a., ph.d., Economics
Hossain, M. A., m.sc., ph.d., Physics
Huda, M. N., m.a., ph.d., Economics
Huq, M. S., ph.d., Applied Physics
Ibrahim, Mrs. N., m.a., ph.d., Bengali
Imamuddin, S. M., m.a., d.phil., Islamic History and Culture
Ishaque, M., ph.d., Arabic and Islamic Studies
Islam, A., m.sc., ph.d., Geography
Islam, A. K. M. N., m.sc., ph.d., Botany
Islam, A. S., m.sc., ph.d., Botany
Islam, M. R., ph.d., Bengali
Islam, M. S., d.phil., Islamic History and Culture
Islam, T., m.a., ph.d., Economics
Jabbar, A., m.sc., ph.d., Pharmacy
Jahan, Miss Rounaq, ph.d., Political Science
Kabir, L., ph.d., Law
Kabir, M., m.a., ph.d., History
Kabir, S. H., ph.d., Zoology
Kamal, A. H. M., ph.d., Bengali
Karim, A. K. N., m.a., ph.d., Sociology
Karim, A. Q. M. B., m.sc., ph.d., Soil Science
Khan, M. N. H., ph.d., Biochemistry
Khan, M. S., ph.d., Botany
Latif, M. A., m.sc., ph.d., Geology
Mahmood, A. N. M., ph.d., Economics
Matin, A., ph.d., Philosophy
Mostafa, M. G., m.sc., ph.d., Statistics
Moniruzzaman, M., m.a., ph.d., Bengali
Moniruzzaman, T., ph.d., Political Science
Murshid, K. S., m.a., ph.d., English
Nabi, S. N., m.sc., ph.d., Chemistry
Nawab, M. A., m.sc., ph.d., Chemistry
Rahim, M. A., m.a., ph.d., History
Rahman, A. H. M. H., m.a., ph.d., Economics
Rahman, M. A., m.a., ph.d., Economics
Rahman, M. M., ph.d., Biochemistry
Rahman, W., m.a., History
Rashid, A. M. H., m.sc., ph.d., Physics
Sardar, M. R. A., m.sc., ph.d., Mathematics
Sarker, A. Q., m.sc., ph.d., Physics
Selim, M., m.a., ed.d., Institute of Education and Research
Sharif, A., m.a., ph.d., Bengali
Siddiq, A. K. M., m.sc., ph.d., Physics
Talukder, M. A. H. ph.d., Statistics
Tarafdar, M. R., m.a., ph.d., Islamic History and Culture

Affiliated Colleges:

There are 151 affiliated colleges and 20 constituent colleges.

JAHANGIRNAGAR UNIVERSITY

SAVAR, DACCA

Telephone: 316071.

Founded 1970.

Languages of instruction: Bengali and English; Academic year: July to June (three terms).

Chancellor: PRESIDENT OF THE PEOPLE'S REPUBLIC OF BANGLADESH.

Vice-Chancellor: Prof. Z. R. SIDDIQUI.

Registrar: A. H. CHAUDHURY, B.A.

Librarian: A. F. FAZLUL MAJID, M.A., M.ED.

Library of 40,000 vols.

Number of teachers: 162.

Number of students: 1,135.

Publications: *Bangla Shahitya Patra of University Studies* (quarterly), *Jahangirnagar Review.*

DEANS:

Faculty of Social Sciences: Prof. M. I. CHOWDHURY, PH.D.

Faculty of Mathematical and Physical Sciences: Dr. SYED SAFIULLAH, PH.D.

Faculty of Mathematical and Physical Sciences: MUSTAFA NURUL ISLAM, PH.D.

Faculty of Arts and Humanities: Prof. MUSTAFA NURAL ISLAM, PH.D.

PROFESSORS:

AHMED, A. F. S., M.A., PH.D., History
AHMED, M., M.SC., PH.D., Chemistry
AHSAN, S. A., M.A., Bengali
CHOWDHURY, M. I., M.A., M.SC., Geography
CHOWDHURY, M. R., PH.D., Mathematics
HOSSAIN, A. M. M., M.A., M.LITT., Engineering
HOSSAIN, K., PH.D., Economics
ISLAM, M. N., PH.D., Bengali
MALLICK, A. R., PH.D., History
MATINUDDIN, S. A. R., M.A., Engineering
RAQIB, M. A., M.SC., PH.D., Physics
SIDDIQUI, Z. R., M.A., English

UNIVERSITY OF RAJSHAHI

RAJSHAHI

Telephone: Rajshahi 2441-9.
Telegraphic Address: University Rajshahi.

Founded 1953.

Language of instruction: English; Academic year: July to June (three terms).

Chancellor: PRESIDENT OF THE PEOPLE'S REPUBLIC OF BANGLADESH.

Vice-Chancellor: Prof. M. A. BARI, M.A., D.PHIL.

Registrar: A. R. JOARDER, M.A.

Librarian: A. RAZZAQUE, M.A., F.L.A.

Library: *see* Libraries.

Number of teachers: 369.

Number of students: 32,630 (including affiliated colleges).

Publications: *University Studies* (annually), *Calendar* (every 2 years).

DEANS:

Faculty of Arts: Prof. A. N. S. HOQUE.
Faculty of Science: Prof. K. A. LATIF.
Faculty of Law: Prof. Z. RAHMAN.
Faculty of Education: Prin. M. ELTASUDDIN.
Faculty of Commerce: Dr. M. A. A. TALUKDER.
Faculty of Medicine: S. ALAUDDIN.
Faculty of Engineering: Prin. R. AHMED.

PROFESSORS:

Arts:

AHMAD, S., M.A., PH.D., English
AHMED, A., M.A., English
AHMED, M., PH.D., Philosophy
AREFIN, S., M.A., LL.B., PH.D., Geography
AWWAL, M. A., PH.D., Bengali
BARI, M. A., Islamic History and Culture
HOQUE, A. N. S., PH.D., Political Science
HOSSAIN, M. M., PH.D., Islamic History and Culture
HUSAIN, Mrs. S., History
HUSAIN, A. M., Islamic History and **Culture**
IMAM, A., History
JOARDER, S., PH.D., Islamic History and Culture
MANNAN, Q. A., Bengali
MIA, A. H., PH.D., Economics
MONDAL, M. S., PH.D., Economics
PATEL, A. M., M.A., Geography
SAKLAYEN, A. T. M. G., M.A., PH.D., Bengali

Science:

CHOUDHURY, F. H., PH.D., Applied Chemistry
CHOWDHURY, S. A., PH.D., Physics
EUNUS, A. M., Botany
HOSSAIN, K. M., Statistics
HUDA, M., Psychology
HUSAIN, A., Physics
KHALIL, F., Mathematics
LATIF, K. A., Chemistry
RAHMAN, M., Mathematics
RAHMAN, M., PH.D., Zoology
SARKAR, M. R., Applied Physics

Law:

CHOUDHURY, Z. I., PH.D.
RAHMAN, Z., PH.D.

Commerce:

HOSSAIN, M., Accounting
MONDAL, M. A., Accounting
TALUKDER, M. A. A., Management

There are 118 affiliated colleges.

ATTACHED INSTITUTE

Institute of Bangladesh Studies: Dir. S. A. AKANDA.

COLLEGES

Bangladesh Textile Institute: Tejgaon, Dacca 8; f. 1950; diploma courses in Jute Technology, Cotton Technology and Textile Chemistry; Principal Dr. M. LUTFUR RAHMAN, M.SC., M.SC.TECH., PH.D.

Chittagong Polytechnic Institute: Chittagong; f. 1962; 1,320 students.

Dacca Polytechnic Institute: Tejgaon Industrial Area, Dacca 8; f. 1955.

Institute of Leather Technology: Dacca.

Institute of Postgraduate Medicine and Research: Dacca 2; f. 1965.

Directors: Prof. N. ISLAM, Prof. M. R. KHAN.

Secretary: M. A. FARAH.

Chief Librarian: M. JASIMUDDIN.

Library of 14,000 vols.

BARBADOS

Population 253,100

LEARNED SOCIETIES

Barbados Astronomical Society: P.O.B. 41, Britton's Hill, St. Michael; f. 1956; Harry Bayley Observatory built 1963; 12½ inch reflector telescope; 85 mems.; library of 200 vols.; Pres. PHILIP STAHL; Sec. JOHN-MICHAEL PETERKIN; publ. *Journal*† (quarterly).

Barbados Pharmaceutical Society: P.O.B. 820 E., St. Michael; f. 1948; 72 mems. (19 students); Pres. HUGH A. MAPP; Sec. ERNEST CHANDLER.

Historical Society: *see under* Barbados Museum.

Library Association of Barbados: P.O.B. 827E, Bridgetown; f. 1968 to unite all persons engaged or interested in library work in Barbados, and to provide opportunities for their meeting together; to promote the active development and maintenance of libraries in Barbados and to foster co-operation between them; to interest the general public in the library services available; 35 mems. Sec. JUDY BLACKMAN; publ. *Bulletin* (annual).

RESEARCH INSTITUTE

Bellairs Research Institute: St. James; f. 1954; attached to McGill University, Canada; research and teaching in all aspects of tropical environment; library of 200 vols.; Dir. Dr. FINN SANDER; Sec. DAVID M. MURRAY.

LIBRARIES

Public Library: Coleridge St., Bridgetown; f. 1847; 191,010 vols.; an island-wide service is provided from the central library in Bridgetown by means of 7 brs., 5 centres, 35 bookmobile stops, and a mobile service to 86 schools; acts as the national copyright repository; Chief Librarian BETTY I. CARRILLO (acting); publs. *West Indian Collection: quarterly additions, Guide to the Barbados Public Library, National Bibliography of Barbados* (quarterly with annual cumulations).

University of the West Indies Library: Bridgetown; f. 1963; 66,000 vols.; Librarian MICHAEL E. GILL, B.SC., DIP.LIB.; publs. *Recent Additions, West Indies Collection* (bi-monthly), *Guide to the Library* (irregular).

MUSEUM

Barbados Museum and Historical Society: St. Ann's Garrison; est. 1933; the museum contains collections illustrating the island's prehistory, history, natural history and marine life; and furniture, silver, china and glass typical of plantation homes; children's gallery; the Society's library specializes in Barbadiana and West Indiana; publ. *Journal* (annually).

UNIVERSITY

UNIVERSITY OF THE WEST INDIES

CAVE HILL CAMPUS

P.O.B. 64, BRIDGETOWN

Founded 1963.

Language of Instruction: English.

Private control; Academic year: October to June (3 terms).

The College is an integral part of the University of the West Indies and is intended to serve Barbados, the Leeward and Windward Islands. The teaching programme covers the Bachelor of Law degree and degrees in arts, general studies, natural sciences and social sciences; the North-Eastern area of the School of Education and the Eastern Caribbean Medical Scheme of the Faculty of Medicine (Barbados) are situated here also.

(*See also* under Jamaica and Trinidad.)

Chancellor: Sir ALLEN MONTGOMERY LEWIS, Q.C., LL.B.
Vice-Chancellor: A. Z. PRESTON, J.P., LL.B., F.C.A., F.C.C.A., F.C.I.S., F.R.ECON.S.
Pro-Vice-Chancellor and Principal: S. L. MARTIN, M.SC., A.R.C.S., D.I.C., F.R.I.C.
Secretary: F. W. BLACKMAN, B.SC.
Librarian: M. GILL, B.SC.

Number of teachers: 270 (57 part-time).
Number of students: 1,380.

DEANS AND VICE-DEANS:

Faculty of Arts and General Studies: K. D. HUNTE, M.A., PH.D.
Faculty of Law: Prof. P. T. GEORGES, B.A. (Dean).
Faculty of Natural Sciences: Prof. R. BINKS, PH.D. (Vice-Dean).
School of Education: R. V. GOODRIDGE, B.A. (Vice-Dean).
Faculty of Social Sciences: F. W. ALLEYNE, B.A., M.SC. (Vice-Dean).
Faculty of Medicine, Eastern Caribbean Medical Scheme (Barbados): Prof. E. R. WALROND, B.SC., M.B., B.S., F.R.C.S. (Vice-Dean).
Extra-Mural Department: Tutor L. L. SHOREY, M.ED., PH.D.

ATTACHED INSTITUTES

Institute of Social and Economic Research: Deputy Dir. Mrs. J. MASSIAH, B.SC.

Caribbean Agricultural Research and Development Institute: Head, Field Unit Dr. D. WALMSLEY, M.SC., PH.D.

COLLEGE

Barbados Community College: "Eyrie", Howell's Cross Rd., St. Michael; f. 1968; library of 26,000 vols.; 78 teachers, 1,800 students; Principal ALVIN F. E. BARNETT.

BELGIUM

Population 9,841,600

ACADEMIES

Académie Royale des Sciences, des Lettres et des Beaux-Arts de Belgique: Palais des Académies, rue Ducale 1, 1000 Brussels; f. 1772.

President: MARCEL MIGEOTTE.
Permanent Secretary: MAURICE LEROY.
Librarian: LOUISE NICOLAS-SERVAIS.
Library: 400,000 volumes.
Number of mems.: 90; 50 correspondents, 150 associate mems.
Publications: *Monthly Bulletin*†, *Memoirs*†, *Year Book*†.

DIRECTORS:

Sciences: MARCEL MIGEOTTE.
Letters and Moral and Political Sciences: GERARD DE MONTPELLIER.
Fine Arts: MARK F. SEVERIN.

MEMBERS:

SCIENCES

Mathematical and Physical Sciences Section:

BRUYLANTS, A.
BUREAU, F.
CAMPUS, F.
D'OR, L.
DUCHESNE, J.
GÉHÉNIAU, J.
GLANSDORFF, P.
HEMPTINNE, M. DE
LAHAYE, E.
LEDOUX, P.
LEPAGE, T.
MIGEOTTE, M.
NICOLET, M.
PRIGOGINE, I.
SWINGS, P.

Natural Sciences Section:

BACQ, Z.
BRACHET, J.
BREMER, F.
DE DUVE, C.
FREDERICQ, H.
HOMÈS, M.
HOMÈS-VAN SCHOOR, G.
LEBRUN, J.
LECLERCQ, S.
LEPERSONNE, J.
MARTENS, P.
MICHOT, P.
PASTEELS, J.
POLL, M.
STOCKMANS, F.

LETTERS AND MORAL AND POLITICAL SCIENCES

History and Letters Section:

DE RUYT, F.
DOSSIN, G.
DRAGUET, R.
GARITTE, G.
GENICOT, L.
HENRY, A.
HERBILLON, J.
JODOGNE, O.
LABARBE, J.
LACROIX, L.
LAMOTTE, E.
LEROY, M.
ROUSSEAU, F.
VAN LOEY, A.
VAN STEENBERGHEN, F.

Moral and Political Sciences Section:

AUBERT, R.
DE VISSCHER, P.
DEL MARMOL, C.
DUPRIEZ, L. H.
GANSHOF VAN DER MEERSCH, W.
HARSIN, P.
JANNE, H.
MONTPELLIER, G. DE
PERELMAN, C.
RENARD, C.
REY, J.
STENGERS, J.
VANLANGENHOVE, F.
WIGNY, P.

FINE ARTS

Painting Section:

ALBERT, J.
BERTRAND, G.
CAMUS, G.
CROMMELYNCK, A.
DASNOY, A.
DELVAUX, P.
LANDUYT, O.
RANSY, J.
VAN LINT, L.

Sculpture Section:

CAILLE, P.
DEBONNAIRES, F.
GRARD, G.
NEUJEAN, N.

Engraving Section:

GORUS, J.
SEVERIN, MARK-F.

Architecture Section:

BASTIN, R.
DE LIGNE, J.
MARTINY, V.
STYNEN, L.

Music Section:

BARBIER, R.
BERNIER, R.
DEFOSSEZ, R.
QUINET, M.
VOUILLEMIN, S.

History and Criticism:

COLMAN, P.
FAIDER-FEYTMANS, Mme G.
GILBERT, P.
ROBERTS-JONES, P.
SNEYERS, R.
VANDEVIVERE, I.

CORRESPONDENTS:

SCIENCES

Mathematical and Physical Sciences Section:

BACKES, F.
BALESCU, R.
DEBEVER, R.
GARNIR, H.
GILLIS, P.
JAUMOTTE, A.
MACQ, P.
PIRENNE, J.
SERPE, J.
VAN MEERSCHE, M.

Natural Sciences Section:

CAHEN, L.
CHANTRENNE, H.
DE BETHUNE, P.
HERLANT-MEEWIS, H.
JEENER, R.
SIRONVAL, C.
THINÈS, G.
THOMAS, R.
UBAGHS, G.

HISTORY AND LETTERS

History and Letters Section:

ARNOULD, M.
BACKVIS, C.
BUYSSENS, E. L.
DELHAYE, Mgr. P.
DELVOYE, C.
HORRENT, J.
LEJEUNE, R.
RENARD, M.
RYCKMANS, J.
VAN RIET, S.

Moral and Political Sciences Section:

ANDRÉ, R.
GODDING, P.
HARMEL, P.
KIRSCHEN, E.-S.
LADRIÈRE, J.
LEBRUN, P.
MOLITOR, A.
PAULUS, J.
TAMINIAUX, J.

FINE ARTS

Painting Section:

COLLIGNON, G.
DELAHAUT, J.
LISMONDE, E.

Engraving Section:

DONNAY, J.

Sculpture Section:

MOESCHAL, J.

Music Section:

FELDBUSCH, E.
HOÉRÉE, A.

Architecture Section:

COSSE, J.

History and Criticism Section:

BALTY, J.
BRAGARD, R.

Koninklijke Academie voor Wetenschappen, Letteren en Schone Kunsten van Belgie (*Royal Academy of Science, Letters and Fine Arts of Belgium*): Paleis der Academiën, Hertogsstraat 1, 1000 Brussels.

President: J. MATON.
Permanent Secretary: G. VERBEKE.

Number of mems. 90, correspondents 30, foreign assocs. 150.

Publications: *Proceedings*†, *Memoirs*†, *Year Book*†, *Reports and Proposals*, *Special Editions*.

DIRECTORS:

Science: J. MATON.
Letters and Moral and Political Sciences: A. GERLO.
Fine Arts: R. VAN DER VELDEN.

MEMBERS:

Sciences:

BILO, J.
BOUCKAERT, L.
BRECKPOT, R.
BUFFEL, K.
DE BEER, E.
DEKEYSER, W.
DE LEY, J.
DE SY, A.
D'HONT, M.
FAUTREZ, J.
GEUKENS, F.
GROSJEAN, C. C.
GULLENTOPS, F.
HIRSCH, G.
KOCH, H.
MARIENS, P.
MATON, J.
PÉTERS, J.
POLSPOEL, G.
PUTZEYS, P.
ROBYNS, W.
SMETS, G.
TAVERNIER, R.
VAN BOUCHOUT, V
VANDENDRIESSCHE, L.
VANDEPITTE, D.
VANDERLINDEN, H. L.
VAN HOOF, A.
VAN MIEGHEM, J.
VELGHE, A. G.

HONORARY MEMBERS:

GOVAERT, F.
RAIGNIER, A.

Letters and Moral and Political Sciences:

COLLIN, F.
COPPENS, Mgr. J.
CRAEYBECKSE, J.
DE LAET, S. J.
DEROLEZ, R.
DE WAELHENS, A.
DONDEYNE, Mgr. A.
EYSKENS, G.
GERLO, A.
GILISSEN, J.
MAST, A.
MATTHYS, J.
MERTENS, J.
NUTTIN, J.
PEREMANS, W.
REEKMANS, C.
RONSE, J.
SANDERS, J.
VANDEN BERGHE, L.
VAN HECKE, G.
VAN HOUTTE, J.
VAN HOUTTE, J. A.
VAN WINDEKENS, A.
VAN'T DACK, E.
VERBEKE, G.
VERGOTE, J.
VERLINDEN, C.
VERVLIET, H.
VICTOR, R.
WYFFELS, C.

HONORARY MEMBERS:

BURSSENS, A.
FREDERICQ, L.
GANSHOF, F. L.

Fine Arts:

AVERMAETE, R.
BOEREBOOM, M.
BONTINCK, G.
BRAEM, R.
DE SMIDT, F.
DHANENS, E.
D'HULST, R. A.
DIELS, H.
DILLE, F.
FELIX, P.
LANGUI, E.
LAUWERS, J. B.
LEBEER, L.
LEGLEY, V.
LENAERTS, R.
LOUËL, J.
MAES, J.
MARIJNISSEN, R.
MENDELSON, M.
MINNE, J.
PAUWELS, H.
PEETERS, Fl.
ROBIJNS, J.
SERVAIS, R.
SLABBINCK, R.
STEPPE, J.
VAN VLASSELAER, J.
VAN DER EYKEN, E.
VAN DER VELDEN, R.
VERMEERSCH, J.

HONORARY MEMBERS:

AUBROECK, K.
POOT, M.
DE BOECK, F.

CORRESPONDING MEMBERS:

Sciences:

CARLIER, A.
COOMANS, A. V.
COTTENIE, A. H.
DE RUYTTERE, A.
FIERS, W.
SOETE, W.
THIJS VAN DEN AUDENAERDE
UYTTERHOEVEN, J. B.
VANHECKE, L.
VERZELE, M.

Letters and Moral and Political Sciences:

DE SMET, D. G.
DUMON, FR.
LIEBAERS, H.
VAN CAENEGEM, R.
VAN DER WEE, H.
VANDEPUTTE, R.
VAN GERVEN, W.

Fine Arts:

BURSSENS, J.
VAN LOOIJ, L. T.
MARTENS, M.

Koninklijke Academie voor Nederlandse Taal- en Letterkunde (*Royal Academy of Dutch Language and Literature*): Koningstraat 18, Ghent; f. 1886; Commissions Middle Dutch, Modern Literature, History of Culture, Education and Dutch Lexicography.

Permanent Secretary: M. HOEBEKE.

Number of mems.: 30; 5 hon. mems., 25 hon. foreign mems.

Library of 40,000 vols.

Publications: *Jaarboek* (annually), *Verslagen en Mededelingen* (2 a year).

MEMBERS:

AERTS, J.
BUCKINX, P. G.
COUPÉ, C.
COUVREUR, W.
DE BELSER, R.
DECORTE, B.
DEMEDTS, A.
DEPREZ, A.
D'HAEN, C.
DESCHAMPS, P.
DRAYE, H.
GILLIAMS, M.
GOOSSENS, J.
GYSSELING, M.
HADERMANN, P.
HOEBEKE, M.
JONCKHEERE, K.
KEERSMAEKERS, A.
LAMPO, H.
LEBEAU, P.
LEYS, O.
LISSENS, R. F.
MOORS, J.
ROELANDTS, K.
ROOSE, L.
VANACKER, V. F.
VAN ELSLANDER, A.
VAN LOEY, A.
WEISGERBER, J.

Académie Royale de Langue et de Littérature Francaises (*Royal Academy of French Language and Literature*): Palais de Académies, 1 rue Ducale, 1000 Brussels; f. 1920.

Director: MAURICE PIRON.
Permanent Secretary: GEORGES SION.
Committee Members: CARLO BRONNE, JOSEPH HANSE, Mme LOUIS DUBRAU.

Publications: *Bulletin*, *Annuaire*, *Mémoires*.

BELGIAN MEMBERS:

Literature

AYGUESPARSE, ALBERT.
BERTIN, CHARLES.
BRONNE, CARLO.
CLOSSON, HERMAN.
DE BOCK, PAUL-ALOÏSE.
DUBRAU, Mme LOUIS.
GOFFIN, ROBERT.
LILAR, Mme SUZANNE.
LOBET, MARCEL.
MOELLER, Mgr CHARLES.
MOULIN, JEANINE.
OWEN, THOMAS.
SIMENON, GEORGES.
SION, GEORGES.
THIRY, MARCEL.
TORDEUR, JEAN.
VANDERCAMMEN, EDMOND.
VERHESEN, FERNAND.
VIVIER, ROBERT.
WILLEMS, PAUL.

Philology:

BAL, WILLY.
DEBOUILLE, MAURICE.
GOOSSE, ANDRÉ.
HANSE, JOSEPH.
MORTIER, ROLAND.
NOULET, EMILIE.
PIRON, MAURICE.
REMACLE, LOUIS.
RUELLE, PIERRE.
VANDEGANS, ANDRÉ.

FOREIGN MEMBERS:

Literature:

CASSOU, JEAN (France).
DE LA ROCHEFOUCAULD, Duchess EDMÉE (France).
GREEN, JULIEN (U.S.A.).
MALLET, ROBERT (France).
YOURCENAR, Mme MARGUERITE (U.S.A.).

Philology:

ELIADE, MIRCEA (U.S.A.).
RAYMOND, MARCEL (Switzerland).
SICILIANO, ITALO (Italy).
VINAVER, EUGÈNE (France).
WAGNER, ROBERT LÉON (France).

Académie Royale de Médecine de Belgique (*Belgian Royal Academy of Medicine*): Palais des Académies, 1 rue Ducale, 1000 Brussels; f. 1841.

President: Prof. Z. M. BACQ.
1st Vice-President: Prof. G. BRUYNOGHE.
2nd Vice-President: Prof. A. LOUSSE.
Permanent Secretary: Prof A. DE SCOVILLE.

66 mems., 38 correspondents, 8 hon. mems., 88 hon. foreign mems., 76 foreign correspondents; competive scientific examinations held open to scientists from foreign countries.

publs. *Monthly Bulletin and Memoirs*†.

MEMBERS:

Anatomy and Physiology, Medical Physics and Chemistry:

AUBERT, X.	HERS, H.
BACQ, Z.	LECOMTE, J.
BRACHET, J.	**LEPLAT, G.**
CHEVREMONT, M.	PASTEELS, J.
DE DUVE, C.	REUSE, J.
FREDERIC, J.	**RIJLANT, P.**
GEREBTZOFF, M.	SCHOFFENIELS, E.
HERLANT, M.	

Human Medicine:

BASTENIE, P.	MERTENS DE WILMARS, CH.
BOBON, J.	NIZET, A.
BREMER, F.	RADERMECKER, J.
DESMEDT, J. E.	**TITECA, J.**
DE VISSCHER, M.	**VAN BOGAERT, Baron L.**
HUGUES, J.	VAN CAUWENBERGE, H.
LAMBERT, P.	**VAN GEHUCHTEN, P.**
LAVENNE, F.	VERNIORY, A.
LEQUIME, Baron J.	

Surgery and Obstetrics:

ALBERT, F.	HONORE, D.
APPELMANS, P. J. M.	LAMBOTTE, R.
BREMER, A.	LORTHIOIR, J.
BUISSERET, J.	ORBAN, F.
CHALANT, CH.	VAN DEN BRANDEN, Baron J.
DELOYERS, L.	VAN GEERTRUYDEN, J.
DE SCOVILLE, A.	VERRIEST, G.
FRANÇOIS, J.	**WEEKERS, R.**

Hygiene, Forensic Medicine:

BEUMER, J.	FREDERICQ, P.
BORDET, P.	VANBREUSEGHEM, R.
BRUYNOGHE, G.	**WELSCH, M.**
FAIN, A.	

Pharmacy:

DUMONT, P.	**MARICQ, L.**
HEUSGHEM, C.	MOLLE, L.
LAPIERE, C. L.	**STAINIER, C.**

Veterinary Medicine:

DERIVAUX, J.	**LOUSSE, A.**
DE VUYST, A.	SCHOENAERS, F.
FLORENT, A.	

Koninklijke Academie voor Geneeskunde van België (*Royal Academy of Medicine of Belgium*): Paleis der Academiën, Hertogsstraat 1, 1000 Brussels; f. 1938.
President: G. PEETERS.
Permament Secretary: Prof. Dr. A. LACQUET.

Library: *see* Libraries.

Number of mems.: 35; also 17 corresp., 3 hon., 13 foreign hon., 52 foreign corresp.

Publications: *Proceedings*, *Year Book*.

MEMBERS:

Anatomy and Physiology, Medical Physics and Chemistry:

BOUCKAERT, J. J.	LAUWERYNS, J. M.
CARMELIET, E.	**LEUSEN, I.**
DE NAYER, P.	**MASSART, L.**
DE SCHAEPDRYVER, A. F.	**VERDONK, G.**
GEPTS, W.	

Human Medicine:

GESSLER, C.	VAN DAMME, J.
GYSELEN, A.	**VANDENBROUCKE, J.**
JOOSSENS, J. V.	VANDER EECKEN, H.
PANNIER, R.	

Surgery and Obstetrics:

GERARD, J.	**SCHOCKAERT, J. A.**
KLUYSKENS, P.	THIERY, M.
LACQUET, A.	**UYTTENBROECK, F.**
RENAER, M.	VAN DE CALSEYDE, P.

Hygiene, Forensic Medicine:

DE MOOR, P.	VAN MECHELEN, V.
DE SOMER, P.	VAN LAERE, J.
JANSSENS, P. G.	VERMEULEN, A.
THOMAS, F.	VERSTRAETE, M.

Pharmacy:

LEMLI, J.

Veterinary Medicine:

PEETERS, G.	**VERSTRAETE, A.**

HONORARY MEMBERS:

CLAUDE, A.	FRANÇOIS, J.
DE DUVE, C.	

Académie Royale d'Archéologie de Belgique/Koninklijke Academie voor Oudheidkunde van België (*Royal Academy of Archaeology of Belgium*): Fondation Universitaire, rue d'Egmont 11, 1050 Brussels; f. 1842; 60 titular mems. of which 18 form the admin. council; 40 corresp. mems.; Pres. JEAN JADOT; Sec. MIREILLE JOTTRAND; publ. *Revue Belge d'Archéologie et d'Histoire de l'Art*.

Académie Royale des Sciences d'Outre-Mer/Koninklijke Academie voor Overzeese Wetenschappen (*Royal Academy of Overseas Sciences*): 1 rue Defacqz, 1050 Brussels; f 1928; the promotion of scientific knowledge of overseas areas, especially those with particular development problems; Perm. Sec. Prof. P. STANER; 10 hon. mems., 43 mems., 66 assocs., 50 corresps.

LEARNED SOCIETIES

Agriculture and Veterinary Science

Alliance Agricole Belge: 82 rue Joseph II, Brussels 4; f. 1930; Pres. R. Noel; Sec. Henri Massaux; publs. *Alliance Agricole, Nos Petits Elevages et Nos Jardins.*

Société Nationale de Laiterie: 49 ave. Charles Verhaegen, Crainhem; f. 1902; concerned with all scientific aspects of the production of milk and its by-products; Pres. L. Martens; Sec. J. Servais.

Architecture and Town Planning

Fédération Royale des Sociétés d'Architectes de Belgique: 537 blvd. de Smet de Naeyer, Brussels 2; Sec.-Gen. E. Draps.

Société Belge des Urbanistes et Architectes Modernistes: 366 ave. Brugmann, Brussels 18; f. 1919; Sec. L. Obizinski.

Société Centrale d'Architecture de Belgique: Hôtel Ravenstein, 3 rue Ravenstein, 1000 Brussels; f. 1872; promotion of architecture and town planning; 225 mems.; Pres. L. J. Baucher; Sec. J. Potvin.

The Arts

Association Belge de Photographie et de Cinématographie: 57 rue Claessens, 1020 Brussels; f. 1874; 130 mems.; Pres. J. Peeters; publ. *Informations* (monthly).

Association des Artistes Professionnels de Belgique: 461 ave. Louise, Brussels 5.

Institut pour le Redressement de l'Art Complet/Instituut voor het Redden der Artistieke Constanten (IRAC): Zandpoortstraat 35B, Ghent; f. 1962; for the defence of aesthetic constants, particularly those of the classical arts, by documentation, lectures and exhibitions; 400 mems.; Pres. Norbert Nojorkam; Sec. Miss M. L. Hamerlinck; publ. *Cahiers de l'IRAC* (in 5 languages).

Société Belge de Musicologie (*Belgian Society of Musicology*): 30 rue de la Régence, 1000 Brussels; f. 1946; encourages the study and progress of the science and history of music; 300 mems.; Pres. R. Wangermee; Sec. H. Vanhulst; publ. *Revue belge de Musicologie* (French, English, German and Flemish) (annually).

Société Royale des Beaux-Arts: 25 avenue Jef. Lambeaux, Brussels; f. 1893; organizes exhibitions of paintings, sculpture and engravings in Brussels; Pres. Baron Albert Houtart; Sec. P. P. Hamesse; publs. exhibition catalogues.

Bibliography, Library Science and Museology

Association Belge de Documentation/Belgische Vereniging voor Documentatie: B.P. 110, B-1040 Brussels 26; f. 1947; 180 mems.; Pres. R. De Backer; Sec. J. C. Sheets; publ. *Cahiers de la Documentation.*

Association des Archivistes et des Bibliothécaires de Belgique/Vereniging van Archivarissen en Bibliothecarissen van België (*Association of Archivists and Librarians*): 4 blvd. de l'Empereur, 1000 Brussels; f. 1907; 450 mems.; Pres. Dr. G. Asaert, Dr. R. Willio; publs. *Archives et Bibliothéques de Belgique—Archief- en bibliotheekwezen in België* (2 a year) (French, Dutch, English, German, Spanish, Italian) and special issues.

Commission Belge de Bibliographie: 80–84 rue des Tanneurs, B-1000 Brussels; f. 1951; Hon. Pres. L. Verniers, E. Vauthier, J. Van Hove; Pres. R.P. H. Ooms; Secs. E. Cosyns-Verhaegen, A. Segers; a sub-committee of UNESCO, studies methods of standardization of bibliography; 68 mems.; publs. *Bulletin* (quarterly), *Bibliographia Belgica, Coll.*

Institut Belge d'Information et de Documentation: rue Montoyer 3, 1040 Brussels; f. 1962; Pres. A. Breyne.

Museumvereniging van de Nederlandse Cultuurgemeenschap in België (*Belgian Museums Association*): c/o L. Daenens, Museum voor Sierkunst, Jan Breydelstraat 7, 9000 Ghent; f. 1968 to defend the interests of museums and museum personnel; 150 mems.; Pres. R. Verstraelen; publ. *Museumleven* (annually).

Service Belge des Echanges Internationaux: 80–84 rue des Tanneurs, B-1000 Brussels; f. 1889; information, documentation, exchange and transmission; Dir. Fr. Vanwijngaerden.

Vereniging der Antwerpsche Bibliophielen (*Antwerp Association of Bibliophiles*): Museum Plantin-Moretus, Vrijdagmarkt 22, 2000 Antwerp; f. 1877; to increase knowledge of books, particularly in Belgium and the Netherlands; 215 mems.; Pres. Dr. G. Schmook and Prof. Dr. H. Liebaers; Sec. Prof. Dr. G. Persoons, Prof. Dr. De Pauw-De Veen; publ. *De Gulden Passer* (annual).

Vereniging van Religieus-Wetenschappelijke Bibliothecarissen (*Association of Theological Librarians*): Minderbroederstraat 5, 3800 St. Truiden; f. 1965; Pres. H. Morlion; Sec. K. van de Casteele; publ. *V.R.B.-Informatie* (quarterly).

Economics, Law and Politics

Institut Belge de Droit Comparé: 14 rue Bosquet, 1060 Brussels; f. 1907; Pres. M. Vauthier, Hon. Pres. of the Conseil d'Etat; Sec. Paul Landrien; 400 mems.; publ. *La Revue de Droit International et de Droit Comparé* (quarterly).

Institut de Science Politique (*Institute of Political Science*): 43 rue des Champs Elysées, 1050 Brussels; f. 1951 to promote the study of political science; 800 mems.; Pres. Charles Goossens; Dir. A Philippart; Sec. Jean Leclercq; publ. *Res Publica* (quarterly).

Institut Belge des Sciences Administratives/Belgisch Instituut voor Bestuurswetenschappen (*Belgian Institute of Administrative Sciences*): rue du Gouvernement Provisoire 15, 1000 Brussels; f. 1936; Pres. F. Meyers; Sec.-Gen. A. François; studies and research in public administration, also studies questions submitted by the International Institute of Administrative Sciences; 150 mems.; publ. *Administration publique*† (quarterly and monthly).

Politologisch Instituut (*Institute of Political Science*): Van Evenstraat 2B, 3000 Louvain; Pres. Hugo Van Hassel; publ. *Res Publica* (French, English, Dutch, German, quarterly), *Belgian Political Yearbook* (Dutch, French).

Société Royale d'Economie Politique de Belgique (*Royal Belgian Society of Political Economy*): c/o CIFOP, 10 blvd. de Fontaine, 6000 Charleroi; f. 1855; for popularisation and progress in political economy; 600 mems.; Pres. Baron Ansiaux; Sec.-Gen. J. van Overbeke; publ. *Comptes rendus des travaux* (7 or 8 a year).

Union Royale Belge pour Les Pays d'Outremer et l'Europe Unie: formerly Union Royale Coloniale Belge; 34 rue de Stassart, 1050 Brussels; f. 1912; 42 mems.; Chair. Raoul Suain; Admin. Pierre Borlee.

EDUCATION

Conférence des Recteurs des Universités Belges: 5 rue d'Egmont, 1050 Brussels; f. 1973; to study the problems of higher education and scientific research; Chair. Mgr. E. MASSAUX.

Fondation Universitaire: 11 rue d'Egmont, 1050 Brussels; f. 1920; Admin. Dir. PIERRE GERITS.

Belgian American Educational Foundation Inc.: *see* U.S.A. chapter.

Fondation Biermans-Lapôtre: *see* French chapter.

Fondation Fernand Lazard: 11 rue d'Egmont, 1050 Brussels; f. 1949; Pres. JULIEN FAUTREZ.

Fondation Francqui: 11 rue d'Egmont, 1050 Brussels; f. 1932; Pres. JOSEPH VAN DER MEULEN; Sec.-Gen. MARCEL GROSJEAN.

Jeunesse Intellectuelle: 11 rue d'Egmont, 1050 Brussels; f. 1945; Admin. Dir. PIERRE GERITS.

The aim of these foundations is to encourage higher education and scientific research in Belgium.

Jeunesse Belge à l'Etranger: 11 rue d'Egmont, 1050 Brussels; Pres. ARMAND HACQUAERT.

HISTORY, GEOGRAPHY AND ARCHAEOLOGY

Association Royale des Demeures Historiques (*Royal Association for Historic Buildings*): 146 blvd. du Souverain, 1160 Brussels; f. 1934; Pres. Prince ALEXANDRE DE MERODE; publ. *La Maison d'Hier et d'Aujourd'hui* (quarterly).

Fondation Egyptologique Reine Elisabeth: Parc du Cinquantenaire 10, 1040 Brussels; f. 1923 to encourage Egyptian and papyrological studies; 650 mems.; library of 30,000 vols.; Pres. E. BONVOISIN; Dirs. J. BINGEN, H. DE MEULENAERE; publs. *Chronique d'Egypte, Bibliotheca Aegyptiaca, Monumenta Aegyptiaca, Papyrologica Bruxellensia, Bibliographie Papyrologique sur fiches.*

Institut Archéologique du Luxembourg: 13 rue des Martyrs, 6700 Arlon (Belgium); f. 1847; Luxembourgeois museum covers prehistoric period, Belgian-Roman period, Frankish period; 800 mems.; library of 50,000 vols.; Pres. ROGER PETIT; Sec./Curator/Librarian LOUIS LEFEBVRE; publs. *Annales, Bulletin* (quarterly).

Institut Archéologique Liégeois: Musée Curtius, 13 quai de Maastricht, Liège; f. 1850; studies of history and archaeology and related sciences in the District of Liège; 450 mems., 40 corresps.; Pres. G. HANSOTTE; Sec. J. PIEYNS; Curator-Dir. Prof. J. PHILIPPE; publ. *Bulletin* (annually).

Institut Géographique National: Abbaye de la Cambre 13, 1050 Brussels; f. 1831; land surveying and cartography; 450 mems.; library of 15,000 vols.; Dir.-Gen. R. VERBERCKT; publ. *Catalog*† (annually).

Société Archéologique: Hotel de Croix, rue Saintraint, Namur; f. 1845; museum and library; approx. 700 mems.; publs. *Annales, Namurcum.*

Société Belge d'Etudes Byzantines: 4 blvd. de l'Empereur, 1000 Brussels; f. 1956; 52 mems.; Pres. A. LEROY-MOLINGHEN; Sec. J. NORET; publ. *Byzantion, Revue internationale d'études byzantines* (2 a year).

Société Belge d'Etudes Géographiques (*Belgian Society for Geographical Studies*): Blandynberg, 2 Ghent; f. 1931; Pres. F. DUSSART; Sec. M. E. DUMONT; centralizes and co-ordinates geographical research in Belgium; 400 mems.; publ. *Bulletin* (2 a year).

Société Royale Belge de Géographie: Institut de Géographie, 87 ave. A. Buyl, 1050 Brussels; f. 1876; 400 mems.; Pres. J. ANNAERT; Sec.-Gen. J. P. GRIMMEAU; publ. *Revue Belge de Géographie*† (3-7 a year).

Société Royale d'Archéologie de Bruxelles: Musée de la Porte de Hal, Brussels; f. 1887; sections for archaeology proper, and the history of art; other collections in Musées Royaux d'Art et d'Histoire (*q.v.*); library of 20,000 vols.; 1,700 mems.; Pres. Lt.-Gen. DE GREEF; Sec.-Gen. Comte J. DE BORCHGRAVE D'ALTENA; Librarian R. LAURENT; publs. *Bulletins, Annales.*

Société Royale d'Archéologie et de Paléontologie (*Royal Society of Archaeology and Palaeontology*): 12 blvd. Jacques Bostrand, Charleroi; f. 1863; 300 mems.; Pres. Baron CARLO HENIN; Sec. S. BRIGODE; publs. *Bulletin* (quarterly), *Documents et Rapports* (every four years).

Société Royale de Géographie d'Anvers/Koninklijk Aardrijkskundig Genootschap van Antwerpen (*Antwerp Royal Geographic Society*): 64 Frankrijklei, B-2000 Antwerp; f. 1876; 455 mems.; Pres. RENÉ DELLA FAILLE DE WAERLOOS; Sec.-Gen. P. VINCENTELLI; publ. *Bulletin—Tijdschrift* (annual).

Société Royale de Numismatique de Belgique: 22 ave. Louise, 1050 Brussels; f. 1841; 50 full mems., 15 hon. mems., 100 national corresp. mems., 100 foreign corresp. mems.; Pres. EMILE BROUETTE; Hon. Pres. PAUL NASTER and JEAN JADOT; Vice-Pres. PAUL DE BAECK; Sec. TONY HACKENS; publ. *Revue Belge de Numismatique et de Sigillographie.*

INTERNATIONAL CULTURAL ORGANIZATIONS

British Council, The: ave. Galilée 5, 1030 Brussels; also serves Luxembourg; library: *see* Libraries; Rep. C. H. WHISTLER, O.B.E.

Fédération Belge des Alliances Françaises et Institutions Associées: 6 Place Quetelet, 1030 Brussels; Pres. Prof. VICTOR DECROYERE.

Goethe Institut: Deutsche Bibliothek, 58 rue Belliard, 1040 Brussels; f. 1959; German language courses, conferences, lectures; library of 30,000 vols.; media centre of 4,500 records and tapes, 1,200 films and 500 slides; Dir. A. REGENBERG.

Institut Danois: ave. Exposition Universelle 9, 1080 Brussels; f. 1948; a branch of Det Danske Selskab in Copenhagen (*q.v.*); organization of summer schools and study trips to Denmark; library of 2,000 vols.; Sec. MICHELINE REVETS; publs. *Contact avec le Danemark, Kontakt met Denemarken, Musical Denmark* and others.

Istituto Italiano di Cultura: 38 rue de Livourne, Brussels; Dir. Prof. AUGUSTO TRAVERSA.

LANGUAGE AND LITERATURE

Association des Ecrivains Belges de Langue Française (*Association of Belgian Writers in the French Language*): Maison des Ecrivains, 150 chaussée de Wavre, Brussels; f. 1902; 500 mems.; library of 7,000 vols.; Pres. ROGER FOULON; Sec.-Gen. PHILIPPE DELABY; publs. *Nos Lettres, Informations* (10 a year).

International PEN Club;

French Branch: f. 1922; 270 mems.; Pres. Baron DE RADZITZKY D'OSTROWICK; Gen. Sec. RAYMOND QUINOT, 76 ave. 11 Novembre, Bte. 7, 1040 Brussels.

International PEN Club;

Flemish Branch: Vooruitgang Straat 225, 1000 Brussels; f. 1935; 103 mems.; Pres. Gov. R. DECLERCK; Gen. Sec. WILLEM M. ROGGEMAN; publ. *PEN-Club Nieuws.*

Société Belge des Auteurs, Compositeurs et Editeurs (SABAM): 75–77 rue d'Arlon, Brussels 1040; f. 1922; collection and distribution of copyrights; 8,000 mems.; Pres. VIC LEGLEY; Man. Dirs. JOSEPH DETHIER (JEAN DARLIER) and ERNEST VAN DER EYKEN; Gen. Man. EDGARD HOOLANTS; publ. *Bulletin trimestriel.*

Société d'Etudes Latines de Bruxelles (*Brussels Society for Latin Studies*): 60 rue Colonel Chaltin, Brussels 1180; f. 1937; 750 mems.; Pres. M. RENARD, G. CAMBIER; publs. *Latomus* (quarterly), *Collection Latomus*.

Société de Langue et de Littérature Wallonnes A.S.B.L. (*Society for Walloon Language and Literature*): Université de Liège, place du XX août 7, Liège; f. 1856; 400 mems.; library of 3,000 vols.; Pres. M. PIRON; Sec. JEAN RATHMES; publs. *Bulletin*†, *Dialectes de Wallonie*† (both annually), etc.

MEDICINE

Association Belge d'Hygiène et de Médecine Sociale: c/o Prof. E. A. Sand, School of Public Health, U.L.B., Campus Erasme, 808 Route de Lennick, B-1070 Brussels; f. 1938; undertakes and promotes research in and outside Belgium; arranges Belgian participation in international conferences; 160 mems.; Pres. Dr. BANDE-KNOPS; Sec. Prof. E. A. SAND; publs. *Archives belges Médecine sociale, d'Hygiene, Médecine du Travail et Médecine légale.*

Association des Sociétés Scientifiques Médicales Belges: Hôtel de Sociétés Scientifiques, 43 rue des Champs Elysées, 1050 Brussels; f. 1945; 4,000 mems.; Pres. Prof. M. VAN DER GHINST; Sec.-Gen. Dr. P. DOR; numerous publs.

Société Belge de Médecine Tropicale/Belgische Vereniging voor Tropische Geneeskunde: Nationalestraat 155, Antwerp; f. 1920; 33 hon. mems. (Belgian and foreign), 71 assoc. mems., 113 titular mems., 344 corresp. mems.; Sec. Prof. L. EYCKMANS; publ. *Annales* (quarterly).

Société Belge d'Ophtalmologie—section francophone (*Belgian Society of Ophthalmology—French-speaking section*): Ave. Maurice 11, bye 3, 1050 Brussels; f. 1896; Sec. Prof. P. DANIS; publ. *Bulletin* (quarterly).

Société Royale Belge de Radiologie/Koninklijke Belgische Vereniging voor Radiologie: 54 blvd. de Waterloo, 1000 Brussels; f. 1906; 500 mems.; library of 2,000 vols.; Pres. Dr. E. PLUYGERS; Secs.-Gen. Prof. L. JEANMART, Prof. A. BAERT; publ. *Journal Belge de Radiologie* (every 2 months).

Société Royale des Sciences Médicales et Naturelles de Bruxelles: 115 blvd. de Waterloo, Brussels; f. 1822; 150 mems.; Sec. Prof. Dr. J. J. REUSE; publ. *Annales* (quarterly).

NATURAL SCIENCES

General

Comité Belge d'Histoire des Sciences: 317 ave. Charles Woeste, 1090 Brussels; f. 1933; 40 mems. and 20 assoc. mems.; Pres. P. BRIEN; Sec.-Treas. G. HIRSCH; publ. *Notes Bibliographiques* (2 a year).

Fédération Belge des Sociétés Scientifiques: 31 rue Vautier, B-1040 Brussels; f. 1949; co-ordination of all scientific activities and publications, and to seek the advancement of pure and applied science; 40 mem. socs.; Pres. A. CAPART; publ. *Le Mouvement Scientifique en Belgique.*

Société Royale des Sciences de Liège (*Royal Society of Sciences*): 15 ave. des Tilleuls, Liège; f. 1835; advancement of mathematical, physical, chemical, mineral and biological sciences; 200 mems.; Pres. J. GODEAUX; Sec.-Gen. H. SAUVENIER; publ. *Bulletin* (every 2 months).

Société Scientifique de Bruxelles: 61 rue de Bruxelles, B-5000 Namur; 244 mems.; Pres. J. MOMIGNY; Sec. C. COURTOY; publs. *Revue des Questions Scientifiques* (quarterly), *Annales* (quarterly).

Biological Sciences

Les Naturalistes Belges: 31 rue Vautier, B-1040 Brussels; f. 1918; 1,000 mems.; library of 5,000 vols.; zoology, botany, geology, nature conservancy, etc.; Pres. ALAIN QUINTART; publ. *Les Naturalistes Belges*† (8 a year).

Société Belge de Biochimie/Belgische Vereniging voor Biochemie: 115 blvd. de Waterloo, 1000 Brussels; f. 1951; 560 mems.; Sec. GISÈLE PRÉAUX.

Société Belge de Biologie: Place Delcour 17, B-4000 Liège; 110 mems.; Sec. J. LECOMTE.

Société Royale de Botanique de Belgique: 236 rue Royale, B-1030 Brussels; f. 1862; 350 mems.; Pres. J. J. SYMOENS; Sec. J. HOMÈS; publs. *Bulletin*† (2 a year), *Mémoires*†.

Société Royale Belge d'Entomologie: 31 rue Vautier, 1040 Brussels; f. 1855; 180 mems.; library of 5,000 vols.; Sec. CH. VERTRAETEN; publs. *Bulletin et Annales, Mémoires, Catalogue des Coléoptères de Belgique.*

Koninklijke Maatschappij voor Dierkunde van Antwerpen/Société Royale de Zoologie d'Anvers: 26 Koningin Astridplein, B2000 Antwerp; f. 1843; Zoological and Botanical Gardens, Aquarium, Nature Reserve, Museums, Laboratories and educational services; 13,500 mems.; library 27,000 vols.; Dir. J. F. GEERAERTS; publs. *Zoo* (quarterly, French and Dutch), *Acta Zoologica et Pathologica Antverpiensia.*

Société Royale Zoologique de Belgique: 50 ave. F. D. Roosevelt, 1050 Brussels; f. 1863; *c.* 300 mems.; Pres. M. VERHEYEN; Sec. J. L. J. HULSELMANS; publ. *Annales*† (quarterly).

Mathematics

Conseil Supérieur de Statistique: 44 rue de Louvain, 1000 Brussels; f. 1841; 51 mems.; Pres. H. PICARD; Sec. E. VAN LANGENDONCK.

Société Mathématique de Belgique: 317 Ave. Ch. Woeste, 1090 Brussels; f. 1921; 800 mems.; Sec. GUY HIRSCH; publ. *Bulletin* (quarterly).

Physical Sciences

Koninklijk Sterrenkundig Genootschap van Antwerpen/Société Royale d'Astronomie d'Anvers (*Royal Astronomical Society of Antwerp*): 24 Minderbroedersstraat, 2000 Antwerp; f. 1905; dissemination, teaching and aid for the promotion of astronomy; 230 mems.; Pres. WILLY DE KORT; Sec. Baron R. DE TERWANGNE; publ. *Rapport annuel*†.

Société Astronomique de Liège (*Liège Society of Astronomy*): c/o Institut d'Astrophysique, ave. de Cointe 5, B-4200 Cointe-Ougrée; f. 1937; brings together amateurs of astronomy, popularizes the science; 475 mems.; library of 450 vols.; Pres. M. GABRIEL; Sec. G. MATHYS; publ. *Bulletin*† (monthly).

Société Belge d'Astronomie, de Météorologie et de Physique du Globe: 3 ave. Circulaire, 1180 Brussels; f. 1899; 750 mems.; Sec. Gen. R. J. DEJAIFFE; publ. *Ciel et Terre* (every 2 months).

Société Belge de Géologie/Belgische Vereniging voor Geologie: 13 rue Jenner, 1040 Brussels; f. 1887; 434 mems.; Pres. F. GULLENTOPS; Sec.-Gen. E. GROESSENS; publs. *Bulletin*† (quarterly), *Mémoires.*

Société Chimique de Belgique: 49 Square Marie-Louise, 1040 Brussels; f. 1887; 7 brs.; 1,000 mems.; library at 48 ave. Depage, Brussels; Pres. Prof. Dr. R. HULS; Gen. Sec. Prof. Dr. G. GEUSKENS; publ. *Bulletin des Sociétés Chimiques Belges* (10–12 a year in collaboration with Vlaamse Chemische Vereniging).

Société Géologique de Belgique (*Belgian Geological Society*): Université de Liège, 7 Place du Vingt-Août, 4000 Liège; f. 1874; 467 mems.; Pres. A. BEUGNIES; Sec. G. UBAGHS; publs. *Annales*† (2 a year), *Mémoires* (irregular).

Vlaamse Chemische Vereniging (*Flemish Chemical Society*): 533 Coupure, B-9000 Ghent; f. 1939; 1,200 mems.; Pres. Dr. M. VANDEWALLE; Sec. Dr. N. SCHAMP; publs. *Chemie Magazine* (monthly), *Bulletins des Sociétés Chimiques Belges* (monthly), *Tijdingen* (every two months).

PHILOSOPHY AND PSYCHOLOGY

Société Belge de Logique et de Philosophie des Sciences: 317 ave. Charles Woeste, 1090 Brussels; Sec. G. HIRSCH.

Société Belge de Philosophie (*Belgian Society of Philosophy*): 143 ave. A. Buyl, Brussels; f. 1920 to bring together people interested in philosophy; 96 mems.; Pres. M. WEYEMBERGH; Sec. G. HOTTOIS.

Société Philosophique de Louvain: c/o Institut Supérieur de Philosophie, Collège Thomas More, SH3, B-1348, Louvain-la-Neuve; f. 1888; 216 mems.; Pres. J. LADRIÈRE; Sec. J. ETIENNE.

RELIGION, SOCIOLOGY, ANTHROPOLOGY

Centre pour l'Etude des Problèmes du Monde Musulman Contemporain (*Study Centre for Problems of the Contemporary Muslim World*): 44 ave. Jeanne, 1050 Brussels; f. 1957; publs. *Correspondance d'Orient—Etudes* (annually), Collections *Correspondance d'Orient* and *Le Monde Musulman Contemporain—Initiations*.

Centrum Voor de Studie van de Mens (*Centre for the Study of Man*): 207-B/4 Italiëlei, 2000 Antwerp; f. 1951; aims to synthesize the scientific and philosophical data about the nature of man both as an individual and as a part of a cultural community; Pres. Prof. Dr. R. DELLAERT; Sec. Mlle L. VERHAVERT; publ. volume of lectures† (annually in Dutch).

Institut Belge des Hautes Etudes Bouddhiques: Chaussée de Louvain 696, B1030 Brussels; f. 1967 to study Buddhist thought and culture; 18 mems.; library of 1,100 vols.; Pres. P. BEAUTRIX; Sec. J. BARUCH; publ. *Cahiers d'études bouddhiques* (quarterly).

Institut Belge des Hautes Etudes Chinoises: c/o Musées Royaux d'Art et d'Histoire, 10 parc du Cinquantenaire, 1040 Brussels; f. 1929; Sinology and Buddhism; lectures, modern and classical Chinese courses; library of *c.* 40,000 vols.; *c.* 250 mems.; Pres. R. DE ROO; publ. *Mélanges Chinois et Bouddhiques*† (annual).

Ruusbroecgenootschap: Prinsstraat 17, 2000 Antwerp; f. 1925; a society of Flemish Jesuits engaged in spiritual studies of the Low Countries; since 1973 incorporated as part of Universitaire Faculteiten Sint-Ignatius (*q.v.*); library of 90,000 vols.; Dir. J. ALAERTS; publs. *Ons Geestelijk Erf*† (quarterly), *Studien en Tekstuitgaven vans Ons Geestelijk Efr*† (series).

Société des Bollandistes: 24 blvd. St. Michel, B-1040 Brussels; f. at Antwerp in 1630, named after Bollandus, who died 1665; medievalist; its members are Belgian Jesuits engaged in the publication of the *Acta Sanctorum* (a critical history of the Saints, with original sources or documents); also publishes the *Analecta Bollandiana* (quarterly) and *Subsidia Hagiographica*; library of 400,000 vols.; Pres. B. DE GAIFFIER.

Société Royale Belge d'Anthropologie et de Préhistoire: 31 rue Vautier, 1040 Brussels; f. 1882; Pres. P. BONENFANT; Sec.-Gen. A. LEGUEBE; 180 mems.; publ. *Bulletin*† (annual).

TECHNOLOGY

Institut Belge de Normalisation (I.B.N.) (*Belgian Standards Institute*): 29 ave. de la Brabançonne, 1040 Brussels; f. 1946; Belgian member of the International Organization for Standardization; 700 mems.; Pres. R. DE PAEPE; Dir.-Gen. J. CROON; publs. *Normes Belges*, *Revue I.B.N.* (every 2 months).

Koninklijke Vlaamse Ingenieursvereniging (*Royal Flemish Association of Engineers*): Ingenieurshuis, Jan van Rijswijcklaan 58, 2000 Antwerp; f. 1928; 7,500 mems.; Pres. ir. L. TEYSEN; Sec.-Gen. ir. R. ALAERTS; publs. *Het Ingenieursblad*† (monthly), *Huishoudelijke Mededelingen*† (fortnightly), *Journal A* (quarterly), *Journal of Computational and Applied Mathematics* (quarterly).

Société Belge de Photogrammétrie (*Belgian Society of Photogrammetry*): 34 blvd. Pachéco (2e étage), 1000 Brussels; f. 1931; 153 mems.; Pres. A. VERDIN; Sec. H. VAN OLFFEN (acting); publ. *Bulletin*† (quarterly).

Société Royale Belge des Electriciens: 54 chaussée de Charleroi, 1060 Brussels; f. 1884; 1,675 mems.; Pres. M. R. VAN DEN DAMME; publs. *Bulletin*, *Revue E* (quarterly).

Société Royale Belge des Ingénieurs et des Industriels: 3 rue Ravenstein, 1000 Brussels; f. 1885; 5,000 mems.; Pres. A. L. JAUMOTTE; Sec.-Gen. J. DUTOY, I.C.A.; publs. *Technical Revue* (monthly), *Bulletin Hebdomadaire*.

RESEARCH INSTITUTES

(*see* also under Universities)

AGRICULTURE AND VETERINARY SCIENCE

Centre de Recherches Agronomiques de Gembloux: 22 ave. de la Faculté d'Agronomie, Gembloux; f. 1872; 68 mems.; Dir. R. LECOMTE; publs. *Rapport d'activité annuel*, *Compte rendu des recherches*, *Notes techniques*; comprises 12 autonomous research stations and a Public Relations Department:

1. **Station de Chimie et de Physique agricoles:** Dir. G. DROEVEN.
2. **Station Laitière:** Dir. P. JAMOTTE.
3. **Station de Phytopathologie:** Dir. G. PARMENTIER.
4. **Station de Zoologie Appliquée:** Dir. J. BERNARD.
5. **Station de Génie Rural:** Dir. V. DUFEY.
6. **Station d'Amélioration des Plantes:** Dir. L. NOULARD.
7. **Station de Technologie Forestière:** Dir. P. ROOSEN.
8. **Station de Haute Belgique:** Dir. L. NYS.
9. **Station de Phytopharmacie:** Dir. L. DETROUX.
10. **Station des Cultures fruitières et maraichères:** Dir. E. DERMINE.
11. **Station de Zootechnie:** Dir. P. VANDENBYVANG.
12. **Station de Phytotechnie:** Dir. L. RIXHON.
13. **Service des Relations Publiques:** Dir. P. CANTILLON.

Institut Economique Agricole: 18 blvd. de Berlaimont, 1000 Brussels; f. 1960; study and research in economics and agricultural sociology; Dir. R. DE SUTTER; publs. *Courriers, Notes et Cahiers de l'I.E.A.*

Institut National de Recherches Vétérinaires: Groeselenberg 99, Uccle, 1180 Brussels; f. 1924; undertakes research in veterinary science, laboratory diagnostics, control of vaccines and production of foot and mouth vaccine; Dir. Dr. LEUNEN; publ. *Rapport d'activité* (annually, French and Dutch).

Arts

Centre National de Recherches "Primitifs Flamands"/ Nationaal Centrum voor Navorsingen over de Vlaamse Primitieven (*National Research Centre of Flemish Primitives*): 1 Parc du Cinquantenaire, B1040 Brussels; f. 1950; research into 15th-century Flemish painting; 12 mems.; library of 5,800 vols.; Pres. E. LANGUI; Dir. R. SNEYERS; Administrator E. BRIES; publs. *Corpus de la Peinture des Anciens Pays-Bas Méridionaux au 15e Siècle, Répertoire des Peintures Flamandes du 15e Siècle, Contributions à l'Etude des Primitifs Flamands* (annually).

Documentation, Information and Library Science

Association Scientifique et Technique pour la Recherche en Informatique Documentaire (ASTRID): ASTRID Bldg., Koningin Astridlaan 89, B9000 Ghent; f. 1971; conducts studies supported by official organizations, by its own funds and by private contributions; Sec. H. K. DE JAEGER; publs. monographs (*ASTRID series on Information Science*).

Centre National de Documentation Scientifique et Technique (*National Centre for Scientific and Technical Documentation*): 4 blvd. de l'Empereur, B-1000 Brussels; f. 1964; aims to inform scientists, university faculties and scientific organizations on the progress of research on special topics in the fields of medicine, fundamental and applied sciences, technology and agriculture; focal point for library, documentation and information networks (national and international); Chair. J. VAN KEYMEULEN; Sec.-Gen. M. WITTEK; Gen. Dir. A. COCKX; publs. *Catalogue Collectif Belge et Luxembourgeois des Périodiques Etrangers en cours de publication, Inventaire permanent de la production scientifique belge, Inventaire permanent des institutions belges de recherche disposant d'une bibliothèque ou d'un centre de documentation, Inventaire Permanent des Congrès Scientifiques et Techniques Nationaux et Internationaux.*

Centre Belge de Traduction (*Belgian National Translation Centre*): 4 blvd. de l'Empereur, 1000 Brussels; f. 1964; works in close co-operation with the Centre National de Documentation Scientifique et Technique; specializes in translations of the less accessible languages and of scientific information; Dir. Mme I. CLEMENS.

Economics, Law and Politics

Centre Interuniversitaire de Droit Comparé (*Inter-university Centre of Comparative Law*): 103 blvd. de Waterloo, 1000 Brussels; f. 1957; research in the field of comparative law (30 research fellows); congresses, colloquia and conferences; 250 mems.; library of 35,000 vols., 200 periodicals; Pres. Prof. W. J. GANSHOF VAN DER MEERSCH; Dir. Prof. G. HORSMANS.

Institut Royal des Relations Internationales: 88 ave. de la Couronne, 1050 Brussels; f. 1947; research in international relations, international economics, international law and international politics; specialized library containing 11,000 vols. and 600 periodicals; archives; lectures and conferences are held; Pres. Baron SNOY ET D'OPPUERS (fmr. Minister of Finance); Vice-Pres. and Treas. Prof. PIERRE ANSIAUX; Dir.-Gen. Prof. EMMANUEL COPPIETERS, DR.ECON., DR.JUR., M.SC.(ECON.); publs. *Studia Diplomatica* (*Chronique de Politique Etrangère*) (bi-monthly), *Internationale Spectator* (monthly).

Medicine

Fondation Born-Bunge pour la Recherche (*Born-Bunge Research Foundation*): Universiteitsplein 1, 2610 Wilrijk-Antwerp; f. 1954; research in neurological sciences; library of 7,000 vols., 150 periodicals; Dir. Dr. L. VAN BOGAERT.

Fondation Médicale Reine Elisabeth: 1 ave. J. J. Crocq, B1020 Brussels; invests money in medical research through a number of laboratories operating at a research institute; Dir. Prof. P. P. LAMBERT.

Institut Neurologique Belge: rue de Linthout 152, Brussels 4; f. 1924; Pres. Comte EDOUARD D'OULTREMONT; publs. *Acta Neurologica* and *Psychiatrica Belgica*.

Institut Pasteur du Brabant: 28 rue du Remorqueur, 1040 Brussels; f. 1900; 199 mems.; scientific research, preparation of serums and vaccines, analyses; Dir. F. DEMEUTER; numerous publs.

Simon Stevin Instituut voor Wetenschappelijk Onderzoek (*Simon Stevin Institute for Scientific Research*): Jerusalemstraat 34, B-8000 Bruges; f. 1959; research in proteins, lipids and hormones; Dir. Dr.Med. H. PEETERS; publ. *Protides of the Biological Fluids.*

Natural Sciences

General

Fonds National de la Recherche Scientifique: 5 rue d'Egmont, B1050 Brussels; f. 1928; to promote scientific research; provides subsidies and grants to research workers and students; Pres. E. BETZ; Sec.-Gen. PAUL LEVAUX; publs. *Rapport annuel*, list of names of academic staff attached to institutions of higher education or research in Belgium. Affiliated institutes:

Institut Interuniversitaire des Sciences Nucléaires: 5 rue d'Egmont, B-1050 Brussels; f. 1951; to subsidize, promote and co-ordinate study and research in nuclear sciences in Belgium; Pres. E. BETZ; Sec.-Gen. PAUL LEVAUX.

Fonds de la Recherche Fondamentale Collective: 5 rue d'Egmont, B-1050 Brussels; f. 1965; to promote basic scientific research, excluding medical and nuclear research; Pres. F. DETHIER; Sec.-Gen. PAUL LEVAUX.

Fonds de la Recherche Scientifique Médicale: 5 rue d'Egmont, B-1050 Brussels; f. 1965; to promote medical research in Belgium; Pres. S. HALTER; Sec.-Gen. PAUL LEVAUX.

Institut Royal des Sciences Naturelles de Belgique/Koninklijk Belgisch Instituut voor Natuurwetenschappen: 31 rue Vautier, 1040 Brussels; f. 1842; library: *see* Libraries; departments for zoology, paleontology, mineralogy, petrography and biology, and general scientific services; Dir. Prof. Dr. X. MISONNE; publs. *Mémoires, Bulletin, Le Gerfaut de Giervalk, Faune de Belgique.*

Biological Sciences

Jardin Botanique National de Belgique/Nationale Plantentuin van België: Domein van Bouchout, B-1860 Meise; f. 1870; botanical taxonomy and geography, especially of African and European plants, including Cryptogams; herbarium with over 2,000,000 specimens; library of *c.* 200,000 vols.; Dir. Dr. E. PETIT; publs. *Bulletin*† (2 a year), *Flore illustrée des champignons d'Afrique Centrale* (annually), *Flore d'Afrique Centrale* (irregularly), *Distributiones plantarum africanarum* (irregularly), *Dumortiera*† (3 a year).

Mathematical Sciences

Institut National de Statistique: 44 rue de Louvain, 1000 Brussels; Dir.-Gen. P. VAN LANDEGHEM; publ. *Bulletin de Statistique* (monthly).

Physical Sciences

Centre d'Etudes de l'Energie Nucléaire/Studiecentrum voor Kernenergie (C.E.N.—S.C.K.): Head Office: 144 ave. Eugène Plasky, 1040 Brussels; Laboratories: Mol-Donk; f. 1952; conducts fundamental and applied research; runs three reactors, two critical assemblies and specialized laboratories; employs about 1,200 people; Gen. Man. S. AMELINCKX.

Institut d'Aéronomie Spatiale de Belgique: Ave. Circulaire 3, 1180 Brussels; f. 1964 to undertake research in aeronomy (physics and chemistry of atmosphere) from information gained from space vehicles; library of 3,000 vols. and 150 periodicals; 60 mems.; Dir. ROGER PASTIELS (acting); Sec. MAURICE HAUTFENNE; publs. *Aeronomica Acta A*† (research), *Aeronomica Acta F*† (information).

Institut de Recherches Chimiques: Ministry of Agriculture. Museumlaan 5, 1980 Tervuren; f. 1928; research in organic chemistry, biochemistry, pedochemistry, geochemistry, and pollution problems; 50 mems.; library of 6,000 vols., 200 periodicals; Dir. J. R. ISTAS.

Institut Royal Météorologique de Belgique: ave. Circulaire 3, Uccle, 1180 Brussels; reorganized 1913; departments for Climatology, Aerometry, Aerology, Applied Meteorology, Geophysics and Numerical Calculus; mems.: scientific 36, assistants 80, technical 32; Dir. Dr. A. VANDENPLAS; publs. *Bulletin Quotidien du temps* (daily), *Observations climatologiques, Observations synoptiques, Observations géophysiques, Observations ionosphériques* (monthly), *Observations d'ozone* (quarterly), *Climatologie, Rayonnement solaire, Magnétisme terrestre, Marées terrestres a Dourbes, Hydrologie* (annual), *Publications de l'I.R.M.* (series A and B) (occasional).

Observatoire Royal de Belgique: ave. Circulaire 3, Uccle, Brussels; f. 1827; astronomy, radioastronomy, geodynamics; 21 scientific, 60 technical staff; Dir. Prof. A. G. VELGHE; publs. *Annuaire, Bulletin Astronomique, Annales, Communications, Monographies, Bulletin séismique, Bulletin d'Observations des Marées Terrestres.*

PHILOSOPHY

Centre National de Recherches de Logique: 32 rue de la Pêcherie, 1180 Brussels; f. 1951; Pres. CH. PERELMAN; Sec.-Gen. P. GOCHET; publ. *Logique et Analyse* (quarterly).

RELIGION, SOCIOLOGY AND ANTHROPOLOGY

Centre National des Hautes Etudes Juives (*National Centre for Jewish Studies*): 44 ave. Jeanne, 1050 Brussels; f. 1959; studies, publications and documentation on contemporary Jewry; library of 2,000 vols. and 160 periodicals; Pres. JEAN BAUGNIET; Dir. WILLY BOK.

Centrum voor Interdisciplinair Antropologisch Onderzoek (*Centre for Interdisciplinary Anthropological Research*): Maria-Christinastraat 8, 3070 Kortenberg; f. 1967; Dir. Prof. Dr. RENÉ DELLAERT.

TECHNOLOGY

Institut des Industries de Fermentation—Institut Meurice Chimie—Institut Supérieur Industriel: 1 ave. Emile Gryzon, Anderlecht, 1070 Brussels; f. 1892; research and training centre for industrial engineers in chemistry, biochemistry and graduates in dietetics; Dir. Dr. J. M. PIÉRARD; publs. *L'Ingénieur Chimiste, Revue des Fermentations et des Industries Alimentaires.*

Institut National des Industries Extractives (INIEX): rue du Chéra 200, B-4000 Liège; f. 1968; scientific research relating to mines and quarries, pollution and polymers; 20 mems.; Pres. J. MEDAETS; Dir. R. LIEGEOIS; publs. *Annales des Mines de Belgique*† (French and Dutch) (monthly).

Institut pour l'Encouragement de la Recherche Scientifique dans l'Industrie et l'Agriculture (I.R.S.I.A.): 6 rue de Crayer, Brussels 5; f. 1944; promotes and encourages, by means of subsidies, scientific and technical research in industry and agriculture; Pres. J. HINNEKENS; Dir. J. VAN KEYMEULEN; Sec.-Gen. A. MARCHAL; publ. *Annual Report, Research Reports.*

Von Karman Institute for Fluid Dynamics: Chaussée de Waterloo 72, 1640 Rhode-St.-Genese; f. 1956; multinational postgraduate teaching and research in aerodynamics, supported by NATO; depts. of aeronautics/aerospace, turbomachinery, general and environmental fluid dynamics, computational fluid dynamics; 80 staff; library of 2,000 vols., 55,000 reports; Dir. JEAN J. GINOUX; publs. *Technical Notes*†, *Lecture Series Notes*, etc.

LIBRARIES AND ARCHIVES

Antwerp

Archief en Museum voor het Vlaamse Cultuurleven (*Archives and Museum of Flemish Culture*): Minderbroedersstraat 22, Antwerp; f. 1933; archives of Flemish literature, arts and politics; files and manuscripts can be seen on application; 55,000 vols., 40,000 files, 35,000 MSS.; Dir. E. WILLEKENS; Sec. D. L. SIMONS; publ. *Mededelingen van de Documentatiedienst.*

Bibliotheek der Nationaal Hoger Instituut en Koninklijke Academie voor Schone Kunsten (*Library of the Nat. Higher Institute and Royal Academy of Fine Arts*): Mutsaertstraat 31, Antwerp; f. 1663; 20,000 vols. and prints, 250 periodicals, etc.; Scientific Librarian G. PERSOONS.

Bibliotheek-Rijksuniversitair Centrum: 1 Middelheimlaan, 2020 Antwerp; f. 1965; 175,000 vols.; (Linguistics: Schildersstraat 41, 2000 Antwerp; Third World Development: 52 ave. Goemaerelei, 2000 Antwerp); Librarian Dr. B. VAN STYVENDAELE.

Bibliotheek-Universitaire Instelling Antwerpen: Universiteitsplein 1, 2610 Wilrijk-Antwerp; f. 1972; 200,000 vols.; University Librarian H. VERVLIET.

Bibliotheek der Universitaire Faculteiten Sint-Ignatius: Prinsstraat 13, 2000 Antwerp; f. 1852; 400,000 vols.; Chief Librarian J. VAN BRABANT.

Rijksarchief te Antwerpen (*Antwerp State Archives*): Door Verstraetepl. 5, B2000 Antwerp; documents from 12th to 20th century; Archivists A. JAMEES, H. DELVAUX.

Stadsarchief (*City Archives*): Venusstraat 11, B-2000 Antwerp; f. 12th century; documents concerning the administration of Antwerp; history, economic history and history of arts of Antwerp; genealogy, heraldry, cartography, sigillography; specialized library of 6,000 vols., 243 periodicals; Archivist Dr. JAN VAN ROEY.

Stadsbibliotheek: Hendrik Conscienceplein 4, Antwerp; f. 1487, reorganized 1834; Dutch literature, history, local press; open to the public; 650,000 vols.; Librarian Dr. E. WILLEKENS.

Arlon

Archives de l'Etat à Arlon: Parc des Expositions, 6700 Arlon; f. 1849; documents concerning the Province of Luxembourg from 11th to 20th century; 62,000 vols.; Archivist R. PETIT.

Bruges

Archives de l'Etat à Bruges: 14 rue de l'Académie; documents on Western Flanders from 12th to 20th century; Archivist J. MERTENS; Scientific Collaborators L. DANHIEUX, M. VANDERMAESEN.

Brussels

American Library, The: Square du Bastion 1c, 1050 Brussels.

Archives de la Ville de Bruxelles: 65 rue des Tanneurs, 1000 Brussels; 6 mems.; collection includes Charles Pergameni historical archives; Archivist for Brussels MINA MARTENS; publ. *Cahiers Bruxellois.*

Archives du Centre public d'aide sociale de Bruxelles: 298A rue Haute, Brussels; archives concerning ancient hospices and places of refuge, 12th century to 1803, 1803–1925, 1925–1977; approx. 20,000 archives; 15,000 vols.; Archivist Mme C. DICKSTEIN-BERNARD.

Archives Générales du Royaume: 2-4 rue de Ruysbroeck, Brussels; f. 1794; 45 kms. documents concerning the Low Countries, Belgium and Brabant from 11th-20th centuries; library of 25,000 vols.; Gen. Archivist C. WYFFELS.

Archives de la Guerre: Brussels; f. 1919; archives concerning World Wars I and II; 25,000 files; also 28,000 vols. and papers; maps, photographs, collections of currency, medals, etc.; open to the public on application.

Bibliothèque des Facultés Universitaires Saint-Louis: 43 blvd. du Jardin Botanique, 1000 Brussels; f. 1858; 100,000 vols.; Librarian G. BRAIVE.

Bibliothèque Centrale du Ministère de l'Education Nationale/Centrale Bibliotheek van het Ministerie van Nationale Opvoeding en Nederlandse Cultuur: 27 rue de Louvain, 1000 Brussels; f. 1879; contains vols. on administration and law, all branches of science and pedagogy, educational books; 450,000 vols., 1,700 periodicals; open only to teachers and mems. of French and Flemish Depts.; Dirs. (French section) MARCEL MAES, (Flemish section) CYRIEL WELLENS.

Bibliothèque de l'Académie Royale des Beaux-Arts: 144 rue du Midi, 1000 Brussels; 17,175 vols.; Librarian JOSÉ GALMACHE.

Bibliothèque de l'Ecole Nationale Supérieure d'Architecture et des Arts Visuels: Fondation I. Errera, 21 abbaye de la Cambre, 1050 Brussels; f. 1918; 42,000 vols.; Librarian PIERRE FRANÇOIS.

Bibliothèque de l'Institut Royal des Sciences Naturelles de Belgique: 31 rue Vautier, B-1040 Brussels; f. 1846; 710,000 vols., 6,000 periodicals; Dir. (vacant).

Bibliothèques de l'Université Libre de Bruxelles: 50 ave. Franklin D. Roosevelt, B-1050 Brussels; f. 1846; 1,310,000 vols. including periodicals and theses; Librarian PAUL DELSEMME.

Bibliothèque, Documentation, Publications du Ministère de l'Emploi et du Travail: 53 rue Belliard, 1040 Brussels; f. 1896 (since the foundation of the Board of Labour); specialized library of 70,000 vols., 1,400 periodicals on sociology and social sciences; Dir. JULIEN SOENEN; publs. *Revue de Travail*† (monthly), *Bulletin bibliographique*† (monthly in Dutch and French), *Arbeidsblad*†.

Bibliothèque du Parlement: Palais de la Nation, 2 place de la Nation, Brussels; f. 1831; *c.* 3,000,000 vols., 2,000 periodicals; Librarian JAN GROOTAERS; publs. acquisitions list (monthly), bibliographical documentation list (fortnightly).

Bibliothèque Fonds Quetelet (*Library of the Ministry of Economic Affairs*): 6 rue de l'Industrie, Brussels; f. 1841; 670,000 vols. on statistics, economic and social sciences, 7,000 periodicals; open to the public; reference and computer-assisted bibliographic services; Chief Librarian J. DE BUCK; publ. *Accroissements de la Bibliothèque Centrale*† (monthly).

Bibliothèque Royale Albert 1er (*The Belgian National Library*): 4 blvd. de l'Empereur, 1000 Brussels; f. 1837; national depository library; 3,000,000 vols., 18,000 periodicals, 35,000 MSS., 35,650 rare printed books, 700,000 prints, 100,000 maps; 160,100 coins and medals; Dir. MARTIN WITTEK; publs. *Bibliographie de Belgique*† (monthly), catalogues† of collections and exhibitions, etc.

British Council Library: Bât. Galilée, 5 ave. Galilée, 1030 Brussels; f. 1946; 16,144 vols., 74 periodicals; Librarian Miss LINDA BULL, B.A., A.L.A.

Library of the Commission of the European Communities: 200 rue de la Loi, 1049 Brussels; f. 1958; a central library linking a system of specialized library/documentation units; with the Documentation Service it forms part of the EEC's Directorate-General IX (Personnel and Administration); its primary task is to supply information to Commission officials; *c.* 250,000 vols. and periodicals on economic and legal subjects, also ex-EURATOM library (scientific and technical); special reading-room for publs. of intergovernmental orgs.; Head ERIC GASKELL; publs. *List of Accessions* (monthly), series of occasional bibliographies, trilingual subject-index to classified catalogue, classification scheme for int. organizations.

Gembloux

Bibliothèque de la Faculté des Sciences Agronomiques de l'Etat: 5800 Gembloux; *c.* 78,000 vols.; Librarian Mme L. WILLAM-ENGELS; publ. *Bulletin des Recherches agronomiques de Gembloux.*

9000 Ghent

Bibliotheek van de Rijksuniversiteit te Gent: 9 Rozier; f. 1797/1817; 2,000,000 vols., 5,060 MSS.; open to the public; Librarian (vacant); publs. *Mededelingen*, etc.

Centrale Bibliotheek Faculteit Landbouwwetenschappen (*Central Library of the Faculty of Agricultural Sciences*): Rijksuniversiteit, Coupure 533; 60,000 vols.; Curator Prof. G. GENIE.

Rijksarchief te Gent: Gerard de Duivelsteen; 12 km. of documents mainly concerning Eastern Flanders from 9th to 20th centuries; Archivist Dr. HILDA COPPEJANS-DESMEDT.

Liège

Archives de l'Etat à Liège: 8 rue Pouplin; documents concerning the Liège district from 9th to 20th centuries; Archivist G. HANSOTTE.

Bibliothèque Publique Centrale de la Ville de Liège: Maison de la Culture, 8 Place des Carmes; f. 1907; general library, history of Liège; *c.* 350,000 vols.; Librarian A. CORDEWIENER.

Bibliothèque de l'Institut Archéologique Liégeois: Musée Curtius, 13 quai de Maastricht; f. 1850; 27,000 vols. (mostly periodicals).

Bibliothèque de l'Université: 1 place Cockerill; f. 1817; 1,650,000 vols. and pamphlets, 3,935 MSS.; open to the public; Librarians P. GORÊT, R. BRAGARD, J. HOYOUX; publ. *Bibliotheca Universitatis Leodiensis*†.

Louvain

Centre Général de Documentation de l'Université Catholique de Louvain: Place Cardinal Mercier 31, 1348 Louvain-La-Neuve; f. 1425; 800,000 vols.; Librarian J. ROELS.

Malines (Mechelen)

Archief en Stadsbibliotheek: Steenweg 1, 2800 Mechelen; f. 1684; the library of the Great Council of the Netherlands; 79,100 vols.; Archivist M. BAFCOP; publs. *Inventaire des Archives de la ville de Malines* (8 vols.), *Catalogue méthodique de la Bibliothèque de Malines* (1 vol.).

Archives de l'Archevêché: Archevêché de Malines, Wollemarkt 15, 2800 Mechelen; f. 1825; archives from 12th to 20th centuries; some MSS. and approx. 500 books; also 1,200 files containing documents, 50,000 photographs, iconographs, souvenirs, etc.; Archivist Dr. C. VAN DE WIEL.

Maredsous

Bibliothèque de l'Abbaye de Saint-Benoît: Maredsous (B-5642-Denée); f. 1872; books of learning, especially history and theology; 200,000 vols., 35,000 brochures; Chief Librarian Dom DANIEL MISONNE; publs. *Revue Bénédictine.*

Mons

Archives de l'Etat: 23 Place du Parc; archives date from 10th century to present day; library contains 25,000 vols.; the buildings were badly damaged during the war and many records lost: at present there is rebuilding and the archives are being added to: the archives of the town of Mons are intact; there are also archives from the Abbeys and noble families of Hainaut; Keeper GABRIEL WYMANS.

Bibliothèque Centrale de la Faculté Polytechnique de Mons: rue de Houdain; f. 1837; 38,000 vols.; Chief Librarian M. LELANGUE.

Bibliothèque de l'Université de l'Etat: 17 Place Warocqué, B7000 Mons; f. 1797; reference and lending sections; rare and early books; 385,000 vols., 500 MSS., 300 incunabula, maps, prints, local documents, periodicals and newspapers; Chief Librarian JOSEPH DELSAUT; Curators RENÉ CLAIX, CHRISTIANE PIERARD.

5000 Namur

Archives de l'Etat à Namur: 45 rue d'Arquet, 5000 Namur; documents concerning the County and Province of Namur from the 8th to 20th centuries; Archivist J. BOVESSE.

Bibliothèque Universitaire Moretus Plantin: 19 rue Grandgagnage; f. 1921; history of Western Europe, Classical, Roman and German philology, philosophy, law, economics, art, sciences; 720,000 vols.; Chief Librarian J. DENIS.

Sint Niklaas Waas

Biblioteek voor Hedendaagse Dokumentatie (*Library on Contemporary Documentation*): Parklaan 2, 2700 Sint Niklaas Waas; private political, social and economic library; *c.* 100,000 vols., 2,500 periodicals, 12,000 maps; special collections on governmental research, public administration; large collections of U.S. government documents; Librarian YVAN VAN GARSSE.

Ypres

Stedelijke Biblioteek (*Public Library*): St. Janstraat 7; f. 1840; general interest; 60,000 vols.; *c.* 300 periodicals; Librarian OCTAAF MUS.

MUSEUMS

Antwerp

Koninklijk Museum voor Schone Kunsten (*Royal Museum of Fine Arts*): Leopold de Waelplein, 2000 Antwerp; f. 1890; collections of Flemish Primitifs, early foreign schools, 16th-17th-century Antwerp School, 17th-century Dutch School, works of Belgian artists of 19th and 20th centuries; important works of Leys, De Braekeleer, Ensor, Wouters, Smits, Permeke; library of *c.* 35,000 vols.; Curator-in-Chief Dr. G. GEPTS; publs. *Jaarboek*† (annually) and catalogues.

Kunsthistorische Musea (*Art History Museums*): Rubenshuis, Wapper 9–11; Curator FRANS BAUDOUIN.

Rubenshuis (*Rubens' House*): Wapper 9–11; f. 1946; reconstruction of Rubens' house and studio; original 17th-century portico and pavilion; paintings by P. P. Rubens, his collaborators and pupils; 17th-century furnishings; Chief Asst. RENÉ PANDELAERS.

Rubenianum: Belgiëlei 91; documentation centre for the study of 17th-century Flemish art; library and photo archives; Dirs. R.-A. D'HULST and FRANS BAUDOUIN; publ. *Corpus Rubenianum Ludwig Burchard.*

Openluchtmuseum voor Beeldhouwkunst (Middelheim) (*Open-air Museum of Sculpture*): Middelheimlaan 61, 2020 Antwerp; f. 1950; important collection of contemporary sculpture, including Rodin, Maillol, Zadkine, Marini, Manzu, Gargallo, Moore, exhibited in a large park; biennial exhibitions devoted to modern sculpture; Asst. Keeper Mrs. MARIE-ROSE BENTEIN-STOELEN.

Museum Smidt van Gelder: Belgiëlei 91; f. 1950; famous collection of Chinese and European porcelains, Dutch 17th-century paintings, and of 18th-century French furniture; Chief Asst. Miss MARIA SNOECKX.

Museum Mayer van den Bergh: Lange Gasthuisstraat 19; f. 1904; unique collection of paintings, including Breughel, Metsys, Aertsen, Mostaert, Bronzino, Heda, de Vos, and medieval sculpture, ivories, etc.; the collections are under the custody of a Board of Regents; Asst. Keeper HANS NIEUWDORP.

Museum Plantin-Moretus: Vrijdagmarkt 22; f. 1876; 16-18th-century patrician house with ancient printing office and foundry, engravings on copper and wood; typography drawings and pictures; illuminated MSS., library of 30,000 books of the 15th to 18th centuries, archives; Dir. Dr. L. VOET.

Oudheidkundige Musea (*Archaeological Museums*): Office: Volkskundemuseum, Gildekamersstraat 2-6; Curator W. VAN NESPEN; publ. *Volkskunde* (quarterly).

Museum Vleeshuis: Vleeshouwersstraat 38; f. 1913; prehistorical finds, local history, Egyptian, Greek and Roman antiquities, numismatics, sculpture, applied art, furniture, arms, musical instruments; Asst. Curator Mrs. J. LAMBRECHTS-DOUILLEZ.

Museum Brouwershuis: Adriaan Brouwerstraat 20; f. 1933; 16th-century installations for water-supply to breweries, rich council chamber; Asst. Curator Mrs. J. LAMBRECHTS-DOUILLEZ.

Nationaal Scheepvaartmuseum (Steen) (*National Maritime Museum*): Steenplein 1; f. 1952; maritime history, especially concerning Belgium; library of 23,000 vols.; Chief Asst. J. VAN BEYLEN.

Volkskundemuseum: Gildekamersstraat 2-6; f. 1907; folklore of the Flemish provinces, especially folk art and craft; Curator W. VAN NESPEN.

Etongrafisch Museum: Internationaal Zeemanshuis, Falconrui 21; arts and crafts of pre-literate and non-European peoples; Asst. Curator A. G. CLAERHOUT; publ. *Verhandelingen.*

Stedelijk Prentenkabinet: Vrijdagmarkt 23; f. 1938; 7,000 vols. in library; ancient and modern collections of prints and drawings; Keeper Dr. L. VOET.

Bouillon

Le Musée Ducal "Les Amis du Vieux Bouillon": f. 1947; archives, historical manuscripts and documents; archaeology, folklore; exhibition of the history of Godefroy de Bouillon; small library; Curator Dr. CLÉMENT; Sec. Mme CLÉMENT BODARD.

Bruges

Arentshuis: Dyver 16; 18th-century manor house, contains paintings which survey the development of Bruges, a collection of 18th- and 19th-century industrial arts and a permanent exhibition of works by Frank Brangwyn; Chief Curator Dr. A. JANSSENS DE BISTHOVEN.

Groeningemuseum (*Municipal Art Gallery*): 12 Dyver; paintings by Jan van Eyck, R. van den Weyden, Hugo van der Goes, Hans Memling, Gerard David, Hieronymus Bosch, etc.; also ancient and modern paintings; Chief Curator Dr. A. JANSSENS DE BISTHOVEN.

Gruuthusemuseum: Dyver 17; municipal archaeological collection in the 15th-century Palace of the Lords of Gruuthuse; furniture, jewellery, paintings, porcelain, tapestries, metals, instruments, Liedts collection of lace; Chief Curator Dr. A. JANSSENS DE BISTHOVEN.

Musée de l'Hospice de la Potterie: 79 quai de la Potterie; f. 1276; church ornaments, furniture, paintings, 16th-century tapestry, etc.

Memling Museum: St. John's Hospital, O.C.M.W., Mariastraat 38; paintings by Jan Memling and other artists, in 12th-14th-century hospital; 17th century pharmacy; Dir. H. LOBELLE (acting).

Stedelijk Museum voor Volkskunde (*Municipal Museum of Folklore*): Balstraat 27; f. 1973; popular art, 19th-century trades and crafts; Curator W. P. DEZUTTER.

Brussels

Koninklijk Museum voor Midden-Afrika/Musée Royal de l'Afrique Centrale: Steenweg op Leuven 13, 1980 Tervuren, near Brussels; f. 1898; large collections in the fields of pre-history, ethnography, native arts and crafts; geology, mineralogy, palaeontology; zoology (entomology, ornithology, mammals, reptiles, etc); history, economics; library of 60,000 vols.; 37 scientific staff; Dir. P. BASILEWSKY; publs. *Annales*, and miscellaneous publications.

Musée des Beaux-Arts d'Ixelles: rue Jean Van Volsem 71, Ixelles, 1050 Brussels; f. 1892; ancient and modern masters, water-colours, drawings, engravings, sculptures, etc.; works of Belgian and foreign schools; 4,000 vols. (bibliography); Curator J. C. COQUELET.

Musée Royal de l'Armée et d'Histoire Militaire: 3 Palais du Cinquantenaire, 1040 Brussels; f. 1910; collection includes military history of Belgium from 18th century onwards; arms, uniforms, decorations, paintings, sculpture, maps, library of 350,000 vols. and archives; Chief Curator E. A. JACOBS; publs. *Revue Belge d'Histoire Militaire/ Belgisch Tijdschrift voor Militaire Geschiedenis*† (quarterly), *AELR* (*Air et Espace, Lucht en Ruimtevaart*)† *Militaria Belgica*† (quarterly).

Musées Royaux d'Art et d'Histoire: 10 Parc du Cinquantenaire, 1040 Brussels; f. 1835; Egyptian, Greek, Roman and pre-historic antiquities; medieval and Renaissance works of art; Flemish tapestries; applied and decorative art; lace; Japanese prints; pre-Columbian art; library of 95,000 vols.; Chief Curator R. DE ROO; publ. *Bulletin*†.

Musée de la Porte de Hal: collection of arms and armour.

Pavillon Chinois: 44 ave van Praet, 1020 Brussels; Chinese art, porcelain and furniture of late period.

Palais de Bellevue: 7 place des Palais, 1000 Brussels; 18th–19th-century applied and decorative art.

Musées Royaux des Beaux-Arts de Belgique: rue du Musée 9; f. 1830; Brussels, medieval, Renaissance and modern pictures and sculpture; Dir. PHILIPPE ROBERTS-JONES; publ. *Bulletin*†.

Musée d'Art Ancien: rue de la Régence 3; paintings and drawings (15th-19th centuries) and old and modern sculpture.

Musée d'Art Moderne: rue de la Régence 3; paintings, drawings and sculpture (19th-20th centuries), temporary exhibitions. (Currently closed for rebuilding.)

Musée Constantin Meunier: rue de l'Abbaye 59; paintings, drawings and sculptures by Constantin Meunier, the artist's house and studio.

Musée Wiertz: rue Vautier 62; paintings by Antoine Wiertz.

Museum Erasmus: Rue du Chapitre 31, B-1070 Brussels; f. 1932; documents, paintings, early editions and manuscripts relating to Erasmus and other Humanists of the 16th century; library of 2,000 vols.; Curator J.-P. VANDEN BRANDEN.

Ghent

Musée des Beaux-Arts: Citadelpark; f. 1902; contains ancient and modern paintings, sculptures, tapestries, drawings and etchings; library; Curator PAUL EECKHOUT; publs. catalogues.

Museum van Hedendaagse Kunst (*Museum of Contemporary Art*): Citadelpark; f. 1975; paintings, sculpture, drawings, etchings; Curator JAN HOET; publs. catalogues.

Oudheidkundig Museum van de Stad Gent: Godshuizenlaan 2; f. 1833; prehistory, local history, applied arts, furniture, arms, numismatics, collection of Chinese art; Dir. Drs. A. VAN DEN KERKHOVE.

Herstal

Fabrique Nationale Museum of Industrial Archaeology: rue en Bois 63, 4400 Herstal; f. 1977 by Fabrique Nationale Herstal with the aim of preserving some of its older tools and equipment; FN was founded in 1889 by a group of Liège gunsmiths, but soon diversified into other fields: bicycles, motorcycles, cars, buses, typewriters, dairy equipment, knitting machines, jet engines, etc.; the museum traces the history of this precision engineering firm from the beginning of the industrial revolution.

Liège

Musées d'Archéologie et des Arts Décoratifs de Liège: Dir. Prof. Dr. JOSEPH PHILIPPE.

Musée Curtius: 13 quai de Maastricht; f. 1909; chief sections: prehistory, Romano-Belgian and Frankish, Liège coins, decorative arts (from the Middle Ages to the 19th century); Annexes: Roman Hypocaust, Place Saint-Lambert, Liège; lapidary collection in Palais de Justice; the museum is the headquarters of the Archaeological Institute of Liège (*q.v.*).

Musée d'Ansembourg: 114 Féronstrée; f. 1905; collections of 18th-century decorative arts of Liège; reconstituted interiors.

Musée du Verre: 13 quai de Maastricht; f. 1959; all the main centres of production, from the earliest times to the 20th century, are represented. Headquarters of the "Association internationale pour l'histoire du Verre"; publs. *Annales*, *Bulletin*.

Musée de la Boverie: 3 parc de la Boverie, 4020 Liège: f. 1819; formerly Musée des Beaux-Arts; modern paintings and abstracts of the Belgian School and French masters; Curator MARIE-MADELEINE SPEHL-ROBEYNS.

Musée de l'Art Wallon: 3 parc de la Boverie; f. 1951; 2,095 ancient and modern paintings of the Walloon School; 145 ancient and modern pieces of sculpture; print room with 20,000 engravings; Curator JACQUES HENDRICK.

Musée de la Vie Wallonne: Cour des Mineurs; f. 1912; varied collection covering south Belgium in the fields of ethnography, folklore, arts and crafts and history; 350,000 documents; library of 23,000 vols.; Curator J. FRAIKIN; publ. *Enquêtes* (annually).

Musée du Fer et du Charbon (*Steel and Coal Museum*).

Service des Collections artistiques: 16 place du 20 août, 4000 Liège; 30,000 prints, 51 paintings of 15th and 16th centuries; 5,483 coins; collection of Zairian art and craft; open to the public; Curator Prof. J. STIENNON.

Malines

Stadsmuseum: Hof van Busleyden-Fred. de Merodestraat 65-67; f. 1844; city museum; paintings, sculptures, history, etc.; section for contemporary painting and sculpture; Dir. M. BAFCOP.

Mariemont

Musée Royal et Domaine de Mariemont: Morlanwelz; f. 1922; contains antiquities from Egypt, Greece, Rome, China, Japan; archaeology; porcelain from Tournai; bookbindings; library of 70,000 vols.; Curator Prof. G. DONNAY; publ. *Les Cahiers de Mariemont*† (annually).

Verviers

Musées Communaux: *Beaux-Arts*: rue Renier 17; f. 1884; sculpture, paintings; ceramics of Europe and Asia; publ. *Guide du Visiteur*. *Archéologie*: rue des Raines, 42; f. 1959; history of art, archaeology, folklore, local history.

UNIVERSITIES

UNIVERSITÉ LIBRE DE BRUXELLES
(Free University of Brussels)

AVE. FRANKLIN ROOSEVELT 50,
1050 BRUSSELS

Telephone: 649-00-30.

Founded 1834.

In 1970 the Université Libre de Bruxelles became independent from the Vrije Universiteit Brussel.

Language of instruction: French; Private control.

President: A. JAUMOTTE.
Vice-President: D. SKALA.
Rector: JEAN MICHOT.
Secretary: C. DEJEAN.
Treasurer-General: G. COOPMANS.
Librarian: P. DELSEMME.

Library: *see under* Libraries.
Number of teachers: 1,800.
Number of students: 14,000.

Publication: *Revue de l'Université.*

DEANS:

Faculty of Philosophy and Letters: HERVÉ HASQUIN.
Faculty of Law: JEAN-J. A. SALMON.
Faculty of Social, Political and Economic Sciences: JACQUES NAGELS.
Faculty of Psychology and Education: PAUL BERTELSON.
Faculty of Sciences: GEORGES VERHAEGEN.
Faculty of Medicine: JEAN-LAMBERT PASTEELS.
Faculty of Applied Sciences: RENÉ WINAND.

INSTITUTES:

Institute of Statistics: Pres. PAUL GILLIS.
Institute of Labour: Dir. MICHEL MAGREZ.
Institute of European Studies: Dir. MICHEL VANDEN ABEELE.
Institute of Phonetics: Dir. MAX WAJSKOP.

ATTACHED INSTITUTES AND SCHOOLS:

Centre Emile Bernheim pour l'Etude des Affaires (*Emile Bernheim Centre for Current Affairs*): f. 1951.
Director: E. DASSEL.

Département d'Economie Appliquée (*Applied Economy Department*): ave. Paul Heger 2, 1050 Brussels.
Director: E. S. KIRSCHEN.

Ecole des Sciences Criminologiques Léon Cornil (*Léon Cornil School of Criminology*): f. 1935.
President: JEAN CORDIER.

Ecole d'Infirmières Annexée à l'Université (*Nursing School attached to the University*): Hôpital Saint Pierre, 322 rue Haute, 1000 Brussels.
Director: MADELEINE LEDOCQUE.

Fondation Archéologique (*Archaeological Foundation*): f. 1930; sculpture casts, photographs, slides and library.
Director: C. DELVOYE.

Institut de Sociologie (*Institute of Sociology*): 44 ave. Jeanne, 1050 Brussels; f. 1901.
Director: ARTHUR DOUCY.

Institut Jules Bordet (*Jules Bordet Institute*): rue Heger-Bordet 1, 1000 Brussels; diagnosis and treatment of tumours.
President: J. HENRY.

VRIJE UNIVERSITEIT BRUSSEL
(Free University of Brussels)

PLEINLAAN 2,
1050 BRUSSELS

Telephone: 648-55-40.

In 1970 the Vrije Universiteit Brussel became independent from the Université Libre de Bruxelles.

Language of instruction: Dutch; Private control

Rector: Prof. B. DE SCHUTTER.
Director-General: LEO PEETERS.
Librarian: M. NAMENWIRTH.

Number of professors: 400.
Number of students: *c.* 4,200.

Publications: *Tijdschrift, Ad Valvas, Academisch Nieuws.*

DEANS:

Faculty of Philosophy and Letters: E. SCHOLLIERS.
Faculty of Law: B. DE SCHUTTER.
Faculty of Science: J. LEMONNE.
Faculty of Medicine: R. VANDEN DRIESSCHE.
Faculty of Applied Science: G. MAGGETTO.
Faculty of Social, Political and Economic Sciences: J. P. BRANS.
Faculty of Psychological and Educational Sciences: T. DE BACKER-BAEKELMANS.

ATTACHED INSTITUTES:

Instituut voor de studie van de Renaissance en het Humanisme (*Institute for the study of the Renaissance and Humanism*): 145 A. Buyllaan, 1050 Brussels.
Director: A. GERLO.

Instituut voor celbiologie (*Institute for cell-biology*): 50 F. D. Rooseveltlaan, 1050 Brussels.
Director: M. MULDER.

Hoger Instituut voor Lichamelijke Opvoeding (*Institute for Physical Training*): 42 P. Hegerlaan, 1050 Brussels.
Director: F. MATTHYS.

RIJKSUNIVERSITEIT TE GENT
(State University of Ghent)

ST.-PIETERSNIEUWSTRAAT 25,
GHENT

Telephone: 23.38.21.

Founded 1817.

Language of Instruction: Dutch; State control.

Academic Year: October to July (October–February, March-July).

Rector: J. HOSTE.
Vice-President of the Board of Directors: H. VAN LOOY.
Pro-Rector: A. DEVREKER.
Administrator: W. DESOT.
Secretary of the Board: M. D'HONDT.

Library: *see under* Libraries.
Number of teachers: 376.
Number of students: 12,876.

Publications: *Studia Philosophica Gandensia, Dessertationes Archaeologicae Gandenses, Didactica classica Gandensia, Travaux de linguistique, Studia Germania Gandensia, Communicatie en cognitie, Orientalia Gandensia, Studia Historica Gandensia, Romanica Gandensia, Uit het seminarie voor Nederlandse literatuurstudie, Uit het seminarie voor Nederlandse taalkunde en Vlaamse dialectologie, Theodisca Gandensia, Uit het seminarie voor Engelse literatuur, Uitgaven van het seminarie voor socio-*

logie, Gentse bijdragen tot de Kunstgeschiedenis en Oudheidkunde, Gids voor de student, Studiegids, Algemene inlichtingen en administratief jaarboek, Verslagen.

DEANS:

Faculty of Philosophy and Letters: J. VEREMANS.
Faculty of Law: R. DE MEYER.
Faculty of Science: P. VAN DER VEKEN.
Faculty of Medicine: A. DE SCHAEPDRYVER.
Faculty of Applied Science: M. VANWORMHOUDT.
Faculty of Economic Sciences: M. VAN VAERENBERGH.
Faculty of Veterinary Sciences: M. DEBACKERE.
Faculty of Psychological and Pedagogical Sciences: P. COETSIER.
Faculty of Agricultural Sciences: M. DE BOODT.
Faculty of Pharmacy: P. DE MOERLOOSE.

PROFESSORS:

Faculty of Philosophy and Letters:

BALTHAZAR, H., Modern History
BOEHM, R., Modern and General Philosophy
BOLCKMANS, A., Modern Scandinavian Languages
BROECKX, J., Music History
BRULEZ, W., Modern Economic History
BURSSENS, H., African Social History
COUVREUR, W., Indo-European Languages
DE GREVE, M., French Literature
DE LAET, S., Archaeology in Western Europe
DE MAEYER, M., History of Plastic Arts in Europe
DE MEYER, L., Cuneiform Philology
DEPREZ, A., Dutch Literature
DEROLEZ, R., English Literature
DE SMET, G., Germanic Philology
ELLEGIERS, D., Chinese and Japanese Language and Literature
JACOBS, J., Negro-African Philology and Literature
JANSSENS, G., Semitic Linguistics
KRUITHOF, J., Ethics and Metaphysics
LOTHE, J., Russian Language and Literature
MOURIN, L., Spanish Language and Literature
MUSSCHE, H., Archaeology and Art History of Classical Antiquity
PLANCKE, M., Islamic Studies
PREVENIER, W., Historic Methodology
SANDERS, G., Juridical and Post-Classic Latin
SCHRICKX W., English Language and Literature and History, American Literature
VANACKER, V., Dutch Philology
VAN CAENEGEM, R., Medieval History
VANDEN BERGHE, Archaeology and Cultural History of the Ancient Near East
VAN EENOO, R., Modern History
VAN ELSLANDER, A., Dutch Literature
VAN LOOY, M., Greek Literature
VEREMANS, J., Classical Latin
VERHOFSTADT, E., German Literature
VERHULST, A., Medieval History
VERMEERSCH, E., Modern Philosophy and Philosophical Anthropology

Faculty of Law:

ADRIAENS, H., Law of Modern States
AMERIJCKX, F., Administrative and Fiscal Law
ANSELIN, M., Surveying and Planning
CALEWAERT, W., General Jurisprudence
CLAEYS BOUUAERT, I., Fiscal Law
DELVA, W., Civil Law
DE MEYER, R., Particular Administrative Law
FREDERICQ, S., Commercial Law
GHYSBRECHT, P., Psychology
KLUYSKENS, P., History of International Relations and Information Media
LENAERTS, H., Applied Social Law
QUINTYN, J., Development of Modern Media
ROELS, W., Roman Law
SCHRANS, G., European Law
SENELLE, R., Legislation concerning Transport and Construction
SPANOGHE, E., International Private Law
STORME, M., Judicial Organization of Authority and Judicature
VAN BILSEN, A., Problems of the Third World
VAN BOGAERT, E., International Law
VANDER STICHELE, A., Administrative Science
VAN OUDENHOVE, G., European Law
VERSICHELEN-TERRYN, M., Sociology

Faculty of Science:

AMERYCKX, J., Agrogeology
ANTEUNIS, M., Organic Chemistry
BILO, J., Analytical Geometry
COOMANS, A., Zoology
DE BREUCK, W., Applied Geology
DE HEINZELIN DE BRAUCOURT, J., Palaeontology
DE LEY, J., Microbiology and Microbial Genetics
DERUYTTER, A., Nuclear Physics
DINGENS, P., Astronomy, Geodesy, Probabilities Calculus
FIERS, W., Molecular Biology
GROSJEAN, C., Mathematical Physics
HOSTE, J., Analytical Chemistry
HUBLÉ, J., Ecology and General Biology
MARÉCHAL, R., Geology
MERTENS, R., Theoretical Mechanics
PHARISEAU, P., Mathematical Physics
SCHELL, J., Genetics
SNACKEN, F., Geography
TAVERNIER, R., Physical Geography
VAN DER KELEN, G., Inorganic Chemistry
VAN DER VEKEN, P., Morphology and Ecology of Plants, Geobotany
VANDEWALLE, M., Organic Chemistry
VANMASSENHOVE, F., Differential and Integral Calculus
VAN SUMERE, C., Botanical Biochemistry
VERBEEK, F., Analytical Chemistry
VERZELE, M., Organic Chemistry

Faculty of Medicine:

BARBIER, F., Internal Medicine
CLAESSENS, H., Physical Therapy and Orthopaedics
CLAEYS, R., Theory and Analysis of Human Movements
DEROM, F., Surgery
DE SCHAEPDRYVER, A., Pharmacology
DIERICKX, K., Embryology
EVRARD, A., Invalid Psychopathology
FAUTREZ, J., Osteology, Anthrology, Myology
KINT, A., Dermatology
KLUYSKENS, P., Oto-Rhino-Laryngology
LACROIX, E., Human Physiology
LEUSEN, I., Physiology and Pathology
MATTON, G., Plastic Surgery
NIHOUL, E., Medical Micro-Biology
PANNIER, R., Cardiology
RINGOIR, S., Internal Medicine
ROELS, H., Pathological Anatomy
SEBRUYNS, M., Histology
STOCKX, J., Physiological Chemistry and General Experimental Physiology applied to Physical Training
THIERY, M., Obstetrics
VANDENDRIESSCHE, L., Physiological Chemistry and Biochemistry
VANDER EECKEN, H., Neuropsychology
VANDERKERCKHOVE, D., Gynaecology
VAN DER STRAETEN, M., Internal Medicine
VAN DE VELDE, E., Radiology
VERBEEK, E., Psychiatry
VERDONK, G., Dietetics and Internal Medicine
VERMEULEN, A., Internal Medicine
VUYLSTEEK, K., Hygiene
WIEME, R., Internal Medicine

Faculty of Applied Sciences:

BOSCH, F., Electro-Metallurgy
COLLE, J., Electronics
DE BEER, E., Mechanics and Foundation Techniques
DECHAENE, R., Cinematics
DE JONG, H., Electric Machines
D'HULST, R., History of Dutch Plastic Arts
FERDINANDE, V., Ship-building
FROMENT, G., Petro-Chemical Technique
KULIASKO, F., Mathematical Analysis
MULLER, H., Industrial Management
RAES, G., Textile Technology
RIESSAUW, F., Ferro-Concrete Construction
SOETE, W., Elasticity
SOMERLING, H., Machines
TISON, G., Hydraulics
VAN BLADEL, J., Electrotechnics
VAN CAUWENBERGHE, A., Control Engineering and Automation
VANDEPITTE, D., Constructional Stability
VAN PETEGHEM, A., Non-ferrous Metallurgy
VANWORMHOUDT, M., Electronics
WILLEMS, J., Electricity

Faculty of Economical Sciences:

BEYAERT, M., History of Commodities
DE PELSEMAEKER, C., Commercial Economy
DE SMET, L., Economic Geography
DEVREKER, A., Social Economy
PICARD, H., Applied Statistics
VAN ACKER, J., Marketing
VAN MEERHAEGHE, M., Economy
VAN VAERENBERGH, M. E., Particular Sociology
VLERICK, A., Applied Economy

Faculty of Veterinary Sciences:

BOUQUET, Y., Animal Genetics
DEBACKERE, M., Pharmacology and Toxicology
DE MOOR, A., Animal Surgery
DEVOS, A., Poultry Pathology, Microbiology and Infectious Diseases
DE VOS, N. B., Animal Anatomy
HOORENS, J., Pathological Anatomy of Animals
MATTHEEUWS, D., Veterinary Medicine (Small Animals)
OYAERT, W., Veterinary Medicine (Large Animals)
PAREDIS, F., Ambulatory Clinic
PEETERS, G., Animal Physiology
VANDEPLASSCHE, M., Veterinary Obstetrics
VERCAUTEREN, R., Physiological Chemistry

Faculty of Psychological and Pedagogical Sciences:
COETSIER, P., Applied Psychology
DE BLOCK, A., Didactics
DE BOCK, G., Welfare of Young People
DE CLERCK, K., Historical and Comparative Pedagogy
DE COSTER, W., Genetic, Differential and Experimental Psychology
MUSSCHOOT, F., Applied Psychology
QUACKELBEEN, J., Applied Psychology
VAN HERREWEGHE, M.-L., Experimental, Psychological, and Social Pedagogy
VERBIST, R., Experimental, Psychological and Social Pedagogy

Faculty of Agricultural Sciences:
BAERT, L., Physical Chemistry
BOESMAN, G., Horticulture
COTTENIE, A., Analytical Chemistry
DE BOODT, M., Soil Physics
DE LEENHEER, L., Geology and Soil Studies
DOORME, H., Cattle Breeding
GILLARD, A., Zoology
HEYNDRICKX, G., Fundamental Technology
HEYNDRICKX, G. A., Cultural Technics
KIPS, R., Phytopharmacy
MOERMAN, J., Agriculture Mechanics
SCHALCK, J., Biology and Technology of Wood
SCHAMP, N., Organic Chemistry
STRYCKERS, J., Plant Breeding
VAN LANCKER, J., Agriculture Mechanics
VAN MIEGROET, M., General and Comparative Forestry
VAN PARIJS, L., Biochemistry
VANSTEENKISTE, G., Mathematics
VERKINDEREN, A., Agricultural Economics
WILSSENS, A., Fermentation Industries

Faculty of Pharmacy:
BRAECKMAN, P., Pharmacognosis and Galenics
CLAEYS, A., Analytical Chemistry
DE MOERLOOSE, P., Pharmaceutical Chemistry
HEYNDRICKX, A., Toxicology
PIJCK, J., Pharmaceutical Microbiology and Hygiene

AFFILIATED INSTITUTES:

Interfacultair Studie- en Vormingscentrum voor Ontwikkelingssamenwerking (*Inter-Faculty Study and Training Centre for Developmental Co-operation*): Universiteitstraat 8; f. 1967; Pres. R. TAVERNIER.

Interfacultair Centrum voor de Studie van Lucht-, Bodem- en Waterverontreiniging (*Inter-Faculty Centre for the Study of Air, Soil and Water Pollution*): Coupure Links 533; f. 1971; Pres. N. SCHAMP.

Interfacultair Centrum voor Informatica (*Inter-Faculty Centre for Informatics*): St.-Pietersnieuwstraat 41; f. 1973; Pres. R. DE CALUWE.

Interfacultair Centrum voor Management (*Inter-Faculty Centre for Management*): Sr. Pietersnieuwstraat 49; f. 1980; Pres. (vacant).

UNIVERSITÉ DE LIÈGE
(University of Liège)

PLACE DU 20-AOÛT 7,
4000 LIÈGE

Telephone: 42.00.80.

Founded 1817.

Language of instruction: French

Rector: E. H. BETZ.
Vice-Rector: N. DEHOUSSE.
Government Commissioner: R. GODEFROID.
Administrator: H. SCHLITZ.
Director-General: J. DELCHEVALERIE.

Library: *see* under Libraries.
Number of teachers: 404.
Number of students: 9,626.

DEANS:

Faculty of Philosophy and Letters: P. DELBOUILLE.
Faculty of Law, Economics and Social Sciences: J. HANSENNE.
Faculty of Science: J. SPORCK.
Faculty of Medicine: R. LAMBOTTE.
Faculty of Applied Science: G. CANTRAINE.
Faculty of Veterinary Medicine: A. LOUSSE.

PROFESSORS:

Faculty of Philosophy and Letters:
ALDENHOFF, J., Modern German Philology
BODSON, A., Latin Language
BOILEAU, A., Comparative Linguistics
COLMAN, P., History of Modern Art
CRAHAY, F., Logic and History of Modern Philology
DELATTE, L., Latin
DELBOUILLE, P., French Stylistics and Analysis of Modern Authors
DEMOULIN, R., Modern History
DEROY, L., Indian Studies and Indo-European Languages
DUBOIS, J., Modern French Authors and Contemporary Literature
DUVIVIER, R., Spanish and American Spanish
DUYCKAERTS, F., History of Philosophy
EVRARD, E., Latin Language and Literature
FONTINOY, CH., Hebrew and Aramaic Languages
FRANÇOIS, G., Ancient Greek Language and Literature
GERARD, A., Comparative Literature
GILLET, L., Dutch Literature
GOCHET, P., Logic and Epistemology
HELIN, E., Economic and Social History
HORRENT, J., Romance Philology
HYART, C., Slavonic Languages and Literatures
JORIS, A., Medieval History
KUPPER, J. R., Assyriology
LABARBE, J., Greek Institutions and Epigraphy, Greek and Latin Literature
LAVIS, G., French Linguistics
MAQUET, A., Italian Language and Literature
MASSAUT, J. P., Modern History
MERTENS, P., Greek Philology and Papyrology
MERTENS-FONCK, Mme. P., Medieval English Language and Literature
MINGUET, J. P., Aesthetics
MOORS, J., Flemish Philology, History of Dutch Language
MUNOT, P., Phonetics and Linguistics
NIVELLE, A., German Literature and Language
NOEL, J., Modern English Philology
RUTTEN, M., Flemish Literature
SERVAIS, J., Greek History
SIMON, Mlle I., English Philology and Literature
STIENNON, J., History of the Art and Archaeology of the Middle Ages
TYSSENS, Mlle M., Old French Linguistics
VANDEGANS, A., History of French Literature
WARNANT, L., French Methodology

Institute of Psychology and Educational Sciences:
DE LANDSHEERE, G., Experimental Pedagogy
DE VISSCHER, P., Social Psychology
FAIDHERBE, J., Psycho-Physiology
HEUCHENNE, C., Mathematics Applied to Psychology and Education
HUSQUINET, A., Educational Psychology
PASQUASY, R., Educational and Professional Orientation
PIRET, R., Psychometry and Industrial Psychology
RICHELLE, M., Experimental Psychology

Faculty of Law, Economics and Social Sciences:
BOURS, E., Fiscal Law
BRAGARD, L., Statistics in Economic and Management Sciences
CLEMENS, R., Sociology, Political Economy
DABIN, L., Commercial Law
DAVID-CONSTANT, Mme. S., Civil Law
DEL MARMOL, CH., Commercial Law
DEMBOUR, J., Administrative Law
DOUCET, J. P., Penal Law
FETTWEIS, A., Civil Procedure
FRANÇOIS, L., Social Law
GAZON, J., Economics
GOOSSENS, CH., Public and Administrative Law
GOTHOT, P., Comparative International Law
GRAULICH, P., Civil and Commercial and Private International Law
HANSENNE, J., Civil Law
HARMEL, P., Public and Administrative Law
JAMOULLE, M., Social Law
JOLIET, R., Commercial and Economic Law
KELLENS, G., Criminology
LAMBERT, P., Economics
LANGASKENS, Y., Economics
LEBRUN, P., Economic History
LEWALLE, P., Public and Administrative Law
MELCHIOR, M., Public International Law
MINGUET, A., Economics
MINON, P., Sociology
MOREAU-MARGRÈVE, Mme I., Private Law
PARTSCH, G., History of Law
PERIN, F., Public Law
PESTIEAU, P., Economic Science
QUADEN, G., Economics
STASSART, J., Economics
STASSEN, J., Administrative Law
VIEUJEAN, E., Civil Law

School of Business Administration:
COMHAIRE, J. J., Market Analysis
DE BRUYN, C., Quantitative Management Methods
DISTER, G., Management Sociology
LANGER, E., Financial Analysis

Faculty of Science:
AGHION, P., Vegetal Biochemistry

ALEXANDRE, J., Physical Geography
BELLIÈRE, J., Geology
BERNIER, G., Vegetal Physiology
BOURGIGNON, P., Minerology
BRENY, H., Probability and Statistics
BRONCHART, R., Vegetal Morphology
COLLIN, J., General Chemistry
DE WILDE, M., Differential Geometry
DISTECHE, A., Oceanography
DUCHESNE, J., Physics and Mathematics
EVRARD, R., Experimental Physics
FREDERICQ, E., Physical Chemistry
GARNIR, H., Analytical Mechanics and Higher Algebra
GOBERT, J., Mathematics
GODEAUX, J., Marine Biology
HAMOIR, G., Biology
HOUZIAUX, L., Astrophysics
HULS, R., Chemistry
HUMBLET, J., Analytical Mechanics
JEUNIAUX, CH., Zoology
JONGMANS, F., Higher Geometry
LAMBINON, J., Vegetal Systematics and Geography
LASZLO, P., Organic Chemistry
LEDOUX, L., Genetics
LEDOUX, P., Astronomy, Analytical Mechanics
LORQUET, J., Physical Chemistry
MAHAUX, C., Theoretical Physics
MIGEOTTE, M., Experimental Physics
MIGNOLET, J., Solid State Chemistry
NIHOUL, J., Analytical Mechanics
NOLLET, L., Analytical Geometry
PIRENNE, J., Quantity Mechanics and Statistical Mechanics
PISSART, A., Geomorphology and Quaternary Geology
RAMAUT, J., Botany
RENSON, M., Organic Chemistry
RUWET, J.-C., Animal Ethology and Psychology
SIMON, R., Analytical Mechanics
SIRONVAL, C., General Botany
SPORCK, J., Economic Geography
STREEL, M., Vegetal Palaeontology
TARTE, P., Mineral Chemistry
TEYSSIE, P., General and Organic Chemistry
TOUSSAINT, J., Crystallography
UBAGHS, G., Zoopalaeontology
VAN DE VORST, A., Experimental Physics
VERLY, W., Biochemistry
WINAND, L., Physical Mechanics

Faculty of Medicine:

ANDRÉ, A., Medical Law
BASSLEER, R., Histology
BETZ, E., Pathological Anatomy
BOBON, J., Psychiatry
BONNAL, J., Neuro-Surgery
BOSLY, J., Medicinal Analysis
CASTERMANS, A., Plastic and Maxillo Facial Surgery
CLOSON, J., Radiotherapy
DE SCOVILLE, A., Anatomy
DRESSE, A., Pharmacology
EISENRING, R., Stomatology
FIRKET, H., General Biology
FREDERIC, J., Genetics
FREDERICQ, P., Hygiene
GEREBTZOFF, M., Anatomy
GEUBELLE, F., Paediatrics
GHUYSEN, J. M., Pharmaceutical Microbiology
GOUTIER, R., Biochemistry
HEUSGHEM, C., Pharmaceutical Chemistry, Hygiene
HONORÉ, D., Surgery
JAMINET, F., Galenic Pharmacy
KOHL, J., Stomatology
LAMBOTTE, R., Gynaecology and Obstetrics
LAMY, M., Anaesthesiology
LAPIÈRE, C. L., Analytical Chemistry Pharmaceutical Chemistry
LAPIÈRE, C. M., Dermatology
LECOMTE, J., Physiology
LEDOUX, A., Oto-Rhino-Laryngology
LEFEBVRE, P., Clinical Medicine
LEJEUNE, G., Clinical and Surgical Semiology
LEROUX, G., Radiography
LUMINET, D., Medical Psychology
MAQUINAY, C., Urology
NIZET, A., Medical Clinic
PETIT, J. M., Medicine and Social Hygiene
SCHOFFENIELS, E., General Biochemistry
VAN CAUWENBERGE, H., Medical Clinic
WEEKERS, R., Ophthalmology
WELSCH, M., General and Medical Microbiology

Institute of Physical Education:

FALIZE, J., Theory and Practice of Physical Education
LIEBECQ, C., Biochemistry and General Physiology

Faculty of Applied Science:

BAUS, R., Civil Engineering Construction
BURNAY, G., Applied Physics, Thermo dynamics and Thermal Machines
CALVAER, A., Electrical Theory
CANTRAINE, G., Electronics
COHEUR, P., Physical Metallurgy
COLLEE, R., Nuclear Materials
DANTHINE, A., Control and Automation
DEHOUSSE, N., Civil Engineering Constructions II
DELVAUX, L., Chemical Engineering
DENDAL, J., Applied Acoustics
DIEU, H., Chemistry
EK, C., Metallurgy
ENGLEBERT, J., Architecture
ETIENNE, J., Mathematics
EVRARD, P., Applied Geology
FAGNOUL, A., Civil Engineering Constructions I
FAWE, A.. Telecommunications
FONDER, G., Structural Mechanics
GAMSKI, K., Civil Engineering Construction Materials
HABRAKEN, L., Metallurgy
LEFEBVRE, A., Industrial Chemistry
LEGROS, W., Electrical Engineering
L'HOMME, G., Chemical Engineering
LINSMAN, M., Applied Mathematics and Information Treatment
MASSONNET, C., The Elasticity of Materials
MEAN, E., Transport and Distribution of Electric Energy
MICHEL, G., Analytical Chemistry
MOMIGNY, J., Chemistry
MONFORT, F., Statistics
PETERS, F., Architecture
RIBBENS, D., Computer Science
RIBBENS-PAVELLA, M., Electrical Circuits
ROBERT, J., Electronics
SANDER, G., Mechanics
SMOLDEREN, J., Applied Aerodynamics
STASSEN, R., Mining Engineering
VAN MELLAERT, L., Automatics
WOLPER, J., Mechanics

Faculty of Veterinary Medicine:

BIENFAIT, J. M., Bioclimatology and Hygiene
BIENFET. V., Medical Pathology
ECTORS, F., Obstetrics and Pathology
FIEVEZ, L., Technology of Foodstuffs derived from Animals
HANSET, R., Genetics
KAECKENBEEK, A., Bacteriology
LASSOIE, L., Surgical Pathology
LOUSSE, A., Physiology and Physiological Chemistry
POUPLARD, L., Histology, Parasitology and Embryology

KATHOLIEKE UNIVERSITEIT LEUVEN
(Catholic University of Louvain)

NAAMSESTRAAT 22,
3000 LOUVAIN
Telephone: 016-22-04-31.

Founded 1425 by Papal Bull.

The University became independent from the French-speaking Université Catholique de Louvain in 1970, and is now a separate legal entity.

Language of instruction: Dutch; Private control; Academic year: October to June.

Rector: PIETER DE SOMER.
Vice-Rector: HERMAN SERVOTTE.
President for Sciences: ALFONS DE BOCK.
President for Humanities: MARCEL JANSSENS.
Rector for Campus at Kortrijk: GUIDO MAERTENS.
General Administrator: GUIDO DECLERCQ.
Librarian: WILLY DEHENNIN.

Library of 700,000 vols.; each faculty has its own library.

Number of teachers: 800.
Number of students: 20,500.

Publications: *Academische Tijdingen*†, *Alumni Leuven*†, *Jaarverslag*, *Collegeroosters*†, *Academische Agenda*, and numerous scientific journals.

DEANS:

Faculty of Theology: M. CAUDRON.
Faculty of Canon Law: R. DILLEMANS (acting).
Faculty of Law: R. DILLEMANS.
Faculty of Economic and Applied Economic Sciences: L. BAECK.
Faculty of Social Sciences: R. MAES.
Faculty of Medicine: P. DE MOOR.
Faculty of Philosophy and Letters: M. PINNOY.
Faculty of Psychology and Education: G. DE COCK.
Faculty of Science: A. CARLIER.
Faculty of Applied Science: P. DE MEESTER.
Faculty of Agriculture: J. B. UYTTERHOEVEN.

INSTITUTES:

Higher Institute of Philosophy: Pres. U. DHONDT.
Higher Institute of Theological Studies: Pres. J. BULCKENS.
Institute of Actuaries: Pres. L. D'HOOGE.
Institute for the Study of Developing Countries: Pres. L. BAECK.
Higher Institute of Business Management: Dir. L. LAGROU.
School of Public Health: Pres. J. BLANPAIN.
Institute of Family and Sex Studies: Pres. E. ROOSENS.

Institute of Pharmaceutical Sciences: Pres. J. LEMLI.
Institute of Physical Training: Pres. M. OSTYN.
Institute of Literary Studies: (vacant).
Institute of Slavic Studies: Pres. A. LATHOUWERS.
Institute of Archaeology and History of Art: Pres. C. HEYMAN.
Institute of Oriental Studies: Pres. E. LIPINSKI.
Institute of Medieval Studies: Pres. G. VERBEKE.
Inter-Faculty Institute of Urban Development and Country Planning: Pres. P. FELIX.
Institute of Preparatory Studies: Pres. W. VAN DYCK.
Institute of Modern Languages: Pres. E. VORLAT.

UNIVERSITÉ CATHOLIQUE DE LOUVAIN

(Catholic University of Louvain)

PLACE DE L'UNIVERSITÉ 1,
1348 LOUVAIN-LA-NEUVE
Telephone: (010) 41-81-81.
Telex: 59037 UCLB.
Founded 1425 by Papal Bull.

Private control, became independent from the Katholieke Universiteit Leuven in 1970.

Language of instruction: French; Academic year: 2 terms (September to December, February to May).

Rector: Mgr. E. MASSAUX.
Vice-Rector: Mgr. J. DEVROEDE.
General Administrator: M. WOITRIN.
Librarian: J. ROELS.

Library: *see* Libraries.
Number of teachers: 927.
Number of students: 17,251.

Publications: *Nouvelles Brèves: Bulletin d'Information de l'Université Catholique de Louvain*†, *U.C.L. Information*†, *Bulletin des Amis de Louvain*†, and various faculty and research reports, etc.

DEANS:

Faculty of Theology: J. PONTHOT.
Higher Institute of Philosophy: J. LADRIÈRE.
Faculty of Law: F. RIGAUX.
Faculty of Economic, Political and Social Sciences: M. NORRO.
Faculty of Medicine: G. SOKAL.
Faculty of Philosophy and Letters: G. MURAILLE.
Faculty of Psychology and Education: J. COSTERMANS.
Faculty of Sciences: P. BERTHET.
Faculty of Applied Sciences: G. DE GHELLINCK.
Faculty of Agriculture: L. DE BACKER.

PRESIDENTS OF INSTITUTES:

Higher Institute of Religious Studies: J. HOUSSIAU.
Institute of Political and Social Sciences: (vacant).
Institute of Economics: H. TULKENS.
Institute of Business and Administration: E. CRACCO.
Institute of Labour Studies: J. DELCOURT.
Institute of Actuarial Studies: A. BEUMIER.
Institute for Developing Countries: J. PH. PEEMANS.
'Open' Faculty of Economic and Social Politics: A. VANDER VORST.
Institute of Physical Education: J. PIEL.
Higher Institute of Archaeology and History of Art: I. VANDEVIVERE.
Oriental Institute: J. RYCKMANS.
Institute of Medieval Studies: R. BULTOT.
Institute of Family Studies and Sexology: J. JASPARD.

UNIVERSITÉ DE L'ÉTAT À MONS

17 PLACE WAROCQUÉ,
7000 MONS
Telephone: 065/31-51-71.
Founded 1965.

Language of instruction: French; State control; Academic year: October to September.

Rector: JACQUES FRANEAU.
Vice-Rector: MARINETTE BRUWIER.
Librarian: JOSEPH DELSAUT.

Number of professors: 146.
Number of students: 1,867.

DEANS:

Faculty of Sciences: PAUL FIERENS.
Faculty of Medicine: YVES VAN HAVERBEKE.
Faculty of Applied Economics: ROGER VERVOORT.
Faculty of Psycho-Educational Sciences: RAYMOND RENARD.

PROFESSORS:

BREUSE, E., Education and Methodology
BRUWIER, M., History of Science
BURION, J., Experimental Education
CARTON, M., Statistics
CEULENEER, R., Mathematical Physics
CORDIER, J., Psychopathology of Children and Adolescents
CRAHAY, R., History of Teaching
DAGONNIER, R., Physical Chemistry
DE GOTTAL, P., Statistical Physics
DELEPINE-MESSE, D., Comparative Education
DELFORGE, J., Physics and Technology
DERSIN, A., Public Economy
DE VRIENDT-DE MAN, M. J., Language Teaching
D'HAINAUT, L., Technology of Formation
D'HOOGH, CH., Financial Economics
DIERKENS, J., Psychology
DIRKX, J., Biological Chemistry
FIERENS, P., General Chemistry
FRANEAU, J., General Physics
FRANEAU, P. H., Private Law
GARSOUX, J., Analytical Mathematics
GEORIS, P., Educational Organization and Guidance
GRARD, F., Theoretical Physics
GROSJEAN, P., General Mechanics
JOLY, R., Philosophy
LAMBERT, F., General Mathematics
LAUDE, L., Solid State Physics
LEFEBVRE, M., Accountancy
LORIS-TEGHEM, J., Mathematics and Operational Research
LUMER, G., Mathematical Analysis
MAQUESTIAU, A., Organic Chemistry
NUYTS, J., Theoretical and Mathematical Physics
POINT, J., Thermodynamics
POUPART, R., Modern Stylistics and Literature
RENARD, R., Phonetics
ROUSSEAU, L., Accountancy
VAN CAKENBERGHE, J., Inorganic Chemistry
VERVOORT, R., Industrial Chemistry

ATTACHED INSTITUTES:

Ecole d'Interprètes Internationaux: Av. du Champ de Mars, 7000 Mons; Dir. LUCIEN COSSON.

Service des Langues: Av. du Champ de Mars, 7000 Mons; Pres. LUCIEN COSSON.

Centre de Calcul et d'Informatique: 17 Place Warocqué, 7000 Mons; Pres. JEAN DIERKENS.

Service d'Instrumentation et de Techniques Audio-Visuelles (S.I.T.A.): Av. du Champ de Mars, 7000 Mons; Pres. LOUIS D'HAINAUT.

INSTITUTIONS WITH UNIVERSITY STATUS

FACULTÉ UNIVERSITAIRE DE THÉOLOGIE PROTESTANTE DE BRUXELLES/UNIVERSITAIRE PROTESTANTSE THEOLOGISCHE FACULTEIT TE BRUSSEL

RUE DES BOLLANDISTES 40,
1040-BRUSSELS
Telephone: (02) 735-67-46.

Founded 1942; closed 1944-50

Languages of instruction: French and Dutch; Private control (United Protestant Church).

Rector: H. R. BOUDIN.
Chairman of Administrative Board: P. MAHILLON.
Dean of Dutch-speaking Section: G. VAN LEEUWEN.
Dean of French-speaking Section: P. LE FORT.
Secretary: C. PEETERS.
Librarian: Mrs. J. BRODSKY.

The library contains 32,746 books.
Number of teachers: 20.
Number of students: 128.

Publication: *Programme et Horaire des Cours*† (annual).

PROFESSORS:

French-speaking Section:

BOUDIN, H., Church History and Methodology
BUSCARLET, J., Practical Theology
CHOPINEAU, J., Old Testament Studies and Hebrew

GABUS, J., Dogmatics, History of Philosophy and Religious Philosophy
LE FORT, P., New Testament Studies and Greek
PIETERS, A., Fundamental Ethics

Dutch-speaking Section:
BAKKER, N. T., Dogmatics, Philosophy, Hermeneutics
BEEKENKAMP, W., History of Church and Dogma, and Latin
GOEDHART, G. L., Practical Theology
JAGERSMA, H., Old Testament Studies, Hebrew, History of Divine Worship
PIETERS, A., The Modern Church
VAN LEEUWEN, G., Ethics and New Testament Studies

FACULTÉ DES SCIENCES AGRONOMIQUES DE L'ÉTAT

5800 GEMBLOUX

Telephone: 081-612961-6.

Founded 1860, university status 1947.

Language of instruction: French; State control.

Rector: C. BONNIER.
Vice-Rector: J. SEMAL.
Secretary: J. BERGANS.

Library: *see* under Libraries.

Number of teachers: 52, including 25 professors

Number of students: 831.

PROFESSORS:

ANTOINE, A., Animal Physiology and Husbandry
BALLIGAND, E., Agricultural Machinery
BONNIER, C., General Microbiology
BRENY, R., Applied Zoology
CASIMIR, J., Organic and Biochemistry
DAGNELIE, P., Statistics
DELTOUR, J., Physics and Physical Chemistry
FRASELLE, J., Phytopharmacy
HANOTIAUX, G., Soil Science
HEINEMANN, P., Plant Biology
LALOUX, R., General Comparative Agriculture
LECLERCQ, J., General Zoology
LEDENT, A., Rural Economy
MOES, A., Genetics and Plant Breeding
MOTTET, A., Forest Technology
NANGNIOT, P., Analytical Chemistry
NEURAY, G., Ornamental Gardening
NISEN, A., Fruit and Market Gardening
NOIRFALISE, A., Ecology
PIERLOT, R., Forestry of Hot Countries
RENARD, M., General and Organic Chemistry
ROISIN, P., Sylviculture
SEMAL, J., Phytopathology
SINE, L., Rural Engineering
TONNARD, V., Geology, Mineralogy

FACULTÉ POLYTECHNIQUE DE MONS

RUE DE HOUDAIN, MONS

Founded 1837.

President of the Board: R. STIÉVENART.
Rector: Prof. R. BALAND.

Library: *see under* Libraries.

Number of teachers: 88, including 67 professors.

Number of students: 526.

DEAN:

Prof. M. MAUROY.

PROFESSORS:

BALAND, J., Applied Mechanics
BALAND, R., Electrotechnology
BARBENSON, W., Mathematical Analysis
BARIGAND, M., General Chemistry
BARTHELEMY, J., Architecture
BERDAL, R., Principles of Building
BERNARDO, J. P., Applied Mechanics
BEUGNIES, A., Mineralogy, Petrography
BLAVE, A., Electronics
BLONDEAU, H., Elasticity, Strength of Materials
BLONDEL, M., Electronics
BOITE, R., Theory of Circuits
BOUCHER, S., Analytical Mechanics
BOUGARD, J., Thermodynamics
BOUQUEGNEAU, C., High Tension Electricity
BROCHE, C., Electrotechnology
BRUXELMANE, M., Chemical Engineering
BRYCH, J., Mining
CARTON, E., Functional and Numerical Analysis
CHAPELLE, P., Physics
CHARLET, J. M., Mineralogy, Petrography
COGNEAUX, M., Electronics
CRAPPE, M., Industrial Applications of Electricity
CRAPPE, R., Electronics
DANGUY, L., Physics of Materials
DEGUELDRE, G., Mining
DE HAAN, A., General Chemistry
DOEHAERD, T., General Chemistry
FRANEAU, J., Physics
GERIN, A., Electricity, Electrical Measurement
GODFRIAUX, J., Geology
GRARD, F., Nuclear Physics
GRÉGOIRE, C., Transport and Distribution of High-Tension Electricity
HANTON, J., Applied Mechanics
HEEMSKERK, J., Mechanical Preparation of Coal and Ore Dressing
HENRIETTE, J., Heat Technology
JACOB, M., Metallurgy of Non-Ferrous Metals
JACOBS, P., Electricity, Electrical Measurement
JADIN, V., Electricity, Electrical Measurement
JADOT, R., Thermodynamics
LABEAU, G., Political Economy
LANNOY, F., Principles of Building
LEDOCQ, J., Construction of Mechanics
LEFEBVRE, S., Chemical Engineering
LEICH, H., Theory of Circuits
LEROY, A., Construction of Machines, Technology, Applied Metrology
LEVERT, J. M., Analytical and Industrial Chemistry
MAQUESTIAU, A., Organic Chemistry
MATHIEU, M., Chemical Engineering
MAUROY, M., Automation
MEUNIER, C., Elasticity, Strength of Materials, Principles of Building
MEUNIER, H., Heat Technology
MOISET, P., Mechanical Preparation of Coal and Ore Dressing
PACQUÉ, C., Metallurgy
PETITJEAN, J., General Chemistry
PETTEAU, C., Physical Mathematics and Use of Combustibles
PILATTE, A., Thermodynamics
QUIVY, R., General Physics
RIQUIER, Y., Metallurgy
ROBASZYNSKI, F., Geology
ROUBENS, M., Mathematics and Operational Research
SAVE, M., Strength of Materials, Stability of Buildings
TRECAT, J., Transport and Distribution of High Tension Electricity
VANDER POORTEN, H., General Chemistry
VANDERSCHUREN, J., Chemical Engineering
VILAIN, A., Metallurgy
VISEUR, A., Construction of Machines

FACULTÉ UNIVERSITAIRE CATHOLIQUE DE MONS

CHAUSSÉE DE BINCHE 151, B7000 MONS

Telephone: 065-121-13.

Institut Supérieur Commercial et Consulaire founded 1896; University founded 1965.

Language of instruction: French; Private control.

Rector: Prof. JACQUES DROUSIE.
Vice-Rector: Prof. JEAN LHOAS.
Secretary-General: A. DURANT.

Number of teachers: *c.* 80.
Number of students: *c.* 600.

FACULTÉS UNIVERSITAIRES NOTRE-DAME DE LA PAIX

61 RUE DE BRUXELLES, NAMUR

Telephone: (081) 229061.

Founded 1831.

Language of instruction: French.

Rector: R. TROISFONTAINES.
Secretary: C. COURTOY.

Library: *see under* Libraries.

Number of teachers: 153.
Number of students: 2,810.

Publications: *Les Etudes Classiques*† (quarterly), *Bibliothèque de la Faculté de Philosophie et Lettres de Namur*† (3 vols. a year), *Travaux de la Faculté des Sciences économiques et sociales*†, *Travaux de la Faculté de Droit*†, *Travaux de l'Institut d'Informatique.*

DEANS:

Faculty of Philosophy and Letters: R. LORIAUX.
Faculty of Law: E. CEREXHE.
Faculty of Economics: L. GEVERS.
Faculty of Sciences: A. BAUCHAU.
Faculty of Medicine: R. WATTIAUX.
Institute of Computer Science: J. BERLEUR.

PROFESSORS:

Faculty of Philosophy and Letters:
DASNOY, A., Archaeology
DE JONG, M., Dutch and Modern Literature, Dutch Language and Philology
GHEQUIERE, A., Art
GOTHOT, P., History of Law
GUILLAUME, J., Modern Literature, French Literature and Romance Philology
HANOT, M., German Philology and Language
HANTSON, A., English Language
LAHAYE, E., Theology and Philosophy
LEGROS, G., Romance Philology
LORIAUX, R., Greek
NOËL, R., History
PAVANI, P., Italian
PETERS, M., German Language
PICHOIS, C., Romance Philology

PIRON, F., History of Music
SOMERS, L.-H., English Philology and Language
WANKENNE, A., Roman History, Latin
WEISSHAUPT, J., Dutch Philology

Faculty of Law:
BAUFAY, J., Philosophy, Metaphysics, Theology
CEREXHE, E., Private Law, Fundamental Legal Principles
CLERFAIJT, G., Economic Principles, Macro-economic Analysis
DETHIER, R. Psychology
DU JARDIN, J., Introduction to Criminology
HANSOTTE, G., Medieval and Modern History
MAES, A., Economic Principles, Microeconomic Analysis
MAON, P., Roman Law, History of Private Law, Theology
TROISFONTAINES, C., General Theory of Knowledge

Faculty of Economics:
ABRAHAM, J. P., International Economics II, Banking, Financial Management
BAUVIGNET, R., Advanced Mathematics
BODART, F., Data Processing Introduction to Analysis, Production Management
COIPEL, M., Introduction to Law, Common Law
COLLARD, R., Management
D'ASPREMONT LYNDEN, C., Decision Theory
DE GROOTE, J., Economics and Finance, Monetary Facts
DEMBLON, L., Public Administration
DE MEESTER DE RAVESTEIN, J. C., Advanced Mathematics for Economists
DESCHAMPS, R., Macro-economics
DULIEU, P., Public Choice Theory
DUPLAT, J.-L., Fiscal Law
GEVERS, L., Micro-Economics
GLEJSER, H., Econometrics
GUILLAUME, M., Business Economics, Budgetary Control, Investment and Capital Expenditures
JAUMOTTE, J.-C., Regional and Sectoral Economic Analysis
JOSET, C.-J., History and International Law
KERVYN DE LETTENHOVE, Baron A. Economics and Finance, Public Finance
LEBRUN, P., Economic Principles
LEGRAND, M., Contemporary Philosophy, Psychology
LEWALLE, P., Belgian and International Public Institutions
NIZET, J., Sociology
PARDON, J., Belgian and International Public Institutions
PELLEMANS, P., Market Management, Market Research, Organization Theory, Personnel Management
QUEVRIN, E., International Economics
RAES, J., Natural Law, Social Philosophy, Contemporary Ideas
SCHEPENS, G., Operations Research
VAN ASSCHE, F., Banking, Finance Management
VAN GINDERACHTER, J., Statistics
VAN WYMEERSCH, C., Managerial Finance, Business Forecasting, Accounting

Institute of Computer Science:
BODART, F., Operations Research in Company Management Operations Research applied to Computer Science
BRUNIN, J., Logical and Switching Circuits, Information Theory and Telecommunication
CHERTON, C., Files Theory
FICHEFET, J., Graph Theory, Numerical Analysis, Mathematical Programming, Simulation languages
GIGOT, R., Management Information systems, Methodology
LEROY, J., Theory of Language
RAMAEKERS, J., Fortran, Computer Logic and Technology, Compilers
VAN BASTELAER, PH., Operating Systems, Teletreatment, Design Configuration

Faculty of Sciences:
ANDRE, J.-M., Chemistry
BAUCHAU, A., Zoology, Animal Biology, Animal Physiology
CARDINAEL, G., Physics, Introduction to Mathematics and Experimental Sciences
CAUDANO, R., Physics
COURTOY, C., Physics, Introduction to Mathematics and Experimental Sciences
DECONNINCK, G., Statistics, Physics, Mechanics
DELANDE, G., Mathematics
DEMORTIER, G., Physics
DENIS, J., Geography
DEPELCHIN, A., Microbiology, Immunology
DEROUANE, E., Chemistry
DE SLOOVER, J.-L., Botany
DURANT, F., Chemistry
FOUREZ, G., Physics, Education
GILLES, J., Physics
GILLET, C., Botany
GRIFFÉ, M., Chemistry
HENRARD, J., Mathematics
KHMELESKAJA, G., Mathematics
KRIEF, A., Chemistry
LUCAS, A., Physics
MENGEOT, J., Zoology
MERSCH, J., Mathematics
OVERLAU, P., Mineralogy, Geology
PANIER, A., Chemistry
RONVEAUX, A., Mathematics
RONVEAUX-DUPAL, M.-F., Cytology, Morphology Analysis Methods
SCHIFFLERS, E., Probabilities, Statistics
SCHONNE, A., Chemistry
THIRAN, J.-P., Numerical Analysis
VERBIST, J., Physical Chemistry
WEXLER, D., Mathematics

Faculty of Medicine:
BERBEN, J., Human Anatomy
DE SCHRYVER, C., Physiology
ELENS, A., General Physiology, Genetics, Human Physiology
LAMMERANT, J., Special Physiology
LELOUP, R., Histology, Embryology
TROISFONTAINES, R., Theology, Psychology and Ethics
WATTIAUX, R., General and Human Biochemistry

ATTACHED RESEARCH INSTITUTES:

Centre for Data Processing: Dir. J. RAMAEKERS.

Centre for Nuclear Research: Dir. G. DECONNINCK.

Inter-Disciplinary Research Unit for Electronic Microscopy: Dir. R. LELOUP.

FACULTÉS UNIVERSITAIRES SAINT-LOUIS

43 BLVD. DU JARDIN BOTANIQUE,
1000 BRUSSELS
Telephone: 02/217-76-53.
Founded 1858.

Language of instruction: French.
Academic year: October to May.

President: Mgr. H. VAN CAMP.
Rector: J. DABIN.
Secretary-General: D. COPPIETERS DE GIBSON.

Library: *see* Libraries.
Number of teachers: 69.
Number of students: 935.

DEANS:

Faculty of Philosophy and Letters: A. KIES.
Faculty of Law: M. VAN DE KERCHOVE.
Faculty of Economic, Social and Political Sciences: L. SIMAR.

PROFESSORS:

Faculty of Philosophy and Letters:
ANGELONI, A., Italian
CELIS, R., Philosophy
COPPIETERS DE GIBSON, D., Greek Philosophy
DELAUNOIS, M., Greek Philology and Linguistics
DE WAELHENS, A., Philosophical Anthropology and German Philosophy
DUHAMEL, R., German Authors, History of German Literature
ENGELBORGHS, M., History of English Literature
GOTHOT-MERSCH, C., Modern French Authors, Theory of Literature, Philology
HEIDERSCHEIDT, J., English Phonetics and Grammar
JONGEN, R., German Phonetics and Grammar
KEERSMAEKERS, A., German Authors, History of German Literature
KIES, A., History of French Literature, Philology
LAVENCY, M., Latin Philology and Linguistics, Latin Translation and Grammar
LENOBLE-PINSON, M., Modern French Grammar, Philology
LEROT, J., Linguistics and Philology
MAICAS, M. P., Spanish
MATTENS, W., Dutch Grammar and Philology
ORBAN, M., Greek Authors, Greek Translation and Grammar
PAQUET, J., Medieval Literature and History
POUCET, J., History of Greek and Latin Literature, and of Greek and Roman Institutions
SEMPOUX, A., Italian
SILVESTRE, H., History
SMEYERS, J., Dutch Authors, History of Dutch Literature
SPITAELS, J., Medieval French Literature
TIHON, A., History
VAREA, P., Spanish
VERMEYLEN, A., Spanish
WARZÉE, P., History of Art and Belgian History
WEBER, P., Moral Philosophy

Faculty of Law:
CAUCHIES, J. M., History of Thought
DABIN, J., Moral Philosophy, Natural Law, Ethics
DILLENS, A. M., Philosophy
GODDING, P., Private Law
JACQUEMIN, A., Political Economics
LORIAUX, C., English
LORY, J., Contemporary History, History of Thought
MACHTENS, O., Dutch Law
MAHIEU, M., Introduction to Law
SILVA LEITON, R., Accountancy

VAN COMPERNOLLE, J., Introduction to Judicial Law
VAN DE KERCKHOVE, M., Introduction to Law

Faculty of Economic, Social and Political Sciences:

BRAGARD, L., Mathematics
CHAUMONT, M., Sociology
CITTA-VANTHEMSCHE, M., Numerical Analysis
D'ASPREMONT LYNDEN, C., Philosophy and Social Sciences
DECLÈVE, H., Philosophy and Ethics
DELPÉRÉE, F., Constitutional Law, Administrative Law
DUHOUX, M., Linear Algebra
FLORENCE, J., Psychology
FONTAINE-DE VISSCHER, L., Philosophy of Language
FROGNIER, A., Political Science
GOFFIN, English
GUÉRET-DE KEYSER, E., History of Thought, Philosophy of Art
HALLOY, P., Accountancy
KLEIBER, M., Philosophy, Ethics
KUMPS, A. M., Political Economy
LECLERCQ, N. C., Civil Law
LOUTE, E., Mathematics
PAULUS-ORTH, N., English
PEETERS, R., Probability and Statistics
REMY, J., Sociology
SERVAIS, E., Sociology
SIMAR, L., Statistics
TULKENS, H., Political Economy
TULKENS, P., Biology
VAN BUNNEN, L., Commercial Law
VAN RILLAER, J., Social and Industrial Psychology
VERHOEVEN, J., International Law
WILMES, P., Informatics
WITTERWULGHE, R., Political Economy

Ecole des Sciences Philosophiques et Religieuses: Founded 1925.

President: Mgr. H. VAN CAMP.
Director: Abbé D. COPPIETERS DE GIBSON.

Number of teachers: 10.
Number of students: 230.

LIMBURGS UNIVERSITAIR CENTRUM

UNIVERSITAIRE CAMPUS, 3610 DIEPENBEEK
Telephone: 011/22.99.61.

Founded 1971.

Private control; State-aided.

Chairman: J. KNAPEN.
Vice-Chairman: P. SCHLUSMANS.
Rector: L. VERHAEGEN.
Vice-Rector: M. VAN POUCKE.
Permanent Secretary: A. GRYPDONCK.

DEANS:

Faculty of Medicine: J. CREEMERS.
Faculty of Sciences: M. BOUTEN.

HEADS OF DEPARTMENTS:

Mathematics-Physics-Physiology: L. STALS.
Chemistry-Biology-Microbiology: H. TEUCHY.
Human and Social Sciences: R. M. BRUYNOOGHE.
Embroylogy - Histology - Anatomy: J. CREEMERS.

RIJKSUNIVERSITAIR CENTRUM TE ANTWERPEN (Antwerp State University Centre)

KASTEEL "DEN BRANDT", 12 BEUKENLAAN, 2020 ANTWERP
Telephone: 03/27-38-07.

Founded 1965.

Language of instruction: Dutch; State control; Academic year: October to July (two semesters).

Rector: Prof. Dr. M. H. A. DE GROODT-LASSEEL.

Deputy Rector: Prof. Dr. E. VANLOMMEL.

Administrator: G. VANSTEENKISTE-LABEAU.

Librarian: Dr. B. VAN STYVENDAELE.

Library: *see* Libraries.

Number of teachers: 170.
Number of students: 2,000.

Publications: *Linguistica Antwerpiensa* (annual), *ALA—Africa Latin-America Asia.*

DEANS:

Faculty of Applied Economic Sciences: Prof. R. VAN ROMPU.

Faculty of Sciences: Prof. Dr. W. DIERICK.

PROFESSORS:

ALDERWEIRELDT, F., Organic Chemistry
AMELINCKX, S., Physics and Solid State Physics
BRUTSAERT, D., Human Physiology
BUTSTRAEN, R., Applied Mathematics (Economics)
COPPIETERS, E., International Organizations
DECLAIR, W., General Biochemistry (animals)
DE CORT, J., German
DE GROODT-LASSEEL, M. H. A., Histology and Microscopic Anatomy
DEPUNT, J., Geometry
DEREYMAEKER, R., Statistics
DEVREESE, J., Applied Mathematics (Sciences)
DIERICK, W., Biochemistry (human body)
DOPPAGNE, A., Spanish
EVENS, F., General Biology
GEVERS, R., Theoretical Mechanics
HERMAN, M., Inorganic Chemistry
HOUVENAGHEL, A., General Physiology (animals)
KENNES, H., Budgetary Policy, with reference to Developing Countries
KREDIET, P., Animal Embryology
KUYK, W., Algebra
LAROCHETTE, J., French
LEVY, L., Financial and Monetary Economics
PEETERS, L., Economic Development
REMAUT, G., Physics
VAKAET, L., Human Anatomy
VANDEWALLE, G., General Economics
VAN HERBRUGGEN, C., Macro-Economics
VANHOORNE, R., General Botany
VANHUYSE, V., Experimental Physics
VAN LERBERGHE, K., Chemical Technology
VAN LEUVEN, P., Theoretical and Mathematical Physics
VANLOMMEL, E., Management (Industrial, Commercial, Financial)
VAN ROMPU, G., Sociology
VERHEYEN, W., General Zoology
VOCHTEN, R., Technology
WERCK, V., Comparative Study of Public, Judicial and Legal Bodies with reference to Developing Countries
WUYTS, P., Mathematical Analysis

ATTACHED INSTITUTES:

Higher Institute for Translators and Interpreters: Pres. Prof. D. GODFRIND.

Institute for Developing Countries: A. Goemaerelei 52, 2000 Antwerp; f. 1920; lectures may be given here in languages other than Dutch.

Institute for Administration Studies: Pres. Prof. H. KENNES.

Institute for Agrarian Economy and Sociology.

UNIVERSITAIRE FACULTEITEN SINT-ALOYSIUS

VRIJHEIDSLAAN 17, 1080 BRUSSELS
Telephone: 02/427.99.60.

Founded 1968.

Language of instruction: Dutch; Private control; Academic year: October to July.

President: JAN LINDEMANS.
Librarian: P. VAN NIEUWENHUYSEN.
Administrative Officer: H. ALLAER.

Library of 60,000 vols.
Number of teachers: 62.
Number of students: 450.

Publications: *Studiegids, Studeren aan de Ufsal.*

DEANS:

Literature and Philosophy: B. F. VAN VLIERDEN.
Law: F. VANHEMELRYCK.
Philosophy: A. WYLLEMAN.
Economic Sciences: R. DONCKELS.

PROFESSORS:

BRAEKMAN, W., History of English Literature
DAEMS, H., Mathematics
DE GEEST, W., Dutch Linguistics
DONCKELS, R., Economics
LINDEMANS, J., Introduction to Law
NELDE, P., German Linguistics
PUTSEYS, Y., English Linguistics
RAYMAEKERS, E., Political Economy
VAN GORP, H., European Literature
VANHEMELRYCK, F., History
VAN VLIERDEN, B., History of Dutch Literature, Introduction to Modern Literature

UNIVERSITAIRE FACULTEITEN SINT-IGNATIUS TE ANTWERPEN

13 PRINSSTRAAT, 2000 ANTWERP
Telephone: 031/31.66.60.

Founded 1852.

Language of instruction: Dutch; Private control; Academic year: October to September.

Rector: Prof. Dr. **Louis Bruyns.**
President of the General Assembly: Prof. L. Wauters.
Chief Administrative Officer: W. Baltussen.
Treasurer: X. Van Meerbeeck.
Librarian: **J. Van Brabant.**

Library: *see under* **Libraries.**
Number of teachers: 160.
Number of students: 2,500.

Publications: *Economisch en Sociaal Tijdschrift*†, *Ons Geestelijk Erf*†, *Bijdragen tot de geschiedenis*†, *Gezelliana*†, *Economische Didactiek*†, *Weekblad voor Nederlandse Didactiek*†, *Info-Frans*†.

Deans:

Faculty of Law: F. Van Neste.
Faculty of Philosophy and Letters: C. Neutjens.
Faculty of Political and Social Sciences: J. Gijssels.
Faculty of Applied Economic Sciences: M. Willems.

Heads of Departments

Philosophy and Religious Studies: W. Thys.
Languages and Literature: J. Gijsel.
History: R. Baetens.
Law: R. Janssens.
Sociology and Social Politics: J. Van Houtte.
Economics: S. Plasschaert.

Affiliated Institutes:

Instituut voor Postuniversitair Onderwijs-IPO (*Institute of Postgraduate Management Studies*): Kipdorp 19, 2000 Antwerp; Dir. E. Durinck.

Instituut voor Didactiek en Andragogiek-'DEA (*Institute of Education*): Prinsstraat 13, 2000 Antwerp; Pres. P. Lenders.

Rekencentrum (*Data Centre*): Prinsstraat 13, 2000 Antwerp; Dir. M Willems.

UNIVERSITAIRE INSTELLING ANTWERPEN

UNIVERSITEITSPLEIN 1,
2610 WILRIJK

Telephone: 031/28-25-28.

Founded 1971.

Private **institution under State** control; Language of instruction: Dutch.

President: **P. van Remoortere.**
Rector: R. Clara.
Vice-President: **C. Paulus.**
Vice-Rector: A. Vermandel.
Secretary: L. **Lambeets.**
Librarian: H. Vervliet.

Library: *see* **Libraries.**

Number of teachers: 188.
Number of students: 1,518.

Publications: Academic Information Guides† (annually).

Deans:

Faculty of Sciences: J. De Greef.
Faculty of Medicine and Pharmacy: W. Eylenbosch.
Faculty of Philosophy and Letters: L. Tasmowski.
Faculty of Law, Political and Social Sciences: J. Van Steenberge.

Heads of Departments:

Physics: F. Verbeure.
Mathematics: J. Haezendonck.
Chemistry: R. Gijbels.
Biological Chemistry: P. Joos.
Biology: F. De Vree.
Medicine: K. Van Camp.
Pharmacy: A. Haemers.
Germanic Philology: A. Lefevere.
Romance Philology: M. Delcroix.
Law: W. Lambrechts.
Political and Social Sciences: J. Lauwers.
Education: S. Maes.

UNIVERSITY LEVEL INSTITUTIONS

COLLEGE OF EUROPE

DYVER 11, B-8000 BRUGES

Telephone: 050/33.53.34.

Telex: 81457 COLEUR B.

Founded **1949; institute of** postgraduate European studies.

Languages of instruction: English and French.

President of Board of Trustees: F X. Ortoli.

Rector: Prof. Dr. J. Lukaszewski.

Librarian: **L. L. Paklons.**

Library of 100,000 vols.
Number of teachers: 85.
Number of students: 150.

Directors:

Law: R. Kovar.
Economics: **G. Denton.**
Administrative Studies: W. Wessels.
Conservation of Historic Towns and Buildings: R. Lemaire.

ÉCOLE DES HAUTES ÉTUDES COMMERCIALES

21 RUE SOHET, LIÈGE

Founded 1898.

Language of instruction: French.

President: **P. Latteur.**
Director: **M. Aldenhoff.**
Librarian: M. A. Collard-Thomas.

The library contains 7,000 vols.
Number of teachers: 60.
Number of students: 520.

HANDELSHOGESCHOOL

KORTE NIEUWSTRAAT 33,
2000 ANTWERP

Telephone: 031/32-74-52.

Founded 1923.

President: A. van Melkebeke.
Librarian: S. de Landtsheer.

The library contains 25,000 vols.
Number of teachers: 50.
Number of students: 325.

HOGER INSTITUUT VOOR BESTUURS-EN HANDELSWETENSCHAPPEN

(Higher Institute for Administration and Commerce)

84 TRIERSTRAAT,
1040 BRUSSELS

Founded 1938.

President: **R. Vandeputte.**
Director: **A. Vander Kerken.**

Publication: ***Tijdschrift*** *voor* ***Bestuurswetenschappen*** *en Publiek recht* (bi-monthly).

INSTITUT CATHOLIQUE DES HAUTES ÉTUDES COMMERCIALES

2 BLVD. BRAND WHITLOCK,
1150 BRUSSELS

Telephone: 735. 91. 44.

Founded 1934.

Language of instruction: French.

Rector: **Prof. P. Dupriez.**
President: **P. Humblet.**
Secretary: Prof. J. Cornez.
Librarian: M. Vanderhoeven. Flahaux.

Library of 14,000 vols.
Number of teachers: 116.
Number of students: 819.

Publication: *Reflets et Persyectives de la Vie Economique.*

Heads of Departments:

Chapel, Y., Economy and Public Management
Humblet, J.-E., Labour
Lurkin, P., Auditing
Mousset, P., Information Science
Smekens, G., Commercial Engineering
Van Nemen, P., Finance
Van Vracem, P., Marketing
Verboomen, A., International Economy

Attached Schools:

Ecole Supérieure des Sciences Fiscales: 30 blvd. Brand Whitlock, 1200 Brussels; f. 1958.
President: **Prof. P. Dupriez.**
Director: P. Sibille.
Librarian: **M. Vanderhoeven-Flahaux.**

The library contains 1,100 volumes.
Number of teachers: 30.
Number of students: 127.

Centre Interdisciplinaire pour la Formation au Marketing et au Merketing Research: 30 blvd. Brand Whitlock, 1200 Brussels.
President: **Prof. P. Dupriez.**
Director: **Prof. P. Van Vracem.**

Centre Didactique des Sciences Economiques:
President: **Prof. P. Dupriez.**

Secretary: Prof. P. VAN VRACEM.

Centre d'Enseignement Supérieur de la Représentation et de la Gestion Commerciale (CERGECO): 72 avenue de Woluwé St. Lambert, 1200 Brussels.

President: Prof. P. DUPRIEZ.
Director: Prof. P. VAN VRACEM.

INSTITUT D'ENSEIGNEMENT SUPÉRIEUR LUCIEN COOREMANS

11 PLACE ANNEESSENS, 1000 BRUSSELS

Founded 1911.

President: P. VAN HALTEREN.
Secretary: L. HARDY.

PRESIDENTS OF FACULTIES:

Faculty of Commerce: J. GOFFIN.
Faculty of Translators and Interpreters: R. BUYCKX.
Faculty of Administrative Science: P. COURTOY.

Number of teachers: 181.
Number of students: 750.

INSTITUT GRAMME LIÈGE

1 QUAI DU CONDROZ, 4900 ANGLEUR (LIÈGE)

Founded 1906.

Language of instruction: French

Director: JULES DUBOIS

Library of 11,528 vols.

Number of teachers: 54.
Number of students: 350.

Courses in industrial engineering.

Publications: *Nouvelles de l'Institut Gramme* (quarterly), *Annuaire*.

INSTITUT SUPÉRIEUR D'ARCHITECTURE VICTOR HORTA DE LA VILLE DE BRUXELLES

144 RUE DU MIDI, 1000 BRUSSELS

Telephone: 513. 59. 68.

Founded 1711.

Language of instruction: French.

Director: RICHARD VANDENDAELE.

Number of teachers: 66.
Number of students: 350.

Publication: *I.S.A.Br.* (monthly).

INSTITUT SUPÉRIEUR DE COMMERCE SAINT-LOUIS

RUE DU MARAIS 113, 1000 BRUSSELS

Telephone: (02) 218.33.52.

President: R. GABRIEL.
Director: H. STASSENS.

Courses in commercial, administrative, diplomatic, and banking sciences.

INSTITUT SUPÉRIEUR DE L'ÉTAT DE TRADUCTEURS ET INTERPRÈTES

RUE JOSEPH HAZARD 34, 1180 BRUSSELS

Telephone: 02. 345. 51. 33.

Founded 1958 to train translators and interpreters at university level.

Director: JEAN NIEULANDT.
Deputy Director: JEAN LECLERCQ-PAULISSEN.
Librarian: J. P. GAHIDE.

Library of over 18,000 vols.

Number of teachers: 69.
Number of students: 780.

Publication: *Equivalences*† (3 a year).

PRINS LEOPOLD INSTITUUT VOOR TROPISCHE GENEESKUNDE/ INSTITUT DE MÉDECINE TROPICALE PRINCE LÉOPOLD

NATIONALESTRAAT 155, 2000 ANTWERP

Telephone: 031/38-58-80.

Founded by Royal Decree in 1931.

Languages of instruction: Dutch and French.

President: R. DECLERCK.
Vice-Presidents: Prof. Dr. R. BORGHGRAEF, M. ZIMMER.
Director: Prof. Dr. L. EYCKMANS.
Secretary: A. GRARE.
Librarian: G. ROELANTS.

The library contains 30,000 books and 15,000 pamphlets.

Number of teachers: 30.

Publication: *Rapport Annuel* (French and Dutch).

PROFESSORS:

EYCKMANS, Dr. L., Tropical Pathology
FAIN, Dr. A., Medical Zoology
GIGASE, Dr. P., Tropical Pathology
HARDOUIN, Dr. J., Tropical Veterinary Pathology
LIMBOS, Dr. P., Tropical Pathology
MERCENIER, Dr. P., Public Health
MORTELMANS, Dr. J., Tropical Veterinary Pathology
VUYLSTEKE, Dr. J., Nutrition
WERY, Dr. M., Protozoology

Clinique Léopold II: Kronenburgstraat 43, Antwerp; forms an annexe to the Prins Leopold Instituut Voor Tropische Geneeskunde; treats patients from tropical countries and seamen.

Dir. Dr. J. DASNOY.

SINT-ALOYSIUS ECONOMISCHE HOGESCHOOL

BROEKSTRAAT 113, 1000 BRUSSELS

A university-level evening school of economics, founded 1925.

Director: K. DE ROOMS.
Secretary: W. VERDOODT.

Number of teachers: 75.

UNIVERSITÉ EUROPÉENNE DU TRAVAIL

3A RUE PAUL-EMILE-JANSON, BOITE 1, 1050 BRUSSELS

Founded 1973.

Faculties of Law, Medicine, Human Sciences, Technology, Sciences, Pharmacy, Veterinary Medicine, Agronomy situated in various European countries; 39 research centres, also experimental stations, etc.

Rector: Prof. A. GIORNELLI.
Vice-Rector: Prof. M. JACOBSON.
Secretary-General: L. DENONNE.

Number of teachers: 1,912.
Number of students: 14,978.

WETENSCHAPPELIJK ONDERWIJS LIMBURG

UNIVERSITAIRE CAMPUS, 3610 DIEPENBEEK

Founded 1964 as a college of economics and postgraduate centre.

Language of instruction: Dutch; Private control (State-aided).

Chairman: H. VANDERMEULEN.
Director: W. VAN LOOY.

Library of 10,000 vols.

Publications: *Kwartaalschrift*† (quarterly), *Extern-Tijdschrift voor Omgevingswetenschappen*† (monthly).

CONSTITUENT COLLEGES:

Economische Hogeschool Limburg (*Business School*): f. 1968; 50 teachers, 500 students (full-time).

PROFESSORS:

BALLON, G., Commercial Law
BERGER, J., French
BOELAERT, R., Public Finance
BORGERS, J., Psychology
BRIERS, R., Statistics
CHRISTIAENS, X., Teacher Training
CLAES, H., Sociology
COONEN, H., Mathematics
CORTHOUTS, F., Psychology
DEGRAEVE, M., Education
DEMIN, P., Fiscal Problems
DESAEYERE, W., Econometrics and Welfare Economics
DIETEREN, H., Technology
FACHÉ, A., Methodology
GEPTS, S., Micro-Economics
HEIRMAN, A., Marketing
JANSSEN, P., Mathematics
KEERIS, H., Economic Geography
LEMEIRE, F., Mathematics
LEUNIS, J., Marketing
OBEN, G., Chemistry
OOMS, A., Mathematics
PAEMELEIRE, R., Accountancy
RAYMAEKERS, R., Banking
RENTMEESTERS, F., Operational Research
ROECK, A., English
ROSIERS, P., International Trade
STEINS, M., German
STUYCK, J., Commercial Law
TOMMISSEN, P., Economic Systems
VANDEN BERGHE, Y., History of Economics
VAN DEN BULCKE, D., Macro-Economics
VANDERLEEN, W., Operational Research

VAN HAEGENDOREN, M., Political Sciences
VAN LEEUWEN, P., Marketing
VAN LEUVEN, J., Statistics
VAN LOOY, W., Financial Sciences
VAN STEENBERGE, J., Social Law
VANTHIELEN, W., Economic Politics
VERAVERBEKE, N., Mathematics
VERMEIRE, A., English
WETHLY, A., Dutch
WILMOTS, J., German

Postuniversitair Centrum Limburg (*Centre for Postgraduate Studies*): f. 1964; organizes post-academic and open university courses; 45 teachers, 425 students (part-time).

COLLEGES

ECOLE ROYAL MILITAIRE/ KONINKLIJKE MILITAIRE SCHOOL

AVE. DE LA RENAISSANCE 30, 1040 BRUSSELS

Telephone: 733.97.94.

Founded 1834.

Education of officers for Army, Navy, Air Force, Medical Service and Gendarmerie. Languages of instruction: French and Dutch.

Commandant: Lt.-Gen. G. RENSON.
Director of Military Instruction: Col. M. BIDLOT.
Director of Studies: Col R. DE BRABANDER.
Library Director: F. DELAET.

Number of teachers: 123, including 28 professors.
Number of students: 730.
Library of 90,000 vols.

PROFESSORS:

ARCHAMBEAU, J. M., Electricity
BELCHE, L. N. N. A., Construction
BOEYNAEMS, M. M., Sociology
BOURGOIS, R. A., Construction
CALLANT, A. A., Rational Mechanics and Aerodynamics
CELENS, E., Armament and Ballistics
CHARLES, J. E., Telecommunications
CHARLES, J. L., History
COEKELBERGS, R. F., General Chemistry
DATH, J., Armament and Ballistics
DAVID, A. H., Statistics and Economics
GENNART, P. E. G., Mathematics and Data Processing
GOBIN, M. A., Mathematics and Data Processing
JACQUES, R., Applied Mechanics
KALITVENTZEFF, B., General Chemistry
LAMINE, T. P. O., Mathematics
LEHOUCK, F. G., Sociology
MEYSMANS ,R. C., Applied Chemistry
PIRET, A. L. G., Applied Mechanics
VAN BUGGENHOUT, J., Psychology
VANDENPLAS, P. E. M., Physics and Director of the Laboratory of Plasma Physics
VAN LAER, R. C. J., Mechanical Transport
VAN PASSEL, F., Methodology of Historical Research and Logics
VAN REMOORTERE, P. P. L., Electricity
VAN TWEMBEKE, U. L., Astronomy, Geodesy, Topography
VAN WAMBEKE, A. E. V., Construction and Soil Mechanics
VERLINDEN, M. R. R., Telecommunications
WULMS, E., Geography and Geology

ÉCOLE ROYALE DU SERVICE DE SANTÉ

AVENUE AUGUSTE RODIN 8, 1050 BRUSSELS

President: P. DEMINE.
Director: Col. Med. P. NIJS.

The library contains 10,000 vols.
Number of teachers: *c.* 30.
Number of students: *c.* 200.

HOGER RIJKSINSTITUUT VOOR TECHNISCH ONDERWIJS MET NORMAALAFDELINGEN

(Higher Institute for Technical and Vocational Education)

ZIJPSTRAAT 14-16, 1810 WEMMEL

Telephone: 02/269.27.04.

Director: K. FONCK.

INSTITUT DES HAUTES ÉTUDES DE BELGIQUE

AVE. JEANNE 44, 1050 BRUSSELS

Founded 1894.

Language of instruction: French.

President: M. LEROY.
General Secretary: P. GOFFIN.

Courses in natural sciences, mechanics, history, philosophy, arts and letters, economics, social and political sciences.

ATTACHED SCHOOL:

Ecole d'Ergologie: Ave. F. D. Roosevelt 50, 1050 Brussels; f. 1925.

Director: G. TOMAS.

MARINE ACADEMIE

(Académie de Marine)

STEENPLEIN 1, ANTWERP

Telephone: 031-320850.

Founded 1935.

President: WALTER DEBROCK.
Secretary-General: JACQUES VYNCKIER
Treasurer: ALEX DE VOS.
Librarian: JULES VAN BEYLEN.

Publications: *Mededelingen, Communications* (annually).

SCHOOLS OF MUSIC, ART AND ARCHITECTURE

Conservatoire Royal de Musique d'Anvers: St. Jacobsmarkt 11, Antwerp.

Conservatoire Royal de Musique de Bruxelles: 30 rue de la Régence; f. 1832; 120 professors, 727 students; library of *c.* 660,000 vols.; museum of instruments; gives symphony concerts; Dir. E. FELDBUSCH; Librarian P. RASPE (acting); Museum Conservator R. DE MAEYER; publ. *Annual Report.*

Conservatoire Royal de Musique de Gand: Hoogpoort 54, Ghent; f. 1879; Dir. G. VERSCHRAEGEN; Admin. Sec. R. LAMBERT.

Conservatoire Royal de Musique de Liège: 14 rue Forgeur; f. 1826; 80 professors; students taken from 15 years of age; all branches of music and theatre; Dir. H. PUOSSEUR; Admin. Sec. Mrs. M. LAHAYE; Librarian M. BARTHELEMY.

Conservatoire Royal de Musique de Mons: 7 rue de Nimy, 7000 Mons; f. 1926; 375 students; library of 25,000 vols.; Dir. J. BAILY.

Académie Royale des Beaux-Arts de Bruxelles (*Brussels Royal Academy of Fine Arts*): 144 rue du Midi, 1000 Brussels; f. 1711; library: *see* Libraries; Dir. CLAUDE LYR.

Ecole Nationale Supérieure d'Architecture et des Arts Visuels: Abbaye de la Cambre 21, 1050 Brussels; f. 1926; 405 students; Dir. R. L. DELEVOY.

Insas (*Institut National Supérieur des Arts du Spectacle et Techniques de Diffusion*): rue Thérésienne 8, 1000 Brussels; f. 1962 for advanced studies in dramatic art, cinema and broadcasting technique, including television; 2-, 3-, 4-year courses; Dir. R. RAVAR.

Koninklijk Vlaams Conservatorium van Antwerpen (*Royal Flemish School of Music*): Desguinlei 25, 2000 Antwerp; f. 1898.

Director: E. TRAEY.
Administrator-Secretary a.i.: ROSY NIETVELT.
Scientific Librarian: MARIE THÉRÈSE BUYSSENS.

Library of 237,686 vols.

Number of professors: 158.
Number of students: 627.
Publication: *Jaarverslag*†.

Nationaal Hoger Instituut voor Bouwkunst en Stedebouw-Antwerpen (*National Higher Institute of Architecture and Town Planning*): Mutsaertstraat 31, Antwerp; developed by successive stages from Royal Academy of Fine Arts; f. by Teniers in 1663; received present statute by Royal Acts of 1946 and 1952; Sections: architecture, urban and regional planning, interior design and industrial design; library: *see* Libraries. Dir. J. DE MOL; Admin. H. GOOSSENS; Scientific Librarian G. PERSOONS.

Nationaal Hoger Instituut en Koninklijke Academie voor Schone Kunsten-Antwerpen (*National Higher Institute and Royal Academy of Fine Arts, Antwerp*): Mutsaertstraat 31, 2000 Antwerp; f. 1663; Dir. L. TH. VAN LOOIJ; Admin. W. CLAESSENS; Scientific Librarian Dr. G. PERSOONS; publs. catalogues of exhibitions†.

BENIN

Population 3,377,000

RESEARCH INSTITUTES

Direction des Mines, de la Géologie et des Hydrocarbures: B.P. 249, Cotonou; f. 1971; 104 mems.; branch of Ministry of Industry, Trade and Tourism; library; Dir. J. J. PEREIRA.

Institut de Recherches du Coton et des Textiles Exotiques (IRCT): B.P. 715, Cotonou; f. 1942; brs. at Abomey, Parakou; Regional Dir. MARC DAESCHNER; library of 200 vols.; publ. *Coton et Fibres Tropicales.*

Institut de Recherches Agronomiques Tropicales et des Cultures Vivrières (IRAT): B.P. 422, Cotonou; f. 1961; station at Niaouli; Dir. R. WERTS.

Institut de Recherches Appliquées: B.P. 6, Porto-Novo; f. 1942; library of 8,000 vols.; Dir. S. S. ADOTEVI; publ. *Etudes.*

Station de Recherches sur le Palmier à l'huile: B.P. 1, Pobé; oil palm station; f. 1977; attached to IRHO (*see* entry under France); Dir. SYLVAIN SALAKO.

Station de Recherches sur le Cocotier: Semé-Podji; coconut research; f. 1977; attached to IRHO (*see* entry under France); Dir. HONORÉ TCHIBOZO.

ARCHIVES, LIBRARY AND MUSEUMS

Archives Nationales de la République Populaire du Benin: B.P. No. 6, Porto Novo; f. 1914, reorganized 1976; conserves and classifies official state documents; Dir. DAMIEN D'ALMEIDA.

Bibliothèque Nationale: Porto Novo; 7,500 vols.

Musée National d'Abomey: Abomey; Curator R.-PH. ASSOGBA.

Musée de Cotonou: Cotonou; Dir. of Museums M. CLÉMENT DA CRUZ, IRA, B.P. 6, Porto-Novo.

UNIVERSITY

UNIVERSITÉ NATIONALE DU BENIN

ABOMEY-CALAVY, B.P. 526, COTONOU

Telephone: 31-49-25, 31-39-26.

Founded 1970.

State control; Language of instruction: French; Academic year: February to December.

Rector: VINCENT DAN.

Secretary-General: MOÏSE HOUNNOU.

Librarian: VALENTINE QUENUM.

Number of teachers: 126.

Number of students: 2,578.

Publications: ***Annuaire*** **and students' guide.**

DEANS:

Faculty of Scientific and Technical Studies: COSME GOUDJO.

Faculty of Arts, Literature and Human Sciences: HONORAT AGUESSY.

Faculty of Medical Studies: HONORÉ ODOULAMI.

Faculty of Law, Economics and Politics: NATHANAEL G. MENSAH.

Faculty of Agriculture: LÉOPOLD FAKAMBI.

BOLIVIA

Population 4,613,400

ACADEMIES

La Paz

Academia Boliviana: fifteenth in order of foundation in Spanish America; correspondent of the Real Academia Española, Madrid; Dir. Porfidio Díaz Machicao; Sec. Moisés Alcázar; publ. *Revista.*

Academia Nacional de Ciencias de Bolivia (*Bolivian National Academy of Sciences*): P.O.B. 5829; f. 1960; 32 mems.; library of 723 vols.; Pres. Dr. Ovidio Suarez Morales; Sec. Ing. Magín Zubieta; Librarian Arq. Teresa G. de Mesa; publs. *Publicaciones*† (irregular), *Boletin Informativo* (monthly), *Revista*† (2 a year).

Academia Nacional de la Historia (*National Academy of History*): Avenida Abel Iturralde 205; f. 1929; 18 mems.; Pres. Dr. David Alvestegui; Sec.-Gen. Dr. Humberto Vázquez-Machicado.

LEARNED SOCIETIES AND RESEARCH INSTITUTES

(*see* also under Universities)

La Paz

Alianza Francesa: Ave. 20 de Octubre 2041, Casilla 1517; f. 1952; French language and culture; library; 1,200 pupils; Dir. Marcel Barthes.

Amigos de la Ciudad (*Friends of the City Assn.*): Plaza del Teatro Núñez del Prado 576, Casilla 911; f. 1916; 518 mems.; Pres. Humberto Muñoz Cornejo; publ. *Boletín Informativo* (weekly).

Anglo-Bolivian Cultural Institute: Calle Bueno, esq. F. Zuazo; library.

Asociación de Arquitectos de Bolivia (*Assn. of Bolivian Architects*): Casilla 1498; f. 1942; 35 mems.; Pres. Arq. Hugo López Videla; Vice-Pres. Arq. Gustavo Knaudt; Sec. Arq. Fernando Calderón.

Asociación de Ingenieros y Geólogos de Yacimientos Petrolíferos Fiscales Bolivianos (AIG—YPFB): Casilla 401, La Paz; f. 1959; 210 mems. in 4 brs.: La Paz, Camiri, Cochabamba, Santa Cruz; Pres. Ing. Juán Carrasco; publ. *Revista Tecnica de Yacimientos Petrolíferos Fiscales Bolivianos* (quarterly).

Centro Nacional de Documentación Científica y Tecnológica (*Bolivian National Scientific and Technological Documentation Centre*): P.O.B. 3383; f. 1967 to provide extensive information service for research and development; depository library for FAO, WHO and ILO, translations from various languages; library of 9,800 vols.; Dir. Lic. Hugo Loaiza Terán; publ. *Actualidades*† (quarterly).

Centro Nacional de Documentación e Información Educativa (*National Centre of Documentation and Educational Information*): c/o Ministerio de Educación y Cultura; f. 1967; Dir. Rosa Melgar de Ipiña.

Círculo de Bellas Artes (*Fine Arts Centre*): Oficina Plaza Teatro; f. 1912; Pres. Ernesto Peñaranda.

Comisión Boliviana de Energía Nuclear: Avda. 6 de Agosto 2905; Postal address: Casilla de Correo 4821; f. 1960; research into peaceful uses of nuclear energy; advises government on nuclear topics; Exec. Dir. Federico Paz Lora; publ. *Publicaciones de la Comisión Boliviana de Energía Nuclear.*

Fundación Universitaria "Simón I. Patiño": Comercio 819, Casilla 1265; awards grants to assist students in Bolivian universities and technical colleges; publishes books by Bolivian authors; also awards prizes in music and literature; Pres. Dr. Luis Ballivián Saracho; Sec.-Gen. Dr. Alberto Salinas López.

Instituto Boliviano de Cultura: Casilla de correo 7846, La Paz; f. 1975 to promote all aspects of Bolivian culture and preserve the national artistic heritage; library of 150,000 vols.; Exec. Dir. Prof. Alfonso Finot; Sec. Gen. Dr. Raúl Gamarra Ortíz; publ. *Fondo de Publicaciones Populares.*

Instituto Boliviano del Petróleo (I.B.P.): Casilla 4722; f. 1959 to support and co-ordinate scientific, technical and economic studies on the oil industry in Bolivia; 50 mems.; library of 1,000 technical vols.; Pres. Ing. José Patiño; Gen. Sec. Ing. Reynaldo Salgueiro Pabón; publs. *Boletin del Instituto Boliviano del Petróleo, Manual de Signos Convencionales.*

Instituto Boliviano de Tecnología Agropecuaria (IBTA): Avenida Camacho 1471, P.O.B. 5783; f. 1975; Dir. Simón Riera G.; publs. *Boletines Experimentales, Boletines de Divulgación Técnica, Boletines Estadisticos.*

Instituto Comercial Superior de la Nación (fmrly. *Instituto Nacional de Comercio*): Campero 94; f. 1944; controls commercial and administrative education; 35 mems.; library of 5,201 vols.; Dir. Tte. Armando de Palacios; publ. *Mercurio* (annually).

Instituto Cultural Boliviano Alemán (*Goethe-Institut*): Casilla 2195; Dir. Dr. Heinrich Heimer.

Instituto Geográfico Militar y de Catastro Nacional (*Inst. of Military Geography*): Cuartel General, Miraflores; Commandant Col. Luis Nicolau Velasco; publ. *Boletín Informativo.*

Instituto Nacional de Arqueología de Bolivia: Calle Tiwanaku 93; Dir. Dr. Carlos Ponce Sanginés; publ. *Publicaciones.*

Instituto Nacional de Estadística (*National Institute of Statistics*): Casilla 6129; f. 1936; national statistics and censuses; library of 14,000 vols.; Dir. Lic. Arturo Valdivieso; publs. *Boletin Estadistico*† (quarterly), *Indice de Precios al Consumidor*†, and various annual reports.

Instituto Nacional de Estudios Lingüísticos (INEL): Junín 608; f. 1965; linguistic, social and educational research and teaching; library of 800 vols.; Dir. Pedro Plaza Martínez; publs. specialized papers, *Yatiñataki, Notas y Noticias Lingüísticas* (monthly).

Observatorio San Calixto: Casilla 5939; f. 1892; meteorology and seismology; Dir. R. P. Ramón Cabré, s. j.; publ. *Seismic Bulletin-Observatorio San Calixto.*

Office de la Recherche Scientifique et Technique Outre-Mer (ORSTOM): Cajon postal 8714; geology, pedology, hydrobiology; Dir. M. SERVANT. (*See* main entry under France.)

P.E.N. Club de Bolivia (Centro Internacional de escritores) (*International P.E.N. Centre*): Calle Goitia 17, Casilla 149; f. 1931; 40 Bolivian mems., 7 from other South American countries; Pres. (vacant); Sec. YOLANDA BEDREGAL DE CÓNITZER.

Servicio Geológico de Bolivia: Federico Zuazo 1673, Casilla 2729; f. 1960 as a national department, reorganized 1966; 10 laboratories, specialized library; Dir. Ing. JOSÉ PONCE VILLAGÓMEZ; publs. geological maps and bulletins.

Sociedad Arqueológica de Bolivia (*Archaeological Soc. of Bolivia*): Av. Chacaltaya 500, Casilla 1487; Pres. Prof. ALBERTO LAGUNA MEAVE; Sec. Prof. ERNESTO ALIAGA SUÁREZ. The Society is divided into the following sections: Geology (Head, Ing. MANUEL V. POSNANSKY), Palaeontology (Head, Dr. LEONARDO BRANISA M.), Anthropology (Head, Dr. GREGORIO LOZA BALSA), Prehistory (Head, Prof. MAX A. BAIRON), Folklore (Head, Prof. BERNABE LEDEZMA V.), Native Affairs (Head, Prof. ALICIA PIZARRO DEL C.), Physics and Mathematics (Head, Prof. ALFREDO P. ARIAS S.), Geography and History (Head, Prof. RAUL BRAVO P.), Law (Head, Dr. JAIME ZEBALLOS PASTEN); publ. *Anales de la Arqueología de Bolivia*.

Sociedad Boliviana de Cirugía: Casilla 1252; f. 1939; 185 mems.; Pres. Dr. HUGO PALAZZI MOSCOSO.

Sociedad Boliviana de Salud Pública: Edif. de Salud Pública, Plaza Franz Tamayo, Casilla Postal 151; f. 1963; Dir. Dr. ANTONIO BROWN LEMA.

Sociedad Geológica Boliviana: Edif. Miniminas, 4° piso, Casilla 2729; f. 1961; Pres. Dr. GUSTAVO DONOSO.

Sociedad Geográfica de La Paz (*La Paz Geographical Soc.*): Casilla 632, Calle Tiahuanaco 12; f. 1889; depts. of Pre-History, History, Folklore, Geography; 580 mems.; Pres. JUAN CABRERA GARCÍA; publ. *Boletín*.

Sociedad Rural Boliviana (*Agricultural Society*): Casilla 786, C. Comercio 979; f. 1934; 31 assoc. mems.; Pres. CARLOS MONTES Y MONTES; publs. *IFAP News*†, *El Surco*†, *Industrias Lacteas*†, *Cotar*†, *Universitas*†.

Cochabamba

Instituto Comercial Superior de la Nación "Federico Alvárez Plate": Ayacucho 6737.

Sociedad de Pediatría de Cochabamba (*Paediatrics Soc.*): Casilla 1429; f. 1945; 14 mems.; Pres. Dr. JULIO CORRALES BADANI; Sec. Dr. MOISÉS SEJAS.

Potosí

Sociedad Geográfica y de Historia "Potosí" (*Geographical and Historical Society*): Casa Nacional de Moneda, Casilla correo 39; f. 1905; 20 mems.; library of 4,000 vols.; Pres. LUIS ALFONSO FERNÁNDEZ; Sec. Prof. EDUARDO ARAUJO VILLEGAS; publs. *Colección de la Boliviana*, 25 vols., *Boletín*.

Santa Cruz de la Sierra

Sociedad de Estudios Geográficos e Históricos (*Geographical and Historical Society*): Plaza 24 de Setiembre; f. 1903; Pres. Dr. HERNANDO SANABRIA FERNÁNDEZ; Vice-Pres. Lic. PLÁCIDO MOLINA B.; Sec. AVELINO PEREDO; publ. *Boletín*.

Sucre

Ateneo de Medicina de Sucre (*Athenaeum of Medicine*): Pres. Dr. AGUSTÍN BENÁVIDES; Vice-Pres. Dr. ALBERTO MARTÍNEZ; Sec.-Gen. Dr. ROMELIO A. SUBIETA.

Instituto de Cancerología "Cupertino Arteaga": Hospital de Clínicas, Plaza de Libertad; f. 1947; Dir. Dr. R. PAREJA F.

Instituto Médico "Sucre" (*Medical Inst.*): San Alberto 8 y 10, Casilla 82; f. 1895; 27 mems., 3 hon., and 130 corresponding; library of 8,000 vols., including *Flora Peruviensis* and 16th-century edition of *Aforismos de Hipocrates*, 6,000 pamphlets; research and production of vaccines and sera; Pres. Dr. EZEQUIEL L. OSORIO; Sec. Dr. JOSÉ AGUIRRE; Librarian Dr. GUSTAVO VACA GUZMÁN; publ. *Revista* (quarterly).

Instituto de Sociología Boliviana (ISBO) (*Inst. of Sociology*): Apdo. 215; f. 1941; investigates economic, juridical and sociological problems; library of 15,000 vols.; Dir. TOMÁS LENZ B.; publ. *Revista del Instituto de Sociología Boliviana*.

Sociedad Geográfica "Sucre" (*Geographical Soc.*): Plaza 25 de Mayo (the old Legislative Assembly); f. 1887; 21 mems.; library; Dir. Dr. JOAQUÍN GANTIER V.; publ. *Boletín*.

LIBRARIES

Cochabamba

Biblioteca Central de la Universidad Mayor de San Simón: Avda. Oquendo-Sucre, Casilla 992; f. 1925; 41,544 vols.; Dir. MARIO ESTENSSORO VASQUEZ; publs. *Letras Bolivianas*†, *Revista de Cultura*†.

La Paz

Biblioteca Central de la Universidad Mayor de San Andrés: C.C. 6548; f. 1930; 121,000 vols.; Dir. Lic. ALBERTO CRESPO RODAS.

Biblioteca de la Dirección General de Cultura: Departamento de Inspección Cultural y Biblioteca: Alacaldía Municipal, Casilla 1856; f. 1832; 130,000 vols.; Dir. EFRAÍN VALDÉS OLAVE.

Biblioteca del Congreso Nacional (*Congress Library*): Palacio Legislativo; f. 1912; 15,000 vols.; shares legal deposit with Nat. Library; newspaper library; rare works on history, travel, theatre, etc.; Dir. RICARDO CORTÉS ARAÑA; Sec. ROSA MARÍA MENDOZA; publ. *Reports of Congress*.

Biblioteca del Instituto Boliviano de Estudio y Acción Social: Avda. Arce 2147; special collections on social science, Boliviana, education and government documents; 12,000 vols.; Dir. ELENA PEDDLE.

Biblioteca del Ministerio de Relaciones Exteriores (*Library of the Ministry of Foreign Affairs*): Ingavi 310; f. 1930; 10,039 vols.; private library; Dir. Prof. PACÍFICO LUNA QUIJARRO.

Biblioteca Municipal "Mariscal Andrés de Santa Cruz" (*Municipal Library*): Plaza Franz Tamayo; f. 1838; 80,000 vols.; 8 brs.; Dir. GABRIEL MONTANO ARANIBAR.

Potosí

Biblioteca Municipal "Ricardo Jaime Freires": f. 1920; 30,000 vols.; Dir. LUIS E. HEREDIA.

Biblioteca Universitaria: Universidad Boliviana "Tomás Frías", Casilla No. 54, Av. del Maestro; f. 1957; 21,135 vols.; Dir. ADOLFO VERA DEL CARPIO; publ. *Boletín*.

Sucre

Biblioteca Central de la Universidad Mayor de San Francisco Xavier: Plaza 25 de Mayo, Apdo. 212; Dir. AGAR PEÑARANDA.

Biblioteca y Archivo Nacional de Bolivia (*Nat. Library and Archives*): Calle Bolívar; f. 1836; 150,000 vols.; Dir. GUNNAR MENDOZA.

MUSEUMS

La Paz

Museo "Casa de Murillo": Calle Jaen 790; f. 1950; folk and colonial art; Dir. JUAN ORTEGA LEYTON.

Museo Nacional de Arqueologia (*National Museum*): Calle Tihuanacu 93, Casilla oficial; f. 1846, reinaugurated 1961; archaeological and ethnographical collections; Lake Titicaca district exhibits; Dir. Prof. GREGORIO CORDERO MIRANDA; publ. *Anales*.

Museo Nacional de Arte: Calle Socabaya 485; f. 1961; Colonial and modern art; Dir. ADOLFO DE MORALES.

Potosí

Museo Nacional de la Casa de Moneda de Potosí (*Nat. Museum of the Potosí Mint*): Casilla 39; f. 1938; housed in "Casa Real de la Moneda", the Royal Mint, founded 1572, now restored, said to be the most outstanding civic monument of the Colonial period in South America; colonial art, 18th-century wooden machinery, coins, historical archives, mineralogy, weapons, Indian ethnography, archaeology, modern art; Dir. LUIS ALFONSO FERNÁNDEZ; publ. *see* under Sociedad Geográfica y de Historia de Potosí.

Sucre

Museo Antropologico: Apdo. Postal 212, Universidad Mayor y Pontificia de San Francisco Xavier de Chuquisaca; f. 1944; sections of archaeology (exhibits of pre-Inca civilizations; Dir. JAIME URIOSTE ARANA), ethnography and folklore (Dir. ELIZABETH ROJAS TORO); publ. *Boletin Antropológico*.

Museo Colonial "Charcas": Universidad de San Francisco Xavier de Chuquisaca, Apdo. 212; Dir. Dr. MANUEL GIMÉNEZ CARRAZANA.

Museo de Bellas Artes (*Museum of Fine Arts*): Apdo. 212.

UNIVERSITIES

Following the law passed in June 1972 the 9 Bolivian universities are administered together as the University of Bolivia, under the National Council for Higher Education. They are divided into three geographical zones (three universities to each zone), the universities in each zone offering complementary courses.

UNIVERSIDAD BOLIVIANA MAYOR, REAL Y PONTIFICIA DE SAN FRANCISCO XAVIER

APDO. 212, SUCRE

Telephone: 3245.

Founded 1624 by Papal Bull of Gregory XV dated 1621 and Royal Charter of Philip III, 1622.

Rector: Dr. ANTONIO PARDO SUBIETA.
Vice-Rector: Dr. JORGE PONCE PAZ.
Administrative Director-General: Lic. CARLOS CHAVEZ CORTÉS.
Librarian: AGAR PEÑARANDA.

Number of teachers: 203.
Number of students: 4,210.

DEANS:

Faculty of Social Sciences: Dr. CARLOS ARCE BROW.
Faculty of Health Sciences: Dr. ALBERTO AGUIRRE SANDOVAL.
Faculty of Pure and Natural Sciences: Dr. ROSENDO CARRERAS.

Institutes of biology, cancer research, nuclear medicine, economics, international law, sociology.

UNIVERSIDAD BOLIVIANA MAYOR DE "SAN ANDRÉS"

CASILLA 6548, LA PAZ

Telephone: 25568.

Founded 1830.

Rector: Ing. HUGO MANSILLA ROMERO.
Vice-Rector: Ing. ORLANDO COSSIO ROMERO.
Administrative Director: Lic. RAMÓN RADA VELASCO.
Librarian: Lic. ALBERTO CRESPO
Ing. ANTONIO SAAVEDRA MUÑOZ.

Library: *see* Libraries.
Number of teachers: 900.
Number of students: 17,000.

DEANS:

Faculty of Pure and Natural Sciences: Ing. ANTONIO SAAVEDRA MUÑOZ.
Faculty of Health Sciences: Dr. MARIO BARRAGÁN VARGAS.
Faculty of Law and Social Sciences: Dr. ABELARDO VILLALPANDO RETAMOSO.
Faculty of Humanities and Education Sciences: LEONARDO SORUCO RIVERO.
Faculty of Technology: Ing. HUGO SILVA FERNÁNDEZ.
Faculty of Architecture and Arts: Arq. JORGE ROMERO PITTARI.
Faculty of Economics and Finance: Lic. EDUARDO NAVA MORALES.
Polytechnic Institute: Ing. RAUL LANZA ORDOÑEZ.

UNIVERSIDAD MAYOR DE "SAN SIMÓN"

CASILLA 992, COCHABAMBA

Telephone: 25501.

Founded 1832.

Language of instruction: Spanish; State control.

Rector: Dr. JORGE TRIGO ANDIA.
Vice-Rector: Dr. MARIO ARGANDOÑA YAÑEZ.
Administrative Director: Lic. JOSÉ ARAMAYO ANTEZANA.
Librarian: MARIO ESTENSSORO V.

Library: *see* Libraries.
Number of professors: 523.
Number of students: 10,000.
Publication: *Anales*.

DEANS:

Faculty of Health Sciences: Dr. EDMUNDO MOSCOSO URQUIDI.
Faculty of Social Sciences: Lic. ANTONIO BORDA PISTERNA.
Faculty of Agriculture and Stockbreeding: Ing. AUGUSTO GONZALES ZAMBRANA.
Faculty of Architecture: Arq. ISRAEL BELTRÁN TORRICO.
Faculty of Sciences: Dr. ADOLFO ADRIÁZOLA BALLIVIAN.
Faculty of Humanities and Education: Lic. RAMÓN DAZA RIVERO.

UNIVERSIDAD TECNICA DE ORURO

C.C. 49, ORURO

Telephone: 50100.

Founded 1892.

Rector: Ing. GUILLERMO ROSSO MENDIETA.
Vice-Rector: Lic. ANTONIO RODRÍGUEZ MENDOZA.
Administrative Director: Lic. LINO ROCHA CÉSPEDES.
Librarian: CLOTILDE CALANCHA CASTÍLLO.

Number of teachers: 260.
Number of students: 6,100.
Publications: *Derecho*†, *Estadísticas Universitarias*.

DEANS:

Faculty of Engineering: Ing. MIROSLAV KLUMMER SNELLER.
Faculty of Economics: Lic. EDUARDO RODRÍGUEZ CÓRDOVA.
Faculty of Law: Dr. FELIX MAURE VARGAS.
Polytechnic Institute: Tec. EDUARDO AYLLÓN VARGAS.

UNIVERSIDAD BOLIVIANA "TOMÁS FRÍAS"

EDIFICIO CENTRAL,
AVENIDA DEL MAESTRO,
CASILLA No. 36, POTOSÍ
Telephone: 3020.
Founded 1892.

Duration of academic year: two semesters.

Rector: Ing. JUAN AITKEN SOUX.
Vice-Rector: Ing. FILIBERTO ZULETA ROMAY.
Administrative Director: Lic. PRIMO VILLALBA LLANO.

Number of teachers: 207.
Number of students: 2,500.
Publication: *Revista Cientifica* and others.

DEANS:

Faculty of Pure and Natural Sciences: Ing. EDUARDO RIOS.
Faculty of Technology: Ing. JOSÉ AHENKE.
Faculty of Social Sciences: Dr. DULFREDO ZAMBRANA.

Departments of Business Administration, Arts, Economics and Law; University Extension Division; Polytechnic Institute.

UNIVERSIDAD BOLIVIANA MAYOR "GABRIEL RENÉ MORENO"

Founded 1880.
C.P. 702, SANTA CRUZ DE LA SIERRA

Rector: Dr. DAVID TERCEROS B.
Vice-Rector: Lic. EFRAÍN BARBERY C.
Administrative Director: GERMAN COIMBRA S.

Library of 35,000 vols.
Number of teachers: *c.* 270.
Number of students: *c.* 1,900.

Publications: *La Universidad, Revista Universitaria* (quarterly).

DEANS:

Faculty of Social and Juridical Sciences: Dr. FAUSTO MEDRANO S.
Faculty of Health Sciences: Dr. MIGUEL JUSTIANIANO L.
Faculty of Pure and Natural Sciences: Dr. MARIO SUÁRES R.
Faculty of Technology: OSCAR ALBORTA V.
Faculty of Tropical Agriculture: Dr. JOSÉ CANDIA Z.

There is also a Department of Arts, a Polytechnic Institute, and a University Extension Division.

UNIVERSIDAD BOLIVIANA "JUAN MISAEL SARACHO"

P.O.B. 51, TARIJA.
Telephone: 3110/11/12
Founded 1946.

Rector: Lic. JAIME A. CASTELLANOS.
Vice-Rector: Dr. EDGAR ORTÍZ LEMA.
Administrative Director: Lic. EDUARDO RUIZ GARCIA.
Librarian: MARCELO OROZA ROMERO.

Number of teachers: 104.
Number of students: 750.

DEANS:

Faculty of Pure and Natural Sciences: (vacant).
Faculty of Technology: ABEL BARROSO.
Faculty of Economics and Social Sciences: Dr. MARIO COSSÍO CEJAS.

There are also Departments of Tourism and Folklore, Dentistry; Polytechnic Institute; University Extension Division.

UNIVERSIDAD BOLIVIANA "MARISCAL JOSE BALLIVIAN"

CASILLA 38, TRINIDAD, BENI
Telephone: 371.
Founded 1967.

State control; Academic year: two semesters.

Rector: Dr. JORGE HURTADO CUÉLLAR.
Vice-Rector: Dr. LUÍS ZAMBRANO IBÁÑEZ.
Administrative Director: Lic. ANGEL VILLAVICENCIO PRUDENCIO.
Librarian: Prof. GUILLERMO HURTADO SUÁREZ.

Number of teachers: 44.
Number of students: 500.
Publ. *Panorama Universitario.*

DEAN:

Faculty of Agriculture and Cattle Breeding: Dr. GERARDO BARBA VILLAVICENCIO.
Institute of Research in Stockbreeding: Dr. CARMELO APONTE VÉLEZ (Dir.).

UNIVERSIDAD CATOLICA BOLIVIANA

C.P. 4805,
LA PAZ
Founded 1966.

Rector: Mgr. GENARO M. PRATA VUOLO.
Administrative Director: Lic. JUAN MARTINEZ CALDERON.

Departments of Business Administration, Communication Sciences, Humanities and Education (at Cochabamba), Economics, and Psychology.

SCHOOLS OF ART AND MUSIC

Conservatorio Nacional de Musica: Avda. 6 de Agosto 2092, La Paz; f. 1908; state control; Dir. HUMBERTO VISCARRA MONJE.

Escuela Superior de Bellas Artes: Calle Rosendo Gutierrez 323, La Paz; f. 1928; 18 teachers, 206 students; Pres. GUSTAVO RIVEROS TEJADA; Registrar WALLY DE MONTALBAN.

BOTSWANA

Population 710,000

LEARNED SOCIETY

British Council: P.O.B. 439, Queen's Rd., Gaborone; f. 1973; reference library of 3,974 vols., 46 periodicals; Rep. S. S. NEWTON.

LIBRARIES

Botswana National Archives: P.O.B. 239, Gaborone; f. 1967; central and district government archives from *c.* 1900; library of *c.* 5,800 items; Government Archivist and Dir. KLAS HAVREN; publ. *Annual Report.*

Botswana National Library Service: P.B. 0036, Gaborone; f. 1968; nation-wide public library service; also acts as a national library (legal deposit); *c.* 160,000 vols.; houses the Gaborone Public Library; reference and children's departments; mobile library service; postal lending service; 11 branch libraries; 3 circulating book box projects; Dir. G. SEAME, A.L.A.; publs. *Annual Report*†, *National Bibliography of Botswana*†, *Annual Bibliography for School and College Libraries.*

MUSEUM

National Museum and Art Gallery: Independence Ave., P.O.B. 114, Gaborone; f. 1968; provides, through dioramas and graphic displays, a visual education in the development of Man in Botswana; runs mobile education service for rural primary schools; repository for scientific collections relating to Botswana; art gallery holds a collection of art of all races of Africa south of the Sahara, and exhibits works from any country; library of 1,900 vols. and numerous journals; Dir. A. C. CAMPBELL; publs. *Annual Report*†, *Botswana Notes and Records*† (annual).

Phuthadikobo Museum: Box 208, Mochudi; f. 1976; ethnography, photographic collections, conservation; Dir. SANDY GRANT; publ. *Annual Report*†.

UNIVERSITY AND COLLEGE

UNIVERSITY COLLEGE OF BOTSWANA

P.B. 0022, GABORONE

Telephone: Gaborone 51155.

Founded 1976.

State control; Language of instruction: English; Academic year: August to May.

Rector: N. O. H. SETIDISHO, M.ED., PH.D.
Registrar: W. D. JOHNSON, M.A.
Librarian: E. K. KORANTENG, F.L.A.

Number of teachers: 117.
Number of students: 860.
Publication: *Calendar*† (annually).

DEANS:

Faculty of Economic and Social Studies: Prof. K. P. VARGHESE.
Faculty of Education: Prof. B. PERKINS.
Faculty of Humanities: Prof. L. D. NGCONGCO.
Faculty of Science: Prof. R. A. AMPOMAH.

HEADS OF DEPARTMENTS:

Faculty of Economic and Social Studies:
AHMAD, N., Economics
DECALO, S., Political and Administrative Studies
PILLAI, R. K., Statistics
PRAH, K. K., Sociology
VARGHESE, K. P., Accountancy

Faculty of Education:
HENDERSON, B. R., Educational Resources Centre
HUGHES, B., Institute of Adult Education
MUELKHE, M., Science Education
OTAALA, B., Educational Foundations
PERKINS, B., Language and Social Science Education

Faculty of Humanities:
HARDIE, A. M., English
KOTEI, S. I. A., Library Studies
MOLOTO, E. S., African Languages and Literature
NGCONGCO, L. D., History
NOKO, I., Theology and Religious Studies
THEROND, M. M. A., French

Faculty of Science:
AMPOMAH, R. A., Mathematics
BLOMBERG, C., Chemistry
COOKE, H. J., Environmental Sciences
HARTLAND-ROWE, R., Biology
MAKHURANE, P. M., Physics
THIJS, G. D., Pre-Entry Science
VINK, B. W., Geology

ATTACHED INSTITUTE:

National Institute of Development and Cultural Research: Dir. Prof. L. D. NGCONGCO (acting).

Botswana Agricultural College: P.B. 0027, Gaborone; f. 1967; courses in agriculture, animal health and community development; 35 teachers, 180 students; Principal E. K. MALOISO.

BRAZIL

Population 119,670,000

ACADEMIES

Brasília, DF

Academia Brasiliense de Letras (*Brasília Academy of Letters*): C.P. 07/245, 70000 Brasília; f. 1968; 40 mems.; Pres. DINAH SILVEIRA DE QUEIROZ.

Rio de Janeiro

Academia Brasileira de Ciências (*Brazilian Academy of Sciences*): CP 229, 20000; f. 1916; 153 senior, 94 junior mems.; Pres. ARISTIDES AZEVEDO PACHECO LEÃO; Vice-Pres. PASCHOAL SENISE, MAURÍCIO MATOS PEIXOTO; Gen. Sec. WALTER BAPTIST MORS; publs. *Anais*, *Revista Brasileira de Biologia*.

Academia Brasileira de Ciência da Administração (*Brazilian Academy of Administration*): Av. 13 de Maio 23, salas 1117 a 1119; f. 1973; 40 mems.; Pres. JORGE OSCAR DE MELLO FLORES; Sec. Gen. ENNOR DE ALMEIDA CARNEIRO.

Academia Brasileira de Letras (*Brazilian Academy of Letters*): Av. Presidente Wilson 203, 20030 Rio de Janeiro, RJ; f. 1897; library, 50,000 vols.; Pres. AUSTREGÉSILO DE ATHAYDE; Sec.-Gen. ABGAR RENAULT; Librarian BARBOSA LIMA SOBRINHO; publ. *Revista* (annals); preparing exhaustive *Dictionary of the Portuguese Language*; annual prizes awarded for best Brazilian works in prose, verse and drama.

Academia Nacional de Farmacia (*National Academy of Pharmacy*): Rua dos Andradas, 96, 10 andar-s 1005 A; f. 1937; publ. *Boletim*.

Academia Nacional de Medicina (*National Academy of Medicine*): Caixa Postal 459, ZC-00; f. 1829; 250 mems.; library of 20,000 vols.; Pres. Acad. EDGARD MAGALHÃES GOMES; Sec.-Gen. FIORAVANTI ALONSO DI PIERO; publ. *Boletim*† (monthly).

Belo Horizonte, Minas Gerais

Academia Mineira de Letras (*Minas Gerais Academy of Letters*): Rua Carijos 150, 6°, 30000 Belo Horizonte; Pres VIVALDI MOREIRA.

Cuiabá, Mato Grosso

Academia Matogrossense de Letras (*Mato Grosso Academy of Letters*): Rua 13 de Junho 173; f. 1921; Pres. JOSÉ DE MERQUITA; publ. *Revista*.

Cachoeiro de Itapemerim, Espírito Santo

Academia Cachoeirense de Letras (*Academy of Letters*): Praça Jerônimo Monteiro 105, 2° andar, 29300 Cachoeiro de Itapemerim; f. 1962; 40 mems.; Pres. EVANDRO MOREIRA.

Florianópolis, Santa Catarina

Academia Catarinense de Letras (*Santa Catarina Academy of Letters*): Edif. José Daux, Rua Vidal Ramos, 88000 Florianópolis; f. 1920; 40 mems., 20 corresp. mems.; library of 4,000 vols.; Pres. THEOBALDO COSTA JAMUNDÁ; Sec.-Gen. SILVIA AMÉLIA CARNEIRO DA CUNHA; Librarian EVALDO PAULI; publ. *Revista*.

Fortaleza, Ceará

Academia Cearense de Letras (*Ceará Academy of Letters*): Rua São Paulo s/n, Palácio Senador Alencar, 60000 Fortaleza; f. 1894; 40 mems., 21 hon. mems.; library of 10,000 vols.; Pres. CLAUDIO MARTINS; Sec.-Gen. RAIMUNDO GIRÃO; publ. *Revista*.

João Pessoa, Paraíba

Academia Paraibana de Letras (*Academy of Letters*): Rua Duque de Caxias 25, C.P. 334, 58000 João Pessoa; f. 1941; 40 mems.; Pres. AFONSO PEREIRA DA SILVA; Gen. Sec. AURÉLIO MORENO DE ALBUQUERQUE; publs. *Revista*†, *Boletim Informativo*†, *Discursos e Ensaios*†.

Luziânia, Goiás

Academia de Letras e Artes do Planalto (*Planalto Academy of Arts and Letters*): Rua Joseph de Mello Alvares 57, 77220 Luziânia; f. 1976; 25 mems.; Pres. Dr. JOSÉ DILERMANDO MEIRELES.

Manaus, Amazonas

Academia Amazonense de Letras (*Amazonas Academy of Letters*): Rua Ramos Ferreira 1009; f. 1918; Pres. DJALMA BATISTA; Sec. GENESINO BRAGA; Librarian MÁRIO YPIRANGA MONTEIRO; 40 mems.; library of 3,500 vols.; publ. *Revista*.

Pôrto Alegre, Rio Grande do Sul

Academia Riograndense de Letras (*Rio Grande Academy of Letters*): Rua Candido Silveira 43; publ. *Revista*.

Recife, Pernambuco

Academia Pernambucana de Letras (*Pernambuco Academy of Letters*): Av. Rui Barbosa 1596, Graças, 50000 Recife; f. 1901; library of 7,000 vols., 40 mems., unlimited number of hon. and corresp. mems. in Brazil and abroad; Pres. Dr. MAURO MOTA; Sec. Dr. ANDRADE LIMA F.; publ. *Revista*.

Salvador, Bahia

Academia de Letras da Bahia (*Academy of Letters*): Praça 15 de Novembro (Terreiro) 15A, 40000 Salvador; f. 1917; 40 mems., 19 corresponding in Brazil, 6 abroad; library of 10,000 vols.; Pres. HÉLIO GOMES SIMÕES; Vice-Pres. EDITH MENDES DA GAMA E ABREU; Sec. ANTÔNIO LOUREIRO DE SOUZA; publ. *Revista* (every 6 months).

São Paulo

Academia de Medicina de São Paulo (*Medical Academy of São Paulo*): Rua Teodoro Sampaio 115, 2°, 05451 São Paulo; f. 1895 as Sociedade de Medicina e Cirurgia; Pres. Dr. PEDRO NAHAS; Secs. Dr. IRANY NOVAH MORAES, Dr. ARMANDO CANGER RODRIGUES.

Academia Paulista de Letras (*São Paulo Academy of Letters*): Largo do Arouche 312, 01219 São Paulo; f. 1909; 40 mems.; library of 16,000 vols.; Pres. FRANCISCO MARINS; publ. *Revista*†.

Teresina, Piauí

Academia de Letras de Piauí (*Piaui Academy of Letters*): 64000 Teresina; Pres. JOSÉ DE ARIMATHÉA TITO FILHO; publ. *Revista*.

Vila Velha, Espírito Santo

Academia de Letras 'Humberto de Campos' (*Academy of Letters*): Rua 23 de Maio, s/n; f. 1948; 122 mems.

Vitória, Espírito Santo

Academia Feminina Espírito Santense de Letras (*Women's Academy of Letters*): Rua Bernardo Horta 30, apto. 1—Jucutuara; f. 1949; 33 mems.

LEARNED SOCIETIES

Agriculture and Veterinary Science

Associação Brasileira de Mecânica dos Solos (*Brazilian Society for Soil Mechanics*): Caixa 7141, 01000 São Paulo, S.P.; Pres. Prof. Dirceu de Alencar Velloso.

Sociedade Nacional de Agricultura (*National Agricultural Society*): Avda. General Justo 171, C.P. 1245, 20021 Rio de Janeiro, R.J.; f. 1897; library, 35,000 vols.; Pres. Octávio Mello Alvarenga; Dir. and 1st Sec. José Motta Maia; publs. *A Lavoura* and pamphlets.

Arts

Associação Nacional de Música: Av. Princesa Isabel 38, Apt. 603, Copacabana, Rio de Janeiro, R.J.

Bibliography and Library Science

Associação dos Arquivistas Brasileiros: Praça Tiradentes 83, S.201, 20.000 Rio de Janeiro; f. 1971; co-operates with the Government, national and international organizations on all matters relating to archives and documentation; organizes study courses, conferences, etc.; hopes to achieve national legislation on archives; 505 mems.; library of 193 vols.; Pres. Marilena Leite Paes; Sec. Eloisa Helena R. Marques; publ. *Arquivo e Administração* (4-monthly).

Conselho Federal de Biblioteconomia—CFB (*Federal Council of Librarianship*): SCLRN, 712/713, Bloco A, Ent. 31, Sobreloja, Sala 2, 70760 Brasília, D.F.; f. 1966 to act as a fiscal body and control professional activities in Brazil; ten regional councils; Pres. Nancy Westphalen Corêra.

Federação Brasileira de Associações de Bibliotecários—FEBAB (*Brazilian Federation of Library Associations*): Rua Avanhandava 40, conj. 110, São Paulo, S.P.; f. 1959 to act for the library associations at a national level; to serve as a centre of documentation and bibliography for Brazil; 21 mem. associations; Pres. Antônio Gabriel; publs. *Revista Brasileira de Biblioteconomia e Documentação, Boletim.*

Instituto Brasileiro de Informação em Ciência e Tecnologia (IBICT): Rua Gen. Argolo 90, São Cristóvão, 20921 Rio de Janeiro, RJ; f. 1954; co-ordinates scientific and technical information services throughout the country; maintains Brazilian Union Catalogue of Serials in microform; supplies microfilms, xerocopies, etc., publishes national current bibliographies on pure and applied sciences using computer (KWIC) index, UDC schedules in Portuguese by automatic processes; carries out studies on offer and demand of information; develops computerized information systems; runs a postgraduate course in Information Science and a special course on scientific documentation; library of 21,170 vols.; Dir. Paulo de Souza Moraes; publ. *Ciência da Informação* (2 a year).

Economics, Law and Politics

Instituto Brasileiro de Economia (*Brazilian Institute of Economics*): Getúlio Vargas Foundation, C.P. 9052, Rio de Janeiro, R.J.; f. 1951; Chair. Octávio Gouvêa de Bulhões; publs. *National Accounts* (annual), *Conjuntura Econômica* (monthly), *Revista Brasileira de Economia* (quarterly).

Instituto Brasileiro de Relações Internacionais (*Brazilian Institute of International Relations*): Praia de Botafogo 186, Gr. B s/213, 22250 Rio de Janeiro, R.J.; f. 1954; 1,000 vols.; Exec. Dir. Cleantho de Paiva Leite; Sec. Eneida Nogueira Rigueira; publ. *Revista Brasileira de Política Internacional* (quarterly).

Instituto dos Advogados Brasileiros (*Institute of Brazilian Lawyers*): Av. Marechal Câmara 210, 5° andar, Castelo, 20020 Rio de Janeiro, R.J.; f. 1843; 756 mems.; Pres. Otto Eduardo Vizeu Gil; library: *see* Libraries; publ. *Revista.*

Instituto Municipal de Administração e Ciências Contábeis (*Municipal Institute of Administration and Business Science*): Parque Municipal, Caixa Postal 1914, Belo Horizonte, Minas Gerais; f. 1954; library of 33,000 vols.; Pres. Raul Lopes Muradas.

Education

Conselho de Reitores das Universidades Brasileiras (*Council of Brazilian University Rectors*): SEP/Norte, Quadra 516, Lote 09, CEP 70770 Brasília, D.F.; f. 1966; study of problems affecting higher education; 78 mems.; library of 10,000 vols.; Pres. Reitor Derblay Galvão; Gen. Sec. Prof. Getúlio de Alencar; publs. *Educação Brasileira, Estudos e Debates, Anais, Documentos Básicos.*

Associação Brasileira de Escolas Superiores Católicas (*Asscn. of Catholic Higher Education Institutions*): Av. Dom José Gaspar 500, Bairro Dom Cabral, Belo Horizonte, M.G.; supervises 11 universities and various faculties; Pres. D. Serafim Fernandes de Araújo.

Associação de Educação Católica do Brasil (*Asscn. for Catholic Education in Brazil*): Rua Martins Ferreira 23, 22271 Rio de Janeiro, R.J.; f. 1945; supervises 27 sections, with a total of 1,750 schools and seminaries; Pres. Ir. Orlando Cunha Lima; publ. *Revista de Educação AEC, Cadernos de Educação.*

Instituto Brasileiro de Educação, Ciência e Cultura (IBECC) (*Brazilian Institute of Education, Science and Culture*): UNESCO National Commission, Avda. Marechal Floriano 196, Palácio Itamaraty, Rio de Janeiro, R.J.; Pres. Prof. Aristides Azevedo Pacheco Leão; Exec. Sec. Dr. Agostinho Olavo Rodrigues.

Educational Foundations

Fundação Educacional de Fortaleza: Av. Capistrano de Abreu 5609, CEP 60000 Fortaleza, Ceará; f. 1974; library of 1,000 vols.; Pres. Antônio Agnelo Neves; Sec.-Gen. José Teixeira Rêgo Neto.

Fundação Getulio Vargas: Praia de Botafogo 190, Rio de Janeiro, R.J.; f. 1944; technical, scientific, educational and philanthropic activities; includes 13 educational institutes; 247 mems. in General Assembly; library of over 80,000 vols.; Pres. Dr. Luíz Simões Lopes.

Instituto "Nami Jafet" Para o Progresso da Ciência e Cultura (*"Nami Jafet" Institute for the Advancement of Science and Culture*): Rua Agostinho Gomes 1455, São Paulo, S.P.; f. 1961; awards annual prizes of three million cruzeiros, a gold medal, diploma and scholarships; established in memory of the late industrialist Prof. Nami Jafet; Chair. of Consultative Council Prof. A. C. Pacheco E. Silva; Chair. of Bd. of Dirs. Prof. Alfredo Buzaid; Exec. Sec. Rone Amorin.

History, Geography and Archaeology

Instituto Arqueológico, Histórico e Geográfico Pernambucano (*Archaeological, Historical and Geographical Institute*): Rua do Hospício 130, Recife, Pernambuco; f. 1862; library of 20,000 vols.; 50 mems., 130 corresp. mems., 5 hon. mems.; Pres. Dr. José Antônio Gonsalves de Melo; First Sec. Dr. Pedro Camelo; Librarian Prof. Fernanda Ivo Neves.; publ. *Revista.*

Instituto do Ceará (*Ceará Institute*): Avda. da Universidade 2431, Fortaleza, Ceará; f. 1887; library, 12,126 vols.; includes the following commissions: History, Manuscripts and Archaeology; Geography, Ethnography and Social Science; Science and Letters; Pres. THOMAZ POMPEU SOBRINHO; Sec.-Gen. Dr. CARLOS STUDART FILHO; Librarian MARIA HILZANIR CALS DE ABREU; publs. *Boletim, Revista, História do Ceará, História e Cultura* (7 vols.).

Instituto Genealógico Brasileiro (*Genealogical Institute*): Rua Dr. Zuquim 1525; São Paulo, S.P.; library of 972 vols.; Pres. Colonel SALVADOR DE MOYA; Sec. Dr. JORGE BUENO DE MIRANDA; publs. *Anuário Genealógico Brasileiro, Anuário Genealógico Latino, Revista Genealógica Brasileira, Biblioteca Genealógica Brasileira, Biblioteca Genealógica Latina, Indices Genealógicos Brasileiros, Subsídios Genealógicos.*

Instituto Geográfico e Histórico da Bahia (*Bahia Geographical and Historical Institute*): Avenida 7 de Setembro, Salvador, Bahia; f. 1894; library of 17,634 vols.; Pres. Dr. FRANCISCO DE MAGALHÃES NETO; Secs. Drs. AUGUSTO A. MACHADO and FRANCISCO DA CONCEIÇÃO MENEZES; publ. *Revista* (annually).

Instituto Geográfico e Histórico do Amazonas: Rua B. Ramos 117131, Manaus, Amazonas; f. 1917; 194 mems.; library 35,961 vols.; Pres. Des. JOÃO REBELO CORRÊA; Sec. JUNOT C. FREDERICO; publs. *Revista, Boletim.*

Instituto Geológico (*Geological Institute*): São Paulo, S.P.; f. 1886; library of 100,000 vols., periodicals and pamphlets; 30,000 maps; map collection, geographical and geological museum; Dir. M. HELENA DE A. MELLO; publs. *Boletim*, reports, maps and monographs.

Instituto Histórico de Alagoas (*Alagoas Historical Institute*): Rua João Pessoa 382, 57000 Maceió, Alagoas; f. 1869; 40 mems.; library of 15,000 vols.; Pres. Dr. JOSÉ LAGES FILHO; Sec. Dr. ABELARDO DUARTE; publ. *Revista.*

Instituto Histórico do Ceará: Avda. Visconde Cauipe, Fortaleza, C.E.; collection of secondary sources on Ceará.

Instituto Histórico e Geográfico Brasileiro (*Brazilian Historical and Geographical Institute*): Avenida Augusto Severo 8, 20021 Rio de Janeiro, R.J.; f. 1838; library of 300,000 vols.; Pres. PEDRO CALMON MONIZ DE BITTENCOURT; Sec. Dr. MANUEL XAVIER DE VASCONCELLOS PEDROSA; publ. *Revista* (quarterly).

Instituto Histórico e Geográfico de Goiás (*Historical and Geographical Institute*): Goiânia; rare collections of letters and newspapers; publ. *Boletim* (quarterly).

Instituto Histórico e Geográfico de Santa Catarina (*Santa Catarina Historical and Geographical Institute*): Rua Vidal Ramos, Ed. José Daux, 11° andar, C.P. D-142, Florianópolis, S.C.; f. 1896; 100 mems.; library of 6,000 vols.; Pres. Prof. Dr. VÍCTOR A. PELUSO JUNIOR; Sec. Prof. JALI MEIRINHO; publs. *Revista*† (quarterly), *Anais*†, *Boletim*†.

Instituto Histórico e Geográfico de São Paulo (*São Paulo Historical and Geographical Institute*): Rua Benjamim Constant 158, 01005 São Paulo, SP; f. 1894; library of 40,000 vols.; Pres. JOSÉ PEDRO LEITE CORDEIRO; Sec. VINICIO STEIN CAMPOS; publ. *Revista.*

Instituto Histórico e Geográfico de Sergipe (*Sergipe Historical and Geographical Institute*): Rua de Itabaianinha 41, 49000 Aracajú; f. 1912; Pres. Prof. MARIA THETIS NUENS; publ. *Revista.*

Instituto Histórico e Geográfico do Espírito Santo (*Historical and Geographical Institute*): Av. República 58, C.P. 227, Vitória; f. 1916; Pres. Prof. ALBERTO STANGE Jr.; Gen. Sec. Prof. PLACIDINO PASSOS; publ. *Revista.*

Instituto Histórico e Geográfico do Maranhão (*Maranhão Historical and Geographical Institute*): Rua Santa Rita 230, 65000 São Luíz, Maranhão; f. 1925; Pres. Dr. JOSÉ RIBAMAR SEGUINS; Sec.-Gen. Dr. FRANCISCO MARIALVA MONT'ALVERNE FROTA; publ. *Revista.*

Instituto Histórico e Geográfico do Pará (*Pará Historical and Geographical Institute*): Rua d'Aveiro-Cidade Irmã 62 (Antiga Thomazia Perdigão), C.P. 547, 66000 Belém; f. 1917; Pres. Dr. JOSÉ RODRIGUES DA SILVEIRA NETTO; First Sec. Dr. ALAÚDIO DE OLIVEIRA MELLO.

Instituto Histórico e Geográfico do Rio Grande do Norte (*Rio Grande do Norte Historical and Geographical Institute*): Rua da Conceição 622, 59000 Natal; f. 1902; library 50,000 vols.; Pres. Dr. ENÉLIO LIMA PETROVICH; Librarian JOÃO CARLOS DE VASCONCELLOS; publ. *Revista.*

Instituto Histórico e Geográfico do Rio Grande do Sul (*Rio Grande do Sul Historical and Geographical Institute*): Rua Riachuelo 1317, 90000 Pôrto Alegre; f. 1920; Pres. Dr. A. MESQUITA DA COSTA; publ. *Revista.*

Instituto Histórico e Geográfico Paraibano (*Paraíba Historical and Geographical Institute*): CP 37, Rua Barão do Abiaí 64, 58000 João Pessoa; f. 1905; library of 10,000 vols.; 40 mems.; 30 corresp.; Pres. ANTÔNIO VITORIANO FREIRE; Sec. EDUARDO MARTINS; publ. *Revista.*

Instituto Histórico, Geográfico e Etnográfico Paranaense (*Historical, Geographical, Ethnographic Institute of Paraná*): Rua José Loureiro 43, 80000 Curitiba; f. 1900; Pres. Gen. LUÍZ CARLOS PEREIRA TOURINHO; Sec. Dr. EDILBERTO TREVISAN; publ. *Boletim.*

Sociedade Brasileira de Cartografia: Rua México 41, Gr. 706-Centro, Rio de Janeiro, R.J.; f. 1958; 2,500 mems.; Pres. CLAUDIO IVANOF LUCAREVSCHI; Dir.-Sec. HANNS J. C. VON STUDNITZ; publs. *Anais, Revista Brasileira de Cartografia.*

Sociedade Brasileira de Geografia (*Brazilian Geographical Society*): Praça da República 54, 1° andar, Rio de Janeiro, R.J.; f. 1883; library 13,712 vols.; 284 mems.; Pres. Prof. JURADYR DE CASTRO PIRES FERREIRA; Sec.-Gen. General HENRIQUE GUILHERME MULLER; publ. *Boletim.*

INTERNATIONAL CULTURAL INSTITUTES

Aliança Francesa: Av. Presidente Antônio Carlos, 58-3°, Rio de Janeiro, R.J.; f. 1886; teaching and spreading French culture; 33 branches; Dir. JEAN ROSE.

British Council: CRN 708/709, Bl. 3, Lote 1 e 3, Brasília; Rep. J. A. BARNETT, O.B.E.; Regional Offices: C.P. 570, Av. Antonio de Goes 240, Pina, 50000 Recife, Reg. Dir. A. P. F. JANSEN; C.P. 2237-ZC-00, Rua Otávio Corrêa 30, 20000 Rio de Janeiro, Reg. Dir. J. D. T. HUGHES; C.P. 1604, Rua Maranhão 416, 01000 São Paulo, Reg. Dir. J. S. ACTON.

Casa Thomas Jefferson (*U.S. International Communication Agency*): C.P. 07-1201, Brasília, D.F.; cultural programmes and language teaching; publ. *CTJ Journal* (2 a year).

Instituto Brasil-Estados Unidos (*Brazil-U.S.A. Institute*): Av. N. S. Copacabana 690, 22050 Rio de Janeiro, R.J.; f. 1937; art gallery; English and Portuguese courses (15,000 students); 1,719 mems.; library of 35,000 vols. and 4,000 records; Pres. Dr. MURILLO BASTOS BELCHIOR; Vice-Pres. MELVIN LEONARD BERG; publ. *Boletim*†.

Instituto Cultural Brasil-Alemanha/Goethe Institut (*Brazil-German Cultural Institute*): Av. Graça Aranha 416, 9° andar, 20030 Rio de Janeiro, R.J.; f. 1957; library of 11,000 vols.; Pres. EDMUNDO DE MACEDO SOARES E SILVA; Exec. Dir. HANS-JOACHIM KOELLREUTTER.

Instituto Cultural Brasil-Japão (*Brazil-Japan Cultural Institute*): Av. Franklin Roosevelt 39, 200021 Rio de Janeiro, R.J.; f. 1957; 700 mems.; library of 15,000 vols.; Pres. Dep. FREDERICO TROTTA.

Instituto Goethe: Rua Augusta 1470, C.P. 30642, 01304 São Paulo, S.P.; f. 1957; German language courses; cultural activities; library of 8,100 vols.; Dir. Dr. H.-J. SCHWIERSKOTT.

Istituto Italiano di Cultura (*Italian Cultural Institute*): Av. Presidente Antônio Carlos, 40° Rua Domingos Ferreira 232/101, Rio de Janeiro, R.J.; f. 1950; library of 6,500 vols.; Dir. Prof. DOMENICO GHIO.

Istituto Italiano di Cultura: Rua Frei Caneca 1071, 01307 São Paulo; Dir. Prof. Dr. PAOLO ANGELERI.

Sociedade Brasileira de Cultura Inglesa (*Anglo-Brazilian Cultural Society*): Rua Raúl Pompeia 231, Caixa Postal 821, Rio de Janeiro, R.J.; f. 1934; brs. at Centro, Jardim Botânico, Copacabana, Botafogo, Brasília, Flamengo, Tijuca, Méier, Madureira, Niteroi, Governador, Petrópolis, Campo Grande, Caxias, Barra do Piraí, Nova Friburgo, Teresópolis and Jacarepaguá; affiliated society at Juiz de Fora; library (*see* Libraries); Pres. R. MARINHO.

União Cultural Brasil-Estados Unidos (*Brazil-United States Cultural Union*): Rua Coronel Oscar Pôrto 208, 04003 São Paulo, S.P.; f. 1938; courses in English and Portuguese and specialized courses; 1,200 mems., 120 teachers, 8,000 students; circulating library of 28,000 vols.; art gallery, concerts, etc.; publs. *Hífen*, *Active English*.

LANGUAGE AND LITERATURE

P.E.N. Clube do Brasil (Associação Universal de Escritores) (*International P.E.N. Centre*): Praia do Flamengo 172, 10°, Rio de Janeiro, R.J.; f. 1936; 225 mems.; monthly free lectures; theatrical performances; Pres. Prof. MARCOS ALMIR MADEIRA; publs. *Boletim*, novels, poetry.

Sociedade Brasileira de Autores Teatrais (*Society of Playwrights*): Av. Almirante Barroso, 97, 3° andar, Rio de Janeiro, R.J.; f. 1917; 4,000 mems.; Pres. RAYMUNDO MAGALHÃES JUNIOR; Communications Dir. DANIEL ROCHA; publ. *Revista de Teatro*.

MEDICINE

Associação Bahiana de Medicina (*Medical Society*): Avda. Sete de Setembro 48, 1°, Salvador, Bahia; f. 1894; Pres. Dr. JOSÉ SILVEIRA; Sec.-Gen. Dr. MENANDRO NOVÃES; publ. *Anais*.

Associação Brasileira de Farmacêuticos (*Brazilian Pharmaceutical Association*): Rua Andradas 96, 10°, ZC-21, Rio de Janeiro, R.J.; f. 1916; comprises the following Comms.: *Econômica e Etica Farmacêutica* (Pharmaceutical Economics and Ethics); *Desenvolvimento Cultural* (Cultural Development); *Propaganda e Intercambio Associativo* (Propaganda and Exchange); *Legislação Comercial* (Commercial Legislation); *Legislação Sanitaria* (Sanitary Legislation); *Legislação Tributaria* (Tax Legislation); *Legislação de Marcas e Patentes* (Trade Marks and Patents); library; 950 mems., hon. and corresponding; Pres. Prof. SALVADOR ALVES PEREIRA; Sec.-Gen. Prof. NUNO ÁLVARES PEREIRA; publ. *Revista Brasileira de Farmácia* (monthly).

Associação Brasileira de Odontologia (*Brazilian Dental Association*): Av. 13 de Maio 13-10°, Rio de Janeiro, R.J.; f. 1937; 1,500 mems.; library 4,000 vols.; Pres. Dr. MÁRIO ARAÚJO; publ. *Revista Brasileira de Odontologia* (monthly).

Subsidiary: Seção Cultural (Advanced School), Rua A. Guanabara 17/21, 8°.

Associação Brasileira de Psiquiatria (*Brazilian Psychiatry Asscn.*): Rua Alvaro Ramos 405, Rio de Janeiro, R.J.; f. 1907; Pres. Dr. JOSÉ LUCENA; publ. *Arquivos Brasileiros de Psiquiatria*.

Associação Médica Brasileira (*Brazilian Medical Association*): Rua São Carlos do Pinhal 324, C.P. 8094, São Paulo; f. 1951; professional association; 35,000 mems.; Pres. Dr. PEDRO KASSAB; Sec.-Gen. Dr. RADION SCHUELER BARBOZA; publs. *Jornal AMB* (weekly), *Boletim AMB* and *Revista AMB* (monthly), *Revista Brasileira de Ortopedia, Arquivos Brasileiros de Endocrinologia e Metabologia, Jornal Brasileira de Nefrologia, Anais Brasileiros de Geriatria e Gerontologia* (quarterly), *Revista Brasileira de Reumatologia* (every 2 months).

Associação Médica do Espírito Santo: Avda. Governador Blay, Edifício Banco Mineiro da Produção, 6 andar, Vitória; f. 1929; 335 mems.; library of 3,800 vols.

Associação Paulista de Medicina (*São Paulo Medical Association*): Av. Brigadeiro Luíz Antônio 278, C.P. 2103, São Paulo; f. 1930; 15,700 active mems.; 432 corresp.; Pres. Dr. ALOYSIO GERALDO F. DE CAMARGO; Sec.-Gen. Dr. SIGISMUNDO J. GOMES AMOROSO; publs. *Revista Paulista de Medicina* (monthly), *Jornal* (fortnightly).

Sociedade Brasileira de Dermatologia (*Brazilian Dermatological Society*): C.P. 389, Rio de Janeiro, R.J.; f. 1912; 1 hon. Pres., 53 hon. mems., 115 corresponding mems., 450 mems.; Dir. Prof. JOÃO B. GONTIFO; Sec.-Gen. Dr. JOSÉ SERRUYA; publ. *Anais Brasileiros de Dermatologia*.

Sociedade de Medicina de Alagoas (*Alagoas Medical Society*): Rua Barão de Anadia 5 (centro), 57000 Maceió; f. 1917; Dir. Dr. ALBERTO EDUARDO COX CARDOSO; publ. *Arquivos*.

Sociedade de Medicina Legal e Criminologia de São Paulo (*Forensic Medicine and Criminological Society*): C.P. 4350, São Paulo; f. 1921; 11 founder mems., 19 hon. mems., 191 mems., 5 associate, 184 corresponding; Pres. Prof. Dr. HILÁRIO VEIGA DE CARVALHO; Sec.-Gen. Dr. JOÃO CARVALHAL RIBAS; publ. *Arquivos* (annually).

Sociedade de Pediatria de Bahia (*Paediatrics Society*): Hospital Martagão Gesteira, Rua José Duarte 114, Salvador, Bahia; f. 1930; 200 mems.; Pres. ELIEZER AUDÍFACE; publ. *Pediatria e Puericultura*.

NATURAL SCIENCES

General

Fundação Moinho Santista (*Moinho Santista Foundation*): Av. M. C. Aguiar 215, Bl. A, São Paulo; f. 1955; capital 30,000 cruzeiros; purpose: to promote the advancement of science, letters and arts in Brazil by granting every year the Moinho Santista prizes consisting of the following: gold medal, diploma of recognition for outstanding service in any of the scientific, literary or artistic fields, plus 300 million cruzeiros; Chair. Prof. ANTÔNIO CARLOS PACHECO E SILVA; Vice-Chair. Prof. MIGUEL REALE; Sec. EUGÊNIO BELOTTI.

Fundação Centro de Pesquisas e Estudos—CPE (*Foundation Centre of Research and Study*): Av. Luíz Viana Filho (Paralela), Centro Administrativo, Salvador, Bahia 40,000; f. 1960; education and further training of state-employed technicians; library of 8,500 vols.; Gen. Dir. Dr. CARLOS VASCONCELOS DOMINGUES DA SILVA; publ. *Planejamento* (monthly).

Sociedade Brasileira para o Progresso da Ciência (*Brazilian Society for Scientific Progress*): C.P. 11008, 01000 São Paulo; f. 1948; 16,271 mems.; Pres. JOSÉ GOLDEMBERG; Sec.-Gen. CAROLINA MARTUSCELLI BORI; publ. *Ciência e Cultura* (monthly).

Sociedade Cientifica de São Paulo (*Scientific Society of São Paulo*): C.P. 1904, C.P. 2679, São Paulo; f. 1939; library of 12,000 vols.; Departments: Law, Chemical Technology, Geology and Mineralogy, Astronomy, Architecture, Genealogy, Philology, Medicine, History and Pre-History, Topography; Pres. Dr. GASTÃO F. DE ALMEIDA; Gen. Secs. Prof. Dr. R. F. MOREIRA, Dr. M. F. DE ALMEIDA.

Biological Sciences

Sociedade de Biologia do Brasil: Caixa Postal 1587, ZC-00, Rio de Janeiro, R.J.; f. 1947.

Sociedade Botânica do Brasil (*Botanical Society of Brazil*): f. 1950; 1,234 mems.; Perm. Sec. Dr. EZEQUIAS HERINGER, Reserva Ecológica do IBGE, Div. Ecologia Vegetal, Ed. Venâncio II, 2° andar, 70302 Brasília, DF; publ. *Anais*† (irreg.).

Sociedade Brasileira de Entomologia (*Brazilian Entomological Society*): C.P. 7172, 01000 São Paulo, S.P.; f. 1937; *c.* 500 mems.; Pres. UBIRAJARA R. MARTINS; Sec. JOSÉ M. S. BARATA; publ. *Revista Brasileira de Entomologia* (quarterly).

Statistics

Fundação Instituto Brasileiro de Geografia e Estatística (*Brazilian Institute of Geography and Statistics*): Av. Franklin Roosevelt 166, Rio de Janeiro, R.J.; f. 1936; produces and analyses statistical, geographical, cartographic, geodetic, demographic, socio-economic, natural resources and environmental information; library of 57,850 vols., 5,083 periodicals; Pres. Prof. JESSÉ MONTELLO; publs. *Revista Brasiliera de Estatística*†, *Anuário Estatístico do Brasil*†, *Boletim Estatístico*†, *Revista Brasileira de Geografia*†.

Physical Sciences

Associação Brasileira de Química (*Brazilian Chemical Association*): Av. Rio Branco 156, C.P. 550, Rio de Janeiro, R.J.; f. 1951; affiliated to IUPAC; 2,500 mems.; library of 2,500 vols.; regional brs. in Amazonas, Campinas, Minas Gerais, Pará, Rio Grande do Sul, São Paulo, Ceará, Maranhão, Rio de Janeiro, Pernambuco; Pres. WALTER B. MORS; publ. *Anais*.

PHILOSOPHY AND PSYCHOLOGY

Sociedade Brasileira de Filosofia (*Brazilian Philosophical Soc.*): Praça da República 54, Rio de Janeiro, R.J.; f. 1927; 80 mems., 8 hon., 5 Brazilian corresp., 12 foreign; Pres. Dr. HERBERT CANABARRO REICHARDT; Sec.-Gen. Prof. ARNALDO CLARO DE SÃO THIAGO; publ. *Anais*.

RELIGION, SOCIOLOGY AND ANTHROPOLOGY

Comissão Nacional de Folclore (*National Folklore Commission*): Palácio Itamaraty, Avenida Marechal Floriano 96, Rio de Janeiro, R.J.; Dept. of the Brazilian Institute of Education, Science and Culture (IBECC); Exec. Sec. AGOSTINHO OLAVO RODRIGUES.

Instituto de Antropologia e Etnologia do Pará (*Institute of Anthropology and Ethnology of Pará*): Caixa Postal 684, Belém; Pres. NAPOLEÃO FIGUEIREDO; publ. *Monografias*.

TECHNOLOGY

Associação Brasileira de Metais (*Brazilian Metals Association*): Av. Paulista 2073, Horsa I 15°, C.P. 22161, 01311 São Paulo, S.P.; f. 1944; 7,139 mems.; library of 1,919 books, periodicals; Pres. Eng. AMARO L. GUATIMOSIM; Vice-Pres. Eng. PAUL D. VILLARES; publ. *Metalurgia—Revista da Associação Brasileira de Metais*.

Associação de Engenharia Química (*Society of Chemical Engineers*): Conjunto das Químicas, Bloco 6, Cidade Universitária, São Paulo, SP; f. 1944; 500 mems.; Pres. PEDRO WONGTSCHOWSKI; Sec. KATSUTOSHI KURATOME.

Instituto de Engenharia de São Paulo: Palácio Mauá, 8° e 9° andares, São Paulo, S.P.; f. 1917; 10,000 mems.; library of 6,500 vols.; Pres. LUÍZ ALFREDO FALCÃO BAUER; publ. *Engenharia* (monthly).

RESEARCH INSTITUTES

(*see* also under Universities)

AGRICULTURE AND VETERINARY SCIENCE

Centro de Energia Nuclear na Agricultura (CENA) (*Centre of Nuclear Energy in Agriculture*): Univ. de São Paulo, C.P. 96, 13400 Piracicaba, S.P.; f. 1966; 34 staff; plant biochemistry, entomology, plant nutrition, radiogenetics, phytopathology, electron microscopy, soil fertility, soil physics, soil microbiology, soil chemistry, immunology, animal nutrition, hydrology, radio chemistry, radiation protection; library of 6,700 vols. and 425 periodicals; Dir. Dr. ADMAR CERVELLINI; publ. *Energia Nuclear e Agricultura*†.

Centro Nacional de Pesquisa de Mandioca e Fruticultura da EMBRAPA: Ministério da Agricultura, 44380 Cruz das Almas, Bahia; f. 1975; research at national level into cassava, citrus fruit, bananas, pineapples and mangoes; 48 staff; library of 3,811 vols.; Dir. MARIO AUGUSTO PINTO DA CUNHA.

Centro Nacional de Pesquisa de Milho e Sorgo: C.P. 151, 35700 Sete Lagoas, M.G.; library of 4,000 vols., 754 periodicals; Dir. Dr. ROLAND VENCOVSKY.

Departamento de Pesquisas e Experimentação Agropecuárias (*Office of Experimentation and Research*): Av. General Justo, 365-4°, Rio de Janeiro, R.J.; f. 1962; Department of Ministry of Agriculture; library of 25,000 vols.; Dir. RULIEN BAZAGLIA.

Divisão de Fitotecnia do D.P.E.A. (*Division of Phytotechnology*): Rodovia Rio-São Paulo, km. 47, Via Campo Grande, Itaguaí, R.J.; Dir. Prof. OTÁVIO DE ALMEIDA DRUMMOND.

EMBRAPA/Centro de Pesquisa Agropecuária do Trópico Úmido: C.P. 48, 66000 Belém, Pará; f. 1976; research in the agricultural resources of the humid tropics; special reference to soil, climate, natural vegetation covering, socio-economic factors, forestry, guaraná, oil palm, black pepper, Brazil nut, tropical fruits, rice, beans, maize, cassava, fibre-producing plants, water buffalo, cattle; 81 staff; library of over 100,000 vols.; Dir. CRISTO BARBOSA DO NASCIMENTO; publs. *Research Bulletins*, *Technical Circulars*, etc.

Emprêsa de Pesquisa Agropecuária da Bahia: Av. Ademar de Barros 967, C.P. 1222, Ondina, 4000 Salvador, BA; f. 1976; 88 staff; library of 2,000 vols.; Dir. RENATO PINHO PEREIRA; publ. *Revista* (2 a year).

Emprêsa de Pesquisa Agropecuária de Minas Gerais (EPAMIG): Av. Amazonas 115, C.P. 515, 30000 Belo Horizonte, M.G.; f. 1974; under State Secretariat of Agriculture; research into animal and crop production, including pisciculture and forestry, agricultural economics and food technology; 2,000 mems.; library of 15,000 vols.; Pres. FLAMARION FERREIRA; Dirs. HÉLIO ANDRADE ALVES, CHRISTIANO ALVES FERREIRA DE MELO NETO; publs. *Informe Agropecuário* (monthly), *Revista do Instituto de Laticinios Cândido Tostes* (every 2 months), *Pesquisando*, *Relatório de Projeto* (irregular).

Emprêsa Pernambucana de Pesquisa Agropecuária: Av. General San Martin 1371, Bonji, 50000 Recife, PE; f. 1935; agricultural research; 120 staff; library of 5,693 vols.; Pres. Eng. Agr. ANTÔNIO CARLOS DE SOUZA REIS; publ. *Pesquisa Agropecuária Pernambucana* (2 a year).

Estação Experimental de Campos: C.P. 131, 28100 Campos; f. 1910; under Ministry of Agriculture; library of 1,300 vols.; Dir. Dr. LENILSON BARBIRATO DE ROSÁRIO.

Estação Experimental de Itaguaí: Rodovia Rio-São Paulo, km. 47, 23460 Seropédica, R.J.; f. 1978, fmrly UEPAE de Itaguaí; animal and horticultural research; 25 staff; library of 11,655 vols.; Dir. PAULO AUGUSTO DA EIRA; publs. *Comunicado Técnico, Boletim Técnico, Sistemas de Produção* (irregular), *Pesquisa em Andamento, Circular Técnica.*

Estação Experimental de Rio Grande: c/o Secretaría da Agricultura, Rua Domingos Petrolini, C.P. 126, Rio Grande, R.G.S.; Dir. APES LIMA PERERA.

Estação Experimental Fitotécnica de Taquari (*Experimental Phytotechnical Station of Taquari*): C.P. 12, 95860 Taquari, R.G.S.; fruit-trees, manioc and beekeeping; Dir. Dr. ENIO CHAVES NUNES.

Fazenda Regional de Criação: Barbacena, M.G.; under Ministry of Agriculture; research in sericulture; Dir. Dr. ANGELO CLOY DUTRA CÂMARA.

Instituto Agronómico (*Institute of Agronomy*): C.P. 28, 13100 Campinas, SP; f. 1887; library of 135,000 vols.; Divisions: Technical Basic and Auxiliary Activities (Dir. J. R. GALLO), Biology (Dir. Dr. N. V. BANZATTO), Experimental Stations (Dir. Dr. C. A. M. FERRAZ), Agricultural Engineering (Dir. H. G. CORREIA) Horticulture (Dir. Dr. O. REGITANO), Basic Food Plants (Dir. Dr. A. CONAGIN), Industrial Plants (Dir. A. J. D'ANDREA PINTO), Soil (Dir. Dr. F. C. VERDADE); Technical Scientific Information Service (Dir. A. G. S. COELHO); 19 experimental stations in the State of São Paulo; 210 research workers; exchange of specimens; Gen. Dir. Dr. FAUSTO J. CORAL; publs. *Bragantia*†, *O Agronômico*†, bulletins and circulars.

Instituto Brasileiro de Desenvolvimento Florestal (IBDF): Palácio do Desenvolvimento, 12°/13° andares, Brasília, DF; f. 1967; library of 4,000 vols.; Pres. Dr. PAULO DE AZEVEDO BERUTTI; Sec.-Gen. Dr. J. F. DE CARVALHO.

Instituto Brasileiro do Café: Av. Rodrigues Alves 129, Térreo, 20081 Rio de Janeiro, R.J.; f. 1952; official organization for the Brazilian coffee industry; library: *see* Libraries; Pres. OCTÁVIO RAINHO DA SILVA NEVES.

Instituto de Economia Agrícola (*Agricultural Economics Institute*): C.P.8.114, 01000 São Paulo; f. 1968; affiliated to S.P. Ministry of Agriculture; *c.* 100 research and technical staff in the fields of economic and sociological agriculture; provides information for state and federal governments and other interested bodies; library of 4,178 vols., 1,500 periodicals; Dir. Eng. Agr. Dr. RUBENS VALENTINI; publs. *Agricultura em São Paulo, Informações Econômicas, Prognóstico*, research results, etc.

Instituto de Pesquisas do Experimentação Agropecuário do Nordeste—IPEANE (*Agricultural and Livestock Research Institute of the Northeast*): C.P. 205, Curado, Pernambuco; Dir. JORGE NETO BRASIL; supports various experimental stations, including:

Estação Experimental de Itapirema and

Estação Experimental de Cana de Açúcar do Curado: C.P. 205; Dir. JOSÉ CLOVIS DE ANDRADE.

Instituto de Pesquisas Veterinárias Desidério Finamor (*Institute of Veterinary Research*): C.P. 2076, 90000 Pôrto Alegre, RGS; f. 1949; research and training in all aspects of animal health; 32 staff; library of 1,395 vols.; Dir. Dr. CARLOS CYPRIANO PIFERO ARTECHE; publ. *Boletim* (irregular).

Instituto de Zootecnia (*Animal Husbandry Institute*): Rua Heitor Penteado 56, C.P. 60, 13460 Nova Odessa, SP; f. 1970; 96 staff; library of 9,211 vols., 4,000 periodicals; Dir.-Gen. Dr. JOSÉ VICENTE SILVEIRA PEDREIRA; publs. *Boletim de Indústria Animal*† (2 a year), *Zootecnia*† (quarterly).

Instituto Florestal—Estado do São Paulo (*São Paulo State Forestry Institute*): Rua do Horto 1197, C.P. 1322, CEP 01000, São Paulo, SP; f. 1896; 75 staff; library of 5,000 vols., 2,000 periodicals; Dir. FRANCISCO JOSÉ DO NASCIMENTO KRONKA: publs. *Silvicultura em São Paulo*†, *Boletim Técnico IF*†, *Publicação IF*†.

Instituto Interamericano de Ciências Agrícolas da OEA: C.P. 16074-ZC-01, 20000 Rio de Janeiro, R.J.; Dir. LUIS A. MONTOYA.

Serviço de Defesa Sanitária Vegetal: Divisão de Defesa SanitáriaVegetal, Ministério da Agricultura, Esplanada dos Ministérios, Bloco 8, 4° andar, Brasília (DF); f. 1920; library of 4,000 vols., pamphlets and periodicals; Dir. HÉLIO TEIXEIRA ALVES; publs. *Boletim Fitossanitário, Monografias.*

Serviço Nacional de Levantamento e Conservação de Solos da EMBRAPA (*National Soil Survey and Soil Conservation Service*): Rua Jardim Botânico 1024, 22460 Rio de Janeiro, R.J.; f. 1975; 47 staff; library of 29,000 vols.; Dir. ABEILARD FERNANDO DE CASTRO; publ. *Comunicado Técnico*†.

Unidade de Execução de Pesquisa de Âmbito Estadual de Pelotas (*Pelotas State Research Unit*): C.P. 553, Pelotas, R.G.S.; f. 1943, re-established 1974; 16 staff; Dir. ALGENOR DA SILVA GOMES; publs. *Relatório Trimestral, Relatório Anual.*

ECONOMICS, LAW AND POLITICS

Centro de Análise Conjuntura Econômica (*Centre for Analysis of Economic Affairs*): Av. Gomes Freire 647, 2° andar, CEP 20231 Rio de Janeiro, RJ.

EDUCATION

Centro Brasileiro de Pesquisas Educacionais (*Brazilian Centre of Educational Research*) of the Instituto Nacional de Estudos Pedagógicos (National Institute of Pedagogical Studies): Palácio de Cultura, Rua de Imprensa 16, Rio de Janeiro, RJ; f. 1955; 5 regional centres in São Paulo, Bahia, Minas Gerais, Rio Grande do Sul and Pernambuco: library: *see* Libraries; Dir. WALTER DE TOLEDO PIZA; Exec. Dir. ELIZA RODRIGUES MARTINS; publs. *Revista Brasileira de Estudos Pedagógicos, Bibliografia Brasileira de Educação, Educação e Ciências Socias*, textbooks, etc.

Centro Regional de Pesquisas Educacionais do Sul (*Southern Centre of Educational Research*): Av. Oswaldo Aranha, 271 (fundos), 8° andar, C.P. 2872, Pôrto Alegre, R.G.S.; library; Dir. Prof. ALVARO MAGALHÃES; publs. *Correio*† (irregular), *Série Pesquisas e Monografias* (irregular), *Boletim* (irregular).

HISTORY, GEOGRAPHY AND ARCHAEOLOGY

Centro de Pesquisas de Geografia do Brasil (*Centre for Geographical Research*): Largo de São Francisco, 24° andar, Rio de Janeiro, R.J.; f. 1952; research work in regional, physical, cultural and economic (including agrarian) geography; 13,000 vols.; Dir. Profa. MARIA DO CARMO CORRÊA GALVÃO; publs. *Bibliografia Geográfica do Brasil, Bibliografia Cartográfica do Brasil* (both annually), monographs.

MEDICINE

Instituto "Adolfo Lutz": Caixa Postal 7027, 01000 São Paulo, S.P.; f. 1892; Central Laboratory of Public Health for the State of São Paulo; library of 40,000 vols., incl. periodicals; Dir. Dr. AUGUSTO E. TAUNAY; publ. *Revista.*

Instituto "Benjamin Constant" (*Institute for the Blind*): Avda. Pasteur 350, Urca, R.J.; f. 1854; the Institute took its present name from its third Director, Benjamin Constant (1869–89); library of 3,200 vols.; Dir. Prof. RENATO MONARD DA GAMA MALCHER; publs. monthly review in Braille, *Revista Brasileira para Cegos.*

Instituto Brasileiro de Estudos e Pesquisas de Gastroenterologia: Rua Dr. Seng 320, Bairro da Bela Vista, C.P.

6209, 01331 São Paulo; f. 1963; study and research in gastroenterology, nutrition and psychosomatic medicine; postgraduate courses; library of 7,000 vols.; Pres. Dr. MOUNIB TACLA; Sec. Dr. OTÁVIO SIQUEIRA NETO; publ. *Arquivos de Gastroenterologia*† (quarterly).

Instituto Butantan (*Butantan Institute*): Avda. Vital Brazil, Caixa Postal 65, Butantan, S.P.; f. 1901; library of 73,120 vols., on ophiology and bio-medical sciences; famous snake farm; Public Health Institute for research and the production of vaccines, sera, etc.; Hospital Vital Brasil (snake, spider and scorpion accidents); publs. *Memórias* (annually), *Coletânea de Trabalhos.*

Instituto de Nutrição (*Institute of Nutrition*): Largo da Misericórdia 24, Rio de Janeiro, R.J.; f. 1946; Dir. Prof. HÉLIO DE SOUZA LUZ; publs. *Arquivos Brasileiros de Nutrição, Trabalhos e Pesquisas.*

Instituto de Saúde: Av. Dr. Eneas Carvalho de Aguiar 188, C.P. 8027, 01000 São Paulo; f. 1969; organization and supervision of study, research and activities in the fields of mother and child care, phthisiology, hansenology, dermatology, ophthalmology and nutrition; library: *see* Libraries; Dir.-Gen. Dr. CÁSSIO MARCONDES DE CARVALHO; publ. *Hansenologia Internationalis*† (2 a year).

Instituto de Tisiologia e Pneumologia da U.F.R.J.: Rua Carlos Seidl 813, Rio de Janeiro, R.J.; library; Dir. Dr. LUIZ MÁRIO JEOLÁS DA MOTTA.

Instituto Evandro Chagas: Avda. Almirante Barroso 492, C.P. 621, 66.000 Belém, Pará; f. 1936; research in bacteriology, parasitology, pathology, virology, mycology; library of 1,000 vols., 130 current periodicals, 10,000 reprints; Dir. Dr. FRANCISCO DE PAULA PINHEIRO.

Instituto "Oscar Freire" (*Oscar Freire Institute*): Rua Teodoro Sampaio 115, Caixa Postal 4350, São Paulo, S.P.; f. 1918; for instruction and research in forensic medicine; assoc. with Univ. of São Paulo; library, 4,200 vols.; Dir. Prof. Dr. AYUSH MORAD AMAR; publ. *Boletim.*

Instituto Oswaldo Cruz (*Oswaldo Cruz Institute*): Av. Brasil, 4365, C.P. 926, CEP 20000 Rio de Janeiro, RJ; f. 1900; library of 180,000 vols.; 130 scientific staff; Pres. Dr. GUILLARDO MARTINS ALVES; Librarian LUCÍLIA MEYER FRIEDMANN; publs. *Memórias* and monographs.

Instituto Pasteur: Avda. Paulista 393, 01311 São Paulo, S.P.; f. 1903; practical measures and theoretical studies aimed at preventing rabies in humans; 15 staff; library of 772 vols. and 1,083 periodicals; Technical Dir. MURILLO PACCA DE AZEVEDO.

Instituto "Penido Bournier": Campinas, S.P.; a leading centre for clinical ophthalmological studies in South America.

Laboratório Central Gonçalo Moniz: Rua Pedro Lessa, Canela, 40.000 Salvador, Bahia; f. 1950, reorganized 1973; research in parasitology, infectious diseases and public health; library of 40,000 vols.; Dir. Dr. A. G. BAPTISTA.

Serviço de Pesquisa e Experimentação de Cancer (*Cancer Research Centre*): Praça Cruz Vermelha 23, Rio de Janeiro, R.J.; library; Dir. Prof. HUGO CASTRO FARIA.

NATURAL SCIENCES

General

Centro de Ciências, Letras e Artes (*Science, Letters and Arts Centre*): Rua Bernardino de Campos 989, C.P. 76, Campinas, S.P.; f. 1901; library, approx. 30,000 vols.; Pres. Dr. JOÃO DE SOUSA COELHO; Gen. Sec. ARISTIDES DA COSTA VERDADE; Librarian G. ZINCK; publ. *Revista*; museum and art gallery attached.

Conselho Nacional de Desenvolvimento Científico e Tecnológico (*National Council of Scientific and Technological Development*): Av. W-3 Norte Quadra 509, Bl. B, Ed. CONTAG, 4° andar, Brasília; f. 1974; Pres. Dr. JOSÉ DION DE MELLO TELLES.

Instituto Nacional de Pesquisas da Amazônia (*National Research Institute for Amazonia*): Estrada do Aleixo, km. 3, 5, C.P. 478, 69000 Manaus; f. 1952; agronomics, biology, medicine, and special projects; library of 141,875 items; herbarium; wood collection; Dir. Dr. WARWICK KERR; publs. *Boletim do INPA* (4 series), *Acta Amazônica* (quarterly).

Biological Sciences

Departamento de Conservação Ambiental (*Department of Environmental Conservation*): Estrada da Vista Chinesa 741, 20531 Rio de Janeiro, R.J.; f. 1955; library of 15,300 vols.; Dir. BENITO PIROPO DA-RIN; publs. *Vellozia*† (annually), *Arboreto Carioca*† (annually).

Estação Experimental de Biologia e Piscicultura (*Experimental Station for Biology and Pisciculture*): Bairro Cachoeira Emas, Pirassununga, S.P.; f. 1938; library; Dir. Dr. ALMIR PERÁCIO.

Herbário "Barbosa Rodrigues": Avda. Marcos Konder 800, 88300 Itajaí, Santa Catarina; f. 1942; botany of Southern Brazil, taxonomy, ecology; 141 mems.; library of 5,500 vols.; Dir. P. RAULINO REITZ; publs. *Sellowia*†, *Flora Ilustrada Catarinense.*

Instituto Biológico (*Biological Institute*): Avda. Cons. Rodrigues Alves 1252, C.P. 7119, São Paulo; f. 1927; animal and plant protection; library of 90,000 vols.; Dir.-Gen. Dr. BENEDICTO BASTOS CRUZ; publs. *Arquivos*† (quarterly), *O Biológico*† (monthly).

Instituto de Biologia e Pesquisas Tecnológicas (*Institute of Biology and Technological Research*): Rua dos Funcionários, Juvevê, Curitiba, PR.; library; Dir. Dr. NELSON ARTUR COSTA.

Instituto de Botânica (*Botanical Institute*): Caixa Postal 4005, 01000 São Paulo; f. 1938; ecology, taxonomy, botanical garden; staff of 56; library of 42,000 vols.; herbarium of 143,500 plants; Dir. Dr. ARMANDO VENTURA (acting); publs. *Hoehnea*† (annual), *Rickia*† (annual), *Flora Brasílica* (irregular).

Instituto "Ezequiel Dias" (Instituto de Biologia e Patologia Médica): C.P. 26, Gameleira, Belo Horizonte; under the Secretariat of Health and Public Welfare; Dir. Dr. LÍVIO RENAULT; publ. *Memórias.*

Instituto Paranaense de Botânica: C.P. 1362, Curitiba, Paraná; f. 1951; herbarium; 5,287 species; botanical statistics, dictionary of botanical terms; library of 1,500 books and 400 periodicals; Dir. Prof. Dr. JOÃO D'ANGELY; publs. *Boletim, Flora of Paraná.*

Jardim Botânico do Rio de Janeiro—IBDF—MA: Rua Jardim Botânico 1008, 22460 Rio de Janeiro, R.J.; f. 1808; botanical research in systematics, wood anatomy (6,094 samples and 16,501 microscope plates) cytomorphology and ecology; library of 7,950 vols., 20,540 periodicals; botanical garden with 7,000 species; Dir. Dr. OSVALDO BASTOS DE MENEZES; publs. *Arquivos do Jardim Botânico*†, *Rodrigésia*†.

Jardim da Praça de República (*Public Gardens*): Rio de Janeiro, R.J.; laid out 1865 by Auguste F. M. Glazion, who collected 23,000 plants; Herbario Glazion forms the most noteworthy exhibit in the Botanical Division of the National Museum.

Physical Sciences

Associação Internacional de Lunologia (*International Association of Lunology*): Caixa Postal 322, Franca, São Paulo; f. 1969; to publish a review on lunar research carried out by all countries.

Centro Brasileiro de Pesquisas Físicas (*Brazilian Centre for Physics Research*): Av. Wenceslau Bráz 71, Rio de Janeiro, RJ; f. 1949; library of 30,860 vols.; Dir. ANTÔNIO CÉSAR OLINTO DE OLIVEIRA; publs. *Notas de Físicas* and Monographs.

Departamento Nacional da Produção Mineral (*National Department of Mineral Production*): Setor de Autarquias Norte, Quadra 1, Projeção E, Bloco B, Esplanada dos Ministérios, Brasília, D.F.; f. 1907; Dept. of Ministry of Mines and Energy; Dir. YVAN BARRETTO DE CARVALHO; publs. *Boletim, Anuário Mineral Brasileiro. Avulso, Boletim de Preços, Balanço Mineral Brasileiro,*

Departamento Nacional de Meteorologia (*Meteorological Office*): Praça 15 de Novembro 2, 5°a., Rio de Janeiro, R.J.; f. 1921; library of 50,109 vols., pamphlets and periodicals; Dir. ROBERTO VENERANDO PEREIRA; publs. *Boletim Diário do Tempo, Boletim Informativo, Boletim Agroclimatólogico, Boletim Climatológico, Boletim Técnico, Pesquisa Meteorológica.*

Instituto Regional de Meteorologia "Coussirat Araújo" (*Regional Meteorological Institute*): Ministério da Agricultura, Pôrto Alegre; f. 1909; Dir. Eng. JOSÉ LUIZ PARANHOS DE ARAÚJO; publ. *Boletim Meteoro-Agrícola do Rio Grande do Sul.*

Laboratório Nacional de Análise (*National Analytical Laboratory*): Avda. Rodrigues Alves, Rio de Janeiro, R.J.; covers organic and inorganic chemistry and biochemistry; library, Dir. YOLANDA QUEIRAGA DE ALBUQUERQUE.

Observatório Nacional do Brasil (*National Observatory*): Rua General Bruce 586, Rio de Janeiro, R.J.; f. 1827; library; astronomical and geophysical research programmes using 7 refractors, a Time Service at Rio de Janeiro and a Time station at Brasília; operates 2 magnetic observatories; a new astrophysical observatory at Brasópolis, MG, operates a 1.60m. telescope equipped with a coude spectrograph; Dir. JOSÉ ANTÔNIO DE FREITAS PACHECO; publs. *Efemérides Astronômicas* (annually), *Contribuições Científicas.*

PHILOSOPHY AND PSYCHOLOGY

Instituto Neo-Pitagórico (*Neo-Pythagorean Institute*): Templo das Musas, Rua Dario Velozo 460, Vila Isabel, C.P. 1047, 80000 Curitiba; f. 1909; 430 mems.; library of 20,000 vols.; Pres. Dr. ROSALA GARZUZE; publs. *A Lâmpada* (quarterly), *Circulares* (annually), *Biblioteca Neo-Pitagórica* (annually), *International Bulletin* (annually), etc.

SOCIOLOGY AND ANTHROPOLOGY

Centro Latino Americano de Pesquisas em Ciências Sociais (*Latin American Centre for Research in the Social Sciences*): Caixa Postal 9012, ZC-02, 20.000 Rio de Janeiro, R.J.; f. 1957; library 10,424 vols.; Dir. MANUEL DIÉGUES, Jr.; publs. *América Latina*† (quarterly).

Fundação Joaquim Nabuco: Irmãos 92, Apipucos, 50000 Recife, Pernambuco; f. 1949; sociological, anthropological and economic studies for agrarian workers in Brazil's north and north-east; specialized library of 30,000 vols. and museum; Dir. FERNANDO DE MELLO FREYRE; publs. *Ciência, Trópico* (2 a year) and various reports and pamphlets.

TECHNOLOGY

Centro de Pesquisas e Desenvolvimento (CEPED) (*Research and Development Centre*): C.P. 09, 42800 Camaçari, Bahia; f. 1969; research in food technology, petrochemistry, metallurgy, ores treatment, environmental engineering, building materials, quality control, materials testing, analysis; library of 13,000 vols., 6,000 pamphlets; 450 staff; Dir. Eng. IRUNDI SAMPAIO EDELWEISS.

Centro de Tecnologia Agrícola e Alimentar da EMBRAPA (*Agricultural and Food Technology Centre*): Rua Jardim Botânico 1024, 22.460 Rio de Janeiro, R.J.; f. 1971; research into grains, cereals, essential and fat oils; 30 staff; Dir. ARLINDO BORBA DE OLIVEIRA; publ. *Boletim Técnico*†.

Comissão Nacional de Energia Nuclear (CNEN) (*Commission for Nuclear Energy*): Rua General Severiano 90, Botafogo ZC-82, 20000 Rio de Janeiro, R.J.; f. 1956; study and proposal of measures relevant to a national policy; issues regulations relating to nuclear facilities and promotes application of nuclear energy for peaceful uses and the training of scientists and experts; 2 nuclear power stations are under construction at Angra dos Reis and 3 research nuclear reactors are in use; Pres. HERVÁSIO GUIMARÃES DE CARVALHO.

Instituto de Energia Atômica (*Atomic Energy Institute*): Caixa Postal 11049; f. 1956; pure and applied research in the peaceful uses of atomic energy; training courses; 250 mems.; library of 10,000 vols., 300 periodicals, reports in full size and in microcards; Dir. Prof. RÔMULO RIBEIRO PIERONI.

Instituto de Engenharia Nuclear (*Nuclear Engineering Institute*): C.P. 2186, Rio de Janeiro, R.J.; f. 1962; pure and applied research and development of uses of atomic energy; Dir. Dr. SILVERIO CARLOS BELLO LISBOA.

Instituto de Pesquisas Radioativas (*Radioactive Research Institute*): C.P. 1941, Belo Horizonte; f. 1953; applied research and industrial development of uses of atomic energy; Dir. Dr. VIRGILIO MATTOS DE ANDRADE E SILVA.

Fundação Instituto Tecnológico do Estado de Pernambuco (ITEP) (*Technological Institute of the State of Pernambuco*): Avda. Conde da Boa Vista 428, Recife, Pernambuco; f. 1942; industrial research; 181 mems.; library of 3,150 vols.; Dir. Dr. PAULO JOSÉ BARBOSA; publ. *Boletim Técnico* (irregular).

Instituto Brasileiro de Petróleo (*Brazilian Institute of Petroleum*): Av. Rio Branco 156-10-S 1035, C.P. 343, CEP 20043, Rio de Janeiro, RJ; f. 1957; holds Brazilian standards for petroleum products and equipment; research in petroleum and petrochemical industries; 940 mems.; Pres. PLÍNIO CANTANHEDE; Dirs. G. C. BARROSO, M. C. RAMOS, R. MIRAGAYA, C. A. S. INSARD.

Instituto de Pesquisas Espaciais—INPE (*Institute for Space Research*): C.P. 515, 12200 São José dos Campos, S.P.; f. 1961, renamed in 1971; space science and technology, satellite communications, systems engineering, remote sensing of natural resources and environment with aircraft and spacecraft, meteorology and climatology and transference of technologies for national development; staff of 1,000; library of 15,000 vols., 500 periodicals, 22,000 specialized papers; Dir. Dr. NELSON DE JESUS PARADA.

Instituto de Pesquisas Tecnológicas (*Institute for Technological Research*): Cidade Universitária Armando de Salles Oliveira, C.P. 7141, 01000 São Paulo, SP; f. 1899 as 'Gabinete de Resistência dos Materiais'; present name since 1934; technological research, materials development, standardization, human resources training; library of 40,000 vols., 2,205 periodicals; Dir. Prof. ALBERTO PEREIRA DE CASTRO; publs. *Relatório*† (annually), *Tecnologia*† (irregular), etc.

Instituto Nacional de Tecnologia (*National Technological Institute*): Av. Venezuela 82, 7° andar, 20081 Rio de Janeiro, RJ; f. 1922; Dir. ROBERTO GOMES DE OLIVEIRA; Admin. Dir. Prof. JÚLIO DE MELLO GARCIA; publ. *Informativo do INT, Relatório*†.

PETROBRÁS Centro de Pesquisas e Desenvolvimento Leopoldo A. Miguez de Mello (*PETROBRÁS Research and Development Centre*): Ilha do Fundão, Quadra 7, C.P. 809, Rio de Janeiro, ZC-00; f. 1966; research into exploitation and refining of petroleum resources; 300 researchers; specialized library of 15,500 vols., 470 periodicals; Dir. Dr. ANTÔNIO SEABRA MOGGI; publs. *Boletim Técnico da PETROBRÁS*†, *Ciência-Tecnologia-Petróleo*†.

LIBRARIES AND ARCHIVES

Brasília, Distrito Federal

Biblioteca Central, Universidade de Brasília: Apdo. 15, 70.910 Brasília, D.F.; f. 1962; 370,000 vols., 2,179 periodicals; Dir. MARIA HELENA DE SÁ BARRETO.

Biblioteca Demonstrativa do Instituto Nacional do Livro: Av. W/3 Sul, Entre Quadras 506/507, 70350/351 Brasília; f. 1970; 23,294 vols., 315 periodicals on general subjects; also maps, microfilms, pictures; Dir. MARIA IRLÂNDIA ALMEIDA FARIAS.

Biblioteca do Exército (*Army Library*): Esplanada dos Ministérios, Bloco 4, 70040 Brasília; f. 1881; 45,000 vols.; general collections to supply cultural needs of the army; Dir. Ten. LUÍZ RIBEIRO; publs. *Boletim da Biblieux* (monthly) and various collections.

Biblioteca do Ministério da Justiça (*Library of Ministry of Justice*): Esplanada dos Ministérios, 70040 Brasília, DF; f. 1941; 100,000 vols., of which many are on law, sociology, labour, and political science; very rare collection of laws of Portuguese colonial period; Dir. JOSÉ PRÓSPERO DANTAS; publ. *Jus Documentação, Arquivos.*

Biblioteca do Ministério das Relações Exteriores (*Library of the Ministry of Foreign Affairs*): Esplanada dos Ministérios, 70040 Brasília, DF; f. 1906; 270,000 vols., including periodicals; law, history, geography, politics, sociology and economics; rare books, including first work printed in Brazil, and only extant copy in S.A. of Richard Flecknoe's *Relation of Ten Years' Travells in Europe, Asia, Africa and America*; Dir. LÍLIAN THOMÉ ANDRADE; publs. *Aquisições bibliográficas* (annually), *Aquisições* (monthly), *Referência de periódicos* (monthly).

Biblioteca do Ministério do Trabalho (*Library of Ministry of Labour*): Esplanada dos Ministérios, Bloco 10, 70040 Brasília, DF; f. 1871; 50,000 vols.; 850 collections of newspapers; Dir. DELSA DE OLIVEIRA ABREU; publs. *Registro Bibliográfico* (annually), periodical catalogues.

Biblioteca do Senado Federal (*Library of the Federal Senate*): Palácio do Congresso Nacional, 70160 Brasília, DF; f. 1826; specializes in social sciences, law, politics, public administration, legislation; also works on literature, pure and applied science, history, geography, etc.; library of 70,000 vols.; Dir. ADÉLIA LEITE COELHO.

Biblioteca Nacional de Agricultura (*National Library of Agriculture*): SCN Q.2. Bloco E, 70710 Brasília; f. 1978 (fmrly Biblioteca Central do Ministério da Agricultura); 45,000 vols., 3,500 serial titles, 17,425 microfiche documents; despository library of the Inter-American Institute of Agricultural Sciences; Dir. JOSÉ ROBERTO BARRETO; publs. *Bibliografia Brasileira de Agricultura, Bibliografias por Produtos e Áreas de Interesse, Guia Brasileiro de Pesquisa Agricola em Andamento* (annually), *Bibliografia Nacionais Retrospectivas* (irreg.), *BINAGRI—Boletim Informativo* (quarterly), *Serie Levantamentos Bibliográficos* (irreg.).

Centro de Documentação e Informação da Câmara dos Deputados (*Documentation and Information Centre of the House of Representatives*): Palácio do Congresso Nacional, Praça dos Três Poderes, 70160 Brasília, DF; f. 1971; 235,000 vols.; 4,569 titles of periodicals; Dir. MÁRIO TELES DE OLIVEIRA; four divisions: (1) Archives (Dir. NILZA TEIXEIRA SOARES), (2) Legislative Studies (Dir. LUÍZ LEITE MARIZ NETO), (3) Library (f. 1866 at Rio de Janeiro, Dir. JURACY ROCHA), (4) Publications (Dir. ARISTEU GONÇALVES DE MELO); Data Processing Centre (vacant); Technical Auxiliary Service (Reprography, Conservation and Restoration, Dir. EURICO DE SOUZA); publs. *Estudos Legislativos* (irregular), *Deputados Brasileiros* (every 4 years), *Anais da Câmara dos Deputados, Documentos Parlamentares, Documentação e Informação.*

Aracajú, Sergipe

Biblioteca Pública do Estado de Sergipe (*Sergipe State Public Library*): f. 1851; Dir. ALFREDO MONTES DE ARAÚJO PINTO; 153,750 vols., including periodicals.

Belém, Pará

Biblioteca Central da Universidade Federal do Pará: Conjunto Universitário Pioneiro-Guamá; f. 1962; 40,000 vols., 2,360 periodicals; Dir. MAGALI RENATA VAN DIJK VERGOLINO.

Biblioteca e Arquivo Público do Pará (*Pará Public Library and Archives*): Rua Campos Sales, f. 1871; Dir. R. MORAES; 45,000 vols., 200,000 MSS.; publ. *Anais da Biblioteca e Arquivo Público.*

Biblioteca do Grêmio Literário e Comercial Portugués (*Library of the Portuguese Literary and Commercial Union*): Rua Senador Manuel Barata 237; f. 1867; Sec. ANÍSIO DE SOARES TEIXEIRA; 29,568 vols.; exchange service.

Belo Horizonte, Minas Gerais

Biblioteca Publica de Minas Gerais (*Public Library*): Praça de Liberdade 21, 30000 Belo Horizonte; f. 1954; 204,000 vols., 2,025 vols. of Braille, 809 periodical titles, 5,763 tapes and discs.

Curitiba, Paraná

Biblioteca Pública do Paraná (*Paraná Public Library*): Rua Cândido Lopes, 80.000 Curitiba; f. 1857; 167,558 vols., 2,860 periodicals; Dir. DANÚSIA ZELAK.

Biblioteca Central da Universidade Federal do Paraná (*University of Paraná Library*): C.P. 441; f. 1956; 185,631 vols.; Dir. MARIA A. DE CASTRO CORREIA.

Florianópolis, Santa Catarina

Biblioteca Pública do Estado de Santa Catarina (*Santa Catarina State Public Library*): Visconde de Ouro Prêto 42; f. 1855; 20,000 vols.; Dir. EDELMIRA RODRIGUES.

Fortaleza, Ceará

Biblioteca Central da Universidade Federal do Ceará: Campus do Pici, C.P. 153-D; f. 1958; 30,000 vols.; Dir. MARIA F. BEZERRA.

Biblioteca Pública do Ceará (*Ceará Public Library*): Rua Solon Pinheiro 76; 15,000 vols.; Librarian HILZANIR CALS DE ABREU.

João Pessôa, Paraíba

Biblioteca Pública do Estado da Paraiba (*Paraíba Public Library*): Av. General Osório 253; f. 1859; Dir. GERALDO EMILIO PÔRTO; 10,000 vols.

Manaus, Amazonas

Biblioteca e Arquivo Público de Manaus (*Manaus Public Library and Archives*).

Niterói, Rio de Janeiro

Biblioteca Pública do Estado do Rio de Janeiro (*Public Library of the State of Rio*): Praça da República; f. 1927; possesses rare early works, newspapers and valuable first editions; 80,000 vols., notably dictionaries, encyclopædias, reference books; Dir. ALBERTINA FORTUNA BARROS.

Ouro Prêto, Minas Gerais

Biblioteca da Escola de Minas e Metalurgia da Universidade Federal de Ouro Prêto (*Library of the Ouro Prêto School of Mines and Metallurgy*): Praça Tiradentes 20; f. 1876; 24,103 vols., 1,175 periodicals; Dir. MARIA DA GLÓRIA RIBEIRO SOARES; publ. *Revista*.

Pelotas, Rio Grande do Sul

Biblioteca Pública Pelotense (*Public Library*): Praça Coronel Pedro Osório 103; f. 1875; 80,000 vols.; museum, cultural exhibition; Pres. HENRIQUE CARLOS DE MORAIS.

Petrópolis, Rio de Janeiro

Biblioteca Municipal (*Municipal Library*): f. 1871; Librarian MARIA HELENA DE AVELLAR PALMA; 100,000 vols.; 2 branches.

Pôrto Alegre, Rio Grande do Sul

Arquivo Histórico do Estado do Rio Grande do Sul: Rua André Puente 318; f. 1954; 5,000 vols., 800,000 documents; Dir. LEOPOLDO COLLOR JOBIM; publs. *Anais*†, *Coleção Descritiva do Acervo*†.

Biblioteca Central da Universidade Federal do Rio Grande do Sul: Av. Paulo Gama 110; f. 1971; 28 branch libraries; 576,839 vols.; Dir. HELOISA BENETTI SCHREINER.

Biblioteca Pública do Estado do Rio Grande do Sul (*Rio Grande do Sul State Public Library*): Rue Riachuelo s/n; f. 1871; 110,941 vols.; Dir. JULIANA VIANNA ROSA.

Recife, Pernambuco

Biblioteca Central da Universidade Federal de Pernambuco: Av. Prof. Moraes Rêgo s/n., Cidade Universitária; f. 1968; 112,535 vols. (including all departmental libraries), 10,365 periodicals; a regional centre for the national bibliographical network organized by the Instituto Brasileiro de Informação em Ciência e Tecnologia (*q.v.*); Dir. IVANILDA FERNANDES DA COSTA ROLIM.

Biblioteca Pública do Estado de Pernambuco (*Pernambuco State Public Library*): f. 1852; Dir. OLYMPIO COSTA JR.; *c.* 80,000 vols.

Rio de Janeiro, R.J.

Arquivo Nacional (*National Archive*): Praça da República 26; f. 1838; Dir. Dr. RAUL LIMA; Librarian MARÍA DE LA ENCARNACIÓN DE ESPAÑA IGLESIAS; specializes in history of Brazil, technique of archives and legislation; 35,000 vols. and 700 periodicals; publ. *Mensário*†.

Biblioteca Bastos Tigre da Associação Brasileira de Imprensa (*Library of Brazilian Printing Association*): Rua Araújo Pôrto Alegre 71, 12° andar; f. 1911; 9,118 vols., over 3,000 periodical titles; Dir. MAURÍCIO AZEDO.

Biblioteca Central do Centro de Ciências da Saúde da Universidade Federal do Rio de Janeiro (*Library of the Health Sciences Centre of the Federal University of Rio de Janeiro*): Cidade Univ., Ilha do Fundão, ZC-32; f. 1833; 185,623 vols.; loan service; Librarian MARIA REGINA AZEVEDO ARBULO URIARTE.

Biblioteca da Sociedade Brasileira de Cultura Inglesa: C.P. 821, Avda. Graça Aranha 327,3° andar; f. 1935; 18 branch libraries; 58,454 vols.; Head Librarian MARIA ILKA BEAUCHAMP; pub. *Library Bulletin*.

Biblioteca do Banco do Brasil (*Library of the Bank of Brazil*): Av. Rio Branco 65-16°; f. 1931; social sciences library of 50,000 vols.; Dir. CARLOS ALTINO MATTOSO.

Biblioteca do Centro Brasileiro de Pesquisas Educacionais (*Library of the Brazilian Centre of Educational Research*): Rua de Imprensa 16; f. 1938; 59,500 vols., including periodicals; specialized semi-public library on Social Sciences; Librarian LYBIA DE MAGALHÃES GARCIA.

Biblioteca do Instituto Brasileiro do Café: Av. Rodrigues Alves 129, Térreo, 20.081; f. 1960; documentation and reference centre for the economics, commerce, statistics, legislation and agricultural aspects of coffee; 19,000 vols.; Head of Documentation Service LENIRA LACERDA DA CÂMARA LIMA; Librarian MARGARIDA MARIA DE MAGALHÃES FIGUEIRA; publs. *Anuário Estatístico do Café*, *Relatório Anual do GERCA*, *Boletim do Documentação*.

Biblioteca do Instituto dos Advogados Brasileiros (*Library of Lawyers' Institute*): Rua Marechal Câmara 210; f. 1843; Dir. Dr. RAUL FLORIANO DA SILVA; 17,000 vols.

Biblioteca do Ministério da Fazenda no Estado do Rio de Janeiro (*Library of the Ministry of Finance of Rio de Janeiro State*): Av. Pres. Antonio Carlos 375, 12° andar, 20020 Rio de Janeiro; f. 1943 by incorporation of various departmental libraries; 69,059 vols., 355 current periodicals; Librarian LÉA ALMEIDA CHAVES; publ. *A Legislação Tributária no Brasil*.

Biblioteca do Mosteiro de S. Bento (*Library of the St. Benedict Monastery*): C.P. 2666, 20000 Rio de Janeiro; f. 1600; Librarian D. MIGUEL VEESER, O.S.B.; 92,000 vols.; also in the towns of São Paulo, Salvador-Bahia and Olinda; publs. *Pergunte e Responderemos*†, *Liturgia e Vida*†.

Biblioteca Estadual: Av. Presidente Vargas 1261; f. 1873; attached to the Division of Libraries and Documentation, State Department of Culture; 161,039 vols.; Dir. HELOISA DE CARVALHO CABRAL LOPES.

Biblioteca Nacional (*National Library*): Av. Rio Branco 219-30; f. 1810, with 60,000 vols. from the Real Biblioteca de Ajuda brought to Brazil by the Royal Family of Portugal in 1808; *c.* 1,800,000 vols., 600,000 MSS., 250,000 engravings, maps, etc., 185 incunabula, 20,000 titles of periodicals; divided into five sections: Acquisition and Processing, General Reference, Special Reference, Divulgation (publications, cultural promotions and exchanges), Conservation; three services: copyright, reprography, administrative. The Library acts as Registo de Direitos Autorais (registration of authors' copyright), and also operates an international exchange service with foreign countries; many rare volumes, including two copies of the Mainz Bible dated 1462; important collections of engravings, MSS. and early Brazilian newspapers; Dir. J. DE MELLO MONTE-MÓR; publs. *Anais da Biblioteca Nacional*† (annual), *Boletim Bibliográfico*† (quarterly), *Publicações*†, catalogue†.

Biblioteca Regional de Copacabana: Av. N.S. de Copacabana 702B, 3° andar; f. 1954; 5,625 mems.; 27,676 vols.; Dir. LIA TEMPORAL AVENA.

Biblioteca Regional da Lagoa: Rua Dias Ferreira 417, Leblon; f. 1954; 15,000 vols.; Dir. LEDA FONSECA.

Fundação Casa de Rui Barbosa (*Rui Barbosa Foundation*): Rua S. Clemente 134; f. 1930, became Foundation 1966; over 60,000 vols. based on author's own collection (35,000 vols.) purchased by the State; includes a centre for research in law and philology, a museum-archive of literature (over 2,500 documents) and a centre for research in history; Pres. Prof. AMÉRICO JACOBINA LACOMBE.

Serviço de Documentação Geral da Marinha (*General Documentation Service of the Navy*): Rua D. Manuel 15, Centro, 20.010 Rio de Janeiro; f. 1802; six divisions: (1) Maritime History of Brazil; (2) Naval Library of approx. 80,000 vols.; (3) Publications: *Subsídios para a História Marítima do Brasil*†, *Revista Marítima Brasileira*†, *Navigator*†, and technical works; (4) Naval Archives; (5) Naval Museum; (6) Administration; Dir. Capt. MAX JUSTO GUEDES.

Rio Grande, Rio Grande do Sul

Biblioteca Rio Grandense (*Rio Grande Library*): Rua General Osório; f. 1846; Dir. FLORA V. DE CASTRO; *c.* 100,000 vols., 2,000 maps.

Rio Negro, Paraná

Biblioteca do Convento dos Franciscanos (*Library of Franciscan Monastery*): f. 1922; Sec. FREI ALFREDO SETÁRO, O.F.M.; 20,000 vols.

Salvador, Bahia

Biblioteca Central do Estado da Bahia (*Bahia State Central Library*): Rua Gen. Labatut 27; f. 1811, name changed 1970; 300,000 vols.; Dir. EURYDICE PIRES DE SANT' ANNA.

Biblioteca do Gabinete Português de Leitura (*Portuguese Reading Room and Library*): Praça 13 de Maio; Librarian JAIME SILVA; 15,000 vols.

Santos, São Paulo

Biblioteca da Sociedade Humanitária dos Empregados no Comércio de Santos (*Library of Cultural Society of Commercial Employees*): Praça José Bonifacio 59, 1° andar, Caixa Postal 9; f. 1888; 20,494 vols.; Librarian RAUL CHRISTIANO SANCHEZ.

São José dos Campos, São Paulo

Biblioteca Pública "Cassiano Ricardo" (*"Cassiano Ricardo" Public Library*): Rua Sebastião Humel 110, 1° andar, C.P. 204; f. 1968; 11,000 vols. and 3,600 periodicals; Dir. MARIA DA FÁTIMA RAMIA MANFREDINI.

São Luis, Maranhão

Biblioteca Pública do Estado (*Public State Library*): Praça de Panteon; f. 1829; 38 mems.; Dir. MARIA JOSÉ VAZ DOS SANTOS; Librarian ROBERTO TAMARA; 45,000 vols.; collections of more than 15,000 engravings, and newspapers dating back to 1821.

São Paulo

Biblioteca Municipal Mário de Andrade (*Municipal Library*): C.P. 8170, Rua Consolação 94; f. 1925; central library 895,320 vols.; 12 branch libraries with 205,774 vols.; incorporates former Biblioteca Pública do Estado de São Paulo (40,000 vols.); a few MSS., collections of old maps, rare editions; arts and micro-film sections, and a Braille library; Dir. NOEMI DO VAL PENTEADO; publ. *Boletim Bibliográfico*.

Biblioteca do Conservatório Dramático e Musical de São Paulo (*Library of Academy of Music and Drama*): Av. São João 269; f. 1906; 30,000 vols.; Dir. Dr. LUÍS CORRÊA FRAGOSO; Sec. JOSÉ RAYMUNDO LOBO.

Biblioteca do Departamento do Arquivo do Estado do São Paulo (*Library of São Paulo State Archives*): Rua Antônia de Queiroz 183; f. 1892; 22,000 vols.; collections of rare books, MSS., periodicals, maps, and plans; private State library; Librarian ARACY FRAGATA; publs. *Boletim, Documentos Interessantes para a História e Costumes de São Paulo, Documentos Avulsos, Inventários e Testamentos*, and, periodically, documents from the Archives.

Biblioteca "George Alexander" (*George Alexander Library*): Rua Itambé 45; f. 1870 as Mackenzie Library, present name 1926; Librarian HELOISA DE ALMEIDA PRADO; 53,473 vols. and children's library; publ. *Boletim Bibliográfico*† (annually).

Biblioteca do Instituto de Saúde (*Health Institute Library*): Av. Enéas Carvalho Aguiar 188, Caixa Postal 8027, 01000 S. Paulo; f. 1969; 40,000 vols., valuable collection of works, reviews, maps on dermatology and leprosy, and rare works dating from 1600; Librarian ASTRID B. WIESEL.

Divisão de Discoteca e Biblioteca de Música de São Paulo (*São Paulo Municipal Music Library*): Rua Catão 611; f. 1935; study and diffusion of Brazilian and international classical folk and popular music; specialized library of 30,057 vols. of music and 6,063 books; collection of 21,458 records, 174 periodical titles; museum of folklore with 1,000 items; Dir. Prof. LAURITA PLATZECK SENRA.

Divisão de Biblioteca e Documentação da Universidade de São Paulo (*São Paulo University Central Library*): Cidade Universitária, Butantan, CEP 05508, C.P. 8191; f. 1947; 40,000 vols.; bibliography information centre; Dir. ROSMARIE APPY; publ. Index of the University Publications, etc.

Vitória, Espírito Santo

Biblioteca Estadual: avda. Pedro Palácios 76; f. 1855; 31,981 vols.

Biblioteca Municipal Vitória: Rua Barão Itapemirim 204, 1° andar; f. 1941; 12,859 vols.

MUSEUMS

Museu Paraense Emilio Goeldi (*Pará Museum*): Av. Magalhães Barata 376, CP 399; f. 1866; natural history, anthropology and ethnography of the Amazon region; zoological and botanical garden; Dir. LUÍZ MIGUEL SCAFF; publs. *Boletim* (four separate series, on anthropology, botany, geology and zoology), *Publicações Avulsas, Guia*.

Belo Horizonte (Minas Gerais)

Museu Histórico (*Historical Museum*): Rua Bernardo Mascarenhas s/n, Cidade Jardim; f. 1941; local collection; Dir. MÁRIO LÚCIO BRANDAO.

Campinas (São Paulo)

Museu de História Natural (*Natural History Museum*): Bosque dos Jequitibás; f. 1939; also historical and folklore museums; Dir. Dr. LUCIO MASELLI ZIGGIATTI.

Campo Grande (Mato Grosso do Sul)

Museu Regional D. Bosco (*D. Bosco Regional Museum*): Rua Barão do Rio Branco 1885, C.P. 415, 79.100 Campo Grande; f. 1951; ethnographic, shell and insect collections; Dir. JOÃO FALCO.

Curitiba (Paraná)

Museu Paranaense (*Paraná Museum*): Praça Generoso Marques s/n; f. 1876; historical, ethnographical and archaeological collections; library of 36,000 vols.; Dir. Prof. OLDEMAR BLASI; publs. *Arquivos do Museu Paranaense, Nova Série*, and special papers.

Fortaleza (Ceará)

Arquivo Público e Museu Histórico do Estado do Ceará (*State Historical Museum*): Praça da Sé 332; public archives and historical museum.

Goiânia (Goiás)

Museu Estadual (*Goiás State Museum*): Praça Cívica; f. 1946; general collection; Dir. REGINA LACERDA.

Itú (São Paulo)

Museu Republicano "Convenção de Itú" (*Itú Convention Republican Museum*): Rua Barão de Itaim 67, CEP 13.300; f. 1923; historical; attached to Museu Paulista da Universidade de São Paulo (*q.v.*); Curator Prof. JONAS SOARES DE SOUZA.

Macapá (Território do Amapá)

Museu Territorial do Amapá (*Amapá Territorial Museum*): Fortaleza de S. José de Macapá; f. 1948: zoology, archaeology, ethnography and numismatics; expeditions.

Olinda (Pernambuco)

Museu Regional de Olinda (*Regional Museum of Olinda*): Rua do Amparo 128; f. 1934; historic and regional art.

Ouro Prêto (Minas Gerais)

Museu da Escola Nacional de Minas e Metalurgia (*Museum of National School of Mines*): f. 1876; affiliated to the Universidade Federal de Ouro Prêto; Dir. Prof. WAGNER COLOMBAROLI.

Museu da Inconfidência (*History of Democratic Ideals and Culture*): Praça Tiradentes 139; f. 1944; documents from the Notary Public's Office during the Colonial Period; library of 3,000 vols.; Dir. RUI MOURÃO.

Petrópolis (Rio de Janeiro)

Museu Imperial (*Imperial Museum*): Av. 7 de Setembro 94 and 220; f. 1940; 16,000 period exhibits of Brazilian Empire and Petrópolis history 1808–89, notably imperial regalia, jewels and apparel; special library on the history of Brazil 21,000 vols.; historical MSS. and D. Pedro II biography; Dir. LOURENÇO LUÍZ LACOMBE; publ. *Anuário*.

Pôrto Alegre (Rio Grande do Sul)

Museu de Arte do Rio Grande do Sul: Praça Barão do Rio Branco; f. 1954; art collection; Dir. LUÍZ INÁCIO MEDEIROS; publ. *Boletim*† (quarterly).

Museu "Julio de Castilhos" (*State Historical Museum*): Rua Duque de Caxias 1931; f. 1903; 4,550 exhibits of national history, including the 1835 Revolutionary period, the Paraguayan War, and collection of Indian pieces; armoury and antique furniture; Dir. JOAQUIM CARLOS DE MORAES.

Recife (Pernambuco)

Museu do Estado (*State Museum*): Av. Rui Barbosa 960; f. 1929; paintings by Teles Juniór; collection of local history; Dir. JOSÉ MARIA CARNEIRO DE ALBUQUERQUE E MELO.

Rio de Janeiro, R.J.

Museu Carpológico do Jardim Botânico do Rio de Janeiro (*Museum of Carpology of the Botanical Garden*): Rua Pacheco Leão 915; specializes in botany; collection of 5,000 fruits, Dir. Dr. FERNANDO TASSO FRAGOSO PIRES.

Museu da Fauna (*Wildlife Museum*): Quinta da Boa Vista; f. 1939; collections include vertebrates, mammals, birds and reptiles from the principal regions of Brazil; part of Tijuca National Park; scientific expeditions; publ. *Monograph*.

Museu da República (*Museum of the Republic*): Rua do Catete, s/n; f. 1960; exhibits of items belonging to former Presidents; library of 3,000 vols.; Dir. Comte. LÉO FONSECA E SILVA; publ. *Anais*.

Museu da Secção de Tecnologia do Serviço Florestal do Ministério da Agricultura (*Museum of the Technological Department of the Forestry Service—Ministry of Agriculture*): Rua Major Rubéns Vaz, 122, Gávea; f. 1938; specializes in wood technology; contains 7,000 samples of wood from Brazil and other countries; display of forestry products and hand-made wood objects; Dir. Dr. NEARCH AZEVEDO DA SILVEIRA; publs. *Arquivos do Serviço Florestal, Revista Florestal e Rodriguésia*.

Museu de Arte Moderna do Rio de Janeiro (*Museum of Modern Art*): Av. Beira Mar, Caixa Postal 44 ZC: f. 1948; library of 7,500 vols.; collections representing different countries; exhibitions, courses, concerts, films; Exec. Dir. HELOISA ALEIXO LUSTOSA.

Museu do Departamento Nacional da Produção Mineral (*Museum of the Mineral Production Division of the Ministry of Mines and Energy*): Av. Pasteur 404, 2° andar, Praia Vermelha; f. 1908; collection of minerals, rocks and fossils of Brazil; Dir. YVAN BARRETO DE CARVALHO.

Museu do Índio (*Museum of the Indian*): rua das Palmeiras 55; f. 1953; ethnology, museology, archaeology, linguistics, anthropology and biology of Brazil; together with the library of 20,000 vols. and the scientific archives (documents, photographs, films and music) it is the technical scientific section of the Divisão de Estudos e Pesquisas do Departamento Geral de Planejamento Comunitário da Fundação Nacional do Índio; Chair. Prof. NEY LAND; publ. *Boletim*†.

Museu do Instituto Histórico e Geográfico Brasileiro (*Museum of the Brazilian Historical and Geographical Institute*): Av. Augusto Severo 8; f. 1838; history, geography and ethnography collection.

Museu e Arquivo Histórico do Banco do Brasil (*Museum and Historical Archives of the Bank of Brazil*): Av. Rio Branco 65-16°; f. 1955; Dir. JOÃO GUIMARÃES VIERA; collection of Brazilian coins of 5,713 pieces in gold, silver and copper, also mint coins and 14,955 coins from other countries; library of 30,000 vols.

Museu Histórico da Cidade do Rio de Janeiro (*Historical Museum of the City*): Estrada Santa Marinha, s/n, Parque da Cidade, Gávea; f. 1934; art and history of the City; library of 2,300 vols.; Dir. BEATRIZ VICQ DE CARVALHO.

Museu Histórico Nacional (*National Historical Museum*): Praça Marechal Ancora s/n, ZC 39; f. 1922; now contains the former Military and Naval Museums; collection of naval prints and paintings, besides historical exhibits; organizes courses in museology; library; Dir. Dr. GERARDO BRITTO RAPOSO DA CÂMARA; publs. guides, catalogues, etc.

Museu Nacional (*National Museum*): Quinta da Boa Vista; f. 1818; departments: geology, botany, entomology, invertebrates, vertebrates, palaeontology and anthropology; *c.* 1,300,000 specimens; library of 310,000 vols.; one of the most important natural history museums in South America; Dir. Dr. LUÍZ EMYGDIO DE MELLO FILHO; publs. *Arquivos, Boletim, Manuais, Publicações Avulsas, Flora ecológica de restingas*, guides, catalogues, pamphlets, etc.

Museu Nacional de Belas Artes (*National Museum of Fine Arts*): Avda. Rio Branco 199; f. 1937; collections of Brazilian and European paintings and sculpture; graphic arts and furniture; primitive art, numismatics, posters, photographs; exhibitions and educational services; library of 8,000 vols.; Dir. Prof. EDSON MOTTA; publ. *Anuário, Boletim*, catalogues†, *Tempo de Arte*†.

Rio Grande (Rio Grande do Sul)

Museu Oceanográfico (*Oceanographic Museum*): Terrapleno Noroeste, C.P. 379, 96200 Rio Grande; f. 1953; oceanography, ichthyology, malacology, algology; large shell collection, cetaceans collection; Dir. Dr. ELIÉZER DE CARVALHO RIOS.

Sabará (Minas Gerais)

Museu do Ouro (*Gold Museum*): Rua da Intendência; f. 1946; museum housed in a building dated 1730; Sections: Technical, Historical, Artistic; antique methods of gold mining and smelting; gold ingots, 18th-century silverware, 18th-century furniture and typical handicrafts of the mining districts; Dir. Dr. RUI MOURÃO.

Salvador (Bahia)

Museu de Arte Antiga: Instituto Femenino da Bahia (*Early Art Museum: Bahia Women's College*): Rua Monsenhor Flaviano 2; f. 1933; Dir. HENRIQUETA MARTINS CATHARINO; collections of religious art, Brazilian art and feminine apparel; also the Museu de Arte Popular; f. 1929; gold, silver, jewelry, clothing, weapons.

Museu de Arte da Bahia (*Bahia Art Museum*): Rua Joana Angélica 198; f. 1918; library of 7,140 vols.; 9,254 exhibits; general collection, with emphasis given to art, particularly Bahian Colonial art; Dir. JOSÉ PEDREIRA; publ. *Publicações do Museu.*

Museu do Instituto Geográfico e Histórico da Bahia: Av. Sete de Setembro 94; f. 1894; Dir. FRANCISCO DA CONCEIÇAO MENEZES; mineralogy section, geography, history and folklore.

Museu do Instituto Nina Rodrigues: Rua Alfredo Brito; f. 1896; forensic medicine and anthropology.

São Paulo

Museu de Arqueologia e Etnologia: Cidade Universitária "Armando de Salles Oliveira", C.P. 8105; Dir. Prof. Dr. ANTÔNIO ROCHA PENTEADO.

Museu de Arte Contemporânea (*Modern Art Museum*): Parque Ibirapuera; f. 1948 to promote the *Bienais*; permanent exhibition of international and Brazilian plastic arts; attached to Univ. of São Paulo; Dir. Prof. Dr. WOLFGANG PFEIFFER.

Museu de Arte de São Paulo: Av. Paulista, 1578; f. 1947; classical and modern paintings, Italian, Spanish, Dutch, Flemish, and French schools; also representative works by Portinari and Lasar Segall; departments of theatre, music, cinema, art history, exhibitions, printing, photography and education; Dir. P. M. BARDI.

Museu da Curia Metropolitana (*Metropolitan Synod Museum*): Praça Clovis Bevilacqua 37; f. 1919; Dir. Padre JOÃO KULAY; religious art, numismatics.

Museu de Zoologia, Universidade de São Paulo (*Museum of Zoology, University of São Paulo*): Av. Nazareth 481, C.P. 7172; formerly Departamento de Zoologia da Secretaria de Agricultura do Estado de São Paulo; f. 1939; 5,000,000 samples of Brazilian and world fauna; library 50,000 vols.; Dir. P. E. VANZOLINI; publs. *Arquivos de Zoologia, Papeis Avulsos de Zoologia.*

Museu de Etnografia "Plínio Ayrosa" da Faculdade de Filosofia, Letras e Ciências Humanas (*Ethnographical Museum of the Faculty of Philosophy, Letters and Human Sciences, São Paulo University*): Caixa Postal 8105; f. 1934; over 4,000 exhibits relating to Brazilian Indian cultures, including fine Canella, Rio Negro and Bororo collections, Tupi, Carajá and Kadiweu ceramics, North Amazon basketry and recent collection of Jê groups; Dirs. LUX VIDAL, RENATE VIERTLER; publs. series on anthropology.

Museu Florestal "Octávio Vecchi" (*Forestry Museum*): Caixa Postal 1322; f. 1931; a dependency of the Forestry Institute of the Sec. of State for Agriculture; forestry and forest technology, collections of local timber; Dir. FRANCISCO JOSÉ DO NASCIMENTO KRONKA.

Museu Paulista da Universidade de São Paulo (*São Paulo Museum*): Parque da Independência, s/n, Ipiranga, C.P. 42.503; f. 1895; archaeological, ethnological, geographical, historical and numismatic specimens; also collections of furniture and stamps; library of 65,000 vols.; Dir. Prof. Dr. SETEMBRINO PETRI; publs. *Anais*†, *Revista*†, *Coleçao Museu Paulista*†, *Catálogos*†.

Pinacoteca do Estado de São Paulo (*State Art Gallery*): Praça da Luz 2; f 1906; specialized library; modern paintings; Dir. ARACY AMARAL; publs. catalogues, lectures on art.

Terezina (Piauí)

Museu Histórico do Piauí, Casa "Anísio Brito" (*Anísio Brito's House*): Rua Coelho Rodrigues 1016; f. 1941; library and public archives and Piauí historical museum.

Vitória (Espírito Santo)

Museu de Arte e História da Universidade Federal do Espírito Santo: Av. P. Müller, Jucutuquara; f. 1939 as State Museum; inc. Jan. 1967 to Federal Univ.; history, sacred art, archaeology and folklore.

UNIVERSITIES

UNIVERSIDADE FEDERAL DO ACRE

AV. GETÚLIO VARGAS 654,
CENTRO, RIO BRANCO,
ACRE

Telephone: 28–26.

Founded 1971.

Rector: ÁULIO GÉLIO ALVES DE SOUZA.
Librarian: VALCI AUGUSTINHO.

Library of 21,858 vols.
Number of teachers: 243.
Number of students: 1,447.

DIRECTORS:

Law: YACUT AYACHE.
Economics: EDSON CARDOSO NUNES.
Education: JAINE MARIA DA SILVA QUEIROZ.
Language and Literature: WANIR DE ALMEIDA HORÁCIO E SILVA.
Geography and History: MANOEL CALAÇA.
Mathematics and Statistics: MARILDA ARAGÃO PRAZERES.
Social Sciences and Philosophy: ANTÔNIO TAVARES MONTEIRO.
Health Sciences, Physical Education and Sports: CLÉLIA SIMPSON LOBATO.
Natural Sciences: CARLOS ALBERTO SIMÃO ANTONIO.
Technological and Agarian Science: ANTÔNIO FRANCISCO DA SILVA.

UNIVERSIDADE FEDERAL DE ALAGOAS

PRAÇA VISCONDE DE
SINIMBU 206,
57.000 MACEIÓ, ALAGOAS

Telephone: 221-3090, 223-4734, 221-3155.

Founded 1961.

State (Federal) control; Language of instruction Portuguese; Academic year: March to December (two semesters).

Rector: Prof. JOÃO FERREIRA AZEVEDO.
Vice-Rector: Prof. AUDÁLIO CÂNDIDO DOS SANTOS.
Chief, Rector's Office: Prof. ELIAS PASSOS TENÓRIO.
Pro-Rector (Academic Affairs): Prof. JOSÉ DAMASCENO LIMA.
Pro-Rector (Community Affairs): Prof. WILD SILVA.
Pro-Rector (Planning Affairs): Prof. RADJALMA JACKSON DE ALBUQUERQUE CAVALCANTE.
Pro-Rector (Postgraduate and Research Affairs): Prof. NABUCO LOPES TAVARES DA COSTA SANTOS.

Number of teachers: 788.
Number of students: 5,244.
Publication: *Boletim da UFAL.*

DEANS:

Centre of Exact and Natural Sciences: Prof. EDMILSON DE VASCONCELOS PONTES.

Centre of Human Sciences, Letters and Arts: Profa. Georgette Castro de Almeida.
Centre of Biological Sciences: Prof. José Márcio Malta Lessa.
Centre of Technology: Prof. Fernando Cardoso Gama.
Centre of Health Sciences: Prof. José Araújo Silva.
Centre of Agrarian Sciences: Profa. Mellia Delabianca Araújo.
Centre of Applied Social Sciences: Prof. Jair Galvão Freire.

UNIVERSIDADE DO AMAZONAS

RUA JOSÉ PARANAGUÁ 200,
C.P. 348,
69000 MANÁUS, AMAZONAS

Founded 1965.

Rector: Octávio Hamilton Botelho Mourão.
Vice-Rector: Roberto dos Santos Vieira.
Sub-Rectors: Afonso Celso Maranhão Nina (Academic Affairs), Adérito da Costa Penafort (Administrative Affairs).

Number of teachers: 764.
Number of students: 6,613.

Faculties of Health Science, Social Science, Education, Technology, Humanities and Letters, Exact Science, Biological Science.

UNIVERSIDADE FEDERAL DA BAHIA

RUA AUGUSTO VIANA S/N,
CANELA, SALVADOR, BAHIA
Telephone: 3-9141/2/3.

Founded 1946.

Rector: Luíz Fernando Seixas de Macedo Costa.
Vice-Rector: Prof. Carlos Brandão da Silva.
Librarian: Lindaura Alban Coruteira.

Libraries: one central and 31 departmental libraries, 231,952 vols.

Number of teachers: 1,642.
Number of students: 15,311.

Publications: *Boletim de Pessoal, Afro-Asia, Universitas, Estudos Baianos.*

Directors:

Faculty of Architecture: Laerte Pedreira Neves.
Faculty of Economics: Dario Ribeiro Cunha.
Faculty of Law: Gerson Pereira dos Santos.
Faculty of Medicine: Renato Tourinho Dantas.
Faculty of Dentistry: João Gonçalves Carvalho.
Faculty of Education: Terezinha Teixeira Guimarães.
Faculty of Pharmacy: Dyrce Franco de Araújo.
Faculty of Philosophy: Eduardo Saback Dias de Moraes.
Polytechnic School: Hernani Savio Sobral.
School of Fine Arts: Ivo José de Sant'Anna Vellame.
School of Librarianship: Antônio Loureiro de Souza.
School of Nursing: Clara Wolfovitch.
School of Administration: Arlindo Braga Senna.
School of Agriculture: Bráulio Luíz Sampaio Seixas.
School of Veterinary Medicine: Geraldo Cézar de Vinhaes Tôrres.
School of Dietetics: Edileuza Nunes Gaudenzi.
School of Music and Scenic Arts: Ernst Widmer.
Institute of Mathematics: José Figueiredo Leal de Araújo.
Institute of Physics: Humberto S. Tanure.
Institute of Chemistry: Antônio Celos Spinola Costa.
Institute of Biology: Cora de Moura Pedreira.
Institute of Geology: Sylvio Carlos Bandeira de Mello e Silva.
Institute of Letters: Hélio Gomes Simões.
Institute of Health Sciences: Edgard Pires da Veiga.
Centre of Afro-Oriental Studies: Guilherme Augusto de Souza Castro.
Centre of Bahian Studies: Consuelo Pondé Senna.
Centre of Inter-disciplinary Studies for Public Services: Margarida Ma. Costa Batista.

UNIVERSIDADE REGIONAL DE BLUMENAU

RUA ANTÔNIO DA VEIGA 140,
CAIXA POSTAL 7E,
89100 BLUMENAU,
SANTA CATARINA
Telephone: 22-4500.

Founded 1968.

Under control of the Fundação Universidade Regional de Blumenau.

Rector: Prof. José Tafner.
Vice-Rector: Prof. Mário Wisintainer.
Registrar: João Schiochet.
Librarian: Sr. Braulio Schloegel.

Library of 46,052 vols., 28,675 periodicals.

Number of teachers: 242.
Number of students: 4,000.

Publications: *Boletim Universitário*†, *Boletim Bibliográfico, FURB-Revista de Divulgação Cultural.*

Directors:

Faculty of Philosophy, Sciences and Letters: Prof. João Joaquim Fronza.
Faculty of Physical Education and Sport: Prof. Lorival Beckhauser.
Faculty of Economic Sciences: Prof. Leo Arno Probst.
Faculty of Law: Prof. Arlindo Bernart.
Faculty of Engineering: Prof. Paulo Oscar Baier.

UNIVERSIDADE DE BRASÍLIA

AGÊNCIA POSTAL 15
70910 BRASÍLIA, D.F.
Telephone: 272-0000.

Founded 1961; inaugurated 1962.

Under the control of the Fundação Universidade Brasília; Language of instruction: Portuguese; Academic year of two terms.

Rector: Prof. José Carlos de Almeida Azevedo.
Vice-Rector: Marco Antônio Rodrigues Dias.
Chief Administrative Officer: Lister de Figueiredo.
Librarian: Maria Helena de Sá Barreto.

Library: *see* Libraries.

Number of teachers: *c.* 730.
Number of students: *c.* 10,000.

Directors and Heads of Departments:

Institute of Exact Sciences: Antônio Carneiro Barbosa.
Physics: Colber Gonçalves de Oliveira.
Geo-sciences: João da Rocha Hirson.
Mathematics: Keti Tenenblat.
Chemistry: Hugo Jorge Monteiro.
Statistics: Henrique Tafuri Malvar.
Institute of Biological Sciences: Cláudio Lúcio Costa.
Cell Biology: Jeferson Bastos Aragão.
Vegetal Biology: Terezinha Isaia Paviani.
Animal Biology: Heloisa Helena Magalhães Castro.
Psychology: Júlia Sursis Nobre Ferro Bucher.
Institute of Human Sciences: Gentil Martins Dias.
Economics: Livio William Reis de Carvalho.
Geography and History: Vamireh Chacon de Albuquerque Nascimento.
Social Sciences: Roque de Barros Laraia.
Institute of Expression and Communication: Moysés Jacob Mandel.
Art: Orlando Vieira Leite.
Communication: Luíz Gonzaga Figueiredo Motta.
Letters and Linguistics: Ulf Gregor Baranow.
Institute of Architecture and Town Planning: Matheus Gorovitz.
Architecture: Matheus Gorovitz.
Town Planning: José Galbinski.
Design: Orlando Luíz de Souza Fragoso Costa.

Faculty of Technology: Nelson Ortegosa da Cunha.

Agricultural Engineering: Roberto Meirelles de Miranda.

Civil Engineering: Oscar Carlos Tápias.

Electrical Engineering: Carlos Lisboa.

Mechanical Engineering: George Raulino.

Faculty of Health Sciences: Zairo Eira Garcia Vieira.

Complementary Medicine: Renato Angelo Saraiva.

General and Community Medicine: Iracema Mathilde Baccarini.

Physical Education: Mario Ribeiro Cantarino.

Specialized Medicine: Aluízio Rosa Prata.

Faculty of Applied Social Studies: José Francisco Rezek.

Administration: Alexandre Assaf Neto.

Library Science: Astério Tavares Campos.

Political Science and International Relations: José Carlos Brandi Aleixo.

Law: José Francisco Paes Landim.

Faculty of Education: Ediruald de Mello.

Theory and Basic Education: José Maria G. de Almeida, Jr.

Methods and Techniques: Elicio Bezerra Pontes.

Planning and Administration: Messias Costa.

PONTIFÍCIA UNIVERSIDADE CATÓLICA DE CAMPINAS

C.P. 317,
RUA MARECHAL DEODORO 1099
13.100 CAMPINAS, SÃO PAULO
Telephone: 0192-41-6766.

Founded 1941.

Private control; Academic year: March to December.

Chancellor: Dom Antônio Maria Alves de Siqueira, Archbishop of Campinas.

Rector: Prof. Dr. Benedito José Barreto Fonseca.

Vice-Rector for Academic Affairs: Prof. Carlos de Aquino Pereira.

Vice-Rector for Administrative Affairs: Prof. Dr. Dom Roberto Pinarello Almeida.

Secretary-General: Dr. José Antônio Trevisan.

Librarian: Profa. Yvone Borçato.

Number of teachers: 928.
Number of students: 20,000.

Periodicals: *Revista da Universidade, Revista Geomorfológica, Notícia Bibliográfica e Histórica, Revista Reflexão.*

DIRECTORS:

Faculty of Law: Prof. Dr. Álvaro Cury.

Faculty of Economic Sciences: Prof. Dr. Cândido F. da Silva.

Faculty of Dentistry: Prof. Dr. Paulo Bianchi.

Faculty of Engineering: Dr. Rubens C. Tocalino.

Faculty of Nursing: Dr. Joaquim de Paula Barreto Fonseca.

Faculty of Social Science: Profa. Madre Maria Mesquita Sampaio.

Faculty of Education: Prof. Antônio Raia.

Faculty of Librarianship: Profa. Ana Lúcia Maia Bonato.

Faculty of Physical Education: Prof. Dorian S. L. Guimarães.

Faculty of Architecture and Town Planning: Prof. Antônio J. de Pinho.

Faculty of Medicine: Prof. Dr. Joaquim de P. B. Fonseca.

Institute of Arts and Communications: Prof. Rosalvo Madeira Cardoso.

Institute of Biological Sciences: Prof. Flavio L. Aranha (acting).

Institute of Exact Sciences: Prof. Ronaldo Passini.

Institute of Philosophy and Theology: Prof. Cônego H. Niero.

Institute of Human Sciences: Prof. Waldyr V. Mayer.

Institute of Letters: Prof. Francisco R. Sampaio.

Institute of Psychology: Profa. Diana Toselo Laloni.

UNIVERSIDADE ESTADUAL DE CAMPINAS

CIDADE UNIVERSITÁRIA,
BARÃO GERALDO,
CAIXA POSTAL 1170,
CAMPINAS, SÃO PAULO
Telephone: 31-4555.

Founded 1962.

State control; Academic year: March to June, August to December; Language of instruction: Portuguese.

Rector: Prof. Zeferino Vaz.

General Co-ordinator: Dr. P. Gomes Romeo.

Secretary-General: Arlinda Rocha Camargo.

Librarian: Maria Alves de Paula Ravaschio.

Number of teachers: 1,400.
Number of students: 8,638.

DIRECTORS:

Institute of Arts: Prof. Dr. Rogério Cézar de C. Leite.

Institute of Biology: Prof. Dr. Walter August Hadler.

Institute of Philosophy and Human Sciences: Prof. Dr. Wilson Cano.

Institute of Physics: Prof. Dr. José E. Ripper Filho.

Institute of Language Studies: Prof. Dr. Antônio Cândido de Mello e Souza.

Institute of Mathematics, Statistics and Computer Science: Prof. Dr. Ubiratan d'Ambrósio.

Institute of Chemistry: Prof. Dr. Giuseppe Cilento.

Faculty of Medical Sciences: Prof. Dr. José A. Pinotti.

Faculty of Education: Prof. Dr. Antônio M. de Rezende.

Faculty of Agricultural and Food Engineering: Prof. Dr. André Tosello.

Faculty of Engineering (Campinas): Prof. Dr. Manoel Sobral, Jr.

Faculty of Engineering (Limeira): Prof. Dr. Morency Arouca.

Faculty of Dentistry (Piracicaba): Prof. Dr. José Merzel.

Logic, Epistemology and History of Science Centre: Prof. Dr. Oswaldo Porchat Pereira da Silva.

Technology Centre: Prof. Dr. Dino Ferraresi.

ATTACHED COLLEGES:

Colégio Técnico Industrial (Campinas): Dir. Prof. Mário Junqueira da Silva.

Colégio Técnico Industrial (Limeira): Dir. Prof. Antônio Prince Rodrigues.

UNIVERSIDADE DE CAXIAS DO SUL

C.P. 1352,
RUA FRANCISCO GETÚLIO VARGAS S/N,
95100 CAXIAS DO SUL, R.S.
Telephone: 21-14-09.

Founded 1967

Private control; Language of instruction: Portuguese.

Rector: Prof. Abrelino Vicente Vazatta.

Vice-Rectors: Profa. Liane Beatriz M. Ribeiro (Graduation); Prof. Ary Nicodemos Trentin (Postgraduates and Research); Prof. Ruy Pauletti (Extension and University Relations).

Administrative Director: Nestor Basso.

Librarian: Beatriz H. Rech.

Number of teachers: 411.
Number of students: 9,027.

Publications: *Revista Chronos*†, *Cadernos, Cadernos de Pesquisa, Jornal, Guia Acadêmico*†.

DIRECTORS AND HEADS OF DEPARTMENTS:

Centre of Sciences and Technology: Dir. Romeo José Hübner.

Department of Exact Sciences: Prof. Renan Ribeiro Mendes.

Department of Engineering: Mauro Rossi.

Centre of Humanities and Arts: Dir. Irmgard Cecília Bornheim.

Department of Letters: Vitalina M. Frosi.

Department of Arts: Carme Maria W. Fávero.

Department of History and Geography: REGINA ANGELA DAL BÓ.
Department of Philosophy, Psychology and Sociology: ISIDORO ZORZI.

Centre of Applied Social Studies: Dir. IVONNE ASSUNTA CORTELLETTI.
Department of Law: PEDRO MYRTES DE LIMA VARGAS.
Department of Education: IVO ADAMATTI.
Department of Economics and Accountancy: MILTON ROSSAROLLA.
Department of Administration: ERNY CASARA.

Centre of Biological Sciences and Health: Dir. ERNANI LOPES PEDONE.
Department of Nursing: ANILEDA BASSO.
Department of Clinical Surgery: FREDDY MARIN.
Department of Clinical Medicine: ADAGOBERTO FORTUNA.
Department of Biological Sciences: CELSO PICCOLI COELHO.
Department of Physical Education: GETÚLIO ASSIS VAZATTA.

UNIVERSIDADE FEDERAL DO CEARÁ

AV. DA UNIVERSIDADE 2853, C.P. 1000, 60000 FORTALEZA, CE

Telephone: 223-0233, 223-0534.

Founded 1955.

Rector: Prof. PAULO ELPÍDIO DE MENEZES NETO.
Vice-Rector: Prof. JOSÉ ANCHIETA ESMERALDO NARRETO.
Administrative Officer: Prof. RUI VERLAINE OLIVEIRA MOREIRA.
Librarian: Profa. MARIA ANTONIETA FIGUEIREDO BEZERRA.

Number of teachers: 1,428.
Number of students: 12,627.

Publications: *Boletim Mensal, Catálogo Anual,* various department publications.

HEADS OF DEPARTMENTS:

Sciences Centre:
Mathematics: Prof. RAIMUNDO TOMPSON GONÇALVES.
Statistics: Prof. FRANCISCO SILVA CAVALCANTE.
Physics: Prof. JOAQUIM HAROLDO PONTE.
***Industrial Chemistry:* Prof. CLÁUDIO S. COUTO.**
Geography: Prof. ANTÔNIO CARLOS GUIMARÃES.
Geology: Prof. JOSÉ VITORIANO DE SOUSA.
Biology: Profa. MARGARIDA MARIA BARROS DE MIRANDA.
Data Processing: Prof. FRANCISCO SILVA CAVALCANTE.

Humanities Centre:
***Social Sciences:* Profa. TEREZINHA HELENA ALENCAR CUNHA.**
Social Communications: Prof. TEOBALDO MOURÃO LANDIN.
History: Prof. JOSÉ TARCÍSIO DINIZ.
Letters: Prof. Fr. FRANCISCO BATISTA LUZ.

Technology Centre:
Civil Engineering: Prof. MOACIR WEYNE FILHO.
Mechanical Engineering: Prof. CARLOS ALBERTO DE CASTRO.
Electrical Engineering: Prof. JESAMAR LEÃO DE OLIVEIRA.
Architecture and Town Planning: Profa. NÍCIA PAES.

Agricultural and Food Sciences Centre:
***Agronomy:* Prof. MÍLTON BOTELHO.**
Fisheries: Profa. FRANCISCA PINHEIRO JOVENTINO.
Domestic Science: Prof. TANIA BARBOSA CABRAL DE ARAÚJO.
Food Technology: Prof. GERALDO ARRAES MAIA LIMA.

Health Sciences:
Medicine: Prof. JOSÉ CARLOS DA COSTA RIBEIRO.
Dentistry: Prof. IRAN BRASIL.
Pharmacy: Prof. FRANCISCO DE ASSIS SILVA FURTADO.

Centre of Applied Social Studies:
Economic Theory: Prof. AGAMENON TAVARES DE ALMEIDA.
Accountancy: Prof. ANTÔNIO ESMERINO PINTO.
Education: Prof. FRANCISCO DE ASSIS MEMDES GÓEZ.
Law: Prof. FÁVILA RIBEIRO.

UNIVERSIDADE FEDERAL DO ESPÍRITO SANTO

AV. FERNANDO FERRARI-GOIABEIRAS,
29.000 VITÓRIA, E.S.

Telephone: 227-0811, 227-4743.

Founded 1961.

Rector: ROMULO AUGUSTO PENINA.
General Secretary: AMAURY COUTO PRADO.
Librarian: NAZIAN MORÃES.

Number of teachers: 1,390.
Number of students: 8,555.

Publications: *Boletim Informativo, Revista de Cultura da UFES.*

DIRECTORS:

Arts Centre: FREDA CAVALCANTI JARDIM.
Biomedical Centre: THOMAZ TOMMASI.
Juridical and Economic Sciences Centre: LUÍZ FLORES ALVES.
General Studies Centre: IRACEMA VIEIRA BOGEA.
Physical Education and Sports Centre: ROBERTO MUSIELLO.
Pedagogic Centre: RITA DE CASSIA REZENDE DIAS.
Technology Centre: JOSÉ ANTÔNIO SAAD ABI-ZAID.
Agricultural and Animal Husbandry Centre: AGOSTINHO MERÇON.

UNIVERSIDADE FEDERAL FLUMINENSE

C.P. 1050,
RUA MIGUEL DE FRIAS 9,
24220 NITERÓI, R.J.

Telephone: 719-5115, 710-0490.

Founded 1960.

Academic year: March to July, August to December.

Rector: ROGÉRIO BENEVENTO.
Vice-Rector: MARIA LÚCIA NOSSAR SIMÕES DE DALGO.
Director of Document Centre: ELISABETH SCHNEIDER DE SÁ.
***Librarian:* Prof. PAULO PY CORDEIRO.**

Number of teachers: 1,987.
Number of students: 16,571.

Publications: *Catálogo Geral, Catálogo de Teses e Disertações, Cursos de Pós-graduação, Pesquisas em Andamento* (annually), *Linguagem: Revista do Instituto de Letras, Revista da Faculdade de Educação, Cadernos de Direito Privado* (2 a year), *Cadernos de Geociências* (irregular).

DEANS AND DIRECTORS:

General Studies Centre: JOSÉ RAIMUNDO MARTINS ROMEO.
Institute of Arts and Social Communications: JOSÉ PEDRO PINTO ESPOSEL.
Institute of Human Sciences and Philosophy: HIDILBERTO RAMOS CAVALCANTI DE ALBURQUERQUE JUNIOR.
Institute of Physics: WILSON LAGALHARD.
Institute of Geosciences: MARIA ALISA FANTOZZI VIEIRA.
Institute of Linguistics and Literature: ELSA SAVINO DE MATTOS.
Institute of Mathematics: RODOLPHO GUILHERME PEDREIRA.
Institute of Chemistry: JORGE JOÃO ABRAÃO.

Applied Social Science Centre: AUSTA GURGEL.
Faculty of Law: ENEAS MARZANO.
Faculty of Economics and Administration: EUTACILIO DA SILVA LEAL.
Faculty of Education: LÚCIA MOLINA TRAJANO DA COSTA.
School of Social Service: CELYR DE PAIVA LESSA DAMÁSCENO FERREIRA.

Medical Sciences Centre: NADIR COELHO.
Biomedical Institute: CELSO DE RESENDE FERREIRA FILHO.
Faculty of Nursing: LEONIA MACHADO BORGES.
Faculty of Pharmacy: SALVADOR ALVES PEREIRA.
Faculty of Medicine: ALOYSIO VEIGA DE PAULA.
Veterinary School: JACINTHO MACHADO MENDONÇA.
Faculty of Dentistry: PAULINO MENEZES PEITERLE.

UNIVERSIDADE DE FORTALEZA

C.P. 1258, FORTALEZA, CEARÁ

Telephone: 227-7910.

Founded 1973; Private control (Fundação Educacional Edson Queiroz).

Rector: Prof. JAIME DA CUNHA REBOUÇAS.

Registrar: JOSÉ RAIMUNDO GONDIM.

Library of 26,767 vols.

Number of teachers: 464.

Number of students: 9,536.

UNIVERSIDADE GAMA FILHO

RUA MANOEL VITORINO 625, PIEDADE, CEP 20.740, RIO DE JANEIRO, R.J.

Telephone: 269 7272.

Founded 1972.

Rector: Prof. JOSÉ MURTA RIBEIRO.

Chancellor: Prof. PAULO GAMA FILHO.

Vice-Chancellor: Prof. PEDRO GAMA FILHO.

Librarian: NELSON AZEVEDO BRANCO.

Library of 60,000 vols.

Number of teachers: 1,500.

Number of students: 23,300.

DEANS:

Sciences and Technology Centre: Prof. Dr. JOÃO CARLOS CORDEIRO DA GRAÇA FILHO.

Biological and Health Sciences Centre: Prof. Dr. ALBERTO GENTILE.

Social Sciences Centre: Prof. HENRIQUE LUÍS ARIENTI.

Human Sciences Centre: Prof. CORINTHO ALVES FILHO.

ATTACHED INSTITUTE

Instituto de Pesquisas Gonzaga da Gama Filho: Dir. Prof. Dr. GOBERT ARAÚJO COSTA

UNIVERSIDADE CATÓLICA DE GOIÁS

PRAÇA UNIVERSITÁRIA, C.P. 86, 74000 GOIÂNIA, GOIÁS

Telephone: 2251188.

Founded 1959.

Academic year: January to December.

Rector: Fr. JOSÉ PEREIRA DE MARIA.

Vice-Rector for Academic Affairs: Prof. JONATHAS SILVA.

Vice-Rector for Administrative Affairs: JOÃO CUPERTINO DE SOUZA CLÍMACO.

Librarian: SÍLVIO JOSÉ RABUSKE.

Number of teachers: 479.

Number of students: 13,624.

Publication: *Estudos Goianienses* (termly).

Faculties of Economics, Law, Philosophy, Sociology.

UNIVERSIDADE FEDERAL DE GOIÁS

CAMPUS II KM. 13, RODOVIA GOIÂNIA, NERÓPOLIS, C.P. 130, 74.000 GOIÂNIA, GOIÁS

Telephone: 261-32-49.

Founded 1960.

Rector: Prof. JOSÉ CRUCIANO DE ARAÚJO.

Vice-Rector: MÁRIO EVARISTO DI OLIVEIRA.

Secretary: EULER DE AMORIM Jr.

Librarian: Profa. MARIETTA TELLES MACHADO.

Number of teachers: 985.

Number of students: 7,645.

Publications: *Boletim do Pessoal*, *A Informação Goiana* (monthly), *Anais da Escola de Agronomia e Veterinária*† (annually), *Boletim Estatistico*† (2 a year), *Revista Goiana de Medicina*† (quarterly).

DEANS AND DIRECTORS:

Faculty of Law: Prof. CID DE ALBERNAZ OLIVEIRA.

Faculty of Education: Prof. NANCY RIBEIRO DE ARAÚJO E SILVA.

Faculty of Medicine: ARY MONTEIRO DO ESPÍRITO SANTO.

Faculty of Pharmacy: HILTON PARANHOS.

Faculty of Odontology: Prof. PEDRO DE ALCÂNTARA NUNES.

School of Engineering: QUINTILIANO AVELAR BLUMENSCHEIN.

School of Agriculture and Veterinary Science: Prof. SALVADOR JORGE DA CUNHA NETTO.

Institute of Mathematics and Physics: Prof. JUAREZ MILANO.

Institute of Tropical Pathology: ROBERTO RUHMAN DAHER.

Institute of Biological Sciences: Prof. OSVALDO VILELA GARCIA.

Institute of Chemistry and Geosciences: Prof. DAVID NICOLAU ISAAK.

Institute of Arts: Prof. MARIA LUIZA PÓVOA CRUZ.

Institute of Human Sciences and Letters: FLAVIO RIOS P. DA SILVEIRA.

HEADS OF DEPARTMENTS:

School of Engineering:

Construction: Prof. BIOLKINO ANTÔNIO PEREIRA DA SILVEIRA.

Machinery and Hydraulics: Prof. CLEBER MALTA DE SÁ (acting).

Structural Engineering: Prof. NESTOR GUIMARÃES.

Electronics: Prof. RUI BARBOSA COELHO.

Electrical Engineering: Prof. EURIDES CURVO (acting).

Institute of Human Sciences and Letters:

Human Sciences: Prof. DALISIA ELIZABETH MARTINS DOLES.

Social Communication: VALQUIRIA BRAGA DOS SANTOS.

Letters: CELENITA AMARAL TURCHI.

Faculty of Pharmacy:

Industrial Pharmacochemistry: MIGUEL JORGE.

Biochemical Control: SEBASTIÃO UNES.

Toxicological Control: LUIZA BARBOSA DE OLIVEIRA.

Institute of Biological Sciences:

Anatomy: Prof. RAUL CONDE.

General Biology: Prof. FERNANDO L. KRATZ.

Biochemistry and Biophysics: Prof. JOSÉ SALUM.

Botany: Prof. JOSÉ ANGELO RIZZO.

Physiology and Pharmacology: Prof. CARLOS ALBERTO TANEZINI.

Histology and Embryology: Prof. DELFINO DA COSTA MACHADO.

Faculty of Medicine:

Surgery: Prof. LUÍZ RASSI.

Medical Clinics: Prof. CELMO C. PÔRTO.

Ophthalmology: Prof. AUGUSTO PARANHOS.

Oto-Rhino-Laryngology: Prof. ALBERANI NITALBERT GONÇALVES LEITE.

Obstetrics and Gynaecology: Prof. GEORTHON RODGRIGUES PHILOCREON.

Orthopaedics: Prof. GERALDO PEDRA.

Paediatrics and Puericulture: Prof. SAULO GUIMARÃES DE SOUZA.

Pathology: Prof. MAURICIO SÉRGIO BRASIL LEITE.

Psychiatry and Forensic Medicine: Prof. GERALDO BRASIL.

Radiology: Prof. NABYH SALUM.

Nursing and Nutrition: Prof. HELENA BEATRIZ BRANDÃO DE ARAÚJO.

Faculty of Odontology:

Oral Medicine: Prof. AMIR NASSAR.

Oral Rehabilitation: Prof. MÁRIO DE ALMEIDA LOYOLA.

Social Odontology: Prof. RAMIRO DE CAMPOS MEIRELES.

Polyclinic: Prof. WILSON BARNABÉ.

Institute of Arts:

Theory: MARIA LUDOVICO DE ALMEIDA E SILVA.

Applied Arts: Prof. ÂNGELOS ANDRÉ KTENAS.

Visual Arts: ANTÔNIO HENRIQUE PECLAT.

Complementary Subjects: ANTÔNIO NÉRI DA SILVA.

Music: Prof. HELOISA BARRA JARDIM.

Materials Applied to Art: DALVA MARIA P. MACHADO BRAGANÇA.

Keyboard and Percussion Instruments: MIRZA PEROTTO.

Institute of Tropical Pathology:

Immunology: Prof. MARIA VITALINA DO NASCIMENTO GUERRA.

Preventive Medicine: Prof. CÉLIO CESAR DE MOURA GOMES.

Tropical Medicine: Prof. SYDNEY SCHMIDT.

Microbiology: Prof. CLEÔMENES REIS.

Parasitology: Prof. MARGARIDA DOBLER KOMMA.

Institute of Chemistry and Geoscience:
Geography: Prof. MARIA DE SOUZA FRANÇA.
Topography and Geodesy: Prof. RENATO BRAZ DE OLIVEIRA E SILVA.
Geology: Prof. ROBERTO LUÍZ FRANCO BUCCI.
Analytical Chemistry: Prof. CARLOS A. DE ARAÚJO.
Organic Chemistry: Prof. MARINHO LINO DE ARAÚJO.
General and Inorganic Chemistry: Prof. MARIA AUXILIADORA ALVES BARBOSA COELHO.

Institute of Mathematics and Physics:
Mathematics: VALDIR VILMAR DA SILVA.
Statistics and Informatics: IAMAMOTO PACHECO.
Technical Design and Geometry: HERMÓGENES COELHO.
Physics: Prof. WALMIR GUEDES MACHADO.

Faculty of Education:
Basic Education: Prof. FLORACY AMARAL REBOUÇAS.
School Administration: Prof. MARGARIDA MARIA DE JESUS.
Educational Practice: Prof. SILVIA ALESSANDRI MONTEIRO DE CASTRO.

Faculty of Law:
Basic Law: Prof. MÁXIMO DOMINGUES.
Comparative Law: Prof. DOMINGOS JULIANO.
Criminal Law: Prof. CLENON DE BARROS LOYOLA.
Private Law: Prof. CARLOS L. DAYRELL.
Civil and Labour Law: Prof. LUÍS FRANCISCO GUEDES DE AMORIM.

School of Agronomy and Veterinary Science:
Pathology: Prof. ROULIEN FONTES.
Agriculture: Prof. JOEL CECILIO.
Animal Husbandry: HÉLIO LOURÊDO DA SILVA.
Horticulture: Prof. RAIMUNDO N. DE MACEDO LIMA.
Clinics: Prof. LOURIVAL PEREIRA NUNES.
Economics: Prof. GABRIEL C. QUIROGA.
Agricultural Engineering: Prof. OLIVAR JOSÉ DA SILVA MORAES LOBATO.
Technology: Prof. HENRIQUE ALFREDO PÉCLAT NERO.
Plant Hygiene: Prof. IVO DE CARVALHO.
Diseases and Inspection: Prof. AUGUSTO SILVA DE CARVALHO.
Veterinary Hospital: Prof. PAULO ROBERTO FIGUEIREDO DA SILVA.

UNIVERSIDADE DE ITAÚNA

RUA CAPITÃO VICENTE 10,
C.P. 100,
35.680 ITAÚNA, M.G.
Telephone: 241-2375.

Founded 1965.

Private control; Academic year: March to July, August to December.

Rector: GUARACY DE CASTRO NOGUEIRA.
Vice-Rector: JOSÉ CAMPOS.
Executive Director: JOSÉ W. TEIXEIRA DE MELO.
Librarian: MARIA DA CONCEIÇÃO APAREDICA CARVALHO C.

Number of teachers: 159.
Number of students: 2,261.

Publication: *Odonto-Itaúna*†, *Cadernos de Extensão*†.

DIRECTORS:

Faculty of Dentistry: JAIR RASO.
Faculty of Engineering: ARILTON LORENZIM.
Faculty of Law: GERALDO DOS SANTOS.
Faculty of Education, Languages and Social Sciences: ANNA ALVES VIERA DOS REIS.
Faculty of Economics: ELOY GRECÓ.

UNIVERSIDADE FEDERAL DE JUIZ DE FORA

RUA BENJAMIM CONSTANT 790,
36100 JUIZ DE FORA,
MINAS GERAIS

Telephone: PABX 212-5966, 212-5122.

Founded 1960.

Federal control; Language of instruction: Portuguese; Academic year: March to July, August to December.

Rector: Prof. SEBASTIÃO DE ALMEIDA PAIVA.
Registrar: Prof. JOSÉ VENTURA.
Librarian: MARIA M. RIBEIRO DE OLIVEIRA.

Number of teachers: 916.
Number of students: 6,345.

Publications: *Boletim da Reitoria*, *Boletim Alemão de Pesquisas* (monthly), *Boletim do Instituto de Ciências Biológicas e de Geociências* (every 2 months), *Revista do Hospital Escola* (quarterly), *Lumina Spargere*, *Tabulae*, *Catálogo Geral dos Cursos* (annually).

DEANS:

Faculty of Medicine: Prof. JOSÉ L. DE OLIVEIRA.
Faculty of Dentistry: Prof. FÁBIO NERY.
Faculty of Economics: Prof. JURANDY ALTOMARE.
Faculty of Pharmacy and Biochemistry: Prof. MÁRCIO LEITE VAZ.
Faculty of Engineering: Prof. EBER LUÍZ HALFELD.
Faculty of Law: Prof. PAULO ROBERTO MEDINA.
Faculty of Education: Profa. DALVA C. DE MENEZES YAZBECK.
Faculty of Social Services: Profa. ALTIVA P. PAIXÃO.
Institute of Biological Sciences and Geosciences: Prof. PAULO TORRES.
Institute of Human Sciences and Letters: Prof. GUILHERME G. M. VAN KEULEN.
Institute of Exact Sciences: Prof. LUCAS M. DO AMARAL.

UNIVERSIDADE ESTADUAL DE LONDRINA

C.P. 2111,
86.100 LONDRINA, PARANÁ
Telephone: 27-3402.

Founded 1971.

Controlled by the Fundação Universidade Estadual de Londrina.

Rector: Prof. JOSÉ CARLOS PINOTTI.
Vice-Rector: Prof. PEDRO DE VASCONCELLOS BARROS.
Secretary-General: Prof. FERNANDO A. C. CAUDURO.
Librarian: Profa. GRAÇA MARIA SIMÕES LOPES PIZA.

Library of 43,000 vols.
Number of teachers: 712.
Number of students: 8,047.

Publications: *Catálogo Geral*† (annually), *Manual do Candidato* (termly), *Boletim Oficial* (monthly), *O Perobal* (monthly), *Semina* (every 2 months).

HEADS OF DEPARTMENTS:

Letters and Human Sciences: Prof. JORGE CERNEV.
Biological Sciences: Prof. MANOEL BARROS DE AZEVEDO.
Exact Sciences: Prof. WILSON DE ARAÚJO CLAUDINO.
Applied Social Studies: Prof. THEOBALDO C. NAVOLAR.
Health Sciences: Prof. ALDO LUIZ HILLE.
Education, Communication and Arts: Profa. MARIA LUZEL CAUDURO.
Rural Sciences and Technology: Prof. GILVAN WOSIACK.

UNIVERSIDADE MACKENZIE*

RUA MARIA ANTONIA 403,
01222 SÃO PAULO
Telephone: 256-6611.

Founded 1952.

Private control; Academic year: March to June, August to December.

Rector: DR. PHILOMENO JOAQUIM DA COSTA.
Secretary-General: DR. PAULO ROBERTO CARVALHO BATISTA.
Librarian: CELINA MUNIZ DE SOUZA.

Number of teachers: *c.* 700.
Number of students: *c.* 11,000.

Publications: ***O Picareta, Revista de Engenharia, Folha Mackenzista, Jornal das Universidades.***

DIRECTORS:

School of Engineering: Prof. M. GIL.
Faculty of Architecture: Prof. J. OKAMOTO.
Faculty of Education, Science and Letters: Prof. FRANCISCO BRANDL HOFFMAN.
Faculty of Economics, Administration and Accountancy: Prof. J. WILSON SARAIVA.
Faculty of Law: Prof. ALFREDO CECÍLIO LOPES.
Faculty of Technology: Prof. AURORA ALBANESE.
Postgraduate Studies: W. CONCEIÇÃO MATTOS.

* No reply received to our questionnaire this year.

UNIVERSIDADE FEDERAL DO MARANHÃO

LARGO DOS AMORES 351,
65000 SÃO LUÍS, MARANHÃO

Founded 1966.

Rector: Prof. JOSÉ MARIA CABRAL MARQUES.

Faculties of Nursing, Physical Education and Sport, Pharmacy and Biochemistry, Medicine, Odontology, Industrial Design, Design, Geography, History, Letters, Mathematics, Chemistry, Librarianship, Accountancy, Communications, Law, Education, Social Service, Industrial Chemistry, Electrical Engineering.

UNIVERSIDADE ESTADUAL DE MARINGÁ

AV. COLOMBO 3960,
C.P. 331,
87100 MARINGÁ, PR
Telephone: 22-4242.

Founded 1970.

Private control; Language of instruction: Portuguese; Academic year: March to December.

Rector: Prof. NEUMAR ADÉLIO GODOY.
Vice-Rector: Prof. AROLDO XAVIER.
Pro-Rectors: Prof. MOACIR COLOMBO (Administration), Prof. JOSÉ GONÇALVES VICENTE (Teaching and Research), Prof. ADILSON IRINAU SCHIAVONI (Extension and Community Affairs).
Librarian: MARIA GRÁZIA ZOLET.

Number of teachers: 517.
Number of students: 4,726.

Publication: *Unimar.*

DIRECTORS:

Socio-Economic Studies Centre: Prof. EURICO MATTANA CAMBOIN.
Human Sciences, Literature and Arts Centre: Prof. ARGEMIRO ALUÍSIO KARLING.
Biological Sciences and Health Centre: Prof. FRANCISCO HERRERO.
Exact Sciences Centre: Prof. MANOEL JACÓ GARCIA GIMENEZ.
Technology Centre: Prof. EVARISTO ATÊNCIO PAREDES.

HEADS OF DEPARTMENTS:

Human Sciences, Literature and Arts Centre:
Geography: EMÍLIO EUGÊNIO NIECE.
Letters: ANGELO SEBASTIÃO DE ANDRADE.
Social Sciences: GILBERTO MATOS SCHMIDT.
Education: BALDUINO MEURER.

Socio-Economic Studies Centre:
Private and Procedural Law: UBIRAJARA FERREIRA.
Public Law: APARECIDO DOMINGOS ERRERIAS LOPES.
Administration and Accountancy: MARCOS IRA RIBAS.

Biological Sciences and Health Centre:
Agrarian Sciences: JOSÉ MARIA DE OLIVEIRA.
Biology: ERASMO RENESTO.
Pharmacy and Biochemistry: BENEDITO PRADO DIAS FILHO.
Physical Education: JOÃO MARIN MECHIA.

Exact Sciences:
Mathematics and Statistics: ELMAR WATERKEMPER.
Chemistry: NILSON EVELÁZIO DE SOUZA.
Physics: WILSON RICARDO WEINAND.

Technology Centre:
Civil Engineering: JOÃO ALBERTO MARCUZZO.
Information: ADEMIR CARNIEL.
Chemical Engineering: NEHEMIAS CURVELO PEREIRA.

DIRECTORS:

Pedagogical Application Centre: MARIA OLGA MALVEZZI PEREIRA LIMA.
Languages Institute: IARA MARIA TELLES MARCOLIN.
Audio-Visual Resource Centre: ANTÔNIO CARLOS LOCATELLI.
Business Development Centre: EDUARDO DE OLIVEIRA LEITE.
Applied Psychology Centre: ANA CAROLINA MANNA BELLASALMA.

UNIVERSIDADE ESTADUAL DE MATO GROSSO DO SUL*

C.P. 649,
CIDADE UNIVERSITÁRIA,
79100 CAMPO GRANDE, MTS
Telephone: 4-8663-5.

Founded 1970.

State control; Language of instruction: Portuguese.

Rector: Dr. EDGARD ZARDO.
Vice-Rector: **HÉLIO MARTINS COELHO.**
Registrar: **ALFREDO BARBOSA FILHO.**
Librarian: **HILDA DE OLIVEIRA LIMA.**

Number of teachers: 300.
Number of students: 2,500.

Publication: ***Boletim Geral.***

Faculties of Pharmacy, Dentistry, Physiology, Pathology, Medicine, Veterinary Science.

* No reply received to our questionnaire this year.

UNIVERSIDADE FEDERAL DE MATO GROSSO

AV. FERNANDO CORRÊA
DA COSTA, 78000 CUIABÁ, M.T.

Founded 1970.

Rector: Prof. GABRIEL NOVIS NEVES.
Administrative Officer: FERNANDO AUGUSTO ALVES PACE.

Number of teachers: 760.
Number of students: 5,485.

Faculties of Agrarian Sciences, Biological and Health Sciences, Letters and Human Sciences, Social Sciences, Exact Sciences and Technology, Technologist Training.

UNIVERSIDADE CATÓLICA DE MINAS GERAIS

AV. DOM JOSÉ GASPAR 500,
C.P. 2686,
30.000 BELO HORIZONTE,
MINAS GERAIS
Telephone: 332-3444.

Founded 1958.

Chancellor: Dom JOÃO RESENDE COSTA.
Rector: Dom SERAFIM FERNANDES DE ARAÚJO.
Vice-Rector: Dr. GAMALIEL HERVAL.
Secretary-General: Profa. NEUSA SATUF REZENDE.
Librarian: **MARIA P. TIMBURIBÁ MACHADO.**

Number of teachers: 713.
Number of students: 11,516.

DIRECTORS:

Department of Law: Prof. AFFONSO HENRIQUES PRATES CORREA.
Department of Portuguese and English: Prof. OSCAR VIEIRA DA SILVA.
Department of History and Geography: Prof. WILSON DE ABREU.
Department of Education: Prof. Pe. ANTÔNIO SÉRGIO PALOMBO DE MAGALHÃES.
Department of Communications: Prof. JOSÉ MILTON DOS SANTOS.
Department of Nursing: Profa. NAHYR RODRIGUES DA CUNHA.
Department of Engineering: Prof. DJALMA FRANCISCO DE CARVALHO.
Department of Dentistry: Prof. EUGÊNIO VILAÇA MENDES.
Department of Biological Sciences: Prof. EDMUNDO PEREIRA RODRIGUES.

UNIVERSIDADE FEDERAL DE MINAS GERAIS

CIDADE UNIVERSITÁRIA, PAMPULHA, C.P. 1621, 1622, 30.000 BELO HORIZONTE, MINAS GERAIS

Telephone: 441-00-66.

Founded 1927.

Rector: Prof. CELSO DE VASCONCELLOS PINHEIRO.

Vice-Rector: Prof. JOSÉ HENRIQUE SANTOS.

Pro-Rectors: Dr. WAGNER SALEME (Administration), Prof. MARCIO QUINTÃO MORENO (Planning and Development), Prof. JARBAS BRUNO (Undergraduates), Profa. MARIA LISBOA DE OLIVEIRA (Graduates), Prof. THEÓFILO ANDRÉ DA COSTA CRUZ (Research), Prof. JENNER PROCÓPIO DE ALVARENGA (Extension).

Director of Libraries: Prof. MARÍLIA JÚNIA DE ALMEIDA GARDINI.

Libraries of 357,356 vols., 10,357 periodicals.

Number of teachers: 2,194.
Number of students: 15,029.

Publications: ***Revista Brasileira de Estudos Políticos, Arquivos da Escola de Veterinária da UFMG, Arquivos do Centro de Estudos da Faculdade de Odontologia da UFMG, Revista Literária do Corpo Docente,*** etc.

DIRECTORS:

School of Fine Arts: BEATRIZ RAMOS DE VASCONCELLOS COELHO.
School of Music: SEBASTIÃO VIANA.
Faculty of Philosophy and Human Sciences: DÉLCIO VIEIRA SALOMON.
Faculty of Letters: EUNICE DUTRA GALERY.
Institute of Biological Sciences: MARCELO VASCONCELOS COELHO.
Institute of Pure Sciences: MANOEL LOPES DE SIQUEIRA.
Institute of Geo-Sciences: WOLNEY LOBATO.
School of Architecture: HENRIQUE OSWALDO DE CAMPOS.
School of Librarianship: ANNA MARIA ATHAYDE POLKE.
Faculty of Economic Sciences: JOÃO BATISTA VIEIRA PÉRET.
Faculty of Law: JOSÉ ALFREDO DE OLIVEIRA BARACHO.
Faculty of Education: MAGDA BECKER SOARES.
School of Physical Education: JOSÉ PEREIRA DA SILVA.
School of Nursing: MARIA NOEMI FERREIRA RIBEIRO.
School of Engineering: HÉLIO ANTONINI.
Faculty of Medicine: LUÍZ DE PAULA CASTRO.
Faculty of Dentistry: HUMBERTO DE CAMPOS.
School of Veterinary Sciences: JADIR JOSÉ FERREIRA DE MIRANDA.
Faculty of Pharmacy: JOSÉ ELIAS MURAD.

AFFILIATED INSTITUTE:

Centro de Desenvolvimento e Planejamento Regional—CEDEPLAR (*Centre for Development and Regional Planning*): Rua Curitiba 832, Belo Horizonte, MG; Dir. CLÉLIO CAMPOLINA DINIZ.

UNIVERSIDADE MINEIRA DE ARTE

AV. AMAZONAS 6252, GAMELEIRA, 30.000 BELO HORIZONTE, MG

Telephone 332-0807, 332-0520 (Plastic Arts), 337-3274 (Music).

Founded 1954.

State control: Language of instruction: Portuguese.

Rector: Prof. RAYMUNDO NONATO FERNANDES.
President: Gen. JOSÉ CARLOS CAMPOS CHRISTO.
Vice-President: Dr. FLAVIO NEVES.
Vice-Rector: JOSÉ OLYMPIO SOARES DE FARIA.
Head of Administration: JOSÉ PIMENTEL BARBOSA.
Librarian: TEREZINHA CARNEIRO DE MOURA.

Number of teachers (Plastic Arts): 54, (Music): 29.
Number of students (Plastic Arts): 955, (Music): 200.

UNIVERSIDADE DE MOGI DAS CRUZES

C.P. 411, AV. CÂNDIDO XAVIER DE ALMEIDA SOUZA 200, 08700 MOGI DAS CRUZES, SP

Telephone: 469-5333.

Founded 1973.

Private control.

Rector: **MANOEL BEZERRA DE MELO.**
Vice-Rector: MILTON DE CARVALHO MELO.
Secretary-General: ADVENIR DE SOUZA LIMA.
Librarian: ANNERIS B. DOMINGUITTO.

Library of 30,000 vols.
Number of teachers: 994.
Number of students: 13,318.

Publications: *Boletim*† (monthly), *Catálogo Geral*† (annually).

DEANS:

Human Sciences: WALTER DE ABREU GARCEZ.
Science and Technology: SEBASTIÃO PEREIRA DE FARIA.
Biomedical Sciences: EDISON KARAM NASSRI.

DIRECTORS:

Institute of Philosophy and Social Sciences: VERA LUCIA PEREIRA LIMA.
Institute of Letters and Arts: VERA LUCIA PEREIRA LIMA.
Faculty of Education: MARIA DE CONCEIÇÃO BERNARDO SILVA.
Faculty of Economics and Administration: WALDIR PEREIRA GOMES.
Faculty of Law: WALTER DE A. GARCEZ.
Faculty of Social Communication: PAULO ROCHA DE OLIVEIRA NETO.
Institute of Sciences: SEBASTIÃO P. DE FARIA.
Faculty of Engineering: WULF WOLKOFF NETO.
Faculty of Operational Engineering: WULF W. NETO.
Faculty of Architecture and Town Planning: SÉRGIO F. G. DE CARVALHO.
Institute of Psychology: FLÁVIO J. R. SARDINHA.
Institute of Biology: JOSÉ ROBINSON DE ARAÚJO NUDI.
Faculty of Medicine: ALDO STACCHINI.
Faculty of Dentistry: EDISON K. NASSRI.
Faculty of Physical Education: JOÃO PEDRO ARANTES.
Higher School of Nursing: ANDRÉ C. GARCIA.

UNIVERSIDADE REGIONAL DO NORDESTE

AV. MAR. FLORIANO PEIXOTO 718, 58100 CAMPINA GRANDE, PARAÍBA

Telephone: 083-321-00-99.

Founded 1966.

Municipal control; Language of instruction: Portuguese; Academic year: March to December

Rector: Prof. JOSÉ CAVALCANTE DE FIGUEIREDO.
Vice-Rector: Prof. MOACI ALVES CARNEIRO.
General Secretary: NILO TAVARES.
Librarian: Profa. MARTA MARIA M. MACHADO.

Library of 65,000 vols.
Number of teachers: 450.
Number of students: 7,200.

Publications: *Catálogo Geral* (annually), *Roteiro, Signun, INFURNE.*

DIRECTORS:

Centre of Humanities, Letters and Arts: Profa. MARGARIDA DA MOTTA ROCHA.
Centre of Sciences and Technology: Prof. JOAQUIM VICTORIANO PEREIRA.
Centre of Biological Sciences and Health: Prof. HUMBERTO MATOS.

HEADS OF DEPARTMENTS:

Centre of Humanities, Letters and Arts:
Department of Letters: Profa. HILMA MARIA LOUREIRO.
Department of Education: Profa. MARIA INÊS DE CASTRO DANTAS.
Department of Social Sciences: Profa. JOSEFA GOMES DE ALMEIDA E SILVA.

Department of Economic Administration and Accountancy: Prof. FRANCISCO NERY LEAL.
Department of Law: Prof. JACKSON ROCHA DUARTE.
Department of Social Communication and Arts: Prof. GILSON SOUTO MAIOR.
Department of Philosophy and Psychology: Prof. JOÃO PEREIRA DE ASSIS.

Centre of Sciences and Technology:
Department of Mathematics and Statistics: Prof. J. ONILDO FREIRE CAVALCANTI.
Department of Physics and Geosciences: Prof. JORGE MARCOS RIBEIRO SILVA.
Department of Chemistry: Prof. JOSÉ FRANCISCO DE MELO NETO.

Centre of Biological Sciences and Health:
Department of Biology: Profa. MARIA DE FÁTIMA S. DE SOUZA LIMA.
Department of Dentistry: Prof. GERALDO DE SÁ SERRÃO.
Department of Nursing: Profa. LALIE ALVES NAVARRO.
Department of Physiotherapy and Physical Education: Profa. SIDILENE GONZAGA DE MELO.

FUNDAÇÃO NORTE MINEIRA DE ENSINO SUPERIOR

VILA MAURICÉIA S/N,
CAIXA POSTAL 126,
39400 MONTES CLAROS,
MINAS GERAIS
Telephone: 221-2340, 221-2118.

Private control, officially recognized; Academic year: March to June, August to December; Language of instruction: Portuguese.

Rector and President of Council: Dr. RAIMUNDO RODRIGUES AVELAR.
Vice-Rector and Executive Director: Profa. ISABEL REBELLO DE PAULA.

Library of 17,366 vols.
Number of teachers: 183.
Number of students: 1,962.

DIRECTORS:

Faculty of Philosophy, Sciences and Letters: Prof. ANTÔNIO JORGE.
Faculty of Law: Dr. AUGUSTO JOSÉ VIEIRA NETO.
Faculty of Administration and Finance: Prof. ALFREDO DOLABELLA PORTELLA FILHO.
Faculty of Medicine: Dr. ITAGIBA DE CASTRO FILHO.

UNIVERSIDADE FEDERAL DE OURO PRÊTO

PRAÇA TIRADENTES 20,
35400 OURO PRÊTO, MG
Telephone: 291, 549

Founded 1969.

Rector: THEODULO PERREIRA.
Chief Administrative Officer: JOÃO C. DE ALMEIDA.
Librarian: MARIA DA G. R. SOARES.

Number of teachers: 178.
Number of students: 1,106.

Publications: *Revista da Escola ue Minas* (monthly), *Revista da Escola de Farmácia, Espeleologia, Boletim de Geologia.*

CONSTITUENT INSTITUTES:

Escola de Minas: f. 1876; courses in Civil Engineering, Mining, Geology, Metallurgy; 158 teachers, 1,050 students; Dir. Prof. WILLIAM L. R. LEITE.

Escola de Farmacia: Dir. JOSÉ C. SOBRINHO.

UNIVERSIDADE FEDERAL DO PARÁ

AV. GOVERNADOR
JOSÉ MALCHER, 1192,
BELÉM, PARÁ
Telephone: 223-25-32.

Founded 1957.

Academic year: March to December; Language of instruction: Portuguese.

Rector: Dr. ARACY AMAZONAS BARRETTO.
Vice-Rector: Prof. GERALDO DE ASSIS GUIMARÃES
Central Library Administrator: MAGALI RENATA VAN DIJK VERGOLINO.

Number of professors: 1,485.
Number of students: 12,329.

Publications: *Revista, Boletim do Serviço, Boletim Informativo* (monthly).

DIRECTORS:

Exact and Natural Sciences Centre: Prof. G. LOPES RAPOSO.
Biology Centre: Prof. J. P. DO VALLE MENDES.
Philosophy and Human Sciences Centre: Prof. D. CRUZ NETO.
Arts and Letters Centre: Prof. R. AUGUSTO DE SOUZA.
Bio-Medical Centre: Prof. R. VELOSO DE CASTRO MENEZES.
Technology Centre: Prof. MÁRIO CARDOSO DE FREITAS GUIMARÃES.
Socio-Economic Centre: Prof. Dr. OPHIR FILGUEIRAS CAVALCANTE.
Education Centre: Profa. ODINÉIA TELLES FIGUEIREDO.
Geophysical and Geological Sciences Centre: Prof. Dr. JOSÉ SEIXAS LOURENÇO.
Advanced Amazonian Studies Centre: Prof. Dr. JOSÉ MARCELINO MONTEIRO DA COSTA.

UNIVERSIDADE FEDERAL DA PARAÍBA

CAMPUS UNIVERSITÁRIO,
58.000 JOÃO PESSOA, PARAÍBA
Telephone: 224-7200.

Founded 1955.

Academic year: March to June, August to December; Language of instruction: Portuguese.

Rector: MILTON FERREIRA DE PAIVA.
Vice-Rector: SERAFIM RODRIGUEZ MARTINEZ.
Chief Administrative Officer: OSCAR SAMPAIO VISGUEIRO.
Librarian: LÊDA MARIA JUREMA DUTRA.

Number of teachers: 2,635.
Number of students: 20,639.

Publications: *Boletim de Notícias*†, *Boletim de Serviços*† (monthly), *Relatório de Atividades*†, *Catálogo de Gradução, Catálogo de Pós-gradução, Catálogo de Serviços* (annually), *Catálogo de Extensão* (2 a year), *Revista de Ciências Humanas, Revista Nordestina de Biologia, Caderno de Estudos Regionais, Documentos (Folclore) e Revista CCS (Saúde), Revista Horizonte*† (quarterly).

Campus I—João Pessoa

58000 JOÃO PESSOA
Telephone: 224-7200.

DIRECTORS AND HEADS OF DEPARTMENTS:

Centre of Health Sciences: Dir. Prof. NOBERTO DE CASTRO NOGUEIRA FILHO.
Surgery: Prof. DOMILSON MAUL DE ANDRADE.
Health Science: Prof. PEDRO MADEIRA DE MELO.
Mother and Child Health: Prof. EDSON PETRUCCI.
Internal Medicine: Prof. FRANCISCO ASSIS DOS ANJOS PALITOT.
Nursing: Profa. REGINA R. BOTTO TARGINO.
Clinical Dentistry: Prof. ESPEDITO DE OLIVEIRA.
Restorative Dentistry: Prof. MARCOS GALVÃO BORGES.
Pharmaceutical Sciences: Profa. CONSUELO SIMÕES LOPES BRANCO.
Morphology: Profa. ANA MARIA SANTOS MACIEL.
Physiology and Pathology: Prof. CLÓCIO BELTRÃO DE ALBUQUERQUE.

Centre of Applied Social Sciences: Dir. Prof. CLAÚDIO SANTA CRUZ COSTA.
Economics: Prof. ANTÔNIO DE PÁDUA CÂMARA.
Administration: Prof. JOSÉ DE CARVALHO COSTA FILHO.
Library Science and Documentation: Profa. MARIA NEUSA DE MORAIS COSTA.
Finance and Accountancy: Prof. ERLON MACHADO GRISI.
Public Law: Prof. RÔMULO RANGEL.
Private Law: Prof. EDIGARDO FERREIRA SOARES.

Centre of Human Sciences, Letters and Arts: Dir. Prof. ALUÍSIO MARIA DE SOUZA.
Classical Literature: Profa. OTÍLIA IDALINA MAIA DE VASCONCELOS.
Modern Languages: Profa. MARIA GLÁUCIA VASCONCELOS COSTA.

Philosophy and History: Prof. Aluísio José Maria de Souza.
Social Sciences: Profa. Maria Lúcia Barbosa de Oliveira.
Social Service: Profa. Lusia Sinval Pinto.
Music: Profa. Ana Lúcia Altino Garcia.
Psychology: Prof. Tereza Neuma Cândido Pereira.
Arts and Communications: José Luíz Warren Jardim Gomes Braga.
History: Profa. Emília Augusta Lins Freire.

Centre of Education: Dir. Prof. Ivanildo Coêlho de Holanda.
Methods of Education: Prof. João Batista Lins Filho.
Introduction to Education: Prof. Carlos Fragoso Filho.
Pedagogic Habilitation: Prof. Lingoya Martins Correia.

Centre of Exact and Natural Sciences: Dir. Prof. Modesto Siebra Coelho.
Mathematics: Prof. Paulo Brito Braz e Silva.
Chemistry: Prof. Josué Eugênio Viana.
Physics: Prof. Júlio de Melo Texeira.
Biology: Prof. Francisco de Assis Fernandes de Carvalho.
Geo-sciences: Profa. Hilarina Maribondo de Araújo.

Technology Centre: Dir. Prof. Antônio Wanderley Moreira.
Civil Engineering: Prof. Geraldo Ramos Borba.
Mechanical Engineering: Prof. José Gonçalves de Almeida.
Chemical and Food Technology: Prof. Paulo Martins de Abreu.
Architecture: Prof. Marco Aurélio Andrade de Filgueiras Gomes.

Campus II—Campina Grande

58100 Campina Grande
Telephone: 321-0655.

Sciences and Technology Centre: Dir. Prof. Geraldo Nunes Sobrinho.
Electrical Engineering: Prof. Marcelo Agra Ramos.
Civil Engineering: Prof. Ademilson Montes Ferreira.
Mechanical Engineering: Prof. Williams Capim de Miranda.
Systems and Computers: Prof. Eratóstenes Edson R. de Araújo.
Mining and Geology: Prof. José Aderaldo M. Ferreira.
Agricultural Engineering: Prof. Hamilton Medeiros de Azevedo.
Atmospheric Sciences: Prof. Mário Adelmo Varejão Silva.
Chemical Engineering: Prof. Edielson de Aquino Santos.
Physics: Prof. Mirabeau Dias.
Mathematics and Statistics: Prof. Samuel Carvalho Duarte.

Human Sciences Centre: Dir. Prof. Ailton Elisiário de Souza.
Arts: Prof. Antonio José Madureira Ferreira.
Administration and Accountancy: Prof. Iraildo Gomes de Abreu.
Economy and Finance: Prof. Paulo Ortiz Rocha de Aragão.
Education and Human Sciences: Profa. Digelma Ribeiro Victor.
Sociology and Anthropology: Prof. Hermano Nepomuceno Araújo.

Biological Sciences and Health Centre: Dir. Prof. Firmino Brasileiro Silva.
Basic and Health Sciences: Prof. Luíz Magno Leite de Almeida.
Social and Preventive Internal Medicine: Prof. Antônio Galdino.
Clinical Surgery: Prof. Sebastião Carlos Coutinho.
Child and Maternal Health: Prof. Patricío Leal de Melo.

Campus III—Areia

58397 Areia
Telephone: 362-2218.

Agricultural Sciences Centre: Dir. Prof. Normando Melquíades de Araújo.
Soil and Rural Engineering: Prof. Carlos Barreto Alcoforado.
Animal Husbandry: Prof. Moacir Omena.
Crop Technology: Prof. Edvaldo Mesquita Beltrão.
Social and Fundamental Sciences: Prof. João José de Oliveira Filho.

Campus IV—Bananeiras

58220 Bananeiras
Telephone: 45-46.

Technologist Training Centre: Dir. Prof. Alírio Trinidade Leite.
Rural Technology: Prof. Paulo José dos Reis.
Basic and Social Sciences: Prof. Anedito Almeida de Freitas.

Campus V—Cajazeiras

58900 Cajazeiras
Telephone: 531-2146.

Teacher Training Centre: Dir. Prof. José Antônio de Albuquerque.
Education and Letters: Profa. Maria Nazaré Lopes Ferreira.
Exact and Social Sciences: Profa. Maria Leonília Albuquerque Machado Amorim.

Campus VI—Sousa

58800 Sousa
Telephone: 521-1816.

Co-ordinator: Prof. Vicente de Paula Nóbrega.
Law Sciences: Prof. Severino Ismael da Costa.

Campus VII—Patos

58700 Patos
Telephone: 421-3397.

Co-ordinator: Prof. José Lenilton de Carvalho.

UNIVERSIDADE CATÓLICA DO PARANÁ

RUA IMACULADA CONCEIÇÃO
1155, C.P. 2293, 80000 CURITIBA
Telephone: 223-0922, 224-9550.
Founded 1959.
Academic year: March to November (two semesters).

Rector: Osvaldo Arns.
Administrative Vice-President: Paulo Wodonos.
Academic Vice-President: José Cordún.
Community Vice-President: Potiguara Acácio Pereira.

Number of teachers: 489.
Number of students: 7,069.

Directors:

Centre for Humanities and Theological Studies: Leopoldo Scherner.
Centre for Judicial and Social Sciences: Francisco Cézar de Luca Pucci.
Centre for Pure and Applied Sciences: Firmino Bonato.
Centre for Biomedical Sciences: José Geraldo Lopes de Noronha.

UNIVERSIDADE FEDERAL DO PARANÁ

RUA 15 DE NOVEMBRO 1299,
CURITIBA, PARANÁ
Telephone: 34-5122.
Founded 1912.

Rector: Prof. Ocyron Cunha.
Vice-Rector: (vacant).
Chief Administrative Officer: Econ. Alcino Miguel de Amorim.
Librarian: Maria Augusta de Castro Correia.

Libraries: *see* Libraries.
Number of teachers: 1,740.
Number of students: 14,393.

Publications: *Acta Biológica Paranaense, Anais de Medicina, Boletim, Cadernos de Artes e Tradições Populares, Fastos Universitários, Floresta, Letras*, etc.

Directors:

Agriculture: Prof. Luiz C. Nascimento Tourinho.
Biological Sciences: Prof. Mílton Miró Vernalha.
Exact Sciences: Prof. Orlando Silveira Pereira.
Humanities, Letters and Arts: Profa. Cecília Maria Westphalen.
Health Sciences: Prof. Ernani Simas Alves.
Applied Social Sciences: Prof. Othelo Werneck Lopes.
Education: Profa. Zélia Milléo Pavão.
Technology: Prof. Antônio dos Santos Segui.

UNIVERSIDADE DE PASSO FUNDO

BAIRRO SÃO JOSÉ, C.P. 566,
99100 PASSO FUNDO,
RIO GRANDE DO SUL

Telephone: 312-3154.

Founded 1968.

Private control; Academic year: March to November (two semesters).

Rector: Dr. BRUNO EDMUNDO MARKUS.
Academic Vice-Rector: ELYDO ALCIDES GUARESCHI.
Administrative Vice-Rector: Dr. MURILO COUTINHO ANNES.
Registrar: Prof. EMILIO TRENTIN.
Librarian: NELCIR ANTONIAZZI.

Number of teachers: 400.
Number of students: 6,300.

Publications: Academic Guide, *Pesquisa sobre Aveia.*

DIRECTORS:

School of Education: Prof. ELLI BENINCÁ.
School of Physical Education: Profa. MARLENE M. F. DE SILVA.
School of Economics and Administration: Prof. BRUNO STEIDL.
School of Law: Prof. JORGE BUAES SOBRINHO.
School of Engineering: Prof. JOSÉ LEONEL THIES DA SILVA.
School of Agronomy: Prof. IRINEO FIOREZE.
School of Dentistry: Prof. ANTÔNIO AUGUSTO PRETTO.
School of Medicine: Prof. ANTÔNIO CARLOS MADALOSSO.
Institute of Philosophy and Humanities: Prof. PEDRO ALCINO BERVIAN.
Institute of Biological Sciences: Prof. JOSÉ CARLOS MORAES.
Institute of Exact and Geosciences: Prof. LUÍS EURICO SPALDING.
Institute of Arts: Profa. IVANILDE ANNA MARINI.

UNIVERSIDADE CATÓLICA DE PELOTAS

RUA FELIX DA CUNHA 412,
96.100 PELOTAS,
RIO GRANDE DO SUL

Telephone: 22-8274.

Founded 1960.

Chancellor: Dom JAYME HENRIQUE CHEMELLO.
Rector: Prof. CARLOS ALBERTO DE SOUZA VIANNA.
Pro-Rector (Academic): Prof. OSMI CUNHA DA ROSA.
Pro-Rector (Administrative): Prof. HENRIQUE WALNER ALVES FEIJÓ.
Librarian: VERA LUCIA MOTA.

Library of 34,800 vols

Number of teachers: 450.
Number of students: 5,182.

DEANS:

Centre of Biological Sciences and Health: Prof. ANTÔNIO ANTUNES PLANELLA.
Centre of Humanities: Prof. ARI DA SILVA DOS SANTOS.
Centre of Exact Sciences and Technology: Prof. ISIDORO HALPERN.

CO-ORDINATORS OF DEPARTMENTS:

Business Administration: Prof. THOMAZ LUCIA.
Biology: Profa. CECÍLIA BRUSQUE ISAACSSON.
Sciences: Profa. CECÍLIA BRUSQUE ISAACSSON.
Accounting: Prof. CARLOS P. SOUZA.
Communications: Prof. JOAQUIM SALVADOR COELHO PINHO.
Civil Engineering: Prof. JOSÉ MABILDE RIPOLL.
Electrical Engineering: Prof. GILBERTO LOPES.
Social Studies: Profa. MAGALI MAYER DOS SANTOS.
Pharmacy and Biochemistry: Profa. MARIA DA GRAÇA DOS SANTOS RESÉM.
Philosophy: Prof. CLÁUDIO NEUTZLING.
Letters: Prof. OSCAR BRISOLARA.
Mathematics: Prof. LINO DE JESUS SOARES.
Medicine: Prof. GIL NEI MEDEIROS PINHEIRO.
Chemistry: Prof. TEODOR PILOWNIC.
Education: Profa. MARIA A. T. DE ARAÚJO.
Psychology: Prof. CARMEM MARIA MOREIRA ENDERLE.
Social Service: Prof. ADELINA BALDISSERA.

UNIVERSIDADE FEDERAL DE PELOTAS

CAMPUS UNIVERSITÁRIO,
96.100 PELOTAS,
RIO GRANDE DO SUL

Telephone: 21-0933, 21-0644.

Founded 1883 as Universidade Federal Rural do Rio Grande do Sul; present name 1969.

Rector: Prof. IBSEN WETZEL STEPHAN.
Vice-Rector: Prof. GUIDO KASTER.

Number of teachers: 849.
Number of students: 5,023.

Publication: *Boletim Administrativo da Reitoria.*

DIRECTORS:

Faculty of Agronomy: Prof. JOSÉ FRANCISCO PATELLA.
Faculty of Veterinary Studies: Prof. LUÍS FERNANDO CUNHA.
Faculty of Law: Prof. SILVINO JOAQUIM LOPES NETO.
Faculty of Dentistry: JÚLIO ELCH SILVEIRA.
Faculty of Medicine: Prof. CLÁUDIO BORBA GOMES.
Faculty of Domestic Science: Prof. ELIDA MINIONI.
School of Physical Education: Prof. PAULO ROBERTO BARCELLOS DE MELLO.
Faculty of Education: Prof. TEÓFILO ALVES GALVÃO.
Conservatory of Music: Prof. MARIA LEDA VERNETTI DOS SANTOS.
Institute of Letters and Arts: Profa. MYRIAM SOUZA ANSELMO.
Institute of Humanities: Prof. SÉRGIO ROMEU VIANNA DA CRUZ LIMA.
Institute of Physics and Mathematics: Prof. MÁRIO CAPANEMA ULYSSEA.
Institute of Chemistry and Geosciences: Prof. CARLOS ALBERTO PETIZ.
Institute of Biology: Prof. FRANCISCO CARLOS FARIA.
Agricultural Technology Team: Prof. FRANCISCO MOREIRA.

UNIVERSIDADE CATÓLICA DE PERNAMBUCO

RUA DO PRÍNCIPE 526,
BOA VISTA, 50000 RECIFE,
PERNAMBUCO

Telephone: PA (B) X 231-3288.

Founded 1951.

Academic year: March to December (two semesters).

Chancellor: Fr. JOSÉ NOGUEIRA MACHADO, S.J.
Rector: Fr. ANTÔNIO GERALDO AMARAL ROSA, S.J.
Pro-Rectors: Fr. ANÍBAL DE SOUSA MELO, S.J. (Academic), Fr. PEDRO ALBERTO CAMPOS, S.J. (Administrative), Fr. FRANCISCUS ANTONIUS HAASEN, S.J. (Community Relations).
Librarian: Mrs. HELENA MARIA DE LOUVOR SOARES BORGES.

Number of teachers: 539.
Number of students: 11,176.

DEANS:

Centre of Social Sciences: Prof. ALUYZIO JOSÉ PEREIRA BRAGA.
Centre of Sciences and Technology: Prof. FERDINANDO PEREIRA RÊGO.
Centre of Theology and Human Sciences: Fr. PAULO GASPAR MENEZES, S.J.

UNIVERSIDADE FEDERAL DE PERNAMBUCO

AV. PROF. MORAES REGO S/N,
CIDADE UNIVERSITÁRIA,
RECIFE, PERNAMBUCO

Telephone: 081-2270444.

Founded 1946.

Academic year: March to December.

Rector: Geraldo Lafayette Bezerra.
Vice-Rector: (vacant).
Pro-Rector for Academic Affairs: Prof. George Browne do Rego.
Pro-Rector for Research and Post-graduate Affairs: Prof. Armando de Alburquer Souto Maior.
Pro-Rector for Planning: Prof. Sebastião Jorge Jatobá Bezerra dos Santos.
Pro-Rector for Administration: Prof. Marcos Dominigues da Silva.
Pro-Rector for Community Affairs: Prof. Merval Jurema.
Pro-Rector for Cultural Affairs and Scientific Exchange: Prof. Ruy João Marques.

Library: *see* **Libraries.**
Number of teachers: *c.* 2,277.
Number of students: *c.* 18,500.
Publication: *Boletim Oficial*†.

Directors and Heads of Departments:

Centre of Arts and Communication: Dir. Zildo Sena Caldas.
Art Theory and Artistic Expression: Carlos Borromeu Limeira de Melo.
Architecture and City Planning: Armindo Ângelo Leal da Costa.
Social Communication: (vacant).
Letters: Geraldo Calábria Lapenda.
Design: Severino José Cavalcanti Aragão Filho.
Librarianship: Maria das Graças de Lima Melo.

Centre of Exact and Natural Sciences: Dir. Roberto Figueiredo Ramalho de Azevedo.
Physics: Edmundo Antônio Soares.
Mathematics: Paulo Figueiredo Lima.
Statistics and Information: José Natal Figueiroa.
Chemistry: Alexandre Ricardo Pereira Schuler.

Centre of Biological Sciences: Dir. Francisco Décio de Andrade Lyra.
Anatomy: João Rodrigues de Sampaio.
Histology and Embryology: Fernando do Rêgo Barros e Albuquerque.
Biochemistry: Marcionilo de Barros Lins.
Biophysics and Radiobiology: Moacir de Almeida Carneiro Leão.
Physiology and Pharmacology: João Ribeiro de Vascolcelos Sobrinho.
General Biology: André Freire Furtado.
Mycology: José Américo de Lima.
Biology of Species: Geraldo Ramos de Almeida.
Antibiotics: Ivan Leôncio d'Albuquerque.

Centre of Philosophy and Humanities: Dir. Paulo da Silva Miranda.
Philosophy: Luíz Gonzage de Albuquerque Brito.
History: Potyguar Figueiredo Mattos.
Social Sciences: Osita Morais Pinto Ferreira.
Psychology: Lúcia Maria Bezerra Menezes.
Geography: Jeronimo Lemos de Freitas.

Education Centre: Dir. Alayde Gouveia Machado.
Socio-Philosophic Bases of Education: Marileide de Carvalho Costa.
Psychology and Educational Orientation: Rubem Eduardo da Silva.
School Administration and Educational Planning: Antônio Carolino Braule Gonçalves da Silva.
Teaching Methods and Techniques: José Alzir Corrêa Leite.

Centre of Applied Social Sciences: Dir. Amílcar de Oliveira Bezeera.
Administrative Sciences: Antônio Cavalcanti Neves.
Accountancy: José Araújo Filho.
Economics: Carlos Osório de Cerqueira.
Social Service: Anita Aline de Albuquerque Costa.

Centre of Health Sciences: Dir. Raimundo de Barros Coelho.
Mother and Child Health: Fernando José Simão dos Santos Figueira.
Clinical Medicine: Carlos Alberto Correia de Araújo.
Surgery: Edvaldo da Silva Telles.
Tropical Medicine: Márcio Lobo Jardim.
Neuro-Psychiatry: Galdino Loreto.
Pathology: Adonis Reis Lyra de Carvalho.
Social Medicine: Manoel Ricardo Costa Carvalho.
Pharmacy: Genisa de Castro Coitinho Bulhões.
Clinical and Preventive Odontology: Romildo Torres e Silva.
Prosthesis and Orofacial Surgery: Francisco de Albuquerque Barbosa.
Nutrition: Fernando José Costa de Aguiar.
Nursing: Maria Nilda de Andrade.
Physical Education: Delza Vasconcelos Pinheiro de Souza.
Rehabilitation: Geraldo Gomes de Freitas.

Technology Centre: Dir. Abelardo Cardoso Montenegro.
Cartographical Engineering: José Jorge de Seixas.
Civil Engineering: José Augusto Pitta Marinho.
Electrical Engineering and Potential Systems: Rômulo Maciel.
Mechanical Engineering: Euler da Silva Maia.
Mining Engineering: Ivan de Albuquerque Loureiro.
Chemical Engineering and Industrial Chemistry: Sebastião Beltrão de Castro.
Geology: Waldir Duarte da Costa.
Nuclear Energy: Clemente José Gusmão Carneiro da Silva.
Oceanography: Olímpio Carneiro da Silva.
Electronics and Systems: Carlos Egberto Andrade de Almeida Albuquerque.

Centre of Juridical Sciences (Faculty of Law): Dir. Francisco de Assis Rosa e Silva Sobrinho.
General and Procedural Law: Luíz Pinto Ferreira.
Public Law: Everardo da Cunha Luna.
General Theory of Law and Private Law: Mário Neves Baptista.

UNIVERSIDADE FEDERAL RURAL DE PERNAMBUCO

RUA D. MANUEL DE MEDEIROS S/N, DOIS IRMÃOS, C.P. 2071, 50.000 RECIFE, PE.
Founded 1954.

Rector: Naldo Halliday Pires Ferreira.

Library of 23,306 vols.
Number of teachers: 360.
Number of students: 4,000.

Heads of Departments:

Agriculture: José Nery da Silva Júnior.
Veterinary Medicine: Fernando Moreira da Silva.
Animal Husbandry: Manoel Francisco de Morais Cavalcanti.
Fishery: Luíz Gonzaga Gomes de Lira.
Education: Emmanuel do Carmo Barreto Campello.
Domestic Science: Inalda Xavier da Silva.
Physics and Mathematics: Milton Tavares Bezerra de Melo.
Chemistry: José Henrique Cavalcanti Pinto de Carvalheira.
Biology: Geraldo Pereira de Arruda.
Morphology and Animal Physiology: Euclides Feitosa Filho.
Letters and Humanities: Roberto Emerson Câmara Benjamim.
Rural Technology: Walderi Ribeiro.
"Dom Agostinho Ikas" Grade 2 College: Marly de Albuquerque Montenegro.

UNIVERSIDADE CATÓLICA DE PETRÓPOLIS

RUA BENJAMIN CONSTANT 213, CENTRO, C.P. 944, 25.600 PETRÓPOLIS, R.J.
Telephone: 42-5062.
Founded 1961.

Private control; Academic year: February to June, August to December.

Rector: JOSÉ FERNANDES VELOSO.
Vice-Rector: Prof. Dr. MANOEL MACHADO DOS SANTOS.
Administrative Officer: Prof. Dr. GETÚLIO CHEHAB.
Librarian: Sra. MARIA DAS NEVES FRANCA LEITE KRÜGER.

Number of teachers: 298.
Number of students: 4,200.

Publication: *Informativo U.C.P.*

DIRECTORS:

Faculty of Law: BENEDITO DE AGUIAR RIBEIRO.
Faculty of Economics, Accounting and Administration: Prof. NICOLAU VIEIRA NUNES.
Faculty of Education: Prof. HANNS LUDWIG LIPPMANN.
School of Engineering: Prof. GILBERTO GOMES DE ANDRADE.
School of Rehabilitation: Prof. Dr. GIORGIO MAZZANTINI.
Institute of Theology, Philosophy and Human Science: Prof. Mgr. GILBERTO FERREIRA DE SOUZA.
Institute of Exact and Natural Sciences: Prof. CARLOS ALBERTO MARTINS PINTO.
Institute of Arts and Communication: Profa. NORMA FONTES DE OLIVEIRA.

UNIVERSIDADE FEDERAL DO PIAUÍ

CAMPUS UNIVERSITÁRIO,
BAIRRO ININGA,
64000 TERESINA, PIAUÍ

Founded 1968.

Controlled by the Fundação Universidade Federal do Piauí.

Rector: Prof. JOSÉ CAMILLO DA SILVEIRA FILHO.
Administrative Director: Dr. BENJAMIN FIÚZA NETO.
Librarian: MARIA DAS GRAÇAS LEITE TARGINO.

Library of 64,812 vols.
Number of teachers: 805.
Number of students: 5,698.

Publication: *Notícias da FUFPI*† (monthly).

Faculties of Medicine, Dentistry, Law, Philosophy, Administration.

UNIVERSIDADE ESTADUAL DE PONTA GROSSA

PRAÇA SANTOS ANDRADE S/N,
84.100 PONTA GROSSA, PARANÁ

Telephone: 24-3966 (0422).

Academic year: March to June, August to November.

Founded 1970.

Rector: DANIEL ALBACH TAVARES.
Vice-Rector: WALDIR SILVA CAPOTE.
Administrative Officer: ALVARO BENEDITO DI PIERO.
Librarian: Prof. FARIS MICHAELE.

Number of teachers: 324.
Number of students: 3,517.

Publications: *Revista Uniletras, Catálogo Geral, Cadernos Universitários.*

DIRECTORS:

Sector of Exact and Natural Sciences: Prof. JOSÉ BITTENCOURT CRAVEIRO DE SÁ.
Sector of Letters and Human Sciences: Prof. JOSÉ HYCZY FONSECA.
Sector of Biological Sciences and Health: Prof. CASEMIRO TIBINKA.

HEADS OF DEPARTMENTS:

Mathematics and Physics: LUIZ RENATO BITTENCOURT.
Chemistry: ALCIONE BORGES DE ANDRADE.
Geosciences: FERNANDO PILATTI.
Engineering: NEY BATISTA ROSAS.
Biology: ALBERTO ESTEFANO GUILHERME KLOTH.
Odontological Sciences: HUMBERTO RENÊ FERNANDES.
Pharmaceutical Sciences and Clinical Analysis: AILTON ELIAS SCHAFRANSKI.
Education: ENI FERREIRA DE SILVA.
Economics and Administration: FLÁVIO JOSÉ CHIBINSKI.
Judicial Sciences: ANTÔNIO JOAQUIM DANTAS.
History: HELCIO DE OLIVEIRA LADEIRA.
Letters: SÉRGIO MONTEIRO ZAN.
Teaching Methods: LAURO FANCHIN.

FUNDAÇÃO UNIVERSIDADE DO RIO GRANDE

RUA LUIZ LORÉA 261,
96.200 RIO GRANDE,
RIO GRANDE DO SUL

Telephone: 2.10.92.

Founded 1969; private control.

Rector: Prof. FERNANDO LOPES PEDONE.
Vice-Rector for Administration: Prof. ALBERTO JOSÉ MEIRELLES LEITE.
Vice-Rector for Teaching and Research: Prof. HENRIQUE DA COSTA BERNARDELLI.
Vice-Rector for Planning and Development: Eng. VIDAL ÁUREO MENDONÇA.

Library of 56,000 vols.
Number of teachers: 490.
Number of students: 3,476.

HEADS OF DEPARTMENTS:

Mathematics: Prof. ALFREDO WEBER.
Physics: Prof. ODILON GOMES.
Chemistry: Prof. JÚLIO CARLOS REGULY.
Geosciences: Prof. WANDER VALENTE.
Letters and Arts: Profa. NÚBIA TOURRUCOO FONSECA.
Economics, Administration and Accountancy: Prof. FELÍCIO LEITE.
Juridical Sciences: Prof. JORGE DA CUNHA AMARAL.
Materials and Construction: Prof. PEDRO SIEDERSBERGER.
Librarianship and History: Profa. CARMEN HELENA BRAZ MIRCO.
Education and Behavioural Sciences: Profa. MARÍLIA RACHE FARAL.
Oceanography: Prof. ANTÔNIO RENATO VIDAL LADEIRA.
Surgery: Prof. AIRTON JORGE VARELA.
Mother and Child Health: Prof. LUÍZ CARLOS DE MELLO ESPERON.
Internal Medicine: Prof. JAIME CUARTAS PALÁCIO.
Morphology (Biology): Prof. JOABER PEREIRA JR.
Physiology: Prof. FERNANDO AMARANTE SILVA.
Pathology: Prof. CARLOS ALBERTO CUELLO LOPES.

UNIVERSIDADE FEDERAL DO RIO GRANDE DO NORTE

CAMPUS UNIVERSITÁRIO
S/N, 59000 NATAL, RN

Telephone: (084) 231-1266.

Founded 1958.

Federal control.

Academic year: March to June, August to December.

Rector: DIOGENES DA CUNHA LIMA FILHO.
Vice-Rector: CLÓVIS GONÇALVES DOS SANTOS.
Administrative Officer: ANA MARIA GUERRA.
Librarian: ZILA DA COSTA MAMEDE.

Number of teachers: 2,000.
Number of students: 14,000.

DEANS:

Exact Sciences: TEREZINHA DE ALMEIDA FREITAS.
Humanities, Letters and Arts: JARDELINO DE LUCENA FILHO.
Technology: FERNANDO ANTÔNIO DA NOBREGA.
Applied Social Sciences: PAULO FERNANDES SOARES DE SOUZA.
Bio-Sciences: JOSÉ ARIBALDO DE CARVALHO.
Health Sciences: CLÁUDIO MOREIRA CAMPOS.

HEADS OF DEPARTMENTS AND PROFESSORS:

Exact Sciences:
FELIPE DA TRINDADE, J., Mathematics
MOACIR SOARES, M., Chemistry
PEREIRA, M., Physics
PESSOA LIRA LINS, F. A., Geology

Humanities, Letters and Arts:
BASTOS PINHEIRO, W. J., Letters
MELQUÍADES MACEDO, J., Centre for Brazilian Studies
MOTA DE LUCENA, R., Social Studies
OLIVEIRA, D. DE, Philosophy, History and Geography
PINTO GALVÃO, C., Arts

Technology:
LAMARTINE NETTO., J. Agriculture
LIMA DE GOIS, R., Architecture

Nóbrega, F. A. da, Mechanical and Chemical Engineering
Silva Filho, H. X. da, Electrical Engineering
Victorio, M., Civil Engineering

Applied Social Sciences:
Dantas, A., Economics
Felippes Oliveira Afonso, D. de, Education
Pires de Azevedo Maia, N., Public Law
Queiroz Aranha, T. de, Social Services
Rios, C., Administration and Accounting
Sampaio Marinho, A., Private Law

Bio-Sciences:
Ferreira Bezerra, J., Biology
Monte, S., Oceanography and Limnology

Health Sciences:
Barbosa Cunha, D., Nutrition
Caldas Moura, E., Orthopaedics
Coelho, O. S., Nursing
Costa, P. G., Physical Education
Costa Ferreira, J. M. da, Surgery
Dantas Cavalcanti, J., General Dentistry
Ferreira Bezerra, H., Paediatrics
Galvão Neto, C., Clinical Dentistry
Januário de Souza, M., Restorative Dentistry
Lemos Vieira, A., Pharmacy
Lourdes Xavier, M. de, Pharmaceutics and Food Technology
Marinho Medeiros de Albuquerque, L., Toxic and Clinical Analyses
Medeiros Rocha, L. V. de, Blood Bank
Morais, L., Gynaecology
Oliveira Sales, G. de, Pathology and Public Health
Pinheiro Wanderley, J. G., Clinical Medicine

UNIVERSIDADE REGIONAL DO RIO GRANDE DO NORTE

PRAÇA MIGUEL FAUSTINO S/N,
59600 MOSSORÓ, RN

Founded 1968.

Rector: Dr. Elder Heronildes da Silva.

Number of teachers: *c.* 120.
Number of students: *c.* 1,800.

Faculties of Economics, Education and Social Services; Institutes of Humanities, Arts and Letters; School of Agriculture.

PONTIFÍCIA UNIVERSIDADE CATÓLICA DO RIO GRANDE DO SUL

AVDA. IPIRANGA 6681,
CAIXA POSTAL 1429,
90.000 PÔRTO ALEGRE

Telephone: 239400.

Founded 1948.

Private control; Academic year: March to December.

Chancellor: Cardinal Alfredo Vicente Scherer.
Vice-Chancellor: **Mgr. Otto Skrsypzak.**
Rector: Prof. Ir. Norberto Francisco Rauch.
Vice-Rector: Prof. Ir. Liberato.
Head of Administration: Prof. Eurico Saldanha de Lemos.
Librarian: **Ir. Dionísio Fuertes Alvarez.**

Number of teachers: 1,540.
Number of students: 21,000.

Publications: *Veritas*†, *Letras de Hoje*†, *Boletim Informativo do IESPE*, *Teocomunicação*† (quarterly), *Anuário*†, *Mundo Jovem* (monthly), *Estudos Ibera-Americanos*† (2 a year), *Direito e Justiça* (2 a year).

DIRECTORS:

Faculty of Education: Prof. Ir. Armando Luíz Bortolini.
Faculty of Economics and Political *Sciences:* Prof. João Pedro Ranquetat Papaléo.
Faculty of Law: Prof. Roberto Geraldo Coelho Silva.
Faculty of Medicine: **Prof. José J. M. Martins.**
Faculty of Dentistry: **Prof. Francisco A. B. Lacroix.**
Faculty of Social Communications Media: **Prof. Antônio F. O. Gonzalez.**
Faculty of Zootechnics: **Prof. Hamilton Vilela.**
Faculty of Social Service: **Prof. Norma Z. Prates.**
Institute of Psychology: **Prof. Ir.** Henrique Justo.
Institute of Philosophy and Humanities: Prof. Pe. Urbano Zilles.
Polytechnic School: Prof. Inácio Vincente Berlitz.
Institute of Geosciences: **Geraldo Hoffmann.**
Institute of Physics: Prof. Antônio Dias Nunes.
Institute of Mathematics: **Prof. Antônio Bianchi.**
Institute of Chemistry: Prof. Ivo Vedana.
Institute of Biosciences: Prof. Francisco Alfredo Jardim.
Institute of Theology: Prof. Pe. Frei Angelo Domingos Salvador.
Institute of Letters and Arts: **Prof. Ir.** Mainar Longhi.
Faculty of Accountancy and Administration: Prof. Roberto Peró de Souza.
Faculty of Philosophy: Prof. Juarez Hernandez.
Institute of Informatics: Profa. Maria Lucia B. Lisbôa.

UNIVERSIDADE FEDERAL DO RIO GRANDE DO SUL

AVENIDA PAULO GAMA S/N,
90.000 PÔRTO ALEGRE,
RIO GRANDE DO SUL

Telephone: 21-70-33.

Founded 1934.

Federal control; Language of instruction: Portuguese; Academic year: March to November (2 semesters).

Rector: Homéro Só Jobim.
Pro-Rectors: Gerhard Jacob (Research and Postgraduates), Luiz Carlos de Mesquita Rothmann (Undergraduates), Francisco Luiz dos Santos Ferraz (Planning), Manoel Marques Leite (Administration), Ernesto Alfredo Preussler (Extension), Jorge Honório M. Brito (University Community).
Registrar: Attico Inacio Chassot.
Librarian: Heloisa Benetti Schreiner.

Number of teachers: 2,247.
Number of students: 17,000.

Publication: *Informativo da UFRGS.*

DIRECTORS:

Faculty of Law: **Fernando Jorge Schneider.**
Faculty of Economic Sciences: Francisco Machado Carrion.
Faculty of Medicine: Carlos Candal dos Santos.
Faculty of Architecture: Newton Silveira Obino.
Faculty of Dentistry: Paulo Pereira Louro Filho.
Faculty of Pharmacy: Sérgio de Meda Lamb.
Faculty of Agriculture: João Ruy Jardim Freire.
Faculty of Veterinary Medicine: João Carlos Athayde Dias.
Faculty of Education: Gilberto Mucilo Medeiros.
Faculty of Librarianship and Communication: Fernando José Pinto Guerreiro.
School of Engineering: Franklin George Gross.
School of Physical Education: Edemundo da Rocha Vieira.
School of Nursing: Vani Maria Chika Faraon.
Institute of Arts: Luiz Paulo Vasconcelos.
Institute of Biological Sciences: Aloy Julius Garcia.
Institute of Chemistry: Solon Vieira Marques.
Institute of Food Technology: Ruth Wiedemann Velloso.
Institute of Geological Sciences: Jorge Alberto Willwock.
Institute of Hydraulic Research: Egydio Hervé Filho.
Institute of Letters: Walter Koch.
Institute of Mathematics: Japyr do Carmo.
Institute of Philosophy and Social Sciences: Dante de Laytano.
Institute of Physics: Milthon José Cunha.

PONTIFÍCIA UNIVERSIDADE CATÓLICA DO RIO DE JANEIRO

RUA MARQUÊS DE SÃO VICENTE 225,
22.453 RIO DE JANEIRO, RJ.

Telephone: 274-9922.

Founded 1940.

Private control; Language of instruction: Portuguese; Academic year: March to July, August to December.

Grand Chancellor: His Eminence D. Eugênio de Araújo Sales, The Cardinal Archbishop of Rio de Janeiro.

Rector: Rev. Fr. João A. Amazonas MacDowell, s.j.

Vice-Rectors: Prof. Luiz Bevilacqua, Rev. Fr. José Carlos de Lima Vaz, s.j., Dr. Ronaldo Barcelos de Pinho, Prof. Heitor Herrera.

Registrar: Prof. Hermes Junqueira Gonçalves.

Librarian: Profa. Suzana Gonçalves.

Library: 122,506 vols.
Number of teachers: 1,030.
Number of students: 10,025.

Publications: *Verbum*† (quarterly), *Boletim da PUC* (weekly), *Anuário*.

Deans:

Social Sciences Centre: Rev. Fr. Spencer Custodio Filho, s.j.

Theology and Human Sciences Centre: Rev. Fr. Manuel Bouzon.

Technical and Scientific Centre: Prof. Alceu Gonçalves de Pinho.

Medical Centre: Prof. Dr. Luiz César Póvoa.

Heads of Departments:

Theology and Human Sciences Centre:

Theology: Rev. Alfonso García Rúbio.

Philosophy: Prof. Carlos Alberto Gomes dos Santos.

Education: Profa. Tereza Penna Firme.

Psychology: Prof. Terezinha Feres Carneiro.

Letters: Profa. Maria Cândida Diaz Bordenave.

Arts: Profa. Irma Arestizábal.

Social Sciences Centre:

History and Geography: Prof. Antônio Edimilson M. Rodrigues.

Sociology and Political Science: Rev. Luiz Garcia de Sousa, s.j.

Economics: Prof. Thomas Schneider.

Law: Rev. Spencer Custodio Filho, s.j.

Communications: Prof. Miguel Serpa Pereira.

Social Work: Profa. Arlete Alves Lima.

Business Administration: Prof. Paulo César Motta.

Technical and Scientific Centre:

Mathematics: Prof. Nathan M. dos Santos.

Physics: Prof. Carlos Mauricio Ferreira Chaves.

Chemistry: Prof. João J. Rotiles Fraústo.

Computer Science: Prof. Carlos José Pereira de Lucena.

Civil Engineering: Prof. Erlane F. Soares.

Electrical Engineering: Prof. Paulo Manassi Osório.

Mechanical Engineering: Prof. Sidney Stuckenbruck.

Metallurgical Engineering: Prof. Fernando Rizzo Assunção.

Industrial Engineering: Prof. Nelio Domingues Pizzolato.

Directors of Attached Institutes:

Institute of Business Administration and Management: Prof. Paulo César Motta.

Centre for the Study of Urbanism and Housing: (vacant).

Institute of International Relations: Prof. Luís Gonzaga Souza Lima.

Institute of Applied Psychology: Profa. Cláudia Garcia.

Centre for Telecommunications Research: Prof. José Paulo de Albuquerque.

Rio Data Centre (Computer Centre): Prof. Leonardo Junqueira Lustosa.

Dentistry Institute (Post-graduate): Prof. Orandino Prado Filho.

Post-graduate Medical School: Prof. Dr. Ivan Lemgruber.

UNIVERSIDADE DO ESTADO DO RIO DE JANEIRO

RUA SÃO FRANCISCO XAVIER 524,
MARACAÑA ZC11 CEP 20,000,
RIO DE JANEIRO, R.J.
Telephone: 234-2130.

Founded 1950.

State control; Language of instruction: Portuguese; Academic year: March to December (two Semesters).

Chancellor: A. P. de Chagas Freitas.

Vice-Chancellor: Arnoldo Niskier.

Rector: Prof. Caio Tácito.

General Administrative Director: Dra. Nira de Castilho.

Librarian: Wanda Coelho da Silva.

Number of teachers: 1,126.
Number of students: 12,059.

Publications: *Jornal*†, *Boletim*†.

Sector Directors:

Bio-medical Centre: Prof. Italo Suassuna.

Education and Humanities Centre: Prof. A. Niskier.

Technology and Science Centre: Prof. João Salim Miguel.

Social Science Centre: Prof. Marcílio Marques Moreira.

Deans:

Training College of Faculty of Philosophy, Sciences and Letters: Profa. Maria Lúcia Weiss.

Faculty of Nursing: Profa. Alaíde Bittencourt Duarte.

Faculty of Education: Profa. Heloisa M. Cardozo da Silva.

Faculty of Social Services: Prof. Aquiles Cortes Guimarães.

Faculty of Administration and Finances: Prof. Moacyr Parente Viana.

Faculty of Economic Sciences: Profa. M. da Conceição Miragaio Pitanga.

Faculty of Medical Sciences: Prof. Italo Suassuna.

Faculty of Law: Prof. Oscar Dias Correia.

Faculty of Engineering: Prof. Darcy Aleixo Deremusson.

Faculty of Dentistry: Prof. Charley Fayal de Lyra.

Institute of Mathematics and Statistics: Prof. Paulo Viveiros.

Institute of Physics: Prof. João Salim Miguel.

Institute of Psychology and Social Communication: Profa. Yonne Moniz Reis.

Institute of Design and Applied Arts: Profa. Carmen Porticulo.

Institute of Social Medicine: Prof. Nelson L. de A. Moraes.

Institute of Biology: Prof. Roberto A. Gomes.

Institute of Philosophy and Letters: Prof. Evanildo Cavalcanti Bechara.

Institute of Humanities: Prof. Pedro Freire Ribeiro.

Institute of Chemistry: Prof. Ayrton Luíz Gonçalves.

Institute of Geosciences: Prof. Miguel Alves de Lima.

UNIVERSIDADE FEDERAL DO RIO DE JANEIRO

ILHA DA CIDADE UNIVERSITÁRIA,
RIO DE JANEIRO
Telephone: 2-607491.

Founded 1920.

Rector: Prof. Luíz Renato Caldas.

Vice-Rector: Prof. George Doyle Maia.

Secretary-General: Dr. Jorge de Freitas Góes.

Director of Central Library: Amélia Rosauro de Almeida.

22 Faculty Libraries.
Number of teachers: 3,241.
Number of students: 37,678.

Publications: *Anais*, *Boletim*.

Deans and Directors:

Mathematics and Natural Sciences Centre: Prof. Paulo Emidio de Freitas Barbosa.

Institute of Biology: Dir. Prof. Aluisio Melo Leitão.

Institute of Physics: Dir. Prof. Eugênio Lerner.

Institute of Geosciences: Dir. Prof. Ignacio Aureliano Machado Brito.

Institute of Mathematics: Dir. Prof. Annibal Parracho Sant'Anna.

Institute of Chemistry: Dir. Prof. Warner Bruce Kover.

Letters and Arts Centre: Prof. ADOLPHO POLILLO.
Faculty of Architecture and Town Planning: Dir. Prof. DARCY BOVE DE AZEVEDO.
Faculty of Letters: Profa. HELENA PARENTE CUNHA (acting).
School of Fine Arts: Dir. Prof. ALMIR PAREDES CUNHA.
School of Music: Dir. Prof. MARIA L DE M. PRIOLLI.

Centre of Philosophy and Human Sciences: Prof. ALBERT EBERT (acting).
Faculty of Education: Dir. LYDINÉA GASMAN.
School of Communications: Dir. Prof. HEITOR PIEDADE DE ASSIS (a.i.).
School of Social Services: Dir. Prof. ANNA S. DE A. FURTADO.
Institute of Philosophy and Social Sciences: Prof. JOSÉ SILVEIRA DA COSTA.
Institute of Psychology: Dir. Prof. ANTÔNIO GOMES PENNA.

Technology Centre: Prof. CARLOS ALBERTO COSENZA.
School of Engineering: Dir. Prof AMARANTO LOPES PEREIRA.
School of Chemistry: Dir. Prof. JOSÉ DE ABREU COUTINHO.
Institute of Electronics: Dir. Prof. PAULO R. LIMA.
Experimental and Metrology Unit: Dir. Prof. GUSTAVO FERRAN LOURENTE.

Law and Economic Sciences Centre: Prof. OSCAR D. CORRÊA.
Faculty of Law: CAIO MARIO MEIRA DE VASCONCELLOS.
Faculty of Economics and Administration: Prof. WINSTON FRITSCHE.
Urban and Regional Planning Unit: Dir. Prof. NESTOR DE OLIVEIRA JUNIOR.

Medical Sciences Centre: Prof. BRUNO ALIPIO LOBO.
Institute of Biomedical Sciences: Dir. Prof. LAURO SOLLERO.
Anna Nery School of Nursing: Dir. Profa. CILEI CHAVES RHODUS.
Faculty of Pharmacy: Dir. Prof EMILIO DINIZ SILVA.
Faculty of Medicine: Dir. Prof. JOSÉ DE PAULA LOPES PONTES.
Institute of Microbiology: Dir. Prof. JOÃO CIRIBELLI GUIMARÃES.
Institute of Nutrition: Dir. Prof. SONIA MOREIRA ALVES DE SOUZA.
Faculty of Dentistry: Dir. Prof. CARLOS DE SOUZA TELES.
School of Physical Education and Sport: Dir. FERNANDA BARRUSO BELTRÃO.
Institute of Biophysics: Dir. Prof. EDUARDO P. FRANCA.
Institute of Gynaecology: Dir. Prof. ALIPIO A. CAMELO.
Institute of Neurology: Dir. Prof. BERNARDO H. DE N. COUTO.
Institute of Psychiatry: Dir. Prof. EUSTACHIO P. NUNES FILHO.
Institute of Child Health: Profa. DALVA COUTINHO SAYEG.
Institute of Phthisiology and Pneumology: Dir. Prof. LUIZ MÁRIO DA MOTA.

UNIVERSIDADE FEDERAL RURAL DO RIO DE JANEIRO

KM.47 DA ANTIGA RODOVIA RIO/SÃO PAULO, 23.460 SEROPÉDICA, ITAGUAÍ, RJ

Founded 1944 as the Universidade Rural do Brazil. State control.

Language of instruction: Portuguese.
Telephone: (021) 767-3134.

Rector: ARTHUR O. LOPEZ DA COSTA.
Vice-Rector: VICENTE DE PAULO GRAÇA.
Secretary: LAFAIETE ARAÚJO.
Dean (Undergraduates): HERCÍLIO VATER FARIA.
Dean (Post-graduates): ALFREDO CÉSAR DO NASCIMENTO FILHO.
Librarian: ALMIRA L. DE ALBUQUERQUE.

Library of 46,343 vols.
Number of teachers: 611.
Number of students: 4,500.
Publications: *Agronomia, Arquivos* (every 2 months).

DIRECTORS:

Institute of Veterinary Science: SIGISMUNDO CARLOS DE ANDRADE.
Institute of Animal Husbandry: NEI QUEIROZ SILVA.
Institute of Biology: ADRIANO LÚCIO PERACCHI.
Institute of Education: GUILHERMINO COSTA DA SOUZA.
Institute of Social Science: HENRIQUE BOSCHI.
Institute of Forestry: LAYETTE E. R. DE MELLO.
Institute of Technology: GLÊNIO CAVALCANTI DE BARROS.
Institute of Exact Sciences: JAMIL CORRÊA MOURÃO.
Institute of Agronomy: DORACY PESSOA RAMOS.

UNIVERSIDADE CATÓLICA DO SALVADOR

PRAÇA 2 DE JULHO 7, 40.000 CAMPO GRANDE, SALVADOR, BAHIA

Telephone: 245-2292.

Founded 1961.

Private control; Languages of instruction: Portuguese, French, English.

Chancellor: Cardinal Dom AVELAR BRANDÃO VILELA.
Rector: Mons. EUGÊNIO DE ANDRADE VEIGA.
Vice-Rector: Prof. Dr. JOSÉ SIMÕES E SILVA, Jr.
Librarian: SONIA RODRIGUES.

Number of teachers: 550.
Number of students: 11,000.

DIRECTORS:

Faculty of Education: Prof. ELZA P. SANTANA.
School of Social Services: Profa. LILIANA MERCURI ALMEIDA.
School of Business Administration: Prof. GYLSON SAMPAIO SILVA.
Faculty of Law: Prof. MANOEL RIBEIRO.
Faculty of Philosophy and Human Sciences: Prof. FRANCISCO P. LIMA Jr.
Faculty of Nursing: Profa. CARMÉLIA S. NEVES.
Institute of Sciences: Prof. JOSÉ S. E SILVA Jr.
Institute of Theology: Prof. Fr. JAN DE BIE.
School of Engineering: Prof. ALCEU R. HILTNER.
Institute of Letters: Prof. RAYMOND VAN DER HAGEN.
Institute of Music: Profa. MARIA D. C. DE B. P. DE ALMEIDA.

UNIVERSIDADE FEDERAL DE SANTA CATARINA

CAMPUS UNIVERSITÁRIO, TRINDADE, C.P. 476, 88.000 FLORIANÓPOLIS, S.C.

Telephone: 33-1000, 33-1001.

Founded 1960.

Federal control; Language of instruction: Portuguese; Academic year: March to June, August to November.

Rector: Prof. CASPAR ERICH STEMMER.
Vice-Rector: Prof. ROLDÃO CONSONI.
Chief Administrative Officer: Prof. JOÃO LINHARES.
Librarian: Profa. AMÉLIA SILVEIRA.

Number of teachers: 1,249.
Number of students: 9,113.
Publications: *Graduate Catalogue*†, *Postgraduate Catalogue*†, *Rector's Annual Report*†, *Personnel Bulletin*†.

DEANS:

Agrarian Sciences Centre: Prof. JOSÉ ANTÔNIO RIBEIRO.
Engineering and Technology Centre: Prof. SÉRGIO ROBERTO ARRUDA.
Bio-Medical Sciences Centre: Prof. ARTHUR PEREIRA E OLIVEIRA.
Social and Economic Sciences Centre: Prof. ANTÔNIO ADOLFO LISBOA.
Education Centre: Prof. ANTÔNIO CÉSAR BECKER.
Physical Education Centre: Prof. ERNESTO VAHL FILHO.
Arts Centre: Prof. MÁRIO FEITEN.
Physics and Mathematics Centre: Prof. PEDRO JOSÉ BOSCO.
Biological Sciences Centre: Prof. CARLOS ARAMI D. DA SILVA.
Human and Social Sciences Centre: Prof. NEREU DO VALLE PEREIRA.

UNIVERSIDADE PARA O DESENVOLVIMENTO DO ESTADO DE SANTA CATARINA

CAMPUS UNIVERSITÁRIO,
RUA MADRE BENVENUTA S/N
ITACOROBI, 88000
FLORIANÓPOLIS, SC
Telephone: 33-2000.

Founded 1966.

Rector: LAURO RIBAS ZIMMER.
Administrative Director: FERNANDO FERNANDES DE AQUINO.

Library of 20,000 vols.

Number of teachers: *c.* 300.
Number of students: 2,523.

DIRECTORS:

Faculty of Education: TERESINHA ISABEL MANSO MUNIZ.
School of Administration: ALEXANDRE FRANCISCO IGNÁCIO EVANGELISTA.
Faculty of Engineering (Joinville): PAULO MALSCHITZKY.
School of Physical Education: ÉRICO STRÄTZ, Jr.
Higher School of Veterinary Medicine (Lages): RHENO ROGÉRIO VIEIRA.

UNIVERSIDADE FEDERAL DE SANTA MARIA

PAIXA DE CAMOBI, KM.9,
EDIF. DA ADM. CENTRAL,
97100 SANTA MARIA, RS
Telephone: (055) 221-16-16.

Founded 1960.

Federal (Government) control; Academic year: March to December (two semesters).

President: Prof. Dr. DERBLAY GALVÃO.
Vice-Presidents: ARMANDO VALLANDRO; ZOZYMO LOPES DOS SANTOS (Postgraduate and Research); SÉRGIO CARVALHO BERNARDES (Graduation); AYRTON VALLANDRO MARÇAL (Students); WALTER ANTONINHO BIANCHINI (Extension); MARIA WARDEREZA SCHMIDT (Planning); JOSÉ ANTÔNIO FERNANDES (Administration).
Chief, President's Office: GEOLAR BADKE.
Librarian: ELOISA FRANZEN.

Library of 61,129 vols.

Number of teachers: 1,378.
Number of students: 9,374.

Publications: *Relatório Geral, Catálogo Geral, O Quero-Quero.*

DIRECTORS OF CENTRES:

Technology: GILBERTO A BENETTI.
Arts and Letters: LIA CECHELLA ACHUTTI.
Rural Sciences: HÉLIO POST.
Education: OLINDO A TOALDO.
Physical Education: HAIMO FENSTERSEIFER.
Health Sciences: ELIAS OLIVEIRA.
Social and Human Sciences: PEDRO L. AGUIRRE.
Natural and Exact Sciences: CLANDIO M. ROCHA.

UNIVERSIDADE FEDERAL DE SÃO CARLOS

VIA WASHINGTON LUÍZ,
KM. 235, C.P. 676,
13560 SÃO CARLOS,
SÃO PAULO
Telephone: (0162) 71-8111.

Founded 1970.

Federal control; Language of instruction: Portuguese; Academic year: March to December.

Rector: Prof. Dr. WILLIAM SAAD HOSSNE.
Vice-Rector: Prof. Dr. EDISON PEREIRA DOS SANTOS.
General Secretary: LUÍZ RENATO SOUZA.
Librarian: CLAUDETE C. SACOMANO.

Number of teachers: 403.
Number of students: 1,798.

DIRECTORS:

Sciences and Technology Centre: Prof. Dr. ODELAR LEITE LINHARES.
Education and Human Sciences Centre: Prof. PAOLO NOZELLA.
Health Science Centre: Prof. Dr. PEDRO MAGALHÃES LACAVA.

HEADS OF DEPARTMENTS:

Computation: T. C. G. LAZZARINI.
Materials Engineering: J. R. G. SILVA.
Chemical Engineering: O. B. DUARTE FILHO.
Production Engineering: L. R. F. COSTA.
Physics: L. C. SANTANNA FILHO.
Mathematics: N. A. MOLFETTA.
Chemistry: A. P. P. TOLEDO.
Education Technology: F. F. SISTO.
Education: B. R. MORAES NETO.
Biology: M. A. MARINS.
Health: H. KRIEGER.

UNIVERSIDADE DE SÃO PAULO

CIDADE UNIVERSITÁRIA,
C.P. 8191, SÃO PAULO, SP
Telephone: 211-00-11.
Telex: 21.519.

Founded 1934.

State control; Academic year: March to November.

Rector: Prof. Dr. WALDYR MUNIZ OLIVA.
Vice-Rector: Prof. Dr. ANTONIO BRITO DA CUNHA.
Secretary-General: Dr. JOSÉ GERALDO SOARES DE MELLO.
Librarian: (vacant).

Library: *see* Libraries.

Number of teachers: 4,461.
Number of students: 44,159.

Publications: *Revista Da Faculdade de Direito*† (annually), *Revista de Farmácia e Bioquímica da USP*† (2 a year), *Revista de História*† *Revista de Saúde Pública*†, *Africa* (quarterly), *Folia Clinica et Biológica*† (bi-monthly), *Revista da Faculdade de Medicina Veterinária e Zootecnia*† (annually), *Revista da Faculdade de Odontologia da USP*† (2 a year), *Revista da Escola de Enfermagem da USP*† (2 a year), *Anais da Escola Superior de Agricultura Luiz de Queiroz*† (annually), *Anuário Astronómico*† (annually).

DEANS:

Faculty of Law: Prof. Dr. ANTÔNIO CHAVES.
Faculty of Medicine: Prof. Dr. MÁRIO RAMOS DE OLIVEIRA.
Faculty of Philosophy, Letters and Human Sciences: Prof. Dr. ERWIN THEODOR ROSENTHAL.
Faculty of Pharmaceutical Sciences: Prof. Dr. DURVAL MAZZEI NOGUEIRA.
Faculty of Dentistry: Prof. Dr. ANTÔNIO ADAMASTOR CORRÊA.
Faculty of Veterinary Medicine and Zootechnics: Prof. Dr. FERNANDO VARELLA DE CARVALHO.
Faculty of Public Health: Prof. Dr. OSVALDO FORATINI.
Faculty of Architecture and Town Planning: Prof. Dr. ARIOSTO MILA.
Faculty of Medicine (Ribeirão Prêto): Prof. Dr. JOSÉ EDUARDO DUTRA DE OLIVEIRA.
Faculty of Dentistry (Bauru): Prof. Dr. LUÍZ CASATI ÁLVARES.
Faculty of Education: Prof. Dr. MOYSÉS BREJON.
School of Communication and Arts: Prof. Dr. ANTÔNIO GUIMARÃES FERRI.
Polytechnic School: Prof. Dr. ANTÔNIO HÉLIO GUERRA VIEIRA.
'Luíz de Queiroz' Higher School of Agriculture: Prof. Dr. ARISTEU MENDES PEIXOTO.
School of Nursing: Prof. CARLOS DA SILVA LACAZ.
School of Nursing (Ribeirão Prêto): Prof. Dr. ALBERTO RAUL MARTINEZ.
School of Engineering (São Carlos): Prof. Dr. SWAMI VILELLA.
School of Physical Education: Prof. Dr. JARBAS GONÇALVES.
Institute of Bio-sciences: Prof. DIVA DINIZ CORRÊA.
Institute of Biomedical Sciences: Prof. Dr. JOSÉ CARNEIRO DA SILVA FILHO.
Institute of Physics: Prof. Dr. MOISÉS NUSSENZVEIG.
Institute of Geophysics and Astronomy: Prof. Dr. ADOLPHO JOSÉ MELFI.
Institute of Mathematics and Statistics: Prof. Dr. CHAIM SAMUEL HÖNNIG.
Institute of Chemistry: Prof. Dr. PASCOAL ERNESTO SENISE.

Institute of Psychology: Profa. Dra. MARIA JOSÉ DE BARROS FORNARI DE AGUIRRE.

Institute of Geosciences: Prof. Dr. REINHOLT ELLERT.

Institute of Mathematical Sciences (São Carlos): Prof. Dr. ANTÔNIO FERNANDES IZÉ.

Institute of Physics and Chemistry (São Carlos): Prof. MILTON FERREIRA DE SOUZA.

Institute of Oceanography: Prof. Dr. ANDRÉ R. CRUZ.

Faculty of Pharmacy and Dentistry (Ribeirão Prêto): Prof. Dr. AYMAR BAPTISTA PRADO.

Faculty of Philosophy, Sciences and Letters (Ribeirão Prêto): Prof. Dr. RENATO HÉLIOS MIGLIORINI.

Centre of African Studies: Prof. Dr. FERNANDO MOURÃO.

Centre of Arab Studies: Prof. Dr. HELMI NASSR.

Centre of Latin-American Studies: Prof. Dr. J. R. FRANCO DE FONSECA.

ATTACHED INSTITUTES:

Instituto de Pesquisas Tecnológicas: see under Research Institutes.

Instituto de Energia Atômica: see under Research Institutes.

Instituto de Eletrotécnica: Dir. Eng. EUCLIDES PASCHOAL CASELLA.

UNIVERSIDADE ESTADUAL PAULISTA "JULIO DE MESQUITA FILHO"

PRAÇA DA SÉ 108,
CEP 01001-CENTRO,
C.P. 30.919, SÃO PAULO, SP
Telephone: 220-0447.

Founded 1976, incorporating previous existing Faculties in São Paulo State.

Rector: Prof. Dr. ARMANDO OCTÁVIO RAMOS.

Head of Administration: Prof. Dr. JUBERT SANCHES CIBANTOS.

Librarian: LEILA MAGALHÃES ZERLOTTI MERCADANTE.

DEANS AND DIRECTORS:

Araraquara Campus: Estrada Araraquara-Jau, Km. 1, C.E.P. 14800, C.P. 174; Pres. Prof. Dr. FRANCISCO DA SILVA BORBA.

Faculty of Pharmaceutical Sciences: Rua Expedicionários do Brasil 1621, CEP 14800, C.P. 331; 50 teachers, 312 students; Dir. Profa. Dra. MARIA APARECIDA POURCHET CAMPOS.

Faculty of Dentistry: Rua Humaitá 1680, CEP 14800; 83 teachers, 332 students; Dir. Prof. Dr. RAPHAEL LIA ROLFSEN.

Institute of Letters, Social Sciences and Education: 113 teachers, 539 students; Dir. Prof. Dr. FRANCISCO DA SILVA BORBA.

Institute of Chemistry: Rua. Prof. Francisco Degne s/n, CEP 14800, C.P. 174; 50 teachers, 221 students; Dir. Prof. Dr. CIRANO ROCHA LEITE.

Botucatu Campus: Distrito Rubião Junior, CEP 18600; Pres. Prof. Dr. HOMERO MORAES BARROS.

Faculty of Agricultural Sciences: 68 teachers, 165 students; Dir. Prof. Dr. JULIO NAKAGAWA.

Faculty of Medicine: 149 teachers, 548 students; Dir. Prof. Dr. JOSÉ CARLOS DE SOUZA TRINDADE.

Faculty of Veterinary Medicine and Animal Husbandry: 59 teachers, 266 students; Dir. Prof. Dr. HOMERO MORAES BARROS.

Institute of Medical and Agricultural Biology: 127 teachers, 179 students; Dir. Profa. Dra. WILMA PEREIRA BASTOS RAMOS.

Rio Claro Campus: Rua Dez 2527, CEP 13500; Pres. Prof. Dr. ANTÔNIO OLIVIO CERON.

Institute of Bio-Sciences: Av. 24-A, s/n, CEP 13500; 63 teachers, 313 students; Dir. Prof. Dr. ALCIDES SERZEDELLO.

Institute of Geo-Sciences and Exact Sciences: 93 teachers, 426 students; Dir. Prof. Dr. ANTÔNIO OLÍVIO CERON.

Franca Campus: Rua Major Claudiano CEP 14400.

Institute of History and Social Service: 53 teachers, 317 students; Dir. Prof. Dr. MANUEL NUNES DIAS.

Jaboticabal Campus: Rodovia Carlos Tonnani s/n, CEP 14870.

Faculty of Agrarian and Veterinary Sciences: 201 teachers, 1,051 students; Dir. Prof. Dr. MARCO ANTÔNIO GIANNONI.

Guaratinguetá Campus: Av. Dr. Ariberto Pereira da Cunha 333, CEP 12500.

Faculty of Engineering: 87 teachers; 507 students; Dir. Prof. DARWIN BASSI.

São Bernardo do Campo Campus: Rua Princess Maria da Gloria 176, CEP 09700.

Planalto Institute of Arts: 37 teachers, 188 students; Dir. Prof. MANOEL LELO BELLOTTO.

São José dos Campos Campus: Rua Eng. Francisco José Longo 777, CEP 12200, C.P. 314.

Faculty of Dentistry: 94 teachers, 152 students; Dir. Prof. Dr. JOSÉ BONIFÁCIO FONSECA.

Assis Campus: Av. Dom Antônio s/n, CEP 19800.

Institute of Literature, History and Psychology: 93 teachers, 809 students; Dir. Prof. Dr. JOÃO DE ALMEIDA.

Marilia Campus: Rua Vicente Ferreira 1298, CEP 17500.

Faculty of Education, Philosophy, Social Sciences and Documentation: 110 teachers, 475 students; Dir. Prof. Dr. JUBERT SANCHES CIBANTOS.

Presidente Prudente Campus: Rua Roberto Simonsen 305, CEP 19100, C.P. 957.

Institute of Planning and Environmental Studies: 75 teachers, 182 students; Dir. Prof. Dr. ALVANIR DE FIGUEIREDO.

Araçatuba Campus: Rua José Bonifácio 1193, CEP 16100, C.P. 533.

Faculty of Dentistry: 94 teachers, 304 students; Dir. Prof. Dr. ROBERTO PANNAIN.

Ilha Solteira Campus: Av. Brasil Centro 56, Municipio de Pereira Barreto, CEP 15378.

Faculty of Engineering: 84 teachers, 270 students; Dir. JOÃO RIBEIRO MATHIAS DUARTE.

São José do Rio Prêto Campus: Rua Cristovão Colombo 2265, CEP 15100.

Institute of Bio-Sciences, Letters and Exact Sciences: Dir. Prof. Dr. AZIZ NACIB AB'SABER.

"Paula Souza" State Centre for Technology: Praçã Coronel Fernando Prestes 74, CEP 01124 São Paulo; faculties in São Paulo and Sorocaba; Dir. Prof. Dr. HELSON ALVES VIANNA.

PONTIFÍCIA UNIVERSIDADE CATÓLICA DE SÃO PAULO

C.P. 7982,
RUA MONTE ALEGRE 984,
BAIRRO PERDIZES,
05014 SÃO PAULO
Telephone: 263-0211.

Founded 1946.

Academic year: March to December (two semesters).

Grand Chancellor: DOM PAULO EVARISTO ARNS, Cardinal Archbishop of São Paulo.

Rector: Profa. NADIR GOUVÊA KFOURI.

Vice-Rector for Academic Affairs: Dr. CASEMIRO DOS REIS FILHO.

Vice-Rector for Administration: Prof. ARMANDO JOÃO CAROPRESO.

Vice-Rector for Community Affairs: Prof. PE. EDÊNIO REIS VALLE.

General Secretary: Dr. José Feliciano Ferreira da Rosa Aquino.

Librarian: Dr. Luíz Kubinszky.

Number of teachers: 1,480.

Number of students: 14,871.

Publications: *Revista, Revista de Psicologia Normal e Patológica.*

Directors:

Centre of Law, Economics and Administration: Prof. Dirceu de Mello.

Faculty of Law: Prof. Hermínio A. Marques Pôrto.

Faculty of Economics and Administration: Prof. Felício Padula Benatti.

Centre of Humanities: Profa. Anna Maria Marques Cintra.

Faculty of Psychology: Dra. Maria do Carmo Guedes.

Faculty of Communications and Philosophy: Profa. Beatriz Berrini.

Faculty of Social Service: Profa. Mariangela Belfiore.

Faculty of Social Sciences: Prof. Dr. Paulo Edgar Almeida Resende.

Centre of Mathematical, Physical and Technological Sciences: Prof. Álvaro Puga Paz.

Faculty of Mathematical and Physical Sciences: Profa. Célia C. L. Cursino.

Centre of Education: Prof. Antônio Joaquim Severino.

Centre of Biological and Medical Sciences: Prof. Dr. José Rosemberg.

Faculty of Biological Sciences: Prof. Newton de Oliveira.

Faculty of Medical Sciences: Prof. Antônio Conti.

UNIVERSIDADE FEDERAL DE SERGIPE

RUA LAGARTO 952,
ARACAJÚ, SERGIPE

Founded 1967.

Rector: Prof. José Aloísio de Campos.

Vice-Rector: Prof. Nestor Piva.

President of Council: Dr. Osman Hora Fontes.

Number of teachers: 277.

Number of students: 2,700.

Directors:

Centre of Biological Sciences and Health: Prof. Gilton Machado Rezende.

Centre of Applied Social Sciences: Profa. Cândida Maria Fontes de Santana.

Centre of Education and Humanities: Profa. Maria de Lourdes Amaral Maciel.

Centre of Exact Sciences and Technology: José Wilson Brito Couto.

UNIVERSIDADE FEDERAL DE UBERLÂNDIA

AV. PARÁ 1720,
JARDIM UMUARAMA, C.P. 593,
38400 UBERLÂNDIA, MG

Telephone: 235-1500.

Founded 1969.

Academic year: February to June, August to November.

Rector: Prof. Ataulfo Marques Martins da Costa.

Vice-Rector: Prof. Sebastião Buiatti.

Pro-Rectors: Prof. Sebastião Buiatti (Administrative); Prof. Antonino Martins da Silva, Jr. (Academic); Profa. Cláudia Lúcia Carneiro de Mattos (Student Affairs and Extension).

Secretary General: Myriam Silva Gonçalves Alvares.

Librarian: Marlene Teodoro Guimarães.

Library of 28,000 vols.

Number of teachers: 647.

Number of students: 6,416.

Heads of Courses:

Centre of Biomedical Sciences:

Physical Education: Prof. Thales de Assis Martins.

Biology: Profa. Ida Damis Rodrigues.

Medicine: Prof. José Côrtes Filho.

Veterinary Medicine: Prof. Wilson Ferreira Lúcio.

Odontology: Prof. Luiz Mário Guimarães Gonçalves.

Centre of Exact Sciences and Technology:

Basic Engineering: Prof. José Peppe Júnior.

Mathematics: Profa. Yone Vicentini Gomes.

Civil Engineering: Prof. Dagoberto Camargo Caria.

Electrical Engineering: Prof. Waldomiro Saliby Junqueira.

Chemical Engineering: Prof. José de Paulo Carvalho.

Mechanical Engineering: Prof. Reny Simão.

Centre of Humanities and Arts:

Plastic Arts: Profa. Myrthes Linhares Lintz.

Music: Profa. Vanilda de Fátima Rezende Garcia.

Administration: Profa. Linda Mar Peixoto de Souza.

Accountancy: Prof. Reinaldo Campos Andraus.

Economics: Profa. Marly Vieira da Silva Melazo.

Law: Prof. Geraldo de Carvalho.

Social Studies: Profa. Miriam Michel Cury Dib.

Letters: Prof. Mariano Parziale.

Education: Profa. Carmelita Vieira dos Santos.

Psychology: Profa. Maria Ignez de Assis Moura.

UNIVERSIDADE DO VALE DO RIO DOS SINOS

PRAÇA TIRADENTES 35,
C.P. 275, 93.000
SÃO LEOPOLDO, R.S.

Telephone: (0512) 92-1613.

Founded 1969.

Private control; Language of instruction: Portuguese.

Rector: Prof. Luíz Marobin, s.j.

Vice-Rector (Academic): Prof. Miron A. Stoffels, s.j.

Vice-Rector (Administrative): Egídio E. Schneider, s.j.

Registrar: Prof. José Marculano.

Librarian: Virgílio Adami, s.j.

Number of teachers: 650.

Number of students: 24,000.

Publications: *Pesquisas*†, *Estudos Leopoldenses*†, *Perspectivas Teológicas*†, *Boletim Informativo, Estudos Jurídicos*†, *ale do Rio dos Sinos*†.

Deans:

Education and Humanism: Prof. Lodomilo Mallmann.

Health Sciences: Prof. Dr. Pedro E. Haeser, s.j.

Communication: Prof. Sérgio Farina.

Law: Prof. Hermann H. de C. Roenick.

Economics: Prof. José F. Kanarzveski.

Positive Sciences: Prof. Arilton P. da Silva.

Technological Sciences: Prof. Dirceu D. Calegari.

Centre for Documentation and Research, Population and Family: Prof. Dr. Pedro C. Beltrão.

UNIVERSIDADE FEDERAL DE VIÇOSA

AV. P.H. ROLFS S/N,
VIÇOSA, MINAS GERAIS

Telephone: 891-1225.

Founded 1948; formerly the Universidade Rural do Estado de Minas Gerais.

Rector: Prof. Paulo Mário del Giudice.

Secretary-General: Prof. Antônio José de Oliveira Baungratz.

Librarian: Prof. Milgar Camargos Loureiro.

Number of teachers: 614.

Number of students: 5,567.

Publications: *Revista Ceres, Experientiae, Seiva, UFV Informa, Boletim Informativo, Revista Brasileira de*

Armazenamento, Revista da Sociedade Brasileira de Zootecnia.

DIRECTORS:

Higher School of Agriculture: Prof. RENATO MÁRIO DEL GIUDICE.

Higher School of Forestry: Prof. HÉRCIO PEREIRA LADEIRA.

Higher School of Domestic Science: Prof. LENY DO VALE CINTRA.

Institute of Exact Sciences: Prof. CID MARTINS BATISTA.

Institute of Biological Sciences: Prof. JOSÉ ALBERTO H. FREIRE.

Graduate Council: Prof. RENATO MÁROI DEL GIUDICE.

Undergraduate Council: Prof. JOSÉ MANSUR NACIF.

Extension Council: Prof. ANTÔNIO LUIZ LIMA.

Research Council: Prof. PETER JOHN MARTYN.

Administrative Officer: Prof. GEORGE TANN DE HOLANDA LIMA.

COLLEGES

GENERAL

Associação de Ensino Unificado do Distrito Federal: SEPS 704 A, Lotes A,B,C, Brasília, DF; f. 1967; controls Instituto de Ciências Sociais; courses in accountancy, administration, economics, education and law; 200 teachers, 7,000 students; library of 21,520 vols.; Pres. REZENDE RIBEIRO DE REZENDE.

Centro de Ensino Unificado de Brasília: EQN 707/9, Brasília, DF; f. 1968; controls Faculdade de Direito do Distrito Federal, Faculdade de Filosofia, Ciencias e Letras do Distrito Federal, Faculdade de Ciências Econômicas, Contábeis e Administrativas do Distrito Federal; 8,229 students; library of 22,000 vols.; Pres. Dr. ALBERTO PÉRES; publ. *Universitas*† (quarterly).

Faculdade Católica de Ciências Humanas: Av. W-3 Norte, Quadra 702 "C", Brasília, DF; f. 1974; courses in administration, economics, education, teaching of literacy classes; library of 19,320 vols.; Dir. IRMA ALMERINDA DOS ANJOS.

Faculdade Católica de Tecnologia: f. 1980; courses in data processing, physics, chemistry, biology, mathematics.

Faculdades Unidas Católicas de Mato Grosso: Av. Mato Grosso 421, Campo Grande, MGS; f. 1961; independent; comprises: Faculdade Dom Aquino de Filosofia, Ciências e Letras, Faculdade de Direito de Campo Grande, Faculdade de Ciências Econômicas, Contábeis e de Administração de Campo Grande, and Faculdade de Serviço Social de Campo Grande; staff of 85; library of 89,207 vols.; Dir.-Gen. Fr. WALTER BOCCHI.

Federação de Escolas Superiores: Rua Cobre 200, 30.000 Belo Horizonte, MG; f. 1967; controlled by the Fundação Mineira de Educação e Cultura; courses in psychology, education, civil engineering, business administration, accountancy; 185 professors; 2,585 students; library of 23,247 vols.; Pres. HÉLIO LOPES.

Fundação Valeparaibana de Ensino: Praça Cândido Dias Castejón 75, 12200 São José dos Campos, SP; library of 26,000 vols.; Dir.-Gen. Dr. CLÉLIO MARCONDES; controls the following:

Faculdade de Ciências Econômicas e Administrativas do Vale do Paraíba: f. 1961; 760 students; Dir. Prof. EIVANY ANTÔNIO DA SILVA.

Faculdade de Direito do Vale do Paraíba: f. 1952; 880 students; Dir. Dr. CLÉLIO MARCONDES.

Faculdade de Engenharia: f. 1968; 820 students; Dir. Profa. THELMA KRUG DE MORAIS.

Faculdade de Filosofia, Ciências e Letras: f. 1967; 670 students; Dir. Profa. ENY DE ALMEIDA E SILVA.

Faculdade de Serviço Social "Ministro Tarso Dutra": f. 1969; 417 students; Dir. Prof. GERALDO VILHENA DE ALMEIDA PAIVA.

Faculdade de Arquitetura e Urbanismo "Elmano Ferreira Veloso": f. 1970; Dir. Prof. ARNALDO CATTARUZZI.

Instituição Universitária "Moura Lacerda": Rua Padre Euclides, 995, Ribeirão Prêto, SP; f. 1923; controls the Faculdade de Ciências Econômicas de Ribeirão Prêto, the Instituto Politécnico de Ribeirão Prêto and the Faculdade de Filosofia, Ciências e Letras Ribeirão Prêto; library of 9,756 vols.; Pres. Dr. OSCAR DE MOURA LACERDA.

BIBLIOGRAPHY AND LIBRARY SCIENCE

Curso de Biblioteconomia e Documentaçao: Rua Xavier Sigaud 290, URCA, Rio de Janeiro; f. 1911; certificate and diploma courses in library science and documentation; Dir. Prof. DÉA SANTOS DE ARAÚJO COUTINHO AMADEO.

Escola de Biblioteconomia e Documentação de São Carlos: Rua São Sebastião 2828, C.P. 382, São Carlos, S.P.; f. 1959; 21 professors; 216 students; library of 6,500 vols.; Dir. ALFREDO A. HAMAR.

ECONOMICS, POLITICAL SCIENCE, SOCIOLOGY

Escola de Administração de Emprêsas de São Paulo da Fundação Getúlio Vargas: Av. 9 de Julho 2029, CEP 01313 Bela Vista, São Paulo; f. 1954; business and public administration; library of 54,854 vols.; 239 teachers, 2,547 students; Dir. FERNANDO GOMEZ CARMONA; publ. *Revista de Administração de Emprêsas*†.

Faculdade de Ciências Contábeis de Santa Cruz do Sul (*Santa Cruz do Sul College of Accountancy*): Rua Cel Oscar R. Jost 1551, C.P. 236, Santa Cruz do Sul; f. 1962; maintained by the Associação Pró Ensino em Santa Cruz do Sul; teaching and research; library of 18,000 vols; Pres. Prof. ERVINO HOELTZ.

Faculdade de Ciências Econômicas de Marília: R. 7 de Setembro no. 35, C.P. 79, Marília, S.P.; f. 1954; library of 3,000 vols.; Dir. Prof. MILTON PÓVOAS.

Faculdade de Ciências Econômicas do Sul de Minas: Rua Padre João Batista Van Royen s/n, Itajubá, Minas Gerais; f. 1965; Dir. Eng. LUÍZ CARLOS TIGRE MAIA.

Faculdade de Ciências Econômicas e Administrativas de Santo André: Av. Príncipe de Gales 821, C. P. 247, Santo André, S.P.; f. 1954; supported by the Fundação Santo André; Dir. Prof. DENIS DONAIRE.

Faculdade de Ciências Econômicas e Administrativas de Taubaté: Rua Visconde do Rio Branco 210, Taubaté, S.P.; f. 1961; courses in Accounting, Economics and Business Administration; Dir. Dr. ULISSES VIEIRA.

Faculdade de Ciências Políticas e Econômicas de Cruz Alta: Rua Andrade Neves 308, Cruz Alta; f. 1955; independent; library of 4,605 vols.; Dir. DARIO SILVEIRA NETTO.

Faculdade de Ciências Políticas e Econômicas de Rio Grande: Rua Luíz Loréa 261, Rio Grande, R.S.; f. 1955; Dir. ALDO LAPOLLI; Sec. JOSÉ CARVALHO FREIRE.

Faculdade Estadual de Ciências Econômicas de Apucarana: Rodovia do Café, BR 376-Km. 3, C.P. 98, 86800 Apucarana, Paraná; f. 1959; state school; Dir. Prof. ADRIANO CORRÊA.

Faculdade Municipal de Ciências Econômicas e Administrativas de Osasco: Rua Mariano Jatahy Marcondes Ferraz 260, Osasco, S.P.; f. 1965; Dir. Prof. CLOVIS GLOEDEN.

Instituto Universitário de Pesquisas do Rio de Janeiro: Rua da Matriz 82, Botafogo, ZC 02; f. 1963; research and graduate courses in sociology and political science; library of 9,500 vols.; Dir. César Augusto Coelho Guimarães; publ. *Dados*† (3 a year and one in English).

Law

Faculdade de Direito Cândido Mendes: Praça 15 de Novembro 101, Rio de Janeiro, RJ.: f. 1953; courses in Law, Sociology and Economics; library of 10,000 vols.; Dir. Prof. Cândido Mendes de Almeida; publ. *Dados*.

Faculdade de Direito de Caruarú: Av. Portugal s/n, 55100 Caruarú, PE; f. 1959; library of 6,027 vols.; Dir. Prof. Luíz Pinto Ferreira; publ. *Revista*.

Faculdade de Direito de São Bernardo do Campo: Rua Java 425, Jardim do Mar, C.P. 180, São Bernardo do Campo, S.P.; f. 1964; library of 8,300 vols.; Dir. Prof. Dr. Horácio de Carvalho, Jr.

Faculdade de Direito de Sorocabana: Rua Dra. Ursulina Lopes Torres 123, 18100 Sorocaba, SP; f. 1957; library of 10,000 vols.; Dir. Dr. José Pereira Cardoso; publ. *Revista*.

Medicine

Escola de Farmácia e Odontologia de Alfenas: Rua Gabriel Monteiro da Silva 714, 37130 Alfenas, M.G.; f. 1914; graduate courses in Odontology, Biochemical and Applied Pharmacy, General Nursing and Obstetrics; Dir. Prof. Hélio de Souza; publ. *Revista*.

Escola Paulista de Medicina: Rua Botucatú 740, São Paulo; f. 1933; medicine and biomedical sciences; library of 21,283 vols., 6,862 journals; 541 teachers, 1,265 students; Dir. Prof. Dr. Jair Xavier Guimarães; Admin. Sidnei Nassif Abdalla.

Faculdade de Ciências Médicas de Pernambuco: Rua Carlos Chagas 112, Recife, PE; supported by the Fundação do Ensino Superior de Pernambuco; Dir. Prof. Dr. Fernando Jorge Simão dos Santos Figueira.

Faculdade de Medicina do Triângulo Mineiro: Praça Manoel Terra s/n, 38100 Uberaba, M.G.; f. 1953; Dir. Prof. Dr. João Francisco N. Junqueira.

Faculdade de Odontologia de Lins: Rua Tenente Florêncio Pupo Neto 300, C.P. 118, 16400 Lins, São Paulo; f. 1954; independent; Dir. Prof. Fernando Ribeiro de Toledo Piza (acting).

Faculdade de Odontologia de Passo Fundo: Rua Paissandú s/n, Passo Fundo, RS.; f. 1961; Dir. Dr. Bruno Edmundo Markus.

Faculdade de Odontologia de Pernambuco: Rua do Hospício 949, Recife, Pernambuco; f. 1955; supported by the Fundação da Ensino Superior de Pernambuco; postgraduate courses; 228 teachers, 1,500 students; Dir. Prof. Edrizio Barbosa Pinto.

Faculdade de Odontologia do Triângulo Mineiro: Avenida Guilherme Ferreira 217, C.P. 93, 38100 Uberaba, Minas Gerais; f. 1947; four-year graduate course in Dentistry; library of 3,500 vols.; Dir. Prof. Jayme Soares Bilharinho Netto; Sec. Dr. André Luíz Martins Coimbra.

Fundação Faculdade Católica de Medicina: Rua Sarmento Leite 245, Pôrto Alegre; f. 1953; library of 5,000 vols.; Dir. Prof. Heitor Cirne Lima; publ. *Pesquisa Médica*†.

Philosophy, Arts and Letters

Faculdade de Filosofia, Ciências e Letras de Santos: Rua Euclides da Cunha 247, Santos, SP; f. 1955; supported by the Sociedade Visconde de São Leopoldo; 135 teachers, 2,500 students; library of 30,000 vols.; Dir. Profa. Maria Helena de Almeida Lambert; Sec.-Gen. Prof. Heitor S. de A. Cardoso; publ. *Leopoldianum*.

Faculdade de Filosofia, Ciências e Letras de Ouro Fino: Rodovia MG 290, Km. 59, Ouro Fino, C.P. 38, Minas Gerais do Sul; f. 1972; run by Associação Sul Mineira de Educação e Cultura; 23 teachers, 1,437 students; library of 8,306 vols., 3,522 periodicals; Pres. Prof. Guilherme Bernardes; publ. *Signum*.

Faculdade de Filosofia , Música e Enfermagem do Sagrado Coração de Jesus: Rua Irmã Arminda, C.P. 511, Bauru, S.P.; f. 1954; teaching and research; library of 114,578 vols.; Dir. Irmã M. Elvira Milani.

Faculdade Estadual de Filosofia, Ciências e Letras: Praça Santos Andrade, s/n, Edifício das Faculdades, Ponta Grossa, Paraná; f. 1950; state school; library of 6,500 vols.; Dir. Joselfredo Cercal de Oliveira; publ. *Minerva* (annual).

Faculdade Salesiana de Filosofia, Ciências e Letras: Rua Dom Bosco 284, 12600 Lorena, São Paulo, C.P. 41; f. 1952; library of 35,183 vols.; Dir. P. Vicente de Paulo Moretti Guedes; Sec. P. José Antenor Velho; publ. *Revista*.

Technical

Escola de Engenharia de Lins: Caixa Postal 103, 16400 Lins, S.P.; f. 1961; Departments of Mathematics, Physics, Structural Engineering, Civil Construction, Hydraulics and Transportation, Electrical Engineering; 63 professors, 1,326 students; Dean Prof. Agarb Cézar de Carvalho; Dir. Eng. Milton Léo.

Escola de Engenharia de Taubaté: Av. Marechal Deodoro, 605, Taubaté, S.P.; f. 1962; courses in Civil, Mechanical and Electrical Engineering; library of 6,000 vols.; Dir. Eng. Adolfo Fernandes Araújo.

Escola Federal de Engenharia de Itajubá: Campus Prof. José Rodrigues Seabra, Bairro Pinheirinho, 37500 Itajubá, MG; f. 1913; undergraduate and postgraduate courses in electrical and mechanical engineering; 124 teachers, 1,253 students; library of 10,000 vols.; Dir. José Abel Royo dos Santos; publ. *EFEI Pesquisa*† (quarterly).

Escola Superior de Desenho Industrial: Rua Evaristo da Veiga 95, Rio de Janeiro; f. 1962; state school, affiliated to Univ. do Estado do Rio de Janeiro; Dir. Carmen Portinho.

Faculdade de Ciências Agrárias do Pará: C.P. 917, 66.000 Belém, Pará; f. 1951; agronomical, forestal and veterinary studies; 110 teachers and 927 students; library of 8,000 vols., 2,500 pamphlets, 800 periodicals; Dir. Francisco Barreira Perreira; publs. *Boletim*, *O Trimestre*†.

Faculdades de Tecnologia e de Ciências: Via Conselheiro Antônio Prado, C.P. 16, Barretos, S.P.; f. 1964; part of the Fundação Educacional de Barretos; Civil and Electrical Engineering, Mathematics, Physics and Chemistry; Pres. João Batista da Rocha.

Instituto Nacional de Telecomunicações de Santa Rita do Sapucaí: Av. João de Camargo 510, C.P. 05, Santa Rita do Sapucaí, MG; f. 1965; electrical engineering (electronics and telecommunications); library of 5,496 vols.; Dir. Prof. Luíz Gomes da Silva Jr.

Instituto Tecnológico de Aeronáutica: São José dos Campos, SP; f. 1947; depts. of electronic, aeronautical, mechanical engineering and data processing; 151 teachers, 806 students; Dean Prof. Dr. Jessen Vidal.

SCHOOLS OF ART AND MUSIC

Conservatório Brasileiro de Música: Av. Graça Aranha 57-12°, Rio de Janeiro; f. 1936; Dir. Profa. Amalia Fernandez Conde.

Conservatório de Canto Orfeônico "Maestro Julião": Universidade Católica de Campinas, Rua Marechal Deodoro 1099, Campinas; f. 1947; Dir. Prof. Luíz Biela de Souza.

Conservatório Dramático e Musical de São Paulo: Av. São João 269, São Paulo; f. 1906; library of 30,000 vols.; Dir. Dr. Alonso A. da Fonseca (acting).

Conservatório Nacional de Canto Orfeônico: Av. Pasteur 350, Rio de Janeiro; f. 1943; Dir. Octálio de Souza Braga.

Escola de Artes Visuais (*School of Visual Arts*): Rua Jardim Botânico 414, Parque Lage, ZC 20, CEP 22461 Rio de Janeiro; f. 1950; linked administratively to the State Department of Culture; courses in plastic arts and their technical and industrial application; library of 6,490 vols.; 75 teachers, 1,114 students; Dir. RUBEM BREITMAN.

Escola de Arte-Fundação Armando Alvares Penteado: Rua Alagoas 903, São Paulo; Dir. FLÁVIO L. MOTTA.

Escola de Comunicações e Artes: Cidade Universitária, 05508 São Paulo; f. 1967; undergraduate and postgraduate training given; mass communication, library and informaation science, journalism, public relations, films, radio ,television, the arts; library of 11,620 vols.; Dir. ANTÔNIO GUIMARÃES FERRI.

Escola de Música e Belas Artes do Paraná: Rua Emiliano Perneta 179, Curitiba, Paraná; f. 1948; library of 1,629 vols., also tapes, records; musical instruments, singing, plastic arts; Dir. FERNANDO CALDERARI.

Escola de Música da Universidade Federal do Rio de Janeiro: Rua do Passeio 98, Rio de Janeiro; f. 1848 as Conservatório Imperial de Música, then Instituto Nacional de Música; library (f. 1890), 280,000 vols. of music; museum of 90 antique instruments; Dir. Profa. ANDRELY QUINTELLA DE PAOLA; Librarian MARIA THEREZA HORA.

Attached to the school:

Centro de Pesquisas Folclóricas: f. 1943; Dir. (Técnico Pesquisador) Sra. DULCE LAMAS; collections of native music on records.

Escola de Teatro: Praia do Flamengo 132, Rio de Janeiro; f. 1953; four-year course in dramatic arts; Dir. PERNAMBUCO G. S. DE OLIVEIRA.

Faculdade de Belas Artes de São Paulo: Praça da Luz 2, andar 2, São Paulo; f. 1925; teaching staff: 56; industrial arts, painting, sculpture, architecture etc.; library of 5,000 vols.; Dir. Prof. Arq. LUCIANO O. F. GOMES CARDIM.

Faculdade de Musica Mãe de Deus: Avenida São Paulo 651, C.P. 106, 86100 Londrina, Paraná; f. 1965; library of 2,650 vols.; Dir. Profa. THEODOLINDA GERTRUDES MORO; publ. *Fôlha de Londrina.*

Faculdade de Música Pio XII: Rua Irmã Arminda 10-50, 17100 Bauru, S.P.; f. 1964; 12 teachers; library of 1,500 vols.; Dir. IRMÃ MARIALICE GAZZETTA.

Faculdade de Música "Sagrado Coração de Jesus": Rua Caraibas 882, C.P. 8383, Villa Pompéia, S.P.; f. 1948; undergraduate, postgraduate and special courses; Dir. IRMÃ CHARITAS CAVALLI; Sec. IRMÃ IDA FRANCHIN; 19 teachers, 142 students.

Faculdade Santa Marcelina: Rua Dr. Emílio Ribas 89, Perdizes, 05013 São Paulo; f. 1929; musical instruments, singing, composition, artistic education; 60 mems.; library of 9,000 vols; Pres. FERNANDA MARTELLINI; Dira. ÂNGELA RIVERO.

Instituto de Letras e Artes: Rua Marechal Floriano 179, 96100 Pelotas, R.G.S.; f. 1969; independent; degree courses in plastic arts and music, postgraduate course in history of arts; 70 teachers; Dira. MYRIAM SOUZA ANSELMO.

Instituto de Música da Bahia: Rua Direito de Piedade 2, Salvador, BA; f. 1897; Sec. MARIA CARMELITA SANTOS AGUIAR.

Instituto Musical de São Paulo: Rua Glicério 245, Liberdade, São Paulo; f. 1927; music, theatre, design, plastic arts; library of 3,000 vols.; 85 teachers, 800 students; Principal NEIDE RODRIGUES GOMES.

BRUNEI

Population 201,000

RESEARCH INSTITUTES

Department of Agriculture Research Sections: B.S. Begawan.

Plant Pathology Laboratory: f. 1970; research into diseases, plant import and export control, seed testing and nematology; Plant Pathologist W. T. H. PEREGRINE, M.SC.; publs. *Annual Reports*†.

Soils Science/Agricultural Chemistry: f. 1970; Chief Officer A. W. ALLEN, O.B.E., M.SC.

Agronomy: f. 1970; rice, vegetables, tree crops and pastures; Chief Officer Dr. MORNI B. OTHMAN.

Entomology: f. 1971; Chief Officer D. J. MCCRAE, B.SC. (until July 1981).

LIBRARY

Language and Literature Bureau Library: Jalan Elizabeth II, Bandar Seri Begawan; f. 1967; *c.* 75,000 vols. in Malay and English; brs. in Kuala Belait, Tutong, Bangar and Seria; children's library and 2 bookmobiles; Chief Librarian Miss THELMA T. SALAZAR; publ. *Bibliografi Perpustakaan* (6 a year).

MUSEUMS

Army Museum: f. 1979; Curator Major Dato S. D. BUTTERELL.

Brunei Museum: Kota Batu; f. 1965; ethnographical, archaeological and natural history collections; reference library of 4,627 vols., Borneo Section of 692 vols., and Brunei State Archives; Dir. P. M. Dato SHARIFFUDDIN, D.P.M.B., P.S.B., A.M.A.; publ. *Brunei Museum Journal*† (annual).

Churchill Memorial Museum: f. 1971; historical and cultural centre; Dir. P. M. Dato SHARIFFUDDIN.

COLLEGES

Sultan Hassanal Bolkiah Teachers' College: P.O.B 601, B.S. Begawan; f. 1956; 400 students; library of 40,000 vols.; Principal ABDUL GHANI BUJANG.

Jeffry Bolkiah School of Engineering: Kuala Belait; f. 1970; 430 staff, 5,200 students; Dir. Haji ABU BAKAR HJ. PAUN.

Building Trades School: Jalan Muara.

Seri Begawan Religious Teachers' College: Bandar Seri Begawan.

There are Adult Education Centres attached to colleges and schools.

BULGARIA

Population 8,804,000

BULGARIAN ACADEMY OF SCIENCES

SOFIA, "7 NOEMVRI" 1

Telephone: 8-41-41.

Founded 1869.

President: Acad. ANGEL BALEVSKI.

Vice-Presidents: Acad. PANTELEJ ZAREV, Acad. DIMITĂR KOSEV, Acad. HRISTO DASKALOV, Acad. GEORGI BRANKOV, Corresp. mem. LJUBOMIR ZELJAZKOV, Corresp. mem. MAKO DAKOV.

General Scientific Secretary: Corresp. mem. GEORGI BLIZNAKOV.

Deputy General Scientific Secretary: Corresp. mem. JORDAN SIMEONOV.

Library: *see* Libraries.

Publications: *Spisanie Na Bălgarskata Akademiya Na Naukite*† (Review of the Bulgarian Academy of Sciences), *Dokladi Bolgarskoj Akademii Nauk* (Reports), *Vestnik* (Journal), *Teoretična i Priložna Mehanika*† (Theoretical and Applied Mechanics), *Tehničeska Misăl*† (Technical Thought), *Fiziko-matematičesko Spisanie*† (Physical-Mathematical Review), *Priroda*† (Nature) and many others.

MEMBERS OF THE PRESIDIUM:

A. ANGELOV
S. ANGELOV
G. ANGELOVA
E. BONČEV
M. BORISOV
S. BOŽKOV
K. BRATANOV
P. DINEKOV
A. FOL
G. GANEV
S. GANOVSKI
V. GEORGIEV
A. GJONOV
H. J. HRISTOV
V. HRISTOV
L. ILIEV
B. KURTEV
A. MALEEV
E. MATEEV
K. MIŠEV
N. NAČEV
J. RADEV
B. SENDOV
K. SERAFIMOV
A. STOJKOV
T. TAŠEV
N. TODOROV

MEMBERS:

BALEVSKI, A. (Mechanical Engineering).
BONČEV, E. (Geology).
BRANKOV, G. (Mechanics).
BRATANOV, K. (Animal Breeding).
BUREŠ, I., (Zoology, Entomology).
CANEV, G. (Literary History and Criticism).
DACEV, A. (Theoretical Physics).
DASKALOV, H. (Plant Breeding).
DINEKOV, P. (Literary History and Criticism).
GANOVSKI, S. (Philosophy, Pedagogy).
GEORGIEV, E. (Theory of Literature).
GEORGIEV, V. (Linguistics).
GEORGIEVA, R. (Genetics and Selection of Plants).
HADŽIOLOV, A. (Histology, Embryology).
HRISTOV, H. A. (History).
HRISTOV, H. J. (Theoretical Physics).
ILIEV, L. (Mathematics).
JOVČEV, J. (Geology).
KAIŠEV, R. (Physical Chemistry).
KAMENOV, E. (Economics).
KARASLAVOV, G. (Literature).
KOSEV, D. (History).
KOSTOV, I. (Mineralogy and Crystallography).
KURTEV, B. (Organic Chemistry).
MATEEV, E. (Economics).
NADŽAKOV, G. (Physics).
PAVLOV, S. (Law).
PETKANČIN, B. (Mathematics).
PLATIKANOV, N. (Animal Breeding).
POPIVANOV, R. (Medical Biology, Genetics).
POPOV, P. (Plant Breeding).
PUHLEV, A. (Cardiology).
STEFANOV, B. (Botany, Dendrology).
STEFANOV, I. (Economics, Statistics).
STOEV, K. (Agronomy).
TAŠEV, T. (Gastroenterology).
TODOROV, I. (Theoretical Physics).
TOPENČAROV, V. (History, Journalism).
UZUNOV, D. (Painting).
VELEV, D. (Hydraulic Engineering).
ZAREV, P. (Literature).

CORRESPONDING MEMBERS:

ANGELOV, D. (History).
BAJLOV, D. (Plant Breeding).
BEŠEVLIEV, V. (Classical Philology).
BLIZNAKOV, G. (Inorganic Chemistry).
BORISOV, M. (Physics).
CANEV, R. (Biochemistry).
CANKOV, V. (Geology).
CONČEV, V. (Cardiology).
DAKOV, M. (Forestry).
DIMOV, I. (Mechanical Engineering).
DIMOV, N. (Microbiology).
DINOV, T. (Cinema Art).
ELENKOV, D. (Chemical Engineering Process and Equipment).
GĂLĂBOV, G. (Anatomy).
GĂLĂBOV, Ž. (Geography).
GEORGIEV, I. (Animal Breeding).
HADŽINIKOLOV, V. (History).
HRISTOV, S. (Physical Chemistry).
IRIBADŽAKOV, N. (Philosophy).
IVANOV, C. (Organic Chemistry).
JANEV, E. (Microbiology).
KABAIVANOV, V. (Organic Chemistry).
KADANOV, D. (Anatomy, Anthropology).
KALEV, L. (Metallurgy).
KAMENOV, B. (Geology).
KASABOV, J. (Physics).
KOJNOV, V. (Soil Science).
KOMITSKI, P. (Animal Husbandry).
KONDAREV, M. (Viticulture).
KOVAČEVSKI, I. (Phytopathology).
LAZAROV, A. (Entomology).
LAZAROV, K. (Economics).
MALEEV, A. (Gastroenterology).
MARKOV, K. (Microbiology).
MARKOV, P. (Physics).
MILKOVSKI, J. (Plant Breeding).
MINKOV, M. (Agricultural Economics).
MIŠEV, K. (Geography).
MITROV, G. (Clinical Oncology).
NAPLATANOV, N. (Electrical Engineering, Automation and Technical Cybernetics).
NESTOROV, G. (Geophysics).
NIKLOV, P. (Pharmacology).
OBRETENOV, A. (Art Criticism).
PAVLOV, P. (Bacteriology).
PENČEV, N. (Chemistry).
PETKOV, V. (Pharmacology).
PIRJOV, G. (Psychology).
POLIKAROV, A. (Philosophy).
POPOV, I. (Electrical Engineering).
RADEV, J. (State Law).

RADEV, T. (Physiology).
RAJNOV, B. (Art Criticism).
ŠABANOV, D. (Agronomy).
ŠELUDKO, A. (Physical Chemistry).
SENDOV, B. (Mathematics).
SERAFIMOV, K. (Outer Space Physics).
SIMEONOV, J. (Civil Engineering).
SPASOV, A. (Organic Chemistry).
STOJKOV, A. (Art Criticism).
TAGAMLICKI, J. (Mathematics).
TODORIEV, N. (Thermoengineering).
TODOROV, N. (History).
TONEV, L. (Architecture).
TOŠKOV, A. (Microbiology).
VANČEV, T. (Agronomy).
VASILEV, I. (Helminthology).
VIKTOROV, J. (Urology).
VLAHOV, T. (History).
ŽELJAZKOV, L. (Pharmaceutical Chemistry).

HONORARY MEMBERS:

BOGOLYUBOV, N. N. (U.S.S.R.), Mathematics.
NESMEYANOV, A. N. (U.S.S.R.), Organic Chemistry.

FOREIGN MEMBERS:

ALEXANDROV, A. P. (U.S.S.R.), Physics.
ALFVÉN, H. O. G. (Sweden), Physics and Astrophysics.
AMBARTSUMYAN, V. A. (U.S.S.R.), Astrophysics.
BASOV, N. G. (U.S.S.R.), Physics.
BERNARD, R. (France), Slavonic and Bulgarian Languages and Literature.
BERNSTEIN, S. B. (U.S.S.R.), Linguistics.
BETHGE, H. (G.D.R.), Physics.
BOGNAR, R. (Hungary), Chemistry.
BORSUK, K. (Poland), Mathematics.
CASTELLAN, G. (France), Modern History and Politics.
CEBERTOWICZ, R. (Poland), Hydraulic Engineering.
CHKLIKVADZE, V. M. (U.S.S.R.), Law.
CONDURACHI, E. (Romania), History.
CORRENS, E. (G.D.R.), Chemistry.
DJERASSI, C. (U.S.A.), Chemistry.
DORODNITSYN, A. A. (U.S.S.R.), Mathematics.
ENGELHARDT, V. A. (U.S.S.R.), Biochemistry and Molecular Biology.
ESCANDE, L. (France), Hydrodynamics.
FEDOSEYEV, P. N. (U.S.S.R.), Philosophy.
GERASIMOV, I. P. (U.S.S.R.), Geography.
GLIGORIČ, V. (Yugoslavia), Literature.
GLUSHKOV, V. M. (U.S.S.R.), Mathematics and Cybernetics.
GRABAR, A. (France), Art Criticism, Byzantine Art.
GROSZKOWSKI, J. (Poland), Electrical Engineering.
HARTKE, W. (G.D.R.), History.
HUNGER, H. (Austria), Byzantology.
IMSHENETSKY, A. A. (U.S.S.R.), Microbiology.
IOVCHUK, M. T. (U.S.S.R.), Philosophy.
KACZMAREK, J. (Poland), Metals and Technology.
KEDROV, B. M. (U.S.S.R.), Philosophy.
KHRAPCHENKO, M. B. (U.S.S.R.), Literature.
KIRILLIN, V. A. (U.S.S.R.), Energy.
KLARE, H. (G.D.R.), Chemistry.
KOTARBINSKI, T. (Poland), Philosophy.
KOŽEŠNIK, J. (Czechoslovakia), Cybernetics.
LAVRENTYEV, M. A. (U.S.S.R.), Mathematics.
LIKHACHEV, D. S. (U.S.S.R.), Literature.
LOBANOV, P. P. (U.S.S.R.), Economics.
LOGUNOV, A. A. (U.S.S.R.), Physics.
MALEK, I. (Czechoslovakia), Microbiology.
MARCHUK, G. I. (U.S.S.R.), Physics.
MARKOV, D. F. (U.S.S.R.), Literature, Bulgarian Studies.
MEVIUS, W. (Fed. Repub. of Germany), Botany.
MILCU, S. (Romania), Endocrinology.
MURGULESCU, I. (Romania), Chemistry.
NEMETH, G. (Hungary), Linguistics.
NOWACKI, W. (Poland), Mechanics.
OLSZAK, W. (Poland), Mechanics.
OPARIN, A. I. (U.S.S.R.), Biochemistry.
OVCHINNIKOV, J. A. (U.S.S.R.), Biochemistry.
PATON, B. E. (U.S.S.R.), Metallurgy.
PAVLÍK, O. (Czechoslovakia), Pedagogy.
PETROV, B. N. (U.S.S.R.), Automation and Telemechanics.
PETROVSKY, B. V. (U.S.S.R.), Medicine.
PIENIAŻEK, S. (Poland), Fruit-growing.
POULIK, J. (Czechoslovakia), Archaeology.
ROCHE, J. (France), Biochemistry.
ROSICKÝ, B. (Czechoslovakia), Parasitology.
RYBAKOV, B. (U.S.S.R.), Archaeology.
SANDERS, I. (U.S.A.), Sociology.
SCHAFF, A. (Poland), Philosophy.
SCHWABE, K. (G.D.R.), Electrochemistry and Physical Chemistry.
SEMENOV, N. N. (U.S.S.R.), Physical Chemistry.
SIDORENKO, A. V. (U.S.S.R.), Geology, Geophysics.
SHIRENDEV, B. (Mongolia), History and Literature.
SKRYABIN, G. K. (U.S.S.R.), Medical Technical Biochemistry.
SOMOS, A. (Hungary), Vegetable-growing.
ŚORM, F. (Czechoslovakia), Chemistry.
STANKOVIČ, S. (Yugoslavia), Biology.
STIEBER, Z. (Poland), Linguistics.
ŠTOLL, L. (Czechoslovakia), Theory of Literature and Criticism.
STUBBE, H. (G.S.R.), Plant Breeding.
SZABÓ, I. (Hungary), Law.
SZENTÁGOTHAI, J. (Hungary), Neuromorphology.
TÁRCZY-HORNOCH, A. (Hungary), Geodesy and Geophysics.
THEOCHARIS, P. (Greece), Mechanics.
TIMAKOV, V. D. (U.S.S.R.), Microbiology, Epidemiology.
TOPCHIBASHEV, M. A. (U.S.S.R.), Medicine.
TRZEBIATOWSKI, W. (Poland), Chemistry and Physics.
ZAKYTHINOS, D. (Greece), History.
ZHUKOV, E. M. (U.S.S.R.), History.

In 1972 a reorganization of the Bulgarian Academy of Sciences aud the University of Sofia took place, which resulted in the integration of some Academy Institutes with the respective Faculties at the University of Sofia, and the creation of ten Centres for Research.

Centre for Research in Mathematics and Mechanics: f. 1971; Dir. Acad. L. ILIEV.

Institute of Mathematics with Computing Centre; f. 1949; Dir. Acad. L. ILIEV.

Institute of Mechanics and Biomechanics: f. 1977; Dir. Acad. G. BRANKOV.

Faculty of Mathematics and Mechanics: see University of Sofia.

Publs. *Seridka. Bălgarsko Matematičesko spisanie, Teoretična i Priložna mehanika, Biomehanika.*

Centre for Research in Physics: f. 1972; Dir. Corresp. mem. M. BORISOV.

Institute of Nuclear Research and Nuclear Energy: f. 1972; Dir. Acad. H. HRISTOV.

Institute of Solid State Physics; f. 1972; Dir. Corresp. mem. M. BORISOV.

Institute of Electronics: f. 1963; Dir. A. SPASOV.

Section of Astronomy and National Observatory: f. 1958; Dir. M. POPOVA.

Central Laboratory of Solar Energy and New Energy Sources: f. 1977; Dir. Prof. S. KĂNEV.

Development and Transfer Centre: f. 1974; Head: Eng. I. DIMOV.

Centre for Automation of Scientific Experiments: f. 1977; Head: L. ANTONOV.

Faculty of Physics: See University of Sofia.

Publs. *Bolgarskij fizičeskij žurnal, Jadrena energija, Astronomičeski Kalendar na Observatorijata v Sofija.*

Centre for Research in Chemistry: f. 1972; Dir. Acad. B. KURTEV.

Institute of General and Inorganic Chemistry: f. 1960; Dir. G. BLIZNAKOV.

Institute of Organic Chemistry with Centre of Phytochemistry: f. 1960; Dir. Acad. B. KURTEV.

Institute of Physical Chemistry: f. 1958; Dir. Acad. R. KAIŠEV.

Central Laboratory of Electrochemical Power Sources: f. 1967; Dir. Prof. E. BUDEVSKI.

Central Laboratory of Pnotographic Processes: f. 1967; Dir. Prof. J. MALINOVSKI.

Central Laboratory of Polymers: f. 1972; Dir. Prof. M. MIHAJLOV.

Central Laboratory for Theoretical Foundations of Chemical Engineering: f. 1972; Dir. Corresp. mem. D. ELENKOV.

Branch Research Laboratory for Chemical Reagents and Preparations: f. 1976; Dir. Prof. D. TRENDAFELOV.
Faculty of Chemistry: see University of Sofia.
Publ. *Izvestija po himija.*

Centre for Research in Earth Sciences: f. 1972; Dir. Corresp. mem. K. MISEV.
Institute of Geophysics: f. 1960.
Institute of Geology: f. 1947; Dir. Acad. I. KOSTOV.
Institute of Geography: f. 1950; Dir. Corresp. mem. Ž. GĂLĂBOV.
Institute of Marine Research and Oceanology: f. 1973; Dir. Z. BELBEROV.
Central Laboratory for Space Research: f. 1969; Dir. Corresp. mem. K. SERAFIMOV.
Central Laboratory of Higher Geodesy: f. 1956; Dir. N. GEORGIEV.
Laboratory for Experimental and Engineering Mineralogy: f. 1977; Head M. MALEEV.
Laboratory for Complex Research and Reinforcement of Weak Ground Foundations: f. 1977; Head. Prof. M. MINKOV.
Research and Coordination Centre for the Protection and Reproduction of the Environment: f. 1972; Dir. Prof. I. ZAHARIEV.
Faculty of Geology and Geography: *see* University of Sofia.
Chair of Meteorology and Geophysics at the Faculty of Physics: *see* University of Sofia.
Publs. *Spisanie na Bălgarskoto Geologičesko Družestvo Bălgarsko Geofizičesko spisanie, Problemi na geografijata, Vissa geodeziaj, Geotektonika, tektonofizika i geodinamika, Geohimija, mineralogija i petrologija, Okeanologija, Space Research in Bulgaria, Fosilite na Bălgarija.*

Research Association on Fundamental Problems of Technical Sciences: f. 1977.
Institute of Technical Cybernetics and Robots: f. 1964; Dir. A. ANGELOV.
Institute of Metal Science and Technology of Metals: f. 1967; Dir. Acad. A. BALEVSKI.
Institute of Water Problems: f. 1960; Dir. Prof. P. IGNATOV.
Central Laboratory of Physical and Chemical Mechanics: f. 1972; Dir. Corresp. mem. J. SIMEONOV.
Publs. *Tehničeska Misăl, Problemi na Tehničeskata Kibernetika, Materialoznanie i Technologija, Vodni Problemi, Fizko-himičeska mehanika.*

Centre for Research in Biology: f. 1972; Dir. Acad. K. BRATANOV.
Institute of Biology and Immunology of Reproduction and Development of Organisms: f. 1939; Dir. Acad. K. BRATANOV.
Institute of Botany and Botanical Gardens: f. 1889; Dir. Prof. V. VELČEV.
Institute of Forestry: f. 1928; Dir. Prof. M. MARINOV.
Institute of Genetics: f. 1940; Dir. M. STOILOV.
Institute of Zoology: f. 1889; Dir. Prof. B. BOTEV.
Institute of Molecular Biology: f. 1960; Dir. Corresp. mem. R. CANEV.
Institute of Microbiology: f. 1947; Dir. Prof. I. GRIGOROV.
Institute of Morphology: f. 1953; Dir. Prof. I. GORANOV.
Institute of General and Comparative Pathology: f. 1948; Dir. Prof. Z. MLADENOV.
Institute of Physiology: f. 1947; Dir. Corresp. mem. V. PETKOV.
"Methodi Popov" Institute of Plant Physiology: f. 1948; Dir. Prof. T. KĂDREV.
Central Laboratory of Biophysics: f. 1967; Dir. G. GEORGIEV.
Central Regeneration Laboratory: f. 1964; Dir. Corresp. mem. G. GĂLĂBOV.
"Acad. G. Uzunov" Central Laboratory for Brain Research: f. 1961; Dir. Prof. A. VĂRBANOVA.
Central Laboratory of Helminthology: f. 1954; Dir. Corresp. mem. I. VASILEV.
Research and Production Laboratory of Algology: f. 1966; Dir. H. DILOV.
Experimental and Breeding Centre for Experimental Animals: Slivnica; Dir. Dr. P. DŽAMBAZOV.
Faculty of Biology: *see* University of Sofia.
Publs. *Obšta i sravnitelna patologija, Fitologija, Ekologija, Genetika i selekciaj, Gorsko-stopanska nauka, Helmintologija, Acta morfologica, Acta microbiologica bulgarica, Acta zoologica bulgarica.*

Centre for Research in Philosophy and Sociology: f. 1972; Dir. Prof. Dr. S. ANGELOV.
"Todor Pavlov" Institute of Philosophy: f. 1945; Dir. Acad. S. GANOVSKI.
Institute of Sociology: f. 1968; Dir. Prof. Dr. V. DOBRIJANOV.
Laboratory of Psychology: f. 1972; Head Prof. Z. IVANOVA.
Faculty of Philosophy: *see* University of Sofia.
Publs. *Filosofska misăl, Sociologičeski problemi, Problemi na logikata.*

Centre for Research in State and Legal Sciences: f. 1972; Dir. Corresp. mem. J. RADEV.
Institute of State and Legal Sciences: f. 1948; Dir. Prof. K. LJUTOV.
Faculty of Law: *see* University of Sofia.
Publs. *Pravna misăl.*

Centre for Research in Linguistics and Literature: f. 1972; Dir. Acad. V. GEORGIEV.
Bulgarian Language Institute: f. 1942; Dir. V. STANKOV.
Institute of Literature: f. 1948; Dir. T. ŽEČEV.
Chair of Foreign Languages: f. 1960; Head K. PEHLIVANOVA.
Faculty of Slavonic Philology: *see* University of Sofia.
Faculty of Western Philology: *see* University of Sofia.
Publs. *Bălgarski ezik, Literaturna misăl, Balkansko ezikoznanie, Bălgarska onomastika, Slavističen sbornik, Literaturen arhiv, Bălgarska dialektologija, Proučvanija i materiali.*

Centre for Research in History: f. 1972; Dir. Prof. I. DIMITROV.
Institute of History: f. 1947; Dir. Acad. H. A. HRISTOV.
Institute of Archaeology and Museum: f. 1921 (Institute), 1879 (Museum); Dir. Corresp. mem. D. ANGELOV.
Institute of Ethnography and Museum: f. 1947 (Institute), 1906 (Museum); Dir. Corresp. mem. V. HADŽINIKOLOV.
Institute of Balkan Studies: f. 1963; Dir. Corresp. mem. N. TODOROV.
Institute of Tracology: f. 1972; Dir. Prof. A. FOL.
Faculty of History: *see* University of Sofia.
Publs. *Istoričeski Pregled, Etudes Balkaniques, Arheologija, Bulgarian Historical Review, Studia Balcanica, Bălgarska etnografija, Studia thracica, Balkani.*

Research Association for the Fine Arts: f. 1972; Dir. Corresp. mem. A. STOJKOV.
Institute of Fine Arts: f. 1949; Dir. Corresp. mem. A. OBRETENOV.
Institute of Musicology: f. 1948; Dir. Prof. V. KRĂSTEV.
Institute of Folklore: f. 1972; Dir. Acad. P. DINEKOV.
Institute of Culture: f. 1971; Dir. Prof. E. NIKOLOV.
Institute for the Theory and History of Town Planning and Architecture: f. 1949; Dir. Prof. P. TAŠEV.
Publs. *Problemi na izkustvoto, Bălgarski folklor, Muzikoznanie, Arhitekturata i žizenata sreda na čoveka, Problemi na bălgarskija folklor.*

SCIENTIFIC UNITS ATTACHED TO THE PRESIDIUM OF THE ACADEMY

Institute of Economics: f. 1949; Dir. Dr. K. KIRJAKOV (acting); publ. *Ikonomičeska misal.*

Institute for Contemporary Social Theories: f. 1969; Dir. Prof. R. AVRAMOV; publ. *Săvremenni socialni teorii.*

Institute for International Relations and Socialist Integration; f. 1976; Dir. Prof. N. CAREVSKI; publs. *Meždunarodni otnošenija, Afrikano-aziatski problemi.*

Science of Science Centre: f. 1968; Dir. Prof. N. STEFANOV.

National Natural Science Museum: f. 1889; Dir. Acad. I. KOSTOV.

BODIES UNDER THE DIRECT SUPERVISION OF THE PRESIDIUM OF THE ACADEMY

Chief Department of Hydrology and Meteorology: f. 1950; Head Senior Scientific Researcher K. STANČEV.

Institute of Hydrology and Meteorology: f. 1954; Dir. Prof. P. BECINSKI; publs. *Hidrologija i meteorologija.*

Scientific Information Centre with Central Library and Scientific Archives: f. 1972; Dir. Corresp. mem. A. POLIKAROV. (For the individual units *see* Information Centres, Libraries and Archives.)

Centre for Bulgarian Studies: f. 1970; Dir. Acad. E. GEORGIEV; publs. *Paleobulgarica, Starobălgaristika.*

Bulgarian Academy of Sciences Publishing House and Printing House: f. 1869; Dir. K. KRĂSTEV; publs. *Bălgarska akademična kniga.*

"Bulgarian Encyclopedia" Service: f. 1955; Dir. H. KRUŠEV.

ACADEMY OF MEDICINE

SOFIA 1431, BUL. D. NESTOROV 15

Telephone 53-501.

Founded 1972.

The Academy of Medicine was founded as a result of the integration of the former Higher Medical Institutes and the medical research institutes.

President: Corresp. mem. Prof. A. MALEEV.

Vice-President for Science and Research: Prof. I. NIKOLOV.

Vice-President for Educational Affairs: Prof. J. JORDANOV.

Vice-President for Therapy: Prof. K. ZAIMOV.

Publication: *Acta Medica Bulgarica.*

HIGHER MEDICAL INSTITUTES:

Higher Medical Institute (Sofia): Sofia, G. Sofijski 1; f. 1979; Rector Prof. HR. HRISTOZOV.

Faculty of Dentistry (Sofia): Sofia, G. Sofijski 1; f. 1942; Dean Prof. J. GEORGIEVA.

Faculty of Pharmacy (Sofia): Sofia, Dunav 2; f. 1952; Dean Prof. D. DANČEV.

Higher Medical Institute (Plovdiv): Plovdiv, V. Aprilov 15A; f. 1945; Rector Prof. V. MITKOV.

Faculty of Dentistry (Plovdiv): Plovdiv, V. Tărnovo 24; f. 1974; Dean Prof. M. VUTOV.

Higher Medical Institute (Varna): Varna, M. Drinov 55; f. 1961; Rector Prof. G. KAPRELJAN.

Higher Medical Institute (Pleven): Pleven, Karl Marx 1; f. 1974; Rector N. KJUČKOV.

LEARNED SOCIETIES

GENERAL

Union of Scientific Workers in Bulgaria: Sofia, Tolbuhin 18; f. 1944; Pres. Acad. K. BRATANOV; publ. *Naučen Zivot*†.

AGRICULTURE AND VETERINARY SCIENCE

Bulgarian Soil Society: Sofia-Pavlovo; f. 1959; Pres. L. RAJKOV; Sec. Assoc. Prof. I. ATANASOV.

Scientific and Technical Union of Agricultural Specialists: Sofia, Rakowski 108; f. 1965; Pres. V. CANOV; Sec. P. LEKOV; publ. *Bjuletin-Vnedreni novosti.*

ARCHITECTURE AND TOWN PLANNING

Union of Architects in Bulgaria: Sofia, D. Poljanov 11; f. 1965; Pres. Prof. M. PISAREV; publs. *Arhitectura, Informacionen buletin*†.

THE ARTS

Union of Actors in Bulgaria: Sofia, Alabin 52; f. 1919; Pres. L. KABAKČIEV; Sec. ŠOMOVA; publ. *Teatăr*†.

Union of Bulgarian Artists: Sofia, Šipka 6; f. 1893; Pres. S. RUSEV; publ. *Izkustvo*†.

Union of Bulgarian Cinema Workers: Sofia, Ruski 8a; f. 1954; Pres. H. HRISTOV; publs. *Kinoizkustvo*†, *Filmovi Novini*†.

Union of Bulgarian Composers: Sofia, Iv. Vazov 2; f. 1947; 160 mems.; library of 21,220 vols.; Pres. Assoc. Prof. D. PETKOV; publ. *Bălgarska Muzika*† (monthly).

Union of Bulgarian Musicians: Sofia, Alabin 52; f. 1965; Pres. Prof. A. NEJNSKI; publ. *Muzikalni horizonti.*

ECONOMICS, LAW AND POLITICS

Bulgarian Association of International Law: Sofia, Rakovski 3; f. 1962; 35 mems.; Pres. E. KAMENOV; Sec. S. PENKOV; publ. *Trudove po Meždunarodno Pravo*†.

Bulgarian Association for Penal Law: Sofia, Benkovski 3; f. 1961; Pres. Acad. S. PAVLOV; Sec.-Gen. Prof. I. NENOV.

Economics Association: Sofia, Rakovski 108; f. 1970; Pres. Prof. I. ILIEV; Sec. D. PRAVOV; publ. *Bjuletin.*

HISTORY, GEOGRAPHY AND ARCHAEOLOGY

Bulgarian Geographical Society: Sofia, Ruski 15; f. 1918; Pres. P. PENČEV; Sec. P. POPOV; publs. *Geografija*†, *Izvestija*†, *Problemi na geografijata*†.

Bulgarian Historical Society: Sofia, Volokolamsko Šose 82; f. 1901; Pres. Acad. D. KOSEV; Sec. E. BUŽASKI; publ. *Izvestija.*

Language and Literature

Society of Aesthetes, Art and Literary Critics: Sofia, P. Evtimij 48; f. 1970; Pres. Prof. A. Stojkov; Sec. Dr. K. Goranov.

Society of Foreign Language Teachers: Sofia, Ruski 15; Pres. Prof. A. Ilieva.

Union of Bulgarian Journalists: Sofia, Graf Ignatiev 4; Pres. V. Josifov; publs. *Pogled, Bălgarski Žurnalist.*

Union of Bulgarian Writers: Sofia, Angel Kančev 5; f. 1913; Pres. Acad. P. Zarev; publs. *Literaturen front*†, *Septemvri*†, *Plamăk*†, *Kinoizkustvo*†, *Teatăr*†, *Kartinna galerija, Slavejče.*

Union of Translators in Bulgaria: Sofia, Neofit Rilsky 5; f. 1974; Pres. A. Todorov; publ. *Bjuletin na SPB: teoretičeski sbornik.*

Medicine

Society of Sport Medicine: Sofia, T. Kirkova 1; f. 1953; *c.* 200 mems.; Pres. Prof. Slănčev; Sec. I. Georgiev; publ. *Vuprosi na fizičeskata kăltura.*

Union of Scientific Medical Societies in Bulgaria: Sofia, Serdika 2; f. 1968; Pres. Prof. G. Gălăbov; Sec.-Gen. Prof. G. Stoimenov.

Natural Sciences

Bulgarian Astronautical Society: Sofia, V. Kolarov 36; f. 1967; 100 mems.; library of 500 vols.; Pres. Corresp. mem. N. Bonev; Sec. G. Asparuhov.

Bulgarian Botanical Society: Sofia, Kv. Geo Milev, Acad. G. Bončev Cl. 1; f. 1923; Pres. Acad. D. Jordanov; Sec. S. Kožuharov.

Bulgarian Geological Society: Sofia, Ruski 15; f. 1925; 12,000 vols. in library; Pres. I. Monahov; Sec. V. Kostadinov; publ. *Spisanie.*

Bulgarian Mathematical Society: Sofia, P.O.B. 373; f. 1971; Pres. Prof. A. Mateev; Sec. Assoc. Prof. G. Gerov.

Scientific and Technical Union of Geodesy and Organization of Land Exploitation: Sofia, Rakowski 108; f. 1949; Pres. Prof. V. Pezevski; publ. *Geodesija, Kartografija i Zemeustrojstvo.*

Society of Bulgarian Chemists: Sofia, Anton Ivanov 1; f. 1971; Pres. Prof. J. Čolakov; Sec. L. Rohova.

Society of Bulgarian Physicists: Sofia, Anton Ivanov 5; f. 1971; Pres. Acad. H. Hristov; Sec. S. Nikolova.

Society of Natural Sciences: Sofia, Ruski 1; f. 1896; Pres. B. Botev; Sec. C. Tačev; publs. *Priroda i Znanie, Problemi na Biologijata.*

Philosophy and Psychology

Bulgarian Philosophical Society: Sofia, P. Evtimij 6; f. 1968; Pres. Acad. S. Ganovski; Sec.-Gen. D. Pavlov.

Society of Bulgarian Psychologists: Sofia, Tolbuhin 18; f. 1968; Pres. Prof. G. Pirjov.

Religion, Sociology and Anthropology

Bulgarian Sociological Society: Sofia, P. Evtimij 6; f. 1959; Pres. Z. Ošavkov; Sec. S. Mihajlov; publ. *Bjuletin Sociologičeski izsledvanija*†.

Technology

Central Council of Scientific and Technical Unions: Sofia, Rakovski 108; f. 1949; Pres. Corresp. mem. Prof. I. Popov; Sec.-Gen. E. Marinova; publ. *Tehničesko delo*†.

Scientific and Technical Union of Civil Engineering: Sofia, Rakovski 108; f. 1965; Pres. Prof. D. Kolarov; Sec. M. Ruseva; publ. *Stroitelstvo*†.

Scientific and Technical Union of Energetics, Electrical Engineering and Communications: Sofia, Rakovski 108; f. 1965; Pres. S. Popadijn; Sec. I. Minčev; publs. *Energetika*†, *Electropromišlenost.*

Scientific and Technical Union of Forest Engineering: Sofia, Rakovski 108; f. 1965; Pres. I. Gruev; Sec. G. Georgiev; publ. *Dărvoobrabotvašta i mebelna Promišlenost*†.

Scientific and Technical Union of Mechanical Engineering: Sofia, Rakovski 108; f. 1965; Pres. Prof. V. Diviziev; Sec. M. Trifonova; publ. *Mašinostroene*†.

Scientific and Technical Union of Mining Engineering, Geology and Metallurgy: Sofia, Rakovski 108; f. 1965; Pres. Prof. H. Popjordanov; Sec. B. Conkov; publs. *Văglišta, Rudodobiv, Metalurgija*†.

Scientific and Technical Union of Textiles and Clothing: Sofia, Rakovski 108; f. 1965; Pres. Prof. G. Dahjanov; Sec. M. Todorova; publ. *Tekstilna Promišlenost*†.

Scientific and Technical Union of Chemistry and the Chemical Industry: Sofia, Rakovski 108; f. 1965; Pres. Corresp. mem. Prof. G. Bliznakov; Sec. S. Džalev; publs. *Himija i Industrija*†, *Koži i Obuvki*†, *Celuloza i hartija.*

Scientific and Technical Union of the Food Industry: Sofia, Rakovski 108; f. 1965; Pres. H. Stojanov; Sec. M. Marinov; publ. *Hranitelna promišlenost.*

Scientific and Technical Union of Transport: Sofia, Rakovski 108; f. 1965; Pres. G. Bajčev; Sec. I. Nastev; publs. *Železopăten Transport*†, *Pătista, Korabostroene i Koraboplavane.*

Scientific and Technical Union of Water Works: Sofia, Rakovski 108; f. 1965; Pres. A. Pašev; Sec. V. Jončev; publ. *Hidrotehnika i Melioracii*†.

RESEARCH INSTITUTES

Agriculture and Veterinary Science

(*The Academy of Agricultural Sciences was dissolved in* 1976. *Its Research Institutes are now attached to the National Agro-Industrial Union.*)

Central Veterinary Institute: Sofia; f. 1901; Dir. N. Belev.

Institute of Animal Husbandry: Kostinbrod, Sofia District; f. 1947; Dir. Prof. Tz. Hinkouski.

Institute of Barley Crops: Karnobat; f. 1925; Dir. T. Stefanov.

Institute of Canning Industry: Plovdiv; f. 1954; Dir. B. Mihov.

Institute of Cattle and Sheep Breeding: Stara Zagora, f. 1942; Dir. H. Kraštanov.

Institute of Cereals and Fodder Industry: Sofia; f. 1965; Dir. P. Hristov.

Institute for the Control of Foot and Mouth Disease and Dangerous Infections: Sofia; f. 1974; Dir. I. Genov.

Institute for the Control of Swine Diseases: Vraca; f. 1942; Dir. K. Mermerski.

Institute of Cotton Crops: Čirpan; f. 1925; Dir. M. Božinov.

Institute of Dairy Industry: Vidin; f. 1959; Dir. I. Ivanov

Institute of Economics and Organization of Agriculture: Sofia; f. 1935; Dir. K. Brusarski.

Institute of Fish Industry: Burgas; f. 1965; Dir. V. Hitilov.

Institute of Fish Resources: Varna; f. 1954; Dir. L. Ivanov.

Institute of Fodder Crops: Pleven; f. 1955; Dir. R. Šentov.

Institute of Fruit-Growing: Kjustendil; f. 1929; Dir. S. Manov.

Institute of Fruit-Growing: Plovdiv; f. 1950; Dir. V. Beljakov.

Institute of Hydrotechnics and Improvement: Sofia; f. 1953; Dir. J. Belčev.

Institute of Immunology: Sofia; f. 1942; Dir. S. Bojadžiev.

Institute of Inland Waters Fisheries: Plovdiv; f. 1978; Dir. A. Bojadžiev.

Institute of Introduction and Plant Resources: Sadovo, Plovdiv District; f. 1976; Dir. Prof. G. Stajkov.

Institute of Maize Crops: Kneža; f. 1925; Dir. N. Tomov.

Institute of Meat Industry: Sofia; f. 1955; Dir. Prof. N. Nestorov.

Institute of Mechanization and Electrification of Agriculture: Sofia; f. 1949; Dir. H. Stojanov.

Institute of Mountain Animal Husbandry and Agriculture: Trojan Lovech District; f. 1978; Dir. P. Dončev.

Institute for the Oil-bearing Rose, Ethereal Oil Plants and Medicinal Plants: Kazanlak; f. 1925; Dir. V. Stajkov.

Institute of Plant Protection: Kostinbrod; f. 1935; Dir. Ja. Ljubenov.

Institute of Soya Bean Growing: Pavlikeni; f. 1925; Dir. H. Goranov.

Institute of Sugar Industry: Gorna Orjahovica; f. 1963; Dir. T. Arabadžiev.

Institute of Swine Breeding: Šumen; f. 1955 (part of the Scientific and Production Unit, Sumen); Dir. J. Dimov.

Institute of Tobacco and Tobacco Products: Markovo, Plovdiv District; f. 1950; Dir. D. Šabanov.

Institute of Viticulture and Oenology: Pleven: f. 1902; Dir. K. Katerovo.

Institute of Wheat and Sunflower Crops: General Toševo, Tolbuhin District; f. 1940; Dir. T. Račinski.

Institute of Wine Industry: Sofia; f. 1951; Dir. D. Dimitrov.

"Marica" Institute of Vegetable Crops: Plovdiv; f. 1930; Dir. V. Karaivanov.

"N. Puškarov" Institute of Soil Science and Yields Programming: Sofia; f. 1947; Dir. L. Glogov.

"Obrazcov Čiflik" Institute of Seed Science, Seed Production and Leguminous Crops: Ruse; f. 1905; Dir. J. Todorov.

"Prof. Iv. Ivanov" Science and Production Complex: Carev Brod, Šumen District; f. 1926; Dir. I. Krumov.

Regional Veterinary Institute: Plovdiv; f. 1933; Dir. K. Nikolaev.

Regional Veterinary Institute: Stara Zagora; f. 1930; Dir. I. Jankov.

Regional Veterinary Institute: V. Tărnovo; f. 1930; Dir. Jo. Denev.

Architecture and Town Planning

Complex Institute for Research and Design "Glavproekt": Sofia, Žendov 6; f. 1949; Dir. V. Njagolov.

Complex Research and Design Institute of Regional and Town Planning and Architecture: Sofia, Rakovski 134; Dir. Assoc. Prof. M. Devedžiev.

Earth Sciences

Institute of Geodesy and Photogrammetry: Sofia, Pavlovo, Bul. Deveti Septemvri 217; f. 1966; Dir. B. Krăstev; publ. *Sbornik Trudove*†.

Economics, Law and Politics

Scientific Centre for Home Trade, Public Utilities and Local Industry: Sofia, Dondlukov 41; f. 1968; Dir. Prof. A. Ljutov.

Education

Research Centre for Education: Sofia 1113, Lenin 125, Bl. 5; f. 1977; Gen. Dir. Dr. D. Cvetkov.

Consists of the following institutes:

- Research Institute of General Education: Sofia 1113, Lenin 125, Bl. 5; f. 1950; Dir. L. Georgiev.
- Research Institute of Vocational Training: Sofia 1113, Lenin 125, Bl. 5; f. 1977; Dir. P. Miševa.
- Research Institute of Higher Education: Sofia 1113, Lenin 125, Bl. 4; f. 1977; Dir. Prof. P. Penčev.
- Research Institute of Russian Language and Literature: Sofia 1113, Lenin 125, Bl. 4; f. 1977; Dir. M. Leonidova.
- State Institute of Stenography: Sofia 1000, Lege 5; Dir. N. Makariev.
- Research Institute of Suggestology: Sofia 1000, Budapešta 9; Dir. Dr. G. Lozanov.

Medicine

Institute of Cardio-Vascular Diseases: Sofia, Mike Papo 65; f. 1972; Dir. Prof. C. Dragojčev.

Institute of Dermatology and Venerology: G. Sofijski 1, Sofia; f. 1973; Dir. Prof. P. Mihajlov.

Institute of Endocrinology, Gerontology and Geriatrics: Sofia, H. Mihajlov 6; f. 1972; Dir. Prof. E. Bozadžieva.

Institute of Gastroenterology: Bjalo More 8, Sofia; f. 1972; Dir. Prof. H. Brailski.

Institute of Haematology and Blood Transfusion: Sofia-Dărvenica, Plovdivsko Pole 6; f. 1973; Dir. Prof. V. Serafimov.

Institute of Health Resort Study, Physiotherapy and Rehabilitation: Sofia, Ovča Kupel; f. 1972; Dir. Prof. D. Kostadinov.

Institute of Hygiene and Occupational Health: Sofia, D. Nestorov 15; f. 1972; Dir. Prof. F. Kalojanova.

Institute of Ideological Problems and Medical Pedagogics: Sofia, G. Sofijski 1; f. 1976; Dir. Prof. G. Vekilov.

Institute of Infectious and Parasitic Diseases: Sofia, V. Zaimov 26; f. 1972; Dir. Prof. L. Šindarov.

Institute of Internal Medicine and Pharmacology: Sofia, G. Sofijski 1; f. 1976; Dir. Assoc. Prof. Sv. Ivanov.

Institute of Nephrology, Urology, Haemodialysis and Kidney Transplantation: Sofia, G. Sofijski 1; f. 1972; Dir. Prof. N. Atanasov.

Institute of Neurology, Psychiatry and Neurosurgery: Sofia, Lenin 4 km; f. 1972; Dir. Prof. I. Georgiev.

Institute of Nutrition: Sofia, D. Nestorov 15; f. 1977; Dir. Acad. T. Tašev.

Institute of Obstetrics and Gynaecology: Sofia, Zdrave 2; f. 1976; Dir. Prof. G. Stoimenov.

Institute of Oncology: Sofia, Plovdivsko Pole 6; f. 1972; Dir. Prof. G. Mitrov.

Institute of Ophthalmology and Oto-Rhino-Laryngology: Sofia, Bjalo More 8; f. 1976; Dir. Prof. V. Pavlov.

Institute of Orthopaedics and Traumatology: Sofia, Bjalo More 8; f. 1973; Dir. Prof. Al. Gerčev.

Institute of Paediatrics: Sofia, D. Nestorov 13; f. 1976; Dir. Prof. S. Ninjo.

Institute of Pneumology and Phthisiology: Sofia, D. Nestorov 17; f. 1972; Dir. Prof. R. Radanov.

Institute of Radiology and Radiobiology: Sofia, Želju Vojvoda 56; f. 1976; Dir. Prof. I. Nikolov.

Institute of Surgery and Anaesthesiology: Sofia, G. Sofijski 1; f. 1976; Dir. Prof. Ja. Dobrev.

Medico-biological Institute: Sofia, G. Sofijski 1; f. 1976; Dir. Prof. K. Ičev.

"Pirogov" Emergency Medical Institute: Sofia, Totleben 21; f. 1965; Dir. Assoc. Prof. M. Vanev.

Institute for State Control of Drugs: Sofia, V. Zaimov 26; f. 1949; Dir. Prof. R. Ovčarov.

Sports

Centre for Research and Training in Physical Culture and Sports: 1000 Sofia, T. Kirkova 1; f. 1973; Dir. Dr. P. Slănčev.

Technology

Institute of Agricultural Machine-building: Ruse, A. Getsov 106; f. 1962; Dir. T. Stamenov.

Research and Design Institute of Health Institutions Construction: Sofia, Budapešta 16; f. 1973; Dir. Ž. Kjučukov.

INFORMATION CENTRES, LIBRARIES AND ARCHIVES

Central Agricultural Library: Sofia, Dr. Cankov 6; f. 1961; 380,173 vols.; Dir. M. Bosilska.

Central Historical State Archives: Sofia, ul. Ždanov 5; under the Central Archive Administration; f. 1952; documents of the period 1878–1944; 549,508 dossiers; Dir. D. Mincev.

Central Institute for Scientific and Technical Information (of the State Committee for Science and Technical Progress): Sofia, G. A. Naša 52A; f. 1959; Dir. S. Arsenov (acting); publs. *Obzori*†, *Bjuletini*†.

Central Library of the Higher Technical Institutes: Sofia, Dr. Cankov 2; f. 1942; 417,307 vols.; Dir. S. Ivanova.

Central Medical Library: Sofia, Boul. G. Sofijski 1; f. 1919; 552,458 vols.; 53 affiliated libraries; Dir. N. Kădreva.

Central Scientific-Technical Library: Sofia, G. A. Nasăr 50; f. 1962; 10,597,468 vols. and materials; Dir. I. Vărbanov.

Central State Archives of the People's Republic of Bulgaria: Sofia, Ul. Slavjanska 4; f. 1952; under the Central Archive Administration; documents on state, co-operative and social establishments, organizations and enterprises since Sept. 1944; 350,000 dossiers; Dir. T. Zaševa.

Centre for Pedagogical Information and Documentation: Sofia, Lenin 125; f. 1965; Dir. R. Todorova; publs. *Bjuletin, Pedagogičeska Informacija.*

Centre for Scientific Information, Central Library and Scientific Archives of the Bulgarian Academy of Sciences: Sofia, 7 Noemvri 1; f. 1972; Dir. Corresp. mem. Prof. A. Polikarov.

Centre for Scientific Information on Natural, Mathematical and Social Sciences: f. 1959; Head S. Gabrovska; publs. *Referativnyj Bjuleten Bolgarskoj Naučnoj Literatury* (in Russian, English, French and German).

Central Library: f. 1869; 47 affiliated institute libraries; 1,176,421 vols.; Dir. E. Savova.

Scientific Archives: f. 1869; historical and other documents relating to the Academy and Academicians; Slavonic MSS; 64,300 scientific dossiers; Head D. Koen.

Centre for Scientific, Technical and Economic Information (at the National Agro-Industrial Union): Sofia, D. Cankov 6; f. 1961; Principal Dir. A. Vărbanov; publs. *Informacionni Bjuletini, Obzori, Abstracts of Bulgarian Scientific Literature: series A—Plant Breeding and Forest Economy; series B—Animal Breeding and Veterinary Medicine.*

City Library of Sofia: Sofia, ul. Gurko 1; f. 1930; 580,000 vols.; Dir. St. Avramova.

Information and Computing Centre of the Ministry of Public Health: Sofia, D. Nestorov 15; f. 1977; Dir. Dr. B. Mihov.

Ivan Vazov National Library: Plovdiv; f. 1879; 1,127,000 vols.; Dir. J. Lautliev.

Narodna Biblioteka "Kiril i Metodij" (*Cyril and Methodius National Library*): 1504 Sofia, Boul. Tolbuhin 11; f. 1878; 1,446,155 vols. books and periodicals, 5,509 MSS, 14,094 old and rare publications, 134,641 maps, prints and portraits, 49,526 scores and gramophone records, 265,551 patents and standards; 2,200,000 archival documents; largest public scientific library in Bulgaria; archives of the Bulgarian production of printed materials and national bibliographic centre; archives of documents from the period of Ottoman domination, feudalism and Bulgarian Revival; national information centre in the field of social administration, science and culture; research institute in library science, bibliography and bibliology; national science and coordination centre in library service; Dir. Konstantinka Kalajdžieva; publs. 17 information periodicals including 8 bulletins forming the current national bibliography.

Military Historical Archives: Sofia, Veliko Tărnovo; f. 1915.

Regional Library: Burgas; f. 1889; 305,565 vols.; Dir. P. Jovčeva.

Regional Library: Ruse; 445,416 vols.; Dir. N. Gančev.

Regional Library: Stara Zagora; f. 1955; 288,291 vols.; Dir. D. Denčeva.

Regional Library: Šumen; f. 1922; 455,603 vols.; Dir. N. Laleva.

Regional Library: Varna; f. 1883; 440,246 vols.; Dir. M. Pandova.

Regional Library: Veliko Tărnovo; f. 1922; 414,750 vols.; Dir. D. Sultova.

Sofia City and District State Archives: Sofia, ul. Vitoša 2; f. 1952; 311,042 dossiers; Dir. T. Tončeva.

There are 26 District State Archives in each of the district centres.

Sofiiski Universitet "Kliment Ohridsky" Biblioteka (*University of Sofia Library*): Sofia, Boul. Ruski 15; f. 1888; 1,116,483 vols.; 16 affiliated libraries; Dir. S. Kănčev.

MUSEUMS AND ART GALLERIES

SOFIA

Alexander Stambolisky Museum: Suhodol 44; f. 1956; exhibits illustrating the life of Stambolisky (1879–1923); documents relating to the Agrarian Union Government of 1920–23 and to the Peasant Uprising in Pazardjik led by Stambolisky; Curator P. PETROVA.

Dimitr Blagoev Museum: L. Košut 34; f. 1948; House of the founder of the Bulgarian Communist Party, containing documents and personal effects; Dir. L. JULZARI.

Boyana Church National Museum: Bǎkston 53; f. 1947; Curator J. GENOVA.

Georgi Dimitrov National Museum: Opǎlčenska 66; f. 1953; Dir. M. ČERVENDINEVA.

Ivan Vazov Museum: Ul. I. Vazov10; f. 1926; attached to the Institute of Literature, Bulgarian Academy of Sciences; the house in which the Bulgarian poet lived; Curator V. VǍLČEV.

Museum of Sofia's History: Sofia, Exarch Yossif 27; f. 1953; Dir. M. BUŽAŠKA.

National Archaeological Museum (attached to the Bulgarian Academy of Sciences): A. Stambolisky 2; f. 1892; Dir. D. DOJNOV.

National Agricultural Museum: Dr. Cankov 8; f. 1971; Dir. Prof. R. BALEVSKA.

National Art Gallery: Moskovska 6; f. 1948; representative collection of national art and foreign art; br. in Cathedral Alexandre Nevsky (museum for icons and medieval ecclesiastical art); Dir. V. GOEV.

National Ethnographical Museum (attached to the Bulgarian Academy of Sciences): Moskovska 6A; f. 1906 (re-formed 1949); ethnography and folklore; librarv of 15,530 vols.; Dir. Prof. V. HADŽINIKOLOV; publ. *Sbornik za Narodni Umotyorenia*†.

National Museum of Bulgarian-Soviet Friendship: K. Gotvald 4; f. 1954; Dir. E. CANOV.

National Museum of Ecclesiastical History and Archaeology: Pl. Lenin 19; Dir. Prof. D. PANDURSKI.

National Museum of Military History: Skobelev 23; f. 1916; branch museum in Varna; Dir. S. PENKOV.

National Museum of the Revolutionary Movement of Bulgaria: Pl. Narodno Sǎbranie 11; f. 1950; Dir. T. TANEV; publ. *Godišnik*†.

National Natural History Museum (of the Bulgarian Academy of Sciences): Ruski 1; f. 1889; Dir. Acad. I. KOSTOV.

National Polytechnic Museum: Rakovski 108; f. 1968; Dir. A. VǍLČEV.

PROVINCIAL MUSEUMS
(in alphabetical order by town)

Regional Cultural and Historical Heritage Management Board: Blagoevgrad, Rila 1; f. 1952; archaeology, national revival, history of capitalism and workers' revolutionary movement, socialist building, ethnography, folklore, cultural monuments, plastic arts, national arts and crafts; Dir. I. JOVKOV. Branches: Archaeological Museum in Sandanski; Workers' Revolutionary Movement Museum in Petrich; "Nikola Parapunov" House Museum in Razlog; "Nikola Vaptzarov" House Museum in Bansko; Historical Museum of National Revival in Melnik; "Ivan Kozarev" House Museum in Dobriniste.

Regional Museum of History: Burgas, Lenin 21; f. 1948; archaeology, ethnology, natural sciences, social history and history of the Revolution; Dir. J. KEREMEDČIEV; publ. *Izvestija*†.

Regional Museum of History: Haskovo, Car Osvoboditel 10; f. 1952; archaeology, national revival, ethnography, history of the Revolution, building of socialism; Dir. E. HADŽIEVA.

Hristo Botev Museum: Kalofer; f. 1945; the birth-place of the revolutionary poet and fighter against Ottoman rule (1848-76); Dir. M. NEDELČEVA.

Vasil Levski Museum: Karlovo; f. 1933; the birth-place of the founder and organizer of the Revolutionary Committee for liberation of Bulgaria (1837-73); Dir. P. TATCHEVA.

Directorate of Museums of Koprivštica: Koprivštica; six museums relating to famous Bulgarians; Dir. D. PIRONKOV.

Regional Museum of History: Loveč, H. Kǎrpačev 17; f. 1895; archaeology, ethnology, history of the Revolution; Dir. H. BORISOV.

Museum of the September Uprising: Mihajlovgrad, V. Kolarov 3; f. 1953; Dir. D. PEKOV.

Regional Museum of History: Pazardžik, A. Zlatarov 5; f. 1924; archaeology, history; Dir. N. GIZDOVA.

Stanislav Dospevsky Museum: Pazardžik, B. G. Dimitrov 50; f. 1952; house where the painter lived and worked, containing documents, personal effects and an exhibition of paintings and icons; Dir. C. RADULOV.

Regional Museum of History: Pernik; f. 1954; archaeology, history, ethnography; Dir. K. VODENIČAROV.

Museum of Military History: Pleven, G. Dimitrov 157; f. 1904–07; eight affiliated museums; Dir. K. BANOVA.

Regional Museum of History: Pleven, G. Dimitrov 104; f. 1903; archaeology, ethnology, history of the Revolution; Dir. K. BANOVA.

Art Gallery: Plovdiv, V. Kolarov 15; Dir. K. VITKOVSKI.

Natural Science Museum: Plovdiv, General Zaimov 34; f. 1955; Dir. L. BASAMAKOV.

Regional Museum of Archaeology: Plovdiv, Pl. Sǎedinenie 1; f. 1882; prehistory, classical and mediaeval archaeology, numismatics; Dir. H. DŽAMBOV; publ. *Godišnik*.

Regional Museum of Ethnology: Plovdiv, Dr. Čomakov 2; f. 1945; Dir. Z. MITROVSKA.

Regional Museum of the Revolutionary Movement: Plovdiv, A. Bukoreštliev 14; f. 1948; history of Capitalism, the Uprising and Socialism; Dir. I. TERZIJSKI.

Rila Monastery National Museum: Rila; f. 1961; historical development of Bulgarian art and architecture during the Ottoman period, Bulgarian history and history of the monastery; Dir. P. MITEV.

Regional Museum of History: Ruse; f. 1904; revival and national liberation, history of Capitalism and workers' revolutionary movement, socialist building; Dir. I. IVANOV; publ. *Izvestija*†.

Sipka-Buzludza National Park Museum: Kazanlǎk; f. 1964; monuments connected with the liberation of Bulgaria from Ottoman rule and the foundation of the Bulgarian Communist party; Dir. P. SINKOV.

Ivan Vazov Museum: Sopot; f. 1933; the birth-place of the writer (1850-1921); Dir. C. NEDELČEVA.

Regional Museum of History: Stara Zagora, Ruski 42; f. 1907; archaeology, history, ethnology; Dir. D. NIKOLOV.

Regional Museum of History: Šumen; f. 1904; Šumen fortress; archaeology, history, ethnology; branches in Madara, Pliska, Preslav; Dir. V. VELIKOV.

Regional Museum of History: Tolbuhin; f. 1956; archaeology, national revival, ethnography, history of the Revolution, building of socialism; Dir. M. PASKALEVA.

Museum of Wood Carving and Mural Paintings: Trjavna, P. Slavejkov 27; f. 1963; Dir. L. BONEVA.

Museum of Applied Arts and Crafts: Trojan, Pl. W. Wlaskovski; f. 1961; Dir. P. SĂJČEVSKI.

Regional Museum of History: Varna; f. 1906; archaeology, history, ethnology; Dir. K. STOJANOV; publ. *Izvestija*†.

Regional Museum of History: Veliko Tărnovo, I. Boteva 1; f. 1884; Dir. N. NURKOV; publ. *Izvestija*†.

Regional Museum of History: Vidin, G. Dimitrov 55; f. 1905; archaeology, ethnology, folklore, history of the Revolution; Dir. J. ATANASOVA.

Regional Museum of History: Vraca, Pl. Hr. Botev 1; f. 1952; archaeology, national revival, ethnography, history of the Revolution, building of socialism; Dir. T. PAVLOVA.

UNIVERSITIES

SOFIISKI UNIVERSITET "KLIMENT OHRIDSKY"

(University of Sofia)

RUSKI 15, SOFIA

Telephone: 85-81.

Founded 1888 as High School; granted charter 1909.

State control; Academic year: September to June (two terms).

Rector: Prof. ILCHO DIMITROV.
Pro-Rectors: Prof. T. HRISTOV, Assoc. Prof. M. MIHAJLOVA, Prof. N. TODOROV, Prof. B. NIKOLOV, Prof. V. VERGILOV.
Secretary: K. TĂRGOVSKA.
Librarian: S. KĂNČEV.

Library: *see* under Libraries.
Number of teachers: 1,195.
Number of students: 12,616.
Publication: *Godišnik*†.

DEANS:

Faculty of Philosophy: Assoc. Prof. K. NEŠEV.
Faculty of History: Prof. N. GENČEV.
Faculty of Slavonic Philology: Prof. G. GERMANOV.
Faculty of Classical and Modern Philology: Assoc. Prof. P. PETKOV.
Faculty of Mathematics: Assoc. Prof. D. DIMITROV.
Faculty of Physics: Assoc. Prof. C. BONČEV.
Faculty of Chemistry: Doc. M. KIRILOV.
Faculty of Biology: Prof. G. KONSTANTINOV.
Faculty of Geology and Geography: Prof. D. KANEV.
Faculty of Law: Doc. J. VEKILOV.
Faculty of Journalism: Assoc. Prof. N. RAČEV.

PROFESSORS:

Faculty of Philosophy:
ATANASOV, Ž., Pedagogics
CONEVSKI, ST., Dialectic Materialism
IRIBADŽAKOV, N., Criticism of Contemporary Bourgeois Philosophy
IVANOVA, Z., Psychology
MIHAJLOV, S., Methods of Social Investigation
NIKOLOV, L., Sociology
PASI, I., Aesthetics
PASI, I., Logistics
PETROV, S., Scientific Communism
RADEV, R., Pedagogic Psychology
SPASOV, D., Logic
TODOROV, G., Psychology
VASILEV, K., Historical Materialism
VASILEV, V., Dialectic Materialism

Faculty of History:
ANGELOV, D., Byzantine History
AVRAMOV, A., History of the Bulgarian Communist Party
CVETKOVA, B., History of the Balkan Peoples
DIMITROV, I., History of Bulgarian Institutions
GENČEV, N., Bulgarian History
MIHOVA, H., General Modern History
MILČEV, A., Archaeology
NESTOROV, H., General Modern History
PETROV, P., Bulgarian History
TIVČEV, P., Byzantine History
TODOROV, N., History of the Balkan Peoples
VELKOV, V., Archaeology

Faculty of Slavonic Philology:
AVDŽIEV, Z., Bulgarian Literature
DINEKOV, P., Bulgarian Literature
DURIDANOV, I., General Linguistics
GERMANOV, G., 19th-century Russian Literature
IVANČEV, S., Slavonic Linguistics
MARKOV, G., Theory of Literature
PARVEV, H., Modern Bulgarian, History of Bulgarian Language
PAŠOV, P., Modern Bulgarian

Faculty of Classical and Modern Philology:
DIMITROV, S., History of Arab Countries
ILIEVA, A., Methods of Teaching German Language
MIHAJLOV, G., History of Ancient Greek Language and Culture
NIČEV, A., Ancient Greek Literature
NIKOLOV, B., French Phonetics
VLAHOV, K., Ancient Greek Syntax, Thracian Language

Faculty of Mathematics:
BRANKOV, G., Fluid Mechanics
ČOBANOV, I., Mechanics
DENČEV, R., Differential Equations
DIMITROV, D., Algebra
ILIEV, L., Differential Equations, Advanced Analysis
KOLAROV, D., Solid Mechanics
MATEEV, A., Differential Geometry, Principles of Mathematics
SENDOV, B., Mathematics of Computation
TAGAMLICKI, J., Differential and Integral Calculus

Faculty of Physics:
ANTNRONOV, A., Biophysics Group
BONČEV, C., Atomic Physics
BORISOV, M., Solid State Physics
DANCEV, A., Physics, Contemporary Theory of Physics
MOLDOVANOVA, M., Semi-conductor Physics
NIKOLOV, N., Astronomy
PANČEV, S., Dynamic Meteorology
PETKOV, I., Geophysics
PETRAKIEV, A., Optics and Spectroscopy
RAEV, A., General Physics
STOJČEV, J., Physical Electronics

Faculty of Chemistry:
ANTONOV, D., Technology of Organic Chemistry
BLIZNAKOV, G., Inorganic Chemistry
BUDUROV, S., Physical Chemistry of Metals and Alloys
GEORGIEV, H., Organic Catalysis
GEORGIEV, M., Organic Synthesis
HRISTOV, H., Organic Chemistry
ŠELUDKO, A., Colloidal Chemistry

Faculty of Biology:
GENČEV, G., Genetics
GEORGIEV, G., Plant Physiology
KALČEV, L., Animal and Human Physiology
KITANOV, B., Botany
KONSTANTINOV, G., Genetics
NIKOLOV, T., Biochemistry
KONSTANTINOV, G., Genetics
NIKOLOV, T., Biochemistry
PENEV, I., Plant Ecology
PEŠEV, C., Zoology of Vertebrates
STEFANOV, S., Histology and Cytology of Vertebrates
VELČEV, V., Botany

Faculty of Geology and Geography:
ATANASOV, G., Petrography
BELMUSTAKOV, E., Dynamic and Historical Geology
DIMITROV, D., Climatology
GEORGIEV, M., Physical Geography of Bulgaria and the Continents
HRISTOV, T., Economic Geography
JORDANOV, M., Dynamic and Historical Geology
KANEV, D., Geomorphology
MANDEV, P., Geology; Mineral Oils Geochemistry
MIŠEV, M., Economic Geography of the Socialist Countries
PENČEV, P., General Hydrology
PENKOV, I., Economic Geography of Bulgaria
VERGILOV, V., Petrography
ŽELJAZKOVA, M., Geochemistry

Faculty of Law:
CONEV, V., Theory of State and Law
DERMENDŽIEV, I., Administrative Law
GOLEMINOV, C., Contract Law
JANEV, J., Theory of State and Law
JANOVSKI, B., Civil Law
KOSTADINOV, G., Administrative Law
LJALEV, T., Civil Law
NENOV, I., Penal Law

POPOV, L., Contract Law
SPASOV, B., Constitutional Law
TADŽER, V., Civil Law
VELINOV, I. Civil Law

Faculty of Journalism:
DIMITROV, G., Scientific Grounds of Propaganda
GEORGIEV, D., Theory and Practice of Newspaper Graphical Design
NINKOV, M., Theory and Practice of Broadcasting/Radio and TV/Journalism
PANAJOTOV, F., History of Bulgarian Journalism
RAČEV, N., Genres of Journalism
TODOROV, D., Foreign Journalism

Scientific Council for Political Economy:
KAMENOV, E.
MILOŠEVSKI, A.
NENOV, I.
POPOV, N.

PLOVDIVSKI UNIVERSITET "PAISIJ HILENDARSKI"

("Paisij Hilendarski" University of Plovdiv)

PLOVDIV, CAR ASEN 24

Telephone: 3-86-61.

Founded 1961 from "Paisij Hilendarski" Higher Pedagogical Institute, Plovdiv.

Rector: Assoc. Prof. D. POBORNIKOV.
Pro-Rectors: Prof. I. PETROV, Assoc. Prof. T. NAKOV, Assoc. Prof. M. GURGULOVA, Assoc. Prof. A. ATANSOV, Assoc. Prof. H. MIHOVSKI.
Registrar: J. BAKALOV.
Librarian: K. AKŠAROV.

Number of teachers: 265.
Number of students: 3,921.
Publication: *Naučni Trudove*†.

DEANS:

Faculty of Mathematics: Assoc. Prof. I. ILIEV.
Faculty of Chemistry and Biology: Assoc. Prof. N. JANEV.
Faculty of Physics: Assoc. Prof. P. KARTALOV.
Faculty of Public Professions: Assoc. Prof. B. JORDANOV.

PROFESSORS:

ANGELOV, P., Zoology
BONEV, Z., Geology
IVANOV, S., Technology of Organic Chemistry
PETROV, J., Human Anatomy and Physiology

VELIKO TARNOVSKI UNIVERSITET "KIRIL I METODII"

(Cyril and Methodius University of Veliko Tărnovo)

Telephone: 26-11.

Founded 1971 from "Kiril i Metodi" Higher Pedagogical Institute.

Rector: Prof. Dr. D. FILIPOV.
Pro-Rectors: Assoc. Prof. A. DAVIDOV, Assoc. Prof. G. DANCEV, Assoc. Prof. R. RUSINOV, Assoc. Prof. J. NIKOLOVA.
Registrar: S. MARKOV.
Librarian: I. PENCEV.

Number of teachers: 240.
Number of students: 5,046.
Publication: *Trudove*†.

HIGHER INSTITUTES

(in alphabetical order by town)

HIGHER INSTITUTE OF CHEMICAL TECHNOLOGY

8010 BURGAS

Telephone: 6-01-19.

Founded 1962.

Rector: Prof. G. ANGELOVA.
Pro-Rectors: Assoc. Prof. D. GROZDEV, Assoc. Prof. A. DIMOV, Assoc.Prof. I. DOBREVSKI.
Register: V. PETROV.
Librarian: M. MURGOVA.

Library of 60,000 vols.
Number of teachers: 160.
Number of students: 1,200.
Publication: *Godišnik*†.

HIGHER MECHANICAL ELECTROTECHNICAL INSTITUTE

GABROVO, HADŽI DIMITĂR, 4

Telephone: 2-19-31.

Founded 1963.

Rector: Assoc. Prof. G. UZUNOV.
Pro-Rectors: Prof. G. STOJANOV, Assoc. Prof. T. TODOROV, Assoc. Prof. P. ČANTOV, Assoc. Prof. C. DŽONOV.
Registrar: I. KAMBUROV.

Number of teachers: 152.
Number of students: 1,797.

HIGHER INSTITUTE OF FOOD AND FLAVOUR INDUSTRIES

PLOVDIV, LENIN 26

Telephone: 4-18-11.

Founded as an independent Institute 1953.

Rector: Prof. L. GJUZELEV.
Pro-Rectors: Prof. S. TANČEV, Prof. J. POPOVA, Assoc. Prof. S. DIČEV.
Registrar: K. PALIKRUŠEV.
Librarian: S. TODOROVA.

Number of teachers: 250.
Number of students: 2,493.
Publication: *Naučni Trudove*†.

PROFESSORS:

ATANASOV, D., Tobacco
BEŠKOV, M., Microbiology
BONEV, S., Fruit and Vegetable Technology
GJUZELEV, L., Tobacco
GEROV, S., Wine Technology
HRISTOV, E., Meat and Fish Technology
IVANOV, I., Mechanics
IVANOV, T., Technology of Fermentation Products
KOSTOV, K., Meat Technology
LAMBREV, B., Public Catering
LUKANOV, K., Economics and Organization
MANČEV, S., Beer Technology
MANEVA, D., Analytical Chemistry
NUŠEV, I., Technology of Spirits
PRODANSKI, P., Milk Technology
ŠIKRENOV, D., Grain Preservation

"VASIL KOLAROV" HIGHER INSTITUTE OF AGRICULTURE

PLOVDIV, D.MENDELEEV 12

Telephone: 34-98.

Rector: Prof. I. RANČEV.
Pro-Rectors: Assoc. Prof. I. TAFRADŽIJSKI, Prof. M. DIRIMANOV, Assoc. Prof. K. DOJKOV, Prof. V. VASILIEV.
Chief Librarian: H. NAJDENOV.

Number of teachers: 239.
Number of students: 1,785.

PROFESSORS:

ANGELIEV, V., Horticulture
BOGDANOV, V., Phytopathology
CANKOV, B., Viticulture
COLOV, C., Fruit Growing
DELČEV, S., Agricultural Organization
DELIPAVLOV, D., Botany
DIMITROV, S., Botany
DIRIMANOV, M., Entomology
DRAGANOV, D., Plant Physiology
ENČEV, J., Genetics
FETVADŽIEVA, N., Farming
GENKOV, G., Horticulture
GJUROV, G., Soil Science
GRIGOROV, S., Entomology
HRISTOV, N., Phytopathology
IVANOV, I., Horticulture
JAKIMOVA, J., Feedstuffs Production
KARTALOV, P., Horticulture
KOEDŽIKOV, H., Plant Breeding
KOJNOV, G., Plant Breeding
KOJNOV, V., Soil Science
KOLEV, D., Plant Breeding
KOLEV, I., Botany
KOLEVA, B., Soil Science
KOVAČEV, S., Agricultural Mechanization
KOZAREV, G., Farming
MASLINKOV, M., Plant Breeding
MURTAZOV, T., Horticulture
NIKOLOV, H., Viticulture
PETKOV, C., Agricultural Economics
PETROV, N., Animal Husbandry
POPOV, S., Fruit Growing,
RANČEV, I., Agricultural Economics
RIZVANOV, K., Microbiology
STANČEV, L., Agricultural Chemistry
TAFRADŽIJSKI, I., Phytopathology
TENEV, P., Viticulture
TOPALOV, V., Plant Breeding
TOREV, A., Plant Physiology

UZUNOV, M., Feedstuff Production
VAKARELSKI, J., Agricultural Mechanization
VAAILEV, V., Agricultural Improvement
ZANKOV, Z., Viticulture
ŽELEV, A., Farming

HIGHER INSTITUTE OF MACHINE-BUILDING, MECHANIZATION AND ELECTRIFICATION OF AGRICULTURE

RUSE,
UL. KOMSOMOLSKA 8
Telephone: 44-71.
Founded 1954.

Rector: Prof. A. SUČKOV.
Pro-Rectors: Assoc. Prof. S. STOJKOV, Assoc. Prof. M. KANEV, Assoc. Prof. G. GATEV.
Registrar: D. DIMITROV.
Librarian: M. FOTEVA.

Library of 135,000 vols.
Number of teachers: 380.
Number of students: 3,800.
Publication: *Naučni Trudove*†.

PROFESSORS:

DIMITROV, I., Machine Elements
GEORGIEV, I., Agricultural Machines
SPIRIDONOV, G., Agricultural Technology
SUČKOV, A., Machine-building
TODOROV, M., Mechanics
VELEV, D., Thermotechnics

"GEORGI DIMITROV" HIGHER INSTITUTE OF PHYSICAL CULTURE

SOFIA, TINA KIRKOVA 1
Telephone: 88-15-11.
Founded 1942.
Academic year: September to June (two terms).

Rector: Prof. Dr. P. SLĂNČEV.
Pro-Rectors: Assoc. Prof. N. PETROVA, Assoc. Prof. S. BOBEV, Dr. I. ILEV.
Registrar: M. RUSEV.
Librarian: N. BLIZNAKOVA.

Number of teachers: 240.
Number of students: 2,405.
Publication: *Trudove*†.

PROFESSORS:

DOBREV, D., Physiology
GEORGIEV, V., Neurophysiology
HADŽIEV, N., Gymnastics
KRĂSTEV, K., Physiology
MOROV, S., Anatomy
PĂRVANOV, B., Psychology of Sport
PETROV, R., Wrestling
SLĂNČEV, P., Sports Medicine
STAJKOV, I., Skiing
ŽELJAZKOV, Z., Research Basis of Training
ZOTOV, S., Physiology

HIGHER INSTITUTE OF CHEMICAL TECHNOLOGY

SOFIA, 56 DĂRVENICA
Telephone: 66-51-21.
Founded as an independent Institute 1953.

Rector: Prof. M. NATOV.
Pro-Rectors: Assoc. Prof. I. BOŽOV, Assoc. Prof. B. SAMUNEVA, Assoc. Prof. P. BOZADŽIEV.
Registrar: A. TRIFONOV.
Librarian: P. HĂŠOVSKA.

Library of 40,000 vols.
Number of teachers: 364.
Number of students: 3,440.
Publication: *Godišnik*†.

DEANS:

Faculty of Organic Technology: Prof. S. IKONOPISOV.
Faculty of Inorganic Technology: Assoc. Prof. D. ŠIŠKOV.
Faculty of Metallurgy: Assoc. Prof. A. AVRAMOV.

PROFESSORS:

Faculty of Organic Technology:
ALEKSANDROV, A., Chemical Engineering
BOŽOV, I., Automatization
CVETKOV, I., Leather Technology
DIMITROV, D., General Chemical Technology
GUROV, R., Economics of Chemical and Metal Production
HRISTOV, C., Chemical Technology of Wood
IVANOV, C., Organic Chemistry
KABAIVANOV, V., Technology of Plastics
KAIŠEV, K., Fuels
MILOŠEV, M., Organization and Protection of the Population and People's Economy
RAJČEVA, S., Physical Chemistry
STOJANOV, A., Organic Synthesis Technology
TODOROV, I., Rubber Technology
TODOROV, K., Chemical Fibres and Textile Chemistry Technology

Faculty of Inorganic Technology:
DONČEV, S., Heat Engineering
ILIEV, I., Mineralogy and Petrography
KARADAKOV, B., Analytical Chemistry
NENOV, I., Technology of Electrochemical Processes
PIRGOV, D., Mathematics
VIDENOV, N., Inorganic Substances

Faculty of Metallurgy:
DŽOGLEV, D., Chemistry and Technology of Semiconductor Materials
ERININ, H., Metallurgy of Ferrous Metals
HRISTOV, L., Physics
JORDANOV, H., Metallurgy of Nonferrous Metals
KOLAROV, N., Inorganic Chemistry
NIKOLOV, T., Metal Casting and Metallurgy
POPOV, K., Mechanics

HIGHER INSTITUTE OF CIVIL ENGINEERING

H. SMIRNENSKI 1, SOFIA
Telephone: 66-17-71.
Founded 1942.

Rector: Prof. I. PATOKOV.
Pro-Rectors: Prof. G. STEFANOV, Prof. G. KOLEV, Assoc. Prof. M. SLAVOV, Assoc. Prof. M. MINEV.
Registrar: T. GRIGOROV.

Number of teachers: 325.
Number of students: 6,700.

DEANS:

Faculty of Civil Engineering: Assoc. Prof. T. CURINSKI.
Faculty of Hydrotechnical Engineering: Prof. G. ILČEV.
Faculty of Geodesy: Prof. I. STANEV.
Faculty of Architecture: Prof. I. SAZDOV.

PROFESSORS:

Faculty of Civil Engineering:
ASENOV, K., Roads
BONČEV, I., Concrete Bridges
BRAJNOV, M., Steel, Steel Bridges and Wooden Constructions
BRANKOV, G., Concrete Constructions
ČAVOV, T., Steel, Steel Bridges and Wooden Constructions
COSTOV, T., Railways
CURINSKI, T., Building Organization
DENČEV, M., Machine-building
DIMITROV, D., Steel, Steel Bridges and Wooden Constructions
DINGOZOV, G., Terrestrial Mechanics
GENOV, G., Surface Building
GENOV, H., Construction Economics
GOČEV, S., Wooden Constructions
IVANOV, G., Railways
KARAMANSKI, T., Theory of Elasticity and Stability
MANOILOV, L., Reinforced Concrete
MARKOV, T., Reinforced Concrete
SIMEONOV, S., Building Statistics
SOTIROV, D., Roads
STAMENOV, S., Building Materials
STEFANOV, G., Soil Mechanics
ŠTILJANOV, G., Roads
TODOROV, T., Roads
TOTOV, G., Advanced Mathematics
VĂLEV, V., Building Technology
VĂRBANOV, H., Theory of Elasticity and Stability
VENKOV, V., Soil Mechanics

Faculty of Hydrotechnical Engineering:
DŽUNINSKI, B., Hydromeliorations
GADŽALSKI, I., Amelioration
GEORGIEV, L., Underground Hydro-Construction
HADŽIEV, H., Water Supplies and Drains Systems of Buildings
IGNATOV, P., Water Supply and Sewerage Systems
ILČEV, G., Hydraulics
IVANČEV, N., Physics
KINAREV, I., Hydraulics
KOTOV, L., Drainage and River Bed Correction
KOZAROV, M., Technical Mechanics
MARINOV, I., Hydraulic Power Utilization
MILOSLAVOV, S., Hydraulic Power Utilization
NIKOLOV, N., Hydraulic and Water Research
NIKOLOV, Ž., Hydrology
NINOV, I., Hydraulics
PATOKOV, I., Hydro-Construction, Waterways and Ports
PENKOV, M., Soil Science
RADEV, N., Hydromelioration
RAJNOV, C., Hydrotechnical Equipments
SĂEV, S., Agrotechnics and Agriculture
SLAVOV, M., Water Supply and Drainage Systems of Buildings
STANČEV, S., Hydraulics
VASILEV, S., Hydraulic Power Utilization
ZACEV, Z., Water Supply and Drainage Systems of Buildings

Faculty of Geodesy:
ATANASOV, ST., Engineering Geodesy
DASKALOVA, M., Geodesy
DIŠEVA, N., Economics and Organization of Socialist Agriculture

Djulgerov, S., Cartography
Hajduški, I., Photogrammetry
Jončev, V., Planning and Organization of Villages
Kolev, G., Land Exploitation
Nakov, N., Photogrammetry
Rusev, B., Geodesy
Stanev, I., Organization of Land Exploitation
Vučkov, P., Organization of Land Exploitation
Zlatanov, G., Computer Technology, Organization and Control of Geodesy Works

Faculty of Architecture:
Angelov, M., Building Construction
Damjanov, A., Building Design
Dorosiev, Al., Interior Design
Ivančev, I., Public Buildings
Ivanova, M., History of Architecture
Kondarev, N., Scientific Communism
Mitev, B., History of the Bulgarian Communist Party
Pisarski, M., Industrial Buildings
Sazdov, I., Public Building
Šterev, C., Building Construction
Stoičkov, A., Town Planning
Stojčev, L., Landscape Design
Tašev, P., Town Planning
Tatarov, I., Public Buildings
Todorova, M., Town Planning

HIGHER INSTITUTE OF FORESTRY

DĂRVENICA, SOFIA
Telephone: 63-01.

Founded as an independent Institute 1953; Academic year: September to June (two terms).

Rector: Prof. A. Iliev.
Pro-Rectors: Assoc. Prof. T. Iliev, Assoc. Prof. P. Karadočev, Assoc. Prof. G. Filipov.
Registrar: B. Popov.

Number of teachers: 164.
Number of students: 1,815.
Publication: ***Naučni Trudove†.***

Deans:

Faculty of Forestry: Prof. I. Dobrinov.
Faculty of Wood Technology: Assoc. Prof. A. Kavalov.

Professors:

Barbutov, G., Electrical Engineering
Biolčev, A., Soil Erosion
Bogdanov, B., Silviculture
Dakov, N., Silviculture
Dobrinov, I., Genetics and Selection
Dončev, G., Woodworking
Donov, V., Forest Fertilization
Enčev, E., Wood Technology
Hristov, S., Forest Utilization and Transport
Iliev, A., Forest Planning
Iliev, T., Mechanization and Automation in Woodworking
Karadocev, P., Economics, Organization and Planning
Nikolov, S., Wood Technology
Nisimov, H., Forest Utilization and Transport
Ribarov, S., Geodesy
Ronkov, B., Chemistry and Physics
Sirakov, H., Economics, Organization and Planning
Statkov, N., Forest Utilization and Transport
Tošev, B., Mathematics, Mechanics and Theory of Elasticity
Vlasev, Vl., Silviculture
Zahariev, B., Silviculture

HIGHER INSTITUTE OF MINING AND GEOLOGY

SOFIA 1156, DĂRVENICA
Telephone: 6-25-81.
Founded 1953.

Academic year: October to June (two terms).

Rector: Prof. Dr. T. Dobrev.
Pro-Rectors: Prof. T. Conkov, Prof. K. Bandov, Prof. B. Strašimirov.
Registrar: C. Angelov.
Librarian: F. Ivanova.

Number of teachers : 236.
Number of students: 1,591.
Publication: ***Godišnik†.***

Deans:

Faculty of Mining: Prof. S. Gajdaržiev.
Faculty of Geology: Prof. S. Stojanov.

Professors:

Faculty of Geology:
Antonov, H., Hydrogeology
Bogdanov, B., Economic Geology
Demirev, A., Engineering Geology
Dobrev, T., Geophysics
Nenkov, N., Drilling Mechanics
Nikolaev, G., Economic Geology
Ognjanov, S., Oil and Gas Drilling
Raškov, R., Economic Geology
Stojanov, S., Mineralogy
Strašimirov, B., Palaeontology
Trošanov, V., Exploration of Oil and Gas Deposits
Zafirov, S., Geotectonics

Faculty of Mining:
Bandov, K., Mechanization of Mines
Conkov, N., Mine Surveying
Čonkov, T., Mining
Danailov, D., Mine Electrification
Denev, S., Mineral Processing
Dimov, I., Theoretical Mechanics
Gajdardžiev, S., Mineral Processing
Hristov, I., Mine Surveying
Irinkov, S., Mine Electrification
Isatkov, S., Mining
Ivanov, I., Higher Mathematics
Kandov, L., Theoretical Mechanics
Konjarov, N., Political Economy
Kovačev, K., Mineral Processnig
Minčev, T., Theoretical Mechanics
Obreškov, D., Theory of Mechanisms
Paraškevov, Mining
Šejretov, K., Mechanization of Mines
Stefanov, T., Mine Ventilation
Stoev, S., Mineral Processing
Stojanov, B., Mine Surveying
Velev, M., Mining

"V. I. LENIN" HIGHER INSTITUTE OF ELECTRICAL AND MECHANICAL ENGINEERING

SOFIA, DĂRVENICA,
19 FEVRUARI 1
Telephone: 88-43-51.
Founded as an independent Institute 1953.

Rector: Prof. N. Načev.
Pro-Rectors: Prof. P. Penčev, Prof A. Pisarev, Assoc. Prof. S. Conkov, Prof. D. Dimitrov, Assoc. Prof. B. Stojnov.
Registrar: **A. Čanev.**
Librarians: S. Vărbanova, E. Nikolova.

Library: ***see*** **under Libraries.**
Number of teachers: 900.
Number of students: 11,000.
Publication: *Izvestija.*

Deans:

Faculty of Radioelectronics: Assoc. Prof. H. Hristov.
Faculty of Electrotechnics: Prof. V. Dinov.
Faculty of Machine Technology: Assoc. Prof. V. Alvasov.
Faculty of Machine Building: Assoc. Prof. I. Kolarov.
Faculty of Energy Machine Building: Prof. G. Mumžijan.
Faculty of Automation: Prof. D. Jordanov.
Faculty of Transport: Prof. S. Nedelčev.
Centre for Ideological Disciplines: Prof. S. Sarkisjan.
Centre for Applied Mathematics: Prof. V. Topenčarov.

"KARL MARX" HIGHER INSTITUTE OF ECONOMICS

SOFIA, RAKOVSKI 114
Telephone: 88-29-02.
Founded 1920.

Rector: Prof. G. Vakliev.
Pro-Rectors: Prof. L. Radulov, Prof. Tr. Georgiev, Assoc. Prof. D. Dimitrov, Assoc. Prof. I. Dobreva.
Registrar: S. Ženkova.
Librarian: S. Ševikova.

Library of 173,184 vols.
Number of teachers: 444.
Number of students: 8,625.
Publication: ***Trudove†.***

Deans:

Faculty of Economic Information: Assoc. Prof. N. Dimitrov.
Faculty of General Economics: Assoc. Prof. I. Bonev.
Faculty of Branch Economics: Prof. I. Dočev.
Faculty of Commerce: Assoc. Prof. C. Jočev.
Faculty of International Economic Relations: Assoc. Prof. L. Karakaševa.

Professors:

Faculty of Economic Information:
Avramov, A., Statistics
Dusanov, I., Book-keeping
Ganev, A., Information Processing
Jordanov, D., Accounting and Bookkeeping
Pergelov, K., Accounting and Bookkeeping
Stanev, S., Statistics

TOTEV, T., Accounting and Book-keeping
VAKLIEV, G., Accounting and Book-keeping

Faculty of General Economics:
ANGELOV, T., Planning
AROJO, J., Political Economy
ATANASOV, A., Finance
BEROV, L., Political Economy
DAVIDOV, D., Labour Economics
DIMOV, N., Marxism-Leninism
GRIGOROV, K., History of Economic Doctrines
HADŽIIVANOV, I., Planning
ILIEV, I., Planning
JORDANOV, I., Political Economy
KOSTOV, I., Political Economy
MATEEV, E., Planning
MEČEV, S., Political Economy
NAUMOV, N., Statistics
PAČEV. T., Sociology
PAVLIDIS, S., Political Economy
PETROV, G., Finance
PETROV, M., Political Economy
RADULOV, L., Political Economy
RUSINOV, M., Finance
SAVOV, S., Political Economy
ŠOPOV, D., Labour Economics
VALEV, N., Planning
VALOV, T., Marxism-Leninism
VELIKOV, N., Political Economy

Faculty of Branch Economics:
ANAČKOV, V., Business Management and Modelling of Agro-Industrial Units
ATANASOV, P., Technology of Agro-Industrial Units
CANKOV, S., Transport
COLOV, J., Business Management and Modelling of Agro-Industrial Units
DOČEV, I., Industrial Economics
GADJAROV, N., Technology of Agro-Industrial Units
GEORGIEV, T., Business Management and Modelling of Agro-Industrial Units
GROZEV, I., Agrarian Economy
IVANOV, I., Technology of Agro-Industrial Units
JORDANOV, T., Regional Economics
KALIGOROV, H., Industrial Economics
KALOJANOV, A., Agrarian Economy
KOVACEVA, Z., Agrarian Economy
LENKOV, L., Agrarian Economy
MANOV, I. Agrarian Economy
MIŠEV, V., Agrarian Economy
PETEV, D., Technology of Agro-Industrial Units
PETKOV, P., Economics and Planning of Agro-Industrial Units
POPOV, T., Agrarian Economy
TANOV, A., Economics and Planning of Agro-Industrial Units
TOPČIJSKI, S., Agrarian Economy
VĂLEV, G., Technology
ZAHARIEV, Z., Agrarian Economy
ZLATANOV, Z., Industrial Economics

Faculty of Commerce:
ALEKSANDROV, K., Home Trade
ANDREEV, A., Science of Commodities
CAUŠEV, A., Home Trade
HADŽINIKOLOV, H., Home Trade
VIDENOV, I., Home Trade

Faculty of International Economic Relations:
CAREVSKI, N., International Monetary and Financial Relations
DIMITROV, D., Law Science
GEORGIEV, L., International Relations
HRISTOFOROV, V., Law
POPISAKOV, G., International Economic Relations
RADKOVSKI, P., Organization and Management of Foreign Trade
SAVOV, M., International Socialist Integration
VASILEV, D., Foreign Trade

HIGHER INSTITUTE OF ZOOTECHNICS AND VETERINARY MEDICINE

STARA ZAGORA, D. BLAGOEV 62
Telephone: 2-80-31.
Founded 1974.

Rector: Prof. V. GRUEV.
Pro-Rectors: Prof. R. KARAIVANOV, Prof. T. TOMOV, Prof. G. KAMBUROV, Assoc. Prof. I. BOŠNAKOV.

Number of teachers: 240.
Number of students: 1,596.

DEANS:

Zootechnical Faculty: Prof. N. KIROV.
Faculty of Veterinary Medicine: Prof. O. NEJČEV.

PROFESSORS:

Zootechnical Faculty:
ALEKSIEV, A., Stock Feeding and Dietetics
BAROV, V., Mathematics
BEREMSKI, S., Swine Breeding
GANOVSKI, H., Stock Feeding and Dietetics
GRUEV, V., Sheep Breeding
IVANOV, N., Biochemistry
KARAIVANOV, R., Horse Breeding
KIREV, P., Economics and Organization of Agriculture
KIROV, N., Dairying and Microbiology
KOSTOV, K., Forage Production
LAZAROV, E., Zoohygiene
RADEV, G., Artificial Insemination
RAJČEV, S., Sheep Breeding
RALČEV, G., Sheep Breeding
RUSEV, V., Physiology of Domestic Animals
STANEV, S., Cattle Breeding
SJAROV, J., Cattle Breeding
STOJANOV, V., Stock Feeding and Dietetics
TANEV, D., Sheep Breeding
TODOROV, A., Anatomy of Domestic Animals
TOŠEV, A., Physiology of Domestic Animals
VALOV, T., Anatomy of Domestic Animals
VANČEV, T., Poultry Raising
VASILEVA, J., Genetics and Livestock Breeding
VLADIMIROV, J., Stock Feeding and Dietetics
ZAHARIEV, Z., Cattle Breeding

Faculty of Veterinary Medicine:
ARSOV, R., Epizootology
BODUROV, N., Surgery
CONKOV, P., Genetics and Livestock Breeding
DJAKOV, L., Pathological Anatomy
DRUMEV, D., Veterinary Pharmacology
DRJANOVSKI, P., Radiobiology
GABRAŠANSKI, P., Internal Medicine
GIGOV, C., Anatomy of Domestic Animals
GIRGINOV, G., Epizootology
GRADINARSKI, G., Veterinary Physiology
IVANOV, I., Parasitology
JOVČEV, E., Epizootology
KAMBUROV, G., Microbiology
KOJČEV, K., Surgery
KRĂSTEV, H., Cytology, Histology and Embryology
NEJČEV, O., Surgery
NESTOROV, N., Physiology of Domestic Animals
NIKOV, S., Internal Medicine
PRANŽEV, I., Obstetrics, Gynaecology, Artificial Insemination
TOMOV, T., Veterinary Physiology
VARBANOVA, S., Chemistry
VASILEV, I., Parasitology
JOCOV, S., Genetics and Livestock Breeding
ZAHARIEV, C., Hygiene and Technology of Foodstuffs
ŽELEV, V., Pathological Anatomy

"D. A. CENOV" HIGHER INSTITUTE OF ECONOMICS AND FINANCE

SVIŠTOV, ČAKĂROV 2
Telephone: 27-21-25.
Founded 1936.

Rector: Prof. Dr. D. PANAJOTOV.
Pro-Rectors: Assoc. Prof. SL. SLAVEV, Assoc. Prof. S. KALČEV, Assoc. Prof. C. KOSEV.
Registrar: K. KALUŠKOV.
Librarian: V. ANTONOV.

Library of 110,000.

Number of teachers: 190.
Number of students: 4,000.
Publication: *Godišnik*†.

DEANS:

Faculty of Finance: Prof. Dr. H. DRAGANOV.
Faculty of Book-keeping: Prof. ST. ALEKSANDROV.

PROFESSORS:

HRISTOV, M., Finance
IVANOV, P., Political Economy
KACAROV, I., Social Affairs
MARINOV, H., Economic Geography and Regional Economics
MUTAFOV, N., Statistics
NANKOV, V., Mechanization of Data Processing
PAMUKČIEV, M., Informatics
PANAJOTOV, D., Economic Planning
PAVLOV, V., Control
PORJAZOV, D., Political Economy of Capitalism
SLAVEV, S., Geography
SPASOV, D., Accounting

"DIMITR BLAGOEV" HIGHER INSTITUTE OF NATIONAL ECONOMY

VARNA, LENIN 77
Telephone: 2-11-81.
Founded 1921.

Academic year: September to June.

Rector: Prof. G. DIMITROV.
Pro-Rectors: Assoc. Prof. N. GRADEV, Assoc. Prof. Z. KOVAČEV, Assoc. Prof. K. BONEV, Assoc. Prof. M. KOLAROVA.
Registrar: I. DŽUTEV.
Librarian: A. TODOROVA.

Library of 159,232 vols.
Number of teachers: 188.
Number of students: 5,300.
Publications: *Trudove*†, *Izvestija*†.

DEANS:

Faculty of Accountancy: Assoc. Prof. L. KOSTOVA.
Faculty of Commerce: Assoc. Prof. A. GEORGIEV.

PROFESSORS:

ANGELOV, R., Finance and Credit
BAZLJANKOV, M., Accountancy
CONEV, S., Economics and Organization of Tourism
DIMITROV, G., Economics of Building
GENČEV, P., Economics of Supply
HADŽIEV, S., Economics of Building
KOVAČEV, Z., Political Economy
STANEV, L., Statistics and Mathematics
TELBIZOV, K., Law
VANKOV, V., Scientific Communism

HIGHER INSTITUTE OF ELECTRICAL AND MECHANICAL ENGINEERING

VARNA, KV. LEVSKI, POST OFFICE 10
Telephone: 8-01-61.
Founded 1962.

Rector: Prof. L. LEFTEROV.
Pro-Rectors: Assoc. Prof. M. MARINOV, Assoc. Prof. S. KOLEV, Assoc. Prof. H. HANŽIJSKI, Assoc. Prof. P. DRAGULEV.
Registrar: G. TEPAVIČAROV.
Librarian: R. VOJNOVA.

Library of 211,890 vols.
Number of teachers: 352.
Number of students: 4,800.
Publication: *Godišnik*†.

DEANS:

Faculty of Electrical Engineering: Assoc. Prof. D. DIMITROV.
Faculty of Mechanical Engineering: Assoc. Prof. V. SEVASTAKIEV.
Faculty of Shipbuilding: Assoc. Prof. S. ALEKSANDROV.

PROFESSORS:

LEFTEROV, L., Machine Elements
VĂTEV, E., Metal Science

SCHOOLS OF ART AND MUSIC

HIGHER PEDAGOGICAL INSTITUTE OF MUSIC

PLOVDIV, T. SAMODUMOV 2
Telephone: 2-83-11.
Founded 1972.

Rector: Prof. A. DIAMANDIEV.
Pro-Rectors: Assoc. Prof. K. DŽENEV, Assoc. Prof. N. TODOROV, Assoc. Prof. N. STOJKOV.
Registrar: I. MATEV.

Number of teachers: 62.
Number of students: 779.

BULGARIAN STATE CONSERVATOIRE

SOFIA, K. GOTVALD 11
Telephone: 44-20-79.
First founded 1904; reorganized as a Conservatoire 1954.

Rector: Prof. A. RAJČEV.
Pro-Rectors: Prof. C. CVETANOV, Prof. B. ELIEZER.
Registrar: B. STAVREV.
Librarian: J. EKSAROVA.

Number of teachers: 181.
Number of students: 870.
Publication: *Godišnik*†.

DEANS:

Faculty of Musical Theory, Composition and Conducting: Assoc. Prof. V. ARNAUDOV.
Faculty of Instrumentation: Prof. P. HRISTOSKOV.
Faculty of Vocal Studies: Assoc. Prof. S. IVANOVA.

"KRASTJU SARAFOV" HIGHER INSTITUTE OF DRAMATIC ART AND CINEMATOGRAPHY

SOFIA, RAKOVSKI 108A
Telephone: 87-98-62.
Founded 1948.

Rector: Prof. K. GORANOV.
Pro-Rectors: Assoc. Prof. N. GEORGIEVA, Assoc. Prof. N. MILEV.
Registrar: N. SOPOV.
Librarian: A. DOKOVA.

Number of teachers: 140.
Number of students: 431.
Publication: *Godišnik*†.

"NIKOLAJ PAVLOVIC" HIGHER INSTITUTE OF FINE ARTS

SOFIA, ŠIPKA 1
First founded 1896; reorganized as an Institute 1954.

Rector: Prof. V. MINEKOV.
Pro-Rectors: Prof. V. JONČEV, Prof. P. ČUHOVSKI, Assoc. Prof. G. PETROV.
Registrar: I. SARČEV.
Librarian: L. HRISTOVA.

Number of teachers: 101.
Number of students: 670.

DEANS:

Faculty of Fine Arts: Prof. D. DOBREV.
Faculty of Applied Arts: Assoc. Prof. S. SERAFIMOV.

BURMA

Population 32,573,000

LEARNED SOCIETIES

Archaeological Department: Ministry of Culture, 32-D Prome Rd., Rangoon; revived in 1946; responsible for the maintenance of ancient monuments, epigraphical research, exploration and excavation of historical sites, maintenance of site museums.

British Council: British Embassy, 80 Strand Rd., Rangoon; Cultural Attaché N. O. Hudson.

Cultural Institute: Ministry of Union Culture, 26/42 Pansodan St., Rangoon; four divisions: National Library; National Museum; Research Division for Indigenous Culture; Library and Museum Centres in the constituent Union States. Collects national publications, MSS. and antiquities; publs. rare literary works and works related to ethnic groups.

Department of Fine Arts: 1 Narawat Yeiktha Rd., Rangoon; standardizes, notates and publishes classical songs; studies and records ancient styles of music and singing.

Sarpay Beikman Division: 529 Merchant St., 361 Prome Rd., Rangoon; f. 1947; translates and publishes books in Burmese and the indigenous languages; encourages research in Burmese literature and fine arts; library (*see* Libraries); Chair. U Mya Maung; publ. *Burmese Encyclopaedia*, over 500 titles of popular reading on science, health, economics, history and general literature; in charge of annual National Literary Awards; runs a Book Club.

RESEARCH INSTITUTES

Burma Educational Research Bureau: Prome Rd., University P.O., Rangoon; f. 1966; 40 staff; curriculum evaluation, teacher education, adult education, community development, statistics; Chair. Ye Aung; publ. *Journal* (quarterly).

Burma Research Society: Universities' Central Library, University Post Office, Rangoon; f. 1910 to promote cultural and scientific studies and research relating to Burma and neighbouring countries; 1,040 mems.; 855 vols.; Pres. U Htin Gyi; Hon. Sec. Dr. Shein; publ. *Journal of the Burma Research Society* (bi-annually).

Central Research Organization: Kanbe, Yankin Post Office, Rangoon; composed of the Analysis Dept., Metallurgy Research Dept., Physics and Engineering Research Dept., Technical Information Centre, Instruments Dept., Applied Chemistry Research Dept., Ceramics Research Dept., Standards and Specifications Dept., Polymer Research Dept., Pharmaceutical Research Dept., Food Technology Research Dept. and the Union of Burma Atomic Energy Centre; library of 11,000 vols., 663 periodicals; Dir.-Gen. Dr. Mehm Thet San.

Department of Historical Research: 1 Narawat Yeiktha Rd., Rangoon; Dir.-Gen. Dr. Khin Mg Nyunt.

Department of Medical Research: 5 Zafar Shah Rd., Rangoon; formerly Burma Medical Research Institute, f. 1963; 19 divisions: animal services, bacteriology, biochemistry, epidemiology, experimental medicine, haematology and clinical research, immunology, instrumentation, library, medical entomology, medical research statistics, nutrition, parasitology, pathology, pharmacology, physiology, publications, radioisotope and virology; Dir.-Gen. Dr. Aung Than Batu; publs. *Annual Report of the Burma Medical Research Council*†, *Burma Medical Research Council Special Report Series*†.

Department of Religious Affairs: Kaba-aye Pagoda compound, Rangoon; a government-supported centre for research and studies in Buddhist and allied subjects; library (*see* Libraries); museum (*see* Museums); Dir.-Gen. U Kyi Nyunt.

Division of Research: Institute of Economics, University Estate, Rangoon; conducts research into various aspects of the Burmese economy; current activities include investigation of problems of modernization and development of agriculture, industrial development, planning and economic management, trade and development, etc.; Head Prof. Dr. Khin Maung Kyi; publs. occasional papers and research monographs†.

National Health Laboratories: f. 1968 by amalgamating the Harcourt-Butler Institute of Public Health, the Pasteur Institute, Office of the Chemical Examiner and Office of the Public Analyst; composed of five divisions: Administration, Public Health, Chemical, Food and Drugs and Clinical; Dir. Dr. Mehm Soe Myint.

United States Information Service Center: 581 Merchant St., Rangoon.

LIBRARIES

National Library: Town Hall, Rangoon; f. 1952; incorporating the Bernard Free Library; 49,123 vols., 4,010 MSS., 46,565 periodicals; open to general public.

Arts and Science University Library: University Estate, Mandalay; 102,596 vols.; Librarian U Maung Maung.

Bassein College Library: Bassein; f. 1964; 19,160 vols.; Librarian U Aung Gyi.

Institute of Agriculture Library: Yezin, Pyinmana; f. 1964; 12,000 vols., 70 periodicals; Librarian U Myint Thein.

Institute of Animal Husbandry and Veterinary Science Library: Insein; f. 1964; 4,110 vols.; Assistant Librarian U Kyaw Hoe.

Institute of Economics Library: University Estate, Rangoon; f. 1964; 31,526 vols.; Librarian Daw Hlaing Hlaing Cho.

Institute of Education Library: University Estate, Rangoon; f. 1964; 36,166 vols. Librarian Daw Gilda Twe.

Institute of Medicine Library: Seiktaramahi Quarters, Mandalay; f. 1964; over 23,000 vols., 114 periodicals; Librarian U. Kaung Nyunt, B.A., M.A.L.S.

Institute of Medicine I Library: 245 Lanmadaw Rd., Rangoon; f. 1964; over 15,000 vols.; Librarian U Mg Mg Win.

Institute of Medicine II Library: Mingaladon, Rangoon; f. 1964; 6,795 vols.; Librarian U Htun Aung.

Institute of Technology Library: Insein P.O., Gyogon, Rangoon; f. 1961; 35,000 vols., 350 periodicals; Librarian Daw Myint Myint Khyn, M.L.S.

Magwe College Library: Magwe; f. 1958; 26,900 vols.; Dir. DAW KHIN KHIN MYINT.

Moulmein College Library: Moulmein; f. 1964; 5,257 vols.; Librarian U THEIN LWIN.

Sarpay Beikman Public Library: 529 Merchant St., Rangoon; f. 1956; 53,506 vols. (30,490 Burmese, 23,016 English).

State Library: Bassein; f. 1963; 1,453 vols.

State Library: Kyaukpyu; f. 1955; 8,651 vols.

State Library: Mandalay; f. 1955; 7,004 vols.

State Library: Moulmein; f. 1955; 13,265 vols.; 1,262 MSS.

Universities' Central Library: University P.O., Rangoon; f. 1929; 200,000 vols.; central library for all higher education institutes; specializes in Burmese books, palm-leaf MSS (over 4,000), and books on Burma and Asia; Librarian U THAW KAUNG, B.A., A.L.A., A.L.A.A.

Workers' College Library: Rangoon; f. 1964; 19,500 vols.; Librarian DAW KHIN THIN KYU.

MUSEUMS

Bogyoke Aung San Museum: 25 Tower Lane, Rangoon; f. 1959; 571 exhibits relating to the life and work of General Aung San.

National Museum of Art and Archaeology: Jubilee Hall, Pagoda Rd., Rangoon; f. 1952; 1,652 antiquities; 354 paintings; replica of King Mindon's Mandalay Palace.

State Museum: Kyaukpyu; f. 1955; the museum contains 104 exhibits (silver coins, costumes, etc.).

State Museum: Moulmein; f. 1955; over 300 exhibits.

State Museum: Mandalay; f. 1955; 350 exhibits.

UNIVERSITIES AND UNIVERSITY INSTITUTES

Universities Administration Office: Department of Higher Education, Prome Rd., University Post Office, Rangoon; f. 1964; university courses now take 2 years, following the opening of the 2-year pre-university programmes in regional colleges; 4-year correspondence courses are now offered in science, arts, economics and law.

Director-General: U SAN THA AUNG.

ARTS AND SCIENCE UNIVERSITY, MANDALAY

UNIVERSITY ESTATE, MANDALAY

Telephone 659.

Founded 1964.

Rector: U KYAW MYINT.
Registrar: U THA SAING.

Number of teachers: *c.* 400.
Number of students: *c.* 7,000.

ARTS AND SCIENCE UNIVERSITY, RANGOON

UNIVERSITY ESTATE, RANGOON, UNIVERSITY POST OFFICE

Telephone: Auto. 31144.

Founded 1920.

Rector: Dr. MAUNG DI.
Registrar: DAW SEIN SEIN.

Number of teachers: *c.* 550.
Number of students: *c.* 12,000.

Institute of Agriculture: Yezin, Pyinmana; f. 1956, autonomous 1964; Dir. U THAN TUN.

Institute of Economics: University Estate, Rangoon; f. 1964.

Rector: Dr. KHIN MG NYUNT.

Number of teachers: 170 full-time, 15 part-time.
Numbers of students: 4,700.

Institute of Education: University Estate, Rangoon; f. 1964.

Rector: U THAUNG HTUT.

Institute of Medicine (I): 245 Godwin Rd., Rangoon; f. 1964.

Rector: Dr. TUN MIN.

Institute of Medicine (II): 13 Mile Prome Rd., Mingaladon, Rangoon; f. 1964.

Rector: Dr. KHIN MAUNG NYEIN.

Institute of Medicine: Seiktaramahi Quarters, Mandalay; f. 1964.

Rector: Dr. PE THEIN.

Rangoon Institute of Technology: Gyogon, Insein; f. 1964; 4-year first degree courses.

President: Dr. AUNG GYI.

A Regional College System provides 2-year arts and science pre-university courses at 18 colleges.

DEFENCE SERVICES ACADEMY

MAYMYO

An independent degree College under the Ministry of Defence, f. 1955; degree courses to cadets training for service as regular commissioned officers in the Burma Army, Navy and Air Force; *c.* 120 staff, *c.* 400 students; Commanding Officer Col. AUNG WIN.

COLLEGES OF ART, MUSIC AND DRAMA

State School of Fine Arts: Mandalay; f. 1953; Principal U KAN NYUNT.

State School of Fine Arts: Rangoon; f. 1952; courses in drawing, fine art, commercial art, sculpture and wood-carving; Principal U LUN KYWE.

State School of Music and Drama: Mandalay; f. 1953; courses in dancing, singing, Burmese harp and orchestra, xylophone, piano, oboe, stringed instruments and stave notation; Principal U KAN NYUNT.

State School of Music and Drama: Jubilee Hall, Shwedagon Pagoda Rd., Rangoon; f. 1952; courses in dancing, singing, Burmese harp and orchestra, piano, oboe, xylophone, stringed instruments, stave notation and Burmese verse; Principal U MYA OO.

BURUNDI

Population 3,987,000

LEARNED SOCIETIES AND RESEARCH INSTITUTES

Centre National d'Hydrométéorologie: Bujumbura; Dir. E. KAYENGAYENGE.

Centre Culturel Français: B.P. 894, Bujumbura.

Département de Géologie et Mines du Burundi: Ministère de la Géologie et des Mines, B.P. 745, Bujumbura; Dirs. R. SAMOYA (geology), M. KAMBIRIGI (Mines).

Institut des Sciences Agronomiques du Burundi (ISABU): B.P. 795, Bujumbura; f. 1962; applied agronomical research and farm management; Dir.-Gen. E. BARADANDIKANYA.

Laboratoire Médicale: Bujumbura; devoted to clinical analyses and physio-pathological research nutritional studies.

LIBRARIES

Bibliothèque de l'Université: B.P. 1320, Bujumbura; f. 1961; 60,000 vols.; Librarian F. KINIGI.

Bibliothèque Publique: B.P. 960, Bujumbura; 26,000 vols.

MUSEUMS

Musée National de Gitega: B.P. 110, Gitega; f. 1955; ethnography; Curator J. MAPFARAKORA.

Musée Vivant de Bujumbura: B.P. 1095, Bujumbura; f. 1977; part of Centre de Civilisation Burundaise attached to Ministry of Youth, Sport and Culture; reflects the life of the Murundi people in all its aspects; includes a reptile house, aquarium, aviary, traditional Urugo dwelling, open-air theatre, fishing museum, botanical garden, musical pavilion, and crafts village; Dir. LÉONIDAS NDORICIMPA.

UNIVERSITY

UNIVERSITÉ DU BURUNDI

B.P. 1550, BUJUMBURA

Telephone: 3288.

Founded 1960, present name 1975.

Academic year: October to June.

President of Administrative Council: ANDRÉ BIBWA.

Rector: BONAVENTURE NICIMPAYE.

Vice-Rector: BARNABÉ KAROLERO.

Administrative Director: GERVAIS HAVYARIMANA.

Academic Director: PASCAL NDAYISHINGUJE.

Librarian: FIRMIN KINIGI.

Number of teachers: *c.* 600.

Number of students: *c.* 1,000.

Publication: *Revue de l'Université* (quarterly).

DEANS:

Faculty of Letters and Humanities: P. NTAHOMBAYE.

Faculty of Economic and Administrative Sciences: M. SINAMENYE.

Faculty of Sciences: J. KATIHABWE.

Faculty of Law: Abbé MARC BARENGAYABO.

Faculty of Medicine: Dr. SEBATIGITA.

Faculty of Psychology and Education: L. NTAWURISHIRA.

Faculty of Agriculture: L. DAK.

Institute of Physical Education: M. RAT.

COLLEGES

Lycée Technique: Bujumbura; f. 1949; training apprentices, craftsmen and professional workers; four workshops; mechanics, masonry, carpentry, electrical assembling; 450 students.

Centre Social et Éducatif—C.S.E.: Bujumbura; f. 1957; courses in crafts, photography, mechanics; 75 students.

CAMEROON

Population 7,663,000

LEARNED SOCIETIES AND RESEARCH INSTITUTES

American Cultural Center: B.P. 817, Yaoundé; branch in Douala.

British Council: Les Galeries, Rue de l'Intendance, Yaoundé (B.P. 818); f. 1971; library of 8,453 vols., 105 periodicals; Rep. Dr. B. H. G. McAdam.

Centre Culturel Allemand: rue de Narvik 4, B.P. 1067, Yaoundé; f. 1960; library of 5,000 vols.; language courses, cultural activities; Dir. Dr. Klaus Stoltz.

Centre Culturel Français: avenue du 27 août, B.P. 513, Yaoundé; f. 1960; 3,500 mems.; 20,000 vols. in library; Dir. Roger Aubry.

Centre d'Edition et de Production de Manuels Scolaires de l'UNESCO: Yaoundé; f. 1962; set up under the African Emergency Programme; provides printing supplies, expert editorial and technical staff; the textbooks cover all educational levels; publications in English and French.

Centre des Recherches Forestières: B.P. 832, Douala; f. 1975; forestry research; Dir. A. M. Maino; publ. *Rapport Annuel.*

Compagnie Française pour le Développement des Fibres Textiles (CFDT): B.P. 302, Garoua; brs. at Garoua, Maroua, Mora, Touboro and Kaele; textile research.

Institut de Formation et de Recherches Démographiques: B.P. 1556, Yaoundé; f. 1972 with the co-operation of the UNDP; basic research on demographic trends and their links with economic and social factors; library of 7,000 vols.; Dir. J. Amegandjin; publ. *Annales.*

Institut de la Recherche Agronomique: B.P. 2067, Yaoundé-Messa; centres at Douala, Ekona, Maroua, Njombe; Dir. Nya-Ngatchou.

Centre des Cultures Vivrières et Fruitières: B.P. 13, Njombé; stations at Njombé, Dschang, Bambui, Bertoua, Santchou; Dir. Dr. J.-P. Eckebil.

Institut de Recherches du Coton et des Textiles Exotiques—IRCT: Section Expérimentation Cotonnière du Cameroun; B.P. 22, Maroua; genetics, agronomy and phytosanitary defence; Dir. P. Jacquemard.

Institut de Recherches pour les Huiles et Oléagineux (IRHO): B.P. 243, Douala; f. 1949; Dir. J. N. Regaud.

Institut Géographique National: Yaoundé, avenue Mgr.-Vogt, B.P. 157; f. 1945; survey office; Dir. J. L. le Floc'h.

Institut Pasteur du Cameroun: B.P. 888, Yaoundé; f. 1959; 4 doctors and 1 biochemist; bio-medical research; Dir. Dr. P. Ravisse.

Institut des Relations Internationales du Cameroun (IRIC): B.P. 1637, Yaoundé; f. 1971 by the Federal Government, the Carnegie Endowment for International Peace, the Swiss Division for Technical Co-operation and others; a bi-lingual establishment for training, research and documentation, and post-graduate studies; Dir. Prof. Joseph Owona.

Laboratoire Interdépartemental: B.P. 4046, Douala; attached to the Ministry of Health; research on hygiene and public health matters.

Météorologie Nationale du Cameroun: B.P. 186, Douala; f. 1934; departments of climatology, hydro-meteorology, agrometeorology, synoptic, aeronautical and marine meteorology, research and training; 34 surface observation stations, 400 rainfall posts; small library; Dir. Samuel Mbele-Mbong; publs. *Bulletin Météorologique Mensuel du Cameroun* (monthly), *Annuaire Hydrométéorologique* (annually), *Annales Climatologiques du Cameroun.*

Office National de la Recherche Scientifique et Technique: B.P. 1457, Yaoundé; soil science, hydrology, nutrition, psycho-sociology, demography, economics, geography, archaeology, botany and vegetal biology, and medical entomology.

LIBRARIES AND ARCHIVES

Archives Nationales: B.P. 1053, Yaoundé; f. 1952; conserves and classifies all documents relating to the Republic; library of 2,071 vols. and 20,000 cases of documents.

Bibliothèque Nationale du Cameroun: B.P. 1053, Yaoundé, 10,000 vols.

UNIVERSITY

UNIVERSITÉ DE YAOUNDÉ

(University of Yaoundé)

B.P. 337, YAOUNDÉ

Telephone: 22-07-44.

Founded 1962.

Academic year: October to July; Languages of instruction: English and French. Regional campuses at Douala (economics), Buea (arts), Dschang (agriculture), Ngaoundéré (sciences).

Chancellor: Robert Mbella Mbappe.

Vice-Chancellor: Victor Anomah Ngu.

Secretary-General: Ebenezer Njoh Mouelle.

Librarian: Peter Chateh.

Library of 68,000 vols.

Number of teachers: 390.

Number of students: 8,245.

Publications: *Guide Bibliographique du Monde Noir, Annales.*

DEANS:

Faculty of Law and Economics: S. MELONE.
Faculty of Arts: MARTIN NJEUMA.
Faculty of Science: M. BOPELET.

AFFILIATED INSTITUTES:

Centre Universitaire des Sciences de la Santé: B.P. 1364, Yaoundé; f. 1969; aid from WHO, UNDP and foreign governments; 53 teachers, 434 students; library of 4,000 vols.; Dir. G. MONEKOSSO.

Ecole Normale Supérieure: B.P. 47, Yaoundé; f. 1961; 57 teachers, 712 students; library of 16,240 vols.; Dir. A. SOPPO N'DONGO; publ. *Revue Camerounaise de Pédagogie.*

Ecole Nationale Supérieure Agronomique: B.P. 138, Yaoundé; f. 1960; 34 teachers, 170 students; library of 4,000 vols.; Dir. G. BOL ALIMA.

Ecole Nationale Supérieure Polytechnique: B.P. 337, Yaoundé; f. 1971; three and five-year courses; Departments of Mechanical and Electrical Engineering; Public Works and Buildings; Electronics and Telecommunications; 32 teachers, 174 students; library being formed; Dir. C. MARTY.

Ecole Supérieure Internationale de Journalisme de Yaoundé (ESIJY): B.P. 1328, Yaoundé; f. 1970; three-year courses open to students from Cameroon, Central African Republic, Gabon, Rwanda, Chad, Togo; library of 3,000 vols.; 7 teachers, 115 students; Dir. JEAN-PAUL NYALENDO.

Institut des Relations Internationales du Cameroun: B.P. 1365, Yaoundé; 70 students; Dir. JOSEPH OWONA.

Institut d'Administration des Entreprises: B.P. 337, Yaoundé; f. 1959; training for public administration;

Ecole Nationale d'Administration et de Magistrature: Yaoundé; f. 1959; training for public administration; library of *c.* 11,000 vols.; 10 full-time, 75 part-time teachers, 500 students; Dir. V. MOUTTAPA.

CANADA

Population 23,671,000

ROYAL SOCIETY OF CANADA

344 WELLINGTON STREET, OTTAWA, ONT. K1A ON4
Telephone: 992-3468.
Founded 1882.

Hon. Patron: HIS EXCELLENCY the GOVERNOR-GENERAL.
President: R. E. BELL, C.C., M.A., PH.D., F.R.S.
Vice-Presidents: A. FAUCHER, M.A., L.SC.SOC., J. M. ROBSON, M.A., PH.D., D. H. COPP, O.C., M.D., PH.D., F.R.S.
Hon. Secretary: FERNAND OUELLET, B.A., L. ÈSL.
Hon. Treasurer: K. U. INGOLD, D.PHIL., F.R.S.
Hon. Editor: A. G. MCKAY, M.A., A.M., PH.D.
Hon. Librarian: G. SYLVESTRE, M.A., L.PH., D.LITT., D.BIBL.

HONORARY FELLOWS

H.R.H. PRINCE PHILIP, THE DUKE OF EDINBURGH.
The Rt. Hon. ROLAND MICHENER, C.C., P.C., C.M.M., C.D., Q.C., D.C.L.
The Rt. Hon. PIERRE ELLIOTT TRUDEAU, P.C., Q.C., M.P., M.A., LL.L.
The Rt. Hon. JULES LÉGER, C.C., P.C., C.M.M., C.D.

FELLOWS

Academy I-Lettres et Sciences Humaines:

ARÈS, R. P. RICHARD, S.J., M.A., L.SC.SOC., PH.D., D.SC.SOC., D.U.P.
AUDET, JEAN-PAUL, D.TH., L.E.S.
AUDET, LOUIS-PHILIPPE, L. ès SC., D.PÉD.
BAUDOUIN, JEAN-LOUIS, DR. EN DROIT.
BEAUDOIN, GÉRALD A., M.A., LL.L.
BEAULIEU, PAUL, LL.L.
BEAULNE, GUY, B.A., B.PH.
BEETZ, JEAN, LL.L., M.A.
BÉLISLE, LOUIS-ALEXANDRE, A.C.B.A.
BESSETTE, GÉRARD, M.A., L. ès L.
BOISSONNAULT, CHARLES-MARIE.
BRAZEAU, JACQUES, M.A., PH.D.
BRETON, RAYMOND, M.A., PH.D.
BROUILLETTE, BENOIT, L.SC., D.U.P., D. ès L.
BRUCHÉSI, JEAN, LL.L., D.SC.POL., D.LITT., D. ès L.
CADIEUX, MARCEL, Q.C., LL.L., LL.D.
CAMPEAU, LUCIEN, S.J., M.A., L.PHIL., L.TH., D.HIST.ECCL.
CAMU, PIERRE, M.A., L. ès L., PH.D.
CARRIER, HERVÉ.
CHABOT, Mlle CECILE.
CHANTAL, RENÉ DE, L. ès L., D.U.P.
COMTOIS, ROGER, LL.L., LL.D.
CORMIER, R. P. CLÉMENT.
DAGENAIS, PIERRE, L. ès SC., L. ès L., D. DE L'U.
DARBELNET, JEAN, L. ès L., AG. DE L'U. (Paris).
DÉCARIE, VIANNEY, L.PHIL., PH.D., D. ès L.
DESCHÊNES, JULES.
DION, M. l'Abbé GÉRARD, O.C., L.TH., L.PHIL., M.SC.SOC.
DION, LEON, M.A., PH.D.
DOAT, JAN, LÉG.D'HON.
DORION, HENRI, M.A., LL.L.
DOUVILLE, RAYMOND, B.A.
DUHAMEL, ROGER, LL.L.
FALARDEAU, JEAN-CHARLES, M.A., L.PH.
FAUCHER, ALBERT, M.A., L.SC.SOC.
FILIATRAULT, JEAN.
FILION, GÉRARD, B.A., L.SC.COM.
GAGNON, JEAN-LOUIS, D.M.
GALARNEAU, CLAUDE, M.A.
GARIGUE, PHILIPPE, PH.D.
GASCON, JEAN, C.C., LL.D., D.C.L., D.LITT.
GAUTHIER, ROBERT, B.PH., L.PH., D.PAED.
GÉLINAS, GRATIEN, D. ès L.
GOUIN, Hon. LÉON-MERCIER, B.A., LL.L., LL.D., C.R., D.SC.POL.
GOUIN-DÉCARIE, Mme THÉRÈSE, O.C., B.A.
GUINDON, HUBERT, L.PH., M.A.
HAMELIN, JEAN, B.A., L. ès L.
HAMELIN, LOUIS-EDMOND, M.A., D.GEO.
HAMELIN, MARCEL, D. ès L.
HÉBERT, GÉRARD, PH.D.
HENRIPIN, JACQUES, L.SC.EC., D.SC.EC.
JUNEAU, Hon. PIERRE, O.C., B.A., L.PH.
KATTAN, NAÏM.
KUSHNER, EVA, M.A., PH.D.
LACOURCIÈRE, LUC, C.C., B.A., L. ès L., D. ès L.
LACROIX, BENOÎT, L.TH., PH.D.
LALANDE, GILLES, L.SC.C.
LAMONTAGNE, LÉOPOLD, B.A., L. ès L., PH.D., D.U.P.
LAMONTAGNE, MAURICE, L.SC.SOC., M.A.
LANGEVIN, GILLES, S.J., D.TH.
LASNIER, RINA.
LAURENCE, JEAN-MARIE, B.A.
LEBEL, MAURICE, O.C., M.A., L. ès L., D.LITT., PH.D.
LEFEBVRE, JEAN JACQUES, B.L.
LÉGARÉ, JACQUES.
LEGAULT, ALBERT.
LEGAULT, LE R. P. EMILE, B.A.
LEMELIN, ROGER.
LÉVESQUE, LE R. P. GEORGES-HENRI, O.P., O.C., L.TH.
LOCKQUELL, Frère CLEMENT, M.A., PH.D.
LORRAIN, LÉON, D.SC.COM.
LORTIE, LÉON, O.C., L. ès SC., D. ès SC.
MACKEY, WILLIAM F.
MAILLET, ANTONINE.
MAILLOUX, LE R. P. NOEL, O.P., O.C., PH.D., S.TH.L.
MAJOR, JEAN-LOUIS, M.A., D.PH.
MARCHAND, CLÉMENT, B.A.
MARION, SÉRAPHIN, M.A., D. ès L., D.U.P.
MIGUE, JEAN-LUC.
MONET, JACQUES, S.J., PH.D.
OUELLET, FERNAND, L. ès L., D. ès L.
PAQUET, GILLES, M.A.
PARENTEAU, ROLAND, B.A., L.S.C.
PARIZEAU, GÉRARD, L.S.C., F.I.I.C.
PILON, JEAN-GUY, LL.L.
RAYNAULD, ANDRÉ, B.A., M.A., D.SC.EC.
ROCHER, GUY, C.C., M.A., PH.D.
ROY, ANTOINE, D. ès L.
ROY, GABRIELLE, C. C.
SABOURIN, LOUIS.
SAVARD, PIERRE.
SÉGUIN, ROBERT LIONEL, D. ès L., L.SC.SOC.
SIMARD, JEAN.
SYLVAIN, PHILIPPE, B.A., L. ès SC., L. ès L., D.U.P.
SYLVESTRE, GUY, M.A., L.PH., D.BIBL.
SZABO, DENIS, L.SC.POL., D.SC.POL.
THÉRIO, ADRIEN, M.A., PH.D.
TOUGAS, GÉRARD, M.A., PH.D.
TREMBLAY, ARTHUR, M.SC.SOC.
TREMBLAY, MARC-ADÉLARD, M.A., PH.D.
TROTTIER, PIERRE, DIP. DR., F.C.I.A.
VACHON, ANDRÉ, L. ès L., D.E.S., D. ès L.
VACHON, Mgr. LOUIS-ALBERT, P.A., D.PH., D.TH.
VALOIS, MARCEL, B. ès L.
VERDIER, PHILIPPE, AG. ès L.
VINAY, J.-P., M.A., L. ès L.
VINETTE, ROLAND, B.A.
WALLOT, JEAN-PIERRE, PH.D., L. ès L.
WYCZNSKI, PAUL, L. ès L., Dip. E.S., D.PH.
ZUMTHOR, PAUL, DR. ÈS L.

Academy II—Humanities and Social Sciences:

AKENSON, DONALD H., M.ED., PH.D.
AKRIGG, PHILIP G., M.A., PH.D.
AMES, MICHAEL M., PH.D.
ANDRUSYSHEN, C. H., M.A., PH.D.
ANGUS, HENRY FORBES, O.C., M.A., B.C.L., LL.D.
ARCHIBALD, G. C., M.A., B.SC.
ARNOLD, ARMIN H., D. ès L.
ASIMAKOPULOS, ATHANASIOS, M.A., PH.D.
BAGNANI, GILBERT F., D.LITT.
BAILEY, A. G., M.A., PH.D.
BARBER, CLARENCE L.
BARKER, ARTHUR E., M.A., PH.D.
BATTS, MICHAEL S., DR.PHIL., D.LIT.
BAYLEY, C. C., M.A., PH.D.
BECK, MURRAY J., M.A., PH.D.
BELSHAW, CYRIL S., M.A., PH.D.
BERGER, CARL.
BERRY, E. G., M.A., PH.D.
BINDRA, DALBIR, PH.D.
BIRD, RICHARD, M., PH.D.
BIRNEY, A. E., O.C., M.A., PH.D.
BISSELL, C. T., M.A., PH.D.
BLADEN, V. W., M.A., LL.D., D.LITT.
BLISSETT, M. A., PH.D.
BOESCHENSTEIN, HERMANN, PH.D.
BOSHER, JOHN F., PH.D.
BOURNE, CHARLES B., S.J.D.
BRADY, ALEXANDER, O.C., M.A., PH.D.
BRECHER, MICHAEL, PH.D.
BRETON, ALBERT A., PH.D.
BRIEGER, P. H., PH.D.
BRYCE, R. B., M.A.
BURRIDGE, KENELM O. L.
CAIRNS, ALAN C., M.A., D.PHIL.
CARELESS, J. M. S., A.M., PH.D.
CASTEL, JEAN-GABRIEL, S.J.D.
CLARK, S. D., M.A., PH.D.
COBURN, Miss K., M.A., B.LITT.
COLLIN, W. E., L. ès L., M.A.
CONACHER, DESMOND J., M.A., PH.D.
CONLON, PIERRE M., M.A., D.DE L'U. (Paris).
COOK, RAMSAY, M.A., PH.D.
CORRY, JAMES A., B.C.L., LL.M., LL.D.
CRAIG, GERALD M., PH.D.
CURTIS, C. A., PH.D.
DALES, JOHN H., M.A., PH.D.
D'ANDREA, ANTONIO, D.FIL.
DAVIES, ROBERTSON, C.C., LL.D., D.LITT., D.C.L.
DOBSON, W. A. C. H., O.C., M.A.
DONNELLY, MURRAY S., M.A., PH.D.
DORLAND, A. G., M.A., PH.D., LL.D.
DRAY, W. H., M.A., D.PHIL.
DRYER, D. P., A.M.
DURRANT, GEOFFREY HUGH.
EASTERBROOK, W. T., M.A., PH.D.
EASTMAN, HARRY CLAUDE M., A.M., PH.D.
EASTON, DAVID, M.A., PH.D.
EAYRS, JAMES G., A.M., PH.D.
EICHNER, HANS, PH.D.
ELLIOTT, GEORGE A., M.A.
FACKENHEIM, EMIL L., PH.D., LL.D., D.D.
FAIRLEY, BARKER, M.A., PH.D., LITT.D., LL.D.
FAIRWEATHER, Rev. E. R., TH.D., D.D.
FERGUSON, GEORGE A., B.ED., PH.D.
FERGUSON, W. K., M.A., PH.D., LITT.D.
FIELDHOUSE, H. NOEL, M.A.
FINCH, R. D. C., B.A.
FITCH, BRIAN T., D.DE L'U.
FORSEY, EUGENE A., O.C., M.A., PH.D., LL.D., LITT.D.
FREDEMAN, WILLIAM EVAN, M.A., PH.D.
FRYE, H. NORTHROP, O.C., M.A., LL.D.
GAUTHIER, DAVID P., A.M., D.PHIL.
GORDON, H. SCOTT.
GOUDGE, T. A., M.A., PH.D.
GRAHAM, J. F., A.M., PH.D.
GRAHAM, V. E., M.A., PH.D.
GRANT, G. P., B.A., D.PHIL.
GRAY, JAMES, PH.D.
GREENE, DONALD J.
GRUBE, GEORGE M. A., M.A.
HALL, OSWALD.
HALPENNY, FRANCESS G.
HAMILTON, ALBERT C.
HANSON, E. J., M.A.
HÄRING, NICHOLAS M., S.T.D., M.S.D.
HARPER, J. RUSSELL.
HAWTHORN, H. B., O.C., M.SC., PH.D.
HAYNE, DAVID M., M.A., PH.D.
HEBB, D. O., M.A., PH.D.
HELLEINER, G. K., PH.D.
HELLEINER, K. F., PH.D.
HELLIWELL, JOHN F., M.A., D.PHIL.
HEMLOW, Miss JOYCE, M.A., A.M., PH.D.
HERISSON, C. D., M.A., L. ès L.
HIGGINS, B. H., M.SC., M.A., M.P.A., PH.D.
HODGETTS, J. E., M.A., PH.D.
HOLLANDER, SAMUEL, M.A., PH.D.
HOLMES, JOHN W.
HOOD, WM. C., M.A., PH.D.
HUBBARD, R. H., M.A., PH.D.
JAFFÉ, WILLIAM, M.A., DR. EN DROIT, LL.D.
JOHNSON, A. H., M.A., PH.D.
JONES, D. G., M.A.
KALISKI, S. F., M.A., PH.D.
KEITH, WILLIAM J., M.A., PH.D.
KEYFITZ, NATHAN, PH.D.
KLIBANSKY, RAYMOND, M.A., D.PHIL.
KLINCK, CARL F., O.C., M.A., PH.D., D.LITT.
KROTKI, KAROL, M.A., PH.D.
LA FOREST, GÉRARD V.
LAMB, W. KAYE O.C., M.A., PH.D., LL.D.
LAMBERT, WALLACE, M.A., PH.D.
LANDER, J. R., M.A., M.LITT.
LA PONCE, JEAN ANTOINE.
LASKIN, BORA, Q.C., M.A., LL.M.
LAURENCE, MARGARET.
LEPAN, D. V., D.LITT., LL.D.
LEDERMAN, WILLIAM R., B.A., B.C.L., LL.D.
LEECHMAN, J. D., M.A., PH.D.
LEVY, K. L., M.A., PH.D.
LLOYD, TREVOR, PH.D., D.SC.
LOCHHEAD, DOUGLAS G., PH.D.
LOWER, A. R. M., C.C., M.A., PH.D., LL.D.
MCFEAT, TOM, A.M., PH.D.
MACGILLIVRAY, JAMES R., M.A., PH.D.
MACGREGOR, D. C., M.A.
MCGREGOR, M. F., M.A., PH.D.
MCIVOR, R. C., A.M., PH.D.
MCKAY, A. G., M.A., A.M., PH.D.
MACKAY, ROBERT A., PH.D., LL.D.
MACKENZIE, NORMAN A. M., C.M.G., M.M., Q.C., LL.D., D.C.L., D.SC.
MACKENZIE, NORMAN H., M.A., PH.D.
MCLEAN, HUGH J.
MACLENNAN, HUGH, M.A., PH.D., D.LITT.
MCLUHAN, H. M., C.C., M.A., PH.D.
MACLURE, MILLAR, M.A., PH.D.
MACPHERSON, C. B., M.SC., D.SC.
MCRAE, KENNETH D.
MALLORY, J. R., LL.B., M.A.
MARANDA, PIERRE, PH.D.
MASTERS, D. C., M.A., D.PHIL.
MAURER, A. A., M.A., PH.D., M.S.
MAYO, H. B., M.A., D.PHIL.
MEISEL, JOHN, M.A., PH.D.
MOLINARO, JULIUS A.
MORTON, W. L., O.C., M.A., LL.D.
NEATBY, H. BLAIR.
O'DONNELL, Rev. J. R., M.A., PH.D.
ORMSBY, MARGARET A., M.A., PH.D., LL.D.
OWEN, WARWICK J. B.
OWENS, Rev. J., M.S.D., M.S.L.
PAINE, ROBERT P. B., D.PHIL.
PAIVIO, ALLAN U., M.SC., PH.D.
PARKER, J. H., PH.D., LL.D.
PENELHUM, TERENCE M.
PINARD, MAURICE, L.L.L., M.A., PH.D.
PORTER, J. A., D.SC.ECON.
PRATT, R. CRANFORD, B.A., B.PHIL.
PRIESTLEY, F. E. L., M.A., PH.D., F.R.S.L.
RADDALL, T. H., LL.D.
RAFTIS, JAMES A., M.A., D. ès SOC. SC., PH.D.
RAJAN, BALACHANDRA.
READY, WILLIAM B., M.A., M.L.S.
REANEY, JAMES C., O.C., M.A., PH.D.
REDFORD, DONALD B.
REUBER, GRANT L., A.M., PH.D.
RIST, JOHN M., M.A.
ROBBINS, WILLIAM, M.A., PH.D.

Robertson, R. Gordon, c.c., m.a., ll.d.
Robson, John M., m.a., ph.d.
Rosenbluth, Gideon, ph.d.
Ross, M. M., m.a., ph.d., d.litt.
Rouillard, C. D., a.m. ph.d.
Saddlemeyer, Ann, m.a., ph.d.
Safarian, A. Edward, ph.d.
Salisbury, Richard F., m.a., a.m., ph.d.
Salmon, E. T., m.a., ph.d.
Savory, Roger M., m.a., ph.d.
Scargill, M.H., ph.d
Schoeck, R. J., m.a., ph.d., f.r.h.s.
Schogt, Henry Gilius.
Scott, A. D., b.comm., m.a., ph.d.
Scott, Francis R., c.c., b.litt., b.c.l., ll.d.
Scott, R. B. Y., m.a., ph.d., d.d.
Sirluck, Ernest, m.b.e., m.a., ph.d.
Skilling, H. Gordon, m.a., ph.d.
Smiley, Donald V., m.ed., m.a., ph.d
Smith, David C., m.a., ph.d.
Smith, Philip E. L., ph.d., d.litt.
Smith, Wilfred C., m.a., ph.d., d.d.
Soward, F. H., d.c.l., b.litt.
Sparshott, Francis Edward.
Stacey, C. P., o.c., o.b.e., a.m., ph.d.
Stairs, Denis, m.a., ph.d.
Stanley, George F. G., m.a., b.litt.
Stedmond, J. M., m.a., ph.d.
Stewart, Andrew, b.s.a., m.a., ll.d., d.econ.
Symons, Thomas H. B.
Talman, James J., m.a., ph.d.
Tarnopolsky, Walter S., a.m., ll.m.
Taylor, Charles.
Taylor, K. W., c.b.e., m.a., ll.d.
Thomas, Lewis G., m.a., ph.d.
Thompson, H. A., m.a., ph.d., ll.d.
Thornton, Archibald P.
Tracy, Clarence, ph.d.
Trethewey, W. H., m.a., ph.d
Trigger, Bruce G., ph.d.
Trueman, A. W., o.c., m.a., d.litt., ll.d.
Tushingham, A. Douglas, b.d., ph.d., f.s.a., f.c.m.a.
Urquhart, M. C., b.a.
Vallee, Frank G., ph.d.
Von Richthofen, Erich.
Waite, Peter B., m.a., ph.d.
Wallace, Elisabeth, ph.d.
Ward, N. M., o.c., m.a., ph.d.
Warntz, William, a.m., ph.d.
Weldon, John C.
Wevers, John W., th.d.
Whalley, George, m.a., ph.d.
Wickens, G. M., m.a.
Wilkinson, B., m.a., ph.d.
Williams, R. J., m.a., b.d., ph.d.
Wilson, Milton T.
Winch, David Monk.
Winnett, F. V., m.a., ph.d.
Wonders, William C., m.a., ph.d.
Woodbury, Leonard E.
Woods, H. D., m.a., ll.d.
Zaslow, Morris.

Academy III—Science:

Aczel, J. D., m.a., ph.d.
Adams, G. A., m.sc., ph.d.
Akcoglu, Mustafa Agah, m.sc., ph.d.
Alty, Thomas, d.sc., ph.d., d.cl., ll.d.
Anderson, J. A., m.sc., ph.d.
Archibald, William J., m.a., ph.d.
Armstrong, J. E., m.a.sc., ph.d.
Armstrong, H. S., m.a., ph.d.
Armstrong, R. L., m.sc., ph.d.
Armstrong, W. McC., b.a.sc.
Atkinson, F. V., d.phil., m.a.
Auger, P. E., ph.d.
Aumento, Fabrizio, ph.d.
Ayer, William A., ph.d.
Babbitt, J. D., d.phil.
Bachynski, M. P., m.sc., ph.d.
Bailey, D. L., m.sc., ph.d.
Baird, D. M., m.s., ph.d.
Banaschewski, Bernhard, ph.d.
Bancroft, G. Michael, m.sc., m.a., ph.d.
Bancroft, J. B., ph.d.
Bannan, M. W., ph.d.
Barbeau, André.
Barnes, William H., m.sc., ph.d.
Barr, Murray L., o.c., m.d., m.sc., ll.d.
Bartholomew, G. A., ph.d.
Basinski, Zbigniew S., d.phil., d.sc.
Bates, David V., m.d., f.r.c.p.
Batten, Alan H.
Beck, J. C., b.sc., m.c., c.m., m.sc.
Bélanger, L.-F., m.d., m.a.(med.sc.).
Bell, John M., o.c., m.sc., ph.d.
Bell, R. E., c.c., m.a., ph.d.
Belleau, B. R., m.sc., ph.d.
Belyea, Helen R., m.a., ph.d.
Benson, G. Campbell, m.a., ph.d.
Bergeron, Robert, m.a., d.sc.
Berlinguet, Louis, o.c., d.sc.
Bernard, Richard, m.sc., ph.d.
Bernstein, H. J., m.a., ph.d.
Berrill, N. J., ph.d., d.sc., f.r.s.
Berry, L. G., m.a., ph.d.
Beveridge, J. M. R., ph.d., m.d.
Bhatia, A. B., m.sc., d.phil., ph.d.
Bidwell, R. G. S., m.a., ph.d.
Biely, J., m.s., m.s.a.
Bishop, C. J., a.m., ph.d.
Bishop, Claude T., ph.d.
Blachut, T. J., m.sc.
Blackwood, A. C., m.sc., ph.d.
Blais, Roger A., m.sc., ph.d.
Blanchard, J. E., m.a., ph.d.
Bloom, Myer, m.sc., ph.d.
Bohn, E. V., dipl.math., dr. rer. nat.
Bois, Pierre, m.d., ph.d.
Boivin, Albéric, d.sc.
Boivin, Bernard, l.sc., ph.d.
Bostock, H. S., m.sc., ph.d.
Boucher, Roger, m.sc., ph.d., f.c.i.c.
Boulet, Lionel, ph.d.
Bourns, A. N., m.a., ph.d.
Bousfield, E. L., ph.d.
Boyd, William, c.c., m.d., ll.d., d.sc.
Boyle, R. W., m.a.sc., ph.d.
Brand, John C. D., ph.d., d.sc.
Brett, J. R., m.a., ph.d.
Brockhouse, B. N., m.a., ph.d.
Brook, Adrian G.
Brown, A. W. A., m.b.e., b.sc.f., m.a., ph.d.
Browne, J. S. L., m.d., c.m., ph.d., ll.d.
Brownell, G. M., m.sc., ph.d.
Bures, Donald J. C., ph.d.
Butler, G. C., ph.d.
Byers, A. R., m.sc., ph.d.
Bywater, Stanley, ph.d.
Caldwell, W. G. E., ph.d.
Cameron, Alastair G. W., ph.d.
Cameron, T. W. M., o.c., t.d., m.a., ph.d., d.sc., m.r.c.v.
Campbell, A. B., m.sc., ph.d.
Campbell, Alan N., m.sc., ph.d., d.sc.
Campbell, F. A., m.a., ph.d.
Campbell, Jack J. R., ph.d.
Campbell, W. R., m.a., m.b., m.d., f.r.c.p.(c.).
Canvin, David Thomas.
Carbotte, Jules P., m.sc., ph.d.
Carmichael, Hugh, m.a., ph.d.
Casselman, William A., ph.d.
Chacon, R. V. S., ph.d.
Chalk, John, ph.d.
Chant, Donald A., m.a., ph.d.
Chapman, J. H., m.sc., ph.d.
Chitty, Dennis H., m.a., d.phil.
Chown, Bruce, o.c., m.c., b.a., m.d., d.sc., f.a.c.o.g., f.r.c.o.g.
Cinader, B., b.sc., f.r.i.c.
Clark, Howard C.
Clark, T. H., a.m., ph.d.
Clermont, Yves W., ph.d.
Cloutier, Gilles G., ph.d.
Coates, D. F., m.a., m.eng., ph.d.
Cobbold, Richard S. C., ph.d.
Collier, H. B., m.a., ph.d.
Colonnier, Marc, m.d., ph.d.
Colter, John Sparby, ph.d.
Common, R. H., d.agr., m.agr., ph.d., d.sc.
Connell, George E.

CONWAY, B. E., PH.D., D.SC.
COOK, W. H., O.C., O.B.E., M.SC., PH.D., LL.D.
COPP, D. HAROLD, O.C., M.D., PH.D.
CORMACK, M. W., M.SC., PH.D.
CORMACK, R. G. H., M.A., PH.D.
COSSINS, EDWIN ALBERT, PH.D.
COSTAIN, CECIL C., D.S.C., M.A., PH.D.
COWAN, IAN MCT., PH.D.
COXETER, H. S. M., PH.D., LL.D., F.R.S.
CRAIGIE, E. HORNE, PH.D.
CRAIGIE, J. H., O.C., M.SC., PH.D., D.SC., LL.D., F.R.S.
CRAMPTON, E. W., M.SC., PH.D.
CURRIE, B. W., C.C., M.SC., PH.D.
CVETANOVIČ, R. J., M.A., PH.D.
DAINTY, JACK, M.A., D.SC., F.R.S.E.
DANIELS, J. M., M.A., D.PHIL.
DANSEREAU, PIERRE, C. C., D.SC.
DARWENT, B. DE B., PH.D.
DATARS, WILLIAM R., M.SC., PH.D.
DAUPHINEE, JAMES A., O.B.E., PH.D., M.D., F.R.C.P.(C.).
DAVENPORT, ALAN G.
DAVEY, KENNETH G.
DAVIAULT, LIONEL, M.SC., PH.D.
DAVIES, F. T., M.SC.
DAVIES, J. A., M.A., PH.D.
DAVISON, EDWARD JOSEPH.
DE LEEUW, JACOB H., PH.D.
DEMAYO, PAUL, PH.D., D. ÈS SC.
DEMERS, PIERRE, L.SC., M.SC., D.SC.
DENCE, MICHAEL R., B.SC.
DENIS, B. T., PH.D.
DERRY, DOUGLAS, PH.D.
DERRY, D. R., M.A., PH.D.
DESLONGCHAMPS, PIERRE, PH.D.
DESMARAIS, ANDRÉ, L.SC., PH.D.
DICKIE, LLOYD M., M.SC., PH.D.
D'IORIO, ANTOINE.
DIXON, GORDON H., PH.D.
DLAB, VLASTIMIL.
DOLMAGE, VICTOR, PH.D.
DOLMAN, C. E., M.B., B.SC., D.P.H., PH.D., F.R.C.P.
DOUGLAS, A. E., M.A., PH.D.
DOUGLAS, R. J. W., PH.D.
DOWNEY, R. KEITH, O.C., M.SC., PH.D.
DREIMANIS, ALEKSIS, MAG.RER.NAT., D.SC.
DUCKWORTH, H. E., PH.D.
DUFF, G. F. D., M.A., PH.D.
DUFFELL, STANLEY, M.A., PH.D.
DUGAL, L.-PAUL, O.B.E., M.SC., PH.D.
DUGDALE, J. S., M.A., D.PHIL.
DUNBAR, M. J., M.A., PH.D.
DUNBAR, MOIRA, M.A.
EAGLES, BLYTHE, M.A., PH.D.
EDWARD, JOHN T., PH.D., D.PHIL., M.A.
EDWARDS, O. E., M.S., PH.D.
ELLIOTT, K. A. C., B.SC., M.SC., PH.D., SC.D.
EMBLETON, TONY F. W., PH.D., D.SC.
ETKIN, B., B.A.SC., M.A.SC.
ETTINGER, G. H., M.B.E., M.D., C.M., D.SC.
EWAN, GEORGE T.
FALLIS, A. MURRAY, PH.D.
FARQUHAR, R. M., M.A., PH.D.
FEINDEL, WILLIAM H., M.D. C.M., D.SC., D.PHIL.
FERGUSON, J. K. W., M.B.E., M.A., M.D.
FERGUSON, ROBERT B., M.A., PH.D.
FERNIE, JOHN D., M.SC., PH.D., F.R.A.S.
FIELD, GEORGE S., M.B.E., M.SC., D.SC.
FILLMORE, PETER A., M.A., PH.D.
FILTEAU, GABRIEL, D.SC.
FINN, D. B., C.M.G., M.SC., PH.D.
FOLINSBEE, R. E., M.S., PH.D.
FORSYTH, P. A., M.A., PH.D.
FORTIER, CLAUDE, L.SC.SOC., M.D., PH.D.
FORTIER, Y. O., M.SC., PH.D.
FOSTER, JOHN S., D.ENG.
FRANKLIN, COLIN A., M.SC., PH.D.
FRAPPIER, ARMAND, O.B.E., M.D., L. ÈS SC.
FRASER, D. A. S., M.A., PH.D.
FRASER, F. CLARKE, M.SC., PH.D., M.D., C.M.
FREBOLD, HANS, D.PHIL.
FREEDMAN, SAMUEL O., M.D.C.M.
FREEZE, R. ALLAN, M.SC., PH.D.
FRIEDMAN, SYDNEY M., M.D., C.M., M.SC., PH.D.
FRIESEN, HENRY G., M.D., F.R.C.P.
FRITZ, MADELEINE A., M.A., PH.D.
FRY, F. E. J., M.B.E., M.A., PH.D.
FURNIVAL, G. M., M.A., PH.D.
FYLES, J. G., M.A.SC., PH.D.
GABRIELSE, HUBERT.
GARLAND, GEORGE D., M.A., PH.D.
GARRETT, CHRISTOPHER.
GAUDRY, ROGER, B.SC.A., D.SC.
GAUVIN, W. H., C.C., PH.D., D.ENG.
GENDRON, PIERRE R., C.C., PH.D., LL.D., D.SC.
GENEST, JACQUES, M.D., F.A.C.P., F.R.C.P.(C)
GIBBARD, JAMES, B.S.A., S.M.
GIBBS, R. DARNLEY, M.SC., PH.D., F.L.S.
GIGUÈRE, PAUL-A., PH.D.
GILL, J. E., PH.D.
GILLESPIE, R. J., PH.D., D.SC.
GISHLER, P. E., M.SC., PH.D.
GLASS, IRVINE I., M.A.SC., PH.D
GLEN, ROBERT, M.SC., PH.D., LL.D.
GODSON, W. L., M.A., PH.D.
GOLD, LORNE W., M.SC., PH.D.
GOLD, PHIL.
GOODWIN, ALAN M., M.SC., PH.D.
GORHAM, PAUL R., M.S., PH.D.
GORING, D. A. I., PH.D.
GORNALL, ALLAN G., PH.D.
GOTLIEB, C. C., M.A., PH.D.
GOUGH, DENIS I., M.SC., PH.D.
GOULDEN, C. H., M.S.A., PH.D., LL.D.
GRAHAM, A. F., PH.D., D.SC.
GRANIRER, EDMOND E.
GRATZER, GEORGE A., DR.RER.NAT., PH.D.
GRAVENOR, C. P., M.S., PH.D.
GREENWOOD, H. J., M.A.SC., PH.D.
GREINER, PETER CHARLES.
GUNNING, H. C., S.M., PH.D.
GUNNING, HARRY E., M.A., PH.D.
GUSSOW, W. C., M.SC., PH.D.
HACHEY, H. B., M.B.E., E.D., M.SC., LL.D.
HACQUEBARD, PETER A., B.SC., M.SC., PH.D.
HAERING, R. R., M.A., PH.D.
HAGE, CONRAD O., B.SC., M.A.
HAIST, R. E., M.D., M.A., PH.D.
HALLIDAY, IAN, M.A., PH.D.
HAM, A. W., M.B.
HANES, C. S., PH.D., SC.D., F.R.S.
HANNA, G. C., M.A.
HARDY, J. C., M.SC., PH.D.
HARDY, R. M., M.SC., D.SC., D.L.S.
HARE, F. K., PH.D., LL.D.
HARRIS, WALTER E.
HARRISON, J. M., M.A., PH.D.
HASLAM, R. N. H., M.A., PH.D.
HATTERSLEY-SMITH, G. F., M.A., D.PHIL.
HAYES, F. R., M.SC., PH.D., D.SC.
HEIMBURGER, E. C., M.SC.F., PH.D.
HENDERSON, GERALD, M.SC., PH.D.
HENDERSON, J. F., PH.D.
HENDERSON, JOHN T., M.B.E., M.SC., PH.D.
HERZ, CARL S., PH.D.
HERZBERG, GERHARD, M.A., DR.ING., LL.D., D.SC., F.R.S.
HEWSON, E. WENDELL, M.A., D.I.C., PH.D.
HILL, PHILIP G., M.SC., SC.D.
HINCKS, E. P., M.A.
HINES, COLIN O., M.A., PH.D.
HITSCHFELD, WALTER F., PH.D.
HOAR, W. S., M.A., PH.D.
HODGINS, J. W., PH.D.
HODGSON, JOHN H., M.A., PH.D.
HOGG, B. G., M.A., PH.D.
HOGG, HELEN S., A.M., PH.D., D.SC.
HOLLAND, G. P., M.A., D.SC.
HOLLING, C. S., M.A., PH.D.
HOLMES, R. H. L., M.SC., A.M., PH.D.
HOPKINS, J. W., M.SC., PH.D.
HOWLETT, L. E., M.B.E., M.A., PH.D.
HUGHES, A., D.SC.
HUGHES, STANLEY, M.SC., D.SC.
HULL, T. E., PH.D.
HURST, D. G., M.SC., PH.D.
HYNES, H. B. NOEL, D.SC., PH.D.
IDLER, DAVID R., M.A., PH.D.
INGOLD, K. U., D.PHIL.
INNES, M. J. S., M.A., PH.D.
IRVING, EDWARD, M.A., M.SC., SC.D.
ISRAEL, WERNER, M.SC., PH.D.

Jacobs, J. A., M.A., PH.D., D.SC.
James, W. F., M.SC., PH.D., D.SC.
Jaques, L. B., M.A., PH.D.
Jasper, Herbert H., O.C., M.A., PH.D., D.ÈS SC., M.D., C.H.
Jeletzky, George, M.SC., PH.D.
Jervis, Robert E., M.A., PH.D.
Johns, H. E., M.A., PH.D.
Johns, Martin W., M.A., PH.D.
Johnson, T., O.C., M.SC., PH.D., D.SC.
Jolliffe, A. W., M.A., PH.D.
Jones, A. V., M.SC., PH.D.
Jones, G. M., M.A., M.B., B.CH.
Jones, R. N., M.SC., PH.D., D.SC.

Kalow, Werner.
Kanasewich, Ernest R., PH.D.
Kates, Morris, M.A., PH.D., F.C.I.C.
Katz, Leon, M.SC., PH.D.
Kay, Cyril M., PH.D.
Kebarle, P., PH.D.
Keen, Michael J., M.A., PH.D.
Kerwin, J. Larkin, M.SC., D.SC.
Kindle, E. D., M.A., PH.D.
King, Gerald W., PH.D., D.SC., F.C.I.C.
Kinsey, B. B., PH.D.
Kirkaldy, John S.
Kranck, E. H., M.SC., PH.D.
Krebs, Charles J., PH.D.
Krnjeyic, Kresimir.
Kuehner, John A.
Kulka, M., M.S., PH.D.
Kupsch, W. O., M.SC., PH.D.

Labarre, Jules, B.PH., L. ès S.
Labrie, Fernand, M.D., PH.D.
Lachlan, Alistair H., M.A., PH.D.
Ladanyi, Branko, D.SC.
Laidlaw, John C.
Laidler, K. J., M.A., PH.D., D.SC.
Lang, A. H., M.A., PH.D.
Langlands, Robert P., M.A., PH.D.
Larkin, P. A., M.A., D.PHIL.
Laurence, G. C., M.B.E., M.SC., PH.D.
Lauzier, L. M., M.SC., D.SC.
Layne, Donald S.
Leblond, C. P., M.D., L. ès SC., PH.D., D.SC.
L'Ecuyer, Philibert, B.SC.A., B.SC., D.PHIL.
Leech, G. B., M.SC., PH.D.
Legget, R. F., B.ENG., M.ENG.
Lehmann, H. E., M.D.
Lemieux, R. U., PH.D.
LeRoy, D. J., M.A., PH.D.
Lewis, W. B., C.B.E., M.A., PH.D., F.R.S.
Lindsay, Casimir C., M.A., PH.D.
List, Roland, DR.SC.NAT.
Litherland, A. E., PH.D.
Llewellyn-Thomas, Edward, B.SC., M.D.C.M.
Lochhead, A. G., PH.D., D.AGR.
Locke, J. L., M.A., PH.D.
Lorch, L. A., M.A., PH.D.
Lord, C. S., M.A.SC., PH.D.
Lorrain, Paul, M.SC., PH.D.
Lossing, F. P., M.A., PH.D.
Lucas, C. C., M.A.SC., PH.D.

McAllister, A. L., M.SC., PH.D.
McCalla, A. G., M.SC., PH.D.
McCallum, K. J., M.SC., PH.D.
McCarter, J. A., M.A., PH.D.
McCulloch, Ernest, M.D., F.R.C.P.(C).
McDiarmid, Ian B., M.A., PH.D.
MacDonald, S. F., M.A., DR.RER.NAT.
McDowell, C. A., M.SC., D.SC.
MacIntosh, F. C., M.A., PH.D., F.R.S.
McIntosh, R. L., M.B.E., M.SC., PH.D.
McKay, A. F., M.SC., PH.D.
MacKay, B. R., C.M., PH.D.
Mackay, J. Ross, M.A., PH.D.
Mackenzie, C. J., C.C., C.M.G., M.C., D.ENG., D.SC., LL.D., D.C.L., F.R.S.
McKinley, D. W. R., O.B.E., M.A., PH.D.
McLachlan, Jack L., M.A., PH.D.
McLaren, D. J., M.A., PH.D.
MacLean, L. D., M.D., PH.D., F.R.C.S.
MacLeod, Robert A., M.A., PH.D.
McLeod, Norman W.
McLennan, H., M.SC., PH.D.

McPhail, M. K., PH.D.
Macphail, M. S., M.A., D.PHIL.
MacRae, D. A., A.M., PH.D.
Mainland, D., M.B., CH.B., D.SC.
March, Beryl E., M.S.A.
Margolis, Leo.
Marion, Léo, M.B.E., PH.D., D.SC., D. ès SC.
Marmet, Paul, D.SC.
Marrian, G. F., D.SC., F.R.I.C., F.R.S.
Marshall, J. S., M.A., PH.D.
Masamune, Satoru.
Mason, S. G., B.ENG., PH.D.
Mathews, W. H., M.A.SC., PH.D.
Maxwell, J. A., M.SC., PH.D.
Mendelsohn, Nathan S., M.A., PH.D.
Mettrick, David F., PH.D., D.SC., F.R.S.A.
Meyerhof, G. G., M.SC., PH.D., D.SC.
Middleton, G. V., PH.D.
Middleton, W. E. K., M.SC., D.SC.
Migicovsky, B. B., PH.D., D.SC., F.C.I.C., F.A.I.C.
Millman, Peter M., A.M., PH.D.
Milner, Brenda, PH.D., D.SC.
Milner, Eric C., M.SC., PH.D.
Milton, J. C. D., M.A., PH.D.
Misener, A. D., M.A., PH.D.
Moens, P. B., M.A., PH.D.
Moloney, P. J., O.B.E., M.A., PH.D.
Moody, N. F., B.E., F.I.E.E.
Mooradian, A. J., M.SC., PH.D.
Morgenstern, Nobert R.
Morley, L. W., M.A., PH.D.
Morrell, C. A., M.A., PH.D.
Morrish, A. H., M.A., PH.D.
Morrison, J. A., M.SC., PH.D.
Munro, L. A., M.A., PH.D.
Munroe, Egene G., M.SC., PH.D.
Murray, R. G. E., M.A., M.D., C.M.
Mustard, Fraser J., M.D., PH.D.

Narang, Saran A., PH.D.
Naylor, J. N., M.SC., PH.D.
Neale, E. R. W., M.S., PH.D.
Neave, Ferris, M.SC., PH.D.
Needler, A. W. H., O.B.E., M.A., PH.D., D.SC.
Newcombe, Howard B., A.I.C.T.A., PH.D.
Newton, Robert, M.C., M.SC., PH.D., D.SC., LL.D.
Nicholls, R. W., PH.D., D.SC., F.I.P., F.A.P.S.
Nickerson, Mark, SC.M., PH.D., M.D.
Noble, R. L., M.D., PH.D., D.SC.
Nobles, Mildred K., M.A., PH.D.
Norman, G. W. H., PH.D.
Nuffield, E. W., PH.D.

Oka, Takeshi.
Okulitch, V. J., M.A.SC., PH.D.
Opechowski, W., MAG.PHIL.
Osborne, F. F., M.A.SC., PH.D.
Ouellet, Cyrias, D.SC.

Panisset, M. G., D.V., D.V.M.
Paquet, Jean-Guy, D.SC.
Parker, R. C., PH.D., D.SC.
Parkin, J. H., C.B.E., B.A.SC., M.E.
Parr, J. G., PH.D.
Parsons, T. R., M.SC., PH.D.
Paterson, Norman R.
Patterson, G. N., M.A., PH.D., LL.D.
Pavilanis, Vytautas, M.D., C.S.P.Q.
Pearce, J. A. P., M.A., D.SC., PH.D.
Pearson, W. B., D.F.C., M.A., D.PHIL.
Perlin, A. S., M.SC., PH.D.
Perrault, Guy, M.SC.A., PH.D.
Perryman, Eric C. W., M.A.
Person, C. O., M.A., PH.D.
Petch, H. E., M.SC., PH.D.
Petrie, William, A.M., PH.D.
Phillips, John Edward.
Pickard, G. L., M.B.E., M.A., D.PHIL.
Pidgeon, L. M., M.B.E., M.SC. PH.D.
Polanyi, J. C., M.SC., PH.D., D.SC.
Pomerleau, René, M.SC., D.SC.
Porter, Arthur, M.SC., PH.D.
Pounder, Elton K., PH.D.
Préfontaine, Georges, B.A., M.D., L. ès SC.
Prest, V. K., M.SC., PH.D.
Preston, M. A., M.A., PH.D.
Price, R. A., M.A., PH.D.
Pringle, Robert, PH.D.

Pritchard, Huw Owen, ph.d., d.sc.
Puddington, I. E., m.sc., ph.d.
Pugsley, L. I., m.sc., ph.d.
Quastel, J. H., a.r.c.s., d.sc., ph.d., f.r.s.
Radforth, Norman W., m.a., ph.d.
Ramsay, D. A., m.a., ph.d.
Ranger, K. B., ph.d.
Rapson, W. H., m.a.sc., ph.d.
Redhead, P. A., m.a.
Ree, Rimhak, ph.d.
Reeves, Leonard W., ph.d., d.sc.
Rhodes, A. J., m.b., ch.b., m.d., f.r.c.p.(Edin.).
Ribenboim, P., ph.d.
Ribner, Herbert S., m.s., ph.d.
Ricker, W. E., m.a., ph.d.
Riddell, J. E., b.eng., m.sc., ph.d.
Riley, Gordon A., ph.d., d.sc.
Risi, Joseph, l.sc., d.sc.
Robertson, R. E., m.sc., ph.d.
Robertson, Rocke, c.c., m.d.c.m., ll.d., d.c.l., d.de l'u., d.sc., f.r.c.s.(ed.), f.r.c.s.(can.).
Robinow, C. F., m.d.
Robinson, Gilbert de B., m.b.e., ph.d.
Robinson, S. C., m.a.sc., ph.d.
Robson, J. M., m.a.
Roliff, W. A., m.sc.
Rooney, P. G., ph.d.
Rose, Bram, b.a., m.d., c.m., m.sc., ph.d.
Rose, D. C., o.b.e., m.sc., ph.d.
Ross, D. M., m.a., ph.d., sc.d.
Russell, L. S., m.a., ph.d., ll.d.
Russell, R. D., m.a., ph.d.
Salter, Robert B., o.c., m.d., m.s.
Samborski, Daniel J.
Sandin, R.B., m.sc., ph.d.
Sandorfy, C., ph.d., d.sc.
Sanwal, Bishnu D., ph.d., dr.nat.sc.
Sargent, B. W., m.b.e., m.a., ph.d.
Satterly, Jack, m.a., ph.d.
Savile, D. B. O., m.sc., ph.d.
Scagel, Robert F., m.a., ph.d.
Schaefer, Theodore, m.sc., d.phil., f.c.i.c.
Scherk, Peter, ph.d.
Schiff, Harold, m.a., ph.d.
Schneider, W. G., m.sc., ph.d.
Schwerdtfeger, H., m.a., ph.d.
Scriver, Charles R., m.d.c.m., f.r.c.p.(c).
Scudder, Geoffrey G. E.
Sehon, A., b.sc., m.sc., ph.d., d.sc.
Selye, Hans, m.d., ph.d., d.sc.
Senn, H. A., m.a., ph.d.
Setterfield, George, ph.d.
Shaw, Denis M., m.a., ph.d.
Shaw, Edgar A. G.
Shaw, Michael, m.sc., ph.d.
Shebeski, L. H., m.sc.
Shinbrot, Marvin, m.a., ph.d.
Shrum, G. M., o.b.e., m.a., ph.d.
Sifton, H. B., m.a., ph.d.
Siminovitch, David, ph.d.
Siminovitch, Louis, m.sc., ph.d.
Sinclair, George, m.sc., ph.d.
Slipper, S. E., b.sc.
Slykhuis, John T.
Smallman, B. N., m.a., ph.d.
Smeltzer, Walter W., ph.d.
Smillie, Lawrence B., m.a., ph.d.
Smith, Charles H., m.sc., m.s., ph.d.
Smith, Harold A., b.sc.
Smith, Ian C. P.
Snider, Robert F.
Solandt, O. M., o.b.e., m.a., m.d., d.sc., m.r.c.p., ll.d.
Solomon, Samuel, m.sc., ph.d.
Sonéa, Sorin.
Sourkes, T. L., m.sc., ph.d.
Spencer, Mary E., m.a., ph.d.
Spinks, J. W. T., m.b.e., d.sc., ph.d., ll.d.
Sprott, David A.
Stavraky, C. W., m.b., m.sc., m.d., c.m.
Stearn, C. W., m.s., ph.d.
Steeves, T. A., m.a., ph.d.
Stelck, C. R., m.sc., ph.d.
Sternberg, C. M., ll.d.
Stevenson, J. S., ph.d.
Stewart, A. T., m.sc., ph.d.
Stewart, R., m.a., ph.d.
Stewart, R. W., m.s., ph.d.
Stockwell, C. H., ph.d.
Stoicheff, B. P., m.a., ph.d., f.r.s.
Stothers, John B., m.sc., ph.d.
Strangway, David, m.a., ph.d.
Suzuki, David Takayoshi, o.c., ph.d.
Swanson, C. O., m.a.sc., ph.d.
Synge, John L., m.a., sc.d., f.r.s.
Tarr, H. L. A., m.s.a., ph.d.(McGill), ph.d.(Cantab.).
Taurins, A., eng.chem., dr.chem.
Templeman, W., o.b.e., m.a., ph.d.
Templeton, Ian M., m.a., d.phil.
Terasmae, Jaan.
Thiessen, G. J., m.sc., ph.d.
Thode, H. G., m.b.e., m.sc., ph.d., d.sc., f.r.s.
Thompson, I. M., m.b., ch.b., f.r.s.e.
Thomson, J. E., m.a., ph.d.
Thorsteinsson, R., m.a., ph.d.
Till, J. E., b.a., m.a., ph.d.
Tomlinson, George H.
Towers, G. H. N., m.sc., ph.d.
Tozer, E. T., ph.d.
Tremblay, J.-L., ph.d., d.s.c.
Trotter, James, ph.d., d.sc.
Tully, John P., m.b.e., c.m., ph.d.
Tutte, W. T., m.a., m.sc., ph.d.
Uffen, Robert J., m.a., ph.d.
Valenta, Zdenek, m.sc., ph.d.
Van Cleave, A. B., m.sc., ph.d.
Van den Bergh, S., m.sc., dr. rer. nat., f.r.a.s.
Van Kranendonk, Jan, ph.d.
Van Rooyen, C. E., d.sc., m.d., f.r.c.p.(lond.), f.r.c.p.(c.), f.r.c.path., m.r.c.p., m.b., ch.b.
Vanterpool, T. C., m.sc.
Venning, Eleanor H. m.sc., ph.d.
Vining, Leo C., m.sc., ph.d.
Vladykov, V. D., ph.d.
Vogt, E. W., m.sc., ph.d.
Volkoff, G. M., m.b.e., m.a., ph.d., d.sc.
Walker, Gordon A. H.
Walker, Norma Ford, ph.d.
Wallace, Philip R., m.a., ph.d.
Ward, Arthur G., m.a.
Warren, H. V., b.a.sc., b.sc., d.phil.
Warren, J. B., ph.d., a.r.c.s.
Watson, J. W., m.a., ph.d.
Watson, W. H., m.a., ph.d.
Waygood, E. R., m.s.a., ph.d., f.c.i.c.
Weld, C. B., m.a., m.d., l.m.c.c.
Welsh, H. L., m.a., ph.d.
Westman, A. E. R., m.a., ph.d.
Whalley, E., ph.d., d.sc.
Wheeler, J. O., ph.d.
Whitehead, J. Rennie, ph.d.
Whitham, K., m.a., ph.d.
Whitmore, Gordon F., m.a., ph.d.
Wickenden, R. T. D., ph.b., m.a., ph.d.
Wiesner, K., d.sc.
Williams, G. R., ph.d., d.sc.
Williams, Harold, m.sc., ph.d.
Wilson, H. D. B., m.s., ph.d.
Wilson, J. Tuzo, c.c., o.b.e., sc.d., ph.d., ll.d., d.sc., f.r.s.
Wilt, John C.
Wolfe, Leonhard S., m.sc., ph.d., m.d.
Woonton, G. A., m.a., d.sc.
Wright, K. O., m.a., ph.d.
Wright, W. J., ph.d., ll.d.
Wyman, Max, ph.d.
Wynne-Edwards, H. R., m.a., ph.d.
Wynne-Edwards, V. C., m.a.
Yaffe, Leo, m.sc., ph.d.
Yates, P., m.sc., ph.d.
Yen, Lin Jui, m.a.sc., ph.d.
Young, Lawrence.
Zassenhaus, H. J., m.a., ph.d.

ROYAL CANADIAN ACADEMY OF ARTS

40 UNIVERSITY AVE., SUITE 530, TORONTO, ONT. M5J 1T1.

Founded 1880

President: JOHN C. PARKIN, C.C.

Executive Vice-President: C. BLAKEWAY MILLAR.

Regional Vice-Presidents: YVES TRUDEAU, BRUNO FRESCHI.

Treasurer: GEORGE CUTHBERTSON.

Executive Director: LOUISE CHÉNIER.

COUNCIL MEMBERS:

BIELER, TED.
DAUDELIN, CHARLES.
DEVISSER, JOHN.
FISHER, BRIAN.
GAGNON, CHARLES.
GERIN-LAJOIE, GUY.
GLADSTONE, GERALD.
GOTTSCHALK, FRITZ.
GREGOR, HELEN FRANCES.
KAISER, ROBERT.
KRAMER, BURTON.
McLOUGHLIN, MICHELE.
MOLINARI, GUIDO.
PRATT, CHRISTOPHER.
SEMAK, MICHAEL.
SISLER, REBECCA.
SMITH, GORDON A.
TANABE, TAKAO.

LEARNED SOCIETIES

GENERAL

Royal Canadian Institute: 191 College St., Toronto; f. 1849; for the promotion of the physical sciences, the arts, and manufactures by research and dissemination of scientific knowledge; 2,200 mems.; Pres. A. HILES CARTER; Exec. Sec. Mrs. RUTH J. BREITHAUPT; publ. *Transactions.*

AGRICULTURE AND VETERINARY SCIENCE

Agricultural Institute of Canada: Suite 907, 151 Slater St., Ottawa, Ontario K1P 5H4; f. 1920 to organize and unite all workers in scientific and technical agriculture and to serve as a medium where progressive ideas for improvements in agricultural education, investigation, publicity and extension work can be discussed and recommended for adoption; 5,000 mems.; Gen. Man. W. E. HENDERSON; publs. *Canadian Journal of Plant Science*†, *Canadian Journal of Soil Science*†, *Canadian Journal of Animal Science*†, *Agrologist*† (all quarterly), *Agronews* (monthly).

Canadian Forestry Association: 185 Somerset St. West, Suite 203, Ottawa, Ont. K2P 0J2; f. 1900; 9 provincial asscns. with a membership of 35,000; educational and other programmes designed to encourage better understanding of forests and related resources, and to encourage their wise use; Pres. D. R. REDMOND; Exec. Dir. A. D. HALL; publ. *C.F.A.News.*

ARCHITECTURE AND TOWN PLANNING

Canadian Society of Landscape Architects: P.O.B. 3304, Station C, Ottawa, Ont. K1Y 4J5; f. 1934; 194 mems.; 24 affiliate mems.

Royal Architectural Institute of Canada: 151 Slater St., Suite 1104, Ottawa, Ont. K1P 5H3; f. 1908; 3,500 mems.; Exec. Dir. ROBBINS ELLIOTT.

The Town Planning Institute of Canada: 80 King St. W., Suite 1507, Toronto 1, Ont.; Pres. M. V. JONES; Sec.-Treas. W. WRONSKI; publ. *Plan.*

THE ARTS

Canada Council/Conseil des Arts: 255 Albert St., Ottawa, Ont. K1P 5V8; f. 1957; the council provides grants to individuals and supports organizations in the arts; it fosters Canadian cultural relations abroad; it administers on behalf of the Canadian Government a programme of cultural exchanges with a number of other countries; it provides the secretariat for the national commission for UNESCO; 21 mems.; Chair. MAVOR MOORE; Dir. CHARLES LUSSIER; publ. *Annual Report.*

Canadian Film Institute: 1105-75 Albert St., Ottawa, Ont. K1P 5E7; f. 1935 to encourage and promote the study, appreciation and use of motion pictures and television in Canada; operates National Film Library, renting 10,000 educational films; National Film Theatre; Canadian Centre for Films on Art; International Animated Film Festival; Exec. Dir. FREDERIK MANTER; publs. *Film Canadiana* (annual), *The Guide to Film and Television Courses offered in Canada* (2 a year)

Canadian Music Centre: 1263 Bay St., Toronto, Ont. M5R 2C1; for the promotion, in Canada and abroad, of music by Canadian composers; Dir.-Gen. J. P. L. ROBERTS.

Canadian Music Council: c/o Secretary-General, 36 Elgin, Ottawa K1P 5K5; f. 1949; mems. from every national and regional organization and individual mems.; Mem. Int. Music Council (UNESCO) and Int. Soc. Contemporary Music; publs. *Musicanada* (quarterly).

Canadian Society of Painters in Watercolour: c/o Visual Arts Ontario, 417 Queen's Quay West, Suite G100, Toronto M5V 1A2; f. 1925; 100 mems.; Pres. JULIUS GRIFFITH; Sec. AIMÉE MILLIN.

Composers, Authors and Publishers Association of Canada Ltd: 1240 Bay St., Toronto, Ont. M5R 2C2; f. 1925; performing rights society; 8,000 mems.; Gen. Man. J. V. MILLS; publ. *The Canadian Composer*† (10 a year).

Contemporary Art Society: 60 St. James's Street West, Montreal; f. 1939; 85 mems.; Sec. ALLAN HARRISON.

National Design Council: 235 Queen St., Ottawa, Ont. K1A 0H5; f. 1961; 17 appointed mems.; Chair. D. DALY (acting); Exec. Dir. PURVIS C. FREDENBURGH.

Print and Drawing Council of Canada: c/o Dept. of Art and Design, University of Alberta, Edmonton, Alta; f. 1977 following merger of the Society of Canadian Painter-Etchers and Engravers and the Graphic Arts Society; Chair. W. JULE.

Sculptors' Society of Canada: 40 Armadale Ave., Toronto M6S 3W8; f. 1928; Pres. MAY MARX.

Visual Arts Ontario: 417 Queen's Quay W., Suite G100, Toronto, Ont. M5V 1A2; f. 1973; federation of professional artists' asscns; 5,000 mems.; Exec. Dir. WILLIAM J. S. BOYLE; publ. *Artviews*† (every 2 months).

BIBLIOGRAPHY, LIBRARY SCIENCE AND MUSEOLOGY

Association pour l'avancement des sciences et des techniques de la documentation (*Association for the advancement of documentation sciences and techniques*): 360 rue Le Moyne, Montreal H2Y 1Y3, Quebec; f. 1943; a professional organization of libraries and librarians; Pres. GUY CLOUTIER; Dir.-Gen. ARTHUR BOUDRIAS.

Bibliographical Society of Canada: P.O.B. 1878, Guelph, Ont.; f. 1946; Pres. Mrs. G. M. STRATHERN; Sec.-Treas. MARION CAMERON.

Canadian Library Association: 151 Sparks St., Ottawa, Ont. K1P 5E3; f. 1946; 5,000 mems.; Pres. ALAN MACDONALD; Exec. Dir. PAUL KITCHEN; publs. *Canadian Library Journal, Feliciter, Canadian Periodical Index, Canadian Materials.*

Canadian Museums Association (*Association des musées canadiens*): 331 Cooper St., Suite 400, Ottawa, Ont. K2P 0G5; f. 1947; advancement of public museum and art gallery services; 1,201 individual, 409 institutional mems.; library of 980 vols.; Pres. Dr. GEORGE MACBEATH; Exec. Dir. R. LYNN OGDEN; Sec.-Treas. PIERRE LACHAPELLE; publs. *Gazette*† (quarterly), *Museogramme*† (monthly).

ECONOMICS, LAW AND POLITICS

Canadian Bar Association: The Varette Bldg., 130 Albert St., Ottawa, Ont. K1P 5G4; f. 1914 to promote the administration of justice and uniformity of legislation throughout Canada; to encourage a high standing of legal education, training and ethics; 28,000 mems.; Pres. A. W. COX, Q.C.; publs. *The National*, *The Canadian Bar Review*.

Canadian Economics Association: Carleton University, Ottawa, Ont.; f. 1967; Pres. E. ROSENBLUTH; Sec.-Treas. Prof. GILLES PAQUET; publs. *Canadian Journal of Economics*, *Canadian Public Policy*, *Analyse de Politiques*.

Canadian Institute of Chartered Accountants: 250 Bloor St. East, Toronto M4W 1G5; f. 1902; professional and examining body; 30,200 mems.; Pres. R. G. HARRIS; Exec. Dir. K. C. FINCHAM; publs. *CA Magazine* (monthly), *Members Directory* (every 2 years).

Canadian Institute of International Affairs: 15 King's College Circle, Toronto, Ont. M5S 2V9; f. 1928; 2,700 mems. in 23 brs.; library of 23,000 vols.; Pres. CLARENCE D. SHEPARD; Exec. Dir. JACQUES RASTOUL; Research Dir. JOHN W. HOLMES; publs. *International Canada* (monthly), *Behind the Headlines* (6 a year), *International Journal*†, *Etudes Internationales* (quarterly), *Annual Report*, *Canada in World Affairs* (every 2 years), *Choix* (irregular) and special research projects.

Canadian Political Science Association/Association canadienne de Science politique: Carleton University, Ottawa, Ont. K1S 5B6; f. 1913; Pres. WALTER D. YOUNG; Sec.-Treas. N. CHI; publ. *Canadian Journal of Political Science*, *The Bulletin* (newsletter), *Annual Meeting/Congrès annuel* (microfiched collection of annual conference papers).

EDUCATION

Association of Canadian Community Colleges: 211 Consumers Rd., Suite 203, Willowdale, Ont. M2J 4G8; national non-profit asscn. of non-degree granting institutions, interested in the growth and potential of community colleges (cégeps, vocational institutions, schools of allied health, etc.); it currently serves Canada's 169 non-degree granting institutions; Exec. Dir. ALLAN GOLDENBERG; publs. *College Canada* monthly), *ACCC Journal* (quarterly), *Directory of College Programmes* (annually), bulletins and newsletters (English and French).

Association of Canadian University Information Bureaux (*l'Association des bureaux de l'information des universités du Canada*): f. 1968; aims to further the development of post-secondary education through the improvement of information exchange between universities; Pres. DOUG WATERSTON, Dir. of Information, University of Guelph, Guelph, Ont. N1G 2W1.

Association of Universities and Colleges of Canada: 151 Slater St., Ottawa, Ont. K1P 5N1; f. 1911; devoted to higher education in Canada and elsewhere; 69 corporate mems.; library of 8,000 vols., 350 periodicals with a special collection on university administration; Pres. A. J. EARP; Exec. Dir. A. GILLMORE; publs. *Directory of Canadian Universities* (annual), *Proceedings* (annual), *University Affairs*† (10 a year), *Select Bibliography on Higher Education*† (quarterly); many other publications, bibliographies, bulletins, directories, specific study reports, etc.; all published in English and French.

Canadian Association for Adult Education: 29 Prince Arthur Ave., Toronto M5R 1B2; Pres. WALTER PITMAN; Exec. Dir. IAN MORRISON.

Canadian Education Association: 252 Bloor St. W, Suite S850, Toronto, Ont. M5S 1V5; f. 1891; 1,200 mems.; Pres. L. R. MOASE; Exec. Dir. G. NASON; publs. *Education Canada* (quarterly), *Newsletter* (9 a year), *Bulletin* (French, 9 a year), *Canadian Education Index* (2 interim issues and annual culumation)

HISTORY, GEOGRAPHY AND ARCHAEOLOGY

Antiquarian and Numismatic Society of Montreal: 280 Notre Dame St. E, Montreal, Que. H2Y 1C5; f. 1862; 200 mems.; Pres. Dr. J. O. W. BRABANDER; Recording Sec. JACQUES POULIN; publ. *Canadian Antiquarian and Numismatic Journal of Montreal*.

Canadian Association of Geographers: Burnside Hall, McGill Univ., 805 Sherbrooke St. W., Montreal, Que. H3A 2K6; f. 1951; Pres. Dr. MARIE SANDERSON; Sec.-Treas. J. D. BOOTH; publs. *The Canadian Geographer* (quarterly), *Directory* (annually).

Canadian Historical Association: Public Archives of Canada, Ottawa K1A 0N3; f. 1922, to encourage historical research and public interest in history; 2,500 mems.; Sec. (English) NORMAN HILLMER; Sec. (French) ANDRÉE LÉVESQUE; publs. *Historical Papers*, *Historical Booklets*, *Newsletter*, *Register of Dissertations*.

Institut d'Histoire de l'Amérique Française: 261 Bloomfield Ave., Montreal H2V 3R6, Quebec, Canada; f. 1947; independent institution; library contains over 10,000 vols., 3,500 documents; Pres. RENÉ DUROCHER; Vice-Pres. ANDRÉE DÉSILETS; Sec. MARCEL CAYA; Treas. JEAN-CLAUDE ROBERT; publ. *Revue d'Histoire de l'Amérique Française*† (quarterly).

Nova Scotia Historical Society: P.O.B. 895, Armdale, Halifax, N.S.; f. 1878; 400 mems.; Sec. L. BERARD; publs. *Collections*, *Genealogical Newsletter*.

Ontario Archaeological Society: Pres. Dr. R. DEAN AXELSON; Sec. Mrs. CECILIA FINNIGAN, 57 Chestnut Park Rd., Toronto 5.

Ontario Historical Society: 78 Dunloe Rd., Toronto, Ont. M5P 2T6; f. 1888; 2,300 mems.; 63 affiliated societies; Sec. U. ERNEST BUCHNER; publs. *Ontario History Bulletin* (quarterly), *Approaching Ontario's Past* (3 a year).

The Royal Canadian Geographical Society: 488 Wilbrod St., Ottawa K1N 6M8; 85,000 mems.; Exec. Sec. D. L. REGAN; Editor DAVID MACLELLAN; publ. *Canadian Geographic* (every 2 months).

Société Généalogique Canadienne-Française: Case postale 335, Place d'Armes, Montreal H2Y 3H1; f. 1943; studies and publications on the origins and history of French Canadian families since 1615; library of *c.* 4,000 vols., and over 1,500,000 cards on marriages; *c.* 2,500 mems.; Pres. Rév. J. DÉZIEL; publ. *Mémoires* (quarterly).

Waterloo Historical Society: P.O.B. 522, Station C, Kitchener, Ont. N2G 4A2; f. 1912; local history; collection at Kitchener Public Library, Ont.; Sec. RICHARD WOELLER; publ. annual volume containing articles on regional history.

INTERNATIONAL CULTURAL INSTITUTES

Académie canadienne-française: 100 rue Notre-Dame est, Montreal; f. 1944; for the promotion of the French language and culture in Canada; Dir. ROGER DUHAMEL; Sec. EDMOND ROBILLARD; publ. *Les Cahiers de l'Académie* (annually).

Alliance Française: 1312 blvd. Mont Royal, Montreal, Que. H2V 2J1; brs. in all major towns.

British Council: c/o British High Commission, 80 Elgin St., Ottawa K2P 0K8; Rep. W. E. BROOK.

Canadian Council for International Co-operation (*Conseil Canadien pour la Coopération Internationale*): 321 Chapel St., Ottawa, Ont. K1N 7Z2; f. 1968 (formerly Overseas Institute of Canada, f. 1961); co-ordination centre for voluntary agencies working in international development; 100 mems.; Pres. THOMAS KINES; Exec. Dir. RICHARD HARMSTON; publs. *Newsletter* (monthly), *Directory of Canadian NGOs*.

Goethe-Institut Montreal: Place Bonaventure, P.O.B. 428, Montreal, Que. H2A 1B8; Dir. HEINZ HUGO BECKER.

Institut Canadien-Français d'Ottawa: 95 York St., Ottawa K1N 7E7; f. 1852; 900 mems.; Pres. L.-PAUL BOUCHER; Sec. HENRI LAPERRIÈRE.

Istituto Italiano di Cultura: 1200 ave. Docteur Penfield, Montreal; Dir. Prof. GIOVANNI BATTAGLIA.

Language and Literature

Canadian Authors' Association: 24 Ryerson Ave., Toronto, Ont. M5T 2P3; f. 1921; 800 mems.; publs. *Author and Bookman* (quarterly), *The Writer's Guide* (irregular).

Canadian Linguistic Association—Association canadienne de Linguistique: Queen's University, Kingston, Ont.; f. 1954 to advance the study of linguistics, languages in Canada; 868 mems.; Pres. NORMAND BEAUCHEMIN; Sec.-Treas. DAN A. WILSON; publ. *The Canadian Journal of Linguistics/La Revue Canadienne de Linguistique*† (2 a year).

International P.E.N.: Suite 417, 3535 Queen Mary Rd., Montreal, Que. H3V 1H8; Pres. EDGAR H. COHEN; Sec. (vacant).

Medicine

Academy of Medicine: 288 Bloor St. W., Toronto, Ont. M5S 1V8; f. 1907; 2,500 fellows; sections of medicine, surgery, paediatrics, pathology, obstetrics and gynaecology, ophthalmology, oto-laryngology, anaesthesia, haematology and gastrointestinal diseases, preventive medicine, cancer, neurological sciences, urology, dermatology, cardiovascular sciences, orthopaedic surgery, history of medicine, aviation, space and underwater medicine, medical archaeology and anthropology; library of 80,000 vols.; Hon. Sec. Dr. B. A. Q. HAMILTON-SMITH; Exec. Sec. M. E. WILSON; publ. *Bulletin*.

Canadian Association of Anatomists: University of Manitoba, Dept. of Anatomy; f. 1956; 265 mems.; Pres. Dr. THEODORE F. LEVEQUE; Sec. Dr. JAMES A. THLIVERIS.

Canadian Association of Optometrists: Suite 2001, 210 Gladstone Ave., Ottawa, Ont. K2P 0Y6; f. 1948; Pres. Dr. JACK HUBER; Exec. Dir. DONALD SCHAEFER; publ. *The Canadian Journal of Optometry* (quarterly).

Canadian Dental Association: 1815 Alta Vista Drive, Ottawa, Ont. K1G 3Y6; f. 1902; 9,500 mems.; Exec. Dir. H. E. DROUIN; publ. *Journal*.

Canadian Lung Association: 75 Albert St., Suite 908, Ottawa, Ont. K1P 5E7; f. 1900; 1,200 mems.; Exec. Dir. Dr. E. S. HERSHFIELD; publs. *Annual Report, Quarterly Bulletin*.

Canadian Medical Association: P.O.B. 8650, Ottawa, Ont. K1G 0G8; f. 1867; 33,500 mems.; Sec.-Gen. Dr. R. G. WILSON; publs. *Canadian Medical Association Journal*†, *Canadian Journal of Surgery*†.

Canadian Paediatric Society (*Société Canadienne de Pédiatrie*): Centre Hospitalier Universitaire de Sherbrooke, Sherbrooke, Quebec J1H 5N4; f. 1923; 875 mems.; Pres. Dr. MARTIN G. WOLFISH; Exec. Vice-Pres. Dr. J. H. V. MARCHESSAULT; publ. *Newsletter* (monthly).

Canadian Pharmaceutical Association, Inc.: 1815 Alta Vista Drive, Ottawa, Ont. K1G 3Y6; f. 1907; 8,000 mems.; Exec. Dir. L. C. FEVANG; publs. *Canadian Journal of Pharmaceutical Sciences* (quarterly), *Canadian Pharmaceutical Journal* (monthly), *Compendium of Pharmaceuticals and Specialities* (annual), *Canadian Self-Medication* (every 2 years).

Canadian Physiological Society: f. 1936; 471 mems.; Pres. Dr. O. HÉROUX; Sec. Dr. D. B. JENNINGS, Dept. of Physiology, Queen's University, Kingston, Ontario; publs. *The Canadian Journal of Physiology and Pharmacology* (monthly), *Physiology Canada* (quarterly).

Canadian Public Health Association: 1335 Carling Ave., Suite 210, Ottawa, Ont. K1Z 8N8; f. 1910; 2,900 mems.; Pres. RALPH E. J. RICKETTS; Exec. Dir. GERALD H. DAFOE; publ. *Canadian Journal of Public Health* (every 2 months).

Nutrition Society of Canada: c/o F. A. Farmer, Box 276, Macdonald Campus of McGill University, Ste. Anne de Bellevue, Que. H9X 1CO; f. 1957 to extend knowledge of nutrition by research, discussion of research reports, and interchange of information; 325 mems.; Pres. J. F. ANGEL; Sec. F. A. FARMER; publ. *Nutrition/Forum de Nutrition* (2 a year).

Pharmacological Society of Canada: f. 1956; 241 mems.; Pres. Dr. J. H. MCNEILL; Sec. Dr. G. D. BELLWARD, Faculty of Pharmaceutical Sciences, University of British Columbia, Vancouver, B.C. V6T 1W5; publ. *Canadian Journal of Physiology and Pharmacology*.

Royal College of Physicians and Surgeons of Canada: 74 Stanley Ave., Ottawa, Ont. K1M 1P4; f. 1929; 18,000 mems.; approves postgraduate medical training programmes; acts as examining body to certify medical, surgical and laboratory specialists; organizes continuing medical education for specialists; Pres. Dr. BERNARD PEREY; Vice-Pres. Dr. G. ROSS LANGLEY (Medicine), Dr. WILLIAM PAUL (Surgery); Exec. Dir. Dr. JAMES H. DARRAGH; publ. *Annals* (quarterly).

Natural Sciences

General

Association Canadienne-Française pour l'Avancement des Sciences Inc.: C.P. 6060, Montreal, P.Q. H3C 3A7; f. 1923; 45 societies as mems.; a federation of French-Canadian learned societies; aims to popularize Science by means of lectures, meetings, awards, publications; Dir.-Gen. and Gen. Sec. DENIS JACOB; publs. *Annales* (yearly), *Le Jeune Scientifique* (monthly).

Nova Scotian Institute of Science: Science Library, Dalhousie Univ., Halifax B3H 4J3; f. 1862; 300 mems.; Sec. ROBERT J. CONOVER; Treas. Dr. JOHN VAN DER MEER; publs. *Proceedings, Supplements*.

Science Council of Canada/Conseil des Sciences du Canada: 100 Metcalfe St., Ottawa K1P 5M1; f. 1966, became a Crown Corporation 1969; a national advisory body to assess Canada's scientific and technological resources, requirements and opportunities; recommendations are made through the Minister of State for Science and Technology and through reports and studies; Chair. Dr. CL. FORTIER, C.C., M.D., PH.D., F.R.C.P.(C.), F.R.S.C.; Sec. LESLIE MILLIN; Exec. Dir. MAURICE L'ABBÉ; publ. *Agenda* (quarterly).

SCITEC: Association of the Scientific, Engineering and Technological Community of Canada: Suite 202, 151 Slater St., Ottawa K1P 5H3; f. 1970; national scientific organization of 55 mem. societies and 450 individuals co-operating with the government, industry and the public to promote understanding of science in everyday life; Pres. Dr. VIVIAN C. ABRAHAMS; Exec. Dir. JUDITH A. STANLEY (acting).

Biological Sciences

Canadian Federation of Biological Societies: f. 1957; Member Societies—Canadian Physiological Society, Pharmacological Society of Canada, Canadian Association of Anatomists, Canadian Biochemical Society, Nutrition Society of Canada, Canadian Society for Cell Biology, Canadian Society for Immunology, Society of Toxicology of Canada; 3,500 mems.; Chair. Dr. K. COOPER; Hon. Sec. Treas. Dr. J. T. HAMILTON, Dept. of Pharmacology, Rm. 274, University of Western Ontario, London, Ont. N6G 2K3; publs. *Canadian Federation News* (annually), *Programme of Annual Meeting* (annually), *Programme and Proceedings* (annually).

Canadian Phytopathological Society: f. 1929; 350 mems.; Pres. W. E. MCKEEN; Sec.-Treas. Dr. R. J. COPEMAN, Plant Science Dept., Univ. of British Columbia, Vancouver, B.C. V6T 1W5; publs. *Proceedings* (annually), *News* (quarterly), *The Canadian Journal of Plant Pathology* (quarterly).

Canadian Society for Cell Biology: Dept. of Biology, York University, Downsview, Ont. M3J 1P3; f. 1966; 320 mems.; Pres. S. BAYLEY; Sec. I. B. HEATH; publ. *Bulletin* (3 a year).

Canadian Society for Immunology/ Société Canadienne d'Immunologie: Dept. of Immunology, University of Manitoba, Winnipeg, Man. R3E 0W3; f. 1966; 400 mems.; Pres. Dr. B. CINADER; Sec.-Treas. Dr. A. FROESE; publ. *Bulletin* (irregular).

Canadian Society of Microbiologists/ Société Canadienne des Microbiologistes: 500-85 Albert St., Ottawa, Ont. K1P 6A4; f. 1951; 800 mems.; Pres. Dr. D. J. KUSHNER; Sec.-Treas. Dr. I. MCDONALD; publ. *C.S.M. Newsletter* (3 or 4 a year), *Programme & Abstracts* (annually).

Cercles des Jeunes Naturalistes: 455 rue Saint-Jean, Montreal, Que. H2Y 2R5; f. 1931; 20,000 mems.; Pres. Gen. BÉATRICE GAUCHER; Dir. MAURICE PROVENCHER; publs. *Bibliothèque des Jeunes Naturalistes* (4 a year), *Les Feuillets du Club* (monthly), *Faune de mon pays* (2 series).

Entomological Society of Canada: 1320 Carling Ave., Ottawa, K1Z 7K9; f. 1868; 900 mems.; 1,100 subscribers; 7 affiliated regional societies; Pres. S. R. LOSCHIAVO; Sec. JOHN E. LAING; publs. *The Canadian Entomologist* (monthly), *Memoirs, Bulletin.*

Manitoba Naturalists Society: 214-190 Rupert Ave., Winnipeg, Man. R3B 0N2; f. 1920; 1,900 mems.; Pres. DENNIS FAST; Sec. EDNA HAATAINEN.

Société Linnéenne de Québec: Aquarium de Québec, Ste-Foy, Quebec 10; f. 1929; 250 mems.; Pres. JEAN GAUTHIER; publ. *Le Linnéen* (2 a year).

Vancouver Natural History Society: P.O.B. 3021, Vancouver, B.C. V6B 3X5; f. 1918; 1,000 mems.; aims to promote interest in nature, conservation of natural resources, protection of plants and animals liable to extinction; Pres. ROBERT M. DUNDAS; Treas. GEORGE SALE; publ. *Bulletin Discovery*†.

Physical Sciences

Canadian Association of Physicists/Association Canadienne des Physiciens: 151 Slater St., Ottawa, Ont. K1P 5H3; f. 1945; 2,000 mems.; Pres. C. C. COSTAIN; Exec. Sec. MONA L. JENTO; publ. *Physics in Canada* (every 2 months).

Canadian Biochemical Society (*La Société Canadienne de Biochimie*): c/o Dept. of Biochemistry, University of Alberta, Edmonton T6G 2H7; f. 1958; 750 mems.; Pres. Dr. D. S. LAYNE; Vice-Pres. Dr. C. M. KAY; Sec. Dr. W. A. BRIDGER; publ. *Bulletin* (quarterly).

Chemical Institute of Canada: 151 Slater St., Ottawa K1P 5H3; f. 1945; 33 local sections, 14 subject divisions, 71 student chapters and two constituent societies—Canadian Society for Chemical Engineering and the Canadian Society for Chemical Technology; 11,000 mems.; Exec. Dir. T. H. G. MICHAEL, F.C.I.C.; official publs. *Chemistry in Canada* (11 a year), *The Canadian Journal of Chemical Engineering* (bi-monthly).

Geological Association of Canada: Dept. of Earth Sciences, University of Waterloo, Waterloo, Ont. N2L 3G1; f. 1947 to advance the science of geology and related fields of study and to promote a better understanding thereof throughout Canada; 2,597 mems.; Pres. W. G. E. CALDWELL; Sec.-Treas. A. V. MORGAN; publs. *Geoscience Canada, Geolog* (quarterly).

Royal Astronomical Society of Canada: 124 Merton St., Toronto, Ont. M4S 2Z2; f. 1890; 18 centres; 29,000 mems.; Nat. Sec. NORMAN GREEN; publs. *Journal* (bi-monthly), *Observers' Handbook* (annual, December).

Society of Chemical Industry (Canadian Section): c/o Emery Industries Ltd., 365 Evans Ave., Toronto, Ont. M8Z 1K2; f. 1902; 250 mems.; Hon. Sec. R. G. PRYMA.

PHILOSOPHY AND PSYCHOLOGY

Canadian Philosophical Association, The (*L'Association Canadienne de Philosophie*): 1390 Sherbrooke St. W., Montreal, Quebec H3G 1K2; f. 1958 to promote philosophical scholarship in Canada and to represent Canadian philosophers; 770 mems.; Admin. Sec. JOANNE S. MCGLYNN; publ. *Dialogue* (quarterly).

Canadian Psychological Association (*Société Canadienne de Psychologie*): 558 King Edward Ave., Ottawa, Ont. K1N 7N6; f. 1939 to promote psychological research and the practical applications of psychology in Canada; 2,506 mems.; Pres. Dr. V. VIKIS-FREIBERGS; Sec.-Treas. Dr. R. F. WILSON; Exec. Officer Dr. T. V. HOGAN; publs. *Canadian Journal of Psychology, Canadian Psychology, Canadian Journal of Behavioral Science* (quarterly).

RELIGION, SOCIOLOGY AND ANTHROPOLOGY

Association for the Advancement of Christian Scholarship: 229 College St., Toronto, Ont. M5T 1R4; f. 1967; Exec. Dir. ROBERT E. VANDER VENNEN. Sponsors:

Institute for Christian Studies: religion and interdisciplinary studies; 9 teachers, 30 students.

Canadian Association of African Studies/Association Canadienne des Etudes Africaines: Dept. of Geography, Carleton University, Ottawa, Ont. K1S 5B6; f. 1970; *c.* 200 mems.; promotion of the study of Africa in Canada; aims to improve the Canadian public's knowledge and awareness of Africa; provides a link between Canadian and African scholarly and scientific communities; Pres. Prof. ROBERT L. MCCORMACK; Sec.-Treas. Prof. D. R. F. TAYLOR; publ. *Canadian Journal of African Studies/Revue Canadienne des Etudes Africaines* (3 a year), *Newsletter/Bulletin*† (2 a year).

Canadian Association of Latin American Studies/Association Canadienne des Etudes Latino-Américaines: c/o Prof. ANTONIO URRELLO, Sec.-Treas. CALAS/ACELA, Room 210, 151 Slater St., Ottawa K1P 5H3; f. 1969; 200 mems.; Pres. J. C. M. OGELSBY; Vice-Pres. CLAUDE MORIN; publs. *North South/Nord Sud/Norte Sur, Canadian Journal of Latin American Studies* (2 a year), *Newsletter* (quarterly), *Directory of Canadian Scholars and Universities interested in Latin American Studies.*

Canadian Society of Biblical Studies: c/o Principal's Office, University College, Univ. of Toronto, Toronto, Ont. M5S 1A1; f. 1933; the promotion of scholarship in Biblical studies; 140 mems.; Pres. VERNON FAWCETT; Exec. Sec. Prof. G. P. RICHARDSON; publs. *Newsletter for Ugaritic Studies, Newsletter for Targum Studies* (2 a year), *Bulletin* (annually).

TECHNOLOGY

Association of Canadian Industrial Designers/Association des Designers industriels du Canada: c/o School of Industrial Design, Carleton University, Ottawa, Ont. K1S 5B6; f. 1948; 200 mems.; Pres. GEORGE LYNN; Vice-Pres. PHILIPPE LALANDE.

Canadian Aeronautics and Space Institute: 60–75 Sparks St., Ottawa, Ont. K1P 5A5; f. 1954; 1,425 mems.; Pres. Dr. J. D. F. MACNAUGHTON; Exec. Sec. P. A. COBBETT; publ. *Canadian Aeronautics and Space Journal* (quarterly).

Canadian Council of Professional Engineers (Co-ordinating Body for 11 Provincial Licensing Bodies): Suite 401, 116 Albert St., Ottawa, Ont. K1P 5G3; total membership of affiliated associations, 100,000; Gen. Man. C. LAJEUNESSE, P.ENG.

Canadian Electrical Association: 320 Tramways Building, 159 Craig St. West, Montreal; f. 1889; 1,600 mems.; Gen. Man. D. C. CAMPBELL; publs. *Reports, Proceedings.*

Canadian Institute of Mining and Metallurgy, The: 400–1130 Sherbrooke St. West, Montreal H3A 2M8; f. 1898; 10,363 mems.; Publisher G. F. SKILLING; publs. *Bulletin* (monthly), *Transactions, CIM Directory* (annually), *Journal of Canadian Petroleum Technology* (quarterly).

Engineering Institute of Canada: 2050 Mansfield St., Montreal H3A 1Y9; f. 1887; 16,000 mems. and 4 constituent societies (*see below*); Gen. Man. ROBERT J. THIBAULT; publs. *Engineering Journal* (bi-monthly), *Canadian Journal of Civil Engineering, CSME Transactions, Canadian Electrical Engineering Journal, Canadian Geotechnical Journal* (quarterly), *EIC Transactions* (irregular).

Canadian Society for Mechanical Engineering: f. 1970.

Canadian Society for Civil Engineering: f. 1972.

Canadian Society for Electrical Engineering: f. 1973.

Canadian Geotechnical Society: f. 1972.

Institute of Electrical and Electronics Engineers Inc., Canadian Regional Office: 7061 Yonge St., Thornhill, Ont. L3T 2A6; Man. GEORGE G. ARMITAGE. (*See* main entry under U.S.A.)

RESEARCH INSTITUTES

(*see* also under Universities)

GENERAL

Alberta Research Council: 11315 87th Ave., Edmonton, Alta. T6G 2C2; f. 1921; scientific and technological research in the areas of energy, natural resources, frontier sciences and industrial and engineering services with the aim of assisting and developing industry in the province of Alberta; library of 10,000 vols. 12,000 reports, 600 periodicals, 500 geological maps; Pres. Dr. GILLES G. CLOUTIER.

British Columbia Research Council: 3650 Wesbrook Mall, Vancouver, B.C. V6S 2L2; f. 1944; independent, non-profit organization; sponsored by government and industry to conduct technological research in fields of applied biology, applied chemistry, engineering-physics and management studies; library of 10,500 monographs, 400 periodicals and 15,000 separates; Dir. P. C. TRUSSELL; publs. *Annual Report*†, *Guidelines to Industrial Progress*†, *Productivity Caselines*†.

Nova Scotia Research Foundation Corporation: 100 Fenwick St., P.O.B. 790, Dartmouth, Nova Scotia B2Y 3Z7; f. 1947; 105 mems.; library of 11,000 vols.; assists economic development of Nova Scotia by promoting effective use of science and technology by government and industry; undertakes research and development to that end; Pres. Dr. J. E. BLANCHARD; Sec.-Treas. T. B. NICKERSON; publ. *Annual Report.*

Ontario Research Foundation: Sheridan Park, Mississauga, Ont. L5K 1B3; f. 1928; Chair. J. S. DEWAR; Pres. W. R. STADELMAN; Sec. J. N. MATTHEWS; library of 24,000 vols.; publs. *Annual Report*†, *Newsletter*† (monthly).

Saskatchewan Research Council: 30 Campus Drive, Saskatoon, Sask. S7N 0X1; f. 1947 to advance the development of the Province through research in chemistry, engineering, geology, physics, industrial services and management consulting; *c.* 175 staff; library (Saskatchewan Information Retrieval Centre) of 9,000 vols. and 400 periodicals; Exec. Dir. Dr. TOM PEPPER.

AGRICULTURE

Canadian Forestry Service: Ottawa, Ont. K1A 0E7; f. 1899; forest production, forest management, tree improvement, forest statistics and the environmental aspects of forestry; supports 2 private research organizations: FORINTEK (fmrly Forest Products Research Laboratories) and the Forest Engineering Research Institute of Canada; also supports research at 6 Canadian forestry schools; budget of *c.* $41 million; 1,200 personnel; Dir.-Gen. Dr. R. J. BOURCHIER; publs. *Bi-Monthly Research Notes*, regional and institute *Information Reports*, departmental publs., etc.

Research establishments:

Pacific Forest Research Centre: 506 West Burnside Rd., Victoria, B.C. V8Z 1M5; Dir. T. G. HONER (acting).

Northern Forest Research Centre: 5320 122nd St., Edmonton, Alta. T6H 3S5; Dir. Dr. G. T. SILVER.

Great Lakes Forest Research Centre: Box 490, 1219 Queen St. East, Sault Ste. Marie, Ont. P6A 5M7; Dir. J. H. CAYFORD.

Laurentian Forest Research Centre: Box 3800, 1080 Route du Vallon, Ste. Foy, Que. G1V 4C7; Dir. Dr. C. WINGET.

Maritimes Forest Research Centre: Box 4000, College Hill, Fredericton, N.B. E3B 5G4; Dir. Dr. M. M. NEILSON.

Newfoundland Forest Research Centre: Box 6028, Bldg. 304, Pleasantville, St. John's, Newfoundland A1C 5X8; Dir. Dr. W. J. CARROLL.

Forest Pest Management Institute: P.O.B. 490, 1195 Queen St. E., Sault Ste. Marie, Ont. P6A 5M7; Dir. Dr. G. W. GREEN.

Petawawa National Forestry Institute: Chalk River, Ont. K0J 1J0; Dir. Dr. R. M. NEWNHAM.

HISTORY, GEOGRAPHY AND ARCHAEOLOGY

Interuniversity Centre for European Studies: 1193 Phillips Square, Pavillon Phillips, 3400, C.P. 8892, Montreal H3C 3P8; f. 1972 to promote contact between those working on European subjects in an historical framework, to augment the scholarly and teaching resources available to them, and to encourage individual and group research; 500 mems.; documentation centre of *c.* 20 periodicals and 20 bulletins, etc.; Dir. Prof. ALEX MACLEOD; publs. *Newsletter*† (2 a month during academic year), *Europa* (2 a year), *Proceedings*, research reports and occasional publications.

MEDICINE

Canadian Dental Research Foundation: 1815 Alta Vista Drive, Ottawa, Ont. K1G 3Y6; f. 1920.

Medical Research Council of Canada: Ottawa, K1A 0W9; f. 1960; function is to promote, assist and undertake basic, applied and clinical research in Canada in the health sciences; Pres. Dr. RENÉ SIMARD; Sec. Miss D. J. WRIGHT; publs. *MRC Newsletter*† (quarterly), *Report of the President*† (annually), *MRC: Grants and Awards Guide*† (annually).

National Cancer Institute of Canada: 77 Bloor St. West, Suite 401, Toronto, Ont. M5S 2V7; Pres. Dr. R. S. BUSH; Exec. Dir. Dr. R. A. MACBETH.

Ontario Cancer Treatment and Research Foundation, The: 7 Overlea Blvd., Toronto M4H 1A8; f. 1943; treatment, diagnosis and research in cancer; Chair. G. R. CUNNINGHAM; Exec. Dir. Dr. J. W. MEAKIN; Sec.-Treas. R. D. GRAY, C.A.; publs. *Cancer in Ontario*†, *Proceedings of the Clinical Conferences*†.

NATURAL SCIENCES

General

Arctic Institute of North America: University Library Tower, 2500 University Drive, N.W., Calgary, Alta. T2N 1N4; f. 1945, became inst. of Univ. of Calgary 1979; multi-disciplinary research on physical, biological and social sciences; 300 fellows, 1,800 mems.; library of 30,000 vols.; Exec. Dir. Dr. PETER SCHLEDERMANN; publs. Special publications, Technical publications, *Arctic*†, *Newsletter* (quarterly).

International Development Research Centre: P.O.B. 8500, Ottawa, Ont., K1G 3H9; f. 1970 by Act of the Canadian Parliament; to support and conduct research in the developing regions of the world in the fields of agriculture, food and nutrition sciences; information sciences; health sciences; social sciences and human resources; Pres. IVAN L. HEAD; Sec. JAMES C. PFEIFER; publs. annual report, *IDRC Reports* (quarterly).

National Research Council of Canada/Conseil national de recherches Canada: Ottawa, Ont. K1A 0R6; f. 1916; laboratory divisions of biosciences, building research, chemistry, Herzberg Inst. of Astrophysics, mechanical engineering, National Aeronautical Establishment, physics, electrical engineering; Prairie Regional Laboratory, Saskatoon and Atlantic Regional Laboratory, Halifax; Pres. W. G. SCHNEIDER, M.SC., PH.D., D.SC., LL.D., F.R.S.C., F.R.S.; publs. *Canadian Journals of Biochemistry, of Botany, of Chemistry, of Civil Engineering, of Earth Sciences, of Geotechnology, of Microbiology, of Physics, of Physiology and Pharmacology, of Zoology, Forest Research, Annual Report, NRC Science Dimension* (bi-monthly), brochures.

Natural Sciences and Engineering Research Council of Canada: Montreal Rd., Ottawa, Ont. K1A 0R6; f. 1978; a crown corporation of the federal Government reporting to Parliament through a designated minister; promotes research in the natural sciences and engineering other than the health sciences; advises the Minister of State for Science and Technology; 22 mems.; Pres. G. M. MACNABB; Sec. M. BROCHU; Exec. Dir. G. JULIEN; publs. *NSERC Awards Guide, NSERC Scholarships and Fellowships Guide, Report of the President, Contact* (newsletter), *The Natural Sciences and Engineering Research Council* (description of NSERC's programmes).

Biological Sciences

Huntsman Marine Laboratory: Brandy Cove, St. Andrews, N.B.; f. 1969 with the co-operation of universities, two Int. Foundations, Fisheries Research Board of Canada and the Province of New Brunswick Dept. of Fisheries; research and teaching in marine sciences; Pres. Dr. K. G. DAVEY; Exec. Dir. Dr. W. B. SCOTT.

Physical Sciences

Algonquin Radio Observatory: Lake Traverse, Ont.; operated by the National Research Council; includes 150 ft.-diameter radiotelescope completed in 1966.

Atmospheric Environment Service: 4905 Dufferin St., Downsview, Ont. M3H 5T4; f. 1839; a service of the Federal Dept. of the Environment; Canadian Meteorological Centre at Montreal; offices at Vancouver, Whitehorse, Edmonton, Regina, Winnipeg, Toronto, Montreal, Halifax and Gander; 60 civil Weather Offices and an Ice Forecast Central; Asst. Deputy Minister Dr. A. E. COLLIN; Dir.-Gen. Canadian Climate Centre M. K. THOMAS; Dir.-Gen. Central Services D. K. SMITH; Dir.-Gen. Field Services J. A. W. MCCULLOCH; Dir.-Gen. Atmospheric Research D. W. L. GODSON; publs. *Monthly Record of Meteorological Observations in Canada, Canadian Weather Review, Monthly Radiation Summary, Snow-Cover Data Canada* (annually), *Supplementary Precipitation Data* (2 a year), *Meteorological Summaries* (monthly and annually), *Ozone Data for the World.*

Canadian 220 MHz NMR Centre: Department of Medical Genetics, University of Toronto Medical Sciences Building, Toronto, Ont. M5S 1A8; f. 1970; a national centre for high field NMR spectroscopy; administered by the representatives of industry, universities and the Government; Dir. Dr. A. A. GREY.

David Dunlap Observatory of the University of Toronto: P.O.B. 360, Richmond Hill, Ont.; f. 1935; 50 mems.; library of 30,000 vols.; Dir. J. D. FERNIE.

Dominion Astrophysical Observatory: RR7, Victoria, B.C. V8X 3X3; f. 1918; 40 mems.; 8,300 vols.; Dir. SIDNEY VAN DEN BERGH, A.B., M.SC., DR.RER.NAT.(ASTRON.), F.R.S.C.; Sec. D. CROWE; publs. *Publications*†, *Contributions*†.

Earth Physics Branch, Department of Energy, Mines and Resources: 1 Observatory Crescent, Ottawa, Ont. K1A 0Y3; f. 1905 as Dominion Observatory, re-organized 1970; global and Canadian solid earth geophysics; 169 staff mems.; library of 52,000 vols.; Dir.-Gen. Dr. J. G. TANNER; publs. *Publications, Contributions, Seismological, Geothermal, Gravity Map, Geodynamics, Geomagnetic* series.

Geological Survey of Canada: 601 Booth St., Ottawa, Ont. K1A 0E8; f. 1842; geological research, mapping and specialized studies throughout Canada; branches: Atlantic Geoscience Centre for research in marine geology and geophysics in Dartmouth, N.S.; Institute of Sedimentary and Petroleum Geology in Calgary, Alta.; Cordilleran Geology Division for West Coast bedrock and marine geology studies in Vancouver, B.C.; library in Ottawa of 150,000 vols., smaller collections in regional centres; Dir.-Gen. D. J. MCLAREN; Chief Geologist J. G. FYLES; publs. *Current Research*, memoirs, bulletins, economic geology, reports, papers and maps.

RELIGION, SOCIOLOGY AND ANTHROPOLOGY

Canadian Federation for the Humanities: 151 Slater St., Suite 415, Ottawa, Ont. K1P 5H3; f. 1943 to promote research in the humanities and to represent the humanities community in Canada; Chair. PIERRE LABERGE; Exec. Dir. VIVIANE LAUNAY-ELBAZ; publs. *Bulletin, Annual Report.*

International Center for Research on Bilingualism—Centre international de recherche sur le bilinguisme: Cité Universitaire, Sainte-Foy, Quebec G1K 7P4; f. 1967; basic research on bilingualism, biculturalism, and related phenomena; Exec. Dir. J. D. GENDRON.

Social Science Federation of Canada: 151 Slater St., Ottawa, Ont. K1P 5H3; Pres. VAIRA VIKIS-FREIBURGS; Dir. JOHN E. TRENT; publs. *Annual Report, Social Sciences in Canada* (quarterly).

Social Sciences and Humanities Research Council of Canada/Conseil de recherches en sciences humaines du Canada: 255 Albert St., Box 1610, Ottawa, Ont. K1P 6G4; f. 1978 to promote and assist excellence in Canadian research and scholarship in the social sciences and humanities; took over programmes formerly administered by the humanities and social sciences division of the Canada Council; administers funds voted by Parliament through a variety of scholarships, fellowships and research grants; 22-mem. Council; Pres. André Fortier; Exec. Dir. J. G. Nicholson.

Technology

Atomic Energy of Canada, Ltd.: 275 Slater St., Ottawa, Ont. K1A DS4; f. 1952; development of economic nuclear power systems, research in nuclear science, exploitation of radiation sources and radio isotopes, nuclear power station marketing; Pres. J. S. Foster.

Establishments:

Chalk River Nuclear Laboratories: Chalk River, Ont.; f. 1944; nuclear reactors (NRU, NRX, Pool Test Reactor PTR and ZED-2), tandem Van de Graaff accelerator, equipment for nuclear research and engineering development; Vice-Pres. A. J. Mooradian.

Commercial Products Division: South March, Tunney's Pasture, Ottawa, Ont.; f. 1946; Radio isotopes and radiation resources; Vice-Pres. J. M. Beddoes.

Power Projects Division: Sheridan Park, Ont.; f. 1958; Design, development, construction of nuclear power stations; consulting services; Vice-Pres. G. A. Pon.

Whiteshell Nuclear Research Establishment: Pinawa, Man.; f. 1960; one nuclear reactor, equipment for nuclear research and engineering development; Vice-Pres. R. G. Hart.

Canada Centre for Inland Waters: P.O.B. 5050, Burlington, Ontario, L7R 4A6; f. 1967; one of the principal research laboratories and survey centres of the Dept. of the Environment; undertakes physical, chemical, biological and social research for the purpose of improved fresh water management; also serves as a base for the conduct of surveys into water quality and quantity, and for hydrographic charting; library of 30,000 vols.; Dir. A. R. Le Feuvre; publs. annual report and various papers.

Institute for Aerospace Studies: 4925 Dufferin St., Downsview, Ont. M3H 5T6; f. 1949; an interdisciplinary institute of the Univ. of Toronto; graduate studies; research in applied and basic fields; serves industrial research and development needs in government and industry; facilities include one of the best-equipped laboratories in Canada; 15 academic staff; library of 72,000 vols.; Dir. Prof. J. H. de Leeuw, ph.d.; publs. *Progress Report*† (annually), series of technical notes, reviews, etc.

Pulp and Paper Research Institute of Canada: 570 St. John's Blvd., Pointe Claire, Que. H9R 3J9; f. 1925; pulp and paper research, contract research and technical services; postgraduate training programme in co-operation with McGill University and University of British Columbia; staff of *c.* 300; library of 14,000 vols.; Pres. B. W. Burgess; Sec. K. M. Thompson; publs. *Annual Report, TREND Magazine* (1–2 a year).

Research and Productivity Council: P.O.B. 6000, Fredericton, N.B. E3B 5H1; f. 1962; independent non-profit organization providing scientific, engineering, technical and management services to governments and companies in primary, manufacturing and service industries; staff of 82; library of 5,500 reference vols., 350 periodicals; Exec. Dir. Dr. Claude Bursill, m.a., m.sc., ph.d.; publ. *Annual Reports*.

LIBRARIES AND ARCHIVES

Alberta

Calgary Public Library: 616 Macleod Trail S.E., Calgary, T2G 2M2; 739,921 vols.; 14 branches; special section on petroleum; Librarian John Dutton.

City of Edmonton Archives: 10105 112th Ave., Edmonton T5G 0H1; f. 1971; reference library of 2,500 vols., also MSS., photographs and maps of the city; Man. Helen Larose.

Edmonton Public Library: 7 Sir Winston Churchill Square, Edmonton, T5J 2V4; f. 1913; 10 brs, 3 book mobiles; 950,000 vols., 25,000 audio-visual items; Librarian Vincent Richards.

Glenbow-Alberta Institute Library and Archives: 9th Ave. and 1st St. S.E., Calgary T2G 0P3; 40,000 vols., 150,000 photographs and a large collection of manuscript materials, chiefly on Western and Northern Canada; Librarian L. J. Gottselig; Archivist William McKee.

Legislature Library: 216 Legislature Bldg., Edmonton, Alberta T5K 2B6; f. 1906; parliamentary library of 117,644 vols. and documents; Librarian D. B. McDougall; publs. *Annual Report, Directory of Alberta Government Libraries* (2 a year).

Provincial Archives of Alberta: 12845 102nd Ave., Edmonton; f. 1963; collections of non-current govt. records, private papers, municipal records, photos, taped interviews and maps pertaining to the history of Alberta; special collection of Western Canadian in Historical Resources Library (17,000 vols.); circulating and recent accession exhibitions; Provincial Archivist Alan D. Ridge; publs. *Information Leaflets, Publication Series*.

University of Alberta Library: Edmonton; f. 1909; 2,000,000 vols., 500,000 government publications, 1,300,000 microforms; Librarian Bruce Braden Peel, m.a., b.l.s.

University of Calgary Library: f. 1966; 1,392,319 vols.; 898,133 microforms; Dir. Alan H. MacDonald.

British Columbia

Fraser Valley Regional Library: Headquarters: 2469 Montrose Ave., Abbotsford, B.C. V2S 3T2; f. 1930; 26 branches, 2 bookmobiles; 365,000 vols.; 1,255 films; maps; music scores; pamphlets; photographs; Dir. W. H. Overend.

Provincial Archives: Victoria; f. 1893; 50,000 vols.; 10,000 feet of MSS. and government records, 250,000 photographs, 5,000 paintings; Provincial Archivist John A. Bovey.

Legislative Library: Victoria; f. 1893; 500,000 vols.; Librarian J. G. Mitchell.

University of British Columbia Library: Vancouver V6T 1Y3; f. 1912; 12 branches; 2,107,500 vols., 2,350,000 microtexts, 960,000 other non-book items; Librarian B. Stuart-Stubbs, b.a., b.l.s.

Vancouver Island Regional Library: Headquarters: 10 Strickland St., Nanaimo, B.C.; f. 1936; 25 branch libraries and bookmobile service; 280,000 vols.; Librarian Fred T. White, m.a., b.l.s.

Vancouver Public Library: Vancouver; f. 1887; 865,000 vols.; 180,000 pamphlets; 18 brs., one bookmobile; Dir. Dr. George Wootton.

Vancouver School of Theology Library: 6050 Chancellor Blvd., Vancouver, B.C. V6T 1X3; f. 1971; 65,000 vols.; Librarian PAUL NATHANSON.

MANITOBA

Law Society of Manitoba Library: Law Courts, Winnipeg 1; f. 1877; 40,000 vols.; Librarian Mrs. DEIRDRE K. HARVEY.

University of Manitoba Libraries: Winnipeg R3T 2N2 f. 1877; collections supporting 13 faculties and 7 schools; 1,187,000 vols. 383,000 government publications, 129,000 other print items (maps, performance music, text book collection), 540,000 microforms, 16,400 audio-visual items, 13,300 serial titles; Dir. M. J. SHARROW.

NEW BRUNSWICK

Bibliothèque Champlain (Université de Moncton): Moncton E1A 3E9; f. 1965; 245,000 vols. and 400,000 micro-units; Librarian ALBERT LÉVESQUE, M.S.L.S.

Harriet Irving Library: University of New Brunswick, Fredericton; f. 1800; 760,981 vols. and 877,214 (equivalent vols.) microforms; Librarian GERTRUDE GUNN, PH.D.

Legislative Library: Box 6000, Fredericton; f. 1841; 50,000 vols.; Librarian JOCELYNE LEBEL.

R. P. Bell Library: Mount Allison University, Sackville, N.B. E0A 3C0; 265,000 vols.; Librarian RUTH MACDONALD (acting).

NEWFOUNDLAND

Memorial University of Newfoundland Library: St. John's; 875,000 vols., 1,260,000 micro-units; Librarian THEODORE D. PHILLIPS.

Provincial Archives of Newfoundland and Labrador: Colonial Bldg., St. John's; Provincial Archivist F. BURNHAM GILL.

NOVA SCOTIA

Acadia University Library: Wolfville; f. 1843; 340,000 vols.; Librarian ISOBEL HORTON, B.A., B.L.S.

Angus L. Macdonald Library: St. Francis Xavier University, Antigonish; 290,000 vols.; Librarian Rev. CHARLES BREWER; publ. *The Antigonish Review* (quarterly).

Dalhousie University Library System: Halifax, N.S. B3H 4H8.

- **University Library:** f. 1868; 744,025 vols., 7,000 periodicals; University Librarian DOROTHY L. COOKE.
- **W. K. Kellogg Health Sciences Library:** f. 1868, reorganized 1915 and 1967; 120,056 vols.; Librarian ANN NEVILL.
- **Sir James Dunn Law Library:** org. 1883; 125,723 vols.; Librarian CHRISTIAN L. WIKTOR.

Legislative Library of Nova Scotia: Province House, Halifax; f. 1862; 65,000 vols.; Librarian SHIRLEY B. ELLIOTT.

Public Archives of Nova Scotia: Coburg Road, Halifax; f. 1931; official records, family and business papers, maps, charts, pictures, microfilmed files of leading newspapers, and a research library of about 45,000 vols.; Archivist HUGH A. TAYLOR.

University of King's College Library: Halifax, B3H 2A1; 68,000 vols.; Librarian Mrs. J. E. LANE.

ONTARIO

Canada Institute for Scientific and Technical Information (CISTI): Montreal Rd., Ottawa K1A 0S2; operated by National Research Council of Canada; f. 1974, fmrly National Science Library; focal point of a national scientific and technical information network; resources of over 1,000,000 vols. are made available through loan, photocopy and consultation; information services include operation of a national computerized current awareness service (CAN/SDI), a national on-line enquiry system (CAN/OLE) for retrospective searching of several large data bases, Unified Literature Search Service providing custom bibliographies on requested topics, Health Sciences Resources Centre which is also the major MEDLINE centre for Canada, Information Exchange Centre for federally supported university research, Translations Information Centre, Depository for Unpublished Data. Dir. (vacant); publs. *Union List of Scientific Serials in Canadian Libraries*†, *Infoscope* (newsletter)†, *Recent Additions to the Library*†, *Canadian Location of Journals Indexed in Index Medicus*†, *Directory of Federally Supported Research in Universities*†, *Health Science Libraries in Canada, Serials, News, Notes*†, *Problems of the North*†, *Scientific and Technical Societies of Canada*†, *Scientific Policy Research and Development in Canada*†.

Carleton University Library: Colonel By Drive, Ottawa K1S 5J7; 1,000,000 vols.; 375,000 microforms, etc.; Librarian GEOFFREY H. BRIGGS, M.A.

Hamilton Public Library: 55 Main St. West, Hamilton, Ont. L8P 1H5; f. 1889; special collections of local history and Canadiana to 1950; 750,000 vols. and 2,700 periodicals; 9 br. libraries; 2 bookmobiles; Librarian FRANK N. HOGG.

Libraries Division, Department of Agriculture: Sir John Carling Bldg., Ottawa K1A 0C5; f. 1910; 550,000 vols., 5,200 journals, 12,000 continuations; specializes in agriculture, biology, biochemistry, plant science, entomology, veterinary medicine, food sciences, economics; serves 22 field libraries; Dir. M. L. MORTON; publs. *Union List of Serials in CDA Libraries, List of CDA Publications, Selected List of Acquisitions* (monthly).

Library of the Geological Survey of Canada: 601 Booth St., Ottawa, K1A 0E8; f. 1842; interlibrary loans, CAN/SDI, on-line retrospective searching; 250,000 vols., 150,000 geological maps; Head of Library Services A. E. BOURGEOIS; publs. *Monthly Accessions List, List of Translations* (irregular), *List of serials titles* (quarterly).

Library of Parliament: Ottawa; f. 1867; 570,000 vols., 21,200 microfilm reels; 116,212 microfiches; Parl. Librarian ERIK J. SPICER, C.D., B.A., B.L.S., M.A.L.S.; publs. *Quorum* (daily, during session), *Selected Additions List* (monthly), *Current Issue Reviews* (monthly), *Selected Periodicals Articles* (2 a month), *This is Your Library* (irregular), *Annual Report*†, *Periodicals and Newspapers in the Collections of the Library of Parliament* (irregular).

Library of the Pontifical Institute of Mediaeval Studies: 113 St. Joseph's St., Toronto M5S 1J4, f. 1929; 59,000 vols., 10,000 folios of MSS. on photostats, 200,000 folios of MSS. on microfilm; Librarian Rev. D. F. FINLAY, C.S.B., B.A., S.T.B., M.A.L.S.

Library of Supreme Court: Ottawa; Librarian R. BOULT, Q.C.

London Public Libraries and Museums: London; f. 1894; libraries and historical museums; 536,806 vols., 23,080 recordings; Dir. E. STANLEY BEACOCK; Curator (Historical Museums) C. SEVERANCE.

McMaster University Libraries: Hamilton L8S 4L6; f. 1887; 1,082,410 vols.; contains among others Samuel Beckett collection and Bertrand Russell archives; Librarian GRAHAM R. HILL; publs. *Library Research News*† (irregular), *Russell: The Journal of the Bertrand Russell Archives*.

Metropolitan Toronto Library: 789 Yonge St., Toronto, Ont. M4W 2G8; f. 1967; Canada's largest public reference library; services to other libraries in its area; 1,058,177 vols. and periodicals; 12 specialized depts.: general reference, fine art, theatre, music, science and technology, social sciences, business, history, Canadian history, literature, languages, municipal reference; Head Mrs. M. ALLEN; publs. *Annual Report*†, *MTLB News*†, etc.

National Library: 395 Wellington St., Ottawa K1A 0N4; f. 1953; a National Union Catalogue is maintained; National Librarian J. GUY SYLVESTRE, M.A., F.R.S.C.; Assoc. National Librarian HOPE CLEMENT, M.A., B.L.S.; Dir. Public Services Branch, F. PATTERSON, B.L.S.; Dir. Library Systems Centre LOUIS FONGET, B.A., B.L.S.; Dir. Collections Development Branch, A. PREIBISH, B.L.S.; Dir. Cataloguing Branch, C. DURANCE; publs. *Canadiana*, national bibliography (monthly, annual cumulations), *Canadian Theses—Thèses Canadiennes* (annual), *Canadian Theses on Microfilm* (numbered), *National Library News—Nouvelles de la Bibliothèque Nationale* (quarterly), *Annual Report*.

Ontario Legislative Library, Research and Information Services: Legislative Bldg., Queen's Park, Toronto M7A 1A2; f. 1867; 150,000 vols.; Dir. R. BRIAN LAND; publs. *Memo to Members, Periodical Contents, Periodical Selections, Selected New Titles* (monthly), *Annual Report of the Director*.

Ottawa City Archives: 174 Stanley Ave., Ottawa, K1M 1P1; f. 1975; repository of public records of civic administration and other historical material; *c.* 10,000 vols. and MSS; City Archivist EDWIN WELCH, M.A., PH.D., F.S.A.

Ottawa Public Library: 120 Metcalfe St., Ottawa; f. 1906; 631,324 vols.; Librarian G. FRAPPIER.

Public Archives of Canada: 395 Wellington St., Ottawa K1A 0N3; f. 1872; depository of public records and historical material; over 5,000,000 photographs, 750,000 maps, pictures, sound tapes and film; 100,000 books and pamphlets; Dominion Archivist W. I. SMITH; publs. *The Archivist/L'Archiviste*† (2 a month), *Annual Report*.

Queen's University Library: Kingston, Ont. K7L 5C4; f. 1842; 1,328,012 vols., 2,664,625 other items; Chief Librarian MARGOT B. MCBURNEY.

Toronto Public Library: 40 Orchard View Blvd., Toronto; f. 1883; 1,216,248 vols.; 28 brs.; library service to 7 hospitals, 8 other institutions and 9 homes for the aged; Osborne Collection of Early Children's Books, Spaced-Out Library; Chief Librarian E. L. FOWLIE; publ. *T.P.L. News*† (monthly).

University of Ottawa Library System: Ottawa; f. 1848; 1,012,000 vols.; University Chief Librarian F. YVON RICHER, M.L.S.

University of Toronto Libraries: Toronto; f. 1842; 5,304,966 vols., 1,409,366 microtexts, 635,607 other non-book items (maps, sheet music, L.P. phonorecords, manuscript titles, aerial photographs, etc.); Chief Librarian R. H. BLACKBURN, M.A., B.L.S., M.S., LL.D.

University of Trinity College Library: Toronto M5S 1H8; 103,000 vols.; Librarian Mrs. L. CORMAN, M.L.S.

University of Western Ontario Libraries: London; f. 1878; 1,382,647 vols.; Librarian ROBERT LEE, M.A., PH.D.

Victoria University Library: 71 Queen's Park Crescent East, Toronto M5S 1K7; 200,000 vols.; Librarian ROBERT C. BRANDEIS, M.L.S., PH.D.

PRINCE EDWARD ISLAND

Confederation Centre Library: incorporating Charlottetown Public Library, Legislative Library of P.E.I. and Public Archives: P.O.B. 1000, Charlottetown; f. 1773; 35,000 vols.; Provincial Archivist NICHOLAS DE JONG; Librarian Mrs. MARGARET ARMITAGE.

Prince Edward Island Provincial Library: University Ave., Charlottetown RR7, P.E.I. C1A 7N9; est. 1933; 191,044 vols. in regional system of 25 rural and town public libraries; Librarian D. SCOTT.

QUEBEC

Archives Nationales du Québec: 1210 ave. du Séminaire, C.P. 10450, Sainte-Foy, Quebec G1V 4N1; f. 1920; 45,000 vols.; regional centres at Hull, Trois-Rivières, Montréal, Chicoutimi, Sherbrooke, Noranda, Rimouski; Archivist FRANÇOIS BEAUDIN; publs. *Rapport* (annual), *Archives en tête* (every 2 months).

Bibliothèque de la Ville de Montréal: 1210 Sherbrooke St. E., Montreal H2L 1L9; f. 1902; 1,546,737 vols., of which 44,274 books, 11,839 pamphlets, 23,894 pictures, 1,540 maps and 39,112 microforms relate to Canada and Canadian history; 18 branches and 1 bookmobile; Dir. JACQUES PANNETON.

Bibliothèque du Barreau de Montréal (*Bar Library of Montreal*): Palais de Justice, Montreal H2Y 1B6; f. 1828; 84,553 vols.; Librarian ARTHUR PERRAULT.

Bibliothèque du Collège de l'Immaculée-Conception (Facultés de Théologie et de Philosophie de la Compagnie de Jésus): 5605 rue Decelles, Montreal, H3T 1W4; 177,500 vols.; Dir. C.-R. NADEAU; Librarian PIERRE LE BRETON.

Bibliothèque Nationale du Québec: (Ministère des Affaires culturelles du Québec): 1700 rue Saint-Denis, Montreal H2X 3K6; f. 1967 (absorbed Bibliothèque Saint-Sulpice); Laurentiana, MSS., old and rare books, 560,150 vols., 14,525 microfilms, 22,363 maps, 6,900 periodicals; Librarian J. R. BRAULT; publs. *Bibliographie du Québec* (printed and machine readable, monthly), *Bulletin* (quarterly), *RADAR* (*Répertoire analytique d'articles de revues du Québec*) (every 2 months).

Bibliothèques de l'Université de Montréal: C.P. 6128, Montreal, H3C 3J7; f. 1928; 2,000,000 vols., 19,000 current periodicals (including those of affiliated schools); Dir. of Libraries (vacant).

Centre Canadien des Recherches Généalogiques: Case postale 845, Haute-Ville, Quebec G1R 4S7; f. 1957; 5,000 vols.; Dir. ROLAND-J. AUGER; publs. *French Canadian and Acadian Genealogical Review* (quarterly), *Cahiers de généalogie québécoise* (twice yearly).

Concordia University Libraries: 1455 de Maisonneuve Blvd. West, Montreal, H3G 1M8; f. 1974; 1,100,000 vols.; Dir. PAUL-EMILE FILION, S.J., LL.D.

Fraser-Hickson Institute, Montreal (Free Library): 4855 Kensington Ave., Montreal H3X 3S6; f. 1885; over 190,000 vols.; Librarian Miss MARGERY W. TRENHOLME, B.A., B.L.S.; publ. *Annual Report*.

Laval University Library: Quebec; f. 1852; 1,621,503 vols., 20,097 periodicals, 3,964 films, 75,547 maps; Dir. CÉLINE R. CARTIER, C.A.F..B, M.A.P., M.L.S.; publs. *Répertoire des vedettes-matière de Laval, Guides bibliographiques, Rapport annual*.

Library of the Legislature of Quebec (*Bibliothèque de la Législature du Québec*): Hôtel du Gouvernement, Quebec G1A 1A5; f. 1867; 856,951 vols.; Chief Librarian JACQUES PRÉMONT, Q.C.; publs. *Bulletin, Bibliographie-documentation*.

McGill University Libraries: 3459 McTavish St., Montreal H3A 1Y1; f. 1855; 23 libraries, 1,938,334 vols., 402,387 microforms, 1,190,231 government documents; Dir. MARIANNE SCOTT, B.L.S.

Osler Library: McGill University, McIntyre Medical Sciences Building, 3655 Drummond St., Montreal H3G 1Y6, Que.; f. 1929; history of medicine and allied sciences; 30,000 vols.; Librarian PHILIP M. TEIGEN; publ. *Newsletter*†.

SASKATCHEWAN

Regina Public Library: 2311 12th Ave., Regina; f. 1909; 4 brs.; 3 bookmobiles; 345,000 vols.; Librarian RONALD YEO.

Saskatchewan Legislative Reference Library: Regina; f. 1878; 90,000 vols.; social sciences, law and history; noted for its collection of government documents and Western Canadiana; Librarian CHRISTINE MACDONALD.

Saskatchewan Provincial Library: 1352 Winnipeg St., Regina; f. 1953; co-ordinates library services in the province; 190,000 vols., specializing in library science, bibliography and Canadiana; Chief Librarian DONALD F. MEADOWS; publs. *Annual Report, Focus on Saskatchewan Libraries* and various subject bibliographies (irregular).

Saskatoon Public Library: 311 23rd St. East, Saskatoon; f. 1913; 4 branches, 3 bookmobiles; 817,000 vols.; local history room; Librarian Mrs. FRANCES MORRISON; Asst. Librarian Miss ALICE TURNER; publ. *Preface* (monthly, Sept. to June).

University of Saskatchewan Library: Saskatoon; f. 1909; 950,000 vols. and Adam Shortt collection of Canadiana; University Librarian N. A. BROWN.

Wapiti Regional Library: 145 12th St. East, Prince Albert, S6V 1B7; f. 1950; 52 brs.; 218,790 vols.; Chief Librarian J. GOLIATH; publ. *Northern Air*† (quarterly).

MUSEUMS AND ART GALLERIES

ALBERTA

Allied Arts Centre: 830 Ninth Ave., S.W., Calgary; f. 1946; Civic Arts Centre, Fine Arts Galleries, Theatre for Children, legitimate theatre; children's programme: creative art, dance, drama, ceramics; headquarters for cultural organizations; group meetings for adults; Dir. E. D. KNOWLES.

Banff National Park Museum: Box 900, Banff; f. 1904; flora and fauna of Banff National Park.

Department of Geology Museum, University of Alberta: Edmonton; f. 1912; geology, meteorites, mineralogy, vertebrate palaeontology, stratigraphy; Curator Dr. J. KRUPICKA.

Edmonton Art Gallery: 2 Sir Winston Churchill Square, Edmonton; f. 1923; Canadian and international paintings and sculpture; courses in art education; library of 2,500 vols., periodicals on art and education, 17,000 slides; Dir. TERRY FENTON; publ. *Update* (every 2 months).

Glenbow Museum: 9th Ave. and 1st St. S.E., Calgary; f. 1966; preserves, and makes available for study, materials relating to the history of Western Canada; museum, art gallery, library and archives; Dir. DUNCAN CAMERON; Chair. Board of Governors Mrs. JANE EDWARDS.

Subsidiary museum:

Luxton Museum: Banff; f. 1953; Indian collection and historical exhibits, natural history.

Medicine Hat Museum and Art Gallery: 1302 Bomford Crescent, Medicine Hat; f. 1967; cutural and natural history, palaeontology, and primitive peoples representative of S.E. Alberta; art gallery; monthly exhibits by Canadian and international artists; Dir. TOM WILLOCK.

Provincial Museum of Alberta: 12845 102nd Ave., Edmonton; f. 1963; collections and exhibits on the natural and human history of Alberta; geology, palaeontology, botany, zoology, archaeology, ethnology, history, fine and decorative arts; circulating exhibitions; educational programmes; Dir. ERIC WATERTON (acting); publs. *Museum* (Notes), *Publication Series, Occasional Papers* and leaflets.

Ring House Gallery: Ring House 1, University of Alberta Campus, Edmonton, TG6 2E2; Curator/Dir. HELEN COLLINSON.

BRITISH COLUMBIA

British Columbia Provincial Museum: 601 Belleville St., Victoria, V8V 1X4; f. 1886; contains reference collections and exhibits pertaining to natural history and human history of B.C.; Dir. R. YORKE EDWARDS; publs. *Annual Report*†, *Occasional Papers, Handbook Series, Anthropology in B.C.* (series), *SYESIS*† (technical journal).

Craigflower Manor Historic Museum: 110 Island Highway, Victoria; maintained by Provincial Archives; Provincial Archivist ALLAN TURNER; Resident Curator Mrs. J. THOMPSON.

Helmcken House Museum: 638 Elliott St., Victoria; four rooms in house built in 1852; maintained by Provincial Heritage Conservation Branch; Curator Mrs. M. PETTIGREW.

Museum of Northern British Columbia: 1st Ave. and McBride St., P.O.B. 669, Prince Rupert; f. 1924; Indian art and artefacts, local and natural history displays; Dir. RON DENMAN.

Vancouver Art Gallery: 1145 West Georgia St., Vancouver, V6E 3H2; f. 1931; paintings, sculpture, graphics, photography, video; Canadian paintings and graphics with emphasis on B.C. artists; Emily Carr Collection; modern American prints; British watercolours; 18th-20th-century British paintings; library of 6,250 vols., 10,000 catalogues, 500 bound vols, periodicals; Dir. LUKE ROMBOUT; publ. *Vanguard* (10 a year).

Vancouver Museums and Planetarium: 1100 Chestnut St., Vancouver V6J 3J9; anthropology, art, B.C. Indian artefacts, history of colonial exploration and settlement; maritime history and astronomy; Sec.-Gen. ROBIN INGLIS; Curator DAVID HURD.

Centennial Museum: f. 1968 as City of Vancouver centennial project; Chief Curator: ROBERT D. WATT.

Maritime Museum: f. 1958; home of R.C.M.P. schooner *St. Roch*; Chief Curator MICHAEL J. DUNCAN.

H. R. MacMillan Planetarium: f. 1968; Curator DAVID A. RODGER.

M.Y. Williams Geological Museum: Dept. of Geological Sciences, University of British Columbia, Vancouver, V6T 2B4; f. 1925; Curator J. NAGEL.

MANITOBA

Manitoba Museum of Man and Nature: 190 Rupert Ave., Winnipeg R3B 0N2; f. 1965; history and natural history of Manitoba; planetarium; Exec. Dir. H. D. HEMPHILL; Museum Dir. C. E. LAMMERS (acting).

Museums of University of Manitoba: Winnipeg; Curators: Mineralogy, I. CERNY; Botany, H. KENNEDY; Zoology, S. LOWRY; Anatomy and Pathology, Dr. L. C. BARTLETT.

Winnipeg Art Gallery: 300 Memorial Blvd., Winnipeg, Man. R3C 1V1; f. 1912; exhibitions, lectures, films, performing arts, education programmes; Dir. ROGER L. SELBY.

NEW BRUNSWICK

Beaverbrook Art Gallery: Fredericton, New Brunswick; f. 1959; 500 paintings and 200 drawings, 500 prints; Pillow collection of English porcelain; English sculptures; Lectures, films, travelling exhibitions, chamber concerts and guided tours, etc.; Curator IAN G. LUMSDEN; publs. *Beaverbrook Art Gallery Quarterly*, exhibition catalogues.

Fort Beauséjour National Historic Park and Museum: Aulac, N.B. E0A 3C0; f. 1926; Superintendent DAVID TAYLOR.

Miramichi Natural History Museum: 149 Wellington St., Chatham; f. 1880; Pres. R. M. WOOD.

New Brunswick Museum: 277 Douglas Ave., St. John, N.B. E2K 1E5; f. (1842) 1930; art gallery, archives, natural and human history museum chiefly relating to New Brunswick; Dir. DAVID ROSS; publs. *Annual Journal*†.

York-Sunbury Historical Society Museum: P.O.B. 1312, Fredericton E3B 58C; Pres. Prof. RICHARD BIRD.

NEWFOUNDLAND

Newfoundland Museum: 285 Duckworth St., St. John's; f. 1887; archaeology, ethnology, marine, natural, native peoples, human and military history; Dir. MARTIN L. BOWE; publ. *N.M. Technical Papers, Notes series.*

NOVA SCOTIA

Art Gallery of Nova Scotia: P.O.B. 2262, 6152 Coburg Rd., Halifax B3J 3C8; f. 1975 to replace the N.S. Museum of Fine Arts; paintings, drawings, sculpture, prints, collection of Nova Scotia folk art; Curator BERNARD RIORDON.

Fort Anne National Historic Park and Museum: Annapolis Royal; Supt. of Fort Anne and Port Royal National Historic Parks J. A. HALL.

Fortress of Louisbourg National Historic Park: Louisbourg; reconstruction and restoration project, including 18th-century period rooms and museum complex; historical and archaeological unit; archives and library; Park Superintendent JOHN FORTIER.

Nova Scotia Museum: 1747 Summer St., Halifax; f. 1868; natural science exhibits relating to N.S.; early N.S. furniture, Indian artifacts; crafts; architecture and maritime exhibits; 20 br. museums throughout N.S.; Dir. J. L. MARTIN.

ONTARIO

Art Gallery of Hamilton: 123 King St. West, Hamilton L8P 4S8; f. 1914; mainly Canadian paintings, sculpture and graphics; also art from the U.S.A., Britain and other European countries; workshops, films and lectures; library of 3,000 vols.; Dir. GLEN E. CUMMING; Curator A. J. OKO; publs. *Bulletin* (monthly), *Calendar of Events*† (monthly), *Catalogue* (annual).

Art Gallery of Ontario: 317 Dundas St. W., Toronto, M5T 1G4; f. 1900; art in Europe and North America, Canadian art; Tintoretto, Hals, Van Dyck, Rembrandt, Reynolds, Rubens, Poussin, Claude, Gainsborough, Chardin, Delacroix, Renoir, Picasso and the Impressionists are represented; library of 25,000 vols.; Dir. WILLIAM J. WITHROW; Chief Curator Dr. ROALD NASGAARD; publs. *The Gallery* (10 a year), *Annual Report*.

Collingwood Museum: Memorial Park, Collingwood, Ont.; f. 1904; Curator J. H. CONNELLY.

Dundurn Castle: Hamilton; former home of Sir Allan MacNab, Prime Minister of United Canada 1854–56, built 1834, restored 1967; guided tours, and outdoor theatre, music etc. in summer; Dir. MARTEN LEWIS.

Jordan Historical Museum of the Twenty: Jordan, Ont.; f. 1953; a collection illustrating life in the Twenty Mile Creek Area after 1776; Dir. HARRY L. CROWFOOT.

Marine Museum of Upper Canada: Stanley Barracks Exhibition Park, Toronto M6K 3C3; f. 1959; operated by the Toronto Historical Board; describes the waterways of Central Canada and the Great Lakes—St. Lawrence Basin, with emphasis on shipping; Curator ALAN N. HOWARD.

National Arts Centre: Confederation Square, Ottawa; opened 1969; opera house, theatre, studio and salon; over 900 performances a year; resident 46-piece orchestra; Dir.-Gen. DONALD MACSWEEN; publs. *Annual Report*†, *Calendars*† (monthly).

The National Museums of Canada: L'Esplanade Laurier, 300 Laurier Ave. West, Ottawa K1A 0M8; f. 1968, incorporating Canada's 4 national museums; also includes Museum Assistance programmes, Canadian Conservation Institute, National Inventory of Museum Collections, Museumobile Programme and International Programme; library of 120,000 vols.; Sec.-Gen. IAN CHRISTIE CLARK; Librarian VALERIE MONKHOUSE.

National Gallery of Canada: Elgin and Slater Streets, Ottawa, K1A 0M8; f. 1913; Old Masters; Modern European paintings and sculpture; world's foremost collection of Canadian art; prints and drawings and decorative arts; library of 46,000 vols.; Dir. Dr. HSIO-YEN SHIH.

National Museum of Man: Victoria Memorial Museum Building, Metcalfe and McLeod Streets, Ottawa, K1A 0M8; f. 1957; archaeology, ethnology, and history of Canada; study collections open to research by properly qualified students; consists of the Archaeological Survey of Canada, Canadian Centre for Folk Culture Studies, the Canadian War Museum, History Division, Canadian Ethnology Service, National Programmes Division, and Education and Cultural Affairs Division; Dir. WILLIAM E. TAYLOR, Jr.

National Museum of Natural Sciences: Victoria Memorial Museum Building, Metcalfe and McLeod Streets, Ottawa, K1A 0M8; f. 1957; geology, mineralogy, palaeontology, zoology and botany; study collections open to research by properly qualified students; Dir. Dr. LOUIS LEMIEUX.

National Museum of Science and Technology: 1867 St. Laurent Blvd., Ottawa; f. 1966; technology of ground transportation, agriculture, meteorology, chemistry, mining, energy and communications; it includes displays and artefacts demonstrating the physical sciences and how man has applied technology to his environment; self-operated experiments and areas designed to show how man has conquered distance and physical hardships; Dir. Dr. D. M. BAIRD. This museum also includes the National Aeronautical Collection; Curator R. W. BRADFORD.

National Postal Museum: 180 Wellington St., Ottawa, Ont. K1A 1C6; f. 1974; Curator C. R. MCGUIRE.

Ontario Science Centre: 770 Don Mills Road, Don Mills, Toronto, Ont. M3C 1T3; f. 1965; over 550 exhibits in all fields of science and technology; library of 10,000 vols.; Dir.-Gen. Dr. TUZO WILSON.

Queen's University Museums: Kingston; geology dept., f. 1901; Curator L. G. Berry; biology dept., f. 1880, Curator J. Webb; anatomy dept., f. 1854, Curator Dr. A. Travill.

Royal Ontario Museum: 100 Queen's Park, Toronto M5S 2C6; f. 1912; library (serving all depts.) of 65,000 vols.; Dir. James E. Cruise, ph.d.; publs. *Annual Report, Art & Archaeology Occasional Papers, Life Science Contributions, Life Sciences Occasional Papers, Rotunda* (quarterly), etc. (Public galleries closed for renovation 1981–82.)

Art and Archaeology Departments: research collections in each of Greek and Roman, Near Eastern, Far Eastern, European, textiles and costume, Canadiana, and ethnology departments. Collections illustrate prehistory, classical civilizations, medieval and modern Europe, Chinese collection of art and archaeology, with large Far Eastern library; extensive ethnology collections with emphasis on American Indians; North American archaeological collections and active research programme; Chief Archaeologist A. D. Tushingham, b.d., ph.d., f.s.a.

Life Sciences Departments: departments and public galleries of entomology, mammalogy, ornithology, herpetology, ichthyology, invertebrates, fossil vertebrates, fossil invertebrates, each with extensive research collections and facilities.

Earth Sciences Departments: departments of geology and mineralogy. Public galleries of physical and applied geology, systematic gallery of mineralogy, gem collection display. Extensive research collections; McLaughlin Planetarium: star theatre and astronomical exhibits and reference library.

Education and Communications: conducts museum educational programme for Ontario schools, and adult groups, film programmes, children's clubs, etc.; Asst. Dir. J. R. DiProfio.

Canadiana Building: 14 Queen's Park Crescent West, Toronto 5; f. 1939; early Canadian paintings, drawings, prints, furniture, silver, 19th-century glass; Curator D. B. Webster.

Stephen Leacock Memorial Home: Old Brewery Bay, Atherley Rd., Orillia; f. 1957; summer home, correspondence, manuscripts, personal effects of Stephen Butler Leacock 1869–1944; Curator Ralph L. Curry.

Tom Thomson Memorial Gallery and Museum of Fine Art: P.O.B. 312, 840 1st Ave. West, Owen Sound, Ont. N4K 5P5; f. 1967; Tom Thomson paintings, memorabilia; also other Canadian artists represented; Dir. James Logan; publ. *Newsletter* (monthly).

Upper Canada Village: P.O.B. 740, Morrisburg K0C 1X0; f. 1961; outdoor museum of regional history; 40 restored buildings portraying a rural community *c.* 1784–1867; library of 3,000 vols.; Dir. W. J. Patterson.

Quebec

Redpath Museum: McGill University; f. 1882; natural history, geology, mineralogy, paleontology, anthropology, vertebrate and invertebrate zoology; Dir. John B. Lewis.

McCord Museum: 690 Sherbrooke St. West, Montreal H3A 1E9; f. 1919; general museum and collections of Canadian ethnology, paintings, drawings, prints, costumes, decorative arts, toys, documents; Notman Photographic Archives containing 600,000 photos; library of 2,500 vols.; Chief Curator David W. Bellman.

Musée des beaux arts de Montréal: 3400 av. du Musée, Montreal H3G 1K3; f. 1860 (paintings), 1916 (museum); library of 54,700 vols.; French, Spanish, Dutch, British, Canadian and other paintings; decorative arts; textiles; Harry A. Norton collection of ancient glass; Lucile Pillow collection of porcelain; Chinese, Near Eastern, Peruvian, Amerindian and Inuit art; classes, tours, lectures, film programmes, boutique, art sales and rental gallery; Pres. Jacques M. Brault; Dir. Jean Trudel; Librarian Miss Juanita Toupin; publs. *Collage* (monthly), *Guide to the Collections*.

Musée du Québec: Parc des Champs de Bataille, Quebec; f. 1933; beaux-arts; Dir. Lyse Picher.

Quebec Seminary Museum: 6 University St., Quebec; paintings of the Canadian, Italian, French, Dutch, Spanish and English schools; old silver and antique furniture, Canadian coins and stamps; Curator J. M. Thivierge.

Saskatchewan

Lund Wild Life Exhibit: Lund Exhibit Building, Prince Albert; Curator Gordon E. Lund.

Mendel Art Gallery and Civic Conservatory (Saskatoon Gallery and Conservatory Corporation): 950 Spadina Crescent East, P.O.B. 569, Saskatoon S7K 3L6; f. 1964; Canadian, Eskimo, international art, exhibitions, permanent collection; library of 4,000 vols.; publ. *Folio* (monthly).

Museum of Ukrainian Culture: 202 Ave. M. South, Saskatoon; f. 1955; affiliated to diocese of Saskatchewan; 200-vol. library of ancient, historical and religious books, available for research; lectures, films, concerts, exhibitions; exhibits of Ukrainian culture of the 18th, 19th, 20th centuries; Curator Mrs. A. Shudlik.

Norman Mackenzie Art Gallery: University of Regina; permanent collection of 15th–19th-century European paintings and drawings, contemporary Canadian and American art, travelling exhibitions; public and academic programmes; Dir. Mrs. Carol Phillips (acting).

Prince Albert Heritage Museum: Prince Albert; f. 1923; run by Prince Albert Historical Society; local historical exhibits, early settlement, pioneers, Indian life, etc.

Saskatchewan Museum of Natural History: Wascana Park, Regina; f. 1906; new building opened 1955; habitat cases depicting wildlife in its natural environment; specimens and maps illustrating the geological history of the earth; archaeological exhibits including artifacts used by early inhabitants of Saskatchewan; electronic tours for individuals and school groups; division of Cultural Activities Branch, Saskatchewan Culture and Youth, Provincial Govt.; Dir. J. E. Storer (acting).

Saskatchewan Western Development Museums: P.O.B. 1910, Saskatoon; f. 1949; brs. at North Battleford, Moose Jaw, Saskatoon, and Yorkton; collection associated with the settlement of the Canadian West; agricultural machinery, early transport and household items; annual summer shows; George Shepherd Library of 15,000 historical vols.; Exec. Dir. Dr. Terrence Heath; publ. *Sparks off the Anvil* (monthly).

University of Saskatchewan Biology Museum: Saskatoon; f. 1917.

UNIVERSITIES AND COLLEGES

ACADIA UNIVERSITY

WOLFVILLE, N.S.

Telephone: (902) 542-2201.

Founded 1838.

Chancellor: (vacant).
President and Vice-Chancellor: A. M. SINCLAIR, LL.M., S.J.D., Q.C.
Academic Vice-President: J. R. C. PERKIN, M.A., D.PHIL.
Vice-President for Administration: F. J. ELDERKIN, LL.B.
Provost and Dean of Student Affairs: E. S. HANSEN, PH.D.
Registrar: D. J. GREEN, M.A.
Librarian: ISOBEL HORTON, B.A., B.L.S.

Library: *see* Libraries.

Number of teachers: 185 full-time, including 49 professors.

Number of students: 2,700.

DEANS:

Faculty of Arts: E. A. EAGLES, B.A., B.ED., M.A.
Faculty of Science: E. E. ZINCK, PH.D.
School of Engineering: T. PETRZYKOWSKA, PH.D.
School of Home Economics: VIRGINIA A. CAMPBELL, M.SC., PH.D.
School of Music: OWEN W. STEPHENS, M.MUS.
Faculty of Theology: HAROLD L. MITTON, B.A., D.D.
School of Education: W. RONALD MACDONALD, M.A., ED.D.
School of Business Administration: D. L. MISENER, B.COMM., B.ED., M.S.
School of Recreation and Physical Education: J. D. BAYER, M.SC.
School of Secretarial Science: J. E. MARSH, M.A.
Department of Extension: W. H. WHITE, M.ED.

PROFESSORS:

BAILET, M. H., D. ÈS L, French
BASARABA, J., M.SC.A., PH.D., Biology
BENT, F. C., PH.D., Biology
BISHOP, R. L., M.SC., PH.D., Physics
BLEAKNEY, J. S., M.SC., PH.D., Biology
BOOTH, A. P., M.A., M.A., Classics
CAMPBELL, V. A., M.SC., PH.D., Home Economics
CASSIDY, I., PH.D., Education
CHERRY, M. R., B.A., TH.D., D.D., Systematic Theology
CONNOR, J., M.A., PH.D., Economics
CURRY, G. M., M.S., A.M., PH.D., Biology
DODDS, D. G., M.SC., PH.D., Biology
DRAPER, W. A., M.A., PH.D., Psychology
ELLIS, V. A., M.MUS., M.MUS.ED, Music
FFRENCH, M. A., PH.D., Economics
FISCHER, G., LL.D., Political Science
FOSTER, J. A., PH.D., Education
FRASER, D. G. L., C.D., M.A., Political Science
GIBSON, M. A., M.SC., PH.D., Biology
GRUND, M. S., PH.D., Biology
HANSEN, E. S., PH.D., Chemistry
HAYES, E. R., M.SC., PH.D., Chemistry
HILLIER, G. A., M.ED., Business
LEWIS, H., M.A., PH.D., Philosophy
LOVESEY, M. R. B., M.A., B.SC., M.TH., D.D., Theology
MANALAYSAY, R. G., M.ED., ED.D., Education
MARSH, J. E., M.A., Secretarial Science
MISENER, D. L., M.S., Business Administration
MOORE, R. G., M.SC., PH.D., Geology
MACDONALD, W. R., M.A., ED.D., Education
MACINTOSH, A. W., M.A., PH.D., History
MACLEAN, A. H., M.A., PH.D., History
MACNEILL, R. H., C.D., M.SC., F.G.A.C., Geology
PEACH, M. E., M.A., PH.D., Chemistry
PEARSON, PH.D., Mathematics
PERKIN, R. J. C., M.A., D.PHIL., Religious Studies
ROTHBERGER, F., PH.D., Mathematics
SHARMA, G. N., M.A., PH.D., English
SHERIFF, J., M.A., English
SNOW, D. O., M.SC., PH.D., Mathematics
STEVENS, G. B., M.A., PH.D., Geology
STILES, D. A., PH.D., Chemistry
STOKESBURY, J. L., M.A., PH.D., History
STUART-KUTZE, R., M.B.A., Business
TAYLOR, C., S.T.M., D.D., Clinical Pastoral Education
TILLEMANS. T., LIT. DRS., Education
TILLOTSON, J. G., M.SC., Physics
TURNER, F. C., M.ENG., Engineering
VELLEK, G. F., PH.D., Classics
WASEEM, G. S., M.A., PH.D., German
WINTER, J., M.A., Economics
ZEMAN, J. K., D.TH., Theology
ZINCK, E. E., PH.D., Chemistry

ASSOCIATED INSTITUTION:

Acadia Divinity College: f. 1968; under direction of Atlantic United Baptist Convention; degrees granted by the University; Principal H. L. MITTON, B.A., D.D.

UNIVERSITY OF ALBERTA

EDMONTON, ALBERTA T6G 2E1

Telephone: 403-432-3113.

Founded 1906.

Provincial control; Language of instruction: English (Collège Universitaire Saint-Jean: English and French); Academic year: September to June (July summer session).

Chancellor: J. FOREST.
President and Vice-Chancellor: M. HOROWITZ, ED.D.
Vice-President (Academic): R. G. BALDWIN, M.A., PH.D.
Vice-President (Finance and Administration): L. C. LEITCH, LL.B., M.B.A.
Vice-President (Campus Planning and Development): R. E. PHILLIPS, B.SC.
Executive Assistant to the President: A. A. RYAN, M.A., LL.D.
Registrar: W. A. BLANCHARD, PH.D.
Librarian: B. B. PEEL, M.A., B.L.S.

Library: *see* Libraries.

Number of teachers: 1,550.

Number of students: 18,075 full-time.

Publications: *The New Trail* (quarterly), *Folio* (weekly), *Report of the Governors of the University of Alberta* (annually), *Calendar*† (annually).

DEANS AND DIRECTORS:

Faculty of Arts: T. WHITE.
Faculty of Engineering: P. F. G. ADAMS, PH.D., P.ENG.
Faculty of Medicine: D. CAMERON, B.A., M.D., F.R.C.P.(C.), F.A.C.A.
Faculty of Agriculture and Forestry: J. P. BOWLAND, M.S., PH.D.
Faculty of Law: F. D. JONES, B.A., LL.M.
Faculty of Dentistry: G. W. THOMPSON, D.D.S., PH.D., F.R.C.D.(C.).
School of Dental Hygiene: J. CONKLIN, M.SC. (Director).
Faculty of Education: W. H. WORTH, M.ED., ED.D.
Faculty of Pharmacy and Pharmaceutical Science: G. E. MEYERS, M.SC., PH.D. (acting).
Faculty of Science: K. B. NEWBOUND, M.SC., PH.D.
Faculty of Graduate Studies and Research: J. FORSTER, M.A., PH.D.
Faculty of Business Administration and Commerce: R. S. SMITH, M.A., PH.D.
Faculty of Library Science: WILLIAM KURMEY.
Faculty of Physical Education and Recreation: H. J. MCLACHLIN, M.SC., PH.D. (acting).
Faculty of Nursing: (vacant).
Faculty of Home Economics: DORIS BADIR, M.SC.
Faculty of Rehabilitation Medicine: F. B. WILSON, PH.D., F.A.S.H.A.
Collège Universitaire St.-Jean: Mme. GAMILA MORCOS.

PROFESSORS:

Faculty of Arts:

ABU-LABAN, B.U.D.R., PH.D., Sociology
ANDERSON, R. F., PH.D., English
AYLING, R. F., PH.D., English
BALDWIN, R. G., M.A., PH.D., English
BARCLAY, H. B., M.A., PH.D., Anthropology
BILSLAND, J. W., M.A., PH.D., English
BLACKLEY, F. D., M.A., PH.D., History
BLANCHARD, W. A., PH.D., Psychology
BLODGETT, E. D., PH.D., Comparative Literature
BOSLEY, R. N., PH.D., Philosophy
BOURASSA, C. M., M.A., PH.D., Psychology
BRAUN, R. E., PH.D., Classics
BRAUSS, H. F., Music
BRYAN, A. L., M.A., PH.D., Anthropology
BUCK, R. J., PH.D., Classics
BUECKERT, F. F., M.A., Drama
BUSE, A., PH.D., Economics
CAHILL, P. J., M.A., S.T.D., Religious Studies
CALDAROLA, C., M.A., PH.D., Sociology
CIRILLO, R. P., D.D., M.SC., Economics
CONNELL, A. B., B.A., D.U., Romance Languages
CRIGHTON, A. B., MUS.BAC., D.M.A., Music
CURTIS, D. W., M.A., PH.D., Psychology
DAVEY, R. A., B.A., Art and Design
DAVIS, A. K., PH.D., Sociology

DAVY, G. R., PH.D., Political Science
DE LUNA, B. N., M.A., PH.D., English
DE LUNA, F. A., M.A., PH.D., History
DI LOLLO, V., PH.D., Psychology
DIMIC, C. A.-M., M.A., PH.D., Romance Languages
DIMIC, M. V., Comparative Literature
ENGELMANN, F. C., A.M., M.A., PH.D., Political Science
EVANS, B. L., PH.D., History
FAUCHER, M., LIC. EN DROIT, Romance Languages
FERRATE, J., LIC. EN DROIT, Romance Languages
FISHER, L. V., M.MUS., Music
FISHWICK, D., M.A., Classics
FORBES, J. A., M.ED., M.A., Art and Design
FORREST, J. F., B.LITT., M.A., A.M., PH.D., English
FORSYTH, M., D.MUS., Music
GAINER, W. D., M.A., PH.D., Economics
GREEN, L. C., LL.D., Political Science
GRUHN-BRYAN, R., PH.D., Anthropology
GUPTA, K. L., PH.D., Economics
HACKLER, J. C., M.A., PH.D., Sociology
HARGREAVES, H. A., PH.D., English
HAYNES, D. H., Art and Design
HIRABAYASHI, G. K., M.A., PH.D., Sociology
HOBART, C. W., M.A., PH.D., Sociology
HODYSH, H. W., M.ED., PH.D., Educational Foundations
HOWARTH, E., M.SC., PH.D., Psychology
JONES, W. J., PH.D., History
JUNGKIND, W., Art and Design
KENNESON, C. E., M.MUS., Music
KING-FARLOW, J., M.R., A.M., PH.D., Philosophy
KORDA, B., D.SC., Economics
KREISEL, H. K., M.A., PH.D., F.I.A.L., F.R.S.A., Comparative Literature
KRISHNAN, P., M.S., PH.D., Sociology
KROTKI, K. J., M.A., PH.D., Sociology
LAUBER, J. F., M.A., PH.D., English
LIEBEL-WECKOWICZ, H. P., M.A., PH.D., History
LINCOLN, E., L.MUS., L.R.A.M., A.R.C.T., Music
MCCAUGHEY, G. S., M.A., English
MCMASTER, J. S., PH.D., English
MCMASTER, R. D., M.A., PH.D., English
MARAHRENS, G., PH.D., Germanic Languages
MATEJKO, A. J., PH.D., Sociology
MEEKISON, J. P., M.A., PH.D., Political Science
MONOD, P. A. R., M.A., PH.D., Romance Languages
MOORE, C. H., D. DE L'U., Romance Languages
MORAVCIK, I., M.A., PH.D., Economics
MOTUT, R. G., PH.D., Romance Languages
MOZEJKO, E., PH.D., Comparative Literature
MUNN, A. M., A.MUS., L.R.S.M., Music
NELSON, T. M., M.A., PH.D., Psychology
NORMAN, M., PH.D., English
ORRELL, J. O., M.A., PH.D., English
PAGE, N. A., PH.D., English
PEACOCK, G. B., M.F.A., M.ED., Drama
PEACOCKE, C. T., M.F.A., Drama
POCKLINGTON, T. C., PH.D., Political Science
POWRIE, T. L., M.A., D.PHIL., Economics
PRIDEAUX, G. D., PH.D., Linguistics
QURESHI, A. H., M.A., PH.D., English
QURESHI, S. M. M., M.A., PH.D., Political Science
REINHOLD, E., M.A., PH.D., Germanic Languages
ROLSTON, T., A.R.A.M., Music
ROSE, E. J., A.M., PH.D., English
ROSE, S., PH.D., English
ROSS, M. L., PH.D., English
ROTHROCK, G. A., PH.D., History
ROZEBOOM, W. W., PH.D., Psychology
RUDNYTSKY, I. L., M.A., PH.D., History and Political Science
RULE, B. G., M.A., PH.D., Psychology
RULE, S. J., M.SC., PH.D., Psychology
RUNQUIST, W. N., PH.D., Psychology
RYAN, A. A., M.A., LL.D., English
SALYZYN, V., M.A., PH.D., Economics
SASONKIN, M., PH.D., Music
SCHAARSCHMIDT, G. H., M.A., PH.D., Slavic Languages
SCHOULS, P. A., M.A., PH.D., Philosophy
SCOTT-PRELORENTZOS, ALISON, PH.D., Germanic Languages
SHINER, R. A., M.A., PH.D., Philosophy
SILVESTER, R., A.R.C.A., A.T.D., Art and Design
SMITH, R. C., PH.D., Classics
STANGELAND, R. A., M.MUS., D.M.A., Music
SWARTZ, P., M.A., PH.D., Psychology
TARVER, J. B., M.A., Drama
TENNESSEN, H., M.A., Philosophy
TERFLOTH, J. H., M.F.A., PH.D., Drama
THIMME, ANNELISE, D.PHIL., History
THOMAS, L. H., M.A., PH.D., LL.D., History
TRUMPENER, U., PH.D., History
VON HOHENBALKEN, B., DR.RER.POL., Economics
WATSON, W., M.A., PH.D., English
WECKOWICZ, T. E., M.B., CH.B., D.P.M., PH.D., Psychology
WHITE, T. H., M.A., PH.D., Sociology
WIEBE, R. H., M.A., English
WILCOCKS, R. W. F., PH.D., Romance Languages
WILKINSON, B. W., PH.D., Economics
WILSON, C. R., PH.D., Anthropology
YATES, E. N., A.O.C.A., Art and Design
ZUJEWSKY, O., M.A., PH.D., Slavic Languages

Faculty of Science:
ABBOTT, H. L., PH.D., Mathematics
ADLER, J. G., PH.D., Physics
AHMED, A., PH.D., Genetics
ALLEN, W. F., PH.D., Chemistry
AL-SALAM, W. A., M.A., PH.D., Mathematics
AYER, W. A., PH.D., Chemistry
BAADSGAARD, H., PH.D., Geology
BAKER, W. J., M.A., PH.D., Linguistics
BEATTY, D. D., M.S., PH.D., Zoology
BERCOV, R. D., PH.D., Mathematics
BERTIE, J. E., PH.D., Chemistry
BHATIA, A. B., M.SC., D.PHIL., PH.D., F.R.S.C., Physics
BIRSS, F. W., M.A., D.PHIL., Chemistry
BLISS, L. C., M.SC., PH.D., Botany
BOAG, D. A., PH.D., Zoology
BURWASH, R. A., M.SC., PH.D., Geology
CAMPBELL, J. N., M.SC., PH.D., Microbiology
CAVELL, R. G., M.SC., PH.D., Chemistry
CHARLESWORTH, M. A., PH.D., Geology
CHIA, F. S., PH.D., Zoology
CLIFFORD, H. F., M.S., PH.D., Zoology
COOK, F. D., PH.D., Microbiology
COSSINS, E. A., PH.D., F.R.S.C., Botany
CRAWFORD, R. J., PH.D., M.SC., Chemistry
CUMMING, G. L., M.A., PH.D., Physics
DAVIS, W. A., PH.D., Computing Science
DAWSON, W. K., M.A., PH.D., Physics
DITZIAN, Z., PH.D., Mathematics
DUNFORD, H. B., M.SC., PH.D., Chemistry
FOX, R. C., PH.D., Geology
FRAGA, S., LIC. EN DROIT, Chemistry
FRANCK, J. P., DIP.PHYS., DR. RER. NAT., Physics
FREEDMAN, H. I., M.A., PH.D., Mathematics
FREEMAN, G. R., M.A., PH.D., D.PHIL., F.C.I.C., Chemistry
FULLER, W. A., M.A., PH.D., Zoology
GARG, K. M., PH.D., Mathematics
GHURYE, S. G., PH.D., Mathematics
GILL, D. A., PH.D., Geography
GORHAM, P. R., B.A., M.S., PH.D., Botany
GOUGH, D. I., M.SC., PH.D., Physics
GRAHAM, W. A. G., M.A., PH.D., Chemistry
GUNNING, H. E., M.A., PH.D., Chemistry
HAGE, K. D., M.A., PH.D., Geography
HARRIS, W. E., M.SC., PH.D., Chemistry
HASTINGS, P. J., PH.D., Genetics
HOLMES, J. C., PH.D., Zoology
HOO, C. S., M.SC., PH.D., Mathematics
HOOZ, J., PH.D., Chemistry
HUGHES, D. G., PH.D., Physics
HUZINAGA, S., M.SC., PH.D., Chemistry
IRONSIDE, R. G., PH.D., Geography
ISRAEL, W., M.SC., PH.D., Physics
JORDAN, R. B., PH.D., Inorganic Chemistry
KAMAL, A. N., M.SC., PH.D., Physics
KANASEWICH, E. R., PH.D., Physics
KEBARLE, P., PH.D., Chemistry
KENNEDY, L. L., M.SC., PH.D., Botany
KLAMKIN, M. S., M.SC., Mathematics
KOPECKY, K. R., PH.D., Organic Chemistry
KOSINSKI, L. A., PH.D., Geography
KRATOCHVIL, B. G., PH.D., Chemistry
KUSPIRA, L., M.SC., PH.D., Genetics
LAMBERT, R. S., M.A., PH.D., Geology
LAUBER, J. K., PH.D., Zoology
LAYCOCK, A. H., PH.D., Geography
LEMIEUX, R. U., PH.D., Chemistry
LERBEKMO, J. F., PH.D., Geology
LEWIN, V., PH.D., Zoology
LOWN, J. W., M.SC., PH.D., A.R.C.S., D.I.C., Chemistry
MCDONALD, W. J., PH.D., Physics
MCGREGOR, J. R., PH.D., B.SC., M.ED., Mathematics
MACKI, J. W., PH.D., Mathematics
MCPHERSON, H., M.SC., PH.D., Geography
MALHOTRA, S. K., PH.D. Botany and Zoology
MASAMUNE, S., PH.D., Chemistry
MEHRA, K. L., PH.D., Mathematics
MEIR, A., M.SC., PH.D., Mathematics
MILLAR, R. F., M.A., PH.D., Mathematics
MOON, J. W., M.A., PH.D., Mathematics
MORTON, R. D., PH.D., Geology
MOSER, W., D.PHIL., Botany
MULDOWNEY, J. S., PH.D., Mathematics
NARAYANA, T. V., M.A., PH.D., Mathematics
NASH, PH.D., Genetics
NEILSON, G. C., M.A., PH.D., Physics
NELSON, J. S., PH.D., Zoology
NELSON, T. M., PH.D., Psychology
NEWBOUND, K. B., M.SC., PH.D., Physics
NURSALL, J. R., M.A., PH.D., Zoology
OGUZTORELI, M. N., PH.D., Mathematics
OLSEN, W. C., M.A.SC., PH.D., Physics
PACKER, J. G., PH.D., Botany
PARANJAPE, B. V., PH.D., Physics
PINNINGTON, E. H., PH.D., Physics
RANKIN, D., M.A., PH.D., Physics
RAZAVY, M., PH.D., Physics
REINELT, E. R., PH.D., M.A., Geography
RHEMTULLA, A. H., PH.D., Mathematics
ROBINS, M. J., PH.D., Chemistry
ROSS, D. M., M.A., PH.D., Zoology
ROY, G., PH.D., Nuclear Physics
RUTH, R. F., PH.D., Zoology
RUTTER, N. W., PH.D., Geology
SAMPLE, J. T., M.A., PH.D., Physics
SCHIFF, H., M.SC., PH.D., Physics
SEHGAL, S. K., M.A., PH.D., Mathematics
SHEININ, S. S., PH.D., Physics
SHARMA, A., M.A., PH.D., Mathematics
SMILLIE, K. W., PH.D., Computing Science
SMITH, D. G. W., M.A., M.SC., PH.D., Geology

SMITH, P. J., M.A., PH.D., Geography
SMITH, W. E., M.SC., PH.D., Genetics
STEINER, A. L., D.SC., Zoology
STELCK, C. R., M.SC., PH.D., Geology
STEMKE, G. W., PH.D., Microbiology
STEWART, W. N., M.S., PH.D., Botany
STRAUSZ, O. P., PH.D., Chemistry
STUART, C. I. J. M., M.A., Zoology
SUBBARAO, M. V., M.A., M.SC., PH.D., Mathematics
TAKAHASHI, Y., D.SC., Physics
TANNER, D. D., PH.D., Chemistry
TARTAR, J., PH.D., Computing Science
THORSON, W. R., PH.D., Chemistry
UMEZAWA, H., PH.D., Theoretical Physics
VON BORSTEL, R. C., PH.D., Genetics
WEICHMAN, F. L., PH,D., Physics
WEIJER, J., M.SC., PH.D., D.SC., Genetics
WESTLAKE, D. W. S., M.SC., PH.D., Microbiology
WILLIAMS, G. D., PH.D., Geology
WONDERS, W. C., M.A., PH.D., Geography
WOODS, S. B., M.A., PH.D., Physics
WOUK, A., PH.D., Computing Science
WYMAN, M., PH.D., F.R.S.C., Mathematics
YAMAMOTO, T., M.SC., PH.D., Microbiology
ZALIK, S. E., M.S., PH.D., Zoology
ZWICKEL, F. C., PH.D., Zoology

Faculty of Engineering:

ADAMS, P. F. G., PH.D., P.ENG., Civil Engineering
ALI, S. M. F., M.SC., PH.D., Mineral Engineering
ANDERSON, K. O., M.SC., P.ENG., Civil Engineering
BAKKER, J. J., M.S.C.E., P.ENG., Civil Engineering
BELLOW, D. G., M.SC., PH.D., P.ENG., Mechanical Engineering
BOUTHILLIER, P. H., S.M., P.ENG., Civil Engineering
BRADFORD, S. A., PH.D., P.ENG., Mineral Engineering
CAPJACK, C. E., M.SC., PH.D., Electrical Engineering
CHENG, K. C., PH.D., Mechanical Engineering
CHRISTENSEN, G. S., M.A.SC., PH.D., P.ENG., Electrical Engineering
CHUTE, F. S., M.A.SC., PH.D., P.ENG., Electrical Engineering
COLBOURNE, J. R., PH.D., P.ENG., Mechanical Engineering
CRAGGS, A., PH.D., Mechanical Engineering
DALLA LANA, I. G., M.SC., PH.D., Chemical Engineering
DRANCHUK, P. M., M.SC., Mineral Engineering
EISENSTEIN, Z., PH.D., P.ENG., Civil Engineering
FISHER, D. G., PH.D., Chemical Engineering
FLOCK, D. L., M.S., PH.D., P.ENG., Mineral Engineering
FORD, G., M.SC., PH.D., P.ENG., Mechanical Engineering
FOWLER, E. L., M.SC., P.ENG., Civil Engineering
GOUD, P. A., PH.D., P.ENG., Electrical Engineering
GOURISHANKAR, V., B.E., M.S., PH.D., P.ENG., Electrical Engineering
HADDOW, J. B., M.SC., PH.D., Mechanical Engineering
HARDING, P. J., M.A.SC., Electrical Engineering
JAMES, C. R., PH.D., P.ENG., Electrical Engineering
KELLY, D. H., PH.D., P.ENG., Electrical Engineering
KENNEDY, J. S., M.SC., PH.D., P.ENG., Mechanical Engineering
KINGMA, Y. L., NAT.ING., Electrical Engineering
KULAK, G. L., M.S., PH.D., P.ENG., Civil Engineering
LOCK, G. S. H., PH.D., P.ENG., Mechanical Engineering
MACGREGOR, J. G., M.S., PH.D., P.ENG., Civil Engineering
MARSDEN, D. J., D.C.AE., PH.D., P.ENG., Mechanical Engineering
MATHER, A. E., M.SC., PH.D., Chemical Engineering
MORGENSTERN, N. R., PH.D., P.ENG., F.R.S.C., Civil Engineering
MURRAY, D. W., M.SC., P.ENG., Civil Engineering
NADER, W., M.SC., DR.PHIL., Chemical Engineering
OFFENBERGER, A. A., M.A.SC., PH.D., Electrical Engineering
OTTO, F. D., M.SC., PH.D., P.ENG., Chemical Engineering
PATCHING, T., B.SC., P.ENG., Mineral Engineering
PETERSON, A. W., M.SC., P.ENG., Civil Engineering
PLITT, L. R., M.SC., Mineral Engineering
QUON, D., M.SC., SC.D., Chemical Engineering
RAJARATNAM, N., PH.D., P.ENG., Civil Engineering
ROBINSON, D. B., M.A.SC., PH.D., Chemical Engineering
RODKIEWICZ, C. M., PH.D., P.ENG., Mechanical Engineering
RYAN, J. T., M.SC., PH.D., Chemical Engineering
SADLER, G. W., M.SC., P.ENG., Mechanical Engineering
SCHMIDT-WEINMAR, H. G., PH.D., Electrical Engineering
SEGUIN, H. J. J., PH.D., Electrical Engineering
SEYER, F. A., M.S., PH.D., Chemical Engineering
SIMMONDS, S. H., PH.D., M.SC., P.ENG., Civil Engineering
SMY, P. R., PH.D., P.ENG., Electrical Engineering
STROMSMOE, K. A., M.SC., PH.D., Electrical Engineering
THOMSON, S., M.SC., PH.D., P.ENG., Civil Engineering
VERMEULEN, F. E., PH.D., M.A.SC., P.ENG., Electrical Engineering
VERSCHUREN, J. P., M.SC., PH.D., P.ENG., Civil Engineering
VITOVEC, F. H., DR.TECH.SC., P.ENG., Mining and Metallurgical Engineering
VOSS, W. A. G., PH.D., C.ENG., Electrical Engineering
WALKER, G. B., M.S., PH.D., P.ENG., Electrical Engineering
WANKE, S. E., M.SC., PH.D., Chemical Engineering
WARWARUK, J., M.S., PH.D., P.ENG. Civil Engineering
WAYMAN, M. L., M.SC., PH.D., Metallurgy
WOOD, R. K., PH.D., Chemical Engineering

Faculty of Medicine:

BAER, H. P., Oncology
BAIN, G. O., B.SC., M.D., Pathology
BECK, R. P., M.D., C.M., F.A.C.S., Oncology, Obstetrics and Gynaecology
BOBERG, E., M.A., PH.D., Audiology and Speech Pathology
BOWEN, P., M.D., F.R.C.P.(C), Paediatrics
BOYD, T. A. S., M.B., CH.B., F.R.S.C., Ophthalmology
BRUCHOVSKY, N., Oncology, Biochemistry and Endocrinology
BRYAN, L. E., Bacteriology
CAMERON, D. F., B.A., M.D., F.R.C.P.(C)., F.A.C.A., Anaesthesia
CHARNOCK, J. S., PH.D., Pharmacology
COLTER, J. S., PH.D., Oncology and Biochemistry
COOKSON, F. B., B.SC., M.B., CH.B., Anatomy
CROCKFORD, P. M., M.D., F.R.C.P.(C)., F.A.C.P., Endocrinology
DEWHURST, W. G., M.A., B.CH., Psychiatry
DIENER, E., PH.D., Immunology
DIXON, J. M. S., M.B., B.CH., M.D., Bacteriology
DOSSETOR, J. B., B.M., C.L.B., M.R.C.S., L.R.C.P., M.R.C.P., F.R.C.P.(C), PH.D., F.A.C.P., Nephrology
DUNLOP, D. L., M.D., M.S., F.R.C.S.(D), Obstetrics and Gynaecology
EDDY, G. E., B.SC., M.D., C.M., F R.C.P.(C)., Paediatrics
FRANK, G. B., M.SC., PH.D., Pharmacology
FRASER, R. S., M.SC., M.D., F.R.C.P.(C), F.A.C.S., Cardiology
GAUK, E. W., Paediatrics
GILBERT, J. A. L., M.D., F.C.R.P., M.R.C.P., Medicine
GOLDSAND, G., Infectious Diseases
GREENHILL, S. E., M.D., HON.S.G., F.R.C.M., F.A.C.P., Community Medicine
GRISDALE, L. C., M.D., Community Medicine
HAYS, P., M.B., Psychiatry
HEATH, C., Pharmacology
HENDERSON, J. F., M.S., PH.D., Oncology and Biochemistry
HÖHN, E. O., M.B., M.SC., PH.D., F.Z.S., Physiology
HUTCHISON, K. J., Physiology
JACKSON, F. L., M.B., B.S., Bacteriology
JAMES, M. N. G., M.SC., D.PHIL., Biochemistry
KAY, C. M., PH.D., Biochemistry
KLING, S., B.A., M.D., F.R.C.S., Surgery
LAKEY, W. H., B.SC., M.D., F.R.C.S., Surgery
LEESON, T. S., M.A., M.D., B.CHIR., Anatomy
LE PAGE, G. A., Oncology and Biochemistry
McCOY, E. E., M.D., Paediatrics
MACDONALD, R. N., M.D., C.M., Oncology and Clinical Haematology
McFADDEN, K. D., Anatomy
McINTYRE, J. W. R., M.R.C.S., L.R.C.P., D.A., F.F.A.R.C.S., Anaesthesia
MADSEN, N. B., M.SC., PH.D., Biochemistry
MEILICKE, C. A., PH.D., Health Services
MIELKE, B. W., M.D., Pathology
MILLER, J. D. R., B.SC., M.D., B.CH., F.R.C.P.(C.), Radiology
MOLNAR, G. D., B.SC., M.D., Medicine and Endocrinology
MONCKTON, G., M.B., B.S., M.D., M.R.C.P., F.R.C.P.(C), Neurology
MORGANTE, O., M.D., M.SC., PH.D., Medical Bacteriology
NIHEI, T., PH.D., Neurology
OVERTON, T. R., Biomedical Engineering
PAETKAU, V. H., M.SC., PH.D., Biochemistry
PARANCHYCH, W., M.SC., PH.D., Biochemistry
PATERSON, A. R. P., M.A., PH.D., Oncology and Biochemistry
PATON, D. M., M.B., CH.B., M.D., F.I.BIOL., Pharmacology
PEARCE, W. G., Ophthalmology
PEARSON, J. G., M.B., CH.B., Oncology
PERCY, J. S., Rheumatology
ROSSALL, R. E., B.SC., M.B., CH.B., M.D., M.R.C.P., F.R.C.P.(C), Cardiology
RUSSELL, A. S., M.A., M.R.C.P., F.R.C.P.(C.), Medicine
SALMON, P. A., M.S., PH.D., M.D., Surgery

SCHACHTER, M., M.D., C.M., M.SC., Physiology
SCOTT, G. W., M.B.B.S., M.S., F.R.C.S.(C.), Surgery
SHNITKA, T. K., Pathology
SMILLIE, L. B., M.A., PH.D., Biochemistry
SPROULE, B. J., M.SC., M.D., F.R.C.P.(C), Medicine
STEIN, R. B., B.SC., M.A., PH.D., Physiology
STINSON, SHIRLEY M., B.SC., M.N.A., ED.D., Health Service
SWALLOW, R. J., B.A., M.D., Pathology
TAYLOR, R. F., M.D., C.M., Medicine
TAYLOR, W. C., M.B., CL.B., Paediatrics
THURSTON, O. G., B.A., M.D., F.R.C.S.(C.), Surgery
VOSS, W. A. G., Biomedical Engineering
WECKOWICZ, T. E., M.B., CH.B., D.P.M., PH.D., Psychiatry
WEGMAN, T. G., Immunology
WEINSTEIN, W. M., M.D., F.R.C.P.(C.), Medicine
WILLIAMS, H. T. G., M.B., CH.B., F.R.C.S., F.R.C.S.(C.), F.A.C.S., Surgery
WILSON, F. B., PH.D., Rehabilitation Medicine
WYATT, H. T., M.D., F.R.C.S., Ophthalmology
YAKIMETS, W. W., M.D., F.R.C.S.(C.), Surgery

Faculty of Agriculture and Forestry:
ANDREW, W. T., M.S., PH.D., Plant Science
BALL, G. E., PH.D., M.S., Entomology
BENTLEY, C. F., M.SC., PH.D., Soils
BERG, R. T., PH.D., Animal Genetics
BOWLAND, J. P., M.S., PH.D., Animal Science
CLANDININ, D. R., M.S.A., PH.D., Poultry Husbandry
COLOTELO, N., M.SC., PH.D., Plant Science
COOK, F. D., PH.D., Soil Microbiology
CORNS, W. G., M.SC., PH.D., Plant Science
DOMIER, K. W., PH.D., Power and Machinery
EVANS, W. G., M.SC., PH.D., Entomology
GILL, D. S., PH.D., Rural Sociology and Agricultural Extension
GOODING, R. H., SC.D., Entomology
GRIEVE, C. M., PH.D., Animal Science
HARDIN, R. T., PH.D., Animal Science
HARRISON, H. P., PH.D., Farm Machinery
HAWKINS, M. H., M.SC., PH.D., Marketing and Business Management
HIRUKI, C., PH.D., Virology
JACKSON, H., M.SC., PH.D., Food Science
KNOWLES, R. H., M.SC., Plant Science
LEROHL, M. L., M.S.A., PH.D., Agricultural Economics and Rural Sociology
MACHARDY, F. V., B.E., M.S., PH.D., Agricultural Engineering
MANNING, T. W., M.SC., PH.D., Agricultural Economy and Farm Management
MILLIGAN, L. P., M.SC., PH.D., Animal Biochemistry
MURPHY, P. J., M.SC.F., Forest Science
NYBORG, M. P. K., PH.D., Soil Science
PAWLUK, S., M.SC., PH.D., Soil Science
PETERSEN, T. A., PH.D., Farm Management
PHILLIPS, W. E., PH.D., Econometrics and Natural Resources Economics
PRESTON, T. A., M.A., Agricultural Engineering
RAPP, E., M.SC., Soil and Water
RICHTER, J. J., DR.RER.POL., Marketing and Trade
ROBBLEE, A. R., M.SC., PH.D., Poultry Husbandry
ROBERTSON, J. A., PH.D., Soil Chemistry
SCHULTZ, W. M., PH.D., Rural Economy
SKOROPAD, W. P., M.SC., PH.D., Plant Science
SPENCER, M. S., M.A., PH.D., Plant Biochemistry
STEPHANSON, B. T., M.SC., Agricultural Engineering
VANDEN BORN, W. H., M.SC., PH.D., Plant Science
WALTON, P. D., PH.D., Plant Breeding
WEBSTER, G. R., PH.D., Soil Chemistry
WOLFE, F. H., PH.D., Food Chemistry
YOUNG, B. A., PH.D., Animal Science
ZALIK, S., M.SC., PH.D., Plant Science

Faculty of Law:
BARKER, B. M., LL.B.
DAVIES, D. C., LL.M.
DAVIES, G. J., B.A., LL.M.
DUNLOP, C. R. B., LL.M., M.A.
FREEMAN, P. L., B.A., M.L.L.S.
HURLBURT, W. H., Q.C., B.A., LL.B.
IRWIN, H. J. L., B.A., LL.B.
JONES, F. D., Q.C., B.A., LL.M.
KHETARPAL, S. P., LL.M., PH.D.
LAUX, F. A., B.A., LL.M.
MIS, W. K. J., B.A., LL.M.
PICARD, E. I., B.ED., LL.B.
POLLOCK, L. J., B.A., LL.B.
WILLIAMS, J. S., B.C.L., LL.M.

Faculty of Dentistry:
CARMICHAEL, D. J., PH.D., Oral Biology
COLLINSON, D. M., D.D.S., Clinical Director
DICK, H. M., D.D.S., M.SC., Oral Biology
FEE, A. D., D.D.S., M.SC., Prosthetic Dentistry
GAU, D. J., M.SC., D.D.S., Oral Biology
GELDART, S. G., D.D.S., Preventive and Community Dentistry
GIBB, G. H., D.D.S., Restorative Dentistry
HARLEY, W. T., D.D.S., M.S.D., Prosthetic Dentistry
HAWRISH, C. E., B.A., D.D.S., M.SC., Oral Diagnosis and Surgery
MCCLELLAND, R. C., D.D.S., Prosthetic Dentistry
MACRAE, P. D., D.D.S., Pedodontics
MEYER, W. C., D.D.S., Operative Dentistry
MYERS, G. W., D.D.S., Operative Dentistry
OSBORN, J. W., PH.D., Oral Surgery
SIMONS, A. J., D.D.S., Paediatric Dentistry
SIMPSON, W. J., D.D.S., M.SC., Pedodontics
SPERBER, G. H., PH.D., M.SC., Oral Biology
THOMAS, N. R., PH.D., Oral Biology
THOMPSON, G. W., D.D.S., PH.D., Dental Science

Faculty of Education:
AFFLECK, M. A., M.ED., ED.D., Elementary Education
ANDERSON, C. C., M.A., ED.P., PH.D., Educational Psychology
AOKI, T., M.ED., PH.D., Secondary Education
ATKINSON, T. P., PH.D., Elementary Education
BACCHUS, M. K., M.A., PH.D., M.P.H., Educational Foundations
BELL, J. B., M.ED., ED.D., PH.D., Secondary Education
BERGEN, J. J., PH.D., Educational Administration
BHATTACHARYA, N. C., M.A., LL.B., M.A., PH.D., Educational Foundations
BOERSMA, F. J., PH.D., Educational Psychology
BOWERS, K. L., PH.D., Secondary Education
BRYCE, R. C., PH.D., Educational Administration
BUMBARGER, C., ED.D., Educational Administration
CARD, B. Y., D.ED., PH.D., Educational Foundations
CHALMERS, J. W., M.A., M.ED., ED.D., Educational Foundations
CHAMBERLIN, C. R., M.A., PH.D., Elementary Education
CHAMBERS, J., PH.D., Educational Psychology
EBERLEIN, E. L., PH.D., Educational Psychology
ENNS, F., M.ED., PH.D., Educational Administration
FAGAN, W. T., PH.D., Elementary Education
FARMER, G. M., M.A., PH.D., Secondary Education
FILIPOWSKI, E. H., M.A., Elementary Education and Music
FRIESEN, D., PH.D., Educational Administration
GALLAGHER, J. E., ED.D., Vocational and Industrial Education
GARFINKLE, H., M.A., PH.D., Educational Foundations
GUE, L. R., PH.D., B.S.W., Educational Administration
HAMPSON, C. G., PH.D., Secondary Education
HODGSON, E. D., M.ED., PH.D., Educational Administration
HOLDAWAY, E. A., M.ED., PH.D., Educational Administration
HOROWITZ, M., ED.D., Elementary Education
HUNKA, S. M., PH.D., M.ED., Educational Psychology
INGRAM, E. J., M.ED., PH.D., Educational Administration
JACKNICKE, K. G., M.ED., PH.D., Secondary Education
JENKINSON, M. D., PH.D., Elementary Education
KASS, H. J., PH.D., Secondary Education
KIEREN, T. E., PH.D., Secondary Education
KIRKPATRICK, J. E., PH.D., Elementary Education
KIRMAN, J. M., PH.D., Elementary Education
KONRAD, A. G., PH.D., Educational Administration
LUPUL, M. R., PH.D., M.A., B.ED., Educational Foundations
MACARTHUR, R. S., M.ED., PH.D., Educational Psychology
MCFETRIDGE, P. A., M.A., PH.D., Elementary Education
MAGUIRE, T. O., M.ED., PH.D., Educational Psychology
MCINTOSH, R. G., M.SC., ED.M., ED.D., Educational Administration
MACKAY, D. A., M.A., PH.D., Elementary Education
MARTIN, R. G., M.A., PH.D., Secondary Education
MASSEY, D. L., M.S.ED., PH.D., Elementary Education
MIKLOS, E., M.ED., PH.D., Educational Administration
MILLER, P. J., PH.D., Educational Foundations
MOWAT, G. L., M.A., ED.D., Educational Foundations
NAY, M. A., M.SC., PH.D., Secondary Education
NELSON, L. D., PH.D., M.ED., Elementary Education
NEUFELD, K. A., PH.D., Elementary Education
NYBERG, V. R., M.ED., ED.D., Educational Psychology

OH, C. Y., M.S., PH.D., Secondary Education
PATERSON, J. G., M.A., ED.D., Educational Psychology
PATTERSON, R. S., M.ED., PH.D., Educational Foundations
PETRUK, M. W., M.ED., PH.D., Industrial and Vocational Education
PREITZ, C. H., ED.D., Industrial and Vocational Education
PRESS, E. C., M.A., PH.D., Elementary Education
PUFFER, K., ED.D., Industrial and Vocational Education
RATSOY, E. W., PH.D., Educational Administration
REESE, W. F., M.A., ED.D., Elementary Education
ROBERTSON, J. E., M.ED., PH.D., Elementary Education
ROMANIUK, E. W., M.ED., PH.D., Educational Research Services
SAWATZKY, D. D., M.ED., PH.D., Educational Psychology
SEGER, J. E., PH.D., Educational Administration
SIGURDSON, S. E., M.A., PH.D., Secondary Education
SMALL, J. M., M.ED., PH.D., Educational Administration
SMITH, A. A., M.MUS., D.M.A., Secondary Education
STEPHENS, R. E., PH.D., Elementary Education
STEWART, L. D., M.ED., ED.D., Secondary Education
TICHENOR, H. D., B.S., M.A., ED.D., Vocational and Industrial Education
WARE, R. L., M.MUS.ED., ED.D., Elementary Education
WHYTE, L., PH.D., Educational Psychology
WIEDRICK, L. G., M.S., ED.D., Elementary Education
WILDE, W. D., M.A., PH.D., Elementary Education
WORTH, W. H., ED.D., Elementary Education
YOUNG, D. R., M.ED., PH.D., Industrial and Vocational Education
ZIEL, H. R., M.S., ED.D., Industrial and Vocational Education
ZINGLE, H. W., M.ED., PH.D., Educational Psychology

Faculty of Pharmacy and Pharmaceutical Sciences:
ANDERSON, A. J., M.S., PH.D.
BIGGS, D. F., PH.D.
CHATTEN, L. G., M.SC., PH.D.
COUTTS, R. T., PH.D.
HENDERSON, R., M.S., PH.D.
MOSKALYK, R. E., PH.D.
MYERS, G. E., PH.D., M.S.
NOUJAIM, A. A., M.S., PH.D.
STEPHENS-NEWSHAM, L. G., PH.D.
VAN PETTEN, G. R., M.SC., PH.D.

Faculty of Business Administration and Commerce:
CHAMBERS, E. J., PH.D., Marketing and Economic Analysis
GILLAM, C., PH.D., Industrial and Legal Relations
HAMEED, S. M. A., PH.D., Industrial and Legal Relations
HARNDEN, B. M., M.B.A., PH.D., Accounting
HOSKINS, C., PH.D., Finance and Management Science
JANSSEN, C., M.B.A., PH.D., Finance and Management Science
LEE, C. A., PH.D., Organizational Analysis
LEMKE, K., M.COMM., Accounting
MCFADYEN, S. M., M.A., PH.D., Marketing and Economic Analysis
MUMEY, G. A., B.SC., M.A., PH.D., Finance and Management Science
NEDD, A., PH.D., Organizational Analysis
RESCHENTHALER, G. B., M.A., PH.D., Marketing and Economic Analysis
ROGERS, R. E., M.A., PH.D., Organizational Analysis
SCHNECK, R. E., PH.D., Organizational Analysis
SHIHADEH, E. S., M.P.A., PH.D., Organizational Analysis
STERLING, R., Professional Accounting
TINIC, S. M., M.B.A., PH.D., Finance and Management Science
TYNDALL, D. G., M.A., PH.D., Finance and Management Science
WILLIAMS, C. B., B.COM., M.B.A., PH.D., Industrial and Legal Relations

Faculty of Physical Education and Recreation:
AFFLECK, A. F., B.PH.E., B.ED., M.S.
ALDERMAN, R. B., M.P.E., ED.D.
ANDERSON, RUBY O., M.ED., Teaching Methods
AUSTIN, PATRICIA L., M.A., PH.D.
BURTON, T. L., PH.D.
COTTLE, W. H., PH.D.
GLASSFORD, R. G., PH.D., History
MACNAB, R. B. J., PH.D., Physiology of Exercise
MCLACHLIN, H. J., M.S., PH.D.
MENDRYK, S., M.S.
SINGH, M., M.A., M.S.
WILBERG, R. B., M.S., PH.D.

Faculty of Home Economics:
ADAMS, W. J., M.S.S.W., PH.D., Home Economics
BADIR, D., M.SC., Home Economics
DONALD, E., M.SC., PH.D.
HADZIYEV, D., PH.D., Food Science
HAWRYSH, Z., PH.D.
KERNALEGUEN, A. P., M.S.W., PH.D., Clothing and Textiles
RENNER, RUTH, M.SC., PH.D., Foods and Nutrition
STILES, M. E., M.S., PH.D.

Faculty of Library Science:
HENDERSON, M. E. P., M.A., LL.D.

Faculty of Nursing:
STINSON, SHIRLEY, M.N.A., ED.D.

Faculty of Rehabilitation Medicine:
WILSON, F. B., PH.D., F.A.S.H.A.

AFFILIATED COLLEGES:

Camrose Lutheran College: Box 1540, Camrose, Alberta; affiliated 1959; second-year university courses.
President: Rev. K. GLEN JOHNSON, B.A., B.D.

Canadian Union College: P.O.B. 466, College Heights, Alberta; affiliated since 1971 to offer first-year courses.
President: N. O. MATTHEWS, B.SC., B.T., M.ED., PH.D.

Concordia Lutheran College: 7128 Ada Blvd., Edmonton, Alberta; affiliated 1967; offers first- and second-year courses.
President: A. R. ROTH, D.ED.

St. Joseph's College: Edmonton, Alberta; affiliated 1926; Roman Catholic; courses in Philosophy and Christian Theology.
Rector: J. B. COURTNEY, C.S.B., S.T.B., S.T.L.

St. Stephen's College: Edmonton, Alberta; affiliated 1909; theological school of United Church of Canada; offers its own courses to degree level and certain courses open to students of the University.
Principal: Rev. G. M. TUTTLE, TH.D.

AFFILIATED RESEARCH INSTITUTES:

Alberta Institute of Pedology: soil survey, research, interpretation of data; Chair. S. PAWLUIK PH.D.

Boreal Institute for Northern Studies: Room CW401, Biological Sciences Bldg., University of Alberta, Edmonton; research in circumpolar regions, especially in northern Canada; Dir. R. S. JAMIESON (acting).

Canadian Institute of Ukrainian Studies: f. 1976; to help meet the academic needs of Ukrainians in Canada; Dir. M. R. LUPUL, PH.D.

Centre for Advanced Study in Theoretical Psychology: programme of education and research connected with the historical and theoretical foundations of psychology, with interdisciplinary and methodological emphases; Distinguished Visiting Scholar Program is co-ordinated with an annual theme and a subsequent conference in Banff; 6 staff mems.; 7 fellows; Dir. J. R. ROYCE, PH.D.

Centre for the Study of Mental Retardation: f. 1967; for conducting studies to understand the nature of intellectual subnormality and to devise methods for its prevention and treatment; Dir. J. P. DAS, PH.D.

Institute of Earth and Planetary Physics: f. 1970; Dir. D. I. GOUGH, PH.D., F.R.S.C.

Institute of Law Research and Reform: f. 1967 by agreement between the Provincial Government, the Law Society of Alberta and the University; submits reports to the Government; Dir. W. H. HURLBURT, Q.C.

Nuclear Research Centre: conducts studies to determine the fundamental properties of the nucleus of atoms; six million volt Van de Graaff accelerator; Dir. G. C. NEILSON, M.A., PH.D.

Population Research Laboratory: f. 1966; Dir. L. W. KENNEDY, PH.D.

Theoretical Physics Institute: f. 1960; Dir. D. D. BETTS, M.SC., PH.D.

University of Alberta Cancer Research Institute: Dr. John S. McEachern Cancer Research Laboratory; f. 1962 in co-operation with Canadian Cancer Society; Dir. Dr. G. A. LEPAGE, M.S., PH.D.

University of Alberta Surgical-Medical Research Institute.

ATHABASCA UNIVERSITY

12352-149 ST.,
EDMONTON, ALBERTA T5V 1G9
Telephone: (403) 452-9990.
Founded 1972.

Provincial control; undergraduate "open university" courses for adult, non-residential students; Language of instruction: English.

Chairman, Governing Council: K. J. CHAPMAN, LL.B.
President: S. GRIEW, PH.D.
Vice-President Learning Services: R. H. PAUL, PH.D.
Vice-President University Services: N. O. HENRY, M.A. (acting).
Director Course Development: C. R. SHOBE, PH.D.
Director Regional and Student Services: A. G. MEECH, M.A.
Registrar: J. R. Y. SCARLETT, B.A.
Librarian: T. A. EDGE, B.A., B.L.S.
Director Computing Services: D. W. COWPER, M.ED.

Number of teachers: 80.
Number of students: 4,800.

Publications: *Annual Report*†, *Ergo*† (5 a year), *Calendar*† (annually).

HEADS OF AREA STUDIES:

Environmental Sciences: T. S. BAKSHI, PH.D.
Humanities: M. G. HAMILTON, M.A. (acting).
Social Sciences: I. C. TAYLOR, PH.D.

BISHOP'S UNIVERSITY

LENNOXVILLE, QUEBEC
Telephone: (819) 569-9551.

Founded 1843, constituted a university by Royal Charter 1853.

Language of instruction: English; Private control; Academic year: September to May (two terms).

Chancellor: Hon. Mr. Justice W. MITCHELL, D.C.L.
Vice-Chancellor and Principal: CHRISTOPHER NICHOLL, PH.D.
Registrar: G. J. MARCOTTE, M.A.
Dean of the Faculty: Dr. KARL J. KUEPPER.
Librarian: G. BELISLE, B. ÈS L., B.A., B.PH., B. ÈS SC.BIBLIO.

Number of teachers: 75 full-time.
Number of students: 1,400.

BRANDON UNIVERSITY

BRANDON, MANITOBA R7A 6A9
Telephone: (204) 728-9520.

Founded 1899; gained full autonomy July 1967.

Public control; Academic year: September to April.

Chancellor: S. H. KNOWLES, M.P., LL.D.
President and Vice-Chancellor: H. J. PERKINS, M.SC., PH.D.
Registrar: C. W. KENNEDY, B.A.
Librarian: T. A. MITCHELL, M.L.S.

Number of teachers: 150.

Number of students 2,044 (full and part-time).

Publications: *President's Report* (bi-annually), *Alumni News* (quarterly), Calendars of several faculties.

DEANS AND DIRECTORS:

Faculty of Arts: M. BLANAR, B.ED., M.A., PH.D.
Faculty of Science: R. A. GILES, PH.D., F.INST.P.
Faculty of Education: D. T. HAYES, M.A., ED.D.
School of Music: L. WATSON, D.MUS., M.A., L.T.C.M.

PROFESSORS:

BLANAR, M., M.A., PH.D., English
BLUE, A. W., M.S., PH.D., Native Studies
BRISTOL, C. C., M.SC., PH.D., Geology
BROCKWAY, R. W., M.DIV., M.A., PH.D., Religion
CHAPLIN, F., MUS.DOC., Music
EASTMAN, D. E., M.SC., PH.D., Mathematics
ENTZ, W. H., PH.D., German
GILES, R. A., PH.D., F.INST.P., Physics
HALAMANDARIS, P. G., M.S., PH.D., Education
HARGREAVES-MAWDSLEY, W. N., M.A., D.PHIL., F.S.A., F.R.HIST.S., History
HAYES, D. T., M.A., ED.D., Education
KING, R. F. B., M.A., PH.D., English
KLASSEN, I. G., M.ED., ED.D., Education
LETKEMAN, P., M.SC., PH.D., Chemistry
LOGAN, LILLIAN, M.S., PH.D., Education
MACDOWELL, G. F., M.A., Economics
MACPHERSON, G. C., M.MUS., L.R.C.T., Music
NAIDU, M. V., M.A., PH.D., Political Science
PEPPER, E. H., M.SC., PH.D., Botany
PERKINS, H. J., M.SC., PH.D., Chemistry
PIPPERT, R. R., M.S., PH.D., Education
STEWART, D. B., B.SC., M.D., F.R.C.S., F.R.C.O.G., Zoology
TYLER, E. J., M.SC., PH.D., Psychology
WATSON, L., M.A., D.MUS., L.T.C.M., Music
WELSTED, J. E., M.SC., PH.D., Geography
WHEELER, D. N., M.A., D.PHIL., Economics
WONG, W. G., M.A., Physics

UNIVERSITY OF BRITISH COLUMBIA

VANCOUVER V6T 1W5, BRITISH COLUMBIA
Telephone: 228-2211.
Founded 1908.

Chancellor: The Hon. J. V. CLYNE, C.C., B.A.
President and Vice-Chancellor: D. T. KENNY, M.A., PH.D.
Vice-Presidents: C. J. CONNAGHAN, M.A. (Administrative Services); M. SHAW, M.SC., PH.D., D.SC., P.AG., F.L.S., F.A.P.S., F.R.S.C. (Academic Development); E. W. VOGT, O.C., M.SC., PH.D., F.R.S.C. (Faculty and Student Affairs); W. WHITE, F.C.G.A. (Bursar).
Registrar: K. YOUNG.
Librarian: **B. STUART-STUBBS, B.A., B.L.S.**

Library: *see* Libraries.
Number of teachers: 1,821.
Number of students: 23,897.

Publications: *University Calendar* (winter and summer), *Canadian Literature, Pacific Affairs, Davidsonia* (quarterly), *B.C. Studies, The Canadian Yearbook of International Law.*

DEANS:

Faculty of Agricultural Sciences: W. D. KITTS, M.S.A., PH.D., F.A.I.C.
Faculty of Applied Science: L. M. WEDEPOHL, PH.D., F.I.E.E., C.ENG., P.ENG.
Faculty of Arts: R. M. WILL, A.M., PH.D.
Faculty of Commerce and Business Administration: P. A. LUSZTIG, M.B.A., PH.D.
Faculty of Dentistry: G. S. BEAGRIE, D.D.S., F.D.S.R.C.S., F.R.C.D.(C.), F.I.C.D.
Faculty of Education: T. R. BENTLEY, PH.D. (acting).
Faculty of Forestry: **J. A. F. GARDNER, M.A., PH.D., F.C.I.C., F.I.A.W.S.**
Faculty of Graduate Studies: P. A. LARKIN, M.A., D.PHIL., F.R.S.C.
Faculty of Law: K. M. LYSYK, Q.C., LL.B., B.C.L.
Faculty of Medicine: W. A. WEBBER, M.D.
Faculty of Pharmaceutical Sciences: B. E. RIEDEL, C.D., M.SC., PH.D.
Faculty of Science: C. V. FINNEGAN, PH.D.

DIRECTORS OF SCHOOLS:

School of Architecture: D. SHADBOLT, D.ENG., F.R.A.I.C.
School of Home Economics: R. H. RODGERS, M.A., PH.D.
School of Nursing: MARILYN D. WILLMAN, M.S.N., PH.D., R.N.
School of Physical Education and Recreation: W. R. MORFORD, M.P.E., ED.D.
School of Social Work: **G. M. HOUGHAM, M.A., PH.D**
School of Librarianship: R. STOKES, M.A., M.PHIL., F.L.A.
School of Rehabilitation Medicine: T. A. CONINE, D.H.S.
School of Community and Regional Planning: BRAHM WIESMAN, M.ARCH.

PROFESSORS:

ABERLE, D. F., PH.D. Anthropology
ADAMOVICH, L., M.F., R.P.F., P.ENG., Forestry
ACTON, A. B., M.A., D.PHIL., Zoology
ADAMS, J. R., M.SC., PH.D., Zoology
ADAMS, R. A., PH.D., Mathematics
AGUZZI-BARBAGLI, D., DOTT., LETT., PH.D., Italian
AHLBORN, B., DR.RER.NAT., MEM.A.S.M.E., Physics
ALDEN, T. H., M.S., PH.D., Metallurgy
ALLDRITT, K., M.A., English
AMES, M. M., PH.D., Anthropology
ANASTASIOU, C. J., M.ED., PH.D., Education

ANDERSON, J. D., M.D., PH.D., F.R.C.PATH., Medical Microbiology
ANDREWS, J. H. M., M.A., PH.D., Education
APPLEGARTH, D. A., PH.D., Paediatrics
ARCHIBALD, G. C., M.A., Economics
ARMSTRONG, R. L., PH.D., Geological Sciences
ATRENS, J. J., M.A., B.C.L., Law
AUBKE, F., DR.RER.NAT., Chemistry
AUERSPERG, N. M.D., PH.D., Anatomy
AUMAN, J. R., PH.D., Geophysics and Astronomy
AVAKUMOVIC, I., M.A., D.PHIL., History
BANDONI, R. J., M.S., PH.D., Botany
BANKSON, D., M.A., PH.D., Creative Writing
BARNARD, A. J., M.SC., PH.D., Physics
BARRIE, R., PH.D., Physics
BATES, D. V., M.D., F.R.C.P., F.R.S.C., F.R.C.P.C., Medicine and Physiology
BATTS, M. S., M.L.S., D.LITT., DR.PHIL., German
BAUDOUIN, D., D.E.S., French
BEAGRIE, G. S., D.D.S., F.D.S.R.C.S., F.R.C.D.(C.), Oral Medicine
BECK, B. E. F., D.PHIL., Anthropology
BEDDOES, M. P., D.I.C., PH.D., P.ENG., M.I.E.E.E., Electrical Engineering
BEEDLE, A., D.LITT., F.C.A., Commerce and Business Administration
BEER, C. T., D.PHIL., A.R.I.C., F.R.I.C., Biochemistry
BELLWARD, G. D. B., PH.D., Pharmaceutical Sciences
BELSHAW, C. S., M.A., PH.D., F.R.S.C., Anthropology
BIESER, M., M.D., Psychiatry
BENNETT, J., B.PHIL., M.A., Philosophy
BENTLEY, T. R., M.A., PH.D., Education
BERRY, W., PH.D., Music
BISALPUTRA, T., M.SC., PH.D., Botany
BLACKORBY, C., PH.D., Economics
BLANK, S. S., M.A., PH.D., Education
BLOOM, M., M.SC., PH.D., F.R.S.C., Physics
BOHM, B. A., M.S., PH.D., Botany
BOHN, E. V., DIPL. MATH., DR. RER. NAT., F.R.S.C., M.I.E.E.E., Electrical Engineering
BOLDT, W., M.A., PH.D., Education
BONGIE, L. L., D.DE L'UNIV. (PARIS), French
BOULBY, M., M.A., PH.D., German
BOURNE, C. B., LL.B., S.J.D., Law
BOYD, D. W., M.A., PH.D., Mathematics
BRADLEY, P. G., PH.D., Economics
BRAGG, D. B., M.S., PH.D., Poultry Science
BRAGG, P. D., PH.D., Biochemistry
BRANION, R. M. R., M.A.SC., PH.D., P.ENG., M.C.I.C., Chemical Engineering
BRAUNER, C. J., A.M., PH.D., Education
BREE, A., PH.D., Chemistry
BRENNAN, M. J., PH.D., Commerce and Business Administration
BRIMACOMBE, J. K., PH.D., P.ENG., D.I.C., Metallurgical Engineering
BRION, C. E., PH.D., Chemistry
BROCKLEY, C. A., PH.D., P.ENG., Mechanical Engineering
BROCKINGTON, J., D.F.A., Theatre
BROSAMLER, G. A., PH.D., Mathematics
BROWN, D. G., M.A., D.PHIL., Philosophy
BROWN, J. C., PH.D., Physiology
BROWN, L. C., PH.D., Metallurgy
BROWN, S. R., M.S., PH.D., Physical Education and Recreation
BRUMELLE, S. L., PH.D., Commerce and Business Administration
BRYANS, F. E., B.SC., M.D., F.R.S.C.(C), F.R.C.O.G., Obstetrics and Gynaecology
BUI, A. T., LI.SC., PH.D., Mathematics
BULLEN, P. S., M.SC., PH.D., Mathematics
BULLOCK, M. H., Creative Writing
BURES, D. J., PH.D., F.R.S.C., Mathematics
BURHENNE, H. J., M.D., F.A.C.R., Diagnostic Radiology
BURLING, R. W., M.SC., PH.D., Oceanography
BURNS, P. T., LL.M., Law
BURRIDGE, K. O. L., M.A., DIP.ANTH., PH.D., Anthropology
CAIRNS, H. A. C., M.A., D.PHIL., Political Science
CALAM, J. H., M.A., PH.D., Education
CALVERT, S. E., PH.D., Oceanography
CAMPANELLA, R. G., M.S., PH.D., P.ENG., M.AM.SOC.C.E., Civil Engineering
CAMPBELL, J. J. R., PH.D., F.R.S.C., Microbiology
CAMPBELL, M. A., M.S., ED.D., R.N., Nursing
CANNON, G. H., M.SC., ED.D., Education
CASSELMAN, W. A., PH.D., Mathematics
CATTERSON, J. H., M.ED., D.ED., Education
CAVERS, S. D., M.A.SC., PH.D., P.ENG., F.C.I.C., Chemical Engineering
CHACON, R. V. S., M.A., PH.D., Mathematics
CHAKLADER, A. C. D., PH.D., Metallurgy
CHANDLER, M. J., PH.D., Psychology
CHAO, C.-Y., B.A., Asian Studies
CHAPMAN, J. D., M.A., PH.D., Geography
CHASE, R. L., PH.D., Geology
CHASE, W. H., M.D., C.M., Pathology
CHERRY, S., M.S., PH.D., P.ENG., F.AM.SOC.C.E., M.C.S.C.E., M.E.I.C., Civil Engineering
CHOW, A. W. C., M.D., F.R.C.P.(C), Medicine
CHUNG, W. B., M.D., C.M., F.R.C.S.C., F.A.C.S., Medicine (Surgery)
CLARK, C. W., PH.D., Mathematics
CLARK, R. M., A.M., PH.D., Economics
CLARKE, B. R., PH.D., Education
CLARKE, G. K. C., M.A., PH.D., Geophysics and Astronomy
CLINGMAN, A. E., M.M.E., M.A., ED.D., Education
COHN, W., PH.D., Sociology
COLE, K. M., PH.D., M.A., F.L.S., Botany
CONINE, T., M.A., Rehabilitation Medicine
CONWAY, J. S., M.A., PH.D., History
COOMBS, J. R., M.A., PH.D., Education
COOPE, J. A. R., M.A., D.PHIL., Chemistry
COPP, D. H., D.SC., B.A., M.D., PH.D., LL.D., F.R.S.C., F.R.C.P.(C)., F.R.S., Physiology
COREN, S., PH.D., Psychology
COVAL, S. C., M.A., PH.D., D.PHIL., Philosophy
CRADDOCK, M. K., M.A., D.PHIL., Physics
CRAGG, J. G., PH.D., Economics
CRAIG, K. D., PH.D., Psychology
CRANE, J., M.S.W., PH.D., Social Work
CRICHTON, A. O. J., M.A., PH.D., Health Care and Epidemiology
CULLEN, W. R., M.SC., PH.D., Chemistry
CURZON, F. L., A.R.C.S., D.I.C., PH.D., Physics
CZAYKOWSKI, B., M.A., Slavonic Studies
DAHLIE, J., PH.D., Education
DALBY, F. W., M.A., PH.D., Physics
DANIELS, L. B., M.A., PH.D., Education
DANNER, W. R., M.SC., PH.D., Geological Sciences
DAVID, C. G., PH.D., Education
DAVIDSON, P. O., M.A., PH.D., Psychology
DEHNEL, P. A., M.A., PH.D., Zoology
DENNISON, J. D., M.P.E., ED.D., Education
DESAI, I. D., M.SC., PH.D., Home Economics
DIEWERT, W. E., PH.D., Economics
DIRKS, J. H., M.D., F.R.C.P.(C.), F.A.C.P., Medicine
DIVINSKY, N. J., M.SC., PH.D., Mathematics
DOLPHIN, D. H., PH.D., Chemistry
DOMMEL, H. W., D.ENG., P.ENG., F.I.E.E.E., Electrical Engineering
DONALDSON, D. J., PH.D., Economics
DONALDSON, R. W., S.M., PH.D., Electrical Engineering
DOWNEY, L. W., PH.D., Education
DOYLE, P. J., M.D., F.R.C.S.(C.), Surgery
D'OYLEY, V. R., ED.D., Education
DRANCE, S. M., M.B., CH.B., M.D., F.R.C.S., F.R.C.S.C., Ophthalmology
DUNCAN, J. P., M.E., D.SC., P.ENG., CH.E., F.I.MECH.E., F.I.PROD.E., A.INST.P., Mechanical Engineering
DUNELL, B.A., M.A.SC., A.M., PH.D., F.C.I.C., Chemistry
DUNN, H. G., M.B., CH.B., M.A., F.R.C.P., F.R.C.P.(C)., D.C.H., Paediatrics
DUNN, W. L., M.D., PH.D., F.R.C.P.(C)., Pathology
DURRANT, G., M.A., D.LITT., English
DUTTON, G. G. S., M.A., M.SC., PH.D., F.R.I.C., F.C.I.C., Chemistry
EATON, B. C., PH.D., Economics
EATON, G. W., PH.D., Horticulture
EGOFF, SHEILA A., F.L.A., Librarianship
ELLIS, R. M., M.SC., PH.D., Geophysics and Astronomy
EPSTEIN, N., M.ENG., ENG.SC.D., P.ENG., F.C.I.C., F.A.I.CH.E., Chemical Engineering
ERDMAN, K. L., M.SC., PH.D., Physics
EVANS, J. A. S., M.A., PH.D., Classics
EVANS, R. G., PH.D., Economics
FARMER, J. B., PH.D., Chemistry
FEAVER, G. A., PH.D., Political Science
FELTHAM, G. A., PH.D., C.A., Accounting and Management Information Systems
FIELDS, D. B., M.B.A., F.C.A., Commerce and Business Administration
FINLAY, D. G., M.S.W., PH.D., Social Work
FINN, W. D., M.SC., PH.D., P.ENG., M.AM.SOC.C.E., M.A.S.E.E., Civil Engineering
FINNEGAN, C. V., M.S., PH.D., Zoology
FISHER, H. D., M.A., PH.D., Zoology
FORD, D. K., M.D., F.R.C.P.(C)., Rheumatology
FORSYTH, J. S., PH.D., P.ENG., A.R.I.C., M.I.CH.E., F.C.I.C., Chemical Engineering
FOSTER, M. I., M.A., Education
FOULKS, J. G., PH.D., M.D., Pharmacology
FOURNIER, J. J. F., PH.D., Mathematics
FOX, I. K., A.B., A.M., Community and Regional Planning
FRANZ, N. C., M.W.T., PH.D., Forestry
FREDEMAN, W. E., F.R.S.C., F.R.S.L., English
FREEMAN, R. D, M.D., D.P.M., Psychiatry
FREEZE, R. A., M.SC., PH.D., Geological Sciences
FRIEDMAN, S. M., B.A., M.D., C.M., M.SC., PH.D., F.R.S.C., Anatomy
FRIESEN, J. D., Education
FRIZ, C. T., M.SC., PH.D., Anatomy
FROST, D. C., PH.D., Chemistry
FUTRELL, M. H., PH.D., Slavonic Studies
GARDNER, J. A. F., M.A., PH.D., F.C.I.C., F.I.A.W.S., R.P.F., Forestry
GARTSHORE, I. S., PH.D., P.ENG., A.F.C.A.S.I., Mechanical Engineering
GERSON, W., A.A.DIPL., F.R.A.I.C., A.R.I.B.A., Architecture
GILBERT, J. H. V., M.S., PH.D., L.C.S.T., Paediatrics and Audiology and Speech Sciences
GILMORE, P. C., M.A., PH.D., Computer Science
GOLD, A. V., PH.D., Physics
GOLDBERG, M. A., M.A., PH.D., Commerce and Business Administration
GOLDBERG, M. K., PH.D., English
GOLDBERG, T., D.M., Education
GOMEL, V., M.D., F.R.C.S.(C), Obstetrics and Gynaecology
GOSE, E. B., M.A., PH.D., English
GOULDSTONE, A. P., A.T.D., Education
GOURLAY, C., M.COM., C.G.A., Commerce and Business Administration
GRACE, J. R., PH.D., Chemical Engineering
GRANIRER, E. E., M.SC., PH.D., F.R.S.C., Mathematics
GRANTHAM, P. R., M.D., C.R.P.C.(F), Family Practice

GRAY, R. F., M.ED., PH.D., Education
GREENWOOD, H. J., M.A.SC., PH.D., Geological Sciences
GRIFFITH, W. S., M.S., PH.D., Adult Education
GRIFFITHS, G. M., M.A., PH.D., Physics
GROVER, F. J., L.ÈS.L., PH.D., French
GRZYBOWSKI, S., CH.B., M.D., M.R.C.P., F.R.C.P.(C), Medicine
GUNN, A. M., B.ED., M.A., Education
GUSH, H. P., M.A., PH.D., Physics
HAERING, R. R., O.C., M.A., PH.D., F.R.S.C., Physics
HAGLER, R. A., A.M.L.S., A.M., PH.D., Librarianship
HAHN, P., M.D., C.SC., D.SC., Obstetrics and Gynaecology
HALL, L. D., PH.D., Chemistry
HALL, N. A., M.B.A., D.B.A., Commerce and Business Administration
HALL, W. F., M.A., PH.D., English
HAMLIN, F. R., PH.D., French
HANNAM, A. G., F.D.S., R.C.S.(ENG.), PH.D., F.A.C.D.S., Oral Biology
HARDWICK, D. F., M.D., F.R.C.P., F.C.A.P., Paediatric Pathology
HARDWICK, W. G., M.A., PH.D., Geography
HARDY, W. N., PH.D., Physics
HARE, R. D., M.A., PH.D., Psychology
HARLOW, R., D.F.C., M.F.A., Creative Writing
HARNETTY, P., A.M., PH.D., Asian Studies
HARRIS, R. C., M.A., PH.D., Geography
HARRISON, L. G., PH.D., Chemistry
HARRISON, R. C., M.D., M.S., F.R.C.S.(C.), F.A.C.S., Surgery
HARROP, T. J., L.D.S., D.D.S., M.S., PH.D., Restorative Dentistry
HARTRICK, W. J., PH.D., Education
HAUPTMAN, E. G., PH.D., P.ENG., M.A.S.M.E., M.C.S.M.E., Mechanical Engineering
HAYWARD, L. D., PH.D., F.C.I.C., Chemistry
HEAVER, T. D., M.A., PH.D., Commerce and Business Administration
HELLIWELL, J. F., M.A., D.PHIL., Economics
HENINGER, S. K., M.A., PH.D., English
HENY, F. W., P.C.E., PH.D., Linguistics
HERBERT, R. G., D.F.C., C.D., LL.B., Law
HERSOM, N., M.ED., PH.D., Education
HICKLING, M. A., PH.D., Law
HIGHTOWER, H. C., PH.D., Community and Regional Planning
HILL, L. E., PH.D., History
HILL, P. G., M.SC., PH.D., P.ENG., M.A.S.M.E., C.S.M.E., Mechanical Engineering
HILLS, R. J., M.A., PH.D., Education
HINDMARCH, R. G., M.S., ED.D., Physical Education
HLYNKA, J. N., M.SC., PH.D., Clinical Pharmacy
HOCHACHKA, P. W., M.SC., PH.D., Zoology
HODGES, J., B.SC., M.A., PH.D., A.M.P., F.R.S.A., Animal Science
HOECHSMANN, K., M.A., PH.D., Mathematics
HOFFMAN, M. M., PH.D., F.R.C.P., Medicine
HOGARTH, J., PH.D., Law
HOGG, J. C., M.D., M.SC., PH.D., F.R.C.P.(C.), Pathology
HOLLING, C. S., M.SC., PH.D., Zoology
HOLSTI, K. J., A.M., PH.D., Political Science
HOOLEY, J. G., M.A., PH.D., F.C.I.C., Chemistry
HOOLEY, R. F., M.SC., PH.D., P.ENG., M.I.A.B.S.E., M.E.I.C., Civil Engineering
HOUGHAM, G. M., M.A., PH.D., Social Work
HOUSEGO, I. E., M.ED., PH.D., Education
HUGHES, G. C., M.S., PH.D., F.L.S., Botany
HULCOOP, J. F., M.A., PH.D., English
HULTBERG, C. R., M.MUS., M.S., Music
HURVITZ, L., M.A., PH.D., Asian Studies
INGRAM, R. W., M.A., PH.D., English
IQBAL, M., PH.D., M.A.S.M.E., M.A.S.H.R.A.E., Mechanical Engineering
JAHNKE, L. G., LL.B., LL.M., Law
JAMES, B. R., M.A., D.PHIL., Chemistry
JAMES, D. G. L., M.A., PH.D., F.C.I.C., Chemistry
JAMIESON, S. M., M.A., PH.D., Economics
JENKINS, L. C., C.M., M.D., F.R.C.P.C., Anaesthesiology
JOHNSON, R. R., PH.D., Physics
JOHNSTONE, F. R. C., M.B., M.SC., F.R.C.S., F.A.C.S., Surgery
JONES, D. R., PH.D., Zoology
JONES, G., M.SC., PH.D., Physics
JONES, R. G., M.A., ED.D., PH.D., Education
JORDAN, R. M., M.A., PH.D., English
KAEMPFFER, F. A., DR.RER.NAT., Physics
KAHNEMAN, D., PH.D., Psychology
KANE, J., PH.D., Zoology
KEELER, R., PH.D., Physiology
KENDALL, D. C., M.A., PH.D., Education
KENNEDY, J. M., M.A., PH.D., Computer Science
KENNY, D. T., M.A., PH.D., Psychology
KHARADLY, M. M. Z., D.I.C., PH.D., C.ENG., M.I.E.E., Electrical Engineering
KILBURN, D. G., PH.D., Microbiology
KIMMINS, J. P., PH.D., Forestry
KINCADE, M. D., M.A., PH.D., Linguistics
KITTS, W. D., M.S.A., PH.D., F.A.I.C., Animal Science
KIYOOKA, R., Fine Arts
KLONOFF, H., M.A., PH.D., Psychiatry
KNOBLOCH, F., M.D., C.SC., F.R.C.P.C., Psychiatry
KNOX, G., M.A., PH.D., Fine Arts
KNUTSON, H. C., M.A., PH.D., French
KOZAK, A., B.S.F., M.F., PH.D., Forestry
KRAINTZ, L., A.B., M.A., PH.D., Oral Biology
KRAUS, A., M.B.A., PH.D., Commerce and Business Administration
KREBS, C. J., M.A., PH.D., Zoology
KRISHNAMURTI, C. R., M.V.SC., PH.D., Animal Science
KUBICEK, R. V., PH.D., History
KUTNEY, J. P., M.SC., PH.D., Chemistry
LAKOWSKI, R., M.A., PH.D., Psychology
LAM, K. Y., PH.D., Mathematics
LANGDON, F. C., A.M., PH.D., Political Science
LAPONCE, J. A., DIPL.I.E.P., PH.D., Political Science
LARKIN, P. A., M.A., D.PHIL., F.R.S.C., Zoology
LAVIN, J. A., B.A., PH.D., English
LAVKULICH, L. M., M.SC., PH.D., Social Science
LAZERSON, M., M.A., PH.D., Education
LEAR, C. S. C., B.D.S., D.M.D., Orthodontics
LEBLOND, P. H., PH.D., Oceanography
LEDSOME, J. R., M.B., CH.B., M.D., Physiology
LEE, M., M.A., PH.D., Home Economics
LEE, S. S., PH.D., Education
LEJA, J., A.R.S.M., PH.D., P.ENG., F.C.I.C., M.I.M., M.C.I.M., Mineral Engineering
LEUNG, S. W., D.D.S., PH.D., F.A.C.D., F.I.C.D., F.R.C.D.(C.), Oral Biology
LEVY, JULIA, PH.D., Microbiology
LEWIS, A. G., M.SC., PH.D., Oceanography
LIELMEZS, J., M.SC., P.ENG., M.A.I.CH.E., F.I.I.C., M.A.C.S., F.N.Y.A.S., Chemical Engineering
LILEY, N. R., D.PHIL., Zoology
LIN, T-Y, M.D., D.MED.SCI., C.R.C.P.C., Psychiatry
LIN, W. C., PH.D., Chemistry
LINK, A. E., M.A., PH.D., Religious Studies
LIOY, F., M.D., PH.D., Physiology
LIPSON, S. L., M.S., F.AM.SOC.E., M.AM.C.I., M.E.I.C., M.C.S.C.E., Civil Engineering
LIRENMAN, D. S., M.D., F.R.C.P., Paediatrics
LIVERMORE, H. V., M.A., Hispanic and Italian
LOBAN, J. A., M.A., Music
LOFFMARK, R. R., M.B.A., C.A., Commerce and Business Administration
LOOS, O., DR.RER.NAT., Mathematics
LOW, M. D., M.D., PH.D., Medicine
LOWE, L. E., M.A., M.SC., PH.D., Soil Science
LUDWIG, D., PH.D., Mathematics
LUFT, E., DR.RER.NAT., Mathematics
LUND, J. A. H., PH.D., P.ENG., Metallurgy
LUSZTIG, P. A., M.B.A., PH.D., Commerce and Business Administration
LYSYK, K. M., Q.C., LL.B., B.C.L., Law
MAAS, H. S., PH.D., Social Work
MCCANN, E. K., M.S.N., R.N., Nursing
MCCLEAN, A. J., LL.B., PH.D., Law
MCCONNELL, R. E., M.A., PH.D., Education
MACCRIMMON, K. R., M.B.A., PH.D., Commerce and Business Administration
MACDONALD, J. A. S., Education
MACDOUGALL, D. J., LL.B., J.D., Law
MCDOWELL, C. A., M.SC., D.SC., F.R.I.C., F.C.I.C., F.R.S.C., Chemistry
MCGEE, T. G., PH.D., Asian and Slavonic Studies
MCGEER, E. G., PH.D., Psychiatry
MCGEER, P. L., PH.D., M.D., Psychiatry
MCINTOSH, H. W., M.B., M.D., C.M., M.SC., F.R.C.P.(C.), Medicine
MACINTYRE, J. M., LL.B., LL.M., Law
MACKAY, J. R., M.A., PH.D., D.U., F.R.S.C., Geography
MACKENZIE, C. J. G., M.D., C.M., D.P.H., F.R.C.P.C., Health Care and Epidemiology
MCKIE, T. D. M., M.A., PH.D., Education
MCLEAN, D. M., M.D., F.R.C.P.(C.), Medical Microbiology
MCLENNAN, H., M.SC., PH.D., F.R.S.C., Physiology
MACMILLAN, J. A., M.SC., PH.D., Agricultural Economics
MCMILLAN, J. M., M.SC., PH.D., Physics
MCNEILL, J. H., M.SC., PH.D., Pharmacology and Toxicology
MCPHAIL, J. D., M.SC., PH.D., Zoology
MCRAE, D. M., LL.M., Law
MCTAGGART, K. C., M.SC., PH.D., F.G.S.A., Geology
MANZALAOUI, M. A., M.A., D.PHIL., PH.D., English
MAO, J. C. T., M.B.A., PH.D., Commerce and Business Administration
MARCH, BERYL E., M.S.A., F.A.I.C., F.R.S.C., F.P.S.A., Poultry Science
MARGETTS, E. L., B.A., M.D., C.M., D.PSYCH., F.R.C.P., F.R.C.P.C., F.A.P.A., F.R.A.I., F.R.M.S., Psychiatry
MARSHALL, A., PH.D., Mathemetics
MATHEWS, W. H., M.A.SC., PH.D., F.G.S.A., F.R.S.C., Geology
MATTESSICH, R. V., DIPLOMKAUFMANN, DR.RER.POL., C.P.A., Commerce and Business Administration
MEASDAY, D. F., M.A., D.PHIL., Physics
MEISEN, A., PH.D., M.C.I.C., P.ENG., Chemical Engineering
MEISSNER, M., PH.D., Sociology
MELZAK, Z. A., M.SC., PH.D., Mathematics
MENON, T. K., D.I.I.C., PH.D., Geophysics and Astronomy
MERER, A. J., M.A., D.PHIL., Chemistry
MERIVALE, PATRICIA, M.A., PH.D., English
MEYER, J., Physics
MILBURN, D., M.SC., M.PHIL., PH.D., Education
MILLER, J. R., M.A., PH.D., F.C.C.M.G., Medical Genetics
MILNE, R. S., M.A., Political Science
MILSUM, J. H., S.M., M.E., SC.D., Health Care and Epidemiology
MITCHELL, C. L., M.B.A., F.C.A., Commerce and Business Administration
MITCHELL, A., D.PHIL., P.ENG., Metallurgy
MITCHELL, A. G., PH.D., M.P.S., Pharmaceutical Sciences

MITCHELL, H., M.A., PH.D., History
MITCHELL, V. F., M.B.A., PH.D., Commerce and Business Administration
MITTEN, L. G., M.S., PH.D., Commerce and Business Administration
MIURA, R. M., PH.D., Mathematics
MODI, V. J., D.I.I.SC., M.S., PH.D., P.ENG., MEM. A.S.M.E., MEM. A.I.A.A., ASSOC. FELLOW C.A.S.I., SEN. MEM. A.A.S., Mechanical Engineering
MONEY, T., PH.D., D.SC., F.R.I.C., F.C.I.C., C.CHEM., Chemistry
MOORE, A. D., M.SC., PH.D., P.ENG., Sen. Mem. I.E.E.E., M.E.I.C., M.C.S.E.E., Electrical Engineering
MOORE, A. M., B.A., A.M., Economics
MORAN, L. J., M.A., PH.D., Psychology
MORFORD, W. R., M.P.E., ED.D., Physical Education and Recreation
MORRIS, R. B., M.S.M., D.V.PAED., Music
MORRISON, B. M., M.A., PH.D., Asian Studies
MORRISON, F. A., M.B.E., C.D., B.S.P., M.SC., PHARM.D., Pharmaceutical Sciences
MORTON, K. S., M.SC., M.D., C.M., F.R.C.S.(C.), F.A.C.S., Orthopaedic Surgery
MOYLS, B., M.A., PH.D., Mathematics
MULAR, A. L., M.SC., P.ENG., M.C.I.M., Mineral Engineering
MUNRO, B. C., M.ED., PH.D., Education
MUNRO, D. D., M.S., PH.D., R.P.F., Forestry
MUNRO, G., PH.D., Economics
MURRAY, FRANCIS E., PH.D., P.ENG., C.P.P.A., M.TECH., Chemical Engineering
MURRY, J. W., M.A., PH.D., Geological Sciences
MYSAK, L. A., M.SC., A.M., PH.D., Mathematics
NADEAU, J. S., M.S., PH.D., P.ENG., Metallurgy
NAGATANI, K., M.A., PH.D., Economics
NAKAI, S., PH.D., Food Science
NASH, S. W., M.A., PH.D., Mathematics
NATHAN, N. D., S.M., PH.D., P.ENG., MEM. A.C.I., MEM. P.C.I., Civil Engineering
NEHER, P. A., PH.D., Economics
NEILL, J. W., M.C., PH.D., F.C.S.L.A., Horticulture
NEVISON, MYRNE, PH.D., Education
NEW, W. H., PH.D., English
NICHOLLS, C. G. W., M.A., Religious Studies
NICHOLLS, W. M., M.SC., Social Work
NODWELL, R., M.A.SC., PH.D., Physics
NORRIS, J. M., M.A., PH.D., History
NORTHCOTE, T. G., M.A., PH.D., Forestry and Zoology
OBERLANDER, H. P., M.C.P., PH.D., Community and Regional Planning
O'DONNELL, V. J., PH.D., Biochemistry
OGILVIE, A. L., D.D.S., M.S., Oral Medicine
OGRYZLO, E. A., M.SC., PH.D., Chemistry
OKE, T. R., PH.D., Geography
OLDRIDGE, O. A., B.D., ED.D., Education
OLSON, M. D., PH.D., P.ENG., M.A.I.A.A., Civil Engineering
OVENDEN, M. W., M.A., PH.D., F.R.S.(EDIN.), F.R.A.S., Geophysics
OWEN, B. D., M.SC., PH.D., Animal Science
OZIER, I., A.M., PH.D., Physics
PADDOCK, N. L., Chemistry
PALATY, V., Ing., PH.D., Anatomy
PARKINSON, G. V., M.S., PH.D., P.ENG., FELLOW C.A.S.I., Mechanical Engineering
PARSONS, T. R., M.SC., PH.D., Zoology and Oceanography
PATE, B. D., M.SC., PH.D., Pharmaceutical Sciences
PATTERSON, F. P., M.D., C.M., F.R.C.S.(C), F.A.C.S., Surgery
PATTON, T. E., M.A., PH.D., Philosophy
PEARCE, R. H., M.SC., PH.D., C.C.C., Pathology
PEARSE, P. H., M.A., PH.D., B.C.R.F., Economics
PEARSON, J. A., PH.D., Physiology
PEARSON, R. J., PH.D., Anthropology and Sociology
PECH, S. Z., M.A., PH.D., History
PECK, J. E. L., M.SC., PH.D., Computer Science
PENDAKUR, V. S., M.SC., M.S.C.E., PH.D., Community and Regional Planning
PERKINS, S., M.ED., ED.D., Education
PERKS, A. M., M.A., PH.D., Zoology
PERRY, T. L., A.B., M.D., Pharmacology
PERSON, C. O., B.A., PH.D., F.R.S.C., Botany
PETERS, E., M.A.SC., PH.D., P.ENG. Metallurgy
PHILLIPS, J. E., M.SC., PH.D., Zoology
PICKARD, G. L., M.B.E., M.A., D.PHIL., F.R.S.C., Physics
PIERS, E., PH.D., Chemistry
PILTZ, H.-K., M.MUS., Music
PINCOCK, R. E., A.M., PH.D., Chemistry
PINDER, K. L., M.ENG., PH.D., F.C.I.C., Chemical Engineering
PINKUS, P., PH.D., English
PITERNICK, A. B., B.A., A.L.A., Librarianship
PITERNICK, G., A.B., B.L.S., Librarianship
PODLECKI, A. J., M.A., PH.D., Classics
POLGLASE, W. J., M.A., PH.D., Biochemistry
POLING, G. W., M.SC., PH.D., P.ENG., M.C.I.M., Mineral Engineering
PORTER, G. B., PH.D., Chemistry
POWRIE, W. D., M.A., PH.D., Agricultural Mechanics and Food Science
PRANG, MARGARET E., M.A., PH.D., History
PRICE, J. D. E., M.D., C.M., F.R.C.P.C., F.A.C.P., Medicine
PRYCE, M. H. L., M.A., PH.D., F.R.S., Physics
PUGH, D. L., B.A., Physical Education and Recreation
PULLEYBLANK, E. G., PH.D., M.A., Asian Studies
QUASTEL, D. M. J., M.D., PH.D., Pharmacology
QUICK, M. C., PH.D., P.ENG., M.AM.SOC.C.E., Civil Engineering
RANDALL, D. J., PH.D., Zoology
RASTALL, P., PH.D., Physics
REE, R., PH.D., F.R.S.C., Mathematics
REID, C., B.SC., A.R.C.S., D.I.C., PH.D., F.C.I.C., Chemistry
REMNANT, P., M.A., PH.D., Philosophy
RENNEY, A. J., M.S., PH.D., Plant Science
RESTREPO, R. A., PH.D., Mathematics
REUBART, D., M.MUS., D.M.A., Music
REYNERTSON, A. JOAN, M.A., PH.D., Theatre
RICHARDS, J. F., M.A., PH.D., Biochemistry
RICHARDS, J. F., M.SC., PH.D., Food Science
RIEDEL, B. E., C.D., M.SC., PH.D., Pharmaceutical Sciences
ROBERTS, C. W., M.S., PH.D., Poultry Science
ROBINSON, G. C., M.D., C.M., F.R.C.P.(C.), Paediatrics
ROBINSON, J. L., M.A., PH.D., Geography
ROBSON, R. A. H., PH.D., Anthropology and Sociology
RODGERS, R. H., M.A., PH.D., Home Economics
ROGATNICK, A., M.ARCH., F.R.A.I.C., Architecture
ROSENBLUTH, G., PH.D., F.R.S.C., Economics
ROSENTHAL, A., M.SC., PH.D., F.C.I.C., Chemistry
ROSS, I. S., M.A., PH.D., English
ROSS, J. V., PH.D., A.R.C.S., D.I.C., Geological Sciences
ROTHSTEIN, S., M.A., PH.D., D.LITT., Librarianship
ROUSE, G. E., M.SC., PH.D., F.L.S., Botany
ROWAN, R. J., M.A., PH.D., Philosophy
ROWLES, C. A., M.SC., PH.D., Soil Science
ROYDHOUSE, R. H., M.S., D.D.SC., Restorative Dentistry
RUEDY, J., M.D., F.R.C.P.(C.), C.S.P.Q., Medicine
RUNECKLES, V. C., PH.D., Plant Science
RUNIKIS, J. O., PH.D., Pharmaceutical Sciences
RUPPENTHAL, K. M., L.L.B., M.BA., PH.D., Commerce and Business Administration
RUSSELL, R. D., M.A., PH.D., F.R.S.C, Gerophysics and Astronomy
RUUS, E., DR.ENG., P.ENG., M.AM.SOC.C.E., M.E.I.C., Civil Engineering
SAINT-JACQUES, B., D. ès L. et SC.HUM., Linguistics
SAMS, J. R., PH.D., Chemistry
SANDERS, D., LL.M., Law
SARNDAL, C. E., M.B.A., PH.D., Commerce and Business Administration
SAWYER, A. R., M.A., D.F.A., Fine Arts
SCAGEL, R. F., M.A., PH.D., F.R.S.C., F.L.S., Botany
SCHOFIELD, W. B., M.A., PH.D., Botany
SCHWAB, B., M.S., M.B.A., PH.D., Commerce and Business Administration
SCHWERDTFEGER, C. F., PH.D., Physics
SCOTT, A. D., A.M., PH.D., F.R.S.C., Economics
SCUDDER, G. G. E., D.PHIL., F.R.E.S., P.E.S.C., F.R.S.C., Zoology
SEGAL, S., M.A., M.D., C.M., F.R.C.P., Paediatrics
SHAW, M., M.SC., PH.D., P.AG., F.A.P.S., F.L.S., F.R.S.C., Agricultural Botany
SHEARER, R. A., M.A., PH.D., Economics
SHEPPARD, A. F., LL.M., Law
SHIM, S. S., M.D., PH.D., F.R.C.S.(C), F.A.C.S., Surgery
SHULMAN, L., M.S.W., ED.D., Social Work
SHUTER, W. L. H., PH.D., Physics
SIGNORI, EDRO, B.A., M.A., PH.D., Psychology
SINCLAIR, A. J., M.A.SC., PH.D., Geological Sciences
SINEL, A. A., A.M., PH.D., History
SION, M., M.S., PH.D., Mathematics
SLADE, H. C., M.D., F.R.C.P.(C), C.R.C.P.(C), Family Practice
SLAWSON, W. F., PH.D., Geophysics and Astronomy
SLONECKER, C. E., D.D.S., PH.D., Anatomy
SMEDLEY, G., Fine Arts
SMITH, G. A., R.C.A., LL.D., Education
SMITH, J. C., LL.B., LL.M., Law
SMITH, J. H. G., M.F., PH.D., R.P.F., Forestry
SMITH, M., PH.D., Biochemistry
SMITH, R H T., M.A., PH.D., Geography
SMITH, R. N., M.A., PH.D., Education
SNIDER, R. F., PH.D., F.R.C.S., Chemistry
SOUDACK, A., M.S., PH.D., Electrical Engineering
SOULE, D. E., M.A., PH.D., Theatre
SPLANE, R. B., M.A., M.S.W., PH.D., Social Work
SPOUGE, J. D., M.D.S., F.D.S., R.C.S., M.R.C.S., L.R.C.P., F.R.C.D.(C.), Dentistry
STAGER, J. K., PH.D., Geography
STALEY, L. M., M.SC., P.ENG., Bio-Resource Engineering
STANKIEWICZ, W. J., M.A., PH.D., Political Science
STANWOOD, P. G., PH.D., English
STEIN, J. R., M.A., PH.D., F.L.S., Botany
STEINBERG, M. W., M.A., PH.D., English
STEPHENS, D. G., M.A., PH.D., English
STEWART, ROSS, M.A., PH.D., F.C.I.C., F.R.S.C., Chemistry
STEWART, W. D., M.D., F.R.C.P.(C), Medicine
STICH, H. F., PH.D., Zoology
STOCK, J. J., M.SC., PH.D., Microbiology
STOKES, R., M.A., M.PHIL., F.L.A., Librarianship
SUEDFELD, P., M.A., PH.D., Psychology
SUMMERS, E. G., M.A., PH.D., Education
SUTHERLAND, N. J., M.A., PH.D., Education
SUTTER, M. C., M.D., PH.D., Pharmacology

SUZUKI, D., PH.D., F.R.S.C., Zoology
SWANSON, C. A., M.A., PH.D., Mathematics
SZASZ, G., M.D., Health Care and Epidemiology
SZIKLAI, O., M.F., PH.D., R.P.F., Forestry
TAYLOR, F. J. R., PH.D., Botany and Oceanography
TAYLOR, J. M., M.A., PH.D., Zoology
TAYLOR, R. L., PH.D., F.L.S., Dir. of Botanical Garden
TEES, R. C., PH.D., Psychology
TEGHTSOONIAN, E., M.A., PH.D., P.ENG., Metallurgy
TENER, G. M., M.S., PH.D., Biochemistry
THOMAS, J. W. P., M.D., C.M., F.R.C.P.(C.), Pathology
THOMPSON, A. R., LL.B., LL.M., J.S.D., Law
THOMPSON, D. W., PH.D., P.ENG., M.C.I.C., M.I.CH.E., M.A.I.CH.E., Chemical Engineering
TICKNER, F. A., M.MUS., Music
TIERS, C. A., M.ARCH., M.R.A.I.C., Architecture
TODD, E. C. E., LL.D., LL.M., Law
TOMKINS, G., M.A., PH.D., Education
TONZETICH, J., PH.D., Oral Biology
TOUGAS, G. R., M.A., PH.D., French
TOWELL, M., M.B., B.S., M.R.C.O.G., F.R.C.S.(C), Obstetrics and Gynaecology
TOWERS, G. H. N., M.SC., PH.D., F.L.S., F.R.S.C., Botany
TOWNSLEY, P. M., M.S., PH.D., Food Science
TREISMAN, A. M., D.PHIL., Psychology
TROTTER, J., PH.D., D.SC., F.R.I.C., F.C.I.C., Chemistry
TROWSDALE, G. C., M.ED., D.ED., Education
TSURUTA, K. M.A., PH.D., Asian Studies
TUNG, M. A., PH.D., Food Science
TURNER, R., M.A., PH.D., Anthropology and Sociology
TURRELL, B. G., M.A., D.PHIL., Physics
TYERS, G. F. O., M.D., F.R.C.S., F.A.C.S., Surgery
TYHURST, J. S., B.SC., M.D., C.M., D.PSYCH., Psychiatry
ULRYCH, T. J., M.SC., PH.D., Geophysics and Astronomy
UPTON, L. F. S., M.A., PH.D., History
VARAH, J. M., M.S., PH.D., Computer Science
VERTINSKY, I., PH.D., Commerce and Business Administration and Animal Resource Ecology
VINCE, D. J., M.D., F.R.C.P.C., Medicine (Cardiology)
VOGT, E. W., O.C., M.SC., PH.D., F.R.S.C., Physics
WADA, J., M.D., D.M.SC., F.A.A.N., F.R.C.P.(C.), Neurological Sciences
WALES, T. J., PH.D., Economics
WALKER, D. C., PH.D., D.SC., Chemistry
WALKER, G. A. H., PH.D., F.R.S.C., Geophysics and Astronomy
WALLIN, J. H. A., M.ED., PH.D., Education
WALSH, J. B., M.A., PH.D., Mathematics
WALTERS, J., M.F., R.P.F., Forestry
WAN, F., PH.D., Mathematics
WARREN, I. H., PH.D., P.ENG., Metallurgy
WARREN, J. B., D.I.C., PH.D., P.ENG., F.INST.P., Physics
WARREN, R. A. J., M.SC., PH.D., Microbiology
WATANABE, T., PH.D., Geophysics and Astronomy
WATKINSON, A. P., PH.D., P.ENG., M.C.I.C., Chemical Engineering
WEBBER, W. A., M.D., Anatomy
WEDEPOHL, L. M., PH.D., F.I.E.E., C.ENG., P.ENG.(Man.), Electrical Engineering
WEETMAN, G. F., M.F., PH.D., Forestry
WEINBERG, F., M.A., PH.D., Metallurgy
WEISGARBER, E., M.MUS., Music
WEISS, D. L., M.S., PH.D., Commerce and Business Administration
WELLINGTON, W. G., M.A., PH.D., Plant Science and Animal Resource Ecology
WESTWICK, R., M.A., PH.D., Mathematics
WHITE, B. L., D.I.C., PH.D., Physics
WHITTAKER, J. V., M.A., PH.D., Mathematics
WHITTLE, H. D., M.S., PH.D., Physical Education
WICKBERG, E., M.A., PH.D., History
WIESMAN, B., M.ARCH., Community and Regional Planning
WIGGINS, J., PH.D., Psychology
WILIMOVSKY, N. J., M.A., PH.D., Zoology
WILL, R. M., A.M., PH.D., Economics
WILLIAMS, D. LL., PH.D., Physics
WILLMAN, M. D., M.S.N., PH.D., Nursing
WILSON, J. D., PH.D., Education
WILSON, J. W., M.S., PH.D., Forestry
WINTER, G. R., M.S., PH.D., Agricultural Economics
WINTER, J. H., PH.D., History
WONG, R., M.A., PH.D., Psychology
WOODLAND, A. D., PH.D., Economics
WOODSIDE, A. B., A.M., PH.D., History
WOOLF, L. I., PH.D., Neurological Sciences
YEO, D. J., D.D.S., M.P.H., F.I.C.D., F.R.C.D.(C.), Public and Community Dental Health
YOUNG, L., M.A., PH.D., SC.D., F.R.S.C., M.I.E.E.E., Electrical Engineering
ZACK, D. T., D.M.D., M.S.D., Oral Surgery
ZAHRADNIK, J. W., M.S., PH.D., Bio-Resource Engineering
ZBARSKY, S. H., M.A., PH.D., Biochemistry
ZIDEK, J. V., M.SC., PH.D., Mathematics
ZIEMBER, W. T., M.B.A., PH.D., Commerce and Business Administration
ZILBER, J., M.A., Creative Writing
ZOLBROD, L. M., M.A., PH.D., Asian Studies

THEOLOGICAL COLLEGES:

Carey Hall: Baptist.
Principal: J. E. RUNIONS, M.D., F.R.C.P.(C.), M.R.C.PSYCH.

Regent College: Trans-denominational.
Principal: CARL E. AMERDING, M.A., TH.D. (acting).

St. Andrew's Hall: Presbyterian.
Dean of Residence: Rev. J. A. ROSS, M.A., PH.D.

St. Mark's College: Vancouver; Roman Catholic.
Principal: Rev. D. MULVIHILL, C.S.B., M.A., PH.D.
Registrar: Rev. N. KELLY, C.S.B., S.T.B., M.A.

Vancouver School of Theology: 6000 Iona Drive, Vancouver, B.C.; an ecumenical school of theology, incorporated 1971; continues work of the Anglican Theological College of B.C. and Union College of B.C.; provides theological education for laymen, for future clergy and for graduates in theology.
Principal: Rev. J. P. MARTIN, TH.M., PH.D.

BROCK UNIVERSITY

MERRITTVILLE HIGHWAY,
ST. CATHARINES, ONTARIO
L2S 3A1
Telephone: (416) 684-7201.

Founded 1964.

Provincial control; Academic year: September to April; Language of Instruction: English.

Chancellor: C. G. SHAVER, M.B., D.SC., F.R.C.P.(C).
President and Vice-Chancellor: A. J. EARP, M.A., M.LITT., LL.D.
Registrar and Dean of Student Services: R. W. MCGRAW, B.A.
Vice-President Administration: T. B. VARCOE, M.B.A., C.A.
Librarian: J. HOGAN, B.A., A.L.A.
Dean of Humanities: M. YACOWAR, M.A., PH.D.
Dean of Social Sciences and Vice-President: W. A. MATHESON, M.B.A., M.A., PH.D.
Dean of Science and Mathematics: M. S. GIBSON, M.A., D.PHIL.
Dean of College of Education: P. J. ATHERTON, PH.D.

Number of teachers: 212.
Number of students: 5,079.
Publication: *Calendar*† (annual).

PROFESSORS:

ADAMCZEWSKI, Z., Philosophy
ADAMS-WEBBER, J. R., Psychology
ATHERTON, P. J., Education
BELL, H. E., Mathematics
BENJAFIELD, J. G., Psychology
BISMUTH, R., French
BOWN, A. W., Biological Sciences
CARLSEN, N., Psychology
CHERNIAK, E. A., Chemistry
EARP, A. J., Classics
EDDS, J. A., Administrative Studies
EVANS, J. R., Physical Education
FIC, V. M., Politics
GIBSON, M. S., Chemistry
GOODSPEED, D. J., History
HANRAHAN, J. R., Administration
HIATT, R., Chemistry
HOOVER, R. C., Urban Studies
HORNYANSKY, M., English
HOUSTON, A. H., Biological Sciences
HULL, W. H. N., Politics
JACKSON, J. N., Applied Geography
KENNEDY, M. J., Geological Sciences
KERNAGHAN, W. D. K., Politics and Administrative Services
KOFFYBERG, F. P., Physics
LAVERY, J., Psychology
LIBERTY, B. A., Geological Sciences
LORDAHL, D. S., Psychology
LOWENBERGER, A. G., Physical Education
MANOCHA, M. S., Biological Sciences
MAYBERRY, J. P., Mathematics
MAYER, J. R. A., Philosophy
MCEWEN, J. M., History
MILLER, J. M., Chemistry
MOASE, R. B., Education
MOULE, D. C., Chemistry
MULLER, E. R., Mathematics
NICHOLLS, P., Biological Sciences
OWEN, C. R., German
PEACH, P. A., Geological Sciences
PLINT, C. A., Physics
RAND, R. P., Biological Sciences
REED, J., Mathematics
ROBERTSON, N. D., Classics
SEWELL, J. P., Politics
SHUKLA, R. C., Physics
SKILTON, F. R., Computer Sciences and Information Processing
TEMKIN, G., Economics
TERASMAE, J., Geological Sciences
THOMAS, P. A. V., Computer Science and Information Processing
THOMPSON, B. W., Geography
TINKLER, K. J., Geography
TREMAIN, R., Music
YACOWAR, M., Drama

UNIVERSITY OF CALGARY

2920, 24TH AVENUE N.W.,
CALGARY, ALBERTA T2N 1N4
Telephone: (403) 284-5110.

Founded in 1945 as a branch of the University of Alberta, gained full autonomy 1966.

Academic year: July 1st to June 30th (four sessions).

Chancellor: J. L. LEBEL, B.A., LL.B.
President and Vice-Chancellor: NORMAN E. WAGNER, PH.D.
Vice-President (Academic): P. J. KRUEGER, M.SC., D.PHIL., F.C.I.C., F.R.I.C.
Vice-President (Finance): H. W. BLISS, F.C.A.
Vice-President (Services): H. A. R. DE PAIVA, M.S., PH.D.
Registrar: J. TURNER.
Librarian: ALAN MACDONALD, B.A., B.L.S.

Number of teachers (full-time): 985, ncluding 317 professors.

Number of students: 10,398 full-time; 3,040 part-time; total 13,441.

Publications: *The University Calendars* (annual), *Annual Report, University Gazette* (monthly), *Ariel*†: a review of international English literature (quarterly), *Calgary University Dept. of Economics, Discussion Papers Series*† (irregular), *Canadian Ethnic Studies*† (biannual), *Journal of Comparative Family Studies*† (biannual), *Journal of Educational Thought*† (3 a year), *Studies in Land-Use History and Landscape Change*† (irregular), *The Big Byte* (Journal of the Data Centre, monthly), *The Gauntlet* (student newspaper), *Canadian Psychologist* (quarterly), *Calum* (5 a year).

DEANS AND DIRECTORS:

Faculty of Continuing Education: R. S. CHAPMAN, PH.D.
Faculty of Education: R. F. LAWSON, M.A., PH.D.
Faculty of Engineering: T. H. BARTON, PH.D., D.ENG., F.I.E.E., F.I.E.E.E.
Faculty of Environmental Design: W. T. PERKS, M.C.D.
Faculty of Fine Arts: A. ROBERTSON, D.A.
Faculty of Graduate Studies: J. B. HYNE, PH.D., F.C.I.C.
Faculty of Humanities: P. C. CRAIGIE, M.A., PH.D.
Faculty of Law: J. P. S. MCLAREN, LL.M.
Faculty of Management: G. S. LANE, PH.D., R.I.A.
Faculty of Medicine: L. E. MCLEOD, M.D., M.SC.
Faculty of Nursing: MARGARET SCOTT-WRIGHT, PH.D.
Faculty of Physical Education: R JACKSON, PH.D.
Faculty of Sciences: T. A. OLIVER.
Faculty of Social Sciences: H. K. BETZ, PH.D.
Faculty of Social Welfare: LEONARD RICHARDS, PH.D.
University College: F. TERENTIUK, M.A., PH.D.

PROFESSORS:

ADAM, I. W., M.A., English
ADAM, J. A., PH.D., Psychology
ADAM, J., C.SC., Economics
AGGARWALA, B. D., M.A., PH.D., Mathematics and Statistics
ALEXANDER, F., M.B., M.D., M.R.C.PATH., Pathology
AL-ISSA, I. A., PH.D., Psychology
ALTMANN, H. A., Educational Psychology
ANDERSON, J. M., M.A., PH.D., Linguistics
ANDERSON, P. K., M.SC., PH.D., Biology
ANGER, C. D., M.A., PH.D., Physics
ANTON, F. R., M.A., PH.D., Economics
ARAI, H. P., PH.D., Biology
ARCHER, CI., PH.D., History.
ARMSTRONG, D. A., PH.D., F.C.I.C., Chemistry
AZIZ, K., M.SC., PH.D., P.ENG., Chemical Engineering
BAKER, W. P., M.A., PH.D., English
BALA, R. M., M.D., F.R.C.P.(C.), Medicine
BALDWIN, B., PH.D., Classics
BARR, B. M., PH.D., Geography
BARTON, T. H., PH.D., D.ENG., F.I.E.E., Electrical Engineering
BASKETT, H. K., M.A., Continuing Education
BAYER, M. B., M.B.A., M.A.SC., PH.D., Management
BAYLISS, P., PH.D., F.M.S.A., Geography and Geophysics
BECK, J. S., PH.D., Medical Bio-Physics
BENDER, E. I., ED.D., A.C.S.W., Social Welfare
BENN, M. H., PH.D., D.I.C., A.R.C.S., Chemistry
BENNION, D. W., M.S., PH.D., Chemical Engineering
BERCUSON, D. J., PH.D., History
BERG, G. J., M.A.SC., Electrical Engineering
BETZ, H. K., M.A., PH.D., Economics
BEWLEY, J. D., PH.D., Biology
BIRD, C. D., M.SC., PH.D., Biology
BLACK, A. J., M.A., PH.D., English
BLACK, D. B., M.ED., ED.D., Educational Psychology
BLAIR, W. R. N., C.D., M.A., PH.D., Psychology
BLAND, C. J., PH.D., A.R.C.S., Physics
BRATTON, R. D., M.SC., PH.D., Physical Education
BRAUN, C., M.ED., PH.D., Curriculum and Instruction
BRESKY, D., M.A., PH.D., Romance Studies
BREUGELMANS, R., M.A., PH.D., Germanic and Slavic Studies
BRINKERHOFF, M. B., PH.D., Sociology
BROSZ, V. R., M.ED., Art
BROWDER, L. W., PH.D., Biology
BROWN, A. M., ED.D., Music
BROWN, R. I., PH.D., Educational Psychology
BRUTON, L. T., M.ENG., PH.D., Electrical Engineering
BRYAN, L. E., PH.D., Pathology
BUCKMASTER, H. A., M.A., PH.D., F.INST.P., P.GEOPHYS., P.ENG., Physics
CAMERON, J. R., M.A., PH.D., Curriculum and Instruction
CAMPBELL, F. A., M.A., PH.D., F.R.S.(C.), Geology
CARNIE, R. H., M.A., PH.D., English
CARSON, R. B., M.ED., ED.D., Educational Administration
CARSWELL, R. J. B., M.A.T., ED.D., Curriculum and Instruction
CHADBOURNE, R. M., M.A., PH.D., Romance Studies (French)
CHALLICE, C. E., PH.D., D.SC., A.R.C.S., D.I.C., F.INST.P., F.R.S.A., P.ENG., Physics
CHAN, W.-C., PH.D., Electrical Engineering
CHANG, K. W., PH.D., Mathematics and Statistics
CHAPMAN, R. S., M.ED., PH.D., Continuing Education
CHIA, C.-Y., PH.D., Civil Engineering
CHIVERS, T., PH.D., Chemistry
CHORNY, M., M.ED., ED.D., Curriculum andInstruction
CHURCH, R. B., M.SC., PH.D., Biology and Medical Biochemistry
COLE, W. K., M.A., ED.D., Music
CONKLIN, R. C., PH.D., Educational Psychology
CONSUL, P. C., M.SC., PH.D., Mathematics and Statistics
COOK, E.-D., M.A., PH.D., Linguistics
COOKE, B. J., M.A., S.TH.L., S.T.D., LITT.D., Religious Studies
COOPER, K. E., M.B.B.S., M.SC., M.A., D.SC., Medical Physiology
COOPER, R. M., M.A., PH.D., Psychology
COSTELLO, C. G., M.SC, PH.D., Psychology
COSTERTON, J. W. F., M.A., PH.D., Biology
CRAGG, J. B., M.SC., D.SC., D.TH.P.T. CEnvironmental Design
CRAIGIE, P. C., PH.D., Religious Studies
CRUICKSHANK, D. A.. LL.M., Law
CRUSE, P. J. E., M.B.CH.B., C.R.C.S.(C.), F.R.C.S.(C.), F.A.C.S., F.R.C.S.(ED.), Surgery
CUMMING, P., Natural Resources Law
DAHLIE, H., M.A., PH.D., English
DAIS, E. E., J.D., Law
DAVIES, W. K. D., PH.D., Geography
DE JUBECOURT, G. S., M.S., PH.D., Romance Studies
DE KRASINSKI, J. S. A., PH.D., Mechanical Engineering
DE PAIVA, H. A. R., M.S., PH.D., Civil Engineering
DETOMASI, D. D., PH.D., Environmental Design (Economics)
DEWAR, R. E., PH.D., Psychology
DHALIWAL, R. S., M.A., PH.D., Mathematics and Statistics
DICKSON, A. D., M.B., M.D., M.A., Morphological Science
DIEMERT, H. M., M.A., D.ED., Art
DILGER, W. H., DR.-ING., Civil Engineering
DIXON, G. H., PH.D., F.R.S.(C.), F.R.S., Medical Biochemistry
DODD, E. M., M.A., Art
DOIGE, A. G., M.SC., PH.D., Mechanical Engineering
DOOLITTLE, J. D., M.A., Drama
DOOLITTLE, Q. D., M.M., A.M.D., Music
DRUMMOND, G. I., M.SC., PH.D., Biochemistry
DUERKSEN, J. D., M.SC., PH.D., Biology
DUGGAN, H. E., M.D., L.M.C.C., C.R.C.P.S.(C.), F.A.C.R., F.R.C.P.(C.), Diagnostic Radiology
DUWORS, R. E., M.A., PH.D., Sociology
ECCLES, P. J., M.S., ED.D., Educational Curriculum and Instruction
EDGINGTON, E. S., M.S., PH.D., Psychology
ELDER, P. S., LL.M., Environmental Design
ELSON, L. B., M.M.A., D.M.A., Music
ENNS, E. G., PH.D., Mathematics and Statistics
ESLER, J. K., B.F.A., B.ED., R.C.A., Art
EYCK, U. F. J., M.A., F.R.HIST.S., History
FARAHAT, H. K., PH.D., Mathematics and Statistics
FATHI, A., M.A., PH.D., Sociology
FINLEY, A. H., M.D., C.M., L.M.C.C., C.R.C.P.(C.), D.A.P.B., F.R.C.P.(C.), F.A.A.P., Paediatrics and Community Health Science
FINN, S. G., M.A., PH.D., Music
FISHER, A. W. F., M.B., M.D., Morphological Science
FISHER, L. A., M.ED., PH.D., Educational Planning and Assessment
FLANAGAN, T. E., PH.D, Political Science
FORBIS, R. G., M.A., PH.D., Archaeology

FRANCIS, R. P., LL.M., Law
FRANKEN, R. E., PH.D., Psychology
FRITZ, J. O., M.A., M.SC., D.ED., Curriculum and Instruction
FROST, B. P., P.G.C.E., M.A., PH.D., F.B.PS.S., Educational Psychology
FRY, P. S., PH.D., Educational Psychology
GALLOWAY, W. A., LL.B., Law
GANDHI, R. S., PH.D , Sociology
GAUCHER. G. M., PH.D., Biochemistry
GEIST, V., PH.D., Environmental Design
GHALI, A., M.SC., PH.D., Civil Engineering
GHENT, E. D., PH.D., Geology
GIBB, A. A., M.A., M.SC., ED.D., Curriculum and Instruction
GILES, T. E., ED.D., Educational Administration
GIBSON, W. M., M.B., CH.B., Family Practice
GILLMOR, R. D., M.ARCH., Environmental Design (Architecture)
GILLOTT, J. E., M.SC., PH.D., Civil Engineering
GIOVINETTO, M. B., M.S., PH.D., Geography
GLOCKNER, P. G., M.SC., PH.D., Civil Engineering
GONZALEZ, A., M.A., PH.D., Geography
GOODMAN, H. J. A., ED.D., Curriculum and Instruction
GOODWIN, L., M.ED., PH.D., Physical Education
GREGORY, G. A., PH.D., Chemical Engineering
GREIG, G. M., M.A., Philosophy
GRETENER, P. E. F., M.SC., PH.D., Geology
GRIPTON, J. M., D.S.W., Social Welfare
GROVES, T. K., M.SC., PH.D., Mechanical Engineering
GUENTER, C. A., M.D., F.R.C.P.(C.), Medicine
GUY, E. F., M.A., PH.D., English
GUY, R. K., M.A., DIP.ED., Mathematics and Statistics
HALLWORTH, H. J., M.A., PH.D., F.B.PS.S., A.K.C., Educational Psychology
HALPERN, J., PH.D., Management
HAMILTON, A. B., ED.D., Continuing Engineering
HAMZA, M. H., D.SC.TECH., PH.D., Electrical Education
HARMS, A., PH.D., Romance Studies
HARRIS, S. A., M.SC., PH.D., Geography
HARRISON, A. W., M.SC., PH.D., Physics
HARTLAND-ROWE, R. C. B., PH.D., Biology
HASLAM, R. H. A., M.D., D.A.B.P., F.A.A.P., Paediatrics
HASLETT, J. W., PH.D., Electrical Engineering
HAWKES, F. J., M.SC., PH.D., Social Welfare
HEIDEMANN, R. A., D.SC., Chemical Engineering
HEINRICH, A. C., M.ED., PH.D., Anthropology
HEINTZ, J. W., PH.D., Philosophy
HENDERSON, N. E., M.SC., PH.D., Biology
HERTZ, T., M.MUS., Music
HILLS, L. V., M.SC., PH.D., Geology
HODGSON, G. W., M.SC., PH.D., Environmental Design (Environmental Science)
HOLLENBERG, M. D., M.D., M.SC., PH.D., Pharmacology and Therapeutics
HOPE, G. S., PH.D., D.I.C., Electrical Engineering
HORNBY, R., PH.D., Drama
HUBER, R. E., PH.D., Biochemistry
HYNE, J. B., PH.D., F.C.I.C., Chemistry
INLOW, E. B., M.A., PH.D., Political Science
IRONS, B. M., D.SC., M.R.A.E.S., P.ENG., Civil Engineering
ISMAEL, T. Y., A.M., PH.D., Political Science
IZZO, H. J., A.M., PH.D., Linguistics
JACKSON, R. C., PH.D., Physical Education
JERRY, L. M., PH.D., F.R.C.P.(C.), F.A.C.P., Medicine
JOHNSTON, A. R., M.MUS., PH.D., Music
JOHNSTON, C. D., PH.D., Civil Engineering
JONES, H. W., PH.D., C.T., P.ENG., F.I.P., Physics and Mechanical Engineering
JORDAAN, I. J., PH.D., Civil Engineering
KAPOOR, M., M.SC., PH.D., Biology
KARIEL, H. G., M.ED., PH.D., Geography
KARIM, G. A., PH.D., D.SC., D.I.C., Mechanical Engineering
KELLEY, D. H., PH.D., Archaeology
KELLEY, N. J. H., PH.D., Archaeology
KENDALL, E. J. M., M.SC., PH.D., P.ENG., F.INST.P., Electrical Engineering
KENTFIELD, J. A. C., PH.D., D.I.C., Mechanical Engineering
KERR, M. G., M.B.CH.B., F.R.C.S.(ED.), F.R.C.O.G.. F.R.C.S.(C.), Obstetrics and Gynaecology
KHER, I. N., PH.D., English
KING, ETHEL M., M.A., PH.D., Curriculum and Instruction
KINGSTON, G. E., PH.D., Physical Education
KINSELLA, T. D., M.D., C.M., F.R.C.P.(C.), Medicine
KIYOOKA, H. M., M.A., M.F.A., Art
KLOVAN, J. E., A.M., PH.D., Geology and Geophysics
KNAFLA, L. A., PH.D., History
KOCH, E. L., ED.M., ED.D., Educational Administration
KROETSCH, R., English
KROUSE, H. R., PH.D., F.INST.P., Physics
KRUEGER, P. J., M.SC., D.PHIL., F.C.I.C., F.R.I.C., Chemistry
KURIAN, G., M.A., M.SC., PH.D., Sociology
LAIDLAW, W. G., M.SC., PH.D., Chemistry
LAMARRE, C. J., M.D., L.M.C.C., F.A.P.A., F.R.C.P.(C.), Psychiatry
LAMBERT, R. A., M.ED., PH.D., Educational Psychology
LANCASTER, P., M.SC., PH.D., Mathematics and Statistics
LANE, G. S., PH.D., R.I.A., Management
LANNIGAN, R., M.B., CH.B., M.D., PH.D., F.R.C.PATH., Pathology
LARSEN, D. E., M.A., PH.D., Community Health Science
LAURENSON, R. D., M.B., CH.B., M.D., Morphological Science
LAWSON, R. F., M.A., PH.D., Educational Foundations
LEDERIS, K., PH.D., D.SC., Pharmacology and Therapeutics
LEE, R. G., M.D., F.R.C.P.(C.), Medicine
LENNAM, T. N. S., M.A., PH.D., Drama
LEVENE, C., M.B., B.CH., B.A.O., M.D., Morphological Science
LEVINSON, A. A., M.S., PH.D., F.G.S.A., F.M.S.A., Geology and Geophysics
LEVY, J. C., LL.M., Law
LEWIS, D. J., M.D., C.R.C.P., F.R.C.P., F.A.P.A., Psychiatry
LIN, C. C., PH.D., Paediatrics and Medical Biochemistry
LINDER, G., M.B.A., C.A., Continuing Education
LOOV, R. E., M.S., PH.D., Civil Engineering
LOVE, E. J., M.D., PH.D., C.R.C.P.(C.), Community Health Science
LOWRY, R. B., M.B., B.A.O., D.C.H., L.M.C.C., F.R.C.P.(C.), Paediatrics and Community Health Science
LUCAS, A. R., LL.M., Law
LUPRI, E., PH.D., Sociology
LYTTON, H., M.A., PH.D., F.B.PS.S., Educational Psychology
MACCANNELL, K. L., M.D., PH.D., L.M.C.C., F.R.C.P.(C.), Pharmacology and Therapeutics
MACDONALD, J., M.A., PH.D., Educational Foundations
MACINTOSH, J. J., M.A., B.PHIL., Philosophy
MACKENZIE, K. R., M.D., F.R.C.P.(C.), Psychiatry
MACKINNON, F., M.A., PH.D., LL.D., O.C., Political Science
MAGEE, W. H., M.A., PH.D., English
MAJUMDAR, S. R., M.A., PH.D., Mathematics and Statistics
MALIK, O. P., M.E., PH.D., D.I.C., Electrical Engineering
MANDIN, H., M.D., F.R.C.P.(C.), Medicine
MARTIN, C. B., PH.D., Philosophy
MARTIN. J. S. T., PH.D., English
MASH, E. J.. PH.D.. Psychology
MATHEWS, T., M.A., PH.D., D.I.C., Physics
MCARTHUR. R. G., M.D., C.R.C.P.(C.), Paediatrics
MCCORMACK, W. C., A.M., PH.D., Anthropology and Linguistics
MCGUGAN, A., M.SC., D.SC., Geology
MCKELLAR, J., M.ARCH., M.C.P., Environmental Design
MCKENNA, M. C., M.A., PH.D., History
MCLACHLAN, D. L., PH.D., Economics
MCLAREN, J. P. S., LL.M., Law
MCLEOD, L. E., M.D., M.SC., F.R.C.P.(C.), F.A.C.P., Medicine
MCMAHON. B. R.. PH.D., Biology
MCMULLEN, A. E., M.SC., PH.D., Civil Engineering
MCPHEDRAN, N. T., M.D., F.R.C.S.(C.), F.A.C.S., Surgery
MEIKLE, A. B. S., M.A., PH.D., Psychology
MCQUITTY. G. D. H., M.C., M.B., CH.B., C.C.F.P.(C.), Family Practice
MEIKLE, A. B. S., M.A., PH.D., Psychology and Psychiatry
MILLER, R. M., M.A.T., M.A., ED.D., Educational Foundations
MILLS, D. L., A.M., PH.D., Sociology
MILNER, E. C., M.SC., PH.D., F.R.S.(C.), Mathematics and Statistics
MITCHELL, V. E., A.M., L.G.S.M., Drama
MOGHADAM, H., M.D., M.P.H., F.R.C.P.(C.), Paediatrics and Community Health Science
MOHTADI, M. F., PH.D., P.ENG., F.I.C.H.E., M.A.I.C.H.E., Chemical Engineering
MOMSEN, R. P., M.A., PH.D., Geography
MOORE-EYMAN, EVELYN R., M.A., Curriculum and Instruction
MORRISH, H. F., M.D., L.M.C.C., C.R.C.P.S.(C.), D.A.B.R., F.R.C.P.(C.), Diagnostic Radiology
NELSON, S. J., M.A.SC., PH.D., Geology and Geophysics
NEWTON, D. M., ED.D., Physical Education
NICHOLS, S. T., M.SC., PH.D., Electrical Engineering
NIELSEN, K. E., PH.D., Philosophy
NKEMDIRIM, L. C., PH.D., Geography
NORRIE, D. H., PH.D., Mechanical Engineering
NORRIS, S., M.A., ED.D., Curriculum and Instruction
OGAWA, J., D.SC., Mathematics and Statistics
OLIVA, F. D., M.ED., ED.D., Educational Administration
OLIVER, T. A., M.SC., PH.D., Geology
OYLER, J. E., M.A., PH.D., Germanic and Slavic Studies (German)
PAREL, A. J., PH.L., S.T.L., PH.D., Political Science
PARKINSON, D., PH.D., Microbiology
PARNEY, F. L., M.D., F.F.A.R.C.S., F.R.C.P.(C), Anaesthesia
PEARCE, K. I., M.B.B.S., C.R.C.P., M.D., M.R.C.S., L.R.C.P., L.M.C.C., M.R.C.(PSYCH), F.R.C.P.(C.), Psychiatry
PEITCHINIS, S. G., M.A., PH.D., Economics
PENELHUM, T. M., M.A., B.PHIL., F.R.S.(CAN.), Religious Studies
PERKS, W. T., M.C.D., Environmental Design (Urbanism)
PETTI, A. G. R., M.A., D.LITT., F.S.A., F.R.HIST.S., English

PHARIS, R. P., M.F., D.F., Biology
PINEO, G. F., M.D., F.R.C.P.(C.), F.A.C.P., Medicine
PLATTOR, E. E., ED.D., Curriculum and Instruction
PRITCHARD, G., PH.D., A.R.C.S., Biology
RAO, N. D., PH.D., Electrical Engineering
RASPORICH, A. W., PH.D., History
READ, J. H., M.D., D.P.H., C.R.C.P.(C.), Community Health Sciences and Paediatrics
REASONS, C. E., PH.D., Sociology
REID, D. M., PH.D., M.I.BIOL., Biology
RENDALL, J. A., LL.M., Law
RICHARDS, L., M.S.W., M.A., PHIL.M., PH.D., Social Welfare
RITCHIE, J. R. B., PH.D., Management
ROBERTS, W. G., M.ED., PH.D., Educational Administration
ROBERTSON, R. E., M.SC., PH.D., F.R.S.(C.), Chemistry
ROBINSON, I. M., M.A., PH.D., Urban Planning
ROBINSON, J. M. A., M.B.A., PH.D., Management
ROCHE, R. S., PH.D., F.R.I.C., F.C.I.C., Chemistry
ROMAN, Z., M.A., PH.D., Music
ROSENBERG, G. M., M.D., C.M., F.R.C.P.(C.), F.A.C.P., Family Practice and Medicine
ROUKES, N. M., M.A., Art
ROWLANDS, S., PH.D., F.I.P., L.R.C.P., M.R.C.S., Medical Biophysics and Physics
SAHNEY, B. N., M.SC., PH.D., Mathematics and Statistics
SANDERSON, K. E., M.SC., PH.D., Biology
SARGIOUS, M. A., M.ENG., PH.D., Civil Engineering
SAUER, N., DR.PHIL., Mathematics and Statistics
SAUNDERS, T. C., M.D., C.M., C.C.F.P.(C.), Family Practice
SCHEINBERG, E., M.S., PH.D., Biology
SCHNELL, R. L., PH.D., Educational Foundations
SCHOFIELD, B., M.B., M.A., M.D., Medical Physiology
SCHONFIELD, A. E. D., M.A., DIP.AB.PSYCH., Psychology
SCHUMACHER, M. E., M.A., ED.M., Nursing
SEASTONE, D., M.A., PH.D., Economics
SHIELDS, R. A. M., PH.D., History
SHINNIE, P. L., M.A., F.S.A., Archaeology
SIMONY, P. S., M.SC., PH.D., D.I.C., Geology
SMEATON, B. H., M.A., PH.D., Linguistics
SORENSEN, T. S., PH.D., Chemistry
SREENIVASAN, S. R., PH.D., Physics
STAMP, R. M., M.A., PH.D., Educational Foundations
STARR, G., M.S.L.S., Law
STEBBINS, R. A., M.A., PH.D., Sociology
STEIN, R. A., M.S., PH.D., Electrical Engineering
STEWART, W. F. M., M.A., PH.D., Philosophy
STRUC, R. S., M.A., PH.D., Germanic and Slavic Studies (German)
SUGARS, E. G. K., PH.D., Management
SVRCEK, W. Y., PH.D., P.ENG., Chemical Engineering
SWADDLE, T. W., PH.D., Chemistry
TAYLOR, D. M., M.ARCH., M.R.A.I.C., Environmental Design
TENER, R. H., M.A., PH.D., English
TERENTIUK, F., M.A., PH.D., Continuing Education
THOMAS, V., D.ED., Curriculum and Instruction
THORPE, T. A., PH.D., Botany
TOEWS, J. B., M.A., PH.D., History
TOLLEFSON, E. L., M.A., PH.D., F.C.I.C., P.ENG., Chemical Engineering
TROFIMENKOFF, F. N., M.SC., DIC., PH.D., Electrical Engineering
TSCHUIKOW-ROUX, M.S., PH.D., Chemistry
TULCZYJEW, W. M., PH.D., Mathematics and Statistics
TYLER, F. H., M.S.W., ED.D., Social Welfare
UNRUH, W. R., PH.D., Educational Psychology
VAN DE PANNE, C., DRS., PH.D., Economics
VAN DE SANDE, J. H., PH.D., Medical Biochemistry
VARADARAJAN, K., PH.D., Mathematics and Statistics
VEALE, W. L., M.S., PH.D., Medical Physiology
VENKATESAN, D., M.SC., PH.D., F.INST.P., Physics
VON MORSTEIN, P., Philosophy
WAGNER, N. E., PH.D., Archaeology and Religious Studies
WALDMAN, E., M.A., PH.D., Political Science
WALKER, G., PH.D., Mechanical Engineering
WARD, M. A., PH.D., D.I.C., Civil Engineering
WARDLAW, N. C., PH.D., Geology and Geophysics
WATANABE, M., M.D., C.M., PH.D., F.R.C.P.(C.), Medicine
WATSON, J. I., M.D., C.M., F.R.C.P.(C.), Medicine
WEYANT, R. G., M.A., PH.D., F.A.P.A., Psychology
WILLIAMS, D., M.A., PH.D., D.PHIL., F.R.HIST.S., F.R.G.S., History
WILLIAMSON, J. H., M.S., PH.D., Biology
WING, G. D., M.A., English
WISEMAN, C. S., PH.D., English
WOODSWORTH, J. G., ED.D., Educational Psychology
WRIGHT, R. W., M.A., PH.D., Economics
ZACHARIAH, M., M.A., PH.D., Educational Foundations
ZAITZEFF, S. I., PH.D., Romance Studies
ZENTNER, H., M.A., PH.D., Educational Administration
ZISSOS, D., B.SC., Computer Science and Electrical Engineering

AFFILIATED COLLEGES:

Medicine Hat College: Medicine Hat, Alberta; f. 1965; affiliated as a Junior College in 1966.

President: ROBERT E. SACKLEY, B.SC.

Mount Royal College: Calgary, Alberta; f. by the late Dr. George W. Kerby; inc. 1910; affiliated as a Junior College in 1966.

President: D. M. LAUCHLAN, B.A., B.D., D.ADMIN.

COLLEGE OF CAPE BRETON

P.O.B. 5300, SYDNEY, N.S.
B1P 6L2

Telephone: 902-539-5300.

Founded 1954.

Private control; Language of instruction: English; Academic year: September to May.

President: DONALD F. CAMPBELL.
Senior Vice-President: J. E. TERRY.
Academic Vice-President: Dr. W. M. REID.
Registrar: DONALD FEWER.
Librarian: RITA MACINNIS.

Library of 120,000 vols.

Number of teachers: 130.

Number of students: 1,061 full-time, 836 part-time, 826 summer school, 157 trades.

Publications: *Calendar*, *President's Report*.

DEANS:

Faculty of Arts and Science: (vacant).
Faculty of Trades and Technology: ROBERT RUDDERHAM.

ATTACHED INSTITUTES:

Bras d'Or Institute: f. 1972 to stimulate research, development and enquiry relevant to Cape Breton Island (agriculture, aquaculture, environment, energy, social studies, etc.); Dir. DONALD ARSENEAU.

Tompkins Institute of Human Values and Technology: f. 1974; Dir. JOSEPH DAWSON.

Bell Institute: Dir. THOMAS KIERANS; f. 1977 to foster research in any matter compatible with the range of interests of Alexander Graham Bell.

Beaton Institute: repository of Cape Breton history and archives of College of Cape Breton; open for research to students and members of the public; Dir. ROBERT MORGAN.

Centre for International Studies: f. 1978; Dir. Dr. BRIAN TENNYSON.

CARLETON UNIVERSITY

OTTAWA, ONTARIO K1S 5B6

Telephone: 613-231-4321.

Founded 1942.

Provincial control; Language of instruction: English; Academic year: September to May.

Chancellor: G. HERZBERG, C.C., DR.ING., D.SC., LL.D., F.R.S., F.R.S.C.
President and Vice-Chancellor: W. E. BECKEL, M.SC., PH.D.
Vice-President (Academic): (vacant).
Vice-President (Administration) and Bursar: A. B. LAROSE, B.COM., C.A.
Registrar: J. I. JACKSON.
Librarian: G. H. BRIGGS, M.A.
Dean of Student Services: NORMAN D. FENN, M.ED.

Library: *see* Libraries.

Number of full-time teachers: 635, including 161 professors.

Number of students: 8,763 full-time, 6,419 part-time.

Publications: *Calendars*† (Undergraduate, Graduate, Summer School, Extension), *The President's Report*†, *The University Report*†, *Research and Studies*†, *The Charlatan* (weekly), *The Raven* (annual), *This Week at Carleton* (weekly).

DEANS:

Faculty of Arts: NAOMI GRIFFITHS.
Faculty of Social Sciences: T. RYAN, M.A., PH.D.
St. Patrick's College Division, Faculty of Arts: G. E. CLARKE, M.A. (acting).
Faculty of Science: J. WOLFSON, M.SC., PH.D.
Faculty of Engineering: M. C. DE MALHERBE, PH.D.

Faculty of Graduate Studies: C. AMBERG, M.A., PH.D.

PROFESSORS:

ABBOTT, R. D., B.A., LL.M., Law
ADJELEIAN, J., S.M., Engineering
AMBERG, C. H., M.A., PH.D., F.C.I.C., Chemistry
ANGLIN, D. G., M.A., D.PHIL., Political Science
APSIMON, J. W., PH.D., Chemistry
BARLOW, C. A., M.A., PH.D., Biology
BARRADAS, R. G., PH.D., F.R.S.C., F.C.I.C., Chemistry
BEESACK, P. R., A.M., PH.D., Mathematics
BELLAMY, J. G., M.A., PH.D., History
BOCIURKIW, B. R., M.A., PH.D., Political Science
BOOTHROYD, A. R., PH.D., F.I.E.E.E., Engineering
BOWEN, B. A., M.SC., PH.D., P.ENG., Engineering
BOWEN D. G., M.A., PH.D., F.R.S.A.I., History
BOWES, W. H., M.E., M.SC., P.ENG., Engineering
BREWIS, T. N., M.COM., PH.D., Economics
BROWNE, G. P., M.A., D.PHIL., History
CHAKRABARTI, C. L., M.SC., PH.D., F.R.S.C., F.C.I.C., Chemistry
CHANT, J. F., PH.D., Economics
CHAO, G. Y., M.SC., PH.D., Geology
CHARI, V. K., PH.D., English
CHUNG, D., PH.D., Religion and History
CHURCHILL, J., B.MUS., F.R.C.O., G.R.S.M., L.R.A.M., A.R.C.M., Music
CLARKE, R. L., PH.D., Physics
CLIVE, H. P., PH.D., French
COLL, D. C., M.ENG., PH.D., P.ENG., Engineering
CONDLMINE, O., M.A., PH.D., French
COOTE, M., M.ARCH., A.R.I.B.A., Architecture
COPELAND, M.A., PH.D., Engineering
COUSE, G. S., PH.D., History
COWAN, W. G., PH.D., Linguistics
CROOK, R. K., A.M., PH.D., Sociology and Anthropology
CSÖRGÖ, M., M.A., PH.D., Mathematics
DALE, D. K., M.SC., F.S.S., Mathematics
DAWSON, D., M.SC., PH.D., Mathematics
DE MALHERBE, M. C., DIPL.ENG., D.I.C., PH.D., Engineering
DIXON, J. D., M.A., PH.D., Mathematics
DLAB, V., R.N.DR., C.SC., PH.D., D.SC., Mathematics
DONALDSON, J. A., PH.D., Geology
DOWNEY, J., M.A., PH.D., English
DUNTON, D. C.C., LL.D., D.SC., Canadian Studies
ELWOOD, R. C., M.A., PH.D., History
ENGLISH, H. E., PH.D., Economics
FARR, D. M. L., M.A., D.PHIL., History
FITZGERALD, P. J., M.A., Law
FLEISCHAUER, C. P., A.M., PH.D., French
FRUMHARTZ, M. C., A.M., Sociology and Anthropology
GEORGE, D. A., M.S., SC.D., P.ENG., Engineering
GILLES, W., Industrial Design
GILLESPIE, W. I., PH.D., Economics
GNAROWSKI, M. A., PH.D., English
GOLDAK, J. A., M.SC., PH.D., Engineering
GREBENSCHIKOV, V. I., M.A., PH.D., Russian
GULLEN, M. A., M.S., P.ENG., Engineering
HAIDER, S. G., M.S., PH.D., Architecture
HARMSTONE, T. R., A.M., PH.D., Political Science
HARP, J., M.SC., PH.D., Sociology and Anthropology
HAY, K. A. J., M.SC., Economics
HETTICH, W., M.A., PH.D., Economics
HILL, P. A., PH.D., F.G.S., F.P.S., F.R.G.S., Geology
HODGE, A. T., M.A., PH.D., Classics
HOLMES, J. M., M.A., PH.D., F.C.I.C., Chemistry
HOWDEN, H. F., M.S., PH.D., Biology
IRVING, G., O.M.I., PH.D., Sociology
IYER, V. N., M.SC., PH.D., Biology
JACKSON, R. J., M.A., D.PHIL., Political Science
JACKSON, R. L., M.A., PH.D., Spanish
JOHNSON, J. K., M.A., History
JOHNSON, JR., J. P., A.M., PH.D., Geography
JOHNSTON, G. B., M.A., English
JONES, B. W., A.M., PH.D., English
JOY, K. W., PH.D., Biology
JURADO, J., DR.FA.Y LETRAS, Spanish
KARDOS, G., M.ENG., PH.D., P.ENG., Engineering
KAYE, E. F., M.A., D.E.S., D.D'UNIV., French
KESSLER, D., M.SC., D. ès SC., Physics
KESTERTON, W. H., B.J., Journalism
KNIGHTS, R. M., PH.D., Psychology
KONINGSTEIN, J. A., D.SC., Chemistry
KRUUS, P., LIC.TECH., PH.D., Chemistry
LANGFORD, C. H., PH.D., Chemistry
LAUGHTON, P. M., M.SC., PH.D., F.C.I.C., Chemistry
LAVER, A. B., M.A., PH.D., Psychology
LEE, P. E., M.SC., PH.D., Biology
LITHWICK, N. H., PH.D., Economics
LOVE, G. R., M.A., PH.D., Physics
LUKASIEWICZ, J., C. DE LA C., D.I.C., DIPL. ING., D.SC., F.A.I.A.A., F.C.A.S.I., F.I.MECH.E., Engineering
LYON, P. V., M.A., D.PHIL., Political Science
MACDOUGALL, H. A., O.M.I., PH.D., History
MANDL, P., M.A., PH.D., Mathematics
MARSHALL, M., M.A., PH.D., Psychology
MATHEWS, R. D., M.A., English
MAULE, C. J., M.A., PH.D., Economics
MCCORMACK, P. D., M.A., PH.D., Psychology
MCCULLY, M. E., M.S.A., PH.D., Biology
MCDOUGALL, R. L., M.A., PH.D., English
MCFARLANE, B. A., M.A., PH.D., Sociology and Anthropology
MCRAE, K. D., A.M., PH.D., Political Science
MEALING, S. R., M.A., History
MERKLEY, P. C., M.A., PH.D., History
MERRILL, G. C., M.A., PH.D., Geography
MILLAR, D. A. J., M.E., SC.D., P.ENG., Engineering
MOIZER, J. D., DIPL.ARCH., A.R.I.B.A., Architecture
MOORE, Jr., J. M., PH.D., Geology
NEATBY, H. B., M.A., PH.D., History
NEELIN, J. M., PH.D., Biology
NEL, L. D., PH.D., Mathematics
NESBITT, H. H. J., M.A., PH.D., D.SC., F.L.S., F.R.E.S., F.Z.S., Biology
NEUWIRTH, G., DR.RER.POL., PH.D., Sociology and Anthropology
NORTH, F. K., M.A., D.PHIL., Geology
NORTHOVER, F. H., M.A., PH.D., D.SC., M.INST.R.E., Mathematics
OLIVER, M., Political Science
OPPENHEIMER, E. M., M.A., PH.D., German
OSBORNE, R. E., S.T.M., PH.D., Religion
PAGUREK, B., M.A.SC., PH.D., Systems Engineering and Computer Science
PALTIEL, K. Z., M.A., PH.D., Political Science
PAQUET, G., M.A., Economics
PODGORECKI, A., Sociology and Anthropology
RAO, J. N. K., PH.D., Mathematics
RAY, D. M., M.A., PH.D., Geography
READ, L. M., M.A., PH.D., Religion
RIORDON, J. S., M.ENG., D.I.C., PH.D., P.ENG., Systems Engineering and Computer Science
ROGERS, J. T., M.ENG., PH.D., P.ENG., Engineering
ROWAT, D. C., A.M., PH.D., Political Science
RYAN, T. J., M.A., PH.D., Psychology
RYMES, T. K., M.A., PH.D., Economics
SARAVANAMUTTOO, H. I. H., PH.D., P.ENG., Engineering
SCANLON, T. J., B.J., M.A., Journalism
SCHIRMER, H. H., M.A., PH.D., Mathematics
SCHNEIDER, W. J., M.S., PH.D., Mathematics
SELUCKY, R., C.SC., Political Science
SETTERFIELD, G., PH.D., Biology
SHARON, H. N., B.ARCH., Architecture
SIDA, D. W., M.SC., PH.D., F.R.A.S., Mathematics
SMITH, A., B.A., B.C.L., International Affairs
STRICKLAND, L. H., PH.D., Psychology
STRONG, J. W., M.A., PH.D., History
STRUTT, J. W., B.ARCH., F.R.A.I.C., Architecture
SUBRAMANIAN, V., M.A., PH.D., Political Science
SUNDARESAN, M. K., M.SC., PH.D., Physics
SWINTON, G., B.A., Art History
SYDENHAM, M. J., PH.D., F.R.S.A., F.R.HIST.S., History
TASSIE, J. S., M.A., PH.D., French
TAYLOR, D. R. F., M.A., PH.D., Geography and International Affairs
THISTLE, M. W., M.A., Journalism
THOMAS, R. E., D.I.C., PH.D., Electronics
TOLLEY, A. T., B.A., English
TOMBAUGH, T. N., M.A., PH.D., Psychology
TSAI, C. S., M.SC., PH.D., Chemistry
TUPPER, W. M., M.SC., PH.D., Geology
ULUG, M. E., M.SC., PH.D., Engineering
UREN, P. E., M.A., PH.D., Geography
VALENTINE, V. F., M.A., Sociology and Anthropology
VALLEE, F. G., PH.D., Sociology and Anthropology
VAN RUTTEN, P., PH.D., French
VON RIEKHOFF, H., M.A., P.D., Political Science
WAKE, F. R., PH.D., Psychology
WAND, B., M.A., PH.D., Philosophy
WEBB, J. A., PH.D., Biology
WENDT, R. A., M.A., Psychology
WERNHAM, J. C. S., M.A., S.T.M., Philosophy
WEST, E. G., M.SC., PH.D., Economics
WESTELL, A., Journalism
WHYTE, D., M.SC., PH.D., Sociology and Anthropology
WIGHTMAN, F., PH.D., Biology
WILES, D. R., M.SC., PH.D., F.C.I.C., Chemistry
WILLIAMS, K. S., M.A., PH.D., Mathematics
WILLIAMS, P. J., M.A., Geography
WISE, S. F., M.A., History
WOLFSON, J. L., M.SC., PH.D., Physics
WOOD, G. J., M.A., English
YAMAZAKI, H., M.S., PH.D., Biology

CONCORDIA UNIVERSITY

Incorporating Sir George Williams University and Loyola College
Telephone: 879-5955.

Established by merger 1974.

Sir George Williams Campus

1455 DE MAISONNEUVE WEST,
MONTREAL, QUEBEC H3G 1M8

Loyola Campus

7141 SHERBROOKE STREET WEST,
MONTREAL, QUEBEC H4B 1R6

Provincial control; Language of instruction: English; Summer term, May to July; Winter term, September to April.

Chancellor: HENRY J. HEMENS, B.C.L., Q.C.
Rector and Vice-Chancellor: J. W. O'BRIEN, M.A., PH.D.
Vice-Rector and Principal of Loyola Campus: J. A. GRAHAM, S.J., M.A., S.T.L.
Vice-Rector, Academic: J. BORDAN, M.SC.ENG.
Vice-Rector, Administration and Finance: G. MARTIN, M.SC.
Registrar: K. D. ADAMS, B.SC., L.MUS.
Director of Libraries: P. E. FILION, S.J., M.S., D.U.L., LL.D.

Library: *see* Libraries.

Number of teachers: 654 full-time, 750 part-time.

Number of students: 23,440.

Publications: *The Georgian, The Loyola News.*

DEANS:

Faculty of Arts and Science:
Division I: (vacant).
Division II: J. CHAIKELSON, M.SC., PH.D.
Division III: M. COHEN, PH.D.
University Faculty of Commerce and Administration: P. SIMON, M.A., PH.D.
University Faculty of Engineering: N. M. S. SWAMY, PH.D.
University Faculty of Fine Arts: C. A. EMERY.
Graduate Studies: S. G. FRENCH, PH.D.
Director of Admissions, Sir George Williams Campus: T. E. SWIFT, B.A.
Director of Admissions, Loyola Campus: GRENDON E. HAINES, B.A., B.PED.

PROFESSORS:

ADAMSON, A. H., PH.D., History
AHMAD, J., M.B.A., PH.D., Finance
AMIT, Z., PH.D., Psychology
ANGEL, R. B., M.A., PH.D., Philosophy
ANTONIOU, A., PH.D., Engineering
ARBUCKLE-MAAG, PH.D., Psychology
ARMSTRONG, MURIEL, M.A., Economics
BAGCHI, S. N., M.SC., D.SC., Physics
BEDFORD, F. W., M.SC., Mathematics
BEISSEL, H. E., M.A., English
BELMORE, N., M.S., PH.D., Linguistics
BESSNER, L., B.COMM., Accountancy
BHATNAGAR, J. K., M.A., PH.D., Education
BHATTACHARYYA, B. B., M.TECH., PH.D., Engineering
BORDAN, J., M.SC., M.ENG., M.E.I.C., Engineering
BRANT, C. S., M.A., PH.D., Sociology and Anthropology
BRINK, G., M.B.A., Management
BRYANT, R. W. G., M.A., M.SC., Geography
BUELL, J., M.A., PH.D., Communication Studies
BUTOVAKY, M., M.A., English
BYERS, V., M.SC., PH.D., Mathematics
CHENG, R. M. H., M.SC., PH.D., Mech. Engineering
CHODAK, S., M.A., PH.D., Sociology
COLEBROOK, L. D., M.SC., PH.D., Chemistry
COOKE, E. F., M.F.A., Fine Arts
CORBO, V., PH.D., Economics
DAVIES, A., M.A., PH.D., Applied Linguistics
DAVIS, C. A., S.T.L., Religion
DESPLAND, M., TH.D., Religion
D'HOLLANDER, P. J., D.D'U., D.ÈS L., French
DICK, J. G., B.SC., Chemistry
DICKIE, A., B.COMM., C.A., Accountancy
DIMOCK, H. G., M.A., ED.D., Applied Social Science
DU PLESSIS, M., M.SC., PH.D., Engineering
ENESCO, H., M.A., PH.D., Biology
ENTWHISTLE, H., M.ED., PH.D., Education
FAZIO, P. P., M.A.SC., PH.D., Engineering
FONDA, C., PH.D., Modern Languages
FOSTER, M. B., M.A., English
FRANCIS, W., M.A., English
FRASER, D. A., PH.D., Geography
FRENCH, S. G., M.A., PH.D., Philosophy
GAUCHER, Y. J., Fine Arts
GRAHAM, Rev. A., M.A., S.T.L., Chemistry
GUINDON, H., PH.L., M.A., Sociology
HABIB, H., M.A., PH.D., Political Science
HAYES, F., PH.D., Economics
IBRAHIM, R., M.SC., PH.D., Biology
INAGAKI, M., M.SC., M.A., PH.D., Economics
JOLY, G. W., M.SC., Engineering
JONASSOHN, K., M.A., Sociology
JOOS, E., M.A., PH.D., Philosophy
KANTER, M., PH.D., Mathematics
KAWCZAK, A., LL.M., M.A., PH.D., Philosophy
KELLY, J., M.ED., PH.D., Management
KETTERER, D., M.A., D.PHIL., English
KIRPALANI, V. H., M.A., D.SC., Marketing
KNELMAN, F. N., M.E., PH.D., Science and Human Affairs
KUBINA, S., M.ENG., PH.D., Engineering
KWOK, C. C. K., M.E., PH.D., Engineering
LABBÉ, G., L.ÈS L., D.DE L'U., French Studies
LADD, H., M.A., PH.D., Psychology
LAFFEY, J., PH.D., History
LAGACE, B., B.A., Music
LASKEY, D., M.A., PH.D., Philosophy
LAURION, G., L. ÈS L., D. DE L'U., French Studies
LAUZIERE, A., M.A., D.U., French Studies
LEUNG, K. V., ING.DR., Computer Science
LOMBOS, B. A., PH.D., Engineering
LOSIQUE, S., L. ÈS L., D. U., Cinematographic Art
MALIK, M., B.A., D.SC., Communication Studies
MALLEN, B., M.SC., M.B.A., PH.D., Marketing
MANN, H., M.B.A., PH.D., Accountancy
MARSH, C., M.A., M.ENG., Engineering
MCCULLOUGH, E. E., M.A., PH.D., History
MCDONALD, R. D., M.S.W., Applied Social Science
MCDONOUGH, S., M.A., PH.D., Religion
MCDOUGALL, D. J., M.SC., PH.D., Geology
MCKAY, J., PH.D., Computer Science
MCQUEEN, H. J., M.S., PH.D, Engineering
MISRA, S., M.SC., PH.D., Physics
MITCHELL, P. D., M.A., PH.D., Education
MOLINARI, G., Fine Arts
NEWMAN, E. B., M.A., PH.D., Biology
NISH, C., M.A., PH.D., History
NOGRADY, T., M.SC., PH.D., Chemistry
O'BRIEN, Rev. J. E., S.T.L., PH.D., Communication Studies
O'BRIEN, J. W., M.A., PH.D., Economics
O'KEEFE, Rev. C. B., S.T.L., M.A., PH.D., History
OSMAN, M. O., DR.SC.TECH., Engineering
PARK, D., M.A., PH.D., Philosophy
PEDERZOLI, G., M.S., M.A., PH.D., Quantitative Methods
PEETS, D. L., B.SC., Human Genetics
PERRY, C., PH.D., Psychology
PINSKY, A., Fine Arts
POTTER, C. C., M.COM., PH.D., Finance
RAMACHANDRAN, V., PH.D., Engineering
RAMAMURTHY, A. S., M.SC., PH.D., Engineering
ROTHKRUG, L. N., M.A., PH.D., History
RUDÉ, G., M.A., PH.D., D.LITT., History
SANDERSON, W., M.A., PH.D., Art History
SANKAR, T., M.E., PH.D., Mech. Engineering
SCHWARTZMAN, A., PH.D., Psychology
SHERMAN, L., M.A., Fine Arts
SIMON, P., M.A., PH.D., Management
SMITH, N. E., M.A., PH.D., Mathematics
SMOLA, J., M.A., PH.D., Management
SPRINGFORD, NORMA, B.A., Theatre Arts
STEWART, J., PH.D., Psychology
SWAMY, M. N. S., M.SC., PH.D., Engineering
SZABO, M. E., M.A., M.SC., PH.D., Mathematics
TAGGART, G. C., M.A., PH.D., French
TOBIAS, R. H., B.A., English
TOUPIN, P., M.A., D.DE L'U., French Studies
TROITSKY, M. S., D.TECH.SC., Engineering
TUTSCH, H., LL.D., Management
UFFORD, J. R., M.A.SC., PH.D., Chemistry
VERSCHINGEL, R. H. C., PH.D., Chemistry
VICTORIA, J., M.S., PH.D., Fine Arts
VIDYASAGAR, M., M.S., PH.D., Electrical Engineering
WALL, R. E., M.A., PH.D., History
WHEELER, D., B.SC., F.I.M.A., Mathematics
WHITELAW, J. H., M.A., Modern Languages
WIDDOWS, P. F., M.A., PH.D., Classics
WILBUR, R., M.A., History
YORKEY, R. C., M.A., ED.D., Applied Linguistics
ZIELINSKI, Z. A., D.TECH.SC., Engineering
ZWEIG, J. P., M.A., PH.D., Psychology

DALHOUSIE UNIVERSITY

HALIFAX, NOVA SCOTIA

Telephone: (902) 424-2211.

Founded 1818.

In association with King's College. Mount Saint Vincent University and Nova Scotia Technical College (*q.v.*).

Private control; Language of instruction: English; Academic year: September to May.

Chancellor: Lady BEAVERBROOK, LL.D.
President and Vice-Chancellor: W. A. MACKAY, Q.C., LL.D.
Registrar: A. J. TINGLEY, PH.D.
Librarian: D. COOKE, B.A., B.L.S.

Library: *see* Libraries.

Number of teachers: 1,250 full- and part-time.

Number of students: 10,963 full- and part-time.

Publications: *Calendars* (annually), *The Dalhousie Review* (quarterly), *Dalhousie Alumni News, University News* (2 a month), *Communications and Information Systems.*

DEANS:

Faculty of Arts and Science: D. BETTS, M.SC., PH.D.
Faculty of Law: WILLIAM CHARLES' M.A., LL.M.
Faculty of Medicine: J. D. HATCHER, M.D., PH.D.
Faculty of Dentistry: I. C. BENNETT, B.D.S., D.D.S., M.SC.
Faculty of Graduate Studies: K. T. LEFFEK, PH.D., F.C.I.C.
Faculty of Health Professions: R. S. TONKS, PH.D.
Faculty of Administrative Studies: T. W. KENT, M.A.

DIRECTORS:

Institute of Public Affairs: G. K. ANTOFT, B.A.

Institute of Oceanography: P. J. WANGERSKY, PH.D.
Institute of Environmental Studies: A. J. HANSON, M.SC., PH.D.
School of Dental Hygiene: KATE MACDONALD, B.S.
Part-time Studies and Extension: J. D. MYERS, M.A., PH.D.

PROFESSORS:

Faculty of Arts and Sciences:

AIKENS, H. F., A.M., Romance Languages
AITCHISON, J. H., B.ED., PH.D., Political Science
ARMSTRONG, A. H., M.A., Classics
ARNOLD, D. R., Chemistry
ATHERTON, J. P., Classics
AUE, W. A., PH.D., Classics
BECK, J. M., M.A., PH.D., Political Science
BEVAN, A. R., PH.D., English
BLUM, E., M.A., Mathematics
BOWEN, A. J., M.A., PH.D., Oceanography
BOYD, C. M., PH.D., Biology and Oceanography
BRAYBROOKE, D., M.A., PH.D., Philosophy and Politics
BROWN, R. G. Biology
BURROUGHS, P., PH.D., F.R.HIST.S., History
CALKIN, M. G., M.SC., PH.D., Physics
CAMERON, M. L., M.SC., PH.D., Biology
CHAVY, P., AGR. DES L., French
CHUTE, W. J., M.A., PH.D., Chemistry
CLAIRMONT, D. H., M.A., PH.D., Sociology
COMEAU, F. L., M.A., PH.D., Economics
COOKE, H. B. S., M.A., D.SC., F.R.S.S.AFR., Geology
CORNWALL, J. L., M.SC., PH.D., Economics
CROSS, M. S., M.A., PH.D., History
COXON, J. A., Chemistry
CROUSE, R. D., S.T.B., M.A., M.TH., PH.D., Classics
DUNHAM, P. J., Psychology
DOULL, J. A., M.A., Classics, German
EDELSTEIN, M., M.SC., D.SC., Mathematics
FARLEY, J., Biology
FENTRESS, J. C., PH.D., Psychology,
FILLMORE, P. A., M.A., PH.D., Mathematics
FLINT, J. E., M.A., PH.D., F.R.HIST.S., History
FORREST, T. P., M.SC., PH.D., Chemistry
FRASER, J. F., M.A., PH.D., English
FRASER, P., PH.D., History
FRIEDENBERG, E. Z., PH.D., Education
GAEDE, F. W., DR.PHIL., German
GELDART, D. J. W., Physics
GEORGE, R. E., M.A., Commerce and Economics
GLAZOV, Y., PH.D., Russian
GODDARD, G. V., M.A., PH.D., Psychology
GRAHAM, J. F., A.M., PH.D., Economics
GRANTER, H. S., A.M., History
GRAY, J., PH.D., F.R.S.A., English
HAINES, R. M., M.A., D.PHIL., F.R.HIST.S., History
HALL, B. K., PH.D., Biology
HALL, J. M., PH.D., Geology
HARE, W. F., Philosophy and Education
HAYES, K. E., PH.D., Chemistry
HEARD, K. A., M.A., PH.D., Political Science
HONIG, W. K., PH.D., Psychology
HOYT, C. K., M.SC., PH.D., Physics
JAMES, P. H. R., PH.D., Psychology
JERICHO, M. H., M.SC., PH.D., Physics
JONES, W. E., M.SC., PH.D., Chemistry
KAMRA, O. P., M.S., PH.D., Radiation Biology
KASDAN, L., PH.D., Sociology
KEMP, W. H., Music
KIANG, D. B. I., Physics
KIMMINS, W. C., PH.D., Biology (Botany)
KING, H. W., PH.D., Engineering and Engineering Physics
KLEIN, E. Economics
KNOP, O., D.SC., Chemistry
KONCZACKI, Z. A., PH.D., Economics
LANGSTROTH, G. F. O., PH.D., Physics
LAWLER, J. R., M.A., PH.D., French
LEFFEK, K. T., PH.D., F.C.I.C., Chemistry
LEVIN, A., M.I.E.E., Physics
LOLORDO, V. M., Psychology
MCALLISTER, R. I., M.A., Economics
MCGWIRE, M. K., B.SC., Maritime and Strategic Studies, Political Science
MCLAREN, I. A., M.SC., PH.D., Biology
MACLEAN, G. R., M.A., PH.D., History
MCNULTY, J. A., M.A., PH.D., Psychology
MALTZAHN, K. E., VON, M.S., PH.D., Biology (Botany)
MANN, K. H., PH.D., D.SC., Biology
MANGALAM, J. J. PH.D., Sociology
MARCH, R. H., M.SC., PH.D., Physics
MARFELS, C. T., Economics
MARGINSON, K. F., B.E., M.SC., M.E.I.C., P.ENG., Engineering
MICHELSEN, P., German
MILLIGAN, G. C., M.SC., PH.D., Geology
MILLS, E. L., PH.D., Biology and Oceanography
MORSE, N. H., M.A., M.A., PH.D., Economics
MYERS, J. D., M.A., PH.D., Education
NAKAJIMA, S., M.A., PH.D., Psychology
OGDEN, J. G., M.S., PH.D., Biology
PAGE, F. H., M.A., D.D., Philosophy
PARKS, M. G., M.A., PH.D., D.SC., English
PIELOU, E., PH.D., Biology
PILLAY, P. D., History
PUCCETTI, R. P., PH.D., Philosophy
RADJAVI, H., M.A., PH.D., Mathematics
RAVINDRA, R., Religion
REGAN, D., D.SC., PH.D., Psychology
RENNER, K. E., M.A., PH.D., Psychology
RODGER, R. S., PH.D., Psychology
ROSEN, R., Mathematics
ROSS, M. M., M.A., PH.D., D.LITT., F.R.C.S., English
RYAN, D. E., M.A., PH.D., D.SC., Chemistry
SCHENK, P. E., M.S., PH.D., Geology
SEGELBERG, E., TH.D., Classics
SINCLAIR, A. M., PH.D., Economics
SMITH, R. J., M.A., PH.D., English
SPROTT, S. E., M.A., B.D., PH.D., English
STAIRS, D. W., PH.D., Political Science
STEPHENS, W. N., M.A., ED.D., Sociology and Anthropology
TINGLEY, A. J., PH.D., Mathematics
UHLMAN, H. J., M.A., M.ED., PH.D., Education
VINING, L. C., PH.D., F.R.S.C., Biology
VARMA, D. P., M.A., PH.D., D.LITT., English
WAITE, P. B., M.A., PH.D., F.R.S.(C.), History
WANGERSKY, P. J., SC.B., PH.D., Chemistry
WEBSTER, J. B., PH.D., History
WINHAM, G. R., Political Science
YOON, M., Psychology

Faculty of Law:

BALOGH, L. V., B.A., LL.B.
BISSETT-JOHNSON, LL.M.
CHRISTIE, I. M., B.A., LL.M.
DARBY, P. E., B.A., LL.B.
FOOTE, A. L., LL.B., B.C.L., LL.M.
HARRIS, E. C., B.COM., LL.M., R.I.A., C.A.
HUTCHINS, C., LL.B.
JOHNSTON, D. M., M.A., M.C.L., LL.M., J.S.D.
MACDONALD, R. St. J., Q.C., B.A., LL.M.
MACKAY, W. A., Q.C., B.A., LL.M.
MEAGHER, A. J., Q.C., B.A., LL.B.
MURRAY, R. G., Q.C., B.A., LL.M.
O'BRIEN, H. L., B.COM., LL.B., LL.M.
RENDALL, J. A., LL.M.
SAMEK, R. A., LL.B., M.A., M.LITT., M.COMM.
TOMBLIN, W. A., LL.B.
YOGIS, J. A. L., B.A., LL.B., LL.M.

Faculty of Medicine:

ALDOUS, J. G., M.A., PH.D., Pharmacology
ANDERSON, R. N., M.D., C.M., F.R.C.P.(C.), F.A.C.S., Medicine
ATERMAN, K., M.D., M.B., CH.B., M.R.C.P., PH.D., D.SC., Pathology
BAILEY, L. E., PH.D., Pharmacology
BETHUNE, G. W., M.D., C.M., F.R.C.S.(C.), Clinical Surgery
BLECHER, S. R., M.B., CH.B., B.SC., Anatomy
BROWN, B. ST. J., M.B., F.R.C.P.(C.), Radiology
CHAPMAN, D. M., M.SC., PH.D., Anatomy
COLLINS, J. A., M.D., F.A.C.S., F.R.C.S.(C.), Obstetrics and Gynaecology
COOPER, J. H., M.B., CH.B., F.R.C.P.(C.), Pathology
DAVIS, G. E., M.D., C.M., Radiology
DOANE, B. K., M.A., PH.D., M.D., F.R.C.P.(C.), Psychiatry
DRESEL, P. E., B.S., PH.D., Pharmacology
EASTERBROOK, K. B., PH.D., Microbiology
EMBIL, J. A., M.S., PH.D., Microbiology
GHOSE, T., M.B.B.S., PH.D., Pathology
GOLDBLOOM, R. B., M.D., C.M., F.R.C.P.(C.), Paediatrics
GORDON, P. C., B.SC., M.D., C.M., D.P.H., C.R.C.P.(C.), F.A.P.H.A., Preventive Medicine
GRANTMYRE, E. B., M.D., C.M., F.R.C.P.(C), Radiology
GWYN, D. G., M.B., B.S., PH.D., Anatomy
HATCHER, J. D., M.D., PH.D., Physiology
HELLEINER, C. W., B.A., PH.D., Biochemistry
HENNEN, B. K. E., M.D., C.C.F.P., Family Medicine
HIRSCH, S., B.SC., M.D., C.M., F.R.C.P.(C.), Psychiatry
HUESTIS, W. S., M.D., C.M., F.R.C.S.(C.).
IRWIN, A. C., M.D., D.P.H., D.S.M., Preventive Medicine
ISSEKUTZ, B., M.D., DR.MED., Physiology & Biophysics
JANIGAN, D. T., B.SC., M.D., C.M., Pathology
JONES, R. O., B.SC., M.D., C.M., F.A.P.A., F.R.C.P.(C.), Psychiatry
JOSENHANS, W., M.D., Physiology
KIND, L. S., PH.D., Microbiology
KLASSEN, G. A., M.D., F.R.C.P.(C), F.A.C.C., Physiology and Biophysics
LANDRIGAN, P. L., B.A., M.D., C.M., F.R.C.P.(C), Medicine
LANGLEY, G. R., M.D., C.M., F.R.C.P.(C.), F.A.C.P., Medicine
LEIGHTON, A. H., M.A., M.D., Psychiatry and Preventive Medicine
MACAULAY, M. A., M.D., F.R.C.P.(C), Pathology
MACDONALD, H. N. A., M.D., C.M. F.R.C.P.(C), Medicine
MACDONALD, R. M., B.S.A., M.B., CH.B., F.R.C.P.(C.), Medicine
MACK, F. G., M.D., C.M., F.R.C.S.(C.), Urology
MANCHESTER, J. S., M.D., C.M., Radiology
MOFFITT, E. A., M.D., C.M., F.R.C.P.(C.), Anaesthesia
MURRAY, T. J., M.D., F.R.C.P.(C), Medicine
NICHOLSON, J. F., M.D., C.M., F.R.C.P.(C.), Psychiatry
NOVOTNY, G. M., M.D., F.R.C.S.(C), Otolaryngology

OZERE, R. L., B.SC., M.D., Paediatrics, Medicine and Microbiology
PATRICK, S. J., PH.D., Biochemistry
PEDDLE, L. T., M.D., F.R.C.S.(C.), Obstetrics and Gynaecology
PURKIS, I. E., M.B., B.S., F.R.C.P.(C.), Anaesthesia
RAUTAHARJU, P. M., M.D., PH.D., Physiology and Biophysics
REYNOLDS, A. K., M.SC., PH.D., Pharmacology
RICHMAN, A., M.D., Preventive Medicine
ROBINSON, S. C., M.D., Obstetrics and Gynaecology
ROSEN, R., B.S., M.A., PH.D., Physiology and Biophysics
ROY, D. L., M.D., C.M., F.R.C.P.(C.), Paediatrics
ROZEE, K. R., M.SC., PH.D., Microbiology
RUBINSTEIN, D., Biochemistry
RUDERMAN, A. P., M.A., PH.D., M.B.A., Preventive Medicine
RUSSELL, D. W., PH.D., D.SC., Biochemistry
SHEARS, A. H., M.D., C.M., F.R.C.P.(C), Medicine
SIDOROV, J. J., M.D., F.R.C.P.(C), Medicine
SPENCE, M. W., M.D., PH.D., Paediatrics
STANDEN, J. R., M.D., F.R.C.P.(C.), Radiology
STEEVES, L. C., B.A., M.D., C.M., F.R.C.P.(C.), F.A.C.P., LL.D., Medicine
STEVENSON, W. D., M.D., C.M., F.R.C.S.(C.), Neurosurgery
SZERB, J. C., M.D., Physiology and Biophysics
TUPPER, W. R. C., B.SC., M.D., C.M., F.A.C.S., F.I.C.S., Obstetrics and Gynaecology
WAINWRIGHT, S. D., PH.D., Biochemistry Research
WOODBURY, J. F. L., M.D., F.R.C.P.(C.), Medicine

Faculty of Dentistry:
BENNETT, I. C., D.D.S., M.SC.
BINGHAM, R. H., D.D.S., F.I.C.D., Oral Diagnosis
CHAYTOR, D. V., D.D.S., M.SC., Prosthodontics
CHRISTIE, P. S., D.D.S., F.I.C.D., Orthodontics
JONES, D. W., PH.D., Dental Materials Science
LILIENTHAL, B., D.D.SC., D.PHIL., Oral Biology
LOVELY, F. W., D.D.S., M.S., F.R.C.D.(C.), Oral Surgery
LUBETSKY, I. K., D.D.S., Oral Surgery
MACCONNACHIE, H. I., M.S.D., D.D.S., Operative Dentistry
MCLEAN, J. D., D.D.S., F.I.C.D., F.A.C.D., Dentistry
PENTZ, D. G., D.D.S., Periodontics
ROGER, A. T., M.B.E., C.D., D.D.S., Dentistry and Clinic Director

Faculty of Health Professions:
College of Pharmacy:
DUFF, J. G., M.SC., PH.D.
JAMES, K. M., M.SC., PH.D.
MEZEI, M., PH.D.
TONKS, R. S., PH.D., F.P.S., F.I.BIOL.
YUNG, D. K., M.SC., PH.D.
School of Physical Education:
MALONEY, T. L. (Director)
YOUNG, A. J., M.A., PH.D.
School of Nursing:
BRADLEY, M. (Director)
School of Physiotherapy:
EGAN, D., M.SC. (Director)
School of Human Communication Disorders:
MENCHER, G. T., M.A., PH.D.
WEBSTER, L. M., M.S., PH.D. (Director)

Faculty of Administrative Studies:
Maritime School of Social Work:
CHELLAM, G., M.A., M.S.W., D.S.W.
CRAIG, R. A., M.S.W.
CUMMINGS, J., M.S.W., D.S.W.
GIFFORD, C. G., M.S.W., (Director).
O'BRIEN, D., D.S.W.
School of Business Administration:
BROOKBANK, C. R., M.A.
CHESLEY, G. R., M.A., PH.D.
DIPCHAND, C. R., M.B.A., PH.D.
GEORGE, R. E., M.A., PH.D.
MARTIN, M. J. C., PH.D.
PARKER, J. E., M.B.A., C.PHIL., C.A.
SCHANDL, C. W., Doctor Juris
SCHEIBELHUT, J. H., M.B.A., D.B.A. (Director).
STOREY, R. G., M.B.A., PH.D.
School of Library Service:
HORROCKS, N., M.L.S., PH.D., F.L.A., A.L.A.A. (Director).
School of Public Administration:
AUCOIN, P., M.A., PH.D.
CAMERON, D. M., M.A., PHIL.M., PH.D.
KIRBY, M. J. L., M.A., PH.D.
PROSS, A. P., M.A., PH.D.

COLLÈGE DOMINICAIN DE PHILOSOPHIE ET DE THÉOLOGIE

96 EMPRESS AVE., OTTAWA, ONT. K1R 7G2
Telephone: 233-5696.

Founded 1909 as 'Studium Generale' of Order of Friars Preachers in Canada; present name 1967.

Chancellor: Most Rev. J. M. GAY.
President and Regent of Studies: G. D. MAILHIOT.
Vice-President and Vice-Regent of Studies: G.-A. VILLEMURE.
Master of Studies and Registrar: A. GAUTHIER.
Secretary-Treasurer: T. R. POTVIN.
Librarian: Y. CAILHIER.

Library of 85,000 vols., 350 periodicals.
Number of teachers: 34.
Number of students: 122 full-time, 603 part-time.

DEANS:

Institute of Pastoral Theology: J.-C. BRETON.
Faculty of Theology: M. GOURGUES.
Department of Philosophy: J. LAVOIE.

UNIVERSITY OF GUELPH

GUELPH, ONTARIO N1G 2W1
Telephone: (519) 824-4120.

Founded 1964 from Ontario Agricultural College, Ontario Veterinary College and Macdonald Institute, formerly affiliated to the University of Toronto.

Private control; Academic year: September to following July (three semesters).

Language of instruction: English.

Chancellor: The Hon. PAULINE M. MCGIBBON, LL.D., D.U., B.A.A.
Vice-Chancellor and President: D. F. FORSTER, A.M.
Vice-President (Academic): H. C. CLARK, M.SC., PH.D., SC.D.
Vice-President (Administration): C. C. FERGUSON, M.A.
Registrar: A. G. HOLMES, B.S.A.
Librarian: MARGARET BECKMAN, B.A., M.L.S.

Library of over 1 million vols.
Number of teachers: 850.
Number of students: 10,000.
Publications: *Graduate Calendar*†, *Undergraduate Calendar*†, *Annual Report*†.

DEANS:

Ontario Agricultural College: C. M. SWITZER, M.S.A., PH.D.
Ontario Veterinary College: D. C. MAPLESDEN, PH.D.
College of Biological Science: K. RONALD, M.SC., PH.D., F.I.BIOL.
College of Family and Consumer Studies: J. M. WARDLAW, M.S., PH.D.
College of Arts: (vacant).
College of Social Science: (vacant).
College of Physical Science: E. B. MACNAUGHTON, M.A., PH.D.
Faculty of Graduate Studies: (vacant).
Office of Research: W. E. TOSSELL, M.S.A., PH.D.

PROFESSORS AND DIRECTORS OF DEPARTMENTS AND SCHOOLS:

ANDERSEN, M., PH.D., Languages
BARHAM, R. M., M.A., PH.D., Family Studies
BARKER, W. G., M.SC., PH.D., Botany and Genetics
BEAMISH, F. W. H., PH.D., Zoology
BLOOMFIELD, B. A., PH.D., Geography
BROOKE, J. D., D.L.C., M.SC., PH.D., Dir. School of Human Biology
DALRYMPLE-ALFORD, E. C., PH.D., Psychology
DEMAN, J. M., CHEM.ENG., PH.D., Food Science
DERBYSHIRE, J. B., PH.D., M.R.C.V.S., Veterinary Microbiology and Immunology
DRAPER, H. H., M.SC., PH.D., Nutrition
DUNCAN, K. J., M.A., Sociology, Anthropology
DWIVEDI, O. P., PH.D., Political Studies
JANZEN, E. G., M.SC., PH.D., Chemistry
JORDAN, D. C., M.S.A., PH.D., Microbiology
KILLAM, G. D., PH.D., English Language and Literature
KING, K. M., M.S., PH.D., Land Resource Science
LINDERS, J. G., M.A.SC., D.I.C., PH.D. Computing and Information Science
MACDONALD, J. R., PH.D., Physics
MAN, C., M.L.A., Landscape Architecture
MCEWEN, F. L., M.SC., PH.D., Environmental Biology
MENZIE, E. L., M.S.A., PH.D., Agricultural Economics
MORRISON, W. D., M.SC., PH.D., Animal and Poultry Science
NONNECKE, I. L., M.SC., PH.D., Horticultural Science
OGILVIE, J. R., M.S.A., PH.D., Engineering

POWERS, T. F., PH.D., School of Hotel and Food Administration
SALMON, E., B.A., Drama
SMITH, W. R., PH.D., Mathematics and Statistics
STRAKA, W. W., M.A., PH.D., History
TANNER, J. W., M.S.A., PH.D., Crop Science
TODD, G. F., M.A., PH.D., Philosophy
TRITSCHLER, T. C., J.D., M.A., PH.D., Fine Art
USBORNE, W. R., PH.D., Food Science
VALLI, V. E., D.V.M., PH.D., Pathology
VANDERKAMP, J., B.EC.SC., M.B.A., PH.D., Economics
VOSBURGH, R. E., M.B.A., D.B.A., Consumer Studies
WILSON, M. R., PH.D., M.R.C.V.S., Clinical Studies

UNIVERSITY OF KING'S COLLEGE

HALIFAX, NOVA SCOTIA
B3H 2A1

Telephone: (902) 422-1271.

Founded 1789 by United Empire Loyalists; granted Royal Charter 1802; entered into association with Dalhousie University 1923.

Language of instruction: English; Academic year: September to May.

Chancellor: Hon. Mr. Justice R. A. RITCHIE, Q.C., D.C.L., LL.D.

President and Vice-Chancellor: J. F. GODFREY, D.PHIL.

Vice-President: H. S. GRANTER, A.M.

Registrar: H. ROPER, M.A., PH.D.

Bursar: D. FRY.

Librarian: Mrs. J. E. LANE, B.A.

Number of professors: 12.

Number of students: 380.

Publication: *Calendar* (annual).

PROFESSORS:

ATHERTON, J. P., M.A., PH.D., Classics
BAIN, G. C. S., Dir., School of Journalism
CROUSE, R. D., PH.D., Classics
DAWSON, R. MACG., M.A., B.LITT., English
GODFREY, J. F., D.PHIL., History
GRANTER, H. S., A.M., History
HANKEY, W. J., M.A., Classics
MEESE, H. E., B.A., Journalism
OANCIA, D., Director, School of Journalism
PAGE, F. H., M.A., D.D., Philosophy
STARNES, C. J., S.T.B., M.A., PH.D., Director Foundation Year Programme
STEFFEN, D., PH.D., German

LAKEHEAD UNIVERSITY

OLIVER RD., THUNDER BAY "P", ONTARIO P7B 5E1

Telephone: 345-2121.

Founded 1965; previously established as Lakehead College of Arts, Science and Technology, 1956, and Lakehead Technical Institute, 1946.

Academic year: September to April; Spring and Summer sessions.

Chancellor: ROBERT JAMES PRETTIE, D.COM.

Vice-Chancellor and President: GEORGE A. HARROWER, M.SC., PH.D.

Secretary: D. E. AYRE, B.A.

Registrar: P. A. PAULARINNE, B.A.

Number of teachers: 250.

Number of students: 2,887 full-time, 2,900 part-time.

DEANS:

Faculty of Arts: ERNEST R. ZIMMERMANN, PH.D.

Faculty of Science: J. S. MOTHERSILL, PH.D.

Dean of University Schools: ROBERT G. ROSEHART, M.A.SC., PH.D., P.ENG.

Faculty of Education: J. J. STAPLETON, M.T.S., M.A., PH.D.

PROFESSORS:

ANGUS, J. T., M.ED., PH.D., Education
ARTHUR, M. E., M.A., PH.D., History
BARCLAY-ESTRUP, P., PH.D., Biology
BLAIR, J. H., R.P.F., Forestry
CHARLES, K. J., M.A., PH.D., Economics
CLARK, S. D., O.C., M.A., PH.D., F.R.S.C., Sociology
CROWE, W. R., M.A., PH.D., A.C.I.S., A.I.S., Business Administration
DAWSON, K. C., C.D.M.A., Anthropology
DAY, R. J., M.A., M.SC.F., R.P.F., Forestry
EAGER, E. L., M.A., PH.D., Political Studies
EAMES, W., M.SC., PH.D., Mathematics
ENGHOLM, G. F., PH.D., Political Science
FLEMING, G. R., M.SC., PH.D., P.ENG., Engineering
FREITAG, R., M.SC., PH.D., Biology
FRENCH, C. L., PH.D., Sociology
FROOD, D. G., PH.D., Physics
GINSBERG, N., PH.D., Psychology
GRIFFITH, J. S., PH.D., Mathematics
HANLEY, W. J., M.COMM., M.A., Business Administration
HART, J., PH.D., Physics
HEARNDEN, K. W., R.P.F., Forestry
HOLAH, D. G., PH.D., Chemistry
HOODLESS, I. M., PH.D., Chemistry
HUGHES, A. N., PH.D., Chemistry
ISHAK, F. M., PH.D., English
JECCHINIS, C., PH.D., Economics
KENT, C. F., PH.D., Mathematics
LINDSAY, D. R., M.S., Biology
LOCKER, J. G., M.SC., PH.D., P.ENG., Engineering
MANOLI, S. H., PH.D., Engineering
MCLEOD, H. N., M.A., PH.D., Psychology
MELNYK, W. T., M.A., PH.D., Psychology
MERCY, E. L. P., PH.D., Geology
MERRILL, G. J., PH.D., English
MILLER, T. B., PH.D., History
MOMOT, W. T., M.S., PH.D., Biology
MOTHERSILL, J. S., PH.D., Geology
MORRIS, W. S., PH.D., Philosophy
NAIMPALLY, S. A., M.A., PH.D., Mathematics
NAVRATIL, S., M.SC.F., PH.D., Forestry
OZBURN, G. W., PH.D., D.I.C., Biology
PAGE, M. R., C.D., M.PUB.H., REG.N., Nursing
PARANJAPE, V. V., M.SC., PH.D., Physics
PATTERSON, M., M.SC., PH.D., P.ENG., Engineering
PETRONE, S. P., A.T.C.M., PH.D., Education
RIDEOUT, J. G., M.S., PH.D., English
ROBINSON, F. J., M.PHIL., P.ENG., Engineering
RODDY, D., M.SC., P.ENG., Engineering
ROSEHART, R. G., M.A.SC., PH.D., P.ENG., Engineering
ROSS, R. A., PH.D., D.SC., Chemistry
RUSHALL, B. S., D.P.E.MS., PH.D., Physical Education
SATINDER, K. P., M.A., PH.D., Psychology
TAYLOR, I. A., M.A., PH.D., Psychology
WALKER, S., D.SC., D.PHIL., Chemistry
WARREN, J., M.SC., PH.D., Physics
WEIR, N. A., PH.D., Chemistry
WIDDOP, J. H., M.A., PH.D., Physical Education
ZAWADOWSKI, L., M.A., PH.D., Languages

LAURENTIAN UNIVERSITY OF SUDBURY

RAMSEY LAKE ROAD, SUDBURY, ONTARIO P3E 2C6

Telephone: (705) 675-1151.

Founded 1960.

Provincially-assisted, non-denominational; Academic year: mid-September to early May; Intersession, mid-April to end of June; Summer session, early July to mid-August.

Teaching is in French and English, certain departments offering parallel courses in both languages.

President: HENRY B. M. BEST, M.A., D.PH.

Vice-President (Administration): T. L. HENNESSY, B.A.SC.

Vice-President (Academic): F. J. TURNER, D.S.W.

Registrar: J. M. PORTER, M.ED.

Librarian: A. H. MROZEWSKI, M.A., M.L.S.

Director, Centre for Continuing Education: G. J. LAFRENIÈRE, B.A., L.PH.

Number of teachers: 274.

Number of students: 2,291 full-time, 2,163 part-time winter session.

Publications: *Laurentian Journal*†, *Laurentian University Review*, *Laurentian University Calendar*†, *Laurentian Gazette*†, *Graduate Studies Calendar*†, *Guide to Laurentian*†.

DEANS:

Humanities: (vacant).

Social Sciences: K. W. SCHWAGER, DRS. SOC.

Science: D. H. WILLIAMSON, PH.D.

Professional Schools: D. J. HILLDRUP, M.SC., M.B.A.

CHAIRMEN OF DEPARTMENTS:

Biology: F. V. CLULOW, M.SC., PH.D.
Canadian Studies: R. DYCK, PH.D.
Classics: E. B. HEAVEN, M.A., L.TH., S.T.B.
Commerce and Administration: D. J. HILLDRUP, M.SC., M.B.A.
Chemistry: D. GOLDSACK, PH.D.
Economics: W. R. COOK, M.A., PH.D.
Education: R. LALLIER, M.ED.
Engineering: F. J. TURNER, D.S.W.
English: D. G. WALLACE, M.A.
Folklore: G. LEMIEUX, S.J., M.A., PH.D.
French: P. SABOURIN, D.U.
Geography: J. P. MARTIN, L. ÈS L.
Geology: R. S. JAMES, PH.D.
History: A. D. GILBERT, M.A., PH.D.
Law: A. W. CRAGG, M.A., D.PHIL.
Mathematics: J. L. DAVISON, PH.D.
Modern Languages: E. GORKY, M.A.
Music: D. WEBB, PH.D., L. J. WINCKEL, D.TH.
Native Studies: T. ALCOZE, M.SC.

Nursing: W. Gerhard, M.SC.N.
Philosophy: V. di Norcia, M.A., PH.D.
Physical Education: R. R. Wallingford, ED.D.
Physics and Astronomy: G. A. Rubin, DR.RER.NAT.
Political Science: E. E. Mahant, M.A., PH.D.
Psychology: M. Moroz, M.A., PH.D.
Religious Studies: L. Winckel, D.TH., M.A., PH.D.
Social Work: J. Lévesque, M.S.W., PH.D.
Sociology: A. Barnett, M.S., PH.D.
Sports Administration: R. S. Wanzel, M.A., PH.D.
School of Translators and Interpreters: A. F. M. Arbuckle, L. ÈS L., D.E.S.
School of Graduate Studies: E. Wright, PH.D.

Federated Universities:

University of Sudbury: Ramsey Lake Road, Sudbury, Ontario (conducted by the Jesuit Fathers); f. 1913.
President: L. Michaud, S.J., B.A., B.PH., ED.D.

Huntington University: Ramsey Lake Road, Sudbury, Ontario (related to United Church of Canada); f. 1960.
President: L. J. Winckel, B.A., TH.M., D.TH.
Registrar: D. Joblin, B.A., B.D.

Thorneloe University: Ramsey Lake Road, Sudbury, Ontario.
Chancellor: Rt. Rev. F. F. Nock, B.A.
Provost and Vice-Chancellor: Rev. E. Heaven, L.TH., S.T.B., M.A.
Registrar: A. McGregor, M.A.

Algoma College: Shingwauk Hall, Sault Ste. Marie, Ontario.
Chairman, Board of Trustees: D. G. Howell, PH.D., M.R.C.V.S.
Dean: R. G. Ewing, M.A., PH.D.
Registrar: R. McCutcheon, M.A.

Collège de Hearst: Hearst, Ontario; f. 1952.
Director: R. Bernard, M.A.
Registrar: D. Coulombe, B.A.

Nipissing College: Gormanville Rd., North Bay, Ontario.
President: G. Zytaruk, B.ED., M.A., PH.D.
Registrar: D. L. Lawrence, B.MATH., B.ED.

University College: Sudbury.
Principal and Registrar: R. M. Bray, M.A., PH.D.

UNIVERSITÉ LAVAL

CITÉ UNIVERSITAIRE,
QUEBEC, QUE. G1K 7P4
Telephone: (418) 656-2131.

Founded 1852; Royal Charter signed December 1852, Pontifical Charter 1876. Provincial Charter 1970.

Language of instruction: French; Academic year: September to January, January to May, May to September.

Rector: J. G. Paquet, D.SC.
Vice-Rectors: A. Dufour, LL.D. (Executive); L. Trotier, L. ÈS L. (Staff and Students); J. Desautels, B.PH., L. ÈS L., D.U. (Teaching and Research); F. Gingras, B.PHIL., L.TH. (Administration).
Secretary-General: L.-M. Babineau, D.SC.
Director of Graduate Studies: C. St.-Pierre, D.SC.
Director of Undergraduate Curriculums: B. Dumais, M.SC.COM.
Director of Extension Division: A. Bouchard, PH.D.
Director of Permanent Education: N. Le Blanc, O.C., B.SC.AGR., M.SC.SOC.
Registrar: M. Boucher, B.SC.
Director of Public Relations: A. Barnard, B.SC.APP.
Librarian: Celine Cartier, M.ADM.P., M.L.S.

Library: *see* Libraries.

Number of teachers: 1,582 full-time, 1,150 part-time.

Number of students: 16,902 full-time, 6,642 part-time.

Publications: *Université Laval—Rapport* (annually), *Laval Théologique et Philosophique* (2 a year), *La Vie Médicale* (monthly), *Les cahiers de droit* (student editors), *Études littéraires* (3 a year), *Relations industrielles—Industrial Relations* (quarterly), *Service Social* (3 a year), *Recherches sociographiques* (3 a year), *Les Archives de Folklore* (2 a year), *Annuaire général, Renseignements généraux, Aide financière, Annuaires des facultés*, various course programmes (annually).

Deans and Directors:

Faculty of Theology: P. Gaudette, D.TH.
Faculty of Agriculture and Food Sciences: G. B. Martin, D.SC.
Faculty of Arts: J. C. Blouin, B.PH., L. ÈS L., L.TH.
Faculty of Administrative and Commercial Sciences: C. Lebon, M.COM., PH.D.
Faculty of Education: H. Saint-Pierre, L.PH., D.PSY.
Faculty of Forestry and Geodesy: B. Bernier, PH.D.
Faculty of Law: C. Belleau.
Faculty of Letters: L. Laforge.
Faculty of Medicine: J. Rochon, PH.D.
Faculty of Philosophy: R. Plante, D.PH.
Faculty of Sciences and Engineering: L. Huot, L.SC.A., D.SC.
Faculty of Social Sciences: A. Beaudoin, PH.D.
School of Architecture: J. Baker. B.A.(ARCH.).
School of Graduate Studies: C. St.-Pierre, D.SC. (Director).
School of Dentistry: R. Vallee, D.D.S. (Director).
School of Fine Arts: B. Jasmin, D.PH. (Director).
School of Music: A. Bouchard, L.TH. (Director).
School of Nursing: T. Fortier, M.NURS. (Director).
School of Pharmacy: J. Dumas, D.PHARM. (Director).
School of Rehabilitation: P. Turcotte, M.SC.
School of Psychology: F.-X. Desrosiers, D.SC. (Director).
School of Social Work: M. Laforest, M.SERV.SOC., D.TH. (Director).

Professors:

Faculty of Theology:
Beaucamp, E., D.TH.
Beaudet, R., B.PH., L.TH.
Beaumont, H., D.D.C., B.PH., L.TH.
Gagné, H., M.S.L., M.A., L.TH.
Gaudette, P., L.PH., D.TH.
Gervais, M., L.TH., L.PH.
Lacouline, P., D.TH., L.E.S., Bible Languages
Langevin, G., L.PH., L.TH.
Langevin, P.-E., M.A., D.TH.
Mathieu, A., D.TH., Dogmatic Theology
Mathieu, J.-P., L.TH.
Page, J.-G., D.TH.
Petit, Mgr. G., D.D.C., Canonical Institutions
Richard, J., D.TH.
Roberge, M., D.TH.
Robitaille, L., D.TH.
Roy, Y., D.TH., L.PH.
Vachon, Mgr. L.-A., D.TH., D.PH., Dogmatic Theology

Faculty of Agriculture and Food Sciences:
Alarie, A., PH.D., Soil Bacteriology
Baril, R., M.SC., Soil Morphology
Bédard, R., PH.D., M.SC.
Belzile, R. R., PH.D., Animal Nutrition
Bouchard, A., PH.D., Agronomy
Boulet, M., PH.D., Science of Foodstuffs
Bourbeau, G. A., PH.D.
Brisson, G., M.SC., PH.D., Animal Nutrition
Carel, M., ING.AGR., D.SC.ECON., Rural Economy
Cescas, M. P., PH.D., Zootechnics
Charette, L., PH.D., Zootechnics
Chartier, Y., B.SC.AGR., Rural Engineering
Chevrette, J.-E., PH.D., Improvement of Plants
Choiniere, J.-A., M.SC., Rural Engineering
Dumais, B., B.SC.AGR., M.SC.COMM., Rural Economics
Gervais, P., M.SC., PH.D., Large Scale Farming
Julien, J.-P., M.SC., Sciences of Foodstuffs
Lachance, Robert, PH.D., Agrobiology
Lavoie, V., D.SC., M.SC.
Lemay, J.-P., D.SC., Zootechnics
Martin, G. B., D.SC., Food Science
O'Grady, L.-J., PH.D., Pedology
Ola'h, G. M., D.SC.
Pare, J.-P., PH.D., Agrobiology
Pauze, F. J., PH.D., Agrobiology
Saint-Hilaire, F., PH.D., Dietetics
Saint-Laurent, G., PH.D., Agriculture
Sevigny, Sister J., PH.D., Nutrition
St-Louis, R., PH.D., Rural Economics
Therrien, H. P., M.SC., D.SC.
Trudel, M.-J., PH.D.
Wampach, J.-P., PH.D., Agriculture

Faculty of Arts:

BEDARD, Y., B.A.
BLOUIN, J.-C., L. ès. L., L.TH.
FICHER, F., Visual Arts
FORTIER, Mgr. E., B.TH., Music
JEAN, M., Visual Arts
LABERGE, P.-A., L. ès L., Greek Literature
LAFRENIÈRE, Mgr. A., L.T., French Literature
LALLIER, H., L. ès L., M.A., Education of Adults
LAMARRE, P.-H., L.LITT, Latin Institutions
LAUZON, Mgr. M., L.TH., L.PED., L.SC.SOC., Scholar Demography
PARENT, C. E., L. ès L., L.PH., Literature

Faculty of Administrative Sciences:

BÉLANGER, F., M.SC.COMM., Management
BELLEHUMEUR, A., D.SC.EC., Administration
BRAULT, R., M.SC.COM., M.SC.COMM.
BROWN, A., L. ès SC., M.A., Mathematics
D'AMBOISE, G., PH.D., C.A., Administration
DUGRE, R., M.B.A., Finance
GAGNON, J. M., M.B.A., PH.D., Finance
HARDY, S., D.SC.COM., Advanced Accountancy
HOULE, A., L.SC.COM., PH.D., Statistics
KHOURY, N., M.A., Economic Politics
LABRECQUE, G., M.A., Economic Politics
LEBON, C., M.COMM., PH.D.
MARTEL, J.-M., D.SC.ECON.
MCGOLDRICK, R., M.SC., Marketing
PELLETIER, C., M.SC.COM., M.SC.COMM.
PETROF, J. V., M.SC., PH.D., Administration,
RASSI, F., D.SC.ECON., Administration
ROBERGE, M., L ès L., M.A., Economics
ROLAND, E., LL.D., Industrial Relations
ST.-PIERRE, J., M.SC.COM., D.SC.ECON.
SYLVAIN, F., B.SC.COM., M.B.A., Accounting
TARDIF, G., M.A.
THOMASSIN, R., M.A., M.SC.COM.
TREMBLAY, D., M.SC.COM., M.SC.COMM., PH.D.
VEZINA, P., M.SC., D.SC.,ECON. Administration
WAYLAND, D.-G., M.SC.COM., PH.D.
YACCARINI, B., LL.L., M.SC.SOC., Administration

Faculty of Education:

BABY, A., L.OR., D.SOC.
BARBEAU, M., LL.L., L.PED., Didactics
BARRETTE, ABBÉ G., Mathematics
BELANGER, J.-D., M.SOC., B.PED.
BELANGER, P.-W., M.A.
BHUSHAN, V., M.SC., M.ED., D.SC.ED.
BOUCHARD, C., M.SC., Physical Education
BRUNELLE, J., D.ED.PHYS., Physical Education
DROLET, J.-Y., L.PED., PH.D., School Administration
DUBE, L., L.BPH., B.TH., L.ÈS L., Education
DUVAL, R., L.ORIENT., Counselling
GAULIN, C., B.SC.APP., B.PH., M.SC.
GODBOUT, P., PH.D., Physical Education
HAMELIN, J. M., L.TH., L.PH., Psychology
HARVEY, V., PH.D., School Administration
JASMIN, B., L.PH., Education
LACHANCE, B., L.PH., D.PSYCH., Psychopedagogy
LACHANCE, J.-M., L.PH., L.TH., L.PSYCH., Education
LANDRY, F., M.SC., PH.D., Physical Education
LANGEVIN, C., L.PÉD., L.SC.ED., Education
L'ARCHEVEQUE, P., M.A., D.PED., Docimology
LEDUC, A., L.PH., L.PSYCH., M.A., Education
LEMAY, F., Mathematics
LESSARD, J.-C., L.PSYCH., D.PH., Psychology of Maladjusted Children
MARANDA, A., L.TH., L.DR., D.PH., Psychology
MARTON, P., D.PÉD., Education
MIVILLE, R., L.PH., Psychology
MOHANNA, M., L. ès L.
MORENCY, C., PH.D., Education
RICHARD, B., D.PSYCH., Education
RICHARD, H., L.DR., D.PSYCH., Psychology
ROBERT, B., M.A., Education
ROBERT, M., L.PED., PH.D.
SCALLON, G., PH.D., Education
SLATER, E., L.DR., Vocational Guidance

Faculty of Forestry and Geodesy:

BELANGER, J., D.SC., Statistics
BELLEFEUILLE, R., I.F., L.SC., Dendrometry
BERNIER, B., PH.D., Forest Pedology
BRANDENBERGER, A.-J., M.SC., D.SC., **Photogrammetry**
FORTIN, J.-A., D.SC., Ecology and Pedology
FRECHETTE, A., M.SC.FOR., D. ès SC., Geodetic Science
GOSSELIN, R., I.F., PH.D., Mathematics
GOULET, M., D.SC., Wood Technology
GRANDTNER, M., M.SC.F., D.SC.A., Botany
HEROUX, R., B.GEOG., L. ès L., 3E. CYCLE, Geography
JONCAS, L., C.E., B.SC.APP., Geodesy
LA CHANCE, P., B.PH., B.ARP.
LA DOUCEUR, G., D.SC., Photogrammety
LAFLAMME, Y., D.SC., Chemistry
LAFOND, A., PH.D., Ecology
LANGEVIN, R., ARP., I.F., Forest Exploitation
MALDAGUE, M., D.SC., Zoology
NAUD, R., M.A., Forest Management
PARROT, L., M.SC., D.ING., Forestry
POLIQUIN, J., M.SC., D.SC.TECH.
RICHARD, A., M.SC., PH.D., Podology
SANCHEZ, R., DIPL.ING., Forestry
ST.-ARNAUD, R., D.SC., Cartography
SASSEVILLE, G., B.SC.APP., Surveying and Cartography
VEZINA, P.-E., D.SC., Forestry

Faculty of Law:

BELLEAU, C., LL.D.
BERNIER, Y., LL.D., PH.D.
BINETTE, S., LL.D.
BRUN, H., LL.D., L. ès L., Public Law
CAPARROS, E., LL.D.
GARANT, P., L. ès L., LL.D.
GOULET, J., LL.D.
GIGUERE, M., LL.D., Commercial Law
HUDON, E.-G., LL.D.
L'HEUREUX, N., LL.D.
OUELLET, R.-L., LL.D., M.SC.COM.
REID, H., LL.L., D.E.S., Civil Procedure
TANCELIN, M., LL.D.
VERGE, P., M.A., LL.D.

Faculty of Letters:

ALVAREZ, G. H., M.A., D. 3E. CYCLE, Languages and Linguistics
BEAULIEU, B., D.ÈS.L., Literature
BELANGER, M., B.PH., L. ès L., Geography
BERGERON, C., PH.D., History
BERNIER, J., L. ès L., Ancient History
BERTHIAUME, A., B.PED., M.A., D. 3E CYCLE, Literature
BLAIS, J., D. ès L., Literature
BOURNEUF, R., D. ès L., Education
CESTRE, G., D. ès L., Literature
CLIBBON, P., M.A., D. ès L., Geography
DENIS, P.-Y., M.A., D.PHIL. & L., Geography
DESAUTELS, J., L. ès L., D.U., Literature
DES GAGNIERS, J., L.PH., Ancient Studies
DOAT, J., Theatre
DORION, H., LL.D., M.A., Geography
DULONG, G., L. ès L., Linguistics
DUPONT, J.-C., D. ès L., History
FRANCOEUR, L., B.TH., M.A., Literature
GAGNE, M., D. ès L., Literature
GALARNEAU, C., L. ès L., Modern History
GENDRON, J.-D., L. ès L., Phonetics
GIROUX, H., D. 3E CYCLE, History
GREIF, H.-J., D. ès L., Literature
GRENIER, F., L. ès L., D.E.S., Geography
HAMELIN, J., L. ès L., History
HAMELIN, L.-E., L.SC.SOC., D.GÉOG. Geography
HIRTLE, W., PH.D., Linguistics
HUFTY, A., L.GÉOG., D.SC., Geography
JARQUE-ANDRES, F., D. ès L., Literature
JAUKSCH-ORLOWSKI, M.A., PH.D., Languages and Linguistics
JENTEL, M. O., D. ès L., D.HIST., History
JOLY, R., L. ès L., D.PHIL., Literature
KONGAS-MARANDA, E., M.PH., PH.D., History
LACOURCIÈRE, L., L. ès L., Folklore
LAFORGE, L., D. ès L., Languages and Linguistics
LAPOINTE, J., L. ès L., French Grammar
LAROCHE, M., L. ès L., Literature
LEBLANC, A., D.U., Literature
LEMIRE, M., L.TH., M.A., D. ès L., Literature
MACKEY, W., M.A., PH.D., English Linguistics
MALONEY, G., L. ès L., Literature
MANIET, A., D. ès L., Philology
MARTINEZ-RISCO, A., D. ès L., Literature
MAURANGES, J.-P., D. 3E. CYCLE, Linguistics
MELANCON, J., L. ès L., L.TH., Literature
MEPHAN, M., D.U., Linguistics
MOISAN, C., L. ès L., D.UNIV., Literature
OUELLET, R., L. ès L., D.UNIV., Literature
PADLEY, G. A., D.UNIV., PH.D., Languages and Linguistics
PAQUETTE, J.-M., D. 3E CYCLE, Literature
POULIN, J.-C., D.HIST., History
REISNER, T.-A., M.A., PH.D., Literure at
RITCHOT, G., M.A., D. 3E CYCLE, Geography
ROBY, Y., L. ès L., PH.D., Languages and Literature
ROCHETTE, C., D. ès L., Languages and Literature
RONDEAU, G., PH.D., Linguistics
ST.-JACQUES, D., L. ès L., Literature
ST.-YVES, M., B.GEOG., L.PED., M.A., Geography
SANFAÇON, R., L ès L., DIPL.S., History
SAVARD, J.-G., L.PÉD., L.ÈS.L., Linguistics
SCHMIDT-MACKEY, I., D. ès L., German Literature
SCHWARTZ, W., M.A., PH.D., Literature
SOLDEVILA-DURANTE, I., D. ès L., Spanish Literature
SYLVAIN, P., B.PED., L. ès SC., L. ès L., Contemporary History
TETU, M., D. ès L., Literature
THERASSE, J., L.PH., L.PHILOL., D. ès L., Literature
TROTIER, L., L. ès L., Geography
VALIN, R., L. ès L., General Linguistics
ZOLTVANY, Y.-F., M.A., PH.D., History

Faculty of Medicine:

ACKERMAN, H.-W., M.D., Microbiology
AWAD, J., M.D., Clinical Surgery
BABINEAU, L. M., B.SC.A., D. ès SC., Biochemistry
BEAUDOIN, J., M.D., Medicine
BELANGER, C., M.D., Medicine
BERGERON, G.-A., M.D., Physiology

BONENFANT, J.-L., M.D., Anatomical Pathology
CAUCHON, R., M.D., Clinical Surgery
CHOUINARD, L., B.SC.A., PH.D., Cytogenetics
COLLET, A. J., M.D., Anatomy
COLONNIER, M., M.SC., M.D., PH.D., Anatomy
COUTURE, J., M.D., Surgery
DINH, B. L., D.SC., Biochemistry
DIONNE, L., M.D., Surgery
DUFOUR, D., M.D., D.SC., Biomedicine
ESTABLE-PUIG, J., M.D., Pathology
FERLAND, J.-J., M.D., Clinical Surgery
FERRERO DE ESTABLE, R., PH.D., Pathology
FORTIER, C., M.D., D.SC., Experimental Physiology
FOURNIER, L., M.D., F.R.C.P.(CAN.), Anaesthesia
FUGERE, P., M.D., Oto-Rhino-Laryngology
GAGNÉ, F., M.D., F.R.C.P., Pathology
GAGNON, PAUL M., M.D., D.SC., Pathology
GARNEAU, R., M.D., Pathological Anatomy
GAUVREAU, L., M.D., Microbiology
GENEST, P., D.V.M., D.SC., Pathological Anatomy
GIRARD, GÉRARD, M.D., D.SC., Anatomy
GOURDEAU, R., M.D., Paediatrics
GRANTHAM, H., M.D., Psychiatry
HOULD, F., M.D.
JEAN, C., M.D., Pathology
LABRIE, F., M.D., B.SC., Physiology
LARUE, A., M.D., Paediatrics
LEBLANC, J., D.SC., Physiology
LEMIEUX, J.-M., M.D., Surgery
LEMONDE, A., D.SC., Biochemistry
LEVASSEUR, L., M.D., Surgery
LOISELLE, J.-M., M.D., D.SC., Biochemistry
LUPIEN, P.-J., M.SC., PH.D., Biochemistry
MOISAN, A., M.SC., M.D., Medicine
MORIN, Y., M.D., Cardiology
MURTHY, M.-R.-V., D.SC., Biochemistry
NICOLE, L., D.SC., Biology
NORMAND, M., D.SC., Physiology
NOSAL, G., D.SC., Pharmacology
PARADIS, B., M.D., Anaesthesia
PELLETIER, G.-H., D.SC., M.D., Physiology
POIRIER, L., M.D., Experimental Neurology
POTVIN, P., M.D., D.SC., Physiology
RADOUCO-THOMAS, C., M.D., Pharmacology
RADOUCO-THOMAS, S., D.SC., Pharmacology
ROUSSEAU, A., M.D., Ophthalmology
ROY, P.-E., M.D., Pathology
SAMSON, E., M.D., Surgery
SAUCIER, G., M.D., Clinical Medicine
SIMARD, R., M.D., Obstetrical Clinic
STERIADE, M., M.D., D.SC., Physiology
WARREN, Y., M.D., Clinical Medicine

Faculty of Philosophy:

BABIN, E., D.PH., Ethics
BLAIS, M., D.PH.
BLANCHET, L.-E., L.TH., D.TH., Philosophy of Mathematics
COTÉ, A., D.PH., Logic
DANEK, J., D.PH.
DE KONINCK, T., M.A., D.PH.
DIONNE, Mgr. M., L.TH., L.PH., Logic
GALLUP, J., B.TH., D.PH.
GODIN, G., L.TH., D.TH., Metaphysics
PLANTE, R., L.TH., D.PH.
ST.-JACQUES, A., L.PH.
TRÉPANIER, E., D.PH., Contemporary Philosophy

Faculty of Sciences and Engineering:

ANGERS, D., D.SC., Electrical Engineering
ANGERS, R., D.SC., Metallurgy
ARDOUIN, P., B.SC.APP., Computer and Information Science
ASSAD, J.-R., M.SC., PH.D., Geology and Mineralogy
ASSAD, J.-R., M.SC., PH.D., Geology and Mineralogy
AUPETIT, B., L.SC., Mathematics
AZZARIA, L.-M., M.A., PH.D., Geology and Mineralogy
BARBEAU, C., D.SC.NAT., Chemistry
BARIL, M., M.SC.APP., D.SC., Physics
BEDARD, J.-H., M.SC., PH.D., Biology
BÉLAND, R., PH.D., Structural Geology
BERNARD, R., PH.D., Physiology
BIBAUD, R.-E., M.SC., PH.D., Chemical Engineering
BLANCHARD, L.-P., D.SC., Chemical Engineering
BOISVERT, MOZART, D.SC., Electrical Engineering
BOIVIN, A., D.SC.PHYS., Optics
BOIVIN, G., D.SC., Physics
BONENFANT, F., M.SC.PHYS., Electro-Magnetism
BONNEAU, L.-P., B.SC.APP., Thermodynamics
BOUILLON, G., M.SC., Mechanical Engineering
BOURQUE, C., D.SC., Mechanical Engineering
BOVET, J., D.SC., Biology
BRASSARD, P., D.SC., Chemistry
BURNELL, R.-H., PH.D., Chemistry
CANONNE, P., D.SC., Chemistry
CARDINAL, A., D.SC., Biology
CARETTE, J.-D., D.SC., Physics
CARON, J.-Y., M.SC., Electrical Engineering
CHASSE, Y., M.SC., Physics
CHOLETTE, A., D.SC., Chemical Engineering
CLAISSE, F., D.SC., Metallurgy
CLOUTIER, L., D.SC., Chemical Engineering
CONSTANTIN, R., D.SC., Chemistry
COTE, A.-G., B.SC.APP., Civil Engineering
CUJEC, B., PH.D., Physics
CUMMINS, J., M.SC., PH.D., Electrical Engineering
DARLING, B. T., M.SC., PH.D., Physics
DE VRIENDT, A., D.ING., Mechanical Engineering
DELISLE, C., D.SC., Physics
DESROCHERS, P., M.SC., D.ING., Mechanical Engineering
DICKINSON, J., M.A., D.SC., Mechanical Engineering
DROUIN, R., PH.D., Chemistry
DUBE, A., D.SC., Mechanical Metallurgy
DUMAS, J., M.SC., Electrical Engineering
DUPRAT, J., M.SC., M.A., Mathematics
ENGEL, C.-R., D.SC., Chemistry
FAUCHER, G., M.SC.APP., PH.D., Mechanical Engineering
FILTEAU, G., D.SC., Zoology
FINLEY, M. R., Jr., M.A., PH.D., Computer and Information Science
FORST, W., PH.D., Chemistry
FRENETTE, M., D.SC., Civil Engineering
GAGNÉ, R., PH.D., Electrical Engineering
GAGNON, A., L.SC., Biology
GALIBOIS, A., D.SC., Mining and Metallurgy
GANGULY, U., D.SC., Electrical Engineering
GERARDIN, H., Mechanical Engineering
GILLE, J.-C., L.SC. ING., Electrical Engineering
GIROUX, Y.-M., D.SC., Structural Analysis
GODIN, C., Biochemistry, D.SC.
GOODSPEED, F., PH.D., Mathematics
GRENIER, P., M.SC., Chemical Engineering
GUAY, F., SURV., B.APPL.SC., Geodesy
GUBELI, O., D.SC., Chemistry
HABASHI, F., D.SC.TECH., Mining and Metallurgy
HATCHER, W. S., D.SC., Mathematics
HENGARTNER, W., D.SC., Mathematics
HERMANN, J. A., D.SC., Chemistry
HO-KIM, Q., M.SC., PH.D., Physics
HUCKA, V., PH.D., Mining and Metallurgy
HUOT, L., D.SC., Biology
ISHAQ, M., D.SC., Mathematics
IZATT, J., PH.D., Physics
JEAN, M., D.SC., Bacteriology
JORDAN, I.-B., D.SC., Electrical Engineering
KERWIN, L., D.SC., Atomic Physics
KOENIG, H.-P., D.SC., Physics
KRIEGER, A.-W., ING.D., Civil Engineering
LACHANCE, L., D.SC., Civil Engineering
LACROIX, G., L.PH., D.SC., Biology
LACROIX, N., PH.D., Mathematics
LAFONTAINE, J.-G., PH.D., Biology
LAGUEUX, R., M.SC., Biology
LANGLOIS, J.-M., D.SC., Biology
LAROCHELLE, P., PH.D., Civil Engineering
LAURENT, R., D.SC., Geology and Mineralogy
LAVALLEE, J., M.SC., Mathematics
LAVOIE, J. L., D.SC., Mathematics
LECOURS, M., PH.D., Electrical Engineering
LEDOUX, R., PH.D., Geology and Mineralogy
LEFRANÇOIS, M., D.SC., Chemistry
LÉONARD, J., M.SC., PH.D., Chemistry
LLAMAS, J., PH.D., Civil Engineering
LOCONG, L., D.SC., Computer Sciences
MARMET, P., D.SC., Physics
METHOT, J.-C., D.SC., Mechanical Engineering
MICHEL, B., D.ENG., Civil Engineering
MONETTE, H., B.ENG., Mining
MOREAU, J. R., PH.D., Chemical Engineering
MORISSET, P., PH.D., Biology
NADEAU, G., M.SC.PHYS., Physics
NETSCH, H., D.ING., Mechanical Engineering
NGUYEN, N. D., D.SC., Mechanical Engineering
ODGERS, J., B.SC., Mechanical Engineering
OUELLET, Y., D.SC., Civil Engineering
PALLOTTA, D., PH.D., Biology
PAQUET, J. G., D.SC., Electrical Engineering
PARADIS, G., B.COM., Actuarial Science
PERRON, J.-M., D.SC., Biology
POTVIN, R., PH.D., M.SC.APP., Electro-Metallurgy
POUSSART, D., M.SC., PH.D., Electrical Engineering
RAMALHO, R., PH.D., Chemical Engineering
RAMAVATARAM, K., M.SC., PH.D., Physics
RIVA, J., M.SC., PH.D., Geology and Mineralogy
ROBERGE, P.-C., D.SC., Chemistry
ROBERT, A., M.SC., Mathematics
ROY, G., D.SC., Mathematics
ROY, J.-C., PH.D., Chemistry
ROY, P.-H., M.SC., PH.D., Chemical Engineering
SABOURIN, R., D.SC., Geology and Mineralogy
ST.-ARNAUD, R., PH.D., Electrical Engineering
ST-JULIEN, P., D.SC., Geology and Mineralogy
ST.-PIERRE, C., D.SC., Physics
SAVOIE, R., D.SC., Chemistry
SCHLADER, A., D.ING., Mechanical Engineering
SIDDIQI, J., M.A., D.SC., PH.D.

SLINGERLAND, F., M.SC., Mechanical Engineering
SLOBODRIAN, R.-J., D.SC., Physics
SOUCY, A., D.ING., Civil Engineering
TAILLEUR, P., D.SC., Biochemistry
TALBOT, G., D.SC., Biochemistry
TAVENAS, F., D.SC., Civil Engineering
THEODORESCU, R., D.SC., Mathematics
THIBOUTOT, M., B.SC.APP., Mathematics
TORDION, G. V., D.ING., Mechanical Drawing
TRAN, K., B.SC.A., B.SC.SOC., Electrical Engineering
TREMBLAY, L.-M., D. DE 3E CYCLE, Physics
TREMBLAY, R., D.SC., Physics
TRUDEL, P., M.SC., Biology
VAN NESTE, A., D.SC., Mining and Metallurgy
VANIER, J., M.SC., PH.D., Electrical Engineering
VERRETTE, J.-L., B.SC.A., Civil Engineering
WILDI, T., Industrial Electronics

Faculty of Social Sciences:

AUTIN, C., M.SC.SOC., Economics
AYOUB, A., LL.L., D.E.S., D.SC.SOC., Economics
BACCIGALUPO, A., D. 3E. CYCLE, Political Science
BEAUDOIN, A., PH.D., Social Work
BÉLANGER, G., B.SC.SOC., Economics
BÉLANGER, L., M.SC.SOC., PH.D., Economics
BELZILE, B., M.SC.SOC., Industrial Relations
BERGERON, G., M.SC.SOC., PH.D., Political Theory
BERNIER, J., D.SC.SOC., Industrial Relations
BRETON, Y., PH.D., Anthropology
CORRIVEAULT, C., M.SC.SOC., Sociology
DANEAU, M., M.SC., Economics
DEHEM, R., D.SC.ECON., Economics
DESCHENES, J.-P., M.SC.SOC., Industrial Relations
DION, G., L.TH., L.PH., L.SC.SOC., Morals
DION, L., D.SC.SOC., Politics
DUBE, Y., B.SC.APP., Economics
DUMAIS, A., D.SC.SOC., Sociology
DUMONT, F., M.SC.SOC., D.SC.SOC., Sociology
FALARDEAU, J.-C., L.PH., L.SOC.SC., Institutional Sociology
FAUCHER, A., L.SC.SOC., M.A., Economic History
FRITERS, G.-M., L.SC.POL., D.SC.POL., Political Sciences
GUAY, D., Sociology
LAFORGE, H., PH.D., Psychology
LEBLANC, N., M.SC.SOC., Popular Education
LEGAULT, A., D.SC.SOC., Politics
LEMIEUX, V., M.SC.SOC., Political Science
LESSARD, M.-A., M.SC.SOC., Sociology
A.LUX, , D.SC.,ECON. Sociology
MASSON, C., M.SC.SOC., Economics
MATUSZEWSKI, T., M.SC., Economics
MONTMINY, J. P., M.SC.SOC., D.TH., Sociology
PAINCHAUD, P., L. ès L., M.A., Political Science
POULIN, M., M.SERV.SOC., M.B.A., Social Work
SALADIN-D'ANGLURE, B., M.A., Anthropology
SANTERRE, R., L. ès L., M.ANT., D. DE 3E CYCLE, Anthropology
SCHWARZ, A., L. ès L., M.A., Sociology
SCHWIMMER, E., Anthropology
SIMONIS, Y., D.SC.SOC., Anthropology
ST.-LAURENT, J., M.SC.SOC., Industrial Relations
THIBAULT, M.-A., M.SC.SOC., Economics
TREMBLAY, M.-A., L.SC.A., PH.D., Applied Anthropology
TREMBLAY, M., M.SC.SOC., M.A., Social and Political Philosophy

School of Architecture:

BAKER, J., B.A.(ARCH.)
BOURQUE, P.-N., M.SC., Architecture

School of Dentistry:

SIMARD, P., D.H.D.P., D.D.S.

School of Music:

BIOT, B.
BOUCHARD, A., L.TH.
BROCHU, L., L.MUS., Religious Song
BROUW, F.
FERLAND, A., L.MUS.
GLOBENSKI, A.-M., M.MUS.
HETU, J., L.MUS.
JEANNOTTE, J.-P.
KNIAZ, A., M.A.
LAGACE, C., B.MUS.
LANDRY, J., M.MUS., Harmony
MASSON-BOURQUE, C.
PARE-TOUSIGNANT, E.
WEISZ, R.

School of Pharmacy:

CLAVEAU, P., D.PHARM.
FAVREAU, G., D.PHARM.
JOLY, L.-P., D.PHARM.
ROY, P.-G., PH.D., Biopharmacy

School of Psychology:

CHENE, H., L.OR.
DAIGLE, G., L.PSYCH.
DESROSIERS, F.-X., L.OR., PH.D.
JOSHI, P., M.A., D.UNIV.
LORTIE, J.-Y., L.ORIENT., PH.D.
MEUNIER, M., L.PSYCH., Psychology
NOELTING, G., D.PSYCH., D.SC., Psychology of Genetics
OUELLET, H.-R., D.PH., History of Psychology

School of Social Work:

BELANGER, G.-M., M.A., Social Encyclicals
LAFOREST, J., M.S.SOC., D.TH., Social Service
PARE, S., M.SERV.SOC., D.SOC.WELF., Group Social Service
ST.-ARNAUD, G., M.S.SOC.
ZAY, N., L.SC.P., LL.D., Social Service

ATTACHED RESEARCH INSTITUTES:

Centre de recherches sur l'eau: Université Laval, Quebec G1K 7P4.
Director: J. LLAMAS, PH.D.

Centre de recherches en nutrition: Université Laval, Quebec G1K 7P4.
Director: JOËL DE LA NOUE, D.SC.

Centre d'études nordiques: Université Laval, Quebec G1K 7P4.
Director: (vacant).

Centre international de recherches sur le bilinguisme: *see* under Research Institutes.

Centre de recherches en sociologie religieuse: Université Laval, Quebec G1K 7P4.
Director: J.-P. ROULEAU, M.A., D.SC.SOC. (acting).

Institut supérieur des sciences humaines: Université Laval, Quebec G1K 7P4.
Director: G. GODIN, D.PH., L.PH., L.TH.

Centre de Recherche en Aménagement et en Développement: Université Laval, Quebec G1K 7P4.
Director: P. CLIBBON, D. ÈS L. (acting).

UNIVERSITY OF LETHBRIDGE

4401 UNIVERSITY DRIVE,
LETHBRIDGE,
ALBERTA T1K 3M4
Telephone: 329-2111.
Founded 1967.

Provincial control; Language of instruction: English; Academic year: September to April (2 semesters), also summer sessions.

Chancellor: ISLAY ARNOLD.
President: Dr. J. WOODS.
***Registrar:* J. D. OVIATT, B.ED.**
Chief Librarian: D. E. WICK.

Number of teachers: 150.
Number of students: 2,000.
Library of 200,000 vols.
Publications: *Annual Calendar, Annual Report of the Board of Governors*†.

DEANS:

Faculty of Arts and Science: O. G. HOLMES, M.A., PH.D. (acting).
Faculty of Education: J. THORLACIUS, M.ED., PH.D.

PROFESSORS:

ANDERSON, R. N., M.A., PH.D., Education
BEATY, C. B., M.A., PH.D., Geography
BLAIR, D. G., M.M., Music
CAMPBELL, G., M.A., PH.D., Education
CASSIS, A. F., PH.D., English
CORMIER, L.-P., M.A., PH.D., Modern Languages
DAYKIN, P. N., M.A., PH.D., Mathematics and Computing Science
DWYER, R. J., M.A., PH.D., Sociology
FALKENBERG, E. E., M.SC., ED.D., Education
FLETCHER, R., M.A., PH.D., Geography
HEPLER, L. G., PH.D., Chemistry
HOLMES, O. G., M.A., PH.D., Chemistry
KUIJT, J. M.A., PH.D., Biological Sciences
LATTA, W. C., M.A., PH.D., English
MCCURDY, K. G., M.A., PH.D., Chemistry
MEINTZER, R. B., M.S., PH.D., Chemistry
MIKHAIL, E. H., D.E.S., PH.D., English
MILLER, E. E., M.A., PH.D., Geography
MOKOSCH, E., PH.D., Education
NEEDHAM, L. A., A.G.S.M., A.R.C.M., Music
PENTON, M. J., M.A., PH.D., History
PETHERBRIDGE, D. L., PH.D., Education
ROOD, J. L., M.A., PH.D., Physics
SCHOTT, C. J., M.A., PH.D., Education
SKOLROOD, A. H., M.A., PH.D., Education
THORLACIUS, J. M., M.ED., PH.D., Education
TWA, R. J., M.ED., PH.D., Education
WAGENAAR, E. B., M.SC., PH.D., Biological Sciences
WHISHAW, I. Q. A., M.SC., PH.D., Psychology
WILLIAMS, A. W., A.M., PH.D., History
WOODS, J. H., M.A., PH.D., Philosophy

McGILL UNIVERSITY

845 SHERBROOKE STREET WEST, MONTREAL, P.Q. H3A 2T5

Telephone: (514) 392-4311.

Founded 1821 by legacy of Hon. James McGill.

Private control; Language of instruction: English; Academic year: September to May (two terms).

Chancellor: CONRAD F. HARRINGTON, C.D., B.A., B.C.L., C.ST.J.

Principal and Vice-Chancellor: DAVID L. JOHNSTON, A.B., LL.B.

Vice-Principal (Academic): E. PEDERSEN, M.A., ED.D.

Vice-Principal (Administration): L. YAFFE, M.SC., PH.D., F.C.I.C., F.A.P.S., F.R.S.C., F.R.S.

Vice-Principal (Finance): J. ARMOUR, A.A.C.C.A.

Vice-Principal (Planning): E. J. STANSBURY, M.A., PH.D.

Vice-Principal (Research): G. A. MACLACHLAN, M.A., PH.D.

Secretary-General: C. M. MCDOUGALL, D.S.O., B.A.

Registrar: J.-P. SCHULLER, B.A.

Director of Libraries: MARIANNE SCOTT, B.L.S.

Library: *see* **Libraries.**

Numbers of teachers: *c.* 1,300 full-time; *c.* 1,400 part-time.

Number of students: *c.* 19,000.

Publications: ***McGill Reporter*** **(weekly),** ***Annual Report†, Calendars†, McGill Journal of Education*** **(quarterly).**

DEANS:

Faculty of Agriculture: L. E. LLOYD, M.SC., PH.D.

Faculty of Arts: R. VOGEL, M.A., PH.D.

Faculty of Science: S. ORVIG, M.SC., PH.D., F.R.S.C., F.R.MET.S.

Faculty of Dentistry: K. C. BENTLEY, D.D.S., M.D.C.M., F.I.C.D., F.A.C.D.

Faculty of Engineering: **G. W. FARNELL, PH.D., F.I.E.E.E.**

Faculty of Graduate Studies and Research: G. A. MACLACHLAN, M.A., PH.D.

Faculty of Law: J. E. C. BRIERLEY, B.A., B.C.L., D.U.

Faculty of Medicine: S. O. FREEDMAN, B.SC., M.D.C.M., F.R.S.C., F.R.C.P.(C.).

Faculty of Religious Studies: J. MCLELLAND, M.A., PH.D., D.D.

Faculty of Music: P. R. PEDERSEN, M.MUS., PH.D.

Faculty of Education: G. E. FLOWER, M A., ED.D.

Faculty of Management: L. PICARD, C.C., B.PHIL. B.SC.A., D.B.A.

Dean of Students: M. HERSCHORN, M.A., PH.D.

DIRECTORS OF SCHOOLS:

Architecture: D. DRUMMOND, B.ARCH.

Communication Disorders: K. CHARAN, M.A., PH.D.

Computer Science: M. M. NEWBORN, PH.D.

Food Science: SHIRLEY M. WEBER, M.S.

Graduate School of Library Science: VIVIAN S. SESSIONS, M.A., M.S.

Physical and Occupational Therapy: M. C. PIPER, PH.D.

Social Work: MYER KATZ, M.S.W., PH.D.

Nursing: JOAN GILCHRIST, M.SC.(A), R.N.

Urban Planning: DAVID FARLEY, M.ARCH., M.C.P.

Centre for Continuing Education: J. A. DUFF, M.A., C.A.

PROFESSORS:

Faculty of Agriculture:

BAKER, B. E., D.SC., Agricultural Chemistry
BIDER, J. R., M.SC., PH.D., Wildlife Biology
BLACKWOOD, A. C., M.SC., PH.D., F.R.S.C., Microbiology
BROUGHTON, R., S.M., PH.D., Agricultural Engineering
BUCKLAND, R. B., M.SC., PH.D., Animal Science
DAVID, J., L.S.A., PH.D., Horticulture
DONEFER, E., M.S., PH.D., Animal Science
DOUGLAS, R. H., M.A., PH.D., Agricultural Physics
ESTEY, R. H., M.S., D.I.C., PH.D., F.L.S., Plant Pathology
FARMER, F., M.SC., PH.D., Food Science
GRANT, W. F., M.A., PH.D., F.L.S., Agronomy
IDZIAK, E. S., D.SC., Microbiology and Food Science
KEVAN, D. K. MCE., PH.D., F.R.S.E., M.I.BIOL., Entomology
KLINCK, H. R., M.SC., PH.D., Agronomy
KNOWLES, R., PH.D., Microbiology
LLOYD, L. E., PH.D., Animal Science
MCFARLANE, J. E., M.A., PH.D., Entomology
MACKENZIE, A. F., M.SC., PH.D., Soil Science
MACLEOD, R. A., M.A., PH.D., F.R.S.C., Microbiology
MOXLEY, J. E., M.SC., PH.D., Animal Science
NEILSON, HELEN R., M.B.E., M.SC., Food Science
PELLETIER, R. L., M.SC., PH.D., Plant Pathology
SACKSTON, W. E., M.SC., PH.D., Plant Pathology
STEPPLER, H. A., M.SC., PH.D., F.A.I.C., Agronomy
STEWART, R. K., PH.D., Entomology
TOUCHBURN, S. P., M.S.A., PH.D., Animal Science
VICKERY, V. R., M.SC., PH.D., Entomology
WEBER, S. M., PH.D., Food Science

Faculty of Arts:

ARNOLD, A. H., D. ès L., F.R.S.C., German
ASIMAKOPULOS, A., M.A., PH.D., F.R.S.C., Economics
BEACH, E. F., A.M., PH.D., Economics
BLAISE, B., M.A., M.F.A., PH.D., English
BOSS, V., C.C.K., PH.D., History
BRACKEN, H. MCF., M.A., PH.D., Philosophy
BRECHER, I., M.A., LL.B., PH.D., Economics
BRECHER, M., PH.D., F.R.S.C., Political Science
BUNGE, M. C., PH.D., Philosophy
CECIL, C. D., M.A., English
COLLET, G.-P., D. ès LET., French
DALY, P., PH.D., German
D'ANDREA, A., D.FIL., F.R.S.C., Italian
DECHÊNE, L., D. ÈS L., History
DEUTSCH, A., PH.D., Economics
DISTEFAND, G., L. ÈS L., D.U., French
DUDEK, L., A.M., PH.D., English
ELLIS, C. D., M.A., PH.D., Linguistics
ETHIER-BLAIS, J., D. ès L., French
FRYE, D. C., M.A., PH.D., English
GALAVARIS, G., M.A., PH.D., Art History
GREEN, C., PH.D., Economics
GUTKIND, P. C. W., M.A., PH.D., Anthropology
HAMILTON, R. F., M.A., PH.D., Sociology
HEMLOW, JOYCE, M.A., PH.D., LL.D., F.R.S.C., English
HEUSER, A., M.A., PH.D., English
HOFFMANN, P. C., PH.D., History
IKAWA-SMITH, F., M.A., PH.D., Anthropology
JUDKINS, W. O., A.M., PH.D., Art History
KIERANS, E. W., B.A., Economics
KLIMA, S., M.A., PH.D., English
KUSHNER, E., M.A., PH.D., F.R.S.C., French
LAUNAY, J. L., L. ès L., DIP.D'ÉTUDES SUP., French
LIPP, S., M.S., PH.D., Hispanic Studies
LUCAS, A., A.M., PH.D., English
MCCULLAGH, P. F., PH.D., Classics
MCKINNON, A. T., M.A., PH.D., Philosophy
MACLENNAN, H., C.C., PH.D., LL.D., D.LITT., F.R.S.C., English
MCPHERSON, H. A., M.A., PH.D., English
MALLOCH, A. E., M.A., PH.D., English
MALLORY, J. R., M.A., LL.D., F.R.S.C., Political Science
MAXWELL, M. P., M.A., PH.D., History
MORISOT, J. C., D. ès L., French
NAYAR, B. R., M.A., PH.D., Political Science
OHLIN, P. H., M.A., PH.D., English
PINARD, M., L.L.L., M.A., PH.D., F.R.S.C., Sociology
RIGAULT, A. A. L., L. ès L., DIP. ÉTUDES SUP., D.PH., Linguistics
ROWLEY, J. C., M.SC., PH.D., Economics
SALISBURY, R. F., A.M., M.A., PH.D., F.R.S.C., Anthropology
SCHACHTER, A., D.PHIL., Classics
SENIOR, H., M.A., PH.D., History
SOLOMON, D. N., M.A., PH.D., Sociology
SUVIN, D., M.SC., PH.D., English
TAYLOR, C., M.A., D.PHIL., F.R.S.C., Political Science
THOMSON, D. C., D.U., Political Science
TRENTMAN, J. A., M.A., PH.D., Philosophy
TRIGGER, B. G., PH.D., Anthropology
VOGEL, R., M.A., PH.D., History
WELDON, J. C., PH.D., F.R.S.C., Economics
WESTLEY, W. A., M.A., PH.D., Sociology
WISSE, RUTH, M.A., PH.D., Jewish Studies
WRIGHT, H. R. C., M.A, PH.D., Economics

Faculty of Dentistry:

BENTLEY, K. C., D.D.S., M.D.C.M., Anaesthesiology
DE VRIES, JOAN, B.A., M.D.C.M., Microbiology
ROSEN, H., B.SC., D.D.S., Operative Dentistry

Faculty of Education:

BIRCH, L. B., M.A.
BUTEAU, M., M.A., PH.D.
CRAM, J. M., ED.D.
EDWARDS, R., M.ED.
FLOWER, G. E., M.A., ED.D.
FRANCOEUR, T. A., M.A., D.ED.
GILLETT, MARGARET, M.A., ED.D.
GREENE, F., M.A., PH.D.
HENCHEY, N., PH.D.

KLISSOURAS, V., M.S., D.P.E.
MAGNUSON, R. P., M.A., PH.D.,
MCKAY, G. H. M.A., ED.D.
MORRISON, H. D., M.A., M.ED.
PEDERSEN, E. M.A., ED.D.
SMITH, D. C., M.A., PH.D.
STINSON, F., M.A., ED.D.
STUTT, H. A., M.ED.
WILKINSON, R. E., M.A., D.P.E.
YOUNG, J. E. M., M.A., PH.D.

Faculty of Engineering:
ADLER, E. L., M.A.SC., PH.D., Electrical Engineering
AXELRAD, D. R., M.ENG., D.ENG.SC., Mechanical Engineering
BÉLANGER, P. R., S.M., PH.D., Electrical Engineering
BLOSTEIN, M. L., M.ENG., PH.D., Electrical Engineering
BRUCE, W., M.A.SC., M.E.I.C., M.A.S.M.E., Mechanical Engineering
CAVADIAS, G. S., M.SC., PH.D., Civil Engineering
COLLINS, P., DIP.ARCH., M.A., L.L.M., F.R.A.I.C., School of Architecture
DAVENPORT, W. G., M.SC., PH.D., Mining and Metallurgical Engineering
DEALY, J. M., PH.D., Chemical Engineering
DOUGLAS, W. J. M., PH.D., Chemical Engineering
FARNELL, G. W., S.M., PH.D., F.I.E.E.E., Electrical Engineering
GUTHRIE, R. I. L., PH.D., Mining and Metallurgical Engineering
HARRIS, P. J., M.ENG., PH.D., M.E.I.C., Civil Engineering and Applied Mechanics
JONAS, J. J., PH.D., Mining and Metallurgical Engineering
KAMAL, M. R., PH.D., Chemical Engineering
LEE, J. H. S., M.SC., PH.D., Mechanical Engineering
LEVINE, M. D., PH.D., Electrical Engineering
MIRZA, M. S., PH.D., Civil Engineering
NEWMAN, B. G., M.A., PH.D., F.R.A.E.S., Mechanical Engineering
OSLER, J. C., S.M., Civil Engineering
PAIDOUSSIS, M. P., PH.D., Mechanical Engineering
PAVLASEK, T. J., M.ENG., PH.D., M.E.I.C., S.M.I.E.E.E., Electrical Engineering
REDWOOD, R. G. M.A.SC., PH.D., Civil Engineering
SAVAGE, S. B., PH.D., Civil Engineering
SCHOENAUER, N., M.ARCH., School of Architecture
SILVESTER, P. P., M.A.SC., PH.D., Electrical Engineering
SMITH, G. W., M.ENG., PH.D., Mining and Metallurgical Engineering
STAFFORD SMITH, B., PH.D., D.SC., Civil Engineering
TELFORD, W. M., M.SC., PH.D., Mining and Metallurgical Engineering
THORPE, W. D., M.A., School of Computer Science
TURKSTRA, C. J., M.S., PH.D., Civil Engineering
WEBER, M. E., SC.D., Chemical Engineering
WILLIAMS, W. M., M.SC., PH.D., M.C.I.M., M.I.M., Mining and Metallurgical Engineering
WILSON, S., B.ARCH., School of Architecture
YONG, R. N., M.ENG., M.SC..E., PH.D., Civil Engineering
ZAMES, G. D., SC.D., Electrical Engineering
ZUK, R., M.ARCH., M.R.A.I.C., Architecture

Faculty of Graduate Studies:
ASTBURY, EFFIE C., M.L.S., School of Library Science
FARLEY, J. D., M.ARCH., M.CITY PLG., Urban Planning
KATZ, MYER, M.S.W., PH.D., Social Work
MARCUS, LOTTE, D.S.W., Social Work
SESSIONS, V. S., M.A., M.S. IN L.S., Library Science
SHINER, E. V., M.S.W., ED.D., Social Work
WOODSWORTH, D. E., M.A., PH.D., Social Work

Faculty of Law:
BRIERLEY, J. E. C., B.A., B.C.L., D.U.
CREPEAU, P. A., Q.C., L.PH., LL.L., D.U., LL.D., F.R.S.C.
DURNFORD, J. W., B.C.L.
FOSTER, W. F., LL.M.
GLENN, H. P., LL.M., DR. EN DROIT
GROFFIER-ATALA, E., D.C.L.
JOHNSTON, D. L., A.B., LL.B.
SCOTT, S. A., D.PHIL.
TETLEY, W., Q.C., LL.L.
VLASIC, I. A., LL.M., J.S.D., Air and Space Law

Faculty of Management:
AMEY, L. R., PH.D.
ARMSTRONG, D. E., PH.D.
BRIANT, P. C., M.B.A., PH.D., C.A.
FALK, H., M.B.A., PH.D., C.A.
KANUNGO, R. N., M.A., PH.D.
LAYBOURN, R. G., M.A., C.A.
MINTZBERG, H., PH.D., F.R.S.C.
MORRISON, R. N., M.A.
PICARD, L., B.PHIL., B.SC.A., D.B.A.
SHAPIRO, S. J., M.B.A., PH.D.
SMITH, J. G., M.A., PH.D.
STEINBERG, C., M.A., PH.D.
WHITMORE, G. A., M.S., PH.D.

Faculty of Medicine:
AGUAYO, A. J., M.D., F.R.C.P.(C.), Neurology, Medicine
ALLEN, F. MOYRA, M.A., PH.D., R.N., Nursing
ANDERMANN, F., M.D., Neurology and Neurosurgery
ATES, D. G., M.D., B.A., History of Medicine
BAXTER, D. W., M.D.C.M., Neurology and Neurosurgery, Medicine
BAXTER, J. D., M.D.C.M., F.R.C.S.(C), Otolaryngology
BEAUDRY, P. H., M.D., Paediatrics
BECKLAKE-MCGREGOR, M. R., M.D., M.R.C.P., Epidemiology and Health, Medicine
BENFEY, B. G., M.D., Pharmacology and Therapeutics
BERTRAND, G., M.D. M.SC., Neurology and Neurosurgery
BIRKS, R. I., PH.D., Physiology
BIRMINGHAM, MARION K., M.SC., PH.D., Psychiatry
BOLANDE, R. P., M.S., M.D., Pathology
BURGESS, J. H., B.SC., M.D.C.M., F.R.C.P. (C.), Medicine
CAMERON, D. G., O.C., M.C., M.D.C.M., F.R.C.P.(C), F.A.C.P., Medicine
CARPENTER, S., M.D., Neurology and Neurosurgery
CHANG, T. M., PH.D., M.D.C.M., F.R.C.P., Physiology, Medicine
CLERMONT, Y. W., PH.D., F.R.S.C., Anatomy and Histology
COHEN, M., PH.D., Radiation Oncology, Physics
COLLE, E., M.D., Paediatrics
COLLIER, B., PH.D., Pharmacology and Theraputics
COOPER, B. A., M.D.C.M., F.R.C.P.(C), Medicine

CORMIER, B. M., B.A., M.D., Psychiatry
CRAWHALL, J. C., PH.D., M.B.B.S., Medicine
CRONIN, R. F. P., M.D.C.M., M.SC., F.R.C.P., F.R.C.P.(C), Medicine
CRUESS, R. L., M.D., Surgery
DE VOE, I. W., PH.D., Microbiology and Immunology
DOBELL, A. R. C., M.D.C.M., Surgery
DOEHRING, D. G., M.A., PH.D., Human Communication Disorders
DONGIER, M., M.D., Psychiatry
DRUMMOND, K., M.D.C.M., F.R.C.P.(C.), Paediatrics
DUGUID, W., M.B.CH.B., Pathology
ECOBICHON, D., M.A., PH.D., Pharmacology and Therapeutics
ERVIN, F., M.D., Psychiatry
ETHIER, R., B.A., M.D., Neurology and Neurosurgery
FEINDEL, W. H., M.SC., M.D.C.M., D.PHIL., F.R.C.S.(C.), F.A.C.S., Neurology and Neurosurgery
FORSEY, R. R., M.D., Medicine
FRASER, M. J., M.SC., PH.D., Biochemistry
FRASER F. C., M.SC., PH.D., M.D.C.M., D.SC., F.R.S.C., Paediatrics
FREEDMAN, S. O., M.D.C.M., F.R.S.C., F.R.C.P.(C.), Medicine
GILCHRIST, JOAN M., M.SC.(A.), Nursing
GLOOR, P., M.D., PH.D., Neurology and Neurosurgery
GOLD, P., M.SC., M.D.C.M., PH.D., F.R.S.C., F.R.C.P.(C.), Medicine
GOLDSMITH, H. L., M.A., PH.D., Medicine
GORESKY, C. A., PH.D., M.D.C.M., F.R.C.P.(C), Medicine
GRAHAM, A. F., M.SC., PH.D., D.SC., F.R.S.C., Biochemistry
GUTTMANN, R. D., B.A., B.S., M.D., Medicine
GUYDA, H., B.SC., M.D., Medicine
HAMPSON, L. G., M.SC., M.D.C.M., F.R.C.S.(C.), Surgery
HAND, R., M.D., Medicine, Microbiology and Immunology
HAWKINS, D. G., M.D., Medicine
HOFFMAN, M., M.SC., PH.D., M.D.C.M., D.SC., Medicine
HOSEIN, E., M.SC., PH.D., Biochemistry
JOHNSON, L. G., M.D.C.M., Medicine
JOHNSTONE-ROSE, M., PH.D., Biochemistry
JONES, G. M., M.A., M.B., M.D., F.R.S., F.R.S.(C.), B.A., M.D.C.M., Medicine
JORON, G. E., B.A., M.D.C.M., Medicine
KAHN, D. S., M.D., L.M.C.C., Pathology
KARPATI, G., M.D., Neurology and Neurosurgery
KAYE, M., M.B.B.S., F.R.C.P.(C.), Medicine
KESSLER, J. I., M.D., F.R.C.P., Medicine
KINCH, R. A. H., M.B.B.S., M.R.C.S.-L.R.C.P., L.M.C.C., F.R.C.S.(C.), F.R.C.O.G., F.A.C.O.G., Obstetrics and Gynaecology
KRAVITZ, H., M.D.C.M., F.A.P.A., Psychiatry
KRNJEVIC, K., PH.D., M.B.CH.B., F.R.S.C., Physiology, Anaesthesia Research
LALA, P., PH.D., M.D., Anatomy
LATOUR, J-P. A., M.D.C.M., F.A.C.S., F.R.C.P.(C.), Obstetrics and Gynaecology
LAWRENCE, D. C., B.SC., M.D.C.M., Neurology and Neurosurgery
LEBLOND, C. P., LIC.SC., M.D., PH.D., D.SC., F.R.S., F.R.S.C., Anatomy and Histology
LEE, S. S., Dr., P.H., M.D., Epidemiology and Health

LEHMANN, H. E., O.C., M.D., F.R.S.C., Psychiatry
LESTER, E. P., M.D., Psychiatry
LEVY, M., M.D., Medicine
LIDDELL, F. D., M.A., Epidemiology and Health
LING, D., M.SC., PH.D., Otolaryngology
LOCKE, J. G., M.D.C.M., MED.SC.D., F.R.C.S.(C.), F.A.C.S., Ophthalmology
LOWENTHAL, J., M.SC., PH.D., Pharmacology and Therapeutics
MCCALLUM, J. L., M.D.C.M., F.R.C.P.(C.), F.A.C.P., Family Medicine
MCGARRY, ELEANOR, M.SC., M.D.C.M., F.R.C.P.(C.), Medicine
MCGREGOR, M., M.B.B.CH., M.D., F.R.C.P., F.R.C.P.(C.), Medicine
MACINTOSH, F. C., M.A., PH.D., LL.D., F.R.S., F.R.S.C., Physiology
MCKENZIE, J. M., M.B.CH.B., M.D., M.D., F.R.S., F.R.S.C., Medicine
MACKINNON, K. J., M.D.C.M., B.SC., Surgery
MACKLEM, P. T., M.D.C.M., F.R.C.P.(C.), Medicine
MACLEAN, L. D., PH.D., M.D., F.R.C.S.(C.), Surgery
MACLEOD, A. W., M.B.CH.B., M.R.C.P., Psychiatry
MCNAUGHTON, F., M.D.C.M., M.SC., Neurology and Neurosurgery
MACPHERSON, A. S., M.D., M.SC., Epidemiology and Health
MANDL, G., PH.D., Physiology
MANN, A. M., M.D.C.M., Psychiatry
MEAKINS, J. F., M.A., M.D.C.M., F.R.C.P.(C.), Medicine
MILIC-EMILI, J., M.D., F.R.S.C., Physiology, Medicine
MILLER, J. E., M.SC., M.D., F.R.C.P.(C.), Surgery
MILNER, BRENDA, PH.D., D.SC., F.R.S., F.R.S.C., Neurology and Neurosurgery
MITCHELL, N. S., B.A., M.D.C.M., Surgery
MORE, R. H., M.D., M.SC., F.R.C.P.(C.), Pathology
MOUNT, B., M.D.C.M., Surgery
MULDER, D. S., M.D., M.SC., Surgery
MURPHY, B. P., M.D., M.SC., PH.D., Medicine
MURPHY, B., M.D., M.SC., PH.D., Medicine
MURPHY, D. R., M.SC., M.D.C.M., Surgery
MURPHY, H. B. M., M.B.CH.B., D.P.H., M.D., PH.D., Psychiatry
MURPHY, S. B., S.B., M.D.C.M., F.R.C.P.(C.), Ophthalmology
NICKERSON, M., SC.M., PH.D., M.D., Pharmacology and Therapeutics
OGILVIE, R. I., M.D., Medicine and Pharmacology
OSEASOHN, R., M.D., Epidemiology and Health
OSMOND, D. G., M.B.CH.B., Anatomy
OSTERLAND, C. K., M.D., Medicine
PALAYEW, M. J., M.D., Diagnostic Radiology
PALMER, W. H., B.SC., M.D.C.M., F.R.C.P.(C.), Family Medicine
PAPPIUS, H., M.SC., PH.D., Biochemistry
PARÉ, J. A. P., B.SC., M.D.C.M., Medicine
PINSKY, L., B.SC., M.D.C.M., Human Genetics
PLESS, I. B., B.A., M.D., Epidemiology and Health
POLOSA, C., M.D., PH.D., Physiology
POSNER, B., M.D., Medicine
PRINCE, R. H., B.A., M.SC., M.D., Psychiatry
RASMUSSEN, T. R., M.B., M.S., M.D., F.R.C.S.(C.), Neurology and Neurosurgery
RICHARDSON, J. B., M.D.C.M., PH.D., Pharmacology and Therapeutics, Pathology
ROBB, J. P., M.D.C.M., Neurology and Neurosurgery
ROBSON, H. G., M.D., Medicine, Microbiology and Immunology
RONA, G., M.D., PH.D., Pathology
ROSE, B., M.SC., PH.D., M.D.C.M., F.R.S.C., Medicine
ROSENTHALL, L., B.SC., M.D.C.M., Diagnostic Radiology
RUF, K., M.D., Obstetrics and Gynaecology
SANDISON, J. W., M.B., Anaesthesia
SCOTT, H. J., M.D.C.M., F.R.C.S.(C.), F.A.C.S., Surgery
SCRIVER, C. R., M.D.C.M., Paediatrics, Human Genetics
SEELY, J., M.D.C.M., Medicine
SHAPIRO, L., M.D.C.M., Medicine
SHELDON, H., M.D., Pathology
SHERWIN, A. L., B.SC., M.D.C.M., PH.D., Neurology
SHIZGAL, H. M., B.SC., M.D.C.M., Surgery
SHUSTER, J., M.D., PH.D., Medicine
SOLOMON, S., M.SC., PH.D., F.R.S.C., Biochemistry, Obstetrics and Gynaecology
SOURKES, T. L., M.SC., PH.D., F.R.C.S., Biochemistry, Psychiatry
SPITZER, W. O., M.D., M.H.A., M.P.H., Family Medicine
STRATFORD, J. G., M.SC., M.D.C.M., F.R.C.S.(C.), F.A.C.S., Neurology and Neurosurgery
STUTZMAN, L., M.D., Medicine
TENENHOUSE, A., PH.D., M.D.C.M., Pharmacology and Therapeutics
THOMPSON, A. G., M.D.C.M., Surgery
TONKS, D. B., PH.D., F.C.I.C., Medicine
TREMBLAY, G., M.D., Pathology
TRIFARO, J. M., M.D., Pharmacology and Therapeutics
TWEEDIE, F. J., M.D.C.M., F.R.C.S., Obstetrics and Gynaecology
WARSHAWSKY, H., PH.D., Anatomy
WATTERS, G., M.D., Neurology and Neurosurgery, Paediatrics
WEISS, GABRIELLE, B.SC., M.D.C.M., Psychiatry
WILKINSON, R. D., M.D.C.M., Medicine
WILLIAMS, H. B., M.D.C.M., Surgery
WINSBERG, F., PH.B., M.D., Diagnostic Radiology
WOLFE, L. S., M.SC., PH.D., M.D., F.R.S.C., Neurology and Neurosurgery
YAPHE, W., PH.D., Microbiology and Immunology

Faculty of Music:

HAMBRAEUS, B., PH.D.
JONES, K., D.MUS.
KONDAKS, S.

Faculty of Religious Studies:

ABU-HAKIMA, A., M.A., PH.D., Gulf History
ADAMS, C. J., PH.D., Islamic Religious Tradition
BOULLATA, I. J., PH.D., Arabic Language and Literature
CULLEY, R. C., PH.D., Old Testament
FROST, S. B., M.TH., DR.PHIL., D.D., D.LITT., Old Testament Language and Literature
HALL, D. J., M.D.I.V., S.T.M., TH.D., Christian Theology
JOHNSTON, G., M.A., PH.D., D.D., New Testament Language and Literature
LANDOLT, H. A., PH.D., Sufism
LITTLE, D. P., M.A. PH.D., Islamic History and Arabic
MCLELLAND, J. C., M.A., PH.D., Philosophy of Religion

Faculty of Science:

BARR, M., PH.D., Mathematics
BELL, R. E., C.C., M.A., PH.D., LL.D., D.SC., F.R.S., F.R.S.C., Physics
BELLEAU, B. R., M.SC., PH.D., F.R.S.C. Chemistry
BINDRA, D., M.A., PH.D., Psychology
BIRD, J. B., M.A., Geography
BOLL, W. G., PH.D., Biology
BOOTHROYD, E. R., M.SC., PH.D., Biology
BREGMAN, A. S., M.A., PH.D., Psychology
BROWN, W., M.A., PH.D., Mathematics
BUTLER, I. S., PH.D., Chemistry
CAVE-BROWN-CAVE, G., M.A., PH.D., F.C.I.C., Chemistry
CHAN, T. H., M.A., PH.D., Chemistry
CHOKSI, J., PH.D., Mathematics
CONNELL, I. G., PH.D., Mathematics
CONTOGOURIS, A. P., PH.D., Physics
CROLL, N. A., PH.D., D.I.C., D.C.C., Parasitology
DAS GUPTA, S., M.SC., PH.D., Physics
DE TAKACSY, N. B., M.SC., PH.D., Physics
DIGBY, P. S., D.SC., Biology
DOIG, R., M.SC., PH.D., Geological Sciences
DONNAY, GABRIELLE, PH.D., Geological Sciences
DOUGLAS, VIRGINIA, M.A., M.S.W., PH.D., Psychology
DUNBAR, M. J., M.A., PH.D., F.R.S.C., F.A.G.S., F.R.G.S., Marine Sciences
EDWARD, J. T., PH.D., D.PHIL.,D., SC. F.R.S.C., Chemistry
EISENBERG, A., M.A., PH.D., Chemistry
ELSON, J. A., M.SC., PH.D., Geological Sciences
EU, B. C., PH.D., Chemistry
FARRELL, P. G., PH.D., Chemistry
FERGUSON, G. A., M.ED., PH.D., F.R.S.C., Psychology
FRASER, F. C., M.SC., PH.D., M.D.C.M., D.SC., F.R.S.C., Biology
GARNIER, B. J., M.A., Geography
GIBBS, SARAH, M.S., PH.D., Biology
GILSON, D. F. R., M.SC., PH.D., Chemistry
GOWRISANKARAN, K., M.A., PH.D., Mathematics
HARPP, D. N., M.A., PH.D., Chemistry
HARROD, J. F., PH.D., Chemistry
HEDGCOCK, F. T., M.SC., PH.D., Physics
HERSCHORN, M., M.A., PH.D., Mathematics
HERZ, C., PH.D., F.R.S.C., Mathematics
HILLS, T. L., M.A., PH.D., Geography
HITSCHFELD, W. F., PH.D., F.R.MET.S., F.R.S.C., Meteorology, Physics
JUST, G., PH.D., Chemistry
KÄFER, E., D.PHIL., Biology
KALFF, J., M.S.A., PH.D., Biology
KAUFMAN, H., PH.D., Mathematics
KITCHING, J. E., PH.D., Physics
LAM, C. S., PH.D., Physics
LAMBEK, J., M.SC., PH.D., F.R.S.C., Mathematics
LAMBERT, W. E., M.A., PH.D., Psychology
LANGLEBEN, M. P., PH.D., Physics
LAROCHE, G., M.SC., PH.D., Marine Sciences
LEGGETT, W. C., M.SC., PH.D., Biology
LEMON, R. E., M.SC., PH.D., Biology
LEWIS, J. B., M.SC., PH.D., Marine Sciences
MACNAMARA, J., PH.D., Psychology
MAKKAI, N., PH.D., Mathematics
MARGOLIS, B., M.SC., PH.D., Physics
MARK, S. K., M.SC., PH.D., Physics
MARSDEN, JOAN R., M.SC., PH.D., Biology
MARTIN, W. M., PH.D., Physics
MASON, S. G., PH.D., F.R.S.C., Chemistry
MATHAI, A., PH.D., Mathematics
MEEROVITCH, E., M.SC., PH.D., Parasitology
MELZACK, R., M.SC., PH.D., Psychology
MILNER, P. M., M.SC., PH.D., Psychology
MOORE, R. B., M.SC., PH.D., Physics
MOSER, W. O. J. M.A., PH.D., Mathematics

MOUNTJOY, E. W., PH.D., Geological Sciences
MUKHERJEE, B. B., PH.D., Biology
OGILVIE, K. K., PH.D., Chemistry
OKUBO, T., M.SC., PH.D., Mathematics
ONYSZCHUK, M., M.SC., PH.D., Chemistry
ORVIG, S., M.SC., PH.D., F.R.S.C., Meteorology
PARRY, J., M.A., M.SC., PH.D., Geography
PATTERSON, D. D., M.SC., Chemistry
PERLIN, A. S., M.SC., PH.D., F.R.S.C., Chemistry
PIHL, R. O., PH.D., Psychology
POSER, E. G., M.A., PH.D., Psychology
POUNDER, E. R., PH.D., Physics
PURDY, W. C., PH.D., Chemistry
RAMSAY, J. O., PH.D., Psychology
RATTRAY, B., M.SC., PH.D., Mathematics
RIGLER, F., M.A., PH.D., Biology
ROBERTSON, R. F., PH.D., Chemistry
ROBSON, J., M.A., SC.D., F.R.S.C., Physics
ROGERS, R. R., S.M., PH.D., Meteorology
ROSENTHALL, E., M.SC., PH.D., Mathematics
RUBEN, H., PH.D., Mathematics
ST. PIERRE, L. E., PH.D., Chemistry
SATTLER, R. O., PH.D., Biology
SAULL, V. A., D.SC., PH.D., Geological Sciences
SESHADRI, V., M.A., PH.D., Mathematics
SHARP, R. T., M.SC., PH.D., Physics
SOLIN, C. D., M.A., PH.D., Mathematics
STAIRS, D. G., M.SC., PH.D., Physics
STANSBURY, E. J., M.A., PH.D., Physics
STEARN, C. W., M.S., PH.D., F.R.S.C., Geological Sciences
STERN, MURIEL, M.SC., PH.D., Psychology
STEVENSON, D. R., M.S.E., SC.D., Physics
TANNER, C., M.SC., PH.D., Parasitology
TAYLOR, J. C., M.A., PH.D., Mathematics
VOWINCKEL, E., PH.D., Meteorology
WALLACE, P. R., M.A., PH.D., Physics
WALSH, D., M.SC., PH.D., Physics
WHITEHEAD, M. A., PH.D., D.SC., Chemistry
WILSON, C. M., M.A., PH.D., Biology
YAFFE, L., M.SC., PH.D., F.C.I.C., F.A.P.S., F.R.P.S., F.R.S.C., Chemistry
ZUCKERMAN, M. J., M.A., D.PHIL., Physics

INCORPORATED COLLEGE:

Royal Victoria College: Montreal; is the Women's College of the University.
Warden: (vacant).

AFFILIATED BODIES:

Diocesan College of Montreal: 3473 University St., Montreal, P.Q. H3A 2A8.
Principal: Canon A. C. CAPON, M.A., B.D.

Presbyterian College: 3495 University St., Montreal, P.Q. H3A 2A8.
Principal: W. J. KLEMPA, M.A., PH.D.

United Theological College: 3521 University St., Montreal, P.Q. H3A 2A8;
Principal: PIERRE GOLDBERGER, B.A.

ATTACHED RESEARCH INSTITUTES:

Bellairs Research Institute: Barbados (*q.v.*); marine biology, geology, geography, tropical climatology; Dir. F. SANDER.

Brace Research Institute: utilization of solar and wind energy to improve living conditions; Dir. of Research T. A. LAWAND.

Institute of Occupational Health and Safety: Dir. G. W. GIBBS.

Industrial Relations Centre: McGill University; Dir. FRANCES BAIRSTOW.

McGill Centre for Northern Studies and Research: Dir. M. P. LANGLEBEN.

Marine Sciences Centre: Dir. R. G. INGRAM.

Allan Memorial Institute of Psychiatry: Montreal, Quebec; Dir. M. DONGIER.

Institute of Air and Space Law: McGill University; Dir. N. M. MATTE.

Institute of Comparative Law: McGill University; Dir. P. A. CRÉPEAU.

Institute of Islamic Studies: McGill University; Dir. C. J. ADAMS.

Management Institute: McGill University; Dir. R. N. MORRISON.

Montreal Neurological Institute: Montreal, Quebec; Dir. W. FEINDEL.

Institute of Parasitology: Macdonald College, Quebec; Dir. E. MEEROVITCH.

Institute of Pathology: McGill University; Dir. J. B. RICHARDSON.

Lyman Entomological Research Laboratory: Macdonald College; Dir. K. McE. KEVAN.

Pulp and Paper Research Institute: *see* under Research Institutes.

McGill Cancer Centre: Dir. P. GOLD.

Foster Radiation Laboratory: McGill University; Dir. S. K. MARK.

Human Genetics Centre: Dir. L. PINSKY.

Artificial Cells and Organs Research Centre: Dir. T. M. S. CHANG.

Geotechnical Research Centre: Dir. R. N. YONG.

McMASTER UNIVERSITY

HAMILTON, ONTARIO L8S 4L8

Telephone: (416) 525-9140.

Established in Toronto 1887, moved to Hamilton 1930.

Private control; Language of instruction: English; Academic year: September to April.

Chancellor: H. A. LEAL, B.A., LL.D., Q.C.
President and Vice-Chancellor: A. A. LEE, M.A., PH.D.
Vice-President (Academic): L. J. KING, PH.D.
Vice-President, Administration: J. A. MACFARLANE, B.A., C.A.
Librarian: G. R. HILL, M.A., M.L.S.
Registrar: A. L. DARLING, B.SC., M.ED.

Library: ***see* Libraries.**

Number of teachers: 914 full-time.

Number of students: 16,000 full- and part-time.

Publications: Staff Directory (annually), Calendars (biennially), *Year I Handbook* (annually), *McMaster Alumni News*, *McMaster University Library Research News*, *Journal of the Bertrand Russell Archives* (quarterly), *The Research Bulletin* (monthly), *Contact* (weekly).

DEANS:

Faculty of Business: A. Z. SZENDROVITS, PH.D.
Faculty of Engineering: J. W. BANDLER, PH.D., D.SC.(ENG.), D.I.C., F.I.E.E.E., F.I.E.E., P.ENG.
Faculty of Humanities: A. BERLAND, M.A., M.LITT.
Faculty of Health Sciences: J. F. MUSTARD, M.D., PH.D., F.R.C.P.CAN.
Faculty of Social Sciences: P. J. GEORGE, M.A., PH.D.
Faculty of Science: D. DAVIDSON, D.PHIL. (acting).
Graduate Studies: D. M. SHAW, M.A., PH.D., F.G.S., F.R.S.C.
Student Affairs: L. R. KURTZ, M.A., PH.D.
Women: **S. SCOTT (Mrs. A. FRANK), B.A.**
Men: B. D. HARRISON, B.A.
Principal of the Divinity College: M. R. HILLMER, B.A., B.D., PH.D.

PROFESSORS:

Faculty of Business:

BANTING, P. M., PH.D., Marketing
ECKEL, L. G., M.B.A., PH.D., Accounting
JAIN, H. C., M.B.A., PH.D., Organizational Behaviour
JOYNER, R. C., M.A., PH.D., Organizational Behaviour
MAHATOO, W. H., M.SC., PH.D., Marketing
SCHLATTER, W. J., A.M., PH.D., C.P.A., Accounting
STIDSEN, B., PH.D., Marketing
SZENDROVITS, A. Z., M.A., PH.D., Production and Management Science
TORRANCE, G. W., M.B.A., PH.D., Production and Management
WESOLOWSKY, G. O., M.B.A., PH.D., Management Science

Faculty of Humanities:

ALESSIO, A. G., D.LETT., Italian
ALLEN, A. R., M.A., PH.D., History
AZIZ, M., D.PHIL., English
BERLAND, A., M.A., M.LITT., English
BRASWELL, L. A., M.A., PH.D., English
BRINK, A. W., M.A., PH.D., English
CAPPADOCIA, E., M.A., PH.D., History
CAIN, T. H., PH.D., English
CASSELS, A., M.A., PH.D., History
CONLON, P. M., M.A., D.DE L'UNIV. (PARIS), F.R.S.C., French
CRO, S., DOTT.LING. E LETT., Italian
DALY, J. W., M.A., PH.D., History
DENNER, K., M.A., PH.D., German
DUNCAN, D. J. M., PH.D., English
GAGAN, D. P., M.A., PH.D., History
GUITE, H. F., M.A., Classics
HEPNER, L. A., PH.D., Music
HIDY, M., M.A., Music
HOEY, T. F., M.A., PH.D., Classics
JACKSON, B. A. W., D.PHIL., English
JOHN, B., M.A., PH.D., English
JOHNSTON, C. M., M.A., PH.D., History
KNIGHT, E. W., A.B., D.U., French
LEE, A. A. B.D., M.A., PH.D., English

McKay, A. G., m.a., a.m., ph.d., f.r.s.(c.), Classics
Morton, R. E., b.litt., English
Noxon, J. H., m.a., ph.d., Philosophy
Owen, W. J. B., m.a., ph.d., f.r.s.c., English
Paul, G. M., m.a., ph.d., Classics
Petrie, G., m.a., b.litt., English
Rempel, R. A., d.phil., History
Rouben, C., m.a., ph.d., French
Russo, D. J., m.a., ph.d., History
Shalom, A., m.a., d. de l'univ., d. ès l., Philosophy
Shein, L. J., m.a., ph.d., Russian
Shepherd, **D. M., m.a., ph.d., Classics**
Shrive, F. N., c.d., m.a., ph.d., English
Slater, W. J., m.a., ph.d., Classics
Thomas, J. E., m.a., ph.d., Philosophy
Trueman, J. H., m.a., ph.d., History
Walker, A., d.mus., a.r.c.m., Music
Wallace, G. B., m.a., Art and Art History
Wallace, W., ph.d., Music
Walton, P. H., a.m., ph.d., Art and Art History
West, G. D., t.d., m.a., ph.d., French
Wightman, E., m.a., d.phl., History
Wilson, N. L., m.a., ph.d., Philosophy
Wood, C., m.a., ph.d., English

Faculty of Health Sciences:

Adset, C. A., m.d., f.r.c.p.(c.), Psychiatry
Anderson, J. E., m.d., Anatomy
Barrows, H. S., m.d., c.r.c.p.(c.), Medicine
Bartolucci, G., m.d., f.a.p.a., Psychiatry
Basmajian, J. V., m.d., Medicine
Bienenstock, J., m.b., b.s., Medicine
Brain, M. C., m.a., d.m., f.r.c.p., Medicine
Brown, G. M., m.a., d.psych., ph.d., f.r.c.p.s.(c.), f.a.p.a., Neurosciences and Psychiatry
Buchanan, W. W., m.d., f.r.c.p.(e.), f.r.c.p.(g.), Medicine
Byles, J. A., d.s.w., Psychiatry
Campbell, E. J. M., m.b., m.d., ph.d., f.r.c.p., c.r.c.p.(c.), Medicine
Carr, D. H., m.d., ch.b., ph.d., Anatomy
Catton, D. V., m.d., f.r.c.p.(c.), Anaesthesia
Cleghorn, J. M., m.d., c.m., Psychiatry
Coates, G., m.b., f.r.c.p.(c.), Radiology
Cockshott, W. P., m.b., ch.b., d.m.r.d., m.d., Radiology
Cornett, R. W., m.d.c.m., m.sc.(med.), f.r.c.p.s.(c.), f.a.c.c.p., Medicine
Cosmos, E., m.sc., ph.d., Neurosciences
Davidson, R. G., m.d., Paediatrics
Diamond, J., m.b., b.s., ph.d., Neurosciences
Dolovich, J., m.d., f.r.c.p.can., Paediatrics
Dunnett, C. W., m.a., d.sc., Clinical Epidemiology and Biostatistics
Epand, R. M., a.b., ph.d., Biochemistry
Epstein, N. B., m.d., c.m., f.a.p.a., Psychiatry
Feldman, W., b.a., m.d.c.m., Paediatrics
Fitzgerald, J. D., b.sc., m.b., b.ch., m.r.c.p., Medicine
Flight, G. H., m.d.c.m., f.r.c.s.(c.), f.r.c.o.g., Obstetrics and Gynaecology
Forrest, J. B., m.b., ch.b., f.f.a.r.c.s., Anaesthesia
French, S. E., b.n., m.s., School of Nursing
Garnett, E. S., m.b., b.s., Radiology
Gent, M., m.sc., Clinical Epidemiology and Biostatistics
Goldsmith, C. H., ph.d., Clinical Epidemiology and Biostatistics
Goldstein, S., m.d., Medicine
Gordon, D. A., m.d., f.r.c.(c.), f.a.c.p., Medicine
Hamilton, J. D., m.b., b.s., m.r.c.p., Medicine
Hay, J., b.a., m.d., c.m., Family Medicine
Hirsh, J., m.a., m.b., b.s., m.d., m.r.a.c.p., r.c.p.s.(c.), Pathology
Hryniuk, W. M., m.d., Medicine
Inman, D. R., ph.d., Neurosciences
Jacobs, J., b.s., m.b., m.d., m.r.c.p., f.r.c.p., Paediatrics
Johnson, A. L., b.a., m.sc., m.d., c.m., Clinical Epidemiology and Biostatistics
Johnson, F. L., m.d., f.r.c.s.(c.), Obstetrics and Gynaecology
Jones, N. L., m.d., f.r.c.p., f.r.c.p.(c.), Medicine
Kay, J. M., m.b., ch.b., m.d., Pathology
Keane, P. M., m.b., ch.b., Pathology
Kristofferson, M. W., ph.d., Psychiatry
Laidlaw, J. C., m.d., m.a., ph.d., Medicine
Levine, L. E., m.s.w., Psychiatry
McCallion, D. J., ph.d., m.a., Anatomy
McComas, A. J., b.sc., m.b., b.s., Medicine
MacMillan, A. B., m.d., c.m., f.r.c.p.(c.), Paediatrics
McNab, A. R., b.a., m.d., ph.d., Medicine
Maudsley, R. F., m.d.c.m., f.r.c.s.(c.), f.a.c.o.g., Obstetrics and Gynaecology
Moore, C. A., m.d., Family Medicine
Moore, S., m.b., b.ch., b.a.o., l.m.c.c., Pathology
Mueller, C. B., m.d., a.b., f.a.c.s., Surgery
Muir, C. F., m.b.b.s., ph.d., f.r.c.p., Medicine
Mustard, J. F., m.d., ph.d., f.r.c.p.(c.), Pathology
Neufeld, V. R., b.a., m.d., m.a., f.r.c.p.s.(c.), Medicine
Nieboer, E., m.sc., ph.d., Toxicology
O'Brien, S. E., m.d., f.r.c.s.(c.), f.a.c.s., Surgery
Offord, D. R., m.d.c.m., f.a.p.a., Psychiatry
Pallie, W., m.b., b.s., d.phil., Anatomy
Rae-Grant, N. I., d.p.m., f.r.c.p.(u.k.), f.r.c.p.s.(c.), Psychiatry
Rawls, W. F., b.a., m.d., m.s., Pathology
Regoeczi, E., m.d., Pathology
Richardson, H., m.d., f.r.c.p.can., Pathology
Roland, C. G., m.d., Family Medicine
Sackett, D. L., b.s., m.d., m.s., Clinical Epidemiology and Biostatistics
Sakinofsky, I., m.d., ch.b., d.p.m., Psychiatry
Sarna, S., m.sc., ph.d., Surgery and Electrical Engineering
Schatz, S., b.a., m.d., b.sc.(med.), f.r.c.s.(c.), f.a.c.s., Surgery
Sibley, J. C., m.d., f.r.c.p., f.r.c.p.(c.), Medicine
Simon, G. T., m.d., Pathology
Sinclair, J. C., b.a., m.sc.(m), m.d., Paediatrics
Singal, D. P., m.sc., ph.d., Pathology
Spaulding, W. B., m.d., f.r.c.p.(c.), f.a.c.p., Medicine
Stewart, I. O., m.b., ch.b., f.r.c.path., f.r.c.p.s.(c.), Pathology
Streiner, D. L., ph.d., Psychiatry
Towell, M. E., m.b.b.s., f.r.c.o.g., f.r.c.s.(c.), Obstetrics and Gynaecology
Uchida, Irene A., ph.d., Paediatrics
Van der Spuy, H. I. J., m.a., ph.d., Psychiatry
Vayda, E., b.s., m.d., c.r.c.p.(c.), Clinical Epidemiology and Biostatistics
Walker, W. H. C., m.b., b.s., Pathology
Walsh, W. J., m.d., f.r.c.p.(c.), f.a.c.p., Medicine
Watters, W. W., m.d., Psychiatry
Wilson, W. W., m.d., f.r.c.p.s.(c.), f.a.a.p., Paediatrics
Witelson, S. F., m.sc., ph.d., Psychiatry
Woolever, C. A., m.d., f.r.c.p.can., Obstetrics and Gynaecology
Wright, F. J., m.d.c.m., f.r.c.p.can., Anaesthesia
Wynn-Williams, A., m.b., ch.b., m.d., ph.d., f.r.c.p.path., f.r.c.p.(ed.), m.r.c.p.a., d.c.p., Pathology
Zipursky, A., m.d., f.r.c.p.(c.), Paediatrics
Zylak, C. J., m.d., f.r.c.a.s.(c.), Radiology

Faculty of Social Sciences:

Ahmad, S., m.a., ll.b., m.sc., Economics
Arapura, J. G., s.t.m., m.a., ph.d., Religious Studies
Bromke, A., m.a., ph.d., Political Science
Brotz, H. M., m.a., ph.d., Sociology
Combs, A. E., m.div., ph.d., Religious Studies
Damas, D. J., a.m., ph.d., Anthropology
Denton, F. T., m.a., Economics
Freeman, M. M. R., ph.d., Anthropology
George, P. J., m.a., ph.d., Economics
Glanville, E. V., ph.d., Anthropology
Goldstein, M. N., ph.d., Political Science
Graham, J. E. L., m.a., b.litt., Economics
Greenland, C., m.sc., Social Work
Hayden, F. J., m.s., ph.d., Physical Education
Hunter, W. D. G., m.a., Economics
Jan, Y.-H., m.a., ph.d., Religious Studies
Johnson, J. A., m.a., ph.d., Economics
Jones, F. E., m.a., ph.d., Sociology
McIvor, R. C., m.a., ph.d., f.r.s.c., Economics
Means, G. P., m.a., ph.d., Political Science
Meyer, B. F., m.a., m.s.t., s.s.l., s.t.d. s.t.l., Religious Studies
Mol, J. J., m.s., ph.d., Religious Studies
Noble, W. C., ph.d., Anthropology
Novak, D., b.a., Political Science
Oksanen, E. H., m.a., ph.d., Economics
Penny, H. L., b.a., m.s.w., Social Work
Pineo, P. C., m.a., ph.d., Sociology
Potichnyj, P. J., m.a., ph.d., Political Science
Preston, A. B., ph.d., Anthropology
Rogers, E. S., m.a., ph.d., Anthropology
Sanders, E. P., b.a., th.d., Religious Studies
Scammell, W. M., ph.d., Economics
Slobodin, R., m.s., ph.d., Anthropology
Smith, A. J., c.d., m.ed., Physical Education
Spencer, B. G., ph.d., Economics
Stein, M. B., m.a., ph.d., Political Science
Thompson, R. W., m.a., ph.d., Economics
Wheeler, M., b.a., m.s.w., Social Work
Williams, J. R., m.a., ph.d., Economics
Winch, D. M., m.a., ph.d., Economics
Younger, P., m.a., th.m., ph.d., Religious Studies

Faculty of Theology:

Ford, M. J. S., m.a., d.rel.
Hillmer, B. A., ph.d.

HOBBS, T. R., M.TH., PH.D., Biblical Studies

Faculty of Science:

BADER, R. F. W., M.SC., PH.D., F.C.I.C., Chemistry
BALLIK, E. A., D.PHIL., Engineering Physics and Physics
BANASCHEWSKI, B., DR. RER. NAT., F.R.S.C., Mathematics
BAYLEY, S. T., PH.D., Biology
BEHRENS, E. A., DR.PHIL.NAT., Mathematics
BELL, R. A., M.SC., PH.D., Chemistry
BHADURI, R. K., M.SC., PH.D., Physics
BILLIGHEIMER, C. E., M.A., PH.D., Mathematics
BIRCHALL, T., A.R.I.C., PH.D., Chemistry
BOURNS, A. N., PH.D., F.R.S.C., F.C.I.C., Chemistry
BRANDA, L. A., D.SC., Biochemistry
BROCKHOUSE, B. N., M.A., PH.D., F.R.S.C., F.R.S., Physics
BROOKS, L. R., M.S., PH.D., Psychology
BROWN, I. D., PH.D., Physics
BRUNS, G. W. A., DR. RER. NAT., Mathematics
BUNTING, B. T., PH.D., Geography
BURGHARDT, A. F., M.S., PH.D., Geography
BURKE, D. G. M.SC., PH.D., Physics
BURLEY, B. J., M.SC., PH.D., Geology
CAMERON, J. A., PH.D., Physics
CARBOTTE, J. P., M.SC., PH.D., Physics
CARMENT, D. W., M.A., PH.D., Psychology
CHAN, U. W., M.A., PH.D., Biochemistry
CHILDS, R. F., B.SC., PH.D., Chemistry
CHOE, T. H., M.A., PH.D., Mathematics
CLARKE, W. B., PH.D., Physics
CLIFFORD, P. M., PH.D., Geology
COLLINS, M. F., M.A., PH.D., Physics
CORSINI, A., PH.D., F.C.I.C., Chemistry
CROCKETT, J. H., PH.D., Geology
CSIMA, J., PH.D., Mathematics
DATARS, W. R., M.SC., PH.D., Physics
DAVIDSON, D., D.PHIL., Biology
DAVIES, D. M., PH.D., Biology
DAVIES, J. A., M.SC., PH.D., Geography
DUNNETT, C. W., M.A., D.SC., Clinical Epidemiology, Biostatics and Applied Mathematics
EATON, D. R., M.A., D.PHIL., Chemistry
EMBURY, J. D., PH.D., Metallurgy and Materials Science
EPAND, R. M., A.B., PH.D., Biochemistry
FIELD, G., PH.D., Applied Mathematics
FORD, D. C., D.PHIL., Geography
FREEMAN, K. B., PH.D., Biochemistry
GALEF, B. G., A.B., M.A., PH.D., Psychology
GARSIDE, B. K., D.PHIL., Physics and Engineering Physics
GENTILCORE, R. L., PH.D., Geography
GHOSH, H. P., M.SC., D.PHIL., Biochemistry
GILLESPIE, R. J., PH.D., D.SC., F.R.S.C., F.R.I.C., F.C.I.C., F.R.S., Chemistry
GOODINGS, D. A., PH.D., Physics
HALL, R. H., M.A., PH.D., Biochemistry
HANNELL, F. G., PH.D., Geography
HEINIG, H. P., M.A., PH.D., Mathematics
HERON, B. R. W., M.A., PH.D., Psychology
HUSAIN, T., M.A., PH.D. .Mathematics
IVES, M. B., PH.D., Metallurgy and Materials Science
JACKSON, H. L., M.A., Mathematics
JENKINS, H. M., PH.D., Psychology
JOHNS, M. W., M.A., PH.D., F.R.S.C., Physics
KAY, D. A. R., PH.D., Metallurgy and Material Sciences
KEECH, G. L., M.SC., PH.D., Applied Mathematics
KENNETT, T. J., M.SC., PH.D., Physics and Engineering Physics
KERSHAW, K. A., PH.D., D.SC., Biology
KING, G. W., PH.D., F.C.I.C., F.R.S.CAN., Chemistry
KING, L. J., M.A., PH.D., Geography
KIRKALDY, J. S., M.A.SC., PH.D., Metallurgy and Material Science and Engineering Physics
KRAMER, J. R., M.SC., PH.D., Geology
KRISTOFFERSON, A. B., M.A., PH.D., Psychology
KUEHNER, J. A., M.A., PH.D., Physics
LANE, N. D., M.A., PH.D., Mathematics
LINK, S. W., PH.D., Psychology
LINTZ, R. G., PH.D., Mathematics
LOCK, C. J. L., A.R.S.C., PH.D., F.C.I.C., Chemistry
LU, W.-K., PH.D., Metallurgy and Material Science
MACLEAN, D. B., PH.D., F.C.I.C., Chemistry
MCCALLA, D. R., M.SC., PH.D., F.C.I.C., Biochemistry
MCCALLION, W. J., M.A., Mathematics
MCCANDLESS, E. L., M.S., PH.D., Biology
MCCANN, S.-B., PH.D., Geography
MCCULLOUGH, J. J., PH.D., Chemistry
MCMULLEN, C. C., M.SC., PH.D., Physics
MAK, S., M.SC., PH.D., Biology
MIDDLETON, G. V., A.R.C.S., PH.D., D.I.C., F.R.S.CAN. Geology
MILLER, J. J., PH.D., Biology
MOHANTY, S. G., M.A., PH.D., Mathematics
MORRISON, G. R., M.SC., PH.D., F.R.S.C., Psychology
MORRISON, J. A., M.SC., PH.D., Chemistry
MÜLLER, B. J. W., M.S., PH.D., Mathematics
NEILSON, T., PH.D., Biochemistry
NEWBIGGING, P. L., M.A., PH.D., Psychology
NICHOLSON, P. S., M.SC., PH.D., Metallurgy and Material Science
NOGAMI, Y., D.SC., Physics
OAKS, B. ANN, M.A., PH.D., Biology
PAPAGEORGIOU, G. J., M.C.P., PH.D., Geography
PIERCY, G. R., M.A.SC., PH.D., Metallurgy and Materials Science
PLATT, J. R., PH.D., Psychology
PRESTWICH, W. V., PH.D., Physics
PREVEC, L. A., PH.D., Biology
PRITCHARD, R. M., PH.D., Psychology
PURDY, G. R., M.SC., PH.D., Metallurgy and Materials Science
RACINE, R. J., M.SC., PH.D., Psychology
REEDS, L. G., M.A., PH.D., Geography
RIEHM, C. R., PH.D., Mathematics
ROBERTS, L. E., PH.D., Psychology
ROSA, A., PH.D., Mathematics
ROUSE, W. R., M.SC., PH.D., Geography
SANTRY, D. P., PH.D., Chemistry
SCHWARCZ, H. P., M.S., PH.D., Geology
SHAW, D. M., M.A., PH.D., F.G.S., F.R.S.C., Geology
SIEGEL, S., M.S., PH.D., Psychology
SMELTZER, W. W., PH.D., Metallurgy and Materials Science
SMITH, G. K., PH.D., Psychology
SORGER, G. J., M.S., PH.D., Biology
SPENSER, I. D., PH.D., D.SC., F.R.I.C., F.C.I.C., Biochemistry and Chemistry
SPRUNG, D. W. L., PH.D., Physics
STAGER, C. V., PH.D., Physics
SUMMERS-GILL, R.-G., M.A., PH.D., Physics and Engineering Physics
TAKAHASHI, I., M.S.A., PH.D., Biology
TAYLOR, D. W., D.PHIL., Physics
THODE, H. G., C.C., M.B.E., M.SC., PH.D., R.M.C., F.R.S., F.R.S.C., F.C.I.C., Chemistry
THRELKELD, S. F. H., M.SC., PH.D., Biology
TIKU, M. L., M.A., M.SC., PH.D., Applied Mathematics
TIMUSK, T., PH.D., Physics
TOMLINSON, R. H., PH.D., F.C.I.C., Chemistry
VOLKOV, A. B., M.S., PH.D., Physics
WADDINGTON, J. C., PH.D., Physics
WALKER, R. G., D.PHIL., Geology
WALTON, D., M.SC., PH.D., Physics
WARKENTIN, J., M.SC., PH.D., F.C.I.C., Chemistry
WEBBER, M. J., PH.D., Geography
WERSTIUK, N. H., PH.D., Chemistry
WESTERMANN, G. E. G., D.SC., Geology
WESTERMANN, J. E. M., PH.D., Biology
WOOD, D., PH.D., Applied Mathematics
WOOD, H. A., PH.D., Geography

Faculty of Engineering:

ALDEN, R. T. H., M.A.SC., PH.D., Electrical Engineering
ANDERSON, R. B., M.S., PH.D., F.C.I.C., Chemical Engineering
BAIRD, M. H. I., PH.D., Chemical Engineering
BANDLER, J. W., D.I.C., PH.D., Electrical Engineering
BANERJEE, S., PH.D., Engineering Physics
BRASH, J. L., PH.D., Chemical Engineering and Pathology
CAMPBELL, C. K., S.M., PH.D., F.R.S.A., Electrical Engineering
CROWE, C. M., PH.D., Chemical Engineering
DAVIES, J. A., M.A., PH.D., Engineering Physics
DE BUDA, R., PH.D., Electrical Engineering
DICENZO, C. D., C.M., C.D., M.SC., F.E.I.C., F.I.E.E.E., Electrical Engineering
DOKAINISH, M. A., M.A.SC., PH.D., Mechanical Engineering
DRYSDALE, R. G., M.A.SC., PH.D., Civil Engineering and Engineering Mechanics
DUNCAN, J. L., M.SC.TECH., PH.D., Mechanical Engineering
GARSIDE, B. K., D.PHIL., Engineering Physics and Physics
GLADWIN, A. S., D.SC., PH.D., Electrical Engineering
HAMIELEC, A. E., M.A.SC., PH.D., Chemical Engineering
HARMS, A. A., PH.D., Engineering Physics
HAYKIN, S. S., PH.D., D.SC., Electrical Engineering
HEIDEBRECHT, A. C., M.S., PH.D., Civil Engineering and Engineering Mechanics
HOFFMAN, T. W., M.SC., PH.D., F.C.I.C., Chemical Engineering
JAMES, W., PH.D., Civil Engineering and Engineering Mechanics
JUDD, R. L., M.ENG., PH.D., Mechanical Engineering
KAY, D. A. R., PH.D., Metallurgy and Material Science
KITAI, R., D.SC., Electrical Engineering
LATTO, B., PH.D., Mechanical Engineering
MURPHY, K. L., M.SC., PH.D., Civil Engineering and Engineering Mechanics and Chemical Engineering
NEWCOMBE, W. R., M.ENG., Mechanical Engineering
ORAVAS, G. A. E., M.S.CIV.ENG., M.S.ENG.MECH., Civil Engineering and Engineering Mechanics
PIERCY, G. R., M.A.SC., PH.D., Metallurgy and Metals Science
ROBINSON, H., PH.D., Civil Engineering and Engineering Mechanics

ROUND, G. F., PH.D., F.C.I.C., Mechanical Engineering
SHEMILT, L. W., M.SC., PH.D., F.C.I.C., F.A.I.CHEM.E., Chemical Engineering
SIDDALL, J. N., S.M., Mechanical Engineering
SINHA, N. K., PH.D., Electrical Engineering
SMELTZER, W. W., PH.D., Metallurgy and Materials Science
SMITH, A. A., PH.D., Civil Engineering and Engineering Mechanics
SOWERBY, R., M.SC., PH.D., Mechanical Engineering
TLUSTY, J., DIPL.ING., PH.D., D.SC., Mechanical Engineering
TSO, W. K., M.S., PH.D., Civil Engineering and Engineering Mechanics
VLACHOPOULOS, J., D.SC., Chemical Engineering
WADE, J. H. T., M.A.SC., PH.D., Mechanical Engineering
WILSON, N. E., M.A., M.A.I., S.M., Civil Engineering and Engineering Mechanics
WOODS, D. A., M.SC., PH.D., Chemical Engineering
WRIGHT, J. D., PH.D., Chemical Engineering

UNIVERSITY OF MANITOBA

WINNIPEG, MANITOBA R3T 2N2

Telephone: 474-8880.

Founded 1877.

Language of instruction: English; Academic year: September to April (two terms).

Chancellor: I. G. AULD, M.A.

President and Vice-Chancellor: D. R. CAMPBELL, M.A. (until July 1981).

Director of Student Records: J. B. SALT.

Vice-President (Administration): D. J. LAWLESS, PH.D.

Vice-President (Academic): J. C. GILSON, PH.D.

Director of Libraries: M. SHARROW, PH.D.

Number of teachers: 1,272.

Number of full-time students: 11,477.

DEANS:

Faculty of Administrative Studies: J. D. MUNDIE, M.B.A., PH.D.
Faculty of Agriculture: R. C. MCGINNIS, PH.D.
Faculty of Architecture: H. E. THOMPSON, M.ARCH.
Faculty of Arts: F. G. STAMBROOK, B.SC., PH.D.
Faculty of Dentistry: A. SCHWARTZ, D.D.S.
***Faculty of Education:* E. D. MACPHERSON, M.A., PH.D.**
Faculty of Engineering: E. KUFFEL, PH.D., D.SC., P.ENG.
Faculty of Graduate Studies: T. P. HOGAN, PH.D.
Faculty of Home Economics: B. E. MACDONALD, M.S.C., PH.D.
Faculty of Law: J. LONDON, LL.M.
***Faculty of Medicine:* A. NAIMARK, M.D., M.SC., F.R.C.P.(C.).**
***Faculty of Pharmacy:* J. R. MURRAY, M.SC., PH.D.**
Faculty of Science: C. BIGELOW, M.SC., PH.D.

DIRECTORS:

***School of Agriculture:* P. STELMASCHUK, B.SC., M.ED.**
School of Art: A. E. HAMMER, M.F.A.
School of Dental Hygiene: S. C. LENZ, M.P.H.
School of Medical Rehabilitation: (vacant).
School of Music: P. W. PATERSON, M.SC.
Natural Resource Institute: T. HENLEY.
School of Nursing: J. M. BRADLEY, M.S.N.
School of Physical Education: HENRY JANZEN, M.P.E., ED.D.
School of Social Work: A. PENNER, PH.D.

PROFESSORS:

Faculty of Agriculture:

BERNIER, C. C., M.SC., PH.D., Plant Science
BRUST, R. A., M.SC., PH.D., Entomology
CHO, C. M., M.SC., PH.D., Soil Science
CLARK, K. W., B.S.A., PH.D., Plant Science
DEVLIN, T. J., M.SC., PH.D., Animal Science
EVANS, L. E., M.SC., PH.D., Plant Science
FRAMINGHAM, C. F., PH.D., Agricultural Economics
GALLOP, R. A., M.SC., PH.D., Food Science
GILSON, J. C., B.S.A., M.SC., PH.D., F.A.I.C., Agricultural Economics
HEDLIN, R. A., B.S.A., M.SC., PH.D., Soil Science
HENDERSON, H. M., PH.D., Food Science
HILL, R. D., PH.D., Plant Science
HOUGEN, F. W., PH.D., Plant Science
INGALLS, J. R., M.S., PH.D., Animal Science
JAY, S. C., M.S.A., PH.D., Entomology
LACROIX, L. J., M.SC., PH.D., Plant Science
LALIBERTE, G. E., B.E., M.SC., PH.D., Agricultural Engineering
LAPP, H. M., B.E., M.S., Agricultural Engineering
LARTER, E. N., M.SC., PH.D., Plant Science
LENZ, L. M., M.SC., Plant Science
LOYNS, R. M. A., M.SC., PH.D., Agricultural Economics
MCCONNELL, M. B., PH.D., Food Science
MARQUARDT, R. R., M.SC., PH.D., Animal Science
MUIR, W. E., M.S., PH.D., Agricultural Engineering
MURRAY, E. D., PH.D., Food Science
NESBITT, J. PH.D., Agriculture
PALMER, W. M., PH.D., M.SC., Animal Science
PARKER, R. J., M.S.A., PH.D., Animal Science
PEREIRA, R. R., M.SC., PH.D., Food Science
PHILLIPS, G. D, B.SC., B.V.SC., PH.D., Animal Science
RACZ, G. J., M.SC., PH.D., Soil Science
RIDLEY, A. O., B.S.A., M.SC., Soil Science
ROBINSON, A. G., M.SC., PH.D., Entomology
SIEMENS, L. B., M.SC., M.A., Agriculture
SOPER, R. J., B.A., B.S.A., M.SC., PH.D., Soil Science
STANGER, N. E., B.S.A., M.SC., D.V.M., Animal Science
STEFANSSON, B. R., M.SC., PH.D., Plant Science
STOBBE, E. H., PH.D., Plant Science
STORGAARD, A. K., M.SC., PH.D., Plant Science
STOTHERS, S. C., B.S.A., M.S., PH.D., Animal Science
STRINGHAM, E. W., M.SC., PH.D., Animal Science
TANGRI, O. P., M.A., PH.D., Agricultural Economics
TOWNSEND, J. S., PH.D., Agricultural Engineering
TRUSCOTT, J. D., M.SC., PH.D., Agriculture
TYRCHNIEWICZ, E. W., M.S., PH.D., Agricultural Economics
WOOD, A. W., B.A (HONS.), B.S.A., M.SC., PH.D., Agricultural Economics
YEH, M. H., M.SC., PH.D., P.D.F., Agricultural Economics
YOUNG, G. M., M.SC., Plant Science

Faculty of Architecture:

ANDERSON, J. M., DIP.ARCH., F.R.I.B.A., F.R.I.A.S., M.S.I.A., Architecture
CARVALHO, M., M.C.P., City Planning
COLLIN, J., D.P.L.G., E.I.U.P., Architecture
DA ROZA, G. U., B.ARCH., F.R.A.I.C., Architecture
DE FOREST, C., M.ARCH., M.R.A.I.C., Environmental Studies
ELLIS, D. A., M.ARCH., Environmental Studies
FONSECA, R., M.ARCH., PH.D., Environmental Studies
FORRESTER, R. A., M.ARCH., M.C., R.P., Architecture
FORSTER, P., C.D., A.R.I.B.A., Environmental Studies
FULLER, G. R., PH.D., M.I.D.I.M., I.D.C., Interior Design
GERECKE, K., M.A., PH.D., City Planning
GRAHAM, J. W., M.I.D.I.M., F.R.A.I.C., Environmental Studies
LEHRMAN, J. B., M.ARCH., A.R.I.B.A., M.C.I.P., M.R.A.I.C., F.R.S.A., Architecture
MARSHALL, G., M.A., M.I.D.I.M., Interior Design
NELSON, JR., C.R., M.ARCH., M.R.A.I.C., Landscape Architecture
RATTRAY, A. E., M.LAND.ARCH., Landscape Architecture
SHAY, J. M., M.SC., PH.D., Landscape Architecture
STYLIARAS, D., PH.D., M.R.A.I.C., M.T.P.I.C., City Planning
VEITCH, R., M.ARCH., Interior Design
WELCH, J. D., Environmental Studies

Faculty of Arts:

ADAIR, J. G., M.SC., PH.D., Psychology
ANNA, T. E., M.A., PH.D., History
BARBER, C. L., M.A., PH.D., Economics
BECKERS, G., DR.PHIL., German
BELLAN, R. C., M.A., PH.D., Economics
BERRY, E. G., M.A., PH.D., F.R.S.C., Classics
BESSASON, H., Icelandic
CATCHPOLE, A. J. W., PH.D., Geography
CHURCHLAND, P., PH.D., Philosophy
CLARK, L. C., M.A., PH.D., History
DALY, P. M., DR.PHIL., German
DEPREZ, P., M.A., PH.D., Economics
DI LOLLO, V., PH.D., Psychology
DOERKSEN, V. G., DR.PHIL., M.A., German
DONNELLY, M. S., M.A., PH.D., Political Studies
FINLAY, J. L., M.A., PH.D., History
FORTIER, P., M.A., PH.D., French
GLASSEN, P., M.A., A.M., Philosophy
GONICK, C. W., PH.D., Economics
GRISLIS, E., PH.D., Religion
GUTKIN, M., M.A., English

HARLAND, G., PH.D., Religion
HARRIS, R. F., B.COMM., M.A., Economics
HELLER, H., PH.D., History
HOGAN, T. P., M.A., PH.D., Psychology
JENSEN, C. A., M.A., PH.D., Romance Languages
JENSEN, V. J. (S.J.), M.A., S.T.L., History
JOUBERT, A. M., L. ès L., D.E.S., French
KENDLE, J. E., PH.D., History
KINNEAR, M. S. R., M.A., D.PHIL., History
KLASSEN, W., B.A., B.D., TH.D., Religion
KLOSTERMAIER, K. K., DR.PHIL., PH.D., Religion
KOULACK, D., M.S., PH.D., Psychology
KRISTJANSON, G. A., M.SC., PH.D., Sociology
LAWLESS, D. J., M.A., PH.D., Psychology
LEBRUN, R. A., M.A., PH.D., History
MARCUSE, F. L., M.A., PH.D., Psychology
MCCARTHY, D. J., M.A., PH.D., L.M.S., Philosophy and Religion
MARTIN, D. G., M.A., PH.D., Psychology
MARTIN, G. L., M.A., PH.D., Psychology
MOULTON, E. C., M.A., PH.D., History
NICKELS, J. B., M.A., PH.D., Psychology
PEAR, J. J., PH.D., Psychology
PRESSEY, A. W., M.A., PH.D., Psychology
REA, J. E., M.A., PH.D., History
RENNIE, D. L., B.SC., M.A., PH.D., Sociology
SCHULDERMAN, E. H., PH.D., Psychology
SCHLUTZ, G. A., M.A., PH.D., History
SHEPHARD, A. H., M.A., PH.D., Psychology
SMITH, W. D., M.A., History
STAMBROOK, F. G., PH.D., History
SWEET, LOUISE E., M.A., PH.D., Anthropology
TEUNISSEN, J. J., M.A., PH.D., English
TURNER, M., PH.D., English
VINCENT, R. H., A.M., Philosophy
WATERMAN, Rev. A. M. C., M.A., PH.D., Economics
WEIL, H. S., PH.D., English
WOLFART, H. C., M.A., PH.D., Anthropology
WRIGHT, M. W., M.A., PH.D., Psychology

Faculty of Education:

BAKER, L. D., M.ED., ED.D., Educational Psychology
FROESE, V., PH.D., Curriculum: Humanities and Social Sciences
GREGOR, A. D., PH.D., Educational Administration and Foundations
HEDLEY, R. L., M.ED., ED.D., Curriculum (Mathematics and Natural Sciences)
HUSBY, P. J., M.ED., PH.D., Educational Administration
MACPHERSON, E. D., M.A., PH.D., Curriculum (Mathematics and Natural Sciences)
MCPHERSON, A. M., M.ED., Curriculum (Mathematics and Natural Sciences)
MAURICE, L. J., PH.D., M.ED., Curriculum (Humanities and Social Sciences)
MAY, H. E., M.S., ED.D., Curriculum (Humanities and Social Sciences)
PEACH, J. W., B.A., M.ED., PH.D., Educational Administration
RIFFEL, A., M.ED., PH.D., Educational Administration
SANDALS, L. H., M.A., PH.D., Educational Psychology
SEALEY, D. B., M.ED., Educational Foundations
SLENTZ, K. R., M.ED., M.S., D.ED., Curriculum (Mathematics and Natural Sciences)
TROSKY, O. S., M.ED., PH.D., Curriculum (Humanities and Social Sciences)
WILLIAMS, H. D., PH.D., Curriculum (Mathematics and Natural Sciences)
WILSON, K., M.A., M.ED., PH.D., Educational Foundations

Faculty of Law:

ANDERSON, D. T., B.A.,
BASS, A. B., LL.M.
BRAID, E. A., LL.M.
DEBICKA, Mrs. J., LL.M.
DILTS, C. G., B.A., LL.B., Q.C.
EDWARDS, C. H. C., LL.B.
GIBSON, R. D., LL.M.
HARVEY, D. A. C., LL.M.
IRVINE, J., M.A., B.C.L.
NEMIROFF, G. LL.M.
NEPON, M. B.
OSBORNE, P. H.
PENNER, R., Q.C., LL.B.
SNEIDEMAN, B.
TURNER, K., Q.C., LL.M.

Faculty of Dentistry (inc. School of Dental Hygiene):

BORDEN, S. M., M.S.D., Periodontology
BRASS, G. A., D.D.S., B.S.D., F.I.C.D.
CHEBIB, F. S., M.SC., PH.D., Preventive Dentistry
DAWES, C., PH.D., Physiology
DOWSE, C. M., B.SC., PH.D.
FORGAY, M. G. E., B.A., B.ED., Dental Hygiene
HAMILTON, I. R., M.S.A., PH.D., Bacteriology
JACKIN, P. M., M.SC.D., Operative Crown and Bridge
KENNETT, S., M.D., F.D.S.R.C.S.
LAVELLE, C. L. B., PH.D., M.D.S., D.SC., Oral Biology
LENZ, S., B.SC., Dental Hygiene
LOVE, W. B., D.M.D., M.SC., Prosthodontics
NEILSON, J. W., B.A., D.D.S., M.SC., F.I.C.D., F.A.C.D., F.R.C.D.(C.)
NICKELS, J. B., PH.D., Dental Hygiene
PRITCHARD, E. T., M.SC., PH.D.
PROCTOR, D. B., D.D.S., Stomatology
ROLLO, I. M., B.SC., PH.D.
SCHWARTZ, A., D.D.S.
STOREY, A. T., D.D.S., PH.D., Preventive Dentistry
WEDGWOOD, D. L., B.D.S., M.B., B.S., Stomatology
ZEBROWSKI, E. J., M.SC., PH.D.

Faculty of Engineering:

AZAD, R. S., PH.D., Mechanical
BARACOS, A., M.SC.(C.E.), M.E.I.C., P.ENG., Civil and Geological
BOOY, C., C.E., P.ENG., Civil
BRIDGES, E., M.SC.(E.E.), P.ENG., Electrical
CAHOON, J. R., M.SC., PH.D., P.ENG., Mechanical
CARLSON, A. J., B.SC.(C.E.), M.A.SC., M.E.I.C., P.ENG., Civil
CHANT, R. E., M.ENG.(MECH.), M.E.I.C., M.A.S.M.E., P.ENG., Mechanical
CHATURVEDI, M. C., M.MET., PH.D., Mechanical
COHEN, H. C., M.SC., PH.D., Civil
HAMID, M. A. K., M.ENG., PH.D., P.ENG., Electrical
HSU, T. R., M.SC., PH.D., Mechanical
JOHNSON, R. A., M.SC., P.ENG., Electrical
KAO, K. C., B.SC.(E.E.), M.S.C., PH.D., Electrical
KIM, H. K., M.SC., PH.D., P.ENG., Electrical
KUFFEL, E., D.SC., PH.D., Electrical
KUIPER, E., B.SC.(C.E.), M.SC.(C.E.), F.ASCE., M.E.I.C., P.ENG., Civil
LANSDOWN, A. M., B.SC.(C.E.), PH.D., M.E.I.C., Civil
MARTENS, G. O., M.A.SC., PH.D., Electrical
MATHUR, R. M., PH.D., P.ENG., Electrical
MORRIS, G. A. ,PH.D., M.SC., Civil
SHAFAI, L., PH.D., Electrical
SHEWCHUK, J., M.SC.(M.E.), PH.D., P.ENG., Mechanical
SIMS, G. E., M.SC., PH.D., C.S.M.E., P.ENG., Mechanical
SWIFT, G. W., M.SC.(E.E.), PH.D., P.ENG., Electrical
TANGRI, K. K., B.SC.(MET.ENG), M.SC., PH.D., P.ENG., Mechanical
TARNAWECKY, M. Z., M.SC.(E.E.), P.ENG., Electrical
TINKLER, J., B.SC.(ENG.), PH.D., P.ENG., Mechanical
WEXLER, A., PH.D., F.R.S.A., Electrical

Faculty of Administrative Studies:

BECKMAN, M. D., M.B.A., PH.D., Business Administration
BECTOR, C. R., M.A., PH.D., Actuarial and Business Mathematics
BLAZOUSKE, J. D., B.A., B.COM., M.B.A., F.C.A., R.I.A., Accounting and Finance
BOOM, H. J., DOCT., A.S.A., F.C.I.A., Actuarial and Business Mathematics
ELIAS, N. S., PH.D., M.S., Accounting and Finance
GOOD, W. S., M.S., M.B.A., PH.D., Business Administration
HERCUS, T. F., M.B.A., Business Administration
MAJOR, T. S., DIPL.ECON., Actuarial and Business Mathematics
MUNDIE, J. D., B.COM., M.B.A., PH.D., Business Administration
ROOS, L. L., PH.D., Business Administration
ROOS, N. P., PH.D., Business Administration
THOMAS, G. D., M.B.A., PH.D., Business Administration
TRACHTENBERG, S., M.A., Public Policy
VOGT, E. R., B.COM. (HONS.), F.S.A., F.C.I.A., A.I.A., Actuarial and Business Mathematics
WAHN, J. D., M.SC., M.A., Public Policy

Faculty of Home Economics:

BROCKMAN, LOIS M., M.SC., PH.D., Family Studies
CARTER, N., M.S.W., Family Studies
ESKIN, N. A. M., PH.D., Foods and Nutrition
FENIAK, ELIZABETH, B.SC.(H.EC.), M.S., PH.D., General Home Economics
JACKSON, E. LOLA, M.SC., PH.D., Family Studies
MCDONALD, B. E., M.SC., PH.D., Foods and Nutrition
MORTON, MARGARET I., B.SC.(H.EC.), M.A., PH.D., Clothing and Textiles
VAISEY GENSER, Mrs. F. MARION, M.SC., Foods and Nutrition

Faculty of Pharmacy:

BILOUS, R., M.SC., PH.D.
MURRAY, J. R., M.SC., PH.D., Pharmacology
SHAW, J. A. M., M.SC., PH.D., A.R.I.C., Pharmaceutics
STEELE, J. W., B.SC.(PHARM.), A.R.C.S.T., PH.D., A.R.I.C., Pharmaceutical Chemistry
TEMPLETON, J. F., M.SC., PH.D., Pharmacy
VITTI, T. G., M.SC., PH.D., Biochemistry

Faculty of Medicine:

ALEXANDER, W., M.D., Otolaryngology
ANTHONISEN, N., M.D., Medicine
BAKER, S., M.D., Medicine
BERTALANFFY, F. D., M.SC., PH.D., F.R.M.S., Anatomy
BIHLER, I., M.SC., PH.D., Pharmacology

BLACK, E. F. E., M.D., F.R.C.S.(C.), F.R.C.O.G., F.A.C.S., Obstetrics and Gynaecology
BLANCHAER, M. C., B.A., M.D., C.M., Biochemistry
BOWDEN, D. H., M.B., CH.B., M.D., Pathology
BOWMAN, J. M., M.D., R.C.P.S.(C.), Paediatrics
BOWMAN, W. D., M.D., F.R.C.P., Paediatrics
BOWNESS, J. M., B.SC., PH.D., Biochemistry
BRIGGS, E. J. N., M.B., B.S., M.D., F.R.C.P., F.R.C.P.(C.), Paediatrics
CARTER, S. A., M.D., M.SC., Physiology
CHERNICK, V., M.D., Paediatrics
CHOI, N. W., M.D., M.PH., PH.D., Preventive Medicine
CRAIG, D. B., M.D.C.M., M.SC., F.R.C.P.(C.), Anaesthesia
CUDDY, T. E., M.D., F.R.C.P.(C), F.A.C.S., Medicine
CUMMING, G. R., M.D., F.R.C.P.(C.), Paediatrics
DAKSHINAMURTI, K., M.SC., PH.D., F.R.I.C., Biochemistry
DHALLA, N. S., M.S., PH.D., Physiology
DOWNS, A. R., M.D., F.R.C.S.(C.), F.A.C.S., Surgery
FAIMAN, C., M.D., M.SC., Physiology
FERGUSON, C. C., M.D., F.R.C.S.(C.), F.A.C.S., Surgery
FISH, D. G., M.A., PH.D., Social and Preventive Medicine
FOERSTER, J., B.SC., M.D., Medicine
FRIESEN, H. G., M.D., F.R.C.P.(C.), Physiology and Medicine
FYLES, T. W., M.D., M.SC., F.R.C.P.(C.), F.A.C.P., Medicine
GASKELL, P., M.D., PH.D., Physiology
GEMMELL, J. P., M.D., M.R.C.P., F.R.C.P.(C.), F.A.C.P., F.R.C.P., Medicine
GOLDENBERG, G. J., PH.D., M.D., Medicine
GREWAR, D. A. I., M.B., D.C.H., M.R.C.P., Paediatrics
HAMERTON, J. L., D.SC., Paediatrics
HAVILCEK, V., PH.D., D.SC., Physiology
HAWORTH, J. C., M.D., F.R.C.P.(C.), Paediatrics
HENDERSON, J. S., M.B., CH.B., Pathology
HILDES, J. A., M.D., M.R.C.P., F.R.C.P.(C.), F.R.C.P., Medicine
HUGHES, J. F. S., M.D., M.SC., Medicine
HUGHES, K. R., PH.D., M.A., Physiology
INNES, I. R., M.B., CH.B., Pharmacology and Therapeutics
ISRAELS, L. G., B.A., M.D., M.SC.(MED.), F.R.C.P.(C.), Medicine
KANFER, J. N., M.S., PH.D., Biochemistry
KIRK, B. W., M.D., F.R.C.P.(C.), Medicine
KIRKPATRICK, J. R., CH.M., F.R.C.S., R.R.C.S., General Surgery
KORDOVA, N., M.D., PH.D., Medical Microbiology
KROLMAN, G. M., B.SC., M.D., F.R.C.S.(C.), F.R.C.S.(E.), Ophthalmology
LABELLA, F. S., M.A., PH.D., Pharmacology
LAMBERD, W. G., D.F.C., M.B., CH.B., M.SC., C.R.C.P.(C.), Psychiatry
LAVELLE, C. L. B., PH.D., F.R.C.D.(C.), Anatomy
MCCULLOUGH, D. W., M.B., B.CH., F.R.C.S.(E.), F.R.C.S.(C.), Otolaryngology
MACDONNELL, J. A., M.D., F.R.C.P., Medicine
MACDOUGALL, J. T., D.S.O., B.A., M.D., C.M., F.R.C.S.(E.), F.R.C.S.(C.), F.A.C.S., Surgery
MACLEAN, J. P., M.D., Medicine
MCRAE, K. N., M.D., F.R.C.P.(C.), Paediatrics
MARTIN, R. M., M.S., PH.D., Psychiatry
MOORHOUSE, J. A., M.D., M.SC., Physiology
NAIMARK, A., M.D., M.SC., F.R.C.P.(C.), Medicine and Physiology
NATHANIEL, E. J. H., M.S., PH.D., Anatomy
PARASKEVAS, F., M.D., M.R.C.P., Medicine
PENNER, D. W., B.A., M.D., F.A.C.P., Pathology
PERSAUD, T. V. N., M.D., PH.D., Anatomy
PINSKY, C., PH.D., Pharmacology and Therapeutics
PROSEN, H., M.D., M.SC., F.A.P.A., F.R.C.P.(C.), Psychiatry
RIESE, K. T., M.D., F.R.C.S.(C.), F.A.C.S., General Surgery
ROLLO, I. M., B.SC., PH.D., Pharmacology and Therapeutics
ROMEYN, J. A., M.D., D.PH., Medical Microbiology
RONALD, A. R., M.D., F.R.C.P., Medical Microbiology and Medicine
ROOS, NORA, PH.D., Preventive Medicine
ROSS, R. T., M.D., M.R.C.P., F.R.C.P.(C.), Medicine
ROULSTON, T. M., M.B., B.CH., B.A.O., F.R.C.O.G., F.A.C.O.G., F.R.C.P.(C.), F.R.C.S.(C.), Obstetrics and Gynaecology
SEHON, A., M.SC., PH.D., D.SC., F.R.S.(C.), Immunology
SISLER, G. C., M.D., F.R.C.P.(C.), F.A.P.A., Psychiatry
SNIDAL, D. P., M.D., M.SC., F.R.C.P.(C.), Medicine
STEPHENS, N. L., M.B., B.S., M.D., Physiology
STEVENS, F. C., PH.D., Biochemistry
THOMSON, A. E., B.A., M.D., M.SC.(MED.), F.R.C.P.(C.), Medicine, and Pharmacology and Therapeutics
THURLBECK, W. M., B.SC., M.B., CH.B., F.R.C.P., F.R.C.P.(C.), Pathology
TYSON, J. E. A., M.D., F.R.C.S.(C.), Obstetrics and Gynaecology, Physiology
WADE, J. G., B.S., M.D., F.R.C.P.(C.), Anaesthesia
WALTON, R. J., M.B., CH.B., D.M.R., D.M.R.T., Radiology
WANG, J. H., PH.D., Biochemistry
WILT, J. C., M.D., M.SC., F.A.C.P., F.R.C.P.(C.), Medical Microbiology
WINTER, J. S. D., M.D., F.R.C.P.(C.), Paediatrics
WISEMAN, G. M., PH.D., Medical Microbiology
YAMADA, Mrs. ESTHER, M.SC., PH.D., Biochemistry

Faculty of Science:

ARSCOTT, F. M., M.SC., PH.D., Applied Mathematics
AYRES, L. D., PH.D., Earth Sciences
BARBER, R. C., M.SC., PH.D., Physics
BETTS, R. H., M.SC., PH.D., Chemistry
BOCK, E., M.SC., PH.D., Chemistry
BRISBIN, W. C., PH.D., Earth Sciences
BURTON, D. N., PH.D., Microbiology
CAMPBELL, N. E. R., M.SC., PH.D., Microbiology
CLARK, G. S., M.SC., PH.D., Earth Sciences
COISH, H. R., M.SC., PH.D., Physics
COLLENS, R. J., PH.D., Computer Science
DUNN, G. E., M.A., PH.D., Chemistry
EALES, J. G., M.SC., PH.D., Zoology
EVANS, R. M., PH.D., Zoology
FALK, W., PH.D., Physics
FERGUSON, R. B., M.A., PH.D., F.R.S.C., Earth Sciences
GAUNT, P., D.PHIL., Physics
GEE, J. H., PH.D., Zoology
GESSER, H., PH.D., Chemistry
GRATZER, G. A., PH.D., Mathematics
GUPTA, N. D., M.A., PHD., Mathematics
HALL, D. H., M.SC., PH.D., Earth Sciences
HALVORSON, H., PH.D., M.SC., Microbiology
HAWIRKO, R. Z., M.SC., PH.D., Microbiology
HENRY, B. R., PH.D., Chemistry
HOLLOWAY, A. F., M.SC., PH.D., Physics
HRUSKA, F. E., M.SC., PH.D., Chemistry
ISAAC, P. K., PH.D., A.R.C.S., D.I.C., F.R.M.S., Botany
JAMIESON, J. C., PH.D., Chemistry
JANZEN, A. F., PH.D., Chemistry
JOHNSON, DIANE, PH.D., M.SC., Mathematics
JOVANOVIC, J. V., PH.D., Physics
KELLY, F. M., M.A., PH.D., Physics
KING, P. R., PH.D., Computer Science
KRAUSE, G., PH.D., Mathematics and Astronomy
LAKSER, H., A.M., PH.D., Mathematics
LEJOHN, H. B., PH.D., Microbiology
LINDSEY, C. C., M.A., PH.D., Zoology
LOSEY, G. O., M.SC., PH.D., Mathematics
MENDELSOHN, N., M.A., PH.D., F.R.S.C., Mathematics
MCKINNON, D. M., PH.D., Chemistry
MORRISH, A. H., M.A., PH.D., Physics
MCKEE, J. S. C., PH.D., Physics
MUZIO, J. C., PH.D., Computer Science
PARAMESWARAN, M. R., M.A., M.SC., D.SC., Mathematics and Astronomy
PAUL, G. I., M.SC., PH.D., Statistics
PRUITT, W. O., Jr., M.A., PH.D., Zoology
QUACKENBUSH, R. W., PH.D., Mathematics and Astronomy
REID, J., M.SC., PH.D., Botany
ROBINSON, G. G. C., PH.D., Botany
SCHAEFER, T., M.SC., D.PHIL., Chemistry
SEARLE, C. W., M.SC., PH.D., Physics
SHAY, Mrs. J. M., M.SC., PH.D., Botany
SHIVAKUMAR, P. N., M.SC., PH.D., Applied Mathematics
SICHLER, J., PH.D., Mathematics
SINHA, S. K., M.A., M.SC., A.M., PH.D., Statistics
STANDIL, S., M.SC., PH.D., Physics
STANDING, K. G., M.A., PH.D., Physics
STANTON, R. G., M.A., PH.D., Computer Science
STEWART, J. M., M.SC., PH.D., Botany
SUBRAHMANIAM, K., M.SC., D.SC., Statistics
SUZUKI, I., PH.D., Microbiology
TURNOCK, A. C., M.SC., PH.D., Earth Sciences
USMANI, R. A., PH.D., Applied Mathematics
VAIL, J. M., M.SC., PH.D., Physics
VAN OERS, W. T. H., PH.D., Physics
VENKATARAMAN, R., M.SC., PH.D., Mathematics
WALLACE, R., PH.D., Chemistry
WARD, F. J., M.A., PH.D., Zoology
WELCH, H. E., M.A., PH.D., Zoology
WESTMORE, J. B., PH.D., Chemistry
WILLIAMS, G., D.I.C., PH.D., Physics
WILSON, H. D. B., M.SC., PH.D., Earth Sciences
WONG, C. M., PH.D., Chemistry
WONG, R. S. C., PH.D., Mathematics and Astronomy
WOODS, R. G., PH.D., Mathematics and Astronomy

School of Art:

ARCHAMBEAU, R., M.F.A.
EYRE, I.
HAMMER, A., M.F.A.
REICHERT, D.
WILLIAMS, R. E., B.A., M.F.A.

School of Music:

TURNER, R., D.MUS.

School of Nursing:
GLASS, HELEN P., R.N., M.A., ED.D.

School of Physical Education:
CORROLL, V. A., M.S., PH.D.
HRENCHUK, E. J., M.A.
JANZEN, H. F., M.P.E., ED.D.
MACDIARMID, J. A., B.P.E., M.A.

School of Social Work:
JEHU, D., B.A., F.B.PS.S.
LAMPE, W., M.S.W., PH.D.
RYANT, J. C., M.A., M.S.W., PH.D.
WOOLLEY, PATRICIA, M.S., B.A.

Continuing Education Division:
LAWLESS, D. J., M.A., PH.D.
MORRISON, T. R., PH.D.

Counselling Service:
EIDE, L. J., PH.D.
FRIDFINNSON, A. M.A.
HUDSON, R. I., M.A., ED.D.

AFFILIATED COLLEGES:

St. Boniface College: 200 Cathedral Ave., St. Boniface, Manitoba; f. 1818 (Roman Catholic); Rector CL. THIBAULT.

St. John's College: Winnipeg, Manitoba R3T 2M5; f. 1866 (Anglican); Warden and Vice-Chancellor Rev. Canon J. R. BROWN, M.A., D.D.

St. Paul's College: 430 Dysart Rd., Winnipeg, Manitoba R3T 2M6; f. 1926 (Roman Catholic); Rector Dr. H. E. KANE.

ASSOCIATED COLLEGE:

St. Andrew's College: 475 Dysart Rd., Winnipeg, Manitoba R3T 2M7; f. 1946 (Ukrainian Greek Orthodox Church); Principal J. R. SOLOMON, LL.B.

MEMORIAL UNIVERSITY OF NEWFOUNDLAND

ELIZABETH AVENUE,
ST. JOHN'S,
NEWFOUNDLAND A1C 5S7

Telephone: 737-8000.

Founded 1925 by Provincial Government as Memorial University College, University status 1949.

Academic year: September to August (three terms); Language of instruction: English.

Chancellor: P. G. DESMARAIS, O.C., LL.D.
President and Vice-Chancellor: M. O. MORGAN, C.C., M.A., LL.D., D.C.L.
Vice-Presidents:
Academic and Pro-Vice-Chancellor: L. G. HARRIS, M.A., PH.D.
Administration: W. H. M. SELBY, LL.B., F.C.C.A., F.C.I.S., M.B.I.M.
Health Sciences: I. E. RUSTED, M.SC., M.D., C.M., F.R.C.P.(C.), F.A.C.P.
Professional Schools and Community Services: A. A. BRUNEAU, D.I.C., PH.D., P.ENG.
Student Affairs and Services: J. D. EATON, M.A., PH.D.
Registrar: R. W. W. THISTLE.
Librarian: T. PHILIPPS.

Number of teachers: 797.

Number of students: 6,658 full-time, 2,717 part-time.

DEANS:

Faculty of Arts: I. A. F. BRUCE, M.A., PH.D.
Faculty of Science: P. J. HEALD, D.SC., PH.D., F.R.S.
Faculty of Education: B. V. PADDOCK, M.ED.
Faculty of Engineering: (vacant).
Faculty of Medicine: A. R. COX, M.D., F.R.C.P.(C.), F.A.C.P.
School of Graduate Studies: F. A. ALDRICH, M.SC., PH.D.

PROFESSORS:

ALDRICH, F. A., M.SC., PH.D., Biology
ALEXANDER, D. G., M.A., PH.D., History
ANDERSON, H. J., M.SC., PH.D., Chemistry
ASHLEY, J. B., M.A., PH.D., Classics
BAL, A. K., M.SC., PH.D., Biology
BARNES, J. G., M.B.A., PH.D., Business Administration
BARNSLEY, E. A., PH.D., Biochemistry
BARTON, D., PH.D., Chemistry
BENNETT, G. F., M.SC., PH.D., Biology
BLUNDON, W. J., M.A., Mathematics
BRACE, A. T., ED.D., Curriculum and Instruction
BRECKON, S. W., PH.D., Physics
BRIGGS, J. L., M.A., PH.D., Anthropology
BROWN-GRANT, K., M.A., M.D., SC.D., Physiology
BROWNRIGG, G. M., M.D., C.M., F.R.C.S.(C.), F.A.C.S., Surgery (Clinical)
BRUCE, I. A. F., M.A., PH.D., Classics
BRUNEAU, A. A., D.I.C., PH.D., P.ENG., Engineering
BULLOCK, E., M.A., PH.D., Chemistry
BURRY, J. H., M.SC., PH.D., Mathematics
CHANDRA, R. K., M.D., F.C.C.P., F.R.C.P.(C.), M.A.M.S., Paediatrics
CHO, C. W., M.A., PH.D., Physics
CHURCH, J. W., M.A.SC., LL.D., P.ENG., Engineering
CLARK, E. R., M.A., French
COLTON, T., M.S., SC.D., Epidemiology, Biostatistics
COOK, D. F., S.S.M., A.R.C.M., A.A.G.O., CL.M., Music
COOPER, G. A., M.ED., ED.D., Educational Foundations
COUVES, C. M., M.D., F.R.C.S., F.R.C.S.(C.), F.A.C.S., F.C.C.P., F.A.C.C., Surgery
COX, A. R., M.D., Medicine
CRAPO, H. H., PH.D., Mathematics
CRASKE, B., PH.D., Psychology
CUFF, H. A., M.A., ED.D., Student Teaching
DAVIS, C. C., M.SC., PH.D., Biology
DEUTSCH, E. R., M.A., PH.D., Physics
DRINKWATER, J. B., M.SC., Physical Education
EDWARDS, W. R., F.R.C.S.ED., Obstetrics and Gynaecology
FACEY, J. M. C., B.SC.(ENG.), M.I.E.E., Engineering
FEDER, Mrs. H., M.A., PH.D., English
FEKETE, A. E., M.SC., Mathematics
FELTHAM, L. A. W., M.A., PH.D., Biochemistry
FIZZARD, G., ED.D., Audio Visual
FODOR, J., M.D., C.S., Epidemiology
FOSTER, M. J., DIP. PHY.ED., M.SC., Physical Education
FRANCIS, C. J., M.A., PH.D., English
GARDNER, P. G., M.A., PH.D., English
GAULT, M. H., M.SC., M.D., C.M., F.R.C.P.(C.), F.A.C.P., Medicine (Nephrology)
GIEN, T. T., PH.D., Physics
GOGAN, N. J., PH.D., Chemistry
GOLDSTEIN, K. S., M.B.A., PH.D., Folklore
GUSHUE, W. J., ED.D., Educational Foundations
HAARD, N. F., M.A., PH.D., Biochemistry
HALPERT, H., M.A., PH.D., Folklore
HARRIS, L., M.A., PH.D., History
HARRIS, R. S., D.M.R.D., PH.D., F.F.R., Radiology
HART, D. S., PH.D., Psychology
HEWSON, J., M. ès A., D. DE L'U., Linguistics
HILLIER, M. J., M.SC.(ENG.), Engineering
HILLMAN, E., M.D., F.R.C.P.(C.), Medicine
HODDER, M. F., B.A., S.T.M., TH.D., Religious Studies
HOENIG, J., M.D., M.R.C.P., D.P.M., Psychiatry
HOUSE, A. M., M.D., C.M., F.R.C.P.(C.), Medicine
HUGHES, C. J., M.A., D.PHIL., Geology
HUNTSMAN, R. G., B.CHIR., M.D., F.R.C.P., Pathology
IDLER, D. R., M.A., PH.D., Biochemistry
INGRAM, D. W., M.B., B.CH., B.A.O., M.S., F.R.C.P.(C.), General Medicine and Therapeutics
JACKSON, F. L., M.A., Philosophy
JACKSON, H. H., LL.D., German and Russian
JANES, E. M., M.S.(ED.), ED.D., Curriculum and Instruction
JOSEPHSON, J. E., M.D., C.M., F.R.C.P.(C.), F.A.C.P., Pathology (Clinical)
KARAGIANIS, L. D., M.A., ED.D., Educational Psychology
KING, E. H., M.A., PH.D., English
KIRWIN, W. J., M.A., PH.D., English
KITCHEN, H. E., M.ED., PH.D., Educational Administration
LAIRD, M., M.SC., PH.D., D.SC., Biology
LAL, M., M.SC., PH.D., Mathematics
LAYMAN, G., M.A., A.I.E., Curriculum and Instruction
MACDONALD, A. A., M.A., B.LITT., PH.D., English
MACHIN, W. D., PH.D., Chemistry
MACLAUGHLIN, E. A., D.M.R.D., F.R.C.P.(C.), Radiology
MCCANN, W. P., PH.D., Educational Foundations
MCLEAN, Miss N., M.D., A.M., Nursing
MANNING, F., M.A., Anthropology
MARSHALL, W. H., M.D., PH.D., M.R.C.P., Immunology
MARTIN, J. R., M.D., C.M., Medicine
MATTHEWS, K., D.PHIL., History
MELLOR, C. S., PH.D., M.D., F.R.C.PSYCH., Psychiatry
MENSINKAI, S. S., M.A., PH.D., Economics
MOOKERJEA, S. S., M.SC., PH.D., Biochemistry
MOWBRAY, R. M., M.A., PH.D., Psychology and Medicine
MUI, H. C., M.A., PH.D., History
MURPHY, G., M.ED., PH.D., Curriculum and Instruction
MUSSELS, L., M.D., C.M., M.SC., Health Care
NEWLANDS, M. J., M.A., PH.D., Chemistry
NOEL, T. C., M.SC., Physics
O'BRIEN, P. J., M.SC., PH.D., Biochemistry
O'FLAHERTY, P. A., M.A., PH.D., English
PAINE, R. P. B., M.A., D.PHIL., Anthropology
PANTING, G. E., M.A., History
PAPEZIK, V. S., M.SC., PH.D., Geology
PARK, G. K., M.A., PH.D., Sociology and Anthropology
PAYTON, B. W., PH.D., Physiology
PETER, E. M., M.B.A., PH.D., C.A., P.S.W., Business Administration
PFEIFFER, C. J., PH.D., Gastrointestinal Physiology
PICCININNI, R., M.A., PH.D., Mathematics
PITT, D. G., M.A., PH.D., English

POOLE, C. F., M.A., PH.D., Philosophy
PRESTON, C. F., M.A., PH.D., L.TH., B.D., Psychology
RABINOWITZ, R. M., M.S., PH.D., Psychology
RALPH, E. K., PH.D., Chemistry
RATZ, A. E., PH.D., German
REDDY, D. V., M.S., D.I.C., PH.D., Engineering
REDDY, S. P., D.SC., F.INST.P., Physics
RENDELL, D. H., PH.D., Physics
REVUSKY, S. H., PH.D., Psychology
ROBERTS, G. D., M.A., PH.D., English
ROBERTS, K. B., M.A., M.B., D.PHIL., M.R.C.S., L.R.C.P., Physiology
ROCHESTER, M. G., M.A, PH.D., Physics
ROSS, J. C., M.S., PH.D., Sociology
ROSS, J. M., M.B., CH.B., Family Practice
RUSTED, I. E., M.SC., M.D., C.M., F.R.C.P.(C.), F.A.C.P., Medicine
RUSTED, N. F. S., M.D., C.M., D.SC., F.A.C.S., C.R.C.S.(C.), Surgery (Clinical)
SCARLETT, M. J., M.A., D.E.S., PH.D., Geography
SCHWARTZ, G. M., M.I.A., D.PHIL., History
SCOTT, J. M. W., PH.D., Chemistry
SELLS, B. H., M.A., PH.D., Molecular Biology
SINGH, B., M.A., M.S., C.F.E.A., PH.D., Economics
SINGH, S. P., M.SC., PH.D., Mathematics
SKANES, G. R., M.A., PH.D., Psychology
SKEVINGTON, D., PH.D., D.SC., Geology
SMITH, F. R., PH.D., Chemistry
SMITH, P. D. D., M.SC., Physics
SNELLEN, J. W., M.D., PH.D., Applied Physiology
SNYDER, H. L., P.ENG., Engineering
SOUTH, G. R., PH.D., Biology
STEELE, D. H., M.SC., PH.D., Biology
STEIN, A. R., PH.D., Chemistry
STORY, G. M., D.PHIL., English
STRONG, D. F., M.S., PH.D., Geology
SULLIVAN, A. M., M.A., PH.D., Psychology
SUMMERS, W. F., M.SC., PH.D., Geography
SUTTIE, B., M.B., CH.B., D.M.S.A., Health Care Delivery
TAGUE, J. A., M.A., PH.D., History
THOMAS, G. W., B.A., M.D., C.M., F.R.C.S.(C.), Surgery (Clinical)
THOMEIER, S., D.PHIL.NAT., Mathematics
THOMPSON, J. V., M.S.W., D.S.W., Social Work
THRELFALL, W., PH.D., Biology
TOMLINSON, J. D. W., M.A., M.B., B.CHIR., Anatomy
TSAGARAKIS, O., PH.D., Classics
TUCK, J. A., PH.D., Anthropology
VETTER, W. J., M.A.SC., PH.D., Engineering
VEYSOGLU, R., M.S., PH.D., Economics
WARREN, P. J., M.ED., PH.D., Educational Administration
WAY, H. H., M.A., M.SC., ED.D., Educational Psychology, Guidance and Counselling
WHALEN, H. J., M.A., Political Science
WHITELEY, W. H., M.A., PH.D., History
WHITTAKER, J., M.A., DR.PHIL., Classics
WILLIAMS, H., M.SC., PH.D., F.R.S.C., Geology
WOLINETZ, S. B., M.A.. PH.D., Political Science

ATTACHED INSTITUTES:

Institute of Social and Economic Research.
Chairman: L. HARRIS, M.A., PH.D.

Institute for Research in Human Abilities.
Director: P. A. JONES, M.ED., PH.D. (acting).

Marine Sciences Research Laboratory: Logy Bay.
Director: D. R. IDLER, D.F.C., M.A., PH.D., F.R.S.C.

Folklore and Language Archive.
Director: NEIL V. ROSENBERG, M.A., PH.D.

Research Unit on Vector Pathology.
Director: M. LAIRD, PH.D., D.SC.

Centre for Cold Ocean Resources Engineering.
Director: H. L. SNYDER, P.ENG.

Centre for Research in Labrador.
Chairman: G. F. BENNETT, M.SC., PH.D.

Institute for Educational Research and Development.
Director: R. K. CROCKER, PH.D.

International Reference Centre for Avian Haematozoa.
Director: G. F. BENNETT, M.SC., PH.D.

Maritime History Group.
Chairman: K. MATTHEWS, D.PHIL.

UNIVERSITÉ DE MONCTON

MONCTON, NEW BRUNSWICK
E1A 3E9
Telephone: 858-4000.

Founded 1864 as St. Joseph's University; name changed 1963.

Language of instruction: French; Private control; Academic year: September to May.

Campuses also in Edmundston (Saint-Louis-Maillet) and Shippagan.

Chancellor: LÉON RICHARD, B.A., M.D., L.M.C.C., D.SC.
Rector: GILBERT FINN, M.A.
Vice-Rectors: B. T. NEWBOLD, D.SC. (Moncton); M. SORMANY, M.SC.SOC. (Saint-Louis-Maillet); J. G. RIOUX, M.A.ED. (Shippagan).
Secretary-General: GILLES LONG, M.SC. COM.
Librarian: A. LEVESQUE, M.S.L.S.

Number of teachers: 309.
Number of students: 3,018 full-time, 1,435 part-time.
Publications: *Revue*, *Annuaire général*.

DEANS:

Faculty of Arts: (vacant).
Faculty of Business Administration: N. ROY, B.SC.COM., M.B.A.
School of Nursing: M. DUMONT, B.SC.N., M.ED.
Faculty of Education: L. MALENFANT, B.ED., M.A.
Faculty of Science and Engineering: L. J. LEBLANC, PH.D.
School of Behavioural and Social Sciences: L. DESJARDINS, PH.D.
School of Home Economics: M. PRÉFONTAINE, M.SC., PH.D.
School of Law: (vacant).

PROFESSORS:

ALLAIRE, G., Music
ARSENAULT, F., Religious Studies
ARSENAULT, G., Home Economics
BOSI, G., Physics, Mathematics
BOUDREAU, P., Accounting
BOURQUE, L., Accounting
CADIEUX, J., Accountancy
CANDELA, R., Biology
CHAMARD, M., French
COLLETTE, J., Finance
CORMIER, G., Psychology
CORMIER, J. B., Chemistry
DAIGLE, L. M., Philosophy
DESJARDINS, R., Psychology
DION, P., Psychology
DIONNE, R., History
GALLANT, C., Philosophy
GALLANT, M., French
GAUDET, A., Education
GAUDET, L., French
JEFFREY, C., Psychology
LEBLANC, L., Physics, Mathematics
LEBLANC, R., Physics, Mathematics
LEGER, J., Nursing
LONGVAL, R., Engineering
MEHRA, M. C., Chemistry
NADEAU, G. G., Education
ROBICHAUD, O., Education
ROSS, V., Engineering
SAJOUS, E., Economics
SRIVASTAVA, N., Engineering
WEIL, F. Mathematics
YOUNG, A., Sociology

UNIVERSITÉ DE MONTRÉAL

C.P. 6128, SUCCURSALE "A",
MONTREAL, QUEBEC H3C 3J7
Telephone: 343-6111.
Founded 1876.

Language of Instruction: French; Private control.

Chancellor: HERVÉ HÉBERT, B.SC.
Rector: PAUL LACOSTE, M.A., L.PH., LL.L., D. DE L'U.
Vice-Rectors: ANDRÉ ARCHAMBAULT, D.PHM., RENÉ J. A. LÉVESQUE, PH.D., JACQUES LUCIER, M.A., JACQUES ST.-PIERRE, M.SC., PH.D., LOUIS-MARIE TREMBLAY, M.SC. SOC., PH.D., J. MÉNARD.
Secretary-General: JACQUES BOUCHER.
Registrar: C. ST-ARNAUD, L.SC.PHYS., M.SC., PH.D.
Director of Finances: R. CHOUINARD, L.SC., C.A.
Librarian: C. AUDET.

Library: *see* Libraries.
Number of professors: 1,916.
Number of students: 37,978.
Publications: *L'Ingénieur*, *L'Actualité économique*, *Annuaire Général*, *La Revue canadienne de Biologie*, *Criminologie*, *Etudes Françaises*, *Chercheurs Pédagogiques*, *Revue des Sciences de l'éducation*.

DEANS:

Faculty of Graduate Studies: (vacant).
Faculty of Theology: L. AUDET, L.S.S., D.TH.
Faculty of Law: R. COMTOIS, LL.D.
Faculty of Medicine: P. BOIS, M.D., PH.D.

Faculty of Arts and Sciences: R. RIVEST, PH.D., D.SC., F.C.I.C., F.A.A.A.S. (CHEM.)
Faculty of Dental Medicine: A. VAILLANCOURT, D.D.S., M.S.
Faculty of Pharmacy: J. BRAUN, D.SC. PHM.
Faculty of Environment Design: C. H. DAVIDSON, M.ARCH.
Faculty of Music: H. FAVRE, ING.CHIM., D.SC., F.C.I.C.
Faculty of Nursing: D. GOYETTE, M.NURS.
Faculty of Education Sciences: M. GAGNON, M.A., PH.D.
Faculty of Veterinary Medicine: G. COUSINEAU, D.M.V.
Faculty of Continuing Education: G. BOURGEAULT, D.PH., D.TH.

PROFESSORS:

Faculty of Education Sciences:
DAOUST, G., D.PH., D.TH.
DE GRANDPRÉ, M., D.PED.
DEMERS, M., M.SC., PH.D.
DUPUIS, P., PH.D.
FARINE, A., M.A., PH.D.
JOFFE-NICODEME, A., L. EN PHIL. ET LETTRES, PH.D.
LEFEBVRE, A., D.ÈS L.
LEMIRE, V., L.TH., L.PS.
LE SIEUR, A., PH.D.
PLOURDE, M., D. ÈS L.
POIRIER, J., D.PED.
TOUSIGNANT, R., D. EN. SC. PED.

Faculty of Environment Design:
School of Architecture
BARACS, J., ING. P.
CHARNEY, M., M.ARCH.
CORBOZ, A., LIC.JUR., L.L.D.
DAVIDSON, C. H., M.ARCH.
DOELLE, L. L., M.ARCH.
LIPP, J.-J., ING.DIPL.
POULIN, J.-L., ARCH.DIPL.
WARSHAW, L.-D., B.ARCH.

School of Landscape Architecture
BEGIN, B., M.SC.A., SC.A.P., M.R.C.P.

Institute of Urbanism
CHARLES, R., D.E.S., D.EN.DROIT
CHEVALIER, M., M.C.P., PH.D.
GABBOUR, I., M.ARCH., M.C.P., PH.D.
MCNEIL, J., L.SC., D.E.S., D.SC.ECON.

Faculty of Theology:
BROSSEAU, R., L.TH., D.PH.
COUTURIER, G., L.TH., M.A., L.S.S.
D'ARAGON, J.-L., L.PH., L.TH., L.S.S.
GRAND'MAISON, J., L.SOC., D.TH.
HAMELIN, L., D.TH.
ROBILLARD, E., D.TH.

Faculty of Law:
BAUDOIN, J. L., LL.D.
BELLEMARE, J., LL.L.
BOHEMIER, A., LL.D.
BOUCHER, J., LL.L., D.E.S.
BROSSARD, J., LL.L.
CARDINAL, J. G., LL.D.
CARIGNAN, P., LL.M., M.A.
CHEVRETTE, F., D.E.S.
COMTOIS, R., D.E.S.
FORTIN, J., LL.D.
LACHAPELLE, R., B.C.L., D.E.S.
LAJOIE, A., M.A.
LORD, G., D.PHIL.
MARTINEAU, P., LL.M.
MOREL, A. LL.L., M.A., LL.D.
MORIN, F., LL.M., D.E.S.
MORIN, J.-Y., LL.M., S.M.U.
OUELLETTE, Y., LL.D.
PEPIN, G., LL.L., LL.D.
PINEAU, J., LL.D., D.E.S.
POPOVICI, A., D.E.S.
SAVOIE, R., LL.M.
TASCHERAU, L. P., LL.M.
TREMBLAY, A., LL.D.

Faculty of Medicine:
Department of Anatomy
BLAIS, J.-M., M.D.
BOIS, P., M.D., PH.D.
DAOUST, R., M.SC., PH.D.
FRANCHEBOIS, P., M.D.
GAGNON, R. P., M.D., PH.D.
JEAN, P., M.D., PH.D.
MESSIER, B., PH.D.
MESSIER, P. E., PH.D.
SAINTE-MARIE, G., M.D., PH.D.
VEILLEUX, R., D.M.V., PH.D.

Department of Biochemistry
DE LAMIRANDE, G., PH.D.
GIANETTO, R., PH.D.
GINGRAS, G., M.SC., DOCT.D'ETAT
SAVARD, K., D.SC.

Department of Occupational and Environmental Health
BRODEUR, J., M.D., PH.D.
Institute of Biomedical Engineering:
ROBERGE, F., PH.D.

Institute of Experimental Medicine and Surgery:
DE LAMIRANDE, G., PH.D.

Department of Health Administration
BLAIN, G., M.D., M.A.H.

Department of Medicine
BAND, P., M.D.
BARBEAU, A., M.D.
BERNIER, J., M.D.
BOLTE, E., M.D.
CARRIÈRE, S., M.D.
CHAPDELAINE, A., M.D., M.SC.
CHARBONNEAU, R., M.D.
COURTOIS, G., M.D., M.SC.
COUTU, L. L., M.D., PH.D.
GENEST, J., M.D., C.C.
GIROUX, J. M., M.D.
JULIEN, P.-P., M.D.
LANTHIER, A., M.D.
LECOURS, A. R., M.D.
LEMIEUX, G., M.D.
MARC-AURELE, J., M.D.
MATHIEU, J., M.D.
NADEAU, P., M.D.
NADEAU, R., M.D.
PESANT, P., M.D.
PROULX, A., M.D.
RASIO, E., M.D., PH.D.
THIBERT, F., M.D.
VAILLANCOURT, G., M.D., D.SC.
VERDY, M., M.D.
VIALLET, A., M.D.

Department of Microbiology and Immunology
ADAMKIEWICZ, V., M.SC., PH.D.
DE REPENTIGNY, J., PH.D.
GYENES, L., PH.D.
JONCAS, J. H., M.D., PH.D.
KURSTAK, E., D.SC.
MARTINEAU, B., M.D.
MATHIEU, L. G., D.M.V., M.SC., PH.D.
SASARMAN, A., M.D.
SONEA, S., M.D.
TURGEON, F., M.D., M.SC.

Department of Nutrition
BEAUDOIN, R., D.SC.H.
DALMÉ, C., M.NS.
MONGEAU, E., M.SC., PH.D.
RENAUD, S., D.M.V., PH.D.

Department of Obstetrics and Gynaecology
AUDET-LAPOINTE, P., M.D.
LEFEBVRE, Y., M.D.
VAN CAMPENHOUT, J., M.D.

Department of Ophthalmology
MATHIEU, M., M.D.

Department of Paediatrics
CHICOINE, L. F., M.D.
DAVIGNON, A., M.D.
DUCHARME, J. R., M.D., M.SC.
GAGNAN-BRUNETTE, M., M.D., M.SC.
JELIU, G., M.D.
MORIN, C. L., M.D., M.SC.
POIRIER, R., M.D.
ROY, C., M.D.
ROYER, A., M.D.

Department of Pathology
CANTIN, M., M.D., PH.D.
JASMIN, G., M.D., PH.D.
ROBERT, F., M.D.
SIMARD, R., M.D., D.SC.
SOLYMOSS, B., M.D.

Department of Pharmacology
BIRON, P., M.D., M.SC.
COTE, M.-G., D.M.V., M.SC., PH.D.
GASCON, A., PH.D.
MARCHAND, C., M.D., PH.D.
PLAA, G. L., M.S., PH.D.

Department of Physiology
BERGERON, M., M.D., M.SC.
COURVILLE, J., M.D., M.SC.
DE CHAMPLAIN, J., M.D., PH.D.
DESCARRIES, L., M.D.
LAMARCHE, G., M.D.
LAMARRE, V., M.D., PH.D.
LEDUC, J., M.D., PH.D.
STERNBERG, J., M.D., M.SC.
VAN GELDER, N., PH.D.

Department of Psychiatry
BEAUDOIN, G., M.D.
BOULANGER, J. B., M.D., M.A.
GAUTHIER, Y., M.D.
HOUDE, L., M.D.
LAURIN, C., M.D.

Department of Radiology
MALTAIS, R., M.D.
SALTIEL, J., M.D.

Department of Surgery
CHOLETTE, J. P., M.D.
COLIN, P.-P., M.D.
DALOZE, P., M.D.
DESJARDINS, J.-G., M.D.
FAUTEUX, J.-P., M.D.
HARDY, J., M.D.
LAURENDEAU, F., M.D.
LAURIN, C. A., M.D.
LAVOIE, P., M.D.
PARENT, M., M.D.

Faculty of Arts and Sciences:
Department of Philosophy
AUDET, J. P., D.TH.
BERNIER, R., D. DE L'U.
BLANCHARD, Y., D.PH.
CAUCHY, V., D.PH.
CROMP, G., L.PH., M.A., D.PH.
DÉCARIE, V., D.PH., D. ÈS L.
GAUTHIER, Y., PH.D.
LACOSTE, P., M.A., L.PH., LL.L., **D. DE L'U.**
LEVESQUE, C., D.PH.
MURIN, C. A., D. EN DROIT, PH.D.
RIOUX, B., D. DE L'U.

Institute of Medieval Studies:
LACROIX, P. B.-M., PH.D.

Department of Psychology

ACHILLE, P. A., M.D.
BELANGER, D., D.PH.
CAOUETTE, C. E., D.PH.
CARDU, B., PH.D.
CLERK, GABRIELLE, D.PH.
CORMIER, D., PH.D.
DÉCARIE, THÉRÈSE, D.PH.
DUCHARME, R., D.PH.
DUDEK, S. Z., PH.D.
FREIBERGS, V., PH.D.
LAPOINTE, R. E., D.PH.
LAROCHE, J. L., D.PS.
LAURENDEAU-BENDAVID, MONIQUE, D.PH.
LAVOIE, G., PH.D.
LUSSIER, A., PH.D.
PINARD, A., S.TH.L., D.PH.
STROBEL, M., PH.D.
TÉTREAU, B., L.PH., D.ED.
ZAVALLONI, M., PH.D.

School of Educational Psychology

ANDRY, R., M.A., PH.D.
GUINDON, J., PH.D.

Department of English Studies

BROWNE, R., M.A., PH.D.
HOOD, H. J., M.A., PH.D.
STRATFORD, P. C., D. DE L'U.
VANCE, E., PH.D.
ZUMTHOR, P., D.E.S., D. ÈS L.

Department of French Studies

BEUGNOT, B., L. ÈS L., D. DE L'U.
BOSCO, M., PH.D.
DE CHANTAL, R., L. ÈS L., D. DE L'U.
DEMERS, J., M.A., D. DE 3E CYCLE
DESCHAMPS, N., D. DE L'U.
DUPRIEZ, B., L. ÈS L., D. DE L'U., D. ÈS L.
MARCOTTE, G., M.A., PH.D.
VACHON, G.-A., L.TH., D. DE L'U.

Department of Geography

BEAUREGARD, L., M.A., PH.D.

Department of History

BLAIN, J., D.E.S., D.ÈS L.
BRUNET, M., M.A., L.SC.SOC., PH.D.
CAMPEAU, L., PH.D.
DIMAKIS, J., D. DE 3E CYCLE
FALMAGNE, J., D. ÈS L.
LAMONTAGNE, R., M.A., PH.D.
OIKONOMIDES, N., D. DE 3E CYCLE
SEGUIN, M., D. ÈS L.
WALLOT, J. P., L. ÈS L., M.A., PH.D.

Institute of History and Sociopolitical Sciences

GAUDRY, R., C.C., D.SC.
LIMOGES, C., D. DE 3E CYCLE
SHROEDER-GUDEHUS, B., D.SC.POL.

Department of Linguistics and Philology

CHARBONNEAU, REV. R., D. DE L'U.
CLAS, A., D.PH.
HANNA, B. T., PH.D.
KULLY, R. M., D.PH., DR. HABIL.
MEL'CUK, I. A., PH.D.
TIFFOU, E., D. ÈS L.

Department of Chemistry

ABRAHAM, M., D. SC.
BEAUCHAMP, A.,PH.D.
BENOIT, R. L., ING.CHIM.
BERSE, C., D.SC.
BOURGON, M., L.SC., PH.D.
DAOUST, H., PH .D.
DUROCHER, G.,PH.D.
FAVRE, H., ING CHIM., D.SC., F.C.I.C.
FLISZAR, S., D. SC.
GRAVEL, D., PH.D.
HANESSIAN, S., PH.D.
MARCHESSAULT, R. H., PH.D.
PICHE, L., SC. CHIM., PH.D., F.C.I.C.
RICHER, J C., PH.D..
RIVEST, R., PH.D., D.S.C., F.C.I.C., F.A.A.A.S.
SANDORFY, C., D.PHIL., F.C.I.C., D.SC.
SICOTTE, Y., PH.D.
ST. JACQUES, M., PH.D.
THEOPHINADES, T., PH.D., DR.CHIM. INDUST.
ZADOR, M., D.SC.

Department of Ancient and Modern Studies

BERTRAND DE MUNOZ, M., D. DE L'U.
CARRASCO, F., D.PHIL.
DROUILLY, J. F., D. ÈS L.
GOMEZ-MORIANA, A., PH.D.
HERMENEGILDO, A., L. ÈS L., D.PHIL.
KRYSINSKI, W., D. DE L'U.
LACH, F., PH.D.
OPULSKI, A., PH.D.

Department of Biology

ALI, M.-A., PH.D., D.SC., D.SC.NAT.
AUCLAIR, J.-L., M.SC., PH.D.
BEAUDRY, J.-R., M.SC., PH.D.
CAILLOUX, M., D.SC.
COUILLARD, P., PH.D
DEMERS, J.-M., D.E.S., D.SC.
ISLER, H., ING. CHIM., D.SC.
JOLICOEUR, P., PH.D.
MCNEIL, R., PH.D.
MAGNIN, E. N., D.E.S., D.SC.NAT.
PHAN, C. T., D.SC.
PILON, J.-G., M.SC., PH.D.
PIRLOT, P., PH.D., D.SC.
ROULEAU, E., D.SC.
VIETH, J., DR.RER.NAT., D.SC.NAT.

Department of Geology

BELAND, J., M.SC.A., PH.D.
HOFMANN, H., PH.D.
HUBERT, C., PH.D.
LAJOIE, J., PH.D.
LESPÉRANCE, P. J., M.SC., PH.D.
MAMET, B. L., M.A., D.SC.
TIPHANE, M., M.SC.

Department of Computing Sciences and Operational Research

BACOPOULOS, A., PH.D.
BRATLEY, P., M.A.
CLEROUX, R., PH.D.
FLORIAN, M., D.ENG.SC.
FOX, B. L., PH.D.
GECSEI, J., CAND.ÈS SC.
HYDER, S., PH.D.
MAAG, U., PH.D.
ROBERT, P., PH.D.
ST.-PIERRE, J., L.SC., M.SC., PH.D.

Department of Mathematics and Statistics

BRUNET, R., PH.D.
DAIGNEAULT, A., PH.D.
DUBUC, S., PH.D.
FOX, G., PH.D.
GIRI, N. C., PH.D.
GRANAS, A., PH.D.
JOFFE, A., PH.D.
KRAFT, C., M.SC., PH.D.
L'ABBÉ, M., M.A., PH.D.
RAHMAN, Q. I., D.I.C., PH.D.
SABIDUSSI, G., PH.D.
TAKAHASHI, S., PH.D.
VAN EEDEN, C., PH.D.
ZAIDMAN, S., D.SC.

Department of Physics

BÖSE, A., M.SC., DR.RER.NAT.
BREBNER, J. L., PH.D.
DE POMMIER, P., D.SC., O.S.C.C.
DEL BIANCO, W., PH.D.
DEMERS, P., M.SC., F.R.S.C.(C.), D.D'ETAT.
DESTRY, J., PH.D.
GOULARD, B., PH.D.
JÉRÉMIE, H., D.SC.
L'ECUYER, J., PH.D.
LETOURNEUX, J., D.PHIL.
LEVESQUE, R. J. A., PH.D.
LORRAIN, P., PH.D., M.S.R.C.
MONARO, S., D.PHYS.
PAQUETTE, G., M.A., PH.D.
PEARSON, M., PH.D.
RACINE, R., PH.D.
TARAS, P., PH.D.
TASSOUL, P., J.-L., D.SC.
TEICHMANN, J., D.SC., PH.D.
VAN VLIET, K., M.SC., PH.D.

Department of Anthropology

BALIKCI, A., PH.D., L.SC.ECON., L.SC.SOC., L.SC.GEOG.
BENOIST, J., M.D., D.SC.
DUBREUIL, G., M.A.
SMITH, P. E., PH.D.
TOLSTOY, P., PH.D.
VALLEE, L., PH.D.

School of Criminology

FRECHETTE, M., PH.D.
NORMANDEAU, A., M.A., PH.D.
RICO, J., D. EN DROIT, D. DE L'INST. DE CRIM.
SZABO, D., D.SC.SOC.

Department of Demography

CHARBONNEAU, H., M.A., D.DEM.
HENRIPIN, J., D.EN SC. ECON.
LEGARE, J., D.DEM.

Department of Economics

BOUCHARD, M., D.SC.ECON.
DAGENAIS, M., M.SC., PH.D.
MARION, G., D.ECON.
MARTIN, F., M.A., PH.D.
TREMBLAY, R., PH.D.
TURCAN, P., D. EN SC. ECON.
VERHULST, M., LL.L., B.LITT., ECON.

Department of Industrial Relations

BRIZARD, L. P., M.A.
GOSSELIN, E., LL.L., M.A., D.E.S.
HÉBERT, G., PH.D.
TREMBLAY, L. M., M.SC.SOC., PH.D.

Department of Politics

BOURASSA, G., M.A., D. DE L'U.
GARIGUE, P., PH.D.ANTH.
ORBAN, E., D.SC.POL. ET SOC.

Department of Sociology

BRAZEAU, J., M.A., PH.D.
CARISSE, C., M.A., PH.D.
DOFNY, L., L. ÈS L., D.SOC.
GAGNON, G., M.A., D.SOC.
LACOSTE, N., D. EN SC. POL. & SOC.
RIOUX, M., L.SC.POL.&SOC., M.A.
ROCHER, G., M.A., PH.D.
SÉVIGNY, R., D.EN SC. POL.

Faculty of Dental Medicine:
Department of Dental Prosthesis

NADEAU, J., D.D.S., F.R.C.D.(C.)
PATENAUDE, C., D.D.S.
ROBICHAUD, H. M., D.D.S.
YERGEAU, J., D.D.S.

Department of Preventive Dentistry

LUSSIER, J.-P., D.D.S., PH.D., F.A.C.D.

Department of Stomatology

BUSSIERES, J., D.D.S.
DEMIRJIAN, A., D.D.S., M.SC.D.
RAYMOND, A., D.D.S., F.R.C.D.(C.)
SIMARD-SAVOIE, S., L.PHARM, M.SC.

Faculty of Pharmacy:
ARCHAMBAULT, A., D.PHARM.
BRAUN, J. E., D.SC.PHARM.
PLOURDE, R., D.PHARM.

SALVADOR, R., PH.D.
SIROIS, G., PH.D.
TAWASHI, R., PH.D.

Faculty of Music:
GARANT, S.
MANNY, G.
PAPINEAU-COUTURE, J., B.MUS., LL.D.H.C.
PREVOST, A.

Faculty of Veterinary Medicine:

Department of Anatomy and Animal Physiology
GARON, O., D.M.V., M.SC., PH.D.
PHANEUF, L., D.M.V., M.SC., PH.D.
PIÉRARD, J., D.M.V., M.S.

Department of Medicine
FLIPO, J., D.V.M.
GUAY, P., D.M.V., M.S.
JACQUES, E., D.M.V.
PANISSET, J. C., D.M.V., PH.D.

Department of Pathology and Microbiology
BARTH, R., D.M.V., D.M.V.T., D.P.H.
BEAUREGARD, M., D.M.V., M.SC.
COUSINEAU, G., D.M.V., D.V.
FRECHETTE, J.-L., D.M.V., M.SC.
HARRISON, R.-J., PH.D.
NADEAU, J. D., D.M.V., M.S.
TEUSCHER, E., D.M.V.

Department of Physical Education:
SHEEDY, A., M.SC.

School of Optometry:
BEALNE, C., L.SC.O., M.SC.
LETOURNEAU, J., PH.D.
PAPINEAU, Y., L.SC.O.

AFFILIATED INSTITUTIONS:

Polytechnic School: 2500 Ch. de Polytechnique, Montreal; f. 1874; Dir. R. P. LANGLOIS, ING. S.M.

School of Higher Commercial Studies: 5255 ave. Decelles, Montreal; f. 1907; Dir. PIERRE LAURIN, D.B.A.

MOUNT ALLISON UNIVERSITY

SACKVILLE, N.B. E0A 3C0
Telephone: 536-2040.
Telegraphic Address: Mt. Allison.
Founded 1840.

Private control: Language of instruction: English; Academic year: September to May.

Chancellor: Very Rev. ANGUS JAMES MACQUEEN, D.D., LL.D.
President and Vice-Chancellor: GUY ROBERTSON MACLEAN, M.A., PH.D.
Provost: BRIAN ASH, M.A., PH.D.
Dean of Arts and Science: A. B. FANCY, M.A.
Registrar: D. A. CAMERON, B.SC., LL.D.
Librarian: RUTH O. MACDONALD, B.COMM., M.L.S. (acting).

Number of teachers: 145.
Number of students: 1,468.

Publications: ***President's Report*** (annually), *Mount Allison Record* **(quarterly alumni production),** ***Mount Allison News Letter*** (bi-monthly).

PROFESSORS:

ADAMS, G. Jr., M.A., PH.D., History
ALLEN, C. M., M.SC., Geology
BARCLAY, L. R. C., M.SC., PH.D., Chemistry
BOORNE, R. A., B.SC., Engineering
BURKE, H. C., M.A., PH.D., English
CALKINS, R. W., M.A., PH.D., English
CRAWFORD, W. S. H., Mathematics
CUNNINGHAM, W. B., M.A., PH.D., Economics
DE VOS, N., B.COM., C.A., Commerce
ELIOT, C. W. J., M.A., PH.D., Classics
FANCY, A. B., M.A., French
FENSOM, D. S., B.A.SC., Biology
FERGUSON, L., PH.D., Geology
HALPERT, H., M.A., PH.D., Maritime Studies
HAMMOCK, V., M.F.A., Fine Arts
HARRIES, H., M.SC., PH.D., Biology
LOCHHEAD, D. G., M.A., F.R.S.C., Canadian Studies
MACFARLANE, J. T., B.A., M.SC., Physics
MANSON, G., M.ED., PH.D., Education
MATTHEWS, J. H., B.SC., M.SC., PH.D., Physics
MOORE, J. C. G., M.SC., PH.D., Geology
MOTYER, A. J., M.A., English
NICHOLS, E. G., M.S.C., PH.D., Psychology
PATRIDGE, D. C., B.S., M.B.A., Commerce
READ, J. F., PH.D., Chemistry
RIMMINGTON, G. T., M.A., M.ED., PH.D., F.C.P., Education
RODDA, M., PH.D., Psychology
ROSS, E. D., M.A., PH.D., Geography
SCOBIE, C. H. H., S.T.M., M.A., B.D., PH.D., Religious Studies
SILVERBERG, D., B.A., Fine Arts
STANWAY, R. A., M.A., PH.D., Philosophy
THORPE, M., M.A.C.T., English
TORY, E. M., PH.D., Mathematics
WELCH, C., M.A., PH.D., Philosophy
WELCH, L., M.A., PH.D., French

MOUNT SAINT VINCENT UNIVERSITY

HALIFAX, NOVA SCOTIA
Telephone: 443-4450
Founded 1925.

Chancellor: **Most Revd. J. M. HAYES, D.D.**
President and Vice-Chancellor: E. MARGARET FULTON, M.A., PH.D.
Registrar: JEAN M. HARTLEY, M.SC.
Academic Vice-President: WALTER SHELTON, PH.D.

Number of teachers: 150.
Number of students: 2,500.

DEANS:

Humanities and Sciences: Sr. PATRICIA MULLINS, M.SC., PH.D.
Human and Professional Development: SUSAN CLARK, M.A., PH.D.

PROFESSORS:

ALBERTUS, Sister MARY, M.A., PH.D., Education
ANTHONY, Sister GERALDINE, M.A., PH.D., English
FULTON, E. MARGARET, M.A., PH.D., English
GERIN, PIERRE, L.ÈS L., C.A.P.E.S., D.E.S., D.T.C., French
MCSHANE, P., D.PHIL., Philosophy
MONAGHAN, D., M.PHIL., PH.D., English
MULLINS, Sister PATRICIA, M.S., PH.D., Chemistry
SHELTON, W. J., PH.D., History
USMIANI, R., M.A., English
VAN HOUTEN, R., M.A., PH.D., Psychology
WAINWRIGHT, L., PH.D., Biology
WHEATON, J. B., PH.D., Religious Studies

UNIVERSITY OF NEW BRUNSWICK

P.O.B. 4400, FREDERICTON, NEW BRUNSWICK E3B 5A3
Telephone: (506) 453-4995.
Telex: 014-46202.
Established 1785.

Provincial control; Language of instruction: English; Academic year: September to May.

Chancellor: Sir MAX AITKEN, Bart., D.S.O., D.F.C., LL.D.
President and Vice-Chancellor: JAMES DOWNEY, M.A., PH.D.
Vice-President (Academic): R. E. BURRIDGE, M.S., PH.D.
Vice-President (Finance and Administration): **J. F. O'SULLIVAN, B.B.A.**
Vice-President (St. John): T. J. CONDON, M.A., PH.D.
Dean (St. John): I. R. CAMERON, PH.D.
Comptroller: J. E. O'BRIEN, R.I.A.
Secretary: J. WOODFIELD, PH.D.
Registrar: B. INGRAM, B.A.
Librarian: GERTRUDE E. GUNN, M.A., M.L.S., PH.D.

Number of teachers: 553.
Number of students: 5,860.

Publications: *Calendar, Summer School Calendar, Graduate Studies and Research Calendar, Faculty of Law Calendar, Freshman Bulletin, Fiddlehead* (short stories and poetry, quarterly), *Acadiensis,* a historical journal of the Atlantic provinces (2 a year), *Research Inventory* (annually), *Studies in Canadian Literature* (3 a year), *International Fiction Review* (2 a year).

DEANS:

Faculty of Administration: E. N. WEST, M.SC., PH.D.
Faculty of Arts: P. G. KEPROS, M.SC., PH.D.
Faculty of Education: D. A. MACIVER, M.ED., PH.D.
Faculty of Engineering: A. M. STEVENS, M.SC. (acting).
Faculty of Forestry: J. W. KER, M.F., D.FOR., D.SC.
Faculty of Science: J. A. MCKENZIE, M.A., PH.D. (acting).
Faculty of Law: E. VEITCH, M.A.
Faculty of Nursing: IRENE LECKIE, B.SC.N., M.S.N.
Faculty of Physical Education and Recreation: W. W. MACGILLIVARY, M.A., PH.D.
School of Graduate Studies and Research: R. J. KAVANAGH, M.A.SC., PH.D., D.I.C.

PROFESSORS (Fredericton Campus):

Faculty of Administration:
MAHER, E. D., M.B.A., M.A., Business Administration
NAIR, K. P. K., M.TECH., PH.D., Business Administration
SHARP, H. A., M.B.A., C.A., R.I.A., Business Administration
WEST, E. N., M.SC., PH.D., Business Administration
WILLINGS, D. R., M.A., PH.D., Business Administration

Faculty of Arts:

Acheson, T. W., m.a., ph.d., History
Ackerman, C. D., ph.d., Anthropology
Allardyce, G. D., m.a., ph.d., History
Bauer, W. A., m.a., ph.d., English
Bosnitch, S. D., m.a., ph.d., Political Science
Bouwer, I. Z., m.sc., ph.d., Mathematics and Statistics
Boxill, H. F. A. m.a., ph.d., English
Brander, J. R. G., m.a., Economics
Brown, W., m.a., ph.d., History
Buckner, P. A., ph.d., History
Chapman, J. K., m.a., ph.d., History
Cockburn, R. H., m.a., English
Coghlan, F. A., m.a., ph.d., History
Cogswell, F. W., m.a., ph.d., English
Colson, T., m.a., ph.d., English
Dalton, W. G., ph.d., Anthropology
Datta, A. K., m.a., ph.d., Economics
Davies, E. B., m.a., ph.d., English
Donaldson, A. R., m.a., English
Downey, J., m.a., ph.d., English
Earl, J. F., m.a., Economics
Easterbrook, J. A., m.a., ph.d., Psychology
Elkhadem, S. E. A., dr.phil., German and Russian
Eppert, F., dr.phil., German and Russian
Erickson, V. Ô., m.a., ph.d., Anthropology
Ferris, G. D., m.a., Romance Languages
Forbes, E. R., m.a., ph.d., History
Forster, J. C., m.a., d.litt., Spanish
Friesen, A., dr.phil., German and Russian
Gair, W. R., m.a., ph.d., English
Galloway, D. R., m.c., m.a., English
Gibbs, R. J., m.a., ph.d., English
Graham, D. S., m.a., ph.d., History
Henheffer, B. W., m.a., Sociology
Howroyd, T. D., m.sc., ph.d., Mathematics and Statistics
Iverson, N. S., m.a., ph.d., Sociology
Kent, P. C., m.sc.econ., ph.d., History
Kepros, P. G., m.sc., ph.d., Psychology
Kinloch, A. M., m.a., ph.d., English
Knight, W. R., m.a., ph.d., Mathematics and Computer Science (also under Faculty of Engineering)
Konishi, H., m.a., ph.d., Classics and Ancient History
Kuun, G. C., ll.d., Political Science
Lane, L., Jr., m.a., ph.d., English
Larsen, H. K., m.sc., Economics
Lee, R. W. M., m.a.sc., ph.d., Mathematics and Statistics
Levine, A. L., m.a., ph.d., Economics
Lusher, H. E. G., m.a., ph.d., German and Russian
MacGill, N. W., m.a., Philosophy
McDonnell, P. M., m.a., ph.d., Psychology
Mason, G. R., m.sc., ph.d., Mathematics and Statistics
Mikaelian, H. H., ph.d., Psychology
Milham, Mary E., m.a., ph.d., Classics and Ancient History
Nicki, R. M., m.a., ph.d., Psychology
Patterson, S. E., m.a., ph.d., History
Pepperdene, B. J., m.a., ph.d., Sociology
Poyatos, F., m.a., ph.d., Romance Languages
Pugh, A. R., m.a., ph.d., Romance Languages
Pullman, D. R., m.a., ph.d., Sociology
Robinson, P. R., m.a., ph.d., Philosophy
Rowan, D. F., m.a., ph.d., English
Shaw, A. J., m.a., Romance Languages
Singh, K., m.a., ph.d., Mathematics and Statistics
Smith, L. C., m.a., ph.d., Classics and Ancient History
Smith, S. A., m.a., ph.d., History
Smith, W. Y., m.a., Economics
Szabo, L., ph.d., German and Russian
Taylor, M. J., ph.d., English
Thomas. D. P.. m.a., ph.d., English
Thompson, K. E., m.a., ph.d., English
Tupper, B. O. J., ph.d., Mathematics and Statistics
Whalen, R. G., b.a., Romance Languages
Wilson, A. J., ph.d., Political Science
Woodfield, J., ph.d., English
Woodward, C. A., ph.d., Political Science
Young, D. M., ph.d., History

Faculty of Education:

Biden, C. W., m.a., Student Teaching
Hamilton, W. D., m.a., Curriculum and Instruction
Hawkes, R. E., m.a., Curriculum and Instruction
Leaman, H. L., m.a., Curriculum and Instruction
Leblanc, D. R., m.ed., ph.d., Vocational Education
Macdougall, Margaret J., c.a., m.s.t., Vocational Education
MacIver, D. A., m.ed., ph.d., Educational Foundations
McNeilly, R. A., m.a., l.c.p., Educational Foundations
Rankine, F. C., m.a., ed.d., Educational Foundations
Stewart, M. F., m.a., ed.d., Curriculum and Instruction
Walter, R. E., m.ed., a.i.e., Educational Foundations

Faculty of Engineering:

Balasubramanian, R., m.e., ph.d., Electrical Engineering
Beattie, I. M., m.sc., Civil Engineering
Bray, D. I., m.sc., ph.d., Civil Engineering
Bremner, T. W., m.sc., d.i.c., Civil Engineering
Burgess, J. P., m.sc., ph.d., d.i.c., Electrical Engineering
Burridge, R. E., m.s., ph.d., Electrical Engineering
Chrzanowski, A. J., m.sc., dr.ing., Surveying Engineering
Davar, K. S., b.e., m.i.e., ph.d., Civil Engineering
Davies, H. G., ph.d., Mechanical Engineering
Derenyi, E. E., m.sc., ph.d., Surveying Engineering
Faig, W., m.sc., dr.ing., Surveying Engineering
Findlay, R.D., m.a. sc., ph.d., Electrical Engineering
Francis, R. M., m.sc., Civil Engineering
Garland, E. C., m.s., Civil Engineering
Grant, E. J., b.sc., d.i.c., Civil Engineering
Hamilton, A. C., m.a.sc., Surveying Engineering
Hill, E. F., m.sc., ph.d., Electrical Engineering
Ireton, V. M., b.sc., Mechanical Engineering
Kavanagh, R. J., m.a.sc., ph.d., d.i.c., Electrical Engineering
Knight, W. R., m.a., ph.d., Computer Science and Mathematics and Statistics (also under Faculty of Arts)
Kristmanson, D. D., ph.d., d.i.c., Chemical Engineering
Landau, J., ph.d., Chemical Engineering
Landva, A. O., b.sc., lic.tech., dr.ing., Civil Engineering
Lenard, J. G., m.a.sc., ph.d., Mechanical Engineering
Lewis, J. E., ph.d., Electrical Engineering
Machin, K. E., m.sc., Mechanical Engineering
McFarlane, H. W., m.s.e., Civil Engineering and Forest Engineering (also under Faculty of Forestry)
McLaughlin, R. H., m.sc., Civil Engineering
Masry, S. E., d.u.c.l., ph.d., Surveying Engineering
Moreland, C., ph.d., Chemical Engineering
Morris, D. R., ph.d., Chemical Engineering
Narraway, J. J., m.sc., ph.d., Electrical Engineering
Picot, J. J. C., s.m., ph.d., Chemical Engineering
Rogers, J. D., b.sc., Electrical Engineering
Ruthven, D. M., m.a., ph.d., Chemical Engineering
Scott, R. N., b.sc., Electrical Engineering
Smolinski, W. J., m.a.sc., Electrical Engineering
Starkermann, R., dr.sc.techn., Mechanical Engineering
Stevens, A. M., m.sc., Civil Engineering and Forest Engineering (also under Faculty of Forestry)
Steward, F. R., s.m., sc.d., Chemical Engineering
Torfason, L. E., m.sc., Mechanical Engineering
Vanicek, P., m.eng., ph.d., Surveying Engineering
Venart, J. E. S., ph.d., Mechanical Engineering
Wasson, W. D., s.m., ph.d., Computer Science
Wilson, F. R., m.sc., ph.d., Civil Engineering

Faculty of Forestry:

Baskerville, G. L., m.f., ph.d.
Bjerkelund, T. C., b.sc.f.
Brown, N. R., m.a.
Dickison, R. B. B., m.a.
Dickson, A., m.s., ph.d.
Hilborn, W. H., b.sc.f., m.a.
Kayll, A. J., m.f., ph.d.
Ker, J. W., m.f., d.for., d.sc.
Kissick, N. L., m.f.
Krause, H. H., ph.d.
Oliver, F. S., m.sc.f.
Powell, G. R., m.sc., ph.d.
Schneider, M. H., m.sc.
Sebastian, L. P., m.sc., ph.d.
Van Slyke, A. L., m.f.

Faculty of Science:

Bottomley, F., m.sc., ph.d., Chemistry
Brewer, D. G., ph.d., Chemistry
Brooks, W. V. F., ph.d., Chemistry
Burke, K. B. S., ph.d., Geology
Burt, M. D. B., ph.d., f.l.s., Biology
Cumming, B. G., ph.d., Biology
De Mille, G. R., m.sc., ph.d., Physics
Dionne, L. A., m.sc., ph.d., Biology
Edwards, M. A., m.sc., ph.d., Physics
Findlay, J. A., ph.d., Chemistry
Grein, F., m.sc., ph.d., Chemistry
Hagen, D. W., m.a., ph.d., Biology
Hale, W. E., m.sc., ph.d., f.g.s.a., Geology
Kaiser, R., dr.rer.nat., Physics
Krause, Margarida O., m.sc., ph.d., Biology
Lajtai, E. Z., m.a.sc., ph.d., Geology
Lees, R. M., m.sc., ph.d., Physics
Linton, C., ph.d., d.i.c., Physics
Livesey, D. L., ph.d., Physics
McAllister, A. L., m.sc., ph.d., f.r.s.c., Geology

McKenzie, J. A., m.a., ph.d., Biology
Noble, J. P. A., ph.d., Geology
Paim, U., ph.d., Biology
Pajari, G. E., m.a., ph.d., Geology
Passmore, J., ph.d., Chemistry
Sastry, K. V. L. N., m.sc., ph.d., Physics
Seabrook, W. D., m.sc., ph.d., d.i.c., Biology
Semeluk, G. P., m.sc., ph.d., Chemistry
Stringer, P., ph.d., Geology
Taylor, A. R. A., ph.d., Biology
Trembath, L. T., m.sc., ph.d., Geology
Unger, I., m.sc., ph.d., Chemistry
Valenta, Z., dipl.ing.chem., m.sc., ph.d., f.r.s.c., Chemistry
van de Poll, H. W., m.sc., ph.d., Geology
Verma, R. D., m.sc., ph.d., Physics
Wein, R. W., m.s., ph.d., Biology
Wiesner, K., d.sc., f.r.s.c., f.r.s., Chemistry
Williams, P. F., m.sc., ph.d., Geology
Yoo, B. Y., m.sc., ph.d., Biology
Young, C., m.a., ph.d., Physics

Faculty of Law:
Bird, R. W., ll.m.
Hurley, D. M., ll.m., ph.d.
Rouse, D. G., b.a., ll.b.
Smith, B. G., b.c.l.
Stapleton, B. D., b.a., b.comm., b.c.l.
Veitch, E., ll.b., m.a.

Faculty of Nursing:
Alcoe, Shirley Y., m.a., m.ed., ed.d.
Cutler, Ryllys M., m.a.
Leckie, Irene, m.s.n.

Faculty of Physical Education and Recreation:
Meagher, J. W., m.sc., d.ed.
MacGillivary, W. W., m.a., ph.d.
Paton, G. A., m.a., ph.d.
Thompson, G. B., m.sc.

Professors (Saint John Campus):

Administration Division:
Jain, H. C., m.s., ph.d., Business Administration

Humanities and Languages Division:
Condon, T. J., m.a., ph.d., History
Jory, D. H., m.a., d.d'univ., Romance Languages
Prouty, W., m.a., English

Mathematics, Engineering and Computer Science Division:
Spinney, F. B., m.sc., Mechanical Engineering

Division of Sciences:
Beckett, B. A., ph.d., Chemistry
Cameron, I. R., ph.d., Physics
Gordon, A. J., ph.d., Geology
Halcrow, K., m.sc., ph.d., Biology
Kelly, R. B., m.sc., ph.d., Chemistry
Logan, A., ph.d., Geology
Stanley, E., ph.d., d.sc., Physics
Thomas, M. L. H., m.s.a., ph.d., Biology

Division of Social Science:
Betts, G. M., m.a., ph.d., Political Science
Willis, P. W., m.a., Economics

Federated University:

St. Thomas University: Fredericton, N.B.; f. 1910.
President: Rev. George W. Martin, b.a., b.th.

NOVA SCOTIA AGRICULTURAL COLLEGE

TRURO, N.S. B2N 5E3
Telephone: Truro 895-1571.
Founded 1905.

Under the direction of the Nova Scotia Department of Agriculture and Marketing.

Principal: H. F. MacRae, m.sc., ph.d.
Vice-Principal: I. M. Fraser, b.sc., m.a.
Dean, Technical and Vocational Training: A. D. Ells, m.a.
Registrar: P. Y. Hamilton, m.sc.
Librarian: B. S. Sodhi, m.a., dip.l.s.

Library of 7,600 vols. (approx.).
Number of teachers: 43.
Number of students: *c.* 460.
Publications: *N.S.A.C. College Calendar.*

NOVA SCOTIA COLLEGE OF ART AND DESIGN

5163 DUKE ST., HALIFAX, N.S., B3J 3J6
Founded 1887.

President: Garry Neill Kennedy, a.o.c.a., m.f.a.
Dean: Alan Barkley, b.a., m.f.a.
Library Director: John Murchie, m.l.s.

The library contains 15,000 vols., 220 art periodicals, 65,000 colour slides.

Number of teachers: 43.
Number of students: 450.

Fine art studios in painting, sculpture, printmaking, ceramics, weaving, video, film, wood and metal working, textiles, jewellery, photography; programmes in communication design and environmental design; art education and history.

TECHNICAL UNIVERSITY OF NOVA SCOTIA

P.O.B. 1000,
HALIFAX, NOVA SCOTIA
Telephone: (902) 429-8300.
Founded 1907.

Academic year: September to May; Language of instruction: English.

Chancellor: C. Norman Simpson, b.sc., ll.d., d.eng.
President: J. Clair Callaghan, m.sc. (eng.)., p.eng.
Registrar: Nelson Ferguson, m.a.sc., p.eng.
Librarian: M. R. Hussain, m.a., m.s.l.s.

Number of teachers: 75.
Number of students: 868.
Publications: *Calendar*†, *Annual Report*†.

Deans:

Engineering: D. A. Roy, m.eng., ph.d., p.eng.
Architecture: P. Manning, ph.d., f.r.a.i.c., a.r.i.b.a.

Heads of Departments:

Civil Engineering: Prof. G. G. Meyerhof, m.sc., ph.d., d.sc., f.r.s.c., p.eng.
Electrical Engineering: Prof. O. K. Gashus, ph.d., p.eng.
Mechanical Engineering: Prof. J. L. Warner, s.m., ph.d., p.eng.
Mining Engineering: Prof. K. V. Gow, m.sc., ph.d., p.eng.
Chemical Engineering: Prof. A. F. MacMillan, m.sc., ph.d., p.eng.
Industrial Engineering: G. P. Wilson, m.sc., p.eng. (acting).
School of Architecture: Prof. P. Manning, ph.d., f.r.a.i.c., a.r.i.b.a.
Applied Mathematics: S. N. Sarwal, m.a. (acting).
Bio-Resources: Prof. J. C. MacKinnon, m.sc., ph.d., p.eng.
Continuing Education: Barbara Watt.

Attached Research Institutes

Atlantic Industrial Research Institute: Halifax, N.S.; Dir. G. P. Wilson.

Centre for Energy Studies.

UNIVERSITY OF OTTAWA

550 CUMBERLAND ST.,
OTTAWA, ONTARIO K1N 6N5
Telephone: (613) 231-3311.
Founded 1848.

Languages of Instruction: French and English, almost generally in parallel courses; Control: Independent, Provincially assisted; Academic year: September to August (undergraduate 2 semesters, graduate 3 terms).

Chancellor: Mme Jules Léger, c.c., d.u.
Rector: Rev. R. Guindon, o.m.i., c.c., b.a., l.ph.d.th., ll.d.
Vice-Rectors:
(*Academic*): Dr. Antoine D'Iorio, ph.d., f.r.s.c.
(*Administration*): A. K. Gillmore, b.a.
Registrar: R. R. Labelle, b.a., l.ph.
Secretary of the University: Rev. Paul-E. Drouin, o.m.i., l.ph., l.th., m.a., m.l.s.
Head Librarian: F. Yvon Richer, m.l.s.

Library: *see under* Libraries.

Number of teachers: 953 full-time, 380 part-time.

Number of students: 10,917 full-time, 7,758 part-time.

Publications: *Revue* (quarterly), *Medical Journal* (quarterly), *Law Review* (2 a year), *Histoire Sociale/Social History* (2 a year), *University of Ottawa Gazette* (2 a month), Calendars of the several Faculties.

Deans and Directors:

Faculty of Health Sciences: Gilles D. Hurteau, b.a., m.d., f.r.c.s.(c.).
School of Human Kinetics: Maxwell L. Howell, m.a., ed.d.
School of Medicine: Gilles D. Hurteau.

School of Nursing: MARIE A. LOYER, M.A., M.P.H., M.ED.
Faculty of Theology: Rev. ANDRÉ GUINDON, O.M.I., L.PH., S.T.L., D.TH.
Faculty of Canon Law: **Rev. F. G. MORRISEY, L.PH., L.TH., PH.D.**
Faculty of Law:
(*Civil Law*): RAYMOND A. LANDRY, B.A., LL.L.
(*Common Law*): H. A. HUBBARD, B.A.
Faculty of Science and Engineering: PETER MORAND, PH.D.
Faculty of Arts: **M. HAMELIN, PH.D.**
Faculty of Social Sciences: **D. CARRIER, M.SC.COM., D.U.**
School of Psychology: JOSEPH M. DEKONINCK, M.A., PH.D.
Faculty of Education: YVES POIRIER, M.ED., PH.D.
Faculty of Administration: J. J. CARSON, M.A.(PS.), D.U.
School of Graduate Studies: **P. B. HAGEN, M.B., F.C.I.C.**

PROFESSORS:

Faculty of Health Sciences:

School of Human Kinetics:

DAVIDSON, S. A., M.A., ED.D., Physical Education
HOWELL, M. L., M.A., ED.D.
JETTÉ, M. J., M.S.P.E., PH.D., Kinanthropology
MÉTIVIER, G. J., M.S., PH.D., Kinanthropology
ORBAN, W. A. R., M.S., PH.D., Kinanthropology

School of Medicine:

ALLEN, D., M.D., C.M., Ophthalmology
BEANLANDS, D. S., M.D., Medicine, Cardiology
BEAULIEU, M., M.SC., PH.D., Microbiology and Immunology
BENOITON, N. L., M.SC., PH.D., Biochemistry
BERKMAN, F., M.D.C.M., F.R.C.P.(C.), Medicine
BROUGHTON, R. J., M.D., PH.D., Medicine, Pharmacology
CHALKE, F. C. R., M.D., M.MED.SC., F.R.C.P.(C.), Psychiatry
COLLINS, W. E., M.D., F.R.C.S.(C.), F.A.C.S., Urology
CONWAY, D. J., M.D., F.R.C.P.(C.), Paediatrics
COPESTAKE, G. G., M.B., F.R.C.P.(C.), Radiology
DEVITT, J. E., M.D., M.SC., F.R.C.ED., F.R.C.S.(C.), Surgery
DON, C. J., M.B., B.S., M.R.C.P., F.F.R., Radiology
FITT, P. S., PH.D., Biochemistry
HAGEN, P. B., M.B.B.S., F.C.I.C., Pharmacology
HALL, E. A., M.D., PH.D., Anatomy
HARRIS, J. E., M.D., F.R.C.P.(C.), Medicine
HEGGTVEIT, H. A., M.D., M.R.C.PATH., F.R.C.P.(C.), F.A.C.C., F.C.A.P., F.A.C.A., D.A.PATH., Pathology
HETENYI, G., M.D., PH.D., Physiology
HILL, D. P., M.D., Pathology
HILTON, J. H. B., M.D., F.R.C.P., Medicine
HIMMS-HAGEN, J., D.PHIL., Biochemistry
HRDINA, P. D., M.D., PH.D., Pharmacology
HURTEAU, G. D., M.D., F.R.C.S.(C.), Obstetrics and Gynaecology
IRVINE, A. H., M.D., F.R.C.S.(C.), Urology
JANDE, S. S., M.SC., PH.D., Anatomy
JAWORSKI, Z. F. G., M.D., F.R.C.P.(C.), Medicine
KAKO, KYOHEI, M.D., Physiology
KALSNER, S., A.B., PH.D., Pharmacology
KAPLAN, H., PH.D., Biochemistry
KATES, M., PH.D., F.C.I.C., F.R.S.(C.), Biochemistry
KEON, W. J., M.D., M.SC., F.R.C.S.(C.), Surgery
KINSON, G. A., M.S., PH.D., F.R.I.C., Physiology
KORANYI, E. K., M.D., Psychiatry
KORECKY, B., M.D., PH.D., Physiology
LAMONT, M. D., Family Medicine
LAST, J. M., M.D., D.P.H., F.R.A.C.P., Epidemiology and Community Medicine
LAYNE, D. S., PH.D., Biochemistry
MACIVER, D. A., M.B., F.C.C.S.(C.), Surgery
MAINWOOD, C. W., PH.D., Physiology
MAZURKIEWICZ-KWILECKI, I. M., M.PHARM., M.SC., PH.D., Pharmacology
MCKEE, J. A., M.D., F.R.C.P.(C.), F.A.A.P., F.C.C.P., Paediatrics
MCKENDRY, B. R., M.D., M.SC., F.R.C.P.(C.), Medicine
METUZALS, J., PH.D., Anatomy
NERI, L. C., M.D., M.SC., Epidemiology and Community Medicine
OXORN, H., M.D.C.M., F.R.C.S.(C.), F.A.C.S., Obstetrics and Gynaecology
PERRY, E., M.D., Microbiology and Immunology
PETERSON, E. W., M.D.C.M., F.R.C.S.(C.), Surgery
PROULX, P. R., PH.D., Biochemistry
RAKUSAN, K. J., M.D., PH.D., Physiology
RICHTER, M., PH.D., M.D.C.M., Pathology
ROBERTS, C. A., M.D., F.R.C.P., Psychiatry
ROBICHON, J., M.D., M.SC., F.R.C.S.(C.), F.A.C.S., Surgery
ROSSIER, E., M.D., Microbiology and Immunology
ROWSELL, H. C., D.V.M., D.V.P.H., PH.D., Pathology
RYAN, M. T., PH.D., Biochemistry
SARWER-FONER, G. J., M.D., F.R.C.P., F.A.G.S., F.A.O.P.A., F.A.C.P., Psychiatry
SIM, M., M.D., F.R.C.ED., F.R.C.P.(C.), Psychiatry
SIMEON, J. G., M.D., Psychiatry
SINGHAL, R. L., M.SC., PH.D., Pharmacology
SMILEY, R. K., M.D., C.M., F.R.C.P.(C.), Medicine
STEWART, T. H. M., M.B., F.R.C.P.(C.), Medicine
STODDART, T. G., M.D., F.R.C.P., Radiology
SZABO, J., M.D., Anatomy
TAYLOR, H. E., M.D., LL.D., F.R.C.P., F.R.C.P.(C.), Pathology
THOMPSON, W. G., M.D., F.R.C.P.(C.), Medicine
TOLNAI, G., M.D., F.R.C.P.(C.), Pathology
TOLNAI, S., M.D., Anatomy
TREMBLAY, P. C., M.D., F.R.C.S.(C.), F.A.C.S., Obstetrics and Gynaecology
UHTHOFF, H. K., M.D., F.R.C.S.(C.), Surgery
VOGELFANGER, I. J., M.D., D.MED.SC., F.A.C.S., F.I.C.S., Surgery
WADDELL, W. G., M.D.C.M., F.R.C.S.(C.), Surgery
WATSON, A. G., M.B., F.R.C.S.(C.), F.A.C.S., Ophthalmology
WESTWOOD, J. C., M.B., B.CHIR., Microbiology and Immunology
WHITAKER, D. R., PH.D., D.SC., Biochemistry

Faculty of Theology:

BELLEMARE, Rev. R., O.M.I., PH.L., S.T.D.
DUMAIS, Rev. M., O.M.I., L.PH., S.T.L., S.S.L., D.TH.
GERVAIS, Rev. J., O.M.I., PH.L., S.T.D.
GUINDON, Rev. A., O.M.I., L.PH., S.T.L., D.TH.
HUDON, Rev. G., O.M.I., S.T.D.
LABERGE, Rev. L., O.M.I., L.PH., S.T.L., S.S.E., S.S.D.
LE MARIER, Rev. J. G., O.M.I., L.PH., L.TH., S.T.D.
PAGANO, Rev. S., O.M.I., D.TH.
QUESNEL, REV. R., S.T.D., L.PH., L.TH.
ROBERGE, Rev. M., O.M.I., L.TH., L.S.S., S.T.D.
VOGELS, Rev. W., P.B., L.E.S., PH.D., D.TH.

Faculty of Civil Law:

BEAUDOIN, G.A., Q.C., LL.L., M.A., D.E.S.D., F.R.S.C.
BERGERON, V., LL.L., D.E.S.D.
BISSON, A.-F., LL.L.
BRIERE, G., LL.L., D.E.S.D.
DES COTEAUX, G., LL.L., D.E.S.P., D.E.S.D.
DUCHARME, L., L.PH., LL.L., DIPL.E.S.D.
LAROUCHE, A., B.A., LL.L.
LILKOFF, L., LL.L., D.E.S.D.
MARQUIS, P. V., LL.L., D.C.L.
PHARAND, D., LL.D., LL.M., S.J.D.

Faculty of Common Law:

ARLIDGE, B. K., LL.M.
BINAVINCE, E., LL.B., M.C.L., LL.M.
CLARENCE SMITH, J. A., M.A.
FEENEY, T. G., Q.C., LL.B.
GRANGER, C., LL.M.
HAYEK, E. J., J.U.DR.
HUBBARD, A., B.A.
KAVANAGH, J. A., LL.B., LL.M.
MCCAUGHEY, W. E., LL.B.
PAYNE, J. D., LL.B.
RATUSHNY, E. J., LL.M.
SUSSMANN, F. B., M.S.(ED.), J.D.

Faculty of Canon Law:

LATRÉMOUILLE, Rev. R., O.M.I., D.D.C., D.PH.
LESAGE, Rev. G., O.M.I., M.A., PH.D., D.S.SC., S.T.D., D. ÈS L., J.C.D., D.D.C.
MORRISEY, Rev. F. G., O.M.I., L.TH., M.A.(REL.), M.D.C., PH.D.

Faculty of Science and Engineering:

AFRIAT, S. N., M.A., D.PHIL., Mathematics
ALPER, H., PH.D., Chemistry
BAER, A. J., L.SC., D.SC., Geology
BAER, H. H., DR. RER. NAT., F.C.I.C., Chemistry
BENOITON, N. L., M.SC., PH.D., Biochemistry
BERWANGER, C., M.SC., Civil Engineering
BISHOP, D. M., PH.D., D.SC., Chemistry
CONWAY, B. E., PH.D., D.SC., F.R.I.C., F.C.I.C., F.R.S.C., Chemistry
DEO, C. M., M.SC., PH.D., Mathematics
DODSON, E. O., PH.D., Biology
FEINGOLD, A., D.ENG., Mechanical Engineering
FITT, P. S., PH.D., Biochemistry
FRASER, R. R., M.SC., PH.D., Chemistry
FYSON, W. K., M.SC., PH.D., Geology
GLYDE, H. R., D.PHIL., Physics
HAGEN, P. B., M.B.B.S., F.C.I.C., Biochemistry
HAYDUK, W., M.A.SC., PH.D., Chemical Engineering
HEBERT, J., M.SC., Physics
HELFENSTEIN, H. G., M.SC., D.SC., Mathematics
HIMMS-HAGEN, J., D.PHIL., Biochemistry
HIRD, B., M.A., D.PHIL., Physics
HOGARTH, D. D., M.A.SC., PH.D., Geology
HOLMES, J. L., PH.D., Chemistry
HOWLAND, J. L., M.A., PH.D., Mathematics
KAPLAN, J. G., M.A., PH.D., Biology
KATES, M., M.A., PH.D., Biochemistry

KESARWANI, R. N., M.SC., PH.D., Mathematics
KOZICKI, W., M.A.SC., PH.D., F.C.I.C., Chemical Engineering
KRAUSZ, A. S., M.SC., PH.D., Mechanical Engineering
KRETZ, R., M.SC., PH.D., Geology
KUSHNER, D. J., M.SC., PH.D., Biology
LA HAM, Q., M.SC., PH.D., Biology
LAIDLER, K. J., M.A., D.SC., PH.D., F.C.I.C., F.R.S.(C.), Chemistry
LAMARCHE, G., M.SC., PH.D., Physics
LAYNE, D. S., M.SC., PH.D., Biochemistry
LE BLANC, M. A. R., M.A., PH.D., Physics
LEE, Y., M.ENG., PH.D., Mechanical Engineering
LINIS, V. M.SC., PH.D., Mathematics
LU, B. C. Y., M.E., M.SC., F.C.I.C., PH.D., Chemical Engineering
MANN, R. S., M.SC., M.CH.ENG., PH.D., F.I.P., F.R.I.C., Chemical Engineering
PROULX, P. R., M.SC., PH.D., Biochemistry
RYAN, M. T., PH.D., Biochemistry
SCOTT, J. D., M.SC., PH.D., Civil Engineering
SHIELDS, D. H., B.SC., D.I.C., PH.D., Civil Engineering
SHIVA, S. G. S., M.S.E.E., Electrical Engineering
STEENAART, W. J. D., E.E.ENG., Electrical Engineering
STUCHLY, S. S., M.ENG., D.SC., Electrical Engineering
TALBOT, F. D. F., M.SC., PH.D., Chemical Engineering
TOMIUK, B. J., M.SC., PH.D., Mathematics
TOWNSEND, D. R., PH.D., Civil Engineering
VARSHNI, Y. P., M.SC., PH.D., Physics
VEIZER, J., R.N.DR., PH.D., Geology
WESTLAND, A. D., M.A., PH.D., F.C.I.C., Chemistry
WHITAKER, D. R., PH.D., D.SC., Biochemistry
WOOLEY, J. C., PH.D., Physics

Faculty of Arts:
ALLARD, J. L., L.PH., D.PH., Philosophy
ARBOUR, R., D.U.P., L.PH., L.TH., PH.D., French Literature
BERNIER, F., B.A., Music
CAMPBELL, A. P., M.A., PH.D., English Literature
CARR, D. T., PH.D., Philosophy
CHARRON, G. J.-M., M.A., D.PH., Philosophy
COLLINS, R. G., M.A., PH.D., English
CROTEAU, Rev. J., O.M.I., M.A., PH.D., S.T.L., Philosophy
DRAY, W. H., M.A., D.PHIL., F.R.S.C., Philosophy
DUBÉ, J.-C., History
DUCHARME, Rev. L., O.M.I., PH.D., S.T.L., Philosophy
DUCHESNEAU, F. B., D.PH., Philosophy
ELDREDGE, L. M., PH.D., English
FOLEJEWSKI, Z., PH.D., Slavic Studies and Modern Languages
GAGNON, C., Visual Arts
GARCEAU, Rev. B., O.M.I., S.T.L., D.PH., Philosophy
GAREAU, Rev. E., PH.B., D.U.P., TH.L. Classical Studies
GERAETS, T., D.PH., Philosophy
GWYN, J., M.A., D.PHIL., History
HARE, J. E., PH.D., French Literature
JAENEN, C. J., PH.D., History
JOST, T., M.PH., PH.D., Geography
KELLY, L., M.A., PH.D., Linguistics
KRESIC, S., D.E.S., Classical Studies
LAFRANCE, L. G., M.A., D.PH., Philosophy
LAFRANCE, Y., D.PH., Philosophy
LAMIRANDE, E., M.PH., M.A., D.TH., S.T.M., Religious Studies
LE MOINE, R., M.A., L. ÈS L., D.ÈS L., French Literature
LE MOYNE, S. R., Visual Arts
LOCHEAD, K. C., Visual Arts
MCGUINTY, D. J., M.A., PH.D., English Literature
MACMILLAN, K., M.A., Music
MAJOR, J.-L., B.A., L.PH., M.A., D.PH., French Literature
MARCOTTE, P., M.A., PH.D., English Literature
MERCIÉ, J.-L., L. ÈS L., PH.D., French Literature
MOSELEY, VIRGINIA, M.A., PH.D., English Literature
O'NEILL, M. J., M.A., PH.D., English Literature
OUELLET, F., L. ÈS L., D.LETT., History
PAQUET, Rev. L., O.M.I., L.TH., D.PH., Philosophy
PAVEL, T., PH.D., Linguistics
PLASKACZ, B., M.A., PH.D., Slavic Studies
POTVIN, G., M.A., Geography
ROBERTO, E. M., D.LETT., French Literature
ROBIDOUX, R., L.PH., S.T.L., L. ÈS L., D.U.P., French Literature
ROBITAILLE, B., L. ÈS L.(GEOG.), D.LETT., Geography
SAVARD, P., D.LETT., F.R.S.C., French Literature
SCULLY, J. E., M.A., PH.D., M.S.L., Philosophy
SRIVASTAVA, H., M.A., PH.D., Geography
STEED, G. P. F., PH.D., Geography
ST. ONGE, D., B.A., D.SC., Geography
THEAU, J. F. L., D.PH., Philosophy
THERIO, J. A., M.A., PH.D., M.A.(POL.SC.), French Literature
THOMSON, G. H., M.A., PH.D., English Literature
TRUDEL, M., D. ÈS L., History
VIGNEAULT, R., L. ÈS L., PH.D., French Literature
WELLS, C. M., PH.D., Classical Studies
WOJCIECHOWSKI, J. A., PH.D., Philosophy
WYCZYNSKI, P., L. ÈS L., PH.D., French Literature
YUZYK, P., M.A., PH.D., History

Faculty of Social Sciences:
AFRIAT, S. N. M.A., D.PHIL., Economics
BODKIN, R. G., M.A., PH.D., Economics
BOREHAM, G., PH.D., Economics
CHOSSUDOVSKY, M., PH.D., Economics
CIALE, J., M.A., PH.D., Criminology
DAGUM, C., PH.D., Economics
DEANDRADE, R. O., L.PH., S.T.L., M.A. (SOCIOL.), Sociology
GOODALE, T. L., M.S., PH.D., Recreology
GRYGIER, T., LL.M., PH.D., F.B.PS.P., Criminology
JAYEWARDENE, C. H. S., A.M., PH.D., Criminology
KIS, T. I., D.SC.POL.SOC., Political Science
KOS-RABCEWICZ-ZUBROWSKI, L., LL.D., Criminology
LAPLANTE, J., M.A., PH.D., Criminology
MIGUELEZ, R. J., M.A., PH.D., Sociology
QUIRION, Rev. J.-M., O.M.I., B.A., L.PH., B.TH., B.COMM., M.SC.(ECON.), A.C.I.S., Economics
ROSS, R. R., M.A., PH.D., Criminology
STOREY, E. H., M.S., PH.D., Recreology
VACHET, A., L.PH., D.U.P., Political Science
WRIGHT, J. R.,, M.S., PH.D., Recreology

School of Psychology:
BARRY, W. F., M.PS., PH.D.
CASAS, E. F., LL.D., PH.D., L.PS.
CELOVSKY, A., PH.D.
CHAGNON, G., M.PS.
CHAGNON, M., L.PH., M.A., PH.D., D.U.
COADY, H., M.A., PH.D.
POREBSKI, O., PH.D.
RUDA, O. J., L.PH., M.A., PH.D.
SIDLAUKAS, AGATHE, M.A., PH.D.
STRETCH, R., PH.D.
SWINGLE, P., M.A., PH.D.
VAILLANCOURT, R., M.A., PH.D.
WYSPIANSKI, J. O., M.A., PH.D.

Faculty of Education:
BABIN, P., M.S.ED., PH.D.
BENISKOS, J. M., M.A., PH.D.
BOSS, M., M.ED., PH.D.
DESJARLAIS, L., M.A., PH.D.
GOLDSTEIN, E. M., B.A., PH.D., B.EC., M.ED., Teacher Education
MULCAHY, SR. MARY T., M.A., PH.D.
SAINT-PIERRE, J. G., B.A., M.A.(ED.), M.A.(ENG.), PH.D.(LING.), Teacher Education

Faculty of Administration:
BAKER, W., M.A., PH.D.
CRAIG, A. W. J., M.B.A., PH.D.
DEBANNE, J., M.SC., PH.D.
FORTIER, G. L., B.COM.
MAHEU, R., B.A., L.SC.COM., L.SC.COMP.
SABOURIN, L., LL.L., PH.D.

FEDERATED UNIVERSITY:

Saint Paul University: 223 Main St., Ottawa K1S 1C4.

Rector: Rev. HENRI GOUDREAULT, O.M.I., L.TH., S.S.L., D.TH.

ATTACHED INSTITUTES:

Institute for International Co-operation: Dir. Rev. J.-M. QUIRION, O.M.I., B.A., L.PH., B.TH., B.COMM., M.SC., A.C.I.S.

UNIVERSITY OF PRINCE EDWARD ISLAND

CHARLOTTETOWN,
PRINCE EDWARD ISLAND
C1A 4P3
Telephone: 892-4121.
Founded 1969.

St. Dunstan's University (f. 1855) and Prince of Wales College (f. 1834) have merged to form the University of Prince Edward Island.

Academic year: September to May (two semesters).

Chancellor: GUSTAVE GINGRAS, C.C., M.D., F.R.S.A., LL.D., F.R.C.P.(C.).
President and Vice-Chancellor: PETER P. M. MEINCKE, PH.D.
Registrar: MICHAEL F. HENNESSEY, B.A., B.ED.
Director of Extension and Summer Sessions: IAN P. MACDONALD, B.SC.
Comptroller: G. DENNIS CLOUGH, B.COM., C.A.
Chief Librarian: MERRITT CROCKETT, B.A., B.L.S.

Library: *see* Libraries.

Number of teachers: 130.
Number of students: 2,057.

DEANS:

Arts: FRANCIS J. LEDWELL, M.A.
Science: J. IVAN DOWLING, M.SC.
Education: D. ROY CAMPBELL, M.A., PH.D.

DEPARTMENTAL HEADS:
Biology: IAN G. MACQUARRIE.
Business Administration: WALTER ISENOR.
Chemistry: LEON LOUCKS.
Classics: J. R. KELLY.
Economics: P. NAGARAJAN.
Education: D. ROY CAMPBELL.
Engineering: DON MACEWEN.
English: BRENDAN O'GRADY.
History: S. ANDREW ROBB.
Home Economics: D. ANDERSON.
Mathematics and Computer Science: G. W. PINEAU.
Modern Languages: F. FALVO.
Music: H. TERSTEEG.
Philosophy: V. SMITHERAM.
Physics: E. L. WONNACOTT.
Political Science: GARY WEBSTER.
Psychology: T. D. WEIDEN.
Religious Studies: THOMAS MACLELLAN.
Sociology and Anthropology: R. H. WILLS.

UNIVERSITÉ DU QUÉBEC

2875 BLVD. LAURIER,
SAINTE-FOY, QUEBEC G1V 2M3
Telephone: (418) 657-3551.
Founded 1968.

Language of instruction: French.

President: GILLES BOULET.
Vice-President: PIERRE CAZALIS.
Vice-President (Teaching and Research): GERMAIN GAUTHIER.
Vice-President (Planning and Communications): PIERRE DECELLES.
Vice-President (Administration and Finance): ROGER LEFRANÇOIS.
Secretary-General: JEAN-PIERRE FORTIN.
Director of Public Relations: SERGE DE LA ROCHELLE.
Librarian: JEAN-PIERRE ROY.

Number of teachers: 1,399.
Number of students: 42,675.

Publication: *Réseau*† (monthly).

CONSTITUENT INSTITUTIONS:

UNIVERSITÉ DU QUÉBEC À CHICOUTIMI

930 RUE JACQUES CARTIER, EST,
CHICOUTIMI,
QUEBEC G7H 2B1
Telephone: 545-5011.
Founded 1969.

State control; Language of instruction: French.

Rector: GÉRARD ARGUIN.
Secretary-General: LUCIEN GENDRON.
Registrar: NOEL TREMBLAY.
Librarian: PAUL E. BOULET.

Number of teachers: 169.
Number of students: 1,975 full-time, 4,200 part-time.

HEADS OF DEPARTMENTS:
Education: PASQUALE PUCELLA.
Economic and Administrative Sciences: ADAM LAPOINTE.
Human Sciences: JEAN DÉSY.
Pure Sciences: CLÉMENT RICHARD.
Applied Sciences: RENÉ CHOUINARD.
Religious Sciences: RAYMOND GIRARD.
Arts and Literature: GLEIDER HERNANDEZ.

UNIVERSITÉ DU QUÉBEC À MONTRÉAL

1187 RUE DE BLEURY,
MONTREAL, QUEBEC H3C 3P8
Telephone: 876-3161.
Founded 1969.

Rector: CLAUDE PICHETTE.
Secretary-General: PIERRE BROSSARD.
Registrar: D. LAFORTE.

Library of 275,000 vols.
Number of teachers: 420.
Number of students: 4,500 full-time, 7,500 part-time.

HEADS OF DEPARTMENTS:
Administration: M. COTE.
Plastic Arts (2D): ANGELE BEAUDRY.
Plastic Arts (3D): P. PICHET.
Chemistry: Y. PEPIN.
Literature: R. ST.-AMOUR.
Geography: C. LEMAY.
History: D. BERTRAND.
Anthropology: P.-G. ROBINEAULT.
Linguistics: G. LABELLE.
Mathematics: C. JANVIER.
Art Education: M. FORTIN.
Philosophy: N. LACHARITE.
Physics: A. BOUTARD.
Psychology: H. NEIDHART.
Biology: Y. PAGEAU.
Earth Sciences: Y. PAGEAU.
Education: G. LUCAS.
Economics: V. LEROY.
Political Sciences: A. BERNARD.
Religion: R. CHAGNON.
Sociology: M. RAFIE.

UNIVERSITÉ DU QUÉBEC À RIMOUSKI

300 AVE. DES URSULINES,
RIMOUSKI, QUEBEC G5L 3A1
Telephone: 723-1986.
Telex: 051-8-6302.
Founded 1969.

Academic year: September to April (2 semesters).

Rector: PASCAL PARENT, D.PHIL.
Vice-Rectors: GABRIEL BÉRUBÉ (Teaching and Research), MARC-ANDRÉ DIONNE (Administration and Finance).
Secretary-General: BERTRAND LEPAGE.
Librarian: CHRISTIAN BIEL.

Library of 137,485 vols.
Number of teachers: 130.
Number of students: 1,185 full-time, 3,041 part-time.

HEADS OF DEPARTMENTS:
Letters and Human Sciences: BENOIT BEAUCAGE.
Administration: MARC LETOURNEAU.
Pure Sciences: A. STRACHAN.
Oceanography: J.-R. BRINDLE.
Education Sciences: ROMAIN ROUSSEAU.

UNIVERSITÉ DU QUÉBEC À TROIS-RIVIÈRES

3351 BLVD. DES FORGES, C.P. 500,
TROIS-RIVIÈRES,
QUEBEC G9A 5H7
Telephone: 376-5011.
Telex: 051-3488.
Founded 1969.

Provincial control; Academic year: September to April.

Rector: LOUIS-EDMOND HAMELIN, PH.D.
President: FRANÇOIS ST.-ARNAUD.
Registrar: HENRI-PAUL MCGEE, B.A., L.PED., L.ADM.SCOL.
Secretary-General: ANDRÉ BROUSSEAU, B.A., L.PED.
Librarian: MAURICE AUGER.

Library of 389,000 vols.
Number of teachers: 315.
Number of students: 3,957 full-time, 3,936 part-time.
Publication: *La Semaine*†.

HEADS OF DEPARTMENTS:
Chemistry-Biology: PIERRE BLANCHET.
Psychology: ERCILIA QUINTIN.
Engineering: ACHILLE LEBLANC.
Mathematics: TOAN NGUYEN KY.
Physics: CHRISTIAN DEMERS.
Philosophy: PAUL GAGNE.
Administration and Economics: ROBERT BEAUDOIN.
Education: ROBERT CHAMPAGNE.
Human Sciences: NORMAND SÉGUIN.
Theology: ARTHUR METTAYER.
French: PAUL BEAUBIEN.
Physical Education: ANDRÉ QUIRION.
Health Sciences: LISETTE ARCAND.
Plastic Arts and Music: NICOLE BOURGET.
Recreation: GILLES PRONOVOST.

Ecole Nationale d'Administration Publique: 625 rue Saint-Amable, Que. G1R 2G5; f. 1969; 340 students; library of 13,000 vols.; Dir.-Gen. LOUIS BRUNEL.

Ecole de Technologie Supérieure: 180 rue St. Catherine est, Montreal, Que. H2X 3M4; f. 1974; *c.* 300 students; Dir. Gen. R. A. DUGRÉ.

Institut Armand-Frappier: 531 blvd. des Prairies, C.P. 100, Laval-des-Rapides, Que. H7N 4Z3; f. 1938, affiliated to the Univ. of Quebec 1972; microbiological research; Dir. A. BEAULNES, M.D.

Institut National de la Recherche Scientifique: 2700 rue Einstein, C.P. 7500, Quebec, Que. G1V 4C7; f. 1969; 60 students; Dir. ANDRÉ LEMAY.

Centre d'études universitaires dans l'Ouest québécois: f. 1970; 7,500 students; Dir.-Gen. JEAN R. MESSIER.

Outaouais Campus: C.P. 1250, succursale "B", Hull, Que. J8X 3X7; f. 1971; administration, accounting, arts, social sciences, education, human sciences, nursing; library of 39,000 vols.

North-West Campus: 435 rue Gagné, C.P. 700, Rouyn, Que. J9X 5E4; f. 1970; administration, accounting, arts, education, human sciences, nursing; library of 31,115 vols.; Dir. REMY TRUDEL.

Télé-Université: 214 ave. Saint-Sacrement, Quebec, Que. G1N 4M6; f. 1972; distant-study programmes; *c.* 12,000 students; Dir. Gen. F. GRENIER.

QUEEN'S UNIVERSITY AT KINGSTON

KINGSTON, ONTARIO K7L 3N6

Telephone: 547-5511.

Founded 1841.

Language of instruction: English; Academic year: September to May (two terms).

Chancellor: A. McC. BENIDICKSON, B.A., LL.D.

Rector: H. CHRISTIE, B.A.

Vice-Chancellor and Principal: Prof. R. L. WATTS, M.A., D.PHIL.

Vice-Principal (Services): H. M. LOVE, PH.D.

Vice-Principal (Development and Information): (vacant).

Vice-Principal (Resources): R. J. HAND, M.B.A.

Vice-Principal (Health Science): H. G. KELLY, M.D.

Registrar: Dr. K. L. S. GUNN.

Secretary of the University: J. W. BANNISTER, B.COM.

Chief Librarian: MARGOT MCBURNEY.

Number of teachers: *c.* 860.

Number of students: *c.* 10,500.

Publications: ***Campus, Queen's Gazette, Journal, Douglas Library Notes, Golden Words.***

DEANS:

Faculty of Applied Science: D. W. BACON, M.S., PH.D.

Faculty of Arts and Sciences: D G. SINCLAIR, D.V.M., V.S., M.S.A., PH.D.

Faculty of Law: B. L. ADELL, D.PHIL.

Faculty of Medicine: T. J. BOAG, M.B., CH.B.

School of Graduate Studies: M. YEATES, M.A., PH.D.

School of Business: J. GORDON, PH.D.

School of Nursing: A. J. BAUNGART, M.SC.

Faculty of Education: T. R. WILLIAMS, M.A., ED.D.

PROFESSORS:

(Some staff teach in more than one faculty)

Faculty of Applied Science:

BACON, D. W., M.S. PH.D., Chemical Engineering
BATCHELOR, B. DE V., PH.D., D.I.C., Civil Engineering
BAUER, A., PH.D., Mining Engineering
BEAL, J. C., PH.D., Electrical Engineering
BECKER, H. A., M.SC., SC.D., Chemical Engineering
BREBNER, B.SC., PH.D., A.M.I.C.E., Civil Engineering
BROWN, J. H., S.M., SC.D., Mining Engineering
CAMPLING, C. H. R., B.SC., S.M., Electrical Engineering
CLARK, R. H., B.SC.(ENG.), PH.D., Chemical Engineering
CORNEIL, E. R., PH.D., D.I.C., Mechanical Engineering
DOWNIE, J., M.A.SC., PH.D., Chemical Engineering
EDWARDS, H. M., M.S.C.E., B.SC., Civil Engineering
GILBERT, W. D., B.SC., S.M., Mechanical Engineering
HAMES, F. A., M.SC., PH.D., Metallurgy
HENRY, W. G., M.A.SC., PH.D., Metallurgy
HILL, P. G., M.SC., Mechanical Engineering
HOGARTH, J. E., M.SC., PH.D., Engineering Mathematics
KAMPHUIS, J. W., M.SC., PH.D., D.H.E., Civil Engineering
KENNEDY, R. J., M.C., M.S., Civil Engineering
KURTZ, E. F., S.M., PH.D., Mechanical Engineering
LAZIER, S. S., M.A.SC., Civil Engineering
MACKAY, W. B. F., M.S., PH.D., Metallurgy
PENSTONE, S. R., M.SC., Electrical Engineering
POLLOCK, H. S., M.SC., Electrical Engineering
RAYMOND, G. P., M.SC., PH.D., D.SC., Civil Engineering
RICE, W. B., M.ENG., D. ès SC.APP., Mechanical Engineering
RUSH, C. K., M.SC., Mechanical Engineering
SMITH, R. W., PH.D., Metallurgy
STINSON, W. C., B.SC., Engineering Drawing
WATT, W. E., M.SC., PH.D., D.I.C., Civil Engineering
WITTKE, P. H., M.SC., PH.D., Electrical Engineering
WOJCIECHOWSKI, B. W., M.A.SC., PH.D., Chemical Engineering
YALIN, S. M., DR.ING., DOZENT, Civil Engineering

Faculty of Arts and Science:

ABRAHAMS, V. C., PH.D., Physiology
AKENSON, D. H. M.ED., PH.D., History
ALLEN, J. R., M.A., PH.D., Physics
ALLEN, R., D.F.A., Art History
ANDREW, G. M., M.SC., PH.D., Physical and Health Education
ANHALT, I., Music
ARDAL, P. S., M.A., PH.D., Philosophy
ARTHUR, A. Z., PH.D., Psychology
ATHERTON, D. L., M.A., Physics
BATER, B. R., M.A., S.T.M., PH.D., Religion
BAXTER, J. S., PH.D., English
BEQUIRAZ, M. A., M.S., PH.D., Sociology
BERRY, L. G., M.A., PH.D., F.G.S.A., F.R.S.C., F.M.S.A., Geology
BESSETTE, G., L. ès L., M.A., D. ès L., F.R.S.C., French
BIDWELL, R. G. S., M.A., PH.D., Biology
BLACK, E. R., M.A., PH.D., Political Studies
BLYTH, C. R., M.A., PH.D., Mathematics
BOND, E. J., M.A., PH.D., Philosophy
BONHAM, D. H., LL.M., C.A., Commerce
BOTTERELL, E. H., O.B.E., M.D., M.S., D.SC., LL.D., F.R.C.S.(C.), Anatomy
BRECK, W. G., M.SC., PH.D., Chemistry
BROWN, N. J. P., M.A., B.PHIL., Philosophy
BROWN, S. R., Biology
BUNCEL, E., PH.D., D.SC., Chemistry
CAMPBELL, D., M.A., PH.D., Psychology
CAMPBELL, L. L., M.S., PH.D., Mathematics
CANVIN, D. T., M.SC., PH.D., Biology
CHADWICK, P. M.B., B.S., Microbiology and Immunology
CLARK, G., M.A., PH.D., English
CLARKE, F. R. C., MUS.DOC., F.C.C.O., A.R.C.T., Music
COLEMAN, A. J., M.A., PH.D., Mathematics
COLPA, J. P., PH.D., Chemistry
CONKIE, W. R., M.SC., PH.D., Physics
CRANDALL, R. H., M.B.A., PH.D., C.A., Commerce
CRAWFORD, D. H., M.A., M.ED., PH.D., Mathematics
CRAWLEY, D. F., M.A., PH.D., English
CROWDER, C. M. D., M.A., D.PHIL., History
DELUCCA, J., M.A., PH.D., Philosophy
DENNIS, D. T., PH.D., Biology
DEUTSCH, J. J., C.C., B.COM., LL.D., F.R.S.C., Economics
DOBELL, A. R., M.A., PH.D., Economics
DODWELL, P. C., M.A., D.PHIL., Psychology
DOWNE, A. E. R., M.A., PH.D., Biology
DUNCAN, A. R. C., M.A., Philosophy
EASTON, D., M.A., PH.D., Political Science
EDWARDS, J. F., M.A.(P.E.), Physical and Health Education
EIDINGER, D., M.D., PH.D., Microbiology and Immunology
ELLIS, H. W., M.SC., M.A., PH.D., Mathematics
EVANS, H. C., M.SC., PH.D., Physics
EWAN, G. T., PH.D., Physics
FAULKNER, P., PH.D., Microbiology and Immunology
FELL, A., P.A.M., Philosophy
FINLEY, G. E., M.A., PH.D., Art History
FISHER, G. R., M.A., Economics
FITZPATRICK, M. M., M.A., PH.D., F.G.A.C., Geological Sciences
FIXMAN, U., M.SC., PH.D., Mathematics
FOX, A. M., M.A., PH.D., Spanish
FULLERTON, H. V., M.A., Commerce
GEORGE, G., MUS.BAC., MUS.DOC., F.C.C.O., Music
GIBSON, F. W., M.A., History
GILES, R., D.SC., Mathematics
GORDON, H. S., M.A., PH.D., Economics
GORMAN, W. A., M.SC., PH.D., F.G.A.C., Geological Sciences
GOOD, PH.D., Biology
GRAHAM, W. R., M.A., PH.D., History
GREER, L. N., M.B.A., C.A., Commerce
GROVE, J. W., D.P.A., Political Studies
GUNN, J. A. W., M.A., D.PHIL., Political Studies
HAMILTON, A. C., M.A., PH.D., English
HAND, R. J., B.COM., M.B.A., Commerce
HATCHER, J. D., M.D., PH.D., Physiology
HELMERS, H. O., B.S.M.E., M.B.A., PH.D., School of Business
HEYDING, R. D., M.SC., PH.D., M.C.I.C., Chemistry
HODGES, H. W. M., M.B., Art
HOGARTH, J. E., M.A., Engineering Mathematics
HUGHES, V. A., M.SC., Physics
HURST, R. O., PH.D., F.C.I.C., Biochemistry
INGLIS, J., M.A., PH.D., D.SC., Psychology
IRELAND, G. W., M.A., D.LITT., French
JARDINE, D. A., M.SC., PH.D., Computing and Information Science
JELLINCK, P. H., M.SC., PH.D., Biochemistry
JENNINGS, D. B., M.D., C.M., M.SC., PH.D., Physiology
JONES, J. K. N., PH.D., D.SC., A.R.I.C., F.C.I.C., F.R.S.C., F.R.S., Chemistry
KALISKI, S. F., M.A., PH.D., Economics

KEAST, J. A., M.SC., M.A., PH.D., Biology
KEMP, R. R. D., PH.D., Mathematics
KEPPEL-JONES, A. M., M.A., PH.D., History
KIRBY, B. J., M.A., PH.D., Mathematics
KNOWLES, J. B., PH.D., Psychology
KRAICER, J., B.A., M.D., PH.D., Physiology
KRAUSSE, H. K., M.A., PH.D., German and Literature
LAW, C. E., B.A., Commerce
LEITH, J. A., M.A., PH.D., History
LELE, J., M.A., PH.D., Political Studies and Sociology
LEONARD, W. G., F.C.A., Commerce
LEVISON, M., PH.D., Computing and Information Science
LEYS, C., M.A., Political Studies
LIPSEY, R. G., M.A., PH.D., Economics
LOEB, E., M.A., PH.D., German
LOUGHEED, W. C., M.A., PH.D., English
LOVE, H. M., PH.D., Physics
MACINTOSH, D. DE F., M.S., PH.D., Physical and Health Education
MCINTOSH, R. L., M.B.E., M.SC., PH.D., Chemistry
MACKENZIE, N. H., M.A., PH.D., English
MACLACHLAN, D. C. L., M.A., PH.D., Philosophy
MACLEAN, A. C., TH.M., PH.D., Religion
MACLEOD, A. M., M.A., PH.D., Philosophy
MARKS, G. S., M.SC., D.PHIL. Pharmacology
MATTHEWS, J. P., M.A., DIP.ED., PH.D., F.R.C.S., English
MEISEL, J., M.A., PH.D., Political Studies
MCGHIEL, A., M.A., PH.D., Psychology
MILAZZO, F. H., M.S., PH.D., Microbiology and Immunology
MOIR, R. Y., M.A., PH.D., Chemistry
MONIESON, D. D., M.B.E., PH.D., Commerce
MONTAGUE, J. H., S.M., PH.D., Physics
MOORE, E. G., M.A., PH.D., Geography
NEATBY, H., M.A., PH.D., LL.D., History
NEILSON, J. M., M.SC., PH.D., Geological Sciences
NEWELL, I., M.A., English
NICHOL, I., M.A., PH.D., Geological Sciences
OBREANU, P. E., LIC., Mathematics
ØRVIK, N., M.A., PH.D., Political Studies
PAGE, J. A., M.SC., PH.D., Chemistry
PALDA, K. S., PH.D., Commerce
PARKER, C. H., PH.D., Hebrew and Religion
PIERCE, R. A., M.A., PH.D., History
POLZER, J., M.A., PH.D., Art History
PRICE, R. A., M.A., PH.D., F.R.S.C., F.G.S.A., F.G.A.G., Geological Sciences
PULLMAN, N. J., M.A., PH.D., Mathematics
PULLEN, C. H., M.A., PH.D., English
RAWLYK, G. A., M.A., PH.D., History
REESOR, M. E., M.A., PH.D., Classics
RIBENBOIM, R., PH.D., Mathematics
RILEY, A. W., PH.D., German
ROBERTS, D. T., PH.D., Physics
ROEDER, P. L., PH.D., Geological Sciences
ROMERO-SIERRA, C., M.A., PH.D., English
RUGGLES, R. I., M.A., PH.D., F.R.G.S., Geography
RUSSELL, J. J., M.A., Philosophy
RUSSELL, K. E., M.A., PH.D., Chemistry
RUTHERFORD, G. K., M.SC., PH.D., Geography
SAYEED, K. B., M.A., PH.D., Political Studies
SAYER, M., PH.D., Physics
SCHURMAN, D. M., M.A., PH.D., History
SEARLE, C., B.SC., S.M., Psychology and Electrical Engineering
SEGEL, S. L., M.S., PH.D., Physics
SEMPLE, R. E., M.A., PH.D., Physiology
SMALLMAN, B. N., M.SC., PH.D., F.R.S.C., Biology
SHERWOOD, J. M., M.A., PH.D., History
SINCLAIR, D. G., D.V.M., V.S., M.S.A., PH.D., Physiology
SMETHURST, S. E., M.A., Classics
SMITH, D. C., M.A., PH.D., Economics
SMITH, V. H., M.S., PH.D., Chemistry
SMITH, W. M., PH.D., Chemistry
SPARKS, G. R., M.A., PH.D., Economics
SPETTIGUE, D. O., M.A., PH.D., English
STEDMOND, J. M., M.A., PH.D., English
STEWART, A. T., M.SC., PH.D., Physics
STEWART, R. B., M.A., PH.D., Microbiology and Immunology
TAYLOR, A. M., M.A., D.PHIL., Geography and Political Studies
THANH, P. C., PH.D., Economics
THOMPSON, W. R., M.A., PH.D., Psychology
THORBURN, H. G., A.M., PH.D., Political Studies
TRAVILL, A. A., M.B., B.S., M.R.C.S.(ENG.), M.SC.(MED.), L.R.C.P., Anatomy
UFFEN, R. J., M.A., PH.D., D.SC., F.R.S.C., F.G.S.A., Geological Sciences
URQUHART, M. C., B.A., F.R.S.C., Economics
USHER, D., M.A., PH.D., Economics
WAN, J. K. S., PH.D., Chemistry
WASAN, M. T., M.A., PH.D., Mathematics
WATTS, D. G., M.A.SC., PH.D., Mathematics
WATTS, R. L., M.A., D.PHIL., Political Studies
WEBSTER, S., M.A., PH.D., History
WHALLEY, A. G. C., C.D., M.A., PH.D., F.R.S.L., F.R.S.C., English
WHEELER, R. C., M.SC. PH.D., Chemistry
WILDE, G. J. S., PH.D., Psychology
WILLETT, T. C., T.D., PH.D., Sociology
WINTLE, H. J., M.A., M.SC., PH.D., Physics
WYATT, G. R., PH.D., Biology
WOLFE, S., M.A., PH.D., Chemistry
WOOD, W. D., M.A., A.M., PH.D., Economics
YEATES, M. H., M.A., PH.D., Geography

Faculty of Education:

APPLEGATE, M., M.A., Continuing Education
ATHERTON, P. J., B.ED., Education Administration
BAILEY, J. C., M.S., Elementary Education
BALANCHUK, M. L., M.ED., Guidance and Counselling
CRAWFORD, D. H., M.A., M.ED., PH.D., Graduate Studies
GRIME, A. R., M.ED., Geography
HENNESSY, P. H., B.A., Student Teaching
HOLOMEGO, H., M.A., Physical and Health Education
KING, A. J. C., M.SC., ED.D., Sociology
LONEY, D. E., B.SC., Technical Education
MASSEY, D. A., M.A., M.A.T., French and German
ORR, A. A., M.A., English
PIEH, R. J., M.SC., Clinical and Field Studies
THOMPSON, L., M.A., English
THUMM, W., B.A., D.ED., B.SC., M.A.T., Physics and Diagnostic Radiology

Faculty of Medicine:

BECK, I. T., M.D., PH.D., F.R.C.P.(C.), F.A.C.P., Physiology
BENCOSME, S. A., M.D., M.SC., PH.D., Pathology
BIRD, C. E., M.D., C.M., PH.D., F.R.C.P.(C.), Medicine
BOAG, T. J., M.B., CH.B., Psychiatry
BOTHERELL, E. H., O.B.E., M.D., M.S., D.SC., F.R.C.S.(C.), Anatomy
BRUCE, A. W., M.B., CH.B., F.R.C.S., F.R.C.S.(C.), Urology
BRYANS, A. M., M.D., F.R.C.P.(C), Paediatrics
CAMPBELL, D., M.A., PH.D., Psychiatry
CONNELL, W. F., M.D., C.M., F.R.C.P. (LOND.), F.R.C.P.(C), F.A.C.P., Medicine and Clinical Medicine
DINSDALE, H. B., M.D., C.M., F.R.C.P.(C.), Medicine
EIDINGER, D., M.D., PH.D., Microbiology
FRANSMAN, S. L., M.D., F.C.C.P., Radiology
GHENT, W. R., M.D., C.M., R.R.C.S.(C.), F.A.C.S., F.I.C.S., Surgery
GULETIUS, J. R., B.A., M.D., C.M., F.R.C.S.(C.), F.A.C.S., Surgery
HAYNES, E. R., M.A., M.B., CH.B., B.A.O., F.R.F.P.(C.), Family Medicine
KAUFMAN, N., M.D., C.M., Pathology
KELLY, H. G., M.D., C.M., F.R.C.P.(C), F.A.C.P., Medicine
KIPKIE, G. F., M.D., C.M., M.SC., Pathology
KRAUS, A. S., M.SC., SC.D., Preventive Medicine
LAVERTY, S. G., B.SC., M.B., CH.B., M.R.C.P., D.P.M., F.R.C.P.(C.), Psychiatry
LOTT, S., M.D., Therapeutic Radiology
LOW, J. A., M.D., F.R.C.S.(C), Obstetrics and Gynaecology
LYNN, R. B., M.D.C.M., F.R.C.S., F.R.C.S. (EDIN.), F.A.C.S., Surgery
MCCORRISTON, J. R., M.D.C.M., M.SC., Surgery
MILLIKEN, J. A., M.D., Medicine
PARTINGTON, M. W., M.B., B.S., PH.D. F.R.C.P., D.C.H., Paediatrics
PICKLES, B., Rehabilitation Therapy
PINKERTON, R. M. H., M.B., B.CH., F.R.C.S., F.R.C.S.(C.), Ophthalmology
POWLES, W. E., B.A., M.D., C.M., F.R.C.P.(C.), Psychiatry
ROBERTSON, D. M., M.D., M.SC., Pathology
ROMERO-SIERRA, C., M.D., D.SC., Anatomy
ROSEN, D. A., M.D.C.M., F.R.C.S.(C.), Ophthalmology
SIMPSON, N. A., M.A., PH.D., Paediatrics
SORBIE, C., M.B., CH.B., F.R.C.S.(C.), Surgery
STEELE, H. D., M.D., C.M., Pathology
STEELE, R., M.D., D.P.H., F.A.P.H.A., Preventive Medicine
STERNS, E. E., M.D., C.M., F.R.C.S.(C.), Surgery
SYMINGTON, D. C., M.B., CH.B., Rehabilitation Medicine
TRAVILL, A. A., M.R.C.S., L.R.C.P., M.SC.(MED.), Anatomy
VANDEWATER, S. L., M.D., F.R.C.P.(C.), Anaesthesia
WAUGH, D. O. W., M.D., C.M., M.SC., PH.D., Pathology
WHITE, D. N., M.A., M.D., M.R.C.P., F.R.C.P.(C), F.A.C.P., Neurology
WILLIAMS, D. M. L., M.R.C.S., F.R.C.S., F.R.C.S.(C.), Otolaryngology
WILSON, D. L., M.A., M.D., C.M., F.R.C.P.(C.), F.A.C.P., Medical Law and Medicine
WRIGHT, F. J., M.D., C.M., F.R.C.P.(C.), Anaesthesiology
YENDT, E. R., M.D., F.R.C.P.(C.), Medicine

Faculty of Law:

ADELL, B. L., LL.B., D.PHIL.
ALEXANDROWICZ, G. W., M.A., LL.D., LL.M.
ASPUND, C. T., B.A., LL.B.
BALE, C. G., M.A., LL.B., LL.M.
BONHAM, D. H., LL.M., C.A.

BESSETTE, IRENE, LIC. EN DROIT, M.S., LL.B.
BAER, M. G., B.A., LL.M.
CARTER, D. D., B.A., LL.B., B.L.L.
CHEN, T. P., M.C.L., LL.M., S.J.D.
ISON, T. G., LL.B., LL.M.
JOHNSON, J. M., B.A., LL.B.
LAWFORD, H. J., B.A., LL.B., B.C.L.
LEDERMAN, W. R., Q.C., B.A., LL.B., B.C.L.
LYON, N., LL.M.
PRICE, R. R., LL.B.
RYAN, H. R. S., Q.C., B.A.
SADINSKY, S., B.A., LL.B.
SIMMONS, C. G., B.A., B.C.L., LL.M.
SOBERMAN, D. A., LL.B., LL.M.

School of Rehabilitation Therapy:
FORREST, W. J., M.D., M.SC.(MED.).

AFFILIATED COLLEGE:

Queen's Theological College: f. 1841.
Principal: Rev. B. R. BATER, M.A., B.D., S.T.M.

UNIVERSITY OF REGINA

REGINA,
SASKATCHEWAN S4S 0A2
Telephone: 584-4111.

Founded 1974 (previously Regina Campus, University of Saskatchewan).
State control; Language of instruction: English; Academic year: September to June (2 terms, plus spring and summer sessions).

Chancellor: A. R. ANDREYCHUK, B.A., LL.B.
Vice-Chancellor and President: L. I. BARBER, O.C., M.B.A., PH.D.
Vice-President: E. B. TINKER, M.SC., PH.D.
University Secretary: D. T. LOWERY, B.COMM., C.A., R.I.A.
Controller: S. G. MANN, B.A., B.COMM.
Registrar: N. A. STABLES, B.COMM., C.A.
Librarian: S. HARLAND, M.A., F.L.A.

Number of teachers: 347.
Number of students: 3,344 full-time, 2,924 part-time.

Publications: *Wascana Review*† (2 a year), *General Calendar*†, *Graduate Studies Calendar*†, *President's Report*† (annually).

DEANS:

Administration: D. E. SHAW, M.A., PH.D.
Arts: R. R. ROBINSON, D.PHIL.
Education: G. E. RICHERT, M.ED., PH.D.
Engineering: W. H. B. COOKE, M.S., PH.D.
Graduate Studies and Research: C. W. BLACHFORD, M.S., PH.D.
Science: W. B. MCCONNELL, M.SC., PH.D.
Social Work: (vacant).

PROFESSORS:

ANDERSON, F. W., M.A., Economics
ANDERSON, M., M.A., LL.D., English
ANDERSON, R. H., C.A., M.B.A., Administration
ARCHER, J. H., M.A., PH.D., Western Canadian History
BARBER, L. I., M.B.A., PH.D., Administration
BERTRAND, H., M.SC., PH.D., Biology
BESSAI, F., M.ED., PH.D., Education
BLACHFORD, C. W., M.S., PH.D., Engineering
BLEWETT, D. B., M.A., PH.D., Psychology
BOAN, J. A., PH.D., Economics
BRANDT, L. W., M.A., PH.D., Psychology
BURGESS, J. O., M.A., D.ED., Education
CHANDLER, W. D., PH.D., Chemistry
CLEVELAND, R. L., M.A., PH.D., History
CONLAN, J., M.A., PH.D., Mathematics
COOKE, W. B. H., M.S., PH.D., Engineering
COSBEY, R. C., M.A., PH.D., English
COWAN, D. F., M.A., ED.D., Education
COWASJEE, S., M.A., PH.D., English
CULLIMORE, D. R., PH.D., Biology
DALE, E. H., M.SC., PH.D., Geography
FULLER, G. A., M.SC., PH.D., Systems Engineering
GEAR, J. R., M.A., PH.D., Chemistry
GODWIN, E. W., Visual Arts
GORDON, W. A., PH.D., Geology
GRAY, G. E., M.S., M.SC., D.ED., Education
GREENBERG, L. H., M.SC., PH.D., Physics
GROOME, AGNES, M.A., PH.D., Education
GUPTA, H. N., M.A., PH.D., Mathematics
HILLABOLD, A. B., M.A., PH.D., Economics
HONTZEAS, S. A., PH.D., Chemistry
JACK, H. H., M.A., PH.D., Philosophy
JOHNSON, K. E., A.R.C.S., PH.D., D.I.C., D.SC., Chemistry
JOHNSON, R. E., M.A., PH.D., Psychology
JONESCU, M. E., M.A., PH.D., Education
KAUL, S. K., M.SC., PH.D., Mathematics
KELLY, A. K., M.A., PH.D., Economics
KENT, D. M. J., M.SC., PH.D., Geology
KLOPOUSHAK, E. L., M.ED., PH.D., Education
KOH, E. L., M.S., M.SC., PH.D., Mathematics
KOVACS, M. L., M.A., M.ED., PH.D., History
LAW, A. G., M.A., PH.D., Computer Science
LEE, D. G., M.A., PH.D., Chemistry
LEYTON-BROWN, H., D.F.E., A.MUS.A., F.G.S.M., D.M.A., Music
LOBAUGH, H. B., M.M., PH.D., Music
MALIKAIL, J. S., M.A., PH.D., Education
MANTLE, J. B., M.S., Engineering
MCBEATH, A. G., M.ED., ED.D., Education
MCCONNELL, W. B., M.SC., PH.D., Chemistry
MCCRORIE, J. N., M.A., PH.D., Sociology
MITCHELL, G. J., M.A., PH.D., Biology
MONTGOMERY, W. D., M.S., PH.D., Mathematics
MUTHUCHIDAMBARAM, S. P., M.A., LL.B., PH.D., Administration
NAQVI, S. I. H., M.SC., PH.D., Physics
NEWTON, J. L., M.A., PH.D., Education
NUGENT, J. C., Visual Arts
NULF, F. A., M.A., PH.D., Art
PACHNER, J., D.TECH.SC., DR. PHYS. MATH.SC., Physics
PAPINI, G. A., DOTTORE IN FISICA, Physics
POPE, R. K., M.A., Anthropology and Social Sciences
RAJU, M. V. S., M.SC., PH.D., Biology
RAO, V. V., M.A., PH.D., Mathematics
RICHERT, G. E., M.ED., PH.D., Education
RIEGERT, P. W., M.SC., PH.D., Biology
ROBERTSON, B. E., M.SC., PH.D., Physics
RUMMENS, F. H. A., D.SC.TU., Chemistry
SATO, D., M.A., PH.D., Mathematics
SCHUBERT, J. J., M.A., PH.D., Psychology
SCHUDEL, T. M., M.A., D.M.A., Music
SEAWELL, O. D., S.M., Systems Engineering
SHAW, D. E., M.A., PH.D., Administration
STALWICK, H., M.S.W., PH.D., Social Work
STEWART, S. E., M.A., Classics
STEWART, W. D., M.SC., PH.D., Systems Engineering
STIRLING, R. M., M.A., PH.D., Sociology
SURES, J. J., M.A., Visual Art
SYMES, L. R., M.S., PH.D., Computer Science
TINKER, E. B., M.SC., PH.D., Engineering
TOMKINS, R. J., M.S., PH.D., Mathematics
TOOMBS, W. N., M.ED., PH.D., Education
VENTRE, A. G. L., M.ED., Physical Education
VIGRASS, L. W., M.SC., PH.D., Geology
WALLACE, W. J., PH.D., Chemistry
WEBER, B. J., M.A., PH.D., English
WILHELM, B. J., D. ÈS L., French
WONG, C. L., M.A., M.SC., PH.D., Mathematics
WOROBY, P., M.SC., PH.D., Economics
ZACHARUK, R. Y., M.SC., PH.D., Biology
ZAGORIN, B., M.A., PH.D., History

ATTACHED INSTITUTES:

Canadian Plains Research Centre: Dir. M. E. JONESCU, M.A., PH.D.

Regina Water Research Institute: Dir. D. R. CULLIMORE, PH.D.

Energy Research Institute: Dir. L. W. VIGRASS, M.SC., PH.D.

FEDERATED COLLEGES:

Campion College: f. 1918; B.A. courses; *President:* Very Rev. J. B. GAVIN, M.A., PH.D.

Luther College.
President: M. A. ANDERSON, M.A., LL.D.

Saskatchewan Indian Federated College.
Director: I. WASACASE.

ROYAL MILITARY COLLEGE OF CANADA

KINGSTON, ONTARIO K7L 2W3
Telephone: (613) 545-7236.
Founded 1876.

Languages of instruction: English and French; Academic year: August to December (fall term); January to May (winter term).

Chancellor and President: The Hon. ALLAN MCKINNON, M.C., C.D., P.C., M.P.
Commandant: Brig.-Gen. A. J. G. D. DE CHASTELAIN, C.D., P.S.C., B.A.
Principal and Director of Studies: D. E. TILLEY, PH.D.
Registrar: R. E. JONES, M.A., PH.D.
Director of Cadets: Lt.-Col. J. A. ANNAND, C.D., P.S.C., R.M.C., B.A.
Director of Administration: Lt.-Col. F. A. HLOHOVSKY, C.D., B.ENG.
Chief Librarian: R. K. C. CROUCH, A.M.

Library of 175,000 vols.
Number of teachers: 145.
Number of cadets: 631.

DEANS AND CHAIRMEN OF DIVISIONS:

Arts: J. P. CAIRNS, N.D.C., M.A., PH.D.
Science: T. S. HUTCHISON, PH.D., F.INST.P., F.A.P.S.
Engineering: A. C. LEONARD, M.B.E., C.D., M.S.E., PH.D.
Graduate Studies and Research, Commdr. (retd.) J. B. PLANT, C.D. N.D.C., PH.D.
Canadian Forces Military College and Extension Division: W. S. AVIS, M.A., PH.D.

PROFESSORS:

ARSENAULT, G. P., R.M.C., PH.D., Chemistry
AVIS, W. S., M.A., PH.D., English
BAIRD, D. C., PH.D., Physics
BARTON, S. S., M.A., PH.D., Chemistry
BINHAMMER, H. H. F., M.A., PH.D., Economics
BUSSIERES, P., M.ENG., PH.D., Mechanical Engineering
CAIRNS, J. P., N.D.C., M.A., PH.D., Economics
CHAUDHRY, M. D., M.A., PH.D., Economics
CHAUDHRY, M. L., M.A., PH.D., Mathematics
DIAPER, D. G. M., M.A., D.PHIL., F.R.I.C., F.C.I.C., Organic Chemistry
EDWARDS, M. H., M.A., PH.D., F.A.P.S., Physics
EGGENBERGER, Lt.-Col. J. C., C.D., O.M.M., M.ED., PH.D., Military Leadership and Management
ELLIS, J. S., M.ENG., PH.D., Civil Engineering
FURTER, W. F., R.M.C., S.M., PH.D., F.C.I.C., Chemical Engineering
HARRIS-LOWE, R. F. B., PH.D., Physics
HUTCHISON, T. S., PH.D., F.INST.P., F.A.P.S., F.R.S.E., Physics
JONES, R. A., M.SC., PH.D., Chemistry
KIRK, D. W., M.SC., PH.D., Civil Engineering
LEONARD, A. C., M.B.E., C.D., M.S.E., PH.D., Mechanical Engineering
MANN, R. F., M.SC., PH.D., Chemical Engineering
MOFFATT, W. C., R.M.C., M.SC., SC.D., Mechanical Engineering
NALDRETT, S. N., M.SC., PH.D., Chemistry
PIKE, J. G., R.M.C., M.SC., PH.D., Mechanical Engineering
PLANT, Commdr. (retd.) J. B., C.D., PH.D., Electrical Engineering
POPE, N. K., M.SC., PH.D., Mathematics
PRESTON, A. W., M.A., PH.D., History
ROGERS, D. H., M.SC., PH.D., Physics
THOMPSON, F. F., M.A., D.PHIL., DIP.ED., History
WILSON, J. D., PH.D., Electrical Engineering

RYERSON POLYTECHNICAL INSTITUTE

50 GOULD ST., TORONTO, ONT. M5B 1E8

Telephone: (416) 595-5000.

Founded 1963; previously Ryerson Institute of Technology.

President: W. G. PITMAN, M.A.
Vice-Presidents: A. GIFFORD, M.A. (Academic), T. G. SOSA, M.A., M.ED. (Administration).
Registrar: J. BRUNZELL, R.P.I.DIP.

Number of teachers: 551.
Number of students: 9,205.

DEANS:

Applied Arts: (vacant).
Arts: T. W. GRIER, M.A.
Business: W. J. L. CLARK, B.A.SC.
Community Services: A. WILKINSON, M.A.
Technology: T. E. WISZ, M.A.SC., M.SC.

SAINT FRANCIS XAVIER UNIVERSITY

ANTIGONISH, NOVA SCOTIA B2G 1C0

Telephone: 863-3300.

Founded 1853.

Language of Instruction: English; Dates of Academic Year: September to May.

Chancellor: Most Rev. W. E. POWER, D.D.
President: Rev. G. A. MACKINNON, PH.D.
Executive Vice-President: J. J. MACDONALD, PH.D.
Administrative Vice-President: J. T. LANGLEY, C.G.A., M.S.
Director of University Extension: Rev. G. TOPSHEE, B.A.
Registrar: B. U. LIENGME, PH.D.
Librarian: Rev. CHARLES BREWER.

Library: *see* Libraries.
Number of teachers: 158, including 24 professors.
Number of students: 2,226.
Publications: *Xaverian Weekly, St. Francis Xavier Yearbook, Contemporary News.*

DEANS:

Dean of Arts and Science: J. T. SEARS, D.B.A.
Dean of Students: BRIAN MACDONALD, M.A.
University Chaplain: Rev. GREGORY CAMPBELL, M.A.
Director of Admissions: J. A. MACLELLAN, M.ED.

FULL PROFESSORS:

BALAWYDER, A., PH.D., History
BRUNELLE, Y. G., PH.D., English
BUNBURY, D. L., PH.D., Chemistry
CHIASSON, L. P., PH.D., Biology
CORMIER, R. F., PH.D., Geology
CUJES, R., PH.D., Sociology
CURRIE, S., PH.D., English
GINIVAN, Rev. F. J., Mathematics
GREENIDGE, K. N., PH.D., Biology
KONTAK, WALTER, M.A., Political Science
LYNCH, B. M., Chemistry
MACDONALD, J. J., PH.D., Chemistry
MACDONELL, Rev. M., M.A., History
MACKINNON, R. J., PH.D., Mathematics
MACLEAN, C., PH.D., French
MACLEAN, R., PH.D., History
MACPHERSON, J. A., PH.D., English
MACSWEEN, Rev. R. J., B.A., English
PINK, D. A., PH.D., Physics
POWER, Rev. G., PH.D., Classics
SEARS, J. T., D.B.A., Business Administration
SECCO, ETALO, D.SC., Chemistry
SHAW, W., Geology
STEWART, J. B., Political Science
WEINGARTSHOFER, A., D.SC., Physics
WOODFINE, WILLIAM J., PH.D., Economics

UNIVERSITÉ SAINTE-ANNE

CHURCH POINT, N.S. B0W 1M0.

Telephone: (902)769-2114.

Founded 1890.

Language of instruction: French.

President: CHARLES J. GAUDET
Registrar: GÉRALD C. BOUDREAU.
Librarian: GUSTAVE DOUCET.

Library of 50,000 vols.
Number of teachers: 30.
Number of students: 800.
Publications: *Calendar, Revue* (annually).

HEADS OF DEPARTMENTS:

Commerce: MARCEL COTTREAU.
Education: Dr. JOHN KENYON.
English: Dr. JAMES QUINLAN.
Extension and Summer School: LÉGER COMEAU.
French: Dr. MOSHÉ STARETS.
Humanities: Dr. ANDRÉAS BUSS.
Science: Dr. JEAN-CLAUDE DOL.

ATTACHED INSTITUTES:

Acadian Research Center: Dir. NEIL BOUCHER.
Educational Resource Center: Dir. JEAN-LOUIS ROBICHAUD.

SAINT MARY'S UNIVERSITY

ROBIE ST., HALIFAX, NOVA SCOTIA B3H 3C3

Telephone: (902)422-7361.

Founded 1802.

Chancellor: Most Rev. JAMES M. HAYES, J.C.D., D.D.
Vice-Chancellor: Rev. COLIN CAMPBELL, M.S.W., V.G., P.P.
President: KENNETH L. OZMON, M.A., PH.D.
Vice-President (Academic): WILLIAM A. STEWART, S.J., B.A., S.T.L., PH.L. (acting).
Registrar: ELIZABETH A. CHARD, M.A., B.ED.
Librarian: RONALD G. LEWIS, M.DIV., M.L.S.

Number of teachers: 174.
Number of full-time students: 2,205.
Number of part-time students: 1,531.

DEANS:

Dean of Arts: T. J. MUSIAL, M.S., PH.D.
Dean of Education: M. MACMILLAN, B.ED., M.A., PH.D
Dean of Science: (vacant).
Dean of Commerce: S. H. JOPLING, B.MECH ENG., M.S., PH.D.

PROFESSORS:

BEAZLEY, H. G., Business Administration
BEIS, R. H., Philosophy
BOBR-TYLINGO, S., History
BOYD, G., Political Science
BRIDGEO, W. J., Chemistry
CARRIGAN, D. O., History
CHADWICK-JONES, J. D., Psychology
CIUCIURA, T. B., Political Science
DAVIES, D. H., Chemistry
DAY, E. E. D., Geography
GILLIS, D. H., Political Science
HAYSOM, J., Education
HOPE-SIMPSON, D., Geology
JAQUITH, J. R., Anthropology
KABE, DATTATRAYA G., Mathematics
KAPOOR, K., Biology
KRUSE, R. L., Mathematics
MACCORMACK, J. R., History
MONAHAN, A. M., Philosophy
MURTY, D. S., Physics
ROJO, A., Biology
SABEAN, A. T., Chemistry
SANBORN, G. A., Management
STIEGMAN, E., Religious Studies
THOMAS, K., Biology
VAUGHAN, K., Chemistry
VORSTERMANS, J. J., Economics
WILES, M., Biology

UNIVERSITY OF SASKATCHEWAN

SASKATOON,
SASKATCHEWAN S7N 0W0

Telephone: 343-2100.

Founded 1907; two-campus institution 1967 (Saskatoon and Regina). Legislation was passed in 1974 creating two separate Universities.

Academic year: September to April.

Chancellor: The Hon. EMMETT M. HALL, C.C., Q.C., LL.B.

Vice-Chancellor and President: L. F. KRISTJANSON, M.A., PH.D.

Vice-President (Academic): M. A. PRESTON, C.D., M.A., PH.D., F.R.S.C.

Vice-President (Administration): J. A. PRINGLE, E.D., C.D., B.ACC.

Vice-President (Planning): (vacant).

Controller: M. G. SHEPPARD, B.COMM., C.A., F.C.A.

University Secretary: N. K. CRAM, C.D., B.A., B.ED.

Registrar: J. A. DORGAN, B.S.A.

Librarian: NANCY BROWN, M.L.S., M.B.A.

Number of teachers: 1,400.
Number of students: 10,300.

DEANS:

College of Agriculture: J. A. BROWN, M.S.

College of Arts and Science: D. R. CHERRY, M.A., PH.D.

College of Commerce: P. H. MAHER, M.B.A., PH.D.

College of Dentistry: E. R. AMBROSE, D.D.S., F.I.C.D., F.A.C.D., R.C.D.(C.).

College of Education: R. H. FARQUHAR, M.A., PH.D., F.C.C.E.A.

College of Engineering: P. N. NIKIFORUK, PH.D., D.SC., F.R.S.A., F.E.I.C.

College of Graduate Studies and Research: K. J. MCCALLUM, M.SC., PH.D., F.R.S.C.

College of Home Economics: D. GIBSON, M.B.E., M.S., PH.D.

College of Law: D. H. CLARK, LL.B.

College of Medicine: R. G. MURRAY, B.A., M.D., F.R.C.S.(C.).

College of Nursing: U. RIDLEY, M.A.

College of Pharmacy: B. R. SCHNELL, M.B.A., PH.D.

College of Physical Education: J. D. DEWAR, M.A., ED.D.

College of Veterinary Medicine: N. O. NIELSEN, D.V.M., PH.D.

DIRECTORS:

School of Physical Therapy: V. J. COTTRELL, M.C.S.P.

School of Religious Studies: R. W. NOSTBAKKEN, TH.M., PH.D.

PROFESSORS:

ABDEL-MALEK, T., M.A., PH.D., Administration
ABRAMSON, E. J., M.A., Sociology
AIKENHEAD, G., M.A.T., ED.D., Curriculum Studies
ALLEN, J. R., M.A., M.V.SC., PH.D., Veterinary Microbiology
AMBROSE, E. R., D.D.S., F.I.C.D., F.A.C.D., R.C.D.(C.), Dentistry
ARMSTRONG, K. R., D.V.M., Veterinary Clinical Studies
ARORA, B. K., M.S., F.R.C.D.(C.), Oral Surgery and Anaesthesia
ASHENHURST, E. M., M.B., B.CH., M.R.C.P., F.R.C.P. (C.), Clinical Neurological Sciences
ASHFORD, R., M.SC., PH.D., Crop Science
AUSTENSON, H. M., M.SC., PH.D., Crop Science
BABIUK, B. S. A., M.SC., PH.D., Veterinary Microbiology
BAILEY, D. A., M.S.ED., P.E.D., Physical Education
BAKER, F. W., M.D., Paediatrics
BAKER, H. R., B.S.A., M.S., PH.D., Extension
BAKHSHI, N. N., M.SC., PH.D., Chemistry and Chemical Engineering
BALA, R. M., M.D., F.A.C.P., F.R.C.P.(C.), Medicine
BARDWELL, J. A. E., M.SC., PH.D., Chemistry
BARR, W., M.A., M.SC., Geography
BASRAN, G. S., M.S., PH.D., Sociology
BAXTER, G. C., M.B.A., PH.D., Accounting
BECK, R. G., PH.D., Economics and Political Science
BECK, R. N., M.B., B.CH., M.D., M.R.C.P., F.R.C.P.(C.), Medicine
BELL, D., M.A., PH.D., Physical Education
BELL, J. M., B.S.A., M.SC., PH.D., Animal Science
BELLAMY, J. E. C., D.V.M., PH.D., Veterinary Pathology
BERGAN, A. T., M.SC., PH.D., Civil Engineering
BERGSTROM, J. C., M.A., PH.D., Physics
BERNHARDSON, C. S., M.A., PH.D., Psychology
BERRY, H., M.A., PH.D., English
BESANT, R. W., M.S.E., Mechanical Engineering
BHARADWAJ, B., M.B., B.S., B.SC., F.R.C.S.(C.), F.A.C.C., Surgery
BIETENHOLZ, C., PH.D., History
BIGLAND, C. H., D.U.M., D.V.C., D.V.P.H., M.SC., Veterinary Microbiology
BIGSBY, F. W., M.SC., PH.D., Agricultural Engineering
BILLINTON, R., PH.D., D.SC., F.R.S.C., Electrical Engineering
BILSON, G., M.A., PH.D., History
BIRNIE, H. H., M.ED., PH.D., Education (Curriculum Studies)
BISHARA, H. I., M.B.A., PH.D., Administration
BLACK, M., M.A., French and Spanish
BLACKBURN, J. L., M.S., PHARM.D., Pharmacy
BLAIR, R. PH.D., Animal and Poultry Science
BLUM, R., PH.D., Mathematics
BOLARIA, B. S., M.A., PH.D., Sociology
BOLLINGER, K. E., M.SC., Electrical Engineering
BONE, R. M., M.A., PH.D., Geography
BORNSTEIN, E., M.S., Art
BOULTON, A. A., PH.D., Psychiatry
BOYLE, A. R., PH.D., Electrical Engineering
BRACK, R. E., M.S., Extension
BRANDELL, M. S., PH.D., Anatomy
BRAUN, W. K., DR.RER.NAT., Geological Sciences
BRENNAN, W. J., M.B.A., PH.D., C.A., Accounting
BREWSTER, E. W., A.M., PH.D., English
BROOKS, E. E., M.SC., Mechanical Engineering
BROWN, J. A., M.S., Agricultural Economics
BROWN, M., M.SC., PH.D., Psychology
BRYNER, J. R., ED.D., Education
BUCHAN, D. J., M.D., F.R.C.P.(C.), Medicine
BUGLASS, R. B., B.A., LL.B., Law
BURGESS, D. L., M.A., Physical Education
BURKHOLDER, G. D., PH.D., Anatomy
BUTLER, H. M.A., M.D., B.CHIR., PH.D., **Anatomy**
BUTLER, R. S., D.V.M., M.C.ED., Continuing Veterinary Education
BUYNIAK, V., M.A., PH.D., Slavic Studies
CALDWELL, W. G. E., PH.D., Geological Sciences
CAPLAN, H. S., PH.D., Physics
CARLSON, R. A., M.S., M.A., PH.D., Continuing Education
CARR, I. A., M.D., PH.D., F.R.C.PATH., F.R.C.P.(C.), Pathology
CARTER, R. C., Q.C., B.A., LL.B., Law
CATES, G. W., M.D., Pathology
CATES, W. F., D.V.M., PH.D., Veterinary Clinical Studies
CHAKRAVARTI, A. K., M.A., M.S., PH.D., Geography
CHAPPELL, E. W., B.A., M.D., F.R.C.S.(C.), Surgery
CHERRY, D. R., M.A., PH.D., English
CHRIST, L. W., M.D., M.A., Family Medicine
CHRISTENSEN, D. A., M.SC., PH.D., Animal Science
CLARK, D. H., LL.B., Law
CLEWES, T. W., M.S., PH.D., Electrical Engineering
COLEMAN, L. G., M.A., PH.D., Geological Sciences
COOKE, J. E., M.SC., D.PHIL., Administration and Computational Science
COOPER, K. D., LL.B., Law
COTTER, W. A., D.D.S., M.S., Dentistry
COUPLAND, R. T., B.S.A., PH.D., Plant Ecology
COURTNEY, J. C., M.B.A., M.A., PH.D., Economics
CRAWFORD, M. E., M.A., Nursing
CRAWFORD, R. D., M.S., PH.D., Poultry Science
CROCKER, K. M., M.D., C.M., F.R.C.O.G., Obstetrics and Gynaecology
CROSSLEY, D. J., M.A., PH.D., Philosophy
CUMING, R. C. C., LL.M., Law
CUNNINGHAM, T. A., M.B., CH.B., F.R.C.P. (E.), F.R.C.P.(C.), M.R.C.PATH., Pathology
CUTTLE, P., M.A., PH.D., Mathematics
DABBS, D. H., M.SC., Horticulture
DAS, C. S., M.A., PH.D., Administration
DASGUPTA, M. L., M.A., D.PHIL., Accounting
DAVIS, E., M.S.E., PH.D., Civil Engineering
DEAN, C., PH.D., English
DECKKER, B. L. E., PH.D., Mechanical Engineering
DECOURSEY, W. J., PH.D., Chemical Engineering
DE JONG, E., PH.D., Soil Science
DEMPSTER G., M.B., CH.B., B.SC., M.D., Microbiology
DEWAR, J. D., M.A., ED.D., Physical Education
DEXTER, D., M.B., CH.B., M.D., F.C.PATH., Pathology
DEY, S. K., M.SC., PH.D., D.I.C., Electrical Engineering
DHAND, H., M.A., ED.D., Education (Curriculum Studies)
DHINGRA, H. L., M.A., PH.D., Administration
DIBSKI, D. J., M.ED., PH.D., Educational Administration
DIMMOCK, J. R., PH.D., Pharmacy
DOIGE, C. E., D.V.M., PH.D., Veterinary Pathology
DOOLEY, P. C., PH.D., Economics
DOROTICH, D., M.A.(ED.), PH.D., Educational Foundations
EAGER, R. L., MS.C., PH.D., Chemistry
EIDINGER, D., PH.D., M.D., Microbiology
EL-SERAFI, A. M., PH.D., DR.ING., Electrical Engineering
EMSON, H. E., M.A., B.CH., M.D., Pathology

Ewing, C. C., M.B., F.R.C.S.(C.), Ophthalmology
Farmer, D. L., M.A., D.PHIL., History
Farquhar, R. H., M.A., PH.D., Education
Fedoroff, S., M.A., PH.D., Anatomy
Fedoruk, S., M.A., Oncology
Fischer, D. G., M.A., PH.D., Psychology
Fleming, R. J., M.SC., PH.D., F.E.I.C., Electrical Engineering
Flood, P. F., M.SC., M.R.C.V.S., Veterinary Anatomy
Forsyth, G. W., M.SC., PH.D., Veterinary Physiological Sciences
Fowke, L. C., PH.D., Biology
Fraser, A. F., M.R.C.V.S., M.V.SC., F.I.BIOL., Veterinary Clinical Studies
Fredlund, D. G., M.SC., PH.D., Civil Engineering
Fretz, P. B., V.M.D., Veterinary Clinical Studies
Gajadharsingh, J. L., M.ED., PH.D., Education (Curriculum Studies)
Genereux, G. P., M.D., C.M., F.R.C.P.(C.), Diagnostic Radiology
Genuist, M., L. ÈS L., D. DE L'U., French
Genuist, P., L. ÈS L., D.DE L'U., French
Gerrard, J. W., B.A., B.M., B.CH., M.R.C.P., Paediatrics
Ghadially, F. N., M.D., PH.D., D.SC., Pathology
Gibson, D. L., M.B.E., B.S.A., M.SC., PH.D., Dairy and Food Science
Gilboe, D. B., D.D.S., M.S., Restorative and Prosthetic Dentistry
Gillott, C., PH.D., Biology
Gilmour, T. H. J., PH.D., Biology
Goodspeed, Georgia M., B.ACC., M.B.A., C.A., Accounting
Grant, D. R., PH.D., Chemistry
Gray, D. M., M.S.A., PH.D., Agricultural Engineering
Green, D. E., M.A., PH.D., History
Green, G. H., B.E., M.S., Mechanical Engineering
Greenough, P. R., F.R.C.V.S., Veterinary Clinical Studies
Gregory, J. B., M.SC., PH.D., Physics
Grodums, E. I., D.D.S., PH.D., Microbiology
Gruen, H. E., M.A., PH.D., Biology
Guenther, H. V., PH.D., Far Eastern Studies
Gupta, M. M., M.SC., PH.D., Mechanical Engineering
Gupta, V. S., M.SC., PH.D., Veterinary Physiological Sciences
Hader, W., M.D., F.R.C.P.(C.), Rehabilitation Medicine
Halstead, E. H., M.SC., PH.D., Soil Science
Hamilton, D. L., D.V.M., PH.D., Veterinary Physiological Sciences
Hamilton, G. F., D.V.M., PH.D., Veterinary Clinical Studies
Hammer, U. T., B.ED., M.S., PH.D., Biology
Harms, V. L., M.S., PH.D., Plant Ecology and Biology
Harvey, B. L., M.SC., PH.D., Crop Science
Hawes, E. M., PH.D., Pharmacy
Hayden, J. M., M.A., PH.D., History
Hayton, R. C., B.SC., M.D., F.R.C.P.(C.), Medicine
Heasman, D. J., B.SC., Political Science
Henry, J. L., M.SC., Soil Science
Hertz, L., M.SC.,aA mynot
Hickie, R. A., M.SC., PH.D., Pharmacology
Hindmarsh, K. W., M.SC., PH.D., Pharmacy
Hirose, A., M.SC., PH.D., Physics
Holmes, I. H., M.D., F.R.C.P.(C.), Medicine
Holmlund, B. A., M.SC., Computer Science
Horlick, L., B.SC., M.D.C.M., M.SC., F.R.C.P.(C.), Medicine
Hosain, M. U., M.SC., PH.D., Civil Engineering
Houston, C. S., M.D., Diagnostic Radiology
Howell, W. E., M.S., PH.D., Animal Science
Hrudka, F., MED.VET.DR., MED.VET. EXOT., DR.SCI., Veterinary Anatomy
Huang, P. M., M.SC., PH.D., Soil Science
Hughes, M. E., LL.M., M.S.W., Law
Humbert, E. S., M.SC., PH.D., Dairy and Food Science
Hunt, D., M.ED., PH.D., Educational Psychology
Ingledew, W. M., PH.D., Dairy and Food Science
Inglis, F. G., M.D., C.M., M.SC., F.R.C.S.(C.), Surgery
Innes, J. E., M.SC., Nursing
Irvin, V. B., PH.D., R.I.A., Accounting
Iversen, J. O., D.V.M., M.P.H., PH.D., Veterinary Microbiology
James, W. H., M.A., PH.D., Psychology
Jeffrey, J. G., B.S.P., M.SC., PH.D., Pharmacy
Johnson, D. D., M.SC., PH.D., Pharmacology
Johnson, G. E., M.A., PH.D., Pharmacology
Johnson, H. C., M.A., PH.D., History
Johnstone, J. K., M.A., PH.D., English
Jones, G. A., M.SC., PH.D., Dairy and Food Science
Kaplan, D. L., M.M., PH.D., Music
Kelm, H., M.A., PH.D., Psychology
Kennedy, J. E., M.SC., Physics
Kennedy, Rev. L. A., C.S.B., M.A., PH.D., Philosophy
Kent, C. A., M.A., D.PHIL., History
Kent, H. P., M.A., M.B., B.CHIR., Diagnostic Radiology
Kerr, T., F.T.C.L., Drama
Kilduff, C. J., M.B., B.CH., Anaesthesia
King, J., M.SC., PH.D., Biology
King, M. S., M.S., PH.D., Geological Sciences
Kirkaldy-Willis, W. H., M.A., M.D. F.R.C.S., Surgery
Klaassen, D., M.D., F.R.C.P.S.(C.), Oncology
Knight, A. R., M.SC., PH.D., Chemistry
Knight, W. L. R., M.ED., Education (Curriculum Studies)
Knott, D. R., M.S., PH.D., Crop Science
Koehler, J. A. R., B.E., M.SC., PH.D., Physics
Krause, A. E., M.SC., Electrical Engineering
Kristjanson, L. F., M.A., PH.D., Economics and Political Science
Kulshreshtha, S. N., M.SC.AG., PH.D., Agricultural Economics
Kupsch, W. O., M.SC., PH.D., F.R.S.C., Geology
Lackie, T. H., M.A.SC., Civil Engineering
Laimon, S., M.B.A., B.COMM., Accounting
Lal, K., M.A., DR.DISC.POL., Economics
Lalli, B. S., M.A., PH.D., Mathematics
Lambi, I. N., M.A., PH.D., History
Lampman, W. P., M.S., Agricultural Engineering
Langford, F. F., M.A., PH.D., Geological Sciences
Latshaw, W. K., D.V.M., M.S., PH.D., Veterinary Anatomy
Lawson, P. A., M.A., PH.D., Physical Education
Laxdal, O. E., B.A., M.D., F.R.C.P.(C.), Continuing Medical Education
Lee, C. C., B.E., M.SC., SC.D., Chemistry
Lee, G. E., M.SC., PH.D., Agricultural Economics
Lehmkuhl, D. M., Biology
Leicester, J. B., C.D., M.ED., Physical Education
Le May, I., PH.D., Mechanical Engineering
Leong, C. K., M.A.(ED.), Education
Llewellyn, E. J., PH.D., Physics
Lopez, J. F., M.D., F.R.C.P.(C.), Medicine
Ludwig, R. E., M.SC., Electrical Engineering
MacCallum, F. J., M.R.C.V.S., Veterinary Anatomy
McCallum, K. J., M.SC., PH.D., F.R.S.C., Chemistry
McConnell, W. H., M.A., PH.D., LL.M., Law
McDonald, I. M., M.D., Psychiatry
MacDonald, W. B., B.A., M.D., F.R.C.P.(C.), Anaesthesia
McDuffie, N. M., M.A., PH.D., Physiology
McEwen, D. J., M.A., PH.D., Physics
MacFadyen, D. J., M.SC., M.D., F.R.C.P.(C.), Clinical Neurological Sciences
McKercher, R. B., M.SC., PH.D., Soil Science
MacLachlan, T. B., M.D., Medicine
McLennan, B. D., M.SC., PH.D., Biochemistry
McLeod, J., PH.D., Education
McMurray, G. A., M.A., PH.D., Psychology
McPhail, C. W. B., D.D.S., M.S.D., M.SC.D., Dentistry
McPherson, G. H., M.A., PH.D., Sociology
McQueen, J. D., M.D., M.A., Clinical Neurological Sciences
Maginnes, E. A., M.S., PH.D., Horticulture
Maher, P. M., M.B.A., PH.D., Commerce
Maher, W. J., M.S., PH.D., Biology
Male, D. H., M.SC., PH.D., Mechanical Engineering
Mann, O., M.S., Mechanical Engineering
Manns, J. G., M.SC., PH.D., Veterinary Physiological Studies
Manohar, R., M.SC., DR.RER.NAT., Mathematics
Manson, A. H., PH.D., Physics
Mapletoft, R. J., D.V.M., PH.D., Veterinary Clinical Studies
Marken, R. G., M.A., PH.D., English
Markham, J. W., M.B., B.S., Social and Preventive Medicine
Marshall, M. A., B.ED., M.A., PH.D., Mathematics
Martin, R. O., PH.D., Biochemistry
Mathews, J. F., M.S., PH.D., Chemical Engineering
Matthews, V. L., M.D., D.P.M. L.M.C.C., Social and Preventive Medicine
Midha, K. K., PH.D., Pharmacy
Millar, J. F. V., PH.D., Anthropology and Archaeology
Miller, J. R., M.A., PH.D., History
Miller, L. G., M.A., PH.D., Philosophy
Mills, D. K., M.D., F.R.C.P.(C.), Psychiatry
Mills, I. M., M.A., ED.D., Music
Mills, J. A., PH.D., Psychology
Mills, J. H. L., D.V.M., M.S., PH.D., Veterinary Pathology
Mitchell, D. M., M.D., F.R.C.P.(C.), Medicine
Montalbetti, R., PH.D., Physics
Moody, R. V., M.A., PH.D., Mathematics
Morrall, R. A. A., M.A., Biology
Morrissey, L. J., M.A., PH.D., English
Mostert, C. E., LL.M., Law
Moysey, E. B., M.S., Agricultural Engineering
Munkacsi, I., M.D., PH.D., Anatomy
Murphy, F. A., M.D., F.R.C.P.(C.), Pathology
Murphy, G. J., PH.D., C.A., Accounting
Murray, J. M., M.S., Agricultural Engineering
Murray, R. G., M.D., F.R.C.S.(C.), Ophthalmology
Nasser, K. W., M.SC., PH.D., Civil Engineering
Naylor, J. M., B.S.A., M.SC., PH.D., Biology
Neis, V. V., M.E., PH.D., Civil Engineering
Nelson, D., B.S., M.A., Music
Nelson, S. H., M.S., PH.D., Horticulture
Newstead, J. D. M., M.A., PH.D., Anatomy

NEWTON, E. E., M.ED., PH.D., Education Administration
NICHOLSON. H. H., M.S.A., PH.D., Animal Science
NICHOLSON, R. C., M.SC., PH.D., Agricultural Economics
NIELSEN, N. O., D.U.M., PH.D., Veterinary Pathology
NIKIFORUK, P., PH.D., Mechanical Engineering
NIXON, H. R., M.S., P.E.D., Physical Education
NJAA, L. J., M.ED., PH.D., Education (Educational Psychology)
NORMAN, K. E., B.A., LL.B., B.C.L., Law
NORUM, D. I., M.SC., PH.D., Agricultural Engineering

OLLEY, R. E., M.A., PH.D., Economics
OSBORNE, A. D., D.V.S.M., M.R.C.V.S., F.R.C.PATH., Veterinary Microbiology
OWEN, J. S., M.B., CH.B., Social and Preventive Medicine

PAINE, K. W. E., M.R.C.S., L.R.C.P., M.B., B.S., F.R.C.S., Clinical Neurological Sciences
PAUL, E. A.. M.SC., PH.D., Soil Science
PAULSON, K. V., M.SC., PH.D., Physics
PEPPER, J. M.. M.A., PH.D., Chemistry and Chemical Engineering
PEREZ, L. A., M.A., D.LL., Spanish
PETERS, H. D., M.A., PH.D., Education (Educational Psychology)
PHILLIS, J. W., PH.D., D.SC., Physiology
POHORECKY, Z. S., M.A., PH.D., Anthropology and Archaeology
POLLAK, V., PH.D., DR.TECH.SCI., Electrical Engineering
PORTER, J. M., M.A., PH.D., Political Science
POSTLETHWAITE, J., M.SC.TECH., PH.D., Chemistry and Chemical Engineering
PRASAD, K., M.D., PH.D., F.I.C.A., F.A.C.C., Physiology
PRESNELL, K. R., D.V.M., M.SC., Veterinary Clinical Studies
PRESTON, M. A., M.A., PH.D., F.R.S.C., Physics
PRITCHET, C. D., M.A., PH.D., Greek and Roman Studies

RADOSTITS, O. M., D.V.M., M.SC., Veterinary Clinical Studies
RAJPUT, A. H., M.S., F.R.C.P.(C.), Clinical Neurological Sciences
RANDHAWA, B. S., M.A., M.ED., PH.D., Education
RANK, G. H., M.SC., PH.D., Biology
REDMANN, R. E., M.S.. PH.D., Plant Ecology
REGEHR, T. D., M.A., PH.D., History
RENNIE, D. A., D.S.A., PH.D., Soil Science
RICHARDS, J. H., M.A., PH.D., Geography
RIDDELL, C., D.V.M.. M.SC., PH.D.. Veterinary Pathology
RIDGWAY, R. S., M.A., D. DE L'UNIV., French
RIDLEY, U., M.A., Nursing
RIEMER, P., B.E., Civil Engineering
RIPLEY, E. A., B.SC., M.A., Plant Ecology
ROBERTS, L. D., M.SC., PH.D., Education
ROBERTSON, R. T., M.A., PH.D., English
ROE, W. E., D.V.M., M.S., Veterinary Physiology
ROGERS, D. O., M.S., Art
ROMERO, L. J., LL.M., Law
ROWE, J. S., M.SC., PH.D., Plant Ecology
ROZDILSKY, B., M.SC., PH.D., Pathology
RUPRECHT, D. D. S., M.SC.D., F.A.A.D.R., F.R.C.D.(C.), Diagnosis and Oral Radiology
RUSNAK, C. H., B.A., M.D., F.R.C.S.(C.), Surgery

ST. ARNAUD, R. O. J., M.SC., PH.D., Soil Science
SACHDEV, M. S., M.SC., PH.D., Electrical Engineering
SAINI, G. L., M.A., PH.D., Mathematics
SALEH, F. A., M.B.A., PH.D., Administration
SARJEANT, W. A. S., PH.D., D.SC., Geological Sciences
SARKAR, A. K., M.COM., M.B.A., PH.D., Administration
SAUER, E. K., M.SC., D.ENG., Civil Engineering
SAUNDERS, J. R., D.V.M., PH.D., Veterinary Microbiology
SAVAGE, H. W., M.ED., ED.D., Education
SCHARF, M. P., M.ED., PH.D., Education
SCHIEFER, H. B., DR.MED.VET., Veterinary Pathology
SCHMEISER, D. A. J., LL.B., LL.M., S.J.D., Law
SCHNEIDER, R. J., M.D., C.M., F.R.C.S.(C), Ophthalmology
SCHNELL, B. R., M.B.A., PH.D., Pharmacy
SCHOTT, L., DR.RER.NAT., Physics
SCOTT, R. I., M.A., PH.D., English
SEARCY, G. P., D.V.M., M.SC., PH.D., Veterinary Pathology
SERVRANCKX, R., D.SC., MATH., Mathematics
SHARGOOL, P. D., M.SC., PH.D., Biochemistry
SHEARD, J. W.. M.SC.. PH.D., Biology
SHIN, Y' M., M.SC., PH.D., Physics
SHOKEIR, M. H. K., M.D., PH.D., F.C.C.M.G., Paediatrics
SHOOK, C. A., PH.D., Chemistry
SILVERSIDES, F. H., B.SC. PH., Administration
SIMPSON, G. M., M.A.SC., PH.D., Crop Science
SINCLAIR, G. E., M.D., Medicine
SINGH, R., M.A., PH.D., Mathematics
SISODIA, C. S., M.S., PH.D., Veterinary Physiological Sciences
SKARSGARD, H. M., M.SC., PH.D., Physics
SKINNER. O. R., M.S., PH.D., Physics
SKINNIDER, L. F., M.B., CH.B., F.R.C.P.(C.), Pathology
SKOPIK, D. M., M.S., PH.D., Physics
SMITH, C. D., M.SC., Civil Engineering
SMITH, D. E., M.A., PH.D., Political Science
SMITH, D. L. T., D.V.M., PH.D., Veterinary Pathology
SMITH, P. J., PH.D., Chemistry
SMITH, R. J. F., M.SC., PH.D., Biology
SOFKO, G. J., PH.D., Physics
SOLEM, R. J., M.A., Music
SOMERVILLE, A. E., M.D., F.R.C.P.(C.), Medicine
SORENSON, P. G., M.SC., PH.D., Computational Science
SOSULSKI, F. W., M.S., PH.D., Crop Science
SPAFFORD, D. S., M.A., Economics
SPOONER, M. A., M.D., M.A., Family Medicine
STABLER, J. C., PH.D., Economics
STAPLES, W. R., M.S., Mechanical Engineering
STAUFFER, M. R., M.SC., PH.D., Geological Sciences
STEAD, S., M.B., CH.B., F.R.C.S.(C.), Social and Preventive Medicine
STEER, R. P., PH.D., Chemistry and Chemical Engineering
STEEVES, T. A., A.M., PH.D., Biology
STEWART, J. W. B., PH.D., Soil Science
STOCKDALE, P. H. G., D.V.M., M.SC., PH.D., Veterinary Microbiology
STONEHAM, M. E., B.SC., Mechanical Engineering
STOREY, G. G., M.SC., M.A., PH.D., Agricultural Economics
SULAKHE, P. V., M.SC., PH.D., Physiology
SULLIVAN, R. D., PH.D., Greek and Roman Studies
SUMMERS, J. L., M.C., B.S.P., M.S., Pharmacy
SUMNER, A. K., M.A., Home Economics
SUTHERLAND, G. B., PH.D., Physiology
SUTHERLAND ,R. G., PH.D., Chemistry
SWAN, P. M., M.A., PH.D., History
SYDIAHA, D., M.SC., PH.D., Psychology

TAN, L. K.-T., B.SC., M.B., B.S., M.A., M.P.H., Social and Preventive Medicine
TATE, E. D., M.A., PH.D., Sociology
TCHANG, S. P. K., M.D., Diagnostic Radiology
TENNANT, H. E., M.B.A., PH.D., Administration
THAIR, P. J., M.SC., PH.D., Agricultural Economics
THOMAS, G. H. M., M.SC., PH.D., Mathematics
TOMUSIAK, E. L., M.SC., PH.D., Physics
TREMBLAY, J. P., M.SC., PH.D., Computer Science
TREW, J. A., M.SC., PH.D., Pathology
TYMCHATYN, E. D., M.A., PH.D., Mathematics
TYRRELL, M. J., M.B., B.S., M.R.C.P., F.R.C.P.(C.), F.A.C.C., Paediatrics

UKRAINETZ, P. R., M.SC., PH.D., Mechanical Engineering

VELLA, F., M.D., M.A., PH.D., F.R.I.C., M.C. PATH., Biochemistry
VERMA, S. P., DR.ING., Electrical Engineering
VERRALL, R. E., PH.D., Chemistry
VICQ, J. G., M.SC., C.A., Accounting

WACKER, A. G., M.SC., PH.D., Electrical Engineering
WAHN, E. V., B.A., LL.B., Administration
WALMSLEY, P. Y., M.A., Administration
WALTZ, W. L., PH.D., Chemistry
WARD, N., O.C., M.A., PH.D., LL.D., F.R.S.C., Political Science
WATSON, L. F., PH.D., Sociology
WEIL, J. A., M.S., PH.D., Chemistry
WENGER, B. S., M.S., PH.D., Anatomy
WHALE, W. B., M.S.A., PH.D., Extension
WIGHAM, J. M., M.SC., Civil Engineering
WILKINSON, A. A., M.A., M.B., M.SC., F.R.C.P.(C.), Diagnostic Radiology
WILLIAMS, C. M., B.S.A., M.SC., PH.D., Animal and Poultry Science
WILLIAMSON, R. G., PH.D., Anthropology and Archaeology
WILLIS, LUCY D., M.A., ED.D., Nursing
WILSON, J. N., M.SC., PH.D., Mechanical Engineering
WILSON, K. A., M.ED., PH.D., Education
WISHART, T. B., M.A., PH.D., Psychology
WITTLIN, C. J., PH.D., French
WOBESER, G. A., M.SC., D.V.M., PH.D., Veterinary Pathology
WOOD, J. A., M.S., PH.D., Pharmacy
WOOD, J. D., PH.D., Biochemistry
WOODS, R. J., PH.D., A.R.C.S., D.I.C., F.R.I.C., Chemistry
WRIGHT, C. J., M.B., CH.B., M.SC., F.R.C.S.(E.), F.R.C.S.(C.), Surgery
WYANT, G. M., M.D., F.F.A.R.C.S., F.A.C.A., Anaesthesia

YOUNG, W. E., M.A., PH.D., Home Economics

ZALESKI, W. A., M.B., CH.B., F.R.C.P.(C.), Paediatrics
ZINK, M., M.SC., PH.D., Biology
ZOERB, G. C., M.S., PH.D., Agricultural Engineering
ZUCK, D. A., M.SC., PH.D., Pharmacy

FEDERATED COLLEGE:

St. Thomas More College: 1437 College Drive, Saskatoon, Sask. S7N 0W6.
President: Rev. L. A. KENNEDY.

UNIVERSITÉ DE SHERBROOKE

CITÉ UNIVERSITAIRE,
SHERBROOKE,
QUEBEC J1K 2R1

Telephone: 565-5970.

Founded 1954.

Private control; Language of instruction: French; Academic year: September to May.

Chancellor: H.E. Mgr. JEAN-MARIE FORTIER, Catholic Archbishop of Sherbrooke.

Rector: YVES MARTIN, L.SC.SOC.

Vice-Rector (Studies and Research): GASTON DENIS, M.SC.

Vice-Rector (Personnel and Students): RICHARD BELAND, M.A., PH.D.

Vice-Rector (Administration): CLAUDE HAMEL, M.SC.A.

Secretary-General: JEAN-GUY FRECHETTE, M.A., L.PH., LL.D.

Registrar: GUY LANGEVIN, B.A.

Librarian: G. CLOUTIER, L. ÈS L., M.L.S,

Library of 800,000 vols.

Number of teachers: 615 full-time, 133 part-time.

Number of students: 6,731 full-time, 4,182 part-time.

DEANS:

Faculty of Administration: A. COUSINEAU, M.SC.COMM.

Faculty of Arts: J. PLAMONDON, L.PH., D. 3E CYCLE.

Faculty of Law: J. J. ANCTIL.

Faculty of Medicine: JEAN DE MARGERIE.

Facility of Science: A. CABANA, M.SC., PH.D.

Faculty of Applied Science: J. DELISLE, M.SC.A., D. 3E CYCLE.

Faculty of Theology: Rev. J. FILLION, B.TH., L.TH.

Faculty of Educational Sciences: (vacant).

Faculty of Physical and Sport Education: R. ROY, M.PHYS.ED., PH.D.

PROFESSORS:

AITCIN, PIERRE, Civil Engineering
ALLARD, JACQUES, Mathematics
ASHIKIAN, BARUIR, Mechanical Engineering
AUBE, GASTON, Electrical Engineering
BASORA, JORDI, Orthopaedics
BAZINET, ANDRÉ, French Studies
BAZINET, JACQUES, Mathematics
BEAUCHEMIN, NORMAND, French Studies
BEAUDOIN, PAUL-HENRI, Operations Management
BEAUDRY, RENÉ, Medicine
BEDARD, ANDRÉ, Theology
BELAND, BERNARD, Electrical Engineering
BENARD, BERNARD, Medicine
BERGERON, ANDRÉ, Theology
BLACHE, PIERRE, Law
BONENFANT, JOSEPH, French Studies
BOUCHER, CLAUDE, Mathematics
BOUNOS, GUSTAVO, General and Plastic Surgery
BOURGAUX, DANIELLE, Microbiology
BOURGAUX, PIERRE, Microbiology
BRODEUR, LÉO-A., French Studies
BROSSEAU, GUY, French Studies
BROWN, GORDON-M., Chemistry
BRUNELLE, PAUL-E., Civil Engineering
BRUNETTE, JEAN-RÉAL, Ophthalmology
CABANA, ALDÉE, Chemistry
CAPPON, CORMAC, English Studies
CARON, Laurent, Physics
CHARRON, CAMILLE, Law
CHEEKE, DAVID, Physics
CHORNET, ESTEBAN, Chemical Engineering
CLEMENT, PIERRE, Geography
CONSTANTIN, JULIEN, Mathematics
COTE, ROGER, Pathology
COUPAL, BERNARD, Chemical Engineering
COURTEAU, BERNARD, Mathematics
COUTURE, GAÉTAN, Marketing
CREPEAU, RICHARD, Law
DE BUJANDA, J.-MARTINEZ, History
DE CERETTI, ELENA, Biophysics
DELISLE, JULES, Electrical Engineering
DE MARGERIE, JEAN, Ophthalmology
DEMERS, PIERRE-P., Paediatrics
DENIS, GASTON, Electrical Engineering
DESILETS, ANDRÉE, History
DESLONGCHAMPS, PIERRE, Chemistry
DESNOYERS, JACQUES E., Chemistry
DESROCHERS, RAYMOND, Biology
DEVROEDE, GHISLAIN, General and Plastic Surgery
DOYON, JACQUES, Theology
DUMAIS, BERTRAND, Medicine
DUNNIGAN, JACQUES, Biology
DUSSAULT, PIERRE, Law
ELHILALI, MOSTAFA, Urology
ELLYIN, FERNAND, Civil Engineering
FRECHETTE, JEAN-GUY, Law
GAGNON, MAURICE, Philosophy
GALLEZ, BERNARD, Civil Engineering
GARANT, J.-PIERRE, Finance
GARNIER, GÉRARD, Finance
GOULET, ROGER, Electrical Engineering
GUERIN, FERNAND, Finance
GUY, MARCEL, Law
HAMEL, CLAUDE, Civil Engineering
HEON, MAURICE, Neurosurgery
HIVON, RENÉ, Pedagogy
HUGON, JEAN, Anatomy
JERUMANIS, STANISLAS, Chemistry
JOLY, RICHARD, Pedagogy
JONES, DOUGLAS, English Studies
JUILLET, JACQUES, Biology
KIMMERLE, FRANK, Chemistry
KOURI, ROBERT, Law
LACASSE, ROBERT, French Studies
LAFOND, RÉAL, Obstetrics and Gynaecology
LALANCETTE, JEAN-MARC, Chemistry
LAMARCHE, YVES, Anaesthesia
LAMY, FRANÇOIS, Biochemistry
LANGLOIS, LÉONARD, Paediatrics
LAROCHELLE, NORMAND, Physics
LAROUCHE, GÉRARD, Medicine
LAVOIE, JEAN-MARIE, Law
LEBEL, ETIENNE, Nuclear Medicine
LEDUC, PIERRE-YVES, Mathematics
LEFEBVRE, GUY, Civil Engineering
LEFEBVRE, RENÉ, Pedagogy
LEGAULT, ALBERT, Biology
LEMIEUX, BERNARD, Paediatrics
LEMIEUX, PIERRE, Civil Engineering
LEROUX, ADRIEN, Electrical Engineering
LEROUX, ARMAND, Economics
LESSARD, JEAN, Chemistry
LEVEQUE, THEODORE, Anatomy
LONGPRE, BERNARD, Medicine
LUSSIER, ANDRÉ, Medicine
MADARNAS, PROMETEO, Pathology
MARCHESSAULT, VICTOR, Paediatrics
MASSOUD, MONIR, Mechanical Engineering
MELANSON, JEAN, Law
MIGNAULT, JEAN, Medicine
MORISSETTE, SARTO, Electrical Engineering
NAAMAN, ANTOINE, French Studies
NEALE, KENNETH, Civil Engineering
O'NEIL, LOUIS-C., Biology
PAQUETTE, ROMAIN, Geography
PARE, CLAUDE, Paediatrics
PAULHUS, EUCHARISTE, Psycho-Education
PELLETIER, GERARD, Chemistry
PELLETIER, GERARD, Economics
PEPIN, JEAN-MARC, Medicine
PEREY, BERNARD, General and Plastic Surgery
PERRON, JULES, Social Service
PIGEON, GILLES, Medicine
PINARD, GILBERT, Psychiatry
PLAMONDON, JACQUES, Philosophy
PLANTE, GÉRARD, Physiology
PREZEAU, CARL, Finance
PROULX, DENIS, Mechanical Engineering
PROVENCHER, LÉO, Accountancy
RAMON-MOLINER, ENRIQUE, Anatomy
REGOLI, DOMENICO, Physiology
REIHER, JEAN, Medicine
RICHARD, SYLVIO, Electrical Engineering
ROBIDOUX, JEAN, Management
ROY, CLÉMENT, Mechanical Engineering
ROY, JEAN-MARIE, Geography
ROY, ROCH, Physical Education
RUEL, PIERRE-H., Psycho-Education
ST-ARNAUD, YVES, Psychology
ST-PIERRE, J. JACQUES, Accountancy
SAUCIER, ROBERT, Biology
SCHANNE, OTTO, Biophysics
SCOTT, HUGH, Medicine
SIROIS, ANTOINE, French Studies
SPIRIDONAKIS, BASIL, History
STANEK, OLEG, Geography
STRINGER, GUY, Pedagogy
SUTHERLAND, ROLAND, English Studies
TCHAO, JOSEPH, Philosophy
TETREAULT, LEON, Medicine
THERIEN, NORMAND, Chemical Engineering
THIBAULT, RICHARD, Electrical Engineering
TRIAS, ANTONI, Orthopaedics
VACHON, LUCIEN, Theology
VALCKE, LOUIS, Philosophy
VANDEN, ABEELE, Physical Education
VOBECKY, JOSEPH, Behavioural Sciences

AFFILIATED INSTITUTIONS:

Collège Militaire Royal de St.-Jean: Que. J0J 1R0; B.Sc., B.A. and B.Admin. courses of the university; Dir./Commandant Col. C.-E. SAVARD.

Ecole de Musique Vincent-D'Indy: 200 rue Vincent-D'Indy, Montreal, Que. H2V 2T3; B.Mus., M.Mus. and Dipl.Concert. courses of the university; Dir. Sr. LORRAINE BOULANGER.

SIMON FRASER UNIVERSITY

BURNABY,
BRITISH COLUMBIA V5A 1S6

Telephone: 291-3111.

Language of instruction: English; Academic year: September to August (3 terms).

Founded 1963.

Chancellor: P. T. COTÉ, M.B.A., P.ENG.

President: G. PEDERSEN, PH.D., F.C.C.T.

Vice-President (Academic): J. M. MUNRO, D.B.A.

Vice-President (Administration): G. SUART, M.B.A.

Registrar: H. M. EVANS, C.D., B.A.

Librarian: T. C. DOBB, B.A., B.L.S.

Number of teachers: 438 (faculty status).

Number of students: 9,707.

Publications: ***Undergraduate Calendar, Graduate Calendar, Report on Scholarly Activities*** (annually), *Glossa—An International Journal of Linguistics* (annually), *West Coast Review* (quarterly), *The Peak, SFU Week* (weekly).

DEANS:

Faculty of Arts: R. C. BROWN, M.SC., PH.D.

Faculty of Science: J. WEBSTER, PH.D.

Faculty of Education: J. W. G. IVANY, M.A., PH.D.

Faculty of Interdisciplinary Studies: T. W. CALVERT, M.S.E.E., PH.D.

Graduate Studies: BRYAN P. BEIRNE, M.A., M.SC., PH.D., M.R.I.A.

PROFESSORS:

Faculty of Arts:

Archaeology:

CARLSON, R. L., M.A., PH.D.
SHUTLER, R., M.A., PH.D.

Business Administration and Economics:

BOLAND, L. A., M.A., PH.D.
BORCHERDING, T. E., PH.D.
CHANT, J. F., PH.D.
CHENG, P. L., M.A., PH.D.
COPES, P., M.A., PH.D.
DE VANY, A. S., M.A., PH.D.
GRUBEL, H. B., PH.D.
HERZOG, J. P., PH.D.
HOLMES, R. A., M.A., PH.D.
HOYT, G. C., M.A., PH.D.
KENNEDY, P. E., PH.D.
KNETSCH, J., M.S., M.P.A., PH.D.
MCDONALD, D. L., C.A., M.B.A., PH.D.
MUNRO, J. M., M.B.A., D.B.A.
PATERSON, T. T., M.A., PH.D.
SCHONER, B., M.B.A., PH.D.
STRAND, K., M.S., PH.D.
VAR, T., M.B.A., PH.D.
VERGIN, R. C., M.S., PH.D.

English:

BLACK, S. A., M.A., PH.D.
BLASER, R. F., M.A., M.L.S.
BUITENHUIS, P. M., M.A., PH.D.
CANDELARIA, F. H., PH.D.
CURTIS, J. R., M.A., PH.D.
DELANY, P., B.COM., A.M., M.A., PH.D.
HARDEN, E. F., A.M., PH.D.
MAUD, R. N., PH.D.
RUDRUM, A., PH.D.
STEIG, M., M.A., PH.D.

Geography:

CRAMPTON, C. B., PH.D.
CUNNINGHAM, F. F., M.A., F.R.G.S.
DAY, J. C., PH.D.
ELIOT-HURST, M. E., PH.D.
MACPHERSON, A., M.A., F.R.MET.S.
WAGNER, P. L., M.A., PH.D.
WILSON, J. W., M.SC., M.R.P.

History:

BUMSTED, J. M., PH.D.
CUNNINGHAM, A. B., M.A., PH.D., F.R.G.S., F.R.HIST.S.
INGRAM ELLIS, E. R.
KITCHEN, J. M., PH.D., F.R.HIST.S.

Languages, Literatures and Linguistics:

BOUTON, C. P., D.E.S., D. ÈS L.
BURSILL-HALL, G. L., M.A., PH.D.
NEWTON, B. E., M.A.
ROBERTS, E. W., M.A., PH.D.

Philosophy:

BRADLEY, R. D., M.A., PH.D.
RESNICK, L., PH.D.
WHEATLEY, J., M.A., PH.D.

Political Science:

CIRIA, A., B.A.
JEWETT, P., M.A., PH.D.
MCWHINNEY, E., Q.C., LL.M., SC.JUR.D.
QUO, F. Q., PH.D.
ROBIN, M., M.A., PH.D.
SOMJEE, A. H., M.A., PH.D.

Psychology:

BAKAN, P., M.A., PH.D.
BURSTEIN, K. R.
DIAMOND, A. L., M.A., PH.D.
MARCIA, J. E., M.A., PH.D.
WEINBERG, H., M.SC., PH.D.

Sociology and Anthropology:

ADAM, H., DIPL.SOC., DR.PHIL.
DICKIE-CLARK., H., PH.D.
WHITAKER, I., M.A., DR.PHIL.

Faculty of Education:

BIRCH, D. R., M.A., PH.D.
EGAN, M. K., PH.D.
ELLIS, J. R., M.A., E.D.D
GIBBONS, M., M.A., ED.D.
IVANY, J. W. G., M.A., PH.D.
KAZEPIDES, A., ED.D.
KIRCHNER, G., M.S., ED.D.
PEDERSEN, K. G., M.A., PH.D., F.C.C.T.
TUINMAN, J. J., M.A., PH.D.
WASSERMANN, S., M.S., ED.D.

Faculty of Interdisciplinary Studies:

Communication:

HARPER, R. J. C., M.A., PH.D., F.R.S.A.
LEISS, W., M.A., PH.D.
MALLINSON, T. J., M.A., PH.D.
MELODY, W. H., M.A., PH.D.
SMYTHE, D. W., PH.D.
WILDEN, A., PH.D.

Computing Science:

CALVERT, T. W., M.S., PH.D.
HARROP, R. B., M.A., PH.D.
STERLING, T. D., M.A., PH.D.

Criminology:

CHAPPELL, D., PH.D.
FATTAH, E. A., LL.L., A.A., PH.D.

Kinesiology:

BANISTER, E. W., M.P.E., PH.D., F.A.C.S.M.
BHAKTHAN, N. M. G., M.SC., PH.D.
CALVERT, T. W., M.S., PH.D.

Faculty of Science:

Biological Sciences:

BARLOW, J. S., M.A., PH.D.
BEIRNE, B. P., M.A., M.SC., PH.D., M.I.R.A.
BORDEN, J. H., M.SC., PH.D.
FINLAYSON, T., B.A.
FISHER, F. J. F., M.SC., PH.D.
GEEN, G. H., M.A., PH.D.
MACKAUER, J. P. M., DR.PHIL.NAT.
NAIR, K. K., M.SC., PH.D.
SADLEIR, R. M. F. S., PH.D.
SRIVASTAVA, L. M., M.SC., PH.D.
TURNBULL, A. L., M.F., D.PHIL.
VIDAVER, W. E., PH.D.
WEBSTER, J. M., PH.D., A.R.C.S., D.I.C.

Chemistry:

ARONOFF, S., PH.D.
BELL, T. N., PH.D.
CHOW, Y. L., PH.D.
EINSTEIN, F. W. B., M.SC., PH.D.
FUNT, B. L., M.SC., PH.D.
MALLI, G. L., M.SC., M.S., PH.D.
OEHLSCHLAGER, A. C., PH.D.
SUTTON, D., PH.D.
UNRAU, A. M., M.S.A., PH.D., F.C.I.C.
VOIGT, E. M., M.SC., PH.D.
WALKLEY, J., PH.D., F.C.I.C.

Mathematics:

BOJADZIEV, G., PH.D.
DAS, A., M.S., PH.D., D.SC.
HARROP, R., M.A., PH.D.
LACHLAN, A. H., M.A., PH.D.
LARDNER, R. W., PH.D.
REILLY, N. R., PH.D.
SHOEMAKER, E. M., M.S., PH.D.
STEPHENS, M. A., A.M., PH.D.
THOMASON, S. K., PH.D.
VILLEGAS, C., ING.IND.

Physics.

ARROTT, A. S., M.S., PH.D.
BALLENTINE, L. E., M.SC., PH.D.
COCHRAN, J. F., M.A.SC., PH.D.
COLBOW, K., M.SC., PH.D.
CURZON, A. E., PH.D., A.R.C.S., D.I.C.
ENNS, R. H., PH.D.
FRINDT, R. F., PH.D.
IRWIN, J. C., PH.D.
RIECKHOFF, K. E., M.SC., PH.D.

UNIVERSITY OF TORONTO

TORONTO, ONTARIO M5S 1A1

Telephone: 928-2011.

Founded 1827.

Language of instruction: English. Provincially supported, assisted by private funds. Academic year: September to May (May to August, summer session).

Chancellor: G. IGNATIEFF, C.C., M.A.

President: J. M. HAM, SC.D.

Vice-President and Provost: D. W. STRANGWAY, M.A., PH.D.

Vice-President, Business Affairs: A. G. RANKIN, B.COM., F.C.A.

Vice-President, Research and Planning, *and Registrar:* H. C. EASTMAN, PH.D., F.R.S.C.

Vice-President, Campus and Community Affairs: W. E. ALEXANDER, M.A., PH.D.

Chief Librarian: R. H. BLACKBURN, M.A., B.L.S., M.S., LL.D.

Library: *see* **Libraries.**

Number of teachers: 5,288, **including** 983 **professors.**

Number of students: total 48,900.

Publications: ***Calendars, Undergraduate Admission Handbook, Bulletin, The Graduate, President's Report.***

DEANS AND DIRECTORS:

Faculty of Arts and Science: A. M. KRUGER, PH.D.

Faculty of Medicine: F. H. LOWY, M.D., F.R.C.P.C.

Faculty of Applied Science and Engineering: G. R. SLEMON, M.A.SC., PH.D., D.SC.

Faculty of Forestry: V. J. NORDIN, PH.D.

Faculty of Dentistry: R. TEN CATE, PH.D.

Faculty of Pharmacy: R. M. BAXTER, M.S., PH.D.

Faculty of Law: F. IACOBUCCI, B.COM., LL.B.

Faculty of Music: G. S. CIAMAGA, M.F.A.

Faculty of Education: J. C. RICKER, M.A.
School of Physical and Health Education: K. A. W. WIPPER, M.ED., M.A.
Faculty of Social Work: R. GARBER, D.S.W.
Faculty of Nursing: P. E. JONES, M.SC.
Faculty of Library Science: K. H. PACKER, A.M.L.S.
Faculty of Management Studies: D. TIGERT, M.B.A., PH.D.
School of Graduate Studies: J. F. LEYERLE, M.A., PH.D.
School of Continuing Studies: J. H. SWORD (acting).

PROFESSORS:

N.B.—In the following list staff members of colleges are indicated thus: Erindale Coll. (E), New Coll. (N), St. Michael's Coll. (M), Scarborough Coll. (S), Trinity Coll. (T), University Coll. (C), Victoria Univ. (V).

Faculty of Arts and Science:

ABOUCHAR, A., A.M., M.A., PH.D., Political Economy
AKCOGLU, M. A., M.SC., PH.D., Mathematics
ALFÖLDI, E., DR.PHIL., PH.D., Fine Arts
ANDERSON, G. M., B.ENG., M.A.SC., PH.D., Geology
ANDREW, D. F., M.SC., PH.D., Statistics
ARMSTRONG, R. L., M.A., PH.D., Physics
ARTHUR, J. G., PH.D., Mathematics
ATKINSON, F. V., D.PHIL., M.A., Mathematics
ATWOOD, H. L., M.A., PH.D., Zoology
AZUMA, R. E., M.A., PH.D., Physics
BARNES, T. G., M.A., D.PHIL., Classics
BARROS, J. A. B., M.I.A., PH.D., Political Economy
BAUM, G. G., M.A., S.T.D., Religious Studies (M)
BAY, C., LL.B., PH.D., Political Economy
BEALES, F. W., M.A., PH.D., Geology
BEATTIE, J. M., M.A., PH.D., History
BEDFORD, G. H., M.A., PH.D., Slavic Languages and Literatures
BELL, N. W., M.A., PH.D., Sociology
BENTLEY, G. E., D.PHIL., F.G.F., F.C.C., English (C)
BERGER, C. C., M.A., PH.D., History
BERGER, J., M.S., PH.D., Zoology
BERMAN, W. C., M.A., PH.D., History
BERNS, W. F., M.A., PH.D., Political Economy
BERRY, A., PH.D., Economics
BEST, E. E., M.A., B.D., PH.D., Religious Studies (V)
BIEDERMAN, G. B., PH.D., Psychology
BIRD, R. M., M.A., PH.D., Political Economy
BILANUIK, P. B., D.TH., DR.PHIL., Religious Studies (M)
BIRNBAUM, E., DIP. OAS., Islamic Studies
BISSELL, C. T., M.A., PH.D., D.LITT., LL.D., F.R.S.C., English (C)
BLAKE, C. R., M.A., PH.D., English (C)
BLISS, J. M., M.A., PH.D., History
BLISSETT, W. F., M.A., PH.D., English (C)
BLOOM, A., A.M., PH.D., Political Economy
BLOOM, T., M.A., PH.D., Mathematics
BORODIN, A., PH.D., Computer Science
BOSNICH, B., PH.D., Chemistry
BOSSONS, J. D., M.A., PH.D., Political Economy
BOUCHARD, D. E., L. ès L., A.M., PH.D., French (V)
BOWMAN, H. E., M.A., PH.D., Slavic Languages and Literatures
BOUISSAC, P. A. R., L. ès L., D.E.S., D. EN PH., French (V)
BOURNE, L. S., M.A., PH.D., Geography
BRAINERD, B. SB., M.S., PH.D., Mathematics
BRETON, A., PH.D., Political Economy
BRETON, R., M.A., PH.D., Sociology
BREWER, A. W., M.SC., PH.D., Physics
BRITTON, J., M.A., PH.D., Geography
BROCK, P., PH.D., D.PHIL., History
BROOK, A. G., PH.D., Chemistry
BROOKS, H. A., M.A., PH.D., Fine Arts
BROWN, R. C., M.A., PH.D., History
BROWNSTONE, M., M.SC., PH.D., Political Economy
BRUCKMANN, Mrs. P. L., M.A., PH.D., English (T)
BRUNS, J. E., M.A., S.T.D., S.S.D., Religious Studies (M)
BRYAN, R. B., PH.D., Geography
BRYDEN, W. K., M.A., PH.D., Political Economy
BUDSROWYCZ, B. B., M.A., PH.D., Slavic Language and Literatures
BURKE, J. F., M.A., PH.D., Hispanic Studies
BURNS, G., A.M., PH.D., Chemistry
BURTON, I., M.A., PH.D., Geography
BUTLER, D. G., M.SC., PH.D., Zoology
CAIRNS, J. C., M.A., PH.D., History
CALLAHAN, W., M.A., PH.D., History
CAMERON, A. F., PH.D., English
CAMERON, M. J., M.A., Literary Studies (M)
CARELESS, J. M. S., A.M., PH.D., F.R.S.C., History
CARR, J. L., M.A., PHD., Political Economy
CARROLL, J. J., M.A., PH.D., English (C)
CARSTENS. W. P., PH.D., Anthropology
CATHOLY, E. K., D.PHIL., German (M)
CHALK, J. H. H., PH.D., Mathematics
CHANDLER, S. B., PH.D., Italian and Hispanic Studies
CHANT, D. A., M.SC., PH.D., Zoology
CHAPMAN, C. H., M.A., PH.D., Physics
CHEW, J. J., M.A., PH.D., Anthropology
CHILDAINE, J. G., A.M., PH.D., French (V)
CHOUDHRY, N. K., Political Economy
CHURCHER, C. S., M.SC., PH D., Zoology
CLARK, G. M., M.SC., PH.D., Zoology
CLARKE, E. G., M.A., B.D., D.LITT., Near Eastern Studies (V)
CLIVIO, G. P., M.A., PH.D., Italian Studies
CLOUTIER-WOJCIECHOWSKA, C., L. ÈS L., D. DE L'U., French
COLE, J. W., M.A., Classics (T)
COLLET, Mme P., PH.D., French (M)
COLMAN, S. J., M.A., Political Economy
CONACHER, D. J., M.A., PH.D., Classics (T)
CONACHER, J. B., M.A., PH.D., History
COOK, S. A., A.M., PH.D., Computer Science
CORBEN, H. C., M.A., M.SC., PH.D., Physics
CRAIG, G. M., PH.D., History
CRAIK, F. I. M., PH.D., Psychology
CRANMER-BYNG, J. L., M.C., M.A., History
CRISPO, J. H. G., PH.D., Political Economy
CURRIE, J. B., M.A., PH.D., Geology
CURRY, L., M.A., PH.D., Geography
DAINTY, J., M.A., D.SC., F.R.S.E., Botany
DALES, J. H., M.A., PH.D., Political Economy
DALZELL, A., M.A., Classics (T)
DANIELS, J. M., M.A., D.LITT., Physics
DAVIES, R., B.LITT., LL.D., D.LITT., English (C)
DAVIS, H. C., M.A., PH.D., Mathematics
DEAN, W. G., M.A., PH.D., Geography
DECKERS, J. M., CAND.SC., LIC.SC.CHEM., Chemistry
DE MONTMOLLIN, D. P., L. ès L., D. ès L., Greek (V)
DENT, J., M.A., PH.D., History
DESAI, R. C., PH.D., Physics
DEWART, L. S., M.A., PH.D., Religious Studies (M)
DIGNAM, M. J., PH.D., Chemistry
DOBSON, W. A. C. H., M.A., East Asian Studies
DOLEŽEL, L., PH.DR., Slavic Languages and Literatures
DOLEZELOVA, M., M.A., PH.D., East Asian Studies
DOOB, A. N., PH.D., Psychology
DOOLEY, D. J., M.A., PH.D., English (M)
DOVE, J. E., M.A., D.PHIL., Chemistry
DREWITT, R. B., PH.D., Anthropology
DRUMMOND, I. M., M.A., PH.D., Political Economy
DRYER, D. P., A.M., Philosophy
DUFF, G. F. D., M.A., PH.D., F.R.S.C., Mathematics
DUNLOP, D. J., M.A., PH.D., Physics
DUNNING, R. W., M.A., PH.D., Anthropology
DUNPHY, W. B., M.A., PH.D., Philosophy (M)
DUPRÉ, J. S., A.M., PH.D., Political Economy
DYCK, H. L., M.A., PH.D., History
EASTMAN, H. C., A.M., PH.D., Political Economy
EASTMAN, S. B., M.A., PH.D., Political Economy
EAYRS, J. G., A.M., PH.D., Political Economy
ECCLES, W. J., M.A., PH.D., History
EDDIE, S., P.HD., Political Economy
EDISON, G., M.A., PH.D., Philosophy (T)
EICHNER, H., M.A., PH.D., F.R.S.C., German (C)
ELLERS, E. N., DR.RER.NAT., Mathematics
ELLIS, K. A. A., M.A., PH.D., Hispanic Studies
EVANS, D. D., PH.D., B.PHIL., D.PHIL., Philosophy
FACKENHEIM, E. L., PH.D., Philosophy
FAIRWEATHER, Rev. E. R., M.A., B.D., TH.D., Religious Studies (T)
FALLE, G. G., M.A., PH.D., English (T)
FALLS, J. B., PH.D., Zoology
FARQUAR, R. M., M.A., PH.D., F.R.S.C., Physics
FAWCETT, J. J., PH.D., Geology
FERNIE, J. D., M.SC., PH.D., Astronomy
FIELD, G. W., M.A., PH.D., German (V)
FIELD, N. C., M.A., PH.D., Geography
FITCH, B. T., D. DE L'U., French (T)
FLAHIFF, F. T., M.A., PH.D., English (M)
FLINN, J. F., M.A., French (C)
FLOYD, J. E., M.A., PH.D., Political Economy
FORRIN, B., M.A., PH.D., Psychology
FOX, D., M.A., PH.D., English (V)
FOX, P. W., M.A., PH.D., Political Economy
FRANCESCHETTI, A., PH.D., Italian Studies
FRANK, M. A., PH.D., English
FRASER, D. A. S., M.A., PH.D., F.R.S.C., Mathematics
FRIEND, W. G., PH.D., Zoology
FRYE, H. N., M.A., D.D., LL.D., D.LITT., L.H.D., F.R.S.C., English (V)
FUREDY, J. J., M.A., PH.D., Psychology
GALE, L. A., Survey Science
GALLOWAY, J., M.A., PH.D., Geography
GAUTHIER, D., A.M., D.PHIL., Philosophy
GIBSON, A. G., D.TH., Religious Studies (M)
GIFFEN, P. J., M.A., Sociology

GILBERT, T., Political Economy
GITTINS, J., M.SC., PH.D., Geology
GLEASON, H. A., PH.D., English (C)
GLICKMAN, R. J., A.M., PH.D., Hispanic Studies
GOFFART, W. A., A.M., PH.D., History
GOODWIN, A. M., M.SC., PH.D., Geology
GORMAN, D. H., PH.D., Geology
GOTLIEB, C. C., M.A., PH.D., Physics
GRACIE, G., PH.D., Geography
GRAHAM, G. M., M.SC., PH.D., Physics
GRAHAM, V. E., M.A., PH.D., French (C)
GRANT, J. R., A.M., PH.D., Classics (V)
GRASHAM, W. E. L., M.A., PH.D., Political Economy
GRAYSON, A. K., M.A., PH.D., Near Eastern Studies
GRAZIANI, R. I. C., M.A., PH.D., English
GREENE, R. A., M.A., PH.D., English (C)
GREINER, P. C., M.A., PH.D., Mathematics
GREUB, W. H., M.A., PH.D., DR. HABIL., M.AG.PHARM., Mathematics
GRENDLER, P. F., M.A., PH.D., History
GRIFFEN, P. A., M.SC., PH.D., Physics
GROSSKURTH, P., M.A., PH.D., English
GUILLET, J. E., PH.D., Chemistry
GULSOY, J., M.A., PH.D., Italian and Hispanic Studies
GUTTMAN, I., M.A., PH.D., Mathematics
HALEWOOD, W. H., M.A., PH.D., English (C)
HANLY, C. M. T., PH.D., Philosophy
HAQUE, W., M.A., M.S., PH.D., Mathematics, Political Economy
HARDEN, A. R., M.A., PH.D., French (V)
HARE, F. K., PH.D., Geography, Physics
HARRISON, A. G., M.SC., PH.D., Chemistry
HARTLE, D. G., M.A., PH.D., Political Economy
HARVEY, H. H., M.SC., PH.D., Zoology
HAYNE, D. M., M.A., PH.D., French (C)
HEIMAN, G., M.A., PH.D., Political Economy
HELLEBUST, J. A., M.A., PH.D., Botany
HELLEINER, G. K., M.A., PH.D., Political Economy
HEMPEL, W., DR.PHIL., German (M)
HERZBERGER, A. G., A.M., PH.D., Philosophy
HEYWORTH, P. L., M.A., English (C)
HIGGS, D. C., M.A., PH.D., History
HODGETTS, J. E., M.A., PH.D., LL.D., D.LITT., F.R.S.C., Political Economy
HOENIGER, F. D., M.A., PH.D., English (V)
HOGAN, J. A., PH.D., Psychology
HOLLADAY, J. S., TH.D., Near Eastern Studies
HOLLANDER, S., M.A., PH.D., Political Economy
HUGGETT, W. J., M.A., PH.D., Philosophy
HUGHES, D. R., PH.D., Anthropology
HULL, T. E., M.A., PH.D., Mathematics
HUME, J. N. P., M.A., PH.D., Physics
HUNTER, J. F. M., M.A., PH.D., Philosophy
HUNTLEY, D. G., M.A., PH.D., Slavic Language and Literatures
HURD, Rev. J. C., B.S., B.D., M.A., PH.D., Religious Studies (T)
HUTCHINSON, T. C., PH.D., Botany
IRIBARNE, J. V., DR.IN CHEM., Physics
IRVING, W. N., PH.D., Anthropology
ISAJIW, W. W., M.A., PH.D., Sociology
IVEY, D. G., M.A., PH.D., Physics
JACKSON, J. R. DE J., M.A., PH.D., English (V)
JAMES, R. L., M.A., PH.D., Sociology (SC)
JEANES, R. W., B.A., D. DE L'U., French (V)
JEFFERIES, R. L., PH.D., Botany
JOBLIN, K. G., TH.M., D.D., Religious Studies (V)
JOHNSON, L., PH.D., Fine Art
JOHNSON, W. M. L. A., M.A., PH.D., Fine Art
JOHNSTON, R. L., M.A., PH.D., Computer Sciences
JONES, C. P., M.A., PH.D., Classics
JONES, J. B., PH.D., D.PHIL., Chemistry
JOPLING, A. V., A.M., PH.D., Geography
JOYCE, D. A., A.M., PH.D., German (T)
KALBACH, W. E., M.A., PH.D., Sociology
KEE, K. O.. M.A., PH.D., English (V)
KEEP, J. L. H., PH.D., History
KEITH, W. J., M.A., PH.D., English (C)
KELLY, J. M., M.A., PH.D., Philosophy (M)
KENNY, L. M., M.A., Middle East and Islamic Studies
KERR, P. D., M.A., PH.D., Geography
KEYES, G. L., M.A., PH.D., Classics (V)
KIRKHAM, M. L., M.PHIL., English
KLEINDIENST, M. R., M.A., PH.D., Anthropology
KNIGHT, D. J., M.A., PH.D., English (V)
KOLERS, P. A., M.A., PH.D., Psychology
KONTOS, A. A., LL.B., PH.D., Political Economy
KOTOWITZ, Y., PH.D., Political Economy
KOVRIG, B., M.A., PH.D., Political Economy
KRESGE, A. J., PH.D., Chemistry (S)
KRONBERG, P. P., M.SC., PH.D., Astronomy
KRUGER, A. M., PH.D., Political Economy
LANCASHIRE, A. C., M.A., PH.D., English
LANG, T. J., M.A., M.SL., Philosophy (M)
LANGAN, T. D., A.M., PH.D., Philosophy
LEE, R. B., M.A., PH.D., Anthropology
LEGGATT, A. M., M.A., PH.D., English
LEHMAN, A. B., PH.D., Mathematics
LEMON, J. T., M.S., PH.D., Geography
LÉON, M. M., D. ès L., D.E.S., D. DE L'U., French (V)
LÉON, P. R. A., L. ès L., PH.D., French (C)
LE PAN, D., M.A., English (C)
LEVY, K. L., M.A., PH.D., Italian and Hispanic Studies
LEYERLE, J. F., M.A., PH.D., English (C)
LIST, R., DR.SC.NAT., Physics
LISTER, M. W., M.A., D.PHIL., Chemistry
LITHERLAND, A. E., F.R.S., PH.D., Physics
LIVERSAGE, R. A., M.A., PH.D., Zoology
LLOYD, T. O., M.A., D.PHIL., History
LOCKHART, J. E., PH.D., Psychology
LOCKHART, R. S., M.A., PH.D., Psychology
LUCKE, H. K., PH.D., Fine Art
LUCKYJ, G. S. N., M.A., PH.D., Slavic Languages and Literatures
LYNCH, L. E. M., M.A., L.M.S., PH.D., Philosophy (M)
LYNEN, J. F., M.A., PH.D., English (C)
MACCALLUM, H. R., M.A., PH.D., English (C)
McCOOL, J., PH.D., Mathematics
MCCREADY, W. T., M.A., PH.D., Italian and Hispanic Studies
MCFEAT, T. F. S., M.A., PH.D., Anthropology (S)
MACLEAN, K., PH.D., English (V)
MCLEAN, S., PH.D., Chemistry
MCLEOD, J. T., M.A., PH.D., Political Economy
MCLEOD, W. E., A.M., PH.D., Classics (V)
MACLURE, M., M.A., PH.D., English (V)
MCNAUGHT, K. W. K., M.A., PH.D., History
MCNEILL, K. G., M.A., D.PHIL., Physics
MACPHERSON, Miss J., PH.D., English (V)
MACRAE, D. A., A.M., PH.D., F.R.S.C., Astronomy
MCRAE, R. F., PH.D., Philosophy
MCSORLEY, H. J., B.S., M.A., D.TH., Religious Studies (M)
MACHIN, J., PH.D., Zoology
MALLON, Rev. H. V., M.A., English (M)
MANCHESTER, F. D., M.SC., PH.D., Physics
MANZER, R., M.A., PH.D., Political Economy
MARGESON J., M. R., M.A., PH.D., English (S)
MARÍN, D., LL.B., M.A., PH.D., Italian and Hispanic Studies
MARINELLI, P. V., M.A., PH.D., English
MARKER, F. J., A.B., English
MARMURA, M. E., M.A., PH.D., Islamic Studies
MARRUS, M. R., PH.D., History
MASSON, D. R., M.SC., PH.D., Mathematics
MASSON, J. M., PH.D., Indian Studies
MASUI, Y., M.SC., PH.D., Zoology
MATILAL, B. K., A.M., PH.D., Sanskrit and Indian Studies
MAURER, Rev. A. A. A., M.A., PH.D., Philosophy (M)
MAY, K. O., M.A., PH.D., Mathematics
MAYCOCK, P. F., M.SC., PH.D., Botany
MEAGER, J. C., M.A., PH.D., English (M)
MERAW, Sister C., PH.D., French (M)
MEREDITH-OWENS, G. M., M.A., Islamic Studies
METTRICK, D. F., PH.D., D.SC., Zoology
MILLGATE, M., M.A., PH.D., English (C)
MILNES, H. N., M.A., PH.D., German (C)
MOFFAT, J. W., PH.D., Physics
MOGGRIDGE, D. E., M.A., PH.D., Economics
MOLINARO, J. A., M.A., PH.D., Italian and Hispanic Studies
MRDSOVSKY, N., PH.D., Psychology, Zoology
MORGAN, P. F., M.A., PH.D., English
MUNRO, J. H. A., M.A., PH.D., Political Economy
MURASUGI, K., D.SC., Mathematics
MURDOCK, B. B., PH.D., Psychology
NALDRETT, A. J., M.SC., PH.D., Geology
NELSON, W. H., M.A., PH.D., History
NIMS, Sister FRANCES, M.A., English (M)
NISHIO, H. K., PH.D., Sociology
NOCE, H. S., M.A., PH.D., Italian and Hispanic Studies
NORRIS, G., M.A., PH.D., Geology
NOWLAN, D. M., M.A., PH.D., Political Economy
NUFFIELD, E. W., B.A., PH.D., F.R.S.C., Geology
NUN, J., LL.M., Political Economy
NYBURG, S. C., PH.D., Chemistry
O'BRIEN, M. J., M.A., PH.D., Classics (C)
O'DONNELL, P. J., PH.D., Physics
O'DRISCOLL, P. R., PH.D., English (M)
O'GORMAN, G. D., PH.D., French (M)
OLIVER, W. A., M.A., PH.D., French
OWEN, Rev. D. R. G., M.A., PH.D., D.D., B.C.L., Religious Studies (T)
OXTOBY, W. G., M.A., PH.D., Religious Studies (T)
OZIN, G. A., PH.D., Chemistry
PALOHEIMO, J. E., M.A., PH.D., Zoology
PARKER, J. H., M.A., PH.D., Italian and Hispanic Studies
PARKER, R. B., M.A., PH.D., F.R.S.C., English (T)
PARSONS, C. R., M.A., PH.D., French (C)
PARSONS, T. S., A.M., PH.D., Zoology
PATRICK, Z. A., PH.D., Botany
PAUL, D. A. L., PH.D., Physics
PEERS, F. W., M.A., PH.D., Political Economy
PEGIS, A. C., M.A., PH.D., F.R.C.S., Philosophy (M)
PERCY, J., M.A., PH.D., Astronomy
POLANYI, J. C., M.SC., PH.D., Chemistry
POWELL, J., PH.D., Chemistry
POWICKE, M. R., M.A., History
POWLES, C. H., A.M., PH.D., Divinity (T)

PRATT, R. C., B.A., PH.D., Political Economy
PRENTICE, J. D., PH.D., Physics
PRITCHARD, A., PH.D., English
PRUGUVECKI, E., PH.D., Mathematics
PUGH, R. E., M.A., PH.D., Physics
QUINN, K. F., M.A., Classics (C)
RANGER, K. B., PH.D., Mathematics
REA, K. J., M.A., PH.D., Political Economy
REDFORD, D. B., M.A., PH.D., Near Eastern Studies
REED, T. E., PH.D., Zoology
REGIER, H. A., M.A., PH.D., Zoology
REVELL, G. J., M.A., PH.D., Near Eastern Studies (V)
REYNOLDS, W. F., PH.D., Chemistry
RICHARDSON, H. W., S.T.B., M.A., PH.D., Religious Studies (M)
RIGG, A. G., M.A., D.PHIL., English (T)
RIST, J. M., M.A., Classics (C)
RITCHIE, J. C., PH.D., D.SC., Botany
ROBERT, P. R., M.A., PH.D., French (C)
ROBINSON, E. A., D.SC., PH.D., Chemistry
ROBINSON, T. M., M.A., PH.D., Philosophy
ROBSON, J. M., M.A., PH.D., English (V)
ROEDER, R. C., M.SC., PH.D., Physics
ROGERS, W. S., M.A., French (T)
ROONEY, P. G., B.SC., PH.D., Mathematics
ROSE, E. E., M.A., History
ROSENBAUM, S. P., M.A., PH.D., English (C)
ROSENTHAL, P., M.A., PH.D., Mathematics
ROSS, A. C. M., C.D., M.A., PH.D., A.T.C.M., French (V)
ROTHFELS, K. H., PH.D., Botany
ROWE, D. J., M.A., D.PHIL., Physics
RUCKLIDGE, J. C., PH.D., Geology
RUSSELL, P. H., M.A., Political Economy
SADDLEMYER, Miss A., M.A., PH.D., English (V)
SAFARIAN, A. E., PH.D., Political Economy
SALUS, P., M.A., PH.D., Linguistics
SAMARIN, W. J., PH.D., Anthropology
SAMUEL, A. E., M.A., PH.D., Classics (C)
SAVAN, D., A.M., Philosophy
SAVORY, R. M., M.A., PH.D., Islamic Studies
SCHIEDER, R. M. K., M.A., PH.D., English (T)
SCHLEPP, N. A., PH.D., East Asian Studies
SCHMID, G. H., PH.D., Chemistry
SCHMITZ, K. L., M.A., M.S.L., PH.D., Philosophy (T)
SCHOGT, H. G., M.A., PH.D., French (C)
SCOTT, G. D., M.A., PH.D., Physics
SEAQUIST, E. R., M.A., PH.D., Astronomy
SEN, D. K., DR.ÈS SC., D.SC., Mathematics
SHATZMILLER, J., M.A., PH.D., History
SHAW, J. W., M.A., PH.D., Fine Art
SHAW, W. D., A.M., PH.D., English (V)
SHEPHERD, R. M. H., M.A., Classics (C)
SHERIDAN, J., M.A., PH.D., Classics (M)
SHOOK, L. K., M.A., PH.D., English (M)
SHORTER, E. L., M.A., PH.D., History
SIDNELL, M. J., M.A., PH.D., English (T)
SIMMONS, J. W., M.A., PH.D., Geography
SKVORECKY, J., PH.D., English
SLAMECKA, N. J., PH.D., Psychology
SMITH, D. W., PH.D., French (V)
SMITH, F. G., M.SC., PH.D., Geology
SMITH, J. E., PH.D., Political Economy
SMITH, L. B., PH.D., Political Economy
SMITH, S. H., PH.D., Mathematics
SMYTH, J. E., M.COMM., F.C.A., Political Economy
SOBELL, J. H., M.A., PH.D., Philosophy
SPARLING, C., PH.D., Botany
SPARSHOTT, F. E., M.A., Ethics (V)
SPELT, J., M.A., PH.D., Geography
SPENCER, R. A., M.A., D.PHIL., History
SRIVASTAVA, M. S., M.SC., PH.D., Mathematics
STOICHEFF, B. P., B.A.SC., M.A., PH.D., Physics
STRANGWAY, D. W., M.A., PH.D., Geology, Physics
STRYLAND, J. C., PH.D., Physics
SUMNER, G. V., M.A., Classics (C)
SYNAN, E. A., M.A., M.S.L., PH.D., S.T.L., Philosophy (M)
TALLAN, I., PH.D., Zoology
TALMAGE, F., PH.D., Near Eastern Studies
TARSHIS, L., PH.D., Political Economy
TAYLOR, H. W., M.SC., PH.D., Physics
TEPPERMAN, L. J., M.A., PH.D., Sociology
THOMSON, R. D. B., M.A., D.PHIL., Slavic Languages and Literature
THORNTON, A. P., M.A., D.PHIL., History
TIDWELL, T. T., A.M., PH.D., Chemistry
TRAINOR, L. E. H., M.A., PH.D., Physics
TREMBLEY, G. F., L. ès L., PH.D., French (C)
TRIANTIS, S., LL.B., M.A., PH.D., Political Economy
TSICHRITZIS, D., M.A., PH.D., Computer Science
TULVING, E., M.A., PH.D., Psychology
TURK, A. T., M.A., PH.D., Sociology
TYREE, M. T., PH.D., Botany
UKAS, M. V., M.A., PH.D., Italian
VALLEAU, J. P., M.A., PH.D., Chemistry
VAN DEN BERGH, S., M.SC., DR.RER.NAT., F.R.A.S., Astronomy
VAN DER EYK, J., M.SC., PH.D., Geography
VAN FOSSEN, R. W., A.M., PH.D., English
VAN FRAASSEN, B. C., M.A., PH.D., Philosophy
VAN KRANENDONK, J., PH.D., Physics
VAN LOON, J. C., PH.D., Geology
VICKERS, G. S., A.M., Fine Art
VANSTONE, J. R., M.A., PH.D., Mathematics
VENKATACHARYA, T., M.A., Sanskrit and Indian Studies
VOSKO, S. H., M.SC., PH.D., Physics
WADE, D. V., M.A., PH.D., Religious Studies (V)
WAGEL, N. K., M.A., PH.D., History
WALKER, J. A., M.A., PH.D., French (C)
WALKER, M. V., D.PHIL., Physics
WALTERS, G. C., PH.D., Psychology
WARDHAUGH, R., M.A., PH.D., Linguistics
WATERHOUSE, D. B., M.A., East Asian Studies
WATKINS, M. H., B.COM., Political Economy
WARDER, A. K., Sanskrit and Indian Studies
WATSON, A. M., M.A., Political Economy
WATSON, G. A. B., M.A., S.T.B., Religious Studies (T)
WATT, F. W., B.LITT., M.A., PH.D., English (C)
WAUGH, W. A. O., M.A., D.PHIL., Mathematics
WAVERMAN, L., M.A., PH.D., Political Economy
WEATHERLEY, A. H., M.SC., PH.D., Biology
WELSH, R. P., M.A., PH.D., Fine Art
WEST, G. F., M.A., PH.D., Physics
WESTGATE, J. A., PH.D., Geology
WETZEL, H., DR.PHIL., German
WEVERS, **J. W., TH.D., Near** Eastern **Studies (C)**
WHITE, P. C. T., M.A., PH.D., History
WHITNEY, J., PH.D., Geography
WICKENS, G. M., M.A., F.R.S.C., Islamic Studies
WILLIAMS, J. P., PH.D., Botany (T)
WILLIAMS, Rev. R. J., M.A., B.D., PH.D., Near Eastern Studies (C)
WILSON, M. T. M.A., PH.D., English (T)
WILSON, T. A., A.M., PH.D., Political Economy
WINDER, J. W. L., M.A., PH.D., Political Economy
WINTER, F. E., PH.D., Fine Arts
WONG, S. S. M., M.S., PH.D., Physics
WOOD, J. S., M.A., D.DE.L'U., French (V)
WOODBURY, L. E., A.M., PH.D., Classics (C)
YATES, K., PH.D., D.PHIL.(C.), Chemistry
YATES, P., M.SC., PH.D., Chemistry
YOON, T. S., M.SC., PH.D., Physics
YORK, D., D.PHIL., Physics
ZAKUTA, L., M.A., PH.D., Sociology
ZEITLIN, I. M., M.A., PH.D., Sociology
ZEKULIN, G., M.A., Slavic Language and Literatures
ZIMMERMAN, A. M., M.S., PH.D., Zoology
ZITNER, S. P., M.A., PH.D., English (T)

Faculty of Medicine:

ALBERTI, P. W. R. M., PH.D., F.R.C.S., Otolaryngology
ALLEMANG, W. H., B.COM., M.D., F.R.S.C.(C), Obstetrics and Gynaecology
ANDERSON, T. W., M.A., B.M., B.CH., D.I.H., PH.D., Epidemiology and Biometrics
ANDERSON, G. H., M.SC., PH.D., Nutrition and Food Sciences
ANWAR, R. A., M.SC., PH.D., Biochemistry
AXELRAD, A. A., B.SC., M.D., C.M., PH.D., Anatomy
BADGLEY, R. F., M.A., PH.D., Behavioural Science and Paediatrics
BAILEY, J. D., M.D., F.R.C.P.C., Paediatrics
BAIN, H. W., M.D., F.R.C.P.(C), Paediatrics
BAINES, A. D., M.D., PH.D., Clinical Biochemistry
BARBER, H. O., M.D., F.R.C.S.(C.), Otolaryngology
BARRON, R. D., M.C., C.D., M.D., D.P.H., D.I.H., Health Administration
BASU, P. K., B.SC., M.D., Ophthalmology
BEAN, I. W., M.D., F.C.F.P., Family and Community Medicine
BEATON, G. H., M.A., PH.D., Nutrition
BEIRNE, P. F., B.CH., F.R.C.S.C., Obstetrics and Gynaecology
BELL, J. S., M.D., C.R.C.P.(C.), D.P.H., F.A.C.P.M., Health Administration
BERRIS, B., M.D., M.S., F.R.C.P.C., Medicine
BERTRAM, E. G., M.SC., PH.D., Anatomy
BORTH, R., D.R.SC., Obstetrics and Gynaecology
BRADSHAW, R. D. F., B.SC., Rehabilitation Medicine
BRIANT, T. D. R., M.D., F.A.C.S., F.R.C.S.(C.), Otolaryngology
BRODER, I., M.D., F.R.C.P.(C.), Medicine
BRYAN, A. C., PH.D., Anaesthesia
BRYCE, D. P., M.D., Otolaryngology
BURROW, G. N., M.D., Medicine
CAMPBELL, J. E., M.D.C.M., F.R.C.P.C., Medicine
CAMPBELL, J. M. R., M.D., F.R.C.P.(C.), Anaesthesia
CARVER, D. H., M.D., Paediatrics
CATHCART, L. M., M.D., Behavioural Science
CHRISTENSEN, L. R., PH.D., Medical Biophysics
CINADER, B., PH.D., D.SC., Medical Genetics, Clinical Biochemistry
CLARKE, D. W., M.SC., PH.D., Physiology
CLARKE, W. T. W., M.D., F.R.C.P.(C), Medicine

CLUTE, K. F., B.A., M.D., F.R.C.P.(C.), Administration
COBBOLD, R. S. C., Biomedical Engineering
COLLINS-WILLIAMS, C., M.D., F.R.C.P.C., Paediatrics
CONN, A. W., M.D., F.R.C.P.C., Anaesthesia
COWAN, D. H., Medicine
CRAPPER, D. R., M.D., F.R.C.P.(C.), Physiology
CRAWFORD, J. S., M.D., C.M., D.O.M.S., Ophthalmology, Rehabilitation Medicine
CRUICKSHANK, B., M.B., C.H.B., PH.D., M.D., F.R.F.P.S., M.R.C.P., F.R.C.P., M.C., Pathology
DEBUBA, Y., M.D., Family and Community Medicine
DORRINGTON, K., PH.D., Biochemistry
DUBISKI, S., M.D., Medical Genetics
DUNCAN, I. B. R., M.D., CH.B., M.C.PATH., Medical Microbiology
DUNN, A. J., M.D., F.R.C.P.(C.), Anaesthesia
EDELIST, G. G., M.D., Anaesthesia
EHRLICH, R. M. E., M.D., F.R.C.P.(C.), Paediatrics
ENDRENYI, L., PH.D., Pharmacology
ENHORNING, G., M.D., Obstetrics and Gynaecology
EYLAR, E. H., M.S., PH.D., Biochemistry
FALLIS, F. B., M.D., F.C.F.P., C.C.F.P., Family and Community Medicine
FARBER, E., M.D., PH.D., Pathology
FEUER, G., M.SC., PH.D., Clinical Biochemistry
FRANCOMBE, W. H., M.D., F.R.C.P.C., Medicine
FRANKLIN, A. E., PH.D., Medical Microbiology, Preventive Medicine
FREDERICKSON, J. M., M.D., F.R.C.S.C., Physiology
FREEMAN, R. S., B.S., M.A., PH.D., Parasitology
FRITZ, I. B., D.D.S., PH.D., Banting and Best Research and Physiology
FUERST, C. R., M.SC., PH.D., Medical Genetics
GEISLER, W. O., M.D., F.R.C.P.C., Rehabilitation Medicine
GLASOR, F. B., M.D., Psychiatry
GODFREY, C. M., Rehabilitation Medicine
GOLD, R., M.D., PH.D., Paediatrics
GOODMAN, W. S., M.D., F.R.C.S.(C.), Otolaryngology
GORNALL, A. G., B.A., PH.D., Clinical Biochemistry
GRAYSON, J., M.D., F.R.C.P.C., Physiology
GREBEN, S. E., M.D., F.R.C.P.(C.), Psychiatry
GRIEW, S., PH.D., Behavioural Science
HALLETT, P. E., M.A., Physiology
HALPERIN, M. L., M.D.C.M., F.R.C.P.C. Medicine
HANNAH, W. J., M.D., F.R.C.S.(C.), Obstetrics and Gynaecology
HARKINS, J. L., M.D., F.R.C.S.(C.), F.A.C.O.G., Obstetrics and Gynaecology
HARRISON, A. W., M.D., F.R.C.S.(C.), Surgery
HASTINGS, J. E. F., M.D., PH.D., Health Administration
HEWITT, D., M.A., Preventive Medicine and Biostatistics
HILL, F. M., M.A. M.D., F.R.C.P.C., Medicine
HILLIARD, I. M., B.A., M.D., Medicine
HINES, R., M.D., C.C.F.P., F.C.B.A., Family and Community Medicine
HINTON, N. A., M.D., C.M., M.SC., C.R.C.P.(C.), Medicine, Microbiology

HOFMANN, T., DIP.CHEM., D.SC.TECH., Biochemistry
HOLLENBERG, C. H., B.SC., M.D., F.R.C.P.(C.), Medicine
HOLMES, R. B., M.D., M.S.C., F.R.C.P.(C), F.A.C.R., Radiology
HORSEY, W. J., B.A., M.D., F.R.C.S.(C), Surgery
HUNT, A., M.SC.D., D.D.S., D.D.P.H., Health Administration
HUNTER, J., M.A., PH.D., Physiology
HUNTER, R. C. A., M.D., D.PSYCH., Psychiatry

ISRAEL, Y., PH.D., Pharmacology

JEEJEEBOY, K. N., M.R.C.P., PH.D., F.R.C.P.C., F.R.C.P.E., Medicine
JIMENEZ, J., M.D., L.M.C.C., L.R.C.P.C., F.R.C.P.C., Rehabilitation Medicine
JOHNSON, D. H., M.D., C.C.F.P., F.C.F.P., Family and Community Medicine
JOY, NANCY, A.O.C.A., Art as Applied to Medicine

KALANT, H., M.D., PH.D., Pharmacology
KALOW, W., M.D., Pharmacology
KHANNA, J. M., M.PHARM., PH.D., Pharmacology
KINSBOURNE, M., Paediatrics

LANE, B. G., PH.D., Biochemistry
LANGER, B., M.D., F.R.C.S., F.A.C.S., Surgery
LANSDOWN, E. L., M.D., F.R.C.P.(C.), Radiology
LERICHE, W. H., M.D., F.A.P.H.A. F.R.C.P.C., Preventive Medicine
LEVINE, S., M.D.C.M., F.R.C.P., Psychiatry
LEVINNE, N. N., M.D., Family and Community Medicine
LITTLE, J. A., M.D., M.A., F.R.C.P.(C)., Medicine
LLEWELLYN-THOMAS, E., B.SC., M.D., C.M., Pharmacology
LOGAN, W. I., M.D., Paediatrics
LOGOTHETOPOULOS, J., M.D., Banting and Best Research
LOWY, F. H., M.D., F.R.C.P.(C.), Psychiatry

MCCULLOCH, J. C., M.D., Ophthalmology
MACLENNAN, D. H., M.A., PH.D., Banting and Best Medical Research
MCLEOD, D. L., M.D., F.R.C.P.(C.), Anatomy
MACMILLAN, R. L., M.D., M.R.C.P., F.R.C.P.(C.), F.A.C.P., Medicine
MACPHERSON, L. W., M.R.C.V.S., D.V.S.M., PH.D., Microbiology
MALKIN, A., M.D., PH.D., F.R.C.P.(C.), Clinical Biochemistry
MARROTTA, J. T., M.D., F.R.C.P.C., Medicine
MILLER, A. B., M.B.B., F.R.C.P., Preventive Medicine
MOODY, N. F., Biomedical Engineering
MOORE, K. L., M.SC., PH.D., Anatomy
MORGAN, R. W., M.D., S.M. HYG., Preventive Medicine
MUNRO, A., M.D., F.R.C.P.E., F.R.C.P., Psychiatry
MURPHY, J. T., M.D., PH.D., Physiology
MURRAY, R. K., M.D., M.S., Biochemistry

NEW, P. K., PH.D., Behavioural Science
NORRIS, J. R., M.D., F.R.C.O.G., F.R.C.S.(C.), Obstetrics and Gynaecology

OGRYZLO, M. A., M.D., F.R.C.P.C., Medicine
OSBORN, R. W., PH.D., Preventive Medicine

PACKHAM, M., PH.D., Biochemistry
PAINTER, R. H., PH.D., Biochemistry
PAPSIN, F., M.D., F.R.C.S.(C.), F.A.C.S., F.A.C.O.G., Obstetrics and Gynaecology
PAUL, W., B.A., PH.D., Clinical Biochemistry

PAUL, W. M., M.D., F.R.C.S.(C), Obstetrics and Gynaecology
PEARSON, F. G., M.D., F.R.C.S.(C.), Surgery
PERKIN, R. L., M.D., F.R.C.P., Family and Community Medicine
PHILLIPS, M. J., M.D., F.C.A.P., F.R.C.P.(C.), Pathology
PINKERTON, P. H., Pathology
PRUZANSKI, W., M.D., Medicine
RAE-GRANT, Q., M.D., F.E.L.C.T., Psychiatry
RAKOFF, V. M., D.PSYCH., F.R.C.P.(C.), Psychiatry
RANCE, C. P., M.D., F.R.C.P.C., Paediatrics
RAPOPORT, A. M., M.D., PH.D., Physiology and Medicine
REID, D. B. W., M.A., M.SC., Biometrics
RITCHIE, A. C., M.B., CH.B., D.PHIL., Pathology
ROBINSON, I. M., B.A., Rehabilitation Medicine
ROSCHLAU, W. H. E., M.D., Pharmacology
ROTHMAN, A. I., B.SC., E.D.D., Medical Education
SALTER, R. B., M.D., M.S., F.R.C.S.(C), Surgery
SCHWENGER, C. W., M.D., D.P.H., Health Administration
SCOTT, A. A., M.D., Anaesthesia
SEEMAN, P., M.SC., M.C., PH.D., M.R.C.P., Pharmacology
SELLERS, E. A., M.D., PH.D., Pharmacology
SEN, A. K., M.D., PH.D., Pharmacology
SHEPHARD, R. J., M.D., PH.D., Physiology
SILVER, M. D., M.D., M.SC., PH.D., F.R.C.P.A., F.A.C.P., M.C.P.A., Pathology
SILVERSIDES, J. L., B.SC., M.D., F.R.C.P.(C.), Medicine
SIMINOVITCH, L., B.SC., PH.D., Medical Genetics
SIREK, A., M.D., M.A., PH.D., Physiology
SIREK, O., M.D., M.A., PH.D., Physiology
SMYTHE, H. A., M.D., F.R.C.P., Medicine
SOWDEN, K. A., M.D., F.R.C.P., Medicine
SPEAKMAN, J. S., B.A., M.D., F.R.C.S.(C.), Ophthalmology
SPENCE, L., M.B., CH.B., D.T.M.&H., DIP. BACT., Medical Microbiology
SUNAHARA, F. A., B.SC., PH.D., Pharmacology
STANACEV, N. Z., M.A., PH.D., Clinical Biochemistry
STEINER, J. W., M.D., Pathology
STEWARD, D., M.B., L.R.C.P., F.R.C.P., Anaesthesia
TALESNIK, J., M.D., Pharmacology
TASKER, R. R., M.D., F.R.C.S.(C.), Surgery
THOMPSON, J. S., M.A., M.D., Anatomy
THOMPSON, MARGARET, PH.D., Medical Genetics
THOMPSON, W., PH.D., Biochemistry
TURNER, J. A. P., M.D., C.R.C.P.C., F.C.C.P., Paediatrics
VAYDA, E., M.D., Health Administration
VOLPE, R., M.D., F.R.C.P.(C.), Medicine
VRANIC, M., M.D., D.SC., Physiology
WALKER, J. F., M.A., L.C.S.T., Speech Pathology
WATTERS, N. A., M.D., Surgery
WHERRETT, J. R., M.D.C.M., F.R.C.P.C., PH.D., Medicine
WIGLE, E. D., Medicine
WILLIAMS, G. R., PH.D., Biochemistry
WILSON, D. R., B.A., M.D., F.R.C.S.(C.), Surgery
WONG, J. T., PH.D., Biochemistry
WOOLF, C. R., M.D., F.C.C.P., M.R.C.P., F.R.C.P.(C.), Medicine
YIP, C., PH.D., Banting and Best Medical Research

Faculty of Applied Science and Engineering:

ABRAMS, J. W., PH.D., Industrial Engineering
ALCOCK, C. B., PH.D., D.SC., A.R.C.S., F.R.I.C., M.I.M.M., Metallurgy and Materials Science
ANDREWS, D. G., M.A., F.R.S.A., Chemical Engineering
AUST, K. T., M.A.SC., PH.D., Metallurgy and Materials Science
BAINES, W. D., M.S., PH.D., Mechanical Engineering
BASMADJIAN, D., M.A.SC., PH.D., Chemical Engineering
BERNHOLTZ, B., B.A., M.A., PH.D., Industrial Engineering
BIRINGER, P. P., M.SC., PH.D., Electrical Engineering
BURGESS, W. H., M.F.S., PH.D., Chemical Engineering
BURKE, P. E., M.A.SC., Electrical Engineering
BUZALOTT, J. A., M.SC., PH.D., Industrial Engineering
CHARLES, M. E., M.SC., PH.D., Chemical Engineering
COBBOLD, R. S. C., M.SC., PH.D., Electrical Engineering
COLLINS, M. P., PH.D., Civil Engineering
CRAIG, G. B., M.A.SC., PH.D., Metallurgy and Materials Science
DAVISON, E. J., M.A., PH.D., Electrical Engineering
DE LEEUW, J. H., M.S. IN AE., PH.D., F.C.A.S.I., Aerospace Studies
DELORY, F. A., M.A.SC., D.I.C., PH.D., Geological Engineering
DEWAN, S. B., M.E., PH.D., Electrical Engineering
ETKIN, B., M.A.SC., D.ENG., F.R.S.C.S., F.C.A.S.I., F.A.I.A.A., Aerospace Studies
FLENGAS, S. N., PH.D., D.I.C., D.SC., F.C.I.C., Metallurgy and Materials Science
FOLEY, P. J., M.A., Industrial Engineering
FRANKLIN, U. M., PH.D., Metallurgy and Materials Science
FRENCH, J. B., M.SC., PH.D., Aerospace Studies
GANCZARLZYK, J., M.SC., D.SC., Civil Engineering
GLASS, I. I., M.A.SC., PH.D., F.A.P.S., F.A.A.A.S., F.C.A.S.I., Aerospace Studies
GRAYDON, W.F., M.A.SC., PH.D., Chemical Engineering
HEINKE, G. W., M.A.SC., PH.D., Civil Engineering
HOEPPNER, D. W., M.S., PH.D., Mèchanical Engineering
HOOPER, F. C., B.A.SC., D.I.C., Mechanical Engineering
HUGHES, P. C., M.A.SC., PH.D., Aerospace Studies
HUMMEL, R. L., PH.D., Chemical Engineering
IIZUKA, K., M.E., M.S., PH.D., Electrical Engineering
JANISCHEWSKYJ, W., M.A.SC., Electrical Engineering
JERVIS, R. E., M.A., PH.D., Chemical Engineering
KEFFER, J. F., M.A.SC., PH.D., Mechanical Engineering
KENNEY, T. C., D.I.C., M.SC., PH.D., Civil Engineering
LEE, E. S., M.ENG., PH.D., Electrical Engineering
LEUTHEUSSER, H. J., M.A.SC., PH.D., Mechanical Engineering
LUUS, R., M.A.SC., M.A., PH.D., Chemical Engineering
MACELHINNEY, W. G., M.A.SC., Chemical Engineering
MACKAY, D., PH.D., Chemical Engineering
MEASURES, R. M., PH.D., Aerospace Studies
MILLS, R. H., B.SC., Civil Engineering
MISSEN, R. W., M.SC., PH.D., Chemical Engineering
NEUMANN, A. W., B.A., DR.RER.NAT., Mechanical Engineering
PHILLIPS, C. R., PH.D., Chemical Engineering
PIGGOTT, M. R., M.SC., PH.D., Aerospace Studies
RAMASWAMI, B., A.M., PH.D., Metallurgy and Materials Science
RIMROTT, F. P. J., M.A.SC., PH.D., DR.ING., Mechanical Engineering
ROBERTSON, S. D. T., M.SC., PH.D., Electrical Engineering
RUBIN, L. J., M.A.SC., PH.D., Chemical Engineering
RUTTER, J. W., M.A., PH.D., Metallurgy and Materials Science
SALAMA, C. A. T., M.A.S.C., PH.D., Electrical Engineering
SANDLER, S., M.A.SC., Chemical Engineering
SCHWAIGHOFER, J., M.S., PH.D., DR.TECH., Civil Engineering
SCOTT, D. S., M.SC., PH.D., Mechanical Engineering
SEDRA, A. S., M.A.SC., PH.D., Electrical Engineering
SEMLYEN, A., D.ENG., PH.D., Electrical Engineering
SENDERS, J. W., A.B., Industrial Engineering
SIMMONS, J. G., M.SC., PH.D., Electrical Engineering
SLEMON, G. R., M.A.SC., D.I.C., PH.D., D.SC., Electrical Engineering
SMITH, H. W., SC.D., Electrical Engineering
SMITH, J. W., M.A.SC., PH.D., Chemical Engineering
SMITH, K. C., M.A.SC., PH.D., Electrical Engineering
SOBERMAN, R. M., PH.D., Civil Engineering
SPINNER, I. H., M.A.SC., PH.D., Chemical Engineering
STOICHEFF, B. P., M.A., PH.D., F.R.S., F.R.S.C., Engineering Science
TABARROK, B., D.PHIL., Mechanical Engineering
TEMPLETON, J. G. C., A.M., PH.D., Industrial Engineering
TENNYSON, R. C., M.A.SC., PH.D., Aerospace Studies
TOGURI, J. M., M.A.SC., PH.D., Metallurgy and Materials Science
TRASS, O., SC.D., Chemical Engineering
UZUMERI, S. M., M.A.SC., Civil Engineering
VANDEVEGTE, J., M.A.SC., PH.D., Mechanical Engineering
WARD, C. A., PH.D., Mechanical Engineering
WAYMAN, M., M.A., PH.D., Chemical Engineering
WILLIAMS, H. L., M.SC., PH.D., Chemical Engineering
WONHAM, W. M., PH.D., Electrical Engineering
WOODHAMS, R. J., M.SC., PH.D., Chemical Engineering
WRIGHT, P. M., M.SC., PH.D., Civil Engineering
YEN, J. L., B.SC., M.A.SC., PH.D., Electrical Engineering

Faculty of Education:

AITKEN, J. L., M.A.
ALEXANDER, D. W. M., B.ED., M.SC.
ANDREWS, W., B.ED., M.SC.
BAINE, R. P., M.A.
BANCROFT, G. W., M.ED., PH.D.
BEDAL, C. L., B.A., M.ED., Counsellor Education
BOYES, G. H., M.A., History, Philosophy and Sociology of Education
CAIRNS, R., B.A.
COMAN, A. C., M.A.
DENT, R. W., M.A., PH.D.
DODD, J. W., B.A., Practice Teaching
EBOS, F., M.SC.
ELLIOTT, Mrs. U., B.ED., M.A.
FAIR, J. W., M.ED., PH.D.
GILBERT, V. K., M.ED.
GOODE, R. C., PH.D.
GRAPKO, M. F., M.A., PH.D., Dir. Institute of Child Study
GREIG, J. W., ED.D., Administrative and Programme Development
HARRIS, R. S., M.A., PH.D.
JONES, R. J., B.A., MUS.BAC., A.R.C.T., Modern Languages
KONG, S. L., M.ED., PH.D.
KUZMICH, Mrs. N., MUS.BAC., M.A.
LA FAVE, L. J., M.B.A.
LANG, H. M., B.A.
LIFE, J. R., M.ED., Physical and Health Education
LONDON, W. G., M.E.
MACDONALD, J. W., M.A., ED.D., English
MCMASTER, R. J., B.A., B.ED., English
REID, G. A., M.A., F.C.C.T., Business Education
RICKER, J. C., M.A.
RIDGE, H. L., M.A., PH.D.
SAGER, W. E., B.A.
SHEPHERD, R. T., B.A.
SMITH, G., M.A.
STEVENS, J. H., M.A., English
STIRLING, JEAN, B.A., Physical and Health Education
WOLFE, T. J. E., M.ED.

Faculty of Library Science:

DENIS, L. G., M.L.S., PH.D.
DONNELLY, F. D., M.L.S., PH.D.
HALPENNY, F. G., M.A., LL.D.
LAND, R. B., M.A., M.L.S.
PACKER, K. H., A.M.L.S.
WILKINSON, J. P., M.L.S., PH.D.

Faculty of Forestry and Landscape Architecture

ANDRESEN, J. W., PH.D.
BALATINECZ, J. J., M.F., PH.D.
BENDELL, F.S., PH.D.
BUCKINGHAM, F. M., M.F., D.F.
FARRAR, J. L., M.F., PH.D.
HUBBES, M., PH.D.
LOVE, D. V., M.F.
NAUTIYAL, J. C., M.F., PH.D.
NORDIN, V. J., PH.D.
ROY, D. N., M.SC., PH.D.
SMITH, V. G., M.S.F., PH.D.

Faculty of Music:

BECKWITH, J., MUS.M., Music
BERMAN, M., M.MUS.
CIAMAGA, G., M.F.A., Musical Theory and Composition
FENYVES, L., Performance
HEFFERNAN, C. W., MUS.M., PH.D., Music Education
HUGHES, A., M.A., D.PHIL.
KENINS, T., B.LITT., Musical Theory and Composition
KLEIN, L. K., M.S., PH.D.
MANIATES, M. R., M.A., PH.D., History and Literature of Music
MORAWETZ, O., MUS.DOC., Musical Theory and Composition
MOREY, C., PH.D.
OLNICK, H. J., M.A., History and Literature of Music
RIDOUT, G., LL.D., History and Literature of Music
SCHABAS, E., M.A., Performance

Faculty of Dentistry:

ANDERSON, D. L., D.D.S., M.SC.D., F.A.I.D., F.R.C.D.(C.), F.A.C.D.
BEAGRIE, G. S., D.D.S., L.D.S., F.D.S., R.C.S., F.R.C.D.(C.), Clinical Sciences
BURGESS, R. C., D.D.C., M.SC., Preventive Dentistry
DAVEY, K. W., D.D.S., M.SC.D., F.R.C.D.(C.), Paedodontics
FISK, R. O., D.D.S., F.R.C.D.(C.)
HORD, A. B., B.SC.D., D.D.S.
HOUSTON, J. B., M.S., D.D.S.
HUNT, A. M., D.D.S., D.D.P.H., M.SC.D., F.R.C.D.(C.) (*Assoc. Dean*)
JACKSON, M., D.D.S., F.R.C.D.(C.), Dentistry
LEVINE, N., D.D.S., M.SC.D., F.R.C.D.
LEWIS, D. W., D.D.S., D.D.P.H., M.SC.D., Community Dentistry
MCADAM, D. B., D.D.S.
MACKAY, W. D., D.D.S., Dental Materials
MADLENER, E. M., D.D.S., M.SC.D., Bacteriology
MAIN, J. H. P., B.D.S., F.D.S., R.C.S., PH.D., M.R.C.PATH., Oral Pathology
MELCHER, A. H., B.D.S., H.D.D., M.D.S., PH.D., Dentistry
MUNROE, C. D., B.CH.D., F.D.S.R.C.S.
NIKIFORUK, G., D.D.S., M.S., F.R.C.D.(C.)
PEDLER, J. A., M.R.C.S., L.R.C.P., M.D.S., F.D.S., R.C.S., F.R.C.D.(C.), Oral Medicine and Pathology
POPOVICH, F., M.SC.D., D.D.S.
SANDHAM, H. J., D.D.S., PH.D.
SESSLE, B. J., M.D.S., PH.D.
SMITH, D. C., M.SC., PH.D., F.R.I.C., Dentistry
SMYLSKI, P. T., D.D.S., F.R.C.D.(C.), Oral Surgery
SPECK, J. E., D.D.S., F.R.C.D.(C.) Periodontics
STONEMAN, D. W., D.D.S.
SYMINGTON, J. M., M.SC., PH.D.
TEN CATE, A. R., PH.D., B.D.S., Biological Sciences
WOODSIDE, D. G., D.D.S., M.SC.D., F.R.C.D.(C.), Orthodontics
ZARB, G. A., B.CH.D., D.D.S., M.SC., M.S., F.R.C.D.(C.), Prosthodontics

Faculty of Pharmacy:

ALEXANDER, W. E., M.SC., PH.D.
BAXTER, R. M., PHM.B., B.S.P., M.S., PH.D., Pharmacognosy
DUNCAN, G. R., M.SC.PHM., D.PHIL.
FREEDMAN, M. H., M.SC.PHM., PH.D.
KANDEL, S., PH.D.
NAIRN, J. G., PH.D., Pharmacy
PATERSON, G. R., PHM.B., B.S.P., M.SC., PH.D., Pharmaceutical Chemistry
STEWART, D. J., B.S.P., M.SC., Hospital Pharmacy
STIEB, E. W., M.SC.PHM., PH.D., History of Pharmacy
TEARE, F. W., M.SC., PH.D.
WALKER, G. C., B.SC., M.S., PH.D., Pharmacy

Faculty of Law:

ALEXANDER, E. R., B.COM., LL.M.
BAXTER, I. F. G., M.A., LL.B.
DUNLOP, J. B., LL.M.
EDWARDS, J., LL.J., M.A., PH.D., LL.D.
FRIEDLAND, L., B.COM., LL.B., PH.D.
GREEN, B., LL.M., S.J.D.
IACOBUCCI, F., DIP.INT.LAW., B.COM., LL.B.
JANISCH, M. C. L., LL.M., J.S.D.
MEWETT, A. W., LL.M., S.J.D.
MORRIS, G. L., LL.M.
MORTON, J. D., Q.C., M.A.
RISK, R. C. B., LL.M.
SCANE, R. E., B.A.
SCHIFF, S. A., LL.M.
SHERBANIUK, D. J., LL.M.
SWAN, J., B.COM., LL.B., B.C.L.
TREBILCOCK, M. J., LL.M.
WADDAMS, S. M., LL.M., S.J.D.
ZIEGEL, J. S., LL.M., PH.D.

School of Architecture:

HOWARTH, T., PH.D., F.R.I.B.A., F.R.A.I.C.
PRANGNELL, P. N., A.A.DIP., M.ARCH., A.R.I.B.A., M.R.A.I.C.
VAN GINKEL, B. L., M.C.P.

School of Physical and Health Education:

DANIEL, JURI, B.PH.E., M.S., PH.D.
FLOWERS, J. F., M.ED., ED.D.
WIPPER, K. A. W., M.ED.

Faculty of Social Work:

BELLAMY, D. F., D.S.W.
BOURKE, W. A., D.S.W.
GANDY, J. M., M.A., M.S.S.A., M.S.W.
GARBER, R., D.S.W.
GODFREY, Miss E. R., B.A., M.A.
LAMBERT, C., M.S., PH.D.
MARKUS, N., D.S.W.
MEEKS, D. E., B.S., D.S.W.
ROSE, A., M.A., PH.D.
SCHLESINGER, B., M.S.W., PH.D.
SHAPIRO, B.-Z., B.A., D.S.W.

Faculty of Nursing:

ALLEMANG, M., M.N., PH.D.
ARPIN, K. E., M.SC.
CAHOON, M. C., M.ED., PH.D.
CUNNINGHAM, R., M.P.H.
JONES, P. E., B.SC.N., M.SC.
KING, M. K., B.A., B.SC.N., M.S.N.
PARKER, N. I., M.A., PH.D.

Faculty of Management Studies:

CLARKSON, M. B. E., M.A.
COUTTS, W. B., B.A., F.C.A., Accounting
CRISPO, J. H. G., B.COM., PH.D., Industrial Relations
DAY, G. S., M.B.A., PH.D., Marketing
EVANS, M. G., M.SC., PH.D.
GORDON, M. J., M.A., PH.D., Finance
HAINES, G. S., M.S., PH.D., Marketing
HOUSE, R., B.S., M.B.A., PH.D., Organizational Behaviour
KALYMON, B. A., M.PHIL., PH.D.
MAIN, O. W., M.A., PH.D., Economics
MAXWELL, S. R., PH.D., Business and Public Policy
MOORE, P. J., M.B.A.
PAULL, A. E., B.A., PH.D., Statistics
POAPST, J. V., M.COM., Finance
QUIRIN, G. D., M.A., A.M., PH.D., Economics
SETHI, S. P., M.B.A., PH.D.
SIEGEL, J. P., PH.D.
SOMMERS, M. S., B.COM., M.B.A., D.B.A., Marketing
TIGERT, D. J., M.B.A., PH.D., Marketing

CONSTITUENT COLLEGES:

University College: Toronto.
Principal: P. RICHARDSON, PH.D.
Registrar: M. G. FINLAYSON, M.A., PH.D.

New College: Toronto.
Principal: R. S. LOCKHART, M.A., PH.D.
Registrar: H. J. MASON, A.M., PH.D.

Innis College: Toronto.
Principal: J. D. DUFFY, M.A., PH.D.
Registrar: D. B. KING, M.A.

Scarborough College: Westhill.
Principal: JOAN E. FOLEY, PH.D.

Erindale College: Missisauga.
Principal: P. FOX, PH.D.

Woodsworth College: Toronto.
Principal: P. SILCOX, M.A., PH.D.
Registrar: A. R. WAUGH, B.A.

FEDERATED UNIVERSITIES AND COLLEGES:

Emmanuel College (the Theological College in Toronto of the United Church of Canada): f. 1928.

Principal: Rev. W. O. FENNELL, S.G.M., D.D. (until July 1981); Rev. D. JAY (from July 1981).

Knox College (Presbyterian).
Principal: Rev. J. C. HAY, PH.D.

Massey College.
Master: R. DAVIES, D.LITT., B.LITT., LL.D., F.R.S.C.

University of St. Michael's College: Toronto 5; f. 1852; conducted by the Basilian Fathers.
President: Rev. P. SWAN, M.A., PH.D. (until July 1981); WILLIAM DUNPHY (from July 1981).

University of Trinity College: Toronto 5; f. 1851; f. as Federated University 1904.
Vice-Chancellor and Provost: F. K. HARE, PH.D.

Victoria University: 73 Queen's Park Crescent, Toronto; f. 1890 as a Federated University.
President: G. S. FRENCH, M.A., PH.D.

Wycliffe College (Anglican).
Principal: Rev. R. F. STACKHOUSE, M.A., B.D., L.TH., PH.D.

AFFILIATED INSTITUTE:

Ontario Institute for Studies in Education: 252 Bloor St. West, Toronto, Ont. M5S 1V6; f. 1965; an independent college, affiliated for degree-granting purposes only; courses lead to certificate of standing and graduate degrees in education; extensive library; Dir. B. SHAPIRO; publs. *Interchange, Curriculum Theory Network, Convergence* (quarterly), *Orbit* (5 a year).

TRENT UNIVERSITY

PETERBOROUGH, ONTARIO K9J 7B8

Founded 1963.

Language of Instruction: English.
Dates of Academic Year: September to May (three terms with reading periods intervening).

Chancellor: WILLIAM L. MORTON, O.C., M.A., LL.D., D.LITT.

President and Vice-Chancellor: DONALD THEALL, M.A., PH.D.

Vice-President: R. D. CHAMBERS, B.A., B.LITT.

Vice-President (Finance): J. E. LEISHMAN, B.COM., C.A.

Registrar: A. O. C. COLE, M.A.

Library Director: BRIAN HEENEY, D.PHIL.

Number of teachers: 175.
Number of students: 2,500.

Publication: *Journal of Canadian Studies.*

DEANS:

Faculty of Arts and Science: DAVID GALLOP, M.A.
Graduate Studies: W. P. ADAMS, PH.D.

PROFESSORS:

ADAMS, W. P., Geography
ALFRED, L. C. R., Physics
BARKER, J. C., History
BAUMGAERTEL, G., German
BERRILL, M., Biology
BEWS, J. P., Classical Studies
BOOTE, M. J., Economics
BOWLES, R. T., Sociology
BROWN, S. A., Chemistry
BURBIDGE, J. W., Philosophy
CARTER, C., Mathematics
CARTER, R. E., Philosophy
CHAKRAVARTTY, I. C., Mathematics
CHAMBERS, R. D., English
CHAPMAN, I. D., Chemistry
CURTIS, D. C. A., Economics
DOXEY, M. P., Politics
EDWARDS, R. L., Biology
GALLAGHER, S. F., English Literature
GALLOP, D., Philosophy
GILCHRIST, J., History
GONZÁLEZ-MARTÍN, J. P., Spanish
HARPER, F. K., French
HEENEY, B., History
HELMUTH, H. S., Anthropology
HODGINS, B. W., History
JOHNSON, R. G., Physics
JOHNSTON, R. B., Anthropology
KETTLER, D., Politics
KITCHEN, H. M., Economics
LODGE, J. I., Physics
MACADAM, J. I., Philosophy
MACMILLAN, D. S., History
MCLACHLAN, I., English Literature
MARCH, R. E., Chemistry
MORRISON, D. R., Political Studies
NADER, G. A., Geography
NIND, T. E. W., Mathematics
OLDHAM, K. B., Chemistry
ORSTEN, E. M., English
POWLES, P. M., Biology
REES, A. H., Chemistry
ROYLE, P., French Studies
RUBINOFF, M. L., Philosophy
SANDEMAN, I. M., Biology
SMITH, S. G. D., Politics
STAIRS, R. A., Chemistry
STEWART, D. D., German
THEALL, D. F., English Literature
TODD, E. M., Anthropology
TRACEY, K. A., Anthropology
VASTOKAS, J. M., Anthropology
WEARING, J., Politics
WHITE, R. F., Sociology
WILSON, A., Canadian Studies
WINNY, J., English Literature
WINOCUR, G., Psychology
WONG, P. T.-P., Psychology
WORTHINGTON, A. G., Psychology

UNIVERSITY OF VICTORIA

P.O.B. 1700, VICTORIA, BRITISH COLUMBIA V8W 2Y2

Telephone: 477-6911.

Founded 1963.

Language of Instruction: English.

Provincial Control: Academic Year: September to April; Summer Studies: May to August, including Summer Session, July and August.

Chancellor: I. MCTAGGART COWAN.
President and Vice-Chancellor: H. E. PETCH.
Vice-President (Academic): A. FISCHER.
Vice-President (Administration): J. T. MATTHEWS.
Vice-President (Finance): R. W. MCQUEEN.
Registrar: R. FERRY.
Librarian: D. W. HALLIWELL.

Number of teachers: 550.

Number of students: 8,362.

Publications: *Calendar*† (annual), *Malahat Review*†.

DEANS:

Faculty of Arts and Sciences: (vacant).
Faculty of Education: ARTHUR KRATZMANN.
Faculty of Fine Arts: DOUGLAS G. MORTON.
Faculty of Graduate Studies: J. M. DEWEY.
Faculty of Human and Social Development: R. W. PAYNE.
Faculty of Law: L. R. ROBINSON.

FULL PROFESSORS AND/OR HEADS OF DEPARTMENTS:

ABRAMSON, J. A., Social Work
ABRIOUX, O. M., French Language and Literature
ALGARD, F. T., Biology
ALKIRE, W. H., Anthropology
ARMSTRONG, R. D., Education
ASHWOOD-SMITH, J. J., Biology
AYERS, J. D., Education
BAKONY, L. I., Economics
BARRODALE, I., Mathematics
BEACH, H. D., Psychology
BEEHLER, R. G., Philosophy
BERTRAM, G. W., Economics
BEST, M. R., English
BIRCH, A. H., Political Science
CABAÑAS, P., Hispanic and Italian Studies
CAMPBELL, D., Classics
CHABASSOL, D. J., Education
CHEFFINS, R. I., Law
CHURCHLEY, F. E., Education
CLEMENTS, R. M., Physics
CLIMENHAGA, J. L., Physics
COCKAYNE, E. J., Mathematics
COLLIS, M. L., Physical Education
COOPERSTOCK, F. I., Physics
COSTA, L. D., Psychology
CORWIN, G. W., Music
CROIZIER, R. C., History
CUTT, J., Public Administration
DAVIDSON, R. R., Mathematics
DEWEY, J. M., Physics
DOBELL, A. R., Public Administration
DOBEREINER, J. P., Visual Arts
DONALD, L. H., Anthropology
DOSSO, H. W., Physics
DOWNING, J. A., Education
DOYLE, C. D., English
EVANS, P. O., Education
FERGUSON, R., Child Care
FISCHER, A., Chemistry
FONTAINE, A. R., Biology
FORWARD, C. N., Geography
FOWLER, R. H., Education
FRASER, F. M., Law
GODFREY, W. D., Creative Writing
GOULSON, C. F., Education
GOWANS, A., History in Art
GRANT, J. P., English
GRIFFITHS, D. A., French Language and Literature
GUNASINGHE, S., History in Art
HAGEDORN, R. B., Sociology
HARE, C., Theatre
HARTWICK, F. D. A., Physics
HARVEY, D., Visual Arts
HAYWARD, J. S., Biology
HEDLEY, R. A., Sociology
HOBSON, G. N., Psychology
HODGKINSON, C. E., Education
HORSBURGH, H. J. N., Philosophy
HOWE, B. L., Education
HUXLEY, H. H., Classics
JACKMAN, S. W., History
JOBSON, K. B., Law
JONES, J. C. H., Economics
KERGIN, D. J., Nursing
KIRK, A. D., Chemistry
KLING, P., Music
KOMOROUS, R., Music
KRATZMANN, A., Education
LAUDADIO, L., Economics
LESLIE, R. F., English
MACGINITIE, W. H., Education
MACKIE, G. O., Biology
MARTENS, F. L., Education
MASON, G. P., Education
MATHESON, A. T., Biochemistry and Microbiology
MCAULEY, A., Chemistry
MCINERNEY, J. E., Biology
MCINTYRE, B., Theatre
MCLEISH, J., Education
MICHELSEN, J. M., Philosophy
MICKELSON, N. I., Education
MILTON, G. A., Psychology
MORGAN, C. G., Philosophy
MORTON, D. G., Visual Arts
NEILSON, W. A. W., Law
O'BRIEN, R. N., Chemistry
ODEH, R. E., Mathematics
O'GRADY, G. N., Linguistics
OLSON, A. V., Education
OWEN, E. E., Education
OWENS. J. N., Biology
PAYNE, R. W., Psychology
PEARCE, R. M., Physics
PETCH, H. E., Physics
PETER, J. D., English
PORTEOUS, J. D., Geography
PRIESTLY, D. M., Law
RANKIN, K. W., Philosophy
RIEDEL, W. E., Germanic Studies
ROBERTSON, L. P., Physics
ROBINSON, L. R., Law
ROY, R. H., History
SATZ, P., Psychology
SCARGILL, M. H., Linguistics
SCHAARSCHMIDT, G. H., Slavonic Studies
SCULLY, S. E., Classics
SEWELL, W. R. D., Geography
SHINBROT, M., Mathematics
SKELTON, R., Creative Writing
SMITH, F., Education
SMITH, H. F., English
SMITH, P. L., Classics
SPREEN, O., Psychology
SPROULE-JONES, M. H., Political Science
SRIVASTAVA, H. M., Mathematics
SWAINSON, N. A., Political Science
TIESSEN, G. W., Visual Arts
VEEVERS, J. E., Sociology
WAELTI-WALTERS, J. R., French Language and Literature
WALLS, J., Pacific and Oriental Studies
WARKENTYNE, H. J., Linguistics
WATERS, D. W. W., Law
WEAVER, J. T., Physics
WHARF, B. W. H., Social Welfare
WICKE, C. R., History in Art
WIKKRAMATILEKE, W. A. R., Geography
WOOD, R., Music
WOOLEY, W. T., History
WUESTER, T. J., Law
YOUNG, P. T., Music
YOUNG, W. D., Political Science

UNIVERSITY OF WATERLOO

WATERLOO, ONTARIO N2L 3G1

Telephone: (519) 885-1211.

Founded 1959.

Provincially supported; Language of instruction: English; Academic year: September to April (Co-operative programmes September to August, Summer Session July to August).

Chancellor: JOSEF KATES, M.A., PH.D.

President and Vice-Chancellor: B. C. MATTHEWS, B.S.A., A.M., PH.D.

Vice-President (Academic): T. A. BRZUSTOWSKI, A.M., PH.D.

Vice-President (Finance and Operations): A. B. GELLATLY, B.A., C.G.A.

Registrar: C. T. BOYES, B.A.

Librarian: M. C. SHEPHERD, B.ED., M.A.

Number of teachers: 730 (full-time).

Number of students: 19,310.

Publications: *U.W. Courier, Gazette, Imprint, Calendars.*

DEANS:

Faculty of Arts: R. K. BANKS, M.A., PH.D.

Faculty of Engineering: W. A. MCLAUGHLIN, M.S., PH.D.

University Graduate Office: L. A. K. WATT, M.S., PH.D.

Faculty of Mathematics: J. A. GEORGE, M.SC., PH.D.

Faculty of Science: R. N. FARVOLDEN, M.SC., PH.D.

Faculty of Human Kinetics and Leisure Studies: G. S. KENYON, B.P.E., M.S., PH.D.

Faculty of Environmental Studies: J. G. NELSON, M.A., PH.D.

DEPARTMENT CHAIRMEN AND DIRECTORS OF PROGRAMMES AND SCHOOLS:

Anthropology: T. S. ABLER, M.S., PH.D.
Architecture: R. H. SIMS, R.I.B.A.
Biology: J. E. THOMPSON, PH.D.
Canadian Studies: S. E. MCMULLIN, M.A., PH.D.
Chemistry: D. E. IRISH, M.SC., PH.D., F.C.I.C.
Chemical Engineering: E. RHODES, M.SC. TECH., PH.D., P.ENG.
Civil Engineering: W. C. LENNOX, M.SC., PH.D., P.ENG.
Classical Studies: P. FORSYTH, M.A., PH.D.
Dance Group: R. PRIDDLE, M.SC., M.A.
Drama and Theatre Arts Group: W. R. CHADWICK, M.A., PH.D.
Earth Sciences: C. R. BARNES, PH.D.
Economics: J. H. HOTSON, M.A., PH.D.
Electrical Engineering: I. F. BLAKE, M.SC., M.A., PH.D., P.ENG.
English: W. R. MACNAUGHTON, M.A., PH.D.
Fine Arts: N. L. PATTERSON, B.A.
French: J. R. DUGAN, M.A., PH.D.
Geography: L. H. RUSSWURM, M.A., PH.D.
Germanic and Slavic Languages and Literatures: J. W. DYCK, M.A., PH.D.
Health Studies: J. A. BEST, PH.D.
History: H. MACKINNON, S.T.L., M.A., D.PHIL.
Kinesiology: N. J. ASHTON, M.S.
Man-Environment Studies: R. F. KEITH, M.A., PH.D.
Management Sciences: D. W. CONRATH, M.S., M.A., PH.D., P.ENG.
Mathematics:
Applied Mathematics: C. F. A. BEAUMONT, M.A.
Computer Science: J. A. BRZOZOWSKI, M.A.SC., PH.D.
Combinatorics and Optimization: J. A. BONDY, D.PHIL.
Pure Mathematics: G. E. CROSS, M.A., PH.D.
Statistics: J. F. LAWLESS, M.SC., PH.D.
Mechanical Engineering: D. J. BURNS, PH.D., P.ENG., C.ENG.
Optometry: M. E. WOODRUFF, O.D., PH.D.
Peace and Conflict Studies: C. G. BRUNK, M.A., PH.D.
Philosophy: R. A. GEORGE, M.A., PH.D.
Physics: N. R. ISENOR, M.SC., PH.D.
Political Science: R. J. WILLIAMS, M.A., PH.D.
Psychology: T. G. WALLER, M.S., PH.D.
Recreation: D. NG, M.A., M.S., RE.D.
Religious Studies: B. J. HUBBARD, M.A., PH.D.
Sociology: A. A. HUNTER, M.A., PH.D.
Spanish: B. THALMAN, M.A., PH.D.
Studies in Personality and Religion: A. L. EVANS, S.T.M., D.MIN.
Systems Design: K. HUSEYIN, PH.D., D.SC., P.ENG.
School of Urban and Regional Planning: D. W. HOFFMAN, M.S.A., PH.D.

FEDERATED COLLEGE:

University of St. Jerome's College (Roman Catholic, conducted by the Congregation of the Resurrection): Waterloo; f. 1864; federated 1960.
President: N. L. CHOATE, C.R., M.A.

AFFILIATED COLLEGES:

Conrad Grebel College (Mennonite): Waterloo.
President: Rev. R. LEBOLD, M.DIV., M.TH.

St. Paul's College (United): Waterloo.
Principal: F. C. GÉRARD, M.A., B.D., S.T.M., PH.D.

Renison College (Anglican): Waterloo; f. 1959, affiliated 1960.
Principal: I. L. CAMPBELL, M.SC.

THE UNIVERSITY OF WESTERN ONTARIO

LONDON, ONTARIO N6A 3K7

Telephone: (519) 679-2111.

Founded 1878.

Charter last revised 1974; Academic year: September to May.

Chancellor: R. M. IVEY, Q.C., LL.D.

President and Vice-Chancellor: G. E. CONNELL, PH.D.

Vice-President (Administration and Finance): A. K. ADLINGTON, B.A.

Vice-President (Academic) and Provost: J. C. LEITH, M.S., PH.D.

Vice-President (Health Sciences): D. BOCKING, M.D., F.R.C.P.(C.), F.A.C.P.

Chief Librarian: **R. E. LEE, M.F.A., PH.D.**

Registrar: D. A. CHAMBERS, M.SC., PH.D.

Number of teachers: 1,410.

Number of students: 16,550 full-time, 10,050 part-time.

Publications: *Medical Journal, Dental Journal, Gazette* (student weekly), *Alumni Gazette, The Business Quarterly,* *The Science Terrapin, The President's Report, Western News* (weekly newsletter), Calendars for all Faculties and Schools.

DEANS:

Faculty of Arts: **JOHN G. ROWE, M.A., PH.D., D.D.**

Faculty of Music: J. BEHRENS, M.S., PH.D.

Faculty of Science: J. B. BANCROFT, PH.D.

Faculty of Social Science: B. B. KYMLICKA, M.A., PH.D.

Faculty of Education: P. B. PARK, M.ED.

Faculty of Physical Education: W. J. L'HEUREUX, M.A., L.L.D.

Faculty of Engineering: G. F. CHESS, M.ENG., PH.D., P.ENG.

Faculty of Dentistry: W. J. DUNN, D.D.S., F.A.C.D.

Faculty of Medicine: M. J. HOLLENBERG, M.D., M.SC., PH.D.

Faculty of Law: P. W. SLAYTON, M.A. (acting).

School of Library and Information Science: W. J. CAMERON, PH.D.

Faculty of Graduate Studies: H. B. STEWART, M.D., PH.D.

Faculty of Nursing: B. A. COX, M.SC., PH.D.

School of Business Administration: C. B. JOHNSTON, M.B.A.

School of Journalism: A. W. MACFARLANE, M.L.S.

PROFESSORS:

Faculty of Arts:
ASENSIO, J., DR.FIL. Y LET., Spanish and Italian
ATANCE, F., M.A., PH.D., French
AVOTINS, I., M.A., PH.D., Classical Studies
BAGULEY, D., M.A., D.U., French
BARRIO-GARAY, J. L., PH.D., Visual Arts
BINKLEY, R. W., PH.D., Philosophy
BOLGAN, A. C., M.A., PH.D., English
BRONAUGH, R. N., M.S., PH.D., Philosophy
BUB, J., PH.D., Philosophy
BUSH, W. S., M.A., D. DE L'UNIV., French
BUTTS, R. E., A.M., PH.D., Philosophy
COLLINS, T. J., M.A., PH.D., English
DALE, W. S. A., M.A., PH.D., Visual Arts
DAVIS, J. W., A.M., PH.D., Philosophy
DE KERGOMMEAUX, D., Visual Arts
DEVEREUX, E. J., M.A., D.PHIL., English

Flint, W., m.a., ph.d., Spanish and Italian
Forsyth, L. H., m.a., ph.d., French
Gerber, D. E., m.a., ph.d., Classics
Graham, J. W., m.a., ph.d., English
Hair, D. S., m.a., ph.d., English
Harper, W. L., m.a., ph.d., Philosophy
Heller, L. M., m.a., ph.d., French
Hieatt, A. K., ph.d., English
Hieatt, C. B., m.a., ph.d., English
Hooker, C. A., ph.d., Philosophy
Issacharoff, M., d.u., French
Johnson, H. J., ph.d., Philosophy
Jones, D. F., m.a., ph.d., French
Kaula, D. C., m.a., ph.d., English
Leach, J. J., m.a., ph.d., Philosophy
Marras, A., ph.d., Philosophy
Marti, A. M., Spanish and Italian
Rajan, B., m.a., ph.d., English
Rans, G., m.a., ph.d., English
Reaney, J., m.a., ph.d., English
Sanborn, C. E., m.a., ph.d., English
Sanders, J. B., m.a., d.u., French
Schluetter, H. J., ph.d., German
Shervill, R. N., m.a., ph.d., Spanish and Italian
Smieja, F. L., m.a., ph.d., Spanish and Italian
Stingle, R. M., m.a., English
Surette, P. L., m.a., ph.d., English
Tracy, G. L., m.a., ph.d., German
Tuchmaier, H., m.a., ph.d., French
Venesoen, C. A., d. ès l.. French
Walters, R. L., m.a., ph.d., French
Woodman, R. G., m.a., ph.d., English

Faculty of Music:

Aldrich, R., mus.bac., l.r.s.m., l.g.s.m.
Bailey, T., m.f.a., ph.d.
Behrens, J., m.s., ph.d.
Bray, K., I., m.m.
Creech, R., b.a.
Downs, P. G., mus.m., ph.d.
Green, J. P., m.m., ph.d., a.r.c.t.
Johnson, D. J., m.a.
McIntosh, J. S., m.m., d.m.a., a.r.c.t., a.a.g.o.
McKellar, D. A., m.m., a.r.c.t., a.mus.
McLean, H. J., m.a., f.r.c.o., a.r.c.m., l.r.s.m., a.mus.
Proctor, G., m.mus., ph.d.
von Kuster, Clifford, mus.bac., l.r.c.t.
Wuensch, G., ph.d.

Faculty of Science:

Alford, W. P., ph.d., Physics
Ali, M. M., m.sc., m.s., ph.d., Mathematics
Allnatt, A. R., ph.d., Chemistry
Baird, N. C., ph.d., Chemistry
Bancroft, G. M., m.sc., ph.d., Chemistry
Bancroft, J. B., ph.d., Plant Sciences
Beck, A. E., ph.d., Geophysics
Blackwell, J. H., m.sc., ph.d., Applied Mathematics
Bolton, J. R., m.a., ph.d., Chemistry
Borwein, D., ph.d., d.sc., Mathematics
Bourns, T. K. R., m.a., ph.d., Zoology
Brand, J. C. D., m.sc., ph.d., d.sc., Chemistry
Brannen, E., m.a., ph.d., Physics
Bruen, A. A., m.sc., ph.d., Mathematics
Carmichael, C. M., m.sc., ph.d., Geophysics.
Carroll, J. M., dr.eng.sci., Computer Science
Cavers, P. B., ph.d., d.i.c., Plant Sciences
Chan, L. K., m.a., ph.d., Mathematics
Cook, F. S., ph.d., Plant Sciences
de Mayo, P., m.sc., ph.d., Chemistry
Dennis, S. C., a.r.c.s., ph.d., Applied Mathematics
Edgar, A. D., m.sc., ph.d., Geology
Ehrman, J. B., a.m., ph.d., Applied Mathematics
Elcock, E. W., ph.d., Computer Science
Ferguson, H. I., m.sc., ph.d., Physics
Fleet, M. E. L., ph.d., Geology
Forsyth, P. A., m.a., ph.d., f.r.s.c., Physics
Fraser, P. A., m.s., ph.d., Applied Mathematics
Fyfe, W. S., ph.d., Geology
Gray, D. F., m.sc., ph.d., Astronomy
Greyson, R. I., m.sc., ph.d., Plant Sciences
Guthrie, J. P., ph.d., Chemistry
Haq, M. S., m.a., ph.d., Mathematics
Hart, J. F., m.a., ph.d., Computer Science
Hay, D. R., m.sc., ph.d., Physics
Hodder, R. W., ph.d., Geology
Howell, W. C., m.sc., ph.d., Chemistry
Hutchinson, R. W., ph.d., Geology
Jacobs, P. W., m.sc., ph.d., d.sc., Chemistry
Jones, J., ph.d., Physics
Judd, W. W., m.a., ph.d., Zoology
Keenleyside, M. H. A., m.a., ph.d., Zoology
King, J. F., ph.d., Chemistry
Landstreet, J. D., m.sc., ph.d., Astronomy
Lenz, A. C., m.sc., ph.d., Geology
Locke, M., m.a., ph.d., Zoology
Lorimer, J. W., m.sc., ph.d., Chemistry
Lowe, R. P., ph.d., Physics
Lyon, G. F., m.a., ph.d., Physics
MacNeill, I. B., m.a., ph.d., Mathematics
Mansinha, L., m.sc., ph.d., Geophysics
Marlborough, J. M., m.a., ph.d., Astronomy
McGowan, J. W., m.sc., d.sc., Physics
McKeen, W. E., m.sc., ph.d., Plant Sciences
McMillan, D. B., m.sc., ph.d., Zoology
Meath, W. J., ph.d., Chemistry
Mereu, R., m.a., ph.d., Geophysics
Moorcroft, D. R., m.sc., ph.d., Physics
Naylor, D., ph.d., Applied Mathematics
Nerenberg, M. A. H., ph.d., Applied Mathematics, Physics
Nuttall, J. H., ph.d., Physics
Orloci, L., m.sc., ph.d., Plant Sciences
Payne, N. C., ph.d., Chemistry
Phipps, J. B., ph.d., Plant Sciences
Puddephatt, R. J., ph.d., Chemistry
Rose, G. S., ph.d., Physics
Sakmar, I. A., m.sc., ph.d., Applied Mathematics
Scott, D. M., ph.d., Zoology
Shawyer, B. L. R., ph.d., Mathematics
Snaith, V. P., m.a., m.sc., ph.d., Mathematics
Starkey, J., ph.d., Geology
Steele, J. E., m.sc., ph.d., Zoology
Stothers, J. B., m.sc., ph.d., Chemistry
Sukava, A. J., m.sc., ph.d., Chemistry
Sullivan, P. J., m.a.sc., ph.d., Applied Mathematics
Talman, J. D., m.sc., ph.d., Applied Mathematics
Thierrin, G., d.math., Mathematics
Tong, B. Y., m.l.s., m.a., ph.d., Physics
Van Huystee, R. B., m.a., ph.d., Plant Sciences
Vogan, E. L., m.sc., ph.d., Physics
Walden, D. B., ph.d., Plant Sciences
Ware, W. R., ph.d., Chemistry
Warnhoff, E. W., ph.d., Chemistry
Wehlau, W. H., ph.d., Astronomy
Wilson, D. G., m.a., ph.d., Plant Sciences
Winder, C. G., ph.d., Geology
Young, G. M., ph.d., Geology

Faculty of Social Science:

Armstrong, F. H., m.a., ph.d., History
Balakrishnan, T. R., m.a., ph.d., Sociology
Barnard, F. M., m.a., ph.d., Political Science
Brainerd, C. J., m.a., ph.d., Psychology
Burch, T. K., m.a., ph.d., Sociology
Burley, K. H., ph.d., Economics
Cartwright, J. R., ph.d., Political Science
Courchene, T. J., ph.d., Economics
Dawson, W. F., m.a., d.phil., Political Science
Ebanks, G. E., ph.d., Sociology
Flaherty, D. H., m.a., ph.d., History
Gardner, R. C., m.sc., ph.d., Psychology
Goodchild, M. F., ph.d., Geography
Hossé, H. A., m.a., ph.d., Geography and Political Science
Jackson, D. N., m.s., ph.d., Psychology
Kimura, D., m.a., ph.d., Psychology
Klapp, O. E., a.m., ph.d., Sociology
Kunkel, J. H., m.a., ph.d., Sociology
Laidler, D. E. W., m.a., ph.d., Economics
Lander, J. R., m.a., m.litt., f.r.h.s., History
Leith, J. C., m.s., ph.d., Economics
Manning, F., m.a., ph.d., Anthropology
McClelland, W. J., m.a., ph.d., Psychology
Melvin, J. R., m.a., ph.d., Economics
Mogenson, G. J., m.a., ph.d., Psychology
Nicholson, N. L., m.sc., ph.d., m.ed., ed.d., f.r.g.s., Geography
Noel, S. J. R., m.a., d.phil., Political Science
O'Brien, A., b.sc., Political Science
Ogelsby, J. C. M., m.a., ph.d., History
Packer, P. W., m.a., f.r.g.s., Geography
Paivio, A. U., m.sc., ph.d., Psychology
Parkin, M., m.a., Economics
Pylyshyn, Z. W., ph.d., Psychology
Reuber, G. L., a.m., ph.d., Economics
Rowe, J. G., m.a., ph.d., History
Singer, B. D., m.a., ph.d., Sociology
Steele, I. K., ph.d., History
Stone, L., ph.d., Sociology
Turner, R. J., ph.d., Sociology
Vanderwolf, C. H., m.sc., ph.d., Psychology
Warntz, W., a.m., ph.d., Geography
Whalley, J., m.a., m.phil., ph.d., Economics
Wonnacott, R. J., a.m., ph.d., Economics
Zaslow, M., m.a., ph.d., History

Faculty of Dentistry:

Brooke, R. I., l.d.s., m.r.c.s., l.r.c.p., f.d.s., r.c.s., Oral Medicine
Dunn, W. J., d.d.s., f.a.c.d., Paediatric and Community Dentistry
Feasby, W. H., d.d.s., m.sc., f.r.c.d.(c.), Paediatric and Community Dentistry
Hunter, W. S., d.d.s., m.s., ph.d., Paediatric Dentistry
Johnson, R. H., d.d.s., m.s.d., Oral Medicine
Jordan, R. E., d.d.s., m.s.d., f.i.c.d., Restorative Dentistry
Moore, D. S., d.d.s., f.r.c.d.(c.), Oral Medicine
Parnell, A. G., f.d.s.r.c.s., Oral Medicine
Stephens, R. G., d.d.s., m.sc., Oral Medicine
Suzuki, M., d.d.s., d.m.d., f.i.c.d., Restorative Dentistry
Wright, G. Z., d.d.s., m.s.d., f.r.c.d.(c.), Paediatric and Community Dentistry

Faculty of Medicine:
ANDERSON, C., M.D., M.R.C.PATH., F.R.C.P.(C.), F.A.C.P., Pathology
ARMSTRONG, D. T., M.S., PH.D., Obstetrics, Gynaecology, Physiology
AUFREITER, J., M.D., Psychiatry
BARNETT, H. J. M., M.D., F.R.C.P.(C.), Neurology, Medicine
BARTON, W. B., M.D., F.R.C.P.(C.), Medicine
BOCKING, D., M.D., F.R.C.P.(C.), F.A.C.P., Medicine
BOLTON, C. F., M.D.C.M., M.S., F.R.C.P.(C.), Clinical Neurological Sciences
BONDY, D. C., M.D., F.R.C.P.(C.), Medicine
BOONE, J. E., M.D., F.R.C.P.(C.), F.A.A.P., Paediatrics
BRENNAN, M., L.R.C.P. & S.I., C.C.F.P., Family Medicine
BROOKS, V. B., M.S., PH.D., Physiology
BROWNSTONE, Y. S., M.SC., PH.D., Clinical Biochemistry
BUCK, CAROL W., M.D., PH.D., D.P.H., Epidemiology, Preventive Medicine
BUCK, R. C., M.D., M.SC., PH.D., Microscopic Anatomy
CALARESU, F. R., M.D., PH.D., Physiology
CAMERON, M. G. P., M.D., F.R.C.P.(C.), Physical Medicine and Rehabilitation
CANHAM, P. B., M.SC., PH.D., Biophysics
CAPE, R. D. T., M.B., CH.B., M.D., F.R.C.P., F.R.C.P.(C.), Medicine
CAREY, L. S., M.D.C.M., M.SC., M.S., F.R.C.P.(C.), Diagnostic Radiology and Nuclear Medicine
CARROLL, K. K., M.SC., M.A., PH.D., Biochemistry
CARROLL, S. E., M.D., F.R.C.S.(C.), F.A.C.C., F.A.C.S., F.A.C.C.P., Surgery
CHAMBERLAIN, M. J., M.R.C.S., L.R.C.P., M.B., CH.B., M.R.C.P., Medicine
CHANCE, G. W., M.B., CH.B., M.R.C.S., L.R.C.P., M.R.C.P., D.C.H., F.R.C.P.(C.), L.M.C.C., F.R.C.P., Obstetrics, Gynaecology and Paediatrics
CHODIRKER, W. B., M.D., F.R.C.P.(C.), Medicine
COLHOUN, E. H., PH.D., Pharmacology
CONNELL, G. E., PH.D., F.R.S.C., F.C.I.C., Biochemistry
DALES, S., M.A., PH.D., Immunology
DEBRUN, G., M.D., C.R.C.P.(C.), Neuro-Radiology, Diagnostic Radiology and Nuclear Medicine
DELLOW, P. G., B.D.S., M.B.B.S., Physiology
DENHARDT, D. T., PH.D., Microbiology and Immunology, Biochemistry
DE VEBER, L. L., M.D., F.R.C.P.(C.), Paediatrics
DRAKE, C. G., M.D., M.SC., D.S., F.R.C.S.(C.), F.R.C.S., Surgery, Clinical Neurology
DUFF, J. H., M.D., Surgery
DUPRE, J., M.A., B.M., B.CH., F.R.C.P., F.R.C.P.(C.), Medicine
EBISUZAKI, K., M.S., PH.D., Microbiology and Immunology, Cancer Research Unit
FITZ-JAMES, P. C., M.S.A., M.D., PH.D., Microbiology and Immunology, Biochemistry
FLUMERFELT, B. A., M.SC., PH.D., Anatomy
FREI, J. V., M.D.C.M., M.SC., PH.D., F.R.C.P.(C.), M.R.C.PATH., Pathology
GAMMAL, E. A., PH.D., Anatomy
GARDNER, D. G., D.D.S., M.S.D., Oral **Pathology**
GOWDEY, C. W., M.SC., D.PHIL., Pharmacology
GREENWAY, R. E., M.D., F.R.C.S.(C.), Otolaryngology
GROOM, A. C., PH.D., Biophysics
GUNTON, R. W., M.D., D.PHIL., F.R.C.P.(C.), F.A.C.P., Medicine
HAMILTON, J. T., PH.D., Pharmacology
HARDING, P. G. R., M.D., M.SC., F.R.C.S.(C.), Obstetrics and Gynaecology
HARTH, M., M.D., F.R.C.P.(C.), Medicine
HAUST, M. D., M.D., M.SC., C.R.C.P.(C.), Pathology, Obstetrics and Gynaecology, Paediatrics
HEAGY, F. C., M.D., M.SC., PH.D., F.R.C.P.(C.), Radiation Oncology, Nuclear Medicine
HEIMBECKER, R., M.D., M.S., F.R.C.S.(C.), Surgery
HESELTINE, G. F. D., D.PSYCH., F.R.C.P. (C.), M.R.C.PSYCH., F.A.P.A., Psychiatry
HINTON, G. G., M.D.C.M., D.C.H., F.R.C.P.(C.), Paediatrics
HIRST, M., PH.D., Pharmacology
HOBKIRK, R., PH.D., D.SC., Clinical Biochemistry
HOLLENBERG, M. J., M.D., PH.D., Anatomy
HUDSON, A. J., Clinical Neurological Sciences, Medicine
INCH, W. R., PH.D., Biophysics, Radiation Oncology
JACO, N. T., M.A., B.SC., B.CH., B.M., M.R.C.P., C.R.C.P.(C.), D.C.H., Paediatrics
KAUFMANN, J. C. E., M.B., CH.B., M.R.C.PATH., Pathology and Clinical Neurological Sciences
KEERI-SZANTO, M., M.D., C.R.C.P.(C.), Anaesthesia
KERTESZ, A., M.D.C.M., B.SC.(MED.), F.R.C.P.(C.), Neurology, Clinical Neurological Sciences
LEFCOE, N. M., M.D., F.R.C.P.(C.), Medicine
LEWIS, J. A., M.D., F.R.C.P.(C.), F.A.C.P., Medicine
LINTON, AL., M.B., CH.B., C.R.C.P.(C.), Medicine
MCANINCH, L. N., M.D., F.R.C.S.(C.), F.A.C.S., Surgery
MCCARTER, J. A., M.A., PH.D., F.R.S.C., Cancer Research
MCCREDIE, J. A., M.B.B.CH., B.A.O., M.CH., F.R.C.S.(C.), F.A.C., Surgery
MACDONALD, J. C. F., M.A., PH.D., Radiation Oncology
MCDONALD, J. W. D., M.D., PH.D., F.R.C.P.(C.), Medicine
MCFARLANE, R. M., M.D., M.SC., F.R.C.S.(C.), F.A.C.S., Surgery
MCKINNA, A. J., M.D.C.M., Ophthalmology
MCLACHLIN, A. D., M.D., M.SC., D.PHIL., M.S., F.R.C.S.(C.), F.R.C.S.(ENG.), F.A.C.S., Surgery
MCMURRAY, W. C., PH.D., Biochemistry
MACPHERSON, C. F. C., M.SC., PH.D., Psychiatry
MCWHINNEY, I. R., M.B., B.CH., M.D., M.R.C.P., Family Medicine
MANNING, G. W., M.A., M.D., PH.D., F.R.C.P.,(C.) Medicine
MARTIN, A. H., M.SC., PH.D., Anatomy
MERCER, P. F., D.V.M., PH.D., Physiology
MERSKEY, H. D., M.A., D.M., M.R.C.P., F.R.C.PSYCH., Psychiatry
MOGENSON, G. J., M.A., PH.D., Physiology
MONTEMURRO, D. G., M.SC., PH.D., Anatomy
MORGAN, W. K. C., M.B.CH.B., M.R.C.S., L.R.C.P., M.R.C.P., M.D., F.R.C.P., F.A.C.P., Medicine
MURRAY, R. G. E., M.D.C.M., M.A., F.R.S.C., Microbiology and Immunology
PEERLESS, S. J., M.D., F.R.C.S.(C.), Surgery and Clinical Neurological Sciences
PERCY, D. H., D.V.M., M.SC., PH.D., Microbiology and Immunology
PHILP, R. B., PH.D., Pharmacology
PLUNKETT, E. R., M.D., PH.D., Obstetrics and Gynaecology
PRATT, G. E., M.D., C.C.F.P., Family Medicine
ROACH, M. R., M.D.C.M., PH.D., Biophysics
ROBINOW, C. F., M.D., F.R.S.C., Microbiology and Immunology
ROBINSON, J., M.SC., PH.D., Microbiology and Immunology
SANWAL, B. D., M.SC., PH.D., Biochemistry
SELLERY, G. R., M.D., D.A., M.R.C.P., Anaesthesia
SHAVER, E. L., M.SC., PH.D., Anatomy
SILVER, M., M.SC., PH.D., M.D., F.R.C.P., F.R.C.P.&S.(C.), Pathology
SINCLAIR, N. R., M.D., PH.D., Microbiology and Immunology
SINGHAL, S. K., PH.D., Microbiology and Immunology
SMITH, D. B., M.A., PH.D., Biochemistry
SMITH, D. R., M.D., F.R.C.P.(C.), Medicine
SOLTAN, H. C., PH.D., M.D., Anatomy
SPOEREL, W. E. G. A., M.D., F.R.C.P.(C.), Anaesthesia
STEELE, J. E., M.SC., PH.D., Physiology
STEWART, H. B., M.D., PH.D., Biochemistry
STREJAN, G. H., M.S., PH.D., Microbiology and Immunology
STRICKLAND, K. P., M.SC., PH.D., Biochemistry
STUART, R. K., M.D., F.R.C.P.(C.), Medicine
THOMPSON, J. M., M.D., F.R.C.P.(C.), Medicine
TILLMAN, W. A., M.D., M.SC., C.R.C.P.(C.), F.A.P.A., Psychiatry
TOOGOOD, J. H., M.D., F.R.C.P.(C.), Medicine
TREVITHICK, J. R., PH.D., Biochemistry
TURNER, R. J., PH.D., Epidemiology and Preventive Medicine
TUSTANOFF, E. R., M.S., PH.D., Clinical Biochemistry
VALBERG, L. S., M.D., M.SC., F.R.C.P.(C.), F.A.C.P., Medicine
VALENTINE, G. H., M.B., CH.B., M.R.C.S., M.R.C.P., D.C.H., F.A.A.P., F.R.C.P.(C.), Paediatrics
WALKER, I. G., M.A., PH.D., Biochemistry
WALKER, J. B., M.D., F.R.C.P.(C.), M.R.C.P., Medicine
WALLACE, A. C., M.D., F.A.C.P., F.R.C.P.(C.), Pathology
WANKLIN, J. M., PH.D., Epidemiology and Preventive Medicine
WARREN, B. A., D.PHIL., M.A., F.R.C.P.A., Pathology
WHITBY, J. L., M.A., M.B., B.CHIR., M.R.C.P., D.T.M. and H., C.R.C.P.(C.), Microbiology and Immunology
WOLFE, B. M., B.M., M.CH., M.SC., F.R.C.P.(C.), Medicine
ZAJIC, J. E., M.S., PH.D., J.D., Microbiology and Immunology
ZARFAS, D. E., M.D.C.M., D.PSYCH., F.R.C.P.(C.), Psychiatry

Faculty of Law:
ARNOLD, B. J., J.D.
BARTON, P. G., LL.M.
BRANDT, G. J., LL.B., M.A.
FRIDMAN, G. H. L., M.A., LL.M.
GORSKY, M. R., B.A., LL.B., LL.M.
HOLLAND, D. C., M.A.
HUNTER, I. A., LL.B.
MACKAY, R. S., Q.C., LL.M.
MCLAREN, R. H., LL.M.

MARTIN, R. I., LL.M.
OOSTERHOFF, A. H., LL.M.
PALMER, E. E., M.A., LL.M.
RAYNER, W. B., LL.M.
SAMUELS, J. W., LL.M.
SLAYTON, P., M.A.

Faculty of Engineering Science:
BEECKMANS, J. M., M.A.S.C., PH.D., P.ENG.
BERGOUGNOU, M. A., PH.D., F.C.I.C., P.ENG.
BROWN, J. D., PH.D., P.ENG.
BULANI, W., M.SC., PH.D., P.ENG.
CASTLE, G. S. P., M.SC., PH.D., D.I.C., P.ENG.
CHESS, G. F., M.ENG., PH.D., P.ENG.
DAVENPORT, A. G., M.A., M.A.SC., PH.D., F.R.S.C., P.ENG.
DICKINSON, S. M., PH.D., C.ENG., P.ENG.
EMMERSON, G. S., M.SC., PH.D., P.ENG.
FOREMAN, J. E. K., M.M.E., P.ENG.
INCULET, I. I., M.SC., F.I.E.E., P.ENG.
KOSARIC, N., M.E.SC., PH.D., P.ENG.
LO, K. Y., M.SC., D.I.C., PH.D., P.ENG.
NOVAK, M., PH.D., P.ENG.
NOWAK, E. S., M.S.M.E., PH.D., P.ENG.
POUCHER, M. P., D.I.C., M.SC., P.ENG.
QUIGLEY, R. M., M.A.SC., PH.D., P.ENG.
SULLIVAN, J. L., M.SC., PH.D., P.ENG.
VICKERY, B. J., M.E.SC., PH.D., M.I.AUST.

School of Business Administration:
ARCHIBALD, T. R., M.B.A., PH.D.
BRITNEY, R. R., D.B.A.
CROOKELL, H., M.B.A., PH.D.
DI STEFANO, J. J., M.B.A., M.A., PH.D.
FRY, J. N., M.B.A., PH.D.
GRINDLAY, A., M.B.A., PH.D.
HAEHLING VON LANZENAUER, C., PH.D.
HODGSON, R. C., M.SC., D.B.A.
JOHNSTON, C. B., M.B.A.
LEENDERS, M., M.B.A., D.B.A.
LITTLE, B., D.B.A.
MARTIN, S. A., M.B.A., D.B.A.
MIKALACHKI, A., M.B.A., PH.D.
NICHOLSON, J. T., D.B.A.
PEACH, D. A., D.B.A.
SHAW, D. C., M.B.A., PH.D., C.A.
THAIN, D. H., M.B.A., D.B.A.
WETTLAUFER, J. J., M.B.A., LL.D.
WOOD, A. R., M.B.A., D.B.A.

Faculty of Education:
BEATTY, H. W., M.E.D., Technological Studies
BOYD, J. A., English and Modern Languages
CASAUBON, T. J., English and Modern Languages
DOW, M. R., M.A., English and Modern Languages
GUTTERIDGE, D., English and Modern Languages
HARPER, F. B., Psychology and Sociology
KALUZA, H. J., Business and Computer Studies
KENNEY, K. W., M.ED., Mathematics
LAMBERT, G. R., M.A., History and Comparative Education
LANGMAN, R. C., M.A., Social Science
LAWSON, G. B., Mathematics
MCMURRAY, J. G., M.A., PH.D., Educational Psychology
MILBURN, G., M.A., Social Science
PROCUNIER, E. R., M.A., English and Modern Languages
SLEMON, A. G., Educational Psychology
SMALLBRIDGE, J. E., M.A., English and Modern Languages
WEBBER, H. D., Science
WEST, N. W., Physical and Health Education
WHITE, J. H., M.M., Fine Arts Education

School of Library and Information Science:
CAMERON, W. J., PH.D.
NEILL, S. D., M.ED.
PRODRICK, R. G., M.A., M.S.
TAGUE, J., PH.D.
WHITE, J. H., M.L.S.

Faculty of Nursing:
COX, B. A., M.SC., PH.D.
MANTLE, J. H., M.NURS.
WOOD, V., E.D.M.

Faculty of Physical Education:
CARRON, A. V., M.A., ED.D.
CUNNINGHAM, D. A., M.S., PH.D.
FAIRS, J. R., M.A.
L'HEUREUX, W. J., M.A., LL.D.
LEYSHON, G. A., M.S., PH.D.
SKINNER, J., M.S., PH.D.
YUHASZ, M. S., M.S., PH.D.
ZEIGLER, E. F., M.A., PH.D.

School of Journalism:
MACFARLANE, A. W., B.A.
WILD, J. L., M.A.
WILSON, H. R., M.A., PH.D.

AFFILIATED INSTITUTIONS:

Huron College: London, Ontario N6G 1H3; f. 1863; Arts and Theological College.
Principal: Rev. J. G. MORDEN, D.TH., D.D., S.T.M.

Brescia College: London, Ontario N6G 1H2; f. 1919; arts subjects.
Dean: Sr. DOLORES KUNTZ, M.A., PH.D.

King's College: London, Ontario N6A 2M3; f. 1912 (Seminary), 1955 (College); Seminary and College of Arts.
Principal: J. D. MORGAN, M.A., PH.D.

WILFRID LAURIER UNIVERSITY

WATERLOO, ONTARIO N2L 3C5

Telephone: (519) 884-1970.

Founded 1911; formerly Waterloo Lutheran University; name changed 1973.

Language of instruction: English; State control; Academic year: September to May (two terms).

Chancellor: The Hon. JOHN B. AIRD.
President and Vice-Chancellor: Dr. NEALE H. TAYLER.
Vice-President (Academic): Dr. JOHN A. WEIR.
Vice-President (Administration and Finance): J. PETER VENTON.
Registrar and Secretary of Senate: J. W. T. WILGAR.
Librarian and Archivist: Rev. E. R. W. SCHULTZ.

Number of teachers: 208 full-time, 232 part-time.

Number of students: 3,436 full-time, 6,000 part-time.

Publications: *Calendars, The Campus* (quarterly), *President's Memo* (weekly), *The Cord* (weekly).

DEANS:

Faculty of Arts and Science: Dr. RUSSELL W. MUNCASTER.
Waterloo Lutheran Seminary: Rev. Dr. DELTON J. GLEBE.
Faculty of Social Work: Dr. SHERMAN MERLE.
Faculty of Graduate Studies: Dr. ANDREW BERCZI.
Faculty of Music: Dr. GORDON GREENE.
School of Business and Economics: Dr. MAX D. STEWART.

DEPARTMENT CHAIRMEN:

BONGART, K. H., PH.D., German
BORRAS, A. A., PH.D, Romance Languages
FINLAY, J. R., PH.D., Economics
GRANSKOU, D., TH.D., School of Religion and Culture
GUENTHER, M. G., PH.D., Sociology and Anthropology
HARKINS, J., PH.D., History
HAYASHIDA, K., PH.D., Biology
HELLER, R. A., PH.D., Chemistry
KILGOUR, D. M., Mathematics
KURUVILLA, P. K., PH.D., Political Science
LIT, J., D.SC., Physics
LITKE, R. F., Philosophy
MACLEAN, H. A., PH.D., Classics
MORGAN, R., PH.D., Psychology
PARSON, HELEN E., PH.D., Geography (acting)
PROUT, H. W., PH.D., Business Administration
WALLER, G. F., PH.D., English

UNIVERSITY OF WINDSOR

WINDSOR, ONTARIO N9B 3P4

Telephone: 253-4232.

Founded 1857.

Provincially assisted; Language of instruction: English; Academic year: September to May (2 semesters).

Chancellor: Maj.-Gen. RICHARD ROHMER, D.F.C., B.A., LL.D.
Vice-Chancellor and President: MERVYN FRANKLIN, PH.D.
Vice-President Academic: P. CASSANO, M.A., PH.D.
Vice-President Administration: J. R. ALLAN, A.M., PH.D.
Registrar: F. L. SMITH, M.ED.
Librarian: A. V. MATE, A.M., A.M.L.S. (acting).

Number of teachers: 515 (full-time).

Number of students: 15,510 (full- and part-time).

Publications: *The Lance*† (weekly), *The Ambassador*†, *Windsor University Magazine*† (quarterly), *Student Handbook*†, *The President's Report*†, *Review*†, *General Calendar*† (annually).

DEANS:

Faculty of Arts: J. F. SULLIVAN, PH.D. (acting).
Faculty of Social Science: W. G. PHILLIPS, M.A., PH.D.
Faculty of Science and Mathematics: C. P. GRAVENOR, M.S., PH.D.
Faculty of Engineering: C. MACINNIS, PH.D.
Faculty of Business Administration: M. ZIN, PH.D.
Faculty of Education: A. STUART NEASE, M.A.

Faculty of Graduate Studies and Research: C. P. J. CROWLEY, M.A., PH.D.
Faculty of Law: R. W. IANNI, Q.C., PH.D.
Faculty of Human Kinetics: R. T. HERMISTON, PH.D.

PROFESSORS:

Faculty of Arts:

BERTMAN, S., PH.D., Classical Studies
BIRD, H. W., PH.D., Classical Studies
BROWN, J. V., PH.D., Philosophy
BUTLER, E. G., D.M.A., Music
CASSANO, P., PH.D., French
CROWLEY, C. P., PH.D., English
CROWLEY, E. J., S.T.L., S.S.L., Religious Studies
CULLITON, J. T., PH.D., Religious Studies
CUNNINGHAM, S. B., PH.D., Philosophy
DELAURO, J. N., M.F.A., Visual Arts
DITSKY, J. M., PH.D., English
DOCTOR, A. P., M.F.A., Visual Arts
DUCHARME, E. W., PH.D., English
FANTAZZI, C., PH.D., Classical Studies, Italian
FLOOD, P. F., PH.D., Philosophy
HOFFMAN, J. C., PH.D., TH.D., Religious Studies
HUANG, R., PH.D., English
JOHNSON, R. H., PH.D., Philosophy
KELLY, D. P., M.A., Dramatic Art
KINGSTON, F. T., D.PHIL., Philosophy
LEDDY, J. F., Q.C., D.PHIL., D.LITT., D. ès L., LL.D., D.C.L., Classical Studies
LEWIS, J. U., PH.D., Philosophy
MCINTYRE, P. P., MUS.DOC., Music
MCNAMARA, E., PH.D., English
NIELSEN, H. A., PH.D., Philosophy
SMEDICK, L., PH.D., English
SMITH, J. C., M.A., English
SMITH, R., PH.D., English
SPELLMAN, J. W., PH.D., Asian Studies
STEVENS, P., PH.D., English
STOLLMAN, S. S., PH.D., English
SULLIVAN, J. F., PH.D., English
SUTTOR, T. L., PH.D., Religious Studies
WIEDEN, F., PH.D., Germanic and Slavic Studies

Faculty of Social Science:

AULD, F., PH.D., Psychology
BALANCE, W. D., PH.D., Psychology
BARNES, J., D.S.W., Social Work
BLACKBOURN, A., PH.D., Geography
BRIGGS, E. D., PH.D., Political Science
BROWN, A. A., PH.D., Economics
BROWN-JOHN, C. L., PH.D., Political Science
BUNT, M. E., PH.D., Psychology
CARNEY, T. F., PH.D., Communication Studies
CERVIN, V. B., PH.D., Psychology
CLARKE, H. D., PH.D., Political Science
EDMUNDS, H. H., M.ED., Communication Studies
FALLENBUCHL, Z. M., PH.D., Economics
FEHR, R. C., PH.D., Psychology
FORTUNE, J. N., PH.D., Economics
GILLEN, W. J., M.A., Economics
GRAVENOR, C. P., M.S., PH.D., Geography
GUCCIONE, A., PH.D., Economics
HALL, NANCY, M.SC., Home Economics
HELLING, R. A., PH.D., Sociology
INNES, F. C., PH.D., Geography
JOWETT, G. S., PH.D., Communication Studies
KAPLAN, M. L., PH.D., Psychology
KOBASIGAWA, A., PH.D., Psychology
KOVACS, A. E., PH.D., Economics
KROEKER, B. J., M.S.W., Social Work
LAGAIPA, J., PH.D., Psychology
LEDUC, L., PH.D., Political Science
LIBBY, W. L., M.B.A., PH.D., Psychology
MCCRONE, K. E., PH.D., History
MALONE, J. A., PH.D., Psychology
MINER, J. N., PH.D., History
MINTON, H. L., PH.D., Psychology
MOORE, S., M.S.W., Social Work
MORROW, HARRY M., M.S.W., Social Work
MOURATIDES, A. I., PH.D., History
NAMIKAS, G. A., PH.D., Psychology
NELSON, R. C., PH.D., Political Science
O'FARRELL, J. K. A., PH.D., History
PHILLIPS, W. G., PH.D., Economics
PRADHAN, M. C., PH.D., Anthropology
PRIMORAC, E., M.COMM., PH.D., Economics
PRYKE, K. G., PH.D., History
RAMACHARAN, S., PH.D., Sociology
RANSOME, J. C., PH.D., Geography
REYNOLDS, D. V., PH.D., Psychology
ROMANOW, W. I., PH.D., Communication Studies
ROURKE, B. P., PH.D., Psychology
SANDERSON, M. E., PH.D., Geography
SAUTTER, U., PH.D., History
SCHNEIDER, F. W., PH.D., Psychology
SELBY, S. A., M.A., ED.D., Communication Studies
SMITH, A. A., PH.D., Psychology
SODERLUND, W. C., PH.D., Political Science
STRICK, J. C., PH.D., Economics
TRENHAILE, A. S., PH.D., Geography
WAGENBERG, R. H., PH.D., Political Science
WHITEHURST, R. N., PH.D., Sociology
WURFEL, D., PH.D., Political Science

Faculty of Science and Mathematics:

(Some professors are also attached to the Faculty of Engineering)

ATKINSON, H. R., PH.D., Mathematics
BAYLIS, W. E., D.SC., Physics
BENEDICT, W. G., PH.D., Biology
CHANDNA, O. P., PH.D., Mathematics
CHANNEN, E. W., PH.D., Computer Science
COTTER, D. A., PH.D., Biology
DEMARCO, F. A., PH.D., Chemistry
DOYLE, R. J., PH.D., Biology
DRAKE, G. W., PH.D., Physics
DRAKE, J. E., PH.D., Chemistry
DUGGAL, K. L., PH.D., Mathematics
FRANKLIN, M., PH.D., Biology
GRAVENOR, C. P., M.S., PH.D., Geology
GUPTA, A., M.SC.N., Nursing
HABOWSKY, J. E. J., PH.D., Biology
HELBING, R. K. B., DR.RER.NAT., Physics
HOLLAND, W. J., PH.D., Chemistry
HOLUJ, FRANK, PH.D., Physics
HUDEC, P. P., PH.D., Geology
KALONI, P. N., PH.D., Mathematics
KRAUSE, L., PH.D., Physics
KREYSZIG, E., M.SC., PH.D., Mathematics
LASKER, G. E., PH.D., Computer Science
LEMIRE, F. W., PH.D., Mathematics
MCCONKEY, J. W., PH.D., Physics
MCCURDY, H. D., PH.D., Biology
MCDONALD, J. F., PH.D., Mathematics
MCGARVEY, B. R., PH.D., Chemistry
MODERWELL, M. K., M.ED., Nursing
PETRAS, M. L., PH.D., Biology
PILLAY, D. T. N., PH.D., Biology
PRICE, S. J. W., PH.D., Chemistry
RUTHERFORD, K. G., PH.D., Chemistry
SABINA, L. R., PH.D., Biology
SCHLESINGER, M., PH.D., Physics
SHENG, C. L., PH.D., Computer Science
SHKLOV, N., M.A., Mathematics
SMITH, A. C., PH.D., Mathematics
SMITH, T. E., PH.D., Geology
SONNENFELD, P., DR.RER.NAT., Geology
SYMONS, D. T. A., PH.D., Geology
SZAMOSI, G., PH.D., D.SC., Physics
TAYLOR, N. F., D.PHIL., Chemistry
THIBERT, R. J., PH.D., Chemistry
TRACY, D. S., PH.D., Mathematics
TUCK, D. G., PH.D., D.SC., Chemistry
TUREK, A., PH.D., Geology
VAN WIJNGAARDEN, A., PH.D., Physics
WARNER, A., PH.D., Biology
WIGLEY, N. M., PH.D., Mathematics
WONG, C. S., PH.D., Mathematics
WOOD, G. W., PH.D., Chemistry
ZISCHKA, K. A., D.SC., Mathematics

Faculty of Business Administration:

BASIC, E. M., PH.D.
BIRCH, C. M., PH.D.
BROWNLIE, J. M., M.B.A.
COWAN, R. K., PH.D.
FIELD, G. A., PH.D.
LAM, W. P., PH.D.
LAU, C., PH.D.
MURRAY, J. A., PH.D.
PATON, W. A., PH.D.
RAGAB, M. A., PH.D.
ROSENBAUM, E., PH.D.
ZIN, M., PH.D.

Faculty of Education:

NEASE, A. S., M.A.

Faculty of Engineering:

ABDEL-SAYED, G., DR. ING., Civil Engineering
BEWTRA, J. K., PH.D., Civil Engineering
BILLINGHURST, R. G., M.A.SC., Engineering Materials
CHEE, S. P., PH.D., Civil Engineering
COLBORNE, W. G., M.SC., Mechanical Engineering
GNYP, A. W., PH.D., Chemical Engineering
HACKAM, R., PH.D., Electrical Engineering
HARTT, J. P., M.S.C.E., Civil Engineering
JULLIEN, G. A., PH.D., Electrical Engineering
KENNEDY, D. J. L., M.S., PH.D., Civil Engineering
KENNEDY, J. B., PH.D., Civil Engineering
LABA, J. T., PH.D., Civil Engineering
MCCORQUODALE, J. A., PH.D., Civil Engineering
MCDONALD, T. W., PH.D., Mechanical Engineering
MACINNIS, C., PH.D., Civil Engineering
MILLER, W. C., PH.D., Electrical Engineering
MONFORTON, G. R., PH.D., Civil Engineering
NORTH, W., PH.D., Mechanical Engineering
NORTHWOOD, D. O., PH.D., Engineering Materials
QURESHI, A., PH.D., Electrical Engineering
RAOUF, A., PH.D., Industrial Engineering
REIF, Z. F., PH.D., Mechanical Engineering
ST. PIERRE, C. C., PH.D., Chemical Engineering
SHRIDHAR, M., PH.D., Electrical Engineering
SRIDHAR, K., PH.D., Mechanical Engineering
STAGER, R. A., PH.D., Chemical Engineering
YOUDELIS, W. V., PH.D., Engineering Materials

Faculty of Human Kinetics:

DUTHIE, J. H., PH.D.
EAVES, C. G., PH.D.
FRACAS, G., B.ED., M.A.
GALASSO, P. J., PH.D.
HERMISTON, R. T., PH.D.
METCALFE, A., PH.D.
MORIARTY, R. J., M.ED., PH.D.
THOMAS, P., PH.D.

Faculty of Law:
BROWN, R. E., Q.C., LL.B.
BUSHNELL, I. S., LL.M.
IANNI, R. W., Q.C., B.COMM., LL.B., PH.D.
KERR, R. W., LL.M.
MCAULIFFE, J. W., B.S., M.B.A., LL.M., J.D.
MANZIG, J. G., DR.IUR.
MARASINGHE, M. L., LL.M.
MARTIN, P., P.C., Q.C., LL.D.
STEWART, G. R., LL.M.
WHITESIDE, J. W., Q.C., B.A.

FEDERATED UNIVERSITY:

Assumption University: 400 Huron Church Rd., Windsor, Ont.
President: D. G. HEATH, C.S.B., B.A., S.T.B., D.ED.

AFFILIATED COLLEGES:

Canterbury College: 172 Patricia Rd., Windsor, Ont.
Principal: Rev. F. T. KINGSTON, M.A., L.TH., B.D., D.PHIL.

Holy Redeemer College: Cousineau Rd., Windsor, Ont.
Principal: Rev. D. L. EGAN, C.SS.R., S.T.L.

Iona College: Sunset Ave., Windsor, Ont.
Principal: Dr. J. C. HOFFMAN, PH.D., TH.D.

UNIVERSITY OF WINNIPEG

515 PORTAGE AVE.,
WINNIPEG, MANITOBA R3B 2E9
Telephone: 786-7811.

Founded 1871; University status 1967.

Controlled jointly by the Government of Manitoba and the United Church of Canada; Language of instruction: English; Academic year: September to April.

Chancellor: R. O. A. HUNTER, LL.D.
President and Vice-Chancellor: H. E. DUCKWORTH, O.C., PH.D., D.SC., LL.D., F.R.S.C.
Vice-President: J. CLAKE, PH.D.
Registrar: R. M. BELLHOUSE, B.SC.
Librarian: R. C. WRIGHT, B.A., B.L.S.

Number of teachers: 175.
Number of students: 2,231 men, 3,246 women, total 5,477.

DEANS:

Arts and Science: D. W. KYDON, M.SC., PH.D.
Collegiate: JOHN VANDERSTOEL, M.ED.
Theology: Rev. A. M. WATTS, PH.D.

DEPARTMENTAL CHAIRMEN:

Faculty of Arts and Science:
ANDREW, W. K., M.A., Psychology
BARTH, F. W., M.SC., PH.D., Chemistry
BEDFORD, A. G., M.A., PH.D., English
BENDOR-SAMUEL, B., M.A., D.U., French
CAMPBELL, W. C., B.A., Mathematics
CHEAL, D. J., PH.D., Sociology
DAMUS, R. S., M.A., Economics
DUFF, J. F. K., M.SC., Physics
GRAHAM, T. E., M.A., PH.D., Religious Studies
HEIDERICH, M. W., M.A., PH.D., German
KEENAN, B. M., M.A., PH.D., Philosophy
MCDOUGALL, J. I., M.A., Classics
MEIKLEJOHN, C., PHIL.M., PH.D., Anthropology
RICHTIK, J. M., M.A., PH.D., Geography
STEIN, W. J., M.A., PH.D., History
VEATCH, S. R., M.A., PH.D., Political Science
WOODS, R. A., M.A., D.PHIL., Biology

PROFESSORS:

BARTH, F. W., M.SC., PH.D., Chemistry
BATZEL, V. M., M.A., PH.D., History
BEDFORD, A. G., M.A., PH.D., English
CAMPBELL, W. C., B.A., Mathematics
CHEKKI, D. A., LL.D., PH.D., Sociology
CLAKE, J., PH.D., Psychology
DUFF, J. F. K., M.SC., Physics
DYCK, D. R., M.S., PH.D., History
EVANS, B. M., M.A., PH.D., Geography
FARAG, F. F., PH.D., English
HAMILTON, K. M., M.A., B.D., TH.M., TH.D., Religious Studies
HOFLEY, J. R., M.A., PH.D., Sociology
HOGG, B. G., M.A., PH.D., F.R.S.C., Physics
HUTTON, H. M., M.SC., PH.D., Chemistry
KERR, D. P., M.SC., PH.D., Physics
KHAN, R. A., M.A., PH.D., Political Science
KRÜÜNER, M. R., M.A., PH.D., English
KYDON, D. W., M.SC., PH.D., Physics
LOEWEN, H., M.A., PH.D., Mennonite Studies
MORRISON, W. A., M.A., PH.D., Sociology
NEWCOMBE, C. R., B.D., S.T.M., PH.D., Religious Studies
REIMER, E. E., M.A., PH.D., English
RUTHERFORD, H. V., PH.D., History
RYAN, J., M.ED., M.A., PH.D., Geography
SIEMENS, L. G., M.A., PH.D., English
STEIN, W. J., M.A., PH.D., History
STEVENS, W. M., M.A., PH.D., History
SWAYZE, W. E., M.A., PH.D., English
THIESSEN, J., PH.D., German
TOMCHUK, E., M.SC., PH.D., Physics
WANAMAKER, M. G., M.A., ED.D., English
WOODS, R. A., M.A., D.PHIL., Biology

ATTACHED INSTITUTE:

Institute of Urban Studies: 515 Portage Ave., Winnipeg; Dir. C. D. MCKEE, B.SC.

YORK UNIVERSITY

4700 KEELE ST., DOWNSVIEW,
ONTARIO M3J 1P3
Telephone: 667-2100.

Founded 1959, independent 1965.

Public control; Language of instruction: English (Glendon College: English and French); Academic year: September to April.

Chancellor: Hon. JOHN P. ROBARTS, Q.C.
President and Vice-Chancellor: H. I. MACDONALD, B.COMM., M.A., B.PHIL., LL.D.
Vice-President (Finance and Development): G. G. BELL, M.B.E., C.D., M.A., PH.D.
Vice-President (University Services): W. W. SMALL, M.A.
Vice-President (Employee and Student Relations): W. D. FARR, M.A.
Vice-President (Academic): W. FOUND, M.A., PH.D.
Registrar: M. A. BIDER, M.A.
Director of Libraries: ANNE WOODSWORTH.

Number of teachers: 1,034.
Number of students: 28,000.

Publications: *Communiqué*† (quarterly), *The Bulletin* (daily), *The York Gazette*† (twice monthly), *Gazette Supplement*† (annually).

DEANS:

Administrative Studies: W. B. CROWSTON, S.M., PH.D.
Arts: H. KAPLAN, PH.D.
Environmental Studies: R. D. SCHWASS, ED.D.
Fine Arts: (vacant).
Graduate Studies: G. F. REED, M.A., M.LITT., PH.D.
Law: S. M. D. BECK, B.A., LL.M.
Science: O. R. LUNDELL, PH.D.
Education: R. L. R. OVERING, M.A., PH.D.
Joseph E. Atkinson College: H. CROWE, M.A.
Glendon College: D. L. MCQUEEN, M.A., PH.D. (Principal).

PROFESSORS:

Faculty of Administrative Studies:
BLACKMORE, W. R., M.SC., PH.D., Management Science
BURKE, R. J., M.A., PH.D., Behavioural Science
CROWSTON, W. B., S.M., PH.D., Management Science
DALY, D. J., M.A., PH.D., Economics
DIXON, B., M.COMM., PH.D., Policy and Environment
FARRIS, G. F., M.A., PH.D., Behavioural Science
FRIEDLAND, S., M.B.A., PH.D., Finance
GILLIES, J. M., M.A., PH.D., Policy and Environment
JORDAN, W. A., M.S., PH.D., Economics
KUHN, T. E., PH.D., Economics
LITVAK, I. A., M.S., PH.D., Policy and Environment
MACDONALD, H. I., M.S., LL.D., Economics
MAYER, C. S., M.B.A., PH.D., Marketing
MOYER, M. S., M.B.A., PH.D., Marketing
PETERSON, R., M.B.A., PH.D., Management Science
READ, W. H., M.A., PH.D., Behavioural Science
ROSEN, L. S., M.B.A., PH.D., Accounting
SHAW, G. C., S.M., PH.D., Management Science
TAYLOR, M. G., M.A., PH.D., LL.D., Policy and Environment
THOMPSON, D. N., M.B.A., PH.D., Marketing
WARNER, S. L., PH.D., Economics
ZOHAR, U., M.A., PH.D., Economics

Faculty of Arts:
AGNEW, N. MCK., M.A., PH.D., Psychology
ANSTIS, S. M., PH.D., Psychology
ARGYLE, B., PH.D., English
BAKAN, D., A.M., PH.D., Psychology
BAR-LEWAW, I., M.A., PH.D., Foreign Literature
BERRY, R. T., M.A., PH.D., English
BLAISE, C. A., M.F.A., Humanities
BLISHEN, B. R., M.A., Sociology
BLOORE, R., A.M., Humanities
BLUM, A. F., M.A., PH.D., Sociology
BOSHER, J. F., PH.D., History
BOURAOUI, H. A., A.M., PH.D., French Literature and Language Studies

BURNS, R. G., PH.D., Mathematics
BUTTRICK, J. A., M.A., PH.D., Economics
CH'EN, J., M.A., PH.D., History
CLUETT, R., A.M., PH.D., English
COLLIE, M., M.A., English
COOK, G. R., M.A., PH.D., History and Social Science
COONS, W. H., M.A., PH.D., Psychology
COSENTINO, F., M.A., PH.D., Physical Education
COWLEY, G. F., M.A., PH.D., Philosophy
COX, R. W., M.A., Political Science
CREAL, K. H. M., M.A., S.T.B., Humanities
CUFF, R. D., A.M., PH.D., History
DANZIGER, K., M.SC., D.PHIL., Psychology
DAVEY, F. W., M.A., PH.D., English
DAVIES, D. I., M.A., PH.D., Sociology
DAVIS, J. T., M.A., PH.D., Geography
DAY, H. I., M.A., PH.D., Psychology
DOXEY, G. V., B.SC., M.A., Economics
EAGLE, M. N., M.A., PH.D., Psychology
EISEN, S., PH.D., History
ELKIN, F., M.A., PH.D., Sociology
ENDLER, N. S., M.SC., PH.D., Psychology
ERNST, J. A., M.A., PH.D., History
FLAKIERSKI, H., D.ECON., Social Science
FLOCK, H. R., A.M., PH.D., Psychology
FOUND, W. C., M.A., PH.D., Geography
FROMKIN, H. L., M.S., PH.D., Psychology
FUSÉ, T., M.A., PH.D., Social Science
GAITO, J., A.M., PH.D., Psychology
GIBSON, J. R., M.A., M.S., PH.D., Geography
GIRLING, H. K., M.A., English
GRANATSTEIN, J. L., M.A., PH.D., History
GRIFFIN, E. G., A.M., PH.D., English
GULLIVER, P. H., PH.D., Anthropology
GUTSELL, B. V., B.A., Geography
HEIDENREICH, C., M.A., PH.D., Geography
HENRY, F., M.A., PH.D., Anthropology
HERTZMAN, L., A.M., PH.D., History
HOCKIN, T. A., M.P.A., PH.D., Political Science
HOWARD, I. P., PH.D., Psychology
ISHWARAN, K., M.A., PH.D., M.S.S., D.LITT., Sociology
JAFFE, W., D. EN D., Economics
JARVIE, I. C., PH.D., Philosophy
KAPLAN, H., PH.D., Political Science
KARRASS, A., M.S., PH.D., Mathematics
KATZ, M., M.A.T., ED.D., History
KAY, M., M.A., Language Arts
KELLMAN, M., M.S., PH.D., Geography
KILBOURN, W. M., M.A., A.M., PH.D., Humanities
KOLKO, G., PH.D., History
LANPHIER, O. M., A.M., PH.D., Sociology
LEFEBER, L., PH.D., Economics
LEISS, W., M.A., PH.D., Political Science
LORCH, L., M.A., PH.D., Mathematics
LOWTHER, G. M. A., Anthropology
MCCORMACK, T. H., B.A., Sociology
MCFARLAND, J. D., M.A., D.PHIL., Philosophy
MCHUGH, P., M.A., PH.D., Sociology
MANDEL, E. W., M.A., PH.D., Humanities
MASSAM, B., M.A., PH.D., Social Science and Geography
MAXWELL, D. E. S., PH.D., English
MEDOW, P., PH.D., Economics
MERRENS, H. R., M.A., PH.D., Geography
MOHR, J. W., M.S.W., PH.D., Sociology
MONTAGUE, J. T., M.A., PH.D., Economics
MORRIS, R., M.SOC.SC., D.PHIL., Sociology
MULDOON, M. E., M.SC., PH.D., Mathematics
MURRAY, A. L., M.A., PH.D., Social Science
MURRAY, V. V., M.A., PH.D., Sociology
NOWELL-SMITH, P. H., A.M., Philosophy
OLIN, P., PH.D., Mathematics
O'NEILL, J., B.SC., M.A., PH.D., Sociology
ONO, H., PH.D., Psychology
PARRY, H., PH.D., Classics and Humanities
PASCUAL-LEONE, J., M.A., M.D., PH.D., Psychology
PIEPENBURG, W. W., M.S., PH.D., History
PRESTHUS, R. V., M.A., PH.D., Political Science
PRICE, J. A., M.A., PH.D., Anthropology
QUARRINGTON, B. J., M.A., PH.D., Psychology
RATHÉ, C. E., M.A., PH.D., French Literature
RAYFIELD, J. R., M.A., PH.D., Anthropology
REED, G. F., M.A., M.LITT., PH.D., Psychology
RICE, L. N., M.ED., PH.D., Psychology
RICHMOND, A. H., M.A., PH.D., Sociology
ROAZEN, P., PH.D., Political Science and Social Science
ROBINSON, A. J., PH.D., Economics
ROCK, V., A.M., PH.D., English
ROWLAND, B., M.A., PH.D., English
RUSSELL, D. C., PH.D., D.SC., Mathematics
SAYWELL, J. T., M.A., PH.D., History
SCHUELER, H. J., M.A., PH.D., Languages, Literatures and Linguistics
SERMAT, V., B.A., M.S., PH.D., Psychology
SHENITZER, A., M.C., PH.D., Mathematics
SILVERMAN, I., PH.D., Psychology
SMITH, M. D., M.S., PH.D., Physical Education and Sociology
SOLITAR, D., M.A., PH.D., Mathematics
STORR, R. J., A.M., PH.D., History
TAYLOR, B. M., D.P.E., Physical Education
THOMAS, C., M.A., PH.D., English
VERNEY, D. V., M.A., PH.D., Political Science
WADDINGTON, M., M.A., M.S.W., English
WARKENTIN, J., M.A., PH.D., Geography
WARWICK, J., M.A., PH.D., French Literature and Social Science
WESTCOTT, M., A.B., M.S., PH.D., Psychology
WHITLA, W. J., M.A., S.T.B., English and Humanities
WOLFE, R. I., M.A., PH.D., Geography
WOOD, N., PH.D., Political Science

Faculty of Education:
BOWERS, J. E., ED.D.
HANDSCOMBE, R. J., M.A.
OVERING, R. L. R., M.A., PH.D.
PARRY, H., PH.D.

Faculty of Environmental Studies:
CAPPON, D., L.M.S.S.A., L.R.C.P., M.R.C.S., M.B.B.S., D.P.M., F.R.C.P. ED., F.R.C.P. CAN.
CARROTHERS, G. A. P., M.ARCH., M.C.P., PH.D., M.R.A.I.C., M.C.I.P., A.I.P., Urban Studies
CHEVALIER, M., M.C.P., PH.D., M.C.I.P., A.I.P.
COMAY, R., B.A., M.C.P., A.I.P.
DIXON, B., M.COMM., PH.D.
ELLIS, J. B., M.SC., D.I.C., PH.D.
FOUND, W. C., M.A., PH.D.
HEFFERON, D. C., B.A., LL.M.
LANG, R. S., M.SC., Environmental Studies
LIVINGSTON, J. A., B.A.
MURRAY, A. L., M.A., PH.D.
PAGE, J. E., M.SC., B.TH., PH.D., M.E.I.C. M.C.I.P., A.I.P.,
SAYWELL, J. T., M.A., PH.D.
SCHWASS, R. D., M.ED., PH.D., Environmental Studies

Faculty of Fine Arts:
BEVERIDGE, J. A., B.A., Film
BLOORE, R., M.A., Visual Arts
GREEN, J. G., M.A., PH.D., Theatre
HEINRICH, T. A., M.LITT., PH.D., LL.D., Visual Arts
HENRY, J., Theatre
MANUPELLI, G., B.S., M.A., ED.D., Visual Arts
MOORE, M., D.LITT., Theatre
MORTON, D., A.R.C.A., Visual Arts
STRATE, G., B.A., LL.B., Dance
VOLAVKA, Z., PH.D., C.SC., Visual Arts

Osgoode Hall Law School (formerly independent):
ANGUS, W. H., B.A., LL.M.
ANISMAN, P., LL.M., J.S.D.
ARTHURS, H. W., B.A., LL.M.
BAUM, D. J., B.A., LL.M., J.S.D.
BECK, S. M. D., B.A., LL.M.
BLANCHARD, J. T., LL.M.
CASTEL, J.-G., B.SC., LIC. EN DROIT, LL.B., S.J.D.
CULLITY, M. C., LL.B., B.C.L.
CUMMING, P. A., LL.M.
EVANS, J. M., B.A., B.C.L.
GLASBEEK, H. J., B.A., LL.B., J.D.
GRANT, A., LL.B.
GRAY, R. J. S., B.A., LL.M.
HALEVY, B. J., LL.B., M.C.L., M.S. IN L.S.
HASSON, R. A., B.A., LL.M.
HEFFERON, D. C., B.A., LL.M.
HOGG, P. W., LL.M., PH.D.
JOHNSON, J. M., B.A., LL.B.
MOHR, J. W., PH.D., M.S.W.
PARKER, G. E., LL.M.
PECK, S. R., LL.B., M.A.
SPENCE, D. B., Q.C., M.A., LL.M.
TARNOPOLSKY, W. S., A.M., LL.M.
WATSON, G. D., LL.M.
WEILER, P. C., M.A., LL.M.
WEISSTUB, D. N., M.A., J.D.
WILSON, H. T., M.A., PH.D.
ZEMANS, F. H., B.A., LL.B.

Faculty of Science:
ASPINALL, G. O., PH.D., D.SC., Chemistry
BOHME, D. K., PH.D., Chemistry
BOYER, M. G., M.S.A., PH.D., Biology
CARRINGTON, T., PH.D., Chemistry
CARSWELL, A. I., M.A., PH.D., Physics
COLMAN, B., PH.D., Biology
DAVEY, K. G., M.SC., PH.D., Biology
DUGAN, C. H., M.A., PH.D., Physics
DULEY, W. W., D.I.C., PH.D., Physics
FORER, A., PH.D., Biology
FOWLE, C. D., M.A., PH.D., Biology
FRIESEN, J. D., M.A., PH.D., Biology
FRISKEN, W. R., M.SC., PH.D., Physics
GOODINGS, J. M., PH.D., Chemistry
HAYNES, R. H., PH.D., Biology
HÉBERT, G. R., M.SC., PH.D., Physics
HEDDLE, J. A. M., PH.D., Biology
HOBSON, R. M., PH.D., Physics
INNANEN, K. A., M.SC., PH.D., P.ENG., Physics
KATZ, M., M.SC., PH.D., D.SC., Chemistry
LAFRAMBOISE, J. G., M.A., PH.D., Physics
LEVER, A. P. B., A.R.C.S., PH.D., D.I.C., Chemistry
LUNDELL, O. R., PH.D., Chemistry
MADRAS, S., PH.D., Chemistry
MCEACHRAN, R. P., M.SC., PH.D., F.INST.P., Physics
MEGAW, W. J., D.SC., Physics
MOENS, P. B., M.A., PH.D., Biology
NICHOLLS, D. M., M.SC., PH.D., M.D., Biology
NICHOLLS, R. W., A.R.C.S., PH.D., D.SC., F.INST.P., Physics
PRITCHARD, H. O., M.SC., PH.D., D.SC., Chemistry
SALEUDDIN, A. S. M., M.SC., PH.D., Biology
SCHIFF, H. I., M.A., PH.D., Chemistry
SHEPHERD, G. G., M.SC., PH.D., Physics
SMYLIE, D. E., M.A., PH.D., Physics
SOKOLOFF, J., M.S., PH.D., Physics

Atkinson College:

- Beattie, E. J., B.ED., M.A., Social Science
- Carter, W. B., M.A., PH.D., Philosophy
- Coleman, W. R., M.A., S.T.M., D.D., Humanities
- Crowe, H. S., M.A., History
- Crysdale, S., TH.M., M.A., PH.D., Sociology
- Davies, J. H., M.A., Economics
- Eaton, G. E., PH.D., Economics and Political Science
- Fann, K. T., M.A., PH.D., Philosophy
- Herren, M., PH.D., Humanities
- Kater, M. H., M.A., D.PHIL., History
- Keehn, J. D., M.A., PH.D., Psychology*
- MacKinnon, V. S., M.A., LL.M., S.J.D., Social Science
- Mann, W. E., M.A., PH.D., Sociology
- Radford, K. J., M.A., Administrative Studies
- Rajagopal, P., M.A., M.SC., PH.D., Computer Science and Mathematics
- Reed, G. F., M.A., M.LITT., PH.D., Psychology
- Smyth, D. McC., M.A., M.PHIL., PH.D., Social Science
- Sowton, I., M.A., English
- Wood, J. D., M.A., PH.D., Geography

* Also affiliated with the Faculty of Science

Glendon College:

- Appathurai, E. R., M.A., PH.D., Political Science
- Bakker, B. A., M.A., PH.D., French
- Baudot, A., D.E.S., French and Humanities
- Burnet, J., M.A., PH.D., Sociology
- Cohen, R. L., FIL.LIC., FIL.DR., Psychology
- Escobar, J., DR. EN FIL. Y LET., Spanish
- Gregory, M. J., M.A., P.D.E.S.L., English
- Handscombe, R. J., M.A., P.D.E.S.L., English
- Harris, H. S., M.A., PH.D., Humanities and Philosophy
- McQueen, D. L., M.A., PH.D., Economics
- Penner, N., M.A., PH.D., Political Science
- Robertson, H. S., A.M., PH.D., French
- Tucker, A. V., M.A., PH.D., History
- Willmott, D. E., M.A., PH.D., Sociology

Attached Institutes:

Institute for Behavioural Research: 242 Administrative Studies Building, York University, 4700 Keele St., Downsview, Ont. M3J 2R6; Dir. A. Richmond.

Centre for Research in Experimental Space Science: 211 Petrie Science Building, York University, 4700 Keele St., Downsview, Ont. M3J 1P3; Dir. Ralph W. Nicholls.

Centre for Research on Environmental Quality: T118 Steacie Science Library, York University, 4700 Keele St., Downsview, Ont. M3J 2R3; Dir. William J. Megaw.

York Transport Centre: 431 Osgoode Hall Law School, York University, 4700 Keele St., Downsview, Ont. M3J 2R5; Dir. William C. Found, M.A., PH.D. (acting).

SCHOOLS OF ART AND MUSIC

Alberta College of Art: 1301 16th Ave. N.W., Calgary, Alta. T2M 0L4; f. 1926; a division of the Southern Alberta Inst. of Technology; 52 teachers, 640 students; library of 6,500 vols. and collection of 52,000 slides; 4-year diploma in visual arts; Head Kenneth Sturdy.

Banff Centre School of Fine Arts: P.O.B. 1020, Banff, Alta. T0L 0C0; f. 1933; a division of Banff Centre for Continuing Education; courses in visual and performing arts, theatre crafts; summer courses: painting, drawing, sculpture, theatre arts, music, photography, ballet, crafts, creative writing; Dir. D. S. R. Leighton.

Conservatoire de Musique de Montréal: 100 est rue Notre-Dame, Montreal H2Y 1C1; f. 1942; a government-controlled institution, largest of a network of seven in Quebec Province; 60 teachers, 300 students; library of 7,100 books, 45,000 scores, 100 rare books, 20 MSS. and 7,300 recordings; Dir. Albert Grenier.

Conservatoire de Musique de Québec: 270 St.-Amable, Quebec, Que. G1R 5G1; f. 1944; Dir. Armando Santiago.

Maritime Conservatory of Music: 5920 Gorsebrook Ave., Halifax, N.S. B3H 1G2; f. 1887.

Secretary: Mrs. Reta Harroun.

Ontario College of Art: 100 McCaul St., Toronto, Ont. M5T 1W1; f. 1876; library of 18,000 vols.; post-secondary education in fine art and design.

Number of teachers: 150.

Number of students: 1,250.

President: Dr. P. D. Fleck.

Royal Canadian College of Organists: f. 1909; Sec./Treas. T. J. Hillier, MUS.BAC., 212 King St. W., Suite 300A, Toronto, Ont. M5H 1K5.

Royal Conservatory of Music: University of Toronto, 273 Bloor St. W., Toronto M5S 1W2, Ont.; f. 1886.

Principal: Ezra Schabas, M.A.

Royal Hamilton College of Music: 126 James St. South, Hamilton, Ont.; f. 1897; vocal, instrumental, dance, art and jazz studies; 6,000 students; Principal Jon Watts.

CENTRAL AFRICAN REPUBLIC

Population 2,370,000

LEARNED SOCIETIES AND RESEARCH INSTITUTES

Centre d'Etudes sur la Trypanosomiase Animale: B.P. 39, Bouar; stations at Bewiti, Sarki; annexe at Bambari.

Centre de Recherche et d'Etude des Populations: B.P. 969, Bangui; affiliated to Union Douanière et Economique de l'Afrique Centrale.

Institut d'Etudes Agronomiques d'Afrique Centrale: Ecole Nationale des Adjoints Techniques d'Agriculture de Wakombo, B.P. 78, M'Baiki; Dir. R. ELIARD.

Institut Français du Café et du Cacao (IFCC): B.P. 44, M'Baiki, Boukoko; regional centres at Nola, Kombo; library shared with *Institut de Recherches Agronomiques:* Dir. M. PICOT.

Institut de Recherches Agronomiques de Boukoko (*Agricultural Research Institute*): B.P. 44, M'Baiki, Boukoko; f. 1948; research into tropical agriculture and plant diseases, fertilization and entomology; library of 2,740 vols.; Dir. M. GONDJIA.

Institut National de Recherches Textiles et Cultures Vivrières: B.P. 995, Bangui; central research station at Bambari; Dir. P. BIANZA.

Institut Pasteur: B.P. 923, Bangui; f. 1961; research on enterovirus and arbovirus, influenza and rabies; 7 scientific staff; Dir. Dr. J. FABRE; publ. *Rapport Annuel*†.

Mission sociologique du Haut-Oubangui: B.P. 68, Bangassou; f. 1954; archaeological discoveries from Nzakara and Zandé districts; historical maps and sociological documents; Head Prof. E. DE DAMPIERRE; publ. *Recherches oubanguiennes* (irregular).

Office de la Recherche Scientifique et Technique Outre-Mer: B.P. 893, Bangui; f. 1948; soil science, geophysics, medical entomology, ethnolinguistics; library of 1,730 vols.; 17 researchers and technicians; Dir. J.-P. COINTEPAS. (*See* main entry under France.)

Station Expérimentale de la Maboké: par M'Baiki; f. 1963 under the direction of the Muséum National d'Histoire Naturelle, Paris; studies in the protection of materials in tropical regions, mycology, entomology, virology, zoology, botany, anthropology, parasitology, protection of natural resources; Dir. ROGER HEIM.

UNIVERSITY

UNIVERSITÉ DE BANGUI

B.P. 1450, BANGUI

Telephone: 61-20 00.

Founded 1969.

Language of instruction: French; Academic year: October to June.

Vice-Chancellor: J. LOUIS MOURALIS.

Secretary-General: FODE KEITA.

Librarian: CHRISTIANE CHASTAINGT.

Number of teachers: 123.

Number of students: 1,489.

Publication: *Annales.*

DEANS:

Faculty of Letters and Humanities: M. F. SEHOULIA.

Faculty of Law and Economic Sciences: J. M. BRETON.

Faculty of Sciences: V. KHARINE.

Faculty of Medicine: M. SIOPATHIS.

DIRECTORS:

University Institute of Business Administration: C. ALBAGLI.

University Institute for Research in Mathematics Teaching: HENRI MAGDALEMA.

University Institute of Mining, Geology and Construction Technology: RADU CIOCARDEL.

University Institute of Agronomy and Forestry: NGUYEN-VU.

Institute of Applied Language Studies: Mme. G. PRIGNITZ.

COLLEGES

Ecole Centrale d'Agriculture: Boukoko.

Ecole Nationale des Arts: B.P. 349, Bangui; f. 1966; music, dance, dramatic art and plastic arts.

Ecole Territoriale d'Agriculture: Grimari.

CHAD*

Population 4,405,000

RESEARCH INSTITUTES

Bureau pour le Développement de la Production Agricole: B.P. 745, N'Djamena.

Centre Culturel Américain: B.P. 3, N'Djamena.

Centre de Documentation Pédagogique: B.P. 731, N'Djamena; f. 1962; library of 2,500 vols. (in French), 670 vols. (in Arabic); Dir. A. SEKIMBAYE; publ. *Revue Pédagogique Tchadienne.*

Institut de Recherches du Coton et des Textiles Exotiques (IRCT): B.P. 764, N'Djamena; f. 1939; cotton research (entomology, agronomy and genetics); Head of station at Bebedja M. LABOUCHEIX; Regional Dir. C. MÉGIE.

Institut National des Sciences Humaines (I.N.S.H.): B.P. 503, N'Djamena; f. 1961; palaeontology, prehistory, proto-history, linguistic history, ethno-sociology, anthropology, geography, demography, economics, oral traditions; archives and museum; library of 3,196 vols. and 3,544 documents; Dir. LAURENT LAOUKISSAM FECKOUA; Gen. Sec. DANYO NABATINGAR ETIENNE; publs. *I.N.S.H.—Informations*†, *Etudes et Documents Tchadiens*† (irregular).

Institut d'Elevage et de Médecine Vétérinaire des Pays Tropicaux: Laboratoire de Farcha, B.P. 433, N'Djamena; f. 1959; veterinary and zootechnical research and production of vaccines; 15 scientists; library of 1,500 vols.; Dir. Dr. Y. CHENEAU; publ. *Rapport annuel*†.

Office de la Recherche Scientifique et Technique Outre-Mer: B.P. 85225, N'Djamena; geology, soil science, hydrology, hydrobiology; library; Dir. A. CHOURET. (*See* main entry under France.)

Station de Recherche Bardai: Tibesti; f. 1965; geographical station of the Free University of Berlin undertaking research in desert geomorphology; assisted by Berlin Research Association; Dir. Dr. J. HÖVERMANN.

MUSEUM

Musée National: B.P. 503, N'Djamena; f. 1963; attached to Institut National des Sciences Humaines (*see* above).

UNIVERSITY

UNIVERSITÉ DU TCHAD

B.P. 1117, N'DJAMENA

Telephone: 21-76.

Founded 1971; State control; Language of instruction French; Academic year: October to June.

Rector: TIMOTHÉE NGAKOUTOU.
Secretary-General: MBAIKILA DJIMASNGAR.
Librarian: NGAOUDANDI DJAOKAMLA.

Library of 12,000 vols.
Number of teachers: 65.
Number of students: 800.
Publications: *Annuaire, Annales.*

DEANS:

Faculty of Letters and Human Sciences: G. B. S. LAUMAI.
Faculty of Sciences: G. MOYA.
Faculty of Law and Economics: (vacant).
University Institute of Stockbreeding: Dr. J. THIBAUD.

COLLEGES

Ecole Nationale d'Administration: B.P. 768, N'Djamena; f. 1963; set up by the Government and controlled by an Administrative Council to train students as public servants; Dir. N. GUELINA.

Ecole Nationale des Télécommunications: Sarh.

*No new information has been received this year.

CHILE

Population 11,010,000

ACADEMIES

Instituto de Chile (*Institute of Chile*): Almirante Montt 453, Clasificador 1349, Correo Central, Santiago; f. 1964 to promote cultural, humanistic and scientific studies at the highest level; it is composed of the following six Academies: Chilean Academy; Academy of History; Academy of Sciences; Academy of Medicine; Academy of Social, Political and Moral Sciences; Academy of Fine Arts (*q.v.*). The Presidency rotates every 3 years between the Presidents of the Academies.

President: Dr. AMADOR NEGHME.

General Secretary: Dr. ALEJANDRO GARRETÓN SILVA.

Publications: *Boletín*†, Monograph series†.

Academia Chilena (*Chilean Academy*): Almirante Montt No. 453, Clasificador 1349, Correo Central, Santiago; f. 1885; sixth in order of foundation in Spanish America; corresp. mem. of the Real Academia Española, Madrid; 24 mems.; Dir. Dr. RODOLFO OROZ SCHEIBE; Sec. FIDEL ARANEDA BRAVO.

Academia Chilena de la Historia (*Academy of History*): Clasificador 1349, Santiago; f. 1933; 36 mems.; Pres. EUGENIO PEREIRA S.; publs. *Boletín*†, Book Series†.

Academia de Ciencias: Instituto de Chile, Clasificador 1349, Santiago; f. 1964; 18 Academicians, 3 corresp., 4 hon. Academicians; promotes research in pure and applied sciences; Pres. JORGE MARDONES RESTAT; Sec. Dr. ADELINA GUTIERREZ ALONSO; publ. *Boletín*† (irregular).

Academia de Medicina (*Academy of Medicine*): Clasificador 1349, Santiago; f. 1964; promotes research in medicine and health sciences education; 31 Academicians, 20 hon. foreign mems.; library of 500 vols.; Pres. Dr. AMADOR NEGHME; publs. *Boletín*†, monographs†.

Academia de Bellas Artes (*Academy of Fine Arts*): Clasificador 1349, Santiago; promotes cultural and creative activities; Pres. DOMINGO SANTA CRUZ W.; publ. *Boletín*.

Academia de Ciencias Sociales, Politicas y Morales (*Academy of Social, Political and Moral Sciences*): Clasificador 1349, Santiago; Pres. ROBERTO MUNIZAGA AGUIRRE; publs. Monographs.

LEARNED SOCIETIES

AGRICULTURE

Sociedad Agronómica de Chile (*Agronomical Society of Chile*): Casilla 4109, Santiago; f. 1910; *c.* 2,000 mems.; library of 1,200 vols.; Pres. ADRIANA PINTO DE TORRES; Sec. FRANCISCO VEGA A.; publ. *Simiente* (quarterly).

Sociedad de Medicina Veterinaria de Chile (*Chilean Veterinary Society*): Clasificador 740, Santiago; f. 1926; 600 mems.; Pres. Dr. Dr. MIGUEL PONCE; Sec. Dr. CAMILO URBINA; publ. *Revista*.

Sociedad Nacional de Agricultura (*National Society of Agriculture*): Casilla 40-D, Santiago; f. 1838; library of 50,000 vols.; research in agricultural, social and economic problems; controls a plant genetics experimental station and a broadcasting chain with stations in three cities; register of pedigree cattle kept; annual industrial and agricultural show since 1869; Pres. GERMÁN RIESCO ZAÑARTU; Sec. RAUL GARCÍA ASTABURUAGA; publ. *El Campesino*.

ARCHITECTURE

Colegio de Arquitectos de Chile (*Chilean College of Architects*): Avda. Libertador Bernardo O'Higgins 115, Casilla 13377, Santiago de Chile; f. 1942 for all Chilean and foreign architects working in Chile; *c.* 3,500 mems.; library of 1,000 vols., 2,000 journals; Pres. Arq. CARLOS ALIAGA LAFRENTZ; Sec.-Treas. Arq. HUGO FERREIRA SEPÚLVEDA; publs. *Revista* (quarterly), *Boletín* (monthly).

BIBLIOGRAPHY AND LIBRARY SCIENCE

Colegio de Bibliotecarios de Chile: Casilla 3741, Santiago; f. 1969; 1,200 mems.; Pres. M. TERESA SANZ; Sec.-Gen. RAQUEL DE LA FUENTE; publs. *Boletín*† (quarterly), monographs and documentation series†, *Noticias* (monthly), *Indices de Publicaciones Periódicas en Bibliotecología* (every 2 months).

Sociedad de Bibliófilos Chilenos (*Society of Chilean Bibliophiles*): Casilla 895, Santiago; f. 1945; Pres. ALAMIRO DE AVILA; Sec. RAMÓN EYZAGUIRRE; 100 mems.; publ. *El Bibliófilo Chileno* (annual).

ECONOMICS, LAW AND POLITICS

Asociación Judicial de Chile (*Law Society of Chile*): Santo Domingo 1373, Santiago.

Instituto Latinoamericano de Planificación Económica y Social (*Latin American Institute for Economic and Social Planning*): United Nations, Avda. Dag Hammarskjöld, Casilla 1567, Santiago; f. 1962; provides technical assistance to Latin American govts., training for govt. officials and research on planning techniques; acts as technical Secretariat of the System of Co-operation among Planning Bodies of Latin American countries; Dir. JORGE MÉNDEZ; publs. *Notebooks, Texts, Planning Bulletin*.

Instituto Médico Legal (*Institute of Forensic Medicine*): Av. La Paz 1012, Santiago.

EDUCATION

Consejo de Rectores de Universidades Chilenas (*Council of Rectors of Chilean Universities*): Moneda 673, 8° piso, Casilla 14798, Santiago; f. 1954; study of higher education problems, university information and co-ordination; Pres. AGUSTÍN TORO DÁVILLA; Gen. Sec. JAIME SANTIBAÑEZ GUARELLO; publs. *Documentos, Cuadernos, Boletines Informativos*.

Oficina Regional de Educación de la Unesco para América Latina y el Caribe (*Unesco Regional Office for Education in Latin America and the Caribbean*): P.O.B. 3187, Enrique Delpiano 2058, Santiago; f. 1969; provides technical assistance to regional member states in preparation and implementation of educational plans; trains teachers and specialists in education and administration; organizes a conference of Ministers of Education of the region; library of 11,834 vols; Dir. GUILLERMO FERNANDEZ S. (acting); publs. *Boletín de Educación* (2 a year), *Boletín Bibliográfico* (monthly), *Informaciones Estadísticas de la Educación y Análisis Cuantitativo* (irregular).

HISTORY, GEOGRAPHY AND ARCHAEOLOGY

Instituto Geográfico Militar (*Military Geographical Institute*): Nueva Santa Isabel 1640, Santiago; f. 1922; official govt. body for maps, geographical surveys, etc.; 507 mems.; library of 3,500 vols., 3,000 maps; Dir. Col. CRISTIAN ALVAREZ SGOLIA; publs. *Anuario* (every 5 years), *Boletín Informativo*† (quarterly).

Sociedad Chilena de Historia y Geografía (*Chilean Society of History and Geography*): Casilla 1386, Santiago; f. 1911; 250 mems., 10 hon., 60 corresponding; library of 12,000 vols.; Pres. HUMBERTO BARRERA VALDEBENITO; Sec.-Gen. MANUEL REYNO GUTIERREZ; publs. *Revista Chilena de Historia y Geografía*, related works.

INTERNATIONAL CULTURAL INSTITUTES

British Council: Casilla 154-D, Santiago; Representative A. C. RAMSAY.

Instituto Chileno-Alemán de Cultura (*Chilean-German Cultural Institute*): Casilla 1050, Santiago; f. 1952; library of 15,773 vols.; Dir. Dr. KLAUS FERKINGHOFF.

Instituto Chileno-Alemán de Cultura (Goethe Institut) (*German-Chilean Cultural Institute*): Casilla 979, Viña del Mar; f. 1960; cultural and language teaching activities; library of 6,800 vols.; Dir. Dr. KLAUS FERKINGHOFF.

Instituto Chileno-Británico: Casilla 929, Viña del Mar; f. 1938; cultural and language teaching activities; library of 9,000 vols.; Dir. PATRICIA MONCKTON.

Instituto Chileno-Francés de Cultura: Agustinas 719, Casilla 3567, Santiago; Dir. JEAN DEDIEU.

Instituto Chileno-Norteamericano de Cultura: Calle Moneda 1467, Casilla 9286, Santiago; f. 1938; library of 18,000 vols.; Admin. Dir. E. VICTOR NIEMEYER, Jr.

Institut Culturel Franco-Chilien: Casilla 3081, Colo Colo 1, Concepción; f. 1950; for the promotion of the French language; arranges films, conferences and lectures; 300 mems.; library of 2,700 vols.; Pres. Dr. RENÉ LOUVEL; Dir. Prof. ROBERT GIANNONI; publ. *Information Bulletin* (half yearly).

Instituto de Estudios Interamericanos (*Institute of Inter-American Studies*): Mesa Central Huérfanos, 1147, pisos 8 and 9, Santiago.

Istituto Italiano di Cultura: Calle Huérfanos, 1828, Santiago; Dir. Prof. FRANCO VENTURINI.

LANGUAGE AND LITERATURE

Sociedad Chilena de Lingüística (*Chilean Linguistics Society*): Casilla 9803, Santiago; f. 1971; over 80 mems.; Pres. AMBROSIO RABANALES; Sec. MARIO BERNALES; publ. *Actas*.

MEDICINE

Colegio de Químico-Farmacéuticos de Chile (*College of Pharmacists*): Casilla 1136, Santiago; f. 1942; Pres. MARIO MARTINEZ AHUMADA; regional councils in Antofagasta, Chillán, Concepción, Iquique, Magallanes, Santiago, La Serena, Talca, Temuco, Valdivia, Valparaíso; 2,500 mems.; publ. *Revista*.

Sociedad Chilena de Cardiología y Cirugía Cardiovascular: Esmeralda 678, Casilla 23-D, Santiago; f. 1949; Pres. Dr. JUAN P. VICUÑA; Sec. Dr. JORGE MERUANE.

Sociedad Chilena de Gerontología (*Chilean Gerontological Society*): Avda. Bulnes 377, Dpto. 605, Santiago; f. 1961; 40 mems.; Pres. Dr. JOSÉ FROIMOVICH S.; Sec. Dr. GUSTAVO ROJAS M.

Sociedad Chilena de Hematología: Esmeralda 678, Casilla 23-D, Santiago; f. 1943; 80 mems.; Pres. Dr. CARLOS REGONESI LONGERI; Sec. Dr. PABLO LIRA VERGARA.

Sociedad Chilena de Nutrición, Bromatología y Toxicología: Vicuña Mackenna 20, Casilla 6084, Santiago; f. 1943; 120 mems.; Pres. IRMA PENNACCHIOTTI M.; Sec. VALENTINA PARRAGUIRRE A.; publs. *Nutrición, Bromatología y Toxicología* (quarterly).

Sociedad Chilena de Parasitología: Esmeralda 678, 2° piso, Casilla Postal 5227, Correo 3, Santiago; f. 1964; 150 mems.; Pres. Dr. WERNER APT B.; Sec. Dr. CARLOS PÉREZ B.; publ. *Revista Médica de Chile* (annually).

Sociedad Chilena de Reumatología: Casilla 23-D, Santiago; f. 1950; Pres. Dr. GONZALO ASTORGA P.; Sec. Dr. ALBERTO VALDÉS S.; publ. *Boletín*† (quarterly).

Sociedad Médica de Concepción (*Medical Society*): Casilla 60-C, Concepción; f. 1886; Pres. Dr. ENRIQUE BELLOLIOZ; publ. *Anales Médicos de Concepción*.

Sociedad Médica de Santiago (*Santiago Medical Society*): Casilla 23-D, Santiago; f. 1869; library 20,000 vols.; Pres. Dr. MARTA VELASCO; Sec. JORGE PFAU; 950 mems.; publ. *Revista Médica de Chile* (monthly).

Sociedad Médica de Valparaíso (*Medical Society of Valparaíso*): Av. Brasil 1689, Valparaíso; f. 1913; library, 3,500 vols.; Pres. Dr. ELIAS BITRAN; Sec. Dr. GUILLERMO RIOS S.; 271 mems.; publ. *Revista Médica de Valparaíso* (quarterly).

Sociedad de Oftalmología de Valparaíso (*Ophthalmological Society of Valparaíso*): Plaza A. Pinto 341, Valparaíso; f. 1928; Pres. Dr. JORGE DUCLOS; Sec. Dr. ARMANDO H. CHAPPARO.

Sociedad de Pediatría de Valparaíso (*Paediatrics Society of Valparaíso*): Avda Brasil 1689, Valparaíso; f. 1932; Pres. Dr. HERNÁN BRITO B.; Sec. Dr. RUY PEYSER; 45 mems.

Sociedad Odontológica de Concepción: Casilla 2107, Concepción; f. 1924; 300 mems.; Pres. Dr. EDUARDO NAVARETE; Sec. Dr. SERGIO ESQUERRÉ S.; publ. *Anuario*†.

NATURAL SCIENCES

General

Academia Chilena de Ciencias Naturales (*Chilean Academy of Natural Sciences*): Medinacelli 1233, Santiago; f. 1926; Pres. Dr. HUGO GUNCKEL L.; Sec. HANS NIEMEYER F.; publ. *Anales*.

Sociedad Chilena de Historia Natural (*Chilean Society of Natural History*): Casilla 787, Santiago; f. 1926; Pres. Dr. RENÉ COVARRUBIAS; Sec. GUMERSINDO REVUELTA; publ. *Revista Chilena de Historia Natural*.

Sociedad Científica de Chile (*Scientific Society of Chile*): Rosa Eguiguren 813, Casilla 696, Santiago; f. 1891; Pres. Prof. Dr. HUGO K. SIEVERS W.; Gen. Sec. Prof. Dr. AGUSTÍN ARRIAGADA V.; publ. *Revista de Ciencias*.

Sociedad Científica Chilena "Claudio Gay" (*Chilean Scientific Society*): Casilla 2974, Santiago; f. 1946; 143 mems.; Dir. LUIS E. PEÑA.

Biological Sciences

Asociación Chilena de Microbiología: Casilla 10409, Santiago; f. 1964; Pres. Dr. MANUEL RODRIGUEZ-LEIVA; Sec. Dr. SILVIA MENDOZA G.

Sociedad Chilena de Entomología (*Entomological Society*): P.O.B. 21132, Santiago 1; f. 1922; Pres. MIGUEL CERDA G.; Vice-Pres. LUIS E. PEÑA G.; Sec. LUIS CARTAGENA; 175 mems.; publ. *Revista Chilena de Entomología*.

Sociedad de Biología de Chile: Casilla 16164, Santiago 9; f. 1928; Pres. Dr. EDUARDO BUSTOS; Sec. Dr. CARLOS VALENZUELA; publs. *Archivos de Biología y Medicina Experimentales.*

Sociedad de Genética de Chile: Instituto de Ecología y Evolución, Universidad Austral de Chile, P.O.B. 57-D, Valdivia; f. 1964; 100 mems.; Pres. Dr. EDUARDO DEL SOLAR; Sec. Dr. HECTOR GARCÍA.

Mathematics and Statistics

Instituto Nacional de Estadísticas (*Statistical Office*): Casilla 7597, Correo 3, Santiago; f. 1843; library of 25,000 vols.; Dir. SERGIO CHAPARRO RUIZ; publs. *Anuarios Estadísticos, Boletín* (2 a year), *Síntesis Estadística* (monthly), *Compendio Estadístico* (annually), censuses and monthly indices.

Physical Sciences

Asociación Chilena de Sismología e Ingeniería Antisísmica (*Chilean Association of Seismology and Anti-seismic Engineering*): Beauchef 851, Casilla 2777, Santiago; f. 1963; Pres. RODRIGO FLORES A.; Sec. PETER WELKNER M.

Comisión Chilena de Energía Nuclear: Salvador 1318, Casilla 188-D, Santiago; f. 1965; library of 5,000 vols., 140,000 reports; Pres. Ing. ROMUALDO PIZARRO SEYMOUR; Exec. Dir. Ing. JUAN MIR DUPOY.

Comité Oceanografico Nacional: Casilla 324, Valparaíso; f. 1971; coordinates all oceanographic activities in the country; Pres. Capt. MARIANO A. SEPULVEDA; Exec. Sec. Ing. BERNARDO UCCELLETTI; publ. *Ciencia y Tecnología del Mar*† (2 a year).

Instituto Hidrográfico de la Armada (*Hydrographic Institute of the Navy*): Casilla 324, Valparaíso; f. 1874; hydrographic surveys, nautical charts, oceanography, maritime safety, coastal marking and lighthouses, national oceanographic data centre; library of 10,000 vols.; Dir. Capt. RAÚL HERRERA A.; publs. *Anuario Hidrográfico, Tablas de Mareas* (annually), *Noticias a los Navegantes* (2 a week), nautical charts, *Ciencia y Tecnología del Mar*, etc.

Liga Marítima de Chile (*Chilean Maritime League*): Avda. Errázuriz 471, Casilla 117-V, Valparaíso; f. 1914; Patron, the Pres. of the Chilean Republic; Pres. Admiral ALEJANDRO NAVARRETE TORRES; Vice-Pres. Admiral RAMÓN BARROS GONZALEZ, BARTOLOMÉ TRAVERSO CAMPOS; Sec. ALVARO RIQUELME VARGAS; 1,350 mems.; brs. in Iquique, Tocopilla, Santiago, Concepción, Tomé, Valdivia, Puerto Montt and Punta Arenas; small sea museum (Museo del Mar "Héctor Vigil"); publ. *Mar* (2 a year).

Sociedad Chilena de Física: Casilla 5487, Santiago; f. 1960; 254 mems.; Pres. CLAUDIO GONZALEZ SAMOHOD.

Sociedad Chilena de Química: Casilla de Correo 2613, Concepción; f. 1945; 1,000 mems.; library of 1,500 vols. and 400 periodicals; Pres. JOSÉ BAABOR; Sec. HERNANDO URRUTIA; publ. *Boletín* (quarterly).

Sociedad de Bioquímica de Concepción: Casilla 237, Escuela de Química y Farmacia y Bioquímica, Concepción; f. 1957; Pres. MARIO POZO LÓPEZ; Sec. FROILÁN HERNÁNDEZ CARTES.

Sociedad Geológica de Chile: Plaza Ercilla 803, Casilla 13518, Correo 21, Santiago; f. 1962; Pres. JOSÉ CORVALÁN D.; Sec.-Gen. HERNE ETCHART K.

TECHNOLOGY

Instituto de Ingenieros de Chile (*Institute of Chilean Engineers*): San Martín 352, Casilla 487, Santiago; f. 1900; publ. *Anales.*

Sociedad Nacional de Minería (*National Society of Mining*): Casilla 1807, Santiago; f. 1883; library of 4,000 vols.; Pres. NORBERTO BERNAL FUENZALIDA; publ. *Boletín Minero.*

RESEARCH INSTITUTES

AGRICULTURE

Estación Experimental "Las Vegas" de la Sociedad Nacional de Agricultura (*National Agricultural Society Experimental Station*): Huelquen-Paine, Santiago; library of 1,000 vols.; f. 1924; Dir. RAUL MATTE VIAL; publ. *El Campesino* (monthly).

Instituto Agrario de Estudios Económicos (INTAGRO): Tenderini 187, Casilla 13907, Santiago; f. 1960; research in agricultural, social and economic problems; gives scientific assistance to farmers and farmers' societies; Dir. BRAULIO FERNÁNDEZ V., J. E. CORREA BULNES; publs. monographs and studies on agro-economic problems.

Instituto de Investigaciones Agropecuarias: Casilla 5427, Santiago; f. 1964; conducts research on soils, plant breeding, animal production, fruit culture, irrigation; 170 research workers; library: *see* Libraries; Exec. Dir. EMILIO MADRID C.; "La Platina" Agricultural Experiment Station, Dir. ANGELA URBINA C.; "Carillanca" Agricultural Experiment Station, Dir. HERNÁN RIQUELME R.; "Quilampu" Agricultural Experiment Station, Dir. CARLOS LAGOS S.; "Remehue" Agricultural Experiment Station, Dir. VIRGILIO COZZI T.; "Kampenaike" Agricultural Experiment Station, Dir. HECTOR DOBERTI N.; publs. *Agricultura Técnica* (quarterly), *Memoria Anual, Investigación y Progreso Agrícola* (annually), *Boletín Técnico, Boletín Divulgativo* (irregular).

Instituto Forestal (*Forestry Institute*): Huérfanos 554, Casilla 3085, Santiago; f. 1961; research and advice in all aspects of forestry; staff of 70; library of 3,800 vols.; Dir. JULIO PONCE LEROU; publs. *Boletín estadístico*† (annual), technical bulletins and notes†, various information sheets, maps and plans† (irregular).

MEDICINE

Fundación Gildemeister: Augustinas esq. Amunátegui 178, 5° piso, Casilla 99-D, Santiago; f. 1947 to co-operate with public or private institutions, universities, etc., in medical research and particularly in the diffusion of the technique of thoracic surgery, cardiology, neurology and neurosurgery; Pres. WALTER PIZA; Hon. Sec. JULIA COHEN; publ. *Revista-Memoria.*

Instituto Bacteriológico de Chile (*Chilean Bacteriological Institute*): Casilla 48, Santiago; f. 1929; headquarters of national health laboratory system; centre for health research and personnel training; 720 mems.; library of 3,360 vols.; Dir. JOAQUÍN LARRAÍN; publ. *Boletín.*

Instituto de Medicina Experimental del Servicio Nacional de Salud (*Institute of Experimental Medicine of the National Health Service*): Av. Irarrázaval 849, Casilla 3401,

Santiago; f. 1937; physiology, neuroendocrinology and cancer research; 15 mems.; library of 6,200 vols.; Dir. Dr. SERGIO YRARRÁZAVAL; Chief Sec. Mrs. BERTA IRIBIRRA.

NATURAL SCIENCES

General

Instituto Científico de Lebu: Apdo. 123, Lebu; f. 1945; research in the field of marine biology, history and geography of Arauco; library of 22,000 vols.; Dir. Prof. A. ZAPATA BARRA; Sec.-Gen. A. SANTOS MUÑOZ.

Instituto de Fomento Pesquero (*Fishery Research Institute*): José Domingo Cañas 2277, Casilla 1287, Santiago; f. 1963 for research into fisheries and development in the fields of Biology, Economy, Technology; 200 staff; library of 2,250 vols.; Exec. Dir. ROBERTO CABEZAS B.; publs. *Boletín Científico, Circular, Publicación, Investigacion Pesquera*†, *Informes Pesqueros*†.

Instituto Nacional de Investigación de Recursos Naturales (*National Institute for Research in Natural Resources*): Casilla 14995, Correo Central, Santiago; f. 1964; a self-financing governmental body, attached to the *Corporación de Fomento de la Producción* (CORFO) of the Ministry of Economic Affairs; provides technical aid for CORFO and similar bodies; draws up plans for the better use of natural resources; maintains a national Information Centre; aims to improve and develop methods of research; 37 staff; library of 3,000 vols., 700 documents; Exec. Dir. Col. ENRIQUE JUNEMANN MARDONES; publ. *Bibliografía de Recursos Naturales*† (annually).

Biological Sciences

Estación de Biología Pesquera: Casilla 492, San Antonio; f. 1961; Dir. SERGIO AVILÉS G.

Physical Sciences

Comité Nacional de Geografía, Geodesia y Geofísica (*National Geographical Geodetic and Geophysical Committee*): Nueva Santa Isabel 1640, Santiago; f. 1935 to encourage and co-ordinate research in the fields mentioned; 119 mems.; Pres. Col. CRISTIAN ALVAREZ SGOLIA; Sec. Col. OCTAVIO FLORES CASTELLI; publ. *Terra Australis*† (annually).

Instituto Antártico Chileno: Luis Thayer Ojeda 814, Casilla 16521, Correo 9, Santiago; f. 1963; a centre for technological and scientific development on matters relating to the Antarctic; 1,350 vols. and 400 periodicals; Dir. HERNAN LORCA FULLER; publs. *Serie Científica*† (annually), *Boletín de Difusión*† (annually).

Instituto de Investigaciones Geológicas—IIG: Agustinas 785, 6° piso, Casilla 10465, Santiago; f. 1957; 147 mems.; geological mapping and research; library of 3,000 vols., 450 periodicals, also unpublished papers, maps, photos; Dir. RAÚL SALAS OLIVARES; publs. *Carta Geológica de Chile*†, *Boletín*†, *Revista Geológica de Chile*†.

Observatorio Astrofísico "Manuel Foster" (*Observatory of the Catholic University of Chile*): Casilla 6014, Santiago; f. 1904; for stellar spectrography, photometry, and mechanics; 8 mems.; 4,500 vols. in library; Dir. ERICH PAUL HEILMAIER; Sub. Dir. BERNADO STARISCHKA.

Observatorio Astronómico Nacional (*National Astronomical Observatory*): Casilla 36-D, Santiago; f. 1853; attached to the Universidad de Chile; Repsold Meridian circle, Transit instrument, Gauthier refractor astrograph, Heyde visual refractor, Danjon astrolabe, Bamberg and Zeiss transit instruments; astronomical station at Cerro El Roble and radio-astronomical observatory at Maipú; library of 6,000 vols.; Dir. Prof. HUGO MORENO; publ. *Publicaciones*†.

Observatorio Europeo Austral (*European Southern Observatory ESO*): Casilla 16317, Correo 9, Santiago; f. 1962; astronomical observatory of the European Organization for Astronomical Research in the Southern Hemisphere; situated on top of Cerro La Silla at an altitude of 2,400 m. in Province of Coquimbo, 600 km. north of Santiago; main field of research is photometry and spectrography of southern hemisphere astronomical objects, especially the Galactic Centre region and the Magellanic Clouds; facilities for member-astronomers and occasionally for non-mems.; equipment: 360-cm. telescope operating in prime focus (f/3), Cassegrain focus (f/8) and coudé focus (f/30); 152-cm. spectrographic telescope with f/15 Cassegrain spectrograph and f/30 coudé spectrograph; 100-cm. f/15 photometric telescope with general purpose photoelectric photometer and polarimeter; 50-cm. f/15 photometric telescope; double 40-cm. astrograph with objective prism; 100/162/300-cm. Schmidt telescope with objective prisms; Swiss 40-cm., Bochum 61-cm. and Danish 150- and 50-cm. telescopes; Dutch 90-cm telescope. (*See* also International—Science.)

Observatorio Interamericano de Cerro Tololo (*Cerro Tololo Inter-American Observatory*): Casilla 603, La Serena; f. 1963; astronomical observation of stars only observable in the southern hemisphere; library of 10,900 vols.; Dir. Dr. VICTOR M. BLANCO.

Oficina Meteorológica de Chile (*Meteorological Bureau*): Dirección Meteorologica de Chile, Casilla 717, Santiago; f. 1884; meteorology, climatology and hydrology; 170 mems.; library of 8,000 vols.; 106 meteorological stations; 66 synoptic stations; 62 termo-rain gain stations; 554 rain grain stations; 4 radiosonde stations, 1 geomagnetic observatory (Easter Island), 12 atmospheric radioactivity observatories; Dir. Col. SERGIO BRAVO FLORES; publs. *Boletín Diario del Tiempo, Boletín Pluviométrico Mensual, Anuarios Meteorológicos*†, occasional scientific publs.

TECHNOLOGY

Comisión Nacional de Investigación Científica y Tecnológica (CONICYT) (*National Commission for Scientific and Technological Research*): Casilla 297-V, Santiago; f. 1969; governmental agency in charge of studying, planning and proposing national scientific and technological policy to the govt. and developing, promoting and improving science and technology; Pres. MANUEL PINOCHET S.; Exec. Sec. GUILLERMO RAMIREZ R.; publs. *La Semana Científica y Tecnológica*† (weekly), irregular study reports, documentation reports and annual reports.

Instituto de Investigaciones y Ensayes de Materiales (IDIEM) Universidad de Chile (*Institute for Materials Research and Testing*): Plaza Ercilla 883, Casilla 1420, Santiago; f. 1898; library of 5,500 vols.; Dr. Ing. Don A. LAMANA POLA; publ. *Revista*† (3 a year).

Instituto Nacional de Normalización (*National Institute of Standardization*): Casilla 995, Correo 1, Santiago; f. 1944; library of 5,000 vols.; Dir. Ing. PEDRO VILASECA P.

LIBRARIES AND ARCHIVES

Santiago

Dirección General de Bibliotecas, Archivos y Museos: Alameda 651; f. 1813; Dir. ENRIQUE CAMPOS MENÉNDEZ.

Archivo Nacional (*National Archives*): Av. Bernardo O'Higgins y MacIver; f. 1927; Historic and Public Administration, comprising collections of related MSS. documents; 150,000 vols.; also repository of 300,000 judicial records; Dir. JAVIER GONZÁLEZ ECHENIQUE; Archivist SERGIO GALLARDO R.; publs. catalogues, inventories, etc.

Biblioteca Central de la Universidad de Chile: Calle Arturo Prat 23, Casilla 10-D; f. 1936; contains more than 200,000 vols., comprising donations from Canada, Great Britain, the United States and Spain, and from private collections, including those of Pedro Montt and Alejandro Fuenzalida Grandón; there are 40 other libraries in the University with an aggregate of 1,000,000 vols.; Dir. of Central Library ALAMIRO DE AVILA MARTEL.

Biblioteca Central del Instituto de Investigaciones Agropecuarias: Casilla 5427; f. 1947; 7,300 vols., 30,000 documents and pamphlets, 619 current periodicals; Librarian SONIA ELSO.

Biblioteca Central de la Universidad Técnica del Estado: Avda. B. O'Higgins 3389; f. 1952; 150,000 vols.; Dir. MARÍA ISABEL BRUCE DE ROGERS.

Biblioteca de la Universidad Católica de Chile: Av. Bernardo O'Higgins 340, Casilla 114-D; f. 1895; 12 faculty libraries; 300,000 vols.; Dir. SOLEDAD FERREIRO SERRANO.

Biblioteca del Congreso Nacional (*Congress Library*): Edificio del Congreso Nacional, Compañía 1175, 2° piso, Clasificador de Correos 1199; f. 1883; 700,000 vols. and 4,000 periodicals on law, social sciences, politics and economics, human sciences and literature; official depository for international organizations, legal depository for national publs.; open to the public; Dir. JORGE I. HUBNER G.; Chief Librarian JOSÉ MIGUEL VICUÑA; publs. *Boletín Bibliográfico*, *Efímeros*, etc.

Biblioteca Nacional de Chile (*National Library*): Avenida B. O'HIGGINS 651; f. 1813; Dir. ENRIQUE CAMPOS MENÉNDEZ; 1,200,000 vols., 4,200 MSS., 83 incunabula; publs. *Mapocho*, *Anuario de la Prensa Chilena*, *Referencias Críticas*.

Centro Nacional de Información y Documentación—CENID (*National Centre for Information and Documentation*): Canadá 308, Casilla 297-V; f. 1963; permanent programme of National Commission for Scientific and Technological Research (*see* Research Institutes); clearing house for scientific documentary and technical information; head of a national system of documentation; national FID mem.; library of 4,000 vols.; Dir. ANNA MARÍA PRAT; publs. *Notas Informativas CENID*† (quarterly), *Serie Información y Documentación*† (irregular), *Serie Bibliografías*†, *Serie Directorios*†.

Concepción

Biblioteca Central de la Universidad de Concepción: Barrio Universitario, Casilla 1807; f. 1919; 300,000 vols., 5,500 periodicals; Dir. JUAN DE LUIGI.

Valparaíso

Biblioteca Central de la Universidad Técnica "Federico Santa María": Avda. España 1680, C.P. 110-V; f. 1926; 71,000 vols., 2,000 periodicals; Dir. BLANCA MATAS; publs. *Scientia*† (quarterly), *Boletín Informativo y Bibliográfico* (monthly), acquisitions list (annually).

Biblioteca de la Universidad Católica de Valparaíso: Casilla 4059; f. 1928; 155,000 vols.; Librarian FRANCISCA MARTÍNEZ; publs. *Boletín Official de la UCV*, *Boletín de Hemeroteca* (monthly), *Boletín Bibliográfico* (irregular), *Resúmenes de Tésis* (2 a year).

Biblioteca Severín de Valparaíso (*Severin Library*): Plaza Victoria; f. 1873; Sections: Chile and General; 101,000 vols.; Dir. G. GAMHAM LÓPEZ.

MUSEUMS

Santiago

Museo de Anatomía Humana "Manuel Villela" (*Anatomical Museum*): Universidad Católica de Chile; f. 1930; Dir. Dr. HUMBERTO GUIRALDES DEL CANTO.

Museo de Arte Colonial de San Francisco: Alameda Bernardo O'Higgins 834; f. 1968 by the Franciscan Order; 16th-19th-century art; includes the most important collection of 17th-century paintings in Chile: the life of St. Francis depicted in 42 pictures; also other religious works of art, furniture, etc.; valuable library; Dir. JOAQUÍN GANDARILLAS INFANTE.

Museo de Arte Contemporáneo (*Contemporary Art Museum*): Universidad de Chile, Parque Forestal frente a Mosqueto; Dir. MARTA BENAVENTE LARRAZABAL.

Museo de Arte Popular Americano (*Art of the American Peoples Museum*): Casilla 10-D, Universidad de Chile; f. 1944; traditional minor arts and industries, ritual, folklore, etc., of the Americas, Araucanian silverware; D. PATRICIO COURT DEL PEDREGAL.

Museo del Carmen de Maipú: Alameda 1691; f. 1956; collection of antiques, historical documents and coaches; Dir. RAMÓN EYZAGUIRRE G.

Museo de Historia Natural de San Pedro Nolasco (*Natural History Museum*): Huérfanos 669, Casilla 525; f. 1912; Dir. Rev. JUAN B. HERRADA.

Museo Histórico Nacional (*National Historical Museum*): Miraflores 50, Casilla 9764, Santiago; f. 1911; sections: Prehispanic, Conquest, Colonial, Independence, Republican periods; library of 5,000 vols.; depts. of painting and textile restoration, archaeological research, military history, architecture, arts and crafts, costumes, iconography; Dir. HERNÁN RODRÍGUEZ VILLEGAS; publ. *Boletín Informativo*† (2 a year).

Museo Nacional de Bellas Artes (*National Museum of Fine Arts*): Parque Forestal, Casilla 3209; f. 1910; library of 15,000 vols.; paintings, engravings, etchings and sculpture; Dir. NENA OSSA.

Museo Nacional de Histório Natural (*National Museum of Natural History*): Casilla 787; f. 1830; Departments: Vertebrates, Invertebrates, Entomology, Hydrobiology, Botany, Cryptogams, Phanerogams, Mineralogy and Geology, Palaeontology, Anthropology, Herpetology; controls Centro Nacional de Museología, the National School for Science Museum personnel; Dir. GRETE MOSTNY G.; publs. *Boletín*, *Noticiario mensual*.

Museo Pedagógico Carlos Stuardo do Ortiz: Cienfuegos 59; f. 1941; records cultural and educational heritage of the country; educational research; translations; bibliographies; library of 25,000 vols.; Dir. Prof. ELENA STOGIANNIS ROMERO; publs. *Guía, Publicación Oficial del Museo*†, *Revista de Educación*†.

Angol

Museo Dillman S. Bullock: Casilla 2-D; f. 1946; general local flora and fauna; extensive local archaeological collection; library of 3,000 vols.; undertakes research, scientific expeditions; Curator JUAN PROVOSTE RETAMAL.

Arica

Museo Regional San Miguel de Azapa: Casilla 287; part of Universidad del Norte dept. of anthropology; f. 1967; study of the southern Andean people, and pre-Colombian history; collection of 22,000 archaeological objects; Dir. GUILLERMO FOCACCI ASTE; publ. *Chungara*.

Cañete

Museo Folklórico Araucano de Cañete "Juan A. Rios M.": Casilla 28; f. 1968; to conserve, exhibit and research the Mapuche culture from its origins to contact with Spanish culture; to recreate the environment which Valdivia saw in 1552 when he built the Tucapel Fort (near the museum); anthropological research of the native Mapuche settlements which still exist; archaeological excavations in the surrounding area; library of 2,000 vols.; Curator MIGUEL V. CERVELLINO GIANNONI.

Concepción

Museo de Concepción (*Concepción Museum*): Edmundo Larenas 420, Casilla 1054; f. 1902; 6,732 vols.; Curator J. E. F. BROUSSE SOTO; publ. *Comunicaciones del Museo de Concepción*†.

Copiapó

Museo Regional de Atacama: Villa El Sol, Block A, 1° piso; f. 1973; archaeology, mineralogy and history; library of 3,000 vols.; Curator MIGUEL CERVELLINO GIANNONI.

Hualpen, near Concepción

Museo de Hualpen (*Hualpen Museum*): f. 1882; Curator Prof. HERNÁN SAN MARTÍN; collections of Greek, Roman and Egyptian Archæology; Chilean arms and numismatic collections; Oriental art; Chilean and American folk arts; Chilean archæology; eighteenth and nineteenth-century furniture.

Iquique

Museo Arqueológico de Iquique, Universidad de Chile: Casilla 121, Baquedano 930; f. 1966; attached to the Dept. of Archaeology and Museums of the University; permanent exhibition showing the cultural development of the people of the region from 10,000 B.C. to 1535; specialized library; Dir. ALFREDO LOAYZA BUSTOS.

La Serena

Museo Arqueológico de la Serena (*La Serena Archaeological Museum*): Casilla 117; f. 1943; sections on archaeology, prehistory, physical anthropology, colonial history, ethnology and palaeontology; library of 13,125 vols., 13,981 slides, 26,108 photographs; Dir. GONZALO AMPUERO B.; specialized library; publs. *Boletín*† (annually), *Notas del Museo*, *Contribuciones Arqueológicas* (irregular), *Fondo Documental*† (2 a year).

Linares

Museo de Arte y Artesania de Linares: Casilla 272; f. 1966; arts and crafts from the Inca period to the present; valuable collections including unique clay miniatures; collection of Huaso implements; ceramics; exhibition of history and people of Linares; exhibition on the sugar industry; conferences, lectures, films, etc.; Dir. PEDRO OLMOS MUÑOZ.

Ovalle

Museo Arqueológico de Ovalle: Calle Vicuña Mackenna 521, Casilla 110; f. 1963; 1,200 archaeological exhibits, including some valuable pottery and ceramics of the Indian culture from the surrounding area; Curator JULIO BROUSSAIN CAMPINO.

Puerto Williams, Magallanes

Museo "Martin Gusinde": f. 1975; situated at the naval base on Navarino Island; history and geography of the southernmost archipelagos of America; aboriginal culture, flora, fauna and minerals of the area; library of 3,600 vols.; Curator OSCAR GÁLVEZ HERREÑA.

Punta Arenas

Museo Regional de los Padres Salesianos (*Salesian Regional Museum*): Instituto "Don Bosco", Av. Bulnes 374, Casilla 347; f. 1893; Dir. Pbro. JUAN CAVAGGION FILIPPI; scientific and ethnographical (notable relics of extreme South American and Tierra del Fuegan tribes).

Museo de la Patagonia: Plaza de Armas, Casilla 97; f. 1967; archaeology, natural sciences (zoology, botany, palaeontology, mineralogy), regional history; specialized library of 1,250 vols.; Curator Sra. DESANKA URSIC V.

San Pedro de Atacama

Museo de Arqueología: f. 1963; affiliated to the Universidad del Norte; exhibits from the paleolithic age; mummies, ceramics, textiles, ornaments, etc. from the neolithic age; research, excavations in the Atacama region; library of 3,500 vols.; Dir. GUSTAVE LE PAIGE, S.J.; publ. *Estudios Atacameños*† (2 a year).

Talca

Museo O'Higginiano y de Bellas Artes: 1 Norte, 2 Oriente No. 875; f. 1925; paintings, sculpture, Chilean history, archaeology, religious artefacts, antique furniture, arms; Curator CÉSAR CUADRADO MERINO.

Temuco

Museo Araucano Regional (*Araucanian Museum*): Avda. Alemania 084, Casilla 481; f. 1940; opened to the public 1943; *c.* 3,000 archaeological, artistic, and folklore exhibits of the Araucanian Indians of South Chile, and others relating to the Conquest and Pacification of Araucania as well as the history of Temuco city itself; specialized library of 500 vols.; Curator Prof. CONSUELO VALDES CHADWICK.

Valdivia

Museo de la Universidad Austral de Chile: Casilla 586; f. 1967; part of university dept. of historical and anthropological studies; undertakes teaching, research, training of museum staff, conservation, museology; library of 3,000 vols.; Dir. Prof. MAURICE VAN DE MAELE.

Vicuña

Museo-Biblioteca Gabriela Mistral: Casilla 50; f. 1971; to preserve the cultural legacy of the poetess, Gabriela Mistral (Nobel prize for Literature 1945); talks, films, music, etc.; library of 6,000 vols.; Dir. MARIO FARIAS ANDRADE; publs. *Guía del Museo*, etc.

Viña del Mar

Museo Comparativo de Zoología Marina: Casilla 13-D; f. 1955; part of Oceanology Dept., Univ. de Chile; fish, birds, crustaceans, echinoderms and molluscs from the coastal regions of the S.E. Pacific; Curator HECTOR ANDRADE V.

Museo de Historia Natural de Valparaíso (*Natural History Museum*): Calle Valparaíso 155, Casilla 925; f. 1876; natural sciences and anthropology; library of *c.* 3,000 vols.; Curator ANA AVALOS VALENZUELA; publ. *Anales*†.

UNIVERSITIES AND TECHNICAL UNIVERSITIES

UNIVERSIDAD AUSTRAL DE CHILE

(Southern University of Chile)

CASILLA 567, VALDIVIA

Telephone: 3911, 3961.

Founded 1954.

Private control; Academic year: March to July, August to December.

Rector: Gen. PEDRO PALACIOS CAMERON.
Vice-Rector for Academic Affairs: Dr. RAFAEL PESSOT ZORICH.
Vice-Rector for Extension and Communications: MAURICIO VAN DE MAELE OLIVIER.
Vice-Rector for Economic and Administrative Affairs: GUIDO MELLER MAYR.
Secretary-General: FELIX URCULLU MOLINA.
Librarian: Sra. ELIZABETH SAELZER.

Number of teachers: 610.
Number of students: 4,752.

Publications†: *Estudios Filológicos, Medio Ambiente, Ciencias de la Salud, Estudios Pedagógicas* (annual), *Agro Sur, Bosque, Archivos de Medicina Veterinaria.*

DEANS:

Faculty of Medicine: Dr. RICHARD RIOS R.
Faculty of Veterinary Medicine: Dr. JUAN J. EBERT K.
Faculty of Agriculture: Dr. JOSÉ MARAMBIO AVARIA.
Faculty of Forestry Engineering: Dr. ROLAND PETERS NARIO.
Faculty of Fine Arts: MAURICIO VAN DE MAELE OLIVIER.
Faculty of Philosophy and Social Sciences: Dr. JORGE MILLAS J.
Faculty of Natural Sciences: Dr. ORLANDO ALARCÓN A.
Faculty of Letters and Education: Dr. ERWIN HAVERBECK O.
Faculty of Physical and Mathematical Sciences: ARIEL GAJARDO A.

UNIVERSIDAD CATÓLICA DE CHILE

(Catholic University of Chile)

AV. BERNARDO O'HIGGINS 340, CASILLA 114-D, SANTIAGO

Telephone: 224516.

Founded 1888.

Asst. Grand Chancellor: Mgr. JORGE MEDINA.
Rector: JORGE SWETT.
Vice-Rectors: HERNÁN RIESCO, HERNÁN LARRAIN, MARIO ALBORNOZ.
General Secretary: RAÚL LECAROS.
Librarian: SOLEDAD FERREIRO.

Library: *see* Libraries.
Number of teachers: 2,393.
Number of students: 15,309.

ACADEMIC UNITS AND DEANS:

Faculty of Theology: Rev. ANTONIO MORENO.
Faculty of Philosophy, Aesthetics, Letters and History: ROQUE E. SCARPA.
Faculty of Exact Sciences: RAFAEL BARRIGA.
Faculty of Biological Sciences: LUIS VARGAS.
Faculty of Architecture, Town Planning and Geography: JORGE LARRAIN.
Faculty of Arts: EUGENIO DITTBORN.
Faculty of Social Sciences: HERNÁN BERWART.
Faculty of Medicine and Health Sciences: PABLO CASANEGRA.
Faculty of Education: RAFAEL HERNANDEZ.
Faculty of Law: SERGIO GAETE.
Faculty of Agronomy: JUAN IGNACIO DOMINGUEZ.
Faculty of Engineering, Civil Engineering; Centre of Computer Sciences, Department of Electrical Engineering: KARL LUDERS.
Faculty of Economics and Management Sciences: JUAN I. VARAS.

BRANCH CAMPUSES:

Sede Regional de Talcahuano: Casilla 127; Dir. HOMERO LARRAÍN.
Sede Regional del Maule: Casilla 617, Talca; Dir. JOAQUIN MONTERO.
Sede Regional de Temuco: Casilla 900; Dir. JUAN G. BALDEIG.
Sede Regional de Villarrica: Casilla 111; Dir. R. F. PAUL WEVERING.

UNIVERSIDAD CATÓLICA DE VALPARAÍSO

AV. BRASIL 2950, CASILLA 4059, VALPARAÍSO

Telephone: 51024.

Founded 1928.

Private control; Academic year: March to July, August to December.

Chancellor: Mgr. EMILIO TAGLE COVARRUBIAS, Archbishop of Valparaíso.
Rector: MATÍAS VALENZUELA LABRA.
Secretary-General: INÉS PARDO DE CARVALLO.
Librarian: FRANCISCA MARTÍNEZ.

Library: *see* Libraries.
Number of teachers: 444 (full-time).
Number of students: *c.* 7,145.

Publications: *Imagen UCV* (annually), several specialist faculty publs.

DEANS:

Faculty of Architecture and Town Planning: HUGO ROJAS SEPÚLVEDA.
Faculty of Engineering: FERNANDO ACEVEDO BONZI.
Faculty of Law and Social Sciences: MAURICIO BEZANILLA BOLOÑA.
Faculty of Philosophy and Education: MANUEL RAMÍREZ ROJAS.
Faculty of Basic Sciences and Mathematics: WALTER ZELLER ALLIER.

DIRECTORS:

Institute of Social Sciences: MANFRED WILHELMY VON WOLF.
Institute of Theology: LUIS OLIVARES MOLINA.
School of Agronomy: FERNANDO COSIO GONZÁLEZ.
School of Commerce: PATRICIO JIMÉNEZ BERMEJO.
School of Civil Engineering: ALFREDO PAVEZ NÚÑEZ.
School of Electricity: JOSÉ RUBIO HORNAUER.
School of Electronics: RAIMUNDO VILLARROEL VALENCIA.
School of Commercial Engineering: RENÉ MANSILLA STEINMEYER.
School of Marine and Food Sciences: GABRIEL DAZAROLA METZGER.
School of Transport: FÉLIX GARCÍA INFANTE.
Centre for Scientific and Technological Research: SAMUEL NAVARRETE CIFUENTES.
Centre for Computer and Information Science: ALDO MIGLIARO OSORIO.
Department of Religious Studies: Mons. JORGE BOSAGNA AGUAYO.

UNIVERSIDAD DE CHILE

(University of Chile)

AV. BERNARDO O'HIGGINS 1058, CASILLA 10-D, SANTIAGO

Telephone: 63656, 86794.

Founded 1738 as Universidad Real de San Felipe; inaugurated 1843 as Universidad de Chile.

State control; Academic year: March to December.

Rector: AGUSTÍN TORO DÁVILA.
Pro-Rector: HERNÁN GARCÍA VIDAL.
Vice-Chancellors: FERNANDO VALENZUELA ERAZO (Academic), FRANCISCO AGUILERA G. (Student Affairs), WILLY HAYES GONZALEZ (Administration), FERNANDO RIQUELME V. (Extension and Communication).

Library: *see* Libraries.

Number of teachers: 10,000 (including all branch institutions).

Number of students: *c.* 54,000.

Publications: *Anales de la Universidad de Chile, Anales* of the different faculties, 75 current publications.

DEANS:

Faculty of Juridical and Social Sciences: HUGO ROSENDE S.
Faculty of Physical and Mathematical Sciences: CLAUDIO ANGUITA C.
Faculty of Medicine (North): Dr. ELÍAS CUMSILLE.
Faculty of Medicine (South): Dr. EDUARDO CASSORLA L.
Faculty of Medicine (East): Dr. GUILLERMO ADRIASOLA E.
Faculty of Medicine (West): Dra. CARMEN VELASCO R.
Faculty of Dentistry: JAIME MERY A.
Faculty of Economic Sciences: MARIO GÓMEZ P.
Faculty of Philosophy and Letters: JOAQUÍN BARCELÓ L.

Faculty of Musical Arts: HERMINIA RACCAGNI.
Faculty of Fine Arts: KURT HERDAN.
Faculty of Architecture: GASTÓN ETCHEVERRY.
Faculty of Forestry Science: MANUEL CONTRERAS SALAS.
Faculty of Education: LUCIA YZOARD.
Faculty of Veterinary Science: SANTIAGO INOSTROZA HOOD.
Faculty of Chemistry and Pharmacy: CARLOS MERCADO S.
Faculty of Agronomy: JOSÉ GARRIDO ROJAS.
Faculty of Sciences: FRANCISCO SANTA MARIA HERRERO.
Faculty of Human Sciences: MARIO CIUDAD V.
Faculty of Mathematics and Natural Sciences (Valparaiso Campus): TATIANA ALVIÑA W.

BRANCH CAMPUSES:

Sede Arica: Gen. Velasquez s/n, Arica; Vice-Rector MAX MONTECINO ROZAS.
Sede Antofagasta: Av. Universidad de Chile s/n, Antofagasta; Vice-Rector RUBEN BUSTOS LYNCH.
Sede Iquique: Serrano 579, Iquique; Vice-Rector FAURD ASSERELLA.
Sede La Serena: Colina "El Pino", La Serena; Vice-Rector EDGARDO ZELAYA CABALLERO.
Sede Valparaíso: Erazuriz esq. Gral. Cruz, Valparaíso; Vice-Rector RAMÓN SALINAS FIGUEROA.
Sede Talca: Camino Lircay s/n, Talca; Vice-Rector PEDRO FELIX DE AGUIRRE LAMAS.
Sede Ñuble: 18 de Septiembre s/n, Chillán; Vice-Rector FERNANDO GONZÁLEZ C.
Sede Temuco: Av. Francisco Salazar s/n, Temuco; Vice-Rector LUIZ ORTIZ L.
Sede Osorno: Fuslocher s/n, Osorno; Vice-Rector VICTOR HUGO VERGARA.

UNIVERSIDAD DE CONCEPCIÓN
(Concepción University)

CASILLA 20-C, CONCEPCION
Telephone: 24467.

Founded 1919.

Private control; Academic year: March to January.

Rector: GUILLERMO CLERICUS.
Academic Vice-Rector: REINALDO GLEISNER EVERSMAN.
Administrative Vice-Rector: HERVI LAGOS CORTÉS.
Vice-Rector (Research): RICARDO REICH ALBERTZ.
Vice-Rector (Communications): HAGEN GLEISNER EVERSMAN.
Secretary-General: GUSTAVO VILLAGRÁN CABRERA.
Library Director: J. DE LUIGI LEMUS.

Number of teachers: 1,800.
Number of students: 12,350.

Publications: *Atenea* (monthly; science, art and letters); *Revista de Derecho* (quarterly); *Gayana* (Institute of Biology); *Paideia* (School of Education); *Informativo de la Rectoria* (Public Relations).

DIRECTORS AND DEANS:

Biological Sciences: Dr. MARCELO MEDINA VARGAS.
Institute of Biology: OSCAR MATTHEI J.
Institute of Medico-Biological Sciences: IVÁN BRAVO R.
School of Medicine: Dr. ABEL OLMOS C.
School of Chemistry, Pharmacy and Biochemistry: Prof. RICARDO WOERNER V.
School of Nursing: Prof. IRENE BOCAZ S.
School of Obstetrics: Prof. ALICIA CASTRO C.
Dental School: Dr. ADOLFO SPICHIGER R.

Physical, Chemical and Mathematical Sciences: Ing. RENATO BECKER D.
School of Civil Engineering: Prof. UWE SCHOTTE S.
School of Building Construction: Prof. JOSÉ B. REYES O.
Institute of Physics: Prof. EDUARDO KRUMM VALENCIA.
Institute of Mathematics: Prof. WALTER STUVEN CONTZEN.
Institute of Chemistry: Prof. MOISÉS SILVA TRIVIÑO.
School of Economics and Administration: JAIME LAVIN INFANTE.
Institute of Computation and Informatics: HÉCTOR RODRÍGUEZ.
El Carbon Centre: Prof. HERNAN CARASCO A.

Education: Prof. MARIO GONZALEZ O.
School of Education: Prof. MARIO GONZALEZ O.
School of Education-Chillán: Prof. HUMBERTO SILVA A.
School of Education-Los Angeles: Prof. FERNANDO HAEMMERLI D.
Physical Education Centre: Prof. RODOLEO FOLCH GARCÍA.

Humanities and Art: Prof. ENRIQUE RUGGERI V.
Institute of Anthropology, History and Geography: Prof. ANTONIO FERNANDEZ V.
Institute of Art: Prof. JOSÉ E. BRITO H.
Institute of Philosophy: Prof. PATRICIO OYANEDER J.
Institute of Languages: Prof. ASTRID RABY B.

Legal and Social Sciences: Prof. JULIO SALAS V.
School of Law: Prof. JULIO SALAS V.
School of Social Service: Prof. MARTA MONTORY T.

Agriculture: Prof. LUIS DEL VILLAR Z.
School of Agronomy: Prof. VICTOR SAELZER R.
School of Veterinary Medicine: Prof. PABLO STROOMAN A.
Centre of Forestry Sciences: Prof. JAIME MILLAN H.
Institute of Agricultural Engineering: ALEJANDRO VALENZUELA.
Graduate School: Prof. CARLOS VON PLESSING B.

UNIVERSIDAD DEL NORTE

CASILLA 1280, ANTOFAGASTA
Telephone: 22040.
Founded 1956.

Language of instruction: Spanish; Private control; Academic year: March to February (two semesters).

Rector: (vacant).
Vice-Rector for Academic Affairs: GERALDO DEL LAGO.
General Secretary: MARIO G. MONTT.
Librarian: Sra. URSULA SCHADLICH.

Library of 60,000 vols.
Number of teachers: 557.
Number of students: 6,521.
Publications: *Anales, Revista,* etc.

DEANS:

Faculty of Sciences: ORLAYER ALCAYAGA.
Faculty of Social Sciences: JOSÉ M. CASASSAS.
Faculty of Humanities: OSVALDO MAYA.
Engineering and Technology: RENZO FOLLEGATI.

(There are branches of the University at Arica and Iquique, and a research centre at Coquimbo).

UNIVERSIDAD TÉCNICA DEL ESTADO
(State Technical University)

AVDA. ECUADOR 3469,
CASILLA 4637, SANTIAGO
Telephone: 97401-08.
Founded 1947.

Rector: Col. EUGENIO REYES TASTEST.
Secretary-General: JORGE SOTO S.

Number of teachers: 590.
Number of students: *c.* 10,000.

Faculties of Sociology and Philosophy; Mathematics, Physics and Chemistry; Electronics, Mechanics and Building; Mining, Metallurgy and Chemistry.

UNIVERSIDAD TÉCNICA "FEDERICO SANTA MARÍA"

CASILLA 110V, VALPARAÍSO
Telephone: 60176.
Founded 1926.

Private control; Language of instruction: Spanish; Academic year: March to December.

Rector: ISMAEL HUERTA DÍAZ.
Vice-Rectors: NELSON LEIVA BLANCO (Academic), Dr. MAX VON BRAND KUHLMANN (Research).
Secretary-General: ENRIQUE PÉREZ SILVA.

Library: *see* Libraries.
Number of teachers: 308.
Number of students: 3,222.

Publications: *Scientia* (quarterly), *Boletín Informativo* (monthly).

DEANS:

Faculty of Civil Engineering: Prof. RAÚL GALINDO URRA.

Faculty of Electrical Engineering: Prof. HUGO PALACIOS FAGERSTROM.

Faculty of Mechanics: Dr. FERNANDO CARVAJAL GUERRA.

Faculty of Chemistry: Dr. FERNANDO AGUIRRE ODE.

COLLEGES

Escuela Agrícola "El Vergel" (*Agricultural School*): Casilla 2-D, Angol; f. 1920; secondary agricultural school; comprises eight sections: plant nursery, orchards, dairy, pig and general farming, reafforestation, vegetable gardening, museum; Rector H. GONZÁLEZ BRAVO; Dir. Agric. School S. E. MOORE; publs. plant catalogue and related scientific publications.

Escuela Militar "General Bernardo O'Higgins": Casilla 174, Las Condes, Santiago; f. 1817 (by General O'Higgins); 56 military instructors and officials, 102 civilian instructors, 1,024 students; Dir. Col. SERGIO CASTILLO ARANGUIZ; publ. *Revista "Cien Aguilas"*.

Facultad Latinoamericana de Ciencias Sociales: Avda. Federico Lacroze 2101, 1426 Capital Federal; f. 1957; postgraduate training and research centre for Latin America; Sec. Gen. ARTURO O'CONNELL.

PEOPLE'S REPUBLIC OF CHINA

Population 958,000,000

Following the decision of the State Council in 1978 to use the Chinese phonetic alphabet as the international standard for romanization of Chinese names and places, the new spelling is used here for the first time. A list of the provinces with their main towns is given below with the old spelling in brackets.

Municipalities directly under the central authorities:
Beijing (Peking)
Shanghai (Shanghai)
Tianjin (Tientsin)
Provinces, autonomous regions for minority nationalities and some well-known cities and other places:

Anhui (Anhwei) Province
Hefei (Hofei)
Bengbu (Pengpu)

Fujian (Fukien) Province
Fuzhou (Foochow)
Xiamen (Amoy)

Gansu (Kansu) Province
Lanzhou (Lanchow)

Guangdong (Kwangtung) Province
Guangzhou (Kwangchow)
Shantou (Swatow)

Guangxi Zhuang (Kwangsi Chuang) Autonomous Region
Nanning (Nanning)
Guilin (Kweilin)

Guizhou (Kweichow) Province
Guiyang (Kweiyang)
Zunyi (Tsunyi)

Hebei (Hopei) Province
Shijiazhuang (Shihchiachuang)
Tangshan (Tangshan)

Heilongjiang (Heilungkiang) Province
Harbin (Harbin)
Daqing Oilfield (Taching Oilfield)
Qiqihar (Chichihar)

Henan (Honan) Province
Zhengzhou (Chengchow)
Luoyang (Loyang)
Kaifeng (Kaifeng)

Hubei (Hupeh) Province
Wuhan (Wuhan)

Hunan (Hunan) Province
Changsha (Changsha)

Jiangsu (Kiangsu) Province
Nanjing (Nanking)
Suzhou (Soochow)
Wuxi (Wuhsi)

Jiangxi (Kiangsi) Province
Nanchang (Nanchang)
Jiujiang (Chiuchiang)

Jilin (Kirin) Province
Changchun (Changchun)

Liaoning (Liaoning) Province
Shenyang (Shenyang)
Anshan (Anshan)
Luda (Luta)

Nei Monggol (Inner Mongolia) Autonomous Region
Hohhot (Huhehot)
Baotou (Paotou)

Ningxia Hui (Ningsia Hui) Autonomous Region
Yinchuan (Yinchuan)

Qinghai (Chinghai) Province
Xining (Sining)

Shaanxi (Shensi) Province
Xian (Sian)
Yanan (Yenan)

Shandong (Shantung) Province
Jinan (Tsinan)
Qingdao (Tsingtao)
Yantai (Yentai)

Shanxi (Shansi) Province
Taiyuan (Taiyuan)
Dazhai (Tachai)

Sichuan (Szechuan) Province
Chengdu (Chengtu)
Chongqing (Chungking)

Xinjiang Uygur (Sinkiang Uighur) Autonomous Region
Urumqi (Urumchi)

Xizang (Tibet) Autonomous Region
Lhasa (Lhasa)

Yunnan (Yunnan) Province
Kunming (Kunming)
Dali (Tali)

Zhejiang (Chekiang) Province
Hangzhou (Hangchow)

ACADEMIES

CHINESE ACADEMY OF SCIENCES

BEIJING

Founded 1949

President: FANG YI.
Secretary-General: YU WEN.

There is a branch of the Academy at Changchun.

INSTITUTES OF THE ACADEMY

Acoustics Institute: Beijing; Dir. WANG DEZHAO.
Astronomical Observatory: Beijing.
Astronomical Observatory: Shanghai; Dir. YE SHUHUA.
Astronomical Observatory: Shaanxi.
Astronomical Observatory: Fenghuangshan, Kunming; Dir. WU MINGZHAN.
Astronomical Observatory: Purple Mountain, Nanjing; Dir. ZHANG YUZHE.
Atmospheric Physics Institute: Beijing.
Atomic Energy Institute: Beijing; Dir. WANG GANCHANG.
Automation Institute: Beijing.
Biochemistry Institute: Shanghai; Dir. WANG YINGLAI.
Biophysics Institute: Beijing; Dir. BEI SHIZHANG.

Botany Institute: Beijing; Dir. TANG PEISONG.
Cell Biology Institute: Shanghai; Dir. ZHUANG XIAOHUI.
Chemical Engineering and Metallurgy Institute: Beijing.
Chemical Physics Institute: Luda; Dir. GU YIJIAN.
Chemistry Institute: Beijing; Dir. LIU DAGANG.
Chemistry Institute: Jinan.
Chemistry Institute of Guangdong: Guangzhou.
Computer Technology Institute: Beijing; Dir. YAN PEILIN.
Computer Technology Institute: Shanghai.
Computer Technology Institute: Shenyang.
Electrical Engineering Institute: Beijing.
Electron Optics Institute: Shanghai.
Electronics Institute: Beijing; Dir. GU DEHUAN.
Engineering Mechanics Institute: Harbin; Dir. LIU HUIXIAN.
Entomology Institute: Shanghai.
Environmental Chemistry Institute: Beijing.
Forestry and Pedology Institute: Shenyang.
Genetics Institute: Beijing; Dir. HU HAN.
Geochemistry Institute: Guiyang.
Geography Institute: Beijing; Dir. HUANG BINGWEI.
Geology and Paleontology Institute: Nanjing; Dir. ZHAO JINKE.
Geology Institute: Beijing; Dir. ZHANG WENYOU.
Geophysics Institute: Beijing; Dir. FU CHENGYI.
Geotectonic Institute: Changsha.
High Energy Physics Institute: Beijing; Dir. ZHANG WENYU.
Hydrobiology Institute: Wuhan.
Materia Medica Institute: Shanghai; Dir. GAO YISHENG.
Mathematics Institute: Beijing; Dir. HUA LUOGENG.
Mechanics Institute: Beijing; Dir. QIAN XUESEN.
Metallurgy Institute: Shanghai.
Metals Institute: Shenyang; Dir. LI XUN.
Microbiology Institute: Beijing.
Nuclear Physics Institute: Shanghai.
Oceanography of the South Seas Institute: Guangzhou; Dir. YONG ZHONG.
Oceanology Institute: Qingdao; Dir. ZENG CHENGKUI; publ. *Studia Marina Sinica*† (2 a year).
Optics and Precision Instruments Institute: Shanghai.
Optics and Precision Instruments Institute: Xian.
Organic Chemistry Institute: Shanghai; Dir. WANG YOU.
Pedology Institute: Nanjing; Dir. XIONG YI.
Photoelectricity Institute of Sichuan.
Photosensitive Chemistry Institute: Beijing.
Physics Institute: Beijing; Dir. SHI RUWEI.
Physics Institute Southwest: Luoshan.
Physiology Institute: Shanghai; Dir. FENG DEPEI.
Plant Physiology Institute: Shanghai: Dir. LUO ZONGLUO.
Psychology Institute: Beijing; Dir. XU LIANCANG.
Rock Soil Mechanics Institute: Wuhan.
Salt Lakes Institute: Xining.
Scientific and Technical Information Institute: Beijing; Dir. NIE ZHONGYONG.
Semiconductors Institute: Beijing; Dir. HUANG KUN.
Shanghai Institute of Ceramics: Shanghai; Dir. YAN DONG-SENG.
Space Physics Institute: Xian.
Structure of Matter Institute of Fujian: Fuzhou; Dir. LU JIAXI.
Systems Science Institute: Beijing; 88 research staff; Dir. GUAN ZHAOZHI.
Technical Physics Institute: Shanghai.
Theoretical Physics Institute.
Tropical Plant Research Institute of Yunnan: Mengla.
Tropical Plant Research Institute of South China.
Vertebrate Palaeontology and Palaeo-Anthropology Institute: Beijing; Dir. YANG ZHONGJIAN.
Zoology Institute: Beijing; Dir. TONG DIZHOU.
Zoology Institute: Shanghai.
Zoology Institute of Yunnan: Kunming.

CHINESE ACADEMY OF SOCIAL SCIENCES

5 JIANGUOMEN NEI DA JIE, BEIJING

Founded c. 1977

President: HU QIAOMU.
Secretary-General: SONG YIPING.

INSTITUTES:

Agricultural Economics Institute: Dir. ZHAN WU.
Archaeology Institute: Beijing; Dir. XIA NAI.
Economics Institute: Beijing; Dir. XU DIXIN.
Foreign Literature Institute: Beijing; Dir. FENG ZHI.
History (Ancient) Institute: Beijing; publ. *Historical Research.*
History (Modern) Institute: Beijing.
History (World) Institute: Beijing.
Industrial Economy Institute: Beijing.
Journalism Institute: Beijing.
Law Institute: Beijing; publ. *Law Research* (every 2 months).
Linguistics and Philology Institute: Beijing; Dir. LU SHUXIANG.
Literature Institute: Beijing; publ. *Discourses on Literature* (series).
Nationalities Institute: Beijing; Dir. YUN BEIFENG; publ. *Nationalities Research.*
Philosophy Institute: Beijing.
Scientific Information Institute: Beijing.
Trade and Commerce Institute: Beijing.
World Economy Institute: Beijing; Dir. QIAN JUNRUI.
World Religion Institute: Beijing; Dir. REN JIYU.

There are branches of the Academy in Nei Monggol and Xinjiang Uygur Autonomous Regions.

CHINESE ACADEMY OF MEDICAL SCIENCES

BEIJING

President: HUANG JIASI.

INSTITUTES:

Basic Medicine Institute: Beijing.
Biomedical Engineering Institute: Sichuan.
Blood Transfusion Institute: Sichuan.
Cardiovascular Diseases Institute: Beijing; Dir. WU YINGKAI.
Clinical Medicine Institute: Beijing.
Dermatology Institute: Jiangsu.
Epidemiology and Microbiology Institute: Beijing.
Experimental Medicine Institute: Beijing.
Haematology Institute: Sichuan.
Hygiene Institute: Beijing.
Materia Medica Institute: Beijing.
Medical Biology Institute: Kunming.
Medical Information Institute: Beijing.
Oncology Institute: Beijing; Dir. WU HUANXING.

Parasitology Institute: Shanghai.
Paediatrics Institute: Beijing.
Radiation Medicine Institute: Sichuan.
Virology Institute: Beijing.

ACADEMY OF CHINESE TRADITIONAL MEDICINE
BEIJING

President: JI ZHONGPU.

INSTITUTES:

Acupuncture Moxibustion Institute.
Traditional Pharmacology Institute.

CHINESE ACADEMY OF AGRICULTURAL SCIENCES
BEIJING

Founded 1957

President: JIN SHANBAO.

INSTITUTES:

Agriculture Institute: Beijing; Dir. YAN JI.
Atomic Energy Utilization in Agriculture Institute: Beijing.
Bees Institute of Jiangxi.
Citrus Fruit Research Institute: Chongqing; Dir. ZENG MIAN.
Crop Breeding and Cultivation Institute: Beijing.
Crops Institute.
Hog Culture Institute.
Plant Protection Institute: Beijing.
Soil Fertilizer Institute.
Tea Institute: Hangzhou.
Vegetable Institute.

CHINESE ACADEMY OF FORESTRY SCIENCES
BEIJING

Founded 1978 from the former Chinese Academy fo Agricultural and Forestry Sciences

INSTITUTES:

Forest Chemical Industry Institute.
Forestry Economics Institute.
Forestry Institute: Dir. HOU ZHIPU.
Forestry Machinery Institute.
Shellac Institute.
Sub-tropical Forestry Institute.
Tropical Forestry Institute.
Wood Industry Research Institute.

ACADEMY OF COAL MINING SCIENCES

President: FAN WEITANG.

INSTITUTE:

Coal Chemistry Institute: Beijing; Dir. WANG YINREN.

ACADEMY OF GEOLOGICAL SCIENCES
BEIJING

President: ZOU JIAYOU.

INSTITUTES:

Institute of Geology: Beijing.
Institute of Geology of Mineral Deposits: Beijing.
Institute of Rock and Mineral Analysis: Beijing.
Institute of Geomechanics: Beijing.
Institute of Geological Information: Beijing.
Geomechanical Comprehensive Research Brigade: Hebei.
Shenyang Institute of Geology and Mineral Resources: Liaoning.
Xian Institute of Geology and Mineral Resources: Shaanxi.
Chengdu Institute of Geology and Mineral Resources: Sichuan.
Yichang Institute of Geology and Mineral Resources: Hubei.
Nanjing Institute of Geology and Mineral Resources: Jiangsu.
Tianjin Institute of Geology and Mineral Resources: Tianjin.
Emei Institute of Multi-purpose Utilization of Mineral Resources: Sichuan.
Institute of Plateau Geology: Chengdu.
Institute of Marine Geology: Qingdao.
Guilin Institute of Karst Geology: Guangxi.
Zhengding Institute of Hydrogeology and Engineering Geology: Hebei.
Geological Museum: Beijing.
National Geological Library: Beijing.

ACADEMY OF METEOROLOGICAL SCIENCES

INSTITUTES:

Atmospheric Soundings Institute.
Meteorological Automatization Institute.
Meteorological Information Institute.
Meteorological Instruments Institute: Changchun.
Metrology, Calibration and Correction of Meteorological Instruments Institute.
Plateau Meteorology Institute.
Synoptic Meteorology and Climatology Institute.
Tropical Meteorology Institute: Guangzhou.
Typhoon Studies Institute: Shanghai.
Weather Modification Institute.

ACADEMY OF SPACE TECHNOLOGY

President: REN XINMIN.

INSTITUTES:

Control Engineering Institute: Beijing; Dir. YANG JIACHI.
Low Temperature and Vacuum Institute: Lanzhou.
Radio Technique Institute: Xian.

NATIONAL SCIENTIFIC COMMISSIONS OF THE STATE COUNCIL (CABINET)

State Scientific and Technological Commission: Minister FANG YI.
National Defence Scientific and Technological Commission: Chair. ZHANG AIPING.

SPECIAL AGENCIES OF THE STATE COUNCIL (CABINET)

Central Meteorological Bureau: Dir. MENG PING.
Foreign Language Publications and Distribution Bureau.
State Aquatic Products Bureau: Dir. ZHANG ZHAO.
State Farm Bureau: Dir. SHEN DIEYUAN.
State Forestry Bureau: Dir. LUO YUCHUAN.
State Geology Bureau: Dir. SUN DAGUANG.
State Museums and Archaeological Data Bureau (Cultural Relics Administrative Bureau): Dir. WANG YEQIU.
State Nationality Languages Translation Bureau.
State Oceanography Bureau: Dir. SHEN ZHENDONG.
State Pharmaceutical Administration.

State Seismological Bureau: Dir. Zou Yu.

State Standardization and Metrology Bureau: Dir. Yue Zhijian.

State Surveying and Cartography Bureau.

Written Chinese Language Reform Committee.

LEARNED SOCIETIES

China Scientific and Technical Association: f. 1958 by an amalgamation of the All-China Federation of Scientific Societies and the All-China Association for the Dissemination of Scientific and Technical Knowledge; Pres. Zhou Peiyuan.

Member Societies:

China Acoustics Society: Pres. Wang Demin.

China Aeronautics and Astronautics Society: Xueyuan Lu' Haidain Qu, Beijing; f. 1964; Pres. Shen Yuan; publ. *Aerospace Knowledge*† (monthly).

China Agricultural Crops Society.

China Agricultural Economy Society: Pres. Cai Ziwei.

China Agricultural Machinery Society.

China Agronomy Society: Pres. Yang Xiandong.

China Animal Husbandry and Veterinary Society.

China Anti-Tuberculosis Society: Pres. Huang Dingchen.

China Aquatic Products Society.

China Architectural Society: Pres. He Guangqian (acting).

China Astronomical Society: Purple Mountain Observatory, Nanjing; Pres. Zhang Yuzhe.

China Automation Society.

China Automotive Engineering Society.

China Biochemistry Society: c/o Shanghai Institute of Biochemistry, 320 Yo-Yang Rd., Shanghai 200031; f. 1979; *c.* 1,000 mems.; holds symposia, congresses, etc.; Pres. Y. L. Wang; Sec.-Gen. C. L. Tsou; publ. *Acta Biochimica et Biophysica Sinica* (quarterly).

China Botany Society: Pres. Tang Peisong.

China Chemical Engineering Society.

China Chemical Society: Pres. Qian Renyuan.

China Civil Engineering Society: 10 Fuxing Rd., P.O.B. 2500, Beijing; f. 1953; Pres. Mao Yisheng; Sec.-Gen. Zhao Xichun; publ. *Civil Engineering Journal*†.

China Coal Mining Society: Pres. He Bingzhang.

China Education Association: Pres. Dong Cuncai.

China Electrical Engineering Society: Pres. Li Daigeng (acting).

China Electronics Society: Pres. Wang Zigang.

China Engineering Thermophysics Society: Chair. Wu Zhonghua.

China Environmental Science Society: Pres. Li Chaobo.

China Fishery Society: Pres. Xiao Peng.

China Forestry Society: Pres. Wu Zhonglun.

China Future Society: Chief Exec. Officer Du Dagong.

China Genetics Society: Pres. Li Ruqi.

China Geography Society.

China Geological Society: Baiwanzhaung, Beijing; f. 1922; 15,000 mems.; over 20 Commissions; Pres. Huang Jiqing; Sec.-Gen. Wang Zejiu; publ. *Acta Geologica Sinica.*

China Geophysics Society: Pres. Gu Gongzu.

China Glaciology and Cryopedology Society: Pres. Shi Yafeng.

China Historical Society.

China Hydraulic Engineering Society: Bai Guang Rd., P.O.B. 2906, Beijing; Pres. Zhang Hanying; publ. *Journal of Hydraulic Engineering.*

China Light Industry Society: Pres. Xie Xinhe.

China Mathematics Society: Pres. Hua Luogeng.

China Mechanical Engineering Society: Pres. Wang Daohan.

China Mechanics and Automation Society: Pres. Qian Xuesen.

China Mechanics Society: Pres. Qian Xuesen.

China Medical Society: Pres. Qian Xinzhong; publs. *Chinese Journal of Oto-rhinolaryngology*, *Chinese Journal of Laboratory Diagnosis* (quarterly).

China Metals Society: Pres. Ye Zhiqiang.

China Meteorology Society: Pres. Zhang Naizhao (acting).

China Metrology Society: Pres. Yue Zhijian.

China Microbiology Society.

China Mineralogical, Petrological and Geochemical Society.

China Naval Architecture and Marine Engineering Society: P.O.B. 817, Beijing; f. 1962; Pres. Zhang Youxuan; publs. *Journal of China Shipbuilding*† (quarterly, English contents and abstracts), *Ship Engineering, Knowledge of Ships* (every 2 months).

China Navigation Society.

China Nuclear Society: Pres. Wang Ganchang.

China Nurses Society: Pres. Chen Kunti.

China Oceanology and Limnology Society: Nanhai Rd., Qingdao; f. 1950; *c.* 1,000 mems.; Pres. C. K. Zeng; Vice-Pres. C. C. Jao, C. P. Ho, B. Z. Jiu; publ. *Oceanologia et Limnologia Sinica*† (quarterly).

China Palaeopalynological Society: Pres. Yin Zanxun.

China Pedology Society: Pres. Li Qingkui.

China Petroleum Society: Pres. Hou Xianglin.

China Pharmacology Society.

China Photography Society.

China Physics Society: Pres. Zhou Peiyuan.

China Physiology Society: Pres. Cai Qiao.

China Precision Machinery Society.

China Psychology Society: Pres. Pan Shu.

China Pulp and Paper Engineering Society: Pres. Wang Yizhi.

China Railway Society: 10 Fuxing Rd., P.O.B. 2499, Beijing; f. 1978; railway transport, construction and rolling stock manufacture; Pres. Liu Jianzhong; Sec.-Gen. Zhao Xichun; publs. *Railway Journal*†, *Railway Knowledge*†.

China Research Society for Modernization of Management.

China Scientific and Technological Information Society.

China Sericulture Society.

China Silicates Society: Pres. Qi Jun (acting).

China Sociological Research Society: c/o Chinese Academy of Social Sciences, 5 Jianguomen Nei Da Jie, Beijing; f. 1979; Pres. Fei Xiaotong; Exec. Sec. Wang Kang.

China Space Flight Society: Pres. Ren Xinmin.

China Study of Religion Society: Pres. Ren Jiyu.

China Technical Economy Research Society.

China Textile and Engineering Society: Pres. Chen Weiji.

China Traditional Medicine Society: Chair. Lu Bingkui.

China West European Economy Society.

LIBRARIES

Library of the Chinese Academy of Sciences: 27 Wangfujing Dajie, Beijing; f. 1951; 4,500,000 vols.; main brs. in Shanghai and Lanzhou.

National Library of Beijing: Beijing 7; f. 1912; contains the imperial collections of the Southern Sung (13th century), Ming (1368–1644) and Ching (Manchu) (1644–1911) dynasties; 10,200,000 vols.; Dir. LIU JI-PING.

PROVINCIAL LIBRARIES

Anhui Library: Hefei, Anhui Province.

Fujian Library: Fuzhou, Fujian Province.

Gansu Library: Lanzhou, Gansu Province.

Guangdong Zhong-shan Library: Guangzhou, Guangdong Province.

Guangxi First Library: Guilian, Guangxi Zhuang Autonomous Region.

Guangxi Second Library: Nanning.

Guizhou Library: Guiyang, Guizhou Province.

Hebei Library: Shijiazhuang, Hebei Province.

Henan Library: Zhengzhou, Henan Province.

Heilongjiang Library: Harbin, Heilongjiang Province.

Hubei Library: Wuhan, Hubei Province.

Hunan Library: Changsha, Hunan Province.

Jiangxi Library: Nanchang, Jiangxi Province.

Jilin Library: Changchun, Jilin Province.

Liaoning Library: Shenyang, Liaoning Province; f. 1948.

Nanjing Library: Nanjing, Jiangsu Province; f. 1933; 4,700,000 vols.; Librarian WANG CHANG-BING.

Nei Monggol Library: Hohhot, Nei Monggol Autonomous Region.

Ningxia Library: Yinchuan, Ningxia Hui Autonomous Region.

Qinghai Library: Xining, Qinghai Province.

Shaanxi Library: Xian, Shaanxi Province.

Shandong Library: Jinan, Shandong Province; f. 1908; 2,800,000 vols.; Librarian LIU JIANFEI; publs. Acquisitions Lists of Chinese books, Bibliography of Foreign Periodicals.

Shanghai Library: Shanghai; f. 1952; 6,926,167 vols.; Librarian GU TING-LONG.

Shanxi Library: Taiyuan, Shanxi Province.

Sichuan Library: Chengdu, Sichuan Province.

Tianjin Municipal Library: 22 Cheng-de Rd., Tianjin; f. 1952; 2,500,000 vols.; Librarian HUANG YU-SHENG; publ. *Library Work Research* (quarterly).

Xinjiang Library: Urumqi, Xinjiang Uygur Autonomous Region.

Yunnan Library: Kunming, Yunnan Province.

Zhejiang Library: Hangzhou, Zhejiang Province.

UNIVERSITIES AND COLLEGES

(In alphabetical order by town, with old-style spelling in brackets).

About 170 institutions of higher education have been re-established, including teacher training colleges. Those listed below include the designated "key" colleges.

ANDA, HEILONGJIANG (HEILUNGKIANG) PROVINCE

Daching Petroleum College.

BEIJING (PEKING)

Aeronautical Engineering College.

Beijing Agricultural University.

Beijing Industrial College.

Beijing Medical College: Xue Yuan Lu, Northern Suburb, Beijing; f. 1912.

President: Dr. MAX XU.

Vice-Presidents: Dr. PENG REI CONG, Prof. HANS MULLER, Prof. FENG CHUAN HAN, Dr. CHEN HUA, Mme ZUO JI, WEI YING.

Library of 200,000 vols., 700 periodicals.

Number of teachers: *c.* 1,000.

Number of students: *c.* 2,800.

Publication: *Journal*† (every 2 months).

DEANS:

Faculty of Basic Medicine: Dr. WANG E.
Faculty of Medicine: Prof. YAN REN YING.
Faculty of Public Health: Prof. LIU SHI JIE.
Faculty of Oral Medicine: Prof. ZHENG LIN FAN.
Faculty of Pharmacy: Prof. WANG XU.

There are 16 research institutes and laboratories, and 6 attached teaching hospitals.

Beijing Teachers University.

Beijing Traditional Medicine College.

Beijing University: f. 1898.

President: ZHOU PEIYUAN.
Director of Foreign Affairs: NI MENG-HSIUNG.

Library of 3,290,000 vols.

Number of teachers: 2,874.

Number of students: 7,404 (including 590 postgraduates).

Publications: *Peking University Academic Journal* (Natural Science edn., quarterly, Social Science edn., every 2 months).

Departments of mathematics, mechanics, physics, technical physics, radio physics and electronics, geophysics, chemistry, biology, geology, geography, computer science and technology, psychology, Chinese language and literature, history, philosophy, economics, law, international politics, library science, oriental languages and literature, Western languages and literature, Russian language and literature. There are also 14 research institutes.

Central Music College.

Central Nationalities Institute: depts. of minority languages, history, Chinese language and literature, art; 2,200 students; Vice-Pres. ZONG QUN.

Chemical Engineering College.

Chinese People's University: Pres. CHENG FANGWU.

Foreign Language College.

Foreign Trade College.

International Relations Institute.

Iron and Steel College.

North China Agricultural Mechanization College.

Northern Jiaotong University.

Physical Culture College: Pres. ZHONG SHITONG.

Posts and Telecommunications College.

Qinghua (Tsinghua) University: 3,000 staff; 6,000 students; Pres. LIU DA.

CHANGCHUN, JILIN (KIRIN) PROVINCE

Jilin Geology College.

Jilin Industrial College.

Jilin University: Pres. TANG AOQING.

CHANGSHA, HUNAN PROVINCE

Changsha Engineering College.

Hunan University: Pres. ZHANG JIAN.

CHENGDU (CHENGTU), SICHUAN (SZECHUAN) PROVINCE

Chengdu Telecommunications Engineering College.

Sichuan Medical College.

Sichuan Mining College.

Sichuan University: Pres. GANG NAIER.

Southwest Jiaotong University.

CHONGQING (CHUNGKING), SICHUAN (SZECHUAN) PROVINCE

Chongqing Construction Engineering College.

Chongqing University.

Southwest Political Science and Law College.

FULAERJI, HEILONGJIANG (HEILUNGKIANG) PROVINCE

Northeast Heavy Machinery College.

FUXIN (FUCHIN), LIAONING PROVINCE

Coal Mining College.

GUANGZHOU (KWANGCHOW), GUANGDONG (KWANGTUNG) PROVINCE

Zhongshan (Sun Yat-Sen) Medical College.

Zhongshan (Sun Yat-Sen) University: Hangzhou; Tel. 51710; f. 1924.

President: HUANG HUANQUI.

Librarian: LIAN ZHEN.

Number of teachers: *c.* 1,000.
Number of students: *c.* 5,000.

Publication: *Journal*† (Social Science, Natural Science edns., quarterly).

HEADS OF DEPARTMENTS:

Chinese Language and Literature: Prof. WU HONGCONG.
History: Assoc. Prof. HU SHOUWEI (acting).
Philosophy: Assoc. Prof. LIU RONG.
Economics: Assoc. Prof. ZHANG ZHICHENG (acting).
Mathematics: Prof. XU SONGQING.
Mechanical Engineering: (vacant).
Computer Science: Assoc. Prof. LI YUESHENG.
Physics: Prof. LI HUAZHONG.
Radio and Electronics: Prof. LIN YIKUN.
Chemistry: Prof. LIN SHANGAN.
Biology: Prof. ZHANG HONGDA.
Geography: Assoc. Prof. SHEN CHANXIN (acting).
Geology: Assoc. Prof. FANG RUILIAN.
Foreign Languages: Prof. DAI LIULING.
Meteorology: Prof. CHEN SHIXUN.
Law: (vacant).

HANGZHOU (HANGCHOW), ZHEJIANG (CHEKIANG) PROVINCE

Hangzhou University: Tian Mu Shan Rd., Hangzhou; f. 1952, university status 1958; library of 800,000 vols.; 1,930 teachers, 3,328 students (77 postgraduate); depts. of Chinese language and literature, history, politics, foreign languages, education, geography, mathematics, physics, chemistry, biology, physical education; Pres. CHEN LI; publ. *Journal—Philosophy and Social Science.*

Zhejiang Agricultural University: Hangzhou; f. 1952.

President: Dr. CHU TSU-SIANG.

Vice-Presidents: JIANG XIONG-FEI, CHEN XICHEN, CHEN ZI-YUAN.

Librarian: YOU XIU-LING.

Library of 400,000 vols.
Number of teachers: 600.

Number of students: *c.* 2,500 (incl. graduate and foreign students).

Publication: *Journal* (2 a year).

HEADS OF DEPARTMENTS:

Agronomy: Prof. JI DAO-FAN.
Soil Science and Agricultural Chemistry: Prof. SUN XI.
Plant Protection: Prof. GE QI-XIN (acting).
Horticulture: Prof. LI SHU-XUAN.
Sericulture: Prof. WU ZAI-DE.
Tea Culture and Processing Technology: Prof. ZHANG TANG-HENG.
Agricultural Machinery: Prof. XU DAO-GUAN.
Animal Husbandry and Veterinary Science: Assoc. Prof. WU LAN-SHANG.
Agricultural Economics: Prof. DU XIU-CHANG.
Basic Sciences: Prof. PENG ZUO-QUAN.

Zhejiang University: Pres. QIAN SANQIANG.

HARBIN, HEILONGJIANG (HEILUNGKIANG) PROVINCE

Harbin Shipbuilding Engineering College.

Harbin University of Science and Technology.

HEFEI (HOFEI), ANHUI (ANHWEI) PROVINCE

China University of Science and Technology: f. 1958 by Academia Sinica.

President: NY TSI-ZÉ.

Vice-Presidents: LI CHANG, HUA LOO-KENG, YANG HAI-BO, TSIEN LING-CHAO, YANG JENG-TSONG, LU GANG-FENG.

Library of 200,000 vols., 500,000 periodicals.
Number of teachers: 655.
Number of students: 2,768 undergraduates, 124 postgraduates.

Departments of mathematics, physics, modern physics, modern chemistry, modern mechanics, radio and electronics, earth and space sciences, biology, precision engineering, management science.

Hefei Industrial University.

HOHHOT (HUHEHOT), NEI MONGGOL (INNER MONGOLIA)

Nei Monggol University.

JINAN (TSINAN), SHANDONG (SHANTUNG) PROVINCE

East China Petroleum College.

Shandong University: Pres. WU FUHENG.

KUNMING, YUNNAN PROVINCE

Yunnan Forestry College.

Yunnan University: Pres. LIU PIYUN.

LANZHOU (LANCHOW), GANSU (KANSU) PROVINCE

Lanzhou University.

LUDA (LUTA), LIAONING PROVINCE

Luda Engineering College.

Marine Transport College: Pres. LI JINGTIAN.

NANCHANG, JIANXI (KIANGSI) PROVINCE

Jiangxi Communist Labour University: Pres. LI CHAO.

NANJING (NANKING), JIANGSU (KIANGSU) PROVINCE

East China Water Conservancy College: Pres. YAN KAI.

Nanjing Aeronautical Engineering College.

Nanjing Engineering College: Pres. SHEN HUA.

Nanjing Meteorology College.

Nanjing University: Han-Kou Rd., Nanjing; f. 1902.

President: KUANG YA-MING.

Vice-Presidents: ZHANG DEI, KAO JI-YU, FAN CUN-ZHONG, XU FU-JI, ZHONG SHI-QIN.

Registrar: YUAN XIANG-WAN.

Chief Administrative Officer: CHENG BO-YANG.

Librarian: FAN CUN-ZHONG.

Number of teachers: 1,651.
Number of students: 4,463.

Publication: *Nanjing Daxue Xuebao* (Journal of Nanjing University).

HEADS OF DEPARTMENTS:

Mathematics: YE YAN-QIAN.
Computer Science: YE NAN-XUN.
Astronomy: QU QUIN-YUE.
Physics: WEI RONG-JUE.
Chemistry: DAI AN-BANG.
Biology: CHEN NE-XUN.
Meteorology: HUANG SHI-SONG.
Geography: REN MEI-E.
Geology: XU KE-QIN.
History: HAN RU-LIN.
Economics: DU WEN-ZHEN.
Philosophy: SUN SHU-PING.
Chinese Language and Literature: CHEN BAI-CHEN.
Foreign Languages and Literature: CHEN JIA.

QINGDAO (TSINGTAO), SHANDONG (SHANTUNG) PROVINCE

Shandong Oceanography College.

SHANGHAI

East China Engineering College.

Foreign Language College.

Fudan University: Shanghai 201903; f. 1905; depts. of liberal arts and sciences; five research institutes; library of 1,650,000 vols.; 2,100 teachers; 4,100 students (300 postgraduate); Pres. SU BUQING; publs. *Journal—Social Science* (every 2 months), *Journal—Natural Science* (quarterly), *University Students*.

Jiaotong University: Pres. ZHU WUHUA.

Shanghai Chemical Engineering College.

Shanghai College of Textile Technology: 1882 Yenan Rd. (West), Shanghai 200051; f. 1951.

President: Prof. QIAN BAO-JUN.

Vice-Presidents: ZHANG ZHUO-RU, XUE XI-MIN, LI DONG-LIN.

Library of 378,800 vols. and bound periodicals.
Publication: *Journal* (quarterly).

HEADS OF DEPARTMENTS:

Textile Engineering: Prof. YAN HAO-JING.
Textile Chemistry: Prof. FANG BAI-RONG.
Mechanical Engineering: Prof. LIU YU-XUAN.
Basic Sciences: Prof. ZHANG JI-CHUAN.
Automation: Assoc. Prof. HONG ZHONG-WEI.

Shanghai First Medical College: 138 Yixueyuan Lu, Shanghai 200032; Pres. SHIH MEIXIN.

Shanghai Teachers University.

Tongji University: Pres. LI GUOHAO.

SHENYANG, LIAONING PROVINCE

Northeast College of Technology: Pres. KANG MINZHUANG.

SHIJIAZHUANG (SHIHCHIACHUANG), HEBEI (HOPEI) PROVINCE

Hebei Electric Power College.

TIANJIN (TIENTSIN)

Nankai University: Balitai, Tianjin; Tel. 2-3083; Telex 0589; f. 1919.

President: S. T. YANG SHIXIAN.

Vice-President: WU DAREN.

Deputy Vice-Presidents: CUI XIMO, LOU PING, HU GUODING, TENG WEIZAO, ZHENG TIANTING.

Chief Administrative Officer: SHI YUMIN.

Librarian: LI GUOBIN.

Number of teachers: 1,263.
Number of students: 3,272.

Publications: *Nankai Journal*† (philosophy and social science edn., every 2 months), *Nankai History* 2 a year), *Collected Essays on Linguistics*† (irregular).

CHAIRMEN OF DEPARTMENTS:

Chinese Language and Literature: Prof. ZHU WEIZHI.
History: Assoc. Prof. WEI HONGYUN.
Economics: Prof. WEI XUN.
Philosophy: Prof. WEN GONGYI.
Foreign Languages and Literatures: Prof. LI JIYE.
Chemistry: Prof. GAO ZHENHENG.
Physics: Prof. HE GUOZHU.
Mathematics: Prof. DENG HANYING.
Biology: CUI CHENG.

PROFESSORS:

Department of Chinese Language and Literature:
ZHU WEIZHI, Foreign Literature, and Foreign Literature in Translation
XING GONGWAN, Linguistics
ZHANG QINGCHANG, Phonology and History of Han Language
HUA CUISHEN, Classical Chinese Opera
WANG DAJIN, History of Criticism of Classical Chinese Literature

Department of History:
ZHENG TIANTING, Ming and Qing Dynasties
WU TINGQIU, Japanese History
WANG YUZHE, Pre-Qin Dynasties
YANG ZHIJIU, Sui, Tang, Song and Yuan Dynasties
YANG SHENGMAO, American History and Modern World History
LI GUOBIN, Historiography of Foreign Countries
YANG YIXIANG, Chinese Historiography and Qin and Han Dynasties

Department of Economics:
JI TAODA, History of Economic Thought
WANG GANYU, Politics, Law and Research on American Economy
FU ZHUFU, Chinese Economic History
TAO JIKAN, American and World Economy
WEI XUN, Monopoly Price Theory
YI MENGHONG, West European and World Economy
YANG JINNIAN, African and World Economy
TENG WEIZAO, Transnational Corporations
QIAN RONGKUN, Modern Western Economic Theory
BAO JUEMIN, Economic Geography
LIU JUNHANG, Chinese Agricultural Economy
CHEN YINFANG, Transnational Corporations

Department of Philosophy:
WEN GONGYI, Logic and History of Chinese Philosophy

Department of Foreign Languages and Literatures:
LI JIYE, Research on Lu Xun and Foreign Literatures in Translation
LI YIXIE, English Poetry and 19th-Century English Literature
GAO DIANSEN, Foreign Literatures in Translation

Department of Chemistry:
GAO ZHENHENG, Structural Theory of Organic Compounds
HE BINGLIN, High Polymer Chemistry
WANG JITAO, Basic Organic Compounds
CHEN RONGTI, Complex Compounds and Catalysis
SHEN PANWEN, Inorganic Synthesis
YU ZHONGJIAN, Organic Analysis
YANG SHIXIAN, Organic Chemistry and Pesticide Chemistry
CHEN RUYU, Pesticide Chemistry

Department of Physics:
JIANG ANCAI, Spectral Analysis
HE GUOZHU, Nuclear Physics and Electron Optics
SHEN SHOUCHUN, Optics and Laser
CHENG JING, Theory of Relativity
ZHAO JINGYUAN, Metallic Physics and Basic Physics

Department of Mathematics:
WU DAREN, Differential Geometry
DENG HANYING, Partial Differential Equations
HU GUODING, Information Theory
YAN ZHIDA, Lie Groups—Lie Algebra
WANG ZIKUN, Probability
ZHOU XUEGUANG, Topology
LI ENPO, Algebra
CHEN SHOU, Geometry

Department of Biology:
CUI CHENG, Plant Physiology
LIU YIRAN, Plant Genetics
QI XIUHUI, Plant Morphology
ZHOU YULIANG, Fungi

Tianjin University.

URUMQI (URUMCHI), XINJIANG (SINKIANG) PROVINCE

Xinjiang University.

WUHAN, HUBEI (HUPEH) PROVINCE

Central China Engineering College: Pres. ZHU JIUSI.

Central China Mining and Metallurgy College.

Hubei Construction Industry College.

Wuhan Geology College.

Wuhan Surveying and Cartography College.

Wuhan University.

Wuhan Water Conservancy and Electric Power College.

XIAMEN (AMOY), FUJIAN (FUKIEN) PROVINCE

Xiamen University: Xiamen, Fujian; Tel. 2080; Telex 0633; f. 1921.

President: ZENG MING.

Vice-Presidents: SI SHOU-XING, CAI QI-RUI, ZHAO YUAN, WEI LI-GONG, PAN MAO-YUAN, TANG ZHONG-ZHANG, FU JIA-LIN.

Chief Administrative Officer: JIN JIAN.

Number of teachers: 1,194.

Number of students: 4,523 undergraduate, 168 postgraduate.

Publications: *Xiamen University Journal*† (philosophy and social sciences edn. and natural sciences edn., both quarterly).

DEANS:

Chinese: Prof. ZHENG CHAO-ZONG.
Foreign Languages: LIN YI-JIN.
History: Prof. CHEN BI-SHENG.
Economics: Prof. YAN ZHEN-YUE.
Philosophy: ZHOU YONG-XIAN.
Mathematics: Prof. FANG DE-ZHI.
Physics: WO BO-XI.
Chemistry: GU XUE-MING.
Biology: HUANG HOU-ZHE.
Oceanography: HOU EN-DIAN.

XIAN (SIAN), SHAANXI (SHENSI) PROVINCE

Northwest Industrial University.

Northwest Light Industry College.

Northwest Telecommunications College.

Northwest University.

Xian Jiaotong University: Xianning Rd., Xian; Tel. 3-1011; Telex 2827 XIAN; f. 1896.

President: CHEN WUYU.

Vice-Presidents: ZHOU HUIJIU, CHEN XUEJUN, ZHUANG LITING, SHI WEIXIANG.

Administrative Officers: SHI WEIXIANG, LIAO CHUNEN.

Librarian: ZHAO FUXIN.

Number of teachers: 1,500.

Number of students: 8,000 (including 180 postgraduates).

Publication: *Journal*†.

DEANS:

Department of Mathematics: XU GUIFANG.
Department of Engineering Mechanics: JIANG YONGQIU.
Department of Mechanical Engineering and Materials Science: TAO ZHONG.
Department of Power Machinery Engineering (1): FU LONGZHOU.
Department of Power Machinery Engineering (2): CHENG NAIJIN.
Department of Electrical Engineering: PAN JI.
Department of Electronic Engineering: HU ZHENGJIA.
Department of Information and Control Engineering: HU BAOSHENG.
Department of Basic Courses: CHEN WENJIAN.

DIRECTORS:

Research Institute of Mechanical Behaviour of Metals: ZHOU HUIJIU.
Mechanical Engineering Research Institute: TAO ZHONG.
Systems Engineering Research Institute.
Research Institute of Engineering Thermophysics: CHEN XUEJUN.

XIANGTAN (SIANGTAN), HUNAN PROVINCE

Xiangtan University.

XIYANG, SHANXI (SHANSI) PROVINCE

Dazhai Agricultural College.

ZHENJIANG (CHENCHIANG), JIANGSU (KIANGSU) PROVINCE

Agricultural Machinery College.

ZHENGZHOU (CHENGCHOW), HENAN (HONAN) PROVINCE

North China Agricultural University.

CHINA (TAIWAN)

Population 17,000,000

ACADEMIES

ACADEMIA SINICA

NANKANG, TAIPEI

Founded 1928.

Directs and promotes scientific research.

President: Dr. SHIH-LIANG CHIEN.
Director-General: Prof. HUA-CHENG KAO.
Secretary-General: SHAO-CHANG WAN.

There are 90 elected members. Library of *c.* 500,000 vols.

Institute of Mathematics: Dir. Dr. KY FAN.
Institute of Physics: Dir. Dr. ER-KANG LIN.
Institute of Chemistry: Dir. Dr. WEI-CHUAN LIN.
Institute of Botany: Dir. Dr. HUNG-PAN WU.
Institute of Zoology: Dir. Dr. KUN-HSIUNG CHANG.
Institute of Biological Chemistry: Dir. Dr. TUNG-BIN LO.
Institute of History and Philology: Dir. Prof. CHU-HSUN KAO.
Institute of Modern History: Dir. Prof. SHIH-CHIANG LU.
Institute of Ethnology: Dir. Prof. CHUNG-I WEN.
Institute of Economics: Dir. Dr. TSONG-SHIAN YU.
Institute of American Culture: Dir. Dr. YEN CHU.
Institute of Earth Sciences Preparatory Office: Dir. Dr. I-BEN TSAI.
Institute of Information Science Preparatory Office: Dir. Dr. T. S. KUO (acting).
Institute of the Three Principles of the People Preparatory Office: Dir. Dr. CHAO-NAN CHEN.

ACADEMIA HISTORICA

225 SEC. 3, PEI YI ROAD, HSINTIEN, TAIPEI

President: HUANG CHI-LU.
Secretary: Prof. LI YUN-HAN.

BOARD OF COUNCILLORS:

Prof. TS'UI CH'UI-YEN, Prof. LENG HSIN, Prof. YANG YUN-PING, Prof. LI CHI, Prof. TSENG HSU-PAI, Prof. LING HUNG-SHUN, Prof. HSIAO I-SHAN, Rev. Prof. MAURUS FANG-HAO, Prof. MAO TSE-SHUI.

Contains national archives, library, documents totalling 2,453,982.

Department of Historical Archives: Dir. CHANG MING-KAI.
Department of Acquisition: Dir. CHIH CHING-TE.
Department of General Affairs: Dir. TAN LONG-PING.

NATIONAL INSTITUTE FOR COMPILATION AND TRANSLATION

247 KEELUNG ROAD, TAIPEI

Founded 1932.

Director: TIEN-MING WANG.

Translates foreign books, examines and approves textbooks and standardizes scientific and technical terms; 49 full-time members; library of 30,000 vols.

Publication: *Counter Attack* (monthly).

Department of Natural Sciences: HAN-CHIH RUI.
Department of Humanities and Social Services: PANG-YUAN CHI.
Department of Textbooks: LIANG-WU CHAO.

LEARNED SOCIETIES

Agricultural Association of China: 14 Wenchow St., Taipei; f. 1917; mems. 116 institutions and 1,856 individuals; Pres. PAUL C. MA; publ. *Journal* (quarterly).

American Cultural Center, American Institute in Taiwan: 54 Nan Hai Rd., Taipei 107; f. 1979; br. in Kaohsiung; promotes understanding and study of America; exhibitions, lectures, etc.; library of 12,300 vols., 280 periodicals, 2,900 microforms, 240 video/audio cassette recordings, 1,300 records.

Asia Foundation, The: 42 Chien Kuo N. Rd., Taipei; one of 12 brs. of the main organization in the U.S.A. (*q.v.*); Representative SHELDON R. SEVERINGHAUS.

Astronomical Society of the Republic of China: c/o Taipei Observatory, Yuan Shan, Taipei 104; f. 1958; to promote the sciences of astronomy and maintain contact with world astronomers; approved by IAU to act as Nat. Cttee. of Astronomy; 200 mems.; Pres. Dr. C. S. SHEN; Gen. Sec. CHANG-HSIEN TSAI.

China Academy: Hwa Kang, Yang Ming Shan; f. 1966; private institution for sinological studies, consisting of 20 academic asscns. and research institutions and Taiwanese and foreign mems.; 251 hon. acads., 517 acads., 1,553 fellows; library of 289,222 Chinese vols., 30,395 Japanese and Korean vols., 89,159 Western vols.; Pres. CHANG CHI-YUN; Sec.-Gen. and Head Research and Development Section PAN WEI-HO; publs. *Sino-American Relations* (quarterly in English), *Beautiful China Pictorial Monthly* (bilingual Chinese and English), *Sinological Monthly* (Chinese), *Sinological Quarterly* (Chinese), *Renaissance Monthly* (Chinese), *Chinese Culture* (quarterly in English).

China National Association of Literature and the Arts: 4 Lane 22, Nuigpo St. W., Taipei.

China Society, The: P.O.B. 13-21, Taipei; f. 1960 as a centre for Chinese studies; *c.* 100 mems.; Pres. Dr. ALBERT R. O'HARA; Vice-Pres. Dr. HERBERT MA; publ. *Journal* (annually).

Chinese Association for the Advancement of Science: 5 Chungshan South Rd., Taipei; f. Nanking 1917, refounded in Taiwan 1954; Pres. CHENG TIEN-FONG; publ. *Science Education.*

Chinese Association for Folklore: 422 Fulin Rd., Shihlin, Taipei, P.O.B. 68-1292; f. 1932; studies Chinese and Asian folklore; 47 mems.; library of over 1,000 vols. and MSS.; Chair. Prof. LOU TSU-K'UANG; Sec. AMY LOU.

Chinese Chemical Society: P.O.B. 609, Taipei; f. 1932; 6,200 mems.; Pres. Dr. T. T. LAI; publs. *Journal*†, *Chemistry* (quarterly).

Chinese Classical Music Association: 1 Lane 3, Linyi St., Taipei 100; f. 1951; 1,100 mems.; Pres. Prof. TSAI-PING LIANG; publs. *Bibliography of Chinese Music, Music of Cheng, Chinese Musical Instruments and Pictures.*

Chinese Forestry Association: 2 Sec. 1, Hang-chou South Rd., Taipei; f. 1948; 1,906 mems.; Pres. HSIOH-HSUIN TSU; publs. *Taiwan's Forestry Monthly, Tables of Volume of Timber in Cubic Feet, Acreage of Forest in Taiwan, Important Wood Species of Taiwan, Quarterly Journal of Chinese Forestry.*

Chinese Institute of Civil Engineering: Room 902, 70 Chunghsiao W. Rd., Sec. I Taipei; f. 1936; Pres. TAO-LUNG WANG; publs. *Civil Engineering, Terms of Civil Engineering, A Series of Codes on Prestressed Concrete.*

Chinese Institute of Engineers: 4th Floor, 1 Jen. Ai Rd., Sec. 2, Taipei; f. 1912; 1,577 mems.; library of 2,000 vols. in Chinese, 11,000 vols. in other languages; Pres. HSIAO-CHANG YEN; publ. *Engineering Journal* (monthly).

Chinese Language Society: c/o Taiwan Normal University, Hop'ing East Road, Taipei; f. 1953; Dir. MAO TZU-SHUI; publ. *Chinese Language Monthly.*

Chinese Mathematical Society: National Taiwan University, Taipei; 185 mems.; Pres. SHIEN-SIU SHU; Sec. LUNG-CHI MIAO.

Chinese Medical Association: 201 Shih-Pai Rd., Sec. II, P.O.B. 3043, Taipei; f. 1915; 1,142 mems.; Pres. Dr. CHI-SHUEN TSOU; Sec.-Gen. Dr. TAO-CHANG HSU; publ. *Chinese Medical Journal* (quarterly).

Chinese National Foreign Relations Association: 3rd Floor, 94, Nanchang St., Sec. 1, Taipei; Pres. HUANG KUO-SHU.

Chinese Statistical Association: 1, Section 1, Nan Chung Rd., Taipei; f. 1941; 1,082 mems.; Pres. C. C. LEE; publ. *Chinese Statistical Journal*.

Committee on Promotion of the Peaceful Uses of Atomic Energy: 110 Yenping South Rd., Taipei; Pres. MILTON J. T. SHIEH.

Confucius-Mencius Society of the Republic of China: 45 Nanhai Rd., Taipei; f. 1960; dedicated to dissemination of knowledge about Confucius and Mencius, the improvement of public morals and the creation of a better society; 3,212 mems.; Chair. Dr. CHEN LI-FU; Sec. JOHNSON C. LU; publs. include *Confucius-Mencius Monthly*, *Journal of Confucius-Mencius Society*.

International House Association, Taipei Chapter: 18 Hsin Yi Rd.; Section 3, Taipei 106; Chair. GEORGE Y. L. WU.

Library Association of China: c/o National Central Library, 43 Nan Hai Rd., Taipei; f. 1953 to assist the Ministry of Education to manage the affairs of the Summer Library Workshop, to compile a librarian's library, promote the exhibition of books, and carry out investigations of libraries of China. The Executive Committee consists of 7 mems.; Sec.-Gen. I TING-CHANG; publs. *Bulletin*, *Newsletter*.

National Bar Association: 124 Chungking South Rd.; Sec. 1, Taipei.

Physical Society of China: c/o Institute of Physics, Academia Sinica, Taipei.

RESEARCH INSTITUTES

(*see also* under Academies and Universities)

Atomic Energy Council: 67 Lane 144, Keelung Rd., Sec. 4, Taipei 107; f. 1955 for the planning and execution of programme for the peaceful application of atomic energy; 15 mems.; library of 10,000 vols. and a deposit library at the National Tsing Hua Univ. with 36,000 vols. and 320,000 microcards; Chair. SHIH LIANG CHIEN; Sec.-Gen. CHEN-HWA CHENG; publs. *Nuclear Science Journal* (quarterly), *Chinese AEC Bulletin* (bi-monthly).

Central Geological Survey: P.O.B. 968, Taipei 100; reorganized from Geological Survey of Taiwan; f. 1946; geological research and mapping; mineral survey; ground water and engineering research; 32 staff; library of over 12,000 vols.; Dir. T. L. HSU (acting); Chief Geologist S. F. TSAN; Chief Mineralogist C. H. CHEN; publs. *Bulletin*† (annually), maps and papers.

Co-operative League of the Republic of China: 11-2 Fu Chow St., Taipei; f. 1928; co-operative business research and education; Chair. KU CHENG-KANG; Exec. Dir./Sec.-Gen. YEN SUNG CHEN.

Council for Agricultural Planning and Development: 37 Nanhai Rd., Taipei; f. 1979 replacing the Sino-American Joint Comm. on Rural Reconstruction (JCRR); an advisory, planning and coordination agency; provides technical and financial assistance in rural reconstruction programmes, aiming to improve living standards, increase agricultural production, strengthen agricultural research and promote international technical co-operation; library of over 14,000 vols.; Chair. Dr. ROBERT C. T. LEE; Sec.-Gen. C. C. KOH; publs. *General Reports*† (annually), technical papers, news releases (irregular).

Industrial Technology Research Institute: 195 Chung Hsing Rd., Sec. 4, Chu-Tung, Hsinchu, Taiwan; f. 1973; *c.* 2,000 staff; library of 100,000 vols.; 4 research laboratories for studying industrial problems; Pres. H. C. FANG; publ. *Industrial Technology*† (monthly in Chinese).

Union Industrial Research Laboratories: f. 1954; 11 research depts.; Dir. PAUL L. C. HAO.

Mining Research and Service Organization: f. 1961; 8 research depts.; Dir. T. T. FENG.

Metal Industrial Research Laboratories: f. 1964; 7 research depts.; Dir. S. K. CHI.

Electronics Research and Service Organization: f. 1977; 3 research depts.; Dir. D. W. HU.

National Bureau of Standards: 61-1 Sung-Chiang Rd., Taipei 104; f. 1947; national standards, weights and measures; patents; trademarks; library of 1,932 vols. in Chinese and Japanese, 2,162 vols. in Western languages, 190 periodicals; Dir.-Gen. C. O. KOU; publs. *Official Gazette for Standards*†, *Official Gazette for Patents*† (monthly), *Official Gazette for Trademarks*† (2 a month), *Chinese National Standards*† (irregular).

National Institute of Education Materials: 41 Nan Hai Rd., Taipei; f. 1956; functions as auxiliary of Ministry of Education; responsible for acquisition, compilation and exhibition of Chinese and foreign educational materials; promotes audio-visual education and produces audio-visual teaching materials; operates educational radio station; Dir. CHIA-YEN CHEN.

National Science Council: 2 Canton St., Taipei, Taiwan; f. 1959; assists and supports general scientific and technological research and development; 207 staff; library of 50,000 vols.; Chair. Dr. SIEN-SIU SHU; publs. *NSC Review*† (annually, in English and Chinese), *Proceedings of NSC*† (quarterly, in English with Chinese abstracts), *Science Bulletin*† (monthly in English), *NSC Monthly*† (in Chinese with English abstracts), *Special Publications* (irregular in Chinese or English), *NSC Symposium Series* (irregular, in Chinese or English).

Taiwan Agricultural Research Institute: 189 Chung-Cheng Rd., Wan-Fen, Wu-Feng, Taichung; f. 1895; research on soils, fertilizers, physiology, pathology and entomology for field and horticultural crops; 235 staff; Dir. Dr. HSIUNG WAN; publ. *Journal of Agricultural Research of China*† (quarterly).

Taiwan Fisheries Research Institute: 199 Hou-ih Rd., Keelung; f. 1909; 306 staff; library of 170,000 vols.; Dir. Dr. TSANN-JAN LEE; publs. *Bulletin*† (annually), reports†.

Taiwan Forestry Research Institute: Botanical Garden, Nan-Hai Rd., Taipei; f. 1945; 145 mems.; library of 30,000 vols.; Dir. SHEN-CHENG LIU; Sec. FAN-SHI KUNG; publ. *Bulletin*† (irregular).

Taiwan Sugar Research Institute: 54 Sheng Chan Rd., Tainan; f. 1932; supported by Taiwan Sugar Corp.; research in sugarcane breeding, agronomy, plant nutrition, plant protection, ground water resources, sugar technology, by-product utilization; 3 experiment stations in Huwei, Hsingying, Pingtun; library of 30,000 vols.; Dir. S. C. SHIH, PH.D.; publs. *Report* (quarterly in Chinese, English summary); *Annual Report* (in English); *Technical Bulletin*, *Extension Bulletin*.

LIBRARIES

National Central Library: 43 Nan Hai Rd., Taipei; f. in Nanking 1933, re-established in Taiwan in 1954; 600,000 items, including rare Chinese collection of 144,467 vols., ancient manuscripts, stone rubbings; the library exchanges books with 969 institutions in 79 nations; Dir. Prof. WANG CHENG-KU; publs. *Chinese National Bibliography* (monthly), *Bulletin* (2 a year), *Index of Chinese Periodicals* (monthly), *NCL Newsletter* (quarterly, English and Chinese edns.), *Guide to Libraries of the Republic of China*, various catalogues and indexes, etc.

Institute of History and Philology Library: Academia Sinica, Taipei 115; 250,000 vols., incl. 21,476 rare books; 30,000 rubbings; 10,000 folk plays; cabinet records of Ming and Ch'ing dynasties and factual files of Ming dynasty.

Kuomintang Central Committee Library: 11 South Chung Shan Rd., Taipei; f. 1934; 226,539 vols. on Dr. Sun Yat-sen's writings and studies on San Min Chu Yih and modern Chinese history; Librarian CHAI CHUN-SHIH; publs.† *Free China Review, China Magazine, Central Monthly.*

National War College Library: Yangmingshan, Taipei; 156,639 vols. on political subjects; Librarian LO MOU-PIN.

Taipei City Library: 46 Chinan Rd., Sec. 2; Taipei; f. 1952; 125,000 vols.; 4 brs., a braille point reading room and 7 mobile units; Dir. CHIH-SHIH YANG; publ. *Taipei Municipal Library Annals.*

Taiwan Branch Library, National Central Library: 1 Hsinshen South Rd., Sec. I, Taipei; f. 1915; 381,704 vols.; special collections of Taiwan and Southern Asian materials; Dir. ANLLEY E. HU; publs. *Catalogue of Books Relating to Taiwan, Catalogue of Western Books on China, Union Catalogue of Chinese Bibliographies, Catalogue of Western Books on Southern Asia, Catalogue of the Periodicals and Newspapers Collected in the NCL, Taiwan Branch.*

MUSEUMS AND ART GALLERIES

Hwa Kang Museum: Ta Yi Bldg., University of Chinese Culture, Yang Ming Shan, Taipei; f. 1963; main collections of folk and modern Chinese arts: bronzes, pottery, porcelain, lacquer ware, calligraphy and paintings; portraits of famous persons in Chinese history; Chinese drama, music, modern handicrafts in Taiwan; exhibitions of pre-historic animals; Taiwan aborigine collection; maps; materials relating to the history of the College of Culture; Dir. CH'EN KUO-NING; publs. *Beautiful China*† (monthly), *Renaissance Monthly*†, *Sinological Monthly*†, *Activities of Hwa Kang Museum*†, *Creative Weekly*†.

National Museum of History: 49 Nan Hai Rd., Taipei; f. 1955; includes collections of Chinese historical objects and artefacts (ritual jades, oracle bones, funerary objects, coins, sculpture, porcelain, wood, ivory, bamboo, calligraphy and paintings); art research; library of 16,000 vols.; Dir. HO HAO-TIEN; publ. *Bulletin*†.

National Museum of Science and Education: Taipei.

National Palace Museum: Wai-shuang-hsi, Shih-lin, Taipei; f. 1925 in Peiping, 1949 in Taiwan as Joint Administration of National Palace and Central Museum in Taichung; moved to Taipei and reorganized under present title 1965; collections consist chiefly of treasures brought from the mainland; bronzes, jade, porcelain, lacquer, enamel ware, carvings, calligraphy, paintings, rare books and documents, dating from the Shang Dynasty (1522–1028 B.C.) to the Ch'ing Dynasty (A.D. 1644–1911); research library of 30,000 vols., 508 periodical titles, 150,000 rare books, over 390,000 documents; Dir. CHIANG FU-TSUNG; publs. *Newsletter*† (monthly in English), *Bulletin*† (every 2 months in English), *Quarterly*† (in English and Chinese), *Palace Museum News Sketches* (monthly in Chinese), illustrated catalogues, handbooks, research monographs, etc.

National Taiwan Arts Center: 47 Nan Hai Rd., Taipei; f. 1957; exhibitions of art; performances of national opera, plays, films, concerts, dancing; Dir. K. K. FENG; publs. *Journal of Arts* (quarterly), *Facial Symbolism in Chinese Opera, Chinese Opera Costumes, Chinese Musical Instruments.*

National Taiwan Science Hall: 41 Nan Hai Rd., Taipei; f. 1958; planetarium, science exhibitions, micro-organism projections; organized Science Clubs of the Republic of China 1962; f. 1956; Dir. CHANG-MO TIEN; publs. *Science Clubs Bulletin* (monthly), *Management Science Thesis* (annually).

Postal Museum: 17 Lane 142, Kwang Ming St., Sintien, Taipei; f. 1966; documents and objects relating to the history of the Chinese postal service and the UPU; complete collection of Chinese postage stamps, original designs of stamps; proofs and engravings; library of books, catalogues and periodicals in connection with philately; Curator F. C. WANG.

Taiwan Provincial Museum: 2 Siangyang Rd., Taipei; f. 1908, renamed in 1946; collections of local Taiwan cultures, natural history, geology, meteorology; spectroscopic dating lab. for fossils; Dir. LIU YEN; publs. *Quarterly Journal*† (in English), *Science Annual*†, *Science Report on the Geology and Paleontology of Ts'o-chen, Tainan* (annually), *Bulletin of Malacology* (annually).

UNIVERSITIES

FU-JEN CATHOLIC UNIVERSITY

HSINCHUANG, TAIPEI

Founded 1963.

President: Most Rev. STANISLAUS LO KUANG.

Colleges of Liberal Arts, Natural Sciences, Business, Foreign Languages and Law; Graduate schools of Chinese literature, history, philosophy, linguistics, mathematics, physics, German language and literature, English language and literature; Evening Division.

Number of teachers: 1,084.
Number of students: 11,680.

NATIONAL CENTRAL UNIVERSITY

CHUNG-LI

Founded 1968 as re-establishment of National Central University (Nanking).

Academic year: February to July, September to January.

President: Prof. SHING-MENG LEE.
Dean of Studies: Prof. GEORGE CHAO SHU.
Dean of Students: Prof. JHY-PING TANG.
Dean of General Affairs: Prof. SHUN-PO LEE.
Librarian: Prof. TSAN-PO YEN.

Number of teachers: 184.
Number of students: 1,388.

Publication: *Bulletin of Geophysics* (2 a year).

DEANS:

College of Liberal Arts: Prof. CHING-MAI YANG.
College of Science: Prof. SAN-CHI HU.
College of Engineering: Prof. SING CHU.

HEADS OF GRADUATE INSTITUTES:

Institute of Mathematics: TSONG-CHIH SHIEH.

Institute of Statistics: Dr. FENG-YI CHUNG.
Institute of Physics and Astronomy: Dr. TSU-WEI NEE.
Institute of Geophysics: Prof. CHIA-HAO YANG.
Institute of Atmospheric Physics: Dr. JER-JIUNN CHEN.
Institute of Chemical Engineering: Prof. LEO-WANG CHEN.

DEPARTMENT HEADS:

Mathematics: Dr. TSONG-CHIH SHIEH.
Physics: Dr. TSU-WEI NEE.
Geophysics: Dr. TSANG-PO YEN.
Atmospheric Physics: Dr. JER-JIUNN CHEN.
Chemical Engineering: Dr. LEO-WANG CHEN.
Civil Engineering: Dr. GUANG-SHI LIN.
Mechanical Engineering: Assoc. Prof. TIEN-I LIU.
Chinese: Prof. TA-CHENG YU.
Foreign Languages: Dr. WEI-HSIN TIEN.

NATIONAL CHENGCHI UNIVERSITY

MUSHAN 116, TAIPEI

Founded 1927 as School of Political Science, university status 1945; Government financed.

Languages of instruction: Chinese and English; Academic year: September to July (two semesters).

President: OU-YANG HSUN.
Dean of Studies: HSIEH-CHI YEH.
Dean of Students: CHIN-HEN YEN.
Dean of Business Affairs: CHENG-FANG CHANG.

Library of 592,051 vols.

Number of teachers: 697 (full-and part-time).

Number of students: 6,031.

DEANS OF GRADUATE SCHOOLS:

Education: PAO-TIEN TSAI.
Political Science: ROLET C. S. CHEN.
International Law and Diplomacy: JEN-CHIEH WANG.
Journalism: CHIN-YAO CHI.
Public Finance: TING-AN CHEN.
Chinese Literature: TZONG-TAO LUO.
Public Administration: LEI-JINN HWA.
Business Administration: SHIH-CHUN HSU.
Land Economics: CHANG-FU YIN.
Law: JHY-MOU SHIH.
East Asian Studies: POI-I TSAO.
Statistics: FRANK F. S. CHI.
Accounting: TING-WONG CHENG.
International Trade: I-KUEI CHOU.
China Border Area Studies: YI-TANG LIU.
Economics: MING-JEN LU.
History: CHIN-HENG YEN.
Dr. Sun Yat-Sen's Doctrine: SHU-FAN YANG.

DEANS OF COLLEGES:

College of Liberal Arts and Sciences: CHIA-SHIH HSU.
College of Law: ROLET C. S. CHEN.
College of Commerce: CHUAN-TING LU.

HEADS OF DEPARTMENTS:

Chinese Literature: TZONG-TAO LUO.
Oriental Languages and Cultures: CHO-HWI WANG.
Western Languages and Literature: BURT LING KING.
Education: SHAN-YUN LIANG.
Journalism: GIN-YAO CHI.
Political Science: CHIH-JEN CHING.
Law: TIEH-GHENG LIU.
Diplomacy: WEI-CHENG LEE.
Sociology and Ethnology: EN-SHEAN LIN.
Public Finance: TING-AN CHEN.
Public Administration: RUENN-SHU CHANG.
Land Economics: CHANG-FU YIN.
International Trade: I-LANG TSOUR.
Statistics: TZO-CZU PENG.
Accounting: TING-WONG CHENG.
Banking: CHING-ING HOU.
Business Administration: IN-FUNG LIN.
History: SHOU-NAN WANG.
Philosophy: ALBERT CHAO.
Economics: MING-JEN LU.
Mathematics: JAU-SHYONG SHIUE.
Psychology: KUO-YANN HUANG.

NATIONAL CHENG KUNG UNIVERSITY

TA-HSUEH ROAD, TAINAN

Telephone: (062) 361111/31.

Founded 1927 as Tainan Higher Technical School, renamed Taiwan Provincial College of Engineering 1946, present name 1971.

Languages of instruction: Chinese and some English; Academic year: September to January, February to June.

President: Dr. WEI-NOON WANG.
Dean of Studies: Dr. YEN-PING SHIH.
Librarian: HSIEN-JU TIEN.

Number of teachers: 733.
Number of students: 9,435.

DEANS:

College of Liberal Arts: Dr. CHUNG-HSIN CHENG.
College of Sciences: Dr. LI-CHUN WANG.
College of Engineering: Dr. LUNG-CHANG CHOW.
College of Business Administration: Dr. CHUEN-TYI CHOW.

Graduate institutes are attached to the College of Engineering.

NATIONAL CHIAO TUNG UNIVERSITY

45 PO AI STREET, HSINCHU

Telephone: (035) 224864.

Founded 1896.

Languages of instruction: Chinese and English; Academic year: September to June (two semesters).

President: Dr. NAN-HUNG KUO.
Dean of Studies: Dr. KUANG-CHIH HUANG.
Dean of Students: Prof. WU KO.
Dean of General Affairs: Prof. SE-SHIANG TZENG.
Secretary: Prof. JIN-CHOU LIN.
Registrar: H. M. WU.
Librarian: SHU LIN.

Library of 113,352 vols.
Number of teachers: 306.
Number of students: 2,434.
Publications: *Journal, Science Bulletin.*

DEANS AND HEADS OF DEPARTMENTS:

College of Engineering: Dr. CHI-FU DEN.
Electronics Engineering: Dr. LONG-ING CHEN.
Control Engineering: Dr. TSU-TIEN LEE.
Communication Engineering: Dr. KUAN-SEN MUNG.
Marine Technology: Dr. TI-LI WAN.
Mechanical Engineering: Dr. CHO-MING CHEN.
Civil Engineering: Dr. CHIA-CHI YAO.
College of Science: (vacant).
Electrophysics: Dr. SHENG-TSI CHOU.
Applied Mathematics: Dr. KUO-SHUNG CHENG.
Information Science: (vacant).
College of Management: Dr. MING-YUEH TARNG.
Management Science: Dr. YING-LIANG CHEN.
Industrial Engineering and Management: Dr. WU-CHENG CHEN.

DIRECTORS OF GRADUATE INSTITUTES:

Electronics: Dr. CHING-YUAN WU.
Management Science: Dr. CHARNG-HORNG HSIEH.
Computer Science: Dr. ZEN CHEN.
Traffic and Transportation: Dr. CHUAN-FANG WANG.
Applied Mathematics: Dr. CHUN-HSIUNG HUANG.
Telecommunication Engineering: Dr. CHI-FU DEN.
Electro-Optical Engineering: (vacant).

NATIONAL CHUNGHSING UNIVERSITY

250 KUOKUANG ROAD, TAICHUNG

Founded 1961.

Includes the former Taiwan Provincial College of Agriculture, Taichung, and the Taiwan Provincial College of Law and Commerce, Taipei.

President: LO YUN-PIN.
Dean of Academic Affairs: LEE CHING-YU.
Dean of General Affairs: LEE CHUN-SHU.
Dean of Students: CHANG NAI-WEI.
Librarian: CHEN CHE-YA.

Number of teachers: 1,107.
Number of students: 9,745.

DEANS:
College of Agriculture: HAN YOU-HSIN.
College of Law and Commerce: CHANG SHU-WEN.
College of Science and Engineering: HAN PAO-TEH.
College of Liberal Arts: HWANG YEONG-WU.

NATIONAL TAIWAN INSTITUTE OF TECHNOLOGY

43 KEELUNG ROAD, SEC. 4, TAIPEI

Founded 1974.

Academic year: August to July (two semesters).

President: KAO-WEN MAO.
Dean of Studies: N. J. CHU.

Library of over 32,000 vols.
Number of teachers: 125.
Number of students: 2,000.

HEADS OF DEPARTMENTS:
Industrial Management: YUAN-CHWEN YOU.
Electronic Engineering: CHING-CHUN HSIEH.
Mechanical Engineering: YIEN-LONG CHEN.
Textile Engineering: WEN-LONG YANG.
Construction Engineering: CHI-TUNG YEH.
Chemical Engineering: CHIEN-TEN LIU.
Electrical Engineering: SHENG-NIAN YEH.

NATIONAL TAIWAN UNIVERSITY

1 ROOSEVELT RD. IV, TAIPEI

Telephone: 351-0231.

Founded in 1928 during the Japanese occupation as the Taihoku Imperial University; taken over and name changed by the Chinese Government in 1954.

Language of instruction: Chinese; Academic year: August to June (two semesters).

President: CHEN-HSING YEN.
Dean of Studies: CHUNG-MO HAN.
Dean of Students: STEVEN KUAN-TSYH YU.
Dean of Business Affairs: KUO-MO CHIAO.
Library Director: YANG ZU-ZAN.

Library of 1,195,547 vols.
Number of teachers: 1,647.
Number of students: 13,519.

Publications: *Acta Geologica Taiwanica, Acta Botanica Taiwanica, History and Chinese Literature Series, Classified Index to Chinese Periodicals, List of Publications of the Faculty and Staff Members of the NTU,* various department publs., etc.

DEANS OF COLLEGES:
College of Liberal Arts: HOU CHIEN.
College of Science: TUNG-PI LO.
College of Law: YAO CHI-CHING.
College of Medicine: MIN-TSUNG PENG.
College of Agriculture: CHAO-CHEN CHEN.

DIRECTORS OF GRADUATE INSTITUTES:
Chinese Literature: CHING-BING YEH.
History: SUN TUNG-HSUN.
Philosophy: HUANG CHENG-HWA.
Archaeology and Anthropology: CHIEN-CHUNG YIN.
Foreign Languages and Literature: JOHN Y. H. HU.
Mathematics: CHEN-UAN HUNG.
Physics: POH-KUN TSENG.
Chemistry: TONG-MING SHEU.
Geology: YUAN WANG.
Zoology: HUANG CHUNG-CHIA.
Botany: CHIU-JUNG LIN.
Psychology: YUNG-HO KO.
Biochemical Science: YEE-HSIUNG CHEN.
Political Science: CHANG CHIAN-HAN.
Law: YANG ZU-ZAN.
Economics: CHENG-CHERNG CHEN.
Business Administration: TING-KO CHEN.
Sociology: CHEN-LOU CHU.
Anatomy: TSUNG-MIN CHENG.
Physiology: T. F. HUANG.
Pathology: SU-WEN HOU.
Biochemistry: LUNG-YAW LIN.
Pharmacology: C. H. OUYANG.
Microbiology: JUI-KUANG CHIU.
Public Health: CHIA-CHIN LIN.
Agronomy: TSAN-LANG LIN.
Agricultural Chemistry: YUAN-CHI SU.
Plant Pathology and Entomology: KAI-KUANG HO.
Horticulture: LIH HUNG.
Oceanography: CHEN JU-CHING.
Civil Engineering: CHIN-LIEN YEN.
Mechanical Engineering: SHUI-SHONG LU.
Electrical Engineering: TE-SON KUO.
Chemical Engineering: SHIH-YOW HUANG.
Agricultural Engineering: YEE-SOONG TSAO.
Forestry: PETER CHÜ-SAN LIN.
Animal Husbandry: CHIN-WEN LIN.
Veterinary Medicine: C. H. CHANG.
Agricultural Economics: YING-CHIH CHIANG
Agricultural Extension: CHENG-HUNG LIAO.
Pharmaceutical Sciences: WANG KUANG-CHAO.
Naval Architecture Engineering: WANG CHIUN-CHONG.
San-Min-Tsu-Yi (Philosophy of Father of the Republic): TAO-CHI CHOU.

NATIONAL TAIWAN NORMAL UNIVERSITY

162 EAST HO PING RD., SECTION 1, TAIPEI

Telephone: 3415101/5.

Founded 1946.

Language of instruction: Chinese; **State control; Academic year: August to July (two semesters).**

President: WEI-FAN KUO.
Registrar: NIE-CHI LIE.
Librarian: TING-CHONG CHANG.

Number of teachers: 1,365.

Dean of Studies: LIANG-TUNG TSUNG.

Number of students: 8,793.

Colleges of Education, Arts, Sciences; Evening Division; 13 affiliated Research Institutes.

Publications: ***Bulletin, Journal of Research Institute of Chinese Literature, Bulletin of Institute of Education Research.***

NATIONAL TSINGHUA UNIVERSITY

855 KUANG FU RD., HSINCHU

Re-founded 1955.

President: MING-CHE CHANG.
Librarian: DANIEL CHANG TUNG-CHE.

Number of teachers: 304.
Number of students: 2,045.

Colleges of nuclear science, engineering and science; 12 graduate institutes.

SOOCHOW UNIVERSITY

WAI SHUANG HSI, SHIHLIN, TAIPEI

Telephone: 881 9471/20.

Founded 1900.

Private control; Languages of instruction: Chinese and English; Academic year: September to June (two semesters).

President: JOSEPH K. TWANMOH.
Dean of Academic Affairs: PEI-YANG CHANG.
Registrar: SHAO-CHANG KOO.
Librarian: MRS. GRACE CHANG.

Library contains 160,400 vols.
Number of teachers: 958.
Number of students: 9,016.

DIRECTORS:
College of Arts: HENG TSE TU.
College of Sciences: YUAN TSUN LIU.
College of Law: ANDREW LEE.
College of Commerce: CHIALIN CHENG.
Graduate School of Chinese Literature: KHAU-TIAO HSO.
Graduate School of Japanese Literature: MAU FENG TSAI.
Graduate School of Law: SHAO-YU WANG.
Graduate School of Economics: CRAIG CHI-YEN WU.
Graduate School of Accounting: T. C. PAN.
Evening School: TENG SHAN HUANG.

TUNGHAI (CHRISTIAN) UNIVERSITY

TAICHUNG

Founded 1955 under the auspices of the United Board for Christian Higher Education in Asia.

Languages of instruction: Chinese and English; Academic year: September to **July (two semesters).**

President: MEI KO-WANG.
Dean of Studies: CH'EN HSIEN-FANG.

Dean of Students: TSENG PO-WEN.
Dean of General Affairs: JOHN CHUANG (acting).
Librarian: CHENG TEH-AN.

Number of teachers: 604.
Number of students: 5,899.
Publications: *Tunghai Journal, Tunghai Bulletin, Tunghai News, The Vineyard.*

DEANS OF COLLEGES:

College of Arts: CHIANG CHU-CH'IEN.
College of Science: PAUL S. ALEXANDER.
College of Engineering: HSU YUNG-SUI.
College of Commerce: BAO ERH-I.

COLLEGES AND INSTITUTES

China Medical College: 91 Hsueh Shih Rd., Taichung City 400; f. 1958; private control; 246 staff, 2,400 students; Pres. TUNG-HO CHENG.

Chingyi (Providence) College of Arts and Sciences: Taichung; private control; 155 teachers, 1,800 students; Pres. KUO FAN.

Chung Yuan Christian College of Science and Engineering: Chung Li, Taiwan 320; f. 1955; 330 staff, 6,600 students; library of 80,000 vols.; Pres. DANIEL YUAN; publs. *C.Y.C.C. News*†, *Chung Yuan Journal*†.

College of Chinese Medicine and Pharmacy: Taipei; f. 1958; Pres. CHOW PANG-TAO; 54 staff, 150 students.

Feng Chia College of Engineering and Business: 100 Wenhwa Rd., Seatwen, Taichung; f. 1961; library of 21,606 vols.; 1,120 teachers; 13,486 undergraduate, 72 graduate students; 4 graduate schools; Pres. YING-MING LIAO; Chief Librarian CHENG-CHANG LI; publ. *Journal*†.

Kaohsiung Institute of Technology: 149 Chien-Kung St., Kaohsiung; f. 1963; depts. of chemical, civil, electrical, electronic and mechanical engineering, tools and die-making; 3,130 students; library of 30,000 vols.; Pres. Dr. NAN-HUNG KUO; publ. *Journal*† (annually).

Kaohsiung Medical College: 100 Shih Chuan 1 Rd., Kaohsiung; f. 1954; private control; 467 teachers, 2,123 students; schools of medicine, dentistry, pharmacy, nursing, and graduate institute of tropical medicine; Pres. HSIEN-CHEN HSIEH.

Taipei Institute of Technology: 3, Sec. 1, Shin-sheng South Rd., Taipei; f. 1912; 8,973 students; library of 112,000 vols.; Pres. Dr. CHIH TANG.

Taipei Medical College: 250 Wu Hsing St., Taipei; f. 1960; private control; 267 teachers; 2,349 students; library of 40,000 vols.; Pres. MUNG-SHIUNG SHIEH, M.D.; Registrar TUNG-KUEI HUNG, M.ED.; Librarian SHERMAN CHIU.

Taiwan Provincial College of Marine and Oceanic Technology: Keelung; f. 1953; 3,743 students; Pres. SIEH CHUN-TAO.

Taiwan Provincial Pingtung Institute of Agriculture: Men-Sheng Rd., Pingtung; f. 1954; depts. of agronomy, agricultural chemistry, food science, animal science, veterinary medicine, forestry, agricultural engineering, water and soil conservation, etc.; 45 professors, 2,052 students; library of 58,507 vols.; Pres. KUO MONG-SHANG; publs. *Bulletin* (annually), etc.

Tamkang College of Arts and Sciences: Main Campus: Tamsui; City Campus: Taipei; f. 1950; private control; library of 250,000 vols.; 15,000 undergraduate (evening school), 205 graduate students; Pres. CLEMENT C. P. CHANG; publs. *Tamkang Journals*†, etc.

Tatung Institute of Technology: 40 Chungshan N. Rd., Sec. 3, Taipei; f. 1956; private control; depts. of chemical, electrical, mechanical engineering, industrial design, business management (research centres attached); 195 teachers; library of 66,129 vols.; Pres. T. S. LIN; Dean of Academic Affairs C. Y. LIN.

University of Chinese Culture: Hwa Kang, Yang Ming Shan; f. 1962; private control; 1,764 teachers, 15,449 students; library of 412,287 vols.; Pres. PAN WEI-HO.

SCHOOL OF ART AND MUSIC

National Taiwan Academy of Arts: Pan-chiao Park, Taipei; f. 1955; cinema, drama, radio, TV, fine arts, graphic arts, industrial arts, Chinese and Western music, dancing; 281 teachers, 1,847 students; Pres. CHU TSUN-I.

COLOMBIA

Population 25,867,000

ACADEMIES

Bogotá

Academia Colombiana de la Lengua (*Colombian Academy*): Apdo. Aéreo 13922; f. 1871; corresponding Academy of the Real Academia Española, Madrid; 29 mems.; 50 corresp. and hon. mems.; library of 40,000 vols.; publs. *Anuario* (12 vols.), *Boletín*.

Director: EDUARDO GUZMÁN ESPONDA.

Secretary: JOSÉ MANUEL RIVAS SACCONI.

Librarian: MANUEL JOSÉ FORERO.

MEMBERS:

ACHURY VALENZUELA, DARÍO
ARCINIEGAS, GERMÁN
AZULA BARRERA, RAFAEL
BATEMAN, ALFREDO D.
BEJARANO DÍAZ, HORACIO
BETANCUR, CAYETANO
BRICEÑO JÁUREGUI, R. P. MANUEL
CABALLERO CALDERON, EDUARDO
CARRANZA, EDUARDO
ECHANDÍA, DARÍO
FLÓREZ, LUIS
FORERO, MANUEL JOSÉ
GUZMÁN ESPONDA, EDUARDO
LEÓN REY, JOSÉ ANTONIO
LLERAS CAMARGO, ALBERTO
LOZANO Y LOZANO, JUAN
MAYA, RAFAEL
MESA, R.P. CARLOS E.
NARANJO VILLEGAS, ABEL
ORTEGA TORRES, R.P. JOSÉ J.
PABÓN NÚÑEZ, LUCIO.
PIÑEROS CORPAS, JOAQUÍN
RIVAS SACCONI, JOSÉ MANUEL
ROCHA ALVIRA, ANTONIO
ROJAS, JORGE
ROMERO, Mons. MARIO GERMÁN
TORRES QUINTERO, RAFAEL
VALENCIA, GERARDO
ZUBIRÍA, RAMÓN DE

Academia Colombiana de Ciencias Exactas, Físicas y Naturales (*Colombian Academy of Exact, Physical and Natural Sciences*): Observatorio Astronómico Nacional, Carrera 8a, Calle 8a, Apdo. Aéreo 2584; 12 hon. mems., 29 mems., 75 corresp. mems.; Pres. Ing. VICENTE PIZANO RESTREPO; Vice-Pres. R. P. LORENZO URIBE; Sec. Dr. AUGUSTO GAST GALVIS; publ. *Revista*.

Academia Colombiana de Historia (*Colombian Academy of History*): Calle 10 No. 8-95, Apdo. Aéreo 14428; f. 1902; library of 40,000 vols.; 40 mems. excluding Colombian and foreign corresp. mems.; Pres. Dr. MANUEL JOSÉ FORERO; Sec. CAMILO RIAÑO; Library Dir. Dr. ALBERTO MIRAMÓN; publs. *Archivos*, *Boletín de Historia y Antigüedades*.

Academia Colombiana de Jurisprudencia (*Colombian Academy of Jurisprudence*): Calle 17 No. 4-95, Oficina 210; f. 1894; Sec. GERARDO MELGUIZO; publs. *Revista*, *Anuario*.

Academia Nacional de Medicina (*National Academy of Medicine*): Carrera 9, No. 20-13, Apdo. Aéreo 23224; f. 1890; 40 mems.; Pres. Dr. SANTIAGO TRIANA; Vice-Pres. Dr. GUILLERMO R. MONTAÑA; Perm. Sec. Dr. LUIS P. CAMARGO; publs. *Boletín* (monthly, Feb. to Nov.), *Temas Médicos* (annual).

Cartagena

Academia de Historia de Cartagena de Indias (*Cartagena Academy of History*): Palacio de la Inquisición; f. 1912; 24 mems., 25 hon., 50 Colombian, and 115 foreign corresponding; Pres. EDUARDO LEMAITRE ROMÁN; Perm. Sec. FRANCISCO SEBÁ PATRÓN; Librarian JOSÉ N. CAVIEDES; publ. *Boletín Historial*.

Medellín

Academia Antioqueña de Historia (*Antioquia Academy of History*): Carrera 53, Nos. 51-65; f. 1903; Pres. EMILIO ROBLEDO, M.D.; publ. *Repertorio Histórico*.

Tunja

Academia Boyacense de Historia (*Boyaca Academy of History*): Casa del Fundador; publication and encouragement of historical, literary and anthropological studies in Boyaca; 30 mems.; library of 1,000 vols., 600 MSS. from the period 1539–1860; Pres. Dr. ULISES ROJAS; Sec. RAMÓN CORREA; publ. *Repertorio Boyacense* (2 a year).

LEARNED SOCIETIES

Bogotá

Alianza Colombo-Francesa: Carrera 3A No. 18-45, Apdo. Aéreo 50-64; Dir. Y. JÉZÉQUEL.

Asociación Colombiana de Bibliotecarios—ASCOLBI (*Colombian Association of Librarians*): Calle 10, No. 3-16, Apdo. Aéreo 30883; f. 1942; 1,200 mems.; Pres. S. CASTRILLÓN DE MIRANDA; Gen. Sec. STELLA CASTILLO SANDOVAL; publ. *Boletín* (quarterly).

Asociación Colombiana de Facultades de Medicina (*Colombian Association of Medical Faculties*): Calle 45A No. 9-77, Pisos 6°, 7°, 8°; f. 1959 to further higher education and research in medicine; divisions of Education and Health; membership 16 medical faculties (Institutional members), 6 associate mems., 1,500 individuals; library of 3,000 vols., 100 periodicals and audiovisual materials; Pres. ERNESTO ZAMBRANO CAMPO; Exec. Dir. ABEL DUEÑAS PADRÓN; publs. research reports.

Asociación Colombiana de Fisioterapía: Hospital Militar, Transversal 5°, No. 49-00, Piso 13; f. 1953; 90 assoc. mems.; Pres. MARGARITA FAJARDO; Exec. Sec. MARTHA T. DE RESTREPO; publs. *Boletín* (monthly), *Revista* (bi-annually).

Asociación Colombiana de Sociedades Científicas: Apdo. Aéreo 6572; f. 1957, present name 1970; mems.: 16 medical and 3 para-medical societies; Exec. Dir. JUAN GAITÁN-DÁVILA, M.D.; Sec. GABRIEL ROZO-ROJAS, M.D.

Asociación Colombiana de Universidades (*Colombian Universities Association*): Apdo. Aéreo 012300, Calle 50, No. 9-32; f. 1957; groups all State and Private Universities; Pres. Dr. FERNANDO HINESTROSA; Dir. Dr.

CARLOS MEDELLÍN; Sec.-Gen. Dr. ULADISLAO GONZÁLEZ-ANDRADE; publs. *ASCUN*, *Mundo Universitario* (quarterly).

British Council (*El Consejo Británico*): Apdo. Aéreo 4682, Calle 11 No. 5-16, Bogotá 1; library (*see* Libraries); Rep. J. A. LAWRENCE.

Centro Brasileiro de Cultura: Calle 35 No. 6-64; f. 1970; attached to Brazilian Embassy; cultural exchange, courses in Portuguese language; library of 300 vols.; Dir. NORMA RAMOS.

Centro Colombo-Americano: Apdo. Aéreo 38-15; f. 1942; to spread North American and Colombian culture; English courses; 5,000 mems.; library of 8,000 vols.; Dir.-Gen. Mrs. SALLY GROOMS.

Centro de Estudios sobre Desarrollo Económico (*Centre for Economic Development Studies*): Universidad de los Andes, Carrera 1 No. 18-A-82, Apdo. Aéreo 4976, Bogotá; f. 1958; Dir. HAROLDO CALVO S.; publs. monographs, books.

Centro Regional para el Fomento del Libro en America Latina (*Regional Centre for the Promotion of Books in Latin America and the Caribbean*): Calle 70 No. 9-52, Apdo. Aéreo 17438, Bogotá; f. by UNESCO and Colombian govt., later joined by most states in the area; provides technical assistance and training; publishes bibliography of countries in the region; organizes seminars, courses, etc.; library of *c.* 1,000 vols.; Dir. Dr. GONZALO CANAL RAMÍREZ; Gen. Sec. Dra. LUCILA MARTÍNEZ DE JIMÉNEZ; publs. *Boletín Bibliográfico* (quarterly), *Noticias Sobre el Libro y Bibliografia* (every 2 months).

Instituto Caro y Cuervo: Apdo. Aéreo 51502; f. 1942; Hispanic Philology and Literature; 25 mems.; library of 50,000 vols.; Dir. Dr. JOSÉ MANUEL RIVAS SACCONI; Sec.-Gen. Dr. FRANCISCO SÁNCHEZ ARÉVALO; publs. *Thesaurus*† (3 a year), *Biblioteca de Publicaciones del Instituto, Series Minor, Clásicos Colombianos, Filólogos Colombianos, Anuario Bibliográfico Colombiano, Serie Bibliográfica, Diccionario de Construcción y Régimen de la Lengua Castellana* vols. 1-3, *Archivo Epistolar Colombiano, Biblioteca Colombiana, La Granada Entreabierta, Noticias Culturales*† (monthly).

Instituto Colombiano de Crédito Educativo y Estudios Técnicos en el Exterior (ICETEX) (*Colombian Institute for Educational Loans and Advanced Studies Abroad*): Carrera 3A, No. 18-24, Apdo. Aéreo 5735, Bogotá; f. 1950; provides undergraduate and postgraduate grants; selects Colombian students for foreign scholarships, and finances foreign students in Colombia; documentation centre; library of 5,000 vols.; Dir. AUGUSTO FRANCO ARBELÁEZ.

Instituto Colombiano de Cultura: Carrera 3-A, 18-24, piso 5°; f. 1968; conservation of the national heritage, organization of the development of arts and letters, promotion of national folklore; administers all cultural activity through 3 main depts.: Cultural Heritage, Cultural Communications, Fine Arts; Dir. GLORIA ZEA DE URIBE; Sec.-Gen. ALFONSO RODRÍGUEZ GUZMÁN; publs. *Colección Popular* (monthly), *Colección de Autores Nacionales* (monthly), *Gaceta Colcultura* (monthly), *Biblioteca Básica Colombiana* (2 a year), *Historia viva*, special publications, children's literature.

Instituto Colombiano de Cultura Hispánica: Calle 12, 2-41; f. 1951; study and conservation of the traditions of Hispanic peoples; contains important editions of "Flora of the Royal Botanic Expedition" of the New Kingdom of Granada in conjunction with the Centro Iberoamericano de Cooperación, Madrid; library of 6,000 vols. (open to public); Dir. EDUARDO MENDOZA VARELA.

Instituto Cultural Colombo-Alemán: Calle 24, No. 6-31; f. 1961; Dir. Dr. H. J. REIN.

Instituto Nacional de Medicina Legal (*National Institute of Forensic Medicine*): Carrera 13, Nos. 7-30 and 7-46; f. 1948; staff of 200; library of 10,000 vols.; Dir. Dr. GUILLERMO RESTREPO ISAZA; publ. *Revista*.

Istituto Italiano di Cultura: Calle 35 No. 15-32, Apdo. Aéreo 51126; Dir. Prof. SALVATORE AMEDEO ZAGONE.

PEN Internacional de Escritores de Colombia: Apdo. Aéreo 51557; f. 1971; 20 mems.; library of 500 vols.; Pres. JOSÉ MARÍA ACOSTA ACOSTA; Sec. HERNANDO TORRES NEIRA; publ. *Política de Hoy* (monthly).

Sociedad Colombiana de Cancerología: Hospital Militar, Piso 13; f. 1964.

Sociedad Colombiana de Cardiología (*Colombian Cardiological Society*): Hospital Militar Central, Piso 13; f. 1944; 101 mems.; Pres. Dr. RAFAEL CASTAÑO A.; Sec. Dr. EDUARDO MAYORGA S.

Sociedad Colombiana de Economista: Calle 25 No. 12-15, Apdo. Aéreo 8429; f. 1957; to promote the improvement of the teaching of economic sciences and economics as a profession, for the economic and social development of the country; 2,000 mems.; library of 15,000 vols.; Pres. Dr. JORGE RAMÍREZ OCAMPO; Sec.-Gen. LUIS EDUARDO GALLEGO V.; publ. *Revista* (bi-monthly).

Sociedad Colombiana de Ingenieros (*Colombian Society of Engineers*): Carrera 4, No. 10-41; f. 1887; 1,520 mems.; library 6,910 vols.; Pres. LUIS HERNANDO PEDRAZA M.; Sec. ANTONIO JOSÉ ANGULO; publ. *Anales de Ingeniería*.

Sociedad Colombiana de Matemáticas: Apdo. Aéreo 2521; f. 1955; 250 mems.; library of 3,000 vols.; Pres. ALONSO TAKAHASHI; publs. *Revista Colombiana de Matemáticas*†, *Boletín de Matemáticas*†, *Notas de Matemáticas*†, *Monografías Matemáticas*†, *Temas de Matemáticas*†.

Sociedad Colombiana de Obstetricia y Ginecología: Apdo. Aéreo No. 14961; f. 1943; 118 mems.; Pres. Dr. EDUARDO CÁCERES; Vice-Pres. Dr. ROBERTO JARAMILLO; Sec.-Gen. Dr. ENRIQUE ARCHILA; publ. *Revista Colombiana de Obstetricia y Ginecología*† (every 2 months).

Sociedad Colombiana de Patología: Depto. de Patología, Hospital San José, Calle 10, No. 18-75; f. 1955; to improve all aspects of pathology studies; 155 mems.; Pres. Dr. DARIO CADENA; Sec. and Treas. Dr. JOSÉ A. DORADO.

Sociedad Colombiana de Pediatría y Puericultura (*Colombian Paediatrics Society*): Hospital Militar Central, Transveral 5, No. 49-00, Piso 13; f. 1917; 92 mems.; library of 1,133 vols.; Pres. EMILIO POSADA-SARMIENTO; Sec. HERNANDO BARRIOS ANGULO; publ. *Pediatría* (quarterly).

Sociedad Colombiana de Psiquiatría: Carrera 18 No. 84-87, Of. 203, Bogotá 8; f. 1961; 198 mems.; Pres. Dr. GILBERTO ARTETA DE LA HOZ; Sec. LIBARDO BRAVO SOLARTE; publ. *Revista Colombiana de Psiquiatría* (quarterly).

Sociedad Colombiana de Químicos e Ingenieros Químicos: Avda. Jimenez 8-74, Ofs. 501-513; f. 1941 to promote chemical research in Colombia, to uphold professional ethical standards, to serve as an advisory body for public and private organizations, to maintain relations with similar institutions at home and abroad; 250 mems.; Pres. Chem. Eng. HERNANDO LÓPEZ CH.; Sec. Chem. Eng. MARTHA LUCÍA DE ESCOBAR; publ. *Química e Industria* (irregular).

Sociedad Colombiana de Radiología (*Radiological Society*): Apdo. Aéreo 5804; f. 1945; Dir. AMIRO TAMARA, M.D.

Sociedad de Agricultores de Colombia (*Colombian Farmers' Society*): Apdo. Nac. 2252, Apdo. Aéreo 3638; f. 1871; consultative body for the Government; 3,500 mems. in Bogotá, 200,000 others in remainder of the country; Dir.-Gen. EDUARDO CASAS CAYCEDO; publ. *Revista Nacional de Agricultura* (monthly).

Sociedad de Biología de Bogotá (*Biological Society*): Carrera 13, No. 48-26; f. 1942; 36 mems.; Pres. Dr. J. HERNANDO ORDÓNEZ; Sec. Dra. BERTHA DE DULCE; publ. *Anales*.

Sociedad Geográfica de Colombia (*Colombian Geographical Society*): Observatorio Astronómico Nacional, Apdo. 2584; f. 1903; 40 mems.; Pres. Ing. LUIS LAVERDE G.; Sec. Ing. DELIO MARULANDA V.; publs. *Boletín* (3 a year), *Cuadernos de Geografía Colombiana*; affiliated societies in Barranquilla, Pasto, Medellín, Tunja, Sibundoy.

Sociedad Jurídica de la Universidad Nacional (*Juridical Society of the National University*): Apdo. Aéreo 14.490; f. 1908; Pres. ALVARO MENESE S.; Vice-Pres. ALBERTO GONZÁLES D.; Administrator LUIS ALBERTO PATIÑO; publs. *Revista Jurídica* and *Gaceta de la Universidad Nacional*.

Manizales

Centro Filosófico-Literario (*Philosophical-Literary Centre*): Apdo. Nacional 298.

Medellín

Sociedad Antioqueña de Ingenieros y Arquitectos (*Society of Engineers and Architects*): Calle 71 No. 65-100, Apdo. 4754; f. 1913; 950 mems.; Pres. Ing. CARLOS IGNACIO RESTREPO A.; Exec. Dir. Ing. ALVARO VÁSQUEZ O.; publs. *Publicaciones Técnicas*† (series, irreg.), *Informador SAI* (monthly), *Revista SAI* (quarterly).

Sociedad de Ciencias Naturales Caldas: Apdo. Aéreo 1180; f. 1938; Pres. EDGAR ISAZA; publs. occasional articles.

Sociedad Odontológica Antioqueña: Carrera 54 No. 48-49; f. 1945; 150 mems.; Pres. Dr. JORGE RAMOS; Sec. Dr. WILLIAM CANO; publ. *Temas Odontológicos*† (3 a year);

RESEARCH INSTITUTES

Bogotá

Departamento Administrativo Nacional de Estadística (*Statistics Office*): Centro Administrativo Nacional, Vía El Dorado, Apdo. Aéreo 80043; f. 1953; library of 18,000 vols., 725 periodicals received; Dir. Dr. ALVARO VELÁSQUEZ COCK; Sec.-Gen. ALFONSO SALAZAR RESTREPO; publs. *Boletín Mensual de Estadística, Anuario General de Estadística, Anuario de Comercio Exterior, Informe al Congreso Nacional*, and others.

Fondo Colombiano de Investigaciones Científicas y Proyectos Especiales "Francisco José de Caldas" (Colciencias): Apdo. Aéreo 29828; f. 1968; to promote scientific and technical development; co-ordinates and finances projects; library of 3,500 vols.; Gen. Dir. EFRAIM OTERO R.; Gen. Sec. EDUARDO SANTA; publ. *Informativo*.

Instituto Colombiano de Administración: Carrera 7 No. 26-20, piso 3°; f. 1959; courses in administration; library of *c.* 100 vols.; Dir. FEDERICO ECHAVARRIA.

Instituto Colombiano Agropecuario (*Colombian Agricultural and Livestock Institute*): Apdo. Aéreo 7984, Calle 37 No. 8-43, 8°; f. 1962 to promote, co-ordinate and carry out research, teaching and development in agriculture and animal husbandry; specialized library (*see* under Libraries); Gen. Man. JOSUE FRANCO MENDOZA; publs. *Revista ICA*† (quarterly), *ICA-Informa*† (every 2 months), *Informe Anual*, bulletins.

Instituto Colombiano de Antropología (*Colombian Institute of Anthropology*): National Museum, Carrera 7A, No. 28-66, Apdo. Nacional 407; f. 1952; Dir. Dr. ALBERTO RIVERA-GUTIÉRREZ; Sec. ELVIRA GÓMEZ DE SALAMANCA; publs. *Revista Colombiana de Anthropología, Revista Colombiana de Folclor*. This Institute also administers the Museo Arqueológico Nacional and the Museo Entnográfico Nacional.

Instituto Colombiano de Normas Técnicas—ICONTEC: Carrera 19, No. 39B-16; f. 1963; *c.* 500 mems.; library of *c.* 80,000 vols.; Exec. Dir. Ing. JAVIER HENAO LONDOÑO; Gen. Sec. GUILLERMO HIGUERA A.; publs. *Boletín Informativo*† (monthly), *Boletín Bibliográfico*† (quarterly), *Standars*† (monthly).

Instituto Colombiano para el Fomento de la Educación Superior: Apdo. Aéreo 6319, Calle 17, No. 3-40; f. 1968 to supersede the Fondo Universitario Nacional; branch of the Ministry of Education; documentation centre specializing in higher education; library of 6,000 vols., 2,000 documents, 2,200 periodicals, 500 films; Dir. Dr. LUIS FERNANDO DUQUE; publs. various.

Instituto de Asuntos Nucleares (*Nuclear Institute*): Avda. Eldorado, Carrera 50, Apdo. Aéreo 8595; f. 1959 to study the applications of atomic and nuclear energy in a pacifist framework; library of 3,000 vols., 180 periodicals, 30,000 documents, *c.* 60,000 microforms; 120 staff; Dir. ERNESTO VILLARREAL SILVA; publs. scientific works, report of activities.

Instituto de Ciencias Naturales—Museo de Historia Natural (*Institute of Natural Sciences—Natural History Museum*): Universidad Nacional de Colombia, Apdo. 7495; f. 1936 to conduct scientific research; four main sections; botany, zoology, geology and anthropology; 35 mems.; library of 6,000 vols.; Dir. POLIDORO PINTO-ESCOBAR; publs. *Caldasia*†, *Lozania*† (Zoology), *Mutisia*† (Botany), *Catálogo Ilustrado de las Plantas de Cundinamarca*†, *Notas Divulgativas*.

Instituto de Investigaciones Tecnológicas (*Institute for Technological Research*): Avenida 30, No. 52-A-77, Apdo. Aéreo 7031; f. 1958, as an autonomous organization, to execute studies in applied research and to provide services of technical information and technical assistance to industry; specializing in food industry, metallurgical and metal-mechanical industries, agricultural and chemical process industries; library of 7,600 vols., 26,000 reports and bulletins, 1,200 periodicals; Dir. JAIME AYALA RAMIREZ; publs. *Tecnología*† (every 2 months), *Informe Anual*† (annually).

Instituto Geográfico "Agustín Codazzi": Avenida Ciudad de Quito 48-51; f. 1935; prepares topographical, cadastral, sectional, national, and agricultural maps of the country, and geophysical, cadastral and geodetic surveys; prepares geographical studies of Colombia; library of 12,000 vols.

Instituto Nacional de Cancerología: Calle 1, No. 9-85; f. 1934; diagnosis, therapy, control, teaching and research in cancer; library of 26,000 vols.; Dir. Dr. JULIO ENRIQUE OSPINA; publ. *Boletín del I.N.C.* (quarterly).

Instituto Nacional de Investigaciones Geológico-Mineras: Apdo. Aéreo 4865; f. 1968, existed formerly as a scientific commission; 480 mems.; library of 3,445 books and 1,718 reports and magazines; Dir. ALBERTO ALVAREZ-OSEJO; publ. *Boletín Geológico* (annually, 16 vols.), official geological studies, maps, reports and magazines.

Instituto Nacional de Salud INPES (*National Institute of Health*): Avenida el Dorado carrera 50, Apdo. Aéreo 80334; f. 1968; Dir. Dr. HERNANDO GROOT.

Observatorio Astronómico Nacional (*National Astronomical Observatory*): Apdo. Aéreo 2584; f. 1803; library of 2,000 vols.; Dir. Ing. EDUARDO BRIEVA BUSTILLO; publs. *Anuario del Observatorio*, occasional publications.

Santa Marta

Instituto de Investigaciones Marinas de "Punta de Betín": Apdo. Aéreo 1016; f. 1965; co-operative venture between COLCIENCIAS (Government Agency), the Justus Liebig-Universität in Giessen and the Univ. Nacional de Colombia to study and preserve the marine and terrestrial wildlife of the adjacent zones; library of 5,000 vols.; 10 staff scientists; Dirs. Dr. JOSÉ A. LOZANO, Dr. B. WERDING; publ. *Anales*†.

LIBRARIES

Bogotá

Archivo Nacional de Colombia: Biblioteca Nacional, Calle 24 No. 5-60, 4° piso; f. 1868; *c.* 40,600 vols. and 3,135 metres of documents; Dir. Fr. ALBERTO LEE LÓPEZ; publs. *Revista*†, *Indices*†, and series of historic documents.

Biblioteca Agropecuaria de Colombia: Inst. Colombiano Agropecuario, Apdo. Aéreo 151123; f. 1954; 25,000 vols. devoted to agriculture and livestock, 35,000 pamphlets, 1,800 journals, 9,000 documents; Dir. Ing. Agr. L. ARMANDO MAYORGA DO.

Biblioteca Central de la Universidad Nacional de Colombia: Ciudad Universitaria, Apdo. Aéreo 14490; f. 1867; 125,000 vols.; Dir. Dra. STELLA M. DE CUÉLLAR; publs. *Universidad Nacional*† (irregular), *Anuario Colombiano de Historia Social y de la Cultura*†, *Ideas y Valores*† (irregular), *Geología Colombiana*† (irregular).

Biblioteca Central de la Pontificia Universidad Javeriana: Carrera 7A, No. 40-62, Apdo. Aéreo 5315; f. 1931; 145,000 vols.; Dir. LINA ESPITALETA DE VILLEGAS.

Biblioteca "Luis-Angel Arango" del Banco de la República (*Bank of the Republic Library*): Apdo. Aéreo 3531, Calle 11 No. 4-14; f. 1958; 250,000 vols., 1,000 MSS.; 3 reading-rooms, research rooms, concert-hall; Dir. JAIME DUARTE FRENCH.

Biblioteca Nacional de Colombia (*National Library*): Calle 24, No. 5-60, Apdo. 27600; f. 1777; 400,000 vols.; 500 MSS.; Dir. PILAR MORENO DE ANGEL.

Biblioteca Seminario Mayor Arquidiocesano (*Library of the Archdiocesan Major Seminary*): Carrera 7 No. 94-80, Bogotá 8, D.E.; f. 1823; 26,500 vols. specializing in philosophy and theology; Dir. Rev. ALVARO J. JARAMILLO E.

British Council Library: Apdo. Aéreo 4682, Calle 11, No. 5-16; f. 1939; 12,300 vols., 70 periodicals; Librarian Sra. M. C. DE BOHORQUEZ.

División de Documentación e Información Educativa, Ministerio de Educación Nacional (*Educational Documentation and Information Division, Ministry of Education*): Avda. El Dorado, CAN, Apdo. 80359; co-ordinates the Educational Documentation and Information Sub-system, the School Libraries National Programme and runs the National Educational Documentation Centre; 10,000 vols., 300 pamphlets, 3,000 documents, 520 periodicals; publs. *Memorias del Ministro de Educación al Congreso Nacional* (annually), *Educar* (monthly), monographs.

Barranquilla

Biblioteca Pública Departamental: Carrera 38-B, No. 38-21; f. 1923; 32,000 vols.; Dir. OLGA CHAMS.

Bello

Biblioteca del Marco Fidel Suárez: public library and regional centre.

Calí

Biblioteca Municipal del Centenario: Carrera 5a, No. 7-10; f. 1910; 22,000 vols.; Dir. ALFONSO ZAWADKY.

Cartagena

Departamento de Bibliotecas, Universidad de Cartagena: Apdo. Aéreo 3210; f. 1968; 26,500 vols.; Librarian LUZ MARIA CABARCAS SANTOYA; publ. *Boletín de Adquisiciones.*

Itagüí

Biblioteca de Itagüí: f. 1945; 15,000 vols.; Dir. MARGARITA ECHAVARRÍA DE URIBE.

Jamundí

Biblioteca Abel Guerrero Vega: Carrera 12, No. 3-03; f. 1962; library of 2,065 vols.; Dir. NOEMI RAMOS PERLAZA.

Manizales

Biblioteca Central, Universidad de Caldas: Apdo. Aéreo 275; 25,000 vols.; Librarian GLORIA L. ESCOBAR DE PÉREZ.

Biblioteca Departamental de Caldas: f. 1954; 14,460 vols.

Medellín

Biblioteca de la Universidad Pontificia Bolivariana: Ap. Nac. 109; Ap. Aéreo 1178; 20,000 vols.; Librarian Lic. BEATRIZ RESTREPO.

Biblioteca Pública Piloto de Medellín para la América Latina (*Pilot Public Library of Medellín for Latin America*): f. 1954 and under the auspices of UNESCO; 50,000 vols.; library extension activities; Dir. Dr., DARÍO ALBERTO RESTREPO G.; publs. *Boletín de labores*, *Manual.*

Departamento de Bibliotecas, Universidad de Antioquia: Apdo. Aéreo 1226; f. 1935; 150,000 vols., 3,385 periodicals; Dir. Dr. JORGE IVÁN CORREA VÉLEZ; publ. *Biblioteca Informa.*

Popayán

Departamento de Bibliotecas, Universidad del Cauca: Apdo. Nacional 113, Calle 5A 4-92; f. 1827; 40,000 vols.; Dir. JOSÉ MARÍA SERRANO PRADA; publs. *Catálogo del Archivo Central del Cauca*†, *Boletín Bibliográfico*†, *Boletín Informativo*†, *Cuadernos de Medicina*, *Boletín del Comité de Investigaciones Científicas*†, *Revista Cátedra*†.

Tunja

Biblioteca Central, Universidad Pedagógica y Tecnológica de Colombia: Apdo. Aéreo 1234; f. 1932; 29 mems.; 68,000 vols.; 1,700 periodical titles; Dir. BARBARA MARTIN MARTIN.

MUSEUMS

Bogotá

Museo Arqueológico Nacional (*National Museum of Archaeology*): Carrera 6, No. 7-43, Apdo. Nacional 407.

Museo Bolivariano (*Bolivar Museum*): Calle 20, No. 3-23; f. 1922 in the country house occupied by Simón Bolívar in 1827, where relics of the Liberator and his epoch are exhibited; is administered by the Sociedad de Mejoras y Ornato de la Cuidad de Bogotá; Dir. NONEMI PARRA.

Museo Nacional (*National Museum*): Carrera 7a, No. 28-66; f. 1824; history and art relating to the foundation of Bogotá, Spanish conquest and colonial period; collections of portraits, arms, banners, medals and coins; fine arts section. The museum also possesses a theatre and an exhibition gallery; Dir. EMMA ARAÚJO.

Museo de Arte Colonial de Bogotá (*Museum of the Colonial Period*): Carrera 6a, No. 9-77; f. 1942; controlled by the *Instituto Colombiano de Cultura*; paintings, sculpture, furniture, gold and silver work, drawings, etc., of the Spanish colonial period (16th, 17th and 18th centuries); it is installed in a building erected by the Jesuits in 1622 to house the first Javeriana University; Dir. FRANCISCO GIL TOVAR.

Museo del Oro (*Gold Museum*): Parque de Santander; f. 1939; 27,000 pre-Colombian gold objects representing the gods, myths, and customs of the Quimbaya,

Musica and other native Indian cultures; Dir. LUIS DUQUE GÓMEZ; publ. *Boletín*.

Museo "Jorge Eliecer Gaitán": Calle 42, No. 15-52; f. 1948; collection relating to the history of Bogotá; Dir. HAROLD DAVID.

Museo Nacional de Antropologia (*National Museum of Anthropology*): Apdo. Nacional 407; f. 1938; ceramics, stone carvings, gold objects, textiles, etc., from all districts of Colombia; is a Department of the Instituto Colombiano de Antropología; Dir. Dr. ALBERTO RIVERA GUTIÉRREZ; Curator Dr. LUCÍA DE PERDOMO.

Manizales

Museo Antropológico de Caldas: Universidad de Caldas, Apdo. 150; f. 1955; archaeology and ethnology; Dir. GIORGIO MARIO MANZINI; publ. *Memorias*†

Medellín

Museo Universitario: Universidad de Antioquia, Apdo. Aéreo 1226; f. 1942; Dir. BEATRIZ RESTREPO.

Anthropology section: 10,000 archaeological exhibits, 600 ethnographical exhibits; 20,000 archaeological fragments for research.

Natural sciences section: 8,000 mineralogical, botanical and zoological exhibits.

Plastic Arts section: temporary art exhibitions.

Museo de Ciencias Naturales del Colegio de San José (*Natural Science Museum*): Apdo. Aéreo 1180; f. 1913; natural history in general, zoology, botany, mineralogy, anthropology; library of 500 vols. and 1,000 magazines; Dir. H. MARCO A. SERNA D.; publs. *Avancemos* (monthly), *El Colombiano* (daily), *Boletín Cultural* (quarterly).

NATIONAL UNIVERSITIES

UNIVERSIDAD DE ANTIOQUIA

APDO. AÉREO 1226,
CIUDAD UNIVERSITARIA,
MEDELLÍN

Telephone: 334740.

Founded 1822.

Rector: Dr. LUIS CARLOS MUÑOZ URIBE.
Secretary-General: Lic. LUZ ELENA ZABALA DE ACEVEDO.
Academic Director: Ing. GABRIEL DARÍO RESTREPO POSADA.
Administrative Director: Dr. RAFAEL ARANGO TORO.
Librarian: Dr. JORGE IVÁN CORREA VÉLEZ.

Library: *see* Libraries.

Number of teachers: *c.* 2,000.
Number of students: 25,000.

Publications: *Revista Universidad de Antioquia, Noticiero Universitario de la Secretaria General.*

DEANS:

Faculty of Sciences and Humanities: Dr. JOSÉ BARRIENTOS ARANGO.
Faculty of Education: Dr. BERNARDO RESTREPO GÓMEZ.
Faculty of Economics: Econ. SAÚL MESA OCHOA.
Faculty of Law and Political Science: Ab. FERNANDO MEZA MORALES.
Faculty of Engineering: Ing. ALVARO GAVIRIA ORTIZ.
Faculty of Medicine: Dr. ANTONIO YEPES PARRA.
Faculty of Veterinary Medicine and Zootechnics: Med. Vet. ANÍBAL RUIZ VELÁSQUEZ.
Faculty of Dentistry: JAIME CÁRDENAS MOLINA.
Faculty of Pharmaceutical Chemistry: ANTONIO MESA ESCOBAR.
School of Public Health: Dr. EMIRO TRUJILLO URIBE (Dir.).

ATTACHED INSTITUTE:

Escuela Interamericana de Bibliotecología de la Universidad de Antioquia (*Interamerican School of Librarianship*): Apdo. Aéreo 1307, Medellín; f. 1956; training in librarianship to postgraduate level; technical assistance on administration and organization of information centres and libraries; 10 full-time, 5 part-time staff; 300 students; library of 16,000 vols.; Dir. RODRIGO VEGA LÓPEZ; publ. *Revista Interamericana de Bibliotecología.*

UNIVERSIDAD DEL ATLÁNTICO

CARRERA 43, No. 50-53,
APARTADO AÉREO 1890,
BARRANQUILLA

Telephone: 13-513.

Founded 1941.

Rector: Lic. CARLOS J. MARIA B.
Secretary-General: Dr. ROBERTO PERSAND BARNES.
Librarian: HILDA DE VENGOECHEA.

Number of teachers: 592.
Number of students: 8,784.
Publication: "*Economia*".

DEANS:

Faculty of Fine Arts: Dr. ALFREDO GÓMEZ-ZUREK.
Faculty of Economics: IVAN ROMERO MENDOZA.
Faculty of Pharmacy and Chemistry: JULIO QUEVEDO.
Faculty of Law and Political Science: NESTOR ISAAC PARDO.
Faculty of Chemical Engineering: CARMELO FUENTES LOZANO.
Faculty of Architecture: WALTER SUAREZ GLASSER.
Faculty of Education: RAMON MOLINARES SARMIENTO.
Faculty of Nutrition and Dietetics: HILDA DE RODRÍGUEZ.

UNIVERSIDAD DE CALDAS

APDO. AÉREO 275,
MANIZALES, CALDAS

Telephone: 552-40.

Founded 1943.

Academic year: February to December (two semesters).

Rector: CARLOS IVAN BUITRAGO MUÑOZ.
Academic Vice-Rector: Dr. ALBERTO GÓMEZ GIRALDO.
Administrative Vice-Rector: Dr. RODRIGO GIRALDO GONZÁLEZ.
Registrar: RUTH LONDOÑO CALLEJAS.
Librarian: GLORIA L. ESCOBAR DE PÉREZ.

Library: *see* Libraries.

Number of teachers: 393.
Number of students: 3,802.

DEANS:

Faculty of Agriculture: Dr. FABIO DIAZ JARAMILLO.
Faculty of Law: Dr. HUMBERTO DE LA CALLE LOMBANA.
Faculty of Home Economics: Lic. MARIA RITA ECHEVERRI.
Faculty of Education: Lic. DAVID VALENCIA CUELLAR.
Faculty of Philosophy and Letters: Lic. LUIS ENRIQUE GARCIA RESTREPO.
Faculty of Medicine: Dr. ROGER GARCIA TOBON.
Faculty of Nursing: Lic. CECILIA MORALES DE CASTAÑO.
Faculty of Social Work: Lic. MARIO GONZALEZ BAENA.
Faculty of Veterinary Medicine and Stockbreeding: Dr. EDELBERTO MULETT CHAVEZ.
Faculty of Fine Arts: Lic. FERNANDO ALVARADO.

UNIVERSIDAD DE CARTAGENA

APARTADO AÉREO 1382,
CARTAGENA

Telephone: 40-180.

Founded 1827.

Academic year: February to December.

President of the Council: Dr. MARUN GOSSAIN JATTIN.

Rector: Dr. LUIS H. ARRAUT ESQUIVEL.

Vice-Rector: HERNANDO THORNE CAMPO.

Administrative Director: Dr. ANTONIO CARLOS MARTINEZ MARRUGO.

Librarian: LUZ MARIA CABARCAS SANTOYA.

Library: *see* Libraries.

Number of teachers: 648.

Number of students: *c.* 4,202.

Publications: *Prospecto Universidad, Revista Facultad de Economía, Revista Facultad de Medicina.*

DEANS:

Faculty of Law: Dr. FABIO MORON DIAZ.

Faculty of Medicine: Dr. OSCAR GUARDO NUÑEZ.

Faculty of Dentistry: Dr. ANTONIO NADER NADER.

Faculty of Pharmaceutical Chemistry: Dr. GONZALO URBINA OSPINO.

Faculty of Engineering: Dr. ISMAEL GUETTE BURGOS.

Faculty of Economics: Dr. JOSÉ MACIA MOSCOTE.

Faculty of Nursing: Lic. NURY TORRES GARCIA.

Faculty of Social Work: Lic. ESTHER PEREZ DE ALVEAR.

UNIVERSIDAD DEL CAUCA

APARTADO NACIONAL 113,
CALLE 5A 4-70, POPAYÁN

Telephone: 30-20.

Founded 1827.

Academic year: January to June, July to December.

Rector: Dr. GERARDO BONILLA FERNÁNDEZ.

General Secretary: Dra. ROCIO DEL PILAR PENAGOS PAZ.

Administrative Director: Dr. RODRIGO BALCAZAR ORDOÑEZ.

Planning Head: Ing. LUIS A. LEMOS BUSTAMANTE.

Library Director: Lic. JOSÉ MARÍA SERRANO PRADA.

Library: *see* Libraries.

Number of teachers: 470.

Number of students: 3,800.

Publications: *Revista*† (quarterly), *Boletín Informativo*† (monthly).

DEANS:

Faculty of Law, Political and Social Sciences: Dr. SAMUEL ERNESTO CONSTAIN GONZALEZ.

Faculty of Civil Engineering: Ing. HUMBERTO GARCÍA DÍAZ.

Faculty of Electrical Engineering and Telecommunications: Ing. PABLO J. GALVIS GARCIA.

Faculty of Medicine: Dr. ALBERTO VALLEJO DURÁN.

Faculty of Accountancy: C. P. T. OTTO ARNULFO BOLAÑOS BOLAÑOS.

Faculty of Education: LIBIO ALFONSO RUALES PAZ.

Faculty of Humanities: Dr. JOSÉ TOMÁS ILLERA LÓPEZ.

Conservatory of Music: MARIO FERNANDO LATORRE (Dir.).

School of Nursing: Lic. MARIA ROCIO RAMIREZ (Dir.).

UNIVERSIDAD FRANCISCO DE PAULA SANTANDER

AVDA. GRAN COLOMBIA,
12E-96, BARRIO COLSAG,
APDO. AÉREO 1055,
CÚCUTA

Telephone: 44252.

Founded 1962.

Affiliated to the Universidad Nacional.

Rector: ADOLFO MORALES VILLAMIZAR.

Secretary-General: LUIS CARLOS RUBIO VELANDIA.

Administrative Director: LUIS QUIROGA CORZO.

Academic Dean: GUSTAVO CARRILLO ALVAREZ.

Librarian: DEBORA DAZA DURAN.

The library contains 4,500 vols.

Number of teachers: 243.

Number of students: 2,314.

DEANS:

Faculty of Humanities: RODRIGO ALZATE.

Faculty of Engineering: RODOLFO DAVILA.

Faculty of Technology: JOSE LUIS TOLOSA.

Faculty of Education: MIGUEL ANDRADE YAÑEZ.

FUNDACIÓN UNIVERSIDAD CENTRAL*

CARRERA 16 No. 24-25,
APDO. AÉREO 5896, BOGOTÁ

Founded 1966.

Rector: Dr. JORGE ENRIQUE MOLINA M.

Secretary-General: Dr. JESÚS ALBERTO PLATA MARTINEZ.

Number of students: *c.* 1,000.

Faculties of Economics, Administration, Accountancy; School of Journalism and Advertising.

* No reply received to our questionnaire this year.

UNIVERSIDAD NACIONAL DE COLOMBIA
(National University of Colombia)

CIUDAD UNIVERSITARIA,
APDO. AÉREO 14.490,
BOGOTÁ

Telephone: 699111.

Founded 1867.

Academic year: January to July, August to December.

Campuses in Manizales, Medellín, Palmira.

Rector: EMILIO ALJURE NASSER.

Vice-Rector: RAMSES HAKIM MURAD.

Secretary-General: FRANCISCO VARELA ANJEL.

Librarian: STELLA MIRANDA DE CUELLAR.

Number of teachers: 3,061.

Number of students: *c.* 25,000 (20,000 at Bogotá).

Publications: Various faculty reviews.

DEANS:

Faculty of Arts: ARTURO ROBLEDO OCAMPO.

Faculty of Science: JAIME RODRÍGUEZ LARA.

Faculty of Agriculture: NILSON LOPEZ.

Faculty of Humanities: ANITA DE BELALCÁZAR.

Faculty of Medicine: JOSÉ MORA RUBIO.

Faculty of Law and Politics: RAMIRO MARTÍNEZ VESGA.

Faculty of Engineering: JUAN M. CORREA GALVEZ.

Faculty of Nursing: LIGIA BARRERA.

Faculty of Dentistry: MIGUEL LOMANTO.

Faculty of Veterinary Science: PEDRO J. LÁZARO BUSTOS.

UNIVERSIDAD DE CÓRDOBA

APDO. AÉREO 354,
CARRETERA A CERETE, KM. 5,
MONTERÍA

Telephone: 33-81.

Founded 1966.

Academic year: April to March.

Rector: Dr. RODRIGO NEGRETE SOTO.

Secretary-General: Dr. JORGE ANAYA HERNÁNDEZ.

Administrative Director: Dr. ANTONIO GARCES HERAZO.

Number of teachers: 221.

Number of students: 2,600.

DEANS:

Faculty of Veterinary Medicine and Animal Husbandry: Dr. NOITIER CANO-GUZMÁN.

Faculty of Agronomy: Dr. SERAFIN VELÁSQUEZ ACOSTA.

Faculty of Education: Dr. LIBARDO GARCÍA GARCÍA.

Faculty of Nursing: Dr. FRANCISCO VILLADIEGO ABUCHAR.

UNIVERSIDAD DISTRITAL "FRANCISCO JOSÉ DE CALDAS"

CARRERA 8, No. 40-78,
APDO. AÉREO 8668, BOGOTÁ

Telephone: 457088, 450440.

Founded 1950.

Rector: DARIO SAMPER.

Secretary-General: ENRIQUE GAUIRIA LIEVANO.

Librarian: MYRIAM MEJÍA E.

The library contains 35,000 vols.

Number of teachers: 350.
Number of students: 4,500.

DEANS:

Faculty of Electrical Engineering: Dr. HUMBERTO SARMIENTO.
Faculty of Forestry: Dr. GONZALO DE LAS SALAS.
Faculty of Land Resources and School of Topography: Dr. RAMUN D'LUYZ.

UNIVERSIDAD DE NARIÑO

CARRERA 22, No. 18-109,
PASTO, NARIÑO
Telephone: 16-52, 16-53.

Founded in 1827 as Colegio Provincial by General Francisco de Paula Santander; later named Colegio Académico; university status 1964.

Rector: Dr. EDUARDO ALVARADO HURTADO.
Secretary: Dr. CLAUDIO PASCUAZA BENAVIDES.
Librarian: LUIS MAYA MONTALVO.

Central library of 10,000 vols.; agronomy library of 15,000 vols.

Number of teachers: 181
Number of students: 2,197.

Publications: *Anales, Foro Universitario, Boletín Informativo y Bibliotecario, Numen Universitario "A", Bibliografías, Meridiano* (Faculty of Education review).

DEANS:

Faculty of Law: Dr. JOSÉ ANTONIO ROSERO REVELO.
Faculty of Education: ALVARO ALMEIDA DELGADO.
Faculty of Agronomy: Dr. BERNARDO MARTÍNEZ SANTACRUZ.
Department of Languages: HÉCTOR MUÑOZ CH.

UNIVERSIDAD DE PAMPLONA

APARTADO AÉREO 1046,
CARRERA 4 No. 4-38,
PAMPLONA
Founded 1960.

Rector: Dr. EDUARDO VILLAMIZAR LAMUS.
General Secretary: Dr. JUAN DE DIOS PELAEZ.

Number of teachers: 100.
Number of students: 1,300.

Publications: *Informativo Biblioteca* (monthly), *Anuario* (yearly).

Departments of Science, Humanities, Education.

UNIVERSIDAD PEDAGÓGICA NACIONAL

(National Pedagogical University)

APDO. AÉREO 53040, APDO. NACIONAL 465/2,
CALLE 72, No. 11-86, BOGOTÁ
Telephone: 2352044.
Founded 1955.

Academic year: January to December (two semesters).

Rector: AUGUSTO FRANCO ARBELAEZ.
Vice-Rector: AUGUSTO RODRIGUEZ MOLANO.
Administrative Secretary: CARLOS JULIO DIAZ MURCIA.
Librarian: ARACELI CARDONA DE MEJIA.

Number of teachers: 746.
Number of students: 4,778 (and 4,250 in attached institutes).

Publications: *Revista Colombiana de Educación, Documentación Educativa.*

HEADS OF DEPARTMENTS:

Fine Arts: DANIEL NIETO SOTOMAYOR.
Biology: GUIDO MONCAYO.
Chemistry: HUMBERTO CAICEDO.
Physics: ALVARO RAMÍREZ QUEVEDO.
Mathematics: SAMUEL MUÑOZ SILVA.
Education: LYDA QUINTERO DE HINCAPIE.
Social Sciences: ALFONSO GÓMEZ ORDUZ.
Physical Education: JUDITH J. DE PALACIO.
Languages: MARÍA CRISTINA DE VÉLEZ.
Industrial Education: JAIME PANQUEVA.
Librarianship and Educational Aids: ARACELI CARDONA DE MEJÍA.

AFFILIATED INSTITUTES:

Instituto Pedagógico Nacional: Calle 127 No. 12-A 20, Bogotá.

Instituto Tecnico Industrial: Calle 2A No. 23–33, Barrio Julio Caro, Zipaquirá.

UNIVERSIDAD DEL QUINDIO

AVDA. BOLÍVAR CALLE 12,
APDO. AÉREO 460, ARMENIA
Telephone: 45896.
Founded 1962.

Rector: Dr. GABRIEL HINCAPIE CARDONA.
Secretary-General: Dr. HENRY GONZALEZ MEZA.
Administrative Director: JESUS ARBELAEZ SALGADO.
Librarian: CECILIA RODRIGUEZ DE CASTELLANOS.

Library of *c.* 10,700 vols.

Number of teachers: 165.
Number of students: *c.* 3,300.

Four-semester courses in Mathematics and Physics, Biology, Chemistry, Topography, Education, Languages, Social Sciences, Engineering.

DEANS:

Faculty of Humanities: MARIO APARICIO CASTAÑEDA.
Faculty of Sciences: HERNANDO ARIZA CALDERÓN.
Faculty of Accountancy and Finance: LIBARDO ROJAS.

UNIVERSIDAD INDUSTRIAL DE SANTANDER

(Industrial University of Santander)

APARTADO AÉREO 678,
BUCARAMANGA, SANTANDER
Telephone: 56141.
Founded 1947.

Rector: Dr. ALVARO RUEDA GÓMEZ.
Vice-Rector: Dr. WILFRIDO MONTAGUT MONTAGUT.
Secretary-General: Dr. LUIS SERRANO GÓMEZ.
Academic Dean: Dr. EDGAR BARRIOS U.
Librarian: Dr. NEVARDO RANGEL MURCIA.

Number of teachers: 380.
Number of students: 5,500.

Publications: *Revista UIS Investigaciones*†, *Landa*†, *Ion*†, *Boletín de Geología*†.

DEANS:

Sciences: JAIME BERNAL.
Physical/Mechanical Sciences: ENRIQUE GONZALEZ C.
Physical Chemistry: ALVARO QUIROGA C.
Health Sciences: PEDRO RUSSI S.
Research: WILSON ORTIZ G.
Humanities: MARIA DEL SOCORRO TROUCHON.
Postgraduate Studies: AUGUSTO LOPEZ.

DIRECTORS:

Biology: PEDRO E. FALCO.
Physical Education: SUSANA GONZÁLEZ C.
Physics: RENÉ SALAZAR.
Mathematics: SERGIO GAMBOA.
Chemistry: GUILLERMO GONZALEZ.
Electricity and Electronics: JULIO RUGELES.
Civil Engineering: GERARDO BAUTISTA.
Mechanical Engineering: ADOLFO LEÓN ARENAS.
Industrial Production: CARLOS ALIRIO RIVERA.
Systems: LUIS E. ARÍAS.
Metallurgy: ROQUE CALDERÓN.
Chemical Engineering: LUIS DAVID SANCHEZ.
Petroleum Engineering: ALBERTO SANTACRUZ.
Arts and Letters: ALICIA MANTILLA.
Economics and Administration: JORGE MONTERO.
Social Sciences: ROSA C. DE MALDONADO.
Education: DUILIO ALTERIO BASSO.
University Extension: LUIS SERRANO GÓMEZ.
Institute of History: ARIEL DÍAZ O.
Morpho-Pathology: REYNEL SANJUÁN.
Physiological Sciences: GERMAN OLIVEROS.
Microbiological Sciences: RODOLFO PEÑA.
Nursing: HORTENCIA DE CIFUENTES.
Internal Medicine: ANTONIO BÁEZ D.
Paediatrics: JORGE GÓMEZ F.
Psychiatry: ROBERTO SERPA.
Surgery: EDUARDO HANSSEN V.

Nutrition and Physical Rehabilitation: Olga Torres de Gomez.
Preventive Medicine and Public Health: Jesus Roberto Cortes.
Drawing: Luis Eduardo León.
Industrial Consultations: Juan Francisco Pedraza.
Social-Economic Studies: Alejandro Parra.
Medical-Biological Studies: Rozo Alfredo Cala.
Chemical Engineering (Graduate): Alvaro Barrera L.
Physics (Graduate): René Salazar.
Metallurgical Engineering (Graduate): Roque Calderón C.

UNIVERSIDAD DEL TOLIMA

APDO. AÉREO No. 546, IBAGUÉ

Telephone: 34218.

Founded 1945, University status 1954.

Academic year: February to June, August to December.

Rector: Dr. Camilo R. Polanco Torres.
Academic Dean: Dr. Mario J. Quintero Gil.
Secretary-General: Dr. J. Hermes Martínez Rodríguez.
Registrar: Lic. Armando Garrido Perez.
Librarian: Lic. Ligia Azuero Peñaranda.

Number of teachers: *c.* 250.
Number of students: 3,500.

Deans:

Faculty of Agricultural Engineering: Dr. Darley Salazar Restrepo.
Faculty of Forestry: Dr. Agustin Vasquez Jimenez.
Faculty of Business Studies: Dr. Francisco Rodriguez Bohorquez.
Faculty of Educational Science: Lic. Bernabe Rowdon Rodriguez.
Institute of Technology: Dr. Antonio Osorio Jaramillo.

UNIVERSIDAD DEL VALLE

CIUDAD UNIVERSITARIA, MELÉNDEZ, APDO. AÉREO 2188, APDO. NACIONAL 439, CALI

Telephone: 391171.

Founded 1945.

Academic year: January to June, August to December.

Rector: Antonio Barberena Saavedra.

General Secretary: Fernando Duque Jaramillo.
Dean of Studies: Jaime López Collazos.
Chief Administration Officer: José J. Serna.
Library Director: Isabel Romero de Dulcey.

Library of 110,000 vols.

Number of professors: 884.
Number of students: 8,056.

Publications: *Boletín del Departamento de Biología*†, *Revista División de Ingeniería*† (irregular), *Acta Médica del Valle*†, *Boletín de Adquisiciones*†, *Logos*† (quarterly), *Revista Universidad del Valle.*

Directors:

Division of Architecture: Armando Velasco.
Engineering Division: Guillermo Valencia M.
Health Division: Alvaro Mercado.
Division of Economics and Social Sciences: Orlando Márquez.
Division of Humanities: Isabel Castellanos.
Division of Education: Myriam Zuñiga E.
Science Division: José Mulett.

Heads of Departments:

Engineering Division:
Department of Agricultural Engineering: Dr. Carlos Piedrahita.
Department of Civil Engineering: Dr. Johanio Marulanda.
Department of Electrical Engineering: Dr. José Antonio Abadia.
Department of Information Systems: Dr. Olga de Calle.
Department of Fluid and Heat Sciences: César Uribe.
Department of Chemical and Biological Processes: Dr. Fernando Naranjo.
Computer Centre: Jaime Taffur.

Health Division:
Department of Morphology: Dr. Jorge Cruz.
Department of Physiology: Dr. Vicente Piazzuelo.
Department of Pathology: Dr. José Edgar Duque.
Department of Radiology: Dr. Tito Javier Sánchez.
Department of Anaesthesiology: Dr. Roberto nel Peláez.
Department of Internal Medicine: Dr. Oscar Bolaños.
Department of Surgery: Dr. Jaime Ruíz.
Department of Paediatrics: Dr. José Eduardo Sanmartin.
Department of Obstetrics and Gynaecology: Dr. Edgar Cobo.
Department of Psychiatry: **Dr. Carlos Climent.**
Department of Social Medicine: Dr. Jaime Rodríguez.
Department of Microbiology: Dr. Alvaro Dueñas.
Department of Stomatology: Dr. José Fernando Barreto.
Department of Nursing: Ceneyda de Jaimes.
Clinical Laboratory: Carmen de Gómez.
School of Physiotherapy: Dr. Jaime Villaquirán.

Division of Architecture and Plastic Arts:
Department of Construction: Dr. Humberto Palau.
Department of Environmental Planning: Dr. Jairo Mazorra.
Department of Design: Dr. Luis H. Ramírez.

Science Division:
Department of Mathematics: Dr. Guillermo Valdés.
Department of Physics: Dr. Jaime Hernández.
Department of Chemistry: Dr. Arnoldo Ramírez.
Department of Biology: Dr. José Mulett.

Division of Social and Economic Sciences:
Department of Economics: Dr. Alberto Corchuelo.
Department of Social Sciences: Dr. Gilberto Aristizabal.
Department of Industrial Administratinn: Dr. Milton Mora.

Humanities Division:
Department of Languages: Dr. Hector Rios.
Department of History: Dr. Germán Colmenares.
Department of Music: Dr. Pilar Lago de Hoyos.
Department of Philosophy: Dr. Juan M. Jaramillo.
Department of Communications: Dr. Jesús Martín B.
Department of Social Work: Dr. Camilo Bautista.
Department of Letters: Dr. Carlos Vásquez.

Education Division:
Department of Education Extension: Dr. Víctor Julio Ortíz.
Department of Psychology: Dr. Elsa Strauss de Gutiérrez.
Department of Curriculum: Dr. Carlos Soto.
Department of Educational Administration: Guillermo Salazar.
Department of Physical Education and Sport: Alberto Calderon.

UNIVERSIDAD PEDAGÓGICA Y TECNOLÓGICA DE COLOMBIA

(Pedagogical and Technological University of Colombia)

APDO. AÉREO 1094, CIUDAD UNIVERSITARIA, TUNJA, BOYACÁ

Telephone: 21-74.

Founded 1953.

Rector: Osmar Correal Cabral.
Head of Administration: Jaime Archila Saenz.

Number of teachers: 415.
Number of students: 4,592.

Deans:

Faculty of Education: Jorge Palacio P.
Faculty of Agronomy: José Joaquín F.
Faculty of Engineering: Eduardo Vargas C. (acting).
Faculty of Economics and Administration: José García J.

UNIVERSIDAD TECNOLÓGICA DEL MAGDALENA

CARRERA 2A, No. 16-44,
SANTA MARTA

Telephone: 31 10, 31 11.

Founded 1958, opened 1966.

Rector: ANTONIO SERRANO ZUÑIGA.
Secretary-General: Dr. LUIS ALFREDO PARIA.

Number of students: *c.* 500.

Faculties of Agricultural Engineering, Farm Management, Sciences.

UNIVERSIDAD TECNOLÓGICA DE PEREIRA
(Pereira Technological University)

APARTADO AÉREO 97,
PEREIRA

Telephone: 32-781.

Founded 1958.

Rector: Ing. GABRIEL JAIME CARDONA O.
Secretary-General: Dra. SONIA DE BERNAL.
Academic Secretary: Lic. HUGO FORERO M.
Academic Dean: Dr. HERNÁN MARTÍNEZ.
Librarian: Lic. SAÚL SÁNCHEZ TORO.

Library of 14,393 vols.
Number of teachers: 269.
Number of students: 3,891.

Publications: *Revista U.T.P.*†, *Noticiero Bibliográfico e Informativo*†, *Serie Arte y Cultura.*

DIRECTORS:

Electrical Engineering: Ing. HECTOR SÁNCHEZ A.
Mechanical Engineering: Ing. JOSELÍN CUADRADO.
Industrial Engineering: Ing. OMAR FLOREZ.
Department of Basic Studies: Ing. FABIO HENAO.
Department of Medicine: Dr. ARTURO CAMPO POSADA.
Institute of Fine Arts: MARÍA TERESA DE LA CUESTA DE SALAZAR.
Education: Lic. NEIYER JAIRO CORREAL.
Polytechnic Institute: Ing. OLMEDO GARCÍA.
Computer Centre: Ing. CÉSAR JARAMILLO N.

ESCUELA SUPERIOR DE ADMINISTRACIÓN PÚBLICA

APDO. AÉREO 29745,
APDO. NACIONAL 2085,
CARRERA 7 No. 6-54, BOGOTÁ

Telephone: 699186.

Founded 1958.

Academic year: February to November.

Director: Dr. HUMBERTO GALLEGO G.
Secretary-General: Dr. RAFAEL H. SERRANO VARÓN.
Librarian: NELLY BELTRÁN DE PORRAS.

Library of 17,330 vols.
Number of teachers: 72.
Number of students: 753.

Publications: *Administración y Desarrollo* (2 a year).

DIRECTORS:

Research and Information Centre: Dr. JORGE ENRIQUE RODRÍGUEZ ROA.
Faculty of Political and Administrative Sciences: Dr. EDUARDO ROZO ACUÑA.

PRIVATE UNIVERSITIES

FUNDACIÓN UNIVERSIDAD DE BOGOTÁ
"Jorge Tadeo Lozano"

APDO. AÉREO 34185, CALLE 23,
No. 4-47, BOGOTÁ

Telephone: 2439771.

Founded 1954.

Academic year: February to December (two semesters).

President-Rector: Dr. JAIME FORERO VALDÉS.
Secretary-General: Dr. JUAN MANUEL CABALLERO PRIETO.
Librarian: AURORA ARCINIEGAS.

Number of teachers: 650.
Number of students: 6,100.

DEANS:

Faculty of Business Administration: Dr. RAFAEL GUTIÉRREZ.
Faculty of Public Accountancy: Dr. ALVARO PINZÓN.
Faculty of Economic Sciences: Dr. EDUARDO SUAREZ.
Faculty of Food Technology: Dr. GABRIEL ACEVEDO.
Faculty of Geographic Engineering: Dr. MARIANO OSPINA R.
Faculty of Agronomy: Dr. ABDÓN CORTÉS.
Faculty of Political Sciences: Dr. DIEGO URIBE VARGAS.
Faculty of International Commerce: Dr. ALBERTO NAVAS.
Faculty of Social Communication: Dr. MANUEL CABRERA T.
Faculty of Industrial Design: Dr. JULIO VINACCIA.
School of Fine Arts: Señora ANA DE JACOBINI.

UNIVERSIDAD AUTÓNOMA LATINOAMERICANA

CARRERA 55 No. 49-51,
APDO. AÉREO 3455, MEDELLÍN

Telephone: 31-11-99.
Telex: UNAULA.

Founded 1966.

Academic year: January to June, July to December.

Rector: Dr. JAIRO URIBE ARANGO.
Secretary-General: Dr. ALVARO OCHOA MORALES.
Librarian: Lic. JAIME MARULANDA VALENCIA.

Number of teachers: 265.
Number of students: 3,018.

Publications: *Revista*† (annually), *Boletín Informativo*†, *Boletín de Bibliotecas* (monthly)†, *Sociología* (annually).

DEANS:

Faculty of Law: Dr. RODRIGO FLOREZ R.
Faculty of Education: Dr. JAIRO SALAZAR R.
Faculty of Sociology: Lic. JAIRO R. SOLANO A.
Faculty of Accountancy: Dr. ARMANDO DURAN G.
Faculty of Economics: Dr. JOSÉ E. ZULUAGA-PINEDA.
Faculty of Industrial Engineering: Dr. JAVIER OSSA M.

UNIVERSIDAD PONTIFICIA BOLIVARIANA

APDO. POSTAL 109, LA PLAYA
40-102, MEDELLÍN

Telephone: 49 71 99

Founded 1936.

Rector: Mons. LUIS ALFONSO LONDOÑO BERNAL.
Vice-Rector: Dr. JUAN MEJÍA URIBE.
Secretary: **Dr. DIEGO VELÁSQUEZ N.**
Administrative Director: **Dr. HUGO LONDOÑO.**

Library: ***see under*** **Libraries.**
Number of teachers: 560.
Number of students: 9,867.

Publications: *Revista Universidad Pontificia Bolivariana*, *Revista de la Academia de Historia Eclesiástica*, and individual faculty reviews.

DEANS:

Faculty of Philosophy and Letters: Lic. GONZALO SOTO POSADA.
Faculty of Education: Lic. PIEDAD HENAO VÁSQUEZ.
Faculty of Design: Arq. ALBERTO URIBE DUQUE.
Faculty of Law: Dr. JORGE BOTERO OSPINA.
Faculty of Social Work: Lic. CECILIA ANGEL.
Faculty of Chemical Engineering: Ing. FABIO MARTÍNEZ URIBE.
Faculty of Architecture and Town Planning: Arq. IVAN ARANGO HERRERA.
Faculty of Electrical and Electronic Engineering: Ing. EVARISTO ARANGO ARCILA.
Faculty of Mechanical Engineering: Ing. ALONSO VÉLEZ COVO.
Faculty of Sociology: Lic. CARLOS OCAMPO GÓMEZ.
Faculty of Social Communication: Lic. YOLANDA OROZCO GIRALDO.
Faculty of Theology: Pbro. ALFONSO LÓPEZ SERNA.
Faculty of Medicine: Dr. MARIO MONTOYA TORO.
Institute of Business Administration: OSCAR JAIME GÓMEZ MONTOYA.

UNIVERSIDAD EXTERNADO DE COLOMBIA

CALLE 12 Nos. 1–17 ESTE, BOGOTÁ
Telephone: 82-60-66.
Founded 1886.

Academic year: February to December.
Rector: Dr. FERNANDO HINESTROSA.
Vice-Rector: Dr. CARLOS MEDELLÍN FORERO.
Secretary-General: Dr. MANUEL CUBIDES ROMERO.
Librarian: Dra. EMILSSEN GONZÁLEZ DE CANCINO.

Number of professors: 445.
Number of students: 6,079.
Publication: *Revista* (quarterly).

DIRECTORS:

Faculty of Law and Political Sciences: FERNANDO HINESTROSA.
Faculty of Economics, Administration and Accountancy: ENRIQUE LOW MURTRA.
Faculty of Educational Sciences: LUIS ALEJANDRO GUERRA.
Faculty of Social Work: FANNY RUBIO.
Faculty of Social Communication: JOSÉ DE RECASENS.

UNIVERSIDAD LA GRAN COLOMBIA

CARRERA 6, No. 13-40, APDO. AÉREO 7909, BOGOTÁ
Telephone: 43 80 47.
Founded 1951.

Academic year: February to December (two semesters).
Rector: Dr. JORGE URIBE RESTREPO.
Secretary-General: Dr. HUMBERTO ALVAREZ RICO.
Librarian: Lic. MARÍA EUGENIA MONCADA GARRIDO.

Number of teachers: 650.
Number of students: 7,257.
Publication: *Revista*† (irregular).

DEANS:

Faculty of Architecture: Arq. EDGAR ERASSO VALLEJO.
Faculty of Education: Dr. ALFONSO RAMOS ZAPATA.
Faculty of Accountancy: Dr. ALVARO PINZÓN PÉREZ.
Faculty of Law: Dr. EDUARDO KRONFLY KRONFLY.
Faculty of Economics: Dr. CARLOS MEDINA ZARATE.
Faculty of Civil Engineering: Dr. CARLOS GONZÁLEZ.

PONTIFICIA UNIVERSIDAD JAVERIANA

CARRERA 7A, No. 40-62, APARTADO AÉREO 5315, BOGOTÁ
Telephone: 32 20 40.

Founded 1622 by the Jesuit Fathers; re-established 1931, present status 1937.

Academic year: January to November (two semesters).
Chancellor: R.P. PEDRO ARRUPE, S.J.
Vice-Grand Chancellor: P. GERARDO ARANGO, S.J.
Rector: R. P. ROBERTO CARO, S.J.
Vice-Rectors: P. JORGE HOYOS, P. HERNAN POSADA, Dr. ALVARO DÁVILA.

Library: *see* Libraries.
Number of teachers: 1,146.
Number of students: 12,512.
Publications: *Theologica Xaveriana*†, *Universitas Médica*† (quarterly), *Universitas Juridica*†, *Universitas Humanística*†, *Universitas Economica*† (2 a year).

DEANS:

Faculty of Theology: P. ALBERTO MÚNERA, S.J.
Faculty of Canon Law: P. LIBORIO RESTREPO, S.J.
Faculty of Social Communication: P. JOAQUÍN SÁNCHEZ, S.J.
Faculty of Medicine: Dr. ALBERTO ESCALLÓN.
Faculty of Law and Socio-Economic Sciences: Dr. JUAN BENAVIDES.
Faculty of Engineering: Dr. FERNANDO MARTÍNEZ.
Faculty of Sciences: Dr. JAIME F. GEORGE.
Faculty of Electrical Engineering: Dr. FERNANDO GARCIA.
Faculty of Architecture: Dr. PEDRO POLO VERANO.
Faculty of Philosophy and Letters: P. JAIME VÉLEZ, S.J.
Faculty of Psychology: P. MARCO TULIO GONZÁLEZ, S.J.
Faculty of Economic and Administrative Sciences: Dr. GABRIEL ROSAS.
Faculty of Dentistry: Dr. ENRIQUE GARCIA MONGE.
Faculty of Education: P. ALFONSO QUINTANA, S.J.
Faculty of Nursing: Dra. MARIA TERESA VERGARA.
Faculty of Interdisciplinary Studies: Dr. HERNANDO ARELLANO.
San Ignacio University Hospital: Dr. AUGUSTO BUENDÍA.
Department of Languages: P. ROBERTO CABRERA, S.J.
Department of Religious Sciences: P. RAÚL POSADA, S.J.

AFFILIATED INSTITUTE:

Instituto Geofísico de los Andes Colombianos (*Geophysical Institute of the Colombian Andes*): f. 1941; Dir. P. JESÚS EMILIO RAMÍREZ S.J.

UNIVERSIDAD LIBRE DE COLOMBIA*
(Free University)

CARRERA 6, No. 8-06, BOGOTÁ
Telephone: 344883.
Founded 1923.

Rector: Dr. DARIO SAMPER.
Secretary-General: JULIO ROBERTO GALINDO H.
Faculties' Secretary: Dr. CARLOS MARTÍNEZ RODRÍGUEZ.
Librarian: LUCREZIA MEDINA.

Number of teachers: *c.* 220.
Number of students: *c.* 2,000.
Faculties of Accountancy, Law and Politics, Metallurgy, Education.

* No reply received to our questionnaire this year.

UNIVERSIDAD DE LOS ANDES

CARRERA 1, No. 18-A-82; APDO AÉREO 4976, BOGOTÁ
Telephone: 824066.
Founded 1948.

Academic year: January to December (two semesters).
President: HUMBERTO VEGALARA.
Rector: MAURICIO OBREGÓN.
Vice-Rector: CARLOS J. AMAYA.
Chief Administrative Officer: FERNANDO ACOSTA.
Secretary-General: GRETEL WERNHER.
Librarian: MARÍA SOLEDAD DE MENÉNDEZ.

Library of 90,000 vols.
Number of teachers: 150 (full-time).
Number of students: 4,000.
Publications: *Razón y Fábula* (every 2 months), *News Bulletin* (technical bulletins on economics, engineering, town planning, biology, anthropology and political sciences).

DEANS:

Faculty of Administration: JUAN MANUEL LLERAS.
Faculty of Economics: Dr. AUGUSTO CANO.
Faculty of Engineering: LASLO SZEKESSY.
Faculty of Architecture: MANUEL CARRIZOSA.
Faculty of Philosophy and Letters: GERMÁN ARCINIEGAS.
Faculty of Arts and Sciences: MANUEL RODRÍGUEZ-BECERRA.
Faculty of Law: EDUARDO ALVAREZ CORREA.

AFFILIATED RESEARCH INSTITUTES:

Centre of Studies on Economic Development (CEDE): Dir. EDGAR REVEIZ.
Centre of Electronic Computation (CCE): Dir. JOAQUÍN ORAMAS.
Centre of Hydraulic Studies and Research (CETIH): Dir. (vacant).
Institute of Genetics: Dir. HUGO HOENISBERG.

UNIVERSIDAD DE MEDELLÍN

APDO. AÉREO 1983, CALLE 31, No. 83-B-150, MEDELLÍN
Telephone: 38-38-06.
Founded 1950.

President: Dr. JAVIER CHICA MOLINA.
Rector: Dr. PEDRO P. CARDONA GALEANO.
Administrative Officer: Dr. JOSÉ JOAQUÍN BOTERO URIBE.

Secretary-General: Dr. IGNACIO CADAVID GOMEZ.
Librarian: Lic. ALBERTO GUTIÉRREZ.

Number of professors: 420.
Number of students: 5,036.

Publications: *Revista U DE M*† (4 a year), *Prospecto Facultad de Derecho*† (annual), *Universidad y Pueblo*† (20 a year).

DEANS:

Faculty of Law: Dr. DÁRIO MUÑOZ BEDOYA.
Faculty of Industrial Economy: Dr. VICENTE CUARTAS MEJÍA.
Faculty of Administrative Sciences: Dr. ALBERTO E. URIBE-MEJÍA.
Faculty of Statistics: Dr. ALBERTO QUIJANO MANCHERI.
Faculty of Civil Engineering: Dr. JAIME ORREGO POSADA.
Faculty of Educational Sciences: Dra. GLORIA C. FAJARDO AVENDAÑO.
Faculty of Public Accountancy: Dr. WALTHER RÍOS MUÑOZ.

AFFILIATED INSTITUTES:

Instituto de Derecho Penal y Criminología: Dir. Dr. GUILLERMO BAENA RESTREPO.

Instituto de Estudios de Postgrado e Investigación: Dir. Dr. RODRIGO SALAZAR PINEDA.

UNIVERSIDAD DEL NORTE

APDO. AÉREO 1569,
BARRANQUILLA
Telephone: 357720-24.
Founded 1966.

Academic year: January to May, August to December.

Rector: JESUS FERRO BAYONA.
Registrar: MARGARITA DE CASTRO.
Dean of Students: ALFONSO FREIDEL DONADO.
Academic Services: CARMEN H. DE PEÑA.
Librarian: MARTHA OROZCO.

The library contains 11,000 vols.
Number of teachers: 296.
Number of students: 2,180.

DEANS:

Faculty of Business Administration: ANTONIO BITAR YANCE.
Faculty of Psychology: BEATRIZ DE TORRES.
Faculty of Engineering: REMIRO BESADA LOMBANA.
Faculty of Health Sciences: FUAD J. RUMIÉ.

UNIVERSIDAD SANTIAGO DE CALÍ*

CARRERA 5 No. 7-2, CALI
Telephone: 89 693–89 699.
Founded 1958.

Rector: LEONIDAS CHAUX MOSQUERA.
Secretary-General: **Dr. PEDRO E. SERRANO.**
Librarian: **Dr. LIBORIO VILLA CANTILLO.**

Number of students: 3,800.

Faculties of Law, Administration, Accountancy, Education.

* No reply received to our questionnaire this year.

UNIVERSIDAD DE SAN BUENAVENTURA

CALLE 73, No. 10-45,
APDO. AÉREO 053746,
BOGOTÁ
Telephone: 352922.
Founded 1715, University status 1964.

Academic year: February to November.

Campuses in Calí and Medellín.

Chancellor: Rev. CONSTANTINO KOSER.
Vice-Chancellor: Rev. ENRIQUE GONZÁLEZ.
Rector: Rev. DARIO CORREA GÓMEZ.
Vice-Rector: Rev. DARÍO MOLINA.
Administrative Officer: Rev. MARIO JARAMILLO.
Librarian: MARÍA T. GARDEAZABAL.

Number of teachers: 110.
Number of students: 1,600.
Publication: *Franciscanum*† (three times yearly).

DEANS:

Faculty of Philosophy: Rev. IGNACIO BURGOS.
Faculty of Theology: Rev. DARÍO MOLINA.

Medellín:

Faculty of Sociology: Rev. ARTURO CALLE.
Faculty of Psychology: Rev. HÉCTOR J. RAMÍREZ.

Calí:

Faculty of Law: Dr. GENARO CHAMORRO.
Faculty of Administration: Rev. PABLO GARCÍA.
Faculty of Education: Dr. OSCAR G. RAMOS.

UNIVERSIDAD DE SANTO TOMÁS

CARRERA 9A, No. 51-23,
APDO. AÉREO 21019,
BOGOTÁ, D.E.
Telephone: 357192.
Founded 1580; restored 1965.

Academic year: February to June, August to December.

Rector: R.P. Dr. ALVARO GALVIS RAMÍREZ, O.P.
Vice-Rectors: R.P. Dr. JOSÉ LUIS SANZ TENA, O.P. (Academic); R.P. Dr. JOSÉ DE J. FARÍAS, O.P. (University Affairs); R.P. Dr. NORBERTO RANGEL ARGUELLO, O.P. (Administration).
Secretary-General: R.P. Ing. JULIO CÉSAR VACA, O.P.
Librarian: R.P. Dr. JOAQUÍN ZABALZA IRIARTE, O.P.

Library of 15,000 vols.
Number of teachers: 800.
Number of students: 3,250.
Publication: ***Universidad Santo Tomás.***

DEANS:

Faculty of Law and Political Science: Dr. JOSÉ A. BONIVENTO F.
Faculty of Public Accounting: Dr. ALBERTO YEPES MORA.
Faculty of Civil Engineering: Ing. FRANCISCO GNECCO CALVO.
Faculty of Philosophy: Lic. ALBERTO CÁRDENAS PATIÑO.
Faculty of Economics and Business Administration: Dr. JAIME CONCHA S.
Faculty of Sociology: Dr. GUILLERMO PÁEZ MORALES.

UNIVERSIDAD SOCIAL CATÓLICA DE LA SALLE

CALLE 11, No. 1-47, BOGOTÁ
Telephone: 34-61-37.
Founded 1965.

Rector: Dr. SVEN ZETHELIUS PEÑALOSA.
Administrative Vice-Rector: Dr. ENRIQUE BEJARANO MORENO.
Academic Vice-Rector: Dr. JAIME GONZÁLEZ SANTOS.
Secretary-General: Dr. GUSTAVO SANDOVAL VALDERRAMA.
Librarian: Dra. YOLANDA HURTADO TOVAR.

Number of teachers: 300.
Number of students: 3,450.

DEANS:

Faculty of Architecture: Dr. JOSÉ IGNACIO SANCLEMENTE V.
Faculty of Civil Engineering: Dr. ARTURO RAMÍREZ MONTUFAR.
Faculty of Economics: Dr. BLAS J. GIFFUNI CABRA.
Faculty of Education: Dr. CAMPO ELIAS GONZALEZ, F.S.C.
Faculty of Philosophy and Letters: Dr. MARTÍN CARLOS MORALES, F.S.C.
Faculty of Information Science: Dr. GASTON LITTON BERRY.
Faculty of Optometry: Dr. GABRIEL MERCHÁN DE MENDOZA.

DIRECTORS:

Department of Social Work: Dra. CLARA I. RODRIGUEZ DE TAMAYO.
Department of Statistics: Dr. JORGE AUGUSTO CELIS SARMIENTO.
Department of Business Administration: Dr. LUIS EDUARDO ILLERA.
Department of Agricultural Administration: Dr. AQUILEO PARRA A.
Department of Biology and Chemistry: Dr. ROQUE CASALLAS L., F.S.C.
Department of Mathematics and Physics: Dr. RICARDO LOSADA MARQUEZ.
Department of Languages: Dr. HUGO NOEL PARRA F.
Department of Religious Studies: Dr. OTTO PANTANO GUEVARA, F.S.C.

Department of Education: Dr. GERARD M. ZIMMERMANN.
Department of Audio-visual Aids: Dr. HERNANDO ALFONSO.
Department of Accounting: Dr. JORGE JIMENEZ.

COLEGIO MAYOR DE NUESTRA SEÑORA DEL ROSARIO

CALLE 14, No. 6-25, BOGOTÁ

Telephone: 2820088.

Founded 1653.

Academic year: February to November.

Rector: Dr. ALVARO TAFUR GALVIS.
Vice-Rector: Dr. ALVARO DAZA ROA.
Secretary-General: Dr. GUSTAVO COMBATT L.
Librarian: LUCÍA BELMONTE.

Number of teachers: 607.
Number of students: 3,007.
Publication: *Revista*†.

DEANS:

Faculty of Law: GUILLERMO CUBILLOS ESCOBAR.
Faculty of Economics: Dr. JORGE GUTIÉRREZ G.
Faculty of Philosophy, Letters and History: Dr. LUIS ENRIQUE RUIZ LÓPEZ.
Faculty of Medicine: Dr. GUILLERMO RUEDA MONTAÑA.
Faculty of Business Administration: Dr. GUILLERMO LLÍNAS A.
School of Translating and Interpreting: PAOLA M. DE VÁSQUEZ R.

ESCUELA DE ADMINISTRACIÓN Y FINANZAS Y TECNOLOGÍAS

APDO. AÉREO 3300, MEDELLÍN

Telephone: 550500.

Founded 1960.

Private control; Academic year: February to June, August to December.

Rector: HECTOR OCHOA DIAZ.
Registrar: LUIS EDUARDO GÓMEZ.
Librarian: LIA CARDENAS.

Library of 12,000 vols.
Number of teachers: 154.
Number of students: 1,735.
Publication: *Temas Administrativos.*

SCHOOLS OF ART AND MUSIC

Conservatorio Nacional de Música (*National Conservatory of Music*): Ciudad Universitaria, Bogotá; f. 1910; included in the Faculty of Arts.

Secretary: Dr. VICENTE R. GAVIRIA.

Number of teachers: 40.
Number of students: 443.
Library of 2,500 volumes, scores and records.

Conservatorio de Música de la Universidad del Atlántico: Calle 68, No. 53-45, Apdo. Aéreo 1890, Barranquilla; f. 1939; 21 teachers, 400 students; Dir. Prof. GUNTER RENZ.

Conservatorio de Música del Tolima: Calle 9, No. 1-18; f. 1906; 57 teachers; library of 1,827 vols.; Gen. Sec. PILAR JARAMILLO LOZANO.

Escuela de Música: Universidad de Nariño, Calle 21 No. 23-90, Pasto, Nariño; Dir. FAUSTO MARTINEZ.

Escuela de Música y Artes Representativas: Universidad de Antioquia, Bloque 25, Medellín; f. 1959; 40 teachers and 350 students; library of 1,000 vols., 4,000 scores; Dir. Dr. HERNAN ROJO FERNANDEZ.

Escuela de Pintura y Artes Plásticas: Universidad del Atlántico, Calle 68, No. 53-45, Barranquilla; f. 1961; teaching of plastic arts; staff of 11; library of 1,900 vols. Dir. Dr. EDUARDO VIDES CELIS.

Instituto de Artes Plásticas: Universidad de Antioquia, Medellín; Dir. Dr. RODRIGO MORALES.

Instituto Musical de Cartagena: Apartado Aéreo No. 17-67, Cartagena; f. 1890; 12 teachers, 340 students; library of 1,500 vols.; Dir. Prof. JIRI PITRO M.

CONGO PEOPLE'S REPUBLIC

Population 1,440,000

LEARNED SOCIETIES AND RESEARCH INSTITUTES

Bureau pour le Développement de la Production Agricole (BDPA): B.P. 2222, Brazzaville; 5 staff give expert technical assistance; main office in France.

Centre Culturel Français: B.P. 2141, Brazzaville; f. 1962; library of 5,000 vols.; Dir. C. HURLOLT.

Centre Technique Forestier Tropical: B.P. 764, Pointe-Noire; f. 1958; forestry research; Dir. J.-C. DELWAULLE.

Conseil National de la Recherche Scientifique et Technique: Brazzaville; f. 1966; special commissions for medical science, agronomic and pastoral sciences, forestry research, marine science and fisheries, hydrology, geology, botany, anthropology, educational and industrial research; Pres. The Commissioner for Planning.

Institut Africain: Mouyondzi; living African languages.

Institut de Recherches pour les Huiles et Oléagineux: Sibiti; Dir. A. MALLA.

Office de la Recherche Scientifique et Technique Outre-Mer: B.P. 181, Brazzaville; soil science, hydrology, botany, medical entomology, sociology and psychosociology, geography, economics, phytopathology and applied zoology; library; Dir. M. MOLINIER. (*See* main entry under France).

Office de la Recherche Scientifique et Technique Outre-Mer: B.P. 1286, Pointe-Noire; f. 1950; biological and physical oceanography; library; Dir. B. PITON. (*See* main entry under France.)

Station Fruitière du Congo: B.P. 27, Loudima; f. 1963; Dir. C. MAKAY.

LIBRARIES

Bibliothèque de l'Organisation mondiale de la Santé, Bureau régional de l'Afrique (*Library of WHO Regional Office for Africa*): B.P. 6, Brazzaville; f. 1952; 40,000 vols.; Librarian A. IKAMA-OBAMBI; publs. bibliographies, catalogues.

Bibliothèque de l'Université de Brazzaville: B.P. 2025, Brazzaville; f. 1959; 70,000 vols.; Chief Librarian F. WELLOT-SAMBA; publs. catalogues, guides.

MUSEUM

Musée National: B.P. 459, Brazzaville; f. 1965; ethnographic collection and national history; library of 285 vols.; Dir. JOSEPH NGOUBELI.

UNIVERSITY AND COLLEGES

UNIVERSITÉ MARIEN-NGOUABI

B.P. 69, BRAZZAVILLE

Telephone: 81-24-36.

Founded 1961 as Centre d'Enseignement Supérieur; University status 1972.

Language of instruction: French.

Rector: ANACLET TSOMAMBET.
Vice-Rector: BERNARD NGANGA.
Secretary-General: FRANÇOIS OKOBO.
Librarian: FRANÇOIS WELLOT-SAMBA.

Number of teachers: 230.
Number of students: 4,336.

Publications: *Annales, Annuaire, DIMI.*

DEANS:

Faculty of Letters and Human Sciences: MICHEL MOWELLE.
Faculty of Sciences: JEAN-FRANÇOIS MIAYOUKOU.

ATTACHED INSTITUTES:

Institut Supérieur des Sciences de l'Education (INSSED): B.P. 237, Brazzaville; f. 1962 under UN Special Fund; Dir. RAYMOND MANG-BENZA.

Institut des Sciences de la Santé (INSSSA): B.P. 69, Brazzaville; f. 1976; Dir. CHRISTOPHE BOURAMOUE.

Institut Supérieur des Sciences Economiques, Juridiques, Administratives et de Gestion (INSSEJAG): B.P. 2469, Brazzaville; f. 1976; Dir. ZACHARIE SAMBA.

Institut de Développement Rural (IDR): B.P. 69, Brazzaville; f. 1976; Dir. CONSTANT MAMPOUYA.

Institut Supérieur d'Education Physique et Sportive (ISEPS): B.P. 1100, Brazzaville; f. 1976; Dir. PAUL EBONDZIBATO.

Centre d'Etudes Administratives et Techniques Supérieures: administrative and judicial centre, school of arts.

Collège d'Enseignement Technique Agricole: B.P. 30, Sibiti; f. 1943; Dir. JEAN BOUNGOU.

Collège Technique, Commercial et Industriel de Brazzaville (et centre d'Apprentissage): Brazzaville; f. 1959; Dir. HUBERT CUOPPEY.

Ecole Supérieure Africaine des Cadres des Chemins de Fer (*Higher School for Railway Engineers*): Brazzaville; f. 1977; 3-year courses in engineering and management.

COSTA RICA

Population 2,125,000

ACADEMIES

Academia Costarricense de la Lengua: Sala de España, Biblioteca Nacional, Apdo. 10008, San José; f. 1923; 9th in order of foundation in Spanish America; corresp. of the Real Academia Española, Madrid; 18 mems.; publ. *Boletín de la Academia Costarricense de la Lengua*.
Director: HERNÁN G. PERALTA.
Secretary: JUAN TREJOS QUIRÓS.

Academia de Geografía e Historia de Costa Rica: Apdo. 4499, San José; 31 mems.; Pres. Lic. CARLOS MELÉNDEZ; Sec. Dr. OSCAR AGUILAR B.; publ. *Anales*†.

LEARNED SOCIETIES AND RESEARCH INSTITUTES

Academia Costarricense de Periodoncia: Apdo. 1435, San José; f. 1965; Pres. Dr. C. MORA.

Alliance Française (*Comité de l'Alliance Française au Costa Rica*): Apdo. 10.195, San José; library of 4,500 vols.

Asociación Costarricense de Bibliotecarios (*Costa Rican Association of Librarians*): Apdo. 3308, San José; f. 1949; responsible for national bibliography; Pres. EFRAIM ROJAS R.; Sec.-Gen. NELLY KOPPER; publs. *Boletín*† (irregular), *Anuario Bibliográfico Costarricense*† (annually).

Asociación Costarricense de Cirugía (*Surgery Association*): Apdo. 2724, San José; f. 1954; 62 mems.; Pres. Dr. RAFAEL A. NUÑEZ HERNÁNDEZ; Sec. Dr. FEDERICO SOSTO PERALTA.

Asociación Costarricense de Pediatría (*Costa Rican Paediatrics Association*): Apdo. 1654, San José; f. 1951; organizes national conference every October; 121 mems.; Pres. Dr. CARLOS A. LEÓN; Sec. Dr. ORLANDO SESÍN.

Asociación de Cardiologia (*Cardiology Association*): Hospital San Juan de Dios, San José.

Asociación de Medicina Interna (*Association of Internal Medicine*): Hospital San Juan de Dios, San José.

Asociación de Obstetricia y Ginecologia (*Obstetrics and Gynaecology Association*): Hospital San Juan de Dios, San José.

Centro Agronómico Tropical de Investigación y Enseñanza (CATIE): Turrialba; f. 1973 by the IICA and the Costa Rican Government as a non-profit-making scientific and educational asscn. for work in the Central American Isthmus and the Caribbean areas; Panama, Nicaragua and Honduras are now mems.; Dir. SANTIAGO FONSECA; publ. *Activities at Turrialba* (quarterly, in English and Spanish), *Memoria Annual*.

Centro Cultural Costarricense-Norteamericano: Apdo. 1489, San Jose; f. 1945; teaches English and Spanish, cultural programmes, etc.; 300 mems.; library: *see* Libraries; Pres. ARMANDO GONZALEZ; Dir. DELORES RICK.

Centro de Estudios Médicos Ricardo Moreno Cañas: Apdo. 10151, San José; f. 1942; 400 mems.; Pres. Dr. E. GARCÍA CARRILLO; Sec. Dr. R. CÉSPEDES FONSECA.

Comisión de Energía Atómica de Costa Rica (*National Atomic Energy Commission*): Apdo. 6681, San José; f. 1967; Pres. JOSÉ F. CARVAJAL.

Dirección General de Estadistica y Censos: Apartado 10163, San José; library of 3,000 vols.

Dirección General de Geologia, Minas y Petróleo: Apdo. 2549, San José; f. 1951; in addition to research in above-named subjects, acts as central science policy-making body for Costa Rica; grants; Dir. LUIS FELIPE SANDOVAL MOLINA; publ. *Informes Técnicos y Notas Geológicas*.

Instituto de Alajuela (*Alajuela Institute*): Alajuela; scientific research station; Dir. JULIO C. SOLERA.

Instituto Centroamericano de Administración Pública (ICAP) (*Central American Institute of Public Administration*): Apdo. 10025, San José; f. 1954; public administration, economic development and integration; library of 25,000 vols.; Dir. CARLOS CORDERO D'AUBUISSON.

Instituto Centroamericano de Extensión de la Cultura: Apdo. 2948, San José; f. 1963 to provide cultural and educational opportunities for those who cannot attend a centre of learning, particularly those in rural areas of Central America; broadcasts six days a week a half-hourly programme "Escuela para Todos"; library of 1,200 vols.; Sec.-Gen. Dr. RODERICH THUN STOTZINGEN; publs. *Escuela para Todos* (annually), newsletter (quarterly in Spanish, German, English).

Instituto Costarricense de Ciencias Politicas y Sociales (*Costa Rican Institute of Social and Political Sciences*): San José, C.9, Ave. 1-3.

Instituto Geográfico Nacional: Apdo. 2272, San José; f. 1944; library of 3,000 vols.; Dir. Ing. FERNANDO MAURO RUDÍN RODRÍGUEZ; publs. *Informe Semestral*, *Geográficas*, etc.

Instituto Interamericano de Ciencias Agrícolas de la OEA (*Inter-American Institute of Agricultural Sciences*): *see* International section.

Instituto Latinoamericano de las Naciones Unidas para la Prevención del Delito y Tratamiento del Delincuente (*UN Latin American Institute for Crime Prevention and Treatment of Offenders*): Apdo. 10.338, San José; f. 1975 as a UN regional agency; provides training, advice and research in the fields of law, public administration, sociology and criminology; projects include the creation of a specialized library and data bank for international use, symposia, ministerial meetings, and a pilot project in San Ramón of research and community participation in crime prevention; Dir. Lic. JORGE A. MONTERO; publ. *Revista Latinoamericana sobre Política Criminal*.

Instituto Meteorológico Nacional: Apdo. 7-3350, San José; f. 1888; climatology, hydrometeorology, synoptic and aeronautical meteorology; 60 mems.; Dir. Lic. NORMAN VEGA.

Organization for Tropical Studies: University of Costa Rica, Ciudad Universitaria, San José; consortium of 29 American and Costa Rican universities and institutions, to provide formal introductory courses at graduate level in tropical studies, seminars, graduate research and independent study.

Tropical Science Centre: Apartado 8-3870, San José; f. 1962; private non-profit assn.; research and training in tropical science; consultation on life zone ecology mapping, land use planning; specialized library; biological reserve and field station at Monteverde Cloud Forest; Administrator J. A. TOSI, Jr., PH.D.; publ. *Occasional Paper Series*† (irregular).

LIBRARIES

Archivo Nacional de Costa Rica: Calle 7, ave. 4, Apdo. 5028, San José; 8,500 vols.; Librarian LUS A. CHACÓN; publ. *Revista* (quarterly).

Biblioteca de la Asamblea Legislativa: Apdo. 10.162, San José; f. 1953; 30,000 vols.; Dir. SALVADOR JIMÉNEZ-CANOSSA.

Biblioteca "Carlos Monge Alfaro" de la Universidad de Costa Rica: Ciudad Universitaria, San José; f. 1946; 300,000 vols.; Dir. Prof. MARÍA JULIA VARGAS B. (acting).

Biblioteca "Alvaro Castro J.": Calle 2, Av. 4-6, Apdo. 10058, San José; f. 1950; 30,163 vols.; Librarian DEYANIRA VARGAS DE BONILLA.

Biblioteca del Centro Cultural Costarricense-Norteamericano: Apdo. 1489, San José; f. 1945; 7,500 vols.; Librarian PRISCILLA LORES.

Biblioteca del Ministerio de Relaciones Exteriores: Calle 11 a 7, San José; f. 1960; 12,500 vols.; Librarian MARITZA RODRÍGUEZ QUESADA.

Biblioteca Nacional: Apdo. 10008, Calle 5, Avenidas 1/3, San José; f. 1888; 175,000 vols.; Dir. MARCO TULIO ZELEDÓN.

MUSEUMS AND GALLERIES

Sala de Conciertos Tassara: Calle 14, No. 944, San José.

Museo Nacional: Apto. 749, San José; f. 1887; general museum: precolumbian art, colonial religious art, natural history, national herbarium; library of *c.* 10,000 vols.; Dir. LUIS D. GÓMEZ; publs. *Brenesia*†, *Vinculos* (2 a year), occasional papers.

Museo de Zoología: Dpto. de Biología, Univ. de Costa Rica; mammals, herpetology, fish; small library.

Museo de Entomología: Faculty of Agronomy, Univ.de Costa Rica.

Galería Teatro Nacional: Apdo. 5015, San José.

Galería Facultad de Bellas Artes: University of Costa Rica, Ciudad Universitaria, San José.

Galería la Casa del Artista: San José.

Museo Indígeno (*Native Museum*): Seminario Central, San José; f. 1890; library of 40,000 vols.; Dir. Rev. WALTER E. JOVEL CASTRO.

Museo de Historia Eclesiastica "Anselmo Llorente y Lafuente": f. 1972; collection of sacred objects, articles owned by the bishops, and important documents on the history of the church in Costa Rica.

UNIVERSITIES AND COLLEGE

UNIVERSIDAD DE COSTA RICA

CIUDAD UNIVERSITARIA RODRIGO FACIO,
SAN PEDRO DE MONTES DE OCA, SAN JOSÉ

Telephone: 25-55-55.

Founded 1843, re-founded 1940.

Autonomous control; Language of instruction: Spanish; Academic year: March to November.

President: Lic. MARÍA EUGENIA DENGO DE VARGAS.
Rector: Dr. CLAUDIO GUTIÉRREZ CARRANZA.
Registrar: Prof. JORGE SALAS GONZÁLEZ.

Number of teachers: 2,662.
Number of students: 28,378.
Publications: faculty reviews†.

DEANS:

Faculty of Agronomy: Ing. GUILLERMO YGLESIAS PACHECO.
Faculty of Fine Arts: Prof. JOSÉ L. MARÍN PAYNTER.
Faculty of Economics: Lic. HERNÁN SÁENZ JIMÉNEZ.
Faculty of Science: Lic. ARMANDO ACUÑA.
Faculty of Arts: Lic. VIRGINIA SANDOVAL SANDOVAL.
Faculty of Law: Dr. FERNANDO MORA ROJAS.
Faculty of Education: Lic. JESÚS UGALDE VÍQUEZ.
Faculty of Pharmacy: Lic. OSCAR RAMÍREZ GUEVARA.
Faculty of Engineering: Ing. RODRIGO OROZCO SABORÍO.
Faculty of Medicine: Dr. RODRIGO GUTIÉRREZ SÁENZ.
Faculty of Microbiology: Dr. EUGENIE RUDÍN DE MONGE.
Faculty of Dentistry: Dr. JOSÉ JOAQUÍN ULLOA GAMBOA.
Faculty of Social Sciences: Dr. MANUEL FORMOSO HERRERA.

AFFILIATED INSTITUTES:

Organización de Estudios Tropicales (*Tropical Studies Organization*).

Centro Latinoamericano de Demografía (*Latin American Demographic Centre*).

Centro de Estudios Sociales y de Población (*Centre for Social and Population Studies*).

Escuela Centroamericana de Geografía (*Central American School of Geography*): sponsored by UNDP, Unesco, OAS.

UNIVERSIDAD ESTATAL A DISTANCIA
(Open University)

APDO. 2, PLAZA GONZÁLEZ VÍQUEZ,
SAN JOSÉ

Telephone: 24-18-33.

Founded 1977.

Rector: Dr. FRANCISCO ANTONIO PACHECO FERNÁNDEZ.
Vice-Rector for Planning: Dr. CHESTER ZELAYA GOODMAN.
Executive Vice-Rector: Dr. RONALD GARCÍA SOTO.
Academic Vice-Rector: Dipl. Math. ENRIQUE GÓNGORA TREJOS.
Administrative Director: Lic. CARLOS LUIS FALLAS MONGE.
Librarian: Br. LIGIA MARÍA LÓPEZ SANCHO.

Number of teachers: 150.
Number of students: 6,095.

There are 21 regional centres where students can register, receive instruction, sit examinations and use library facilities.

UNIVERSIDAD NACIONAL AUTÓNOMA DE HEREDIA

APDO. 86,
HEREDIA

Founded 1973; in process of formation.

Campuses in Guanacaste, San Ramón, San Isidro de El General.

Faculties of agriculture, education, geography, philosophy and letters, religion, veterinary sciences; *c.* 8,000 students.

Instituto Tecnológico de Costa Rica: Apdo. Postal 159, Cartago; f. 1971; depts. of engineering, agriculture and forestry; 2,500 students; library of 25,000 vols.; Rector Eng. VIDAL QUIRÓS; publs. *Tecnología en Marcha, Comunicación* (quarterly).

CUBA

Population 9,738,000

ACADEMIES

ACADEMIA DE CIENCIAS DE CUBA

CAPITOLIO NACIONAL,
HAVANA 2

Founded 1962.

Scientific research in agricultural, biological, chemical earth, physical, technical and social sciences.

President: Dr. WILFREDO TORRES YRIBAR.

Vice-Presidents: Ing. TIRSO SÁENZ SÁNCHEZ, Dr. JOSÉ B, ALTSHULER GUTWERT, Dr. JOSÉ A. BUSTAMENTE O'LEARY, Ing. EDDY SOSA ARTÍZ, Lic. MARIO ZORRILLA MONTEQUÍN.

Secretary-General: Dr. ISMAEL CLARK ARXER.

Publications: *Ciencias Agrícolas, Ciencias Biológicas-Ciencias de la Tierra, Ciencias Físico-Técnicas y Matemáticas, Ciencias Sociales, Boletín del Archivo Nacional, Boletín del Centro para el Estudio de la Neurosis, Boletín L/L* (Literature and Linguistics). Occasional papers: *Poeyana, Informes Científico-Técnicos.*

INSTITUTES:

Archivo Nacional: *See* under Libraries and Archives.

Centro de Estudios Filosóficos: Calzada No. 251 esq. J., Havana 4; Dir. Dr. MARIANO RODRIGUEZ SOLVEIRA.

Centro de Estudios de Historia y Organizacion de la Ciencia: Cuba No. 460, Havana 1; f. 1861; Dir. Dr. ANTONIO MORENO LUNA.

Instituto de Botánica: Calzada del Cerro No. 1257, esq. a Buenos Aires, Havana 6; the botanical gardens of Havana and Cienfuegos and the natural reserves of the Academy are under the direction of the institute; Dir. Lic. ONANEY MUÑIZ GUTIÉRREZ.

Instituto de Ciencias Sociales: Capitolio Nacional, Havana 2; research in anthropology, archaeology, ethnology, history, social psychology; Dir. Lic. NURIA GREGORY TORADA.

Instituto de Documentación e Información Científica y Técnica: Calle C, No. 351, Havana 4; national centre for scientific information; incorporates a series of provincial centres; Dir. Ing. ALEJANDRO RODRÍGUEZ.

Instituto de Geofísica y Astronomía: Calle 212 No. 2906 entre 29 y 31, Reparto Cubanacan, Havana 16; incorporates a series of seismic and radioastronomic stations; Dir. Dr. Lic. ROSENDO ALVAREZ MORALES.

Instituto de Geografía: Calle 11, No. 514 entre D y E, Havana 4; incorporates a Laboratory of Biospeleology in Santiago de Cuba; Dir. Prof. Dr. PEDRO CAÑAS ABRIL.

Instituto de Geología y Paleontología: Calzada No. 851, esq. a calle 4, Havana 4; Dir. Lic. LENIA MONTERO ZAMORA.

Instituto de Investigaciones de la Caña de Azúcar: Ave. Van Troi No. 17203, Rancho Boyeros; incorporates experimental stations at Güines, Jovellanos, Florida, Ciego de Avila, Morón, Nuevitas, Guaro and Cristino Naranjo; Dir. Ing. RICARDO CAMPOS ZABALA.

Instituto de Investigaciones Fundamentales en Agricultura Tropical "Alejandro de Humboldt": Calle 2, esq. a 1, Santiago de las Vegas; research in plant genetics and physiology and on pest control; incorporates an experimental station at Güira; Dir. Ing. ROMÁN M. GARCÍA GONZÁLEZ.

Instituto de Investigaciones Fundamentales del Cerebro: Calle Loma y 37, Nuevo Vedado, Havana 4; research on neurosis and neurophysiology; Dir. Prof. Dr. JOSÉ A. BUSTAMANTE O'LEARY.

Instituto de Investigaciones Nucleares: Managua, Havana; Dir. Ing. RAIMUNDO FRANCO PARELLADA.

Instituto de Investigación Técnica Fundamental: Calle O No. 8, Havana 4; research on electronic circuits, lasers, solar energy; Dir. Ing. JOSÉ B. ALTSHULER GUTWERT.

Instituto de Literatura y Lingüística: Ave. Salvador Allende No. 710, Havana 3; f. 1793; library; Dir. Prof. Dr. MIRTA AGUIRRE CARRERAS; publ. *Boletín L/L.*

Instituto de Matemática, Cibernética y Computación: Academia de Ciencias, Havana 1; incorporates the computing centre of the Academy; Dir. Ing. JESÚS MARTÍNEZ MARTÍNEZ.

Instituto de Meteorología: Casablanca, Havana 11; national meteorological research centre and 60 meteorological stations on the island are under its control; Dir. Met. MANUEL RODRÍGUEZ NÚÑEZ.

Instituto de Oceanología: Ave. 1ra. No. 18406, Reparto Flores, Cubanacán, Havana 16; Dir. Lic. RODOLFO CLARO MADRUGA.

Instituto de Suelos: Carretera de Vento, Km. 8½, Capdevila, Havana 19; incorporates a laboratory on saline soil research in Guantánamo; Dir. Ing. ABILIO CÁRDENAS GARCÍA.

Instituto de Química y Biología Experimental: Ave. 26, No. 1605, entre Calzada de Puentes Grandes y Boyeros, Havana 6; Dir. Prof. Dr. RUTH D. HENRIQUES RODRÍGUEZ.

Instituto de Zoología: Calle 214, esq. a Ave. 19, No. 17A O9, Reparto Atabey, Havana 16; Dir. Lic. ISRAEL GARCÍA AVILA.

Academia Cubana de la Lengua: Av. 5 No. 608, Vedado; f. 1951; corresponds with the Real Academia Española.

Director: ANTONIO IRAIZOZ.

Secretary: JUAN FONSECA.

Librarian: RAIMUNDO LASO.

LEARNED SOCIETIES AND RESEARCH INSTITUTES

(*see* also under Universities)

Ateneo de La Habana (*Havana Athenaeum*): Av. 5 No. 608, Vedado, Havana; f. 1902; Pres. Dr. JOSÉ M. CHACÓN Y CALVO; Sec. Dr. JOSÉ ENRIQUE HEYMANN Y DE LA GÁNDARA.

Casa de la Cultura Checoslovaca: Calle 23 y O, La Rampa, Vedado; Czechoslovakian culture; Dir. Dr. ZDENEK SUCHOMEL.

Casa de las Américas: G y Tercera, Vedado, Havana; f. 1959; cultural institution dedicated to the promotion of understanding between the Latin American countries and to inform the Cuban public of events in this field; sponsors literary and music festivals, publishing works selected by an international jury; holds festivals in Havana of Latin American drama; organizes exhibitions of Latin American art; arranges conferences on literary, artistic and scientific themes; documentary centre attached; maintains the public library "José A. Echevarría" (*q.v.*); Dir. HAYDÉE SANTAMARÍA; publs. *Casa de las Américas*† (bi-monthly), *Conjunto*† (quarterly), *Boletín de Música*† (bi-monthly).

Centro de Investigaciones y Capacitación Forestales del INDAF: Calle 174 No. 1723 e/17B y 17C, Siboney, Havana; f. 1969; forestry research; 250 researchers; library of 3,000 vols.; Dir. JOSÉ R. GÓMEZ RICAÑO; publ. *Baracoa*† (3 a year).

Centro de Investigaciones para la Industria Minero Metalúrgica: Finca "La Luisa" km. 1, Carretera Varona, Arroyo Naranjo, Havana; including the development of substitute materials where necessary; Dir. OMELIO SÁNCHEZ SERRÚ.

Centro de Investigaciones Pesqueras (*Fisheries Research Centre*): Av. 1 y 26, Miramar, Marianao, Havana; f. 1959; fisheries research, oceanography, marine biology, aquaculture, pollution control; 330 staff; library of 3,551 vols., 1,500 periodicals; Dir. RENÁN PÉREZ FERNÁNDEZ; publ. *Revista Cubama de Investigaciones Pesqueras* (quarterly).

Centro Nacional de Información de Ciencias Médicas: 23 No. 177, entre N y O, Vedado, Havana; scientific and technical information in biomedical sciences, odontology and pharmacy; Dir. VICENTE OSORIO ACOSTA; publs. *Revista Cubana de Medicina*, and other specialized medical journals.

Centro Nacional de Investigaciones Científicas—CNIC: Ave. 25, Calle 158, Reparto Cubanacán; f. 1964; dependent on University of Havana; postgraduate research, related to economic and industrial growth of the country, conducted in fields of biological sciences, chemistry, physics; 225 researchers; 5 service laboratories; documentation and information section; library of 7,000 vols.; Dir. Dr. WILFREDO TORRES I.

Consejo Nacional de Universidades (*National University Council*): Ministerio de Educación, Obispo 160, Havana 1; f. 1960; co-ordinating body for educational and scientific activities and for the administration of the four national universities; Pres. JOSÉ RAMÓN FERNÁNDEZ; Sec. Ing. MIGUEL MARRERO VALLET.

Grupo Hidráulico de Desarrollo Agropecuario del País: Humboldt 106 esq. P., Vedado, Havana; planning the use of water resources; construction of hydraulic and irrigation systems; research in hydraulics, geo-hydrology, general hydrology; Dir. Ing. PEDRO LUIS DORTICOS DEL RÍO; publs. *Voluntad Hidráulica*†, *Boletín de la Lluvia*† (quarterly), *Boletín Hidrométrico* (annual).

Grupo Nacional de Radiologia (*National Radiological Group*): Ministerio de Salud Pública, 23 y N, 3° piso, Vedado, Havana 4; f. 1968; Pres. Dr. EDUARDO RIVERO VALDES-CASTRO; Sec. Dr. RAFAEL MARTORELL GARCIA.

Instituto Cubano de Investigaciones de los Derivados de la Caña de Azúcar—ICIDCA (*Cuban Institute for Research on Sugar Cane By-Products*): Vía Blanca y Carretera Central 804, Apdo. 4026, Guanabacoa, Havana; f. 1963; covers technical-economic aspects, mainly sugar, cellulose and fermentation technologies; 500 staff; library of 5,000 vols.; Dir. LUIS GÁLVEZ TAUPIER; publ. *Sobre los derivados de la Caña de Azúcar*† (4 bulletins a year).

Instituto Cubano de Investigaciones Mineras y Metalúrgicas (*Cuban Institute of Mineral and Metallurgical Research*): Aguiar 207 e/Empedrado y Tejadillo, Havana; technical-economic evolution; Dir. CARLOS COCA OLIVER.

Instituto de Administración: Miguel E. Capote 351, Bayamo, Oriente; Dir. AIDA RAMÍREZ.

Instituto de Oncologia y Radiobiología de La Habana (*Institute of Oncology and Radiobiology*): 29 y F, Vedado, Havana; f. 1961; cancer research, virology, radiobiology, genetics, surgery, immunology and related fields; 400 researchers and technicians; library of 2,500 vols.; Dir. Prof. Dr. ZOILO MARINELLO VIDAURRETA.

Instituto de Política Internacional (*Institute of International Politics*): Ministerio de Relaciones Exteriores, Calzada y G, Vedado, Havana; f. 1962; 11 mems.; Dir. RENÉ ALVÁREZ RÍOS.

Instituto de Superación Educacional—ISE (*Institute of Educational Advancement*): Ciudad Libertad, Marianao, Havana; Dir. Dra. MARÍA LUISA RODRÍGUEZ CÓLOMBIÉ.

Instituto Nacional de Desarrollo y Aprovechamiento Forestales (INDAF): Virtudes 680, Havana; f. 1967; forestry development; Dir. JOSÉ PONCE DÍAZ.

Instituto Nacional de Higiene: Infanta y Crucero de Ferrocarril, Havana; administered by the Ministerio de Salud Pública; Dir. Dr. FRANCISCO BÁEZ SABLÓN.

Instituto Nacional de la Reforma Agraria—INRA: Calzada de Bejucal y calle 100, Havana; f. 1961; consists of 10 main research centres for coffee and cocoa, cereals and vegetables, citrus and other fruits, rice, tobacco, irrigation, plant breeding, plant protection, soils, and fertilizers and agricultural machinery; various experimental stations and laboratories.

Centro de Información y Documentación Agropecuaria (CIDA—INRA): Gaveta Postal 4149, Havana 4; f. 1971; Dir. Lic. ELENA BLANCO DÍAZ; publs. *Revista Cubana de Ciencia Veterinaria*, *Revista Agrotecnia de Cuba*, monographs, pamphlets, catalogues.

Instituto Tecnológico de la Caña de Azúcar "Carlos M. de Cespedes": La Inagua, Apdo. de correos 164, Guantánamo, Oriente; Dir. MIGDONIO CAUSSE.

Instituto Tecnológico "Mártires de Girón": 5a Ave. 16607 esq. 170, Marianao, Havana; Dir. MARTA ORTEGA SUÁREZ.

Instituto Tecnológico de Electrónica "Fernando Aguado Rico": Belascoaín y Maloja, Havana; Dir. Ing. GONZALO IGLESIAS Y RODRÍGUEZ-MENA.

Jardin Botánico Nacional de Cuba (*National Botanical Gardens of Cuba*): Havana University, Calabazar; f. 1968; library of 2,600 vols.; Herbarium: *c.* 45,000 items mostly of Cuban flora; Dir. Lic. ANGELA LEIVA; publs. *Revista*† (3 a year), *Index Seminum*† (annually).

Sociedad Cubana de Historia de la Medicina (*Cuban Society of the History of Medicine*): Cuba No. 460, Havana 1; Pres. Dr. JOSÉ LÓPEZ SÁNCHEZ; Sec.-Gen. Dr. LUIS F. LE ROY; publ. *Cuadernos*.

Sociedad Cubana de Ingenieros (*Cuban Engineers' Association*): Avda. de Bélgica 258, Havana; f. 1908; library of 9,000 vols.; 500 mems.; Pres. Ing. GUSTAVO STERLING; Sec. Ing. HONORATO COLETE; publ. *Revista* (bi-monthly).

Sociedad Cubano-Mexicana de Relaciones Culturales: Calles 19 y J, Vedado; Mexican culture; Pres. Dr. JUAN MARINELLO VIDAURRETA.

Unión de Escritores y Artistas de Cuba: Calle 17 No. 351, Vedado, Havana; f. 1961; 600 mems.; Pres. NICOLÁS GUILLÉN; Admin. Sec. BENVENIDO SUAREZ; publs. *Gaceta de Cuba* (monthly), *Unión* (quarterly).

LIBRARIES AND ARCHIVES

Havana

Academia de Ciencias de Cuba: Biblioteca Central: Capitolio Nacional; f. 1962; collective catalogue, reference service, library school, distribution of scientific and technical literature; 20,000 vols.; Dir. MARÍA ISABEL ALVAREZ CANTO.

Archivo Nacional: Compostela No. 1, esq. a San Isidro, Havana; national historical archives; incorporates a series of provincial archives; Dir. Dr. VICENTE DE LA O. GUTIÉRREZ.

Biblioteca Central "Rubén Martínez Villena" de la Universidad de la Habana (*Havana University Library*): f. 1728; 202,881 vols. and numerous periodicals; there are specialised libraries attached to the Faculties and Laboratories; separate collection of Cuban authors; complete copy of *Historia Física, Política y Natural de la Isla de Cuba*, in Spanish, printed in Paris 1837-57 by Ramón de la Sagra; contains the Dr. Néstor Carbonell y Rivera and Fernández de Castro collections; Dir. Dr. BLANCA BAHAMONDE.

Biblioteca del Consejo Nacional de Tuberculosis "Paulina Aldina" (*Library of the National Council of Tuberculosis*): Calzada de Colombia y Octava, Marianao; f. 1946; 5,000 vols., partly for patients' loan service and partly scientific for use of doctors; periodicals library; Dir. Dr. ERNESTO BELLO.

Biblioteca del Instituto de Literatura y Linguistica: Salvador Allende, 710; f. 1793; 61,083 vols.; 7,152 periodicals; collection of Havana newspapers prior to 1878; Librarian Lcda. ISABEL FERNÁNDEZ SANTANA.

Biblioteca del Instituto Pre-universitario de La Habana (*Library of the Pre-University Institute of Education*): Zulueta y San José; f. 1894; 32,000 vols.; rare works dating from 1605; newspaper library; Dir. JOSÉ MANUEL CASTELLANOS RODILES.

Biblioteca Histórica Cubana y Americana (*Cuban and American Historical Library*): Municipio de La Habana, Oficina del Historiador de la Ciudad; f. 1938; lending library based on the private collections of Emilio Roig de Leuchsenring, Fermín Preaza y Sarausa, Enrique Gay Galbó, Mario Guiral Moreno, Raquel Catalá, José Luciano Franco, Emeterio S. Santovenia, Gerardo Castellanos, Félix Lizaso, Elias Entralgo, Julio Volloldo, Joaquín Llaverías, Federico Córdova, Manuel Bisbé, Roberto Agramonte, Federico Castaneda, and Mario Sánchez Roig.

Biblioteca "José Antonio Echevarría": Casa de las Americas, Tercera y G, Vedado; 77,000 vols.; Dir. Dra. MARTA TERRY GONZÁLEZ; publ. *Bibliographies*† (irregular).

Biblioteca "Manuel Sanguily": Ministerio de Relaciones Exteriores, Calzada y G., Vedado; f. 1960; 29,512 vols.; Dir. Dra. ASUNCIÓN DIAZ CUERVO.

Biblioteca Nacional "José Martí" (*National Library*): Apdo. Oficial No. 3, Plaza de la Revolución José Martí; f. 1901; 531,329 vols., 56,680 pieces (maps, drawings, engravings, records, printed music, posters and slides). The library includes the following Departments: Book Selection, Acquisition and Exchange, Cataloguing and Classifying, Scientific and Technical Information (National Union Catalogue of Technical Publications), Reading and Reference Rooms (General and Technical), Cuban Collections and Rare Books, Periodicals and Humanistic Information (National Union Catalogue of Periodicals—humanistic aspects), Art, Music, Juvenile; circulation library; also theatre, exhibition rooms, accommodation for research workers, book deposit, binding and preservation; Dir. LUIS SUARDÍAZ; publs. *Revista, Bibliografía Cubana, Bibliografía Técnico Científicas, Indice general de Publicaciones Periódicas Cubanas, Boletín Polillita, Anuario Martiano, Textos para narradores* (adaptations of national and universal folklore tales), and historical and literary research work undertaken by the library.

Biblioteca "Raul Cepero Bonilla": Banco Nacional de Cuba, Amargura 158; f. 1950; 22,500 vols. and large collection of periodicals on economics, finance and banking; Librarian PAULA GARCÍA GONZÁLEZ.

Biblioteca "Ruben Martinez Villena": Obispo 160; 34,213 vols.; Dir. GUIDO DÍAZ.

Santa Clara, Las Villas

Biblioteca General de la Universidad Central de las Villas: f. 1953; 75,000 vols.; Librarian Prof. ESTHER CALCINES RUÍZ.

Santiago

Biblioteca Central de la Universidad de Oriente: Carretera de Cuabitos; f. 1947; 118,000 vols.; Librarian Dr. JOSÉ A. B. JOANES.

Biblioteca Provincial "Elvira Cape": Calle Heredia 259; f. 1898; 114,800 vols.

MUSEUMS

Havana

Museo Nacional (*National Museum*): Palacio de Bellas Artes, Animas entre Zulueta y Monserrate; f. 1913; includes examples of works of art from Egypt, Greece, Rome, Italy (Renaissance and XVII–XVIII centuries), Low Countries, France, England and Spain and an exhibition of Cuban art from the colonial period to the present day; includes a specialized library and a theatre; Dir. MARTA ARJONA PÉREZ.

Museo Antropológico Montané (*Anthropological Museum*): Universidad de La Habana; some collections date from 1847; exhibits include objects relating to American and Cuban ethnology, the primitive (pre-discovery) cultures of Cuba and the Antilles, deriving from archaeological expeditions; also collections relating to Asia, Africa, Oceania and the Americas; notable collections of Aborigen pottery of Taino and sub-Taino cultures; Dir. Dr. MANUEL RIVERO DE LA CALLE.

Museo Agricola y Exposición Permanente (*Agricultural Museum*): Ministerio de Agricultura; exhibits show the main products of the country, as well as those devoted to agriculture and mining; Curator ARCHIBALD DURLAND Y NIETO.

Museo Colonial de la Habana: Plaza de la Catedral; Dir. MARGARITA SUÁREZ.

Museo de Artes Decorativas: Calle 17 No. 502, Vedado; f. 1964; porcelain, bronzes, gold and silver work, tapestries, European and Oriental furniture and fans of 15th–19th century; specialized library of 2,500 vols.; Dir. Dra. MARÍA DEL CARMEN SAN PEDRO LÓPEZ; publs. *Boletín semestral*, monthly catalogues.

Museo Hemingway: Finoa La Vigía, San Francisco de Paula; books and personal items of Ernest Hemingway who lived here 1939–60; Dir. JULIO PÉREZ BELTRÁN.

Museo Histórico de las Ciencias Médicas "Carlos J. Finlay" (*Carlos J. Finlay Historical Science Museum*): 460 Calle Cuba, P.O.B. 70; controlled by the Comisión Nacional de la Academia de Ciencias de la República de Cuba; f. 1962; library of 300,000 titles and 50,000 vols.; permanent exhibition of items relating to Cuban scientists, history of medicine and history of science; Dir. Dr. ANTONIO MORENO LUNA.

Museo Histórico de Guanabacoa: Martí 108, Guanabacoa; 19th-century and Afro-Cuban relics, including a voodoo collection; Dir. JOSÉ LUIS LLERENA.

Museo José Martí: Leonor Pérez 314; relics of José Martí, his works, iconography and bibliography; f. 1925 by Arturo R. de Carricarte, who purchased the martyr's birthplace to make it a national monument; Curator MANUEL I. MESA RODRÍGUEZ.

Museo Nacional de la Campaña de Alfabetización: Ciudad Libertad, Marianao; illustrates national literacy campaign; Dir. Dra. NIEVES VALMAÑA.

Museo Napoleónico: San Miguel y Ronda; f. 1961; paintings, sculptures, furniture, bronzes, porcelain, weapons, clothing and other historical objects and works of art of Revolutionary, Imperial and Directorate France.

Museo Numismatico: Banco Nacional de Cuba, Aguiar 456, Havana; f. 1975; collection of Cuban coins from 1536, medals, orders and decorations; Spanish, French, U.S. and Latin American coins; counterfeits and forgeries; numismatic library.

Museo Poey (*Poey Museum*): Facultad de Ciencias, Universidad de la Habana; f. 1902; 100,000 exhibits, primarily zoological; library of 80,520 vols.; Dir. Dr. MIGUEL L. JAUME.

Museo y Archivo Histórico Municipal de la Ciudad de La Habana: Oficina del Historiador, Palacio de los Capitanes Generales, Plaza Carlos Manuel Céspedes; f. 1947; historical items from 1550 to the present.

Camagüey

Museo Ignacio Agramonte: paintings, furniture, remnants from the colonial period.

Cárdenas

Museo Municipal Oscar M. de Rojas: Avda. de José Martí; f. 1903; exhibits relating to Martí; library; Curator OSCAR M. DE ROJAS Y CRUZAT.

Matanzas

Museo Municipal de Matanzas (*Municipal Museum*): Dir. Dr. ISRAEL M. MOLINER.

Pinar del Río

Museo de Pesca de la Escuela Naval del Mariel (*Museum of Marine Fauna*): Naval Academy, Mariel, Pinar del Río; f. 1943; rare specimens of deep-sea fish; Dir. LUIS HOWELL RIVERO, D.S.

Remedios

Museo de Remedios "José Maria Espinosa": Maceo 32; f. 1933; history, science, and art; Pres. Dr. CARLOS A. MARTÍNEZ-FORTÚN; Dir. ALBERTO VIGIL Y COLOMA.

Santiago

Museo "Emilio Bacardi Moreau": Aguilera y Pio Rosado, Apdo. 759; f. 1899; natural history, art, archaeology; Dir. ANTONIO FERRER CABELLO.

UNIVERSITIES AND UNIVERSITY CENTRES

UNIVERSIDAD DE LA HABANA

CALLE 1 No. 302, ESQ. A 15, VEDADO, HAVANA 4

Telephone: 7-3231, 70-5863.

Founded 1728, reorganized 1863, 1943 and 1962.

Rector: FERNANDO ROJAS AVALES (acting).
Secretary-General: Dr. REINALDO CASÍN GONZÁLEZ.

Library: *see* Libraries.

Number of teachers: 3,066.
Number of students: 53,682.

Publications: *Universidad de la Habana, Boletín Universitario*, and various scientific and technical publs.

DEANS:

Faculty of Technology: Ing. ORLANDO OLIVERA MARTÍN.
Faculty of Medicine: Dr. ANGEL FERNÁNDEZ VILA.
Faculty of Sciences: Dr. ARNALDO AGUIAR CASTRO.
Faculty of Agriculture: Ing. ROBERTO IGLESIAS ALBERNI.
Faculty of Humanities: Lic. ESTEBAN MORALES DOMÍNGUEZ.
Institute of Economics: Lic. ÁLEXIS CODINA JIMÉNEZ.
Education Institute: Prof. LUIS GUZMÁN DE ARMAS.

ATTACHED RESEARCH INSTITUTES:

Centro Nacional de Investigaciones Científicas: see under Research Institutes.

Instituto de Ciencia Animal: Dir. Dr. RAMIRO ORTÍZ RODRÍGUEZ.

Instituto de Ciencias Agrícolas: Dir. Ing. SOLEDAD DÍAZ.

Estación Experimental de Pastos y Forrajes "Indio Hatuey": Dir. Ing. FÉLIX BLANCO RODRÍGUEZ.

UNIVERSIDAD DE ORIENTE*

AVDA. PATRICIO LUMUMBA S/N, SANTIAGO DE CUBA, ORIENTE

Telephone: 8050 and 8996.

Founded 1947.

Rector: Arq. RAFAEL ALMEIDA.
Secretary: LUIS JOVER PUIG.
Librarian: Dr. JOSÉ A. B. JOANES.

Number of teachers: *c.* 800.
Number of students: 16,000.
Publication: *Mambí*.

DEANS:

Faculty of Humanities: Lic. MIGUEL A. SÁNCHEZ MARIÑO.
Faculty of Technology: Ing. ENRIQUE MARAÑÓN.
Faculty of Medicine: Dr. JOSÉ AVALO.
Preparatory Faculty for Rural Workers: Dr. JOSÉ GARCÍA FERNÁNDEZ.
Faculty of Science: Lic. NIDIA SÁNCHEZ PIUGBERT.
Institute of Economics: Lic. RENÉ POMBO.
"Frank Pais" Institute of Education: EUGENIO MONTENEGRO.
Faculty of Agriculture and Animal Husbandry: Ing. ABELARDO IGLESIAS EGEA.

* No reply received to our questionnaire this year.

UNIVERSIDAD DE LAS VILLAS

CARRETERA DE CAMAJUANÍ Km.10,
SANTA CLARA, LAS VILLAS

Telephone: 5481.

Founded 1948.

Rector: Dr. E. REMEDIOS DE LOS CUETOS.

Vice-Rector: FRANCISCO SORI MORO.

Library: *see* Libraries.

Number of teachers: *c.* 400.

Number of students: 8,200.

Publications: *Islas, Revista, Boletín Militante, Boletín Informativo, Centro, Memoria Anual.*

DEANS:

Faculty of Technology: Ing. EVELIO DE LA SOTA CONTRERA.

Faculty of Agriculture and Animal Husbandry Studies: Ing. EFRAÍN ABREU HEREDIA.

Faculty of Science: C. P. GONZÁLO PALENCIA MÉNDEZ.

Faculty of Humanities: Dra. STHEL GARCÍA DOMÍNGUEZ.

Faculty of Medicine: Dr. JUÁN M. DIEGO COBELO.

Institute of Economics: C. P. ANDRÉS FUENTES GONZÁLEZ.

UNIVERSIDAD DE CAMAGÜEY

CARRETERA DE CIRCUNVALACIÓN, CAMAGUEY

Founded as branch of University of Havana, present name 1974.

Number of students: *c.* 5,000.

Depts. of agriculture, economics, education, medicine, technology.

Centro Universitario de Matanzas: Calle Medio 100 e/Zaragoza y Manzaneda, Matanzas; Dir. CARLOS QUINTANA.

Centro Universitario de Pinar del Rio: Martí 270 esq. a 27 de Noviembre, Pinar del Rio; Dir. RICARDO ABREU.

Centro Universitario de Holguín: Miró No. 125 e/Frexes y Aguilera, Holguín.

SCHOOLS OF ART AND MUSIC

Havana

Conservatorio Alejandro García Caturla: Avenida 31 y Calle 82, Marianao.

Conservatorio de Música Amadeo Roldán: Rastro y Lealtad.

Escuela Nacional de Bellas Artes "San Alejandro" (*National School of Fine Arts*): Dragones 308; f. 1818 as Academia de San Alejandro; formerly Escuela de Pintura, organised by the French painter, Jean Baptiste Vermay; 800 students; Dir. DOMINGO RAMOS ENRÍQUEZ.

CYPRUS

Population 616,000

LEARNED SOCIETIES AND RESEARCH INSTITUTES

British Council: 3 Museum St., P.O.B. 1995, Nicosia; Rep. D. S. Marler; library: (*see* Libraries).

Centre Culturel Français: 3 Jean Moreas St., Nicosia; f. 1959; cultural activities include films, drama, music, language courses; library of 8,000 vols.; Dir. Paul Pouradier Duteil.

Cyprus Geographical Association: P.O.B. 3656, Nicosia; f. 1968; research and study of the geography of Cyprus; aims to improve the teaching of geography, and safeguard professional interests of geographers; 200 mems.; library of 500 vols.; Pres. Andreas Cl. Sophocleous; Gen. Sec. Phrosoula Christofidoy; publ. *The Geographical Chronicles*† (2 a year).

Cyprus Research Centre (*Kentron Epistemonikōn Erevnōn*): P.O.B. 1436, Nicosia; under the jurisdiction of the Ministry of Education; f. 1967; aims: the promotion of scientific research in Cyprus with special reference to the historico-philological disciplines and the social sciences; research library; sections: (a) Historical Section: edition and publication of the sources of the history of Cyprus; (b) Ethnographic Section: collection, preservation, and publication of materials relating to the local culture of the island; (c) Philological and Linguistic Section: collection of lexicographic materials, the preparation of a historical dictionary of the Cypriot dialect, and the edition of literary and dialectic texts; (d) Oriental Section: promotion of oriental studies in Cyprus, with special reference to Arab, Turkish, Jewish, and African studies; (e) Sociological Section; Dir. Theodore Papadopoullos; publs. *Texts and Studies of the History of Cyprus, Publications, Epeteris* (annually).

Etaireia Kypriakon Spoudon (*Society of Cypriot Studies*): P.O.B. 1436, Nicosia; f. 1936; aims: the collection, preservation and study of material concerning all periods of the history, dialect and folklore of Cyprus; the Society maintains a Museum of Cypriot Folk Art; 250 mems.; library of Kypria 4,000 vols.; Pres. G. Papacharalambous; Sec. K. Nicolaou; Editor Th. Papadopoullos; publs. *Demosievmata, Kypriakai Spoudai* (Cypriot Studies, annually).

Goethe Institut: P.O.B. 1813, 21 Markos Drakos Ave., Nicosia; f. 1959; library of 5,000 vols.; Dir. Dr. R. Rauschenbach.

Library Association of Cyprus: P.O.B. 1039, Nicosia; f. 1962; promotes library science and professional activities; 45 mems.; Pres. Costas D. Stephanou; Sec. Paris G. Rossos.

LIBRARIES

British Council Library: 3 Museum St., P.O.B. 1995, Nicosia; f. 1940, re-established 1955; 30,200 vols., 50 periodicals; Librarian T. Thomas.

Library of the American Center: 33B Homer Ave., Nicosia; f. 1962; lending and reference; 5,934 vols.; Librarian D. Akkides.

Library of the Archbishopric: P.O.B. 1130, Nicosia; f. 1821; 5,000 vols.; Librarian Chr.Theodotou.

Library of the Cyprus Museum: P.O.B. 2024, Nicosia; f. 1883; incorporated in Dept. of Antiquities 1934; 13,500 vols.; Librarian Mrs. L. Ieromonachou.

Library of the Famagusta Greek Gymnasium: P.O.B. 80, Famagusta; f. 1937; 9,500 vols.; Librarian D. A. Kyprianou-Skourou.

Library of the Institute of Education: c/o Ministry of Education, Nicosia; f. 1972; 13,000 vols. Greek, English, German and French; Librarian Paris G. Rossos.

Library of Phaneromeni: P.O.B. 1637, Nicosia; f. 1934; 45,000 vols.; books and periodicals relating to medieval, Byzantine and post-Byzantine studies; Librarian Constantine Hadjipsaltis.

Ministry of Education Library: Didaskalikon Megaron, Archbishop Makarios III Ave., Nicosia; f. 1962; incorporates Cyprus Public Library; 25,000 vols.; Librarian Costas D. Stephanou.

Municipal Library: P.O.B. 41, Famagusta; f. 1954; reference and lending sections, including many books on Cyprus and in several languages; the Famagusta Municipal Art Gallery, with a historical maps section, is attached; 18,000 vols.; Librarian and Curator Ch. Christofides.

Municipal Library: Limassol; f. 1945; 12,000 vols.; Librarian Miss A. Kyriakides.

Sultan's Library: Evcaf, Nicosia; f. by Sultan Mahmud II; collection of Turkish, Persian and Arabic books.

Turkish Public Library: 49 Mecediye St., Nicosia; f. 1955; about 4,000 vols.; Librarian M. Nesdjet.

MUSEUMS

Cyprus Historical Museum and Archives: Pentelis 50, Strovolos, Nicosia; f. 1975; a private enterprise to create a cultural centre; aims to tape-record accounts of historical events in Cyprus, to photocopy all existing historical material about Cyprus, to liaise with the Ministry of Culture and Greek historians, to find and publicize historical treasures in private collections; library of 3,000 vols.; Pres. Petros Stylianou; Gen. Sec. Cleitos Symeonides.

Cyprus Museum, The: P.O.B. 2024, Nicosia; f. 1883; inc. in Dept. of Antiquities 1934; Curator (vacant).

Collection of (1) pottery from the Neolithic and Chalcolithic periods to the Graeco-Roman Age; (2) terracotta figures of the Bronze Age to Graeco-Roman times, including the Ayia Irini group; (3) limestone and marble sculpture from the Archaic to the Graeco-Roman Age; (4) jewellery from the Bronze Age, and especially the Mycenaean period (1400–1200 B.C.) to early Byzantine times, and coins from the 6th century to Roman times; (5) miscellaneous collections, including inscriptions (Cypro-Minoan, Phoenician, Cypro-syllabic and Greek), bronzes, glass, alabaster, bone, etc. An interesting feature is the room of reconstructed tombs. Extensive reserve collections are available for students.

An archaeological library (*see above*) is housed in the Cyprus Museum building and is open to students.

Publs. *Report of the Department of Antiquities*, *Annual Report of the Director of Antiquities*, monographs.

Folk Art Museum: P.O.B. 1436, Nicosia; f. 1950; Cyprus arts and crafts from early to recent times; mainly Cypriot Greek items.

Lapidary Museum: Nicosia; medieval tombstones, marble lintels, carved stones of palaces, churches, etc.

District Museums: Famagusta, Larnaca, Limassol and Paphos; site museums: Kourion (Espiskopi) and Palaipaphos (Kouklia). These are archaeological museums housing antiquities from Neolithic to Byzantine times.

COLLEGES

Cyprus College of Art: Kato Paphos; one-year post-graduate course in painting; also part-time courses and summer school; Dir. STASS PARASKOS.

Cyprus Forestry College: Prodromos; f. 1951; technical-level training in forestry; 5 teachers, 36 students; Principal S. THEOPHANOUS.

Higher Technical Institute: P.O.B. 2423, Nicosia; f. 1968; 3-year courses in civil, electrical, mechanical and marine engineering.

Paedagogiki Academia (*College of Education*): P.O.B. 1039, Nicosia; f. 1959; 3-year courses for elementary school and kindergarten teachers and short course for training in the preservation of old documents; 25 teachers, 110 students; Principal MICHAEL J. MARATHEFTIS, B.A., M.ED.; publs. *Epetiris Paedagogikis Academias* (yearbook), *Deltion Paedagogikis Enimeroseos* (Educational Bulletin) (quarterly), *Spoudastis* (Student) (2 a year).

CZECHOSLOVAKIA

Population 15,280,148

ACADEMIES

ČESKOSLOVENSKÁ AKADEMIE VĚD
(Czechoslovak Academy of Sciences)

NÁRODNÍ TŘ. 3, 111 42 PRAGUE 1

Telephone: 243441.

Founded 1952.

President: Acad. Jaroslav Kožešník.

Vice-Presidents: Acad. Vladimír Hajko, Acad. Bohumil Kvasil, Acad. Vladimír Pokorný, Acad Zdeněk Snítil.

Scientific Secretary: Acad. Josef Říman.

Administrative Director: Ing. Miroslav Havel.

Publs. include: *Acta entomologica bohemoslovaca, Acta technica, Acta virologica, Folia zoologica, Aplikace matematiky, Archeologické rozhledy, Archiv orientální, Biologia Plantarum, Biologické listy, Bulletin of the Astronomical Institutes of Czechoslovakia, Byzantinoslavica, Collection of Czechoslovak Chemical Communications, Czechoslovak Journal of Physics, Czechoslovak Mathematical Journal, Časopis pro mineralogii a geologii, Časopis pro pěstováni matematiky, Česká literatura, Česká mykologie, Československá fysiologie, Československá psychologie, Československá rusistika, Československý časopis historický, Československý časopis pro fysiku, Český lid, Dějiny věd a techniky, Ekonomicko-matematický obzor, Estetika, Filosofický časopis, Folia biologica, Folia geobotanica et phytotaxonomica, Folia microbiologica, Folia morphologica, Folia parasitologica, Hudební věda, Chemické listy, Kybernetika, Lidé a země, Listy filologické, Naše řeč, Nový orient, Památky archeologické, Pedagogika, Philologica Pragensia, Photosynthetica, Physiologia bohemoslovaca, Pokroky matematiky, fysiky a astronomie, Politická ekonomie, Právník, Preslia, Přírodovědné práce ústavů ČSAV v Brně, Rozpravy Československé akademie věd, Sborník Čs. společnosti zeměpisné, Silikáty, Slavia, Slezský sborník, Slovanský přehled, Slovo a slovesnost, Sociologický časopis, Studia geophysica et geodaetica, Umění, Vesmír, Věstník Československé akademie věd, Věstnik Čs. společnosti zoologické, Věstník Ústředního ústavu geologického, Zdravotniechnika a vzduchotechnika, Ziva.*

Academicians:

Bačkovský, Jindřich.
Benda, Břetislav.
Blaškovič, Dionýz.
Borůvka, Otakar.
Charvát, Josef.
Čirlič, Jovan.
Filip, Jan.
Filkorn, Vojtech.
Hajko, Vladimír.
Heller, Bedřich.
Houštěk, Josef.
Hovorka, Ján.
Hrbek, Jaromír.
Jakubík, Ján.
Katětov, Miroslav.
Kellö, Vojtech.
Klečka, Antonín.
Knapp, Viktor.
Kolbenheyer, Tibor.
Kořínek, Vladimír.
Koutek, Jaromír.
Kožešník, Jaroslav.
Kratochvíl, Josef.
Kudrna, Karel.
Kvasil, Bohumil.
Laco, Karol.
Laufberger, Vilém.
Macek, Josef.
Mahel, Michal.
Málek, Ivan.
Němec, Jaroslav.
Novák, Josef.
Pavlík, Ondrej.
Pokorný, Vladimír.
Poulík, Josef.
Prát, Silvestr.
Richta, Radovan.
Rosický, Bohumír.
Ryš, Přemysl.
Ryšavý, Bohumil.
Říman, Josef.
Schwarz, Štefan.
Servít, Zdeněk.
Sirácky, Andrej.
Snítil, Zdeněk.
Stránský, Josef.
Šiška, Karol.
Šorm, František.
Špaldon, Emil.
Štoll, Ladislav.
Švestka, Bedřich.
Thurzo, Viliam.
Vaněček, Václav.
Veverka, Antonín.
Votruba, Václav.
Wichterle, Otto.
Zachar, Jozef.
Záruba, Quido.
Zátopek, Alois.
Zoubek, Vladimír.

Corresponding Members:

Antal, Juraj.
Balaš, Ján.
Balaš, Vladimír.
Baruš, Vlastimil.
Benda, Oldrich.
Bílek, Jan.
Blažej, Anton.
Boda, Koloman.
Borecký, Ladislav.
Bretschneider, Rudolf.
Bucha, Václav.
Bumba, Václav.
Cambel, Bohuslav.
Chmelař, Vilém.
Cirbes, Vladimír.
Čábelka, Jaroslav.
Čabelka, Jozef.
Čadek, Josef.
Češka, Zdeněk.
Čůta, František.
Dekan, Ján.
Delong, Armin.
Dostálek, Ctibor.
Faltus, František.
Fiala, František.
Friml, Karel.
Gažo, Ján.
Gonda, Ján.
Haas, Štefan.
Hadač, Emil.
Hajkr, Oldřich.
Hála, Eduard.
Haňka, Ladislav.
Hašek, Milan.
Hejný, Slavomil.
Herout, Vlastimil.
Hloucal, Ludvík.
Holotík, L'udovít.
Holub, Antonín.
Horálek, Karel.
Hořejší, Jaroslav.
Hrabák, Josef.
Hrivňák, Ivan.
Ilkovič, Dionýz.
Janíček, Gustav.
Jerie, Jan.
Jeřábek, Jaroslav.
Juliš, Karel.
Jůza, Jan.
Kašpar, Jan.
Karpfel, Zdeněk.
Klesnil, Mirko.
Klíma, Arnošt.
Klíma, Jiří.
Kneppo, L'udovít.
Kochanovská, Adéla.
Konček, Mikuláš.
Kopecký, Miloslav.
Koritta, Josef.
Kotalík, Jiří.
Kotásek, Alfréd.
Kováćik, Anton.
Kroupa, František.
Kubíček, Ladislav.
Kubík, Stanislav.
Kunc, Zdeněk.
Kunz, Emil.
Kurzweil, Jaroslav.
Kusák, Vlastimil.
Kvěš, Václav.
Landa, Stanislav.
Landa, Vladimír.
Linhart, Josef.
Löbl, Karel.
Macůrek, Josef.
Majer, Jaroslav.
Málek, Prokop.
Mareček, František
Martinec, Theodor.
Mašek, Josef.
Maštovský, Otakar.
Matejiček, Emil.
Matěna, Štěpán.
Matyáš, Miloš.
Mazanec, Karel.
Mazúr, Emil.
Merhaut, Josef.
Mostecký, Jiří.
Myslivec, Alois.
Navrátil, Jan.
Nechleba, Miroslav.
Nedoma, Jiří.
Nekolný, Jaroslav.
Nemec, Pavol.
Neumann, Jaromír.
Niederland, **Rudolf.**
Novák, Vladimír.
Okáč, Arnošt.
Oliva, Pavel.
Pastýrik, L'udovít.
Patočka, František.
Pavlovič, Gustáv.
Perek, Luboš.
Pešek, Rudolf.
Petr, Rudolf.
Píchal, Miroslav.
Pilous, Václav.
Pješčak, Ján.

PLESNÍK, JÁN.
PLEVZA, VILIAM.
PLUHAŘ, JAROSLAV.
PRASLIČKA, MILAN.
PROCHÁZKA, JAROSLAV.
PUCHNER, ONDREJ.
PURŠ, JAROSLAV.
PŮST, LADISLAV.
RAŠKA, KAREL.
RAŠKOVÁ, HELENA.
REPÁŠ, MILAN.
RUML, VLADIMÍR.
RYPÁČEK, VLADIMÍR.
SCHNELLER, JIŘÍ.
SEDLÁČEK, KAREL.
SEKANINA, JOSEF.
SKALIČKA, VLADÍMIR.
SKALKOVÁ-PROCHÁZKOVÁ, JARMILA.
SKRÚCANÝ, RUDOLF.
STARÝ, OLDŘICH.
STEHLÍK, VÁCLAV.
STEINHART, LEO.
SVOBODA, JOSEF.
ŠEBOR, GUSTAV.
ŠIŠKA, LUBOMIR.
ŠORMOVÁ, ZORA.
ŠPAČEK, BOHUMIL.
ŠTAFL, MILOŠ.
ŠTELCL, JINDŘICH.
ŠTERZL, JAROSLAV.
ŠTOLL, ČESTMÍR.
ŠTOURAČ, LADISLAV.
TRLIFAJ, LADISLAV.
TRLIFAJ, MIROSLAV.
VACHTL, JOSEF.
VLČEK, ANTONÍN A.
VRTIAK, OTO JAROSLAV.
VYKLICKÝ, LADISLAV.
VYSKOT, MIROSLAV.
WEISER, JAROSLAV.
WEISMANN, LUDOVÍT.
WHEELER, GEORGE SHAW.
ZACHAR, DUŠAN.
ZACHOVAL, LADISLAV.
ZIMA, VÁCLAV.
ZVÁRA, IVO.

FOREIGN MEMBERS:

ALEXANDROV, ANATOLI P.
AMBARTSUMIAN, VIKTOR A.
BALEVSKI, ANGEL TONČEV.
BASOV, NIKOLAI G.
BORISEVICH, NIKOLAI A.
ENGELHARDT, VLADIMIR ALEXANDROVICH.
FEDOSEJEV, PETR NIKOLAYEVICH.
GLASS, HIRAM BENTLEY.
GROSZKOWSKI, JANUSZ.
ISHLINSKY, ALEXANDR J.
JABLOŃSKI, HENRYK.
JIMÉNEZ, ANTONIO NÚÑEZ.
KAISHEV, ROSTILAV ATANASOV.
KLARE, HERMANN.
KOTELNIKOV, VLADIMIR ALEXANDROVICH.
LAVRENTIEV, MIKHAIL ALEXEYEVICH.
MARCHUK, GURI I.
MONOD, JACQUES.
MURGULESCU, ILIE.
NOWACKI, WITOLD.
PATON, BORIS JEVGENIEVICH.
PETROV, BORIS NIKOLAYEVICH.
ROMPE, ROBERT.
RUSNYAK, ISTVÁN.
RYBAKOV, BORIS ALEXANDROVICH.
SEMENOV, NIKOLAI NIKOLAYEVICH.
SIDORENKO, ALEXANDR V.
SKRIABIN, GEORGI K.
ŠIRENDYB, BAZARYN.
THOMSON, GEORGE.
TRAPEZNIKOV, VADIM ALEXANDROVICH.
TRZEBIATOWSKI, WŁODZIMIERZ.
ZHAVORONKOV, NIKOLAI M.

SCIENTIFIC INSTITUTES:

Analytical Chemistry Institute: Brno.
Animal Physiology and Genetics Institute: Prague.
Archaeology Institute: Brno.
Astronomical Institute: Prague.
Atmospheric Physics Institute: Prague.
Basic Chemical Technology Institute: Prague.
Biophysics Institute: Brno.
Botanical Institute: Průhonice.
J. A. Comenius Education Institute: Prague.
Czech and World Literatures Institute: Prague.
Czech Language Institute: Prague.
Czechoslovak-Soviet Institute: Prague.
Czechoslovak and World History Institute: Prague.
Department of Foreign Languages: Prague.
Economics Institute: Prague.
Electrical Engineering Institute: Prague.
Entomology Institute: Prague.
Ethnography and Folklore Institute: Prague.
Experimental Botany Institute: Prague.
Experimental Medicine Institute: Prague.
Geography Institute: Brno.
Geology and Geotechnics Institute: Prague.
Geophysics Institute: Prague.
Greek, Roman and Latin Studies Institute: Prague.
Hydrodynamics Institute: Prague.
J. Heyrovský Physical Chemistry and Electrochemistry Institute: Prague.
Industrial Landscape Ecology Institute: Prague.
Information Theory and Automation Institute: Prague.
Inorganic Chemistry Institute: Prague.
Instrument Engineering Institute: Brno.
Joint ČSAV and VŠCHT Laboratory for Silicates Research: Prague.
Isotope Laboratory of the Biological Institutes: Prague.
Landscape Ecology Institute: Průhonice.
Law Institute: Prague.
Macromolecular Chemistry Institute: Prague.
Mathematics Institute: Prague.
Metallurgical Processes Institute: Ostrava.
Microbiology Institute: Prague.
Molecular Genetics Institute: Prague.
Nuclear Physics Institute: Řež, nr. Prague.
Organic Chemistry and Biochemistry Institute: Prague.
Oriental Institute: Prague.
Parasitology Institute: Prague.
Pharmacology Institute: Prague.
Philosophy and Sociology Institute: Prague.
Physical Metallurgy Institute: Brno.
Physics Institute: Prague.
Physiology Institute: Prague.
Physiological Regulations Institute: Prague.
Plasma Physics Institute: Prague.
Psychology Institute: Prague.
Psychology Laboratory: Brno.
Radiation Dosimetry Institute: Prague.
Radio Engineering and Electronics Institute: Prague.
Scientific Atheism Institute: Brno.
Silesian Institute: Opava.
Theoretical and Applied Mechanics Institute: Prague.
Thermomechanics Institute: Prague.
Vertebrate Zoology Institute: Brno.

ASSOCIATED INSTITUTIONS:

Academia Publishing House.
Cabinet of Marxism-Leninism.
Central Archives.
Designing Department.
Encyclopaedic Institute.
General Computing Centre.
Inventions and Scientific Discoveries Department.
Main Library—Centre for Scientific Information: *see* under Libraries.
Main Administration for Buildings.
Technical Services Administration.

SCIENTIFIC SOCIETIES OF THE CZECHOSLOVAK ACADEMY OF SCIENCES

Česká společnost pro estetiku (*Czech Society for Aesthetics*): Prague 1, Haštalská 6; f. 1969; Pres. PhDr. S. ŠABOUK; Sec. PhDr. L. GAWLIK.

Česká společnost pro mezinárodní právo (*Czech Society for International Law*): Prague 1, Národní tř. 18; f. 1969; 109 mems.; Pres. Prof. JUDr. V. KOPAL; Sec. JUDr. V. MIKULKA.

Československá astronomická společnost (*Czechoslovak Astronomical Society*): Prague 7, Královská obora 233; f. 1917; Pres. Dr. V. LEFTUS, C.SC.; Sec. Prof. O. HLAD.

Československá biologická společnost (*Czechoslovak Biological Society*): Brno, Obránců míru 10; f. 1922; 1,400 mems.; Pres. Prof. Dr. M. DVOŘÁK; Sec. MUDr. R. JANISCH.

Československá botanická společnost (*Czechoslovak Botanical Society*): 128 01 Prague 2, Benátská 2; f. 1912; 800 mems.; library of 30,000 books; Chair. Dr. S. HEJNÝ;

Sec. J. Holub; publs. *Preslia*† (quarterly), *Zprávy ČSBS*† (irregular).

Československá demografická společnost (*Czechoslovak Society for Demography*): 130 67 Prague 3, nám. A. Zápotockého 4; f. 1964; 330 mems.; Pres. Doc. Ing. Z. Pavlík, c.sc.; Sec. Doc. Ing. V. Roubíček, c.sc.

Československá geografická společnost (*Czechoslovak Geographical Society*): Prague 1, Na příkopě 29; f. 1894; 1,000 mems.; Pres. Dr. J. Demek; Sec. Dr. S. Řehák; publ. *Sborník* (journal, quarterly).

Československá historická společnost (*Czechoslovak Historical Society*): Prague 1, Staroměstské nám. 12; f. 1934; 500 mems.; Pres. Prof. V. Král; Sec. PhDr. O. Novák.

Československá kybernetická společnost (*Czechoslovak Society for Cybernetics*): Prague 8, Pod vodárenskou věží 4; f. 1966; 500 mems.; Pres. Corresp. Mem. J. Nedoma; Sec. RNDr. M. Ullrich, c.sc.

Československá lékařská společnost J. E. Purkyně (*Czechoslovak J. E. Purkyne Medical Society*): 120 26 Prague 2, Vítězného února 31; f. 1949; 45,000 mems.; Pres. Prof. Dr. B. Špaček, dr.sc.; Sec. Prof. Dr. J. Homolka, dr.sc.

Československá limnologická společnost (*Czechoslovak Society for Limnology*): 151 05 Prague 5, Vltavská 17; f. 1966; 280 mems.; Pres. Doc. Dr. J. Lellák; Sec. Dr. P. Punčochář.

Československá meteorologická společnost (*Czechoslovak Society for Meteorology*): Prague 5, Holečkova 8; f. 1958; 200 mems.; Pres. RNDr. V. Vítek; Sec. RNDr. O. Zikmunda, c.sc.

Československá pedagogická společnost při ČSAV (*Czechoslovak Society for Education*): 116 77 Prague 1, Purkyňova 2; f. 1964; 582 mems.; Pres. Doc. Dr. J. Skalka; Sec. Dr. J. Semrád, c.sc.

Československá sociologická společnost (*Czechoslovak Sociological Association*): Prague 1, Na příkope 29; f. 1964; 709 mems.; Pres. Prof. Dr. J. Zvara; Sec. Ing. PhDr. V. Dubský.

Československá spektroskopická společnost (*Czechoslovak Spectroscopic Society*): Prague 6, Kozlovská 1; f. 1949; 980 mems.; Pres. Dr. J. Kuba; Sec. Dr. I. Rubeška.

Československá společnost antropologická (*Czechoslovak Anthropological Association*): 659 37 Brno, nám. 25 února 7; f. 1964; 180 mems.; Pres. RNDr. J. Jelínek; Sec. Doc. Dr. V. Novotný; publ. *Zprávy* (quarterly).

Československá společnost archeologická (*Czechoslovak Society for Archaeology*): Prague 1, Letenská 4; f. 1919; 250 mems.; Pres. Prof. Dr. B. Chropovsky; Sec. Doc Dr. R. Pleiner.

Československá společnost biochemická při ČSAV (*Czechoslovak Biochemical Society*): 101 00 Prague 10, Hradešínská 66; f. 1956; 800 mems.; Pres. Prof. Jan Škoda; Sec. Dr. Jiří Kraml.

Československá společnost bioklimatologická (*Czechoslovak Society for Bioclimatology*): Prague 10, Šrobárova 48; f. 1965; 220 mems.; Pres. Prof. MUDr. K. Symon; Sec. Doc. Ing. V. Pasák.

Československá společnost ekonomická (*Czechoslovak Economic Association*): 113 73 Prague 1, tř. Politickych vězňu 7; f. 1962; 700 mems.; Pres. Doc. Ing. V. Wacker; Sec. Ing. M. Hrnčíř.

Československá společnost entomologická (*Czechoslovak Society for Entomology*): 128 00 Prague 2, Viničná 7; f. 1904; 1,200 mems.; library of 15,000 vols.; Pres. Dr. A. Pfeffer; Sec. Dr. M. Chvála; publ. *Acta entomologica bohemoslovaca*† (6 a year).

Československá společnost histo- a cytochemická (*Czechoslovak Society for Histochemistry and Cytochemistry*): 142 20 Prague 4, Vídenska 1083; f. 1962; 210 mems.; Pres. Prof. MUDr. Z. Lojda, dr.sc.; Sec. RNDr. J. Faltin, c.sc.

Československá společnost chemická (*Czechoslovak Chemical Society*): 118 29 Prague 1, Hradčanské nám. 12; f. 1866; 3,100 mems.; Pres. Prof. Ing. J. Pick; Sec. Ing. Dr. V. Chvalovský; publ. *Chemické Listy*† (monthly).

Československá společnost mikrobiologická (*Czechoslovak Society for Microbiology*): Prague 2, Viničná 5; f. 1930; 1,000 mems.; Pres. T. Martinec; Sec. M. Rýc; Exec. Sec. V. Havel; publ. *Bulletin of the Czechoslovak Society for Microbiology* (Czech, bi-monthly).

Československá společnost orientalistická při ČSAV (*Czechoslovak Society for Eastern Studies*): 118 000 Prague 1, Lázeňská 4; f. 1958; 150 mems.; Pres. JUDr. B. Doubrava; Sec. PhDr. J. Marek.

Československá společnost parasitologická (*Czechoslovak Society for Parasitology*): Prague 6, Flemingovo nám. 2; f. 1959; 200 mems.; Pres. Acad. J. Hovorka; Secs. RNDr. K. Samšiňák, RNDr. L. Červa; publ. *Zpráry Československé Společnosti Parasitologické* (quarterly).

Československá společnost pro dějiny věd a techniky (*Czechoslovak Society for the History of Science and Technology*); Prague 2, Mikovcova 5; f. 1965; 380 mems.; Pres. Dr. L. Nový; Sec. Dr. S. Štrbáňová; publ. *Dějiny věd a techniky*† (quarterly).

Československá společnost pro mechaniku (*Czechoslovak Society for Mechanics*): 128 00 Prague 2, Vyšehradská 49; f. 1966; 510 mems.; Pres. J. Valenta; Sec. R. Dvořák.

Československá společnost pro mineralogii a geologii (*Czechoslovak Society for Mineralogy and Geology*): Prague 2, Albertov 6; f. 1923; 800 mems.; Pres. Prof. Z. Pouba; Sec. RNDr. J. Zeman.

Československá společnost pro nauku o kovech při ČSAV (*Czechoslovak Metals Society*): Prague 1, Křemencova 10; f. 1966; 200 mems.; Pres. Prof. Ing. Dr. V. Sedláček; Sec. Doc. Ing. L. Lakatoš.

Československá společnost pro politické vědy (*Czechoslovak Society for Political Sciences*): Prague 1, Jilská 1; f. 1967; Pres. Prof. Dr. Milan Matouš, c.sc.; Sec. Dr. M. Narta, c.sc.

Československá společnost pro vědeckou kinematografii (*Czechoslovak Scientific Film Association*): Brno, Zemědělská 1; f. 1923, reorganized 1966; 250 mems.; Pres. Prof. Dr. J. Calábek; Sec. RNDr. M. Nováček.

Československá společnost pro vědy zemědělské, lesnické, veterinární a potravinářské (*Czechoslovak Society for Agriculture, Veterinary Science and Food Technology*): Prague 6-Suchdol VŠZ; f. 1968; 750 mems.; Pres. Prof. Ing. F. Hron; Sec. Doc. Dr. M. Valla.

Československá vědecká společnost pro mykologii (*Czechoslovak Scientific Society for Mycology*): Prague 1, Krakovská 1; f. 1923; 350 mems.; Pres. Prof. Dr. Vl. Rypáček, dr.sc.; Sec. Dr. Z. Pouzar, c.sc.

Československá vědecká společnost pro psychologii (*Czechoslovak Psychological Society*): Prague 2, nábř. B. Engelse 6; f. 1927; 850 mems.; Pres. Doc. Dr. J. Čepelák, c.sc.; Sec. Dr. S. Fraňková, c.sc.

Československá zoologická společnost (*Czechoslovak Zoological Society*): Prague 2, Viničná 7; f. 1927; 400 mems.; Pres. Acad. J. Kratochvil; Sec. Doc. Dr. J. Buchar; publ. *Acta Societatis Zoologicae Bohemoslovenicae* (quarterly).

Chirurgická Společnost (*Czechoslovak Surgical Society*): 120 26 Prague 2, Tř. Vítězného února 31; f. 1920; mem. of the J. E. Purkyně Medical Society; 700 mems.;

Pres. Prof. EMIL MATEJÍČEK; Sec. VLADIMÍR HOLEC; publ. *Rozhledy v chirurgii*†.

Jazykovědné sdružení (*Linguistic Asscn.*): Prague 1, Letenská 4; f. 1956; 332 mems.; Pres. Dr. MILAN ROMPORT; Sec. Dr. J. ŠTĚPÁN, C.SC.

Jednota čs. matematiků a fyziků (*Society of Czech Mathematicians and Physicists*): Prague 1, Spálená 26; f. 1862; 3,000 mems.; Pres. Acad. J. NOVÁK; Sec. M. JELÍNEK.

Jednota filosofická (*Philosophical Union*): Prague 1, Valdštejnská 14; f. 1881; 150 mems.; Pres. PhDr. V. RUML; Sec. Doc. Dr. J. MUŽÍK.

Jednota klasických filologů (*Classical Philology Union*): Prague 2, Lazarská 8; f. 1868; 357 mems.; library of 26,870 vols.; Pres. Prof. PhDr. K. JANÁČEK; Sec. PhDr. L. VIDMAN; publ. *Zprávy Jednoty klasických filologů* (2 or 3 a year).

Kruh modernich filologů (*Modern Philology Association*): 128 00 Prague 2, Engelsovo nábř 6; f. 1911; 320 mems.; Pres. Prof. Dr. O. NOVÁK; Sec. Doc. Dr. A. TIONOVÁ.

Literárněvědná společnost (*Literary Society*): Prague 1, Nové zámecké schody 4; f. 1934; 250 mems.; Pres. Corresp. Mem. J. HRABÁK; Sec. PhDr. K. HYRŠLOVÁ-ELZNICOVÁ.

Národopisná společnost československá (*Czechoslovak Ethnography Society*): Prague 1, Všehrdova 2; f. 1891; 506 mems.; Pres. Dr. H. JOHNOVÁ; Sec. Dr. J. VAŘEKA.

SLOVENSKÁ AKADÉMIE VIED
(Slovak Academy of Sciences)

UL. OBRANCOV MIERU 41, BRATISLAVA

Founded 1953; since 1960 a part of the Czechoslovak Academy of Sciences and the supreme national and regional scientific institution in Slovakia.

President: Acad. VLADIMÍR HAJKO.
Vice-Presidents: Acad. VOJTECH FILKORN, Acad. JOZEF ZACHAR, Corr. Mem. MILAN REPÁŠ.
General Secretary: Acad. VOJTECH KELLÖ.
Members of the Presidium: Acad. OLDRICH BENDA, Acad. TIBOR KOLBENHEYER, Acad. RUDOLF TEOFIL NIEDERLAND, Acad. ŠTEFAN SCHWARZ, Acad. OTO JAROSLAV VRTIAK, Corresp. Mems. JÁN BALAŠ, VLADIMÍR CIRBES, JÁN DEKAN, JAROSLAV MAJER, EMIL MAZÚR, RUDOLF SKRÚCANÝ, NORBERT SZUTTOR.

Publications: *Acta Virologica, Architektúra a Urbanizmus, Biológia, Bratislavské lekárske listy, Ekonomicky časopis, Elektrotechnicky časopis, Endocrinologia Experimentalis, Filozofia, Fyzikálny časopis, Geografický sbornik, Historický časopis, Chemické zvesti, Jazykovedný časopis, Kovové materiály, Kultura slova, Lesnícky časopis, Matematický časopis, Neoplasma, Polnohospodárstvo, Právny obzor, Studia psychologica, Slavia Slovaca, Slovenská archeológia, Slovenská literatura, Slovenská reč, Slovenské divadlo, Slovensky národopis, Sociologia, Stavebnícky časopis, Strojnicky časopis, Vedecký Ateizmus, Vodohospodársky časopis, Zivotné prostredie.*

ACADEMICIANS:

ANTAL, JURAJ.
BENDA, OLDRICH.
BLAŠKOVIČ, DIONÝZ.
ČABELKA, JOSEF.
CAMBEL, BOHUSLAV.
ČERNÁČEK, JOZEF.
FILKORN, VOJTECH.
GONDA, JÁN.
HAJKO, VLADIMÍR.
HOVORKA, JÁN.
ILKOVIČ, DIONÝZ.
JAKUBÍK, JÁN.
KELLÖ, VOJTĚCH.
KNEPPO, L'UDOVÍT.
KOLBENHEYER, TIBOR.
LACO, KAROL.
MAHEL, MICHAL.
MUCHA, VOJTĚCH.
NIEDERLAND, TEOFIL.
PAVLÍK, ONDREJ.
PAVLOVIČ, GUSTÁV.
RAPANT, DANIEL.
SCHWARZ, ŠTEFAN.
SIRÁCKY, ANDREJ.
ŠIŠKA, KAROL.
ŠPALDON, EMIL.
THURZO, VILIAM.
VRTIAK, OTO.
ZACHAR, JOZEF.

CORRESPONDING MEMBERS:

BALAŠ, JÁN.
BLAŽEJ, ANTON.
BODA, KOLOMAN.
BODNÁR, JÁN.
BORECKÝ, LADISLAV.
ČATÁR, GUSTÁV.
CIRBES, VLADIMÍR.
DEKAN, JÁN.
DUBINSKÝ, JURAJ.
FUSÁN, OTTO.
GAŽO, JÁN.
GUTH, VLADIMÍR.
HOLOTÍK, L'UDOVÍT.
HRIVŇÁK, IVAN.
CHMEL, LADISLAV.
CHROPOVSKÝ, BOHUSLAV.
JEŘÁBEK, JAROSLAV.
KALAŠ, VÁCLAV.
KONČEK, MIKULÁŠ.
KRESÁK, L'UBOR.
KROPILÁK, MIROSLAV.
MACHO, LADISLAV.
MAJER, JAROSLAV.
MATEJIČEK, EMIL.
MAZÚR, EMIL.
MICHALIČKOVÁ, JAROSLAVA.
NEMEC, PAVOL.
PASTÝRIK, L'ÚDOVÍT.
PAULÍNY, EUGEN.
PLESNÍK, JÁN.
PLEVZA, VILIAM.
PRASLIČKA, MILAN.
PUCHNER, ONDREJ.
REPÁŠ, MILAN.
RUŽIČKA, JOZEF.
SITAJ, ŠTEFAN.
SKRÚCANÝ, RUDOLF.
SZUTTOR, NORBERT.
ŠALAMON, MIROSLAV.
TESÁR, ARPÁD.
VÁROSS, MARIAN.
VARSIK, BRANISLAV.
VAŠEČKA, FÉLIX.
WEISMANN, LUDOVÍT.
ZACHAR, DUŠAN.

SCIENTIFIC INSTITUTES

Department of Earth and Space Sciences, Mathematics, Physics and Technical Sciences:

Mathematics Institute: Bratislava.
Physics Institute: Bratislava.
Experimental Physics Institute: Košice.
Electrotechnical Institute: Bratislava.
Technical Cybernetics Institute: Bratislava.
Institute of Measurement: Bratislava.
Astronomy Institute: Skalnaté Pleso.
Geophysics Institute: Bratislava.
Geography Institute: Bratislava.
Geology Institute: Bratislava.
Mechanical Engineering Institute: Bratislava.
Metals Materials Institute: Bratislava.
Experimental Metallurgy Institute: Košice.
Building and Architecture Institute: Bratislava.
Hydrology and Hydraulics Institute: Bratislava.

Department of Chemistry, Biology, Medicine and Biological Agricultural Sciences:

Chemistry Institute: Bratislava.
Inorganic Chemistry Institute: Bratislava.
Polymer Institute: Bratislava.
Molecular Biology Institute: Bratislava.
Neurobiology Institute: Košice.
Experimental Oncology Institute: Bratislava.
Experimental Pharmacology Institute: Bratislava.
Virology Institute: Bratislava.
Normal and Pathological Physiology Institute: Bratislava.
Experimental Endocrinology Institute: Bratislava.
Experimental Surgery Institute: Bratislava.
Experimental Biology and Ecology Institute: Bratislava.
"Mlyňany" Arboretum—Dendrology Institute: Vieska nad Žitavou.
Helminthology Institute: Košice.
Experimental Phytopathology and Entomology Institute: Bratislava.
Animal Physiology Institute: Košice.

Department of Social Sciences and Humanities:

Philosophy and Sociology Institute: Bratislava.
Scientific Atheism Institute: Bratislava.
Experimental Education Institute: Bratislava.
Experimental Psychology Institute: Bratislava.
Archaeology Institute: Nitra-Hrad.
History Institute: Bratislava.
Institute of European Socialist Countries: Bratislava.
Ethnography Institute: Bratislava.
Oriental Institute: Bratislava.
Economics Institute: Bratislava.

Law Institute: Bratislava.
"L. Štúra" Linguistics Institute: Bratislava.
Literature Institute: Bratislava.
Institute of Arts: Bratislava.

SCIENTIFIC SOCIETIES OF THE SLOVAK ACADEMY OF SCIENCES

Jednota klasických filologov (*Union for Classical Philology*): f. 1969; 56 mems.; Pres. Prof. Dr. M. OKÁL; Sec. Dr. D. ŠKOVIERA.

Jednota slov. matematikov a fyzikov (*Union of Slovak Mathematicians and Physicists*): f. 1862; 2,000 mems.; Pres. Prof. RNDr. V. MEDEK; Sec. Doc. Dr. J. ELIÁŠ.

Krúžok moderných filologov (*Union for Modern Philology*): f. 1959; 205 mems.; Pres. Prof. Dr. V. SCHWANZER; Sec. Dr. J. MARKO.

Slovenská antropologická spoločnost (*Slovak Anthropological Society*): f. 1961; 127 mems.; Pres. Doc.RNDr. M. POSPÍŠIL; Sec. Doc. Dr. J. DROBNÝ.

Slov. archeologická spoločnost (*Slovak Archaeological Society*): f. 1960; 215 mems.; Pres. Dr. JOSEF VLADÁR; Sec. Dr. P. ROMSAUER.

Slov. astronomická spoločnost (*Slovak Astronomical Society*): f. 1959; 242 mems.; Pres. RNDr. A. HAJDUK; Sec. Dr. J. SVOREN.

Slov. biochemická spoločnost (*Slovak Biochemical Society*): f. 1962; 350 mems.; Pres. Doc. Ing. J. ZELINKA; Sec. Doc. MUDr. J. PECHÁŇ.

Slov. bioklimatologická spoločnost (*Slovak Bioclimatology Society*): f. 1966; 80 mems.; Pres. Dr. ROBERT INTRIBUS; Sec. MUDr. V. BALÁŽ.

Slov. biologická spoločnost (*Slovak Biological Society*): f. 1967; 145 mems.; Pres. Prof. MUDr. V. VRŠANSKÝ; Sec. MUDr. M. KARASOVÁ.

Slov. botanická spoločnost (*Slovak Botanical Society*): f. 1955; 350 mems.; Pres. Dr. J. MICHALKO; Sec. Dr. F. HINDÁK.

Slov. demograficko-štatistická spoločnost (*Slovak Demographic-Statistical Society*): f. 1968; 174 mems.; Pres. Doc. Ing. D. VOJTKO; Sec. Dr. J. GRUND.

Slov. ekonomická spoločnost (*Slovak Economics Society*): f. 1965; 400 mems.; Pres. Prof. Dr. J. CHORVÁT; Sec. Ing. G. BRHLOVIČ.

Slov. entomologická spoločnost (*Slovak Entomology Society*): f. 1957; 100 mems.; Pres. Doc. Dr. O. STEPANOVIČOVÁ; Sec. Dr. L. JEDLIČKA.

Slov. filozofická spoločnost (*Slovak Philosophical Society*): f. 1965; 140 mems.; Pres. Doc. R. ŠÍMA; Sec. PhDr. D. HAJKO.

Slov. geografická spoločnost (*Slovak Geographical Society*): f. 1955; 305 mems.; Pres. Dr. JÁN DRDOŠ; Sec. Dr. M. STANKOVJANSKY.

Slov. geologická spoločnost (*Slovak Geological Society*): f. 1955; 700 mems.; Pres. OTTO FUSÁN; Sec. Ing. S. KONEČNÝ.

Slov. historická spoločnost (*Slovak Historical Society*): f. 1957; 450 mems.; Pres. Corresp. Mem. L. HOLOTÍK; Sec. Dr. J. BARTL.

Slov. chemická spoločnost (*Slovak Chemical Society*): f. 1940; 938 mems.; Pres. Prof. Dr. Ing. J. TOMKO; Sec. Doc. Ing. J. MALINOVSKÝ.

Slov. jazykovedná spoločnost (*Slovak Linguistics Society*): f. 1967; 200 mems.; Pres. Dr. ŠT. PECIAR; Sec. Dr. ST. LIPTÁK.

Slov. kybernetická spoločnost (*Slovak Cybernetics Society*): f. 1965; 200 mems.; Pres. Doc. Ing. ŠT. NEUSCHL; Sec. Ing. B. VYKOUK.

Slov. literárnovedná spoločnost (*Slovak Literary Society*): f. 1957; 200 mems.; Pres. Prof. Dr. M. PIŠÚT; Sec. Dr. K. TOMIŠ.

Slov. meteorologická spoločnost (*Slovak Meteorological Society*): f. 1959; 140 mems.; Pres. Doc. RNDr. F. ŠAMAJ; Sec. Dr. J. LUKÁČ.

Slov. národopisná spoločnost (*Slovak Ethnography Society*): f. 1961; 400 mems.; Pres. Dr. EMA DRÁBÍKOVÁ; Sec. G. KILIÁNOVÁ.

Slov. orientalistická spoločnost (*Slovak Society for Oriental Studies*): f. 1965; 35 mems.; Pres. PhDr. L. DROZDÍK; Sec. PhDr. K. BAŇÁK.

Slov. pedagogická spoločnost (*Slovak Education Society*): f. 1965; 326 mems.; Pres. Prof. Dr. J. KOTOČ; Sec. Dr. J. LIHOCKÝ.

Slov. psychologická spoločnost (*Slovak Psychological Society*): f. 1956; 500 mems.; Pres. DAMIÁN KOVÁČ; Sec. Dr. J. RUISER.

Slov. sociologická spoločnost (*Slovak Sociological Society*): f. 1962; 220 mems.; Pres. Dr. JANČOVIČOVÁ; Sec. J. KOŠTA.

Slov. spoločnost pre dejiny vied a techniky (*Slovak Society for History of Science and Technology*): f. 1966; 124 mems.; Pres. Acad. JÁN GONDA; Sec. Dr. M. BOKESOVÁ.

Slov. spoločnost pre medzinárodné právo (*Slovak Society for International Law*): f. 1970; Pres. Prof. Dr. JURAJ GUTH; Sec. Dr. V. STRÁZNICKÁ.

Slov. spoločnost pre mechaniku (*Slovak Society for Mechanics*): f. 1967; 206 mems.; Pres. Prof. Dr. J. BRILLA; Sec. Ing. S. LICHARDUS.

Slov. spoločnost pre vedy polnohospodarné, lesnické, potravinárské (*Slovak Society for Agriculture, Forestry and Food*): f. 1967; 820 mems.; Pres. Ing. J. KRÁLOVIČ; Sec. Ing. J. DEMEČKO.

Slov. zoologická spoločnost (*Slovak Zoological Society*): f. 1957; 250 mems.; Pres. Doc. RNDr. S. VILČEK; Sec. RNDr. D. MATIS.

ČESKOSLOVENSKÁ AKADEMIE ZEMĚDĚLSKÁ

(Czechoslovak Academy of Agriculture)

TESNOV 65, 110 06 PRAGUE 1

Telephone: 619 28.

Founded 1924.

President: Acad. KAREL KUDRNA.

Vice-Presidents: Acad. OTTO VRTIAK, Prof. Ing. JIRI DAVIDEK, DR.SC.

Scientific Secretary: Ing. JAROSLAV KUNC, C.SC.

Publs. *Rostlinná výroba* (Plant Production), *Živočičná výroba* (Animal Production), *Veterinární medicína* (Veterinary Medicine), *Zemědělská technika* (Agricultural Technology), *Zemědělská ekonomika* (Agricultural Economy), *Lesnictví* (Forestry), *Ochrana rostlin* (Plant Protection), *Meliorace* (Melioration), *Sociologie zemědělství* (Agricultural Sociology), *Genetika a šlechtění* (Genetics and Breeding), *Zahradnictví* (Gardening), *Scientia agriculturae bohemoslovaca* (articles in English, German or Russian), *Věstník Československé akademie zemědělské* (Bulletin of the Czechoslovak Academy of Agriculture).

MEMBERS

ADAM, Ing. MILOSLAV.
BAIER, Ing. JAN.
BENDA, Asst. Prof. Ing. JOSEF.
BENETÍN, Prof. Ing. JAN.
BODA, Prof. Dr. KOLOMAN.
DAVÍDEK, JIŘÍ.
DĚDEK, MIROSLAV.
DUŠEK, Asst. Prof. Ing. JAROMÍR.
FIŠERA, Prof. Dr. ŠTEFAN.
GROLIG, Prof. Dr. Ing. ALOIS.
HALAJ, Prof. Dr. Ing. JÁN.
HEJNÝ, Dr. SLAVOMIL.
HOLUB, Prof. Dr. ANTONÍN.
HOMOLKA, Ing. JAROSLAV.
HRAŠKO, JURAJ.
CHUDÍK, IGOR.

JAKUBEC, Asst. Prof. Ing. VÁCLAV.
JANÍČEK, Prof. Dr. Ing. GUSTAV.
KABRHEL, Prof. JAROSLAV.
KAŠPAR, FRANTIŠEK.
KLESNIL, ANTONÍN.
KLIMENT, Prof. Ing. JOZEF.
KOVÁČIK, Prof. Ing. ANTON.
KRUPAUER, Prof. Ing. VLADIMÍR.
KUBAS, PAVOL.
KUČERA, Ing. VLADIMÍR.
KUDRNA, Acad. KAREL.
KUNC, Ing. JAROSLAV.
KYZLINK, Prof. Ing. VLADIMÍR.
LEDL, Prof. Ing. CTIBOR.
LEKEŠ, Ing. JAROSLAV.
MACHEK, JIŘÍ.
MAJERČIAK, PAVOL.
MAREČEK, Ing. FRANTIŠEK.
MARKO, ALFONZ.
MARTÍNEK, Ing. MIROSLAV.
MINAŘÍK, Ing. FRANTIŠEK.
NIKL, Asst. Prof. Ing. JOSEF.
NOVÁK, Asst. Prof. Ing. BOHUMÍR.
PAVLOVIČKOVÁ, AURÉLIA.
PEŘINA, VLADIMÍR.
PLESNÍK, Prof. Ing. JÁN.
PODANÝ, JAN.
POTOČNÝ, VOJTĚCH.
RAPOŠ, Ing. PAVOL.
ROD, Asst. Prof. Dr. Ing. JÁN.
RUPRICH, JIŘÍ.
SEDLÁK, Ing. EMIL.
SLABÝ, Asst. Prof. Ing. ALOIS.
SOMMER, ALEXANDER.
ŠORMAN, LADISLAV.
ŠPALDON, Acad. EMIL.
ŠPOLINA, Ing. MIROSLAV.
URBAN, KAREL.
VELEBIL, Asst. Prof. Ing. MILOSLAV.
VEREŠ, ALOJZ.
VESELÝ, VÁCLAV.
VRTIAK, Prof. Dr. OTTO.
ZACHAR, Prof. Ing. DUŠAN.
ZAJÍČEK, Ing. PAVEL.

SCIENTIFIC SECTIONS

Section for Land Improvement and Protection: Chair. Ing. JURAJ HRAŠKO, D.SC.
Section for Crop Production: Chair. Prof. Ing. ANTON KOVÁČIK.
Section for Livestock Production: Chair. Prof. Ing. JÁN PLESNÍK.
Section for Veterinary Medicine: Chair. Prof. Dr. ANTONÍN HOLUB.
Section for Farm Technology, Construction and Energy: Chair. Ing. JIŘÍ FIALA, D.SC.
Section for Nutrition and the Food Industry: Chair. Ing. VÁCLAV VESELÝ, C.SC.
Section for Economics, Organization and Management: Chair. Dr. EMIL BORÁK.
Section for Forestry: Chair. Ing. KAREL URBAN.
Section for Water Conservancy in Agriculture: Chair. Ing. VLADIMÍR ŠVEHLA.
Central Commission for Feedstuffs: Chair. Asst. Prof. Ing. JOSEF BODA, C.SC.
Central Commission for Environmental Protection: Chair. Prof. Ing. DUŠAN ZACHAR.
Central Commission for Scientific-Technical Information: Chair. Ing. OTO ŠILHÁN, C.SC.

LEARNED SOCIETIES

British Council: British Embassy, Prague 1, Jungmannova 30; Cultural Attaché W. G. PREEN.

Český spolek pro komorní hudbu (*Czech Society for Chamber Music*): 152 00 Prague 5, Barrandov 327; f. 1894; 3,500 mems.; Chair. Dr. V. ČELAKOVSKÝ.

Divadelní ústav (*Theatre Institute*): 110 01 Prague 1, Celetná 17; f. 1956; research and documentation on contemporary theatre; central theatre library containing 100,000 vols.; Czechoslovak centre of the International Theatre Institute (ITI); Dir. Dr. EVA SOUKUPOVÁ; publs. *Scénografie* (irregular), *Interscena*† (irregular), *Světové divadlo* (irregular), *Premiéry československých divadel* (monthly), *Technický bulletin* (irregular).

Matice moravská (*Moravian Society of History and Literature*): Brno, Gorkého 14; f. 1849; 560 mems.; Pres. Prof. Dr. BEDŘICH ŠINDELÁŘ; Sec. Dr. RUDOLF FIŠER; publ. *Časopis Matice moravské* (quarterly).

Národni muzeum: Ústřední muzeologický Kabinet (*National Museum—Central Office of Museology*): Prague 1, Malá Strana, U Luzického semináře 13; f. 1956; experimental documentary and advisory centre for museums; 13 staff; library of 11,500 vols. (museological and regional literature); Dir. FRANTIŠKA HYNDRÁKOVÁ; publs. *Muzejní práce* (Museum Work), *Muzejní a vlastivědná práce* (Museum and Regional Work), *International Museological Bibliography* (with UNESCO/ICOM documentation centre), *Metodické listy* (Methodical Papers), *Informace* (Information), *Bibliografie české muzeologické literatury* (Czech Museological Bibliography).

Svaz architektů ČSR (*Union of Architects of ČSR*): Prague 1, Letenská 5; Pres. Ing. arch. ZDENĚK STRNADEL; publs. *Architektura ČSR* (10 a year), *Čs. architekt* (fortnightly).

Svaz československých dramatických umělců (*Union of Czechoslovak Dramatists*): Prague 1, Pod nuselskými schody 3; f. 1978; 2,000 mems.; theatre, film, television, radio; publ. *Scéna*† (2 a month).

Svaz československých skladatelů (*Union of Czechoslovak Composers*): Prague 1, Valdštejnské nám. 1; f. 1978; Pres. Prof. ANDREJ OČENÁŠ.

Svaz československých spisovatelů (*Union of Czech Writers*): Prague 1, Národni 11; Prse. JAN KOZÁK; publ. *Literární měsíčnik* (Literary monthly).

Svaz československých výtvarných umělců (*Union of Czechoslovak Creative Artists*): 11000 Prague 1, Gottwaldovo nábr. 250; Pres. JOSEF MALEJOVSKÝ; publ. *Výtvarná kultura* (Prague), *Výtvarný život* (Bratislava).

Svaz českých dramatických umělců (*Union of Czech Dramatists*): Valdštejnské nám. 3, Prague 1; f. 1972; theatre, TV, film, radio; 1,000 mems.; Pres. JIŘINA ŠVORCOVÁ; publ. *Scéna 81* (fortnightly).

Svaz českých skladatelů a koncertnich umělců (*Union of Czech Composers and Concert Artists*): Prague 1, Valdštejnské nám. 1; Pres. JAN SEIDEL; punl. *Hudební rozhledy*.

Ústav pro kulturně výchovnou činnost (*Institute for Culture and Education*): Prague 2, Vinohrady, Blanická 4; f. 1906 as Union of Culture, in 1925 became the Masaryk Institute for People's Education, is today an institution of the Ministry of Culture, and organizes adult education and cultural research; Dir. MIROSLAV BUKOVSKÝ.

Zväz slovenských architektov (*Union of Slovak Architects*): Nálepkova 15, 80100 Bratislava; Pres. Ing. arch. VLADIMIR FAŠANG; Sec. Acad. arch. Ing. JOZEF SMIDA; publ. *Projekt* (monthly).

Zväz slovenských dramatických umelcov (*Union of Slovak Dramatists*): Gorkého 4, Bratislava; Pres. VILIAM ZÁBORSKÝ.

Zväz slovenských spisovatel'ov (*Union of Slovak Writers*): 890 08 Bratislava, Obrancov Mieru 14; Pres. ANDREJ PLÁVKA; publ. *Slovenské pohl'ady* (Slovak Review).

Zväz slovenských skladatelov (*Union of Slovak Composers*): Bratislava, Sladkovičova 11; f. 1955; 233 mems.; Pres. Prof. EUGEN SUCHOŇ; Sec. Dr. ŠTEFAN KLIMO.

RESEARCH INSTITUTES

Federální statistický úřad (*Federal Statistical Office*): Prague 8, Sokolovská 142; f. 1919; Pres. Ing. JAN KAZIMOUR; publs. *Statistical Yearbook of Czechoslovakia, Statistika, Statistické přehledy* (monthly), *Demografie* (quarterly), *Demosta* (quarterly).

Hydrometeorologický ústav (*Hydrometeorological Institute*): 151 29 Prague 5, Holečkova 8; f. 1920; library of 40,000 vols.; Dir. Ing. V. RICHTER; publs. *Annual of Meteorological Observations at the Meteorological Stations*†, *Annual of Atmospheric Precipitations*†, *Annual of Instrument Records at Prague-Karlov Observatory*†, *Annual of Air Pollution*†, *Bi-monthly Review of Radiation Observations*†, *Transactions*†, *Meteorologické zprávy*† (Bulletin—every 2 months), *Monthly Review of Meteorological Observations at Prague-Karlov Observatory*†, *Monthly Synoptic Weather Report, Daily Weather Report.*

Institut hygieny a epidemiologie (*Institute of Hygiene and Epidemiology*): 100 42 Prague 10, Srobárova 48; library of 92,000 vols.; Dir. Prof. Dr. B. ROSICKÝ, D.SC.; publs. *Československá hygiena, Pracovní lékařství*†, *Československá epidemiologie mikrobiologie imunologie*†, *Journal of Hygiene, Epidemiology, Microbiology and Immunology*†.

Státní ústav pro kontrolu léčiv (*State Institute for the Control of Drugs*): 100 41 Prague 10, Šrobárova 48; Dir. J. BURIÁNEK, PH.D.

Úřad pro normalizaci a měřeni (*Office for Standards and Measurements*): Prague 1, Václavské nám. 19; Pres. Ing. TIMOTEJ HILL; publs. *Československá standardizace, Věstník Úřadu pro normalizaci a měření* (monthly).

Ústav mezinárodních vztahů (*Institute of International Relations*): Nerudova 3, Prague 1.

Ústav pro výzkum, výrobu a využití radioisotopů (*Institute for Research, Production and Application of Radioisotopes*): Prague 7, Přístavní 24; f. 1919; 240 mems.; library of 15,000 vols.; Dir. J. HOKR; Deputy Dir. K. CHORVÁT; publs. monographs, *Radioisotopy* (bimonthly), *Reports.*

Ústav sér a očkovacích látek (*Institute of Sera and Vaccines*): Wilhelma Piecka 108, Prague 10; Gen. Dir. JIŘÍ MÁLEK, M.D.

Ústřední ústav geologický, Praha (*Geological Survey, Prague*): 118 21 Prague 1, Malostranské náměstí 19; f. 1919; library of 125,000 vols.; Dir. Dr. J. VACEK; publs. *Sborník geologických věd*† (Geological Sciences Journal—series: Geology, Palaeontology, Anthropozoics, Economic Geology and Mineralogy, Applied Geophysics, Hydrogeology and Engineering Geology, Technology and Geochemistry), *Rozpravy*† (palaeontological monographs), *Věstník*† (Bulletin 6 times a year), *Knihovna*† (Library—methodical papers or comprehensive reports), *Mineralogicko-geologická bibliografie ČSSR*† (annual), *Geological Guides*†, geological maps.

Vojenský zeměpisný ústav (*Military Geographical Institute*): Prague 6, Rooseveltova 23; f. 1919.

Výzkumný ústav geodetický, topografický a kartografický v Praze (*Research Institute of Geodesy, Topography and Cartography*): 250 66 Zdiby 98; f. 1954; library of 70,000 vols.; Dir. Ing. JAROSLAV KOUBA; publ. *Bibliographical Journal.*

Výzkumný ústav pedagogický (*Research Institute of Education*): Bratislava, Štúrova 5; f. 1947; departmental institute of the Ministry of Education of the Slovak Socialist Republic; research in educational and related scientific fields; 139 mems.; library of 27,000 vols.; Dir. Prof. Dr. EMIL STRAČÁR, DR.SC.; publ. *Jednotná škola.*

Výzkumný ústav pedagogický (*Research Institute of Education*): Prague 1, Mikulandská 5; f. 1945; departmental institute of the Czech Ministry of Education; research in educational theory and psychology in all fields of general education and instruction; part of the Institute forms the J. A. Comenius Pedagogic Museum; 196 mems.; Dir. Doc. Dr. VLADIMÍR ČÁRA; library of 27,000 vols.; publ. *Reports.*

Výzkumný ústav vodohospodářský (*Water Research Institute*): 16062 Prague 6, Podbabská 30; f. 1920; research into hydrology, applied hydraulics, water pollution, water supply; Dir. Ing. MILOSLAV BOHÁČ; publs. *Práce a studie*†, *Bibliography of Hydrology.*

LIBRARIES

PRAGUE

Knihovna Archeologického ústavu ČSAV (*Library of the Archaeological Institute of the Czechoslovak Academy of Sciences—research centre Prague*): Prague 1, Letenská 4; 47,130 vols.; Chief Librarian Dr. Z. KRUMPHANZLOVÁ; publs. *Památky Archeologické, Archeologické Rozhledy, Archeologické studijní materiály, Výzkumy v Čechách, Crania Bohemica.*

Knihovna Bedřicha Smetany (*Bedřich Smetana Library*): Prague 1, Dr. V. Vacka 1; f. 1893; Musical dept. of Public City Library; 190,000 vols.; Dir. Dr. ALEŠ KŘIČKA.

Knihovna Husova domu (*Hus House Library*): Prague 1, Jungmannova 9; Central Library of the Evangelical Church, containing books on religious subjects.

Knihovna Komenského fakulty (*Library of Comenius Faculty of Theology*): 115 55 Prague 1, Jungmannova 9.

Knihovna Národní galerie (*Library of the National Gallery*): Prague 1, Hradčanské nam. 15; f. 1887; 40,000 vols.; Dir. VLASTA MUCHKOVÁ.

Knihovna Národního musea (*National Museum Library*): 115 79 Prague 1, Václavské nám. 1700; f. 1818; *c.* 2,400,000 vols.; Departments: Central Museum Library, Bohemian Literature and the Czechoslovak Book Museum at Ždar n.S., historical libraries of Bohemian and Moravian castles, periodicals and 19th-century literature; Dir. Dr. JAROSLAV VRCHOTKA, C.SC.; publ. *Acta Musei Nationalis Pragae*, Series C† (5 a year).

Knihovna Národního technického musea (*National Technical Museum Library*): Prague 7, Kostelní 42; f. 1835; 200,000 vols.; Chief Librarian J. ŠKOP.

Knihovna Orientálního ústavu Československé akademie věd (*Library of Oriental Institute of Czechoslovak Academy of Sciences*): 118 37 Prague 1, Lázeňská 4; Chinese library of 62,000 vols., general library 186,398 vols.; Librarian HELENA LINHARTOVÁ.

Knihovna Ústředního ústavu geologického (*Geological Institute Library*): Prague 1, Hradební 9; f. 1919; geology and related branches; 125,000 vols.; Librarian MARIE MEZEROVÁ.

Knihovny fakult a ústavů University Karlovy (*Libraries of Faculties and Institutes of Charles University*): 116 36 Prague 1, Ovocný trh 5; f. 1366; altogether 2,745,199 vols.; 226,830 documents; 10,335 periodicals; separate library for each faculty and institute; many publs.†

Archiv University Karlovy: 116 36 Prague 1, Ovocný trh 5; 22,000 vols., 62 periodicals; Librarian PhDr. MARIE ŠTEMBERKOVÁ.

Městská knihovna v Praze (*Prague City Library*): 115 72 Prague 1, nám. primátora dr. V. Vacka 1; f. 1891; 2,318,815 vols.; 10 district libraries, 74 brs., 3 bibliobuses, also 46 libraries added recently to the Prague area; special departments: music, drama and films, local history, People's Science University; Dir. ANNA BIMKOVÁ.

Státní knihovna České socialistické republiky (*State Library of the Czech Socialist Republic*): 113 07 Prague 1, Klementinum 190; f. 1958 by merger of various libraries; 5,000,000 vols.; central research library of Bohemia and Moravia, agent for Czechoslovak International Exchange Service, national centre for restoration of books; collection of microfilms; Dir. K. KOZELEK; publs. *Bibliografický katalog ČSR* (weekly); *Česká bibliografie* (bi-annually); *Novinky literatury* (monthly); *Ročenka Státní knihovny ČSR* (annually); *Novinky knihovnické literatury* (quarterly).

Státní pedagogická knihovna Komenského při Ústavu školských informací ministerstva školství ČSR (*Comenius State Library*): Prague 1, Mikulandská 5; f. 1919; 355,000 vols. on education; youth branch (Suk Library), 38,000 vols.; Chief Librarian IVANA HUTAŘOVÁ; publs. *Přehled pedagogické literatury* (survey of pedagogic literature, 6 a year), *Výběr knih SPKK* (selection of books, quarterly).

Státní technická knihovna (*State Technical Library*): 113 07 Prague 1, Klementinum 190; f. 1718; Library Division of the Centre for Scientific, Technical and Economic Information; lending research library and documentation centre; 836,348 vols., 5,974 periodicals, 586,563 items of trade literature, collections of microfilms and photo-duplicating service; Exchange Department dealing with 700 foreign institutions in 40 countries; Dir. Dr. E. SOŠKOVÁ; publs. *Technická knihovna*† (The Technical Library—monthly), *Czechoslovak Scientific Technical Periodical Contents*† (10 a year), and various bibliographies, acquisitions lists, etc.

Ústav vědeckých lékařských informací (*Institute for Medical Information*): 121 32 Prague 2, Nové Město, Vít února 31; f. 1961; scientific information for medical research institutes and for the network of health care institutions; Czechoslovak medical literature and Excerpta Medica databases; demand searches and SDI service; central lending services, international exchange of publications; publication of bibliographies, abstracts and information periodicals; 230,000 vols., 1,470 current periodicals; Dir. JAN PEŠKA; Chief Librarian DANA BABOROVÁ; publs. *Bibliographia Medica Čechoslovaca*† (12 a year), *Annual of Czechoslovak Medical Literature*†, *Novinky Literatury-Zdravotnictví*† (10 a year), *Referátové Výběry*† (122 a year), *Zdravotnická Dokumentace*† (4 a year), *Seznam Literárních rešersí*† (list of literature searches, irregular), *Soupis Lékarských devizových časopisů docházejících do ČSSR*† (list of foreign medical periodicals in Czechoslovak libraries, yearly).

Ústřední knihovna fakulty všeobecného lékařství, Universita Karlova (*Central Library of the Faculty of General Medicine, Charles University*): Prague 2, Kateřinská 32; f. 1949; 403,000 vols., 1,450 current periodicals; xeroxing service; Dir. EVA HOLADOVÁ; publs. *Acta Universitatis Carolinae-Medica*†, *Monografia*†, *Proceedings of the Scientific Conferences*†.

Ústřední knihovna patentové literatury (*Central Library of Patent Literature*): 160 68 Prague 6, Uhřbitova 2; 22 million vols.; Dir. Ing. JAROSLAV OPAR.

Ústřední knihovna pedagogické fakulty Univerzity Karlovy —Oborové informační středisko (*Central Library, Information and Reference Centre of the Faculty of Pedagogy, Charles University*): 116 39 Prague 1, M. D. Rettigové 4; Dir. PhDr. PAVLA LIPERTOVÁ.

Ústřední tělovýchovná knihovna (*Central Library of Physical Training*): Prague 1, Újezd 450; f. 1927; 213,000 vols.; Dir. JITKA PETROVOVÁ; publ. *Acta Gymnica University Karlovy*.

Ústřední zemědělská a lesnická knihovna (*Central Agricultural and Forestry Library*): 120 56 Prague 2, Slezská 7; f. 1924; since 1961 a section of the Institute of Scientific and Technical Information for Agriculture; *c.* 935,000 vols.; lending library, reading-room, reprographic information service, bibliographical section, all open to the public; all Czechoslovak publications exchanged with foreign countries; Dir. Ing. OTTO ŠILHAN; Chief Librarian JAROSLAVA STAŇKOVÁ, C.SC.; publs. *Výběr nových přírůstků zahr.zem.lit. ve fondu ÚZLK-ÚVTIZ* (bi-monthly, selection of new accessions), *Prehled rešerší a tém. bibliografií* (quarterly list of latest them. bibl. and spec. searches), *Výběry literatury* (thematic bibliography, irregular), *Světové zemědělství v cestovních zprávách* (2 a year, annotations from Czechoslovak experts' journeys abroad), *Agricultural Literature of Czechoslovakia* (quarterly, also in Russian, German and French, annotations of the largest Czechoslovak agriculture and forestry publs.), catalogues.

Základní knihovna—Ústředí vědeckých informací Československé akademie věd (*Main Library—Scientific Information Centre of the Czechoslovak Academy of Sciences*): 115 22 Prague 1, Národní tř. 3; f. 1952; 824,600 vols., 4,000 periodicals; collection of microfilms; a research and lending library; exchange with 1,200 foreign institutions in 74 countries; Dir. JIŘÍ ZAHRADIL; publ. *Vedecké informace*† (Scientific Information), *Společenské vědy v ČSAV* (Social Sciences, monthly).

PROVINCES

Archiv hlavného mesta SSR Bratislavy, Regionálna knižnica (*Bratislava Regional Library*): 886 23 Bratislava, Primaciálne nám. č. 1; f. 1923; 82,500 vols.; Dir. VLADIMÍR HORVÁTH.

Československá akademie věd, Slezský ústav, Vědecká knihovna (*Silesian Institute of the Czechoslovak Academy of Sciences, Special Library*): Opava, Nádrazní okruh 31; f. 1945; 174,982 vols.; Dir. EVA MALÁ; publ. *Slezký sborník* (Acta Silesiaca).

Knihovna Moravské galerie (*Library of the Moravian Gallery*): 66 22 6 Brno, Husova 14; f. 1873; 65,500 vols.; Dir. KAREL HOLEŠOVSKÝ; publs. art catalogues, *Bulletin*†.

Knihovna Vaclava Kopeckeho (*Scientific and Public Library*): nám. Bojovníků za mír 23, 460 53 Liberec; 650,000 vols.; special section on the textile, glass and plastic industries; sudetica; Dir. R. BRZOBOHATÝ.

Krajská knižnica (*Regional Library*): 042 64 Košice, Leninova 59; f. 1657; 163,000 vols.; Dir. V. ČAP.

Matica slovenská (*Slovak National Library*): 036 52 Martin Hostihora; f. 1863; 4,500,000 vols.; contains literary archives and museum documents; Dir. Dr. ŠTEFAN KRIVUŠ; publs. *Slovenská národná bibliografia—Knihy, Članky, Hudobniny, Čitatel'* (monthly), *Knižnice a vedecké informácie* (every 2 months), *Bibliografický zborník, Knižničný zborník, Kniha, Literárny archív, Hudobný archív, Literárnomúzejný letopis Biografické štúdie, Slováci v zahraničí* (yearbooks).

Mestská knižnica Bratislava (*Bratislava Municipal Library*): Bratislava, Obchodná č. 2; f. 1900; 200,000 vols.; Dir. MILAN SCHWARZ.

Slovenská lekárska knižnica (*Slovak Medical Library*): Bratislava, ul. Čs. armády 24; f. 1951; 112,000 vols.; research service; methodical centre for health library organization; Dir. MÁRIA CHRÁSTKOVÁ; publs. *Prírastky zahraničných kníh—Séria F* (bi-monthly), *Zoznam rešerší* (annually), *Metodický informátor* (quarterly), *Zoznam časopisov dochádzajúcich na Slovensko* (annually).

Slovenská pedagogická knižnica a Ústav Školských informacií (*Slovak Pedagogic Library*): 886 44 Bratislava, Klariská ulica 5; f. 1978; education, psychology, sociology, librarianship, information science; 220,000 vols.; Dir. Dr. JÚLIUS LIHOCKÝ; publ. *Pedagogický bibliografický spravodaj*†, *Skolské knižnice*†.

Slovenská technická knižnica (*Slovak Technical Library*): Bratislava, Gottwaldovo nám. 2; f. 1938; 2,200,000 vols.; general reference and bibliography; special collections of trade literature 800,000; standards 145,493; patents 854,091; micro-films 310,279; photo-duplication service; international exchange of publications; 3,500 current periodicals; Dir. GABRIEL KUKORELLI; publs. *Novinky zahraničnej literatúry, Zoznam dochádzajúcich časopisov, Zoznam prekladov, Zoznam rešerší, Bulletin špeciálnych druhov technickej literatúry, Súborné bibliografie, Metodické listy, Studijné príručky, Učebné pomôcky, Klasifikačné pomôcky, Rozvoj vedy a techniky, Novosti vedy a techniky.*

Štátna vedecká knižnica (*State Scientific Library*): Košice, Leninova 10; f. 1657, re-opened 1946; 1,911,206 vols.; general reference and bibliography; Dir. Ing. PAVEL DZIAK; bibliographical publications.

Štátna vedecká knižnica (*State Scientific Library*): Prešov; f. 1952; 255,000 vols.; Dir. J. REŠOVSKÝ.

Státní vědecká knihovna (*State Scientific Library*): Brno, Leninova 5; f. 1958 (merger of Universitní knihovna, Státní technická knihovna and Státní pedagogická knihovna); humanities, social and natural sciences; special technical and pedagogical collections; 4,000,000 vols., 2,250 MSS., 7,300 periodicals; microfilm and xerox services, international exchange of publications; Dir. J. TRAUTMANN; publs. various catalogues and bibliographies.

Státní vědecká knihovna (*State Scientific Library*): 370 59 České Budějovice, Riegrova ul. 3; f. 1885; 1,467,000 vols.; Dir. K. CEMPÍRKOVÁ.

Státní vědecká knihovna (*State Scientific Library*): Olomouc, Bezručova 2; f. 1566; open to the public; 1,237,380 vols., including 1,800 incunabula and 1,447 MSS.; Librarian Dr. ANTONÍN PŘICHYSTAL.

Státní vědecká knihovna (*State Scientific Library*): Ostrava, Nová radnice; f. 1951; 632,000 vols.; general library and special library on mining and metallurgy; Dir. Z. JURDOVA.

Státní vědecká knihovna (*State Scientific Library*): Plzeň, ul. B. Smetany 14; f. 1950; 1,494,400 vols.; Dir. Dr. A. POSLEDNÍ.

Státní vědecká knihovna (*State Scientific Library*): 500 49 Hradec Králové; f. 1949; 634,860 vols.; Dir. MILOSLAV HROMÁDKA.

Státní vědecká knihovna Maxima Gorkého (*Maxim Gorky State Scientific Library*): 400 21 Ústí nad Labem, Velká hradební 49; 349,000 vols.; Dir. L. ZOUBEK.

Univerzitná knižnica (*University Library*): Bratislava, Michalská 1; f. 1919; special collections: social and natural sciences; 1,500,000 vols.; Dir. Dr. V. KÚTIK; numerous publs.

Ústredná ekonomická knižnica (*Central Economic Library*): 886 32 Bratislava, Palisády 22; f. 1940; 360,000 vols.; Dir. Ing. B. PROCHÁZKA; publs. *Informačný spravodaj* (quarterly), *EKO-Index* (monthly), *Prírastky zahraničných kníh* (*PZK*) (new foreign acquisitions, monthly).

Ústredná knižnica Slovenskej akadémie vied (*Central Library of the Slovak Academy of Sciences*): Bratislava, Klemensova 19; 475,000 vols.; functions of the library include the international exchange of publications; Dir. Dr. J. BOLDIŠ.

Ústredná lesnícka a drevárska knižnica (*Central Library for Forestry and Wood Technology*): 960 02 Zvolen, Marxova 8; f. 1952; 522,000 vols.; attached to the Univ. College of Forestry and Wood Technology; Dir. J. DANIEL; publs. *Acta Facultatis Forestalis*†, *Collection of Scientific Works*† (annually).

Ústredná pôdohospodárska knižnica—Študijného a informačného centra Vysokej školy pol'nohospodárskej (*Central Library of the Study and Information Centre of the University of Agriculture*): 949 59 Nitra, Štúrova 9; f. 1946; 400,000 vols.; Dir. LUDMILA BENETINOVÁ; publ. *Prírastky zahraničných kníh* (monthly).

Ústrední knihovna Vysoké školy báňské (*Central Library of the State College of Mining and Metallurgy*): 710 10 Ostrava 10, Michálkovická 109; f. 1849; 450,000 vols.; Dir. Dr. JIŘINA ZLÁ; publ. *Sborník vědeckých prací Vysoké školy banské v Ostravě*† (Transactions).

Ustredni knihovna Vysoké školy veterinární (*Central Library of the School of Veterinary Medicine*): 612 42 Brno 12, Palackého 1–3; f. 1919; 169,377 vols.; Librarian Dr. FRANTIŠEK ŠPIRK; publ. *Acta veterinaria Brno.*

MUSEUMS AND ART GALLERIES

PRAGUE

Hrdličkovo muzeum člověka (*Hrdlička Museum of Anthropology*): Prague 2, Viničná 7; f. 1930; attached to the Faculty of Natural Sciences, Charles University; evolution of man, comparative anatomy, primatology, ontogenetic evolution, racial differences, postmortal body changes, osteotraumatology, pathology, artificial deformations of skull, postmortal casts; Dir. Doc. Dr. CHRUDOŠ TRONÍČEK, C.SC.

Muzeum Aloise Jiráska a Mikoláše Alše (*Alois Jirásek and Mikoláš Aleš Museum*): Prague 6, Liboc, letohrádek Hvězda; f. 1951; contains works and documents of Czech writer A. Jirásek and the Czech painter M. Aleš; library of 10,000 vols.; Dir. JAROSLAV HLÁSEK.

Muzeum hl. m. Prahy (*Museum of the Capital City of Prague*): Prague 8, Sady Jana Švermy 1554; f. 1883; collection of fine art works and items relating to the history of the city; library of 10,749 vols.; Dir. Z. MÍKA; publs. *Acta musei pragensis, Archeologica pragensia* (annually).

Muzeum Klementa Gottwalda (*Klement Gottwald Museum*): Prague 1, Rytířská 29; f. 1954; history of the Czechoslovak Communist Party and of the Czechoslovak Revolutionary Labour Movement; Dir. J. POSPÍŠIL.

Muzeum tělesné výchovy a sportu (*Museum of Physical Training and Sport*): Prague 1, Ujezd 40; f. 1885, re-organized 1953; a department of the National Museum;

collections of documents about the development of physical training and sport; Dir. JAROMÍR KOUBA.

Muzeum V. I. Lenina (*V. I. Lenin Museum*): Prague 1, Hybernská 7; history of International Labour Movement and Leninism; Dir. PhDr. ALEXANDR JEŽEK.

Náprstkovo muzeum asijských, afrických a amerických kultur (*Náprstek Museum of Asian, African and American Cultures*): Prague 1, Betlémské náměstí 1; f. 1862; a dept. of the National Museum; ethnological and archaeological objects, Oriental art; library of 100,000 vols.; Dir. Dr. JANA SOUČKOVÁ; publs. *Annals* (annually), *Papers* (irregular).

Národní galerie (*National Gallery*): Prague 1-Hradčany, Hradčanské námestí 15; f. 1796; Departments of Ancient Art, Modern Art, Drawings and Prints, Oriental Art in various buildings both in and outside Prague; Dir. Prof. Dr. JIŘÍ KOTALÍK.

Národní muzeum (*National Museum*): 115 79 Prague 1, Central Bldg., Tr. Vítězného února 74; f. 1818, present building erected 1891; consists of six institutions: 1. Museum of Natural History (depts of mineralogy and petrography, palaeontology, mycology, botany, entomology, zoology, anthropology and chemical research); 2. Historical Museum (depts of pre-history, history, numismatics, theatre, archives and ethnography) and Museum of Physical Education and Sports); 3. Naprstek Museum of Asian, African and American cultures; 4. Museum Library: *see* Libraries; 5. Museum of Czech Music (instruments, Bedřich Smetana Museum, Antonin Dvořák Museum); 6. Central Office of Museology; Dir. Dr. ADOLF ČEJCHAN, C.SC; publs. *Sborník Národního muzea v Praze*† (*Acta Musei Nationalis Pragae*†), *Časopis Národního muzea*†, *Acta Entomologica*†, *Acta Faunistica*†, *Fontes Archaeologici Pragenses*†, *Muzejní a vlastivědná práce, Metodické listy, Muzejni práce, Numismatické listy*†, *Lynx*†, *Sylvia*.

Národní technické muzeum (*National Technical Museum*): Kostelní 42, Prague 7; f. 1908; permanent exhibition of engineering, transport, mining, metallurgy, cinematography, photography, broadcasting, television, astronomy, building industry, atomic energy, etc.; temporary exhibitions, educational and documentation section; library: *see* Libraries; foreign department; Dir. Dr. JOSEF KUBA, C.SC.; publs. *Sborník Národního technického muzea v Praze, Rozpravy Národního technického muzea, Katalog sbírek Národního technického muzea, Bibliografie a prameny Národního technického muzea, CIMUSET—Informační Bulletin, Národní technické muzeum.*

Památník národního písemnictví na Strahově (*Museum of Czech Literature*): Strahovské nám. 132, Prague 1; f. 1953; exhibition of the development of Czech literature; library of the Strahov monastery containing 900,000 vols.; literary archives containing 4 million objects; Dir. Dr. JIŘÍ SEDLÁČEK; publs. *Strahovská knihovna, Literární archiv.*

Pedagogické muzeum J. A. Komenského (*J. A. Komenský Pedagogical Museum*): 118 00 Prague 1, Valdštejnské nám. 4; documents illustrating the development of Czechoslovak education and the life and work of Comenius; Dir. Doc. Dr. RUDOLF OPATA.

Poštovní muzeum (*Post Museum*): Prague 5, Smíchov, Holečkova ul. 10; documents of the history of the post and stamp collections; Dir. Dr. PAVEL ČTVRTNÍK.

Státní židovské muzeum (*State Jewish Museum*): 110 01 Prague 1, Jáchymova 3; f. 1950; contains collection of silver liturgical objects, synagogue textiles of historic interest, library of ancient books and Hebrew MSS., archives of Bohemian and Moravian Jewish communities, children's drawings from the concentration camp in Terezín/Theresienstadt, collection of paintings, Jewish cemetery of the 15th century and oldest synagogue in gothic style of the 13th century; Dir. Dr. MIROSLAV JAROS; publ. *Judaica Bohemiae*† (2 a year).

Středočeská Galerie v Praze (*Gallery of Central Bohemia in Prague*): Prague 1, Old Town, Husova ul. 19/21; f. 1963; regular exhibitions; permanent exhibition of 14th to 19th century European art in Nelahozeves Manor near Kralupy n. Vetavou; Dir. JOSEF SCHLESINGER.

Uměleckoprůmyslové muzeum (*Museum of Decorative Arts*): Prague 1, Ulice 17 listopadu 2; f. 1885; one of the largest collections of glass in the world; ceramics, porcelain, textiles, furniture, gold and silver work, prints; library of 100,000 vols.; Dir. Dr. DAGMAR HEJDOVÁ.

Vojenské muzeum (*Military Museum*): Prague 3, U. Památníku 2; f. 1918; comprises three permanent exhibitions: 1. development of Czech and Slovak military history from 10th century onwards (Schwarzenberg Palace, Prague 1, Hradčanské nám. 2); 2. development of the Czechoslovak army from 1917 onwards (Prague 3, U. Památníku 2); 3. development of Czechoslovak military and civil air force, development of aircraft production (Prague 9, Kbely Airport); Dir. Dr. M. ŠÁDA.

Zemědělské muzeum (*Museum of Agriculture*): Prague 2, Makarenkova 46; f. 1891; exhibition of agriculture and food industry located in Kačina Castle near Kutná Hora; of forestry, hunting, fishery in Ohrada Castle near České Budejovice and of hunting, horticulture in Lednice Castle near Břeclav; 65,000 photographic archives; library of 74,000 vols.; Dir. Ing. Dr. ZDENĚK KUTTELVAŠER, C.SC.; publs. *Vědecké práce ZM.*† (Scientific Studies), *Acta museorum agriculturae*†, *Prameny historie zemědělství a Lesnictví*† (Sources of Agricultural and Forestry History).

PROVINCES

Alšova Jihočeská galerie (*Aleš South Bohemian Gallery*): Hluboká nad Vltavou; f. 1953; contains collection of Gothic and Baroque art of South Bohemia, 17th-century Flemish and Dutch painting, world ceramics and modern 20th-century Czech art; Dir. BOŘIVOJ LAUDA.

Galéria hlavného mesta Slovenskej socialistickej republiky Bratislavy (*Gallery of the Capital of the Slovak Socialist Republic, Bratislava*): Mirbachov palác, Dibrovovo nám. 11, Bratislava; comprises three exhibitions: Ancient European Art, Primaciálny palác; 18th- to 20th-century Art, Mirbachor palác; Gothic painting and plastic art, Klarisky; library of 5,000 vols.; Dir. PhDr. MILAN JANKOVSKY.

Historické muzeum ve Slavkově (*Slavkov Historical Museum*): 684 11 Slavkov u Brna-zámek; f. 1901; collections from the Napoleonic wars with a special exhibition of the battle of Slavkov (Austerlitz) and of the deserted medieval villages of Moravia; history of Slavkov and environs; memorial hall to Dr. Václav Graf von Kaunitz; Dir. PhDr. PAVEL KOUŘIL.

Jihočeské muzeum České Budejovice (*Museum of South Bohemia*): České Budejovice, Dukelská 2; collections of natural sciences, archaeology, theatre and music, arts and crafts, history, art and literature from the region of South Bohemia; Dir. E. SCHNEIDER; publs. *Jihočeský sborník historický* (Historical Sciences), *Sborník JčM-Přírodní vědy* (Natural Sciences).

Jihomoravské muzeum Znojmo (*Znojmo South Moravian Museum*): Znojmo, Přemyslovců 6; collections of natural sciences and history from South Moravia; installed in castle with 11th-century chapel; collections of ceramics of South Moravia and furniture; Dir. Dr. V. VILDOMEC.

Karlovarské muzeum (*Karlovy Vary Museum*): Karlovy Vary, Zámecký vrch 22; collections of natural sciences, art and industry, history and documents from the history of the Spa Karlovy; Dir. KAMILA PEŠTÁKOVÁ.

Krajské muzeum Východních Čech (*Regional Museum of Eastern Bohemia*): 531 34 Pardubice, Zámek č. 1; f. 1880; natural sciences, history and arts from the Pardubice region; special collections: arms, glass, numismatics; library of 32,000 vols.; Dir. MILAN KOUBEK.

Krajské muzeum v Teplicích (*Teplice Regional Museum*): 415 01 Teplice, 14 Zámecké nám.; f. 1896; collections of natural sciences, archaeology, history, ethnography, art and literature from the region of North-West Bohemia; library of 60,000 vols.; Dir. ROBERT ŠTAFFA; publs. *Zprávy a studie, Monografické studie.*

Krajské vlastivědné muzeum (*Regional Museum*): 771 73 Olomouc, nám. Republiky 5-6; f. 1874; collections of natural sciences, archaeology, history, ethnography and arts; Dir. PhDr. JAROSLAV VÁŇA; publs. *Zprávy*†, *Práce odboru přírodních věd*†, *Prácé odboru společenských věd.*

Moravská galerie v Brně (*Moravian Gallery in Brno*): Brno, Husova 14; f. 1818; collections of historic and modern European pictures, sculptures, graphic art, applied art, oriental art; art library; Dir. JIŘÍ HLUŠIČKA.

Moravské muzeum v Brně (*Moravian Museum in Brno*): Brno 1, nám. 25, února 6; f. 1818 as Museum Franciscеum; comprises sixteen sections, including geology, mineralogy, palaeontology, Karst geomorphology, botany, history, entomology, zoology, genetics, anthropology, archaeology, ethnography, numismatics, music-theatre-, literature-archives, museology; 170 mems.; Dir. Doc. Dr. J. SEJBAL, C.SC.; publs. *Acta Musei Moraviae, Anthropologie, Folia Mendeliana, Ethnographica, Numismatica Moravica,* monographs.

Muzeum J. A. Komenského v Uherském Brodě (*Uherský Brod Comenius Museum*): 688 12 Uherský Brod, ul. Přemysla Otakara II 38/39; f. 1894; Dir. ZDENĚK VRBA; exhibition of the life and work of Comenius, and collections of ethnography, archaeology and history; publ. *Studia Comeniana et historica.*

Mestské muzeum v Bratislave (*Bratislava Municipal Museum*): 80100 Bratislava, Primaciálny palác-Stará Radnica; f. 1868; collections of prehistoric weapons, sculpture, ceramics, pharmaceutical equipment, furniture, costumes, instruments of medieval justice, etc., records of guilds and viniculture; rooms devoted to writer Janko Jesenský and composer Johan Nepomuk Hummel; Folk Museum in Vajnory; Dir. ŠIMON JANČO; publ. *Acta.*

Muzeum města Brna (*Brno Municipal Museum*): Brno, Hrad 1; f. 1904; Dir. O. TOMAN.

Muzeum husitského revolučního hnutí (*Museum of the Hussite Revolutionary Movement*): Tábor, Žižkovo nám. 1; f. 1878; district museum specializing in the Hussite movement and traditions; library of 32,000 vols.; Dir. PhDr. MILOŠ DRDA; publ. *Husitský Tábor*† (annually).

Muzeum skla (*Glass Museum*): Harrachov; exhibits include blown glass from one of the oldest Czechoslovak glass-works, founded in 1712, and other unique blown glass examples; also modern exhibits.

Muzeum skla a bižuterie (*Museum of Glass and Jewellery*): Jablonec nad Nisou, Jiráskova 4; f. 1950; exhibition of glass products of all kinds illustrating the development of Czech glass-making and of Jablonec jewellery; Dir. Ing. LUBOMÍR ŠKORPÍK; publ. *Ars vitraria.*

Muzeum ukrajinskej kultúry (*Museum of Ukrainian Culture*): Svidník, Leninova 258; Dir. Dr. J. ČABIŇÁK.

Muzeum Vysočiny Jihlava (*Jihlava Regional Museum*): Jihlava, nám. Míru 57; collections of zoology, archaeology, history, botany and mineralogy-petrography; connected to Museums in Polná, Telč and Roštejn castle; library of 20,000 vols.; Dir. Dr. OLDŘICH TAUBR.

Národopisné muzeum horního Pojizeří (*Ethnographical Museum of Pojizeří*): Železný Brod; f. 1870; ethnographic collection, glass products illustrating the development of local glass-making; library of 205 vols.; Dir. J. JELÍNKOVÁ.

Oblastní muzeum jihovýchodní Moravy v Gottwaldově (*Regional Museum of South-Eastern Moravia in Gottwaldov*): Gottwaldov, Soudní 1; collections of natural sciences, archaeology, ethnography, history; Dir. MILAN SMÝKAL; publs. *Zprávy OMG,* catalogues, etc.

Památník Terezín (*Terezín Memorial*): Malá pevnost Terezín; documents and other material on the German concentration camp and the Jewish ghetto at Terezín during the Second World War; Dir. VÁCLAV NOVÁK.

Severočeská galerie výtvarného umění (*North Bohemian Gallery of Fine Arts*): Michalská 7, Litoměřice; f. 1956; 13th–20th century painting and sculpture, special collections of Roman, Gothic and 13th–16th century North-West Bohemian paintings and sculptures; special collections of naive paintings and sculptures; library of 9,000 vols.; Dir. BOHUMIL HORČIC.

Severočeské muzeum v Liberci (*Liberec North Bohemian Museum*): Liberec, Leninova 11; historical and contemporary collection of European and Bohemian glass and industrial arts; Dir. BERTA VELEŠÍKOVÁ.

Slezské muzeum (*Silesian Museum*): 746 46 Opava, Tyršova 1; f. 1814; collections of natural sciences, archaeology, history, ethnography, musicology, literature, theatre, colour photography, dendrology, applied arts and documents from the Silesian region; arboretum at Nový Dvůr; Dir. Dr. VILÉM PLAČEK; publs. *Index Seminum* (annually), *Vlastivědné listy Severomoravského kraje* (2 a year), *Časopis Slezského muzea* (natural sciences and historical sciences series, 3 a year).

Slovenská národná galéria (*Slovak National Gallery*): Bratislava, Rázusovo nábrežie 2; f. 1948; paintings, sculpture, prints, drawings, applied art, facsimiles; scientific library of 50,000 vols.; Dir. Doc. PhDr. ŠTEFAN MRUŠKOVIČ, C.SC.

Slovenské bánske múzeum (*Slovak Mining Museum*): 969 00 Banská Štiavnica; f. 1927; library of 14,430 vols.; Dir. Ing. MILAN HOCK; publs. *Zborník SBM*† (bulletin).

Slovenské národné múzeum (*Slovak National Museum*): 885 36 Bratislava, Vajanského nábrežie 2; f. 1924; archaeology, history, natural science, museology; Dir. PhDr. ALOJZ HABOVŠTIAK; publs. *Zborník*† (yearbook), *Fontes*† (various publs. on history, archaeology, natural science), *Annotationes Zoologicae et Botanicae*†, etc.

Slovenské národné múzeum—Etnografický ústav (*Slovak National Museum—Ethnographical Institute*): 036 80 Martin; f. 1893; ethnographic section; 114,354 objects; library of 38,071 vols.; Dir. IGOR KRIŠTEK, C.SC.; publs. *Zborník, Fontes.*

Technické muzeum Tatra Kopřivnice (*Tatra Technical Motor Car Museum*): 742 21 Kopřivnice; f. 1947; special museum of motor cars; Dir. KAREL ROSENKRANZ.

Valašské muzeum v přírodě (*Wallachian Open-air Museum*): Rožnov pod Radhoštěm; f. 1925; open-air museum in the form of village with 60 original buildings; library of 8,500 vols.; Dir. JAROSLAV ŠTIKA.

Východoslovenské muzeum (*Museum of Eastern Slovakia*): 04136 Košice, Leninova ul. 27; f. 1872; collections and exhibitions of history, history of art, zoology, geology, archaeology and ethnography; library of 31,000 vols.; Dir. VILIAM ŠULC; publs. *Historica Carpatica*†, *Zborník*† (annually).

Západočeská galerie v Plzni (*West Bohemian Gallery*): Pilsen, Kopeckého sady 2; gallery of national art, pictures and sculptures from XIVth century to the present time; Dir. O. KUBA.

Západočeské muzeum v Plzni (*West Bohemian Museum*): Pilsen, Kopeckého sady 2; depts. of archaeology, the middle ages, recent history, natural history, applied art, ethnography and the history of brewing in West Bohemia; Dir. PhDr. J. MELŠA.

UNIVERSITIES

UNIVERZITA KOMENSKÉHO BRATISLAVA
(Comenius University of Bratislava)

BRATISLAVA,
ŠAFÁRIKOVO NÁMESTIE 6
Telephone: 580-41.
Founded 1919.

State control; Language of instruction: Slovak; Academic year: September to January, February to June.

Rector: Prof. PhDr. J. KVASNIČKA, C.SC.

Pro-Rectors: Prof. PhDr. S. CAMBEL, DR.SC., Prof. RNDr. V. SUTORIS, C.SC., Prof. MUDr. J. ŠTEFANOVIČ, C.SC., Doc. RNDr. O. ŠTEPANOVIČOVÁ, C.SC., Doc. JUDr. R. TRELLA, C.SC.

Questor: JUDr. J. BURAJ.

Number of teachers: 2,032.

Number of students: 18,100.

Publications: Numerous faculty publications.

DEANS:

Faculty of Law: Prof. JUDr. J. FILO, C.SC.
Faculty of Medicine at Bratislava: Prof. MUDr. G. ČATÁR, D.SC.
Faculty of Medicine at Martin: Prof. MUDr. O. HAL'ÁK, C.SC.
Faculty of Philosophy and Arts: Prof. PhDr. R. ŠTEPANOVIČ, C.SC.
Faculty of Natural Sciences: Prof. RNDr. S. USAČEV, C.SC.
Faculty of Pharmaceutics: Prof. RNDr. PhMr. M. MANDÁK, C.SC.
Faculty of Physical Education and Sport: Prof. PhDr. I. MACÁK, D.SC.
Teacher Training College at Trnava: Doc. PhDr. J. VIDA, C.SC.

PROFESSORS:

Faculty of Law:
BAVORSKÝ, J., Civil Law
CHORVÁT, J., Political Economy
CÚTH, J., International Law
FILO, J., Labour Law
HUSÁR, E., Penal Law
LACO, K., Constitutional Law
MATOUŠEK, S., Constitutional Law
PLANK, K., Civil Law
REBRO, K., Roman Law
SCHUBERT, L., Penal Law
SLOVINSKÝ, A., Financial Law
TOMKO, J., International Law

Faculty of Medicine:
ANDRIK, P., Stomatology
BARTKO, D., Neurology
BROZMAN, M., Pathological Anatomy
BRUCHÁČ, D., Obstetrics and Gynaecology
ČATÁR, G., Parasitology
ČERNÁČEK, J., Neurology
ČIERNY, G., Anatomy
CHMEL, L., Dermatology
DEMJÉN, Š., Operative Plastic Surgery
GUENSBERGER, E., Psychiatry
HALMOŠ, J., Stomatology
HANDZO, P., Physical Medicine
HAVIAR, V., Internal Medicine
HEGYI, E., Dermatology
HENSEL, J., Balneology
HOREČNÝ, K., Paediatrics
HRÚZIK, J., Infectious Medicine
HUDCOVIČ, A., Obstetrics and Gynaecology
HURAJ, E., Orthopaedics
KAPELLER, K., Anatomy
KOKAVEC, M., Judicial Medicine
KOLESÁR, J., Balneology
KOSTOLNÝ, I., Surgery
KUBIS, J., Chemistry
KUKURA, J., Hygiene
MICHALIČKOVÁ, J., Paediatrics
NÁDVORNÍK, P., Neurosurgery
NIEDERLAND, R., Biochemistry
NOSÁL, M., Occupational Diseases
ONDREJIČKA, M., Internal Medicine
PONT'UCH, A., Obstetrics and Gynaecology
REHÁK, A., Dermatology
ŠIŠKA, K., Surgery
ŠTEFANOVIČ, J., Microbiology
ŠUSTER, J., Ophthalmology
TURSKÝ, T., Biochemistry
VELGOS, Š., Stomatology
VRŠANSKÝ, V., General Biology
ZVARA, V., Urology

Faculty of Philosophy and Arts:
BORÍSEK, J., Journalism
BUTVIN, J., Czechoslovak History
CAMBEL, S., History
CSANDA, A., Hungarian Language
FILKORN, V., Logic
GAŠPARÍK, M., Slovak Language
GOSIOROVSKÝ, M., History
HANZEL, L., Philosophy
HRUŠOVSKÝ, I., Philosophy
KOTOČ, J., Pedagogics
KRESÁNEK, J., Music
MÁTEJ, J., Pedagogy
MICHALIDES, P., History of Art
NOVOTNÝ, B., Prehistory
OKÁL, M., Classical Philology
ONDRUŠ, P., Slovak Language
ONDRUŠ, Š., Slovak Language
PARDEL, T., Psychology
PASIAR, Š., Librarianship
PAULÍNY, E., Slovak Language and Literature
PAVLÍK, O., Pedagogy
PIŠÚT, M., History of Czech and Slovak Literature
RUTTKAY, F., Journalism
SCHWANZER, V., German Language
ŠKULTÉTY, J., Romance Philology
ŠPAŇÁR, J., Latin
STAVROVSKÝ, E., History
SÝKORA, E., Pedagogy
ŠTEPANOVIĆ, R., Pedagogy
ŠTEVČEK, J., Slovak Language
TERRAY, E., German Language

Faculty of Natural Sciences:
BÖHMER, M., Geology
BRILLA, J., Mathematics
CAMBEL, B., Geochemistry
DUBOVSKÝ, J., Genetics
GOREK, A., Geology
GREGUŠ, M., Mathematics
HUT'A, A., Mathematics
IVANIČKA, K., Economic Geography
KAMENICKÝ, J., Mineralogy and Petrography
KODĚRA, M., Mineralogy
KOLIBIAR, M., Mathematics
KONČEK, M., Meteorology
KORBEL, L., Zoology
KOSMÁK, L., Mathematics
KRIST, E., Mineralogy
LUKÁČ, RUDOLF, Mineralogy and Petrography
LUKNIŠ, M., Physical Geography
MASÁR, J., Inorganic Chemistry
MATULA, M., Geology
MIŠÍK, M., Geology
PASTÝRIK, M., Physiology of Plants
PETROV, I., Agrobiology
PLESNÍK, P., Geography
ŠALÁT, M., Mathematics
STANKOVIANSKÝ, S., Analytical Chemistry
SUTORIS, V., Organic Chemistry
ŠVAGROVSKÝ, J., Palaeontology
ŠVEC, M., Mathematics
ŤAVODA, O., Geology
TOMLAIN, J., Meteorology
TREINDL, L., Physical Chemistry
USAČEV, S., Physics
VARČEK, C., Geology
VEIS, Š., Physics

Faculty of Pharmaceutics:
CHALABALA, M., Galenic Pharmacy
JINDRA, A., Pharmaceutical Botany
KRASNEC, L., Organic Chemistry
MAJER, J., Analytical Chemistry
MANDÁK, M., Galenic Pharmacy
TOMKO, J., Pharmacognosy

Faculty of Physical Education and Sport:
ČERNUŠÁK, V., Physical Culture
KILÁR, L., Physical Culture
KUCHEN, A., Physical Culture
MACÁK, I., Psychology, Pedagogy and History of Physical Education
ROVNÝ, M., Theory and Methodology of Play
STRÁŇAI, K., Physical Culture
SÝKORA, F., Physical Culture

Teachers' Training College at Trnava:
BRT'KA, J., Education
GREGOREC, J., Slovak Language
STOJKA, O., Education

Faculty of Medicine at Martin:
GALANDA, V., Paediatrics
HALÁK, O., Internal Medicine
KORPÁŠ, J., Experimental Pathology
KUKURA, A., Surgery
LÁNYI, A., Radiology
MATULAY, K., Neurology
MÉZEŠ, V., Biochemistry
PÉČ, J., Urology

Department of Marxism-Leninism:
BOGÁR, M., Scientific Communism
JIRGES, M., Political Economy
KVASNIČKA, J., Scientific Communism
PLEVA, J., Czechoslovak History
TOPOLSKÝ, M., Philosophy

UNIVERZITA J. E. PURKYNĚ
(Purkyně University)

601 77 BRNO, A. NOVÁKA 1

Telephone: 59711.

Founded 1919.

State control; Language of instruction: Czech; Academic year: October to July.

Rector: Prof. Dr. VOJTĚCH KUBÁČEK.
Prof. Dr. JAROSLAV SÝKORA.

Vice-Rectors: Prof. Dr. FRANTIŠEK HEJL, Prof. Dr. MILOSLAV MÁŠA, Prof. Dr. JAROSLAV SÝKORA, Prof. Dr. JINDŘICH ŠTELCL.

Registrar: JUDr. Ing. ANTONÍN BRZOBOHATÝ.

Library of *c.* 1,000,000 vols.

Number of teachers: 911.

Number of students: 10,600.

Publications: *Universitas, Scripta Medica, Archivum mathematicum, Scripta naturalia, Folia Fac. Scientarium Naturalium, Sborník prací filozofické fakulty, Sborník prací pedagogické fakulty, Sborník prací právnické fakulty, Spisy filozofické fakulty, Spisy právnické fakulty, Spisy pedagogické fakulty, Spisy lékařské fakulty.*

DEANS:

Faculty of Philosophy: Prof. Dr. BEDŘICH ŠINDELÁŘ.
Faculty of Natural Sciences: Prof. Dr. KAREL HODÁK.
Faculty of Law: Prof. Dr. JOSEF MACUR.
Faculty of Medicine: Prof. Dr. BOHUMIL BEDNAŘÍK.
Faculty of Pedagogics: Doc. Dr. JAROSLAV HADAČ.
Institute of Marxism-Leninism: Prof. Dr. W. SMRČKA.

UNIVERZITA KARLOVA
(Charles University)

116 36 PRAGUE 1, OVOCNY TRH 5

Telephone: 228 441.

Founded 1348.

State control; Language of instruction: Czech; Academic year: October to January, February to September.

Rector: Prof. Dr. Z. ČEŠKA, C.SC.

Vice-Rectors: Prof. Dr. V. PROSSER, Prof. Dr. V. RZOUNEK, Prof. Dr. A. SEHR, Prof. Dr. J. SKOŘEPA, Prof. Dr. B. SÝKORA, DR.SC., Prof. L. NOVOTNÝ, C.SC.

Questor: Dr. Z. JEZERSKÝ.

Library: *see* Libraries.

Number of teachers: 2,764.

Number of students: 22,558.

Publications: *Acta Universitatis Carolinae*†—series: *Mathematica et Physica, Biologica, Geologica, Geographica, Oeconomica, Medica, Gymnica, Philosophica et Historica, Iuridica, Philologica, Historia Universitatis Carolinae Pragensis, Prague Bulletin of Mathematical Linguistics*†, *Psychologie v ekonomické praxi*† (quarterly).

DEANS:

Faculty of Mathematics and Physics: Prof. Dr. K. VACEK, DR.SC.
Faculty of Sciences: Prof. Dr. F. ČECH, C.SC.
Faculty of Medicine: Prof. Dr. V. BALAŠ.
Faculty of Medicine, Branch in Plzeň: Prof. Dr. F. MACKŮ.
Faculty of Medicine in Hradec Králové: Prof. P. NAVRÁTIL.
Faculty of Paediatrics: Prof. J. HOUŠTĚK.
Faculty of Medical Hygiene: Prof. Dr. V. VÍŠEK.
Faculty of Philosophy: Prof. V. RÁB.
Faculty of Law: Prof. Dr. V. DELONG.
Faculty of Journalism: Prof. Dr. V. HUDEC.
Faculty of Physical Training and Sport: Prof. Dr. V. KOSTKA.
Faculty of Education: Doc. Dr. J. FIŠER.
Faculty of Pharmacy in Hradec Králové: Prof. Dr. J. KVĚTINA.
Institute of Marxism-Leninism: Prof. L. NOVOTNÝ.

PROFESSORS:

Faculty of Law:
ČERVINKA, A., Economics
ČEŠKA, Z., Civil Judicial Procedure
DELONG, V., Administrative Law
FÁBRY, V., Agricultural Co-operative Law
KINCL, J., History of State and Law
KNAPPOVÁ, M., Civil Law
KUČERA, E., Theory of State and Law
LUKEŠ, Z., Administrative Law
PJEŠČAK, J., Criminal Law
PLUNDR, O., Civil Judicial Procedure
RŮŽEK, A., Criminal Law
VANĚČEK, V., Legal History
ZDOBINSKÝ, S., Constitutional Law

Faculty of Medicine:
BALAŠ, V., Surgery
BEDNÁŘ, B., Pathological Anatomy
BLAŽEK, O., Roentgenology and Radiology
BOROVANSKÝ, V., Stomatology
CHARVÁT, J., Internal Medicine
ČIHÁK, R., Anatomy
DIENSTBIER, Z., Nuclear Medicine
DOBIÁŠ, J., Psychiatry
DOBIÁŠ, J., Pathological Anatomy
DONNER, L., Internal Medicine
FUČÍK, M., Internal Medicine
HERFORT, K., Internal Medicine
HEŘMANSKÝ, F., Internal Medicine
HOMOLKA, J., Medical Chemistry
HRADEC, E., Surgery
JIRÁSEK, L., Dermatology
JIROUT, J., Neurology
KÁBRT, J., Latin
KLIKA, E., Histology and Embryology
KOBILKOVÁ, J., Obstetrics and Gynaecology
KONOPÍK, J., Dermatology
KOUBA, K., Infectious Diseases
LICHTENBERG, J., Surgery
LOJDA, Z., Pathological Anatomy
MACÚCH, P., Hygiene
PACOVSKÝ, V., Internal Medicine
PAPEŽ, L., Obstetrics and Gynaecology
RABOCH, J., Internal Medicine
REINIŠ, Z., Cardiology
RIPKA, O., Internal Medicine
RUBÍN, A., Internal Medicine
SCHREIBER, V., Internal Medicine
SEDLÁČEK, K., Phonology
SKOŘEPA, J., Internal Medicine
ŠTARK, O., Medical Biology
ŠTÁVA, Z., Dermatology
ŠTORK, A., Pathology and Therapy of Internal Diseases
ŠULA, J., Oncology
TESAŘ, J., Forensic Medicine
TOMAN, J., Stomatology
TRÁVNÍČEK, T., Physiology
URBAN, F., Stomatology
VACEK, Zd., Histology and Embryology
VANĚČEK, F., Pathology
VENCOVSKÝ, E., Psychiatry
VYMAZAL, J., Neurology
WENKE, M., Pharmacology

Faculty of Paediatrics:
GREGOR, O., Internal Medicine
HAVLÍK, J., Internal Medicine
HLOUŠKOVÁ, Z., Paediatrics
HOUŠTĚK, J., Paediatrics
HRODEK, O., Paediatrics
KOMÍNEK, J., Surgery
KOTÁSEK, A., Gynaecology and Obstetrics
LESNÝ, I., Paediatrics
LOMÍČKOVÁ, H., Ophthalmology
MÁČEK, M., Physiotherapy
NAHODIL, V., Pathology and Surgery
SVATÝ, J., Internal Medicine
SVOBODA, Z., Internal Medicine
VANEČEK, J., Pharmacology

Faculty of Medical Hygiene:
BÍLEK, V., Medical Organization
CHLÁDEK, V., Oto-rhino-laryngology
FÁTA, M., Plastic Surgery
HÁJEK, S., Forensic Medicine
HANZLÍČEK, L., Psychiatry
JANDA, F., Hygiene
PROKOPEC, J., Nuclear Medicine
PUZANOVÁ, L., Anatomy
SEHR, A., Roentgenology and Radiology
ŠPAČEK, B., Surgery
STÝBLOVÁ, V., Neurology
ŠVESTKA, B., Professional Medicine
SYMON, K., Hygiene
VÍŠEK, V., Internal Medicine

Faculty of Medicine in Plzen:
CHUDÁČEK, Z., Radiology
KARLÍČEK, V., Pathology and Therapy of Internal Diseases
KOS, J., Anatomy
LUKEŠ, J., Paediatrics
MACKŮ, F., Gynaecology
PALISA, V., Infectious Diseases
PODZIMEK, A., Surgery
ŠEDIVEC, V., Psychiatry
SLABÝ, O., Histology and Embryology
SOBOTKA, P., Pathological Physiology
VANĚK, J., Pathological Anatomy

Faculty of Medicine in Hradec Kralové:
KOUŘÍLEK, J., Political Economy
NAVRÁTIL, P., Urology
PEREGRIN, J., Pathological Physiology
PETR, R., Surgery
PLACHÝ, V., Paediatrics
PROCHÁZKA, J., Surgery
ŘEHÁK, S., Ophthalmology
STEINHART, L., Radiology
ŠVÁB, J., Surgery
TUŠL, M., Hygiene
VÁCHA, K., Gynaecology and Obstetrics

Faculty of Sciences:
BENDOVÁ, O., Microbiology
ČECH, F., Mineralogy and Petrography
ČÍHALÍK, J., Analytical Chemistry
DOLEŽAL, Analytical Chemistry
GRUNTORÁD, J., Geophysics
HÄUFLER, V., Economic Geography
HENDRYCH, R., Botany
HRADÍLEK, L., Applied Geophysics
KALOUSEK, M., Physical Chemistry
KONTA, J., Petrography
MÍSAŘ, Z., Geology
POKORNÝ, V., Palaeontology
POUBA, Z., Geology and Mineralogy
ROST, R., Mineralogy and Petrography
RYŠAVÝ, B., Parasitology
SEIFERT, J., Soil Biology
SLÁDEČEK, F., Zoology
ŠPINAR, Z., Palaeontology
STANĚK, J., Organic Chemistry
VANĚČEK, M., Geology
VYSTRČIL, A., Organic Chemistry
ZÝKA, J., Analytical Chemistry

Faculty of Philosophy:
ANGELIS, K., Pedagogy
BARNET, V., Russian Language
BĚLIČ, O., Spanish Studies
BRŮŽEK, M., Social Sciences
BURIÁNEK, F., Modern Czech Literature
ČERNÝ, F., History of Czech Theatre
CIPRO, M., Pedagogy
FISCHER, J., French Literature
HÁJEK, J., Literary Criticism
HAUSENBLAS, K., Czech Language
HOŠEK, R., Classical Philology
JEDLIČKA, A., Czech Language
KOUŘIL, M., Theory of the Theatre
KRÁL, V., History
KŘÍSTEK, V., Czech Language
KRPATA, M., Scientific Communism
LINHART, J., Psychology
PAROLEK, R., Russian Literature
PETRÁČEK, K., Philology
POLDAUF, I., English Philology
POLIŠENSKÝ, J., Ethnography
RÁB, V., Social Sciences
ROMPORTL, M., Phonetics
RZOUNEK, V., Czech Literature
ŠABRŠULA, J., French Language
SOMMER, V., History of Music
SEDLÁŘ, R., Pedagogy
SYLLABA, T., Philosophy
URBAN, Z., Slavistics
VOLEK, J., Aesthetics

Faculty of Mathematics and Physics:
DRBOHLAV, K., Mathematics
FABIAN, F. Applied Mathematics
KLIER, E., Experimental Physics
MAREK, I., Mathematics
NOŽIČKA, F., Mathematics
PROSSER, V., Experimental Physics
STŘÍBRNÝ, Z., Mathematical Linguistics
UTEHLA, I., Theoretical Physics
VACEK, K., Experimental Physics
VALENTA, L., Theoretical Physics
VANÝSEK, V., Astrophysics
ZÁTOPEK, A., Geophysics

Faculty of Education:
BUREŠ, J., Art Education
FIŠER, J., Pedagogy
KLÍMOVÁ, M., Pedagogy
KLÍMA, A., History
KOŘÍNEK, M., Education
KRAEMER, E., Geometry
KUBÍK, M., Russian
MUSIL, Z., Art
PLCH, J., Theory of Czech Literature Teaching

Faculty of Journalism:
BARTOŠ, B., Theory and Practice of Journalism
HLADKÝ, M., Publicity
HUDEC, V., Theory of Journalism
TECHNIK, A., Theory and History of Journalism

Faculty of Physical Education and Sport:
BOSÁK E., Theory and Method of Exercises
ČELIKOVSKÝ, S., Physical Training
FLEISCHMANN, J., Anatomy
KOBRLE, J., Para-military Physical Training
KOSTKA, V., Theory and Didactics
SELIGER, V., Physiology
SÝKORA, B., Theory of Instruction
VANĚK, M., Psychology

Faculty of Pharmacy in Hradec Kralové:
JOKL, V., Chemistry
KVĚTINA, J., Pharmacology

Institute of Marxism-Leninism:
KLUSÁKOVÁ, Z., Political Economy
NOVOTNÝ, L., Political Economy
REINER, J., Scientific Communism
SOUKUPOVÁ, D., Political Economy

UNIVERZITA PALACKÉHO V OLOMOUCI
(Palacký University)

771 47 OLOMOUC, KŘÍŽKOVSKÉHO 10

Telephone: 22441.

Founded 1576, re-opened 1946.

State control; Language of instruction: Czech; Academic year: October to July.

Rector: Prof. MUDr. FRANTIŠEK GAZÁREK, C.SC.

Pro-Rectors: Prof. MUDr. JIŘÍ HARTL, DR.SC., Prof. RNDr. MIROSLAV LAITOCH, C.SC., PhDr. JAROSLAV ZEZULA, C.SC., Doc. Dr. MILAN GRÉGR.

Administrative Officer: Dr. FRANTIŠEK KRAVEC.

Number of students: 7,000.

Publication: *Acta Universitatis Palackianae* (quarterly).

DEANS:

Faculty of Philosophy: Prof. PhDr. JAN NAVRÁTIL, C.SC.
Faculty of Natural Sciences: Prof. Dr. LADISLAV SEDLÁČEK.
Faculty of Medicine: Prof. MUDr. VÁCLAV ŠVEC, C.SC.
Faculty of Pedagogics: Prof. RNDr. JOSEF KLEMENTA, C.SC.

UNIVERZITA PAVLA JOZEFA ŠAFÁRIKA
(Šafárik University)

040 00 KOŠICE, ŠROBÁROVA 57

Telephone: 22610.

Founded 1959.

State control; Language of instruction: Slovak; Academic year: October to July.

Rector: Prof. Ing. MICHAL BARAN.

Pro-Rectors: Prof. Dr. IVAN BAJCURA, Prof. Dr. MICHAL DANILÁK, Prof. Dr. VLADIMÍR DRAHOVSKÝ, Doc. Ing. SLAVOMÍR CHALUPKA.

Registrar: Dr. ŠTEFAN MOŠON.

Number of students: 7,100.

DEANS:

Faculty of Philosophy: Prof. Dr. MIKULÁŠ ŠTEC.
Faculty of Natural Sciences: Prof. Dr. JURAJ DANIEL-SZABÓ.
Faculty of Law: Asst. Prof. Dr. JOZEF SUCHOŽA.
Faculty of Medicine: Prof. Dr. JOZEF LUKÁČI.
Faculty of Pedagogics: Asst. Prof. Dr. ONDREJ STREČKO.

TECHNICAL UNIVERSITIES AND COLLEGES

ČESKÉ VYSOKÉ UČENÍ TECHNICKÉ V PRAZE
(Technical University of Prague)

PRAGUE 6, ZIKOVA 4

Founded 1707; reorganized 1806, 1863, 1920, 1960.

State control; Language of instruction: Czech; Academic year: September to June.

Rector: Prof. Ing. J. KLÍMA.

Vice-Rectors: Prof. Ing. V. PIRKL, Prof. Ing. J. VLADAŘ, Prof. Ing. Arch. E. KOVAŘÍK, Prof. Ing. Z. CAHA, Doc. Ing. J. PECHAR, Prof. S. JÄGERMANN.

Chief Administrative Officer: Dr. V. LUHAN.

Number of teachers: 1,500.
Number of students: 13,000.

Publication *Acta Polytechnica-Práce ČVUT v Praze.*

DEANS:

Faculty of Civil Engineering: Prof. Ing. Dr. M. HOLÝ, D.SC.
Faculty of Mechanical Engineering: Prof. Ing. J. KAMARÁD, C.SC.
Faculty of Electrical Engineering: Prof. Ing. Z. KOTEK, C.SC.
Faculty of Nuclear Physics: Doc. Ing. I. ŠTOLL, C.SC.
Faculty of Architecture: Prof. Ing. Arch. J. SEDLÁČEK, C.SC.

SLOVENSKÁ VYSOKÁ ŠKOLA TECHNICKÁ BRATISLAVA
(Slovak Technical University in Bratislava)

880 43 BRATISLAVA, GOTTWALDOVO NÁM. 17

Telephone: 566-21.

Founded 1938.

State control; Language of instruction: Slovak; Academic year: September to July.

Rector: Prof. Ing. A. BLAŽEJ, DR.SC.

Pro-Rectors: Prof. Ing. B. BUŠOVÁ, C.SC., Prof. Ing. J. SOUČEK, C.SC., Prof. Ing. A. SUCHÁNEK, C.SC., Doc. Ing. J. HULLA, C.SC., Doc. Ing. M. HUCL, C.SC., DOC. Ing. G. ONDREJOVIČ, C.SC.

Chief Administrative Officer: JUDr. J. VALENTOVIČ.

Number of teachers: 1,400.
Number of students: 17,000.

Publication: *Revue Technika.*

DEANS:

Faculty of Electrical Engineering: Prof. Ing. L. HRUŠKOVIČ, C.SC.

Faculty of Architecture: Prof. Ing. D. MAJZLÍK, C.SC.

Faculty of Chemical Engineering: Prof. Ing. A. LODES, C.SC.

Faculty of Civil Engineering: Prof. Ing. M. BIELEK, DR.SC.

Faculty of Mechanical Engineering: Prof. Ing. S. LABUZA, DR.SC.

VYSOKÁ ŠKOLA BÁŇSKÁ
(State College of Mining and Metallurgy)

OSTRAVA—PORUBA, TŘÍDA VÍTEZNÉHO ÚNORA, 708 33

Telephone: 448560-69.

Founded 1716.

Rector: Prof. RNDr. O. HAJKR, DR.SC.

Pro-Rectors: Prof. Ing. HORYMÍR SRP, Doc. Ing. ALEŠ MUČKA, Doc. Ing. LUMÍR KUCHAŘ, Prof. Ing. STANISLAV SLOVÁK.

Registrar: Ing. VALERIAN LUKSZA.

Librarian: JIŘINA ZLÁ.

Number of teachers: 461.
Number of students: 6,200.

Publication: *Sborník vědeckých prací VSB.*

DEANS:

Faculty of Mining and Geology: Prof. Ing. LUBOMÍR ŠIŠKA, DR.SC.

Faculty of Metallurgy: Prof. Ing. KAREL MAZANEC, DR.SC.

Faculty of Mechanical and Electrical Engineering: Doc. Ing. VLADIMÍR PODHORNÝ.

Faculty of Economics: Prof. Judr. MILOŠ SVOBODA.

VYSOKÁ ŠKOLA CHEMICKOTECHNOLOGICKÁ V PRAZE
(Prague Institute of Chemical Technology)

166 28 PRAGUE 6, SUCHBÁTAROVA 5

Telephone: 332.

Telex: 122744.

Founded 1807.

State control; Language of instruction: Czech; Academic year: September to July.

Rector: Prof. JIŘÍ MOSTECKÝ, M.SC., PH.D., D.SC.

Pro-Rectors: Prof. VÁCLAV DĚDEK, M.SC., PH.D., Prof. JAROSLAV EGER, M.SC., PH.D., Prof. JAROSLAV KRÁLÍČEK, M.SC., PH.D., Prof. PETR GRAU, PH.D., D.SC.

Registrar: Dr. JAN MRÁZEK.

Librarian: Dr. KVĚTUŠE SGALLOVÁ.

Library of 225,000 vols.

Number of teachers: 400.
Number of students: 3,900.

Publication: *Sborník.*

DEANS:

Faculty of Chemical Technology: Assoc. Prof. JOSEF MATOUŠEK, M.SC., PH.D.

Faculty of Fuel and Water Technology: Assoc. Prof. JOSEF PELIKÁN, M.SC., PH.D.

Faculty of Food and Biochemical Technology: Prof. JIŘÍ DAVÍDEK, M.SC., PH.D., D.SC.

Faculty of Chemical Engineering: Assoc. Prof. SVATOPLUK VALENTA, M.SC., PH.D.

PROFESSORS:

ADÁMKOVÁ, H., Political Economics
BRETSCHNEIDER, R., Chemistry and Technology of Saccharides
ČELEDA, J., Radiochemistry
ČERNÝ, Č., Physical Chemistry
DAVÍDEK, J., Food Chemistry and Technology
DĚDEK, V., Organic Chemistry
DOLEŽÁLEK, J., Milk and Fat Technology
EGER, J., Political Economics
ELIÁŠEK, J., Power Engineering
FERLES, M., Organic Chemistry
GRAU, P., Water Technology and Environmental Engineering
GRÉGR, V., Fermentation Chemistry and Technology
HÁJEK, B., Inorganic Chemistry
HAMPL, J., Chemistry and Technology of Saccharides.
HOLUB, R., Physical Chemistry
HOLZBECHER, Z., Analytical Chemistry
HORÁK, J., Organic Technology
JANÍČEK, G., Food Chemistry and Technology
KLEIN, S., Food Preservation and Meat Technology
KRÁLÍČEK, J., Polymer Technology
KUBÍČEK, L., Chemical Technology of Metals
KUTHAN, J., Organic Chemistry
KYZLINK, V., Food Preservation and Meat Technology
MACÁK, J., Coke and Gas Technology
MADĚRA, V., Water Technology
MOSTECKÝ, J., Petroleum Technology and Petrochemistry
MUSIL, J., Economics and Management of the Chemical Industry
PICK, J., Physical Chemistry
RŮŽIČKA, V., Organic Technology
SKŘIVÁNEK, J., Chemical Engineering
STANĚK, J., Technology of Silicates
STEIDL, H., Chemical Engineering
ŠEŠULKA, V., Fuel Technology
VALENTA, S., Technical Physics and Electrical Engineering
VOSOLSOBĚ, J., Inorganic Technology

VYSOKÁ ŠKOLA CHEMICKO-TECHNOLOGICKÁ V PARDUBICÍCH
(College of Chemical Technology in Pardubice)

PARDUBICE, LENINOVO NÁM 565

Telephone: 25111.

Founded 1950.

Rector: Prof. Ing. FRANTIŠEK LÉBR, C.SC.

Pro-Rectors: Doc. Ing. VLADIMÍR LIŠKA, C.SC., Doc. Ing. STANISLAV KOLDA, C.SC., Prof. Ing. JAROSLAV POSKOČIL, C.SC.

Administrative Officer: Dr. ZDENĚK BENEŠ.

Library: 104,000 vols.

Number of teachers: 156.
Number of students: 1,830.

Publication: *Scientific Papers*† (twice yearly).

HEADS OF DEPARTMENTS:

Mathematics: Doc. Ing. S. KOLDA, C.SC.

Physics: Prof. Ing. Dr. VÁCLAV HUSA, DR.SC.

General and Inorganic Chemistry: Prof. Ing. Dr. J. KLIKORKA.

Organic Chemistry: Prof. Ing. Dr. M. VEČEŘA, DR. SC.

Analytical Chemistry: Doc. Ing. J. CHURÁČEK, C.SC.

Physical Chemistry: Prof. RNDr. A. TOCKSTEIN, C.SC.

Processes and Apparatus of Chemical Technology: Doc. Ing. ZDENĚK LECJAKS, C.SC.

Automation of Chemical Processes: Prof. Ing. J. KOMŮRKA.

Organization, Economics and Planning of Chemical Industry: Doc. Ing. M. FILKA, C.SC.

Inorganic Technology: Doc. Ing. M. KUCHLER, C.SC.

Organic Technology: Doc. Ing. J. POSKOČIL, C.SC.

Technology of Plastics: Prof. Dr. Ing. J. MLEZIVA.

Chemical Technology of Fibred Materials: Prof. Ing. Dr. FRANTIŠEK KREJČÍ, C.SC.

Chemical Technology of Paper and Cellulose: Prof. Ing. F. LÉBR, C.SC.

VYSOKÁ ŠKOLA DOPRAVY A SPOJOV
(University of Transport and Telecommunications)

010 88 ŽILINA, MOYZESOVA 20

Telephone: 20392, 23408.

Founded 1953.

State control; Language of instruction: Slovak; Academic year: September to July.

Rector: Prof. Ing. JAROSLAV JEŘÁBEK, DR.SC.

Pro-Rectors: Prof. Ing. PETER HERMAN, C.SC., Doc. RNDr. JOZEF MORAVČÍK, C.SC., Prof. Ing. LADIS-

LAV SKÝVA, DR.SC., Doc. Ing. MILAN KEJZLAR.

Registrar: JUDr. CTIBOR BLEY.

Librarian: PhDr. M. KRCHO, C.SC.

Library of *c.* 250,000 vols.

Number of teachers: 517.

Number of students: 5,460.

Publications: *Práce a štúdie VSD*†, *Zborník vedeckých konferencii VSD* (every 3 years)†.

DEANS:

Faculty of Exploitation and Economy of Transport and Telecommunications: Doc. Ing. CYRIL KUBJATKO, C.SC.

Faculty of Mechanical and Electrical Engineering: Prof. Ing. MIROSLAV ZAFKA.

VYSOKÁ ŠKOLA EKONOMICKÁ

(School of Economics)

BRATISLAVA, UL. ODBOJAROV 10

Telephone: 605-61.

Founded 1940, became State School 1945; Academic year: October to January, February to June.

Rector: Prof. Dr. LADISLAV RENDOŠ, DR. SC.

Pro-Rectors: Prof. Ing. VLADIMÍR HÁČIK, DR., SC., Prof. Ing. ŠTEFAN DURINA, C.SC., Prof. Ing. ADAM LAŠČIAK, C.SC., Doc. RNDr. JÚLIA ŽILINKOVÁ, Doc. Ing. VLADISLAV STRAČÁR, C.SC.

Registrar: LUDMILA SASINKOVÁ.

Librarian: Ing. BORIS PROCHÁDZKA.

Number of teachers: 426.

Number of students: 5,892.

DEANS:

Faculty of National Economy: Doc. Ing. VLADIMÍR ZAPLETAL, C.SC.

Faculty of Economics and Management of Industry: Doc. Ing. MICHAL LEŠČIŠIN, C.SC.

Faculty of Management: Doc. Ing. DANIEL VOJTKO, C.SC.

Faculty of Trade: Doc. Ing. VÍT'AZOSLAV BALHAR, C.SC.

PROFESSORS:

Faculty of National Economy:

FRANCE, K., C.SC.
HÁČIK, V., DR.SC.
PETER, O., C.SC.
RAPOŠ, P., C.SC.

Faculty of Management:

FECANIN, J., C.SC.
KRÁLIČEK, V., DR.SC.
LAŠČIAK, A., C.SC.
LAUČÍK, Z., DR.SC.
PARTYK, B., DR.SC.
SOJKA, J., C.SC.
UNČOVSKY, L., C.SC.

Faculty of Trade:

BALHAR, V., C.SC.
KULČÁKOVÁ, M., C.SC.
RAČEK, P., C.SC.
RENDOŠ, L., DR.SC.
SLOBODA, Š., C.SC.
SOPIRA, A., DR. SC.

Faculty of Economics and Management of Industry:

DURINA, Š., C.SC.
FIŠERA, S., DR.SC.
HUTNÍK, F., DR.SC.
LEŠČIŠIN, M., C.SC.
RAŠKO, A., C.SC.
SEDLÁK, M., C.SC.
ŠVANTNER, M., C.SC.

Faculty of Economics of Services and Tourism:

KOPŠO, E., C.SC.

Institute of Marxism-Leninism:

NOVOTNY, Č., C.SC.
PECHO, M., C.SC.

VYSOKÁ ŠKOLA EKONOMICKÁ

(School of Economics)

130 67 PRAGUE, NÁM. ANT. ZÁPOTOCKÉHO 4

Telephone: 26-16-41.

Founded 1953.

State control; Language of instruction: Czech; Academic year: October to July.

Rector: Prof. Ing. S. HRADECKÝ, C.SC.

Pro-Rectors: Prof. Ing. VÁCLAV LOHR, Prof. Ing. LIBUŠE MIKOVÁ, C.SC., Prof. Ing. LUBOMÍR CYHELSKÝ, C.SC., Prof. Ing. FRANTISEK VALENTA, DR.SC.

Registrar: Ing. IVO BLAŽEK.

Number of teachers: 651.

Number of students: 15,000.

Publications: *Acta Oeconomica Pragensia, Informační Bulletin* (both irregular).

DEANS:

Faculty of Economics: Prof. Ing. J. PETŘÍVALSKÝ.

Faculty of Production Economics: Prof. Ing. V. LÍBAL, C.SC.

Faculty of Commerce: Prof. Ing. Inf. JAROSLAV MALÝ, C.SC.

Faculty of Management: Prof. Dr. JAROSLAV KOHOUT.

VYSOKÁ ŠKOLA LESNÍCKA A DREVÁRSKA

(College of Forestry and Wood Technology)

ZVOLEN, ŠTUROVA 14

Telephone: 3772.

Founded 1807, reorganized 1952.

State control; Languages of instruction: Slovak, Czech; Academic year: October to June.

Rector: Prof. ADOLF PRIESOL.

Vice-Rectors: Assoc. Prof. LADISLAV ŠEBÍK, Prof. MARTIN SIVÁK, Prof. JOZEF PALOVIČ, Asst. Prof. JOZEF MARKO.

Registrar: Ing. J. UHLIAR.

Librarian: MARTA LENDVAYOVÁ.

Library of 110,000 vols.

Number of teachers: 185.

Number of students: 2,050.

Publication: *Symposium of Scientific Works of the University College of Forestry and Wood Processing in Zvolen.*

DEANS:

Faculty of Forestry: Prof. JOZEF PORUBIAK.

Faculty of Wood Technology: Assoc. Prof. FRANTIŠEK KRUTEL.

VYSOKÁ ŠKOLA POLITICKÁ ÚV KSČ

(College of Political Studies, Central Committee of the Czechoslovak Communist Party)

160 00 PRAGUE—VELESLAVÍN

Telephone: 369941.

Founded 1953.

Rector: Prof. Ing. VÁCLAV KVĚŠ.

Pro-Rectors: Doc. Dr. JOZEF BOBOK, Dr. STANISLAV JÄGERMAN, Doc. Dr. MILOSLAV ŠPAČEK.

VYSOKÁ ŠKOLA POLNOHOSPODÁRSKA

(College of Agriculture)

949 76 NITRA, NÁBREŽIE MLÁDEŽE

Telephone: 262-41.

Founded 1946.

State control; Language of instruction: Slovak; Academic year: October to January, March to June.

Rector: Prof. Ing. J. KLIMENT, DR.SC.

Pro-Rectors: Doc. Ing. M. KOVÁČ, C.SC., Doc. Ing. Š. HRAŠKA, C.SC., Prof. Ing. V. SIDOR, DR.SC., Doc. Ing. M. BRANICKÝ, C.SC.

Registrar: Ing. R. ŠIŠKA.

Library: *see* "Ústredná pôdohospodárska knižnica", under Libraries.

Number of teachers: 430.

Number of students: 6,400.

Publications: *Acta Fytotechnica*†, *Acta Zootechnica*†, *Acta Operativo-Oeconomica*†, *Acta Technologica Agriculturae*†.

DEANS:

Faculty of Agricultural Economics: Prof. Ing. J. ŠEVČÍK, C.SC.

Faculty of Agronomy: Prof. Ing. J. BENETÍN, DR.SC.

Faculty of Mechanics: Prof. Ing. PETER DUCHO, C.SC.

PROFESSORS:

Faculty of Agronomy:

ANDRAŠČÍK, M., Crop Production
BENETIN, J., Agricultural Amelioration
BOHÁČ, J., Plant Breeding and Plant Protection
GROM, A., Poultry Keeping and Zoology

KLIMENT, J., Genetics and Breeding Biology
KRESAN, J., Physiology and Anatomy of Farm Animals
LABUDA, J., Nutrition and Feeding of Farm Animals
SIDOR, V., Special Zootechnics
SOTÁKOVÁ, S., Agricultural Chemistry and Soil Science
ŠPALDON, E., Crop Production

Faculty of Agricultural Economics:
ŠEVČÍK, J., Organization of Agricultural Enterprises
ŠPYRKA, M., Agricultural Economy

Faculty of Mechanics:
DUCHO, P., Mechanization and Electrification of Animal Production
KNAPO, A., Farm Buildings
MINÁRIK, I., Farm Buildings

VYSOKÁ ŠKOLA STROJNÍ A ELEKTROTECHNICKÁ V PLZNI
(College of Mechanical and Electrical Engineering in Plzeň)

306 14 PLZEN,
NEJEDLÉHO SADY 14

Telephone: 37461-5.

Founded 1949 (reconstituted 1953–60).
State control; Language of instruction: Czech; Academic year: October to September.

Rector: Prof. Ing STANISLAV KUBÍK, D.SC.
Pro-Rectors: Doc. Ing. JINDŘICH STRAKA, C.SC., Prof. Ing. LUDĚK BĚLÍK, D.SC.
Registrar: Dr. ANTONÍN VYŠINKA.
Librarian: EVA ŠTUDENTOVÁ.

Library of 150,000 vols.
Number of teachers: 300.
Number of students: 2,100.
Publication: *Sborník prací VSSE v Plzni* (Annals of Scientific Research).

DEANS:
Faculty of Mechanical Engineering: Doc. Ing. MIROSLAV ČAPEK, C.SC.
Faculty of Electrical Engineering: Doc. Ing. ZBYNĚK KRAUS, C.SC.

VYSOKÁ ŠKOLA STROJNÍ A TEXTILNÍ V LIBERCI
(College of Mechanical and Textile Engineering in Liberec)

461 17 LIBEREC, HÁLKOVA 6

Telephone: 25441-5.

Founded 1953.
State control; Language of instruction: Czech; Academic year: September to July.

Rector: Prof. Ing. Dr. JOVAN ČIRLIČ.
Pro-Rectors: Doc. Ing. JÁN ALAXIN, C.SC., Doc. Ing. OLDŘICH KREJČÍŘ, C.SC., Doc. Ing. JAROSLAV TMĚJ, C.SC.
Registrar: Ing. EVA PETROVSKÁ.

Number of teachers: 199.
Number of students: 2,500.
Publication: *Sborník vědeckých prací VSST* (Annals of Scientific Research).

DEANS:
Faculty of Mechanical Engineering: Doc. RNDr. BOHUSLAV STŘÍŽ, C.SC.
Faculty of Textiles: Doc. Ing. JÁCHYM NOVÁK, C.SC.

VYSOKÁ ŠKOLA TECHNICKÁ V KOŠICIACH
(Košice Technical University)

KOŠICE, ŠVERMOVA 9

Founded 1952.
State control; Language of instruction: Slovak; Academic year: October to June.

Rector: Prof. Dr. Ing. A. PAŽÁK.
Pro-Rectors: Doc. Dr. J. BADIDA, Doc. RNDr. P. GALAJDA, Prof. L. ROZLOŽNÍK, Prof. Ing. PAVOL VELES.

Number of professors: 31.
Number of students: 7,200.

DEANS:
Faculty of Mining: Prof. Ing. JÁN PUZDER, C.SC.
Faculty of Metallurgy: Prof. Ing. J. KOCICH, C.SC.
Faculty of Engineering: Prof. Ing. J. BUDA, DR.SC.
Faculty of Electrotechnical Engineering: Prof. Ing. M. RÁKOŠ, DR.SC.
Faculty of Building: Prof. Ing. JURAJ SÜTTI, DR.SC.

VYSOKÁ ŠKOLA VETERINÁRNÍ V BRNĚ
(University School of Veterinary Medicine in Brno)

612 42 BRNO 12, PALACKÉHO 1-3

Telephone: 445.

Founded 1918.

Rector: Prof. MVDr. JAROSLAV DRAŽAN, C.SC.
Pro-Rectors: Prof. MVDr. PŘEMYSL JAGOŠ, C.SC., Prof. MVDr. JAROSLAV NEUMANN, C.SC., Prof. MVDr. KAREL HEJLÍČEK, DR.SC., Prof. MVDr. ZDENĚK VESELÝ, C.SC.
Questor: JUDr. RUDOLF KNĚŽÍNEK.

Library of 165,855 vols.
Number of teachers: 130 (including professors and docents).
Number of students: *c.* 1,300.
Publication: *Acta Veterinaria.*

VYSOKÁ ŠKOLA VETERINÁRSKA V KOŠICIACH
(College of Veterinary Medicine in Košice)

041 81 KOŠICE,
KOMENSKÉHO 73

Telephone: 32111, 26611.

Founded 1949.
State control; Language of instruction: Slovak; Academic year: October to July.

Rector: Prof. MVDr. OTO JAROSLAV VRTIAK.
Pro-Rectors: Doc. MVDr. MICHAL SITKO, Doc. Ing. JÁN ŠÁNDOR, Prof. MVDr. LEOPOLD VRZGULA.

Number of teachers: 264.
Number of students: 1,150.

VYSOKÁ ŠKOLA ZEMEDĚLSKÁ
(University of Agriculture)

662 65 BRNO, ZEMEDELSKÁ 1

Founded by State Law in 1919.

Rector: Prof. Ing. et Ing. Z. ŠTEFFL, C.SC.
Pro-Rectors: Prof. Ing. E. HALVA, C.SC., Prof. Ing. JIŘÍ RUPRICH, C.SC., Prof. RNDr. PhMr. M. PENKA, DR.SC., Prof. Ing. J. KUBÍČEK, C.SC., Prof. Ing. J. KREJČÍŘ, C.SC.
Chief Administrative Officer: Ing. V. BULLA.
Chief Librarian: RNDr. VÁCLAV ZATLOUKAL.

Library of 395,000 vols.
Number of teachers: 367.
Number of students: 5,900.
Publications: *Acta Universitatis agriculturae Brno*† (Annals of the University of Agriculture), *Information Bulletin.*

DEANS:
Faculty of Agronomy: Prof. Ing. R. VACULÍK, C.SC.
Faculty of Agricultural Economics and Management: Prof. Ing. J. TRUKSA, C.SC.
Faculty of Forestry: Doc. Ing. A. ČÍHAL, C.SC.

VYSOKÁ ŠKOLA ZEMEDĚLSKÁ V PRAZE
(Prague Agricultural University)

161 21 PRAGUE, SUCHDOL,
POŠTA SUCHDOL 2

Telephone: 323640-9.

Founded 1906.
State control; Language of instruction: Czech; Academic year: October to July.

Rector: Prof. Ing. CTIBOR LEDL, DR.SC.
Pro-Rectors: Prof. Ing. JAROMÍR HUBÁČEK, C.SC., Prof. MVDr. ZDENĚK SOVA, DR.SC., Prof. Ing. KAREL NEUBAUER, C.SC., Doc. Ing. MIROSLAV PECHÁČ, C.SC., Prof. Ing. Dr. JAN DVOŘÁK, C.SC.
Registrar: JOSEF SVOBODA.
Librarian: Ing. FRANTIŠEK HUBÁČEK.

Library of 120,000 vols.

Number of teachers: 530.

Number of students: 7,000.

Publication: *Scientific Papers.*

DEANS:

Faculty of Agronomy: Prof. Ing. ANTONÍN KLESNIL, C.SC.
Faculty of Mechanics: Prof. Ing. BOHUMIL KRUPIČKA, C.SC.
Faculty of Agricultural Economics and Management: Prof. Ing. JAROSLAV PÍČ, DR.SC.
Faculty of Agricultural Economics and Management in České Bdějovice: Prof. Ing. VLADIMÍR KRUPAUER, C.SC.

VYSOKÉ UČENÍ TECHNICKÉ V BRNĚ
(Technical University of Brno)

601 90 BRNO, OPLETALOVA 6

Telephone: 25831-3.

Founded 1899.

State control; Language of instruction: Czech; Academic year: October to July.

Rector: Prof. Ing. FRANTISEK KOUŘIL.

Pro-Rectors: Prof. JUDr. VLASTIMIL HALAXA, Prof. Ing. MILOSLAV HODINKA, Prof. Ing. arch. Dr. FRANTIŠEK KORVAS, Prof. Ing. arch. ANTONÍN KRASICKÝ, Asst. Prof. Ing. BLANKA SIROKORADOVÁ.

Registrar: Dr. MILOSLAV SOVADINA.

Number of students: 14,600.

Publication: *Bulletin of the Technical University of Brno* (quarterly).

DEANS:

Faculty of Civil Engineering: Prof. Ing. MATĚJ POKORA.
Faculty of Mechanical Engineering: Prof. Ing. Dr. JAN ŽIŽKA.
Faculty of Electrical Engineering: Prof. Ing. ZDENĚK ERTINGER.
Faculty of Technology: Prof. Ing. MILAN MLÁDEK.
Faculty of Architecture: Asst. Prof. Ing. FRANTIŠEK BARTEK.

SCHOOLS OF ART AND MUSIC

Akademie múzických umění (*Academy of Arts*): Prague 1, Smetanovo nábřeží 2; faculties of music, theatre and dramatic art (including puppetry), film and television art; Rector Prof. KAREL MARTÍNEK.

Akademie výtvarných umění (*Academy of Fine Arts*): 170 22 Prague 7, U Akademie 4; f. 1799; 18 staff; library of 29,000 vols.; Rector Prof. MILOŠ AXMAN; publ. *Almanach.*

Janáčkova akademie múzických umění (*Janáček Academy of Music and Dramatic Art*): Brno, Komenského nám 6; f. 1947; 152 staff; 230 students; Rector Prof. F. ŠOLC.

Konservatoř v Brně (*Conservatoire in Brno*): Brno, Třída kpt Jaroše 43-45; f. 1881, from 1919 known as Leoš Janáček State School; music department, drama and ballet departments; specialist preparatory school; 121 professors, 550 students; Dir. J. BROŽ.

Konservatoř v Praze (*Conservatoire of Music in Prague*): Prague 1, Na rejdišti 1; f. 1811; 170 professors, 670 students; library of 124,448 books; Dir. Prof. FRANTIŠEK MARTINÍK; Chief of Library (Archives) OLDŘICH ČENĚK.

Konzervatórium: Košice, Leninova 89; f. 1951; 100 teachers, 343 students; library of 21,000 vols. and 3,000 records; Dir. PhDr. ŠTEFAN MEREŠŠ, C.SC.; publ. *Hudobný život na východnom Slovensku* (Musical Life in East Slovakia).

Konzervatórium: Žilina, ul. Marxa-Engelsa 12; f. 1952; 53 teachers, 335 students; library of 17,500 vols.; Dir. MILAN SEIDL.

Konzervatórium: 801 00 Bratislava, Tolsteho 11; sections for singing, wind instruments, strings, keyboard instruments, composing and conducting, dancing; 112 teachers, 500 students; Dir. Z. NOVÁČEK.

Vysoká škola muzických umení (*Academy of Arts*): 883 01 Bratislava, Jiráskova ul. 3; faculties of music, dramatic arts; Rector Prof. PhDr. RUDOLF MRLIAN, DR.SC.

Vysoká škola uměleckoprůmyslová (*Academy of Applied Arts*): Prague 1, nám. Krasnoarmějců 80; f. 1885; 250 students; Rector Prof. JAN SIMOTA.

Vysoká škola výtvarných umení (*High School of Fine Arts*): 885 37 Bratislava, Hviezdoslavovo nám. 18; f. 1949; 49 teachers, 195 students; library of 15,200 vols.; Rector Prof. JÁN KULICH; Pro-Rectors Doc. OTO LUPTÁK, Doc. Dr. L. PETERAJOVÁ, Prof. Ing. arch. D. KUZMA; Questor Doc. F. BOLLO.

DENMARK

Population 5,118,000

ACADEMIES

DET KONGELIGE DANSKE VIDENSKABERNES SELSKAB
(The Royal Danish Academy of Sciences and Letters)
H. C. ANDERSENS BOULEVARD 35, DK-1553
COPENHAGEN V.
Founded 1742.

President: P. J. RIIS.
Vice-President, Chairman of History and Philosophy Section: HENRIK GLAHN.
Vice-President, Chairman of Mathematics and Natural Sciences Section: OLE MAALØE.
Secretary: CHRISTIAN CRONE.

Publications: *Oversigt*† (annual), *Meddelelser*† and *Skrifter*† (Hist. & Philos., Maths. & Phys., Biol.).

DANISH MEMBERS:

History and Philosophy Section:

ANDERSEN, POUL.
ASMUSSEN, JES P.
BACH, H.
BAGGE, POVL.
BECH, GUNNAR.
BECKER, C. J.
BJERRUM, ANDERS.
BJØL, ERLING.
BLEGVAD, MOGENS.
BLINKENBERG, ANDREAS.
BRØNDSTED, MOGENS.
CHRISTENSEN, A. E.
CHRISTENSEN, JOHNNY C.
CHRISTENSEN, TORBEN.
CHRISTIANSEN, SOFUS E.
DAL, ERIK.
DALGÅRD, SUNE.
EGEROD, SØREN.
ELLEHØJ, SVEND.
ESTRUP, HECTOR.
FAVRHOLDT, DAVID.
FISCHER, ERIK.
FISCHER-JØRGENSEN, E.
FROM, FRANZ.
GELTING, JØRGEN.
GJØDESEN, MOGENS.
GLAHN, HENRIK.
GLAMANN, KRISTOF.
GLOB, P. V.
GOMARD, BERNHARD.
HALD, KRISTIAN.
HAMMERSHAIMB, E.
HANSEN, AAGE.
HELGASON, JÓN.
HENDRIKSEN, HANS.
HJORTH, P. LINDEGÅRD
HVIDTFELDT, ARILD.
JACOBSEN, ERIC.
JANSEN, F. J. BILLESKOV.
JENSEN, POVL JOHS.
JOHANSEN, H. FRIIS.
JOHANSEN, K. FRIIS.
KABELL, AAGE.
LARSEN, JENS PETER.
LIDIN, O. G.
LÆSSØE, JØRGEN.
MONBERG, TORBEN.
MOUSTGAARD, IB K.
NIELSEN, THØGER.
NYKROG, PER.
OLSEN, OLAF H.
PETERSEN, E. LADEWIG.
PINBORG, JAN.
RASMUSSEN, HOLGER.
RASMUSSEN, P. NØRREGAARD.
RIIS, P. J.
RISCHEL, JØRGEN.
RAASTED, JØRGEN.
SASS, ELSE KAI.
SCHIØRRING, NILS.
SKAUTRUP, J. PETER A.
SKRUBBELTRANG, FRIDLEV S.
SKYUM-NIELSEN, NIELS.
SPANG-HANSSEN, H.
STEENSBERG, AXEL.
STIEF, CARL.
SVANE, GUNNAR O.
SØRENSEN, BENGT ALGOT.
SØRENSON, JOHN KOUSGÅRD.
SØRENSEN, SØREN.
THOMSEN, NIELS J.
THOMSEN, RUDI.
WAABEN, KNUD.

Mathematics and Natural Sciences Section:

ANDERSEN, EINAR A.
ANDERSEN, ERIK SPARRE.
ANDERSEN, SV. O.
ANDERSEN, SV. TH.
ANDERSEN, TORKILD
ASMUSSEN, ERLING.
ASMUSSEN, ROBERT W.
BAK, BØRGE N.
BAK, THOR A.
BALLHAUSEN, C. J.
BANG, THØGER.
BARNDORFF-NIELSEN, O.
BEHNKE, OLAV.
BERTHELSEN, AS.
BERTHELSEN, OLE
BIRKELUND, TOVE.
BJERRUM, JANNIK.
BJØRNHOLM, SV.
BOHR, AAGE N.
BUCHTHAL, FRITZ.
BUCHWALD, VAGN F.
BÖCHER, TYGE W.
BØGGILD, J. K.
CHRISTENSEN, BENT.
CRONE, CHRISTIAN.
DAHL, JENS PEDER.
DANSGAARD, WILLI.
ELLITSGAARD-RASMUSSEN, K.
ENGBERG, INGEMAR.
FENCHEL, M. WERNER.
FENCHEL, TOM.
FINK, TROELS.
FORCHHAMMER, JES.
FUGLEDE, B.
HALD, ANDERS H.
HANSEN, HANS JØRGEN.
HOLMSGAARD, ERIK.
HOLSTENER-JØRGENSEN, H.
HOLTER, HEINZ.
HUUS, TORBEN.
JENSEN, AKSEL TOVBORG.
JENSEN, H. HØJGAARD.
JENSEN, KAI ARNE.
JESSEN, BØRGE CHRISTIAN.
JÓNASSON, P. M.
JØRGENSEN, C. C. BARKER.
KJAER, ANDERS C.
KJELDGAARD, NIELS OLE.
KLENOW, HANS.
KOFOED-HANSEN, OTTO M.
KRISTENSEN, LEIF.
KRISTENSEN, MARTIN K.
KRUHØFFER, POUL.
KULLENBERG, GUNNAR.
LARSEN, KAI
LARSEN, PEDER OLESEN.
LASSEN, NIELS A.
LASSEN, N. O.
LASSEN, ULRIK.
LINDHARD, JENS.
LUND, BODIL JERSLEV.
LUND, EBBA.
LUND, HENNING
LUNDQUIST, FRANK.
MAALØE, OLE URBAN.
MACKINTOSH, A. R.
MADSEN, IB.
MARCKER, KJELD A.
MAUNSBACH, ARVID.
MICHELSEN, AXEL A.
MOHR, J.
MOTTELSON, BEN.
MUNCH-PETERSEN, AGNETE
MØLLER, C. KNAKKERGÅRD.
MØLLER, H. BJERRUM.
NATHAN, OVE.
NIELSEN, CHR. OVERGAARD.
NIELSEN, H. E. STEEMANN.
NIELSEN, NIELS.
NISSEN, POUL ERIK
NOE-NYGAARD, ARNE.
NØRLUND, NIELS ERIK
OLESEN, POUL.
OTTESEN, MARTIN.
PEDERSEN, G. KJAERGÅRD.
PEDERSEN, KAI J.
PEDERSEN, OLAF.
PETERS, B.
PIHL, MOGENS.
REHBERG, POUL BRANDT.
REIZ, S. ANDERS T.
RUDKJØBING, MOGENS H.
SCHÄFFER, CLAUS.
SEIDENFADEN, GUNNAR.
SIIM, J. CHR.
SIMONSEN, M.
SKOU, J. C.
STEN-KNUDSEN, O.
STRID, ARNE K.
STRÖMGREN, BENGT.
SVEJGAARD, ARNE.
SØRENSEN, HENNING.
THAYSEN, J. HESS.
TORNEHAVE, HANS M. N.
TROELS-SMITH, JØRGEN A.
USSING, HANS H.
VON WETTSTEIN, DITER H.
WIETH, JENS OTTO.
WINGSTRAND, KARL GEORG.
WINTHER, AA.

Akademiet for de skønne Kunster (*Academy of Fine Arts*): Charlottenborg, Kongens Nytorv 1, 1050 Copenhagen K; f. 1754; up to 72 mems. elected for 6 years.

President: PETER BONNÉN.

Vice-President: MOGENS BREYEN.

Akademiet for de tekniske Videnskaber (*Danish Academy of Technical Sciences*): 266 Lundtoftevej, 2800 Lyngby; f. 1937; 539 mems., of which roughly half represent science and half industry and agriculture. Members belong to one of 8 science groups: basic sciences, chemical, mechanical, civil, electrical and agricultural engineering, industrial economy, biology and hygiene; 26 research institutes and associations are affiliated to ATV; Technical Dir. NIELS GRAM; Gen. Sec. VIBEKE Q. ZEUTHEN.

AFFILIATED INSTITUTIONS

Asfaltindustriens Vejforskningslaboratorium (***Asphalt Industries' Laboratory for Road Construction***).
Bioteknisk Institut (*Biotechnical Institute*).
BKF-centralen (*Danish Structural Research and Development Centre*).

Carbon 14 Centralen (*International Agency for 14C Determination*).
Danatom (***Danish Association for Industrial Development of Atomic Energy***).
Danmedia (*Danish Research Society for Mass and Telecommunication*).
Danfip (***Danish Federation for Information Processing and Management***).
Dansk Automationsselskab (***Danish Automation Society***).
Dansk Datamatic Center (*Danish Centre for Datamatics*).
Dansk Hydraulisk Institut (*Danish Hydraulic Institute*).
Elektronikcentralen (***Danish Research Centre for Applied Electronics***).
Emballageinstituttet (***Danish Packaging Research Institute***).
Geoteknisk Institut (***Danish Geotechnical Institute***).
Isotopcentralen (***Danish Isotope Centre***).
Korrosionscentralen (***Danish Corrosion Centre***).
Lydteknisk Laboratorium (***Acoustical Laboratory***).
Lysteknisk Laboratorium (*Illuminating Engineering Laboratory*).
Medicoteknisk Institut (*Institute of Biomedical Engineering*).
Nordisk Forskningsinstitut for Maling og Trykfarver (*Scandinavian Paint and Printing Ink Research Institute*).
Optisk Laboratorium (***Laboratory for Technical Optics***).
Proteinkemisk Institut (***Danish Institute for Protein Chemistry***).
Skibsteknisk Laboratorium (*Danish Ship Research Laboratory*).
Skovteknisk Institut (*Danish Institute of Forest Technology*).
Svejsecentralen (***Danish Welding Institute***).
Træraadet (***Danish Wood Council***).
Vandkvalitetsinstituttet (*Water Quality Institute*).

LEARNED SOCIETIES

Agriculture and Veterinary Science

Dansk Agronomforening (*Danish Agronomy Society*): Gammeltorv 22, postboks 2172, 1017 Copenhagen K; f. 1896; 2,556 mems.; Chief Sec. G. Fredslund Nielsen; publ. *Ugeskrift for Jordbrug*†.

Dansk Mejeristforening (*Danish Dairy Society*): Hestehaven 3, 5260 Odense S.; f. 1887; 1,505 mems.; Dir. K. Mark Christensen; publ. *Maelkeritidende*† (weekly).

Dansk Skovforening (*Danish Forestry Society*): Vester Voldgade 86, 1552 Copenhagen V; f. 1888; Chair. I. Estrup; Gen. Man. Ole Fog; publ. *Dansk Skovforenings Tidsskrift & Skoven*.

Dansk Veterinærhistorisk Samfund (*Danish Veterinary History Society*): Søvang 14, 3460 Birkerød; f. 1934; 500 mems.; Pres. H. H. Sass; publ. *Dansk Veterinærhistorisk Årbog* (annually).

Kongelige Danske Landhusholdningsselskab (*Royal Danish Agricultural Society*): Rolighedsvej 26, 1958 Copenhagen V; f. 1769; Presidents A. S. Olufsen, A. Neimann-Sørensen, E. A. Tesdorpf; Sec. Jørgen Christophersen.

Architecture and Town Planning

Dansk Byplanlaboratorium (*Danish Town Planning Institution*): Tordenskjoldsgade 10, 1055 Copenhagen; f. 1921; educational services and seminars; library of 12,000 vols.; Chair. Arne Gaardmand; Dir. Tage Drabye; publ. *Byplan*† (6 a year).

Danske Arkitekters Landsforbund/Akademisk Arkitektforening (*Federation of Danish Architects*): Bredgad. 66, 1260 Copenhagen K; f. 1951; 3,700 mems.; Pres. Søren Nielsen; Man. Dir. Jørgen Pers; publs. *Arkitekten, Arkitektur*.

The Arts

Dansk Billedhuggersamfund (*Danish Sculptors' Society*): Billedkunstnernes Forbund, Klareboderne 16, 1115 Copenhagen K; f. 1905; 120 mems.; Chair. Johan Galster.

Dansk Komponist-Forening (*Danish Composers' Society*): Valkendorfsgade 3, 1151 Copenhagen K; f. 1913; 115 mems.; Chair Per Nørgård; Sec. Käthie Kirk.

Dansk Korforening (*Danish Choral Society*): Absalonsgade 3, 4180 Sorø; f. 1911; mems.: 27 choirs; Pres. Asger Larsen.

Dansk Tonekunster Forening (***Danish Musical Society***): Radhusstraede 1, Copenhagen K; f. 1903; Sec. S. Heering.

Danske Kunsthåndværkeres Landssammenslutning—D.K.L. (*Danish Arts and Crafts Association*): Gothersgade 80, 1123 Copenhagen K; f. 1976; arranges exhibitions; professional advice for schools, museums, etc.; 250 mems.; 8 regional groups of artist-craftsmen; Sec.-Gen. Kai Strandgaard; publ. *Orientering fra D.K.L.* (quarterly).

Foreningen for National Kunst (***Society for National Art***): Landemarkt 3, Copenhagen; f. 1900; Dir. P. C. J. Stagsted; Sec. O. Haase.

Kunstnerforeningen af 18 de November (*Artists' Association of the 18th November*): Frederiksgade 8, Copenhagen K; f. 1842; Chair. Jørn Glob; Sec. Adv. Arne Pedersen.

Kunstforeningen i København (***Copenhagen Art Society***): Gl. Strand 48, 1202 Copenhagen K; f. 1825; exhibitions, publishers of art books for mems.; 5,000 mems.; Dir. Charlotte Christensen.

Malende Kunstneres Sammenslutning (***Painters' Association***): f. 1909; 300 mems.; Chair. Folmer Bendtsen; Sec. Erik M. Goldschmidt, Nørregade 33, Copenhagen.

Ny Carlsbergfondet (*New Carlsberg Foundation*): Brolæggerstræde 5, 1211 Copenhagen K; f. 1902; supports art and history of art in Denmark; Pres. Dr. phil. Torben Holck Colding.

Samfundet til Udgivelse af Dansk Musik (*Society for Publishing Danish Music*): Valkendorfsgadec3, 1151 Copenhagen K; f. 1871; Chair. Svend Erik Tarp; Sec. Käthie Kirk.

Sammenslutningen af Danske Kunstforeninger (*National Committee of Danish Art Societies*): "Lillebo" Niverød, 2990 Nivå; f. 1942; arranges touring art exhibitions with government support; 15,000 mems.; Pres. Bjørn Harder; Sec. Edith Dam.

Bibliography, Library Science and Museology

Bibliotekscentralen: Telegrafvej 5, 2750 Ballerup; f. 1939; provides bibliographical services for Danish libraries, including centralized cataloguing, national bibliographies, book lists and special bibliographies; Dir. Leo Alster; publs. *Dansk Bogfortegnelse* (The Danish National Bibliography, Books), *Dansk Periodica Foregnelse* (The Danish National Bibliography, serials), etc.

Danmarks Biblioteksforening (*Danish Library Association*): Trekronergade 15, DK-2500 Copenhagen Valby; f. 1905; Sec. F. Ettrup; publ. *Bogens Verden* (World of Books).

Danmarks Forskningsbiblioteksforening (*Danish Research Library Association*): Det Kongelige Bibliotek, Christians Brygge 8, DK-1219 Copenhagen K; f. 1978; publ. *DF-revy*.

Dansk Kulturhistorisk Museumsforening: P.O.B. 26, 4000 Roskilde; f. 1929; annual assemblies and study meetings; 147 institutional mems.; Pres. JENS OLE LEVEVRE; Sec. HENRIK VENSILD; publs. *Arv & Eje* (annual), *STOF* (3 a year).

Foreningen af Danske Kunstmuseer (*Union of Danish Art Museums*): P.O.B. 26, DK-4000 Roskilde; f. 1978; 36 institutional mems.; Chair TROELS ANDERSEN; publ. *Kunst og Museum*† (2 a year).

Foreningen af Danske Museumsmaend (*Association of Danish Museum Curators*): Kobenhavns Bymuseum, Vesterbrogade 59, 1620 Copenhagen V; f. 1928; 240 mems.; Pres. JOHN ERICHSEN; Sec. METTE BLIGAARD.

ECONOMICS, LAW AND POLITICS

Danmarks Jurist- og Økonomforbund (*Danish Lawyers and Economists Association*): Gothersgade 133, 1123 Copenhagen K; f. 1972; 15,000 mems.; Chair JENS N. CHRISTIANSEN; Sec.-Gen. BENT NYLØKKE JØRGENSEN; publ. *Juristen, Økonomen* (2 a month).

Dansk Kriminalistforening: Gl. Torv 18, Copenhagen; f. 1899; Sec. E. L. J. HØGH.

International Law Association: Danish Branch: c/o Hon. Sec. A. KAUFMANN, Skoubogade 1, Copenhagen K; f. 1925; Pres. Prof. ALLAN PHILIP.

Juridisk Forening: Amaliegade 4, 1256 Copenhagen K; f. 1851; 550 mems.; Sec. N. J. J. KLERK.

Nationalekonomisk Forening (*Danish Economic Association*): Danmarks National Bank, Havnegade 5, 1093 Copenhagen K; f. 1872; 2,000 mems.; Chair. Prof. Dr. NIELS THYGESEN; Sec. BENT ANDERSEN; publ. *Nationaloekonomisk Tidsskrift* (3 a year).

Det Udenrigspolitiske Selskab (*Foreign Policy Society*): Vandkunsten 8, DK-1467 Copenhagen K; f. 1946; studies, debates, courses and conferences on international affairs; Dir. JOHAN WILHJELM; Chair KJELD OLESEN; publs. *Fremtiden. Udenrigspolitiske Skrifter, Økonomisk Kronik.*

EDUCATION

Dansk Forening for Hjem og Skole (*Danish Society for Home and School*): V. Vedsted, Copenhagen; f. 1887; Dir. Dr. HOLGER KJOER.

Folkeuniversitetsudvalget (*Committee for University Extension Services in Denmark*): University of Odense, 5230 Odense M; f. 1898; Chair. Med. Dr. PER FROM HANSEN; Man. Dir. HARALD KREBS, M.A.

Mellemfolkeligt Samvirke (*Danish Association for International Co-operation*): Hejrevej 38, DK-2400 Copenhagen NV; administration of Danish Volunteers and International Work Camps; public information service on the problems of the developing countries and international co-operation.

Rektorkollegiet (*Conference of Danish Rectors*): Vester Voldgade 117, 1552 Copenhagen V; f. 1967; consulting authority for co-operation and communication between institutions of higher education and the Ministry of Education; mems.: the rectors of the 18 institutions of higher education in Denmark; Chair. Prof. CARL F. WANDEL; Sec. ULLA BARNECHOW JACOBSEN.

Tuborgfondet (*The Tuborg Foundation*): Strandvejen 50, DK-2900 Hellerup; f. 1931; financed by grants from The United Breweries' shareholders; interest from assets used for educational and scientific grants, especially in support of commerce and industry; Chair. POUL J. SVANHOLM.

HISTORY, GEOGRAPHY AND ARCHAEOLOGY

Arktisk Institut (*Arctic Institute*): L. E. Bruuns Vej 10, 2920 Charlottenlund; f. 1954; library of 6,000 vols. and over 50,000 photographs, mainly of Greenland; Dir. N. O. CHRISTENSEN; publ. *Acta Arctica*†.

Dansk Selskab for Oldtids- og Middelalderforskning (*Danish Society for Research of Ancient and Medieval Times*): Nationalmuseet, 1220 Copenhagen K; f. 1934; 120 mems.; Pres. SVEND GISSEL; Sec. JØRGEN STEEN JENSEN; publ. *Classica et Mediaevalia*, Vols. 1-31.

Danske Historiske Forening (*Danish Historical Society*); Njalsgade 102, Trappe 15, DK-2300 Copenhagen S: f. 1839; Chair. Prof. Dr. SVEND ELLERHØJ; Secs. Prof. Dr. E. LADEWIG PETERSEN and Dr. INGA FLOTO; publ. *Historisk Tidsskrift* (historical review, 2 a year).

Jysk Arkaeologisk Selskab (*Jutland Archaeological Society*): Moesgård, 8270 Højbjerg; f. 1951; lectures and publication of primary archaeological and ethnological investigations; 1,800 mems.; Pres. P. V. GLOB; Sec.-Gen. P. KJAERUM; publs. *KUML*† (annually), *Jysk Arkaeologisk Selskabs Skrifter I-XIII*† (monographs, irregular), *Handbooks 1-2*† (irregular).

Jysk Selskab for Historie (*Jutland Historical Society*): Vester Allé 12, 8000 Århus C; f. 1866; 2,000 mems.; Pres. Dr. Phil. VAGN DYBDAHL; Sec. cand. mag. IB GEJL; publs. *Historie*† (2 a year), *Nyt fra Historien* (quarterly).

Det Kongelige Danske Geografiske Selskab (*The Royal Danish Geographical Society*): Haraldsgade 68-70, Copenhagen; f. 1876; 450 mems.; the library contains *c.* 100,000 vols.; Protector H.M. QUEEN MARGRETHE; Pres. H.R.H. PRINCE HENRIK; Vice-Pres. Vice-Adm. S. THOSTRUP, Prof. Dr. EINAR ANDERSEN; Sec. Prof. Dr. N. KINGO JACOBSEN; publs. *Geografisk Tidsskrift*†, *Folia Geographica Danica*†, *Kulturgeografiske Skrifter*† and *Atlas of Denmark.*

Det Kongelige Danske Selskab for Fædrelandets Historie (*The Royal Danish Society for National History*): H. C. Andersens Blvd. 35, Copenhagen; f. 1745; 40 mems.; 15 foreign correspondents; Pres. SVEND ELLEHØJ; Sec. VIGGO SJØQVIST; publ. *Danske Magazin.*

Det Kongelige Nordiske Oldskriftselskab (*Royal Society of Northern Antiquaries*): Prinsens Palais, 1220 Copenhagen; f. 1825; *c.* 1,600 mems.; library in the National Museum; Vice-Pres. P. V. GLOB; Sec. J. STEEN JENSEN; publs. *Aarboger for Nordisk Oldkyndighed og Historie*†, *Nordiske Fortidsminder*†.

Samfundet for Dansk Genealogi og Personalhistorie (*The Danish Genealogical and Biographical Society*): Grysgårdsvej 2, DK2400 Copenhagen NV; f. 1879; 1,100 mems.; Chair. HANS H. WORSØE; Sec. FINN ANDERSEN; publ. *Personalhistorisk Tidsskrift* (2 a year), *Hvem forsker Hvad*† (yearly).

Selskabet for Dansk Kulturhistorie (*Society for the History of Danish Culture*): Nationalmuseet, 1220 Copenhagen K; f. 1936; 30 mems.; Pres. HANS STIESDAL; Sec. BREDO GRANDJEAN; publ. *Kulturminder.*

Selskabet for Historie og Samfundøkonomi (*Society of History and Economics*): Rosenborggade 15, Copenhagen K; f. 1960; Chair. Prof. Dr. SVEN HENNINGSEN; Editor H. HANSEN; publ. *Ökonomi og Politik* (quarterly).

INTERNATIONAL CULTURAL INSTITUTES

Alliance Française: 141 Tordenskjoldsgade TV, 1055 Copenhagen K.

British Council: Møntergade 1, 1116 Copenhagen K; library: *see* Libraries; Rep. Dr. W. N. BROWN.

Det Danske Selskab (*Danish Institute for Information about Denmark and Cultural Co-operation with other Nations*): Kultorvet 2, 1175 Copenhagen K; f. 1940; has delegates in the United Kingdom (Edinburgh), Benelux (Brussels), France (Rouen), Fed. Repub. of Germany (Dortmund), Italy (Milan), Switzerland (Zürich); study tours, annual summer seminars on education, social welfare, architecture, arts and crafts, libraries, regionalism, etc.; publs. *Danish Information Handbooks,*

Danish Reference Papers (educational and social topics), *Contact with Denmark* (in English, French, German, Flemish, Italian, twice yearly), *Musical Denmark* (annual), etc.

Deutsches Kulturinstitut (Goethe-Institut): Nörre Voldgade 106, DK-1358 Copenhagen K; f. 1961; cultural arrangements, German language courses, etc.; library of 15,000 vols.; Dir. FRIEDRICH SCHMÖE.

Foreningen Norden (*Danish Association for Nordic Collaboration*): Malmøgade 3, 2100 Copenhagen Ø; f. 1919 for strengthening Nordic cultural, legal and economic collaboration; 35,000 individual mems. and also national organizations; Pres. ERIK ANDERSEN; Man. Dir. TORBEN STAUBO.

Institut Français: Rosenvængetsallé 34-38, 2100 Copenhagen Ø; Dir. J. C. TERRAC.

Istituto Italiano di Cultura: Gjørlingsvej 11, 2900 Hellerup, Copenhagen; Dir. Prof. MARIO NATI.

U.S. International Communication Agency: Dag Hammarskjölds Alle 24, 2100 Copenhagen Ø.

LANGUAGE AND LITERATURE

Dansk Forfatterforening (*Danish Authors' Society*): Forfatternes hus, Nyhavn 21, Copenhagen K; f. 1894; Chair. HANS JØRGEN LEMBOURN; publ. *Forfatteren* (8 a year).

Det Danske Sprog- og Litteraturselskab (*Danish Language and Literature Society*): Frederiksholms Kanal 18A, DK-1220 Copenhagen; f. 1911; *c.* 50 mems.; Administrator Dr. ERIK DAL.

Det Filologisk-Historiske Samfund (*Philological Society*): Kastelsvej 1, 2100 Copenhagen Ø; f. 1854; 450 mems.; Pres. Prof. J. E. SKYDSGAARD; publ. *Studier fra Sprog-og Oldtidsforskning*.

Íslenzka fraédafélag (*Icelandic Literary Society*): Helsevej 21, Hillerød; f. 1912; Sec. P. JÓNASSON.

Samfund til Udgivelse af Gammel Nordisk Litteratur (*Society for the Publication of Old Norse Literature*): Kjaerstrupvej 33, 2500 Valby; Chair. JON HELGASON; Sec. AGNETE LOTH.

MEDICINE

Den Almindelige Danske Lægeforening (*Danish Medical Association*): Kristianiagade 12A, 2100 Copenhagen Ø; f. 1857; professional and educational activities; 13,939 mems.; Dir. B. SØRENSEN; publs. *Ugeskrift for Laeger* (weekly), *Danish Medical Bulletin* (English—6 a year).

Danmarks Farmaceutiske Selskab (*Danish Pharmaceutical Society*): c/o Danmarks farmaceutiske Højskole, 2 Universitetsparken, 2100 Copenhagen Ø; f. 1912; to encourage the scientific and practical development of Danish pharmacy; 675 mems.; Pres. H. GJELSTRUP KRISTENSEN; publ. *Archiv. Pharm. Chem. Sci. Ed.*†

Dansk Farmaceutforening (*Danish Pharmacists' Association*): Toldbodgade 36, DK-1253 Copenhagen K; f. 1873; library of 16,000 vols.; 2,200 mems.; Pres. LARS CLEMMENSEN; publ. *Farmaceutisk Tidende* (weekly).

Dansk Medicinsk Selskab (*Danish Medical Society*): Rygårds Allé 55, 2900 Hellerup; f. 1919; an asscn. of 54 socs. covering all aspects of medical science; Pres. OLE MUNCK; Sec. KARSTEN JENSEN.

Dansk Tandlægeforening (*Danish Dental Association*): Amaliegade 17, Postboks 143, 1004 Copenhagen K; f. 1873; 5,192 mems.; publ. *Tandlaegebladet* (22 a year).

Medicinske Selskab i København (*Medical Society of Copenhagen*): Kristianiagade 12A, 2100 Copenhagen Ø; f. 1772; 1,441 mems.; Pres. Dr. POUL A. PEDERSEN; Sec. MARIANNE PONTOPPIDAN.

NATURAL SCIENCES

Astronomisk Selskab (*Astronomical Society*): Observatoriet, Øster Voldgade 3, DK-1350 Copenhagen K; f. 1916; Dir. L. HJARVARD.

Biologisk Selskab (*Biological Society*): Arvebiologisk Institut, Tagensvej 14, DK-2200 Copenhagen N; f. 1896; 535 mems.; Pres. AGNETE MUNCH-PETERSEN; Sec. SØREN NØRBY.

Carlsbergfondet: H. C. Andersens Boulevard 35, 1553 Copenhagen V; f. 1876; Pres. KRISTOF GLAMANN; three Departments:

Carlsberg Laboratoriet: Gl. Carlsbergvej 8-10, 2500 Copenhagen Valby; scientific work in chemistry and physiology; Dirs. Prof. M. OTTESEN, PH.D. (chemistry), Prof. D. VON WETTSTEIN, PH.D. (physiology); publ. *Carlsberg Research Communications*†.

General Department for promoting studies in Natural Science, Mathematics, Philosophy, History, Social Science and Languages; also controls:

Carlsbergfondets Biologiske Institut: Tagensvej 16, 2200 Copenhagen N; Dir. (vacant).

Det Nationalhistoriske Museum paa Frederiksborg: Hillerød (*see* under Museums).

Danmarks Naturfredningsforening (*Danish Society for Nature Preservation*): Frederiksberg Runddel 1, 2000 Copenhagen F; f. 1911; 60,000 mems.; library of 5,000 vols.; Pres. Prof. V. M. MIKKELSEN; Dir. H. SUNE EBBESEN; publ. *Tidsskriftet natur og miljø* (annually).

Danmarks Naturvidenskabelige Samfund (*Danish Association of Natural Sciences*): Danmarks Tekniske Højskole, Bygning 101, Lyngby; f. 1911; 212 mems.; Pres. E. JACOBSEN; Vice-Pres. H. C. ASLYNG, CHRISTIAN F. ROVSING; Sec. PAUL CARPENTIER.

Dansk Botanisk Forening (*Danish Botanical Society*): Øster Farimagsgade 2D, 1353 Copenhagen K; f. 1840; 850 mems.; Pres. J. KRISTIANSEN; publs. *Botanisk Tidsskrift*† (Botanical Journal), *Dansk Botanisk Arkiv*† (Danish Botanical Archives).

Dansk Geologisk Forening (*Geological Society of Denmark*): Øster Voldgade 10, DK-1350 Copenhagen K; f. 1893; *c.* 720 mems.; Sec. HENRIK STENDAL; publ. *Meddelelser*† (Bulletin).

Dansk Naturhistorisk Forening (*Danish Natural History Society*): Universitetsparken 15, Copenhagen Ø; f. 1833; 907 mems.; Dir. CLAUS NIELSEN; publs. *Videnskabelige Meddelelser*† (annually), *Danmarks Fauna*.

Dansk Ornithologisk Forening (*Danish Ornithological Society*): Vesterbrogade 140, 1620 Copenhagen V; f. 1906; 6,000 mems.; Pres. L. FERDINAND; publs. *Tidsskrift*†, *Feltornithologen* (quarterly), *Meddelelser*†, *Fugleværn*† (annually).

Entomologisk Forening (*Entomological Society*): Zoological Museum, Universitetsparken 15, Copenhagen; f. 1868; 510 mems.; Pres. NIELS HAARLØV; Sec. OLE LOMHOLDT; publ. *Entomologiske Meddelelser* (3 a year).

Kemisk Forening (*Danish Chemical Society*): H. C. Ørsted Institutet, Universitetsparken 5, 2100 Copenhagen Ø; f. 1879; 600 mems.; Chair. R. MOSS; Sec. O. MØNSTED.

Selskabet for Naturlærens Udbredelse (*Society for the Promulgation of Natural Science*): Kemisk Laboratorium III, Universitetsparken 5, 2100 Copenhagen Ø; f. 1824 by H. C. ØRSTED; 200 mems.; Pres. Prof. THOR A. BAK; Sec. Dr. SVEND ERIK NIELSEN; publ. *Fysisk Tidsskrift* (six annually).

PHILOSOPHY AND PSYCHOLOGY

Dansk Psykologforening (*Danish Psychologists' Association*): Pilestraede 43, 1112 Copenhagen K; f. 1947; Chair. ELSA SCHMIDT; Sec.-Gen. JENS ERIK LUND.

Religion, Sociology and Anthropology

Det Danske Bibelselskab (*Danish Bible Society*): Købmagergade 67, 1150 Copenhagen K; f. 1814; editing and distributing Bibles; 5,550 mems.; Chair. B. Hancke Rossel; Gen. Sec. Rev. N. J. Cappelørn; publ. *News* (quarterly), *Annual Report*.

Det Grønlandske Selskab (*The Greenland Society*): Kraemer Hus, L. E. Bruuns Vej 10, 2920 Charlottenlund; f. 1905; 1,500 mems. with interest in Greenland and its people; Chair. Chr. Berthelsen; publ. *Gronland* (10 a year).

Kirkeligt Centrum (*Church Centre*): Vinstrups Allé 64, 2900 Hellerup; f. 1899; Chair. Rev. Gunner Tjalve; publ. *Kirkeligt Centrum* (quarterly).

Orientalsk Samfund (*Institute of East Asian Studies*): University of Copenhagen, 2 Kejsergade, Copenhagen K; f. 1915; 72 mems.; Pres. Prof. Søren Egerod; Sec. Prof. J. P. Asmussen; publ. *Acta Orientalia*.

Technology

Byggecentrum (*The Building Centre*): Gyldenløvesgade 19, 1600 Copenhagen V; f. 1956; to promote the productivity of the building trade with a view to reducing building costs and introducing improved techniques; Man. Dir. Poul Damkjaer Olesen; publ. *Bygge orientering*.

Dansk Husflidsselskab (*Danish Society of Domestic Crafts*): Haarlev; f. 1873; promotes domestic crafts on an artistic and craftsmanship basis.

Dansk Ingeniørforening (*Danish Society of Chemical, Civil, Electrical and Mechanical Engineers*): Ingeniørhuset, Vester Farimagsgade 31, 1606 Copenhagen V; f. 1892; to promote professional matters and advance scientific technical education and research; 12,100 mems.; Gen. Sec. Bjørn Andersen; publ. *Ingeniøren* (weekly).

Elektroteknisk Forening (*Electro-Technical Society*): Rådhusstrade 6 st., 1466 Copenhagen K; f. 1903; Dir. H. C. Peitersen.

Nordisk Byggedag (*Nordic Building Conference*): c/o FDBS arkitektkontor, Roskildevej 65, DK-2620 Albertslund; also in Helsinki, Reykjavik, Oslo and Stockholm; f. 1927; arranges congresses on building problems every third year alternately in the Nordic Countries; next congress in Iceland, 1983; 222 mems., official and private institutions; Sec.-Gen. Svend Hansen; publ. Congress literature.

RESEARCH INSTITUTES

General

Forskningssekretariatet (*Danish Research Administration*): Holmens Kanal 7, 1060 København K.; joint secretariat for all the under-mentioned councils; cooperates with the other Nordic research councils; publs. Annual Reports.

Planlægningsrådet for Forskningen (*Danish Council for Scientific Policy and Planning*): f. 1972, to replace *Forskningens Fællesudvalg.*; 15 mems. appointed by the Minister of Education; advisory body to government in science policy matters; makes proposals on resources, structures, etc. required for the development and exploitation of Danish research; provides comprehensive R & D statistics and necessary planning and forecasts; Chair. Prof. Dr. phil. Flemming Woldbye.

Statens naturvidenskabelige Forskningsråd (*Danish Natural Science Research Council*): f. 1968; 15 mems. appointed by the Minister of Education; advisory body to public authorities and institutions in the natural sciences; initiates, supports and co-ordinates research, national and international; awards grants and fellowships for scientific research; Chair. Prof. Dr. phil. Henning Sørensen.

Statens lægevidenskabelige Forskningsråd (*Danish Medical Research Council*): f. 1968; 15 mems. appointed by the Minister of Education; advisory body to public authorities and institutions in medical sciences, including odontology and pharmacy; initiates and supports research, co-ordinates research, national and international; awards grants and fellowships to scientific research; Chair. Prof. Dr. med. Niels Tygstrup.

Statens jordbrugs- og veterinærvidenskabelige Forskningsråd (*Danish Agricultural and Veterinary Research Council*): f. 1968; 14 mems. appointed by the Minister of Education; advisory body to public authorities and institutions in the agricultural and veterinary sciences; initiates and supports national and international research; awards grants and fellowships for scientific research; Chair. Lektor Dr. med. vet. Birthe Palludan.

Statens samfundsvidenskabelige Forskningsråd (*Danish Social Science Research Council*): f. 1968; 15 mems. appointed by the Minister of Education; advisory body to public authorities and institutions in the social sciences; initiates and supports national and international research; awards grants and fellowships for scientific research; Chair. Prof. Dr. phil. Erling B. Andersen.

Statens humanistiske Forskningsråd (*Danish Council for the Humanities*): f. 1968; 15 mems. appointed by the Minister of Education; advisory body to public authorities and institutions in the humanities; initiates and supports national and international research; awards grants and fellowships for scientific research; Chair. Prof. Dr. phil. Knud Rahbek Schmidt.

Statens teknisk-videnskabelige Forskningsråd (*Danish Council for Scientific and Industrial Research*): f. 1973, to replace *Danmarks teknisk-videnskabelige Forskningsrad and Statens teknisk-videnskabelige Fond.*; 15 mems. appointed by the Minister of Education; advisory body to public authorities in the technical sciences; initiates and supports national and international research; awards grants and fellowships for scientific research; Chair. Udviklingschef O. Gram Jeppesen.

DANDOK (*Danish Committee for Scientific and Technical Information and Documentation*): f. 1970; 7 mems.; advisory body to public and private authorities and institutions in scientific and technical information and documentation; prepares and evaluates Danish participation in international co-operation in the field; Chair. Overbibliotekar Vibeke Ammundsen.

Agriculture and Veterinary Science

Hedeselskabet (*Danish Land Development Service*): P.O.B. 110, 8800 Viborg; forestry, soil improvement, land reclamation, drainage, irrigation, hydrology and research; 350 staff; specialists carry out practical assignments and research; technical projects designed and administered for farmers, foresters, industry, government authorities in Denmark and abroad; Dir. K. Sandahl Skov.

Statens Husdyrbrugsforsøg (*National Institute of Animal Science*): Rolighedsvej 25, 1958 Copenhagen V; f. 1882; research in animal husbandry and connected subjects; Pres. P. CHR. OTTOSEN; Dir. MOGENS MUNCH; publs. *Beretning* (reports, *c.* 15 a year), *Meddelelse* (bulletins, 60–70 a year).

ECONOMICS, LAW AND POLITICS

Center for Udviklingsforskning (*Centre for Development Research*): 9 Ny Kongensgade, 1472 Copenhagen K; f. 1969; library of 7,000 vols.; promotes and undertakes research in the economic and social development of developing countries; Dir. Prof. KNUD ERIK SVENDSEN; publs. *Den Ny Verden* (quarterly), *CDR Papers*†, *CDR Library Service Papers*†, *Annual Report*† (English).

EDUCATION

Danmarks Paedagogiske Institut (*Danish Institute for Educational Research*): Hermodsgade 28, DK-2200 Copenhagen N; Dir. JESPER FLORANDER; publs. *Beretning* (annual report), research reports.

HISTORY, GEOGRAPHY AND ARCHAEOLOGY

Den Danske Komité for Historikernes Internationale Samarbejde (*Danish Committee for International Historical Co-operation*): Aarhus University; f. 1926; 44 mems.; Chair. Prof. RUDI THOMSEN.

MEDICINE

Finseninstitutet: Strandboulevarden 49, 2100 Copenhagen Ø; f. 1896; cancer hospital and institute for research into the action of radiation on living organisms; Pres. J. H. ZEUTHEN.

NATURAL SCIENCES

Biological Sciences

Danmarks Fiskeri- og Havundersøgelser (*Danish Institute for Fisheries and Marine Research*): Charlottenlund Slot, DK-2920 Charlottenlund; f. 1952; research into the biological aspects of fishing; staff of 25 scientists and 58 technicians; large specialist library of fisheries and biology texts; Dir. Dr. J. MØLLER CHRISTENSEN; publs. *Fisk og Hav*† (annually), *Meddelelser*† (irregular).

Statens Seruminstitut: Amager Boulevard 80, 2300 Copenhagen; f. 1902; microbiological institute; 110 scientists; the library contains *c.* 17,000 vols.; Scientific Dir. J. CHR. SIIM, M.D.; Man. Dir. O. FORSTING, LL.B.

Arctic Station, University of Copenhagen: 3953 Godhavn, Greenland; f. 1906 for study of Arctic nature; laboratory, library, research cutter "Porsild"; Governors: Dr. BENT FREDSKILD, Dr. NIELS NIELSEN, Dr. G. HØPNER PETERSEN, Prof. HENNING SØRENSEN; correspondence to: Bestyrelsen for Universitetets Arktiske Station, 1168 Frue Plads, Copenhagen.

Zoologisk Have (*Zoological Gardens*): Sdr. Fasanvej 79, 2000 Copenhagen F; f. 1859; Dir. BENT JORGENSEN.

Mathematics and Statistics

Danmarks Statistik: Sejrøgade 11, 2100 Copenhagen Ø; f. 1849; central institution for all Danish statistics; the library contains 130,000 vols.; Dir. N. V. SKAK-NIELSEN; publs. *Statistik Årbog* (annually), *Danmarks vare indfoersel og- udfoersel* (annually), *Statistiske Efterretninger* (*c.* 110 a year), *Konjunkturoversigt*† (quarterly), *Kvartalsstatistik over Udenrigshandelen* (quarterly), *Kvartalsstatistik for industrien* (quarterly), *Detailpriser* (Retail Prices, quarterly), *Nyt fra Danmarks Statistik* (*c.* 250 a year), *Månedsstatistik over udenrigshandelen* (monthly), *Statistik Tabelvaerk* and *Statistiske Meddelelser* (irregular and annually), *Statistiske Undersøgelser* (special items, irregular), *Statistisk Ti-årsoversigt* (statistical ten-year survey, annually), and other statistical publications.

Physical Sciences

Astronomisk Institut, Aarhus Universitet: Langelandsgade, 8000 Aarhus C; f. 1956; photoelectric and electronographic stellar and extra-galactic photometry, interstellar medium, stellar atmospheres, fundamental co-ordinate system.

Danmarks Geologiske Undersøgelse (*Geological Survey of Denmark*): 31 Thoravej, DK-2400 Copenhagen NV; f. 1888; library of 25,000 vols.; Dir. OLE BERTHELSEN; publs. *Danmarks Geologiske Undersøgelse, Series I-V, Series of Reports, Yearbook, Series A and B.*

Danske Meteorologiske Institut (*Danish Meteorological Institute*): Gamlehavealle 22, Charlottenlund; f. 1872; library contains 30,000 vols.; Dir. KARL O. ANDERSEN; publs. include *Annuaire Météorologique* (Part 1 Denmark, Part 2 Greenland), *Magnetic Results* (Rude Skov, Denmark; Godhavn and Thule, Greenland), oceanographical observations from Danish light vessels and coastal stations, monthly surface temperatures of North Atlantic, *Daily Weather Reports.*

Geodetic Institute: Rigsdagsgaarden 7, DK-1218 Copenhagen K; f. 1816; reconstructed 1928; geodetical and geophysical research institute; responsible for geodetic surveying in Denmark, Faeroe Isles and Greenland; operates 4 seismological stations; 300 mems.; library of 20,000 vols.; Dir. FLEMMING WIINBLAD, LL.B.; publs. *Mémoires*† *Communications*†.

Nordisk Institut for Teoretisk Atomfysik (NORDITA) (*Nordic Institute for Theoretical Atomic Physics*): Blegdamsvej 17, DK-2100 Copenhagen Ø; f. 1957; member countries: Denmark, Finland, Iceland, Norway and Sweden; Chair. of Board HAAKON OLSEN; Dir. AAGE BOHR.

Universitetets Astronomiske Observatorium (*Astronomical Observatory of Copenhagen University*): Øster Voldgade 3, 1350 Copenhagen K; f. 1642; observatory, f. 1950, is at Brorfelde, Tølløse; library of *c.* 10,000 vols.; Dir. Dr. J. V. CLAUSEN.

RELIGION, SOCIOLOGY AND ANTHROPOLOGY

Socialforskningsinstituttet (*Danish National Institute of Social Research*): Borgergade 28, 1300 Copenhagen K; f. 1958; independent research body under Ministry of Social Affairs; library of 32,500 vols.; Dir.-in-Chief JACOB VEDEL-PETERSEN.

TECHNOLOGY

Førsogsanlæg (*Risø National Laboratory*): P.O.B. 49, DK-4000 Roskilde; f. 1958; research in reactor technology and safety, the nuclear fuel cycle, radiation technology, environmental research, non-nuclear energy and safety and agriculture research; library of 300,000 vols., 1,800 current periodicals; Dir. Fil. dr. NIELS W. HOLM; publs. *Risø Reports*†, *Annual Reports*†.

LIBRARIES AND ARCHIVES

Århus Kommunes Biblioteker (*Århus Public Library*): Mølleparken, 8000 Århus C; f. 1934; 1,600,000 vols.; Chief Librarian P. DAUGAARD; publ. *Beretning* (Annual Report).

Biblioteket for Vejle By og Amt (*Vejle County and Central Library*): Vestre Engvej 55, 7100 Vejle; f. 1895; 289,000 vols.; Chief Librarian EGON KNUDSEN.

British Council Library: Møntergade 1, 1116 Copenhagen K; f. 1946; 11,949 vols., 84 periodicals; Librarian Mrs. J. TEIK HANSEN.

Centralbiblioteket for Sydvestjylland (*South-west Jutland Central Library*): Esbjerg, Nørregade 25; f. 1897; 505,000 vols.; Chief Librarian JOHS. PETERSEN; publ. *Årsberetning* (annual).

Danmarks Farmaceutiske Højskoles Bibliotek (*Royal Danish School of Pharmacy Library*): Universitetsparken 2, 2100 Copenhagen Ø; f. 1892; 40,000 vols.; Librarian HELGA THOMSEN.

Danmarks Laererhøjskoles Bibliotek (*Library of the Royal Danish School of Educational Studies*): Emdrupvej 101, Copenhagen NV; f. 1895; 232,621 vols., 2,593 periodicals; Chief Librarian METTE STOCKMARR.

Danmarks Paedagogiske Bibliotek (*National Library of Education*): 101 Lersø Parkallé, DK-2100 Copenhagen Ø; f. 1887; 280,000 vols., *c.* 250,000 microfiches and films; Dir. ROBERT HELLNER.

Danmarks Tekniske Bibliotek (*National Technological Library*): Anker Engelunds Vej 1, DK-2800 Lyngby; f. 1942; the national technical library, devoted to applied science (except medicine and agriculture) 491,920 vols., 8,560 current periodicals; Dir. VIBEKE AMMUNDSEN.

Danmarks Veterinaer- og Jordbrugsbibliotek (*Danish Veterinary and Agricultural Library*): Bülowsvej 13, 1870 Copenhagen V; f. 1783; 310,000 vols.; Chief Librarian INGE BERG HANSEN.

Erhvervsarkivet. Statens Erhvervshistoriske Arkiv (*Danish National Business History Archives*): Vester Allé 12, 8000 Århus; f. 1948; also a research institute for economic and social history; Chief Archivist Dr. VAGN DYBDAHL.

Frederiksberg Kommunes Biblioteker (*Public Library*): Solbjergvej 21-25, 2000 Copenhagen F; f. 1887; 300,000 vols.; 4 brs.; also a children's library and school libraries (f. 1937), 370,000 vols.; Chief Librarian SVEND ESBECH.

Gentofte Kommunebibliotek (*Public Library*): Øregaards Allé 7, DK-2900 Hellerup; f. 1918; 657,327 vols.; 5 brs.; also an art library; Chief Librarian HELGE STENKILDE.

Handelshøjskolens Bibliotek (*Library of the Copenhagen School of Economics and Business Administration*): Julius Thomsens Plads 10, 1925 Copenhagen V; 180,000 vols.; Librarian OLE HARBO.

Københavns Kommunes Biblioteker (*Copenhagen Municipal Libraries*): Kultorvet 2, DK-1175 Copenhagen K; f. 1885; 2,151,026 vols.; Librarian BRITA OLSSON; publs. *Arsberetning* (annually), *Boger i satsamlingen* (annually).

Københavns Stadsarkiv (*Copenhagen City Archives*): Rådhuset, 1599 Copenhagen V; first mentioned 1563; Dir. HELLE LINDE; Archivists EGIL SKALL, HANS KOFOED; publ. *Historiske Meddelelser om København 1907* ff. (annually).

Kongelige Bibliotek (*Royal Library*): Christians Brygge 8, DK-1219 Copenhagen; f. between 1657 and 1664; acts as the Danish National Library, principal research library and university library for Theology, the Humanities and the Social Sciences; is the largest library in Scandinavia; *c.* 2,300,000 vols., 5,000 incunabula, 56,000 western MSS., 30,000 vols. and MSS. in Oriental dept., 3,000,000 maps and prints, 750,000 musical items, 70,000 vols. in Dept. of Judaica and Hebraica; open to the public; Chief Librarian PALLE BIRKELUND; publs. bibliographies.

Kongelige Garnisonsbibliotek (*Royal Army Library*): 42 Kastellet, 2100 Copenhagen Ø; f. 1785; Army central research library; 130,000 vols.; Librarian Lt.-Col. S. HANSEN.

Kunstakademiets Bibliotek (*Academy of Fine Arts Library*): Kgs. Nytorv 1, 1050 Copenhagen K; f. 1758; 93,000 vols. on history of art and architecture, 91,000 architectural drawings, 333,000 photographs, 81,500 slides; Dir. HAKON LUND; publ. *Bibliografi over Dansk Kunst*†.

Landsarkivet for Fyn (*Provincial Archives of Funen*): 5000 Odense; f. 1893; the archives include records of local administration of Funen and neighbouring islands and collections of private papers. The Karen Brahe Library, the only nearly complete private Danish library from the 17th century, with about 3,400 printed books and 1,153 MSS., is deposited in the Archives; Dir. ANNE RIISING, PH.D.

Landsarkivet for Nørrejylland (*Provincial Archives of Northern Jutland*): 8800 Viborg; f. 1889, opened 1891; Dir. JENS HOLMGAARD, M.A.

Marinens Bibliotek: Overgaden oven Vandet 62B, 1415 Copenhagen K; f. 1765; naval affairs and Greenland literature; 30,000 vols.; Librarian Commdr. A. HOLM.

Det Nordjyske Landsbibliotek (*Central Library for the County of North Jutland*): Ved Vor Frue Kirke, 9000 Ålborg; f. 1895; 825,000 vols., 1,125 current periodicals; 21 brs. and 3 mobile libraries; also a medical library; Chief Librarian BIRGER KNUDSEN.

Odense Centralbibliotek (*County Library, Odense*): DK-5000 Odense; f. 1924; 534,700 vols.; Chief Librarian POUL MUNCH; publs. *Skraeppebladet*† (monthly bulletin), *Aarsberetning* (annual report).

Odense Universitetsbibliotek (*Odense University Library*): Campusvej 55, 5230 Odense M; f. 1965; humanities, social sciences, medicine, science; 540,000 vols.; Chief Librarian TORKIL OLSEN.

Rigsarkivet (*National Record Office*): Rigsdagsgården 9, 1218 Copenhagen K; f. 1582; consists of a Central Record Office in Copenhagen and four Provincial Record Offices (*Landsarkiver*), situated in Copenhagen, Odense, Viborg and Aabenraa. The Central Record Office contains most of the medieval documents (1200-1559), the archives of the Central Administration, and the armed forces, and the papers of the Royal family and of famous statesmen; Dir. VAGN DYBDAHL; publs. historical series; *Arkiv* (2 a year).

Silkeborg Bibliotek (*Public Library*): 8600 Silkeborg; f. 1900; 177,000 vols., plus 100,000 in the Children's Dept. and 146,000 in school libraries; Chief Librarian POVL SKOV.

Statsbiblioteket i Århus (*Århus State and University Library*): Universitetsparken, DK-8000 Århus C; f. 1902; 1,538,700 vols., including special collections of books on foreign missions, music and books on Schleswig-Holstein, also collection of Friesland and Friesian literature from all Friesian areas; Chief Librarian KARL V. THOMSEN.

Universitetsbiblioteket: Copenhagen; f. 1482; Section 1 (Humanities): Fiolstraede 1, 1171. K.; campus branch: Njalsgade 80, 2300. S.; 500,000 vols., 40,000 vols. Danish newspapers; Chief Librarian TORBEN NIELSEN; Section 2 (Science and Medicine): Nørre Allé 49, 2200. N.; 1,200,000 vols.; Chief Librarian KELL PREHN.

MUSEUMS

Aalborg Historiske Museum: Aalgade 48, 9000 Aalborg; f. 1863; archaeology, history, ethnology; Dir. Torben Witt.

Aarhus Kunstmuseum (*Aarhus Art Museum*): Vennelystparken, 8000 Aarhus C; f. 1858; Dir. Kristian Jakobsen.

Botanisk Have (*Botanical Gardens*): Øster Farimagsgade 2B, 1353 Copenhagen K; Curator Olaf Olsen.

Danmarks Tekniske Museum (*Danish Museum of Science and Industry*): Office: Ole Roemers Vej, 3000 Elsinore; Exhibition Hall: Ndr. Strandvej 23, 3000 Elsinore; f. 1911; more than 12,000 items, particularly relating to Danish inventions; library of 18,000 vols.; Dir. K. O. B. Joergensen; publ. *Årbog* (Yearbook).

Forhistorisk Museum (*Prehistoric Museum*): Moesgård, DK-8270 Højbjerg; f. 1861; collections of Danish prehistoric antiquities; research organization in environmental, Danish and Oriental archaeology and ethnology; Dir. Prof. Ole Klindt-Jensen.

Geologisk Museum: Østervoldgade 5, 1350 Copenhagen K; minerals, rocks, meteorites and fossils; geology of Denmark and Greenland.

Handels- og Søfartsmuseet (*Danish Maritime Museum*): Kronborg Castle, 3000 Elsinore; f. 1914; maritime library of 20,000 vols.; Dir. Henning Henningsen, ph.d.; publs. Year books, Guides, and a series of maritime studies *Söhistoriske skrifter*.

Jagt- og Skovbrugsmuseet (*Museum of Hunting and Forestry*): DK-2970 Hørsholm; f. 1942; Curator P. O. Olesen.

Københavns Bymuseum (*Copenhagen City Museum*): Vesterbrogade 59; history of Copenhagen including pictures, architecture, models. Also houses the collection of Kierkegaard relics; Curator S. Linvald.

Kronborg: Elsinore; fortified royal castle dating from the end of the 16th century; contains the Royal Apartments (furniture, tapestry, etc.), banqueting hall, chapel.

Kunstindustrimuseet (*The Danish Museum of Applied Art*): Bredgade 68, 1260 Copenhagen K; f. 1890; European applied art from the Middle Ages to modern times, Chinese and Japanese art, and a library of 58,000 vols. on applied art; Pres. J. Trolle; Dir. Erik Lassen.

Landbrugsmuseet (*The Agricultural Museum*): Gl. Estrup, 8963 Auning, Jutland; f. 1889; Pres. H. J. Kristensen; Sec. J. Elling; Curator Svend Nielsen, m.a.

Louisiana: Gl. Strandvej 13, 3050 Humlebæk; f. 1958; neo-classic villa and estate transformed into a modern museum of art; collection of Danish and international art; temporary exhibitions of modern art; cinema, concerts, theatre; Founder and Dir. Knud W. Jensen; publ. *Louisiana Revy*.

Museet for Danmarks Frihedskamp 1940-1945 (*The Museum of Denmark's Fight for Freedom 1940-1945*): Churchill Parken, 1263 Copenhagen K; f. 1957; objects, photographs and other materials from the period of the German occupation during World War II; also archives and library; Dir. Jørgen Barfod; publ. *Yearly Publication for the Friends of the Museum*.

Musikhistorisk Museum og Carl Claudius' Samling (*Musical History Museum and Carl Claudius Collection*): Åbenrå 34, 1124 Copenhagen K; f. 1898; collection of musical instruments; concerts, library, archives; Dir. cand. mag. Mette Müller.

Det Nationalhistoriske Museum paa Frederiksborg (*The Museum of National History at Frederiksborg Castle*): Frederiksborg Slot, DK-3400 Hilleröd; castle built in 1560s and 1600–20 and endowed as museum in 1878; contains a chronological collection of portraits and paintings illustrating the history of Denmark, all arranged in rooms, the furniture and appointments in keeping with the period of the paintings; *c.* 10,000 exhibits; library contains 15,000 vols.; Pres. M. O. Olufsen, Chamberlain; Dir. Dr. Phil. Povl Eller; Curators Mette Bligaard, Stefefn Heiberg; publs. various catalogues and illustrated guides.

Nationalmuseet (*The National Museum*): Prinsens Palæ, Frederiksholms Kanal 12, Copenhagen; f. 1807 on basis of the older Royal Collections; consists of 10 divisions; Dir. Prof. Dr. P. V. Glob; Keepers: Danish Prehistoric Collection Mogens Ørsnes; Danish Historical Collection Harald Langberg; Danish Folk Museum H. Rasmussen; Ethnographic Collection Dr. Torben Monberg; Collection of Classical Antiquities Dr. M. L. Buhl; Royal Collection of Coins and Medals Otto Mørkholm; Open-air Museum at Sorgenfri P. Michelsen; Department of Natural Science Dr. J. Troels-Smith; Museum of Denmark's Fight for Freedom 1940-1945 Jørgen Barfod; Department for Public Relations and Publications Birte Friis; publs. *Arbejdsmark* (yearbook), *Skrifter* (in 3 series), *Nyt fra Nationalmuseet* (quarterly), catalogues.

Naturhistorisk Museum (*Natural History Museum*): Universitetsparken, DK-8000 Århus C; f. 1921; permanent field laboratory: "Molslaboratoriet", Femmöller, 8400 Ebeltoft; the museum laboratories are open to scientists, and specialize in terrestrial ecology, limnology, ornithology and bio-acoustics; the library contains 15,000 vols.; Pres. V. Nedergaard Jørgensen; Dir. A. G. Holm Joensen; publs. *Natura Jutlandica* (in English), *Natur og Museum* (in Danish).

Nordjyllands Kunstmuseum (*North Jutland Arts Museum*): Kong Christians alle 50, 9000 Aalborg; f. 1972; painting, sculpture, graphics, especially since 1900; library on art; Dir. Else Bülow.

Ny Carlsberg Glyptotek: Dantes Plads, 1556 Copenhagen V; f. 1888; Danish and French sculpture and painting, Egyptian, Greek, Roman and Etruscan art, mainly sculpture; Pres. Dr. Torben Holck Colding; Dir. Flemming Johansen; Curators Hans Edvard Nørregård-Nielsen (Danish and French art), Jette Christiansen and Mette Moltesen (ancient art).

Odense Bys Museer (*Odense City Museums*): Jernbanegade 13, 5000 Odense C.

Fyns Stiftsmuseum: archaeology.

Kulturhistorisk Museum: Montergaarden, Overgade 48-50; historical museum; collection of coins and medals; publ. *Fynske Minder*† (Bygone Funen, annually).

Den fynske Landsby (*Funen Village*): Sejerskovvej, 5260 Hjallese; open-air museum.

Fyns Kunstmuseum: art gallery.

H. C. Andersens Hus (*Hans Christian Andersen Museum*): Hans Jensensstrade; includes library (8,000 vols.) of works by the author; publ. *Anderseniana*† (annually).

H. C. Andersens Barndomshjem: Munkemøllestrade; the poet's childhood home.

Carl Nielsens Barndomshjem: Nr. Lyndelse, 5652 Nr. Søby; the composer's childhood home.

Ordrupgaardsamlingen: Vilvordevej 110, 2920 Charlottenlund; f. 1918; museum and art gallery for Danish and French 19th- and early 20th-century works; Dir. Hanne Finsen, m.a.

Orlogsmuseet (*Royal Naval Museum*): Quinti Lynette, Refshalevej, Copenhagen; ship-models, weapons, illustrations and other souvenirs of the history of the Danish navy; Dir. B. von Munthe af Morgenstierne.

Rosenborg Slot (*Rosenborg Castle*): Øster Voldgade 4A, 1350 Copenhagen K; contains "The Chronological Collections of the Danish Kings"; the collection was founded by Frederik III about 1660, and consists of arms, apparel, jewellery, and furniture from 1470 to 1863; the Crown Jewels are also here; Dir. Chamberlain M. Olufsen; Curator Mogens Bencard, M.A.

Rudolph Tegners Museum og Statuepark: Villingerød Pr. Dronningmøll; f. 1938; Dir. Elna Tegner.

Statens Museum for Kunst (*Royal Fine Arts Museum*): Sølvgade, 1307 Copenhagen K; contains the main collection of Danish paintings and sculpture; a number of works by other 19th- and 20th-century Scandinavian artists; J. Rump collection of modern French art; about 1,000 paintings by old masters of the Italian, Flemish, Dutch and German Schools (chiefly derived from the old royal collection, which was organized as an art gallery in the 1760s). The print room includes about 200,000 Danish and foreign prints and drawings. Library of about 50,000 vols. Dir. Lars Rostrup Bøyesen, M.A.; Curators (Painting and Sculpture): Bente Skovgaard, M.A., Harald Olsen, M.A., Ph.D., Olaf Koester, M.A., Hanne Westergaard, M.A., Hanne Jönsson, M.A.; (Prints and Drawings): Erik Fischer, M.A., Jan Garff, M.A., Jan Würtz Frandsen, M.A., Vibeke Knudsen, M.A.; publs. *Kunstmuseets Aarsskrift* (annual) and catalogues.

Teatermuseet: Christiansborg Palace, 10 Ridebanen, Copenhagen K; f. 1912; illustrates the development of the Danish theatre from the Middle Ages to the present day; approx. 1,000 mems. of supporting society (Danish Society for Theatre Research); library and MSS. collection; Dir. Karen Neiiendam.

Thorvaldsens Museum: Porthusgade 2, 1213 Copenhagen K; f. 1839-48; sculpture and drawings by the Danish sculptor Bertel Thorvaldsen (1770–1844), his collections of contemporary European paintings, drawings and prints, classical antiquities and his library of 2,655 vols.; museum library of *c.* 5,000 vols.; Dir. Dyveke Helsted; publs. catalogues in Danish, English, French and German, *Meddelelser*† (Bulletin).

Tøjhusmuseet (*Royal Danish Arsenal Museum*): Frederiksholms Kanal 29 (Administration) and Tøjhusgade 3 (main entrance), Copenhagen; f. 1838; central State museum for arms and armour; history of arms in Europe, from the introduction of gunpowder till the present time; history and development of international military materials; Dir. Finn Askgaard, M.A.; Chief Curator Arne Orloff, M.A.

Vikingeskibshallen I Roskilde (*The Viking Ship Museum*): Strandengen, 4000 Roskilde; f. 1969; exhibits the five Viking ships found at Skuldelev in 1962, and aims to promote research in ship-building history in general; research on maritime subjects is carried out by the Institute of Maritime Archaeology of the National Museum, housed in the same building; Dir. Ole Crumlin-Pedersen.

Zoologisk Museum (*University of Copenhagen Zoological Museum*): Universitetsparken 15, 2100 Copenhagen; f. 1770; Danish and large international collection includes Arctic and deep-sea animals, Danish and South American quaternary fossils; Dir. Jørgen Nielsen; publs. *Steenstrupia*†, *Atlantide Report*, *Galathea Report*, *Dana Report*.

UNIVERSITIES AND TECHNICAL UNIVERSITIES

AALBORG UNIVERSITETSCENTER

P.O.B. 159, LANGAGERVEJ 2,
9100 AALBORG
Telephone: 08-159111.

Founded 1974; in process of formation.

State control; Academic year: September to July.

Courses in the humanities, social sciences, sciences and technology.

Rector: Sven Caspersen.
Administrative Officer: Peter Plenge.
Librarian: Bent Jørgensen.

Number of teachers: 330.
Number of students: 2,900.
Publication: *Center Nyt*†.

Deans:

Faculty of Humanities: Hans Siggaard Jensen.
Faculty of Social Sciences: Carsten Heyn-Johnsen.
Faculty of Technology and Sciences: Jørgen Østergaard.

Attached Research Institutes:

Institute of Social Studies, Public Administration and Political Institutions.
Institute of Education and Socialization.
Institute of Languages, Communication and History of Civilization.
Institute of Development and Planning.
Institute of Civil Engineering.
Institute of Building Technology and Structural Engineering.
Institute of Industrial Constructions and Energy Technology.
Institute of Electronic Systems.
Institute of Production and Production Processes.

AARHUS UNIVERSITET

NDR. RINGGADE, 8000 AARHUS C
Telephone: (06) 134311.
Founded 1928.

State controlled; Academic year: September to June.

Rector: Prof. Carl F. Wandel.
Pro-Rector: (vacant).
Director: Stig Møller.

Library: *see* Libraries.
Number of professors: 170.
Number of students: 15,000.
Publications: *Acta Jutlandica Årsberetning* (yearbook).

Deans:

Faculty of Arts: P. Mortensen.
Faculty of Medicine: P. Juul-Jensen.
Faculty of Law and Economics: Niels Amstrup.
Faculty of Divinity: P. Nepper-Christensen.
Faculty of Natural Sciences: H. H. Andersen.

Professors:

Faculty of Arts:
Albertsen, L. L., Germanic Philology
Christensen, N. E., Philosophy
Dahlerup, T., History
Dittmer, E., German Philology
Due, O. S., Classical Languages
Engberg, Jens, History
Hannah, D. W., English Philology.
Jensen, J. F., Comparative Literature
Jensen, J. S., Romance Philology
Jeppesen, K., Classical Archaeology
Johansen, H. F., Classical Languages
Juul Jensen, Uffe, Philosophy
Kabell, Aa., Nordic Literature
Mathiassen, F., Musicology
Nielsen, N. Å., Nordic Languages
Nykrog, P., Romance Philology
Olsen, O., Archaeology
Poulsen, H., Modern History
Ringgaard, K., Nordic Philology
Schmidt, K. R., Russian Language and Literature
Sørensen, K., English Language
Sørensen, S., Musicology
Svane, G., Slav Languages and Literature
Thomsen, R., Ancient History

TOLL, G. G., Semitic Philology
ULSIG, E., Medieval History
WESTERGÅRD-NIELSEN, CHR., Western Nordic Language and Literature

Faculty of Medicine:
AMDRUP, E., Surgery
ANDERSSON, K.-E., Clinical Pharmacology
BASTRUP-MADSEN, P., Internal Medicine
BOLUND, L., Clinical Genetics
BONDE, G. J., Hygiene
BRODERSEN, R., Biochemistry
CLAUSEN, T., Physiology
DALGAARD, J. B., Forensic Medicine
EHLERS, N., Ophthalmology
ELBRØND, O., Oto-rhino-laryngology
ENGBERG, B. I., Physiology
ESMANN, V., Internal Medicine
FREUNDT, E., Comparative Pathology
GLIEMANN, J., Physiology
GOETTZSCHE, H., Internal Medicine
HEIMAR, L., Anatomy
HOLM-NIELSEN, P., Surgery
IVERSEN, T., Paediatrics
JENSEN, O. M., Pathology
JUHL, B., Anaesthesiology
KAAE, S., Radiology
KEIDING, R., Clinical Chemistry
KISSMEYER, F., Immunology
MAUNSBACH, A., Anatomy
NERSTROM, B., Urology
OLIVARIUS, B. DE FINE, Neurology
OLSEN, S., Pathological Anatomy
PETERSEN, V. P., Internal Medicine
RASMUSSEN, P., Neurosurgery
REHFELD, J. F., Biochemistry
SCHOU, M., Psychiatry
SKOU, J. C., Biophysics
SNEPPEN, O., Orthopaedic Surgery
STENDERUP, A., Bacteriology
SØNDERGAARD, T., Surgery
THERKELSEN, A. J., Human Genetics
VIIDIK, A., Anatomy
ZACHARIAE, H., Dermatology and Venereal Diseases

Faculty of Law and Economics:
ANDERSEN, C. J., Economic Planning
BECH, R., Jurisprudence
BEFRING, E., Psychology
BJOL, E., Political Science
BORRE, O., Political Science
CARSTENSEN, V. U., Jurisprudence
CLAUSEN, H. P., Political Science
FENGER, O., Jurisprudence
FREDENS, S., Economic Planning
GAD, H., Social Science
GELTING, J., National Economy
GERMER, P., Jurisprudence
HARSAAE, E., Statistics
JEPSEN, G. T., National Economy
JESPERSEN, H. K., Jurisprudence
JØRGENSEN, S., Jurisprudence
KATZENELSON, BOJE, Psychology
LARSEN, B. U., Jurisprudence
LAURSEN, K., National Economy
MADSEN, V., Economic Planning
MATHIASSEN, JORGEN, Jurisprudence
MEYER, P., Political Science
MOORE, T., Psychology
MYRUP, H. P., Economic Planning
NØRGAARD, C. A., Jurisprudence
NØRGAARD, J. H., Jurisprudence
PETERSEN, E., Psychology
POULSEN, B. B., Psychology
POULSEN, H., Psychology
RASMUSSEN, E., Political Science
ROERSTED, B., Economic Planning
SCHMIDT, T. S., Jurisprudence
VIBE-PEDERSEN, J., National Economy
YNDGAARD, E., National Economy

Faculty of Divinity:
BALLING, J. L., Church History
GIVERSEN, S., Theology
LINDHARDT, P. G., Church History
OTZEN, B., Old Testament Exegesis
SIMONSEN, H., New Testament Exegesis
SLOK, J., Theology
THODBERG, C., Practical Theology

Faculty of Natural Sciences:
ANDERSEN, J. U., Experimental Physics
ANDERSEN, T., Physics
BALSLEV, E., PH.D., Mathematics
BARNDORFF-NIELSEN, O., Mathematics
BRODERSEN, S., Chemistry
BUNDGAARD, S., Mathematics
CARSTENS, H., Geology
CLARK, B., Chemistry
FENCHEL, T., Zoology
HANSEN, P. G., Physics
HUMLUM, J., Geography
JOHANSEN, K., Zoophysiology
KJELDGAARD, O., Molecular Biology
KRISTENSEN, L., Mathematics
KRISTENSEN, P. V., Physics
LARSEN, G., Geology
LARSEN, K., Botany
LINDERBERG, J., Chemistry
LINDHARD, J., Physics
MARCKER, K., Biological Biochemistry
MAYOH, B. H., Mathematics
MUUS, L. T., Chemistry
MØLLER, J. T., Geography
NIELSEN, K. O., Physics
PEDERSEN, O., History of Exact Sciences
POULSEN, E. T., Mathematics
RASMUSSEN, S. E., Chemistry
RUDKJØBING, M., Astronomy
SAXOV, S., Geology
SPJELDNAES, N., Geology
TORSSELL, K., Chemistry
WANDEL, C. F., Physics

ATTACHED INSTITUTES:

School of Post-Basic Nursing: f. 1938.
Institute of Occupational Therapy and Physiotherapy: f. 1959.
Institute of Home Economics: f. 1945.

KØBENHAVNS UNIVERSITET

FRUE PLADS,
1168 COPENHAGEN K
Telephone: Copenhagen 01-110828.
Founded 1479.

Rector: Prof. Dr. med. E. SKINHØJ.
Director: V. SYLVEST LARSEN.
Number of professors: 249.
Number of students: 26,361.

DEANS:

Faculty of Theology: L. GRANE.
Faculty of Social Sciences: H. GAMMELTOFT-HANSEN.
Faculty of Medicine: O. BEHNKE.
Faculty of Arts: B. MUNK OLSEN.
Faculty of Mathematics and Natural Science: C. NIELSEN.

PROFESSORS:

Faculty of Theology:
ANDERSEN, N. K., Danish Church History
CHRISTENSEN, T., Church and Dogmatic History
FORELL, U., Systematic Theology
GRANE, L., Church History
HOLM-NIELSEN, S., Old Testament Exegesis
HYLDAHL, N. C., New Testament Exegesis
JØRGENSEN, T., Dogmatics
NIELSEN, E., Old Testament Exegesis
THEISSEN, G., New Testament Exegesis
THULSTRUP, N., Systematic Theology

Faculty of Social Sciences:
ANDERSEN, E., Economics
ANDERSEN, E. B., Theoretical Statistics
CHRISTENSEN, B., Law
DANØ, S., Business Economy
ESPERSEN, O., Law
ESTRUP, H., Economics
EYBEN, W. E. VON, Law
FOIGHEL, I., Law
GAMMELTOFT-HANSEN, H. T., Law
GOMARD, B., Law
GRODAL, B. K., Economics
HANSEN, SV. AA., Statistics and Economic History of Denmark
KOKTVEDGAARD, M., Law
KRARUP, O. Law
KRUSE, A. V., Law
LAURIDSEN, P. S., Law
MATTHIESSEN, P. C., Demography
NIELSEN, T., Law
NICOLAISEN, A. J., Ethnology and Anthropology
ØLGAARD, A., Economics
RASMUSSEN, P. N., Economics
SIESBY, E., Law
SVALASTOGA, K., Sociology
TAKSØE-JENSEN, F., Law
TAMM, D., Law
THYGESEN, N. C., Economics
VIND, K., Economics
WAABEN, K., Law

Faculty of Medicine:
ANDERSEN, S. R., Ophthalmology
ANDREASSEN, M., Surgery
ARNOLDI, C. C., Orthopaedic Surgery
ASBOE-HANSEN, G., Skin and Venereal Diseases
ASTRUP, P., Clinical Chemistry and Laboratory Technique
BADEN, H., Surgery
BACKER, P., General Medicine
BEHNKE, O., Cytology
BENDIXEN, G., Internal Medicine
CHRISTENSEN, L., KORSGAARD, Internal Medicine
CRONE, U. C., Physiology
DIAMANT, B., Pharmacology
FABER, J. V., Epidemic Diseases
FABER, M., Medical Radiobiology
FREIESLEBEN, E., Blood-Type Serology
FRIIS-HANSEN, B. J., Paediatrics
GAMMELGAARD, P. A., Surgery
GORMSEN, H., Forensic Medicine
GREGERSEN, E., Eye Diseases
HANSEN, A. T., Internal Medicine
HASNER, E. M., Surgery
HJORTH, N., Skin and Venereal Diseases
HOLMA, B. O. A., Hygiene
HOLST, E. K., Social Medicine
HVIDBERG, E. F., Clinical Pharmacology
JOHANSEN, S. H., Anaesthesiology
JOSEFSSON, L., Biochemistry
KIILMANN, S. A., Internal Medicine
KLENOW, H., Biochemistry
KOCH, F., Pathological Anatomy
KRISTENSEN, H. K., Oto-Rhino-Laryngology
KRUHØFFER, P. W., Physiology
LARSEN, H. W., Eye Diseases
LARSEN, J. F., Midwifery and Gynaecology
LAURSEN, A. M., Behavioural Physiology
LORENZEN, I., Internal Medicine
LUND, F., Surgery
LUNDQUIST, F., Biochemistry
LUNN, V., Psychiatry
MELCHIOR, J. C., Paediatrics
MELLERGÅRD, M. J., Psychiatry
MOE, H., Anatomy

Mohr, J., Genetics
Müllertz, S. C., Clinical Chemistry and Laboratory Technique
Nielsen, A. E., Medical Chemistry
Norn, M. S., Eye Diseases
Pakkenberg, H., Neurology
Petersen, O., Radiology
Philip, J., Midwifery and Gynaecology
Poulsen, H. E., Pathological Anatomy
Quaade, F., Internal Medicine
Rafaelsen, O. J., Psychiatry
Riis, P., Internal Medicine
Riishede, J., Neuro-Surgery
Riskaer, N., Oto-Rhino-Laryngology
Rovsing, H. C., Radiology
Ruben, H. M., Anaesthesiology
Schiødt, T., Pathological Anatomy
Schou, J., Pharmacology
Schulsinger, F. M., Psychiatry
Secher, O. W., Anaesthesiology
Siggaard-Andersen, O., Clinical Chemistry and Laboratory Technique
Simonsen, M., Immunobiology
Skinhøj, E., Neurology
Snorrason, E. S. H., Physical Medicine
Søndergaard, J., Skin and Venereal Diseases
Sørensen, B., Surgery
Sørensen, H., Oto-Rhino-Laryngology
Sørensen, H. R., Surgery
Stakemann, G., Obstetrics and Gynaecology
Sten-Kundsen, O., Biophysics
Thaysen, J. H., Internal Medicine
Thomsen, G., Radiology
Thorn, N. A., Physiology
Thygesen, P., Neurology
Tolstrup, K., Children's Psychiatry
Trolle, D., Midwifery and Gynaecology
Tygstrup, N., Internal Medicine
Vesterdal, J., Paediatrics
Visfeldt, J., Pathological Anatomy
Volkert, M., Pathology
Zachau-Christiansen, B., Paediatrics

Faculty of Arts

Asmussen, J., Iranian Philology
Asplund, K. J., Psychology
Becker, C. J., Prehistoric Archaeology
Blegvad, M., Philosophy
Bredsdorff, H. T., Danish Literature
Brunius, J. A. T., History of Art
Christensen, J., Classical Philology
Egerod, S. C., East Asian Languages
Ejskjaer, I., Danish Dialectology
Ellehøj, S., History
Fafner, J., Metrics and Recitation
Fischer-Jørgensen, E., Phonetics
From, F., Psychology
Glahn, H., Music
Glamann, K., History
Hansen, E., Danish Language
Hendriksen, H., Indian and Eastern Philology
Henningsen, S., Modern History
Henriksen, Aa., Nordic Literature
Hjorth, P. V. Lindegård, Nordic Languages
Hvidtfeldt, A., Sociology of Religion
Hyldgaard-Jensen, K., German Language
Jacobsen, E., English Language and Literature
Johansen, J. Prytz, History of Religion
Johansen, K. Friis, Ancient and Medieval Philosophy
Johansen, M. V., Normal Psychology
Jørgensen, S. Aa., German Philology
Kristensen, S. Møller, Nordic Literature
Kvam, K., Theatre Studies
Levine, P., American Language and Literature
Lidin, O., East Asian Languages
Louis-Jensen, J., Icelandic Language and Literature
Lundquist, L. H. S., Social Sciences
Læssøe, J., Assyriology
Løkkegaard, F., Oriental Philology
Madsen, P., Literary History
Maegaard, J., Music
Moustgaard, I. K., Psychology
Nordhjem, B., English Language and Literature
Nylander, C. R. L., Archaeology
Nørretranders, B. F., East European History
Olsen, B. M., Romance Languages and Literature
Osing, J., Egyptology
Østergaard, A. E., Clinical Psychoogy
Pedersen, J., Romance Languages and Literature
Pedersen, O. Karup, International Politics
Petersen, R. K. F., Eskimo Language and Literature
Pinborg, J. B., Classical Philology
Rischel, J., Linguistics
Schiørring, N., Music
Sjöblom, G., Social Science
Skydsgaard, J. E., Ancient History
Skyum-Nielsen, N., History
Spang-Hanssen, E., Romance Languages and Literature
Spang-Hanssen, H., Mathematical Linguistics
Steensgaard, N. P., History
Steffensen, S., German Philology
Stief, C., Slavonic Philology
Stoklund, B., European Ethnology
Stybe, J. E., Philosophy
Sørensen, H., Chr. Slavonic Languages
Sørensen, H. Steen, English Language and Literature
Sørensen, J. Kousgaard, Danish Language
Thomsen, N. J., History
Vikner, C., Romance Languages and Literature
Willanger, R., Psychology
Zettersten, A., English Language and Literature

Faculty of Mathematics and Natural Science

Andersen, E. S., Mathematics
Andersen, S. O., Zoo-Physiology
Bak, B., Molecular Spectroscopy
Bak, T. A., Chemistry
Ballhausen, C. J., Chemistry
Bang, T., Mathematics
Berg, C., Mathematics
Berthelsen, S. A., Geology
Birkelund, T., Historical Geology
Böcher, T. W., Botany
Bohr, A., Physics
Brøns, H., Mathematical Statistics
Buchardt, O., Chemistry
Chadderton, L. T., Physics
Christensen, B., Zoology
Christiansen, S., Geography
Dahlgreen, R., Botany
Dansgaard, W., Physical Glaciology
Egel, R., Genetics
Elbek, B., Physics
Eliasen, E., Meteorology
Foltmann, B., Genetics
Fuglede, B., Mathematics
Grimby, L. C., Theory of Gymnastics
Hald, A., Statistics
Hansen, O., Physics
Hansen, V. O., Ethnogeography
Hoem, J. M., Actuarial Science
Huus, T., Physics
Jacobsen, N. K., Geography
Jensen, C. U., Mathematics
Jensen, H. Højgaard, Physics
Johansen, P., Computer Science
Jónasson, P. M., Freshwater Biology
Jørgensen, C. B., Animal Physiology
Jørgensen, E. G., Plant Physiology
Koie, M., Botanical Ecology
Kullenberg, G. E. B., Oceanography
Lange, M., Botany
Lassen, N. O., Physics
Lassen, U. V., Animal Physiology
Maaløe, O., Microbiology
Mackintosh, A. R., Experimental Solid State Physics
Micheelsen, H. I., Mineralogy
Munch-Petersen, I. A., Biochemistry
Muus, B. J., Zoology
Nathan, O., Physics
Naur, P., Computer Science
Nielsen, C. O., Zoology
Pedersen, G. K., Mathematics
Poulsen, V. J., Geology
Reiz, A., Astronomy
Saltin, B., Theory of Gymnastics
Schmidt, O. H., History of Exact Sciences
Sharma, P. V., Geophysics
Smith, H., Physics
Sørensen, H., Geology
Strid, A., Botany
Svensson, S. A. H., Geomorphology
Tornehave, H., Mathematics
Ussing, H. H., Biochemistry
Wingstrand, K. G., Anatomy and Morphology
Winther, A., Theoretical Physics

Attached Institute:

Institute for Studies in Higher Education: f. 1969.

KONGELIGE VETERINÆR- OG LANDBOHØJSKOLE
(Royal Veterinary and Agricultural University)

BÜLOWSVEJ 13,
DK 1870 COPENHAGEN V
Telephone: (01) 351788.
Founded 1856.

Rector: Prof. Dr. H. C. Aslyng.
Pro-Rector: Dr. Folke Rasmussen.
Administrator: J. E. Høibye Hansen.
Head of the College Arboretum in Hørsholm: Dr. agro. Bent Søegaard.

Number of teachers: 278, including 59 professors.

Number of students: 1,928.

Deans:

Faculty of Basic Science: Hanne Flyge.
Faculty of Veterinary Science: Dr. Preben Willeberg.
Faculty of Agricultural Science: Prof. Henning Staun.
Faculty of Forestry Science: Finn Helles.
Faculty of Horticultural Science: Poul Karlsen.
Faculty of Dairy and Food Science: Aage Jart.

Professors:

Adler, H. C., Forensic Medicine
Andersen, S., Agricultural Plant Culture
Aslyng, H. C., Agricultural Hydrotechnology
Bisgaard, K. M., Physics
Björkmann, N., Anatomy

BRUMMERSTEDT, E., Pathology and Pathological Anatomy
CHRISTENSEN, J. V., Horticulture
CHRISTENSEN, N. O., Polyclinic and Veterinary Practice
DAHL, N. J., Agricultural Civil Engineering
DALGAARD-MIKKELSEN, Sv., Pharmacology
ESPERSEN, G. J., Veterinary Surgery
FLENSTED-JENSEN, M., Mathematics and Statistics
FLINK, J., Food Science
HAARLØV, N., Zoology
HENNINGSEN, K. W., Genetics
HENRIKSEN, H. A., Forestry
HERMANSEN, J. E., Plant Pathology
JAKOBSEN, P. E., Animal Physiology
JENSEN, A. T., Chemistry
JENSEN, J. F., Breeding and Feeding of Poultry
JENSEN, V., Microbiology
JØRGENSEN, J., Zoology
KJELDSEN-KRAGH, S., Political Economy
KLOUGART, A., Horticulture
LANGE, J., Botany
LARSEN, H. E., Veterinary Microbiology and Hygiene
LARSEN, P. O., Chemistry
LARSEN, S., Soil Fertility and Plant Nutrition
LUND E., Virology and Immunology
MARTHEDAL, H. E., Diseases of Poultry
MIKKELSEN, V. M., Botany
MOLTESEN, P., Forestry
MOUSTGAARD, J., Endocrinology and Physiology
NEIMANN-SØRENSEN, A., Animal Husbandry
NIELSEN, K., Special Pathology and Therapeutics
OVERBY, J. A., Dairy Chemistry and Bacteriology
PEDERSEN, TH. T., Farm Machinery
RAJAGOPAL, R., Physiological Botany
RASBECH, N. O., Gynaecology and Obstetrics
RASMUSSEN, K., Agricultural Chemistry and Soil Science
RUDEMO, M., Mathematics and Statistics
SAMUELSSON, E.-G., Dairy Science
SCHMIDT, J. P., Horticulture
SKOVGAARD, N., Food Microbiology and Hygiene
STAUN, H., Animal Husbandry
SØRENSEN, P. H., Animal Husbandry
THOMSEN, C., Agricultural Policy
THORDAL-CHRISTENSEN, A., Veterinary Medicine
VEDEL, H., Botany
VOLDUM, A., Surveying
WISMER-PEDERSEN, J., Meat Technology
WULFF, H., Agricultural Law
AALUND, O., Internal Medicine

ODENSE UNIVERSITET

CAMPUSVEJ 55,
5230 ODENSE M.
Telephone: (09) 158600.

Founded 1964 (teaching commenced September 1966).

State control; Academic year: September to June (two semesters).

Rector: AAGE TROMMER.
Pro-Rector: ANNELISE BACH.
Chief Administrative Officer: BENT EGEDE FICH.

Library: *see under* Libraries.
Number of teachers 294.
Number of students: 5,000.

DEANS:

Faculty of Arts: JØRN MOESTRUP.
Faculty of Natural Sciences: CARL TH. PEDERSEN.
Faculty of Medicine: JØRGEN RINGSTED.

PROFESSORS:

Faculty of Arts:
BASBØLL, H., Scandinavian Language
BRØNDSTED, M., Scandinavian Literature
DANIELSEN, N., German Language and Literature
FAVRHOLDT, D., Philosophy
GØRTZ, E., National Economics
HAARDER, A., English Language and Literature
HANSEN, PETER, Political Science
HARTVIGSON, H., English Language and Literature
JENNERGREN, L. P., Business Economics
JENSEN, S. S., Classical Philology
JOHANSEN, H. C., History
JOHANSEN, JØRGEN DINES, Comparative Literature
KAARSTED, T. H., History
KNUDSEN, N. C., National Economics
MATTHIESEN, LARS, Economics
MEY, J. L., Linguistics
MOESTRUP, J., Romance Philology
NIELSEN, H. B., Scandinavian Languages
NØJGAARD, M., Romance Philology
PEDERSEN, M. N., Political Sciences
PETERSEN, E. L., History
PETERSEN, J. H., Social Sciences
SØRENSEN, B. A., German Language and Literature

Faculty of Natural Sciences:
BALSLEV, I., Physics
BOLL, P. M., Chemistry
KARLOG, O. B., Biology
MICHELSEN, A., Biology
MØLLER, C. K., Chemistry
NORDSTRØM, KURT, Experimental Microbiology
PERRAM, JOHN WILLIAM, Applied Mathematics
PLESNER, P., Molecular Biology
SCHAMBYE, P. A., Biochemistry
SIGMUND, H. P., Physics
WEBER, R. E.

Faculty of Medicine:
ANDERSEN, D., Surgery
BIERRING, F., Anatomy
CHAKRAVARTY, N. K., Pharmacology
CHRISTENSEN, H. E., Pathology
FABRICIUS, J., Clinical Physiology
GARBY, G., Physiology
GOLDSCHMIDT, E.
GRAM, L. F., Pharmacology
HANSEN, ERIK, Neurology
HARVALD, B., Internal Medicine
HAUGE, M., Hereditary Pathology
JUEL-NIELSEN, N., Psychiatry
JØRGENSEN, S., Anaesthesiology
KEMP, E., Internal Medicine
KILDEBERG, P. A., Paediatrics
KRISTOFFERSEN, K., Obstetrics and Gynaecology
RASMUSSEN, L.
SCHMIDT, H., Dermatology and Venereal Diseases
SIBONI, K., Microbiology
SIMONSEN, J., Forensic Medicine
STOKSTED, P., Oto-rhino-laryngology
SVEHAG, S. E., Microbiology

ROSKILDE UNIVERSITETSCENTER

P.O.B. 260, MARBJERGVEJ 35,
DK-4000 ROSKILDE
Telephone: (03) 36-36-11.
Founded 1970.

State controlled; Academic year: September to June (two semesters).

Rector: BOEL JØRGENSEN.
Pro-Rector: HENNING SALLING OLESEN.
Administrative Officer: ERNST GRAVESEN.
Librarian: MORTEN LAURSEN-VIG.

Library of 197,300 vols.
Number of teachers: 155 full-time, 55 part-time.
Number of students: *c.* 2,000.

PROFESSORS:

Humanities:
BAGGESEN, S., Science of Texts, Scandinavian and American Literature
BJERG, J., Educational Psychology
BLATT, T., English
BRASK, P., Science of Texts, Theory and Methodology of Literary Analysis
GEMZELL, C.-A., Modern History
GLEBE-MØLLER, J., Philosophy
HAASTRUP, N., Danish
HANNEBORG, K. Ø., Philosophy
JENSEN, J. P., Psychology
JENSEN, J. AA., Educational Psychology
KJØRUP, SOREN, Philosophy
MORTENSEN, A. T., Philosophy
OLSEN, MICHEL, French
PEDERSEN, STIG ANDUR, Science
PRÆSTGAARD, EIGIL, Chemistry
TELEMAN, U., General and Nordic Linguistics
WEBB, T. W., Sociology of Education

Natural Sciences:
ANDERSEN, FRODE SØGÅRD, Ecology
BONDESEN, E., Geology
CLAUSEN, JØRGEN, Biochemistry
FERNHOLM, BO, Biology
HANSEN, H. B., Computer Sciences

Social Sciences:
ADLER-KARLSSON, G., Social Science Theory
BENTZON, A. W., Sociology of Law
DYBBROE, K. O., Development and Planning Theory
NISSEN, G., Social Conditions of Education
OLSEN, E., International Economics
RERUP, L., History
SVENDSEN, K. E., Development Economics

DEN POLYTEKNISKE LAEREANSTALT, DANMARKS TEKNISKE HØJSKOLE (Technical University of Denmark)

2800 LYNGBY, COPENHAGEN
Telephone: (02) 88-22-22.
Founded 1829.

President: Lektor PETER LAWÆTZ.
Vice-President: Lektor BENT KNUDSEN.
Secretary: P. CARPENTIER.

Number of professors: 84.
Number of students: 3,391.

DEANS:

Faculty of Common Sciences: Prof. Dr. NIELS MEYER.

Faculty of Civil Structural Engineering: Lektor KNUD CHRISTENSEN.

Faculty of Electrotechnics: Lektor TORBEN JOHANSSON.

Faculty of Chemical Science: Prof. AAGE FREDENSLUND.

Faculty of Mechanical Science: Prof. F. NIORDSON.

PROFESSORS:

ALTING, L., Mechanical Engineering
ANDERSEN, A. L., Physics
ASKEGAARD, V., Structural Engineering
BJÖRKMAN, A. E. G., Technical Chemistry
BJØRNER, D., Computer Science
BOE, C., Engineering Design
BRAMSNÆS, F., Technical Bio-Chemistry
BRO-RASMUSSEN, F., Environmental Science and Ecology
BRUUN, G., Electronics
BRØNDUM-NIELSEN, T., Structural Engineering
BUCH, K. R., Mathematics
BUSK, T., Applied Mathematics
CARLSEN, T., Physics
COTTERILL, R. M. J., Materials Science
DAHL, J. P., Chemical Physics
DJURTOFT, R., Biochemistry and Nutrition
ENGELUND, F., Hydraulics
FANGER, P. O., Heating and Air Conditioning
FRANK, V., Physics
FREDENSLUND, AA., Chemical Engineering
FREDERIKSEN, E., Machinery
GIMSING, N. J., Structural Engineering
GOLDSCHMIDT, V., Social Science
GRAM, C., Computer Science
GUDMANDSEN, P. E., Microwave Techniques
GUDNASON, C. H., Machine Technics
GAARSLEV, A., Construction Management
HANNERZ, N. E., Thermal Processsing
HANSEN, B., Soil Mechanics
HANSEN, E. B., Applied Mathematics
HANSEN, E., Hydrology
HANSEN, J. R., Electric Power Supply
HANSEN, T. C., Structural Engineering
HANSEN, V. L., Mathematics
HARBOE, K. P., Building Design
HARREMOES, P., Sanitary Engineering
HARVALD, S. A., Shipbuilding
INGERSLEV, F. H. B., Acoustics
JACOBI, O., Surveying and Photogrammetry
JENSEN, A., Mathematics
JENSEN, J. R., Servomechanisms
JENSEN, L. B., Acoustics
JENSEN, P. G., Impulses
JUSTESEN, J., Telecommunication
JØRGENSEN, N. O., Traffic
JØRGENSEN, O. B., Applied Biochemistry
KJAER, A., Organic Chemistry
KNUDSEN, H. L., Electro-magnetic Theory
KOPS, J., Polymer Chemistry and Engineering
KORSGAARD, V., Thermal Insulation
KRABBE, U. H., Electrical Circuit and Machines
LANGER, E. W., Metallurgy
LUNDGREN, H., Harbour Building and Foundations
MEYENBURG, H. K. VON, Microbiology
MEYER, N., Physics
MUNCH-PETERSEN, J. F., Industrial Building
NIELSEN, A., Physics
NIELSEN, M. P., Structural Analysis
NIORDSON, F., Machinery
NORRESTAM, R., Chemistry
OTT, S., Town Planning
PAULY, H. J., Crystallography and Mineralogy
PEDERSEN, B. E., Structural Engineering
PEDERSEN, C., Organic Chemistry
PEDERSEN, P. T., Strength of Materials
PEULICKE, H., Industrial Electronics
QVALE, B., Mechanical Engineering
REFSLUND, K., Fluid Mechanics
RUZICKA, J., Analytical Chemistry
SIMONSEN, K. A., Technical Chemistry
SKOVGAARD, H. E., Mathematics
SÆRMARK, K., Physics
SØRENSEN, E. V., Circuit Theory and Electronics
THAGESEN, B. M., Road Building
THÖLÉN, A. R., Physics
TROSTMANN, E., Control Engineering
TRUMPY, G., Physics
WANHEIM, T., Machine Technics
WOLDBYE, F., Inorganic Chemistry
WORSØE-SCHMIDT, P., Power Current
ØLGAARD, P. L., Reactor Physics and Nuclear Engineering
ØSTERGAARD, K., Chemical Engineering

DANMARKS INGENIØRAKADEMI (Engineering Academy of Denmark)

BYGNING 101,
2800 LYNGBY, COPENHAGEN

Founded 1957.

Rector: Dr. P. LAWÆTZ.
Deputy Rector: L. ALFRED HANSEN.

Number of professors: 37.
Number of students: 1,300.

DEANS:

Faculty of Civil Engineering: KATE ESROM LARSEN.

Faculty of Electronics: OTTO MORTENSEN.

Faculty of Chemical Science: J. D. MONRAD.

Faculty of Mechanical Science: OVE BOGØ.

OTHER INSTITUTIONS OF HIGHER EDUCATION

Arkitektskolen i Aarhus (*Aarhus School of Architecture*): Nørreport 20, 8000 Aarhus C; f. 1965.

Rector: Prof. NILS-OLE LUND.
Administrator: ARNE SØRENSEN.

Number of teachers: 83, including 7 professors.

Publications: *Årsberetning, Skolehåndbogen* (annually).

Danmarks Journalisthøjskole (*Danish School of Journalism*): Halmstadgade 11, 8200 Århus N.; Telephone: 06.16.11.22; f. 1971.

Dean: ARNE EJBYE-ERNST.
Vice-Dean: HANS VEIRUP.
Administrator: BIRGER SØRENSEN.

Number of teachers: 26.
Number of students: 637.

Handelshøjskolen i Århus (*The Århus Graduate School of Economics, Business Administration and Modern Languages*): Fuglesangs Allé 4, 8210 Århus V; f. 1939.

Rector: Prof. NIELS NIELSEN.
Secretary: CHR. LORENZEN.
Librarian: A. M. FRANDSEN.

Number of teachers: 125 full-time including professors, 134 part-time.

Number of students: 3,200.

PROFESSORS:

BALLING, M., Finance
BLOK, P., Business Law
GAMMELGÅRD, S., Macroeconomics
HERBORG NIELSEN, TH., Business Organization and Management
JACOBSEN, BENT, English Language
NIELSEN, N., Microeconomics
NIELSEN, OLE, Mathematical Statistics and Computer Science
POULSEN, S.-O., German Language
PRINTZ, L., Managerial Data Processing
PROVSTGAARD, B., Accountancy
RASMUSSEN, K., Foreign Trade
SLOTH CARLSEN, P., Statistical Description
ÖLANDER, FOLKE, Economic Psychology

Handelshøjskolen i København (*The Copenhagen School of Economics and Business Administration*): Fabrikvej 7, 2000 Copenhagen F; Telephone (01) 19-19-19; f. 1917; State control; Academic year: September to July.

Rector: Prof. LAUGE STETTING.
Secretary: POUL FLINDHARDT.

Library: *see* under Libraries.

Number of teachers: 662 including 21 professors.

Number of students: 8,589.

Publications: *Handelshøjskolens Shriftrækker* (series of publications).

Københavns Tandlægehøjskole (*Royal Dental College*): Universitetsparken 4, 2100 Copenhagen Ø; Telephone: 01-37-17-00; f. 1888.

Dean: J. JAKOBSEN.
Vice-Dean: Prof. E. KISLING.
Administrator: M. SCHULTZER-NIELSEN.

Number of teachers: 190, including 14 professors.

Number of students: 700.

PROFESSORS:

BJÖRK, A., D.D.S., DR.ODONT.
DABELSTEEN, S. E., D.D.S., DR.ODONT.
FRANDSEN, A., D.D.S., DR.ODONT.
HELM, S., D.D.S., DR.ODONT.
HJØRTING-HANSEN, E., D.D.S., DR.ODONT.
JØRGENSEN, K. D., D.D.S., M.S., DR.ODONT.
KISLING, E., D.D.S., DR.ODONT.
MØLLER, E., D.D.S., DR.ODONT.
PINDBORG, J. J., D.D.S., DR.ODONT.
POULSEN, H., M.D.
POULSEN, K., M.D.
THYLSTRUP, A., D.D.S., DR.ODONT.
ZELANDER, T., M.D.

ATTACHED INSTITUTE:

Skolen for Klinikassistenter og Tandplejere: Møllegade 26, 2200 Copenhagen N.
Director: A. C. LØGSTRUP, D.D.S.

Århus Tandlaegehøjskole (*Royal Dental College, Århus*): Vennelyst Boulevard, 8000 Århus C; f. 1958.
Dean: Prof. OLE FEJERSKOV.
Administrator: PETER MONDRUP BRAAD.
Librarian: P. JUNKER JACOBSEN.
Number of teachers: 125, including 11 professors.
Number of students: 485.

Danmarks Farmaceutiske Højskole (*Royal Danish School of Pharmacy*): Universitetsparken 2, DK-2100 Copenhagen Ø; Telephone: 45-137 08 50; f. 1892.
Rector: Prof. J. RASSING, DR.PHIL.
Administrator: G. BRILL JENSEN.
Library: *see under* Libraries.
Number of teachers: 71, including 11 professors.
Number of students: 660 (men and women).

PROFESSORS:

AAES-JØRGENSEN, E., Biochemistry
DRENCK, K., Physics
JENSEN, V. GAUNØ, Pharmaceutics
JERSLEV, B., Chemistry
JUUL, P., Pharmacology
KOFOD, H., Chemistry
KRISTENSEN, H. G., Pharmaceutics
RASSING, J., Chemistry
SKADHAUGE, K., Microbiology

Danmarks Laererhøjskole (*Royal Danish School of Educational Studies*): Emdrupvej 101, 2400 Copenhagen NV; 8 local branches in provincial cities; Telephone: 01-69 66 33; f. 1856.
Rector: HENNING ANDERSEN.
Pro-Rector: KAJ SPELLING.
Administrator: ERIK JENSEN.
Chief Librarian: METTE STOCKMARR.
Library: *see* Libraries.
Number of teachers: 165 (*c.* 1,800 part-time), including 25 professors.
Number of students: *c.* 17,500.

CHAIRMEN OF INSTITUTES:

Pedagogics and Psychology: KENNY JÖRGENSEN.
Religious Studies: KAI MOGENSEN.
Danish Language and Literature: ERIK LARSEN.
Foreign Languages: POUL STELLER.
History and Social Sciences: HELGE GAMRATH.
Danish Educational History: VAGN SKOVGAARD-PETERSEN.
Geography: TROELS RAADAM.
Music and Musicology: FINN EGELAND HANSEN.
Mathematics: THOMAS KYED.
Physics: NILS HORNSTRUP.
Chemistry: HABS CHR. HELT.
Biology: CHR. U. CHRISTENSEN.
Nutrition and Biochemistry: BODIL HANSEN.

Jydske Musikkonservatorium, Det (*Royal Academy of Music, Århus*): Fuglesangs Allé 26, 8210 Århus V; f. 1927.
President: Prof. T. NIELSEN.
Secretary: Dr. S. ANGELSÖ.
Number of teachers: 100.
Number of students: 200.

Kongelige Danske Kunstakademi (*Royal Danish Academy of Fine Arts*): Charlottenborg, Kgs. Nytorv 1,1050 Copenhagen K.
Rectors: Prof. T. FABER (School of Architecture), Prof. H. BERTRAM (School of Painting, Sculpture and Graphic Arts), H. P. PEDERSEN (School of Conservation).
Administrator: Cand. Jur. O. RØDER.
Number of professors: 27.
Number of students: 2,000.

Kongelige Danske Musikkonservatorium (*Royal Danish Academy of Music*): Niels Brocksgade 1, 1574 Copenhagen V; f. 1867.
President: ANNE-KARIN HØGENHAVEN.
Administrator: TORBEN WISKUM.
Librarian: TOVE KRAG.
Library of 50,000 vols.
Number of teachers: 150.
Number of students: *c.* 600.

COLLEGES

Danmarks Biblioteksskole (*Royal School of Librarianship, Copenhagen*): Birketinget 6, 2300 Copenhagen S; f. 1956; 120 teachers including 51 part-time; 1,269 students; library of 83,892 vols.

Danmarks Biblioteksskoles Aalborgafdeling (*Royal School of Librarianship, Aalborg Branch*): Langagervej 4, 9220 Aalborg Øst.
Rector: P. KIRKEGAARD.

Fynske Musikkonservatorium (*Academy of Music*): Islandsgade 2, 5000 Odense C.; f. 1929.
President: SVEN ERIK WERNER.
Number of teachers: 50.
Number of students: 80.

Jydsk Teknologisk Institut (*Jutland Technological Institute*): Marselis Boulevard 135, 8000 Århus C; f. 1943; short courses and service to industry in technology and management.
Director: JØRGEN LADEGAARD.

Københavns tekniske Skole (*Copenhagen Technical School*): Rebslagervej 11, 2400 Copenhagen NV; formerly Tekniske Selskabs Skoler; *c.* 300 staff, *c.* 6,000 students.
Director: Dr. H. HORNBY.

Nordjysk Musikkonservatorium (*Academy of Music, Aalborg*): Ryesgade, 9000 Aalborg; f. 1930; 74 students; Rector ERIK BACH.

Teknologisk Institut (*The Technological Institute*): Hagemannsgade 2, 1607 Copenhagen V; f. 1906; advisory services and vocational training to collect, adapt and distribute professional knowledge; teachers 450, students 10,000.
Director: MORTEN KNUDSEN.

Vestjysk Musikkonservatorium (*Academy of Music, Esbjerg*): Islandsgade 50, 6700 Esbjerg; f. 1946; 73 students.
Director: ANETTE FAABORG.

THE FAEROE ISLANDS

LEARNED SOCIETIES AND RESEARCH INSTITUTES

Felagid "Vardin" ("*Vardin*" *Literary Society*): 3800 Tórshavn; f. 1919; Pres. JOHAN HENDRIK W. POULSEN; publ. *Varđin* (The Cairn) (quarterly).

Fiskirannsóknarstovan (*Marine Research Institute*): Debesartrøð, Tórshavn; f. 1951; fishery biology; Dir. JAKUP SVERRI JOENSEN; publ. *Tiđindi frá Fiskirannsóknarstovuni* (3 a year).

Føroya Búnadarfelag (*Faeroese Agricultural Society*): Yviri við Strond 8, Tórshavn; f. 1924; to promote the agricultural industry; advisory service; 1,500 mems.; Chair. HANUS JOHANNESEN.

Føroya Forngripafelag (*Faeroese Archaeological Society*): Foroya Fornminnissavn, 3800 Tórshavn; f. 1898; works in conjunction with the National Museum; 300 mems.; Pres. HEINI OLSEN.

Föroya Fródskaparfelag/Societas Scientiarum Færoensis (*Faeroese Society of Science and Letters*): P.O.B. 209, 3800 Tórshavn; f. 1952; aims to procure scientific and scholarly literature and to work for the establishment of a fund which would form the economic basis for a future institute of research and education; *c.* 65 mems.; Pres. Dr. HÖGNI DEBES JOENSEN; publs. *Fróđskaparrit* (Annals), *Supplementa*.

Føroya Náttúra—Føroya Skúli (*Natural History Society*): Debesartrøð, 3800 Tórshavn; f. 1951; 150 mems.; Pres. ÁSMUNDUR JOHANNESEN.

Føroya Verfrødingafelag (*Chartered Engineers Asscn.*): Eystara Bryggya, 3800 Tórshavn; f. 1967; 100 mems.; Pres. HJARNAR DJURHUUS; publ. *Verkfrøđi* (2 a year).

Føroyskt-Bretskt Felag (*Faeroese-British Asscn.*): í Brekkuni 7, 3800 Tórshavn; f. 1973; promotion of friendship and co-operation between the two countries; 95 mems.; Chair. FINNBJØRN DAM; Sec. FRED BRODERICK.

Heilsufrødiliga Starvsstovan (*Hygiene Institute*): Debesartrøð, 3800 Tórshavn; f. 1975; research and services for the fish industry; quality control, etc.; government dept.; Dirs. JÁKUP MØRKØRE, JUSTINES OLSEN; publ. *Ársfrágreiđing* (annual report).

Norrøna Felagid i Føroyum (*Nordic Society*): Brattabrekka 11, 3800 Tórshavn; f. 1952; co-operation between the Nordic countries; 325 mems.; Chair. KYARTAN HOYDAL; Sec. HANNA MORTENSEN.

Rithøvundafelag Føroya (*Faeroese Writers Union*): 3800 Tórshavn; f. 1957; to promote the growth of Faeroese literature and to protect authors' rights; 53 mems.; Pres. KARSTEN HOYDAL.

LIBRARIES AND MUSEUMS

Býarbókasavnid (*Public Library*): Niels Finsensgøta 7, P.O.B. 358, 3800 Tórshavn; f. 1969; 42,398 vols.; Dir. ANNA BRIMNES.

Føroya Landsbókasavn (*National Library*): P.O.B. 61, Tórshavn; f. 1828; 82,000 vols. (14,000 scientific); open to the public; Dir. SVERRI EGHOLM; publs. *Føroyskur Bókalisti* (annual list of Faeroese publs.), *Samskrá* (quarterly accession catalogue).

Landsskjalasavnid (*National Archives*): Debesartrøð, Tórshavn; f. 1932; Dir. PALL J. NOLSØE.

Føroya Fornminnissavn (*National Museum*): Debesartrøð, 3800 Tórshavn; f. 1898 by Føroya Forngripafelag, taken over by State 1952; Antiquary SVERRI DAHL; publ. *Mondul*.

Føroya Náttúrugripasavn (*Natural History Museum*): Debesartrøð, 3800 Tórshavn; f. 1955; depts. of geology, botany, zoology; Dir. JÓANNES RASMUSSEN.

COLLEGE

Fródskaparsetur Føroya/Academia Færoensis (*Faeroese Academy*): Debesartrøð, 3800 Tórshavn; f. 1965; depts. of Faeroese, natural sciences, theology; 8 full-time staff, 35 full-time students; also evening classes and public lectures; Pres. of Board HANS J. JOENSEN; Sec. MAUD HEINESEN.

DOMINICAN REPUBLIC

Population 5,275,000

ACADEMIES

Santo Domingo

Academia Dominicana de la Lengua (*Dominican Academy*): Félix Mariano Lluberes 18, Santo Domingo; correspondent of the Real Academia Española, Madrid; 17th in order of foundation in Spanish America; library of 50,000 vols.; Pres. D. FABIO A. MOTA; Vice-Pres. D. PORFIRO HERRERA; Sec. MARIANO LEBRÓN SAVIÑÓN.

MEMBERS:

AVELINO, ANDRÉS.
BALAGUER, JOAQUÍN.
BONELLY, RAFAEL F.
GARRIDO, VÍCTOR (*elected*).
GONZÁLEZ, MANUEL RUEDA.
HENRÍQUEZ UREÑA, Dr. MAX.
INCHÁUSTEGUI CABRAL, HÉCTOR (*elected*).
LEBRÓN SAVIÑÓN, MARIANO.
PACHECO, ARMANDO OSCAR.
PÉREZ, CARLOS FEDERICO.
PIETER, HERIBERTO.
ROBLES TOLEDANO, OSCAR.
RODRÍGUEZ DEMORIZI, EMILIO.
TRONCOSO SÁNCHEZ, PEDRO.

Academia Dominicana de la Historia (*Academy of History*): Calle Mercaderes, 50; f. 1931; Pres. Lic. E. RODRÍGUEZ DEMORIZI; Sec. Dr. V. ALFAU DURÁN; Librarian Lic. F. E. BERAS; publ. *Clio* (quarterly).

MEMBERS:

AMIAMA, Lic. MANUEL, A.
BALAGUER, Dr. JOAQUÍN.
CAMPILLO PÉREZ, J. G.
GOICO, M. DE J.
HERRERA, Lic. CESAR, A.
MAÑÓN ARREDONDO, M. DE J.
MOYA PONS, Dr. FRANK.
POLANCO BRITO, Monseñor H.E.
TRONCOSO SÁNCHEZ, Lic. PEDRO.
12 national corresponding mems., 55 foreign.

LEARNED SOCIETIES AND RESEARCH INSTITUTES

(*see* also under Universities)

Santo Domingo

Alliance Française: Calle Dr. Horacio Vicioso 103, Centro de los Héroes, Apdo. 1300; f. 1914; propagation of French culture; 400 mems., *c.* 1,400 pupils; library of 5,000 vols.; Dir. GUY RONDREUX.

Asociación Dominicana de Bibliotecarios, Inc. (ASODOBI) (*Librarians' Association*): c/o Biblioteca Nacional, Plaza de la Cultura; f. 1974 to develop library services in the Republic, increase the standing of the profession and encourage the training of its members; 64 mems.; Pres. PRÓSPERO J. MELLA CHAVIER; Sec.-Gen. VERÓNICA REGÚS DE TOSCA; publ. *El Papiro* (quarterly).

Asociación Médica Dominicana (*Dominican Medical Association*): Apartado de Correos No. 1,237, Santo Domingo; f. 1941; 1,551 mems.; Pres. Dr. ANGEL S. CHAN AQUINO; Sec. Dr. CARLOS LAMARCHE REY; publ. *Revista Médica Dominicana.*

Instituto Azucarero Dominicano (*Dominican Sugar Institute*): Centro de los Héroes, Apdo. 667.

Instituto Cartográfico Militar de las Fuerzas Armadas (*Military Cartographic Institute*): f. 1950; Dir. Lt.-Commdr. JOSÉ J. HUNGRÍA M.

Instituto Cristóbal Colón (*Christopher Columbus Institute*): Miami 50.

Instituto Cultural Dominicano-Americano: Abraham Lincoln 21, Apdo. 147; f. 1947.

Instituto de Cultura Dominicano: Biblioteca Nacional, César Nicolás Penson; f. 1971; to promote the cultural tradition of the country, encourage artistic creation in general, and the expression of the spirit of the Dominican people; Pres. ENRIQUE APOLINAR HENRÍQUEZ; Sec. PEDRO GIL ITURBIDES.

Instituto de Investigaciones Históricas (*Institute of Historical Research*): José Reyes 24 (altos); f. 1936; library of 10,000 vols.; Pres. Dr. GUSTAVO ADOLFO MEJÍA RICART; Vice-Pres. Lic. CARLOS SÁNCHEZ S.; Sec.-Gen. (*ad hoc*) Lic. MÁXIMO COISCOU H.; Curator Lic. LEONTE GUZMÁN S.; publ. *Revista de Historia.*

Santiago de los Caballeros

Asociación Médica de Santiago (*Santiago Medical Association*): Apartado 445; f. 1941; library of 821 vols.; 65 mems.; Pres. Dr. OCTAVIO R. ALMONTE; Sec. Dr. JOSÉ COROMINAS P.; publs. *Boletín Médico* (quarterly), *Boletín Informativo* (fortnightly).

LIBRARIES

Santo Domingo

Archivo General de la Nación: Calle M. E. Diaz; f. 1935; 3,000 vols.; Dir. MARISOL FLORÉN; publ. *Boletin*† (quarterly).

Biblioteca de la Cámara de Comercio, Agricultura e Industria del Distrito Nacional (*Library of the Chamber of Commerce, Agriculture and Industry*): Arzobispo Nouel No. 206, altos, Apdo. 815; f. 1910; 4,000 vols.

Biblioteca de la Secretaría de Estado de Relaciones Exteriores (*Library of the Secretariat of Foreign Affairs*): Estancia Ramfis; special collections relating to international law; Dir. Dr. PRÓSPERO J. MELLA CHAVIER.

Biblioteca de la Universidad Autónoma de Santo Domingo (*Library of Santo Domingo University*): Ciudad Universitaria, Apdo. 1355; f. 1458; 104,441 vols. (Dominicana, historical archives, prints, maps, microfilms, etc.), 782,795 reviews (chiefly foreign, relating to the different faculties), microfilms, gramophone records; Dir. Dra. MARTHA MARÍA DE CASTRO COTES; publ. *Boletín de Adquisiciones*.

Biblioteca Dominicana: housed in a chapel of the Dominican Order dating from 1729; f. 1914; over 6,000 vols., of which Dominican authors comprise 700; collections of periodicals; also contains a students' reading-room, text-books, maps; Dir. JOSÉ RIJO.

Biblioteca Municipal de Santo Domingo (*Municipal Library of Santo Domingo*): Padre Billini No. 18; Librarian LUZ DEL CARMEN RAPOZO.

Biblioteca Nacional: César Nicolás Penson; f. 1971; collects government publs.; houses National Bibliography; exhibitions, conferences, research and documentation; 153,955 vols.; Dir. PEDRO GIL ITURBIDES.

Servicio de Documentación y Biblioteca (*Library and Documentation Service*): Palacio de Educación; f. 1958; under the auspices of UNESCO; Dir. Señora NIDIA TEJEDA DE RUIZ.

Baní

Biblioteca "Padre Billini": Calle Duarte No. 6; f. 1926; *c.* 38,000 vols.; Dir. Lic. FERNANDO HERRERA.

Moca

Biblioteca Municipal "Gabriel Morillo": Calle Antonio de la Maza esq. Independencia; f. 1942; 6,422 vols.; Dir. Lcdo. ADRIANO MIGUEL TEJADA E.

San Pedro de Macorís

Biblioteca del Ateneo de Macoris (*Library of the Athenaeum of Macoris*): f. 1890; 6,274 vols.; Pres. Lic. JOSÉ A. CHEVALIER.

Santiago de Los Caballeros

Biblioteca de la Sociedad Amantes de la Luz: España esq. Av. Central; f. 1874; public library of cultural society; 18,000 vols.; Dir. Lic. BERENI ESTRELLA DE INOA.

MUSEUMS AND ART GALLERIES

Santo Domingo

Galería Nacional de Bellas Artes (*National Fine Arts Gallery*): f. 1943; contains the later paintings and sculptures previously exhibited in the Museo Nacional; controlled by the Dirección General de Bellas Artes (*Fine Arts Council*); Dir. Dr. JOSÉ DE J. ALVAREZ VALVERDE.

Museo de las Casas Reales (*Museum of the Royal Houses*): Mercedes Esq. Las Damas, Apdo. postal 2664; f. 1976; buildings used to be the headquarters of the colonial government; exhibition of items from that period (1492–1821); library of 7,000 vols.; Dir. Dr. Arq. CÉSAR IVÁN FERIS IGLESIAS; publ. *Casas Reales*† (3 a year).

Museo del Hombre Dominicano (*Museum of Dominican Man*) (fmrly. Museo Nacional): Calle Pedro Henríquez Ureña, Plaza de la Cultura; f. 1973; 19,000 exhibits: *Pre-Columbian* (Indian archaeological; anthropological and ethnographical exhibits; ceramics, wooden objects, idols, amulets, charms, weapons and tools, pots, osseous remains); *Colonial* (weapons and armour, parts of ships, Spanish religious objects, ceramics, bells, etc.); *Contemporary* (photographs); library of 3,000 vols.; Dir. Lic. BERNARDO VEGA BOYRIE; publ. *Boletin*.

Oficina de Patrimonio Cultural: Alcázar de Colón; Dir. OCTAVIO AMIAMA CASTRO. Controls:

Alcázar de Diego Colón (*Columbus Palace*): museum f. 1957; the castle, built in 1510, was the residence of Don Diego Columbus, son of Christopher Columbus, and Viceroy of the island; period furniture and objects, tapestries, musical instruments, ceramics.

Museo Virreinal (*Viceregal Museum*): f. 1968; a house in the grounds of the Palace, displaying a valuable collection of paintings of the Spanish and Flemish schools.

Museo de la Familia Dominicana Siglo XIX (*Museum of the Dominican Family*): f. 1973; a 19th-century house displaying household items for a noble family of that period.

Casa-Fuerte de Ponce de León (*Ponce de León's Fort*): Yuma; museum f. 1972; the residence of Ponce de León who discovered Florida and Puerto Rico; authentic furniture and household items from a house of the period.

Sala de Arte Prehispánico: Apdo. 723; f. 1973; run by the García Arévalo Foundation; studies and exhibits culture of pre-Hispanic times; library of 6,000 vols. on anthropology and the history of Santo Domingo and the Caribbean; Dir. MANUEL ANT. GARCÍA ARÉVALO; publs. *Salida Semestral, Caney*.

UNIVERSITIES

UNIVERSIDAD AUTÓNOMA DE SANTO DOMINGO (Santo Domingo University)

CIUDAD UNIVERSITARIA, APDO. 1355, SANTO DOMINGO
Telephone: 533-1694, 533-1954.

Founded 1538 by Papal Bull of Paul III, closed 1801–15; reopened as a lay institution in 1815, reorganized in 1914. It is the oldest university in the Americas.

Rector: Dr. GUAROCUYA BATISTA DEL VILLAR.

Vice-Rector: Dra. JOSEFINA PADILLA Vda. SÁNCHEZ.

Secretary-General: Dr. ANTONIO LOCKWARD ARTILES.

Number of teachers: 1,178.
Number of students: 28,628.

Publications: *Anuario, Catálogo General, Memoria Anual de la Oficina de Planificación.*

DEANS:

Faculty of Humanities: Dr. VIRGILIO BELLO ROSA.
Faculty of Law: Dr. RAFAEL RICHIEZ ACEVEDO.
Faculty of Medicine: Dr. JOSÉ A. GARCÍA RAMÍREZ.
Faculty of Sciences: Dra. YOLANDA LAGARES DE MARCHENA.
Faculty of Engineering and Architecture: Ing. ROLANDO A. ROQUE MARTÍNEZ.
Faculty of Agronomy and Veterinary Science: Ing. Agr. RAFAEL MARTÍNEZ RICHIEZ.
Faculty of Economic and Social Sciences: Lic. FRANCISCO A. DE MOYA ESPINAL.

UNIVERSIDAD CATÓLICA MADRE Y MAESTRA

AUTOPISTA DUARTE, SANTIAGO DE LOS CABALLEROS
Telephone: 582-5105.
Founded 1962.

Private control; Academic year: August to May (two semesters) and a summer session June to July.

Rector: Mgr. AGRIPINO NÚÑEZ COLLADO.

Academic Vice-Rector: Lic. RADHAMÉS MEJÍA.

Vice-Rector (Administration and Finance): Lic. PEDRO PABLO CORDERO.

Registrar: Lic. RICARDO LORA.

Librarian: Lic. LEOVIGILDO RODRÍGUEZ.

Number of teachers: 465.
Number of students: 5,095.

Publications: *Eme Eme Estudios Dominicanos*†, *Nóvitas—Boletín de Noticias*†, *Revista de Ciencias Jurídicas*†, *Magister*† (monthly).

DEANS:

Faculty of Engineering: Ing. NELSON GIL GIL.
Faculty of Social and Administrative Sciences: Rev. Fr. Dr. JOSÉ LUIS ALEMÁN.
Faculty of Sciences and Humanities: Dr. EDUARDO LUNA.
Faculty of Health Sciences: Dr. ANDRÉS PERALTA.
Dean of Students: Lic. PEDRO PICHARDO.

UNIVERSIDAD CENTRAL DEL ESTE

CALLE DUARTE 36, SAN PEDRO DE MACORÍS
Telephone: 529-2830.
Founded 1970.

Private control; Academic year: January to December (3 terms).

President: Dr. JOSÉ A. HAZIM AZAR.
Vice-President: FRAY GUMERSINDO DE GRANADA.
Rector: Dr. JOSÉ E. HAZIM FRAPPIER.
Secretary General: Lic. PIEDAD L. NOBOA MEJÍA.
Librarian: Dr. EDGARDO HERNÁNDEZ MEJÍA.

The library contains 20,000 vols.
Number of teachers: 370.
Number of students: 15,000.

Publications: *Anuario Científico*†, *UCE*†, *Publicaciones Periódicas.*

DEANS:

Faculty of Medicine: Dr. JUAN A. SILVA SANTOS.
Faculty of Engineering: Lic. ROGER ACOSTA SEGURA.
Faculty of Humanities: Dr. EMILIO MEYER FRIAS.
Faculty of Economics and Social Sciences: Dr. RAFAEL MOREY VALDEZ.
Faculty of Law: Dr. LUIS E. CABRERA.
General Course: Dr. ANTONIO LEÓN SASSO.

UNIVERSIDAD NACIONAL "PEDRO HENRÍQUEZ UREÑA"

SANTO DOMINGO
Telephone: 565-6651.
Founded 1966.

Private control; Academic year: August to June.

Rector: Dr. JUAN TOMÁS MEJÍA FELIÚ.
Administrative Dean: Dr. RAYMUNDO AMARO GUZMÁN.
Dean of Academic Affairs: Dr. SALVADOR IGLESIAS B.
Dean of Students: Lic. EDGAR SENIOR.
Librarian: Dr. PRÓSPERO J. MELLA CHAVIER.

The library contains 30,000 vols.
Number of teachers: 500.
Number of students: 7,000.

Publications: *Biblionotas*†, *Publicaciones UNPHU*†, *Aula, Cuadernos Jurídicos.*

DEANS:

Faculty of Agronomy and Veterinary Science: Ing. Agr. RAMÓN E. TIÓ.
Faculty of Humanities: Dr. JOSÉ HENRÍQUEZ ALMANZAR.
Faculty of Law and Politics: Dr. BERNARDO FERNÁNDEZ PICHARDO.
Faculty of Engineering and Technology: Ing. MANUEL TRONCOSO.
Faculty of Health Science: Dr. RENÉ PUIG BENZ.
Faculty of Architecture and Arts: Arq. ROBERTO BERGÉS.
Faculty of Education: Dr. LUIS A. DUVERGÉ MEJÍA.
Faculty of Science: Dr. JAIME A. VIÑAS ROMÁN.
Faculty of Economics and Social Sciences: Lic. GUSTAVO BENEDICTO.

AFFILIATED INSTITUTES:

Instituto de Investigaciones Folklóricas: Dir. Prof. MANUEL RUEDA.

Centro de Información de Drogas: Dir. Dra. SOCORRO PERROTA DE VÁSQUEZ.

Centro de Investigaciones: Dir. Ing. EZEQUIEL GARCÍA.

Instituto de Estudios Biomedicos: Dir. SERGIO BENCOSME.

UNIVERSIDAD TECNOLÓGICA DE SANTIAGO

685 SANTIAGO
Telephone: 582-7156.
Founded 1974.

Rector: Dr. PRIAMO A. RODRÍGUEZ.

Vice-Rector (Academic): Dra. MARTHA GARCÍA.

Vice-Rector (Development): Lic. JUAN JOSÉ DE LA CRUZ.

Administrative Director: Lic. MANUEL R. CASTILLO.

Librarian: Lic. INGRID GONZÁLEZ.

Library of 15,000 vols.
Number of teachers: 90.
Number of students: 4,000.

DEANS:

Faculty of Social and Economic Science: Lic. MIGUEL ANGEL PUIG MESSON.

Faculty of Engineering and Architecture: Ing. VINICIO SORIANO.

Secretarial Studies: Lic. DILIA DE GARCÍA.

Languages School: Lic. PUBLIO GARCÍA BAKER.

COLLEGES

Instituto de Estudios Superiores Commerciales (*Institute of Advanced Commercial Studies*): Avda. Máximo Gómez 72, Santo Domingo; f. 1965; schools of business administration, English, pedagogy, secretarial science and electronics; library of 12,000 vols.; 9 staff; Chair. Prof. ANTONIO CUELLAS; Rector Dr. OSCAR G. BERGÉS; publ. *El Mundo del IES*.

Instituto de Formación Integral: Apdo. 1497, Santo Domingo; commerce.

Instituto Superior de Agricultura (ISA) (*Higher Institute of Agriculture*): Apdo. 166, Santiago; f. 1962; independent institution but operates joint programme in agriculture with the Universidad Católica Madre y Maestra; training in agricultural sciences at high school and undergraduate level; subjects for degree course: horticulture, food technology, forestry, agricultural education, mechanization, irrigation, agrarian reform, agricultural economics, administration; library of 12,948 vols.; Pres. Lic. VÍCTOR M. ESPAILLAT; Dir. Gen. Ing. NORBERTO A. QUEZADA; publs. occasional research papers.

Instituto Tecnológico de Santo Domingo: Av. de los Próceres, Galá, Apdo. 249, Zona 2, Santo Domingo; f. 1972; undergraduate and postgraduate teaching and research; schools of science and technology, social sciences and humanities, health sciences.

Rector: EDUARDO LATORRE.

Administrative Director: ILDEFONDO GUÉMEZ.

Number of students: 2,700.

Centro de Asistencia Técnica: serves as a link between university and industry; since 1975 UNDP and Dominican Government have supported a project to create an Industrial Management Consultation Unit.

Centro de Estudios de la Educación: f. 1975 for in-service training and postgraduate work in all branches of education, including child and adult education in rural areas; Exec. Dir. NATACHA CALDERÓN.

SCHOOLS OF ART AND MUSIC

Dirección General de Bellas Artes (*Fine Arts Council*): Santo Domingo; Dir. JOSÉ DELMONTE PEGUERO; controls the following:

Academias de Música (*Academies of Music*): Villa Consuelo and Villa Francisca, Santo Domingo, and in 19 provincial towns.

Conservatorio Nacional de Música (*National Conservatoire of Music and Elocution*): Santo Domingo.

Escuela de Arte Escénico (*School of Scenic Art*): Santo Domingo.

Escuela Nacional de Bellas Artes (*Fine Arts School*): Santo Domingo.

Escuelas de Artes Plásticas (*School of Plastic Arts*) at Santiago and La Vega.

Escuelas de Bellas Artes (*Schools of Fine Arts*) at San Francisco de Macorís and San Juan de la Maguana.

ECUADOR

Population 7,814,000

ACADEMIES

Quito

Academia Ecuatoriana (*Academy of Ecuador*): Apdo. 3460; f. 1875; 2nd in order of foundation in Spanish America; correspondent of the Real Academia Española, Madrid; the library, with over 2,000 vols., forms part of the National Library.

Director: Don JULIO TOBAR DONOSO.
Secretary: Doña MARTHA MONTENEGRO L.

Publications: *Memorias*† (quarterly), *Obras de la Literatura Ecuatoriana*† (quarterly).

Academia Ecuatoriana de Medicina (*Ecuadorian Academy of Medicine*): Casa de la Cultura Ecuatoriana, Apdo. 67; f. 1958.

LEARNED SOCIETIES AND RESEARCH INSTITUTES

(*see* also under Universities)

Quito

Alliance Française: Eloy Alfaro 1900 y 6 de Diciembre, Casilla 6275; f. 1953; 1,300 students; library of 8,000 vols.; Pres. Dr. JOSÉ VARGAS; Dir. YVES PÉREZ.

British Council: Apdo. 1197, Avda. Amazonas 1615 y Orellana; Rep. J. H. G. FOLEY.

Casa de la Cultura Ecuatoriana: Apdo. 67, Avda. 6 Diciembre 332; f. 1944; covers all aspects of Ecuadorian culture; 25 staff; Dir. Dr. GALO RENE PÉREZ; Sec. Dr. TEODORO VANEGAS ANDRADE; publs. 15 regular journals in sciences, culture, art, etc.

Comisión Ecuatoriana de Energía Atómica (*Atomic Energy Commission of Ecuador*): Calle Cordero 779 y Avda. 6 de Diciembre, Casilla 2517; f. 1958; 40 mems.; library of 3,000 vols.; Exec. Dir. FAUSTO MUÑOZ RIBADENEIRA; publ. *Noticias Trimestrales.*

Dirección General de Geología y Minas (*General Directorate of Geology and Mines*): c/o Ministerio de Recursos Naturales y Energía; f. 1964, as Servicio Nacional de Geología y Minería; supervises enforcement of laws relating to general and gold mining and sets standards for mining industry; 150 mems.; Dir. RODRIGO B. ALVARDO; Sec. JAIME CORDERO; publs. *Geological Map of Ecuador, Mining Statistics* (annually), *Metalliferous Map of Ecuador, Revista de Geología y Minas.*

Dirección General de Hidrocarburos (*General Directorate of Hydrocarbons*): Avda. 10 de Agosto 321; f. 1969; supervises enforcement of laws relating to petroleum exploration and development, and sets standards for mining-petroleum industry; 210 mems.; Dir. Gen. Ing. GUILLERMO BIXBY; Sec. ERNESTO CORRAL; publs. *Estadística Petrolera, Reporte Geológico de la Costa Ecuatoriana, Indice de Leyes y Decretos de la Industria Petrolera.*

Federación Nacional de Médicos del Ecuador (*National Federation of Ecuadorian Doctors*): Avda. de los Estadios e Iñaquito; f. 1942; 1,435 mems.; Pres. Dr. LEONARDO MALO BORRERO; Sec. Dr. ALFREDO PÉREZ RUEDA.

Instituto de Ciencias Nucleares (*Institute of Nuclear Science*): Escuela Politécnica Nacional, P.O.B. 2759; f. 1957; library with department of microcards and microfilms; equipment for application of radioisotopes to Chemistry, Agriculture, Medicine and Radiation control; cobalt source-60 2,400 curies; 4 departments: Department of Application to Chemistry and Agriculture, Dir. RICARDO A. MUÑOZ; Department of Biomedical Applications, Dir. RODRIGO FIERRO B.; Department of Natural Resources, Dir. Dr. ERNESTO GROSSMAN; Department of Radiation Control, Dir. Ing. FREDDIE ORBE M.

Instituto Ecuatoriano de Antropología y Geografía (*Ecuadorean Institute of Anthropology and Geography*): Casilla 2258; f. 1950; research in Anthropology, Ethnology, Folk-lore, Linguistics and national questions; 20 mems.; 80 hon. mems.; library of 3,000 vols.; Dir. Dr. ALBERTO FLORES GONZÁLEZ; publ. review *Llacta* (twice yearly).

Instituto Ecuatoriano de Ciencias Naturales (*Ecuadorian Institute of Natural Sciences*): P.O.B. 408; f. 1940; 52 founder mems.; 50 corresponding.; library; Dir. Prof. Dr. MISAEL ACOSTA-SOLÍS; publs. *Flora* (official organ), contributions and monographs.

Instituto Interamericano Agricultural Experimental (*Inter-American Experimental Agricultural Institute*): Conocoto, Línea 63; part of OAS Interamerican Agricultural Institute.

Instituto Latinoamericano de Investigaciones Sociales (ILDIS) (*Latin-American Social Sciences Research Institute*): Casilla 367-A; f. 1974; affiliated to the Friedrich-Ebert Foundation (*q.v.*); research in economics, sociology, political science and education; library of 5,000 vols.; Dir. Dr. HANS PETERSEN; publs. *ILDIS—Nueva Sociedad* (2 a month), *Materiales de Trabajo* (series).

Instituto Nacional de Estadística y Censos (*National Statistics and Census Institute*): Junta Nacional de Planificación y Coordinación, Avda. 10 de Agosto 229; f. 1944; Dir. Gral. Econ. GASTÓN ACOSTA; publs. *Anuario de Estadísticas Vitales, Anuario de Estadísticas Hospitalarias, Anuario de Estadísticas de Transporte, Anuario de Estadísticas Educacionales*, etc.

Instituto Nacional de Investigaciones Agropecuarios (*National Institute of Agricultural Research*): San Javier 295 y Orellana, apdo. 2600; f. 1959; Dir.-Gen. Dr. ENRIQUE AMPUERO P.; publs. scientific articles, annual report, bulletins.

Instituto Nacional de Meteorología e Hidrología (*Meteorological Office*): Calle Daniel Hidalgo 132; f. 1961; 133 mems.; library of 5,000 vols.; Dir. VICENTE L. GÓMEZ ANDRADE; publs. *Anuario Meteorológico, Anuario Hidrológico, Boletín Climatológico* (monthly).

Instituto Nacional de Nutrición (*National Institute of Nutrition*): Apdo. 3806; f. 1950; training courses and surveys; Dir. Dr. LUIS VALLEJO C.

Observatorio Astronómico de Quito (*Astronomical Observatory*): Apdo. 165, Parque Alameda; f. 1873; Astronomy, Seismology and Meteorology; Admin. Dir. (vacant); publs. *Boletín Trimestral, Resumen de Observaciones Meteorológicas, Boletín Sismológico* Series A, B and *Boletín Astronómico* Series A, B.

Office de la Recherche Scientifique et Technique Outre-Mer (ORSTOM): Apdo. Postal 099-B; pedology, hydrology, botany and vegetal biology, geography, economics; Dir. F. VICARIOT. (*See* main entry under France.)

Guayaquil

Centro de Investigaciones Históricas (*Centre of Historical Research*): Apdo. 7.110; f. 1930; 15 mems.; library of 6,000 vols.; Pres. Dr. ABEL ROMEO CASTILLO; Sec.-Gen. JULIO ESTRADA YCAZA; publ. *Revista*†.

Centro Ecuatoriano-Norteamericano (*Ecuador-U.S. Center*): Apdo. 5717, Luis Urdaneta y G. Cordova; f. 1957; 681 mems.; library of 3,710 vols.; Chief Officer EUGENE HARTER.

Instituto de Investigaciones Veterinarias del Litoral (*Veterinary Research Institute*): f. 1954; Dir. Dr. GONZALO SOTOMAYER NAVAS.

Instituto Nacional de Higiene "Leopoldo Izquieta Pérez" (*National Institute of Hygiene*): Apdo 3961; f. 1941; 24 departments and sections; library of 5,000 vols.; Dir. Dr. F. PARRA GIL; Sec. Abogado JUAN RIVERA ZÚÑIGA; publ. *Revista Ecuatoriana de Higiene y Medicina Tropical.*

Instituto Nacional de Pesca (*National Fishery Institute*): Casilla 5918; f. 1960; fishing research and development; library of 20,000 vols.; Dir. Dr. RAUL ICAZA GOMEZ; publs. *Boletín Científico Técnico*†, *Serie Informes Pesqueros*†.

Instituto Oceanográfico de la Armada (*Naval Oceanographic Institute*): Avda. 25 de Julio, P.O.B. 5940; f. 1972 to study oceanography and hydrography; 200 staff; library of 2,000 vols.; Dir. Capt. FERNANDO ALFARO ECHEVERRÍA; publ. *Acta Oceanográfica del Pacífico* (2 a year).

Sociedad Ecuatoriana de Pediatría (*Paediatrics Society of Ecuador*): Casilla 5865; f. 1945; scientific extension courses and lectures; Pres. Dr. ISIDORO MARTÍNEZ MCKLIFF; Sec. Dr. ARTURO VALERO ROJAS; publ. *Revista Ecuatoriana de Pediatría.*

Sociedad Médico-Quirúrgica del Guayas (*Medical and Surgical Society*): publ. *Anales.*

Galapagos Islands

Charles Darwin Research Station: Pto. Ayora, Santa Cruz; f. 1964 under the auspices of the Ecuadorian Government, UNESCO and the Charles Darwin Foundation to study and preserve the flora and fauna of the Archipelago; Dir. HENDRIK HOECK; the headquarters of the organization are at Greensted Hall, Ongar, Essex, England (*see* under International Organizations—Science); publ. *Noticias de Galápagos* (bi-annual).

LIBRARIES

Quito

Archivo-Biblioteca de la Función Legislativa: Palacio Legislativo, Quito; f. 1886; scientific and cultural; 20,000 vols.; Dir. Lcdo. RAFAEL A. PIEDRA SOLÍS; publs. *Clave de la Legislación Ecuatoriana*†, *Diario de Debates de la Legislatura*†.

Archivo Nacional de Historia (*National Historical Archives*): Av. 6 de Diciembre, No. 332; Apdo. 67; f. 1938; 2,500 vols.; colonial documents of the 16th to 19th centuries; Dir. JORGE A. GARCÉS Y GARCÉS; Sec. JUAN R. FREKE-GRANIZO; publ. *Arnahis.*

Biblioteca Nacional del Ecuador (*National Library*): García Moreno y Sucre, Apdo. 163; f. 1792; 55,000 vols. of which 7,000 date from the 16th to 18th centuries; shares legal deposit with municipal libraries; Dir. JORGE CARRERA ANDRADE; Sec. MERCEDES ALVAREZ M.

Biblioteca de la Casa de la Cultura Ecuatoriana (*Library of Ecuadorean Culture*): Apdo. 67, Avda. Colombia; f. 1944; 12,000 vols. and over 20,000 periodicals; Dir. LAURA DE CRESPO TORAL.

Biblioteca de la Universidad Central del Ecuador (*Central University Library*): f. 1826; 170,000 vols.; Dir. ALONSO ALTAMIRANO, M.L.S.; publ. *Anales*†, *Bibliografía Ecuatoriana*†, *Anuario Bibliográfico*†.

Biblioteca Ecuatoriana "Aurelio Espinosa Pólit": Apdo. 160; f. 1928; Ecuadorian library, archive, Ecuadorian art and history museum; 65,000 vols.; Librarian JULIAN G. BRAVO, S.I.

Biblioteca Municipal (*Municipal Library*): Casa de Montalvo, Apdo. 75; f. 1886; 12,500 vols., 300 MSS., 4 incunabula.

Cuenca

Biblioteca "Juan Bautista Vázquez" de la Universidad de Cuenca (*Cuenca University Library*): Apdo. 168; f. 1882; 62,185 vols.; Dir. CELIANO A. VINTIMILLA V.

Biblioteca de Autores Nacionales "Fray Vicente Solano": Apdo. 222; f. 1929; 39,569 vols.; Founder-Dir. Prof. DANIEL A. VINTIMILLA RAMÍREZ.

Biblioteca Publica Municipal (*Public Municipal Library*): Apdo. 202; f. 1927; 50,000 vols.; Dir. JUAN TAMA MÁRQUEZ.

Biblioteca Hispano-Americana (*Hispanic-American Library*): Mariscal Sucre 338, Apdo. 133; f. 1934; 54,700 vols.; Dir. CELIANO A. VINTIMILLA V.

Biblioteca Panamericana (*Pan-American Library*): Apdo. 57; f. 1912; 28,000 vols.; Dir. B. ALBÓRNOZ C.

Guayaquil

Biblioteca "Angel Andrés García" de la Universidad "Vicente Rocafuerte": Vélez 2203, Apdo. 330; f. 1847; 13,000 vols.; Dir. HERNÁN CABEZAS CANDEL; publs. *Revista de la Universidad "Vicente Rocafuerte"* and students' periodicals.

Biblioteca de Autores Nacionales "Carlos A. Rolando" (*Library of Ecuadorian Writers*): Palacio Municipal; f. 1913; 12,000 vols., 15,000 pamphlets, 17,000 leaflets, 3,000 MSS. relating to Ecuadorian authors and foreign works about Ecuador; Dir. Dr. CARLOS A. ROLANDO.

Biblioteca de la Casa de la Cultura Ecuatoriana: Nucleo de Guayas, 9 de Octubre y Pedro Moncayo, Apdo. 3542; f. 1945; 15,000 vols.; Dir. MARÍA LOLA CASTRO TOLA.

Biblioteca General, Universidad de Guayaquil: Apdo. 3834; f. 1901; 25,000 vols.; Dir. Lic. CONSTANTINO VINUEZA M.; publ. *Revista.*

Biblioteca Histórica y Archivo Colonial (*Historical Library and Colonial Archives*): Palacio de la Municipalidad, P.O.B. 75; f. 1930; Dir. Dr. CARLOS A. ROLANDO; Sec. Prof. GUSTAVO MONROY GARAICOA.

Biblioteca Municipal "Pedro Carbo" (*Public Library*): Avda. 10 de Agosto, Calle Pedro Carbo; f. 1862; 120,000 vols.; Dir. PATRICIA DE QUEVEDO (*see* also under Museums).

MUSEUMS

Quito

Museo Antropológico "Antonio Santiana": Universidad Central del Ecuador; f. 1925; sections of anthropology, archaeology, ethnography; library of 2,000 vols.; Dir. MARÍA ANGÉLICA C. DE SANTIANA; publ. *Humanitas*†, *Boletín Ecuatoriano de Antropología* (irregular).

Museo Arqueológico y Galerías de Arte del Banco Central del Ecuador: Apdo. 339, Banco Central, Avda. 10 de Agosto; f. 1969; pre-historical archaeological exhibits; colonial and modern art (sculpture, paintings, etc.); library of 3,000 vols.; Dir. Arq. HERNÁN CRESPO TORAL; publs. *Pieza del mes, Folletos didácticos sobre culturas precolombinas ecuatorianas.*

Museo de Arqueología y Etnología (del Instituto Ecuatoriano de Antropología y Geografía) (*Museum of Archaeology and Ethnology*): Casilla 2258; f. 1950; precious stones, ceramics, prehistoric sculptures.

Museo de Arte Colonial: Apdo. 25–55, Calle Cuenca Mejía; f. 1914; many examples of art from the *Escuela Quiteña* of the colonial epoch—17th and 18th centuries, 19th-century art and some contemporary art exhibitions (the latter in conjunction with the Casa de la Cultura Ecuatoriana); Dir. CARLOS A. RODRÍGUEZ T.

Museo de Arte e Historia de la Ciudad (*Civic Museum of Arts and History*): Calle Espejo 1147, Apdo. 399; f. 1930; sculptures, paintings, documents; Dir. HUGO MONCAYO; Sec. JUDITH PAREDES Z.

Museo de Ciencias Naturales de la Escuela Militar "Eloy Alfaro": Avda. Orellana, La Pradera 400; f. 1937; geological specimens and fauna from the Galapagos Islands; taxidermy and anatomy illustrated, especially of mammals and birds; Taxidermist LUIS ALFREDO PÉREZ VACA; publ. *Revista Anual del Plantel.*

Museo Jijón y Caamaño de Arqueología e Historia (*Jijón y Caamaño Archaeological and Historical Museum*): 12 de Octubre y Ladrón de Guevara, Apto. 2184.

Museo Petrográfico de la Dirección General de Geología y Minas: c/o Ministerio de Recursos Naturales y Energía; minerals found in the country; Dir. Ing. JULIO CÉSAR GRANTA VACA.

Guayaquil

Museo Antropológico del Banco Central del Ecuador: f. 1974; archaeology of the Ecuadorian coast; ethnography of whole of Ecuador; research; small library; Dir. OLAF HOLM; Research Dir. JORGE G. MARCOS, PH.D.

Museo Municipal (*Municipal Museum*): Avda. 10 de Agosto, Calle Pedro Carbo; f. 1862; historical, ethnographical, palaeontological, geological exhibits; colonial period and modern paintings and numismatics; (*see also* Libraries).

UNIVERSITIES AND TECHNICAL UNIVERSITIES

UNIVERSIDAD CENTRAL DEL ECUADOR

CIUDADELA UNIVERSITARIA, APDO. 166, QUITO

Telephone: 524714.

Founded 1769, from the Seminary of San Luis, founded 1594; the University of San Gregorio Magno, founded 1622; and the Dominican University of Santo Tomás de Aquino. Reorganized 1822, 1926.

State control; Language of instruction: Spanish.

Rector: Ing. CARLOS OQUENDO.

Vice-Rector: Prof. EDMUNDO RIBADENEIRA.

Librarian: ALONSO ALTAMIRANO.

Number of teachers: 2,500.
Number of students: 60,000.

Publications: *Anales*†, *Bibliografía Ecuatoriana.*

DEANS:

Faculty of Jurisprudence: Dr. FRANCISCO J. SALGADO.
Faculty of Economics: Econ. FAUSTO GUERRERO.
Faculty of Medical Sciences: Dr. CARLOS MOSQUERA.
Faculty of Chemistry: Dr. XAVIER BUSTOS.
Faculty of Odontology: Dr. CARLOS LASSO.
Faculty of Architecture and Town Planning: Arq. MARIO SOLIS.
Faculty of Philosophy: Lic. JORGE GUZMÁN.
Faculty of Engineering: Ing. VÍCTOR HUGO OLALLA P.
Faculty of Agricultural Engineering: Ing. NELSON PENAFIEL R.
Faculty of Administration: Lic. MARCO SILVA.
Faculty of Arts: Arq. LENIN OÑA.
Faculty of Psychology: Dr. LUIS A. RIOFRIO.

PONTIFICIA UNIVERSIDAD CATÓLICA DEL ECUADOR

AVDA. 12 DE OCTUBRE 1076 Y CARRIÓN, APDO. 21-84, QUITO

Telephone: 529-240, 529-280.

Founded 1946.

Private control; Language of instruction: Spanish. Academic year: October to July.

GOVERNING COUNCIL:

Grand Chancellor: Cardinal PABLO MUÑOZ VEGA, Archbishop of Quito.
Vice-Chancellor: Rev. JULIO TOBAR GARCÍA, S.J.
Rector: Dr. HERNÁN ANDRADE TOBAR, S.J.
Vice-Rector: Dr. JULIO TERÁN DUTARI, S.J.
Registrar: Lcdo. GUSTAVO RIOFRIO.
Librarian: Dr. MANUEL NIETO, S.J.

Number of teachers: 573.
Number of students: 14,924.

Publication: *Revista*†.

DEANS:

Faculty of Law: Dr. JOSÉ VICENTE TROYA JARAMILLO.
Faculty of Engineering: Ing. JOSÉ CHACÓN TORAL.
Faculty of Economics: Econ. LIONEL LÓPEZ PINTO.
Faculty of Education: Dr. MANUEL CORRALES, S.J.
Faculty of Human Sciences: Lcdo. JOSÉ LASSO.
Faculty of Nursing: Sister FRANCISCA LÓPEZ, H.C.
Faculty of Theology: Dr. JULIO TERÁN DUTARI, S.J.
Faculty of Administration (Cuenca): Dr. JOSÉ CUESTA.
Faculty of Philosophy (Cuenca): Dr. JUAN CORDERO.
Faculty of Administration (Ibarra): Pro-Rector: Dr. ERNESTO PROAÑO, S.J.
Faculty of Languages (Ibarra): Dir. Econ. GUILLERMO LANDÁZURI.

ATTACHED INSTITUTE:

Higher Institute of Philosophy: Avda. 12 de Octubre y Madrid; Dir. Rev. Father JORGE UGALDE PALADINES.

UNIVERSIDAD CATÓLICA DE CUENCA

P.O.B. 19A, CUENCA

Telephone: 824-365.

Founded 1970.

Private control; Academic year: October to July (2 terms).

Rector: Dr. CÉSAR CORDERO MOSCOSO.
Academic Vice-Rector: Dr. HUGO DARQUEA LÓPEZ.
Administrative Vice-Rector: Dr. JOSÉ VEGA DELGADO.
Chief Administrative Officer: Dr. RENÉ ZEA OCHOA.
Dean of Studies: Dr. ALBERTO AYORA PAZÁN.
Librarian: Lcdo. JOSÉ ESCANDÓN MEJÍA.

Library of 5,000 vols.
Number of teachers: 300.
Number of students: 2,910.

Publications: *Panoramas*†, *Estudios*†, *Retama, Presencia, Diálogo.*

DEANS:

Faculty of Law and Social Sciences: Dr. HUGO DARQUEA L.
Faculty of Education and Psychology: Dr. LEOPOLDO PEÑAHERRERA MOSQUERA.
Faculty of Medicine and Health Sciences: Dr. FLAVIO LOYOLA MERCHÁN.
Faculty of Civil Engineering: Ing. MARCELO DARQUEA LÓPEZ.
Faculty of Economics: Econ. LUIS ORELLANA CORREA.
Faculty of Chemical Engineering: Dr. ALEJANDRO VÁSQUEZ CH.
Faculty of Agricultural Engineering: Ing. Agr. JUAN PALACIOS VINTIMILLA.

School of Social Service: Dr. CLAUDIO PEÑAHERRERA M.
Bilingual Secretarial School: Econ. LUIS CISNEROS GONZÁLEZ.
Extension University at Macas: Dr. RODRIGO PATIÑO LEDESMA.
School of Drama: Lic. MAURO BRAVO BRAVO.
School of Physical Education: Lcdo. EDUARDO CORONEL DÍAZ.
Centre of Communication and Television: Lcdo. JORGE ILLESCAS BRAVO.

UNIVERSIDAD DE CUENCA

(also called Universidad del Azuay)
APDO. 168, CUENCA
Telephone: 82-75-56.
Founded 1868.

Rector: Ing. MARIO VINTIMILLA ORDÓÑEZ.
Vice-Rector: Dr. RAÚL CORDERO RODAS.
Secretary-General: Dr. ALFREDO ABAD GÓMEZ.
Librarian: MARTA AGUILAR DE CARRASCO.

Number of teachers: 470.
Number of students: 14,212.

Publications: *Anales de la Universidad de Cuenca, Revista de la Facultad de Jurisprudencia, Revista de la Facultad de Ciencias Médicas.*

DEANS:

Faculty of Law: Dr. TEODORO COELLO VÁZQUEZ.
Faculty of Medicine: Dr. VICENTE RUILOVA SÁNCHEZ.
Faculty of Engineering: Ing. VLADIMIRO CORDERO ORDÓÑEZ.
Faculty of Philosophy and Letters: Dr. FRANCISCO OLMEDO LLORENTE.
Faculty of Chemistry: Dr. MARCO JARAMILLO MORALES.
Faculty of Dentistry: Dr. JORGE ABAD GÓMEZ.
Faculty of Architecture: Arq. ALCIBIADES VEGA MALO.
Faculty of Economics: Econ. OSWALDO LARRIVA ALVARADO.

UNIVERSIDAD ESTATAL DE GUAYAQUIL*

CASILLA 471, GUAYAQUIL
Telephone: 15422.
Founded 1867.

Rector: Dr. ANTONIO ANDRADE.
Vice-Rector: Ing. NICOLÁS LEÓN PIZARRO.
Secretary-General: **Dr. ALBERTO SÁNCHEZ BALDA.**

Number of teachers: *c.* **400.**
Number of students: *c.* **4,500.**

Publications: *Anales, Boletín Universitario, Revista.*

Faculties of Agriculture and Veterinary Science, Architecture, Chemical Engineering, Dentistry, Natural Sciences, Economics, Education, Law, Mathematics, and Medicine.

*** No reply received to our questionnaire this year.**

UNIVERSIDAD NACIONAL DE LOJA

CASILLA LETRA "S", LOJA
Telephone: 961-841.
Telex: 4135 UNLOJA ED.
Founded 1869 as the Junta Universitaria; university status 1943.

State control; Academic year: October to July.

Rector: Ing. GUILLERMO FALCONI ESPINOSA.
Vice-Rector: Ing. NELSON YÉPEZ MONTENEGRO.
Secretary-General: Dr. GONZALO AÑASCO.

Library contains 3,500 volumes.
Number of teachers: 245.
Number of students: 7,536.

Publications: *Revista Universitaria*†, and various faculty bulletins.

DEANS:

Faculty of Law, Social Sciences, Economics and Politics: Dr. HARTMAN MONTEROS ULLAURI.
Faculty of Philosophy, Arts and Educational Science: Lic. JAIME JARAMILLO GUZMÁN.
Faculty of Agronomy and Veterinary Science: Ing. EDUARDO SAMANIEGO VÉLEZ.
Faculty of Medicine: Dr. JORGE BURNEO RIOFRÍO.
Faculty of Veterinary Science: Dr. VICENTE CUEVA CUEVA.

UNIVERSIDAD CATÓLICA DE SANTIAGO DE GUAYAQUIL

CASILLA 4671, GUAYAQUIL,
Telephone: 391058.
Founded 1962.

Private control; Academic year: April to December.

Rector: Ing. EUDORO CEVALLOS DE LA JARA.
Vice-Rector: Dr. GALO GARCÍA FERAUD.
Secretary-General and Registrar: Ab. GUILLERMO VILLACRES SMITH.
Librarian: Lcda. CLEMENCIA MITE DE SANTILLÁN.

Number of teachers: 500.
Number of students: 4,290.
The library contains 10,000 volumes.

Publications: *Revista Universidad, Revista Cuadernos.*

DEANS:

Faculty of Law: Dr. GUSTAVO NOBOA BEJARANO.
Faculty of Economics: CÉSAR ROBALINO GONZAGA.
Faculty of Engineering: Ing. JORGE BAQUERIZO CARBO.
Faculty of Architecture: Arq. WALTER VITERI ILLINGWORTH.
Faculty of Philosophy: Dra. CECILIA VERA DE GÁLVEZ.
Faculty of Medicine: Dr. GUSTAVO CORNEJO MONTALVO.
Faculty of Technical Education for Development: Dr. FAUSTO ROMERO GRANDA.

UNIVERSIDAD TÉCNICA DE BABAHOYO

VIA FLORES, BABAHOYO, LOS RÍOS
Telephone: 730208.
Founded 1971.

Rector: Dr. VICENTE VANEGAS LÓPEZ.
Vice-Rector: Dr. EDGAR UNDA AGUIRRE.
Librarians: LUIS VARGAS, MERCEDES HY-FONG.

The library contains 1,673 vols.
Number of teachers: 80.
Number of students: 1,168.

DEANS:

Faculty of Agronomy: Ing. LUIS CUENCA A.
Faculty of Education: Arq. ALBERTO MORENO C.

UNIVERSIDAD TÉCNICA PARTICULAR DE LOJA

APDO. 608, LOJA
Telephone: 960-375.
Founded 1971.

Private control; Academic year: October to February, April to August.

Chancellor: Hno. TICIANO CAGIGAL GARCÍA.
Rector: Ing. GUSTAVO TRUEBA BARAHONA.
Vice-Rector: Lic. MIGUEL VALAREZO SIGCHO.
Librarian: Lic. AMADA JARAMILLO, L.

Library of 3,000 vols.
Number of teachers: 120.
Number of students: 4,232.

Publications: *Revista Universitaria*† (2 a year), *Universidad* (monthly).

DEANS:

Faculty of Civil Engineering: Ing. JORGE AGUIRRE ASANZA.
Faculty of Economics: Econ. JORGE PIEDRA ARMIJOS.
Faculty of Agricultural Engineering: Ing. HERMÁN BRAVO PIEDRA.
Faculty of Education: Dr. CARLOS MONTALVO JARAMILLO.

DIRECTORS:

Institute of Languages: Lcdo. LUIS VARELA ESTÉVEZ.

Institute of Human Sciences: Lic. LUIS ERIQUE ORTEGA.
School of Fine Arts: Hno. TICIANO CAGIGAL GARCÍA.
Institute of Sciences: Ing. MAX TORRES GUZMÁN.
Institute of Computer Science: Hno. CÉSAR ORTIZ VIGIL.
General Programme: Hno. ANGEL PASTRANA CORRAL.

UNIVERSIDAD TÉCNICA DE MACHALA

CASILLA 466,
MACHALA
Telephone: 920-856.
Founded 1969.

State control; Language of instruction: Spanish; Academic year: March to January.

Rector: Dr. GERARDO FERNÁNDEZ CAPA.
Vice-Rector: Dr. JAIME PALACIOS PERALTA.
Secretary-General: ROBERTO POMBO.
Librarian: MARÍA UNDA SERRANA DE BARREZUETA.

Library of 3,000 vols.
Number of teachers: 182.
Number of students: 2,743.

Publication: *Revista de la Facultad de Agronomia y Veterinaria*†.

DEANS:

Faculty of Agronomy and Veterinary Science: Dr. JOSÉ ALVAREZ ALVARADO.
Faculty of Sciences: Dr. MANUEL MUÑOZ LECARO.
Faculty of Sociology: GERMÁN PARRA ALBARRACÍN.
Faculty of Civil Engineering: Ing. JORGE GAVILÁNEZ ORDÓÑEZ.
Faculty of Business Administration and Accountancy: Ing. Com. ROBERTO WONG CHÍA.

UNIVERSIDAD TÉCNICA DE MANABÍ*

(Manabí Technical University)
CASILLA 82, PORTOVIEJO,
MANABÍ
Telephone: 665.
Founded 1952.

State control; Academic year: May to January (two semesters).

Rector: Ing. IGNACIO HIDALGO VILLAVICENCIO.
Secretary: **RAÚL ANDRADE GUILLEM.**
Librarian: **MARÍA ANGELA CEDEÑO.**

Number of teachers: *c.* 60.
Number of students: *c.* 300.

Publication: *Revista.*

Faculties of Mathematics, Physics and Chemistry, and Agriculture and Veterinary Medicine.

*** No reply received to our** questionnaire **this year.**

UNIVERSIDAD TÉCNICA "LUIS VARGAS TORRES"

APDO. 179, ESMERALDAS
Telephone: 711-851.
Founded 1970.

Rector: Lic. ARCESIO APARICIO BENAVÍDEZ.
Vice-Rector: Ing. For. LUIS COLÓN GÓVEZ LEMOS.
Secretary-General: Dr. CARLOS ARCE ALVARADO.
Librarian: MARÍA PAZMIÑO DE H.

Number of teachers: 144.
Number of students: 757.

DEANS:

Faculty of Agrarian Sciences: Ing. LUIS QUIÑÓNEZ QUIÑÓNEZ.
Faculty of Education: Lic. SEGUNDO ESTUPIÑÁN E.
Faculty of Administrative Sciences: Lic. LENIN SOLIS CULTER.
Faculty of Sociology: Lic. CARLOS OJEDA SAN MARTÍN.

UNIVERSIDAD LAICA "VICENTE ROCAFUERTE" DE GUAYAQUIL

AVENIDA DE LAS AMÉRICAS,
APDO. 11-33, GUAYAQUIL
Telephone: 3-92-121.

Founded 1847; university status 1966.

Rector: Econ. CELSO EGAS ASTUDILLO.
Vice-Rector: Dr. ANA RODRÍGUEZ DE GÓMEZ.

Faculties of Architecture, Economics, Business Administration, Education, Civil Engineering, Law and Social Sciences.

ESCUELA POLITÉCNICA NACIONAL

(National Polytechnic School)
ISABEL LA CATÓLICA
Y VEINTIMILLA,
APDO. 2759, QUITO
Founded 1869.

Autonomous control; Language of instruction: Spanish; Academic year: October to July (two semesters).

Rector: Ing. RUBÉN ORELLANA.
Vice-Rector: Ing. FAUSTO CÁRDENAS.
Secretary: Dr. ALEJANDRO JARAMILLO.

Number of teachers: 391.
Number of students: 18,605.

Institutes of Engineering, Technological and Nuclear Research (*see* under Research Institutes).

DEANS:

Faculty of Civil Engineering: Ing. MARCELO HIDALGO.
Faculty of Electrical Engineering: Dr. KANTI HORE.
Faculty of Geology, Mines and Petroleum: Ing. GASTÓN VÁSCONEZ.
Faculty of Mechanical Engineering: Ing. STALIN SUÁREZ.
Faculty of Chemical Engineering: Ing. EDGAR PROAÑO.

ESCUELA SUPERIOR POLITÉCNICA DE CHIMBORAZO

CASILLA 4703, RIOBAMBA
Telephone: 61969.
Founded 1969.

Rector: Ing. IVÁN MORENO GALÁRRAGA.
Secretary-General: Dr. ARMANDO VINUEZA.

Library of 7,000 vols.

Number of teachers: 82.
Number of students: 1,615.

Publication: *El Chasqui.*

Faculties of Mechanical and Agricultural Engineering, Nutrition and Dietetics; Language Institute.

ESCUELA SUPERIOR POLITÉCNICA DEL LITORAL

ROCAFUERTE 101 Y
JULIÁN CORONEL,
CASILLA 5863, GUAYAQUIL
Telephone: 303733.
Founded 1958.

State control; Language of instruction: Spanish.

Rector: Ing. GUSTAVO GALINDO VELASCO.
Vice-Rector: Ing. EDUARDO RIVADENEIRA.
Administrative Officer: Ing. MARIO GONZÁLEZ.
Librarian: ELOISA PATIÑO LARA.

Number of teachers: 84 full-time; 53 part-time.
Number of students: 2,500.
Library of 15,000 vols.

Publications: *Boletin Informativo Polipesca, Tecnológica, Informes de Actividades.*

DIRECTORS:

Department of Electrical and Electronic Engineering: Ing. JUAN DEL POZO.
Department of Geology, Mines and Petroleum Engineering: Ing. FERNANDO REPETTO.
Department of Maritime Engineering: Ing. CRISTOBAL MARISCAL.
Department of Mechanical Engineering: Ing. ANTONIO VITERI.
Institute of Physics: JAIME VÁSQUEZ.
Institute of Chemistry: Dr. GUSTAVO SAMANIEGO.

Institute of Mathematics: Ing. HOMERO ORTIZ.

Institute of General Studies: Dr. HUGO ARIAS.

COLLEGES

Colegio Nacional de Agricultura "Luis A. Martínez": Casilla 286, Ambato; f. 1913; Dir. Dr. CÉSAR VÁSCONEZ S.; Sec. CÉSAR EDUARDO COBO N.; 500 students; publ. *Germinación.*

Colegio Nacional "24 de Mayo", Quito: Quito; f. 1934; an experimental institution for women's higher education; assisted by UNESCO; departments of modern humanities for students preparing for universities and commerce, administration and professional training; Rector Dra. MARÍA A. CARRILLO DE MATA M.; number of teachers 122; number of students 3,388.

Centro Internacional de Estudios Superiores de Comunicación para América Latina (*International Centre for Advanced Studies in Communications for Latin America*): Diego de Almagro s/n, Andrade Marín, Apdo. 584, Quito; f. 1960 with UNESCO aid; training, documentation and research; 31 staff; library of 5,000 vols.; Dir.-Gen. MARCO ORDÓÑEZ ANDRADE.

Escuela de Agricultura: Daule.

Escuela de Agricultura: Ibarra.

SCHOOLS OF ART AND MUSIC

Conservatorio Nacional de Música (*National Academy of Music*): Ministerio de Educación Publica, Quito; f. 1900; library of 4,000 vols.; Dir. LUIS H. SALGADO T.; Sec. RODOLFO JARRÍN A.; number of students: 434 men, 332 women.

Academia de Bellas Artes "Remigio Crespo Toral": Cuenca; Dir. Dr. LAURO ORDÓÑEZ ESPINOZA; teaching staff 4.

Conservatorio de Música "José Maria Rodriguez": Cuenca; Dir. Prof. RAFAEL SOJOS JARAMILLO; teaching staff 11.

EGYPT

Population 41,000,000

ACADEMIES

Academy of the Arabic Language: 26 Sharia Dr. Taha Hussein, Giza; f. 1932; 40 mems.; library of 27,675 vols.

President: Dr. Ibrahim Madkour.
Vice-President: Dr. Ahmad Ammar.
Secretary-General: Dr. Mahdi Allam.
Director-General: Abdalla Ismail Nabeeh.

Publications: *Review*† (2 a year), *Councils and Conferences Proceedings*†, *A Collection of Technical and Scientific Terms*†.

Institut d'Egypte: 13 Sharia Sheikh Rihane, Cairo; f. 1798 by Napoleon Bonaparte, reconstituted 1859; studies literary, artistic and scientific questions relating to Egypt and neighbouring countries; 60 mems., 50 assoc. mems., 50 corresp. mems.; publs. *Bulletin* (annual) and *Mémoires*.

President: Dr. Sileman Hazien.
Secretary-General: Mahmoud Hafez.

LEARNED SOCIETIES

Agriculture and Veterinary Science

Egyptian Society of Dairy Science: 1 Ouziris St., Garden City, Cairo; f. 1972; Pres. Dr. Ismael Yousry; publ. *Egyptian Journal of Dairy Science*.

The Arts

Armenian Artistic Union: 3 Sharia Soliman, El-Halaby, P.O.B. 1060, Cairo; f. 1920; aims: promotion of Armenian and Arabic culture; 300 mems.; Pres. Vahag Depoyan.

L'"Atelier": 6 Victor Bassili St., 6 Pharaohs St., Porte de Rosette, Alexandria; society of artists and writers; f. 1934; 130 mems.; library of 5,000 vols.; Hon. Pres. R. Lackany; Hon. Sec.-Gen. Sayed Kortam; publ. *Bulletin*.

High Council of Arts and Literature: 9, Sharia Hassan Sabri, Zamalek, Cairo; f. 1956; publs. books on literature, arts and social sciences.

Institute of Arab Music: Alexandria, 2 Sharia Tewfik; Pres. Ahmed Bey Hassan; Hon. Sec. Aly Saad.

Institute of Arab Music: Cairo, 22 Sharia Ramses.

Bibliography, Documentation, Library Science

Egyptian Association for Archives, Librarianship and Information Sciences: c/o Dept. of Archives, Librarianship and Information Science, Faculty of Arts, Univ. of Cairo, Cairo; f. 1956; 538 mems.; Pres. Dr. S. M. Hagrassy.

National Information and Documentation Centre: Al-Tahrir St., Dokki, Cairo; f. 1955; accumulates and disseminates information in all languages and in all branches of science and technology; comprises six depts.: Libraries, Bibliography, Translations, Reprography, Editing and Publishing, and Printing; Dir. Dr. Ahmed M. Gad; publs. *Arab Science Abstracts*, 18 scientific journals.

Economics, Law and Politics

Egyptian Society of International Law: 16 Avenue Ramses, Cairo; f. 1945; objects: to promote the study of international law and to work for the establishment of international relations based on law and justice; Pres. Prof. Dr. Hafez Ghanem; Vice-Pres. Dr. Boutros B. Ghali, Dr. Fouad A. Reyad; 410 mems.; library contains 3,200 books and 200 periodicals; publ. *Revue Egyptienne de Droit International* (annual).

Egyptian Society of Political Economy, Statistics and Legislation: 16 Avenue Ramses, Cairo, P.O.B. 732; f. 1909; Pres. Dr. Gamal El Oteifi; Gen.-Sec. Dr. Ibrahim Ali Saleh; 1,520 mems.; library contains 15,250 vols.; publs. *L'Egypte Contemporaine* (quarterly, in Arabic, English and French), and numerous other publications on economics and law.

History, Geography and Archaeology

Egyptian Geographical Society: Sharia Kasr El-Aini (Jardin du Ministère d'Irrigation); P.O. Garden City, Cairo; f. 1875, reorganized 1917; library of 29,000 vols.; Pres. Soliman A. Huzzayn; Sec.-Gen. Muhammad M. Alsayyad; publ. *Bulletin*†.

Hellenic Society of Ptolemaic Egypt: 20 Avenue Fouad I, Alexandria; f. 1908; Pres. Dr. G. Partheniadis; Sec. Costa A. Sandi.

Office for the Preservation of Arabic Monuments (*Idarit Hifx el-Assar el-Arabia*): 1 Sharia el-Walda (Qasr-el-Doubara), Cairo; f. 1882; Pres. of the Higher Council H.E. the Egyptian Minister of Education; Dir. Muhammad Abdel Fattah Helmy; Pres. of the Permanent Cttee. Muhammad Aly Namazy; publ. *Bulletin*.

Société Archéologique d'Alexandrie: 6 Sharia Mahmoud Moukhtar, Alexandria; f. 1893; 100 mems.; Pres. Dr. A. Sadek; Sec.-Gen. and Editor D. A. Daoud; Treas. M. F. Mansour; publs. *Bulletins*, *Mémoires*, *Monuments de l'Egypte Gréco-Romaine*.

Society for Coptic Archaeology: 222 Sharia Ramses, Cairo; f. 1934, for the study of Coptology in archaeology, linguistics, papyrology, church history, liturgy and art; 360 mems.; library of 10,000 vols.; Pres. Mirrit Boutros Ghali; Librarian Dr. L. S. B. MacCoull; Sec. Dr. Norman Daniel; publs. *Bulletin* (annually), monographs: *Fouilles*, *Textes et documents*, MSS., etc.

International Cultural Institutes

American Center, The: 4 Ahmed Ragheb St., Garden City, Cairo; f. 1974; cultural programmes and information services; library of 10,000 vols., 240 periodicals, 15,000 microfiche; Dir. Mrs. Sheila W. Austrian; publ. accessions list.

British Council: 192 Sh. El-Nil, Agouza, Cairo; library: *see* Libraries; Representative M. S. Dalziel.

Centro Cultural Hispánico (*Hispanic Cultural Institute*): Sharia Gamal Abdel Nasser 101, Alexandria.

Deutsches Kulturinstitut (*German Cultural Institute/Goethe Institute*): 10 rue des Ptolémées, Alexandria; Dir. Dr. Adolf Tüllmann.

Istituto Italiano di Cultura (*Italian Cultural Institute*): 3 Sharia Sheikh El Marsafi (Zamalek), Cairo; Dir. Prof. Manrico Fiore.

Österreichisches Kulturinstitut Kairo (*Austrian Cultural Office of Cairo*): 1103 Sharia Corniche el Nil, Apt. 7,

Qasr el Doubara, Cairo; f. 1958; science, research, educational and cultural activities; Dir. OTTO A. ZUNDRITSCH.

MEDICINE

Alexandria Medical Association, The: 4 G. Carducci Street, Alexandria; f. 1921; 860 mems.; Pres. Prof. M. L. DOWIDAR; Sec. Dr. ALI NOFAL; publ. *The Alexandria Medical Journal* (English, French and Arabic, quarterly).

Cairo Odontological Society: 39 Kasr El-Nil, Cairo; Pres. Dr. ABULNAGA M. ABDEL-AZIM; Sec. Dr. J. ALCÉE.

Egyptian Medical Association: 42 Sharia Kasr El-Aini, Cairo; f. 1919; 2,142 mems.; Pres. Prof. Dr. A. EL-KATEB; Sec.-Gen. Prof. Dr. A. H. SHAABAN; Vice-Pres. Prof. Dr. M. IBRAHIM; publ. *Journal* (monthly, in Arabic and English).

Egyptian Society of Medicine and Tropical Hygiene: 2 Sharia Fouad I, Alexandria; f. 1927; Hon. Pres. Dr. AHMED HELMI; Pres. Dr. IBRAHIM ABDEL-SAYED; Sec.-Gen. and Treas. Dr. J. KHOURI.

Ophthalmological Society of Egypt: Dar El Hekma, 42 Sharia Kasr El Ainy, Cairo; f. 1902; Pres. Prof. Dr. EL-SAID KHALIL ABOU SHOUSA; Hon. Sec. Dr. AHMAD EZ EL-DIN NAIM; 480 mems.; publ. *Annual Bulletin*.

NATURAL SCIENCES

Société Entomologique d'Egypte: 14 Sharia Ramses, P.O.B. 430, Cairo; f. 1907; 502 mems.; publs. bulletins and Economic Series; library of 28,000 vols.; Pres. MAHMOUD HAFEZ; Vice-Pres. Dr. ABDEL AZIZ HAFEZ SOLIMAN, Dr. ABDEL AZIZ KAMEL; Sec.-Gen. Dr. ABDEL HAKIM M. KAMEL.

Zoological Society of Egypt: Giza Zoo, Giza; f. 1927; aims to promote zoological studies and to foster good relations between zoologists in Egypt and abroad; field courses, lectures, etc.; library of 2,500 vols.; 260 mems.; Pres. Dr. HASSAN A. HAFEZ; Sec. Prof. A. MAHER ALI; publ. *The Zoological Society of Egypt*†.

PHILOSOPHY AND PSYCHOLOGY

Egyptian Association for Mental Health: 1 Sharia 'Ilhami, Qasr al-Doubara, Cairo; f. 1948; 630 mems.

Egyptian Association for Psychological Studies: Faculty of Education, Ain Shams University, Abbasiyah, Cairo; f. 1948; 683 mems.

RELIGION, SOCIOLOGY AND ANTHROPOLOGY

Institut Dominicain d'Etudes Orientales: Priory of the Dominican Fathers, 1 Sharia Masna al-Tarabish, Abbasiyah, Cairo; f. 1952; library of 34,000 vols.; Dir. Père G. C. ANAWATI; publ. *Mélanges* (annually).

Social Sciences Association of Egypt: Cairo; f. 1957; 1,234 mems.

TECHNOLOGY

Egyptian Society of Engineers: 28 Sh. Ramses, Cairo; f. 1920; Pres. Prof. Dr. IBRAHIM ADHAM EL-DEMIRDASH; Sec. Dr. MOHAMED M. EL-HASHIMY.

RESEARCH INSTITUTES

GENERAL

Academy of Scientific Research and Technology: 101 Sharia Kasr El-Aini, Cairo; f. 1971; the national body responsible for science and technology; Pres. Prof. Dr. HASSAN ISMAIL; Vice-Pres. Prof. Dr. GAMAL ABDEL SAMIE, Prof. Dr. MOHAMED B. FAYEZ; Sec.-Gen. Prof. Dr. ABU EL FOTUOH ABDEL LATIF.

Affiliated institutions (*see* also below): National Research Centre, Central Metallurgical Research and Development Institute, Institute of Oceanography and Fisheries, Institute of Astronomy and Geophysics, National Institute for Standards, Petroleum Research Institute, Remote Sensing Centre, Scientific Instrument Centre, National Information and Documentation Centre.

National Research Centre: Al-Tahrir St., Dokki, Cairo; f. 1939; began functioning in 1947 and laboratory work started in 1956; fosters and carries out research in both pure and applied sciences; the 46 laboratories are divided into 14 sections: textile industries, metallurgy, food industries and nutrition, pharmaceutical industries, chemical industries, engineering, agriculture, animal welfare, medical, applied organic and inorganic chemistry, physics, basic sciences, environment; library of 12,000 vols.; Dir. Prof. Dr. MOHAMED KAMEL MAHMOUD; Sec.-Gen. Prof. Dr. FAHMEY RAMADAN.

AGRICULTURE AND VETERINARY SCIENCE

Agricultural Research Centre, Ministry of Agriculture: Giza. Attached research institutes:

Agricultural Economy Research Institute: Giza; f. 1973; Dir. Dr. MD. KAMEL HINDY.

Agricultural Guidance Research Institute: Nadi El Said St., Dokki; f. 1977; Dir. Dr. TAHER HASSAN DORRAH.

Animal Health Research Institute: Nadi El Said St., Dokki; f. 1928; Dir. Dr. OMAR LOTFI AHMED.

Animal Production Research Institute: Nadi El Said St., Dokki; f. 1938; Dir. Dr. ABDEL MONEM ABDEL HAMID MEKKI.

Central Laboratory for Design and Statistical Analysis Research: Cairo University St., Giza; Dir. Dr. ABDEL RAHMAN AHMED EL SAID.

Cotton Research Institute: Cairo University St., Giza; f. 1919; Dir. Dr. MOHSEN ABBASS EL DIDY.

Desert Research Institute: Mataria, Cairo; f. 1949; four divisions: water resources, soil, botany, animal health; Dir. Prof. Dr. ABDOU ALI SHATA.

Field Crops Research Institute: Cairo University St., Giza; f. 1971; Dir. ABDEL LATIF MD. HASSAN.

General Department of Agricultural Research Stations: Cairo University St., Giza; f. 1961; Dir. IBRAHIM BOULOS IBRAHIM.

Horticultural Research Institute: Cairo University St., Giza; f. 1948; Dir. Dr. AHMED TALAAT EL WAKEEL.

International Centre for Rural Development: Mariut; P.O. 1023, Alexandria; f. 1971; Dir. SALAH EZZAT ZAGLOUL.

Plant Pathology Research Institute: Cairo University St., Giza; f. 1919; research in various aspects of disease survey: ecology, biology, epidemiology and control measures; staff of *c.* 170 research staff; library of 1,098 vols.; Dir. Dr. M. FAHMY; publs. *Agricultural Research Review*, *Egyptian Phytopathology*, *Journal of Applied Microbiology*.

Plant Protection Research Institute: Cairo University St., Giza; f. 1971; Dir. Dr. HASSAN HAMED ATIA.

Soil and Water Research Institute: Cairo University St., Giza; f. 1969; Dir. Dr. ALI HASSAN SERRY.

ARCHITECTURE AND TOWN PLANNING

General Organization for Housing, Building and Planning Research: P.O.B. 1770, Cairo; attached to the Ministry of Housing; carries out basic and applied research work on building materials and means of construction; also provides technical information and acts as consultant to the different authorities concerned with building and construction materials; seven specialized laboratories; Chair. Dr. MOSTAFA M. EL-HIFNAWI; publs. bulletins, reports.

ECONOMICS, LAW AND POLITICS

Institute of Arab Research and Studies: 1 Tolombat St., Garden City, Cairo; f. 1953; affiliated to the Arab League Educational, Cultural and Scientific Organization (ALECSO); library of *c.* 60,000 vols., 800 periodicals; for specialization by graduates of Arab univs.; national and international affairs, economics, social studies, history, law, literature; Dir. Prof. M. S. ABULEZZ, PH.D.; publs books on Arab subjects and *Bulletin* (annually).

Institute of National Planning: Salah Salem St., Nasr City, Cairo; f. 1960; research, training and publication in planning and development; organized in 8 centres; computing unit in charge of research and training; library of 28,000 vols.; Dir. Prof. Dr. ISMAIL SABRY ABDALLAH; Sec.-Gen. MOHAMED FAHMY; publ. *Memoranda* (irregular).

EDUCATION

National Centre for Educational Research: Central Ministry of Education, 33 Sharia Falaky, Cairo; f. 1972; co-ordinates current educational policy with that of the National Specialized Councils; exchanges information with like institutions throughout the world; provides local and foreign documents on education; Dir. Dr. YOUSSEF KHALIL YOUSSEF; publs. *Contemporary Trends in Education* (2 a year), *Educational Information Bulletin* (monthly), and various works on education in Egypt and the Arab world.

HISTORY, GEOGRAPHY AND ARCHAEOLOGY

Deutsches Archäologisches Institut (*German Institute of Archaeology*): 22 Sharia Gezira al Wusta, Cairo- Zamalek; Dir. Prof. Dr. WERNER KAISER.

Institut Français d'Archéologie Orientale (*French Institute of Oriental Archaeology*): 37 rue Mourira, Cairo; f. 1880; excavations, research and publications intended to widen knowledge of Egyptian history from the Pharaohs to the Islamic period; 6 scientific mems.; library of 60,000 vols.; Dir. J. VERCOUTTER; Sec.-Gen. Mme. G. VIVENT-BATAILLE; publs. *Bulletin*, *Annales Islamologiques* (annually).

MEDICINE

Theodor Bilharz Research Institute: Al-Tahrir St., Giza; f. 1978 in co-operation with Federal Germany; deals with national health problems; Dir. Prof. ALI ZEIN EL ABIDIEN.

Egyptian Organization for Biological Products and Vaccines: 51 Sharia Wezarat El Zeraa, Agouza, Giza.

Memorial Institute for Ophthalmic Research: Sharia Al-Ahram, Giza, Cairo; f. 1925; library of 2,800 vols.; Dir. Dr. ABDEL MEGID ABDEL RAHMAN; publ. *Report.*

National Organization for Drug Control and Research: 6 Abou Hazem St., Giza; f. 1976; 300 staff; Chair. Dr. ALI HIGAZI.

Nutrition Research Institute: 16 Kasr El Einy St., Cairo; f. 1944; 180 staff; Dir. Dr. HIKMAT EL SAID ALI.

Public Health Laboratories: Ministry of Public Health, 19 Sharia Sheikh Rehan, Cairo; f. 1885; Dir.-Gen. Dr. H. S. YUSEF; Diagnostic Laboratories: Dr. M. ROUSHDI; Production Laboratories: Dr. A. H. WAHBA; Public Health Services: Dr. H. M. EL KASSAS; Drug Control Laboratories: Dr. H. EL HAKIM; Virology Dept.: Dr. I. ZAGLOOL; Library of 2,000 vols.; publs. *Bacteriology, Virology, Sera and Vaccines Production.*

Research Institute for Tropical Medicine: 10 Sharia Kasr El-Aini, Cairo; f. 1932; sections: clinical parasitology, helminthology, entomology, biochemistry, physiology and pharmacology, radiology, radiotherapy and radio isotopes, bacteriology, pathology, haematology, endoscopy, serology, urology, immunology, malacology, animal house and field research units; library of 4,000 vols.; Dir.-Gen. M. SAIF.

NATURAL SCIENCES

Alexandria Institute of Oceanography and Fisheries: Kayed Bey, Alexandria; f. 1931; library: *see* Libraries; Dir. Prof. Dr. SAAD K. EL-WAKEEL; Sec. Sheik EL-ARAB SADEEK; publ. *Bulletin*† (annually).

Geological Survey and Mining Authority: 3 Salah Salem St., Abbassia, Cairo; f. 1898; regional geological mapping, mineral prospecting, evaluation of mineral deposits, preparation of techno-economic reports, mine and quarry designs, and granting mineral exploration and exploitation rights; 280 research workers; library of 30,000 vols.; Chair. Board GALAL EL DIN ALY MOSTAFA; publs. occasional papers†, *Annals*†.

Institute of Astronomy and Geophysics: Helwan, Cairo; f. 1903; carries out research studies in geophysics and astronomy; comprises the Helwan Observatory, the Kottamyia Observatory, the Misallat geomagnetic observatory, the seismic stations at Helwan, Aswan, Matrouh, and the satellite tracking stations at Helwan and Abu Simbel; attached to the Academy of Scientific Research and Technology; library of 10,594 vols.; Dir. Prof. M. FAHIM MAHMOUD; publs. bulletins.

Institute of Freshwater Fishery Biology: 10 Hassan Sabry St. (Fish Garden), P.O. Zamalik, Cairo; f. 1954; undertakes research in fish biology and culture; 7 scientists; Dir. Prof. A. R. EL BOLOCK.

Institute of Oceanography and Fisheries: 101 Sharia Kasr El-Ainy, Cairo; f. 1920 in connection with the Faculty of Science, Cairo; undertakes oceanographical and fisheries research; attached to the Academy of Scientific Research; contains a library and a museum; regular correspondence is kept up with more than 350 scientific institutions; Dir. Prof. Dr. A. AL-RIFAI BAYOUMI; publ. *Al Ghardaqa* (Red Sea).

Remote Sensing Center: 101 Kasr El-Eini St., Cairo; f. 1971 by Academy of Scientific Research in co-operation with the U.S.A.; covers geology, mineral and energy resources, hydrogeology, agriculture, soils, geophysics, photogrammetry, engineering, physics and data processing; one of the few centres which applied LANDSAT imagery interpretations from an early stage; 65 specialist scientists, as well as technical staff; Dir. Dr. MOHAMED ABDEL HADY; publs. *Proceedings* of various conferences and symposiums, technical reports.

TECHNOLOGY

Central Metallurgical Research and Development Institute: Sharia al-Tahrir, Dokki, Cairo; set up by the Industrial Research Executive Organization; attached to the Academy of Scientific Research and Technology; sections for Ore Metallurgy, Physical Metallurgy and General Services; Dir. Dr. AHMED ADEL ABD EL AZIM.

Egyptian Atomic Energy Establishment: 101 Kasr El Einy St., Dokki, Cairo; f. 1957; Chair. I. F. HAMOUDA.

Nuclear Research Centre (NRC): Inshas; main facilities include a 2 MW research reactor, a 2.5 Van de Graff accelerator, a radio-isotope production laboratory, nuclear fuel research and development laboratory, laboratories for application of radio-isotopes, electronic instrumentation laboratory and radiation protection laboratory; Dir. S. HASHISH.

National Centre for Radiation Research and Technology (NCRRT): Nasr City, Cairo; main facilities include a 400,000 Ci, Co-60 unit and an electron accelerator; Dir. H. M. ROUSHDY.

Hydraulics and Sediment Research Institute: Delta Barrage; f. 1949; technical and scientific research using scale models; 26 scientific staff; Dir. M. El-Moatassem Kotb; publ. *Technical Report* (annual).

Middle Eastern Regional Radioisotope Centre for the Arab Countries: Dokki, Giza; f. 1963; trains specialists in the applications of radioisotopes, particularly in the medical, agricultural and industrial fields; conducts research in hydrology, tropical and sub-tropical diseases, fertilizers, and entomology; promotes the use of radioisotopes in the Arab countries; Dir. Dr. Salah El Din El Said Hashish.

National Chemical Research Centre: c/o Industrial Research Executive Organization, Dokki, Cairo.

National Institute for Standards: Sharia al-Tahrir, Dokki, Cairo; attached to the Academy of Scientific Research and Technology; responsible for maintenance of national standards for physical units and their use for purposes of calibration; research on scientific metrology, to develop new techniques for measurements, calibrations, and development of new standards; consists of the following laboratories: electricity, photometry, frequency, thermometry, radiation, acoustics, mass, length metrology, engineering metrology, testing of materials, safety tests and textile testing; Dir. M. M. Ammar.

Petroleum Research Institute: P.O.B. 2130, Cairo; set up by Egyptian General Petroleum Authority; attached to the Academy of Scientific Research and Technology; ten sections, dealing with all aspects of petroleum research; Dir. Dr. Fathy Mosaad Ebaid.

Textile Consolidation Fund: El-Syouf, Alexandria; Gen. Man. Nabil El-Nozahi. Attached centres:

Textile Quality Control Centre: f. 1967; central laboratories for testing and quality control; 300 staff.

Textile Development Centre: f. 1975; applied research on all technical problems.

Textile Information Centre: f. 1978; library of 5,000 vols., 80 periodicals.

Unesco Regional Office for Science and Technology in the Arab States (ROSTAS): 8 Abdul Rahman Fahmy St. (ex. Salamlek), Garden City, Cairo; f. 1947; advisory services, trains personnel, undertakes studies and research; co-ordination at regional level for Unesco activities; 16 staff; depository library for Unesco publs.; Dir. and Unesco Rep. for Egypt and Sudan Dr. Saad Al-Rawi; publ. *Rostas Bulletin*† (quarterly).

LIBRARIES

Al-Azhar University Library: Nasr City, Cairo; 80,000 vols., including 20,000 MSS.; Librarian M. E. A. Hady.

Alexandria Municipal Library: 18 Sharia Menasha Moharrem Bey, Alexandria; f. 1892; 22,390 Arabic vols., 35,399 European vols., 4,086 MSS.; Chief Librarian Sheikh Beshir el-Shindi.

Alexandria University Library: 22 Al-Gueish Ave., Shatby, Alexandria; f. 1942; consists of the Central Library (122,225 vols.), 7 Faculty libraries, and the Library of the Institute of Chemical Technology; over 1,000,000 vols.; Dir. Essmat El-Ashry.

American University in Cairo Library: 113 Sharia Kasr El-Aini, Cairo; f. 1919; 175,000 vols.; 1,200 periodicals; Librarian Jesse E. Duggan.

Arab League Information Centre (Library): Midan Al-Tahir, Cairo; f. 1945; 30,000 vols., 250 periodicals.

Assiut University Library: Assiut; 25,000 vols.; Dir. Mrs. W. J. Skellie.

British Council Library: 192 Sh. El-Nil, Agouza, Cairo; f. 1963; 32,357 vols., 147 periodicals; Regional Librarian V. Forshaw, a.l.a.

Cairo University Library: Orman, Giza; f. 1908; 1,000,000 vols., 7,000 periodicals; Librarian Ahmad Issa.

Centre of Documentation and Studies on Ancient Egypt: 3 El-Adel Abou Bakr St., Zamalek, Cairo; f. 1956; scientific and documentary reference centre for all Egyptian Pharaonic monuments; 205 mems.; 3,484 vols.; Dir.-Gen. Dr. Abdel-Meguid Elrabii; publs. a wide range of specialist material on ancient Egypt.

Damanhour Municipal Library: Damanhour; 13,431 vols.

Egyptian Library: Abdin Palace, Cairo; over 20,000 vols.; Dir. Abdel Hamid Hosni.

Egyptian National Library (*Dar-ul-Kutub*): Kornish El-Nil St., Bulaq, Cairo; f. 1870; 1,500,000 vols. (400,000 European); 11 brs. with 250,000 vols., including fine arts library; deposit library; Dir. Hassan Rashad.

Helwan Observatory Library: Helwan; f. 1903; 10,600 vols.; Dir. Prof. M. Fahim; publ. *Bulletin.*

Library of the Central Bank of Egypt: 31 Kasr El-Nil St., Cairo; over 5,000 vols.; Dir. Muhammad Rouchdy.

Library of the Greek Orthodox Patriarchate of Alexandria: P.O.B. 2006, Alexandria; f. 10th century; 40,000 vols., 539 MSS., 2,210 rare editions; Librarian Dimitrios Th. Mosconas, b.a., m.l.s.; publ. *Analecta* (yearly); houses an Institute for Oriental Studies.

Library of the Institut d'Egypte: 13 Sharia Sheikh Rihane, Cairo; f. 1859; over 160,000 vols.; Librarian M. Mostafa; publs. *Bulletin, Mémoires.*

Library of the Ministry of Agriculture: Giza-Orman; f. 1920; 25,000 vols.; Dir. Latif Ibrahim.

Library of the Ministry of Education: 16 Sharia El-Falaki, Cairo; f. 1927; 55,966 vols. (European and Arabic).

Library of the Ministry of Health: Sharia Sultan Hussein, Cairo; over 27,000 vols.

Library of the Ministry of Justice: Midan Lazoghli, Cairo; f. 1929; over 90,000 vols. and periodicals in Arabic, French and English (law and social science); private library for the use of judges and members of the Parquet (public prosecution and criminal investigation authority); a centre attached to the library contains the latest texts of local and comparative legislature on Personal Status; Dir. F. Abou-El-Kheir.

Library of the Ministry of Trade: Sharia Ismail Abaza Pasha, Cairo; over 20,048 vols.

Library of the Ministry of Waqfs: Qoubbih al-Ghoury, Cairo; f. 1942; 20,219 vols.

Library of the Monastery of St. Catherine: Mount Sinai; f. 327; over 3,300 MSS.; the Codex Sinaiticus was discovered in this library in 1856.

Mansoura Municipal Library: contains 17,984 vols. (Arabic 13,036, European 4,948).

National Archives: Al-Qalcah, Cairo; f. 1954; 37,800 archives from the ex-Royal Family, Turkish and Foreign; Dir. M. Z. Reihan.

National Assembly Library: Palace of the National Assembly, Cairo; f. 1924; over 50,000 vols.; Dir. Antoun Matta.

Sharkia Provincial Council Library: Zagazig; contains 12,238 vols. (Arabic 7,861, European 4,377).

Tanta Municipal Library: contains 20,943 vols.

MUSEUMS

Agricultural Museum: Dokki, Cairo; f. 1938; exhibits of Egyptian agriculture, horticulture, irrigation; botanical and zoological sections; library of 8,023 vols.; Dir. Dr. M. H. El Ghawas.

Al-Gawhara Palace Museum: The Citadel, Cairo; f. 1954, refurnished 1956; built in 1811 in the Ottoman style, the Palace retains much of its original interior, contains Oriental and French furniture, including gilded throne, Turkish paintings, exhibitions of clocks, glass, 19th-century costumes.

Anderson Museum: Beit el-Kretlia, Cairo; f. 1936; private collections of Oriental art objects bequeathed to Egypt by R. G. Gayer Anderson Pasha in 1936; Curator YOUNES MAHRAN.

Cairo Geological Museum: 15 Sheikh Rihan Street, Cairo, Dawawin Post Office; a section of the Geological Survey; f. 1899; 50,000 specimens, mostly Egyptian; exhibits illustrating all branches of geology, especially recent acquisitions connected with revival of industrialization; Dir. RAGI A. EISSA.

Cairo Museum of Hygiene: Midan-el-Sakakini, Daher, Cairo; Dir. Dr. FAWZI SWEHA.

Coptic Museum: Old Cairo, Cairo; f. 1910; sculpture and frescoes, MSS., textiles, icons, ivory and bone, carved wood, metalwork, pottery and glass; library of 6,587 vols.; Dir. MOUNIR BASTA; publs. *The Coptic Museum* (general guide), *Catalogue of the Coptic and Arabic Manuscripts in the Coptic Museum and the Patriarchate, Cairo's Ancient Coptic Churches* (guide book), *The Monasteries of Egypt* (Arabic), etc.

Cotton Museum: Gezira, Cairo; f. 1923; established by the Egyptian Agricultural Society; all aspects of cotton growing, diseases, pests, and methods of spinning and weaving are shown; Dir. M. EL-BAHTIMI.

Egyptian (National) Museum: Midan-el-Tahrir, Kasr El-Nil, Cairo; f. 1900; exhibits from prehistoric times until the 6th century A.D.; excludes Coptic and Islamic periods; houses the Department of Antiquities; established by decree in 1835 to conserve antiquities; the Department administers the archaeological museums and controls excavations; library of 35,650 vols.; Dir. ABD EL-KADER SELIM; Chief Curator MOHAMMED A. MOHSEN; publs. museum catalogue, *Annals of the Antiquities Service of Egypt*†, etc.

Greco-Roman Museum: Museum St., Alexandria; f. 1892; exhibits from the Byzantine, Roman, and Greek eras; library of 7,184 vols., Omar Tousson collection of 4,000 vols.; Dir. YOUSSEL EL GHERIANY; publ. *Annuaire du Musée Gréco-Romain.*

Museum of Islamic Art: Ahmed Maher Sq., Bab al-Khalq, Cairo; f. 1882; collection representing the evolution of Islamic art up to 1879; Dir.-Gen. ABD AL-RAUF A. YOUSUF; library of 14,060 vols.; publs. *Islamic Archaeological Studies* (annually), catalogues and Islamic decorative arts.

Museum of Modern Art: 4 Sharia Kasr El-Nil, Cairo; f. 1920; Curator SALAH E. TAHER.

Railway Museum: Cairo Station; f. 1933; contains models of foreign and Egyptian railways, and technical information and statistics of the evolution and development of the Egyptian railway services; library of 5,595 vols. (Arabic 2,694, European 2,901); Curator NAGUIB NASR GEORGE.

War Museum: The Citadel, Cairo; library of 6,000 vols.

UNIVERSITIES

AIN SHAMS UNIVERSITY

KASR-EL-ZAAFRAN,
ABBASIYAH, CAIRO

Telephone: 821455.

Founded 1950.

President: ABDEL AZIZ HAFEZ SOLAYMAN.

Vice-President for Undergraduate Studies: Prof. Dr. NASR EL SAYED NASR.

Vice-President for Graduate Studies and Research: Prof. Dr. ZAGLOUL YOUNIS MAHRAN.

Secretary-General: ABDEL HAMID IBRAHIM.

Number of teachers: 3,755.
Number of students: 86,324.
Publications: Faculty reviews.

DEANS:

Faculty of Medicine: Prof. Dr. AHMED ZAKY EL-BANHAWY.

Faculty of Arts: Prof. Dr. GAMAL EL-DIN ZAKARIA KASSEM.

Faculty of Science: Dr. ABDEL HAFEZ HELMY M. ABDEL HAFEZ.

Faculty of Engineering: Prof. Dr. MOHD. M. EL-HASHIMY.

Faculty of Agriculture: Prof. Dr. SAAD ALY ZAKY.

Faculty of Commerce: Prof. Dr. IBRAHIM ABDEL REHIM HOUMENY.

Faculty of Law: Prof. Dr. SOLAYMAN MOHAMED SOLAYMAN EL-TAMAWI.

Women's College: Dr. SAMIHA M. ABDEL WAHAB.

Faculty of Education: Prof. Dr. ABDEL SALAM ABDEL KADER.

Al Alsun Faculty: Prof. Dr. ABD EL-SAMEIE MOHAMED.

UNIVERSITY OF ALEXANDRIA

3 AL-GUEISH AVENUE,
SHATBY, ALEXANDRIA

Telephone: 71675/8.

Telex: 54467 UNIVY UN.

Founded 1942.

State control; Academic year: September to May; Languages of instruction: Arabic and English.

President: Prof. Dr. ALI REDA EL-HENEIDY.

Vice-President for Undergraduate Studies: Prof. Dr. MOUSTAFA KHALIL.

Vice-President for Graduate Studies and Research: Prof. Dr. MOHAMED EMARY OKAIL.

Secretary-General: MOHAMED Z. EL-RAFFAH.

Chief Librarian: KHALID EL-RAMADY.

Library: *see* Libraries.

Number of teachers: 3,195.
Number of students: 80,837.

Publications: Faculty Bulletins, *University Monthly Gazette* (for staff and personnel), *Collection of Public Affairs Lectures.*

DEANS:

Faculty of Arts: Prof. Dr. MOHAMED ATEF GEITH.

Faculty of Laws: Prof. Dr. TAWFIK FARAG.

Faculty of Commerce: Prof. Dr. ABDEL EL-FATTAH EL-SAHN.

Faculty of Science: Prof. Dr. ABD EL-SALLAM SHALABY.

Faculty of Medicine: Prof. Dr. RAFEK A. ZAHER.

Faculty of Engineering: Prof. MOHAMED M. MEAHID.

Faculty of Agriculture: Prof. Dr. KHALID EL-SHAZLY.

Faculty of Pharmacy: Prof. Dr. MOHAMED RASHAD SALEH.

Faculty of Dentistry: Prof. Dr. MAHMOOD EL-HADARY.

Faculty of Education: Prof. Dr. EBRAHIM WAGEH.

Faculty of Veterinary Medicine: Prof. Dr. EBRAHIM ABU EL-AZM.

Higher Institute of Public Health: Prof. Dr. MOHAMED HUSSEIN KHALIL (*see* also under Colleges).

Institute of Medical Research: Dir. Prof. Dr. ABD EL-MONEIM KABIL.

Higher Institute of Nursing: Dir. Dr. SOHAER MOKABEL.

ATTACHED INSTITUTES:

Centre for Advancement of Postgraduate Science Studies: f. 1972 with Unesco and UNDP aid; Dir. Prof. Dr. ABDEL-RAHMAN EL-SADR.

Computation Science Centre: Dir. Dr. KHALIL MOHAMED AHMED.

AL-AZHAR UNIVERSITY
CAIRO

Telephone: 904051, 706097, 906154.

Founded 970, modernized and expanded 1961.

President: Prof. Dr. AWDALLAH HIGAZY.
Vice-Presidents: Prof. Dr. IBRAHIM M. NAGA, Prof. Dr. AHMED FATHY EL-ZAYAT.

Library: *see* Libraries.
Number of teachers: 3,604.
Number of students: *c.* 43,439.

Publications: *Annual Report*, University and Faculty Calendars.

DEANS:

Faculty of Islamic Theology: Dr. MOUSSA SHAHIN LASHIN.
Faculty of Islamic Jurisprudence and Law: Dr. M. EL-SAID ABD RAPPOH.
Faculty of Arabic Studies: Dr. HASSAN GAD HASSAN.
Faculty of Engineering: Prof. Dr. AHMED A. MOUGHTAR.
Faculty of Medicine: Dr. KHALIFA ABDEL LATIF KAMALY.
Faculty of Commerce: Dr. EZZAT M. EL-SHEIK.
Faculty of Agriculture: Prof. Dr. AHMED M. OMAR.
Islamic Women's College: Prof. Dr. MOHAMED M. GABR NASSAR.
Faculty of Arabic and Islamic Studies: Dr. AHMED MEGAHID MISBAH.
Faculty of Language and Translation: Prof. Dr. MAHMOUD SHOKRY MOUSTAFA.
Faculty of Science: Prof. Dr. YANZA M. EZZAT.

AMERICAN UNIVERSITY IN CAIRO
113 SHARIA KASR EL-AINI, CAIRO

Telephone: 22969.

American Address: 866 United Nations Plaza, New York, N.Y. 10017.

Founded 1919.

Private control; Academic year: September to June; Language of instruction: English.

President: Dr. RICHARD F. PEDERSEN.
Vice-Presidents: Dr. MOHAMMED ABDEL KHALEK ALLAM, Dr. THOMAS A. LAMONT, JAMES B. ROBINSON.
Dean of the Faculties: Dr. THOMAS AQUINAS LAMONT.

Library: *see* Libraries.
Number of teachers: 130.
Number of students: 1,200 undergraduates, 500 graduates.

Fifteen undergraduate degrees. Master degrees in Management, Economics, Political Economy, Solid State Science, English Literature, Teaching English as a Foreign Language, Islamic History, Islamic Art and Architecture, Arabic Literature, Arabic as a Foreign Language, Sociology-Anthropology, Mass Communication.

ATTACHED UNITS:

Division of Public Service: non-credit study programme for 8,500 students per semester; Dir. Dr. HERBERT REAS.

Social Research Centre: Current research projects on demography and human resettlement; Dir. Dr. SAAD GADALLA.

English Language Institute: diploma and M.A. degree in teaching English as a Foreign Language; Dir. Dr. YEHIA EL-EZABI.

UNIVERSITY OF ASSIUT
ASSIUT

Telephone: Assiut 3000.

Founded 1957.

Languages of instruction: Arabic and English.

President: Prof. Dr. HASSAN HAMDY IBRAHIM.
Vice-President for Undergraduate Studies: Prof. Dr. ABDEL RAZEK R. HASSAN.
Vice-President for Graduate Studies and Research: Prof. Dr. AHMED MOUSTAFA YASSEIN.

Number of teachers: 1,717.
Number of students: 30,355.

DEANS:

Faculty of Science: Prof. Dr. ABDEL AAL HASSAN MEBASHIR.
Faculty of Engineerng: Prof. Dr. OMAR EL KHATTAB TEWFIK.
Faculty of Agriculture: Prof. Dr. MOHAMED HELMY ZEIN-EL-ABDINE EL-GUIBALY.
Faculty of Law: Prof. Dr. MAHMOUD SALLAM ZENATI.
Faculty of Medicine: Prof. Dr. MAHMOUD FAHMY FATH ALLAH.
Faculty of Pharmacy: Prof. Dr. AHMED MOHAMED EL-MOGHAZY SHOUEIB.
Faculty of Veterinary Medicine: Prof. Dr. ABDEL RAHMAN M. EL-TAHER.
Faculty of Commerce: Prof. Dr. MOUSTAFA M. BAGHAT.
Faculty of Education: Prof. Dr. HASSAN SALAMA EL FEKY.
Faculty of Arts (in Sohag): Prof. Dr. M. HELMY MOUSTAFA.
Faculty of Science (in Sohag): Prof. Dr. SAID M. EMMARA.
Faculty of Education (in Sohag): Prof. Dr. IBRAHIM BASSYOUNI.
Faculty of Science (in Kena): Prof. Dr. TAWFIK M. ALY BARAKAT.
Faculty of Science (in Aswan): Prof. Dr. M. KAMEL SAAD EL DIN SHEREIF.

Further faculties are in preparation in Aswan and Kena.

UNIVERSITY OF CAIRO
ORMAN, GHIZA, CAIRO

Telephone: 845186.

Founded 1908.

State control; Language of instruction: Arabic (English in practical faculties); Academic year: October to June.

President: Dr. IBRAHIM BADRAN.
Vice-President for Undergraduate Studies: Prof. Dr. M. SOBHY ABDEL HAKIM.
Vice-President for Graduate Studies and Research: Prof. Dr. MOHAMED F. HOUSSAIN.
Secretary-General: (vacant).

Library: *see* Libraries.

Number of teachers: 4,639.
Number of students: 90,781.

DEANS:

Faculty of Arts: Dr. HUSSAIN MOHAMED NASSER.
Faculty of Law: Dr. MAHMOUD N. HOSENY.
Faculty of Medicine: Dr. Y. TAHER MOHAMED.
Faculty of Economic and Political Science: Dr. MAHMOUD K. ESSA.
Faculty of Science: Dr. EZZAT M. KAIRY.
Faculty of Commerce: Dr. ADEL ABDEL HAMID EZZ.
Faculty of Engineering: Dr. Y. HASSAN KABEEL.
Faculty of Dentistry: Dr. M. EL SAYED AL SEDDEK.
Faculty of Pharmacy: Dr. FAYEK M. M. HASHEM.
Faculty of Agriculture: Dr. M. T. ABD EL-HAMED KIRA.
Faculty of Daral-Ulum: Dr. ABDALLAH ABD EL FATTAH DARWISH.
Faculty of Veterinary Medicine: Dr. KAMAL EL DIN M. ZAKI.
Faculty of Mass Communication: Dr. ABDEL MALIK OUDAH.
Faculty of Archaeology: Dr. ABD EL AZIZ SALEH MOHAMED.
Higher Institute of Nursing: Dr. IMAN M. MOURAD.
National Institute of Cancer Research: Dr. SALAH ABD EL RAHMAN SHAHBANDER.
Higher Institute of Physical Therapy: Dr. AMIN AL-BATAWY.
Institute of Research and Statistical Studies: Dr. SAAD EL DIN EL SHAYAL.
Institute of African Research Studies: Dr. MOHAMED EL SAID GALLAB.
University College of Education (in Fayoum): Dr. A. IBRAHIM KALIL.
Faculty of Agriculture (in Fayoum): Dr. ALI ABDEL FATTAH EL BASIL.
Faculty of Commerce (in Beni-Suef): Dr. ADEL ABDEL HAMID EZZ.
Statistics Centre: Dr. AHMED AZIZ KAMAL.

HELWAN UNIVERSITY

7 MODERIET EL-TAHRIR ST.,
GARDEN CITY, CAIRO
Telephone: 32043.

Founded 1975, incorporating existing institutes of higher education.

State control; Languages of instruction: Arabic, English and some French and German; Academic year: October to May.

President: MOHAMED ISMAEL ALAM ELDIN.
Vice-President: Prof. MOHAMED LOTFY EL-SAYED.
Registrar: FAWZY A. Z. KHAMIS.
Librarian: Mrs. SAMIRA A. BADAWI.

Library of 250,000 vols.

Number of teachers: 1,089.
Number of students: 31,468.

Publication: *Research Studies*† (quarterly).

DEANS:

Faculty of Engineering and Technology (Helwan): Prof. MONIR AZZOUZ.
Faculty of Engineering and Technology (Mataria): Prof. Dr. FATHY S. EL SHEREEF.
Faculty of Commerce and Business Administration: Prof. AHMED SOROUR.
Faculty of Art Education: Prof. Dr. FATHEL BAB A. HALEEM.
Faculty of Musical Education: Prof. AWATTIF ABDEL KAREEM.
Faculty of Fine Arts (Cairo): Prof. SALAH NAYEL.
Faculty of Fine Arts (Alexandria): Prof. YEHYA HAMMOUDA.
Faculty of Applied Arts: Prof. TAHA HESSEIN.
Faculty of Physical Education for Boys (Cairo): Prof. IBRAHIM KANDEEL.
Faculty of Physical Education for Girls (Cairo): Prof. Dr. ENAYAT FARAG.
Faculty of Physical Education for Boys (Alexandria): Prof. KAMAL ELDIN SHALABY.
Faculty of Physical Education for Girls (Alexandria): Prof. AFAF ABDEL KAREEM.
Faculty of Social Work: Prof. ABDEL FATTAH OSMAN.
Faculty of Home Economics: Prof. ENSAF NASR.
Faculty of Tourism and Hotel Management: Prof. MOHYI ELDIN IBRAHIM.
Faculty of Cotton Sciences (Alexandria): Prof. FATHALLA REHAB.

HEADS OF DEPARTMENTS:

Faculty of Engineering and Technology (Helwan):
Communications and Electronic Engineering: Prof. NABIL NAAOUM.
Electrical Engineering: Prof. MONIR AZZOUZ.
Production Engineering: Prof. REDA SWAILEM.
Physics: KAMEL ELDEHEIMI.
Mathematics: MOHAMED ELSEMARY.

Faculty of Engineering and Technology (Mataria):
Architecture: Prof. MAHMOUD SAMY.
Cars and Tractors: Prof. REFAAT SHAFEIK.
Mechanical Design: Prof. FATHY ELSHERIEF.
Mechanical Power: Prof. AHMED SABER.
Chemistry: Prof. WAGIH KABEEL.

Faculty of Commerce and Business Administration:
Law and Political Sciences: Prof. AFAF MAHFOUZ.
Business Administration: Prof. AHMED SOROUR.
Accountancy: Prof. IBRAHIM ASHMAWI.
Economics: Prof. ABDEL NABY YOUSSEF.
Foreign Trade: Prof. Dr. HAMDIA ZAHRAN.
Postal Affairs: Prof. ABDEL NABY YOUSSEF.
Languages: Prof. AMIN AZIZ.

Faculty of Art Education:
Educational Theory: Prof. FATHEL BAB A. HALEEM.
Curriculum and Methods of Teaching: Prof. KAWSAR KOJOK.
Psychology and Educational Technology: Prof. AMAL SADEK.
Drawing and Artistic Appreciation: Prof. AISHA ELARAMANY.
Sculpture and Ceramics: Prof. AIDA ABDEL KAREEM.
Design in Art Education: Prof. NADIA KHAFAGI.
Artistic and Popular Work: Prof. ABDEL RAZEK SOLIMAN.

Faculty of Musical Education:
Music Theory: Prof. AWATTIF ABDEL KAREEM.
Oriental Music: Prof. ISIS FATHALLA.
Piano: Prof. BOTHYNA ELZENATY.
Aural Training: Prof. SOAAD HASSANEIN.
Orchestral Instruments: Prof. ISMAEL ZAKY.
Singing: Prof. ENAYAT WASFY.

Faculty of Fine Arts (Cairo):
Photography: Prof. ZAKARIA ELZEINY.
Graphics: Prof. HESSEIN ELGEBALY.
Sculpture: Prof. SOBHY SAAD.
Interior Decoration: Prof. SALAH ABDEL KAREEM.
Architecture: Prof. GALAL MOMEN.
Construction: Prof. HASSAN ELESSEILY.

Faculty of Fine Arts (Alexandria):
Architecture: Prof. YEHYA HAMMOUDA.
Photography: Prof. FATMA ARARGI.
Interior Decoration: Prof. AHMED ABDALLAH.
Sculpture: Prof. AHMED ABDEL WAHAB.
Printed Design: Prof. MARIEM AFIFI.

Faculty of Applied Arts:
Industrial Design (Ceramics and Glass): Prof. AMEEN RAAFAT.
Interior Design and Furniture: Prof. ABDEL HADY ZAGHLOUL.
Textile Design: Prof. ABDEL MONEIM.
Photography and Printing: Prof. MOHAMED KAMEL.

Faculty of Physical Education for Boys (Cairo):
Combat and Aquatic Sports: Prof. ABBAS ELRAMLY.
Athletics: Prof. IBRAHIM KANDIL.
Exercises and Gymnastics: Prof. MOSAAD FARAGHALLY.
Principles of Physical Education and Recreation: Prof. HASSAN MOAWAD.
Games: Prof. HANAFY MOKHTAR.
Hygiene: Prof. ZENAB KHALIFA.

Faculty of Physical Education for Girls (Cairo):
Athletics: Prof. MADIHA SAMY.
Combat and Aquatic Sports: Prof. NEMAT SABER.
Games: Prof. ZENAB FAHMY.
Exercises, Gymnastics and Rhythm: Prof. SAFEYA ABOU OAF.
Methods: Prof. NAFIESSA BAHGAT.

Faculty of Physical Education for Boys (Alexandria):
Methods of Teaching and Training: Prof. AMEEN NAYEL.
Hygiene: Prof. MOHAMED SHATA.
Games: Prof. BOTROS RISK.
Athletics: Prof. SABER KHEIRALLA.
Exercises and Gymnastics: Prof. MOUSSA FAHMY.
Combat and Aquatic Sports: Prof. SOROUR MANSOUR.

Faculty of Physical Education for Girls (Alexandria):
Education: Prof. KAMAL SHALABY.
Principles of Physical Education: Prof. SHOUKRIA KHALIL.
Exercises, Gymnastics and Rhythm: Prof. AWATIF ABDEL KAREEM.
Athletics: Prof. DALAL H. FAHMY.
Games: Prof. ELEN W. FAHMY.
Combat and Aquatic Sports: Prof. EFFAT SHAFEIK.

Faculty of Social Work:
Group Service: Prof. MOHAMED SHAMS.
Community Organization: Prof. ABDEL HALEEM REDA.
Social Planning: Prof. ABDEL FATTAH OSMAN.
Individual Service: Prof. ABDEL FATTAH OSMAN.
Social Work Training: Prof. MOHAMED HESSEIN.

Faculty of Home Economics:
Nutrition and Food: Prof. BOTHYNA MAHRAN.
Home Management: Prof. LOULOU DAWOUD.
Clothing and Textiles: Prof. ENSAF NASR.

Faculty of Tourism and Hotel Management:
Hotel Studies: Prof. SANYA ABDEL HAMID.
Tourism Studies: Prof. MOHAMED OMAR.

History, Geography and Archaeology: Prof. MOHYI ELDIN IBRAHIM.

Faculty of Cotton Sciences (Alexandria):
Cotton Production: Prof. ABDEL FATTAH SAYED.
Cotton Technology: Prof. A. MOHAMED ELSARDY.
Cotton Economics: Prof. MOHAMED K. AHMED.

MANSOURA UNIVERSITY

SHARIA AL-COMHORIA, MANSOURA

Telephone: 7054/5.

Founded 1972 from the Mansoura branch of Cairo University.

State control; Languages of instruction: Arabic and English.

President: Prof. SHAFIK IBRAHIM BALBAA.
Vice-President: Prof. Dr. MOHAMED MOHIEY EL-DIN AWAD.
Chief Administrative Officer: MOHAMED SAFWAT EL BASYOUNY.
Librarian: SHAFIK GONENA.

Number of teachers: 500.
Number of students: 26,000.

DEANS:

Faculty of Pharmacy: Prof. ABUL MALIK ABOU OOF.
Faculty of Law: Prof. Dr. ABD EL FATTAH MOHAMED HASSAN.
Faculty of Science: Prof. Dr. HUSSEIN GHALEB OSMAN.
Faculty of Education: Prof. Dr. SAID HASSAN KHEIR ALLAH.
Faculty of Engineering: Prof. Dr. RASHAD EL BADRAWY.
Faculty of Commerce: Prof. ABD EL LATIF ABD EL FATTAH.
Faculty of Agriculture: Prof. YEHIA AHMED MASOUD.
Faculty of Medicine: Prof. KAMAL EL DIN AHMED.
Faculty of Dentistry: Prof. RADWAN YOUSEFF EL HAK.
Faculty of Arts: Prof. Dr. MOHAMED ABD EL KADER MOHAMED.

MENIA UNIVERSITY

MENIA

Founded 1976, incorporating existing faculties of University of Assiut.

President: Prof. Dr. YAHYA ALY SHAHIN.
Vice-President: Prof. Dr. MAHMOUD ISMAIL TAHA.

Number of teachers: 527.
Number of students: 10,102.

DEANS:

Faculty of Arts: Prof. Dr. ABDEL MONEM HUSEIN SHAWKI.
Faculty of Science: Prof. Dr. M. ABOU EL FATH RAMADAN.
Faculty of Engineering and Technology: Prof. H. MOUSTAFA ASFOUR.
Faculty of Agriculture: Prof. Dr. NASR HANAFY METWALLY.
Faculty of Education: Dr. Prof. IBRAHIM M. EL SHAFEY.

Faculties of Fine Arts and Medicine are in preparation.

MENUFIA UNIVERSITY

MENUFIA

Founded 1976.

President: Prof. Dr. ZAKI MAHMOUD SHABANA.
Vice-President: Prof. Dr. MOHAMED R. ABOU EL GHAR.

Number of teachers: 519.
Number of students: 11,801.

DEANS:

Faculty of Engineering and Technology: Dr. SAAD M. MOUSTAFA WAHEBAH.
Faculty of Electronic Engineering (in Monouf): Dr. ABDEL SALAM ALY Z. EL HAMALAWY.
Faculty of Agriculture: Dr. MOHAMED M. TAHA EL KADY.
Faculty of Education: Dr. SAAD ZAGLOUL EL NAGGAR.

SUEZ CANAL UNIVERSITY

Founded 1976.

President: Prof. Dr. ABD EL-MEGEID OSMAN.
Vice-President: Prof. Dr. AHMED ABOU SHADY.

Number of teachers: 371.
Number of students: 6,642.

DEANS:

Faculty of Commerce and Administration (in Port Said): Dr. ABDEL HAMID EL-HOUSEINY HASHIM.
Faculty of Petroleum and Mining Engineering (in Suez): Dr. ALY HOUMEIDA ALY GOMAA.
Faculty of Engineering and Technology (in Port Said): Dr. M. KAMEL EL-RAYISS.

Other faculties are in preparation.

TANTA UNIVERSITY

TANTA

Telephone: 2785-4985.

Founded 1972 from the Tanta branch of the University of Alexandria.

State control; Language of instruction: English.

President: Prof. Dr. ABDEL HAIY AHMED MASHHOUR.
Vice-President for Undergraduate Studies: Prof. Dr. AHMED M. AMIN.
Vice-President for Graduate Studies and Research: Prof. Dr. MOHAMED KAMAL EL AKKAD.

Number of teachers: 887.
Number of students: 21,840.

DEANS:

Faculty of Medicine: Prof. H. MOSTAFA.
Faculty of Science: Prof. Dr. M. WAGDI EL-SAWAH.
Faculty of Education: Prof. Dr. IBRAHIM ESMAT M. MOTAWEI.
Faculty of Commerce: Prof. A. GENEID.
Faculty of Agriculture: Prof. M. ABOU ELGHAR.
Faculty of Engineering: Prof. S. WEHEBA.
Faculty of Electronics: Prof. Y. TANTAWI.
Faculty of Arts: Prof. A. WEHEBA.
Faculty of Agriculture (at Kafr El Sheikh): Prof. AHMED SAYED EL NAWAWY.
Faculty of Pharmacy: Prof. M. A. ELDAWY.

ZAGAZIG UNIVERSITY

ZAGAZIG

Founded 1974, incorporating existing faculties of Ain-Shams University.

President: Prof. Dr. MOHAMED TOLBA OWEIDA.
Vice-President for Undergraduate Studies: Prof. Dr. IBRAHIM ALY ESHMAWY.
Vice-President for Graduate Studies and Research: Prof. Dr. M. FATHY EL SAID EL SHENEITY.

Number of teachers: 1,225.
Number of students: 35,522.

DEANS:

Faculty of Arts: Prof. Dr. M. EL HEFNY ZOHNY.
Faculty of Law: Prof. Dr. AHMED ABDEL AZIZ SALEM.
Faculty of Commerce: Prof. Dr. ABBAS MAHDY SHERAZY.
Faculty of Science: Prof. Dr. ABDEL AZIM ABDALLAH SHALABY.
Faculty of Medicine: Prof. Dr. M. ABDEL LATIF IBRAHIM.
Faculty of Pharmacy: Prof. Dr. AFAF ABOU EL KHAIR.
Faculty of Engineering: Prof. Dr. RAMZY HABIB DAWOUD.
Faculty of Agriculture: Prof. Dr. M. BAKR MOUSTAFA.
Faculty of Veterinary Medicine: Prof. Dr. ABDEL TAWAB M. BAHGAT.
Faculty of Education: Prof. Dr. KAMAL M. DESOUKI.
Faculty of Commerce (in Banha): Prof. Dr. HENRY ANIS.
Faculty of Engineering (in Choubra): Prof. Dr. ABDEL AZIZ MORSY EL MAHDY.
Faculty of Agriculture (in Moshtohor): Prof. Dr. ABDEL MONEM M. SOLAYMAN.

COLLEGES

Arab States Regional Centre for Functional Literacy in Rural Areas (ASFEC): Sirs-el-Layyan, Menoufia; f. 1952 by UNESCO; training of specialists, production of prototype educational material, research in community development problems; advisory service to member states; Dir. Dr. ABDEL FATTAH GALAL.

Cairo Polytechnic Institute: 108 Shoubra Street, Shoubra, Cairo; f. 1961; Engineering, Agriculture, Commerce; Dir. H. H. MOHAMED.

Higher Industrial Institute: Aswan; f. 1962; state control; courses in mechanical, electrical and chemical engineering, mining and natural sciences.

Higher Institute of Public Health: an autonomous unit of the Univ. of Alexandria, 165 Gamal Abd El Nasser Ave., El-Hadra P.O., Alexandria; f. 1955; undertakes fundamental teaching and applied public health research; 53 staff mems. and 50 instructors; departments of Public Health Administration, Biostatistics, Nutrition, Epidemiology, Tropical Health, Microbiology, Occupational and Environmental Health, Family Health; library of 10,000 vols.; Dean Prof. MOHAMMED HUSSEIN MOHAMMED; publ. *Bulletin*†.

Mansoura Polytechnic Institute: Mit-Khamis St., Mansoura; f. 1957; 147 teachers, 2,290 students; library of 21,400 vols.; Dir. Dr. ESSAYED SELIM ELMOLLA.

SCHOOLS OF ART AND MUSIC

Academy of Arts: Pyramids Rd., Giza; f. 1969; organized in seven institutions:

Higher Institute of Ballet: f. 1958; Dean ENZYAH AZMY.

Higher Institute of Cinema: f. 1959; depts. of scriptwriting, directing, editing, camerawork, scene design, sound, production; 50 staff, 300 students; library of 3,000 vols.; Dean Prof. MAHMOUD EL SHERIF.

Higher Institute of Dramatic Art: f. 1959; Dean Dr. IBRAHIM HAMADA.

Higher Institute of Arab Music: f. 1967; Dean RATIBA M. EL-HEFNY.

Higher Institute of Artistic Criticism: f. 1970; Dean Dr. FAWZY FAHMY AHMED.

Higher Institute of Music (Conservatoire): f. 1959; Dean Dr. SAMHA AMIN EL KHOULY.

Folklore Studies Centre: f. 1957; Dir. Dr. AHMED MORSY.

EL SALVADOR

Population 4,255,000

ACADEMIES

San Salvador

Academia Salvadoreña (*El Salvador Academy*): 4th in order of foundation in Spanish America; correspondent of the Real Academia Española, Madrid.
Director: Enrique Córdova.
Secretary: Alberto Rivas Bonilla.

Academia Salvadoreña de la Historia (*El Salvador Academy of History*): f. 1925; Dir. Manuel Castro Ramírez; Sec. Julio Enrique Avila; correspondent of the Real Academia de la Historia, Madrid.

LEARNED SOCIETIES AND RESEARCH INSTITUTES

San Salvador

Alianza Francesa: Apdo. postal (01) 175; f. 1954; diffusion of French culture; language courses, exhibitions, conferences, etc.; 150 mems.; library of 9,000 vols.; Pres. Dr. Ernesto Lima; Acad. Dir. Paul Fieschi.

Ateneo de El Salvador: 13a C.P. Centro de Gobierno; f. 1912; library of 2,600 vols.; 37 mems., 95 corresponding mems.; Pres. Doña Eva Alcaine de Palomo; Sec.-Gen. Gen. José María López Ayala.

Centro de Estudios e Investigaciones Geotécnicas: P.O.B. 109; reorganized 1964; Departments of Seismology, Soil Mechanics, Building Materials, Minerals, Geological Surveys; Dir. Eng. Edgar Parker Escolán.

Centro Nacional de Tecnología Agropecuaria (CENTA): Final 1a. Avenida Norte; f. 1942; research and development of seeds; 400 staff; library of 6,500 vols., incl. periodicals; publs. *Agricultura en El Salvador*† (irregular), *Boletín Técnico*† (occasional), *Circular*† (occasional).

Colegio Médico de El Salvador: Final Pasaje 10, Col. Miramonte; f. 1943; promotes medical research and co-operation; Pres. Dr. Benjamín Valdez H; publ. *Archivos*.

Comisión Salvadoreña de Energia Nuclear (COSEN): c/o Ministerio de Economía, 4 Avda. Norte 233; f. 1961; to consider the applications in medicine, agriculture and industry of radio-isotopes and nuclear energy.

Dirección General de Estadística y Censos (*Statistical Office*): Calle Arce 953; f. 1881; Dir. Cnel. y Lic. Hector Fermín Aguila; publs. *Anuario Estadístico, Boletín Estadístico, Indice de Precios al Consumidor Obrero, El Salvador en Cifras*.

Instituto Salvadoreño de Investigaciones del Café: Ministerio de Agricultura, 23 Avda. Norte No. 114; f. 1956; administered by the Ministry of Agriculture; publs. monographs, *Boletín Informativo* (6 a year).

Servicio Meteorológico de El Salvador, C.A.: Ministerio de Agricultura y Ganaderia, 23 Avda. Norte No. 114; f. 1953; formerly Observatorio Nacional Meteorológico y Sismológico, f. 1889; sections: synoptic and aeronautical meteorology, climatology, agrometorology, red meteorology; library of 634 vols.; publs. *Anuario Meteorológico de El Salvador y Almanaque de El Salvador*†, *Carta del Tiempo*† (daily), *Revista Climatológica de 2 Meses Consecutivos* †(6 a year), *Publicaciones Técnicas*†.

Sociedad de Anestesiología de El Salvador: Gustavo Guerrero 640; f. 1958; Pres. Dr. J. Coto; publ. Report.

Sociedad de Ginecología y Obstetricia de El Salvador: Colegio Médico de El Salvador, Final Pasaje 10, Col. Miramonte; f. 1947; 46 mems.; library of 2,000 vols.; Pres. Dr. Ricardo J. Burgos; Sec. Dr. Ramiro Martínez Pérez.

Sociedad Médica de Salud Pública: Colegio Médico, Final Pasaje 10, Col. Miramonte; f. 1960; 50 mems.; Pres. Dr. R. Lucio Fernández.

LIBRARIES

San Salvador

Archivo General de la Nación: Palacio Nacional; Dir. Ofilio Gómez Posada; publ. *Repositorio*.

Biblioteca Ambulantes, Ministerio de Educación: 8a Ave. Sur No. 15; f. 1951; 25,000 vols.; Librarian Valentín Amaya.

Biblioteca Central de la Universidad de El Salvador: Apdo. Postal 143; f. 1847; 91,000 vols.; Dir. Lic. Ana Aurora de Kapsalis, a.l.a.

Biblioteca del Ministerio de Economía: Departamento de Estudios Económicos; f. 1950; 14,000 vols.; Librarian Roberto Galeano y Somoza.

Biblioteca del Ministerio de Relaciones Exteriores (*Library of the Ministry of Foreign Affairs*): 10,000 vols.; Librarian Manuel Antonio López.

Biblioteca Nacional (*National Library*): 8a Avenida Norte y Calle Delgado; f. 1870; 95,000 vols., 994 periodicals; collection of early 19th-century works relating to Central and South American States; Dir. Rosa Velásquez de Doumakis; publ. *Anaqueles* (irregular).

MUSEUMS

San Salvador

Museo Nacional "David J. Guzmán" (*National Museum*): Avda. la Revolución, Colonia San Benito; f. 1883; specializes in history, archaeology, ethnology, library science and restoration; Dir. Arq. Julia Mercedes A. de Quintanilla; publs. *Anales, Colección Antropología e Historia, La Cofradia, El Xipe*. Also administers:
Museo Tazumal: Chalchuapa, Dpto. de Santa Ana; f. 1951; archaeology.

Parque Zoológico Nacional y Jardin Botánico: Calle Modelo; f. 1961; houses natural science museum; Dir. Carlos Hidalgo.

UNIVERSITIES

UNIVERSIDAD DE EL SALVADOR

CIUDAD UNIVERSITARIA,
FINAL 25 AV. NORTE,
SAN SALVADOR
Telephone: 25-1490.

Founded 1841; branches at Santa Ana and San Miguel.

Rector: Ing. SALVADOR ENRIQUE HOVEL.
Secretary-General: Dr. RAFAEL ANTONIO OVIDIO.
Librarian: Lic. ANA AURORA DE KAPSALIS.

Number of teachers: 1,108.
Number of students: 24,303.

Publications: *La Universidad, Comunicaciones, Economía Salvadoreña.*

DEANS:

Faculty of Dentistry: Dr. MIGUEL ANTONIO BARRIOS.
Faculty of Medicine: Dr. MAURICIO SALAZAR.
Faculty of Chemistry and Pharmacy: Dr. AMÍLCAR AVENDAÑO Y ORTIZ.
Faculty of Law and Social Sciences: Dr. FRANCISCO VEGA.
Faculty of Engineering and Architecture: Arq. MANUEL ENRIQUE ALFARO.
Faculty of Sciences and Humanities: Lic. ROBERTO L. PAREDES.
Faculty of Agricultural Sciences: Ing. RUBEN GONZALEZ OLMEDO.
Faculty of Economics: Dr. CARLOS A. RODRIGUEZ.
Faculty of Agriculture: Ing. SALVADOR ENRIQUE JOVEL.
Faculty of Economics: Dr. CARLOS RODRÍGUEZ.

UNIVERSIDAD CENTROAMERICANA "JOSÉ SIMEÓN CAÑAS"

APDO. (01) 168, SAN SALVADOR
Telephone: 24-0011.
Telex: 30018 PROCA.

Founded 1965.
Private control.

Language of instruction: Spanish; Academic year: March to December.

Rector: Dr. IGNACIO ELLACURÍA.
Vice-Rector (Academic): Dr. LUIS DE SEBASTIÁN.
Vice-Rector (Administration): Ing. AXEL SODERBERTG.
Secretary-General: Lic. JOSÉ MARÍA GONDRA.
Librarian: Sra. MÉLIDA ARTEAGA.

Number of teachers: 179.
Number of students: 4,972.

Publications: *Estudios Centroamericanos (ECA), Tecnología y Ciencia, Administración y Empresa, Boletín de Ciencias Económicas y Sociales, Boletín Proceso.*

DEANS:

Faculty of Economics: FRANCISCO J. IBISATE.
Faculty of Engineering: Ing. FREDY VILLALTA.
Faculty of Human and Natural Sciences: Dr. JESÚS DELGADO.
Theology: Dr. JON SOBRINO.

UNIVERSIDAD "DR. JOSÉ MATIAS DELGADO"

CALLE ARCE 1114,
SAN SALVADOR
Telephone: 22-13-38.

Founded 1977; private control.

Language of instruction: Spanish; Academic year: January to May, June to November.

Rector: Dr. GUILLERMO TRIGUEROS H.
Academic Vice-Rector: Dr. DAVID ESCOBAR GALINDO.
Secretary-General: Dr. FRANCISCO JOSÉ BARRIENTOS.

Number of teachers: 120.
Number of students: 1,640.

DEANS AND DIRECTORS:

School of Law: Dr. SALVADOR N. GARCÍA CÓRDOVA.
School of Liberal and Fine Arts: Dr. HUGO LINDO.
School of Applied Arts: ROBERTO GALICIA.
School of Public Accountancy: Dr. SALVADOR MELARA GONZÁLEZ.
School of Business Administration and Marketing: Ing. VÍCTOR MANUEL VALDÉS.
School of Public Administration: Dr. ARTURO ZELEDÓN CASTRILLO.
School of Foreign Exchange: Lic. MARÍA E. AMORY DE MARÍN.
School of Insurance and Bank Administration: Lic. JOSÉ HERNÁNDEZ Y HERNÁNDEZ.

COLLEGES

Central American Technical Institute: Apdo. 33, Santa Tecla; opened 1969; a joint British-Salvadorian programme in which Britain has equipped the workshops and laboratories; 4 British, 80 Salvadorian staff, 900 students; library of 3,000 vols.; Dir. R. K. SIMMONDS, O.B.E.

Departamento de Música del Centro Nacional de Artes: 6A Avda. Norte 319, San Salvador; Dir. Prof. LUIS MARIO FLAMENCO SEVILLA.

Escuela de Trabajo Social (*School of Social Work*): 37 Calle Oriente 255, San Salvador; f. 1953; 25 teachers, 116 students; Dir. Srta. T. S. R. DEL CARMEN R. V. DE CASTRO.

Escuela Nacional de Agricultura "Roberto Quiñónez": San Andrés, Ciudad Arce, La Libertad, Apdo. 2139, San Salvador; f. 1956; 500 students, 40 teachers; library of 6,500 vols.; Dir. CARLOS TADEO CAÑAS.

ETHIOPIA

Population 29,707,000

LEARNED SOCIETIES AND RESEARCH INSTITUTES

British Council: P.O.B. 1043, Artistic Building, Adwa Ave., Addis Ababa; f. 1959; library: *see* Libraries; Rep. D. A. Bell.

Desert Locust Control Organization for Eastern Africa: P.O.B. 4255, Addis Ababa; f. 1962; mems.: Ethiopia, France, Kenya, Somalia, Sudan, Tanzania, Uganda; Dir. Alto Mulugetta (acting); publs. *Annual Report, Technical Reports.*

Ethiopian Library Association: P.O.B. 30530, Addis Ababa; f. 1961; to promote the interests of libraries, archives, documentation centres, etc., and to serve those working in them; 150 mems.; Pres. Degife Gabre Tsadik; Sec. Yonas Telahun; publ. *Bulletin* (2 a year).

Ethiopian Mapping Agency: P.O.B. 597, Addis Ababa; f. 1955; conducts geodetic and cadastral surveying, mapping and geographical research; 250 mems.; under the Ethiopian Central Planning Commission.

Ethiopian Medical Association: P.O.B. 2179, Addis Ababa; f. 1961; Pres. Dr. Mesfin Demissie; publ. *Ethiopian Medical Journal (quarterly).*

Forestry Research Institute: University of Addis Ababa, P.O.B. 1176, Addis Ababa; f. 1962; Dir. (vacant); publ. *Timbers of Ethiopia* (irregular).

Geological Survey of Ethiopia: P.O.B. 486, Addis Ababa; f. 1968; department of Ministry of Mines and Energy; Dir. Dr. John S. Tooms.

Geophysical Observatory: University of Addis Ababa, P.O.B. 1176, Addis Ababa; f. 1958; located on the magnetic equator, for study of geomagnetic transients and the equatorial electrojet; also for study of the seismicity, geotectonics and gravity anomalies of the Ethiopian Rift System; library of 500 vols. and 50 periodicals; Dir. P. Gouin, M.Sc., F.R.A.S.; publs. *Bulletin, Contributions* (irregular).

Goethe-Institut (*German Cultural Institute*): P.O.B. 1193, Addis Ababa; f. 1962; Dir. S. Reile.

Institut d'Archéologie: P.O.B. 1907, Addis Ababa; conducts archaeological excavations in the Soddo region and at Axum, Yeha and Matara; undertakes preservation work at Axum, Gondar and Tana; Dir. Dr. Berhanou Abbébé; publ. *Annales d'Ethiopie.*

Institut de Recherches Agronomiques Tropicales et des Cultures Vivrières (IRAT): Awassa Agronomical and Experimental Station, P.O.B. 6, Awassa (Sidamo); f. 1967; general agronomy, food crops for medium tropical altitudes, maize husbandry and breeding; Dir. Gebre Selassie Kahsay. *See* main entry under France.

Institute of Agricultural Research: P.O.B. 2003, Addis Ababa; f. 1966 as an autonomous public authority of the Government under the Ministry of Agricultural Reform; aid from UNDP/FAO and other sources; 8 research stations; library of *c.* 1,000 vols. and 99 journals; Gen. Man. Zemedu Worku; publs. *Summary Report*†, *Progress Reports*†, *Proceedings of the IAR Research Seminar*†, results of national crop trials, etc.†

Institute of Ethiopian Studies: University of Addis Ababa, P.O.B. 1176, Addis Ababa; f. 1963; advanced study and documentation centre; library and ethnological-historical museum; Dir. Dr. Taddesse Tamrat; Librarian Dr. Metikou Ourgay; Curator Dr. Girma Kidane; publs. include *Journal of Ethiopian Studies* (bi-annually), *Register of Research on Ethiopia and the Horn of Africa* (annual), *List of Periodical Publications in Ethiopia* (every two years), *Publications in Ethiopia* (annual).

International Livestock Centre for Africa (ILCA): P.O.B. 5689, Addis Ababa; f. 1974, with the support of the Consultative Group on International Agricultural Research, as an interdisciplinary research and information centre to promote and improve livestock production in tropical Africa; 60 staff; field programmes in Ethiopia, Botswana, Kenya, Mali, Nigeria; library of *c.* 12,000 vols.; Dir. Gen. D. J. Pratt; publs. *Systems Studies, Monographs, Bulletin,* progress reports.

LIBRARIES

Asmara Public Library: 20 Adua Ave., Asmara; f. 1955; 5,200 vols.

British Council Library: P.O.B. 1043, Addis Ababa; f. 1959; 21,858 vols., 133 periodicals; Librarian Ato Mulugeta Hunde, B.A., B.Lib.; Asmara: f. 1971; 9,311 vols., 46 periodicals; Librarian A. G. G. Medhin, D.L.Sc.

National Library and Archives: P.O.B. 717, Addis Ababa; f. 1944; 100,000 vols.; includes Public Library section; Dirs. Tsegaye Solomon, Bekele Negussie.

University of Addis Ababa Library: P.O.B. 1176, Addis Ababa; f. 1950; 375,000 vols.; collection includes rare books, pamphlets, maps and microfilms on Ethiopia published abroad; special attention is paid to the collection of books in the Amharic language; central library, six branch libraries and specialist libraries in Alemaya and Gondar; Librarian Getachew Birru.

MUSEUMS

Musée Archéologique: c/o Institut Ethiopien d'Archéologie, P.O.B. 1907, Addis Ababa.

Museum of the Institute of Ethiopian Studies: University of Addis Ababa, P.O.B. 1176, Addis Ababa; f. 1963; sections: material culture (household artefacts, clothing, handicrafts, etc.); ethno-musicology (all types of Ethiopian musical instruments, religious and secular music and poetry, record archive of oral tradition and folklore; cultural history (photographic documents); traditional art (church paintings and furnishings, icons, etc.), 14th century to the present); Curator Dr. Girma Kidane.

UNIVERSITIES

ADDIS ABABA UNIVERSITY

P.O. BOX 1176, ADDIS ABABA

Telephone: 110844

University College founded 1950, University 1961; extension centres in Addis Ababa, Alemaya, Gondar, Awassa, Bahir Dar and Debre Zeit. Closed 1974; reopened 1976 under Commission for Higher Education.

President: Dr. DURI MOHAMMED.

Academic Vice-President: Ato BILLILIGN MANDEFRO.

Vice-President for Business and Development: Dr. ASMELASH BEYENE.

Registrar: Ato AYELE MESHESHA.

Librarian: Ato GETACHEW BIRU (acting).

Number of teachers: *c.* 750.
Number of students: *c.* 11,200.

Publications: *Journal of Ethiopian Studies, SINET: An Ethiopian Journal of Science, Ethiopian Journal of Development Research, Ethiopian Journal of Education, Register of Current Research on Ethiopia and the Horn of Africa, Ethiopian Publications.*

DEANS:

College of Agriculture (Alemaya): Dr. EPHREM MAMO.

College of Social Sciences: Dr. MEKETE BELACHEW.

Faculty of Science: Ato BISRATE DELNESSAHU.

Faculty of Technology: Dr. ALEMAYEHU TEFERRA.

College of Pedagogical Sciences: Dr. ZEWDNEH YIMTATTU.

Faculty of Law: Dr. FASSIL NAHOM.

Faculty of Medicine (Addis Ababa): Dr. MESEL GEDDEBU.

Faculty of Medicine (Gondar): Dr. MALEDE MAROU.

School of Pharmacy: Dr. MULATOU DJOTE.

Division of Continuing Education: Ato LAKEW MULAT.

Awassa Junior College of Agriculture: Dr. GEREMEW HAILE.

Debre Zeit Junior College of Agriculture: Dr. TAYE BEZUNEH.

Bahir Dar Academy of Pedagogy: Ato ABRAHAM HUSSEN.

School of Graduate Studies: Dr. ABRAHAM BISRAT.

College of Veterinary Science, Debre Zeit: Dr. FISSEHA GEBREAB.

Directors:

Institute of Ethiopian Studies: Dr. TADDESSE TAMRAT.

Institute of Pathobiology: Dr. TEKLE MARIAM AYELE.

Institute of Development Research: Dr. ALULA ABATE.

Institute of Language Studies: Dr. HAILU ARAYA.

UNIVERSITY OF ASMARA*

P.O.B. 1220, ASMARA

Telephone: 113600

Italian section founded 1958; English section received charter 1968.

Private control (Roman Catholic); language of instruction: English (official languages English and Amharic); Academic year: October to July.

Vice-Chancellor: Rev. Mother FEDERICA BETTARI.

President: (vacant).

Academic Vice-President: Sr. MANNA GHEBREMEDHIN.

Administrative Vice-President: Sr. MARY ROSE SOMETTI.

Registrar: Sr. ANNA MARIA MARIANI.

Librarian: Rev. R. K. LE FLEUR, M.L.S.

The library contains 32,000 volumes.
Number of teachers: *c.* 60.
Number of students: *c.* 600.

DEANS:

Faculty of Arts: Sr. GABRIELA CARTONCINI.

Faculty of Commerce: Sr. MARISA RANZATO.

Faculty of Science: Sr. ANNA MARIA SORIOLO.

Evening Division: Sr. ELENA BINETTI.

* No reply received to our questionnaire this year.

COLLEGES

Awassa Community Development Training and Demonstration Centre: Addis Ababa University at Awassa, Junior College of Agriculture, P.O.B. 5, Awassa, Sidamo; f. 1977; depts. of agronomy, animal science, agricultural engineering; 650 students; Dean Dr. MELAKU WOREDE.

Jimma Agricultural Institute: P.O.B. 307, Jimma; f. 1966; library of 13,205 vols.; 23 teachers, 156 students; Pres. Ato ABRAHAM WOLDU; Registrar Ato LEMMA DESALEGU; Librarian TESHOME NEGERO.

National School of Music: c/o Ministry of Education, Addis Ababa.

Polytechnic Institute: P.O.B. 26, Bahar-Dar; f. 1963; agricultural mechanics, industrial chemistry, electrical technology, wood-working and processing technology, textile technology and metal technology; 370 students; Dir. Ato BEYENE BEKELE; Dean of Students Ato YETNA BEYENE; Librarian Ato TESFAI BERHANE.

FIJI

Population 607,000

LEARNED SOCIETIES

Fiji Society, The: Box 1205, Suva; f. 1936; is concerned with subjects of historic and scientific interest to Fiji and other islands of the Pacific; Pres. IVAN WILLIAMS; publ. *Transactions* (irregular).

Fiji Law Society, The: P.O.B. 144, Ba; Pres. K. N. GOVIND; Sec. G. P. SHANKAR.

LIBRARIES AND MUSEUM

Library Service of Fiji: Western Regional Library, P.O.B. 150, Lautoka; 7 brs.; 112 Bookbox stations, postal loan service, 13 Government department libraries; certificate course in librarianship; Chief Librarian KANTILAL JINNA, A.L.A.A.

National Archives of Fiji: P.O.B. 2125, Government Bldgs., Suva; f. 1954 as the Central Archives of Fiji and the Western Pacific High Commission; Government records, mission records, 5,000 vols. of monographs, newspapers, official publications; Archivist SETAREKI TUINACEVA, B.A.

Ramkrishna Mission Library: Nadi; f. 1927; books, periodicals, Braille literature, gramophone records, films, film strips, microfilms; Librarian Rev. SWAMI DAMODARANANDA.

Suva City Library: P.O.B. 176, Suva; f. 1909; public lending library; 46,218 vols.; mobile library service for children; Librarian M. ALIM AKBAR, B.A.

Fiji Museum: P.O.B. 2023, Suva; f. 1906; contains archaeological, ethnological and ornithological collections relating to Fiji, the Solomon Islands, and other islands of the South-West Pacific; archives of Fijian oral traditions; Dir. FERGUS CLUNIE; publs. *Bulletin*, *Journal*.

UNIVERSITY

THE UNIVERSITY OF THE SOUTH PACIFIC

P.O.B. 1168, SUVA
Telephone: 27131.
Founded 1968.

Academic year: February to November (two semesters); extension centres in the Cook Islands, Fiji, Kiribati, Niue, Solomon Islands, Tonga, Western Samoa; link arrangements with Nauru, New Hebrides, Tuvalu; the South Pacific Regional College of Tropical Agriculture in Alafua, Western Samoa, is now the university's second campus.

Chancellor: Gen. Sir BADDELEY DEVESI (Solomon Islands).
Pro-Chancellor and Chairman of Council: S. LANGI KAVALIKU, M.A., PH.D.
Vice-Chancellor: JAMES A. MARAJ, M.O.M., PH.D.
Deputy Vice-Chancellor: R. W. HOPKINS, M.COM., PH.D.
Registrar: M. GRIFFITH, LL.B., B.A.
Librarian: H. HOLDSWORTH, O.B.E., M.A., F.L.A.

Library of 170,000 vols.
Number of teaching staff: 139.
Number of students: 1,427.
Publication: *Calendar*.

HEADS OF SCHOOLS:

School of Education: Prof. W. MAXWELL, ED.D.
School of Natural Resources: N. J. SKINNER, PH.D.
School of Social and Economical Development: D. E. PATERSON, LL.M., J.S.D.
School of Agriculture (Alafua Campus): Prof. F. WENDT, PH.D.

PROFESSORS:

BROSNAHAN, L. F., M.A., D.LITT. AND PHIL., English
CROCOMBE, R. G., PH.D., Pacific Studies
DANDY, A. J., PH.D., Chemistry
HOPKINS, R. W., PH.D., F.C.A., C.M.A., Accounting
MAXWELL, W., B.S., Education
PATERSON, D. E., LL.M., J.S.D., Public Administration
RYLAND, J. S., PH.D., Biology
WENDT, F., PH.D., Agriculture

COLLEGES

Fiji College of Agriculture: Koronivia, Nausori; f. 1954, reorganized 1962; three-year diploma course in tropical agriculture; 130 students; Principal V. NATH.

Fiji Institute of Technology: P.O.B. 3722, Samabula; f. 1964; courses in building and civil engineering, business studies, agricultural, electrical and mechanical engineering, maritime studies, general studies, printing, catering; 150 full-time teachers, 2,500 students; library of 20,000 vols.; Principal K. F. CALLIGAN.

Fiji School of Medicine: Tamavua, Suva; f. 1886, reorganized as Central Medical School 1928; courses in all branches of medical and dental science and technology; postgraduate courses.
Principal: Dr. B. PATHIK.
Number of students: 266.

FINLAND

Population 4,764,000

ACADEMY

Suomen Akatemia (*Academy of Finland*): Ratamestarinkatu 12, SF 00520 Helsinki 52; f. 1947 and reorganized 1970 to promote scientific research and to develop national science policy by maintaining research fellowships, sponsoring projects, and publishing reports; a central governmental organ for research administration, reporting directly to the Ministry of Education and submitting its annual budget to Parliament for approval.

President: KAI OTTO DONNER.

Head of Administration: HEIKKI KALLIO.

Research Director: ELISABETH HELANDER.

Members of Central Board of Research Councils:

AHLSTRÖN, ANTTI (Research Council for Agriculture and Forestry)
ALHO, OLLI (Research Council for the Humanities)
GRAEFFE, GUNNAR (Research Council for the Natural Sciences)
KAILA, MARTTI M. (Research Council for Technology)
KETTUNEN, PERTTI (Research Council for the Social Sciences)
MIKKONEN, VALDE (Government appointee)
PAUNIO, ILKKA (Government appointee)
PUSKA, PEKKA (Government appointee)
SANTTI, RISTO (Medical Research Council)

ACADEMICIANS:

ITKONEN, ERKKI (Finno-Ugric Philology)
KOKKONEN, JOONAS (Art of Music)
LAURILA, ERKKI (Physics)
VON WRIGHT, GEORG HENRIK (Philosophy)

RESEARCH PROFESSORS:

AARNIO, AULIS (Law)
ENARI, TOR-MAGNUS (Biotechnology)
HÄNNINEN, OSMO (Physiology)
HINTIKKA, JAAKKO (Philosophy)
KIVIRIKKO, KARI (Medical Chemistry)
KOHONEN, TEUVO (Technical Physics)
LAGERSPETZ, KIRSTI (Psychology)
LOUNASMAA, OLLI (Technical Physics)
OKSMAN, JUHANI (Theoretical Electrical Engineering)
PAASIVIRTA, JUHANI (Political History)
POLVINEN, TUOMO (General History)
SEPPÄLÄ, MARKKU (Gynaecology)
TAKALA, ANNIKA (Educational Sciences)
TAWASTSTJERNA, ERIK (Musicology)
VAHERI, ANTTI (Virology)

LEARNED SOCIETIES

GENERAL

Societas Scientiarum Fennica/Finska Vetenskaps-Societeten/Suomen Tiedeseura (*Finnish Scientific Society*): Snellmaninkatu 9-11, 00170 Helsinki 17; f. 1838; *c.* 150 mems.; Pres. Prof. J.-M. JANSSON; Sec. Prof. H. THESLEFF; publs. *Årsbok—Vuosikirja* (Yearbook), *Commentationes physico-mathematicae, humanarum litterarum, Scientiarum socialium, Bidrag till kännedom av Finlands natur och folk.*

Suomalainen Tiedeakatemia (*Finnish Academy of Science and Letters*): Snellmaninkatu 9-11, 00170 Helsinki 17; f. 1908; 279 Finnish mems., 132 foreign; Pres. OSMO JÄRVI; Sec.-Gen. LAURI A. VUORELA; publs. *Annales Academiae Scientiarum Fennicae*†, *F. F. Communications*†, *Documenta Historica*†, *Yearbook*†, etc.

AGRICULTURE AND VETERINARY SCIENCE

Suomen Maataloustieteellinen Seura (*Scientific Agricultural Society of Finland*): Rukkila 00001, Helsinki 100; f. 1909; 480 mems.; Pres. Prof. LIISA SYRJÄLÄ; Sec. Dr. J. ROUHIAINEN; publ. *Journal*†.

Suomen Metsätieteellinen Seura (*Society of Forestry in Finland*): Unioninkatu 40B, SF-00170 Helsinki 17; f. 1909 to encourage forest research work in Finland; is composed of persons devoting themselves to the study of forestry and its underlying theory; 460 mems.; Pres. KUSTAA SEPPÄLÄ; Sec. EINO MÄLKÖNEN; publs. *Acta Forestalia Fennica, Silva Fennica* (quarterly).

THE ARTS

Suomen Näytelmäkirjailijaliitto (*Dramatists' League of Finland*): Vironkatu 12B, Helsinki; f. 1921; Pres. INKERI KILPINEN-BENSON; Sec. KAIJU SAREVA.

Suomen Säveltäjät ry (*Society of Finnish Composers*): Runeberginkatu 15 A 11, 00100 Helsinki 10; f. 1945; 67 mems.; Pres. OLAVI PESONEN; Vice-Pres. USKO MERILÄINEN; Sec. TAIMI KYYRÖ.

Suomen Taideyhdistys (*Fine Arts Society of Finland*): Helsingin Taidehalli, Nervanderinkatu 3, 00100 Helsinki 10; f. 1846; 5,500 mems.; Pres. GÖRAN STJERNSCHANTZ; Sec. SEPPO NIINIVAARA.

Suomen Taiteilijaseura/Konstnärsgillet i Finland (*Artists' Association of Finland*): Ainonkatu 3, Helsinki; f. 1864; mem. socs. consist of the Painters' Union of Finland, the Sculptors' Union of Finland, the Association of Graphic Artists in Finland and the Federation of the Fine Arts Associations in Finland; promotes professional interests of artists and holds an annual exhibition; Chair. RAIMO HEINO; publs. *Taide* (Art), *Suomen taide* (Art of Finland), *Taiteilijamatrikkeli* (Dictionary of Finnish Artists).

Turun Soitannollinen Seura (*Turku Music Society*): Sibelius Museum, Piispankatu 17, Turku; f. 1790; 250 mems.; Pres. Prof. Dr. ARNE ROUSI; Sec. HEIKKI LANG, M.D.

BIBLIOGRAPHY, LIBRARY SCIENCE AND MUSEOLOGY

Suomen Kirjastoseura (*The Library Association of Finland*): Museokatu 18 A 5, 00100 Helsinki 10; f. 1910; 2,500 mems.; Pres. TELLERVO KOIVISTO; Sec. HILKKA M. KAUPPI, M.A.; publ. *Kirjastolehti* (Bulletin).

Suomen Museoliitto/Finlands Museiförbund (*Finnish Museums Association*): Museokatu 5, 00100 Helsinki 10; f. 1923; 200 museums; library of 5,000 vols.; publs. *Osma, Julkaisuja, Tiedottaa* (newsletter).

Suomen Tieteellinen Kirjastoseura (*Finnish Research Library Association*): c/o Eduskunnan kirjasto, SF-00102 Helsinki 10; f. 1929; 542 mems.; Pres. IRJA-LEENA SUHONEN; Sec. JORMA HIRSIVUORI; publ. *Signum* (Bulletin).

Tieteellisen Informoinnin Neuvosto (*Finnish Council for Scientific Information and Research Libraries*): P.O.B. 312, SF-00171 Helsinki 17; f. 1972; attached to the Ministry of Education; 16 mems.; Chair. EEVA-MAIJA TAMMEKANN; Sec. MARKETTA LEHTO-TOIVAKKA.

ECONOMICS, LAW AND POLITICS

Ekonomiska Samfundet i Finland (*Economic Society of Finland*): Observatoriegatan 4 A 9, Helsinki; f. 1894; 650 mems.; Pres. GÖSTA MICKWITZ; Sec. BÖRJE WIKSTEDT; publ. *Tidskrift* (Journal, quarterly).

International Law Association: Finnish branch: f. 1946; 107 mems.; Pres. Prof. BENGT BROMS; Vice-Pres. Prof. HEIKKI JOKELA, Prof. TOIVO SAINIO; Hon. Sec. KARI HAKAPÄÄ, Kadetintie 18 A5, 00330 Helsinki 33.

Juridiska Föreningen i Finland (*Law Society of Finland*): Helsinki; f. 1862; 841 mems.; Pres. CURT OLSSON, Granfeltsv.-8B, Helsinki; Sec. ANDERS CROHNS, Mechelinikatu 26 A20, Helsinki 10; publs. *Tidskrift utgiven av Juridiska Föreningen i Finland*, various legal publications.

Kansantaloudellinen Yhdistys (*Finnish Economic Association*): Helsinki School of Economics, Runeberginkatu 22–24, 00100 Helsinki 10; f. 1885; 1,020 mems.; Pres. PENTTI VARTIA; Sec. ASKO LINDQVIST; publs. *Kansantaloudellinen Aikakauskirja* (The Finnish Economic Journal) and *Kansantaloudellisia Tutkimuksia* (Economic Studies).

Suomalainen Lakimiesyhdistys (*The Society of Finnish Jurists*): Annankatu 16B, Helsinki 12; f. 1898; 3,150 mems.; Pres. Prof. Dr. ANTTI SUVIRANTA; Sec. MARTTI LEISTEN; publs. *Lakimies, Suomalaisen Lakimiesyhdistyksen Julkaisuja*, series A-D, *Lakimies-aikakauskirja*.

Suomen Väestötieteen Yhdistys (*Finnish Demographic Society*): Dept. of Economic and Social History, Univ. of Helsinki, Aleksanterinkatu 7, 00100 Helsinki 10; f. 1973; population studies; 130 mems.; Chair. Lic. ALTTI MAJAVA; Sec. Lic. KARI PITKÄNEN; publ. *Publications*.

Taloushistoriallinen Yhdistys (*Economic History Society*): Dept. of Economic and Social History, University of Helsinki; f. 1952; studies economic and social history; 83 mems.; Chair. Prof. SVEN-ERIC ÅSTRÖM; Hon. Sec. Prof. ERKKI PIHKALA; publ. *Scandinavian Economic History Review* (in co-operation with other Scandinavian societies for the advancement of the study of economic history).

EDUCATION

Suomen Kasvatusopillinen Yhdistys/Pedagogiska Föreningen i Finland r.y. (*Educational Association of Finland*): Kasarminkatu 23A, 00130 Helsinki 13; f. 1863; 150 mems.; Pres. JOUKO HAAVISTO, M.A.; Sec. SIRPA RAUANHEIMO, M.A.

Educational Foundation

Suomen Kulttuurirahasto (*Finnish Cultural Foundation*): Bulevardi 5A, Helsinki 12; f. 1939; promotes cultural life in Finland, grants scholarships of 3,000 to 20,000 Finnish Marks usually for one year to students of Finnish nationality; Chair. LAURI SAXÉN; Gen. Sec. ERKKI SALONEN; Exec. Sec. MATTI ILMANEN.

HISTORY, GEOGRAPHY AND ARCHAEOLOGY

Historian Ystäväin Liitto (*Society for the Friends of History*): Viljelijantie 4-6 A 8, 00410 Helsinki 41; 1,000 mems.; Sec. TAPIO KOSKIMIES.

Suomen Historiallinen Seura (*Finnish Historical Society*): Säätytalo, Snellmaninkatu 9-11, 00170 Helsinki 17; f. 1875; 320 mems.; the library contains 8,500 vols.; Pres. Prof. MATTI KLINGE; Sec. Prof. OSMO JUSSILA; publs. *Historiallinen Arkisto*† (Historical Archives), *Historiallisia Tutkimuksia*† (Historical Researches), *Suomen historian lähteitä*† (Sources of the History of Finland), *Käiskirjoja*† (Handbooks), *Studia Historica*† (Historical Studies in German, French and English).

Suomen Kirkkohistoriallinen Seura (*Finnish Society of Ecclesiastical History*): Säätytalo, Snellmanink. 9-11, 00170 Helsinki 17; f. 1891; 1,250 mems.; Pres. Prof. Dr. M. PARVIO; Sec. Theol. lic. E. KOSKENVESA; publs. *Vuosikirja-Årsskrift* (Yearbook), *Toimituksia-Handlingar* (research papers).

Suomen Maantieteellinen Seura/Geografiska Sällskapet i Finland (*Geographical Society of Finland*): Snellmanink. 9-11, 00170 Helsinki 17; f. 1888; 1,300 mems.; the library contains approx. 53,000 vols.; Pres. A. NYYSSÖNEN; Sec. O. HEIKKINEN; publs. *Fennia*† and *Terra*†.

Suomen Muinaismuistoyhdistys/Finska Fornminnesföreningen (*Archaeological Society of Finland*): P.O.B. 913, 00101 Helsinki 10; f. 1870; about 500 mems.; Pres. HENRIK LILIUS; Sec. TEPPO KORHONEN; publs. *Suomen Museo, Finskt Museum, Suomen Muinaismuistoyhdistyksen Aikakauskirja-Finska Fornminnesföreningens Tidskrift, Kansatieteellinen Arkisto.*

Suomen Sukututkimusseura/Genealogiska Samfundet i Finland (*Genealogical Society of Finland*): Snellmaninkatu 9-11, 00170 Helsinki 17; f. 1917; *c.* 900 mems.; library of *c.* 30,000 vols.; Pres. Lic. PENTTI J. VOIPIO; Sec. MANU HERNA; publs. *Vuosikirja—Årsskrift*† (Yearbook), *Genos*† (quarterly), *Julkaisuja—Skrifter*† (monographs).

INTERNATIONAL CULTURAL INSTITUTES

America Center: P.O.B. 256, Kaivokatu 10A, 00100 Helsinki 10.

British Council: Etelaesplanadi 22A, 00130 Helsinki 13/06; library: *see* Libraries; Rep. A. R. PAYNE.

Goethe Institut: Mannerheimintie 14A, SF-00100 Helsinki 10; Dir. BERTHOLD DOBIESS; also at Tuomiokirkonkatu 34B, SF-33100 Tampere 10; Dir. Dr. KLAUS LANKISCH.

Istituto Italiano di Cultura: Ullankatu 3A 2, 00140 Helsinki 14; Dir. Prof. CLAUDIA VELICOGNA NAIT.

LANGUAGE AND LITERATURE

Finlands Svenska Författareförening (*Asscn. of Swedish-speaking Authors in Finland*): Runebergsgatan 32 C 27, 00100 Helsinki 10; f. 1919; 190 mems.; library of 600 vols.; Pres. CLAES ANDERSSON (author); Vice-Pres. INGMAR SVEDBERG (critic); Sec. METTE C. JENSEN.

Kirjallisuudentutkijain Seura (*Research Society Literary*): Suomen Kirjallisuuden Tiedotuskeskus, Liisankatu 16 A 5, 00170 Helsinki 17; f. 1927; serves as a link between literary research workers and promotes their work in Finland; 190 mems. (incl. 10 foreign corresp. mems.); Pres. Prof. KAI LAITINEN; Vice-Pres. Prof. ANNAMARI SARAJAS, Prof. KERTTU SAARENHEIMO; Sec. ANNA MATTONEN; publ. *Vuosikirja* (Annual).

Klassillis-filologinen Yhdistys (*Society for Classical Philology*): Saariseläntie 2 C 36, 00970 Helsinki 97; f. 1882; promotes the study of classical philology and classical antiquity in general; *c.* 100 mems.; Pres. Prof. IIRO KAJANTO; Sec.-Treas. M. TYNI; publs. *Arctos*†, *Acta*

Philologica Fennica†, *Nova Series I* (1954)—*IX* (1975), *Supplementum I* (1968).

Kotikielen Seura (*Mother-Tongue Society*): Fabianinkatu 33, 00170 Helsinki 17; f. 1876; Finnish linguistics, especially dialectology, sociolinguistics, language planning; 200 mems.; Pres. TERHO ITKONEN; Sec. TAPANI LEHTINEN; publ. *Virittäjä*† (quarterly).

Suomalaisen Kirjallisuuden Seura (*Finnish Literature Society*): Hallituskatu 1, P.O.B. 259, 00171 Helsinki 17; f. 1831 to promote study of folklore, ethnology, literature and Finnish language; 1,000 mems.; Pres. of Council Prof. LAURI HONKO; Chair. Exec. Cttee. Prof. PERTTI VIRTARANTA; Gen. Sec. URPO VENTO; *see also* under Libraries; publs. *Studia Fennica*† (yearly), *Suomi*, *Tietolipas*, *Toimituksia* (irregular).

Suomalais-ugrilainen Seura (*Finno-Ugrian Society*): Snellmaninkatu 9-11, 00170 Helsinki 17; f. 1883; 650 mems.; Pres. Prof. Dr. L. POSTI; Sec. Prof. Dr. SEPPO SUHONEN; publs. *Journal*†, *Mémoires*†, *Lexica Societatis F.U.*†, *Travaux ethnographiques*†.

Suomen englanninopettajat r.y. (*Association of Teachers of English in Finland*): Annankatu 22 A 1, 00100 Helsinki 10; f. 1948; 2,600 mems.; Pres. Miss PIRKKO-SISKO HÄKINEN; Sec. Mrs. LEENA LEVANTO.

Suomen Kirjailijaliitto (*Association of Finnish Authors*): Helsinki, Runebergink. 32C; f. 1897; allied to the Scandinavian Authors' Council; 475 mems.; Pres. JAAKKO SYRJÄ; Exec. Sec. PIRKKO PESOLA; publs. *Suomen Runotar*, *Suomalaiset kertojat*.

Svenska Litteratursällskapet i Finland (*Swedish Literary Society in Finland*): Snellmansg. 9-11, 00170 Helsinki 17; f. 1885; 1,100 mems.; library of 10,000 vols.; Pres. Prof. CARL-ERIC THORS; Sec. Prof. LARS HULDEN; publ. *Skrifter*.

Uusfilologinen Yhdistys (*Modern Language Society*): Porthania, The University, Helsinki 10; f. 1887; 420 mems.; Pres. Prof. VEIKKO VÄÄNÄNEN; Hon. Sec. Mrs. KIRSTI KEKÄLÄINEN; Editorial Sec. Miss LEENA KAHLAS; publs. *Mémoires*† (irregular), *Mitteilungen*† (Bulletin, quarterly).

MEDICINE

Cancer Society of Finland: Liisankatu 21 B 9, 00170 Helsinki 17; Sec.-Gen. NIILO VOIPIO.

Tasavallan Presidentti J. K. Paasikiven Rahasto Syöpätautien Tieteellistä Tutkimustyötä Varten (*President J. K. Paasikivi Foundation for Cancer Research*): f. 1950; grants fellowships to scientists for cancer research and to institutions supported by the Society; Pres. ERNST PALMÉN, PH.D.

Syöpätautien Tutkimussäätiö (*Foundation for Cancer Research*): f. 1969; grants fellowships to scientists for cancer research and to institutions supported by the Society; Pres. LAURI RAURAMO, M.D.

Finska Läkaresällskapet (*Medical Society of Finland*): Helsinki, Ständerhuset; f. 1835; 800 mems.; the library contains 30,000 vols.; Pres. TOR PETTERSSON; Sec. T. WEBER; publ. *Finska Läkaresällskapets Handlingar*.

Suomalainen Lääkäriseura Duodecim (*Finnish Medical Society Duodecim*): Helsinki 26, Runeberginkatu 47A; library Haartmaninkatu 4, Helsinki 29; f. 1881; 8,200 mems.; the library contains 17,000 vols.; Pres. KIMMO MUSTAKALLIO; Sec. S. TARPILA; publs. *Duodecim*†, *Medical Biology*†, *Annales chirurgiae et gynaecologiae*, *Annals of Clinical Research*†.

Suomen Hammaslääkäriseura (*Finnish Dental Society*): Rautatieläisenkatu 6 (library: Haartmaninkatu 4), 00520 Helsinki 52; f. 1892; 3,300 mems.; Librarian Dr. AULI RAHKAMO; library of 4,000 vols.; Pres. Dr. LASSI ALVESALO; Sec. Dr. HEIKKI LEIKOMAA; publ. *Toimituksia*† (Proceedings, 6 a year).

NATURAL SCIENCES

Biological Sciences

Societas Amicorum Naturae Ouluensis (*Oulun Luonnonystäväin Yhdistys*): Kasarmintie 8, SF-90100 Oulu 10; f. 1925; 600 mems.; Pres. Dos. E. ERKINARO; Sec. K. KUUSELA; publs. *Aquilo, Ser. Botanica*, *Aquilo, Ser. Zoologica*.

Societas Biochemica, Biophysica et Microbiologica Fenniae (*Biochemical, Biophysical and Microbiological Society of Finland*): P. Hesperiankatu 3B 10, 00260 Helsinki 26; f. 1945; 950 mems.; Pres. Prof. VELI KAUPPINEN; Sec. ILKKA PALVA.

Societas Biologica Fennica Vanamo (*Suomen Biologian Seura Vanamo*): P. Rautatiekatu 13, 00100 Helsinki 10; f. 1896; Pres. LIISA SIMOLA; Sec. RISTO A. VÄISÄNEN; Exchange Librarian ILMARI VALOVIRTA; publs. *Atlas Florae Europaeae*, *Luonnon Tutkija* (The Naturalist, 5 a year).

Societas Entomologica Fennica (*Suomen Hyönteistieteellinen Seura*): P. Rautatiek. 13, S-F 00100 Helsinki 10; f. 1935; library; Pres. Prof. M. MARKKULA; Vice-Pres. Dr. E. KARPPINEN; Sec. Lic. A. PEKKARINEN; publs. *Annales Entomologici Fennici*†, *Acta Entomologica Fennica*†, *Notulae Entomologicae*†.

Societas pro Fauna et Flora Fennica: Snellmansg. 9-11, 00170 Helsinki 17; f. 1821; 600 mems.; the library contains 44,000 vols.; Pres. Prof. H. WALLGREN; Sec. B. FEDERLEY, M.SC.; publs. *Acta Botanica Fennica*†, *Acta Zoologica Fennica*†, *Memoranda Societatis pro Fauna et Flora Fennica*†.

Suomen Lintutieteellinen Yhdistys (*Finnish Ornithological Society*): P. Rautatiek. 13, SF-00100 Helsinki 10; f. 1924; Pres. PD. JUHANI RINNE; Sec. TORSTEN STJERNBERG; publ. *Ornis Fennica*† (quarterly).

Physical Sciences

Finska Kemistsamfundet/Suomen Kemistiseura (*Chemical Society of Finland*): N. Hesperiagatan 3 B 10, 00260 Helsinki 26; f. 1891; 400 mems.; Pres. GÖRAN NORDMAN; Sec. HARRIET WALLIN.

Suomalaisten Kemistien Seura (*Finnish Chemical Society*): P. Hesperiankatu 3B, SF-00260 Helsinki 26; f. 1919; 2,400 mems.; Pres. OSMO MÄKITIE; Sec. MARJATTA KIVIMÄKI.

Suomen Geologinen Seura (*Geological Society of Finland*): Kivimiehentie 1, 02150 Espoo 15; f. 1886; 900 mems.; Pres. I HAAPALA; Sec. KALEVI KORSMAN; publs. *Bulletin*† (1 or 2 a year), *Geologi* (10 a year).

PHILOSOPHY AND PSYCHOLOGY

Suomen Filosofinen Yhdistys (*Philosophical Society of Finland*): Department of Philosophy, Unioninkatu 40B, 00170 Helsinki 17; f. 1873; promotes the study of philosophy and related disciplines in Finland; 450 mems.; Pres. Prof. ILKKA NIINILUOTO; Sec. LEILA TAIMINEN; publs. *Acta Philosophica Fennica*, *Ajatus*.

RELIGION, SOCIOLOGY AND ANTHROPOLOGY

Suomalainen Teologinen Kirjallisuusseura (*Finnish Society for Theological Literature*): Neitsytpolku 1B, 00140 Helsinki 14; Chair. Prof. K. TAMMINEN.

Suomen Itämainen Seura (*Finnish Oriental Society*): Helsinki, Vuorikatu 3 A 15; f. 1917; 200 mems.; Pres. Dr. E. SALONEN; Sec. Dr. TAPANI HARUIAINEN; publ. *Studia Orientalia*.

TECHNOLOGY

Suomen Teknillinen Seura (*Engineering Society in Finland*): Ratavartijankatu 2, 00520 Helsinki 52; f. 1896; serves as a link between engineers and architects, promotes technical sciences and industry, fosters Finnish economic life; 16,000 mems. (incl. 6,900 junior mems.); Pres. PEKKA KAINULAINEN; Sec. MATTI KAARIO; publs. *Insinööriuutiset, Talouselämä, Tekniikka.*

Svenska Tekniska Vetenskapsakademien i Finland (*Swedish Technical Science Academy in Finland*): Apollogatan 8, 00100 Helsingfors 10; f. 1921; 108 mems.; Sec. F. STENMAN; publs. *Forhandlingar*† (Proceedings), *Meddelanden*† (Reports).

Tekniikan edistämissäätiö (*Technological Foundation*): Aleksanterinkatu 10, 00170 Helsinki 17; f. 1949 to provide yearly fellowships for the advancement of technology; Pres. FREDRIK CASTRÉN; Sec.-Gen. HAKON GUVENIUS; Sec. URPO J. SALO.

Teknillisten Tieteiden Akatemia/Akademin för Tekniska Vetenskaper r.y. (*Finnish Academy of Technical Sciences*): Kansakoulukatu 10 A, 00100 Helsinki 10; f. 1957 to promote technical-scientific research; 204 mems.; Pres. Prof. PENTTI LAASONEN; Man. Dir. Prof. OLLI LOKKI; publs. *Acta Polytechnica Scandinavica* (monographs)†, *Tutkimus ja tekniikka—Forskning och teknik* (5 issues per year).

Tekniska Föreningen i Finland (*The Engineering Society in Finland—TFiF*): Georgsgatan 30, Helsinki 10; f. 1880; 2,310 mems.; Pres. ERIK MORING; Man. Dir. FREJ GUSTAFSSON; publ. *Forum för ekonomi och teknik.*

RESEARCH INSTITUTES

(*see* also under Universities)

AGRICULTURE AND VETERINARY SCIENCE

Maatalouden Tutkimuskeskus (*Agricultural Research Centre*): Erottajank. 15-17, Helsinki; f. 1898; Dir.-Gen. Prof. JUHANI PAATELA, DR.SC.AGRIC.; consists of 9 institutes, 15 experimental stations and 4 offices; publs. *Annales Agriculturae Fenniae* (Journal of the Agricultural Research Centre), *Koetoiminta ja Käytäntö* (Experimental work and Practice newspaper), *Kehittyvä Maatalous* (Advancement in Agriculture).

Maatalouden Tutkimuskeskus, Kasvinjalostuslaitos (*Agricultural Research Centre, Institute of Plant Breeding*): Jokioinen; f. 1909; the library contains 15,000 vols.; gene bank; special collections of seeds of cultivated plants; 90,000 trial plots per year; Dir. Prof. ROLF MANNER, DR.SC.AGRIC.

Maatalouden Tutkimuskeskus, Kasvinviljelylaitos (*Agricultural Research Centre, Institute of Plant Husbandry*): Jokioinen; f. 1898; the library contains 3,500 vols.; Dir. Prof. J. MUKULA, DR.SC.AGRIC.

Maatalouden Tutkimuskeskus, Kasvitautien tutkimuslaitos (*Agricultural Research Centre, Institute of Plant Pathology*): Vantaa; f. 1911; research into diseases of cultivated plants; the library contains 7,000 vols.; Dir. Prof. A. YLIMÄKI, DR.SC.AGRIC.

Maatalouden Tutkimuskeskus, Kotieläinhoidon tutkimuslaitos (*Agricultural Research Centre, Institute of Animal Husbandry*): Jokioinen; f. 1924; the library contains 2,900 vols.; Dir. Prof. MARTTI LAMPILA, DR.SC.AGRIC.

Maatalouden Tutkimuskeskus, Kotieläinjalostuslaitos (*Agricultural Research Centre, Institute of Animal Breeding*): Vantaa; f. 1924; the library contains 1,600 vols.; Dir. Prof. ULF LINDSTRÖM, DR.SC.AGRIC.

Maatalcuden Tutkimuskeskus, Maantutkimuslaitos (*Agricultural Research Centre, Institute of Soil Science*): Vantaa; f. 1918; the library contains 7,000 vols.; Dir. Prof. MIKKO SILLANPÄÄ, DR.SC.AGRIC.

Maatalouden Tutkimuskeskus, Maanviljelyskemian jafysiikan laitos (*Agricultural Research Centre, Institute of Agricultural Chemistry and Physics*): Jokioinen; f. 1898; the library contains 2,261 vols.; Dir. PAAVO ELONEN, DR.SC.AGRIC.

Maatalouden Tutkimuskeskus, Puutarhantutkimuslaitos (*Agricultural Research Centre, Institute of Horticulture*): 21500 Piikkiö; f. 1927; the library contains 1,500 vols.; collection of cytological slides; Dir. Prof. J. SÄKÖ, DR.SC.AGRIC.

Maatalouden Tutkimuskeskus, Tuhoeläintutkimuslaitos (*Agricultural Research Centre, Institute of Pest Investigation*): Vantaa; f. 1898; the library contains 15,000 vols.; entomological collections on Coleoptera, Lepidoptera, Hemiptera and Hymenoptera; Asst. Dir. Prof. UNTO TULISALO, DR.SC.AGRIC.

Metsäntutkimuslaitos (*Finnish Forest Research Institute*) Helsinki 17, Unioninkatu 40A; f. 1918; 150 mems.; library contains about 13,000 vols.; Pres. (vacant); Sec. KARI SOHKANEN; publs. *Julkaisuja* (*Communicationes*), *Folia Forestalia.*

Department of Forest Economics: f. 1928; Dir. Prof. LAURI HEIKINHEIMO, D.SC.FOR.

Department of Forest Genetics: f. 1968; Dir. Prof. MAX HAGMAN, D.SC.FOR.

Department of Forest Inventory and Yield: f. 1917; Dir. Prof. YRJÖ VUOKILA, D.SC.FOR.

Department of Forest Protection: f. 1972; Dir. Prof. PAAVO JUUTINEN, D.SC.FOR.

Department of Forest Technology: f. 1931; Dir. Prof. PENTTI HAKKILA, D.SC.FOR.

Department of Mathematics: f. 1967; Dir. Dr. RISTO SEPPÄLÄ, D.POL.SC.

Department of Peatland Forestry: f. 1928; Dir. Prof. OLAVI HUIKARI, D.SC.FOR.

Department of Silviculture: f. 1917; Dir. (vacant).

Department of Soil Sciences: f. 1917; Dir. Prof. ERKKI LÄHDE.

Kolari Forest Research Station: 95900 Kolari; . 1965; Dir. ERKKI NUMMINEN, LIC.SC.FOR.

Parkano Forest Research Station: 39700 Parkano; f. 1961; Dir. Dr. OLAVI LAIHO.

Pyhåkoski Forest Research Station: 91500 Muhos; f. 1969; JUKKA VALTANEN, B.FOR.

Rovaniemi Forest Research Station: Eteläranta 55, 96300 Rovaniemi 30; f. 1970; Dir. Dr. ELJAS POHTILA.

Suonenjoki Experimental Station for Forest Regeneration: 77600 Suonenjoki; f. 1968; Dir. PAAVO PELKONEN, LIC.SC.FOR.

Valtion Maatalouskoneiden Tutkimuslaitos (*Finnish Research Institute of Agricultural and Forestry Engineering*): 03450 Olkkala; f. 1949; 40 staff; library of 400 vols.; Dir. Prof. ALPO REINIKAINEN; Sec. THELMA KIVINIEMI; publs. various reports.

ECONOMICS, LAW AND POLITICS

Liiketaloustieteellinen Tutkimuslaitos (*Helsinki Research Institute for Business Economics*): Runeberginkatu 15A, 00100 Helsinki 10; f. 1938; 21 staff; Dir. Prof. AATTO PRIHTI, D.SC.(ECON.).

EDUCATION

Suomen Kasvatustieteellinen Seura r.y./Samfundet för Pedagogisk Forskning (*Finnish Society for Educational Research*): Fabianinkatu 28, 00100 Helsinki 10; f. 1967; 161 mems.; Pres. Prof. JUKKA LEHTINEN; publ. *Kasvatus.*

MUSEOLOGY

Museovirasto (*National Board of Antiquities and Historical Monuments*): Box. 913, 00101 Helsinki 10; f. 1884 as *The Archaeological Commission*, reorganized 1972; supervises prehistoric, historic and ethnographic monuments, conducts excavations and restorations, etc., administers *Suomen kansallismuseo* (*see under* Museums); library, including that of Finnish Archaeological Society, of 100,000 vols.; Dir.-Gen. C. J. GARDBERG, PH.D.

NATURAL SCIENCES

Mathematics

Tilastokeskus (*Central Statistical Office of Finland*): Annankatu 44, 00100 Helsinki 10; f. 1865; library: *see* Libraries; Dir. Dr. OLAVI E. NIITAMO; chief publs. *Suomen Tilastollinen Vuosikirja*† (Statistical Yearbook of Finland), *Tilastokatsauksia*† (Bulletin of Statistics, monthly), *Suomen* (*Virallinen Tilasto*)† (Official Statistics of Finland, irregular), *Tilastotiedotus*† (Statistical Reports), *Indeksitiedotus*† (Index Report, monthly), *Tilastollisia tiedonantoja*† (Statistical Surveys), *Tutkimuksia*† (Studies, irregular).

Physical Sciences

Biokemiallinen Tutkimuslaitos (*Biochemical Research Institute*): 00180 Helsinki 18, Kalevankatu 56B; f. 1929; labs. of the Foundation for Chemical Research and of Valio Finnish Co-operative Dairies' Association; the library contains about 11,000 vols.; Dir. Prof. MATTI KREULA, PH.D.; publ. *Kemiantutkimus-Säätiön vuosikertomus* (Annual Report of the Foundation for Chemical Research).

Goedeettinen Laitos (*Geodetic Institute*): Ilmalankatu 1 A, SE-00240 Helsinki; f. 1918; 21 mems.; the library contains 28,000 vols.; Dir. Prof. Dr. JUHANI KAKKURI; heads of departments Prof. Tech. Dr. JUHANI HAKKARAINEN, Prof. Dr. ERKKI HYTÖNEN, Dr. AIMO KIVINIEMI, Prof. Dr. TEUVO PARM; publs. *Suomen Geodeettisen laitoksen julkaisuja*† (Publications of the Finnish Geodetic Institute) (also in German), *Suomen Geodeettisen laitoksen tiedonantoja*† (Reports of the Finnish Geodetic Institute).

Geologinen Tutkimuslaitos (*Geological Survey of Finland*): 02150 Espoo 15; f. 1885; 725 mems.; the library contains 92,577 vols. and 23,335 pamphlets; Dir. Prof. L. K. KAURANNE (acting); Dir. of Research Prof. K. KORPELA; publs. *Vuosikertomus* (Annual Report), *Geological Survey of Finland, Bulletin*†, *Geoteknillisiä julkaisuja, Geological Maps*†, *Report of Investigation*†.

Ilmatieteen laitos (*Finnish Meteorological Institute*): P.O.B. 503, Vuorikatu 24, 00101 Helsinki 10; f. 1838; 322 staff; library of *c.* 30,000 vols. and *c.* 10,000 offprints; Dir. (vacant); publs. *Year-Books, Kuukausikatsaus Suomen Ilmastoon* (Monthly Weather Bulletin), *Toimituksia* (Contributions), *Maamagneettisia tutkimuksia* (Studies in Earth Magnetism), *Radioaktiivisuushavaintoja* (Observations of Radioactivity), *Nurmijärven geofysikaalisen observatorion magneettisia mittauksia* (Magnetic Results from Nurmijärvi Geophysical Observatory), *Havaintoja maan lämpötilasta* (Soil Temperature Measurements), *Technical Report, Ilmatieteen laitoksen tiedonantoja, Tutkimusseloste* (only in Finnish).

Säteilyturvallisuuslaitos (*Institute of Radiation Protection*): P.O.B. 268, SF-00101 Helsinki 10; f. 1958; Government Institute for radiation protection and reactor safety, including inspection and research in the field; 197 mems.; library of 10,000 vols.; Chief Dir. Prof. AULIS ISOLA; Dir. Prof. ANTTI VUORINEN; publ. *STL-A Reports*†.

TECHNOLOGY

Oy Keskuslaboratorio-Centrallaboratorium Ab (*Finnish Pulp and Paper Research Institute*): P.O.B. 136, SF-00101 Helsinki 10; f. 1916; technical and scientific research in the pulp, paper and board industry; 271 staff; library of 28,000 vols.; Man. Dir. Prof. W. JENSEN; publs. *Annual Report*†, *Teollisuuden Keskuslaboratorion Tiedonantoja—Meddelanden från Industrins Centrallaboratorium*†.

Valtion teknillinen tutkimuskeskus (*Technical Research Centre of Finland*): Vuorimiehentie 5, 02150 Espoo 15; f. 1942; 1,557 mems.; library of 42,000 vols.; consists of general division, 3 research divisions (with 30 laboratories) and technical information service; Dir.-Gen. Prof. PEKKA JAUHO; publs. *Vuosikertomus*† (Annual Review), *Valtion teknillinen tutkimuskeskus, Publication*†, *Julkaisu, Tiedonanto* (Report, Finnish and English).

LIBRARIES AND ARCHIVES

Åbo Akademis Bibliotek (*Library of Åbo Academy*): 20500 Åbo 50, Domkyrkogatan 2-4; f. 1918; general library; 1,050,000 vols. (excluding pamphlets and MSS.); Chief Librarian OLOF MUSTELIN, PH.D.

British Council Library: Etelaesplanadi 22A, 00130 Helsinki 13/06; f. 1945; lending and reference collection of 13,878 vols., 98 periodicals, primarily for teachers and students of English language and literature and British studies; Librarian PIA SUNDELL, B.A.

Eduskunnan Kirjasto (*Library of Parliament*): 00102 Helsinki 10; f. 1872; 400,000 vols. on administration, law, political and social sciences; Chief Librarian EEVA-MAIJA TAMMEKANN; the library is open to the public; publs. *Eduskunnan kirjaston julkaisuja*† (Library of Parliament Publications 1-5), *Valtion virallisjulkaisut*† (Government publications in Finland 1961–).

Helsingin Kauppakorkeakoulun Kirjasto (*Library of the Helsinki School of Economics*): Runeberginkatu 22-24, 00100 Helsinki 10; f. 1911; 170,000 vols.; Librarian HENRI BROMS, PH.D.; publs. *Bibliography of Economics, Bibliography of Business Administration* (annually).

Helsingin Kaupunginkirjasto (*Helsinki City Library*): Helsinki, Rikhardinkatu 3; f. 1860; 26 br. libraries; total 873,829 vols. (591,812 Finnish, 203,794 Scandinavian, 78,223 foreign); Chief Librarian SVEN HIRN, PH.D.; publ. *Helsingin kaupunginkirjaston toimintakertomus* (Annual Report of Helsinki City Library).

Helsingin Teknillisen Korkeakoulun Kirjasto (*Library of Helsinki University of Technology*): Otaniementie 9, SF-02150 Espoo 15; f. 1849; 900,000 vols., 10,000 periodicals on engineering and allied sciences, mathematics, environmental sciences, architecture, urban planning and industrial economy; Dir. E. TÖRNUDD, M.SC.CHEM.ENG.; publs. *Programme*†, *Catalogue of Staff and Students*†, *Annual Report*†, *Research Papers*†, dissertations†, Library Occasional Papers†, index to Finnish technical periodicals, index to theses† (annually), index to dissertations, monthly bulletin of accessions.

Helsingin Yliopiston Historiallis-Kielitieteellinen Kirjasto (*Helsinki University Library of History and Philology*):

Hallituskatu 11-13, 00100 Helsinki 10; f. 1904; *c.* 105,000 vols.; Librarian KAARINA KIVIKATAJA, M.A.

Helsingin Yliopiston Kirjasto (*Helsinki University Library*): Unioninkatu 36, P.O.B. 312, SF-00171 Helsinki 17; f. 1640 in Turku (Åbo), removed to Helsinki 1828; general library of the University of Helsinki and national library of Finland; comprehensive collection of books printed in Finland, large foreign collection, and comprehensive collection of books printed in Russia between 1828 and 1917; approx. 2,000,000 vols., *c.* 1,200 shelf metres MSS., and 350 incunabula; Librarian ESKO HÄKLI; publs. *Suomen kirjallisuus* (The Finnish National Bibliography)†, *List of Academic Publications of the University of Helsinki*†, *Yhteisluettelo Suomen tieteellisten kirjastojen ulkomaisesta kirjallisuudesta* (Union catalogue of foreign literature in the research libraries in Finland)†, *Finuc-S.* (Union catalogue of foreign serials in the research libraries of Finland)†, *Helsingin yliopiston kirjaston julkaisuja* (Publications of the Helsinki University Library)†.

Helsingin Yliopiston Maatalouskirjasto (*Helsinki University Library of Agriculture*): Viiki 00710 Helsinki 71; f. 1929; depository library for FAO publications; 200,000 vols., 2,800 serial titles on agriculture, food and nutrition, household and environmental sciences; Librarian ANNIKKI KAIVOSOJA.

Helsingin Yliopiston Oikeustieteellisen Tiedekunnan Kirjasto (*The Law Library of the University of Helsinki*): Helsinki, Porthania, Hallituskatu 11-13; f. 1910; 40,000 vols.; Librarian JUHANI WIRILANDER; the library is open to University teachers and students.

Helsingin Yliopiston Valtiotieteellisen Tiedekunnan Kirjasto (*The Social Sciences Library, University of Helsinki*): Aleksanterinkatu 7, Helsinki 10 and Franzéninkatu 13, Helsinki 50; f. 1950; 75,000 vols.; Librarian HILKKA SISKO LAMMINEN, M.A.; the library is open to University teachers and students.

Jyväskylän Yliopiston Kirjasto (*Jyväskylä University Library*): 40100 Jyväskylä 10; f. 1912; 600,000 vols.; Chief Librarian OILI KOKKONEN.

Lääketieteellinen Keskuskirjasto (*Central Medical Library*): Haartmanink. 4, 00290 Helsinki 29; f. 1966; the national medical library and the medical library of Helsinki University; *c.* 300,000 vols., 2,500 periodicals; Dir. RITVA SIEVÄNEN-ALLEN, M.A., M.L.S.; publs. *Lääketieteellinen Keskuskirjasto Julkaisuja* (Central Medical Library publications), *Jatkuvasti tulevat aikakauslehdet* (list of current serials).

Maatalouden Tutkimuskeskuksen Kirjasto (*The Agricultural Research Centre Library*): P.O.B. 18, 01301 Vantaa 30; f. 1935; 75,000 vols.; Librarian kirj hoit. T. TUOMINEN; publ. *Annales Agriculturae Fenniae*†.

Oulun Yliopiston Kirjasto (*Oulu University Library*): Kasarmintie 7, 90100 Oulu 10; f. 1959; 774,000 vols.; special collections: theses, textbooks, old Finnish literature; material concerning Finland's attaining independence and the civil war; music library, collections of pictures, maps; Chief Librarian (vacant); publs. *Publications of Oulu University Library*†, *Acquisitions list*†, *Guide to the Library.*

Sibelius-Akatemian Kirjasto (*Sibelius Academy Library*): Pohj. Rautatiek. 9, Helsinki; f. 1882; 50,000 scores, 3,500 records, 6,600 books; Librarian PENTTI SOINI, M.A.; Keeper of Scores Mrs. TUULIKKI KOLEHMAINEN.

Suomalaisen Kirjallisuuden Seuran Kirjasto (*Library of the Finnish Literature Society*): Hallituskatu 1, P.O.B. 259, 00171 Helsinki 17; f. 1831; 185,000 vols. on folklore, ethnology, Finnish literature, history and language; Librarian RAUNI PURANEN, M.A.

Suomalaisen Kirjallisuuden Seuran Kansanrunousarkisto (*Folklore Archives of the Finnish Literature Society*): 2,500,000 documents, 5,600 hours of recordings; Archivist PEKKA LAAKSONEN, LIC.PHIL.

Suomalaisen Kirjallisuuden Seuran Kirjallisuusarkisto (*Literary Manuscript-Archives of the Finnish Literature Society*): about 16,500 MSS. and photographs on Finnish literature, history and language; Librarian KAARINA LAMPENIUS, M.A.

Svenska Handelshögskolans Bibliotek (*Library of the Swedish School of Economics and Business Administration*): 00100 Helsinki 10, Arkadiagatan 22; 120,000 vols.; Librarian T. W. HOLM.

Tampereen keskussairaalan lääketieteellinen kirjasto (*Medical Library of Tampere Central Hospital*): SF-33520 Tampere 52; f. 1962; 21,000 vols.; 382 periodicals; Librarian Mrs. MAIJA POHJAKALLIO.

Tampereen teknillisen korkeakoulun kirjasto (*Tampere University of Technology Library*): P.O.B. 537, 33101 Tampere 10; f. 1956; 90,000 vols., 1,300 periodicals; Librarian V. KAUTTO.

Tampereen Yliopisto: Kirjasto (*Library of the University of Tampere*): P.O.B. 617, 33101, Tampere 10; f. 1925 in Helsinki; 500,000 vols.; Chief Librarian HANNELE SOINI.

Tilastokirjasto (*Statistics Library*): Central Statistical Office of Finland, P.O.B. 504, Annankatu 44 (2nd Floor), 00101 Helsinki 10; f. 1865; 127,500 vols., over 800 periodicals; Librarian Miss H. YRJÖLÄ.

Turun Kauppakorkeakoulun Kirjasto (*Library of the Turku School of Economics*): SF-20500 Turku 50, Rehtorinpellontie 3; f. 1950; 56,000 vols.; Librarian SIRKKA SALORANTA, M.A.; various publications†.

Turun Yliopiston Kirjasto (*Turku University Library*): SF-20500 Turku 50; f. 1922; 1,120,000 vols., 280,000 pamphlets, 1,000 MSS.; Chief Librarian HEIKKI ESKELINEN, LIC.PHIL.; publs. *Turun Yliopiston kirjaston julkaisuja, Suomen aikakauslehti-indeksi* (Index to Finnish periodicals).

Valtionarkisto (*National Archives*): P.B. 274, 00171 Helsinki 17; f. 1869; library of 52,800 vols., 34,000 metres of documents; central office for public archives; controls seven Provincial Archives at Turku, Hämeenlinna, Mikkeli, Vaasa, Oulu, Jyväskylä and Joensuu; holds historical documents and archives of the Government, Supreme Court and other court records, and private papers of statesmen and politicians; the Provincial archives contain documents relating to Regional and Local Administration; Dir. Prof. Dr. TOIVO J. PALOPOSKI; publs. series of historical documents and guides.

Helsingin Kaupunginarkisto (*Helsinki City Archives*): 00530 Helsinki 53, 2 linja 4 F; f. 1945; central archive repository for City Administration; Dir. S. IMPOLA, M.A.

Sota-arkisto (*Military Archives*): P.B. 223, 00171 Helsinki 17; f. 1918; central archive repository of the Defence Forces; Dir. Dr. RISTO ROPPONEN.

MUSEUMS

Ålands Museum: Box 60, SF-22101 Mariehamn, Åland Islands; f. 1933; 27,376 exhibits; conducts archaeological excavations and ethnological field examinations on Åland Islands; library of 15,000 vols.; Man. STIG DREIJER; publ. *Åländsk Odling* (annual), *Ålands Folkminnesförbund, Bygdeserien.*

Ålands Sjöfartsmuseum: Mariehamn; f. 1935; 3,000 exhibits; contains ships' documents, model ships, etc.; Pres. EDGAR ERIKSON; Dir. Capt. KARL KÄHRE.

Helsingin Yliopiston Eläinmuseo (*Zoological Museum of the University of Helsinki*): P. Rautatiekatu 13, SF-00100 Helsinki 10; Dir. W. HACKMAN.

Helsinki City Museum: Karamzininkatu 2, SF-00100 Helsinki 10; f. 1911; cultural historical museum; permanent exhibition on the history of Helsinki; special exhibitions to highlight various features of the city's past; collection of objects; documentation and inventory pertaining to different eras; photographs of the Helsinki scene; library of 6,000 vols.; photo archive of 300,000 photos from 1860s to the present; Dir. MARJA-LIISA LAMPINEN; publs. *Narinkka*, Guide books†.

Pohjois-Pohjanmaan Museo: Oulu; f. 1896; 15,000 exhibits; specializes in historical-ethnological research on Ostrobothnia and Lapland; Dir. AIMO KEHUSMAA.

Satakunnan Museo: Pori; f. 1888; 45,000 archaeological and historical exhibits and 96,000 photographs relating to the history of the province of Satakunta; 10,000 vols. in reference library and 6,000 old books; Dir. RISTO KOSKINEN.

Sibeliusmuseum (Musikvetenskapliga Institutionen vid Åbo Akademi) (*Sibelius Museum at Åbo Akademi*): Biskopsgatan 17, Turku; f. 1926; contains archives and library relating to Sibelius and to Finnish music, and possesses a collection of musical instruments; Curator M. A. ILPO TOLVAS; Principal Prof. FABIAN DAHLSTRÖM, FIL.DOKT.; publs. *Acta Musica, Källskrifter och studier utg. av Musikvetenskapliga institutionen vid Åbo Akademi.*

Suomen kansallismuseo (*National Museum of Finland*): Mannerheimintie 34, 00100 Helsinki 10; in 1893 the Historical-Ethnographical Museum of the Helsinki University, the Collections of the Finnish Archaeological Society and the Ethnographical Museum of the Finnish Undergraduates' Corporation were united to form the State Historical Museum, from 1916 the National Museum of Finland; it comprises a Prehistoric Department with Finnish and Comparative Collections, a Historical Department, a Collection of Coins and Medals and an Ethnographical Department with Finnish, Finno-Ugrian and Comparative Ethnographic Collections, the Open-Air Museum at Seurasaari, the museums at Suomenlinna, Louhisaari Manor in Askainen and Pukkila Manor in Piikkiö, Yli-Laurosela Farmhouse in Ilmajoki, Paikkari Cottage in Sammatti; controlled by the National Board of Antiquities and Historial Monuments (*see under* Research Institutes); Dir. OSMO VUORISTO.

Tampereen Kaupungin Museolautakunta (*Tampere Museums*): Hatanpään kartano, 33100 Tampere 10; Dir. MARTTI HELIN.

Tampereen Teknillinen Museo (*Tampere Technical Museum*): Itsenäisyydenkatu 21, 33500 Tampere 50: f. 1958; technical history of Finland; reference library of 2,000 vols., notably works on early aviation and watch-making; Dir. MARTTI HELIN.

Tampereen Kaupunginmuseo (*Tampere City Museum*): Hatanpään kartano, 33100 Tampere 10; f. 1970; history of Tampere; reference library of 4,000 vols.; Dir. MARTTI HELIN; publ. *Tampereen kaupungin museot* (annually).

Tampereen Luonnontieteellinen Museo (*Tampere Natural Science Museum*): Pirkankatu 2, 33210 Tampere 21; f. 1961; flora and fauna of northern Satakunta and northern Häme provinces; nature conservation service; Curator TUULA KALLIO.

Hämeen Museo (*Häme Museum*): Näsilinna, 33210 Tampere 21; f. 1904; prehistory and folk art of the cultural district of Tampere and the old Häme province; Dir. MARTTI HELIN.

Suomen Koulumuseo (*Finnish School Museum*): Tammelan kansakoulu, 33500 Tampere 50; f. 1960; the development of the Finnish school system; Curator MARTTI HELIN.

Turun kaupungin historiallinen museo (*Historical Museum of Turku/Åbo*): office: Kalastajankatu 4, SF-20100 Turku 10; f. 1881; consists of the Castle of Turku with the collections of the Historical Museum, the Handicraft Museum at Luostarinmäki, the Pharmacy Museum, Qwensel House and the Biological Museum; furniture, paintings, costumes, textiles, porcelain, glass, silver, copper, fire-arms, weapons, coins; Dir. KNUT DRAKE; publs. *Vuosijulkaisu/Årsskrift*†, museum guides.

Turun Taidemuseo (*Turku Art Museum*): Puolalanpuisto, 20100 Turku 10; f. 1904; collection of modern paintings and sculpture, prints and drawings, mainly of Finnish and Scandinavian art; international print collection; Pres. Asst. Prof. LEIF B. SOURANDER; Vice-Pres. OSMO LAINE; Dir. ERIK BERGH.

Väinö Tuomaalan Museosäätiö: Väinöntalo-Evijärvi, 62540 Vasikka-aho; f. 1960; exhibits illustrate the rural life of the Järviseutu district; library of 2,500 vols.; Pres. JUHANI TUOMAALA; Sec. JUOKO TUOMAALA; publs. *Järviseudun Joulu, Evijärven Väinöntalo, Runo Soinin kirkosta, Pietersaaren ylämaalaisten käräjäjutut vuosilta 1543-1600, Erkki Lahti, pohjalainen kuvanveistäjä 1816-58, Kotiseututyön opas.*

UNIVERSITIES

ÅBO AKADEMI
(The Swedish University of Åbo)

20500 ÅBO 50,
DOMKYRKOTORGET 3
Telephone: 33-51-33.
Founded 1917.

Language of instruction: Swedish; Private control, with State subventions; Academic year: September to May.

Chancellor: S. LINDMAN, PH.D.
Rector: B. WIDÉN, PH.D.
Vice-Rector: B. QVIST, PH.D.
Director of Administration: ROGER BROO.
Treasurer: J. LAGSTRÖM, LL.B.
Librarian: S. O. A. MUSTELIN, PH.D.

Number of teachers: 205, including 52 professors.
Number of students: 4,000.
Publications: *Årsskrift* (Annual Review)†, *Acta Academiae Aboensis*†.

DEANS:

Faculty of Humanities: Prof. N. STORÅ.
Faculty of Mathematics and Natural Science: Prof. B.-J. WIKGREN.
Faculty of Economics and Political Sciences: Prof. L. NORDBERG.
Faculty of Chemical Technology: Prof. R. VON SCHALIER.
Faculty of Theology: Prof. G. NYGREN.
Faculty of Education: V. HANNUS.

PROFESSORS:

Faculty of Humanities:
BRUUN, P., History
DAHLSTRÖM, F., Musicology
DAVIDSSON, C., Russian
ENKVIST, N. E., English Language and Literature
JUNGAR, S. H., Scandinavian History
LAGERSPETZ, K. M. J., Psychology
LÍNNÉR, S. G., Literature
LOMAN, B. R. C., Swedish Language
NYHOLM, K. R., German Philology
RINGBOM, S. I. A., History of Art
STORÅ, N. E., Scandinavian Ethnology and Folklore
WESTMAN, R. R. O. R., Greek and Roman Literature

Faculty of Mathematical and Natural Sciences:
BRENNER, M. W., Physics
DANIELSSON, I., Physical Chemistry
EDELMAN, N. H., Geology and Mineralogy
FOGEL, K. G., Theoretical Physics
GAHMBERG, C., Pharmaceutical Chemistry and Biochemistry
PENSAR, G., Organic Chemistry
QVIST, K. B. M., Applied Mathematics
SJÖBERG, B. H., Mathematics
WIKGREN, B.-J. P., General Biology

Faculty of Economics and Political Science:
ANCKAR, D. B. B., Political Science
ANCKAR, O., Economics
BÄCKMAN, G. M., Social Policy
ERIKSSON, G. A., Commercial Geography
LINDSTRÖM, C.-G., Business Administration
NORDBERG, L. B., Statistics and Econometrics
PIPPING, K. G., Sociology
STÅHLBERG, K., Public Administration

Faculty of Chemical Technology:
BRUUN, H. H., Wood Chemistry
HUMMELSTEDT, L. I., Chemical Technology
KARLSSON, K. H., Inorganic Chemistry
MYREEN, B., Chemical Engineering
STENLUND, B., Polymer Technology
VON SCHALIEN, S. N. R., Heat Engineering
WALLER, K. V. T., Automatic Control
WÄNNINEN, E. V., Analytical Chemistry

Faculty of Theology:
ILLMAN, K.-J., Old Testament Exegesis and Jewish Studies
NYGREN, G. A. T. S., Systematic Theology
SANDHOLM, Å. S., Practical Theology
THURÉN, J. T., New Testament Exegesis
WIDÉN, B. E. A., Church History

HELSINGIN YLIOPISTO/ HELSINGFORS UNIVERSITET
(University of Helsinki)

FABIANINKATU 33,
00170 HELSINKI 17
Telephone: 1911.
Founded 1640 Turku (Åbo), 1828 Helsinki.

Languages of instruction: Finnish and Swedish; State control; Academic year: September to May (two terms).

Chancellor: Prof. E. PALMÉN.
Rector: Prof. N. C. E. OKER-BLOM.
Vice-Rector: Prof. E. W. ANDERSSON.
Director of Administration: N. G. FELLMAN.
Librarian: E. A. HÄKLI.

Number of teachers: 2,190.
Number of students: 23,958.

DEANS:

Faculty of Theology: Prof. M. L. PARVIO.
Faculty of Law: Prof. T. HOLOPAINEN.
Faculty of Medicine: Prof. K. A. ACHTÉ.
Faculty of Philosophy:
Faculty of Arts: Prof. J. O. W. WREDE.
Faculty of Science: Prof. O. E. LEHTO.
Faculty of Education: Prof. E. A. NISKANEN.
Faculty of Social Sciences: Prof. P. A. SEPPÄNEN.
Faculty of Agriculture and Forestry: Prof. R. K. RYHÄNEN.

PROFESSORS:

Faculty of Theology:
MURTORINNE, E. J., Church History
PARVIO, M. L., Practical Theology
PENTIKÄINEN, J. Y., Study of Religions
PIRINEN, K. A., General Church History
RÄISÄNEN, H. M., Biblical Exegesis
SOISALON-SOININEN, K. O. I., Old Testament Exegesis
TAMMINEN, K. R., Practical Theology
TEINONEN, S. A., Dogmatics

Faculty of Law:
AALTO, J. S., Judicial Procedure
AARNIO, A. A., Civil Law
ANDERSSON, E. W., Public Law
ANTTILA, S. INKERI, Criminal Law
ARO, P.-L., Commercial Law
BROMS, B. H. G. A., International and Constitutional Law
HALILA, J. J., Judicial Procedure
HIDÉN, M. J. V., Constitutional and International Law
HOLOPAINEN, T., Administrative Law
HOPPU, E. H., Law of Insurance and Damages
HYVÖNEN, V. O., Land Partition, Land Reform and Water Law
JOKELA, H. E., Jurisprudence and International Civil Law
MAKKONEN, K. A., Jurisprudence
MODEEN, T. G. W., Municipal Law and Economy
SARKKO, K., Labour Law
SUVIRANTA, A. J., Labour Law
TIKKA, K. S., Financial Law
VILKKONEN, E. A., Administrative Law
YLIKANGAS, H. E., Legal History and Roman Law
YLÖSTALO, M. V., Civil Law

Faculty of Medicine:
ACHTÉ, K. A., Psychiatry
ADLERCREUTZ, C. H. T., Clinical Chemistry
AINAMO, J. K., Paediatrics
ALHA, A. R., Forensic Chemistry
ARAJÄRVI, T. M., Child Psychiatry
BERGSTRÖM, R. A. M., Physiology
DE LA CHAPELLE, A. F., Medical Genetics
ERÄNKÖ, E. O., Anatomy
HAATAJA, J., Pedodontics and Orthodontics
HALLMAN, N. O. B., Paediatrics
HALONEN, P. I., Internal Medicine
HOLSTI, L.-R. M., Medical Radiology
JÄRNEFELT, J., Medical Chemistry
LAMBERG, B. A., Endocrinology
LANDTMAN, B., Paediatrics
LANGENSKIÖLD, A. F., Orthopaedics and Traumatology
MATTILA, K. J., Dental Radiology
MATTILA, M. J., Pharmacology
MIETTINEN, T. A., Internal Medicine
MOTTONEN, M. K., Forensic Medicine
MUSTAKALLIO, K. K., Skin and Venereal Diseases
MÄKELÄ, V. E. O., Bacteriology and Serology
NEVAKARI, K. M., Dental Prosthetics
NIKKILÄ, E. A., Internal Medicine
OKER-BLOM, N. C. E., Virology
PAASONEN, M. K., Pharmacology
PALVA, T. K., Otolaryngology
PAUNIO, I. K., Cardiology
PÄTIÄLÄ, J. S., Tuberculosis
PELTOLA, P. J., Clinical Pharmacology
PENTTINEN, K. J., Virology
PIRILA, V. P., Skin and Venereal Diseases
RANTASALO, V. I., Public Health Service
SARIS, N.-E. L., Medical Chemistry
SAXÉN, A. E., Pathological Anatomy
SAXÉN, L. O., Experimental Pathology
SCHEININ, TH. M., Surgery
SETÄLÄ, K. M. E., Pathological Anatomy
SOILA, A. P., Diagnostic Radiology
TALA, P. M., Surgery
TAMMISTO, A. T., Anaesthesiology
TROUPP, H. E., Neurosurgery

TURUNEN, M. I., Surgery
VANNAS, SALME FR., Ophthalmology
WASZ-HÖCKERT, B. O., Paediatrics
WEGELIUS, C. O., Internal Medicine
WIDHOLM, O. E. B., Obstetrics and Gynaecology

Faculty of Philosophy:

I. Faculty of Arts

AALTO, P., Comparative Linguistics
ARO, J. T., Oriental Literature
BLOMSTEDT, Y. R. E., Finnish and Scandinavian History
HULDÉN, L. E., Scandinavian Philology
ITKONEN, T. K., Finnish Language
KAIMIO, MAARIT, Greek Literature
KAJANTO, I. I., Latin Literature
KIVINIEMI, E. O., Finnish Language
KLINGE, M., History
KORHONEN, V.-M., Finno-Ugric Linguistics
KOSKINEN, A. A., General Ethnology
KURVINEN, A., English Philology
KUUJO, E. O., General History
KUUSI, M. A., Finnish and Comparative Folklore
LEHTONEN, H. M., Comparative Literature and Aesthetics
LINDGREN, K. BR., German Philology
MEINANDER, C. F. V., Finnish and Scandinavian Archaeology
NÄÄTÄNEN, R. K., General Psychology
PETTERSSON, L. K. J., History of Art
POLVINEN, T. I., General History
PÖRN, I., Philosophy
RISSANEN, M. J., English Philology
SARAJAS, ANNAMARI, Finnish Literature
SUOLAHTI, J. W., History
TAWASTSTJERNA, E. W., Music
THESLEFF, B. H., Greek Philology
TIUSANEN, T., Dramatic Art
THORS, C.-E., Scandinavian Philology
TOMMILA, J. P., Finnish History
VAHROS, I., Russian Language and Literature
VIITAMAKI, R. O., Psychology
VIRTARANTA, E. P. I., Finnish Language
VÄLIKANGAS, O. M. J., Romance Philology
WIS, M., German Philology
WREDE, J. O. W., Swedish Literature

II. Faculty of Science

AARTOLAHTI, T. Y. A., Geography
AHTEE, L. M., Pharmacy
DONNER, J. J., Geology and Palaeontology
DONNER, K. O., Zoology
HALMEKOSKI, J. J., Pharmaceutical Chemistry
VON HAARTMAN, L. A. A., Zoology
HAMBERG, U. M., Biochemistry
HIRSJÄRVI, H. P., Organic Chemistry
HOLOPAINEN, E. O., Meteorology
ILLMAN, S. A., Mathematics
JAATINEN, S. T. HJ., Geography
JALAS, A. J. J., Botany
KAJANTIE, K. O., Physics
KOSKIKALLIO, J. U., Physical Chemistry
KROGERUS, V. E., Pharmaceutical Technology
KURKISUONIO, K. V. J., Physics
KURTÉN, B. O. L., Palaeontology
LAURIKAINEN, K. V., Nuclear Physics
LEHTO, O. E., Mathematics
LINDBERG, J. J., Wood and Polymer Chemistry
LUMME, P. O., Inorganic Chemistry
LUTHER, H. E., Botany
LUUKKALA, M. V., Physics
MIETTINEN, J. K., Radiochemistry
MYRBERG, L. J., Mathematics
MÄKELAINEN, T. O. T., Applied Mathematics
MÄKITIE, O. A., Analytical Chemistry
NIEMI, Å. A., Ecology
PALMÉN, E. PH., Zoology
PERTTUNEN, V. H. J., Experimental Entomology
RANKAMA, K. K., Mineral Chemistry
RENKONEN, H. M. O., Lipid Chemistry
RIKKINEN, K. V., Geography
ROOS, M. G. V., High Energy Physics
VON SCHANTZ, M. F. E., Pharmacognosy
SIIVOLA, A. T., Physics
SIMOLA, L. K., Botany
SIMONS, K. L., Biochemistry
SPRING, E. A., Applied Physics
SUNDMAN, A. VERONICA, General Microbiology
SUNDMAN, K. J., Chemistry
TAMMI, E. O., Mathematics
TIENARI, M. J., Computer Science
TUOMINEN, H. V., Geology and Mineralogy
VIRTANEN, K. I., Mathematics
VÄISÄLÄ, J. I., Mathematics
VÄLIAHO, H. S., Applied Mathematics
WALLGREN, L. H., Zoology

III. Faculty of Education

NISKANEN, E. A., Pedagogics

Faculty of Social Sciences:

ALLARDT, E. A., Sociology
BONSDORFF, G. E. VON, Political Science
HEISKANEN, I. J., Political Science
LAAKKONEN, V. E., Social Politics
MICKWITZ, G., Economics
MOLANDER, A. I., Economics
MUSTONEN, S. J., Statistics
PAUNIO, J. J. K., Economics
PESONEN, P. A., Political Science
PÖYHÖNEN, P. K., Economics
PUROLA, T., Social Politics
RAINIO, K., Social Psychology
RIIHINEN, E. O., Social Politics
SEPPÄNEN, P. A., Sociology
SOIKKANEN, H. V., Social History
TENKKU, J. A., Practical Philosophy
TERÄSVIRTA, T. L., Statistics
TUOMELA, R. H., Practical Philosophy
VALKONEN, Y. T., Sociology
ÅSTRÖM, S.-E. R., Economic and Social History

Faculty of Agriculture and Forestry:

AHLSTRÖM, A. G., Nutrition
ANTILA, M. T., Dairy Science
ERVASTI, S. M., Forest Products Marketing
GRANVIK, B.-A., Forest Technology
GYLLENBERG, H. H. G., Microbiology
HAHTOLA, K. H., Land Use Economics
HEIKURAINEN, L. O., Peatland Forestry
HONKANEN, M. I., Household Economics
HÅRDH, J. E., Horticulture
IHAMUOTILA, R. V. A., Agricultural Policy
JOKELAINEN, I. A., Household Technology
KAILA, A. K., Agricultural Chemistry and Physics
KELTIKANGAS, M., Business Economics in Forestry
KOIVISTOINEN, P. E., Food Chemistry and Technology
MAIJALA, K. J., Animal Breeding
MAKKONEN, O. J., Forest History
NIINIVAARA, P. F., Meat Technology
NUORTEVA, M. K., Agricultural and Forest Zoology
NVORTEVA, P. O., Environmental Conservation
NYYSSÖNEN, A. O., Forest Mensuration and Management
POUTIAINEN, E. K., Animal Husbandry
PUTKISTO, K., Forest Technology
RIIHINEN, P., Social Economics of Forestry
RYHÄNEN, R. K., Limnology
RYYNÄNEN, V. A., Agricultural Economics
SÄRKISILTA, M. S., Agricultural Marketing Economics
TAPIO, E., Plant Pathology
TIGERSTEDT, P. M. A., Plant Breeding
VARIS, E. A., Plant Husbandry
WECKMAN, K. J. B., Agricultural Economics

JOENSUUN KORKEAKOULU
(University of Joensuu)

P.O.B. 111,
80101 JOENSUU 10
Telephone: Joensuu 26211.
Founded 1969.

Language of instruction: Finnish; State control; Academic year: August to July (three terms).

Rector: HEIKKI KIRKINEN.

Vice-Rector: JORMA TAHVANAINEN.

Director of Administration: MATTI HALONEN.

Librarian: TUULIKKI NURMINEN.

Number of teachers: 164.

Number of students: 2,862.

Publications: *Julkaisuja*† (Publications), *Tiedote*†.

PROFESSORS:

ANTIKAINEN, ARI, Sociology of Education
HIRVONEN, PEKKA, English Language
HULT, JUHANI, Geography
HYVÄRINEN, HEIKKI, Biology
HÄMÄLÄINEN, RAUNO, Physics
HÄYRYNEN, YRJÖ-PAAVO, Psychology
KIRKINEN, HEIKKI, History
LAINE, ILPO, Mathematics
MÄLKÖNEN, PENTTI, Chemistry
OJANEN, MUUSA, Russian Language
PULLIAINEN, KYÖSTI, Political Economy
RÄISÄNEN, ALPO, Finnish Language
SIHVO, HANNES, Literature
TAKALA, ANNIKA, Educational Sciences
WIKSTRÖM, KAI, Swedish Language

ATTACHED INSTITUTE:

Karjalan Tutkimuslaitos (*Karelian Research Institute*): Joensuun korkeakoulu, PL 111, 80101 Joensuu 10; Dir. Prof. KYÖSTI PULLIAINEN.

JYVÄSKYLÄN YLIOPISTO
(University of Jyväskylä)

SEMINAARINKATU 15,
SF 40100 JYVÄSKYLÄ 10
Telephone: 35 841/291 211.

Founded as Teacher Training School 1863, became University 1966.

Language of instruction: Finnish; State control; Academic year: September to July (three terms).

Rector: Prof. KALEVI HEINILÄ.

Pro-Rectors: Prof. MIKKO RAATIKAINEN, Prof. TIMO MÄKINEN.

Administrative Director: MATTI HIETALA, LL.M.

Chief Librarian: OILI KOKKONEN, M.A. (acting).

Number of teachers: 538, including 100 professors.

Number of students: 6,914.

Publications: *Studia Historica Jyväskyläensia, Studia Philologica Jyväskyläensia, Jyväskylä Studies in Education, Psychology and Social Research, Jyväskylä Studies in the Arts, Jyväskylä Studies in Sport, Physical Education and Health, Kasvatus, Biological Research Reports.*

DEANS:

Faculty of Education (including Teacher Training College): Prof. ERKKI VILJANEN.
Faculty of Social Sciences: Prof. PERTTI KETTUNEN.
Faculty of Humanities: Prof. HEIKKI LESKINEN.
Faculty of Mathematics and Natural Sciences: Prof. JORMA ELORANTA.
Faculty of Physical and Health Education: Prof. EINO HEIKKINEN.

PROFESSORS:

Faculty of Education:
HEINONEN, VEIKKO, Education
PESONEN, JAAKKO, Special Education
PÄIVÄNSALO, PAAVO, Education
VILJANEN, ERKKI, Education

Faculty of Social Sciences:
JYRKILÄ, FAINA, Sociology
KETTUNEN, PERTTI, Business Administration
PAUKKUNEN, LEO, Social Politics
PELTOLA, EERO, Data Processing
RUOPPILA, ISTO, Developmental Psychology
SARETSALO, LAURI, Statistics
TAKALA, MARTTI, Psychology
TANSKANEN, ANTTI, National Economics
WILENIUS, REIJO, Philosophy

Faculty of Humanities:
JOKIPII, MAUNO, History
KEMILÄINEN, AIRA, History
LESKINEN, HEIKKI, Finnish Language
LÖFSTEDT, LEENA, Romance Philology
MÄKINEN, TIMO, Musicology
OJALA, AATOS, Literature
PEKKANEN, TUOMO, Latin
PELTOLA, NIILO, English Philology
PÖYKKÖ, KALEVI, Art Research
SAJAVAARA, KARI, English Philology
TARVAINEN, KALEVI, German Philology
VILKUNA, ASKO, Ethnology

Faculty of Mathematics and Natural Sciences:
ARSTILA, ANTTI, Biology
BAGGE, PAULI, Hydrobiology
ELORANTA, JORMA, Chemistry
KANTELE, JUHANI, Physics
LIPAS, PERTTI, Theoretical Physics
MARTIO, OLLI, Mathematics
PAASIVIRTA, JAAKKO, Chemistry
PERKO, AARNI, Applied Mathematics
RAATIKAINEN, MIKKO, Biology
VALLI, KALEVI, Physics

Faculty of Physical and Health Education:
HEIKKINEN, EINO, Hygiene of Exercise and Public Health
HEINILÄ, KALEVI, Sociology of Sport
KOMI, PAAVO, Biology of Exercise

ATTACHED INSTITUTES:

Department of Teaching Technology: Dir. OLAVI NÖJD, M.ED.

Language Centre: Dir. VALTER MAKELA, M.A.

Computing Centre: Dir. SEPPO SAARI, M.SC.

Institute for Educational Research: Dir. JOUKO KARI, DR.ED.

KUOPION KORKEAKOULU
(University of Kuopio)

BOX 138, 70101 KUOPIO 10

Telephone: 971-162211.

Founded 1966.

State control; Language of instruction: Finnish; Academic year: August to June.

Rector: T. P. J. VANHA-PERTTULA, M.D.
Vice-Rector: P. M. KAURANEN, PH.D.
Administrative Director: T. T. TEITTINEN, M.A.
Librarian: P. K. TIAINEN, M.A.

Number of teachers: 158, including 31 professors.
Number of students: 1,450.

PROFESSORS:

AIRAKSINEN, M. M., Pharmacology
CASTRÉN, O. M., Gynaecology and Obstetrics
COLLAN, Y. U. I., Pathology
HÄNNINEN, O. O. P., Physiology
HEINONEN, O. P., Community Health (Epidemiology)
HORSMANHEIMO, M. T., Dermatology
JUSLIN, M. J., Pharmaceutical Technology
KALLIOKOSKI, P. J., Environmental Hygiene
KAURANEN, P. M., Chemistry
KETTUNEN, K. O., Surgery
KÄRENLAMPI, L. V., Environmental Hygiene (Ecology)
KÄRJÄ, J. A., Oto-rhino-laryngology
LAAMANEN, A. T., Environmental Hygiene (Chemical-Physical Analytics)
LAUNIALA, K. A., Paediatrics
LUOMA, H., Preventive Dentistry
MÄENPÄÄ, P. H., Biochemistry
MÄNTYJÄRVI, R. A., Clinical Microbiology
PATOMÄKI, L. K., Medical Physics
PYÖRÄLÄ, P. K., Internal Medicine
RAINA, A. M., Physiological Chemistry
RIEKKINEN, P. J., Neurology
SINKKOKEN, S. E., Nursing Administration
TÄHKÄ, V. A., Psychiatry
TUOMISTO, J. J., Toxicology and Pharmacokinetics
TUOVINEN, E. E. J., Ophthalmology
VANHA-PERTTULA, T. P. J., Anatomy
VUORI, H. V., Community Health
WIDEN, C.-J. V., Pharmaceutical Chemistry
WILJASALO, M. A., Diagnostic Radiology

ATTACHED INSTITUTE:

Institute of Public Health.

LAPPEENRANNAN TEKNILLINEN KORKEAKOULU
(Lappeenranta University of Technology)

BOX 20, SF-53851
LAPPEENRANTA 85

Telephone: 953-27570.
Telex: 58290.

Founded 1969.

Language of instruction: Finnish; State control; Academic year: August to July (two terms).

Rector: Prof. JUHANI JAAKKOLA.
Vice-Rector: Prof. LAURI AURA.
Secretary: ARTO OIKKONEN.
Librarian: SAARA RAAKKULA.

Number of teachers: 88, including 9 professors.
Number of students: 1,100.

Publications: *Tieteellisiä julkaisuja*† (research papers).

PROFESSORS:

AURA, LAURI, Electrical Systems
HUOVILAINEN, REINO, Power Plants
JAAKKOLA, JUHANI, Industrial Engineering
KAUPPINEN, VEIJO, Mechanical Technology
NIEMI, ERKKI, Steel Structures
ORPANA, VEIKKO, Materials Handling and Logistics
PALOSAARI, SEPPO, Chemical Engineering
SARKOMAA, PERTII, Technical Thermodynamics
WILSKA, SEPPO, Chemical Technology

OULUN YLIOPISTO
(University of Oulu)

KIRKKOKATU 11A,
SF-90101 OULU 10

Telephone: 35881-222700.

Founded 1958.

Language of instruction: Finnish; State control; Academic year: September to May (two terms).

Rector: Prof. M. MANNERKOSKI, DR. TECH.
Vice-Rector: P. HAVAS, PH.D.
Administrative Director: P. HEIKKINEN, LL.B.

Number of teachers: 650.
Number of students: 7,300.

DEANS:

Faculty of Humanities: Prof. K. JULKU, PH.D.
Faculty of Education: Asst. Prof. P. SAARINEN, PH.D.
Faculty of Science: Prof. E. PULLIAINEN.
Faculty of Technology: Prof. E. HYTTINEN, DR.TECH.
Faculty of Medicine: Prof. L. K. KORHONEN, M.D.

PROFESSORS:

Faculty of Humanities:
FORSSELL, O., D.SOC.SC., Economics
JULKU, K., PH.D., General History
KARKAMA, P., Literature
KORHONEN, J., German Language
MANNINEN, J., History of Ideas and Learning
SAUKKONEN, P., PH.D., Finnish Language
WIKSTRÖM, K., Scandinavian Philology

Faculty of Education:
JUSSILA, M., Didactics
NURMI, V., Education

Faculty of Science:
AARIO, R., PH.D., Soil Geology
ARJAS, E., PH.D., Applied Mathematics and Statistics

HAAHTI, H., PH.D., Mathematics
HAVAS, P., PH.D., Botany
HÄMEEN-ANTTILA, K. A., PH.D., Astronomy
KALLIO, A., PH.D., Theoretical Physics
KILPI, Y., PH.D., Mathematics
KRIEGER, H., PH.D., DR.RER.NAT., Organic Chemistry
KUPILA-AHVENNIEMI, S., PH.D., Plant Physiology
LAAJOKI, K., Geology and Mineralogy
LAKOVAARA, S., PH.D., Genetics
MELA, M., Biophysics
NAUKKARINEN, A., Regional Planning
PIHA, S., PH.D., Biochemistry
PORKKA, M., PH.D., Geophysics
PULLIAINEN, E., Zoology
RAHKAMAA, E., Structure Elucidation in Chemistry
TANSKANEN, P., PH.D., Physics
TURAKAINEN, P., PH.D., Mathematics
VARJO, U., PH.D., Geography
VIRTANEN, O., PH.D., Physical Chemistry

Faculty of Technology:
HALME, A., Control and Systems Engineering
HARTIKAINEN, J., Soil Mechanics and Foundations
HYTTINEN, E., DR.TECH., Statics and Bridge Engineering
JULKUNEN, T., LIC.TECH., Machine Construction.
JÄRVENTAUS, E., ARCH., History of Architecture
KALLIOMÄKI, K., Measurement Technology
KARRAS, M., PH.D., Electronic Measurement Technology
KIIRAS, M., Construction Economics
KURRONEN, S., Mechanical Process Engineering
LAPPALAINEN, P., Electrical Instrumentation
LEINONEN, T., DR.TECH., Machine Design
LÄHTEENKORVA, E., PH.D., Technical Physics
MÄKINEN, M., Building Construction
MANNERKOSKI, M., DR.TECH., Physical Metallurgy
MÄÄTTÄNEN, M., Technical Mechanics
NIEMINEN, J., Mathematics
OKSMAN, J., DR.TECH., Theoretical Electricity
PUTKONEN, A. I., DR.TECH., Structural Engineering
SEPPÄLÄ, V., PH.D., Applied Mathematics
SOHLO, J., LIC.TECH., Heat and Mass Transfer Processes
SÄYNÄJÄKANGAS, S., Electronics
TUPAMÄKI, P. A., DR.TECH., Construction of Shells and Plates
UKKONEN, A., Road Construction
URONEN, P., DR.TECH., Process Control and Dynamics
VALJUS, S., ARCH., Architecture
VEIJOLA, V., DR.TECH., Chemical Process Engineering

Faculty of Medicine:
DAMMERT, K., M.D., Pathological Anatomy
FORSIUS, H., M.D., Ophthalmology
HANNUKSELA, M., Dermatology and Venereal Diseases
HIRVONEN, J., M.D., Forensic Medicine
HIRVONEN, L., M.D., Physiology
HOKKANEN, E., M.D., Neurology
HOLLMÉN, A., M.D., Anaesthesiology
JÄRVINEN, P. A., M.D., Obstetrics and Gynaecology
KAIPAINEN, W. J., M.D., Internal Medicine
KARI-KOSKINEN, O., M.D., Public Health
KIVIRIKKO, K., M.D., Medical Biochemistry
KORHONEN, L. K., M.D., Anatomy
KOUVALAINEN, K., M.D., Paediatrics
KÄRKI, N., M.D., Pharmacology
LARMAS, M., Dentistry
LARMI, T., M.D., Surgery
NYSTRÖM, S., Neurosurgery
PALVA, A., Oto-Rhino-Laryngology
RÖNNING, O., Dentistry
SALMINEN, A., M.D., Microbiology
TASKINEN, P., M.D., Radiotherapy
TIENARI, P., M.D., Psychiatry
TIILIKAINEN, A., Clinical Microbiology and Immunology
VIHKO, R., M.D., Clinical Chemistry
VIRTANEN, K., Dental Prosthetics
VUORIA, P., M.D., Diagnostic Radiology

ATTACHED INSTITUTES:

Institute of Data Processing: Head Prof. P. KEROLA.

Pohjois-Suomen Tutkimuslaitos (*Northern Finland Research Institute*): Torikatu 7, 90100 Oulu 10; Dir. Prof. B. SEGERSTÅHL.

TAMPEREEN TEKNILLINEN KORKEAKOULU
(Tampere University of Technology)

BOX 527, SF-33101 TAMPERE 10

Telephone: 931-162111.
Telex: 22-313 TTKTR-SF.

Founded 1965.

Language of instruction: Finnish; State control; Academic year: September to May.

Rector: Prof. OSMO HASSI.
Vice-Rector: Prof. ILMARI KURKI-SUONIO.
Director of Administration: SEPPO LOIMIO.
Librarian: VESA KAUTTO.

Number of teachers: 423, including 27 professors.

Number of students: *c.* 2,600.

DEANS:

Department of Architecture: Asst. Prof. E. HELAMAA.
Department of Civil Engineering: Prof. R. SALOKANGAS.
Department of Electrical Engineering: Prof. J. KÄRNÄ.
Department of Mechanical Engineering: Prof. I. LAPINLEIMU.

PROFESSORS:

AHO, K., Machine Design
AITTOMÄKI, A., Refrigeration Technology
AUMALA, O., Measurement Engineering
GRAEFFE, G., Physics
HANSSON, O., Design of Buildings
HARTIKAINEN, O. P., Road and Traffic Engineering
HASSI, O., Electrical Power Engineering
HELAMAA, E., Methods and Materials of Building Construction
KARTTUNEN, P., Control Engineering
KEINONEN, L., Soil Mechanics and Foundation Engineering
KESKINEN, R., Hydraulic Machines
KETTUNEN, P., Materials Science
KURKI-SUONIO, I., Thermal Engineering
KÄRNÄ, J., Electrical Power Engineering
LAPINLEIMU, I., Production Engineering
LEPISTÖ, T., Mathematics
MAULA, J., Urban Planning
MEHTO, L., Building Construction
NEUVO, Y., Electronics
PARLAND, H., Theory of Structures
REIJONEN, A., Textile Technology
SAARI, J., Labour Protection
SALOKANGAS, R., Construction Economics
STENROS, H., Architectural Theory I
SUNDQUIST, J., Textile Technology
VIITASAARI, M., Water Supply and Sewage

TAMPEREEN YLIOPISTO
(University of Tampere)

PL.607, 33101 TAMPERE 10,
KALEVANTIE 4

Telephone: 931-156111.

Founded 1925.

Language of instruction: Finnish; State control; Academic year: September to May.

Chancellor: Prof. A. NIEMINEN, PH.D.
Rector: Prof. R. ERMA, LL.D.
Vice-Rectors: Prof. J. VISAKORPI, M.D., Prof. O. BORG, PH.D.
Administrative Director: Y. SILO, M.POL.SC.
Librarian: H. SOINI, L.PHIL.

Number of teachers: 407, including 62 professors.

Number of students: 11,000.

Publication: *Acta Universitatis Tamperensis*†.

DEANS:

Faculty of Social Sciences: Prof. O. APUNEN.
Faculty of Humanistic Studies: Prof. V. RASILA.
Faculty of Economics and Administration: Prof. S. SIIRILÄ.
Faculty of Medicine: Prof. T. NIKKARI.
Faculty of Education: Prof. J. LEHTINEN.

PROFESSORS:

Faculty of Social Sciences:
APUNEN, O., PH.D., International Politics
BORG, O., PH.D., Politics
ESKOLA, A., PH.D., Social Psychology
HEMANUS, P., PH.D., Mass Communication
NORDENSTRENG, K., PH.D., Mass Communication
NUMMENMAA, T., PH.D., Psychology
OKKO, M., PH.D., Library and Information Science
RANDELL, S., PH.D., Sociology
SALO, R., PH.D., Social Policy and Social Welfare
TYRNI, I., PH.D., Economics

Faculty of Humanistic Studies:
HOLSTI, K., PH.D., Literature
PAUNONEN, H., PH.D., Finnish Language
PETTERSSON, B., PH.D., Nordic Philology
RASILA, V., PH.D., Finnish History
SEPPÄNEN, A., PH.D., English Philology
SEPPÄNEN, L., PH.D., Germanic Philology
VEHVILÄINEN, O., PH.D., History

Faculty of Economics and Administration:
AHTIALA, P., PH.D., Economics
ERMA, R., LL.D., Civil Law
HAUTAMÄKI, L., PH.D., Regional Science

Hyyrö, S., ph.d., Mathematics
Kauppi, R., ph.d., Philosophy
Keskumäki, O., ph.d., Economics
Kiiskinen, A., ph.d., Economics
Kurki-Suonio, R., ph.d., Computer Science
Pystynen, E., ph.d., Municipal Policy
Siirilä, S., ph.d., Regional Science
Uotila, J., ll.d., Public Law

Faculty of Medicine:

Anttinen, E., m.d., Social Psychiatry
Hakama, M., ph.d., Epidemiology
Hasan, J., l.m., Work Health
Heikkinen, E., m.d., Gerontology
Isokoski, M., m.d., Public Health
Jansson, E., m.d., Microbiology and Immunology
Karma, P., m.d., Oto-Rhino-Laryngology
Koivisto, E., X-ray Diagnostics
Krohn, K., m.d., Pathology
Nikkari, T., m.d., Medical Biochemistry
Niskanen, P., m.d., Psychiatry
Oja, S., m.d., ph.d., Physiology
Pasternack, A., m.d., Internal Diseases
Pystynen, P., m.d., Obstetrics and Gynaecology
Rokkanen, P., m.d., Surgery
Tuohimaa, P., m.d., Anatomy
Vapaatalo, H., m.d., Pharmacology
Visakorpi, J., m.d., Paediatrics

Faculty of Education:

Heikkinen, V., ph.d., Education
Lehtinen, J., ph.d., Education
Peltonen, M., ph.d., Adult Education

Affiliated Institutes:

Yhteiskuntatieteiden tutkimuslaitos (*Research Institute for Social Sciences*): f. 1945; Dir. Y. Littunen, ph.d.

Tietokonekeskus (*Computer Centre*): f. 1966; Dir. H. Sinervo, l.sc.

Täydennyskoulutuskeskus (*Institute for Extension Studies*): f. 1970; Dir. P. Salmelin, ph.d.

Kansanperinteen laitos (*Institute for Folk Tradition*): f. 1965; Dir. E. Ala-Könni, ph.d.

Puheopin laitos (*Institute for Speech Studies*): f. 1973; Dir. T. Leino, l.phil.

Kielikeskus (*General Language Teaching Centre*): f. 1975; Dir. L. Kurki-Suonio, m.a.

TEKNILLINEN KORKEAKOULU
(Helsinki University of Technology)

02150 ESPOO 15

Telephone: 460144.

Founded 1908.

Language of instruction: Finnish, with some lectures in Swedish; State control; Academic year: September to May.

Rector: Prof. Paul A. Wuori.
Vice-Rectors: Prof. J. M. J. Hyyppä, E. Voipio.
Administrative Director: M. Liesto.
Librarian: E. M. Törnudd.

Number of teachers: 590, including 80 professors.

Number of students: 7,137.

Deans:

Department of Technical Physics: Prof. J. Routti.
Department of Civil Engineering: Prof. J. Hooli.
Department of Mechanical Engineering: Prof. V. Kostilainen.
Department of Electrical Engineering: Prof. S. J. Halme.
Department of Wood and Paper Engineering: Prof. R. Juvonen.
Department of Chemistry: Prof. P. Linko.
Department of Mining and Metallurgy: Prof. V. Lindroos.
Department of Surveying: Prof. P. Virtanen.
Department of Architecture: Prof. J. Laapotti.
Department of General Sciences: Prof. M. A. Ranta.

Professors:

Blomberg, H., Theoretical Electrical Engineering
Bredenberg, J., Industrial Chemistry
Byckling, E., Technical Physics
Ebeling, K., Paper Technology
Enkvist, E., Naval Architecture
Halme, S., Communication Engineering
Holappa, L., Chemical Metallurgy
Hollo, E., Economic Jurisprudence
Hooli, J. E., Water Resource Development
Huhtamo, O. E., Mechanical Technology
Hyyppä, J. M. J., Civil Engineering
Häkkinen, S., Industrial Psychology and Personnel Management
Jaatinen, M., Architecture
Jahkola, A., Energy Economics and Power Plants
Jaskari, O., Economics
Jokinen, T., Electrical Engineering
Juvonen, R. J., Mechanical Technology of Wood
Jääskeläinen, P., Applied Electronics
Kaila, M. M., Strength of Materials
Kajosaari, E. T., Water Supply and Sewerage
Kanerva, P., Building Structures and Technology
Kauppinen, V. S., Biochemistry
Kilpelä, O. E., Photogrammetry
Kivinen, M. O., Regional and Urban Planning
Kohonen, T., Technical Physics
Korhonen, A., Regional and Urban Planning
Korhonen, K.-H., Foundation Engineering and Soil Mechanics
Kostilainen, V., Naval Architecture
Laapotti, J., Architecture II
Laine, S., Aeronautical Engineering
Lappo, O., Architecture
Lehti, R., Mathematics
Lilius, H., History of Architecture
Lindroos, V. K., Physical Metallurgy
Linko, E. P., Food Technology
Lounasmaa, M., Organic Chemistry
Lundsten, B. V., Materials and Construction Methods
Lyly, S., Traffic and Transportation Engineering
Martikainen, M., Geodesy
Mikkola, A., Mineralogy and Geology
Mikkola, M., Theory of Structures
Mörsky, J., Electrical Engineering
Niemi, A. J., Automatic Control
Niinistö, L., Inorganic Chemistry
Nordén, H. V., Chemical Engineering
Ojala, L., Electrical Engineering
Olkkonen, T., Industrial Engineering
Paavola, H. P., Bridge Construction
Perilä, O., Printing Technology
Pietikäinen, J., Metals Technology
Pitkänen, J., Machine Building
Puhakka, L. Y. V., Steam Technology
Rahko, K. J. S., Telephone Engineering
Ranta, M. A., Mechanics
Routti, J., Technical Physics
Ryti, K. J. H., Heat Engineering and Machinery
Saarsalmi, E., Construction Economy and Management
Sahlberg, P.-H., Steam Technology
Sistonen, H., Hydraulics
Sjöström, O. G., Wood Chemistry
Stubb, T., Electronics
Sulonen, M. Metallography
Sundholm, G., Physical Chemistry
Tiuri, M., Radio Engineering
Virkola, N. E., Pulping Technology
Virtanen, P., Real Estate Law
Voipio, E., Theoretical Electrical Engineering
Vuorelainen, O. M., Heating and Ventilation, Sanitary Engineering
Wuori, P., Hydraulic Machines

TURUN YLIOPISTO
(University of Turku)

20500 TURKU 50

Telephone: 921-645111.

Founded 1920.

Language of instruction: Finnish; State control; Academic year: August to July (two semesters).

Chancellor: K. J. W. Hartiala, m.d.
Rector: O. K. Ikola, ph.d.
Vice-Rectors: E. Euranto, K. Paunio.
Head of Administration: E. Välimäki, m.l.
Librarian: H. Eskelinen, lic.phil.

Number of teachers: 957, including 93 professors and 87 assoc. professors.

Number of students: 9,445.

Publication: *Annales Universitatis Turkuensis*†.

Deans:

Faculty of Humanities: Prof. L. Lindgren.
Faculty of Mathematics and Natural Sciences: Prof. U. Pursiheimo.
Faculty of Medicine: Prof. P. Virtama.
Faculty of Law: Prof. H. Klami, d.l.
Faculty of Social Sciences: Prof. O. Vuori.
Faculty of Educational Sciences: Prof. E. Lahdes, d.ed.

Professors:

Faculty of Humanities:

Alhoniemi, A. E. V., Finno-Ugrian Linguistics
Erämetsä, E., ph.d., Germanic Philology
Fortelius, B. G. G., ph.d., Nordic Philology
Honko, L. O., ph.d., Folkloristics and Comparative Religion
Ikola, O. K., ph.d., Finnish Language
Koskenniemi, H. K. J., ph.d., Classical Philology
Kangasmaa-Minn, E., ph.d., Finno-Ugrian and General Linguistics
Koskenniemi, I. K., ph.d., English Philology
Lauerma, M., ph.d., General History
Lindgren, L. B., ph.d., Romance Philology
Litzén, V., ph.d., Cultural History
Niemi, I., ph.d., General Literature

SAARENHEIMO, K. K., PH.D., Finnish Literature
SALO, U. O., PH.D., Finnish and Comparative Archaeology
TALVE, I., PH.D., Finnish and Comparative Ethnology
VIRRANKOSKI, P., PH.D., History of Finland
WIIK, K. K., PH.D., Phonetics

Faculty of Mathematics and Natural Sciences:
ENNOLA, V., PH.D., Mathematics
EURANTO, E. K., Organic Chemistry
GRANÖ, O. J., PH.D., Geography
HAUKIOJA, E., PH.D., Zoology
HELLMAN, O. B., D.TECH., Applied Mathematics
JÄRVI, T. H. J., PH.D., Computer Science
KANKARE, J., PH.D., Analytical Chemistry
KRUSIUS, F. M., D.TECH., Physics
LAGERSPETZ, K. Y. H., PH.D., Zoology
LAPPALAINEN, V., PH.D., Quaternary Geology
MANSIKKA, K. A., PH.D., Theoretical Physics
NEUVONEN, K. J., PH.D., Geology and Mineralogy
NORTIA, T. A. O., D.TECH., Inorganic Chemistry
NURMIKKO, V. T., PH.D., Biochemistry
PIHLAJA, K., PH.D., Physical Chemistry
PORTIN, P., PH.D., Genetics
PUNKKINEN, M., PH.D., Physics
PURSIHEIMO, U. J., PH.D., Applied Mathematics
PÖYHÖNEN, J. U., PH.D., Physics
ROUSI, A. H., PH.D., Botany
SALOMAA, A. K., PH.D., Mathematics
SUONINEN, E. J., PH.D., Materials Research
TIETÄVÄINEN, A. A., PH.D., Mathematics
VALANNE, N., PH.D., Botany
VALTONEN, M., PH.D., Astronomy
YLI-JOKIPII, P., PH.D., Geography

Faculty of Medicine:
ALANEN, Y. O., M.D., Psychiatry
HALONEN, P. E., M.D., Virology
HARTIALA, K. J. W., M.D., Physiology
HAVU, V. K., M.D., Dermatology and Venereal Diseases
KALLIOMÄKI, J. L., M.D., Internal Medicine
KOIVUMAA, K. K., D.D.S., Dental Prosthetics
KOSKI, P. K., D.D.S., Pedodontics and Orthodontics
KULONEN, E. I., M.D., Medical Chemistry
MEURMAN, O. H., M.D., Oto-Rhino-Laryngology
NIEMI, M. I., M.D., Anatomy
NORDMAN, E., M.D., Oncology
OKSALA, A. A., M.D., Ophthalmology
OKSALA, E. J., D.M.D., Dental Surgery
PAUNIO, K., D.D.S., Parodontology
PEKKARINEN, A. I., M.D., Pharmacology
PELTONEN, T. E., M.D., Paediatrics
RAEKALLIO, J. A. J., M.D., Forensic Medicine
RAURAMO, M. L., M.D., Obstetrics and Gynaecology
RINNE, U. K., M.D., Neurology
SCHEININ, A. N., D.D.S., Operative Dentistry
TALA, E. J., M.D., Lung Diseases
TAMMISALO, E. H., D.D.S., Dental Radiology
TOIVANEN, P. U., M.D., Medical Microbiology
VAPAAVUORI, M. J., M.D., Anaesthesiology
VIIKARI, S. J., M.D., Surgery
VIRTAMA, P. E. J., M.D., Roentgenology
VUORI, I., M.D., Public Health

Faculty of Law:
BJÖRNE, L., D.L., History of Law and Roman Law
HUTTUNEN, A. A., D.L., Civil Law III
JYRANKI, A., D.L., Constitutional and International Law
KARTIO, L., D.L., Civil Law
KLAMI, H. T., D.L., Jurisprudence and International Private Law
KYLÄKALLIO, R. J., D.L., Civil Law I
RYTKÖLÄ, V. O., D.L., Administrative Law
VESANEN, T. I., D.L., Financial Law

Faculty of Social Sciences:
ASP, E. K., PH.D., Sociology
HILPINEN, R., PH.D., Theoretical Philosophy
NOUSIAINEN, J. I., D.POL.SC., Political Science
PAASIVIRTA, J., PH.D., Political History
PIETARINEN, V. J., D.POL.SC., Practical Philosophy
PULKKINEN, T. U., D.POL.SC., Social Politics
VON WRIGHT, J. M., PH.D., Psychology
VUORELA, E., D.POL.SC., Political Economy
VUORI, O. Y., D.POL.SC., Political Economy

Faculty of Educational Sciences:
KARVONEN, J., D.ED., Education
LAHDES, E. L. K., D.ED., Education (Teacher Training)

ATTACHED INSTITUTES:

Archipelago Research Institute: Head T. JUUSTI, M.A.

Cardiovascular Research Unit: Head Assoc. Prof. I. VÄLIMÄKI.

Computer Centre: Head H. AALTO, M.A.

Language Centre: Head Prof. K. WIIK.

Subarctic Research Institute Kevo: Head Prof. M. SULKINOJA, M.A.

Wihuri Physical Laboratory: Head Assoc. Prof. L. NIEMELÄ.

COLLEGES OF UNIVERSITY STANDING

ELÄINLÄÄKETIETEELLINEN KORKEAKOULU
(College of Veterinary Medicine)

HÄMEENTIE 57, HELSINKI 55

Founded 1945.

Languages of instruction: Finnish and Swedish; State control; Academic year: September to May.

Rector: Prof. K. KALLELA.
Secretary: T. IJÄS.
***Librarian:* A. SETÄLÄ.**

Number of teachers: 55, including 11 professors.

Number of students: 260.

PROFESSORS:

KALLELA, K., Animal Hygiene
LINDBERG, P., Biochemistry
OKSANEN, H., Medicine
PAATSAMA, S., Surgery
PEKKANEN, T., Food Hygiene
RAHKO, T., Pathology
ROINE, K., Obstetrics and Gynaceology
SANDHOLM, M., Pharmacology and Toxicology
SARAJAS, S., Physiology
TALANTI, S., Anatomy and Embryology
TUOMI, J., Microbiology and Epizootology

HANDELSHÖGSKOLAN VID ÅBO AKADEMI
(Åbo Swedish University School of Economics)

20500 ÅBO 50,
HENRIKSGATAN 7
Telephone: 33-51-33.
Founded 1927.

Language of instruction: Swedish; Private control; Academic year: September to May.

Rector: C.-G. LINDSTRÖM.
Vice-Rector: A. TÖRN.
Secretary: ULLA ACHRÉN.
Librarian: INGER SÖDERLUND.

Number of teachers: 28, including 7 professors.

Number of students: 640.

Publications: *Skriftserie A & B*†, *Årsberättelse* (Annual Review)†, *Meddelanden & Memoranda från Företagsekonomiska Institutionen*†, *Meddelanden & Memoranda från Nationalekonomiska Institutionen*†, *Meddelanden & Memoranda från Ekonomisk-geografiska Institutionen*†.

PROFESSORS:

ANCKAR, O., D.ECON., Economics
ERIKSSON, G. A., FIL.D., Commercial Geography
LINDSTRÖM, C.-G., D.ECON., Business Administration

ATTACHED INSTITUTES:

Företagsekonomiska Institutionen (*Institute of Microeconomics and Management Science*): Dir. C.-G. LINDSTRÖM.

Nationalekonomiska Institutionen (*Institute of Economics*): Dir. O. ANCKAR.

Ekonomisk-geografiska Institutionen (*Institute of Commercial Geography*): Dir. G. A. ERIKSSON.

HELSINGIN KAUPPAKORKEAKOULU
(Helsinki School of Economics)

00100 HELSINKI 10,
RUNEBERGINKATU 14-16
and 22-24
Telephone: 440211.
Founded 1911.

Language of instruction: Finnish; State control; Academic year: September to May.

Chancellor: J. HONKO, D.ECON., PH.D.
Rector: V. LEIVO, D.TECH.
Vice-Rector: M. KASKIMIES, ECON.D.
Head of Administration: O. TARPILA, B.L.
Librarian: H. BROMS, PH.D.

Number of teachers: 210, including 19 professors.
Number of students: 3,800.
Publications: *Acta Academiae Oeconomicae Helsingiensis*†, Series B, C, D.

PROFESSORS:

AALTIO, E., D.TECH., Commodity Studies and Technology
HELLE, R., PH.D., Economic Geography
HONKO, J., ECON.D., PH.D., Business Economics
KALLIO, M., PH.D., Management Systems
KASKIMIES, M., ECON.D., Marketing
LAAKSONEN, O., D.POL.SC., Business Administration
LEHTOVUORI, J., ECON.D., Business Economics
LEIVO, V., D.TECH., Marketing
LEPONIEMI, A., D.POL.SC., Econometrics
MATTILA, S., PH.D., Mathematics and Statistics
MUUKKONEN, P., LL.D., Business Law
NYBERG, A., D.POL.SC., Research
PAAKKANEN, J., ECON.D., Economics
PIHKALA, E., D.POL.SC., Economic History
SALO, S., D.TECH., Mathematics
TELARANTA, K., LL.D., Business Law
VAIVIO, F., ECON.D., Economics
VOIPIO, J., LL.D., Public Law

SVENSKA HANDELSHÖGSKOLAN
(Swedish School of Economics)

00100 HELSINKI 10,
ARKADIAGATAN 22
Telephone: 440291.
Founded 1909.

Language of instruction: Swedish; Academic year: September to May.

Rector: L. WAHLBECK, ECON.D.
Vice-Rector: J. FELLMAN, PH.D.
Secretary: G. WESTERLUND, B.L.
Librarian: T. W. HOLM, LIC.POL.SC.

Number of teachers: 77, including 11 professors.
Number of students: 1,605.
Publications: *Ekonomi och Samhälle* (main series), Reports, Working Papers (Swedish or English).

PROFESSORS:

BERNDTSON, H., D.ECON., Economics (acting)
EKHOLM, B.-G., D.ECON., Business Administration (acting)
FELLMAN, J., PH.D., Statistics
GRÖNROOS, CHR., D.ECON., International and Industrial Marketing (acting)
HELENIUS, R., D.POL.SC., Politics
JÄGERHORN, R., D.ECON., Accountancy
KOCK, S., D.ECON., Administration
LERVIKS, A., D.ECON., Marketing
LINDBERG, O., PH.D., Economic Geography
RISKA, O., D.L., Commercial Law
WAHLBECK, L., ECON.D., Business Administration

TAIDETEOLLINEN KORKEAKOULU
(University of Industrial Arts)

KAIVOKATU 2-4B,
00100 HELSINKI 10
Founded 1842.

Principal: Y. KUKKAPURO.

HEADS OF DEPARTMENTS:

LAAKSO, T., Product and Environmental Design
LIPASTI, T., Visual Communication
LYYTIKÄINEN, L., Training Centre
PARKO, S., General Studies
SALMINEN, A., Art Education

Number of teachers: 225.
Number of students: 973.
Library of 13,237 vols.
Publication: *Vuosikertomus* (annual report).

TURUN KAUPPAKORKEAKOULU
(Turku School of Economics)

20500 TURKU 50,
REHTORINPELLONTIE 3
Telephone: 33-55-35.
Founded 1950.

Language of instruction: Finnish; State control; Academic year: September to June.

Rector: R. KANERVA, D.ECON.
Vice-Rector: V. REINIKAINEN, D.ECON.
Chief Administrative Officer: A. LEINO, B.L.
Librarian: S. SALORANTA, M.A.

Number of teachers: 100, including 13 professors.
Number of students: 1,300.
Publication: *Julkaisuja.*

PROFESSORS:

AALTONEN, A. O., LL.D., Commercial Law
HALME, V., PH.D., Economics
KANERVA, R., D.ECON., Business Administration and Marketing
MAJALA, R., D.ECON., Business Administration and Accounting
MALASKA, P., D.ENG., Mathematics and Statistics
MÄKINEN, E. H., LIC.ECON., International Marketing (acting)
NURMI, R. W., D.POL., Business Administation and Management.
PIHA, K., PH.D., Business Administration and Management
PIHLANTO, P. H., D.ECON., Business Administration and Accountancy (acting)
REINIKAINEN, V., D.ECON., Economics
REPONEN, T., D.ECON., Computer Science
SALO, M., M.SC.ECON., Business Administration and Marketing
SAVIRANTA, J., PH.D., Economic Geography

VAASAN KAUPPAKORKEAKOULU
(Vaasa School of Economics)

VAASA, RAASTUVANK 31
Telephone: 242-511.
Founded 1966.

Rector: M. PALOMAKI.
Vice-Rector: R. RUUHELA.
Secretary: L. NYQVIST.
Librarian: R. FAVORIN.

Library of 55,000 vols.
Number of teachers: 60.
Number of students: 1,150.
Publications: *Acta Wasaensia*†, *Proceedings.*

PROFESSORS:

HÄMÄLÄINEN, R., D.ENG., Mathematics
LAURÉN, C., PH.D., Swedish
PALOMÄKI, M., PH.D., Economic Geography
ROUTAMO, E., LL.D., Business Law
RUUHELA, R., ECON.D., Business Administration and Accountancy

OTHER COLLEGES AND INSTITUTES

HELSINGIN TEKNILLINEN OPPILAITOS
(Technical Institute of Helsinki)
HELSINKI
Founded 1881.

Rector: AULIS ESKOLA.
Vice-Rector: J. TEINONEN.

Number of teachers: 300.
Number of students: 2,900.
Library of 20,000 vols.

SVENSKA SOCIAL- OCH KOMMUNALHÖGSKOLAN
(Swedish School of Social Work and Local Administration)
TOPELIUSGATAN 16,
00250 HELSINKI 25
Telephone: 407272.
Founded 1943.

President: GUNVOR BRETTSCHNEIDER.

Library of 20,000 vols.
Number of teachers: *c.* 25.
Number of students: *c.* 350.

TEKNISKA LÄROVERKET I HELSINGFORS
(Helsinki College of Technology)
APOLLOGATAN 8,
00100 HELSINKI 10
Founded 1916.

Dean: P. BREMER.

Library of 11,000 vols.

TURUN TEKNILLINEN OPPILAITOS
(Turku Institute of Technology)
SEPÄNKATU 1,
SF-20700 TURKU 70

Rector: YRJÄNÄ K. VUORI.
Vice-Rector: KALEVI KOPONEN.

TYÖTERVEYSLAITOS
(Institute of Occupational Health)
HAARTMANINKATU 1,
00290 HELSINKI 29
Founded 1951.

Director-General: JORMA RANTANEN, M.D.
Scientific Director: SVEN HERNBERG, M.D.

Library of 18,000 vols. and *c.* 400 journals.

Number of teachers: 200.

Publications: *Scandinavian Journal of Work, Environment and Health* (4 a year), *Työ-Terveys-Turvallisuus* (16 a year).

Regional Institutes in Kuopio, Lappeenranta, Oulu, Tampere, Turku and Uusimaa.

SCHOOLS OF ART AND MUSIC

SIBELIUS-AKATEMIA
(Sibelius Academy)
00100 HELSINKI 10,
POHJOIS-RAUTATIEKATU 9
Telephone: 444 999.

Founded 1882.

Languages of instruction: Finnish and Swedish; Private control but with State financial support; Academic year: September to May.

Chancellor: J. KOKKONEN.
President: E. TAWASTSTJERNA.
Rector: V. HELASVUO.
Vice-Rector: Mrs. ELLEN URHO.
Chief Administration Officer: SEPPO SUIHKO.

Number of teachers: 70 full-time, 96 part-time.
Number of students: 900.
Library: *see* Libraries.
Publication: *Vuosikertomus*† (annual report).

DEANS:

School Music Department: R. ASPLUND (acting).
Church Music Department: H. ANDERSÉN.
General Department: Mrs. E. URHO.
Junior Department: Mrs. SEIJA-SISKO RAITIO.

PROFESSORS:

FORSBLOM, E., Organ
HAAPANEN, T., Violin
LEHTINEN, M., Singing
NORAS, A., Cello
PANULA, J., Conducting
POHJOLA, Mrs. L., Piano
RAUTAVAARA, E., Composition
RAUTIO, E., Cello
SALOMAA, P., Opera (acting)
VALSTA, T., Piano

SUOMEN TAIDEAKATEMIAN KOULU
(Academy of Fine Arts)
ATENEUM B,
00100 HELSINKI 10
Founded 1848.

Rector: JAAKKO SIEVÄNEN.

Four-year courses in painting, sculpture and graphics.

Number of teachers: 13.
Number of students: *c.* 70.

FRANCE

Population 53,373,000

ACADEMIES

L'INSTITUT DE FRANCE

23 QUAI DE CONTI, PARIS 6e

Founded 1795.

BOARD FOR 1980:

President: PAUL-LOUIS WEILLER (Académie des Beaux-Arts).

Vice-Presidents: JEAN MISTLER (Académie française), PIERRE DEMARGNE (Académie des Inscriptions et Belles-Lettres), ROGER GAUTHERET (Académie des Sciences), ANDRÉ PIETTRE (Académie des Sciences morales et politiques).

Secretary: EMMANUEL BONDEVILLE (Académie des Beaux-Arts.

Chancellor: EDOUARD BONNEFOUS.

Librarian: Mme HAUTECOEUR-MILLIEZ.

Director of Services: PHILIPPE BRISSAUD.

Prizes of the Institute: Prix Osiris, d'Aumale, Jaffé, Berthault, etc.

The Institute is composed of the following five Academies:

(1) **Académie française:** f. 1635 by Louis XIII; Dir. elected quarterly; Permanent Sec. JEAN MISTLER; Sec. Adm. CECILE DE BOSSON; 40 elected members; Prizes: Grand prix de littérature, Grand prix du roman, Grand prix de poésie-Roucoules, Grand prix du Rayonnement français, Prix Gobert for historical works and others.

MEMBERS:

LACRETELLE, JACQUES DE (1936).
BROGLIE, LOUIS, Duc de (1944).
GENEVOIX, MAURICE (1946).
GAXOTTE, PIERRE (1953).
LEVIS MIREPOIX, ANTOINE, Duc de (1953).
CHAMSON, ANDRÉ (1956).
DELAY, JEAN (1959).
TROYAT, HENRI (1959).
HUYGHE, RENÉ (1960).
CLAIR, RENÉ (1960).
GUITTON, JEAN (1961).
MAULNIER, THIERRY (1964).
BRION, MARCEL (1964).
LEPRINCE-RINGUET, LOUIS (1966).
MISTLER, JEAN (1966).
DRUON, MAURICE (1966).
ARLAND, MARCEL (1968).
EMMANUEL, PIERRE (1968).
IONESCO, EUGÈNE (1970).
GREEN, JULIEN (1971).
WOLFF, ETIENNE (1971).
CASTRIES, RENÉ, Duc de (1972).
GAUTIER, JEAN-JACQUES (1972).
ROUSSIN, ANDRÉ (1973).
LÉVI-STRAUSS, CLAUDE (1973).
D'ORMESSON, JEAN (1973).
SCHUMANN, MAURICE (1974).
BERNARD, JEAN (1975).
CARRÉ, Rév. Père (1975).
MARCEAU, FÉLICIEN (1975).
RHEIMS, MAURICE (1976).
PEYREFITTE, ALAIN (1977).
DÉON, MICHEL (1978).
FAURE, EDGAR (1978).
DUMEZIL, GEORGES (1978).
DUTOURD, JEAN (1978).
GOUHIER, HENRI (1979).
DECAUX, ALAIN (1979).
DROIT, MICHEL (1980).
YOURCENAR, MARGUERITE (1980).

(2) **Académie des Inscriptions et Belles-Lettres:** f. 1663 by Louis XIV; 45 members, 10 free members, 20 foreign associates, 30 French and 40 foreign correspondents; Permanent Sec. ANDRÉ DUPONT-SOMMER; Pres. PIERRE DEMARGNE; Vice-Pres. MICHEL FRANÇOIS; publs. *Comptes Rendus, Mémoires,* and various on Orientalism, Classical Antiquity and the Middle Ages.

MEMBERS:

SAMARAN, CHARLES (1941).
ROBERT, LOUIS (1948).
SCHAEFFER, CLAUDE (1953).
GRABAR, ANDRÉ (1955).
LEBÈGUE, RAYMOND (1955).
FESTUGIÈRE, JEAN (1958).
MAROT, PIERRE (1958).
DUPONT-SOMMER, ANDRÉ (1961).
PUECH, HENRI-CHARLES (1962).
LEJEUNE, MICHEL (1963).
PARROT, ANDRÉ (1963).
HUBERT, JEAN (1963).
COURCELLE, PIERRE (1965).
LEMERLE, PAUL (1966).
FILLIOZAT, JEAN (1966).
LECOY, FÉLIX (1966).
FLACELIÈRE, ROBERT (1967).
HEURGON, JACQUES (1968).
DEMARGNE, PIERRE (1969).
POSENER, GEORGES (1969).
FRANÇOIS, MICHEL (1969).
PEZARD, ANDRÉ (1970).
DUMEZIL, GEORGES (1970).
SESTON, WILLIAM (1970).
DAUX, GEORGES (1971).
DUVAL, PAUL-MARIE (1971).
CAHEN, CLAUDE (1973).
MARICHAL, ROBERT (1974).
LECLANT, JEAN (1974).
DUBY, GEORGES (1974).
LAOUST, HENRI (1974).
BAUTIER, ROBERT-HENRI (1974).
ROMILLY, JACQUELINE DAVID (dite DE) (1975).
CHASTEL, ANDRÉ (1975).
MARTIN, ROLAND (1975).
GRIMAL, PIERRE (1977).
SALET, FRANCIS (1977).
CAQUOT, ANDRÉ (1977).
MOLLAT DU JOURDIN, MICHEL (1978).
POUILLOUX, JEAN (1978)
LEROI-GOURHAN, ANDRÉ (1980).
VERNET, ANDRÉ (1980).

Free Members:

SCHNEIDER, JEAN (1968).
PALANQUE, JEAN-RÉMY (1968).
SIMON, MARCEL (1969).
OURLIAC, PAUL (1970).
LAROCHE, EMMANUEL (1972).
IMBS, PAUL (1972).
AMANDRY, PIERRE (1972).
WOLFF, PHILIPPE (1973).
WILL, ERNEST (1973).
BOÜARD DE LA FOREST, MICHEL DE (1973).

(3) **Académie des Sciences:** f. 1666 by Louis XIV; 130 ordinary members; at most 80 foreign associates and 160 correspondents; Permanent Secs. PAUL GERMAIN (Mathematical and Physical Sciences and their applications) and ROBERT COURRIER (Chemical, Natural, Biological and Medical Sciences and their applications); Pres. ROGER GAUTHERET; Vice-Pres. PIERRE JACQUINOT; publs. *Comptes rendus, Exposés, Annuaire.*

MEMBERS:

Section I. Mathematics:
GARNIER, RENÉ (1952).
MILLOUX, HENRI (1959).
DIEUDONNÉ, JEAN (1968).
MANDELBROJT, SZOLEM (1972).
CARTAN, HENRI (1974).
SCHWARTZ, LAURENT (1975).
CHOQUET, GUSTAVE (1976).
THOM, RENÉ (1976).
SERRE, JEAN-PIERRE (1976).
MALLIAVIN, PAUL (1979).
TITS, JACQUES (1979).

Section II. Physics:
LEPRINCE-RINGUET, LOUIS (1949).
DUPOUY, GASTON (1950).
NÉEL, LOUIS (1953).
PERRIN, FRANCIS (1953).
TRILLAT, JEAN-JACQUES (1959).
PONTE, MAURICE (1963).
KASTLER, ALFRED (1964).
LUCAS, RENÉ (1964).
JACQUINOT, PIERRE (1966).
BLANC-LAPIERRE, ANDRÉ (1970).
ROUARD, PIERRE (1970).
GUINIER, ANDRÉ (1971).
GORODETZKY, SERGE (1971).
GRIVET, PIERRE (1972).
ABRAGAM, ANATOLE (1973).
BROSSEL, JEAN (1977).
CASTAING, RAIMOND (1977).
AUGER, PIERRE (1977).
FRIEDEL, JACQUES (1977).
GENNES, PIERRE GILLES DE (1979).
BERTAUT, FELIX (1979).
MICHEL, LOUIS (1979).

Section III. Mechanics:
ROY, MAURICE (1949).
LERAY, JEAN (1953).
ESCANDE, LÉOPOLD (1954).
LICHNEROWICZ, ANDRÉ (1963).
BASTIEN, PAUL (1967).
LEGENDRE, ROBERT (1968).
LIONS, JACQUES-LOUIS (1973).
FAVRE, ALEXANDRE (1977).
DAUTRAY, ROBERT (1977).
MALAVARD, LUCIEN (1979).
CHOQUET-BRUHAT, YVONNE (1979).

Section IV. Science of the Universe:
PIVETEAU, JEAN (1956).
WYART, JEAN (1959).
COULOMB, JEAN (1960).
DECAUX, BERNARD (1966).
DENISSE, JEAN-FRANÇOIS (1967).
FEHRENBACH, CHARLES (1968).
GLANGEAUD, LOUIS (1968).
THELLIER, EMILE (1968).
LACOMBE, HENRI (1973).
WLERICK, GÉRARD (1977).
PECKER, JEAN-CLAUDE (1977).
MILLOT, GEORGES (1977).
LEHMAN, JEAN-PIERRE (1979).
BLAMONT, JACQUES (1979).

Section V. Chemistry:
VELLUZ, LÉON (1961).
ROCHE, JEAN (1963).
NORMANT, HENRI (1966).
LAFFITTE, PAUL (1969).
CHARLOT, GASTON (1970).
GALLAIS, FERNAND (1973).
HOREAU, ALAIN (1977).
DESNUELLE, PIERRE (1977).
JULIA, MARC (1977).
BENARD, JACQUES (1979).
EBEL, JEAN-PIERRE (1979).
FRÉJACQUES, CLAUDE (1979).

Section VI. Cellular and Molecular Biology:
BUVAT, ROGER (1965).
WURMSER, RENÉ (1969).
LATARJET, RAYMOND (1972).
LWOFF, ANDRÉ (1976).
JACOB, FRANÇOIS (1976).
GROS, FRANÇOIS (1979).
DOUZOU, PIERRE (1979).
PULLMAN, BERNARD (1979).

Section VII. Animal and Plant Biology:
GRASSÉ, PIERRE-PAUL (1948).
VANDEL, ALBERT (1956).
FONTAINE, MAURICE (1957).
PLANTEFOL, LUCIEN (1957).
GAUTHERET, ROGER (1958).
WOLFF, ETIENNE (1963).
FESSARD, ALFRED (1963).
MONOD, THÉODORE (1963).
BALACHOWSKY, ALFRED (1967).
AUBRÉVILLE, ANDRÉ (1968).
VAGO, CONSTANTIN (1971).
THOMAS, ANDRÉ (1972).
DORST, JEAN (1973).
PÉRÈS, JEAN-MARIE (1973).
BENOIT, JACQUES (1977).
BOUREAU, EDOUARD (1977).
CAUDERON, ANDRÉ (1977).
JOST, ALFRED (1979).
DURANTON, HENRI (1979).

Section VIII. Human Biology and Medical Sciences:
LÉPINE, PIERRE (1961).
TURPIN, RAYMOND (1962).
PRÉVOT, ANDRÉ-ROMAIN (1963).
MERLE D'AUBIGNÉ, ROBERT (1966).
TRUHAUT, RENÉ (1968).
VERNEJOUL, ROBERT DE (1970).
BERNARD, JEAN (1972).
HAMBURGER, JEAN (1974).
LAZORTHES, GUY (1975).
DUBOST, CHARLES (1975).
DAUSSET, JEAN (1977).
BARGETON, DANIEL (1977).
JOUVET, MICHEL (1977).
OUDIN, JACQUES (1979).
BESSIS, MARCEL (1979).
KARLI, PIERRE (1979).

(4) **Académie des Beaux-Arts:** f. 1803; 50 ordinary members, 15 foreign associates, 50 correspondents; Perm. Sec. EMMANUEL BONDEVILLE; Pres. PAUL-LOUIS WEILLER; Vice-Pres. FELIX LABISSE; publ. *Annuaire de l'Académie des Beaux-Arts.*

MEMBERS:

Section I. Painting:
SOUVERBIE, JEAN (1946).
BRAYER, YVES (1957).
CHEYSSIAL, GEORGES (1958).
PLANSON, ANDRÉ (1960).
LABISSE, FELIX (1966).
ROHNER, GEORGES (1968).
CHASTEL, ROGER (1968).
DESPIERRE, JACQUES (1969).
BUFFET, BERNARD (1974).
MATHIEU, GEORGES (1975).
HARTUNG, HANS (1977).
CARZOU, JEAN (1977).

Section II. Sculpture:
BELMONDO, PAUL (1960).
MARTIN, RAYMOND (1961).
CARTON, JEAN (1964).
LEYGUE, LOUIS (1969).
ÉTIENNE-MARTIN (1970).
YENCESSE, HUBERT (1973).
HILBERT, GEORGES (1973).

Section III. Architecture:
Le Maresquier, Noël (1961)
Beaudouin, Eugène (1961).
Gillet, Guillaume (1968).
Bernard, Henry (1968).
Saltet, Marc (1972).
Couëlle, Jacques (1976).
Langlois, Christian (1977).
Novarina, Maurice (1979).
Remondet, André (1979).

Section IV. Engraving:
Decaris, Albert (1943).
Clairin, Pierre-Eugène (1967).
Corbin, Raymond (1970).
Trémois, Pierre-Yves (1978).

Section V. Musical Composition:
Bondeville, Emmanuel (1959).
Auric, Georges (1962).
Messiaen, Olivier (1967).
Aubin, Tony (1969).
Landowski, Marcel (1975).
Sauguet, Henri (1975).
Gallois-Montbrun, Raymond (1980).

Section VI. Free Members:
Weiller, Paul-Louis (1965).
Palewski, Gaston (1968).
Van Der Kemp, Gérald (1968).
Wildenstein, Daniel (1971).
Dehaye, Pierre (1975).
Gavoty, Bernard (1975).
Bazin, Germain (1976).
Dux, Pierre (1978).

(5) **Académie des Sciences morales et Politiques:** f. 1832 by Louis-Philippe; 50 members, 12 foreign associates, 60 correspondents; Pres. André Piettre; Vice-Pres. Henri Guitton; Perm. Sec. Bernard Chenot; Hon. Perm. Sec. Pierre Clarac; publs. *Revue des Travaux de l'Académie et Comptes Rendus de ses Séances, Ordonnances des Rois de France, Notices biographiques et bibliographiques.*

Members:

Section I. Philosophy:
Poirier, René (1956).
Gouhier, Henri (1961).
Aron, Raymond (1963).
Schuhl, Pierre-Maxime (1970).
Alquié, Ferdinand (1975).
Lacombe, Olivier (1977).
Stoetzel, Jean (1977).

Section II. Moral and Sociological Sciences:
Clarac, Pierre (1964).
Martin-Chauffier, Louis (1964).
Debray, Jean-Robert (1965).
Kaplan, Jacob (1967).
Fourastié, Jean (1968).
Cazeneuve, Jean (1973).
Castex, Pierre-Georges (1974).
Lhermitte, François (1975).

Section III. Legislation, Public Law and Jurisprudence:
Rousselet, Marcel (1959).
Chevallier, Jean-Jacques (1964).
Mazeaud, Henri (1969).
Ancel, Marc (1970).
Waline, Marcel (1970).
Bastid, Suzanne (1971).
Batiffol, Henri (1977).
Brunois, Albert (1977).

Section IV. Political Economy, Statistics and Finance:
Moreau-Néret, Olivier (1946).
Giscard d'Estaing, Edmond (1960).
James, Emile (1966).
Piettre, André (1970).
Guitton, Henri (1971).
Massé, Pierre (1977).
Guindey, Guillaume (1979).

Section V. History and Geography:
Baumont, Maurice (1957).
Duroselle, Jean-Baptiste (1975).
Laloy, Jean (1975).
Le Lannou, Maurice (1975).
Mousnier, Roland (1977).
Amouroux, Henri (1978).
George, Pierre (1980).

Section VI. General Section:
Noël, Léon (1944).
Bonnefous, Edouard (1958).
de Lubac, Henri (1958).
Lapie, Pierre Olivier (1969).
Cullmann, Oscar (1972).
Gambiez, Gén. Fernand (1974).
Chenot, Bernard (1976).
Wormser, Olivier (1978).
Triboulet, Raymond (1979).
Joxe, Louis (1980).

Foreign Associate Members:
Papi, Giuseppe Ugo, Italy (1958)
Erkin, Feridun Cemal, Turkey (1959).
Amoroso Lima, Alceu, Brazil (1967).
Senghor, Léopold, Senegal (1969).
Habsbourg, Otto de (1970).
Balthasar, Hans-Urs von, Switzerland (1974).
Weizsäcker, Carl-Friedrich von, Germany (1974).
Raymond, Marcel, Switzerland (1977).
Tsatsos, Constantin, Greece (1979).

Académie d'Agriculture de France: 18 rue de Bellechasse, Paris 7e; f. 1761; 100 mems. (and 165 Corresp.) attached to sections on Arable Farming, Sylviculture, Animal Economy, Agricultural Economics and Rural Sociology, Physical and Chemical Science, Natural History and Agricultural Engineering; Pres. Gustave Drouineau; Perm. Sec. Pierre Rouveroux; library of 80,000 vols., 500 periodicals; publ. *Comptes rendus des Séances.*

Académie d'Architecture: 9 place des Vosges, 75004 Paris; f. 1840 as Société Centrale des Architectes, name changed 1953; 100 elected mems.; Pres. Robert Auzelle; Gen. Sec. Robert Boitel.

Académie de Chirurgie: 26 blvd. Raspail, 75007 Paris; f. 1935; 88 mems.; library of *c.* 6,000 vols.; Sec.-Gen. Philippe Monod-Broca; publ. *Chirurgie (Mémoires de l'Académie de Chirurgie).*

Académie de Marine: 3 ave. Octave Gréard, Paris 7e; f. 1752; 65 members attached to sections on History, Law, Naval Equipment, Navigation, Military Affairs, Economics, Yachting, Mercantile Marine; Pres. Amiral Rosset; Sec. Amiral Sala.

Académie de Nîmes: 16 rue Dorée, 30000 Nîmes; f. 1682; 60 mems.; library of 7,000 vols.; Pres. Joachim Durand; Perm. Sec. Pierre Hugues; publs. *Bulletin Trimestriel, Mémoires.*

Académie des Jeux Floraux: Hotel d'Assézat, 31000 Toulouse; f. 1323; composed of 40 "mainteneurs" and 25 "Maitres ès Jeux Floraux"; Permanent Sec. Pierre de Gorsse; publ. *Recueil* (annually).

Académie des Lettres et des Arts: c/o Musée de Montmartre, 17 rue Saint Vincent, Paris 18e; f. 1947; 11 mems.; awards the Prix de Paris; Pres. Romain Delahalle.

Académie des Sciences, Agriculture, Arts et Belles-Lettres d'Aix: 2A rue du 4-Septembre, 13100 Aix-en-Provence; f. 1808; library of 100,000 vols.; collections of ceramics, paintings, sculpture and mineral specimens; Pres. Jean Macqueron; Perm. Sec. Georges Souville; publ. *Bulletin*†.

Académie des Sciences, Arts et Belles-Lettres de Dijon: 5 rue de l'Ecole de Droit, 21 Dijon; f. 1740; 50 mems.; small library; Pres. Doyen Jean Richard; Sec. M. Rigault; publs. *Mémoires de l'Académie, Mémoires de la Commission des Antiquités de la Côte d'Or.*

Académie des Sciences, Belles-Lettres et Arts de Lyon: Palais Saint-Jean, 4 ave. Adolphe Max, 69005 Lyons;

f. 1700; 52 elected mems.; library of 60,000 vols.; Pres. MOREL-JOURNEL; Librarian R. WASMER; publ. *Mémoires*† (annually).

Académie des Sciences d'Outre-mer: 15 rue La Pérouse, Paris 16e; f. 1922; 100 mems. attached to sections on Geography, Politics and Administration, Law, Economics and Sociology, Science and Medicine, Education; Pres. RENÉ PLEVEN; Perm. Sec. ROBERT CORNEVIN; publ. *Comptes Rendus*.

Académie du Monde Latin: 217 blvd. Saint-Germain, 75 Paris 7e; aims to encourage contact between leading personalities of countries whose language, culture and civilization are of Latin origin; 100 co-opted mems.; Pres. PAULO DE BERREDO CARNEIRO (Brazil).

Académie Goncourt: Société des gens de Lettres, 38 rue du Faubourg St. Jacques, Paris 14e; f. 1896 by Edmond de Goncourt; composed of 10 members. The prize (5,000 francs) awarded at the end of each year by the Academy is regarded as a very high literary distinction; Pres. HERVÉ BAZIN; Sec.-Gen. ARMAND LANOUX.

Académie Mallarmé: Hôtel de Massa, 38 rue du Faubourg Saint-Jacques, 75014 Paris; 30 mems., 10 corresp.; awards an annual prize in conjunction with the Fondation Yves Rocher; Pres. EUGÈNE GUILLEVIC; Sec.-Gen. MAX-POL FOUCHET.

Académie Montaigne: Le Doyenné, 72140 Sillé-le-Guillaume; f. 1924; for the study of literature; awards an annual prize for research; 20 mems.; Sec. CONSTANT HUBERT.

Académie Nationale de Médecine: 16 rue Bonaparte, 75006 Paris; f. 1820 by Louis XVIII; library of 300,000 vols.; 130 mems. attached to sections on Medicine, Surgery, Hygiene, Science, Social Sciences, Veterinary Medicine, and Pharmacy; Pres. GUILLAUME VALETTE; Perm. Sec. ANDRÉ LEMAIRE; publ. *Bulletin*.

Académie Nationale de Pharmacie de Paris: 4 ave. de l'Observatoire, 75006 Paris; f. 1803; 325 mems.; Pres. A. QUEVAUVILLER; Gen. Sec. Prog. G. VALETTE; publ. *Annales Pharmaceutiques Françaises*.

Académie Vétérinaire de France (CSSF): 60 blvd. Latour-Maubourg, 75007 Paris; f. 1844; 44 mems.; Sec. Prof. J. GUILHON; publ. *Bulletin* (4 a year).

Euskaltzaindia/Académie de la Langue Basque: 15 rue Port-Neuf, 64100 Bayonne. *See also* under Spain, Academies.

LEARNED SOCIETIES

AGRICULTURE AND VETERINARY SCIENCE

Association Centrale des Vétérinaires: 10 place Léon Blum, 75011 Paris; f. 1889; 3,000 mems.; Pres. Prof. C. BRESSOU.

Association Française pour l'Etude du Sol: Centre National de Recherches Agronomiques, Route de St.-Cyr, 78000 Versailles; f. 1934; pedology, agronomy; 760 mems.; Pres. N. LENEUF; publ. *Bulletin* (quarterly).

Société Française d'Economie Rurale: 4 rue Hardy, 78000 Versailles; f. 1949; two study sessions a year; 400 mems.; Pres. Prof. P. MAINIÉ; Sec.-Gen. F. CLERC; publ. *Economie Rurale* (every 2 months).

Société française d'Ichtyologie: 43 rue Cuvier, 75231 Paris Cedex 05; f. 1976; biology and systematics of fish, sea and freshwater fisheries; Pres. J. DAGET; Secs. J. C. HUREAU, J. ALLARDI; publ. *Cybium*† (quarterly).

Société Nationale d'Horticulture de France (SNHF): 84 rue de Grenelle, 75007 Paris; f. 1827; 13,000 mems., 800,000 affiliated mems.; library of 10,000 vols.; Pres. PIERRE SCHNEITER; Gen. Sec. GUY CUENOT; publ. *Jardins de France* (10 a year).

Société Vétérinaire Pratique de France: 10 place Léon Blum, 75011 Paris; f. 1879; 1,800 mems.; Pres. Dr. JACQUES ROZIER; Sec.-Gen. LUCIEN PIGOURY; publ. *Bulletin* (monthly).

ARCHITECTURE AND TOWN PLANNING

Association Nationale pour la Protection des Villes d'Art: 39 ave. de La Motte-Picquet, Paris 7e; f. 1963; an association of local societies in 85 cities for the protection and restoration of historic and artistic buildings; Pres. J. de SACY.

Compagnie des Experts Architectes: près la Cour d'Appel de Paris, 140 ave. Victor Hugo, 75116 Paris; f. 1928; Pres. CHARLES RAMBERT; Gen. Sec. O. LESNE.

Office Général du Bâtiment et des Travaux Publics: 55 ave. Kléber, 75784 Paris Cedex 16; f. 1918; combines the majority of societies, unions and federations of architects and contractors; Pres. P. ALEXANDER.

Ordre des Architectes: 140 ave. Victor Hugo, 75116 Paris; f. 1940 as the official regulating body for the architectural profession; Pres. of Conseil Supérieur ALAIN GILLOT; Sec.-Gen. GUY ROBINE; council of 12 mems.; publ. *Bulletin* (monthly).

Société Française des Architectes: 100 rue du Cherche-Midi, 75270 Paris Cedex 06; f. 1877; 2,000 mems.; Pres. GÉRARD BENOIT; Gen. Sec. GILBERT PICQUENARD; publs. *Architecture, Mouvement, Continuité* (quarterly).

Société Nationale des Architectes de France: f. 1872; professional union; 500 members; Pres. J.-F. BELLAT, Membre du Conseil Régional de l'Ordre de Paris, 8 rue Albert Samain, 75017 Paris; Gen. Sec. ROGER LAINE; publ. *Le Moniteur des Architectes—Bulletin de la Société Nationale*.

Société pour la Protection des Paysages et de l'Esthétique de la France: 39 ave. de La Motte-Picquet, Paris 7e; f. 1901; publ. *Sites et Monuments* (quarterly).

THE ARTS

Académie de Philatélie: 66 blvd. Raspail, Paris 6e; publ. *Documents Philatéliques*.

Association Française pour la Recherche et la Création Musicales: 9 rue Chaptal, Paris 9e; f. 1971 to encourage and sustain musical research and innovation; Pres. FRANÇOIS BAYLE; Vice-Pres. ANDRÉ JOUVE; Sec.-Gen. FRANÇOIS DELALANDE.

Jeunesses Musicales de France: 14 rue François-Miron, 75004 Paris; f. 1944; encourages young audiences, promotes concerts, etc.; Pres. LOUIS LEPRINCE-RINGUET; Dir. JEAN-PIERRE DE LAVIGNE; 38,000 mems.; publ. *J.M.F. Informations*.

Ordre des Musiciens: 121 rue la Fayette, Paris 10e; Pres. A. EHRMANN; Sec.-Gen. Mme. VIGUÉE.

Société d'Histoire du Théâtre: 98 blvd. Kellermann, 75013 Paris; f. 1948; *c.* 1,000 mems.; library of 40,000 vols.; Pres. JEAN-LOUIS BARRAULT; Sec. Gen. ROSE MARIE MOUDOUES; publ. *Revue d'Histoire du Théâtre*† (quarterly).

Société de l'Histoire de l'Art Français (CSSF): Pavillon de Marsan, 107 rue de Rivoli, 75001 Paris; f. 1870; 800 mems.; Pres. SYLVIE BEGUIN; Gen. Sec. BRUNO FOUCART; publs. *Bulletin* and *Archives de l'Art Français*.

Société des Amis du Louvre: 107 rue de Rivoli, 75001 Paris; f. 1897; 18,500 members; Pres. JACQUES DUPONT; Sec.-Gen. PHILIPPE GANGNAT; publ. *Chronique*.

Société des Artistes Décorateurs (SAD): ave. Winston Churchill, Paris 8e; f. 1901 to promote modern art; 350 mems.; Pres. JEAN-PIERRE KHALIFA.

Société des Artistes Français: Grand Palais des Champs-Elysées, Paris 8e; f. 1882; 4,000 members; its exhibition is held at the beginning of the spring; Pres. G. MUGUET; Gen. Sec. J. GUERIS; publ. *Bulletin*.

Société des Artistes Indépendants: Grand Palais des Champs-Elysées, Ave. Winston Churchill, Porte H, Paris 8e; f. 1884; 2,500 members; unites the majority of artists of modern tendency; annual exhibition of painting, sculpture, engravings and decorative art; Pres. JEAN MONNERET; Gen. Sec. MARGUERITE FELLOWS SHARON D'OBREMER.

Société des Auteurs, Compositeurs et Editeurs de Musique: 10 rue Chaptal, 75441 Paris, Cedex 09; f. 1851; 28,000 mems.; deals with collection and distribution of performing rights; Pres. HENRI CONTET; Dir.-Gen. JEAN-LOUP TOURNIER.

Société du Salon d'Automne: Grand Palais, porte H, Paris 8e; f. 1903; sections: painting, sculpture, architecture; Pres. MAC AVOY.

Société Française de Musicologie: 2 rue Louvois, 75002 Paris; f. 1917; 550 mems.; Pres. MARC HONEGGER; Sec.-Gen. NICOLE SEVESTRE; publs. *Revue* (semi-annually), *Publications* (37 vols.).

Société Française de Photographie et Cinématographie: 9 rue Montalembert, Paris 7e; f. 1854; 1,200 mems.; library of 4,600 vols.; Pres. Prof. J.-J. TRILLAT.

Société Nationale de Musique: 45 rue de la Boétie, Paris 8e; f. 1871; 135 members; Pres. P. LE FLEM; Sec. HENRI MARTELLI.

Société Nationale des Beaux-Arts: Fondation S. de Rothschild, 11 rue Berryer, Paris 8e; f. 1890; organizes art exhibitions; Pres. FRANÇOIS BABOULET; Gen. Sec. JEAN NAVARRE; Treas. JEAN-PIERRE ALAUX.

Union Centrale des Arts Décoratifs: Pavillon de Marsan, 107 rue de Rivoli, Paris 1er; f. 1882; 3,000 members; library of 80,000 vols.; Pres. ROBERT BORDAZ; Curator of Museum F. MATHEY; Sec.-Gen. PIERRE MEILHAC; Librarian G. PICON.

BIBLIOGRAPHY, LIBRARY SCIENCE AND MUSEOLOGY

Association de l'Ecole Nationale Supérieure de Bibliothécaires: 17–21 blvd. du 11 novembre 1918, 69100 Villeurbanne; f. 1967; organizes conferences, study groups, study tours, etc. and collaborates with other similar bodies to further research and training in all aspects of librarianship; 600 mems.; Pres. J.-M. ARNOULT; Secs. Y. VALIN, P.-J. LAMBLIN; publ. *Annuaire*.

Association des Archivistes Français: 60 rue des Francs-Bourgeois, 75141 Paris Cedex 03; f. 1904; 600 mems.; Pres. H. CHARNIER; Secs. Mme A.-L. REY, Mlle G. ETIENNE; publ. *La Gazette des Archives* (quarterly).

Association des Bibliothécaires Français (CSSF): 65 rue de Richelieu, 75002 Paris; f. 1906; 2,500 mems.; Gen. Sec. Mlle M. BEAUDIQUEZ; publs. *A. B. F. Bulletin d'Informations* (quarterly), *Documents A.B.F.*

Association Générale des Conservateurs des Collections Publiques de France: Palais du Louvre, Pavillon Mollien, Paris 1er; f. 1932 to promote and improve museums and museums' administration; 850 mems.; Gen. Sec. FRANÇOISE AMANIEUX.

Centre d'Archives et de Documentation Politiques et Sociales: 86 blvd. Haussmann, 75008 Paris; f. 1949; Dir. Dr. G. ALBERTINI; publs. *Informations Politiques et Sociales* (weekly in France, Africa and Asia), *Est et Ouest* (monthly), *Le Monde des Conflits* (monthly).

Société Internationale de Bibliographie Classique: 11 ave. René Coty, Paris 14e; f. 1948; Gen. Sec. JULIETTE ERNST; Admin. P. PETITMENGIN; publs. *L'Année Philologique* (*Bibliographie de l'antiquité gréco-latine 1923 ss.*).

ECONOMICS, LAW AND POLITICS

Association d'Etudes et d'Informations Politiques Internationales: 86 blvd. Haussmann, Paris 8e; f. 1949; Dir. G. ALBERTINI; publs. *Est & Ouest* (Paris, twice monthly), *Documenti sul Comunismo* (Rome), *Este y Oeste* (Caracas).

Centre d'Etudes de la Socio-Economie: 19 blvd. de Courcelles, Paris 8°; f. 1961; Pres. JACQUES BASSOT; Sec. R. GAZAGNE.

Fondation Nationale des Sciences Politiques: 27 rue Saint Guillaume, 75341 Paris Cedex 07; f. 1945; administers the Institut d'Etudes Politiques de Paris (*q.v.*), promotes research centres and political science studies, documentation service; library of 500,000 vols.; Pres. FRANÇOIS GOGUEL; Admin. J. CHAPSAL; Gen. Sec. S. HURTIG; publs. *Revue Française de Science Politique* (every 2 months), *Bulletin Analytique de Documentation* (monthly).

Institut des Actuaires Français: 5 rue de Rome, 75008 Paris; f. 1890; 385 mems.; library of 5,000 vols.; Pres. JEAN LAMSON; Gen. Sec. CLAUDE BEBEAR; publ. *Bulletin trimestriel*.

Institut d'Histoire Sociale: 15 ave. Raymond Poincaré, 75116 Paris; library of 22,000 vols. specializing in political sciences and history of workers' movements since beginning of 19th century, trade union periodicals and political reviews; Librarian P. HUMBERT-DROZ.

Institut Français des Relations Internationales: 6 rue Ferrus, 76014 Paris; f. 1979; 500 mems.; library of 28,000 vols.; Dir. THIERRY DE MONTBRIAL; publ. *Politique Etrangère*† (quarterly).

Société d'Economie et de Science Sociales: 4 place de Breteuil, Paris 15e; f. 1856; concerned with social reforms and sociology; 300 mems.; Pres. EDOUARD SECRETAN; publ. *Les Etudes Sociales*† (quarterly).

Société d'Economie Politique: c/o Librairie Sirey, 22 rue Soufflot, Paris 5e; Pres. D. VILLEY; publ. *Annales d'Economie Politique*.

SEDEIS (Société d'Etudes et de Documentation Economiques, Industrielles et Sociales): 44 rue François I, 75008 Paris; f. 1948; economic, industrial and social studies; Pres. JACQUES PLASSARD; publs. *Chroniques d'Actualité*, *Analyses de la SEDEIS*.

Société d'Etudes Jaurésiennes: 131 rue de l'Abbé-Groult, 75015 Paris; f. 1959 to promote all aspects of the life and works of Jean Jaurès; promotes the publication or re-edition of his speeches and writings; Sec.-Gen. JEAN-PIERRE RIOUX; publ. *Bulletin* (quarterly).

Société d'Etudes pour le Développement Economique et Social: 84 rue de Lille, Paris 7e; f. 1958; 215 mems.; library of 15,000 vols.; Pres. R. MERCIER; Gen. Man. J. BOULARD.

Société d'Histoire du Droit (CSSF): 158 rue Saint Jacques, 75005 Paris; f. 1913; 450 mems.; Pres. Prof. ROBERT VILLERS; Sec. O. GUILLOT; publs. *Chartes de franchises de la France*, *Recueils de jurisprudence du Moyen-Age*, works on the history of law, institutions, political thought.

Société de Législation Comparée (CSSF): 28 rue St. Guillaume, 75007 Paris; f. 1869; comparative law; library of 100,000 vols.; 1,700 mems.; Pres. ROLAND DRAGO; Gen. Sec. XAVIER BLANC-JOUVAN; publ. *Revue Internationale de Droit Comparé*† (quarterly).

Sociétés de Statistique de Paris et de France (CSSF): 29 rue de Rome, 75008 Paris; f. 1860; 1,040 mems.; library of 60,000 vols.; Gen. Sec. JACQUES-MICHEL DURAND; Librarian Mlle LEBLANC; publs. *Journal, Revue trimestrielle internationale des statisticiens d'expression française.*

EDUCATION

Association Française pour le Développement de l'Enseignement Technique: 42 rue de Bellechasse, Paris 7e; publ. *L'Enseignement Technique.*

Association Francophone d'Education Comparée: 1 ave. Léon Journault, 92310 Sèvres; f. 1973 to promote comparative education in French-speaking countries; organizes three seminars a year and participates in meetings of the Comparative Education Society in Europe and the World Council of Comparative Educational Societies; Pres. MICHEL DEBEAUVAIS; Sec.-Gen. JACQUES POUJOL; publs. *Bulletin, Proceedings of Seminars* (3 a year).

Association Universitaire pour la Diffusion Internationale de la Recherche: Presses de la Fondation nationale des sciences politiques, 27 rue Saint-Guillaume, 75341 Paris Cedex 07; f. 1972 to circulate scientific information in the field of human sciences by publishing (in micro-fiche) hitherto unpublished research work of all kinds; 25 mems.; Pres. PIERRE DEYON; Sec.-Gen. FRANÇOIS FURET; publs. catalogues.

Conférence des Présidents d'Université: 12 rue de l'Ecole de Médecine, 75006 Paris; f. 1971; consultative body at the disposition of the Minister of Education; also studies questions of interest to all universities and co-ordinates the activities of various commissions on all aspects of education; mems.: 74 Presidents of universities and State institutions; Pres. The Minister for Universities.

Fondation Biermans-Lapôtre: 9A blvd. Jourdan, 75690 Paris Cedex 14; f. 1924; promotes academic and scientific exchanges between France and Belgium; offers grants, etc.; affiliated to Fondation Universitaire (*see* Belgium chapter); Pres. Baron PATERNOTTE DE LA VAILLÉE; Dir. HENRI VAN ZEVEREN.

Fondation Calouste Gulbenkian: 51 ave. d'Iéna, Paris 16e; f. 1955; non-profit-making; awards grants in the fields of education, art, science and charity; attached to Calouste Gulbenkian Foundation in Lisbon (*q.v.*); library of 40,000 vols.; Dir. Prof. JOSÉ V. DE PINA MARTINS.

Ligue Internationale de l'Enseignement, de l'Education et de la Culture Populaire: *see* under International.

Office National d'Information sur les Enseignements et les Professions: 50 rue Albert, 75013 Paris; f. 1970; Dir. C. VIMONT; publs. *Avenirs, Communiqué, Bulletin d'Information et de Documentation Scolaire et Professionnelle, Réadaption.*

Société Française de Pédagogie: I.N.R.D.P., 29 rue d'Ulm, 75005 Paris; f. 1902; 10,000 mems.; studies educational theories and teaching methods; Pres. M. BONISSEL; Gen. Sec. M. GEVREY; publ. *Bulletin Trimestriel.*

Société Générale d'Education et d'Enseignement: 14 *bis* rue d'Assas, Paris 6e; f. 1868; publ. *L'Enseignement Libre.*

Union des Professeurs de Spéciales (Mathématiques et Sciences Physiques): O.F.R.A.T.E.M., 29 rue d'Ulm, 75230 Paris Cedex 05; f. 1928; 1,000 mems.; Pres. M. SIMON; Sec. M. SELLIER.

HISTORY, GEOGRAPHY AND ARCHAEOLOGY

General

Comité Scientifique du Club Alpin Français: 9 rue La Boétie, 75008 Paris; f. 1874; 20 mems.; Dir. J. MALBOS.

Fédération Française de Spéléologie: 130 rue Saint-Maur; Paris 11e; f. 1963; 6,000 mems.; library of 2,000 vols., publs. *Spelunca Bulletin, Mémoires.*

Société d'Ethnographie de Paris: 6 rue Champfleury, 75007 Paris; 400 mems.; publ. *L'Ethnographie* (2 a year).

Société d'Ethnologie Française: 6 route du Mahatma Gandhi, 75116 Paris; 300 mems.; Pres. C. MARCEL-DUBOIS; Sec.-Gen. M. SEGALEN; publ. *Ethnologie Française* (quarterly).

Société Française de Numismatique: Bibliothèque Nationale, Cabinet des Médailles, 58 rue de Richelieu, 75084 Paris Cedex 02; f. 1865; 700 mems.; Pres. DANIEL NONY; Gen. Sec. XAVIER LORIOT; publs. *Revue Numismatique, Bulletin Mensuel*†.

Société Historique, Archéologique et Littéraire de Lyon: Mairie Centrale de Lyon, 69000 Lyon; f. 1807; Pres. H. HOURS; Sec. Mlle J. ROUBERT; publ. *Bulletin.*

Archaeology

Société Française d'Archéocivilisation et de Folklore: Ecole des Hautes Etudes en Sciences Sociales, 54 blvd. Raspail, Paris 6e; f. 1946; Pres. ANDRÉ VARAGNAC; Gen. Sec. Mme CHOLLOT-VARAGNAC; publ. *Archéocivilisation* (semi-annually).

Société Française d'Archéologie (CSSF): Musée National des Monuments Français, Palais de Chaillot, Paris 16e; f. 1834; 2,800 mems.; Pres. JEAN CHATELAIN; Dir. FRANCIS SALET; Gen. Sec. PIERRE MACHERAS; publs. *Bulletin Monumental* (quarterly), *Congrès Archéologiques de France* (annually).

Société Française d'Egyptologie: Collège de France, place Marcelin-Berthelot, 75231 Paris Cedex 05; f. 1923; 850 mems.; Pres. J. YOYOTTE; Sec. P. VERNUS; publs. *Bulletin, Revue d'Egyptologie.*

Société Nationale des Antiquaires de France (CSSF): Palais du Louvre, Pavillon Mollien, 75001 Paris; f. 1803; 55 elected mems. and 350 correspondents; history, philology and archaeology of Antiquity and the Middle Ages; publs. *Bulletin de la Société nationale des Antiquaires de France* (annual), *Mémoires de la Société nationale des Antiquaires de France* (irregular).

Geography

Association de Géographes Français (CSSF): 191 rue St. Jacques, Paris 5e; f. 1920; 700 mems.; Pres. P. BIROT; Sec. J. DEMANGEOT; publs. *Bulletin Mensuel, Bibliographie géographique annuelle.*

Comité National Français de Géographie: 191 rue Saint-Jacques, Paris 5e; co-ordinates French geographical activity and participates in the work of the International Geographical Union; 250 mems.; Pres. A. JOURNAUX; Sec.-Gen. E. DALMASSO; publ. *Bibliographie Géographique Internationale* (published jointly with the International Geographical Union).

Institut Géographique National: 136 *bis* rue de Grenelle, 75700 Paris; f. 1940; aerial and ground surveys, map printing; national map and aerial photograph library; administers *Ecole Nat. des Sciences Géographiques (q.v.)*; 2,500 staff mems.; Dir.-Gen. RENÉ MAYER; publ. *Bulletin d'Information* (quarterly).

Société de Biogéographie: 57 rue Cuvier, 75231 Paris Cedex 05; f. 1924; 350 mems.; Sec.-Gen. Dr. CL. SASTRE; publs. *Compte Rendu des Séances, Mémoires hors série.*

Société de Géographie: 184 blvd. St.-Germain, Paris 6e; f. 1821; library of 500,000 vols. at 8 rue des Petits Champs, Paris 2e (Librarian Mlle DE LA RONCIÈRE); 900 mems.; Pres. M. BLAIS; Sec.-Gen. M. CHARTIER; publ. *Acta Geographica*† (quarterly).

Société de Géographie Commerciale de Paris: 8 rue Roquépine, Paris 8e; f. 1873; Pres. JULIEN BRUNHES; Vice-Pres. Dr. ROBERT PIROT; library 2,000 vols.; publ. *Revue Economique Française* (quarterly).

Société des Amis de la Revue de Géographie de Lyon: 74 rue Pasteur, Lyon 7e; f. 1923; Pres. JACQUES BETHEMONT; publ. *Revue de Géographie de Lyon*† (quarterly).

Société des Océanistes: Musée de l'Homme, Palais de Chaillot, 75116 Paris; f. 1938; 560 mems.; Pres. JEAN GUIART; Sec.-Gen. JOSÉ GARANGER; publs. *Journal*† (quarterly), *Publications*.

History

Association Marc Bloch: 54 blvd. Raspail, 75006 Paris; f. 1949; for the study of the history of civilization; Pres. F. FURET; Vice-Pres. G. FRIEDMANN, P. LEUILLIOT; publ. *Annales Economies Sociétés Civilisations*, jointly with Centre de Recherches Historiques, Ecole des Hautes Etudes en Sciences Sociales.

Centre International d'Etudes Romanes: 43 rue Boissonade, Paris 14e; f. 1952; 1,000 mems.; Pres. Prof. MARCEL GUILLOT; Sec.-Gen. Mlle M. CHAVANON; publ. *Bulletin* (quarterly).

Deutsches Historisches Institut: 9 rue Maspéro, 75016 Paris; f. 1958; library of 42,000 vols.; publs. *Francia* (annually), *Pariser Historische Studien, Dokumentation Westeuropa, Documentations et Recherches, Beihefte der Francia* (all monograph series).

Institut des Sciences Historiques: Société Archéologique de France, 169 rue St.-Jacques, Paris 5e; f. 1816; 150 mems.; Dir.-Gen. JEAN-PASCAL ROMAIN; Dir.-Gen.-Adj. HENRY DE SERVIGNAT; publ. *La Science Historique* (3 a year).

Institut Français d'Etudes Byzantines: 8 rue François-1er, Paris 8e; f. 1897; Byzantine research, particularly on sources of ecclesiastical history; 4 mems.; library of 50,000 vols.; publ. *Revue des Etudes Byzantines*† (annually).

Institut Français d'Histoire Sociale: Archives Nationales, Hôtel de Rohan, 87 rue Vieille-du-Temple, 75003 Paris; f. 1948; 142 mems.; library of 8,000 vols., 20,000 pamphlets, large collection of periodicals and manuscripts; Pres. PHILIPPE VIGIER; Vice-Pres. HENRI BARTOLI; Sec. D. FAUVEL-ROUIF.

La Demeure Historique: Hôtel de Nesmond, 55 quai de la Tournelle, Paris 5e; f. 1924; 1,400 members; study, research and conservation of historic buildings, châteaux, etc.; Pres. Prince de BEAUVEAU-CRAON; publ. *La Demeure Historique* (quarterly).

Société d'Emulation du Bourbonnais: Hôtel de Ville, 03000 Moulins; f. 1846; 600 mems.; library of 11,000 vols.; Pres. Mme H. DUSSOURD; publ. *Bulletin* (quarterly).

Société d'Etude du XVIIe Siècle: c/o Collège de France, 11 place Marcelin-Berthelot, 75231 Paris Cedex 05; f. 1948; 1,000 mems.; Pres. J. MESNARD; publ. *XVIIe Siècle* (quarterly).

Société d'Histoire Générale et d'Histoire Diplomatique: 13 rue Soufflot, Paris 5e; f. 1887; publ. *Revue d'Histoire Diplomatique*.

Société d'Histoire Moderne (CSSF): 5 Villa Poirier, 75015 Paris; f. 1901; Pres. F.-G. PARISET; Sec.-Gen. PHILIPPE GUT; 1,100 mems.; 16th–20th century French and foreign history; publs. *Bulletin-Revue d'Histoire Moderne et Contemporaine* (4 parts a year).

Société de l'Histoire de France: Ecole des Chartes, 19 rue de la Sorbonne, Paris 5e; f. 1834; Pres. Général GAMBIEZ; Sec. MICHEL FRANÇOIS; publs. *Annuaires-Bulletins, Mémoires, Textes inédits de l'histoire de France*.

Société des Etudes Historiques (CSSF): 44 rue de Rennes, Paris 6e; f. 1833; Pres. CHRISTIAN SCHAFFER; Sec.-Gen. M. DEBORDE DE MONTGORIN; Dir. EMM. RODOCANACHI; publ. *Revue des Études Historiques*.

Société Française d'Histoire d'Outre-Mer (formerly Société de l'Histoire des Colonies Françaises): B.P. 107, 75022 Paris Cedex 01; f. 1912; 500 mems.; Pres. JEAN DEVISSE; Sec.-Gen. MARC MICHEL; publ. *Revue Française d'Histoire d'Outre-Mer* (quarterly).

Société Internationale d'Etudes Historiques Cercle Louis XVII: Hôtel des Sociétés Savantes, 28 rue Serpente, Paris 6e.

Vieilles Maisons Françaises: 93 rue de l'Université, 75007 Paris; the society seeks to bring together all those who own buildings of historical interest and those who help to preserve them; 16,000 mems.; Hon. Pres. Marquise de AMODIO; Pres. Y. DE LACRETELLE; publ. *Revue* (quarterly).

INTERNATIONAL CULTURAL INSTITUTES

Alliance Française: 101 blvd. Raspail, 75270 Paris Cedex 06; f. 1883; the oldest-established French language school for foreigners; affiliated to the University of Paris; 34,000 students; library of 10,000 vols.; Pres. MARC BLANCPAIN; Sec.-Gen. PHILIPPE GREFFET; Dir. of the School MAURICE BRUÉZIÈRE; publ. *Bulletin Pédagogique* (quarterly).

Association France-Amérique: 9-11 ave. Franklin-Roosevelt, Paris 8e; f. 1909; 4,500 mems.; 2,500 vols.; Pres. HUBERT MARTIN; publ. *France-Amérique* (quarterly).

Association France-Grande-Bretagne: 17 rue Philibert Delorme, 75017 Paris; f. 1916; Pres. H. E. GEOFFROY DE COURCEL; Sec.-Gen. Prof. ROBERT WIEDER.

Association France-Yemen: 1 *bis* rue Saint-Julien le Pauvre, 75005 Paris; f. 1969; 100 mems.; Pres. J. CHELHOD; publ. *Bulletin France-Yemen*.

Association Internationale pour la Culture Française: 32 rue de Babylone, 75007 Paris; f. 1952; 400 mems.; Pres. A. VIATTE; Gen. Sec. R. LACOMBE; publ. *Culture Française*† (quarterly).

British Council: 9 rue de Constantine, 75007 Paris; libraries (*see* Libraries); Rep. B. W. SWINGLER, C.B.E.

Bureau International de Liaison et de Documentation (BILD): 50 rue de Laborde, Paris 8e; f. 1945 to promote international exchanges and social and cultural studies; French branch of Gesellschaft für Übernationale Zusammenarbeit (*q.v.*); organizes conferences, study groups, exchange holidays, etc. between France and Germany; Pres. FRANÇOIS BOUREL; Sec.-Gen. ROLAND MAGER; publs. *Documents, Revue des questions allemands*.

Goethe Institut: 17 ave. d'Iéna, 75116 Paris; German language courses, cultural programme; library of 40,000 vols.; Dir. Dr. GÜNTER BÄR.

Institut Autrichien: 30 blvd. des Invalides, Paris 7e; f. 1954; library of 12,000 vols.; Dir. ALEXANDER AUER.

Institut Collégial Européen, dit de Royaumont: Secretariat: Logis des Montains, 37600 Loches; f. 1950; Chair. Prof. A. LICHNÉROWICZ; Dir. Prof. G. GADOFFRE; research seminars and conferences at Loches, Versailles, and the College de France.

Institut Néerlandais: 121 rue de Lille, Paris 7e; f. 1956 by F. LUGT; library of 22,000 vols.; cultural activities; Dir. J. VAN PRAAG; Librarian Mme M. FRANÇOIS.

Istituto Italiano di Cultura: 50 rue de Varenne, Paris 7e; library of 14,000 vols.; Dir. Prof. FERNANDO CARUSO; publ. *Notiziario Culturale Italiano* (quarterly).

Société d'Etudes Hispaniques et de Diffusion de la Culture Française à l'Etranger: 65 rue Solférino, 24000 Périgueux; publ. *Gallia-Hispania*.

Language and Literature

Association des Ecrivains Combattants: 8 rue Roquépine, Paris 8e; f. 1919; 470 mems.; Pres. Pierre Chanlaine; Sec. Maurice-Ch. Renard; publ. *Bulletin.*

Association des Ecrivains de langue française (Mer et Outre-Mer) (*Association of Writers in the French Language*): 38 rue du Faubourg-Saint-Jacques, 75014 Paris; f. 1926 as "Société des romanciers et auteurs coloniaux français" to bring together writers outside France who use the French language; awards 13 literary prizes; 1,600 mems. in 59 countries; Pres. Robert Cornevin; Sec.-Gen. André Teulières; publ. *Annuaire.*

Association Française des Professeurs de Langues Vivantes: c/o INRDP, 29 rue d'Ulm, Paris 5e; f. 1902; 5,800 mems.; Pres. M. Hardin; Gen. Sec. M. Arrouays; publ. *Les Langues Modernes*† (two-monthly).

Association Guillaume Budé (CSSF): 95 blvd. Raspail, 75006 Paris; f. 1917; 5,000 mems.; publishes ancient Greek, Latin, Byzantine, Indian, Arabic, Chinese, French and English classical texts with French translations and studies on history, philology and archaeology; Pres. F. Robert; Vice-Pres. J. Heurgon, Mme. J. de Romilly; periodical publs. *Bulletin* and *Lettres d'Humanité.*

Centre National des Académies et Associations Littéraires et Savantes des Provinces Françaises: Musée des Arts et Traditions Populaires, Route de Madrid, Paris 16e.

Centre National des Lettres: 6 rue Dufrénoy, 75116 Paris; f. 1946, present name 1973, to uphold and encourage the work of French writers; to give financial help to writers, editors and public libraries; to promote translation into French; Pres. M. Vandevoorde; Sec.-Gen. M. Charpillon.

Maison de Poésie (*Fondation Emile Blémont*): 11 *bis* rue Ballu, Paris 9e; f. 1928; Pres. Mme George-Day; library of 16,000 vols.; annual prizes: Prix Petitdidier (300 francs), Prix Emile Blémont (100 francs), Prix Paul Verlaine (100 francs), Prix Edgar Poe (100 francs), Prix Gabriel Vicaire (100 francs), Prix Léon Riotor (100 francs), Prix Van Lerberghe (100 francs), Prix Fernand Dauphin (150 francs).

Organisation de la Jeunesse Esperantiste Française (J.E.F.O.): 4 *bis* rue de la Cerisaie, 75004 Paris; f. 1970; promotes Esperanto among young people; 218 mems.; Pres. François Lo Jacomo; Sec. Marie-Christine Fouchereau; publ. *Koncize* (every 2 months).

PEN International (Centre français): 6 rue François Miron, 75004 Paris; f. 1921; Pres. René Tavernier; Sec. Dimitri Stolypine; publ. *Bulletin* (every 2 months).

Société d'Etudes Dantesques: Centre Universitaire Méditerranéen, 65 Promenade-des-Anglais, Nice; f. 1935; Sec.-Gen. Simon Lorenzi; publ. *Bulletin.*

Société d'Histoire Littéraire de la France (CSSF): 14 rue de l'Industrie, 75013 Paris; f. 1894; 300 mems.; Pres. R. Pomeau; publs. *Revue d'Histoire Littéraire de la France* (alternate months); *Bibliographie de la Littérature française* (annually).

Société de Linguistique de Paris (CSSF): Ecole Pratique des Hautes Etudes, 4e section, Sorbonne, 47 rue des Ecoles, Paris 5e; f. 1864; 750 mems.; Sec. Prof. J. Perrot; Admin. Prof. A. Crépin; publs. *Collection Linguistique, Bulletin.*

Société des Anciens Textes Français (CSSF): 19 rue de la Sorbonne, Paris 5e; f. 1875; 800 mems.; Pres. Prof. A. Vernet; Dir. Prof. F. Lecoy; Gen. Sec. Prof. J. Monfrin.

Société des Auteurs et Compositeurs Dramatiques: 11 *bis* rue Ballu, Paris 9e; f. 1791; Pres. Alain Decaux; publ. *Bulletin.*

Société des Etudes Latines (CSSF): 1 rue Victor-Cousin, 75230 Paris Cedex 05; f. 1923; Dir. P. Grimal; publs. *Revue des Etudes Latines, Collection d'études latines.*

Société des Gens de Lettres: Hôtel de Massa, 38 rue du Faubourg St. Jacques, 75014 Paris; f. 1838; Pres. Paul Mousset; Gen. Sec. Jacques Bens.

Société des Poètes Français: 38 rue du Faubourg St. Jacques, Paris 14e; f. 1902; 1,600 mems.; presents prizes annually; Hon. Pres. Marthe-Claire Fleury; publ. *Bulletin trimestriel.*

Syndicat des Critiques Littéraires: 58 rue Claude Bernard, 75005 Paris; f. 1949; 165 mems.; Pres. Michel Décaudin; Sec. R. André; publ. *Bulletin du Syndicat* (quarterly).

Union Culturelle et Technique de Langue Française: 47 blvd. Lannes, Paris 16e; f. 1954; to promote the French language and co-operation amongst French-speaking organizations and individuals throughout the world; small library; Pres. Mme Jaudoin-Prom; publ. *Lisez et Choisissez.*

Union des Ecrivains et Artistes Latins: 11 rue de l'Estrapade, Paris 5e; f. 1957 to preserve Latin culture and civilization in all its forms, maintains regional traditions and the "Langue d'Oc"; Pres. L. Amargier; Sec. M. Decremps; publs. *France Latine* and books in Langue d'Oc.

Medicine

Association des Anatomistes (CNRS): B.P. 184, 54500 Vandoeuvre-les-Nancy; f. 1899; 1,003 mems.; Gen. Sec. Prof. E. Legait; publ. *Bulletin* (triennially).

Association Française d'Urologie: c/o 60 blvd. Latour-Maubourg, 75327 Paris Cedex 07; f. 1896; 403 mems.; Hon. Pres. R. Gouverneur; Pres. J. Cibert; Vice-Pres. R. Couvelaire; Sec.-Gen. P. Delinotte; publ. *Mémoires* (annually).

Association Française pour l'Etude du Cancer: 26 rue d'Ulm, 75231 Paris Cedex 05; f. 1920; 255 mems.; quarterly meetings, annual symposium; offers grants to doctors from abroad or French doctors for work abroad; publ. *Bulletin du Cancer.*

Association Générale des Médecins de France: 60 boulevard de Latour-Maubourg, Paris 7e; Pres. P. Baudouin; Sec. Dr. Touchard; publ. *Bulletin.*

Association pour le Développement des Relations Médicales entre la France et les Pays Etrangers: 12 rue Ecole de Médecine, Paris 6e.

Centre d'Etude de l'Expression: Clinique des Maladies Mentales et de l'Encéphale, 100 rue de la Santé, 75014 Paris; f. 1973 to develop psychopathological and psychological studies of various forms of expression: plastic, verbal, mimic, body-language, musical, theatrical; Pres. Prof. P. Pichot; Sec.-Gen. C. Wiart.

Centre d'étude et d'enseignement de la Méthode Naturelle en Médecine: 27 rue Casimir Périer, 75007 Paris; f. 1962; study and teaching of the natural method in medicine, hygiene, education, agriculture; Founder-Pres. Dr. André Schlemmer; publs. *Les Cahiers de la Méthode Naturelle en Médecine* (quarterly), *Réunion d'Etudes Médicales.*

Comité National contre la Tuberculose et les Maladies Respiratoires: 66 blvd. Saint-Michel, Paris 6e; f. 1916; 600 mems.; Dir.-Gen. H. Coudreau; publ. *Bulletin* (quarterly).

Confédération des Syndicats Médicaux Français: 60 boulevard de Latour-Maubourg, Paris 7e; f. 1930; 30,000 members; Pres. Dr. J. Monier; Sec.-Gen. Dr. J. Beaupere; publs. *Bulletin, Le Médecin de France.*

Ecole Française d'Acupuncture (E.F.A.): 2 rue du Général de Larminat, 75015 Paris; f. 1945 as Société d'Acupuncture; 1,000 mems.; Pres. Dr. Georges Cantoni; Sec.-Gen. Dr. Olivo; publ. *Méridiens* (quarterly).

Fédération des Gynécologues et Obstétriciens de Langue Française: Clinique Baudelocque, 123 blvd. de Port Royal, 75014 Paris; f. 1950; 2,000 mems.; Pres. Prof. P. MAGNIN (Lyon); Sec.-Gen. Prof. C. SUREAU (Paris); publ. *Journal de Gynécologie Obstétrique et Biologie de la Reproduction* (8 a year).

Fédération Nationale des Syndicats Départementaux de Médecins Electro-Radiologistes Qualifiés: 60 blvd. Latour-Maubourg, 75327 Paris Cedex 07; f. 1907; 2,300 mems.; Pres. Dr. J. MOINARD; publ. *Bulletin.*

Société d'Electroencéphalographie et de Neurophysiologie, Clinique de Langue Française: 120 blvd. St.-Germain, 75280 Paris Cedex 06; f. 1948; 400 mems.; Pres. Dr. J. RADERMECKER; Sec.-Gen. Prof. J. CADILHAC; publ. *Revue d'E.E.G.* (quarterly).

Societe d'Histoire de la Pharmacie: 4 ave. de l'Observatoire, 75270 Paris Cedex 06; f. 1913; 1,300 mems.; Pres. M. VALETTE; Sec. M. BONNEMAIN; publ. *Revue d'Histoire de la Pharmacie* (quarterly).

Société d'Ophtalmologie de Paris: 108 rue du Bac, 75007 Paris; f. 1888; Sec. Gen. Dr. JEAN-PAUL BOISSIN; publ. *Bulletin.*

Société de chirurgie thoracique et cardio-vasculaire de langue française: 129 rue de Tolbiac, 75013 Paris; Sec.-Gen. J. LANGLOIS.

Société de Dermatologie et Syphilographie: 37 rue Galilée, Paris 16e; Pres. M. GASTINEL; Sec. M. DEGOS.

Société de Gastronomie Médicale: 5 rue Berryer, Paris 8e.

Société de Médecine de Paris: 109 rue de Bellevue 92100 Boulogne Billancourt; f. 1796; Sec.-Gen. Dr. G. CARRAUD; publs. *Bulletin, Mémoires.*

Société de Médecine de Strasbourg: Faculté de Médecine, 4 rue Kirschleger, 67085 Strasbourg Cedex; f. 1919; 450 mems.; organizes medical conferences; Sec.-Gen. E. FORSTER; Secs. Dr. GANDAR, Dr. MOISE; publ. monthly bulletin.

Société de Médecine Légale et de Criminologie de France: 2 place Mazas, 75012 Paris; f. 1868; Pres. P. MICHAUX; Sec. A. HADENGUE; publs. *Médecine légale, Toxicologie.*

Société Médico-Chirurgicale des Hôpitaux et Formations Sanitaires des Armées: 277 *bis* rue St. Jacques, Paris 5e; f. 1969; publ. *Bulletin.*

Société de Neurochirurgie de Langue Française: 60 blvd. Latour-Maubourg, 75007 Paris; f. 1948; 500 mems.; Pres. P. JANNY; Sec. C. LAPRAS; publ. *Neurochirurgie* (every 2 months)†.

Société de Pathologie Exotique: 25 rue du Docteur-Roux, Paris 15e; f. 1908; 350 mems.; Pres. Prof. M. PAYET; Secs.-Gen. Prof. A. DODIN, Prof. L. LAMY; publ. *Bulletin* (quarterly).

Société de Stomatologie de France: 20 passage Dauphine, Paris 6e; Sec. Gen. Dr. R. BATAILLE.

Société des Chirurgiens de Paris: 60 blvd. de Latour-Maubourg, Paris 7e; f. 1909; 300 mems.; Sec. Gen. GILBERT SCHULSINGER; publ. *Bulletin et Mémoires* (every two months).

Société Française d'Allergologie: 1 rue du Val-de-Grace, 75005 Paris; f. 1947; Sec.-Gen. Prof. P. GERVAIS; publ. *Revue Française d'Allergologie et d'Immunologie clinique* (5 a year).

Société Française d'Anesthésie, d'Analgésie et de Réanimation: 185-187 rue Saint Maur, 75010 Paris; 1,860 mems.; Pres. Dr. CHARLES ROUET; Sec.-Gen. Prof. WINCKLER; publ. *Anesthésie, Analgésie, Réanimation* (6 a year).

Société Française d'Angéiologie: 3 rue Jacques Dulud, 92200 Neuilly; f. 1947; 350 mems.; Sec. Dr. LOUIS GERSON; publ. *Angéiologie* (8 a year).

Société Française d'Electroradiologie Médicale: 12 rue de Seine, Paris 6e; f. 1909; 950 members; Sec. M. DARIAUX; publ. *Journal de Radiologie d'Electrologie et de Médecine Nucléaire.*

Société Française d'Endocrinologie: c/o Masson Edit., 120 blvd. St.-Germain, 75280 Paris Cedex 06; f. 1939; 550 mems.; Pres. PR. BAULIEU; Sec. PR. MORNEX; publ. *Annales* (6 a year).

Société Française d'Histoire de la Médecine: 52 rue de Garches, 92210 St. Cloud; f. 1902; 600 mems.; library; Pres. Prof. SOURNIA; Gen. Sec. Dr. VALENTIN; publ. *Histoire des Sciences médicales*† (quarterly).

Société Française d'Hydrologie et de Climatologie Médicales: 1 rue Monticelli, 75014 Paris; 413 mems.; Pres. Dr. DUBOIS; Sec.-Gen. Dr. GENEVIÈVE GIRAULT; publ. *La Presse Thermale et Climatique.*

Société Française d'Hygiène, de Médecine Sociale et de Génie Sanitaire: f. 1877; *c.* 400 mems.; Sec.-Gen. Dr. H. POULIZAC, Institut régional d'hygiène, 40 rue Lionnois, 54000 Nancy; publs. congress reports (annually).

Société Française d'Ophtalmologie: 9 rue Mathurin-Régnier, 75015 Paris; f. 1883; 4,000 mems.; Sec.-Gen. Prof. M. MASSIN; publs. *Bulletins et Mémoires, Rapport* (annually).

Société Française d'Oto-Rhino-Laryngologie et de Pathologie Cervico-Faciale: 10 Villa Scheffer, 75016 Paris; f. 1880; 1,300 mems.; Pres. Dr. YVES LALLEMANT; Sec. Dr. J. BOUCHE; publs. *Comptes Rendus* and *Rapports Discutés au Congrès.*

Société Française d'Urologie: 6 ave. Constant Coquelin, Paris 7e; f. 1919; 50 mems.; Pres. Dr. BOISSONNAT; publ. *Journal d'Urologie.*

Société Française de Biologie Clinique: Laboratoire de Chimie Clinique et Biologie Moléculaire, 15 rue de l'Ecole de Médecine, 75270 Paris Cedex 06; Sec. Prof. L. HARTMANN.

Société Française de Chirurgie Infantile: Hôpital Brettonneau, 2 rue Carpeaux, 75018 Paris; f. 1959; Pres. J. BIENAIMÉ; Sec.-Gen. P. MOLLARD; publ. *Chirurgie Pédiatrique.*

Société Française de Chirurgie Orthopédique et de Traumatologie: Secrétariat: Pavillon Ollier, Hopital Cochin, 27 rue du Faubourg Saint-Jacques, Paris 14e; 1,250 mems.; Pres. M. POSTEL; publ. *Revue de Chirurgie Orthopédique.*

Société Française de Chirurgie Plastique et Reconstructive: 40 rue Bichat, 75010 Paris; f. 1953; Pres. Dr. G. JOST; Sec.-Gen. Prof. P. BANZET.

Société Française de Gynécologie: 20 rue Clément Marot. 75008 Paris; 552 mems.; Pres. Prof. P. MULLER; Sec.-Gen. ANDRÉ GORINS; publ. *Gynécologie* (6 a year).

Société Française de Mycologie Médicale: 25 rue du Docteur-Roux, Paris 15e; f. 1956; 325 mems.; Sec.-Gen. Prof. E. DROUHET; publ. *Bulletin.*

Société Française de Neurologie: 120 blvd. Saint Germain, 75280 Paris; f. 1899; Pres. F. ROHMER; Sec.-Gen. J. CAMBIER; publ. *Revue Neurologique* (monthly).

Société Française de Pédiatrie: 149 rue de Sèvres, Paris 15e. f. 1929; Pres. Prof. GUY FONTAINE; Sec.-Gen. Prof. JEAN FREZAL.

Société Française de Phlébologie: 52 ave. de la Bourdonnais, 75007 Paris; f. 1947; 1,200 mems.; Pres. H. CHATARD; Sec.-Gen. P. WALLOIS; publ. *Bulletins*† (quarterly).

Société Française de Physiologie et de Médecine Aéronautiques et Cosmonautiques: Hôpital Dominique Larrey,

78013 Versailles; f. 1960; publishes papers on experimental and clinical studies; 550 mems.; Sec.-Gen. Prof. DELAHAYE; publs. *Médecine Aéronautique et Spatiale, Médecine Subaquatique et Hyperbare* (quarterly).

Société Francaise de Phytiatrie et de Phytopharmacie: C.N.R.A., Route de Saint Cyr, 78000 Versailles; f. 1951; 1,000 mems.

Société Française de Thérapeutique et de Pharmacodynamie: Doin, Editeurs, 8 place de l'Odéon, Paris 6e; therapeutics, experimental and clinical pharmacology; 1,270 mems.; Pres. M. DUCHÊNE-MARRULAZ; Sec.-Gen. F. C. HUGHES; publ. *Thérapie.*

Société Française de la Tuberculose et des Maladies Respiratoires: 66 blvd. Saint-Michel, 75006 Paris; Pres. Prof. P. RENAULT; Secs. Gen. Prof. H. BROCARD, Prof. C. SORS; publ. *Revue Française des Maladies Respiratoires.*

Société Médicale des Hôpitaux de Paris: 26 blvd. Raspail Paris 6e; Sec. M. PESTEL; publ. *Annales de Médecine Interne.*

Société Médico-Chirurgicale des Hôpitaux Libres: 1 place d'Iéna, Paris 16e; Pres. L. MICHELET; Secs. J. A. HUET, A. D. HERSCHBERG, J. VALLETTA.

Société Médico-Psychologique: Hôpital de Jour, 26 rue du Général Sarrail, 94000 Créteil; f. 1852; 675 mems.; Pres. J. M. SUTTER; Sec.-Gen. Dr. LIONEL VIDART; publ. *Annales médico-psychologiques* (monthly).

Société Nationale Française de Gastro-Entérologie: 33 blvd. Picpus, 75571 Paris Cedex 12; Sec.-Gen. Prof. YVES LE QUINTREC; publ. *Gastroentérologie clinique et biologique.*

Société Odontologique de Paris (S.O.P.): 11 Cité Charles Godon, 75009 Paris; 1,400 mems.; Pres. Dr. P. SAFAR; Sec.-Gen. Dr. M. CORDIER; publ. *Revue Française d'Odonto-Stomatologie* (every 2 months).

Société Scientifique d'Hygiène Alimentaire (CSSF): 16 rue de l'Estrapade, Paris 5e; f. 1904; 1,182 mems.; Pres. Dr. GUY EBRARD; publ. *L'Alimentation et la Vie* (quarterly).

NATURAL SCIENCES

General

Association Française pour l'Avancement des Sciences (AFAS): 250 rue Saint-Jacques, 75005 Paris; f. 1872; 1,500 mems.; Pres. Prof. CORDIER; Sec. of the Council Prof. J. VERNE; publ. *Sciences* (quarterly).

Centre International de Synthèse (*Foundation for International Scientific Co-ordination*): 12 rue Colbert, Paris 2e; f. 1924 by Henri Berr; Admin. Council of 36 mems.; Pres. GEORGES LE RIDER; Dir./Sec.-Gen. JACQUES ROGER; publs. *Revue de Synthèse, Semaines Internationales de Synthèse, Revue d'Histoire des Sciences, L'Evolution de l'Humanité.*

Comité National Français des Recherches Antarctiques: 39 ter rue Gay-Lussac, 75005 Paris; 100 mems.; Pres. G. LACLAVÈRE; Sec.-Gen. G. PILLET; publ. *Rapport* (annually).

Confédération des Sociétés Scientifiques Françaises: 11 rue Pierre Curie, Paris 5e; f. 1919 to protect the interests of scientific research in its five branches, documentation, bibliography, research proper, publication and discussion. It is divided into four federations, covering mathematics, chemistry, physics and the natural sciences; Pres. M. BLONDEL; Gen. Sec. Prof. JEAN VERNE. (The societies affiliated to it are marked CSSF in this section.)

Fédération Française des Sociétés de Sciences Naturelles: 57 rue Cuvier, 75231 Paris Cedex 05; f. 1919; groups 110 societies; Pres. Prof. J. F. LEROY; Gen. Sec. Ing. R. F. PUJOL; publs. *L'Année Biologique, Bulletin.*

Union des Travailleurs Scientifiques: 20 rue Ecole Polytechnique, Paris 5e; Pres. E. SCHATZMANN; Sec.-Gen. P. AVERBUCH.

Biological Sciences

Naturalistes Parisiens, Les: 57 rue Cuvier, 75231 Paris Cedex 05; f. 1904 to undertake research in natural history and deepen the scientific knowledge of its members; 600 mems.; Sec. C. DUPUIS; publs. *Cahiers des Naturalistes*†, *Bulletin des Naturalistes Parisiens* (quarterly).

Société Botanique de France (CSSF); 4 ave. de l'Observatoire, 75270 Paris Cedex 06; f. 1854; 900 mems.; Gen. Sec. G. DEYSSON; publs. *Bulletin* (every 2 months), *Actualités botaniques* (quarterly), *Mémoires* (annual).

Société d'Etudes Ornithologiques: 46 rue d'Ulm, Paris 5e; f. 1929; scientific study of wild birds; 1,100 mems.; library of 4,000 vols.; Secs. H. HEIM DE BALSAC, J. VIELLIARD; publs. *Alauda*†, *Revue Internationale d'Ornithologie* (quarterly).

Société de Biologie: Collège de France, 75231 Paris Cedex 05; f. 1848; 140 hon. mems., 50 elected mems., 130 associates, 190 corres.; Pres. Prof. R. GAUTHERET; Sec. Prof. J. ROCHE; publ. *Comptes Rendus.*

Société de Pathologie Végétale et d'Entomologie Agricole de France (CSSF): Institut Pasteur, 25 rue Dr. Roux, Paris 15e; f. 1914; 650 mems.; Pres. C. JACQUIOT; Secs. A. BALACHOWSKY, G. REMAUDIERE.

Société Entomologique de France: 45 *bis* rue de Buffon, Paris 5e; f. 1832; Gen. Sec. J. D'AGUILAR; 800 mems.; specialized entomological library; 80 entomological periodicals, 40,000 vols.; publs. *Annales* (quarterly) and *Bulletin*† (5 a year).

Société Française de Génétique (CNRS): Institut de Génétique, 91190 Gif-sur-Yvette; f. 1947; Sec.-Gen. G. PRÉVOST; publ. *Annales de Génétique* (quarterly).

Société Française de Physiologie Végétale: 4 Place Jussieu, 75230 Paris Cedex 05; f. 1955; 500 mems.; Pres. G. DUCET; Sec.-Gen. Prof. MAZLIAK; publ. *Physiologie végétale* (quarterly).

Société Mycologique de France (CSSF): 36 rue Geoffroy St. Hilaire, 75005 Paris; f. 1884; Pres. JACQUES BUIDIN; Sec. Gen. HENRI ROMAGNESI; 2,000 mems.; publ. *Bulletin Trimestriel.*

Société Nationale de Protection de la Nature et d'Acclimatation de France (CSSF): 57 rue Cuvier, Paris 5e; f. 1854; 8,500 mems.; Pres. FRANÇOIS BOURLIÈRE; Gen. Sec. CHRISTIAN JOUANIN; publs. *La Terre et la Vie, Le Courrier de la Nature.*

Société Ornithologique de France: Secretariat and Library, 55 rue de Buffon, Paris 5e; f. 1909; Pres. C. JOUANIN; publs. *L'Oiseau et La Revue Française d'Ornithologie, Bulletin de la Société* and *Mémoires.*

Société Zoologique de France (CSSF); 195 rue St. Jacques, Paris 5e; f. 1876; 798 mems.; Pres. Prof. M. LAMOTTE; Gen. Sec. Prof. A. BEAUMONT; publs. *Bulletin* (quarterly).

Mathematics

Association des Professeurs de Mathématiques de l'Enseignement Public (APMEP): 29 rue d'Ulm, 75230 Paris Cedex 05; f. 1910; 13,000 mems.; Pres. Mme. ZEHREN; publ. *Bulletin* (5 a year).

Comité National Français de Mathématiciens: 11 rue Pierre et Marie Curie, 75231 Paris Cedex 05; f. 1950; Pres. J. NEVEU; Sec. A. BRUNEL.

Société Mathématique de France (CSSF): 11 rue Pierre et Marie Curie, 75231 Paris Cedex 05; f. 1872; 1,400 mems.; Pres. M. BERGER; publs. *Bulletin, Mémoires* (both quarterly), *Circulaire d'informations, Astérisque* (both monthly).

Physical Sciences

Association Française d'Observateurs d'Etoiles Variables: Observatoire de Lyon, 69230 St. Genis Laval; f. 1927; 70 mems.; Pres. E. SCHWEITZER; Sec.-Gen. M. PROUST.

Association Française pour l'Etude du Quaternaire: Laboratoire de Géologie I, Tour 16, 4e étage, 4 place Jussieu, 75230 Paris Cedex 05; f. 1962 to prepare scientific publications and exchange information on the Quaternary; 650 mems.; Pres. Prof. J. CHALINE; Sec. Prof. J. MISKOVSKY; publ. *Bulletin* (quarterly).

Association Scientifique et Technique pour l'Exploitation des Océans: 19 ave. Pres. Wilson, 75016 Paris; f. 1967; oil technology and allied activities, pollution control, polymetallic nodules, sand and gravel workings, fishing technology and fish farming; 90 mem. industries; Pres. Y. LA PRAIRIE; Sec.-Gen. C. MELLAC; publ. *Annuaire Technique et Industriel.*

Comité National Français de Géodésie et Géophysique: 39 ter rue Gay-Lussac, 75005 Paris; 470 mems.; Pres. J. GOGUEL; Sec.-Gen. J. DE BEAUREGARD; publ. *Comptes Rendus* (annual).

Fédération Nationale des Associations de Chimie de France (CSSF): 28 rue St. Dominique, Paris 7e; 11 affiliated socs., 12,000 mems.; Sec.-Gen. Prof. R. DELABY.

Société Astronomique de France: 3 rue Beethoven, 75016 Paris; f. 1887; 6,000 mems.; Pres. A. DOLLFUS; Gen. Sec. P. DE LA COTARDIÈRE; publ. *L'Astronomie* (monthly).

Société Chimique de France: 250 rue St. Jacques, 75005 Paris; f. 1857; 4,600 mems.; Pres. F. GALLAIS; Sec.-Gen. R. GUILLAUMONT; Exec. Sec. G. PERREAU; publs. *Bulletin* (monthly), *L'Actualité chimique* (10 a year).

Société de Chimie Biologique (CSSF): 4 ave. de l'Observatoire, 75270 Paris Cedex 06; f. 1914; 1,467 mems.; Pres. G. DIRHEIMER; Gen. Secs. R. PERLES, J. P. EBEL; publs. *Biochimie*†, *Regard sur la Biochimie.*

Société de Chimie Industrielle (CSSF): 28 rue Saint-Dominique, 75007 Paris; f. 1917; 4,000 mems.; Pres. L. DENIVELLE; Dél.-Gén. R. GUILLET; publs. *L'actualité chimique, Informations Chimie/Chimie et Industrie, Analysis.*

Société de Chimie Physique: Ecole de Physique et de Chimie, 10 rue Vauquelin, Paris 5e; f. 1908; 1,400 mems.; Sec.-Gen. Dr. C. TROYANOWSKY; publ. *Journal de Chimie physique* (monthly).

Société des Experts-Chimistes de France: 42 *bis* rue de Bourgogne, Paris 7e; f. 1912; 1,250 mems.; Pres. RENÉ TRUHAUT; Sec.-Gen. GUY JANSSENS; publ. *Annales des falsifications et de l'Expertise Chimique.*

Société Française de Minéralogie et de Cristallographie (CSSF): 4 Place Jussieu, Tour 16, 75230 Paris Cedex 05; f. 1878; 700 mems.; Sec. M. LAGACHE; publ. *Bulletin de Minéralogie.*

Société Française de Physique (CSSF): 33 rue Croulebarbe, 75013 Paris; f. 1873; 3,200 mems.; Pres. BERNARD CAGNAC; Gen. Sec. MARCEL BARRERE; publs. *Bulletin, Catalogue de l'Exposition de Physique, Journal de Physique, Revue de Physique Appliquée, Colloques.*

Société Géologique de France: 77 rue Claude Bernard, 75005 Paris; f. 1830; 2,500 mems.; Pres. ALAIN PERRODON; publs. *Bulletin, Mémoires.*

Société Météorologique de France (CSSF): 73-77 rue de Sèvres, 92100 Boulogne-Billancourt; f. 1852; 950 mems.; Sec.-Gen. A. MILLEVIEILLE; publ. *La Météorologie.*

Union des Physiciens (CSSF): 44 blvd. Saint-Michel, 75270 Paris Cedex 06; f. 1906; 13,000 mems.; Pres. Prof. M. GIÉ; publ. *Bulletin* (monthly).

PHILOSOPHY AND PSYCHOLOGY

Société Française d'Etude des Phénomènes Psychiques: 1 rue des Gâtines, Paris 20e; conducts experiments in psychic clairvoyance and undertakes research to prove the immortality of the soul; publ. *La Tribune Psychique.*

Société Française de Philosophie (CSSF): 12 rue Colbert, 75002 Paris; f. 1901; 180 mems.; Pres. JACQUES MERLEAU-PONTY; Vice-Pres. HENRI GOUHIER, JACQUES BRUNSCHWIG; Sec.-Gen. SUZANNE DELORME; publs. *Bulletin, Revue de Métaphysique et de Morale* (quarterly).

Société Française de Psychologie: 28 rue Serpente, 75006 Paris; f. 1901, reorganized in 1920; 1,600 mems.; Sec.-Gen. C. BONNET; publ. *Psychologie Française.*

RELIGION, SOCIOLOGY AND ANTHROPOLOGY

Association Française des Arabisants: 40 ave. d'Iéna, 75116 Paris; f. 1973 to promote Arabic studies, to study questions of doctrine and practice relative to teaching and research in Arabic; to keep its members informed of ideas and activities of interest to teachers, researchers and students of Arabic; 300 mems.; Pres. BRUNO HALFF; Sec. ARLETTE NEGRE; publ. *L'Arabisant*†.

Association pour l'Enseignement des Sciences Anthropologiques, Ecole d'Anthropologie: 95 blvd. St.-Michel, Paris 5e; f. 1875; Dir. Dr. J. A. HUET; Deputy Dir. Mme F. LOUIS MARIN.

Société Asiatique: 3 rue Mazarine, Paris 6e; f. 1822; library of 80,000 vols.; 650 mems.; Pres. C. CAHEN; Vice-Pres. J. FILLIOZAT, A. CAQUOT; publs. *Journal Asiatique* (quarterly), *Cahiers.*

Société d'Anthropologie de Paris (CSSF): 1 rue René Panhard, 75013 Paris; f. 1859; biological anthropology; 550 mems.; Pres. HENRI PINEAU; Sec.-Gen. D. FEREMBACH; publ. *Bulletins et Mémoires* (quarterly).

Société d'Histoire Ecclésiastique de la France: 28 rue d'Assas, 75006 Paris; f. 1910; 900 mems.; Pres. J.-R. PALANQUE; Sec.-Gen. PIERRE MAROT; publ. *Revue d'Histoire de l'Eglise de France.*

Société de l'Histoire du Protestantisme Français: 54 rue des Saints-Pères, 75007 Paris; f. 1852; 120,000 vols., 12,000 MSS. in library; Pres. FRANÇOIS MEJAN; Sec.-Gen. HENRI DUBIEF; Librarian Pasteur DENIS VATINEL; publs. *Bulletin Historique et Littéraire*†, *Cahiers de Généalogie Protestante*† (quarterly).

Société de Mythologie Française: Lycée Félix Faure, 175 rue de Pontoise, 60000 Beauvais; f. 1949; 200 mems.; Pres. H. DONTENVILLE; Dir. H. FROMAGE; publ. *Bulletin* (quarterly).

Société des Africanistes (CSSF): Musée de l'Homme, place du Trocadéro, 75116 Paris; f. 1931; 350 mems.; Sec. Mme G. CALAME-GRIAULE; publ. *Journal des Africanistes.*

Société des Américanistes: Musée de l'Homme, place du Trocadéro, 75116 Paris; f. 1896; 500 mems.; Pres. M. SOUSTELLE; Gen. Sec. M. BECQUELIN; publs. *Journal, Bibliographie américaniste* (annually).

Société Française de Sociologie: 82 rue Cardinet, 75017 Paris; f. 1962; Pres. JEAN CARBONNIER; Sec.-Gen. JACQUES LAUTMAN.

TECHNOLOGY

Association Aéronautique et Astronautique de France (AAAF): 80 rue Lauriston, 75116 Paris; f. 1972; 1,800 mems.; formed by merger of Association Française des Ingénieurs de l'Aéronautique et de l'Espace and Société Française d'Astronautique; Pres. P. CONTENSOU; publ. *L'Aéronautique de l'Astronautique* (6 a year).

Association des Anciens Elèves de l'Ecole Nationale Supérieure des Industries Agricoles et Alimentaires: 9-11 ave. Franklin D. Roosevelt, 75008 Paris; 1,300 mems.; Pres. ETIENNE ESPIARD; Sec.-Gen. ALAIN GEORGE; publ. *Industries Alimentaires et Agricoles* (monthly).

Association des Chimistes de l'Industrie Textile: 12 rue d'Anjou, 75008 Paris; f. 1910; 1,300 mems.; publs. *Chronique* (monthly), *Revue Teintex*.

Association des Chimistes, Ingénieurs et Cadres des Industries Agricoles et Alimentaires: 156 blvd. de Magenta, 75010 Paris; f. 1883; 2,000 mems.; library of 8,000 vols.; Sec. M. BIROLAUD; publ. *Industries Alimentaires et Agricoles* (monthly).

Association Française des Ingénieurs, Chimistes et Techniciens des Industries du Cuir: 181-203 ave. Jean Jaurès, 69007 Lyon; f. 1939; 400 mems.; Sec.-Gen. J. BARADUC; publ. *Technicuir*.

Association Française du Froid: 129 blvd. St.-Germain, 75279 Paris Cedex 06; f. 1908; Pres. ANDRÉ GAC; Sec.-Gen. HENRI MINAULT; publ. *Revue Générale du Froid* (monthly).

Association Nationale de la Recherche Technique: 101 ave. Raymond Poincaré, 75116 Paris; f. 1953 to promote technical research and organizations, and to foster contact with technical research institutions abroad; 134 titular, 57 associate and 73 corresp. mems.; Pres. M. B. DELAPALME; publ. *Le Progrès Technique* (quarterly).

Institut Français de l'Energie: 3 rue Henri-Heine, 75016 Paris; f. 1952; organises teaching (l'Ecole de Thermique), documentation, and information; library of 15,000 vols.; Pres. JEAN COUTURE; Gen. Dir. EDOUARD MAINTRIEU; publs. *Actualité Combustibles—Energie* (monthly), *Revue Générale de Thermique* (monthly), *Comptes Rendus des Journées Internationales de l'I.F.E.*, *Cahiers de la Thermique*.

Société d'Encouragement pour l'Industrie Nationale: 4 place Saint-Germain-des-Prés, Paris 6e; f. 1801; Sec. M. PASCAULT; publ. *L'Industrie Nationale*.

Société des Ingénieurs Civils de France: 19 rue Blanche, Paris 9e; f. 1848; 11,000 mems.; library of 100,000 vols.; Dir. CLAUDE HERSELIN; publ. *Sciences et Techniques* (10 times a year).

Société Française de Métallurgie: 5 rue Paul Cézanne, 75008 Paris; f. 1945; 2,000 mems.; Pres. LUCIEN COCHE; Sec.-Gen. HUMBERT DE VILLOUTREYS.

Société Française de Microscopie Electronique: Ecole Normale Supérieure, Laboratoire de Botanique, 24 rue Lhomond, 75231 Paris Cedex 05; f. 1959; to further electron microscopy, electronic optics and electronic diffraction, spectroscopy, microprobe, cellular biology; 2,300 mems.; Pres. Prof. JEAN PHILIBERT; publs. *Biologie Cellulaire* (9 a year), *Journal de Microscopie et de Spectroscopie Electroniques* (6 a year).

Société Française de Photogrammétrie et de Télédétection: 2 ave. Pasteur, 94160 St. Mandé; f. 1959; photogrammetry and photo-interpretation; 615 mems.; Pres. R. CHEVALLIER; Sec.-Gen. G. DUCHER; publ. *Bulletin*† (quarterly).

Société des Electriciens, des Electroniciens et des Radioélectriciens (SEE): 48 rue de la Procession, 75724 Paris Cedex 15; f. 1883; 9,000 mems.; Pres. L. MALAVARD; Gen. Sec. V. BERTRAND.

Société Hydrotechnique de France: 199 rue de Grenelle, Paris 7e; f. 1912; hydrotechnics and mechanics of fluids; 300 mems.; library of 500 vols.; Pres. M. BANAL; Sec.-Gen. G. REMENIERAS; publs. *La Houille Blanche* (8 a year), *Proceedings*, *Journées de l'Hydraulique* (every 2 years).

RESEARCH INSTITUTES

(*see* also under Universities)

CENTRE NATIONAL DE LA RECHERCHE SCIENTIFIQUE (CNRS)

15 QUAI ANATOLE FRANCE, 75700 PARIS

Founded 1939.

Organization. The CNRS proposes to the Government means of doing research and how to allocate funds. It controls over 1,300 laboratories and research centres, covering the Natural Sciences and the Humanities. The total annual budget for 1980 was 3,800 million francs, and the number of research workers was 8,700.

Objects.

1. To co-ordinate and promote scientific research.
2. To make grants-in-aid to scientific bodies and to individuals to enable them to carry out research work.
3. To subsidise or set up laboratories for scientific research.

President: CHARLES THIBAULT.

Director-General: J. DUCUING.

Secretary-General: GEORGES ROLIX.

Scientific Directors: J. YOCCOZ (Nuclear and Particle Physics), J. WINTER (Mathematics, Physics), Y.-A. ROCHER (Physical Sciences for Engineers), R. MAUREL (Chemistry), MICHEL PETIT (Earth and Space Sciences), A. BERKALOFF (Life Sciences), E. LISLE (Human Sciences).

I. NUCLEAR AND PARTICLE PHYSICS

Centre de Spectrométrie nucléaire et de Spectrométrie de Masse (I.N2.P3.): Bâtiment 104 CNRS Campus, 91406 Orsay; f. 1946; Dir. ROBERT KLAPISCH.

Centre de Recherches Nucléaires de Strasbourg Cronenbourg (I.N2P3): B.P. 20 CR, 67037 Strasbourg Cedex; f. 1960; Dir. ANDRÉ GALLMANN.

Laboratoire d'Annecy de Physique des Particules (I.N2P3): B.P. 909, 74019 Annecy le Vieux Cedex; f. 1975; Dir. M. VIVARGENT.

II. MATHEMATICS AND PHYSICS

Laboratoire de Physique Théorique: École normale supérieure, 24 rue Lhomond, 75231 Paris Cedex 05; f. 1974; Dir. JEAN-LOUP GERVAIS.

Laboratoire de Photophysique Moléculaire: Université de Paris XI, Bâtiment 213, 91405 Orsay; f. 1972; Dir. SYDNEY LEACH.

Centre de Physique Théorique: 31 chemin Joseph Aiguier, 13274 Marseille Cedex 2; f. 1967; Dir. EDUARDO DE RAFAEL.

Laboratoire Aimé Cotton: Bâtiment 505, CNRS II campus, 91405 Orsay; f. 1938; Dir. SERGE FENEUILLE.

Service National des Champs Intenses: 166X, 38042 Grenoble Cedex; f. 1971; Dir. GUY AUBERT.

Laboratoire d'Optique Quantique: Laboratoire de l'école polytechnique, route de Saclay, 91120 Palaiseau; f. 1971; Dir. CHRISTOS FLYTZANIS.

Laboratoire des Interactions Moléculaires et des Hautes Pressions: Rue Jean Baptiste Clément, 93430 Villetaneuse; f. 1947; Dir. JACQUES ROMAND.

Laboratoire de Physique des Solides: 1 place Aristide Briand, 92190 Meudon; f. 1970; Dir. YVES MARFAING.

Laboratoire de Magnétisme de Bellevue: 1 place Aristide Briand, 92190 Meudon; f. 1970; Dir. NINO BOCCARA.

Laboratoire de Physique des Matériaux: 1 place Aristide Briand, 92190 Meudon; f. 1938; Dir. JEAN PHILIBERT.

Centre de Recherches sur les très Basses Températures: 166X, 38042 Grenoble Cedex; f. 1962; Dir. ROBERT TOURNIER.

Laboratoire Louis Neel: 166X, 38042 Grenoble Cedex; f. 1971; Dir. JEAN-CLAUDE BARBIER.

Laboratoire des Propriétés Mécaniques et Thermodynamiques des Matériaux: Université de Paris-Nord, ave. Jean-Baptiste Clément, 93430 Villetaneuse; f. 1973; Dir. GEORGES SAADA.

Centre de Recherches sur les Solides à Organisation Cristalline Imparfaite: 1B rue de la Férollerie, 45045 Orléans Cedex; f. 1969; Dir. JEAN-JOSÉ FRIPIAT.

Laboratoire de Cristallographie: 166X, 38042 Grenoble Cedex; f. 1971; Dir. ERWIN BERTAUT.

Laboratoire d'Optique Electronique: 29 rue Jeanne Marvig. B.P. 4347, 31055 Toulouse Cedex; f. 1949; Dir. BERNARD JOUFFREY.

Centre de recherches sur les Mécanismes de la Croissance Cristalline: Université de Provence, Centre St.-Jérome, rue Henri Poincaré, Traverse de la Barasse, 13397 Marseille Cedex 4; f. 1975; Dir. RAYMOND KERN.

Laboratoire "Léon Brillouin": Centre d'Etudes Nucléaires de Saclay, B.P. 2, 91190 Gif-sur-Yvette; f. 1974; Dir. DANIEL CRIBIER.

Service de Diffusion de la Technologie des Matériaux: Université de Paris XI, Bâtiment 490, 91405 Orsay; f. 1946; Dir. JEAN-PIERRE CHAPELLE.

Laboratoire pour l'utilisation du rayonnement électromagnétique: Université de Paris XI, Bâtiment 200, 91405 Orsay; f. 1976; Dir. Y. FARGE.

III. PHYSICS FOR ENGINEERS

Laboratoire d'Aérothermique: 4 *ter* route des Gardes, 92190 Meudon; f. 1938; Dir. JEAN-JOSEPH BERNARD.

Laboratoire d'Automatique et d'Analyse des Systèmes: LAAS, complexe aérospatial de Toulouse, Lespinet, 7 ave. du Colonel Roche, 31400 Toulouse; f. 1967; Dir. GEORGES GRATELOUP.

Laboratoire d'Energétique Solaire: B.P. 5 Odeillo-Via, 66120 Font-Romeu; f. 1950; Dir. ANDRÉ VIALARON.

Laboratoire de Mécanique et d'Acoustique: 31 chemin Joseph Aiguier, 13274 Marseille Cedex 2; f. 1941; Dir. BERNARD NAYROLES.

Laboratoire de Physique et de Métrologie des Oscillateurs: 32 ave. de l'Observatoire, 25000 Besançon; f. 1973; Dir. JEAN-JACQUES GAGNEPAIN.

Laboratoire des Signaux et Systèmes "L25": École supérieure d'électricité, Plateau du Moulon, 91190 Gif-sur-Yvette; f. 1974; Dir. BERNARD PICINBONO.

Laboratoire des Verres: Université de Montpellier II, 2 place Eugène Bataillon, 34060 Montpellier Cedex; f. 1961; Dir. JERSY ZARZICKI.

Centre de Recherches sur la Physique des Hautes Températures: 1D ave. de la recherche scientifique, 45045 Orléans Cedex; f. 1968; Dir. FRANÇOIS CABANNES.

Laboratoire d'Electrostatique: 166X, 38042 Grenoble Cedex; f. 1971; Dir. NOËL FELICI.

Laboratoire d'Informatique pour la Mécanique et les Sciences de l'Ingénieur: Université de Paris XI, Bâtiment 508, B.P. 30, 91405 Orsay; f. 1945; Dir. LUCIEN MALAVARD.

Centre de Documentation scientifique et technique: 26 rue Boyer, 75971 Paris Cedex; f. 1939; Dir. J. D'OLIER.

COMPUTER CENTRES

Centre Inter-Régional de Calcul Electronique: Bâtiment 506, CNRS III campus, 91405 Orsay; f. 1969; Dir. Mme JANINE CONNES.

Centre de Calcul de Strasbourg: 23 rue de Loess, B.P. 20 CR, 67037 Strasbourg Cedex; f. 1968; Dir. GEORGES MONSONEGO.

Centre de Calcul de l'INAG: 5 place Jules Janssen, 92190 Meudon; f. 1968; Dir. MICHEL DREYFUS.

Centre de Calcul de Physique Nucléaire de l'IN2P3: 11 quai St. Bernard, 75230 Paris Cedex 05; f. 1966; Dir. JACQUES COHEN-GANOUNA.

Service de Calcul en Sciences Humaines: 54 blvd. Raspail, 75260 Paris Cedex 06; Dir. MONIQUE RENAUD.

Centre de Calcul du Pharo: Jardin Emil Duclaux, 58 blvd. Charles Livon, 13007 Marseille; f. 1972; Dir. COLETTE CONNAT.

IV. CHEMISTRY

Centre de Biophysique Moléculaire: 1A ave. de la recherche scientifique, 45045 Orléans Cedex; f. 1967; Dir. CLAUDE HELENE.

Institut de Recherche sur la Catalyse: 79 blvd. du 11 novembre 1918, 69626 Villeurbanne; f. 1958; Dir. BORIS IMELIK.

Centre de Recherches sur la Chimie de la Combustion et des Hautes Températures: 1C ave. de la recherche scientifique, 45045 Orléans Cedex; f. 1969; Dir. RALPH DELBOURGO.

Centre d'Etudes de Chimie Métallurgique: 15 rue Georges Urbain, 94400 Vitry; f. 1936; Dir. MICHEL FAYARD.

Centre d'Etudes et de Recherches de Chimie Organique Appliquée: CERCOA, 2–8 rue Henri Dunant, B.P. 28, 94320 Thiais; f. 1938; Dir. FRANÇOIS LE GOFFIC.

Laboratoire de Chimie Macromoléculaire sous Rayonnement: 1 place Aristide Briand, 92190 Meudon; f. 1938; Dir. ADOLPHE CHAPIRO.

Laboratoire de Chimie du Solide: Université de Bordeaux I, 351 cours de la Libération, 33405 Talence Cedex; f. 1974; Dir. PAUL HAGENMULLER.

Centre de Recherches de Chimie Structurale "Paul Pascal": "Domaine Universitaire", 33405 Talence; f. 1963; Dir. ADOLPHE PACAULT.

Institut de Chimie des Substances Naturelles: 91190 Gif-sur-Yvette; f. 1959; Dir. Sir DEREK BARTON.

Laboratoire de Recherches sur les Interactions Gaz-Solides "Maurice Letort": route de Vandoeuvre, B.P. 104, 54600 Villers-les-Nancy; f. 1963; Dir. ALBERT CASSUTO.

Service du Cyclotron: 3A rue de la Ferollerie, 45045 Orléans Cedex; f. 1974; Dirs. ROLAND MUXART, PHILIPPE ALBERT.

Laboratoire d'Electrochimie Interfaciale: 1 place Aristide Briand, 92190 Bellevue; f. 1958; Dir. ROGER PARSONS.

Centre de Recherches sur les Macromolécules: 6 rue Boussingault, 67083 Strasbourg Cedex; f. 1947; Dir. CONSTANT WIPPLER.

Centre de Recherches sur les Macromolécules Végétales: B.P. 53, 38041 Grenoble Cedex; f. 1967; Dir. DIDIER GAGNAIRE.

Centre de Mécanique Ondulatoire Appliquée: 23 rue du Maroc, 75019 Paris; f. 1957; Dir. RAYMOND DAUDEL.

Service Central d'Analyse: B.P. 22, Autoroute Lyon-Vienne, Echangeur de Solaize, 69390 Vernaison; f. 1958; Dir. ALAIN LAMOTTE.

Centre de Recherches de Microcalorimétrie et de Thermodynamique: 26 rue du 141e R.I.A., 13003 Marseille; f. 1959; Dir. JEAN-CLAUDE MATHIEU.

Centre de Recherches sur la Physico-chimie des Surfaces Solides: École supérieure de chimie, 24 ave. du Président Kennedy, 68200 Mulhouse; f. 1967; Dir. JEAN-BAPTISTE DONNET.

Laboratoire d'Analyse par Activation "Pierre Sue": Bâtiment 37, B.P. 2, 91190 Gif-sur-Yvette; f. 1969; Dir. GILLES REVEL.

Laboratoire de Spectrochimie Infrarouge et Raman: Laboratoire Case 5, B.P. 36, 59650 Villeneuve d'Ascq; f. 1965; Dir. MICHEL DELHAYE.

Laboratoire des Ultra-Réfractaires: B.P. 5, Odeillo-Via, 66120 Font-Romeu; f. 1963; Dir. GEORGES URBAIN.

Laboratoire des Sciences du Génie Chimique: 1 rue Granville, 54042 Nancy; f. 1975; Dir. M. J. VILLERMAUX.

Laboratoire de Chimie de Coordination: B.P. 4142, 31030 Toulouse Cedex; f. 1974; Dir. RENÉ POILBLANC.

Laboratoire des Matériaux Organiques: B.P. 22, Autoroute Lyon-Vienne, Echangeur de Solaize, 69390 Vernaison; f. 1977; Dir. ALAIN GUYOT.

Groupe d'Etude et de Synthèse des Microstructures: Ecole Supérieure de Physique et Chimie industrielle de la ville de Paris, 10 rue Vauquelin, 75231 Paris Cedex; f. 1970; Dir. MAX PAULUS.

V. EARTH AND SPACE SCIENCES

Services Généraux du groupe des Laboratoires de Verrières-le-Buisson: B.P. 11, 91370 Verrières-le-Buisson; Admin. MICHEL FILLERON.

Service d'Aéronomie: B.P. 3, 91370 Verrières-le-Buisson; f. 1958; Dir JACQUES BLAMONT.

Laboratoire d'Astronomie Spatiale: traverse du Siphon, les Trois Lucs, 13012 Marseille; f. 1965; Dir. GEORGES COURTES.

Institut d'Astrophysique: 98 *bis* blvd. Arago, 75014 Paris; f. 1936; Dir. JEAN AUDOUZE.

Centre Géologique et Géophysique: Université de Montpellier II, place Eugène Batallion, 34060 Montpellier Cedex; f. 1974; Dir. PIERRE LOUIS.

Laboratoire de Géologie du Quaternaire: Centre Universitaire de Marseille-Luminy, 70 route Léon Lachamp, 13288 Marseille Cedex 2; f. 1958; Dir. HUGUES FAURE.

Centre de Recherches Géophysiques: Garchy, 58150 Pouilly-sur-Loire; f. 1953; Dir. JEAN-PAUL MOSNIER.

Laboratoire de Glaciologie: 2 rue Très-Cloîtres, 38031 Grenoble Cedex; f. 1942; Dir. LOUIS LLIBOUTRY.

Centre de Recherches en Physique de l'Environnement terrestre et planétaire: 3A ave. de la recherche scientifique, 45045 Orléans Cedex; f. 1975; Dir. JAMES HIEBLOT.

Laboratoire de Météorologie Dynamique: Ecole Polytechnique, Route départementale 36, 91128 Palaiseau; f. 1939; Dir. ANDRÉ BERROIR.

Observatoire de Haute-Provence: Saint-Michel l'observatoire, 04300 Forcalquier; f. 1937; Dir. CHARLES FEHRENBACH.

Centre d'Etudes d'Océanographie et de Biologie Marine: Station biologique, place Georges Teissier, 29211 Roscoff; f. 1946; Dir. JOSEPH BERGERARD.

Centre de Pédologie Biologique: 17 rue Notre-Dame-des-Pauvres, B.P. 5, 54500 Vandoeuvre-les-Nancy; f. 1961; Dir. BERNARD SOUCHIER.

Centre de Recherches Pétrographiques et Géochimiques: 15 rue Notre-Dame-des-Pauvres, C.O. 1, 54500 Vandoeuvre-les-Nancy; f. 1953; Dir. HUBERT DE LA ROCHE.

Centre des Faibles Radioactivités: 91190 Gif-sur-Yvette; f. 1961; Dir. JACQUES LABEYRIE.

Centre de Sédimentologie et de Géochimie de la Surface: 1 rue Blessig, 67084 Strasbourg Cedex; f. 1963; Dir. GEORGES MILLOT.

Centre Armoricain d'Etude Structurale des Socles: Institut de géologie, B.P. 25A, 35031 Rennes Cedex; f. 1974; Dir. JEAN COGNE.

Laboratoire Souterrain de Moulis: 09410 Moulis; f. 1948; Dir. CLAUDE DROGUE.

Mission Permanente en Afghanistan: c/o French Embassy, Kabul; (Université de Picardie, Dept. Géologie, 33 rue St. Leu, 80039 Amiens Cedex;) f. 1974; Dir. JEAN-PIERRE CARBONNEL.

Centre de Recherches sur la Synthèse et la Chimie des Minéraux: 1A rue de la Férollerie, 45045 Orléans Cedex; f. 1969; Dir. ZDENEK JOHAN.

VI. LIFE SCIENCES

Centre de Recherches de Biochimie Macromoléculaire: route de Mende, B.P. 5051, 34033 Montpellier Cedex; f. 1973; Dir. NGUYEN VAN THOAI.

Centre Régional d'Elevage et de Production d'Animaux de Laboratoire: chemin départemental 56, 13790 Le Rousset; f. 1974; Dir. PIERRE LUCCIANI.

Centre de Sélection et d'Elevage d'Animaux de Laboratoire: 3B rue de la Férollerie, 45045 Orléans Cedex; f. 1953; Dir. MICHEL SABOURDY.

Centre d'Etudes Biologiques des Animaux Sauvages: forêt de Chizé, Villiers-en-Bois, 79360 Beauvoir-sur-Niort; f. 1968; Dir. JEAN-CLAUDE BOISSIN.

Centre de Biochimie et de Biologie Moléculaire: 31 chemin Joseph Aiguier, 13274 Marseille 9e Cedex 2; f. 1967; Dir. PIERRE DESNUELLE.

Centre de Recherches de Biochimie et de Génétique Cellulaires: 118 route de Narbonne, 31077 Toulouse Cedex; f. 1972; Dir. JEAN-PIERRE ZALTA.

Centre d'Etudes Bioclimatiques: 21 rue Becquerel, 67087 Strasbourg Cedex; f. 1962; Dir. BERNARD METZ.

Institut de Recherches en Biologie Moléculaire: Université de Paris VII, 2 place Jussieu, tour 43, 75221 Paris Cedex 05; f. 1966; Dir. BERNARDI GIORGIO.

Institut de Biologie Moléculaire et Cellulaire: 15 rue René Déscartes, 67084 Strasbourg Cedex; f. 1973; Dirs. JEAN-PIERRE EBEL, LÉON HIRTH.

Institut de Recherches Scientifiques sur le Cancer: 7 rue Guy Mocquet, B.P. 8, 94800 Villejuif; f. 1947; Dir. ROGER MONIER.

Laboratoire de Chimie Bactérienne: 31 chemin Joseph Aiguier, 13274 Marseille 9e Cedex 2; f. 1962; Dir. JACQUES SENEZ.

Institut d'Embryologie: 49 *bis* ave. de la Belle-Gabrielle, 94130 Nogent-sur-Marne; f. 1947; Dir. NICOLE LE DOUARIN.

Laboratoire d'Enzymologie: 91190 Gif-sur-Yvette; f. 1959; Dir. JEKISIEH SZULMAJSTER.

Centre de Génétique Moléculaire: 91190 Gif-sur-Yvette; f. 1946; Dir. PIERRE SLONIMSKI.

Centre de Génétique des Virus: 91190 Gif-sur-Yvette; f. 1946; Dir. GILBERT BRUN.

Centre d'Hémotypologie: C.H.U. Purpan, ave. de la Grande-Bretagne, 31300 Toulouse; f. 1962; Dir. GEORGES LARROUY.

Centre de Morphologie Expérimentale: Institut de biologie animale, ave. des Facultés, 33400 Talence; f. 1946; Dir. ANDRÉ HAGET.

Centre de Neurochimie: 11 rue Humann, 67085 Strasbourg Cedex; f. 1965; Dir. GUY VINCENDON.

Institut de Neurophysiologie et Psychophysiologie: 31 chemin Joseph Aiguier, 13274 Marseille 9e Cedex 2; f. 1961; Dir. JACQUES PAILLARD.

Centre de Recherches sur la Nutrition: 9 rue Jules Hetzel, 92190 Meudon; f. 1946; Dir. ALAIN RERAT.

Centre National de Coordination des Etudes et Recherches sur la Nutrition et l'Alimentation: 72 rue de Sèvres, 75007 Paris; f. 1945; Dir. ANDRÉ FRANÇOIS.

Laboratoire de Pharmacologie et Toxicologie Fondamentales: 205 route de Narbonne, 31078 Toulouse Cedex; f. 1960; Dir. CLAUDE PAOLETTI.

Laboratoire de Physiologie des Organes Végétaux après Récolte: 4 *ter* route des Gardes, 92190 Meudon; f. 1942; Dir. DANIEL CÔME.

Laboratoire de Photosynthèse: 91190 Gif-sur-Yvette; f. 1953; Dir. JEAN LAVOREL.

Laboratoire de Cytophysiologie de la Photosynthèse: 91190 Gif-sur-Yvette; f. 1969; Dir. Mme MARCELLE LEFORT-TRAN.

Laboratoire de Physiologie Comparée des Régulations: 23 rue du Loess, B.P. 20 CR, 67037 Strasbourg Cedex; f. 1960; Dir. PIERRE LAURENT.

Laboratoire de Physiologie Respiratoire: 23 rue Becquerel, 67087 Strasbourg Cedex; f. 1969; Dir. PIERRE DEJOURS.

Laboratoire de Physiologie du Travail: 91 blvd. de l'Hôpital, 75634 Paris Cedex 13; f. 1945; Dir. HUGUES MONOD.

Centre d'Etudes Phytosociologiques et Ecologiques Louis-Emberger: route de Mende, B.P. 5051, 34033 Montpellier Cedex; f. 1947; Dir. SANE DE PARCEVAUX.

Ecothèque Méditerranéenne du CNRS: B.P. 5051, 34033 Montpellier Cedex; Dir. GILBERT LONG.

Laboratoire du Phytotron: 91190 Gif-sur-Yvette; f. 1957; Dir. ROGER JACQUES.

Laboratoire de Primatologie et d'Ecologie des Forêts Equatoriales: Makokou (Gabon), B.P. 18; 4 ave. du Petit-Château, 91800 Brunoy; f. 1969; Dir. ANDRÉ BROSSET.

Services Techniques Communs de Villejuif: 16 *bis* ave. Vaillant-Couturier, B.P. 3, 94800 Villejuif; f. 1970; Admin. Dr. M. CAUBEL.

Centre d'Etudes du Système Nerveux: Laboratoire de physiologie nerveuse: 91190 Gif-sur-Yvette; f. 1972; Dir. ROBERT NAQUET; Laboratoire de neurobiologie cellulaire: 91190 Gif-sur-Yvette; Dir. LADISLAV TAUC.

Service de la Carte de la Végétation: 29 rue Jeanne Marvig, B.P. 4009, 31055 Toulouse Cedex; f. 1947; Dir. PAUL REY.

Laboratoire de Biologie et de Génétique Evolutive: 91190 Gif-sur-Yvette; f. 1947; Dir. JEAN DAVID.

Centre d'Ecologie de Camargue: Le Sambuc, 13200 Arles; f. 1975; Dir. PIERRE HEURTAUX.

Laboratoire de Biologie et Technologie des Membranes: 43 blvd. du 11 Novembre 1918, 69621 Villeurbanne; f. 1976; Dir. DANIELLE GAUTHERON.

Centre d'Immunologie: 70 route Léon Lachamp, 13288 Marseille Cedex 02; f. 1976; Dir. FRANÇOIS KOURILSKY.

Laboratoire de Génétique et Physiologie du Développement des Plantes: 91190 Gif-sur-Yvette; f. 1976; Dir. JEAN PERNES.

Centre de Cytologie Expérimentale: 67 rue Maurice Günsbourg, 94200 Ivry; f. 1969; Dir. PIERRE FAVART.

Centre d'Epidémiologie: Hôpital Edouard Herriot, Pavillon H bis, 5 place d'Arsonval, 69374 Lyon Cedex 2; f. 1978; Dir. RENÉ LAMBERT.

Laboratoire de Génétique Moléculaire des Eucaryotes: 11 rue Humann, 67085 Strasbourg Cedex; f. 1977; Dir. PIERRE CHAMBON.

VII. HUMANITIES

Centre de Recherches Archéologiques: Sophia-Antipolis, 06560 Valbonne; f. 1970; Dir. ROLAND MARTIN.

Service d'Architecture Antique: Institut d'art et d'archéologie, 3 rue Michelet, 75006 Paris; f. 1957; Dir. ROLAND MARTIN.

Centre d'Etudes de Géographie Tropicale: CEGET, Domaine Universitaire, 33405 Talence; f. 1968; Dir. GUY LASSERRE.

Centre de Géomorphologie: Université de Caen, rue des Tilleuls, 14000 Caen; f. 1963; Dir. ANDRÉ JOURNAUX.

Service de Recherches Juridiques Comparatives: 27 rue Paul Bert, 94200 Ivry-sur-Seine; f. 1952; Dir. MICHEL LESAGE.

Centre d'Etudes Sociologiques: 82 rue Cardinet, 75017 Paris; f. 1946; library of 23,000 vols.; Dir. RENAUD SAINSAULIEU.

Institut de Recherche et d'histoire des Textes: 40 ave. d'Iéna, 75116 Paris; f. 1937; Dir. JEAN GLENISSON.

Laboratoire d'Economie et de Sociologie du Travail: 33 chemin du coton rouge, 13100 Aix-en-Provence; f. 1969; Dir. ALAIN D'IRIBARUE.

Institut de la Langue Française: 44 ave. de la Libération, 54000 Nancy; f. 1960; Dir. BERNARD QUEMADA.

Centre de Documentation Sciences Humaines: 54 blvd. Raspail, 75260 Paris Cedex 06; f. 1970; Dir. ROGER BRUNET.

Mission Permanente en Egypte: Centre franco-égyptien d'étude des temples de Karnak, CNRS, Luxor, Egypt; f. 1974; Dir. JEAN-CLAUDE GOIVIN.

Mission Permanente en Israël: Centre de recherches préhistoriques français de Jérusalem, B.P. 547, Jerusalem; f. 1974; Dir. JEAN PERROT.

Laboratoire de Langues et Civilisations à Traditions Orales: 27 rue Paul Bert, 94200 Ivry; Dir. Mlle THOMAS.

Laboratoire d'Information et de Documentation en Géographie "INTERGEO": 191 rue St. Jacques, 75005 Paris; f. 1976; Dir. ROGER BRUNET.

Centre d'Etudes et de Réalisations cartographiques géographiques: 191 rue St. Jacques, 75005 Paris; f. 1976; Dir. FERNAND JOLY.

Institut de Recherche sur la Pédagogie de l'Economie et sur l'Audiovisuel pour la Communication dans les Sciences sociales: 29 chemin des Mouilles, 69130 Ecully; f. 1975; Dir. JEAN-MARIE ALBERTINI.

Centre de Sociologie des Organisations: 88 rue de Lille, 75007 Paris; f. 1975; Dir. MICHEL CROZIER.

Laboratoire d'Informatique pour les Sciences de l'Homme: 31 chemin Joseph Aiguier, 13274 Marseille Cedex 2; f. 1976; Dir. M. BORILLO.

Centre de Recherches sur l'Afrique Orientale: Sophia-Antipolis, B.P. 6, 06560 Valbonne; f. 1977; Dir. J. TUBIANA.

NATIONAL INSTITUTES

Institut National d'Astronomie et de Géophysique (INAG): 77 ave. Denfert-Rochereau, 75014 Paris; f. 1967; 76 mems.; to promote and co-ordinate research in astronomy and geophysics and to conduct large projects in these fields; Dir. MICHEL PETIT; publ. annual report.

Institut National de Physique Nucléaire et de Physique des Particules (I.N2.P3.): 11 rue Pierre et Marie Curie, 75231 Paris Cedex 05; Dir. JEAN YOCCOZ.

AGRICULTURE AND VETERINARY SCIENCES

Centre National de Recherches Agronomiques: Etoile de Choisy, route de Saint Cyr, 78000 Versailles; linked to INRA (*see* below); library of 4,500 vols., 2,000 current periodicals; Dirs. of Central Stations: R. BETREMIEUX (soil science), A. PERRIER (bioclimatology), B. SCHWEISGUTH (plant breeding), F. RAPILLY (plant pathology), J. P. MOREAU (zoology), M. HASCOET (phytopharmacy), A. HENTGEN (experimentation and information services), C. DUBY (biometry), C. GOILLOT (teledetection), M. JAMAGNE (cartography), J. MOSSE (proteins), E. JOLIVET (intermediate metabolism), J. P. BOURGIN (cellular biology), J. MARGARA (morphogenesis).

Centre National de Recherches Forestières: Champenoux, 54280 Seichamps; library of 2,000 vols.; linked to INRA (*see* below); Admin. M. BONNEAU.

Centre Technique du Génie Rural, des Eaux et des Forêts: Groupement d'Antony, Parc de Tourvoie, 92160 Antony; Dir. D. MÉRIAUX.

Centre Technique Forestier Tropical (C.T.F.T.): 45 *bis* ave. de la Belle-Gabrielle, 94130 Nogent-sur-Marne; state-owned; applied research relating to waterways and forests in inter-tropical and sub-tropical regions; trains experts; research centres in Cameroon, Congo People's Republic, Gabon, Ivory Coast, Madagascar, Niger, Senegal, Upper Volta and New Caledonia; Gen. Dir. LOUIS HUGUET.

Groupement d'Etudes et de Recherches pour le Développement de l'Agronomie Tropicale (G.E.R.D.A.T.): 42 rue Scheffer, 75016 Paris; f. 1970; groups the eight French overseas agricultural research organizations which have in common: short- and medium-term research with the object of practical application as soon as possible; specialization in one or a group of products so as to ensure maximum efficiency; close contact with professional circles interested in their work; Pres. JEAN-PIERRE BENARD; Administrator JACQUES ALLIOT; publ. *Agritrop* (2 a year), *Machinisme agricole et tropical* (quarterly), annual report†.

Consists of: C.T.F.T. (*see* above), I.E.M.V.T., I.F.C.C., I.R.A.T., I.R.C.A., I.R.C.T., I.R.F.A., I.R.H.O. (*see* below), and **Centre D'Etudes et d'Expérimentation du Machinisme Agricole et Tropical (C.E.E.M.A.T.):** Parc de Tourvoie, 92160 Antony; common to all eight institutes; deals with all matters concerning problems of agricultural mechanization in developing countries in the tropical zone; Dir. CLAUDE UZUREAU.

Institut d'Elevage et de Médecine Vétérinaire des Pays Tropicaux (IEMVT): 10 rue Pierre Curie, 94700 Maisons-Alfort; f. 1948; research and missions to countries of Africa, Asia and South America; library of 15,000 vols.; Dir. A. PROVOST; publs. *Revue d'Elevage et de Médecine Vétérinaire des Pays Tropicaux*† (quarterly).

Institut de Recherches Agronomiques Tropicales et des Cultures Vivrières (I.R.A.T.): 110 rue de l'Université, 75007 Paris; f. 1960; works in numerous stations in Senegal, Mauritania, Mali, Upper Volta, Niger, Ivory Coast, Benin, Togo, Cameroon, Ethiopia, Madagascar, Comores, Réunion, Antilles, Tahiti, Guyana, Brazil; research into general agronomy, the cultivation of food crops, tobacco, sugar cane, forages, spices, etc.; 220 research workers and technicians; library of 28,000 vols.; Dir. F. BOUR; publ. *L'Agronomie Tropicale* (quarterly).

Institut de Recherches pour les Huiles et Oléagineux (I.R.H.O.) (*Research Institute for Oils and Oilseeds*): 8, 11-13 square Pétrarque, 75016 Paris; f. 1942; scientific and technical research; experimental stations, industrial plantations; technical assistance in 30 tropical countries; Pres. M. BOURGES-MAUNOURY; Dir.-Gen. J. FLEURY; publ. *Oléagineux* (monthly).

Institut de Recherches sur le Caoutchouc en Afrique (I.R.C.A.): 42 rue Scheffer, 75016 Paris; to introduce and develop heveaculture in Africa; central laboratories in Paris and Le Mans in association with the Institut Français du Caoutchouc; maintains a station in the Ivory Coast and a research centre in Cameroon; Pres. RAYMOND DE PADIRAC; Dir.-Gen. C. J. DU PLESSIX.

Institut de Recherches sur les Fruits et Agrumes (I.R.F.A.): 6 rue du Général Clergerie, 75116 Paris; f. 1945; brs. in Martinique, Guadeloupe, Réunion, Corsica, Ivory Coast, Cameroon, French Guyana; missions in Niger, Senegal, Benin, Upper Volta and Algeria; publ. *Fruits*.

Institut Français du Café et du Cacao (I.F.C.C.): 34 rue des Renaudes, 75017 Paris; f. 1957; research and technical assistance in 6 countries; Dir. J. BRAUDEAU; publ. *Café Cacao Thé* (quarterly).

Institut National de la Recherche Agronomique (INRA): 149 rue de Grenelle, 75007 Paris; f. 1946; agricultural research, including forestry; administers and subsidizes a large number of centres, laboratories and experimental farms in France; Dir.-Gen. J. POLY; Dir.-Gen. Adj. R. BOUCHET, F. RINVILLE; publ. *Annales*.

Laboratoire Central de Recherches Vétérinaires: B.P. 67, 22 rue Pierre Curie, 94703 Maisons-Alfort Cedex; f. 1901; study of contagious diseases in domestic and wild animals; supervises sanitary regulations for import and export of livestock; Dir. Dr. LOUIS DHENNIN; Asst. Dir. Dr. C. QUINCHON.

ECONOMICS, LAW AND POLITICS

Centre de Recherches sur l'U.R.S.S. et les Pays de l'Est: Université des Sciences Juridiques, Politiques, Sociales et de Technologie de Strasbourg, place d'Athènes, 67084 Strasbourg Cedex; f. 1959; research on law and government, international relations, economics and sociology; library of 13,000 vols.; Dir. ALEXANDER KISS; Sec. J. C. ROMER; publ. *Annuaire de l'U.R.S.S. et des Pays socialistes européens* (annually).

Fondation pour la Recherche Sociale: 14 rue St.-Benoît, 75006 Paris; f. 1965; sociology and economics; 15 mems.; publ. *Recherche Sociale*† (quarterly).

Institut de Sciences Mathématiques et Economiques Appliquées: 11 rue Pierre et Marie Curie, 75005 Paris; f. 1944; 20 mems.; study of economic problems and exchange of ideas with other countries; Chair. FRANÇOIS PERROUX; publs. *Economies et Sociétés* (monthly), *Economie Appliquée—Archives de l'I.S.M.E.A.* (quarterly), *Mondes en Développement* (quarterly).

Institut National d'Etudes Démographiques: 27 rue du Commandeur, 75675 Paris Cedex 14; f. 1945; 45 research staff; library of 30,000 vols.; Dir. GÉRARD CALOT; publs. *Population* (bi-monthly), *Population et Sociétés* (monthly), *Cahiers de Travaux et Documents de l'INED* (4–6 a year).

Institut National de la Statistique et des Etudes Economiques: 18 blvd. Adolphe Pinard, 75675 Paris Cedex 14; f. 1946; statistical research: population census, economic indices and forecasts; library: *see* Libraries; Dir.-Gen. EDMOND MALINVAUD; publs. *Annuaire Statistique*, *Bulletin Mensuel de Statistique*, *Economie et Statistique* (monthly), *Documentation Economique* (6 a year), *Annales* (quarterly), *Tendance de la Conjoncture* (monthly), *Courrier des Statistiques* (quarterly).

EDUCATION

Institut National de Recherche Pédagogique: 29 rue d'Ulm, 75230 Paris Cedex 05; f. 1879; 500 mems.; library contains 1,200,000 vols., mainly in the field of education; Dir. G. SEPTOURS; publs. *Revue Française de Pédagogie*† (quarterly), *Recherches Pédagogiques* (irregular).

Attached Institute:

Centre International d'Etudes Pédagogiques de Sevres: 1 ave. Léon-Journault, 92310 Sevres; research and studies in education; training overseas teachers; pilot experimental school; Dir. J. AUBA; publ. *Les Amis de Sèvres* (3 a year).

HISTORY, GEOGRAPHY AND ARCHAEOLOGY

Centre d'Études Supérieures de la Renaissance: 59 rue Néricault-Destouches, B.P. 1328, 37013 Tours Cedex; f. 1956; also a specialized library of 30,000 vols.; Dir. Prof. J. C. MARGOLIN; Sec. P. LALLAZ.

Centre de Recherches sur les Monuments Historiques: Palais de Chaillot, 75 Paris 16e; f. 1942; Dir. M. PARENT.

Centre de Recherches Historiques: Ecole des Hautes Etudes en Sciences Sociales et CNRS, C.P. 321, 54 blvd. Raspail, 75006 Paris; f. 1950; joint research in economic and social history; 115 mems.; Dir. J. GOY.

Comité Technique de la Recherche Archéologique en France: 16 rue Pierre et Marie Curie, 75005 Paris; publs. *Gallia, Gallia Préhistoire* and supplements.

Sous-Direction des Fouilles et Antiquités: 3 rue de Valois, 75001 Paris; f. 1964; attached to the Ministry of Culture and Communication; Dir. R. DELAROZIERE.

MEDICINE

Institut Alfred-Fournier: 25 boulevard Saint-Jacques, 75014 Paris; research into sexually transmitted illnesses; Dir. Dr. COULON.

Institut National de la Santé et de la Recherche Médicale: 101 rue de Tolbiac, 75645 Paris Cedex 13; f. 1941 as Institut National d'Hygiène, renamed 1964; assisted by eight scientific commissions; Gen. Dir. PHILIPPE LAUDAT; publs. *Répertoire des Services et Laboratoires, Bulletin de liaison, Symposium, Statistiques en Morbidité et Mortalité.*

Institut Pasteur: 25-28 rue du Dr. Roux, Paris 15e; f. 1888; Pres. PIERRE ROYER; Dir. FRANÇOIS GROS; Gen. Sec. J. MERY; publs. *Annales, Bulletin* (monthly).

Institut Prophylactique: 36 rue d'Assas, Paris 6e; f. 1916; Dir. ARTHUR VERNES.

NATURAL SCIENCES

General

Office de la Recherche Scientifique et Technique Outre-Mer (ORSTOM): 24 rue Bayard, 75008 Paris; f. 1943; a public corporation charged to aid developing countries by means of research, both fundamental and applied, in the non-temperate regions, with special application to human environment problems and food production; library and documentation centre; Dir.-Gen. Prof. G. CAMUS. Maintains the following services:

Services Scientifiques Centraux: 70–74 route d'Aulnay, 93140 Bondy; geophysics, geology, hydrology, soil biology, plant amelioration, biochemistry, botany, vegetable biology, phytopathology, applied zoology, virology, medical entomology, geography; cartographic workshop, study centre for musicology and oral traditions; remote sensing bureau; Dir. M. LAMOUROUX.

Service Hydrologique: 19 rue Eugène Carrière, 75018 Paris; Dir. M. ROCHE.

Services Extérieures:

Laboratoire de Géochronologie commun ORSTOM/ Université de Nice: Parc Valrose, 06000 Nice; geology.

Laboratoire de Tropicalisation: 2 place de la Gare de Ceinture, 78210 St-Cyr l'Ecole.

Antenne ORSTOM auprès du CNEXO: Centre Océanologique de Bretagne, B.P. 337, 29273 Brest Cedex; oceanography.

Antenne ORSTOM auprès de l'INRA: Station d'Hydrobiologie Lacustre de Thonon, Ave. de Corzent, 74203 Thonon les Bains; hydrobiology.

Antenne ORSTOM auprès du Laboratoire de Phanérogamie, Muséum National d'Histoire Naturelle, 16 rue de Buffon, 75231 Paris Cedex 05; botany.

Antenne ORSTOM auprès du CEA: Centre d'Etudes Nucléaires de Cadarache, Service de Radio-agronomie, B.P.1, 13115 St. Paul lez Durance; nuclear agronomy.

Antenne ORSTOM, Station Météorologique: Nouveau Sémaphore, Quai des Abeilles, 76600 Le Havre Océanographie.

Biological Sciences

Centre National de Recherches Zootechniques: Domaine de Vilvert, 78350 Jouy-en-Josas; library of 8,000 vols., 1,250 periodicals; publs. *Annales de Biologie Animale, Biochimie, Biophysique, Annales de Zootechnie, Annales de Génétique Animale* (fortnightly), *Bulletin Signalétique* (weekly).

Institut de Biologie Physico-chimique: 13 rue Pierre et Marie Curie, 75005 Paris; f. 1927; Dir. Prof. B. PULLMAN; Dirs. of Laboratories: Dr. D. HAYES (Cellular Chemistry), Dr. R. BANERJEE (Biophysics), Mrs. M. GRUNBERG MANAGO (Biochemistry), Prof. P. DOUZOU (Biospectroscopy), Dr. P. JOLIOT (Photosynthesis), Dr. A. M. MICHELSON (Physical Biochemistry), B. PULLMAN (Theoretical Chemistry).

Muséum National d'Histoire Naturelle: *see* under State Colleges.

Station Biologique de Roscoff: 29211 Roscoff; f. 1872; marine biology, oceanography; 35 mems.; Dir. Prof. J. BERGERARD; publs. *Cahiers de Biologie marine* (quarterly), *Travaux*† (annually).

Physical Sciences

Association pour l'Etude de la Neige et des Avalanches (ANENA): 46 ave. Félix Viallet, 38000 Grenoble; f. 1971; to aid research and study by public or private organizations, and facilitate co-operation with other countries; 500 mems.; library; Pres. PHILIPPE TRAYNARD; Dir. GUY DE MARLIAVE; Sec. G. BRUGNOT; publ. *Neige et Avalanches* (quarterly).

Bureau de Recherches Géologiques et Minières: B.P. 6009, 45060 Orléans; f. 1944; 2,300 mems.; library of 50,000 vols.; publs. *Bulletin du BRGM*† (4 sections on Geology of France, Economic Geology, Hydrology-Engineering Geology and General Geology, quarterly), *Mineral Prospecting Review, Mémoires du BRGM*, geological maps, Bibliographies, SDI and retrospective searches.

Bureau des Longitudes: Palais de l'Institut, 3 rue Mazarine, Paris 6e; f. 1795 by Convention Nationale; 50 mems, and corresp.; Pres. J. TERRIEN; Vice-Pres. J. DELHAYE; Sec. J. LÉVY; publs. *Annuaire, Connaissance des Temps, Ephémérides Nautiques et Ephémérides Aéronautiques* (annually).

Centre d'Etudes Géologiques et Minières: 103 rue de Lille, 75007 Paris; f. 1932; geological documentation centre; library of 2,500 vols., 200 periodicals; Dir. M. VIGNEAUX; Sec.-Gen. L. BURNOL; publ. *Chronique de la Recherche minière*† (6 a year).

Centre d'Etudes Marines Avancées: 149 Plage de l'Estaque, 13016 Marseille; f. 1953; underwater exploration, study and research; Pres. Commdr. J. Y. COUSTEAU; Sec.-Gen. A. SIVIRINE.

Centre de Recherches Atmosphériques Henri Dessens: Cidex B47, 65300 Lannemezan; f. 1960; cloud physics, weather modification; 20 mems.; library of 2,000 vols.; Dirs. H. SAUVAGEOT, J. DESSENS; publs. *Journal de Recherches Atmosphériques* (quarterly).

Centre de Recherches et d'Etudes Océanographiques: 73-77 rue de Sèvres, 92100 Boulogne; Dir. V. ROMANOVSKY; publ. *Travaux*.

Centre National pour l'Exploitation des Océans: 66 ave. d'Iéna, 75116 Paris; f. 1967; research in all fields of oceanography and ocean technology; small library; Pres., Dir.-Gen. GÉRARD PIKETTY; publs. *Bulletin d'Information* (monthly), *Rapport Annuel*, series of scientific and technical publs.

Centre Océanologique de Bretagne: B.P. 337, 29273 Brest Cedex; f. 1968; Dir. J. VICARIOT.

Base Océanologique pour la Méditerranée: Zone Portuaire de Brégaillon, B.P. 2, 83501 La Seyne Cedex; Dir. BRUNO CHOMEL DE VARAGNES.

Centre Océanologique pour le Pacifique: B.P. 7004, Taravao, Tahiti; Dir. JEAN DE CHAZEAUX.

Centre Technique et du Matériel de la Météorologie Nationale: 196 rue de l'Université, Paris 7e; Dir. M. MARC.

Commissariat à l'Energie Atomique: 29-33 rue de la Fédération, Paris 15e; f. 1945; fundamental and applied nuclear research, energy generator studies; library; four affiliated study centres; Pres. of Atomic Energy Cttee. The Minister of Industry and Research; Gen. Administrator A. GIRAUD; publs. *Bulletin d'Information Scientifique et Technique, Les Echos du CEA, Notes d'Informations CEA, Rapport Annuel.*

Etablissement d'Etudes et de Recherches Météorologiques: 196 rue de l'Université, Paris 7e; f. 1946; Dir. L. FACY.

Institut Curie: 26 rue d'Ulm, 75231 Paris Cedex 05; f. 1978 (fmrly. Fondation Curie—Inst. du Radium); 940 staff; three sections: Physics-Chemistry (Dir. M. DUQUESNE), Biology (Dir. J. M. LHOSTE), Medicine (Dir. R. CALLE); 940 mems.; Pres. F. CABANNE.

Institut et Observatoire de Physique du Globe du Puy de Dôme: 12 ave. des Landais, Clermont-Ferrand; f. 1871; specializes in atmospheric physics: radiometeorology, weather modification and terrestrial magnetism; Dir. SERGE GODARD; publ. *Journal de Recherches Atmosphériques* (quarterly).

Laboratoire d'Astronomie de l'Université de Lille I: 1 impasse de l'Observatoire, 59000 Lille; f. 1934; Dir. P. BACCHUS.

Météorologie Nationale: 73-77 rue de Sèvres, 92106 Boulogne-Billancourt Cedex; f. 1945; Dir. R. MITTNER; Asst. Dir. B. GOSSET; publs. *Bulletins quotidiens de Renseignements, Mémorial, Monographies, Résumé mensuel du temps.*

Observatoire de l'Université de Bordeaux: ave. P. Sémirot, 33270 Floirac; f. 1880; 50 mems.; 1,600 vols.; Dir. FERNAND POUMEYROL; publs. *Rapport*†, *Publications*†.

Observatoire de Lyon: 69230 Saint-Genis-Laval; f. 1880; specialises in photometry and spectroscopy, polarimetry and studies in the upper atmosphere; library of 14,000 vols.; Dir. M. MONNET.

Observatoire de Marseille: 2 place Le Verrier, 13004 Marseille; Dir. Y. GEORGELIN.

Observatoire National: 41 *bis* ave. de l'Observatoire, 25000 Besançon; f. 1882; theoretical and observational research (stellar dynamics, galactic structure, planetary atmospheres, astronomy); 35 staff; library of *c.* 15,000 vols.; Dir. MICHEL CRÉZÉ.

Observatoire de Nice: B.P. 252, 06007 Nice Cedex; f. 1881; affiliated to the University of Nice; astronomy and astrophysics; 6,000 vols.; Dir. J.-P. ZAHN.

Observatoire de Paris: 61 ave. de l'Observatoire, 75014 Paris; f. 1667; library of 60,000 vols.; Pres. J. BOULON; publs. *Catalogues d'Etoiles*†, *Circulaires et Rapport du Bureau International de l'Heure.*

Observatoire de Strasbourg: 11 rue de l'Université, Strasbourg; f. 1882; specializes in stellar data and spectroscopy; library of 16,000 vols.; 11 astronomers; Dir. ALPHONSE FLORSCH; publ. *Publication du Centre de Données Stellaires.*

Observatoires du Pic du Midi et de Toulouse:

Headquarters: 65200 Bagnères-de-Bigorre; 100 mems.; library of 50,000 vols.; solar, planetary and stellar astrophysics, physics of the atmosphere, cosmic physics; Dir. Prof. J. RÖSCH; publs. *Travaux des Observatoires du Pic du Midi et de Toulouse*†.

Observatoire du Pic du Midi: 65200 Bagnères-de-Bigorre; f. 1878; high altitude observatory (2,860 m.).

Observatoire de Toulouse: 1 ave. Camille Flammarion, 31500 Toulouse; f. 1733.

Station de Radioastronomie de Nancay: administered by the Observatoire de Paris, Département de Radioastronomie, 92190 Meudon; f. 1953; study of the sun, comets, planets and radio sources; radio telescopes; 85 mems.; Dir. J. GUIBERT; many publs. on astronomy.

RELIGION, SOCIOLOGY AND ANTHROPOLOGY

Institut des Etudes Augustiniennes: 3 rue de l'Abbaye, 75006 Paris; f. 1943; research into life, thought and times of St. Augustine; specialized public library of 20,000 vols.; publs. *Revue des Etudes Augustiniennes* (quarterly), *Oeuvres Complètes de St. Augustin* and others.

Institut d'Ethnologie: Musée de l'Homme, Palais de Chaillot, place du Trocadéro, 75116 Paris; f. 1925; social anthropology, archaeology, linguistics; Dirs. Prof. A. LEROI-GOURHAN and J. GUIART; publ. *Travaux et Mémoires, Archives et documents.*

Institut National d'Etude du Travail et d'Orientation Professionnelle: 41 rue Gay-Lussac, Paris 5e; f. 1928; undertakes research and trains vocational guidance officers; library of 13,000 vols., 350 periodicals; Dir. Prof. M. REUCHLIN; publ. *l'Orientation Scolaire et Professionnelle.*

Maison des Sciences de l'Homme: 54 blvd. Raspail, 75270 Paris Cedex 06; f. 1963 to support research in the social sciences; Administrator F. BRAUDEL.

TECHNOLOGY

Association Française pour l'Etude des Eaux: 21 rue de Madrid, 75008 Paris; f. 1949; 450 mems.; documentation centre on water problems; Pres. F. BLAIZOT; Dir. X. DAGALLIER; Gen. Sec. Mme ANNA VINCENT; publ. *Information Eaux* (monthly).

Association Nationale pour la Protection des Eaux: Institut Océanographique, 195 rue Saint-Jacques, Paris 5e; f. 1960; brings to public notice the necessity of protecting and preserving the quality and quantity of water-supplies, studies problems of water pollution and its prevention; 800 mems.; Pres. ED. BONNEFOUS; Vice-Pres. P. L. TENAILLON; publ. *L'Eau Pure* (every 2 months).

Centre d'Etudes Nucléaires de Cadarache: B.P. 1, 13115 St. Paul lez Durance; technological study of modern nuclear reactors; Dir. ANDRÉ JUNCA.

Centre d'Etudes Nucléaires de Fontenay-aux-Roses—CENFAR (*Nuclear Research Centre, Fontenay-aux-Roses*): B.P. 6, 92260 Fontenay-aux-Roses; f. 1945; first French reactor; Zoé natural uranium, heavy water moderated; twin swimming-pool reactor Triton, and laboratories specializing mainly in chemical and metallurgical research on plutonium, controlled fusion, chemistry analysis, corrosion studies, mineralogy, concentration of uranium ores, health physics and sanitary protection; Dir. J. ASTY.

Centre d'Etudes Nucléaires de Saclay—CENS (*Saclay Nuclear Research Centre*): B.P. 2, 91190 Gif-sur-Yvette; f. 1949; equipped with two high-flux experimental reactors, six particle accelerators and special laboratories: spent fuel study facility, isotope and labelled molecule production laboratories, activation analysis centre, ionizing radiations applications centre; laboratories specializing in research on reactors, nuclear metallurgy and chemistry, nuclear physics, biology, radioactivity measurement and electronics; library of 48,000 vols., 400,000 reports; Dir. C. CHAUVEZ.

Centre National d'Etudes Spatiales: 129 rue de l'Université, Paris 7e; f. 1961; prepares national programmes of space research, provides information, promotes international co-operation; Pres. HUBERT CURIEN; Dir.-Gen. YVES SILLARD.

Institut d'Hydrologie et de Climatologie: Faculté de Médecine, Pitié-Salpétrière, 91 blvd. de l'Hôpital, 75013 Paris; 5 main laboratories in Paris, and further laboratories at the principal spas; Gen.-Sec. Prof. P. DESGREZ; publ. *Les Annales de l'Institut d'Hydrologie et de Climatologie*.

Institut de Recherches du Coton et des Textiles Exotiques (IRCT) (*Research Institute for Cotton and Tropical Textiles*): 34 rue des Renaudes, Paris 17e; experts stationed in the Ivory Coast, Chad, Togo, Benin, Upper Volta, Mali, Senegal, Cameroon, Paraguay; Dir. J. DEQUECKER.

Institut de Recherches sur le Caoutchouc: 42 rue Scheffer, Paris 16e; f. 1936; scientific and technical research, introduction and development of heveaculture; Pres. R. DE PADIRAC; Dir.-Gen. C. J. DU PLESSIX.

Institut Français de Pétrole: 1 and 4 ave. de Bois-Préau, B.P. 311, 92506 Rueil Malmaison Cedex; f. 1945; scientific and technical organization for the purpose of training specialists at the Ecole Nationale Supérieure du Pétrole et des Moteurs; research, development and industrialization, information and documentation, international technical assistance in the different fields of the oil industry; library of 163,400 vols.; Gen. Man. J. C. BALACEANU; publs. *Revue*†, scientific treatises and monographs, practical handbooks, etc.

Institut Max von Laue-Paul Langevin (ILL): 156x, 38042 Grenoble Cedex; f. 1967 by France and Fed. Repub. of Germany, U.K. became third equal partner in 1973; research on fundamental and nuclear physics, solid state physics, metallurgy, chemistry and biology by using reactor neutrons; receives *c.* 1,700 guest scientists a year and carries out *c.* 900 experiments on 50 different instruments; central facility is high flux beam reactor producing maximum flux of 1.2 x 10^{15}n/cm^2/s.; 430 staff; Dir. Prof. TASSO SPRINGER (Fed. Repub. of Germany); Asst. Dirs. Prof. BRIAN FENDER (U.K.), Prof. JACQUES JOFFRIN (France); publs. *Annual Report*, scientific and technical reports, etc.

Institut National de Recherche en Informatique et en Automatique (INRIA): Domaine de Voluceau, Rocquencourt, 78150 Le Chesnay; f. 1967; 400 mems.; library of 14,000 vols.; Pres. J. L. LIONS; publs. *Bulletin de liaison de la Recherche en Informatique et en Automatique, Rapports de Recherche, Rapports Techniques, Séminaires*.

Institut National des Sciences et Techniques Nucléaires—INSTN (*National Institute of Nuclear Science and Technology*): B.P. 6, 91190 Gif-sur-Yvette; f. 1956; provides, in co-operation with the Universities, courses at Saclay in nuclear engineering, reactor physics, mechanics of structures, analytical chemistry, use of radioisotopes, special metallurgy, economy of research and development; Dir. A. HERPIN; Pres. Council of Instruction J. TEILLAC.

Institut Technique du Bâtiment et des Travaux Publics: 9 rue Lapérouse, 75784 Paris Cedex 16; f. 1933; Lecture and Documentation Centre for engineers, building contractors, architects, and students, for study of architecture, building construction and public works; 5,000 mems.; Dir. Y. AUBERT; publ. *Annales* (monthly).

Office National d'Etudes et de Recherches Aérospatiales—ONERA: 29 ave. de la Division Leclerc, 92320 Châtillon-sous-Bagneux; f. 1946 to develop, direct, and co-ordinate scientific and technical research in the field of space and aeronautics; Dir. ANDRÉ AURIOL; publ. *La Recherche Aérospatiale* (every 2 months).

Station d'Oenologie et de Technologie Végétale—INRA: B.P. 72, blvd. Général de Gaulle, 11104 Narbonne Cedex; f. 1895; 42 mems.; library of 5,000 vols.; Dir. CLAUDE JOURET; publ. *Annales de Technologie Agricole de l'INRA*.

LIBRARIES AND ARCHIVES

(University libraries are listed in a separate section at the end.)

The administrative control of the libraries and archives of France is vested in the three following organizations:

Service des Bibliothèques: 61-65 rue Dutot, 75732 Paris Cedex 15; f. 1975; under the Ministry for Universities; Dir. PIERRE TRINCAL; publ. *Bulletin des bibliothèques de France* (monthly).

Direction du Livre: 4 rue de la Banque 75002 Paris; f. 1976; under the Ministry of Culture and Communication; Dir. PIERRE VANDEVOORDE.

Direction des Archives de France: 60 rue des Francs-Bourgeois, Paris 3e; f. 1897; Dir.-Gen. JEAN FAVIER; under the Ministry of Culture and Communication.

NATIONAL ARCHIVES

Archives Nationales: 60 rue des Francs-Bourgeois, Paris 3e; f. 1789; approx. 1,500 million documents; Dir.-Gen. JEAN FAVIER.

NATIONAL LIBRARY

Bibliothèque Nationale: 58 rue de Richelieu, Paris 2e; f. by Charles V; Gen. Admin. GEORGES LE RIDER; Gen. Sec. THÉRÈSE KLEINDIENST; publs. *Bulletin, Bibliographie de la France* (weekly), *Bulletin des Bibliothèques de France* (containing *Bulletin de Documentation bibliographique*). The library consists of the following three depts. and four technical centres for inter-library co-operation:

1. *Administration:* legal depository, photographic laboratory, conservation and restoration services;

2. *Dept. of Printed Books:* acquistions, printed books (9 million vols.), periodicals (500,000), official publs., *Bibliothèque de l'Arsenal* (*q.v.*).

3. *Specialized Depts.:* maps and plans (800,000), stamps (12 million) and photography (2 million), MSS. (180,000 bound vols.), coins and medals (700,000) and antiques,

music (inc. *Bibliothèque du Conservatoire, Bibliothèque de l'Opéra*) (500,000 items), national record library and audio-visual aids (360,000 records, 1,600 tape recordings, etc.), theatre arts (3 million items).

Centre bibliographique national.
Centre national des Echanges.
Centre national de Prêt.
Centre national du Livre ancien et des Documents rares et précieux.

PARIS

The American Library in Paris Inc.: 10 rue Général Camou, Paris 7e; Provincial branches in Toulouse, Montpellier, Grenoble, Nancy and Nantes; f. 1920; 7,000 mems.; 150,000 vols.; reference and lending library; Chair. MARIA-HÉLÈNE DE LAIRE.

Bibliothèque Administrative de la Marine: 2 rue Royale, Paris 8e; 50,000 vols.; admin. section of the Service Historique de la Marine; Libr. Mme MACAREZ.

Bibliothèque Centrale de l'Ecole Polytechnique: Plateau de Palaiseau, 91128 Palaiseau Cedex; f. 1794; 300,000 vols.; Chief Librarian Mme G. FEUILLEBOIS.

Bibliothèque de l'Académie Nationale de Médecine: 16 rue Bonaparte, 75006 Paris; f. 1847; over 300,000 vols.; Librarian Mme CATHERINE LUPOVICI.

Bibliothèque de l'Arsenal: 1 rue de Sully, 75004 Paris; f. by the Marquess of Paulmy, became public library in 1797; department of the Bibliothèque Nationale; specializes in literature and theatre; open to students; contains 1,500,000 vols.; 250,000 vols. of theatrical collection, 15,000 MSS., many autographs, 120,000 prints; Dir. JACQUES GUIGNARD.

Bibliothèque de l'Assemblée Nationale: Palais Bourbon, Paris 7e; f. 1796; 600,000 vols., 1,800 MSS., and 80 incunabula; Dir. MADELEINE MOINOT.

Bibliothèque de l'Ecole des Langues Orientales: 2 rue de Lille, 75007 Paris; f. 1868; over 500,000 vols.; Chief Librarian Mme. MARION DEBOUT.

Bibliothèque de l'Ecole Nationale Supérieure des Mines: 60 blvd. Saint-Michel, 75272 Paris Cedex 06; f. 1783; 500,000 vols., 2,500 periodicals; earth sciences, materials science and applied mathematics; Chief Librarian Mme B. GAUTHIER.

Bibliothèque de l'Ecole Normale Supérieure: 45 rue d'Ulm, 75230 Paris Cedex 05; f. 1795; 600,000 vols.; Dir. JEAN BOUSQUET; Chief Librarian PIERRE PETITMENGIN.

Bibliothèque de Linguistique: Sorbonne, Galerie Richelieu, Esc. F, 2e étage, 12 rue Cujas, 75005 Paris; general and applied linguistics; 5,000 vols.; Dir. ANDRÉ MARTINET.

Bibliothèque de l'Institut Catholique: 21 rue d'Assas, Paris 6e; f. 1875; over 600,000 vols.; Chief Librarians Mlle C. LEHMANN and M. ROCHAIS.

Bibliothèque de l'Institut de France: 23 quai de Conti, Paris 6e; f. 1795; 1,500,000 vols.; Chief Curator Mme LOUIS HAUTECOEUR.

Bibliothèque de l'Institut National de la Statistique et des Etudes Economiques: 18 blvd. Adolphe Pinard, 75675 Paris Cedex 14; f. 1946; 150,000 vols., 6,000 periodicals; Dir. BERNARD CHEVALIER; publ. *Bulletin* (weekly).

Bibliothèque de la Cour des Comptes: 13 rue Cambon, 75100 Paris RP; f. 1807 by Napoleon I; 50,000 vols. on finance, law and economy; Librarian MARIE-FRANCE BOUGIE; publs. *Bulletin de la Bibliothèque* (quarterly).

Bibliothèque des Avocats à la Cour d'Appel: Palais de Justice, Paris 1er; f. 1708; confiscated during the Revolution, but refounded in 1810; 160,000 vols.; not open to the public; Librarian MICHEL BRICHARD.

Bibliothèque du Conseil d'Etat: Place du Palais-Royal, Paris 1er; f. 1871; 150,000 vols. on jurisprudence, history, political science and legislation; Librarian Mlle RABANT; publ. *Etudes et Documents.*

Bibliothèque du Conservatoire National des Arts et Métiers: 292 rue St. Martin, 75141 Paris Cedex 03; 170,000 vols. on science, technology, political economy; Librarian Mme CLAUDE MICHEL.

Bibliothèque du Conservatoire National Supérieur de Musique: 14 rue de Madrid, 75008 Paris; f. 1795; 80,000 vols.; music, musicology and music teaching; part of the music dept. of the National Library; Chief Curator FRANÇOIS LESURE.

Bibliothèque du Ministère des Affaires Etrangères: 37 quai d'Orsay, Paris 7e; f. in 18th century; over 400,000 vols.; in charge of the Asst. Curator of the Archives Dept.; Librarian GEORGES DETHAN.

Bibliothèque du Ministère des Armées: 231 blvd. Saint-Germain, Paris 7e; over 350,000 vols.; f. 1823; science and military history; Librarian Mlle M. LENOIR.

Bibliothèque du Muséum National d'Histoire Naturelle: 38 rue Geoffroy-Saint-Hilaire, 75005 Paris; f. 1635; 800,000 vols.; Chief Librarian Y. LAISSUS.

Bibliothèque du Sénat: Palais du Luxembourg, Paris 6e; f. 1818; 520,000 vols., chiefly on history and law, 1,343 MSS. and 40,000 prints; open to members of Parliament; Dir. JEAN BÉCARUD.

Bibliothèque Espagnole: 11 ave. Marceau, 75116 Paris; f. 1952; library of 20,000 vols.; Dirs. ARTURO MORALES, M. CAMPOS ORIOLA; publ. *Mélanges* (annually).

Bibliothèque et Archives du Louvre et des Musées Nationaux: Palais du Louvre, 34 quai du Louvre, 75041 Paris; f. 1871; contains books, files and MSS. connected with the Louvre and the National Museums; open only to authorized persons; 250,000 vols.; Archivist and Librarian NICOLE VILLA.

Bibliothèque Forney: 1 rue du Figuier, Paris 4e; f. 1886; 120,000 vols., 250,000 specimens of decorative art, furniture, silverwork, etc.; Librarian Mme J. VIAUX.

Bibliothèque Georges Duhamel: square Brieussel Bourgeois, 78200 Mantes-la-Jolie; f. 1797; encyclopaedic library; 60,000 vols.; record library: 2,000 records; permanent exhibitions in Georges Duhamel gallery; Dir. PAUL JOLAS; publ. *Rencontres Artistiques et Littéraires.*

Bibliothèque Historique de la Marine: 3 avenue Octave Gréard, Paris 7e; f. 1922; 60,000 vols. on naval history; Librarian J. P. BUSSON.

Bibliothèque Historique de la Ville de Paris: 24 rue Pavée, 75004 Paris; f. 1871; 650,000 vols., 15,000 MSS. on history of Paris; Curator HÉLÈNE VERLET.

Bibliothèque Mazarine: 23 quai de Conti, Paris 6e; f. 1643 by Cardinal Mazarin, since 1945 attached to Institut de France; 400,000 vols., 4,600 MSS., 1,500 incunabula; Dir. PIERRE GASNAULT.

Bibliothèque-Musée de l'Opéra: place Charles Garnier, Paris 9e; f. 1875; 200,000 vols., 30,000 scores, 80,000 libretti, 100,000 drawings, 100,000 lithographs, 100,000 photographs, 40,000 periodicals; Librarian MARTINE KAHANE.

Bibliothèque Pédagogique (*Institut National de Recherche et de Documentation Pédagogiques*): 29 rue d'Ulm, Paris 5e; f. 1879; 1,000,000 vols.; Dir. G. PALMADE.

Bibliothèque Polonaise: 6 quai d'Orléans, 75004 Paris; 8,000 maps (16th to 20th centuries); Curator EUGÈNE ZALESKI.

Bibliothèque Publique d'Information: Centre Georges-Pompidou, 75191 Paris Cedex 04; f. 1976; reference library, open to the public; 463,900 documents on all subjects (books, newspapers, audio-visual documents, slides); also language laboratory, children's library (32,700 documents), newsroom (9,500 documents) and exhibitions; Dir. RENÉ FILLET. (*See* also *Centre Georges-Pompidou*, under Museums).

Bibliothèque Thiers: 27 place Saint-Georges, Paris 9e, f. 1905; attached to Institut de France; 80,000 vols. and 2,300 MSS. on 19th-century history; Librarian Mlle H. MICHAUD.

British Council Library: 9 rue de Constantine, 75007 Paris; f. 1946; 47,773 vols, 182 periodicals; reference and lending library, open to the public; brs. in Bordeaux, Lille, Lyon, Marseille and Toulouse; Librarian (Paris) Mrs. FRANCES SALINIÉ.

Centre de Documentation Benjamin Franklin/Benjamin Franklin Reference Library: 2 rue Saint-Florentin, 75001 Paris; f. 1945; sponsored by International Communications Agency; reference library specialized in all aspects of American civilization except scientific and technical subjects; 8,000 vols.; Dir. CHRISTIANE LAUDE.

Centre de Documentation Economique de la Chambre de Commerce et d'Industrie de Paris: 16 rue de Châteaubriand, Paris 8e; f. 1821; 300,000 vols., 13,000 periodicals; Dir. DOMINIQUE BAGGE; publs. various documentary guides.

Centre Pédagogique de Documentation de l'Ecole nationale des Ponts et Chaussées: 28 rue des Saints-Pères, 75007 Paris; f. 1747; over 200,000 vols. on building, civil engineering; Dir. J. MICHEL.

Direction des Services d'Archives de Paris: 30 quai Henri IV, 75004 Paris, and Hôtel de Saint-Aignan, 71 rue du Temple, 75003 Paris; f. 1971; collections of various kinds of documents relating to the history of Paris; library of 20,000 vols. specializing in history of Paris and administrative publications of the Paris prefecture; Dir. J.-Y. RIBAULT.

PROVINCIAL LIBRARIES

(In alphabetical order according to place name.)

Bibliothèque Municipale: Jardin d'Emonville, place Clémenceau, 80101 Abbeville; f. 1643; 104,000 vols.; Librarian M. AGACHE-LECAT.

Bibliothèque Municipale: Hôtel de Ville, 13100 Aix-en-Provence; f. 1810; 310,000 vols.; Chief Librarian S. ESTEVE.

Bibliothèque Municipale: 28 rue Rochegude, 81000 Albi; f. during the French Revolution; 200,000 vols.; Librarian JACQUES PONS.

Bibliothèque Municipale: 50 rue de la République, 80037 Amiens Cedex; f. during the French Revolution; 160,000 vols.; Chief Librarian GENEVIÈVE TOURNOVER.

Bibliothèque Municipale Classée: 49 rue Toussaint, 49000 Angers; f. during the French Revolution; 325,000 vols.; Librarian Mlle ISABELLE BATTEZ.

Bibliothèque Calvet: 65 rue Joseph Vernet, 84000 Avignon; f. 1810; 270,000 vols., 6,400 MSS., 700 incunabula, 12,600 musical scores, 40,000 engravings and maps, 30,000 coins; Chief Librarian GEORGES DE LOYE.

Bibliothèque Municipale: 1 rue de la Bibliothèque, 25000 Besançon; f. 1694; 300,000 vols., 3,000 MSS., 1,000 incunabula, etc.; Chief Librarian J. MIRONNEAU.

Bibliothèque Municipale: 3 rue Mably, 33075 Bordeaux Cedex; f. 1736; 723,346 vols.; 3,964 MSS.; Chief Librarian PIERRE BOTINEAU.

British Council Library: c/o British Consulate-General, 15 Cours de Verdun, 33000 Bordeaux; f. 1950; 10,318 vols., 48 periodicals.

Bibliothèque Municipale: 109 rue Félix-Adam, 62200 Boulogne-sur-Mer; f. during the French Revolution; 150,000 vols., 1,100 MSS.; Librarian LOUIS SEGUIN.

Bibliothèque Municipale: place Louis-Guillouard, 14034 Caen Cedex; f. 18th century; 460,000 vols., 671 periodicals; special Normandy collection; Librarian GENEVIÈVE LE CACHEUX.

Bibliothèque Municipale Classée: 37 rue St. Georges, 59400 Cambrai; f. 1791; 70,000 vols., 1,400 MSS., 600 incunabula; Librarian MICHEL BOUVY.

Bibliothèque Inguimbertine: 234 blvd. Albin-Durand 84200 Carpentras; f. 1745; 210,906 vols.; Librarian H. DUBLED.

Bibliothèque Municipale: passage Henri-Vendel, 51000 Châlons-sur-Marne; f. 1803; 300,000 vols.; Chief Librarian A. LIEUTAUD.

Bibliothèque de la Ville de Colmar: place des Martyrs de la Résistance, 68000 Colmar; f. 1803; 350,000 vols.; Chief Librarian FRANCIS GUETH.

Bibliothèque Municipale: 5 rue de l'Ecole-de-Droit, 21000 Dijon; f. 1701; 250,000 vols.; Chief Librarian PIERRE GRAS.

Bibliotheque Municipale: rue de la Fonderie, 595000 Douai; f. 1767; 136,000 vols.; Librarian Mlle FRANÇOISE BRUNO.

Bibliothèque Municipale: blvd. Maréchal Lyautey, 38000 Grenoble; f. 1772; 761,119 vols., 654 incunabula, 20,437 MSS., 80,000 prints, 2,560 maps; Dir. CÉCIL GUITART.

Bibliothèque et Musée de la Ville: 9 rue du Maréchal Foch, 67500 Haguenau; f. 1839; 120,000 vols.; also museum of protohistory and folk-lore; Dir. A. M. BURG; publ. *Etudes Haguenoviennes* (every 3 years).

Bibliothèque Municipale: 28 rue Gargoulleau, 17025 La Rochelle Cedex; f. 1750; 215,000 vols.; Librarian Mlle OLGA BERNARD DE SAINT-AFFRIQUE.

Bibliothèque Municipale: 17 rue Jules Lecesne, 76600 Le Havre; f. 17th/18th century; 250,000 vols.; Librarians Mlle M.-F. ROSE, M. P. DUREAU, M. BERARD.

Bibliothèque Municipale: 34 rue Edouard Delesalle, 59043 Lille Cedex; f. 1726; 550,000 vols.; Librarian Mlle ODETTE CROMBEZ.

British Council Library: c/o British Consulate-General, 10 rue du Pont Neuf, 59000 Lille; f. 1966; 8,834 vols., 50 periodicals.

Bibliothèque Municipale: 6 place de l'Ancienne-Comédie, 87032 Limoges Cedex; f. 1804; 270,000 vols.; collection of books on ceramic porcelain; enamels; Librarian Mlle M.-M. ERLEVINT.

Bibliothèque Municipale: 30 blvd. Vivier-Merle, 69431 Lyon Cedex 3; f. 1693; 850,000 vols., *c.* 9,000 MSS. and archives; Dir. JEAN-LOUIS ROCHER.

British Council Library: c/o British Consulate-General, 24 rue Childebot, 69288 Lyon Cedex 1; f. 1948; 10,647 vols., 82 periodicals.

Bibliothèque Municipale: 38 rue du 141e R.I.A., 13331 Marseille Cedex 3; f. 1800; 400,000 vols.; Chief Librarian MICHEL GERNET.

British Council Library: c/o British Consulate-General, 24 ave. du Rado, 13008 Marseille; f. 1974; 3,487 vols., 31 periodicals.

Bibliothèque Municipale: 1 cour Elie Fleur, 57000 Metz; f. 1811; 200,000 vols., 1,195 MSS., 5,000 engravings, 463 incunabula; Chief Librarian GERARD BRIAND.

Bibliothèque de la Ville et du Musée Fabre: blvd. Bonnes Nouvelles, 34000 Montpellier; f. during the French Revolution; 500,000 vols.; Librarian Mlle F. MOURGUE-MOLINES.

Bibliothèque Municipale: 43 rue Stanislas, 54042 Nancy Cedex; f. 1750; 500,000 vols.; Chief Librarian RENE CUENOT.

Bibliothèque Municipale: 37 rue Gambetta, 44041 Nantes Cedex; f. 1753; 350,000 vols.; Chief Librarian LUCE COURVILLE.

Bibliothèque Municipale d'Etudes: 21 *bis* blvd. Dubouchage, 06047 Nice Cedex; f. 1802; 372,410 vols.; Chief Librarian MADELEINE CAMBUZAT.

Bibliothèque Municipale: 19 Grande-Rue, 30000 Nîmes; f. 1794; 234,000 vols., 865 MSS.; Chief Librarian Mlle COTTON.

Bibliothèque Municipale: 1 rue Dupanloup, 45043 Orléans Cedex; f. 1714; 380,000 vols.; 2,361 MSS.; Librarian FRANÇOIS HAUCHECORNE.

Bibliothèque Municipale: place Paul-Lafond, 64000 Pau; 270,000 vols.; includes municipal archives; special collections on Henri IV and Béarn; Librarian XAVIER LAVAGNE.

Bibliothèque Municipale: 20 cours Tourny, 24000 Périgueux; f. 1781; 130,000 vols.; Librarian Mme D. ROBIN.

Bibliothèque Municipale: 43 place Charles-de-Gaulle, 86000 Poitiers; f. during the French Revolution; 350,000 vols., 1,771 MSS., 272 incunabula; Librarian JEANNE CONDAMIN.

Bibliothèque Municipale: 2 place Carnegie, 51095 Reims; f. 1809; 245,000 vols., 2,502 MSS.; Librarian ROGER LASLIER.

Bibliothèque Municipale: 1 rue de la Borderie, 35042 Rennes Cedex; f. 1790; 350,000 vols.; Librarian LOUIS ROUSSEAU.

Bibliothèque Municipale: 3 rue Jacques-Villon, 76000 Rouen; f. 1791; 350,000 vols.; Chief Librarian C. SIMONNET.

Bibliothèque Municipale: 1 rue du Périgord, 31070 Toulouse Cedex; f. 1782; 500,000 vols.; Chief Librarian JEAN GOASGUEN.

British Council Library: 56 rue du Taur, 31000 Toulouse; f. 1970; 6,262 vols., 42 periodicals.

Bibliothèque Municipale: place Anatole France, 37042 Tours Cedex; f. 1791; old library destroyed in 1940; 460,000 vols.; Librarian M. SANSEN.

Bibliothèque Municipale: 21 rue Chrestien de Troyes, 10042 Troyes Cedex; f. 1651; 300,000 vols.; Chief Librarian Mlle FRANÇOISE BIBOLET.

Bibliothèque Municipale: 4 place des Ormeaux, 26000 Valence; f. 1775; 100,000 vols.; Librarian ELISABETH CADIC.

Bibliothèque Municipale: 2-6 rue Ferrand, 59300 Valenciennes; f. 1765; 151,673 vols.; Librarian FRÉDÉRIC BARBIER.

Bibliothèque Municipale: 5 rue de l'Indépendance Américaine, 78000 Versailles; f. 1803; 450,000 vols.; Chief Librarian ALICE GARRIGOUX.

UNIVERSITY LIBRARIES

AIX-EN-PROVENCE

Bibliothèque Interuniversitaire d'Aix-Marseille (Direction-Administration): 3 ave. Robert Schuman, B.P. 331, 13606 Aix-en-Provence; Dir. Mlle GENEVIÈVE KOEST.

Bibliothèque Interuniversitaire d'Aix-Marseille (Droit): 3 ave. Robert Schuman, 13626 Aix-en-Provence; f. 1879; 140,000 vols.; Librarian Mlle GUIEU.

Bibliothèque Interuniversitaire d'Aix-Marseille (Lettres): Chemin du Moulin de Testas, 13626 Aix-en-Provence; f. 1967; 250,000 vols.; Librarian HENRY LECOMTE.

AMIENS

Bibliothèque de l'Université de Picardie: f. 1966; 120,000 vols.; 1,200 periodicals; Dir. PHILIPPE DUPONT.

Section Droit-Lettres: rue Solomon Mahlanghu, Campus, 80025 Amiens Cedex; Librarians J. KAMOWSKI and A.-M. DUCROCQ.

Section Médecine: 12 rue Frédéric Petit, 80036 Amiens; Librarian C. DEGRUTERE.

Section Sciences: 33 rue St. Leu, 80039 Amiens; Librarian N. DIEZ.

Section Scientifique de St. Quentin: 48 rue Raspail, 02100 St. Quentin; Librarian M. A. CARDOT.

ANGERS

Bibliothèque Universitaire: blvd. Lavoisier, 49045 Angers Cedex; Dir. J.-C. BROUILLARD.

Section Sciences-Droit-Lettres: blvd. Lavoisier, 49045 Angers Cedex.

Section Médecine-Pharmacie: 16 blvd. Daviers, 49000 Angers.

AVIGNON

Bibliothèque du Centre Universitaire: Librarian Mlle FRANÇOISE FEBVRE.

Section Lettres: 5 rue Violette, 84000 Avignon; f. 1978; 25,000 vols., 196 periodicals.

Section Sciences: 33 rue Louis Pasteur, 84000 Avignon; f. 1968; 6,000 vols., 130 periodicals.

BESANÇON

Bibliothèque de l'Université: f. 1880; Dir. CHRISTIAN PIERDET.

Section Centrale (Droit-Lettres-Médecine): 32 rue Mégevand, B.P. 1057, Besançon Cedex 25001.

Section Sciences: Ave. de l'Observatoire, La Bouloie, 25030 Besançon Cedex.

BORDEAUX

Bibliothèque Interuniversitaire de Bordeaux (Direction-Administration): ave. des Arts, Domaine Universitaire, 33405 Talence; f. 1879; 910,000 vols.; Dir. Mlle ELISABETH TRAISSAC.

Section Lettres: ave. des Arts, Domaine Universitaire, 33405 Talence.

Section Droit et Sciences Economiques: allée Maine de Biran, Domaine Universitaire, 33405 Talence.

Section Sciences: ave. des Facultés, Domaine Universitaire, 33405 Talence.

Section Médecine: 146 rue Léo-Saignat, 33076 Bordeaux.

Section Pharmacie-Odontologie: place de la Victoire, 33076 Bordeaux.

BREST

Bibliothèque Universitaire: 10 ave. Victor Le Gorgeu, 29283 Brest Cedex; Medical Section: 22 rue Camille Desmoulins, 29200 Brest; Librarian Mlle DE SALLIER DUPIN.

CAEN

Bibliothèque Universitaire: Université, Esplanade de la Paix, 14032 Caen; 600,000 vols.; Chief Librarian T. TORCHY.

CHAMBÉRY

Bibliothèque du Centre Universitaire de Savoie: B.P. 143, 1 rue Marcoz, 73011 Chambéry; Librarian Mlle J. GRELLIER.

CLERMONT-FERRAND

Bibliothèque Municipale et Universitaire: Dir. M.-TH. SART.

Section Lettres: 1 blvd. Lafayette, B.P. 27, 63001 Clermont-Ferrand Cedex; Librarian H. CHALAS.

Section Municipale: Librarian S. MONTAGNE.

Section Droit: 41 blvd. Gergovia, 63037 Clermont-Ferrand Cedex; Librarian G. SEMONSOUS.

Section Lettres 1er cycle: 29 blvd. Gergovia, Clermont-Ferrand; Librarian Mme SERANDON.

Section Sciences: Campus Universitaire des Cézeaux, 63170 Aubière; Librarian A. JOBERT.

Section Médecine-Pharmacie-Odontologie: 28 place Henri Dunant, 63039 Clermont-Ferrand Cedex; Librarian R. PERRIN.

DIJON

Bibliothèque de l'Université: Dir. J.-C. GARRETA.

Section Droit-Lettres: Campus de Montmuzard, 21100 Dijon; Librarian (vacant).

Section Sciences: 2 rue Sully, 21100 Dijon; Librarian Mlle F. HAGENE.

Section Médecine-Pharmacie: 7 blvd. Jeanne d'Arc, 21100 Dijon; 370,000 vols.; Librarian (vacant).

GRENOBLE

Bibliothèque Interuniversitaire: Dir. G. NIGAY.

Section Droit et Section Lettres: B.P. 36, 38401 St. Martin-d'Hères Cedex.

Section Sciences: B.P. 22, 38402 St.-Martin-d'Hères Cedex.

Section Médecine-Pharmacie: Domaine de la Merci, 38700 La Tronche.

LE MANS

Bibliothèque de l'Université du Maine: route de Laval "Vaurouzé", 72017 Le Mans Cedex; f. 1965; 50,000 vols., 500 periodicals; Dir. N. RICHTER.

LILLE

Bibliothèque Interuniversitaire:

Section Droit-Lettres: Domaine Universitaire Littéraire et Juridique, B.P. 99, 59652 Villeneuve d'Ascq Cedex.

Section Sciences: ave. Henri Poincaré, 59650 Villeneuve d'Ascq.

Section Médecine: place de Verdun, 59045 Lille Cedex.

Section Pharmacie: rue du Prof. Laguesse, 59045 Lille Cedex.

LIMOGES

Bibliothèque de l'Université de Limoges: f. 1965; 50,000 vols.

Section des Sciences: 123 rue Albert Thomas, 87060 Limoges Cedex; Librarian M. GAUMY.

Section des Lettres: 39 rue Camille Guérin, 87031 Limoges Cedex; Librarian Mlle GASC.

Section du Droit: 39 rue Camille Guérin, 87031 Limoges Cedex; Librarian Mlle C. BOUTTEAUX.

Section Médecine-Pharmacie: 2 rue du Docteur Marcland, 87031 Limoges Cedex; Librarian Mlle BOIS.

LYON

Bibliothèque Interuniversitaire: 43 blvd. du 11 Novembre 1918, 69622 Villeurbanne; f. 1964; Chief Librarian ROGER THOUMIEUX.

Bibliothèque Interuniversitaire (Droit-Lettres): 16 quai Claude Bernard, 69365 Lyon Cedex 2; f. 1896; 450,000 vols.

Bibliothèque Interuniversitaire (Droit-Lettres): ave. de l'Université, 69500 Bron; f. 1972; 60,000 vols.

Bibliothèque Interuniversitaire (Médecine): 8 ave. Rockefeller, 69373 Lyon Cedex 2; f. 1930; 350,000 vols.

Bibliothèque Interuniversitaire (Sciences): 43 blvd. du 11 November 1918, 69622 Villeurbanne; f. 1964; 186,000 vols.

MARSEILLE

Bibliothèque Interuniversitaire d'Aix-Marseille:

Section C.H.U. Nord: Chemin des Bourrely, 13326 Marseille Cedex 3; f. 1970; 15,000 vols.; Librarian Mme MICHELLE BESNARD.

Section Luminy: 70 route Léon Lachamp, 13288 Marseille Cedex 2; f. 1967; 25,000 vols.; Librarian Mlle MARIE-HÉLÈNE BOURNAT.

Section Médecine: 27 blvd. Jean Moulin, 13385 Marseille Cedex 4; f. 1891; 250,000 vols.; Librarian Mlle C. PERRIN.

Section Pharmacie: 27 blvd. Jean Moulin, 13385 Marseille Cedex 4; f. 1974; 4,500 vols.; Librarian Mme MICHELINE EMERY.

Section Sciences St. Charles: 1 place Victor Hugo, 13331 Marseille Cedex 3; f. 1880; 240,000 vols.; Librarians J. BILLIOUD, F. LAPÈLERIE, G. HAZZAN.

Section Sciences St. Jérôme: rue Henri Poincaré, 13397 Marseille Cedex 4; f. 1967; 18,000 vols.; Librarian Mlle MICHELE TERRAS.

METZ

Bibliothèque Universitaire: Ile du Saulcy, 57000 Metz; f. 1972; 70,000 vols., 450 periodicals; Librarian JEAN MARIE DILIGENT.

MONTPELLIER

Bibliothèque Interuniversitaire: Administration: 4 rue de l'Ecole Mage, 34060 Montpellier Cedex; f. 1890; *c.* 850,000 vols.; Dir. Mlle DELRIEU.

Section Droit et Sciences Economiques: 4 rue de l'Ecole Mage, 34060 Montpellier Cedex; Librarian Mlle LAMURE.

Section des Lettres et Sciences Humaines: route de Mende, 34060 Montpellier Cedex; Librarian M. BERNARD.

Section Médecine: 2 rue de l'Ecole de Médecine, 34060 Montpellier Cedex; Librarian Mme. FONTAINE-LEVENT.

Section Pharmacie: ave. Charles Flahault, 34060 Montpellier Cedex; Librarian Mme NICQ.

Section Sciences: Place Eugène Bataillon, 34060 Montpellier Cedex; Librarian Mlle JUSTRABO.

MULHOUSE

Bibliothèque de l'Université de Haute Alsace:

Section Lettres: 31 Grand'Rue, 68090 Mulhouse Cedex.

Section Sciences: 6 rue des Frères Lumière, 68093 Mulhouse Cedex; Dir. HUBERT CHOPIN.

NANCY

Bibliothèque Interuniversitaire: 11 place Carnot, 54042 Nancy Cedex; Chief Librarian GÉRARD THIRION.

Section Droit-économie: 11 place Carnot; Librarian Mlle NELLY VINGTDEUX.

Section Lettres-Sciences Humaines: 46 ave. de la Libération, 54000 Nancy; Librarian Mme. FRANCINE HEDDESHEIMER.

Section Médecine: ave. de la Forêt de Haye, Brabois, 54500 Vandoeuvre; Librarian Mlle MARIE-FRANÇOISE BESSE.

Section Sciences et techniques: blvd. des Aiguillettes, 54600 Villers les Nancy; Librarian CLAUDE GERARD.

Section Pharmacie: rue Albert Lebrun, 54000 Nancy; Librarian EMILE RIMLINGER.

NANTES

Bibliothèque Universitaire:

Section Droit-Lettres: Domaine du Tertre, Chemin de la Sensive du Tertre, 44072 Nantes Cedex.

Section Sciences: 2 Chemin de la Houssinière, 44072 Nantes Cedex; Librarian G. LABBÉ.

Section Médecine-Pharmacie: 1 rue Gaston-Weil, 44000 Nantes.

NICE

Bibliothèque Universitaire:

Section Lettres: 100 blvd. Edouard Herriot, 06200 Nice.

Section Droit et Sciences Economiques: 28 ave. Emile Henriot, 06000 Nice.

Section Sciences: 28 ave. Valrose, 06100 Nice.

Section Médecine: Chemin de Vallombrose, 06000 Nice.

ORLÉANS

Bibliothèque Universitaire: Domaine de la Source, 45045 Orléans Cedex; f. 1965; 74,000 vols. 713 periodicals, 14,450 theses; Dir. Mme BONNEFOY.

Section Droit: Librarian Mme CORGIER.

Section Lettres: Librarian Mme OJALVO.

Section Sciences: Librarian M. CORGIER.

PARIS

Bibliothèques des Universités de Paris: comprises the libraries of the 13 universities of Paris, eight main libraries and the libraries attached to the various institutes and research centres of the universities. The eight main constituent libraries are as follows:

Bibliothèque de la Sorbonne: 47 rue des Ecoles, 75230 Paris Cedex 05; formed in 1762; over 2,200,000 vols., 6,500 periodicals; Chief Librarian ANDRÉ TUILIER.

Bibliothèque de la Faculté de Droit: 127 rue Saint-Jacques, Paris 5e; f. 1876; over 350,000 vols.; Chief Librarian Mme RAMBAUD.

Bibliothèque de la Faculté de Médecine: 12 rue de l'Ecole-de-Médecine, Paris 6e; f. 1733; 490,000 vols.; Chief Librarian Mlle DUMAITRE.

Bibliothèque de la Faculté de Pharmacie: 4 ave. de l'Observatoire, Paris 5e; f. 1570; 120,000 vols.; 1,077,000 patents; Chief Librarian PAUL ROUX-FOUILLET.

Bibliothèque Sainte-Geneviève: 10 place du Panthéon, Paris 5e; f. 1624 by Cardinal F. de la Rochefoucauld; 1,500,000 vols., 30,000 prints, 1,500 incunabula and 4,000 MSS.; comprehensive library specializing in philosophy, theology, ancient law, medicine, science; Dir. Mme FRANÇOISE GASTINEL.

Bibliothèque de Documentation Internationale Contemporaine: Centre Universitaire de Nanterre, 92001 Nanterre; f. 1914; over 400,000 vols., 26,610 series of periodicals, 4,000 pamphlets and theses; Dir. V. BLUM; the Musée des Deux Guerres Mondiales is attached to this library.

Bibliothèque de l'Institut de Géographie: 191 rue Saint-Jacques, Paris 5e; 16,000 vols., 70,000 maps, 7,000 photographs; Librarian Mme SOMMER.

Bibliothèque d'Art et d'Archéologie (Fondation Jacques-Doucet): 3 rue Michelet, Paris 6e; f. 1918; 250,000 vols.; Chief Librarian Mlle DENISE GAZIER.

PAU

Bibliothèque de l'Université de Pau et des Pays de l'Adour: Domaine Universitaire, ave. Philippon, B.P. 550 Pau-Université, 64010 Pau Cedex; f. 1971; 70,000 vols., 750 periodicals; Dir. M. BOSC.

Section Lettres: Librarian M. VIANÈS.

Section Sciences: Librarian Mme VIANÈS.

Section Droit: Librarian Mlle MASSIAS.

PERPIGNAN

Bibliothèque Universitaire: B.P. 1062, Moulin à Vent, ave. de Villeneuve, 66010 Perpignan; f. 1962; 35,000 vols., 387 periodicals; Dir. F. BELLEDENT.

POITIERS

Bibliothèque Universitaire de Poitiers: B.P. 605, 86022 Poitiers Cedex; Dir. SUZANNE GUYOTAT.

Section Droit-Lettres: 93 ave. du Recteur Pineau.

Section Sciences: 40 ave. du Recteur Pineau.

Section Médecine-Pharmacie: 34 rue du Jardin des Plantes.

REIMS

Bibliothèque de l'Université de Reims: ave. François Mauriac, 51100 Reims; Dir. JEAN-PIERRE CASSEYRE.

Section Lettres: ave. François Mauriac, 51100 Reims.

Section Droit: ave. François Mauriac, 51100 Reims.

Section Sciences: Moulin de la Housse, rue des Crayères, 51100 Reims.

Section Médecine-Pharmacie-Odontologie: 51 rue Cognacq Jay, B.P. 477, 51066 Reims Cedex.

RENNES

Bibliothèque Interuniversitaire de Rennes: Administration and Law section: 1 rue de la Borderie, 35000 Rennes; Letters section: 5 ave. du Professeur Léon Bernard; Science section: 18 ave. des Buttes de Coësmes; Medical section: 13 ave. du Professeur Léon Bernard; f. 1855; 550,000 vols.; Chief Librarian B. DOUBLET.

ROUEN

Bibliothèque Universitaire de Rouen: Dir. Mlle F. MARIE-CARDINE.

Section Droit-Lettres: rue Lavoisier, 76130 Mont Saint Aignan; f. 1964.

Section Sciences: blvd. Maurice de Broglie, 76130 Mont Saint Aignon; f. 1964.

Section Médecine-Pharmacie: blvd. Maurice de Broglie, 76130 Mont Saint Aignan; f. 1967.

SAINT-ETIENNE

Bibliothèque Universitaire:

Section Droit-Lettres: 1 place Desnoëttes, 42100 St.-Etienne;

Section Sciences-Médecine: 21 rue du Dr. Paul Michelon, 42100 St.-Etienne Cedex.

STRASBOURG

Bibliothèque Nationale et Universitaire:

Affaires Générales: 5 rue du Maréchal Joffre, B.P. 1029/F, 67070 Strasbourg Cedex; 25,000 coins and medals, 4,678 papyri, 3,024 ostraca; Chief Librarian Mlle L. GREINER.

Section Sciences Humaines: 6 place de la République, B.P. 1029/F, 67070 Strasbourg Cedex; literature, human and social sciences; 2,300,000 vols., 5,837 MSS., 2,018 incunabula, 31,000 maps; Librarian Mme M. LEIPP.

Section des Alsatiques: 3 rue du Maréchal Joffre, B.P. 1029/F, 67070 Strasbourg Cedex; publications relating to Alsace; 100,000 vols.; Librarian G. LITTLER.

Section Droit: 5 rue du Maréchal Joffre, B.P. 1029/F, 67070 Strasbourg Cedex; 150,000 vols.; Librarian D. BRANDENBERGER.

Section Médecine: 6 rue Kirschleger, 67085 Strasbourg Cedex; 220,000 vols.; Librarian Mlle S. SCHLUMBERGER.

Section des Sciences: 34 blvd. de la Victoire, B.P. 1037/F, 67070 Strasbourg Cedex; 250,000 vols.; Chief Librarian E. GEISS.

TOULON

Bibliothèque de l'Université—Centre Universitaire de Toulon: Château Saint-Michel, R.N. 98, 83130 La Garde; f. 1971; 14,000 vols., 400 periodicals; law, economics, business, sciences, electrical and mechanical engineering, general culture; Dir. Mme F. BERGÉ.

TOULOUSE

Bibliothèque Interuniversitaire: 11 rue des Puits-Creusés, 31070 Toulouse Cedex (Sections of Gen. Admin., Law and Letters); f. 1879; 900,000 vols.; Literary Library at 12 rue de l'Université de Mirail; Medical Library at 37 allées Jules-Guesde; Scientific Library: 118 route de Narbonne; Chief Librarian P. TRAINAR.

TOURS

Bibliothèque Universitaire:

Section Lettres: 5 rue des Tanneurs, 37000 Tours.

Section Droit: 5 rue des Tanneurs, 37000 Tours.

Section Sciences: Parc de Grandmont, 37200 Tours.

Section Médecine-Pharmacie: 2 bis blvd. Tonnelle, 37000 Tours.

MUSEUMS AND ART GALLERIES

Direction des Musées de France: Palais du Louvre, 75041 Paris Cedex 01; Dir. HUBERT LANDAIS.

Réunion des Musées Nationaux: Palais du Louvre, 75001 Paris; comprises:

Conseil Administratif de la Réunion des Musées Nationaux: Pres. HUBERT LANDAIS.

Conseil Artistique de la Réunion des Musées Nationaux: Pres. RENÉ HUYGHE; Vice-Pres. GASTON PALEWSKI.

Direction de l'Action Culturelle et de la Jeunesse et des Sports: 17 blvd. Morland, Paris 4e; Dir. A. TRAPENARD; Asst. Dir. F. DEBIDOUR.

PARIS

CEDIAS Musée Social: 5 rue Las-Cases, 75007 Paris; f. 1894; social information and documentation; public library containing 100,000 vols.; Curator PIERRE CHARBONNEAU; publs. *Vie Sociale* (monthly), *Manuel de Placement.*

Centre National d'Art et de Culture Georges-Pompidou (Centre Beaubourg): 75004 Paris; f. 1975; Pres. JEAN-CLAUDE GROSHENS; publs. *Revue Traverses* (*CCI*), *Lettre d'Information*†; comprises:

Bibliothèque Publique d'Information: see under Libraries.

Musée National d'Art Moderne: 20th-century paintings, sculptures, prints and drawings, photographs and art films; reference material; Dir. PONTUS HULTEN; Dir.-Designate DOMINIQUE BOZO.

Centre de Création Industrielle: covers all aspects of the design and evolution of modern life-style; exhibitions, reference material, information facilities for specialists and general public; Dir. FRANÇOIS MATHEY.

Institut de Recherche et coordination Acoustique/Musique: interdisciplinary research centre for musicians and scientists; data processing, electro-acoustics, instrumental and vocal research; Dir. PIERRE BOULEZ.

Galerie du Jeu de Paume: place de la Concorde, Paris 1er; administered by the Musée du Louvre (*q.v.*); exhibition of Impressionist art; Chief Curator MICHEL LACLOTTE.

Maison de Balzac: 47 rue Raynouard, Paris 16e; museum and library of 3,000 books and periodicals; documents relating to life and work of Honoré de Balzac; Curator JACQUELINE SARMENT.

Maison de Victor Hugo: 6 place des Vosges, Paris 4e; f. 1902; personal belongings, correspondence, first editions; library of 3,000 vols.; drawings by Victor Hugo, etc.; Curator HENRI CAZAUMAYOU.

Musée Astronomique de l'Observatoire de Paris: 61 ave. de l'Observatoire, 75014 Paris; f. 1667; astronomical instruments of the 16th, 17th, 18th and 19th centuries; statutes and pictures of celebrated astronomers; Pres. J. BOULON; Librarian Mme DE NARBONNE.

Musée Carnavalet: 23 rue de Sévigné, 75003 Paris; f. 1866; history of Paris and of the Revolution, dept. of prints and drawings; Chief Curator BERNARD DE MONTGOLFIER; publ. *Bulletin* (2 a year).

Musée Cernuschi: 7 ave. Velasquez, Paris 8e; f. 1896; ancient and contemporary Chinese art; Dir. VADIME ELISSEEFF.

Musée Cognacq-Jay: 25 blvd. des Capucines, Paris 2e; f. 1929; 18th century works of art, English and French paintings, porcelain, furniture, etc.; Curator THÉRÈSE BUROLLET.

Musée d'Art Moderne de la Ville de Paris: 11 ave. du Président-Wilson, Paris 16e; Postal address: 9 rue Gaston de Saint-Paul, 75016 Paris; f. 1961; modern painting and sculpture; Curator BERNADETTE CONTENSOU.

Musée d'Ennery: 59 avenue Foch, Paris 16e; f. 1903; Chinese and Japanese furniture, china, and objets d'art; Curator JEAN-PAUL DESROCHES.

Musée de l'Air: 8 rue des Vertugadins, 92190 Meudon, and Aéroport du Bourget, 93350 Le Bourget; f. 1919; aeronautics, representative collection of aircraft; Curator Général LISSARRAGUE.

Bureaux et Service Documentation: 91 blvd. Péreire, 75017 Paris; library of 17,000 vols.; collection of photographs.

Musée de l'Armée: Hôtel des Invalides, Paris 7e; f. 1905; collections of artillery, armour, uniforms, banners; history of French Army from its origin to present day; library of 30,000 vols., 60,000 prints, 35,000 photographs; Dir.-Gen. G. LE DIBERDER; publ. *Revue de la Société des Amis du Musée de l'Armée*† (annually).

Musée de l'Histoire de France: 60 rue des Francs-Bourgeois, Paris 3e; f. 1867; frequent exhibitions showing original documents from the National Archives tracing the principal events in the history of France from Merovingian times to the 20th century; also historical objects and iconography; Curator MARTINE GARRIGUES; publ. *Catalogue* (four parts).

Musée de l'Homme: Palais de Chaillot, 75016 Paris; f. 1878; library of 250,000 vols., 4,500 periodicals; ethnography, anthropology, prehistory; attached to the Muséum National d'Histoire Naturelle (*q.v.*); also a research and education centre; Profs. JEAN GUIART, ROBERT GESSAIN DE LUMLEY; publ. *Objets et Mondes* (4 a year).

Musée de l'Orangerie: place de la Concorde/Angle Seine, 75007 Paris; permanent exhibition of the "Nymphéas" murals by Claude Monet; Chief Curator MICHEL HOOG.

Musée de la Marine: Palais de Chaillot, Place du Trocadéro et du 11 novembre, 75116 Paris; f. 1827; collection of models of the navy; oceanographic research; Dir. Capt. FRANÇOIS BELLEC.

Musée de la Mode et du Costume: Palais Galliéra, 10 ave. Pierre 1er de Serbie, 75116 Paris; French costumes from 1725; Curator MADELEINE DELPIERRE.

Musée des Antiquités Nationales: 78100 Saint-Germain-en-Laye; f. 1862; Prehistoric, Bronze Age, Celtic, Gallo-Roman and Merovingian antiquities; Chief Curator RENÉ JOFFROY.

Musée des Arts Décoratifs: Palais du Louvre, Pavillon de Marsan, 107 rue de Rivoli, 75001 Paris; f. 1883; collection from Middle Ages to 1900; woodwork, furniture, tapestries, textiles, jewels, ceramics, sculpture, painting, gold and silver work, glass, collections of Western and Oriental art, Dubuffet Bequest; includes a national arts information and documentation centre; library of 80,000 vols.; Curator FRANÇOIS MATHEY.

Musée des deux Guerres Mondiales (Universités de Paris—Bibliothèque de Documentation Internationale Contemporaine): Hôtel National des Invalides, 75007 Paris; f. 1914; 400,000 documents (paintings, engravings, posters, cartoons, etc.); Photographic Archives, B.D.I.C., Centre Universitaire, 92001 Nanterre; Chief Curator V. BLUM.

Musée des Plans-Reliefs: Hôtel National des Invalides, 75007 Paris; f. 1668; models of fortified towns, archives and photographs; Curators G. COSTA, C. BRISAC.

Musée des Thermes et de l'Hôtel de Cluny: 6 place Paul Painlevé, Paris 5e; f. 1844; sculpture, tapestry, armour, ivory, enamels and furniture of Middle Ages; Curator A. ERLANDE BRANDENBURG.

Musée du Château: 78600 Maisons-Laffitte; Château dates from 1642; contains paintings, sculptures, tapestries and furniture; it is available for hire to organizations and private persons; Curator FLORENCE DE LA RONCIERE.

Musée du Louvre: Palais du Louvre, 75001 Paris; f. 1793; Dir. ANDRÉ CHABAUD; depts. and curators: Oriental Antiquities (PIERRE AMIET), Egyptian Antiquities (CHRISTIANE DESROCHES-NOBLECOURT), Greek and Roman Antiquities (FRANÇOIS VILLARD), Medieval, Renaissance and Modern Sculpture (JEAN-RENÉ GABORIT), *Objets d'art* (vacant), Paintings (MICHEL LACLOTTE), Drawings (MAURICE SERULLAZ), Orangerie and Jeu de Paume Galleries (HÉLÈNE ADHEMAR).

Musée du Petit Palais: ave. Churchill, Paris 8e; Municipal Museum, f. 1902; ancient and modern paintings and works of art; library of 10,000 vols.; Curator Mme CACAN DE BISSY.

Musée Guimet (*Asiatic Dept. of National Museums*): 6 place d'Iéna, 75116 Paris; f. 1889; library of 100,000 vols.; art, archaeology, religions, history, literature and music of India, Central Asia, Tibet, Afghanistan, China, Korea and Japan, Khmer, Thailand and Indonesia; Chief Curator Mlle J. AUBOYER; Librarian F. MACOUIN; publ. *Annales du Musée Guimet*†.

Musée Gustave Moreau: 14 rue de la Rochefoucauld, Paris 9e; f. 1902 from a bequest by the painter Gustave Moreau of his house and contents, including paintings, watercolours, sketches, and designs; Dir. JEAN PALADILHE.

Musée Jacquemart-André: 158 blvd. Haussmann, Paris 8e; f. 1912; painting, tapestry and furniture of Renaissance and 18th century; Dir. RENÉ HUYGHE.

Musée Marmottan: 2 rue Louis Boilly, Paris 16e; f. 1932; Primitives, Renaissance, Empire and Impressionists; permanent exhibition "Monet et ses Amis"; affiliated to the *Académie des Beaux-Arts;* Curator YVES BRAYER.

Musée Monétaire: Hotel de la Monnaie, 11 quai de Conti, Paris 6e; f. 1771; collections of ancient and modern medals, coins and dies; Dir. P. DEHAYE; publs. *Catalogues expositions, Bulletin du Club Français de la Médaille.*

Musée National de Céramique: place de la Manufacture, 92310 Sèvres; f. 1824; ancient and modern ceramic art; Curator HENRY-PIERRE FOUREST.

Musée National de Fontainebleau: 77300 Château de Fontainebleau; buildings 12th-19th centuries; paintings, interior decoration and furniture of the Renaissance, 17th and 18th centuries, 1st Empire and 19th century; Curators JEAN-PIERRE SAMOYAULT, Mme SAMOYAULT-VERLET.

Musée National des Arts et Traditions Populaires: 6 route du Mahatma Gandhi, 75116 Paris; f. 1937; 110,000 objects; library of 60,000 books, 2,000 periodicals; 160,000 photographic documents, 50,000 tape records; Curator JEAN CUISENIER; publs. *Archives d'Ethnologie Française, Guides Ethnologiques, Catalogues des Expositions, Ethnologie française.*

Musée National des Granges de Port-Royal: Magny-les-Hameaux, 78470 St.-Remy-les-Chevreuse; f. 1952; history of Port-Royal and Jansenism; presented in the house of "Petites Ecoles" where Racine studied; Curator Mme T. PICQUENARD.

Muséum National d'Histoire Naturelle: *see* under State Colleges.

Musée National de la Légion d'Honneur et des Ordres de Chevalerie: 2 rue de Bellechasse, 75007 Paris; f. 1925; contains histories of National Orders and Awards of all countries; unique collection of decorations, costumes, arms, documents, etc.; Centre de Documentation International de l'Histoire des Ordres et des Décorations; also collection and documents relating to Napoleon I; Curator Mme CLAUDE DUCOURTIAL, Mme ANABELLE DU PASQUIER.

Musée National de Malmaison (Musée d'art et d'histoire de l'époque napoléonienne): 92500-Rueil-Malmaison; f. 1906; historical collection of Napoleon I and Josephine; Chief Curator GÉRARD HUBERT.

Musée National de Bois-Préau: 1 ave. de l'Impératrice Joséphine, 92500 Rueil-Malmaison; f. 1958; Napoleonic history; court and military clothes and weapons; souvenirs of St. Helena; Chief Curator GÉRARD HUBERT.

Musée National des Monuments Français (fmrly. Musée de Sculpture Comparée): Palais de Chaillot, place du Trocadéro, Paris 16e; f. 1882; library: 10,000 works on history of art, 200,000 photographs (including those belonging to the Archives des Monuments Historiques), collection of scale reproductions of murals of the Middle Ages and materials connected with building and decoration; casts of portions of monuments and sculptures from beginning of Christianity to 19th century; Curator PHILIPPE CHAPU; Keepers FRANÇOISE HILAIRE, CHRISTIAN DE MERINDOL; publ. *Guides.*

Musée National des Techniques: 292 rue St. Martin, Paris 3e; f. 1794; evolution of industrial technique from 18th century to present day.

Musée National du Château de Versailles: 78000 Château de Versailles; f. 1837 by Louis-Philippe; historical painting and sculpture from 16th to 20th centuries, furniture of the 17th to 19th centuries; Grand Trianon, Petit Trianon châteaux, Hameau de la Reine, park and carriage museum; Cur. PIERRE LEMOINE.

Musée Nissim de Camondo: 63 rue de Monceau, Paris 8e; f. 1936; branch of Musée des Arts Décoratifs; 18th-century furniture and works of art; Savonnerie carpets; china; silver work; Curator Mme NADINE GASC; publ. *Catalogue.*

Musée Rodin: Hôtel Biron, 77 rue de Varenne, Paris 7e; f. 1916; sculpture and drawings by Rodin and objects from his collections; Curator Mme MONIQUE LAURENT.

Palais de la Découverte: ave. Franklin D. Roosevelt, 75008 Paris; f. 1937 as a scientific centre for the popularization of science; experiments explained to the public; departments of mathematics, astronomy, physics, chemistry, biology, medicine, history of science, earth sciences; also includes a Planetarium and cinema; library of 7,000 vols.; Dir. A. J. ROSE; publs. *Revue*†, *Monographies.*

PROVINCIAL MUSEUMS

(In alphabetical order according to place name.)

Musée des Beaux-Arts: place de l'Hôtel-de-Ville, 47000 Agen; f. 1876; local, Roman and mediaeval archaeology; paintings of Corneille de Lyon, Goya and the Impressionists; ceramics; Curator Mlle ANNE-MARIE LABIT.

Musée Granet: place St. Jean de Malte, 13100 Aix-en-Provence; f. 1765; Egyptian, Greek, Celto-Ligurian, Roman and Gallo-Roman archaeology; pictures of Cézanne and the French Schools, with special emphasis on Provence; Italian, Spanish, Flemish, Dutch and German Schools; modern painting; sculpture; furniture of 16th, 17th and 18th centuries; Curator LOUIS MALBOS.

Musée d'Ozé: place Lamagdelaine, 61000 Alençon; f. 1857; works of art from Cambodia; local history; numismatics; archaeology.

Musée de l'Hôtel de Ville: 37400 Amboise; collection includes tapestries, and autographs of the kings of France; Curator Mme PINOT.

Musée de la Poste: rue Joyeuse, 37400 Amboise; f. 1971; collection includes material on historic postal services and transport.

Musée de Picardie: rue de la République, 80000 Amiens; f. 1854; acquired by the municipality in 1869; fine collection of paintings of Northern and French Schools; murals by Puvis de Chavannes; Egyptian, Greek and Roman antiquities; objets d'art of Middle Ages and Renaissance; Curator VERONIQUE ALEMANY.

Musée des Beaux-Arts: 10 rue du Musée, 49000 Angers; f. 1797; housed in 15th-century "logis Barrault"; paintings of 18th-century French School and 17th-century Dutch and Flemish Schools; sculpture, including busts by Houdon and complete works of David d'Angers; Cur. Mme VIVIANE HUCHARD.

Musée Picasso: 06600 Antibes; f. 1928; works by Picasso, abstract paintings, archaeology, history; archives, library and photographs.

Musée d'Arras: Ancienne Abbaye Saint-Vaast, 22 rue Paul Doumer, 62000 Arras; f. 1825; sculpture, painting and porcelain, also temporary exhibitions each year; Curator Mlle FRANÇOISE MAISON.

Exposition Permanente du Débarquement (*Permanent Exhibition of the Landings*): 14117 Arromanches; f. 1954; exhibition of the Normandy landings of D-Day, 6th June 1944; comprises artificial port and museum of relief maps, working models, photographs, diorama and films.

Musée Calvet: Fine Arts Section, 65 rue Joseph Vernet, 84000 Avignon; Lapidary Section, 27 rue de la République; f. 1810; rich archaeological collection; antique sculpture; paintings of the French, Italian, Flemish and Dutch Schools; collection of ironwork; lapidary collection of the region; Chief Curator GEORGES DE LOYE.

Musée du Petit Palais: place du Palais des papes, 84000 Avignon; f. 1976; in the old archbishop's palace (14th–15th-century); medieval paintings of the Avignon and Italian Schools, medieval sculpture from Avignon; Chief Curator GEORGES DE LOYE.

Musée Basque de Bayonne: 1 rue Marengo, 64100 Bayonne; f. 1924; four sections covering the history and folklore of the town of Bayonne, the French Basque country, the Spanish Basque country, and the Basques in the New World; Dir. Dr. J. HARITSCHELHAR; publ. *Bulletin* (quarterly).

Musée des Beaux-Arts: 1 place de la Révolution, 25000 Besançon; f. 1694, moved to present buildings 1843; prehistoric, Greek, Roman, Gallo-Roman, and Burgundian antiquities, paintings, sculpture, ceramics and objets d'art; special section of old clocks and watches; drawings (Pâris, Gigoux and Besson collections), 15th–20th centuries and 18th-century French in detail; Curators F. SOULIER-FRANÇOIS, P. LAGRANGE.

Musée Granvelle: Palais Granvelle, 96 Grande rue, 25000 Besançon; built 1534, museum since 1945; history of Franche-Comté; Curator DENIS COUTAGNE.

Musée Lapidaire de l'Abbatiale St.-Paul: 2 rue d'Alsace, 25000 Besançon; f. 1956; collection from the Gallo-Roman period to the 18th century; Curator Mme FRANÇOISE SOULIER-FRANÇOIS.

Musée Populaire Comtois: La Citadelle, 25000 Besançon; folklore of Franche-Comté; f. 1960; Curator Abbé JEAN GARNERET; publs. *Barbizier*, Annual bulletin.

Musée National Fernand Léger: 06410 Biot; f. 1960; permanent exhibition of tableaux, drawings, lithographs, ceramics, gouaches, bronzes, tapestries.

Musée National de la Coopération Franco-Américaine: Château de Blérancourt, 02300 Chauny; f. 1927 to contain collections presented to the State by Mrs. Anna Murray Dike, Miss Anne Morgan, and other French and American benefactors, relating to the history of Franco-American relations; the castle, formerly the ancestral home of the Ducs de Gesvres, is classed as an historical monument.

Musée des Beaux-Arts: Cours d'Albret, 33000 Bordeaux; f. 1801; paintings, sculpture, prints and drawings; Curator GILBERTE MARTIN-MERY.

Musée de Normandie: Château de Caen, 14000 Caen; f. 1946; history, archaeology and ethnology of Normandy; Curator (vacant); publ. *Annales de Normandie*† (quarterly).

Musée et Château de Chantilly (Musée Condé): 60500 Chantilly; f. 1885; paintings, miniatures, drawings, 70,000 books, 3,000 MSS., etc.; Curator R. CAZELLES.

Musée National de la Voiture et du Tourisme: 60200 Château de Compiègne; f. 1927 with the co-operation of the Touring Club de France; old carriages, sedan chairs, survey of development of the bicycle and the automobile; 180 vehicles; Curator JEAN-MARIE MOULIN.

Musée National du Château de Compiègne: 60200 Compiègne; royal palace of the first kings of France, reconstructed under Louis XV and Louis XVI and partly redecorated under the First Empire; furniture of 18th and 19th centuries, mostly First Empire period; tapestries of 18th century; collections from the Second Empire period; souvenirs of the Empress Eugénie; Curator JEAN-MARIE MOULIN.

Musée des Beaux-Arts: place de la Sainte-Chapelle, 21000 Dijon; f. 1799 and housed in the Palace of the Dukes of Burgundy and the Palace of the States of Burgundy; Swiss primitives; paintings of Franco-Flemish School of 15th century and of other French and foreign schools; prints and drawings; sculptures from tombs of the Dukes of Burgundy; marble, ivory, armour; modern art section; Granville collection; Curator MARGUERITE GUILLAUME (acting); publ. *Bulletin de la Société des Amis des Musées de Dijon* (every 3 years).

Musée Magnin: 4 rue des Bons-Enfants, 21000 Dijon; Curators PIERRE QUARRÉ, A. BREJON DE LAVERGNÉE.

Musée des Trois Guerres: Diors, 36130 Déols; f. 1920; museum of the wars of 1870, 1914, 1939, Indochina, Suez, Algeria; Curator Comte R. DE LA ROCHEFOUCAULD.

Musée des Beaux-Arts: place de Verdun, 38000 Grenoble, f. 1798; fine collection of 16th-, 17th- and 18th-century paintings; Italian, French, Spanish, Flemish schools; modern collection; Egyptology collection; library of 2,500 vols., 6,500 catalogues; Curator PIERRE GAUDIBERT.

Musée Stendhal: Ancienne Mairie, Jardin de Ville, 38000 Grenoble; f. 1933; documents relating to Stendhal's life; 18th-century setting; Dir. P. HAMON.

Château de Langeais: 37130 Langeais; built in 15th century and given to the Institut de France in 1904; furniture and tapestries of the 13th-15th centuries and 15th-century architecture.

Musée des Beaux-Arts "André Malraux": blvd. J. F. Kennedy, 76600 Le Havre; f. 1845; rebuilt 1961; permanent collection from 14th to 20th centuries; exhibitions; Dir. Mme G. TESTANIÈRE.

Musée de l'Abbaye de Graville: rue Elisée Reclus, 76000 Le Havre; f. 1926; sculpture from the 12th to 18th centuries; models of old houses; exhibitions.

Musée de l'Ancien Havre: rue Jérôme Bellarmato, 76000 Le Havre; f. 1955; drawings and documents on the foundation of Le Havre by François I; ancient pottery and glass; naval models.

Musées: 72000 Le Mans; Dir. M. DE LASSÉE.

Musée de l'Automobile: circuit permanent de la Sarthe; cars, cycles and motorcycles.

Musée de la Reine Bérengère: 9–13 rue de la Reine Bérengère; 16th-century architecture, folklore, ceramics, etc.

Musée de Tesse: 2 ave. de Paderborn; paintings and sculpture.

Musée Saint-Pierre-la-Cour: 4 rue des Fosses-St.-Pierre, 72000 Le Mans; 14th-century Gothic church; tapestries and sculpture.

Musée des Beaux-Arts: place de la République, 59000 Lille; f. 1801; paintings of Flemish, Italian, Spanish, French and Dutch Schools; exceptional collection of drawings; sculpture, ceramics and archaeological exhibits; Curator HERVÉ OURSEL.

Musée Adrien Dubouché: place Winston Churchill, 87000 Limoges; f. 1900; ceramics; Chief Curator H. P. FOUREST.

Musée Municipal: place de la Cathédrale, 87000 Limoges; Limoges enamels; Egyptian collection; archaeological and lapidary collection; mineralogical collection; Curator MADELEINE MARCHEIX.

Musée des Beaux-Arts: place des Terreaux, 69001 Lyon; f. 1801 and housed in the former Benedictine Abbey of the Dames de Saint-Pierre, built in 1659; the important collection contains paintings of French, Flemish, Dutch, Italian and Spanish Schools, and sections devoted to local painters, modern art, and murals by Puvis de Chavannes; ancient, medieval and modern sculpture; French, Italian, Oriental and Hispano-Moorish ceramics; drawings, prints, furniture, numismatic collection; Chief Curator MADELEINE ROCHER-JAUNEAU; publs. *Bulletin des Musées et Monuments Lyonnais* (quarterly), illustrated guides.

Musée Cantini: 19 rue Grignan, 13006 Marseille; f. 1936; faïence, Oriental and modern art; Curator Mme M. LATOUR.

Musées d'Archéologie: Château Borély, 13008 Marseille; Curator SIMONE BOURLARD-COLLIN.

Musée Borély: f. 1863; Egyptian, Greek, Cypriot, Gallic, Roman and Gallo-Roman antiquities; 200 drawings by Fragonard, Hubert Robert and Boucher; library of 4,000 vols.

Musée des Docks Romains: place Vivaux, 13002 Marseille; ancient commerce; exhibits include amphorae, ingots and marine archaeology.

Musée de la Marine de Marseille: Chambre de Commerce et d'Industrie de Marseille, Palais de la Bourse, La Canebière, B.P. 826 bis, 13222 Marseille Cedex 1; f. 1932; history of Marseille and Mediterranean shipping; models of ships, paintings, drawings, plans, etc.; 25,000 tape recordings; Nossof, Cantelar and Grimard collections (history of steam ships); Curator F. REYNAUD.

Musée des Beaux-Arts: Palais de Longchamp, Marseille; f. 1801; paintings, French, Foreign and Provençal schools; murals by Puvis de Chavannes; collection of drawings and paintings relating to Puget; sculptures and lithographs by Daumier; Curator Mme J. LATOUR.

Musée Atger: Faculté de Médecine, 2 rue de l'Ecole de Médecine, 34000 Montpellier; f. 1823; drawings and paintings of French, Italian and Flemish schools, 16th to 18th centuries (Fragonard, Natoire, Tiepolo); Curator Mlle S. DELRIEU.

Musée Fabre: rue Montpellieret, 34000 Montpellier; f. 1825 by the painter Fabre; paintings of French (Greuze, Delacroix, Courbet, Bazille, Géricault), Italian, Spanish and Flemish Schools; drawings, sculpture (Houdon), furniture, tapestries, porcelain, silver.

Musée de l'Impression sur Etoffes: 3 rue des Bonnes-Gens, 68100 Mulhouse; f. 1858; 12 million documents, international collection and specialist library of *c.* 1,000 examples; Curator J. JACQUÉ.

Musée des Beaux-Arts: place Stanislas, 54000 Nancy; f. 1793; paintings, drawings and prints from 15th to 20th century; temporary exhibitions; Curator SIMONE GUILLAUME.

Musée des Beaux-Arts: 10 rue Georges-Clémenceau, 44000 Nantes; f. 1804; 2,000 paintings; Curator CLAUDE-PIERRE SOUVIRON.

Direction des Musées de Nice: c/o 164 ave. des Arènes de Cimiez, 06000 Nice; f. 1921; Dir. M. BATIER (acting).

Musée Massena: 65 rue de France, 06000; art and history; Curator C. A. FIGHIERA.

Musée des Beaux-Arts: 33 ave. des Beaumettes, 06000; painting and sculpture; works of Jules Chéret; Curator (vacant).

Musée d'Archéologie: 164 ave. des Arènes de Cimiez, 06000; Curator Mlle D. MOUCHOT.

Musée Matisse: 164 ave. des Arènes de Cimiez, 06000; collection of paintings by Henri Matisse; Curator Mlle C. AUDIBERT.

Musée du Vieux-Logis: 59 ave. Saint Barthélemy, 06100; antique furniture; Curator R. P. THIVET.

Muséum d'Histoire Naturelle: 60 *bis* blvd. Risso, 06300; f. 1823; Curator G. THOMEL.

Palais Lascaris: 15 rue Droite, 06300; 17th- and 18th-century frescoes and furniture; Curator Mlle C. AUDIBERT.

Galerie des Ponchettes: 77 quai des Etats-Unis, 06300; temporary exhibitions.

Galerie de la Marine: 59 quai des Etats-Unis, 06300; temporary exhibitions.

Musée National Message Biblique Marc Chagall: Ave. du Dr. Ménard, 06000 Nice; f. 1973; permanent collection of the artist's biblical works; temporary exhibitions; library of 300 vols.; Curator PIERRE PROVOYEUR.

Musée Archéologique: blvd. Amiral Courbet, 30000 Nîmes; f. 1823; protohistoric and Gallic and Roman archaeology; Curator VICTOR LASSALLE.

Musée des Beaux-Arts: rue Cité Foulc, 30000 Nîmes; f. 1823; paintings and sculpture of all European countries from the 15th century to modern times; Curator VICTOR LASSALLE.

Musée du Vieux Nîmes: place de la Cathédrale, 30000 Nîmes; f. 1921; local history, folklore and traditional employments; Asst. Dir. Mme CHRISTIANE LASSALLE.

Musée des Beaux-Arts: 1 place de la République, 45000 Orléans; f. 1823 and housed in the former Hôtel de Ville of the 15th and 16th centuries; sculpture; French, Flemish, Italian, Dutch, German and Spanish paintings and drawings (especially of 17th and 18th centuries); Max Jacob Room; Curator D. OJALVO.

Musée Historique et Archéologique de l'Orléanais: Hôtel Cabu, place Abbé Desnoyers, Orléans; f. 1855; Roman bronzes, Gallo-Roman collection from Neuvy-en-Sullias, ivories and enamels from Middle Ages to 18th century; popular prints and ceramics from Orléans; Curator D. OJALVO.

Musées de Pau:

Musée Bernadotte: 8 rue Tran, 64000 Pau; f. 1952; pictures and documents tracing the career of Jean Baptiste Bernadotte, Marshal under Napoleon, later King of Sweden; Swedish pictures; Curator PH. COMTE; publ. *Bulletin* (annually).

Musée des Beaux Arts: f. 1864; pictures by French, Flemish, Dutch, English, Italian and Spanish artists; sculptures, engravings and drawings; numismatic collections; Curator PH. COMTE.

Musée National du Château de Pau: f. 1927; 16th- and 17th-century collection of tapestries; Cur. JACQUES DE LAPRADE.

Musée Régional Béarnais: a collection relating to the Bearnese country; Curator J. CAZAURANG.

Conservation des Musées de Poitiers: 3 *bis* rue Jean Jaurès, 86000 Poitiers; f. 1820; Curators MICHEL REROLLE, MARIE-CHRISTINE PLANCHARD.

Baptistère Saint-Jean: rue Jean Jaurès; f. 1836; Merovingian archaeology.

Hypogée des Dunes: rue Père-Delacroix; f. 1909; 7th to 8th century archaeology.

Musée Sainte-Croix: 3 *bis* rue Jean Jaurès; f. 1974; fine arts, history of Poitou (archaeological, ethnographical collections, sculpture).

Musée des Augustins: Hôtel Rupert de Chièvres, 9 rue Victor Hugo; f. 1887; industrial and decorative art.

Musée de Bretagne: 20 quai Emile Zola, 35100 Rennes; f. 1960; geology, prehistory, Armorica at the Roman period, medieval art, historical documents, popular art, furniture, 19th-century costumes, contemporary regional art and history; Curator J. Y. VEILLARD.

Musée des Beaux-Arts: 20 quai Emile Zola, 35100 Rennes; f. 1799; paintings of French and foreign Schools from the 15th century, archaeology, drawings, regional ceramics; Curator NICOLE BARBIER.

Musée Saint-Denis: 8 rue Chanzy, 51100 Reims; f. 1795; paintings (especially French School, 17th-century Le Nain, and 19th-century Corot-Delacroix), and Cranach drawings; 15th- and 16th-century "Toiles Peintes"; Curator FRANÇOIS POMARÈDE.

Musée Saint-Remi: 53 rue Simon, 51100 Reims; the old Abbey of St. Remi (12th to 18th centuries), Prehistoric, Celtic, Gallo-Roman, Romanesque and Gothic antiquities and sculptures; tapestries of St.-Remi life (1530); old weapons; Curator MARC BOUXIN.

Musée des Beaux-Arts et de Céramique: 26 bis rue Thiers, 76000 Rouen; f. 1800; paintings, drawings and sculpture; ceramics from Rouen and elsewhere; Curator FRANÇOIS BERGOT.

Musée d'Art et d'Industrie: place Louis Comte, 42000 St.-Etienne; f. 1833, at Palais des Arts since 1850; ancient and modern paintings, sculpture, and ceramics; natural history; armaments; fabrics; Regional Centre for Contemporary Art; library; Curator BERNARD CEYSSON.

Musée de Saint-Malo: Château de Saint-Malo, 35400; f. 1950; history of Saint-Malo and temporary contemporary exhibitions; Curator DAN LAILLER.

Musée International du Long Cours: Tour Solidor, St.-Servan, 35400 Saint-Malo; f. 1969; international history of sailing around the world, 16th to 20th centuries; Cur. D. LAILLER.

Fondation Maeght: 06570 St.-Paul-de-Vence; f. 1964; modern paintings and sculpture; contemporary music; library on modern arts and daily films on art and artists; Curator JEAN-LOUIS PRAT.

Musée de L'Annonciade: place George Grammont, 83990 St. Tropez; f. 1955; French paintings from 1890 to 1940; Curator ERIC HILD.

Musée d'Arts Décoratifs: Le Château, 49400 Saumur; f. 1829 and reorganized 1960; local archaeology, the collection of Comte Charles Lair of decorative arts, including tapestries, furniture, wood carvings, liturgical ornaments; fine porcelain of 16th to 18th centuries; Curator Mlle MONIQUE JACOB.

Musée de l'Ile de France: Château de Sceaux, 92330 Sceaux; f. 1935; old and modern paintings, sculpture, engravings, furniture, decorative art, tapestries, history and popular traditions of the environs of Paris; exhibitions, concerts, documentation centre on the Paris region; educational services; annexes: Orangerie and Pavillon de l'Aurore (Parc de Sceaux); Chief Curator GEORGES POISSON.

Musée Municipal: 2 rue de la Congrégation, 02200 Soissons; f. 1857; antiquities, medieval sculpture, paintings of 17th to 20th centuries, local history; Cur. J. DEPOUILLY.

Musée Archéologique: Château des Rohan, 2 place du Château, 67000 Strasbourg; prehistoric, Gallo-Roman and Merovingian collections; results of excavations in Alsace; Curator J. J. HATT.

Musée des Augustins: 21 rue de Metz, 31000 Toulouse; f. 1795 and housed in the former Augustine Convent, of which parts date from the 14th and 15th centuries; medieval sculptures, paintings; Curator D. MILHAU.

Musée des Beaux-Arts: place François-Sicard, 37000 Tours; f. 1793 and moved in 1910 to the former Archbishop's palace dating from the 17th and 18th centuries; paintings by Mantegna, Rubens, Rembrandt, Terborch, Vignon, Lancret, Boucher, Delacroix, Degas; sculpture by Le Moyne, Houdon, Bourdelle; furniture, tapestries and objets d'art; Curators Mme PINOT DE VILLECHENON, Mme LEGRAND, Mlle GUILLOT DE SUDUIRAUT; affiliated museums:

Château d'Azay-le-Ferron: 36290 Mézières-en-Brenne; buildings, objets d'art and furniture of the 16th to early 19th century.

Château de Plessis-lès-Tours: La Riche, 37000 Tours; contains collection of souvenirs of Louis XI and St. Francis of Paula.

Musée du Compagnonnage: 8 rue Nationale, 37000 Tours; f. 1968; archives and historical masterpieces; Curator ROGER LECOTTÉ.

Musée des Vins de Touraine: 16 rue Nationale (parvis Saint-Julien), 37000 Tours; f. 1975; Curator ROGER LECOTTÉ.

Musée de Richelieu: Hôtel de Ville, 37120 Richelieu; f. 1961; objects of art, historical souvenirs relating to Cardinal Richelieu and the castle and town of Richelieu.

Musée de la Société Archéologique de Touraine: Hôtel Gouin, 25 rue du Commerce, 37000 Tours; gallic and roman archaeology, medieval and 16th-century sculptures; iconography of Tours, 18th- and 19th-century pottery.

Musée des Beaux-Arts: place Verte, 59300 Valenciennes; painting, sculpture, tapestry, etc.; Curator M. HARDY.

Musée National Picasso de Vallauris "La Guerre et la Paix": 06220 Vallauris; f. 1959; works by Picasso; Curator Mme GUYNET-PECHADRE.

Musée Archéologique: Quartier de Puymin, 84110 Vaison-la-Romaine; f. 1920; archaeological collection from excavations at Vaison.

STATE UNIVERSITIES

UNIVERSITÉ D'AIX-MARSEILLE I (UNIVERSITÉ DE PROVENCE)

PLACE VICTOR HUGO,
13331 MARSEILLE CEDEX 3
Telephone: 95-90-71.
Founded 1970.

Rector: YVES DURAND.
President: CLAUDE MESLIAND.
Secretary-General: AUGUSTE HAMM.
Librarian: Mlle G. KOEST.

Library: *see* Libraries.

Number of students: 15,691.

Publication: *Guide de l'Etudiant.*

TEACHING AND RESEARCH UNITS:

History: Dir. M. BOURREL DE LA RONCIÈRE.
Anglo-American Languages, Literature and Civilization: Dir. RENÉ RIVARA.
Oriental and Slavonic Studies: Dir. PIERRE BACCHERETTI.
Romance Languages, Literature and Civilization and Latin American Studies: Dir. ROGER SIMON.
Germanic Languages, Literature and Civilization: Dir. RENÉ GÉRARD.
Classics: Dir. LUDOVIC GRAVAGNE.
Arts, Letters, Expression: Dir. Mme MARGUERITE ROSSI.
Psychology: Dir. J. C. ABRIC.
Sociology and Ethnology: Dir. JACQUES PAILLARD.
Philosophy: Dir. LOUIS FREY.
Mediterranean Research: Dir. J.-L. MIEGE.
Mathematics: Dir. FERNAND BOREL.
Physics: Dir. MICHEL GIRAUD.
Chemistry: Dir. (vacant).
Natural Sciences: Dir. CLAUDE ROUSSET.
Observatory: 2 place Le Verrier, 13004 Marseille; Dir. YVON GEORGELIN.

UNIVERSITÉ D'AIX-MARSEILLE II

JARDIN DU PHARO,
58 BLVD. CHARLES LIVON,
13007 MARSEILLE
Telephone: 52-90-34.

Rector: YVES DURAND.
President: GEORGES SERRATRICE.
Secretary-General: J. FIOL.

TEACHING AND RESEARCH UNITS:

Economic Science: ave. Jules Ferry, 38 cours Mirabeau, 13100 Aix-En-Provence; Dir. M. PARODI.
Institute of Labour, Economic and Social Research: 12 traverse Saint-Pierre, 13100 Aix-En-Provence; Dir. F. HORDERN.
Institute of Geography: 29 ave. Robert Schuman, 13100 Aix-En-Provence; Dir. M. WOLKOWITSCH.
Institute of Technology: ave. Gaston Berger, 13100 Aix-En-Provence; Dir. A. GALICHON.
Medicine: 27 blvd. Jean Moulin, 13385 Marseille Cedex 4; Dir. Prof. TOGA.
Pharmacy: blvd. Jean Moulin, 13385 Marseille Cedex 4; Dir. C. GREBUS.
Dental Surgery: blvd. Charles Livon, 13007 Marseille; Dir. R. SANGIULO.
Tropical Medicine: Hôpital Michel Levy, 84 rue de Lodi, 13006 Marseille; Dir. Prof. P. PENE.
Institute of Physical Education: 70 route Léon Lachamp, 13288 Marseille Cedex 2; Dir. S. HOLSTEIN.
Experimental Unit, Luminy: 70 route Léon Lachamp, 13288 Marseille Cedex 2; Dir. M. MEBKHOUT.
Oceanic Sciences: rue Batterie des Lions, 13288 Marseille Cedex 2; Dir. A. BOURDILLON.
Institute of Fluid Mechanics: 1 rue Honnorat, 13003 Marseille; Dir. J. VALENSI.
Institute of Turbulence Statistics Mechanics: 12 ave. du Gén. Leclerc, 13003 Marseille; Dir. A. FAVRE.

UNIVERSITÉ D'AIX-MARSEILLE III (UNIVERSITÉ DE DROIT, D'ECONOMIE ET DES SCIENCES)

3 AVE. ROBERT SCHUMAN,
13628 AIX-EN-PROVENCE
Telephone: 59-99-20.
Founded 1973.

Rector: Y. DURAND.
President: L. FAVOREU.
Vice-Presidents: F. BOULAN, R. GRANIER, J. C. MAIRE, J. METZGER.
Secretary-General: A. YAGUES.

Number of teachers: 452.
Number of students: 13,364.

Publications: *Bulletin d'information* (monthly), *Flash mensuel* (monthly), *Livret de l'Etudiant* (annually).

DEANS:

Faculty of Law and Political Science: F. BOULAN.
Faculty of Applied Economics: C. BENSOUSSAN.

TEACHING AND RESEARCH UNITS:

Institute of Penal Sciences and Criminology: Dir. F. BOULAN.
Institute of Business Law: Dir. C. LOUIT.
Legal Research Unit: Dir. J.-L. MESTRE.
Institute of Regional Development: Dir. Y. PRATS.
Institute of Business Management: Dir. P. EIGLIER.
Institute of Political Studies: Dir. Y. DAUDET.
Institute of French Studies for Foreign Students: Dir. O. DEBBASCH.
Preparatory Science Unit: Marseille; Dir. M. GILLET.
Teacher Training Unit: Marseille; Dir. J.-P. PETRAKIAN.
Professional Training Unit: Marseille; Dir. G. LESGARDS.
Scientific and Technical Research Unit: Marseille; Dir. M. DUSSARDIER.
Institute of Petrochemistry and Organic Industrial Synthesis: Marseille; Dir. J. METZGER.
Higher School of Physics: Marseille; Dir. P. BOUSQUET.
University Institute of Technology: Marseille; Dir. J. VALLIER.

UNIVERSITÉ D'ANGERS

30 RUE DES ARENES, B.P. 3532,
49035 ANGERS CEDEX
Telephone: 88-58-43.

Founded 1971; formerly Centre Universitaire d'Angers.

Rector and Chancellor: YVES SAUDRAY.
President: J.-C. REMY.
Vice-President: PH. SEJOURNE.
Secretary-General: C. SATOUR.
Librarian: J.-C. BROUILLARD.

Number of teachers: 327.
Number of students: 6,796.

Publication: *Plantes médicinales et phytothérapie*†.

DEANS:

Faculty of Medicine and Pharmacy: M. EMILE.
Faculty of Exact and Natural Sciences: M. GOUIN.
Faculty of Law and Economic Sciences: M. DEBENEST.
Faculty of Letters and Human Sciences: M. SEJOURNE.
University Institute of Technology: M. MAGNIEN.
Technical Sciences: Mlle ASTIE.

CENTRE UNIVERSITAIRE D'AVIGNON

35 RUE JOSEPH VERNET,
84000 AVIGNON
Telephone: (90) 82-68-10.

Founded 1973; formerly U.E.R. Lettres et Sciences at the University of Provence.

President: JOËL MAHÉ.
Vice-President: ALBERT FAVRE.
Secretary-General: CAMILLE ALLUÉ.
Librarian: Mlle FRANÇOISE FEBVRE.

Number of teachers: 85.
Number of students: 1,487.

DEANS:

Faculty of Sciences: JACQUES NOUGIER.
Faculty of Arts: GUY CHEYMOL.

PROFESSORS:

Faculty of Sciences:
COULOMB, P., Mathematics
ESPAGNAC, H., Plant Biology
DI GUGLIELMO, Computer Science
MAHE, Geology

MICHEL, Mathematics
NOUGIER, Geology
PAVIA, Chemistry
PECAUT, Mme, Mathematics
REIDENBACH, Animal Biology
ROGGERO, Chemistry
TESTARD, Physics
VIVES, Physics

Faculty of Arts:
BRUN, Mlle, Geography
DUMAS, Provençal Studies
FAVRE, English
JONIN, Medieval French Literature
LE REVEREND, Provençal Studies
MAGNIER, Mlle, English
MALAVIE, French

UNIVERSITÉ DE BORDEAUX I

351 COURS DE LA LIBERATION,
33405 TALENCE CEDEX

Rector and Chancellor: J. VERGUIN.
President: M. RIMPAULT.
Chief Administration Officer: A. PICARD.

Number of teachers: 500.
Number of students: 14,580.

TEACHING AND RESEARCH UNITS:

Juridical Sciences (First Cycle): Dir. E. DRAVASA.
Private Law: Dir. J. DERRUPPE.
Public Law and Political Science: Dir. J. C. GAUTRON.
Fundamental Economic Studies: Dir. C. LACOUR.
Higher Economic Studies: Dir. A. LABOURDETTE.
Regional Institute of Business Studies: Dir. G. MERIGOT.
Land and Regional Development: Dir. J. LAJUGIE.
Scientific Studies (First Cycle): Dir. B. DE MATHAN.
Mathematics: Dir. G. GARANDEL.
Physics: Dir. A. CHARRU.
Chemistry: Dir. H. GASPAROUX.
Biology: Dir. C. CHAPRON.
Geological Studies and Research of Aquitaine: Dir. A. KLINGEBIEL.
Higher School of Electronics and Radio-electricity: Dir. G. BOUSSEAU.
Observatory: Dir. F. POUMEYROL.
University Institute of Technology: Dir. P. DESCAURION.

AFFILIATED TEACHING AND RESEARCH UNITS:

Institute of Political Sciences: Dir. C. EMERI.
Higher National School of Chemistry: Dir. R. LALANDE.
Research Institute on Mathematics Teaching: Dir. J. COLMEZ.
Pine Research Institute: Dir. J. VALADE.
Fats Research Laboratory: Dir. J. VALADE.
Metal Assaying Laboratory: Dir. R. NASLAIN.
University Institute of Marine Biology: Dir. J. BOISSEAU.
Electronic Microscopy Centre: Dir. R. CAMBAR.
Institute of Quaternary and Prehistoric Geology: Dir. F. BORDES.
Institute of Labour: Dir. M. PENOUIL.
Institute of Legal Studies: Dir. P. ROBINO.
Institute of Comparative Law: Dir. M. TREILLARD.
Institute of Criminal Studies: Dir. J. P. DELMAS-SAINT-HILAIRE.
Périgueux Municipal Institute of Legal and Economic Studies: Dir. P. JAUBERT.
Regional Institute of Management: Dir. J. DERRUPPE.

UNIVERSITÉ DE BORDEAUX II

146 RUE LÉO-SAIGNAT,
33076 BORDEAUX CEDEX
Telephone: (56) 90-91-24.

Rector and Chancellor: J. VERGUIN.
President: J. LATRILLE.
Secretary-General: Mme M.-C. LEGLISE.

TEACHING AND RESEARCH UNITS:

Medical Sciences I: Dir. D. DUCASSOU.
Medical Sciences II: Dir. J. TAVERNIER.
Medical Sciences III: Dir. A. QUINTON.
Pharmacy: Dir. M. CROCKETT.
Odontology: Dir. P. FOURTEAU.
Tropical Medicine: Dir. G. MORETTI.
Biology and Physiopathology: Dir. M. VARENE.
Psychiatry: Dir. M. BLANC (acting).
Biochemistry and Cellular Biology: Dir. B. GUERIN.
Social and Psychological Sciences: Dir. F. CHAZEL.
Institute of Applied Human Sciences: Dir. M. SAINGOLET.
Regional Institute of Physical Education: Dir. J. THIBAULT.
Institute of Oenology: Dir. J. RIBEREAU-GAYON.

AFFILIATED RESEARCH INSTITUTES:

Unité de Recherches sur les Applications Médicales et Biologiques des Isotopes Radio-Actifs: Domaine de Carreire, rue Camille Saint-Saens, Bordeaux; Dir. Prof. P. BLANQUET.

Unité de Recherches sur l'Immunologie des Affections Parasitaires: Domaine de Carreire, rue Camille Saint-Saens, Bordeaux; Dir. Prof. R. PAUTRIZEL.

Unité de Recherches de Cardiologie: Hôpital du Tondu, Bordeaux; Dir. Prof. H. BRICAUD.

Unité de Recherches de Radiobiologie Experimentale et de Cancérologie: Fondation Bergonié, 180 rue de Saint-Genès, Bordeaux; Dir. Dr. DUPLAN.

Equipe de Recherche Associée au C.N.R.S. de Neurobiologie des Hormones et Comportement: 24 rue Paul-Broca, annexe Broca II, Bordeaux; Dir. Prof. J. D. VINCENT.

Centre d'Etudes Biologiques des Animaux Sauvages (C.N.R.S.): Villiers en Bois, 79360 Beauvoir sur Niort; Dir. M. BOISSIN.

Equipe de Recherche C.N.R.S. "Laboratoires d'Enzymologie": 351 cours de la Libération, 33405 Talence; Dir. Mme LABOUESSE.

Equipe de Recherche Associée an C.N.R.S. "Laboratoire de Génétique": 351 cours de la Libération, 33405 Talence; Dir. Prof. J. BERNET.

Station de Physiologie et de Biochimie Végétales (I.N.R.A.): La Grande Ferrade, 33 Pont-de-la-Maye; Dir. M. BOVÉ.

UNIVERSITÉ DE BORDEAUX III

ESPL. MICHEL-MONTAIGNE,
DOMAINE UNIVERSITAIRE,
33405 TALENCE CEDEX
Telephone: (56) 80-84-83.

Rector and Chancellor: J. VERGUIN.
President: J. PEREZ.

TEACHING AND RESEARCH UNITS:

Letters and Arts: Dir. CL. DUBOIS.
Philosophy: Dir. J.-C. FRAISSE.
History: Dir. B. GUILLEMAIN.
Geography: Dir. C. HUETZ DE LEMPS.
Language, Literature and Civilization of Anglophone countries: Dir. P. SPRIET.
Foreign Languages and Literature "A": Dir. F. LOPEZ.
Foreign Languages and Literature "B": Dir. J. ROUCHETTE.
Iberian Studies: Dir. M. CHEVALIER.
Pluridisciplinary Unit of Techniques of Expression and Communication: Dir. M. PERROT.
University Institute of Technology: Dir. Mme. EYSSAUTIER.
Geology: Dir. M. CLIN.
Research Unit "Man and His Environment": Dir. J. KOECHLIN.

UNIVERSITÉ DE BRETAGNE OCCIDENTALE

RUE DES ARCHIVES,
B.P. 137, 29279 BREST CEDEX
Telephone: (98) 03-24-83.

Rector: YVES MARTIN.
President: MICHEL QUESNEL.
Secretary-General: PAUL CADIOU.
Librarian: Mlle E. DE SALLIER DUPIN.

Number of teaching staff: 514.
Number of students: 8,486.

TEACHING AND RESEARCH UNITS:

Letters and Social Sciences: 20 ave. Victor Le Gorgeu, B.P. 860, 29279 Brest Cedex; Dean EDMOND MONANGE.
Science and Technology: 6 ave. Victor Le Gorgeu, 29283 Brest Cedex; Dean YANN QUENTEL.
Medicine: 22 ave. Camille Desmoulins, B.P. 815, 29279 Brest Cedex; Dean GABRIEL LE MENN.
Law and Economics: ave. Foch, B.P. 331, 29273 Brest Cedex; Dean BERNARD LANDAIS.

Dentistry: 22 ave. Camille Desmoulins, 29271 Brest; Pres. Mme. CHRISTIANE CASTEL.

University Institute of Technology (Brest): rue de la Grandière, 29283 Brest Cedex; Dir. CLAUDE CHEZE.

University Institute of Technology (Quimper): rue de l'Université, B.P. 319, 29191 Quimper; Dir. LUCIEN LE CAM.

University Institute of Technology (Lorient): rue Jean Zay, 56100 Lorient; Dir. JEAN-JACQUES QUEMENER.

UNIVERSITÉ DE CAEN

ESPL. DE LA PAIX,
14032 CAEN CEDEX
Telephone: 94-59-10.

Founded 1432; reorganized 1970.

Chancellor: G. LESCUYER.

President: M. ROBBA.

Vice-President: Mme JACQUELINE GENET.

Secretary-General: Mme JOSETTE MARTIN.

Librarian: Mlle THÉRÈSE TORCHY.

Library: *see* Libraries.

Number of teachers: 740.
Number of students: 13,070.

TEACHING AND RESEARCH UNITS:

Droit et Sciences Politiques: Dir. P. GOYARD.

Sciences Economiques: Dir. M. GOERGEN.

Médecine: ave. de la Côte de Nacre, 14032 Caen Cedex; Dir. M. LEVY.

Sciences Pharmaceutiques: 1 rue Vaubénard, 14032 Caen Cedex; Dir. M. FOUCHER.

Sciences de l'Homme: Dir. J. GUGLIELMI.

Sciences de la Vie et du Comportement: Dir. M. STREIFF.

Sciences de la Terre et de l'Aménagement Régional: Dir. Mme BABONAUX.

Langues Vivantes Etrangères: Dir. PHILIPPE BOUQUET.

Histoire: Dir. HENRY-PAUL LONGUET.

Sciences: Dir. MAX EBEL.

Préparation aux Affaires: Dir. R. LE DUFF.

Institut des Sciences de la Matière et du Rayonnement: Dir. N. LOZAC'H.

Sciences de l'Alimentation et de la Nutrition: Dir. PIERRE BOIVINET.

Institut Universitaire de Technologie: blvd. Maréchal-Juin, 14032 Caen Cedex; Dir. J. P. LEROUX.

Institut Régional d'Education Physique et Sportive: blvd. Maréchal-Juin, 14032 Caen Cedex; Dir. R. LEMONNIER.

UNIVERSITÉ DE CLERMONT-FERRAND I

34 AVE. CARNOT, B.P. 179,
63005 CLERMONT-FERRAND CEDEX
Telephone: (73) 92-97-32.

Founded 1810; present status 1977.

Rector and Chancellor: JEAN-CLAUDE DISCHAMPS.

President: LOUIS JOYON.

Secretary-General: JEAN ORTOLI.

Librarian: Mlle SART.

Number of teachers: 500.
Number of students: 7,860.

TEACHING AND RESEARCH UNITS:

Médecine: 28 place Henri Dunant, 63001 Clermont-Ferrand Cedex; Dir. G. MEYNIEL.

Pharmacie: 28 place Henri Dunant, 63001 Clermont-Ferrand Cedex; Dir. M. COULET.

Sciences Juridiques et Politiques: 41 blvd. Gergovia, 63002 Clermont-Ferrand Cedex; Dir. R. CHIROUX.

Sciences Économiques et Sociales: 41 blvd. Gergovia, 63002 Clermont-Ferrand Cedex; Dir. J. P. VEDRINE.

Institut Universitaire de Technologie de Clermont-Ferrand: Ensemble universitaire des Céseaux, B.P. 29, 63170 Aubiére; Dir. J. ROCHE.

Odontologie: 11 blvd. Charles de Gaulle, 63005 Clermont-Ferrand Cedex; Dir. P. ROUSSENQUE.

UNIVERSITÉ DE CLERMONT-FERRAND II

34 AVE. CARNOT, B.P. 185,
63006 CLERMONT-FERRAND CEDEX
Telephone: (73) 92-97-32.

Founded 1810, present status 1977.

Rector and Chancellor: JEAN-CLAUDE DISCHAMPS.

President: P. CABANES.

Secretary-General: J. SENESI.

Librarian: Mlle SART.

Number of teachers: 568.
Number of students: 7,038.

TEACHING AND RESEARCH UNITS:

Sciences Exactes et Naturelles (Enseignement): 24 ave. des Landais, B.P. 45, 63170 Aubière; Dir. R. COMBE.

Sciences Exactes et Naturelles (Recherche): 24 ave. des Landais, B.P. 45, 63170 Aubière; Dir. A. KERGOMARD.

Lettres et Sciences Humaines: 29 blvd. Gergovia, 63037 Clermont-Ferrand Cedex; Dir. M. PARIENTE.

Institut et Observatoire de Physique du Globe du Puy-de-Dôme: 12 ave. des Landais, 63001 Clermont-Ferrand Cedex; Dir. PH. WALDTEUFEL.

Education Physique et Sportive: Complexe Scientifique des Cézeaux, 63170 Aubière; Dir. P. BOYER.

Institut Universitaire de Technologie de Montluçon: ave. Aristide Briand, 03107 Montluçon; Dir. M. MERCIER.

Ecole Nationale Supérieure de Chimie: 71 blvd. Côte Blatin, 63000 Clermont-Ferrand; Dir. R. VESSIERE.

Technologie: rue des Meuniers, B.P. 48, 63170 Aubière; Dir. J. FONTAINE.

UNIVERSITÉ DE TECHNOLOGIE DE COMPIÈGNE

CENTRE B. FRANKLIN, B.P. 233,
RUE ROGER COUTTOLENC,
60206 COMPIÈGNE CEDEX
Telephone: 420-99-77.

Founded 1972.

Academic year: September to August (2 semesters).

President: GUY DENIELOU.

Secretary-General: CLAUDE CADIERGUES.

Librarian: LILIANE VEZIER.

Number of teachers: 120.
Number of students: 1,000.

Publications: *Guide de l'Etudiant*†, *Annuaire des Enseignants-Chercheurs*† (annually), *Informations U.T.C.* (weekly).

DIRECTORS:

Department of International Affairs: GILBERT KARPMAN.

Department of Mechanical Engineering: DOMINIQUE FRANÇOIS.

Department of Biological Engineering: GEORGES BROUN.

Department of Chemical Engineering: MAURICE GELUS.

Department of Applied Mathematics and Computer Science: ROBERT COLCOMBET.

Department of Pedagogy: PAUL GAILLARD.

ATTACHED INSTITUTES:

Institut d'Informatique et de Management de l'Information: Dir. PIERRE MATHELOT.

Institut de Technologie des Surfaces Actives, Biologiques et Chimiques: Dir. EMILE SEGARD.

UNIVERSITÉ DE CORSE
(Università di Corti)

4 PLACE DE GAULLE, B.P. 24,
20250 CORTE
Telephone: (95) 46-04-47.

Founded 1976; scheduled to open for the 1981 academic year.

Rector: PIERRE FERRARI.

President: PASCAL ARRIGHI.

Secretary-General: PAUL MARCELLI.

Four departments are planned: literature, economics, sciences, law. An intake of *c.* 800 students is planned for the first year.

UNIVERSITÉ DE DIJON

CAMPUS DE MONTMUZARD,
B.P. 138,
21004 DIJON CEDEX
Telephone: (80) 66-64-13.

Rector and Chancellor: J. FAIVRE-LAMBERT.

President: J. VAUDIAUX.

Secretary-General: R. ROSEZ.

Librarian: J. C. GARRETA.

Number of students: 13,432.

Publications: *Annuaire*†, *Bulletin d'Information*†, *Publications de l'Université*† (irregular series of monographs).

TEACHING AND RESEARCH UNITS:

Droit et Science Politique: Dir. D. TRICOT.
Science Economique et Gestion: Dir. J. M. HURIOT.
Lettres et Philosophie: F. PRUNER.
Langues, Littérature et Civilisation Etrangères: Dir. N. JONARD.
Sciences Humaines: Dir. J. SURATTEAU.
Mathématiques, Informatique, Physique, Chimie: M. PERSON.
Sciences de la Vie et de l'Environnement: Dir. J. PAGÈS.
Sciences Pharmaceutiques et Biologiques: Dir. Mme ZOLL.
Institut des Relations Internationales: Dir. G. BURDEAU-BASTID.
Institut des Sciences de la Terre: Dir. P. FEUILLÉE.
Recherches sur la Nutrition: Dir. J. BÉZARD.
Education Physique et Sportive: Dir. J. LABICHE.
Médecine: Dir. J. GUERRIN.
Institut Universitaire de Technologie de Dijon: Dir. P. HARTMANN.
Institut Universitaire de Technologie Le Creusot: Dir. M. BIZOUARD.
E.N.S.B.A.N.A.: Dir. Mlle D. SIMATOS.
Centre d'Expérimentation Viticole et Oenologique: Dir. J. BERGERET.

PROFESSORS:

Arts Faculties:
ANDRÉ, Latin Language and Literature
BRUN, Philosophy
CHARDONNET, Geography
CHASTAING, Psychology
COLIN, Russian
COLLINET, French Literature
DONDAINE, Mme, French Philology
DUBOIS, Geography
DUCROCQ, English
GRANGE, Comparative Literature
GRIVELET, English Language and Literature
JONARD, Italian Language and Literature
LIGOU, Modern History
MATUS-ROMO, Spanish
MILNER, French Literature
MONTEIL, Philology of Classical Languages
PAGNEY, Human Sciences
PRUNER, F., French Language and Literature
RICHARD, Burgundian History, Literature and Dialect
SURATTEAU, Contemporary History

Science Faculties:
BARON, Biological Chemistry
BARRET, Chemistry
BEZARD, Animal Physiology
BUGNON, Plant Biology
CHAUDONNERET, Zoology
FEUILLÉE, P., Geology
FLATO, Mathematics
GODEFROY, Radioelectricity and Electronics
GODEFROY, Mme, Physics
GRAF, General Biology
HENRY, Botany
JOUBERT, Mathematics
LABESSE, Mathematics
LENEUF, Geology
MORET-BAILLY, Physics
NOIROT, Zoology
PERSON, Chemistry
PIGEAUD, Mathematics
RAT, Geology
ROUSSARIE, Mathematics
TINTANT, Palaeontology
TIROUFLET, General Chemistry
VERNIER, Physics
WATELLE, Mme, Chemistry

Faculties of Law and Economic Science:
BALESTRA, Economic Sciences
BART, Law, Roman Law
BLAISE, Private Law
BOLARD, Private Law
BURDEAU, Mme, International Law
COURVOISIER, Political Sciences
COUTURIER, Private Law
DOMARCHI, Political Economy
DRAN, Public Law
EICHER, Political Economy
FROMONT, Public Law
PIERI, History of Law
PONSARD, C., Political Economy
PROU, Political Economy
SCHAPIRA, Private Law
TRICOT, Private Law

Faculties of Medicine and Pharmacy:
ALISON, Paediatrics
AUPECLE, Surgical Semiology
BARRY, Anatomy
BOUHEY, Medical Semiology
BRALET, Physiology
CABANNE, Pathological Anatomy
COMPAGNON, Pharmacy (Organic Chemistry)
CORTET, Medical Pathology
DESTAING, Infectious Diseases
FERRY, Surgical Pathology
JAHIER, Obstetrics
KLEPPING, C., Hepatology, Gastroenterology
KLEPPING, J., Physiology
MARIN, Forensic Medicine
MICHIELS, Pathological Anatomy
NOUVEL, Pharmacy
PADIEU, Biological Chemistry
PUTELAT, Medical Pathology
TRUCHOT, Pharmaceutical Biochemistry
VIARD, Clinical Surgery
ZAHND, Embryology
ZOLL, Mme, Pharmacognosy

University Institute of Technology:
BIZOUARD, M., Thermodynamics
HARTMANN, P., Physics
KORNPROBST, B., Public Law

Higher National School of Applied Biology:
SIMATOS, M.

UNIVERSITÉ DE FRANCHE-COMTÉ

30 AVE. DE L'OBSERVATOIRE,
25030 BESANÇON CEDEX
Telephone: 50-81-21.

Founded 1422 at Dôle, 1691 at Besançon.

Rector and Chancellor: H. LEGOHÉREL.

President: P. LÉVEQUE.

Vice-Presidents: JACQUES PETIT, JACQUES ROBERT.

Secretary-General: GEORGES LAMBERT.

Librarian: (vacant).

Number of teachers: 734.
Number of students: 11,123.

Publications: *Annales Littéraires de l'Université, Journal de Médecine de Besançon, Annales Scientifiques de l'Université, Revue Géographique de l'Est, Annales de l'Observatoire de Besançon.*

TEACHING AND RESEARCH UNITS:

Lettres et Sciences Humaines: Dean M. GILLI.
Sciences et Techniques: Dean J. BULABOIS.
Droit, Sciences Economiques et Politiques: Dean M. GERMAIN.
Médecine et Pharmacie: Dean J. BERTHELAY.
Institut Universitaire de Technologie de Besançon: Dir. C. DEVIN.
Institut Universitaire de Technologie de Belfort: Dir. J. M. KAUFFMANN.
Ecole Nationale Supérieure de Chronométrie et de Micromécanique: Dir. R. CHALEAT.
Institut de Chimie: Dir. E. CERUTTI.
Recherches Biologiques et Médicales: Dir. J.-P. MAURAT.
Observatoire de Besançon: Dir. M. CREZE.
Education Physique: Dir. J. M. BONNARD.

PROFESSORS:

Sciences et Techniques:
BANTEGNIE, ROBERT, Mathematics
BENILAN, PHILIPPE, Mathematics
BERNARD, JEAN, Physical Chemistry
BIDAULT, MICHEL, Taxonomy
BROQUET, PAUL, Geology
BRUCKERT, SYLVAIN, Plant Ecology
BULABOIS, JEAN, General Physics
CAPODANNO, PIERRE, Mechanics
CERUTTI, ERNEST, Applied Chemistry
CHALÉAT, RAYMOND, Applied Mechanics
CHARDON, J. CLAUDE, Spectroscopy
CHAUVE, PIERRE, Geology, Mineralogy
COUGNARD, JEAN, Mathematics
DEVIN, CLAUDE, Chemistry
DUBOUCHET, JACQUES, Plant Physiology
GALATRY, LOUIS, Molecular Physics
GAUDEMER, YVES, Biochemistry
GOMOT, LUCIEN, Zoology
GOUARNE, RENÉ, Mathematics
GRAS, GEORGES, Mathematics
GREMILLARD, JEAN, Mathematics
KARCHE, J. PAUL, Petrography
LALLEMENT, GÉRARD, Applied Mechanics
LAUDE, B., Organic Chemistry
LESAINT, PIERRE, Mathematics
LHOTE, F., Automation
MÉRIGOUX, HENRI, Crystallography
MIELLOU, J.-C., Numerical Analysis
MILLET, BERNARD, Botany
MONTAGNER, HUBERT, Psychophysiology
MOREELS, GUY, Astronomy

Olivier, Marcel, Electronics
Parizet, Jean, Applied Mathematics
Perrot, Roger, General Chemistry
Pluvinage, P., Theoretical Physics
Potier, Robert, Solid State Physics
Rangheard, Yves, Geology
Real, Pierre, Biology
Ripplinger, Jean, Zoology
Robert, Daniel, Molecular Physics
Robert, G., Electrochemistry
Robert, Jacques, Mathematics
Théobald, J. Gérard, Spectroscopy
Thiebaut, Jean, Geology, Mineralogy
Trehel, Michel, Numerical Analysis
Verneaux, Jean, Zoology
Vienot, Jean-Charles, Physics
Weil, Michel, Mathematics

Lettres et Sciences Humaines:
Alhinc, Jean, English
Baroin, J., Medieval and Renaissance French
Bernand, E., Greek
Bois, G., Medieval History
Clavel-Lévêque, Mme M., Roman History
Derozier, A., Spanish
Deschoux, Marcel, Philosophy
Doignon, Jean, Latin
Dunand, Mlle Françoise, Ancient History
Gilli, M., German
Gresset, M., Modern History
Hamard, J., English
Lantz, P., Sociology
Leveque, P., Ancient History
Millotte, J., Pre-Historic Archaeology
Petit, J., French
Peytard, Jean, Linguistics
Robin, P., Latin
Varet, G., Philosophy
Vergez, André, Philosophy

Médecine et Pharmacie:
Agache, P., Dermatology
Bechtel, Pierre, Pharmacology
Benabdeljlil, Mme C., Biochemistry
Berthelay, J., Physiology
Bittard, M., Urology
Bugnon, C., Histology
Colette, C., Obstetrics and Gynaecology
Cotte, Louis, Forensic Medicine, Toxicology
Duvernoy, H., Anatomy
Gille, P., Surgical Pathology
Gillet, Michel, General Surgery
Gisselbrecht, H., Medical Practice
Grandmottet, P., Therapeutics
Lafon, J.-Cl., Oto-rhino-laryngology
Leboeuf, M., Materia Medica
Henry, Jean-Charles, Biochemistry
Leconte des Floris, R., Medical Practice
Lenys, Mme D., Histology
Levillain, R., Pathological Anatomy
Maurat, Jean-Pierre, Cardiology
Michel-Briand, Y., Bacteriology, Virology
Milleret, P., External Medicine
Oppermann, A., Pathological Anatomy
Panouse, J., Chemical Pharmaceutics
Peters, André, Haematology
Raffi, A., Paediatrics
Robert, J.-F., Chemical Pharmacy
Royer, J., Ophthalmology
Steimle, Raoul, Neuro-surgery
Tran Ba Loc, P., Zoology
Vichard, P., Traumatology
Volmat, R., Neurology and Psychiatry
Warnet, M., Toxicology
Weill, Francis, Electro-radiology

Droit, Sciences Economiques et Politiques:
Becet, J. M., Public Law
Drakidis, Philippe, Private Law
Louis-Lucas, P., Public Law
Mougeot, M., Economics
Schütz, B., Private Law

Attached Institutes:

Centre Universitaire d'Etudes Régionales: 18 rue Chifflet, 25030 Besançon Cedex; Dir. M. Bidault.

Institut d'Etudes Comtoises et Jurassiennes: 18 rue Chifflet, 25030 Besancon Cedex; Dir. R. Locatelli.

Centre de Documentation et de Bibliographie Philosophiques: 18 rue Chifflet, 25030 Besançon Cedex; Dir. G. Varet.

Centre de Linguistique Appliquée: 47 rue Mégevand, 25030 Besançon Cedex; Dir. J. Petit.

Centre de Formation des Psychologues Scolaires: 2 rue Granvelle, 25030 Besançon Cedex; Dir. C. Bried.

Centre de Formation et de Recherches Psycho-Pédagogiques: 2 rue Granvelle, 25030 Besançon Cedex; Dir. C. Bried.

Centre de Recherches Spécialisées en Littérature Française: 30 rue Mégevand 25030 Besançon Cedex; Dir. J. Petit.

Centre de Recherches Spécialisées en Histoire Ancienne: 30 rue Mégevand, 25030 Besançon Cedex; Dir. P. Leveque.

Centre de Recherches Socio-Economiques et d'Initiation aux Responsabilités dans les Entreprises Publiques ou Privées: 18 rue Chifflet, 25030 Besançon Cedex; Dir. J. P. Massonie.

Institut de Formation de Conseillers d'Orientation: 2 rue Granvelle, 25030 Besançon Cedex; Dir. C. Bried.

Centre Universitaire d'Environnement et d'Urbanisme: Faculté des Sciences, La Bouloie, Route de Gray, 25030 Besançon Cedex; Dir. P. Broquet.

Centre d'Hydrobiologie et d'Hydrologie: Institut des Sciences Naturelles, pl. Leclerc, 25030 Besançon Cedex; Dir. P. Chauve.

Institut de Recherche sur l'Enseignement des Mathématiques: route de Gray, 25030 Besançon Cedex; Dir. J. C. Fontaine.

Institut Universitaire de Formation Continue: 30 ave. de l'Observatoire, 25030 Besançon Cedex; Dir. M. Collette.

Centre de Télé-Enseignement Universitaire: 30 rue Mégevand, 25030 Besançon Cedex; Dir. M. Gavoille.

Centre Universitaire de Calcul: route de Gray, 25030 Besançon Cedex; Dir. M. Lacroix.

UNIVERSITÉ DE GRENOBLE I (UNIVERSITÉ SCIENTIFIQUE ET MÉDICALE)

B.P. 53, 38041 GRENOBLE CEDEX
Telephone: (76) 54-81-52.

President: Gabriel Cau.

Vice-President: Jean-Louis Koszul.

Secretary-General: Jacques Rambaud.

Number of students: 10,784.

Teaching and Research Units:

Sciences Biologiques et Médicales (1er cycle): Dir. Prof. Tanche.
Sciences Biologiques et Médicales (2e et 3e cycles): Dir. Prof. R. Sarrazin.
Sciences Pharmaceutiques: Dir. Prof. Carraz.
Recherches Biomédicales et Pharmaceutiques: Domaine de la Merci, 38 La Tronche; Dir. Prof. Lacharme.
Géographie Générale et Alpine: rue Maurice Gignoux, 38 Grenoble; Dir. J. David.
Sciences Exactes et Naturelles: Dir. R. Dufournet.
Formation des Cadres Techniques: Dir. J.-Cl. Fanton.
Formation des Enseignants de Second Degré: Dir. Prof. P. Ducros.
Formation Scientifique Fondamentale et d'Initation à la Recherche: Dir. Ch. Deportes.
Institut de Recherche de Mathématiques Avancées: Dir. Prof. van Cutsem.
Mécanique: Dir. D. Cordary.
Physique des Solides et Thermodynamique: Dir. Prof. A. Lacaze.
Géophysique et Physique des Plasmas: Dir. G. Perrier.
Spectrométrie et Cristallographie: Dir. M. Minier.
Institut des Sciences Nucléaires: Dir. Prof. Longequeue.
Chimie et Physico-Chimie des Matériaux: Dir. Prof. Cauquis.
Chimie Physique Organique: Dir. Prof. A. Rassat.
Biologie Physiologique et Ecologique: Dir. Prof. F. Barnoud.
Sciences de la Terre: Dir. Prof. Perriaux.
Institut Universitaire de Technologie A.: Dir. Prof. Sibille.
Institut Régional d'Éducation Physique et Sportive: Domaine Universitaire, 38 Saint-Martin-d'Hères; Dir. Prof. Chifflet.

UNIVERSITÉ DE GRENOBLE II (UNIVERSITÉ DES SCIENCES SOCIALES)

47X, 38040 GRENOBLE CEDEX
Telephone: (76) 54-81-78.
Founded 1970.

President: Michel Rousset.
Secretary-General: R. Poirier.

Library: *see* Libraries.

Number of staff: 410.
Number of students: 10,590.

Publications: *Bulletin d'Information* (quarterly), *Flash* (weekly), *Livret de l'Etudiant*.

TEACHING AND RESEARCH UNITS:

Droit: Dir. M. ROUSSET.
Institut d'Etudes Politiques: 17X, 38040 Grenoble Cedex; Dir. C. DOMENACH.
Sciences Economiques: Dir. B. MERIAUX.
Institut d'Etudes Commerciales: Dir. J.-P. VICARIO.
Histoire et Histoire des Arts: 25X, 38040 Grenoble Cedex; Dir. R. BORNEQUE.
Philosophie et Sociologie: Dir. P. SANSOT.
Psychologie et Sciences de l'Education: Dir. N. GALIFRET-GRANGEON.
Institut Universitaire de Technologie II: Place Doyen Gosse, 38000 Grenoble; Dir. D. PANEL.
Institut d'Administration des Entreprises: Dir. A. PAGE.
Urbanisation et Aménagement: 2 rue François-Raoult, 38000 Grenoble; Dir. C. LACROIX.
Institut de Recherche Economique et de Planification: Dir. J.-F. TROUSSIER.
Informatique et Mathématiques en Sciences Sociales: Dir. G. ROMIER.
Institut d'Administration Economique et Sociale: Dir. P. MAURICE.

PROFESSORS:

ALTER, M., Private Law
BARREYRE, P.-Y., Management
BAUMGARTNER, G., Management
BAUDIN, H., Literature
BERR, C., Private Law
BERTHIER, P., Applied Mathematics
BILLAUDOT, B., Political Science
BLIGNY, B., Medieval History
BOLLIET, L., Informatics
BORELLY, R., Economics
BORNECQUE, R., History
BRODEAU, F., Applied Mathematics
BROUE, P., Political Science
CHALARON, Y., Private Law
CHAPAL, P., Public Law
CHATELIN, F., Economics
CHATELUS, M., Economics
CHEVALLIER, P., Legal History
CHRISTIN, Y., Economics
CLAUSTRE, H., Education
COURBON, J.-C., Management Informatics
COURTIN, J., Informatics
CROISAT, M., Political Science
D'ARCY, F., Political Science
DE BERNIS, G., Economics
DEJEAN DE LA BATIE, N., Private Law
DESSAU, Y., Economics
DOMENACH, C., Political Science
DUBOUIS, L., Public Law
DUC-JACQUET, M., Economics
DURAND, G., Sociology
FLIGITTER, R., Management
FREYSSINET, J., Economics
GALIFRET-GRANJON, N., Genetic Psychology
GANGNEUX, G., History
GIROD, P., Management
GIVERDON, C., Private Law
GIVORD, F., Private Law
GUILHAUDIS, M., Public Law
GUILLEN, P., Modern History
GLEIZAL, J. J., Public Law
HATWELL, Y., Experimental Psychology
HEIDSIECK, F., Moral Philosophy
HOLLAR, M., Economics
JOLY, H., Philosophy
KELKEL, A., Philosophy
LACROIX, C., Urban Studies
LARGUIER, J., Private Law
LECA, J., Public Law
LEFEBVRE, D., Private Law
LE MEN, J., Psychology
LEROY, P., Public Law
LONGEOT, F., Psychology
MAISONNEUVE, B., Economics
MARTIN, C., Management
MAURICE, P., Economics
MENDEGRIS, R., Private Law
MERIAUX, B., Economics
MILLET, L., Philosophy
NIZARD, L., Public Law and Political Science
PAGE, A., Economics
PASCAL, G., Philosophy
PEISER, G., Public Law
PECCOUD, F, Informatics
PERCEBOIS, J., Economics
PETIT, P., Ancient History and Latin Epigraphy
PHILIBERT, M., Philosophy
REBOUD, L., Economics
ROMIER, G., Applied Mathematics
ROUAULT, J., Applied Mathematics
ROUSSET, M., Public Law
SAMUELSON, A., Economics
SANSOT, P., Philosophy
SCHEMEIL, G., Political Science
VERJUS, J. P., Applied Mathematics

UNIVERSITÉ DE GRENOBLE III (UNIVERSITÉ DES LANGUES ET LETTRES)

B.P. 25 X,
38040 GRENOBLE CEDEX
Telephone: 44-82-18.
Founded 1810.

President: J. H. DONNARD.
Vice-Presidents: M. MONNIER, M. LUCIANI.
Secretary-General: M. MARTIN.

Number of teachers: 130.
Number of students: 4,500.
Publication: *Livret de l'étudiant.*

DIRECTORS:

Languages:
BERNHARD, German
BOURMESYTER, Russian
CREISSELS, Linguistics
CRINEL, Italian
DABENE, Mme., Language teaching
EXTRAMIANA, Spanish
FAVRAT, German
PERRIN, English

Letters:
BERTRAND, Institute of French Language and Linguistics
CAUNE, Phonetics Institute
DEL LITTO, Institute of General and Comparative Literature
JACQUEMIN, Mme, Expression and Communications Institute
MONNIER, French Studies Centre
SGARD, Institute of French Literature

Classical Studies:
LANCEL, Latin
MARTIN, Greek

UNIVERSITÉ DE HAUTE-ALSACE

61 RUE ALBERT CAMUS.
68093 MULHOUSE CEDEX
Telephone: (89) 42-68-82.
Founded 1970.

Rector and Chancellor: P. MAGNIN.
President: JEAN-BAPTISTE DONNET.
Secretary-General: BERNARD SCHUB.
Librarian: HUBERT CHOPIN.

Number of students: 2,300.

TEACHING AND RESEARCH UNITS:

Letters and Humanities: Dir. R. EICHENLAUB.
Sciences: Dir. A. JUNG.
Institute of Technology: Dir. R. STEIN.
Higher National School of Chemistry: Dir. J.-P. FLEURY.
Higher National School of the Textile Industries: Dir. R.-A. SCHUTZ.
International Transport Institute: f. 1980.

UNIVERSITÉ DES SCIENCES ET TECHNIQUES DE LILLE (UNIVERSITÉ DE LILLE I)

59655 VILLENEUVE D'ASCQ
Telephone: 91-92-22.

Founded 1855 as Faculty of Sciences; present status 1971.

Rector and Chancellor: H. TOUCHARD.
President: M. MIGEON.
Secretary-General: S. KUBIAK.

Number of teachers: 861.
Number of students: 11,908.

TEACHING AND RESEARCH UNITS:

Mathématiques Pures et Appliquées: Dir. M. ROGALSKI.
Informatique, Électronique, Électrotechnique et Automatique: Dir. M. CORDONNIER.
Physique: Dir. M. DUBOIS.
Chimie: Dir. (vacant).
Biologie: Dir. M. LACOSTE.
Sciences de la Terre: Dir. M. PROUVOST.
Sciences Exactes et Naturelles (Calais): Dir. M. DEBOUDT.
Géographie et Aménagement Spatial: Dir. Mme BATTIAU-QUENEY.
Sciences Economiques et Sociales: Dir. M. SIMON.
Institut Universitaire de Technologie de Lille: Dir. M. BECART.
Institut Universitaire de Technologie de Béthune: Dir. M. BRIDOUX.
Institut de Préparation aux Affaires: Dir. M. DEBOURSE.
Institut Agricole: Dir. M. BOURIQUET.
Institut de Mécanique des Fluides: Dir. M. GOBELTZ.
École Nationale Supérieure de Chimie de Lille: Dir. M. LABLACHE-COMBIER.
Institut Universitaire de Technologie du Littoral: M. HOUDART.
Centre Université, Économie d'Éducation Permanente: Dir. M. LEBRUN.
Ecole Universitaire d'Ingénieurs de Lille: Dir. F. LOUAGE.

PROFESSORS:

BACCHUS, P., Calculus and Information Science
BEAUFILS, J.-P., Catalysis
BYAYS, P., Climatology, Hydrology and Biogeography
BONNOT, E., Plant Cytology

BOUGHON, P., Algebra, Theory of Numbers and Algebraic Geometry
BOURIQUET, R., Vegetal Physiology
CELET, P., Applied Geology
COEURE, G., Pure and Applied Mathematics
CONSTANT, E., Electronics
CORDONNIER, V., Calculus and Information Science
DEBOURSE, J.-P., Specialized Education
DELATTRE, C., Regional Geology
DURCHON, M., Endocrinology of Annelida and Molluscs
FAURE, R., Mechanics
FOURET, R., Solid Physics
GABILLARD, R., Electronics
GRANELLE, J.-J., Specialized Education
GUILLAUME, J., Microbiology
HECTOR, J., Mathematics
HEUBEL, J., Chemistry
LAVEINE, J.-P., Palaeobotany
LENOBLE, Mme., Atmospheric Optics
LOMBARD, J., Sociology
LHOMME, J., Organic Chemistry
LOUCHEUX, C., Macromolecular Chemistry
MONTREUIL, J., Biological Chemistry
PAQUET, J., Applied Geology
PROUVOST, J., Mineralogy
SCHWARTZ, Mme, Geometry and Topology
SEGUIER, G., Electro-Technology
STANKIEWICZ, F., Specialized Education
TILLIEU, J., Theoretical Physics
TRIDOT, G., Applied Mineral Chemistry
VIDAL, P., Automation
VIVIER, E., Electronic Microscopy
WERTHEIMER, R., Hertzian Spectroscopy
ZEYTOUNIAN, R., Mechanics

UNIVERSITÉ DE LILLE II (DROIT ET SANTÉ)

42 RUE PAUL DUEZ,
59800 LILLE
Telephone: 52-56-29.
Founded 1969.

State control; Language of instruction: French; Academic year: October to June.

President: E. CUINGNET.
Secretary-General: P. MICHEL.

Number of teachers: 600.
Number of students: 15,075.

DIRECTORS OF TEACHING AND RESEARCH UNITS:

Médecine 1: M. VERGNES.
Médecine 2: M. FOURRIER.
Médecine 3: M. GUERRIN.
Pharmacie: M. TRAISNEL.
Odontologie: M. LEPERS.
Sciences Juridiques: M. ROYER.
Education Physique et Sportive: M. VANLERENBERGHE.
Institut des Sciences du Travail: M. SOINNE.
Institut Universitaire de Technologie: M. GODÉ.

ATTACHED INSTITUTES:

Institut de Médecine Légale et Sociale: Dir. M. MULLER.

Institut de Chimie Pharmaceutique: Dir. M. LESPAGNOL.

Institut d'Education Permanente: Dir. M. DEPREUX.

Institut de la Construction, de l'Environnement et de l'Urbanisme: Dir. M. SAVOYE.

UNIVERSITÉ DE LILLE III (SCIENCES HUMAINES, LETTRES ET ARTS)

S.P. 18, D.U.L.J.V.A.,
59650 VILLENEUVE D'ASCQ
Founded 1560, present status 1970.

Rector and Chancellor: M. TOUCHARD.
President: (vacant).
Vice-Presidents: H. TOUZARD, J. DECOBERT.
Secretary-General: R. MATHA.
Librarian: M. S. DE NUCÉ.

Number of teachers: 318.
Number of students: 10,038.

Publications: *Revue du Nord* (history, quarterly), *Revue des Sciences Humaines, Etudes Irlandaises.*

TEACHING AND RESEARCH UNITS:

History, History of Art and Archaeology: Dir. Mme DEYON.
English: Dir. M. LILLY.
German Studies: Dir. Mme. HERMENT.
Romance, Semitic, Slav and Hungarian Studies: Dir. M. PICOCHE.
Classical Languages: Dir. Mlle VIARRE.
French Linguistics and Literature: Dir. M. BILLAZ.
Mathematics, Economics, Social Sciences: Dir. M. GRESLE.
Philosophy: Dir. M. TROTIGNON.
Psychology and Social Sciences: Dir. M. TOUZARD.
Readaptation Techniques: Dir. M. FRACKOWIAK.
University Institute of Technology: Dir. M. ALLUIN.

PROFESSORS:

BOLLACK, J., Greek
CODACCONI, F., Contemporary History
DECOTTIGNIES, J., Modern and Contemporary French Literature
DEYON, P., Modern and Contemporary Social and Economic History
DUMONT, J.-P., History of Philosophy
FOURQUIN, G., Regional and Medieval History
DE LA GENIERE, Mme J., Ancient Theology
GILLET, M., Regional and Contemporary History
MOULOUD, N., Logic and Philosophy of Science
NAERT, Mlle E., Philosophy
NAUDOU, J., Indian Studies
RAFROIDI, P., Contemporary English and Irish Literature
TRENARD, L., Modern and Regional History
TROTIGNON, P., Moral and Political Philosophy
VIARRE, Mlle S., Latin Language and Literature

UNIVERSITÉ DE LIMOGES

ALLÉE ANDRÉ MAUROIS,
ZUP DE L'AURENCE,
87100 LIMOGES
Telephone: 01-60-55.
Founded 1808, suppressed 1840, re-opened 1965.
Academic year: October to June.

Rector and Chancellor: D. QUIVY.
President: R. JULIEN.
Secretary-General: ETIENNE MICHAU.
Librarian: J. P. BITARD.

Library: *see* Libraries.
Number of teachers: 450.
Number of students: 7,600.

TEACHING AND RESEARCH UNITS:

Law and Economic Sciences: Dir. R. ARCHER.
Medicine and Pharmacy: Dir. M. CAIX.
Sciences: Dir. J.-L. TEYSSIER.
Letters and Social Sciences: Dir. J.-C. VAREILLE.
University Institute of Technology: Dir. J. MEXMAIN.

AFFILIATED INSTITUTES:

Centre Limousin d'Administration des Entreprises.
Director: G. CHAMBON.

Centre Limousin Associé au Conservatoire des Arts et Métiers.
Director: J.-L. TEYSSIER.

UNIVERSITÉ CLAUDE-BERNARD (LYON I)

86 RUE PASTEUR,
69365 LYON CEDEX 2
Telephone: 858-05-46.
Founded 1970.

State control; Language of instruction: French; Academic year: October to June.

Rector and Chancellor: MAURICE NIVEAU.
President: DANIEL GERMAIN.
Vice-President: MAURICE DUFAY.
Secretary-General: FRANÇOIS MARIANI.

Number of teachers: 417.
Number of students: 22,013.

Publications: *Bulletin de Liaison* (monthly), *Livret de l'Etudiant* (annual), *Annuaire sur la Recherche* (annually).

DIRECTORS OF TEACHING AND RESEARCH UNITS:

Médecine "Grange-Blanche": PAUL ZECH.
Médecine "Alesis-Carrel": R. MORNEX.
Médecine "Lyon-Nord": YVES MINAIRE.
Médecine "Sud": J. NORMAND.
Sciences Pharmaceutiques: C. A. BIZOLLON.
Techniques de Réadaptation: A. MORGON.
Biologie Humaine: J.-P. REVILLARD.
Sciences Odontologiques: JEAN PARRET.
Institut régional d'éducation physique et sportive: A. MILLON.
Mathématiques: P. PICARD.
Physique: J. DELMAU.
Chemistry and Biochemistry: ANNICK VARAGNAT.
Sciences de la Nature: YVES LEMOIGNE.
Sciences Physiologiques: J.-F. WORBE.
Physique Nucléaire: M. GUSAKOW.
Mécanique: G. COMTE-BELLOT.
Observatoire de Lyon: G. MONNET.
Institut Universitaire de Technologie I: A. VILLE.

Institut Universitaire de Technologie II: J. GALLET.

PROFESSORS:

Médecine "Grange-Blanche":
AMIEL, M., Radiology
AYMARD, M., Bacteriology, Virology
BRUNE, Pneumo-phthisiology
CIER, J. F., Physiology
COLIN, Forensic Medicine
COUDERT, Parasitology and Tropical Diseases
CREYSSEL, Biological Chemistry
CZYBA, Histology
DEJOUR, H., Orthopaedics and Traumatology
DESCOS, L., Hepato-gastro-enterology
FEROLDI, Pathological Anatomy
FAUCON, Medical Biology and Pharmacodynamics
FLANDROIS, Physiology
GALY, Psycho-Pathology
GERMAIN, Haematology-Immunology
GUILLET, Surgery
HUGONNIER, Ophthalmology
JOUVET, General and Experimental Pathology
LAMBERT, Hepato-gastro-enterology
LECUIRE, Neuro-Surgery
MAGNIN, Obstetrics
MICHAUD, Clinical Heart Surgery
MONNET, Bacteriology
MORGON, A., Oto-Rhino-Laryngology
MOTIN, Anaesthesiology
NOEL, Internal Medicine
PAPILLON, Radiology
PASQUIER, Internal Medicine
PEYRIN, Biological Physics
SALLE, B., Paediatrics
SCHOTT, Neuro-Psychiatry
THIVOLET, Clinical Dermato-Syphilography and Allergology
VIGNON, Hydrology
ZECH, P., Nephrology

Médecine "Alexis-Carrel":
BERGER, Biological Physics
BERTRAND, J.-A., Biochemistry
BOUCHET, Anatomy
BOURRET, Industrial Medicine
COMTET, J.-J., Orthopaedics, Traumatology
DELAHAYE, J. P., Cardiology
DELEUZE, Anaesthesiology
DESCOTES, J., Therapeutics and Surgical Technology
DEVIC, Neuro Psychiatry
DUMAS, Clinical Stomatology
FLEURETTE, Bacterio-Virology
FRANCOIS, Paediatrics
FRANÇOIS, B., Internal Medicine
GARMIER, Gynaecology and Obstetrics
GIROD, Histology
GONIN, Therapeutics
GUYOTAT, Adult Psychiatry
HERMIER, M., Paediatrics
MAILLET, P., Surgery
MARTIN, Clinical Oto-Rhino-Laryngology and Audio-Phonology
MEUNIER, P., Rheumatology
MORNEX, Endocrinology
DE MOURGUES, Orthopaedics
PAUPERT-RAVAULT, Ophthalmology
PELLET, M., Physiology
ROCHE, Forensic Medicine and Deontology
ROCHET, Clinical Gynaecology
TOMMASI, Pathological Anatomy
TOURAINE, Phthisiology
VIALA, Medical Semeiology
VIGNAL, J., General Surgery

Médecine "Lyon-Nord":
ALLEGRE, Neuro-Surgery
BEL, A., Clinical Medicine
BERTOYE, Bacteriology
BETHENOD, Paediatrics
BONNET, M., Ophthalmology
BRAILLON, G., Surgical Pathology
BRETTE, R., Digestive Diseases
BOURRAT, C., Neurology
CHABAL, Surgery
CHARVET, Gynaecology and Obstetrics
CHATONNET, Physiology
COURJON, Neurology
DELAYE, J., Cardiology
DUMONT, Gynaecology
DUQUESNEL, J., Electro-radiology
FREDERICH, Pharmacology
GAILLARD, Clinical Oto-Rhino-Laryngology
GARIN, Parasitology
JAUBERT DE BEAUJEU, Paediatrics
KALB, Pneumo-Phthisiology
LARBRE, Paediatrics
LEJEUNE, Rheumatology
MARION, Thoracic and Cardio-Vascular Surgery
MOULIN, Dermatology, Venereology
PINET, A., Radiology
PONT, Cardiology
REBOUD, J.-P., Biological and Medical Chemistry
SEPETJIAN, Hygiene and Social and Sanitary Action
TRAEGER, Nephrology
TOURNIAIRE, J., Endocrinology, Metabolism, Nutrition
VAUZELLE, J.-L., Pathological Anatomy
VINCENT, P., Bacteriology, Virology

Médecine "Lyon-Sud":
AMARD, G., Neurology
ARCHIMBAUD, J.-P., Urology
BOUVIER, M., Rheumatology
COLOMB, Dermatology
CROISILLE, M., Electro-radiology
DUBOIS, P., Histology
FAVRE-GILLY, J., Clinical Haematology
GILLY, Paediatrics
GUILLEMIN, Surgery
GUINET, P., Endocrinology
LAPRAS, C., Neurosurgery
LATARJET, Surgery
LOUISOT, P., Biochemistry
MAYER, Clinical Carcinology
MOLLARD, P., Children's Surgery
MORET, Biophysics
NORMAND, Cardiology
NOTTER, Gynaecology
PALIARD, P., Hepato-gastro-enterology
PERRIN-FAYOLLE, M., Pneumo-phthisiology
PINET, Electro-Radiology
ROBERT, Medical Genetics
SITE, Statistical Mathematics
TERMET, H., Thoracic and Cardio-vascular Surgery
TETE, R., Internal Medicine
TOLOT, Labour Medicine
TRILLET, M., Neurology

Pharmacie:
BIZOLLON, Physics
CARRAZ, M., Immunology
CHAMBON, P., Toxicology
COLLET, Pharmacy
COTTE, J. M., Galenic Pharmacy
GRAS, Biological Chemistry
MALLEIN, Analytical Biochemistry
NETIEN, Botany and Cellular Biology
ODDOUX, Cryptogamy and Phytopharmacy
QUINCY, C., Analytical Chemistry, Bromatology
REVOL, A., Pharmaceutical Biochemistry
ROLLET, M., Galenic Pharmacy
SASSARD, J., Physiology
VALLON, J. J., Analytical Chemistry

Institut universitaire de technologie Lyon I
BACQUES, Physiology
BOUCHE, Informatics
POUYET, Chemistry
VILLE, A., Biochemistry

Institut universitaire de technologie Lyon II
GAILLARD, Physics

Mathématiques:
BETHOUX, Mathematics
BRACONNIER, Mathematics
BUCHWALTER, Mathematics
COMBET, Mathematics
COROMINAS, Mathematics
DAZORD, Mathematics
FERON, Mathematics
FLAMANT, M., Mathematics
HACQUE, Mathematics
JANIN, P., Mathematics
LEFEBVRE, Mathematics
MALECOT, Rational and Applied Mechanics
MARTEL, Mechanics
MAURY, Mathematical Methods in Physics
PICARD, Mathematics
PONASSE, D., Mathematics
ROT, Mathematics

Physique:
ASCH, Electronics
BERGEON, Spectroscopy and Luminescence
BESSIS, Spectroscopy
BOUVIER, A., Luminescence Spectroscopy
DELMAU, Spectroscopy
DI BARTOLO, Spectroscopy
DUFAY, Atmospheric Physics
DUPUY, Electronics
ERBEIA, Spectroscopy
FONTAINE, Spectroscopy
GAUME, Physics
MAITROT, Electronics
MESNARD, Electronics
MICHEL, Generalogy
PAVAGEAU, Physics
SCHMITT, Physics
SERUGHETTI, J., Mineralogy
UZAN, Electronics

Chimie-Biochimie:
CHASTRETTE, Physical Organic Chemistry
CHOPIN, Biochemistry
COHEN-ADAD, Chemistry
DESCOTES, Chemistry
DREUX, Chemistry
EYRAUD, Chemical Engineering
GAUTHERON, (Mlle.), Biochemistry
GAUTHIER, Chemistry
GERMAIN, Chemistry
GORE, Organic Chemistry
GOT, R., Biochemistry
HUET, Organic Chemistry
LAURENT, Chemistry
MERLIN, Chemistry
MICHEL, Biochemistry
PARIS, J., Inorganic Chemistry
PORTHAULT, Chemistry
ROUX, R., Applied Chemistry
TEICHNER, Industrial Chemistry
THOMAS-DAVID, (Mme), Analytical Chemistry
TOUSSET, Chemistry
VALLET, Macromolecular Chemistry

Sciences de la Nature:
BERTHET, Plant Biology
BOIDIN, Microbiology and Mycology
BRUN, Biology
CHENEVOY, Petrography
COTILLON, P., Geology
DAILLIE, Biology
DAVID, L., Geology
DEMARCQ, Geology
ELOUARD, Geology
ENAY, Earth Sciences
GEVIN, Geology
GINET, Zoology
LAMOURE, (Mlle.), Biology

LEBRETON, Microbiology
LEGAY, Biology
LEMOIGNE, Botany
NIGON, Experimental Zoology
PAVANS DE CECCATTY, Zoology
ROUX, Animal Biology and Zoology

Sciences Physiologiques:
CHANEL, Psychophysiology
COSNIER, J., Animal and Comparative Psychology
HOLLEY, Electrophysiology
PERES, Physiology
WORBE, Metabolic Physiology

Physique Nucléaire:
BERKES, Nuclear Physics
BURQ, Nuclear Physics
CHERY, Nuclear Physics
DEPRAZ, Nuclear Physics
EL BAZ, Nuclear Physics
ERICSON, (Mme.), Nuclear Physics
GUSAKOW, Nuclear Physics
LAFOUCRIERE, Theoretical Nuclear Physics
LAMBERT, Nuclear Physics
PHILIBERT, Nuclear Physics
RUHLA, Nuclear Physics

Odontologie:
BERTOIN, Pathology and Dental Therapeutics
BLANC-BENON, J., Operative Dentistry
BOIS, D., Prosthetics
BONIN, P., Operative Dentistry
BRUGIRARD, Prosthetics
BRUNNER, Dental Orthopaedics
CAUDMONT, M., Children's Dentistry
CHAMBAZ, Operative Dentistry
CHASSIGNOL, Dento-Facial Orthopaedics
DEPLAGNE, Dental Orthopaedics
DOURY, J., Parodontology
DUCLOS, P., Pathology
DUMONT, Biology
DUMONT, A., Prosthetics
HESKIA, Dental Orthopaedics
LABE, Operative Dentistry
LALLICH, Prosthetics
LIBOUREL, Biology
MAGLOIRE, Biology
MALQUARTI, Prosthetics
PARRET, Biology
PERDRIX, G., Para-dentistry
PEROL, Operative Dentistry
PIREL, C., Prosthetics
POULARD, Operative Dentistry
THOMAS, Operative Dentistry
TOURTET, L., Prosthetics
VINARD, H., Biology
VINCENT, Pathology and Dental Therapeutics

Observatoire:
HAYLI, A.
MONNET, G.

Mécanique:
BATAILLE, Mechanics

ATTACHED INSTITUTES:

Institut Cardiovasculaire: 8 ave. Rockefeller, 69373 Lyon Cedex 2; Dir. P. MARION.

Institut de Pharmacie Industrielle: 8 ave. Rockefeller, 69373 Lyon Cedex 2; Dir. Prof. J. COTTE.

Institut d'Audiophonologie: Hôpital Edouard-Herriot, Pavillon U, 5 place d'Arsonval, 69003 Lyon; Dir. A. MORGON.

Institut de Stomatologie: Hôpital Edouard-Herriot, Pavillon B, 5 place d'Arsonval, 69003 Lyon; Dir. Prof. P. DUMAS.

Institut de Médecine du Travail: 8 ave. Rockefeller, 69373 Lyon Cedex 2; Dir. F. TOLOT.

Institut d'Hydrologie et Climatologie: 8 ave. Rockefeller, 69373 Lyon Cedex 2; Dir. Prof. G. VIGNON.

Institut de Médecine et d'Hygiène Tropicales: 8 ave. Rockefeller, 69373 Lyon Cedex 2; Dir. Prof. J. COUDERT.

Institut de Science Financière et d'Assurance: 43 blvd. du 11 Novembre 1918, 69622 Villeurbanne; Dir. Prof. G. MALECOT.

Institut Michel-Pacha: Laboratoire Maritime de Physiologie, 83000 Tamaris-sur-Mer; Dir. Prof. G. PERES.

Institut de Météorologie et Sciences Climatiques: 43 blvd. du 11 Novembre 1918, 68622 Villeurbanne; Dir. (vacant).

Institut de Recherche sur l'Enseignement des Mathématiques (I.R.E.M.): 43 blvd. du 11 Novembre 1918, 69621 Villeurbanne; Dir. M. BRAEMER.

UNIVERSITÉ LYON II

86 RUE PASTEUR,
69365 LYON CEDEX 02
Telephone: 869-24-45.

Rector and Chancellor: M. NIVEAU.
President: P. LUCAS.
Secretary-General: Mlle C. FRANCHI.

Number of teachers: 342 (full-time).
Number of students: 12,500.

TEACHING AND RESEARCH UNITS:

Economic Sciences and Management: Dir. M. VATE.
Institute of Political Studies: Dir. M. PACAUT.
Psychology and Social Sciences: Dir. A. HENRI.
Sciences of Man and his Environment: Dir. F. DELPECH.
Classical and Modern Letters and Civilizations: Dir. P. RETAT.
Mediterranean Languages and Literatures (Spanish, Arabic, Portuguese): Dir. L. COMBET.
Practical Psychology Training Institute: Dir. G. BROYER.
Juridical Sciences: Dir. Mlle RONGERE.
Linguistics, German and Scandinavian Languages: Dir. M. LEGUERN.
Foreign Literature and Civilization (English): Dir. P. FONTANEY.

UNIVERSITÉ JEAN MOULIN (LYON III)

B.P. 155,
69224 LYON CEDEX 1
Telephone: 869-24-93.

Founded 1973.

President: JACQUES GOUDET.
Vice-Presidents: LAURENT BOYER, BERNARD BOURGEOIS.
Secretary-General: P. CHIAVERINI.
Librarian: CHANTAL BROS.

Number of teachers: 230.
Number of students: 10,014.
Publication: *Annales.*

DEANS:

Faculty of Law: PIERRE VIALLE.
Faculty of Languages: JEAN-PIERRE PETIT.
Faculty of Letters and Civilizations: MICHEL RAMBAUD.
Faculty of Philosophy: FRANÇOIS DAGOGNET.
Institute of Business Administration and Management: ANDRÉ VARINARD.
Institute of Work and Social Security Studies: JOSEPH FROSSARD.

PROFESSORS:

Faculty of Law:

Private Law:
AZEMA, J.
CHAVANNE, A.
GUIHO, P.
GUINCHARD, S.
LAMBERT-FAIVRE, Y.
LANDRAUD, D.
NERSON, R.
ROBERT, A.
ROLAND, H.
RUBELLIN, Mme J.
SCHWARZ-LIEBERMANN, H. A.
VARINARD, A.
VINCENT, J.

Public Law:
BOURDONCLE, R.
DEBENE, M.
GARAGNON, J.
MONTAGNIER, G.
PELLOUX, R.
SIMONNET, M.
TAY, H.
UNTERMAIER, J.
VIALLE, P.

History Section:
BASTIER, J.
BOYER, L.
CHEVAILLER, L.
DOCKES, Mme.
GENIN, J.-C.

Economics Section:
LAMBERT, D.-C.

Faculty of Languages:
ALEXANDRE, D., Russian
BAILLET, R., Italian
DELADRIERE, R., Arabic
GOUDET, J., Italian
HEITZLER, P., German
LANNE, J. C., Russian
LUST, C., Modern Greek
PETIT, J. P., English
PETIT, Mme, Spanish
SANINE, Mlle KYRA, Russian
TERRIER, M., English
THOMAS, L., English, Chinese
WEIL, M., Hebrew

Faculty of Letters and Civilizations:
ANTONIOLI, M., French Renaissance Literature
BONJOUR, M., Latin
BOUCHER, J.-P., Latin
FEDOU, R., Medieval History

FREDOUILLE, J. C., Latin
FROSTIN, C., Modern History
GADILLE, J., Modern History
GADILLE, Mme ROLANDE, Regional and Rural Geography
HAUDRY, J., Sanskrit and Comparative Grammar
LAFFERRERE, M., Urban and Industrial Geography
MERAD, A., Arabic
MINGRET, P., Economic Geography
MOTTET, G., Physical Geography
PROST-VANDENBROUCKE, B., Regional Geography
RAMBAUD, M., Latin
SCHAETTEL, M., Modern French Literature
TOUPET, C., Tropical Geography
TURCAN, R., National Antiquities
VERNIERE, Y., Ancient Greek

Faculty of Philosophy:
BOURGEOIS, B., History of Philosophy
COURT, R., Aesthetics
DAGOGNET, F., History and Philosophy of Science, Arts and Technology
GAUDIN, C., History of Philosophy
MALDINEY, H., Aesthetics and Anthropology
TRICAUD, F., Morality and Pedagogy

ATTACHED INSTITUTES:

Institut des Assurances de Lyon: Dir. M. GUINCHARD.

Institut d'Etudes Judiciaires: Dir. M. VARINARD.

Institut d'Etudes Administratives: Dir. M. VIALLE.

Institut du Droit Comparé: Dir. M. NERSON.

Institut du Droit de l'Environnement: Dir. M. UNTERMAIER.

Centre d'Etudes Juridiques de l'Ain: Dir. M. HARTEMANN.

Centre de Documentation et de Recherche Européenne: Dir. M. MONTAGNIER.

Centre Lyonnais d'Etudes de Securité Internationale et de Défense: Dir. M. VIALLE.

Centre d'Etudes Romaines et Gallo-Romaines: Dirs. M. RAMBAUD, M. TURCAN.

Institut de Droit et d'Economie des Affaires: Dir. M. CROCHAT.

Institut d'Etudes de la Population et des Relations Internationales: Dir. M. LAFFERRERE.

Institut d'Etudes Rhodaniennes: Dir. M. LAFFERRERE.

Institut d'Histoire du Christianisme: Dir. M. GADILLE.

Centre d'Etudes sur l'Humanisme et la Communication: Dir. M. ANTONIOLI.

Groupe Rhône-Alpes de Recherche et d'Etudes en Gestion: Dir. M. FAYETTE.

Centre Linguistique Appliquée et Comparée et de Néo-Dialectologie: Dir. M. GOUDET.

Centre d'Etudes du Milieu Naturel: Dir. M. MOTTET.

Institut de Recherche sur le Cadre de Vie et l'Economie: Dir. M. LAFFERRERE.

Centre de Recherches et d'Application en Ergonomie: Dir. M. RICHARD.

Centre d'Etudes Orthodoxes: Dir. M. GOUDET.

Institut Néo-Hellénique: Dir. Mme LUST.

UNIVERSITÉ DU MAINE

ROUTE DE LAVAL, B.P. 535,
72017 LE MANS CEDEX
Telephone: 24-70-37.
Founded 1969.

Rector and Chancellor: Y. SAUDRAY.
President: C. PHILIP.
Secretary-General: Mme LANDRY.

Number of teachers: 202.
Number of students: 3,700.

Publications: *Livret de l'Etudiant* (annually), *La Vie de l'Université du Maine* (2 or 3 a year).

DEANS:

Faculty of Sciences: M. VARRET.
Faculty of Letters and Human Sciences: M. ROULEAU.
Faculty of Economic, Legal and Social Sciences: M. VIDAL.
University Institute of Technology: M. LEHMANN.

DIRECTORS OF DEPARTMENTS:

Faculty of Sciences:
BROWN, Organic Chemistry
BRUNEAU, Macromolecular Physical Chemistry
CASALS, Physical Chemistry, Photochemistry
CUPCIC, Materials Physics
DE PAPE, Solid State Chemistry
EL KAROUI, Mme, Mathematics
LEHMANN, Physics
LEJUEZ, Natural Sciences
MORET-BAILLY, Computer Science
PINAZZI, Organic Macromolecular Chemistry
ROUESSAC, Organic Chemistry

Faculty of Letters and Human Sciences:
BERTHELOT, Spanish
BOUCHE, Mme, Modern Literature
BRUN, German
COGNY, Mme, Classical Languages
COUSSY, Mme, English
GENGOUX, French
PHILIPPE, History
ROULEAU, Geography
THILL, Psychology

Faculty of Economic, Legal and Social Sciences:
ANCEL, Law
PASQUIER, Economics

University Institute of Technology:
LALOS, Mechanical Engineering
RACOIS, Chemistry
THOMAS, Business and Administration

UNIVERSITÉ DE METZ

ILE DU SAULCY, 57000 METZ
Telephone: 730-26-63.
Founded 1971.

Rector and Chancellor: B. SAINT-SERNIN.
President: J. DAVID.
Vice-President: D. CAGNIANT.
Secretary-General: J. DIEBOLT.
Librarian: J.-M. DILIGENT.

Number of teachers: 242.
Number of students: 5,306.

DEANS:

Letters and Human Sciences: Prof. GÉRARD NAUROY.
Exact and Natural Sciences: Prof. DOMINIQUE DURAND.
University Institute of Technology: Prof. RAYMOND BARO.
Law: ANDRÉE BRUNET.
Ecology: Prof. J.-C. PIHAN.

PROFESSORS:

Letters and Human Sciences:
CHARPENTIER, English
CHRISTOPHE, German
HENNEQUIN, Literature
POIDEVIN, History
REITEL, Geography

Exact and Natural Sciences:
BAUDELET, Technology
BLOCH, Chemistry
LONCHAMP, Physics
SEC, Mme, Mathematics

UNIVERSITÉ DE MONTPELLIER I

5 BLVD. HENRI IV,
34060 MONTPELLIER CEDEX
Telephone: 41-20-90.
Founded 1970.

State control; Language of instruction: French; Academic year: September to June.

President: J. MIROUZE.
Vice-Presidents: J. OUSSET, H. ORZALESI.
Secretary-General: R. BÉGON.
Librarian: Mlle S. DELRIEU.

Number of teachers: 751.
Number of students: 17,649.

Publications: *L'Economie Méridionale, Revue de la Société d'Histoire du Droit, Journal de Médecine, Le Ligament.*

TEACHING AND RESEARCH UNITS:

Law and Social Sciences: Dir. M. DONNIER.
Economics: Dir. A. DUMAS.
Business Management: Dir. J.-M. MOUSSERON.
Juridical Information and Economics: Dir. M. ROUZIER.
Medicine: Dir. P. RABISCHONG.
Pharmacy: Dir. H. ORZALESI.
Industrial Pharmacy: Dir. H. DELONCA.
Dentistry: Dir. P. PARGUEL.
Alimentary and Biological Studies: Dir. Mme S. BRUN.

UNIVERSITÉ DE MONTPELLIER II (UNIVERSITÉ DES SCIENCES ET TECHNIQUES DU LANGUEDOC)

PLACE EUGÈNE BATAILLON, 34060 MONTPELLIER CEDEX

Telephone: (67) 63-91-44.

Telex: USTMONT 490944F

Rector and Chancellor: JACQUES FARRAN.

President: LOUIS THALER.

Secretary-General: ETIENNE SIAU.

Librarian: Mlle JACQUELINE JUSTRABO.

Number of teachers: 685.
Number of students: 7,500.

Publications: *Naturalia Monspelianesia, Paléobiologie Continentale—Paléovertebrata, Cahiers de Mathématiques.*

TEACHING AND RESEARCH UNITS:

General and Scientific Training (1st Cycle): Dir. BERNARD BRUN.

Pedagogic and Scientific Teacher Training (2nd cycle): Dir. MAURICE MAURIN.

Basic Science and Introduction to Research (2nd cycle): Dir. JEAN-FRANÇOIS REGNIER.

Institute of Engineering Sciences: Dir. CHRISTIAN DURANTE.

Mathematics: Dir. ARTIBANO MICALI.

Physics: Dir. CLAUDE GOUT.

Chemistry: Dir. PHILIPPE VIALLEFONT.

Biological Sciences and Basic Geology: Dir. Mme NICOLE PARIS.

Natural Resources and Regional Planning (including Botanical Institute): Dir. JACQUES AVIAS.

Higher National School of Chemical Engineers: 8 rue de l'Ecole Normale, 34075 Montpellier Cedex; Dir. ROBERT JACQUIER.

University Institute of Technology of Montpellier-Nîmes: 99 ave. d'Occitanie, Montpellier Cedex; Dir. RENÉ CANO.

Business School: Dir. RENÉ MAURY.

UNIVERSITÉ PAUL VALÉRY (MONTPELLIER III)

PLACE DE LA VOIE DOMITIENNE B.P. 5043, 34032 MONTPELLIER CEDEX

Telephone: 63-91-10.

Rector and Chancellor: A. SAUNIER-SEITÉ.

President: A. MARTEL.

Secretary-General: R. ROUQUAIROL.

Number of students: 8,913.

TEACHING AND RESEARCH UNITS:

Letters, Philosophy and Arts.
Mediterranean Languages, Literatures and Civilizations.
Psychology.
Human Sciences.
American, Germanic and Slavonic Languages and Literatures.
Classics.
Applied Mathematics.
Applied Economics.
Institute of Medical-Social Psychology.
Geography and Environmental Planning.
Sociology and Ethnology.

UNIVERSITÉ DE NANCY I

24 RUE LIONNOIS, B.P. 3153, 54013 NANCY CEDEX

Telephone: 35-81-81.

Founded 1970.

Rector and Chancellor: B. SAINT-SERNIN.

President: MICHEL BOULANGÉ.

Secretary-General: J. F. PIOCHE.

Number of teachers: 853.
Number of students: 12,120.

TEACHING AND RESEARCH UNITS:

Medical Sciences A: Dir. M. STREIFF.
Medical Sciences B: Dir. M. GRIGNON.
Pharmaceutical and Biological Sciences: Dir. M. BENE.
Dental Surgery: Dir. M. VADOT.
Material Sciences: Dir. M. ROCCI.
Biological Sciences: Dir. M. GARNIER.
Mathematical Sciences: Dir. M. NOVERRAZ.
Earth Sciences, Metallurgy and Mineral Chemistry: Dir. M. HERTZ.
Physics, Chemistry and Biology: Dir. M. LEHR.
Nutrition and Alimentation: Dir. M. BONALY.
Institute of Engineering Sciences: Dir. M. MARI.
University Institute of Technology: Dir. M. PROST.
Sport and Physical Education: Dir. M. NOEL.
University Centre for Economic and Social Co-operation: Dir. M. AUBRUN.

PROFESSORS:

Faculty of Medicine:

ARNOULD, G., Neuro-Psychiatry
ARNOULD, P., Physiology
BEAU, Clinical Infant Surgery
BENICHOUX, Surgery
BERTRAND, A., Medicine
BEUREY, Dermato-Syphilography
BOULANGE, Human Physiology and Aeronautical Medicine
BURG, Biophysics
CAYOTTE, Anatomy
CHARDOT, Cancerology
CORDIER, Ophthalmology
CUNY, Gerontology
DEBRY, Nutrition
DOLLANDER, Embryology
FAIVRE, Therapeutics
FRISCH, R., Surgery
GAUCHER, A., Rheumatology
GOSSEREZ, Stomatology
GRIGNON, Histology, Embryology
GRILLIAT, Internal Medicine
GROSDIDIER, Surgery
GROSS, Renal Physio-pathology
GUILLEMIN, Urology
HARTEMANN, P., Medical Pathology
HERBEUVAL, Clinical Medicine
LACOSTE, Experimental Functional Surgery
LAMARCHE, Medical Hydrology
LAMY, Tuberculosis
LARCAN, Medicine
DE LAVERGNE, Bacteriology, Virology, Immunology
LEGAIT, Histology
LEPOIRE, Neuro-Surgery
LOCHARD, Surgical Pathology
MANCIAUX, Preventive Paediatrics
MARTIN, Medical Computer Science
MICHON, Orthopaedics
NEIMANN, Clinical Paediatrics
PAYSANT, Biological Chemistry
PERNOT, Cardiology
PICARD, Anaesthesiology
PIERQUIN, Industrial Medicine and Rehabilitation
PIERSON, Puericulture and Genetics
PREVOT, Surgery
RAUBER, Pathological Anatomy
RICHON, Obstetrics
DE REN, Forensic Medicine, Toxicology
RIBON, Gynaecology, Obstetrics
SADOUL, Psycho-Pathological Respiration
SENAULT, Hygiene and Social Medicine
SOMMELET, General Surgery
STREIFF, Haematology
TREHEUX, Clinical Electro-radiology
TRIDON, Child Psychiatry
WAYOFF, M., Oto-rhino-laryngology

Faculty of Sciences:

ALAIS, Applied Biochemistry
BARETH, Animal Biology
BASTICK, Mme, Chemistry
BAUMANN, Theoretical Physics
BESSIERE, Animal Biology
BOLFA, Mineralogy
BURDIN, Bacteriology, Virology
CASTRO, Organic Chemistry
CAUBERE, Organic Chemistry
CHAPON, Biological Chemistry
CONDE, Zoology
DAVRAINVILLE, General Physiology
DELPUECH, Organic Physio-Chemistry
DEPAIX, Mathematics
DEXHEIMER, Botany
DUVAL, Applied Chemistry
EYMARD, Differential and Integral Calculus
FELDEN, Physics of Ionised Mediums
FERRIER, Mathematics
FLECHON, Physics
FRENTZ, Animal Biology
FRUHLING, Electricity and Automatics
GADAL, Plant Biology
GAGNY, Regional Geology
GARNIER, Plant Physiology
GAY, Biological Chemistry
GAYET, General Physiology
GERL, Solid State Physics
GROSS, Organic Chemistry
HADNI, Solid State Physics, Infra-red Optics
HEROLD, Applied Inorganic Chemistry
HILLY, Sedimentology
HILY, Propaedeutic Mathematics
HORN, Biophysics
HUET, Mme, Propaedeutic Mathematics
JANOT, Solid State Physics
KRAFFT, Psychophysiology
LEGRAS, Rational Mechanics
LUMER, Pure Mathematics
MAINARD, Thermo-magnetism
MANGENOT, Botany and Microbiology
MARTIN, Chemistry of Radicals
MORLET, Pure Mathematics
NOVERRAZ, Pure Mathematics
PROTAS, Mineralogy and Crystallography
PUJOL, Physical Mechanics
RIVAIL, Theoretical Chemistry
ROCCI, Petrology
ROQUES, Inorganic Chemistry
SOUCHIER, Pedology
STEPHAN, General Zoology

TAKAHASHI, Analysis
TOSSER, Electronics
VEILLET, Animal Biology
VUILLAUME, Psycho-Physiology
WEISLINGER, Quantum Physics

Faculty of Pharmacy:
BENE, Natural Science
BERNANOSE, Physics
BESSON, Mlle, Pharmacodynamics
GIRARD, Mlle, Hygiene
HAYON, J.-C., Cryptogamy
LEMAY, General Pharmacy
MIRJOLET, Analytical Chemistry
PIERREFITTE, Biological Chemistry
SCHWARTZBROD, Microbiology
SIEST, G., Biological Chemistry
SOLEIL, Pharmaceutical Chemistry

University Institute of Technology:
AUBRUN, Automatic Electronics
DURAND, Civil Engineering
FOUSSE, Thermo-energetics
GEORGES, Biology, Biochemistry
HERTZ, Organic Chemistry

Institute of Engineering Sciences:
GILORMINI, Numerical Analysis
GRANGE, Optics, Atomic Physics
HUMBERT, Automatic Electronics
MARI, Applied Material Chemistry

UNIVERSITÉ DE NANCY II

25 RUE BARON LOUIS,
B.P. 454, 54001 NANCY CEDEX
Telephone: 20-47-48.
Founded 1970.

Rector and Chancellor: B. SAINT-SERNIN.
President: J.-C. BONNEFONT.
Secretary-General: C. GUILLERME.

Library: *see* Libraries.
Number of teachers: 450.
Number of students: 9,442

TEACHING AND RESEARCH UNITS:

Faculty of Law and Economic Sciences: Dir. JACK LANG.
Institute of Labour (Nancy): Dir. CLAUDE COLLOT.
Administrative and Political Studies: Dir. GEORGES-PHILIPPE BLOCH.
Institute of Commerce (Nancy): Dir. JEAN LACOMBE.
European University Centre: Dir. GEORGES BONET.
Regional Research: Dir. JEAN LANHER.
Literature: Dir. RENÉ GUISE.
Foreign Languages and Literature: Dir. WAHIB ATALLAH.
Historical and Geographical Sciences: Dir. GUY CABOURDIN.
Philosophy, Psychology, Sociology and Educational Sciences: Dir. JEAN-LÉON BEAUVOIS.
Applied Linguistics: Dir. GUY BOURQUIN.
Mathematics and Informatics: Dir. COLETTE ROLLAND.
University Institute of Technology: Dir. ROBERT MAINARD.

UNIVERSITÉ DE NANTES

1 QUAI DE TOURVILLE,
B.P. 1026,
44035 NANTES CEDEX
Telephone: 47-83-16.

Rector and Chancellor: YVES SAUDRAY.
President: JACQUES VILAINE.
Secretary-General: J. SAILLARD.

TEACHING AND RESEARCH UNITS:

Economic Sciences: Dir. J. C. LEBOSSE.
Law: Dir. J. C. COLLIARD.
Business Administration: Dir. M. LE GALL.
Medicine: Dir. P. MALVY.
Pharmacy: Dir. A. FOUCAUD.
Dentistry: Dir. M. HAMEL.
Chemistry: Dir. M. CHABANEL.
Mathematics: Dir. M. PHAM THE LAÏ.
Physics: Dir. G. GOUREAUX.
Natural Sciences: Dir. J. P. MARGEREL.
Industrial Engineering: Dir. Mme Y. DE ROECK HOLTZHAUER.
Institute of Technology: Dir. M.
School of Mechanical Engineering: Dir. R. PIRONNEAU.
French: Dir. M. RIVIÈRE.
Geography: Dir. M. PINOT.
History: Dir. J. FIERAIN.
Ancient Languages: Dir. M. RIEDINGER.
Modern Languages "A": Dir. M. JOLICOEUR.
Modern Languages "B": Dir. M. RESANO.
Human Sciences: Dir. M. MALHERBE.
Institute of Technology (St.-Nazaire): Dir. M. BECLE.

PROFESSORS:

Faculty of Medicine and Pharmacy:
AUVIGNE, J., Urology
BARBIN, J.-Y., Anatomy
BARRIERE, H., Dermatology
BERNARD, S., Medical Biochemistry
BOITEAU, H., Hygiene and Toxicology
CHARBONNEL, A., Neurology
COLLET, L., Neurosurgery
CORNET, E., Thoracic and Cardiovascular Surgery
COTTIN, S., Therapeutics
COURTIEU, A., Bacteriology and Hygiene
DELAIRE, J., Clinical Stomatology
DESCUNS, P., Neurosurgery
DUMORTIER, L., Social Medicine
DUPON, H., Cardio-Vascular Surgery
FOUCAUD, A., Botany and Cryptogamy
GILLOT, F., Children's Medicine
GUENEL, J., General Medicine
GUIHARD, R., Physics
GUILLON, J., Medical Pathology
HEAVOUET, D., General Medicine
HOULNE, M., Clinical Obstetrics
KERNEIS, J.-P., Pathological Anatomy
LEGENT, F., Oto-rhino-laryngology
LOUSSOUARN, E. P., Pharmaceutical Chemistry
MALVY, P., Surgical Pathology
MINICONI, P., Gastro-enterology
MONNET, R., Materia Medica and Pharmacy
MOUSSEAU, M., Clinical Surgery
MUSINI, J., Pathology
NICOLAS, G., Cardiology
PLOQUIN, J., Chemical Pharmacy
QUERE, M., Ophthalmology
ROUZET, M., Galenic Pharmacy
SOURDILLE, J., Traumatology
TUSQUES, J., Histology and Embryology
VERMEIL, C., Parasitology and Exotic Pathology
VIOLETTE, F., Physiology
WELIN, L., Pharmacodynamics

Faculty of Sciences:
AVIGNON, P., Physics
BOULLOUD, A., Physics
BRILLOUET, G., Mathematics
CAVET, P., Geology
COLLET, L.-H., Physics
GARRIGUES, R., Biology
GRAFF, Y., Chemistry
IBISCH, H., Mathematics
LE DOUARIN, G., Biology
LE DOUARIN, NICOLE, Biology
MARTIN, G., Chemistry
MEZENCEV, R., Physics
MINN, S., Physics
MOUTON, H., Physics
OFFRET, SUZANNE, Physics
PAUC, C., Mathematics
PETRESCO, J., Mathematics
PIERI, J., Biology
PIRONNEAU, Y., Engineering
QUINIOU, H., Chemistry
RAFFIN, Mathematics
ROUXEL, J., Chemistry
SELLIER, R., Biology
WOJTKOWIAK, B., Chemistry

Faculty of Letters and Human Sciences:
DURAND, Y.
GARDIES, J.-L.
GRAS, J., Geography
MAVROCORDATO, A., English
VIGARIE, A., Geography and Regional Development

UNIVERSITÉ DE NICE

PARC VALROSE,
06034 NICE CEDEX
Telephone: 51-91-00.

Rector and Chancellor: P. PASTOUR.
President: MARCEL AZZARO.
Secretary-General: A. DELIAU.

Publications: *Annuaire, Annales du Centre Universitaire Méditerranéen, Bulletin de la Société d'Etudes Dantesques, Guide des Laboratoires de Recherche, Revue ETHNIES.*

TEACHING AND RESEARCH UNITS:

Droit et Sciences Economiques: ave. Emile Henriot; Dir. R. CHARVIN.
Institut d'Administration des Entreprises: ave. Emile Henriot; Dir. J. LEBRATY.
Droit de la Paix et du Développement: ave. Emile Henriot; Dir. P. ISOART.
Médecine: Chemin de Vallombrose; Dir. H. RICHELME.
Odontologie: chemin de Vallombrose; Dir. P. CIOSI.
Mathématiques et Sciences Physiques: Parc Valrose; Dir. F. ROCCA.
Sciences et Techniques: Parc Valrose; Dir. B. LAHLOU.
Institut Polytechnique Méditerranéen: Parc Valrose; Dir. M. ROUILLARD.
Lettres et Sciences Humaines: 98 blvd Edouard Herriot; Dir. Mme C. MARTINEAU.

Civilisations: 117 rue de France; Dir. P. CASTELA.

Observatoire: Mont Gros; Dir. J.-P. ZAHN.

Institut Universitaire de Technologie: 95 Chemin de Fabron; Dir. X. BOISSELIER.

ATTACHED INSTITUTES:

Centre Universitaire Mediterranéen: 65 Promenade des Anglais; Sec.-Gen. J. POIRIER.

Institut d'Etudes Scientifiques de Cargese (Corsica): Dir. M. LEVY.

Institut d'Etudes et de Recherches Interethniques et Interculturelles: 34 rue Verdi; Dir. M. ORIOL.

Institut de Recherche sur l'Enseignement des Mathématiques: Dir. M. MERIGOT.

UNIVERSITÉ D'ORLÉANS

CHÂTEAU DE LA SOURCE,
B.P. 6057,
45017 ORLEANS CEDEX
Founded 1971.
Telephone: 63-22-16.

Rector and Chancellor: P. DELORME.
President: NORBERT GRELET.
Secretary-General: R. MOISSIN.

Number of students: 6,000.

TEACHING AND RESEARCH UNITS:

Law and Economics: Dir. M. LEUREGANS.

Letters and Human Sciences: Dir. Mlle MAGNOU.

Theoretical and Applied Sciences: Dir. M. ROYER.

Institute of Technology (Orleans): Dir. M. TATIBOUET.

Institute of Technology (Bourges): Dir. M. LASSAU.

Advanced Science and Technology: Dir. M. PLAN.

Ligerian Studies: Dir. M. DUPIN.

UNIVERSITÉ DE PARIS I (PANTHÉON-SORBONNE)

12 PLACE DU PANTHÉON,
75231 PARIS CEDEX 05
Telephone: 329-21-40.
Founded 1971.

State control; Language of instruction: French; Academic year: October to June.

Rector and Chancellor: P. TABATONI.
President: Mme H. AHRWEILER.
Vice-President: G. DUPUIS.
Secretary-General: J. GEOFFROY.
Librarian: M. RAUX.

Number of teachers: 610.
Number of students: 28,368.

TEACHING AND RESEARCH UNITS:

General Economics: business administration: Dir. Prof. MERCILLON.

Economic Analysis and Politics, Econometrics, Labour and Human Resources: Dir. Prof. HENIN.

Public Administration and Public Law: Dir. Mme. DREYFUS.

Business Law: Dir. Prof. AZOULAI.

Development, International, European and Comparative Studies: Dir. Prof. COLLIARD.

Geography: Dir. Prof. SOPPELSA.

History: Dir. Prof. FOLHEN.

Philosophy: Dir. Prof. BLOCH.

Labour and Social Sciences: Dir. M. STEUDLER.

Political Science: Dir. Prof. CONAC.

Plastic Arts and Science of Art: Dir. Prof. BAQUE.

Art and Archaeology: Dir. Prof. GARANGER.

INSTITUTES:

Institute of Business Administration: Dir. Prof. TRIOLAIRE.

Institute of Demography: Dir. M. GROSSAT.

Institute of Economic and Social Development: Dir. Prof. MORAZE.

Institute of Social Sciences: Dir. Prof. FREYSSINET.

DEPARTMENTS:

Applied Modern Languages: Dir. Prof. DUCROS.

Social Sciences: Dir. (vacant).

Mathematics, Informatics and Statistics: Dir. Prof. GIRAULT.

PROFESSORS:

Public Administration and Public Internal Law:

CHATELAIN, J., Constitutional Law
DEBEYRE, G., Regional and Local Administration
DUPUIS, G., Administrative Law and Institutions
LALUMIERE, P., Finance
LAVIGNE, P., Constitutional Law
LEGENDRE, P., Administrative Law and History of Law
LUCHAIRE, F., Institutions, International Law

Economic Analysis and Politics, Econometrics, Labour and Human Resources:

BARTOLI, H., Economic Analysis, Economy in Developing Countries
BAUCHET, P., Accountancy
BENARD, J., Public Economy, Theory of Political Economy
BOUZITAT, J., Mathematics
BROCHIER, H., Financial Economics
BUQUET, L., Demography
COULBOIS, P., Political Economy
DENIS, H., History of Economy, Economic Theory in Socialist Countries
DUCROS, B., Economic Analysis
FARDEAU, Mme M., Health Economics, Social Economics
FAU, Mme J., Economic Analysis
FAUVEL, L., Agricultural Economics
FOURGEAUD, C., Statistics
GOUX, C., Applied Macro-economics
LECAILLON, J., Incomes and Techniques of Remuneration
MOUCHEZ, P., General Health Economics
PASSET, R., Economic Analysis
ROTTIER, G., Econometrics
VERNIERES, M., Economic Analysis

Art and Archaeology:

DENTZER, J. M., Archaeology and History of Roman Art
GARANGER, J., Prehistory and Ethnology
LE BOT, M., Contemporary Art
MARCADE, J., Greek Art

Plastic Arts:

BAQUE, P., Plastic Arts
GUIOMAR, M., Music
LAUDE, J., History and Theory of Art
RUDEL, J., Plastic Arts
TEYSSEDRE, B., Graphic Art and Science of Art

Business Law:

AZOULAI, M., Penal Law, Civil Law, Criminal Procedure
BADINTER, R., Penal Procedure
BIGOT, J., Civil and Insurance Law
BREDIN, J.-L., Civil and Judicial Law
GAVALDA, C., Banking and Commercial Law
GHESTIN, J., Civil Law
GUYON, Y., Commercial Law
SCHMIDT, J., Fiscal Law
TUNC, A., Comparative Business Law
VINEY, G., Civil Law

General Economics and Business:

CAPET, M., Business Control and Organization
FLAMANT, M., Modern Economic and Social History
GIRAULT, M., Mathematics and Statistics
JOBARD, J. P., Finance
KREWERAS, M., Mathematics and Statistics
LASSEGUE, P., Scientific Methods Applied to Commerce
MERCILLON, H., Commercial Politics
NGUYEN HUU, C., Economics of Education
PARENT, J., Industrial Politics
PERCEROU, R., Business Law
POUPARD, Y., Mathematics
ROLLAND, C., Informatics
WOLFF, J., Sociology and Social Psychology

Development, International, European and Comparative Studies:

ALLIOT, M., African Institutions
BROCHIER, H., Financial Economics, Asian Economics
COLLIARD, C., International Public Law
FLOUZAT, D., Economic Analysis
GUGLIELMI, J., European Economics
LAGARDE, P., International Private Law
LASSUDRIE DUCHENE, B., International Economy
MANIN, P., International Public Law
MORRISSON, C., Development Economics
PINTO, R., International Public Law
VERGES, J., European Community Law

Geography:

BABONAUX, Y., Urban and Industrial Geography
BEAUDET, G., Physical Geography
BEAUJEU-GARNIER, J., Land Use, Urban Geography
BONNAMOUR, J., Human Geography
COQUE, R., Physical Geography
GODARD, A., Physical Geography
NOIN, D., Population Geography
PINCHEMEL, P., Introduction to Geography, Human and Historic Geography
ROCHEFORT, M., Urban and Human Geography
SAUTTER, G., Human, Tropical and Regional Geography
SOPPELSA, J., Regional Geography

History:
- AGULHON, M., Modern History
- AHRWEILER, HÉLÈNE, History of Byzantine Civilization
- BOUVIER, J., Modern Economic History
- CHEVALLIER, F., Latin American History
- DUROSELLE, J., History of Contemporary International Relations
- FOHLEN, C., North American History
- FOSSIER, R., Medieval History
- GARELLI, P., Near Eastern History
- GOUBERT, P., Modern History
- GUENEE, B., Medieval History
- JACQUART, J., Modern History
- LE GALL, J., Roman History
- NICOLET, C., Roman History
- PEDRONCINI, G., Contemporary Military History
- PERSON, Y., Contemporary African History
- PROST, A., Contemporary History
- ROGER, J., History of Science
- SERRES, M., History of Science and Technology
- SOBOUL, A., History of the French Revolution
- TOUBERT, P., Medieval History
- VAN EFFENTERRE, H., Greek History

Philosophy:
- BACHELARD, SUZANNE, Epistemology
- BLOCH, O., History of Philosophy
- CONCHE, M., General Philosophy
- DEPRUN, J., General Philosophy
- DESANTI, J., History of Modern Philosophy
- MISRAHI, B., Moral Philosophy
- REVAULT-D'ALLONES, O., Aesthetics
- SALA-MOLINS, L., Political Philosophy
- THILLET, P., Philosophy of Antiquity
- ULMANN, J., Philosophy of Education
- VEDRINE, H., History of Philosophy

Political Science:
- CONAC, G., Comparative Political Institutions
- COT, J.-P., Political Science
- COTTERET, J.-M., Political Communication
- DABEZIES, P., Constitutional Law
- DUVERGER, M., Comparative Political Systems
- GONIDEC, P., Third World Politics
- LAGROYE, J., History of Law
- LESAGE, M., Theory of Organizations
- MERLE, M., International Relations
- PISIER KOUCHNER, E., History of Political Science

Labour and Social Studies:
- BLANC, J., Labour Law
- DAVID, M., Labour Law
- DEBBASCH, Y., Economic History of Under-Development
- LYON CAEN, G., Labour Law and Social Policy
- OLLIER, P., Professional Organization

UNIVERSITÉ DE PARIS II (UNIVERSITÉ DE DROIT, D'ÉCONOMIE ET DES SCIENCES SOCIALES)

12 PLACE DU PANTHÉON,
75231 PARIS CEDEX 05

Telephone: 329-21-40.

Founded 1970.

Rector and Chancellor: P. TABATONI.

President: J. ROBERT.

Secretary-General: B. WICKER.

Librarian: Mme RAMBAUD.

Number of teachers: 135.

Number of students: 15,225.

Publication: *Travaux et recherches* (5–6 a year).

TEACHING AND RESEARCH UNITS:

General Private Law and Judicial Law: Dir. Prof. JAMBU-MERLIN.

Business Law: Dir. Prof. SAINT ALARY.

Public Law and Public Administration: Dir. Prof. MATHIOT.

Political Science: Dir. Prof. CADART.

Penal, Criminological and Social Adjustment Studies: Dir. Prof. LEAUTE.

Legal and Economic Studies in International, European and Comparative Law: Dir. Prof. VIRALLY.

Institutional and Economic History and Sociology: Dir. Prof. J. GAUDEMET.

Judicial Studies: Dir. Prof. RAYNAUD.

Economic Science: Dir. Prof. JESSUA.

Information Sciences (French Press Institute): Dir. Prof. BALLE.

Institute of Judicial Studies: Dir. Prof. RAYNAUD.

Advanced International Studies: Dirs. Profs. ROUSSEAU and WEIL.

Comparative Law: Prof. PEDAMON.

Centre for Studies and Research in International Law: Dir. Prof. LOUSSOUARN.

Centre of Philosophy of Law: Profs. BATIFFOL and VILLEY.

PROFESSORS:
- ALBERT, P., Sociology
- ALPHANDERY, E., Economic Sciences
- AUSTRUY, J. J., Economic Sciences
- ARDANT, P., Public Law
- BALLE, F., General History
- BARDONNET, D., Public Law
- BENOIT, F. P., Public Law
- BIACABE, P., Economic Sciences
- BONGERT, Mlle Y., History of Law
- BOULET SAUTEL, Mme M., History of Law
- BOULOUIS, J., Public Law
- BOUREL, P., Private Law
- BOURCIER DE CARBON, L., Economic Sciences
- BRIMO, A., Political Science
- CADART, J., Public Law
- CARDASCIA, G., History of Law
- CATALA, Mme N., Private Law
- CATALA, P., Private Law
- CHAPUS, R., Public Law
- CHARLIER, R., Public Law
- DECOCQ, A., Private Law
- DE CORAIL, J. L., Public Law
- DISCHAMPS, J. C., Management
- DRAGO, R., Public Law
- CORNU, G., Private Law
- DUPEYROUX, J. J., Private Law
- DURRY, G., Private Law
- FLOUR, J., Private Law
- FOYER, J., Private Law
- FRANCON, A., Private Law
- GARRISSON, F., History of Law
- GAUDEMET, J., History of Law
- GAUDEMET, P., Public Law
- GOBERT, Mme M., Private Law
- GOLDMAN, B., Private Law
- GORE, F., Private Law
- HEMARD, J., Private Law
- HOUIN, R., Private Law
- IMBERT, J., History of Law
- JAMBU MERLIN, R., Private Law
- JESSUA, C., Economic Sciences
- DE JUGLART, M., Private Law
- LABROUSSE C., Economic Sciences
- DE LAUBADERE, A., Public Law
- LEAUTE, J., Private Law
- LEVY, D., Public Law
- LEVY, J. PH., History of Law
- LOUSSOUARN, Y., Private Law
- MAGDELAIN, A., History of Law
- DE MALAFOSSE, J., History of Law
- MALAURIE, P., Private Law
- MALINVAUD, P., Private Law
- MATHIOT, A., Public Law
- NEME, Mme C., Economic Sciences
- DEMOURGUES, Mme M., Economic Sciences
- PATARIN, J., Private Law
- PEDAMON, M., Private Law
- PERROT, R., Private Law
- DE PONTAVICE, E., Private Law
- RAYNAUD, P., Private Law
- REUTER, P., Private Law
- RIVERO, J., Public Law
- ROBERT, J., Public Law
- RODIERE, R., Private Law
- ROUVIER, J., Political Science
- SAINT ALARY, R., Private Law
- SAUTEL, G., History of Law
- SCHWARTZENBERG, R. G., Public Law
- DE SOTO, J., Public Law
- SOYER, J., CI., Private Law
- TALLON, D., Private Law
- TERRE, F., Private Law
- TIMBAL, P., History of Law
- TURLAN, Mlle J., History of Law
- VANDENBOSSCHE, A., History of Law
- VASSEUR, M., Private Law
- VEDEL, C., Economic Sciences
- VEDEL, G., Public Law
- VILLERS, R., History of Law
- VILLEY, M., History of Law
- VIRALLY, M., Public Law
- WEIL, P., Public Law

UNIVERSITÉ DE PARIS III (SORBONNE-NOUVELLE)

17 RUE DE LA SORBONNE,
75230 PARIS CEDEX 05

Rector and Chancellor: P. TABATONI.

President: J. CHOUILLET.

Vice-President: M. DUFOURNET.

Secretary-General: Mme. LAGARDE.

TEACHING AND RESEARCH UNITS:

Theatre Studies.

General and Comparative Literature.

Language, Literatures and Civilizations of English-Speaking Countries.

National Institute of Oriental Languages and Civilizations.

German Institute.

Phonetics and Speech.

Latin American Languages and Civilizations.

Institute of Teachers of French Abroad.

Oriental and North African Languages and Civilizations.

Higher School of Interpreters and Translators.

French Language and Literature.

Italian and Romanian.

Iberian Studies.

Department of Cinematography.

Department of Juridical, Economic and Political Sciences.

Department of Techniques of Expression and Communication.

Department of Physical Education, Sports and Open-air Activities.

UNIVERSITÉ DE PARIS IV (PARIS-SORBONNE)

1 RUE VICTOR-COUSIN,
75230 PARIS CEDEX 05
Telephone: 329-12-13.
Founded 1970.

State control; Language of instruction: French; Academic year: October to June.

President: R. POLIN.
Secretary-General: C. CARRIERE.

Number of students: 18,700.

TEACHING AND RESEARCH UNITS:

French Literature.
French Language.
Latin Language and Literature.
Greek.
Philosophy.
History.
History of Art.
Geography.
English.
Germanic Studies.
Iberian Studies.
Italian and Romanian.
Slavonic Studies.
Musicology.
Modern Western Civilization.
Institute of Applied Humanities.
Centre of Applied Literary and Scientific Studies.

ATTACHED DEPARTMENTS:

Department of Science of Religions.
Department of Islamic Studies.
Experimental Department of French Civilization.
Department of Information Science applied to Humanities.
Department of Classical Civilizations.
Department of Applied Modern Languages.

UNIVERSITÉ DE PARIS V (RENÉ DESCARTES)

12 RUE DE L'ÉCOLE DE MÉDECINE,
75270 PARIS CEDEX 06
Telephone: 329-21-77.
Founded 1970.

Academic year: October to June.

Rector and Chancellor: P. TABATONI.
President: F. DELBARRE.
Secretary-General: J. LENA.
Librarian: G. ACHOUR.

Number of teachers: 1,612.
Number of students: 30,641.

Publications: *Bulletin* (monthly), *Annuaire Paris V.*

TEACHING AND RESEARCH UNITS:

Institute of Psychology: Dir. Mme C. LEVY-LEBOYER.
Social Sciences: Dir. A. ADAM.
Psychology: Dir. Mme G. DE MONTMOLIN.
Educational Sciences: Dir. G. SNYDERS.
Mathematics, Formal Logic and Information Science: Dir. M. BARBUT.
General and Applied Linguistics: Dir. F. FRANÇOIS.
University Institute of Technology: Dir. P. LECOINTE.
Medicine: Cochin—Port-Royal: Dir. G. CREMER.
Medicine: Necker—Enfants Malades: Dir. J. PAUPE.
Medicine: Paris-Ouest: Dir. M. GOULON.
Forensic Medicine, Medical Law and Deontology: Dir. L. DEROBERT.
Biomedicine: Dir. A. DELMAS.
Medical and Biological Studies: Dir. P. HUARD.
Dentistry: Dir. B. TUCAT.
Pharmaceutical and Biological Sciences: Dir. J. FLAHAUT.
Effects of Medicines and Toxics: Dir. R. BOULU.
Human and Experimental Biology: Dir. J. SAVEL.
Physical Education and Sports: Dir. C. HAMOT.
Faculty of Law: Dir. J. HILAIRE.

UNIVERSITÉ DE PARIS VI (PIERRE ET MARIE CURIE)

4 PLACE JUSSIEU,
75230 PARIS CEDEX 05
Telephone: 329-12-21.

Rector and Chancellor: P. TABATONI.
President: J. DRY.
Secretary-General: R. POULLAIN.

TEACHING AND RESEARCH UNITS:

Institute of Pure and Applied Mathematics: Dir. Prof. M. COMBES.
Analysis, Probability and Application: Dir. Prof. PRIOURET.
Institute of Theoretical and Applied Mechanics: Dir. Prof. DUVAUT.
Computer Science, Statistics and Application: Dir. Prof. ROBINET.
Applied Physics: Dir. Prof. GARNIER.
Optics, Atomic, Molecular and Crystalline Physics: Dir. Prof. ABELÈS.
Condensed State Physics: Dir. Prof. AUTHIER.
Theoretical Physics: Dir. Prof. BRIAND.
Physical Chemistry: Dir. Prof. CHEMLA.
Organic Chemistry: Dir. Prof. CASADEVALL.
Inorganic Chemistry: Dir. Prof. Mme. HERPIN.
Biochemistry: Dir. Prof. LE PECQ.
Institute of Plant Biology: Dir. Prof. Mme. LEJAL-NICOL.
Genetics: Dir. Prof. FAVARD.
Animal Physiology: Dir. Prof. Mme ALBE-FESSARD.
Zoology: Dir. Prof. Mme RACCAUD.
Earth Sciences: Dir. Prof. POIGNANT.
Geophysics Institute: Dir. Prof. ALLEGRE.
Statistics Institute of Paris: Dir. Prof. DUGUE.
National Higher School of Chemistry of Paris: Dir. Prof. COUSSEMANT.
Medicine: Saint-Antoine: Dir. Prof. PICARD.
Medicine: Pitié-Salpêtrière: Dir. Prof. LEGRAND.
Medicine: Broussais Hôtel-Dieu: Dir. Prof. DIEBOLD.
Institute of Stomatology: Dir. Prof. VAILLANT.
Department of Modern Languages: Dir. M. INNOCENT.
Department of Geography: Dir. Prof. ROGNON.
Department of Physical, Sporting and Outdoor Activities: Dir. Mme DUMONTAUX.

UNIVERSITÉ DE PARIS VII

2 PLACE JUSSIEU,
75221 PARIS CEDEX 05
Telephone: 336-25-25.
Telex: Pariset 270075 F Paris
Founded 1970.

Rector and Chancellor: P. TABATONI.
President: Y. LE CORRE.
Secretary-General: CLAUDE BELOT.

Number of teachers: 1,645.
Number of students: 35,000.
Publication: *Cahiers Jussieu* (2 a year).

TEACHING AND RESEARCH UNITS:

Anthropology, Ethnology and Religious Studies: Dir. R. JAULIN.
Biochemistry: Dir. G. GONZY-TREBOUL.
Biology and Genetics: Dir. J. SCHAEVERBEKE.
Chemistry: Dir. G. LAPLUYE.
Didactics of Disciplines: Dir. J. DE FELICE.
Environment: Dir. J. VIGNERON.
Dental Surgery: Dir. G. PENNE.
Medicine Lariboisière-Saint-Louis: Dir. R. HOUDART.
Medicine Xavier-Bichat: Dir. F. DE PAILLERETS.
Geography and Social Sciences: Dir. M. NICOLAS.
Haematology: Dir. J. BERNARD.
General Computer Science: Dir. H. BESTOUGEFF.
Institute of English: Dir. J. SUREL.
Eastern Asian Languages and Literature: Dir. Y. HERVOUETT.
Modern Languages for Non-Specialists: Dir. M. MERLE.
Mathematics: Dir. M. KAROUBI.
Physics: Dir. J. KLEIN.
Linguistic Research: Dir. A. CULIOLI.
Clinical Human Sciences: Dir. P. FEDIDA.
Earth Sciences: Dir. C. ALLEGRE.
Sciences of Texts and Documents: Dir. M. SARRAZIN.
Sociology: Dir. P. ANSART.
Audiovisual: M. BERDOT.

UNIVERSITÉ DE PARIS VIII

93200 ST. DENIS

Rector and Chancellor: P. TABATONI.
President: CH. ELMARY (acting).
Secretary-General: G. ROUX.

Number of teachers: 600.
Number of students: 31,500.

Publications: *Revue "Littérature"*†, *Bulletin de linguistique allemande*†, *Bulletin de la R.D.A.*†, *Bulletin de la France au XXe siècle*†, *Travaux sur le capitalisme et l'économie politique*†, *"Art et Info"*†.

Teaching and Research Units:

Slav, Oriental and Asiatic Studies: Dir. M. Zafrani.
Spanish, Italian and Portuguese: Dir. M. Bouissy.
Anglo-American Languages, Literatures and Civilizations: Dir. B. Cassen.
German: Dir. M. Rovan.
History and Sociology: Dir. M. Debouzy.
Geography: Dir. C. Thayer.
Psychology and Educational Sciences: Dir. J. F. Richard.
General Literatures: Dir. Mme Kaufolz.
Linguistics and Information Science: Dir. J. Donio.
Sociology and Mathematics: Dir. M. Chevalley.
Philosophy and Psychoanalysis: Dir. J. A. Miller.
Juridical Administrative and Political Sciences: Dir. G. Lapassade.
Arts: Plastic, Dir. F. Popper; Cinema, Dir. Mme Eizyckman; Music, Dir. D. Charles; Theatre, Dir. A. Veinstein.
Political Economy: Dir. M. Bellon.
Town Planning: Dirs. F. Choay, M. Coquery, F. Mellet.

UNIVERSITÉ DE PARIS IX (PARIS-DAUPHINE)

PLACE DU MARÉCHAL DE LATTRE DE TASSIGNY, 75016 PARIS

Telephone: 505-14-10.

President: H. Tézenas du Montcel.
Secretary-General: Aimé Salfati.
Librarian: M. Guilbaud.

Number of teachers: 600.
Number of students: 5,500.

Teaching and Research Units:

Business Studies: Applied Economics: Dir. Prof. C. Gauvin.
Business Studies: Dir. M. Jarniou.
Applied Economics: Dir. M. Poix.
Organization Sciences: Dir. Prof. E. Levy.
Business Information Science: Dir. Prof. G. Levy.
Mathematics: Dir. Prof. H. Moulin.

UNIVERSITÉ DE PARIS X (PARIS-NANTERRE)

200 AVE. DE LA RÉPUBLIQUE, 92000 NANTERRE

Telephone: 725-92-34.

Rector and Chancellor: P. Albarede.
President: J. M. Verdier.
Vice-Presidents: P. Larivaille, P. Derycke, F. Gerbod, G. Schneilin, M. Couchez.
Secretary-General: G. Laurent.
Librarian: M. Hue.

Number of teachers: 669.
Number of students: 22,087.

Teaching and Research Units:

Economic Sciences: Dir. M. Seller.
Juridical Sciences: Dir. M. Couchez.
History: Dir. M. Levy-Leboyer.
Geography: Dir. M. Burgel.
Psychology and Education Sciences: Dir. M. Filloux.
Sociology: Dir. M. Lautman.
Philosophy: Dir. M. Reznikoff.
Letters: Dir. M. Canivet.
English: Dir. M. Guillaume.
German, Romance Languages, Slav and Applied Foreign Languages: Dir. M. Schneilin.
Administration: Dir. M. Berstein.
Institute of Technology (Ville d'Avray): Dir. M. Dufour.
Science and Techniques of Physical and Sporting Activities: Dir. M. Neaumet.

UNIVERSITÉ DE PARIS XI (PARIS-SUD)

15 RUE G. CLÉMENCEAU, 91405 ORSAY

Telephone: 941-67-50.

Rector and Chancellor: P. Albarede.
President: Roland Omnes.
Secretary-General: Gilbert Pons.
Librarian: Mme Bonnet.

Number of teachers: 1,750.
Number of students: 20,800.

Teaching and Research Units:

First Cycle: Scientific and Medical Orientation: Dir. J. Roussel.
Second Cycle: Exact and Natural Sciences: Dir. C. Chabbert.
Third Cycle: Exact and Natural Sciences: Dir. G. Ruget.
Institute of Nuclear Physics: Dir. M. Riou.
Linear Accelerator: Dir. J. Perez y Jorba.
University Institute of Technology (Orsay): Dir. M. Donadieu.
University Institute of Technology (Cachan): Dir. A. Leblond.
Pharmaceutical and Biological Sciences (Chatenay-Malabry): Dir. Y. Cohen.
Therapeutic Chemistry (Chatenay-Malabry): Dir. J. Mestre.
Hygiene and Protection of Man and his Environment (Chatenay-Malabry): Dir. C. Pellerin.
Hospital and University Centre at Kremlin-Bicêtre: Dir. J. Dormont.
Law and Economics (Sceaux): Dir. C. Zorgbibe.
University Institute of Technology (Sceaux): Dir. F. Hamon.

UNIVERSITÉ DE PARIS XII (PARIS-VAL-DE-MARNE)

AVE. GÉNÉRAL DE GAULLE, 94010 CRÉTEIL CEDEX

Rector and Chancellor: J. Dehaussy.
President: M. Guillou.

Number of teachers: 545.
Number of students: 10,000.

Teaching and Research Units:

Institute of Town Planning: Dir. M. Houin.
Medicine: Dir. M. Rapin.
Law and Politics: Dir. M. Matringe.
Economic Sciences: Dir. M. Bresson.
Letters and Humanities: Dir. M. Pergnier.
Science: Dir. M. Buvet.
Institute of Technology: Dir. M. Chappey.

UNIVERSITÉ DE PARIS XIII (PARIS-NORD)

AVE. J.-B. CLEMENT, 93430 VILLETANEUSE

Rector: J. Dehaussy.
President: M. Nisard.

Publications: *Psychologie clinique, Annales du C.E.S.E.R.E., Cahiers de Linguistique Hispanique Médiévale.*

Teaching and Research Units:

Saint-Denis Scientific and Polytechnic Centre: Dir. M. Glass.
Law and Political Science: Dir. M. Dufau.
Letters and Humanities: Dir. M. Jaisson.
University Institute of Technology (Saint-Denis): Dir. J. Bodin.
University Institute of Technology (Villetaneuse): Dir. H. Charpentier.
Medicine and Human Biology Experimental Centre: Dir. P. Cornillot.
Economic Sciences and Business Administration: Dir. Duc Loi Phan.
Expression and Communications Sciences: Dir. F. Dumont.

UNIVERSITÉ DE PAU ET DES PAYS DE L'ADOUR

68 RUE MONTPENSIER, B.P. 576 PAU-UNIVERSITÉ, 64010 PAU CEDEX

Telephone: (59) 32-56-47.

Founded 1970.

Rector and Chancellor: M. Verguin.
President: D. Levier.
Secretary-General: Mlle Dagues-Bie.
Librarian: M. Bosc.

Number of teachers: 192.
Number of students: 5,058.

Teaching and Research Units:

Faculty of Law and Economic Sciences: Dean Jean-Claude Douence.
Faculty of Exact Sciences: Dean M. Xans.
Faculty of Letters and Human Sciences: Dean M. Manso.
University Institute of Scientific Research: Dir. M. Delfaud.
University Institute of Technology (in Bayonne): Dir. M. Verdun (acting).

UNIVERSITÉ DE PERPIGNAN

AVE. DE VILLENEUVE,
66025 PERPIGNAN CEDEX
Telephone: (68) 50-08-01.
Founded 1971.

Rector and Chancellor: JACQUES FARRAN.
President: YVES SERRA.
Secretary-General: BERNARD BIAU.
Librarian: FERNAND BELLEDENT.

Number of teachers: 172.
Number of students: 2,643.

Publications: *L'ordinaire du Mexacaniste, Bulletin du Centre d'Etudes et d'administration des Collectivités locales.*

TEACHING AND RESEARCH UNITS:
Humanities and Social Sciences: Dir. MICHEL PRALUS.
Exact and Natural Sciences: Dir. PIERRE BERÇOT.
University Institute of Technology: Dir. GEORGES RIERA.

UNIVERSITÉ DE PICARDIE

RUE SOLOMON MAHLANGU,
80025 AMIENS CEDEX
Telephone: 95-13-14.
Founded 1965.

Rector and Chancellor: LOÏC SPARFEL.
President: BERNARD ROUSSET.
Secretary-General: MAX ARNIAUD.

TEACHING AND RESEARCH UNITS:
Law: Dir. JACQUES CHEVALLIER.
Economics: Dir. M. CERISIER.
Modern Languages: Dir. Prof. CREPIN.
Literature: Dir. Prof. RIBARD.
Philosophy and Human Sciences: Dir. TRINH VAN THAO.
History and Geography: Dir. M. REGRAIN.
Medicine: 12 rue Frédéric Petit, Amiens; Dir. Prof. BERNASCONI.
Pharmacy: 3 place Louis Dewailly, 80037 Amiens Cedex; Dir. Prof. PERDU.
Sciences: 33 rue Saint-Leu, Amiens; Dir. PAUL PERSONNE.
Mathematics: 33 rue Saint Leu, 80039 Amiens Cedex; Dir. Prof. A. CHEVALIER.
University Institute of Technology: ave. des Facultés, Le Bailly, Amiens; Dir. Prof. TUDO.
U.E.R. (Saint-Quentin): 48 rue Raspail, 02109 Saint-Quentin Cedex; Dir. M. BAUER.

UNIVERSITÉ DE POITIERS

15 RUE DE BLOSSAC
86034 POITIERS CEDEX
Telephone: (49) 88-26-32.
Founded 1432.

Rector and Chancellor: JEAN-CLAUDE MAESTRE.
President: JACQUES BORZEIX.
Secretaries-General: JEAN-ALFRED ARNÉODO, ANDRÉ MÉSA.
Librarian: Mlle S. GUYOTAT.

Number of students: 13,000.

TEACHING AND RESEARCH UNITS:
Sciences Exactes et Naturelles: Dir. GUY RENAULT.
Sciences Fondamentales et Appliquées: Dir. (vacant).
Médecine et Pharmacie: Dir. DOMINIQUE PATTE.
Langues et Littératures: Dir. AARON LAWTON.
Sciences Humaines: Dir. JACQUES MARCADÉ.
Centre d'Etudes Supérieures de Civilisation Médiévale: Dir. PIERRE BEC.
Sciences Juridiques et Sociales: Dir. PIERRE COUVRAT.
Sciences Economiques: Dir. PIERRE ZLATIEV.
Institut Régional d'Education Physique et Sportive: Dir. JEAN-JACQUES BAINCHET.
Institut Universitaire de Technologie de Poitiers: Dir. CLAUDE GASC.
Institut Universitaire de Technologie de La Rochelle: Dir. ANDRÉ BALLAGE.
Ecole Nationale Supérieure de Mécanique et d'Aérotechnique: Dir. JACQUES DE FOUQUET.
Centre d'Etudes Aérodynamiques et Thermiques: Dir. THIERRY ALZIARY DE ROQUEFORT.
Sciences et Techniques: Dir. MICHEL BLANCHARD.

UNIVERSITÉ DE REIMS

23 RUE BOULARD, 51100 REIMS
Telephone: (26) 40-04-98.
Founded 1969.

Rector and Chancellor: JEAN-LOUIS BOURSIN.
President: LUCIEN BERNARD.
Vice-Presidents: JACQUES BUR, JEAN-CLAUDE ETIENNE.
Secretary-General: (vacant).

Library: *see* Libraries.
Number of teachers: 700.
Number of students: 12,600.

Publications: *Livret de l'Université, Publications du département d'anglais* (annually), *Etudes Champenoises* (annually), *Revue de l'Institut de Géographie* (termly), *Jurisprudence Cour d'appel* (quarterly).

TEACHING AND RESEARCH UNITS:
Exact and Natural Sciences: Dir. BERNARD GASTAMBIDE.
Medicine: Dir. SERGE KOCHMAN.
Pharmacy: Dir. JEAN LEVY.
Letters and Human Sciences: Dir. CLAUDE FIEROBE.
Law and Economic Sciences: Dir. BERNARD TOURET.
Odontology: Dir. GUY DUCROT.
University Institute of Technology of Reims: Dir. CLAUDE COLLOT.
University Institute of Technology of Troyes: Dir. ALAIN RIGOLOT.

UNIVERSITÉ DE RENNES I

2 RUE DU THABOR,
35000 RENNES
Telephone: (99) 36.28.54.

Rector and Chancellor: J. GARAGNON.
President: J. P. CURTES.

Number of teaching staff: 980.
Number of students: 16,476.

TEACHING AND RESEARCH UNITS:
Legal Sciences: 9 rue Jean Macé, 35042 Rennes Cedex; Dir. M. JUGAULT.
Economic Sciences and Business Economy: 7 place Hoche, 35000 Rennes; Dir. M. J. C. HARDOUIN.
Institute of Management: 9 rue Jean Macé, 35042 Rennes Cedex; Dir. M. C. CHAMPAUD.
Physical Chemistry, Fundamental and Applied Biology: Ave. du Professeur Léon Bernard, 35043 Rennes Cedex; Dir. M. F. PICARD.
Medical Therapeutics: Ave. du Professeur Léon Bernard, 35043 Rennes Cedex; Dir. M. J. GOUFFAULT.
Pharmacy: Ave. du Professeur Léon Bernard, 35043 Rennes Cedex; Dir. M. HUET.
Public Health: Ave. du Professeur Léon Bernard, 35043 Rennes Cedex; Dir. M. KERISIT.
Odontology: 2 place Pasteur, 35000 Rennes; Dir. M. BIGARRE.
Material Sciences: Campus de Beaulieu, 35042 Rennes Cedex; Dir. M. VEZZOZI.
Mathematics and Information Science: Campus de Beaulieu, 35042 Rennes Cedex; Dir. M. G. BOULAYE.
Life and Environmental Sciences: Campus de Beaulieu, 35042 Rennes Cedex; Dir. M. HUON.
Philosophy: Campus de Beaulieu, 35042 Rennes Cedex; Dir. M. JACQUES.
School of Chemical Engineering: Ave. du Général Leclerc, 35000 Rennes; Dir. M. KERFANTO.
Institute of Technology (Rennes): Rue du Clos Courtel, Buttes de Coësmes, 35000 Rennes.
Institute of Technology (Lannion): Route de Perros Guirrec, B.P. 112, 22302 Lannion.

UNIVERSITÉ DE RENNES II (UNIVERSITÉ DE HAUTE BRETAGNE)

6 AVE. GASTON BERGER,
35043 RENNES CEDEX
Telephone: 59-20-33.

Rector and Chancellor: J. J. GARAGNON.
President: (vacant).
Secretary-General: Mme H. LE MARRE.

Number of teaching staff: 276.
Number of students: 8,078.

TEACHING AND RESEARCH UNITS:

Arts: Dir. Mme D. DELOUCHE.
Literature: Dir. CHARLES FOULON.

Geography: Dir. M. MOUNIER.
History and Political Sciences: Dir. M. THOBIE.
English: Dir. M. NOEL.
Modern Languages: Dir. M. GUERIN.
Psychology and Sociology: Dir. M. POSTIC.
Language and Culture: Dir. M. GAGNEPAIN.
Ancient and Modern Civilization of West Amorica: Dir. M. LEBRUN.
Physical Education and Sport: Dir. M. POIRIER.
Science and Technology: Dir. M. LE CALVE.
University Institute of Technology at Vannes: B.P. 1104, 56008 Vannes; Dir. M. KERGUERIS.

UNIVERSITÉ DE ROUEN-HAUTE NORMANDIE

RUE THOMAS BECKET, 76130 MONT-SAINT-AIGNAN
Telephone: 74-03-32.
Founded 1966.

Academic year: October to June.

Rector and Chancellor: JOEL BOURDIN.
President: P. ROLLIN.
Vice-Presidents: JACQUES LECLAIRE, JEAN-MARIE HELBERT.
Secretary-General: BERNARD BARRAULT.
Librarian: Mlle F. MARIE-CARDINE.

Number of teachers: 670.
Number of students: 12,500.

TEACHING AND RESEARCH UNITS:

Medicine and Pharmacy: Dir. H. PIGUET.
Sciences and Technology: Dir. J. GALLOT.
Letters and Humanities: Dir. A. SADOURNY.
Law and Economic Sciences: Dir. P. GELARD.
University Institute of Technology (Rouen): Dir. J. GOUAULT.
University Institute of Technology (Le Havre): Dir. J. RIPOCHE.
Institute of Behavioural and Educational Sciences: Dir. H. LEHALLÉ.
Scientific Institute of Upper Normandy: Dir. G. CONRAD.
Science and Technology (Le Havre): Dir. G. LARCHER.
International Affairs (Le Havre): Dir. P. GELARD.

PROFESSORS:

Medicine and Pharmacy:

BOHOUN, C., Pharmaceutical Chemistry
BORDE, J., Child Surgery
BOURREILLE, J., Clinical Medicine
DAILLY, R., Paediatrics
DALION, J., Histology-Embryology
DESHAYES, P., Rheumatology
DUVAL, C., Clinical Obstetrics
FAUGERAS, G., Materia Medica and Pharmaco-dynamics
FILLASTRE, J. P., Nephrology
FRIGOT, P., Galenic Pharmacy
GARNIER, Mme J., Botany and Cryptogamy
HELLOUIN DE MENIBUS, C., Experimental Pathology
HILLEMAND, B., Therapeutics
HUMBERT, G., Tropical and Infectious Diseases
LAUMONIER, R., Pathological Anatomy
LAURET, P., Dermatology
LEFRANÇOIS, R. Physiology
LEMELAND, J.-F., Bacterio-Virology
LEMERCIER, J. P., Pneumo-phthisiology
LETAC, B., Cardiology
MAISONNET, M., Hygiene
MATRAY, F., Medical Biochemistry
MICHON, R., Legal and Social Medicine
MITROFANOFF, P., Infantile Surgery
MORÈRE, P., Medical Pathology
PASQUIS, P., Physiology
PELLERIN, F., Pharmaceutical Chemistry
PIGUET, H., Immuno-haematology
ROPARTZ, C., Genetics
SAMSON, M., Neurology
SCHRUB, J. C., Therapeutics
SEYER, J., Anatomy
SORIA, Mlle C., Pharmaceutical Biochemistry
TARDIF, B., Anatomy
TESTART, J., Clinical Surgery
THOMINE, M., Orthopaedic and Traumatological Surgery
WINCKLER, C., Anaesthesiology
WOLF, L., Therapeutic Internal Medicine

Sciences and Technology:

BANEGE, A., Physics
BOUAZIZ, R., Chemistry
BOUIX, M., Mathematics
BOULARD, B., Vegetal Biology
CAULLET, C., Chemistry
DERRIDJ, M., Mathematics
DESAMLAZARO, J., Mathematics
DUHAMEL, P., Chemistry
GALLOT, J., Physics
GOUAULT, J., Chemistry
GRAF, R., Physics
GRIBENSKY, A., Animal Biology
HANSEL, G., Mathematics
HAYMANN, P., Physics
HELBERT, J. M., Physics
HOMMERIL, P., Geology
LARCHER, G., Physics
PEREZ, G., Chemistry
PERRIN, D., Mathematics
QUEGUINER, G., Chemistry
RIPOCHE, J., Electronics, Electrotechnics and Automatism
ROLLIN, P., Vegetal Biology
ROUSSEAU, Mme M., Physics
SELEGNY, E., Chemistry
SURIN, Mme A., Mathematics
THELLIER, M., Vegetal Biology
VAILLANT, R., Animal Physiology
VALENTIN, P., Physics
VAUTIER, C., Physics
WINOGRADZKI, Mme J., Physics

Letters and Humanities:

BAILBE, J., Modern French Literature
CORVISIER, A., Modern and Contemporary History
DEGHAYE, P., German
DREYFUS, GINETTE, Philosophy
DUBOIS, H., History
DUMONT, R., Comparative Literature
EDIGHOFFER, R., German
GALLAIS, J., Geography
GRANIER, J., Philosophy
GUILLEMAIN, B., Philosophy
HENRIOT, J., Philosophy
JOUKOVSKY, Mme, F., French Language and Literature
LECLAIRE, J., English
MARCELLESI, J., French Grammar and Philology
NIDERST, A., French
PERPILLOU, J. L., Latin
PIERROT, J., Modern French Literature and Language
PONS, G., German
RENUCCI, Mlle J., Geography
VENARD, M., Modern and Contemporary History
VERNIER, M., English
VIDALENC, J., Modern and Contemporary History

Law and Economic Sciences:

BAZEX, M., Public Law
CEDRAS, J., Economic Sciences
DEBOISSIEU, C., Economic Sciences
GELARD, P., Public Law
GOY, R., Public Law
MERCADAL, B., Private Law
PEYREFITTE, L., Private Law
VESPERINI, J.-P., Economic Sciences

AFFILIATED INSTITUTES:

Institut National Supérieur de Chimie: place Emile Blondel, 76 Mont-Saint-Aignan; Dir. R. DARRIGO.

Ecole Supérieure de Commerce et d'Administration des Entreprises: blvd. Siegfried, 76 Mont-Saint-Aignan; Dir. G. MOREL.

Ecole Supérieure de Commerce et d'Administration des Entreprises du Havre: 1–9 rue Emile Zola, 76 Le Havre; Dir.-Gen. J. CAMUS.

UNIVERSITÉ DE SAINT-ÉTIENNE

34 RUE FRANCIS BAULIER, 42023 SAINT-ETIENNE CEDEX
Telephone: 25-22-02.

President: C. FORESTIER.
Vice-Presidents: L. ROUX, C. LONGEON, D. IMBERT.
Secretary-General: R. ROUQUAIROL.
Librarian: Mme. ACHARD.

Number of teachers: 326.
Number of students: 6,717.

TEACHING AND RESEARCH UNITS:

Law: Dir. A. JEAMMEAUD.
Economics: Dir. P. MIFSUD.
Letters and Human Sciences: Dir. M. ARGOUD.
Sciences: Dir. R. ROUGNY.
Medicine: Dir. P. QUENEAU.
University Institute of Technology: Dir. J. MARCHAND.

UNIVERSITÉ DE SAVOIE (CHAMBÉRY)

DOMAINE UNIVERSITAIRE DE JACOB-BELLE COMBETTE, B.P. 143, 73011 CHAMBÉRY CEDEX
Telephone: (79) 69-27-18.
Founded 1970.

President: DOMINIQUE PACCARD.
Registrar: MONIQUE BELLEMIN.
Librarian: Mlle FRANCE MESMIN (acting).

Number of teachers: 125.
Number of students: 2,540.

Publications: *Annales* (annual), *C.I.R.C.E.* (annual), *Etudes maistriennes.*

TEACHING AND RESEARCH UNITS:

Lettres, Sciences Humaines et Sciences Sociales: Dir. L. TERREAUX.

Sciences et Techniques: Dir. M. MARTIN-BOUYER.
Institut Universitaire de Technologie: Chemin du Bray à Annecy-le-Vieux, B.P. 900, 74019 Annecy Cedex; Dir. (vacant).

UNIVERSITÉ LOUIS PASTEUR (UNIVERSITÉ DE STRASBOURG I)

4 RUE BLAISE PASCAL,
67070 STRASBOURG CEDEX
Telephone: (88) 614830.
Founded 1971.

Rector and Chancellor: PIERRE MAGNIN.
President: FRANÇOIS MARCOUX.
Vice-Presidents: Prof. JACQUES-HENRI WEIL, Prof. PHILIPPE ROPARTZ, PHILIPPE GAERTNER.
Secretary-General: GILBERT KIEHL.

Number of teachers: 920.
Number of students: 13,013.

TEACHING AND RESEARCH UNITS:

Medical Sciences I: 4 rue Kirschleger, 67085 Strasbourg Cedex; Dir. M. DORNER.
Biomedical Sciences: 4 rue Kirschleger, 67085 Strasbourg Cedex; Dir. A. KIRN.
Dentistry: 4 rue Kirschleger, 67085 Strasbourg Cedex; Dir. R. FRANK.
Pharmacy: 74 route du Rhin, B.P. 10, 67048 Strasbourg Cedex; Dir. P. METAIS.
Mathematics: 7 rue René Descartes, 67084 Strasbourg Cedex; Dir. X. FERNIQUE (acting).
Physics and Chemistry: 4 rue Blaise Pascal, B.P. 1032/F, 67070 Strasbourg Cedex; Dir. H. BENOIT.
Materials Sciences: 4 rue Blaise Pascal, B.P. 1032/F, 67070 Strasbourg Cedex; Dir. J. J. FRIED.
Earth and Life Sciences: 28 rue Goethe, 67083 Strasbourg Cedex; Dir. Y. BOULANGER.
Behavioural and Environmental Sciences: 14 rue Goethe, 67000 Strasbourg; Dir. B. WILL.
Economic Sciences: 4 rue Blaise Pascal, 67070 Strasbourg Cedex; Dir. J. L. GAFFARD.
Geography: 43 rue Goethe, 67000 Strasbourg; Dir. P. MICHEL.
School of Polymer Science: 4 rue Boussingault, 67000 Strasbourg; Dir. C. WIPPLER.
National School of Chemical Engineering: 1 rue Blaise Pascal, 67008 Strasbourg Cedex; Dir. M. DAIRE.
Observatory: 11 rue de l'Université, 67000 Strasbourg; Dir. A. FLORSCH.
Institute of Geophysics: 5 rue René Descartes, 67084 Stasbourg Cedex; Dir. R. SCHLICH.

UNIVERSITÉ DE STRASBOURG II (SCIENCES HUMAINES)

22 RUE RENÉ DESCARTES,
67084 STRASBOURG
Telephone: 61-39-39.
Founded 1538.

Rector and Chancellor: PIERRE MAGNIN.
President: LUCIEN BRAUN.
Secretary-General: PAUL HELMS.

Number of teachers: 310.
Number of students: 6,775.

Publications†: *Recherches anglaises et nord-américaines, Travaux de l'Institut d'Etudes Latino-américaines, Recherches germaniques, Bulletin analytique d'histoire romaine, Revue des sciences sociales de la France de l'Est, Travaux de l'Institut de Phonétique, Civilisations Anciennes, Revue de Droit Canonique* (annually), *Revue d' Histoire et de Philosophie religieuses, Revue des Sciences Religieuses* (quarterly).

DIRECTORS OF TEACHING AND RESEARCH UNITS:

Langues Classiques: HUBERT ZEHNACKER.
Lettres Modernes: PAUL HOFFMAN.
Langues, Littératures et Civilisations Etrangères: ROLAND MARX.
Sciences Historiques: EDMOND FREZOULS.
Philosophie: LUCIEN BRAUN.
Sciences Sociales: CHRISTIAN DE MONTLIBERT.
Théologie Catholique: BERNARD RENAUD.
Théologie Protestante: ROGER MEHL.

PROFESSORS:

Classics:
FUGIER, Mlle H., Latin Philology
JOUANNA, J., Greek Language and Literature
SCHILLING, R., Latin Language and Civilization
SCHWARZ, J., Greek Language and Papyrology
ZEHNACKER, H., Latin Language and Literature

Modern Literature:
HEPP, Mlle N., 17th- and 18th-century French Literature
MANSUY, M., Modern French Literature
MULLER, C., French Philology
PARENT, Mlle M., History of the French Language
SIMON, Mme P., Phonetics
STRAKA, G., Romance Philology
VERNOIS, P., 20th-century French Literature

Foreign Languages, Literature and Civilisation:
CHARIER, J., Germanic Philology
FAHD, T., Arabic Language and Literature, Islamology
FINK, G.-L., German Literature and Civilisation
MELIKOFF, Mme I., Turkish
NANDRIS, O., Romanian
NEVEUX, J., German Literature and Civilisation
PERROUD, R., Italian Language and Literature
PHILIPP, Mlle M., German Linguistics
VOGELWEITH, G., Scandinavian Literature

Philosophy:
BRAUN, L., History of Philosophy and Aesthetics
CANIVEZ, A., Ethics
REBOUL, O., Philosophy

Historical Sciences:
CHATELET, A., History of Art
FREZOULS, E., Roman History
HATT, J. J., National Antiquities
LIVET, G., Modern History
PAVIS D'ESCURAC, Mme H., Ancient History
RAPP, F., Medieval History
SIMON, M., History of Religions
THIRIET, F., Auxiliary Historical Sciences

Social Sciences:
FREUND, J., Ethics and Sociology
PAQUES, Mme V., Ethnology

Catholic Theology:
AUBERT, J. M., Moral Theology
BARBOTIN, E., Philosophy
BERNHARD, J., Canon Law
JAVELET, R., Philosophical Introduction to Theology
MENARD, J., History of Religions
MUNIER, C., Church History
SCHMITT, J., Scriptural Studies
VOGEL, C., History of the Liturgy and Archaeology
WACKENHEIM, C., Apologetics
WINLING, R., Special Dogmatics

Protestant Theology:
BENOIT, A., History of Christian Antiquity
CHEVALLIER, A., New Testament
HONEGGER, M., Musicology
JACOB, E., Old Testament
MEHL, R., Religious Ethics and Sociology
PHILONENKO, M., History of Religion
PRIGENT, P., Biblical Philology
SIEGWALT, G., Dogmatics
TROCME, E., New Testament
VOELTZEL, R., Practical Theology

UNIVERSITÉ DE STRASBOURG III

PLACE D'ATHÈNES,
67084 STRASBOURG CEDEX
Telephone: (88) 61-18-18.

Rector and Chancellor: PIERRE MAGNIN.
President: JEAN-MARC BISCHOFF.
Vice-President: MAURICE GROSS.
Secretary-General: ALEXANDRE MARY.

Number of students: 5,900.

TEACHING AND RESEARCH UNITS:

Law and Political Sciences: Dir. M. JACQUÉ.
Legal, Political and Social Research: Dir. Mme D. HUET.
Institute of Labour: Dir. M. BABINET.
Institute of Political Studies: Dir. M. KNAUB.
Institute of Business Economics: Dir. M. FRUIT.
Centre for International Patent Rights: Dir. M. BURST.
University Centre for Journalistic Studies: Dir. M. IRJUD.
Applied Research and Technology: Dir. M. SOGUEL.
European Institute for Advanced Commercial Studies: Dir. Mme S. URBAN.
University Institute of Technology: Dir. M. GROSS.
Institute of Advanced European Studies: Dir. F. G. DREYFUS.
Language Centre: Dir. M. ARNOLD.
Adult Education Service: Dir. M. CUBAYNES.
Local Communities in Europe: Dir. Mlle M. LOMBARD.

PROFESSORS:

BABINET, F., History of Law
BAUD, J. P., History of Law
BELLANGER, F., Public Law
BISCHOFF, J. M., Private Law
BURST, J. J., Private Law
COHEN-JONATHAN, G., Public Law
CONSTANTINESCO, V., Public Law
DREYFUS, F. G., Modern History and Political Science
DUPEUX, L., Modern History and Political Science
DUPRAT, J. P., Political Science
FRUIT, R., General Economics and Statistics
GANGHOFFER, R., Legal History
HERTZOG, R., Public Law
HUET, Mme D., Private Law
HUET, A., Private Law
JACQUE, J. P., Public Law
JEANCLOS, Y., History of Law
KNAUB, G., Public Law
KOENIG, P., Public Law
KOERING, Mme R., Private Law
KOVAR, R., Public Law
LEMOINE, P., Chemistry
PRIEUR, M., Public Law
PUECH, M., Private Law
RIEG, A., Private Law
SCHMIDT, D., Private Law
SIMLER, P., Private Law
SINAY, Mme H., Private Law
TANIELIAN, C., Chemistry
THOMANN, M., History of Law
URBAN, Mme S., Management
WALINE, J., Public Law
WIEDERKEHR, G., Private Law

UNIVERSITÉ DE TOULON ET DU VAR

CHÂTEAU ST. MICHEL,
83130 LA GARDE

Telephone: (94) 75-90-50.

Founded 1970.

Rector and Chancellor: PAUL PASTOUR.
President: Prof. PIERRE BROCHE.
Secretary-General: GUY SLAWY.
Librarian: Mme FRANÇOISE BERGÉ.

Number of teachers: 114.
Number of students: 2,475.

TEACHING AND RESEARCH UNITS:

Sciences and Technology: Dir. JEAN-FRANÇOIS CAVASSILAS.
Law and Economic Sciences: Dir. JEAN-CLAUDE ESCARRAS.
University Institute of Technology: Dir. JEAN-LOUIS VERNET.

UNIVERSITÉ DE TOULOUSE I (SCIENCES SOCIALES)

PLACE ANATOLE FRANCE,
31042 TOULOUSE CEDEX

Telephone: 23-11-45.

Rector and Chancellor: C. CHALIN.
President: M. DESPAX.
Secretary-General: Mme D. ROULLAND.
Librarian: Mlle G. ROGÉ.

Number of teachers: 195.
Number of students: 10,832.

Publications: *Livret de l'Etudiant, Annales.*

TEACHING AND RESEARCH UNITS:

Law, First Cycle: Dir. G. SICARD.
Law, Second Cycle: Dir. L. BOYER.
Economics: Dir. GEORGES MOLINS YSAL.
Practical Studies in Law: Dir. GABRIEL ROUJOU DE BOUBÉE.
International Studies, Development and Modern Languages: Dir. P. VELLAS.
Research on Organization of Societies: Dir. FERNAND BOUYSSOU.
Informatics: Dir. G. BAZERQUE.
Business Studies: Dir. P. SPITERI.
Politics: Dir. P. OURLIAC.

UNIVERSITÉ DE TOULOUSE II (LE MIRAIL)

109 *BIS* RUE VAUQUELIN,
31081 TOULOUSE CEDEX

Telephone: (61) 41-11-05.

Rector and Chancellor: C. CHALIN.
President: B. BENNASSAR.
Secretary-General: J. L. PERILLIER.

TEACHING AND RESEARCH UNITS:

Etudes Philosophiques et Politiques: Dir. M. SOL.
Sciences Sociales: Dir. R. LEDRUT.
Sciences du Comportement et de l'Education: Dir. C. FRONTY.
Langues, Littératures, Civilisations Étrangères et Linguistique Générale: Dir. F. LAGARDE.
Lettres et Langues Anciennes: Dir. P. NESPOULOUS.
Lettres Françaises et Littérature Comparée: Dir. J. EYMARD.
Histoire, Archéologie et Histoire de l'Art: Dir. J. GODECHOT.
Géographie: Dir. M. BERTRAND.
Sciences Économiques et Gestion: Dir. A. LEFEBVRE.
Département de Mathématiques, Informatique et Statistiques: Dir. G. HEUZÉ.
Etudes Hispaniques et Hispano-Américaines: Dir. M. FONQUERNE.
Institut Universitaire de Technologie: Dir. G. HEUZE (acting).

UNIVERSITÉ PAUL SABATIER (TOULOUSE III)

118 ROUTE DE NARBONNE,
31062 TOULOUSE CEDEX

Telephone: 53-11-20.

Rector and Chancellor: C. CHALIN.
President: J.-C. MARTIN.
Secretary-General: M. PRINEAU.

TEACHING AND RESEARCH UNITS:

Mathematics, Information Science, Management: Dir. Prof. CUPPENS.
Physics and Chemistry: Dir. Prof. BLANC.
Natural Sciences: Dir. Prof. HOLLANDE.
Physical Education and Sport: Prof. MOULIN.
University Institute of Technology: Dir. Prof. REME.
Modern Languages: Dir. Prof. MAGNIONT.
Pic du Midi/Toulouse Observatory: Dir. Prof. ROSCH.
Dental Surgery: Dean Prof. LODTER.
Medical Sciences (Purpan): Dean Prof. GUIRAUD-CHAUMEIL.
Medical Sciences (Rangueil): Dean Prof. PUEL.
Pharmaceutical Sciences: Dean Prof. CROS.
Readaptation Technology: Dir. Prof. BEC.

UNIVERSITÉ DE TOURS (UNIVERSITÉ FRANÇOIS RABELAIS)

3 RUE DES TANNEURS,
37041 TOURS CEDEX

Telephone: (47) 20-47-62.

Founded 1970.

Rector and Chancellor: P. DELORME.
President: MARC MAILLET.
Secretary-General: Y. COTTEREAU.
Librarian: Mme C. GROUAS.

Number of teachers: 600.
Number of students: 13,000.

DIRECTORS OF TEACHING AND RESEARCH UNITS:

Law and Economics: M. BOURJOL.
Medicine: A. GOUAZE.
Pharmacy: P. MAUPAS.
University Institute of Technology: P. BACHELARD.
Exact and Natural Sciences: H. ZAMARLIK.
Centre for Renaissance Studies: J. C. MARGOLIN.
Town Planning, Geography, Informatics: R. PERRIN.
Science of Man: M. SARTRE.
Classical and Modern Languages, Literatures, Civilizations: R. FRANCIS.
Language, Literature and Civilization of English-speaking Countries: J. ATHERTON.

UNIVERSITÉ DE VALENCIENNES ET DU HAINAUT-CAMBRESIS

MONT HOUY,
59326 VALENCIENNES CEDEX

Telephone: (16.27) 46-66-08.

Founded 1969.

State control; Language of instruction: French; Academic year: September to June.

Rector and Chancellor: M. TOUCHARD.
President: N. MALVACHE.
Vice-President: J. MARCOU.
Librarian: Mlle G. SIMONOT.

Library of 6,000 vols.
Number of teachers: 270.
Number of students: 2,900.

Publications: *Cahiers de l'UER Froissart* (annually), *Guide d'étudiant* (annually), *Rapport d'activité des laboratoires de recherche* (annually).

TEACHING AND RESEARCH UNITS:

Exact and Natural Sciences: Dir. M. LERAY.
Institute of Technology: Dir. Mme C. MORIAMEZ.
Letters, Human Sciences and Arts: Dir. R. BOURGOIS.
Law, Economics and Management: M. TAISNE.
National College of Mechanical Engineering and Energetics: Dir. M. TORGUET.

POLYTECHNIC INSTITUTES

INSTITUT NATIONAL POLYTECHNIQUE DE GRENOBLE

46 AVE. FELIX VIALLET,
38031 GRENOBLE CEDEX
Telephone: 47-98-55.
Founded 1970.

President: P. TRAYNARD.

TEACHING AND RESEARCH UNITS:

Ecole Nationale Supérieure d'Electronique et de Radio-électricité: Ave. des Martyrs, 38031 Grenoble Cedex; Dir. MAURICE BUYLE-BODIN.

Ecole Nationale Supérieure d'Electrochimie et d'Electrométallurgie: Domaine Universitaire, 38401 Saint-Martin-d'Hères; Dir. JEAN-CHARLES PARIAUD.

Ecole Nationale Supérieure d'Ingénieurs Electriciens de Grenoble: B.P. 46, 38402 Saint-Martin d'Hères; Dir. DANIEL BLOCH.

Ecole Nationale Supérieure d'Informatique et de Mathématiques Appliquées: B.P. 53, Centre de Tri, 38041 Grenoble Cedex; Dir. GÉRARD VEILLON.

Ecole Nationale Supérieure d'Hydraulique: Domaine Universitaire, B.P. 53X, Centre de Tri, 38041 Grenoble Cedex; Dir. PHILIPPE LE ROY.

AFFILIATED INSTITUTES:

Centre Universitaire d'Education et de Formation des Adultes: Domaine Universitaire, 38400 Saint-Martin-d'Hères; Dir. P. ARNAUD.

Ecole Française de Papeterie: B.P. 3, 38400 Saint-Martin-d'Hères; Dir. CLAUDE FOULARD.

INSTITUT NATIONAL POLYTECHNIQUE DE LORRAINE

PORTE DE LA CRAFFE, B.P. 3308,
54014 NANCY CEDEX
Telephone: (83) 36-46-25.

Founded 1970.

President: CLAUDE PAIR.
Vice-President: C. COGNET.
Secretary-General: C. CARON.

Number of teachers: 168.
Number of students: 1,893.

TEACHING AND RESEARCH UNITS:

Agronomy and Food Industry: Dir. F. JACQUIN.
Electricity and Mechanics: Dir. M. LUCIUS.
Applied Geology and Mine Prospecting: Dir. P. BLAZY.
Chemical Engineering: Dir. J. BORDET.
Metallurgy and Mining: Dir. B. DEVIOT.

INSTITUT NATIONAL POLYTECHNIQUE DE TOULOUSE

PLACE DES HAUTS-MURATS,
B.P. 354,
31006 TOULOUSE CEDEX
Telephone: 52-21-37.
Founded 1970.

President: GÉRARD MONTEL.

Number of teachers: 173.
Number of students: 1,430.

TEACHING AND RESEARCH UNITS:

Ecole Nationale Supérieure Agronomique: 145 ave. de Muret, 31076 Toulouse 03; Dir. M. RAYNAUD.

Ecole Nationale Supérieure d'Electrotechnique, d'Electronique, d'Informatique et d'Hydraulique: 2, rue Camichel, 31071 Toulouse Cedex; Dir. M. NOUGARO.

Ecole Nationale Supérieure de Chimie: 118 rue de Narbonne, 31077 Toulouse Cedex; Dir. M. VOIGT.

Institut de Génie Chimique: Chemin de la Loge, 31078 Toulouse Cedex; Dir. M. GARDY.

STATE COLLEGES AND INSTITUTES

GENERAL

COLLÈGE DE FRANCE

11 PLACE MARCELIN-BERTHELOT, 75005 PARIS
Telephone: 329-12-11.
Founded 1530 by François I.

President: A. HOREAU.

The library consists of 85,000 vols.
Number of teaching staff: 52 professors.

Publications: *Annuaire, Leçons inaugurales et terminales des professeurs.*

PROFESSORS:

Science:

ABRAGAM, Nuclear Magnetism
AJURIAGUERRA, J. DE, Neuropsychology of Development
CHANGEUX, J.-P., Cellular Communications
COHEN-TANNOUDJI, Atomic and Molecular Physics
DAUSSET, J., Experimental Medicine
FROISSART, Particle Physics
DE GENNES, Solid State Physics
GROS, Cellular Biochemistry
HOREAU, Organic Chemistry of Hormones
JACOB, Cellular Genetics
JOST, Physiology of Development
LAPORTE, Neurophysiology
LEHN, Chemistry of Molecular Interaction
LICHNEROWICZ, Mathematical Physics
LIONS, Mathematical Analysis of Systems
MOREL, Cellular Physiology
PECKER, Theoretical Astronomy
PRENTKI, Theoretical Physics of Particles
RUFFIÉ, Anthropology
SERRE, Algebra and Geometry
TITS, Theory of Groups

Letters

BAREAU, Buddhist Studies
BERNOT, South-East Asian Sociology
BERQUE, Social History of Modern Islam
BLIN, French Modern History
BOULEZ, Invention, Technique and Language in Music
CAQUOT, Hebrew and Aramaic
CHASTEL, Art and Civilization of Renaissance Italy
CHEVALIER, History and Social Structure of Paris and the Parisian Region
COURCELLE, Latin Literature
DAGRON, Byzantine History
DELUMEAU, History of Religious Attitudes in the Modern West
DUBY, History of Medieval Societies
DUPUY, International Law
DUVAL, Archaeology and History of Gaul
FOUCAULT, History of Systems of Thought
FRANK, Japanese Civilization
GERNET, J., Social and Intellectual History of China
GUILLAUMONT, A., Christianity and Gnosticism in the Pre-Islamic East
LAROCHE, Languages and Civilisations of Asia Minor
LECLANT, Egyptology
LEROI-GOURHAN, Prehistory
LE ROY LADURIE, History of Modern Civilisation
LÉVI-STRAUSS, Social Anthropology
MIQUEL, Classical Arabic
DE ROMILLY, Greece and the Formation of Moral and Political Philosophy
STEIN, Institutions and Concepts of Chinese Civilization
THUILLIER, History of French Art
VERNANT, Comparative Study of Ancient Religions
VEYNE, Roman History
VUILLEMIN, Philosophy of Knowledge

Ecole Pratique des Hautes Etudes: 45–47 rue des Ecoles, Paris 5e; f. 1868; library of 50,000 vols.

Five divisions:

Mathematical Sciences: 11 rue Pierre Curie, Paris 5e; f. 1868; Pres. R. DEHEUVELS; publ. *Bulletin des Sciences Mathématiques.*

Physical and Chemical Sciences: 46 rue Saint-Jacques, 75005 Paris; f. 1868; Pres. A. GUINIER.

Natural Sciences: 46 rue Saint-Jacques, 75005 Paris; f. 1868; Pres. J. CARAYON; publ. *Annuaire de la 3ème Section.*

Historical and Philological Sciences: 45–47 rue des Ecoles, Paris 5e; f. 1868; Pres. M. FLEURY; publ. *Annuaire de la 4ème Section*, etc.

Religious Sciences: Sorbonne, 45-47 rue des Ecoles, Paris 5e; f. 1886; Pres. R. STAUFFER; publ. *Annuaire de la 5ème Section.*

ADMINISTRATION

Ecole Nationale d'Administration: 56 rue des Saints-Pères, Paris 7e; f. 1945 to provide training for the higher ranks of the Civil Service; Dir. PIERRE-LOUIS BLANC; Gen. Sec. R. CHELLE.

Ecole Supérieure de Commerce et d'Administration des Entreprises: 4 blvd. Trudaine, 63037 Clermont-Ferrand; f. 1919; dependent on the Direction de l'Enseignement Supérieur du Ministre de l'Education; 100 teachers, 420 students; library of 3,500 vols.; Dir. H. VERDIER; publs. *Revue* (annually), *Point Zéro* (bi-monthly), *Bulletin* (quarterly).

Institut International d'Administration Publique: 2 ave. de l'Observatoire, Paris 6e; f. 1966 to train high-ranking civil servants at the request of governments from Europe, Africa, America, Asia and the Middle East; research in comparative administration; Five sections: administrative, social, diplomatic, economic and legal; research and documentation services; library of 90,000 vols.; scholarships can be granted.

Director: HENRI ROSON.

Publications: *Revue française d'Administration publique* (quarterly), *Annuaire international de la fonction publique*†, *Bibliothèque de l'Institut International d'Administration Publique*†, *Encyclopédie Politique et Constitutionnelle*, *Encyclopédie Administrative.*

AGRICULTURE, FORESTRY, VETERINARY SCIENCE

Centre de Recherches Agronomiques de Rennes: 65 rue de Saint-Brieuc, 35042 Rennes Cedex; f. 1830; library of 24,000 vols.; Dir. C. MOULE; publ. *Sciences Agronomiques*† (annual).

Ecole Nationale du Génie Rural des Eaux et des Forêts: Centre de Nancy, 14 rue Girardet, 54 Nancy; f. 1965 by the fusion of the Ecole Nationale du Génie Rural and the Ecole Nationale des Eaux et Forêts; library of 32,000 vols., 1,100 periodicals; Dir. M. GUILLARD; publ. *Revue Forestière française* (bi-monthly).

Ecole Nationale Supérieure Agronomique de Montpellier: place Viala, 34060 Montpellier Cedex; f. 1872; 250 students; library of 45,000 vols., 600 periodicals; Dir. J. F. BRETON.

Ecole Nationale Supérieure d'Horticulture: 4 rue Hardy, 78000 Versailles; f. 1873; library of 13,000 vols.; Dir. R. CHAUX.

Ecole Nationale Supérieure des Industries Agricoles et Alimentaires: 1 ave. des Olympiades, 91305 Massy (Essonne); f. 1893; Dir. M. CLEMENT; research centre, rue de l'Université, 59509 Douai (Nord); publ. *Industries Alimentaires et Agricoles* (monthly).

Ecole Nationale Supérieure Féminine d'Agronomie: 65 rue de Saint-Brieuc, 35000 Rennes; f. 1964; public establishment under the Ministry of Agriculture; 150 students; Dir. C. MOULE.

Ecole Nationale Vétérinaire d'Alfort: 7 ave. Général de Gaulle, 94704 Maisons-Alfort Cedex; f. 1965; Dir. CHARLES PILET; 47 teachers; library of 150,000 vols.

Ecole Nationale Vétérinaire de Lyon: Marcy-l'Etoile 69260 Charbonniers-les-Bains; f. 1762; library of 10,000 vols.; Dir. Prof. COTTEREAU; teaching personnel 52; publs. *Revue de Médecine Vétérinaire* (monthly), *Bulletin des Sciences Vétérinaires de Lyon* (bi-monthly).

Ecole Nationale Vétérinaire de Toulouse: 23 chemin des Capelles, 31076 Toulouse Cedex; f. 1828; library of 50,000 vols.; Dir. R. LAUTIE; Sec.-Gen. A. CHAMAYOU; Librarian Prof. PH. DORCHIES; teaching personnel 54; publ. *Revue de Médecine Vétérinaire* (monthly).

Ecole Supérieure d'Agronomie Tropicale: 45 *bis* ave. de la Belle Gabrielle, 94130 Nogent-sur-Marne; f. 1902; courses in tropical agricultural development; 55 teachers; library of 10,000 vols., 80 periodicals; Dir. A. GUINARD.

Institut National Agronomique Paris-Grignon: 16 rue Claude Bernard, 75231 Paris Cedex 05; f. 1876 (Paris), 1826 (Grignon), 1972 (Paris-Grignon); teaching personnel 129; library of 50,000 vols. and 800 periodicals; Dir. J. DELAGE.

ECONOMICS, LAW AND POLITICS

Centre de Hautes Etudes sur l'Afrique et l'Asie Modernes: 13 rue du Four, 75006 Paris; f. 1936; affiliated to the Fondation Nationale des Sciences Politiques (*q.v.*); library of 14,000 vols.; Dir. G. R. MALÉCOT; publs. *L'Afrique et L'Asie Modernes* (quarterly), *Cahiers de l'Afrique et l'Asie, Langues et Dialectes d'Outre-Mer, Recherches et Documents du CHEAM, Cahiers du CHEAM* (irregular).

Centre Français de Droit Comparé: 28 rue Saint-Guillaume, Paris 7e; f. 1951; library of 100,000 vols.; Pres. M. MARC ANCEL; Sec.-Gen. M. RENÉ RODIERE; publs. *Revue Internationale de Droit Comparé, Revue de Science Criminelle et de Droit Pénal Comparé* (quarterly), *Bulletin des Organismes Français de Droit Comparé* (annually).

Ecole des Hautes Etudes en Sciences Sociales: 54 rue de Varenne, 75007 Paris; f. 1947; 8,000 students; Pres. JACQUES LE GOFF.

Ecole Nationale de la Statistique et de l'Administration Economique: 3 ave. Pierre Larousse, 92240 Malakoff; f. 1960, formerly Ecole d'Application; attached to the Institut National de la Statistique et des Etudes Economiques (*see* Research Institutes); 430 students; Dir. J. MAIRESSE.

Institut d'Etudes Politiques de Paris: 27 rue Saint-Guillaume, 75341 Paris Cedex 07; f. 1945 as successor to l'Ecole Libre des Sciences Politiques; library of 500,000 vols.; Dir. M. GENTOT.

EDUCATION

Ecole Normale Supérieure: 45 rue d'Ulm, Paris 5e; f. 1794 by the National Convention; library: *see* Libraries; 525 students; Dir. J. BOUSQUET; publs. *Presses de l'Ecole Normale Supérieure, Annales Scientifiques de l'École Normale Supérieure.*

Ecole Normale Supérieure de Jeunes Filles: 48 blvd. Jourdan, 75014 Paris; f. 1881; library of 125,000 vols.; 44 teaching staff; 383 students; one of the two university-level women's colleges for academic and research positions in France Dir.; Mme JOSIANE SERRE.

GEOGRAPHY

Ecole Nationale des Sciences Géographiques: 2 ave. Pasteur, 94160 Saint-Mandé; f. 1941; administered by Institut Géographique National; 300 students (including part-time); specialized library of 36,000 books, 950,000 maps, 2,100,000 aerial photographs; Dir. R. D'HOLLANDER.

PROFESSORS·

AFFHOLDER, J. G., Programming
BROSSIER, R., Remote Sensing
CAGNET, M., Optics
DENIS, P., Photogrammetry
GAMBIN, Mme. M. T., Thematic Cartography
HOTTIER, P., Numerical Analysis
JOLY, F., Geomorphology
LAFOND, L., Oceanography
LAPOIX, F., Ecology
LAVILLE, G., Applied Mathematics
LE MENESTREL, J., Astronomy, Geodesy
LOISEAU, J., Cosmography
MOSCHETTI, J., Topography
VUILLECOT, C., Cartography
WEIL, G., Town Planning

HISTORY

Ecole Nationale des Chartes: 19 rue de la Sorbonne, 75005 Paris; f. 1821, reorganized 1846; library of 150,000 vols.

Director: J. MONFRIN.
Secretary: M.-C. HUBERT.
Librarian: C. HUSTACHE.

Number of students: 80.

Publication: *Bibliothèque de l'Ecole des Chartes*†.

PROFESSORS:

BARBICHE, B., History of French Institutions
BAUTIER, R.-H., Diplomatics
BOURGAIN, P., Literacy Manuscripts
DELMAS, B., Modern Archival Sciences and Technology
DUPARC, P., History of Law
MARTIN, H. J., Bibliography and History of Books
MONFRIN, J., Romance Philology
POULLE, E., Palaeography
THIRION, J., Archaeology

LIBRARIANSHIP

Ecole Nationale Supérieure des Bibliothèques: 17/21 blvd. du 11 Novembre 1918, 69100 Villeurbanne; f. 1964; 11 teachers, 60 full-time students; library of 15,000 vols.; Dir. MICHEL MERLAND.

MEDICINE

Ecole d'Application du Service de Santé des Armées: 1 place Alphonse Laveran, 75230 Paris Cedex 05; f. 1851; mainly one-year graduate courses; important medical library; Dir. Med.-Gen. NOSNY; publ. *Médecine et Armées*.

Ecole Nationale de la Santé Publique: ave. du Professeur Léon Bernard, 35043 Rennes Cedex; Bureau de liaison: 1 place de Fontenoy, 75700 Paris; f. 1945; 500 students; Dir. L. PICARD; Sec.-Gen. M. F. LE BARBIER.

SCIENCES

Ecole Nationale de la Météorologie: 2 ave. Rapp, Paris 7e; f. 1948; library of 40,000 vols.; Dir. M. DADY.

Institut National des Sciences Appliquées de Lyon: 20 ave. Albert Einstein, 69621 Villeurbanne Cedex; f. 1957; library of 100,000 vols.; 450 teachers, 3,500 students; applied biochemistry, computer science, civil, electrical and mechanical engineering, material science, energy; 32 research laboratories; Dir. Prof. R. HAMELIN.

Institut National des Sciences Appliquées de Rennes: 20 ave. des Buttes de Coësmes, B.P. 14A, 35031 Rennes Cedex; f. 1961; physical and electrical engineering, civil engineering and town planning, informatics; 103 teachers, 620 students; Dir. Prof. J.-C. CUBAUD.

Muséum National d'Histoire Naturelle: 57 rue Cuvier, 75281 Paris Cedex 05; f. 1635; teaching and research in natural history; administers the Zoological Garden and the *Musée de l'Homme* (*q.v.*); Dir. Prof. JEAN DORST; Gen. Sec. A. BERTHELOT.

PROFESSORS:

ANTHONY, J., Comparative Anatomy
BRYGOO, M. E. R., Zoology (Reptiles and Amphibians)
CARAYON, J., Entomology
CHABAUD, A., Vermicology
COINEAU, Y., Arthropods
COPPENS, Y., Anthropology
DAGET, J., Ichthyology
DELAMARE DEBOUTTEVILLE, C., General Ecology
DOUMENGE, F., Ethology and Conservation
DORST, J., Zoology of Mammals and Birds
DOUZOU, P., Physical Chemistry
FABRIES, J., Mineralogy
FONTAINE, M., General and Comparative Physiology
GUIART, Ethnology
HAMEL, J.-L., Applied Vegetal Biology
HELENE, C., Biophysics
JOVET, S., Cryptogamy
LACOMBE, H., Physical Oceanography
LAFFITTE, R., Geology
LEFEUVRE, J. C., Evolution of Natural Systems
LEHMAN, J.-P., Palæontology
LEROY, J.-F., Phanerogamy
LEVI, C., Biology of Marine Invertebrates and Malacology
DE LUMLEY, H., Prehistory
MOLHO, D., Applied Organic Chemistry

TECHNOLOGY

Centre d'Etudes Supérieures de Mécanique: 12 rue Marie Bonaparte, 92210 St. Cloud; postgraduate courses in aero-thermodynamics (attached to University Paris VI).

Conservatoire National des Arts et Métiers: 292 rue St. Martin, Paris 3e; f. 1794; library of 100,000 vols.; Mathematics, Mechanics, Chemistry, Industrial Arts, Economics, Statistics, Organisation of Labour; 60 teachers; Library: *see* Libraries; Dir. F. CAMBOU; Sec.-Gen. J. LARCEBEAU.

ATTACHED INSTITUTES:

Institut d'Etudes Supérieures des Techniques d'Organisation: f. 1956; Dir. GERBIER.

Institut d'Informatique d'Entreprise: f. 1968; Dir. E. PICHAT.

Institut Français du Froid Industriel: Dir. J. J. VEYSSIÉ.

Institut National de Formation des Cadres Supérieurs de la Vente: f. 1956; Dir. A. DAUGER.

Institut National des Techniques de la Documentation: f. 1950; Dir. (vacant).

Institut Technique de Prévision Economique et Sociale: f. 1962; Dir. R. SAINT-PAUL.

Institut Scientifique et Technique de l'Alimentation: Dir. H. DUPIN.

Institut de la Construction et de l'Habitation: Dir. G. LIET-VEAUX.

Institut National des Techniques Economiques et Comptables: Dir. C. PEROCHON.

Institut National d'Etude du Travail et d'Orientation Professionnelle: Dir. M. REUCHLIN.

Centre de Formation de Formateurs d'Adultes: Dir. M. LESNE.

Institut de Topométrie et Ecole Supérieure des Géomètres et Topographes: Dir. (vacant).

Centre d'Actualisation des Connaissances et de l'Etude des Matériaux Industriels: Dir. B. HOCHEID.

Ecole Nationale d'Assurances: Dir. J. LAMSON.

Institut Français d'Ingénierie: Dir. J. GIRERD.

Centre de Préparation au Diplôme d'Etat d'Audioprothésiste: Dir. A. DIDIER.

Institut Technique de Banque: Dir. J. MONTGAILLARD.

Centre de Recherche Science Technologie et Société: Dir. R. SAINT-PAUL.

Institut National de Métrologie: Dir. A. ALLISY.

Ecole Centrale des Arts et Manufactures: Grande Voie des Vignes, 92290 Châtenay-Malabry; f. 1829; higher degrees in engineering; library of 50,000 vols. and 440 periodicals; 1,000 students; Dir. D. GOURISSE.

Ecole Nationale Arts et Métiers: f. 1806; 151 blvd. de l'Hôpital, 75013 Paris; Dir. M. FEUVRAIS.

Ecole Nationale de l'Aviation Civile: P.O.B. 107, 94310 Aéroport d'Orly; f. 1948; Dir. M. MANUEL.

Ecole Nationale de l'Aviation Civile: B.P. 4005, 31000 Toulouse; dependent on Ministry of Transport; 245 teachers.

Ecole Nationale d'Ingénieurs de Belfort: 8 blvd. Anatole France, 90016 Belfort Cedex; f. 1962; library of 3,000 vols.; Dir. R. FLORENTIN.

Ecole Nationale des Ingénieurs des Travaux des Eaux et Forêts: Les Barres, 45290 Nogent-sur-Vernisson; f. 1884; library of 6,000 vols.; Dir. D. AUBERTIN.

Ecole Nationale de la Marine Marchande: rue Pierre Loti, 22500 Paimpol; f. 1863, new school opened 1962; dependent on the Ministry of Industry; library of 1,700 vols.; Dir. M. RAPIDEL.

Ecole Nationale des Ponts et Chaussées: 28 rue des Saints-Pères, 75007 Paris; f. 1747; civil engineering, town and country planning, transport; library of 170,000 vols.; 500 students, 300 teachers; Dir. J. TANZI; Sec.-Gen. A. THOMASSIN.

Ecole Nationale Supérieure de l'Aéronautique et de l'Espace: B.P. 4032, 31055 Toulouse Cedex; f. 1909; library of 15,000 vols.; 550 students; Dir. M. FLOURENS.

Ecole Nationale Supérieure des Arts des Industries Textiles de Roubaix: B.P. 69, 2 place des Martyrs de la Résistance, 59100 Roubaix; f. 1883; library of 18,000 vols.; Dir. P. PIGACHE.

Ecole Nationale Supérieure d'Arts et Métiers: 8 blvd. Louis XIV, 59046 Lille Cedex; f. 1881; 300 students; Dir. M. OUZIAUX.

Ecole Nationale Supérieure de Céramique Industrielle: 47-73 rue Albert Thomas, 87065 Limoges Cedex; f. 1893; library of 2,600 vols.; 60 teachers, 120 students; Dir. P. BOCH; publ. *Annuaire*.

Ecole Nationale Supérieure de l'Electronique et de ses Applications (ENSEA): Impasse des Chênes Pourpres, 95000 Cergy; f. 1975; electronics, telecommunications, biomedical engineering; Dir. M. WATTEAU.

Ecole Normale Supérieure de l'Enseignement Technique: 61 ave. du Président Wilson, 94230 Cachan; f. 1912; library of 23,000 vols.; Dir. M. THUREAU.

Ecole Nationale Supérieure de Mécanique: see under University of Nantes.

Ecole Nationale Supérieure des Mines de Paris: 60 blvd. St. Michel, 75272 Paris Cedex 06; f. 1783; library of 500,000 vols. and 2,500 periodicals; 274 students; Pres. R. FISCHESSER; Dir. P. LAFFITTE; Sec.-Gen. R. JANIN; Librarian Mme GAUTHIER; publ. *Rapport* (annually).

Ecole Nationale Supérieure du Pétrole et des Moteurs à Combustion Interne: B.P. 311, 92506 Rueil-Malmaison Cedex; five centres: geological and geophysical prospecting, drilling and exploitation, chemical engineering and refining, internal combustion engines and application of petroleum products, petroleum economics; Dir. J. CHAPELLE.

Ecole Nationale Supérieure de Techniques Avancées: 32 blvd. Victor, 75015 Paris; f. 1765, refounded 1969; naval architecture and construction, oceanology, mechanics, nuclear techniques, chemical engineering, electronics; 3-year curriculum; 120 students a year; library of 9,000 vols.; Dir. H. BOUCHER.

Ecole Nationale Supérieure des Télécommunications: 46 rue Barrault, 75634 Paris Cedex 13; f. 1942; Dir. M. FAUVET.

Ecole Polytechnique: Plateau de Palaiseau, 91128 Palaiseau Cedex; f. 1794; 180 teachers, 600 students; library of 300,000 vols.; Dir. Général JACQUES SAUNIER; Dean of Scientific Studies Ing. Général FERRANDON; Librarian Mme G. FEUILLEBOIS.

Ecole Supérieure de Physique et de Chimie Industrielles de la Ville de Paris: 10 rue Vauquelin, Paris 5e; f. 1882; library of 5,000 vols.; Dir. P. G. DE GENNES.

Institut Supérieur du Béton Armé: 110 blvd. de la Libération, 13004 Marseille; f. 1952; courses for qualified engineers; Dir. BERNARD SUSSMANN.

Institut Supérieur des Matériaux et de la Construction Mécanique: 3 rue Fernand Hainaut, 93400 St. Ouen; f. 1948; 200 students, 110 research workers; Dir. PIERRE AZOU.

CATHOLIC COLLEGES AND INSTITUTES

GENERAL

INSTITUT CATHOLIQUE DE PARIS

21 RUE D'ASSAS,
75270 PARIS CEDEX 06
Telephone: 222-41-80.
Founded 1875.

Academic year: October to June.

Chancellor: H.E. Cardinal FRANÇOIS MARTY.
Rector: Mgr. PAUL POUPARD.
Vice-Rector: R.P. MICHEL LEGRAIN.
General Secretary: M. GOURIOU.
Head Librarian: H. ROCHAIS.

Library: *see* Libraries.

Number of teaching staff: 892, including 57 professors.

Number of students: 15,840.

Publication: *Nouvelles* (quarterly).

CONSTITUENT UNITS:

Biblical and Systematic Theology: Dir. Abbé C. WIÉNER.
Institut Supérieur d'Etudes Oecuméniques: Dir. M. CARREZ.
Institut Supérieur de Liturgie: Dir. Rev. P.-M. GY.
Institut Supérieur de Pastorale Catéchetique: Dir. Rev. R. MARLÉ.
Institut de Science et de Théologie des Religions: Dir. Rev. J. VIDAL.
Studies for Doctorate in Theology: Dir. Rev. C.-J. GEFFRÉ.
Ecole des Langues Orientales Anciennes: Dir. J. TRINQUET.
Institut de Musique Liturgique: Dir. M. l'Abbé BIHAN.

DEANS:

U.E.R. of Theology: Abbé J. BRIEND.
Faculty of Canon Law: J. PASSICOS.
Faculty of Philosophy: P. COLIN.
Faculty of Letters: Y. MARCHASSON.

PROFESSORS:

U.E.R. of Theology:
AUDINET, Pastoral Theology
BRIEND, Exegesis
CORBIN, Dogmatics
COTHENET, Holy Scripture
COUDREAU,
DELZANT, Dogmatics
DORÉ, Dogmatics
GEFFRÉ, C.-J., General Dogmatics
GELINEAU, Liturgy
GERMAIN, History
GRELOT, Holy Scripture
GY, Liturgy
HRUBY, Rabbinical Hebrew
JOUNEL, Liturgy
KANNENGIESSER, History of the Origins of Christianity
LAFON, Christian Anthropology
LAVALETTE, DE, Dogmatic Theology
LE GUILLOU, Ecumenical Theology
LEVEQUE, Holy Scripture
MARCHASSON, Ecclesiastical History
MARLÉ, Dogmatics
MOINGT, Dogmatics
MOUBARAC, Arabic
PERROT, Holy Scripture
TRINQUET, Ethiopian Studies
WOLINSKI, Patristics

Faculty of Canon Law:
CORTEEL
GUIBAL
LEGRAIN
LE ROY
PASSICOS
SORIA-VASCO

Faculty of Philosophy:
BRETON, Ontology and Theodicy
CHÂTILLON, Medieval History
COLIN, Anthropology
LEDURE, German Language and German Philosophers
MADEC, History of Patristic Theology
MILET, History of Philosophy

Faculty of Letters:
CLAVAUD, Greek
GOBRY, Philosophy
LEBREC, French Literature
LOLOUM, English Language and Literature
MARCHASSON, History
PIERRARD, History
PLATELLE, History
PLONGERON, History
SAULNIER, History
TESTARD, Latin
WARTELLE, Greek

AFFILIATED SCHOOLS AND INSTITUTES:

Institut d'Etudes Sociales: Dir. Rev. P. DE DINECHIN.

Institut d'Etudes Religieuses: Dir. Rév. P. G. ESPIE.

Année de Formation aux Ministères: Dir. M. LE CHANOINE P. BARRAU.

Centre de Formation Pédagogique pour l'Enseignement Spécialisé: Dir. Mlle A. M. AUDIC.

Ecole de Formation Psycho-Pédagogique: Dir. J. UGHETTO.

Institut Supérieur de Pédagogie: Dir. M. l'Abbé J. M. DI FALCO.

Ecole de Psychologues-Praticiens: Dir. M. l'Abbé J. BESSON.

Centre d'Etudes et de Recherches Ibéro-Américaines: Pres. Mlle DE COURLON.

Centre de Recherches d'Histoire Religieuses: Pres. Mgr. P. POUPARD.

Centre d'Etudes de Madrid: Dir. Sr. BUISSON.

Ecole Supérieure des Sciences Economiques et Commerciales: B.P. 105, 95001 Cergy; Dir. J. COUDY.

Institut Supérieur d'Interprétariat et de Traduction: Dir. Mme DE DAX.

Ecole de Bibliothécaires-Documentalistes: Dir. R. Marichal.

Institut Supérieur d'Electronique de Paris: Dir. M. l'Abbé J. Vieillard.

Ecole Supérieure de Chimie Organique et Minérale: 12 rue Cassette, 75006 Paris; Dir. R. P. Mastagli.

Institut Géologique Albert-de-Lapparent: Dir. M. P. Bordet.

Institut de Langue et Culture Françaises: 21 rue d'Assas, 75006 Paris; f. 1948; Dir. Mme E. Soriano.

Cours Universitaires d'Eté: Dir. Y. Marchasson.

Institut Supérieur Agricole de Beauvais: rue Pierre Waguet, 60000 Beauvais; f. 1855; Dir. M. J. Hurier.

Institut Libre d'Education Physique Supérieure: 277 rue St.-Jacques, 75005 Paris; Dir. (vacant).

Ecole Normale d'Education Physique Féminine: 17 rue de l'Assomption, 75016 Paris; Dir. Soeur Anne-Cécile Lestienne.

FÉDÉRATION UNIVERSITAIRE ET POLYTECHNIQUE DE LILLE

60 BLVD. VAUBAN,
59046 LILLE CEDEX
Telephone: (20) 30.88.27.

Founded 1875 as Faculty of Law, became university institution in 1877.

Rector: M. Falise.
Librarian: G. Mathon.

Library: nearly 500,000 volumes.

Number of teachers: over 600.
Number of students: 7,863.

Publications: *Journal des Sciences Médicales de Lille*, *Mémoires et Travaux*, *Mélanges de Sciences Religieuses* (3 a year), *Ensemble*.

Deans:

Faculty of Theology: M. Derousseaux.
Faculty of Law: (vacant).
Faculty of Medicine and Pharmacy: J. Liefooghe.
Faculty of Letters: R. Sansen.
Faculty of Science: A. Defebvre.

Attached Institutes:

Institut de Hautes Etudes Industrielles (H.E.I.): 13 rue de Toul, 59 Lille; f. 1885; civil engineering, chemistry and electronics; 55 teachers, 705 students; Dir. G. Leroy.

Institut Technique Roubaisien (I.T.R.): 37 rue du College, 59100 Roubaix; f. 1895; technology, engineering; 40 teachers, 168 students; Dir. B. Avrin.

Institut Supérieur d'Agriculture (I.S.A.): 39 *bis* rue du Port, 59 Lille; f. 1963; independent administration; four-year course; 273 students; Dir. R. Dusautois.

Institut Supérieur d'Electronique du Nord (I.S.E.N.): 3 rue François Baës, 59 Lille; f. 1956; electrical engineering; 35 teachers, 440 students; Dir. G. Vandecandelaere.

Institut Catholique d'Arts et Métiers (I.C.A.M.): 6 rue Auber, 59 Lille; f. 1898; 357 students; Dir. M. Debeunne.

Institut d'Economie d'Entreprise et de Formation Sociale pour Ingénieurs (I.E.F.S.I.): 41 rue du Port, 59 Lille; f. 1962; 15 students; Dir. P. Verstraete.

Ecole de Hautes Etudes Commerciales du Nord (E.D.H.E.C.): 58 rue du port, 59 Lille; f. 1920; 339 students; Dir. D. Leroux.

Institut d'Economie Scientifique et de Gestion (I.E.S.E.G.): 1 rue François Baës, 59 Lille; f. 1964; 174 students; Dir. F. Calcoen.

Centre de Recherches Economiques, Sociologiques et de Gestion (C.R.E.S.G.E.): 1 rue François Baës, 59 Lille; f. 1964.

Institut d'Expertise Comptable (I.E.C.): 60 blvd. Vauban, 59 Lille; 660 students; Dir. G. Duytschaever.

Ecole des Secrétaires et Attachées de Direction (E.S.A.D.): 60 blvd. Vauban, 59 Lille; f. 1964; 249 students; Dir. B. Charron.

Ecole Supérieure de Traducteurs, Interprètes, et de Cadres du Commerce Extérieur (E.S.T.I.C.E.): 60 blvd. Vauban, 59 Lille; f. 1961; 50 students; Dir. J. M. Dejonghe.

Ecole de Secrétariat Bilingue et Trilingue (E.S.B.T.): 60 blvd. Vauban, 59 Lille; f. 1961; 148 students; Dir. J. M. Dejonghe.

Ecole de Service Social de la Région Nord (E.S.S.R.N.): 68 blvd. Vauban, 59 Lille; f. 1932; 277 students; Dir. Cl. Durondeau.

Ecole de Formation d'Animateurs Sociaux (E.F.A.S.): 31 rue Patou, 59 Lille; f. 1973; 68 students; Dir. J. D. Vernier.

Ecole de Professeurs (E.D.P.): 60 blvd. Vauban, 59 Lille; f. 1962; 108 students; Dir. Ph. Crémer.

Ecole d'Infirmières et de Puéricultrices (E.I.P.): 70 rue du Port, 59 Lille; f. 1927; 629 students; Dir. Mère Marie de la Providence.

Ecole de Masso-Kinésithérapie et de Pédicurie: 56 rue du Port, 59 Lille; f. 1964; 352 students; Dir. R. Joseph.

Ecole Supérieure Professionnelle OZANAM: 50 rue Saint Gabriel, 59 Lille; Dir. R. d'Halluin.

Institution Saint Pierre: 18 rue Saint Jean Baptiste de la Salle, 59 Lille; 391 students; Dir. A. Lebon.

FACULTÉS CATHOLIQUES DE LYON

25 RUE DU PLAT, 69 LYONS 2E
Telephone: 842-10-30.
Founded 1875.

Rector: Mgr. Paul Chevallier.
Vice-Rector: Abbé J. Massot.
Secretary-General: Chanoine Alban-Ray.
Librarian: P. F. Desramaut.

Library: 240,000 volumes.

Number of teachers: 175, including 76 professors.

Number of students: 1,315 men, 1,770 women, total 3,085.

Publication: *Bulletin*†.

Deans:

Faculty of Theology: M. Bourgeois.
Faculty of Philosophy: R. le Troquer.
Faculty of Letters: M. Vericel.
Faculty of Science: R. Mouterde.
School of Engineering: A. Dufour.
School of Agriculture: E. Carrière.

Affiliated Institutions:

Ecole de Biochimie Pratique: f. 1952; 16 teachers, 86 students; Dir. M. Delsol.

Ecole Supérieure de Secrétaires-Traducteurs: f. 1968; 15 teachers, 65 students; Dir. M. Perrin.

Institut de Chimie et Physique Industrielles: f. 1919 as Institut de Chimie; 41 teachers, 243 students; Dir. A. Dufour.

Institut Supérieur d'Agriculture Rhône-Alpes: f. 1968; 21 teachers, 240 students; Dir. E. Carrière.

Institut des Sciences Sociales appliquées: f. 1944; 15 teachers, 250 students; Dir. G. Blardonne.

Institut des Sciences de la Famille: f. 1974; 10 teachers, 150 students; Dir. Mlle E. Gounot.

INSTITUT CATHOLIQUE DE TOULOUSE

31 RUE DE LA FONDERIE,
31068 TOULOUSE CEDEX
Telephone: (61) 52-62-35.

Founded 1877 and administered by a Council of Bishops of the region.

Chancellor: H.E. Mgr. André Collini, Archbishop of Toulouse.
Rector: Mgr. Pierre Eyt.
Registrar: Jean Mompha.

Library: over 200,000 vols.

Number of teachers: 125, including 74 professors.

Number of students: 1,610 (full-time), 2,000 (part-time).

Publication: *Bulletin de Littérature ecclésiastique*† (quarterly).

DEANS:

Faculty of Theology: P. DUTHEIL.
Faculty of Canon Law: J. PASSICOS.
Faculty of Philosophy: P. COURTES.
Faculty of Letters: F. BUFFIERE.
College of Science: J. GUITTARD.

UNIVERSITÉ CATHOLIQUE DE L'OUEST

3 PLACE ANDRÉ LEROY,
B.P. 808, 49005 ANGERS CEDEX
Telephone: 88-33-12.

Founded 1876, under the patronage of the Bishops of the western region of France.

Rector: Mgr. LOUIS COLLIN.
Vice-Rector: Rev. P. OUVRARD.
Secretary-General: Rev. H. HOUARD.

Publications: *Annuaire, Impacts* (quarterly).

DEANS:

Faculty of Theology: R.P. J. STARCK.
Teacher Training Institute: Rev. P. OUVRARD.
Modern Languages Institute: Mme MARTIN.
Psychology Centre: G. LE BOUÉDEC.
Applied Mathematics Institute: Y. L'HOSPITALIER.
Basic and Applied Research Institute: Rev. R. CORILLION.

AFFILIATED SCHOOLS:

Ecole Supérieure d'Electronique de l'Ouest: 4 rue Merlet de la Boulaye, 49 Angers; f. 1956; Dir. P. GUÉNÉ.

Ecole Supérieure des Sciences Commerciales d'Angers: 1 rue Lakanal, 49 Angers; Dir. D. WAQUET.

Ecole Technique Supérieure de Chimie de l'Ouest: 50 rue Michelet, 49 Angers; Dir. M. THIBAUD.

Institut féminin d'éducation physique et sportive: 3 place André-Leroy, 49005 Angers Cedex; Dir. M. F GRANDIÈRE.

INDEPENDENT INSTITUTES

AGRICULTURE

Ecole Supérieure d'Ingénieurs et Techniciens pour l'Agriculture: 27100 Le Vaudreuil; f. 1919; four-year diploma courses for agricultural engineers; Dir. G. BASTIEN.

COMMERCE, ADMINISTRATION AND STATISTICS

Centre Européen d'Education Permanente (CEDEP): blvd. de Constance, 77305 Fontainebleau Cedex; f. 1971; management development courses in business administration for member companies (6 French, 3 Danish, 4 British, 2 Swedish, 2 Belgian, 1 Swiss, 1 Italian, 1 Dutch); affiliated to the Institut Européen d'Administration des Affaires; Gen. Dir. SALVATORE TERESI.

Centre d'Enseignement Supérieur des Affaires: 78350 Jouy-en-Josas; run by the Chamber of Commerce; library of 33,000 vols.; 100 full-time staff; Del.-Gen. D. HOURI; publ. *Management Research.* Includes 4 management education or development programmes:

Ecole des Hautes Etudes Commerciales: Dir. C. VULLIEZ.

Institut Supérieur des Affaires: Dir. J. SCARINGELLA.

Internat de Gestion: Dir. R. REITTER.

Centre de Formation Continue: Dir. J. L. VIARGUES.

Centre d'Enseignement et de Recherche de Statistique Appliquée: 4 place Jussieu, Tour 45-55, E.2, 75230 Paris Cedex 05; f. 1952; Dir. D. DUGUE; publ. *Revue de Statistique Appliquée* (quarterly).

Centre Parisien de Management: 108 blvd. Malesherbes, 75017 Paris; Del.-Gen. B. LEBLANC; run by the Paris Chamber of Commerce and Industry; comprises:

Centre de Perfectionnement dans l'Administration des Affaires: 108 blvd. Malesherbes, 75017 Paris; f. 1930; 80 students; Dir. P. MECHIN; Sec.-Gen. A. COURCIER.

Ecole des Affaires de Paris: European training programme in management; three-year diploma course; Dir. M. LEBLANC.

Ecole Supérieure de Commerce de Paris: 79 ave. de la République, 75011 Paris; f. 1820; three-year diploma courses, continuing education programmes; Dean J. PERRIN.

Institut de Formation d'Animateurs Conseillers d'Entreprises: 79 ave de la République, 75011 Paris; two-year course, continuing education programmes; Dir. M. FUROIS.

Ecole du Chef d'Entreprise—E.C.E.: 24–26 rue Hamelin, 75116 Paris; f. 1944; business administration; 50 teachers; Pres. M. Y. CHOTARD; Dir. A. CALLU; Sec.-Gen. Mlle M. JANNOR.

Ecole Nouvelle d'Organisation Economique et Sociale (E.N.O.E.S.): 62 rue de Miromesnil, Paris 8e; f. 1937; courses in business administration and accountancy; Gen. Administrator J. DESMYTTERE; Dir. of Studies P. LE GO; publ. *La Vie de l'E.N.O.E.S.*

Ecole Supérieure de Commerce et d'Administration des Entreprises de Lille: ave. Gaston Berger, 59 Lille; f. 1892; 400 students; Dir. B. MAIRE.

Ecole Supérieure de Commerce de Lyon: 23 route de Dardilly, 69130 Ecully; f. 1872; library of 5,000 vols.; Dir. J. LAGARDE.

Centre d'Etudes Supérieures du Marketing (CESMA): f. 1970; Dir. P. ALBERT.

Ecole Supérieure de Commerce et d'Administration des Entreprises de Marseille-Luminy: Domaine de Luminy, 13288 Marseille Cedex 02; f. 1872; library of 8,000 vols.; 200 teachers; Dir. G. MURAT.

Ecole Supérieure de Commerce et d'Administration des Entreprises de Montpellier: ave. des Moulins, 34030 Montpellier Cedex; f. 1897; Dir. J. DUVAUX; 60 professors, 300 students; three-year courses in environmental sciences, business administration, market research, information science.

Ecole Supérieure de Commerce et d'Administration des Entreprises de Poitiers: 62 rue Jean Jaurès, B.P. 5, 86001 Poitiers; f. 1961; diploma courses; *c.* 40 teachers; library of *c.* 1,800 vols.; Dir. GÉRARD ROUSSEAU.

Ecole Supérieure des Sciences Economiques et Commerciales: B.P. 105, 95021 Cergy Pontoise Cedex; f. 1913; business administration and management; 35 full-time, 150 part-time teachers, 750 students; Dir. D. XARDEL.

European Institute of Business Administration: blvd. de Constance, 77305 Fontainebleau; f. 1958; post-graduate management education, executive development programmes; 45 professors; library of 22,000 vols.; Chair. Board of Govs. Jonkheer J. H. LOUDON; Dir.-Gen. PIERRE CAILLIAU; Dean HEINZ THANHEISER.

LAW AND POLITICAL SCIENCE

Académie Internationale de Science Politique et d'Histoire Constitutionnelle en Sorbonne: 88 blvd. Péreire, Paris 17e; f. 1936; Pres. M. PRELOT; Gen. Sec. G. LANGROD; publ. *Politique* (3rd series).

Ecole de Hautes Etudes Internationales: 44 rue de Rennes, Paris 6e; f. 1924; Pres. J. ROLLAND; Dir. A LE JULES.

Ecole de Notariat d'Amiens: 3 place Louis Dewailly, 80000 Amiens; f. 1942; Dir. M. DUBAR.

Ecole de Notariat de Bordeaux: 8 rue Mably, Bordeaux; f. 1905; under the patronage of the Chambre des Notaires de la Gironde; two-year course.

Ecole de Notariat de Clermont-Ferrand: 41 blvd. Gergovia, 63000 Clermont-Ferrand; f. 1913; Diploma course; library of 1,641 vols.; Dir. F. DUTOUR.

Ecole de Notariat de Paris: 9 rue Villaret-de-Joyeuse, 75017 Paris; f. 1896; Dir. M. P. MATHIEU.

Ecole Supérieure de Journalisme: 44 rue de Rennes, Paris 6e; f. 1899; Pres. J. ROLLAND; Dir. A. LE JULES.

Ecoles Polytechniques de Notariat, de Droit et d'Assurances: 76 rue Bonapart, Paris 6e; Dir. Mme GENEVIÈVE JAQUET.

Institut International des Droits de l'Homme (*International Institute of Human Rights*): 1 quai Lezay-Marnésia, 67000 Strasbourg; f. 1969 by René Cassin; postgraduate teaching in international and comparative law of human rights; annual study session during July; Pres. EDGAR FAURE.

International Training Centre for University Human Rights Teaching: f. 1973 at the request of UNESCO; six-week courses for university teachers.

MEDICINE

Centre Français de Documentation Odonto-Stomatologique: 45 rue de la Tour d'Auvergne, 75009 Paris; f. 1879; library of 30,000 vols., 20,000 pamphlets; Dir. L. VERCHERE.

Ecole de Chirurgie Dentaire et de Stomatologie de Paris: 45-47 boulevard Voltaire, Paris 11e; f. 1927; Dir. M. J.-F. ROBERT.

Ecole Dentaire Française: 29 blvd. Saint-Martin, Paris 3e; Dir. P. PRETTO.

Ecole Supérieure d'Optométrie: 134 route de Chartres, 91440 Bures-sur-Yvette; f. 1942; Dir. of Studies T. THIEBAUT; Adm.-Dir. J. P. ROOSEN.

Institut d'Optique Théorique et Appliquée: B.P. 43, 91406 Orsay Cedex; attached to Univ. Paris XI; research in fundamental and applied optics; Dir.-Gen. A. MARÉCHAL.

RELIGION

Faculté Libre de Théologie Protestante de Paris: 83 boulevard Arago, Paris 14e; f. 1877; Religious History, Old and New Testament, Ecclesiastical History, Systematic Theology, Philosophy, Practical Theology, Hebrew, Greek, German, English; library of 50,000 vols.; 10 professors, 160 students; Dean J.-L. KLEIN; Sec. M. CARREZ.

Institut de Théologie Orthodoxe: 93 rue de Crimée, Paris 19e; f. 1925; 12 professors and 33 students; library of 20,000 vols; Rector Dean Arch. A. KNIAZEFF; publ. *Pensée Orthodoxe* (annual).

Institut Orthodoxe Français de Paris (Saint-Denis): 96 blvd. Auguste-Blanqui, Paris 13e; f. 1944; 12 professors and 35 students; library of 5,000 vols.; Faculties of Theology and Philosophy; Rector Bishop G. BERTRAND-HARDY; publ. *Présence Orthodoxe*†.

Séminaire Israélite de France (Ecole Rabbinique): 9 rue Vauquelin, Paris 5e; f. 1829; Talmud, Bible, Jewish history, Hebrew language and literature studies; library of 20,000 vols.; Dir. Grand Rabbi EMMANUEL CHOUCHENA.

SCIENCES

Ecole d'Anthropologie: 1 place d'Iéna, 75116 Paris; f. 1876 by Prof. Broca; Pre-History, Anatomical Anthropology, Ethnology, Biology, Genetics, Endocrinology, Immunology, Ethnography, Demography, Third World Problems, Psychology, Criminology, Anthropotechnics, Biometeorology; Dir. Prof. J. A. HUET; Publ. *Nouvelle revue anthropologique*† (annually).

Ecole Supérieure de Biochimie et de Biologie: 31 bis blvd. de Rochechouart, 75009 Paris; Dir. R. CASTAN.

Ecole Supérieure Libre de Chimie de Paris: 21 rue Joubert, Paris 9e; Dir. of Studies R. DAUDEL.

Institut de Biologie Sociale et d'Hygiène Mentale: 1 rue Cabanis, Paris 14e; Dir. J. J. RONDEPIERRE.

Institut de Paléontologie Humaine: 1 rue René Panhard, 75013 Paris; f. 1914 by Prince Albert I of Monaco; library of 25,000 vols.; 3 professors; palaeontology, prehistory, quaternary geology; Dir. L. BALOUT; publ. *Archives*.

Institut Océanographique: 195 rue Saint Jacques, 75005 Paris; f. 1906 by Prince Albert I of Monaco; library of 5,000 vols.; Pres J. DELORME; Dir. M. FONTAINE; Sec. J. F. COLLINET; publs. *Annales*, *Oceanis*.

Musée Océanographique: Monaco; library of 7,000 vols.; Dir. Cdr. J. COUSTEAU; publ. *Bulletin*.

SOCIAL AND ECONOMIC SCIENCES

CNOF—Centre d'Enseignement du Management: 3 rue Cassette, 75006 Paris; with the Collège des Sciences Sociales et Economiques, provides executive, managerial, administrative and secretarial training; Dir. SERGE VÉZON-DAUNIS.

Collège Libre des Sciences Sociales et Economiques: 184 boulevard Saint-Germain, Paris 6e; f. 1895; composed of six sections: social, economic, international and public relations; evening and correspondence courses; diplomas conferred after two or three years' study, and submission of thesis on some aspect of applied economics; Pres. J. RUEFF; Dir. L. DE SAINTE-LORETTE.

Ecole de Hautes Etudes Sociales: 44 rue de Rennes, Paris 6e; f. 1899; Pres. J. ROLLAND; Dir. A. LE JULES.

Faculté des Lettres et Sciences Sociales: B.P. 800, 29200 Brest; Tel.: 80-19-87; f. 1960.

President and Dean: Prof. MICHEL QUESNEL.

Library of 18,000 vols.

Number of teachers: 105.

Number of students: 2,752.

Institut Européen des Hautes Etudes Internationales: Palais de Marbre, 9 ave. de Fabron, 06200 Nice; f. 1965; 40 teachers, 70 students; uses library of University of Nice; Dir. Prof. G. MICHAUD; Sec.-Gen. C. NIGOUL.

TECHNOLOGY

Centre de Perfectionnement Technique: 9 ave. Alexandre-Maistrasse, 92500 Rueil Malmaison; f. 1934; Dir. P. C. DU FRAYSSEIX.

Ecole Catholique des Arts et Métiers: 40 montée Saint-Barthélemy, 69321 Lyon Cedex 1; f. 1900; 280 students, 30 professors; courses in electrotechnics, mechanics, metallurgy, chemistry and physics; library of 3,000 vols.; Dir. R. BONNETAIN; publ. *Bulletin* (quarterly).

Ecole Centrale de Lyon: 36 route de Dardilly, 69130 Ecully; f. 1857; cultural, scientific and technical training for engineers in all branches of industry; library of 7,000 vols.; 500 students; Dir. M. MOIROUX.

Ecole d'Electricité et de Mécanique Industrielles (Ecole Violet): 115 ave. Emile Zola, 75739 Paris, Cedex 15; f. 1902; Pres. Dir.-Gen. Mme SIMONNE RICHARD.

Ecole d'Electricité Industrielle de Paris (Ecole Charliat): 11 rue Nully d'Hécourt, 60000 Beauvais; f. 1901; courses in electronic, electrotechnical and mechanical engineering; Dir. M. L. GRAILLAT.

Ecole Française de Tannerie: 181-203 ave. Jean-Jaurès, 69007 Lyon; f. 1899; diploma courses in chemical engineering, leather technology, painting and varnishing technology, plastics; Dir. L. VILLA.

Ecole de Thermique: 3 rue Henri Heine, Paris 16e; teaching centre for the Institut Français de l'Energie (IFE); Dir. R. GUYONNET.

Ecole Nationale Supérieure de Meunerie et des Industries Céréalières (*Grain-milling Technology*): 16 rue Nicolas-Fortin, Paris 13e; f. 1924; Dir. M. DENIS.

Ecole Française de Radioélectricité, d'Electronique et d'Informatique: 10 rue Amyot, 75005 Paris; f. 1936; courses in telecommunications and electronic engineering; Dir. J. BOUCHARD.

Ecole Polytechnique Féminine: 3 *bis* rue Lakanal, 92330 Sceaux; Dir. M. Berthaume.

Ecole Spéciale de Mécanique et d'Electricité A.-M.-Ampère: 4 rue Blaise-Desgoffe, Paris 6e; Dir. P. Doceul.

Ecole Spéciale des Travaux Aéronautiques: 151 blvd. de l'Hôpital, Paris 13e; f. 1930; Technical Dir. M. Schweisch.

Ecole Spéciale des Travaux Publics, du Bâtiment et de l'Industrie: 57 blvd. Saint-Germain, Paris 5e; f. 1891; civil engineering for private enterprise; 2,000 students; library of 5,000 vols.; Dir. M. Eyrolles.

Ecole Supérieure d'Electricité: Plateau du Moulon, 91190 Gif sur Yvette; f. 1894; two- or three-year courses in electrical engineering, radio engineering and electronics; 760 students; attached to Univ. Paris XI; Dir.-Gen. J. L. Delcroix.

Ecole Supérieure des Industries du Caoutchouc: 12 rue Carvès, 92120 Montrouge; f. 1941; Dir. M. J. Curchod.

Ecole Supérieure d'Ingénieurs en Electrotechnique et Electronique: 81-91 rue Falguière, Paris 15e; f. 1967; library of 2,500 vols.; Pres. M. Bertrandias; Dir. M. Monzat; publ. *Recherches et Echanges* (3 a year).

Ecole Supérieure d'Ingénieurs de Marseille: 2 rue des Electriciens, 13012 Marseille; f. 1907; training of civil, thermal and electrical engineers; library of 1,650 vols.; 35 teachers, 250 students.

Ecole Supérieure de Fonderie: 278–284 ave. Aristide Briand, 92220 Bagneux; f. 1923; library of 1,850 vols.; Dir. J. Duflot.

Ecole Supérieure de Soudure Autogène (*Welding Engineering*): 32 blvd. de la Chapelle, 75018 Paris; f. 1930; 19 teachers; Dir. H. Granjon.

Ecole Supérieure du Bois: 6 avenue de Saint-Mandé, 75012 Paris; f. 1934; Dir. B. Tonnet.

Ecole Supérieure des Industries du Vêtement: 73 blvd. Saint-Marcel, 75013 Paris; Dir. M. Boudry.

Ecole Supérieure des Industries Textiles d'Epinal: 85 rue d'Alsace, 88000 Epinal; f. 1905; training of industrial textile engineers; library of 1,500 vols.; Dir. P. Lecoanet.

Ecole Supérieure des Techniques Aéronautiques et de Construction Automobile: 5 rue Pablo-Néruda, 92300 Levallois-Perret; f. 1925; private school offering 5-year courses; 400 students; Dir. M. Plan; publ. *De l'Aéronautique et de l'Automobile.*

Ecole Supérieure Textile: 43 cours Général-Giraud, 69001 Lyon; f. 1884; general tuition in mechanics, machinery technology and in all aspects of the textile industry; library of 21,500 vols., 18,400 patents, 80 current periodicals; Dir. G. Démortier.

Ecole Technique Scientia: 23 rue François-Gérard, Paris 16e; f. 1909; Dir. Mlle Le Chevalier.

Ecole Technique Supérieure du Laboratoire: 93 et 95 rue du Dessous-des-Berges, Paris 13e; f. 1934; Dir. J. Chomienne.

Institut Textile de France: 35 rue des Abondances, B.P. 79, 92105 Boulogne Billancourt Cedex; f. 1946; library of 15,000 vols. and documents; Dir. D. Marcé; publ. *Bulletin.*

SCHOOLS OF ART AND MUSIC

Conservatoire National d'Art Dramatique: 2 bis rue du Conservatoire, 75009 Paris; f. 1946; *c.* 100 students; Dir. J. Rosner.

Conservatoire National Supérieur de Musique: 14 rue de Madrid, 75008 Paris; f. 1795; the library forms part of the Music Section of the National Library.

Director: R. Gallois-Montbrun.
Assistant Director: Mme Claude Perrin.

Number of teachers: 134.
Number of students: *c.* 1,000 French, *c.* 150 foreign.

Unité Pédagogique d'Architecture de Lille: rue Verte, quartier de l'Hotel de Ville, 59650 Villeneuve d'Ascq; f. 1755 as Ecole d'Architecture, reorganized 1968; library of 2,700 vols.; 45 teachers, 450 students; Dir. Gérard Engrand.

ECOLE DU LOUVRE

34 QUAI DU LOUVRE,
75001 PARIS
Telephone: 260-3926.
Founded 1882.

Principal: H. Landais.
Librarian: Mlle H. Rouit.
Director of Studies: M. D. Ponnau.
Secretary-General: Mme L. Lanfranchi.

Library of 20,000 vols.
Number of students: 5,000.

Professors:

Amiet, P., Oriental Archaeology
Baratte, F., Greek and Roman Archaeology
Chatelain, J., Museology
Cuisenier, J., Ethnography
Cuzin, J.-P., History of Painting from its Origins to the 18th Century
Desroches-Noblecourt, Mme, Egyptian Archaeology
Forestier, J., Ethnography
Guiart, Mme B., History of Africa and Oceanic Arts
Hoog, M., History of 19th and 20th Century Art
Hours, Mme, M., Museology
Joffroy, R., Pre-History and National Antiquities
Landais, H., Museology
Le Bonheur, M., Archaeology and Art in India and the Far East
Pasquier, A., Ancient Ceramics
Taylor, J. P., History of Islamic Art

Ecole Nationale Supérieure des Arts Décoratifs: 31 rue d'Ulm, Paris 5e; f. 1766; Dir. M. Tourliere.

Ecole Nationale Supérieure des Beaux-Arts: 17 quai Malaquais, 75006 Paris; f. 1648 as Académie Royale de Peinture et de Sculpture, and in 1671 as Académie Royale d'Architecture; includes *Centre d'études et de recherches architecturales*; library of 110,000 vols.; 85 teachers, 2,500 students; Dir. Jean Musy.

Ecole Régionale des Beaux-Arts et des Arts Industriels de Clermont-Ferrand: 11 rue Ballainvilliers, 6300 Clermont-Ferrand; f. 1824; Dir. S. Helias.

Ecole Régionale des Beaux-Arts de Lille: 97 blvd. Carnot, 59000 Lille; f. 1775; 13 teachers; library of 14,000 vols.; Dir. J. Rozo.

Ecole Spéciale d'Architecture: 254 blvd. Raspail, 75014 Paris; f. 1865; 1,200 students, 82 teachers; library of 5,500 vols.; Dir. F. Wehrlin; publ. *Bulletin d'Information Pédagogique* (weekly).

Schola Cantorum, Ecole Supérieure de Musique, de Danse et d'Art Dramatique: 269 rue St. Jacques, Paris 5e; f. 1896 by Vincent d'Indy; Dir. J. Chailley.

FRENCH OVERSEAS DEPARTMENTS AND TERRITORIES

OVERSEAS DEPARTMENTS

FRENCH GUIANA

SOCIETIES AND RESEARCH INSTITUTES

Association des Etudiants en Droit: 97300 Cayenne; law.

Institut Pasteur: B.P. 304, 97300 Cayenne; f. 1940; medical and biological research; Dir. Y. Robin.

Mission I.R.A.T./Guyane: B.P. 60, 97301 Cayenne Cedex; f. 1962; agricultural research; library of 1,300 vols.; Dir. R. L. P. Vanbercie; publ. *Rapport annuel*†. (*See* main entry under France).

Office de la Recherche Scientifique et Technique Outre-Mer Centre ORSTOM de Cayenne: B.P. 165, 97301 Cayenne Cedex; f. 1947; pedology, hydrology, botany and vegetal biology; medical entomology, agricultural entomology, phytopharmacology, musicology, ethnology, sociology; library; Dir. J. Hervieu. (*See* main entry under France).

LIBRARY AND MUSEUM

Bibliothèque Franconie: 97300 Cayenne; general lending library.

Musée Local: 2 ave. Géneral de Gaulle, 97300 Cayenne; flora and fauna of Guiana; historical documents.

COLLEGE

Centre Universitaire Antilles-Guyane: (*see* also under Guadeloupe); 85 rue Léopold Héder, B.P. 718, 97300 Cayenne; 236 students; library of 1,000 vols.; first- and second-year courses in law.

GUADELOUPE

RESEARCH INSTITUTES

Centre INRA Antilles Guyane: 97170 Petit-Bourg; f. 1948; part of the Institut National de la Recherche Agronomique (France); controls eight research stations, four laboratories, two experimental farms and a Documentation Service throughout French Antilles and French Guiana; publs. *Nouvelles Agronomiques des Antilles et de la Guyane*† (quarterly).

Institut de Recherches sur les Fruits et Agrumes (I.R.F.A.): Station de Neufchâteau, 97135 Sainte Marie. (*See* main entry under France.)

Institut Pasteur de la Guadeloupe: B.P. 484, 97159 Pointe-à-Pitre; f. 1948; medical and microbiological analysis laboratories; leprosy research centre; international vaccination centre; bilharziasis immunology centre; departmental blood transfusion centre; haemoglobinopathy centre; small library; Dir. Dr. Y. Le Corroller; publ. *Archives*† (annually).

Office de la Recherche Scientifique et Technique Outre-Mer (ORSTOM)/Bureau des Sols: B.P. 504, 97165 Pointe-a-Pitre Cedex; f. 1960; pedology, hydrology; Dir. M. Gautheyrou. (*See* main entry under France.)

ARCHIVES AND LIBRARY

Archives départementales de la Guadeloupe: B.P. 74, 97102 Basse-Terre; f. 1951; library of 4,000 vols.; Dir. Jean-Paul Hervieu; publ. *Caribbean Archives*† (2 a year), *Bulletin de la Société d'Histoire de la Guadeloupe*† (quarterly).

Bibliothèque Universitaire Antilles Guyane (Section Guadeloupe): B.P. 32, 97151 Pointe-à-Pitre Cedex; f. 1972; 8,500 vols., 220 periodicals; Dir. M. F. Bernabe.

MUSEUM

Musée Schoelcher: 26 rue Peynier, 97110 Pointe-à-Pitre.

COLLEGE

Centre Universitaire Antilles-Guyane: (*See* also under Martinique); B.P. 771, 97173 Pointe-à-Pitre Cedex; f. 1970; 80 teachers; 3,700 students; library: *see* Libraries; Pres. Roland Thesauros; Sec.-Gen. Claude Roubinowitz.

Teaching and Research Units:

Law and Economics: B.P. 810, 97174 Pointe-à-Pitre Cedex; Dir. C. Edinval.

Sciences: Campus Universitaire de la Pointe Fouillole, B.P. 592, 97167 Pointe-à-Pitre Cedex; Dir. M. Bourgeois.

Caribbean Research Centre: B.P. 771, 97173 Pointe-à-Pitre; research in criminology; Dir. E. Lepointe.

MARTINIQUE

RESEARCH INSTITUTES

Institut de Recherches Agronomiques Tropicales et des Cultures Vivrières (IRAT): B.P. 427, 97204 Fort de France Cedex; f. 1963; stations in Martinique (Lamentin): Dir. P. J. Daly; and Guadeloupe (Petit-Bourg): Dir. J. C. Mauboussin.

Institut de Recherches sur les Fruits et Agrumes (I.R.F.A.): B.P. 153, 97200 Fort de France. (*See* main entry under France.)

Laboratoire Départemental d'Hygiène de la Martinique: blvd. Pasteur, B.P. 628, 97261 Fort de France Cedex; f. 1977; hygiene research and analysis, entomology, immunology of parasitic diseases; Dir. Dr. J. F. Magnaval.

Office de la Recherche Scientifique et Technique Outre-Mer. Centre ORSTOM des Antilles: B.P. 81, 97201 Fort de France Cedex; f. 1958; hydrology, soil science, economy, sociology, demography; library of 1,000 vols.; Dir. F. Colmet-Daage.

ARCHIVES AND LIBRARIES

Archives départementales de la Martinique: Quartier Tartenson, route de la Clairière, B.P. 649, 97262 Fort de France Cedex; f. 1950; 8,693 vols.; Dir. Mlle Liliane Chauleau.

Bibliothèque Schoelcher: B.P. 640, rue de la Liberté, Fort de France; f. 1893; 101,700 vols.; Dir. Mme Jacqueline Leger.

Bibliothèque Universitaire Antilles-Guyane (Section Martinique): B.P. 675, 97262 Fort de France Cedex; f. 1972; 30,000 vols., 470 periodicals on law and economics, letters and human sciences; specializes in Caribbean bibliography; branches in Guadeloupe, Martinique and French Guiana serve the needs of students at those univ. centres; Dir. Mme M. F. BERNABE.

MUSEUMS

Musée Départemental de la Martinique: B.P. 720, 97207 Fort de France; f. 1970; history, customs and costumes of Martinique; archaeological collections; Dir. M. MATTIONI.

Musée du Père Pinchon: Fort de France Seminary, 97207 Fort de France.

COLLEGE

Centre Universitaire Antilles-Guyane: (*see* also under Guadeluope); Campus de Schoelcher, B.P. 675, 97262 Fort de France Cedex; library: *see* Libraries; Vice-Pres PHILIPPE SAINT-CYR.

TEACHING AND RESEARCH UNITS:

Law and Economics: Campus de Schoelcher, B.P. 511, 97206 Fort de France; Dir. N. MONTOUT.

Letters and Huaman Sciences: B.P. 601, 97200 Fort de France; Dir. M. BORNECQUE.

Creole Studies: B.P. 601, 97200 Fort de France; Co-ordinator J. BERNABE.

REUNION

SOCIETIES AND RESEARCH INSTITUTES

Académie de la Réunion: c/o Bibliothèque Centrale de Prêt, place Joffre, 97400 Saint-Denis; f. 1913; 25 mems.; Pres. SERGE YCARD; Sec. Y. DROUHET; publ. *Bulletin*.

Association Historique Internationale de l'Océan Indien: c/o Archives Départementales, Le Chaudron, 97490 Sainte-Clotilde.

Société des Sciences et Arts: 22 rue la Bourdonnais, 97400 Saint-Denis; Pres. Mme MAS.

Institut de Recherches Agronomiques Tropicales et des Cultures Vivrières (IRAT): Agence de la Réunion, 97487 Saint-Denis; f. 1962; library of 5,000 vols.; Dir. M. HOARAU.

Institut de Recherches sur les Fruits et Agrumes (I.R.F.A.): 97455 Saint-Pierre Cedex; stations in Cilaos and Saint-Pierre; Dir. B. MOREAU.

LIBRARIES AND MUSEUMS

Archives Départementales: Le Chaudron, 97490 Sainte-Clotilde; specializes in the history of the Indian Ocean; 5,000 vols.; Dir. MICHEL CHABIN.

Bibliothèque Centrale de Prêt: place Joffre, 97400 Saint-Denis; f. 1956; 120,000 vols.; Dir. YVES DROUHET.

Bibliothèque Départementale: rue Roland Garros, 97400 Saint-Denis; f. 1856; 90,000 vols.; Dir. ALAIN VAUTHIER.

Bibliothèque Municipale: blvd. Hubert-Delisle, 97410 Saint-Pierre; f. 1967; 21,000 vols.; Dir. JULES VOLIA.

Bibliothèque Universitaire:

Section Sciences et Administration Centrale: Campus Universitaire du Chaudron, 97490 Ste.-Clotilde.

Section Lettres et Droit: 12 rue de la Victoire, 97489 St.-Denis; f. 1971 as autonomous unit; 34,000 vols.; 200 current periodicals; special collections on the Mascarene islands, oceanography, and tropical botany; Dir. JEAN-CLAUDE RODA; publs. *Bourbon médical*†, *Les Cahiers du Centre Universitaire de la Réunion*†.

Muséum d'Histoire Naturelle: Jardin de l'Etat, 97400 Saint-Denis; f. 1854; library of 2,000 vols.; zoology collection; Dir. H. GRUCHET; publ. *Info-Nature*† (annually).

Musée Historique: 97435 Saint-Gilles-les-Hauts; f. 1976; Curator S. GREFFET-KENDIG.

Musée Léon-Dierx: 97400 Saint-Denis; f. 1911; history and fine arts; Curator S. GREFFET-KENDIG.

COLLEGE

Centre Universitaire de la Réunion: 12 rue de la Victoire 97489 Saint-Denis; f. 1950; library: *see* Libraries attached to the Universities of Aix-Marseille and Nice; Pres. Y. POIRIER.

OVERSEAS TERRITORIES

NEW CALEDONIA

SOCIETY AND RESEARCH INSTITUTES

Institut Pasteur de la Nouvelle-Calédonie: B.P. 61, Nouméa; f. 1959; medical analysis laboratory; regional blood bank; research laboratory; library of 150 vols.; Dir. G. CHANALET; publ. *Rapport technique*† (annually).

Office de la Recherche Scientifique et Technique Outre-Mer Centre ORSTOM de Nouméa: B.P. A5, Nouméa; f. 1948; geology, geophysics, pedology, hydrology agronomy, botany and vegetal biology, phytopathology and applied zoology, physical and biological oceanography, ethnology, geography, sociology, archaeology; 140 staff; library of 2,000 vols.; Dir. P. DE BOISSEZON. (*See* main entry under France.)

Société des Etudes Mélanésiennes: Nouméa.

LIBRARIES

Bibliothèque Bernheim: B.P. G1 Nouméa Cedex; f. 1905; 38,000 vols., 120 periodicals; public library (adults and children); historical, ethnological collections dealing with New Caledonia and the Pacific Islands; Librarian Mme H. COLOMBANI-SAVOIE; publ. *List of Acquisitions and Information Review*† (quarterly).

South Pacific Commission Library: South Pacific Commission H.Q., P.O.B. D5, Nouméa Cedex; reference library on health, and economic and social development in S. Pacific; 16,000 vols.

COLLEGE

Conservatoire National des Arts et Métiers: B.P. H3, Nouméa Cedex; f. 1971; attached to the Conservatoire National des Arts et Métiers in Paris; 12 staff, 150 students; Pres. J. CHALIER; Dir. ROGER MAISONNEUVE.

FRENCH POLYNESIA

SOCIETIES AND RESEARCH INSTITUTES

Office de la Recherche Scientifique et Technique Outre-Mer Centre ORSTOM de Papeete: B.P. 529, Papeete; f. 1963; geophysics, climatological station, hydrology, geography, ethnology, archaeology, museology, linguistics, oceanography, pedology, medical entomology, economics, demography; library; Dir. J. FAGES. (*See* main entry under France.)

Société d'Etudes Océaniennes: Rue Lagarde, B.P. 110, Papeete; f. 1917; 550 mems.; library; Pres. Dr. P. MOORTGAT; publ. *Bulletin* (quarterly).

Institut de Recherches Médicales "Louis Malardé": B.P. 30, Papeete; f. 1949; parasitology (in particular lymphatic filariasis), virology, pulmonary diseases, leprosy, medical oceanography (ciguatera fish poisoning) and entomology; 95 staff: library of 1,442 vols.; Dir. Dr. JACQUES LAIGRET.

MUSEUM

Musée Paul Gauguin: P.O.B. 536, Papeari, Tahiti; f. 1965; 1,000 documents on Gauguin's life and work; library of unpublished documents; collection of paintings by R. Delaunay, S. Delaunay, Buffet and others; 20 original works by Gauguin (paintings, sculptures, watercolours); Curator G. ARTUR.

COLLEGE

Collège d'Enseignement Technique: Papeete; depts. of carpentry, general engineering, mechanical engineering, electricity and masonry.

FRENCH SOUTHERN AND ANTARCTIC TERRITORIES

RESEARCH STATIONS

Meteorological and Geophysical Research Station: Port-aux-Français, Kerguelen Island, South Indian Ocean.

Meteorological Station: New Amsterdam Island, South Indian Ocean.

GABON

Population 1,000,000

LEARNED SOCIETY AND RESEARCH INSTITUTES

Bureau de Recherches Géologiques et Minières: B.P. 175, Libreville; f. 1960; Dir. M. BERTUCAT.

Centre Technique Forestier Tropical: Section Gabon: B.P. 149, Libreville; f. 1958; silviculture, technology, genetic improvement; library of 500 vols.; Dir. J. LEROY DEVAL.

Laboratoire de Primatologie et d'Ecologie des Forêts Equatoriales (C.N.R.S.): B.P. 18, Makokou; f. 1970; study of the 17 species of primate living in the wild state; research on the general ecology of the equatorial forest; Dir. A. BROSSET; publ. *Biologia Gabonica* (3 a year).

Institut de Recherches Agronomiques Tropicales et des Cultures Vivrières (IRAT): B.P. 43, Libreville; Dir. G. COURS D'ARNE.

Office de la Recherche Scientifique et Technique Outre-Mer Mission ORSTOM auprès du CENAREST: B.P. 13115, Libreville (Gros-Bouquet); f. 1960; hydrology, pedology, psychosociology, ethnology; Dir. EDMOND GUICHARD.

LIBRARY

Bibliothèque du Centre d'Information: Libreville; f. 1960; 6,000 vols.; 80 current periodicals.

UNIVERSITY

UNIVERSITÉ OMAR BONGO

B.P. 13 131,
BLVD. LÉON M'BA,
LIBREVILLE
Telephone: 73 25 06.

Founded 1970, renamed 1978.

State control; Language of instruction: French; Academic year: October to July.

Rector: MOÏSE OLIVEIRA.
Vice-Rector: DJOHOU BOMA.
Secretary-General: LÉONARD ANDJEMBE.
Librarian: M. ABOGHE-OBIANG.

Number of teachers: 135.
Number of students: 600.

DEANS:

Faculty of Law: AGONDJO OKAWE.
Faculty of Letters: ALHIANGA MARTIN.
Faculty of Sciences: DJOHOU BOMA.
National Law School: M. GUER'CH.
Higher Teacher Training School: M. GAHILA.
Higher Technical Teacher Training School: M. RAUCY.
National Higher School of Engineering: M. DOUSSAINT.
Health Science Centre: (vacant).
National School of Administration: M. AMPRIMOZ.
National School of Forestry and Hydraulics: J. AKEWA.

GERMAN DEMOCRATIC REPUBLIC

Population 16,751,000

ACADEMIES

Akademie der Wissenschaften der DDR (*German Democratic Republic Academy of Sciences*): 108 Berlin, Otto-Nuschke-Str. 22/23; f. 1700.

President: Prof. Dr. WERNER SCHELER.

Vice-Presidents: Prof. Dr. ULRICH HOFMANN, Prof. Dr. WERNER KALWEIT, Prof. Dr. HERMANN KLARE; Prof. Dr. HEINRICH SCHEEL, Prof. Dr. KURT SCHWABE.

Secretary-General: Prof. Dr. CLAUS GROTE.

Library: *see under* Libraries.

Publications: ***Sitzungsberichte, Abhandlungen, Vorträge und Schriften, Jahrbuch, Monatsberichte, Deutsche Literaturzeitung.***

ORDINARY MEMBERS:

ALBRECHT, ROSEMARIE
ALBRING, WERNER
ALEXANDER, KARL FRIEDRICH
AUTH, JOACHIM
BAHNER, WERNER
BARTEL, HORST
BAUMANN, RUDOLF
BECKER, HEINZ
BEHRENS, FRIEDRICH
BERTSCH, HEINRICH
BETHGE, HEINZ
BIELFELDT, HANS HOLM
BIELKA, HEINZ
BILKENROTH, GEORG
BOBETH, WOLFGANG
BÖHME, HELMUT
BUDACH, LOTHAR
BUHR, MANFRED
BUNKE, OLAF
CORRENS, ERICH
DAVID, HEINZ
DIEHL, ERNST
DIETZE, WALTER
DREFAHL, GÜNTHER
DUTZ, HARALD
EICHHORN, WOLFGANG
EMONS, HANS-HEINZ
ENGELBERG, ERNST
FRATSCHER, WOLFGANG
FRÜHAUF, HANS
FUCHS, KLAUS
GERSCH, MANFRED
GÖRLICH, PAUL
GOERTTLER, VIKTOR
GRAFFI, ARNOLD
GROSSE, RUDOLF
GROTE, CLAUS
HAENEL, HELMUT
HÄRTIG, HELMUT
HARTKE, WERNER
HENKEL, OTTO
HERFORTH, LIESELOTT
HERRMANN, JOACHIM
HINTZE, FRITZ
HÖFER, KARL-HEINZ
HOFMANN, ULRICH
HORZ, HERBERT
JANTE, ALFRED
JONAS, ERNST-WOLFGANG
JUNG, FRIEDRICH
KALWEIT, WERNER
KAUTZSCH, EBERHARD
KEIL, GERHARD
KELBG, GÜNTER
KIRCHBERG, HELMUT
KIRSCHE, WALTER
KLARE, HERMANN
KLIX, FREIDHART
KNEPLER, GEORG
KÖHLER, KARL
KÖHLER, WERNER
KOHLMEY, GUNTHER
KOLDITZ, LOTHAR
KOSING, ALFRED
KOSSOK, MANFRED
KOZIOLEK, HELMUT
KRAATZ, HELMUT
KUCZYNSKI, JÜRGEN
KYANK, HELMUT
LANGE, WERNER
LANIUS, KARL
LAUTER, ERNST-AUGUST
LAUTERBACH, ROBERT
LEHMANN, EDGAR
LEHNERT, MARTIN
LEIBNITZ, EBERHARD
LICHTENHELDT, WILLIBALD
LOHS, KARLHEINZ
LÖSCHE, ARTHUR
MARKOV, WALTER
MATTHIES, HANSJÜRGEN
MEBEL, MORITZ
MITTENZWEI, WERNER
MONTAG, GERHARD
MOTHES, KURT
MOTTEK, HANS
MÜLLER, ARNO-HERMANN
MÜLLER, HANS JOACHIM
MÜLLER-STOLL, WOLFGANG R.
NAUMANN, MANFRED
NEUBERT, ALBRECHT
NEUNER, GERHART
NOWAK, SIEGFRIED
ÖHLMANN, GERHARD
PASTERNAK, GÜNTER
PEEK, WERNER
PFEIFFER, HARRY
PHILIPP, BURKART
PIETSCH, ALBRECHT
POMMER, KURT
POPPE, EBERHARD
PROKOP, OTTO
RAETZSCH, MANFRED
RAMMLER, ERICH
RAPOPORT, SAMUEL MITJA
REICHARDT, HANS
REINHOLD, OTTO
RIECHE, ALFRED
RIEGER, RIGOMAR
RIENÄCKER, GÜNTHER
ROHRER, HEINZ
ROMPE, ROBERT
ROSENKRANZ, OTTO
ROSENTHAL, SINAIDA
RUBEN, WALTER
RŮŽIČKA, RUDOLF
SANKE, HEINZ
SCHEEL, HEINRICH
SCHELER, WERNER
SCHIRMER, WOLFGANG
SCHMELOWSKY, KARL-HEINZ
SCHMITZ, GERHARD
SCHOBER, RITA
SCHREIBER, KLAUS
SCHWABE, KURT
SEIDEL, KARL
STEENBECK, MAX
STERBA, GÜNTHER
STERN, LEO
STILLER, HEINZ
STUBBE, HANS
TAUBENECK, UDO
THIEHLE, HELMUT
THIESSEN, PETER ADOLF
TREDER, HANS-JÜRGEN
UHLMANN, ARMIN
VOJTA, GÜNTER
WATZNZUER, ADOLF
WEISS, CARL-FRIEDRICH
WEISSMANTEL, CHRISTIAN
WERNER, ERNST
WINKLER, RUDOLF
WINTER, EDUARD
WOLLENBERGER, ALBERT
ZIEGENBALG, SIEGFRIED

CORRESPONDING MEMBERS:

ALBRECHT, GÜNTER
ASSER, GÜNTER
BLUMENAUER, HORST
BÖHME, WOLFGANG
BRÜNING, EBERHARD
CORNU, AUGUSTE
DONDA, ARNO
EBELING, WERNER
ENGST, RUDOLF
FEIST, PETER
FINK, WILHELM
FLACH, GÜNTER
FLEISCHER, WOLFGANG
FRATZSCHER, WOLFGANG
FRIEDRICH, GERD
FROMMELT, HORST
GLASER, ROLAND
GOELDNER, HANS
GRUNZE, HERBERT
HAHN, ERICH
HEUER, UWE-JENS
HOFMANN, EBERHARD
IRMSCHER, JOHANNES
JUNGE, KLAUS
KAUTZLEBEN, HEINZ
KERSTAN, JOHANNES
KLENNER, HERRMANN
KLEIN, HELMUT
KOCH, HELMUT
KÖHLER, WERNER
KÖNIG, OTTO
KRÖBER, GÜNTER
KUTZSCHE, WERNER
LANGE, FRANZ HEINRICH
LASSNER, GERD
LEKSCHAS, JOHN
MARKWARDT, FRITZ
MATTHES, KLAUS
MEISSNER, HERBERT
MERKEL, GERHARD
MOSCH, WOLFGANG
MÜHLENPFORDT, JUSTUS
MÜLLER, KARLHEINZ
MÜNZE, RUDOLF
OCKLITZ, HANS-WOLFGANG
PESCHEL, MANFRED
RAMBUCH, KARL
RATHMANN, LOTHAR
RÄTZSCH, MANFRED
REINISCH, GERHARD
RICHTER, JOACHIM
RINGPFEIL, MANFRED
SCHATT, WERNER
SCHMIDT, KARL
SCHMITZ, ERNST
SCHUBERT, MANFRED
SCHUBERT, MAX
SCHUBERT, RUDOLF
SPANGENBERG, HANS-JOACHIM
SPIES, KONSTANTIN
STEINBRÜCK, PAUL
STRZODKA, KLAUS
TEMBROCK, GÜNTER
TÖPFER, EDELHARD
TRIEBEL, HANS
UHLIG, EGON
WEBER, HORST
WOLF, FRIEDRICH
WOSCHNI, EUGEN-GEORG

CENTRAL INSTITUTES OF THE ACADEMY

Zentralinstitut für Astrophysik: 1502 Potsdam-Babelsberg, Rosa-Luxemburg-Str. 17A.

Zentralinstitut für anorganische Chemie: 1199 Berlin-Adlershof, Rudower Chaussee 5.

Zentralinstitut für organische Chemie: 1199 Berlin-Adlershof, Rudower Chaussee 5.

Zentralinstitut für physikalische Chemie: 1199 Berlin-Adlershof, Rudower Chaussee 5.

Zentralinstitut für Elektronenphysik: 108 Berlin-Mohrenstr. 40/41.

Zentralinstitut für Ernährung: 1505 Bergholz-Rehbrücke, Arthur-Scheunert-Allee 114.

Zentralinstitut für Festkörperphysik und Werkstofforschung: 8027 Dresden, Helmholtzstr. 20.

Zentralinstitut für Genetik und Kulturpflanzenforschung: 4325 Gatersleben.

Zentralinstitut für Geschichte: 108 Berlin, Clara-Zetkin-Str. 26.

Zentralinstitut für Alte Geschichte und Archäologie: 108 Berlin, Leipziger Str. 3/4.

Zentralinstitut für Herz- und Kreislauf-Regulationsforschung: 1115 Berlin-Buch, Wiltbergstr. 50.

Zentralinstitut für Isotopen- und Strahlenforschung: 705 Leipzig, Permoserstr. 15.

Zentralinstitut für Kernforschung: 8051 Dresden, Postfach 19.

Zentralinstitut für Krebsforschung: 1115 Berlin-Buch, Lindenberger Weg 70.

Zentralinstitut für Kybernetik und Informationsprozesse: 1199 Berlin-Adlershof, Rudower Chaussee 5.

Zentralinstitut für Literaturgeschichte: 108 Berlin, Otto-Nuschke-Str. 22/23.

Zentralinstitut für Mathematik und Mechanik: 108 Berlin, Mohrenstr. 39.

Zentralinstitut für Mikrobiologie und experimentelle Therapie: 69 Jena, Beuthenbergstr. 11.

Zentralinstitut für Molekularbiologie: 1115 Berlin-Buch, Lindenberger Weg 70.

Zentralinstitut für Optik und Spektroskopie: 1199 Berlin-Adlershof, Rudower Chaussee 5.

Zentralinstitut für Philosophie: 108 Berlin, Otto-Nuschke-Str. 22/23.

Zentralinstitut für Physik der Erde: 15 Potsdam, Telegrafenberg A 43.

Zentralinstitut für solar-terrestrische Physik: 1199 Berlin-Adlershof, Rudower Chaussee 5.

Zentralinstitut für Sprachwissenschaft: 108 Berlin, Otto-Nuschke-Str. 22/23.

Zentralinstitut für Wirtschaftswissenschaften: 108 Berlin, Leipziger Str. 3/4.

INSTITUTES OF THE ACADEMY

Forschungsinstitut für Aufbereitung: 92 Freiberg, Strasse des Friedens 40.

Institut für Biochemie der Pflanzen: 401 Halle, Weinberg 2.

Institut für Polymerenchemie: 153 Teltow-Seehof, Kantstr. 55.

Institut für technische Chemie: 705 Leipzig, Permoserstr. 15.

Institut für Technologie der Fasern: 801 Dresden, Hohe Str. 6.

Institut für Elektronik: 1199 Berlin-Adlershof, Rudower Chaussee 5.

Institut für Festkörperphysik und Elektronenmikroskopie: 401 Halle, Am Weinberg 2.

Institut für Geographie und Geoökologie: 701 Leipzig, Georgi-Dimitroff-Platz 1.

Institut für Hochenergiephysik: 1615 Zeuthen, Platanenallee 6.

Institut für Meereskunde: 253 Rostock-Warnemünde, Seestr. 15.

Institut für Theorie des Staates und des Rechts: 108 Berlin, Otto-Nuschke-Str. 22/23.

Institut für Physik der Werkstoffbearbeitung: 1166 Berlin-Rahnsdorf, Seestr. 82.

Institut für Theorie, Geschichte und Organisation der Wissenschaft: 108 Berlin, Otto-Nuschke-Str. 22/23.

Institut für Wirkstofforschung: 1136 Berlin, Wilhelmstr. 4.

Institut für Wirtschaftsgeschichte: 108 Berlin, Clara-Zetkin-Str. 26.

RESEARCH DEPARTMENTS OF THE ACADEMY

Zentrum für Wissenschaftlichen Gerätebau: 1199 Berlin-Adlershof, Rudower Chaussee 6.

Zentrum für Rechentechnik: 1199 Berlin-Adlershof, Rudower Chaussee 5.

Forschungsstelle für chemische Toxikologie: 701 Leipzig, Johannesallee 20.

Forschungsstelle für Wirbeltierforschung: 1136 Berlin-Friedrichsfelde, Am Tierpark 41.

Forschungsstelle für Akademiegeschichte: 1199 Berlin, Rudower Chaussee 5.

National Committees:
(with affiliations to International Organizations)

Nationalkomitee für den Internationalen Rat der wissenschaftlichen Unionen.
Nationalkomitee für Astronomie.
Nationalkomitee für Geodäsie und Geophysik.
Nationalkomitee für Geographie und Kartographie.
Nationalkomitee für Mathematik, Kybernetik und Informationsprozesse.
Nationalkomitee für Geologische Wissenschaften.
Nationalkomitee der Historiker.
Nationalkomitee für Kristallographie.
Nationalkomitee für Krebsforschung.
Nationalkomitee für Biowissenschaften.
Nationalkomitee für medizinische Physik.
Nationalkomitee für Elektronenmikroskopie.
Nationalkomitee für Philosophie und Geschichte der Wissenschaften.
Nationalkomitee für Physik.
Nationalkomitee für Radiophysik und Radiotechnik.
Nationalkomitee der Slawisten.
Nationalkomitee für Soziologie.
Nationalkomitee für Südosteuropäische Studien.
Nationalkomitee der Byzantinisten.
Nationalkomitee für Wirtschaftswissenschaften.
Nationalkomitee der Wirtschaftshistoriker.
Nationalkomitee für Ur- und Frühgeschichte.
Nationalkomitee für Chemie.

SCIENTIFIC SOCIETIES ATTACHED TO THE ACADEMY

Astronautische Gesellschaft der DDR: 102 Berlin, Poststrasse 4-5; f. 1960; 214 mems.; Pres. Prof. Dr. J. Hoppe; Sec. H. Pfaffe; publs. *Astronomie und Raumfahrt, Kosmos-Kurier.*

Biologische Gesellschaft der DDR: 104 Berlin, Friedrichstrasse 129, Block F; f. 1959; 1,470 mems.; Pres. Prof. Dr. G. Sterba; Sec. Dr. G. Kretschmar; publs. *Mitteilungen der Sektion Schulbiologie, Mitteilungen der Sektion Anthropologie, Mitteilungen der Sektion Geobotanik und Phytotaxonomie, Avifauna DDR.*

Gesellschaft für physikalische und mathematische Biologie der DDR: 108 Berlin, Am Kupfergraben 7; f. 1962; 323 mems.; Pres. Prof. Dr. E. Geissler; Sec. M. Koch; publ. *Studia Biophysica.*

Chemische Gesellschaft der DDR: 108 Berlin, Clara-Zetkin-Strasse 105; f. 1953; 3,246 mems.; Pres. Prof. Dr. H.-J. Bittrich; Sec. D. Schoenberg; publs. *Journal für* *praktische Chemie, Acta hydrochimica et hydrobiologica, Journal für Signalaufzeichnungsmaterialien, Zeitschrift für Chemie, Zeitschrift für physikalische Chemie.*

Geographische Gesellschaft der DDR: 701 Leipzig, Georgi-Dimitroff-Platz 1; f. 1953; 2,511 mems.; Pres. Prof. Dr. A. ZIMM; Sec. Dr. F. HÖNSCH; publs. *Geographische Berichte, Petermanns Geographische Mitteilungen, Wissenschaftliche Abhandlungen.*

Gesellschaft für Geologische Wissenschaften der DDR: 104 Berlin, Invalidenstrasse 43; f. 1954; 1,109 mems.; Pres. Prof. Dr. R. DABER; Sec. J. LAMPRECHT; publs. *Zeitschrift für Geologische Wissenschaften, Mitteilungen der Gesellschaft für Geologische Wissenschaften der DDR.*

Historiker Gesellschaft der DDR: 108 Berlin, Unter den Linden 2; f. 1958; 1,526 mems.; Pres. Prof. Dr. H. SCHEEL; Sec. Dr. M. LAHNE.

Mathematische Gesellschaft der DDR: 1071 Berlin, Willi-Bredel-Strasse 46; f. 1962; 1,262 mems.; Pres. Prof. Dr. ENGEL; Sec. I. BAUSCH; publ. *Zeitschrift für Elektronische Informationsverarbeitung und Kybernetik.*

Meteorologische Gesellschaft der DDR: 15 Potsdam, Luckenwalder Strasse 42-44-46; f. 1957; 203 mems.; Pres. Prof. A. MÄDE; Sec. K. RICHTER; publ. *Zeitschrift für Meteorologie.*

Parasitologische Gesellschaft der DDR: 104 Berlin, Hannoversche Strasse 28/29; f. 1961; 135 mems.; Pres. Prof. Dr. TH. HIEPE; Sec. Dr. R. BUCHWALDER; publ. *Angewandte Parasitologie.*

Physikalische Gesellschaft der DDR: 108 Berlin, Am Kupfergraben 7; f. 1952; 1,106 mems.; Pres. Prof. Dr. R. ROMPE; Sec. R. LINKE; publs. *Fortschritte der Physik, Experimentelle Technik der Physik.*

Gesellschaft für Psychologie der DDR: 108 Berlin, Am Kupfergraben 7; f. 1962; 588 mems.; Pres. Prof. Dr. F. KLIX; Sec. J. SIEBENBRODT; publs. *Probleme und Ergebnisse der Psychologie, Zeitschrift für Psychologie mit Zeitschrift für Angewandte Psychologie.*

OTHER INSTITUTES ATTACHED TO THE ACADEMY

Akademie-Archiv: 108 Berlin, Otto-Nuschke-Str. 22/23.

Akademie-Verlag G.m.b.H.: 108 Berlin, Leipziger Str. 3/4.

Alexander-von-Humboldt-Forschungsstelle: 108 Berlin, Leipziger Str. 3/4.

Wissenschaftliches Informationszentrum: 104 Berlin, Schiffbauerdamm 19.

Hauptbibliothek: 108 Berlin, Unter den Linden 8.

Zentrale Leitung für gesellschaftswissenschaftliche Information und Dokumentation: 108 Berlin, Universitätsstr. 8.

Akademie der Landwirtschaftswissenschaften der DDR (*Academy of Agricultural Sciences of the GDR*): 1086 Berlin, Krausenstrasse 38/39; f. 1951; organized into three departments, each with its own scientific secretary, and into 8 scientific sections; 25 research units; library of 280,000 vols.; number of members: 39 ord., 20 emer., 36 candidate, 44 corresp.; Pres. Prof. Dr. E. RÜBENSAM; Vice-Pres. Prof. Dr. D. SPAAR; publs. *Tagungsberichte*†, *Landwirtschaftliches Zentralblatt*†, *Informationen für industriemassige Tierproduktion*†, *Referatekarteien*†, 8 archives and 5 magazines on agricultural matters.

Deutsche Akademie der Naturforscher Leopoldina (*Leopoldine German Academy of Researchers in Natural Sciences*): 401 Halle/Saale, August-Bebel-Str. 50A; f. 1652 in Schweinfurt.

President: Prof. Dr. HEINZ BETHGE.

Vice-Presidents: Prof. Dr. HORST SACKMANN, Prof. Dr. HELMUT RENNERT, Prof. Dr. KLAUS BETKE.

General Secretary: Prof. Dr. HANS-ALBRECHT FREYE.

Director Ephemeridum: Prof. Dr. Dr. JOACHIM-HERMANN SCHARF.

Archive Director: Prof. Dr. GEORG USCHMANN.

Secretaries, Medical Section: Doz. Dr. GOTTFRIED GEILER, Prof. Dr. PETER-FRIEDRICH MATZEN.

Secretaries, Natural Sciences Section: Prof. Dr. ROLAND PAETZOLD, Prof. Dr. BENNO PARTHIER.

Number of members: 1,000.

Library: *see* Libraries.

Publs. *Nova Acta Leopoldina (Neue Folge)*†, *Leopoldina*†, *Struktur und Mitgliederbestand*†, *Acta historica Leopoldina*†, *Informationen*†.

Sächsische Akademie der Wissenschaften zu Leipzig (*Saxon Academy of Sciences in Leipzig*): 701 Leipzig, Goethestr. 3-5, I; f. 1846.

President: Prof. Dr.-Ing. Drs. h.c. KURT SCHWABE.

Vice-President: Prof. Dr. Phil. Dr.-Ing. e.h. EDGAR LEHMANN.

Secretary, Mathematics and Natural Science Section: Prof. Dr. Phil. ERNST NEEF.

Secretary, Philology and History Section: Prof. Dr. Phil. RUDOLF GROSSE.

Number of members: 134.

Publs. *Abhandlungen, Sitzungsberichte, Jahrbücher, Festschriften.*

Akademie der Künste der Deutschen Demokratischen Republik (*Academy of Arts of the German Democratic Republic*): 104 Berlin, Hermann-Matern-Strasse 58/59; f. 1950; 97 ordinary mems., 1 hon. mem., 86 corresp. mems.

President: KONRAD WOLF.

Vice-Presidents: Prof. Dr. ROBERT WEIMANN, Dr. HELMUT BAIERL, Prof. FRITZ CREMER, Prof. Dr. JOHANN CILENSEK, WIELAND FÖRSTER, Prof. Dr. MANFRED WEKWERTH.

Secretary, Fine Arts Section: Prof. WERNER KLEMKE.

Secretary, Visual Arts Section: RUTH BERGHAUS.

Secretary, Literature and Philology Section: GÜNTHER RÜCKER.

Secretary, Music Section: SIEGFRIED MATTHUS.

Director-General: HEINZ SCHNABEL.

Publs. *Sinn und Form, Mitteilungen, Arbeitshefte.*

Bauakademie der Deutschen Demokratischen Republik (*Academy of Building of the GDR*): 1125 Berlin, Plauener Str.; f. 1951; research programmes for the development of the building industry and socialist town planning; laboratory and testing facilities; central specialist library and centre for information and scientific publications; 25 ordinary mems., 30 candidate mems., *c.* 80 corresponding mems.; library of 150,000 vols.

President: Prof. Dr. HANS FRITSCHE.

Research Director: Prof. Dr. Sc. JOACHIM TESCH.

Vice-Presidents: Prof. RUDOLF SCHÜTTAUF, Prof. Dr. ULE LAMMERT.

Publs. *Bauforschung-Baupraxis*† (*c.* 25 titles a year), *Standardisierung*† (10 a year), *Baurecht*† (6 a year), *Bauinformation*† (6 a year), *Mitteilungsblatt Staatliche Bauaufsicht*† (monthly), etc.

LEARNED SOCIETIES

Berliner Gesellschaft für Innere Medizin (*Berlin Society of Internal Medicine*): 104 Berlin, Schumannstr. 21; Chair. Prof. Dr. med. habil. FRIEDRICH-HORST SCHULZ, Prof. Dr. med. RUDOLF BAUMANN; Sec. Prof. Dr. H.-G. HEINRICH.

Bibliotheksverband der Deutschen Demokratischen Republik (*Library Assn.*): 1040 Berlin, Hermann-Matern-Str. 57; f. 1964; mems.: 1,623 libraries and information organizations; Pres. GOTTHARD RÜCKL; Sec. WILFRIED KERN; publs. *Jahrbuch der Bibliotheken, Archive und Informationsstellen der Deutschen Demokratischen Republik*† (2 a year), *Bibliotheksverband aktuell*† (every 2 months), monographs†.

Gesellschaft für Gerontologie der DDR: 104 Berlin, H. Matern-Str. 13A; Chair. Dr. WOLFGANG RÜHLAND; Sec. Dr. UDO JÜRGEN SCHMIDT.

Goethe Gesellschaft in Weimar: 53 Weimar, Hans-Wahl-Strasse 4; Pres. Prof. Dr. KARL-HEINZ HAHN; Vice-Pres. Dr. JÖRN GÖRES; publs. *Goethe-Jahrbuch, Schriften der G.G.*

Institut für Literatur "Johannes R. Becher": Leipzig C.1, Karl-Tauchnitzstr. 8; f. 1955 to further aims and aid development of young writers; library of 30,000 vols.; Dir. Prof. MAX WALTER SCHULZ.

Montanwissenschaftliche Gesellschaft der Deutschen Demokratischen Republik: in der Kammer der Technik, 102 Berlin, Wallstrasse 68; publs. *Neue Bergbautechnik, Neue Hütte, Giessereitechnik* (monthly).

Wissenschaftlich-Technische Gesellschaft für Energiewirtschaft der Kammer der Technik: 108 Berlin, Clara-Zetkin-Str. 115/117; f. 1972; solid fuels, electricity, gas, utilization of energy; Sec. D. KOTHE; publ. *Energietechnik* (monthly).

RESEARCH INSTITUTES

(*see* also under Universities)

Akademie der Pädagogischen Wissenschaften der Deutschen Demokratischen Republik (*Academy of Pedagogical Sciences of the German Democratic Republic*): 108 Berlin, Otto-Grotewohl-Strasse 11; f. 1970; educational research and development; library of 900,000 vols.; Pres. Prof. Dr. Sc. GERHART NEUNER; publs. *Pädagogik, Vergleichende Pädagogik.*

Meteorologischer Dienst der Deutschen Demokratischen Republik: 1500 Potsdam, Albert-Einstein-Str. 42-46, Alfred-Wegener-Haus; f. 1950; Dir. Prof. Dr. W. BÖHME; affiliates meteorological observatories and institutes including a libraries and publications division (central library of *c.* 50,000 vols.), also Meteorologisches Hauptobservatorium, Potsdam; Hauptamt für Klimatologie, Potsdam; Ämter für Meteorologie Schwerin, Halle, Dresden und Weimar; Instrumentenamt, Potsdam; Forschungsinstitut für Hydrometeorologie, Berlin; Forschungsinstitut für Agrarmeteorologie, Halle; Forschungsinstitut für Bioklimatologie, Berlin; Zentrale Wetterdienststelle, Potsdam; Wetterdienststelle, Leipzig; Seewetterdienststelle, Warnemünde, Flugwetterwarte, Berlin-Schönefeld; observatories at Wahnsdorf and Lindenberg; publs. *Meteorologisches Jahrbuch der Deutschen Demokratischen Republik*†, *Abhandlungen*†, *Veröffentlichungen*†.

Ministerrat der Deutschen Demokratischen Republik, Staatliche Zentralverwaltung für Statistik (*The Council of Ministers of the German Democratic Republic, State Central Administration for Statistics*): 102 Berlin, Hans-Beimler-Str. 70-72; Dir. Prof. Dr. A. DONDA; publs. *Statistische Praxis*† (every 2 months), *Statistisches Jahrbuch der DDR*† (annual), *Statistisches Taschenbuch*† (annual, in German, Russian, English, French, Spanish, Arabic).

Universitäts-Sternwarte: Jena, Schillergässchen 2; Dir. Dr. H. ZIMMERMANN.

Zentrales Geologisches Institut: 104 Berlin, Invalidenstrasse 44; f. 1960; library of 150,000 vols.; Dir. Prof. KARL SCHMIDT; publs. *Zeitschrift für angewandte Geologie* (monthly), *Abhandlungen des Zentralen Geologisches Institutes* (5 times yearly), *Jahrbuch für Geologie* (yearly).

Zentralinstitut für Kernforschung (*Central Institute for Nuclear Research*): 8051 Dresden, Postfach 19; f. 1956; Dir. Prof. Dr.-Ing. HELMUTH FAULSTICH; WWR-S (M) 10,000 kW. reactor, cyclotron 120 cm. diameter argonaut-type zero power reactor.

LIBRARIES AND ARCHIVES

BERLIN

Berliner Stadtbibliothek: C.2, Breitestrasse 37; f. 1900; 800,000 vols.; Dir. HEINZ WERNER.

Bibliothek des Obersten Gerichts der Deutschen Demokratischen Republik: Wilhelm-Pieck-Str. 109; f. 1879; contains 300,000 vols.; Chair. U. GERICKE.

Deutsche Staatsbibliothek (originally Preussische Staatsbibliothek): 1086 Berlin, Unter den Linden 8; f. 1661; 5,047,990 vols. (1.8 million vols. of the original collection are at present deposited in the Staatsbibliothek in West Berlin), 10,212 periodicals, 31,776 serials, 1,083,734 maps, portraits, musical scores, records, etc.; departments: Acquisition, Catalogues, Lending, MSS., Oriental Books, Incunabula, Music, Cartography, Children's Literature, Rare and Precious Books, Reprography, *Institut für Leihverkehr und Zentralkataloge;* connected with Deutsche Fotothek in Dresden; Gen. Dir. Dr. FRIEDHILDE KRAUSE; Deputy Dir. Dr. HEINZ GITTIG; publs. *Berliner Titeldrucke, Jahresberichte der Deutschen Staatsbibliothek*†, *Zeitschriftenbestandsverzeichnisse, Gesamtkatalog der Wiegendrucke, Beiträge zur Inkunabelkunde, Zentralkatalog der DDR—Zeitschriften und Serien des Auslands, Fontane-Blätter,* catalogues and bibliographies.

Landwirtschaftliche Zentralbibliothek: 1086 Berlin, Krausenstr. 38–39; f. 1952; library of the Akademie der Landwirtschaftswissenschaften der DDR; information and documentation centre; 326,900 vols.

Pädagogische Zentralbibliothek-Deutsche Lehrerbücherei: 1020 Berlin, Alexanderplatz, Haus des Lehrers; f. 1876, reorganized 1950; 540,000 vols.; Dir. Oberstudienrat Dr. RENATE MEWES.

Universitätsbibliothek: 108 Berlin, Clara-Zetkin-Str. 27; f. 1831; library of the Humboldt University; *c.* 2,000,000 vols., 1,800,000 vols. in Institute libraries; Dir. Dr. WALTRAUD IRMSCHER.

Wissenschaftliches Informationszentrum der Akademie der Wissenschaften der DDR: 104 Berlin, Schiffbauerdamm 19; f. 1973; Dir. Dr. WERNER RICHTER.

Hauptbibliothek: 108 Berlin, Unter den Linden 8; f. 1700; 290,000 vols.; Dir. Dr. JOACHIM REX.

Zentralbibliothek im Hause der Ministerien: W.1, Leipziger Strasse 5-7; 180,000 vols.; Dir. A. PRITZBUER.

Zentralbibliothek der Staatlichen Museen zu Berlin: 102 Berlin, Bodestrasse 1–3; f. 1830; *c.* 126,000 vols.; Dir. Dr. ALBRECHT DOHMANN; publ. *Forschungen und Berichte* (annually).

Zentralinstitut für Information und Dokumentation der Deutschen Demokratischen Republik: 102 Berlin, Köpenicker Str. 80-82; f. 1963; organization and co-ordination of scientific and technical information; Dir. HANS OCH; publs. *Informatik* (every 2 months), *Information/Dokumentation* (monthly).

DESSAU

Stadtbibliothek Dessau: Strasse der DSF 10; f. 1897; 194,000 vols., 109 incunabula, 900 MSS., 211 current periodicals; Dir. IRMGARD LANGE.

DRESDEN

Bibliothek der Hochschule für Verkehrswesen "Friedrich List": 8010 Dresden, Friedrich-List-Platz 1; f. 1952; 305,000 vols.; Dir. Dr.-Ing. HELMUT ZESEWITZ; publ. *Wissenschaftliche Zeitschrift der Hochschule für Verkehrswesen*†, *Forschungshefte zur Verkehrssicherheit.*

Sächsische Landesbibliothek: 806 Dresden, Marienallee 12; f. 1556; contains about 1,400,000 vols.; Dir. Prof. Dr. sc. BURGHARD BURGEMEISTER; publs. *Sächsische Bibliographie*†, *Bibliographie Bildende Kunst*†, *Bibliographie Illustrierte Bücher der DDR*†, *Bibliographie Geschichte der Technik*†, *Bibliographie Musik der DDR*†, *Sozialistisches Musikschaffen der DDR*† (all annually), *Neuerwerbungen und Nachrichten*† (monthly).

Staatsarchiv Dresden: 8060 Dresden, Archivstr. 14; f. 1834; 53,000 vols.; Dir. Dr. REINER GROSS; publ. *Schriftenreihe des Staatsarchivs Dresden*† (Vols. 1–11).

Stadt- und Bezirksbibliothek: Pf. 58, Dresden, Elsa-Fenske-Str. 11; f. 1910; 622,000 vols.; Dir. WERNER SCHÄFER.

Universitätsbibliothek der Technischen Universität: 8027 Dresden, Mommsenstr. 13; f. 1828; DDR and BRD patents; industrial and commercial literature; 1,150,000 vols., incl. 5,500 periodicals, 110,000 theses; Dir. Prof. Dr. phil. H. FELKE; publs. *Bibliographische Informationen—Neuerwerbungsverzeichnis*†, *Veröffentlichungen von Wissenschaftlern der Tech. Universität, Bibliographische Arbeiten*†.

ERFURT

Wissenschaftliche Bibliothek: Michaelisstr. 39; f. 1407; 450,000 vols., 1,514 MSS., 616 incunabula; Dir. W. STROBEL.

FREIBERG I. SA.

Wissenschaftliches Informationszentrum der Bergakademie —Bibliothek "Georgius Agricola": Agricola-Strasse; f. 1765; 460,000 vols., 800 MSS., 4,764 trade pamphlets, 2,093 records, 30,078 standards, 16,041 cards, 730,262 patents; Dir. Dr. DIETER SCHMIDMAIER; publ. *Veröffentlichungen.*

GOTHA

Forschungsbibliothek Gotha: Schloss Friedenstein; f. 1647; contains 502,505 vols., *c.* 8,935 MSS.; Dir. Dr. HELMUT CLAUS (acting).

GREIFSWALD

Universitätsbibliothek: 2200 Greifswald, Rubenowstr. 4; f. 1604; 1,940,102 vols., including 606,407 theses, 2,104 autographs, 350 incunabula; Dir. ILSE HÖCHEL.

HALLE

Bibliothek der Deutschen Akademie der Naturforscher Leopoldina: 401 Halle/S., August-Bebel-Str. 50A; f. 1731; 190,000 vols., 18,500 theses; Dir. WOLFGANG HEESE.

Universitäts- und Landesbibliothek Sachsen-Anhalt: August-Bebel-Strasse 13 and 50; f. 1696; 3,562,000 vols., 527,000 theses; Ponickau collection on Thuringian and Saxon history and folklore; Dir. Prof. Dr. JOACHIM DIETZE.

ILMENAU

Bibliothek der Technischen Hochschule Ilmenau: Strasse der Jungen Techniker 26; f. 1953; 167,000 vols., 1,858 periodicals; Dir. HANS GESSNER; publs. *Wissenschaftliche Zeitschrift*†, *Internationales Wissenschaftliches Kolloquium*†, *Schriftenreihe "Information/Dokumentation"*† (all annually), *Bibliographie der Veröffentlichungen von Angehörigen der Technischen Hochschule Ilmenau* (every 2 years).

JENA

Universitätsbibliothek: Goetheallee 6; f. 1558; 2,417,778 vols., 745,540 pamphlets, 56,867 MSS., 123,960 patents, 7,208 current periodicals; Dir. Prof. Dr. LOTHAR BOHMÜLLER.

KARL-MARX-STADT

Bibliothek der Technischen Hochschule: 901, Postfach 964, Strasse der Nationen 62; f. 1836; 546,463 vols., 3,318 periodicals; Dir. Dr. DIETER SCHEFFEL; publ. *Wiss. Zeitschrift der Technischen Hochschule Karl-Marx-Stadt.*

Stadt- und Bezirksbibliothek: Haus am Schillerplatz; 235,000 vols.; Dir. WOLFGANG SCHIEFER.

LEIPZIG

Comenius-Bücherei: 703 Leipzig, Schenkendorfstr. 34; f. 1871; branch of Pädagogische Zentralbibliothek in Berlin; 254,000 vols.; 130 periodicals; Head Dr. G. FEHLING.

Deutsche Bucherei: 7010, Deutscher Platz; f. 1912; 6,900,000 vols.; Gen. Dir. Prof. Dr. HELMUT ROETZSCH; Deputy Dirs. Dr. HELMUT LOHSE, Dr. GERHARD POMASSL; Accession (Dr. H. LOHSE), Bibliographies (Dr. G. POMASSL), Catalogues (Dr. HEINZ HOEHNE), Reference (KÄTE SCHROETER), Lending (Dr. KARL-HEINZ WENKEL), Deutsches Buch- und Schriftmuseum (Dr. FRITZ FUNKE); publs. *Deutsche Nationalbibliographie und Bibliographie des im Ausland erschienenen deutschsprachigen Schrifttums, Deutsche Musikbibliographie, Bibliographie der Kunstblätter, Bibliographie der Übersetzungen deutschsprachiger Werke, Bibliographie fremdsprachiger Germanica, Jahresverzeichnis der Verlagsschriften und einer Auswahl der ausserhalb des Buchhandels erschienenen Veröffentlichungen der DDR, der BRD und Westberlins sowie der deutschsprachigen Werke anderer Länder, Jahresverzeichnis der Musikalien und Musikschriften, Jahresverzeichnis der Hochschulschriften der DDR, der BRD und Westberlins, Deutsches Bücherverzeichnis, Bibliographie der Bibliographien, Sonderbibliographien der Deutschen Bücherei, Bibliographischer Informationsdienst der Deutschen Bücherei, Informationsdienst Bibliothekswesen, Jahrbuch, Neujahrsgabener, Bibliographie aktuell;* Collaborating in: *Jahresberichte für deutsche Geschichte, International Bibliography of Historical Sciences, International Bibliography of Social and Cultural Anthropology.*

Institut für Geographie und Geoökologie der Akademie der Wissenschaften der DDR: Arbeitsgruppe Geographische Zentralbibliothek: 701 Leipzig, Georgi-Dimitroff-Platz 1; f. 1892; 168,000 vols.; Chief Librarian Dipl.-Bibl. HANS-PETER WEINHOLD; publs. *Beiträge zur Geographie*† (annually), *Acta Hydrophysica*† (monthly), *Literaturinformation Territorialplanung-Territorialforschung*† (monthly), *Nachrichten Mensch-Umwelt*† (quarterly), *Werte unserer Heimat*† (irregular), *Schnellinformation über Neuerwerbungen der Geographischen Zentralbibliothek*† (monthly), *Wissenschaftliche Nachrichten aus dem Institut für Geographie und Geoökologie* (quarterly).

Musikbibliothek der Stadt Leipzig: 7010 Leipzig, Ferdinand-Lassalle-Str. 21; f. 1894; 110,895 vols., 23,005 recordings; numerous special collections of printed and handwritten music from 15th century onwards; Dir. ELLEN ROESER; publ. *Bibliographische Veröffentlichungen.*

Stadt- und Bezirksbibliothek Leipzig: 7010 Leipzig, Mozartstr. 1; f. 1914; 629,158 vols.; Dir. HELGA LAUE.

Stadtarchiv: 7010 Leipzig, Burgplatz 1; f. about 1100; Dir. Dr. HORST THIEME.

Universitätsbibliothek der Karl-Marx-Universität Leipzig: 7010 Leipzig, Beethovenstrasse 6; f. 1543; approx. 3,050,000 vols.; Dir. Dr. FRITZ SCHAAF.

MAGDEBURG

Staatsarchiv Magdeburg: 301 Magdeburg, Hegelstr. 25; f. 1823; archives of the former states of Saxony and Anhalt and their territories; public record office for Magdeburg and Halle; attached institutes of capitalist and socialist economics; 38,000 vols., 47,500 documents, 31,000 metres of records, 50,000 maps; Dir. R. ENGELHARDT.

Stadt- und Bezirksbibliothek: Weitlingstr. 1A; f. 1525; 265,000 vols.; Dir. MARTIN WIEHLE.

MEININGEN

Max-Reger-Archiv: Schloss Elisabethenburg; 1947 moved to Meiningen from Weimar; special department of the Staatliche Museum, Meiningen; musical history, MSS., collection of instruments; Dir. (vacant).

POTSDAM

Bibliothek der Akademie für Staats- und Rechtswissenschaft der DDR: 1502 Potsdam-Babelsberg, August-Bebel-Str. 89; f. 1948; 355,000 vols., 1,200 periodicals; Chief Librarian URSULA DIX.

Staatsarchiv Potsdam: 15 Potsdam, Sanssouci-Orangerie; 35,000 vols. in library; Dir. Dr. FRIEDRICH BECK.

Wissenschaftlichen Allgemeinbibliothek des Bezirkes Potsdam: 1500 Postdam, Heinrich-Rau-Allee 47; f. 1969 (formerly Brandenburgische Landes- und Hochschulbibliothek and Stadt- und Bezirksbibliothek); 650,000 vols.; pedagogy and Brandenburg collections; district medical library; Dir. ILSE SCHUMANN.

Zentrales Staatsarchiv: 15 Potsdam, Berliner Str. 98-101; f. 1946; preserves records of the central administration of the German Reich (1867-1945), the central administration of Prussia and the central organs and institutions of the G.D.R.; library of 140,000 vols.; Dir. Dr. HELMUT LÖTZKE.

ROSTOCK

Universitätsbibliothek: 25 Rostock, Universitätsplatz 5; f. 1569; 1,758,818 vols., 4,692 MSS., 725 incunabula, 4,472 journals; Dir. Dr. Phil. KARL-HEINZ JÜGELT; publs. *Wissenschaftliche Veröffentlichungen der Wilhelm-Pieck-Universität* (annually), *Rostocker Dissertationen und Diplomarbeiten* (annually).

SCHWERIN I. MECKL

Wissenschaftliche Allgemeinbibliothek des Bezirkes Schwerin: 2700 Schwerin, Schlossstrasse 15; f. 1779; formerly Mecklenburgische Landesbibliothek and Stadt- und Bezirksbibliothek; 720,000 vols.; Dir. Dr. H. U. KLOTH.

WEIMAR

Bibliothek der Hochschule für Architektur und Bauwesen Weimar: Karl-Marx-Platz 2; f. 1947; 155,000 vols., 1,200 periodicals; Dir. Dr. J. SCHILD.

Nationale Forschungs- und Gedenkstätten der klassischen deutschen Literatur—Zentralbibliothek der deutschen Klassik: 53 Weimar, Platz der Demokratie 1; f. 1691; German literature, art and music, and Faust studies in world literature; 780,000 vols.; Dir. Dr. HANS HENNING; publs. *Internationale Bibliographie zur deutschen Klassik*†, *Personal-Bibliographien zur deutschen Klassik*†, *Thüringen-Bibliographie*†, *Faust-Bibliographie*†.

Staatsarchiv Weimar: 53 Weimar, Marstallstr. 2; f. 1547; brs. in Altenburg, Gotha, Greiz and Meiningen; 61,900 vols., 28,000 documents, 21,300 maps, 29,500 MSS.; Dir. GOTTFRIED BÖRNERT.

MUSEUMS AND ART GALLERIES

BERLIN

Staatliche Museen zu Berlin: 102, Bodestrasse 1/3; f. 1830; Gen. Dir. Prof. Dr. EBERHARD BARTKE; publ. *Forschungen und Berichte, Jahrbuch*†. Comprises the following museums and collections:

- **National-Galerie:** f. 1876; paintings and sculptures from the end of the 18th century to the present day; Dir. Prof. Dr. EBERHARD BARTKE.
- **Vorderasiatisches Museum:** Dir. Dr. LIANE JAKOB-ROST.
- **Islamisches Museum:** Curator VOLKMAR ENDERLEIN.
- **Antiken-Sammlung:** Dir. Dr. ELISABETH ROHDE.
- **Ostasiatische Sammlung:** Dir. BRUNO VOIGT.
- **Museum für Volkskunde:** Dir. Prof. Dr. WOLFGANG JACOBEIT.
- **Museums-Bibliothek:** Dir. Dr. ALBRECHT DOHMANN.
- **Ägyptisches Museum und Papyrus-Sammlung:** Dir. Dr. WOLFGANG MÜLLER.
- **Frühchristlich-byzantinische Sammlung:** Dir. Dr. ARNE EFFENBERGER.
- **Skulpturen-Sammlung:** Dir. Dr. EDITH FRÜNDT.
- **Gemälde-Galerie:** Dir. Dr. IRENE GEISMEIER.
- **Kupferstichkabinett und Sammlung der Zeichnungen:** Dir. Dr. HANS EBERT.
- **Münzkabinett:** Dir. Dr. HEINZ FENGLER.
- **Museum für Ur- und Frühgeschichte:** Dir. Dr. ERIK HÜHNS.
- **Kunstgewerbe-Museum:** 117 Berlin, Schloss Köpenick; Dir. Dr. GÜNTER SCHADE.

Märkisches Museum, kultur-historisches Museum der Stadt Berlin: 102 Berlin, Am Köllnischen Park 5; f. 1874; illustrates history of Berlin, its culture and its art; library of 15,000 vols.; Dir. Dipl. phil. HERBERT HAMPE; publ. *Jahrbuch*†.

Museum für Deutsche Geschichte (*History Museum*): DDR-108 Berlin, Unter den Linden 2; Dir. Prof. Dr. WOLFGANG HERBST; publ. *Beiträge und Mitteilungen*†.

Museum für Naturkunde an der Humboldt-Universität zu Berlin (*Natural History Museum*): DDR, 104 Berlin,

Invalidenstr. 43; f. 1889; Dir. Prof. Dr. HOPPE. Comprises the following institutions:

Paläontologisches Museum (*Palaeontological Museum*): DDR, 104 Berlin, Invalidenstr. 43; f. 1810; library of 30,000 vols.; Dir. Dr. HERMANN JAEGER.

Mineralogisches Museum (*Mineralogical Museum*): DDR, 104 Berlin, Invalidenstr. 43; f. 1770 as Royal Prussian Institute of Minerals; has collections of minerals, meteorites and specimens of ore deposits; 8,000 vols. in library; Dir. Prof. Dr. GUNTER HOPPE.

Zoologisches Museum (*Zoological Museum*): DDR, 104 Berlin, Invalidenstr. 43; f. 1810; library of *c.* 150,000 vols.; Dir. Dr. HANS-JOACHIM HANNEMAN; publs. *Mitteilungen aus dem Zoologischen Museum in Berlin*†, *Deutsche Entomologische Zeitschrift*†.

Bereich Botanik und Arboretum (*Botanical Institute and Arboretum*): DDR, 1195 Berlin-Baumschulenweg, Späthstr. 80–81; library of 8,500 vols.; Dir. Prof. Dr. WALTER VENT; publs. *Feddes Repertorium*†, *Gleditschia*.

Bereich Anthropologie (*Anthropological Institute*): DDR, 104 Berlin, Invalidenstr. 43; research and instruction; library of 3,000 vols.; Dir. Prof. Dr. HANS GRIMM; Rudolf-Virchow collection.

DRESDEN

Armeemuseum der Deutschen Demokratischen Republik: Dr.-Kurt-Fischer-Platz 3; f. 1972; military history from 1400 to 1945, and contemporary military history of the G.D.R.; over 6,000 exhibits include weapons, equipment, documents, uniforms and combat vehicles; open-air exhibition of aeroplanes, helicopters, rockets, cannons and tanks; also films of military events, models, dioramas, paintings and sculptures; library of *c.* 120,000 vols.; Dir. Konteradmiral Dipl. rer. mil. JOHANNES STREUBEL.

Barockmuseum: Schloss Moritzburg bei Dresden, 08105 Moritzburg bei Dresden; f. 1947; furniture, paintings, statues, porcelain, glasswork, principally of the 18th century; Dir. GERHARD THÜMMLER.

Landesmuseum für Vorgeschichte: Japanisches Palais; Dir. Dr. COBLENZ.

Museum für Geschichte der Stadt Dresden (*Dresden History Museum*): 801 Dresden, Ernst-Thälmann-Str. 2; f. 1966; library of 18,000 vols.; Dir. Dr. RUDOLF FÖRSTER; publ. *Jahrbuch zur Geschichte der Stadt Dresden*. The Museum zur Dresdner Frühromantik, J. I. Kraszewski-Museum and the Martin-Andersen-Nexö-Gedenkstätte are attached to this Museum.

Schloss Weesenstein: Müglitztal, Kreis Pirna; 18th- and 19th-century rooms.

Staatliche Kunstsammlungen Dresden: Head Office: 8012 Dresden, PSF 450, Georg-Treu-Platz Albertinum; f. 1560; Gen. Dir. Prof. Dr. MANFRED BACHMANN; publs. *Jahrbuch*†, *Dresdener Kunstblätter*† (every 2 months); comprise:

Gemäldegalerie Alte Meister: 8010 Dresden, Semperbau Zwinger; Dir. Dr. ANNALIESE MAYER-MEINTSCHEL.

Gemäldegalerie Neue Meister: 8010 Dresden, Georg-Treu-Platz Albertinum; Dir. JOACHIM UHLITZSCH.

Kupferstichkabinett: 8019 Dresden, Güntzstrasse 34; Dir. Dipl. phil. WERNER SCHMIDT.

Skulpturensammlung: 8010 Dresden, Georg-Treu-Platz Albertinum; Dir. Dipl. phil. MARTIN RAUMSCHÜSSEL.

Grünes Gewölbe: 8010 Dresden, Georg-Treu-Platz Albertinum; Dir. Dr. JOACHIM MENZHAUSEN.

Porzellansammlung: 8010 Dresden, Zwinger, Sophienstrasse; Dir. Dipl. phil. INGELORE MENZHAUSEN.

Historisches Museum: 8010 Dresden, Semperbau/Osthalle; Dir. Dipl. phil. JOHANNES SCHÖBEL.

Münzkabinett: 8019 Dresden, Güntzstr. 34; Dir. Dr. PAUL ARNOLD.

Museum für Kunsthandwerk: 8057 Dresden, Schloss Pillnitz, Wasserpalais; Dir. Dr. GÜNTER REINHECKEL.

Museum für Volkskunst: 8060 Dresden, Köpckestr. 1; Dir. Dr. JOHANNES JUST; also a puppet theatre collection: Radebeul Barkengasse 6; Dir. Dr. päd. ROLF MÄSER.

Zentrale Kunstbibliothek: 8019 Dresden, Güntzstrasse 34; 45,000 vols.; Dir. Dipl. bibl. KÄTHE NEUMANN.

Abgusswerkstatt: 801 Dresden, Georg-Treu-Platz Albertinum.

Technisches Museum Dresden: 806 Dresden, Fr.-Engels-str. 15; f. 1966; library of 2,500 vols.; Dir. Dr. LEUSCHNER.

Staatlicher Mathematisch-Physikalischer Salon (*Natural Sciences*): 801 Dresden, Zwinger; f. 1560; library of *c.* 5,000 vols.; Dir. Dr. SCHILLINGER; publ. *Veröffentlichungen* (annually).

Staatliches Museum für Mineralogie und Geologie: 801 Dresden, Augustusstr. 2; f. 1560; library of 32,742 vols.; Dir. Dr. PRESCHER; publ. *Abhandlungen*† (1–2 a year).

Staatliches Museum für Tierkunde (*Zoology*): 801 Dresden, Augustusstr. 2; f. 1560; library of 45,000 vols.; Dir. Dr. HERTEL; publs. *Entomologische Abhandlungen*†, *Zoologische Abhandlungen*†, *Malakologische Abhandlungen*†, *Faunistische Abhandlungen*†, *Reichenbachia Zeitschrift für entomolog. Taxonomie*† (annually).

Staatliches Museum für Völkerkunde (*Ethnology*): 806 Dresden, Japanisches Palais; f. 1875; library of 33,646 vols.; Dir. Dr. NEUMANN; publs. *Abhandlungen und Berichte*†, *Kleine Beiträge*† (annually).

Verkehrsmuseum (*Museum of Transport*): 801 Dresden, Augustusstrasse 1; f. 1952; library of 16,000 vols.; Dir. Dr. Ing. CHRISTA GÄRTNER.

GÖRLITZ

Oberlausitzische Bibliothek der Wissenschaften bei den Städtischen Kunstsammlungen Görlitz: Neiss Str. 30; f. 1950 (original library 1779); scientific, historical and general library including rare book collection; 100,000 vols.; Librarian ANNEROSE KLAMMT.

GOTHA

Museen der Stadt Gotha: Dir. H. WIEGAND; comprise:

Museum für Regionalgeschichte und Volkskunde: Schloss Friedenstein; exhibition of local history, with *Ekhof-Theater* (baroque theatre); publ. *Abhandlungen und Berichte zur Regionalgeschichte*.

Schlossmuseum: Schloss Friedenstein; art collections, historical rooms, coin collections, Egyptological exhibition.

Museum der Natur: Parkallee 15; animal and mineral exhibitions, with exhibition of local natural history; publ. *Abhandlungen und Berichte des Museums der Natur, Gotha*.

Gedenkstätte: Gothaer Parteitag 1875: Strasse der Pariser Kommune; historical exhibition of the labour movement.

HALLE

Landesmuseum für Vorgeschichte (*Prehistory Museum*): Richard-Wagner-Str. 9/10; f. 1823; pre- and medieval history; library of 30,000 vols.; Dir. Dr. HERMANN BEHRENS; publs. *Jahresschrift für mitteldeutsche Vorgeschichte* (annual), *Veröffentlichungen*†.

JENA

Goethe-Gedenkstätte (im Inspektorhaus des Botanischen Gartens): Goetheallee 26; f. 1921, revived 1965; Admin. Friedrich-Schiller-Universität, Kustodie.

Optisches Museum der Carl-Zeiss-Stiftung: 69 Jena, Am Planetarium 7; f. 1965; history of optical instruments; Dir. (vacant).

Schiller-Gedenkstätte (Schillerhäuschen und -garten): Schillergasschen 2; f. 1924; biographical and literary museum; Admin. Friedrich-Schiller-Universität, Kustodie.

Stadtmuseum Jena: Am Planetarium 12; Dir. MARIA SCHMID.

LEIPZIG

Deutsches Buch- und Schriftmuseum der Deutschen Bücherei (*German Book Museum*): 7010 Deutscher Platz; f. 1884; exhibits relate to history of books, writing and paper; library of *c.* 83,800 vols.; Dir. Dr. FRITZ FUNKE.

Georgi-Dimitroff-Museum: 701, Georgi-Dimitroff-Platz 1; f. 1952, reorganized 1965; history of the international working-class movement with regard to Georgi Dimitroff, special collection of posters and newspaper cuttings; library of 50,000 vols.; Prof. HANS-JOACHIM BERNHARD; publ. *Schriftenreihe des Georgi-Dimitroff-Museums*†.

Museum der Bildenden Künste: 701 Leipzig, Georgi-Dimitroff-Platz 1; f. 1837; Dir. Prof. Dr. GERHARD WINKLER; Curators K.-H. MEHNERT (graphics), Dr. SUSANNE HEILAND (paintings and sculpture).

Museum für Völkerkunde Leipzig, Staatliche Forschungsstelle (*Ethnographical Museum and State Research Centre*): 701 Leipzig, Täubchenweg 2; f. 1869; ethnographical collections from Asia, Pacific Islands, Africa, America, Europe; library of 60,000 vols.; Dir. Dr. LOTHAR STEIN; publs. *Jahrbuch* (Year Book), *Veröffentlichungen* (Publications), *Mitteilungen*.

Museum für Geschichte der Stadt Leipzig: Altes Rathaus, 7010 Leipzig, Markt 1; f. 1909; 45,000 items; publ. *Jahrbuch zur Geschichte der Stadt Leipzig*.

Museum des Kunsthandwerks Leipzig Grassi-Museum (*Museum of Industrial Art*): Johannisplatz; f. 1874; textiles, ceramics, glass, wood, and metal objects; collection of etchings and woodcuts relating to ornament (*c.* 1,100 prints); library of 23,000 vols.; Dir. Dr. FRITZ KÄMPFER; Keeper Dr. ANNELIESE HANISCH.

MAGDEBURG

Kulturhistorisches Museum: Otto von Guerickestr. 68-73; f. 1892; art gallery, sculptures, handicrafts, graphics, bibliophilia, costumes, sociology, natural history and prehistory collection and technological museum; library of 50,000 vols.; Dir. GÜNTER LANGE; publs. *Abhandlungen und Berichte Naturkunde und Vorgeschichte, Kataloge der Sonderausstellungen der Abteilungen Kunst und Stadtgeschichte*.

POTSDAM

Museum für Ur- und Frühgeschichte (*Pre- and Early History*): Forschungsstelle für die Bezirke Potsdam, Frankfurt/O. und Cottbus, DDR-1502 Potsdam-Babelsberg, Schloss Babelsberg; f. 1953; Dir. Dr. B. GRAMSCH; publ. *Veröffentlichungen des Museums für Ur- und Frühgeschichte Potsdam*† (annually).

SCHWERIN

Museum für Ur- und Frühgeschichte (Forschungsstelle): 27 Schwerin, Schloss; f. 1953; library of 11,500 vols.; Dir. Prof. Dr. EWALD SCHULDT; publs. *Bodendenkmalpflege in Mecklenburg Jahrbuch*†, *Beiträge zur Ur- und Frühgeschichte der Bezirke Rostock, Schwerin und Neubrandenburg*†, *Bild- und Ausstellungskataloge*† (annually).

STRALSUND

Kulturhistorisches Museum Stralsund: Mönchstr. 25–27; f. 1858; prehistory, ecclesiastical art, folklore, local history, furniture, history of navigation, modern art, handicrafts, 18th-century products; Dir. Dipl. phil. PETER HERFERT.

53 WEIMAR

Kunstsammlungen zu Weimar: Burgplatz 4; f. 1809 by Goethe; Dir. L. HONIGMANN-ZINSERLING; comprises: (1) Schlossmuseum; (2) Graphische Sammlung; (3) Kunstbibliothek; (4) Rokokomuseum Belvedere; (5) Münzkabinett; (6) Kunsthalle am Theaterplatz.

Museum für Ur- und Frühgeschichte Thüringens in Weimar: Humboldtstr. 11; f. 1888; Dir. Dr. habil. RUDOLF FEUSTEL; publs. *Jahresschrift "Alt-Thüringen"*†, *Veröffentlichungen*†, *Weimarer Monographien zur Ur- und Frühgeschichte*†, *Restaurierung und Museumstechnik*†, *Urgeschichte und Heimatforschung*†.

Nationale Forschungs- und Gedenkstätten der klassischen deutschen Literatur in Weimar: Am Burgplatz 4; Gen. Dir. Prof. Dr. WALTER DIETZE; directs the following:

Goethe- und Schiller-Archiv: Hans-Wahl-Str. 4; 800,000 MSS. of German writers; Dir. Prof. Dr. K.-H. HAHN.

Goethe-Nationalmuseum: Am Frauenplan; Goethehaus; Goethemuseum; Goethes Gartenhaus; Schillerhaus; Kirms-Krackow-Haus; Wittumspalais; Goethe- und Schiller-Gruft; Schloss Tiefurt; Dornburger Schlösser; Schloss Kochberg; Jagdhaus Gabelbach; Goethehaus Stützerbach; Römisches Haus; Lisztnaus; Wielandgut Ossmannstedt; Schillerhaus Bauerbach; Dir. Dr. D. ECKARDT.

Zentralbibliothek der deutschen Klassik: Platz der Demokratie; Dir. Dr. H. HENNING.

Institut für klassische deutscher Literatur: Am Burgplatz 4; Dir. Prof. Dr. H.-D. DAHNKE.

Direktion Öffentlichkeitsarbeit: Frauentorstrasse; Dir. Stud.-R. M. KAHLER.

Direktion Bau und Denkmalpflege: Am Burgplatz 4; Dir. Dr. J. SEIFERT.

Direktion Gärten und Parke: Am Burgplatz 4, Dir. Dipl.-Gartenarch. J. JÄGER.

Direktion Verwaltung und Werkstätten: Am Burgplatz 4; Dir. J. STILL.

WITTENBERG

Lutherhalle, Reformationsgeschichtliches Museum (*History of the Reformation Museum*): DDR-46-Lutherstadt Wittenberg, Collegienstr. 54; f. 1883; portraits, MSS., pictures, woodcuts, copperplates, medallions and original works on the history of the Reformation; library of *c.* 12,000 vols.; Dir. ELFRIEDE STARKE.

UNIVERSITIES

HUMBOLDT-UNIVERSITÄT ZU BERLIN

1086 BERLIN
UNTER DEN LINDEN 6
Telephone: 2030.

Founded 1809.

State control; Academic year: October–February, March–July.

Rector: Prof. Dr. Dr. h.c. HELMUT KLEIN.

Pro-Rectors: Prof. Dr. WILLI EHLERT, Prof. Dr. JOACHIM AUTH (Natural Sciences), Prof. Dr. DIETER KLEIN (Social Sciences), Prof. Dr. SIEGFRIED SCHWAHNKE (Education).

Library: *see* Libraries.

Number of teachers: *c.* 5,000.

Number of students: *c.* 12,000; also 7,000 external students.

Publication: *Wissenschaftliche Zeitschrift.*

DIRECTORS OF DEPARTMENTS:

Marxism-Leninism: Prof. Dr. H. ZAPF.
Theory and Organization of Science: Prof. Dr. SCHULZE.
Foreign Languages: Dr. HELGA WÜSTENECK.
Physical Education: Prof. Dr. A. HUNOLD.
Mathematics: Prof. Dr. H. FRANK.
Physics: Prof. Dr. R. ENDERLEIN.
Chemistry: Prof. Dr. L. KOLDITZ.
Biology: Prof. Dr. B. GÖRING.
Geography: Prof. Dr. A. ZIMM.
Animal Husbandry and Veterinary Medicine: Prof. Dr. D. LÖTSCH.
Nutrition and Food Technology: Prof. Dr. E. MANZKE.
Horticulture: Prof. Dr. KRAMER.
Plant Production: Prof. Dr. W. BREUNIG.
Psychology: Prof. Dr. F. KLIX.
Marxist-Leninist Philosophy: Prof. Dr. F. KUMPF.
History: Prof. Dr. E. NICKEL.
Law: Prof. Dr. E. BUCHHOLZ.
Criminology: Prof. Dr. E. STELZER.
Economics: Prof. Dr. W. EHLERT.
Education: Prof. Dr. E. MÄDICKE.
Rehabilitation and Communications Science: Prof. Dr. K.-P. BECKER.
Germanic Studies: Prof. Dr. P. HERDEN.
Aesthetics and Arts: Prof. Dr. H. OLBRICH.
Asian Studies: Prof. Dr. D. WEIDEMANN.
Medicine: Prof. Dr. R. SCHORR.
Faculty of Theology: Prof. Dr. K.-H. BERNHARDT (Dean).
Electronics: Prof. Dr. H. WARNKE.
American, English and Romance Studies: Prof. Dr. H.-D. PAUFLER.
Slavonic Studies: Prof. Dr. M. JÄHNICHEN.
Institute of Library Science and Scientific Information: Prof. Dr. H. KUBITSCHEK.
Control and Computer Centre (ORZ): Prof. Dr. B. WENZLAFF.
Institute of Higher Education: Prof. Dr. H.-G. SCHULZ.
Natural Science Museum: Prof. Dr. HOPPE.

TECHNISCHE UNIVERSITÄT DRESDEN

8027 DRESDEN,
MOMMSENSTRASSE 13
Telephone: Dresden 463 4312.

Founded 1828, University status 1961.

Rector: Prof. Dr. RUDOLF KNÖNER.

Pro-Rectors: Prof. Dr. FRITZ DEUMLICH, Prof. Dr. HERMANN PLANKENBICHLER (Education), Prof. Dr. WERNER LOTZE (Natural Sciences and Engineering), Prof. Dr. MARTIN RUHNOW (Social Sciences).

Library: *see* Libraries.

Number of teachers: 2,700.

Number of students: 9,400 and 2,200 external students.

Publication: *Wissenschaftliche Zeitschrift.*

DEANS:

Faculty of Social Sciences: Prof. Dr. GERHARD SPEER.
Faculty of Natural Sciences and Mathematics: Prof. Dr. KLAUS SCHWETLIK.
Faculty of Electrical Engineering and Electronics: Prof. Dr. WOLFGANG MOSCH.
Faculty of Mechanical Engineering: Prof. Dr. WERNER SCHATT.
Faculty of Civil Engineering, Hydraulics and Forestry: Prof. Dr. GÜNTER RICKENSTORF.

DIRECTORS OF DEPARTMENTS:

Marxism-Leninism: Prof. Dr. GÜNTER SCHNEIDER.
Philosophy and the Humanities: Prof. Dr. LOTHAR STRIEBING.
Teacher Training at Vocational Schools: Prof. Dr. HORST REIBETANZ.
Socialist Industrial Management: Prof. Dr. WOLFGANG HEYDE.
Physics: (vacant).
Chemistry: Prof. Dr. Dr. WINFRIED PIPPEL.
Mathematics: Prof. Dr. KARL-HEINZ KÖRBER.
Data Processing: Prof. Dr. DIETRICH SCHUBERT.
Information Techniques: Prof. Dr. PETER VIELHAUER.
Electronics and Precision Apparatus Engineering: Prof. Dr. DIETER STÜNDEL.
Electrical Engineering: Prof. Dr. HARRY CONRAD.
Energy Transformation: Prof. Dr. ERNST ADAM.
Basic Mechanical Engineering: Prof. Dr. KURT LUCK.
Production Techniques and Machine Tools: Prof. Dr. WOLFGANG ROCKSTROM.
Manufacturing and Processing Technology: Prof. Dr. EBERHARD HEIDENREICH.
Automotive, Agricultural and Transport Engineering: Prof. Dr. GÖTZ IHLE.
Construction Engineering: Prof. Dr. KARL THOMAS.
Architecture: Prof. Dr. KARL-HEINZ LANDER.
Surveying and Cartography: Prof. Dr. RUDI OGRISSEK.
Hydraulic Engineering: Prof. Dr. KARL-FRANZ BUSCH.
Forestry: Prof. Dr. HARALD THOMASIUS.
Labour Studies: Prof. Dr. FRIEDRICH MACHER.
Institute of Socialist Control of Economy: Prof. Dr. RUDI WEIDAUER.
Institute for Industry: Prof. Dr. KARL FRIEDRICH.
Computer Centre: Prof. Dr. HENRY STAHL.
Institute of Applied Linguistics: Dr. EDGAR BAUMANN.
Institute of Physical Education: Dr. ERHARD ECKERT.

ERNST-MORITZ-ARNDT-UNIVERSITÄT

2200 GREIFSWALD,
DOMSTRASSE 11
Telephone: 630.

Founded 1456.

Rector: Prof. Dr. Sc. nat. DIETER BIRNBAUM.

Pro-Rector: Prof. Dr. Sc. nat. GERHARD STEINICH.

Library: *see* Libraries.

Number of teachers: *c.* 140 professors.

Number of students: *c.* 3,000.

Departments of Philosophy, History, Fine Arts, Languages, Mathematics, Natural Sciences, Electronics, Medicine, Pharmacy, Geography, Geology, Marxism-Leninism, Music, Education, Physical Education, Theology.

Publications: *Wissenschaftliche Zeitschrift*†, *Gesellschafts- und sprachwissenschaftliche Reihe*†, *Mathematisch-Naturwissenschaftliche Reihe*† *Medizinische Reihe*†.

MARTIN LUTHER-UNIVERSITÄT HALLE-WITTENBERG

401 HALLE (SAALE), UNIVERSITÄTSPLATZ 10

Telephone: 8320.

Founded 1502 (Wittenberg), 1694 (Halle), 1817 (Halle-Wittenberg).

Rector: Prof. Dr. DIETER BERGNER.

Pro-Rector: Prof. Dr. JOSEF SCHUH.

Librarian: JOACHIM DIETZE.

Library: *see* Libraries.

Number of teachers: 345, including 188 Ordinary Professors.

Number of students: 8,642.

Publications: *Wissenschaftliche Zeitschrift der Martin-Luther-Universität* (monthly)†, *Hallesches Jahrbuch für Geowissenschaften*†, *Zeitschrift "Hercynia", Beiträge zur Erforschung und Pflege der naturlichen Ressourcen* (quarterly)†.

DEANS:

Faculty of Philosophy: WOLFGANG JAHN.
Faculty of Law and Economics: HANS SPILLER.
Faculty of Natural Sciences: LOTHAR REPPEL.
Faculty of Medicine: LEO ZETT.
Faculty of Agriculture: GEORG MÜLLER.

DIRECTORS OF DEPARTMENTS:

Marxism-Leninism: DIETRICH NOSKE.
Biological Sciences: HORST REINBOTHE.
Chemistry: MANFRED AUGUSTIN.
Education: ERNST GORNY.
Geography: ERWIN MÜCKE.
German and Arts Studies: EBERHARD STOCK.
History and Political Science: HANS HÜBNER.
Philosophy: REINHARD MOCEK.
Mathematics: WERNER WALSCH.
Medicine: HARALD AURICH.
Classical and Oriental Studies: HORST GERICKE.
Agriculture: WERNER ISBANER.
Pharmacy: LOTHAR REPPEL.
Physics: KURT STECKER.
Polytechnics: MARTIN KLEINAU.
Physical Education: GERHARD MÖSER.
Modern Languages and Literatures: HORST SCHMIDT.
Law: ROLF SCHÜSSELER.
Theology: GERHARD WALLIS.
Economics: HELMUT DIETRICH.

FRIEDRICH-SCHILLER-UNIVERSITÄT

69 JENA, GOETHEALLEE 1

Telephone: 820.

Founded 1548 as an academy; university status 1558. Language of instruction: German; Academic year: September to August.

Rector: Prof. Dr. sc.med. Dr.h.c. FRANZ BOLCK.

Pro-Rectors: Prof. Dr. H. KESSLER, Prof. Dr. M. WEGNER, Prof. Dr. D. UNANGST, Prof. Dr. H. O. SCHÜTZENMEISTER, Prof. Dr. H. BRAÜNLICH.

Librarian: Prof. Dr. L. BOHMÜLLER.

Library: *see* Libraries.

Number of teachers: 546.

Number of students: 5,355 (incl. 683 external students).

Publications: *Wissenschaftliche Zeitschrift*†, *Jenaer Reden und Schriften, Bibliographische Mitteilungen der Universitätsbibliothek Jena*†.

Section of Marxism-Leninism.
Section of Pedagogics.
Section of History.
Section of Literature and Arts.
Section of Marxist-Leninist Philosophy.
Section of Psychology.
Section of Physical Education.
Section of Languages and Philology.
Section of Law.
Section of Economics.
Section of Classical Studies and Archaeology.
Section of Biology.
Section of Chemistry.
Section of Mathematics.
Section of Physics.
Section of Instrument Technology.
Department of Medicine (*incl. Dentistry*)
Medical Care Training School.
Section of Theology (*Protestant*).
Computer Centre.

ATTACHED INSTITUTES:

Botanical Garden: *see under* Museums.

Ernst-Haeckel-Haus: history of medicine and natural science.

Schiller-Gedenkstätte: *see under* Museums.

Herbarium Haussknecht.

KARL-MARX-UNIVERSITÄT LEIPZIG

701 LEIPZIG, KARL-MARX-PLATZ

Telephone: 7190.

Founded 1409.

Rector: Prof. Dr. GERHARD WINKLER.

First Pro-Rector: Prof. Dr. STEIN.

Pro-Rector for Social Sciences: Prof. Dr. T. KIESSIG.

Pro-Rector for Scientific Development: Prof. Dr. S. HAUPTMANN.

Librarian: Dr. F. SCHAAF.

Library: *see* Libraries.

Number of teachers: *c.* 2,481, including 250 Professors.

Number of students: 14,818.

DEANS:

Faculty of Economics and Law: Prof. Dr. HEINZ SUCH.
Faculty of Philosophy and History: Prof. Dr. DIETER WITTICH.
Faculty of Culture, Languages and Education: Prof. Dr. GERHART HELBIG.
Faculty of Mathematics and Natural Sciences: Prof. Dr. H. PFEIFER.
Faculty of Medicine: Prof. Dr. JOACHIM WEISKOPF.
Faculty of Agriculture: Prof. Dr. GUNTHER GEBHARDT.

DIRECTORS:

Marxism-Leninism: Prof. Dr. H. NIEMANN.
Marxist-Leninist Philosophy and Scientific Communism: Prof. Dr. FRANK FIEDLER.
Economics: Prof. Dr. GERHARD TEUSLAU.
History: Prof. Dr. WERNER LOCH.
Law: Prof. Dr. R. HÄHNERT.
Pedagogics: Prof. Dr. G. DIETRICH.
Psychology: Prof. Dr. MANFRED VORWARK.
Journalism: Prof. Dr. E. DUSISKA.
Liberal Arts and German Studies: Prof. Dr. WILLI BEITZ.
Theoretical and Applied Linguistics: Prof. Dr. R. ECKERT.
African and Near Eastern Studies: Prof. Dr. MANFRED VOIGT.
Mathematics: Prof. Dr. HORST SCHUMANN.
Physics: Prof. Dr. WOLFGANG WINDSCH.
Chemistry: Prof. Dr. R. SCHÖLLNER.
Biological Sciences: Prof. Dr. ARMIN ERMISCH.
Animal Husbandry and Veterinary Medicine: Prof. Dr. HANS-JOACHIM SCHWARK.
Medicine: Prof. Dr. H. KÖHLER.
Theology: Prof. Dr. H. MORITZ.
Franz-Mehring Institute: Prof. Dr. G. HANDEL.
Institute of International Studies: Prof. Dr. W. POEGGEL.
Herder Institute: Prof. Dr. J. RÖSSLER.
Institute of Tropical Agriculture and Veterinary Medicine: Prof. Dr. G. FRÖHLICH.
Institute of Physical Education: W. KUPPER.

WILHELM-PIECK-UNIVERSITÄT ROSTOCK

25 ROSTOCK, UNIVERSITÄTSPLATZ

Telephone: 3690.

Founded 1419.

Rector: Prof. Dr. sc. phil. W. BRAUER.

Library Director: Dr. phil. K.-H. JÜGELT.

Library: *see* Libraries.

Number of teachers: 285.

Number of students: 6,060.

Publications: *Wissenschaftliche Zeitschrift, Ges.-Sprachwissenschaftliche Reihe, Math.-Naturwissenschaftliche Reihe, Semesterberichte der Sektion, Lateinamerikawissenschaften, Rostocker Phil. Manuskripte, Archiv der Naturfreunde Mecklenburgs, Rostocker Universitätsreden.*

DEPARTMENTS:

Technical Electronics.
Marine Engineering.
Mathematics.
Physics.
Chemistry.
Biology.
Animal Husbandry.
Agriculture.
Agricultural Techniques.
Latin American Studies.
History.
Linguistics and Literature.
Pedagogics and Psychology.
Social Industrial Management.
Marxism-Leninism.
Science of Physical Education.
Theology.
Medicine.

COLLEGES

‡ *Indicates that the College is of University standing*

AGRICULTURE

Hochschule für Landwirtschaft und Nahrungsgüterwirtschaft: 435 Bernburg/Saale, Mitschurinstr. 48; f. 1961; Rector Prof. Dr. PHILIP KIRIAN.

Hochschule für Landwirtschaftliche Produktionsgenossenschaften: Freiheit 13, 825 Meissen.

ARTS, ARCHITECTURE

Hochschule für Bildende Künste: Günzstrasse 34, 8016 Dresden A 16.

Hochschule für Film und Fernsehen der DDR (*College of Cinematography and Television of the GDR*): 1502 Potsdam-Babelsberg, Karl-Marx-Strasse 27; f. 1954; Rector PETER ULBRICH; Vice-Chancellor Dr. MANFRED GERBING; 90 lecturers, 250 students; library of 80,000 vols.; publs. *FWB* (*Filmwissenschaftliche Beiträge*) (2 a year), *Annual Report on Film Biography*.

Hochschule für Grafik und Buchkunst in Leipzig (*State Academy of Graphic Arts and Book Production*): 701 Leipzig C.1, Dimitroffstr. 11; f. 1764; Rector Prof. BERNHARD HEISIG.

Kunsthochschule Berlin: 112 Berlin, Strasse 203 Nr. 20.

Theaterhochschule "Hans Otto", Leipzig: 7010 Leipzig, Schwagrichenstr. 3; f. 1953; drama, choreography, theatre management; information and documentation on theatre development; 40 teachers, 210 students; Rector Prof. Dr. ROLF ROHMER; publ. *Theaterwissenschaftlicher Informationsdienst*†.

ECONOMICS, POLITICAL AND SOCIAL SCIENCES, PUBLIC ADMINISTRATION

‡**Akademie für Staats- und Rechtswissenschaft der DDR:** 1502 Potsdam-Babelsberg, August-Bebel-Str. 89; f. 1948; library: *see* Libraries; Rector Prof. Dr. G. SCHÜSSLER; publs. *Staat und Recht, Deutsche Aussenpolitik, Organisation, Spezialbibliographien, Bibliographien und Referateblätter Staat und Recht, Schriftenreihe Aktuelle Beiträge der Staats- und Rechtswissenschaft.*

Institut für Internationale Beziehungen an der Akademie für Staats- und Rechtswissenschaft der DDR (*Institute for International Relations*): 1502 Potsdam-Babelsberg, August-Bebel-Str. 89; f. 1964; research and training in international law and international relations; Dir. Prof. Dr. STEFAN DOERNBERG; publs. *Jahrbuch Internationale Politik und Wirtschaft* (annually), *Deutsche Aussenpolitik* (monthly), *Bibliographie Völkerrecht und internationale Beziehungen, Blickpunkt Weltpolitik* (5–7 a year).

Hochschule für Ökonomie "Bruno Leuschner", Berlin: 1157 Berlin, Hermann-Duncker-Str. 8; f. 1950; library of 200,000 vols.; Rector Prof. Dr. sc. R. SIEBER; publ. *Wissenschaftliche Zeitschrift*† (quarterly).

MEDICINE

‡**Medizinische Akademie "Carl Gustav Carus" Dresden:** 8019 Dresden, Fetscherstrasse 74; f. 1954; 29 teachers, 1,237 students.

Rector: Prof. Dr. sc. med. H. G. KNOCH.
Pro-Rector: Doz. Dr. sc. med. K. KÖHLER.
Registrar: Dipl. jur. H. SCHWARZENBERG.
Librarian: Dipl.-Phil. W. PRASSE.

‡**Medizinische Akademie Erfurt:** 5060 Erfurt, Nordhäuser Str. 74; f. 1954; 62 teachers, 676 students.

Rector: Prof. Dr. W. USBECK.
Pro-Rector: Prof. Dr. W. SCHUNK.
Administrative Officer: Dipl.-Jur. oec. H. WEDERMANN.
Librarian: M. SAHR.

Library of 70,000 vols.

‡**Medizinische Akademie Magdeburg:** 3090 Magdeburg, Leipziger Str. 44; f. 1954; 38 teachers, 600 students.

Rector: Prof. Dr. R. D. KOCH.
Pro-Rectors: Prof. Dr. H. WALTHER, Dr. HEINZ GAHSE.

MUSIC

Hochschule für Musik "Hanns Eisler": 108 Berlin, Otto-Grotewohl-Str. 19; f. 1950; Rector Prof. DIETER ZECHLIN; departments of composition, conducting, production, opera, orchestra and choir school.

Hochschule für Musik "Carl Maria von Weber" Dresden: 801 Dresden, Blochmannstrasse 2/4; f. 1856; Rector Prof. Dr. sc. S. KÖHLER; Pro-Rectors Dr. D. JAHN, Dr. G. STEPHAN, Prof. G. BERGE; 250 teachers, 700 students.

Hochschule für Musik "Franz Liszt": 53 Weimar, Platz der Demokratie; f. 1872; 600 students, 200 teachers; library of 60,000 vols. and 45,000 tapes; Rector Prof. Dr. H. R. JUNG; Pro-Rectors Prof. Dr. E. HARTWIG, Prof. Dr. H. SLOMMA, Prof. K. HÜBENTHAL; Admin. Dir. G. ROKOSCH; instruction in: keyboard, string and wind instruments, accordion, guitar, conducting, singing and music teaching; advanced classes in composition and violin.

Hochschule für Musik "Felix Mendelssohn Bartholdy" Leipzig: Leipzig 701, Grassistr. 8; f. 1843; Rector Prof. GUSTAV SCHMAHL.

TECHNOLOGY

‡**Bergakademie Freiberg:** 92 Freiberg, Akademiestr. 6; mathematics, natural sciences, mining, metallurgy and engineering economics; 800 teachers, 2,500 students; library: *see* Libraries; Rector Prof. K. STRZODKA; publ. *Freiberger Forschungshefte.*

‡**Hochschule für Architektur und Bauwesen Weimar:** 53 Weimar, Geschwister-Scholl-Str. 8; f. 1860.

Rector: Prof. Dr. h.c. KARL-ALBERT FUCHS.
Pro-Rectors: Prof. Dr. paed. ROLF FRITSCH, Prof. Dr. rer. oec. ERICH MARTH, Prof. Dr. Ing. HANS GLISSMEYER, Prof. Dr.-Ing. habil. FRITZ HENNECKE.
Librarian: Dr. phil. JOHANNES SCHILD.

Number of teachers: 334; students: 1,969.

Publication: *Wissenschaftliche Zeitschrift*† (6 a year).

DEANS:

Faculty of Building Engineering: Prof. Dr.-Ing. WILHELM WÖLFEL.
Faculty of Natural Sciences/Methodology: Prof. Dr. rer. nat. habil. OTTO HENNING.

Hochschule für Industrielle Formgestaltung Halle: Burg Giebichenstein, 402 Halle/Saale.

‡**Hochschule für Verkehrswesen "Friedrich List" Dresden:** 801 Dresden, Friedrich-List-Platz; f. 1952.

Rector magnificus: Prof. Dr.-Ing. EDGAR MEIER.
Librarian: Dr.-Ing. HELMUT ZESEWITZ.

Ingenieurhochschule Cottbus: 75 Cottbus, Sielower Str. 10; f. 1969; 50 teachers, 1,500 students; library of 70,000 vols., 932 periodicals, 50,000 patents and standards; Rector Prof. Dr. Ing. H. PRÄSSLER; publs. *Wissenschaftliche Zeitschrift, Informationen f.d. Leiter des Bauwesens* (2 a month), *Kennzahlen, Daten, Fakten* (twice annually).

‡Technische Hochschule Karl-Marx-Stadt: 9001 Karl-Marx-Stadt, Strasse der Nationen 62; f. 1836.

Rector: Prof. Dr. H. WEBER.
Vice-Rector: Prof. Dr. H. BRENDEL.
Vice-Rector (Science): Prof. Dr. F. KUHNERT.
Vice-Rector (Training and Education): Dr. A. BOITZ.
Vice-Rector (Social Sciences): Prof. Dr. E. JOBST.
Librarian: Dr. D. SCHEFFEL.

Library: *see* Libraries.

DIRECTORS:

Department of Marxism-Leninism: Dr. H. MEYER.
Department of Economics: Dr. U. HOFFMANN.
Department of Teacher Training: Prof. CH. BÜHRDEL.
Department of Foreign Languages: Prof. Dr. G. FISCHER.
Department of Mathematics: Prof. Dr. V. FRIEDRICH.
Department of Physics and Electronic Components: Prof. Dr. C. HAMANN.
Department of Metal-cutting and Metal-forming Manufacturing Processes and Machinery: Prof. Dr. E. HERLING.
Department of Textile and Leather Engineering: Prof. Dr. H. VIETH.
Department of Processing Technology: Prof. Dr. H. AURICH.
Department of Automation Technology: Prof. Dr. P.-K. BUDIG.
Department of Information Technology: Prof. Dr. M. KRAUSS.
Department of Chemistry and Materials Technology: Prof. Dr. G. MARX.
Department of Metal Production Engineering: Dr. WOLF.
Department of Data Processing and Computer Technology: Dr. K. MÄTZEL.
Department of Machine Elements: Prof. Dr. J. HEYMANN.
Institute of Socialist Economic Management: Prof. Dr. K. LEITERT.

‡Technische Hochschule Ilmenau: 6300 Ilmenau, P.O.B. 327; f. 1953.

Rector: Prof. Dr.-Ing. GERHARD LINNEMANN.
Pro-Rector: Prof. Dr. jur. habil. Ing. FELIX WEBER.

Library: *see* Libraries.

Number of teachers: 127.
Number of students: 2,231.

Publications: *Wiss. Zeitschrift der T.H.I.*†, *Tagungsberichte über das alljährliche Internationale Wissenschaftliche Kolloquium der T.H.I.*†, *Information/Dokumentation*†.

DEANS:

Faculty of Social Sciences: Prof. Dr. sc. oec. ERICH GLÄSER.
Faculty of Technology: Prof. Dr. sc. techn. EBERHARD FORTH.
Faculty of Mathematics and Natural Sciences: Prof. Dr. rer. nat. habil. JOHANNES VOGEL.

‡Technische Hochschule Leipzig: 7030 Leipzig, Karl-Liebknecht-Strasse 132; f. 1977 (fmrly. Hochschule für Bauwesen); 4-year or 4 half-year degree courses in all branches of science and technology.

Rector: Prof. dr. sc. techn. WOLFGANG ALTNER.
Pro-Rector: Prof. Dr. jur. JOHANNES WIESSFLOG.
Librarian: Dr. phil. GERHARD SCHRÖER.

Number of teachers: 65.
Number of students: 1,350.

Publication: *Wissenschaftliche Zeitschrift*† (6 a year).

‡Technische Hochschule Otto von Guericke Magdeburg: 3010 Magdeburg, Boleslaw-Bieurt-Platz 5, Pf. 124; f. 1953.

Rector: Prof. Dr. REINHARD PROBST.
Pro-Rector: Prof. Dr. UDO FISCHER.

Library of 150,000 vols.
Number of teachers: 140.
Number of students: 5,000 (inc. 1,500 external).

Publication: *Wissenschaftliche Zeitschrift*† (8 a year).

‡Technische Hochschule "Carl Schorlemmer" Leuna-Merseburg: 42 Merseburg, Geusaer Str.; f. 1954; depts. of Marxism-Leninism, applied chemistry, engineering, economics, mathematics and data processing, social sciences, physics and materials engineering.

Rector: Prof. Dr.-Ing. habil. G. NAUE.
Pro-Rector: Prof. Dr. sc. oec. H. J. AUST.
Pro-Rector (Sociology): Prof. Dr. sc. oec. D. GRAICHEN.
Pro-Rector (Science and Technology): Prof. Dr. rer. nat. habil. H. BREMER.
Pro-Rector (Education): Prof. Dr. sc. nat. H. ERFURTH.
Librarian: R. MACK.

Number of teachers: 670.
Number of students: 3,900.

Publication: *Wissenschaftliche Zeitschrift* (quarterly).

FEDERAL REPUBLIC OF GERMANY

Population 61,322,000

ACADEMIES

Bayerische Akademie der Wissenschaften (*Bavarian Academy of Sciences*): Munich 22, Marstallplatz 8; f. 1759.

President: Prof. Dr. HERBERT FRANKE.

Secretaries for Philosophy and History: Prof. Dr. ANTON SPITALER, Prof. Dr. JOACHIM WERNER.

Secretaries for Mathematics and Natural Sciences: Prof. Dr. HANSJOCHEM AUTRUM, Prof. Dr. KARL STEIN.

MEMBERS:

Philosophy and History:

BECK, HANS-GEORG
BENGTSON, HERMANN
BISCHOFF, BERNHARD
BOCKELMANN, PAUL
BOESSNECK, JOACHIM
BORCHARDT, KNUT
BOSL, KARL
CLEMEN, WOLFGANG
DEMPF, ALOIS
EILERS, WILHELM
FIKENTSCHER, WOLFGANG
FRANKE, HERBERT
FRITZ, KURT VON
FROMM, HANS
FUHRMANN, HORST
GNEUSS, HELMUT
HOFFMANN, KARL
HOLTHUSEN, JOHANNES
HROUDA, BARTHEL
KAUFMANN, ARTHUR
KISSLING, HANS-JOACHIM
KOSSACK, GEORG
KRAUS, ANDREAS
KRETZENBACHER, LEOPOLD
KRINGS, HERMANN
KUNKEL, WOLFGANG
KUNZE, EMIL
LERCHE, PETER
LOEWENICH, WALTHER VON
MAURER, WILHELM
MEDICUS, DIETER
MÖLLER, HANS
MÖRSDORF, KLAUS
MÜLLER, HANS WOLFGANG
MÜLLER, THEODOR
MÜLLER-SEIDEL, WALTER
NÖRR, DIETER
NOYER-WEIDNER, ALFRED
PANNENBERG, WOLFHART
PETSCHOW, HERBERT
RAUPACH, HANS
RITTER, GERHARD
RUH, KURT
SAUERLÄNDER, WILLIBALD
SCHEFFCZYK, LEO
SCHMAUS, MICHAEL
SENGLE, FRIEDRICH
SPINDLER, MAX
SPITALER, ANTON
STEGMÜLLER, WOLFGANG
STIMM, HELMUT
STRAUBE, HELMUT
STRUNK, KLAUS A.
ULMER, EUGEN
VOGT, ERNST
WAGNER, FRITZ
WEIS, EBERHARD
WERNER, JOACHIM
WITTE, EBERHARD
ZANKER, PAUL
ZIEGLER, JOSEPH

Mathematics and Natural Sciences:

ANGENHEISTER, GUSTAV
AUMANN, GEORG
AUTRUM, HANSJOCHEM
BAUER, FRIEDRICH L.
BAUER, HEINZ
BETKE, KLAUS H.
BIERMANN, LUDWIG F. B.
BOPP, FRITZ
BRAUNITZER, GERHARD
BÜCHER, THEODOR
BÜDEL, JULIUS
BUTENANDT, ADOLF
DEHM, RICHARD
DUDEL, JOSEF
EHLERS, JÜRGEN
ERNST, THEODOR
FISCHER, ERNST OTTO
FLEISCHMANN, RUDOLF
FORST, AUGUST WILHELM
FREYBERG, BRUNO VON
FRISCH, KARL RITTER VON
GEIGER, RUDOLF
GRIGULL, ULRICH
HAGEDORN, HORST
HAUPT, OTTO
HESSE, GERHARD
HÜNIG, SIEGFRIED
HUISGEN, ROLF
JAGODZINSKI, HEINZ
KIPPENHAHN, RUDOLF
LANGE, OTTO L.
LENSE, JOSEF
LOUIS, HERBERT
LÜST, REIMAR
LUND, OTTO-ERICH
MAIER-LEIBNITZ, HEINZ
MAUCHER, ALBERT
MENZER, GEORG
MERXMÜLLER, HERMANN
MÖLLER, FRITZ
MOLLWO, ERICH
MÖSSBAUER, RUDOLF
NEUBER, HEINZ
NÖBELING, GEORG
NÖTH, HEINRICH
PLOOG, DETLEV
ROLLWAGEN, WALTER
SCHLAG, EDWARD
SCHLÜTER, ARNULF
SCHMIDT, HERMANN
SCHNEIDER, DIETRICH
SCHÜTTE, KURT
SCHWAB, GEORG-MARIA
SIGL, RUDOLF
SIZMANN, RUDOLF
STEIN, KARL
VOITLÄNDER, JÜRGEN
WELKER, HEINRICH
WELLMANN, PETER
ZACHTAU, HANS GEORG
ZANDER, JOSEF
ZIEGLER, HUBERT

Akademie der Wissenschaften in Göttingen (*Göttingen Academy of Sciences*): Gottingen, Theatrestr. 7; f. 1751.

President: Prof. Dr. JOSEF FLECKENSTEIN.

Vice-President: Prof. Dr. HANS HEINRICH VOIGT.

Secretary: Prof. HEINZ GEORG WAGNER.

Number of members: 243, incl. corresponding mems.

Publications: *Jahrbuch, Nachrichten, Abhandlungen, Göttingische Gelehrte Anzeigen.*

MEMBERS:

Philology and History:

ABEL, WILHELM.
ANDRESEN, CARL.
ARNDT, KARL.
BECHERT, HEINZ.
BLEICKEN, JOCHEN.
BORGER, RIEKELE.
BUEHLER, WINFRIED
CONZELMANN, HANS.
DIETRICH, ALBERT.
DREIER, RALF
DÜRR, ALFRED.
ERDMANN, KARL DIETRICH.
FLECKENSTEIN, JOSEF.
FLUME, WERNER
FRIEDRICH, WOLF-HARTMUT.
GROSS, WALTER H.
HAEBLER, CLAUS.
HAUCK, KARL.
HEIMPEL, HERMANN.
HEUSS, ALFRED.
HORN, RUDOLF.
HUBER, ERNST RUDOLF.
JANKUHN, HERBERT.
KASER, MAX.
KELLENBENZ, HERMANN.
KILLY, WALTHER.
KROESCHELL, KARL.
LAUER, REINHARD
LAUSBERG, HEINRICH.
LOHSE, EDUARD.
LORENZEN, PAUL.
MICHAELIS, KARL.
MOELLER, BERND.
MÖLK, ULRICH
NEUMANN, GÜNTER.
NEUMANN, HANS.
NÜRNBERGER, RICHARD.
PATZE, HANS.
PATZIG, GÜNTHER.
PLESSNER, HELMUTH.
RANKE, KURT.
SCHABRAM, HANS.
SCHAFFSTEIN, FRIEDRICH.
SCHEIBE, ERHARD.
SCHIEFFER, THEODOR.
SCHLACHTER, WOLFGANG.
SCHLESINGER, WALTER.
SCHÖNE, ALBRECHT.
SCHÖNE, WOLFGANG.
SCHÜTZEICHEL, RUDOLF.
SEHRT, ERNST THEODOR.
SMEND, RUDOLF.
SNELL, BRUNO.
STACKMANN, KARL.
WALDSCHMIDT, ERNST.
WENSKUS, REINHARD.
WESTENDORF, WOLFHART.
WIEACKER, FRANZ.
WOLPERS, THEODOR.
ZIMMERLI, WALTHER.

Mathematics and Physics:

BIRUKOW, GEORG.
BORCHERS, HANS-JÜRGEN.
BRETSCHNEIDER, HANS-JÜRGEN.
BROCKMANN, HANS.
CORRENS, CARL WILHELM.
CREMER, LOTHAR.
DEURING, MAX.
DRESCHER-KADEN, FRIEDRICH KARL.
EIGEN, MANFRED.
ELLENBERG, HEINZ.
FLAMMERSFELD. ARNOLD.
GLEMSER, OSKAR.
GOTTSCHALK, GERHARD.
GRAUERT, JOHANNES.
HAASEN, PETER.
HECKMANN, OTTO.
HEINZ, ERHARD.
HUND, FRIEDRICH.
INHOFFEN, HANS-HERLOFF.
JOST, WILHELM.
KERTZ, WALTER.
KIPPENHAHN, RUDOLF.
KLEMM, WILHELM.
KNESER, MARTIN.
KRAMER, KURT.
LENKEIT, WALTER.
LINZBACH, JOHANNES
LÜDERS, GERHART.
LÜTTKE, WOLFGANG.
MAAK, WILHELM.
MAGNUS, WILHELM.
MARTIN, HENNO.
MAYER, HERBERT.
MENSCHING, HORST.
MINNIGERODE, GUNTHER VON.
PIRSON, ANDRÉ.
POSER, HANS.

Raether, Heinz.
Schlegel, Hans-Günter.
Schmalzried, Hermann.
Schöllkopf, Ulrich.
Schroeder, Manfred Robert.
Siegel, Carl Ludwig.
Voigt, Erhard.
Voigt, Hans Heinrich.
von Weizsäcker, Carl Friedrich.
Wagner, Heinz Georg.
Wannagat, Ulrich.
Wedepohl, Karl Hans.
Weller, Albert.
Winkler, Helmut G. F.
Witt, Ernst.
Woermann, Emil.

Heidelberger Akademie der Wissenschaften (*Heidelberg Academy of Sciences*): 6900 Heidelberg 1, Karlstrasse 1, Pf. 102769; f. 1909.

President: Prof. Dr. Viktor Pöschl.

Secretary of the Mathematics and Natural Sciences Section: Prof. Dr. Dieter Puppe.

Secretary of the Philosophy and History Section: Prof. Dr. Peter Classen.

Akademie der Wissenschaften und der Literatur (*Academy of Sciences and Literature*): Mainz, Geschwister Scholl-str. 2; f. 1949.

President: Prof. Dr. Heinrich Otten.

Vice-President Mathematics and Natural Science Section: Prof. Dr. Dr. Gerhard Thews.

Vice-President Philosophy and Social Science Section: Prof. Dr. Wolfgang P. Schmid.

Vice-President Literature Section: Dieter Hoffmann.

Secretary-General: Dr. Günter Brenner.

Publications: *Jahrbuch, Abhandlungen, Forschungsreihen.*

Members:

Mathematics and Natural Sciences:

Ax, Peter.
Becker, Friedrich.
Bredt, Heinrich.
Dabelow, Adolf.
Deuring, Max.
Ehrenberg, Hans.
Erben, Heinrich Karl.
Gräff, Gernot.
Hachenberg, Otto.
Haupt, Otto.
Henn, Walter.
Inhoffen, Hans Herloff.
Jentschke, Willibald.
Jordan, Pascual.
Jung, Richard.
Justi, Eduard.
Klingenberg, Wilhelm.
Klöppel, Kurt.
Kuhn, Hans.
Lauer, Wilhelm.
Lautz, Günter.
Lenz, Widukind.
Lindauer, Martin.
Patat, Franz.
Rauh, Werner.
Reichardt, Werner.
Ringsdorf, Helmut.
Rohen, Johannes.
Seibold, Eugen.
Thews, Gerhard.
Wedepohl, Karl Hans.
Wezler, Karl.
Woermann, Emil.
Zahn, Rudolf.
Zimmer, Karl Gunter.

Philosophy and Social Science:

Bellen, Heinz.
Benzing, Johannes.
Bischoff, Karl.
Bittel, Kurt.
Born, Karl Erich.
Bräuer, Herbert.
Brunner, Otto.
Dahlmann, Hellfried.
Eggebrecht, Hans Heinrich.
Einem, Herbert von.
Funke, Gerhard.
Haussherr, Reiner.
Heitsch, Ernst.
Isele, Hellmut Georg.
Iserloh, Erwin.
Jedin, Hubert.
Kühn, Herbert.
Lange, Hermann.
Loos, Erich.
Mann, Gunter.
Müller, Gerhard.
Oppel, Horst.
Otten, Heinrich.
Rau, Wilhelm.
Schalk, Fritz.
Schieder, Theodor.
Schmid, Wolfgang P.
Schmitz, Arnold.
Schmölders, Günter.
Schröder, Werner.
Vogt, Joseph.
Zimmermann, Harald.
Zintzen, Clemens.

Literature:

Bender, Hans.
Borchers, Elisabeth.
Emrich, Wilhelm.
Fritz, Walter Helmut.
Härtling, Peter.
Hausmann, Manfred.
Heissenbüttel, Helmut.
Hillebrand, Bruno.
Hoffmann, Dieter.
Kessel, Martin.
Koch, Werner.
König, Barbara.
Leonhard, Kurt.
Meckel, Christoph.
Mehnert, Klaus.
Schirmbeck, Heinrich.
Schwedhelm, Karl.
Usinger, Fritz.
Vormweg, Heinrich.
Wellershoff, Dieter.
Wickert, Erwin.
Zeller, Bernhard.

Rheinisch-Westfälische Akademie der Wissenschaften (*Rheinland-Westphalia Academy of Sciences*): Düsseldorf, Palmenstrasse 16; f. 1950 (renamed 1970).

President: Prof. Dr. Franz Grosse-Brockhoff.

Vice-President and Secretary of Philosophical Section: Prof. D. Wilhelm Schneemelcher.

Secretary of Natural, Engineering and Economic Sciences Section: Prof. Dr. Werner Schreyer.

Managing Secretary: Prof. Dr. Gerhard Kegel.

Number of members: 138, corresponding 22.

Publications: *Sitzungsberichte, Abhandlungen, Jahresprogramm, Jahrbuch.*

Members:

Philosophical Section:

Dassmann, Ernst.
Dörrie, Heinrich.
Edel, Elmar.
Einem, Herbert von.
Esch, Arno.
Ewig, Eugen.
Fellerer, Karl Gustav.
Flume, Werner.
Goepper, Roger.
Gollwitzer, Heinz.
Hegel, Eduard.
Heissig, Walther.
Hermann, Siegfried.
Himmelmann, Nikolaus.
Hinck, Walter.
Höffner, Joseph Kardinal.
Honecker, Martin.
Hübinger, Paul Egon.
Hübner, Heinz.
Jedin, Hubert.
Kassel, Rudolf.
Kauffmann, Georg.
Kaufmann, Armin.
Kegel, Gerhard.
Klauser, Theodor.
Kluxen, Wolfgang.
Kötting, Bernhard.
Koselleck, Reinhart.
Landgrebe, Ludwig.
Lausberg, Heinrich.
Lewin, Bruno.
Luhmann, Niklas.
Menze, Clemens.
Merkelbach, Reinhold.
Mikat, Paul.
Narr, Karl J.
Niemöller, Klaus Wolfgang.
Önnerfors, Alf.
Ohly, Friedrich.
Otremba, Erich.
Petrikovits, Harald von.
Pieper, Josef.
Pöggeler, Otto.
Rengstorf, Karl Heinrich.
Rothe, Hans.
Rothschuh, Karl Eduard.
Schadewaldt, Hans.
Schalk, Fritz.
Schelsky, Helmut.
Scheuner, Ulrich.
Schieder, Theodor.
Schieffer, Theodor.
Schirmer, Walter Franz.
Schneemelcher, Wilhelm.
Schott, Rüdiger.
Seiler, Hansjakob.
Skalweit, Stephan.
Stern, Klaus
Stökl, Günther.
Straub, Johannes.
Untermann, Jürgen.
Weber, Wilhelm.
Wehr, Hans.
Weisgerber, Joh. Leo.
Wendland, Heinz-Dietrich.
Westermann, Harry.
Wiese und Kaiserswalda u Benno von.

Corresponding Members:

Beierwaltes, Werner.
Böckenförde, Ernst Wolfgang.
Conze, Werner.
Dihle, Albrecht.
Dinkler, Erich.
Grimm, Tilemann.
Holthusen, Johannes.
Kauffmann, Hans.
Lübbe, Hermann.
Nörr, Dieter.
Ratzinger, Joseph Kardinal.
Scholem, Gershom.
Weinrich, Harald.
Widengren, Geo.

Natural, Engineering, and Economic Sciences Section:

Albach, Horst.
Aschoff, Volker.
Bayer, Otto.
Becker, Friedrich.
Bogdandy, Ludwig von.
Bollenrath, Franz.
Breuer, Heinz.
Dettmering, Wilhelm.
Döring, Herbert.
Domenjoz, Robert.
Domke, Helmut.
Effert, Sven.
Eichhorn, Friedrich.
Engell, Hans-Jürgen.
Engl, Walter L.
Feinendegen, Ludwig E.
Fettweis, Alfred.
Flegler, Eugen.
Flohn, Hermann.
Fucks, Wilhelm.
Gärtner, Erwin.
Grosse-Brockhoff, Franz.
Grundmann, Ekkehard.
Hachenberg, Otto.
Hauss, Werner Heinrich.
Helferich, Burckhardt.
Hess, Benno.
Hirzebruch, Friedrich.
Jaenicke, Lothar.
Kick, Hermann.
Kneller, Eckart.
Knipping, Hugo Wilhelm.
Knoche, Karl F.

Krelle, Wilhelm.
Meixner, Josef.
Meyer-Schwickerath, Gerd.
Micheel, Fritz.
Mückenhausen, Eduard.
Müller, Claus.
Naumann, Alexander.
Paul, Wolfgang.
Peschl, Ernst.
Potthoff, Erich.
Priester, Wolfgang.
Quick, August Wilhelm.
Remmert, Rinhold.
Rensch, Bernhard.
Roik, Karlheinz.
Rollnik, Horst.
Schäfer, Harald.
Schenck, Günther Otto.
Schenck, Hermann.
Schmeisser, Martin.
Schmidt, Carl Gottfried.
Schmidt, Fritz A. F.
Schneider, Hans Karl.
Schreyer, Werner.
Schulten, Rudolf.
Schwartzkopff, Johann.
Steiner, Maximilian.
Straub, Joseph.
Vogel, Emanuel.
Wasserrab, Theodor.
Weizel, Walter.
Welte, Dietrich.
Wever, Franz.
Wicke, Ewald.
Wilke, Günther.
Winterhager, Helmut.
Zahn, Helmut.
Zenk, Meinhart H.
Zerna, Wolfgang.

Corresponding Members:

Danneel, Rolf.
Hermes, Hans.
Hlawka, Edmund.
Hubert, Franz.
Klaudy, Peter.
Klemm, Wilhelm.
Prigogine, Ilya.
Wijn, Henricus P. J.

Akademie der Künste (*Academy of Arts*): Berlin 21, Hanseatenweg 10; f. 1696.

President: Prof. Werner Düttmann.

Vice-President: Dr. Rudolf Hartung.

Number of members: 134, extraordinary 67, honorary 3.

Members:

Fine Arts:

Altenbourg, Gerhard.
Antes, Horst.
Bill, Max.
Camaro, Alexander.
Geiger, Rupprecht.
Goller, Bruno.
Graubner, Gotthard.
Grieshaber, H. A. P.
Hauser, Erich.
Heerich, Erwin.
Heiliger, Bernhard.
Höch, Hannah.
Hoflehner, Rudolf.
Janssen, Horst.
Kaus, Max.
Kirchner, Heinrich.
Koenig, Fritz.
Küchenmeister, Rainer.
Mack, Heinz.
Marcks, Gerhard.
Matschinsky-Denninghoff, Brigitte.
Muche, Georg.
Oelze, Richard.
Schultze, Bernard.
Schumacher, Emil.
Stadler, Toni.
Szymanski, Rolf.
Trökes, Heinz.
Wimmer, Hans.

Architecture:

Baumgarten, Paul.
Böhm, Gottfried.
Deilmann, Harald.
Despotopoulos, Jan.
Düttmann, Werner.
Fehling, Hermann.
Gutbrod, Rolf.
Guther, Max.
Hämer, Hardt-Waltherr.
Hermkes, Bernhard.
Hillebrecht, Rudolf.
Kammerer, Hans.
Leo, Ludwig.
Linde, Horst.
Moldenschardt, H. H.
Müller, Hans.
Mutschler, Carlfried.
Nestler, Paolo.
Oesterlen, Dieter.
Pfau, Bernhard.
Poelzig, Peter.
Posener, Julius.
Rossow, Walter.
Ruf, Sep.
Spengelin, Friedrich.
Wirsing, Werner.

Music:

Ahrens, Joseph.
Bialas, Günter.
Boulez, Pierre.
Chemin-Petit, Hans.
David, Johann Nepomuk.
Egk, Werner.
Einem, Gottfried von.
Fortner, Wolfgang.
Genzmer, Harald.
Höller, Karl.
Jarnach, Philipp.
Klebe, Giselher.
Liebermann, Rolf.
Ligeti, György.
Orff, Carl.
Pepping, Ernst.
Reimann, Aribert.
Reutter, Hermann.
Stockhausen, Karlheinz.
Stuckenschmidt, H. H.
Tal, Josef.
Vogel, Wladimir.
Yun, Isang.
Zemanhek, Heinz.

Literature:

Aichinger, Ilse.
Becker, Jürgen.
Bender, Hans.
Böll, Heinrich.
Canetti, Elias.
Goes, Albrecht.
Grass, Günter.
Härtling, Peter.
Hartung, Rudolf.
Hausmann, Manfred
Heissenbüttel, Helmut.
Hildesheimer, Wolfgang.
Höllerer, Walter.
Hohoff, Curt.
Holthusen, Hans Egon.
Huchel, Peter.
Jens, Walter.
Johnson, Uwe.
Kessel, Martin.
Kluge, Alexander.
Koeppen, Wolfgang.
Lenz, Siegfried.
Mayer, Hans.
Rinser, Luise.
Scholz, Hans.
Tumler, Franz.

Performing Arts:

Barlog, Boleslaw.
Becker, Maria.
Benrath, Martin.
Berger, Erna.
Bergner, Elisabeth.
Fischer-Dieskau, Dietrich.
Gobert, Boy.
Gsovsky, Tatjana.
Hasse, O. E.
Held, Martin.
Hinz, Werner.
Hoppe, Marianne.
Ivogün, Maria.
Lietzau, Hans.
Lindtberg, Leopold.
Mosheim, Grete.
Noelte, Rudolf.
Raeck, Kurt.
Rennert, Günther.
Rose, Jürgen.
Schellow, Erich.
Schmidt, Willi.
Schuh, Oscar Fritz.
Stroux, Karlheinz.
Wimmer, Maria.

Honorary Members:

Bloch, Ernst.
Reichhold, Henry H.
Schmidt-Rottluff, Karl.

LEARNED SOCIETIES

General

Stifterverband für die Deutsche Wissenschaft (*Donors Association for the Promotion of Sciences and Humanities in Germany*): 4300 Essen (Bredeney), Brucker Holt 56-60, Postfach 230 360; f. 1921; raises funds within the German business community and administers 72 trusts; capital of DM 102.7 million; runs a science service centre in Bonn-Bad Godesberg; 5,550 mems.; Pres. Dr. Hans-Helmut Kuhnke; Sec.-Gen. Dr. H. Niemeyer; publs. *Wirtschaft und Wissenchaft* (quarterly), *Materialien aus dem Stiftungszentrum, Materialien zur Bildungspolitik, FORUM Stifterverband, Arbeitsschriften Forschung und Entwicklung in der Wirtschaft, Schriftenreine zum Stiftungswesen, Vademecum Deutscher Lehr- und Forschungsstätten.*

Agriculture and Veterinary Science

Agrarsoziale Gesellschaft (ASG): 34 Göttingen, Kurze Geismarstr. 23–25; f. 1947; 396 mems., plus 151 corporate mems.; Pres. Dr. T. Tröscher; Dir. Prof. Dr. F. K. Riemann; publs. *Rundbrief der ASG, Schriftenreihe für landliche Sozialfragen, Materialsammlung der ASG, Arbeitsbericht der ASG, Kleine ASG-Reihe.*

Dachverband Wissenschaftlicher Gesellschaften der Agrar-, Forst-, Ernährungs-, Veterinär- und Umweltforschung e.V.: 8000 Munich 22, Bürkleinstr. 12; f. 1973; advancement and co-ordination of research; information; contacts; representation; 25 mems.; Pres. Prof. Dr. H. Haushofer; Man. Dir. G. Blank.

Deutsche Landwirtschafts-Gesellschaft (*German Agricultural Society*): D-6000 Frankfurt a.M., Zimmerweg 16, DLG-Haus; originally f. 1885, re-founded 1947; 12,000 mems.; Pres. Konrad Jacob; Dir. Hermann-Adolf Ihle; publs. *Mitteilungen der DLG, Archiv der DLG, Arbeiten der DLG, Das wirtschaftseigene Futter,*

Zeitschrift für Agrargeschichte und Agrarsoziologie, Zeitschrift für ausländische Landwirtschaft.

Deutsche Veterinärmedizinische Gesellschaft: 63 Giessen, Frankfurter Str. 85; f. 1952; 1,600 mems.; Pres. Prof. Dr. A. MAYR; Sec. Prof. Dr. H. GEISSLER; publ. *Kongressbericht* (every 2 years).

Deutscher Forstwirtschaftsrat e.V.: 5308 Rheinbach bei Bonn, Münstereifeler Strasse 19; Pres. Bürgermeister HANS-GEORG PRIMUS; Man. Forstoberrat PETER STAHL.

Verband Deutscher Landwirtschaftlicher Untersuchungs- und Forschungsanstalten e.V. (*Association of German Agricultural Research Institutes*): 6100 Darmstadt, Bismarckstrasse 41A; f. 1888; Pres. Prof. Dr. H. VETTER; publs. *Landwirtschaftliche Forschung* (annual vol.), *Handbuch der landwirtschaftlichen Versuchs- und Untersuchungsmethodik, Mitteilungen, Presseinformationen.*

ARCHITECTURE AND TOWN PLANNING

Deutscher Architekten- und Ingenieurverband e.V. (DAI): 5300 Bonn 2, Theaterplatz 2; f. 1871; 5,500 mems.; Chair. Ltd. Senatsrat Dipl.-Ing. J. DARGE; Dir. H. KUHLMEY; publ. *DAI-Verbandszeitschrift BAUKULTUR.*

Deutscher Verband für Wohnungswesen, Städtebau und Raumplanung e.V. (*German Federation for Housing and Planning*): 5 Köln-Mülheim, Wrangelstr. 12; f. 1946; independent research in housing, town and country planning; 1,300 mems.; library of 9,000 vols.; Pres. Senator a.D. ROLF SCHWEDLER, MD.B.; Sec.-Gen. Dr. HANS KAMPFFMEYER; publs. *Stadtbau-Informationen, Schrifttumsnachweis Bau-, Wohnungs- und Siedlungswesen, Dokumentation laufender und abgeschlossener Forschungsarbeiten*, etc.

Gesellschaft des Bauwesens e.V. (IRB): 6000 Frankfurt-am-Main 1, RKW-Haus, Gutleutstrasse 163–167.

Informationsverbundzentrum Raum und Bau der Fraunhofer-Gesellschaft (*Planning and Construction Information Centre*): 7000 Stuttgart 1, Silberburgstr. 119A; f. 1977; documentation on building, planning, architecture and civil engineering; standard and individual SDIs, bibliographies, data base services; library of *c.* 55,000 vols., research reports, standards, information on tests and licences; Dir. Dr.-Ing. W. WISSMANN; publs. *Schrifttum Bauwesen*†; *Schrifttum Raumordnung, Städtebau, Wohnungswesen*; *Kurzberichte aus der Bauforschung*† (all monthly), *Schrifttum Wohnungswesen/Wohnungswirtschaft* (quarterly), etc.

THE ARTS

Bayerische Akademie der Schönen Künste: 8 Munich 22, Max Joseph Platz 3; Pres. Prof. Dr.-Ing. GERD ALBERS; Gen. Sec. Dr. KARL SCHUMANN.

Deutsche Gesellschaft für Photographie e.V. (*German Society for Photography*): 5 Cologne 1, Neumarkt 49; f. 1951; 700 mems.; library of 4,000 books; Pres. Dr. HANS FRIDERICHS; Gen. Sec. GERT KOSHOFER.

Deutsche Mozart-Gesellschaft e.V. (*German Mozart Society*): 8900 Augsburg, Karlstr. 6/4; f. 1951; 2,000 mems.; Pres. Prof. Dr. E. VALENTIN; Sec. Dr. F. VON PHILIPP; publ. *Acta Mozartiana.*

Deutscher Komponisten-Verband e.V. (*German Composers' Association*): 1 Berlin 38, Bergengruenstrasse 28; f. 1954; 800 mems.; Pres. RAIMUND ROSENBERGER; Dir. MARIANNE AUGUSTIN.

Deutscher Verein für Kunstwissenschaft (*Society for the Study of German Art*): 1 Berlin 12 (Charlottenburg), Jebensstr. 1; f. 1908; 1,600 mems.; Chair. Prof. Dr. PETER BLOCH; publs. *Denkmäler deutscher Kunst, Zeitschrift, Schrifttum zur deutschen Kunst, Forschungen zur deutschen Kunstgeschichte.*

Gesellschaft für Neue Musik e.V. Mannheim: 68 Mannheim 1, N7, 13-15 c/o Musik-Heckel; f. 1963 to promote concerts of modern music and lectures; 400 mems.; Chair. Prof. HANS VOGT; Sec. Dr. CLAUS MEISSNER.

Institut für den Wissenschaftlichen Film (*Scientific Film Institute*): 3400 Göttingen, Nonnenstieg 72; f. 1956; 100 mems.; library of 5,500 films; Dir. Dr. H.-K. GALLE; Man. Dr. A. LUTHARDT; publs. *Forschungsfilm, Gesamtverzeichnis der wissenschaftlichen Filme, Encyclopaedia Cinematographica, Publikationen zu wissenschaftlichen Filmen, IWF aktuell.*

Kestner-Gesellschaft: 3000 Hanover 1, Warmbuechenstrasse 1; f. 1916; 4,000 mems.; activities concerned with the promotion of modern art; Pres. Dr. WOLFGANG WAGNER; Dir. Dr. CARL HAENLEIN.

Stiftung Preussischer Kulturbesitz (*Prussian Cultural Foundation*): c/o Staatliche Museen, 1000 Berlin 30, Stauffenbergstr. 41; f. 1961 to preserve and augment the Prussian cultural heritage; comprises the 14 state museums, the state library, the state Privy Archives, the Iberian-American Institute and the State Institute for Research in Music with the Museum for Musical Instruments; it is preparing to complete the Kulturforum in the Tiergarten district; Pres. Prof. Dr. WERNER KNOPP.

Verband Deutscher Kunsthistoriker e.V. (*Assn. of German Art Historians*): f. 1948; Pres. Prof. Dr. DIETRICH ELLGER; Sec. Dr. HILDA LIETZMANN, 8000 Munich 40, Bauerstr. 12.

BIBLIOGRAPHY, LIBRARY SCIENCE AND MUSEOLOGY

Arbeitsgemeinschaft der Spezialbibliotheken e.V.: c/o Senckenbergische Bibliothek, Bockenheimer Landstr. 135, D-6 Frankfurt a.M.; f. 1946; service to specialized libraries; 350 mems.; Pres. (vacant); publs. *Arbeitsgemeinschaft der Spezialbibliotheken* (every 2 years), reports.

Deutsches Bibliotheksinstitut: 1000 Berlin 31, Bundesallee 184/185; f. 1978; provides services, research publs. and advanced training for librarians; Dir. Prof. GÜNTER BEYERSDORFF; publs. *Bibliotheksdienst*† (monthly), *dbi—materialien* (irregular).

Deutsche Gesellschaft für Dokumentation e.V.: 6000 Frankfurt a.M. 1, Westendstr. 19; f. 1948; promotion of information and documentation, information science and practice; 850 mems.; Pres. Prof. PETER CANISIUS; publs. *Nachrichten für Dokumentation*† (5 a year), *Internationale Aufgaben der DGD*† (10 a year).

Deutscher Museumsbund, e.V. (*German Museums Association*): 6000 Frankfurt a.M., Senckenberg-Anlage 25; f. 1906; to promote museums, their development and museology; 600 mems.; Pres. Dr. W. KLAUSEWITZ; Sec. Dr. G. GALL; publ *Museumskunde* (3 a year).

Internationale Vereinigung der Musikbibliotheken (AIBM) Deutsche Gruppe BRD (*International Assn. of Music Libraries, F.R.G. Branch*): Universität Bremen, Postfach 330160, 28 Bremen 33; f. 1952; 183 mems.; Pres. Prof. Dr. WOLFGANG KRUEGER; Sec.-Gen. BRIGITTE KOHL.

Leitstelle Politische Dokumentation, Freie Universität Berlin (*Political Documentation Clearing-house*): 1 Berlin 45, Paulinenstr. 22; f. 1965; collates political information from *c.* 200 German-language publications, reports research in progress, information and documentation activities in politics and political science; Dir. Prof. Dr. WALTER KRUMHOLZ; publs. *Politische Dokumentation, Politikwissenschaftliche Forschung.*

Verein Deutscher Bibliothekare e.V.: Universitätsbibliothek Stuttgart, Holzgartenstr. 16, 7000 Stuttgart 1; f. 1900, re-f. 1948; Pres. JÜRGEN HERING; Sec. EBERHARD ZWINK; publs. *Zeitschrift für Bibliothekswesen* *und Bibliographie, Jahrbuch der Deutschen Bibliotheken.*

Württembergische Bibliotheksgesellschaft (*Society of Friends of the Württemberg State Library*): 7000 Stuttgart 1, Konrad-Adenauer-Strasse 8; f. 1946 to support the reconstruction of the Wurttemberg State Library, to hold lectures, meetings, exhibitions, etc.; 700 mems.; Pres. Prof. Dr. JOSEF EBERLE; Chair. WILHELM HOFFMANN, PH.D.; Sec. (vacant).

ECONOMICS, LAW AND POLITICS

Akademie für Führungskräfte der Wirtschaft e.V. (*Academy for Leadership Studies in Economics*): 3388 Bad Harzburg 1, Amsbergstr. 9A; f. 1956, independent 1976; Pres. Prof. Dr. KARL MARTIN BOLTE; Dir. Prof. Dr. REINHARD HÖHN.

Akademie für Fernstudium e.V. (*Academy for Distance Study*): 3388 Bad Harzburg 1, An den Weiden 15; f. 1961, independent 1975; Pres. Prof. Dr. REINHARD HÖHN; Dir. GISELA BÖHME.

Deutsche Gesellschaft für Auswärtige Politik e.V. (*German Society for Foreign Affairs*): 53 Bonn, Adenauerallee 133; f. 1955; 1,100 mems.; discusses and promotes research on problems of international politics; research library of 30,000 vols.; Pres. Dr. Dr. h.c. KURT BIRRENBACH; Exec. Vice-Pres. Dr. GEBHARDT VON WALTHER; Dir. Research Institute, Prof. Dr. KARL KAISER; publs. *Die Internationale Politik* (yearbook), *Europa-Archiv—Zeitschrift für internationale Politik* (fortnightly).

Deutsche Gesellschaft für Betriebswirtschaft e.V. (*Industrial Administration*): 1000 Berlin 30, Rankestr. 23; f. 1936; 600 mems.; Pres. Prof. Dr.-Ing. HANS BLOHM; Dir. Dipl.-Betriebswirt Dr. GERHARD KOCH; publ. *Report* (monthly).

Deutsche Gesellschaft für Osteuropakunde e.V. (*German Society for Eastern European Studies*): 1 Berlin 15, Schaperstr. 30; f. 1913; 700 mems.; Pres. OTTO WOLFF VON AMERONGEN; Dir. Dr. jur. ERNST VON EICKE; publs. *Osteuropa* (monthly), *Osteuropa-Recht, Osteuropa-Wirtschaft* (quarterlies).

Deutsche Gesellschaft für Versicherungsmathematik (Deutscher Aktuarverein): Neue Rabenstr. 15–19, D-2000 Hamburg 36; Gen. Dir. HORST BECKER.

Deutsche Gesellschaft für Völkerrecht (*International Law*): 5000 Cologne 41, Gottfried-Keller-Str. 2; f. 1917 re-f. 1949; 190 mems.; Pres. Prof. Dr. Dr. IGNAZ SEIDL-HOHENVELDERN; publ. *Berichte* (every 2 years).

Deutsche Statistische Gesellschaft: 62 Wiesbaden, Gustav-Stresemann-Ring 11; f. 1911; 691 mems.; Pres. Dr. HILDEGARD BARTELS; Sec. WALTER HÖRNER; publs. *Allgemeines Statistisches Archiv* (quarterly), *Einzelschriften der Deutschen Statistischen Gesellschaft* (irregular).

Deutsche Vereinigung für Politische Wissenschaft: 2000 Hamburg 13, Von-Melle-Park 15; f. 1951; 900 mems.; Pres. Prof. Dr. THOMAS ELLWEIN; Vice-Pres. Prof. Dr. UDO BERMBACH. Prof. Dr. MANFRED HÄTTICH; Dir. Dipl. Pol. BERND ANDRESEN; publ. *Politische Vierteljahresschrift* (quarterly).

Deutsche Volkswirtschaftliche Gesellschaft e.V. (*German Society for Political Economy*): 3388 Bad Harzburg, Amsbergstr. 9A; f. 1946; Pres. Dipl.-Eng. W. CORDES; Dir. Prof. Dr. REINHARD HÖHN; publ. *Management Heute-Harzburger Hefte* (monthly).

Deutscher Juristentag e.V.: 53 Bonn, Oxfordstr. 10; f. 1860; furthers discussion among jurists; 7,400 mems.; Sec. F. BUSSE.

Gesellschaft für öffentliche Wirtschaft und Gemeinwirtschaft e.V. (*Society for Public and Co-operative Economy*): 1000 Berlin 21, Gotzkowskystr. 8; f. 1951; 80 corporative, 20 individual mems.; research and information on public and co-operative enterprises; library of 1,000 vols.; Pres. Dr. WALTER KLIEMT; Dir. Dipl.-Volksw. WOLF LEETZ; publ. *ÖWG-Öffentliche Wirtschaft und Gemeinwirtschaft* (quarterly).

Gesellschaft für Rechtsvergleichung (*Comparative Law*): 78 Freiburg im Breisgau, Werthmannplatz, Universität; f. 1950; 1,000 mems.; Chair. Prof. Dr. Dr. h.c. HANS-HEINRICH JESCHECK; Sec.-Gen. Prof. Dr. UWE BLAUROCK; publs. *Arbeiten zur Rechtsvergleichung, Mitteilungen, Ausländische Aktiengesetze.*

Gesellschaft für Sozial- und Wirtschaftsgeschichte (*Society for Social and Economic History*): c/o The Pres. Prof. Dr. H. KELLENBENZ, 8500 Nurnberg, Seminar für Wirtschafts- u. Sozialgeschichte, Univ. Erlangen-Nürnberg, Findelgasse 7; f. 1961; 210 mems.; Sec. Prof. Dr. H. POHL.

Gesellschaft für Wirtschafts- und Sozialwissenschaften (Verein für Sozialpolitik) (*Society for Economic and Social Sciences*): Gosslerstr. 1B, 3400 Göttingen; 1,500 mems.; Pres. Prof. Dr. HELMUT HESSE.

Institut für Auslandsbeziehungen: 7 Stuttgart, Charlottenplatz 17; f. 1917; library of 264,135 vols.; Pres. Dr. Dr. h.c. WILHELM HAHN; Gen. Sec. Dr. MICHAEL REHS; publs. *Literarisch-Künstlerische Reihe, Wissenschaftlich-Publizistische Reihe, Deutsch-Ausländische Kulturbeziehungen, Geistige Begegnung, Zeitschrift für Kulturaustausch, Ländermonographien, Reihe Dokumentation.*

Kommission für Geschichte des Parlamentarismus und der Politischen Parteien (*Commission for History of Parliamentarism and Political Parties*): Poppelsdorfer Allee 55, 5300 Bonn 1; f. 1951; Pres. Prof. Dr. R. MORSEY; Gen. Sec. Dr. M. SCHUMACKER; publs. *Beiträge zur Geschichte des Parlamentarismus und der politischen Parteien, Quellen zur Geschichte des Parlamentarismus und der politischen Parteien, Bibliographien.*

Wirtschaftsakademie für Lehrer e.V. (*Economics Academy for Teachers*): 3388 Bad Harzburg 1, An den Weiden 15; f. 1959, independent 1975; Pres. Prof. Dr. REINHARD HÖHN; Dir. GISELA BÖHME.

Wirtschaftspolitische Gesellschaft von 1947: 6 Frankfurt a.M., Holzhausenstr. 15; Pres. ULRICH VON PUFFENDORF; publ. *Offene Welt* (irregular).

EDUCATION

Deutscher Akademischer Austauschdienst (DAAD) (*German Academic Exchange Service*): 5300 Bonn 2, Kennedyallee 50; branch offices: 11-15 Arlington St., London, SW1A 1RD. U.K.; 15 rue de Verneuil, 75007 Paris, France; 6A Sharia Ismail Mohamed, Cairo-Zamalek, Egypt; 176 Golf Links, New Delhi 110003, India; 535 Fifth Avenue, Apt. 1107, New York, N.Y. 10017, U.S.A.; C.P. 64, ZC-00 Rio de Janeiro, Brazil; P.O.B. 25275, Nairobi, Kenya; Akasaka 7-5-56, Minato-ku, Tokyo 107, Japan; f. 1925; exchange of professors, lecturers in German for foreign universities, IAESTE—student-trainees, scholarships, etc.; Pres. Prof. Dr. HANSGERD SCHULTE; Gen. Sec. Dr. HUBERTUS SCHEIBE.

Deutscher Volkshochschul-Verband e.V. (*German Adult Education Association*): 53 Bonn-2, Konstantinstr. 100; f. 1953; 11 regional associations of 1,000 Volkshochschulen with 4,000 branches; f. 1979; Pres. Dr. DIETER SAUBERZWEIG; Dir. HELMUTH DOLFF; publ. *Volkshochschule im Westen* (2 a month), *Adult Education and Development* (2 a year, English, French and Spanish).

Humboldt Gesellschaft für Wissenschaft, Kunst und Bildung e.V. (*Humboldt Society for Science, Art and Education*): 6800 Mannheim 31, Riedlach 12; f. 1962; 550 mems.; Pres. Prof. Dr. ERWIN STEIN.

Katholischer Akademischer Ausländer-Dienst: 53 Bonn, Reuterstrasse 39; f. 1956; Pres. Dr. PAUL BECHER; Dir. HANS REINER LIMBACH; co-ordinates activities of Catholic organizations concerned with foreign students in Germany and grants scholarships.

Westdeutsche Rektorenkonferenz (*West German Rectors' Conference*): 53 Bonn 2, Ahrstrasse 39; f. 1949; the central voluntary body representing the universities and higher education institutes; mems.: 158 insts.; Pres. Prof. Dr. GEORGE TURNER; Sec.-Gen. (vacant).

Educational Foundations

Alexander von Humboldt-Stiftung (*Humboldt Foundation*): D-5300 Bonn-2, 12 Jean Paul Strasse; f. 1860, re-f. 1925, 1953; provides *c.* 500 research fellowships annually for young foreign scholars and scientists for post doctoral research at universities and other research institutes in the Federal Republic of Germany; Pres. Prof. Dr. WOLFGANG PAUL; Sec.-Gen. Dr. HEINRICH PFEIFFER.

Carl Duisberg-Gesellschaft e.V. (*The Carl Duisberg Society*): 5 Cologne 1, Hohenstaufenring 30-32; f. 1949; a non-profit making organization for worldwide trainee exchange from developing and industrialized countries for business and industry; mems.: 730 firms; Chair. Board Trustees Dr. HERBERT GRÜNEWALD; Exec. Secs. Dr. RUDOLF SCHUSTER, KLAUS RACHWALSKY; publ. *Duisberg-Hefte* (irregular).

Cusanuswerk Bischöfliche Studienförderung: 5300 Bonn 2, Annaberger Str. 283; f. 1956; scholarships are awarded for undergraduate (*c.* 450 a year) and postgraduate studies (*c.* 80 a year) to German Roman Catholic students specially qualified in their fields; Dir. Prof. DDr. KARL DELAHAYE; Gen. Sec. Dr. KARL-WILHELM MERKS.

Friedrich-Ebert-Stiftung e.V. (*The Friedrich Ebert Foundation*): Godesberger Allee 149, 5300 Bonn 2; f. 1925; there are five departments: Adult Education, Scholarship programme for students and postgraduates, International Relations, Research, Political Information; library of 300,000 vols.; Pres. ALFRED NAU; Gen. Sec. Dr. G. GRUNWALD; publs. *Archiv für Sozialgeschichte, Schriftenreihe des Forschungsinstituts der Friedrich-Ebert-Stiftung, Vierteljahresberichte des Forschungsinstituts der Friedrich-Ebert-Stiftung.*

Fritz Thyssen Stiftung: 5 Cologne 1, Postfach 180346; f. 1959 to promote academic and scientific research; donations of *c.* 19 million marks in 1979; Chair. KURT BIRRENBACH; Dir. RUDOLF KERSCHER; publ. *Annual Report.*

Pestalozzi-Fröbel-Haus: 1 Berlin, 30, Karl Schrader Strasse 7/8; f. 1874; Depts. of Social Pedagogy, Social Welfare, Child Guidance; 640 students; library of 18,165 vols.

Stiftung Mitbestimmung: D-4000 Düsseldorf 30, Hans-Böckler-Str. 39; f. 1954; awards grants to persons recommended by unions, and finances research relevant to the union movement; Head of Curatorium MARIA WEBER; Chair. of Dirs. RUDOLF JUDITH; Educational Dir. Dr. ERHARD LENK; publ. *Mitteilungen.*

Stiftung Volkswagenwerk: 3000 Hannover 81, Kastanienallee 35; f. 1961; promotes science, technology and the humanities by sponsoring research and university teaching; Sec.-Gen. Dr. W. BORST; publs. *Annual Report*†, *Schriftenreihe*†.

Studienstiftung des deutschen Volkes (*German National Scholarship Foundation*): 5300 Bonn 2, Mirbachstr. 7; f. 1925, re-established 1948; sponsors mainly highly gifted university students; 4,000 scholarships a year; Pres. Prof. Dr. WERNER MAIHOFER; Gen. Sec. Dr. HARTMUT RAHN.

History, Geography and Archaeology

Arbeitsgemeinschaft Historischer Kommissionen und Landesgeschichtlicher Institute e.V. (*Association of Historic Councils and Regional History Institutes*): Domplatz 20–22, 4400 Münster; f. 1898; controls 50 societies and institutes; Pres. Prof. Dr. HEINZ STOOB.

Deutsche Gesellschaft fur Kartographie e.V.: 4600 Dortmund-Brunninghausen, Klusenerskamp 10; f. 1950; promotes scientific and practical cartography; 1,380 mems.; Pres. Prof. Dr. HEINZ PAPE; Sec. Dipl. Geog. Dr. KARL-HEINZ MEINE; publ. *Kartographische Nachrichten* (6 a year).

Deutsche Gesellschaft für Ortung und Navigation e.V. (*German Institute of Navigation*): 4 Düsseldorf, Am Wehrhahn 94, Postfach 2622; f. 1951 as Ausschuss für Funkortung, 1961 under present title; to promote the investigation and development of methods of determining position by radar or navigation; Pres. Prof. Dr. DIEHL; publ. *Ortung und Navigation* (quarterly).

Deutsche Quartärvereinigung (*Quaternary Union*): 3000 Hannover 51, P.O.B. 510153; f. 1950; 650 mems.; Pres. Prof. Dr. O. FRÄNZLE; publ. *Eiszeitalter und Gegenwart.*

Deutscher Nautischer Verein von 1868 e.V. (*German Nautical Association of 1868*): 2 Hamburg 36, Esplanade 6; f. 1868; 4,000 mems. of which 3,940 in local Nautical Associations; Pres. ERICH EBERS; Sec. Capt. ALFRED MARGNER.

Fränkische Geographische Gesellschaft: 8520 Erlangen, Kochstr. 4; f. 1954; library of 8,000 vols.; 1,039 mems.; Dir. Prof. Dr. EUGEN WIRTH; Gen. Sec. FRIEDRICH LINNENBERG; publs. *Mitteilungen*† (annual), *Erlanger Geographische Arbeiten* (irregular).

Geographisch-Kartographische Gesellschaft: Rendsburg, Alte Kieler Landstr. 147; Dir. KLAUS KRIEGER.

Gesamtverein der Deutschen Geschichts- und Altertumsvereine (*Union of German Historical and Archaeological Societies*): Marburg/L, Krummbogen 28c; f. 1852; 121 affiliated asscns.; Pres. Prof. Dr. W. HEINEMEYER; Treas. Dr. E. KITTEL; publ. *Blätter für deutsche Landesgeschichte.*

Gesellschaft für Erd- und Völkerkunde (*Geographical and Anthropological Society*): 5300 Bonn, Franziskanerstr. 2; f. 1910; 250 mems.; Pres. Prof. Dr. GERHARD AYMANS; Sec. Dr. GÜNTER THIEME.

Gesellschaft für Erdkunde zu Berlin (*Berlin Geographical Society*): Berlin 41, Arno-Holzstr. 14; 577 mems.; f. 1828; Pres. Prof. Dr. KARL LENZ; Gen. Sec. Prof. Dr. FRIDO BADER; publ. *Die Erde (Zeitschrift der Gesellschaft für Erdkunde zu Berlin).*

Görres-Gesellschaft zur Pflege der Wissenschaft: 5000 Cologne 1, Postfach 100 905; f. 1876; over 2,300 mems.; Pres. Prof. Dr. PAUL MIKAT; Gen. Sec. Prof. Dr. HERMANN KRINGS.

Monumenta Germaniae Historica: Munich, Ludwigstrasse 16; f. 1819; *c.* 75,000 vols. in library; Pres. Prof. Dr. HORST FUHRMANN; Sec. Dr. WOLFRAM SETZ; Librarian Dr. HILDA LIETZMANN; publ. *Deutsches Archiv für Erforschung des Mittelalters.*

Verband der Historiker Deutschlands (*Union of German Historians*): f. 1893; re-founded 1949; 950 mems.; Pres. Prof. Dr. GERHARD A. RITTER; Gen. Sec. Prof. Dr. KARL OTMAR Frh. VON ARETIN, Institut für Europäische Geschichte, 65 Mainz, Alte Universitätsstrasse 19.

Zentralausschuss für Deutsche Landeskunde (*Central Council for Geography of Germany*): D-55 Trier, Tarforst; f. 1882, re-f. 1946; study of German regional geography; Pres. Prof. Dr. GEROLD RICHTER; Sec. Prof. Dr. HELLMUT SCHROEDER-LANZ; publs. *For-*

schungen zur deutschen Landeskunde (2-3 a year), *Berichte zur deutschen Landeskunde* (2 a year).

Zentralverband der deutschen Geographen: 8700 Würzburg, Geographisches Institut der Universität, Am Hubland; Pres. Prof. Dr. H. HAGEDORN; Sec.-Gen. Prof. Dr. K. GIESSNER.

INTERNATIONAL CULTURAL INSTITUTES

Amerika Haus Berlin/U.S. Cultural Center: 1 Berlin 12, Hardenbergstr. 22–24; f. 1946 as part of USIS (now International Communication Agency); centre for cultural and information exchange; lectures, seminars, etc. on int. relations and economic policy, social affairs, education, scientific research; cultural activities; library of 7,500 vols., 440 journals; Dir. ROBERT P. MILTON.

British Council: Head Office: 5 Cologne 1, Hahnenstr. 6; libraries; *see* Libraries; Rep. D. BEARD; Regional offices: 1 Berlin 12, Hardenbergstr. 20, Regional Dir. J. F. GREEN; 2 Hamburg 36, Neuer Wall 86, Regional Dir. D. A. HANDFORTH; 8 Munich 22, Bruderstr. 7/111, Regional Dir. D. J. RUNDLE.

Dänisches Institut: 4600 Dortmund, Westfalendamm 174; the Institute is a branch of Det Danske Selskab (*q.v.*).

Gesellschaft für Übernationale Zusammenarbeit e.V.: 5000 Cologne 1, Hohenstaufenring 11; f. 1945; German branch of Bureau International de Liaison et de Documentation (BILD) (Paris) (*q.v.*); to promote exchanges and social and cultural studies between France and Federal Germany, organizes conferences, study groups, exchange holidays, etc.; Pres. FRANÇOIS BOUREL (Paris); Gen. Secs. JOSEF WINKELHEIDE (Cologne), ROLAND MAGER (Paris); publs. *Dokumente, Zeitschrift für übernationale Zusammenarbeit, Documents, Revue des questions allemandes.*

Goethe-Institut: 8000 Munich 2, Lenbachplatz 3; f. 1932 to foster German language and culture; 18 colleges for foreigners; 113 branches abroad; library of 25,000 vols.; Pres. KLAUS VON BISMARCK.

Institut Français: 5300 Bonn, Adenauerallee 35; Dir. P. FANCHINI; brs. at Berlin, Cologne, Frankfurt a.M., Freiburg, Hamburg, Mainz, Munich, Stuttgart.

Instituto de España en Munich: Marstallplatz 7, 8000 Munich 22; Dir. Dr. MANUEL MUÑOZ CORTÉS.

Inter Nationes: 5300 Bonn-2, Kennedyallee 91-103; f. 1952; non-profit organization with the object of strengthening cultural relations between foreign countries and the Federal Republic of Germany; Dir. Dr. HORST SCHIRMER; publs. *German Review of Education and Science*, articles on political, economic, social and technical developments and events in the Fed. Repub. of Germany, audio-visual media, etc.

Istituto Italiano di Cultura: 5 Cologne, Universitätsstrasse 81; Dir. Prof. LORENZO GABETTI; Hansastrasse 6, Hamburg; Dir. Prof. LIVIO OLIVIERI.

Japanisches Kulturinstitut: 5000 Cologne, Postfach 270346, Universitätsstrasse 98; f. 1969; library of 10,000 vols.; Dir. Prof. Dr. M. WATANABE; publs. *Jahresbericht* (annual report), *Monatsprogramme* (monthly programmes).

LANGUAGE AND LITERATURE

Deutsche Gesellschaft für Sprachwissenschaft (*German Society for Linguistics*): c/o Prof. Dr. M. Reis, Institut für deutsche Sprache und Literatur, Universität Köln, Albertus-Magnus-Platz, 5000 Köln 41; f. 1978 for the advancement of the scientific investigation of language, and the support of linguists engaged in this; 300 mems.; Pres. Prof. Dr. WOLFGANG KLEIN; Sec. Prof. Dr. MARGA REIS; publ. *Bulletin*† (3 a year).

Deutsche Shakespeare-Gesellschaft West: Rathaus, 4630 Bochum 1; f. 1963; 1,580 mems.; Pres. Prof. Dr. HABICHT; Chair. Prof. Dr. SUERBAUM; publ. *Shakespeare-Jahrbuch.*

Gesellschaft für deutsche Sprache e.V. (*Society for the German Language*): 6200 Wiesbaden 1, Taunusstr. 11, P.O.B. 2669; f. 1947; 2,200 mems.; library of 3,400 vols.; Dir. OTTO NUESSLER; publs. *Muttersprache*† (bi-monthly), *Der Sprachdienst*† (monthly).

Hölderlin-Gesellschaft e.V.: 74 Tübingen, Hölderlinhaus; f. 1943, reconstituted 1946; 1,250 mems.; Pres. Prof. Dr. Uvo HÖLSCHER; publs. *Hölderlin-Jahrbuch* (every two years), *Schriften der Hölderlin-Gesellschaft* (irregular).

Mommsen-Gesellschaft: 2000 Hamburg 13, Universität (Seminar für Klassische Philologie); association of classical scholars; Pres. Prof. Dr. WALTHER LUDWIG; Sec. Dr. WIDU-W. EHLERS.

P.E.N. Zentrum Bundesrepublik Deutschland: 61 Darmstadt, Sandstrasse 10; f. 1951; 460 mems.; Pres. Prof. Dr. WALTER JENS; Sec.-Gen. MARTIN GREGOR-DELLIN.

MEDICINE

Anatomische Gesellschaft (*Anatomical Society*): D-5100 Aachen, Abteilung Anatomie der Rheinisch-Westfälischen Technischen Hochschule; f. 1886; 812 mems.; Sec. Prof. Dr. Med. WOLFGANG KÜHNEL; publ. *Anatomischer Anzeiger.*

Berliner Medizinische Gesellschaft (*Berlin Medical Society*): 1 Berlin 41, Fregestr. 73; Pres. Prof. Dr. HANS HERKEN; Sec. Prof. Dr. K.-O. HABERMEHL.

Deutsche Dermatologische Gesellschaft: 5 Cologne 41, Univ.-Hautklinik; f. 1888; 1,100 mems.; Pres. Prof. Dr. G. STÜTTGEN; Sec.-Gen. Prof. Dr. G. K. STEIGLEDER; publ. *Hatarzt* (monthly).

Deutsche Gesellschaft für Anästhesiologie und Intensivmedizin: 8500 Nürnberg, Flurstr. 17; f. 1953; 2,400 mems.; Pres. Dr. J. SCHARA; Sec. Priv. Doz. Dr. H. W. OPDERBECKE; publ. *Anästhesiologie und Intensivmedizin* (monthly), etc.

Deutsche Gesellschaft für Angewandte Optik (*German Society for Applied Optics*): c/o Ernst Leitz Wetzlar GmbH, 6330 Wetzlar, Postfach 2020; f. 1923; 540 mems.; Pres. Dr. H. WALTER; Sec. H.-J. PREUSS; publ. *Optik* (monthly).

Deutsche Gesellschaft für Arbeitsschutz e.V.: 6 Frankfurt a.M., Schumannstr. 1-3; f. 1908; industrial medicine; library of 3,000 books and 5,000 pamphlets; Pres. Dr. G. BÖHME; Dir. W. ASTHEIMER; publ. *Zentralblatt für Arbeitsmedizin und Arbeitsschutz.*

Deutsche Gesellschaft für Chirurgie (*German Surgical Society*): 1000 Berlin 15, Kurfürstendamm 179; f. 1872; 2,850 mems.; Pres. Prof. Dr. E. UNGEHEUER; Sec. Prof. Dr. h.c. H. JUNGHANNS; publs. *Langenbecks Archiv für Chirurgie.*

Deutsche Gesellschaft für Endokrinologie: 3000 Hannover 61, Karl-Wiechert-Allee 9; f. 1953; 609 mems.; Sec. Prof. Dr. A. VON ZUR MÜHLEN; publ. *Endokrinologie-Mitteilung* (every 2 months).

Deutsche Gesellschaft für Ernährung e.V. (*Nutrition*): 6000 Frankfurt/Main, Feldbergstr. 28; f. 1953; Pres. Prof. Dr. HANS JOACHIM BIELIG; Exec. Sec. GUSTAV KOBBE; publ. *Ernährungs-Umschau* (monthly).

Deutsche Gesellschaft für Geschichte der Medizin, Naturwissenschaft und Technik e.V.: 2000 Hamburg 13, Universitat Hamburg, Inst. für Geschichte der Naturwissenschaften, Mathematik und Technik, Bundesstr. 55; f. 1901, reorganized 1949; 700 mems.; Pres. Prof. Dr. rer. nat. CHRISTOPH J. SCRIBA; Sec. Prof. Dr. phil. CHRISTIAN HÜNEMÖRDER.

Deutsche Gesellschaft für Gynäkologie und Geburtshilfe: 6000 Frankfurt 70, Theodor-Stern-Kai 7, Universitäts Frauenklinik; Pres. Prof. Dr. H. Schmidt-Matthiesen.

Deutsche Gesellschaft für Hals-Nasen-Ohren-Heilkunde, Kopf- und Hals-Chirurgie (*Otorhinolaryngology*): c/o Frau A. Karwel, 5300 Bonn-Venusberg, Univ. Hals-Nasen-Ohrenklinik; Pres. Prof. Dr. H.-G. Boenninghaus; Sec. Prof. Dr. J. Berendes.

Deutsche Gesellschaft für Hygiene und Mikrobiologie: 2400 Lübeck 1, Ratzeburger Allee 160; f. 1900; 1,000 mems.; Chair. Prof. Dr. Gottschalk; Sec. Prof. Dr. med. W. Henkel.

Deutsche Gesellschaft für innere Medizin (*Internal Medicine*): 6200 Wiesbaden, Med. Klinik 1 der Kliniken der Landeshauptstadt, Schwalbacher Str. 62; f. 1882; 3,000 mems.; Sec. Prof. Dr. Bernhard Schlegel; publ. *Verhandlungen der Deutschen Gesellschaft für innere Medizin* (annually).

Deutsche Gesellschaft für Kinderheilkunde (*Paediatrics*): 4300 Essen 1, Hufelandstr. 55; f. 1883; 3,500 mems.; Pres. Prof. Dr. Herman Olbing.

Deutsche Gesellschaft für Neurochirurgie: 43 Essen 1, Hufelandstr. 55; f. 1950; 244 mems.; Pres. Prof. Dr. med. W. Grote; Gen. Sec. Prof. Dr. med. H. Dietz.

Deutsche Gesellschaft für Nuklearmedizin: 3000 Hanover, Karl Wiechert Allee 9; f. 1970; 150 mems.; Pres. Prof. Dr. H. Hundeshagen.

Deutsche Gesellschaft für Orthopädie und Traumatologie: 3500 Kassel W., Uhlenhorststr. 21; f. 1901; 1,300 mems.; Pres. Prof. Dr. H. H. Matthiass; Sec. Prof. Dr. H. Cotta; publ. *Verhandlungen* (annually).

Deutsche Gesellschaft für Pathologie: 665 Homburg (Saar), c/o Pathologisches Institut der Universität des Saarlandes; f. 1897; 900 mems.; Sec. Prof. Dr. G. Dhom.

Deutsche Gesellschaft für Physikalische Medizin und Rehabilitation: 3470 Höxter, Weserbergland-Klinik; physical medicine and rehabilitation, balneology and medical bioclimatology; Pres. Prof. Dr. E. A. Zysno; Hon. Sec. Prof. Dr. R. Fricke.

Deutsche Gesellschaft für Plastische und Wiederherstellungs-Chirurgie (*German Society for Plastic and Reconstructive Surgery*): 1000 Berlin 33, Clay Allee 229, Oskar Helene Heim; f. 1961; 280 mems.; Sec. Priv. Doz. Dr. H. Zilch.

Deutsche Gesellschaft für Psychiatrie und Nervenheilkunde: 8000 München 2, Beethovenpl. 4; f. 1842; *c.* 1,100 mems.; Pres. Prof. Dr. Dr. H. Helmchen; Sec. Dr. P. W. Schulte; publs. *Spektrum, Nervenarzt.*

Deutsche Gesellschaft für Psychotherapie, Psychosomatik und Tiefenpsychologie e.V. (DGPPT): 2 Hamburg 13, Heimhuder Str. 69; f. 1949 to train psycho-therapists; 800 mems.; Pres. Prof. Dr. med. Helmut Bach; Dir. Dr. med. Ulrich Ehebald.

Deutsche Gesellschaft für Rechtsmedizin: 8700 Würzburg, Versbacher Str. 3; Pres. Prof. W. Schwerd.

Deutsche Gesellschaft für Rheumatologie: 2357 Bad Bramstedt, Rheumaklinik; f. 1927; 320 mems.; Sec. Dr. G. Josenhans; publ. *Zeitschrift für Rheumatologie.*

Deutsche Gesellschaft für Sozialmedizin (*German Society for Social Medicine*): 6900 Heidelberg, Im Neuenheimer Feld 368; f. 1964; 300 mems.; Pres. Prof. Dr. Maria Blohmke; publs. *Arbeitsmedizin, Sozialmedizin, Präventivmedizin.*

Deutsche Gesellschaft für Zahn-, Mund- und Kieferheilkunde (*German Society for Oral Surgery*): 4 Düsseldorf, Lindemannstrasse 96; f. 1859; 7,500 mems.; Gen. Sec. Dr. Karl Heinz Tiegelkamp.

Deutsche Gesellschaft zur Förderung der Rehabilitation e.V.: 5100 Aachen, Im Gruental 59; f. 1955; theory and practice of rehabilitation; Pres. Prof. Dr. Kh. Woeber; publ. *Rehabilitation.*

Deutsche Ophthalmologische Gesellschaft Heidelberg: 69 Heidelberg, Bergheimerstrasse 20; f. 1857; 1,600 mems.; Pres. Prof. Dr. W. Böke; Sec. Prof. Dr. W. Jaeger; publ. *Jahresbericht.*

Deutsche Physiologische Gesellschaft e.V.: 8000 Munich 2, Pettenkoferstr. 12; f. 1904; 570 mems.; Pres. Prof. Dr. med. P. Deetjen; Sec. Prof. Dr. med. G. ten Bruggencate.

Deutsche Psychoanalytische Gesellschaft: 8035 Gauting/Munich, Hildegradestr. 30 f. 1910; psycho-analytic training, education and research; 200 mems.; Pres. Dr. med. Wolfgang Zander; Vice-Pres. Dr. med. Friedrich Beese; Sec./Treas. Dr. med. Gerhard Mentzel; publs. *Zeitschrift für Psychosomatische Medizin und Psychoanalyse, Praxis der Kinderpsychologie und Kinderpsychiatrie, DPG-Mitteilungen.*

Deutsche Psychoanalytische Vereinigung e.V.: D-1000 Berlin 33 (Grunewald), Sulzaer-Strasse 3; br. of the International Psychoanalytical Association: Pres. Prof. Dr. H. Henseler; Sec. Dr. A. Kuchenbuch.

Deutsche Röntgengesellschaft für Medizinische Radiologie, Strahlenbiologie und Nuklearmedizin e.V. (*Radiological Society*): 8000 Munich 70, Klinikum Grosshadern, Marchioninistr. 15; Pres. Prof. Dr. med. Josef Lissner.

Deutsche Tropenmedizinische Gesellschaft: 5600 Wuppertal 1, Postfach 101709; f. 1962 to bring together persons interested in medical and veterinary questions relating to the tropics; 355 mems.; Pres. Prof. Dr. H. J. Diesfeld; First Sec. Dr. A. Haberkorn.

Vereinigung Westdeutscher Hals-, Nasen- und Ohrenärzte (*Association of West-German Oto-Rhino-Laryngologists*): 5000 Cologne 41, Universitäts-HNO-Klinik Köln, Joseph-Stelzmann-Str. 9; f. *c.* 1920; 1,370 mems.; Sec. Prof. Dr. K.-G. Rose.

Natural Sciences

General

Georg-Agricola Gesellschaft zur Förderung der Geschichte der Naturwissenschaften und der Technik e.V.: 4300 Essen 1, Postfach 230 343; f. 1926; promotes study of the history of science and technology; 80 mems.; 27 mem. asscns.; Pres. Dr.-Ing. W. Fries; Sec. Dr.-Ing. F. Benthaus.

Gesellschaft Deutscher Naturforscher und Ärzte (*German Society for Scientists and Doctors*): 5600 Wuppertal 1, Friedrich-Ebert-Str. 217; f. 1822; 6,900 mems.; Pres. Prof. Dr. P. Sitte; Gen. Sec. Prof. Dr. E. Auhagen.

Joachim-Jungius-Gesellschaft der Wissenschaften e.V.: 2 Hamburg 13, Edmund-Siemers-Allee 1; f. 1947; 55 individual mems., 6 mem. asscns.; Pres. Prof. Dr. W. Walter; Vice-Pres. Prof. Dr. D. Gerhardt; publs. *Tagungsvorträge, Veröffentlichungen.*

Wissenschaftsrat (*Science Council*): 5000 Cologne 51, Marienburgerstr. 8; f. 1957 through co-operation of Land and Federal Governments; advisory and co-ordinating body for science policy; makes recommedations on the structural and curricular development of the universities and on the organization and promotion of science and research; 39 nominated mems. in two commissions (Scientific and Administrative); Chair. Prof. Dr. jur. Andreas Heldrich.

Biological Sciences

Bayerische Botanische Gesellschaft (*Bavarian Botanical*

Society): 8000 Munich 19, Menzinger Str. 67; f. 1890; 800 mems.; library of 10,000 vols.; Pres. Dr. W. LIPPERT; publs. *Berichte*†, *Mitteilungen der Arbeitsgemeinschaft zür floristischen Kartierung Bayerns*†.

Deutsche Botanische Gesellschaft: 3400 Göttingen, Untere Karspüle 2; f. 1882; 1,050 mems.; Pres. Prof. Dr. W. HAUPT; publ. *Berichte* (3 a year).

Deutsche Gesellschaft für allgemeine und angewandte Entomologie e.V. (*German Society for General and Applied Entomology*): 6300 Lahn 1-Giessen, Ludwigstr. 23/1; 453 mems.; Pres. Prof. Dr. H. SCHMUTTERER; Dir. H. HOLST.

Deutsche Gesellschaft für Züchtungskunde e.V.: 5300 Bonn, Adenauerallee 174; f. 1905; livestock breeding, animal housing, reproduction, hygiene, nutrition; *c.* 1,600 mems.; Man. Dr. HARTWIG TEWES; publ. *Züchtungskunde*† (6 a year).

Deutsche Malakozoologische Gesellschaft: 6000 Frankfurt am Main 1, Senckenberg-Anlage; f. 1868; study of Mollusca; 250 mems.; library of 20,000 vols.; Pres. Dr. HARTWIG SCHÜTT; publs. *Archiv für Molluskenkunde* (2 a year), *Mitteilungen* (1–2 a year).

Deutsche Ornithologen-Gesellschaft e.V.: 7760 Möggingen/Radolfzell (Bodensee); f. 1850; 2,200 mems.; Pres. Prof. Dr. K. IMMELMANN; publs. *Journal für Ornithologie, Die Vogelwarte.*

Deutsche Phytomedizinische Gesellschaft e.V. (*German Phyto-medical Society*): Grisebachstr. 6, 3400 Göttingen; f. 1949; 944 mems.; Pres. Prof. Dr. R. HEITEFUSS; Sec. Dr. K. RUDOLPH.

Deutsche Zoologische Gesellschaft e.V. (*German Zoological Society*): 2000 Hamburg 50, Olbersweg 24; f. 1890; 1,160 mems.; Chair. Prof. Dr. SCHWARTZKOPFF; Sec. Dr. GABRIELE PETERS; publ. *Verhandlungen.*

Gesellschaft für Biologische Chemie: 1000 Berlin 65, Müllerstr. 170-178; 2,250 mems.; Chair. Prof. Dr. H. G. WITTMANN; Sec. Prof. Dr. H. GIBIAN.

Münchner Entomologie Gesellschaft e.V. (*Munich Entomological Society*): 8000 Munich 19, Maria-Ward-Str. 1B; f. 1905; 650 mems.; library of 10,000 vols., 457 periodicals (attached to library of the State Zoological Collection); Pres. Dr. WALTER FORSTER; publs. *Mitteilungen*†, *Nachrichtenblatt der Bayerischen Entomologen*†.

Naturhistorische Gesellschaft in Hannover (*Hanover Society of Natural History*): 3000 Hannover 51, Alfred-Bentz-Haus, Postfach 510153; f. 1797; 361 mems.; Pres. Dr. J. D. BECKER-PLATEN; publ. *Berichte*†.

Naturwissenschaftlicher Verein in Hamburg (*Hamburg Natural Science Association*): c/o Zoologisches Museum, Martin-Luther-King-Platz 3, 2000 Hamburg 13; f. 1837; *c.* 450 mems.; Chair. Prof. Dr. K. KUBITZKI; Gen. Man. Dr. FR. E. MEISTER; publ. *Abhandlungen und Verhandlungen*†, *Sonderbände.*

Naturwissenschaftlicher Verein zu Bremen (*Bremen Natural Science Association*): 28 Bremen, Übersee-Museum; f. 1864; Sec. Dr. TH. KRUCKOW; about 400 mems.; publ. *Abhandlungen*†.

Verein Naturschutzpark e.V. (*Nature Reserves Federation*): 2 Hamburg 1, Ballindamm 2-3; f. 1909; 8,000 mems.; Pres. Dr. h.c. ALFRED TOEPFER; publs. *Naturschutz- und Naturparke, Natur- und Nationalparke.*

Gesellschaft für Naturkunde in Württemberg: 7 Stuttgart 1, Schloss Rosenstein; f. 1844; 835 mems.; Pres. Prof. Dr. W. GOTTHARD; publ. *Jahreshefte* (Editor Dr. H. JANUS).

Vereinigung für angewandte Botanik e.V. (*Applied Botany*): 34 Göttingen, Grisebachstr. 6; f. 1902; *c.* 400 mems.; Pres. Prof. Dr. S. REHM; Sec. Prof. Dr. J. ULLRICH; publ. *Angewandte Botanik* (quarterly).

Mathematics

Berliner Mathematische Gesellschaft e.V. (*Berlin Mathematical Society*): 1 Berlin 12, Str. des 17 Juni 135; f. 1899; Chair. Prof. Dr. H.-J. TÖPFER; publ. *Sitzungsberichte.*

Deutsche Gesellschaft für Kybernetik (DGK) (*German Society of Cybernetics*): 8131 Seewiesen, Max-Planck-Institut für Verhaltensphysiologie; f. 1962; co-ordinates the activities of its 13 member societies and promotes national and international exchange of research results; Pres. Dr. H. MITTELSTAEDT; Sec. H. MÄUSL.

Deutsche Gesellschaft für Operations Research—DGOR (*German Society for Operational Research*): Kurt-Schumacher-Str. 38, 6361 Niddatal 2; fusion of *Deutsche Gesellschaft für Unternehmensforschung* and *Gesellschaft für Operations Research* (earlier *AKOR*); f. 1972; 710 mems.; promotes development of operational research and encourages co-ordination of theoretical and practical branches of the subject; library of 4,000 vols.; Pres. Prof. Dr. D. B. PRESSMAR; Sec. MARGRIT PETERS; publ. *ZOR "Zeitschrift für Operations Research".*

Deutsche Mathematiker Vereinigung e.V. (*German Mathematical Association*): Albertstr. 24, 7800 Freiburg; Pres. Prof. Dr. G. FISCHER; Sec. Prof. Dr. R. WALLISSER; publ. *Jahresbericht der DMV* (quarterly).

Gesellschaft für angewandte Mathematik und Mechanik (*Society for Applied Mathematics and Mechanics*): f. 1922; advancement of scientific work and international co-operation in applied mathematics, mechanics and physics; 1,800 mems.; Pres. Prof. Dr. K. KIRCHGÄSSNER; Sec. Prof. Dr. BROSOWSKI, 6 Frankfurt a.M., Johann-Wolfgang-Goethe-Universität, Fachbereich Mathematik, Robert-Mayer-Str. 6–10.

Gesellschaft für Mathematik und Datenverarbeitung m.b.H. Bonn (GMD) (*Society for Mathematics and Data Processing Ltd.*): 5205 St. Augustin 1, Schloss Birlinghoven; f. 1968; research and development of data processing and its utilization in the public sector; library of 50,000 vols.; Dirs. Prof. Dr. rer. nat. FRITZ KRÜCKEBERG, LORENZ KNESER, FRIEDRICH WINKELHAGE; publs. *Berichte der GMD, GMD-Studien*†.

Gesellschaft für Programmierte Instruktion und Mediendidaktik e.V.: c/o Seminar Anglistik/Didaktik, Justus Liebig-Universität, Otto Behagel Str. 10, 6300 Lahn/Giessen; f. 1964; 600 mems.; to promote development of automated instruction methods and computers; Chair. Prof. H.-E. PIEPHO; publ. *Neue Unterrichtspraxis.*

Physical Sciences

Astronomische Gesellschaft: f. 1863; Pres. Prof. Dr. TH. SCHMIDT-KALER; Sec. Prof. Dr. HORST MAUDER, 7400 Tübingen, Astronomisches Institut, Waldhäuser-Str. 64.

Deutsche Bunsen-Gesellschaft für Physikalische Chemie e.V.: 6 Frankfurt a.M., Varrentrappstr. 40-42; f. 1894; 1,500 mems.; Dir. Prof. E. U. FRANCK; Sec. Dr. H. BEHRET.

Deutsche Geologische Gesellschaft: 3000 Hannover, Alfred-Bentz Haus, Stilleweg 2; f. 1848; 1,900 mems.; Pres. Prof. Dr. W. KREBS; publs. *Zeitschrift*†, *Nachrichten*†.

Deutsche Geophysikalische Gesellschaft e.V.: 3392 Clausthal, Postfach 230; f. 1922; 617 mems.; Chair. Prof. H. BERCKHEMER; Sec. Dr. R. VEES; publ. *Zeitschrift für Geophysik, Journal of Geophysics.*

Deutsche Gesellschaft für Biophysik e.V.: 63 Giessen, Leihgesterner Weg 217; f. 1961; 300 mems.; Pres. Prof. Dr. KREUTZ; Sec. Prof. Dr. LOHMANN.

Deutsche Gesellschaft für Elektronenmikroskopie e.V.: p.Adr. Battelle-Institut e.V., 6000 Frankfurt/Main 90,

Postfach 900160; f. 1949; c. 1,000 mems.; Pres. Dr. FRIEDRICH LENZ; Sec. Dr.-Ing. G. SCHIMMEL.

Deutsche Meteorologische Gesellschaft e.V.: 8 Munich 2, Bavariaring 10, Wetteramt München; f. 1974; 960 mems.; brs. in various towns; Pres. Prof. Dr. J. VAN EIMERN; Sec. W. HELLMISS; publs. *Meteorologische Rundschau* (6 a year), *Beiträge zur Physik der Atmosphäre* (12 a year).

Deutsche Mineralogische Gesellschaft (*German Mineralogical Society*): 84 Regensburg, Universität; f. 1908; Sec. Prof. Dr. H. VON PHILIPSBORN; c. 1,400 mems.; publ. *Fortschritte der Mineralogie.*

Deutsche Pharmakologische Gesellschaft: c/o Klinge Pharma, Postfach, 8000 Munich 40; 1,300 mems.; Chair. Prof. Dr. E. HABERMANN; Sec. Dr. G. HOFRICHTER.

Deutsche Pharmazeutische Gesellschaft e.V.: 61 Darmstadt, Frankfurterstr. 250; f. 1890; 5,000 mems.; Pres. Prof. Dr. H. J. ROTH; Sec.-Gen. Dr. ADOLF ILTGEN; publs. *Archiv der Pharmazie* (monthly), *Pharmazie in unserer Zeit* (6 issues a year).

Deutsche Physikalische Gesellschaft e.V.: Hauptstr. 5, 5340 Bad Honnef; f. 1845; 6,500 mems.; Pres. Prof. Dr. H. ROLLNIK; Sec. Dr. W. HEINICKE; publs. *Physikalische Berichte, Physikalische Blätter* (monthly), *Verhandlungen der D.P.G.* (c. 10 a year).

Deutscher Zentralausschuss für Chemie: 6000 Frankfurt a.M. 90, P.O.B. 90 04 40, Carl Bosch-Haus, Varrentrappstrasse 40-42; Chair. Prof. Dr. phil. HELLMUT BREDERECK; Sec. Dr.rer.nat. WOLFGANG FRITSCHE.

Deutsches Atomforum e.V.: 53 Bonn, Allianzplatz, Haus X, Heussallee 2-10; f. 1959; 620 mems.; library of 1,100 vols.; promotes the peaceful uses of atomic energy; Pres. Prof. Dr. KARL WINNACKER.

Geologische Vereinigung (*Geological Association*): 5442 Mendig; f. 1910; 2,800 mems.; Chair. Prof. Dr. W. VON ENGELHARDT; publ. *Geologische Rundschau* (quarterly).

Gesellschaft Deutscher Chemiker: 6000 Frankfurt a.M. 90, Carl Bosch-Haus, Varrentrappstr. 40-42; f. 1946; 18,000 mems.; Gen.-Sec. Dr. rer. nat. WOLFGANG FRITSCHE; publs. *Angewandte Chemie* (fortnightly, International Edn. in English, monthly), *Chemie-Ingenieur-Technik* (fortnightly), *Chemie in unserer Zeit* (two-monthly), *Chemische Berichte* (monthly), *Chemischer Informationsdienst* (weekly), *Nachrichten aus Chemie, Technik und Laboratorium* (monthly).

Paläontologische Gesellschaft: c/o Geol. Paläont. Institut, Gievenbeckerweg 61, 44 Münster; f. 1912; Pres. Prof. Dr. K. VOGEL; Treas. Prof. Dr. M. J. KAEVER; publ. *Paläontologische Zeitschrift.*

PHILOSOPHY AND PSYCHOLOGY

Allgemeine Gesellschaft für Philosophie in Deutschland e.V.: f. 1948; 450 mems.; Pres. Prof. Dr. WOLFGANG KLUXEN; Sec. Prof. Dr. HANS-MARTIN SASS, 4630 Bochum 1, Institut für Philosophie, Ruhr-Univ. Bochum, Postfach 10 21 48.

Deutsche Gesellschaft für Psychologie e.V.: 5500 Trier, Universität Fachgebiet Psychologie; f. 1904 for the advancement of scientific psychology; 590 mems.; Pres. Prof. Dr. ERWIN ROTH; Sec. Prof. Dr. WOLFGANG MICHAELIS; publ. *Kongressberichte* (every 2 years).

Frobenius-Gesellschaft e.V. (Deutsche Gesellschaft für Kulturmorphologie): 6 Frankfurt a.M., Liebigstrasse 41; f. 1938; African cultures and history; c. 500 mems.; library of 62,000 vols.; Pres. ERNST A. TEVES; Dir. Prof. Dr. EIKE HABERLAND; publ. *Paideuma*† (annually).

Gesellschaft für Geistesgeschichte e.V. (*Society for the History of Ideas*): 852 Erlangen, Kochstr. 4; f. 1958; 130 mems.; Pres. Prof. Dr. JOACHIM SCHOEPS; Sec. Dr. KURT TÖPNER; publ. *Zeitschrift für Religions- und Geistesgeschichte.*

Gottfried-Wilhelm-Leibniz-Gesellschaft: 3000 Hannover 1, Waterloostr. 8 (Niedersaechsische Landesbibliothek); f. 1966; 250 mems., 12 mem. asscns.; Pres. Prof. Dr. R. HILLEBRECHT; Gen. Sec. Dr. W. TOTOK; publs. *Studia Leibnitiana*†, *Studia Leibnitiana Supplementa, Mitteilungen.*

Kant-Gesellschaft: 5301 Röttgen, Am alten Forsthaus 16; f. 1904; 600 mems.; Dir. Prof. Dr. G. MARTIN.

RELIGION, SOCIOLOGY AND ANTHROPOLOGY

Albertus Magnus-Institut: 53 Bonn, Adenauerallee 19; f. 1931; critical editions of the works of Albertus Magnus; 6 mems.; Dir. Prof. Dr. W. KÜBEL.

Berliner Gesellschaft für Anthropologie, Ethnologie und Urgeschichte (*Berlin Society for Anthropology, Ethnology and Prehistory*): 1 Berlin 19, Schloss Charlottenburg. Langhansbau; f. 1869; 350 mems.; Pres. Dr. G. HARTMANN; Sec. Dr. KLAUS GOLDMANN; publ. *Mitteilungen.*

Deutsche Gesellschaft für Anthropologie und Humangenetik: 3400 Göttingen, Bürgestr. 50; Pres. Prof. Dr. C. VOGEL.

Deutsche Gesellschaft für Bevölkerungswissenschaft e.V. (*German Society for Population Studies*): 6200 Wiesbaden, Postfach 55 28; f. 1952 to promote all fields of demographic research and co-ordinate research work undertaken by demographers, inc. non-Germans; meetings and publs.; 227 mems.; Pres. Prof. Dr. KARL SCHWARZ; Vice-Pres. Prof. Dr. MAX WINGEN; publ. information bulletin†.

Deutsche Gesellschaft für Ost- und Südostasienkunde e.V. (*German Association for East and Southeast Asian Studies*): 2 Hamburg 13, Rothenbaumchaussee 32; f. 1967; promotion and co-ordination of contemporary East and Southeast Asian research; 630 mems.; Pres. GÜNTER DIEHL; publ. *Mitteilungen der Koordinierungsstelle für gegenwartsbezogene Ost- und Südostasienforschung*† (3 a year).

Deutsche Gesellschaft für Soziologie: 8000 Munich 40, Konradstr. 6; Pres. Prof. K. M. BOLTE.

Deutsche Gesellschaft für Volkskunde e.V. (*German Society for European Ethnology*): Schloss, 74 Tübingen; f. 1904; 600 mems.; Pres. Prof. Dr. HERMANN BAUSINGER; publs. *Zeitschrift für Volkskunde, Internationale Volkskundliche Bibliographie, Mitteilungen der Deutschen Gesellschaft für Volkskunde (dgv-Informationen).*

Deutsche Morgenländische Gesellschaft (*German Oriental Society*): Postfach 1407, 1000 Berlin 30; f. 1845; 531 mems.; library of 50,000 vols.; Sec. Dr. DIETER GEORGE; publs. *Zeitschrift, Abhandlungen für die Kunde des Morgenlandes, Bibliotheca Islamica, Wörterbuch der Klassischen Arabischen Sprache, Beiruter Texte und Studien, Verzeichnis der orientalischen Handschriften in Deutschland.*

Deutsche Orient-Gesellschaft (*German Oriental Society*): 1 Berlin 19, Schloss Charlottenburg, Museum für Vor- und Frühgeschichte, Langhansbau; f. 1898; 560 mems.; Pres. Prof. Dr. BARTHEL HROUDA; Sec. Prof. Dr. VOLKMAR FRITZ; publs. *Mitteilungen, Wissenschaftliche Veröffentlichungen, Abhandlungen.*

Deutsches Orient-Institut: 2000 Hamburg 13, Mittelweg 150; f. 1960; to study modern Near and Middle East; library of 18,000 vols.; Dir. Dr. UDO STEINBACH; Deputy Dir. THOMAS KOSZINOWSKI; publs. *Orient*† (quarterly), *Mitteilungen* (irregular).

Gesellschaft für Anthropologie und Humangenetik (*Society for Anthropology and Human Genetics*): 2000 Hamburg, Anthropologisches Institut der Universität; Pres. Prof. Dr. R. Knussmann.

Gesellschaft für Evangelische Theologie: 3400 Göttingen, Merkelstr. 49; f. 1940; *c.* 800 mems.; Pres. Prof. Dr. F. Vogel, Prof. Dr. E. Wolf; publ. *Verkündigung und Forschung* (twice yearly).

Institut für Asienkunde (*Institute of Asian Affairs*): 2000 Hamburg 13, Rothenbaumchaussee 32; f. 1956; research and documentation into all aspects of contemporary South, South-East and East Asia; 35,000 books; Pres. Dr. W. Röhl; Dir. Dr. W. Draguhn; publs. *China aktuell, North Korea Quarterly, Official Activities and Monthly Bibliography, Japan* (annually in German).

Rheinische Vereinigung für Volkskunde: 5300 Bonn, Am Hofgarten 22; f. 1947; *c.* 200 mems.; Pres. Prof. Dr. H. L. Cox; publs. *Rheinisches Jahrbuch für Volkskunde*†, *Rheinisch-westfälische Zeitschrift für Volkskunde*† (quarterly).

Soziographisches Institut an der Johann Wolfgang Goethe Universität: Frankfurt University, 6 Frankfurt a.M., Schaumainkai 35; Pres. Dr. Carl Schweyer; Dir. Prof. Dr. Ludwig Neundörfer.

Wissenschaftliche Gesellschaft für Theologie: 34 Göttingen, Auf dem Hagen 23; f. 1973; 300 mems. in Federal Germany, Switzerland and Austria; six sections: Old Testament, New Testament, Church History, Systematic Theology, Practical Theology, Missions and Religion; Pres. Prof. Dr. Dr. W. Lohff.

Technology

DECHEMA (Deutsche Gesellschaft für chemisches Apparatewesen e.V.) (*Chemical Engineering*): 6 Frankfurt a.M. 97, Theodor-Heuss-Allee 25; f. 1926; 3,100 mems.; Pres. Prof. Dr. rer. nat. Heinz-Gerhard Franck; Prof. Dr. rer. nat. Dieter Behrens; publs. *Chemie-Ingenieur-Technik, Werkstoffe und Korrosion, Zeitschrift für Werkstofftechnik* (all monthly), *Dechema-Werkstoff-Tabelle, Dechema Monographien, Dechema-Erfahrungsaustausch, Achema-Jahrbuch, Thesaurus der Chemischen Technik, Dechema Chemistry Data Series.*

Deutsche Gemmologische Gesellschaft e.V. (*Gemmological Association of Germany*): 6580 Idar-Oberstein 2, P.O.B. 2260; f. 1932; administers the German Gemmological Training Centre; 2,500 mems.; library of 1,500 vols.; Dir. Dr. G. Lenzen; publ. *Zeitschrift* (quarterly).

Deutsche Gesellschaft für Bauingenieurwesen e.V. (*Constructional Engineering*): 75 Karlsruhe, Barbarossaplatz 2; f. 1946; 490 mems.; Pres. Prof. Dr. Wilhelm Strickler; Sec. Dipl. Ing. Gerhart Bochmann.

Deutsche Gesellschaft für Luft- und Raumfahrt e.V. (DGLR) (*German Society for Aeronautics and Astronautics*): 5 Köln 51, Goethestr. 10; f. 1968; 3,500 mems.; support of aeronautics and astronautics for all scientific and technical purposes; Pres. Prof. Dr.-Ing. G. Brüning; Vice-Pres. Prof. Dr. -Ing. B. Laschka; Dr. M. Bodenschatz; Sec.-Gen. H. Schwäbisch; publs. *Zeitschrift für Flugwissenschaften und Weltraumforschung* (every 2 months), *Luft- und Raumfahrt* (quarterly).

Deutsche Gesellschaft für Metallkunde (*Metallurgy*): 637 Oberursel/Taunus, Adenauerallee 21; f. 1919; *c.* 2,000 mems.; Pres. Prof. B. Liebmann; Sec. Dr. V. Schumacher; publ. *Zeitschrift für Metallkunde.*

Deutsche Gesellschaft für Mineralölwissenschaft und Kohlechemie e.V. (*German Society for Petroleum Sciences and Coal Chemistry*): 2 Hamburg 1, Nordkanalstr. 28; f. 1948; 1,100 mems.; Pres. Dr. W. von Ilsemann; Sec. Dr. K. Klinksiek; publs. *Erdöl und Kohle, Erdgas, Petrochemie.*

Deutsche Gesellschaft für Zerstörungsfreie Prüfung e.V. (*Non-Destructive Testing*): 1 Berlin 45, Unter den Eichen 87; f. 1933; 800 mems.; Pres. Prof. Dr. rer. nat. H. J. Kopineck; Sec. Dipl.-Ing. W. Bock; publ. *Materialprüfung* (monthly).

Deutsche Gesellschaft für Photogrammetrie: 3 Hanover, Institut für Photogrammetrie, Nienburger Str. 1; f. 1909; 550 mems.; Pres. Prof. Dr. Gottfried Konecny; publ. *Bildmessung und Luftbildwesen*† (two monthly).

Deutsche Glastechnische Gesellschaft e.V. (*German Society of Glass Technology*): 6 Frankfurt a.M., Mendelssohnstr. 75-77; f. 1922; 1,100 mems.; library of 16,175 vols., 14,492 patents; Chair. Dr. O. Stehl; Sec. Prof. Dr. Ing. Wolfgang Trier; publ. *Glastechnische Berichte* (monthly).

Deutsche Keramische Gesellschaft e.V. (*Ceramic Society*): 5340 Bad Honnef/Rhein, Menzenberger Str. 47, Postfach 1226; f. 1919; 1,250 mems.; Pres. H. Lehmann; Sec. G. Rechenberger; publ. *Berichte der Deutschen Keramischen Gesellschaft*† (monthly).

Deutscher Beton-Verein e.V. (*German Concrete Association*): 6200 Wiesbaden 1, Bahnhofstr. 61; f. 1898; quality control, research, standardization and construction advice; 255 mems.; Pres. Dr.-Ing. Georg Lücking; Secs. Dr. Ing.-Manfred Stiller, Dr.-Ing. Hans Seiler; publs. *Vorträge, Betontag, Beton-Handbuch, Bemessungsbeispiele.*

Deutscher Kälte- und Klimatechnischer Verein (*Refrigerating Association*): 7 Stuttgart 1, Seidenstr.36; f. 1909; 4 sections for production and industrial application of refrigeration, food science and technology, storage, transport and air conditioning; 700 mems.; Pres. Prof. Dr.-Ing. F. Steimle; Sec. Dr.-Ing. R. Wallner; publs. *DKV-Abhandlungen, DKV-Forschungsberichte*† (irregular), *DKV-Tagungsbericht* (annually).

Deutscher Markscheider Verein e.V. (*Mining Surveyors*): Gelsenkirchen-Buer, Horster Str. 165; Pres. Dr.-Ing. Herbert Spickernagel.

Deutscher Verband für Materialprüfung e.V. (DVM) (*Materials Testing*): 1 Berlin 45, Unter den Eichen 87; f. 1896; 300 mems.; Pres. Prof. Dr.-Ing. C. Razim; Secs. Dipl.-Ing. W. Bock, Dipl.-Ing. W. Raue; publ. *Materialprüfung* (monthly).

Deutscher Verband für Schweisstechnik e.V. (*German Welding Asscn.*): 4 Düsseldorf, Postfach 2725, Aachener Str. 172; f. 1947; 12,000 mems.; Pres. Dr.-Ing. Joseph Mennen; Dir. Dr.-Ing. Heinz Sossenheimer; publs. *Schweissen und Schneiden*†, *Schriftenreihe Schweissen und Schneiden*†, *Der Praktiker—Schweissen und Schneiden*†, *Fachbuchreihe Schweisstechnik*†, *DVS-Berichte*†, *Die Schweisstechnische Praxis*†, *Referateorgan Schweissen und verwandte Verfahren*†, *DVS Merkblätter*†, *DVS Richtlinien*†.

Deutscher Verband technisch-wissenschaftlicher Vereine (*Union of Technical and Scientific Asscns.*): 4 Düsseldorf 1, Graf-Recke-Str. 84; f. 1916; Chair. Bundesminister a.D. Prof. Dr.-Ing. S. Balke; Sec. Dr. F. W. Lehmann; publ. *VDI-Nachrichten.*

Deutscher Verein des Gas- und Wasserfaches e.V. (*Gas and Water Engineers*): 6236 Eschborn/Ts., Frankfurter Allee 27; f. 1859; technical regulations, scientific research work and training for public gas and water supply; 3,725 mems.; 3,000 books; Pres. Dipl.-Ing. Helmut Zander; Sec.-Gen. Dr.-Ing. Werner Feind and Dr.-Ing. Wolfgang Merkel; publs. *DVGW—Regelwerk Gas und Wasser, DVGW—Schriftreihen Gas und Wasser*†.

Deutscher Verein für Vermessungswesen e.V. (*Surveying*): 28 Bremen, An der Gete 47; f. 1871; *c.* 3,300 mems.; Pres.

Dr.-Phil. H. RÖHRS; publ. *Zeitschrift für Vermessungswesen* (monthly).

Deutscher Wasserwirtschafts- und Wasserkraftverband (*Water Power Asscn.*): 1 Berlin 12, Str. des 17 Juni 140-142-144; f. 1891; 30 mems.; Chair. TOCKUSS; publ. *Die Wasserwirtschaft* (monthly).

Deutsches Institut für Normung e.V. (DIN) (*Institute of Standardization*): 1 Berlin 30, Burggrafenstr. 4/10; f. 1917; Pres. Prof. Dipl.-Ing. H. KOCH; Dir. Dr.-Ing. H. REIHLEN; publ. *DIN-Mitteilungen* (monthly).

Institut für gewerbliche Wasserwirtschaft und Luftreinhaltung e.V. (*Industrial Water Supply and Clean Air*): 5000 Cologne 51, Oberländer Ufer 84-88; f. 1956; 2,500 mems.; Dir. Dr. WILLI GÄSSLER; publs. *IWL Kurzberichte* (monthly), *IWL Forum* (irregular).

Lichttechnische Gesellschaft e.V.: 1000 Berlin 30, Burggrafenstr. 4-7; Sec. D. ULFFERS.

Nachrichtentechnische Gesellschaft im VDE (NTG) (*Telecommunication Association*): 6 Frankfurt a.M. 70, Stresemann Allee 21; f. 1954; 9,000 mems.; Chair. Apraes. Dipl.-Ing. HEINZ KUNZE; Sec. Dr.-Ing. FRIEDRICH COËRS; publ. *Nachrichtentechnische Zeitschrift* (*NTZ*) (monthly).

Rationalisierungs-Kuratorium der Deutschen Wirtschaft e.V. (RKW) (*German Productivity and Management Association*): 6236 Eschborn, Düsseldorfer Str. 40; f. 1921; 9,000 mems.; Pres. Prof. ERICH POTTHOFF; Secs. Dr. H. W. BÜTTNER, Prof. H. RÜHLE VON LILIENSTERN; publ. *Rationalisierung* (monthly).

Verband Deutscher Elektrotechniker (VDE) e.V. (*German Association of Electrical Engineers*): 6 Frankfurt a.M. 70, Stresemann Allee 21; f. 1893; 30,000 mems.; Chair. Dr.-Ing. e.h. Dipl.-Ing. GÜNTER NIEHAGE; Sec. Prof. Dr. phil. nat. PAUL DIETRICH; publs. *Elektrotechnische Zeitschrift, Nachrichtentechnische Zeitschrift, VDE-Vorschriften, VDE-Fachberichte, VDE-Buchreihe, VDE-Schnellberichte, NTZ-Report, ETZ-Report, NTG-Fachberichte, VDE-Schriftenreihe.*

Verein der Zellstoff- und Papier-Chemiker und -Ingenieure e.V. (*Association of Pulp and Paper Chemists and Engineers*): Darmstadt, Berliner Allee 56; f. 1905; 1,436 mems.; Pres. Dipl.-Ing. D. WAUBERT DE PUISEAU; Sec. Dipl.-Ing. R. WEIDENMÜLLER; Librarian Prof. Dr. TH. KRAUSE; publs. *Das Papier.*

Verein Deutscher Eisenhüttenleute (*Association of German Iron Metallurgists*): 4000 Düsseldorf 1, Breite Str. 27; f. 1860; promotion of research, literature, education and training; 10,500 mems.; library of 90,000 vols.; Pres. Dr. G. KLOTZBACH; Gen. Sec. Dr. H. KEGEL; publs. *Stahl und Eisen, Archiv für das Eisenhüttenwesen, Zeitschriften-und Bücherschau "Stahl und Eisen"*†.

Verein Deutscher Giessereifachleute (*Asscn. of German Foundry Engineers*): 4000 Düsseldorf 1, Sohnstr. 70; f. 1909; 3,500 mems.; library of 25,000 vols.; Chair. WILLI FINGER; Sec. Dr.-Ing. G. ENGELS; publs. *Giesserei* (fortnightly), *Giessereiforschung* (quarterly).

Verein Deutscher Ingenieure (*Asscn. of German Engineers*): 4 Düsseldorf 1, Graf-Recke-Str. 84; f. 1856; technical and scientific co-operation in 15 engineering sections concerning all fields of technology; training courses for professional engineers; over 70,000 mems.; library of c. 90,000 vols., 450 German and 350 foreign technical journals; complete documentation in various branches of engineering and prevention of air pollution and noise; Dir. Dr.-Ing. REINHARD MENGER; publs. *VDI-Zeitschrift* (fortnightly), *VDI-Nachrichten* (weekly), *Forschung im Ingenieurwesen* (6 a year), *Umwelt* (6 a year), etc.

Wissenschaftlicher Verein für Verkehrswesen e.V. (WVV) (*Transport Asscn.*): 43 Essen, Zweigerstr. 34; f. 1971; 200 mems.; Pres. ERICH THIEMER.

RESEARCH INSTITUTES

(*see* also under Universities)

GENERAL

Deutsche Forschungsgemeinschaft (*German Research Society*): 5300 Bonn 2, Kennedyallee 40; f. 1920, re-established 1949 for the area of the Federal Republic; provides financial and other assistance for research; in 1979 distributed DM. 739,000,000 (including special funds); members: universities, the Academies of Sciences, certain scientific and teaching institutions: mem. of the International Council of Scientific Unions; Pres. Prof. Dr. EUGEN SEIBOLD; Gen. Sec. Dr. CARL-HEINZ SCHIEL.

MAX-PLANCK-GESELLSCHAFT ZUR FÖRDERUNG DER WISSENSCHAFTEN E.V.

(Max Planck Society for the Advancement of Science)

P.O.B. 647, 8000 MUNICH 2,
REZIDENZSTRASSE 1A

Supersedes the former Kaiser-Wilhelm-Gesellschaft, Berlin (f. 1911).

The Society maintains 49 self-administering Research Institutes and 1 Project Group.

President: Prof. Dr. REIMAR LÜST.

Vice-Presidents: Prof. Dr. HELMUT COING, Prof. Dr. BENNO HESS, Prof. Dr. h.c. HANS L. MERKLE, Prof. Dr. GÜNTHER WILKE.

General Secretary: DIETRICH RANFT.

Research Institutes:

Max-Planck-Institut für Aeronomie (*Aeronomy*): 3411 Katlenburg-Lindau 3, Postfach 20; Man. Dir. Prof. Dr. W. IAN AXFORD.

Max-Planck-Institut für Astronomie (*Astronomy*): 6900 Heidelberg 1, Königstuhl; Man.-Dir. Prof. Dr. HANS ELSÄSSER.

Bibliotheca Hertziana (Max-Planck-Institut) (*Research Library for Art History*): 00187 Rome, Palazzo Zuccari, via Gregoriana 28; Man. Dir. Prof. Dr. MATTHIAS WINNER. *See under* Italy—Libraries).

Max-Planck-Institut für Bildungsforschung (*Education Research*): 1000 Berlin 33, Lentzeallee 94; Dir. Prof. D. GOLDSCHMIDT.

Max-Planck-Institut für Biochemie (*Biochemistry*): 8033 Martinsried bei München; Man. Dir. Prof. Dr. PETER HANS HOFSCHNEIDER.

Max-Planck-Institut für Biologie (*Biology*): 7400 Tübingen, Corrensstr. 38; Man. Dir. Prof. Dr. ULF HENNING.

Max-Planck-Institut für Biophysik (*Biophysics*): 6000 Frankfurt a.M. 70, Kennedyallee 70; Man. Dir. Prof. Dr. KARL JULIUS ULLRICH.

Max-Planck-Institut für Chemie (Otto-Hahn-Institut) (*Chemistry*): 6500 Mainz, Saarstr. 23, Postfach 3060; Man. Dir. Prof. Dr. FRIEDRICH BEGEMANN.

Max-Planck-Institut für biophysikalische Chemie (Karl-Friedrich-Bonhoeffer-Institut) (*Biophysical Chemistry*): 3400 Göttingen-Nikolausberg, Am Fassberg, Postfach 968; Man. Dir. Prof. Dr. ALBERT WELLER.

Max-Planck-Institut für Eisenforschung GmbH (*Iron*):

4000 Düsseldorf, Max-Planck-Strasse 1, Postfach 140 260; Head Manager and Dir. Prof. Dr. HANS JÜRGEN ENGELL.

Max-Planck-Institut für experimentelle Endokrinologie (*Endocrinology*): 3000 Hanover 61, Karl-Wiechert-Allee 9, Postfach 610309; Dir. Prof. Dr. PETER W. JUNGBLUT.

Max-Planck-Institut für Ernährungsphysiologie (*Nutrition*): 4600 Dortmund, Rheinlanddamm 201; library of 10,500 vols.; Dir. Prof. Dr. BENNO HESS.

Max-Planck-Institut für Festkörperforschung (*Solid State*): 7000 Stuttgart 80, Heisenbergstr. 1.; Man. Dir. Prof. Dr. ARNDT SIMON.

Max-Planck-Institut für molekulare Genetik (*Molecular Genetics*): 1000 Berlin 33 (Dahlem), Ihnestrasse 63–73; Man. Dir. Prof. Dr. HEINZ-GÜNTER WITTMANN.

Max-Planck-Institut für Geschichte (*History*): 3400 Göttingen, Hermann-Föge-Weg 11, Postfach 619; library of 27,300 vols.; Man.-Dir. Prof. Dr. RUDOLF VIERHAUS.

Gmelin-Institut für anorganische Chemie und Grenzgebiete der Max-Planck-Gesellschaft (*Inorganic Chemistry*): 6000 Frankfurt a.M. 90, Varrentrappstr. 40-42, Carl Bosch-Haus, Postfach 900467; Dir. Prof. Dr. EKKEHARD FLUCK.

Fritz-Haber-Institut der Max-Planck-Gesellschaft (*Physical Chemistry*): 1000 Berlin 33, Faradayweg 4-6; Man. Dir. Prof. Dr. HEINZ GERISCHER.

Max-Planck-Institut für Hirnforschung (*Brain Research*): 6000 Frankfurt/Main-Niederrad, Deutschordenstr. 46, Postfach 710 409; Man. Dir. Prof. Dr. ROLF HASSLER.

Max-Planck-Institut für Immunbiologie (*Immunology*): 7800 Freiburg, Stübeweg 51, Postfach 1169; Man. Dir. Prof. Dr. OTTO WESTPHAL.

Max-Planck-Institut für Kernphysik (*Nuclear Physics*): 6900 Heidelberg I, Saupfercheckweg, Postfach 103980; Man. Dir. Prof. Dr. HUGO FECHTIG.

Max-Planck-Institut für Kohlenforschung (*Coal*): 4330 Mülheim/Ruhr, Kaiser-Wilhelm-Platz 1; Dir. Prof. Dr. GÜNTHER WILKE.

Max-Planck-Institut für biologische Kybernetik (*Biological Cybernetics*): 7400 Tübingen, Spemannstr. 38; Man. Dir. Prof. Dr. WERNER REICHARDT.

Projektgruppe für Laserforschung (*Laser Research*): 8046 Garching bei München; Man. Dir. Prof. Dr. HERBERT WALTHER.

Max-Planck-Institut für Limnologie (*Limnology*): 2320 Plön/Holstein, August-Thienemann-Strasse 2, Postfach 165; Man. Dir. Prof. Dr. HANS JÜRGEN OVERBECK.

Max-Planck-Institut für experimentelle Medizin (*Experimental Medicine*): 3400 Göttingen, Hermann-Rein-Str. 3; Man. Dir. Prof. Dr. WALTHER VOGT.

Max-Planck-Institut für medizinische Forschung (*Medical Research*): 6900 Heidelberg 1, Jahnstr. 29; Man. Dir. Prof. Dr. HEINZ A. STAAB.

Max-Planck-Institut für Metallforschung (*Metallurgy*): 7000 Stuttgart 80, Heisenbergstr. 1; Man. Dir. JÖRG DIEHL.

Max-Planck-Institut für Meteorologie (*Meteorology*): 2000 Hamburg 13, Bundesstr. 55; Dir. Prof. Dr. KLAUS HASSELMANN.

Friedrich-Miescher-Laboratorium in der Max-Planck-Gesellschaft: 7400 Tübingen, Spemannstr. 39, Postfach 2109; biological research groups; Man. Dr. REINHARD KURTH, Dr. WILFRIED SEIFERT, Dr. MATTHIAS WABL, Dr. HEINZ WÄSSLE.

Max-Planck-Institut für ausländisches und internationales Patent-, Urheber- und Wettbewerbsrecht (*Foreign and International Patent, Copyright and Competition Law*): 8000 Munich 80, Siebertstr. 3; library of 20,000 vols.; Man. Dir. Prof. Dr. FRIEDRICH-KARL BEIER; publs. *Gewerblicher Rechtsschutz und Urheberrecht, Internationaler Teil* (monthly), *International Review of Industrial Property and Copyright* (quarterly).

Max-Planck-Institut für Physik und Astrophysik (*Physics and Astrophysics*): 8000 Munich 40, Föhringer Ring 6, Postfach 401212; Man. Dir. Prof. Dr. HANS-PETER DÜRR.

Max-Planck-Institut für physiologische und klinische Forschung, W. G. Kerckhoff-Institut (*Physiological and Clinical Research*): 6350 Bad Nauheim, Parkstrasse 1; Man. Dir. Prof. Dr. WOLFGANG SCHAPER.

Max-Planck-Institut für Plasmaphysik (*Plasma Physics*): 8046 Garching bei München; Scient. Dir. Prof. Dr. RUDOLF WIENECKE.

Max-Planck-Institut für ausländisches und internationales Privatrecht (*Foreign and International Private Law*): 2000 Hamburg 13, Mittelweg 187; Man. Dir. Prof. Dr. HEIN KÖTZ.

Max-Planck-Institut für Psychiatrie (Deutsche Forschungsanstalt für Psychiatrie) (*Psychiatry*): 8000 Munich 40, Kraepelinstrasse 2 and 10; Man. Dir. Prof. Dr. DETLEV PLOOG.

Max-Planck-Institut für Psycholinguistik (*Psycholinguistics*): 6522 Nijmegen, Berg en Dalseweg 79, Netherlands; Dir. Prof. Dr. WILLEM J. M. LEVELT.

Forschungsstelle für Psychopathologie und Psychotherapie in der Max-Planck-Gesellschaft (*Psychopathology and Psychotherapy*): 8000 Munich 40, Montsalvatstr. 19; Man. Prof. Dr. Dr. PAUL MATUSSEK.

Max-Planck-Institut für Radioastronomie (*Radioastronomy*): 5300 Bonn 1, Auf dem Hügel 69; Man. Dir. Prof. Dr.-Ing. PETER G. MEZGER.

Max-Planck-Institut für ausländisches öffentliches Recht und Völkerrecht (*Foreign Public and International Law*): 6900 Heidelberg, Berliner Str. 48; Dirs. Prof. Dr. RUDOLF BERNHARDT, Prof. Dr. HERMANN MOSLER.

Max-Planck-Institut für europäische Rechtsgeschichte (*European Legal History*): 6000 Frankfurt/Main 1, Freiherr-vom Stein-Str. 7; Man. Dir. Prof. Dr. WALTER WILHELM.

Max-Planck-Institut für ausländisches und internationales Sozialrecht (*International and Comparative Social Law*): 8000 Munich 40, Akademiestr. 7; Dir. Prof. Dr. HANS F. ZACHER.

Max-Planck-Institut für Sozialwissenschaften (*Research into the Essentials of the Scientific-Technological World*): 8130 Starnberg, Riemerschmidstrasse 7, Postfach 1529; Dir. Prof. Dr. JÜRGEN HABERMAS.

Max-Planck-Institut für ausländisches und internationales Strafrecht (*Foreign and international penal law*): 7800 Freiburg i. Br., Günterstalstr. 73; library of 64,000 vols.; Dirs. Prof. Dr. HANS-HEINRICH JESCHECK, Prof. Dr. GÜNTHER KAISER; publ. *Zeitschrift für die gesamte Strafrechtswissenschaft* (quarterly).

Max-Planck-Institut für Strömungsforschung (*Fluid Dynamics*): 3400 Göttingen, Böttingerstrasse 6-8; Man. Dir. Prof. Dr. HEINZ-GEORG WAGNER.

Max-Planck-Institut für Systemphysiologie (*Systems Physiology*): 46 Dortmund, Rheinlanddamm 201; Dir. Prof. Dr. DIETRICH WERNER LÜBBERS.

Forschungsstelle Vennesland: 1000 Berlin 33, Harnackstr. 23; Man. Prof. Dr. BIRGIT VENNESLAND.

Max-Planck-Institut für Verhaltensphysiologie (*Physiology of Behaviour*): 8131 Seewiesen über Starnberg, Obb.; Man. Dir. Prof. Dr. FRANZ HUBER.

Max-Planck-Institut für Virusforschung (*Virology*): 7400 Tübingen, Spemannstr. 35, Postfach 2109; Man. Dir. Dr. ULI SCHWARZ.

Max-Planck-Institut für Zellbiologie (*Cell Biology*): 6802 Ladenburg bei Heidelberg, Rosenhof; Man. Dir. Prof. Dr. HANS-GEORG SCHWEIGER.

Max-Planck-Institut für Züchtungsforschung (Erwin-Baur-Institut) (*Plant Breeding*): 5000 Cologne 30, Egelspfad; Dir. Prof. Dr. JOZEF ST. SCHELL.

OTHER INSTITUTIONS

Bibliothek und Archiv zur Geschichte der Max-Planck-Gesellschaft: 1000 Berlin 33, Garystr. 32; Dir. Dr. ROLF NEUHAUS.

Garching Instrumente Gesellschaft zur industriellen Nutzung von Forschungsergebnissen m.b.H.: Leonrodstr. 56, 8000 Munich 19; Man. Dr. HEINRICH KUHN.

Minerva Gesellschaft für die Forschung m.b.H.: 8000 Munich 2, Residenzstr. 1A; Man. DIETRICH RANFT.

Kerckhoff-Klinik: 6350 Bad Nauheim, Benekestr. 6–8; Dir. Prof. Dr. MARTIN SCHLEPPER.

Gesellschaft für wissenschaftliche Datenverarbeitung m.b.H. Göttingen: 3400 Göttingen-Nikolausberg, Am Fassberg; Mans. Dr. DIETER WALL, Dr. KURT PFUHL.

Zentrum für Interdisziplinäre Forschung: Universität Bielefeld, Wellenberg 1; f. 1968; interdisciplinary research in the fields of basic research, law and social sciences, behaviour and communications, natural sciences; 40 mems.; reference library of 15,000 vols.; Man. Dir. Prof. Dr. WILHELM VOSSKAMP.

AGRICULTURE AND VETERINARY SCIENCE

Bundesforschungsanstalt für Fischerei (*Federal Research Centre for Fisheries*): 2000 Hamburg 50, Palmaille 9; f. 1948; research into inland and sea fishing; 234 mems.; library of 46,500 vols.; Dir. Prof. Dr. W. SCHREIBER; publs. *Archiv für Fischereiwissenschaft*†, *Schriften der Budnesforschungsanstalt für Fischerei*, *Informationen für die Fischwirtschaft*†.

Institut für Seefischerei: Dir. Prof. Dr. DIETRICH SAHRHAGE; publ. *Mitteilungen aus dem Institut für Seefischerei*†.

Institut für Küsten- und Binnenfischerei: Dir. Prof. Dr. KLAUS TIEWS; publ. *Veröffentlichungen des Instituts für Küsten- und Binnenfischerei*†.

Institut für Fangtechnik: Dir. Prof. Dr. ROLF STEINBERG; publ. *Protokolle zur Fischereitechnik*†.

Institut für Biochemie und Technologie: Dir. Prof. Dr. WOLFGANG SCHREIBER.

Isotopenlaboratorium: Dir. Prof. Dipl.-Phys. WERNER FELDT.

Informations- und Dokumentationsstelle: Dir. Dr. WULF PETER KIRCHNER.

Also at Bremerhaven, Cuxhaven, Kiel, Langballigau and Ahrensburg.

Bundesforschungsanstalt für Landwirtschaft (*Federal Research Centre for Agriculture*): Braunschweig-Völkenrode (FAL), 33 Braunschweig, Bundesallee 50; f. 1947; library of 100,000 vols.; Pres. Prof. Dr. JOACHIM PIOTROWSKI; Gen. Sec. (vacant); 14 institutes for specialized agricultural research; publs. *Landbauforschung Völkenrode* (2 or 3 per year), *Annual Report*.

Deutsche Gesellschaft für Holzforschung e.V. (*Wood Research*): 8000 Munich 2, Prannerstr. 9; f. 1942; Pres. Prof. Dr. H. SCHULZ; Man. HEINRICH FREIHERR VON BODMAN; publs. *DGfH-Nachrichten* (quarterly), *Informationsdienst Holz der Entwicklungsgemeinschaft Holzbau*†, and several annual reports, etc.

Deutsche Gesellschaft für Hopfenforschung (*Hops Research*): Wolnzach, Preysingstr. 10/1; Pres. Sen. H. BOEHM; Dir. H. SCHLICKER.

Forschungsgesellschaft für Agrarpolitik und Agrarsoziologie: 53 Bonn, Meckenheimer Allee 125; f. 1952; 60 mems.; Pres. Prof. Dr. H. KÖLTER; Dir. Prof. Dr. B. VAN DEENEN.

ARCHITECTURE AND TOWN PLANNING

Akademie für Raumforschung und Landesplanung (*Academy of Regional Research and Land Planning*): 3000 Hannover, Hohenzollernstr. 11; f. 1935, re-founded 1946; 300 mems.; library of 15,000 vols.; Pres. Dr. KLAUS MAYER; Scientific Sec. Dr. K. HAUBNER; publ. *Raumforschung und Raumordnung*† (every 2 months).

Deutsche Akademie für Städtebau und Landesplanung (*Town and Country Planning*): 3000 Hannover 1, Friedrichswall 4; f. 1922; 450 mems.; library of 3,000 vols.; Pres. Prof. Dr.-Ing. E. h. R. HILLEBRECHT; publ. *Mitteilungen*† (once or twice annually).

THE ARTS

Gesellschaft für Musikforschung: 3500 Kassel-Wilhelmshöhe, Heinrich-Schütz-Allee 35; f. 1946; 1,500 mems. Pres. Prof. Dr. CARL DAHLHAUS; Treas. Dr. WOLFGANG REHM; publ. *Die Musikforschung* (quarterly).

Staatliches Institut für Musikforschung Preussischer Kulturbesitz: 1 Berlin 30, Stauffenbergstr. 14; f. 1935; collects musicological material, instruments, records, phonograms and tape recordings; conducts research into the development and history of musicology, inc. acoustics, musical instruments and the style and practice of executing music of the past; archival and documentary research and comparative musicological research; research in German folk music; 48 mems.; open to the public; library of over 35,000 vols.; lectures, concerts and exhibitions; Dir. Prof. Dr. HANS-PETER REINECKE; Representative Dr. DAGMAR DROYSEN-REBER; publs. *Veröffentlichungen*†, *Bibliographie des Musikschrifttums*†, *Jahrbuch*†, etc.

Zentralinstitut für Kunstgeschichte in München (*History of Art*): 8 Munich 2, Meiserstr. 10; f. 1946; 195,000 vols.; 500,000 photographs; Dir. Prof. Dr. WILLIBALD SAUERLÄNDER; Vice-Dir. Dr. JÖRG RASMUSSEN; publs. *Veröffentlichungen*, *Kunstchronik*† (monthly), *Reallexikon zur deutschen Kunstgeschichte*, *Münchner Jahrbuch der bildenden Kunst*† (annually) (with the Bavarian State Museums).

BIBLIOGRAPHY AND LIBRARY SCIENCE

Gutenberg-Gesellschaft (*Gutenberg Society*): 65 Mainz, Liebfrauenplatz 5; f. 1901; for the publication of research work on the art of book printing from Gutenberg until the present day; 1,700 mems.; Pres. The Lord Mayor of the City of Mainz; Chair. Prof. Dr. H.-J. KOPPITZ; publs. *Gutenberg-Jahrbuch*, *Kleine Drucke*, *Veröffentlichungen*, etc.

ECONOMICS, LAW AND POLITICS

Arbeitsgemeinschaft deutscher Wirtschaftswissenschaftlicher Forschungsinstitute e.V. (*Association of German Economic Science Research Institutes*): 43 Essen, Hohenzollernstr. 1-3; f. 1949; 27 mem. institutes; co-ordinates programmes of the institutes and provides a permanent base for research exchange and co-operation; Chair. Prof. Dr. H. GIERSCH; publ. *Gemeinschaftsdiagnose* (every 6 months); affiliates the following:

Deutsches Institut für Wirtschaftsforschung (Institut für Konjunkturforschung) (*German Institute for*

Economic Research): 1000 Berlin 33, Königin-Luise-Str. 5; f. 1925; Pres. Prof. Dr. HANS-JÜRGEN KRUPP; publs. *Wochenbericht*† (weekly), *Vierteljahreshefte zur Wirtschaftsforschung* (quarterly), *Economic Bulletin*† (monthly).

Abteilung Wirtschaftswissenschaft im Osteuropa Institut an der Freien Universität Berlin (*Economics Department of the East European Institute at the Free University, Berlin*): 1000 Berlin 33, Garystr. 55; f. 1950; economic research on CMEA-countries; 13 mems.; library of 30,000 vols. and 200 periodicals; Dir. Prof. Dr. ERICH KLINKMÜLLER; publs. *Wirtschaftswissenschaftliche Veröffentlichungen, Berichte des Osteuropa Instituts/Reihe Wirtschaft und Recht.*

Forschungsinstitut der Friedrich-Ebert-Stiftung (*Research Department of Friedrich-Ebert-Stiftung*): 5300 Bonn 2, Godesberger Allee 149; Dir. Dr. HORST HEIDERMANN.

Institut für landwirtschaftliche Marktforschung der Bundesforschungsanstalt für Landwirtschaft Braunschweig-Völkenrode (FAL) (*Institute for Agricultural Market Research of the Federal Research Centre for Agriculture*): 3300 Braunschweig, Bundesallee 50; Dir. Prof. Dr. H. E. BUCHHOLZ.

Bremer Ausschuss für Wirtschaftsforschung (*Bremen Economic Research Institute*): 2800 Bremen 1, Domshof 14–15/IV; f. 1947; library of 30,000 vols.; Dir. Dr. FRANK HALLER; publs. *Wirtschaftsdaten*† (annually), *Die Wirtschaftsstruktur Bremens*† (every 3 years).

Rheinisch-Westfälisches Institut für Wirtschaftsforschung (*Rheinland-Westphalian Institute for Economic Research*): 4300 Essen, Hohenzollernstr. 1-3; f. 1943; study of the structure and development of the West German economy; special research facilities, advice on administration and economics for firms and students; 20 mems.; library of 45,000 vols.; Dirs. Dr. GREGOR WIMKELMEYER, Dipl.-Volksw. BERNHARD FILUSCH, Dr. WILLI LAMBERTS; publs. *Konjunkturberichte*†, *Mitteilungen*† (quarterly), *Die Konjunktur im Handwerk*† (annually), *Konjunkturbriefe, Schriftenreihe, RWI-Papiere* (all irregular).

Schmalenbach-Gesellschaft—Deutsche Gesellschaft fur Betriebs-Wirtschaft e.V.: 5000 Köln 51, Tiberiusstr. 4; f. 1978; economic research; 1,500 mems.; Pres. Dr. MAX GUENTHER; Man. Dr. GERTRUD FUCHS-WEGNER; publ. *Schmalenbachs Zeitschrift für betriebswirtschaftliche Forschung* (*ZfbF*) (monthly).

Institut für Allgemeine Überseeforschung der Stiftung "Deutsches Übersee-Institut" (*Institute for General Overseas Research*): 2 Hamburg 36, Neuer Jungfernstieg 21; f. 1964; 10 mems.; library of 1,800 vols. and periodicals; Dir. Prof. Dr. J. LÜBBERT.

HWWA-Institut für Wirtschaftsforschung-Hamburg (*Hamburg Institute for International Economics*): 2000 Hamburg 36, Neuer Jungfernstieg 21; f. 1908; economic systems, trade cycles and statistics, public finance and regional policy, economic integration, development policies and international monetary policy; 250 mems.; library of 700,000 vols., 9,000 reference books, 3,600 periodicals; depository library for UN, FAO, GATT, OECD, EEC; Dir. Prof. Dr. H. D. ORTLIEB; publs. *Wirtschaftsdienst*†, *Bibliographie der Wirtschaftspresse*† (monthly), *Konjunktur von Morgen*† (fortnightly), *Intereconomics*† (every 2 months in English), *Weltkonjunkturdienst, Finanzierung und Entwicklung* (quarterly).

Institut für Weltwirtschaft an der Universität Kiel: (*see under* Christian-Albrechts-Universität).

Deutsches Institut zur Förderung des industriellen Führungsnachwuchses (*German Institute for the Promotion of Industrial Management Training*): 5000 Köln 51, Ulmenallee 140; f. 1955; library of 10,000 vols.; Dir. Dr. H. HELLWIG.

Energiewirtschaftliches Institut an der Universität zu Köln: 5000 Köln 41; Albertus Magnus Platz, Dir. Prof. Dr. HANS K. SCHNEIDER.

Institut für Handelsforschung an der Universität zu Köln: 5000 Köln 41, Säckinger Str. 5; Dir. Prof. Dr. E. SUNDHOFF.

Institut für Wirtschaftspolitik an der Universität zu Köln: 5000 Köln 41, Lindenburger Allee 32; Dirs. Profs. Dr. H. WILLGERODT, Dr. CHR. WATRIN.

Wirtschafts- und Sozialwissenschaftliches Institut des Deutschen Gewerkschaftsbundes GmbH (*Trade Unions' Economic Research Institute*): 4000 Düsseldorf, Hans-Böcklerstr. 39; Dirs. Dr. H. MARKMANN, R. A. Dr. WOLFGANG SPIEKER.

Forschunginstitut für Wirtschaftspolitik an der Universität Mainz: (*see under* Johannes Gutenberg-Universität).

IFO-Institut für Wirtschaftsforschung (*IFO-Institute for Economic Research*): 8000 Munich 86, Poschingerstrasse 5; f. 1949; empirical economic research; 230 staff; library of 80,000 vols.; Chair. Dr. K. H. OPPENLÄNDER; publs. *IFO-Schnelldienst*† (3 a month), *Wirtschaftskonjunktur*† (monthly), *IFO Digest*† (quarterly, English), *IFO-Studien* (quarterly).

Deutsches Wirtschaftswissenschaftliches Institut für Fremdenverkehr an der Universität München (*German Institute for Economic Research in Tourism and Travel, University of Munich*): 8000 Munich 2, Herman-Sack-Strasse 2; f. 1950; 60 staff; Dirs. Prof. Dr. E. V. BÖVENTER, Prof. Dr. K. RUPPERT, Dr. A. KOCH; publ. *Jahrbuch für Fremdenverkehr.*

Forschungsstelle für allgemeine und textile Marktwirtschaft an der Universität Münster (*Research Institute for General and Textile Economics*): 4400 Münster i.W., Alter Fischmarkt 21; f. 1941; 25 mems.; library of 15,000 vols.; Dir. Prof. Dr. ERNST HELMSTÄDTER.

G.f.K.—Nürnberg, Gesellschaft für Konsum-, Markt- und Absatzforschung e.V. (*Society for Consumer and Market Research*): 8500 Nuremberg, Burgschmietstrasse 2; 775 mems.; library of 3,000 vols.; Dirs. Dipl. Kfm. PAUL BECK, Dipl. Kfm. W. OTT, R. RADLER; publs. *Yearbook of Marketing and Consumer Research, Europe Basic Market Data, GFK Press Release.*

Institut für Angewandte Wirtschaftsforschung Tübingen (*Institute for Applied Economic Research*): Ob dem Himmelreich 1, 7400 Tübingen; f. 1957; analysis of applied politics; econometric macromodels; 18 mems.; library of 6,000 vols.; Dir. Prof. Dr. A. E. OTT.

Statistisches Bundesamt (*Federal Statistical Office*): 6200 Wiesbaden 1, Gustav-Streseman-Ring 11; f. 1950; 2,700 mems.; library of 205,000 vols.; Pres. Dr. FRANZ KROPPENSTEDT.

Institut der deutschen Wirtschaft e.V.: 5000 Cologne 51, Oberländer Ufer 84/88; f. 1951; economic and social sciences; library and archives include 140,000 monographs; Dir. Prof. B. FREUDENFELD.

Osteuropa-Institut München: 8000 Munich 80, Scheinerstr. 11; Dir. Prof. Dr. G. HEDTKAMP.

Institut für Wirtschafts- und Gesellschaftspolitik (*Institute for Economic and Social Policy*): 5300 Bonn 2, Ahrstr. 45; Dir. Dr. MEINHARD MIEGEL.

Institut für Arbeitsmarkt- und Berufsforschung der Bundesanstalt für Arbeit: 85 Nürnberg, Regensburger Str. 104; f. 1967; employment and labour market research; library of *c.* 15,000 vols.; Dir. Dr. D. MERTENS; publ. *Mitteilungen aus der Arbeitsmarkt- und Berufsforschung* (quarterly).

Institut für Seeverkehrswirtschaft (*Institute of Shipping Economics*): 2800 Bremen 1, Werderstr. 73; f. 1954; shipping, shipbuilding, sea-port economics, seaborne trade; library of about 60,000 bibliographical units; 500 periodicals; Dir. Dr. H. L. BETH; publs. *Lectures and Contributions to International Shipping Research, Shipping Statistics* (monthly figures of shipping, shipbuilding, sea-ports and sea-borne trade), *Statistical Yearbook Facts and Figures.*

Arbeitsgemeinschaft Sozialwissenschaftlicher Institute e.V. (*Association of Social Science Institutes*): 5300 Bonn 1, Lennéstr. 30; f. 1947 to promote research in social sciences; 83 mems.; Pres. Prof. Dr. MAX KAASE; Man. Dir. Dr. J. HAGENA; publ. *Soziale Welt* (quarterly).

Arnold Bergstraesser Institut für kulturwissenschaftliche Forschung (ABI): 78 Freiburg im Breisgau, Windausstr. 16; f. 1960; socio-political research particularly on education and administration in Africa, Asia, Near East and Latin America; depts. of overseas education and overseas admin.; four regional depts.; Africa Asia, Latin America, Middle East/North Africa; 50 mems.; library of *c.* 50,000 vols.; Dirs. Prof. Dr. T. HANF, Prof. Dr. D. OBERNDÖRFER.

Deutsche Gesellschaft für Friedens- und Konfliktforschung (*German Society for Peace and Conflict Research*): 5300 Bonn 2, Theaterplatz 28; f. 1970; promotion of Peace and Conflict research and diffusion of the idea of Peace; Dir. KARLHEINZ KOPPE; publ. *DGFK-Informationen*† (2 a year).

Gesellschaft für Deutschlandforschung e.V. (*Society for Research on Germany*): Roonstr. 14, 1000 Berlin 37; f. 1979; contemporary research on Germany; promotes and finances interested researchers; seminars and conferences; *c.* 125 mems.; Pres. Prof. Dr. SIEGFRIED MAMPEL; Vice-Pres. Prof. Dr. GERNOT GUTTMANN.

Informationszentrum Sozialwissenschaften (*Social Science Information Centre*): 5300 Bonn 1, Lennéstr. 30; f. 1969; collection and dissemination of information in the social sciences; Pres. Prof. Dr. MAX KAASE; publ. *Forschungsarbeiten, Dokumentation* (annually).

Institut Finanzen und Steuern e.V. (*Finance and Taxation Institute*): 53 Bonn, Markt 14; f. 1939; Dir. Prof. Dr. H. VOGEL.

Institut für Afrika-Kunde (*Institute of African Studies*): 2000 Hamburg 36; Neuer Jungfernstieg 21, f. 1963; research, documentation, discussion groups, international contact with organizations and individuals with specialized knowledge of African affairs; library of 22,000 vols. and *c.* 500 periodicals; Dir. Dr. ROLF HOFMEIER; publs. *Afrika Spectrum*† (3 a year), *Dokumentationsdienst Afrika*†, *Ausgewählte neuere Literatur* (quarterly), *Aktueller Informationsdienst Afrika*† (2 a month), *Hamburger Beiträge zur Afrika-Kunde, Arbeiten*, monographs†.

Institut für international vergleichende Wirtschafts- und Sozialstatistik an der Universität Heidelberg: 6900 Heidelberg, Grabengasse 14; 5 mems.; library of *c.* 20,000 vols.; Dir. Prof. G. MENGES.

Internationales Forschungsinstitut für Staatssoziologie und Politik: 78 Freiburg, Postschliessfach 1622; f. 1950; 5 mems.; library of 6,000 vols.; Dirs. Dr. M. VAERTING, Dr. E. ELMERICH; publ. *Zeitschrift für Staatssoziologie.*

Johann-Gottfried-Herder-Institut: 3550 Marburg/Lahn 1, Gisonenweg 5-7; f. 1950; research on countries and peoples of Eastern Central Europe; library: *see* Libraries; Dir. Prof. Dr. RODERICH SCHMIDT; publs. *Zeitschrift für Ostforschung*† (quarterly), *Dokumentation Ostmitteleuropa*† (every 2 months).

Stiftung Wissenschaft und Politik—Forschungsinstitut für Internationale Politik und Sicherheit (*Foundation for Science and Politics—Research Institute for International Politics and Security*): 8026 Ebenhausen/Isartal; f. 1962; government-sponsored research; *c.* 110 staff; library of 40,000 vols., 600 periodicals, 1,000 yearbooks; Pres. Prof. Dr. h.c. H. L. MERKLE; Dir. Prof. Dr. K. RITTER.

EDUCATION

Bildungstechnologisches Zentrum G.m.b.H. (BTZ): 62 Wiesbaden, Bodenstedtstr. 7; f. 1970; research into technologically supported teaching procedures and instructional systems; development, testing and implementation of prototypes, instructional programmes, other teaching materials and complex instructional systems for school, university, vocational training and adult education; support of education and advanced training of teachers; 48 mems.; library of 5,400 vols. and 111 periodicals; Exec. Dir. EDGAR SCHMIDT; publs. *Beitrage zur Bildungstechnologie*†, *BTZ Information,*† *BTZ Gutachten u. BTZ Monographien I–V*†.

Deutsches Institut für Internationale Pädagogische Forschung: 6000 Frankfurt am Main 90, Schloss-Str. 29; f. 1952; educational research; 100 mems.; library of 110,000 vols.; Dir. Prof. Dr. WOLFGANG MITTER; publ. *Mitteilungen und Nachrichten*†.

Gesellschaft zur Förderung Pädagogischer Forschung e.V. (*Society for the Promotion of Educational Research*): 6000 Frankfurt am Main 90, Schloss-Str. 29, Postfach 900280; f. 1952; dissemination of research results, organization of communication processes between educational research and school practice; *c.* 600 mems.; Pres. Prof. Dr. E. STEIN; Sec. Prof. Dr. H. BARTENWERFER; publ. *Mitteilungen und Nachrichten*†.

HISTORY, GEOGRAPHY AND ARCHAEOLOGY

Bundesforschungsanstalt für Landeskunde und Raumordnung (*Federal Research Institute for Regional Geography and Regional Planning*): P.O.B. 200130, 5300 Bonn 2; f. 1941; library of 150,000 vols., 650 periodicals, 200,000 maps, 1,500 atlases; Dir. Dr. KARL GANSER; Head of Library Dept. Dr. J. WEBER; publ. *Referateblatt zur Raumentwicklung* (quarterly and special numbers).

Deutsches Archäologisches Institut (*Archaeological Institute*): 1 Berlin 33, Podbielskiallee 69-71; f. 1829; Pres. Prof. Dr. WERNER KRÄMER; Dir. Prof. Dr. VOLKER MICHAEL STROCKA; brs. in Rome (Prof. Dr. THEODOR KRAUS), Athens (Prof. Dr. HELMUT KYRIELEIS), Istanbul (Prof. Dr.-Ing. W. MÜLLER-WIENER), Madrid (Prof. Dr. WILHELM GRÜNHAGEN), Cairo (Prof. Dr. W. KAISER), Baghdad (Prof. Dr. H. J. SCHMIDT), and Teheran (Prof. Dr. WOLFRAM KLEISS); also Römisch-Germanische Kommission, Frankfurt am Main (Prof. Dr. HANS SCHÖNBERGER) and Kommission für Alte Geschichte und Epigraphik, München (Prof. Dr. E. BUCHNER); publs. *Jahrbuch, Archäologischer Anzeiger, Archäologische Bibliographie, Berichte der Römisch-Germanischen-Kommission, Germania, Chiron, Athenische Mitteilungen, Römische Mitteilungen, Istanbuler Mitteilungen*, monographs (40-50 a year) and others.

Institut für Europäische Geschichte (*Institute for European History*): 6500 Mainz, Alte Universitätsstr. 19; f. 1953; history of religion in Europe at the time of Humanism and the Reformation, European history since 1648; library of 100,000 vols.; Dirs. Prof. Dr. PETER MEINHOLD (Abt. Religionsgeschichte), Prof. Dr. K. O. VON ARETIN (Abt. Universalgeschichte); publ. *Veröffentlichungen.*

Institut für Zeitgeschichte (*Institute of Modern History*): 8 Munich 19, Leonrodstr. 46b; f. 1949; German history research since 1918, particularly Weimar Republic, National Socialism and post 1945 history; library of 79,000 vols.; Dir. Prof. Dr. M. BROSZAT; publs. *Vierteljahrshefte für Zeitgeschichte* (quarterly), *Schriftenreihe* (2 a year), *Studien zur Zeitgeschichte, Quellen und Darstellungen zur Zeitgeschichte.*

Vereinigung zur Erforschung der Neueren Geschichte e.V. (*Modern History Research Association*): 53 Bonn, Argelanderstr. 59; f. 1956; 17th century to present-day history; Dir. Prof. Dr. KONRAD REPGEN; Man. Dr. G. BUCHSTAB; publs. *Acta Pacis Westphalicae* (Sources of the Westphalian Peace Conference), *Schriftenreihe.*

LANGUAGE AND LITERATURE

Arbeitsstelle für Robert-Musil-Forschung/Centre de Recherches Robert Musil: 6600 Saarbrücken 11, FR. 8.1 Germanistik, Universität des Saarlandes, St. Johanner Stadtwald; f. 1970; library of 600 vols.; archives; study programmes, publications, collections, symposia, bibliography; Dirs. Prof. Dr. MARIE-LOUISE ROTH, Dr. MARIE-CHRISTINE PILA, WOLFGANG VOGT; publs. research reports. (*See also* International Robert Musil Society).

Institut für Deutsche Sprache: 68 Mannheim, Friedrich-Karl-Str. 12; f. 1964; scientific study of present-day German; 90 mems.; library of *c.* 40,000 vols.; Pres. Prof. Dr. HUGO MOSER; Dir. Dr. GERHARD STICKEL; publs. *Sprache der Gegenwart, Heutiges Deutsch, Forschungsberichte, Deutsche Sprache, Germanistik.*

MEDICINE

Bernhard-Nocht-Institut für Schiffs- und Tropenkrankheiten (*Nautical and Tropical Medicine*): 2 Hamburg 4, Bernhard-Nocht-Strasse 74; f. 1900; tropical medicine and parasitology; field research station in Liberia; library of 19,000 vols. and 47,000 reprints; Dir. Prof. Dr. HANS-HARALD SCHUMACHER; publ. *Tropenmedizin und Parasitologie.*

Chemotherapeutisches Forschungsinstitut Georg-Speyer-Haus: 6000 Frankfurt a.M. 70, Paul-Ehrlich-Strasse 42/44; f. 1906; 30 mems.; Dir. Prof. Dr. H. D. BREDE.

C. u O. Vogt-Institut für Hirnforschung, Universität Düsseldorf (*Brain Research*): 4 Düsseldorf, Moorenstr. 5; f. 1937; morphometry, neuroanatomy, neuropathology, psychopharmacology, neurochemistry, neuropsychology; Dir. Prof. Dr. A. HOPF; publ. *Journal für Hirnforschung.*

Deutsche Gesellschaft für Allergieforschung (*Allergy Research*): 74 Tübingen, Liebermeisterstr. 8; Dir. Prof. Dr. E. LETTERER.

Deutsche Gesellschaft für Herz- und Kreislaufforschung (*Cardiovascular Research*): 6350 Bad Nauheim, Max-Planck-Institut für physiologische und klinische Forschung, W. G. Kerckhoff-Institut; f. 1927; 1,000 mems.; Sec. W. SCHAPER; publ. *Verhandlungen* (annual).

Deutsche Gesellschaft für Sexualforschung e.V. (*German Association for Sex Research*): 6000 Frankfurt a.M. 70, c/o Abteilung für Sexualwissenschaft, Klinikum der Universität, Theodor-Stern-Kai 7; f. 1950; 220 mems.; Pres. Prof. Dr. VOLKMAR SIGUSCH; publ. *Beiträge zur Sexualforschung.*

Deutsche Krebsgesellschaft e.V. (*German Cancer Society*): 43 Essen, Hufelandstrasse 55; f. 1951; co-ordinates activities of regional cancer research institutions; Pres. Prof. Dr. C. G. SCHMIDT; Sec.-Gen. Prof. Dr. A. GEORGII.

Forschungsvereinigung Feinmechanik und Optik e.V. (*Precision Mechanics and Optic Research Association*): 5000 Cologne, Pipinstrasse 16; f. 1963; Dir. Prof. Dr. W. ZIEGLER.

Geomedizinische Forschungsstelle der Heidelberger Akademie der Wissenschaften: 69 Heidelberg, Karlstr. 4; f. 1952; 50 mems.; library of 3,000 vols.; Dir. Prof. Dr. JUSATZ; publs. *World Atlas of Epidemic Diseases* (3 vols. 1952-1961), *World Maps of Climatology, Geomedical Monographs Series*† 6 (vols.).

Gesellschaft für Strahlen- und Umweltforschung m.b.H. (*Society for Radiation and Environmental Research*): 8042 Neuherberg, Post Oberschleissheim, Ingolstädter Landstr. 1; f. 1964; controls 27 institutes and departments of biology, radiation-botany, biochemistry, haematology, medical data processing, ecological chemistry, toxicology, health physics, radiohydrometry, applied optics and underground storage; central library of 8,000 vols. and 300 journals; Commercial Dir. Dr. R. GEROLD; Scientific and Technical Dir. Prof. Dr. R. WITTENZELLNER.

Gollwitzer-Meier-Institut: 497 Bad Oeynhausen, Herforder Strasse; f. 1955; cardiovascular diagnosis and rehabilitation; 110 mems.; library of 2,000 vols.; Dir. Prof. Dr. U. GLEICHMANN.

Institut für Wasserchemie und Chemische Balneologie der Technischen Universität München: 8000 Munich 70, Marchioninistr. 17; f. 1951; water chemistry, chemical hydrology, hydrogeology; 40 mems.; Dir. Prof. Dr. K. E. QUENTIN; publ. *Journal for Water and Wastewater Research* (every two months).

Max von Pettenkofer-Institut (*Institute of Hygiene and Medical Microbiology*): 8 Munich 2, Pettenkoferstr. 9a; Institute of Ludwig-Maximilians-Universität, Munich.

Medizinisches Institut für Umwelthygiene an der Universität Düsseldorf: 4000 Düsseldorf, Gurlittstr. 53; f. 1962; research into air pollution and pneumoconiosis; 220 mems.; library of *c.* 3,500 vols.; Dir. Prof. Dr. H. W. SCHLIPKÖTER; publ. *Umwelthygiene, Jahresberichte*†.

Paul-Ehrlich-Institut, Bundesamt für Sera und Impfstoffe: 6000 Frankfurt a.M. 70, Paul-Ehrlich-Strasse 42/44; f. 1899; 160 mems.; library of 30,000 vols.; Pres. Prof. Dr. H. D. BREDE; publ. *Arbeiten aus dem Paul-Ehrlich-Institut, dem Georg-Speyer-Haus und dem Ferdinand-Blum-Institut*† (irregular).

Wissenschaftliche Vereinigung für Ultraschallforschung e.V. (*Supersonic Research*): 51 Aachen, Luisenhospital; Dir. Prof. Dr. REIMAR POHLMAN; Sec. Prof. Dr. K. WOEBER; publ. *Rehabilitation.*

NATURAL SCIENCES

General

Forschungsinstitut und Natur-Museum Senckenberg (*Research institute and Natural History Museum*): Frankfurt a.M., 25 Senckenberg-Anlage; f. 1817; systematics, anatomy, distribution, ecology, evolution in zoology, botany, palaeozoology, palaeobotany, marine biology and geology, palaeoanthropology; 35 scientists; Dir. Prof. Dr. W. SCHÄFER; publs. *Abhandlungen der SNG*†, *Senckenbergiana biologica*†, *Senckenbergiana lethaea*†, *Senckenbergiana maritima*†, *Archiv für Molluskenkunde*†, *Senckenberg-Bücher*†, *Aufsätze und Reden der Senckenbergischen Naturforschenden Gesellschaft*†, *Natur und Museum*†, *Kleine Senckenberg-Reihe*†, *Courier Forschungsinstitut Senckenberg*†.

Fraunhofer-Gesellschaft zur Förderung der angewandten Forschung: 8 Munich 19, Leonrodstr. 54; f. 1949; 450 mems.; Pres. Prof. Dr. HEINZ KELLER.

Biological Sciences

Biologische Anstalt Helgoland (*Biological Institution Helgoland*): Central Laboratory 2000 Hamburg; Marine Station, 2192 Helgoland; Littoral Station, 2282 List/Sylt; f. 1892; research in marine biology; 163 mems.;

library of 36,000 books and journals; Dir. Prof. Dr. O. KINNE; publ. *Helgoländer wissenschaftliche Meeresuntersuchungen.*

Deutsche Gesellschaft für Moor- und Torfkunde (*German Society for Bog and Peat Research*): 3 Hannover-Buchholz, Alfred-Bentz-Haus, Stille-Weg 2; f. 1970; 150 mems.; Pres. Prof. Dr. G. LÜTTIG; publ. *TELMA.*

Forschungsinstitut Borstel, Institut für Experimentelle Biologie und Medizin (*Borstel Research Institute for Experimental Biology and Medicine*): 2061 Borstel, Parkallee 1; f. 1947; research in fields of biology, chemistry, and medicine; library of 15,000 vols.; Pres. Dr. H. LEMKE; Dir. Prof. Dr. J. MEISSNER.

Institut für Meeresforschung (*Marine Research*): 2850 Bremerhaven-G, Am Handelshafen 12; f. 1948; library of 10,000 vols.; Dir. Prof. Dr. SEBASTIAN GERLACH; publ. *Veröffentlichungen des Instituts für Meeresforschung in Bremerhaven*†.

Institut für Vogelforschung Vogelwarte Helgoland (*Ornithological Research*): 2940 Wilhelmshaven, Rüstersiel; f. 1910, re-opened 1947; biology, migration studies, ringing centre, ecology, morphology, ethology of birds and biology of sea-birds, etc.; Dir. Priv.-Doz. Dr. J. NICOLAI.

Naturforschende Gesellschaft Bamberg e.V.: 8600 Bamberg, Hegelstrasse 83; f. 1834; 160 mems.; 18,000 vols.; Dirs. Dr. E. UNGER, Dr. J. JÄGER; publ. *Berichte*†.

Naturforschende Gesellschaft Freiburg i. Br.: 78 Freiburg i. Br., Albertstr. 23B; f. 1821; 250 mems.; Pres. Prof. Dr. ERNST BECKSMANN; publ. *Berichte* (1–2 a year).

Institut für Allgemeine Botanik und Botanischer Garten der Universität (*Institute for General Botany and Botanic Garden of the University*): 2 Hamburg 36, Jungiusstrasse 6; f. 1821; research in botany and microbiology; botanical garden and herbarium comprising *c.* 800,000 specimens; *c.* 150 mems.; library of 22,250 vols. and 49,000 reprints; Man. Dir. Prof. Dr. W. O. ABEL; publs. *Mitteilungen*†, *Institut für Allgemeine Botanik Hamburg*†.

Institut für Angewandte Botanik (*Institute of Applied Botany at Hamburg University*): 2 Hamburg 36, Marseiller Strasse 7; f. 1885; *c.* 145 mems.; library of 130,000 vols.; research on plant products, agriculture and horticulture; Dir. Prof. Dr. K. VON WEIHE; publ. *Jahresberichte*† (every 2 years).

Mathematics

Mathematisches Forschungsinstitut (*Mathematical Research Institute*): 762 Oberwolfach-Walke, Schwarzwald, Lorenzenhof; Dir. Prof. Dr. MARTIN BARNER.

Physical Sciences

Astronomisches Institut der Universität Münster und Sternwarte: 44 Münster (Westf.), Steinfurterstr. 107; f. 1912; photometry, spectroscopy; 10 staff; library of *c.* 14,000 books; Dir. W. SEITTER; publ. *Mitteilungen*† (irregular).

Astronomisches Institut der Universität Tübingen: 7400 Tübingen, Waldhäuserstr. 64; EUV- and X-ray astronomy, optical astronomy, solar physics; library of 4,300 vols.; Dir. Prof. M. GREWING.

Astronomisches Rechen-Institut (*Astronomical Institute*): 6900 Heidelberg, 12-14 Mönchhofstrasse; f. 1700; theoretical astronomy; 20 mems,; library of 20,000 vols.; Dir. Prof. Dr. W. FRICKE; publs. *Apparent Places of Fundamental Stars, Astronomy and Astrophysics Abstracts, Veröffentlichungen.*

Bundesanstalt für Geowissenschaften und Rohstoffe (*Federal Institute for Geosciences and Natural Resources*): 3000 Hannover 51, Postfach 51 0153; f. 1958; mapping, geological and geophysical prospecting, mineral surveys and marine geology; employs 725 scientists throughout world; geoscientific collections of *c.* 100,000 specimens; 250,000 vols.; Pres. Prof. Dr. FRIEDRICH BENDER; publ. *Geologisches Jahrbuch.*

Deutsches Hydrographisches Institut: Postfach 220, 2000 Hamburg 4, Bernhard-Nocht-Str. 78; f. 1945 (1861); under the Federal Ministry of Transport; oceanography, tides and currents, geomagnetism, gravimetry, time service for sea-going vessels, nautical technics, navigating methods, hydrographic surveying and nautical geodesy, bathymetry, sea-bed geology, pollution control, ice information service, nautical charts and publications; library of 100,000 vols.; hydrographic information service; 800 mems.; Pres. Prof. Dr. G. ZICKWOLFF; publs. *Deutsche Hydrographische Zeitschrift* (six per annum), *Der Seeward* (6 a year), *Jahresberichte, Nachrichten für Seefahrer* (weekly), *Eisberichte*, etc.

Deutscher Wetterdienst (*German Meteorological Service*): 6050 Offenbach, Frankfurter Str. 135; f. 1952; central office for the Federal Republic; 2,200 mems.; library of 125,000 vols.; Pres. Prof. Dr. ERNST LINGELBACH; publs. *Europäischer Wetterbericht*†, *Monatlicher Witterungsbericht*†, *Die Grosswetterlagen Europas*† (monthly), *Jahresbericht*†, *Deutsches Meteorologisches Jahrbuch*† (annually), *promet-Meteorologische Fortbildung* (quarterly, *Annalen der Meteorologie*†, *Berichte*†, *Bibliographien*†, *Leitfäden für die Ausbildung.*

Forschungsgemeinschaft Explorations-Geophysik e.V. (*Geophysical Research Association*): 3007 Gehrden, Th. Fontane-Str. 9; f. 1954; Dir. Dr. W. DÖDERLEIN.

Fraunhofer-Institut für Bauphysik: 7000 Stuttgart 70, Königsträssle 74; f. 1929; acoustics, noise control, thermal insulation, heating, ventilation; 75 mems.; field-research station at Holzkirchen (Upper Bavaria); Dir. Prof. Dr. F. P. MECHEL; publs. *Veroffentlichungen* (irregular), *Kurzmitteilungen aus dem IBP*†.

Geologisch-Paläontologisches Institut (*Geological and Palaeontological Institute*): 2 Hamburg 13, Bundesstr. 55; f. 1907; 16 scientific mems.; 70,000 vols.; Man. Dir. Prof. Dr. E. T. DEGENS; publ. *Mitteilungen aus dem Geologisch-Paläontologischen Institut der Universität Hamburg* (annual).

Hahn-Meitner-Institut für Kernforschung Berlin GmbH (*Nuclear Research*): 1000 Berlin 39, Glienicker Str. 100; f. 1957; 619 mems.; 31,000 vols. and 295,000 reports; Mans. Dr. MARTIN NETTESHEIM, Prof. HANS WOLFGANG LEVI; Librarian JOBST FISCHER.

Hamburger Sternwarte: 2 Hamburg 80, Gojenbergsweg 112; f. 1830; astrometry, photometry, spectroscopy, stellar structure and interstellar medium; library of 50,000 vols.; Dir. Prof. A. WEIGERT, Prof. H. J. WENDKER.

Institut für Astronomie und Astrophysik der Universität Würzburg: 8700 Würzburg, Am Hubland; f. 1967; astronomy, theoretical physics; library of 5,000 vols., 50 journals; Dir. Prof. Dr. ROLF EBERT.

Institut für Spektrochemie und angewandte Spektroskopie e.V.: 4600 Dortmund 1, Bunsen-Kirchhoff-Strasse 11; f. 1952; various aspects of spectro-physics; 100 staff mems.; Dir. Dr. K. MÜLLER-GLIEMANN.

Institute für Chemie und Pharmazie (*Chemical and Pharmaceutical Institutes of Hamburg University*): 2 Hamburg 13, Martin-Luther-King-Platz 6; f. 1878; Institute of Organic Chemistry and Biochemistry, Dir. Prof. Dr. W. WALTER; Institute of Inorganic and Applied Chemistry; Dir. Prof. Dr. H. SINN; Institute of Physical Chemistry, Prof. Dr. B. KASTENING; Institute of Pharmaceutical Chemistry, Dir. Prof. Dr. N. KREUTZKAMP.

Kernforschungszentrum Karlsruhe G.m.b.H. (*Nuclear Research Centre*): 75 Karlsruhe, Weberstr. 5, Postfach

3640; f. 1956; fast breeder reactors, reprocessing, nuclear safety, uranium enrichment, fusion technology, low temperature technology, data processing, basic research; 3,300 mems.; library of 120,000 vols., 1,600 periodical titles, 400,000 reports; Man. Dirs. Prof. Dr. HARDE, Dr. WAGNER, Prof. Dr. BÖHM, Prof. Dr. KLOSE, Dr. HENNIES.

Kiepenheuer-Institut für Sonnenphysik: 78 Freiburg i.Br., Schöneckstr. 6; observatories at Freiburg/Schauinsland and Anacapri; f. 1942; optical investigation of the solar atmosphere; 48 mems.; Dir. Prof. Dr. EGON H. SCHRÖTER; publ. *Mitteilungen.*

Landessternwarte auf dem Königstuhl bei Heidelberg: 6900 Heidelberg, Königstuhl; f. 1897; astronomical scientific research; 26 mems.; library of 16,000 vols.; Dir. Prof. Dr. I. APPENZELLER; publs. *Veröffentlichungen der Landessternwarte, Mitteilungen der Landessternwarte.*

Remeis-Sternwarte (*Remeis Observatory*): 86 Bamberg, Sternwartstr. 7; f. 1889; attached to Erlangen University; Dir. Prof. Dr. J. RAHE.

Sternwarte Bochum—Institut für Weltraumforschung (*Bochum Observatory—Institute of Space Research*): 4630 Bochum, Blankensteinerstr. 200a; 14 mems.; development and testing of electronic equipment for tracking and reception of satellite data, development of display and reproduction systems for satellite imagery, photo-interpretation of satellite imagery for geo-scientific and environmental studies; remote sensing; Dir. Prof. HEINZ KAMINSKI.

Universitäts-Sternwarte, Institut für Astronomie und Astrophysik und Sonnenobservatorium Wendelstein: 8 Munich 80, Scheinerstr. 1; f. 1817; Dir. Prof. Dr. P. WELLMANN; publs. *Veröffentlichungen*†, *Mitteilungen*†.

Universitäts-Sternwarte Göttingen: 34 Göttingen, Geismarlandstr. 11; f. 1748; solar physics, stellar photometry and theoretical astrophysics; Dirs. W. DEINZER, R. KIPPENHAHN, E. H. SCHRÖTER, H. H. VOIGT.

PHILOSOPHY AND PSYCHOLOGY

Institut für Gerichtspsychologie Bochum (*Institute of Forensic Psychology*): 463 Bochum, Gilsingstr. 5; f. 1951; 41 mems.; Dir. Dr. FRIEDRICH ARNTZEN.

TECHNOLOGY

Arbeitsgemeinschaft Industrieller Forschungsvereinigungen e.V.: 5 Köln-Marienburg, Bayenthalgürtel 23; f. 1954; co-operation in scientific research of industrial importance; 76 mems.; Pres. Dipl.-Ing. GÜNTER PEDDINGHAUS; Dir.-Gen. Dipl. agr. ERNST JOHN VON FREYEND.

Battelle-Institut e.V., Forschung, Entwicklung, Innovation: 6 Frankfurt a.M., Am Römerhof 35; f. 1952; sponsored research, development and innovation in bio-sciences, chemistry, physics, systems engineering, materials technology, information processing, energy technology and economics and social sciences; 870 staff mems.; library of 40,000 vols.; Dir. Dr. HORST HAESKE; publ. *Battelle-Information.*

Bergbau-Forschung G.m.b.H., Forschungsinstitut des Steinkohlenbergbauvereins (*Mining Research*): 4300 Essen 13 (Kray), Franz-Fischer-Weg 61; f. 1918; library of 180,000 vols.; Dir. Dr. rer. nat. KURT-GÜNTHER BECK.

Bundesanstalt für Materialprüfung (*Federal Institute for Material Testing*): 1000 Berlin 45, Unter den Eichen 87; f. 1870; 1,200 mems.; library of 50,000 vols.; Pres. Prof. Dr. G. W. BECKER; publs. *Jahresbericht d. Bundesanstalt f. Materialprüfung, Amts- u. Mitteilungsblatt d. Bundesanstalt f. Materialprüfung* (quarterly), *BAM-Berichte* (scientific reports, irregular).

Bundesforschungsanstalt für Ernährung (*Federal Research Centre for Nutrition*): 7500 Karlsruhe, Engesserstr. 20; f. 1936; 240 mems.; library of 30,000 vols.; Dir. Prof. Dr. H. K. FRANK; incorporates: *Institute for Biology:* Dir. Prof. Dr. H. K. FRANK; *Institute for Food Chemistry:* Dir. Prof. Dr. A. FRICKER; *Institute for Biochemistry:* Dir. Prof. Dr. J. F. DIEHL; *Institute for Home Economics:* Dir. Prof. Dr. ELFRIEDE STÜBLER; *Institute for Food Technology:* Dir. Prof. Dr. H. SCHUBERT; *Central Laboratory for Isotope Techniques:* Dir. Dr. E. FISCHER.

Deutsche Forschungsanstalt für Lebensmittelchemie (*German Kesearch Institute for Food Chemistry*): 8 Munich 40, Leopoldstrasse 175; f. 1918; Dir. Prof. Dr. H.-D. BELITZ; publ. *Annual Research Report.*

Deutsche Forschungs- und Versuchsanstalt für Luft- und Raumfahrt e.V. (DFVLR) (*German Aerospace Research Establishment*); 5000 Cologne 90 (Porz), Box 906058, Linder Höhe; f. 1969; flight mechanics, guidance and control, fluid mechanics, structure and materials, communication technology and remote sensing, energetics; *c.* 130 mems.; Chair. Prof. Dr.rer.nat. Dr. HERMANN L. JORDAN; publs. *Deutsche Luft- und Raumfahrt, Forschungsberichte* (irregular), *DFVLR-Nachrichten*† (irregular), *Zeitschrift für Flugwissenschaften und Weltraumforschung* (every 2 months).

Deutsches Textilforschungszentrum Nord-West e.V.: 200 mems.; comprises the following:

Textilforschungsanstalt Krefeld: 4150 Krefeld, Frankenring 2; Dir. Prof. Dr. G. VALK.

Wäschereiforschung Krefeld: 4150 Krefeld, Adlerstr. 44; Dir. Dr. H. KRÜSSMANN.

Institut für textile Messtechnik M'Gladbach: 4050 Mönchengladbach 1, Voltastr. 2; Dir. Dr. W. STEIN.

Forschungsbereich Denkendorf: 7306 Denkendorf, Körschtalstr. 26; 65 mems.; Dir. Prof. Dr.-Ing. GERHARD EGBERS.

Forschungsgemeinschaft Bauen und Wohnen (*Buildings*): 7000 Stuttgart 1, Hohenzollernstr. 25; f. 1947; Dir. K. BRANDSTETTER; publ. *FBW-Schriftenreihe.*

Forschungsinstitut für Edelmetalle und Metallchemie (*Precious and Rare Metals*): 707 Schwäbisch Gmünd, Katherinenstr. 17; Dir. Dr. CH. J. RAUB.

Forschungsinstitut für Internationale Technisch-Wirtschaftliche Zusammenarbeit (*Research Institute for International Techno-Economic Co-operation*): Rheinisch-Westfälische Technische Hochschule Aachen, 5100 Aachen, Henricistr. 50; f. 1957; 30 mems.; library of 40,000 vols.; Dir. Prof. Dr.-Ing. HANS A. HAVEMANN; publs. *Internationale Kooperation, intertechnik*†, *Forschungsberichte und Gutachten*†, *Veröffentlichungen der Dokumentation*† and others.

Forschungsinstitut für Wärmeschutz e.V. München (*Thermal Insulation, Testing, Research*): 8032 Gräfelfing Lochamer Schlag 4; f. 1918; 140 mems.; Scientific Dir. Dr. W. F. CAMMERER.

Fraunhofer-Institut fur Lebensmitteltechnologie und Verpackung (*Food Technology and Packaging*): 8000 Munich 50, Schragenhofstrasse 35; f. 1942; food preservation and packaging, general packaging; 206 mems.; library of 2,800 vols.; Man. Dir. Dr. G. SCHRICKER; publ. *ILV-Mitteilungen* (monthly).

Gesellschaft für Schwerionenforschung, m.b.H.: 61 Darmstadt 11, P.O.B. 110 541; f. 1969; carries out basic research with heavy ions in nuclear physics and chemistry, solid state and atomic physics, radiation biology, etc.; heavy ion linear accelerator and laboratory; library of 3,000 vols.; Dirs. G. ZU PUTLITZ, H. O. SCHUFF; publ. *GSI-Bericht*†.

Institut für Bauforschung e.V. (*Building Research*): 3000 Hanover 1, An der Markuskirche 1; f. 1946; Dir. Dr.-Ing. HERBERT MENKHOFF.

Institut für Erdölforschung (*Petroleum Research*): 3000 Hanover, Am Kleinen Felde 30; f. 1942; oil recovery, reservoir engineering, refinery technology, research in petroleum products; 70 mems.; library of 5,000 vols.; Dir. Prof. Dr. H. H. OELERT; Vice-Dir. Prof. Dr. H. J. NEUMANN; publ. research report† (annual).

Institut für Textiltechnik der Institute für Textil- und Faserforschung Stuttgart (*Textiles*): 7410 Reutlingen, Burgstr. 29; f. 1921; 75 staff; library of 2,500 vols.; Dir. Prof. Dr. G. EGBERS.

Forschungsbereich Reutlingen: 7410 Reutlingen, Burgstr. 29; 70 staff; library of 2,500 vols.

Forschungsbereich Denkendorf: 7306 Denkendorf, Körschtalstr. 26; 70 staff.

Institut für Werkstoffkunde der Technischen Hochschule Darmstadt (*Raw Materials Institute*): 6100 Darmstadt, Grafenstr. 2; Dir. Prof. Dr.-Ing. K. H. KLOOS.

Landesanstalt für Immissionsschutz des Landes Nordrhein-Westfalen: 4300 Essen, Wallneyer Str. 6; f. 1963; research and advice in the fields of air pollution and noise control; 380 mems.; library of 13,500 vols.; Pres. Prof. Dr. rer.nat. H. STRATMANN; publ. *Schriftenreihe der Landesanstalt*†.

Physikalisch-Technische Bundesanstalt (*National Institute for Science and Technology*): 3300 Braunschweig, Bundesallee 100; f. 1887; divisions for mechanics, electricity, heat, optics, acoustics, atomic physics, reactor radiation, long-term storage and final disposal of radioactive waste, general technical and scientific services; 1,400 staff mems.; library of 80,000 vols.; Pres. Prof. Dr.-Ing. D. KIND; incorporates the **Institut Berlin:** 1000 Berlin 10 (Charlottenburg), Ernst-Abbe-Str. 2–12; Dir. Prof. Dr. G. SAUERBREY; publs. *PTB-Mitteilungen* (every 2 months), *Jahresbericht*, *PTB-Berichte* (scientific reports, irregular), *PTB Prüfregeln* (irregular).

Versuchsanstalt für Wasserbau und Wassermengenwirtschaft—Oskar von Miller Institut: 8111 Obernach, Post Walchensee; laboratory and open-air research station for hydraulic engineering; affiliated to the Munich Technical University; f. 1924; 7 academic staff; library of *c.* 5,000 vols.; Dir. Prof. Dr. H. BLIND; publ. *Berichte.*

LIBRARIES

51 AACHEN

Bibliothek der Technischen Hochschule: Templergraben 61; f. 1870; 740,000 vols.; Dir. Dr. ULRICH FELLMANN.

Oeffentliche Bibliothek: Couvenstr. 15; f. 1828; specialises in literature of the Benelux countries and historical works (medieval and classical); 380,000 vols.; Dir. H. FRINGS.

89 AUGSBURG

Staats- und Stadtbibliothek: Schaezlerstr. 25; f. 1537; 370,000 vols., 3,540 MSS., 3,070 incunabula, 16,000 drawings and engravings; Dir. Dr. JOSEF BELLOT.

Universitätsbibliothek: Memminger Str. 6; f. 1970; 635 vols., 58,300 theses, 21,000 maps, 20,000 items of AV material; Dir. Dr. RUDOLF FRANKENBERGER.

86 BAMBERG

Staatsbibliothek Bamberg: Domplatz 8, Neue Residenz; f. 1803; contains 300,000 vols., including a special collection of old manuscripts (4,500), incunabula (3,400), and graphics; Chief Librarian Dr. WILHELM SCHLEICHER; publ. *Katalog der MSS.*

Universitätsbibliothek: Postfach 1549, An der Universität 2; f. 1973; 350,000 vols. on theology, humanities and social sciences; Dir. Dr. DIETER KARASEK.

BAYREUTH

Universitätsbibliothek: 8580 Bayreuth, Justus-Liebig-Str. 8, Postfach 3008; f. 1973 to serve the university and the public; 500,000 vols.; Dir. Dr. K. WICKERT.

1000 BERLIN

Amerika-Gedenkbibliothek: Berliner Zentralbibliothek (*American Memorial Library*): 1–61, Blücherplatz; f. 1952; central public library of West Berlin; 700,000 vols., 2,700 periodicals; Dir. PETER K. LIEBENOW.

Berliner Medizinische Zentralbibliothek: Berlin 12, Str 17 Juni 112; 110,000 vols.; Dirs. Dr. Dr. M. STÜRZBECHER, K. WOLLITZ; publs. *Monatl. Zss-Rundschau: Gesundheitsfürsorge, Gesundheitserziehung.*

British Council Library: 1000 Berlin 12, Hardenbergstr. 20; f. 1946; 22,254 vols., 78 periodicals; Librarian D. A. HANDLEY.

Ibero-Amerikanisches Institut Preussischer Kulturbesitz: 1000 Berlin 30, Potsdamer Str. 37; f. 1930; research institute and library dedicated to Latin America, Spain and Portugal; 500,000 vols.; Dir. Dr. WILHELM STEGMANN; publs. *Quellenwerke zur alten Geschichte Amerikas, aufgezeichnet in den Sprachen der Eingeborenen, Monumenta Americana, Bibliotheca Ibero-Americana, Stimmen Indianischer Völker, Miscellanea Ibero-Americana, Indiana, Ibero-Amerikanisches Archiv.*

Kunstbibliothek (Staatliche Museen Preussischer Kulturbesitz): Berlin 12, Jebens-Str. 2; f. 1867; 160,000 vols., including the Lipperheidesche Kostümbibliothek; Dir. Prof. Dr. EKHART BERCKENHAGEN.

Staatsbibliothek Preussischer Kulturbesitz: 1000 Berlin 30, Potsdamer Str. 33, Postfach 1407; f. 1661; 3,000,000 vols., 30,800 current periodicals, 30,560 Eastern, 9,150 Western, 20,290 musical MSS., 368,200 maps, 305,880 autographs, 3,030 incunabula, 370 legacies, 5 million pictures and Mendelssohn-Archiv; international exchange of official publications; International ISBN Agency; Gen. Dir. Dr. EKKEHART VESPER; Deputy Dir. Dr. GÜNTER BARON; publs. *Jahresbericht*† (irregular), *Mitteilungen*† (quarterly).

Universitätsbibliothek der Freien Universität Berlin: 1000 Berlin 33, Garystr. 39; 1,295,871 vols., 335,337 theses; Dir. Dr. phil. WERNER LIEBICH.

Universitätsbibliothek der Technischen Universität Berlin: Berlin 12 (Charlottenburg), Str. des 17. Juni 135; 1,000,000 vols., 8,600 periodicals, 40,000 architectural drawings, complete German patents and standards; Dir. HELMUT SONTAG.

4630 BOCHUM

Universitätsbibliothek: 4630 Bochum-Querenburg, P.O.B. 102148; f. 1963; 966,559 vols., 197,000 theses; EDP Dept. for Processing; Dir. B. ADAMS.

Stadtbücherei: Rathausplatz 2–6; f. 1905; 480,000 vols.; Dir. Dr. phil. J. SCHULTHEIS.

53 BONN

Bibliothek der Deutschen Bundespost: Adenauerallee 81; f. 1945; 783,465 vols.; publs. *Vierteljährliche Zugangslisten der Fachliteratur, Sonderkataloge für Belletristik und Jugendschrifttum.*

Bibliothek des Deutschen Bundestages: Bundeshaus, Görresstr. 15; 500,000 vols., 5,400 periodicals, 3,900 official periodicals, 420 newspapers and pamphlets; special collections: 17,000 photographs, 15,000 vols. law archives, 19,000 maps, 3,700,000 press cuttings, 2,300,000 tape recordings, parliamentary records, election propaganda records; Dir. K. G. WERNICKE.

Bibliothek und Geographisch-Kartographischer Dienst des Auswärtigen Amts: Koblenzerstr. 99-103; 145,000 vols., 68,000 maps.; Dir. K.-H. GRUNDMANN.

Universitätsbibliothek: Adenauerallee 39-41; f. 1818; contains 1,400,000 vols., 7,500 current periodicals; Dir. Dr. HARTWIG LOHSE.

Zentralbibliothek der Landbauwissenschaft (*Central Agricultural Library*): Meckenheimer-Allee 172, Postfach 264; f. 1848; agriculture, horticulture, forestry, nutrition, fresh water fisheries; 230,000 vols., 2,600 current periodicals; Dir. Dr. W. GÖCKE.

2800 BREMEN

Bibliothek des Instituts für Seeverkehrswirtschaft: Werderstr. 73; f. 1954; about 60,000 bibliographical units; Librarian C. HEIDELOFF (acting).

Universitätsbibliothek (mit Staatsbibliothek): Bremen 33, Bibliothekstr.; f. 1660; 1,650,000 vols., 14,000 current periodicals; Dir. GERRY WENSKE; publ. *Jahresbericht.*

3300 BRUNSWICK

Bibliothek Braunschweig der Biologischen Bundesanstalt für Land- und Forstwirtschaft: Messeweg 11/12; f. 1950; *c.* 50,000 vols., 1,200 periodicals, 44,000 reprints, 2,200 microfilms; Head Dr. WOLFGANG KOCH; publs. *Nachrichtenblatt des Deutschen Pflanzenschutzdienstes* (monthly), *Jahresbericht der Biologischen Bundesanstalt, Jahresberichte des Deutschen Pflanzenschutzdienstes, Pflanzenschutzmittel-Verzeichnis, Merkblätter* (irregular).

Stadtarchiv und Stadtbibliothek: Steintorwall 15; f. 1861; 260,000 vols., 1,366 medieval MSS., 423 incunabula, 8,100 documents, special collection on the history of the town; Dir. WOLF-DIETER SCHUEGRAF; publ. *Braunschweiger Werkstücke*† (irregular).

Universitätsbibliothek der Technischen Universität: Pockelsstr. 13; f. 1748; 600,000 vols.; Dir. Prof. Dr. JOSEF DAUM.

3392 CLAUSTHAL-ZELLERFELD

Universitätsbibliothek der Technischen Universität: 2 Leibnizstrasse; f. 1811; *c.* 250,000 vols., 2,500 periodicals, 5,000 geological maps; Dir. Dr. H. O. WEBER; publs. *Mitteilungen* (irregular), *Clausthaler Zeitschriftenverzeichnis, Katalog der Calvörschen Bibliothek.*

863 COBURG

Landesbibliothek: Schlossplatz 1; f. *c.* 1775; *c.* 300,000 vols.; Dir. Dr. JÜRGEN ERDMANN.

5 COLOGNE

British Council Library: Hahnenstr. 6; f. 1946; government publications, music collection, language records; 37,503 vols., 193 current periodicals; Librarian Mrs. M. WILLIAMS.

Erzbischöfliche Diözesan- und Dombibliothek: Gereonstr. 2-4; f. 1738; 215,000 vols.; Librarian Direktor WILHELM SCHÖNARTZ.

Kunst- und Museumsbibliothek (Wallraf-Richartz-Museum): An der Rechtschule; f. 1957; 130,000 vols.; Curator Dr. A. SCHUG.

Universitäts- und Stadtbibliothek: 5000 Köln 41, Universitätsstr. 33; f. 1920; *c.* 1,750,000 vols.; Dir. Prof. Dr. S. CORSTEN.

Zentralbibliothek der Medizin (*Central Medical Library*): 5000 Köln 41, Joseph-Stelzmannstr. 9; f. 1908, became Central Library 1969; 520,000 vols.; Dir. Dr. F. J. KÜHNEN.

61 DARMSTADT

Hessische Landes- und Hochschulbibliothek Darmstadt: Schloss; f. 16th century; 1,110,000 vols., 4,220 MSS., 2,063 incunabula, 3,325 musicalia, 2.5 million German patent papers; Dir. Dr. YORCK HAASE.

493 DETMOLD

Lippische Landesbibliothek Detmold: Hornschestr. 41; f. 1614; 320,000 vols., 5,789 MSS.; Dir. Dr. K. A. HELLFAIER.

4600 DORTMUND

Hochschulbibliothek der Pädagogische Hochschule Ruhr: Vogelpothsweg (Universitätsgelände); f. 1946; 408,000 vols., 1,620 periodicals; Dir. GEESCHE WELLNER-BRENNECKE; publ. *Geschäftsstelle der Arbeitsgemeinschaft pädagogischer Bibliotheken.*

Stadt- und Landesbibliothek Dortmund: Hansaplatz; f. 1907; *c.* 400,000 vols.; special collection of MSS. and autographs and material on Westphalia; music dept.; Dir. Dr. ALOIS KLOTZBÜCHER; publs. *Westfälische Bibliographie*† (annually), *Mitteilungen aus dem Literaturarchiv Kulturpreis der Stadt Dortmund*† (every 2 years), *Mitteilungen*† (irregular), *Autographenausstellungen*† (irregular).

Universitätsbibliothek Dortmund: 4600 Dortmund 50, Vogelpothsweg 76; f. 1965; 560,000 vols., complete set of German patents; Dir. Dr. VALENTIN WEHEFRITZ.

4100 DUISBURG

Stadbibliothek: Düsseldorfer Str. 5–7; f. 1901; public library; 1,113,000 vols., 1,669 periodicals; Dir. F. RAKOWSKI.

4 DÜSSELDORF

Heinrich-Heine-Institut: Bilkerstr. 14; f. 1970; *c.* 30,000 vols., 300 manuscripts, 30,000 autographs of 19th and 20th centuries, 130 bequests of literature, music, art and science and a special collection relating to the poet Heine; Dir. Dr. J. A. KRUSE; publs. *Heine-Jahrbuch, Heine-Studien,* etc.

Universitätsbibliothek Düsseldorf: Universitätstr. 1; f. 1970; 1,300,000 vols.; Dir. Prof. Dr. G. GATTERMANN; publ. Catalogue of current periodicals held†.

8833 EICHSTÄTT

Staats- und Seminarbibliothek (*Federal and Departmental Library*): Am Hofgarten 1; f. 15th century; special collection: early theological works; 297,395 vols.; Dir. Dr. A. BAUCH.

852 ERLANGEN

Universitätsbibliothek: Universitätsstr. 4; f. 1743; *c.* 1,616,000 vols., 698,000 theses, 2,600 MSS., 150 papyri, 2,100 incunabula; Dir. Dr. B. SINOGOWITZ.

43 ESSEN

Stadtbibliothek: Hindenburgstr. 25; 609,000 vols.; f. 1902; Dir. Dr. H. J. KUHLMANN.

6 FRANKFURT A.M.

Bibliothek des Freien Deutschen Hochstifts: Grosser Hirschgraben 23-25; 120,000 vols., 25,000 MSS.; Dir. Dr. DETLEV LÜDERS.

Deutsche Bibliothek: Zeppelinallee 4–8; f. 1946; 2,700,000 vols., 57,641 periodicals published since 1945; special collection of German exile literature 1933–1945; acts as a deposit library for all of Germany since 1945 and has adopted the functions of a national library; is the first library in the world to compile its national bibliography by computer; Dir.-Gen. Prof. Dr. GÜNTHER PFLUG; publs. *Deutsche Bibliographie* (weekly, half-yearly and five-yearly issues; special lists of periodicals, official publications, theses, records, printed music and selected new books).

Stadt- und Universitätsbibliothek/Senckenbergische Bibliothek: Bockenheimer Landstr. 134–138; Dir. KLAUS-DIETER LEHMANN.

Stadt- und Universitätsbibliothek: f. 1668; collection of vols. on the humanities and medicine; 2,100,000 vols.

Senckenbergische Bibliothek: f. 1763; natural sciences; 850,000 vols.

78 FREIBURG I. BR.

Universitätsbibliothek: Rempartstr. 15; f. 1976; *c.* 1,176,700 vols., 566,700 dissertations; Dir. Prof. Dr. WOLFGANG KEHR.

64 FULDA

Hessische Landesbibliothek Fulda: Heinrich von Bibra-Platz 12; f. 1778; 180,000 vols., 822 MSS and 428 incunabula; Dir. Dr. A. BRALL.

63 GIESSEN

Universitätsbibliothek der Justus Liebig-Universität Giessen: Bismarckstr. 37; f. 1612; 600,000 vols.; 290,000 dissertations; 2,000 MSS.; 873 incunabula; 3,000 papyri; Dir. Dr. HERMANN SCHÜLING.

34 GÖTTINGEN

Niedersächsische Staats- und Universitätsbibliothek: Prinzenstr. 1, Postfach 318; f. 1734; contains 2,650,000 vols., 13,400 MSS., 6,000 incunabula, 14,000 periodicals; Dir. H. VOGT; publ. *Arbeiten.*

2000 HAMBURG

Bibliothek des Max-Planck-Instituts für Ausländisches und Internationales Privatrecht: Hamburg 13, Mittelweg 187; f. 1926; 200,000 vols., 4,000 periodicals, of which 1,800 current; Dir. Dr. RALPH LANSKY.

British Council Library: Hamburg 36, Neuer Wall 86; 7,455 vols., 18 periodicals; Librarian Miss A. GREGORY.

Commerzbibliothek (Bibliothek der Handelskammer Hamburg): Börse; f. 1735; 100,000 vols. on law, economics, social science and geography; Dir. HUBERT H. KELTIER.

Staats- und Universitätsbibliothek Hamburg: Hamburg 13, Moorweidenstrasse 40 (the former book holdings in Speersort were to a large extent destroyed); f. 1479; deposit library for literature published in Hamburg; special collections: political science, fishing, literature on Portugal and Spain; approx. 186,000 vols. and 8,000 MSS.; Dir. Prof. Dr. HORST GRONEMEYER; publs. *Katalog der Handschriften der Staats- und Universitätsbibliothek Hamburg, Mitteilungen aus der Hamburger Staats- und Universitätsbibliothek, Veröffentlichungen aus der Hamburger Staats- und Universitätsbibliothek, Hamburger Bibliographien.*

3 HANOVER

Universitätsbibliothek Hannover und Technische Informationsbibliothek (TIB): Welfengarten 1B; f. 1831; library of 1,500,000 vols., over 15,000 current periodicals; German research reports, patent specifications, standards; conference proceedings; American doctoral dissertations and American reports (microforms); special emphasis on technical and scientific literature in Eastern languages; acts as central technical library of Federal Republic; provides an express information service by issuing title lists and abstracts of selected newly acquired Eastern literature. Translations available are announced by the Übersetzungstelle; acts as national translations centre in co-operation with the International Translations Centre at Delft; Dir. Dr.-Ing. G. SCHLITT.

Niedersächsische Landesbibliothek: Waterloostr. 8; f. 1665; 1,000,000 vols., 4,279 MSS., 80,000 autographs, 293 incunabula, several thousand maps, etchings, woodcuts; collection of coats of arms and seals; Dir. Dr. WILHELM TOTOK.

Stadtbibliothek: Hildesheimer Str. 12; f. 1440; general information about the city and region; 530,000 vols., 2,900 periodicals; Dir. Dr. J. EYSSEN.

69 HEIDELBERG

Bibliothek des Max-Planck-Instituts für Ausländisches Öffentliches Recht und Völkerrecht: Berlinerstr. 48; f. 1924; 230,000 vols.; Dir. J. SCHWEITZKE.

Universitätsbibliothek: Plöck 107-109; f. 1386; about 1,200,000 vols., 6,000 MSS., 1,689 incunabula, 2,500 documents; Dir. Dr. WALTER KOSCHORRECK; publs. *Bibliothek und Wissenschaft, Facsimilia Heidelbergensia.*

75 KARLSRUHE

Badische Landesbibliothek: Am Nymphengarten, Lammstr. 16; f. 1500; 805,000 vols.; 5,406 MSS.; 1,245 incunabula; Dir. Dr. GERHARD RÖMER.

Bibliothek des Bundesgerichtshofes: Herrenstr. 45; f. 1950; 230,000 vols.; Dir. Dr. H. KIRCHNER.

Universitätsbibliothek: Kaiserstr. 12, Postfach 6920; f. 1832; 500,000 vols.; Dir. Dr. D. POGGENDORF.

35 KASSEL

Murhardsche Bibliothek der Stadt Kassel und Landesbibliothek: Brüder Grimm-Platz 4A; f. 1580; contains 350,000 vols., 4,500 MSS., 7,400 music, 10,000 maps, 700,000 patent specifications; Dir. Dr. DIETER HENNIG.

23 KIEL

Schleswig-Holsteinische Landesbibliothek: Schloss; f. *c.* 1870; 140,000 vols. and literary bequests of *c.* 1,000 authors and scholars; Dir. Prof. Dr. KLAUS FRIEDLAND.

Universitätsbibliothek: Olshausenstr. 29; f. 1665; 1,300,000 vols., 490,000 theses; Dir. Dr. G. WIEGAND.

Zentralbibliothek der Wirtschaftswissenschaften: Düsternbrooker Weg 120–122; f. 1914; 1,500,000 vols.; Librarian Dr. E. HEIDEMANN.

775 KONSTANZ

Bibliothek der Universität: Universitätsstr. 10; f. 1965; 745,000 vols., 70,000 theses; Dir. J. STOLTZENBURG.

24 LÜBECK

Bibliothek der Hansestadt Lübeck: Hundestr. 5-17; *c.* 750,000 vols.; Dir. K. BOCK.

65 MAINZ

Stadtbibliothek: Rheinallee 3B; f. 1477 as University Library, taken over by the City of Mainz in 1806; 452,152 vols., 2,362 incunabula, 1,135 MSS.; Dir. G. WELLMER-BRENNECKE; publs. *Mainzer Zeitschrift*†, *Beiträge zur Geschichte der Stadt Mainz*†.

Universitätsbibliothek: Saarstr. 21, Postfach 4020; 782,000 vols., 815 MSS.; Dir. Dr. J. SCHUBERT.

68 MANNHEIM

Universitätsbibliothek: Schloss-Ostflügel, Postfach 2428; 1,200,000 vols.; Dir. Dr. MANFRED KLEISS.

7142 MARBACH A. NECKAR

Schiller-Nationalmuseum/Deutsches Literaturarchiv: Schillerhöhe 8-10; German literature since 1750; large collection of autographs and documents, 530 legacies, 230,000 vols.; Dir. Prof. Dr. Dr. h.c. BERNHARD ZELLER; publ. *Jahrbuch der Deutschen Schillergesellschaft* and others.

355 MARBURG

Bibliothek des Johann-Gottfried-Herder-Instituts: Gisonenweg 5-7; f. 1950; East Central European library of 190,000 vols.; Chief Librarian Dr. HORST VON CHMIELEWSKI; publs. *J. G. Herder-Institut-Bibliothek: Neuerwerbungen Ostmitteleuropa*† (quarterly).

Universitätsbibliothek: Krummbogen 29; f. 1527; contains about 740,890 vols., 590,631 theses, 3,000 manuscripts; Dir. Prof. Dr. FRANZ-HEINRICH PHILIPP.

405 MÖNCHENGLADBACH

Bibliothek Wissenschaft und Weisheit (*Library of Theology and Philosophy*): Bettratherstr. 79; f. 1929; 70,000 vols.; Dir. Father O. GIMMNICH, O.F.M.; publ. *Wissenschaft und Weisheit: Zeitschrift für Augustinischfranziskanische Theologie und Philosophie in der Gegenwart*†.

Stadtbibliothek: Blücherstr. 6; f. 1904; 400,000 vols.; special collection on social and political questions, 1890-1933; Dir. Dr. ERNST M. WERMTER.

8000 MUNICH

Bayerische Staatsbibliothek: Ludwigstr. 16; f. 1558; more than 4,300,000 vols.; *c.* 50,000 MSS., *c.* 20,000 incunabula; deposit library for Bavaria; library school; Dir. Dr. FRANZ GEORG KALTWASSER; publ. *Jahresbericht*.

Bibliothek des Deutschen Museums: 8000 Munich 22, Museumsinsel 1; f. 1903; 650,000 vols.; Dir. Dr. ERNST H. BERNINGER; publ. *Abhandlungen und Berichte*.

Bibliothek des Deutschen Patentamtes: Munich 2, Zweibrückenstr. 12; f. 1877; 760,000 vols.; Dir. Dr. UTZ-FRIEDEBERT TAUBE.

British Council Library: 8 Munich 22, Bruderstr. 7/111; f. 1950; 2,226 vols. for reference only; 46 periodicals; Librarian Miss M. UTZ.

Städtische Bibliotheken: Munich 2, Schwanthalerstr. 68; f. 1843; 1,800,000 vols.; Dir. Dr. PETER J. THANNABAUR.

Universitätsbibliothek: Munich 22, Geschw.-Scholl-Platz 1; f. 1472; 1,862,690 vols., 2,988 MSS.; Dir. (vacant).

Universitätsbibliothek der Technischen Universität: Arcisstr. 21; f. 1868; 520,000 vols., 280,000 reports; Dir. Dr. P. SCHWEIGLER; publ. catalogue of current periodicals held†.

4400 MÜNSTER

Universitätsbibliothek: Krummer Timpen 3-5; f. 1773, refounded 1902; 1,147,500 vols., 394,000 theses, 900 incunabula, 32,000 autographs, 8,400 periodicals; Dir. Dr. ROBERT REICHELT; publs. *Münsterisches Zeitschriftenverzeichnis*† *Bibliotheksnachrichten*† (monthly).

85 NUREMBERG

Bibliothek des Germanischen Nationalmuseums: Kornmarkt 1; 415,000 vols.; f. 1852; Dir. Dr. ELISABETH RÜCKER.

Stadtbibliothek Nürnberg: Egidienplatz 23; f. 1370; 754,000 vols., 3,132 MSS., 2,500 incunabula, 10,400 recordings; Dir. Dr. ROBERT FRITZSCH.

Universitätsbibliothek Erlangen-Nürnberg, Wirtschafts- und Sozialwissenschaftliche Zweigbibliothek, Nürnberg: Egidienplatz 23; f. 1919; 140,000 vols.; Dir. Dr. JUTTA JUST.

OLDENBURG I. O.

Landesbibliothek: Ofenerstr. 15, Postfach 3480; f. 1792; *c.* 340,000 vols., 541 MSS.; Dir. Dr. A. DIETZEL; Librarians J. BEUTIN, DR. E. KOOLMAN.

839 PASSAU

Staatliche Bibliothek: Michaeligasse 11; f. 1612 as Jesuit library, refounded 1803 as national library; special collections: philosophy, theology, regional history and literature; 170,000 vols.; Dir. Prof. Dr. J. OSWALD.

Universitätsbibliothek: Innstr. 40, Postfach 2540; f. 1976; 300,000 vols., 40,000 theses; Dir. Dr. HEINRICH WIMMER; publ. *Jahresbericht*.

84 REGENSBURG

Bischöfliche Zentralbibliothek: St. Petersweg 11-13; f. 1972; 173,000 vols., 230 journals, with special collections on ascetics and sacred music; includes the library of St. Jacob's Irish monastery and Proske's music library; Dir. PAUL MAI.

Staatliche Bibliothek: Gesandtenstr. 13; f. 1816; special collection of regional history; 176,800 vols.; Dir. Dr. GISELA URBANEK.

Universitätsbibliothek: Universitätsstr. 31-33, Postfach 409; f. 1964; 1,700,000 vols., 160,000 theses; Dir. Dr. MAX PAUER.

66 SAARBRÜCKEN

Universitätsbibliothek: St. Johanner Stadtwald (medical library in Homburg, Saar); f. 1950; 825,000 vols., 242,000 theses; Dir. Dr. OTWIN VINZENT.

672 SPEYER

Pfälzische Landesbibliothek: Johannesstr. 22A; f. 1921; 454,631 vols. on all subjects, with special reference to the Palatinate and the Saar; Dir. Prof. Dr. WOLFGANG METZ.

7 STUTTGART

Bibliothek des Instituts für Auslandsbeziehungen: Charlottenplatz 17; f. 1917; 275,000 vols., 11,000 maps, 4,900 periodicals regularly, 3,200 microfilms, Dir. GERTRUD KUHN; publs. *Reihe, Dokumentation* (new acquisitions).

Bibliothek für Zeitgeschichte-Weltkriegsbücherei: Konrad Adenauer Str. 8; f. 1915; current history, political sciences, military sciences, especially concerning World Wars I and II; 210,000 vols. and special collections (photographs, maps, leaflets, stamps, etc.): Dir. Prof. Dr. JÜRGEN ROHWER; publs. *Jahresbibliographie*†, *Schriftenreihe*†, *Dokumentationen*†.

Bücherei der Staatlichen Hochschule für Musik und Darstellende Kunst: Urbansplatz 2; f. 1857; 12,699 vols., 51,000 musical scores, 12,158 records, 12,464 periodicals; Librarian Frau ERIKA KELLNER.

Landesgewerbeamt Baden-Württemberg, Bibliothek für Berufliche Bildung: Kanzleistr. 19; f. 1848; 20,000 vols., 450 periodicals; Dir. Dip.-Ing BERGER.

Patentschriften und Normblattauslegestelle: f. 1869; German, Swiss and Austrian patents and American abstracts.

Betriebswirtschaftliche Dokumentation: f. 1970.

av-Forum, Informationsstudio für audiovisuelle Medien in der beruflichen Aus- und Fortbildung: f. 1974.

Universitätsbibliothek Hohenheim: Stuttgart-Hohenheim, Garbenstr. 15; f. 1818; 160,000 vols.; agricultural and biological sciences; Dir. Dr. JÖRG MARTIN.

Universitätsbibliothek: Holzgartenstr. 16, P.O.B. 506; f. 1829; contains *c.* 580,000 vols., including 117,000 theses, and 3,940 German and foreign periodicals; Dir. JÜRGEN HERING.

Württembergische Landesbibliothek: Konrad Adenauerstr. 8, Postfach 769; f. 1765; *c.* 1,551,000 vols., *c.* 6,680 incunabula; large collection of old Bibles; more than 11,000 MSS.; Dir. HANS-PETER GEH.

5500 TRIER (TRÈVES)

Bibliothek des Priesterseminars Trier: Jesuitenstr. 13, Postfach 1330; f. 1805; *c.* 215,000 vols. on philosophy and theology, 243 theological manuscripts, and 72 incunabula; Librarian Dr. FRANZ R. REICHERT.

Stadtbibliothek Trier: Weberbach 25; f. 1804; developed from the former Jesuit and University Library and opened to the public in 1775; contains 295,000 books, 4,000 manuscripts and about 2,500 incunabula; scientific library; Chief Librarian Prof. Dr. RICHARD LAUFNER; publ. *Kurtrierisches Jahrbuch*.

74 TÜBINGEN

Universitätsbibliothek: Wilhelmstr. 32; f. in last quarter of 15th century; 1,890,000 books and journals, 588,000 dissertations, 1,654 incunabula, 5,507 MSS.; Dir. Dr. R. LANDWEHRMEYER.

79 ULM

Stadtbibliothek Ulm: Weinhof 12; f. 1516; special collections: the arts, regional history; 198,000 vols.; Dir. Dr. KRAUSS.

4973 VLOTHO

Bibliothek des Gesamteuropäischen Studienwerks: Südfeldstr. 2–4, Postfach 145; f. 1954; information on the political, ideological, economic, sociological and educational development in the East European states, primarily the German Democratic Republic; 47,679 vols., 377 periodicals; Dirs. Prof. Dr. W. HILDEBRANDT, Dipl. Bibl. K. SCHOLLE; publs. *Aktuelle Ostinformationen*†, *Aktuelle Politik*†.

6200 WIESBADEN

Bibliothek-Dokumentation-Archiv Statistisches Bundesamt: Gustav-Stresemann-Ring 11; f. 1948; 205,000 vols., 3,000 statistical periodicals; Chief Librarian Dr. H. K. KULLMER; publ. *Zugangsverzeichnis*.

Hessische Landesbibliothek: Rheinstr. 55-57; f. 1813; contains about 600,000 vols., manuscripts and incunabula; Dir. Dr. HELMUT SCHWITZGEBEL.

334 WOLFENBÜTTEL

Herzog August Bibliothek: Lessingplatz 1, P.O.B. 1227; f. 1572; cultural history from the Middle Ages to the Enlightenment; 600,000 vols., 11,000 manuscripts, 4,000 incunabula; Dir. Prof. Dr. PAUL RAABE; publs. *Ausstellungskataloge*†, *Kleine Schriften*†, *Wolfenbütteler Beiträge*, *Wolfenbütteler Barocknachrichten*, *Wolfenbütteler Notizen zur Buchgeschichte*, *Wolfenbütteler Renaissance-Mitteilungen*, *Wolfenbütteler Forschungen*.

652 WORMS

Stadtbibliothek: Marktplatz 10; f. 1881; 200,000 vols., 160 incunabula; special collections on Luther and Kant; Dir. Dr. GEORG ILLERT; publ. *Der Wormsgau*.

56 WUPPERTAL-ELBERFELD

Stadtbibliothek (*Public Library*): Kolpingstr. 8; f. 1852; special collections: theology, early Socialism; 589,817 vols.; Dir. HORST ERNESTUS.

87 WÜRZBURG

Universitätsbibliothek: Domerschulstr. 16; f. 1619; *c.* 927,708 vols., 260,462 theses, 2,940 incunabula, 1,922 manuscripts, 73 papyri; special Franconian collection; Dir. Dr. G. MÄLZER.

ARCHIVES

AMBERG

Staatsarchiv Amberg: Archivstr. 3; f. 1437, became state archive in 1921; 2 million items in archives, 13,000 vols.; Dirs. Dr. K. O. AMBRONN, Dr. A. FUCHS.

296 AURICH

Niedersächsisches Staatsarchiv Aurich: Oldersumer Str. 50; f. 1872; 14,000 vols.; Dir. Dr. WALTER DEETERS.

86 BAMBERG

Staatsarchiv Bamberg: Hainstrasse 39, Postfach 2668; f. *c.* 1007, became state archive in 1803; special collections: Frankish history, maps, plans, manuscripts, documents; library of 27,300 vols.; Dir. Dr. K. Freiherr v. ANDRÍAN-WERBURG.

1 BERLIN

Geh. Staatsarchiv Preuss. Kulturbesitz: Berlin 33, Archivstr. 12/14; f. 1598; material and research on Prussian history; *c.* 100,000 vols.; Dir. Dr. F. BENNINGHOVEN; publ. *Veröffentlichungen* (1–2 vols. yearly).

Landesarchiv Berlin: Kalckreuthstr. 1–2, 1000 Berlin 30; f. 1948; legal documents, etc. for the Berlin area, and important material of all kinds on the history of Berlin; library of 40,500 vols. and 4,000 film rolls; Dir. Dr. HANS J. REICHHARDT.

53 BONN

Archiv der sozialen Demokratie-Friedrich-Ebert-Stiftung (*Friedrich Ebert Archive of Social Democracy*): 5300 Bonn 2, Godesberger Allee 149; f. 1969; contains material formerly in archives of the Sozialdemokratische Partei Deutschlands (SPD) concerning the history of the party since its formation in 1882; 200,000 vols., 405,000 photographs, 15,000 pamphlets, 11,000 posters, also newspaper cuttings and film-track; Dir. WERNER KRAUSE.

Beethoven-Archiv: Bonngasse 18; f. 1927; books, periodicals, documents on Beethoven and his times; Dir. Prof. Dr. M. STAEHELIN; publs. *Gesamtausgabe der Musikalischen Werke Beethovens*, *Gesamtausgabe der Skizzen Beethovens*, *Beethoven-Jahrbuch*, *Schriften zur Beethoven-Forschung*.

Dokumentationsabteilung und Bibliothek der Westdeutschen Rektorenkonferenz: Bonn 2, Ahrstr. 39 (Westdeutsche Rektorenkonferenz); f. 1954; 33,056 vols., *c.* 700 periodicals, 84,441 records and acts; Head Dr. WOLFGANG KALISCHER.

Politisches Archiv des Auswärtigen Amts: Adenauerallee 99–103; f. 1920; Foreign Office archives; documents for the period 1867–1945; Dir. Dr. WEINANDY; publ. *Akten zur deutschen auswärtigen Politik 1918–1945* (series).

Stadtarchiv und Wissenschaftliche Stadtbibliothek: Stadtverwaltung; f. 1899; *c.* 80,000 vols.; Archivist and Librarian Dr. DIETRICH HÖROLDT; publ. *Bonner Geschichtsblätter* (annually), *Veröffentlichungen des Stadtarchivs Bonn*, *Studien zur Heimatgeschichte des Stadtbezirkes Bonn-Beuel*.

28 BREMEN

Staatsarchiv: Präsident-Kennedy-Platz 2; Dir. Dr. H. MÜLLER; publs. *Veröffentlichungen*†, *Bremisches Jahrbuch*† (annually).

4967 BÜCKEBURG

Niedersächsisches Staatsarchiv: Schloss; f. 1947 in Hanover, 1961 in Bückeburg; archives of the old county, later principality, of Schaumburg-Lippe and the district of Schaumberg; 10,000 documents, 15,000 vols., 15,000 maps; Dir. Dr. BRIGITTE POSCHMANN; publs. *Schaumburger Studien*, *Schaumburg-Lippische Mitteilungen*.

863 COBURG

Staatsarchiv Coburg: Schloss Ehrenburg; f. 13th century, present title since 1939; archives of the duchy and republic of Saxe-Coburg, since 1920 the rural district of Coburg; 215,800 documents; library of 5,000 vols.; Dir. Dr. K. Frhr. v. ANDRIAN-WERBURG.

5 COLOGNE

Archivberatungsstelle Rheinland: Constantinstr. 5; f. 1929; muicipal, church and private archives of the Rheinish region of Nordrhein-Westfalen; 9,000 vols.; Dir. Dr. phil. KURT SCHMITZ; publs. *Landschaftsverband Rheinland, Inventare nichtstaatlicher Archive, Archivberatungsstelle Rheinland, Archivhefte.*

Historisches Archiv: Severinstr. 222-228; f. 1322; records date back to A.D. 875; 43,000 vols.; Dir. Dr. H. STEHKÄMPER; publ. *Mitteilungen aus dem Stadtarchiv von Köln*†.

Rheinisch-Westfälisches Wirtschaftsarchiv zu Köln e.V.: Unter Sachsenhausen 10–26; f. 1906; economic records of the region; research and publication of research results; lending and reference library of business documents; *c.* 13,000 vols.; Dirs. Dr. KLARA VAN EYLL, Prof. Dr. Dr. FRIEDRICH-WILHELM HENNING; publs. *Schriften zur rheinisch-westfälischen Wirtschaftsgeschichte.*

61 DARMSTADT

Hessisches Staatsarchiv: Staatsarchiv, Schloss; f. 1567; Dir. Dr. ECKHART G. FRANZ.

493 DETMOLD

Staatsarchiv (Personenstandsarchiv): Willi-Hofmann-Strasse 2; f. 1957 (formerly Lippisches Landesarchiv, f. 16th century); archives of former regions of Lippe (12th century to 1947) and Minden (1815 to 1947), Dominion of Vianen (Netherlands), Detmold (since 1947); special collections: genealogy, French Citizens' Registers, Parish Registers, Jewish and Dissenters' Registers of Westphalia (1808 to 1874); copies of registers of births, deaths and marriages (1874-1938); library of 42,000 vols.: Dir. Dr. ENGELBERT.

41 DUISBURG

Stadtarchiv Duisburg: Am Burgplatz 19 (Rathaus); f. 12th century; administration, research into local and city history; reference library on local history and customs of Duisburg and Lower Rhine; *c.* 25,000 vols.; Dir. Dr. J. MILZ; publs. *Duisburger Forschungen, Schriftenreihe für Geschichte und Heimatkunde Duisburgs*†, *Duisburger Geschichtsquellen.*

4 DÜSSELDORF

Hauptstaatsarchiv Düsseldorf: Mauerstr. 55; f. 1822; Dir. Prof. Dr. W. JANSSEN; Zweigarchiv Kalkum: Schloss Kalkum über Düsseldorf-Kaiserswerth; publs. *Der Archivar, Mitteilungsblatt für deutsches Archivwesen.*

6 FRANKFURT A.M.

Stadtarchiv Frankfurt am Main: Karmeliterkloster, Karmelitergasse 5; f. 1366; municipal records; documents from the 9th century, registers from the 13th century, deeds from the 14th century; records on Frankfurt from other archives; historical records in writings, pictures and sound; over 40,000 vols. and 750 current periodicals; Dir. Dr. DIETRICH ANDERNACHT; publs. various.

78 FREIBURG I. BR.

Bundesarchiv-Militärarchiv: Wiesentalstr. 10; f. 1955 in Koblenz, 1967 in Freiburg; military documents of the Prussian army, the north German and Imperial navies, and the German army of the 2nd World War, and the present army; 10,100 metres of documentation, 33,740 metres of microfilm, *c.* 96,500 maps, *c.* 24,900 pictures, *c.* 270,000 technical drawings; library of 17,900 vols. and 16,500 official publications; Dir. Dr. FRIEDRICH-CHRISTIAN STAHL.

Deutsches Volksliedarchiv (*German Folksong Archive*): Silberbachstr. 13; f. 1914; 33,000 vols.; Dir. Prof. Dr. LUTZ RÖHRICH; publs. *Deutsche Volkslieder mit ihren Melodien, Jahrbuch für Volksliedforschung, Landschaftliche Volkslieder mit ihren Weisen, Handbuch des Volksliedes, Gottscheer Volkslieder.*

Stadtarchiv Freiburg i. Br.: Grünwälderstr. 15; f. 1840; 45,000 vols.; Dir. Dr. FRANZ LAUBENBERGER; publs. *Veröffentlichungen*†, *Schau-ins-Land*†.

2 HAMBURG

Deutsches Bibel-Archiv: Hamburg 13, Von Melle Park 6; f. 1931; biblical traditions in German literature and art; Bible translations; 5,000 vols.; Dir. HEIMO REINITZER; publs. *Bibel und deutsche Kultur, Abhandlungen und Vorträge*†, *Vestigia bibliae, Naturalis historia bibliae.*

Staatsarchiv: ABC-Str. 19, Eingang A; f. 13th century; history of Hamburg; over 1,000,000 vols.; Dir. Dr. HANS-DIETER LOOSE; publs. *Hamburgisches Urkundenbuch, Veröffentlichungen.*

3 HANOVER

Niedersächsisches Hauptstaatsarchiv in Hannover: Am Archiv 1; f. 16th century; 22,000 metres shelf-space; Dir. (vacant).

75 KARLSRUHE

Generallandesarchiv Karlsruhe: Nördliche Hildapromenade 2; f. 1803; 130,000 documents, 42,000 MSS., 3,500,000 report files; library of 50,000 vols. on Baden history; Dir. Dr. HANS GEORG ZIER; publ. *Zeitschrift für die Geschichte des Oberrheins*† (annually).

54 KOBLENZ

Bundesarchiv: Am Wöllershof 12; f. 1952; central archives of the Federal Republic; Pres. Prof. Dr. HANS BOOMS.

Landeshauptarchiv: Karmeliterstrasse 1–3; f. 1832; 42,000 vols.; Dir. Dr. F. J. HEYEN; publ. *Veröffentlichungen der Landesarchivverwaltung Rheinland-Pfalz.*

83 LANDSHUT

Staatsarchiv: Burg Trausnitz; f. 1753; library of 10,000 vols.; Dir. Dr. E. STAHLEDER.

24 LÜBECK

Archiv der Hansestadt Lübeck: Mühlendamm 1–3; f. 1298; municipal archives and documents of the churches, recognized public bodies, institutions and private persons; *c.* 28,000 vols.; Dir. Dr. A. GRASSMANN; publs. various on the history of Lübeck.

714 LUDWIGSBURG

Staatsarchiv: Schloss; f. 1868; archives for the administrative district of Stuttgart (Nordwürttemberg); 20,000 metres of deeds, documents and books; 29,000 vols.; Dir. Dr. ALOIS SEILER.

6800 MANNHEIM

Deutsches Spracharchiv im Institut für deutsche Sprache (*German Language Archives*): Friedrich-Karl-Str. 12; f. 1932; library of 8,642 tape recordings of spoken German; publ. *Phonai.*

3550 MARBURG

Deutsches Adelsarchiv: Friedrichsplatz 15; f. 1945; genealogy of German nobility; 12,000 vols.; Dir. Dr. phil. WALTER VON HUECK; publ. *Genealogisches Handbuch des Adels.*

Hessisches Staatsarchiv Marburg: Friedrichsplatz 15; f. 1502; 60,000 books, 125,000 charts; 36 kms. of records of the Electorate of Hesse-Kassel, the abbeys of Fulda, Hersfeld, the principality of Waldeck, etc.; Dir. Dr. HANS PHILIPPI; publ. *Repertorien des Staatsarchivs Marburg*†.

8000 MUNICH

Bayerisches Hauptstaatsarchiv: Schönfeldstr. 5; f. 13th century, reorganized 1978; comprises five departments: (1) Ältere Bestände: 360,000 charters, 450,000 documents and vols., 46,000 maps and plans; (2) Neuere Bestände (19th and 20th centuries): 3,000 charters, 420,000 documents; (3) Geheimes Hausarchiv: 9,600 charters, 105,000 documents and vols., 8,000 maps and plans; (4) Kriegsarchiv: 280,000 documents and vols., 490,000 maps and plans, 600,000 pictures; (5) Nachlässe und Sammlungen: collections of private papers, publications, etc.; Dir. Dr. HILDEBRAND TROLL; publs. *Archivalische Zeitschrift, Bayerische Archivinventare, Mitteilungen für die Archivpflege in Bayern, Nachrichten, Ausstellungskataloge.*

Deutsches Bucharchiv München (Institut für Buchwissenschaften): Munich 5, Erhardtstr. 8; f. 1948; documentation and scientific and technical information about books and periodicals; 15,000 vols., 170 periodicals; Dir. Dr. LUDWIG DELP.

Landeskirchliches Archiv: Munich 19, Birkerstr. 22.

Staatsarchiv: Munich 22, Schönfeldstr. 3; 5,304,000 files and vols., 9,367 documents, 18,445 maps and plans; Dir. (vacant).

Stadtarchiv: Winzererstr. 68; f. 1893; 62,000 vols., 75,000 documents, 21,000 maps and plans, 84,000 photos and post-cards, 3,050 soundtracks, 1,200 films, 26,629 posters; Dir. Dr. M. SCHATTENHOFER.

44 MÜNSTER

Staatsarchiv: Bohlweg 2; f. 1829 as Provinzialarchiv, present title since 1867; 110,000 documents dating from 9th century A.D.; library of 120,000 vols.; Dir. Dr. HANS-JOACHIM BEHR; publ. *Das Staatsarchiv Münster und seine Bestände*†.

Westfälisches Landesamt für Archivpflege Münster im Landschaftsverband Westfalen-Lippe: Warendorfer Str. 24; f. 1927; non-state archives; training of archivists; 10,000 vols.; Dir. Dr. HELMUT RICHTERING; publs. *Ivventare nichtstaatlicher Archive Westfalens, Archivpflege in Westfalen und Lippe* (*Mitteilungsblatt mit Beilage Westfälische Quellen im Bild*).

8858 NEUBURG

Staatsarchiv Neuburg a.d. Donau: Schloss; f. 1830; f. 1,800,000 files, vols. and charters; Dir. Dr. R. H. SEITZ.

85 NUREMBERG

Landeskirchliches Archiv der Evangelisch-Lutherischen Kirche in Bayern: Veilhofstrasse 28; f. 1930; *c.* 100,000 vols.; Dir. Dr. H. BAIER.

Staatsarchiv: Archivstr. 17; under general administration of Bavarian State Archives, Munich; f. 1806; archives of middle Franconia; includes Nuremberg trial documents; library of 30,000 vols.; Dir. Dr. GÜNTHER SCHUHMANN.

Stadtarchiv Nürnberg: Egidienplatz 23; f. 1865; reference library of 14,000 vols.; Dir. Dr. GERHARD HIRSCHMANN; publs. *Quellen zur Geschichte und Kultur der Stadt Nürnberg, Nürnberger Werkstücke zur Stadt und Landesgeschichte.*

29 OLDENBURG

Niedersächsisches Staatsarchiv in Oldenburg: Damm 43; f. 1626; public record office for the former district of Oldenburg; library of 30,000 vols.; record repository with 8,000 metres of files; Dir. Dr. ALBRECHT ECKHARDT; contributes to *Veröffentlichungen der Niedersächsischen Archivverwaltung.*

45 OSNABRÜCK

Niedersächsisches Staatsarchiv: Schloss Str. 29; f. 1869; 43,700 vols.; Dir. Dr. H. R. JARCK.

66 SAARBRÜCKEN

Landesarchiv Saarbrücken: Am Ludwigsplatz 7; f. 1948; 3,000 metres of archives, 7,000 vols.; Dir. Dr. HANS-WALTER HERRMANN; 167 official publs.

238 SCHLESWIG

Landesarchiv Schleswig-Holstein: Schloss Gottorf; f. 1870; 17,500 metres of documents, 35,000 vols.; Dir. Prof. Dr. WOLFGANG PRANGE; publ. *Veröffentlichungen*†.

748 SIGMARINGEN

Staatsarchiv: Karlstrasse 3; f. 1865; archives of Regierungsbezirk Tübingen dating from 11th century; family archives of ex-prince of Hohenzollern, barons of Stauffenberg, Enzberg, etc.; *c.* 9,700 metres of archives; library of *c.* 36,000 vols.; Dir. Dr. W. SCHÖNTAG; publ. *Arbeiten zur Landeskunde Hohenzollerns.*

672 SPEYER

Landesarchiv: Domplatz 6; f. 1817; historical archives of the Palatinate (1400–1798), of the French administration until 1815 and the Bavarian administration until 1945; current accessions of administrations in the Palatinate and Rheinhesse; Dir. Dr. A. DOLL.

D-7000 STUTTGART

Hauptstaatsarchiv Stuttgart: Konrad-Adenauer-Str. 4; f. 15th century; ministerial and historical archives of Baden-Württemberg; 73,000 vols.; Dir. Dr. EBERHARD GÖNNER.

Rathausbücherei der Stadt Stuttgart: Im Rathaus, Marktplatz 1; archives f. 1928; 151,000 vols., thousands of documents; large collection of maps, pictures and drawings, coins and medallions; Dir. Dr. HEINZ SCHMITT; publ. *Veröffentlichungen des Archives der Stadt Stuttgart.*

62 WIESBADEN

Hessisches Hauptstaatsarchiv Wiesbaden: Mainzer Str. 80; Dir. Dr. WOLF-ARNO KROPAT; publ. *Nassauische Annalen* (annual).

344 WOLFENBÜTTEL

Niedersächsisches Staatsarchiv: Forstweg 2; f. 16th century; contains documents and records of the province of Brunswick; library of *c.* 54,000 vols.; Dir. Dr. GÜNTER SCHEEL.

652 WORMS

Stadtarchiv: Marktplatz 10; large collection of records, documents and maps; Head Archivist FRITZ REUTER.

87 WÜRZBURG

Staatsarchiv Würzburg: Residenzplatz 2; f. 1764; archives of Lower Franconia dating from Middle Ages; library of 26,388 vols., 4,654,273 documents; Man. Dir. Prof. W. SCHERZER.

MUSEUMS AND ART GALLERIES

51 AACHEN

Internationales Zeitungsmuseum der Stadt Aachen (*International Newspaper Museum*): Pontstr. 13; f. 1885; over 120,000 newspapers; Dir. Dr. HERBERT LEPPER.

Suermondt-Ludwig-Museum: Wilhelmstrasse 18; f. 1882; antiques, sculpture of Middle Ages, paintings, particularly 17th-century Dutch School and modern collection; history of art library of 10,000 vols.; Dir. Dr. E. G. GRIMME; publ. *Aachener Kunstblätter*.

757 BADEN-BADEN

Staatliche Kunsthalle: Lichtentaler Allee 8A; f. 1909; exhibitions of contemporary art; Dir. Dr. HANS ALBERT PETERS; publ. catalogues†.

858 BAYREUTH

Richard-Wagner-Museum: Richard-Wagner-Str. 48; f. 1976; museum and archive of the life and works of Richard Wagner; Dir. Dr. MANFRED EGER.

Richard-Wagner-Gedenkstätte: Wahnfriedstr. 1; f. 1924; archive of the life and works of Richard Wagner; Dir. Dr. MANFRED EGER.

1 BERLIN

Botanischer Garten und Botanisches Museum Berlin-Dahlem: Berlin 33, Königin-Luise-Str. 6–8; f. 1679, 1815; Dir. Prof. Dr. W. GREUTER; library of 47,000 vols.; 85,100 reprints; publs. *Willdenowia*†, *Englera*†.

Brücke-Museum: Berlin 33, Bussardsteig 9; f. 1967; German expressionism, paintings, sculptures and graphic art of the Brücke group; Dir. Prof. Dr. L. REIDEMEISTER; publ. *Brücke Archiv* (yearly).

Staatliche Museen Preussischer Kulturbesitz (West Berlin): Berlin 30, Stauffenbergstrasse 41; f. 1957; Gen. Dir. Prof. Dr. STEPHAN WAETZOLDT; supervises the following museums and collections:

Ägyptisches Museum (*Egyptian Museum*): Dir. Prof. Dr. J. SETTGAST.

Antikenmuseum (*Greek and Roman Antiquities*): Dir. Prof. Dr. WOLF-DIETER HEILMEYER.

Gemäldegalerie (*Gallery of Old Masters' Paintings*): Dir. Prof. Dr. HENNING BOCK.

Kunstbibliothek (*Art Library*): (*see* under Libraries).

Kunstgewerbemuseum (*Applied Arts Museum*): Dir. Prof. Dr. FRANZ-ADRIAN DREIER.

Kupferstichkabinett (*Department of Prints and Drawings*): Dir. Prof. Dr. FEDJA ANZELEWSKI.

Museum für Deutsche Volkskunde (*Museum of German Folklore*): Dir. Prof. Dr. THEODOR KOHLMANN.

Museum für Indische Kunst (*Museum of Indian Art*): Dir. Prof. Dr. H. HÄRTEL.

Museum für Islamische Kunst (*Islamic Art and Antiquities*): Dir. Prof. Dr. KLAUS BRISCH.

Museum für Ostasiatische Kunst (*Museum of Far Eastern Art*): Dir. Prof. Dr. B. VON RAGUÉ.

Museum für Völkerkunde (*Ethnographical Museum*): Dir. Prof. Dr. KURT KRIEGER.

Museum für Vor- und Frühgeschichte (*Museum of Pre- and Early History*): Dir. Prof. Dr. A. VON MUELLER.

Museumsbibliothek (*Museum Library*): Dir. Dr. F. STEENBOCK.

Neue Nationalgalerie (*National Gallery*): Potsdamerstrasse 50, 1 Berlin 30; Dir. Prof. Dr. DIETER HONISCH.

Skulpturengalerie (*Sculpture Gallery*): Dir. Prof. Dr. PETER BLOCH.

Verwaltung der Staatlichen Schlösser und Gärten, West-Berlin (*Administration of State Castles and Gardens*): Schloss Charlottenburg Luisenplatz; f. 1926; the administration controls Charlottenburg Castle, Grunewald Hunting Castle (with collection of paintings), Glienicke Castle and Peacock Island (Castle and Park); 5,000 vols.; Chief Officers Prof. Dr. MARTIN SPERLICH, Dr. HELMUT BÖRSCH-SUPAN.

53 BONN

Beethoven-Haus: Bonngasse 20; f. 1889; Beethoven's birthplace; Beethoven archives; 700 mems.; 5,000 vols.; Pres. HERMANN J. ABS.

Rheinisches Landesmuseum in Bonn (*Rhineland Museum in Bonn*): Colmantstr. 16; f. 1820; prehistoric, Roman and Frankish antiquities of the Rhineland; Rhenish sculpture, painting and applied arts up to the 20th century; Dutch paintings; 70,000 vols.; Dir. Dr. CHRISTOPH B. RÜGER; publs. *Bonner Jahrbücher des Rheinischen Landesmuseums und des Vereins von Altertumsfreunden im Rheinlande* (since 1842), *Das Rheinische Landesmuseum Bonn* (2 a month).

Städtisches Kunstmuseum Bonn: Rathausgasse 7; f. 1882, restored 1954; collection of 20th-century art; German expressionist painting, with important August Macke collection; contemporary international graphic art, contemporary German art; library of *c.* 15,000 vols.; Dir. Dr. DIERK STEMMLER; publs. catalogues†.

Zoologisches Forschungsinstitut und Museum Alexander Koenig (*Zoological Research Institute and Alexander Koenig Museum*): Adenauerallee 150-164; f. 1912; zoology—vertebrates and insects; library of 76,266 vols.; Dir. Prof. Dr. G. NOBIS; publs. *Bonner Zoologische Beiträge*†, *Bonner Zoologische Monographien*†.

28 BREMEN

Focke-Museum (*District Museum for Art and Culture*): Schwachhauser Heerstr. 240; Dir. Dr. ROSEMARIE POHL-WEBER.

Kunsthalle Bremen: Am Wall 207; f. 1823; 15th–20th-century European paintings, prints and drawings; 17th–20th-century sculpture; Japanese drawings and prints, illustrated books; Dir. Dr. GÜNTER BUSCH.

Übersee-Museum Bremen: Bremen, Bahnhofsplatz 13; f. 1896; ethnology, commerce, natural history; library of 60,000 vols.; Dir. Dr. HERBERT GANSLMAYR; publ. *Veröffentlichungen* (scientific and cultural series, irregular).

33 BRUNSWICK

Herzog Anton Ulrich-Museum (former Landesmuseum): Museumstr. 1; f. 1754; collection includes old pictures, prints and drawings, medieval art, ceramics, 16th-century French enamels, carvings in ivory, bronzes, collection of lace, old clocks, etc.; art library of *c.* 40,000 vols.; Dir. Dr. R. KLESSMANN; publs. *Geschichte, Verzeichnis der Gemälde*†, *Zeichnungen alter Meister, Die Braunschweiger Elfenbeinsammlung, Spitzen von der Renaissance bis zum Empire, Corpus vasorum antiquorum, Kunsthefte 1-10, Meisterwerke im Herzog Anton Ulrich-Museum*†, *Bilderhefte 1-5*†.

Städtisches Museum: Am Löwenwall 14; f. 1861; collections illustrate topography, history and culture of the town; 19th- and 20th-century paintings, cabinet of medals (all periods and territories, with about 80,000 pieces); ethnographical collection of Dukedom of Brunswick; 28,000 vols.; Curator Dr. G. SPIES; publs. *Braunschweiger Werkstücke*†, *Arbeitsberichte*†, *Miszellen*†, catalogues†.

5 COLOGNE

Museen der Stadt Köln (*Museums of the City of Cologne*): An der Rechtsschule; Gen. Dir. Dr. GERHARD BOTT; publs. *Museen in Köln, Bulletin*. The General Director supervises the following museums:

Kölnisches Stadtmuseum im Zeughaus: Zeughausstr. 1-3; f. 1888; Dir. Prof. Dr. HUGO BORGER.

Kunstgewerbemuseum: Eigelsteintorburg; f. 1888; Dir. Prof. Dr. BRIGITTE KLESSE; Curator Dr. G. REINEKING VON BOCK.

Kunsthalle: Joseph-Haubrich-Platz; f. 1967.

Museum Ludwig: An der Rechtschule; f. 1976; paintings, modern sculpture, prints; library: *see* Libraries; Dir. Dr. KARL RUHRBERG.

Museum für Ostasiatische Kunst: Universitätsstr. 100; f. 1911; 7,000 vols.; Dir. Prof. Dr. ROGER GOEPPER; Curator Dr. E. DITTRICH.

Rautenstrauch-Joest-Museum: Ubierring 45; f. 1901; ethnological museum; 20,000 vols.; Dir. Dr. AXEL VON GAGERN; Curators Dr. I. BOLZ, Dr. W. STÖHR, Dr. K. VOLPRECHT; publ. *Ethnologica*.

Römisch-Germanisches Museum: Roncalliplatz (Domhof) 2; library of 8,000 vols.; Dir. Prof. Dr. HUGO BORGER; publ. *Kölner Jahrbuch für Vor- und Frühgeschichte*.

Schnütgen-Museum: Cäcilienkloster 29; f. 1906; 8,000 vols.; Dir. Prof. Dr. ANTON LEGNER.

Wallraf-Richartz-Museum: An der Rechtschule; f. 1824; paintings, sculpture, prints; library: *see* Libraries; Dir. Dr. GERHARD BOTT; publ. *Wallraf-Richartz-Jarhbuch*.

61 DARMSTADT

Grossherzogliche Porzellansammlung: Prinz-Georg-Palais, Im Schlossgarten 7; f. 1907; European porcelain, paintings, furniture, faïence; Owner Princess MARGARET VON HESSEN UND BEI RHEIN; Dir. GUDRUN ILLGEN.

Hessisches Landesmuseum Darmstadt: Friedensplatz 1; f. 1820; archaeology, prehistory, zoology, geology-palaeontology, mineralogy; art collections and cultural history from 9th to 20th centuries, inc. crafts, prints and drawings, stained glass, sculptures, painting, post-1945 European and American art and Karl Ströher collection; library of 55,000 vols.; Dir. Dr. W. BEEH; publs. *Kunst in Hessen und am Mittelrhein* (annual).

Jagdmuseum Schloss Kranichstein: 61 Darmstadt, Schloss Kranichstein; f. 1918; pictures, hunting trophies and weapons, furnished rooms; owned by Stiftung Hessischer Jägerhof; Dir. ERNST HOFMANN.

Schlossmuseum: Residenzschloss; f. 1920; Holbein Madonna, 18th-century uniforms, furnished rooms, ceremonial carriages and harness; Owner Princess LUDWIG VON HESSEN UND BEI RHEIN; Dir. ERNST HOFMANN; Custodian Dr. VOLKER ILLGEN.

46 DORTMUND

Museum für Kunst und Kulturgeschichte Dortmund (*Dortmund Museum of Art and Cultural History*): D-4714 Selm, Schloss Cappenberg bei Lünen/Westf.; f. 1883; collections include medieval Westphalian sculpture, Westphalian furniture of 15th–19th centuries, German and European *objets d'art*, paintings, etc.; 12,000 vols.; Dir. Dr. HORST APPUHN; publs. Catalogues†.

4 DÜSSELDORF

Kunstmuseum Düsseldorf: Ehrenhof 5; f. 1913; old masters, modern art, sculpture, glass, engraving; 50,000 vols.; Dir. Dr. HANS ALBERT PETERS; publs. *Düsseldorfer Museumsbulletin* (quarterly), Catalogues†. (Closed for renovation from 1980 until further notice.)

Kunstsammlung Nordrhein-Westfalen: Schloss Jägerhof, Jacobistr. 2; f. 1962; 20th-century art; Dir. Prof. Dr. WERNER SCHMALENBACH; Curator Dr. VOLKMAR ESSERS.

Löbbecke-Museum und Aquarium: Postfach 1120, Brehmstrasse; f. 1904; natural science museum and large aquarium; 5,000 books; Dir. Dr. M. ZAHN; publs. *Jahresberichte* (annually), *Mitteilungen der Arbeitsgemeinschaft rheinischwestfälischer Lepidopterologen* (2 a year).

Neandertal Museum (*Museum of Pre-history: Ice-Age Preserve*): 402 Mettmann, Düsseldorfer Str. 26, Kreishaus-Zimmer 306.

Städtische Kunsthalle Düsseldorf: Grabbeplatz 4; re-opened 1967; exhibitions of contemporary art; Dir. J. HARTEN; publs. *Catalogues*.

43 ESSEN

Museum Folkwang: Bismarckstr. 64 166; f. 1902; 19th- and 20th-century art, including posters and photography; 12,000 vols.; Dir. Prof. Dr. P. VOGT.

239 FLENSBURG

Städtisches Museum (*Municipal Museum*): f. 1876; contains about 23,700 exhibits, mainly arts and crafts, peasant art, and prehistory of Schleswig; library of *c.* 12,000 vols.; Dir. Dr. R. ZÖLLNER; publs. *Nordelbingen, Beiträge zur Kunst- und Kulturgeschichte* (Vols. 1-46, 1923-77).

6 FRANKFURT A.M.

Bundespostmuseum: Frankfurt 70, Schaumainkai 53; f. 1872; items on history of Post and Telecommunication, special exhibitions of stamps; library of 10,000 vols.; Curator GOTTFRIED NORTH.

Freies Deutsches Hochstift-Frankfurter Goethemuseum (Goethes Elternhaus): Gr. Hirschgraben 23-25; f. 1859; German literature of the Romantic period and of Goethe's time; selected works of 19th and 20th centuries; 25,000 MSS. of German poetry of Goethe period; 400 paintings, 15,000 etchings; library of 120,000 vols.; Dir. Dr. DETLEV LÜDERS; publs. *Jahrbuch des Freien Deutschen Hochstifts, Reihe der Schriften des Freien Deutschen Hochstifts*†, guides, literary editions, etc.

Städelsches Kunstinstitut: Frankfurt 70, Dürerstr. 2; f. 1816; paintings, drawings, prints, sculpture; library of 40,000 vols.; Dir. Dr. KLAUS GALLWITZ; publ. *Städeljahrbuch*.

Städtische Museen: comprise:

Städtische Galerie: Schaumainkai 63 (Painting), Schaumainkai 71, Liebieghaus (Sculpture); f. 1907; Dir. Dr. KLAUS GALLWITZ.

Museum für Kunsthandwerk: Schaumainkai 15; European furniture: gothic to art nouveau; f. 1877 (medieval, renaissance, baroque, 19th-century, Islamic and Far Eastern arts are stored); Dir. Dr. ANNALIESE OHM.

Historisches Museum: Untermainkai 14; History of Frankfurt, relics, art and culture; f. 1878; Dir. Dr. H. STUBENVOLL.

Museum für Völkerkunde: Schaumainkai 29; f. 1904; Dir. Prof. Dr. H. NIGGEMEYER.

Museum für Vor- und Frühgeschichte: Justinianstr. 5; f. 1937; Prehistoric, Roman and Early Middle Age objects from the Frankfurt area; Mediterranean and Oriental archaeology; Dir. Dr. ULRICH FISCHER.

78 Freiburg im Breisgau

Städtische Museen (*Municipal Collections*): Salzstr. 32; f. 1862; the collections comprise Augustinermuseum, Folk-lore, Natural History, and early and pre-History; library of *c.* 25,000 vols.; Dir. Dr. Hans H. Hofstätter.

63 Giessen

Burgmannenhaus, Das: Georg-Schlosser-Str. 2; f. 1978; originally the seat of the Junkers of Rodenhausen; now museum of local history and culture; exhibits of material culture of Giessen and surrounding area; portraits, pictures, maps, engravings, textile manufacture and handicraft; furniture, farm implements, costumes, pottery; special exhibitions on the political thinkers Georg Büchner and Wilhelm Liebknecht (founder of the German Social Democratic Party).

Oberhessisches Museum und Gailsche Sammlungen der Stadt Giessen: Asterweg 9; f. 1879; palaeolithic collection, first Middle European flint tools: archaeological collections and treasures of Roman-German and Hessian Franconian culture; oil paintings, watercolours and copperplate engravings of present century; Sec. K. F. Ertel.

34 Göttingen

Städtisches Museum (*Municipal Museum*): Ritterplan 7; f. 1889; prehistory and early history, ecclesiastical art, history of Göttingen and the University, crafts, modern art, etc.; library of 4,000 vols.; Dir. (vacant).

2 Hamburg

Altonaer Museum in Hamburg/Norddeutsches Landesmuseum: Hamburg 50 (Altona), Museumstrasse 23; f. 1863; collections on art and cultural history, folk art, navigation and fishing, geology of northern Germany; library of 40,000 vols.; Dir. Prof. Dr. G. Kaufmann; publs. *Altonaer Museum in Hamburg*†, *Jahrbuch* (Yearbook), catalogues of collections and exhibitions†.

Hamburgisches Museum für Völkerkunde: Binderstr. 14; f. 1879; ethnological collections from Africa, America, Asia, Australia, Europe and the Pacific; library of 55,000 vols.; Dir. Prof. Dr. Jürgen Zwernemann; publs. *Mitteilungen*†, *Monographien zur Völkerkunde*, *Wegweiser zur Völkerkunde*†, *Beiträge zur mittelamerikanischen Völkerkunde*†.

Hamburger Kunsthalle: Glockengiesserwall; f. 1869; paintings from 14th to 20th centuries, sculpture of 19th and 20th, drawings and engravings from 14th to 20th, Greek and Roman coins, medals from 14th to 20th centuries; library of 80,000 vols.; Dir. Prof. Dr. Werner Hofmann; publ. *Jahrbuch der Hamburger Kunstsammlungen*.

Museum für Hamburgische Geschichte: Holstenwall 24; f. 1839; political history of Hamburg, library, coins, handicrafts, models, etc.; Dir. Dr. Jörgen Bracker; publs. *Mitteilungen*, *Hamburger Beiträge zur Numismatik*, *Numismatische Studien*, *Beiträge zur deutschen Volks- und Altertumskunde*.

Museum für Kunst und Gewerbe Hamburg: Steintorplatz 1; f. 1877; 7 mems.; 60,000 books; European sculpture and art from the Middle Ages onward, ancient art, art of the Near and Far East, European popular art, graphic collections; Dir. Prof. Dr. Axel von Saldern; publs. *Jahrbuch der Hamburger Kunstsammlungen*, catalogues.

3 Hanover

Historisches Museum am Hohen Ufer: Pferdestr. 6; f. 1903 as Fatherland Museum, 1937-50 Niedersächsisches Volkstumsmuseum, 1950-66 as Niedersächsisches Heimatmuseum; three sections: Lower Saxon Folklore, History of the City of Hanover, History of the Kingdom of Hanover up to 1866; library of 8,000 vols.; Dir. Dr. W. R. Röhrbein.

Kestner-Museum: Trammplatz 3; opened 1889; Egyptian, Greek, Etruscan and Roman *objets d'art*, and medieval art; illuminated MSS., incunabula, handicrafts of Middle Ages to 20th century; ancient, medieval and modern coins, medals; Dir. Dr. Peter Munro; Curator Dr. Helga Hilschenz; Asst. Curator Dr. Margildis Schlüter.

Niedersächsisches Landesmuseum Hannover: Am Maschpark; f. 1852; art, natural history, prehistory and ethnology sections; libraries attached to each section; Dirs. Dr. Hans W. Grohn (also Dir. art section), Dr. H. Schirnig (pre-history), Dr. G. Boenigk (natural history), Dr. H. Becher (ethnology).

69 Heidelberg

Kurpfälzisches Museum der Stadt Heidelberg: Hauptstr, 97; f. 1879; Dir. Dr. Jörn Bahns.

32 Hildesheim

Roemer- und Pelizæus-Museum: Am Steine 1-2; comprises:

Pelizæus-Museum: f. 1911; collection of Egyptian and Græco-Roman antiquities; library of 5,000 vols.; Dir. Dr. Arne Eggebrecht.

Roemer-Museum: f. 1844; geology, palaeontology, zoology, botany, prehistory, ethnography, etc.; library of 5,000 vols.; Dir. Dr. Walter Konrad.

75 Karlsruhe

Badisches Landesmuseum: Schlossplatz 1; f. 1919; collection includes prehistoric, Egyptian, Greek and Roman antiquities, mediaeval, renaissance and baroque sculpture, works of art from the middle ages to the 20th-century, weapons, folklore and coins, collection of Turkish trophies; library of 38,000 vols.; Dir. Prof. Dr. Ernst Petrasch.

Landessammlungen für Naturkunde (*State Natural History Collections*): D-75 Karlsruhe 1, Erbprinzenstr. 13; f. 1751; research and exhibitions in botany, zoology, mineralogy, geology, entomology, palaeontology, vivarium; library of *c.* 50,000 vols.; Dir. Prof. Dr. S. Rietschel; publ. *Beiträge zur naturkundlichen Forschung in Südwestdeutschland*† (annually).

Oberrheinisches Dichter-Museum: Röntgenstr. 6; f. 1965; exhibition of the works, manuscripts and pictures of various authors; *c.* 4,000 vols.; Pres. Dr. Traugott Bender; Dir. Dr. Beatrice Steiner.

Staatliche Kunsthalle: Hans-Thoma-Strasse 2-6; f. 1803; German, Dutch, Flemish, Italian and French paintings and sculpture, 14th to 20th century; print room; *c.* 50,000 prints and drawings; library of *c.* 65,000 vols.; Dir. Prof. Dr. Horst Vey.

35 Kassel

Brüder Grimm-Museum: Brüder Grimm-Platz 4A; f. 1960; preservation of works of Jacob, Wilhelm and Ludwig Emil Grimm; collection of works by the brothers; original paintings, autographs, letters, drawings, etchings; Dir. Dr. Dieter Hennig.

Staatliche Kunstsammlungen Kassel (*Federal Art Collection*): Schloss Wilhelmshöhe; f. 16th century; classical antiquities, drawings and engravings, paintings from 14th century to 1750; library of 50,000 vols.; Dir. Prof. Dr. E. Herzog; publ. *Kunst in Hessen und am Mittelrhein*† (annually).

Hessisches Landesmuseum: Brüder-Grimm-Platz 5, pre- and early history; scientific instruments, arts-handicraft; folklore.

Neue Galerie: Schöne Aussicht 1; paintings and sculpture from 1750 to present day.

Schloss Friedrichstein: Bad Wildungen; 15th-19th-century military and hunting exhibits.

775 KONSTANZ

Hus-Museum: Hussenstrasse 64; f. 1965; house of Jan Hus with documents of Jan Hus and Hieronymus of Prague; Dir. SIGRID VON BLANCKENHAGEN.

Rosgarten Museum: Rosgartenstr. 3-5; f. 1871; central museum for Lake Constance area; prehistoric, early historic and Roman collection; arts and crafts from the middle ages to 19th century, coins, etc.; library of *c.* 1,000 vols.; Curator S. v. BLANCKENHAGEN.

Bodensee-Naturmuseum: Katzgasse 5-7; f. 1967; geology, palaeontology, zoology and botany of Lake Constance; Curator SIGRID VON BLANCKENHAGEN.

24 LÜBECK

Museum für Kunst und Kulturgeschichte (*Museum for Art and Cultural History*): Verwaltung, Düvekenstr. 21; f. 1800; library of 18,000 vols.; Dir. WULF SCHADENDORF; publs. *Kataloge des St. Annen-Museums, Katalog des Behnhauses, Lübecker Museumshefte, Kataloge.*

St. Annen-Museum: St. Annenstr. 15; Late Gothic convent, built 1502-1515; medieval ecclesiastical art from Lübeck; domestic art from Lübeck, from Middle Ages to modern times.

Museum Behnhaus: Königstr. 11; museum of 19th- and 20th-century art in a late 18th-century patrician house.

Museum Holstentor: built 1464–1478; history of the city.

Katharinenkirche: 14th century; formerly Franciscan monasteries church; casts of medieval sculptures of Lübeck artists in Scandinavia.

Völkerkunde-Sammlung (*Ethnographic Collection*): (no exhibitions at present).

65 MAINZ

Gutenberg-Museum: Liebfrauenplatz 5; f. 1900; world museum of typography; library of 50,000 vols.; Dir. Prof. Dr. HANS A. HALBEY.

Mittelrheinisches Landesmuseum Mainz: Grosse Bleiche 49–51; f. 1806; library of 4,000 vols.; Dir. Prof. WILHELM WEBER; publ. *Mainzer Zeitschrift.*

Münzsammlung (*Coin Collection*): Rheinallee 3B; f. 1784; Dir. (vacant).

Naturhistorisches Museum Mainz (*Natural History Museum*): Mitternachtsplatz; f. 1834; palaeontology and geology of the Mainz basin, zoology, mineralogy, botany; library of 2,000 vols. and 10,000 pamphlets; Dir. Dr. rer. nat. Fr. O. NEUFFER; publs. *Mainzer Naturwissenschaftliches Archiv, Museumsführer* 1–5, *Museumsheft.*

Römisch-Germanisches Zentralmuseum-Forschungsinstitut für Vor- und Frühgeschichte: Ernst-Ludwig-Platz 2; f. 1852; studies in European archaeology and prehistory, conservation of prehistoric, Roman and early medieval antiquities; library of 45,000 vols.; Dir. Prof. Dr. K. BÖHNER; publs. *Kataloge*†, *Ausstellungskataloge*†, *Führer durch die Ausstellungen*†, *Führer zu vor- und frühgeschichtlichen Denkmälern, Jahrbuch*†, *Archäologie und Naturwissenschaften, Arbeitsblätter für Restauratoren, Archäologisches Korrespondenzblatt, Studien zu den Anfängen der Metallurgie*, and various monographs†.

68 MANNHEIM

Städtische Kunsthalle: Moltkestr. 9; f. 1909; Dir. Dr. HEINZ FUCHS.

Reiss-Museum: Zeughaus, C.5; f. 1763; art museum and museums of ethnology, archaeology, prehistory and local history; 40,000 books; Dir. Dr. ERICH GROPENGIESSER.

355 MARBURG/LAHN

Universitätsmuseum für Kunst und Kulturgeschichte: Biegenstr. 11, im Ernst von Hülsen-Haus; f. 1927; Dir. Dr. CARL GRAEPLER.

8 MUNICH

Bayerisches Nationalmuseum: Prinzregentenstr. 3; f. 1855; European fine arts, especially sculpture, decorative art and folk art; library of 60,000 vols.; Schloss Lustheim in Schleissheim (Meissen porcelain, Ernst Schneider collection); Gen. Dir. Dr. LENZ KRISS-RETTENBECK; publs. *Kataloge Vol. I–XV, Führer durch die Schausammlung, Bildführer, Forschungshefte, Bayerische Blätter für Volkskunde.*

Bayerische Staatsgemäldesammlungen (*Bavarian State Art Galleries*): Meiserstr. 10; Gen. Dir. Prof. Dr. E. STEINGRÄBER; Dir. Doerner Institute Dr. H. F. VON SONNENBURG.

Alte Pinakothek: Barerstr. 27; f. 1836; Old Masters.

Neue Pinakothek: Barerstr. 29; f. 1853; 19th-century European art.

Staatsgalerie moderner Kunst: Prinzregentenstr. 1; 20th-century European and American art.

Schackgalerie: Prinzregentenstr. 9; f. 1865; late Romantic German art.

Olaf Gulbransson Museum in Kurpark: Tegernsee.

Also art galleries in the following towns: Ansbach, Aschaffenburg, Augsburg, Bamberg, Bayreuth, Burghausen, Füssen, Kulmbach, Landshut, Ottobeuren, Tegernsee and Würzburg.

Deutsches Museum: Museumsinsel 1; f. 1903; machines, demonstrations, models, etc., on subjects relating to science and technology; library of 630,000 vols.; Chair. Board of Trustees Dr.-Ing. HANS H. MOLL; Dir.-Gen. THEO STILLGER; publs. *Veröffentlichungen des Forschungsinstituts*† (History of the Natural Sciences and Technology), *Abhandlungen und Berichte*†, *Kultur und Technik*† (quarterly).

Generaldirektion der Staatlichen Naturwissenschaftlichen Sammlungen Bayerns, München (*State Scientific Collections, Munich*): 19 Menzingerstr. 71; Gen. Dir. Prof. Dr. WOLFGANG ENGELHARDT. The following institutions are under the control of this body:

Anthropologische Staatssammlung: 2 Karolinenpl. 2A; f. 1886; Dir. (vacant).

Bayerische Staatssammlung für allgemeine und angewandte Geologie: 2 Luisenstrasse 37; f. 1924; Dir. Prof. Dr. KLAUS SCHMIDT.

Bayerische Staatssammlung für Paläontologie und historische Geologie: 2 Richard-Wagner-Str. 10/11; f. 1759; Dir. Prof. Dr. DIETRICH HERM; publs. *Mitteilungen, Zitteliana.*

Botanische Staatssammlung: 19 Menzinger Str. 67; f. 1813; Dir. Prof. Dr. HERMANN MERXMÜLLER; publ. *Mitteilungen.*

Botanischer Garten: 19 Menzinger Str. 67; f. 1914; Dir. Prof. Dr. HERMANN MERXMÜLLER.

Jura-Museum: 8833 Eichstätt, Willibaldsburg; Man. Dr. GÜNTHER VIOHL.

Mineralogische Staatssammlung: 2 Theresienstr. 41; f. 1823; Dir. Prof. Dr. HEINZ JAGODZINSKI.

Naturkundliches Bildungszentrum: Planungsstab 19, Menzinger Str. 69; Man. Dr. EGON POPP.

Zoologische Staatssammlung: 19 Maria-Wardstr. 1B; f. 1807; Dir. Dr. ERNST JOSEF FITTKAU; publs. *Veröffentlichungen, Opuscula Zoologica.*

Neue Sammlung: Prinzregentenstr. 3; modern industrial arts and crafts, architecture, urban planning; f. 1925; Dir. Dr. HANS WICHMANN.

Prähistorische Staatssammlung: Lerchenfeldstr. 2; f. 1885; prehistoric, Roman and early medieval antiquities from Southern Germany; Dir. Dr. HANS-JÖRG KELLNER; publ. *Kataloge*† (irregular).

Staatliche Antikensammlungen: Königsplatz 1; Greek and Etruscan vases and bronzes, Greek and Roman terra-cottas and bronzes, glass, jewellery.

Glyptothek: Königsplatz 3; Greek and Roman sculpture.

Staatliche Graphische Sammlung: Munich 2, Meiserstr. 10; f. 1758; collection of 14-20th-century prints and drawings; Dir. Dr. DIETER KUHRMANN.

Staatliche Münzsammlung (*State Coin Collection*): Residenzstrasse 1; f. 1807; coins from different countries and centuries; special collections: Greek coins from Southern Italy and Sicily, German and Italian Renaissance medals, Bavarian coins, precious stones from antiquity, Middle Ages and Renaissance; specialized library of 13,500 vols.; Dir. Dr. KÜTHMANN.

Staatliche Sammlung Ägyptischer Kunst (*State Collection of Egyptian Art*): Hofgartenstr.; (postal address: Meiserstr. 10;) f. 1966; small specialized library; Dir. Dr. DIETRICH WILDUNG.

Staatliches Museum für Völkerkunde (*State Museum of Ethnology*): Maximilianstrasse 42; f. 1868; collections on Asia, America, Africa and the Pacific Islands; library of 20,000 vols.; Dir. Dr. WALTER RAUNIG.

Städtische Galerie im Lenbachhaus: Luisenstr. 33; f. 1925; Munich artists including paintings by Kandinsky, Klee and the Blaue Reiter group; Dir. Dr. ARMIN ZWEITE.

44 MÜNSTER

Westfälisches Landesmuseum für Kunst und Kulturgeschichte (*Westphalian Museum of Art and Cultural History*): Domplatz 10; f. 1908; German history, numismatics, goldsmith work, Old German and modern paintings, graphic art, plastic art; 60,000 books; Dir. P. BERGHAUS.

85 NUREMBERG

Albrecht-Dürer Haus: Albrecht-Dürer Strasse 39; f. 1828; life and works of Albrecht-Dürer, cultural history of Nürnberg; Dr. KARL-HEINZ SCHREYL.

Germanisches Nationalmuseum: Kornmarkt 1; f. 1852; German art and civilization from prehistoric times to about 1920, folk art, public library, archives, print room, musical instruments; Chief Dir. Dr. ARNO SCHÖNBERGER; publs. *Anzeiger des Germ. Nationalmuseums, Archiv für bildende Künst, Schrifttum zur deutschen Kunst*, catalogues and guides.

Kunsthalle, Stadt Nürnberg: Lorenzer Strasse 32; collection of international modern art (not on permanent show); changing exhibitions; publs. catalogues of exhibitions; Dir. CURT HEIGL.

Stadtmuseum Fembohaus: Burgstrasse 15; f. 1958; art and cultural history of Nuremberg; Dir. Dr. KARL-HEINZ SCHREYL.

605 OFFENBACH A.M.

Klingspor-Museum der Stadt: Herrnstr. 80; f. 1953; collection and exhibition of modern books and MSS.; Dir. CHRISTIAN SCHEFFLER.

753 PFORZHEIM

Reuchlinhaus: Heimatmuseum; f. 1897; Dir. DIETER ESSIG; Schmuckmuseum Pforzheim und mod. Schmuckschau; f. 1938; Dir. Dr. FRITZ FALK; Kunst-und Kunstgewerbverein (Kunst-Wechselausstellungen); f. 1961; Pres. DIETER FREYMARK.

435 RECKLINGHAUSEN

Museen der Stadt Recklinghausen (*Recklinghausen City Museums*): Platz am Hauptbahnhof; Dir. Dr. ANNELIESE SCHRÖDER.

Städtische Kunsthalle (*City Art Gallery*): paintings, drawings, prints and sculptures by contemporary artists.

Ikonenmuseum (*Ikon Museum*): Russian, Byzantine and Balkan ikons, miniatures, metal work, Coptic sculpture and textiles.

Vestisches Museum: Westphalian arts and crafts.

238 SCHLESWIG

Schleswig-Holsteinisches Landesmuseum: Schloss Gottorf; f. 1875; exhibits of art and culture of Schleswig-Holstein and surrounding area; library of 15,000 vols.; Dir. Prof. Dr. GERHARD WIETEK; publ. *Kunst in Schleswig-Holstein.*

Schleswig-Holsteinisches Landesmuseum für Vor- und Frühgeschichte der Universität Kiel (*Provincial Museum of Pre- and Early History*): D-2380 Schleswig, Schloss Gottorf; f. 1834; library of 12,000 vols.; Dir. Prof. Dr. K. W. STRUVE; publs. *Offa* (annually), *Offa Bucher* (irregular), *Archäologie in Schleswig-Holstein* (annually), reports, monographs.

672 SPEYER

Historisches Museum der Pfalz (*Historical Museum of the Palatinate*): Grosse Pfaffengasse 7; f. 1869; art and cultural history of the Palatinate, includes wine museum; library of 15,000 vols.; Curator Dr. OTTO ROLLER; publs. *Mitteilungen des Historischen Vereins der Pfalz* (annually), *Pfälzer Heimat.*

7 STUTTGART

Bibelausstellung der Württembergischen Bibelanstalt (*Bible Exhibition*): Balinger Str. 31; f. 1952; Dirs. Dr. GERNOT WINTER, Dr. SIEGFRIED MEURER; publ. *Bibelreport.*

Galerie der Stadt Stuttgart: Schlossplatz 2, Kunstgebäude; f. 1925; paintings, drawings, graphics and sculptures of 19th and 20th-century artists in Baden-Württemberg; Dir. EUGEN KEUERLEBER.

Linden-Museum Stuttgart, Staatliches Museum für Völkerkunde: Hegelplatz 1; f. 1889; ethnographical museum; library of *c.* 15,000 vols.; Dir. Dr. F. KUSSMAUL; publs. *Tribus*† (Yearbook), catalogues, etc.

Staatliche Kunstsammlungen: comprise:

Württembergisches Landesmuseum: Altes Schloss; f. 1862; collections from prehistoric to modern times of textiles, costumes, European decorative art, Swabian sculpture, clocks and watches, coins, musical instruments, Württemberg crown jewels; Roman lapidarium; Dir. Prof. Dr. C. ZOEGE VON MANTEUFFEL; Chief Curator Dr. M. SCHRÖDER; publ. *Jahrbuch.*

Staatliches Museum für Naturkunde in Stuttgart: Schloss Rosenstein; f. 1791; library of 68,000 vols.; Dir. Prof. Dr. B. ZIEGLER; publ. *Stuttgarter Beiträge zur Naturkunde*†.

Staatsgalerie Stuttgart: Konrad-Adenauerstr. 32; f. 1843; paintings from middle ages to the present, 20th-century plastic art, graphic art; Dir. Prof. Dr. PETER BEYE.

55 TRIER (TRÈVES)

Rheinisches Landesmuseum: Ostallee 44; f. 1877; prehistoric, Roman and early medieval exhibits excavated in Trier and district; library of 35,000 vols.; Dir. Dr. HEINZ CÜPPERS; publs. *Trierer Zeitschrift*†, *Funde und Ausgrabungen im Bezirk Trier*† (annually), *Trier Grabungen und Forschungen, Ausstellungskataloge*†.

79 ULM

Ulmer Museum: Neue Str. 92; f. 1875; collections of Ulm and Swabian Arts from 14th-18th century, 20th-century arts; Dir. Dr. ERWIN TREU.

WORMS

Museum der Stadt Worms: Weckerlingplatz 7; f. 1881; palaeontology, archaeology, town history of Worms; Dir. Dr. MATHILDE GRÜNEWALD; publs. *Der Wormsgau, Zeitschrift der Kulturinstitute der Stadt Worms und des Altertumsvereins Worms.*

Stiftung Kunsthaus Heylshof: Stephansgasse 9; f. 1923, 15th-19th century paintings, sculptures, porcelains; glass; Curator Dr. LUDWIG VON BASSERMANN-JORDAN.

UNIVERSITIES

FERNUNIVERSITÄT
(Open University)

FEITHSTRASSE 152,
5800 HAGEN, P.O.B. 940.

Telephone: 02331/8041.
Telex: 823 137 feuni d
Founded 1974.
36 Regional Study Centres.

State control; Academic year: October to September.

Rector: Prof. Dr. OTTO PETERS.
Chancellor: RALF BARTZ.
Librarian: DIETMAR WEGNER.

Number of teachers: 240.

Number of students: *c.* 22,600 (full- and part-time).

Publications: *Bericht des Gründungsrektors* (Yearbook), *Personal- und Kursverzeichnis* (annually), *Con-tacte—Zeitschrift für die Studenten der Fernuniversität* (quarterly).

DEANS:

Department of Mathematics: Prof. Dr. STETTER.
Department of Economics: Prof. Dr. BITZ.
Department of Education: Prof. Dr. LÜCK.

ATTACHED INSTITUTES:

Zentrales Institut für Fernstudienforschung: Dir. Prof. Dr. HOLMBERG.

Zentrum für Fernstudienentwicklung: Dir. Dr. JÜRGEN WURSTER, M.A.

Rechenzentrum: Dr. STERNBERGER.

RHEINISCH-WESTFÄLISCHE TECHNISCHE HOCHSCHULE AACHEN

5100 AACHEN,
TEMPLERGRABEN 55

Telephone: (0241) 801.

Founded 1870 as Polytechnikum, attained university status 1880.

Rector: Prof. Dr. phil. G. URBAN.
Pro-Rectors: Prof. Dr. techn. O. KNOTEK, Prof. Dr. rer. nat. O. KNACKE.
Registrar: B. MÜLLER.
Librarian: U. FELLMANN.

Library: *see* Libraries.

Number of teachers: 1,976, including 471 Professors.

Number of students: 27,500.

Publications: *Vorlesungsverzeichnis, Alma Mater Aquensis* (annual report), *RWTH—Themen* (quarterly).

DEANS:

Faculty of Mathematics and Natural Science: Prof. Dr. rer. nat. H. NIEMEYER.
Faculty of Architecture and Civil Engineering: Prof. Dr.-Ing. W. LEINS.
Faculty of Mechanical Engineering: Prof. Dr.-Ing. W. KÖNIG.
Faculty of Mining and Metallurgy: Prof. Dr.-Ing. R. KOPP.
Faculty of Electrical Engineering: Prof. Dr. rer. nat. D. HAUPT.
Faculty of Philosophy: Prof. Dr. rer. pol. K. G. ZINN.
Faculty of Medicine: Prof. Dr. med. G. KALFF.

PROFESSORS:

Faculty of Mathematics and Natural Science:

Department of Mathematics and Physics:

ADOMEIT, G., General Mechanics
BUTZER, P. L., Mathematics
DEUTSCHMANN, M., Experimental Physics
DIETZE, H. D., Theoretical Physics
ERWE, F., Mathematics
FAISSNER, H., Experimental Physics
FELDERHOFF, U., Theoretical Physics
GROSSE, P., Experimental Physics
HABETHA, K., Mathematics
HEILAND, G., Experimental Physics
HEINZ, C., Mechanics
HELLWIG, G., Mathematics
IBACH, H., Experimental Physics
INDERMARK, K., Informatics
KASTRUP, H. A., Theoretical Physics
KRAFFT, O., Statistics
LÜBELSMEYER, K., Experimental Physics
MERKWITZ, J., Informatics
MÜLLER, C., Mathematics
NEUBÜSER, J., Mathematics
NIEMEYER, H., Mathematics
NOLTEMEIER, H., Information Science
OBERSCHELP, W., Applied Mathematics, Informatics
RAUHUT, B., Statistics and Mathematics of Economics
RIEDER, G., Technical Mechanics
SANDER, W., Experimental Physics
SCHILLING, W., Experimental Physics
SCHLÖGL, F., Theory of Physics
SCHMITZ, D., Experimental Physics
SCHÖNEBORN, H., Mathematics
SCHNAKENBERG, J., Theoretical Physics
SPRINGER, T., Experimental Physics
WENZL, H., Experimental Physics

Department of Chemistry and Biology:

AACH, H.-G., Botany
BRONGER, W., Inorganic Chemistry
EMEIS, C.-C., Applied Biology
FRANCK, U. F., Physical Chemistry
HAASE, R., Physical Chemistry
HAMMER, H., Fuel Chemistry
HERBERICH, G., Inorganic Chemistry
KAISER, H., Ecology
KEIM, W., Engineering Chemistry and Oil Chemistry
KLESPER, E. G., Macromolecular Chemistry
PAETZOLD, P., Inorganic Chemistry
REISENER, H.-J., Physical Biology
SCHARF, D., Organic Chemistry
SCHLOTE, F.-W., Zoology
STETTER, H., Organic Chemistry
STIEVE, H., Zoology
ZAHN, H., Textile Chemistry

Faculty of Architecture and Civil Engineering:

Department of Architecture:

BÖHM, G., Design and Craftsmanship
CURDES, G., Town and Regional Planning
DÖRING, W., Building Design
ELLER, F., Industrial Building Design
FEHL, G., Theory of Planning
HILLEBRAND, E., Sculpture
HOLLÄNDER, H., History of Art
KRAUSS, F., Building Design
PFLUG, W., Ecology and Landscape Design
SCHILD, E., Building Design
SCHÖNWALD, R., Drawing and Painting
URBAN, G., History of Architecture and Conservation of Monuments

Department of Structural and Civil Engineering:

BÖHNKE, B., Hydrology, Housing Estates
DOMKE, H., Building Construction
HEKTOR, E., Theoretical Geodesy
KAMMENHUBER, J., Statics
LEINS, W., Road and Tunnel Engineering
MÄCKE, P. A., City Engineering
POHLE, G., Building Machinery and Organization
ROUVÉ, G., Hydraulic Engineering and Water Supply
SCHWANHÄUSSER, W., Transport and Railway Engineering
SEDLACEK, G., Structural Engineering (Steel)
TROST, H., Structural Engineering (Concrete)
WESCHE, K., Building Materials
WITTE, B., Geodesy
WITTKE, W., Waterway Engineering, Foundation and Soil Mechanics

Faculty of Mechanical Engineering:

BACKÉ, W., Hydraulic and Pneumatic Power and Control Systems
DAVID, O., Turbines and Motors
DECKEN, CL.-B. VON DER, Reactor Construction
DIBELIUS, G., Steam and Gas Turbines
DITTRICH, G., Kinetics and Dynamics
EICHHORN, F., Welding
EVERSHEIM, W., Production Engineering
HACKSTEIN, R., Industrial Engineering
HARTMANN, H., Process Engineering
HELLING, J., Automotive Engineering
KNOCHE, K.-F., Technical Thermodynamics
KNOTEK, O., Engineering Materials
KOLLER, R., Machine Design
KÖNIG, W., Manufacturing Techniques
KRAUSE, E., Aerodynamics
LÜNENSCHLOSS, J., Textile Technology
MENGES G., Plastics Technology
NICKEL, H., Reactor Materials and Fuels
ÖRY, H., Aircraft Construction
PEEKEN, H., Machine Elements and Machine Design
PISCHINGER, F., Applied Thermodynamics
RAKE, H., Automatic Control
RAUTENBACH, R., Process Engineering
RENZ, U., Heat Transfer and Air Conditioning
SCHNEEKLUTH, H., Naval Architecture
SCHULTEN, R., Reactor Techniques
SCHULTZ, H.-G., Naval Architecture
STAUFENBIEL, R., Aeronautics and Space Travel
THOMAE, H., Dynamics of Missiles
TROOST, A., Engineering Materials
WECK, M., Tool Machine Design

Faculty of Mining and Metallurgy:

Department of Mining:

FAUSER, H., Mining and Metallurgical Machinery

GOERGEN, H., Mining
HOBERG, H., Mineral Dressing (Coal), Coking and Briquetting
REUTHER, E.-U., Mining
SPETTMANN, J., Surveying

Department of Geo-Sciences:
FRIEDRICH, G., Mineralogy and Petrography
HAHN, T., Crystallography
HEITFELD, K.-H., Engineering Geology and Hydrogeology
WALTER, R., Geology and Palaeontology
WELTE, D., Geology of Solid Fuels

Department of Metallurgy:
BUNK, W., Applied Non-Ferrous Metallurgy
DAHL, W., Ferrous Metallurgy
KNACKE, O., Theoretical and Atomic Fuel Metallurgy
KOPP, R., Metal Forming
KRÜGER, J., Non-ferrous and Electrolytical Metallurgy
LÜCKE, K., Physical Metallurgy
REYNEN, P., Glass and Ceramics
WILHELMI, H., Construction and Thermodynamics of Industrial Furnaces

Faculty of Electrical Engineering:
AMELING, W., General Electro-technology and Data Processing
ARLT, G., Electrical Engineering and Materials
BALK, P., Semiconductor Electronics
BASEL, C. VON, Measuring Technique
BENEKING, H., Transistor Engineering
EDWIN, K., Power Generation and Distribution
ENGL, W., Theoretical Electro-Technology
HAUPT, D., Operating Systems
HEMPEL, K.-A., Electrical Engineering and Materials
KUTTRUFF, H., Technical Acoustics
LUEG, H., Technical Electronics
LÜKE, H. D., Telecommunications Engineering
MEYR, H., Electrical Control Engineering
MÖLLER, K., General Electro-Technology and High-Tension Engineering
RAU, G., Biomedical Engineering
SATTLER, P. K., Electrical Machines
SCHREIBER, F., General Electrotechnology and Data Processing
SKUDELNY, H. C., Rectifier Engineering
TAFEL, H. J., Signalling Equipment and Statistical Evaluation

Faculty of Philosophy:
Department of Philosophy and History:
AHNERT, F., Physical Geography
BALD, W.-D., English Philology
BAUM, R., Romance Languages and Literature
BAYERDÖRFER, H.-P., German Literature
BUCK, T., German Literature
CRAMER, T., German Literature
DYSERINCK, H., Comparative Literature
FEGER, H., Psychology
HÖRNING, K.-H., Sociology
KLAUER, K. J., Education
KLINKENBERG, H. M., Medieval History
LENK, K., Political Science
LÜER, G., Psychology
MEYER, H. D., Ancient History
MONHEIM, F., Geography
MÜLLGES, U. Pedagogy
SCHON, P., Romance Languages and Literature
SPINNER, K., English Literature
STANG, F., Geography
THIEL, C., Philosophy and Theory of Science
WEINSTOCK, H., English Literature
WOLANDT, G., Philosophy

Department of Commercial Studies:
FRESE, E., Industrial Management
HAVEMANN, H. A., International Technical Co-operation
KÖHLER, R., Industrial Management
RÖPER, B., Economics and Commerce
SCHINZINGER, F., Social and Economic History
VORMBAUM, H., Industrial Management
ZIMMERMANN, H.-J., Operational Research
ZINN, K. G., Political Economy

Faculty of Medicine:
ALTHOFF, H., Forensic Medicine
BEIER, H., Anatomy
BERNUTH, G. VON, Paediatric Cardiology
EFFERT, S., Internal Medicine
EINBRODT, H. J., Hygiene
FRIK, W., Radiology and Radiotherapy
GILLISSEN, G., Medical Microbiology
GREILING, H., Clinical Chemistry
HEIDENREICH, O., Pharmacology
JUNG, H., Obstetrics and Gynaecology
KALFF, G., Anaesthesiology
KLAGES, W., Psychiatry
KOBERG, W., Dental, Maxillary, and Plastic Surgery
KRENKEL, W., Neuro-Surgery
KÜHNEL, W., Anatomy
LANGE, W., Anatomy
LUTZEYER, W., Urology
MEINHOF, W., Dermatology
MESSMER, B., Cardiovascular Surgery
OHLENBUSCH, H., Physiological Chemistry
OHNSORGE, J., Orthopaedics
PLOEGER, A., Medical Psychology
POECK, K., Neurology
REIFFERSCHEID, M., Surgery
REIM, M., Ophthalmology
REPGES, R., Medical Statistics and Documentation
SCHLÖNDORFF, G., Oto-Rhino-Laryngology
SCHMID-SCHÖNBEIN, H., Physiology
SCHOENMACKERS, J., Pathology
SCHÖNENBERG, H., Paediatrics
WAGENER, K., Biophysics

ATTACHED INSTITUTES:

Haus der Technik e.V., Essen: 43 Essen, Hollestrasse 1; Dir. Prof. Dr.-Ing. E. STEINMETZ.

Technische Akademie e.V., Wuppertal: 56 Wuppertal-Elberfeld, Hubertus-Allee 16-18; Dir. Prof. Dr.-Ing. W. HOLSTE.

Institut für Kunststoffverarbeitung in Industrie und Handwerk (*Institute of Plastics Technology*): 51 Aachen, Pontstrasse 49; Dir. Prof. Dr.-Ing. G. MENGES.

Deutsches Wollforschungsinstitut (*German Wool Research Institute*): 51 Aachen, Veltmanplatz 8; Dir. Prof. Dr.-Ing. H. ZAHN.

Versuchsanstalt für Binnenschiffbau e.V., Duisburg (*Experimental Station for Inland Ship Building*): 41 Duisburg, Klöcknerstrasse 77; Heads: Prof. Dr. Ing. H. SCHNEEKLUTH, Prof. Dr.-Ing. H. H. HEUSER.

Forschungsinstitut für Rationalisierung (*Institute for Research in Rationalization*): 51 Aachen, Pontdriesch 14–16; Dir. Prof. Dr.-Ing. R. HACKSTEIN.

Helmholtz-Institut für Biomedizinische Technik: 51 Aachen, Goethestrasse 27–29; Heads Prof. Dr. S. EFFERT, Prof. Dr. G. RAU.

UNIVERSITÄT AUGSBURG

D8900 AUGSBURG, MEMMINGER STRASSE 6

Telephone: 0821-598-1.
Telex: 53830.

Founded 1970.

President: Prof. Dr. KARL MATTHIAS MEESSEN.
Vice-Presidents: Prof. Dr. H. LEROY, Prof. Dr. FRANZ SCHAFFER.
Chancellor: Dr. DIETER KÖHLER.
Registrar: HARTMUT ARNHOLZ.
Librarian: Dr. RUDOLF FRANKENBERGER.

Library of 755,700 vols.
Number of teachers: 328.
Number of students: 4,100.

DEANS:

Faculty of Economics and Social Science: Prof. Dr. H. HARTMANN.
Faculty of Catholic Theology: Prof. Dr. J. LISTL.
Faculty of Jurisprudence: Prof. Dr. W. JAKOB.
Faculty of Philosophy I: Prof. Dr. A. BARUZZI.
Faculty of Philosophy II: Prof. Dr. K. FILSER.

PROFESSORS:

Faculty of Catholic Theology:
BRANDMÜLLER, W., Ecclesiastical History and Patrology
GESSEL, W., Ecclesiastical History and Patrology
FORSTER, K., Pastoral Theology
HALDER, A., History of Philosophy
HERZ, M., Catholic Religion and Religious Pedagogics
KILIAN, R., Old Testament Exegesis
LEROY, H., Biblical Studies and Hermeneutics
LISTL, J., Church Law
MÖLLER, J., Systematic Philosophy I
PAUL, E., Religious Pedagogics
PIEGSA, Moral Theology
RAUH, F., Theology and Science
RAUSCHER, A., Christian Sociology
ZIEGENHAUS, A., Dogmatics

Faculty of Economics and Social Science:
ATTESLANDER, P., Sociology
BAMBERG, G., Statistics
BLUM, R., Economics
COENENBERG, A., Economics
GAHLEN, B., Economics
HAEGERT, L., Economics
HANUSCH, H., Economics
HARTMANN, H. A., Psychology
HOFFMANN, F., Economics
LAMPERT, H., Economics
MEYER, P.-W., Economics
NEUBERGER, O., Psychology
OPITZ, O., Mathematical Methods of Economics
PERRIDON, L., Economics
PFAFF, M., Economics
REIMANN, H., Sociology

Faculty of Jurisprudence:
BIRK, R., Civil Law

BUCHNER, H., Civil Law
DÜTZ, W., Civil Law
HÄBERLE, P., Public Law
HERRMANN, J., Penal Law
JAKOB, W., Public Law
KNÖPFLE, F., Public Law
MEESSEN, K. M., Public Law, International Law, European Law
RÜPING, H., Criminal Law and Criminal Procedure
SCHLOSSER, H., Civil Law
SCHMIDT, R., Public Law
SIMSHÄUSER, W., Civil Law with Roman Law
SONNENBERGER, H.-J., Civil Law

Faculty of Philosophy I:
BARUZZI, A., Philosophy
FRAAS, H.-J., Protestant Religion and Religious Pedagogics
GRAML, K., Musical Training
HAMPEL, J., Didactics of Social Science
JUNG, J., Biology
KUNTZE, K., Didactics of Mathematics
LICHTENSTEIN-ROTHER, I., Pedagogics
MÄRZ, F., Pedagogics
OBLINGER, H., School Pedagogics
OERTER, R., Psychology
SANDTNER, H., Art Education
SCHMITT, H.-C., Protestant Theology with Biblical Theology
STAMMEN, TH., Political Studies
WALDMANN, P., Sociology
WEBER, E., Pedagogics

Faculty of Philosophy II:
ABEL, F., Didactics of French
BECKER, J., Modern History
FILSER, K., Didactics of History
FINKENSTAEDT, TH., English Language
FISCHER, K., Physical Geography
GOTTLIEB, G., Ancient History
HAENSCH, G., Applied Linguistics
HAUSMANN, W., Didactics of French
KOOPMANN, H., German Literature
KRAUSS, H., Romance Literature
REINHARD, W., Early Modern History
SHÄFER, J., English Literature
SCHAFFER, F., Social and Economic Geography
SCHRÖDER, K., Didactics of English
STOPP, H., Germanic Language
WEBER, A., Didactics of German Language and Literature
WELLMANN, H., German Language
WOLF, L., Romance Philology

UNIVERSITÄT BAMBERG

8600 BAMBERG,
PROMENADESTR. 5
Telephone: 0951/23754.
Founded 1648.

State control; Languages of instruction: French, German, English; Academic year: October to September (two terms).

President: Prof. Dr. SIEGFRIED OPPOLZER.
Vice-Presidents: Prof. Dr. ANNEGRET BOLLÉE, Prof. Dr. LASZLO VASKOVICS.
Chancellor: ALFRED HEMMERLEIN.
Librarian: Dr. DIETER KARASEK.

Number of teachers: 152.
Number of students: 2,233.

Publications: *AULA*† (3 a year), *Bamberger Hochschulschriften* (irregular), *Pressemitteilungen, Informationen* (1 or 2 a week), *Personal- und Vorlesungsverzeichnis*† (1 a term), *Bericht des Präsidenten, Forschungsbericht* (annually).

DEANS:
Faculty of Catholic Theology: Prof. Dr. NORBERT GLATZEL.
Faculty of Pedagogy, Philosophy and Psychology: Prof. Dr. HORST WEIGELT.
Faculty of Language and Literature: Prof. Dr. WOLFGANG THEILE.
Faculty of History and Earth Sciences: Prof. Dr. WERNER HUSS.
Faculty of Social and Economic Sciences: Prof. Dr. GUSTAV DIECKHEUER.
Faculty of Mathematics: (vacant).
Faculty of Social Work: Prof. Dr. MANFRED NÜCHTERLEIN.

PROFESSORS:
Faculty of Catholic Theology:
EID, V., Moral Theology
ESCRIBANO-ALBERCA, I., Fundamental Theology
GÖRG, M., Old Testament
HEPP, J., Catholic Doctrine and Pedagogy
HOFFMANN, P., New Testament
JACOB, H., Pastoral Theology
STÖHR, J., Dogmatics

Faculty of Pedagogy, Philosophy and Psychology:
BECK, H., Philosophy
DÖRNER, D., Psychology II
ERLER, L., Elementary Education
FABER, W., Adult Education
HASTENTEUFEL, P., Pedagogy
KOLB, A., Biology
LACHMANN, R., Evangelical Theology
LIEBEL, H., Psychology
MÜHLFELD, C., Social Pedagogics
MÜLLER, G., Pedagogy, Philosophy
ORTNER, R., Elementary School Didactics
SELG, H., Psychology I
WEIGELT, H., Evangelical Theology

Faculty of Language and Literature:
BERGMANN, R., German Philology and Medieval German Literature
BOLLÉE, A., Romance Philology and Medieval Studies
GOCKEL, H., Modern German Literature
JOCHUM, K. P., English Literature
LEHMANN, J., German Language and Literature
PÜTZ, M., American Literature
RIEKS, R., Classical Philology, Latin
SUDHOF, S., Modern German Literature
THEILE, W., Romance Literature
TIETZ, M., Romance Literature
VIERECK, W., English Language and Medieval Studies
WUTTKE, D., Medieval and Early Modern German Philology

Faculty of History and Earth Sciences:
BECKER, H., Geography
DENZLER, G., Ecclesiastical History
GARLEFF, K., Physical Geography
HUSS, W., Ancient History
MÖCKL, K., Modern History
ROTH, E., Folklore
SCHMITT, E., Modern History
SUCKALE, R., Art History
TREUDE, E., Economic Geography
ZIMMERMANN, G., Medieval History

Faculty of Social and Economic Sciences:
BLEY, H., Social and Business Law
DERLIEN, H.-U., Administrative Law
DIECKHEUER, G., General Political Economy
FRIEDRICH, P., Finance
GROSS, P., Sociology
HEINHOLD, M., General Management Economy
KUPSCH, P., Business Administration and Accounting
OTT, G., Political Science
SCHÄFER, D., Social and Economic Policy
SCHULZE, G., Social Research
VASKOVICS, L., Sociology
VOGEL, F., Statistics

Faculty of Social Work:
BOTT, W., Political Science
CYPRIAN, G., Sociology
FREY, P., Sociology
HAIDL, M., Pedagogy
HEYER, H., Methodology
KLAPPROTT, J., Methodology
NÜCHTERLEIN, M., Law
PLESSEN, H., Psychology
RANK, T., Psychology
RIEBER, A., Philosophy, Social Ethics
SPINDLER, W., Methodology

UNIVERSITÄT BAYREUTH

8580 BAYREUTH,
POSTFACH 3008
Telephone: 0921-608-1.

Founded 1972; first student intake 1975–76.

President: Dr. KLAUS DIETER WOLFF.
Vice-Presidents: Prof. Dr. HANS LUDWIG KRAUSS, Prof. Dr. HELMUT RUPPERT.
Chancellor: Reg.-Dir. WOLF-PETER HENTSCHEL.
Librarian: Dr. KONRAD WICKERT.

Number of teachers: 82.
Number of students: 1,800.

Publication: *Personen- und Vorlesungsverzeichnis*† (2 a year).

DEANS:
Department of Mathematics and Physics: Prof. LORENZ KRAMER, PH.D.
Department of Biology, Chemistry and Geo-sciences: Prof. Dr. ERWIN BECK.
Department of Law and Economics: Prof. Dr. HARRO OTTO.
Department of Language and Literature: Prof. Dr. ROBERT HINDERLING.
Department of Cultural Studies: Prof. Dr. WERNER S. NICKLIS.

PROFESSORS:
Department of Mathematics and Physics:
BÜTTNER, H., Theoretical Physics
DORMANN, E., Experimental Physics
IRLE, A., Mathematics
KALUS, J., Experimental Physics
KERBER, A., Mathematics
KERNER, H., Pure Mathematics
KIEFER, W., Experimental Physics
KRAMER, L., Theoretical Physics
KRÄMER, M., Mathematics
KRAMM, B., Mathematics
LAUBEREAU, A., Experimental Physics
LEMPIO, F., Mathematics
MERTENS, F.-G., Theoretical Physics
MÜLLER, W., Pure Mathematics

PESCH, W., Theoretical Physics
RAINER, D., Theoretical Physics
SCHNEIDER, M., Mathematics
SCHWOERER, M., Experimental Physics
SIMADER, C. G., Mathematics
STRASSER, H., Mathematics
VON WAHL, W., Mathematics
WIEGNER, M., Mathematics
ZEITLER, H., Mathematics
ZOWE, J., Mathematics

Department of Biology, Chemistry and Geosciences:
BECK, E., Plant Physiology
DETTMANN, K., Cultural Geography
GERLACH, H., Organic Chemistry
HERBERHOLD, M., Inorganic Chemistry
HERRMANN, R., Hydrology
HÖCKER, H., Macromolecular Chemistry
HOFFMANN, H., Physical Chemistry
VON HOLST, D., Animal Physiology
HÜSER, K., Geomorphology
KLINGMÜLLER, W., Genetics
KLAUTKE, S., Biology
KLEINER, D., Microbiology
KOMOR, E., Plant Physiology
KRAUSS, H. L., Inorganic Chemistry
MAYER, J., Economic Geography
MONHEIM, R., Cultural Geography
MORYS, P., Inorganic Chemistry
MÜLLER-HOHENSTEIN, K., Biogeography
NICKEL, H., Cultural Geography
RUPPERT, H., Geography
SCHÄFER, K., Geology
SCHULZE, E.-D., Plant Ecology
SPITELLER, G., Organic Chemistry
SPRINZL, M., Biochemistry
STOLP, H., Microbiology
TOPP, W., Animal Ecology
VON WILLERT, D. J., Plant Ecology
ZECH, W., Geography
ZWÖLFER, G., Animal Ecology

Department of Law and Economics:
BERG, W., Public Law
FRETER, H., Economics, Marketing
FRICKE, D., Economics
GITTER, W., Civil Law
GÖRGENS, E., Economics
GOTTWALD, P., Civil Law
GRÖNER, H., Economics
KÖHLER, H., Civil Law
OTTO, H., Criminal Law
SCHMITT GLAESER, W., Public Law
SIGLOCH, J., Economics
SPELLENBERG, U., Civil Law
WOSSIDLO, P. R., Economics

Department of Language and Literature:
GEBHARD, W., Modern German Literature, Teaching of German
HINDERLING, R., German Language Studies
RIESZ, J., Romance Studies
TAYLOR, R. D., Afro-English Studies

Department of Cultural Studies:
ALBRECHT, W., Philosophy
DAUER, A., Catholic Religious Teaching
DIETRICH, TH., Education
HERRMANN, E., History
KASCH, W., Evangelical Religious Teaching
LÖW, K., Politics
NICKLIS, W., Education
TRAXEL, W., Psychology
WEIDMAN, F., Catholic Religious Teaching
WINTER, J. C., Ethnology
ZIESCHANG, K., Sport Science and Physical Education
ZÖLLER, M., Extramural Studies

FREIE UNIVERSITÄT BERLIN

1000 BERLIN 33 (DAHLEM), ALTENSTEINSTRASSE 40
Telephone: 8381.
Founded 1948.

President: Prof. Dr. phil. EBERHARD LÄMMERT.

Vice-Presidents: Prof. Dr. iur. DIETER HECKELMANN, Prof. Dr. phil. HANS JÖRG NISSEN, Prof. Dr. phil. BERNHARD SCHWENK, Prof. Dr. rer. nat. HELMUT GABRIEL.

Librarian: Dr. phil. WERNER LIEBICH.

Library: *see* Libraries.

Number of teachers: 3,093.
Number of students: 36,879.

Publications: *University Calendar*, *FU-Info* (2 a month), annual reports, etc.

DIRECTORS OF DEPARTMENTS:

Basic Medicine and Medical Ecology: Prof. Dr. R. WINAU.
University Hospital Steglitz: Prof. Dr. J. CERVÒS-NAVARRO.
University Hospital Charlottenburg: Prof. Dr. H. G. BEGER.
Dentistry: Prof. Dr. D. HERRMANN.
Veterinary Medicine: Prof. Dr. G. BÖHME.
Law: Prof. Dr. G. BAUMERT.
Economics and Business Administration: Prof. Dr. H. EGNER.
Philosophy and Social Sciences: Prof. Dr. JOHANNA FISCHER.
Education: Prof. Dr. H. MERKENS.
History: Prof. Dr. D. KURZE.
Classics and Archaeology: Prof. Dr. J. RENGER.
Political Science: Prof. Dr. J. FIJALKOWSKI.
German Literature and Philology: Prof. Dr. H. H. LIEB.
Modern Languages and Literatures: Prof. Dr. W. FÜGER.
Mathematics: Prof. Dr. H. SCHEERER.
Physics: Prof. Dr. E. MATTHIAS.
Chemistry: Prof. Dr. J. SIMON.
Pharmacy: Prof. Dr. R. HÄNSEL.
Biology: Prof. Dr. W. DOHLE.
Geo-Sciences: Prof. Dr. G. STÄBLEIN.

CENTRAL ATTACHED INSTITUTES:

John F. Kennedy-Institut für Nordamerikastudien (*J.F.K. Institute of North American Studies*): 1000 Berlin 33, Lansstr. 7-9; Chair. Prof. Dr. H. ICKSTADT.

Lateinamerika-Institut (*Central Institute of Latin American Studies*): 1000 Berlin 33, Breitenbachplatz 2; Chair. Prof. Dr. M. NITSCH.

Osteuropa-Institut (*East European Institute*): 1000 Berlin 33, Garystr. 55; Chair. Prof. Dr. H. J. TORKE.

Zentralinstitut für Sozialwissenschaftliche Forschung (*Central Institute of Social Science Research*): 1000 Berlin 31, Babelsberger Str. 14-16; Chair. Prof. Dr. T. PIRKER.

Institut für Bibliothekarausbildung: 1000 Berlin 33, Hohenzollerndamm 56; Dir. Prof. Dr. H.-D. HOLZHAUSEN.

TECHNISCHE UNIVERSITÄT BERLIN

1000 BERLIN 12, STRASSE DES 17 JUNI 135
Telephone: (030) 31-41.

The Bauakademie (Building Academy) of Berlin (f. 1799) and the Bauakademie und Gewerbeakademie (f. 1821) were amalgamated in 1879 as the Technische Hochschule Berlin, which was opened under its present name in 1946.

President: Dr. JÜRGEN STARNICK.
Chancellor: MICHAEL HÖBICH.
Librarian: HELMUT SONTAG.

Library: *see* Libraries.
Number of professors: *c.* 780.
Number of students: *c.* 22,000.

Publications: *Humanismus und Technik* (3 a year), *Mitteilungsblatt der TUB* (fortnightly), *Vorlesungsverzeichnis* (2 a year), *Universitätsführer* (annually).

UNIVERSITÄT BIELEFELD

4800 BIELEFELD, UNIVERSITÄTSSTRASSE
Telephone: 0521-106-1.
Telex: 932 362 UNIBI.
Founded 1969.

State control; Academic year: April to July, October to February.

Rector: Prof. Dr. K.-P. GROTEMEYER.
Pro-Rectors: Prof. Dr. T. DORFMÜLLER, Prof. Dr. D. STORBECK.
Chancellor: Dr. E. FIRNHABER.
Librarian: Dr. H. HEIM.

Number of teachers: 267.
Number of students: 10,000.

Publications: *Forschungsbericht*† (annual), *Bielefelder Universitätszeitung*† (12 a year), *Jahresbericht des Rektors*† (annual), *Schriften zum Aufbau einer Universität*† (irregular), *Personalverzeichnis/Lehrveranstaltungen* (2 a year).

DEANS:

Faculty of Law: Prof. Dr. H.-J. PAPIER.
Faculty of Mathematics: Prof. Dr. WALTER DEUBER.
Faculty of Sociology: Prof. Dr. H.-D. EVERS.
Faculty of Education: Prof. Dr. K. HURRELMANN.
Faculty of History and Philosophy: Prof. Dr. N. BULST.
Faculty of Linguistics and Literature: Prof. Dr. ROLF GRIMMINGER.
Faculty of Physics: Prof. Dr. DIETER BECK.
Faculty of Economics: Prof. Dr. WOLFGANG SCHÜLER.
Faculty of Biology: Prof. Dr. WOLFGANG KOWALLIK.

Faculty of Chemistry: Prof. Dr. ACHIM MÜLLER.
Faculty of Psychology and Sport Science: Prof. Dr. U. SCHULZE.
Centre for Interdisciplinary Research: Prof. Dr. W. VOSSKAMP.

RUHR-UNIVERSITÄT BOCHUM

4630 BOCHUM,
UNIVERSITÄTSSTR. 150
Telephone: 700-1.
Founded 1962.

Rector: Prof. Dr. KNUT IPSEN.
Pro-Rectors: Prof. Dr. MANFRED BORMANN, Prof. Dr. HERMANN KORTE, Prof. Dr. WOLFGANG MERZKIRCH.
Chancellor: Dr. jur. W. SEEL.
Librarian: B. ADAMS.

Number of teachers: 427.
Number of students: 24,274.

DEANS:

Department of Protestant Theology: Prof. Dr. THEO SUNDERMEIER.
Department of Catholic Theology: Prof. Dr. ARNOLD ANGENENDT.
Department of Philosophy, Pedagogy, Psychology: Prof. Dr. BERNHARD WALDENFELS.
Department of History: Prof. Dr. HELMUT PLECHL.
Department of Philology: Prof. Dr. GÜNTER AHRENDS.
Department of Law: Prof. Dr. KLAUS FRIEDRICH RÖHL.
Department of Economics: Prof. Dr. PETER HAMMAN.
Department of Social Sciences: Prof. Dr. GÜNTER ENDRUWEIT.
Department of East Asian Studies: Dr. KLAUS MÜLLER.
Department of Mechanical Engineering: Prof. Dr.-Ing. FRIEDRICH KOHLER.
Department of Civil Engineering: Prof. Dr.-Ing. WOLFGANG TEICHGRÄBER.
Department of Electrical Engineering: Prof. Dr.-Ing. SIEGFRIED BLUME.
Department of Mathematics: Prof. Dr. EDVARD ZEHNDER.
Department of Physics and Astronomy: Prof. Dr. DETLEF KAMKE.
Department of Geo-sciences: Prof. Dr. NIVANJAN DEB CHATTERJEE.
Department of Chemistry: Prof. Dr. OLAF PONGS.
Department of Biology: Prof. Dr. HELMUT LANGER.
Department of Medicine: Prof. Dr. HOLGER PREUSCHOFT.
Department of Theoretical Medicine: Prof. Dr. KONRAD MORGENROTH.

PROFESSORS:

Department of Protestant Theology:
BAHR, H.-E., Practical Theology
BALZ, H., Theology and New Testament History
BRAKELMANN, G., Christian Sociology
HERRMANN, S., Old Testament
HORNIG, G., Systematic Theology
REVENTLOW, H., Exegesis and Theology of the Old Testament
SCHREIBER, J., Practical Theology
TETZ, M., Church History, Patristics
WALLMANN, J., Church History

Department of Catholic Theology:
ANGENENDT, A., Church History
BITTER, G., Religious Education and Catechism
HEINEMANN, H., Church Law
HÖDL, L., Dogmatics
KRAMER, H., Moral Theology
POTTMEYER, H. J., Fundamental Theology
RUPPERT, L., Old Testament
SCHAEFFLER, R., Philosophy and Theology
SCHNEIDER, G., New Testament
STEGMANN, F. J., Christian Sociology

Department of Philosophy, Pedagogy, Psychology:
ANWEILER, O., Pedagogy
FLASCH, K., Philosophy
GAWLICK, G., Philosophy
GRAEFE, O., Psychology
HECKHAUSEN, H., Psychology
HÖRMANN, H., Psychology
KNOLL, J. H., Practical Pedagogy
KÖNIG, G., Philosophy
KRÜSKEMPER, G., Medical Psychology
MUTH, J., Practical Pedagogy
PÖGGELER, O., Philosophy
SCHAEFFLER, R., Philosophy and Theology
SCHALLER, K., Pedagogy
SCHÖNBACH, P., Social Psychology
SCHULTE, D., Psychology
STRATMANN, K., Vocational Pedagogy
WALDENFELS, B., Philosophy
WOTTAWA, H., Psychology, Methodology

Department of History:
BECKER, H., History of Music
IMDAHL, M., History of Art
KIECHLE, F., Early History
KÖLLMANN, W., Social and Economic History, Demography
LAUTER, H., Archaeology
MEIER, C., Early History
MILDENBERGER, G., Prehistory and Early History
MOMMSEN, H., Modern History
PETZINA, D., Social and Economic History
PLECHL, H., Historical Auxiliary Sciences
RÜSEN, J., Modern History
SCHMALE, F.-J., Medieval History
SCHMIDT, G., Political Science
SCHULZE, W., Modern History
SEIBT, F., Medieval History
TIMM, A., Economic and Industrial History

Department of Philology:
AHRENDS, G., English Philology
BAUSCH, K.-R., Romance Philology
BONNEKAMP, U., Linguistics
DILLER, H.-J., English Philology
EIMERMACHER, K., Slavonic Studies
ENDRESS, G., Arabic and Islamic Studies
FIGGE, U., Romance Philology
FLASHAR, H., Classical Philology
GALLOWAY, D., English Philology
GROSSE, S., Germanic Philology
GUMBRECHT, H. U., Romance Philology
HARWEG, R., Linguistics
HOFFMANN, A., Chinese Language and Literature
JACHNOW, H., Slavonic Studies
KEMPER, H.-G., History of Modern German Literature
KESTING, MARIANNE, General and Comparative Literature
KLUSSMANN, P. G., History of Modern German Literature
KOCH, W., English Philology, Semiotics
LEWIN, B., Language and Literature of Japan
MAURER, K., Romance Philology and General and Comparative Literature
MÜLLER-MICHAELS, H., Literature
NELLMANN, E., Germanic Philology
NEU, E., General and Comparative Philology
SCHNELLE, H., Structural Linguistics and Philology
SCHRIMPF, H. J., History of Modern German Literature
SCHRÖTER, R., Classical Philology
SEEBER, H. U., English Philology
STIERLE, K., Romance Philology and General Literature
STRATMANN, G., English Philology
STROHSCHNEIDER-KOHRS, INGRID, History of Modern German Literature
SUERBAUM, U., English Philology

Department of Law:
BIEDENKOPF, K. H., Civil, Commercial, Economic and Labour Law
BLAU, G., Criminology
BÖKELMANN, E., Civil Procedural Law and Civil Law
DILCHER, H., Modern History of Law and Civil Law
ERICHSEN, H.-U., Public Law
FABRICIUS, F., Civil, Labour, Commercial and Economic Law
GEILEN, G., Penal and Penal Procedural Law
GRAWERT, R., Public Law and Constitutional History
HERZBERG, R. D., Penal and Procedural Law
IPSEN, K., Public Law
KRUSE, H. W., Tax Law, Civil and Commercial Law, General Theory of Law
MIKAT, P., History of German Law, Canon Law
RÖHL, K. F., Civil Law, Civil Procedural Law, Sociology of Law
SANDROCK, O., Commercial and Economic Law, German and International Civil Law and Comparison of Law
SCHMIEDEL, B., Civil Law, Classical History of Law, Roman Law
SCHWIND, H.-D., Criminology
WARDA, G., Penal and Penal Procedural Law
WERTENBRUCH, W., Constitutional Law, Public Law
ZEISS, Procedural Law, Civil Law and Labour Law

Department of Economics:
BESTERS, H., Economic Policy
BUSSE VON COLBE, W., Theoretical Industrial Economics
CHMIELEWICZ, K., Theoretical Industrial Economics
ENGELHARDT, W., Applied Industrial Economics
HAMMANN, P., Applied Industrial Economics
JAEGER, A., Methods of Quantitative Analysis
KLEMMER, P., Economic Policy
KÖLLMANN, W., Economic and Social History, Demography
KRAUS, W., Economy of East Asia, Developmental Policy
KUHN, A., Theoretical Industrial Economics
LASSMANN, Applied Industrial Economics
MAG, W., Theoretical Industrial Economics
MEYER-DOHM, P., Economic Policy
PAHLKE, J., Theory of Finance
PEFFEKOVEN, R., International Economic Relations
REICHARDT, H., Methods of Quantitative Analysis

SCHMITT-RINK, G., Theoretical Political Economy
SCHNEIDER, D., Applied Industrial Economics
SEITZ, T., Theoretical Political Economy
SÜCHTING, J., Applied Industrial Economics
THIEME, H. J., Theoretical Political Economy

Department of Social Sciences:
BUCHHOLZ, E.-W., Sociology
NEUMANN, L. F., Social Politics and Economy
NOLTE, H., Social Psychology
PAPALEKAS, J. C., Sociology
PETZINA, D., Social and Economic History
SCHMIDT, G., Political Science
THIEMEYER, TH., Social Politics
TREINEN, H., Methodology in Social Sciences
VIEFHUES, H., Social Medicine
WEBER-SCHÄFER, P., Political Sciences, East Asian Politics

Department of Mechanical Engineering:
BERNS, H., Material Shaping Technology
BILLET, R., Heat Separation Processes
FASOL, K. H., Measurement and Control
FIEBIG, M., Heat and Matter Transfer
FISTER, W., Fluid Mechanics
GERSTEN, K., Fluid Mechanics
HORNBOGEN, E., Mechanical Properties of Materials
JARCHOW, F., Mechanics and Dynamics of Machinery
KOHLER, F., Thermodynamics
KREMER, H., Energy Storage Technology
MASSBERG, W., Production Systems
SCHNEIDERSMANN, E.-O., Mechanics
SEIFERT, H., Mechanics and Construction of Machinery
ZIEGLER, A., Reactor Techniques

Department of Civil Engineering:
JESSBERGER, H. L., Civil Engineering
KRÄTZIG, W. B., Construction Engineering
LEHMANN, T., Mechanics
MAIDL, B., Construction Engineering
MÖLLER, V., Civil Engineering
ROIK, K., Construction Engineering
SCHULZ, G. A., Civil Engineering
STUMPF, H., Mechanics
TEICHGRÄBER, W., Civil Engineering
WUNDERLICH, W., Construction Engineering
ZERNA, W., Construction Engineering

Department of Electrical Engineering:
BLAUERT, J., General Electrical Engineering and Electro-acoustics
BLUME, S., Theoretical Electrotechnology
BOSCH, B., Electronics
DEPENBROCK, M., Electrical Energy
FETTWEIS, A., Communication Techniques
KLEIN, J. W., Electronics
KNELLER, E., Raw Materials in Electrotechnology
POPP, H.-P., General Electrotechnology and Electro-optics
SEVERIN, H., High-Frequency Techniques
UNBEHAUEN, H., Electric Regulation and Control
WEBER, W., Data Processing

Department of Mathematics:
ALBEVERIO, S.
BAUMANN, V.
BÖHME, R.
BRAESS, D.
EHLICH, H.
EWALD, G.
GERRITZEN, L.
JAEGER, A., Economics
REISSIG, R.
SOMMER, F.
SPALLEK, K.
ZEHNDER, E.
ZIESCHANG, H.

Department of Physics and Astronomy:
BORMANN, M., Teaching of Physics
BUTTLAR, H. VON, Experimental Physics
ECKER, G., Theoretical Physics
HINTZ, E., Experimental Physics
KAMKE, D., Experimental Physics
KÜMMEL, H., Theoretical Physics
KUNZE, H.-J., Experimental Physics
METHFESSEL, S., Experimental Physics
REDHARDT, A., Biophysics
ROHLFS, K., Astronomy
ROSENBERG, M., Experimental Physics
SCHINDLER, K., Theoretical Physics
SCHLÜTER, Experimental Physics
SCHMIDT-KALER, T., Astronomy
WAGNER, D., Theoretical Physics

Department of Geo-sciences:
FLÖRKE, O. W., Mineralogy and Crystallography
FÜCHTBAUER, H., Geology
HOEPPENER, R., Geology
HOTTES, K. H., Geography
JOHN, K., Geology, Geotechnics
KLINK, H.-J., Geography
LIEDTKE, H., Geography
SCHÖLLER, P., Geography
SCHREYER, W., Mineralogy and Petrology
SPECKER, H., Inorganic Chemistry

Department of Chemistry:
BAERNS, M., Technical Chemistry
BERGMANN, G., Analytical Chemistry
HAAS, A., Inorganic Chemistry
KIRMSE, W., Organic Chemistry
KUTZELNIGG, W., Theoretical Chemistry
PONGS, O., Biochemistry
RICHTERING, H., Physical Chemistry
ROTH, W., Organic Chemistry
SCHNEIDER, G., Physical Chemistry
SNATZKE, G., Structural Chemistry
SPECKER, H., Inorganic Chemistry
WILKE, G., Organic Chemistry

Department of Biology:
ESSER, K., General Botany
KEYL, H.-G., Genetics
LANGER, H., Animal Physiology
LÜTTGAU, H., Cell Physiology
MERGNER, H., Special Zoology
PONGS, O., Biochemistry
REDHARDT, A., Biophysics
RUTHMANN, A., Cell Morphology
SCHWARTZKOPFF, J., General Zoology
TREBST, A., Plant Biochemistry
WINKLER, U., Microorganisms
ZENK, M. H., Botanical Physiology

Department of Medicine:
ANDRES, K., Anatomy
HEILMEYER, L., Physiological Chemistry
HINRICHSEN, K., Anatomy
HOLLDORF, A. W., Physiological Chemistry
KEYL, H.-G., Genetics
KRÜSKEMPER, G., Medical Physiology
LOESCHCKE, H. H., Physiology
LÜTTGAU, H. C., Cell Physiology
MARÉES, H. DE., Medicine in Sport
TRINCKER, D., Physiology

Department of Theoretical Medicine:
BRINKMANN, W., Surgery
DAWEKE, H., Internal Medicine
DELANK, H. W., Neurology
FORTH, W., Pharmacology and Toxicology
FRITZE, E., Internal Medicine
HARTUNG, W., Pathology
KÖNN, G., Pathology
KOZUSCHEK, W., Surgery
LAUSBERG, G., Neurosurgery
LEGERLOTZ, C., Obstetrics and Gynaecology
MIETENS, C., Paediatrics and Clinical Virology
MORGENROTH, K., Pathology
MULLER, E., Neurology
OPFERKUCH, W., Medical Microbiology-Bacteriology
REHN, J., Surgery
RICKEN, D., Internal Medicine
ROSENTHAL, A., Surgery
SELENKA, F., General and Environmental Hygiene
STURM, A., Internal Medicine
ULMER, W. T., Internal Medicine
VIEFHUES, H., Social Medicine
WERCHAU, H., Medical Microbiology-Virology

Department of East Asian Studies:
DETTMER, H. A., Japanology
KRAUS, W., East African Economics and Development Politics
LEWIN, B., Japanese Language and Literature
MARTIN, H., Sinology
WEBER-SCHAFER, P., Political Science, East Asian Politics
WIETHOFF, B., Sinology

RHEINISCHE FRIEDRICH-WILHELMS-UNIVERSITÄT BONN

5300 BONN, REGINA-PACIS-WEG 3
Telephone: 731.
Founded 1786, refounded 1818.
State control; Academic year: October to March, April to September.

Rector Magnificus: Prof. Dr. HANS-JACOB KRÜMMEL.
Pro-Rector: Prof. Dr. ALOYS HEUPEL.
Chancellor: Dr. WILHELM WAHLERS.
Librarian: Dr. H. LOHSE.

Number of teachers: 1,850, including 303 Ordinary Professors.

Number of students: 32,585.

Publications: *Bonner Akademische Reden, Politeia; Alma Mater, Academica Bonnensia, Bonner Universitäts-Nachrichten.*

DEANS:
Faculty of Evangelical Theology: Prof. Dr. HANS JÜRGEN HERMISSON.
Faculty of Catholic Theology: Prof. Dr. FRANZ BÖCKLE.
Faculty of Law and Economics: Prof. Dr. HORST HEINRICH JACKOBS.
Faculty of Medicine: Prof. Dr. FRIEDRICH KRÜCK.
Faculty of Philosophy: Prof. Dr. WOLF-DIETER LANGE.
Faculty of Mathematics and Natural Sciences: Prof. Dr. THEO MAYER-KUCKUCK.
Faculty of Agriculture: Prof. Dr. KLAUS ULRICH HEYLAND.
Faculty of Education: Prof. Dr. HEINZ DENK.

PROFESSORS:

Faculty of Evangelical Theology:

GOETERS, J. F., Church History
GRÄSSER, E., New Testament
GUNNEWEG, A., Old Testament
HERMISSION, H.-J., Old Testament
HONECKER, M., Systematic Theology, Social Ethics
KARPP, H., Religious Education
KRAUSE, G., Practical Theology
KRECK, W., Systematic Theology
PLÖGER, O., Old Testament
ROTHERT, H. J., Protestant Theology, Systematic Theology
SAUTER, G., Systematic Theology
SCHÄFERDIEK, K., Church History
SCHNEEMELCHER, W., Church History, New Testament
SCHRAGE, W., New Testament
SCHRÖER, H., Practical Theology
WINTZER, F., Practical Theology

Faculty of Catholic Theology:

ADRIÁNYI, G., Church History
BAUS, K., Ancient Church History
BÖCKLE, F., Moral Theology
BOTTERWECK, G. J., Old Testament
BREUNING, W., Dogmatics
DASSMANN, E., Church History, Patrimony
DELAHAYE, K., Theological Encyclopaedia
DOLCH, H., Religious Philosophy and Fundamental Theology
FLATTEN, H., Canon Law
GRONER, F., Christian Sociology
HEGEL, E., Modern Church History
JEDIN, H., Modern Church History
JORISSEN, Dogmatics, Propaedeutics
KLAUSER, T., Church History
LINDEN, P., Canon Law
NUSSBAUM, K.-O., Liturgy
ROOS, L., Christian Sociology
SCHÖLLGEN, W., Moral Theology
SCHÜTTE, H., Systematic Theology
STASIEWSKI, B., Contemporary Church History
WALDENFELS, H., Fundamental Theology
ZIMMERMANN, H., New Testament

Faculty of Law and Economics:

ALBACH, H., Industrial Administration
BEITZKE, G., Civil, Commercial, Private International Law
BÖS, D., Political Economy
BOSCH, F. W., Civil Law, Law of Proceedings
BRACHER, K. D., Political Science
EISERMANN, G., Sociology
FENN, H., Civil Law
FIEDLER, H., Juridical Information
FLUME, W., Taxation Law, Roman Law and Civil Law
FRIESENHAHN, E., Public Law
GAUL, F., Civil Law
GERHARDT, W., Civil Law
GRÜNWALD, G., Penal Law, Law of Criminal Proceedings
HELLWIG, M., Political Economy
HILDENBRAND, W., Political Economics
HUBER, U., Commercial Law
ISENSEE, J., Civil and Administrative Law
JAKOBS, H. H., Civil and Roman Law
KAMP, E., Political Economy, Finance
KAUFMANN, A., Penal Law, Philosophy of Law
KLEINHEYER, G., Legal History
KNOBBE-KEUK, B., Civil Law, Commercial, Economic, and Taxation Law
KNÜTEL, R., Roman and Civil Law
KORTE, B., Operational Research
KRELLE, W., Political Economy
KRÜMMEL, H.-J., Industrial Administration
LUTTER, M., Civil Law, Commercial and Economic Law.
MARQUARDT, H., Criminology
MARSCHALL V. BIEBERSTEIN, W., Civil Law
MEYER, F., Economics of Political Science
OSSENBÜHL, F., Civil and Administrative Law
PARTSCH, K. J., Civil and Administrative Law
RUBERG, C., Industrial Economics
RUDOLPHI, H. J., Science of Execution of Punishment
SABEL, H., Company Management
SALZWEDEL, J., Political Economy
SCHEUNER, U., Public Law
SCHLAICH, K., Civil and Administrative Law, Ecclesiastical Law
SCHÖNFELD, P., Political Economy
SCHRÖDER, J., Civil Law and International and Foreign Private Law
SONDERMANN, D., Statistics
TOMUSCHAT, C., Public Law
VOGT, H., Roman Law, German Civil Law
VOIGT, F., Political Economy
WEIDNER, V., Civil Law, Commercial Law, Law of Economy, Labour, and Social Security
VON WEIZSÄCKER, C. C., Political Economy

Faculty of Medicine:

BECKER, W., Oto-Rhino-Laryngology
BEST, W., Ophthalmology
BRANDIS, H., Medical Microbiology and Immunology
BREUER, H., Physiological and Clinical Chemistry
BURMEISTER, W., Paediatrics
DENGLER, H. J., Internal Medicine
DIRSCHERL, W., Physiological Chemistry
DOMENJOZ, R., Pharmacology and Toxicology
EGLI, H., Experimental Haematology
v. EIFF, A.-W., Internal Medicine
ELBEL, H., Medical Jurisprudence
FLEISCHHAUER, K., Anatomy
FÖDISCH, H., Child Pathology
GEDIGK, Pathology and Pathological Anatomy
GÜTTGEMANN, A., Surgery
HAAS, H.-G., Physiology
HABS, H., Hygiene
HEIFER, U., Forensic Medicine
HUBER, G., Psychiatry and Neurology
HUNGERLAND, M., Child Medicine
HUPFAUF, L., Dental Prosthetics
JACOBI, H., Obstetrics and Gynaecology
KERSTING, G., Neuropathology
KIRCHHOFF, P., Heart and Vascular Surgery
KREYSEL, H.-W., Dermatology and Venerology
KRÜCK, F., Internal Medicine
LEHNERT, S., Dentistry
LEINBROCK, A., Skin and Venereal Diseases
MANI, N., History of Medicine
OBERHOFFER, G., Statistics
PENIN, H., Neurology and Psychiatry
PICHOTKA, J., Physiology
PIEKARSKI, G., Medical Parasitology
PLOTZ, E.-J., Gynaecology
RENSCHLER, H., Didactics
RÖSSLER, H., Orthopaedics
RÖTTGEN, P., Neuro-Surgery
SAUERWEIN, E., Dentistry
SCHAEDE, A., Internal Medicine
SCHMIDT, K., Ophthalmology
SCHMUTH, G., Dentistry
SCHWABE, U., Pharmacology and Toxicology
STELZNER, F., Surgery
STOECKEL, H., Anaesthesiology
THOFERN, E., Hygiene
THURN, P., X-Ray and Radiation Therapeutics
TIEMANN, F., Internal Medicine
VAHLENSIECK, W., Urology
WARTENBERG, H., Anatomy
WEICKER, H., Human Genetics
WEIGELIN, E., Experimental Ophthalmology
WINKLER, C., Nuclear Medicine
WÜLLENWEBER, R., Neurosurgery
ZILLIKEN, F., Physiological Chemistry

Faculty of Philosophy:

ALLEMANN, B., Modern German Literature
BARION, J., Philosophy
BECK, H., Germanic Studies
BERGLER, R., Psychology
BESCH, W., Germanic Studies
BIERBRAUER, V., Pre- and Primitive History
BOESLER, C.-A., Geography
BRACHER, K. D., Political Science
BUDDENSIEG, T., History of Art
COX, H. L., Folklore
DÄUMLING, A., Psychology
DERBOLAV, J., Philosophy, Pedagogy
DROEGE, G., Medieval and Modern History
EDEL, E., Egyptology
EGGERS, P., Pedagogics
EINEM, H. VON, History of Art
EMGE, M., Sociology
ENNEN, E., Medieval and Modern History
ERBEN, J., German Language and Literature
ERBSE, H., Classical Philology
ESCH, A., English Philology
EWIG, E., Medieval and Modern History
FEHN, K., Historical Geography
GEISSLER, E., Education
GUTIÉRREZ-GIRARDOT, Hispanic Studies
HAHN, H., Geography of Economics
HASENJAEGER, G., Logistics
HEISSIG, W., Central Asiatic Studies
HERTER, H., Classical Philology
HIMMELMANN-WILDSCHÜTZ, Classical Archaeology
HIRDT, W., Romance Philology
HÖLLERMANN, P., Geography
HOENERBACH, W., Islamic Culture and Semitics
HÖNNIGHAUSEN, Z., English Philology
HUBATSCH, W., Medieval and Modern History
HÜBINGER, P. E., Medieval History
JACOBSEN, H.-A., Political Science
KAISER, F., Eastern European History
KEIPERT, H., Slavonic Studies
KLEEMANN, D., European Prehistory and Primitive History
KLIMKEIT, H.-J., Comparative Religion
KLUXEN, W., Philosophy
KNOBLOCH, J., Comparative Linguistics
KOPPEN, E., Comparative Literature
KOTTJE, R., Medieval and Modern History
KREINER, J., Japanology
KULS, W., Geography
LANGE, W. D., Romance Philology
LAUER, W., Geography
LEHR, U., Psychology
LENGLER, R., English Philology
LEUBE, E., Romance Philology
LÜTZELER, H., Art History
MASSENKEIL, G., Music
MEHL, D., English Philology
MEIER, H., Romance Philology
MEISSBURGER, G., Germanic Studies
MOSER, H., Germanic Studies
OBEREM, U., Ethnology
OLBRICHT, P., Sinology

PAPAJEWSKI, H., English Philosophy
PERPEET, U., Philosophy
PETRI, F., Medieval and Modern History
POHL, H., Constitutional History, Economics, Social History
POLHEIM, K. K., Modern German Language and Literature
PÜTZ, P., Modern German
REICHL, K., English Philology
REPGEN, K., Medieval and Modern History
RITZEL, Pedagogy
ROTHE, H. Slavonic Philology
RUDIGER, H., Comparative Literature
SCHALLER, D., Vulgar Latin Philology
SCHETTER, W., Classical Philology
SCHIRMER, W., English Philosophy
SCHMID, W., Classical Philology
SCHMIDT, G., Philosophy
SCHMIDT, K. H., Indo-German Comparative Linguistics
SCHMIDT-GÖRG, J., Music
SKALWEIT, ST., Medieval and Modern History
SPIES, O., Semitic Philology
STRAUB, J., Ancient History
THOMAE, H., Psychology
TRAUZETTEL, R., Sinology
TRIER, E., Art History
TRIMBORN, H., Folklore
UNGEHEUER, G., Phonetics and Communication
VOGEL, C., Indology
WAGNER, H., Philosophy
WEISGERBER, L., Linguistics
WIESE VON, B., Modern German
WILD, ST., Semitic Philology
WILLEMSON, G., Medieval and Modern History
WIRTH, G., Ancient History
WOLF, H. J., Romance Philology
WOLTNER, M., Slavonic Philology
ZENDER, M., German Folklore
ZWIERLEIN, O., Classical Philology

Faculty of Mathematics and Natural Sciences:

ALTHOFF, K.-H., Experimental Physics
APPEL, R., Inorganic Chemistry
BECKER, F., Astronomy
BECKEY, H.-D., Physical Chemistry
BETZ, A., Botany
BLEULER, K., Theoretical Atomic Physics
BODENSTEDT, E., Nuclear Physics
BOESLER, K.-A., Geography
BÖHLING, K. H., Data Processing
BRIESKORN, E., Mathematics
BRINKMANN, R., Geology
COMSA, G., Vacuum Physics
DANNEEL, R., Zoology and Genetics
DIETZ, K., Physics
ERBEN, H., Palaeontology
EVERLING, W., Information Science
FLOHN, H., Meteorology
FRECHEN, J., Petrology
FREHSE, J., Applied Mathematics
GLOMBITZA, K., Pharmaceutical Biology
GOTTSCHALK, W., Genetics
HACHENBERG, O., Radioastronomy
HAHN, H., Geography of Economics
HASENJAEGER, G., Logistics
HELFERICH, B., Chemistry
HILDEBRANDT, ST., Mathematics
HIRZEBRUCH, F., Mathematics
HÖLLERMANN, P., Geography
KATING, H., Pharmaceutical Biology
KELLER, R., Zoology
KLINGENBERG, W., Mathematics
KLOFT, W., Applied Zoology
KNOP, G., Experimental Physics
KRAUS, H., Meteorology
KRÜCKEBERG, F., Applied Mathematics
KULS, W., Geography
LAUER, W., Geography
LEIS, R., Applied Mathematics
LIEB, I., Mathematics
MAYER-BÖRICKE, C., Nuclear Physics
MAYER-KUCKUK, TH., Radiation and Nuclear Physics
MEETZ, K., Theoretical Physics
MÜCKENHAUSEN, E., Study of Soils
MÜLLER, F., Pharmaceutical Technology
MÜLLER, K., Applied Palaeontology
NÖLDEKE, G., Physics
PALLASCHKE, D., Mathematics
PAUL, W., Experimental Physics
PENSELIN, S., Applied Physi cs
PESCHL, E., Mathematics
PEYERIMHOFF, S., Theoretical Chemistry
PHILIPSBORN, VON, H., Applied Mineralogy
PRIESTER, W., Astrophysics and Extraterrestrial Studies
PUFF, H., Inorganic Chemistry
ROLLNIK, J., Physics
ROTH, H., Pharmacy
RÜCKER, G., Pharmacy
SANDHAS, W., Theoretical Physics
SANDHOFF, K., Biochemistry
SCHMIDT, H., Astronomy
SCHMITZ-DUMONT, O., Inorganic Chemistry
SCHNEIDER, H., Zoology
SIEVERS, A., Botany
SPIES, P. P., Informatics
STEGLICH, W., Organic Chemistry
STEINER, M., Pharmaceutical Research
TRÜPER, H. G., Microbiology
TSCHESCHE, R., Organic Chemistry
UNGER, H., Applied Mathematics
VIELSTICH, W., Physical Chemistry
VÖGTLE, F., Chemistry
VOGEL, W., Applied Mathematics
VOLL, G., Petrology
WANDREY, CHR., Biotechnology
WEIZEL, W., Theoretical Physics
WILL, G., Mineralogy
WOHLFAHRTH-BOTTERMANN, K.-E., Cytology and Micromorphology
WURSTER, P., Geology
ZAKOSEK, H., General Pedology
ZIMA, H., Information Science
ZYMALKOWSKI, F., Pharmacy

Faculty of Agriculture:

BAITSCH, B., Country Planning
BICK, H., Zoology
BOEKER, P., Plant Breeding
BORCHARD, K., Housing and Town Planning
BRINKMANN, W., Agricultural Technology
FRANKE, W., Botany
GASSNER, E., Housing and Town Planning
HENRICHSMEYER, W., Political Economy, Agricultural Politics and Information
HESMER, H., Forestry
HEUPEL, A., Cartography, Topography, Technical Science of Reproduction
HEYLAND, K.-U., Special Plant Breeding
HÖTZEL, D., Nutrition
HOFMANN, W., Geodesy
KICK, H., Agricultural Chemistry
KOCH, K.-R., Theoretical Geodesy
KÖTTER, H., Agricultural Sociology
KUPFER, G., Geodesy
LENZ, F., Breeding of Fruit and Vegetables
MÖHLE, A., Geodesy
MÜCKENHAUSEN, E., Pedology
MÜLLER, R., Animal Nutrition
PFEFFER, E., Animal Nutrition
PFEILSTICKER, K., Food Chemistry
SCHMITTEN, F., Animal Breeding
SEEGER, H., Geodesy
SEELE, W., Soil Classification and Cultivation
SKOMROCH, W., Agricultural Economy
SOMMER, H., Anatomy
STEFFEN, G., Agricultural Economy
ULRICH, H., Agricultural Botany
WELTZIEN, H., Phytopathology
WENDT, H., Mathematics
WOLF, H., Theoretical Geodesy
WOLFRAM, R.-E., Market Research
ZAKOSEK, H., General Pedology

ATTACHED INSTITUTES:

Institut für das Recht der Wasserwirtschaft (*Institute for Water Conservation Law*): Dir. Prof. Dr. SALZWEDEL.

Franz Josef Dölger-Institut: Dir. Prof. E. DASSMANN.

Max Planck-Institut für Radioastronomie: *see* under Research Institutes.

Institut für das Spar-, Giro- und Kreditwesen: Dir. Prof. Dr. KRÜMMEL.

TECHNISCHE UNIVERSITÄT CAROLO WILHELMINA ZU BRAUNSCHWEIG

33 BRAUNSCHWEIG,
POCKELSSTRASSE 14

Telephone: (0531) 3911.
Telex: 9 52 526.

Founded in 1745 as the Collegium Carolinum, was established as a humanistic, mercantile and technical teaching centre in 1835, and was expanded in 1862 as the Herzogliche Polytechnische Schule. It was known as the Technische Hochschule from 1877 until 1968 when it acquired its present title as a technical university.

State control; Academic year: October to July (two terms).

President: Prof. Dr. agr. GERHARD SCHAFFER.

Vice-Presidents: Prof. Dr.-Ing. HANS JÜRGEN MATTHIES, Prof. Dr. rer. nat. JOACHIM KLEIN.

Chancellor: ERNST VOGEL.

Librarian: Prof. Dr. rer. nat. JOSEF DAUM.

Library: *see* Libraries.

Number of teachers: 254 full-time professors.

Number of students: 10,281.

Publications: *Mitteilungen* (1 or 2 a year), *TU-aktuell* (monthly), *Forschungsberichtsband* (*c.* every 5 years).

DEANS AND HEADS OF DEPARTMENTS:

Faculty of Natural Sciences: Prof. Dr. FRITZ MÜNNICH.

Mathematics, Physics and Geosciences: Prof. Dr. rer. nat. KLAUS ALBERT.

Chemistry, Pharmacy and Biosciences: Prof. Dr. phil. HANS CHRISTOPH MICKO.

Faculty of Building Construction: Prof. Dr.-Ing. BERTHOLD GOCKELL.

Architecture: Prof. Dipl.-Ing. ROLAND OSTERTAG.

Building Engineering: Prof. Dr.-Ing. KNUT HERING.

Faculty of Mechanical and Electrical Engineering: Prof. Dipl.-Phys. Dr.-Ing. HANS JÜRGEN LÖFFLER.
Mechanical Engineering: Prof. Dr. rer. nat. FRANK HAESSNER.
Electrical Engineering: Prof. Dr.-Ing. HELMUT SCHÖNFELDER.

Faculty of Philosophy and Social Science: Prof. Dr. phil. HERIBERT BOEDER.

Faculty of Educational Science: Prof. Dr.-Ing. WALTER E. THEUERKAUF.

AFFILIATED INSTITUTES:

Wilhelm-Klauditz-Institut für Holzforschung der Fraunhofer-Gesellschaft: Bienroderweg 54E; Dir. Dr.-Ing. GERT KOSSATZ.

Institut für Landwirtschaftliche Technologie und Zuckerindustrie: Langer Kamp 5; Dir. Prof. Dr. rer. nat. ERICH REINEFELD.

Amtliche Materialprüfanstalt für das Bauwesen: Beethovenstr. 52; Dirs. Prof. Dr.-Ing. KARL KORDINA, Prof. Dr.-Ing. FERDINAND S. ROSTÁSY.

UNIVERSITÄT BREMEN

2800 BREMEN 33,
BIBLIOTHEKSSTRASSE
Telephone: (0421) 2181.
Founded 1971.

State control; Academic year: April to March (two terms).

Rector: Dr.-Ing. ALEXANDER WITTKOWSKY.

Chancellor: Dr. HANS-HEINRICH MAASS.

Librarian: Dipl. Chem. GERRY WENSKE.

Number of teachers: 345.
Number of students: 7,100.

Publications: *Veranstaltungsverzeichnis*† (2 a year), *Studienführer*† (annually), *Research Report*† (annually), *Bremer-Universitäts-Zeitung*† (fortnightly).

PROFESSORS:

Department of Employment/Politics:
ALBERS, D., Labour Relations
BAHRENBERG, G., Geography
BARTH, H.-K., Physical Geography
CAMRA, J., Management Economics
EICHWEDE, W., History and Political Systems of Socialist Countries
FISCHER, W. C., Home Economics
FRIESE, H., Home Economics
GEISS, I., Modern and Third World History
HÄGERMANN, D., Medieval History
HARDERS, N., Leisure Education
HOLL, K., Contemporary German History
JAROSLAWSKI, J., Political Theory of Government
KLOFT, H., Ancient History
KURTH, U., Religious Knowledge
LEITHÄUSER, G., Economic and Development Policy
LEUZE. E., Geography
LOTT, J., Religious Knowledge
LUDWIG, K.-H., Social and Technical History
MEINKEN, U., Textile Technology
MILNERA, S., Textile Technology
MÜLLER, R., Physiology and Psychology of Working Conditions and Organization
SCHÄFER, W., Political Sociology and Political Science
SCHAFMEISTER, P., Theoretical Sociology
SCHMIDT, A., Geography Teaching
SCHMIDT, J., Curricula in Economic and Social Studies
SCHRÖDER, A., Textile Technology
SCHWARZWÄLDER, H., History
SEIBT, P., Political Science
TAUBMANN, W., Geography
VON DER VRING, T., Social Sciences
WAGNER, W., Politics
WESSELS, B., Elementary Technical Education
WIRTH, M., Parliamentary System of Federal Germany
ZOLL, R., History and Theory of Trade Unions

Department of Labour Relations:
BRAUN, S., Industrial Sociology
CONCERT, H.-G., Political Science and Education
ELSNER, R., Social Medicine
KALMBACH, P., Economics and Microeconomics
OSTERLAND, M., Sociology
SCHUMANN, M., Techniques of Social Research
WAHSNER, R., Labour and Social Law

Department of Biology:
BERNDT, H., Microbiology
CORDES, H., Biology
ENTRICH, H., Theory and Practice of Education in the Natural Sciences
FLOHR, H., Biology
GRIMME, L. H., Biology
HEYSER, W., Botany
HILDEBRANDT, A., Biology
HUBNER, W., Teaching of Biology
KASCHE, V., Physical Biology
KNOLL, J., Teaching of Biology
KREEB, K., Biology
MOSSAKOWSKI, D., Evolutionary Biology
NEHRKORN, A., Microbiology
PFEIFFER, K., Teaching of Biology
RENSING, L., Cell Biology
ROTH, G., Biology, Ethology
SCHAUZ, K., Biology
SCHLIWA, W., Biology
SCHLOOT, W., Genetics
WALTER, H., Anthropology and Human Biology
WEIDEMANN, G., Ecology
WITTE, H., Zoology

Department of Chemistry:
BEYERSMANN, D., Biochemistry
GABEL, D., Organic Chemistry
JAEGER, N., Physical Chemistry
JASTORFF, B., Chemistry
JUST, E., Chemistry
LEIBFRITZ, D., Chemistry
RIEKENS, R., Chemistry
RÖSCHENTHALER, G., Inorganic Chemistry
SCHROER, U., Physical Chemistry
SCHULZ-EKLOFF, G., Physical Chemistry
THIEMANN, W., Physical Chemistry
WANCZEK, K.-P., Inorganic Chemistry
WILLE, R., Teaching of Chemistry
WÖHRLE, D., Chemistry

Department of Electronics/Cybernetics:
ARNDT, F., High Frequency Technology
BESSLICH, P., Electronics and Cybernetics
BODDEN, H., Theoretical Electronics
DÖPP, K., Computers
HÖNERLOH, H., Electronics and Cybernetics
LUDYK, G., Theory of Regulation
MARTE, G., Electronics
MÜLLER, W., Analysis of the Engineering Professions
NAKE, F., Electronics
POPOVIC, D., Electronics
ROY, S. C., Electronics
WASILJEFF, A., Mathematical Methods of Information Science

Department of Education:
BECK, J., General Education
BUSCH, D. W., Sociology of Education
DIETZE, L., Public Law
DRECHSEL, W., Social History of Education
GABELLE, P., Education
HAFERKORN, H., General Education
HEINZ, W. R., Sociology and Social Psychology
HÜBNER, W., Theory of Learning
HUISKEN, F., Political Economy
JANTZEN, W., Medical Education
MADER, W., Extracurricular Education
MILHOFFER, P., Socialization Theory
PETRAT, G., Teaching
PREUSS, O., Sociology of Education
REHLING-SALFFNER, R., Primary Education
RICHARD, J., Education through Play
ROHR, B., Medical Education
ROTH, L., Theory of Teaching
SCHIFF, B., Comparative Education
SCHÖNWÄLDER, H. G., Educational Planning and Economics
STRAKA, G., Extracurricular Education
UBBELOHDE, R., Education
ZIECHMANN, J., Psychology of Learning

Department of Law:
BACKES, O., Criminal Law
BACKMANN, L., Criminal Law
BILLERBECK, R., Political Sociology
BRÜGGEMEIER, G., Civil and Economic Law
DAÜBLER, W., Labour, Commercial and Economic Law
DERLEDER, P., Civil Law
DUBISCHAR, R., Civil Law
FEEST, J., Criminal Law
FRANCKE, R., Legal Didactics
GOTTHOLD, J., Labour and Social Law
HART, D., Economic Law
HINZ, M., Public Law and Political and Legal Sociology
HOFFMANN, R., Public Law, Labour Law and Political Science
JOERGES, C., Civil Law
KNIEPER, R., Civil and Economic Law
LAUTMANN, R., General and Legal Sociology
LICHTENBERG, H., Labour Law
MEYER, J., Labour and Social Law
PREUSS, U.-K., Public Law
RINKEN, A., Public Law
RÜSSMANN, H., Civil Law
SCHMIDT, E., Civil Law
SCHMINCK, C., History of Law
SCHUMANN, K. F., Criminology
STUBY, G., Public Law and Political Science
TEUBNER, G., Sociology of Law
THOSS, P., Criminal Law
WINTER, G., Civil Law

Department of Arts and Music:
BRECKOFF, W., Musical Education
BUDDEMEIER, H.
DUWE, G., Fine Arts
KLEINEN, G., Music
LEMMERMANN, H., Music
MÄVERS, K., Music
MATTHIES, K., Visual Communications
MÜLLER, M., Architecture
NUTBOHM, H.-W., Fine Arts

Department of Communication:
ALFF, W., Comparative Social History of Germany
BECHERT, J., Linguistics
BÜRGER, P., French and Comparative Studies
DAHLE, W., Language and Literature
DRÖGE, F., Communications
EMMERICH, W., German Literature
FRANZBACH, M., Literature and Social History of Spain and Latin America
GALLAS, H., Literature
HAUPT, H.-G., Social History of France
HERMS, D., History of American Literature
HOERDER, D., Social History of the U.S.A.
JÄGER, H.-W., History of German Literature
KREYE, H., General Linguistics
KROGMANN, W., German
LIEBE-HARKORT, K., German as a Foreign Language
MENK, A.-K., Linguistics
METSCHER, T., English Literature
NAVARRO, J., Applied Linguistics
PAUL, L., Applied Linguistics
RICHTER, D., Critical History of Literature
SAUTERMEISTER, G., History of Literature
STRECKERT, L.-L., German Literature and Language
WAGNER, K.-H., Linguistics
WALTZ, M., French Literature

Department of Education (II):
BOEHM, U., Structure and Development of Education
DRECHSEL, R., Education
GRONWALD, D., Electrical Engineering Education
LITTEK, W., Theory and Practice of Vocational Education
MÜLLER-KRÜGER, H., Sociology of the Family
PETER, H.-U., Social Education
ORTMANN, H., M.A., Educational Sciences
RAVNER, F., Technical Professions

Department of Mathematics:
ARNOLD, L.
BECKER, G.
BEHNEN, K.
DENNEBERG, D.
DEUTSCH, M.
DOMBROWSKI, H.-D.
FISCHER, H. W.
GAMST, J.
HENNING, J.
HERRLICH, H.
HINRICHSEN, D.
HOFFMANN, R.-E.
HORNEFFER, K.
HUPPERTZ, H.
KINDER, H.-P.
KRAUSE, U.
KURTH, I.
LINDENAU, V.
MÜNZNER, H.-F.
OELJEKLAUS, E.
OSIUS, G.
ROOS, P.
PEITGEN, H.-O.
PORST, H.-E.
SCHÄFER, R.
SCHINDLER, M.
TIMM, J.
WISCHNEWSKY, M.

Department of Physics:
AUFSCHNAITER, S. VON, Physics
BLECK, J., Experimental Physics
BOSECK, S., Experimental Physics
DIEHL, H., Biophysics
DREYBRODT, W., Experimental Physics
EHRENSTEIN, D. VON, Experimental Physics
HAEFNER, K., Computer Technology in Educational Sciences
MAYER, A., Biophysics
NIEDDERER, H., Theory and Practice of Teaching of Natural Sciences
NOACK, C., Physics
RYDER, P., Physics
SCHEER, J., Physics
SCHMITZ-FEUERHAKE, I., Experimental Physics
SCHWEDES, H., Physics
SCHWEGLER, H., Theoretical Physics
SIEGERT, W., Physics
SIMHAN, K., Physics
STAUDE, W., Experimental Physics

Department of Social Education:
AMENDT, G., Sub-cultures
BAVER, R., Sub-Culture Theory
BLANDOW, J., Social Education
BROCKMANN, A.-D., Town and Regional Planning
DIESSENBACHER, H., Social Education
KEIL, A., General Education
LANGE, H., Sociology
LEIBRFIED, S., Social Planning
MARZAHN, C., Social Education
MERKEL, J., Pre-School Education
ZANDER, H., Anti-Social Behaviour Research

Department of Social Sciences:
BAHR, H.-D., Theory of Cognition and Society
FREYHOLD, M. V., Development Politics
HAFERKAMP, H., Sociology
HAHN, M., History of Middle-class Society
HAÜSSERMANN, H., Town and Regional Planning
KRÄMER-BADONI, T., Social Sciences
KRAUSE, D., Social Sciences
KRÜGER, M., Social Analysis
PETER, L., Industrial and Management Sociology
QUENSEL, S., Rehabilitation
REICHELT, H., Dialectics in Political Economy
SANDKÜHLER, J.-J., Theory of Cognition
SENGHAAS, D., Development Politics
STEINBERG, J.-J., History of the Labour Movement
STRUBELT, W., Town and Regional Planning

Department of Physical Education:
ANYZEWSKI, J., Anthropology
ARTUS, H. G., Theory and Practice of Teaching Physical Education
BERNDT, J., Biological and Medical Factors in Physical Training
HAGEDORN, G., Physical Development
JONAS, B., Theory and Practice of Teaching Physical Education
SASSENRATH, I., Science of Sport
UNGERER, D., Study of Movement

Department of Economics:
BIESECKER, A., Economic Theory
BUDÄUS, D., Economics
DWORATSCHEK, S., Economics
GERSTENBERGER, H., Middle-class Society and the State
GRENZDÖRFFER, K., Applied Economic Theory
HEIDE, H., Town and Country Planning
HICKEL, R., Political Economy
HOITSCH, H. J., Economics
HÜTTNER, M., Management Economics
HUFFSCHMID, J., Political Economy of the Federal Republic
JAROSLAWSKA, H., Economics
KURZ, H., Economics
LEITHÄUSER, G., Politics of Economic Development
LEMPER, A., Foreign Trade Theory and Politics
REHKUGLER, H., Economics
ROLOFF, O., Theory of State Revenue and Expenditure
SCHÄFER, H., Economics
SCHUI, H., Economics
SCHWIERING, D., Economics
STEIGER, O., General Economic Theory
STEINER, M., Management Economics
WOHLMUTH, K., Comparison of Economic Systems

Department of Psychology:
BAUMGÄRTL, F., Psychological Diagnosis
DONATH, H., Psychology
ESTERS, E.-A., Sociology and Social Psychology
GRABITZ-GNIECH, G., Psychology
HEINZ, W.-R., Sociology and Social Psychology
LEITHÄUSER, T., Developmental Psychology
STEIN, R., Psychology
STEMME, F., Clinical Psychology
VETTER, G., Theory of Learning
VINNAI, G., Analytical Social Psychology

Department of Adult Education:
ALHEIT, P., Adult Education
GERL, H., Adult Education
HINDRICHS, W., Workers' Education
HOLZAPFEL, G., Curricular Planning
KUHLENKAMP, D., Educational Planning
MADER, W., Adult Education
SCHLUTZ, E., Adult Education
THOMSSEN, W., Adult Education
VOIGT, W., Job Training Programmes
WEYMANN, A., Sociology of Adult Education
WOLLENBERG, J., Adult Education in Political Science

Department of Engineering:
BAUCKHAGE, K., General Engineering
LUCZAK, M., Ergonomics

TECHNISCHE UNIVERSITÄT CLAUSTHAL

3392 CLAUSTHAL-ZELLERFELD, ADOLF-RÖMER-STR. 2A
Telephone: 721.

Founded 1775 as Bergakademie Clausthal, attained university status 1963.

State control; Academic year: April to following March (two terms).

Rector: Prof. Dr.-Ing. R. JESCHAR.
Chancellor: V. VON BECKERATH.
Vice-Chancellor: H. RAWALD.
Librarian: Dr. H.-O. WEBER.

Number of teachers: 93, including 49 Ordinary Professors.

Number of students: 3,000.

Publications: *Mitteilungsblatt*, *Informationen*.

DEANS:

Faculty of Natural Sciences and Philosophy: Prof. Dr. rer. nat. HORST QUADE.

Faculty of Mining and Mechanical Engineering: Prof. Dr. rer. nat. H. W. HENNICKE.

HEADS OF DEPARTMENTS:

Faculty of Natural Sciences and Philosophy:

ALBRECHT, J., Mathematics
BAUER, E. G., Experimental Physics
BECKMANN, H., Applied Geology, Petroleum Geology
BOBERG, F., Organic Chemistry
BREHLER, B., Mineralogy, Crystallography
BUES, W., Inorganic Chemistry
DOEBNER, H.-D., Theoretical Physics
FRITSCHE, L., Theoretical Physics
GUNDERMANN, K.-D., Organic Chemistry
HORNFECK, B., Mathematics
JANTSCHER, L., Applied Mathematics
KRAUSE, H., Economic Geology
KÜHNE, G., Mining and Law
LABUSCH, R., Theoretical Metallurgy
MÜLLER, G., Mineralogy and Petrography
REHAGE, G., Physical Chemistry
ROSENBACH, O., Geophysics
SCHOTTLAENDER, ST., Mathematics
SCHWAB, K., Geology, Palaeontology
STUMPP, E., Inorganic Chemistry
WEINERT, H. J., Mathematics

Faculty of Mining and Mechanical Engineering:

BRETTHAUER, K., Electrotechnics
BUNGE, H.-J., Metallurgy, Physics of Metals
CLEMENT, M., Mineral Dressing
DRAUGELATES, U., Theoretical Metallurgy
FUNKE, P., Rolling, Pressing and Drawing of Materials
GRIESE, F. W., Plant Engineering
HAUPT, W., Mine Surveying
HENNICKE, H. W., Glass and Ceramics
HEUSLER, Corrosion Prevention
HEYE, Materials Testing
HOLLAND, J., Friction Studies in Mechanical Engineering
JESCHAR, R., Heat Economy and Furnace Construction
KNISSEL, W., Mining
KUXMANN, U., Non-ferrous Metallurgy
LAMBERTS, K., Electronics and Control Engineering
LESCHONSKI, K., Powder Technology
LÜRIG, H. J., Mining
MARX, C., Petroleum Engineering, Drilling and Production
ODLER, I., Binding and Building Substances
OELERT, H., Chemical Technology
SCHÄFER, M., Technical Machines
SCHÜRMANN, E., Foundry Technology
TELLKAMP, T., Welding Techniques
VOGELPOHL, A., Welding Techniques
WILKE, L., Welding Techniques

TECHNISCHE HOCHSCHULE DARMSTADT

6100 DARMSTADT,
KAROLINENPLATZ 5
Telephone: 06151-161.
Telex: 419579 TH D.

Founded 1836 as Höhere Gewerbeschule, acquired university status in 1895.

President: Prof. Dr. phil. HELMUT BÖHME.
Vice-President: Prof. Dr. rer. nat. WERNER KRABS.
Chancellor: Dr. jur. HANS-GEORG WILKE.

Number of professors: 345.
Number of students: 11,462.

HEADS OF DEPARTMENTS:

Department 1 (*Law and Economics*): Prof. Dr. rer. pol. CHRISTIAN FLÄMIG.
Department 2 (*Cultural and Political Sciences*): Prof. Dr. phil. EVELIES MAYER.
Department 3 (*Education and Psychology*): Prof. Dr. phil. BERNHARD SEILER.
Department 4 (*Mathematics*): Prof. Dr. rer. nat. ERHARD MEISTER.
Department 5 (*Physics*): Prof. Dr.-Ing. GERD HERZIGER.
Department 6 (*Mechanics*): Prof. Dr. rer. nat. WALTER SCHNELL.
Department 7 (*Physical Chemistry*): Prof. Dr.-Ing. JOHANN GAUBE.
Department 8 (*Inorganic and Nuclear Chemistry*): Prof. Dr. rer. nat. HERBERT SCHÄFER.
Department 9 (*Organic and Macromolecular Chemistry*): Prof. Dr. rer. nat. HANS NEUNHOEFFER.
Department 10 (*Biology*): Prof. Dr. rer. nat. WOLFRAM ULLRICH.
Department 11 (*Geosciences and Geography*): Prof. Dr. rer. nat. OTMAR SEUFFERT.
Department 12 (*Surveying*): Prof. Dr.-Ing. OTFRIED WOLFRUM.
Department 13 (*Civil Engineering*): Prof. Dr.-Ing. GÜNTER RINCKE.
Department 14 (*Construction Engineering*): Prof. Dr.-Ing. HORST G. SCHÄFER.
Department 15 (*Architecture*): Prof. Dr. phil. GEORG FRIEDRICH KOCH.
Department 16 (*Mechanical Engineering*): Prof. Dr. rer. nat. ERWIN KRÄMER.
Department 17 (*Power Engineering*): Prof. Dr.-Ing. WOLFGANG PFEIFFER.
Department 18 (*Electrotechnics*): Prof. Dr.-Ing. HANS L. HARTNAGEL.
Department 19 (*Control and Data Engineering*): Prof. Dr. rer. nat. HANS STRACK.
Department 20 (*Computer Science*): Prof. Dr. phil. HELMUT JÜRGENSEN.

PROFESSORS:

Law and Economic Sciences:

AZZOLA, A., Public Law
BECKS, R., Political Economy
FLÄMIG, CH., Finance and Taxation Law
HIELSCHER, U., Industrial Economy
HOFMANN, P., Civil, Economic and Labour Law
HORVÁTH, P., Industrial Economy
KÖRNER, H., Political Economy
MÜLLER-MERBACH, H., Industrial Economy
NICKEL, E., Civil, Economic and Labour Law
OHSE, D., Industrial Economy
PETZOLD, H.-J., Industrial Economy
PODLECH, A., Public Law
POSER, G., Political Economy
RÜRUP, B., Political Economy
SCHLICHT, E., Political Economy
SCHMIDT, R. H., Political Science
SCHNEIDER, U. H., Civil, Economic and Labour Law
SÖHN, H., Finance and Taxation Law
SPECHT, G., Industrial Economy

Cultural and Political Sciences:

v. ARETIN, K., Modern History
BERGMANN, J., Sociology
BÖHME, G., Philosophy
BRINGMANN, K., Ancient History
DAHMER, H., Sociology
zu DOHNA, L. C., Medieval History
EGLOFF, G., Philology and Literature
FLEISCHER, H., Philosophy
HAAS, N., Literature
HEBEL, F., Didactics of German
HOBERG, R., Philology
KALLENBERG, F., Modern History
KELLNER, H., Sociology
KOHLER, BEATE, Political Science
MAYER, E., Sociology
NIXDORFF, P., Political Science
PAULINYI, A., Technological and Economic History
PODLECH, A., Public Law
PROMIES, W., Philology and Literature
SCHMIDT, R. H., Political Science
SCHRÖDER, H.-C., Modern History
SCHUMANN, W., Political Science
SIEGRIST, L., English Language
STROBEL, G., Political Science
TESCHNER, M., Sociology
TREUHEIT, W., Political Science
VIEFHAUS, E., Modern History
VOGT, M., Modern History
WILLE, R., Mathematics

Education and Psychology:

FENGER, H., Vocational Education and Educational Planning
FERTIG, L., Education
GAMM, H.-J., Education
GRÜNER, G., Vocational Education and Educational Planning
HARTMANN, H., Sport
KOCH, J.-J., Psychology
KONEFFKE, G., Education
LEICHNER, R., Psychology
MICHELSEN, U., Vocational Education
PETERSEN, G., Didactics of Natural Sciences
RÜTTINGER, B., Psychology
SEILER, B., Psychology
SINGER, R., Sport
VOSS, H.-G., Psychology
WANDMACHER, J., Psychology

Mathematics:

ARTMANN, B.
BRUHN, G.
BURMEISTER, P.
VON FINCKENSTEIN, Graf K.
GANTER, B.
GROH, H.
HEIL, E.
HOSCHEK, J.
KALF, H.
KEIMEL, K.
KLINGBEIL, E.
KRABS, W.
LAUGWITZ, D.
LEHN, J.
LUH, W.
MÄURER, H.
MEISTER, E.
NOLTE, W.
OSÔRIO, V.
SCHEFFOLD, E.
SCHELLHAAS, H.
SPELLUCI, P.
STEIN, G.
TÖRNIG, W.
TREBELS, W.
WEGMANN, H.
WENDLAND, W.
WILLE, R.

Physics:
BECK, F., Nuclear Physics
CLERC, H.-G., Nuclear Physics
ELSCHNER, B., Solid State Physics
FICK, E., Solid State Physics
FINKENRATH, H., Applied Physics
FRANK, H., Nuclear Physics
HEBER, J., Solid State Physics
HERZIGER, G., Applied Physics
HILF, E., Nuclear Physics
KANKELEIT, E., Nuclear Physics
KÖRDING, A., Nuclear Physics
MANAKOS, P., Nuclear Physics
PAGNIA, H., Applied Physics
RICHTER, A., Nuclear Physics
ROSE, H., Applied Physics
SAUERMANN, G., Solid State Physics
SAUERMANN, H., Solid State Physics
SEELIG, W., Applied Physics
STEGLICH, F., Solid State Physics
THEOBALD, J., Nuclear Physics
WEBER, G., Solid State Physics
WIEN, K., Nuclear Physics

Mechanics:
BECKER, E., Mechanics
GROSS, D., Mechanics
HAGEDORN, P., Mechanics
HAUGER, W., Mechanics
HAUPT, P., Mechanics
KLUG, W., Meteorology
MANIER, G., Meteorology
ROESNER, K., Mechanics
SCHNELL, W., Mechanics
WIPPERMANN, F., Meteorology
WOERNLE, H.-TH., Mechanics

Physical Chemistry:
BRICKMANN, J., Physical Chemistry
EICHENAUER, W., Physical Chemistry
FETTING, F., Chemical Technology
GAUBE, J., Chemical Technology
GÖTTLICHER, S., Structure Research
HAASE, W., Physical Chemistry
HOMANN, K.-H., Physical Chemistry
LUFT, G., Chemical Technology
WEIL, K., Physical Chemistry
WEISS, A., Physical Chemistry
WENDT, H., Chemical Technology
WÖLFEL, E., Structure Research

Inorganic and Nuclear Chemistry:
BÄCHMANN, K., Nuclear Chemistry
BUCHLER, J. W., Inorganic Chemistry
ELIAS, H., Inorganic Chemistry
GROBE, J., Inorganic Chemistry
JOPPIEN, G., Inorganic Chemistry
KOBER, F., Inorganic Chemistry
LIESER, K. H., Inorganic and Nuclear Chemistry
MÜNZEL, H., Nuclear Chemistry
SCHÄFER, H., Inorganic Chemistry

Organic and Macromolecular Chemistry:
BRAUN, D., Organic and Macromolecular Chemistry
EILBRACHT, P., Organic Chemistry
GASSEN, H., Biochemistry
GIESE, B., Chemistry in the Technical Professions
HABERMEHL, G., Organic Chemistry
HAFNER, K., Organic Chemistry
HEIDEMANN, E., Tannic Chemistry
KRAUSE, TH., Macromolecular Chemistry
LICHTENHALER, F. W., Organic Chemistry
LINDNER, H. J., Organic Chemistry
NEUNHOEFFER, H., Chemistry in the Technical Professions
RIESNER, D., Biochemistry

Biology:
BUSCHINGER, A., Zoology
EMMERICH, H., Zoology
FEKETE, MARIA, Plant Biochemistry
GASSEN, H., Biochemistry
GROSSE-BRAUCKMANN, G., Geobotany
HIMSTEDT, W., Zoology
KAISER, W., Zoology
KLUGE, M., Botany
KÖHLER, D., Botany
KUTZNER, H. J., Microbiology
LÜTTGE, U., Botany
MAGNUS, D. B. E., Zoology
MARTIN, H. H., Microbiology
MILTENBURGER, H. G., Zoology
NIXDORFF, KATHRYN, Microbiology
PREUSSER, H.-J., Microbiology
SCHEICH, H., Zoology
STEWART, UTE, Zoology
ULLRICH, W., Botany
WEIGL, J., Botany
WOLLENWEBER, E., Botany
ZIMMERMANN, F., Microbiology

Geosciences and Geography:
BACKHAUS, E., Geology and Palaeontology
EBHARDT, G., Geology and Palaeontology
FAHLBUSCH, K., Geology and Palaeontology
KLEINSCHMIDT, G., Geology and Palaeontology
MAY, H.-D., Geography
MÜLLER, W. F., Petrography and Stratigraphy
PAULITSCH, P., Mineralogy and Applied Geognosy
SCHETELIG, K., Geology and Palaeontology
SCHICK, M., Geography
SCHUMANN, D., Geology and Palaeontology
SEUFFERT, O., Geography

Surveying:
DEKER, H., Photogrammetry and Cartography
EICHORN, G., Geodesy
GERSTENECKER, C.-E., Experimental Physical and Astronomical Geodesy
GROSSE, H., Geodetic Surveying
GROTEN, E., Physical and Satellite Geodesy
PAUL, G., Planning and Soil Classification
WOLFRUM, O., Surveying

Civil Engineering:
DURTH, W., Traffic
EULER, G., Hydraulics and Hydrology
JACOBITZ, K., Water Supplies, Sewage, Municipal Engineering
LACHER, H., Hydraulics and Hydrology
MOCK, J., Hydraulic Engineering
MÜHLHANS, E., Traffic
PAULMANN, G., Traffic
RETZKO, H.-G., Traffic
RINCKE, H., Water Supplies, Sewage, Municipal Engineering
SCHRÖDER, R., Hydraulics and Hydrology
SCHRÖDER, W., Hydraulic Engineering
TIEDT, W., Hydraulics and Hydrology
WOLTERS, N., Water Supplies, Sewage, Municipal Engineering

Construction Engineering:
EBEL, H., Statics
FRIEMANN, H., Steel Construction
JUNGBLUTH, O., Steel Construction
KÖNIG, G., Solid Engineering
MEHLHORN, G., Solid Engineering
SAAL, H., Statics
SCHÄFER, H., Solid Engineering
SCHARDT, R., Statics
SCHUBERT, E., Construction Engineering
SCHWARZ, H., Construction Engineering, Data Processing
SEEGER, T., Steel Construction and Mechanics of Materials
UHLMANN, W., Steel Construction
WEIGLER, H., Technology and Experiment in Engineering

Architecture:
BÄCHER, M., Architectural Design
BEHNISCH, G., Industrial Buildings
BELZ, W., Design and Surface Engineering
BÖHM, H., Drawing, Painting and Graphic Art
BREDOW, J., Design, Housing Construction and Specialized Subjects
EINSELE, M., Town Planning and Design
EMDE, H., Mathematics for Architects and Geometric Data Processing
FÄRBER, P., Architectural Design
FESEL, G., Design and Technology in Surface Engineering
FÜHRER, H., Design and Industrial Construction
GRZIMEK, W., Sculpture
HAAS, W., Architectural History
KNELL, H., Classical Archaeology
KOCH, G. F., History of Art
KÖRTE, A., Planning and Construction in Developing Countries
MANN, W., Statics of Surface Engineering
MÜRB, R., Landscape Architecture
SEELINGER, F., Design and Visual Communication
SIEVERTS, TH., Town Planning and Design
STEIGER, P., Surface Engineering
STÖFFLER, J., Supporting Structures
STRIFFLER, H., Design and Structures
WAECHTER, H.-G., Design, Structures and Country Planning
WIEDEBUSCH, INGEBORG, Science of Colour
WILKES, W., Typography

Mechanical Engineering:
BEER, H., Technical Thermodynamics
BRANDT, F., Heat Technology
BREUER, B., Vehicle Technology
ECKSTEIN, F., Machine Tools, Manufacturing Technology
GÖTTSCHING, L., Paper Technology
HAFER, X., Flight Systems
HUMBACH, W., Reactor Engineering
KAST, W., Heat Process Technology
KLOOS, K.-H., Materials
KRÄMER, E., Machine Dynamics
MÜHLBERG, E., Combustion Engines
MÜLLER, H. W., Mechanics and Dynamics of Machines
NEUGEBAUER, R., Conveying and Lifting Machinery
OSTERWALDER, J., Hydraulic Machinery and Installations
PAHL, G., Machine Elements and Construction
PFEIL, H., Steam Turbines and Installations
RAAB, W., Machine Elements and Mechanics
ROHMERT, W., Kinetics
SCHEUTER, K., Printing Technology
SCHMOECKEL, D., Transformer Technology
SPECKHARDT, H., Materials
SPURK, J. H., Fluid Dynamics
WAZELT, F., Flight Propulsion
WISSMANN, J., Light-weight Structures

Power Engineering:
ANDRESEN, E., Electric Energy Transformation
HASSE, K., Transformer-powered Propulsive Mechanisms
JÖTTEN, R., Transformer Technology and Propulsion Control
KOGLIN, H.-J., Power Systems and Grids
KÖNIG, D., High Voltage Technology

MÜLLER, W., Electric Energy Transforming Fields
OEDING, D., Electric Energy Transformation
PFEIFFER, W., Electrical Measurement
ZÜRNECK, H., Foundations of Electrotechnology

Electrotechnics:
BRADER, C., Electromechanical Apparatus
BUSCHMANN, H., Electromechanical Apparatus
HARTNAGEL, H. L., High Frequency Technology
HOFFMANN, K., Telecommunications
KESSLER, A., High Frequency Technology
PIEFKE, G., Theoretical Electrotechnics
SESSLER, G., Electrical Acoustics
VLCEK, A., High Frequency Technology
WEISSMANTEL, H., Electromechanical Apparatus
ZSCHUNKE, W., Telecommunications

Control and Data Engineering:
BOSSE, G., Foundations of Electrotechnology
HÄNSLER, E., Theory of Signals
HILBERG, W., Digital Circuits and Memories
ISERMANN, R., Theory of Control Systems
KOSTKA, A., Semiconductor Electronics
LANGHEINRICH, W., Semiconductor Technology
PILOTY, R., Computer Science and Engineering
STRACK, H., Semiconductor Technology
TOLLE, H., Theory of Control Systems

Computer Science:
ENCARNAÇAO, J., Data Processing
HÄRDER, TH., Data Administration Systems
HENHAPL, W., Programming Languages and Compilers
HOFFMANN, H.-J., Programming Languages and Compilers
HOFFMANN, R., Micro Programming
JÜRGENSEN, H., Automation Theory and Formal Languages
LUSTIG, G., Data Administration Systems
PILOTY, R., Computer Science and Engineering
SCHINZEL, B., Automation Theory and Formal Languages
STRASSER, W., Graphic Interactive Systems
TZSCHACH, H., Operating Systems
WALDSCHMIDT, H., Operating Systems
WALTER, H., Automation Theory and Formal Languages

UNIVERSITÄT DORTMUND

46 DORTMUND-EICHLINGHOFEN,
AUGUST-SCHMIDT-STRASSE
Telephone: 755-1.
Founded 1966.

Rector: Prof. Dr. P. VELSINGER.
Vice-Rectors: Prof. Dr. M. MÜLLER, Prof. Dr. J. GRIESE, Prof. Dr. R. JÜNEMANN.
Chancellor: Dr. H. RÖKEN.
Librarian: Dr. V. WEHEFRITZ.

Library of 600,000 vols.
Number of students: 6,200.

DEANS:

Department of Mathematics: Prof. Dr. W. HAZOD.
Department of Physics: Prof. Dr. M. KEITER.
Department of Chemistry: Prof. Dr. B. BODDENBERG.
Department of Chemical Engineering: Prof. Dr. G. HINRICHSEN.
Department of Urban and Regional Planning: Prof. Dr. A. BLOCH.
Department of Mechanical Engineering: Prof. Dr. E. VON FINCKENSTEIN.
Department of Computer Sciences: Prof. Dr. H.-D. EHRICH.
Department of Statistics: Prof. Dr. S. SCHACH.
Department of Electrical Engineering: Prof. Dr. K. OBERRETL.
Department of Building Construction and Architecture: Prof. Dipl.-Ing. J. EIBL.
Department of Economic and Social Sciences: Prof. Dr. W. BÜHLER.

PROFESSORS:

Department of Mathematics:
ALBRECHT, P., Applied Mathematics
DANZER, L., Geometry
ERLE, D., Topology
FRANK, H., Differential Geometry
HAZOD, W., Measurement and Integration Theory
JOUSSEN, J., Geometry
KABALLO, W., Analysis
MAYER, K. H., Topology
MENKE, K., Analysis
MITTELMANN, D., Applied Mathematics
MÜLLER, M. W., Applied Mathematics
REIMER, M., Applied Mathematics
SCHNEIDER, A., Analysis
THEDY, A., Algebra
VESELIĆ, K., Applied Mathematics
WALTER, R., Geometry

Department of Physics:
BAACKE, J., Theoretical Physics
BONSE, M., Experimental Physics
BRANDT, U., Theoretical Physics
EISELE, F., Experimental Physics
FRÖHLICH, D., Experimental Physics
KAAT, E. TE., Theoretical Physics
KANERT, O., Experimental Physics
KEITER, H., Theoretical Physics
KLEINKNECHT, K., Experimental Physics
MEHRING, M., Experimental Physics
PASCHOS, E. A., Theoretical Physics
TREUSCH, J., Theoretical Physics
ULBRICH, R. G., Experimental Physics
WEGENER, D., Experimental Physics

Department of Chemistry:
BODDENBERG, B., Physical Chemistry
EICHER, T., Organic Chemistry
GRABKE, H.-J., Physical Chemistry
HUBER, F., Inorganic Chemistry
KLOCKOW, D., Inorganic Chemistry
MINKWITZ, R., Inorganic Chemistry
MITCHELL, T. N., Organic Chemistry
NEUMANN, W. P., Organic Chemistry
RICKERT, H.-P., Physical Chemistry
SCHMEISSER, M., Inorganic Chemistry

Department of Chemical Engineering:
GIESEKUS, H., Fluid Mechanics
HAPKE, J., Chemical Apparatus
HINRICHSEN, G., Synthetics
ONKEN, U., Technical Chemistry
SCHAARWÄCHTER, W., Science of Materials
SCHECKER, H.-G., Physical Chemistry, Processing Science
SCHULZ, S., Thermodynamics
SCHWIND, H., Plant Technology
SIMMROCK, K. H., Technical Chemistry
WEINSPRACH, P.-M., Thermal Process
WERNER, U., Mechanical Process

Department of Urban and Regional Planning:
BLOCH, A., Country Planning
D'ALLEUX, H.-J., Town Building and Water Economy
BARON, P., Traffic
DAVID, C.-H., Planning Law
DIETERICH, H., Surveying and Soil Construction
FINKE, L., Landscape Ecology and Planning
HALSTENBERG, F., Law
JENKIS, H. W., Housing
KREIBICH, V., Geography
KROES, G., Political Economy
KUNZMANN, R., Regional Planning
RÖDDING, W., System Theory and Techniques
SCHOOF, A., Town and Regional Planning
VELSINGER, P., Economics
ZLONICKY, P., Construction Supervision and Town Planning

Department of Mechanical Engineering:
CRONJÄGER, L., Cutting Production Methods
VON FINCKENSTEIN, E., Production Methods
GERLACH, H. H., Factory Organization
HEINZ, K., Manufacturing Preparation
JÜNEMANN, R., Mechanical Handling and Storage
KAUDER, K., Machine Elements
KESSEL, S., Mechanics
LINDNER, G., Factory Organization
RÖPER, R., Machine Elements
STEFFENS, H.-D., Physical Production Methods

Department of Computer Science:
BEILNER, H.
BÖRGER, E.
CLAUS, V.
EHRICH, H. D.
REUSCH, B.
RICHTER, L.
SCHLAGETER, G.
UNGER, C.

Department of Statistics:
EICKER, F., Mathematical Statistics
HEILER, S., Statistics of Economics and Sociology
HERING, F., Experimental Design
SCHACH, S., Mathematical Statistics
SONNEMANN, E., Scientific Statistics

Department of Economics and Sociology:
BÜHLER, W., Investment and Finance
GRIESE, J., Business Data Processing
HOLLÄNDER, H., Economics
HUMMEL, S., Business Administration
MÄNNEL, W., Factory Economics
MEISSNER, H.-G., Marketing
NEUENDORFF, H., Sociology
REICHMANN, TH., Business Administration
SCHUMM-GARLING, U., Sociology
STAHL, K., Economic Theory
TEICHMANN, U., Manufacturing Preparation
ZOHLNHÖFER, W., Political Economy
ZSCHOCKE, D., Management—Operations Research

Department of Building Construction and Architecture:

BAUER, H., Construction, Management, Machinery and Equipment
VON BUSSE, B., Construction and Design
DEILMANN, H., Architectural Design and Town Planning
EIBL, J., Concrete and Reinforced Concrete Structures
FISCHER, M., Steel Structures
KLEIHUES, J. P., Architectural Theory and Design
KLOPPER, H., Physics of Buildings
NALBACH, G., Graphic Communication and Design
POLÓNYI, ST., Building Structures
SZILARD, R., Building Mechanics-Statics

Department of Electrical Engineering:

FISCHER, A. G.
HANDSCHIN, E.
HÖFFLINGER, B.
KIENDL, H.
LÜTZE, W.
OBERRETL, K.
PONNER, F.
SCHERER, R.
VOGES, E.
WALDSCHMIDT, K.
WENDLAND, B.

ATTACHED INSTITUTES:

Institut für Arbeitsphysiologie: Ardeystrasse 67; Dir. Prof. Dr. med. phil. J. RUTENFRANZ.

Institut für Umweltschutz und Umweltgüteplanung: Dir. Prof. Dr.-Ing. H. J. KARPE.

Landesinstitut Sozialforschungsstelle: Rheinlanddamm 199.

UNIVERSITÄT DUISBURG GESAMTHOCHSCHULE

41 DUISBURG,
LOTHARSTRASSE 65
Telephone: 3051.

Founded 1972 by amalgamation and extension of the Pädagogische Hochschule and the Fachhochschule.

Academic year: April to March (two semesters).

Rector: Prof. Dr. ADAM WEYER.

Co-Rectors: Prof. Dr.-Ing. HEINZ LUCK, Prof. Dr. rer. nat. WINFRIED MÖNCH, Prof. Dr. phil. REINHARD STACH.

Chancellor: Dr. RUDOLF BAUMANNS.

Librarian: Dr. ULRICH PFLUGK.

Number of teachers: *c.* 500.

Number of students: *c.* 7,000.

Publications: *Amtliche Mitteilungen*†, *Gesamthochschul-Informationen*†, *Vorlesungsverzeichnis*†.

DEANS:

Department 1 (*Philosophy, Evangelical and Catholic Theology, Social Sciences*): Prof. Dr. FRITZ RUDOLPH.

Department 2 (*Education, Psychology, Physical Education*): Prof. Dr. WOLFGANG FISCHER.

Department 3 (*Linguistics*): Prof. Dr. KARL KOHUT.

Department 4 (*Arts and Crafts, Music*): Stud. Prof'in. MARIANNE RUHLOFF.

Department 5 (*Economics*): Prof. Dr. KLAUS TIEPELMANN.

Department 6 (*Biology, Chemistry and Geography*): Prof. Dr. ALFONS SAUS.

Department 7 (*Construction Engineering*): Prof. Dr. DIETRICH ELBRACHT.

Department 8 (*Metallurgy and Ceramics*): Prof. Dr. GÜNTER DIETZEL.

Department 9 (*Electrical and Control Engineering*): Prof. Dr. ERICH KUBALEK.

Department 10 (*Physics and Technology*): Prof. Dr. HELMUT SANFLEBER.

Department 11 (*Mathematics*): Prof. Dr. KLAUS-WERNER WIEGMANN.

PROFESSORS:

Department 1:

BIRKE, E., History
BRÖCKER, H., Philosophy
CHRISTADLER, M., Political Science
DANCKWERTS, D., Sociology
HENNING, H., Social History
HESSE, J.-J., Political Science
HÜBNER, H., Social Work and Education
HUMMELL, H.-J., Sociology
KREMERS, H., Protestant Theology
KRÜGER, J., Sociology
LANGE, G., Roman Catholic Theology
NUSCHELER, F., Political Science
PETERS, I., Protestant Theology
RUDOLPH, F., Sociology
SCHALLENBERGER, E. H., Political Science
SCHATZ, H., Political Science
SCHÖRKEN, R., Modern History
SIEP, L., Philosophy
STRASSER, H., Sociology
WEYER, A., Protestant Theology

Department 2:

ADOLPHS, L., Pedagogics
FISCHER, W., Pedagogics
HEILAND, H., Pedagogics
HOLTHOFF, F., Pedagogics
LÖWISCH, D.-J., Pedagogics
MEIS, R., Psychology
MIETZEL, G., Psychology
RAATZ, U., Psychology

Department 3:

BORNSCHEUER, L., German Philology
BRIX, G., German Philology
FRIED, V., English Philology/Linguistics
GEISSLER, R., German Philology
HAACK, D., English and American Philology
HORTMANN, W., English Philology
JÄGER, S., German Philology/Linguistics
KOHUT, K., Romance Philology
MIHM, A., German Philology
SCHREY, H., English Philology
SPILLNER, B., Romance Philology/Linguistics
THEIS, R., Romance Philology

Department 4:

BRÖG, H., Art
LINKE, N., Music
MENNING, W., Art

Department 5 (*Economics*):

BODENSTEIN, G.
CASSEL, D.
CLAASSEN, E.-M.
COX, H.
GRAVE, G.
HABERSTOCK, L.
KATH, D.
LANGE, W.
LEUER, H.
MULLER-LINDENBERG, H.-H.
NIERHAUS, H.
PLACHETKA, M. G.
SCHENK, H.-O.
SCHIRA, J.
SCHUBERT, W.
STAUDT, E.
STROSCHEIN, F.-R.
THIELE-WITTIG, M.
TIEPELMANN, K.

Department 6:

BECK, F., Electrical Chemistry
BONNET, P.-H., Organic Chemistry
DOPP, D., Organic Chemistry
DÜLL, R., Biology
GEISMAR, G., Inorganic Chemistry
GÜRTLER, O., Applied Chemistry
VON HAGEN, F., Biology
HAGENMAIER, H., Biology
HEMMER, E.-A., Physical Chemistry
KOSFELD, R., Chemistry
METZE, R., Chemistry
SARTORI, P., Inorganic Chemistry
SAUS, A., Applied Chemistry
STRÄSSER, M., Geography
WAGNER, K., Geography

Department 7:

BAUR, U., Machinery
BRÜGGEMANN, B., Technical Mechanics
DEESE, F., Technical Mechanics
DREES, B., Machinery
ELBRACHT, D., Manufacturing
ELFERT, J., Foundry Machinery
ENGELHARDT, G., Technical Mechanics
FRIK, M., Technical Mechanics
HAGEN, P., Shipbuilding
KLEIN, K., Construction
KLING, B., Transport and Construction
KUGELER, K., Energy Technology
LUCAS, K., Thermodynamics
MOSLÉ, H.-G., Raw Materials
OSER, J., Transport
VON PETIT, E., Construction
ROBIE, H., Raw Materials
ROTH, U., Construction
SAEGLER, O., Transport and Construction
SCHLÜNKES, F., Dynamics
SCHULTE, A., Surveying
SCHWARZ, H., Surveying
SPERLICH, V., Energy Technology
WIENKOOP, J., Manufacturing
WIETASCH, K. W., Shipbuilding
WÜNSCH, D., Construction
ZIETZ, J., Technical Mechanics

Department 8:

AGST, J., Metallurgy
DIETZEL, G., Foundry Materials
FRANKE, E.-P., Metallurgy
GESELL, W., Foundry Operation
HASENKOX, H., Science of Metals
HERRN, P., Science of Metals
VON KAMPTZ, H. T., Glass Technology
JAEGER, E., Foundry Operation
LEMPER, H.-O., Plastics
QUADE, G., Metallurgy
SANGER, F., Plastics
STAHLHACKE, W., Foundry Materials

Department 9:

CONFURIUS, H.-W., Electromechanical Construction
DICKOPP, G., Communications
FISCHER, W., Electrical Energy
FRANK, P., Surveying
FRITZ, W., Electrical Energy
GEISSELHARDT, W., Manufacturing
HEIME, K., Electrical Energy
HENKEL, B., Electrical Surveying
KAYSER, G.-A., Communications

KUBALEK, E., Electrotechnical Materials
LUCK, H., Communications
MANN, H., High Frequency Technology
RASQUIN, W., Electrical Energy Transmission
RUMPEL, D., Electrical Engineering
SCHÜRMANN, H., Electrical Energy Transmission
SCHULTE, K., Electrical Energy Technology
SELBACH, G., Technical Management
WAGNER, H.-G., General and Theoretical Electrotechnics
WENDT, K., Electro-acoustics
WOLFF, I., General and Theoretical Electrotechnics

Department 10:
BORN,, G., Physics
HARREIS, H., Physics
HEBER, G., Theory of Physics
MITBAUER, H., Applied Physics
MÖNCH, W., Experimental Physics
PFANNES, H.-D., Applied Physics
PUTZER, D., Applied Physics
SANFLEBER, H., Technology
USADEL, K., Theory of Physics
WASSERMANN, E., Experimental Physics
WEINHOLD, W., Physics
WERHEIT, H., Experimental Physics
WERNER, E., Building Techniques

Department 11 (Mathematics):
ARNOLD, H.-J.
BAUER, J.
EBERHARD, W.
EBERSOLDT, F.
GERNER, H.
HAUSSMANN, W.
LEPPIG, M.
MOHN, K.-H.
PITTNAUER, F.
SCHLECHTWEG, H.
SIMM, G.
TÖRNER, G.
WAGNER, K.
WIEGMANN, K.-W.

UNIVERSITÄT DÜSSELDORF

4000 DÜSSELDORF,
UNIVERSITÄTSSTRASSE 1
Telephone: 3111.

Founded 1965; formerly Medizinische Akademie, f. 1907.

State control; Language of instruction: German; Academic year: Summer, April to September, Winter, October to March.

Rector: Prof. Dr. P. HÜTTENBERGER.
Pro-Rector: Prof. Dr. H. W. SCHLIPKÖTER.
Chancellor: Dr. C. F. CURTIUS.
Head of Student Secretariat: H. WONSAK.
Librarian: Prof. Dr. G. GATTERMANN.

Library: *see* Libraries.
Number of teachers: *c.* 1,200.
Number of students: 12,500.

Publications: *Personen- und Vorlesungsverzeichnis*† (twice yearly), *Universitätszeitung*† (5 times yearly), *Jahrbuch der Universität*† (annual), *Amtliche Bekanntmachungen*† (4 times a year).

DEANS:

Faculty of Mathematics and Natural Sciences: Prof. Dr. J. UHLENBUSCH.
Faculty of Philosophy: Prof. Dr. G. KAISER.
Faculty of Medicine: Prof. Dr. M. STRASSBURG.

PROFESSORS:

Faculty of Mathematics and Natural Sciences:
BASUCH, R., Theoretical Physics
BERGMANN, A., Mathematics
BIRKOFER, L., Organic Chemistry
DECKER, G., Experimental Physics
DÖRING, B., Applied Mathematics
GERSTENHAUER, A., Geography
HEBER, U., Botany
HESS, O., General Biology
HUSTON, J. P., Psychology
JANKE, W., Psychology
JANSSEN, H.-K., Theoretical
KLINGER, H., Statistics and Documentation
KRANZ, J., Applied Physics
KRAUTH, J., Psychology
KUCHEN, W., Inorganic Chemistry
LARENZ, R.-W., Theoretical Physics
LIPPOLD, B., Pharmaceutical Technology
MEISE, R., Mathematics
MÖHRLE, H., Pharmacy
MOOTZ, D., Molecular Chemistry and Inorganic Chemistry
OTTO, A., Experimental Physics
PERKAMPUS, H.-H., Physical Chemistry
PETERS, W., Zoology
PETRY, W., Instrumental Mathematics
ROTHER, K., Geography
SAHM, H., Biotechnology
SANTARIUS, K. A., Botany
SCHMIDTKE, H.-H., Theoretical Chemistry
SCHNEIDER, G., Zoology
SCHUBERT, H., Mathematics
STEFFEN, K., Mathematics
STEINBERG, H. G., Geography
STUBBE, W., Botany
SUCHY, K., Theoretical Physics
UHLENBUSCH, J., Experimental Physics
WILLUHN, G., Pharmaceutical Biology

Faculty of Philosophy:
ANTON, H., Modern German Literature
BENNING, H. A., English Literature
DIEMER, A., Philosophy
HARDACH, K., Economic History
HIESTAND, R., Medieval History
HÖFLER, M., Romance Philology
HÜTTENBERGER, P., Modern History
KAISER, G., Ancient German Literature
KIENAST, D., Ancient History
KRAMP, W., Education
KRUMM, V., Education
LENGELER, R., English Literature
MOMMSEN, W. J., Modern History
MÜLLER, K., Modern History
MÜNCH, R., Social Science
NICKEL, H., Developmental and Educational Psychology
NIES, F., Romance Philology
OPELT, I., Classical Philology
RAUTER, H., English and American Literature
SCHRADER, L., Romance Philology
SCHULTE HERBRUGGEN, H., English Literature
STÖTZEL, G., German Philology and Linguistics
WEHLE, G., Education
WINDFUHR, M., Modern German Literature
WUNDERLI, P., Romance Philology
WUNDERLICH, D., General Linguistics

Faculty of Medicine:
ARNOLD, G., Anatomy
BECK, L., Obstetrics and Gynaecology
BIRCKS, W., Surgery
BOCK, W., Neurosurgery
BÖTTGER, H., Dentistry
BREMER, H.-J., Paediatrics
BRÜSTER, H. T., Paediatrics and Haematology
DETTMAR, H., Surgery and Urology
FEINENDEGEN, L. E., Nuclear Medicine
VON FERBER, C., Medical Sociology
FREUND, H.-J., Neurology
GOSLAR, H. G., Anatomy
GREEFF, K., Pharmacology and Toxicology
GREITHER, A., Dermatology and Venerology
GRIES, F. A., Internal Medicine
HAASE, J., Physiology
VON HARNACK, Paediatrics
HEIGL-EVERS, A., Psychotherapy
HEINRICH, K., Psychiatry
HOPF, A., Brain Research and Anatomy
HORT, W., General Pathology and Pathological Anatomy
JANSEN, Industrial Medicine
JESDINSKY, H. J., Medical Statistics and Biomathematics
KAUFMANN, R., Clinical Physiology
KREMER, K., Surgery
KRÜSKEMPER, H.-L., Internal Medicine
LOOGEN, F., Internal Medicine, Cardiology
NAUMANN, P., Microbiology and Virology
OHNESORGE, F. K., Toxicology and Pharmacology
PAU, H., Optics
REINAUER, H., Clinical Biochemistry
RICK, W., Clinical Chemistry
RÖHRBORN, G., Human Genetics and Anthropology
ROSENBAUER, K., Anatomy
SCHADEWALDT, H., History of Medicine
SCHLIPKÖTER, H.-W., Hygiene
SCHMIDT, E., Paediatrics
SCHNEIDER, W., Internal Medicine
SCHÜBEL, F., Dentistry
SCHULITZ, K.-P., Orthopaedics
SCHWEITZER, H., Forensic Medicine
STAIB, W., Physiological Chemistry and Biochemistry
STEINGRÜBER, H.-J., Medical Psychology
STRASSBURG, M., Dentistry
STROHMEYER, G., Internal Medicine
VIETEN, H., Rontgenology and Medical Radiology
VOGELL, W., Biophysics and Electronmicroscopy
VOSTEEN, K.-H., Oto-rhino-laryngology
WECHSLER, W., Neuropathology
WEISE, W., Dentistry
ZIMMERMANN, H., Internal Medicine, Metabology and Dietetics
ZINDLER, M., Anaesthesiology

ATTACHED INSTITUTES:

Medizinisches Institut für Umwelthygiene (*Environmental Health Research*): Düsseldorf, Gurlittstr. 53; f. 1962; 97 mems.; Dir. Prof. Dr. med. H.-W. SCHLIPKÖTER.

Diabetes-Forschungsinstitut an der Universität Düsseldorf: 4 Düsseldorf, Auf'm Hennekamp 65; Dirs. Prof. Dr. F. A. GRIES, Prof. Dr. H. REINAUER.

Institut für Biotechnologie an der Kernforschungsanlage Jülich GmbH: 517 Jülich; Dir.-Prof. Dr. H. SAHM.

Institut für Ernährung und Diätetik: 4 Düsseldorf, Moorenstr. 5; Dir. Prof. Dr. H. ZIMMERMANN.

Institut für Medizin an der Kernforschungsanlage Jülich GMBH: 517 Jülich; Dir. Prof. Dr. L. FEINENDEGEN.

Deutsches Krankenhausinstitut: 4 Düsseldorf, Tersteegenstr. 9; Dir. Prof. Dr. EICHHORN.

KATHOLISCHE UNIVERSITÄT EICHSTÄTT

D-8833 EICHSTÄTT,
OSTENSTRASSE 26-28
Telephone: (08421) 201.

Founded 1972 by amalgamation of former Philosophisch-Theologische Hochschule and Pädagogische Hochschule.

President: Prof. Dr. RUDOLF MOSIS.
Chancellor: CARL HEINZ JACOB.
Librarian: Dr. HERMANN HOLZBAUER.

Library of 550,000 vols.
Number of teachers: 159.
Number of students: 1,500.
Publications: *Eichstätter Hochschulreden*† (6 a year), *Vorlesungsverzeichnis*† (2 a year).

DEANS:

Faculty of Catholic Theology: Prof. Dr. theol. PHILIPP KAISER.
Faculty of Philosophy and Education: Prof. Dr. med. Dr. phil. RUDOLF KAUSEN.
Faculty of Arts: Prof. Dr. phil. WINFRIED WEHLE.
Faculty of History and Social Sciences: Prof. Dr. phil. HEINZ HÜRTEN.
Faculty of Mathematics and Geography: Prof. Dr. rer. nat. HELMUT STINGL.
Faculty of Religious Education: Prof. Dr. theol. RUDOLF HASENSTAB.
Faculty of Social Studies: Prof. Dr. phil. HORST SING.

PROFESSORS:

Faculty of Catholic Theology:
BAUCH, A., Church History and Christian Art
BAUMGARTNER, K., Pastoral Theology
BEHRINGER, J., Natural Philosophy
DÖRR, F., Systematic Philosophy
EDMAIER, A., Practical Philosophy and History of Philosophy
ELSÄSSER, A., Moral Theology
FLEISCHMANN, A., Pastoral Theology
GLÄSSER, A., Fundamental Theology
HELLER, A., Religious Teaching and Catechetics
HÜBNER, R., Church History and Patristics
KAISER, P., Philosophy
KÜRZINGER, J., New Testament
LODUCHOWSKI, H., Religious Teaching and Catholic Theology
MATTES, A., Christian Spirituality and Homiletics
MAYER, B., New Testament
MOSIS, R., Old Testament
OTT, L., Dogmatics
REHM, M., Old Testament
REITER, E., Medieval and Modern Church History
SEYBOLD, M., Dogmatics

Faculty of Philosophy and Education:
HISCHER, E., Social Pedagogics
KAUSEN, R., Psychology
KNOPP, W., History of Art
KRAUS, J., Pedagogics
NEUKUM, J., Didactics
PAULIG, P., Pedagogics in Schools
PROKOP, E., Adult Education
SCHLEISSHEIMER, B., Philosophy
TSCHAMLER, H., General Pedagogics
UNVERRICHT, H., History of Music
WEHNER, E. G., Psychology

Faculty of Arts:
BAMMESBERGER, A., English Linguistics
BLAICHER, G., English Literature
GSELL, O., Romance Languages
HAGENBÜCHLE, R., American Literature
HUBER, W., German Philology
HUNFELD, H., Teaching of English
KRAFFT, P., Classical Philology
NIGGL, G., German Literature
RENK, H. E., Teaching of German Language and Literature
WEHLE, W., Romance Literature

Faculty of History and Social Sciences:
DICKERHOF, H., Medieval History
FINA, K., History and its Teaching
HÜRTEN, H., Modern and Contemporary History
LUTHE, H. O., Sociology
ROSEN, K., Ancient History
SUTOR, B., Didactics of Social Education
WITETSCHEK, H., Political Science

Faculty of Mathematics and Geography:
GRÖTZBACH, E., Geography
STINGL, H., Geography

Faculty of Religious Education (vocational courses):
BÄRENZ, R., Pastoral Discourse and Theological Ethnics
BURGEY, F., Theology, Philosophy
HASENSTAB, R., Theological Ethics and Fundamental Theology
HERTLE, V., Religious Teaching and Catechetics
HILBER, W., Pedagogics
LOUIS, B., Psychology
RENKER, J., Theory and Practice of Church Work
SALLER, M., Dogmatics
SEIFERMANN, H., Old Testament
WIMMER, G., Church History and New Testament
WOLF, M., Music and Voice Training

Faculty of Social Studies (vocational courses):
BABINSKY, G., Sociology
BECHER, H., Sociology
DORSCHEL, P., Law
GÖPPNER, H.-J., Psychology
KREISSL, R., Social Work
MERKEL, C. M., Psychology
SING, H., Political Science
SPANHEL, D., Pedagogics
WEHRL, F., History and German Literature

FRIEDRICH-ALEXANDER-UNIVERSITÄT ZU ERLANGEN-NÜRNBERG

8520 ERLANGEN,
SCHLOSSPLATZ 4
Telephone: (09131) 851.

Founded 1743; merged with Universität Altdorf 1809.

President: Prof. N. FIEBIGER.
Vice-Presidents: Prof. H. KÖSSLER, Prof. G. WANKE.
Chancellor: KURT KÖHLER.
Librarian: Dr. B. SINOGOWITZ.

Number of teachers: 570, including 222 Ordinary Professors.
Number of students: 18,300.
Publications: *Unikurier—Informationsorgan der Friedrich-Alexander-Universität, Jahresbibliographie und Forschungsbericht, Personal- und Vorlesungsverzeichnis, Erlanger Bausteine zur fränkischen Heimatforschung, Erlanger Forschungen, Geologische Blätter für Nordost-Bayern und angrenzende Gebiete, Jahrbuch für fränkische Landesforschung, Sitzungsberichte der Physikalisch-Medizinischen Societät zu Erlangen.*

DEANS:

Faculty of Theology: Prof. Dr. K. BEYSCHLAG.
Faculty of Law: Prof. Dr. K. H. GÖSSEL.
Faculty of Medicine: Prof. Dr. W. KERSTEN.
Faculty of Philosophy, History and Social Sciences: Prof. Dr. H. WINTERSTEIN.
Faculty of Languages and Literatures: Prof. Dr. P. KLOPSCH.
Faculty of Mathematics and Physics: Prof. Dr. E. FINCKH.
Faculty of Economic and Social Sciences: Prof. Dr. M. MEYER.
Faculty of Technology: Prof. Dr. H. NIEMANN.
Faculty of Education: Prof. Dr. M. LIEDTKE.
Faculty of Biology and Chemistry: Prof. Dr. E. NÜRNBERG.
Faculty of Geosciences: Prof. Dr. M. BAUSCH.

PROFESSORS:

Faculty of Theology:
BEYSCHLAG, K., Historical Theology
FOHRER, G., Old Testament
JOEST, W., Systematic and New Testament Theology
KLAUS, B., Practical Theology
KUTSCH, E., Old Testament Theology
LILIENFELD, F. VON, Theology of the Christian East
MERK, O., New Testament
MILDENBERGER, F., Systematic Theology
MORITZEN, N.-P., Ecumenical Theology, Science of Missions and Religion
MÜLLER, G., Historical Theology
POSCHARSKY, P., Christian Archaeology and History of Art
ROLOFF, J., New Testament
SEITZ, M., Pastoral Theology
STAEDTKE, J., Reformed Theology

Faculty of Law:
ARZT, G., Penal and Criminal Law
BARTLSPERGER, R., State and Administrative Law
BLOMEYER, W., Private, Commercial, Labour and Comparative Law
GÖSSEL, K. H., Penal and Criminal Law
HERRMANN, J., Roman and German Common Law

HUBMANN, H., Common, International, Commercial Law, Philosophy of Law
LEISER, W., German and Bavarian Legal History and Civic Law
LEISNER, W., National Administrative and International Law
OBERMAYER, K., Church, State and Administrative Law
SCHWAB, K. H., Civil Law
ZIPPELIUS, R., Civil Administrative and Canon Law

Faculty of Medicine:
BACHMANN, K., Internal Medicine
BECKER, V., Pathological Anatomy
BRAND, K., Physiological Chemistry
DEMLING, L., Internal Medicine
ESTLER, C.-J., Toxicology and Chemotherapy
FLECKENSTEIN, B., Virology
FLEISCHER-PETERS, A., Orthodontics
GALL, F., Surgery
GRÄF, W., Hygiene and Bacteriology
HOFMANN, M., Dentistry
HOHMANN, D., Orthopaedics
HORBACH, I., Biomathematics, Medical Statistics, Documentation and Data Processing
HORNSTEIN, O., Dermatology, Venerology
KALDEN, J. R., Immunology and Rheumatology
KEIDEL, W.-D., Physiology
KERSTEN, W., Physiological Chemistry
KESSLER, M., Physiology and Cardiology
KNAPP, W., Hygiene and Microbiology
KRÖNCKE, A., Dentistry
OBER, K.-G., Obstetrics
PAULY, H., Biophysics
PFEIFFER, R. A., Human Genetics and Anthropology
PLATT, D., Gerontology
ROHEN, J. W., Human Morphology and Embryology
RÜGHEIMER, E., Anaesthetics
SAUER, R., Radiotherapy
SCHEIFFARTH, F., Internal Medicine
SCHIEFER, W., Neurosurgery
SCHRECK, E., Optics
SIGEL, A., Urology
SIMMER, H. H., History of Medicine
STEHR, K., Paediatrics
STEINHÄUSER, E., Dentistry
VALENTIN, H., Social and Industrial Medicine
WIECK, H., Neurology, Psychiatry
WIGAND, M. E., Oto-Rhino-Laryngology
WOLF, F., Nuclear Medicine
WUERMELLING, H.-B., Forensic Medicine

Faculty of Philosophy, History and Social Sciences:
BECKMANN, H. K., Education
DIWALD, H., History
ENDRES, R., History
FREUND, GISELLA, Pre- and Early History
GANSLANDT, H. R., Political Science
GEBHARDT, J., Political Science
GOEZ, W., Medieval and Contemporary History
HOSS, J., History
JASPER, G., Politics
KLUXEN, K., Modern History
LORENZEN, P., Philosophy
MANGOLD, W., Sociology
MATTHES, J., Sociology
PARLASCA, K., Classical Archaeology
RIEDEL, M., Philosophy
RUFFMANN, K.-H., East European History
RUHNKE, M., Music
RUMPEL, H., History
RUPPRECHT, B., History of Art
SCHOEPS, H. J., Religion and Philosophy
STÜRMER, M., Medieval and Modern History
SÜNKEL, W., Education
TOMAN, W., Psychology
WENDEHORST, A., Bavarian and Frankish History
WERBIK, H., Psychology
WERNER, R., Ancient History
WINTERSTEIN, H., Politics

Faculty of Languages and Literatures:
BERTAU, K., Germanic Philology
BONATH, G., German
BRUNNER, H., German
FISCHER, W., Oriental Philology
FÜLLEBORN, U., Modern German Literature
HEYDENREICH, T., Romance Philology
HOFFMANN, K., Comparative Indo-european Linguistics
HÖLTGEN, K., English Philology
KLOPSCH, P., Middle Latin Philology
LANG, H.-J., North-American Philology and Cultural History
LIPPERT, Chinese
MÜNSKE, H.-H., German
NARTEN, J., Classical Philology
NEUMANN, G., Modern German Literature
POLLMANN, L., Romance Philology
SCHÜTZ, J., Slavonic Philology
STEFENELLI, A., Romance Philology
STIEWE, K., Classical Philology
VOITL, H., English Philology
WÖLFEL, K., Modern German Literature
WOLFF, E., English Philology

Faculty of Mathematics:
BARTH, W., Mathematics
BAUER, H., Mathematics
BERENS, H., Applied Mathematics
BURZLAFF, H., Crystallography
CHRISTIANSEN, J., Experimental Physics
DEJON, B., Applied Mathematics
FIEBIGER, N., Experimental Physics
FINCKH, E., Experimental Physics
GEYER, E.-D., Mathematics
HOFMANN, A., Physics
HUBER, M., Nuclear Physics
ISCHENKO, G., Physics
JACOBS, K., Mathematical Statistics
KÖLZOW, D., Mathematics
LOHMANN, A., Applied Optics
MÜLLER, K., Solid State Physics
RAHE, J., Astronomy
SCHULZ, M., Applied Physics
STRAMBACH, K., Mathematics
WEGENER, H., Experimental Physics
WEINITSCHKE, Applied Mathematics

Faculty of Biology and Chemistry:
ARNOLD, C. G., Botany and Pharmaceutical Biology
BEHRENS, H., Inorganic and General Chemistry
BESTMANN, H. J., Organic Chemistry
BRODERSEN, K., Inorganic and Analytic Chemistry
DANN, O., Applied Chemistry
HAUPT, W., Botany
HELVERSEN-HELVERSHEIM, O. VON., Zoology
HEUMANN, W., Microbiology
JAENICKE, W., Physical Chemistry
KESSLER, E., Botany
LADIK, J., Theoretical Chemistry
NÜRNBERG, E., Pharmaceutical Technology
SCHLEYER, P. VON RAGNÉ, Organic Chemistry
SCHWEIZER, E., Biochemistry
SEITZ, G., Neurophysiology
SIEWING, R., Zoology
WEDLER, G., Physical Chemistry

Faculty of Geosciences:
FLÜGEL, E., Palaeontology
GROISS, J. TH., Palaeontology
HABBE, K. A., Geography
HÜTTEROTH, W.-D., Geography
KÜHNE, I., Geography
KUZEL, H.-J., Mineralogy
NOLLAU, G., Geology and Mineralogy
SCHWAB, R., Geology and Mineralogy
SCHWAN, W., Geology
TICHY, F., Geography
WIRTH, E., Geography
ZEISS, Palaeontology

Faculty of Economic and Social Sciences:
BERKE, R., Pedagogics
BEREKOVEN, L., Business Economics
BUTTLER, G., Statistics
DÜRR, E., Economics
EICHHORN, P., Business Administration
FRANKE, J., Psychology, Social Psychology
HAHN, O., Banking and Insurance
HEIGL, A., Business Economics
HELM, J., Public and Private Law
HENKE, W., National and Administrative Law
HEUSS, E., Economics
KELLENBENZ, H., Economic and Social History
KLAUS, J., Economics
MERTENS, P., Business Economics
MEYER, M., Business Economics
NEUMANN, M., Political Economics
PAGENSTECHER, U., Statistics and Social Sciences
PFEIFFER, W., Business Economics
RECKTENWALD, H. O., Economics
RITTER, W., Economic and Social Geography
RONNEBERGER, F., Political Science
SCHÄFER, W., Anglo-Saxon Language and Culture
SCHICK, W., German and International Taxation Law
SCHNEEBERGER, H., Statistics
SPECHT, K. G., Sociology
STEGER, H.-A., Romance Languages and Foreign Culture
STEINMANN, H., Economics
WEIGT, E., Social Science

Faculty of Technology:
BRAND, H., High Frequency Techniques
EUTENEUER, C.-A., Fluid Dynamics
HÄNDLER, W., Mathematical Machines and Data Processing
HERZOG, U., Mathematical Machines and Data Processing
HOFMANN, F., Operating Systems
HOFMANN, H., Technical Chemistry
HOSEMANN, G., Energy Techniques
ILSCHNER, B., Materials Science, General Material Properties
KAESCHE, H., Corrosion
KLAPP, E., Mechanical Engineering
LEEB, K., Automatic Theory and Formal Languages
MERTENS, P., Computing and Planning Systems
MOLERUS, O., Mechanical Engineering
MÜLLER, H., Mathematical Machines and Data Processing
NIEMANN, H., Mathematical Machines and Data Processing
OEL, H. J., Raw Materials
PETER, S., Technical Chemistry
PFAFF, G., Electrical Engineering
SCHLITT, H., Regulation Techniques
SCHNEIDER, H.-J., Programming Languages
SCHÜSSLER, H.-W., Communication Techniques
SCHWARZL, F., Raw Materials
SEITZER, D., Technical Electronics
UNBEHAUEN, R., Electrical Engineering

WEISS, H., Raw Materials
ZWICKER, H. U., Materials Science, Metals Technology

Faculty of Education:
ASSEL, H.-G., Political Science
BRANDTSTÄDTER, J., Psychology
BRECHTKEN, J., Catholic Theology
FISCHER, W. L., Mathematics Teaching
FUCKNER, H., Geography
FÜRNROHR, W., History Teaching
GLÖCKEL, H., Education
HIERDEIS, H., Education
KÖHLER, H., Lutheran Theology
KÖSSLER, H., Philosophy
LIEDTKE, M., Education
LIENERT, G., Psychology
RABENSTEIN, R., Elementary Education

UNIVERSITÄT ESSEN-GESAMTHOCHSCHULE

4300 ESSEN,
UNIVERSITÄTSSTRASSE 2,
POSTFACH 6843
Telephone: 0201/1831.
Founded 1972.

State control; Academic year: January to March, April to September.

Rector: Prof. Dr. PETER NEUMANN-MAHLKAU.
Chancellor: Dr. DIETER LEUZE.
Co-Rector (Administration): Prof. Dipl.-Ing. WOLFGANG THOMAS.
Co-Rector (Academic): Prof. Dr. K. D. BÜNTING.
Co-Rector (Research): Prof. Dr. H. G. SCHMITT.
Librarian: Dr. AHMED HELMI HELAL.

Number of teachers: 391.
Number of students: 10,800.

Publications: *Amtliche Bekanntmachungen*†, *GH-Integrale*.

DEPARTMENTS AND DEANS:

Philosophy, Religious Studies and Sociology: Prof. Dr. L. NIETHAMMER.
Educational Sciences: Prof. Dr. HANS HEID.
Languages and Literature: Prof. Dr. E. LEHMANN.
Art and Design: Stud.-Prof. H. A. HEINDRICHS.
Economic Sciences: Prof. Dr. F. BISANI.
Mathematics: Prof. Dr. H. WALK.
Theoretical Medicine: Prof. Dr. H. SCHRIEFERS.
Practical Medicine: Prof. Dr. CH. REIDEMEISTER.
Architecture, Bio- and Geosciences: Prof. Dipl.-Ing. P. HILLIGES.
Construction Engineering: Prof. Dipl.-Ing. R. RÜBENER.
Mechanical Engineering: Prof. Dipl.-Ing. G. WYCISK.
Energy, Systems and Electrotechnology: Prof. Dr. F. STEIMLE.
Surveying: Prof. Dipl.-Ing. K. HERTEL.
Physics: Prof. Dr. R. GRAHAM.
Chemistry: Prof. Dr. F. BANDERMANN.

JOHANN WOLFGANG GOETHE-UNIVERSITÄT FRANKFURT

6000 FRANKFURT AM MAIN,
SENCKENBERGANLAGE 31
Telephone: 7981.
Founded 1914.

Academic year: October to September (2 semesters).

President: Prof. Dr. H. KELM.
Chancellor: G. STROBEL.
Librarian: K.-D. LEHMANN.

Number of teachers: *c.* 1,800, including 583 professors.

Number of students: *c.* 23,000.

Publications: *Vorlesungs u. Personenverzeichnis*, *Studienführer*, *Rechenschaftsbericht* (annually), *Uni-Report* (fortnightly in term-time).

DEANS:

Department of Law: Prof. H. JÄGER.
Department of Economics: Prof. G. GEHRIG.
Department of Social Science: Prof. H. BOSSE.
Department of Education: Prof. P. RÖTHIG.
Department of Psychology: Prof. H. M. TRAUTNER.
Department of Religious Studies: Prof. H. RÖHR.
Department of Philosophy: Prof. U. ALTWICKER.
Department of History: Prof. E.-H. GREFE.
Department of Classical Languages and Arts: Prof. O. SCHÜTZ.
Department of Modern Languages: Prof. K. GARSCHA.
Department of East European and Non-European Languages and Cultures: Prof. A. GOLDBERG.
Department of Mathematics: Prof. H. BEHR.
Department of Physics: Prof. W. MARTIENSSEN.
Department of Chemistry: Prof. M. WILK.
Department of Biochemistry and Pharmacy: Prof. G. SCHNEIDER.
Department of Biology: Prof. H.-M. JAHNS.
Department of Geo-Sciences: Prof. M. KOREKAWA.
Department of Geography: Prof. K. VORLAUFER.
Department of Human Medicine: Prof. H. J. MÜLLER.
Department of Information Science: Prof. G. MÜLLER.
Department of Economics: Prof. W. MÜLLER.

PROFESSORS:

Department of Law:
ARNDT, K. F., Administrative Sciences and Common Law
COING, H., Roman and Civil Law
DENNINGER, E., Common Law
DIESTELKAMP, B., Civil Law and Legal History
DILCHER, G., History of German Law, Canon and Civil Law
GEERDS, F., Criminology, Penal Law and Procedure
GILLES, P., Legal Procedure, Civil and Comparative Law
HASSEMER, W., Theory of Law
KOHL, H., Civil Law
JÄGER, H., Criminal Law
JAENICKE, G., Public Law
KÜBLER, F., Economic and Civil Law
LOEWENHEIM, U., Civil, Commercial and Industrial Law
LÜDERSSEN, K., Criminal Law
MERTENS, H., Civil Law, Commercial Law, Comparative Law and International Private Law
MEYER, H., Public Law
NAUCKE, W., Criminal Law
PAUL, W., Legal Theory and Methodology
REHBINDER, E., Business, Civil, International Private Law
RUHWEDEL, E., Civil, Industrial and Labour Law
SCHMIDT, W., Public Law
SIMITIS, S., Industrial and Civil Law
SIMON, D., Roman and Civil Law
STAFF, I., Criminal Law
STOLLEIS, M., Public Law
TROJE, H. E., Roman Law, History of German Law
WEISS, M., Business and Civil Law
WEYERS, H.-L., Civil Law
WIETHÖLTER, R., Civil, Industrial and Economic Law
WOLF, M., Civil Law
WOLFF, E. A., Criminal Law
ZULEEG, M., Civil, European and Common Law

Department of Economics:
ABB, F., Political Economics
BARTELS, N., Industrial Economics
CZAYKA, L., Political Science
ENGELS, W., Economic Management, especially Bank Management
FLEISCHMANN, G., Political Economics
GÄBLER, J., Political Economy
GEHRIG, G., Economics
GROHMANN, H., Statistics
GÜMBEL, R., Economic Management, especially Commerce
HANSEN, G., Statistics
HÄUSER, K., Political Economy
HAUSER, R., Social Legislation
HOCHSTÄDTER, D., Statistics
KAAS, U., Industrial Economics
KASTEN, H., Political Economy
KLAVEREN, J. J. VAN, History of Economics and Social Science
KOLBECK, R., Business Economics
KOSTA, H. G., Theory
KREIKEBAUM, H., Business Economics
KRUPP, H.-J., Social Legislation and Political Science
LAUX, H., Business Economics
MEINHOLD, H., Political Economy
MEISSNER, W., Political Economics
MELLWIG, WINFRIED, Industrial Economics
MITSCHKE, J., Political and Industrial Accountancy
MOXTER, A., Industrial Economy
MÜLLER, G., Programming
NIEDEREICHHOLZ, J., Business Economics
RIEBEL, P., Economics
RITTER, U., Political Science
ROMMELFANGER, H., Mathematics for Economists
RUDOLPH, B., Business Management
SCHEFOLD, B., Political Economy
TANGERMANN, ST., Agrarian Politics
TIETZ, R., Political Economy

WITTMANN, W., Industrial Economics
WURDACK, E., Politics (Education)

Department of Sociology:

BOSSE, H., Theory of Socialization
BRANDT, G., Sociology
BREDE, H., Regional Town and Community Research
CLEMENZ, M., Sociology of Education
COMBE, A., Sociology
CZEMPIEL, E.-O., Political Science
FETSCHER, I., Political Science
GRESS, F., Political Education
HENNIG, E., Mass Communication
HIRSCH, J., Political Education
HOFMANN, G., Methods of Social Research, Statistics
HONDRICH, K. O., Sociology
JAHN, E., Socio-economic Structure
KÜCHLER, M., Statistical Methods
KUHN, H. W., Political Education
LORENZER, A., Sociology
MANS, D., Methods of Social Research
MUELLER, H., Sociology
NICKLAS, H., Political Science
NITZSCHKE, V., Didactics
OEVERMANN, U., Sociology, Social Psychology
RITSERT, J., Sociology
SANDMANN, F., Didactics
SCHMIDT, L., Political Education
SCHUMM, W., Sociology
SHELL, K., Political Education
SOCHATZY, K., Sociology of Education
STEINERT, H., Sociology
VOGEL, R., Sociology of Education
WENZEL, U., Sociology and Social Psychiatry

Department of Education:

BALLREICH, R., Physical Education
BECK-SCHLEGEL, G., Primary Education
BECKER, E., Education
BECKER, H., Pedagogics
BETHKE, H., Education
BÖHME, G., History of Education
BÖHMER, D., Physical Education
BOLSCHO, D., Primary Education
BRAKEMEIER-LISOP, I., Economic Pedagogics
DEPPE, H., Special Education
DIEDERICH, J., Teacher Training
DIGEL, H., Physical Education
ECKEL, K., Secondary Education
ELZER, H.-M., Education
HAARMANN, D., Primary Teacher Training
HAASE, H., Sports
HORN, H., Primary Teacher Training
HORTLEDER, G., Sociology of Sports
IBEN, G., Health and Special Education
JACOBS, K., Special and Remedial Education
JÜTTEN, D., Education
KALLERT, H., Pedagogics
KRENZER, R., General Education
KUHLOW, A., Teacher Training
LEBER, A., Health Education and Psychology
LINGELBACH, K., Pedagogics
MEIER, R., Primary Teacher Training
NYSSEN, F., Teacher Training
RADIGK, W., Health Education
REISER, H., Education
ROETHIG, P., Physical Education
RUMPF, H., General Education
SCHRIEWER, J., Comparative Education
SCHWARTZ, E., Primary School Training
TENORTH, H.-E., Educational Theory and Methodology
WARWEL, K., Teacher Training
ZANDER, H., Education

Department of Psychology:

ARGELANDER, H., Psychoanalysis
BAUER, W., General Psychology
BURKARDT, F., Applied Psychology
DEGENHARDT, A., Diagnostic Psychology
DEUSINGER, I., Psychology
GIESEN, H., Educational Psychology
HEINERTH, K., Educational Psychology
HERRIG, G., Educational Psychology
KUTTER, P., Psychoanalysis
MATTHAEI, F. K., Educational Psychology
MOOSBRUGGER, H., Psychological Methodology, Statistics
OESTREICH, G., Educational Psychology
PFEIFFER, H., Educational Psychology
PREISER, S., Educational Psychology
SARRIS, V., Psychology
SCHWANENBERG, E., Psychoanalysis
SENNEWALD, H., Educational Psychology
SUELLWOLD, F., Psychology
TRAUTNER, H., Clinical Psychology
WERTHMANN, H.-V., Psychoanalysis
ZOLTOBROCKI, J., Psychology

Department of Religious Studies:

BARTSCH, H.-W., Evangelical Theology
DENINGER, J., Philosophy of Religion
DENINGER-POLZER, G., Catholic Theology
HOFFMANN, J., Moral Theology, Social Ethics
KESSLER, H., Catholic Theology
PESCH, R., Catholic Theology
RASKE, M., Catholic Theology
ROEHR, H., Evangelical Theology
SCHMIDT, H., Evangelical Theology and Religious Pedagogy
SCHMIDT, H. P., Evangelical Theology
SCHOTTROFF, W., Evangelical Theology
SCHRÖDTER, H., Philosophy of Religion
SILLER, H., Catholic Theology and Teaching of Dogma
SPIEGEL, Y., Protestant Theology
STOODT, D., Evangelical Theology
WEBER, E., Evangelical Theology

Department of Philosophy:

ALTWICKER, N., Philosophy
APEL, K. O., Philosophy
BECKER, W., Philosophy
BUBNER, R., Philosophy
ESSLER, W., Philosophy, Logic and Educational Theory
KULENKAMPFF, A., Philosophy
RÖTTGES, H., Philosophy
SCHEER, B., Philosophy
SCHMIDT, A., Philosophy and Sociology

Department of History:

EHLERS, J., Medieval and Modern History
FISCHER, A., Modern History
GALL, L., Medieval and Modern History
GEMBRUCH, W., Medieval and Modern History
GREFE, E.-H., History Teaching
HABERLAND, E., Culture and Folklore
HAMMERSTEIN, N., Medieval and Modern History
JOCKENHÖVEL, A., Pre-history
KRONENBERG, A., Folklore
LAMMERS, W., Medieval and Modern History
LINDIG, W., Folklore
MÜLLER, K., Folklore
MÜLLER-KARPE, H., Pre-history
MUHLACK, U., General History
NIEDERQUELL, T., History Teaching
RADNOTI-ALFÖLDI, M., Ancient Numismatics
RUSCHENBUSCH, E., Ancient History
SCHWABE, K., Medieval and Modern History
SMOLLA, G., Pre-history
WENDE, P., Medieval and Modern History

Department of Classical Philology and Arts:

ABEL-STRUTH, S., Music Teaching
BERAN, T., Archaeology and History of Art
BRANDT, H.-J., Cinema
EIMER, G., History of Art
EISENBERGER, H., Classical Philology
FELGNER, K., Music Teaching
FINSCHER, L., Music
GREVERUS, I.-M., European Ethnology
HEILMANN, W., Classical Philology
HÖRNER, H., Classical Philology
HOFFMANN-ERBRECHT, L., Music
HORTSCHANSKY, K., Music
HUCKE, H., Music
KIEFER, A., Art Teaching
KIRSCH, W., Music
NEUMEISTER, C., Classical Philology
PRINZ, W., Medieval and Modern History of Art
RAHN, H., Classical Philology
SCHLINK, W., European History of Art
SCHÜTZ, O., Art Teaching
SPEMANN, W., Art Teaching
VON STEUBEN, H., Classical Archaeology
WEISMANTEL, G., Art Teaching
WIRTH, H. W., Fine Arts and Art Teaching

Department of Modern Languages:

ALTENHOFER, N., German
BAMBECK, M., Romance Philology
BOHN, V., Modern German
BRACKERT, H., German
BÜRGER, CH., German Language and Literature
CHRISTADLER, M., American
DEGENHARDT, I., German Language and Literature
DODERER, K., German Language and Literature
EULER, A., French Language and Literature
FIEDLER, L. M., Modern German
FISCHER-LICHTE, E., German Language and Literature
FREY, W., German
GARSCHA, K., Romance Philology
GOMPF, G., Teaching of English Language
HERRMANN, W., Teaching of German Language and Literature
HOFMANN, K., English
IVO, H., German Language and Literature
JEZIORKOWSKI, K., Modern German
KARNEIN, A., German
KELLER, U., English
KIMPEL, D., Modern German
KLEIN, H. G., Romance Philology
KLEIN, W., German Philology
KÖNNEKER, B., German
KÜHNEL, W., English and American
LENZ, G., English and American
LEPPER, G., German
MERKELBACH, V., German Language and Literature Teaching
METZNER, E., German
MITTENZWEI, I., Modern German
OSIENDORF, B., English and American Studies
QUETZ, J., English Teaching
RAITZ, W., History of German Literature
REICHERT, K., English/American Language
RIEMENSCHNEIDER, D., English
RÜTTEN, R., French Language and Literature
SCHÄFER, R., German Teaching
SCHARLAU, B., Romance Philology
SCHEIBLE, H., German Language and Literature
SCHLIEBEN-LANGE, B., Romance Philology, Linguistics
SCHLOSSER, H. D., German
SCHNEIDER, G., Romance Philology

VON SEE, K., Germanic Philology
SEITZ, D., German
SOLMECKE, G., Teaching of English Language
STAMMERJOHANN, H., French Teaching
STOLL, A., Romantic Literature
WEBER, G., Germanic and Scandinavian Philology
WEISE, W.-D., English Teaching
WELSLAU, E., Romance Philology
WUTHENOW, R.-R., German
ZIMMERMANN, H.-D., History of Modern German Literature

Department of East European and Non-European Languages and Cultures:
BRANDS, H., Turkish
CHANG, T.-T., Sinology
GOLDBERG, A., Hebrew Studies
HORBATSCH, O., Slavonic Languages
SELLHEIM, R., Oriental Studies
THOMAS, W., Indo-Germanic Languages
WERNST, P., Arabic
WODARZ, H., Phonetics and General Linguistics

Department of Mathematics:
ADASCH, N.
BAUER, F.-W.
BAUMEISTER, J. B., Optimum and Convex Functions
BEHR, H., Pure Mathematics
BLIEDTNER, J., Pure Mathematics
BOLTHAUSEN, E., Probability Theory and Statistics
BORGES, R.
BROSOWSKI, B.
BURDE, G.
CONSTANTINESCU, F.
DINGES, H., Probability Theory and Statistics
ENGEL, A.
GÜTING, R. K.
HOMAGK, F.
KULZE, R.
LUCKHARDT, H., Fundamental Mathematics
METZLER, W.
MÜLLER, K. H., Applied Mathematics
REICHERT, M.
RÖHRL, E.
SCHNORR, C., Applied Mathematics
SCHWARZ, W.
SIEVEKING, M., Applied Mathematics
STUMMEL, F., Applied and Instrumental Mathematics
WEIDMANN, J.
WOLFART, J.

Department of Physics:
BARTH, N., Didactics of Physics
BASS, R., Physics
BECKER, R., Applied Physics
BETHGE, K., Nuclear Physics
VON DECHEND, H., History of Science
DREIZLER, R., Theoretical Physics
ELZE, T., Nuclear Physics
GERHARDT, U., Physics
GRANZER, F., Physics
GREINER, W., Theoretical Physics
GROENEVELD, K.-O., Nuclear Physics
HAUG, H., Theoretical Physics
HILLENKAMP, F., Physics for Medical Students
HIRST, L. L., Theoretical Physics
JELITTO, R., Theoretical Physics
JUNG, W., Didactics of Physics
JUNIOR, P., Physics
KEGEL, W., Theoretical Physics
KLEIN, H., Applied Physics
KUMMER, J., Physics
LÜTHI, B., Experimental Physics
MARTIENSSEN, W., Experimental Physics
MARUHN, J., Theoretical Physics
MAUCK, G., Physics
MOHLER, E., Experimental Physics
MÜLLER, B., Theoretical Physics
POHLIT, W., Biophysics
RAUCH, F., Physics
SALTZER, W., History of Science
SCHAARSCHMIDT, A., Applied Physics
SCHLÖGL, R., Biophysics
SCHOPPER, E., Nuclear Physics
SCHUSTER, H., Theoretical Physics
SEZGIN, F., History of Science
STELZER, K., Physics
WÄCHTER, F., Experimental Physics
WELTNER, K., Didactics of Physics
WOLF, D., Physics

Department of Chemistry:
BECKER, F., Physical Chemistry
BOCK, H., Inorganic Chemistry
BRAUER, E., Physical Chemistry
BRAUER, H.-D., Chemistry
CHUN, H.-U., Physical Chemistry
COMES, F., Physical Chemistry
FRIES, E., Didactics of Chemistry
FRITZ, H.. Organic Chemistry
HARTMANN, H., Physical Chemistry
HENSEN, K., Inorganic and Theoretical Chemistry
HEYDTMANN, H., Physical Chemistry
KESSLER, H., Organic Chemistry
KÖNIG, K.-H., Inorganic and Analytical Chemistry
KOHLMAIER, G., Theoretical and Physical Chemistry
QUINKERT, G., Organic Chemistry
REHM, D., Physical and Organic Chemistry
REINSCH, E. A., Theoretical and Physical Chemistry
RIED, W., Organic Chemistry
ROESKY, H., Inorganic Chemistry
ROSENMUND, P., Inorganic Chemistry
SCHLEIP, A., Chemistry Teaching
STERZEL, W., Inorganic Chemistry
TEUBER, H.-J., Chemistry
TRÖMEL, M., Inorganic Chemistry
WILK, M., Organic Chemistry

Department of Biochemistry and Pharmacy:
FASOLD, H., Biochemistry
GLASL, H., Pharmaceutical Biology
HOFFMANN, H., Pharmaceutical Chemistry
LINDE, H., Pharmaceutical Chemistry
MUTSCHLER, E., Pharmacology
NIEBERGALL, H., Food Chemistry
OELSCHLÄGER, H., Pharmaceutical Chemistry
SCHNEIDER, G., Pharmacognosy
THOMA, K., Galenic Pharmacy

Department of Biology:
BARTH, F., Zoology
BEIER, W., Biology Teaching
BEREITER-HAHN, J., Cell Research
BRÄNDLE, K., Zoology
BRENDEL, M., Microbiology
BUTTERFASS, T., Botany
DÖHLER, G., Botany
FIEDLER, K., Zoology
GAHL, H., Biology Teaching
GIES, T., Biology Teaching
GNATZY, W., Zoology
HALBACH, U., Zoology
HELDMAIER, G., Zoology
HILGENBERG, W., Botany
JAHNS, H.-M., Botany
KAHL, G., Botany
KOHLENBACH, H.-W., Botany
KRANZ, A.-R., Botany
LANGE, H., Botany
LANGE, V., Human Genetics
LEISTIKOW, K.-U., Botany
LESCHIK, G., Biology Teaching
LÖTSCHERT, W., Botany
MASCHWITZ, U., Zoology
MENNIGMANN, H.-D., Microbiology
NEUWEILER, G., Zoology
PONS, F., Microbiology
PROTSCH, R., Anthropology
RHAESE, H.-J., Microbiology
RIED, A., Botany
ROSENSTOCK, G., Botany
RUTTNER, F., Zoology
SAUERLAND, H., Biology
SCHAUB, H., Botany
STEIGER, H., Microbiology
WILTSCHKO, W., Zoology
WINTER, C., Zoology
ZIEGLER, R., Botany

Department of Geosciences:
BARTL, H., Crystallography and Mineralogy
BERCKHEMER, H., Geophysics
BRINKMANN, W. L. F., Geophysics, Hydrology
FUESS, H., Mineralogy and Crystallography
VON GEHLEN, K., Petrology, Geochemistry and Stratigraphy
GEORGII, H.-W., Physics of the Atmosphere
HÄNEL, G., Meteorology
JACOBY, W., Geophysics
KOREKAWA, M., Crystallography and Mineralogy
KRUMM, H., Mineralogy and Petrology
MARTINI, E., Geology and Palaeontology
MURAWSKI, H., Geology
NAGEL, G., Geography
PLASS, W., Soil Science
SCHRÖDER, R., Palaeontology
SEMMEL, A., Geography
URBAN, H., Petrology and Stratigraphy
VOGEL, K.-P., Palaeontology
WINTER, J., Geology and Palaeontology
ZIGAN, F., Crystallography

Department of Geography:
ALBRECHT, V., Geography Teaching
FICK, K., Geography Teaching
FREUND, B., Cultural Geography
GRUBER, G., Geography
JÄGER, H., Geography Teaching
LAMPING, H., Economic Geography
LUTZ, W., Geography
MATZNETTER, J., Economic Geography
NIEMZ, H.-G., Geography Teaching
SEMMEL, A., Geography
SULGER, E., Geography Teaching
VORLAUFER, K., Geography
WERLE, O., Geography Teaching
WOLF, K., Cultural Geography

Department of Medicine:
ABRAHAM, R., Clinical Chemistry
ABT, K., Biomathematics
BALL, F., Paediatrics
BALZER, H., Pharmacology
BOCHNIK, H., Psychiatry
BREDDIN, H-K., Internal Medicine
BRETTEL, H-F., Forensic Medicine
BROCK, R., Industrial Medicine
CHANDRA, P., Therapeutic Biochemistry
CHOU, J. T., Biochemistry and Cytology
DEGENHARDT, K-H., Human Genetics
DEPPE, H.-U., Medical Sociology
DODEN, W., Ophthalmology
DUDZIAK, R., Anaesthesiology
DUFKOVÁ, J., Forensic Medicine
EHRLY, A., Internal Medicine
ENCKE, A., General and Abdominal Surgery
FISCHER, P., Neurology
FÖRSTER, H., Applied Biochemistry
FRENKEL, G., Maxillo-facial Surgery
FUCHS, H., Röntgenology
GEBAUER, A., Internal Medicine
GERCHOW, J., Forensic Medicine
GIERE, W., Documentation and Data Processing
GLÄTZNER, H., Obstetrics and Gynaecology
GROSS, W., Physiological Chemistry

HACKER, H., Neuro-radiology
HALBERSTADT, E., Obstetrics and Gynaecology
HARBAUER, H., Child Psychiatry
HEIPERTZ, W., Orthopaedics
HÖR, G., Nuclear Medicine
HÖVELS, O., Child Health
HOFMANN, D., Child Health
HOHMANN, W., Materials in Dentistry
HOHORST, H-J., Physiological Chemistry
HÜBNER, K., Pathology
VON ILBERG, CH., Oto-rhino-laryngology
JACOBI, G., Child Health
KAHLE, W., Neuropathology
KALTENBACH, M., Internal Medicine
KIRSTEN, R., Clinical Pharmacology
KLIMA, M., Anatomy
KLINKE, R., Physiology
KNOTHE, H., Hygiene and Bacteriology
KOBER, G., Cardiology
KOCH, K., Internal Medicine
KOLLATH, J., Radiation Medicine
KORNHUBER, B., Child Health
KRETER, F., Maxillo-facial Surgery
LACKO, L., Chemical Physiology
LEIBER, B., Child Health
LEMMER, B., Pharmacology
LEONHARDI, G., Physiology and Dermatology
LEUSCHNER, U., Gastroenterology
VON LOEWENICH, V., Child Health
VON LOH, D., Physiology
LORENZ, W., Radio-therapy
LUFF, K., Forensic Medicine
MAIER, W., Anatomy
MAKABE, R., Ophthalmology
MARTIN, H., Internal Medicine
MAY, G., Hygiene
MEIER-SYDOW, J., Internal Medicine
MENTZOS, S., Psychiatry and Neurology
MILBRADT, R., Dermatology
MONDORF, A., Internal Medicine
MÜLLER, H., Anatomy
MÜLLER, H., Physiology
NAUJOKS, H., Gynaecology
OFFENLOCH, K., Neurophysiology
OVERBECK, G., Psychosomatics
PALM, D., Pharmacology and Toxicology
PANNIKE, A., Surgery
PIESCHL, D., Psychiatry
PIRLET, K., Physiotherapy
PITTRICH, W., Psychiatry
PREISER, G., History of Medicine
RAUDONAT, H., Forensic Medicine
REDHARDT, R., Forensic Medicine
REUTHER, J., Maxillo-facial Surgery
RICHTER, J., Anatomy
RIEMANN, H., Radiation Medicine
RIETBROCK, N., Pharmacology
RING, K., Physiological Chemistry
RISTOW, W., Oto-rhino-laryngology
RÖCKEMANN, W., Physiology
RÖSER, D., Audiology
ROSEMANN, G., Oto-rhino-laryngology
SATTER, H., Chest and Heart Surgery
SCHAUPP, H., Oto-rhino-laryngology
SCHLÜTER F., Physiology
SCHMIDT-MATTHIESEN, H., Obstetrics and Gynaecology
SCHMITT, E., Orthopaedics
SCHNEIDER, E., Neurology
SCHNEIDER, R., Anatomy
SCHÖFFLING, K., Internal Medicine
SCHOEPPE, W., Nephrology
SCHOPF, P., Maxillo-facial Surgery
SCHUBERT, R., Hygiene
SEIFFERT, U., Clinical Medicine
SIEDENTOPF, H-G., Gynaecology
SIEFERT, H., History of Medicine
SIGUSCH, V., Sexology
SINN, W., Physiology
SPIELMANN, W., Immuno-haematology
SPRANGER, H., Paradontology
STÄRK, N., Ophthalmology
STILLE, W., Internal Medicine
STOLL, L., Medical Microbiology
STÖRIG, E., Social Orthopaedics
SÜLLWOLD, L., Clinical Psychology
SVEJCAR, J., Human Genetics
TAUBERT, H-D., Endocrinology
THOMALSKE, G., Neuro-surgery
THOMAS, E., Neuro-pathology
TRÄGER, L., Therapeutic Biochemistry
VETTERMANN, H., Child Cardiology
WACKER, A., Therapeutic Biochemistry
WEBER, W., Surgery and Urology
WILHELM, G., Child Health
WILLERT, H-G., Orthopaedics
WINCKLER, J., Anatomy
WINDECKER, D., Dentistry
WINKELMANN, O., History of Medicine
WOENCKHAUS, C., Biochemistry

ALBERT-LUDWIGS-UNIVERSITÄT FREIBURG

7800 FREIBURG I. BR., WERTHMANNPLATZ

Telephone: 0761-2031.

Founded 1457.

Rector: Prof. Dr. BERNHARD STOECKLE.

Pro-Rectors: Prof. Dr. R. DEGKWITZ, Prof. Dr. F. ECKSTEIN, Prof. Dr. C. RUECHARDT.

Director of Administration: Dr. F. W. SIBURG.

Librarian: Prof. Dr. W. KEHR.

Number of teachers: 2,200.

Number of students: 17,000.

DEANS:

Faculty of Theology: Prof. Dr. REMIGIUS BÄUMER.

Faculty of Law: Prof. Dr. KARL KROESCHELL.

Faculty of Economics: Prof. Dr. ALOIS OBERHAUSER.

Faculty of Medicine: Prof. Dr. HUGO STEIM.

Faculty of Philosophy I: Prof. Dr. MARTIN BÜHRLE.

Faculty of Philosophy II: Prof. Dr. WOLFGANG KUHLMANN.

Faculty of Philosophy III: Prof. Dr. HUGO STEGER.

Faculty of Philosophy IV: Dr. ERNST SCHULIN.

Faculty of Mathematics: Prof. Dr. ROLF SCHNEIDER.

Faculty of Physics: Prof. Dr. ERWIN RÖSSLE.

Faculty of Chemistry and Pharmacology: Prof. Dr. HORST RIMPLER.

Faculty of Biology: Prof. Dr. PETER SCHOPFER.

Faculty of Geosciences: Prof. Dr. JÖRG KELLER.

Faculty of Forestry: Prof. Dr. HELMUT BRAUN.

PROFESSORS:

Faculty of Theology:

BÄUMER, R., Medieval and Modern Church History
BIEMER, G., Pedagogics, Catechism
DEISSLER, A., Old Testament Literature
FRANK, S., Old Church History
FÜRST, C. G., Canon Law
GRAMLICH, R., History of Religion
HENNING, R., Christian Sociology
LEHMANN, K., Dogmatics and Ecumenical Theology
RIEDLINGER, H., Dogmatics
SCHUMACHER, W. N., Christian Archaeology and History of Art
STOECKLE, B., Moral Theology
VÖGTLE, A., New Testament Literature
VÖLKL, R., Philanthropy

Faculty of Law:

ARENS, P., Civil Law and Procedure
BULLINGER, M., State and Administrative Law
CAEMMERER, E. VON, Foreign and International Private Law
DIECKMANN, A., Civil Law
HESSE, K., Political, Administrative and Canon Law
HOLLERBACH, A., History of Law, Church Law, Philosophy of Law
JESCHECK, H.-H., German and Foreign Penal Law, Criminal and Civil Procedure, Forestry Law
KAISER, J. H., German and Foreign Public Law, International Law, Ecclesiastical Law
KROESCHELL, K., German History of Law
LIEBS, D., History of Modern Law
LÖWISCH, M., Civil, Labour, Social Insurance and Commercial Law
MÜLLER-FREIENFELS, W., International Civil Law
RITTNER, F., Town, Trade, Business and Labour Law
SCHMITT, R., Penal Law
SIMSON, W. VON, State Law, European Law, Public Law
STOLL, H., Civil Law
TIEDEMANN, K., Criminal Law and Procedure
WAHL, R., Administrative Law
WOLF, J. G., Roman Law

Faculty of Economics:

BLÜMLE, G., Mathematical Economics
BRANDT, K., Political Economy
BRINK, J. H., Commercial Economics
DAMS, T., Political Economy and Agricultural Politics
EHRLICHER, W., Financial Economics
HILKE, W., Commercial Economics
HOPPMANN, E., Political Economy
KÜLP, B., Social Politics
LÜDEKE, D., Statistics
MÜLLER, J. H., Political Economy
OBERHAUSER, A., Political Economy
SCHMIDT, R.-B., Commercial Economics

Faculty of Medicine:

ANTONI, H., Physiology
BECK, C., Oto-rhino-laryngology
BECKMANN, R., Paediatrics
BRECKWOLDT, M., Gynaecology
BREDT, W., Hygiene and Bacteriology
CREMERIUS, J., Psychoanalysis
DECKER, K., Biochemistry
DEGKWITZ, R., Psychiatry and Neurology
VON DEIMLING, O., Chemical Pathology
FAUST, C., Neuropsychology and Rehabilitation
FLECKENSTEIN, A., Physiology
FORSTER, B., Insurance Medicine
GEROK, W., Internal Medicine
GOEPPERT, S., Medical Psychology
GÖPFERT, H., Applied Physiology
ZUR HANSEN, H., Virology
HERTTING, G., Pharmacology
HILLEMANS, H.-G., Gynaecology
HOFFMANN, G., Nuclear Medicine
HOLM, C., Phoniatrics
HOLZER, H., Biochemistry
HUMMEL, K., Blood Serology
JUNG, R., Neurology
KEIP, J., Internal Medicine

KERILMES, P., Neuropathology
KEUL, J., Sport and Leisure Medicine
KOMMERCLE, G., Optics
KREUTZ, W., Biophysics and Radiobiology
KUNER, E., Surgery
KÜNZER, W., Paediatrics
LAEBNER, H. A., Gynaecological Radiology
LOHR, G.-W., Internal Medicine
MACKENSEN, G., Optics
MATTHYS, H., Internal Medicine
MUNDINGER, F., Nuclear Medicine
PFEIDERER, A., Gynaecology
POHL, K. D., Forensic Chemistry
RAKOSI, TH., Orthopaedics
REICHELT, A., Surgery
REITHER, W., Dentistry
SANDRITTER, W., Pathology
SARRE, H., Internal Medicine
SASSE, D., Anatomy
SCHILLI, W., Maxillo-facial Medicine
SCHLOSSER, V., Surgery
SCHOLLER, K. L., Anaesthesiology
SCHOLLMEYER, P., Internal Medicine
SCHÖPF, E., Dermatology
SCHREIBER, S., Dentistry
SCHULETHE, H., Internal Medicine
SCHWAIGER, M., Surgery
SEEGER, W., Neurosurgery
SEIDLER, E., History of Medicine
SOMMERKAMP, H., Surgery
STAUBESAND, J., Anatomy
STEIN, H., Internal Medicine
STRUNK, P., Psychiatry
VON TROSCHKE, J., Medical Sociology
VOGT, A., Immunology
WALTER, E., Medical Statistics and Documentation
WARMENMACHER, M., Radiology
WENZ, W., Radiology
WIEMERS, K., Surgery and Anaesthesiology
WITTEKIND, D., Anatomy
WOLF, U., Human Genetics and Anthropology

Faculty of Philosophy I:
AURIN, K., Philosophy and Pedagogics
BEIERWALTOS, W., Philosophy
BÜHRLE, M., Sports
BUGGLE, F., Psychology
EGGEBRECHT, H. H., Music
EIGLER, G., Philosophy and Pedagogics
FAHRENBERG, J., Psychology
FORSSMAN, E., History of Art
HILTMANN, H., Psychology
MARX, W., Philosophy
MISEHO, J., Psychology
WEBER, H., Classical Archaeology

Faculty of Philosophy II:
AUTENRIETH, J., Medieval Latin Philology
GAUGER, H.-M., Romance Philology
HESS, R., Romance Philology
KIENAST, B., Assyriology
KÖHLER, E., Romance Philology
KULLMANN, W., Classical Philology
LEFÈIRE, E., Classical Philology
RAIBLE, W., Romance Philology
ROEMER, H. R., Islamic Studies
STAUB, H., Romance Philology
SZEMERÉNYI, O., Indo-german Linguistics
WEIHER, E., Slavonics
WUNDERLI, P., Romance Philology

Faculty of Philosophy III:
BAUMANN, G., Modern German Literature
BOESCH, B., German Philology
ERZGRÄBER, W., English Literature
GABRIEL, E., German Philology
GOETSCH, P., English Philology
KAISER, G., Modern German Literature
LINK, F., English Philology, American Language and Literature
MAUSER, W., Modern German Literature
OHL, H., Modern German Literature
PILCH, H., English Philology
PÖRKSEN, U., German Philology
RÖHRICH, L., Folklore and German Philology
SCHLÜTER, K., English Philology
SCHOPF, A., English Philology
STEGER, H., German Philology
WERNER, O., German Philology
WOLF, A., German Philology
ZUTT, H., German Philology

Faculty of Philosophy IV:
AUTENRIETH, J., Medieval Latin Philology
DUX, G., Sociology
HENNIS, W., Political Science
HERDING, O., Medieval History
JÄGER, W., Political Science
OBERNDÖRFER, D., Political Science
OTT, H., Economic and Social History
POPITZ, H., Sociology
ROSEN, K., Ancient History
SANGMEISTER, E., Pre-History
SCHMID, K., Medieval History
SCHMITTHENNER, W., Ancient History
SCHRAMM, G., Modern and East European History
SCHULIN, Modern History
STRASBURGER, H., Ancient History
WINKLER, H. A., Modern History
ZMARZLIK, H.-G., Modern History

Faculty of Mathematics:
BARNER, M., Mathematics
KEGEL, O., Mathematics
KLINGEN, H., Mathematics
NITSCHE, J., Applied Mathematics
SCHNEIDER, R., Mathematics
WALTER, E., Medical Statistics and Documentation
WITTING, H., Mathematics
WOLKE, D., Mathematics

Faculty of Physics:
HONERKAMP, J., Physics
MARSCHALL, H., Theoretical Physics
MEHLHORN, W., Physics
OSBERGHAUS, O., Physics
REIK, H. G., Theoretical Physics
RÖSSLE, E., Physics
RUNGE, K., Physics
SCHLIER, C., Physics
STIER, H.-E., Physics

Faculty of Chemistry and Pharmacy:
ACKERMANN, T., Physical Chemistry
BAUER, K., Pharmaceutical Technology
BRAUER, G., Inorganic Chemistry
CANTOW, H.-J., Physical Chemistry
KREUTZ, W., Biophysics
NITSCHE, R., Crystallography
POHL, R., Pharmacognosy
PREUSS, F. R., Pharmaceutical Chemistry
PRINZBACH, H., Organic Chemistry
RIMPLER, H., Pharmaceutical Biology
RÜCHARDT, CH., Chemical Laboratories and Organic Chemistry
SCHNEIDER, W., Pharmaceutical Chemistry
VAHRENKAMP, H., Inorganic Chemistry
WALLENFELS, K., Chemistry
WEGNER, G., Molecular Chemistry
WEISZ, H., Analytical Chemistry
ZIMMERMANN, H., Physical Chemistry

Faculty of Biology:
BRESCH, C., Genetics
DREWS, G., Botany
GRISEBACH, H., Biochemistry of Plants
HASSENSTEIN, B., Biology
HERTEL, R., Molecular Biology
KESSLER, A., Meteorology
MOHR, H., Botany
OSCHE, G., Biology
SANDER, K., Biology
SCHÖN, G., Microbiology
SITTE, P., Botany
SPATZ, H.-C., Biophysics
TILZER, M., Limnology
WILMANNS, O., Geobotany

Faculty of Geosciences:
HERZOG, R., Ethnology
KELLER, R., Geography
MANSHARD, W., Geography
NITSCHE, R., Crystallography
PFLUG, R., Geology, Palaeontology
SICK, W.-D., Geography
WEISCHET, W., Geography
WIMMENAUER, W., Mineralogy
ZÖTTE, H.-W., Soil Science

Faculty of Forestry:
ABETZ, P., Forest Production
BRAUN, H., Biological Wood Research
GRAMMEL, R., Forest Management
MARQUARDT, H., Forest Botany
NIESSLEIN, E., Forest Policy
SCHMIDT-VOGT, H., Forestry
SPEIDEL, G., Forest Management
STEINLIN, H. J., Forest Management
VITÉ, J. P., Forest Zoology
ZÖTTL, H. W., Soil Science

JUSTUS LIEBIG-UNIVERSITÄT GIESSEN

6300 GIESSEN, LUDWIGSTRASSE 23

Telephone: 0641-7021.

Founded 1607.

Academic year: October to September (two terms).

President: Prof. Dr. K. ALEWELL.
Vice-President: Prof. Dr. H. GRABES.
Chancellor: L. WOLF.
Librarian: Dr. H. SCHUELING.

Number of teachers: 690.
Number of students: 14,360.

PROFESSORS:

Law:
BLAUROCK, U., Civil, Commercial and Economic Law, Tax and Comparative Law
CRAMER, P., Criminal, Procedural, Labour and Social Law
HEINZE, M., Civil and Procedural Law
KISKER, G., Public Law
KÖBLER, G., History of German Law, Civil and Canon Law
KREUZER, A., Criminology, Juvenile Criminal Law
LANGE, K., Administration Law
RAISER, TH., Commercial and Economic Law, Civic Law and Comparative Law
RIDDER, H. K. J., Public Law and Political Science
SCHAPP, J., Civil Law and Philosophy of Law
SÖLLNER, A., Roman Law and Civil Law, Labour and Social Law
STEIGER, H., Public Law
VOGLER, TH., Criminal Law
WEICK, G., Civil and Labour Law
WIESER, E., Civil and Procedural Law
ZEZSCHWITZ, F. VON, Public and Tax Law

Economics:
ABERLE, G., Political Economy
ALEWELL, K., Industrial Economy
ANDEL, N., Political Economy

BLEICHER, K., Industrial Economy
BOHNET, A., Political Economy
DEMMLER, H., Political Economics
FRANKE, G., Industrial Economics
HAHN, D., Industrial Economics
HEMMER, H. R., Political Economy and Developing Countries
KROMPHARDT, J., Political Economy
MONISSEN, H. G., Political Economy
MÜLLER, H., Political Economy
PAUSENBERGER, E., Industrial Economics
RINNE, H., Statistics
SEEGER-LUCKENBACH, H., Political Economy
SELCHERT, F. W., Industrial Economics
WEBER, K., Industrial Economy

Social Sciences:
DÖRR, M., Politics
ERB, G., Politics
FISCHER, K. G., Didactics of Sociology
FRITZSCHE, K., Political Science
GAHLINGS, I., Sociology
GEORGE, S., Didactics of Sociology
GRONEMEYER, R., Sociology
GROSS, E., Sociology of Education
HILLIGEN, W., Didactics of Sociology
KLIEM, K., Politics
KRÖGER, K., Constitutional Law
KRÜGER, H. J., Sociology
MERTEN, K., Empiric Sociology
NEUMANN, F., Politics
REIMANN, B., Sociology
SCHMIDT-RELENBERG, N., Sociology of Education
VARAIN, H. J., Political Science

Education:
BACHMANN, W.
BUNK, G.
DAUZENROTH, E.
FLEHINGHAUS, K.
HELFENBEIN, K.-A.
HEMBERGER, A.
KLASSEN, TH.
LASSAHN, R.
MIESKES, H.
MÖLLER, H.
SCHULZ, M.
SEIDENFADEN, F.
WIDMANN, H.
WILLAND, H.

Arts, Music, Sport:
BIERHOFF-ALFERMANN, D., Sports
DISTLER-BRENDEL, G., Music Education
EHMER, H., Art and Work Education
JOST, E., Music
KOTTER, E., Music Education
MEUSEL, H., Sports
NEUMANN, H., Sport
NOWACKI, P., Sports Medicine
PAPE, W., Music
STAGUHN, K., Art and Work Education
WASMUND, U., Sports

Psychology:
CORRELL, W., Programmed Learning
HAJOS, A., Psychology
HAUBENSAK, G., Psychology
KÖNIG, R., Psychology
NETTER, P., Differential Psychology
OLBRICH, E., Psychology of Evolution
SCHERER, K., Social Psychology
SCHMIDT, R., Methodology
SCHOTT, F., Pedagogic Psychology
SPITZNAGEL, A., Pedagogic Psychology
TODT, E., Pedagogic Psychology
VAITL, D., Psychology
WENDELER, J., Pedagogic Psychology

Religion:
BARTH, H.-M., Systematic Theology
DAUTZENBERG, G., Bible Studies
HAMPEL, A., Moral Theology
JENDORFF, B., Religious Education
KRIECHBAUM, F., Systematic Theology
LINK, E., Catholic Theology
REDHARDT, J., Psychology of Religion
SCHERING, E., Evangelical Theology
VEIT, M., Religious Instruction

History:
BAUMGARTNER, H.-M., Philosophy
BERDING, H., Modern History
BERGMANN, K., Didactics of History
BOEHM, G., European History of Art
BRÜHL, C., Medieval History
BUCHHOLZ, H. G., Classical Archaeology
GESCHE, H., Ancient History
KAHL, H.-D., Medieval History
KAMINSKY, H., Medieval History
MEINHARDT, H., Philosophy
MENKE, M., Pre- and Early History
MORAW, P., Medieval History
PRESS, V., Modern History
QUANDT, S., History Teaching
WERNER, N., Modern History
ZERNACK, K., East European History

German:
ARENDT, D., Didactics of German Language and Literature
EHRISMANN, O., German Language
ENGELS, H., German Philology
v. ERTZDORFF, X., Germanic Philology
GAST, W., German Language Teaching
HESELHAUS, C., Modern German Literature and General Literature
INDERTHAL, K., German Literature
KAISER, G., Modern German Literature
KARTHAUS, U., German Language Teaching
KLUGE, W., Didactics of German Language and Literature
LEIBFRIED, E., General Literature
MARQUARD, O., Philosophy
OESTERLE, G., Modern Literature
RAMGE, H., Linguistics
RÖTZER, G., Didactics of German Language and Literature
SCHWENK, H., German Language Teaching
WIEDEMANN, C., Modern Literature
WILKENDING, G., German Language Teaching

English:
BERGNER, H., English Language
BORGMEIER, R., Modern English and American Literature
BREDELLA, L., English Language and Literature Teaching
BRINKMANN, H., Modern English and American Literature
GERATHS, A., Modern English and American Literature
GRABES, H., Modern English and American Literature
PIEPHO, H. E., English Language Teaching
PREUSCHEN, K. A., English Language Teaching

Mediterranean and East European Studies:
ADAMIETZ, J., Classical Philology
BUCHHEIT, V., Latin Philology
CAUDMONT, J., Romance Linguistics
CHRIST, H., French Language and Literature Teaching
HIERSCHE, R., Comparative Linguistics
JELITTE, H., Slavonic Philology
PÖHLMANN, E., Greek
RIEGER, D., Romance Literature
RÖHRBORN, K., Islamic and Turkish Studies
WAGNER, E., Languages and Culture of North Africa
WENDT, M., French Language Teaching
WOLFZETTEL, F., French Literature

Mathematics:
BRAUNSS, G.
ENDL, K., Pure and Applied Mathematics
FENSKE, C.
FILIPPI, S., Numeric and Instrumental Mathematics
FRICKER, F.
GAIER, D., Applied Mathematics
HOISCHEN, L.
HOLLAND, G., Didactics of Mathematics
JAENISCH, S.
PICKERT, G., Mathematics
PROFKE, L., Mathematics Teaching
SCHMIDT, R., Mathematics Teaching
SCHWARTZE, H., Mathematics Teaching
WAGEMANN, E. B., Mathematics Teaching
WALK, H., Stochastics

Physics:
BIEM, W., Theoretical Physics
BOLTERAUER, H., Theoretical Physics
CLAUSNITZER, G., Nuclear Physics
GRÜN, N., Theoretical Physics
HEIDEN, CHR., Applied Physics
HERMANN, G., Experimental Physics
KANITSCHEIDER, B., Philosophy of Science
KIEFER, J., Biophysics
KNEISSL, U., Nuclear Physics
KUHN, W., Didactics of Physics
LÖB, H., Experimental Physics
LOHMANN, W., Biophysics
MOSEL, U., Theoretical Physics
SALZBORN, E., Nuclear Physics
SCHARTNER, K.-H., Experimental Physics
SCHARMANN, A., Experimental Physics
SCHEID, W., Theoretical Physics
SCHNEIDER, H., Experimental Physics
SCHWARZ, G., Physics Teaching
SEIBT, W., Experimental Physics
WOLLNIK, H., Experimental Physics

Chemistry:
AHLBRECHT, H., Organic Chemistry
ASKANI, R., Organic Chemistry
GEBELEIN, H., Chemistry Teaching
GRUEHN, R., Inorganic Chemistry
HEBECKER, C., Inorganic Chemistry
HOPPE, R., Inorganic Chemistry
MAIER, G., Organic Chemistry
SEIDEL, W., Physical Chemistry
WINNEWISSER, M., Physical Chemistry
WOLLRAB, A., Didactics of Chemistry

Biology:
ANDERS, F., Genetics
BERCK, K.-H., Biology Teaching
CLEFFMANN, G., Zoology
EICHELBERG, D., Zoology
FREY, W., Botany
GLASER, H. S. R., Biology Teaching
GÖTTING, K.-J., Zoology
HOLL, A., Zoology
KILIAN, E. F., Zoology
KLEE, R., Biology Teaching
KNAPP, R., Botany
KUNTER, M., Anthropology
KUNZE, C., Botany
PAHLICH, E., Botany
RINGE, F., Botany
SATTLER, E. L., Nuclear Biology
SCHAEFER, U., Anthropology
SCHERF, H., Zoology
SCHIPP, R., Zoology
SCHNETTER, R., Botany
SCHULTE, E., Zoology
SCHWANTES, H. O., Botany
SCHWARTZ, E., Zoology
SEIFERT, G., Zoology
SPRANKEL, H., Neuro-biology
STEUBING, L., Botany
WESSING, A., Zoology
ZETSCHE, K., Botany

Applied Biology and Environment Conservation:
AHRENS, E., Agricultural Microbiology
ALKÄMPER, J., Tropical Plants
ATANASIU, N., Agriculture
BREBURDA, J., Soil Science
GRUPPE, W., Fructiculture
HARRACH, T., Applied Soil Science
JAHN, W., Plant Cultivation
KOWALD, R., Cultivation
KRANZ, J., Phytopathology
KÜSTER, E., Agricultural Microbiology
MOLL, W., Soil Science
NIESE, G., Agricultural Microbiology
PREUSSE, H.-U., Soil Science
SÄNGER, H. L., Molecular Biology
SCHLÖSSER, E., Plant Pathology
SCHMUTTERER, H., Plant Pathology
SCHUSTER, W., Plant Cultivation
SIMON, U., Pasture and Fodder Growing
STEIN, W., Stock Protection and Applied Zoology
VÖMEL, A., Plant Cultivation
WOHLRAB, B., Agriculture and Applied Hydrology
ZOSCHKE, M., Plant Ecology

Veterinary Medicine and Stockbreeding:
BECHT, H., Microbiology and Immunology
BLOBEL, H. G., Bacteriology and Immunology
EDER, H., Veterinary Physiology
EIKMEIER, H., Internal Veterinary Medicine
FINGER, K. H., Animal Breeding
FISCHER, H., Tropical and Sub-tropical Veterinary Medicine
FRESE, K., Pathological Anatomy
FRIMMER, M., Pharmacology and Toxicology
GEHRING, W., Physiology and Pathology
GEISSLER, H., Poultry Diseases and Hygiene
GOLLER, H., Veterinary Anatomy
GOTHE, R., Parasitology
GRÜNDER, H.-D., Internal Medicine (Ruminants)
HABERMEHL, K. H., Veterinary Anatomy
HADLOK, R., Animal Feeding
HERZOG, A., Comparative Genetics
HOFMANN, R. R., Veterinary Anatomy
KIELWEIN, G., Food Hygiene and Bacteriology
KÖSTERS, J. M., Poultry Diseases
KRAUSS, H., Poultry Diseases
LÄMMLER, G., Parasitology and Parasitic Diseases in Domestic Animals
LANG, K., Animal Feeding Hygiene
LUTZ, F., Pharmacology
MÜLLER, H., Veterinary Surgery and Ophthalmology
RENNER, E., Dairying
RIECK, G.-W., Hereditary Diseases
ROTT, R., Virology
RUDOLPH, R., Pathology
RUFEGER, H., Nutrition
SCHLIESSER, TH., Hygiene and Infectious Diseases in Animals
SCHNORR, B., Veterinary Anatomy
SCHOLTISSEK, C., Biochemistry
SCHONER, W., Biochemistry
SENFT, E. B., Animal Breeding and Dairying
SERNETZ, M., Applied Biochemistry
STEINBACH, J., Ecology of Domestic Animals
TILLMANN, H., Obstetrics
VICTOR, N., Bio-mathematics
WASSMUTH, R., Breeding and Genetics of Domestic Animals
WEISS, E., General Pathology, Pathological Anatomy and Histology of Animals
WELS, A., Veterinary Physiology
WENGLER, G., Virology and Cellular Biology

Nutrition:
BITSCH, I., Nutrition
BRUNE, H., Animal Nutrition
HÖFNER, W., Plant Nutrition
KÜBLER, W., Human Nutrition
LEITZMANN, C., Nutrition
MENDEN, E., Nutrition
MENGEL, K., Plant Nutrition
NEUMANN, K.-H., Plant Nutrition
PALLAUF, J., Animal Nutrition
REHNER, G., Nutrition
TOLCKMITT, W., Nutrition applied to Child Health

Food Economics:
BESCH, M., Agricultural Market Research
BODENSTEDT, A., Agrarian Sociology
BOTTLER, J., Home Economics
EICHHORN, H., Agricultural Machinery
HARSCHE, E., Agricultural Sociology
KUHLMANN, F., Agricultural Management
SCHINKE, E., Agricultural Economics of Socialist Countries
v. SCHWEITZER, R., Household Management
SEUSTER, H., Agricultural Management
SPITZER, H. Regional Science
THIMM, H.-U., Agrarian Politics
WÄDEKIN, K.-E., International Agrarian Politics
WIGGERT, K., Home Economics
WÖHLKEN, E., Market Research
ZILAHI-SZABO, M. G., Computation and Data Processing

Geology and Geography:
BLIND, W., Palaeontology and Geology
ERNST, E., Didactics of Geography
GIESE, E., Economic Geography
HAFFNER, W., Geography
JAHN, G., Geography Teaching
KLITZSCH, E., Geology and Palaeontology
KNOBLICH, K., Geology
MEYER, R., Geography
MOEWES, W., Applied Geography
NEUKIRCH, D., Geography Teaching
PFLUG, H. D., Geology and Palaeontology
SCHULZE, W., Didactics of Geography
SEIFERT, V., Applied Geography
STIBANE, F., Geology and Palaeontology
STRÜBEL, G., Mineralogy and Petrology
UHLIG, H., Geography
WEISE, O., Geography

Medicine:
ADELSTEIN, F., Ophthalmology
ALTARAS, J., Radiology
ALTLAND, K., Human Genetics
BARTH, G., Medical Radiology
BAUER, H., Virology
BAUMANN, CH., Physiology
BAYINDIR, S., Radiology
BECK, E. G., Hygiene
BECKMANN, D., Medical Psychology
BENEDUM, J., History of Medicine
BIKFALVI, A., Surgery
BRÜCK, K., Physiology
DAVIES-OSTERKAMP, S., Medical Psychology
DEGKWITZ, E., Biochemistry
DORNDORF, W., Neurology
DREYER, F., Pharmacology
DUDECK, J., Medical Statistics and Documentation
DUNCKER, H. R., Anatomy
EBNER, H., Surgery
ECKE, H., Surgery
FEDERLIN, K., Internal Medicine
FLEISCHER, K., Oto-Rhino-Laryngology
FRIIS, R., Virology
FUHRMANN, W., Human Genetics
GIERHAKE, F., Surgery
GLASER, E., Internal Medicine
GLOSSMANN, H., Pharmacology
GRAEF, V., Clinical Chemistry
GREBE, S., Clinical Radiology
GROTE, E., Neurosurgery
GUNDLACH, G., Biochemistry
HABERMANN, E. R., Pharmacology
HAGER, H., Pathology
HARTWIG, H.-G., Anatomy
v. HATTINGBERG, H. M., Child Health
HEERD, E., Physiology
HEHRLEIN, F. W., Surgery
HEISING, G., Clinical Psychosomatics
HEMPELMANN, G., Anaesthesiology
HERGET, H. F., Anaesthesiology
HUNDEIKER, M., Dermato-Venerology
ILLIG, L., Dermatology and Venereal Diseases
IRNICH, W., Biomedical Electronics
JACOBI, K. W., Ophthalmology
JESSEN, C.-U., Physiology
KALUZA, G., Virology
KAUFMANN, H., Ophthalmology
KEPP, R. K., Obstetrics and Gynaecology
KIRSCHNER, H., Dentistry
KLENK, H.-D., Virology
KNORPP, K., Internal Medicine
KREY, H., Ophthalmology
KRAUSE, W., Dermatology
KRACHT, J., Pathology
KÜBLER, W., Human Nutrition
KUNZE, K., Neurology
LAMMERS, H.-J., Psychiatry
LAMPERT, F., Paediatrics
LANGE, R. H., Anatomy
LASCH, H. G., Internal Medicine
LAUBE, H., Internal Medicine
LEBER, H.-W., Internal Medicine
LÖFFLER, H., Internal Medicine
LORBER, C. G., Maxillo-facial Surgery
LORENZ, R., Neuro-surgery
LUMPER, L., Biochemistry
MATTHES, K., Internal Medicine
MEYHÖFER, W., Dermatology
MOELLER, M. L., Psycho-hygiene
MÖLLER, W., Anatomy
MÜHLENDYCK, H., Ophthalmology
MÜLLER, H., Clinical Radiology
MÜLLER-BERGHAUS, G., Experimental Medicine
MÜLLER-BRAUNSCHWEIG, H., Clinical Psychosomatics
MUELLER-ECKHARDT, C., Internal Medicine
NEUBÜSER, D., Gynaecology and Obstetrics
NEUHÄUSER, G., Neuropaediatrics
NEUHOF, H., Clinical Pathophysiology
NÖSKE, H.-D., Urology
NOWACKI, P., Sports Medicine
OEHMKE, H.-J., Anatomy
OKSCHE, A., Anatomy
PANTKE, H., Dentistry
PATSCHKE, D., Anaesthesiology
PAUL, F., Internal Medicine, Gastroenterology
PETERS, TH. F., Anatomy
PFÜTZ, E., Dentistry
PIA, H. W., Neurosurgery
PRÜLL, G., Neuro-psychiatry
RAUSCH, L., Radiation Biology
RAUTENBURG, H.-W., Child Health
RETTIG, H., Orthopaedics
RICHTER, H. E., Psychosomatics
RINGLEB, D., Clinical Radiology
RÓKA, L., Clinical Chemistry
ROTHAUGE, C. F., Urology
SCHATZ, H., Internal Medicine (Endocrinology)
SCHEER, J. W., Medical Psychology

SCHEWE, G., Forensic Medicine
SCHIEFER, H.-G., Cell Physiology and Medical Microbiology
SCHMAHL, F. W., Internal Medicine
SCHMIDT, G.-W., Child Health
SCHMIDT, K.-L., Physical Medicine and Balneology
SCHMIDT, P., Hygiene
SCHÜTTERLE, Internal Medicine
SCHULZE, H.-U., Biochemistry
SCHUSTER, W., Paediatric Roentgenology
SCHWEMMLE, K., Surgery
SCHWETLICK, W., Orthopaedics
SOKOLOVSKI, A., Oto-rhino-laryngology
SPRANKEL, H., Comparative Neuropathology
STIRM, S., Biochemistry
TAMMOSCHEIT, U.-G., Orthopaedics
TESCHEMACHER, H., Pharmacology
TOLCKMITT, W., Nutrition
UECK, M., Anatomy
VAHRSON, H., Obstetrics and Gynaecology
VOGEL, W., Physiology
WALTER, P., Cardiovascular Surgery
WEIS, W., Biochemistry
WEISE, M., Internal Medicine
WELLENSIEK, H. J., Microbiology
WESEMANN, W., Clinical Neurochemistry, Experimental Neurosurgery
WETZEL, W. E., Dentistry
WOITOWITZ, H.-J., Industrial Medicine
WOLF, H., Paediatrics
WOLFF, C.-H., Gynaecology and Obstetrics
ZEISBERGER, E., Physiology

GEORG-AUGUST-UNIVERSITÄT ZU GÖTTINGEN

3400 GÖTTINGEN, WILHELMSPLATZ 1

Telephone: 39-1.

Founded 1737.

Academic year: April to March (two terms).

Rector: Prof. Dr. NORBERT KAMP.

Pro-Rector: Prof. Dr. rer. pol. JÜRGEN BLOECH.

Co-Rector: Prof. Dr. rer. nat. HANS JÜRGEN BEUG.

Curator: HANS-LUDWIG SCHNEIDER.

Number of teachers: 724, including 218 Professors.

Number of students: 19,438.

Publications: *Vorlesungsverzeichnis* (2 a year), *Jahresforschungsbericht* (every 2 years), *Georgia-Augusta, Nachrichten* (2 a year).

DEANS:

Faculty of Theology: Prof. Dr. GEORG STRECKER.
Faculty of Law: Prof. Dr. RALF DRIER.
Faculty of Medicine: Prof. Dr. DIETRICH KETTLER.
Faculty of Philosophy: Prof. Dr. CARL JOACHIM CLASSEN.
Faculty of Mathematics and Natural Sciences: Prof. Dr. RAINER KRESS.
Faculty of Forestry: Prof. Dr. SIEGFRIED BOMBOSCH.
Faculty of Agriculture: Prof. Dr. Dr. GERD KOBABE.
Faculty of Economics and Social Sciences: Prof. Dr. KLAUS HELBERG.

PROFESSORS:

Faculty of Theology:
GEYER, H.-G., Systematic Theology
JOSUTTIS, M., Practical Theology
KRAUS, H.-J., Theology of the Reformed Churches
LUZ, U., New Testament
MOELLER, B., Church History
PERLITT, L., Old Testament
SMEND, R., Old Testament
STRECKER, G., New Testament
WIESSNER, G., General History of Religion

Faculty of Law:
BEHRENDS, O., Roman Law, Civil Law, History of Modern Private Law
BOGS, H., Public Law
DEUTSCH, E., Civil Law, Commercial Law, International Private Law and Comparative Law
DIEDERICHSEN, U., Civil Law, Civil Action Law, Commercial Law and Judicial Procedure
DREIER, R., General Theory of Law
GAMILLSCHEG, F., Civil Law, Commercial and Industrial Law, International Private Law
GÖTZ, V., Public Law
HENCKEL, W., Civil Law, Commercial and Process Law
IMMENGA, U., Civil Law, Commercial and Economic Law, Judicial Procedure
KLEIN, H.-H., Public Law
KNOBBE-KEUK, B., Civil Law, Commercial, Economic and Fiscal Law
MAIWALD, M., Criminal Law, Criminal Case Law and Criminology
RAUSCHNING, D., Public Law
SCHÖCH, H., Criminology, Criminal Law and Execution of Punishment
SCHREIBER, H.-L., Criminal Law and General Theory of Law
SELLERT, W., History of German Law and Civil Law
STARCK, C., Public Law

Faculty of Medicine:
BAUER, H., Neurology
BERG, S., Legal Medicine
BEUREN, A., Cardiology
BOMMER, W., General Hygiene
BRETSCHNEIDER, H.-J., Physiology
BRUNNER, E., Medical Statistics
CREUTZFELDT, W., Internal Medicine
EHLERS, C.-T., Medical Documentation and Data Processing
EMRICH, D., Nuclear Medicine
ENGEL, W., Human Genetics
ERDMANN, W.-D., Toxicology and Neuropharmacology
EULNER, H.-H., History of Medicine
FRISCHKORN, R., Gynaecological Radiology
HARDER, D., Medical Physics and Biophysics
HASSELBLATT, A., Pharmacology and Toxicology
HENATSCH, H. D., Physiology
IPPEN, H., Dermatology
KETTLER, D., Anaesthesiology
KIRSCH, T., Dentistry
KOBES, L., Denture Science
KONCZ, J., Surgery
KREUZER, H., Internal Medicine (Cardiology)
KUHN, H.-J., Anatomy
KUHN, W., Obstetrics and Gynaecology
MEYER, J.-E., Psychiatry
MIEHLKE, A., Oto-Rhino-Laryngology
MOTSCH, A., Dentistry
PEIPER, H.-J., Surgery
POHLMEIER, H., Medical Psychology
POPPE, H., Radiology
SCHAUER, A., General and Specialized Pathology
SCHELER, F., Nephrology
SCHRÖTER, W., Paediatrics
SCHULTE, F. J., Paediatrics
SÖLING, H.-D., Clinical Biochemistry
SPOERRI, O., Neurosurgery
STALDER, K., Industrial and Social Medicine
STOFFREGEN, J., Anaesthesiology
THOMSSEN, R., Medical Microbiology
TRUSS, F., Urology
VOGEL, M., Ophthamology

Faculty of Philosophy:
ARNDT, K., History of Art
BAHRDT, H. P., Sociology
BECHERT, H., Indology
BLEICKEN, J., Ancient History
BORGER, R., Assyriology
CLASSEN, C. J., Classical Philology
DIETRICH, A., Arabic Philology
DOERFER, G., Turkology
ENGELBERT, M., Romance Philology
FITTSCHEN, K., Classical Archaeology
FLECHSIG, K.-H., Education
FRANK, A. P., English Philology (North American Literature)
GARDNER, T., English Philology
GREBING, H., Modern History
GULYA, J., Philology
HENZE, W., Teaching of Sport
HERING, G., East European History
HERRLITZ, H.-G., Pedagogy
HOFFMANN, H., Medieval and Modern History
INEICHEN, G., Romance Philology
LAUER, R., Slavonic Philology
MACKENZIE, D. N., Oriental Philology
MÖLK, U., Romance Philology
MOLLENHAUER, K., Education
NICKAU, K., Classical Philology
NITZ, H.-J., Geography
NÜRNBERGER, R., Medieval and Modern History
PATZE, H., History of Lower Saxony, Medieval and Modern History
PATZIG, G., Philosophy
RADDATZ, K., Pre-history
SCHABRAM, H., English Philology and Medieval Literature
SCHEIBE, E., Philosophy
SCHENDA, R., Folklore
SCHINDEL, U., Classical Philology
SCHLESIER, E., Ethnology
SCHMID, W. P., Comparative Indo-Germanic Philology
SCHÖNE, A., German Philology
STACKELBERG, J. Frhr. von, Romance Philology
STACKMANN, K., Germanic Philology
STELLMACHER, D., North German Language and Literature
THADDEN, R. von, Medieval and Modern History
THIEL, M., Auxiliary Science of History
THÜMMEL, W., Germanic Philology
TURK, H., Germanic Philology
DE VINCENZ, A., Slavic Philology
WAGENKNECHT, C.-J., Germanic Philology
WENSKUS, R., Medieval and Modern History
WESTENDORF, W., Egyptology
WIELAND, W., Philosophy
WOLPERS, T., English Philology

Faculty of Mathematics and Natural Sciences:
AX, P., Zoology
BEHR, H.-J., Geology
BINGEL, W., Theoretical Chemistry
BIRUKOW, G., Zoology

Borchers, H.-J., Theoretical Physics
Bredenkamp, J., Psychology
Deuring, M., Mathematics
Dieck, T., Mathematics
Duhm, E., Clinical Psychology
Ellenberg, H., Geobotany
Ertel, S. A., Psychology
Flammersfeld, A., Physics
Fricke, K., Astronomy and Astrophysics
Glemser, O., Inorganic Chemistry
Gottschalk, G., Microbiology
Grauert, H., Mathematics
Grossbach, U., Zoology
Haasen, P., Metallography
Hagedorn, J., Geography
Harder, H., Sediment Petrography
Harten, H.-U., Physics
Heinz, E., Mathematics
Hövermann, J., Geography
Kneser, M., Mathematics
Kohler, M., Theoretical Physics
Kraus, H., Bioclimatology
Krengel, U., Mathematical Statistics
Kress, R., Applied Mathematics
Kupčik, V., Mineralogy and Crystallography
Lüders, G., Theoretical Physics
Lüttke, W., Organic Chemistry
Maak, W., Mathematics
Meller, A., Inorganic Chemistry
Minnigerode, G. von, Physics
Müller, E.-A., Applied Mathematics and Aerodynamics
Nitz, H.-J., Geography
Schaback, R., Numerical and Applied Mathematics
Schlegel, H.-G., Microbiology
Schöllkopf, U., Organic Chemistry
Schroeder, M. R., Applied Physics
Siebert, M., Geophysics
Smith, L., Mathematics
Troe, J., Physical Chemistry
Vogel, C., Anthropology
Voigt, H.-H., Astronomy and Astrophysics
Wagenitz, G., Botany
Wagner, H.-G., Physical Chemistry
Walliser, O., Palaeontology
Wedepohl, K. H., Geochemistry

Faculty of Forestry:
Bombosch, S., Forest Zoology
Brabänder, H. D., Forest Industrial Economics
Eschrich, W., Forest Botany
Festetics, A., Game Biology and Hunting
Haberle, S., Forest Labour Science
Hattemer, H. H., Forest Genetics and Plant Breeding
Knigge, W., Forest Utilization
Kramer, H., Forest Productivity, Management and Wood Surveying
Kraus, H., Bioclimatology
Lamprecht, H., Tropical and Sub-Tropical Forest Research and Cultivation
Röhrig, E., Forest Cultivation and Protection
Ulrich, Pedology and Plant Nourishment
Zundel, R., Forest Politics, Timber Marketing Research, Forest History and Nature Preservation

Faculty of Agriculture:
Baeumer, K., Tillage and Plant Cultivation
Brandes, W., Agricultural Economy
Glodek, P., Stock-breeding
Günther, K.-D., Animal Physiology and Feeding
Heidhues, T., Agricultural Economy
Heitefuss, R., Plant Pathology and Protection
Köhne, M., Agricultural Economy
Kuhnen, F., Foreign Agriculture
Meyer, B., Pedology
Mitscherlich, E., Veterinary Science
Rehm, S., Tropical and Sub-Tropical Plant Cultivation
Röbbelen, G., Applied Genetics and Plant Breeding
Schaefer-Kehnert, W., Agricultural Management
Schlegel, H.-G., Microbiology
Schmitt, G., Agricultural Politics
Welte, E., Agricultural Chemistry
Wieneke, F., Agricultural Machinery

Faculty of Economics and Social Science:
Achtenhagen, F., Economic Education
Aufermann, J., Journalism and Communications
Bahrdt, H. P., Sociology
Bartke, G., Industrial Economics
Bloech, J., Industrial Economics
Brede, H., Political Economy for Students of Law III
Deppe, H.-D., Industrial Economics
Euchner, W., Political Science
Fassheber, P., Commercial and Social Psychology
Gerth, E., Industrial Economics
Hesse, H., Political Economy
Jarchow, H.-J., Political Economy
Kaufhold, K.-H., Economic and Social History
Kern, H., Sociology
Knoblich, H., Industrial Economics
Kricke, M., Statistics and Econometrics
Kucera, G., Political Economy for Students of Law
Kuhn, H., Political Economy
Linhart, H., Statistics and Econometrics
Lösche, P., Political Science
Lücke, W., Industrial Economics
Noltemeier, H., Operations Research and Economic Data Processing
Pollak, H., Political Economy
Roloff, E.-A., Didactics of the Social Sciences
Schlieper, U., Political Economy
Schlotter, H.-G., Political Economy, Economic Political Science
Wacker, W. H., Industrial Economics
Weber, H. K., Industrial Economics
Windisch, R., Political Economy for Students of Law

UNIVERSITÄT HAMBURG

2000 HAMBURG 13,
EDMUND-SIEMERS-ALLEE 1

Telephone: 41-23-1.

Telex: 214732 UNIHH D.

President: Dr. Peter Fischer-Appelt.

Vice-Presidents: Prof. Dr. Wolfgang Bachofer, Prof. Dr. Klaus Glashoff.

Chief Administrative Officer: Dr. Hugbert Flitner.

State and University Librarian: Prof. Dr. Horst Gronemeyer.

Number of teachers: 2,353.
Number of students: 32,095.

Heads of Departments:

Protestant Theology: Prof. Dr. Peter Cornehl.
Law: Prof. Dr. Ingo von Münch.
Law II: Prof. Dr. Norbert Reich.
Economic Sciences: Prof. Dr. Harald Scherf.
Medicine: Prof. Dr. Karl-Heinz Hölzer.
Philosophy and Social Sciences: Prof. Dr. Joachim Raschke.
Pedagogics: Prof. Dr. Hans-Jürgen Krumm.
Philology: Prof. Dr. Johannes Kibelka.
History: Prof. Dr. Peter Herrmann.
History of Culture: Prof. Dr. Martin Warnke.
Oriental Studies: Prof. Dr. Lambert Schmithausen.
Mathematics: Prof. Dr. Carl Geiger.
Physics: Prof. Dr. Harry Lehmann.
Chemistry: Prof. Dr. Fritz Thieme.
Biology: Prof. Dr. Rainer Knussmann.
Geographical Sciences: Prof. Dr. Günter Fischer.
Psychology: Prof. Dr. Detlef Rhenius.
Computer Science: Prof. Dr. Joachim Schmidt.
Physical Education: Prof. Dr. Knut Dietrich.

Professors:

Department of Protestant Theology:
Cornehl, P., Practical Theology
Fischer, H., Systematic Theology
Grünberg, W., Practical Theology
Gülzow, H., Church History and Dogma
Hunzinger, C.-H., New Testament and Religions
Koch, K., Old Testament
Koch, T., Systematic Theology
Kroeger, M., Church History and Dogma
Lindner, W. V., Practical Theology
Lohse, B., Church History and Dogma
Margull, J., Missions and Oecumenics
Müller, H.-P., Old Testament
Otto, E., Old Testament
Pesch, O. H., Systematic Theology
Schramm, T., New Testament
Wilckens, U., New Testament

Department of Law:
Baur, J., Civil, Commercial, Economic and International Private Law
Bernstein, H., Comparative and International Private Law
Bühnemann, B., Informatic Law
Buschendorf, E., Philosophy of Law
Damkowski, W., Administrative Law
Erlinghagen, P., Commercial and Business Law
Fezer, G., Criminal Law
Geilke, G., Eastern Law
Hansen, U., Criminal Law
Hruschka, J., Philosophy of Law
Kerner, H. J., Juvenile and Criminal Law, Criminology
Landwehr, G., German Private Law, Nordic Law
Martens, K. P., Civil Law
Martens, W., Public Law
v. Münch, I., Constitutional Law, Administrative Law
Nicolaysen, G., Public and State Law
Pick, E., Civil Law
Schilling, G., Criminal Law
Schmidhäuser, E., Criminal Law
Schmidt, K., Civil, Commercial and Economic Law, Civil Procedure
Schwabe, J., Public Law
Seiler, H. H., Roman Law, Civil Law
Selmer, P., Public Law, Law of Finance, Law of Taxes
Thieme, H. W., Administrative Law, Public Law
Walter, M., Juvenile and Criminal Law, Criminology

Werber, M., Civil and Insurance Law
Winter, G., Civil and Insurance Law
Zeuner, A., Civil Procedure, Civil Law, Labour Law
Ziegler, K.-H., Roman Law, Civil Law
Zweigert, K., Conflict of Laws and Comparative Law

Department of Law II:

Giehring, H., Criminal Law
Haag, F., Sociology
Hoffmann-Riem, W., Administrative, Criminal and Economic Law
Koch, H.-J., Public Law, Philosophy of Law
Moritz, K., Civil and Labour Law, Sociology of Law
Ott, C., Civil, Commercial and Business Law, Sociology of Law
Paech, N., Political Science, State Theory
Pfarr, H., Civil and Labour Law
Pongratz, L., Sociology, Criminology
Reich, N., Civil Law
Rittstieg, H., Public Law
Randzio, R., Civil Law
Schäfer, H. B., Political Economy
Sonnen, B.-R., Criminal Law
Struck, G., Civil Law
Villmow, B., Criminology
Walz, R., Commercial, Economic and Civil Law

Department of Economic Sciences:

Aldrup, D., Political Economy
Altrogge, G., Business Administration
Engelhardt, G., Political Economy
Erlinghagen, P., Economic Law
Fischer, L., General Business Administration
Fischer, O., Business Administration
Fleischmann, B., Business Administration
Ghaussy, A. G., Political Economy
Gollnick, H., Political Economy, Statistics
Hansmann, K.-W., Business Administration
Hasenkamp, G., Political Economy
Hofmann, H., Theoretical Political Economy
Jacob, H., Business Administration
Jürgensen, H., Political Economy
Kantzenbach, Erhard, Political Economy
Karrenberg, R., Business Administration
Karten, W., Business Administration
Koch, H., Economic Law
Kossbiel, H., Business Administration
Layer, M., Business Administration
Lipfert, H., Business Administration
Lorenzen, G., Political Economy
Lübbert, J., Political Economy
Lüder, K., Business Administration
Mühlenberg, F., Political Economy
Pokropp, F., Statistics and Mathematical Business Theory
Pressmar, D., Business Administration
Schachtsneider, K. A., Economic Law
Scheer, Chr., Finance
Schenk, K. E., Political Economy
Scherf, H., Political Economy, Statistics
Schmidt, H., Business Administration
Seelbach, H., Business Administration
Streidtferdt, L., Business Administration
Strobel, W., Business Administration
Theisen, P., Business Administration
Timmermann, V., Political Economy
Todt, H., Political Economy
Tolkemitt, G., Political Economy
Westphal, U., Political Economy

Department of Medicine:

Arnold, W., Forensic Toxicology
Baumann, K., Physiology
Baumgarten, H.-G., Anatomy
Begemann, F., Internal Medicine
Benthe, H., Experimental Pharmacology
Berger, J., Mathematic and Computer Applications of Medicine
Bettendorf, G., Gynaecology
Bläcker, F., Paediatrics
Bleichert, A., Physiology
Bleifeld, W., Internal Medicine
Boecker, W., General Pathology and Pathological Anatomy
Braun, W., Pharmacology and Toxicology
Brinkmann, B., Forensic Medicine
Bromm, B., Physiology
Bücheler, E., Roentgenology
Burchard, J. M., Psychiatry and Neurology
Busch, H., Transfusion Medicine
Colmant, H. J., Neuro-Pathology
Czok, G., Biochemical Pharmacology
Czygan, P.-J., Gynaecology
Dahm, K., Surgery
Dahme, B., Medical Psychology
Dahmen, G., Orthopaedics
Delling, G., General Pathology and Pathological Anatomy
Effenberger, E., Hygiene
Ewerwahn, V., Surgery
Fischer, K., Paediatrics
Frahm, H., Internal Medicine
Franke, H., Radiology
Franke, J., Facial Maxillary Surgery
Friedrich, W., Physiological Chemistry
Frischbier, H.-J., Gynaecology
Garweg, G., Anatomy
Goedde, H. W., Human Genetics
Götze, W. E., Maxillary Surgery
Grässlin, D., Experimental Endocrinology
Grensemann, H., History of Medicine
Gross, J., Psychiatric Clinic
Grüttner, R., Paediatrics
Gülzow, H. J., Dental Medicine
Halata, Z., Anatomy
Hellner, K.-A., Applied Neurophysiology
Heinrich, H., Physiological Chemistry
Herberhold, C., Oto-rhino-laryngology
Hiller, Chr., Microbiology and Serology
Hilz, H., Physiological Chemistry
Höhne, G., Gynaecology
Höhne, K., Medical Data Processing
Hölzer, K. H., Internal Medicine and Dietetics
Holstein, A.-F., Anatomy
Horatz, K., Anaesthesiology
Jänner, M., Dermatology and Venerology
Janssen, W., Forensic Medicine
Jung, H., Biophysics and Radiobiology
Jungbluth, K.-H., Accident Surgery
Jungmann, H., Balneology and Medical Climatology
Kahlke, W., Internal Medicine
Kalmar, P., Vascular Surgery
Kanz, E., Hospital Hygiene
Kaufmann, P., Anatomy
Kaupen-Haas, H., Medical Sociology
Keck, E., Cardiology
v. Kerékjártó, M., Medical Psychology
Klosterhalfen, H., Urology
Koch, G., Physiological Chemistry
Krause, W. ,Criminal Psychiatry
Kuhlencordt, F., Internal Medicine
Kühnau, J., Internal Medicine
Landbeck, G., Paediatrics
Lassrich, M., Paediatrics
Laufs, R., Medical Microbiology and Immunology
Lehnert, G., Occupational Medicine
Leichtweiss, H.-P., Physiology
Lentrodt, J., Dental Medicine, Dental Surgery
Lichtenthaeler, C., History of Medicine
Lierse, W., Anatomy
Linden, W., Biophysics and Radiobiology
Lindner, J., Pathology
Lisboa, B., Steroid Biochemistry
Löhr, H., Roentgenology
Marquardt, H., General Toxicology
Meigel, W., Dermatology
Meyer, A., Psychosomatic Medicine
Müke, R., Neurosurgery
Müller, D., Neurosurgery
Müller-Wieland, K., Internal Medicine
Nasemann, Th., Dermatology
Neth, R.-D., Experimental Medicine
Otto, H. F., General Pathology and Pathological Anatomy
Pascher, W., Oto-rhino-laryngology
Pfeifer, G., Maxillary Surgery
Puff, H.-K., Neurology
Ranke, B., Experimental Dentistry
Richter, P., Physiological Chemistry
Ritze, H., Dental Prosthesis
Rodewald, G., Cardiology
Rollin, H., Oto-rhino-laryngology
Rottke, B., Maxillary Surgery
Rumberger, E., Physiology
Sautter, H., Ophthalmology
Schäfer, H., General Pathology and Pathological Anatomy
Schassan, H.-H., Microbiology
Schirren, C., Dermatology
Schmidt, G., Sexology
Schneider, C., Radiology
Schönfelder, T., Psychiatry
Schorsch, E., Sexology
Schreiber, H.-W., Surgery
Schulz, K.-H., Dermatology
Schumacher, H.-H., Tropical Medicine and Parasitology
Seifert, G., General Pathology and Pathological Anatomy
Stegner, H.-E., Obstetrics and Gynaecology
Szadkowski, D., Occupational Medicine
Tänzer, A., Radiology
Tamm, J., Internal Medicine
Tarnowski, W., Physiological Chemistry
Thiele, H.-G., Internal Medicine
Thomsen, K., Obstetrics and Gynaecology
Tilsner, V., Internal Medicine
Trams, G., Gynaecology
Von Torklus, D., Orthopaedics
Voigt, K.-D., Clinical Chemistry
Wallis, H., Paediatrics
von Wichert, P., Internal Medicine
Winkler, K., Paediatrics
Wiskemann, A., Skin Diseases

Department of Philosophy and Social Sciences:

Ahrens, G., Social Sciences
Axelos, Chr., Philosophy
Bartuschat, W., Philosophy
Bermbach, U., Political Science
Deichsel, A., Sociology
Detel, W., Philosophy
Friedrichs, J., Sociology
Gantzel, K.-J., Political Science
Hartwich, H. H., Political Science
Hetzler, H. W., Sociology
Hilger, D., Social Sciences
Hilger, M. E., Social Sciences
Hoffmann-Riem, Ch., Sociology
Kleining, G., Sociology
Kleinsteuber, H. J., Political Science
Kob, J., Sociology
Kristof, W., Sociology
Oehler, K., Philosophy
Opp, K.-D., Sociology

RASCHKE, J., Political Science
RENN, H., Sociology
RICHTER, E., Philosophy
RUNDE, P., Sociology
SCHÄFER, L., Philosophy
SCHNÄDELBACH, H., Philosophy
SIEFER, G., Sociology
STEFFANI, W., Political Science
TETSLAFF, R., Political Science
TRAUTMANN, G., Political Science
TROITZCH, U., Social Sciences

Department of Pedagogics:
AHLBORN, H.
BÄRSCH, W.
BAUSCH, H.
BEIER, U.
BELSER, H.
BETZ, O.
BLEIDICK ,U.
BOLLMANN, H.
BORRIES, B. VON
BRAND, W.
BRUHN, J.
BRUMLIK, M.
BÜRGER, W.
BUTH, M.
CLAUSEN, R.
CLAUSSEN, B.
DAHRENDORF, M.
DEHN, M.
DIEL, A.
EHNI, H. W.
ETTL, H.
FIEDLER, U.
FILIPP, K.
FREISE, G.
FURCK, C.-L.
GLÜCKLICH, D.
GRIESING, W.
HAGEMEISTER, U.
HAMPE, R.
HEMMER, K.
HOEBERL-MÄVERS, M.
JUNG, H. W.
KAHL, P. W.
KAMINSKI, H.
KATH, F. M.
KIESSWETTER, K.
KLEBER, E. W.
KLEIN, P.
KLOSTER-JENSEN, M.
KOCH, F.
KOKEMOHR, R.
KREFT, J.
KRÖHNERT, O.
KRÜGER, E.
KÜNNE, W.
LANGE, H.
LAUFF, W.
LECKE, B.
LEHMANN, R.
LOEWER, H.
MARTENS, E.
MARTIN, W.
MARX, N.
MOHS, H.-J.
MYSCHKER, H.
OPASCHOWSKY, H.
OTTO, G.
PFEIFFER, E.
PLICKAT, H.-H.
POSTLETHWAITE, T. N.
PRIOR, H.
RATH, W.
RAUHE, H.
REETZ, L.
RÜNGER, H.
SARRIS, I.
SCARBATH, H.
SCHÄFER, H.-P.
SCHERLER, K.
SCHEUERL, H.
SCHLEICHER, K.
SCHNEIDER, W.
SCHORR, K.-E.
SCHOTTMAYER, G.
SCHREIER, H.
SCHULZ, E.
SCHULZ, W.
SCHWAGER, K.-H.
SEYD, W.
VON STAEHR, G.
STEFFENSKY, F.
STRUCK, P.
STÜTZ, G.
TEUMER, J.
THIELE, J.
TILLMANN, K.-J.
TYMISTER, H. J.
WALLRABENSTEIN, W.
WEICHERT, W.
WITT, R.
WILKENING, F.
WORM, H.

Department of Philology:
BACHOFER, W., German Linguistics and Literature
BERK, C. VAN DEN, Slavonic Philology
BEYERLE, D., Romance Philology
BÖHME, H., German Literature
BÖRNER, W., Linguistics
BOETERS, M., German Linguistics
BORCK, K.-H., German Philology
BRAUNECK, M., German Literature
BRIEGLEB, K., German Philology
BRINKER, K., German Linguistics
BURKHARDT, G., German Literature
DAMMANN, G., German Literature
FINK, E. O., English Philology
FISCHER, L., German Literature
FREYTAG, H., German Philology
FREYTAG, W., German Literature
GERKE, E.-O., German Linguistics
GUTKNECHT, C., English Language
HAAS, R., English Language and Culture
V. HAHN, W., German Linguistics
HENNIG, J., German Linguistics
HILLMANN, K., German Philology
IBANEZ, R., Hispanic Linguistics
KIBELKA, J., German Philology
KLEINSTÜCK, J., English Philology
KÖSTER, U., German Literature
KRATZEL, G., Slavonic Philology
KROGOLL, J., German Literature
KRUMM, H. J., Historiography
KRUSE, MARGOT, Romance Philology
LEHMANN, V., Historiography
LORENZ, E., Romance Philology
MAHER, J. P., English Philology
MANDELKOW, K. R., Literature
MARTENS, G., German Literature
MARTENS, P., German Phonetics
MEIER, J., German Linguistics
MEYER-MINNEMANN, K., Romance Philology
MÖHN, D., German Philology, esp. Low German
MÜLLER, H.-H., German Literature
NOWIKOWA, I., Slavonic Studies
OKSAAR, E., Comparative Language Studies
PRESCH, G., German Linguistics
PRILLWITZ, S., German Linguistics
RÜHL, D., Romance Philology
SCHLUMBOHM, D., Romance Philology
SCHMID, W., Slavonic Literature
SCHMITT, CHR., Romance Philology
SCHNEIDER, K.-L., German Philology and Modern Literature
SCHULTZE, B., English Philology
SCHWANITZ, D., English Philology
SETTEKORN, W.
STEMPEL, W.-D., Romance Philology
TERNES, E., Phonetics
TIEDJE, E., English Philology
VEENKER, W., Finno-Ugrian Philology
WALTER, H. A., Literature of German Exiles
WINTER, H.-G., German Literature
WITTSCHIER, H. W., Romance Philology
WOLLENBERG, F., German Literature

Department of Historiography:
ALPERS, K., Classical Philology
ANGERMANN, M., Medieval and Modern History
BÜHLER, W., Classical Philology
BUISSON, I., Medieval and Modern History
BUISSON, L., Medieval and Modern History
DEININGER, J., Ancient History
EHLERS, W.-W., Classical Philology
GROTHUSEN, K., Modern East European History
HERRMANN, P., Ancient History
HERZIG, A., Modern History
HOFFMANN, D., Ancient History
KAMBYLIS, A., Byzantine and Modern Greek Philology
KNEBEL, G., Classical Philology
KRAUSE, H.-G., Medieval and Modern History
LANGEWIESCHE, D., Modern History
LUDWIG, W., Classical Philology
MEJCHER, H., Modern History
MOLTMANN, G., Medieval and Modern History
SEIDENSTICKER, B., Classical Philology
SYWOTTEK, A., Modern History
THEUERKAUF, G., Medieval and Modern History
VOIGT, E.-M.
WENDT, B. J., Medieval and Modern History
WOHLFEIL, R., Medieval and Modern History

Department of Cultural History:
ALTENMÜLLER, H., Egyptology
DÖMLING, W., Music
FISCHER, H., Folklore
FLOROS, C., Music
HERDING, K., Medieval and Modern History of Art
HINZ, E., Ancient American Language and Culture
HÜBENER, W., European Pre-history
JENSEN, J., Folklore
JÜRGENS, J., Music
KARBUSICKY, V., Music
KÜMMEL, H. M., Cuneiform Characters
LAUBSCHER, H.-P., Classical Archaeology
LUTZ, G., German Archaeology and Folklore
MARX, H. J., Music
PERRIG, A., History of Art
WARNKE, M., History of Art
ZAZOFF, P., Classical Archaeology
ZIEGERT, H., Pre-history

Department of Oriental Studies:
ALTENMÜLLER, H., Egyptology
BENL, O., Japanology
BRAKEL, L., Austronesian Languages and Cultures
EMMERICK, R., Iranian Studies
ENDE, W., Islamic
GERHARDT, L., African Languages and Cultures
HAMMERSCHMIDT, E., African Languages and Cultures
KAPPERT, P., Turkish Studies
KÜMMEL, H. M., Cuneiform Characters
RALL-NIU, J., Sinology
ROSENBERG, K., Thai Philology
SCHMITHAUSEN, L., Indology
SRINIVASAN, S. A., Indology
WENK, K., Thailand Language and Culture
WEZLER, A., Indology

Department of Mathematics:
ANSORGE, R.
BEHNEN, K.
BENZ, W.

BERNDT, R.
BRAUN, H.
BRÜCKNER, H.
ECKHARDT, U.
GEIGER, C.
GLASHOFF, K.
HALIN, R.
HASS, R.
HOFMANN, W. D.
HÜBNER, G.
HÜNEMÖRDER, CH.
KERBY, W.
KLEINERT, A.
KÖHLER, E.
KRÄMER, H.
LEGRADY, K.
MICHALICEK, J.
MÜLLER, H.
NEUHAUS, G.
OPFER, G.
RIEMENSCHNEIDER, O.
SCHAEFFER, H.
SCHRÖDER, E.
SCRIBA, C.
SEIER, W.
STRADE, H.
WERNER, B.
WEYER, J.

Department of Physics:

ANDERSSON-LINDSTRÖM, G., Experimental Physics
APPEL, J., Theoretical Physics
BARTELS, J., Theoretical Physics
BLOBEL, V., Experimental Physics
BRÜCKMANN, M., Experimental Physics
BUCHHOLZ, D., Theoretical Physics
BÜSSER, F.-W., Experimental Physics
DANIELMEYER, H. G., Experimental Physics
DUHM, H., Experimental Physics
FAY, D., Theoretical Physics
GEISSLER, D., Theoretical Physics
GERAMB, H. V. VON, Theoretical Physics
GERDAU, E., Experimental Physics
HAAG, R., Theoretical Physics
HARSDORF, M., Applied Physics
HAUG, U., Astronomy
HAZLEHURST, J., Astronomy
HEYSZENAU, H., Theoretical Physics
HOLDER, M., Experimental Physics
HUBER, G., Experimental Physics
JENTSCHKE, W., Physics
KOTTHAUS, J., Applied Physics
KRAMER, G., Theoretical Physics
KUNZ, CHR., Experimental Physics
LANGKAU, R., Experimental Physics
LAUTERBORN, D., Astronomy
LEGLER, W., Applied Physics
LEHMANN, H., Theoretical Physics
LINDNER, A., Theoretical Physics
LOHRMANN, E., Experimental Physics
MACK, G., Theoretical Physics
REFSDAL, S., Astronomy
SCHARNBERG, K., Theoretical Physics
SCHMIDT, H., Theoretical Physics
SCHMÜSER, P., Experimental Physics
SCHÖNHAMMER, K., Theoretical Physics
SCHOPPER, H., Physics
SCOBEL, W., Experimental Physics
SONNTAG, B., Experimental Physics
SPITZER, H., Fundamental Physics
STÄHELIN, P., Experimental Physics
STEINER, F., Theoretical Physics
STROHBUSCH, U., Experimental Physics
TEWORDT, L., Theoretical Physics
DE VEGT, CH., Astronomy
WEBER, G., Fundamental Physics
WEIGERT, A., Astronomy
WENDKER, H., Astronomy
ZIMMERER, G., Experimental Physics

Department of Chemistry:

TOM DIECK, H., Inorganic Chemistry
FISCHER, R. D., Inorganic Chemistry
FÖRSTER, H., Physical Chemistry
GERCKEN, G., Biochemistry
GUNSSER, W., Physical Chemistry
HANEFELD, W., Pharmaceutical Chemistry
JENTSCH, J., Organic Chemistry
KAMINSKY, W., Inorganic Chemistry
KASTENING, B., Electrical Chemistry
KLAR, G., Inorganic Chemistry
KNAPPWOST, A., Physical Chemistry
KÖNIG, W., Organic Chemistry
KÖSTER, H., Organic Chemistry and Biochemistry
KRAMOLOWSKY, R., Inorganic Chemistry
KREBS, A., Organic Chemistry
KREUZKAMP, N., Pharmaceutical Chemistry
KROPF, H., Organic Chemistry
LECHERT, H., Physical Chemistry
LIEMANN, F., Biochemistry
LÜHRS, K., Pharmaceutical Chemistry
MATTHIES, D., Pharmaceutical Chemistry
DE MEIJERE, A., Inorganic Chemistry
MESSINGER, P., Pharmaceutical Chemistry
MIELK, J., Pharmaceutical Technology
MONTAG, A., Food Chemistry
NAGORNY, K., Physical Chemistry
PAULSEN, H., Organic Chemistry
SCHAUMANN, E., Inorganic Chemistry
SCHNEIDER, E., Food Chemistry
SINN, H., Inorganic Chemistry
STEINBACH, F., Physical Chemistry
THIEM, J., Inorganic Chemistry
THIEME, F., Physical Chemistry
THORN, W., Biochemistry
VOSS, J., Inorganic Chemistry
WALTER, W., Theoretical Chemistry
WEISS, E., Inorganic and Analytical Chemistry
ZACHMANN, G., Inorganic and Analytical Chemistry

Department of Biology:

ABEL, W., Botany
ABRAHAM, R., Entomology
BAUCH, J., Timber Biology
BECKER, W., Zoology
BOCK, E., General Microbiology
BÖTTGER, M., General Botany
BRAUM, E., Fishery Biology
BRÜNIG, E. F., International Forestry
CHOPRA, V., Zoology
DEUTSCHMANN, F., Market Research
DÖRFFLING, K., General Botany
DÜVEL, D., Botany
DZWILLO, M., Zoology
ECKSTEIN, D., Timber Biology
FORTNAGEL, P., Botany
FRANCK, D., Zoology
FRÜHWALD, A., Mechanical Processing of Timber
HARTMANN, G., Zoology
HEINRICH, G., General Botany
IHLENFELDT, H., Botany
KAISER, P., Zoology
KAMINSKY, G., Timber Economics
KIES, L., General Botany
KNÖSEL, D., Phytopathology and Preservation of Plants
KNUSSMANN, R., Anthropology
KOEPCKE, H.-W., Zoology
KRAUS, L., Pharmacognosy
KRAUS, O., Zoology
KRISTEN, U., General Botany
KUBITZKI, K., Systematic Botany
LIESE, W., Timber Biology
LILLELUND, K., Hydrobiology
MERGENHAGEN, D., Cell Biology
MIX, M., Electromicroscopy
NOACK, D., Timber Technology
PARZEFALL, J., Zoology
PATT, R., Chemical Timber Technology
PETERS, N., Zoology
RENWRANTZ, L., Zoology
RÜHM, W., Zoology
SCHLIEMANN, H., Zoology
SCHMIDT, A., General Botany
SCHNACK, D., Hydrobiology
SPRECHER, E., Pharmacognosy
STRÜMPEL, H., Zoology
THIEL, H., Hydrobiology
VILLWOCK, W., Zoology
WEBER, A., General Botany
v. WEIHE, K., Botany
WENZEL, F., Zoology
WIEBECKE, C., Forestry
WILKENS, H., Zoology
ZANDER, C.-D., Zoology

Department of Earth Sciences:

ALBERTI, G., Geology and Palaentology
BEHLE, A., Geophysics
BORCHERT, G., Geography and Palaeontology
DEGENS, E. T., Geology
DUDA, S. J., Geophysics
FIEDLER, K., Geology
FISCHER, G., Geophysics
GRIMMEL, E., Geography
HASSE, L., Geophysics
HILLMER, G., Geology and Palaeontology
HINZPETER, H., Geophysics
JARCHOW, O., Mineralogy
JUNG, D., Mineralogy
LEHMANN, U., Geology
MAKRIS, J., Geophysics
MENSCHING, H., Geography
MIEHLICH, G., Biology
NUHN, H., Economic Geography
OBERBECK, G., Geography
POHL, D., Mineralogy
RATH, R., Mineralogy
SAALFELD, H., Mineralogy
SANDNER, G., Economic Geography
SCHARPENSEEL, H. W., Biology
SENDLER, G., Geography
SPAETH, CH., Geology and Palaeontology
SPIELMANN, H.-O., Geography
STILKE, G., Geophysics
SÜNDERMANN, J., Oceanography
TARKIAN, M., Mineralogy
THIEDIG, F., Geology
VALETON, I., Mineralogy
VOSS, F., Geography
WONG, H. K., Geology

Department of Psychology:

CROPLEY, A.
HEINZE, B.
KREBS, G.
PAWLIK, K.
LANGER, I.
RHENIUS, D.
SCHMALE, H.
SCHMIDTCHEN, S.
SCHULZ, VON THUN, F.
TAUSCH, R.
WIECZERKOWSKI, W.
WITT, H.
WITTE, E.

Department of Computer Sciences:

BRAUER, W., Computer Theory
BRUNNSTEIN, K., Computer Applications
FLESSNER, H., Computer Applications
GRASS, W., Digital Technology
JESSEN, E., Computer Organization
KUDLEK, M., Computer Theory
KUPKA, I., Computer Theory
LAGEMANN, K., Computer Technology
NAGEL, H.-H., Computer Science
SCHMIDT, J., Computer Science
SCHWENKEL, F., Computer Programming
VALK, R., Computer Theory

Department of Physical Education:

CZWALINA, C.
DIETRICH, K.

EICHLER, G.
KRÜGER, A.
LANGE, J.
SCHRÖDER, W.
STRIPP, K.
TIEDEMANN, C.
TIWALD, H.

ATTACHED INSTITUTES:

Interdisciplinary Centre for University Didactics
Computer Centre
Institute for Shipbuilding
Centre for Socio-Pedagogical Studies
Central Institute for Foreign Languages (in the Department of Languages)
Audio-Visual Centre (in the Department of Education)
Contact-Institute for Scientific Continuing Education

MEDIZINISCHE HOCHSCHULE HANNOVER*
(Hanover University of Medicine)

3000 HANNOVER 61,
KARL-WIECHERT-ALLEE 9
Founded 1961.

Rector: Prof. Dr. HEINZ HUNDESHAGEN.
Dean of Student Affairs: Prof. Dr. med. K. ALEXANDER.
Librarian: Dr. rer. nat. G. KUSKE.

Library of 90,000 vols.
Number of teachers: 170.
Number of students: 1,100.

* No reply received to our questionnaire this year.

UNIVERSITÄT HANNOVER

3 HANNOVER,
WELFENGARTEN 1
Telephone: 762-1.
Founded 1831.

Rector: Prof. HINRICH SEIDEL.
Library Director: Dr.-Ing. G. SCHLITT.

Number of teachers: 1,390.
Number of students: 18,000.

DEANS:

Faculty of Mathematics and Sciences: Prof. Dr. rer. nat. HENNINGSEN.
Faculty of Civil Engineering and Architecture: Prof. Dr.-Ing. PARTENSCKY.
Faculty of Mechanical and Electrical Engineering: Prof. Dipl.-Ing. WANGERIN.
Faculty of Horticulture and Agriculture: Prof. Dr. agr. WRICKE.
Faculty of Arts and Social Sciences: Prof. Dr. jur. SEIFERT.
Faculty of Law: Prof. Dr. jur. KILIAN.
Faculty of Economics: Prof. Dr. oec. publ. GEIGANT.

PROFESSORS:

Faculty of Mathematics and Sciences:

Department of Mathematics:

BERTRAM, G., Applied Analysis
EPHESER, H., Mathematical Stochastics
KALUZA, T., Higher Mathematics
MORGENSTERN, D., Informatics
MÜLLER, D., Mathematics
RIEGER, G. J., Geometry
TIETZ, H., Mathematics

Department of Physics:

BÖTTICHER, W.
BREHM, B.
EVERTS, H.-U.
MIKESKA, H. J.
STEUDEL, A.
WELLING, H.
WERNER, E.

Department of Chemistry:

BERTHOLD, H. J., Inorganic Chemistry
BODE, H., Inorganic and Analytical Chemistry
HAUL, R., Physical and Electrical Chemistry
HERRMANN, K., Food Chemistry
HOFFMANN, H. M. R., Organic Chemistry
SCHÜGERL, K., Technical Chemistry
SCHMALZRIED, H., Physical and Electrical Chemistry
SEIDEL, H., Inorganic Chemistry
WINTERFELDT, E., Organic Chemistry

Department of Earth Sciences:

EBERHARD, E., Mineralogy
GRÖTZBACH, E., Culture Geography
HENNINGSEN, D., Geology
VOPPEL, G., Economic Geography

Faculty of Civil Engineering and Architecture:

Department of Architecture:

HOFMANN, W., Building Construction Theory
KAPPELER, D., Drawing and Painting
LAAGE, G., Construction
LANDZETTEL, W., Town and Country Planning
LINDINGER, H., Industrial Design
LUZ, W., Planning and Housing
MECKSEPER, C., History of Architecture
SCHWEGER, P., Design and Industrial Art
SCHWERDTFEGER, S., Modelling
SPECKMANN, W., Work Methods and Processing of Wood and Artificial Materials
SPENGELIN, F., Town and Country Planning
TOKARZ, B., Construction

Department of Civil Engineering:

BIEGER, K.-W., Building Construction
GRABE, W., Building and Road Construction
HAKE, G., Topography and Cartography
JEBE, H., Building Technology
KEJWAL, K., Building Technology
KONECNY, G., Photogrammetry and Engineering Surveying
KRACKE, R., Railways and Roads
LACKNER, E., Foundations, Dams
LECHER, K., Hydrology
PARTENSCKY, H.-W., Hydroengineering
PFLÜGER, A., Statics
SCHEER, J., Steel Construction
SEYFRIED, C.-F., Water Supply
STEIN, E., Building Mechanics
TORGE, W., Theoretical Geodesy
WEINHOLD, J., Building Materials

Faculty of Mechanical and Electrical Engineering:

Department of Mechanical Engineering:

BAMMERT, K., Electrical Machines
BUXMANN, J., Thermodynamics
DOEGE, E., Transformer Technology
EHRLENSPIEL, K., Machine Elements
ERDMANN-JESNITZER, F., Materials
GAUSS, FR., Motor Engines
GROTH, K., Piston Engines
KETTNER, H., Industrial Machinery and Factory Plants
KIPER, G., Machine Elements and Factory Techniques
MAHRENHOLTZ, O., Mechanics
MAYINGER, F., Methodology
MÜNCH, W. VON, Materials
OEHMEN, H., Production Technology
PESTEL, E., Mechanics
RÖGENER, H., Thermodynamics
SCHWERES, M., Machine Construction
STEGEMAN, D., Nuclear Technology
TÖNSHOFF, H., Automated Machines
VOSS, G., Railway Machines

Department of Marine Engineering:

GEISLER, O., Marine Machinery
PETERSHAGEN, H., Ship Construction
WANGERIN, A., Auxiliary Machinery
WENDEL, K., Ship Design and Theory

Department of Electrotechnics:

BEYER, M., High Tension
FROHNE, H., Electrotechnics
FUNK, G., Electricity Supply
KINDLER, H., General Communications Technology
LANGE, K., Theoretical Electronics
LÖCHERER, K.-H., High Frequency Technology
MUSMANN, H.-G., Theoretical Communications Technology
RUMMEL, T., Electrical Heating
THOMA, M., Control Technology

Faculty of Horticulture and Agriculture:

Department of Horticulture:

BÜNEMANN, G., Fructiculture and Nursery Gardening
CARLSSON, N., Gardening Economy
KRUG, H., Horticulture
STORCK, H., Gardening Economy
WEHRMANN, J., Plant Nutrition
WRICKE, G., Applied Genetics
ZABELITZ, C. VON, Gardening Technology
ZIMMER, K., Ornamental Plants

Department of Soil Husbandry:

BUCHWALD, K., Soil Husbandry
KISTENMACHER, H., Landscape Gardening
ZEIDLER, H., Science of Vegetation

Department of Biology and Meteorology:

DIEKMANN, H., Microbiology
GLUBRECHT, H., Biophysics
REICHENBACH, Graf VON, Soil Sciences
RICHTER, G., Botany
ROTH, R., Meteorology and Climatology

Faculty of Arts and Political Sciences:

Department of Philology and History:

GRAU, G.-G., Philosophy
KÖNIG, E., English Language
KREUTZER, L., German Literature and Language
LEUSCHNER, J., History
LUDWIG, O., German Language
MÜLLER, R. W., Politics
SEIFERT, J., Politics
TREUE, W., History
WEBER, R., English Literature and Language
WILDE, H.-O., English Philology

Department of Education:

AMMEN, A., Education
AURIN, K., Education
BRÜCKNER, P., Psychology
JUNGK, D., Vocational Education
KERN, H., Social Sciences
MENCK, P., Education
NEGT, O., Social Sciences
TREBELS, A. H., Sports
TSCHAMMER-OSTEN, B., Domestic Sciences
WELLENDORF, F., Psychology

Faculty of Law:
CALLIESS, R.-P., Criminal Law
DORNDORF, E., Civil Law
GILLES, P., Civil Law
HESSE, H. A., Teaching of Law
HUHN, D., Teaching of Law
KAUPEN, W., Sociology
KILIAN, W., Civil Law
MASSING, O., Politics
OERTZEN, P. VON, Politics
PIEPER, H., Law
SACK, F., Sociology
SCHNEIDER, H.-P., Politics
WALTHER, M., Teaching of Law

Faculty of Economics:
BERGER, K.-H., Management Economics
ECKARDSTEIN, D., Management Economics
HÜBL, L., Economics
JÖHNK, M.-D., Econometrics and Statistics
MÜHLER, U., Economics

TIERÄRZTLICHE HOCHSCHULE HANNOVER
(Hanover School of Veterinary Medicine)

3000 HANNOVER 1,
BISCHOFSHOLER DAMM 15
Telephone: (0511) 81131.
Telex: 922034 tiho D.

Founded 1778 as Königliche Rossarzneischule, attained university status 1913.

Rector: Prof. Dr. W. SCHULZE.
Pro-Rector: Prof. Dr. H. FRERKING.
Administrative Officer: HANS LINNEMANN.
Librarian: Dr. KLAUS BARESEL.

Number of teachers: 132.
Number of students: 1,321.

DIRECTORS:

Institute of Anatomy: Prof. Dr. WILKENS.
Institute of Pathology: Prof. Dr. L.-C. SCHULZ.
Institute of Physiology: Prof. Dr. v. ENGELHARDT.
Institute of Physiological Chemistry: Prof. Dr. J. SCHOLE.
Institute of Microbiology and Animal Diseases: Prof. Dr. BISPING.
Institute of Chemistry: Prof. Dr. RÜSSEL.
Institute of Botany: Prof. Dr. STROTMANN.
Institute of Animal Breeding and Genetics: Prof. Dr. C. GALL.
Institute of Parasitology: Prof. Dr. M. ROMMEL.
Institute of Zoology: Prof. Dr. M. RÖHRS.
Institute of Food Science and Technology: Prof. Dr. S. WENZEL.
Institute of Milk Hygiene and Technology: Prof. Dr. H.-U. WIESNER.
Institute of Pharmacology, Toxicology and Pharmacy: Prof. Dr. K. KAEMMERER.
Poultry Clinic: Prof. Dr. O. SIEGMANN.
Institute of Virology: Prof. Dr. LIESS.
Institute of Animal Nutrition: Prof. Dr. H. MEYER.
Institute of Animal Hygiene: Prof. Dr. H. G. HILLIGER.
Institute of Statistics and Biometry: Prof. Dr. H. RUNDFELDT.
Clinic for Small Hoofed Animals, Forensic Medicine and Ambulatory Clinic: Prof. Dr. W. SCHULZE.
Horse Clinic: Prof. Dr. R. ZELLER.
Clinic for Domestic Pets: Prof. Dr. W. BRASS.
Clinic for Cattle Obstetrics and Gynaecology: Prof. Dr. E. GRUNERT.
Clinic for Cattle Diseases: Prof. Dr. STÖBER.
Clinic for Pet Andrology and Breeding: Prof. Dr. H. MERKT.

RUPRECHT-KARL-UNIVERSITÄT HEIDELBERG

6900 HEIDELBERG,
GRABENGASSE 1,
POSTFACH 105760
Telephone: 541.
Founded 1386.

Rector: Prof. Dr. ADOLF LAUFS.
Pro-Rectors: Prof. Dr. K. ROTHER, Prof. Dr. A. HÖPFNER.
Chancellor: SIEGFRIED KRAFT.
Librarian: Dr. E. MITTLER.

Number of teachers: 1,210.
Number of students: 21,588.

Publications: *Unispiegel* (monthly during term), *Mitteilungsblatt des Rektors* (irregular), *Ruperto Carola* (2 a year), *Pressemitteilungen Forschung* (irregular), *Pressmitteilungen Personalia* (irregular), *Pressespiegel* (monthly), *Heidelberger Jahrbücher* (annually).

DEANS:

Faculty of Theology: Prof. Dr. LOTHAR STEIGER.
Faculty of Law: Prof. Dr. PETER ULMER.
Faculty of Scientific Medicine: Prof. Dr. W. KRIZ.
Faculty of Theoretical Medicine: Prof. Dr. H. IMMICH.
Faculty of Clinical Medicine I: Prof. Dr. E. WEBER.
Faculty of Clinical Medicine II: Prof. Dr. W. JANZARIK.
Faculty of Philosophy and History: (vacant).
Faculty of Oriental and Classical Studies: (vacant).
Faculty of Modern Philology: (vacant).
Faculty of Economic and Social Sciences: (vacant).
Faculty of Mathematics: (vacant).
Faculty of Chemistry: Prof. Dr. K. SCHÄFER.
Faculty of Physics and Astronomy: (vacant).
Faculty of Biology: Prof. Dr. M. BOPP.
Faculty of Geosciences: Prof. Dr. D. BARSCH.
Faculty of Clinical Medicine (Mannheim): (vacant).
Faculty of Pharmacy: Prof. Dr. G. SCHWENKER.

PROFESSORS:

Faculty of Theology:
BOHREN, R., Practical Theology
BURCHARD, C., New Testament Theology
EISINGER, W., Practical Theology
GENSICHEN, H. W., History of Religion
PHILIPPI, P., Practical Theology
PICHT, G., Philosophy of Religion
RENDTORFF, R., Old Testament Exegesis
SCHINDLER, A., Historical Theology
SLENCZKA, R., Systematical Theology
STEIGER, L., Systematic Theology
TÖDT, H. E., Social Ethics
WESTERMANN, C., Old Testament Exegesis
WOLFF, H., Old Testament Theology

Faculty of Law:
BERNHARDT, R., German and Foreign Public Law and International Law
DOEHRING, K., German and Foreign Public Law and International Law
HÄSEMEYER, L., Civic and Civil Procedural Law
JAUERNIG, O., Civil and Procedural Law
KÜPER, W., Criminal Law, Criminal Court Law, History of Criminal Law
LACKNER, K., Penal Law, Procedural Law
LAUFS, A., History of German Law, Private Law, Civil Law
LEFERENZ, H., Criminology
MIEHE, O., Penal Law, Procedural Law, Criminology, Juvenile Law
MISERA, K., Roman Law, Civil Law, Labour Law
MOSLER, H., Public, International and Foreign Public Law
MÜLLER, F., Constitutional, Administrative, Canon Law, Constitutional and Law Philosophy
NICKLISCH, F., Civil Law, Commercial and Economic Law, Civil Court Law
NIEDERLÄNDER, H., Civil, Roman and Comparative Law
SCHNEIDER, H., Public Law
SERICK, R., Civil, Comparative and Commercial Law, Foreign Private Law
ULMER, P., Commercial and Economic Law, Civil Law
WEITNAUER, H., Civil Law, Labour Law, International Private Law

Faculty of Scientific Medicine:
BROSSMER, R., Biochemistry
FAHIMI, H. D., Anatomy
FORSSMANN, W., Anatomy
HARDEGG, W., Vivisection
HASSELBACH, W., Physiology
KRIZ, W., Anatomy
RÜEGG, C., Physiology
SCHIMASSEK, H., Biochemistry
SCHIPPERGES, H., History of Medicine
SCHMÄHL, D., Treatment of Tumours
SELLER, H., Physiology

Faculty of Theoretical Medicine:
BRAUSS, F., Hygiene and Bacteriology
DOERR, W., General Pathology and Pathological Anatomy
GOERTTLER, K., Comparative Pathology
GROSS, F., Pharmacology
IMMICH, H., Medical Documentation and Statistics
MUNK, K., Virology
QUADBECK, G., Pathological Chemistry, General Neuro-Chemistry
ROTHER, K., Immunology and Serology
SCHMIDT, G., Legal Medicine
ULE, G., Neuropathology
VOGEL, F., Anthropology and Human Genetics
WAGNER, G., Medical Documentation and Statistics

Faculty of Clinical Medicine I:
BAHNER, F., Endocrinology
BICKEL, H., Paediatrics
CHRISTIAN, P., Internal Medicine and Neurology
COTTA, H., Orthopaedics
DAUM, R., Paediatric Surgery
HUNSTEIN, W., Internal Medicine
JUST, O., Anaesthesiology
KOMMERELL, B., Internal Medicine
KUBLI, F., Gynaecology
KÜBLER, W., Internal Medicine
LINDER, F., Surgery
PAESLACK, V., Orthopaedics
PENZHOLZ, H., Neurosurgery
RÖHL, L., Urology
SCHETTLER, G., Internal Medicine
SCHMITZ, W., Special Thoracic Surgery
WEICKER, H., Internal Medicine

Faculty of Clinical Medicine II:
BOENNINGHAUS, H., Oto-Rhino-Laryngology
BRÄUTIGAM, W., Psychosomatic Medicine
GÄNSHIRT, H., Neurology
JAEGER, W., Ophthalmology
JANZARIK, W., Psychiatry
KRISTEN, K., Dentistry, especially Dental and Jaw Surgery
MÜLLER-KÜPPERS, M., Paediatric and Juvenile Psychiatry
OVERDIECK, H.-F., Dentistry
SCHEER, K.-E., Nuclear Medicine
SCHNYDER, U., Dermatology and Venereal Diseases
SCHWINDLING, R., Dentistry, especially Denture Science
STAHL, A., Dentistry, especially Jaw Orthopaedics
ZUM, WINKEL K., Radiology

Faculty of Philosophy and History:
ARNDT, H.-J., Political Science
BELTING, H., History of Art
VON BEYME, K., Political Science
CLASSEN, P., Medieval and Modern History
CONZE, W., Modern History
HAMMERSTEIN, R., Music
HENRICH, D., Philosophy
JAKOBS, H., Medieval and Modern History
LEDDEROSE, L., History of East Asian Art
NEUBAUER, H., East European History
RIEDL, P., Contemporary and Modern History of Art
ROTHERMUND, D., Contemporary South Asian History
THEUNISSEN, M., Philosophy
WIEHL, R., Philosophy
WOLGAST, E., Modern History

Faculty of Oriental and Classical Studies:
ALBRECHT, M. V., Classical Philology
ALFÖLDY, G., Ancient History
BERGER, H., Indology
DEBON, G., Sinology
DELLER, K., Assyriology
DIHLE, A., Classical Philology
GÖRGEMANNS, H., Classical Philology
GSCHNITZER, F., Ancient History
HÖLSCHER, T., Classical Archaeology
MILOJČIĆ, V., Prehistory
PÖSCHL, V., Classical Philology
SARKISYANZ, E., Political Science
SCHALL, A., Semitic and Islamic Studies

Faculty of Modern Philology:
BALDINGER, K., Romance Philology
BERSCHIN, W., Latin Philology of the Middle Ages
BROCKHAUS, K., Applied Philology
HEGER, K., Comparative Philology
HEITMANN, K., Romance Philology
HENKEL, A., History of Modern German Literature
KÄSMANN, H., English Philology
MICHELSEN, P., History of Modern German Literature
MÜLLER, B., Romance Philology
OTTEN, K., English Philology
PANZER, B., Slavic Philology
v. POLENZ, P., German Philology
REICHMANN, O., German Philology, especially History of Language
RIESE, T. A., English Philology, especially History of Language
ROTHE, A., Romance Philology
WISNIEWSKI, R., German Philology
ZIMMERMANN, H.-J., English Philology, especially Science of Literature

Faculty of Economic and Social Sciences:
AMELANG, M., Psychology
ANGERMANN, A., Commercial Law
BASTINE, R., Clinical Psychology
BECKER, O., Theoretical Economics
v. CUBE, F., Pedagogics
FABER, M., Political Economics
GRAUMANN, C. F., Psychology
JAKSCH, H. J., Economics
KNALL, B., Political Economy
LENHART, V., Pedagogics
MENGES, G., Economics
RÖHRS, H., Pedagogics
ROSE, M., Political Economics
SCHLUCHTER, W., Sociology
SCHREMMER, E., History of Sociology and Economics
SOHMEN, E., Economics
WEINERT, F., Psychology
WILLEKE, F.-U., Political Economy

Faculty of Mathematics:
BÖGE, W., Applied Mathematics
DOLD, A., Mathematics
JÄGER, W., Applied Mathematics
JANKO, Z., Mathematics
KRIEGER, W., Applied Mathematics
MAASS, H., Mathematics
MÜLLER, G. H., Mathematics and Mathematical Logic
PUPPE, D., Mathematics
ROQUETTE, P., Mathematics
ROST, H., Laws of Probability and Statistics
v. WALDENFELS, W., Applied Mathematics

Faculty of Chemistry:
EBERT, K., Applied Physical Chemistry
JANDER, J., Inorganic Chemistry
KELLER, H., Inorganic Chemistry
OPRITZ, G., Organic Chemistry
PLIENINGER, H., Organic Chemistry
SCHÄFER, K., Physical Chemistry
SCHILDKNECHT, H., Organic Chemistry
SIEBERT, H., Structural Chemistry
STAAB, H., Organic Chemistry
SUNDERMEYER, W., Inorganic Chemistry

Faculty of Physics and Astronomy:
APPENZELLER, I., Astronomy
BASCHEK, B., Theoretical Astrophysics
BRIX, P., Physics
DOSCH, G., Theoretical Physics
ELSÄSSER, H., Astronomy
FRICKE, W., Astronomy
HAXEL, O., Physics
HEINTZE, J., Physics
HÜFNER, J., Theoretical Physics
MÜNNICH, K. O., Physics
NACHTMANN, O., Theoretical Physics
POVH, B., Physics
ZU PUTLITZ, G., Physics
SOERGEL, V., Physics
SPECHT, H. J., Physics
STECH, B., Theoretical Nuclear Physics
TAMM, K., Applied Physics
TITTEL, K., Physics
TRAVING, G., Theoretical Astrophysics
WEGNER, F., Theoretical Physics
WEIDENMÜLLER, H.-A., Theoretical Nuclear Physics

Faculty of Biology:
BAUTZ, E., Biology
BOPP, M., Botany
HECKER, E., Biochemistry
HOFFMANN-BERLING, H., Molecular Biology
KNAPPE, J., Biochemistry
MÜLLER, W., Zoology
RAUH, W., Systematic Botany
SCHACHNER-CAMARTIN, M., Neuro-Biology
SCHALLER, H., Microbiology
SCHNEPF, E., Cell Biology and Biological Electron Microscopy

Faculty of Geosciences:
AMSTUTZ, G., Mineralogy and Petrology
BARSCH, D., Geography
FRICKE, W., Geography
KIRCHHEIMER, FR., Geology and Palaeontology
MÜLLER, G., Mineralogy and Petrology
SIMON, W., Geology and Palaeontology

Faculty of Clinical Medicine (Mannheim):
BLEYL, U., General Pathology and Pathological Anatomy
FRIEDBERG, K. D., Pharmacology and Toxicology
HÄFNER, H., Social Psychiatry
HALLEN, O., Neurology
HENNEMANN, H. H., Internal Medicine
HOFFMEISTER, W., Internal Medicine
HUTH, E., Paediatrics
JENTSCHURA, G., Orthopaedics
JUNG, E., Dermatology and Venereal Diseases
v. KEISER, D., Radiology
LEGLER, U., Oto-Rhino-Laryngology
LIESENHOFF, H., Ophthalmics
LUTZ, H., Anaesthesiology and Reanimation
POTEMPA, J., Urology
SCHEPANK, H., Psychosomatic Medicine and Psychoanalysis
SCHMIDT, W., Dermatology and Venereal Diseases
STOLL, P., Gynaecology
TREDE, M., Surgery
WUNDT, W., Hygiene and Medical Microbiology

Faculty of Pharmacy:
NEIDLEIN, R., Pharmaceutical Chemistry
VOGT, H., Pharmaceutical Technology

ATTACHED INSTITUTES:

Südasien-Institut (*South Asian Institute*): Im Neuenheimer Feld 330; Dir. Prof. Dr. J. DIESFELD.

Institut für Sport und Sportwissenschaft: Im Neuenheimer Feld 700, 7 Akad.; Dir. R. VIERNEISEL.

HOCHSCHULE HILDESHEIM

3200 HILDESHEIM,
MARIENBURGER PLATZ 22
Telephone: 05121/81061-3.
Founded 1978.

Rector: Prof. Dr. HEINZ-WILHELM ALTEN.

Administrative Officer: HERMANN FISCHER.

Librarian: Dr. WOLFGANG EISOLD.

Library of 140,000 vols.

Number of teachers: 103.
Number of students: *c.* 1,000.

Courses in teacher training for elementary and secondary schools; degree courses in education, cultural pedagogy and technical and scientific translation; open university courses for graduate and postgraduate studies; doctoral course. Basic studies: pedagogy, psychology, philosophy, political science, sociology; optional studies: Evangelical theology, Catholic theology, fine arts, biology, chemistry, general studies, German, English, geography, history, mathematics, music, physics, social science, sport, technology, management.

UNIVERSITÄT HOHENHEIM

7000 STUTTGART 70
(HOHENHEIM),
POSTFACH 70 05 62
Telephone: 45011.
Founded 1818.

Academic year: October to September.

President: Prof. Dr. G. TURNER.

Vice-Presidents: Prof. Dr. K. LOEFFLER, Prof. Dr. F. MECHELKE.

Administrative Director: K. STAHLECKER.

University Librarian: Dr. J. MARTIN.

Number of teachers: 450.
Number of students: 3,500.

Publications: *Hohenheimer Arbeiten, Daten und Dokumente zum Umweltschutz, Rechenschaftsbericht*† (annually), *Hochschulführer*† (annually), *Vorlesungsverzeichnis*† (2 a year), *Forschungsbericht*† (every 2 years), *Informationsblatt* (monthly), *Amtliche Mitteilungen*†.

DEANS:

Faculty of General Natural Sciences: Prof. Dr. W. KRAUS.

Faculty of Biology: Prof. Dr. W. FRANK.

Faculty of Agricultural Sciences I (*Plant Production and Ecology*): Prof. Dr. F. GROSSMANN.

Faculty of Agricultural Sciences II (*Agricultural Economics, Agricultural Technology and Animal Production*): Prof. Dr. J. ZEDDIES.

Faculty of Economics and Social Sciences: Prof. Dr. E. HANF.

PROFESSORS:

Faculty of General Natural Sciences:

BACH, G., DR.RER.NAT., Mathematics
BOSCH, K., DR.RER.NAT., Mathematics
BRUCHMANN, E.-E., DR.RER.NAT., Technical Biochemistry
CLASSEN, H.-G., DR.MED., Toxicology and Pharmacology
CHRIST, W., DR.RER.NAT., Food Technology
FISCHER, A., DR.MED.VET., Food Technology
GEIGER, H., DR.RER.NAT., Chemistry
GIERSCHNER, K., DR.RER.NAT., Food Technology
HAUBOLD, H., DR.-ING., Inorganic and Physical Chemistry
HOLTMEIER, H.-J., DR.MED., Nutrition
KOCH, J., DR.RER.NAT., Biochemistry
KRAUS, W., DR.RER.NAT., Organic Chemistry
PFAENDER, P., DR.RER.NAT., Biochemistry
PIEPER, H.-J., DR.RER.NAT., Food Technology
RAU, H., DR.RER.NAT., Physics
RENZ, P., DR.RER.NAT., Biochemistry
SCHREIBER, H., DR.RER.NAT., Physics
SEILER, H., DR.RER.NAT., Physics
THÖNI, H., Biometry

Faculty of Biology:

BAYREUTHER, K., DR.RER.NAT., Genetics
EHRLEIN, H., DR.RER.NAT., Zoophysiology
VON FABER, H., DR.RER.NAT., DR.PHIL., Zoophysiology
FRANK, W., DR.RER.NAT., Zoology
FRENZEL, B., DR.RER.NAT., Botany
HESEMANN, C. U., DR.RER.NAT., Genetics
HESS, D., DR.RER.NAT., Botany
HORNICKE, H., DR.MED.VET., Physiology
KOERBER-GROHNE, U., DR.RER.NAT., Botany
LINGENS, F., DR.RER.NAT., Microbiology and Molecular Biology
MECHELKE, F., DR.RER.NAT., Genetics
RAHMANN, H., DR.RER.NAT., Zoology

Faculty of Agricultural Sciences I:

ACHTNICH, W., DR.SC.AGR., Tropical Plant Production
ALLEWELDT, G., DR.AGR., Viticulture
ARNDT, V., DR., Plant Ecology
AUFHAMMER, W., DR.AGR., Special Plant Production
BABEL, V., DR.SC.AGR., Soil Pedology
BANGERTH, F., DR.AGR., Applied Botany
BUCHLOH, G., DR.RER.NAT., Botany
GEIGER, H., DR.AGR., Genetics
GROSSMANN, F., DR.AGR., Phytopathology and Plant Protection
JACOB, H., Crop and Plant Production
KAHNT, G., DR.SC.AGR., Crop and Plant Production
KOCH, W., DR.AGR., Plant Pathology
KOHLER, A., DR.RER.NAT., Ecology
MARSCHNER, H., DR.AGR., Plant Nutrition and Soil Biology
MARTIN, P., DR.AGR., Plant Nutrition
MUELLER, F., DR.RER.NAT., Plant Protection
MÜLLER, W. A., DR.PHIL., Climatology
OHNESORGE, B., DR.RER.NAT., Applied Zoology
OTTOW, J. C. G., DR.AGR., Soil Chemistry
POLLMER, W. G., DR.AGR., Plant Cultivation
SARKAR, S., DR.RER.NAT., Plant Protection
SCHLICHTING, E., DR.AGR., Soil Science
SCHNELL, F. W., DR.AGR., Genetics and Plant Cultivation
STEINER, A., DR.RER.NAT., Plant Physiology
STOESSER, R., DR.SC.AGR., Applied Botany
WINTER, F., DR.AGR., Applied Botany

Faculty of Agricultural Sciences II:

ALBRECHT, H., DR.AGR., Communications Research and Agricultural Extension
BERGMANN, T., DR.AGR., International Agricultural Politics
BISCHOFF, T., DR.AGR., Agricultural Economics
BÖCKENHOFF, E., DR.AGR., Agricultural Economics
FEWSON, D., DR.AGR., Animal Husbandry
HENZE, A., DR.RER.POL., Agricultural Politics
HINRICHSEN, J. K., DR.AGR., Animal Husbandry
KUTZBACH, H.-D., DR. ING., Agricultural Technology
LOEFFLER, K., DR.MED.VET., Anatomy of Domestic Animals
MENKE, K.-H., DR.AGR., Animal Nutrition
MOSER, E., DR.-ING., Agricultural Technology
MÜLLER, H.-M., DR.RER.NAT., Animal Nutrition
MÜLLER, W., DR.MED.VET., Veterinary Hygiene
PLANCK, V., DR.AGR., Rural Sociology
RABOLD, K., DR.AGR., Animal Breeding
REICHL, J., DR.PHIL., Animal Nutrition
REISCH, E., DR.AGR., Farm Management
RUTHENBERG, H., DR.AGR., Overseas Agriculture
SCHOLTYSSEK, S., DR.AGR., Animal Husbandry
STRAUCH, D., DR.MED.VET., Veterinary Hygiene
STROPPEL, A., DR.-ING., Plant Production Technology
WEINSCHENCK, G., DR.SC.AGR., Agricultural Economics
ZEDDIES, J., DR.SC.AGR., Agricultural Economics

Faculty of Economics and Social Sciences:

BEA, F. X., DR.RER.POL., Management Studies
BLOSSER-REISEN, LORE, DR.AGR., Household Management
BOELCKE, W., DR.PHIL., Social and Economic History
EISELE, W., DR.RER.POL., Micro-economics
FOLKERS, C., DR.RER.POL., Political Economy
FOLLERT, B., DR., Production and Working Science
FROTSCHER, W., DR.JUR., Law
HANF, E., DR.OEC., Mathematical Economics and Operations Research
HÖRSCHGEN, H., DR.OEC. PUBL., Economics
MACHARZINA, K., DR.OEC.PUBL., Management and Organizational Research
MEHLER, F., DR.RER.POL., General Economics
PIESCH, W., DR.RER.POL., Statistics and Econometry
ROHRMOSER, G., DR.PHIL., Social Philosophy
RÜHL, M., DR.RER.POL., Communication Science
SCHERHORN, G., DR.RER.POL., Consumer Economics and Policy
SCHMIDT, J., DR.RER.POL., Competitive Politics
SCHULTZ-KLINKEN, K.-R., DR.AGR., Rural History
STEIN, J. H. VON, DR.OEC.PUBL., Commercial Economy and Banking Management
WAGNER, F. W., DR.OEC.PUBL., DR.RER.-POL.HABIL., Commercial Economy
WALTER, H., DR.RER.POL., Political Economy
WERNER, J., DR.OEC., General Economic and Social Science
WINKEL, H., DR.RER.POL., Economic and Social History

UNIVERSITÄT KAISERSLAUTERN

6750 KAISERSLAUTERN,
PFAFFENBERGERSTRASSE 95,
POSTFACH 3049
Telephone: 0631-8541.

Founded 1970 as Universität Trier-Kaiserslautern, separated 1975.

Academic year: October to September.

President: Prof. Dr. rer. nat. HELMUT EHRHARDT.

Vice-Presidents: Prof. Dr. rer. nat. HORST BECKER, Prof. Dr. rer. nat. MANFRED REGITZ.

Administrative Officer: Dr. HERMANN FAHSE.

Librarian: Dipl.-Ing. DIETER JOHANNES.

Number of teachers: 80.
Number of students: 2,500.

DEANS:

Faculty of Mathematics: Prof. Dr. EBERHARD SCHOCK.

Faculty of Physics: Prof. Dr. WOLFGANG DEMTRÖDER.

Faculty of Chemistry: Prof. Dr. JÜRGEN FUHRMANN.

Faculty of Biology: Prof. Dr. HEINRICH KAUSS.

Faculty of Mechanical Engineering: Prof. Dr. HANS GEORG HAHN.

Faculty of Electrical Engineering: Prof. Dr.-Ing. WERNER FREISE.

Faculty of Architecture, Environment Studies, Education: Prof. Dipl.-Ing. ALBERT SPEER.

Faculty of Computer Science: Prof. Dr. OTTO MAYER.

UNIVERSITÄT FRIDERICIANA KARLSRUHE (Technische Hochschule)

7500 KARLSRUHE,
KAISERSTRASSE 12

Telephone: 6081.

Founded 1825.

The Universität Fridericiana (Technische Hochschule) was the first technical institute in Germany and the first to acquire university status.

State control; Academic year: October to September.

Rector: Prof. Dr. H. DRAHEIM.

Pro-Rectors: Prof. Dr. H. KAHLE, Prof. Dr. G. ERNST.

Chancellor: Dr. G. SELMAYR.

Librarian: Dr. D. POGGENDORF.

Number of teachers: 1,000.
Number of students: 12,000.

Publications: *Personal- und Vorlesungsverzeichnis*†, *Fridericiana*†, *Uni-Information.*

DEANS:

Faculty of Mathematics: Prof. Dr. U. KULISCH.

Faculty of Physics: Prof. Dr. G. FALK.

Faculty of Chemistry: Prof. Dr. W. SEELMANN-EGGEBERT.

Faculty of Biological and Geo-Sciences: Prof. Dr. R. EMMERMANN.

Faculty of Art and Social Sciences: Prof. Dr. E. OLDEMEYER.

Faculty of Architecture: Prof. Dipl.-Ing. P. SCHÜTZ.

Faculty of Construction Engineering: Prof. Dr. H. H. HAHN.

Faculty of Mechanical Engineering: Prof. Dr. R. HALLER.

Faculty of Chemical Engineering: Prof. Dr. K. GRIESBAUM.

Faculty of Electrical Engineering: Prof. Dr. H. WOLF.

Faculty of Information Sciences: Prof. Dr. P. LOCKEMANN.

Faculty of Economics: Prof. Dr. G. HAMMER.

PROFESSORS:

Faculty of Mathematics:

BÜRGER, W., Theoretical Mechanics
FIEGER, W., Mathematical Statistics
HEUSER, H., Mathematics
HINDERER, K., Mathematical Statistics
KULISCH, U., Applied Mathematics
KUNLE, H., Mathematics, especially Geometry
LEOPOLDT, H.-W., Mathematics
MARTENSEN, E., Mathematics
NIEDHAMMER, W., Practical Mathematics
WALTER, W., Mathematics
WEISSINGER, J., Applied Mathematics
WITTICH, H., Mathematics

Faculty of Physics:

BUCKEL, W., Experimental Physics
CITRON, A., Experimental Nuclear Physics
FALK, G., Physics Education
FIEDLER, F., Meteorology
FUCHS, K., Geophysics
HEINZ, W., Experimental Nuclear Physics
HÖHLER, G., Theoretical Nuclear Physics
KAHLE, H. G., Experimental Physics
RUPPEL, W., Applied Physics
SCHMATZ, W., Experimental Nuclear Physics
SCHMID, A., Condensed Matter Physics
STÖCKMANN, F., Applied Physics
WESS, J., Theoretical Physics
WONDRATSCHEK, H., Crystallography
ZEITNITZ, B., Experimental Nuclear Physics

Faculty of Chemistry:

AHLRICHS, R., Theoretical Chemistry
BÄRNIGHAUSEN, H., Inorganic Chemistry II
FITZER, E., Chemical Technology
FRANCK, E. U., Physical Chemistry
FRITZ, G., Inorganic Chemistry
HEIMANN, W., Chemistry of Foodstuffs
HERTZ, G., Physical Chemistry
KROGMANN, K., Analytical Chemistry
MUSSO, H., Organic Chemistry
RETEY, J., Biochemistry
SCHINDEWOLF, U., Physical Chemistry
SCHRÖDER, G., Organic Chemistry II
SEELMANN-EGGEBERT, W., Radio-Chemistry
VOLLMERT, B., Macromolecular Chemistry

Faculty of Biological and Geo-Sciences:

ALTHAUS, E., Mineralogy
HANKE, W., Zoology
HERRLICH, P., Genetics and Toxicology
ILLIES, H., Geology
KILCHENMANN, A., Geography
KÜHLWEIN, H., Botany and Pharmacology
KÜMMEL, G., Zoology
LICHTENTALER, H., Botany
MAURIN, V., Geology, especially Applied Geology
PUCHELT, H., Petrography
WIRTHMANN, A., Geography

Faculty of Arts and Social Sciences:

BUSSMANN, History
LENK, H., Philosophy
LINDE, H., Sociology
ROTHE, G., Teacher Training
SCHULTE, Law
STEINER, J., Literature
WAPNEWSKI, Mediaeval German Literature

Faculty of Architecture:

BLEY, W., Interior Design
HALLER, F., Building Construction
LANKHEIT, K., History of Art
LEDERBOGEN, R., Basic Architecture
MARTINSSON, G., Landscaping and Landscape Gardening
SCHIRMER, W., History of Building
SCHÜTZ, P., Building Construction and Design
SELG, K., House Construction and Design
UHL, O., Building Planning and Design
WENZEL, F., Building Construction

Faculty of Construction Engineering and Surveying:

BAEHRE, W., Building Construction
DRAHEIM, H., Geodesy
GUDEHUS, G., Soil Mechanics and Foundation Construction
HAHN, H. H., Waterworks
HARTMANN, L., Engineering Biology
HEIDEMANN, C., Town and Country Planning
HILSDORF, H., Building Materials
HOFMANN, W., Topography
KREBS, H. G., Road and Railway Construction
KÜHN, G., Machines in the Building Industry
KUNTZ, E., Astronomical and Electronic Measurement
LAMMERS, G., Town and Country Planning
LEUTZBACH, W., Transport
MÖHLER, K., Building Construction
MÜLLER, F. P., Steel and Cement Construction
NATAU, O., Rock Mechanics
NAUDASCHER, E., Waterworks Construction and Hydrology
PLATE, E., Waterworks
SCHWEIZER, G., Transport and Traffic Systems
VOGEL, U., Construction Statics

Faculty of Mechanical Engineering:

BAHKE, E., Haulage
BECKER, E. W., Nuclear Engineering
ERNST, G., Technical Thermodynamics
GRABOWSKI, H., Use of Computers in Machine Construction
HALLER, R., Machine Construction and Heavy Vehicles
JUNGBLUTH, G., Combustion Engines
MACHERAUCH, E., Raw Materials I
MESCH, F., Measurement and Regulation Techniques in Machine Construction and Operating Techniques
SMIDT, D., Reactor Technique
THÜMMLER, F., Raw Materials II
VICTOR, H., Machine Tools, Workshop Technique
WEIDENHAMMER, F., Technical Mechanics
WITTIG, S., Thermal Electric Machines
ZIEREP, J., Theoretical Doctrine of Flow

Faculty of Chemical Engineering:

BIER, K., Technical Thermodynamics
BUGGISCH, N., Mechanical Engineering

GRIESBAUM, K., Petrochemical and Organic Technology
GÜNTHER, R., Heating Technology
HEDDEN, K., Chemistry and Technology of Gas, Petroleum and Coal
LONCIN, M., Food Processes
RIEKERT, L., Chemical Processes
SCHLÜNDER, E. U., Thermotechnics
SONTHEIMER, H., Hydro-Chemistry

Faculty of Electrical Engineering:
BODMANN, H. W., Applied Light Techniques
FÖLLINGER, O., Control and Steering Methods
FRIEDBURG, H., Electronics
GERTHSEN, P., Technology of Electrical Engineering
GRAU, G. K., High Frequency Technique
JUTZI, W., Electronics in Computer Engineering
KRONMÜLLER, H., Process Measuring Techniques
LAU, H., High-Voltage Technique, Electrical Equipment, Drives
MLYNSKI, D., Theoretical Electronic and Measuring Techniques
SCHULZ, P., Lighting
STEINBUCH, K., Communications
VOSSIUS, G., Biological Cybernetics and Physiology
WOLF, H., Communication Systems

Faculty of Information Sciences:
DEUSSEN, P.
GÖRKE, W.
GOOS, G.
KRÜGER, G.
LOCKEMANN, P.
MENZEL, W.
REMBOLD, W.
SCHMID, D.
SCHMITT, A.
SCHREINER, A.
WETTSTEIN, H.

Faculty of Economics:
EICHHORN, W., Economics
FUNCK, R., Economics
GÖPPL, H., Industrial Management
HAMMER, G., Operations Research
HENN, R., Political Economy
NEUMANN, K., Operations Research
ROSENMÜLLER, J., Operations Research and Economic Theory
RÜHL, G., Industrial Economics
RUTSCH, M., Econometrics and Statistics
STUCKY, W., Computer Sciences and Formal Description Methods

UNIVERSITÄT KASSEL

ZENTRALVERWALTUNG,
35 KASSEL,
MÖNCHEBERGSTR. 19
Telephone: 0561-8041.

Founded 1970; courses began October 1971.

State control; Academic year: April to March (two terms).

President: Prof. Dr. E. v. WEIZSÄCKER.
Chancellor: Dr. H. SAUER.
Librarian: Dr. H.-J. KAHLFUSS.

Number of teachers: 485.
Number of students: 7,255.

Publication: *Prisma.*

DEANS:

Educational Sciences: Prof. Dr. D. KRAUSE-VILMAR.
Vocational Training, Polytechnic Sciences: Prof. Dr. K. ANDERSECK.
Psychology, Sport, Music: Prof. Dr. K. ZIMMERMANN.
Social Work: Prof. Dr. D. OHLMEIER.
Social Sciences and History: Prof. Dr. L. DÖHN.
Applied Social Sciences, Law, Geography: Prof. G. RUCKERT.
Economics: Prof. E. LUCZKOWSKI.
Foreign Languages: Prof. Dr. H.-W. DECHERT.
German Language: Prof. Dr. W. BUDDECKE.
Fine Arts: Prof. F. SALZMANN.
Design: Prof. H. OESTREICH.
Architecture: Prof. Dr.Ing. S. KELLER.
City and Landscape Planning: Prof. K. PFROMM.
Civil Engineering: Prof. F. WALTER.
Mechanical Engineering: Prof. H. KLOSNER.
Electrical Engineering: Dr.-Ing. W. KLEINKAUF.
Mathematics: Prof. Dr. K. BURG.
Physics: Prof. Dr. K. SCHÄFER.
Biology and Chemistry: Prof. Dr. H. J. SEIFERT.
Agriculture: Prof. Dr. P. RZEPKA.
International Agriculture: Prof. Dr. H. WALTER.

CHRISTIAN-ALBRECHTS-UNIVERSITÄT KIEL

2300 KIEL, NEUE UNIVERSITÄT, OLSHAUSENSTRASSE 40/60
Telephone: 8801.
Founded 1665.

State control; Academic year: October to July (two terms).

President: Prof. Dr. GERD GRIESSER.
Vice-Presidents: Prof. Dr. WERNER KALTEFLEITER, Prof. Dr. OTMAR WASSERMANN.
Chancellor: HORST NEUMANN.
Librarian: Dr. GÜNTHER WIEGAND.

Number of teachers: 565.
Number of students: 13,392.

Publications: *Personal- und Vorlesungsverzeichnis* (every 6 months), *Christiana-Albertina* (every 6 months), *Jahresbericht* (annually), *Universitätsreden* (irregular).

DEANS:

Faculty of Theology: Prof. Dr. GOTTFRIED MARON.
Faculty of Law: Prof. Dr. JOST DELBRÜCK.
Faculty of Economics and Social Sciences: Prof. Dr. DIETRICH BARTELS.
Faculty of Medicine: Prof. Dr. WILHELM BÖKE.
Faculty of Philosophy: Prof. Dr. HARTMUT BOOCKMANN.
Faculty of Mathematics and Natural Sciences: Prof. Dr. OTTO KLAUS ALLKOFER.
Faculty of Agriculture: Prof. Dr. CLAUS-HENNING HANF.

PROFESSORS:

Faculty of Theology:
BECKER, J., New Testament
BIRKNER, H.-J., Systematic Theology
DONNER, H., Old Testament Studies and Biblical Archaeology
KRAFT, H., Church History and Dogma
LUCK, U., New Testament
MARON, G., Church History and Dogma
METZGER, M., Old Testament and Palestine Area Studies
SCHARFENBERG, J., Practical Theology
STECK, W., Practical Theology
WÖLFEL, E., Systematic Theology

Faculty of Law:
DELBRÜCK, J., Public Law
FIEDLER, W., Public Law
GRAUE, E. D., Civil, International and Comparative Law
HATTENHAUER, H., History of German Law, Civil and Commercial Law
HELLMER, J., Penal Law and Procedure, Criminology
HENKE, H.-E., Civil and Criminal Law
HORN, E., Penal Law and Procedure, Philosophy of Law
KEWENIG, W., Public Law
LOEBER, D. A., Oriental Law
VON MUTIUS, A., Public Law and Administration
SAMSON, E., Penal Law and Procedure
SCHMID, W., Penal Law and Procedure
SCHUBERT, W., Civil and Criminal Law
SONNENSCHEIN, J., Civil and Commercial Law
THIELE, W., Civil Law, Labour Law, Commercial Law
UNRUH, G.-C. VON, Public Law
WAGNER, H., Penal Law and Procedure
WUNNER, S. E., Roman Law and Civil Law

Faculty of Economics and Social Sciences:
ALBERS, W., Economics
BARTELS, D., Geography
BROCKHOFF, K., Industrial Economics
CLAUSEN, L., Sociology
DELLMANN, K., Industrial Economics
GIERSCH, H., Economic Structure
HANSEN, G., Econometrics
HAUSCHILDT, J., Industrial Economics
HERBERG, H., Political Economy
JECK, A., Theoretical Political Economics
KALTEFLEITER, W., History of Politics and Political Science
KNOLMAYER, G., Theoretical Management Studies
PAPPI, F. U., Sociology
PEFFEKOVEN, R., Management and Financial Studies
PESCHEL, K., General Economic Theory
PROSI, G., Political Economics
RÖHRICH, W., Political Science
ROHWEDDER, J., Theoretical Political Economics
SCHMIDT, R., Industrial Economics
WETZEL, W., Statistics and Econometry
WILLMS, M., Economic Structure

Faculty of Medicine:
BERNHARD, A., Surgery
BERNSMEIER, A., Internal Medicine
BLAUTH, W., Orthopaedics
BÖKE, W., Optics
CHRISTOPHERS, E., Dermatology and Venereology
DE DECKER, W., Ophthalmology
DOOSE, H., Paediatrics
GRAHMANN, H., Psychiatry and Neurology

GREMMEL, H., Radiology
GROTE, W., Human Genetics
GRÜNER, O., Legal and Social Medicine
GUNDERMANN, K.-O., Hygiene and Health
HAMELMANN, H., Surgery
HARBERS, E., Biophysics
HÄRLE, D., Dental Surgery
HARMS, D., General Pathology and Pathological Anatomy
HAUSS, K., Experimental Psychopathology
HAVSTEEN, B., Physiological Chemistry
HEINTZEN, P., Paediatrics
HOPPE, W., Dentistry
JENSEN, H.-P., Neurosurgery
KLINK, F., Physiological Chemistry and Molecular Biology
KÖRBER, K., Dentistry
KUDLIEN, F., History of Medicine
LENNERT, K., Pathology and Pathological Anatomy
LEONHARDT, H., Anatomy
LÜLLMANN, H., Pharmacology
MALYUSZ, M., Physiology
MÜLLER-RUCHHOLZ, W., Microbiology and Immunology
NIEDERMAYER, W., Internal Medicine
PEHLEMANN, F.-W., Biology for Doctors
PIRTKIEN, R., Medical Data Processing
REGENSBURGER, D., Surgery
RIECKERT, H., Sports Medicine
RUDERT, H., Oto-Rhino-Laryngology
RUDOLPH, G., History of Medicine
SACHS, V., Haematology and Transfusions
SAUTER, K., Medical Informatics and Statistics
SCHAEFER, J., Internal Medicine
SCHAUB, J., Paediatrics
SCHAUER, R., Physiological Chemistry
SCHIMMELPENNING, G. W., Psychiatry
SCHMIDT, R. F., Physiology
SEMM, K., Obstetrics and Gynaecology
SIMON, C., Paediatrics
SOYKA, D., Neurology
SPRENGER, E., General Pathology and Zytopathology
TILLMANN, B., Anatomy
TOLKSDORF, M.-E., Paediatrics and Medical Cytogenetics
ULBRICHT, W. W., Physiology
ULLMANN, U., Medical Microbiology
VÖLKEL, H., Psychiatry and Neurology
WAND, H., Urology
WASSERMANN, O., Toxicology
WAWERSIK, J., Anaesthesiology
WEISS, CH., Physiology
WELSCH, U., Histology and Cytology
WERNER, H., Radiology
WILLE, R., Geriatric and Social Medicine
WITZLEB, E., Bio-Climatology
ZILLES, K., Anatomy

Faculty of Philosophy:

BÄHR, J., Geography
BAUMANN, U., Psychology
BLÜHER, K. A., Romance Philology
BÖHM, R., English Philology
BOOCKMANN, H., Medieval and Modern History
BUCHLOH, P. G., English Philology
BUSCH, U., Slavonic Philology
BUSSE, H., Oriental Studies
DEBUS, F., German Philology
DOBLHOFER, E., Classical Philology
EDLER, A., Music
FEHLING, D., Classical Philology
FRÄNZLE, O., Geography
FREY, D., Psychology
FREY, K., Pedagogics
GRAU, U., Psychology
GROSS, K., English Philology
HAAG, H., Physical Education
HÄNSEL, B., Archaeology and Prehistory
HAUSMANN, K. G., East European History
HAUSSHERR, R., History of Art
HINZ, H., Archaeology and Prehistory
HOFFMANN, E., Medieval and Modern History
HOFMANN, D., Old German, Nordic and Frisian Philology
HÜBNER, K., Philosophy
JÄGER, D., English Philology
JUHNKE, H., Classical Philology
KOHLER, K., Phonetics
KOLB, F., Ancient History
KÖLVER, B., Indology and Religions
KRAMER, K.-S., Folklore
KRUMMACHER, F., Music
LEHMANN, H., Medieval and Modern History
LOCH, W., Pedagogics
LÜDTKE, H., Romance Philology
MÄHL, H.-J., Modern German Language and Literature
MANNACK, E., History of Modern German Literature
MAYER, H. E., Medieval and Modern History
MÜLLER, K.-D., German Philology
NITSCHE, P., East European History
OBERHOLZER, O., Nordic Philology
OTT, K. A., Romance Philology
PRANGE, K., Pedagogics
PRIESEMANN, G., Pedagogics
QUADLBAUER, F., Middle Latin Philology
REBAS, H., Northern History
RECKOW, F., Music
RUDOLPH, G., History of Medicine
SCHAUENBURG, K., Classical Archaeology
SCHIRMER, K.-H., German Philology
SCHMITZ, H., Philosophy
SCHWINGE, E.-R., Classical Philology
SIEVERS, K. D., Folklore
SJÖLIN, B., Friesian Philology
WEGENER, H., Psychology and Education
WENDT, D., Psychology
WESTPHAL, W., Physics Education
WINTER, W., Indo-German Phonetics
WINTERFELD, D., History of Art
WODE, H., English Philology

Faculty of Mathematics and Natural Sciences:

ACHENBACH, H., Geography
ADELUNG, D., Marine Zoology
AHRENS, J., Applied Mathematics
ALLKOFER, O. C., Physics
AMELUNXEN, F., Pharmaceutical Biology
BAGGE, E., Physics
BÄHR, I., Geography
BARTELS, D., Geography
BAUMANN, U., Psychology
BENDER, H., Mathematics
BETTEN, D., Mathematics
BINDING, H., Botany
BÖGER, H., Geology and Palaeontology
BÖTTGER, K., Zoology
BOHLKEN, H., Zoology
BRODOWSKY, H., Technical Chemistry
DIERSSEN, K., Botany
DREIZLER, H., Physical Chemistry
DUPHORN, K., Quaternary Geology
FLÜGEL, H., Zoology
FRÄNZLE, O., Geography
FREY, K., Pedagogics
FROHNE, D., Pharmacognosy
GASCHÜTZ, W., Mathematics
GÖTZKY, M., Mathematics
GRASSHOFF, K., Oceanology
GUARNIERI, A., Physical Chemistry
GÜNZLER, H., Mathematics
HAENSEL, R., Experimental Physics
HALBSGUTH, W., Botany
HALLER, R., Pharmaceutical Chemistry
HANSEL, B., Prehistory and Early History
HASSE, L., Meteorology
HEMPEL, G., Ichthyology
HEYDEMANN, B., Zoology
HINKELMANN, H., Physics
HINZ, H., Prehistory and Early History
HIRSCH, P., Microbiology
HÖRMANN, P. K., Mineralogy and Petrography with Geochemistry
HOLWEGER, H., Astronomy and Theoretical Physics
HORMANN, K., Geography
HUNGER, K., Theoretical Astrophysics
JAMMEL, A., Informatics
JANKOWSKY, H.-D., Zoology
JÜRGENS, H. W., Anthropology
KANDZIA, P., Practical Mathematics
KARSTENSEN, F., Physics
KERN, H., Mineralogy and Petrography and Geochemistry
KÖSTER, R., Geology
KOLLMANN, R., Botany
KOPPE, H., Theoretical Physics
KRAUSS, W., Theoretical Oceanography
KÜPPERS, H., Crystallography
LAGALY, G., Inorganic Chemistry
LANGMAACK, H., Informatics
LAUDIEN, H., Zoology
LIEBAU, F., Mineralogy and Crystallography
LINCKE, R., Physics
LUTZE, G., Geology and Palaeontology
MATTHESS, G., Geology
MEISSNER, R., Geophysics
MÜLLER, B., Pharmaceutical Technology
MÜLLER-BUSCHBAUM, H., Inorganic Chemistry
NOODT, W., Zoology
OBERSCHELP, A., Logic and Science
POHL, P., Pharmaceutical Biology
PREETZ, W., Inorganic Chemistry
PSCHORN-WALCHER, H., Ecology
RHEINHEIMER, G., Microbiology
RICHTER, J., Experimental Physics
RUDOLPH, H., Botany
SARNTHEIN-LOTICHIUS, J. M., Geology and Palaeontology
SAUTER, J., Botany
SCHIEMENZ, G. P., Organic Chemistry
SCHINDLER, R. N., Physical Chemistry
SCHLENDER, B., Information Sciences
SCHLOSSER, K., Folklore
SCHLÜTER, D., Astrophysics
SCHMIDT, R., Mathematics
SCHNEKENBURGER, J., Pharmaceutical Chemistry
SCHULTZ, W., Zoology
SCHULZ-DUBOIS, E. O., Applied Physics
SEIBOLD, E., Geology and Palaeontology
SEIFERT, F., Petrology and Mineralogy
SIEDLER, G., Geophysics
STEWIG, R., Geography
STRAKA, H., Botany
THIELHEIM, K., Physics
TOCHTERMANN, W., Organic Chemistry
ULLERICH, F.-H., General Zoology
VANSELOW, K., Physics
VOWINKEL, E., Organic Chemistry
WALGER, E., Geology and Palaeontology
WASSERMANN, O., Toxicology
WEGENER, H., Psychology and Pedagogics
WEIDEMANN, V., Astrophysics and Astronomy
WENDT, D., Psychology
WESTPHAL, W., Didactics of Physics
WIBBERENZ, G., Physics and Geophysics
WILHELM, H., Theoretical Oceanography
WLOKA, J., Mathematics
WOODS, J. D., Regional Oceanography
WÜNNENBERG, W., Zoology
ZEITZSCHEL, B., Oceanography

Faculty of Agriculture:
BÖRNER, H., Phytopathology
BOHLKEN, H., Zoology
BRÜMMER, G., Soil Science
DREPPER, K., Physiology, Physiological Chemistry, Animal Nutrition
ERNST, E., Animal Husbandry
FELDHEIM, W., Nutrition
FINCK, A., Plant Feeding and Pedology
GEISLER, G., Agriculture
HALBSGUTH, W., Botany
HANF, C.-H., Agricultural Economics
HANUS, H., Agriculture
HENKEL, H., Animal Nutrition
HESSE, K., Home Economics
HOFFMANN, W., Plant Nutrition and Soil Science
ISENSEE, E., Plant Production
KALM, E., Animal Husbandry and Genetics
KNAUER, N., Crop and Plant Science
KOESTER, U., Agricultural Economics
KOLLMANN, R., Botany
LANGBEHN, C., Agricultural Economics
RIEBE, K., Farm Management
SCHEPER, W., Commercial Politics
SCHROEDER, D., Plant Feeding and Pedology
STAMER, H., Agrarian Economics and Marketing
WEBER, A., Agrarian Economics and Marketing
WIDMOSER, P., Water Conservation

ATTACHED INSTITUTES:

Institut für die Pädagogik der Naturwissenschaften an der Universität Kiel (*Institute for Science Education*): 2300 Kiel 1, Neue Universität, Olshausenstr. 40/60, Haus N30; Dir. Prof. Dr. K. FREY.

Institut für Meereskunde an der Christian-Albrechts-Universität Kiel (*Institute of Oceanography*): 23 Kiel, Düsternbrooker Weg 20; Dir. Prof. Dr. B. ZEITZSCHEL.

Institut für Weltwirtschaft (*Institute for World Economics*): 2300 Kiel, Düsternbrooker Weg 120/122; Dir. Prof. Dr. GIERSCH.

Lorenz-von-Stein-Institut für Verwaltungswissenschaften (*Lorenz von Stein Institute for Management Sciences*).

Max-Planck-Institut für Limnologie zu Plön (*Max-Planck Institute of Limnology*): (*see* under Research Institutes).

Schleswig-Holsteinisches Landesmuseum für Vor-und Frühgeschichte (*Schleswig-Holstein Museum of Prehistory and Ancient History*): (*see* under Museums).

UNIVERSITÄT ZU KÖLN

D-5000 KÖLN 41,
ALBERTUS-MAGNUS-PLATZ
Telephone: 4701.
Founded 1388.

Rector Magnificus: Prof. Dr. iur. HERBERT WIEDEMANN.
Pro-Rector: Prof. Dr. rer. pol. RAINER WILLEKS.
Librarian: Ltd. Bibl.-Direktor Prof. Dr. S. CORSTEN.

Number of teachers: 1,097.
Number of students: 29,885.

DEANS:

Faculty of Economics and Social Sciences: Prof. Dr. H.-P. SCHWARZ.
Faculty of Law: Prof. Dr. P. HANAU.
Faculty of Medicine: Prof. Dr. A. BOLTE.
Faculty of Philosophy: Prof. Dr. G. BINDING.
Faculty of Mathematics and Natural Sciences: Prof. Dr. H. BUDZIKIEWICZ.

PROFESSORS:

Faculty of Economics and Social Sciences:
ANGER, H., Economic and Social Psychology
BIHN, W. R., Statistics and Economics
BÖSSMAN, EVA, Political Economy
BÜSCHGEN, H. E., Industrial Management
DÖRSCHEL, A., Pedagogics
ELLINGER, TH., Economics
FARNY, D., Insurance
GROCHLA, E., Economics
GUTENBERG, E., Economics
GUTMANN, G., Political Economy
HANSMEYER, K.-H., Political Economy
HAX, H., Economics
HENNING, F.-W., Economic and Social History
HERDER-DORNEICH, PH., Social Politics
HERMENS, F., Political Science
KERN, W., Economics
KLEIN-BLENKERS, F., Economics
KLOOCK, J., Economics
KÖHLER, R., Economics
KÖNIG, R., Sociology
KOPPELMANN, U., Economics
KUTZELNIGG, A., Economics
MACKSCHEIDT, K., Political Economy
MANN, F. K., Finance
MANN, G., Economics
MATZ, U., Political Science
MAYNTZ, R., Sociology
MÜNSTERMANN, H., Economics
NEIDHARDT, F., Sociology
OTREMBA, E., Economic Geography
RETTIG, R., Economics
RITTERSHAUSEN, H., Economics
ROSE, G., Economics
SCHÄFFER, K.-A., Economic and Social Statistics
SCHEUCH, E. K., Sociology
SCHLIEPER, F., Education
SCHMIEL, M., Economic and Vocational Instruction
SCHMITZ, P., Information Science
SCHMÖLDERS, G., Political Economy
SCHNEIDER, H. K., Political Economics
SCHWARZ, H.-P., Political Science
SIEBEN, G., Economics
SUNDHOFF, E., Industrial Management
SZYPERSKI, N., Economics
TWARDY, M., Economic and Social Pedagogics
VOPPEL, G., Economic Geography
WATRIN, CH., Political Economics
WEISSER, G., Sociology
WILLEKE, R., Political Economy
WILLGERODT, H., Political Economy
ZERCHE, J., Social Politics

Faculty of Law:
BAUMGÄRTEL, G., Civil Law
BECKER, H.-J., History of German Law, Civil and Canon Law
BÖCKSTIEGEL, K.-H., International and Constitutional Law, German and International Economic Law
BÖRNER, B., Civil Law, Economic Law
CARSTENS, K., Public and International Law
ERMAN, W., Civil Law
FRIAUF, K. H., State and Administration Law, Financial Law and Law of Taxation
HANAU, P., Labour and Economic Law
VON HIPPEL, E., International Law, Public Law, Law and State Philosophy
HIRSCH, H.-J., Penal Law, Process Law, Philosophy of Law
HÜBNER, H., Civil Law, Roman Law
JAHRREISS, H., International and Public Law, Law and State Philosophy
KAUFMANN, H., Criminology
KEGEL, G., Private International Law
KLINGMÜLLER, E., Insurance, Civil, and Commercial Law
KLUG, U., Penal Law, Process Law, Civil Process Law, Philosophy of Law, Banking Law
KOHLMANN, G., Penal Law, Philosophy of Law
KRIELE, M., Civil Law and Public Law
LANGE, R., Penal Law, Civil and Penal Procedure
LIEB, M., Civil and Labour Law
LÜDERITZ, A., Civil Law
MEINECKE, J. P., Civil Law, Roman Law, Law of Taxation
MEISSNER, B., East German Law
OEHLER, D., Penal Law, Penal Process Law, Foreign and International Penal Law, Protestant Church Law
PIRSON, D., International Law
PLEYER, K., Civil, Commercial and Labour Law
SEIDL, E., Roman and German Civil Law
SEIDL-HOHENVELDERN, I., Civil Law
STERN, K., State and Administration Law
TIPKE, K., Law of Taxation
WACKE, A., Roman Law, Civil Law
WEIDES, P., Public Law
WIEDEMANN, H., Labour Law, Commercial and Economic Law

Faculty of Medicine:
BOLT, W., Occupational Medicine, Social Medicine, Social Hygiene
BOLTE, A., Obstetrics and Gynaecology
BONHOEFFER, K., Anaesthesiology
DALICHAU, H., Cardio-surgery
DEBUCH, H., Physiological Chemistry
DOTZAUER, G., Forensic Medicine
EGGERS, H. J., Virology
EIFINGER, F., Dentistry
ENGELKING, R., Urology
FISCHER, R., General Pathology and Pathological Anatomy
FRIEDMANN, G., Clinical Radiology
FROWEIN, R., Neurosurgery
GLADTKE, E., Paediatrics
GROSS, R., Internal Medicine
HACKENBROCH, M. H., Orthopaedics
HEIMANN, K., Ophthalmology
HILGER, H.-H., Internal Medicine
HIRCHE, H., Physiology
HIRSCH, H., Physiology
IMHÄUSER, G., Orthopaedics
ISSELHARD, W., Experimental Surgery
JETTER, D., History of Medicine
KAISER, R., Gynaecology
KATNER, W., History of Medicine
KAUFMANN, C., Obstetrics and Gynaecology
KAUFMANN, W., Internal Medicine
KLAUS, W., Pharmacology and Toxicology
KLUSSMANN, F., Physiology
KNIPPING, H. W., Internal Medicine
KÖHLER, J. A., Dentistry
KUMMER, B., Anatomy

KUTZIM, H., Nuclear Medicine
LENTZE, F., Hygiene and Bacteriology
NEUBAUER, H., Ophthalmology
PAPE, H.-D., Dental Surgery
PETERS, U.-H., Neurology and Psychiatry
PICHLMAIER, H., Surgery
PULVERER, G., Hygiene and Microbiology
ORTMANN, R., Anatomy
SACK, H., Radiotherapy
SCHEID, W., Neurology and Psychiatry
SCHINK, W., Surgery
SCHNEIDER, M., Physiology
SCHWARZE, C., Dentistry
SEIFERTH, L., Oto-rhino-laryngology
STADTMÜLLER, F., Anatomy
STAMMLER, A., Neurology and Psychiatry
STEIGLEDER, G. K., Dermatology
STOFFEL, W., Physiological Chemistry
VOSS, R., Dental Prosthetics
WEIDTMAN, V., Medical Documentation and Statistics
WUSTROW, F., Oto-rhino-laryngology

Faculty of Philosophy:
ANGERMANN, E., Anglo-American History
ANGERMEIER, W. F., Psychology
BADENHAUSEN, R., Theatricals
BINDING, G., Art History and Urban Conservation
BÖCKMANN, P., History of Modern German Literature
BONHEIM, H., Anglo-American Philology
BORK, H.-D., Romance Philology
BRÄUER, H., Slavonic Philology
BREMER, H., Geography
BUCK, E., Theatre, Film and Television Studies
BUMKE, J., German Philology
CONRADY, K. O., History of Modern German Literature
DAHLMANN, H., Classical Philology
DERCHAIN, PH., Egyptology
DIEM, W., Oriental Philology
DOMBRADY, G. S., Japanese
ECK, W., Ancient History
ENGELS, O., Medieval and Modern History
FAUTZ, B., Geography
FELLERER, K.-G., Musicology
GERHARD, D., American Science
GERMER, R., English Philology
GIMM, M., Sinology
GREIVE, A., Romance Philology
GROENKE, U., Nordic Philology
GROOTHOFF, H.-H., Pedagogy
GRZESIK, J., Pedagogy
HEIKE, G., Phonetics
HEINE, B., African Studies
HELLER, K., Pedagogy
HERRMANN, H.-V., Archaeology
HILLGRUBER, A., Medieval and Modern History
HINCK, W., Modern German Language and Literature
HÜSCHEN, H., Musicology
IRMSCHER, H. D., History of Modern German Literature
JACHMANN, G., Classical Philology
JANERT, K., Indology
JOHANSEN, ULLA, Ethnology
KAEGBEIN, P., Library Science
KAHLE, G., Medieval and Modern History
KASACK, W., Slavonic Literatures
KASSEL, R., Classical Philology
KAYSER, K., Geography
KELLER, W., History of Modern German Literature
KIRCHHOFF, R., Psychology
KÖHLER, O., African Studies
KOLB, E., Medieval and Modern History
KUNISCH, J., Medieval and Modern History
LADENDORF, H., Art History
LANDGREBE, L., Philosophy
LANGOSCH, K., Middle Latin Philology
LEHMANN, G. A., Ancient History
LINKE, H., German Philology
MAIER, J., Hebraic Studies
MENZE, C., Pedagogy
MERKELBACH, R., Classical Philology
MEUTHEN, E., Medieval and Modern History
MÜLLER-BOCHAT, E., Romance Philology
OLESCH, R., Slavonic Philology
ÖNNERFORS, A., Middle Latin Philology
OST, H., Art History
OSTHEEREN, K., English Philology
PETRI, H., Ethnology
PIEL, J., Romance Philology
RATHOFER, J., German Philology
REIS, M., German Philology
RUBIN, B., Byzantine Studies
SALBER, W., Psychology
SCHALK, F., Romance Philology
SCHIEDER, T., Medieval and Modern History
SCHIEFFER, T., Medieval and Modern Art History
SCHREINER, P., Byzantine Studies
SCHWABEDISSEN, H., Prehistory, Early History
SCHWEIZER, G., Geography
SEILER, H., Comparative Philology
STÖKL, G., East European History
STRÖKER, ELISABETH, Philosophy
TAUTE, W., Prehistory, Early History
TIMMERMANN, O. F., Geography
UNDEUTSCH, U., Psychology
UNTERMANN, J., Comparative Philology
VATER, H., German Philology
VEKEMAN, H., Dutch Philology
VITTINGHOFF, F., Old History
VOLKMANN-SCHLUCK, K. H., Philosophy
WERNER, D. J., Geography
WICKERT, L., Old History
WOLLMANN, A., Philology
WÜRZBACH, NATASCHA, English Philology
ZIMMERMANN, A., Philosophy
ZINTZEN, C., Classical Philology
ZWIRNER, E., Phonetics and Theory of Language

Faculty of Mathematics and Natural Sciences:
ANGERMEIER, W. F., Psychology
BAUDLER, M., Inorganic and Analytical Chemistry
BAZLEY, N. W., Mathematics
BERGMANN, L., Botany
BINDER, K., Theoretical Physics
BISCHOFF, G., Geology
BREMER, H., Geography
VON BRENTANO, P., Experimental Physics
BRUNNACKER, K., Palaeontology
BUDZIKIEWICZ, H., Organic Chemistry
BURGER, E., Mathematical Statistics and Economic Mathematics
BURKARD, R. E., Mathematics
CAMPAGNA, M., Experimental Physics
DOERFLER, W., Genetics
DOMBROWSKI, P., Mathematics
EGELHAAF, A., Zoology
EHHALT, D. H., Geophysics
EILENBERGER, G., Theoretical Physics
FAUTZ, B., Geography
FEHÉR, F., Inorganic Chemistry
HAJDU, J., Theoretical Physics
HAPP, H., Experimental Physics
HARTE, CORNELIA, Physiology of Adolescents
HAUSER, U., Experimental Physics
HAUSSÜHL, S., Crystallography
HERR, W., Nuclear Chemistry
HOHLNEICHER, G., Theoretical Chemistry
HUMMEL, D., Physical Chemistry
JAENICKE, L., Biochemistry
JASMUND, K., Mineralogy and Petrography
JEHNE, W., Mathematics
JOHANSEN, U., Ethnology
JUX, U., Palaeontology
KAYSER, K., Geography
KIRCHHOFF, R., Psychology
KRUCK, TH., Inorganic Chemistry
LAMOTKE, K., Mathematics
LANDERS, D., Mathematics
LAUTERJUNG, K. H., Nuclear Physics
MEIS, TH., Mathematics
MEYER, C., Mathematics
MITTELSTAEDT, P., Theoretical Physics
MÜHLSCHLEGEL, B., Theoretical Physics
MÜLLER-HARTMANN, E., Theoretical Physics
MÜLLER-HILL, B., Genetics
NEUMANN, Dr., Zoology and Physiological Ecology
PAETZOLD, H. K., Geophysics and Meteorology
PETRI, H., Ethnology
PFANZAGL, J., Mathematics
POBELL, F., Experimental Physics
RAJEWSKI, K., Molecular Genetics
RASCHKE, E., Meteorology
REZNIK, H., Botany
SALBER, W., Psychology
SAUTER, F., Theoretical Physics
SCHRÖDER, J., Mathematics
SCHULT, O., Nuclear Physics
SCHUSTER, H.-U., Inorganic Chemistry
SCHWABEDISSEN, H., Prehistory, Early History
SCHWARZBACH, M., Geology
SCHWEIZER, G., Geography
STARLINGER, P., Genetics and Radiation Biology
STÖCKLIN, G., Nuclear Chemistry
STRAUB, J., Botany
TIMMERMANN, O. F., Geography
UNDEUTSCH, U., Psychology
VIELMETTER, W., Genetics and Microbiology
VOGEL, E., Organic Chemistry
WENDLER, G., Zoology, Animal Physiology
WERNER, D., Geography
WILLENBRINK, J., Botany
WINNEWISSER, G., Experimental Physics
WOERMANN, D., Physical Chemistry
WOHLLEBEN, D., Applied Physics
ZINN, W., Experimental Physics
ZITTARTZ, J., Theoretical Physics

UNIVERSITÄT KONSTANZ

D 7750 KONSTANZ,
POSTFACH 5560
Telephone: (07531) 881.

Founded 1966.

Academic year: October to September.

Rector: Prof. Dr. H. SUND.
Pro-Rectors: Prof. Dr. D. LORENZ, Prof. Dr. H. RABE, Prof. Dr. W. RATHMAYER.
Registrar: G. SCHLENSAG.
Librarian: Dr. jur. J. STOLTZENBURG.

Number of teachers: 136.
Number of students: 3,516.

Publications: *Personal- und Veranstaltungsverzeichnis* (annually), *Konstanzer Blätter für Hochschulfragen, Konstanzer Universitätszeitung und Hochschulnachrichten, Uni-info.*

DEANS:

Faculty of Mathematics: Prof. Dr. H.-B. BRINKMANN.
Faculty of Physics: Prof. Dr. H. BÖMMEL.
Faculty of Chemistry: Prof. Dr. E. DALTROZZO.
Faculty of Biology: Prof. Dr. P. BÖGER.
Faculty of Social Sciences: Prof. Dr. LEHMBRUCH.
Faculty of Economics and Statistics: Prof. Dr. G. GÄFGEN.
Faculty of Law: Prof. Dr. R. STÜRNER.
Faculty of Arts: Prof. Dr. P. L. SCHMIDT.

PROFESSORS:

Faculty of Mathematics:
BOHL, E.
BRINKMANN, H.-B.
FORST, W.
FRITSCH, R.
HOFFMANN, D.
KAUP, L.
NEUBAUER, G.
PRESTEL, A.
PUPPE, V.
SCHÄFKE, F. W.
STOSS, H.-J.
WATZLAWEK, W.

Faculty of Physics:
AUDRETSCH, J.
BÖMMEL, H.
BUCHER, E.
DEHNEN, H.
DIETRICH, W.
JÄCKLE, J.
KLEIN, R.
KORN, D.
RECKNAGEL, E.
SCHATZ, G.
WEBER, R.

Faculty of Chemistry:
BRINTZINGER, H.
DALTROZZO, E.
FELSCHE, J.
HUTTNER, G.
JOCHIMS, J.
METZ, F.
PFLEIDERER, W.
SCHMIDT, R. R.

Faculty of Biology:
ADAM, G.
BADE, E.
BÖGER, P.
BOOS, W.
BRDICZKA, D.
FLOREY, E.
GHISLA, S.
HEMMERICH, P.
HOFER, H.-W.
KNIPPERS, R.
KUTSCH, W.
LÄUGER, P.
MALCHOW, D.
MARKL, H.
MENDGEN, K.
MÜLLER, D. G.
PETTE, D.
PFENNIG, N.
PLATTNER, H.
POHL, F.
RATHMAYER, W.
SCHWOERBEL, J.
STARK, G.
SUND, H.
TILZER, M.
WEILER, E.

Faculty of Social Sciences:

Department of Sociology:
BAIER, H.
KANTOWSKY, D.
LUCKMANN, T.
LÜSCHER, K.
VORBERG, D.
WALTER, H.
WIEHN, E.

Department of Psychology:
COHEN, R.
FREEMAN, R.
FISCH, R.

Department of Political Science and Administration:
BADURA, B.
ELLWEIN, T.
ELSENHANS, H.
FACH, W.
LEHMBRUCH, G.
MÄDING, K.
NEIDHART, L.
TIMMERMANN, M.

Department of Science of Education:
BREZINKA, W.

Faculty of Economics and Statistics:
BONUS, H., Economics
GÄFGEN, G., Economics
GERFIN, H., Economics
KEMPF, W., Statistics
LAÜFER, N., Economics
MORTON, G., Statistics
PACK, L., Economics
RAMSER, H. J., Economics
ROGGE, L., Statistics
RONNING, G.

Faculty of Law:
ARNDT, H.-J.
BROHM, W.
DAMRAU, J.
EBENROTH, C.-T.
HAILBRONNER, K.
HÜBNER, U.
KREUZER, K.
LEIBINGER, R.
LORENZ, D.
MAURER, H.
PFISTER, B.
RÜTHERS, B.
SEITER, H.
STEIN, E.
STRÄTZ, H. W.
STÜRNER, R.
VOLK, K.
WALTER, G.

Faculty of Arts:

Department of Philosophy:
KAMBARTEL, F.
MITTELSTRASS, J.
SCHLEICHERT, H.

Department of History:
BORST, A.
BURCHARDT, L.
GROH, D.
RABE, H.
SCHULLER, W.
WELLMER, A.
WUNDER, B.

Department of Literature:
EFFE, B.
FUHRMANN, M.
GAIER, U.
ISER, W.
JAUSS, H.-R.
NEWIGER, H.-J.
OETTINGER, K.
PICARD, R.
PREISENDANZ, W.
SCHLÄGER, J.
SCHMIDT, P. L.
VERWEYEN, T.
WEBER, H.-J.

Department of Languages:
DI LUZIO, A.
EGLI, U.
FAUST, M.
HARTMANN, P.
LEHFELDT, W.
PAUSE, E.
SCHWARZE, CH.
STECHOW, V. A.
WIENOLD, G.

MEDIZINISCHE HOCHSCHULE LÜBECK

2400 LÜBECK,
RATZEBURGER ALLEE 160
Telephone: (49) 451-5001.

President: Prof. ERHARD D. KLINKE.
Chancellor: WOLF-DIETER v. DETMERING.

JOHANNES GUTENBERG-UNIVERSITÄT MAINZ

6500 MAINZ, SAARSTRASSE 21
Telephone: 391.

Founded 1477; closed 1816; re-opened 1946.

President: Prof. Dr. M. HARDER.
Vice-Presidents: Prof. Dr. K. BEYERMANN, Prof. Dr. L. SCHENKE.
Librarian: J. SCHUBERT.

Library: *see* Libraries.
Number of teachers: 1,256.
Number of students: 21,000.
Publications: *Bericht des Präsidenten, Vorlesungsverzeichnis, Universitätszeitung "JOGU"*.

DEANS:

Faculty of Catholic Theology: Prof. Dr. J. SCHMITZ.
Faculty of Evangelical Theology: Prof. Dr. F. BEISSER.
Faculty of Law and Economics: Prof. Dr. E. HÄRTTER.
Faculty of Medicine: Prof. Dr. H. LEITHOFF.
Faculty of Philosophy and Pedagogics: Prof. Dr. R. WISSER.
Faculty of Social Sciences: Prof. Dr. F. LANDWEHRMANN.
Faculty of Philology I: Prof. Dr. W. H. VEITH.
Faculty of Philology II: Prof. Dr. K. FAISS.
Faculty of Philology III: Prof. Dr. D. JANIK.
Faculty of History: Prof. Dr. M. MUELLER-WILLE.
Faculty of Mathematics: Prof. Dr. W. BUEHLER.
Faculty of Physics: Prof. Dr. G. GRAEFF.
Faculty of Chemistry: Prof. Dr. W. LIPTAY.
Faculty of Pharmacy: Prof. Dr. F. MOLL.
Faculty of Biology: Prof. Dr. H. RISLER.
Faculty of Geo-sciences: Prof. Dr. M. DOMROES.

Faculty of Applied Linguistics: Prof. Dr. K. POERTL.
Faculty of Fine Arts: Prof. F. MÜLLER.
Faculty of Music: Prof. Dr. G. TOUSSAINT.
Faculty of Physical Training: Prof. D. AUGUSTIN.

PROFESSORS:

Faculty of Catholic Theology:
BAUMEISTER, TH., Ancient Church History and Patrology
BECKER, H., Liturgy and Homiletics
GAULY, H., Pastoral Theology
GROSS, W., Old Testament
HAUBST, R., Dogmatics
JUERGENSMEIER, F., Church History and Religious Folklore
MAY, G., Church Law
PESCH, W., New Testament
ROCK, M., Christian Anthropology and Social Ethics
SCHENKE, L., New Testament
SCHMITZ, J., Fundamental Theology and Religious Knowledge
STACHEL, G., Catechisms and Pedagogics
WEISS, B., Dogmatics
ZIEGLER, J. G., Moral Theology

Faculty of Evangelical Theology:
BARTH, CH., Old Testament
BEISSER, F., Systematic Theology
BENRATH, G. A., Church History and Dogmatics
BÖCHER, O., New Testament
BRANDENBURGER, E., New Testament
FRITZ, V., Old Testament
KAMLAH, E., New Testament
KOHLER, W., General Divinity and Missions
MAYER, G., History of Jewdom
OTTO, G., Practical Theology
PÄSCHKE, B., Practical Theology
RITSCHL, D., Systematic Theology
SCHOTTROFF, L., New Testament

Faculty of Law and Economics:
ARMBRUSTER, H., Public Law
BALLWEG, O., Philosophy of Law
BARTLING, H., Economics
BARTMANN, H., Economics
BÖHM, A., Criminology, Penal Law and Execution System
DIEDERICH, H., Business Administration
GUDIAN, G., History of German Law and Civil Law
HADDING, W., Civil Law, Commercial, Economic and Civil Procedural Law
HANACK, E.-W., Penal and Procedural Law, Criminology
HARDER, M., Roman Law, Civil Law, History of Modern Private Law
HÄRTTER, E., Statistics
HOERSTER, N., Jurisprudence, Social Philosophy and Sociology
JOHN, U., Civil Law, Roman Law, Commercial Law
KARGL, H., Business Administration
KNOTH, J., Business Administration
KRAFT, A., Civil, Commercial, Labour and Civil Procedural Law
KRÜMPELMANN, J., Penal and Procedural Law
LENEL, H. O., Economics
MERGEN, A., Criminology
MONTANER, A., Economics and Public Finance
MÜHL, O., Civil Law, Commercial, Economic and Procedural Law
MÜLLER, K., Civil Law, Commercial Law, Foreign and International Private Law, Comparative Law
VON MUTIUS, A., Public Law
PEEGE, J., Economic Pedagogy
ROSE, K., Economics
RUDOLF, W., Public Law
RUPP, H. H., Public Law
SCHEUERLE, W., Civil Law, Labour, Commercial and Civil Procedural Law
SCHMIDT, K., Economics and Public Finance
SCHNEIDER, P., Public Law
SCHULZE, P., Statistics, Econometrics
SCHWANTAG, K., Business Administration
SCHWEITZER, M., International Law
TEICHMANN, A., Civil Law, Commercial Law, German and European Economic Law
WEHRLE, H., History of German Law

Faculty of Medicine:

Department of Theoretical Medicine:
BARNIKOL, W., Physiology
BÄSSLER, K.-H., Physiological Chemistry
VON BAUMGARTEN, R., Physiology
EHRENBRAND, F., Anatomy
GROTE, J., Physiology
HARTH, O., Physiology
HUTTEN, H., Physiology
MAYET, A., Anatomy
MÜLLER, G., Anatomy
MÜLLER, W., Physiological Chemistry
NETTER, P., Psychology
ROMER, F., Medical Biology
SCHMIDT, B., Physiological Chemistry
THEWS, G., Physiology
VAUPEL, P., Physiology
VOLLRATH, L., Anatomy
WEINBLUM, D., Physiological Chemistry
ZAHN, R., Physiological Chemistry
ZANDER, R., Physiology
ZÖLLNER, J., Physiological Chemistry

Department of Clinical Theoretical Medicine:
BITTER-SUERMANN, D., Medical Microbiology
BORNEFF, J., Hygiene and Bacteriology
DIERICH, M., Medical Microbiology
FALKE, D., Medical Microbiology
HADDING, U., Medical Microbiology
JAEHNCHEN, E., Pharmacology and Toxicology
KAHL, G. F., Pharmacology and Toxicology
KILBINGER, H., Pharmacology and Toxicology
KLEIN, P., Medical Microbiology
KÜMMEL, W., History of Medicine
LEITHOFF, H., Forensic Medicine
LOEFFELHOLZ, K., Pharmacology and Toxicology
LOOS, M., Medical Microbiology
MANN, G., History of Medicine
MUSCHOLL, E., Pharmacology
OESCH, F., Pharmacology and Toxicology
PETERSOHN, F., Forensic Medicine
PFEIFFER, E., Hygiene
ROELLINGHOFF, M., Medical Microbiology
RÜDE, E., Immunology
WAGNER, H., Medical Microbiology
WALTHER, G., Forensic Medicine
WOLLERT, Z., Pharmacology and Toxicology

Department of Clinical Institutes:
EISSNER, D., Radiology and Nuclear Medicine
FREY, R., Anaesthesiology
GERBERSHAGEN, H.-U., Anaesthesiology
HAHN, K., Radiology
HALMAGYI, M., Anaesthesiology
HOEHN, P., Pathology
KUTZNER, J., Radiology
LANGER, K.-H., Cytobiology
MEYER, W., Pathology
MICHAELIS, J., Medical Statistics and Documentation
MUENTEFERING, H., Pathology of Children
PAULINI, K., Pathology
SCHRÖDER, J. M., Neuropathology
SEHHATI-CHAFAI, G., Anaesthesiology
STOSSECK, K., Anaesthesiology
THOENES, W., Pathology
WENDE, S., Neuroradiology
WOLF, R., Medical Physics

Department of Conservative Medicine:
BEYER, J., Internal Medicine (Endocrinology)
DISTLER, G.-A., Internal Medicine
EMMRICH, P., Paediatrics
ERDMANN, G., Paediatrics
EWE, K., Internal Medicine
FERLINZ, R., Internal Medicine (Pneumology)
FISCHER, J., Internal Medicine (Haematology)
GILFRICH, H.-J., Internal Medicine
GLATZEL, J., Neuropsychiatry
HAFERKAMP, G., Neurology
HOLTERMÜLLER, K. H., Internal Medicine
HOLZMANN, H., Internal Medicine
HOPF, H. CH., Neurology
JÜNGST, B.-K., Paediatrics
KORTING, G., Skin and Venereal Diseases
LANGEN, D., Physiotherapy and Medical Psychology
LEMMEL, E.-M., Internal Medicine
LOWITZSCH, K., Neurology
MORSCHES, B., Skin and Venereal Diseases
OHLER, W., Internal Medicine
PRELLWITZ, W., Clinical Chemistry
RIEGER, H., Neuropsychiatry
SCHÖLMERICH, PAUS, Internal Medicine
SCHÖNBERGER, W., Paediatrics
SCHUSTER, H.-P., Internal Medicine
SPITZBARTH, H., Internal Medicine
SPRANGER, J., Paediatrics
STRAUB, E., Paediatrics
THEILE, U., Internal Medicine
WANITSCHKE, R., Internal Medicine
WOLFF, H. P., Internal Medicine

Department of Operative Medicine:
ALTWEIN, J. E., Urology
BIESALSKI, P., Phoniatrics, Audiology
BRÜNNER, H., Surgery
BUSCH, G., Neurosurgery
BRUSSATIS, F., Orthopaedics
DRAF, W., Oto-Rhino-Laryngology
FRIEDBERG, V., Obstetrics and Gynaecology
GÄRTNER, J., Ophthalmics
HELMS, J., Oto-Rhino-Laryngology
HOFMANN, K. S., Surgery
HOHENFELLNER, R., Urology
KEMPF, P., Surgery
KESSLER, E., Surgery
KNAPSTEIN, P. G., Obstetrics and Gynaecology
KUMMERLE, F., Surgery
LANGENDORF, H., Surgery
MARBERGER, M., Urology
MELCHERT, F., Gynaecology
NOVER, A., Ophthalmics
OTTE, P., Orthopaedics
RATHGEN, G., Obstetrics and Gynaecology
RITTER, G., Accident Surgery
ROTHMUND, M., Surgery
SCHÜRMANN, K., Neurosurgery
VOTH, D., Neurosurgery
WERNITSCH, W., Surgery

Department of Dental Sciences:
FESSELER, A., Hygiene
FUHR, K., Prosthetics

KETTERL, W., Hygiene
MARX, H., Materials and Technology
SCHEUNEMANN, H., Surgery
SCHMIDSEDER, R.
SERGL, H.-G., Jaw Orthopaedics
SIEBERT, G.
TETSCH, P.

Faculty of Philosophy and Pedagogics:
BALLAUFF, T., Pedagogics
BRÜNING, W.
BUCHER, A., Philosophy
FUNKE, G., Philosophy
HAMBURGER, F., Pedagogics
HETTWER, H., Pedagogics
KOPPER, J., Philosophy
KRON, F. W., Pedagogics
MALTER, R., Philosophy
PEEGE, J., Pedagogics
SPRENGARD, K. A.
STALLMACH, J., Philosophy
TEICHNER, W.
WISSER, R.

Faculty of Social Sciences:
BENESCH, H., Psychology
BUCHHEIM, H., Political Sciences
CHRISTIANSEN, E., Psychology
DE WOLF, P., African Philology
EWERT, O., Psychology
FRÖHLICH, W., Psychology
GILLESSEN, G., Journalism
GROHS, G., Sociology
LANDWEHRMANN, F., Sociology
MOLS, M., Political Science
MÜLLER, E. W., Ethnology
NOELLE-NEUMANN, E., Public Communications
SCHOECK, H., Sociology
SCHWÄGLER, G., Sociology
WEIDENFELD, W., Political Science
WERMUTH, N., Psychology

Faculty of Philology I:
BELLMANN, G., German Language
DICK, M., Modern German Literature
HILLEBRAND, B., Modern German Literature
KLEIBER, W., German Philology and Ethnology
KRUMMACHER, H.-H., Modern German Literature
MENNEMEIER, F., Comparative Studies
ROTERMUND, E., Modern German Literature
SCHWEDT, H., German Ethnology
SEGEBRECHT, W., Modern German Literature
VEITH, W., German Language

Faculty of Philology II:
BUSCH, F., English and American Philology
ERLEBACH, P., English Philology
FAISS, K., English Linguistics
HELMCKE, H., American Philology
HERGET, W., American Philology
HUMBACH, H., Comparative Indo-germanic Philology
LUBBERS, K., English and American Philology
ROLLE, D., English Philology
SCHULZE, F., English Philology

Faculty of Philology III:
ANDRIANNE, R., French Literature
BENZING, J., Islamic Philology and Studies
BIERMANN, H., History of Art
BLÄNSDORF, J., Classical Philology
BRINGMANN, M., History of Art
BUDDRUSS, G., Indology
FISCHER, F., History of Art
FLEISCHER, R., Classical Archaeology
GIRKE, W., Slavonic Philology
VON HINUEBER, O., Indology
HORST, H., Islamic Philology
JANIK, D., Romance Philology
KRÖLL, H., Romance Philology
LATACZ, J., Classical Philology
NICOLAI, W., Classical Philology
REISSNER, E., Slavonic Literature
RINGGER, K., Romance Philology
SALLMANN, K., Classical Philology
SPIRA, A., Classical Philology
VENZLAFF, H., Islamic Philology
WESENBERG, B., Classical Archaeology
WLOSOK, A., Classical Philology

Faculty of History:
BANTELMANN, N., Pre- and Proto-history
BAUMGART, W., Modern and Contemporary History
BECKER, A., Medieval History
BELLEN, H., Ancient History
DOTZAUER, W., Modern History, Comparative Regional History
DUCHHARDT, H., Modern History, Comparative Regional History
FUCHS, K., Modern History, Comparative Regional History, Economy and Social History
GERLICH, A., Medieval and Modern History, Comparative Regional History
KODER, J., Byzantine Studies
KOPPITZ, H.-J., Books and Printing, German Philology
MENZEL, J. J., Medieval History
MÜLLER-WILLE, M., Pre- and Proto-history
RHODE, G., East European History, Medieval and Modern History
RIEDEL, F. W., History of Music
UNVERRICHT, H., History of Music
WEBER, H., Medieval and Modern History
WILD, G., East European History

Faculty of Mathematics:
AMBERG, B. Mathematics
BÖRSCH-SUPAN, W., Applied Mathematics
BÜHLER, W., Mathematical Statistics
DOERK, K., Mathematics
GOTTSCHLING, E., Mathematics
GRAMSCH, B., Mathematics
HELD, D., Mathematics
HERZER, A., Mathematics
HOFMEISTER, G., Mathematics
HUPPERT, B., Mathematics
KALB, K., Mathematics
KONDER, P. P., Mathematics
KRAFFT, F., History of Natural Sciences
KRECK, M., Mathematics
MÜLTHEI, H., Applied Mathematics
PFISTER, A., Mathematics
RÜSSMANN, H., Mathematics
SCHEIBA, K.-J., Mathematics
SCHLEINKOFER, G., Mathematics
STAUDE, U., Mathematics
STULOFF, N., Mathematics

Faculty of Physics:
ALT, E., Physics
ANDRESEN, H. G., Physics
ARENHOEVEL, H., Physics
BECKMANN, P., Theoretical Physics
DRECHSEL, D., Theoretical Physics
EHRENBERG, H., Physics and Nuclear Physics
EIDEN, R., Meteorology
FISCHER, E., Physics
FRICKE, G., Experimental Nuclear Physics
GRÄFF, G., Experimental Physics
HERMINGHAUS, H., Physics
HINKELMANN, K.-H., Theoretical Meteorology
HUFNAGEL, F., Experimental Physics
INTHOFF, W., Theoretical Physics
KLAGES, G., Experimental Physics
KLEMPT, E., Experimental Physics
KLUGE, H.-J., Experimental Physics
KNORR, K., Experimental Physics
KRETZSCHMAR, M., Theoretical Physics
MEINHOLD-HEERLEIN, L., Theoretical Physics
NEUHAUSEN, R., Physics
OTTEN, E. W., Experimental Physics
REICHERT, E., Physics
SCHECK, F., Theoretical Physics
SCHILCHER, K., Theoretical Physics
SCHUBERT, G., Theoretical Physics
TRUEBENBACHER, E.,Theoretical Physics
WALTHER, V., Physics
WERTH, G., Experimental Physics
ZDUNKOWSKI, W., Meteorology

Faculty of Chemistry:
BAUMGÄRTNER, F., Nuclear Chemistry
BEYERMANN, K., Analytical Chemistry
DENSCHLAG, H. O., Nuclear Chemistry
DOSE, K., Biochemistry
FAHR, E., Organic Chemistry
FISCHER, E., Physics
FLESCH, P., Biochemistry
GATTOW, G., Inorganic Chemistry
GEYER, E., Organic Chemistry
GÜTLICH, PH., Inorganic and Analytical Chemistry
HERRMANN, G., Inorganic Chemistry and Nuclear Chemistry
HORNER, L., Organic Chemistry and Biochemistry
KAFFRELL, N., Nuclear Chemistry
KIRSTE, R., Physical Chemistry
LIPTAY, W., Physical Chemistry
MEYERHOFF, G., Physical Chemistry
NEEB, R., Inorganic and Analytical Chemistry
RINGSDORF, H., Macromolecular and Organic Chemistry
SCHULZ, R. C., Organic Chemistry
SILLESCU, H., Physical Chemistry
SINGER, H., Inorganic Chemistry
STROBL, G., Physical Chemistry
STUHRMANN, H., Physical Chemistry
UNGER, K., Inorganic Chemistry
VOGT, W., Organic and Macromolecular Chemistry
WOLF, B., Physical Chemistry

Faculty of Pharmacy:
KREUTZBERGER, A., Pharmaceutical Chemistry
MOLL, F., Pharmaceutical Technology
SCHUNACK, W., Pharmaceutical Chemistry
STOPP, K., Pharmaceutical Biology

Faculty of Biology:
ANDRES, G., Zoology
BAUER, L., Botany
BERNHARD, W., Anthropology
BRAUN, R., Zoology
VON CAMPENHAUSEN, C., Zoology and Biophysics
DORN, A., Zoology
DORN, E., Zoology
HARTL, D., Botany
HARTMANN, E., Botany
HEMMER, H., Zoology
KINZELBACH, R., Zoology
LAVEN, H., Genetics and General Biology
MARTENS, J., Zoology
RADLER, F., Microbiology and Viticulture
REINBOTH, R., Zoology
RISLER, H., Zoology
ROMER, F., Zoology
ROTHE, G., Botany
RUPPRECHT, T., Zoology
SACHSSE, W., Genetics
SCHLEIERMACHER, E., Anthropology

von Seelen, W., Biomathematics
Siegert, A., Botany
Thomas, E., Zoology
Urich, K., Zoology and Biochemistry
Wegener, G., Zoology
Wild, A., Botany

Faculty of Geo-sciences:
Abele, G., Geography
Berg, D. E., Geology and Palaeontology
Boy, J., Palaeontology and Geology
Domrös, M., Geography
Dosch, W., Mineralogy and Petrography
Eggers, H., Geography
Fürst, M., Geology and Palaeontology
Gormsen, E., Geography
Heim, D., Geology and Palaeontology
Helke, A., Mineralogy and Petrography
Hildebrandt, H., Geography
Kandler, O., Geology
Keesmann, I., Mineralogy and Petrography
Klaer, W., Geography
Kröner, A., Geology and Palaeontology
Lorenz, V., Geology and Palaeontology
Pense, J., Mineralogy and Palaeontology
von Platen, H., Mineralogy and Petrography
Rothausen, K., Geology and Palaeontology
Tillmanns, E., Mineralogy and Crystallography
Tobschall, H.-J., Mineralogy
Uthoff, D., Geography

Faculty of Applied Linguistics:
Briesemeister, D., Romance Studies
Drescher, H. W., English Studies
Forstner, M., Arabic Language and Culture
Mayer, G., German Studies
Pörtl, K., Hispanic and Latinamerican Studies
Sachse, A., Philosophy
Schunck, P., Romance Studies
Singer, H.-R., Arabic Language and Culture
Stoll, K.-H., English Studies
Vermeer, H., General and Applied Linguistics

Faculty of Fine Arts:
Brembs, D., Drawing
Hellmann, U., Metal
Hilgner, I., Textiles
König, G., Art Education
Lambert, G., Art Education
Loerincz, P., Graphic
Müller, F., Writing
v. Saalfeld, H., Drawing
Volz, H., Sculpture
Weber, K., Cine-film and Television

Faculty of Music:
Bamberger, F., Piano
Börner, K., Piano, Pedagogics
Ihle, T., Musical History, Phrasing
Jekeli, L., Piano
Köhler, F., Composition
Liebl, K., Singing and Voice Training
Meier, A., Musical History, Phrasing
Schubert, G. H., Phrasing
Seidel, E., Composition
Stadtmüller, P. A., Organ, Church Music
Toussaint, G., History of Music
Volk, E., Musical Training
Wollitz, E., Singing and Voice Training

Faculty of Physical Education:
Augustin, D., Athletics
Letzelter, H., Athletics and Training
Letzelter, M., Movement and Training
Müller, N., Athletics
Petter, W., Sport Education
Rösch, H. E., History of Sport
Salomon, H., Sport Education
Schöpe, H. G., Didactics
Ulmer, H. V., Physiology
Zipf, K. E., Sport Medicine

ATTACHED INSTITUTE:

Forschungsinstitut für Wirtschaftspolitik (*Institute for Economic Research*): 6500 Mainz, Universität, Haus Recht und Wirtschaft; Dirs. Prof. Dr. Erich Welter, Prof. Dr. Helmut Diederich.

UNIVERSITÄT MANNHEIM

6800 MANNHEIM, SCHLOSS
Telephone: (0621) 2921.

Founded 1907 as Städtische Handelshochschule, attached to Heidelberg University 1933, re-opened as Wirtschaftshochschule 1946, University status 1967.

Academic year: April to July, October to February.

Rector: Prof. Dr. Heinz König.
Pro-Rectors: Prof. Dr. Christoph Jentsch, Prof. Dr. Karl-Heinz Schindler.
Chancellor: Dr. iur. Winfried Benz.
Librarian: Dr. rer. nat. Manfred Kleiss.

Number of teachers: *c.* 165.
Number of students: *c.* 5,800.

DEANS:

Faculty of Law: Prof. Dr. Wolfgang Frisch.
Faculty of Economics: Prof. Dr. Robert Buchner.
Faculty of Political Economy and Statistics: Prof. Volker Böhm.
Faculty of Social Sciences: Prof. Dr. Martin Irle.
Faculty of Philosophy, Psychology and Pedagogy: Prof. Dr. Harald Delius.
Faculty of Languages and Literature: Prof. Dr. Burkhart Cardauns.
Faculty of History and Geography: Prof. Dr. Wolfgang Schiering.
Faculty of Mathematics and Information Sciences: Prof. Dr. Hans-Peter Blatt.

PROFESSORS:

Faculty of Law:
Frisch, W., Penal Law and Theory of Law
Laubinger, H.-W., Public Law and Administration
Lorenz, E., Civil Law, Labour Law, International Private Law, History of Modern Private Law
Pawlowski, H.-M., Civil and Procedural Law, Philosophy of Law
Roellecke, G., Public Law and Philosophy of Law
Schenke, W.-R., Public Law
Scherner, K. O., Civil Law and History of German Law
Schindler, K.-H., Civil and Roman Law
Schünemann, B., Penal Law and Philosophy of Law
Steinberger, H., Public Law, European Law
Weber-Fas, R., Public Law, German and International Fiscal Law
Wiese, G., Civil, Labour and Trade Law
Wüst, G., Civil, Commercial and Labour Law

Faculty of Economics:
Bergner, H.
Buchner, R.
Dichtl, E.
Gaugler, E.
Geist, M.
Helten, E.
Ihde, G.-B.
Jacobs, O. H.
Kieser, A.
Kortzfleisch, G. von
Phillipp, F.
Raffée, H.
Steffens, F. E.

Faculty of Political Economy and Statistics:
Böhm, V., Political Economy and Econometry
Kirchgässner, B., Economic and Social History
König, H., Political Economy and Econometry
Nachtkamp, H. H., Political Economy
Schachtschabel, H. G., Political Economy
Schlieper, U., Political Economy
Schröder, J., Political Economy
Siebert, H., Political Economy and Foreign Economy
Stenger, H., Statistics and Econometry
Streit, M. E., Political Economy, Economic and Social Politics
Wille, E., Political Economy
Winckler, K., Statistics and Econometry
Zeitel, G., Political Economy, esp. Finance

Faculty of Social Sciences:
Albert, H., Sociology and Philosophy
Boldt, H., Politics and State Law
Hirsch-Weber, W., Politics
Irle, M., Social Psychology
Kaase, M., Politics
Lepsius, M. R., Sociology
Matthias, E., Politics and Modern History
Müller, W., Methods of Empirical Social Research and Applied Sociology
Weber, H., Politics and Modern History
Wildenmann, R., Politics
Zapf, W., Sociology

Faculty of Philosophy, Psychology and Education:
Arndt, H. W., Philosophy
Delius, H., Philosophy
Groffmann, K. J., Psychology
Groth, G., Education
Herrmann, T., Psychology
Höhn, E., Education and Psychology of Education
Hopf, B., Education
Lössl, E., Psychology
Michel, L., Psychology
Specht, R., Philosophy
Zabeck, J., Education

Faculty of Languages and Literature:
Bauer, G., German Linguistics and Old German Literature
Brockmeier, P., Romance Philology
Cardauns, B., Classical Philology
Fischer, H., English
Funke, H., Classical Philology
Halfmann, U., English

HOFFMANN, W., Old German
HORN, H.-J., Classical Philology
JÖNS, D., History of Modern German Literature
KLOEPFER, R., Romance Philology
LÄGREID, A., Slavic Philology
MATEŠIĆ, J., Slavonic Philology
MEIXNER, H., History of Modern German Literature
ROHR, R., Romance Philology
STEMMLER, T., English
URELAND, P. ST., Linguistics

Faculty of History and Geography:
CHANTRAINE, H., Ancient History
GAEBE, W., Economic Geography
HIPPEL, W. VON, Modern History
HÖHL, G., Geography
JENTSCH, CH., Geography
ROTHE, P., Geology
SCHIERING, W., Archaeology
SCHLENKE, M., Modern History
TRAUTZ, F., History

Faculty of Mathematics and Information Sciences:
BINZ, E.
BLATT, H.-P.
KIEHL, R.
MEINARDUS, G.
OETTLI, W.
POPP, H.
RAMSPOTT, R. J.
STÖRMER, H.
WENZEL, G. H.

ATTACHED INSTITUTES:

Institut für Aufbaustudien: Dir. Prof. Dr. K.-H. SCHINDLER.

Europa-Institut: Dir. Prof. Dr. MANFRED SCHLENKE.

Institut für Empirische Wirtschaftsforschung: Dir. Prof. Dr. R. BUCHNER.

Otto-Selz-Institut für Psychologie und Erziehungswissenschaft: Dir. Prof. Dr. KARL GROFFMANN.

Rechenzentrum: Dir. Prof. Dr. HANS W. MEUER.

Institut für Sozialwissenschaften: Dir. Prof. Dr. H. BOLDT.

Institut Sprachlabor: Dir. Prof. Dr. RUPPRECHT ROHR.

Institut für Volkswirtschaftslehre und Statistik: Dir. Prof. Dr. HEINZ KÖNIG.

PHILIPPS-UNIVERSITÄT MARBURG

3550 MARBURG,
BIEGENSTRASSE 10
Telephone: 281.

Founded 1527.

State control; Academic year: October to July (two terms).

President: Prof. WALTER KRÖLL.
Vice-President: Prof. Dr. WILLI WOLF.
Chancellor: K. EWALD.
Librarian: F.-H. PHILIPP.

Number of students: 13,004.

Publication: *Marburger Universitätszeitung* (fortnightly).

DEANS:

Department of Law: Prof. Dr. REINHARD VON HIPPEL.
Department of Economics: Prof. Dr. ALFRED SCHÜLLER.
Department of Social Sciences: Prof. Dr. MICHAEL TH. GREVEN.
Department of Psychology: Prof. Dr. HANS SCHAUER.
Department of Theology: Prof. Dr. REINER PREUL.
Department of History: Prof. Dr. DIETER FLACH.
Department of Antiquities: Prof. Dr. THOMAS KÖVES-ZULAUF.
Department of General Linguistics and German Philology: Prof. Dr. HANS FRIEBERTSHÄUSER.
Department of Modern German Literature and Arts: Prof. Dr. BURGHARD DEDNER.
Department of Modern Languages and Literature: Prof. Dr. HANS-BERND HARDER.
Department of Non-European Languages and Cultures: Prof. Dr. BERNHARD FORSSMANN.
Department of Mathematics: Prof. WERNER SCHAAL.
Department of Physics: Prof. Dr. FALK PÜHLHOFER.
Department of Physical Chemistry: Prof. Dr. HEINZ BÄSSLER.
Department of Chemistry: Prof. Dr. DIRK REINEN.
Department of Pharmacy and Food Chemistry: Prof. Dr. BERNARD UNTERHALT.
Department of Biology: Prof. Dr. DIETRICH WERNER.
Department of Geo-sciences: Prof. Dr. WERNER FISCHER.
Department of Geography: Prof. Dr. ECKART EHLERS.
Department of Human Medicine: (vacant).
Department of Education: Prof. Dr. WOLFGANG KLAFKI.

PROFESSORS

Department of Law:
v. ARNIM, H. H., Public Law
BALTZER, J., Procedural, Civil, Commercial and Economic Law
BEUTHIEN, V., Civil, Commercial, Economic and Labour Law
BICKEL, D., General Law, Civil and Labour Law
FOLZ, H. E., Public Law
GÖRG, H., Public Law
HAGER, G., Civil and Comparative Law
v. HIPPEL, R., Criminal and Procedural Law
HOFFMANN, G., Public Law
HUPE, E., Criminal Law
KAUFMANN, E., German Legal History, Civil, Commercial and Church Law
KIESSLING, E., Papyrology
LANGER, W., Criminal and Procedural Law
LECHELER, H., Public Law
LESER, H. G., Civil and Comparative Law
LESSMANN, H., Civil, Commercial and Economic Law
MEURER, D., Criminal and Procedural Law, Philosophy of Law
MÜLLER-VOLBEHR, J., Public Law
RUPPRECHT, H.-A., Papyrology
SCHWINGE, E., Public Law, Criminal Law and Procedure
SIMON, D., Civil Law and History of Law
VOLKOMMER, M., Civil and Procedural Law
WERKMÜLLER, D., History of Law
WOLF, E., Civil and Labour Law, Philosophy of Law

Department of Economics:
BRAEUER, W., Political Economy
DÜLFER, E., Commerce
FÖRSTER, W., Statistics
GRUNAU, J., Finance
HAMM, W., Political Economy
HAMPE, A., Statistics
HANEL, A., Economic Problems of Developing Countries
KRÜSSELBERG, H.-G., Political Economy
KUHN, J., Agrarian Economics
MEYER, W., Political Economy—Methods and Hypothesis
MÜNKNER, H.-H., Business Economics
PRIEWASSER, E., Banking
REIGROTZKI, E., Political Economy
RÖPKE, J., Economic Theory
SCHIEMENZ, B., Commerce
SCHÜLLER, A., Economic Theory
STING, K., Political Economy
WAGNER, A., Statistics
ZIMMERMANN, H., Political Economy

Department of Social Science:
ABENDROTH, W., Political Science
ASSION, P., European Ethnology
BORIS, H.-D., Sociology
BRANDT, R., Philosophy
BREDOW, W. VON, Political Science
DEPPE, F., Political Science
EBBINGHAUS, J., Philosophy
ELSENHANS, H., Political Science
FOLTIN, H.-F., European Ethnology
FÜLBERTH, G., Political Science
GÄBE, L., Philosophy
GIEGEL, H. J., Sociology
GREVEN, M. TH., Sociology
HEILFURTH, G., Cultural Sociology and Cultural Anthropology
JANICH, P., Philosophy
KÜHNL, R., Political Science
LANGER-EL SAYED, I., Political Science
NACHTIGALL, H., Folklore and Ethnosociology
RAUSCH, R., Sociology
REICH, K., Philosophy
RÖMER, P., Political Science
RUPP, H.-K., Political Science
SCHILLER, TH., Political Science
SCHUON, K. TH., Political Science
TUSCHLING, B., Philosophy
WEBER-KELLERMANN, I., Folklore and Ethno-sociology
WYNIGER, W., Sociology

Department of Psychology:
EHLERS, T.
FLORIN, I.
LANC, O.
LIEBHART, E.
MERZ, F.
RITTER, M.
SCHAUER, H.
SCHEIBLECHNER, H.
SCHNEIDER, K.
SCHULZE, H.-H.
SOMMER, G.
STELZL, I.
TENT, L.

Department of Theology:
BOUMANN, J., History of Religion
CONRAD, D., Hebrew, Archaeology of Palestine
DAMMANN, E., History of Religion

FUCHS, E., New Testament and Hermeneutics
GRASS, H., Systematic Theology and Social Ethics
GRESCHAT, H.-J., History of Religion
HÄRLE, W., Systematic Theology, History of Theology
HARNISCH, W., New Testament
HUBER, W., Social Ethics
JEREMIAS, G., New Testament
KAISER, O., Old Testament
KAWERAU, P., History of the Eastern Church
KOHLS, E.-W., Historical Theology
KÜMMEL, W., New Testament
LEIPOLD, H., Systematic Theology
LIEBING, H., Church History
MAHLMANN, T., Systematic Theology
OPPEN, D. VON, Social Ethics
PFÜRTNER, ST., Social Ethics
PREUL, R., Practical Theology
RATSCHOW, C.-H., Systematic Theology, History of Theology
RITTER, A. M., Church History
SCHMIDT, W. H., Old Testament
SCHUNACK, G., New Testament
SCHWEBEL, H., Religious Communication
STOLLBERG, D., Practical Theology
SURKAU, H.-W., Practical Theology
WÜRTHWEIN, E., Old Testament
ZELLER, W., Church History

Department of History:
BEUMANN, H., Medieval History
BOG, I., Social and Economic History
CHRIST, K., Ancient History I
CLAUDE, D., Medieval History
ERRINGTON, R. M., Ancient History
FLACH, D., Ancient History
HARDACH, G., Social and Economic History
KLEIN, T., Modern History
KRÜGER, P., Modern History
MALETTKE, K., Modern History
RITTER, H.-W., Ancient History
RÜCK, P., Historical Auxiliary Sciences
SCHULZE, H. K., Medieval History
SEIER, H., Modern History

Department of Antiquities:
ABEL, K., Classical Philology
ANDREAE, B., Classical Archaeology
FREY, O. H., Prehistory
KÖVES-ZULAUF, T., Classical Philology
LENDLE, O., Classical Philology
ROTH, H., Prehistory, Early Medieval Archaeology
SCHMALTZ, B., Classical Archaeology
SCHMIDT, P. G., Medieval and Renaissance Latin
WIMMEL, W., Classical Philology

Department of General Linguistics and Germanic Philology:
BERTHOLD, L., German Philology
BRANDT, W., German Linguistics and Medieval German Philology
FREUDENBERG, R., German Philology
FRIEBERTSHÄUSER, H., German Philology
GÖSCHEL, J., German Linguistics and Phonetics
HILDEBRANDT, R., German Linguistics and Philology
KESELING, G., Germanic and German Philology
KETTNER, B.-U., German Linguistics
LOMNITZER, H., German Language and Old German Philology
PUTSCHKE, W., German Linguistics and Linguistic Informatics
RÖSSING-HAGER, M., German Linguistics and Philology
SCHANZE, H., German Language and Old German Philology
SCHMITT, L. E., Germanic and German Philology
SCHRÖDER, W., Germanic and German Philology
SEIDENSTICKER, P., German Linguistics
WOLF, H., German Philology

Department of Modern German Literature and Arts:
BÄNSCH, D., Modern German Literature
BERNS, J. J., Modern German Literature
DEDNER, B., Modern German Literature
FALK, W., Modern German Literature
GANSBERG, M. L., Modern German Literature
GIESENFELD, G., Modern German Literature
GLÜCK, A., Modern German Literature
HABEL, R., Modern German Literature
HEUSSNER, H., Music
KLOTZ, H., History of Art
KUNST, H.-J., History of Art
MATTENKLOTT, G., Theory of Literature
PERRIG, A., History of Art
PICKERODT, G., Modern German Literature
SCHÄFER, G., Graphics and Painting
SOLMS-HOHENSOLMS-LICH, W., PRINZ ZU, Communication Sciences and Media Teaching
VOGT, G., German Language Teaching
VOSS, E. TH., Modern German Literature
WEYER, M., Theory and Practice of Music

Department of Modern Languages and Literature:
BREUER, H., English Literature
EBERT, K., English, Linguistics
FREIDHOF, G., Slavic Linguistics
GUTHMÜLLER, B., Romance Philology
HARDER, H.-B., Slavic Philology
HOFER, H., Romance Philology
JÄNICKE, O., Romance Philology
LOPE, H. J., Romance Philology
UHLIG, C., English and American Philology
ZIMMERMANN, R., English Linguistics

Department of Non-European Languages and Cultures:
DAMMANN, E., History of Religion
FORSSMAN, B., Comparative Linguistics
JACOBSOHN, H., Egyptology and General History of Religion
JUNGRAITHMAYR, H., African Studies
KAPLONY-HECKEL, U., Egyptology
KÜMMEL, H. M., Ancient Ornamental Studies
MÜLLER, W. W., Semitic Studies
OTTEN, H., Ancient Oriental Studies
RAU, W., Indian Philology
RÖSSING, H., Comparative Linguistics
RÖSSLER, C., Semitic Studies
STEINER, G., Ancient Oriental Studies
WEISWEILER, J., Comparative Linguistics

Department of Mathematics:
AVAKUMOVIĆ, V. G.
BÖHMER, K.
BREUER, M.
DRESSLER, A.
GROMES, W.
GUNDLACH, K.-B.
HANEKE, W.
HEROLD, H.
KNÖLLER, F. W.
KÖRLE, H.-H.
MAMMITZSCH, V.
MIESNER, W.
PORTENIER, C.
REUFEL, M.
SCHAAL, W.
SCHMIDT, P. G.
TARGONSKI, G.

Department of Physics:
ACKERMANN, H., Experimental Physics
BESTGEN, W., Theoretical Physics
BOCK, R., Experimental Physics
CAPPELLER, U., Experimental Physics
ELBEL, M., Experimental Physics
FICK, D., Experimental Physics
FISCHER, R., Experimental Physics
FISCHER, W., Experimental Physics
FUHS, W., Experimental Physics
GANSSAUGE, E., Experimental Physics
GRAWERT, G., Theoretical Physics
GROSSMANN, S., Theoretical Physics
HÜHNERMANN, H., Experimental Physics
JENC, F., Theoretical Physics
KERLER, W., Theoretical Physics
LUDWIG, G., Theoretical Physics
MAAS, W., Theoretical Physics
MADELUNG, O., Theoretical Physics
MELSHEIMER, O., Theoretical Physics
MOVAGHAR, B., Theoretical Physics
NEUMANN, H., Theoretical Physics
PETZOLD, J., Theoretical Physics
PÜHLHOFER, F., Experimental Physics
REITBÖCK, H., Applied Physics
RICHTER, F.-W., Experimental Physics
STÖCKMANN, H.-J., Experimental Physics
STUKE, J., Experimental Physics
THOMAS, P., Theoretical Physics
WALCHER, W., Experimental Physics
WASSMUTH, H.-W., Experimental Physics
WEINER, R., Theoretical Physics
WEISER, G., Experimental Physics
WISSEL, C., Theoretical Physics
ZICKENDRAHT, W., Theoretical Physics
ZIMMERMANN, W., Experimental Physics

Department of Physical Chemistry:
BÄSSLER, H., Physical Chemistry
BRANDT, R., Nuclear Chemistry
EBERT, G., Biopolymers
FÖRSTERLING, H.-D., Physical Chemistry
HEITZ, W., Polymer Chemistry
HENSEL, F., Physical Chemistry
LUCK, W., Physical Chemistry
MÜLLER, F. H., Polymer Chemistry
PATZELT, P., Nuclear Chemistry
RULAND, W., Polymer Physics
SCHWEIG, A., Physical Chemistry
STARKE, K., Nuclear Chemistry

Department of Chemistry:
AURICH, H. G., Organic Chemistry
BABEL, D., Inorganic Chemistry
BECKER, G., Inorganic Chemistry
BERNDT, A., Organic Chemistry
BOCHE, G., Organic Chemistry
DEHNICKE, K., Inorganic Chemistry
ELSCHENBROICH, CHR., Inorganic Chemistry
FOLLMANN, H., Biochemistry
HOFFMANN, R. W., Organic Chemistry
KADENBACH, B., Biochemistry
KINDL, H., Biochemistry
KLAMBERG, H., Inorganic and Analytical Chemistry
LORBERTH, J., Chemistry
MÜLLER, U., Inorganic Chemistry
PERST, H., Organic Chemistry
REETZ, M. T., Organic Chemistry
REICHARDT, C., Organic Chemistry
REINEN, D., Inorganic Chemistry
SIEBERT, W., Inorganic Chemistry
STEUBER, F.-W., Organic Chemistry
STORK, G., Inorganic and Analytical Chemistry
WENTRUP, C., Organic Chemistry

Department of Pharmacy and Nutrition:
BÖHME, H., Pharmaceutical and Food Chemistry
DILG, P., History of Pharmacy
EBEL, S., Pharmaceutical Chemistry
EGER-HUMMEL, G., Pharmaceutical Microbiology
HAAKE, M., Pharmaceutical Chemistry
HARTKE, K., Pharmaceutical Chemistry
HÖLZL, J., Pharmaceutical Biology
KRIEGLSTEIN, J., Pharmacology and Toxicology
KUCKLÄNDER, U., Pharmaceutical Chemistry
LIST, P. H., Pharmaceutical Chemistry and Technology
SCHMITZ, R., History of Pharmacy
SEITZ, G., Pharmaceutical Chemistry
UNTERHALT, B., Pharmaceutical Chemistry
WICHTL, M., Pharmaceutical Biology

Department of Biology:
BERTSH, A., Botany
BUCHHOLTZ, C., Zoology
GEYER, E., Zoology
HAGEN, H.-O. VON, Zoology, Evolution and Human Biology
HENSSEN, A., Systematic Botany
KALMRING, J., Zoology
KIRCHNER, C., Zoology
KOCH, P., Genetics (Zoology)
KOECKE, H.-U., General Zoology
KRÖGER, A., Microbiology
KÜTHE, H. W., Developmental Physiology
LENSKI, I., Morphology
NULTSCH, W., Botany
REMANE, R., Systematics and Evolution of Animals
REMMERT, H., Ecology
SCHÖNBOHM, E., Botany
SEITZ, K.-A., Comparative Anatomy
SENGER, H., Botany
STOSCH, H.-A. VON, Botany
THAUER, R., Microbiology
THROM, G., Botany
WEHRMEYER, W., Botany
WERNER, D., Botany and General Biology

Department of Geological Studies:
ALLMANN, R., Mineralogy and Crystallography
ANDERSON, H.-J., Palaeontology and Geology
BUCK, P., Crystallography
FISCHER, R., Geology and Palaeontology
FISCHER, W., Crystallography and Mineralogy
HAFNER, S., Crystallography and Mineralogy
HAHN, G., Palaeontology
HELLNER, E., Mineralogy
HUCKRIEDE, R., Geology and Palaeontology
LINDSTRÖM, M., Geology
LOHSE, H.-H., Mineralogy
RENNINGER, M., Crystallography
SCHERINGER, CH., Crystallography
ZANKL, H., Geology and Sedimentology
ZIEGLER, W., Palaeontology and Geology

Department of Geography:
ANDRES, W.
BUCHHOFER, E.
DICKEL, H.
DONGUS, H.
EHLERS, E.
LEISTER, I.
MERTINS, G.
PLETSCH, A.
SCHOTT, C.

Department of Medicine:
AHRENS, G., Dentistry
AMON, H., Anatomy
AUMULLER, G., Anatomy
AZIZ, O., Physiology
BALTZER, G., Internal Medicine
BAUER, B., Neurosurgery
BEATO, M., Physiological Chemistry
BERNHARDT, H., Dentistry
BLANKENBURG, W., Psychiatry and Psychopathology
BODE, CH., Internal Medicine
BRAASCH, D., Physiology
BUCHHOLZ, R., Obstetrics and Gynaecology
DAUME, E., Obstetrics and Gynaecology
DITTRICH, J., Paediatrics
DOMBROWSKI, H., Roentgenology
DOSS, M., Clinical Biochemistry and Biochemical Microbiology
EGBRING, R., Internal Medicine
EHRHARDT, H., Forensic and Social Psychiatry
EISSNER, H., Dermatology
ENGEL, P., Physiology and Rehabilitation Research
ESCHENBACH, C., Paediatrics
EXNER, G., Orthopaedics
FLORES DE JACOBY, L., Paradontology
FRIEDERICH, H., Dermatology and Venerology
FRUHSTORFER, H., Physiology
FUHRMANN, G. F., Pharmacology and Toxicology
GALLWITZ, D., Physiological Chemistry
GEUS, A., History of Medicine
GOLENHOFEN, K., Physiology
GRAUL, E., Radiology
GRUNDNER, H.-G., Radiology
HABERICH, F. J., Applied Physiology
HABERMEHL, A., Medical Data Processing
HARDEWIG, A., Internal Medicine
HARTMANN, K., Immunology
HAVEMANN, K., Internal Medicine
HEENE, R., Psychiatry, Neurology
HENNIS, I., Dentistry
HENSEL, H., Physiology
HERING, H.-J., Maxillo-facial Surgery
HESS, F., Roentgenology and Radiology
HILDEBRANDT, G., Physiology of Labour and Rehabilitation Research
HILGERMANN, R., Forensic Medicine
HUFFMANN, G., Neurology and Psychiatry
IHM, P., Medico-Biological Statistics and Documentation
JOSEPH, K., Experimental Nuclear Medicine
KAFFARNIK, H., Internal Medicine
KALBFLEISCH, H., Pathological Anatomy
KARLSON, P., Physio-Chemistry
KERN, H. F., Cytobiology and Cytopathology
KLEINE, T. O., Neurobiochemistry and Physiological Chemistry
KLEINSASSER, O., Oto-Rhino-Laryngology
KLÖTZER, W., Dentistry
KNAUFF, H. G., Internal Medicine
KNOLL, K. H., Hygiene
KOCH, H., Surgery
KOHLHAGE, H., Microbiology
KORANSKY, W., Toxicology and Pharmacology
KUNL, H., Experimental Nuclear Medicine
LANGE, H., Internal Medicine
LAUER, H. H., History of Medicine
LEHMANN, F.-G., Internal Medicine
LEHMANN, K., Dentistry
LENNARTZ, H., Anaesthesiology
LORENZ, W., Experimental Surgery and Pathological Biochemistry
LUDWIG, G., Anatomy
LÜTCKE, A., Psychiatry and Neurology
MANNHEIM, W., Medical Microbiology and Bacterio-Physiology
MANNHERZ, H.-G., Anatomy
MAROSKE, D., Surgery
MARTINI, G. A., Internal Medicine
MASSARAT, S., Internal Medicine
MÜLLER, I., History of Medicine
NETTER, K. J., Pharmacology and Toxicology
NEURATH, F., Orthopaedics
NIEMEYER, W., Oto-Rhino-Laryngology
NIESSING, J., Physiological Chemistry
OEPEN, H., Human Genetics
OEPEN, I., Forensic Medicine
PETRY, G., Anatomy
POHLEN, M., Psychotherapy
PORTIG, J., Pharmacology and Toxicology
POTS, P., Obstetrics and Gynaecology
PRIEBE, L., Biophysics
RODECK, G., Urology
RÖHER, H.-D., Surgery
RUPEC, M., Dermatology
SCHACHTSCHABEL, D., Physiological Chemistry
SCHAUMLÖFFEL, E., Nuclear Biology
SCHIFF, W., Medical Microbiology and Immunology
SCHMIDT, HELMUT, Dentistry
SCHMITZ-MOORMAN, P., General Pathology and Pathological Anatomy
SCHNEIDER, F., Physiological Chemistry and Biochemistry
SCHÖNHÄRL, E., Oto-Rhino-Laryngology
SCHÜFFEL, W., Psychosomatics
SCHULTE-HERMANN, R., Pharmacology and Toxicology
SEIFART, K., Physiological Chemistry
SIEGERT, R., Hygiene and Bacteriology
SIEGRIST, J., Medical Sociology
SLENCZKA, W., Medical Microbiology
SODOMANN, C.-P., Internal Medicine
SOLCHER, H., Neurology and Neuropathology
STOFFT, E., Institute of Anatomy
STRAUB, W., Eye Clinic
STURM, G., Clinical Chemistry and Microscopy
STUTTE, H., Child Psychiatry
THOMAS, C., Institute of Pathology
TURSS, R., Ophthalmology
UNSICKER, K., Institute of Anatomy
WEBER, D., Child Neuro-psychiatry
WELGE-LÜSSEN, L., Ophthalmology
WENDT, G. G., Anthropology
WESEMANN, W., Physiological Chemistry
WIEGANDT, H., Physiological Chemistry
WILLENBOCKEL, U., Paediatrics

Department of Education:
AUERNHEIMER, G.
BERG, H.-C.
BÖNNER, K.-H.
VON BRACKEN, H.
FREUDENSTEIN, R.
FROESE, L.
FUCHS, W.
HILDENBRANDT, E.
KASZTANTOWICZ, U.
KLAFKI, W.
KLIMT, F.
KUTZER, R.
PIPPERT, R.
PROBST, H.
REHBEIN, K.
SACK, H.-G.
SCHILLING, F.
WOLF, W.

LUDWIG-MAXIMILIANS-UNIVERSITÄT MÜNCHEN

8000 MUNICH 2,
GESCHWISTER-SCHOLL-PLATZ 1
Telephone: 21801.
Founded 1471.

President: Prof. Dr. phil. NIKOLAUS LOBKOWICZ.

Vice-Presidents: Prof. Dr. phil. HANS-DIETRICH STACHEL, Prof. Dr. rer. nat. KLAUS STIERSTADT, Prof. Dr. med. ROLF BURKHARDT.

Chief Administrative Officer: FRANZ FRIEDBERGER.

Director of Library: Dr. H. LESKIEN.

Number of teachers: 3,000.
Number of students: 41,000.

Publications: *Vorlesungsverzeichnis* (half-yearly), *Chronik der Ludwig-Maximilians-Universität* (annual), *Informationsdienst* (monthly), *Veranstaltungskalendar*.

DEANS:

Department of Catholic Theology: Prof. Dr. HANS SCHILLING.
Department of Evangelical Theology: Prof. Dr. HARALD HEGERMANN.
Department of Law: Prof. Dr. BRUNO RIMMELSPACHER.
Department of Business Administration: Prof. Dr. ROBERT WITTGEN.
Department of Economics: Prof. Dr. HANS FECHER.
Department of Medicine: Prof. Dr. W. SPANN.
Department of Veterinary Science: Prof. Dr. BERND VOLLMERHAUS.
Department of History and Art: Prof. Dr. THEODOR GÖLLNER.
Department of Philosophy, Science and Statistics: Prof. Dr. STEPHAN OTTO.
Department of Mathematics: Prof. Dr. BODO PAREIGIS.
Department of Physics: Prof. Dr. RUDOLF SIZMANN.
Department of Chemistry and Pharmacy: Prof. Dr. RUDOLF GOMPPER.
Department of Biology: Prof. Dr. HARTWIG CLEVE.
Department of Geosciences: Prof. Dr. HEINRICH SOFFEL.
Department of Forestry: Prof. Dr. WERNER KROTH.
Department of Psychology and Pedagogics: Prof. Dr. HANS SCHIEFELE.
Department of Ancient Cultures: Prof. Dr. WINFRIED BARTA.
Department of Language and Literature I: Prof. Dr. WOLFGANG WEISS.
Department of Language and Literature II: Prof. Dr. HANS G. TILLMANN.
Department of Social Sciences: Prof. Dr. OTTO B. ROEGELE.

PROFESSORS:

Department of Catholic Theology:
DETLOFF, W. R., History of Christian Belief
DÜRIG, W., Liturgy
FEIFEL, E., Pedagogy and Catechetics
FINKENZELLER, J., Dogmatics
FRIES, H., Fundamental Theology
GIERS, J., Christian Social Teaching
GNILKA, J., New Testament
GRÜNDEL, J., Moral Theology
HUBENSTEINER, B., Bavarian Church History
MÖRSDORF, K., Church Law
RICHTER, W., Old Testament and Biblical Oriental Languages
SCHARBERT, J., Old Testament
SCHEFFCZYK, L., Dogmatics
SCHILLING, H., Pastoral Theology
SCHMITZ, H., Medieval and Modern Church History
SCHWAIGER, G., Ecclesiastical and Art History, Archaeology

Department of Evangelical Theology:
BALTZER, K., Old Testament
BÄUMLER, C., Practical Theology II
BAUR, J., Systematic Theology
BÜRKLE, H., Missionary Work
HAHN, F., New Testament
HEGERMANN, H., New Testament II
JEREMIAS, J., Old Testament II
KRETSCHMAR, G. Church History and New Testament
KRUSCHE, P., Practical Theology
PANNENBERG, W., Systematic Theology
RENDTORFF, T., Systematic Theology and Ethics
SCHWARZ, R., Church History II

Department of Law:
BADURA, P., Public Law
CAMPENHAUSEN, A. VON, Public Law and **Church Law**
CANARIS, C.-W., Civil Law
FIKENTSCHER, W., Civil Law
GAGNÉR, S., History of Comparative Law
HELDRICH, A., Civil Law
HUECK, G., Labour Law
JAMEY, E., Civil, International Private, and Comparative Law
KAUFMANN, A., Penal Law and Philosophy of Law
LERCHE, P., Public Law and Public Social Law
LORENZ, W., Civil Law
NEHLSEN, H., German Law History, Civil Law
NÖRR, D., Roman and Civil Law
RIMMELSPACHER, B., Civil Law
ROXIN, C., Penal Law
SCHRICKER, G., Civil and Commercial Law
SCHÜLER-SPRINGORUM, H., Penal Law, Criminology
STEINDORFF, E., International Private Law
VOGEL, K., Financial Law
ZACHER, H., Public Law

Department of Economics:
BOEVENTER, E. VON, Industrial Economy
BORCHARDT, K., Economics and History of Economics
FECHER, H., National Economy and Finance
GRUBER, Mrs. U., National Economy and Finance
GUMPEL, W., Economy and Society of South East Europe
HEDTKAMP, G., Economy and Society of Eastern Europe
MÖLLER, H., Political Economy

Department of Business Administration:
BAUMGARDT, J., Economic and Social Teaching
BIERGANS, E., Business Economy
HANSSMANN, F., Market Research and Techniques
HEINEN, E., Commercial Economics
KIRSCH, W., Business Economics
LEITHERER, E., Business Economics
OETTLE, K., Business Economics
RUPPERT, K., Economic Geography
WITTE, E., Business Economy
WYSOCKI, K. VON, General Business Economy

Department of Forestry:
AMMER, U., Landscape Planning and Management
BAUMGARTNER, A., Bioclimatology and Applied Meteorology
BURSCHEL, P., Wood and Forest Organization
FRANZ, F., Forest Growing
KROTH, W., Forest Economics
LÖFFLER, H. D., Forest Surveying
PECHMANN, H. VON, Forest Biology
PLOCHMANN, R., Forest Policy and History
REHFUESS, K. E., Soil Chemistry
SCHÖNBORN, A. VON, Forest Genetics
SCHULZ, H., Wood Science
SCHÜTT, P., Plant Pathology
SCHWENKE, W., Zoology
SPEER, J., Forest Economics

Department of Medicine:
ASCHER, F., Dentistry
BETKE, K., Paediatrics
BRAUN-FALKO, O., Dermatology and Venereology
BRENDEL, W., Experimental Surgery
BRUGGENCATE, H. G. TEN, Physiology
BUCHBORN, E., Internal Medicine
BÜCHER, T., Physiological Chemistry
DEINHARDT, F., Hygiene and Microbiology
DREXEL, H., Physical Medicine and Balneology
EDER, M., General Pathology and Pathological Anatomy
FRICK, H., Macroscopic Anatomy
FRUHMANN, G., Labour Medicine
GERLACH, E., Physiology
GOERKE, H., History of Medicine
HEBERER, G., Surgery
HECKER, W., Child Surgery
HELLBRÜGGE, TH., Social Paediatrics
HIPPIUS, H., Psychiatry and Neurology
HOLLE, F., Special Surgery
HUG, O., Radiation Biology
KIESE, M., Pharmacology and Toxicology
KLINGENBERG, M., Physical Biochemistry
KLINNER, W., Heart Surgery
KNEDEL, M., Clinical Chemistry
KRAFT, E., Dentistry
LISSNER, J., Physiotherapy, Radiology
LUND, O. E., Ophthalmology
MARGUTH, F., Neurosurgery
MILLER, F., Zytopathology
NAUMANN, H.-H., Oto-Rhino-Laryngology
PETER, K., Anaesthesiology
POPPEL, E., Medical Psychology
RICHTER, K., Obstetrics and Gynaecology
RIECKER, G., Internal Medicine
SCHIMERT, G., Prophylaxis of Circulatory Disease
SCHLEGEL, Dentistry
SCHMIEDT, E., Urology
SCHRADER, A., Neurology
SONNABEND, E., Dentistry
SPANN, W., Forensic Medicine
STOCHDORPH, O., Neuropathology
THURAU, K., Physiology
UBERLA, K., Medical EDV, Statistics and Biomathematics
WETZSTEIN, R., Histology
WITT, A., Orthopaedics
ZACHAU, H., Physiological Chemistry
ZANDER, J., Obstetrics and Gynaecology
ZÖLLNER, N., Internal Medicine

Department of Veterinary Science:
BAKELS, F., Genetics
BOCH, J., Comparative Tropical Medicine
BOESSNECK, J., Palaeoanatomy, Domestication Research and History of Veterinary Science
DAHME, E., Oncology and Neuropathology
DIRKSEN, G., Internal Medicine
GYLSTORFF, I., Poultry Breeding
HEGNER, D., Pharmacology, Toxicology, Pharmacy
KALICH, J., Hygiene
KOTTER, L., Food
KRAEUSSLICH, H., Animal Breeding
LEIDL, W., Andrology
MAYR, A., Microbiology and Contagious Diseases
MERKENSCHLAGER, M., Physiology
RÜSSE, M., Physiology and Pathology of Reproduction
SANERSLEBEN, J., General Pathology and Pathological Anatomy
SCHEBITZ, H., Surgery
TERPLAN, G., Hygiene and Milk Technology
VOLLMERHAUS, B., Anatomy
WALTER, P., Histology and Embryology
ZUCKER, H., Physiology of Nutrition

Department of History and Art:
ACHT, P., Auxiliary Historical Science
BAUER, H., History of Art
BENGTSON, H., Ancient History
BOEHM, L., History
BRAUNFELS, W., Ancient and Modern History of Art
GÖLLNER, TH., Music
HLAWITSCHKA, E., History
HÖSCH, E., History of East and South-East Europe
KRAUS, E., History
LAUFFER, S., Ancient History
LAZAROWICZ, K., Theatre
NIPPERDEY, T., History
PRINZ, F., History
RITTER, G., History
WEIS, E., History

Department of Philosophy, Science and Statistics:
ANDERSON, O., Statistics
BISER, E., Christian Ideology and Philosophy of Religion
FERSCHL, F., Statistics
KRINGS, H., Philosophy
OTTO, ST., Philosophy
SCHNEEWEISS, H., Statistics
SPAEMANN, R., Philosophy
STEGMÜLLER, W., Philosophy
WEICHSELBERGER, K., Statistics

Department of Psychology and Pedagogics:
BUTOLLO, W., Psychology
LUKASCZYK, K., Psychology, Social Psychology
MÜLLER, K., Psychology
ROSENSTIEL, L. VON, Psychology
SCHIEFELE, H., Pedagogy
SCHNEEWIND, K., Psychology
SCHWARZ, R., Pedagogy

Department of Ancient Cultures:
BARTA, W., Egyptology
BAUER, W., East Asian Culture and Language
BRUNHÖLZL, F., Medieval Latin Philology
EDZARD, D. O., Assyriology
FRANKE, H., Civilization and Languages of East Asia
GANSCHOW, G., Finno-Ugrian Studies
HOHLWEG, A., Byzantine and Modern Greek Philology
HOLTHUSEN, J., Slavonic Philology
HROUDA, B., Pre- and Early Far Eastern History
KISSLING, H., Oriental History
KOSSACK, G., Early History
KRETZENBACHER, L., Folklore
NAUMANN, W., Japanology
SCHRENK, J., Slavonic Philology
SPITALER, A., Semitic Philology
STRAUBE, H., Folklore and African Culture
ZANKER, P., Classical Archaeology

Department of Language and Literature I:
BROICH, U., English Philology
GNEUSS, H., English Philology
HÖLSCHER, U., Classics
LIPKA, L., English Philology
NOLTING-HAUFF, I., Romance Philology
NOYER-WEIDNER, A., Romance Philology
SCHLINGLOFF, D., Indology and Iranian Studies
STIMM, H., Romance Philology
STROH, W., Classics
STRUNK, K., General and Indo-European Linguistics
VOGT, E., Classics
WARNING, R., Romance Philology
WEISS, R., English Philology

Department of Language and Literature II:
BAUER, R., History of Modern German Literature
BETZ, W., German Philology
FROMM, H., German Philology
FRÜHWALD, W., History of Modern German Literature
KOLB, H., German Philology
KUHN, H., German Philology
MÜLLER-SEIDEL, W., History of Modern German Literature
SCHIER, K., Northern Philology
SENGLE, F., History of Modern German Literature
TILLMANN, H.-G., Phonetics
VENNEMANN, TH., German Philology

Deartment of Social Sciences:
BOLTE, K.-M., Sociology
BÜHL, W., Sociology
FRIEDMANN, F. G., History of North American Culture
HELLE, H. J., Sociology
KINDERMANN, K. G., International Politics
LOBKOWICZ, N., Political Theory and Political Philosophy
LUDZ, P. C., Political Science
MAIER, H., Political Science
POENICKE, H., History of American Literature
ROEGELE, O. B., Journalism
SONTHEIMER, K., Political Science
ZORN, W., Social and Commercial History

Department of Mathematics:
BATT, J., Practical Mathematics
GERICKE, H., History of Natural Sciences
HÄMMERLIN, G., Practical Mathematics
KASCH, F., Mathematics
KELLERER, H. G., Mathematics
PAREIGIS, B., Mathematics
ROELCKE, W., Mathematics
SEEGMÜLLER, G., Information Sciences
STEIN, K., Mathematics
WIENHOLTZ, E., Practical Mathematics

Department of Physics:
BOER, J. DE, Experimental Physics
BOPP, F., Theoretical Physics
BRANDMÜLLER, J., Experimental Physics
BROSS, H., Theoretical Physics
HOFMANN, G., Meteorology
MEYER-BERKHOUT, U., Experimental Physics
PEISL, H., Experimental Physics
SALECKER, H., Theoretical Physics
SIZMANN, R., Experimental Physics
SKORKA, S., Experimental Physics
SÜSSMANN, G., Theoretical Physics
WAIDELICH, W., Physics
WALTHER, H., Experimental Physics
WELLMANN, P., Astronomy
ZUPANČIĆ, C., Experimental Physics

Department of Chemistry and Pharmacy:
BECK, W., Inorganic Chemistry
BINSCH, G., Organic Chemistry
BOEHM, H.-P., Inorganic Chemistry
EIDEN, F., Pharmacy
ERTL, G., Physical Chemistry
GOMPPER, R., Organic Chemistry
HARTMANN, G., Biochemistry
HUISGEN, R., Organic Chemistry
LYNEN, F., Chemistry
NÖTH, H., Inorganic Chemistry
SEVERIN, TH., Food Chemistry
STACHEL, H. D., Pharmacy
VOITLÄNDER, J., Physical Chemistry
WAGNER, H., Pharmacology
WEISS, A., Inorganic Chemistry

Department of Biology:
BECKER, J. H., Zoology and Genetics
CLEVE, H., Anthropology and Human Genetics
KANDLER, O., Botany
KAUDEWITZ, F., Genetics
JAKOBS, J., Zoology
LINZEN, B., Biology
MERXMÜLLER, H., Botany
RÜDIGER, W., Phytochemistry

Department of Geosciences:
ANGENHEISTER, G., Geophysics
GIERLOFF-EMDEN, H. G., Geography
HERM, D., Geology and Palaeontology
HUCKENHOLZ, H. G., Mineralogy
JAGODZINSKI, H., Crystallography and Mineralogy
SCHMIDT, K., Geology
WILHELM, F., Geography

Department of Education:
BAIER, H., Education for Slow Learners and Physically Handicapped
BIRKENHAUER, J., Geography
BRAUN, A., Education for Slow Learning Children
DAUCHER, H., Art
DIETRICH, G., Psychology
FEIL, E., Catholic Theology
GLASER, H., History
GLEISSNER, A., Catholic Theology
GROSSER, D., Political Science
HECHT, K., English Language and Literature
KILLERMANN, W., Biology
KOTTEN-SEDERQUIST, A., Education for the Speech-Handicapped
LUCHNER, K., Physics
LÜCKERT, H.-R., Psychology
MORDSTEIN, F., Philosophy
MÜLLER-BARDORFF, J., Evangelical Theology
NEUHÄUSLER, A., Philosophy
NOACK, R., Political Science
REIN, K., German Language and Literature
SCHNEIDER, F., Political Science
SCHORB, A. O., Science of Education
SEEBACH, K., Mathematics
SPECK, O., Education for the Mentally Retarded and Disturbed
STOCKER, K., German Language and Literature

WAGNER, R., Music Pedagogics
WASEM, E., Pedagogics
ZÖPFL, H., School Pedagogics

TECHNISCHE UNIVERSITÄT MÜNCHEN

8000 MUNICH 2,
ARCISSTRASSE 21
Telephone: 21051.
Founded 1868.

Academic year: October to September.

President: Prof. Dr. rer. nat. WOLFGANG WILD.

Vice-Presidents: Prof. Dr. RUPPRECHT ZAPF, Prof. Dr. JOHANN RASTETTER.

Chancellor: HEINRICH LAMPERSBERGER.

Librarian: Dr. P. SCHWEIGLER.

Number of teachers: 2,489.

Number of students: 16,163.

Publications: *Personen- und Vorlesungsverzeichnis* (2 a year), *Jahrbuch*† (annually).

DEANS:

Faculty of Mathematics: Prof. Dr. RUDOLF BAYER.

Faculty of Physics: Prof. Dr. WOLFGANG WILD.

Faculty of Chemistry, Biology and Geosciences: Prof. Dr. rer. nat. HUBERT SCHMIDBAUR.

Faculty of Economics and Social Sciences: Prof. Dr. RUDOLF KRASSER.

Faculty of Civil Engineering and Surveying: Prof. Dr. HARRY GRUNDMANN.

Faculty of Architecture: Prof. Dipl.-Ing. CHRISTOPH OTTOW.

Faculty of Mechanical Engineering: Prof. Dr. HORST LIPPMANN.

Faculty of Electrical Engineering: Prof. Dr.-Ing. RUDOLF SAAL.

Faculty of Agriculture and Horticulture: Prof. Dr. WERNER ROTHENBURGER.

Faculty of Brewing, Food Technology and Dairy Science: Prof. Dr. WILHELM POSTEL.

Faculty of Medicine: Prof. Dr. MELCHIOR REITER.

PROFESSORS:

Faculty of Mathematics:

BAUER, F. L., Mathematics and Informatics
BAUMANN, R., Mathematics
BAYER, R., Informatics
BECKMANN, M., Applied Mathematics and Mathematical Statistics
BULIRSCH, R., Mathematics
EICKEL, J., Informatics
GAEDE, K. W., Mathematical Statistics
GIERING, O., Geometry
HEINHOLD, J., Applied Mathematics and Mathematical Statistics
HELWIG, K.-H., Mathematics and Analytical Mechanics
KARZEL, H., Geometry
KÖNIGSBERGER, K., Mathematics
PAUL, M., Informatics
SAMELSON, K., Mathematics and Informatics
SIEGERT, H.-J., Informatics
THOMA, E., Mathematics and Analytical Mechanics

Faculty of Physics:

ALEFELD, G., Physics
BRENIG, W., Theoretical Physics
DANIEL, H., Experimental Physics
DIETRICH, K., Theoretical Physics
FISCHER, S., Theoretical Physics
GLÄSER, W., Experimental Physics
GÖTZE, W., Theoretical Physics
KAISER, W., Experimental Physics
KALVIUS, G., Physics
KIENLE, P., Experimental Physics
KINDER, H., Experimental Physics
KOCH, F., Physics
KÖRNER, H. J., Experimental Physics
LÜSCHER, E., Experimental Physics
MANG, H.-J., Theoretical Physics
MENZEL, D., Physics
MÖSSBAUER, R. L., Experimental Physics
MORINAGA, H., Experimental Physics
WILD, W., Theoretical Physics

Faculty of Chemistry, Biology and Geosciences:

BELITZ, H.-D., Food Technology
DIALER, K., Technical Chemistry
DÖRR, F., Physical Chemistry
FISCHER, E. O., Inorganic Chemistry
FLECKENSTEIN, J. O., History of Science and Technology
FRITZ, H. P., Inorganic Chemistry
HAASE, G., Scientific Photography
HOFACKER, G. L., Theoretical Chemistry
KERBER, R., Macromolecular Materials
KÖHLER, F., Inorganic Chemistry
KRESZE, G., Organic Chemistry
NITSCH, W., Technical Chemistry
QUENTIN, K. E., Hydrogeology and Hydrochemistry
SCHLAG, E. W., Physical Chemistry
SCHLEIFER, K.-H., Microbiology
SCHMIDBAUR, H., Inorganic and Analytical Chemistry
SIMON, H., Organic Chemistry and Biochemistry
UGI, I., Organic Chemistry
ZIEGLER, H., Botany

Faculty of Economics and Social Sciences:

BÄUMLER, G., Physical Education (Psychology)
BERG, J., Philosophy
BUSSMANN, K. F., General and Industrial Management
EBERLEIN, G. L., Sociology
FUCHS, R., Pedagogy and Pedagogical Sociology
GEIPEL, R., Geography
GRÖSSING, S., Physical Education Teaching
HEINRITZ, G., Geography
HOLZHEU, F., Social Economics
HOYOS, GRAF C., Psychology
KRASSER, R., Private and Patent Law
SCHMIDTKE, H., Ergonomics
SCHUSTER, R., Political Science

Faculty of Civil Engineering and Surveying:

BISCHOFSBERGER, W., Hydraulics and Sanitary Engineering
BLIND, H., Hydraulic Engineering
BURKHARDT, G., Tunnel Construction, Building Management
EBNER, H., Photogrammetry
EISENMANN, J., Highway Construction
FINSTERWALDER, R., Cartography and Reproduction
FRANKE, P.-G., Hydraulics and Hydrology
GRUNDMANN, H., Theoretical Mechanics
HEIMESHOFF, B., Building Construction and Wood Structures
HOISL, R., Rural Reorganization
JELINEK, R., Soil Mechanics and Foundation Engineering
KNITTEL, G., Building Statics
KUPFER, H., Massive Construction
NATHER, F., Steel Construction
SCHAECHTERLE, K., Transport and Town Planning
SCHNÄDELBACH, K., Geodesy
SIGL, R., Astronomical and Physical Geodesy
SPRINGENSCHMID, R., Technology of Building Materials

Faculty of Architecture:

ALBERS, G., Town and Country Planning
ANGERER, F., Town Planning and Design
DIETRICHS, B., Regional Research, Policy and Country Planning
GEBHARD, H., Architectural Planning in Rural Areas
GRUBEN, G., History of Building
HUGUES, T., Building Construction and Materials
KOENIG, F., Plastic Arts
KRÜGER, W., House Technology
KURRENT, F., Design, Interior Decorating and Sacred Building
KÜTTINGER, G., Building Construction and Materials
MEITINGER, O., Architectural Design and Preservation of Monuments
MEYER, K., Statics of Rising Structure
OTTOW, J. C., Introduction to Design
SCHMID, T., Design and Industrial Building
SCHMOLL, Gen. EISENWERTH, J. A., History of Art
SCHRÖDER, H., Design
WIENANDS, R., Design and Method of Presentation
WINKLER, B., Project Design

Faculty of Mechanical Engineering:

BLASS, E., Chemical Engineering
BÖTTCHER, S., Materials Handling and Machine Technology
BRÜNING, G., Flight Mechanics and Control
EHRLENSPIEL, K., Machine Design Methods
FISCHER, F., Product Engineering
HABENICHT, G., Joining Technics (Welding, Soldering and Bonding)
HEINZL, J., Precision Mechanics and Kinematics
LIPPMANN, H., Mechanics
MAGNUS, K., Engineering Mechanics
MERSMANN, A., Chemical Engineering
MEYER-JENS, R., Lightweight Structures
MÜLLER-LIMMROTH, W., Ergonomics
MÜNZBERG, H.-G., Propulsion
RAABE, J., Hydraulic Machines and Plants
RUPPE, H. O., Space Technology
SCHMITT-THOMAS, K. G., Metallurgy
SÖHNE, W., Agricultural Engineering
STROHMEIER, K., Apparatus and Reactor Construction
THOMAS, H.-J., Heat Generation Engineering
TRUCKENBRODT, E., Fluid Mechanics
VORTMEYER, D., Thermodynamics
WINTER, E. R. F., Thermodynamics (Cryogenics and Refrigeration Engineering)
WINTER, H., Machine Elements and Laboratory for Gear Research (FZG)
WOSCHNI, G., Internal Combustion Engines and Vehicle Construction

Faculty of Electrical Engineering:

ANTREICH, K., Computer-aided Design
BIRKHOFER, A., Nuclear Reactor Dynamics and Reactor Safety

Boeck, W., High Voltage Engineering and Power Plants
Einsele, T., Data Processing
Färber, G., Process Control Computer
Groll, H., Microwave Engineering
Harth, W., Electrical Engineering
Kessler, G., Electrical Drive Engineering
Lorenzen, H. W., Electrical Machinery (Electrical Machines, Static Converters)
Marko, H., Communication Technics
Meinke, H. H., High Frequency Technology
Müller, R., Technical Electronics
Ruge, I., Integrated Circuits
Saal, R., Network Theory and Circuit Design
Schaefer, H., Energy Technology and Power Plant Engineering
Schmidt, G., Control Engineering
Schrüfer, E., Measurement Engineering
Zwicker, E., Electroacoustics

Faculty of Agriculture and Horticulture:
Amberger, A., Plant Nutrition
Feucht, Fruit Culture
Fischbeck, G., Agriculture and Plant Breeding
Fritz, D., Vegetable Crops
Groth, W., Hygiene and Anatomy of Domestic Animals
Grzimek, G., Landscape Architecture
Haber, W., Landscape Ecology
Hock, B., Botany
Hoffmann, G. M., Phytopathology
Horn, W., Floriculture
Karg, H., Physiology of Reproduction and Lactation
Kirchgessner, M., Nutrition Physiology
Korte, F., Ecological Chemistry
Pirchner, F., Animal Breeding
Rothenburger, W., Economics in Horticulture
Schmidt, H.-L., Chemistry and Biochemistry
Schwertmann, U., Soil Science
Steinhauser, H., Agricultural Economics
Urff, W., Agricultural Policy and Marketing Analysis
Voigtländer, G., Grassland Research
Wenner, H.-L., Agricultural Technology
Wolfram, G., Nutrition
Zapf, R., Applied Agricultural Economics

Faculty of Brewing, Food Technology and Dairy Science:
Berg, F., Brewery Equipment
Denk, V., Mechanics
Drawert, F., Chemical Analysis and Chemical Food Technology
Engerth, H., Brewing Machinery and Energy Economics of Breweries
Kessler, H.-G., Food and Dairy Technology
Klostermeyer, H., Dairy Science
Krüger, R., Brewing Economics
Narziss, L., Technology of Brewing
Postel, W., General Food Technology
Schöffel, F., Mechanical Engineering
Vogel, H., Physics

Faculty of Medicine:
Anacker, H., Radiodiagnostics
Bernett, P., Traumatology of Sports
Blömer, H., Internal Medicine
Blümel, G., Experimental Surgery
Borelli, S., Dermatology and Venereal Diseases
Brachmann, F., Dentistry
Breit, A., Radiotherapy
Dudel, J., Physiology
Eggerer, H., Physiological Chemistry
Fruhmann, G., Industrial Medicine
Görres, A., Medical Psychology and Psychotherapy
Gössner, W., General Pathology and Pathological Anatomy
Hammersen, F., Anatomy
Hipp, E., Orthopaedics
Kolb, E., Anaesthesia
Lange, H.-J., Medical Statistics and Epidemiology
Lauter, H., Psychiatry
Ley, H., Internal Medicine
Liebermeister, K., Hygiene and Medical Microbiology
Mauermayer, W., Urology
Merté, H.-J., Ophthalmology
Oberdorfer, A., Clinical Chemistry and Pathobiochemistry
Pabst, H. W., Nuclear Medicine
Reiter, M., Pharmacology and Toxicology
Soost, H.-J., Clinical Cytology
Struppler, A., Neurology and Clinical Neurophysiology
Waidl, E., Gynaecology

UKRAINISCHE FREIE UNIVERSITÄT

8 MUNICH 80,
PIENZENAUERSTRASSE 15
Telephone: 98-69-28.
Founded 1921.

Private, State recognized; Languages of instruction: Ukrainian, English, German; Academic year: October to August (including Summer Courses July–August).

Rector: Prof. Dr. Wolodymyr Janiw.
Pro-Rector: Prof. Dr. Zenowij Sokoluk.
Registrar: Wolodymyr Didowycz.
Librarian: Marussia Zajac-Sydir.

Number of teachers: 60.
Number of students: 500.

Publications: *Naukovi Zbirnyky UVU*†, *Naukovi Zapysky UVU*† (annually), *Specimina dialectorum ucrainorum*†, and monographs.

Deans:

Faculty of Philosophy: Prof. Dr. Hryhorij Waskowycz.
Faculty of Law and Economics: Prof. Dr. Bohdan Kordiuk.
Summer Courses: Dir. Prof. Dr. H. Waskowycz.

Professors:

Faculty of Philosophy:
Bilaniuk, P., History of Ukrainian Church
Chorney, S., History of Ukrainian Theatre and Drama
Cymbalisty, P., Slavonic Philology
Goy, P., History of Ukraine
Hocij, M., History of Ukrainian Culture and Arts
Horbatsch, O., Slavonic Philology
Hrynioch, I., History of the Ukrainian Church
JHurskyj, J., Slavonic Philology
aniw, W., Psychology and Sociology
Joukovsky, A., History of Ukraine
Kaczurowskyj, I., Ukrainian Literature
Kratochvil, J., Animal Psychology and Sociology
Kulczyckyj, J., East European History
Lew, W., Slavonic Philology
Rudnyckyj, J., Slavonic Philology
Rudnytzky, L., Comparative Literature
Shevelov, G., Slavonic Philology
Stepanenko, M., History of Ukrainian Literature
Waskowycz, H., Pedagogics
Wirsta, A., History of Ukrainian Music

Faculty of Law and Economics:
Bej, E., Political Philosophy
Bohatiuk, N., Political Economy
Ciuciura, T. B., Commercial and Industrial Law
Horn, G., Political Economy, International Law
Kordiuk, B., Economic Geography
Kuschpeta, O., Finance
Lewytzkyj, B., Sociology
Meyer-Laurin, Roman and Civil Law
Osadczuk, B., Sociology
Padoch, J., History of Ukrainian Law
Potichnyj, P. J., Political Sciences
Sokoluk, Z., Constitutional Law
Witochynskyj, B., International Law

WESTFÄLISCHE WILHELMS-UNIVERSITÄT MÜNSTER

4400 MÜNSTER, SCHLOSSPLATZ 2
Telephone: 4901.

Founded 1780; became Academy in 1818; University status again in 1902.

Rector: Prof. Dr. Werner Müller Warmuth.
Chancellor: Dr. Klaus Triebold.
Librarian: Prof. Dr. G. Liebers.

Number of students: 29,807.

Publications: *Personal- und Vorlesungs-Verzeichnis der WWU*† (2 a year), *Jahresschrift der Gesellschaft zur Förderung der WWU*† (annual), ***Nachrichten und Berichte der Universität***† (irregular), *Dissertationen der Mathematischen-Naturwissenschaftlichen Fakultät in Referaten*† (irregular), ***Struktur der Studierenden der WWU***† (1 a term), *Amtliche Bekanntmachungen der WWU* (irregular).

Deans:

Department of Protestant Theology: Prof. Dr. P. Hauptmann.
Department of Catholic Theology: Prof. Dr. H. Steinkamp.
Department of Law: Prof. Dr. R. Battes.
Department of Economic and Social Sciences: Prof. Dr. H. Wagner.
Faculty of Medicine: Prof. Dr. D. Habeck.
Department of Clinical and Theoretical Medicine: Prof. Dr. E.-J. Speckmann.
Department of Clinical Medicine: Prof. Dr. G. Brune.
Faculty of Philosophy: Prof. Dr. M. E. Brockhoff.
Department of Philosophy: Prof. Dr. G. Wiegelmann.
Department of Psychology: Prof. Dr. A. Mummendey.

Department of Education, Sociology and Communications: Prof. Dr. A. MANNZMANN.

Department of History: Prof. Dr. G. W. WITTKÄMPER.

Department of Germanic Studies: Prof. Dr. K. GRUBMÜLLER.

Department of English Studies: Prof. Dr. K. TETZELI VON ROSADOR.

Department of Romance and Slavonic Studies: Prof. Dr. G. RESSEL.

Department of Classical and Non-European Studies: Prof. Dr. K. HECKER.

Faculty of Mathematics and Natural Sciences: Prof. Dr. K.-F. SCHREIBER.

Department of Mathematics: Prof. Dr. H.-G. TILLMANN.

Department of Physics: A. BENNINGHOVEN.

Department of Chemistry: Prof. Dr. H. U. BAMBAUER.

Department of Biology: Prof. Dr. W. BARZ.

Department of Earth Sciences: Prof. Dr. L. BISCHOFF.

UNIVERSITÄT OLDENBURG

D-2900 OLDENBURG, AMMERLÄNDER HEERSTRASSE 67-99, POSTFACH 2503

Telex: 25655 unol d.

Telephone: (0441) 798-1.

Founded 1974.

Academic year: October to September (two terms).

President: Dr. HORST ZILLESSEN.

Vice-Presidents: Prof. Dr. HANS-DIETRICH RAAPKE, Prof. Dr. PETER KÖLL.

Administrative Officer: JÜRGEN LÜTHJE.

Librarian: HERMANN HAVEKOST.

Number of teachers: 153.

Number of students: 5,100.

Publications: *Uni-info* (*c.* 20 a year), *Veranstaltungsverzeichnis*† (2 a year).

CHAIRMEN:

Department I (*Education and Socialization*): Prof. Dr. ENNO FOOKEN.

Department II (*Communication and Aesthetics*): Prof. Dr. FRED RITZEL.

Department III (*Social Sciences*): Prof. Dr. KLAUS LENK.

Department IV (*Mathematics and Natural Sciences*): Prof. Dr. JOACHIM LUTHER.

PROFESSORS:

Department I (*Education and Socialization*):

Pedagogics:

BUSCH, F.-W., General Education
FISCHER, H.-J., General Education
FÜLGRAFF, B., Development
HASLER, H., Education, School Teaching
HOPF, A., Education
LANGE, O., General Education
MAYDELL, J. VON, Education
MAYER-KULENKAMPFF, I., Education, Social Teaching
MERGNER, G., General Education
MEYER, H., Education, School Teaching
MÖLLER, B., Education
NITSCH, W., Theory of Knowledge
PETERS, H., Theory of Deviant Behaviour
RAAPKE, H.-D., General Education
SENSKY, K., Development
TOPSCH, W., Education
WITTIG, H., General Education
WOLFF, J., Social Work Theory

Special Pedagogics:

FOOKEN, E., Education
SCHLEE, J., Pedagogics
SCHRÖDER, U., Special Pedagogics
TIMM, W., General Social Pedagogics
WESTPHAL, E., Education of Backward Children

Philosophy:

BÜTTEMEYER, W., Philosophy
LENGERT, R., Philosophy

Psychology:

BELSCHNER, W., Psychology
FILIPP, S.-H., Development Psychology
GOTTWALD, P., Psychology
GRUBITZSCH, S., Psychology
LAUCKEN, U., Social Psychology
MEES, U., General Psychology
NACHREINER, F., Applied Psychology
SCHEERER, E., General Psychology
SCHICK, A., Psychology
WALCHER, K.-P., Psychology
ZIMMER, A., General Psychology

Sport:

DIECKERT, J., Physical Education
PETERSEN, U., Sport
RIGAUER, B., Sport
SCHMÜCKER, B., Medicine in Sport

Department II (*Communication and Aesthetics*):

German, including German as a foreign language:

DIERKS, M., Literature
GLÜCK, Linguistics
HELMERS, H., German
MALER, A., Literature
ROHDE, W., German, Linguistics
STÖLTING, W., German as a Foreign Language
THIERGARD, U., German
UEDING, G., Literary History

English:

BOEDER, W., Linguistics, Communications Theory
CALBERT, J. P., Comparative Philology
HILLGÄRTNER, R., Literature
VOGT, H., Teaching of English

Fine Arts, Visual Communication:

KIMPEL, D., Architectural History
LIPPE, R. ZUR, Theory of Aesthetics
SPRINGER, P., Theory and History of Art
TESKE, U., Fine Arts and Visual Communication
THIELE, J., Fine Arts and Visual Communication

Music:

GÜNTHER, U., Music
HEIMANN, Music
RITZEL, F., Auditive Communication
STROH, W. M., Theory of Music

Russian:

HANSEN-LÖWE, Russian Literature
THELIN, N. B., Russian Language

Department III (*Social Sciences*):

Social Sciences:

AICH, P., Sociology and Social Politics
DRÖGE-MODELMOG, I., Sociology
FREIWALD, H., Political Science
HOLTMANN, A., Theory and Practice of Political Structures
KRAFFT, A., Organizational Research and Planning
KRAIKER, G., Social and Political Theory
LENK, K., Administration
MEYER, A., Political Science and Theory
MÜLLER-DOOHM, S., Sociology of the Mass Media
NASSMACHER, K.-H., Politics
NAVE-HERZ, R., Sociology of Youth, Family and Leisure
RUDZIO, W., Politics, Political Sociology
SCHMIDT, E., Politics, Parties and Associations
SCHULENBERG, W., Sociology
VONDERACH, G., Industrial Sociology
WOESLER, C., Sociology

Law:

BLANKE, T., Labour Law
STERZEL, D., Public Law

Economics:

BEHRENS, G., General Business Economy
FEHL, U., General Economic Theory
FREYTAG, H.-L., Statistics, Empirical Social Research
KÜPPER, W., Business Economy
KUTSCHA, G., Teaching of Economics and Business
KUTSUPIS, A., Planning
ORTMANN, G., Business Theory
OSSORIO-CAPELLA, C., Political Economics
PETERS, H.-R., Political Economy
PETHIG, R., Political Economy, Finance
PFAFFENBERGER, W., Political Economy
RAVASANI, S., Social Economy of Developing Countries

Planning:

BRAKE, K., Structural Planning
KUMMERER, K., Regional Planning
SIEBEL, W., Sociology, City and Regional Sociology
WINDELBERG, J., Regional Planning

Vocational Studies:

HENSELER, K., Technology Teaching
KAMINSKI, H., Vocational Studies Teaching
RUFFMANN, M., Domestic Science
SELLIN, H., Technology
SIEMANN, G., Textiles and Clothing

Religion:

ROTH, G., Evangelical Theology, Religious Education
VIERZIG, S., Religious Education

History:

HINRICHS, E., Early Modern History
LUCAS, E., Social History
SAUL, K., Social History with emphasis on the 19th & 20th centuries
SCHMIDT, H., Medieval Social History

Department IV (*Natural Sciences, Mathematics*):

Biology:

EBER, W., Botany, Morphology
ESCHENHAGEN, D., Biology Teaching
GEBHARDT, H., Geosciences, Soil Sciences
HAESELER, V., Zoology
HÖPNER, T., Biochemistry, Enzymology
JANSSEN, S., Microbiology
KRUMBEIN, W., Geomicrobiology
MEGNET, R., Applied Biology
SCHMINKE, H. K., Zoology, Morphology
STABENAU, H., Plant Physiology
WILLIG, A., Zoology, Physiology
ZIMMERMANN, H., Biology, Ethology, Neurobiology

Chemistry:

HAMANN, C. H., Applied Physical Chemistry
JANSEN, W., Chemistry, Theory and Practice of School Teaching
KÖLL, P., Organic Chemistry
SCHULLER, D., Analytical and Physical Chemistry
WEIDENBRUCH, M., Inorganic Chemistry
ZEECK, E., General Chemistry

Geography:

JANSSEN, G., Geography and Teaching
JUNG, G., Geography
KRÜGER, R., Geography
STRASSEL, J., Social Geography

Mathematics:

BESUDEN, H., Mathematics
BRUCKER, P., Mathematics, Mathematical Economics
EBENHÖH, W., Mathematics, Analysis
EIFRIG, B., Mathematics
EMRICH, O., Mathematics
FOLKERTS, M., Mathematics, Professional Practice and History of Mathematics
GORNY, P., Applied Informatics
HERZBERGER, J., Applied Mathematics, Instrumental Mathematics
KNAUER, U., Mathematics, Algebraic Methods
LEISSNER, W., Mathematics, Geometry
MÖBUS, C., Applied Informatics
PIEPER-SEIER, I., Mathematics, Algebra
SCHMALE, W., Mathematics, Analysis
SPÄTH, H., Mathematics and Computer Science
SPROCKHOFF, W., Mathematics

Physics:

HAUBOLD, K., Experimental Physics, Solid State Physics
HINSCH, K., Experimental Physics
LUTHER, J., Experimental Physics, Physical Measuring Techniques
MAIER, K.-H., Experimental Physics
MELLERT, V., Applied Physics
RUTH, V., Teaching of Physics
SCHMIDT, W., Physics, Experimental Physics

UNIVERSITÄT OSNABRÜCK

4500 OSNABRÜCK,
POSTFACH 4469

Telephone: 0541-608-1.
Telex: 944850 uni os d.
Founded 1970.
Campus at Vechta.

Academic year: October to September (two terms).

Rector: Prof. Dr. MANFRED HORSTMANN.
Vice-Rectors: Prof. Dr. HEINZ TRAPP, Prof. Dr. GÜNTER C. BEHRMANN.
Registrar: Dr. jur. KLAUS VOLLE.
Librarian: Dr. EILHARD CORDES.

Number of teachers: *c.* 450.
Number of students: *c.* 4,000.

Publications: *Veranstaltungsverzeichnis* (1 a term), *Amtliches Mitteilungsblatt* (irregular), *Betrifft* (monthly during term).

DIRECTORS OF DEPARTMENTS:

Social Sciences (Production and Distribution, Employment and Training): Prof. Dr. RAINER KÜNZEL.
Social Sciences (Political Organization and International Relations): Prof. Dr. URSULA SCHMIEDERER.
Social Sciences (Education and Socialization): Dr. MANFRED TÜCKE.
Natural Sciences (Physics): Prof. Dr. GERHARD MEYER-EHMSEN.
Natural Sciences (Mathematics and Biology): Prof. Dr. ECKHARD WERRIES.
Natural Sciences (Mathematics and Philosophy): Prof. Dr. ELMAR COHORS-FRESENBORG.
Communications/Aesthetics: Prof. Dr. BERND SCHWISCHAY.
Economics: Prof. Dr. THOMAS WITTE.
Law: (vacant).
Catholic Theology: Prof. Dr. RALPH SAUER.
Vechta Campus:
Education and Socialization: Prof. Dr. STEPHANIE KRENN.
Communications and Aesthetics: Prof. Dr. ASTRID SCHMITT VON MÜHLENFELS.
Natural Sciences/Mathematics: Prof. Dr. Dr. HEINRICH E. WEBER.
Social Sciences: Prof. Dr. HILDEGARD WIEGMANN.

GESAMTHOCHSCHULE PADERBORN

4790 PADERBORN,
WARBURGER STRASSE 100

Telephone: 05251-601.
Founded 1972.

State control; Academic year: October to September.

Rector: Prof. Dr. rer. pol. FRIEDRICH BUTTLER.
Co-Rectors: Prof. Dr. rer. nat. RINKENS, Prof. Dr.-Ing. DRAEGER, F.H.L., Prof. Dr. phil. STEINHOFF.
Chancellor: ULRICH HINTZE.
Librarian: KLAUS BARCKOW.

Number of teachers: 314.
Number of students: 6,517.

Publications: *Mitteilungen und Berichte*† (quarterly), *Amtliche Mitteilungen*†.

DEANS:

Department of Philosophy, Religious and Social Sciences: Prof. Dr. ULRICH LOHMAR.
Department of Education, Psychology, Physical Education: Prof. Dr. ECKARD KÖNIG.
Department of Languages and Literature: Prof. Dr. JOHANNES ASSHEUER.
Department of Art and Music Teaching: Prof. NIEDERAU.
Department of Economics: Prof. Dr. WOLFGANG WEBER.
Department of Natural Sciences I: Prof. Dr. WOLFGANG KLEEMANN.
Department of Natural Sciences II: Prof. Dr. Dr. ECKHARD SCHLIMME.
Department of Architecture: Prof. Dipl.-Ing. HELMUT RINGE.
Department of Construction Engineering: Prof. Dipl.-Ing. HANS-ERICH GADIEL.
Department of Agriculture: Prof. RÖPER.
Department of Machine Engineering I: Prof. Dr.-Ing. JOACHIM LÜCKEL.
Department of Machine Engineering II: Prof. Dipl.-Ing. HELMUT FRICK.
Department of Machine Engineering III: Prof. HAVENSTEIN.
Department of Electrical Engineering and Electronics: Prof. Dr.-Ing. WOLFGANG LATZEL.
Department of Telecommunications Technology: Prof. SIEGFRIED REICHE.
Department of Electric Power Engineering: Prof. GRÜNEBERG.
Department of Mathematics and Data Processing: Prof. MELTZOW.

PROFESSORS:

Department of Philosophy, Religious and Social Sciences:

BENSELER, F., Sociology
EICHER, P., Catholic Theology
HÜSER, K., Westphalian History and Teaching of History
LOHMAR, U., Politics
OELMÜLLER, W., Philosophy
SCHELLONG, D., Evangelical Theology and its Teaching
SCHLEGEL, W., Geography and its Teaching
STACHOWIAK, H., Philosophy
STAUDINGER, H., Political Education and Teaching of History

Department of Education, Psychology and Physical Education:

FRANK, H., Education
FRANZ, J., Education
HEICHERT, C., Education
KEIM, W., Adult Education
KRAMER, H.-J., Sport
SCHLÜTER, J., Psychology
TULODZIECKI, G., Education

Department of Languages and Literature:

ASSHEUER, J., German
BROCKHAUS, W., English
CARSTENSEN, B., English
KIENECKER, F., Modern German Literature
LAUSBERG, H., Latin and Romance Philology
MÜLLENBROCK, H.-J., English
PASIERBSKY, F., German
PROFITLICH, U., 16th-18th century German Literature
STEINECKE, H., Modern German Literature
THOMAS, J., Romance Philology

Department of Art and Music Teaching:

KÖTTERS, P., Music

Department of Economics:

BRONNER, R., Business Management
BUTTLER, F., Political Economy
DOBIAS, P., Political Economy
KAISER, F.-J., Economics
LOISTL, O., Business Management
NASTANSKY, L., Business Management
SKALA, H.-J., Statistics, Econometry
STEINMANN, G., Political Economy
WEINBERG, P., Marketing

Department of Natural Sciences I:

ERBER, M., Biology
HOLZAPFEL, W., Experimental Physics
MÜLLER I., Theoretical Physics
OSTEN, W. VON DER, Experimental Physics
SCHMITZ, J., Physics
SCHRÖTER, J., Theoretical Physics
SPAETH, J.-M., Experimental Physics

Department of Natural Sciences II:
KETTRUP, A., Chemistry
LANGEMANN, H., Technical Chemistry
SELLMANN, D., General Analytical and Inorganic Chemistry
STEGEMEYER, H., Physical Chemistry
SUCROW, W., Organic Chemistry

Department of Electrical Engineering and Electronics:
DÖRRSCHEIDT, F., Regulation Techniques
HARTMANN, G., Basic Electrotechnology
KUMM, W., Telecommunications
LATZEL, W., Theory of Electrical Engineering

Department of Machine Engineering I:
HAHN, O., Materials Science
HERMANN, K., Technical Mechanics
JORDEN, W., Mechanical Engineering
LÜCKEL, J., Automation

Department of Mathematics and Data Processing:
BIERSTEDT, K.-D., Mathematics
DEIMLING, K., Mathematics
FUCHSTEINER, B., Mathematics/Analysis
KANIUTH, E., Mathematics
KIYEK, K.-H., Mathematics/Algebra
LANSKY, M., Information Science
LENZING, H., Mathematics
MONIEN, B., Theory of Information Science
RAUTMANN, R., Mathematics
RINKENS, H.-D., Didactics of Mathematics

UNIVERSITÄT PASSAU

RESIDENZPLATZ 8,
8390 PASSAU
Telephone: 0851-2077.
Founded 1972.

State control; Language of instruction: German; Academic year: October to September.

President: Prof. Dr. K.-H. POLLOK.
Vice-President: Prof. Dr. FRANZ ESER.
Administrative Officer: Dr. K. A. FRIEDRICHS.
Librarian: Dr. H. WIMMER.

Number of professors: 39.
Number of students: 681.
Library of 230,000 vols.
Publications: *Personen- und Vorlesungsverzeichnis*† (every term), *Nachrichten und Berichte*†, *Passauer Universitätsreden*†.

DEANS:

Faculty of Catholic Theology: Prof. Dr. AUGUST LEIDL.
Faculty of Law: Prof. Dr. HERBERT BETHGE.
Faculty of Business Sciences: Prof. Dr. GERHARD KLEINHENZ.
Faculty of Language and Literature: Prof. Dr. SASCHA W. FELIX.
Faculty of Cultural Studies: Prof. Dr. EGON BOSHOF.

PROFESSORS:

Faculty of Catholic Theology:
BEER, R., Philosophy
ESER, F., Natural Sciences and Theology
KAMMERMEIER, E., Church Law
KLEBER, K.-H., Moral Theology
KNOCH, O., Preliminary Biblical Studies
KRINETZKI, G., Old Testament Exegesis and Hebrew
LEIDL, A., Church History
MÜHLEK, K., Education and Catechetics
NEUNER, P., Fundamental Theology
SCHINDLER, H., History of Art and Christian Archaeology
SCHRÖGER, F., New Testament Exegesis
ZULEHNER, P. M., Christian Sociology and Pastoral Theology

Faculty of Law:
BETHGE, H., State and Administrative Law
BEULKE, W., Penal Law
FINCKE, M., Penal Law
KOBLER, M., Civic Law and German Legal History
KOLLER, I., Civic Law and Labour Law
KOPP, F., Public Law
LUIG, K., Civic and Roman Law
MUSIELAK, H. J., Civil and Civic Law
SCHMIEDEL, B., Commercial and Business Law
SÖHN, H., State and Administrative Law
WILHELM, J., Civic and Commercial Law

Faculty of Business Sciences:
BÜHNER, R., Management, Organization and Personnel
GERKE, W., Management and Finance
HAASE, K. D., Management and Tax Studies
KLEINHENZ, G., Economic Policy
LÜDEKE, R., Economics and Finance
MÜCKL, W., Economics and Business Theory
SCHMALEN, H., Management and Marketing
SCHWEITZER, W., Statistics

Faculty of Language and Literature:
FELIX, S., General and Applied Linguistics
LAUFHÜTTE, H., Modern German Literature
PFISTER, M., English Literature

Faculty of Cultural Studies:
BOSHOF, E., Medieval History
HARTINGER, W., Folklore
LILL, R., Modern History
OBERREUTER, H., Political Science
WOLFF, H., Ancient History

UNIVERSITÄT REGENSBURG

8400 REGENSBURG,
UNIVERSITÄTSSTRASSE 31
Telephone: 0941/9431.
Founded 1962.

Academic year: October to September.

President: Prof. Dr. D. HENRICH.
Vice-Presidents: Prof. Dr. J. BARTHEL, Prof. Dr. H. BUNGERT.
Administrative Officer: H.-H. ZORGER.
Librarian: Dr. M. PAUER.

Number of teachers: 750, including 200 professors.
Number of students: *c.* 10,000.

Publications: *Universitäts-Zeitung* (monthly), *Informationen* (monthly), *Personen- und Vorlesungsverzeichnis* (every 6 months), *Schriftenreihe.*

DIRECTORS OF DEPARTMENTS:

Catholic Theology: Prof. Dr. J. RIEF.
Law: Prof. Dr. P. LANDAU.
Economics: Prof. Dr. L. HOFFMANN.
Philosophy, Sport and Arts: Prof. Dr. J. TRAEGER.
Pedagogy and Psychology: Prof. Dr. K. ERLINGHAGEN.
History, Social Sciences and Geography: Prof. Dr. R. HOFMANN.
Literature and Language: Prof. Dr. B. GAJEK.
Mathematics: Prof. Dr. R. MENNICKEN.
Physics: Prof. Dr. W. GEBHARDT.
Biology and Basic Medicine: Prof. Dr. A. BRESINSKY.
Chemistry and Pharmacy: Prof. Dr. K. J. RANGE.

PROFESSORS:

Department of Catholic Theology:
BEINERT, W., Dogmatics
BENZ, K.-J., Church History
BROX, N., Ancient Church History and Patrology
GROSS, H., Old Testament
HOFMEIER, J., Catechetics
KAISER, M., Church Law
KLEINHEYER, B., Liturgy
KRENN, K., Philosophical and Theological Propadeutics
MUSSNER, F., New Testament Exegesis
NASTAINCZYCK, W., Religious Education
PETRI, H., Fundamental Theology
RIEF, J., Moral Theology
SCHMUTTERMAYR, G., Introductory Studies
SCHÜTZ, P. CHR., Dogmatics
SCHURR, A., Philosophical and Theological Propadeutics
WINKLER, G. B., Church History

Department of Law:
ARNOLD, R., Public Law, Foreign Public Law, Comparative Law
FIRSCHING, K., Civil Law, Law Procedure and International Private Law
HENRICH, D., Civil Law and Comparative Law
JAKOBS, G., Criminal Law and Procedure
KIMMINICH, O., Civil Law, National Law, State Law and Politics
KNÖPFLE, R., Civil Law, Commercial and Industrial Law
LANDAU, P., History of Canons, History of Private and Civil Law
PICKER, E., Civil and Roman Law
RICHARDI, R., Labour Law, Social Law
ROLINSKI, K., Penal Law
SCHROEDER, F.-C., Criminal Law, Criminal Procedural Law, Eastern Law
SCHUMANN, E., Procedural Law, Civil Law
SCHWAB, D., Civil Law and History of German Law
STEINER, U., Public Law, German and Bavarian State and Administration Law
SOELL, H., Public Law
STEINMÜLLER, W., Church Law, History of Church Law and Philosophy of Law

Department of Economics:
BLAICH, F., History of Economics
BÖCKER, F., Business Economics
BOHR, K., Business Economics
DRUKARCZYK, J., Business Economy
DRUMM, H. J., Business Economy
FAHRMEIR, L., Statistics
HEUBES, J., Political Economy
HOFFMANN, L., Political Economy
JOHN, G., Business Economics
KULLMER, L., Political Economy and Public Finances
MIETH, W., Political Economy
NIEMEYER, G., Business Economics and Information Science
OBERHOFER, W., Political Economy and Econometry

SCHERRER, G., Business Economy
STECKHAN, H., Business Economy
VOGT, W., Political Economy
WIDMAIER, H.-P., Political Economy

Department of Philosophy, Sport and Arts:
BECK, H., Music
HOMMES, U., Philosophy
KUTSCHERA, F., Philosophy
LUTTER, H., Sport
REITER, J., Philosophy
SCHIFFERS, N., Religion
STURM, W., Religion
TOTH, I., History of Science
TRAEGER, J., History of Art
ULRICH, F., Philosophy

Department of Pedagogy and Psychology:
DRÖSLER, J., Psychology
ERLINGHAGEN, K., Pedagogy
FAHN, K., Didactics of Elementary Education
GROSSMANN, K., Psychology
HEID, H., Pedagogy
IPFLING, H.-J., School Education
LUKESCH, H., Psychology
MAIER, K. E., Education
RÜDIGER, D., Psychology
THOMAS, A., Psychology
TRÖGER, W., Education
VUKOVICH, A., Psychology
WITTE, W., Psychology

Department of History, Social Sciences and Geography:
ABELEIN, M., Political Science and Public Law
ALBRECHT, D., History
ANGERMEIER, H., History
BERGER, H., Didactics of Geography
EHRIG, F. R., Geography
FUHRMANN, H., History
GOETZE, D., Sociology
HERMES, K., Geography
HOFMANN, R., Political Science
KLUG, H., Geography
KÖHLE, K., Didactics of Social Studies
LIPPOLD, A., History
OBST, J., Geography
REINDEL, K., History
RUBNER, H., History of Population and Social Affairs
SCHMITZ, M., Political Science
STIEGLITZ, H., Sociology
TORBRÜGGE, W., History
VÖLKL, E., History
VOLKERT, W., History
ZENNER, M., Didactics of History

Department of Language and Literature:
BREKLE, H. E., General Philology
BUNGERT, H., English Philology
ERNST, G., Romance Philology
GAJEK, B., German Philology
GÄRTNER, H., Classical Philology
GAUER, W., Classical Archaeology
GIEHRL, H., Didactics of German Language and Literature
GÖLLER, K. H., English Philology
HAHN, G., German Philology
HEITSCH, E., Classical Philology (Greek)
HIETSCH, O., English Philology
HÖSLE, J., Romance Philology
KREUTZER, H. J., German Philology
MATZEL, K., German Philology
POLLMANN, L., Romance Philology
RIX, H., Indo-Germanic Philology
SIMMLER, F., German Philology
THRAEDE, K., Classical Philology (Latin)
TROST, K., Slavonic Philology
WEDEL, E., Slavonic Studies

Department of Mathematics:
BIERLEIN, D.
BRÖCKER, TH.
HACKENBROCK, W.
JÄNICH, K.
KNEBUSCH, M.
KNORR, K.
KUNZ, E.
MAIER, H.
MENNICKEN, R.
NEUKIRCH, J.
TAMME, G.
WARLIMONT, R.

Department of Physics:
BONART, R.
CREUZBURG, M.
GEBHARDT, W.
HOFFMANN, H.
KELLER, J.
KREY, U.
MAIER, M.
OBERMAIR, G.
PHILIPSBORN, H. VON
RENK, K.
RÖSSLER, U.
SCHRÖDER, U.
STRAUCH, D.
WEISE, W.

Department of Biology and Basic Medicine:
ALBERS, C., Physiology
ALTNER, H., Zoology
BAUER, CH., Physiology
BOECKH, J., Zoology
BRESINSKY, A., Botany
BURKHARDT, D., Zoology
DARNHOFER-DEMAR, B., Zoology
ERNST, K.-D., Zoology
FRIESS, A., Anatomy
HANSEN, K., Zoology
HAUSKA, G., Botany
HÜTTERMANN, J., Biophysics
JAENICKE, R., Biochemistry
KRAMER, B., Zoology
LINDNER, E., Morphology and Anatomy
LÖFFLER, G., Biochemistry
MOLITORIS, H. P., Botany
MOLL, W., Physiology
MÜLLER-BROICH, A., Biophysics
RENG, G., Didactics of Biology
SCHMITT, R., Genetics
SCHNELL, K., Physiology
SPEIERER, G. W., Medical Psychology
SUMPER, M., Biochemistry
TANNER, W., Botany
WROBEL, K.-H., Morphology and Anatomy

Department of Chemistry and Pharmacy:
BARTHEL, J., Physical Chemistry
BRUNNER, H., Inorganic Chemistry
DAUB, J., Organic Chemistry
FRANZ, G., Pharmaceutical Biology
FREISE, V., Physical Chemistry
GLIEMANN, G., Theoretical Chemistry
GROBECKER, H., Pharmacology of Natural Sciences
HECKMANN, K. D., Physical Chemistry
HERMANN, W. A., Inorganic Chemistry
HEUMANN, K. G., Inorganic Chemistry
LIEFLÄNDER, M., Physiological Chemistry
MANNSCHRECK, A., Organic Chemistry
MÄRKL, G., Organic Chemistry
RANGE, K.-J., Inorganic Chemistry
RUPPRECHT, H., Pharmaceutical Technology
SAUER, J., Organic Chemistry
SCHÖNENBERGER, H., Pharmaceutical Chemistry
STEINBORN, O., Theoretical and Physical Chemistry
VOGLER, A., Inorganic Chemistry
WACHTER, R., Physical Chemistry
WIEGREBE, W., Pharmaceutical Chemistry

UNIVERSITÄT DES SAARLANDES

66 SAARBRÜCKEN, IM STADTWALD

Telephone: 3021.

Founded 1948.

President: Prof. Dr. PAUL MÜLLER.
Administrator: Dr. iur. H. J. SCHUSTER.
Librarian: Dr. O. VINZENT.

Number of teachers: 850,
Number of students: 13,599.

Publications: *Annales Universitatis Saraviensis* (quarterly), *Rechts und Wirtschaftswissenschaften, Philosophie, Medizin, Scientia, Vorlesungsverzeichnis.*

DEANS:

Faculty of Law and Economics: Prof. Dr. BRUNO TIETZ.
Faculty of Medicine (at Homburg/Saar): Prof. Dr. HERMANN-JOSEF HAAS.
Faculty of Philosophy: Prof. Dr. GERT HUMMEL.
Faculty of Natural Sciences: Prof. Dr. FRIEDRICH TOMI.

PROFESSORS:

Faculty of Law and Economics:
ALBECK, H., Political Economy
AUBIN, B., German and Comparative Civil Law
BARATTA, A., Sociology of Law and Social Philosophy
BAUER, J.-P., Civil Law
BRECHER, F., Civil Law
BURMEISTER, J., Constitutional and Administrative Law, General Political Science
DINKELBACH, W., Management, Commerce
DOMES, J., Politics
GECK, W. K., Constitutional Law, Foreign Public Law, International Law
HÜFFER, U., Civil Law
JAHR, G., Roman and Civil Law, International Private Law, Comparative Law
JUNG, H., Penal and Procedural Law
KIELWEIN, G., German and Foreign Criminal Law, Criminal Procedure and Criminology
KILGER, W., Industrial Economics
KNIES, W., Public, Administrative and Financial Law
KROEBER-RIEL, W., Management, Commerce
LÜKE, G., Procedural Law
MARETTEK, A., Management
MÜLLER-DIETZ, Penal and Procedural Law, Criminology
NEUBAUER, W., Statistics
POENSGEN, O., Industrial Economy
RESS, G., Public Law
RICHTER, R., National Economy, with special reference to Economic Theory
RÜFNER, W., Public Law
SCHEER, A.-W., Industrial Economics
SCHIEDERMAIR, H., Public Law, Philosophy of Law
SCHMIDTCHEN, D., National Economics
SCHÖN, K., Political Science
SCHULTZ, D., Public Law, Business and Economic Law
SIEVERT, O., National Economics
STEINMETZ, V., Statistics and Econometrics
STÜTZEL, W., Economics
TIETZ, B., Industrial Economics

WADLE, E., History of German Law Civil Law
WILL, M. R., Public Law, Business and Economic Law
WÖHE, G., Industrial Economics, especially Taxation

Faculty of Medicine:
BALDAUF, J., Pharmacology and Toxicology
BERGER, W., Physiology
BETTE, L., Internal Medicine
BOCK, R., Anatomy
BOOZ, K. H., Anatomy
BRAEDEL, H.-U., Clinical Radiology
BÜCH, H. P., Pharmacology and Toxicology
DHOM, G., General Pathology and Pathological Anatomy
DRASCHE, H., Industrial Medicine
EHRICH, W., Ophthalmology
FARTHMANN, E., Surgery
FREITAG, V., Dentistry
FRITSCHE, P., Anaesthesiology
GRILLMAIER, R., Biophysics and Physical Basis of Medicine
HAAS, H. J., Physiological Chemistry
HARBAUER, G., Experimental Surgery
HEPP, H., Gynaecology
HORN, H.-J., Psychiatry and Neurology
HUTSCHENREUTER, K., Anaesthesiology
JELASIC, F., Neurology
JURNA, I., Pharmacology and Toxicology
JUTZLER, G. A., Internal Medicine
KELLER, H. E., Clinical Chemistry
KIENECKER, E.-W., Anatomy
KINDERMANN, W., Sports Medicine
LEETZ, H.-K., Biophysics and Physical Basis of Medicine
LINDEMANN, B., Physiology
LOEW, F., Neurosurgery
LUTHE, R., Psychiatry and Neurology
MEISER, R. J., Internal Medicine
MEVES, H., Physiology
MITTELMEIER, H., Orthopaedics
MOHN, G., Physiological Chemistry
MOOTZ, W., Oto-Rhino-Laryngology
MORGENSTERN, E., Cytology and Electro-Microscopy
MUTH, H., Biophysics
NACIMIENTO, A., Physiology
OBERHAUSEN, E., Biophysics and Physical Basis of Medicine
PAPPAS, A., Internal Medicine
PEPER, K., Physiology
PFLEGER, K., Pharmacology and Toxicology
PIEPGRAS, U., Clinical Radiology
RACENBERG, E., Anaesthesiology
RINDT, W., Gynaecological Endocrinology
RUMMEL, W., Pharmacology and Toxicology
SCHÄTZLE, W., Oto-rhino-laryngology
SCHEURLEN, P. G., Internal Medicine
SCHIEFFER, H. J., Internal Medicine
SCHIMRIGK, K., Neurology
SCHLEGEL, H.-J., Ophthalmology
SCHMEISSNER, H., Dentistry
SCHMIDT, H., Physiology
SCHMITT, W., Psychiatry and Neurology
SCHRENK, M., Psychotherapy
SCHWEIBERER, L., Surgery
SCHWEISFURTH, R., Microbiology
SEELIGER, H., General Pathology and Pathological Anatomy
SITTE, H., Cytology and Electro-Microscopy
SITZMANN, F. C., Paediatrics
SOMMER, F., Medical Radiology
SPECHT, W., Anatomy
STAPENHORST, K., Heart and Chest Surgery
STEGER, E., Dentistry
STÜBEN, J., Dentistry
TIESLER, E., Medical Microbiology
TRAUB, W., Microbiology and Tropical Medicine
TRAUTWEIN, W., Physiology
TRENDELBURG, F., Internal Medicine, especially Pulmonary Diseases
UHLMANN, K., Anatomy
ULLRICH, V., Physiological Chemistry
WAGNER, H.-J., Forensic Medicine
WANKE, K., Neurology, Psychiatry
WEINGES, K., Internal Medicine
WENZEL, E., Haemostasiology and Blood Transfusion Medicine
WERNER, G., Cytology and Electro-Microscopy
WIGAND, R., Microbiology and Tropical Medicine
WITTER, H., Forensic Psychiatry
ZANG, K., Human Genetics
ZIEGLER, M., Urology
ZOCH, E., Physiological Chemistry

Faculty of Philosophy:
APFEL, E., Musicology
BANULS, A., Modern German Literary Criticism
BAUS, M., Sociology
BLANK, J., Biblical Theology
BLICKLE, P., Modern History and National History
BOESCH, E., Psychology
BRAUN, W., Musicology
BRAY, B., Modern French Literature
BREITENBACH, D., Psychology
BRÜCHER, W., Geography
DITTMANN, L., History of Art
ECK, W., Ancient History
ECKENSBERGER, L., Comparative Cultural Psychology
ENGELKAMP, J., Psychology
ERDMANN, P., English Philology
FEHRENBACH, E., Modern History
FLIEDNER, D., Economic Geography
FRANKE, P. R., Ancient History
GÄTJE, H., Eastern Studies
GESEMANN, W., Slavic Languages
GÖRLER, W., Classical Philology
GÖTZ, W., History of Art
HACHMANN, R., Prehistory
HASENHÜTTL, G., Systematic Theology
HAUBRICHS, W., Medieval German Literature
HEINE, K., Geography
HELFER, C., Comparative European Societies and Culture
HILLER, F., Archaeology
HOENSCH, J. K., East European History
HUMMEL, G., Systematic Theology
ILTING, K.-H., Philosophy
ITSCHERT, H., American Studies
JACOBI, R., Islamic Studies
JÄSCHKE, K.-U., Medieval History
JÖRG, H., Education
JUNG, K. O., Art Education
KLEIN, E., Economic and Social History
KLEIN, K., English Philology and Literature
KNAUF, K., Pedagogics of Sport
KORNADT, H.-J., Education and Educational Psychology
KÖTTER, L., Pedagogics
KRÄMER, H.-L., Sociology
KRAUSE, R., Psychology
KURUCZ, J., Sociology
LEIS-SCHINDLER, I., Historical Pedagogics
LICHTENBERGER, S., German Literature
LIPGENS, W., Modern History
LORENZ, K., Philosophy
MAHLING, C.-H., Music
MAHNKEN, I., Slavonic and Balkan Studies
MANGOLD, M., Phonology and Phonetics
MANN, U., Systematic Theology
MAXEINER, J., Education
MEISTER, H., Psychology
MÜLLER, C. W., Classical Philology
MÜLLER, P., Biogeography
MÜLLER-BLATTAU, W., Musicology
NEUSCHÄFER, H., Romance Philology and Literature
NIVELLE, A., Comparative Literature
OHLIG, K.-H., Theology
ORLIK, P., Psychology
ORTHMANN, W., Asian Archaeology
PAUL, H. O., Musicology
PFISTER, M., Romance Philology
RAASCH, H., Applied Linguistics
RATH, R., Modern German Language
REINIG, R., Education
RICHTER, K., Modern German Philology
RISSE, W., Philosophy, especially History of Logic
ROTH, M.-L., Modern German Literature
RUPP, A., Religious History of Ancient Orient
SANDER, A., Education
SANDIG, B., Modern German Language
SANDVOSS, E., History of Philosophy
SAUDER, G., Modern German Philology and Literature
SCHEEL, H. L., Romance Philology and Literature
SCHLOBACH, J., Romance Philology
SCHMIDT-HENKEL, G., Modern German Philology and Literature
SCHMITT, R., Comparative Indo-Germanic Languages
SCHMITZ, J. N., Physical Education
SCHUSTER, H., Theology
SIEBEL, W., Sociology
SIEBURG, H.-O., Modern History
STEIN, F., Prehistory
STEINMETZ, P., Classical Philology
STRITTMATTER, P., Education
TACK, W., Psychology
VEAUTHIER, F., Philosophy
WILSS, W., Applied Linguistics, especially Theory of Interpreting
ZIMMERMANN, H., Medieval History

Faculty of Natural Sciences:
ALBRECHT, E., Mathematics
ALTMANN, G., Zoology
ANDRE, J., Mathematics
ASHWORTH, M., Analytical Chemistry
BECKER, K.-D., Theoretical Electronics
BERGER, R., Mathematics
BLASIUS, E., Inorganic Analytical Chemistry
BLUM, A., Electrotechnics
BREUER, H. D., Physical Chemistry
BROSAMLER, G.-A., Mathematics
DICKENSCHEID, W., Physics
DÜRR, H., Organic Chemistry
ENGELHARDT, H. R., Applied Physical Chemistry
FAILLARD, H., Biochemistry
FISCHER, K., Crystallography
FREY, G., Mathematics
FRISCH, B., Technology of Materials
GLEITER, H., Technology of Materials
GONSER, U., Metallurgy
GRÄSER-CAPUANO, L., Organic Chemistry
HALASZ, I., Applied Physical Chemistry
HARDT, H.-D., Chemistry
HÄUSLER, E., Experimental Physics
HECK, L., Inorganic Chemistry
HÖLLER, P., Applied Physics
HOLZ, A., Theoretical Physics
HOTZ, G., Applied Mathematics
HÜFNER, S., Experimental Physics
ISMAR, H., Applied Physics
JASCHEK, H., Theory of Electronic Systems
JORK, H., Pharmacognosy and Analytical Phytochemistry
KALDEWEY, H., Botany
KALLMEYER, H. J., Pharmaceutical Chemistry
KALTWASSER, H., Microbiology

KNABE, J., Pharmaceutical Chemistry
KÖNIG, H., Mathematics
KROEGER, H., Genetics
KUHN, W., Biology
LAMPRECHT, E., Mathematics
LEIBENGUTH, F., Genetics
LENSCH, G., Mineralogy
LOECKX, J., Information Sciences
LOTH, H., Pharmaceutical Technology
MAURER, R., High Frequency Technology
MEHLHORN, K., Applied Mathematics and Informatics
MEISSNER, G., Theoretical Physics
MOESTA, H., Physical Chemistry
MOSBACHER, G., Zoology
MÜSER, H., Experimental Physics
NACHTIGALL, W., Zoology
NATTERER, F., Applied Mathematics
PATT, H. J., Experimental Physics
PETERSSON, J., Experimental Physics
RUPPERSBERG, H., Physics and Crystallography
SCHANK, K., Organic Chemistry
SCHEIDIG, H., Informatics
SCHLOEMER, H., Mineralogy
SCHMIDT, G., Mathematics
SCHNEIDER, E., Geology
SCHNEIDER, H., Geology
SCHNEIDER, H.-J., Organic Chemistry
SCHULTE, H., Mathematics
SCHULZ, G., Physics
SCHUPP, H., Mathematics
SCHWITZGEBEL, G., Physical Chemistry
SEEL, F., Inorganic Chemistry
SIEMS, R., Theoretical Physics
STAHL, E., Pharmacognosy
TOMI, F., Mathematics
UNRUH, H.-G., Experimental Nuclear Physics
WALISCH, W., Instrumental Chemical Analytics
WARTENBERG, A., Botany
WETTER, C., Botany, Virology
WILHELM, R., Information Science
WITTSTOCK, G., Mathematics
ZEPPEZAUER, M., Biochemistry
ZIMMER, H. G., Mathematics
ZINSMEISTER, H.-D., Botany

ATTACHED INSTITUTES:

Institut für Entwicklungshilfe (*Institute for Development Aid*): Dir. Prof. Dr. E. E. BOESCH.

Institut für empirische Wirtschaftsforschung (*Institute for Economic Research*): comprises:

Institut für Konsum- und Verhaltensforschung (*Consumer Research Institute*): Dir. Prof. Dr. W. KROEBER-RIEL.

Handelsinstitut (*Institute of Commerce*): Dir. Prof. Dr. B. TIETZ.

Abteilung für Struktur- und Regionalforschung (*Department of Structural and Regional Research*): Dir. Prof. Dr. OLAV SIEVERT.

Institut für Wirtschaftsinformatik (*Institute for Economics Information*): Dir. Prof. A. W. SCHEER.

UNIVERSITÄT-GESAMTHOCHSCHULE SIEGEN

5900 SIEGEN 21,
HÖLDERLINSTRASSE 3, AVZ
Telephone: 0271-740-1.

Founded 1972.

Rector: Prof. Dr. ARTUR WOLL.
Co-Rectors: Prof. Dipl.-Ing. GERHARD RIMBACH, Prof. Dr. EDGAR REIMERS, Prof. Dr. KARL WALTER BONFIG.
Chancellor: Dr. HANS-JOACHIM HERRMANN.
Librarian: Dr. WALTER BARTON.

Number of teachers: *c.* 555.
Number of students: *c.* 6,400.
Publications: *Research Report*†, *Reihe Siegen*†.

DEANS:

Department of Philosophy, Religion and History: Prof. Dr. HERMANN BECK, F.H.L.
Department of Education, Psychology and Physical Education: Prof. Dr. ADOLF KELL.
Department of Languages and Literature: Prof. Dr. JOHANNES JANOTA.
Department of Art and Design: Prof. HARTMOT KAPTEINA.
Department of Economics: Prof. Dr. JÜRGEN BERTHEL.
Department of Mathematics: Prof. Dr. VOLKER KLOTZ, F.H.L.
Department of Natural Sciences I (Physics): Prof. Dr. GÜNTER ZECH.
Department of Natural Sciences II (Chemistry, Biology): Prof. Dr. ROGER BLACHNIK.
Department of Architecture: Prof. Dipl.-Ing. DIEDRICH PRAECKEL, F.H.L.
Department of Construction Engineering: Prof. Dr. EBERHARD KELLER, F.H.L.
Department of Mechanical Engineering I: Prof. Dr. HANS SCHULZE, F.H.L.
Department of Mechanical Engineering II (at Gummersbach): Prof. Dipl.-Ing. ERICH BOOS, F.H.L.
Department of Electrical Engineering I: Prof. Dr. PAUL KÜHN.
Department of Electrical Engineering II (at Gummersbach): Prof. Dipl.-Ing. PAUL KALBHEN, F.H.L.

UNIVERSITÄT STUTTGART

7000 STUTTGART,
KEPLERSTRASSE 7
Telephone: 20731.

Founded 1829 as Gewerbeschule, attained University status 1967.
Academic year: October to September.

Rector: Prof. Dr.-Ing. K.-H. HUNKEN.
Pro-Rectors: Prof. Dr. rer. nat. W. WEIDLICH, Prof. Dr. rer. nat. H. ZWICKER.
Chancellor: JÜRGEN BLUM.

Number of teachers: 1,160, including 520 Professors.
Number of students: 11,500.
Publication: *Universitätsnachrichten—Mitteilungen* (monthly during term).

DEANS

Faculty of Architecture and Town Planning: Prof. Dr. H. RITTEL.
Faculty of Civil Engineering and Surveying: Prof. Dr. HEIMERL.
Faculty of Chemistry: Prof. BRÖTZ.
Faculty of Electrotechnics: Prof. KAISER.
Faculty of Energetics: Prof. KUSSMAUL.
Faculty of Production Technology: Prof. K. LANGENBECK.
Faculty of Biological and Geo-Sciences: Prof. M. GWINNER.
Faculty of History, Sociology and Economics: Prof. ZAHN.
Faculty of Aeronautics and Astronautics: Prof. A. FROHN.
Faculty of Mathematics and Information Science: Prof. K.-W. ROGGENKAMP.
Faculty of Philosophy: Prof. OSWALD.
Faculty of Physics: Prof. M. WAGNER.
Faculty of Hydraulics and Transport: Prof. SORG.

PROFESSORS:

Architecture and Town Planning:
HERNANDEZ, A., History of Building
JOEDICKE, J., Fundamentals of Modern Architecture
KAMMERER, H., Interior Design
KAULE, G., Country Planning
KOSSAK, E., Town Planning
RITTEL, H., Planning

Civil Engineering and Surveying:
DIMITROV, N., Construction
GÖTZ, L., Building Materials, Technical Organization and Design
KNOLL, W., Technical Drawing and Planning
KÜSGEN, H., Building Economics
SEIDLEIN, P. VON, Building Construction and Design
SULZER, P., Building Construction and Design

Chemistry:
ALLENSTEIN, E., Inorganic Chemistry
BERGNER, K. G., Chemistry of Foodstuffs
BRÖTZ, W., Technical Chemistry
EFFENBERGER, F., Organic Chemistry
GEROLD, V., Metallurgy
HERLINGER, H., Textile Chemistry
PFLEIDERER, G., Biochemistry
PREDEL, B., Metallurgy
PREUSS, H., Theoretical Physical Chemistry

Electrotechnics:
BLOSS, W., Gas Technology
BÖCKER, H., High Tension Technology
BOEHRINGER, A., Power Electronics
EGGER, A., High Frequency Technology
KAISER, W., Communications
KOHN, G., Telecommunications
LAUBER, R., Electric Installations
LEHNER, G., Theory of Electronics
LOTZE, A., Transmission
LÜDER, E., Theory of Networks and Systems
VON MÜNCH, W., Semi-Conductor Technology
WIENECKE, R., Plasma Physics
ZWICKER, H., Plasma Physics

Energetics:
ESSERS, U., Machine Dynamics and Combustion Engines
HAHNE, E., Thermodynamics
HÖCKER, K.-H., Nuclear Energy
LEIN, G., Hydraulic Power and Pumps
WACHTER, J., Thermal Electric Machines

Production Technology:
BEISTEINER, F., Machinery
GLASER, G., Watch-Making and Precision Tools
LANGE, K., Conversion Techniques
LANGENBECK, K., Machine Elements

LECHNER, G., Machine Elements
SCHIELEN, W., Mechanics
STUTE, G., Machine Tools
TIZIANI, H., Technical Optics
TUFFENTSAMMER, K., Machine Tools
WARNECKE, H.-J., Industrial Manufacture

Biological and Geo-Sciences:

BORCHERDT, H.-C., Economic Geography
GEYER, Geology
GWINNER, M., Geology and Palaeontology
KÖHLER, K., Zoology
KUNZE, P., Animal Physiology
MECKELEIN, W., Geography
MUNDRY, K.-W., Botany
STROBACH, K., Geophysics
ZIEGLER, B., Geology and Palaeontology

History, Sociology and Economics:

ACKERMANN, K.-F., Business Economics
BIERFELDER, W., Business Economics
GREIFFENHAGEN, M., Political Science
HERMANN, A., History of Natural Sciences and Technology
JÄCKEL, E., History
KORNBLUM, U., Law
KRUSE-RODENACKER, A., Political Economy
NITSCHKE, A., History
OLSHAUSEN, History
REMBECK, M., Economics
ZAHN, Business Administration

Aeronautics and Astronautics:

ARGYRIS, J., Statics and Dynamics
BÜHLER, R., Space Propulsion
FROHN, A., Thermodynamics
HÜTTER, U., Aircraft Construction
OTTO, F., Institute for Light Aircraft Wing Assembly
WORTMANN, F.-X., Aerodynamics and Gas Dynamics

Mathematics and Information Science:

BURHHARDT, W., Information Science
DEGEN, W., Mathematics
GUNZENHÄUSER, R., Information Science
KIRCHGÄSSNER, K., Mathematics
KNÖDEL, W., Information Science
LAGALLY, K., Information Science
LEICHTWEISS, K., Mathematics
LESKY, P., Mathematics
MEYER-KÖNIG, W., Mathematics
NEUHOLD, E. J., Information Science
RITTER, K., Mathematics
ROGGENKAMP, K.-W., Mathematics
SCHWABHÄUSER, W., Information Science
VOLKMANN, B., Mathematics
WERNER, P., Mathematics

Philosophy:

BAUMGÄRTNER, K., Linguistics
BENSE, M., Philosophy and Scientific Theory
BIEN, G., Philosophy
BUCK, G., Education
FIETZ, L., English Language
KLOTZ, V., Modern German Literature
NICKEL, G., English Language
ROHRER, C., Romance Languages
SCHLAFFER, H., Modern German Literature
SCHRÖDER, G., Romance Literature
SCHULZ, D., American Literature
SCHWEIKLE, G., German Philology
SOMMER, K.-H., Education

Physics:

EISENMENGER, W., Experimental Physics
HAKEN, H., Theoretical Physics
HOFFMANN, K.-W., Experimental Physics
KRÖNER, E., Theoretical and Applied Physics
PICK, H., Experimental Physics
PILKUHN, M., Physics
SEEGER, A., Solid State Physics
WAGNER, M., Theoretical Physics
WEIDLICH, W., Theoretical Physics
WOLF, H. C., Experimental Physics

Hydraulics and Transport:

GIESECKE, J., Hydraulics
HANISCH, B., Sanitary Engineering
HEIMERL, G., Railway and Transport Systems
HUNKEN, K.-H., Sanitary Engineering
PETRIKAT, K., Technical Hydromechanics
STEIERWALD, G., Road and Transport Systems
TABASARAN, O., Hydraulics
TREUNER, P., Country Planning

UNIVERSITÄT TRIER

5500 TRIER, SCHNEIDERSHOF

Telephone: 0651-7161.

Founded 1970.

President: Prof. Dr. ARND MORKEL.

Vice-President: Prof. Dr. BERNHARD KÖNIG.

Chancellor: IGNAZ BENDER.

Librarian: Prof. Dr. PETER BÖHM.

Number of teachers: 84.

Number of students: 3,469.

Publications: *Unijournal* (monthly in term time), *Studienführer*†, *Vorlesungsverzeichnis*, *Trierer Beiträge* (2 a year), *Trierer Universitätsreden* (6 a year).

DEANS:

Faculty of Pedagogy, Philosophy aud Psychology: Prof. Dr. GISELAR MÜLLER-FOHRBRODT.

Faculty of Language and Literature: Prof. Dr. LOTHAR PIKULIK.

Faculty of Geography, History, Political Science, Classical Archaeology and Egyptology: Prof. Dr. GEROLD RICHTER.

Faculty of Management Economics, Sociology and Political Economy: Prof. Dr. HARTMUT WÄCHTER.

Faculty of Law: Prof. Dr. MICHAEL KLOEPFER.

PROFESSORS:

Faculty of Pedagogy, Philosophy and Psychology:

BARTUSSEK, D., Psychology
BECKER, P., Psychology
HINSKE, N., Philosophy
MINSEL, W.-R., Pedagogy
MONTADA, L., Psychology
ORTH, E.-W., Philosophy
PFAFFENBERGER, H., Pedagogy
RADNITZKY, G., Philosophy
REINERT, G., Psychology
RIES, H., Pedagogy
SCHELLER, R., Psychology
SEILER, H., Pedagogy
STEPHAN, E., Psychology

Faculty of Language and Literature:

AHRENS, R., English Literature and Didactics of English
ALTHAUS, H. P., German Linguistics
BARRERA-VIDAL, A., Romance Philology
BENDER, K.-H., Romance Literature
BERGSON, L., Classical Philology, especially Greek
DIRVEN, R., English Language
DÜSING, W., Modern German Literature
EIBL, K., Modern German Literature
GELHAUS, H., German Linguistics
HASLER, J., English and American Literature
HÖLZ, K., Romance Literature
KÖNIG, B., Romance Literature
KÖSTER, J.-P., Applied Philology, Phonetics
KREMER, D., Romance Philology
KRÖNER, H.-O., Classical Philology, especially Latin
KÜHLWEIN, W., English Philology
NIEDEREHE, H.-J., Romance Philology
VON POLENZ, P., German Linguistics
RIESNER, D., English Literature
RÖLL, W., German Philology
STRAUSS, J., English Philology
ZIRKER, H., English Literature

Faculty of Geography, History, Political Science, Classical Archaeology and Egyptology:

ANTON, H. H., Medieval History
BECKER, C., Applied Geography
BIRTSCH, G., Modern History
DÜWELL, K., Modern and Recent History
FAUL, E., Political Science
GRIMM, G., Classical Archaeology
HAUNGS, P., Political Science
HAVERKAKP, A., Medieval History
HECKLAU, H., German Folklore and Economic Geography
HEINEN, H., Ancient History
IRSIGLER, F., Historical Folklore
JÄTZOLD, R., Regional Geography
KERNIG, C. D., Political Science
LINK, W., Political Science
MORKELL, A., Political Science
SCHIEDER, W., Modern History
SPERLING, W., Geography
URBAN, R., Ancient History
WINTER, E., Egyptology

Faculty of Management Economics, Sociology and Political Economy

ECKERT, R., Sociology
EIRMBTER, W., Sociology
HAHN, A., Sociology
HAMM, B., Sociology
HECHELTJEN, P., Political Economy
HEINEMANN, K., Sociology
KROMSCHRÖDER, B., Management Economics
KRUG, W., Statistics
KUBICEK, H., Management Economics
MÜLLER-HAGEDORN, L., Management Economics
SPEHL, H., Political Economy

Faculty of Law

AMELUNG, K., Criminal Law
EHMANN, H., Civil and Business Law
KRAUSE, P., Public and Social Law, Philosophy of Law
KREY, V., Criminal Law
LINDACHER, W., Civil, Economic and Commercial Law
MARBURGER, P., Civil, Economic and Commercial Law
SCHRÖDER, M., Public, International and European Law
WIELING, H., Civil Law, History of Law

EBERHARD-KARLS-UNIVERSITÄT TÜBINGEN

7400 TUBINGEN 1, WILHELMSTRASSE 7

Telephone: 07071-291.

Telex: 07262867 RZTU D.

Founded 1477.

Academic year: October to July.

President: ADOLF THEIS.

Vice-Presidents: Prof. Dr. TILEMANN GRIMM, Prof. Dr. WALTER GRAUMANN, Prof. Dr. HANNA WEISCHEDEL.

Chief Administrative Officer: Dr. GEORG SANDBERGER.

Librarian: Dr. R. LANDWEHRMEYER.

Number of teachers: 1,678.

Number of students: 19,408.

Publications: *Attempto, Amtliche Mitteilungen, Studienführer, Vorlesungsverzeichnis, Tübinger Universitätszeitung.*

DEANS:

Protestant Theology: Keplerstr. 17; KARL ERNST NIPKOW.

Catholic Theology: Keplerstr. 17; WOLFGANG BARTHOLOMÄUS.

Law: Wilhelmstr. 7; WOLFGANG ZÖLLNER.

Economics: Keplerstr. 17; EBERHARD SCHAICH.

Theoretical Medicine: Geissweg 3; HELMUT HASELMANN.

Clinical Medicine: Geissweg 3; HANS HEIMAN.

Philosophy: Alte Burse; JOSEF SIMON.

Social and Behavioural Sciences: Keplerstr. 19; GERHARD KAMINSKI.

Modern Languages: Wilhelmstr. 50; THEO SCHUMACHER.

History: Keplerstr. 19; DIETRICH GEYER.

Cultural Sciences: Keplerstr. 19; FRANZ FISCHER.

Mathematics: Auf der Morgenstelle 10; MANFRED WOLFF.

Physics: Keplerstr. 17; WOLFRAM PRANDL.

Chemistry and Pharmacy: Keplerstr. 17; MICHAEL HANACK.

Biology: Keplerstr. 19; WILHELM SEYFERT.

Geosciences: Keplerstr. 19; HANS FRIEDRICHSEN.

PROFESSORS:

Department of Protestant Theology:

ABRAMOWSKI, L., Church History
BEYERHAUS, S., Missions, Ecumenical Studies
DONNER, H., Old Testament
GESE, H., Old Testament
HENGEL, M., New Testament and Classical Jewish Studies
JETTER, W., Practical Theology
JÜNGEL, E., Systematic Theology
KUSCHKE, A., Biblical Archaeology
LANG, F., New Testament
MOLTMANN, J., Systematic Theology
MÜLLER, H. M., Practical Theology
NIPKOW, K. E., Practical Theology
OBERMAN, H., Church History
RÖSSLER, D., Practical Theology
SCHOLDER, K., Liturgy
STUHLMACHER, P., New Testament

Department of Catholic Theology:

AUER, A., Moral Theology
GREINACHER, N., Practical Theology
HAAG, H., Old Testament
KASPER, W., Dogma
KORFF, W., Moral Theology
KÜNG, H., Dogma and Ecumenical Theology
OEING-HANHOFF, L., Basic Philosophical Questions of Theology
REINHARDT, R., Medieval and Modern Church History
SCHELKLE, K. H., New Testament
SECKLER, M., Fundamental Theology
VOGT, H. J., Old Church History, Patrology and Christian Archaeology

Department of Law:

BAUMANN, J., Penal Law and Procedural Law
DÜRIG, G., Public Law
ELSENER, F., German Law and Church Law
ESER, A., Criminal and Procedural Law
ESSER, J., Civil Law
GERNHUBER, J., History of German Law, Civil Law, Commercial Law
GÖPPINGER, H., Criminology
HECKEL, M., Public Law and Canon Law
HOPT, K., Civil, Trade, Labour and Commercial Law, International Private Law and Comparative Law
LANGE, H., Roman Law
LENCKNER, T., Penal Law and Procedural Law
MÖSCHEL, W., Civil, Trade and Commercial Law
MÜNZBERG, W., Civil and Procedural Law, International Private Law
NÖRR, W., Civil, Roman and Commercial Law
OPPERMANN, T., Public Law
SCHEYHING, R., Civil Law
SCHNUR, R., Public Law
WILLOWEIT, D., Church Law
ZÖLLNER, W., Civil Law, Trade, Labour and Commercial Law

Department of Economics:

ARNDT, E., Economics
BORN, E. K., Economic and Social History
CANSIER, D., Economics
LANGEN, H., Commerce
MENRAD, S., Commerce
MOLSBERGER, J., Economics
OTT, A., Economics
POHMER, D., Industrial Economics
SCHAICH, E., Economics and Statistics
SCHEELE, E., Economics
SCHWEITZER, M., Commerce
STRECKER, H., Statistics and Mathematics for Economics

Department of Theoretical Medicine:

ARNOLD, M., Anatomy
BADER, R.-E., Hygiene
BETZ, E., Physiology
BOHLE, A., Pathology
DIETZ, K., Medical Biometry
DREWS, U., Anatomy
FICHTNER, G., History of Medicine
GRAUMANN, W., Anatomy
HASELMANN, H., Microscopy
HÖFLER, W., Tropical Medicine
JACOB, R., Physiology
MALLACH, H. J., Legal Medicine
MAYER, K., Medical Psychology
PEIFFER, J., Neuropathology
REMMER, H., Toxicology
RITTER, H., Anthropology and Genetics
SCHLOTE, W., Submicroscopic Pathology and Neuropathology
SIESS, M., Pharmacology
WEICHARDT, H., Labour Medicine

Department of Clinical Medicine:

ADAM, W., Mycology
APITZ, J., Paediatric Cardiology
AULHORN, E., Ophthalmology
BICHLER, K.-H., Urology
BIERICH, J., Paediatrics
BREITLING, G., Radiography
BREUNINGER, H., Phoniatrics and Audiology
DAUSCH-NEUMANN, D., Maxillo-Orthopaedics
DICHGANS, H., Neurology
DÖLLE, Internal Medicine
DRIESEN, W., Neurosurgery
EGGSTEIN, M., Clinical Chemistry
FEINE, Nuclear Medicine
FISCHER, H., Dermatology
FLACH, A., Child Surgery
FROMMHOLD, W., Radiography
GÖBEL, P., Experimental Endocrinology
GUPTA, D., Diagnosis of Hormone Deficiencies and Changes
HAMMACHER, K., Obstetrics and Gynaecology
HEIMANN, H., Psychiatry
HIRSCH, J., Obstetrics and Gynaecology
HIRSCHMANN, J., Neurology
HOFFMEISTER, H. E., Chest and Heart Surgery
JESCHKE, D., Physiology and Sport Therapy
KOCHSIEK, K., Internal Medicine
KÖNIG, P. A., Preventive Gynaecology
KÖRBER, E., Maxillo-Facial Medicine
KOSLOWSKI, L., Surgery
KUMMER, D., Surgery
LEMPP, R., Child and Youth Psychiatry
LOCH, W., Psychoanalysis
MAU, H., Orthopaedics
MAYER, K., Neuropsychology
MICHAELIS, R., Child Development Problems
NAUMANN, G., Ophthalmology
MENTZEL, H., Neonatal Medicine
PETERS, K. W., Radiobiology
PLESTER, D., Oto-Rhino-Laryngology
OLDENKOTT, P., Neurosurgery
RASSNER, G., Dermatology
RIETHE, P., Dentistry
RIETMÜLLER, G., Experimental Surgery
SCHNEIDER, W., Transfusion
SCHORER, R., Anaesthesiology
SCHULTE, W., Dentistry
SCHWENZER, R. N., Maxillo-Facial Surgery
VOIGT, K., Neuroradiology
WALLER, H. D., Internal Medicine
WESSING, A., Ophthalmology

Department of Philosophy:

FAHRENBACH, H.
HARTMANN, K.
SIMON, J.

Department of Social and Behavioural Sciences and Pedagogics:

BAUSINGER, H., German Folklore
BERGIUS, R., Psychology
BIRBAUMER, N., Psychology
DOHMEN, G., Pedagogics
FLITNER, A., Pedagogics
GRUPE, O., Theory of Physical Education
HRBEK, R., Political Studies
KAMINSKI, G., Psychology
LEHMBRUCK, H. G., Political Studies
NEUMANN, B., Sociology of Religion and Law
REUENSTAR, F. D., Psychology
RITTBERGER, V., Political Studies
SPRONDEL, W., Sociology
STAPF, K., Psychology
TENBRUCK, F. H., Sociology
THIERSCH, H., Social Pedagogics
ZIFREUND, W., Pedagogics

Department of Modern Languages:

BARNER, W., German Philology
BRINKMANN, R., German Philology
CHRISTMANN, H. H., Romance Philology
COSERIU, E., Romance Philology and General Philology

DRUBIG, H. B., English Philology
FICHTE, J., English Philology
HAUG, W., German Philology
HEMPEL, W., Romance Philology and Comparative Literature
HERINGER, H.-J., German Philology
HOFFMANN, P., German Philology
JENS, W., General Rhetoric
KUNERT, ILSE, Slavonic Philology
LEINER, W., Romance Philology
LUDWIG, H. W., English Philology
MÜLLER, L., Slavonic Philology
MÜLLER-SCHWEFE, G., English Philology
REIBEL, D. A., English Philology
SCHRÖDER, J., German Language and Literature
SCHUMACHER, T., German Language and Literature
STRASSNER, E., German Philology
WACHINGER, B., German Philology
WEBER, A., American Philology

Department of History:
DECKER-HAUFF, H., Medieval and Modern History
ENGEL, J., Medieval and Modern History
GEYER, D., East European History
LÖWE, H., Medieval and Modern History
PETZOLD, K.-E., Ancient History
SCHULZ, G., Contemporary History
STROHEKER, K. F., Ancient History
ZEEDEN, E. W., Medieval and Modern History
ZIMMERMANN, H., Medieval and Modern History

Department of Cultural Sciences:
BARTHEL, T., Folklore
BRUNNER, H., Egyptology
v. DADELSEN, G., Music
ESS, J. VAN, Semitic and Islamic Studies
FEIL, A., Music Science
FISCHER, F., Pre- and Early History
GAISER, K., Classical Philology
GRIMM, T., East Asian Philology
HAUSMANN, U., Classical Archaeology
HOFFMANN, K., History of Art
KANNICHT, R., Classical Philology
RÖLLIG, W., Oriental Studies
SCHENKEL, W., Egyptology
SCHMID, M., Art
SCHMIDT, E. A., Classical Philology
SCHWAGER, K., History of Art
v. STIETENCRON, H., Indology and Comparative Religion
TOVAR, A., Comparative Philology
WILLE, G., Classical Philology, Linguistics
ZINN, E., Classical Philology

Department of Mathematics:
FELSCHER, W.
HERING, C.
HEYER, H.
KAUP, W.
SALZMANN, H.
SCHAEFER, H. H.
SCHEJA, G.
SCHÖNHAGE, A.
WOLFF, M.
ZELLER, K.

Department of Physics:
ELWERT, G., Theoretical Physics and Astrophysics
GREWING, M., Mathematics
GÜTTINGER, W., Data Processing
HÜBENER, R., Experimental Physics
KRÜGER, H., Physics
LENZ, F., Theoretical Electron Physics
MÖLLENSTEDT, G., Applied Physics
PRANDL, W., Crystallography
SCHMID, E., Theoretical Atomic and Nuclear Physics
SCHRAMM, M., History of Natural Sciences
STUMPF, H., Theoretical Physics
WILDERMUTH, K., Theoretical Atomic and Nuclear Physics

Department of Chemistry and Pharmacy:
AMMON, H., Pharmacology
AUTERHOFF, H., Pharmaceutical Chemistry
BAYER, E., Organic Chemistry
GRAF, E., Pharmaceutical Technology
GUGLIEMLI, J., Biochemistry
HANACK, M., Organic Chemistry
LINDER, E., Inorganic Chemistry
MECKE, D., Biochemistry
METZNER, H., Chemical Plant Physiology
REINHARD, E., Pharmaceutical Biology
STRÄHLE, J., Inorganic Chemistry
WEITZEL, G., Physiological Chemistry
ZEIL, W., Physical Chemistry

Department of Biology:
AMMERMANN, D., Biology
BENTRUP, F. W., Biophysics
BRAUN, V., Microbiology
ENGELS, W., Developmental Physiology
GRELL, K. G., Zoology
HADELER, F.-P., Biomathematics
HAGER, A., Botany
MÖHRES, F. P., Zoology
OBERWINKLER, F., Botany
SCHWEMMLE, B., Botany
SEYFFERT, W., Genetics
SPERLICH, D., Population Genetics
VARJÚ, D., Biological Cybernetics
ZÄHNER, H., Microbiology

Department of Geosciences:
BAYH, W., Crystallography and Mineralogy
BLUME, H., Physical Geography
EINSELE, G., Applied Geography
ERNST, W., Geology
FRIEDRICHSEN, H., Geochemistry
HERM, D., Micropalaeontology
KARGER, A., Eastern European Geography
KOHLHEPP, C., Anthropogeography
LUTERBACHER, H., Micropalaeontology
MÜLLER-BECK, H., Early Pre-History
SCHÖNENBERG, R., General and Applied Geology
SCHRODER, K.-H., European Geography
SEILACHER, A., Geology and Palaeontology
WENDT, J., Geology and Palaeontology

ATTACHED INSTITUTES:

Deutsches Institut für Fernstudien (*German Institute for Distance Studies*): Dir. Prof. Dr. G. DOHMEN.

Goethe-Wörterbuch: Dir. of Commission: Prof. Dr. K. GAISER.

UNIVERSITÄT ULM

7900 ULM,
OBERER ESELSBERG
Telephone: 0731-1781.

Founded 1967 as Medizinische-Naturwissenschaftliche Hochschule, University charter 1967.

State control; Language of instruction: German; Academic year: October to September.

Rector: Prof. Dr. DETLEF BÜCKMANN.
Pro-Rectors: Prof. Dr. rer. nat. HELMUT SCHRAUDOLF, Prof. Dr. med. HELMUT THOMAS.
Chancellor: Dr. DIETRICH EBERHARDT.
Chief Librarian: Dr. phil. MARGARETE REHM.

Number of teachers: 163.
Number of students: 1,386.
Publication: *Mitteilungen des Rektors* (monthly).

DEANS:

Faculty of Natural Sciences and Mathematics: Prof. Dr. rer. nat. OTTO KORNER.
Faculty of Theoretical Medicine: Prof. Dr. med. THEODOR M. FLIEDNER.
Faculty of Clinical Medicine: Prof. Dr. med. WILLI-ERNST ADAM.

PROFESSORS:

Faculty of Natural Sciences and Mathematics:
BALLSCHMITER, K., Analytical Chemistry
BRUNE, H.-A., Organic Chemistry
BÜCKMANN, D., Zoology
FUNKE, W., Zoology
JURKAT, W., Mathematics
KILIAN, H.-G., Experimental Physics
NONNENMACHER, TH., Theoretical Physics
PECHOLD, W., Experimental Physics
PEYERIMHOFF, A., Mathematics
RICHERT, H.-E., Mathematics
RISKEN, H., Theoretical Physics
ROTHE, M., Organic Chemistry
RUDOLPH, H.-D., Physical Chemistry
SACKMANN, E., Experimental Physics
SAWODNY, W., Inorganic Chemistry
SCHRAUDOLF, H., Botany
WALTHER, J. B., Zoology
WEBERLING, F., Morphology and Systematic Botany
WEIS, O., Physics
WIRSING, E., Mathematics
WITSCHEL, W., Theoretical Chemistry

Faculty of Theoretical Medicine:
BADER, H., Pharmacology
BAITSCH, H., Anthropology and Human Genetics
ENKE, H., Clinical Social Psychology
FLIEDNER, T. M., Clinical Physiology
HAFERKAMP, O., Pathology
HENNING, R., Physiological Chemistry
HERRMANN, M., Anatomy
KLEINSCHMIDT, A. K., Microbiology
KRONE, W., Human Genetics
PILGRIM, C., Anatomy
THOMAS, H., Biochemistry

Faculty of Clinical Medicine:
AHNEFELD, F. W., Anaesthesiology
BARGON, G., Radiology
BURRI, C., Surgery
HERFARTH, C., Surgery
KLEIHAUER, R., Paediatrics and Haematology
KNÖRR, K., Gynaecology and Obstetrics
KORNHUBER, H., Neurology
LAURITZEN, C., Gynaecology and Obstetrics
PFEIFFER, E. F., Internal Medicine, Endocrinology and Metabolism
TELLER, W., Endocrinology and Metabolism
THOMÄ, H., Psychotherapy
VOLLMAR, J., Surgery

GESAMTHOCHSCHULE WUPPERTAL

5600 WUPPERTAL 1,
GAUSS-STRASSE 20
Telephone: 0202/439-1.
Founded 1972.

Rector: Prof. RAINER GRUENTER.
Co-Rectors: Prof. GÜNTER STURM, Prof. WILFRIED ECKEY, Prof. GERHARD DEIMLING.
Chancellor: Dr. KLAUS PETERS.
Librarian: Dr. DIETER STÄGLICH.

Number of teachers: 260.
Number of students: 7,000.

DIRECTORS:

Faculty I (Sociology): Prof. HERBERT KRUPPE.
Faculty II (Philosophy and Theology): Prof. Dr. theol. HELMUT MERKLEIN.
Faculty III (Education): Prof. Dr. phil. JÜRGEN LANGEFELD.
Faculty IV (Languages and Literature): Prof. Dr. phil. HANS WEBER.
Faculty V (Art and Design, Music): Prof. WOLFGANG KÖRBER.
Faculty VI (Economics): Prof. Dr. rer. pol. WOLFGANG SODEUR.
Faculty VII (Mathematics): Prof. Dipl.-Math. Dr. rer. nat. KLAS DIEDERICH.
Faculty VIII (Sciences I: Physics): Prof. Dipl.-Phys. Dr. rer. nat. HEINRICH MEYER.
Faculty IX (Sciences II: Chemistry, Biology): Prof. Dr. rer. nat. Dipl.-Chem. DIRK GOTTHARDT.
Faculty X (Architecture): Prof. Dipl.-Ing. BERNHARD CARDINAL VON WIDDERN.
Faculty XI (Construction Engineering): Prof. Dr.-Ing. SIEGFRIED VELSKE.
Faculty XII (Mechanical Engineering): Prof. Dipl.-Ing. ROLF SEYBOLD.
Faculty XIII (Electrical Engineering): Prof. Dipl.-Phys. Dr. rer. nat. Fr. JOSEF IN DER SMITTEN.
Faculty XIV (Safety and Accident Prevention): Prof. Dr.-Ing. REINALD SKIBA.

BAYERISCHE-JULIUS-MAXIMILIANS-UNIVERSITÄT WÜRZBURG

8700 WÜRZBURG,
SANDERRING 2
Telephone: 0931-311.
Founded 1582.

State control; Academic year: 1 October to 30 September.

President: Prof. Dr.phil. TH. BERCHEM.
Chancellor: R. GÜNTHER.
Chief Librarian: Dr. G. MÄLZER.

Number of teachers: 554.
Number of students: 13,282.

Publications: *Personal- und Vorlesungsverzeichnis* (twice yearly), *Jahresbericht, Informationsblatt* (monthly).

DEANS:

Faculty of Catholic Theology: Prof. Dr. theol. R. ZERFASS.
Faculty of Law: Prof. Dr. jur. K. H. NEUMAYER.
Faculty of Medicine: Prof. Dr. med. K.-H. WULF.
Faculty of Philosophy I (Antiquity, Cultural Studies): Prof. Dr. phil. H. STEININGER.
Faculty of Philosophy II (Philology, History, History of Art): Prof. Dr. phil. H. LAITENBERGER.
Faculty of Philosophy III (Philosophy, Education, Social Sciences): Prof. Dr. phil. F. WIEDMANN.
Faculty of Biology: Prof. Dr. rer. nat. H. W. SAUER.
Faculty of Chemistry and Pharmacy: Prof. Dr. Ing. S. HÜNIG.
Faculty of Geosciences: Prof. Dr. rer. nat. H.-G. WAGNER.
Faculty of Mathematics: Prof. Dr. rer. nat. H. W. KNOBLOCH.
Faculty of Physics and Astronomy: Prof. Dr. rer. nat. M. SCHEER.
Faculty of Economics: Prof. Dr. rer. oec. H. H. WEBER.

PROFESSORS:

Faculty of Catholic Theology:

DREIER, W., Christian Sociology
GANOCZY, A., Dogmatics
GANZER, K., Medieval and Modern Church History
KLINGER, E., Basic Theology and Comparative Religion
LANGGÄRTNER, G., Liturgical Studies
MÜLLER, K.-H., Biblical Introduction
NEUENZEIT, P., Religious Instruction
SCHNACKENBURG, R., New Testament Exegesis
SCHREINER, J., Old Testament Exegesis and Biblical Oriental Languages
SCHULZ, H.-J., Theology and History of the Bible Lands
SPEIGL, J., Church History
WEIGAND, R., Church Law, History of Church Law
WILLEKE, H., Missionary Studies
WITTSTADT, K., History of the Frankish Church
ZERFASS, R., Pastoral Theology

Faculty of Law:

BLUMENWITZ, D., International Law and Political Science
BRUNNER, G., Political Science
FORKEL, H., Civil Law, Commercial Law, Industrial Law, Copyright
FUSS, E.-W., Public Law
GRASMANN, G., Civil Law, German, Foreign and International Labour Law
HABSCHEID, W., Civil and Process Law
HAHN, H. J., Public and International Law
HOFMANN, H., Philosophy of Law, Political and Administrative Law
JUST, M., Roman Law, Ancient Law, Civil Law
KNEMEYER, F.-L., Public and Administrative Law
KRAUSE, F.-W., Criminology and Penal Law
KUCHINKE, K., Civil, Roman and Procedural Law
MERZBACHER, F., History of German Law, Civil Law and Commercial Law
NEUMAYER, K., Comparative Law, Civil Law, International Civil Law and Commercial Law
SPENDEL, G., Criminal Law and Procedure
TIEDTKE, K., Law of Finance and Economics
TRUSEN, W., German and Comparative Legal History, Civil Law, Canon Law

Faculty of Medicine:

ALTMANN, H. W., Pathology and Pathological Anatomy
BAUEREISEN, E., Physiology
BOHNDORF, W., Roentgenology
BUSHE, K.-A., Neurosurgery
FROHMÜLLER, H., Urology
HAMPRECHT, B., Physiological Chemistry
HELMREICH, E., Physiological Chemistry
HENSCHLER, D., Pharmacology and Toxicology
HÖHN, H., Human Genetics
KEIL, G., History of Medicine
KELLERER, A. M., Medical Radiology
KERN, E., Surgery
KLEY, W., Oto-Rhino-Laryngology
KOCHSIEK, K., Internal Medicine
KÜHL, W., Dental and Facial Medicine
LANG, J., Anatomy
LEYDHECKER, W., Ophthalmology
MERTENS, H. G., Neurology
TER MEULEN, V., Clinical Virology and Immunology
NAUJOKS, R., Dentistry
NISSEN, G., Child Psychiatry
RÖCKL, H., Dermatology, Venereal Disease
RÜTT, A., Orthopædics
SCHIEBLER, T., Anatomy
SCHRAPPE, O., Psychiatry
SCHWERD, W., Social Medicine
SEELIGER, H., Hygiene, Microbiology
SIEBERT, G., Experimental Dentistry
TRENDELENBURG, U., Pharmacology and Toxicology
WECKER, E., Virology
WEIS, K. H., Anaesthesiology
WITT, E., Dental and Facial Surgery
WULF, K.-H., Obstetrics and Gynaecology
WYSS, D., Psychotherapy and Medical Psychology

Faculty of Philosophy I:

AITZEMÜLLER, R., Slavic Philology
NEUMANN, G., Comparative Indo-Germanic Linguistics
OSTHOFF, W., Music
SCHOLZ, U., Classical Philology
SCHULER, E. VON, Oriental Philology
SIEGMANN, E., Classical Philology
SIMON, ERIKA, Classical Archæology
STEININGER, H., Oriental Philology

Faculty of Philosophy II:

AHRENS, TH., Didactics of English Language and Literature
BAUMGART, P., Modern History
BAUMGÄRTNER, A. C., German Language and Literature
BERCHEM, TH., Romance Philology
BRÜCKNER, W., German Philology and Folklore
HABICHT, W., English Philology
HERDE, P., History
HOFFMANN, G., English Philology
HUBALA, E., History of Art
KUCHINKE, ANNELIESE, History of Modern German Literature
LAITENBERGER, H., Romance Philology
RUHE, E., Romance Philology
SCHINGS, H.-J., Modern German Literature
SPRANDEL, R., History
STANDOP, E., English Philology
TIMPE, D., Ancient History
WOLF, N. R., German Linguistics

Faculty of Philosophy III:

BITTNER, G., Education
BÖHM, W., Education
BOSSLE, L., Sociology
BUSSHOFF, H., Politics
HELLER, O., Psychology
HENZ, H., Education
HOJER, E., Pedagogy
KAPUSTIN, P., Sport
LIPP, W., Sociology

Möckel, Special Education
Müller, G., Theology
Müller, H. A., Psychology
Neuhaus, E., Elementary Education
Pongratz, L., Psychology
Rombach, H., Philosophy
Schöpf, A., Philosophy
Schröder, H., Education
Thalhammer, M., Special Education
Weinacht, P.-L., Didactics of Sociology and Political Science
Wiedmann, F., Philosophy

Faculty of Biology:

Czygan, F. C., Pharmaceutical Biology
Goebel, W., Microbiology
Heber, U., Botany
Heisenberg, M., Genetics
Lange, O., Botany
Lindauer, M., Zoology and Comparative Physiology
Linsenmair, K. E., Zoology
Sauer, H. W., Zoology

Faculty of Chemistry and Pharmacy:

Adam, W., Organic Chemistry
Brieskorn, C. H., Pharmacy and Food Technology
Gross, H. J., Biochemistry
Hünig, S., Chemistry
Riehl, J., Pharmacy
Schmidt, M., Inorganic Chemistry
Schneider, F., Physical Chemistry
Strohmeier, W., Physical Chemistry
Werner, H., Inorganic Chemistry

Faculty of Geosciences:

Boehn, D., Geography Teaching
Hagedorn, H., Geography
Jäger, H., Cultural and Economic Geography
Lindemann, H., Crystallography
Matthes, S., Mineralogy
Rutte, E., Geology and Palaeontology
Schnitzer, W., Geology
Sdzuy, K., Palæontology
Wagner, H.-G., Geography

Faculty of Mathematics:

Barthel, W., Mathematics
Heineken, H., Mathematics
Knobloch, H.-W., Mathematics
Ruschewyh, S., Mathematics
Stoer, J., Applied Mathematics
Uhlmann, W., Statistics
Velte, W., Applied Mathematics
Vollrath, H.-J., Mathematics Teaching

Faculty of Physics and Astronomy:

Deubner, F.-L., Astronomy
Ebert, R., Theoretical Physics
Häfele, H.-G., Experimental Physics
Heuer, D., Physics Teaching
Hink, W., Experimental Physics
Landwehr, G., Experimental Physics
Scheer, M., Experimental Physics
Steinwedel, H., Theoretical Physics

Faculty of Economics:

Freericks, W., Industrial Management
Issing, O., Political Economy
Klatt, S., Political Economy
Koller, H., Industrial Management
Meyer, C. W., Industrial Management
Molitor, B., Political Economy
Noll, W., Economics
Ohm, H., Political Economy
Petermann, G., Industrial Economics
Vollrodt, W., Industrial Management
Weber, H. H. Industrial Management

COLLEGES

General

Schiller International University: 6900 Heidelberg, Friedrich-Ebert-Anlage 4; f. 1964; undergraduate and graduate degree programmes in liberal arts, business administration, international relations, fine arts and theatre; language of instruction: English; Pres. Dr. Walter W. Leibrecht; Academic Dean J. G. Eggert; Dir. of Admissions Dr. Lutz B. Hoernecke.

The University maintains the following four campuses in other countries:

London Campus: Wickham Court, West Wickham, Kent, U.K.; Dir. Mrs. Catherine Ballester.

Madrid Campus: Calle de Rodriguez San Pedro 10, Madrid 15, Spain; Dir. Dr. Wilfred O. Reiners.

Paris Campus: 103 rue de Lille, 75007 Paris, France; Dir. Mrs. Eva Faure.

Strasbourg Campus: Château Pourtalès, rue Melanie, 67 Strasbourg, France; Dir. Kendrick Baker.

Art, Architecture

Akademie der bildenden Künste (*Academy of Fine Arts*): Munich, Akademiestr. 2; f. 1770 (Charter conferred 1808 and 1953); 20 professors; 533 students; Pres. Prof. Schneider-Wessling; Chancellor Dr. Valentin.

Akademie der bildenden Künste in Nürnberg: 8500 Nuremberg, Bingstr. 60; f. 1662; 243 students; library of 12,000 vols.; Pres. Prof. G. Voglsamer; Vice-Pres. Prof. St. Eusemann.

Deutsche Film- und Fernsehakademie (*German Film and Television Academy*): 1000 Berlin 19, Pommernallee 1; f. 1966; Dir. Dr. H. Rathsack; library of 25,000 vols.

Hochschule der Künste Berlin: Ernst-Reuter-Platz 10, 1000 Berlin 10; f. 1975 by amalgamation of the fmr. *Staatliche Hochschule für Bildende Künste* and *Staatliche Hochschule für Musik und Darstellende Kunst*; *c.* 2,500 students; Pres. Ulrich Roloff; Vice-Pres. J. W. Erdmann, Prof. Saschko Gawnloff; publ. *HdK—Information*† (monthly during term).

Hochschule für bildende Künste: 3300 Brunswick, Broitzemer Str. 230; f. 1963; depts. of art (painting, graphics, sculpture, film and photography), design (industrial and graphic), art teaching, experimental environmental design; 719 students; library of *c.* 17,000 vols.; Rector Prof. Gerhard Büttenbender.

Hochschule für bildende Künste Hamburg: 2000 Hamburg 76, Lerchenfeld 2; depts. of architecture, industrial design, visual communication, education; Pres. Prof. Dr. phil. Carl Vogel.

Staatliche Akademie der bildenden Künste: 75 Karlsruhe-1, Reinhold-Frank-Str. 81-83; f. 1854; Rector Prof. Klaus Arnold.

Staatliche Akademie der bildenden Künste: 7 Stuttgart 1, Am Weissenhof 1; f. 1761; art, graphics, sculpture, interior design, ceramics, textiles, etc.; teaching staff 80; Rector Prof. Dr. Wolfgang Kermer; Pro-Rector Prof. H. G. von Stockhausen; publ. *Akademie-Mitteilungen* (2 a year).

Staatliche Hochschule für Bildende Künste—Städelschule: 6000 Frankfurt 70, Dürerstr. 10; f. 1817; Rector Prof. Dr. Reimer Jochims.

Staatliche Kunstakademie Düsseldorf, Hochschule für Bildende Künste (*State Acad. of Art*): 4000 Düsseldorf, Eiskellerstr. 1; f. 1773; 72 teachers, 785 students; library of 60,000 vols.; Dir. Prof. Norbert Kricke.

Economics, Political and Social Sciences, Public Administration

Hochschule für Politik: Munich 22, Ludwigstr. 8; f. 1973; 800 students; library of 28,500 vols.; Rector Prof. Dr. F. Knöpfle; publ. *Zeitschrift für Politik* (quarterly).

Hochschule für Verwaltungswissenschaften: D-672 Speyer, Freiherr-vom-Stein-Strasse 2, P.O.B. 1409; f. 1947; postgraduate studies, in-service training and research in public administration, public law, social sciences; 17 professors, 30 part-time teachers; library of 135,000 vols.; Rector Prof. Dr. Dieter Duwendag.

Languages

Akademie für Fremdsprachen GmbH: Schlueterstrasse 37, 1000 Berlin 12; f. 1971; translators' and interpreters' courses in German, English, French, Spanish, Italian, Russian, and courses in German as a foreign language; 1,600 students; Sec. Norbert Zänker.

Music

Hochschule für Musik: 8000 Munich 2, Arcisstr. 12; f. 1846; 160 teachers; *c.* 700 students; Pres. Prof. Fritz Schieri, Prof. Diethard Hellmann, Prof. Dr. Günther Weiss.

Hochschule für Musik: 8700 Würzburg, Hofstallstr. 6-8; f. 1804; Pres. Prof. B. Hummel.

Hochschule für Musik und Darstellende Kunst: Frankfurt a.M., Eschersheimer Landstrasse 29-39; f. 1878 as Konservatorium, Hochschule since

1938; Rector Prof. HANS-DIETER RESCH.

Hochschule für Musik und Theater Hannover: 3000 Hanover, Emmichplatz 1; f. 1961; 170 teachers, 650 students; library of 95,000 vols.; Dir. Prof. Dr. R. JAKOBY.

Hochschule für Musik und darstellende Kunst Hamburg: 2 Hamburg 13, Harvestehuder Weg 12; f. 1950; teaching staff of 170, 700 students; Pres. Prof. Dr. HERMANN RAUHE.

Internationales Musikinstitut Darmstadt (formerly *Kranichsteiner Musikinstitut*): 61 Darmstadt, Nieder-Ramstädter Str. 190; f. 1946; summer international holiday course for new music; international music lending library of 27,847 vols.; Dir. E. THOMAS.

Leopold Mozart Konservatorium: 8900 Augsburg, Maximilianstrasse 59.

Musikhochschule des Saarlandes: 6600 Saarbrücken 3, Bismarckstrasse 1; f. 1947; 75 teachers, 250 students; library of 80,000 vols.; Rector Prof. Dr. DIETER LOSKANT.

Musikhochschule Lübeck: 24 Lübeck, Jerusalemsberg 4; f. 1933; musical training on all instruments, opera singing and performing, training of music teachers, sacred music (Protestant and Catholic), preparatory training of professional musicians and music teachers; 350 students, 120 teachers; library of 30,000 vols.; Pres. Dr. MANFRED TESSMER; Admin. HANS KLOSE; publ. *Vorlesungsverzeichnis* (2 a year).

Richard-Strauss Konservatorium: 8000 Munich 80, Ismaninger Str. 29; f. 1962; courses in vocal and instrumental studies, composition; 97 teachers, 600 students; library of 10,000 vols.; Dir. P. J. KORN.

Staatliche Hochschule für Musik: 78 Freiburg im Breisgau, Münsterplatz 30; f. 1946; 134 teachers, 598 students; Rector Prof. Dr. J. G. SCHAARSCHMIDT.

Staatliche Hochschule für Musik: 6500 Mainz, Binger Str. 26.

Staatliche Hochschule für Musik Westfalen-Lippe (Nordwestdeutsche Musikakademie): 4930 Detmold, Allee 22 (Palais); f. 1946; 90 teachers; 650 students; Dir. Prof. M. STEPHANI.

Staatliche Hochschule für Musik Heidelberg-Mannheim: 6800 Mannheim L15, 16; f. 1899; 125 teachers, 410 students; Rector Prof. H.-H. SCHWARZ.

Staatliche Hochschule für Musik Karlsruhe: Jahnstr. 11, 75 Karlsruhe 1; f. 1884; library of 50,000 vols.; 95 teachers, 354 students; Rector Prof. W. WIDMAIER.

Staatliche Hochschule für Musik Rheinland: 5 Cologne, Dagobertstrasse 38; f. 1925; teaching staff of 160; 1,400 students; Dir. Prof. Dr. FRANZ MÜLLER-HEUSER.

Staatliche Hochschule für Musik Rheinland Robert Schumann Institut Düsseldorf: 4000 Düsseldorf 30, Fischerstrasse 110; f. 1935; 130 teachers, 700 students; library of 35,000 vols.; Dean Prof. Dr. H. KIRCHMEYER.

Staatliche Hochschule für Musik und Darstellende Kunst: Stuttgart, Urbansplatz 2; f. 1857; 160 teachers, about 650 students; Dir. Prof. WOLFGANG GÖNNENWEIN.

PHILOSOPHY, THEOLOGY

Augustana Hochschule: 8806 Neuendettelsau, Waldstr. 11; f. 1947; 20 teachers; 300 students; Rector Prof. Dr. J. TRACK.

Hochschule für Philosophie: 8000 München 22, Kaulbachstrasse 33; Rector H. ZWIEFELHOFER; Librarian G. KRESS; library of 130,000 vols.; publs. *Theologie und Philosophie* (quarterly), *Pullacher Philosophische Forschungen.*

Kirchliche Hochschule Berlin: 1 Berlin 37, Teltower Damm 120/122; f. 1935.
Rector: Prof. Dr. PETER VON DER OSTEN-SACKEN.
Ephorus: Prof. Dr. R. HENTSCHKE.
Number of teachers: 28.
Number of students: 500.

Kirchliche Hochschule Bethel: 4800 Bielefeld 13; f. 1905; 29 teachers, 320 students; library of 77,000 vols.; Rector Prof. Dr. H. BRAUN; publ. *Jahrbuch—Wort und Dienst* (biannually).

Kirchliche Hochschule Wuppertal: 5600 Wuppertal 2, Missionstr. 9a-17; f. 1935; library of 85,000 vols.; 320 students; Evangelical; Rector Prof. Dr. B. KLAPPERT; Ephorus Pastor SIEGWARD KUNATH; Pro-Rector Prof. Dr. K. HAACKER.

Lutherische Theologische Hochschule Oberursel: 637 Oberursel im Taunus, Altkönigstrasse 150.

Philosophisch-Theologische Hochschule Fulda (Päpstlich Errichtete Theologische Fakultät): 6400 Fulda, Domplatz 2; f. 1748; 20 teachers; 50 students; Rector Prof. Dr. REINELT.

Philosophisch-Theologische Hochschule Sankt Georgen: Frankfurt am Main 70, Offenbacher Landstr. 224; f. 1926 (since 1950 combined with Jesuit Theological Faculty, f. 1863); Rector Prof. Dr. J. BEUTLER; Librarian Prof. Dr. G. SWITEK; library of 300,000 vols.; 34 teachers, including 21 professors; 280 students; publs. *Theologie und Philosophie* (quarterly), *Frankfurter Theologische Studien.*

Theologische Fakultät Paderborn: 4790 Paderborn, Kamp 6; f. 1615; Rector Prof. DDr. WINFRIED SCHULZ; Pro-Rector Prof. Dr. LEO LANGEMEYER; number of teachers 26; students 280; publ. *Theologie und Glaube* (quarterly).

Theologische Fakultät Trier: 5500 Trier; Jesuitenstr. 13; f. 1950; Chancello, Dr. B. STEIN, Bishop of Trier; Rector Prof. Dr. E. HAAG; 20 Ordinary Professors; library of 130,000 vols.: 200 students.

GHANA

Population 10,309,000

ACADEMY

GHANA ACADEMY OF ARTS AND SCIENCES

P.O.B. M.32, ACCRA

Founded 1959.

Aims to promote the study, extension and dissemination of knowledge of the arts and sciences.

Patron: H.R.H. The Prince PHILIP, Duke of EDINBURGH, K.G., P.C., G.B.E., F.R.S.

COUNCIL OF THE ACADEMY:

President and Chairman: Prof. C. O. EASMON.

Vice-President and Chairman of the Humanities Section: Prof. L. H. OFOSU-APPIAH.

Vice-President and Chairman of the Science Section: Prof. F. G. T. TORTO.

Secretary: Prof. E. LAING.

Publications: *Proceedings*† (annually), *J. B. Danquah Memorial Lectures*† (annually).

FELLOWS:

ABRAHAM, Prof. W. E.
ACKAH, Dr. C. A.
ADDAE, Prof. S. K.
AKYEAMPONG, Prof. D. A.
ALLOTEY, Prof. F. K. A.
AMONOO, Prof. R. F.
AMPOFO, Prof. D. A.
ARCHAMPONG, Prof. E. Q.
ASANTE, Dr. S. K. B.
ASOMANING, Dr. E. J. A.
AYENSU, Dr. E. S.
BADOE, Prof. E. A.
BAETA, Prof. C. G.
BAFFOUR, Dr. R. P.
BANNERMAN, Dr. R. H. O.
BEKOE, Prof. D. A.
BOAHEN, Prof. A. A.
BOATENG, Prof. E. A., G.M.
CHAPMAN NYAHO, D. A., C.B.E.
CHRISTIAN, Dr. E. C.
CLERK, Prof. G. C.
CUDJOE, J. E.
DE GRAFT-HANSON, Prof. J. O.
DE GRAFT-JOHNSON, Prof. J. W. S.
DE GRAFT-JOHNSON, Dr. K. T.
DE GRAFT-JOHNSON, Dr. (Mrs.) SUSAN
DICKSON, Prof. K. A.
DICKSON, Prof. K. B.
DODOO, Prof. S. R. A.
EASMON, Prof. C. O.
EVANS-ANFOM, Dr. E.
EWUSIE, Prof. J. Y.
FRIMPONG-ANSAH, J. H.
GARDINER, Dr. R. K. A., G.M.
GILBERT, Dr. C.
GILLMAN, Prof. J.
HUNWICK, Prof. J. O.
JACKSON, Lady BARBARA
KONOTEY-AHULU, Dr. F. D.
KOSTER, Rev. Prof. J. R.
KWAPONG, Prof. A. A.
LA-ANYANE, Prof. S.
LAING, Prof. E.
LAING, Prof. W. N.
LAMB, J., O.B.E.
LARTEY, Dr. E., G.M.
MAY, Prof. A. N.
NKETIAH, Prof. J. H.
OBENG, Dr. (Mrs.) LETITIA.
OBENG, Dr. B. B.
OFOSU-APPIAH, Prof. L. H.
OLLENNU, Dr. N. A., C.D.
OFUSU-AMAAH, Prof. S.
OPPONG, Prof. E. N. W.
QUARTEY, Prof. J. A. K.
SAI, Prof. F. T.
STOUGHTON, Dr. R. H.
TACKIE, Prof. A. N.
TORTO, Prof. F. G. T.
TWUM-BARIMA, Prof. K.
WIREDU, Prof. K.
WRIGHT, Prof. R. W. H.

HONORARY FELLOWS:

CAINE, Sir SYDNEY, K.C.M.G.
CEAUŞESCU, ELENA.
DIKE, Prof. K. O.
HODGKIN, DOROTHY CROWFOOT, O.M., F.R.S.
NICOL, Dr. DAVIDSON S. H. WILLOUGHBY, C.M.G.
TODD OF TRUMPINGTON, Baron, F.R.S.

AFFILIATED BODY:

Encyclopaedia Africana Secretariat: P.O.B. 2797, Accra; f. 1962 to organize the production of an encyclopaedia of African life and history; works through national co-operating committees in various parts of Africa; Dir. Prof. L. H. OFOSU-APPIAH.

AFFILIATED ACADEMIC SOCIETIES AND ASSOCIATIONS:

Classical Association of Ghana.
Economic Society of Ghana.
Historical Society of Ghana.
Ghana Geographical Association.
Ghana Institute of Architects.
Ghana Institution of Engineers.
Ghana Medical Association.
Ghana Science Association.
Ghana Sociological Association.
Ghana Theological Association.
Sarbah Society (Law).

LEARNED SOCIETIES

Alliance Française: P.O.B. 1573, Accra; f. 1958; library of 3,000 vols., 300 mems.; brs. in Kumasi and Takoradi; Pres. THOMAS BOATIN; Dir. PHILIPPE KOEUL.

Arts Council of Ghana: P.O.B. 2738, Accra; f. 1958; to promote and develop the arts and preserve traditional arts; Chair. Prof. J. H. NKETIA; Exec. Sec. C. E. PHILLIPS.

British Council, The: P.O.B. 771, Accra; Rep. A. D. JOHNSON; Regional Offices: P.O.B. 1996, Kumasi; Regional Dir. T. D. EDMUNDSON; library: *see* Libraries.

Classical Association of Ghana: University of Ghana, P.O.B. 25, Legon; f. 1952; 17 mems.; Chair. Dr. J. H. O. MACQUEEN; Treas. and Sec. DAPHNE HEREWARD.

Economic Society of Ghana: P.O.B. 22, Legon, Accra; f. 1957; about 500 mems.; Chief Officers Prof. S. SEY, J. B. ABBAN, J. E. A. MANU, C. D. JEBUNI; publs. *Economic Bulletin of Ghana, Social and Economic Affairs* (quarterly).

Ghana Association of Writers: P.O.B. 4414, Accra; aims at bringing together all the writers of the country, to protect and champion the interests of writers, and to foster the development of Ghanaian literature; literary evenings, annual congress, etc.; Chair. Dr. ROBERT GARDINER; Sec. ATUKWEI OKAI; publs. *Takra* (fortnightly newsletter), *Angla* (anthology, annually).

Ghana Bar Association: P.O.B. 4150, Accra; Pres. W. A. N. ADUMUA-BOSSMAN, LL.B.; Gen. Sec. C. A. LOKKO, LL.B.

Ghana Geographical Association: University of Ghana; f. 1955; Pres. Prof. E. V. T. ENGMANN; Hon. Sec. Dr. L. J. GYAMFI-FENTENG; publ. *Bulletin* (annually).

Ghana Library Association: P.O.B. 4105, Accra; f. 1962; Pres. G. C. O. LAMPTEY, F.L.A.; Sec. Mrs. P. G. AMONOO, M.A., A.L.A.; publ. *Ghana Library Journal* (2 a year).

Ghana Science Association: P.O.B. 7, Legon; f. 1959; Hon. Pres. Dr. E. A. KWEI; Hon. Sec. Dr. J. K. B. ATA; publ. *The Ghana Journal of Science.*

Ghana Sociological Association: P.O.B. 6, Legon; f. 1961; financial aid from University of Ghana; academic activities, conferences, etc.; 215 mems.; Pres. Mr. Justice NII AMAA OLLENNU; Sec. Dr. PATRICK TWUMASI; publ. *Ghana Journal of Sociology*†.

Goethe Institut: P.O.B. 3196, Accra: Dir. DIETER VOLLPRECHT.

Historical Society of Ghana: P.O.B. 12, Legon; f. 1952; formerly Gold Coast and Togoland Historical Soc.; *c.* 600 mems.; Pres. T. A. OSAE; Sec. J. G. K. TENGEY; publs. *Transactions*† (2 a year), *West African Journal for History Teachers*† (annually).

Pharmaceutical Society of Ghana: 268A North Kaneshie Estates, P.O.B. 2133, Accra; f. 1935; aims to advance chemistry and pharmacy and maintain standards of the profession; 7 regional branches; library of 250 vols.; 482 mems.; Pres. AGO SIMMONDS, M.P.S.G.; Hon. Gen. Sec. H. K. ABUTIATE, M.P.S.G.

West African Examinations Council: Headquarters Office, P.O.B. 125, Accra, Ghana; other offices in Lagos, Nigeria; Freetown, Sierra Leone; London, England; Banjul, The Gambia; Monrovia, Liberia; f. 1952 by the four West African Commonwealth countries; conducts School Certificate, Higher School Certificate Examinations in Nigeria; School Certificate/GCE Examinations in The Gambia, Ghana and Sierra Leone; also selection of examinations for entry into secondary schools and similar institutions, the Public Services, entrance and final examinations for teacher training colleges at the request of the various Ministries of Education; holds examinations on behalf of the U.K. examining authorities and the Educational Testing Service, Princeton, New Jersey, U.S.A.; Chair. Prof. E. A. BOATENG; Registrar Dr. JOHN TAYLOR-PEARCE; publs. *Annual Report, Regulations and Syllabuses* (annually).

West African Science Association: c/o Botany Dept.; P.O.B. 7, University of Ghana, Legon; f. 1953; mems.: Ghana, Nigeria, Sierra Leone, Ivory Coast, Senegal, Togo, Niger; observers: Benin, Liberia; Pres. Prof. O. AWE; Sec. Dr. J. M. HYDE; publ. *Journal* (annually).

RESEARCH INSTITUTES

Cocoa Research Institute, Ghana: P.O.B. 8, Tafo; f. 1944; research on cocoa, cola and coffee; 86 staff; library of 10,955 vols., 1,207 pamphlets, 431 journals; Dir. Dr. AGATHA VERONICA MARTINSON (acting); Sec. D. K. LOVE-DARKO (acting); publs. *Annual Report*†, *Technical Bulletin*†, library lists†.

Council for Scientific and Industrial Research: P.O.B. M.32, Accra; f. 1958, incorporated in its present form by legislation in 1968; functions include advice to the Government, encouragement of scientific and industrial research relevant to national development, coordination of research in all its aspects in Ghana, and collation, publication and dissemination of research results; central library: *see* Libraries; Chair. Prof. A. N. TACKIE; Sec. V. AMMAH-ATTOH; Librarian J. A. VILLARS; publs. *CSIR Handbook, CSIR Recorder, Ghana Journal of Science, Ghana Journal of Agricultural Science, Annual Report.*

ATTACHED RESEARCH INSTITUTES:

Animal Research Institute: P.O.B. 20, Achimota; f. 1957; Dir. Dr. E. D. OFFORI.

Building and Road Research Institute: Univ. P.O.B. 40, Kumasi; f. 1952; library of 8,000 vols.; Dir. Dr. M. D. GIDIGASU (acting).

Crops Research Institute: P.O.B. 3785, Kumasi; Dir. Dr. W. K. AGBLE.

Food Research Institute: P.O.B. M.20, Accra; f. 1964; food processing, preservation, storage, analysis marketing, etc.; Dir. Mrs. J. M. KORDYLAS; publ. *Bulletin.*

Forest Products Research Institute: Univ. P.O.B. 63, Kumasi; f. 1963; library of 500 vols.; Dir. F. W. ADDO-ASHONG; publ. *Quarterly Newsletter.*

Institute of Aquatic Biology: P.O.B. 38, Achimota; Dir. Dr. M. A. ODEI.

Industrial Research Institute: P.O.B. M.32, Accra; Dir. Dr. M. N. B. AYIKU (acting).

National Atlas Project: P.O.B. M.32, Accra; Hon. Dir. Prof. K. A. DICKSON.

Scientific Instrumentation Centre: P.O.B. M.32, Accra; f. 1976; Man. Dr. R. G. J. BUTLER.

Soil Research Institute: P.M.B., Academy P.O., Kwadaso, Kumasi; f. 1951; Dir. Dr. H. B. OBENG.

Water Resources Research Unit: P.O.B. M.32, Accra; Dir. N. B. AYIBOTELE.

Geological Survey of Ghana: P.O.B. M.80, Accra; f. 1913; geological mapping and geophysical surveying of the country, research and evaluation of mineral resources; library of 30,216 vols.; Dir. G. O. KESSE, M.SC., M.I.M.M.; publs. *Annual Report*†, memoirs and bulletins†.

Ghana Meteorological Services Department: P.O.B. 87, Legon; f. 1937; serves civil and military aviation, agriculture, forestry, engineering and medical research; 409 mems.; Dir. N. A. GBECKOR-KOVE; publs. numerous regular and irregular reports.

Health Laboratory Services: Ministry of Health, P.O.B. 300, Accra; f. 1920; laboratory services, public health reference laboratory, reference haematology laboratory, training of laboratory technicians; research on public health microbiology, abnormal haemoglobins and allied subjects; library of 8,000 vols. combined with that of the Ghana Medical School; Head E. C. MARBELL, B.SC., M.B., CH.B., D.PATH.

LIBRARIES

Accra Central Library: Thorpe Road, P.O.B. 663, Accra; central reference library; union catalogues.

Ashanti Regional Library: Bantama Rd., P.O.B. 824, Kumasi.

British Council Library: P.O.B. 771, Accra; f. 1963; 21,000 vols., 90 periodicals; Librarian R. DRURY; br. at Kumasi; f. 1950; 10,612 vols., 47 periodicals.

Central Reference and Research Library (C.S.I.R.): P.O.B. M.32, Accra; f. 1964; 6,500 vols., 800 current periodicals; Librarian J. A. VILLARS, F.L.A.; publs. *CRRL Bibliographical Bulletins* (irregular), *Union List of Scientific Journals in Ghana Libraries, Ghana Science Abstracts* (quarterly).

Ghana Library Board: P.O.B. 663, Accra; f. 1950; comprises Accra Central Library (1956), regional libraries at Kumasi (1954), Sekondi (1955), Ho (1960), Tamale (1959), Research Library, Accra (1961), Bolgatanga (1969); branches at Cape Coast, Dunkwa, Hohoe, Obuasi, Takoradi, Tarkwa, Koforidua, Jasikan, Keta, Konongo, Oda, Kpandu, Sunyani, Nkawkaw and Tema; mobile libraries, children's libraries; 800,000 vols.; Dir. of Library Services ADOLFUS OFORI.

National Archives of Ghana: Headquarters: P.O.B. 3056, Accra; f. 1946, legal recognition 1955; charged with the collection, custody, rehabilitation and reproduction of all Public Archives, including valuable private and family papers; regional offices, which serve as record centres and cater for local history, in Kumasi, Cape Coast, Sekondi, Tamale, Sunyani, Koforidua and Ho; library of 2,000 vols.; Chief Archivist J. M. AKITA; staff of 116; publs. *Annual Report*†, exhibition catalogues†, etc.

Research Library on African Affairs: P.O.B. 2970, Accra; f. 1961; collection, processing and dissemination of recorded literature, history and culture of all Africa; 26,300 vols., 770 periodicals; Librarian A. N. DE HEER, F.L.A.; publs. *Bi-monthly Current Bibliography*†, *Annual Ghana National Bibliography*†, Special Subject Bibliographies† (irregular).

Sekondi Regional Library: Old Axim Rd., P.O.B. 174, Sekondi.

University of Ghana Library (Balme Library): P.O.B. 24, Legon; f. 1948; 293,000 vols., 5,210 current periodicals; Librarian J. M. WALPOLE, B.A., A.L.A.

University of Science and Technology Library: University P.O., Kumasi; 85,000 vols., 1,620 periodicals; Librarian (vacant).

MUSEUMS

Ghana National Museum: Barnes Rd., P.O.B. 3343, Accra; f. 1957; controlled by the Ghana Museums and Monuments Board; archaeological and ethnological finds from all over Ghana and West Africa; modern works by Ghanaian artists; the preservation and conservation of ancient forts and castles and traditional buildings; the achievement of man in Africa; Chairman of the Board Dr. OKU AMPOFO; Dir. Prof. R. B. NUNOO.

Ghana National Museum of Science and Technology: P.O.B. 3343, Accra; f. 1965; a temporary exhibition hall with an open-air cinema is used for the display of working models, charts, films and other exhibits on science and technology; collection of exhibits for permanent galleries has begun; temporary exhibitions are taken to the regions, films shown to colleges and schools and Regional and National Science Fairs are organized; Officers-in-Charge E. A. ASANTE, Miss JOSEPHINE QUAINOO, N. A. DAGADU.

West African Historical Museum: P.O.B. 502, Cape Coast; f. 1971; sponsored by the Ghana Museums and Monuments Board and the University of Cape Coast; it is intended that the museum will play a fundamental role in a new education system for Ghana in which "participation" techniques are of increasing importance in schools; research facilities will be developed; library in course of construction; Research Officer DOIG SIMMONDS, M.S.I.A., F.R.A.I., A.M.A.

UNIVERSITIES

UNIVERSITY OF GHANA

P.O.B. 25, LEGON, NR. ACCRA

Telephone: Accra 75381.

Founded 1948 as the University College of Ghana (then Gold Coast); raised to University status 1961.

Language of instruction: English; Academic year: October to June; State control.

Vice-Chancellor: Prof. D. A. BEKOE, D.PHIL.
Pro-Vice-Chancellor: Prof. E. LAING, PH.D.
Registrar: E. A. K. EDZII, B.A.
Librarian: J. M. WALPOLE, B.A., A.L.A.

Number of teachers: 497.
Number of students: 4,000.

Publications: Annual Reports, *University of Ghana Reporter, Calendar*†, *Newsletter*†.

DEANS:

Faculty of Administration: K. E. ADJEI, PH.D.
Faculty of Agriculture: E. N. W. OPPONG, PH.D.
Faculty of Arts: I. K. CHINEBUA, M.A.
Faculty of Law: W. C. EKOW-DANIELS, PH.D.
Faculty of Science: E. LAING, PH.D.
Faculty of Social Studies: J. OFORI-ATTAH, PH.D.
Faculty of Medicine: H. H. PHILLIPS, M.B., B.SC., PH.D.

PROFESSORS:
ACQUAYE, D. K., PH.D., Crop Science
AMPOFO, D. A., M.B., B.S., M.P.H., M.R.C.P., Obstetrics and Gynaecology
ASANTE, G. S., PH.D., Biochemistry
BADOE, E. A., M.B., CH.B., D.T.M.&H., F.R.C.S., Surgery
BENTSI-ENCHILL, K. K. O., B.A., M.B., B.CH., F.R.C.O.G., Obstetrics and Gynaecology
BOAHEN, A. A., PH.D., History
DICKSON, K. A., B.A., B.LITT., Religions
DICKSON, K. B., M.A., PH.D., Geography
DODU, S. R. A., M.B., CH.B., M.D., F.R.C.P., Medicine and Therapeutics
DUCKWORTH, R. B., PH.D., Nutrition and Food Science
FOSTER, E. F. B., CH.B., B.A.O., L.M., M.D., M.A., M.R.C.PSYCH., Psychiatry
HARDIE, A. M., M.A., English
KOSTER, J. R., PH.D., Computer Science
NKETIA, J. H., B.A., African Studies
ODURO, K. A., M.B., CH.B., F.F.A.R.C.S., Anaesthetics
OKONJO, C., DR.RER.NAT., Regional Institute of Population Studies
QUARCOOPOME, C. O., M.B., CH.B., Surgery
QUARTEY, J. A. K., M.A., PH.D., F.R.I.C., Chemistry
SMIT, A. F. J., GEOL.DRS., Geology
SUTTON, J. E. G., M.A., PH.D., Archaeology
TORTO, F. G. T. O'B., PH.D., Chemistry
TWUM-BARIMA, K., M.A., Statistics

ATTACHED INSTITUTES:

Institute of Adult Education: P.O.B. 31, Legon; Dir. E. AMPENE, PH.D.

Institute of African Studies: P.O.B. 73, Legon; Dir. Prof. J. H. NKETIA, B.A.

Institute of Journalism and Communication: P.O.B. 53, Legon; Dir. P. A. V. ANSAH, M.A., PH.D. (acting).

Institute of Statistical, Social and Economic Research: P.O.B. 74, Legon; Dir. Prof. K. TWUM-BARIMA, M.A.

Noguchi Memorial Institute for Medical Research: f. 1979.

Regional Training Centre for Archivists: P.O.B. 60, Legon; Head Prof. S. I. A. KOTEI, M.A., M.PHIL.

Regional Institute for Population Studies: P.O.B. 96, Legon; f. 1972 with UN aid; Dir. Prof. C. OKONJO, DR.RER.NAT.

Volta Basin Research Project: Dir. E. K. OBENG-ASAMOA, M.S., PH.D.

AGRICULTURAL RESEARCH STATIONS:

Agricultural Research Station: P.O.B. 43, Kade.
Officer-in-Charge: S. K. KARIKARI, M.SC.

Agricultural Research Station: P.O.B. 9, Kpong.
Officer-in-Charge: A. N. ARYEETEY, M.SC.

Agricultural Research Station: P.O.B. 38, Legon.
Officer-in-Charge: M. BAFI-YEBOAH, M.V.S., DR.MED. VET.

UNIVERSITY OF SCIENCE AND TECHNOLOGY

UNIVERSITY P.O.,
KUMASI

Telephone: 5351-5360.

Founded 1951 as College of Technology, University status 1961.

Language of instruction: English; State control; Academic year: October to June (2 semesters).

Vice-Chancellor: Prof. E. BAMKO KWAKYE, DR.ING., F.GH.I.E., M.O.V.
Registrar: A. S. Y. ANDOH, M.A.
Librarian: (vacant).

Number of teachers: 352.
Number of students: 2,870.

Publications: *University Calendar, Annual Report, Recorder, Newsletter.*

DEANS:
Faculty of Agriculture: J. C. NORMAN.
Faculty of Architecture: P. A. TETTEH.
Faculty of Art: Prof. E. V. ASIHENE.
Faculty of Engineering: F. O. KWAMI.
Faculty of Medicine: Prof. W. N. LAING.
Faculty of Pharmacy: Assoc. Prof. E. A. GYANG.
Faculty of Science: Prof. F. K. A. ALLOTEY.
Faculty of Social Sciences: E. ACQUAYE.
Institute of Mining and Mineral Engineering: Dr. K. A. B. ASIHENE.
Institute of Postgraduate Studies: Prof. F. A. KUFUOR.

PROFESSORS:
ALLOTEY, F. K. A., Mathematics
ASIHENE, E. V., Painting, Sculpture and Rural Art and Industry
KUFUOR, F. A., Chemistry and Chemical Technology
LAING, W. N., Pathology

UNIVERSITY OF CAPE COAST

CAPE COAST

Telephone: Cape Coast 2440-2449.

Founded 1962.

Language of Instruction: English; State control; Academic year: September/October to June/July (3 terms).

Chancellor: MIGUEL A. RIBEIRO, B.A.
Vice-Chancellor: Prof. K. B. DICKSON, PH.D.
Registrar: (vacant).
Librarian: S. A. AFRE, F.L.A. (acting).

Number of teachers: 206.
Number of students: 1,398.

Publications: *Asemka* (journal), *Bulletin, Calendar*†, *Information Brochure, Annual Report*†, *University Gazette*, etc.

DEANS:
Faculty of Science: K. N. EYESON, PH.D.
Faculty of Arts: KOFI AWOONOR, PH.D.
Faculty of Education: G. O. COLLISON, PH.D.
Faculty of Economic and Social Studies: L. A. DEI, PH.D.

COLLEGES

Accra Polytechnic: P.O.B. 561, Accra.

Accra Technical Training Centre: P.O.B. M.177, Accra; f. 1966, attached to Ministry of Education; to train tradesmen for industry and civil service; number of students: 350; library of *c.* 3,500 vols.

Principal: J. BUDU-SMITH.

Government Technical Institute: P.O.B. 206, Sunyani; f. 1967; technical and business education; 65 teachers; 1,300 students; library of *c.* 4,500 vols.; Librarian J. N. AGYEI; Pres. F. A. BAIDEN.

Ho Technical Institute: 217 Ho, Volta Region; telephone Ho 456; f. 1968.

Principal: J. A. KORLEY.

Librarian: Mr. AGRA.

Library: 2,000 vols.

Number of teachers: *c.* 50.
Number of students: *c.* 620.

Takoradi Polytechnic: P.O.B. 256, Takoradi.

Tamale Technical Institute: P.O.B. 67, Tamale.

Koforidua Technical Institute: P.O.B. 323, Koforidua; f. 1960.

Principal: P. C. NOI.

Library: 2,000 vols.

Number of teachers: 9.
Number of students: 206.

Kpandu Technical Institute: Technical Division, P.O.B. 76, Kpandu, Volta Region; telephone Kpandu 22; f. 1956.

Principal: J. Y. VODZI.

Vice-Principal: S. T. OFEI.

Librarian: V. E. Y. ATIASE.

Library: 4,000 vols.

Number of teachers: 70.
Number of students: 689.

National Film and Television Institute: c/o Broadcasting House, P.O.B. 1633, Accra; f. 1978 by Government decree; 3-year courses in film and television technology, with special emphasis on the production of educational programmes and feature, informative, scientific, documentary and industrial films; receives financial help from public funds and technical assistance from the Friedrich Ebert Foundation; 16 staff (incl. 3 from Federal Republic of Germany), 15 students; library in process of formation; Dir. H. M. HEMANS-MENSAH.

GREECE

Population 9,360,000

ACADEMY

Akadimia Athinon (*Academy of Athens*): Odos Panepistimiou; f. 1926.

President: GEORGE MYLONAS.

Vice-President: IOANNIS CARMIRIS.

Secretary-General: I. THEODORKAOPOULOS.

Secretary for Proceedings: MENELAOS PALLANTIOS.

Secretary for Publications: I. XANTHAKIS.

PRESIDENTS OF SECTIONS:

Positive Sciences: GEORGE MERICAS.

Literature and Fine Arts: ATH. PETSALIS-DIOMIDIS.

Moral and Political Sciences: PAN. CANELLOPOULOS.

Library of 50,000 vols.

Number of members: 65.

Publications: *Praktika*† (*Proceedings*—annually), *Pragmatie* (Papers), *Mnimeia Ellinikis Historias* (Documents of Greek History).

SECTION I

Positive Sciences:

MEMBERS:

XANTHAKIS, IOANNIS (1955).
ALEXOPOULOS, CAESAR (1963).
MARIOLOPOULOS, ELIAS (1966).
LOUROS, NICOLAOS (1966).
PYLARINOS, OTHON (1966).
VASSILIOU, PHILON (1966).
THEOCHARIS, PERICLIS (1973).
TSATSAS, GEORGE (1974).
MOUSSOULOS, LOUCAS (1977).
MERICAS, GEORGE (1977).
TOUMPAS, IOANNIS (1979).
VASSILIADIS (1980).

RESIDENT MEMBER:

GEORGALAS, GEORGIOS (1939).

FOREIGN MEMBERS:

KÜHN, OTHMAR (1964).
KANAZIR, DUSAN (1975).
SAVIC, PAVLE (1975).
WAERDEN, BARTEL LEENDEERT VAN DER (1976).
BALEVSKI, ANGEL TONCHEV (1977).
FEHRENBACH, CHARLES (1978).

CORRESPONDING MEMBERS:

GATOS, CHARALAMBOS (1964).
CARAGOUNIS, GEORGE (1965).
ANASTASSIADIS, IOANNIS (1970).
KATSOYANNIS, PANAYOTIS (1970).
KARABATSOS, GERASSIMOS (1970).
GYPHTOPOYLOS, ELIAS (1970).
ZAÏMIS, ELEONORE (1971).
MOURATOV, GEORGES (1971).
CURIEN, HERBERT (1971).
ARGIRIS, IOANNIS (1973).
PAPADAKIS, JEAN (1975).
CEAUŞESCU, ELENA (1976).
CONSTANTINIDIS, PARIS (1976).
BOURODIMOS, EFSTATHIOS (1976).
ARGYRIS, PETROS (1976).
MELISSINOS, ANDRIANOS (1976).
KORAL, ZDENEK (1976).
SJABO, ARPAD (1976).
CANELLAKIS, EV. (1978).
ALEXOPOULOS, CONST. (1978).
SEVASTICOGLOU, IOANNIS (1978).
ANTONIADIS, CHAR. (1979).
MOSCOVAKIS, IOANNIS (1980).
HELIOPOULOS, IOANNIS (1980).
CHRISTOFOROU, LOUCAS (1980).
RETZEPIS, PAN. (1980).

SECTION II

Literature and Fine Arts:

MEMBERS:

ATHANASSIADIS NOVAS, GEORGIOS (1955).
ZAKYTHINOS, DIONYSIOS (1966).
HARIS, PETROS (1969).
MYLONAS, GEORGIOS (1970).
PALLANDIOS, MENELAOS (1970).
CHATZIKYRIAKOS-GIZAS, N. (1974).
TRYPANIS, C. (1974).
PETSALIS-DIOMIDIS, THANASSIS (1977).
KYDONIATIS, SOLON (1977).
PREVELAKIS, PANTELIS (1977).
POLITIS, LINOS (1980).
CHADZIDAKIS, MAN. (1980).
ROMAIOS, CONST. (1980).
PAPAS, IOANNIS (1980).

FOREIGN MEMBERS:

ROHLFS, GERHARD (1966).
ROBERT, LOUIS (1966).
LEMERLE, PAUL (1967).
LESKY, ALBIN (1967).
MERITT, BENJAMIN (1967).
LEVI, DORO (1974).
LAVAGNINI, BRUNO (1974).
BECK, HANS GEORG (1975).
HUNGER, HERBERT (1975).
RADOJVCIT, SVETOZAR (1976).
DEMARGNE, PIERRE (1977).
PEEK, WERNER (1977).
GEORGIEV, VLADIMIR (1978).
SENGHOR, LEOPOLD SEDAR (1979).
THOMPSON, HOMER (1979).

CORRESPONDING MEMBERS:

EITREM, SAM (1951).
TANAKA, HIDENAKA (1951).
LEJEUNE, LOUIS AIMÉ (1951).
VICOMTE DE ROTON (MARIE ALEXANDRE GABRIEL) (1953).
TURIN, ALEXANDER (1954).
VON DER MUHL, PETER (1964).
DAKIN, DOUGLAS (1971).
CARAGIORGIS, VASSILIOS (1973).
CATAUDELLA, QUINTINO (1974).
TRENDALL, ARTHUR DALE (1974).
RUNCIMAN, Sir STEVEN (1974).
PONTANI, FILIPPO MARIA (1974).
TOMPSON, STITH (1974).
SCHIRO, GIUSEPPE (1975).
POUILLOUX, JEAN (1975).
ROMILY, JACQUELINE DE (1975).
GIGON, ORLOF (1975).
AHRWEILER-GLYKATZI, HELENE (1976).
OLIVIER, GABRIEL (1976).
BRONEER, OSKAR (1976).
DJURIC, VOJISLAV (1976).
MONTALE, EUGENIO (1976).
CRANIDIOTIS, NICOLAOS (1977).
JONES, HUGH LLOYD (1978).
ANASTOS, MILT. (1978).
CHARANIS, PETROS (1978).

REVERDIN, OLIVIER (1978).
OBOLENSKY, DIMITRI (1979).
VAFOPOULOS, GEORGE (1980).
MANOUSSACAS, MAN. (1980).
CRIARAS, EMM. (1980).
LEIGH FERMOR, PATRICK (1980).
ANDRONICOS, EMM. (1980).
MOUTSOPOULOS, NICOLAOS (1980).
BACALAKIS, GEORGE (1980).

SECTION III
Moral and Political Sciences:
MEMBERS:

ZOLOTAS, XENOPHON (1952).
BRATSIOTIS, PANAGIOTIS (1955).
KANELLOPOULOS, PANAGIOTIS (1959).
THEODORAKOPOULOS, IOANNIS (1960).
TSATSOS, CONSTANTINOS (1961).
STASSINOPOULOS, MICHAEL (1968).
CASSIMATIS, GREGORIOS (1969).
ZEPOS, PANAYOTIS (1970).
KARMIRIS, IOANNIS (1974).
MICHAILIDIS-NOUAROS, G. (1974).
ANGELOPOULOS, ANGELOS (1976).
BONIS, CONST. (1978).
SONTIS, IOANNIS (1980).

HONORARY MEMBER:

GISCARD D'ESTAING, VALERY (1980).

FOREIGN MEMBERS:

KUNKEL, WOLFGANG (1963).
GADAMER, HANS GEORG (1970).
RAMSAY, MICHAEL (1974).
CALOGERO, GUIDO (1976).
SCHELTEMA, HERMA JAN (1978).

CORRESPONDING MEMBERS:

VLACHOS, GEORGIOS (1964).
FRANTZESKAKIS, PHOKION (1964).
KLIBANSKY, RAYMOND (1970).
DEL PRETE, PASQUALE (1970).
HENDERSON, GEORGE PATRICK (1974).
SCIACCA, MICHELE (1974).
DE ROBERTIS, FRANCESCO MARIA (1975).
WOLFF, HANS JULIUS (1975).
GAUDEMET, JEAN (1975).
VOLTERRA, EDUARDO (1975).
WOLF, ERIK (1976).
CHLOROS, ALEXANDROS (1976).
GEORGESCU, VALENTIN (1977).
ROUGEMONT, DENIS DE (1977).
CARBONNIER, JEAN (1977).
OEHLER, KLAUS (1977).
BALANDIER, GEORGES (1977).
VALTICOS, NICOLAOS (1978).
VLAVIANOS VASS. (1980).

RESEARCH INSTITUTES UNDER THE SUPERVISION OF THE ACADEMY OF ATHENS

Kentron Erevnis Ellinikis Laographias (*Centre for research in Greek Folklore*): *see* under Research Institutes.

Kentron Syntaxeos Historikou Lexikou (*Centre for the compilation of the Historical Dictionary of the Modern Greek Language*): f. 1914; Dir. DIK. VAYAKAKOS; publs. *Historical Dictionary of the Modern Greek Language* (Vols. I–IV), *Lexicographicon Deltion* (Vols. I–XII).

Kentron Erevnis Messeonikou kai Neou Ellinismou (*Centre for research into Mediaeval and Modern Hellenism (up to 1821)*): f. 1930; Dir. L. VRANOUSSIS; publ. *Epetiris* (annual).

Kentron Erevnis Neoterou Ellinismou (*Centre for research in Contemporary Hellenism (from 1821)*): f. 1957; Dir. EL. PREVELAKIS.

Kentron Erevnis Historias Ellinikou Dikeou (*Centre for Research in the History of the Greek Law*): Akadimia Athinon Anagnostopoulou 14, Athens 136; f. 1929; collects, studies and publishes Greek legal customs, as well as the legal material contained in the literary texts of Byzantine and post-Byzantine times; Dir. MEN. TOURTOGLOU; publ. *Epetiris* (annual).

Kentron Ekdoseos Ellinon Sygrafeon (*Centre for the publication of Ancient Greek Authors*): f. 1955; Dir. CHAR. FLORATOS.

Kentron Erevnon Astronomias kai Ephirmosmenon Mathimatikon tis Akadimias Athinon (*Research Centre for Astronomy and Applied Mathematics, Academy of Athens*): f. 1959; Supervisor Acad. Prof. J. XANTHAKIS; publs. *Contributions from the Research Centre for Astronomy and Applied Mathematics, Annual Report.*

COMMITTEES UNDER THE AUSPICES OF THE ACADEMY OF ATHENS

Greek National Committee for Astronomy: Pres. Acad. J. XANTHAKIS.

Greek National Committee for Space Research: Pres. Acad. J. XANTHAKIS.

Greek National Committee for the Quiet Sun International Years: Pres. Acad. J. XANTHAKIS.

LEARNED SOCIETIES

ARTS

Enosis Hellinon Mousourgon (*League of Greek Composers*): Odos Karageorghi Servias 8, Athens; f. 1931; Pres. A. EVANGELATOS; Sec.-Gen. TH. KARIOTAKIS.

Kallitechnikon Epimelitirion (*Culture Chamber*): Odos Mitropoleos 38, Athens; Pres. KOSTAS MALAMOS; Gen. Sec. G. FOTIS SARRIS.

Pan-Hellenic Musical Association: Odos Halkokondyli 24, Athens; f. 1914; 1,098 mems.; supports School of Modern Music, which houses the library; Pres. E. M. CHYTYRIS; Gen. Sec. COSTOS CLAVVAS.

Society for Byzantine Studies: Odos Aristeidou 8, Athens 122; f. 1919; 250 mems.; library of 5,000 vols.; Pres. A. ORLANDOS; Sec.-Gen. N. B. TOMADAKIS; publ. *Epetiris Etairias Byzantinon Spoudon* (*EEBS*)† (annual).

BIBLIOGRAPHY AND LIBRARY SCIENCE

Enosis Hellinon Bibliothekarion (*Greek Library Association*): Skoyleniou 4, Athens TT 124; f. 1968; 520 mems.; Pres. KATHERINE THANOPOULOU; Gen. Sec. I. CHOREMI; publ. circular letter.

EDUCATION

Hellenic Association of University Women: 44 Voulis St., Athens 118; Pres. AMALIA FLEMING; Sec.-Gen. ASPASIA PAPATHANASSOPOULOU.

Syllogos pros Diadosin ton Hellenikon Grammaton (*Society for the Promotion of Greek Education*): Odos Pindarou 15 (136), Athens; f. 1869; 9 mems.; Pres. PHILIP DRAGOUMIS; Sec.-Gen. ALEXANDRATOS PANAYIOTIS.

HISTORY, GEOGRAPHY AND ARCHAEOLOGY

Archaeologiki Hetairia (*Archaeological Association*): Odos Panepistimiou 22, Athens; f. 1837; library of 60,000 vols.; publs. *Archaeologiki Ephimeris*, *Praktika* (annually), *Archaeological Library* (series of 90 vols.), *Ergon* (annually).

Hellenic Geographical Society: 11 J. Smuts (Voucourestiou) St., Athens 134; f. 1919; 95 mems.; Pres. D. T. NOTI BOTZARIS; Gen. Sec. ANAST ALEXOPOULOS; publ. *Bulletin*.

Historical and Ethnological Society: Old Parliament, Stadiou St., Athens; f. 1882; Pres. D. T. NOTI BOTZARIS; Sec.-Gen. STEPHEN C. AGELASTO.

International Cultural Institutes

British Council: Philikis Etairias 17, P.O.B. 488, Athens 138; Rep. J. M. E. Took, m.b.e.; Regional Dir. (Thessaloniki) T. Aitken; libraries at Athens and Thessaloniki: *see* Libraries.

Goethe Institut: P.O.B. 1022, Omonia Phidiou 14/16, Athens 143; f. 1952; library of 15,000 vols.; lectures, language courses, concerts and exhibitions; Dir. H. A. Oehler; br. in Salonika.

Institut Français d'Athènes: 29–31 Odos Sina, Athens 144; Dir. J. Fauve; publ. *Bulletin Analytique de Bibliographie Hellénique* (irregular).

Istituto Italiano di Cultura: Patission 47, Athens; library of 18,000 vols.; Dir. Prof. Domenico Gardella.

Language and Literature

Association of Arts and Letters: f. 1938; 1,500 mems.; Pres. G. Kornoutos; Gen. Sec. Stef. Xefloudas.

Hetairia Hellinon Logotechnon (*Society of Greek Men of Letters*): Odos Mitropoleos 38, Athens; f. 1934; 300 mems.; Pres. Z. Skaros; Sec. P. Zambatha-Pagoulatos.

Hetairia Hellinon Theatricon Syngrapheon (*Greek Playwrights' Association*): Asklipiou St. 33, Athens; f. 1908; 120 mems.; Pres. Dimitri Ioannopoulos; Sec. Dimitri Yanoukakis.

Sciences

Enosis Ellinon Chimikon (*Association of Greek Chemists*): 27 Odos Kanningos, Athens 147; f. 1924; 3,000 mems.; publ. *Chimika Chronika* (Scientific Edition, twice monthly; General Edition—monthly).

Helliniki Epitropi Atomikis Energhias (*Greek Atomic Energy Commission*): Aghia Paraskevi-Attikis, Athens; f. 1954; Pres. K. Dokas.

Helliniki Mathimatiki Eteria (*Greek Mathematical Society*): Odos Panepistimiou 34, Athens 143; f. 1918; 6,500 mems.; library of 2,000 vols.; seminars, lectures, summer schools, educational policy; Pres. Prof. S. Kounias; Gen. Sec. D. Chassapis; publs. *Euclides* (5 a year), *Mathimatiki Epitheorissi* (Review, quarterly), *Deltion*† (Bulletin, annually), *Enimerossi* (News, quarterly).

RESEARCH INSTITUTES

Athens Center of Ekistics (ACE): P.O.B. 471, 24 Strat. Syndesmou St., Athens 136; research, education, collaboration and documentation in the development of human settlements; secretariat of World Society for Ekistics; library of 22,300 vols.; Dir. P. Psomopoulos; publs. *Ekistics*†, *Ekistic Index*†, special research reports† and monographs†.

Benakion Phytopathologikon Institouton (*Benaki Phyto-Pathological Institute*): 8 Odos Delta, Kifissia, Athens; f. 1930; phyto-pathology, entomology, agricultural zoology, plant pharmaceutics; 23 laboratories; staff of 42 scientists; library of 13,000 books, 40,000 pamphlets and 700 current periodicals; museum of zoological and entomological specimens, including 22,000 insects; Dir. D. Vassilopoulos; publ. *Annales de l'Institut Phytopathologique Benaki*†.

Centre of International and European Economic Law: Plateia Morihovou 1, Thessaloniki; f. 1977; national documentation and research centre, specializing in European Community law; European Documentation Centre by decision of the EEC; library of 3,000 vols., 100 periodicals; Dir. and Pres. of Admin. Council Prof. Phocion Francescakis; Sec. Prof. Dimitrios Evrigenis; publ. *Revue hellénique de droit européen*†.

Centre of Planning and Economic Research: Hippokratous 22, Athens 144; f. 1961; prepares development plans and conducts economic research; library of 15,000 vols., 550 periodical titles, 220 statistical bulletins; Gen. Scientific Dir. Prof. Reghinos D. Theocharis; publs. various monographs, studies, lectures, seminars and surveys on the Greek economy.

'Democritos' Nuclear Research Centre: Aghia Paraskevi-Attikis, Athens; f. 1961; study and research into the peaceful uses of atomic energy; library and nine laboratories; 657 mems.; library of 11,000 vols. and over 1,000 periodicals; Dirs. K. Dokas (Scientific), G. Papadatos (Technological); Librarian Miss Noria Christophoridou; publs. *DEMO Reports*†, *Annual Reports*†, *Progress Reports*†.

Ethnikon Idryma Erevnon (*National Hellenic Research Foundation*): 48 Vassileos Constantinou Av., Athens; Chair. A. Natsinas.

Hellenikon Kentron Paragochikotitos (*Greek Productivity Centre*): 28 Kapodistriou St., Athens; aims at dissemination of principles of productivity and their implementation in the national economy; Dir.-Gen. D. Mavrokordatos.

Hellenic Institute of International and Foreign Law: 73 Solonos St., Athens; f. 1939; library of 20,000 vols.; Dir. Prof. Andreas Gazis; Sec.-Gen. Basil Lambadarios; publ. *Revue Hellénique de Droit International* (quarterly) (English, French and German).

Institouton Geologikon kai Metalleutikon Ereunon (*Institute of Geology and Mineral Exploration*): 70 Messoghiou St., Athens 608; activities include mineral surveys, mapping and exploration, ground-water and petroleum exploration, engineering geology, geophysical investigation; library and four laboratories; Dir.-Gen. Dr. N. Apostolidis; publs. *Geological and Geophysical Research*† (irregular), *The Geology of Greece*†, *Bulletin*, *Annual Report*.

Institut Pasteur Hellénique: Vassilissis Sofias Ave. 127, Athens 618; f. 1919; study and research of microbiology, immunology and virology; staff of 48; library of 2,681 books and 150 periodicals; Dir. Prof. Charles Serie; publ. *Archives*† (annually).

Institute for Balkan Studies: 45 Tsimiski St., Thessaloniki; f. 1953; research centre concerned with the historical, literary, political, economic and social development of the Balkan peoples from their early times to the present day; library of 30,000 vols.; Dir. Prof. K. Mitsakis; Chair. Prof. D. Delivanis; publs. *Balkan Studies* (2 a year).

Institute of Oceanographic and Fisheries Research (formerly the *Hellenic Hydrobiological Institute*): Aghios Kosmas, Hellinikon, Athens; f. 1945; activities include fishing research, fresh-water and marine biological research, oceanographic and technological research and surveys, and development of new fishing grounds; Pres. Prof. Dr. V. Kiortsis; Gen. Dir. Dr. C. Vamvakas; publ. *Thalassographica*†.

International Centre for Classical Research (*of the Hellenic Society for Humanistic Studies*): 47 Alopekis St., Athens 140; study of and research into ancient Greek culture, scientific research and promotion of popular education through conferences and publications; f. 1959; 700 mems.; library of 20,000 vols.; Pres. Prof. Aristoxenos D. Skiadas; Sec.-Gen. George Babiniotis; publs. *Antiquity and Contemporary Problems*†, *Studies and Research*†.

Kentron Erevnis Ellinikis Laographias (*Research Centre for Greek Folklore*): Odos Anagnostopoulou 14, Athens; f. 1918; 5,748 vols., 3,852 MSS., 19,500 songs and proverbs, customs, etc.; Dir. Dr. Stephanos Imellos; publ. *Yearbook*†.

National Centre of Social Research (EKKE): 1 Sophocleous St., Athens 122; f. 1960; operates under the Ministry of Culture and Sciences; aims to promote the development of the social sciences in Greece, to organize and conduct social research and to act as a link between Greek and foreign social scientists, to promote international co-operation in this field; Pres. ANDREAS GAZIS; Dir.-Gen. (vacant); publ. *Epitheorissis Koinonikon Erevnon* (Greek Review of Social Research) (3 a year).

National Observatory: Lophos Nymphon, Athens; f. 1842; library contains 50,000 vols.; Pres. of the Administration Board Prof. E. MARIOLOPOULOS; Directors: Astronomical Institute, Prof. G. CONTOPOULOS, D.SC.; Meteorological Institute, Prof. D. LALAS, D.SC.; Geodynamical Institute, Prof. A. GALANOPOULOS, D.SC.; Ionospheric Institute, Prof. C. CAROUBALOS, D.SC.; publs. *Annals of the National Observatory of Athens*, Vols. I–XII; *Mémoires*, Series I—Astronomy, Series II—Meteorology; bulletins of the Astronomical, Meteorological, Ionospheric and Seismological Institutes.

Patriarchal Institute for Patristic Studies: 64 Eptapyrgiou St., Moni Vlatadon, Akropolis, Thessaloniki; f. 1968; research centre with depts. of patrology, palaeography, history of Byzantine art, history of worship and ecclesiastical history; library of 13,000 vols., 120 periodicals, 115 codex MSS., 450 rare books, 10,000 MSS. on microfilm, colour slides of illuminated MSS.; Dir. Prof. P. K. CHRISTOU; publs. *Kleronomia* (2 a year), *Analekta Vlatadon* (monograph series).

LIBRARIES

American Library (U.S. International Communications Agency): Odos Massalias 22, Athens 144; f. 1945; 12,000 vols., 2,000 pamphlets and U.S. govt. documents; information on U.S. culture and society; collection on international relations, economics, social and political sciences, energy, environment and pollution; reference service; Librarian Mrs. MARY TSERONI.

Athens Academy Library: Odos Venizelou, Athens; 50,000 vols.

Benaki Library: Odos Anthimou Gazi, Athens; f. 1924; 45,000 vols. donated by Emmanuel Benakis.

British Council Library: P.O.B. 488, Athens; f. 1946; 25,679 vols., 200 periodicals; Librarian Miss J. A. CARPENTER, B.LIB.

British Council Library: 49 Proxenou Koromila St., Thessaloniki; f. 1960; 14,065 vols., 60 periodicals; Librarian Miss M. NOUSKALI.

Gennadius Library (*Rare book and research library attached to American School of Classical Studies*): Odos Souidias 61, Athens; f. 1926; 70,000 vols.; specialized library on Greece, the Near East, the Balkans, and travel accounts; Librarian SOPHIE PAPAGEORGIOU; publs. *Gennadeion Monographs I, II, III, and IV*; *Catalogues of Travels I and II*; *Catalogue of the Gennadius Library*, 7 vols., *First Supplement*; *The Griffon* (occasional).

Library of Chamber of Deputies: Paleà Anaktora, Athens; f. 1844; burnt 1859, rebuilt 1875; 1,500,000 vols.; Dir. SPYROS MOURELATOS; Librarian THOMAS PAPADOPOULOS.

Library of the National Polytechnic University of Athens: Odos 28 Octovriou 42, Athens; 120,000 vols.; Librarian MARIA SAVVA.

Library of the Technical Chamber of Greece: Odos Karageorgi Servias 4, Athens; f. 1926; approx. 17,000 vols. on mechanics, engineering and other technical subjects.

Library of the Three Hierarchs: Odos Demetriados-Ogl, Volos; f. 1907; 20,000 vols.; theological and literature library; Librarian ATHINA SOUSLIDOU.

Library of the University of Thessaloniki: Thessaloniki; f. 1927; 750,000 vols.; Dir. DIMITRIOS DIMITRIOU.

National Library: Odos Venizelou, Athens; f. 1828; 1,000,000 vols.; Hon. Gen. Dir. EVANGELOS PHOTIADES.

Pan Library ("Circle of the Friends of Progress"): Odos Giorgios 43, Tripolis, Arcadia; vols. on all subjects.

MUSEUMS AND ART GALLERIES

ATHENS

Acropolis Museum: f. 1878; contains the sculptures discovered on the Acropolis; illustrates the origins of Attic art, pedimental compositions, Korai and sculptures of the Parthenon, Temple of Niké, Erechtheion, etc.; Dir. G. DONTAS.

Benaki Museum: Odos Koumbari 1, Athens 138; f. 1931; collections of ancient Greek art with special emphasis on jewellery; Byzantine and post-Byzantine icons and ecclesiastical vestments, embroideries, metal objects, wood carvings and jewellery; Greek folk art and costumes; historic memorabilia 1821 (War of Independence) to present, memorabilia of politician E. Venizelos; 18th–19th-century paintings; Coptic and Islamic art; textiles and embroidery from Far East and Western Europe; neolithic to modern Chinese porcelain; library of 18,000 vols., 500 MSS., 2,000 water-colours, engravings, drawings; historical archives dept., photographic archives dept.; Dirs. NIKITA PARISSIS, ANGELOS DELIVORRIAS.

Byzantine Museum: Hotel de la Duchesse de Plaisance, Leoforos Vasilissis Sophias 22; f. 1914; contains a large collection of icons and sculptures, carvings in wood, ivory and bronze, religious embroidery, jewellery and enamels of the Byzantine era; also post-Byzantine work of art; Dir. P. LAZARIDIS.

Museum of Decorative Arts: Mosquée de Monastiraki; f. 1916; Dir. Mrs. ZORAS.

National Archaeological Museum: Odos Patission 44; f. 1874; contains rich collections of original Greek sculptures of all kinds and Roman copies of Greek originals; sculptures of the Roman period; Neolithic objects from Thessaly; Bronze Age relics from the mainland and the Aegean Islands; Mycenaean treasures; frescoes and pottery from Thera; rich collections of Greek vases and terracottas; collections of jewels and bronzes; (under preparation) Egyptian antiquities; Dir. GR. CONSTANTINOPOULOS; Curator of Sculpture Mrs. C. CRYSTALI-VOTSI; Curator of Vases Mrs. O. ALEXANDRI; Curator of Prehistoric Collection CHR. DOUMAS; Curator of Bronzes P. G. CALLIGAS.

National Picture Gallery and Alexander Soutzos Museum: 50 Vassileos Konstantinou Ave., Athens 516; f. 1900; 17th–20th-century Greek paintings, sculptures and prints; 14th–20th-century European paintings, including El Greco, Caravaggio, Jordaens, Poussin, Tiepolo, Delacroix, Mondrian, Picasso; engravings; drawings; library of 4,500 vols.; Dir. Dr. DIMITRIOS PAPASTAMOS.

Stoa of Attalos: f. as a museum in 1956; the design of the original building of the 2nd century B.C. has been exactly reproduced in the reconstruction carried out 1953–56 by the American School of Classical Studies; collections include all material found in the excavations of the Athenian Agora, illustrating 5,000 years of Athenian history; Dir. G. DONTAS.

Zoological Laboratory and Museum: Panepistimiopolis (Kouponia), Athens 621; f. 1858; research into developmental biology, regeneration, marine ecology and pollution; Dir. Prof. V. KIORTSIS; publ. *Biologia Gallo-Hellenica* (3–4 a year).

Provincial Museums

Archaeological Museum: Corinth; (postal address: American School of Classical Studies, 54 Souidias, Athens;) f. 1932; findings from excavations made by the American School; Dir. K. Krystallis-Votsi; publs. *Hesperia* (annually), *Corinth*.

Archaeological Museum: Heraklion, Crete; f. 1951; three sections; tourists, students, systematic storage of antiquities; traces the development of the Minoan and early Greek civilizations; branches at: Chania (Mycenaean, Greek and Roman antiquities from West Crete); Rethymnon (Mycenaean, Greek and Roman antiquities); St. Nikolaos (Minoan, Greek and Roman antiquities); Dir. Prof. Dr. J. A. Sakellarakis.

Archaeological Museum: Delphi; f. 1903; findings from the Delphic excavations; continuous excavation; restoration and conservation; library of 2,000 vols.; Dir. Dr. Petros Themelis.

Archaeological Museum: Olympia; contains largest single collection of Greek geometric and archaic bronzes in the world; two pediments from Temple of Zeus, Hermes of Praxiteles, Victory of Paionios; Dir. Alice Triantis; publs. on history and remains of Olympia.

Archaeological Museum: Rhodes; in the Hospital of the Knights; f. 1440; library of 14,000 vols.; Rhodes sculpture, vases and other objects from Ialysos and Kamiros dating from Geometric to late Classical times, stele and weapons dating from Middle Ages; Dir. Dr. Christos Doumas.

UNIVERSITIES

ATHINISIN ETHNIKON KAI KAPODISTRIAKON PANEPISTIMION
(National Capodistrian University of Athens)

ODOS PANEPISTIMIOU,
ATHENS 143

Telephone: 3620-003.

Founded 1837.

Rector: F. Mitsis.
Pro-Rector: G. Paraskevopoulos.
Vice-Rector: E. Theodorou.
Secretary-General: C. Satras.

Number of students: 48,800.

Deans:

Faculty of Theology: V. Dentakis.
Faculty of Law: P. Pavlopoylos.
Faculty of Letters: N. Livadaras.
Faculty of Medicine: K. Papadatos.
Faculty of Mathematics and Physics: A. Apostolakis.
Faculty of Dentistry: K. Kopsiaftis.

ARISTOTELION PANEPISTIMION THESSALONIKIS
(Aristotelian University of Thessaloniki)

UNIVERSITY CAMPUS,
THESSALONIKI

Telephone: 9911.

Founded 1925.

State control; Language of instruction: Greek; Academic year: September to August.

Rector: G. Ch. Stergiadis.
Pro-Rector: B. A. Petropoulos.
Vice-Rector: J. Ch. Hatziotis.
General Secretary: (vacant).
Librarian: D. Dimitriou.

Number of professors: 307.
Number of students: 29,500.
Publications: Catalogue, scientific annals and faculty periodicals.

Deans:

Faculty of Theology: A. G. Geromihalos.
Faculty of Philosophy: E. Th. Tsolakis.
Faculty of Science: D. Iannakoudakis.
Faculty of Law and Economics: K. D. Kerameus.
Faculty of Agriculture and Forestry: M.-E. Taznakakis.
Faculty of Medicine: N. Candreviotis.
Faculty of Veterinary Medicine: A. G. Spais.
Faculty of Technology: G. Tsagas.
Faculty of Dentistry: E. Stasinopoulos.

Professors:

Faculty of Theology:

Anastasiou, E. I., General Church History
Dhoikos, D., Old Testament
Fountoulis, I., Homilectics and Liturgy
Frangos, C., Catechetics and Encyclopedia of Theology
Galitis, G., History of the New Testament Period and New Testament Exegesis
Geromihalos, A. G., Ecclesiastical History of Greece
Kalogirou, J., History of Dogma and the Ecumenical Movement
Kalokyris, C., Christian and Byzantine Archaeology
Karavidopoulos, I., New Testament
Mantzaridis, G., Ethics and Christian Sociology
Matsoukas, N., Dogmatic and Symbolic Theology
Pseutongas, B., Ecclesiastic Literature
Rodopoulos, Most Rev. P., Canon Law and Pastoral Theology
Romanides, J. S., Dogmatic and Symbolic Theology
Simotas, P., Old Testament
Tachiaos, A.-A., History of the Slavic and Autocephalous Orthodox Churches
Tsamis, D., Patrology
Ziakas, G., History of Religion

Faculty of Philosophy:

Andronikos, E., Archaeology
Angelou, A., General and Comparative Literature of Modern Europe
Atsalos, V., Ancient Greek Literature
Avghelis, N., Philosophy
Bayonas, Av.-K., History of Philosophy
Bousoulas, N. I., Philosophy
Charitou-Fatourou, M.-M., General Psychology
Chassiotis, I., Medieval and Modern History
Chourmouziadis, N., Ancient Greek Literature
Conomis, N. C., Greek Language and Literature
Dhespinis, G., Archaeology
Grollios, C., Latin
Houssiadas, L., General Psychology
Hristou, H., History of Art
Karayannopulos, J., Byzantine History
Kyriadou-Nestoros, A., Folklore
Lipourlis, D., Ancient Greek
Manoussacas, M. I., Medieval and Modern History
Maronitis, D., Ancient Greek Literature
Megas, A., Latin
Michaelides-Nouaros, A., Education
Moullas, P., Modern Greek Literature
Pandermalis, D., Archaeology
Papoulia, W., History of the Countries of the Aemos Peninsula
Patrinelis, Ch., History of Modern Greece
Petrochilos, N., Latin
Sahinis, A., Modern Greek Literature
Savvides, G., Modern Greek Literature
Setatos, M., Glossology
Sifakis, G. M., Ancient Greek Literature
Tsantsanoghlou, K., Ancient Greek Literature
Tsolakis, E. Th., Medieval Greek Literature
Valala-Pentzopoulou, A.-T., Philosophy
Wokotopoulos, P., Byzantine Archaeology
Xochellis, P., Pedagogics

Institute of Foreign Languages and Literature:

Aitken, T., English Language and Literature
Eustathiadis, E., English Language and Literature
Malaxou-Samara, Z., French Language and Literature
Saunier, G., French Language and Literature

Faculty of Science:

Alexandrou, N. K., Organic Chemistry
Beis, I., Animal Physiology
Bozis, G., Theoretical Mechanics
Charalambous, S., Nuclear Physics
Eliopoulos, H. A., Mathematics
Georganopoulos, G., Mathematics
Georgatsos, I., Biochemistry
Georgeakopoulos, P., Pharmaceutical Technology

GRYPEOS, M., Theoretical Physics
HADJIDEMETRIOU, J. D., Theoretical Mechanics
IANNAKOUDAKIS, D., Physical Chemistry
IKONOMOU-PETROVICH, N., Pharmaceutics and Pharmaceutical Technology
KARYMBAKAS, K., Electronic Physics
KASTRITSIS, C. D., General Biology
KATTOULAS, M., Zoology
KOUKOLI, E., Botany
KOUNIAS, E., Mathematics
KOUROUNAKIS, P., Pharmaceutical Chemistry and Pharmacognosy
LAKKIS, C., Mathematics
LAVRENTIADES, G., Plant Taxonomy and Plant Geography
MANOUSSAKIS, G. E., Inorganic Chemistry
MARGARIS, N., Ecology
MELENTIS, J. K., Geology and Palaeontology
OECONOMIDIS, N., Mathematics
OECONOMOU, N., Physics
PAPADHAKIS, A.-GH., Mineralogy and Petrology
PAPADIMITRAKI-CHLICHLIA, HELENA, Physics
PAPAZACHOS, B., Geophysics
PERSIDHIS, S., Astronomy
PHOKAS, G. K., Pharmaceutical Chemistry and Pharmacognosy
RENTZEPERIS, P., Applied Physics
SAPOUNTZIS, E., Systematic Mineralogy and Petrology
SIPITANOS, K., General and Inorganic Chemical Technology
SOLDATOS, K., Mineralogy and Petrology
SOTIRIADIS, L., Physical Geography
SPYRIDELIS, I., Physics
STALIDHIS, G., Physical Chemistry
STEPHANIDIS, N. K., Mathematics
STOEMENOS, I., Physics
TSATSARONIS, G. C., Organic Chemical Technology and Food Chemistry
TSEKOS, I., Botany
VARVOGLIS, A., Organic Chemistry
VASILIKIOTIS, G. S., Analytical Chemistry

Faculty of Law and Economics:
ARGYRIADIS, A., Commercial Law
BENDERMACHER-GEROUSSIS, E., Private International Law
CONSTANTOPOULOS, D. S., Public International Law
DELIYANNIS, J., Civil Law
EVRIGENIS, D. J., Private International Law
FILIPPIDIS, T., Criminal Law
GEORGIADIS, A., Civil Law
KERAMEUS, K. D., Civil Procedure
KIANTOU-PAMPOUKI, A. L., Commercial Law
KOTSIRIS, Commercial Law
KOUKIADIS, I., Labour Law
MANESSIS, A., Constitutional Law
MANOLEDAKIS, I., Criminal Law
MARMATAKIS, N., Political Economy
METALLINOS, S., Comparative Law
PAMPOUKIS, K., Commercial Law
PAPANIKOLAIDIS, D., Administrative Law
PAPANTONIOU, N. S., Civil Law
PAPAPOLITIS, N., Commercial Law
RAFTIS, T., Political Economy
THEOCHAROPOULOS, L., Public Finance and Fiscal Law
TSAKLANGANOS, A., Business Administration
TSATSOS, D., General Public Law
VAVOUSKOS, C., Civil (Property) Law
VOUYOUCAS, C., Criminal Procedure
YANNIOTIS, A., Applied Economics

Faculty of Agriculture and Forestry:
ARVANITIS, I., Forest Management and Biometry
ASTERIS, K., Forest Biometrics
ATHANASSIADIS, N., Forest Botany
DAFIS, S. P., Silviculture
FASOULAS, A. C., Genetics and Plant Breeding
GAVRILIDES, S., Farm Machinery
GERAKIS, P.-A., Ecology
KAILIDES, D., Forest Protection
KALOVOULOS, J. M., Applied Soil Science
KANDARTZIS, N., Horticulture and Pomology
KITSOPANIDIS, G. J., Agricultural Economics Research
KOTOULAS, D., Mountain Water Management and Control
LIACOS, L. G., Range Management
LIAKOPOULOS, A., General and Agriculture Hydraulics and Reclamation
MAKRIS, K. J., Forest Policy and Economics
MANOLKIDES, K., Dairy Technology
MATSOUKAS, I., Animal Husbandry
MOURKIDES, G. A., Agricultural Chemistry
PANERAS, E. D., Agricultural and Food Technology
PANETSOS, C., Forest Genetics and Forest Tree Breeding
PAPAMICHOS, N., Forest Soils
POLYZOPOULOS, N., Soil Science
PORLINGIS, I. C., Plant Biology
PSARROS, E., Phytopathology
RAPTOPOULOS, T., Horticulture and Pomology
SFIKAS, A., Agronomy
SKIPITARIS, CH. N., Physiology of Nutrition and Applied Animal Nutrition
STERGIADIS, G. CH., Mechanical Sciences and Topography
TERZIDIS, G., General and Agricultural Hydraulics and Reclamation
TSOUMIS, G., Forest Utilization and Technology
TZANAKAKIS, M. E., Applied Zoology and Parasitology
VLACHOS, M., Viticulture
ZACHOS, D. G., Plant Pathology
ZERVAS, N. P., Animal Husbandry

Faculty of Medicine:
ALETRAS, H. A., Propaedeutic Surgical Department
APOSTOLAKIS, M., Experimental Physiology
AREALIS, E., Surgery
CANDREVIOTIS, N., Anatomy
CASSIMOS, CH., Paediatric Clinic
CHRISTOFORIDIS, A. J., Radiology
CONCOURIS, L., Medical Clinic
DIACOYIANNIS, A., Neurology and Psychiatry
DOZI-VASSILIADOU, I., General Biology
EDIPIDIS, TH., Hygiene
FOROGLOU, G., Neurosurgery
GHOULIS, G., Pathological Clinic
GRANITSAS, A. N., General Biology
HATZICRISTOU, G., Urology
IERODIAKONOU, CH., Psychiatry
KANITAKIS, C., Skin and Venereal Diseases
KARPOUSAS, I., Paediatrics
KERAMEOS-FOROGLOU, CH., Histology and Embryology
LAZARIDES, D. P., Surgery
LOGOTHETIS, J., Neurology and Psychiatry
MANDALENAKIS, S., Obstetrics and Gynaecology
MADENA-PIRGAKI, K., Physiology
MANOLIDIS, L., Ear, Nose and Throat Clinic
MARKANTONATOS, A., Paediatric Surgery and Orthopaedics
MARSELOS, A.-A., Surgery
METAXAS, P., Propaedeutic Clinic of Internal Medicine
PANAYIOTOPOULOS, S., Pathology
PAPALOUCAS, A., Obstetric and Gynaecological Clinic
PAPANICOLAOU, N., Obstetrics and Gynaecology
PAPAPANAGIOTOU, J., Microbiology
PAPAZOGLOU, O., Surgery
PARADHELIS, A., Experimental Pharmacology
PETROPOULOS, B. A., Paediatric Surgery and Orthopaedics
POLYZONIS, V.,-M. Anatomy
PROUKAKIS, C., Medical Physics
ROUTSONIS, K., Neurology
SFOUNGARIS, K., Surgery
SKLAVOUNOY-TSOUROUKTSOGLOU, S., Paediatrics
STAVROPOULOS, C., Tuberculosis and Chest Diseases
TAVRIDIS, G., Neuro-Surgery
THEODOSSIOU, A., Legal Medicine and Toxicology
TOURKANTONIS, A., Pathological Clinic
TRAKATELLIS, A., Biochemistry
TSOURAS, S., Histology and Embryology
TSOUROUKTSOGLOU, W., Medical Propaedeutics

Faculty of Veterinary Medicine:
ELEZOGLOU, V., Physiology and Pharmacology
GEORGAKIS, S., Food Hygiene
HIMONAS, C. A., Applied Helminthology and Entomology
KARAMANLIDIS, A.-N., Anatomy and Histology
KATSAOUNIS, N., Animal Husbandry
LEONTIDIS, S., Pathology
MICHAIL, SOT., Anatomy and Histology
PANETSOS, AC. G., Food Hygiene
PAPADOPOULOS, PH., Surgery
PNEUMATIKATOS, G., Ichthyology
SPAIS, A. G., Medicine
TSAKALOF, P., Bovine and Swine Clinical Pathology
TSIROYANNIS, E., Pathology
VASSILOPOULOS, VASSILIOS, Nutrition

Faculty of Technology:
ALEXIADES, C., Analytical Chemistry
ANAGNOSTOPOULOS, AV., Inorganic Chemistry
ARGYROPOULOS, TH., Town Planning
BADELAS, A., Geodetics
BEKIAROGLOU, P., Physical Chemistry
DAPONTE, I., Construction and Building Materials
DEMIRIS, K., Engineering Geology
DOKOPOULOS, P., Electrical Power Systems
EFTHIMIATOS, D., General Electrotechnics
FATOUROS, A., Design and Industrial Aesthetics
FLYTJANIS, E., Mathematics
FRANGAKIS, C. N., Mathematics
GANOULIS, G., Hydraulics
GREKOUSIS, R.-G., Machine Elements
KARABELAS, A., Technology of Chemical Installations
KOMIS, D., Hydraulics
KOURIS, S., Telecommunications
KRIEZIS, E., Theoretical Electrotechnics
LAGOPOULOS, A.-PH., Town Planning
LAVVAS, G., History of Architecture
LAZARIDES, P., Architecture
LIANIS, G., Applied Mechanics
MAVRIDIS, L. N., Geodetic Astronomy
MITTAS, I., Mathematics
MOUTSOPOULOS, N. K., Architectural Morphology and Rhythmology
NICHAS, S., Chemical Engineering
NITSIOTAS, G., Structural Analysis

PANAGIOTOPOULOS, N., Construction Equipment
PANAGIOTOPOULOS, P., Iron Construction
PAPADOPOULOS, M., Construction and Building Materials
PARTHENIADES, E., Hydraulic Construction
PATTAS, K., Applied Thermodynamics
PENELIS, G., Reinforced Concrete
PETROPAKIS, H., Technology of Agricultural and Food Industries
PETROPOULOS, P. G., Production Technology
PSOÏNOS, D., Production and Business Administration
SAGREDOS, A. N., Organic Chemistry
SAHINIS, N., Visual Arts
SOTIROPOULOS, G., Construction of Processing Equipment
SPYROPOULOS, P., Reinforced Concrete
TJAVARAS, A., Metallurgy
TRIANTAFILLIDIS, J. D., Architectural Design
TSAGAS, G., Mathematics
TZIMOPOULOS, CH., Agricultural Hydraulics
TZONOS, P. P., Architectural Design
VALALAS, D., Soil Mechanics and Foundations
VLACHOS, D., Topography
YIANNOPOULOS, G., Transportation Engineering and Planning

Faculty of Dentistry:
AZARIA, H., Removable Dentures
HARALAMBAKIS, B., Orthodontics
HATZIFOTIADIS, D., Minor Oral Surgery and X-Ray Diagnosis
HATZIOTIS, J. CH., Stomatology
KALOYIANNIDIS, A., Removable Dentures
KARAKASSIS, D., Oral Surgery
LAMBROU, D. B., Preventive Dentistry and Periodontics
MARTIS, CH., Oral Surgery
PAPANAYIOTOU, P., Stomatology
PISSIOTIS, L., Operative Dentistry
STAMOULIS, S., Prosthetics
STASINOPOULOS, E., Pathology and Therapeutics
THEODOROU, T., Prosthetics

ATTACHED INSTITUTES:

University Experimental School: Platonos and Filippou St., Thessaloniki.

Centre for Byzantine Research: 30 Navarinou St., Thessaloniki.

Institute for Modern Greek Studies: University Central Building, Thessaloniki.

University Experimental Farm: Gheorghikis Scholis St., Thessaloniki.

University Forests: Building of the Faculty of Agriculture and Forestry, University Campus, Thessaloniki.

DIMOKRITEION PANEPISTIMION THRAKIS

(University of Thrace)

KOMOTINI

Telephone: 0531/26111.

Founded 1973.

Rector: Prof. Dr. L. N. MAVRIDIS.
Administrative Officer: CH. EVGENIDIS.
Librarian: O. PAPOUTSI.

Library of 10,000 vols.

Number of teachers: 89.
Number of students: 650.

DEANS:

Faculty of Law: Prof. Dr. C. VAVOUSCOS.
Faculty of Engineering: Prof. Dr. L. N. MAVRIDIS.

ETHNIKON METSOVION POLYTECHNEION

(National Technical University of Athens)

ODOS 28 OCTOVRIOU 42, ATHENS

Telephone: 3616922.

Founded 1836.

Rector: P. THEOCHARIS.
Vice-Rector: G. PARISAKIS.
General Secretary: A. PAPAPANAYOTOU.
Librarian: A. NIKOYANNI.

The library contains 150,000 vols.

Number of teachers: 450, including 94 professors.

Number of students: 5,200.

Faculties of Civil, Mechanical, Electrical, Chemical, Mining and Metallurgical Engineering, Architecture, Surveying, Naval Architecture and Marine Engineering.

ORDINARY PROFESSORS:

ABACOUMKIN, G., Railways and Transport
ALEXANDRIDIS, N., Digital Systems and Computers
ANASTASSAKIS, E., Physics
ANGELOPOULOS, M., Nuclear Engineering
ANTONIOU, A., Ship Design and Construction
ARAVANTINOS, A., City Planning
ARGYRAKOS, J., General Astronomy
ARMENAKAS, A., Theory of Structures
ATHANASSIADIS, N., Fluid Mechanics and Turbo-machines
AUGOUSTIDIS, S., Mineralogy, Petrology, Geology
BACOPOULOS, A., Numerical Analysis
BADEKAS, I., Photogrammetry
BALODIMOS, D., General Geodesy
BOUDOURIS, G., Physics
BOURAS, CH., History of Architecture
CANIARIS, VL., Drawing and Painting
CARYDIS, P., Earthquake Engineering
CHAINIS, I., Mathematics
CHALKIAS, CH., Electronics
CHRISTOULAS, G., Sanitary Engineering
CORONEOS, N., Highway Engineering
DASKALOPOULOS, D., Mathematics
DERGALIN, I., Regional Planning and Housing Development
DIAMESIS, I., Electrical Engineering
ECONOMOPOULOS, J., Mining
EPHRAIMIDIS, CH., Mechanical Engineering
FIKIORIS, J., Wireless and Long Distance Communications
FILIPPAS, T., Physics
FRANGISKOS, A., Mineral Processing
GALANIS, E., Higher Mathematics
GROSS, G., Structural Mechanics
KAGARAKIS, C., Science and Technology of Electrical Materials
KAMPOURIS, E., Special Chemical Technology
KORONEOS, E., Materials of Construction
KOUMOUTSOS, N., Mechanical Engineering for Chemical Engineers
KOUREMENOS, D., Thermodynamics Refrigeration
KOUTSOPOULOS, K., Geography
KRIKELIS, N., Automatic Control Systems
KYRIAKOPOULOS, G., Fuels and Lubricants Technology
LADOPOULOS, P., Descriptive and Projective Geometry
LIAPIS, J., Interior Architecture
LOÏZOS, A., Foundation Engineering—Arched and Timber Bridges
LOUKAKIS, T., Ship Theory
MARANGOZIS, J., Chemical Process Engineering
MARKETOS, E., Structural Mechanics and Fundamentals of Technical Works
MOURIKI, D., General History of Art
MYLONAS, C., Mechanics
NIANIAS, D., Philosophy
NICOLAOU, S., Hydro-electric Engineering—Hydraulic Structures, Dams
NIKOLOPOULOS, P., High-Voltage Engineering and Measurement Techniques
NOUTSOPOULOS, G., Theoretical and Applied Hydraulics
PANTELIDIS, G., Mathematics
PAPADANIEL, E., Mechanical Engineering Workshop
PAPADIAS, B., Electric Energy Systems
PAPAGEORGAKIS, J., Mineral Deposits and Applied Geology
PAPAGEORGIOU, A., Rural Architecture and Building Design
PAPAGEORGIOU, N., Steam Generators and Thermal Plants
PAPAILIOU, K., Thermal Turbomachines
PAPPAS, I., Industrial Management
PARISAKIS, G., Inorganic and Analytical Chemistry
PROTONOTARIOS, E., Basic Electrical Engineering
ROGAN, A., Harbour Works
SAKELLARIDIS, P., General Chemistry
SANDRIS, C., Organic Chemistry
SARAVACOS, G., Physical Process Engineering
SERAFIM, P., Electrical Engineering
SINOS, ST., Morphology and Aesthetics of Architecture
SKOULIKIDIS, TH., Physical Chemistry and Applied Electrochemistry
STEFANOPOULOS, G., Technical Economic Studies of Chemical Industry
TASSIOS, T., Reinforced Concrete Structures
TEGOPOULOS, J., Electrical Machines
THEOCARIS, P., Mechanics
THEOPHANOPOULOS, N., Machine Design
THOMOPOULOS, CH., Agricultural and Food Industries
TIKTOPOULOS, G., Theoretical Physics
TSOUTRELIS, C., Mining Engineering
VALKANAS, G., Organic Chemical Technology
VEIS, G., Higher Geodesy and Cartography
YANNOPOULOS, J., Non-Ferrous Metallurgy
XANTHOPOULOS, T., Hydrology and Hydraulics Works
XEROCOSTAS, D., Operational Research
ZACHOS, K., Mining Engineering
ZANNOS, A., Building Construction
ZIVAS, D., Architectural Design

UNIVERSITY OF IOANNINA

IOANNINA

Telephone: 25915.

Founded 1964 as a section of the Aristotelion Panepistimion Thessalonikis; established as an independent university 1970.

State control; Language of instruction: Greek; Duration of academic year: October to June.

Rector: Prof. S. Papadopoulos.

Pro-Rector: Prof. G. Tzivanides.

Vice-Rector: Prof. C. Polydoropoulos.

The library contains over 139,000 vols.

Number of teachers: 96.

Number of students: 2,905.

Publications: *Epetiris* (Annual Prospectus), *Dodoni* (annual) and technical reports.

DEANS:

Faculty of Philosophy: Prof. M. Meraklis.

Faculty of Physics and Mathematics: Prof. D. Metaxas.

Faculty of Medicine: Prof. G. Kallistratos.

PROFESSORS:

Faculty of Philosophy:

Dakaris, S., Classical Archaeology
Dedoussi, C., Classics
Frangos, C., Education
Kakoulidou-Panou, H., Modern Greek Literature
Kakridis, T., Classics
Kambitsis, I., Classics
Marangou, E., Classical Archaeology
Meraklis, M., Folklore
Nystazopoulou-Pelekidou, M., History of the people of the Balkan peninsula
Panagiotakis, N., Medieval Greek Literature
Paraskevopoulos, I., Child Development
Papadopoulos, S., Modern History
Papathomopoulos, E., Classics
Stergiopoulos, C., Modern Greek Literature
Thavoris, A., Linguistics
Tsirpanlis, Z., Medieval and Modern History
Veikos, T., History of Philosophy

Faculty of Physics and Mathematics:

Alexandropoulos, N., Physics
Andritsopoulos, G., Physics
Assimakopoulos, P., Physics
Banos, G., Astronomy
Bozonis, P.-D., Geometry
Gangas, N., Physics
Gounaris, G., Theoretical Physics
Hatzidemos, A., Numerical Analysis
Katsaras, A., Mathematical Analysis
Kosmatos, A., Organic Chemistry
Koutroufiotis, D., Mathematical Analysis
Metaxas, D., Meteorology
Miliotis, D., Applied Physics
Papageorgopoulos, C., Physics
Papaioannou, P., Mathematics
Polidoropoulos, C., Physical Chemistry
Sdoukos, A., Industrial Chemistry
Smyrnelis, E., Mathematical Analysis
Sphikas, I., Mathematics
Staikos, V., Mathematical Analysis
Tsangaris, I., General Chemistry
Tzivanidis, G., Mechanics
Vergados, I., Theoretical Physics
Voudouris, E., Food Chemistry

Faculty of Medicine:

Kallistratos, G., Physiology
Kotoulas, O., Anatomy
Pagoulatos, G., General Biology
Tsolas, O., Biochemistry

UNIVERSITY OF PATRAS

PATRAS

Telephone: (061) 991-822.

Founded 1964.

State control; Language of instruction: Greek; Academic year: October to June.

Rector: Prof. A. Theodossiou.

Pro-Rector: Prof. G. Galanos.

Vice-Rector: Prof. A. Grammaticos.

Administrative Officer: S. Papathanassopoulos.

Number of teachers: 80.

Number of students: *c.* 5,300.

Publication: *Bulletin* (annually).

DEANS:

Faculty of Natural Sciences: Prof. D. Fitros.

Faculty of Engineering: Prof. J. Nicolis.

Faculty of Medicine: Prof. Ch. Koutsogeorgopoulos.

PROFESSORS:

Faculty of Natural Sciences:

Actipis, S., Biochemistry
Artemiadis, N., Mathematics
Balcana, T., Human and Animal Physiology
Barbanis, B., Astronomy
Christodoulou, C., Biology
Christodoulou, G., Palaeontology and Historical Geology
Deligiannis, T., Electronics
Demotakis, P., Radiochemistry
Dokas, L., Mathematics
Fitos, D., Botany
Galinos, A., Inorganic Chemistry
Gavalos, N., Plant Physiology
Giannoussis, S., Theoretical Physics
Georgatsos, J., Biochemistry
Goudas, C., Mechanics
Ilias, D., Physics of Atmosphere
Katsanos, N., Physical Chemistry
Katsoulakos, P., Pharmaceutical Chemistry
Mitakides, G., Set Theory and Logic
Ontrias, J., Zoology
Panagos, A., Geology
Pelekanos, M., Genetics
Rigopoulos, R., Physics
Roilos, M., Physics
Roussas, G., Applied Mathematics
Theodoropoulos, D., Organic Chemistry
Theodossiou, A., Physics
Tsolis, A., Chemical Technology
Zoumpos, A., Philosophy

Faculty of Engineering

Demarogonas, A., Machine Design
Dodos, A., Organic Chemical Technology
Drakatos, P., Mechanical Engineering
Galanos, G., Power Systems
Grammaticos, A., General Electronics
Iconomou, A., Structural Analysis, Earthquake Engineering
Kermanides, T., Material Science and Strength of Materials
Kokkinakis, G., Wire Telecommunication
Kontaratos, A., Industrial Management
Kouskoulas, B., Engineering Economics and Project Management
Lainiotis, D., Pattern Recognition
Lazaris, E., Construction Equipment
Lefas, C., Mechanical Engineering
Makios, B., Theoretical Electrotechnology
Mavromatis, A., Machine Design and Theory
Nikolis, J., Wireless Telecommunication
Papadopoulos, G., Applied Electronics
Papailiou, D., Technical Mechanics and Application
Papamantelos, D., Metal Science
Papanikas, D., Fluid Mechanics and Application
Safakas, A., Electronical Energy Conversion
Syros, C., Nuclear Technology
Theodoridis, G., Theoretical Electronics
Tzannes, N., Information Theory

Faculty of Medicine:

Androulakis, J., Surgery
Beratis, N., Paediatrics
Bonicos, D., Pathology
Demopoulos, J., Radiology
Kondakis, G., Public Health
Koutsogergopoulos, C., Biological Chemistry
Maniatis, G., General Biology
Vagenakis, A., Internal Medicine

COLLEGES OF UNIVERSITY STANDING

American School of Classical Studies at Athens: Odos Souidias 54, Athens; f. 1881; research institute and postgraduate school for students of classical literature and history and classical archaeology; controlled by a committee representing 113 American and Canadian universities; library of 43,000 vols.; Dir. H. Immerwahr; publ. *Hesperia.*

Anotati Geoponiki Scholi Athinon (*College of Agriculture*): Votanikos, Athens; f. 1920.

Rector: C. Niavis.

Secretary-General: K. Tsakoumakis.

Anotati Scholi Economikon Kai Emborikon Epistimon (*The Athens Graduate School of Economics and Business Science*): Odos Patission 76, Athens 104; f. 1920; 28 teachers, 7,000 students; Rector Prof. J. Chryssokeris.

Anotati Scholi Kalon Technon (*Higher School of Fine Arts*): 42 Odos Patission, Athens; Tel. 616930; f. 1836; comprises a preparatory section for drawing and sections for painting, sculpture, engraving and applied arts; 10 teachers, *c.* 300 students; library of 10,706 vols.; Dir. G. Mavroidis.

Anotati Biomichaniki Scholi Pireos (*Graduate School of Industrial*

Studies): 40 Karaoli and Dimitriou St., Piraeus; f. 1938, since 1958 has university status; 4-year degree courses in economics, business administration, statistics; a Ph.D. degree can also be awarded following the submission of a suitable thesis.

Rector: Prof. E. GEORGANDOPOULOS.

Vice-Rector: Prof. S. SARANTIDIS.

Secretary-General: E. PARASKEVAÏDIS.

Number of teachers: 85.

Number of students: 6,000.

Library of 10,000 vols., 200 periodicals.

Publication: *Spoudai*† (quarterly).

Anotati Viomichaniki Scholi Thessalonikis (*Graduate School of Industrial Studies at Thessaloniki*): 3 Agias Sophias St., Thessaloniki; f. 1958; economic and industrial studies; 15 professors, 6,600 students; Rector Prof. J. LIAKIS; Sec.-Gen. A. NIKIFOROU-KAMPOURI.

Panteios School of Political Sciences: Leoforos A. Syngrou 136, Athens 404; f. 1930.

Rector: A. YOTOPOULOS-MARANGOPOULOS.

Vice-Rector: D. KARAYORGAS.

Sec.-Gen. V. KOUGEA.

Number of students: 8,500.

Deree College: American College of Greece, Aghia Paraskevi, Attiki; f. 1875; American-sponsored co-educational, independent undergraduate college with divisions of Arts and Sciences, Business Administration, Secretarial Studies; evening courses; 100 teachers, 1,900 students; library of 32,000 vols.; Pres. JOHN S. BAILEY; publ. *Bulletin* (2 a year).

COLLEGES

ARCHAEOLOGY, GREEK STUDIES

British School at Athens: Odos Souedias 52, Athens 140, and 31-34 Gordon Square, London, WC1H 0PY; f. 1886; library of over 30,000 vols. (ancient, medieval and post-medieval Greek studies and archaeological research) including the Finlay Library (Greek travel and modern Greek literature, etc.); Chair. Prof. P. M. WARREN; Dir. H. W. CATLING; London Sec. Mrs. S. BICKNELL; publs. *British School Annual*, *Archaeological Reports*.

Deutsches Archäologisches Institut, Abteilung Athen (*German Archaeological Institute*): Odos Fidiou 1, Athens 142; f. 1874; library of 60,000 vols.; Dirs. Prof. Dr. H. KYRIELEIS, Prof. Dr. K. KILIAN; publ. *Athenische Mitteilungen* (annual), *Beihefte*†.

Ecole Française d'Athènes (*French Archaeological School*): Odos Didotou 6; f. 1846; excavations, historical and archaeological publications; library of approx. 50,000 vols; Dir. P. AMANDRY; Sec.-Gen. P. AUPERT; 15 mems. and architects; publs. *Bulletin de correspondance hellénique* (annual; f. 1877), *Bibliothèque des Ecoles françaises d'Athènes et de Rome, Fouilles de Delphes, Exploration archéologique de Délos, Etudes thasiennes, Etudes crétoises, Travaux et mémoires, Etudes péloponnésiennes, Etudes chypriotes*.

Italian School of Archaeology: 14 Parthenonos, Athens; f. 1909; postgraduate studies in classical archaeology, epigraphy and antiquities, ancient architecture, research and excavations; library of 19,403 vols.; Dir. Prof. ANTONINO DI VITA; publ. *Annuario della Scuola Archeologica di Atene e delle Missioni Italiane in Oriente* (annual), monographs.

Svenska Institutet i Athen (*Swedish Institute*): 9 Mitseon St., Athens 402; f. 1946; 15 mems.; library of 15,000 vols.; research into Greek antiquity and archaeology, and cultural exchange between Sweden and Greece; Dir. Dr. ROBIN HÄGG; publs. *Skrifter utgivna av Svenska Institutet i Athen* (*Acta Instituti Atheniensis Regni Sueciae*)†, including *Opuscula Atheniensia*.

ARTS, DRAMA, MUSIC

Dramatiki Scholi (*Drama School*): National Theatre, Odos Menandrou 65; f. 1924; open to actors who desire to improve their art and to young people who desire to take up the stage as a career. The staff comprises the Director, 11 professors, and 2 teachers.

Kratikon Odeion Thessaloniki (*State Conservatory of Music*): Odos Olympiou Diamanti 7, Thessaloniki; f. 1915; instrumental, vocal and theoretical studies; library of *c.* 6,000 vols. including collection in Braille; 35 teachers, 850 students; Dir. Dr. DIMITRIOS THEMELIS.

Odeion Athenon (*Odeon of Athens*): Odos Rigillis and Vassileos Georgiou 17/19; f. 1871; comprises a music section, a drama section, a section for military music, and a section for Byzantine Church music; 53 professors, 40 teachers, and 1,000 students; Dir. M. G. PALLANDIOS.

Odeion Ethnikon: Odos Maizonos 8, Athens 108; f. 1926; sections for music, opera, dance and drama; Dirs. KRINO KALOMIRI and LEONIDAS ZORAS.

GUATEMALA

Population 6,835,000

ACADEMIES

Guatemala City

Academia Guatemalteca de la Lengua (*Guatemala Academy of Languages*): 12 Calle 6-40, Zona 9, Edificio Plazuela; 8th in order of foundation in Spanish America; is a correspondent of the Real Academia Española, Madrid.
Director: LUIS BELTRANENA SINIBALDI.
Secretary-General: Prof. DANIEL ARMAS.
Librarian: PEDRO PÉREZ VALENZUELA.
Publication *Boletín de la Academia Guatemalteca.*

Academia de Ciencias Médicas, Físicas y Naturales de Guatemala (*Academy of Medical, Physical and Natural Sciences*): 13 Calle 1-25, Zona 1, Aptdo. Postal 569; f. 1945; 69 mems.; library of *c.* 4,000 vols.; Pres. Dr. CARLOS COSSICH M.; Sec. Lic. RUBÉN MAYORGA; publs. *Annals* (irregular), monographs, research summaries.

LEARNED SOCIETIES AND RESEARCH INSTITUTES

(*See* also under Universities)

Guatemala City

Asociación Guatemalteca de Historia Natural (AGHN): Jardín Botánico, Universidad de San Carlos, Mariscal Cruz 1-56, Zona 10; f. 1960; 86 mems.; Pres. Dr. MARIO DARY RIVERA.

Asociación de Ortodoncistas de Guatemala: 13 Calle 3-43, Zona 10; f. 1946; Pres. Dr. MAX BURAK.

Asociación Pediátrica de Guatemala: 12 Avda. 12-72, Zona 1; f. 1945; Pres. Dr. MARIO CASTEJÓN; publ. *Guatemala Pediátrica.*

Colegio de Ingenieros de Guatemala: 7A Avda. 39-60, Zona 8; f. 1947; 1,342 mems.; Pres. Ing. MANUEL DE J. CASTELLANOS DUBÓN; publ. *Ingeniería.*

Instituto de Antropología e Historia: Edificio 6, 'La Aurora', Zona 13; f. 1946; library of 10,000 vols.; research on Middle-American archaeology, ethnology, philology, and Spanish Colonial history; supervises archaeological sites, monuments, Indian villages and museums; Dir. FRANCIS POLO SIFONTES; publs. *Antropología e Historia de Guatemala* (annually), occasional bulletins, books and special publs.

Instituto de Nutrición de Centro América y Panamá—INCAP (*Institute of Nutrition of Central America and Panama*): Carretera Roosevelt, Zona 11, Guatemala City; f. 1949; represents the following countries: Costa Rica, El Salvador, Guatemala, Honduras, Nicaragua, Panama; administered by Pan American Health Organisation (PAHO)/World Health Organisation (WHO); Divisions of Education, Applied Nutrition (School of Nutrition and 5 postgraduate courses in Nutrition and allied fields), Agricultural and Food Sciences, Biology and Human Nutrition, Statistics, Human Development; library of *c.* 70,000 vols.; Dir. CARLOS TEJADA V., M.D.; publs. scientific articles, monthly nutrition education leaflets, quarterly information bulletin, periodic compilations of scientific publications for member governments, annual reports, monographs, various other documents.

Instituto Centroamericano de Investigación y Tecnología Industrial (ICAITI) (*Central American Research Institute for Industry*): P.O.B. 1552, Avda. La Reforma 4-47, Zona 10; f. 1956; research on marketing, development of new industries and manufacturing techniques, establishment of Central American standards, information services to industry, and professional advice; library of 20,000 vols.; Dir. Lic. FRANCISCO AGUIRRE.

Instituto Geográfico Nacional: Avda. Las Américas 5-76, Zona 13; f. 1964; 411 mems.; Dir. Col. RENÉ AGUILUZ MORALES.

Instituto Guatemalteco-Americano (IGA): Apdo. Postal 691, Ruta 1, 4-05, Zona 4; cultural centre with classes in English and Spanish, and bilingual secretarial course; library of 15,000 vols., Dir. J. D. PARKER.

Instituto Indigenista Nacional (*National Institute of Indian Affairs*) (*Ministerio de Educación Pública*): 6a Avenida 1-22, Zona 1; f. 1945; library of 3,500 vols.; social research undertaken for the advice of the Government in economic conditions and the education of the Indians; affiliated to the Inter-American Indian Institute, Mexico; Dir. EPAMINONDAS QUINTANA; publs. *Guatemala Indígena* (quarterly), and special works.

Instituto Nacional de Energía Nuclear: 3 Avda. 'A' 2-68, Zona 1, Apdo. Postal 1421; Dir. Ing. N. CARAZO ORELLANA.

Instituto Nacional de Sismología, Vulcanología, Meteorología e Hidrología (*National Institute of Seismology, Vulcanology, Meteorology and Hydrology*): f. 1976; Dir. CLAUDIO URRUTIA EVANS; publs. *Anuario Hidrológico* (annually), *Boletín Meteorológico* (monthly), *Boletín Sismológico* (daily), *Reporte Meteorológico* (daily).

Academia de Geografía e Historia de Guatemala (*Geographical and Historical Academy of Guatemala*): 3A Av. 8-35, Zona 1; f. 1923; 275 mems.; library of 30,000 vols.; Pres. Lic. ERNESTO VITERI BERTRAND; publs. *Anales* (annually), *Biblioteca Goathemala*, *Viajeros*, *Publicaciones Especiales.*

Sociedad Pro-Arte Musical (*Musical Society*): 12 Calle 2-09, Zona 3, Apdo. 980; f. 1945; 200 mems.; Pres. LULÚ C. DE HERRARTE; Exec. Sec. DORA G. DE MENDIZÁBAL.

Quezaltenango

Academia de la Lengua Maya Quiché (*Academy of the Maya-Quiché Languages and Culture*): 7a, Calle 11-27, Zona 1; f. 1959; to study the philologies of and preserve the most important indigenous languages, especially the Quiché; 20 mems.; Pres. Prof. ADRIÁN INES CHÁVEZ; Sec. Prof. VÍCTOR SALVADOR DE LEÓN TOLEDO; publ. *El Idioma Quiché y su Grafía.*

Casa de la Cultura de Occidente: 7a Calle 11-35, Zona 1; f. 1958; comprises: a Bibliographical Department, controlling 3 libraries; a Museums Department (natural history, archaeology, local history); an Art Department; an auditorium and exhibition hall; also directs *Escuela Regional de Artes Plasticas* (*q.v.*); Exec. Dir. JULIO CÉSAR ALVAREZ; Pres. GERARDO MUÑOZ MÉNDEZ; publs. *Juegos Florales Centroamericanos*†.

LIBRARIES

Guatemala City

Archivo General de Centro América (*National Archives*): 4A Avda. 7-16, Zona 1; f. 1846; comprises two sections: La Colonia, with 8,427 files of 99,157 documents relating to Guatemala, Chiapas, El Salvador, Honduras, Nicaragua and Costa Rica; library contains ancient and modern historical volumes; periodicals pertaining to the colonial epoch and the period of independence; microfilm and photocopying service for researchers; Dir. ARTURO VALDÉS OLIVA; publ. *Boletín*.

Biblioteca Central de la Universidad de San Carlos: Ciudad Universitaria, Zona 12; f. 1965; faculty libraries; central library formation planned; Dir. (vacant).

Biblioteca de la Corte Suprema de Justicia (*Library of the Supreme Court of Justice*) 9a Avenida 14-31, Zona 1; f. 1881; 10,000 vols.; Dir. ALBERTO LUNA CASTELLANOS.

Biblioteca de la Tipografía Nacional (*Library of the Government Printers*): f. 1892; the greater part of the contents of the Library was destroyed by the earthquakes of 1917 and 1918; modern works printed by them now form the collection.

Biblioteca del Congreso Nacional: 9a Ave. 9-42; f. 1823; 7,000 vols.; Dir. CARLOS H. GODOY Z.

Biblioteca "José Batres Montufar": 12 Avda. Sur No. 1; f. 1921 by the Liberal Party; 15,984 vols., of which 7,099 scientific, 1,397 fiction, with 7,488 reviews and periodicals; open to the public; recently incorporated with the State library service; Librarian Br. JORGE JUÁREZ GARCÍA.

Biblioteca Nacional de Guatemala: 5a Avda. 7-26, Zona 1; f. 1879; *c.* 352,000 vols.; Dir. EVA EVANS V. DE SAGASTUME.

Biblioteca y Sala de Lectura de la Sociedad El Porvenir de los Obreros (*Library and Reading Room of the Workmen's Benefit Society*): Edificio Social, 24 Avda. Sur 13; f. 1896; 3,018 vols.; Dir. RICARDO DOMÍNGUEZ P.

Biblioteca del Banco de Guatemala: f. 1946; 25,000 vols.; Librarian ROSARIO DOMÍNGUEZ.

Quezaltenango

Biblioteca Pública de Quezaltenango: a/c Casa Cultura Occidente 7a, Calle 11-35, Zona 1; reopened 1958; 25,000 vols.; Dir. JULIO CÉSAR ALVÁREZ.

MUSEUMS

Antigua Guatemala

Museo Colonial: 5a Calle O. 5; f. 1936; housed in the old San Carlos University building; period furniture, paintings, sculpture; Dir.-Librarian RAFAEL DE LA HOZ.

Museo del Libro Antiguo: Portal Municipal, Plaza Mayor de Antigua; f. 1956; controlled by the Instituto de Antropología e Historia; books, documents relating to the history of Guatemala; Sec.-Librarian MANUEL REYES.

Musee de Santiago: Portal Municipal, Plaza Mayor de Antigua; f. 1956; arms, furniture, Spanish colonial art; Sec.-Librarian JOSÉ F. MÉNDEZ.

Chichicastenango

Musee Regional de Chichicastenango: Plaza Central; f. 1950; articles of the Maya-Quiché culture; Dir. RAÚL PÉREZ MALDONADO.

Guatemala City

Jardín Botánico: Apdo. 1120; f. 1924; comprises a botanical and zoological collection, including animals from several continents; Exec. Dir. Dr. JUAN DE DIOS CALLE.

Museo de Artes e Industrias Populares: 10a. Avda. 10-72, Zona 1; f. 1959; collections of metal and wooden objects belonging to indigenous races, also costumes; Dir. RICARDO TOLEDO PALOMO.

Museo Nacional de Arte Moderno: Edif. No. 6, Finca La Aurora, Zona 13; f. 1975; paintings, sculpture, engravings, drawings, etc.; Dir. J. OSCAR BARRIENTOS.

Museo Nacional de Historia Natural: 7A Ave. y 6A Calle, Zona 13, Apdo. 987; f. 1950; collection of geological, botanical and zoological specimens; library of 2,000 vols.; Dir. and Founder JORGE A. IBARRA; publ. *Historia Natural y Pro Natura* (quarterly).

Museo Nacional de Historia (*National Museum of History*): 11 Calle 6-33, Zona 1; f. 1975; Dir. ITALO MORALES HIDALGO; publ. *Revista* (quarterly).

Museo Nacional de Arqueología y Etnología de Guatemala (*Archaeological and Ethnographical Museum*): Edificio No. 5, La Aurora, Zona 13; f. 1948; Collection of some 3,000 archaeological pieces, mainly Mayan art, and 1,000 ethnological exhibits, all from Guatemala; Dir. Licda. DORA GUERRA DE GONZALEZ; publ. *Revista* (half-yearly).

UNIVERSITIES

UNIVERSIDAD DE SAN CARLOS DE GUATEMALA

(San Carlos University of Guatemala)

CIUDAD UNIVERSITARIA,
GUATEMALA 12

Telephone: 460611.

Founded 1676 by King Carlos II, established in its present form 1927, autonomous 1944. Branches also at Quezaltenango and Chiquimula.

Language of instruction: Spanish; Academic year: January to November.

Rector: Ing. RAÚL MOLINA MEJÍA.
Secretary-General: JUAN PALOMO.
Librarian: Lic. MARIA LUISA M. DE CEREZO.

Number of teachers: 3,007.
Number of students: 38,000.
Publications: *Alero*† (every 2 months), *Revista* (annually).

DEANS:

Agronomy: Dr. ANTONIO SANDOVAL.
Architecture: Arq. GILBERTO CASTAÑEDA.
Law and Social Sciences: Lic. ROMEO ALVARADO POLANCO.
Economics: Lic. ALFONSO VELÁSQUEZ.
Chemistry and Pharmacy: Lic. LEONEL CARRILLO REEVES.
Medicine: Dr. ROLANDO CASTILLO MONTALVO.
Humanities: Dr. RAÚL OSEGUEDA PALALA.
Engineering: Ing. RAÚL MOLINA MEJÍA.
Dentistry: Dr. FRANCISCO CABARRÚS POITEVIN.
Veterinary Medicine and Zoology: Dr. LUIS FELIPE ROSALES.

DIRECTORS:

School of Biology: Lic. MARIO DARY.
School of Political Science: Lic. JORGE ROMERO YMERI.
School of History: Lic. JULIO GALICIA.
School of Social Work: T. S. FELIPE DE JESÚS CALDERÓN.
School of Communication Studies: Lic. MARIO RENÉ CHÁVEZ.
School of Education: Lic. OSCAR EDUARDO PALACIOS.

There are 8 regional centres in Huehuetenango, Cobán, Quetzaltenango, Chiquimula, Escuintla, Mazatenango, Jalapa, Monterico.

UNIVERSIDAD DEL VALLE DE GUATEMALA

APARTADO POSTAL No. 82, GUATEMALA

Telephone: 692-563/776.

Founded 1966.

Language of instruction: Spanish; Private control; Academic year: February to November.

Rector: (vacant).
Vice-Rector and Executive Secretary: Dr. ROBERT B. MACVEAN.
Librarian: GERTRUDE HUNT.

Library of 20,000 vols.

Number of teachers: 75.
Number of students: 500.

CO-ORDINATORS:

School of Science and Humanities: Dr. JORGE ANTILLÓN.
School of Social Sciences: Dr. ALFREDO MÉNDEZ.
School of Education: Licda. GLORIA AGUILAR.
Research Institute: Ing. JORGE ARIAS DE BLOIS.
University College: Lic. FRANCISCO NIEVES.

UNIVERSIDAD FRANCISCO MARROQUIN

6 AV. 0-28, ZONA 10, GUATEMALA CITY

Telephone: 313888, 316922.

Founded 1971.

Language of instruction: Spanish; Private control; Academic year: January to May, July to November.

Rector: Dr. MANUEL F. AYAU.
Academic Vice-Rector: Dr. RIGOBERTO JUÁREZ-PAZ.
Secretary: ROBERTO SÁNCHEZ LAZO.
Librarian: ELIZABETH HANCKEL.

Library of 10,000 vols.

Number of teachers: 100.
Number of students: 1,838.

DEANS:

Faculty of Law: Lic. FRANCISCO J. CASTILLO.
Faculty of Architecture: Arq. ADOLFO LAU.
Faculty of Economics: Lic. LUCY SCHWANK.
Faculty of Medicine: Dr. RODOLFO HERRERA-LLERANDI.
Faculty of Humanities: RIGOBERTO JUÁREZ-PAZ.

DIRECTORS:

Graduate School of Economics and Business Administration: Ing. RICARDO ALVARADO.
Institute of Informatics and Computer Science: Dr. EDUARDO SUGER.
Graduate School of Social Science: Dr. ARMANDO DE LA TORRE.

UNIVERSIDAD MARIANO GÁLVEZ DE GUATEMALA
(Mariano Gálvez University of Guatemala)

APDO. POSTAL 1811, GUATEMALA

Telephone: 51-08-46.

Founded 1966.

Language of instruction: Spanish; Private control; Academic year: February to November.

Rector: Lic. ADALBERTO SANTIZO ROMÁN.
Vice-Rector: Dr. ALFREDO SAN JOSÉ GONZÁLEZ.
Secretary: Lic. ALVARO R. TORRES MOSS.
Registrar: Sr. FRANCISCO MÉRIDA RODRÍGUEZ.
Librarian: Sr. ALEJANDRO VAQUERANO ROMERO.

Library of 9,000 vols.

Number of teachers: 92.
Number of students: 4,000.

Publication: *Boletín Mensual* (monthly).

DIRECTORS:

Schools of Economics, Public Auditing and Accounting: Lic. RENÉ ARTURO ORELLANA GONZÁLEZ.
School of Law: HUGO CÉSAR MORALES Y MORALES.
School of Civil Engineering: Ing. EMILIO R. SOLIS HEGEL.
School of Business Administration: Lic. JOSÉ MARÍA CARRANZA.
School of Theology: Lic. ARNALDO RUMPH KWANT.
School of Structural Engineering: Ing. LUIS JACINTO QUÁN CHU.
School of Education: Lic. LEOPOLDO COLOM MOLINA.
School of Education (Extramural Branch): Lic. CARLOS ESCOBAR M.

UNIVERSIDAD RAFAEL LANDÍVAR*

VISTA HERMOSA III, ZONA 16, APDO. POSTAL 39 "C", GUATEMALA, C.A.

Telephone: 692151.

Founded 1961.

Language of instruction: Spanish; Private control; Academic year: January to November.

Rector: Dr. SANTOS PÉREZ.
Registrar: Lic. CARLOS AMANN.
Librarian: Dr. SEBASTIÁN MANTILLA.

Number of teachers: *c.* 250.
Number of students: *c.* 3,000.

Publications: *Estudios Sociales*† (monthly).

DEANS:

Faculty of Economic Sciences: Lic. JOSÉ LIZARRALDE.
Faculty of Juridical and Social Sciences: Lic. MARIO QUIÑONEZ.
Faculty of Humanities: Lic. ARNOLDO ESCOBAR.
Institute of Political and Social Sciences: Lic. JOSÉ MIGUEL GAITÁN.
Faculty of Industrial Engineering: Ing. RODOLFO HERMOSILLA.
Faculty of Architecture: Arq. CLAUDIO OLIVARES.

* No reply received to our questionnaire this year.

SCHOOLS OF ART AND MUSIC

Conservatorio Nacional de Música (*National Academy of Music*): Guatemala City; f. 1880; oldest in Central America; 36 teachers; 700 students; Dir. ERNESTO J. ALBERT MENDOZA.

Escuela Nacional de Artes Plásticas: Guatemala City; f. 1920; Dir. MAX SARAVIA GUAL.

Escuela Regional de Artes Plásticas: Quezaltenango; f. 1963; drawing, painting; Dir. RAFAEL MORA.

GUINEA

Population 5,143,000

LEARNED SOCIETIES AND RESEARCH INSTITUTES

Centre de Recherches Rizicoles: Kankan.

Institut de Recherches Fruitières: B.P. 36, Kindia; f. 1961; Dir. C. KEITA.

Institut National de Recherches et Documentation: B.P. 561, Conakry; Dir. S. BOUNAMA SY.

Institut de Recherches et de Biologie Appliquée Pastoria: B.P. 146, Kindia; former **Institut Pasteur**, nationalized 1965; research on anthropoid apes; production of various vaccines; Dir. Dr. T. CAMARA.

Secrétariat d'Etat à la Recherche Scientifique: B.P. 561, Conakry; f. 1969; formerly the Guinea branch of the Institut Français d'Afrique Noire; administers the National Archives, the National Library and Museum, l'Institut des Traditions Populaires, la Section des Sciences Sociales, la Section des Sciences Exactes, l'Institut de Recherche Fruitière de Foulaya, l'Institut de Recherches et de Biologie Appliquée, le Secrétariat d'UNESCO; Minister for Scientific Research SIKÉ CAMARA; publs. *Recherches Africaines* (quarterly), *Cahiers*.

LIBRARIES

Bibliothèque Nationale: B.P. 561, Conakry; f. 1960; 10,000 vols., also special collection on slavery (about 500 books, pamphlets and MSS.); 300 current periodicals; courses in librarianship; Dir. KEITA SIDIKI KOBÉLÉ.

Archives Nationales.

MUSEUMS

Musée National: B.P. 561, Conakry; f. 1960; Curator MAMADOU SAMPIL.

Mount Nimba National Reserve: nature reserve for wild animals.

There are regional museums at Youkounkoun, Kissidougou and N'Zérékoré.

COLLEGES

Institut Polytechnique Gamal Abdul Nasser de Conakry: B.P. 1147, Conakry; f. 1963; est. by the Soviet Union, with teaching staff drawn principally from U.S.S.R. France and Belgium; trains engineers and teachers; library of 15,000 vols.; faculties of Science, Civil Engineering, Geology and Mining, Letters, Agriculture, Medicine and Pharmacy, Chemistry, Electrical Engineering; *c.* 120 students; Rector ALI BADR DOUKOURÉ.

Ecole Nationale des Arts et Métiers: Conakry; f. 1966.

Ecole Supérieure d'Administration: Conakry; f. 1964.

GUYANA

Population 820,000

LEARNED SOCIETIES

Guyana Institute of International Affairs: P.O.B. 812, 189 Charlotte St., Lacytown, Georgetown; f. 1965; 175 mems.; library of 5,000 vols.; Dir. DONALD A. B. TROTMAN; publs. *Annual Journal of International Affairs*, occasional papers.

Guyana Society: Company Path, Georgetown; fmrly. Royal Agricultural & Commercial Society.

U.S. International Communication Agency: P.O.B. 657, Georgetown; f. 1955 to promote international understanding through cultural and information exchanges; includes the John F. Kennedy Library of 8,000 vols.

LIBRARIES

Guyana Medical Science Library: Georgetown Hospital Compound, Georgetown; f. 1966; attached to the Ministry of Health; provides medical information to doctors, nurses, and health personnel; 5,000 vols., 300 journals, 1,000 pamphlets; Librarian Miss MAUREEN WREN; publs. *Bulletin* (quarterly), *Annual Report*.

National Library: P.O.B. 110, Georgetown; f. 1909; combines the functions of a National Library and Public Library; legal depository for material printed in Guyana; 151,879 vols.; Librarian AGNES MCMURDOCH, A.L.A.; publs. *Guyanese National Bibliography*† (quarterly), *New Books* (quarterly).

MUSEUM

Guyana Museum: Company Path, North St., Georgetown; f. 1853 by the Royal Agricultural and Commercial Society; subjects covered include Industry, Art, History, Anthropology, Zoology; Dir. GEORGE E. BURNHAM; publ. *Journal* (annual).

Guyana Zoo, an adjunct of the Museum, specializes in the display, care and management of South American fauna; Dir. GEORGE E. BURNHAM.

UNIVERSITY AND COLLEGES

UNIVERSITY OF GUYANA

P.O.B. 841, GEORGETOWN

Telephone: 54841.

Founded 1963.

Language of instruction: English; Academic year: September to July (three terms).

Chancellor: WILLIAM DEMAS, M.A.

Vice-Chancellor and Principal: DENNIS H. IRVINE, PH.D., D.SC.

Registrar: D. D. KARRAN, LL.B., M.A., Barrister-at-Law.

Librarian: Y. STEPHENSON, M.L.S.

Number of teachers: 183.

Number of students: 732.

Publication: *University of Guyana Bulletin*† (annual).

DEANS:

Faculty of Agriculture: Prof. KRISHNA PRASAD.
Faculty of Arts: RANDOLPH CHOO-SHEE-NAM.
Faculty of Social Sciences: Dr. PAIRAUDEAU MARS.
Faculty of Natural Sciences: Dr. GEORGE WALCOTT.
Faculty of Education: Mrs. BELLE TYNDALL.
Faculty of Technology: JEROME BACCHUS.

PROFESSORS:

CARR, W. I., English
JAMES, R. W., Law
LEDERER, G., Natural Sciences
LUTCHMAN, H., Political Science and Law
ODLE, M., Development Studies
PRASAD, S. K., Biology
THOMAS, C. Y., Economics and Business Administration

ATTACHED INSTITUTE:

Institute of Development Studies: Dir. Dr. M. ODLE.

Guyana School of Agriculture Corporation: Mon Repos, East Coast Demerara; f. 1963; 185 students; library of *c.* 3,000 vols.; Principal WINSLOW A. DAVIDSON.

Guybau Technical Training Complex: Mackenzie, Linden; f. 1958; City and Guilds of London Institute courses in electrical trades, automotive and heavy duty equipment, welding, fitting, machining, driver-training; Principal JOHN HAMMOND, O.B.E.; 17 teachers, 100 full-time and 200 part-time students.

New Amsterdam Technical Institute: New Amsterdam, Berbice; f. 1971; City and Guilds courses in electrical trades, agricultural mechanics, automotive engineering, wood trades, fitting, welding, etc.; secretarial and business studies; Ordinary Technician diploma, Mechanical Engineering Technician course; library of 1,050 vols.; 41 teachers, 1,500 students; Principal C. A. GUISHARD.

HAITI

Population 4,918,000

LEARNED SOCIETIES

Alliance Française: P.O.B. 131, Port-au-Prince; branches in Cap-Haïtien, Jacamel, Gonaïves, Cayes, Jérémie, Port-de-Paix; libraries of 5,000 vols.

Le Bibliophile: Cap Haïtien; f. 1923 to extend and increase knowledge of world literature and love of good books; 28 mems.; Pres. SILVIO FASCHI; Sec. LOUIS TOUSSAINT; publs. *La Citadelle* (weekly), *Stella* (monthly).

Bureau d'Ethnologie: Place des Héros de l'Indépendance, Port-au-Prince; f. 1941; Departments: African-Haitian Ethnography, pre-Columbus Archaeology; Dir.-Gen. EMMANUEL C. PAUL; Sec.-Gen. and Asst. in the Archaeological Section JACQUES M. ORIOL; Hon. Dir. and Asst. in the Africo-Haitian Ethnographical Section GERSON ALEXIS; publ. *Bulletin* (quarterly).

Conseil National des Recherches Scientifiques (*National Council for Scientific Research*): Département de la santé publique et de la population, Port-au-Prince; f. 1963; to co-ordinate scientific development and research, particularly in the field of public health; Pres. Prof. VICTOR NOËL; Sec. M. DOUYON.

Institut Français d'Haiti: Cité de l'Exposition, P.O.B. 131, Port-au-Prince; f. 1945; 1,962 mems.; library of 30,000 vols.; Dir. JACQUES BARROS; publs. *Conjonction*† (quarterly), *Recherches Haïtiennes.*

Institut Haïtiano-Américain: angle rue Capois et rue Saint-Cyr, Port-au-Prince; f. 1942; 1,800 students; English studies, cultural events including lectures on Haitian art; library of 4,500 vols.; Exec. Dir. MILLIE McCOO.

LIBRARIES

Bibliothèque Nationale d'Haïti: rue Hammerton Killick, Port-au-Prince; f. 1940; 19,000 vols.; 12 brs.; Dir. Mme MAX ROSALIE ADOLPHE.

Bibliothèque du Petit Séminaire: Port-au-Prince.

Bibliothèque Saint Louis de Gonzague: Port-au-Prince.

MUSEUMS

Musée Archéologique: Place de l'Indépendance, Port-au-Prince.

Musée National: Turgeau, C.S., Port-au-Prince; f. 1938; sited in former President's mansion; documents, numismatics, paper money, paintings, stones, utensils, arms; Dir. GÉRARD M. LAURENT.

Le Centre d'Art: rue de la Révolution, Port-au-Prince; f. 1944; Dir. DEWITT PETERS; arranges representative exhibitions of Haitian art in the Americas and Western Europe.

UNIVERSITY

UNIVERSITÉ D'ÉTAT D'HAITI

25 RUE BONNE FOI, BOX 2279,
PORT-AU-PRINCE

Telephone: 2-3210; 2-1146.

Founded 1920.

Language of instruction: French; Academic year: October to June.

Rector: LÉONCE VIAUD.
Secretary-General: JEAN-BAPTISTE ROCKEFELLER.
Librarian: JEAN-CLAUDE GERLUS.

The library contains 7,000 vols.
Number of teachers: 384.
Number of students: 2,926.

DEANS:

Faculty of Law and Economics: Dr. VILVERT CELESTIN.
Faculty of Medicine: Dr. FRANTZ MEDARD.
Faculty of Odontology: Dr. SOSTHÈNE DANIEL.
Faculty of Ethnology: Dr. J. B. ROMAIN.
Faculty of Science: FRITZ PIERRE-LOUIS.
Faculty of Human and Social Sciences: PIERRE-LOUIS SALMON.
Faculty of Agronomy and Veterinary Science: LOUIS BLANCHET.
Ecole Normale Supérieure: Dir. RENÉ PIQUION.
Institut National d'Administration, de Gestion et des Hautes Etudes Internationales: Dir. GERARD DORCELY.

COLLEGES

Ecole Polytechnique d'Haïti: Port-au-Prince; f. 1947; Dean MAURICE LATORTUE.

Ecole de Droit: Cap Haitien; Dir. L. BERNARDIN.

Ecole de Droit de Cayes: Cayes; Dir. R. MORPEAU.

Ecole de Droit de Jérémie: Jérémie; f. 1906; Dir. L. BELIZAIRE.

Ecole de Droit de Gonaïves: Gonaïves; f. 1922; Dir. E. GUILLAUME.

Institut National d'Administration de Gestion et des Hautes Etudes Internationales (INAGHEI): 47 ave. Christophe, Port-au-Prince; f. 1958; library of 3,500 vols.; 350 students; Dir. GERARD DORCELY; publ. *Les Cahiers de l'INAGHEI* (irregular).

Institut Supérieur Technique d'Haïti: 22 Ave. du Chili, P.O.B. 992, Port-au-Prince; f. 1962 as Ecole Privée de Génie; Dir. RICHARD LECONTE; Sec.-Gen. Mme LECONTE.

HONDURAS

Population 3,140,000

ACADEMIES

Academia Hondureña (Honduran Academy): Tegucigalpa; 18th in order of foundation in Spanish America; correspondent of the Real Academia Española, Madrid.

Director: ALEJANDRO ALFARO ARRIAGA.
Secretary: JORGE FIDEL DURÓN.
Librarian: JUAN VALLADARES R.

Academia Hondureña de Geografía e Historia: Apdo. Postal 619, Tegucigalpa; f. 1968; 21 mems.; library of 1,535 vols.; Pres. Dr. RAMÓN E. CRUZ; Sec. PM. FERNANDO FERRARI BUSTILLO; publ. *Revista.*

LEARNED SOCIETIES AND RESEARCH INSTITUTES

Asociación de Bibliotecarios y Archivistas de Honduras: 11a Calle, 1a y 2a Avdas. No. 105, Comayagüela, D.C., Tegucigalpa; f. 1951; 53 mems.; library of 3,000 vols.; Pres. FRANCISCA DE ESCOTO ESPINOZA; Sec.-Gen. JUAN ANGEL AYES R.; publ. *Catálogo de Préstamo* (monthly).

Instituto de Ingenieros y Arquitectos de Honduras: Tegucigalpa; f. 1951; 150 mems.; publ. *Revista.*

Instituto Geográfico Nacional (IGN) (*National Geographic Institute*): Barrio La Bolsa, Tegucigalpa, D.C.; f. 1945; delineates natural and mineral resources, their evaluation and their exploitation; 130 staff; library of 1,250 vols.; Dir.-Gen. JOSÉ EDMUNDO ALCERRO PRUDOTH; publs. *Boletín de la Comisión Geográfica Especial de la Secretaría de Marina y Aviación, Boletín de la Dirección General de Cartografía, Secretaría de Fomento, Boletín de la Dirección General de Cartografía del Ministerio de Comunicaciones y Obras Públicas, Boletín del Instituto Geográfico Nacional.*

Instituto Hondureño de Cultura Interamericana: 2a Avda. 511, Comayagüela, D.C., Apdo. 201, Tegucigalpa; f. 1939; 400 active, 500 associate mems.; library of 6,000 vols.; Dir. MARIANA ZEPEDA R.

Instituto Hondureño de Antropología e Historia: Apdo. Postal 1518, Villa Roy, Barrio Buenos Aires, Tegucigalpa; f. 1952; library of 5,000 vols.; research and conservation of cultural property, archaeology, history, ethnography, linguistics; Dir. Dr. J. ADÁN CUEVA; publ. *Yaxkin*† (2 a year).

LIBRARIES

TEGUCIGALPA

Archivo Nacional de Honduras: 6a Ave. No. 408; f. 1880; 40,000 vols.; Dir. Lic. ADYLIA CARDONA DE ANGULO; publ. *Anales del Archivo Nacional de Honduras.*

Biblioteca Nacional de Honduras: 6a Ave. "Salvador Mendieta"; f. 1880; 55,000 vols.; co-ordinates national and international exchange; shares legal deposit with other centres; Dir. MIGUEL ANGEL GARCÍA; publ. *Anuario Bibliográfico.*

Biblioteca 'Wilson Popenoe': Escuela Agricola Panamericana, Apdo. 93; f. 1946; 16,000 vols.; Librarian Prof. HERNAN ISAIAS GALO; publs. *Ceiba* (2 a year), *Boletín Bibliográfico.*

Biblioteca del Instituto Hondureño de Cultura Interamericana: Biblioteca 'James G. Blaine', Apdo. 201; f. 1939; 6,500 vols.; Librarian MARIANA ZEPEDA.

Biblioteca del Ministerio de Relaciones Exteriores: f. 1913; 5,000 vols.; Dir. ERNESTO ALVARADO GARCÍA.

Biblioteca de la Universidad Nacional: Ciudad Universitaria, Suyapa; f. 1847; 89,827 vols.; Librarian Lic. LILIANA CAÑADAS MEJIA; publ. *Boletín del Sistema Bibliotecario*† (quarterly).

MUSEUMS

Museo Nacional: Apdo. 1518, Villa Roy, Barrio Buenos Aires, Tegucigalpa; natural history, political history, archaeology, ethnology, colonial art; part of the *Instituto Hondureño de Antropología e Historia* (*q.v.*); Dir. Prof. JOSÉ LUIS LÓPEZ NOL.

Museo Arqueología y Histórico de Comayagua: Ciudad de Comayagua; f. 1946; archaeological and colonial collections, the former dating back to 1,000 B.C.; some contemporary items; Dir. Prof. HECTOR VALLADARES.

Museo Histórico "Miguel Paz Baraona": Aldea de Pinalejo, Município de Quimistán; f. 1953; archaeological, colonial and contemporary art items of the region; Dir. ESTEBÁN MADRID.

Museo Regional de Arqueologia Maya: Ciudad de Copán; f. 1939; objects relate exclusively to Maya culture; Dir. Prof. OSMIN RIVERA.

Museo Nacional de Historia Colonial: Puerto de Omoa, Cortés; f. 1959 in former prison; colonial and historical items; Cur. RAMÓN ZÚÑIGA ANDRADE.

UNIVERSITY

UNIVERSIDAD NACIONAL AUTÓNOMA DE HONDURAS

CIUDAD UNIVERSITARIA,
BLVD. SUYAPA,
TEGUCIGALPA, D.C.
Telephone: 22-9101.
Founded 1847.

State control; Language of instruction: Spanish; Academic year: February to November.

Rector: Lic. JORGE ARTURO REINA.
Vice-Rector: Dr. DAGOBERTO ESPINOZA MOURRA.
Secretary-General: Lic. RAMÓN IZAGUIRRE.

Library: *see* Libraries.

Number of teachers: 763.
Number of students: 15,404.

Publications: *Revista de la Universidad*†, *Revista de la Facultad de Derecho*†, *Boletín de la Facultad de Medicina*†, *Catálogo de Estudios*†, *Guías para los Estudiantes*†, *Boletín del Instituto de Investigaciones Económicas y Sociales*†, etc.

DEANS:

Faculty of Juridical and Social Sciences: Ab. OSWALDO RAMOS SOTO.

Faculty of Economics: Lic. ROMAN VALLADARES R.

Faculty of Medicine: Dr. DAGOBERTO ESPINOZA MOURRA.

Faculty of Chemistry and Pharmacy: Dr. RENE SAGASTUME.

Faculty of Dentistry: Dr. EDUARDO VILLELA SOTO.

Faculty of Engineering: Ing. SALVADOR A. MEJIA PARDO.

DIRECTORS:

University Centre of the North (San Pedro Sula): Lic. ANIBAL DELGADO FIALLOS.

Atlantic Coast University Centre (La Ceiba): Ing. MIGUEL ALVARADO.

General Studies Centre: Lic. IBRAHIM PINEDA.

COLLEGES

Escuela Agrícola Panamericana: Apdo. 93, Tegucigalpa; f. 1943; 30 teachers, 250 students; library of 18,000 vols.; Dir. Dr. SIMÓN E. MALO; publ. *Ceiba*.

Escuela Nacional de Música: 2a Av. 307, Tegucigalpa.

HUNGARY

Population 10,700,000

ACADEMY

Magyar Tudományos Akadémia (*Hungarian Academy of Sciences*): 1361 Budapest V, Roosevelt-tér 9; Telephone 113-400; f. 1825.

President: JÁNOS SZENTÁGOTHAI.

Vice-Presidents: ZSIGMOND PÁL PACH, KÁROLY POLINSZKY, ANDRÁS SOMOS.

General Secretary: LÉNÁRD PÁL.

Deputy General Secretaries: BÉLA KÖPECZI, ISTVÁN LÁNG.

Presidium: GYULA EÖRSI, JÓZSEF FÜLÖP, ZSUZSA HOLLÁN, FERENC MÁRTA, ERNŐ NEMECZ, JÁNOS PROHÁSZKA, BRUNÓ STRAUB, KÁLMÁN SZABÓ, BÉLA SZŐKEFALVI-NAGY, PÁL TÉTÉNYI, JÓZSEF UJFALUSSY.

Library: *see* Libraries.

Publications: *Acta Agronomica*, *Acta Alimentaria*, *Acta Antiqua*, *Acta Archeologica*, *Acta Biochemica et Biophysica*, *Acta Biologica*, *Acta Botanica*, *Acta Chimica*, *Acta Chirurgica*, *Acta Ethnographica*, *Acta Geodaetica, Geophysica et Montanistica*, *Acta Geologica*, *Acta Historiae Artium*, *Acta Historica*, *Acta Juridica*, *Acta Linguistica*, *Acta Litteraria*, *Acta Mathematica*, *Acta Medica*, *Acta Microbiologica*, *Acta Morphologica*, *Acta Oeconomica*, *Acta Orientalia*, *Acta Paediatrica*, *Acta Physica*, *Acta Physiologica*, *Acta Phytopathologica*, *Acta Technica*, *Acta Veterinaria*, *Acta Zoologica*, *Studia Musicologica*, *Studia Scientiarum Mathematicarum*, *Studia Slavica* (all available for exchange), *Problems of Control and Information Theory*, *Reaction Kinetics and Catalysis Letters*, *Analysis Mathematica*, *Magyar Tudományos Akadémia Osztályközleményei* (Bulletins of the Sections of the Academy, in twelve series), *Magyar Tudomány* (Review of the Hungarian Academy of Sciences) and other publications in Hungarian.

SECTION I

Linguistic and Literary Sciences:

President: MIKLÓS SZABOLCSI.

Honorary Members:

ARISTE, PAUL.
COLLINDER, BJÖRN.
FLAKER, ALEXANDER.
HARTKE, WERNER.
HO TON TRINH.
HRAPCHENKO, MIHAIL BORISOVICH.
ITKONEN, ERKKI ESAIAS.
KONONOV, ANDREI NIKOLAYEVICH.
LARSEN, JENS PETER.
LIHACHOV, DMITRI SERGEYEVICH.
MAYRHOFER, MANFRED.
MORTIER, ROLAND.
PERROT, JEAN.
SAUVAGEOT, AURELIEN.
SHACKLETON, ROBERT.
SHIRENDEB, BAZARIN.
SINOR, DENIS.
VASOLI, CESARE.
VOISINE, JACQUES.

Ordinary Members:

BENKŐ, LÓRÁND.
HADROVICS, LÁSZLÓ.
HAJDU, PÉTER.
HARMATTA, JÁNOS.
KARDOS, LÁSZLÓ.
KIRÁLY, ISTVÁN.
KLANICZAY, TIBOR.
KÖPECZI, BÉLA.
LAKÓ, GYÖRGY.
LIGETI, LAJOS.
SŐTÉR, ISTVÁN.
SZABOLCSI, MIKLÓS.
TAMÁS, LAJOS.
TOLNAI, GÁBOR.

Corresponding Members:

BARTA, JÁNOS.
IMRE, SAMU.
KÁLMÁN, BÉLA.
KERESZTURY, DEZSŐ.
NAGY, PÉTER.
PÁNDI KARDOS, PÁL.
PAPP, FERENC.
TÁLASI, ISTVÁN.
TŐKEI, FERENC.
TÓTH, DEZSO.
UJFALUSSY, JÓZSEF.

SECTION II

Philosophy and Historical Sciences:

President: T. IVÁN BEREND.

Honorary Members:

FEDOSEYEV, PIOTR NIKOLAYEVICH.
HOBSBAWN, ERIC.
HUNGER, HERBERT.
KEDROV, BONIFATI MIHAILOVICH.
KIENIEWICH, STEFAN.
OKLEDNIKOV, ALEKSEI PAVLOVICH.
SOBOUL, ALBERT.

Ordinary Members:

ANDICS, ERZSÉBET.
BEREND, T. IVÁN.
ELEKES, LAJOS.
EMBER, GYŐZŐ.
GEREVICH, LÁSZLÓ.
MÁTRAI, LÁSZLÓ.
MÉREI, GYULA.
NEMES, DEZSŐ.
PACH, ZSIGMOND PÁL.
ZSIGMOND, LÁSZLÓ.

Corresponding Members:

GARAS, KLÁRA.
HAHN, ISTVÁN.
HERMANN, ISTVÁN.
LUKÁCS, JÓZSEF.
MÓCSY, ANDRÁS.
RÁNKI, GYÖRGY.
SZABÓ, ÁRPÁD.
SZÉKELY, GYÖRGY.
SZIGETI, JÓZSEF.

SECTION III

Mathematical and Physical Sciences:

President: IMRE TARJÁN.

Honorary Members:

ALEXANDROV, ANATOLI PETROVICH.
AMBARTSUMYAN, VIKTOR A.
BOGOLYUBOV, NIKOLAI N.
DIRAC, PAUL A. M.
HALMOS, R. PAUL.
HERZBERG, GERHARD.
KASTLER, ALFRED.
KOLMOGOROV, ANDREI NIKOLAEVICH.
KURATOWSKI, KAZIMIERZ.
KÜRTI, MIKLÓS.
MAZUR, STANISLAW.
NIKOLSKY, SERGEI MIKHAILOVICH.
PÓLYA, GYÖRGY.
PONTRJAGIN, LEV SEMYONOVICH.
PROHOROT, A. M.
SAVIC, PAVLE.
SZEGŐ, GÁBOR.
TIHONOV, ANDREI N.
VINOGRADOV, IVAN MATVEEVICH.

Ordinary Members:

CSÁSZÁR, ÁKOS.
ERDŐS, PÁL.
FEJES TÓTH, LÁSZLÓ.
GÁSPÁR, REZSŐ.
KÓNYA, ALBERT.
KOVÁCS, ISTVÁN.
PÁL, LÉNÁRD.
RÉDEI, LÁSZLÓ.
SZALAY, SÁNDOR.
SZŐKEFALVI-NAGY, BÉLA.
TANDORI, KÁROLY.
TARJÁN, IMRE.

Corresponding Members:

BERÉNYI, DÉNES.
BOZÓKY, LÁSZLÓ
CSIKAI, GYULA.
HAJNAL, ANDRÁS.
KÁTAI, IMRE.
KISS, DEZSŐ.
LEINDLER, LÁSZLÓ.
LOVAS, ISTVÁN.
LOVÁSZ, LÁSZLÓ.
MARX, GYÖRGY.
NAGY, ELEMÉR.
NAGY, KÁROLY.
PRÉKOPA, ANDRÁS.
RAPCSÁK, ANDRÁS.

SECTION IV

Agricultural Sciences:

President: ISTVÁN TAMÁSSY.

HONORARY MEMBERS:

BREZHNIEV, DMITRI DANILOVICH.
CICIN, NIKOLAI VASILYEVICH.
CLAUSEN, HJALMAR.
DASKALOV, HRISTO.
DOBRZANSKI, BOHDAN.
LOBANOV, PAVEL PAVLOVICH
MELEHOV, IVAN S.
SCHEFFER, FRITZ.
STUBBE, HANS.
VAVILOV, PETR P.

ORDINARY MEMBERS:

CSELŐTEI, LÁSZLÓ.
CSIZMADIA, ERNŐ.
HORN, ARTUR.
KOZMA, PÁL.
KURNIK, ERNŐ.
MÁTHÉ, IMRE.
SOMOS, ANDRÁS.
STEFANOVITS, PÁL.
SZENT-IVÁNYI, TAMÁS.
TAMÁSSY, ISTVÁN.

CORRESPONDING MEMBERS:

KERESZTESI, BÉLA.
KIRÁLY, ZOLTÁN.
KOVÁCS, FERENC.
LÁNG, ISTVÁN.
MAGYAR, JÁNOS.
MÉSZÁROS, JÁNOS.
RAJKI, SÁNDOR.
SÁLYI, GYULA.

SECTION V

Medical Sciences:

President: GÁBOR PETRI.

HONORARY MEMBERS:

BERNARD, JEAN.
CHUMAKOV, MIKHAIL P.
HADZIOLOV, ASSEN.
HALPERN, BERNARD.
LWOFF, ANDRÉ.
MILCU, STEPHAN MARIUS A.
ORLOWSKI, TADEUS.
PETROVSKY, BORIS.
SABIN, ALBERT B.
VAHLQUIST, BO.

ORDINARY MEMBERS:

BABICS, ANTAL.
BÁLINT, PÉTER.
DONHOFFER, SZILÁRD.
GEGESI KISS, PÁL.
IVÁNOVICS, GYÖRGY.
KERPEL-FRÓNIUS, ÖDÖN.
KNOLL, JÓZSEF.
KÖRNYEI, ISTVÁN.
LAPIS, KÁROLY.
LISSÁK, KÁLMÁN.
PÁLOS, A. LÁSZLÓ.
RADNÓT, MAGDA.

CORRESPONDING MEMBERS:

ANTONI, FERENC.
HALÁSZ, BÉLA.
HOLLÁN, ZSUZSA.
NÁSZ, ISTVÁN.
PÁSZTOR, EMIL.
PETRÁNYI, GYULA.
PETRI, GÁBOR.
STARK, ERVIN.
WEISZFEILER, GYULA.

SECTION VI

Technical Sciences:

President: P. OTTO GESZTI.

HONORARY MEMBERS:

BALEVSKI, ANGEL TONCHEV.
GROSZKOWSKI, JANUSZ.
KALMAN, RUDOLF EMIL.
KERISEL, JEAN LEHUÉROQ.
OLSZAK, WACLAW.
PETROV, BORIS NIKOLAYEVICH.
ROMPE, ROBERT.
SEINDLIN, ALEXANDER Y.
SIFOROV, VLADIMIR IVANOVICH.
STUMPERS, F. LOUIS.
TRAPESNYKOV, VADIM. ALEXANDROVICH.

ORDINARY MEMBERS:

BOGÁRDI, JÁNOS.
BOGNÁR, GÉZA.
BORBÉLY, SAMU.
GÁBOR, LÁSZLÓ.
GESZTI, P. OTTO.
HELLER, LÁSZLÓ.
KÉZDI, ÁRPÁD.
KOVÁCS, K. PÁL.
KOZMA, LÁSZLÓ.
LÉVAI, ANDRÁS.
MAJOR, MÁTÉ.
MILLNER, TIVADAR.
SZABÓ, JÁNOS.
VÁMOS, TIBOR.
VERŐ, JÓZSEF.

CORRESPONDING MEMBERS:

CSIBI, SÁNDOR.
CZIBERE, TIBOR.
KOVÁCS, GYÖRGY.
LUKÁCS, JÓZSEF.
PROHÁSZKA, JÁNOS.
SIMON, SÁNDOR.
STEFÁN, MIHÁLY.
SZENDY, KÁROLY.
VAJDA, GYÖRGY.

SECTION VII

Chemical Sciences:

President: MIHÁLY BECK.

HONORARY MEMBERS:

BARTON, DEREK.
DUBININ, MIHAIL MIHAJLOVICH.
EMANUEL, N. M.
FRUMKIN, ALEXANDER NAUMOVICH.
MANGINI, ANGELO.
MURGULESCU, I. G.
NOWOTNY, HANS.
RIENÄCKER, GÜNTHER.
SEMYONOV, NIKOLAY NIKOLAYEVICH.
SIMON, WILHELM.
ŠORM, FRANTISEK.
ZHAVORONKOV, NIKOLAI MIHAILOVICH.

ORDINARY MEMBERS:

BECK, MIHÁLY.
BOGNÁR, REZSŐ.
FÖLDI, ZOLTÁN.
FREUND, MIHÁLY.
GERECS, ÁRPÁD.
HOLLÓ, JÁNOS.
LENGYEL, BÉLA.
MÁRTA, FERENC.
POLINSZKY, KÁROLY.
PUNGOR, ERNŐ.
SCHAY, GÉZA.
SZABÓ, ZOLTÁN.
TÉTÉNYI, PÁL.

CORRESPONDING MEMBERS:

BENEDEK, PÁL.
FARKAS, LORÁND.
HARDY, GYULA.
LEMPERT, KÁROLY.
MARKÓ, LÁSZLÓ.
NAGY, FERENC.
SZÁNTAY, CSABA.
TÜDŐS, FERENC.
VAS, KÁROLY.

SECTION VIII

Biological Sciences:

President: JÓZSEF TIGYI.

HONORARY MEMBERS:

BAEV, A. A.
BRAUNSTEIN, ALEXANDER Y.
FRANK, GLEB M.
GAILLARD, PIETER JOHANNES.
GILYAROV, M. S.
HOTCHKISS, ROLLIN D.
MOTHES, KURT.
PULLMANN, BERNARD.
RAPAPORT, SAMUEL M.
ROCHE, JEAN.
SZENT-GYÖRGYI, ALBERT.

ORDINARY MEMBERS:

ÁBRAHÁM, AMBRUS.
ÁDÁM, GYÖRGY.
BALOGH, JÁNOS.
ERNST, JENŐ.
FARKAS, GÁBOR.
KASZAB, ZOLTÁN.
KROMPECHER, ISTVÁN.
STRAUB, F. BRUNÓ.
SZABOLCSI, GERTRUD.
SZENTÁGOTHAI, JÁNOS.
TIGYI, JÓZSEF.
TÖRŐ, IMRE.
ZÓLYOMI, BÁLINT.

CORRESPONDING MEMBERS:

DÉNES, GÉZA.
FLERKÓ, BÉLA.
JAKUCS, PÁL.
JERMY, TIBOR.
KELETI, TAMÁS.
SALÁNKI, JÁNOS.
SZABÓ, GÁBOR.

SECTION IX

Economics and Law:

President: KÁLMÁN KULCSÁR.

HONORARY MEMBERS:

ANCEL, MARC.
BALOGH, THOMAS.
HACHATUROV, TIGRAN SERGEYEVICH.
HEADY, EARL O.
KAHN-FREUND, OTTO.
KALDOR, NICHOLAS.
KANTOROVICH, LEONID VITALYEVICH.
KOHLMEY, GUNTHER.
LUKIC, R. D.
KUDRYAVCHEV, VLADIMIR M.
MYRDAL, KARL GUNNAR.

ORDINARY MEMBERS:

BIHARI, OTTÓ.
BOGNÁR, JÓZSEF.
EÖRSI, GYULA.
ERDŐS, PÉTER.
KOVÁCS, ISTVÁN.
OSZTROVSZKI, GYÖRGY.
SZABÓ, IMRE.
SZABÓ, KÁLMÁN.
SZALAI, SÁNDOR.

CORRESPONDING MEMBERS:

FALUSNÉ, SZIKRA KATALIN.
KIRÁLY, TIBOR.
KORNAI, JÁNOS.
KULCSÁR, KÁLMÁN.
PESCHKA, VILMOS.
SIMAI, MIHÁLY.
SIPOS, ALADÁR.

SECTION X

Geo- and Mining Sciences:

President: FERENC MARTOS.

HONORARY MEMBERS:

FINK, JULIUS.
GERASIMOV, INNOKENTY PETROVICH.
KOLBENHEYER, TIBOR.
KRASTANOV, LJUBOMIR.
MELNIKOV, N. V.
PETRASCHEK, WALTER.
RINNER, KARL.
SIDORENKO, ALEXANDER V.

ORDINARY MEMBERS:

FÜLÖP, JÓZSEF.
HAZAY, ISTVÁN.
HOMORÓDI, LAJOS.
MARTOS, FERENC.
NEMECZ, ERNŐ.
PÉCSI, MÁRTON.
SZÁDECZKY-KARDOSS, ELEMÉR.
TÁRCZY-HORNOCH, ANTAL.
TARJÁN, GUSZTÁV.
ZAMBÓ, JÁNOS.

CORRESPONDING MEMBERS:

BARTA, GYÖRGY.
BÉLL, BÉLA.
CZELNAI, RUDOLF.
GRASELLY, GYULA.
KAPOLYI, LÁSZLÓ.
KLIBURSZKYNÉ VOGL, MARIA.

LEARNED SOCIETIES

* *Denotes member societies of Műszaki és Természettudományi Egyesületek Szövetsége (q.v.).*

Műszaki és Természettudományi Egyesületek Szövetsége (*Federation of Technical and Scientific Societies*): 1055 Budapest, Kossuth L. tér 6-8; f. 1948; Pres. JENŐ FOCK; Exec. Pres. GYULA HORGOS; Sec.-Gen. JÁNOS TÓTH; publs. *Müszaki Élet* (Technical Life), *Forum*. There are thirty-two member societies, marked below with asterisk.

AGRICULTURAL AND VETERINARY SCIENCE

***Magyar Agrártudományi Egyesület** (*Hungarian Society of Agricultural Sciences*): 1055 Budapest, Kossuth Lajos tér 6-8; f. 1951; 18,000 mems.; Pres. JENŐ VÁNCSA; Sec.-Gen. ANDRÁS KLENCZNER; publ. *Tudomány és Mezőgazdaság* (Science and Agriculture).

***Magyar Élelmezésipari Tudományos Egyesület** (*Hungarian Scientific Society for Food Industry*): 1054 Budapest, Akadémia u. 1-3; f. 1949; Pres. ZOLTÁN BABOS; Sec. ISTVÁN TÓTH ZSIGA (acting); publs. include *Élelmezési Ipar* (Food Industry) and journals on many branches of the food industry.

***Országos Erdészeti Egyesület** (*Hungarian Forestry Association*): 1061 Budapest, Anker-köz 1; f. 1866; 6,000 mems.; library of 20,000 vols.; Pres. Prof. Dr. IMRE HERPAY; Sec.-Gen. PÁL KIRÁLY; publ. *Az Erdő* (Forest).

ARCHITECTURE AND TOWN PLANNING

***Építőipari Tudományos Egyesület** (*Scientific Society of Building*): 1055 Budapest, Kossuth Lajos tér 6-8; f. 1949; 9,600 mems.; Pres. REZSŐ TRAUTMANN; Sec.-Gen. ZOLTÁN NAGY; publs. *Magyar Építőipar* (Hungarian Building Industry), *Épületgépészet* (Sanitary and Installation Engineering), *Városépités* (Town Planning).

THE ARTS

Liszt Ferenc Társaság (*F. Liszt Society*): 1061 Budapest, Liszt Ferenc tér 8; f. 1893, re-formed 1973; to foster the cult of Liszt, to further the interest of audiences in live music; concerts, competitions, annual Liszt Record Grand Prix, setting up Liszt memorials; 870 mems.; Pres. D. KOVÁCS; Gen. Sec. M. FORRAI.

Magyar Szinházi Intézet (*Hungarian Theatre Institute*): 1016 Budapest, Krisztina-krt. 57; f. 1957; to research into theatre history and theory, information on world drama and theatre; 35 mems.; Dir. MIKLÓS ALMÁSI; publs. *Dramaturgiai Hiradó, Hungarian Theatre News*†, *Szinházelméleti Füzetek, Szinháztörténeti Könyvtár*; controls the National Historical Museum of the Theatre.

Magyar Zenemüvészek Szövetsége (*Association of Hungarian Musicians*): Budapest V, Vörösmarty tér 1; f. 1949; Sec.-Gen. ISTVÁN LÁNG; Exec. Sec. KÁLMÁN STRÉM.

Múzeumi Restaurátor- es Módszertani Központ (*Institute of Conservation and Methodology of Museums*): 1087 Budapest, Kőnyves Kálmán krt. 40, P.O.B. 54; f. 1974; experimental, documentary and advisory centre for museum conservation and education; 40 staff; library of 12,000 vols.; Dir. ISTVÁN ERI; publs. *Múzeumi Műtárgyvédelem*† (Conservation of art objects), *A magyar múzeumok kiadványainak bibliográfiája*† (Bibliography of Hungarian museum publications).

Országos Magyar Cecilia Társulat (*National Hungarian Cecilia Society*): 1027 Budapest, Mártirok u. 64/B; f. 1897; Ecclesiastical Chair. I. KISBERK; Secular Chair. L. BÁRDOS; 2,800 mems.

BIBLIOGRAPHY, LIBRARY SCIENCE

Magyar Könyvtárosok Egyesülete (*Hungarian Library Asscn.*): 1827 Budapest, P.O.B. 486; f. 1935; Pres. J. ZSIDAI; Sec. D. KOVÁTS.

ECONOMICS AND POLITICS

Magyar Külügyi Intézet (*Hungarian Institute of International Relations*): 1016 Budapest, Bérc u. 23; f. 1972; prepares analytical material and information for foreign policy institutions; holds round-table conferences and public lectures; organizes study tours; 41 staff, 23 researchers; reference library; Dir. GYULA GYOVAI; publs. *Külpolitika*† (quarterly, English version of selected articles annually), foreign policy documents, essays, scientific articles.

EDUCATION

Népmüvelési Intézet (*Institute of Culture*): 1251 Budapest, I, Corvin-tér 8; f. 1951; centre for scientific research in cultural development, for life-long education, cultural activities, amateur artistic and leisure pursuits; Dirs. IVÁN VITÁNYI, LIVIA ÁCS; publ. *Kultúra és Közösség*† (Culture and Community).

HISTORY, GEOGRAPHY AND ARCHAEOLOGY

***Geodéziai és Kartográfiai Egyesület** (*Society for Geodesy and Cartography*): 1061 Budapest, Anker-köz 1; f. 1956;

2,400 mems.; Pres. LAJOS HOMORÓDI; Sec.-Gen. ÁKOS DETREKŐI; publs. *Geodézia és Kartográfia*† (Geodesy and Cartography).

Magyar Földrajzi Társaság (*Hungarian Geographical Society*): Budapest VI, Népköztársaság u. 62; f. 1872, reorg. 1953; Pres. SÁNDOR RADÓ; Gen.-Sec. SÁNDOR SOMOGYI; 2,300 mems.; library of 29,000 vols.; publ. *Földrajzi Közlemények* (quarterly), *Geografia Medica* (annually).

Magyar Irodalomtörténeti Társaság (*Society of Hungarian Literary History*): Budapest V, Pesti Barnabás u. 1; f. 1912; Pres. GÁBOR TOLNAI; Vice-Pres. IMRE BÁN; Gen. Sec. ANTAL WÉBER; publs. *Irodalomtörténet* (Literary History, quarterly).

Magyar Régészeti és Művészettörténeti Társulat (*Hungarian Society of Archaeology and History of Fine Arts*): Budapest, VIII, Múzeum-krt. 14; Pres. GÉZA ENTZ, Sec. TIBOR KOVÁCS; publs. *Archaeológiai Értesítő, Művészettörténeti Értesítő, Numizmatikai Közlöny, Érem.*

Magyar Történelmi Társulat (*Hungarian Historical Society*): Budapest I, Uri u. 51-53; f. 1867; Pres. IVAN T. BEREND; Vice-Pres. H. VASS, P. HANÁK, J. KANYAR; E. LIPTAI, I. SINKOVICS; Gen. Sec. OTTO SZABOLCS; publs. *Századok, Magyarország újabbkori történetének forrásai* (*Fontes historiae Hungaricae aevi recentioris*).

INTERNATIONAL CULTURAL INSTITUTES

British Council: British Embassy, Budapest V, Harmincad u. 6; library of 10,054 vols., 53 periodicals; Cultural Attaché G. H. FISHER.

Institut Français: Budapest, VI, Szegfü-utca 6; f. 1947; 1,400 mems.; library of 27,000 vols.; Dir. JEAN-MICHEL LECLERCQ.

Istituto Italiano di Cultura: 1088 Budapest, Bródy Sándor u. 8; f. 1935; maintains cultural relations between Italy and Hungary; 4,000 mems.; library of 10,000 vols.; Dir. Prof. GIUSEPPE RACCA.

Kulturális Kapcsolatok Intézete (*Institute of Cultural Relations*): Budapest, V, Dorottya u. 8; government agency for co-ordination of international cultural, educational and scientific relations; Pres. RUDOLF RÓNAI.

LANGUAGE AND LITERATURE

Magyar Írók Szövetsége (*Association of Hungarian Writers*): Budapest, VI, Bajza u. 18; f. 1945; Pres. IMRE DOBOZY; Gen. Sec. GÁBOR GARAI.

Magyar Nyelvtudományi Társaság (*Hungarian Linguistic Society*): Budapest, V, Pesti Barnabás u. 1; f. 1904; Gen. Sec. ISTVÁN SZATHMÁRY.

Magyar P.E.N. Club (*Hungarian P.E.N. Club*): Budapest, V. Vörösmarty-tér 1; f. 1926; 340 mems.; Pres. IVÁN BOLDIZSÁR; Gen. Sec. LÁSZLÓ KÉRY; publs. *The Hungarian P.E.N., Le P.E.N. Hongrois* (yearly bulletin).

MEDICINE

Magyar Gyógyszerészeti Társaság (*Hungarian Pharmaceutical Society*): 1092 Budapest, IX, Hőgyes Endre u. 4; f. 1924; 2,700 mems.; Pres. Dr. K. ZALAI; Gen. Sec. Dr. E. STENSZKY; publs. *Acta Pharmaceutica Hungarica, Gyógyszerészet.*

Magyar Orvostudományi Társaságok és Egyesületek Szövetsége (*Federation of Hungarian Medical Societies*): Budapest V, Kossuth Lajos tér 4; f. 1966; 60 mem. societies; Pres. IMRE ZOLTÁN; Gen. Sec. GÁBOR NYERGES.

NATURAL SCIENCES

General

Tudományos Ismeretterjesztő Társulat (*Society for Popularization of Scientific Knowledge*): Budapest, VIII, Bródy Sándor u. 16; f. 1841; library of 20,000 vols.; 27,600 mems.; Pres. ÁDÁM GYÖRGI; Gen. Sec. Dr. IMRE KURUCZ; publs. *Élet és Tudomány* (Life and Science) (weekly), *Természet Világa* (World of Nature) (monthly), *Valóság* (Reality) (monthly), *Egészség* (Health), *Föld és Ég* (Earth and Sky) (every 2 months), *Műemlékvédelem* (Care of Ancient Monuments) (quarterly), *Borsodi Szemle* (Borsodi Review) (quarterly), *Békési Élet* (Békés Life) (quarterly).

Biological Sciences

***Magyar Biofizikai Társaság** (*Hungarian Biophysical Society*): 1055 Budapest, Kossuth Lajos tér 6-8; f. 1961; 329 mems.; Pres. JÓZSEF TIGYI; Sec.-Gen. Mme. GYÖRGYI RONTÓ.

***Magyar Biokémiai Társaság** (*Hungarian Biochemical Society*): 1055 Budapest, Kossuth Lajos tér 6-8; f. 1962; Pres. FERENC GUBA; Sec.-Gen. DÁNIEL BAGDY; publ. *Biokémia.*

***Magyar Biológiai Társaság** (*Hungarian Biological Society*): 1055 Budapest, Kossuth Lajos tér 6-8; f. 1952; 2,100 mems.; Pres. IMRE TÖRŐ; Sec.-Gen. TIBOR GÁNTI.

Magyar Rovartani Társaság (*Hungarian Society of Entomology*): H-1088, Budapest, Baross u. 13; f. 1910; 250 mems.; Pres. Dr. L. GOZMÁNY; Vice-Pres. Dr. L. MÓCZÁR, Dr. B. NAGY; Sec. Dr. L. PAPP; publs. *Folia Entomologica Hungarica ser. nov.* (*Rovartani Közlemények*)†.

Mathematics

***Bolyai János Matematikai Társulat** (*Bolyai János Mathematical Society*): 1061 Budapest, Anker-köz 1; f. 1891; 2,200 mems.; Pres. J. SURÁNYI; Gen. Sec. A. CSÁSZÁR; publs. *Matematikai Lapok* (Mathematical Gazette) (annually), *Középiskolai Matematikai Lapok* (Mathematical Gazette for Secondary Schools), *A Matematika Tanitása* (Teaching of Mathematics).

Physical Sciences

***Eötvös Loránd Fizikai Társulat** ("*Roland Eötvös*" *Physical Society*): 1061 Budapest, VI, Anker-köz 1; f. 1891; 2,560 mems.; Pres. GYÖRGY MARX; Sec.-Gen. GYULA CSIKAI; publ. *Fizikai Szemle* (Physics Review).

***Magyar Geofizikusok Egyesülete** (*Assn. of Hungarian Geophysicists*): 1368 Budapest, P.O.B. 240; f. 1954; 820 mems.; Pres. KÁROLY MOLNÁR; Gen. Sec. JÁNOS DERES; publ. *Magyar Geofizika*†.

***Magyar Hidrológiai Társaság** (*Hungarian Hydrological Society*): 1372 Budapest, V, Kossuth L. tér 6-8; f. 1917; 3,735 mems.; Pres. Dr. GYÖRGY ILLÉS; Sec.-Gen. Dr. GYÖRGY SZALAI; publs. *Hidrológiai Közlöny* (Hydrological Journal, monthly), *Hidrológiai Tájékoztató* (Circular on Hydrology) (twice a year).

***Magyar Karszt- és Barlangkutató Társulat** (*Hungarian Speleological Society*): H-1055 Budapest, Kossuth Lajos tér 6-8; f. 1910; Pres. Dr. SÁNDOR LÁNG; Sec.-Gen. Dr. TIVADAR BÖCKER; publs. *Karszt és Barlang, Karszt- és Barlangkutatás* (Cave Research, annually in English, German, French).

***Magyar Kémikusok Egyesülete** (*Hungarian Chemical Assn.*): 1061 Budapest, Anker-köz 1; f. 1909; 6,000 mems.; Pres. BARNA MEZEY; Sec.-Gen. MIKLÓS PREISICH; publs. *Magyar Kémikusok Lapja* (Hungarian Chemistry Journal, monthly), *Magyar Kémiai Folyóirat* (Journal of Hungarian Chemists, monthly).

***Magyar Meteorológiai Társaság** (*Hungarian Meteorological Society*): Budapest, VI, Anker-köz 1; f. 1925; 570 mems.; Pres. BÉLA BÉLL; Gen. Sec. JÓZSEF SZAKÁLY.

***Magyarhoni Földtani Társulat** (*Hungarian Geological Society*): H. Budapest 1061, Anker-köz 1; f. 1848; 1,600 mems.; Pres. V. DANK; Sec. GÉZA HÁMOR; publ. *Földtani Közlöny*† (Bulletin, quarterly).

***Optikai, Akusztikai és Filmtechnikai Egyesület** (*Optical, Acoustical and Filmtechnical Society*): 1061 Budapest,

Anker-köz 1; f. 1933; 1,800 mems.; Pres. István Kondor; Sec.-Gen. T. Barna; publs. *Kép és Hangtechnika* (Picture and Audio Techniques), *Finommechanika-Mikrotechnika* (Precision Mechanics- Microtechnics).

Psychology

Magyar Pszichológiai Társaság (*Hungarian Psychological Society*): Budapest 1124, Meredek u. 1; f. 1928; Pres. E. Moussong; Gen. Sec. Jenő Ranschburg; publ. *Pszichológiai Szemle* (Psychological Review).

Sociology

Magyar Néprajzi Társaság (*Hungarian Ethnographical Society*): H-1055 Budapest, Kossuth Lajos tér 12; f. 1889; 942 mems.; Pres. István Tálasi; Sec.-Gen. Bertalan Andrásfalvy; publs. *Ethnographia* (quarterly), *Néprajzi Hirek* (newsletter).

Technology

***Bőr-, Cipő-, és Bőrfeldolgozóipari Tudományos Egyesület** (*Scientific Society of the Leather, Shoe and Allied Industries*): 1053 Budapest, Kossuth Lajos u. 6; f. 1930; Pres. Mrs. E. Vermes; Sec.-Gen. Dr. Péter Weitzner; publ. *Bőr és Cipőtechnika* (Leather and Shoemaking).

***Energiagazdálkodási Tudományos Egyesület** (*Scientific Society for Energetics*): Budapest, V, Kossuth Lajos tér 6-8; f. 1949; 5,050 mems.; Pres. Dr. Imre Lőrinc; Sec.-Gen. István Varga; publs. *Energia és Atomtechnika*† (Energy and Nuclear Engineering), *Energiagazdálkodás*† (Energy Economics) (both monthly).

***Faipari Tudományos Egyesület** (*Scientific Society of the Timber Industry*): 1061 Budapest, Anker-köz 1; f. 1950; 3,300 mems.; Pres. Kálmán Strobl; Sec.-Gen. László Somogyi; publ. *Faipur* (Timber Industry).

***Gépipari Tudományos Egyesület** (*Scientific Society of Mechanical Engineers*): 1372 Budapest, 5, P.O.B. 451; f. 1949; 18,000 mems.; library of 1,500 vols.; Pres. Prof. Dr. Ing. József Varga; Sec.-Gen. Ing. Lajos Kuti; publs. *Gép* (Machine), *Járművek, Mezőgazdasági Gépek* (Vehicles and Agricultural Machines), *Gépgyártástechnológia* (Production Engineering), *Műanyag és Gumi* (Plastics and Rubber), *Gépipar* (Machinery).

***Hiradástechnikai Tudományos Egyesület** (*Scientific Society for Telecommunications*): 1372 Budapest, (P.f. 451) Kossuth tér 6-8; f. 1949; 2,570 mems.; Pres. Aurél Komporday; Sec.-Gen. György Almássy; publ. *Hiradástechnika* (Telecommunication).

***Közlekedéstudományi Egyesület** (*Scientific Society for Transport*): 1055 Budapest, Kossuth Lajos tér 6-8; f. 1949; 13,500 mems.; Pres. Dipl. Oec. László Földvári; Sec.-Gen. Dr. Ing. Prof. Endre Kerkápoly; publs. *Közlekedéstudományi Szemle* (Communications Review), *Mélyépítéstudományi Szemle* (Civil Engineering Review), *Városi Közlekedés* (Urban Transport).

***Magyar Elektrotechnikai Egyesület** (*Hungarian Electrotechnical Association*): 1055 Budapest, Kossuth Lajos tér 6-8; f. 1900; 5,000 mems.; Pres. János Sebestyén; Gen. Sec. Sándor Szepessy; publs. *Electrotechnika* (Electrical Engineering, monthly), *Villamosság* (Electricity).

***Magyar Iparjogvédelmi Egyesület** (*Hungarian Association for the Protection of Industrial Property*): 1055 Budapest, V, Kossuth Lajos tér 6-8; f. 1962; 1,600 mems.; Pres. Dr. Jenő Szilbereky; Sec.-Gen. Gyula Horváth; publs. *Újitók Lapja* (Innovators' Journal).

***Méréstechnikai es Automatizálási Tudományos Egyesület** (*Scientific Society for Measurement and Automation*): 1372 Budapest, V, Kossuth tér 6-8, p.f. 457; f. 1952; 2,400 mems.; Pres. Andor Frigyes; Gen. Sec. Dr. I. Martos; publ. *Mérés és Automatika* (Measurement and Control).

***Neumann János Számitógéptudományi Társaság** (*John v. Neumann Society for Computer Science*): 1061 Budapest, Anker köz 1; f. 1968; 3,100 mems.; Pres. Tibor Vámos; Sec.-Gen. Győző Kovács.

***Országos Magyar Bányászati és Kohászati Egyesület** (*Hungarian Mining and Metallurgical Society*): Budapest, VI, Anker köz 1; f. 1892; Pres. Gábor Kreffly; Gen. Sec. Dr. Zoltán Nagy; 9,500 mems.; publs. *Bányászat* (Mining), *Kohászat* (Metallurgy), *Öntöde* (Foundry), *Kőolaj és Földgáz* (Oil and Gas).

***Papír- és Nyomdaipari Műszaki Egyesület** (*Technical Association of the Paper and Printing Industry*): 1055 Budapest, Kossuth Lajos tér 6-8; f. 1949; 3,300 mems.; Pres. György Vámos; Sec.-Gen. Péter Gáti; publs. *Papíripar* and *Magyar Grafika* (Paper Industry and Hungarian Graphics).

***Szervezési és Vezetési Tudományos Társaság** (*Society for Organization and Management Science*): 1368 Budapest, Anker köz 1; f. 1970; 1,350 mems.; Pres. József Drecin; Sec.-Gen. G. Bérci; publ. *Ipargazdaság* (Industrial Economy, monthly).

***Szilikátipari Tudományos Egyesület** (*Scientific Society of the Silicate Industry*): H-1061 Budapest, Anker köz 1; f. 1949; 2,100 mems.; library of *c.* 2,500 vols.; Pres. Lajos Szokúp; Sec.-Gen. Elemér Grofcsik; publ. *Építőanyag* (Building Materials).

***Textilipari Müszaki és Tudományos Egyesület** (*Society of* (*Textile Technology and Science*): 1061 Budapest, Anker-Köz 1; f. 1948; 9,300 mems.; Pres. István Rusznák; Gen. Sec. Pál Füsti; publs. *Magyar Textiltechnika*† (Hungarian Textile Engineering), *Textilipari Tervgazdaság* (Planned Economy in the Textile Industry).

RESEARCH INSTITUTES

(*See* also under Universities)

Agriculture and Veterinary Science

Állattenyésztési Kutatóintézet (*Research Institute for Animal Husbandry*): 2053 Herceghalom; f. 1896; animal breeding, physiology and reproductive biology, nutrition; 52 research workers; library of 12,000 vols.; Dir. János Keserü; publs. research papers.

Gabonatermesztési Kutató Intézet (*Cereal Research Institute*): Alsókikötősor 5, Szeged; f. 1924; wheat, barley, oats, maize, sorghum, sunflower, oil-flax, winter coleseed breeding and genetical research; library of 12,000 vols.; Dir. Dr. Imre Széniel; publs. *Cereal Research Communications*† (quarterly), *Annual Report*.

Magyar Tudományos Akadémia Állatorvostudományi Kutatóintézete (*Research Institute for Veterinary Science*): Budapest, XIV, Hungária-krt. 21; f. 1949; research in infectious and parasitic diseases of domestic animals; library of 5,800 vols.; Dir. János Mészáros.

Magyar Tudományos Akadémia Mezőgazdasági Kutató Intézete (*Agricultural Research Institute of the Hungarian Academy of Sciences*): H-2462 Martonvásár; f. 1949; research in plant genetics, plant physiology, plant breeding and plant cultivation; library of 16,000 vols.; Dir. Dr. Sándor Rajki.

Magyar Tudományos Akadémia Talajtani és Agrokémiai Kutató Intézete (*Research Institute for Soil Science and Agricultural Chemistry of the Hungarian Academy of Sciences*): 1022 Budapest, II, Herman Ottó u. 15; f.

1949; research in soil physics, chemistry, genesis, geography and cartography, reclamation of salt-affected and sandy soils, irrigation, conservation, fertilization, soil mineralogy, soil microbiology, soil ecology, recultivation; isotope laboratory; 200 staff; library of 22,516 vols.; Dir. Prof. Dr. I. SZABOLCS; publs. *Agrokémia és Talajtan*† (Agrochemistry and Soil Science, quarterly).

Növényvédelmi Kutató Intézet (*Hungarian Research Institute for Plant Protection*): Budapest, II, Herman Ottó u. 15; f. 1880, reorganized 1950; research into virus, bacterial and fungal plant diseases, insect and weed control methods; 154 mems.; library of 10,000 vols.; Dir. Z. KIRÁLY; publ. *Annales Instituti Protectionis Plantarum Hungarici* (Yearbook).

Országos Állategészségügyi Intézet (*Central Veterinary Institute*): 1149 Budapest, XIV, Tábornok u. 2; f. 1928; diagnostic examinations and scientific research work on the infectious, parasitic and metabolic diseases of animals, also veterinary toxicology and diseases of wild animals; 177 mems.; library of 5,343 vols.; Dir. Dr. Cs. SZENTMIKLÓSSY.

Országos Gyapjú- és Selyemminősítő Intézet (*National Institute for Grading of Wool and Silk*): Budapest, II, Kitaibel Pál u. 1; f. 1898; Dir. JÓZSEF SCHANDL.

Országos Vetőmag és Szaporitóanyag Felügyelőség (*National Inspectorate for Seed and Plant Reproduction Material*): H-1525 Budapest 114, P.O.B. 93; f. 1881; 442 mems.; library of 18,000 vols.; Dir. Dr. B. SZALÓCZY.

Szőlészeti és Borászati Kutató Intézet (*Research Institute for Viticulture and Oenology*): 6000 Kecskemét, Katona József tér 8; f. 1898; library of 10,000 vols.; Dir. J. GODÓR; publs. *Szőlészeti és Borászati Kutató Intézet Évkönyve*† (Yearbook), *Szőlészet és Borászat*† (Viticulture and Oenology).

Tejgazdasági Kisérleti Intézet (*Hungarian Dairy Experimental Institute*): Mosonmagyaróvár, Lucsony u. 24; f. 1903; brs. in Budapest and Pécs; scientific research of raw materials, technology, engineering, chemistry, microbiology, economics; Dir. Dr. FERENC KETTING; Deputy Chief GYÖRGY BABELLA; publ. *Dairy Research Communications* (yearly).

Vizgazdálkodási Tudományos Kutatóközpont (*Research Centre for Water Resources Development*): 1095 Budapest, Kvassay Jenő ut. 1; f. 1952; basic, applied and development research associated with hydrological data collection, processing, storage, information; hydrology of ground-, karstic water, regional soil moisture control; hydromechanics of hydraulic structures; pollution and quality control of water; hydrological and hydraulic problems in agricultural water management (irrigation); 900 staff; library of *c.* 12,000 vols.; Dir.-Gen. Dr. GYÖRGY KOVÁCS, D.SC.; publs. *Hydrological Yearbook of Hungary, Hydrological Atlases of Hungarian Catchments, VITUKI Proceedings*† (research reports, etc., mostly with summaries in a world language).

THE ARTS

Magyar Tudományos Akadémia Művészettörténeti Kutatócsoportja (*Research Institute for Art History*): Budapest 1014, Uri-utca 62; f. 1969; Dir. NÓRA ARADI, D.SC.

Magyar Tudományos Akadémia Zenetudományi Intézete (*Institute for Musicology of the Hungarian Academy of Sciences*): H-1014 Budapest, I, Országház u. 9; f. 1961; incorporates the *Bartók Archives*, the *Hungarian Museum of History of Music*, and depts. of Sociology of Music, Folk Music, Folk Dances, Theory of Music, History of Music; library of 35,590 vols., 100,000 recorded melodies; publs. *Documenta Bartókiana*†, *Musicologia Hungarica*† (annually), *Corpus Musicae Popularis Hungaricae*†.

ECONOMICS, LAW AND POLITICS

Magyar Tudományos Akadémia Világgazdasági Kutató Intézete (*Institute for World Economics of the Hungarian Academy of Sciences*): Budapest, XII, Kálló esperes u. 15; f. 1965; research in world economics; library of 40,000 vols.; Dir. JÓZSEF BOGNÁR; publ. *Tanulmányok a fejlődő országokról*† (Studies on Developing Countries, irregular in Hungarian, English, French, German, Spanish and Russian).

Magyar Tudományos Akadémia Állam- és Jogtudományi Intézete (*Institute for Legal and Administrative Sciences of the Hungarian Academy of Sciences*): Budapest, I, Országház u. 32; f. 1949; departments of political and legal theory, international law, constitutional and administrative law, civil law, criminal law, comparative law, documentation; library of 30,000 vols.; Dir. Prof. IMRE SZABÓ.

Magyar Tudományos Akadémia Ipargazdaságtani Kutatócsoportja (*Research Institute for Industrial Economics of the Hungarian Academy of Sciences*): 1112 Budapest, Budaörsi ut 43-45; f. 1960; Dir. ZOLTÁN ROMÁN, C.SC.; publ. *Ipargazdasági Szemle*.

Magyar Tudományos Akadémia Közgazdaságtudományi Intézete (*Institute of Economics of the Hungarian Academy of Sciences*): 1112 Budapest, Budaörsi ut 43-45; f. 1954; research in the economic problems of the socialist system and of modern capitalism; 113 mems.; 69 research workers; library of 40,000 vols.; Dir. REZSŐ NYERS; publs. *Közgazdasági Szemle*† (Economic Review, monthly, with English and Russian summaries), *Acta Oeconomica*† (bi-monthly, in English, French, German and Russian), *Szigma*† (quarterly, with English and Russian summaries), *Bulletin*† (irregular in Hungarian with English and Russian summaries), *Studies of the Institute of Economics*† (irregular in English), *Reprint Series* (mainly in English and Russian).

EDUCATION

Magyar Tudományos Akadémia Pedagógiai Kutatócsoportja (*Hungarian Academy of Sciences Research Group of Pedagogy*): H-1014 Budapest, Uri-utca 62; f. 1972; 44 mems.; library of 5,000 vols.; Dir. MÁRTON HORVÁTH; publ. *Neveléstudomány és társadalmi gyakorlat* (Educational Science and Social Practice, irregular).

HISTORY, GEOGRAPHY AND ARCHAEOLOGY

Magyar Tudományos Akadémia Dunántuli Tudományos Intézete (*West Hungarian Research Institute of the Hungarian Academy of Sciences*): 7601 Pécs, Kulich u. 22; f. 1943; research into regional planning, geography, ethnography, and history; library of 30,000 vols.; Dir. Prof. Dr. OTTO BIHARI; publs. *Dunántuli Tudományos Gyűjtemény*†, *Értekezések*†, *Dunántuli Tudományos Intézet Közlemények*†.

Magyar Tudományos Akadémia Földrajztudományi Kutató Intézet (*Geographical Research Institute, Hungarian Academy of Sciences*): 1388 Budapest, VI, Népköztársaság u. 62; f. 1950, reorg. 1952; research in physical and economic geography; 80 mems.; library of 58,000 vols. and maps; Dir. Prof. MÁRTON PÉCSI; publs. *Földrajzi Értesítő*† (quarterly), *Földrajzi Tanulmányok*, Studies in Geography in Hungary, Geographical Abstracts, monographs.

Magyar Tudományos Akadémia Régészeti Intézet (*Archaeological Institute of the Hungarian Academy of Sciences*): Budapest, I, Uri u. 49; f. 1958; 25 mems.; library of 20,000 vols.; Dir. LÁSZLÓ GEREVICH; publs. *Studia Archaeologica*† (irregularly in foreign languages), *Magyarország Régészeti Topográfiája*†, *Mitteilungen des Archäologischen Instituts*† (yearbook, in German).

Magyar Tudományos Akadémia Történettudományi Intézete (*Institute of Historical Research of the Hungarian Academy of Sciences*): 1250 Budapest, I, Uri-u. 53; f. 1949; departments of Hungarian history, world history, documentation and bibliography; library of 91,161 vols.; Dir. Zs. P. PACH; Man. Dir. GYÖRGY RÁNKI; publs. *Torténelmi Szemle*†, *Világtörténet*.

LANGUAGE AND LITERATURE

Magyar Tudományos Akadémia Irodalomtudományi Intézete (*Institute of Literary Studies of the Hungarian Academy of Sciences*): 1118 Budapest, XI, Ménesi u. 11-13; f. 1955; research in Hungarian and world literature; 57 mems.; library of 120,000 vols.; Dir. Prof. ISTVÁN SŐTÉR; publs. *Irodalomtörténeti Közlemények* (Proceedings), *Helikon* (quarterly), *Literatura* (quarterly), *Irodalomtörténeti Füzetek* (studies), etc.

Magyar Tudományos Akadémia Nyelvtudományi Intézete (*Institute of Linguistics of the Hungarian Academy of Sciences*): 1014 Budapest 1, Szentháromság u. 2; f. 1949; library of 28,000 vols.; 100 mems.; Dir. P. HAJDÚ.

MEDICINE

Magyar Tudományos Akadémia Kisérleti Orvostudományi Kutató Intézete (*Institute of Experimental Medicine of the Hungarian Academy of Sciences*): 1083 Budapest, Szigony u. 43; f. 1952; research work in experimental morphology, pathophysiology, pharmacology, etc.; library of *c.* 15,300 vols.; Dir. ERVIN STARK, M.D., D.SC.

Országos Közegészségügyi Intézet (*National Institute of Hygiene*): H-1966 Budapest, Gyáli u. 2-6; f. 1927; research in environmental health, epidemiology, microbiology; 160 research staff; library of 30,000 vols.; Dir. Dr. B. TÓTH; publ. *Évi Müködés*† (Annual Report).

Országos Onkológiai Intézet (*National Institute of Oncology*): 1125 Budapest XII, Ráth György u. 7/9; f. 1952; experimental and clinical activities; 130 staff; library of 12,020 vols., 253 periodicals, service for reprints of all publs. available; Dir. Dr. S. J. ECKHARDT; publ. *Magyar Onkologia*† (quarterly), *Anti-Tumour Drug Reports*† (every 2 months, in English and Russian).

NATURAL SCIENCE

Biological Sciences

Magyar Madártani Intézet (*Hungarian Institute of Ornithology*): Budapest, XII, Költő u. 23; f. 1893; 5 mems.; 6,700 vols.; Dir. Dr. ISTVÁN STERBETZ (acting); library; publ. *Aquila* (Yearbook).

Magyar Tudományos Akadémia Biológiai Kutató Intézete (*The Biological Research Institute of the Hungarian Academy of Sciences*): 8237 Tihany; f. 1927; research particularly in experimental biology, hydrobiology, and experimental zoology; 22 scientists; library of 15,000 vols.; Dir. Prof. Dr. JÁNOS SALÁNKI; publ. *Annales Instituti Biologici (Tihany) Hungaricae Academiae Scientiarum*.

Magyar Tudományos Akadémia Botanikai Kutató Intézete (*Botanical Research Institute of the Hungarian Academy of Sciences*): H-2163 Vácrátót; theoretical and experimental research; library of 1,600 vols.; Dir. Dr. ÁRPÁD BERCZIK.

Magyar Tudományos Akadémia Mikrobiológiai Kutatócsoportja (*Microbiological Research Group of the Hungarian Academy of Sciences*): Budapest, XII, Pihenő u. 1; f. 1963; oncogenic viruses, virus tumours, interferon, mycobacteria and mycobacteriophages; library of 2,000 vols.; Dir. ISTVÁN FÖLDES.

Magyar Tudományos Akadémia Szegedi Biológiai Központja (*Biological Research Centre of the Hungarian Academy of Sciences*): H-6701 Szeged, Odesszai-krt. 62, P.O.B. 521; f. 1971; library of 25,000 vols.; Dir. LAJOS ALFÖLDI.

Institutes:

Biofizikai Intézet (*Institute of Biophysics*): f. 1971; Dir. LAJOS KESZTHELYI.

Biokémiai Intézet (*Institute of Biochemistry*): f. 1950; Dir. M. WOLLEMANN.

Enzimológiai Intézet (*Enzymology Institute*): Budapest, XI, Karolina u. 29; Dir. F. BRUNO STRAUB.

Genetikai Intézet (*Institute of Genetics*): f. 1942; Dir. LAJOS ALFÖLDI.

Növényélettani Intézet (*Institute of Plant Physiology*): f. 1970; Dir. G. L. FARKAS.

Mathematics

Magyar Tudományos Akadémia Matematikai Kutató Intézete (*Mathematical Institute of the Hungarian Academy of Sciences*): Budapest, V, Reáltanoda u. 13-15; f. 1950; research in fields of pure and applied mathematics; 80 mems.; library of 28,000 vols.; Dir. Prof. LÁSZLÓ FEJES TÓTH.

Physical Sciences

Magyar Tudományos Akadémia Csillagvizsgáló Intézet (*Observatory of the Hungarian Academy of Sciences*): Budapest, XII, Szabadsághegy, Konkoly Thege Miklós u. 13-17; f. 1899; 52 staff; library of 30,000 vols.; Mountain Station: Piszkéstető, u.p. Galyatető; f. 1962; Schmidt telescope and Cassegrain-reflector; Station for tracking artificial satellites: Baja (Southern Hungary); Dir. BÉLA SZEIDL; publs. *Mitteilungen der Sternwarte der Ungarischen Akademie der Wissenschaften*, *Information Bulletin on Variable Stars of Commission 27 of the I.A.U.*

Magyar Állami Eötvös Loránd Geofizikai Intézet (*Loránd Eötvös Hungarian Geophysical Institute*): H-1145 Budapest XIV, Columbus u. 17-23; f. 1919; geophysical exploration of hydrocarbons, coal, bauxite, water, ores; engineering geophysics; Dir. PÁL MÜLLER; Deputy Dir. FERENC HONFI; library of 40,000 vols.; publs. *Geofizikai Közlemények* (Geophysical Transactions, annually), *Évi Jelentés* (Annual Report); attached to the Institute:

Geophysical Observatory: Tihany; f. 1954; Dir. ZOLTÁN SZABÓ; publ. *Annual Report*.

Magyar Állami Földtani Intézet (*Hungarian State Geological Institute*): Budapest, XIV, Népstadion u. 14; f. 1869; conducts a geological survey of Hungary; over 700 mems.; library of 155,000 vols.; Dir. Prof. G. HÁMOR; publs. *Évi jelentés*† (Annual Report), *Évkönyv*† (Yearbook), *Geologica Hungarica: (a) Series Geologica*†, *(b) Series Palaeontologica*†, and geological maps† and explanatory notes.

Magyar Tudományos Akadémia Atommag Kutató Intézete (*Institute of Nuclear Research of the Hungarian Academy of Sciences*): H-4001 Debrecen, Bem-tér 18/c; f. 1954; basic research in low-energy nuclear physics and applications of nuclear methods in other sciences; 255 staff; 35,000 vols. in library; Dir. Prof. DÉNES BERÉNYI; publ. *ATOMKI Közlemények* (quarterly bulletin).

Magyar Tudományos Akadémia Geodéziai és Geofizikai Kutató Intézete (*Geodetical and Geophysical Research Institute of the Hungarian Academy of Sciences*): H-9400 Sopron, Múzeum u. 6; f. 1955 as two separate laboratories, merged as one institute 1971; research in advanced problems of geodesy and in general and applied geophysics including seismology; library of 25,000 vols.; Dir. Dr. J. SOMOGYI; publs. *Institute Reports*† (irregular), *Geophysical Observatory Reports*† (annual).

Magyar Tudományos Akadémia Izotópintézete (*Institute of Isotopes of the Hungarian Academy of Sciences*): H-1525 Budapest, P.O.B. 77; f. 1959; research in the field of isotope techniques and chemistry; library of 12,000 vols.; Dir. ÁRPÁD VERES; publ. *Izotóptechnika* (every 2 months, with abstracts in Russian and English).

Magyar Tudományos Akadémia Központi Fizikai Kutató Intézete (*Central Research Institute for Phsyics of the Hungarian Academy of Sciences*): H-1525 Budapest, P.O.B. 49; f. 1950; comprises high energy physics and cosmic rays, optics, nuclear physics, reactor physics, solid state physics, chemistry, engineering, measuring and computing techniques; library of 100,000 vols.; Dir. Dr. FERENC SZABÓ; publs. *Yearbook*, *KFKI Reports*, *List of Publications*†, *Catalogue of Equipment*.

Magyar Tudományos Akadémia Központi Kémiai Kutató Intézete (*Central Research Institute for Chemistry of the Hungarian Academy of Sciences*): 1025 Budapest, II, Pusztaszeri u. 59/67; f. 1952; fundamental research in organic, bio-organic and physical chemistry, chemistry and structure of biologically active compounds, catalytic reactions of hydrocarbons, polymerization kinetics and polymer degradation, study of molecular structure; 230 research staff; library of 30,000 vols.; Dir.-Gen. Prof. Dr. FERENC MÁRTA.

Magyar Tudományos Akadémia Műszaki Fizikai Kutató Intézete (*Research Institute for Technical Physics of the Hungarian Academy of Sciences*): 1325 Budapest, P.O.B. 76; f. 1958; fundamental research in the field of technical physics; library of 18,000 vols.; Dir. Dr. ELEMÉR NAGY; publ. *Yearbook*†.

Magyar Tudományos Akadémia Műszaki Kémiai Kutató Intézete (*Research Institute for Technical Chemistry of the Hungarian Academy of Sciences*): Veszprém, Schönherz Zoltán u. 2; f. 1960; Dir. Dr. TIBOR BLICKLE.

Magyar Tudományos Akadémia Napfizikai Obszervatóriuma (*Heliophysical Observatory of the Hungarian Academy of Sciences*): H-4010 Debrecen, P.O.B. 30; f. 1958; mainly solar activity studies; Dir. LORÁNT DEZSŐ; publ. *Publications*†.

Nehézvegyipari Kutató Intézet (*Research Institute for Heavy Chemical Industries*): Veszprém, Wartha Vince u. 1-3; f. 1949; applied research in agricultural pesticides and fertilizers, air pollution, electronic systems, radioisotopes, corrosion and the application of chemicals in agriculture; library of 16,000 vols. and 10,800 periodicals; Dir. Dr. ANDRÁS SZÁNTO; publs. *Közleményei*† (Communications, irregular), *Hungarian Journal of Industrial Chemistry*† (joint publication of the Veszprém Scientific Institutions of the Chemical Industry) (quarterly).

Uránia Bemutató Csillagvizsgáló (*Urania Public Observatory*): H-1016 Budapest, I, Sánc u. 3B; f. 1947; 5 mems.; 8-inch Heyde-Merz refractor; library of 1,100 vols.; Dir. AURÉL PONORI THEWREWK; publs. *Föld és Ég*† (Earth and Sky, monthly), *Meteor*† (bi-monthly).

PHILOSOPHY AND PSYCHOLOGY

Magyar Tudományos Akadémia Filozófiai Intézete (*Institute for Philosophy of the Hungarian Academy of Sciences*): 1054 Budapest, Szemere u. 10; f. 1957 for research into problems of epistemology, philosophy of science, methodological problems of social sciences, philosophy of religion, history of modern philosophical thought, studies in the life and work of György Lukács; Lukács archives and library; 57 mems.; institute library of 14,000 vols.; Dir. JÓZSEF LUKACS.

Magyar Tudományos Akadémia Pszichológiai Intézete (*Institute of Psychology of the Hungarian Academy of Sciences*): 1068 Budapest, Szondy u. 83-85; f. 1902; basic research on experimental psychology, psychophysiology, developmental psychology, social psychology and personality, research on educational psychology and clinical psychology; 55 staff; library of 15,000 vols.; Dir. FERENC PATAKI, PH.D.; publ. *Pszichologia*† (quarterly).

SOCIOLOGY AND ANTHROPOLOGY

Magyar Tudományos Akadémia Néprajzi Kutatócsoportja (*Ethnographical Research Group of the Hungarian Academy of Sciences*): Budapest, I, Országház u. 30; f. 1967; Dir. Dr. TIBOR BODROGI.

Magyar Tudományos Akadémia Szociológiai Kutató Intézete (*Sociological Institute of the Hungarian Academy of Sciences*): 1014 Budapest, Uri u. 49; f. 1963; study of social structure, sociology of organizations and urban and rural sociology, sociology of science and problems of quality of life; 43 mems.; library of 7,000 vols.; Dir. KÁLMÁN KULCSÁR; publs. *Szociológia (quarterly)*, *Szociológiai tanulmányok* (Social Studies, 3–4 issues a year).

TECHNOLOGY

Magyar Tudományos Akadémia Olajbányászati Kutatólaboratóriuma (*Reservoir Engineering Research Laboratory of the Hungarian Academy of Sciences*): Miskolc, Egyetemváros; f. 1957; 60 mems.; library of 3,000 vols.; Dir. JÓZSEF TÓTH; publ. *Tanulmányok a rezervoármechanika tárgykörébõl* (Papers of the Reservoir Engineering Department).

Magyar Tudományos Akadémia Számitástechnikai és Automatizálási Kutató Intézete (*Computer and Automation Institute of the Hungarian Academy of Sciences*): H-1111 Budapest, Kende u. 13/17; f. 1972; conducts research and development in computer applications for production, engineering, economic and environmental systems; 780 mems.; library of 28,000 vols.; Dir. Prof. Dr. TIBOR VÁMOS; publs. *Reports of the Institute* (irregular), *Users' Handbook*† (irregular), *Studies*† (irregular), *Computational Linguistics*†.

Szilikátipari Központi Kutató és Tervező Intézet (*Central Research and Design Institute of the Silicate Industry*): H-1300 Budapest, P.O.B. 112; f. 1953; research and technological design in the silicate sciences and building materials industry; 900 mems.; library of 19,000 vols., 5,800 periodicals; Dir. Prof. Dr. JÓZSEF TALABÉR; publs. *Tudományos Közlemények*† (irregular, summaries in English, German, French, Russian), *Transactions*† (irregular, in English, German, French, Russian).

LIBRARIES AND ARCHIVES

Agrártudományi Egyetem Könyvtára—Gödöllő (*Library of the University of Agricultural Sciences at Gödöllő*): 2100 Gödöllő, Páter Károly u. 1; f. 1945; 260,000 vols., 1,400 current periodicals; Dir. Dr. GY. LŐRINCZ; publs. bibliographies and studies.

Agrártudományi Egyetem Könyvtára—Keszthely (*Library of the Agricultural University—Keszthely*): 8361 Keszthely, Deák F. u. 16; f. 1954; 75,000 vols.; Dir. Mrs. ZSUZSA TÓSZEGI.

Állami Gorkij Könyvtár (*Gorky State Library*): Budapest, V, Molnár u. 11; f. 1956; Hungarian Foreign Language Library; collection of music scores and records; 75 staff; 260,000 vols.; houses and services Central Catalogue of Foreign Literature in Hungarian Libraries; Dir. GYULA TÓTH; publs. Accession List (quarterly), Music Accession List (twice yearly), Periodical and Newspaper Accession List (annually), *News of World Literature*, *Abstracts of Music Literature* (quarterly).

Budapest Főváros Levéltára (*Budapest City Archives*): Budapest, V, Városház u. 9/11; f. 1777; 15,000 metres of bookshelves; Dir. Dr. ÁGNES SÁGVÁRI.

Budapesti Műszaki Egyetem Központi Könyvtára (*Central Library of Budapest Technical University*): Budapest, H-1111, Budafoki u. 4-6; f. 1848; 350,000 vols., 83,000 periodicals; Dir. Dr. KÁROLY HÉBERGER; publs. *Évkönyvek*† (Yearbook) (every 4 or 5 years), *Műszaki Egyetemi Könyvtáros*† (Technical University Librarian) (2 a year), *Felsöoktatási Szakirodalmi Tájékoztato. A sor. Műszaki és Természettudományok*† (Special Literature Review in Higher Education; Ser. A. Science and Technology) (2 a year), *Európai Műszaki Egyetemek és Főiskolák Szakositási Rendje*† (Specialization Systems at European Technical Universities and Colleges) (series), *A Budapesti Műszaki Egyetem Könyvtári Hálózata Külföldi Folyóiratainak Lelőhelyjegyzéke*† (every 2 years).

Eötvös Lóránd Tudományegyetem, Egyetemi Könyvtár (*Eötvös Lóránd University Library*): 1372 Budapest, Károlyi Mihály u. 10, P.O.B. 483; f. 1635; 1,301,362 vols., 191 codices, 1,136 incunabula, 2,615 old Hungarian printed works (to 1711); Dir.-Gen. Prof. BÉLA G. NÉMETH; publ. *Yearbook of the University Library*.

Eötvös Lóránd Tudományegyetem Állam- és Jogtudományi Kar Könyvtára (*Faculty of Law Library of Eötvös Lóránd University*): 1053 Budapest, Egyetem tér 1-3; f. 1957; 28,766 vols., 6,265 periodicals, 10,929 MSS., 7,010 sundry; Dir. KATALIN DIÓSZEGHY-SZÉPE; publs. *Tájékoztató* (Bulletin), *Acta Facultatis Politico-Juridicae, Annales Univ. Sci. Budapestinensis Sect. Juridica*.

Erdészeti és Faipari Egyetem Kőzponti Kőnyvtára (*Central Library of the University of Forestry and of the Timber Industry*): 9401 Sopron, Bajcsy-Zsilinszky u. 4; f. 1735; 180,000 vols.; Dir. Dr. ISTVÁN HILLER.

Főszékesegyházi Könyvtár (*Library of Esztergom Cathedral*): 2500 Esztergom, Bajcsy-Zsilinszky u. 28; f. in the 11th century; 200,000 vols.; Dir. Canon Dr. ZOLTÁN KOVÁCH.

Fővárosi Szabó Ervin Könyvtár (*Ervin Szabó Municipal Library*): 1371 Budapest, Pf. 487, VIII, Szabó Ervin tér 1; f. 1904; sociology, humanities; 3,499,467 vols. (809,186 vols. in central library); 97 brs.; Dir. JENŐ KISS; publ. *Yearbook*, and numerous publs. on sociology†.

Hadtudományi Könyvtár (*Library of Military Science*): H-1014 Budapest, Kapisztrán tér 2; 120,000 vols.

Hittudományi Akadémia Könyvtára (*Library of the Catholic Theological Academy*): Budapest, V, Eötvös L. u. 7; f. 1635; history, theology and linguistics; 30,000 vols. (books from *c.* 1880, older material kept in the Library of the University); also houses the Collection of the Brothers of St. Paul (f. 1775; 12,000 vols.; incunabula and MSS. from the 15th and 16th centuries), Központi Papnevelő Intézet Könyvtára and the Library of the Central Catholic Seminary (f. 1805; 17,300 vols.); Dir. Dr. JÓZSEF FÉLEGYHÁZY.

Iparművészeti Múzeum Könyvtára (*Library of the Museum of Applied Arts*): Budapest, IX, Üllői u. 33-37; f. 1872; scientific research library for the decorative arts; 30,000 vols.; 7,176 periodicals; Dir. Dr. IMRE JAKABFFY; publ. *Ars Decorativa*† (annual).

József Attila Tudományegyetem Központi Könyvtára (*Central Library of the Attila József University*): H-6701 Szeged, Dugonics-tér 13; f. 1921; 693,389 vols.; Dir. Dr. BÉLA KARÁCSONYI; publs. *A Szegedi Egyetemi Könyvtár Kiadványai*†, *Acta Universitatis Szegediensis de Attila József Nominatae: Acta Bibliothecaria*†, *Dissertationes ex Bibliotheca Universitatis de Attila József nominatae*†.

Kertészeti Egyetem Könyvtára (*Library of the University of Horticulture*): 1502 Budapest, XI, Villányi u. 35-43; f. 1860; horticulture, viticulture, pomology, oenology, nursery, food technology, tobacco growing, garden and landscape; 207,000 vols., 1,300 current periodicals; Dir. Dr. GUSZTÁV GEDAY; publs. *A Kertészeti Egyetem Közleményei*† (University of Horticulture Publications), *A "Lippai János" Tudományos Ülésszak Előadásai*† (every 2–3 years), etc.

Kossuth Lajos Tudományegyetem Könyvtára (*Lajos Kossuth University Library*): 4010 Debrecen; f. 1916; 939,953 vols.; Dir. Dr. ISTVÁN CSÜRY; publ. *Könyv és Könyvtár* (annually).

Központi Statisztikai Hivatal Könyvtár és Dokumentációs Szolgálat (*Library and Documentation Service of the Central Statistical Office*): H-1525 Budapest, Pf. 10, II, Keleti Károly u. 5; f. 1869; 513,431 books and periodicals; exchange centre for official statistical publications; Dir. Dr. D. DÁNYI; publs. *Statisztikai Irodalmi Figyelő* (monthly), *Számok és Történelem* (irregular), *Történeti Statisztikai Tanulmányok* (irregular), etc.

Kulturális Minisztérium Levéltári Osztály (*National Board of Archives*): 1014 Budapest, I, Uri u. 54-56; f. 1950; functions as supervising board of all archives in Hungary; Gen. Dir. JÓZSEF MOLNÁR.

Liszt Ferenc Zenemüvészeti Főiskola Könyvtára (*Library of the Ferenc Liszt Academy of Music*): 1391 Budapest, Liszt Ferenc tér 8, P.O.B. 206; f. 1875; 108,000 musical scores plus 30,000 books and periodicals; collection of Liszt mementoes; Dir. JÁNOS KÁRPÁTI.

Magyar Irók Könyvtára (*Library of Hungarian Writers*): 1062 Budapest, Bajza u. 18; f. 1950; maintained by the Hungarian Writers Federation; collection of belles-lettres, history of literature, linguistics and allied sciences by Hungarian and foreign authors, translated and/or in original languages; 90,000 vols., 52 foreign and 108 Hungarian periodicals; Dir. Mrs. ISTVÁN KENDE.

Magyar Izraeliták Országos Könyvtára (*Library of the Hungarian Jews*): Budapest, VIII, József-krt. 27; comprises:

Library of the Jewish Community: Budapest, VIII, József-krt. 27; public circulating library for Jews; *c.* 22,000 vols.; Librarian Prof. Dr. SÁNDOR SCHEIBER.

Library of the Jewish Theological Seminary of Hungary: Budapest, VIII, Rökk Szilard u. 26; f. 1877; 40,000 vols.; Librarian Prof. Dr. SÁNDOR SCHEIBER.

Magyar Nemzeti Galéria Könyvtára (*Library of the Hungarian National Gallery*): 1250 Budapest, Budavári Palota, Pf. 31; f. 1957; books on art from all over the world, specializing in Hungarian sculpture, wood-carvings, panel paintings, Baroque art, art from the 12th century onwards; 25,000 vols., 18,000 catalogues, 5,000 periodicals, 12,000 slides; Dir. Dr. ÉVA RÓZSA; publ. *A Magyar Nemzeti Galéria Evkönyve*† (Annals), catalogues†.

Magyar Nemzeti Múzeum Régészeti Könyvtára (*Archaeological Library of the Hungarian National Museum*): 1088 Budapest, Múzeum-körút 14-16; f. 1952; 95,000 vols. of Hungarian and foreign archaeology, numismatics and history; Dir. Dr. SÁNDOR SOPRONI; publs. *List of Exchange Publications*, *Folia Archaeologica* (annually), *Folia Historica* (annually), *Régészeti Füzetek* (*Fasciculi Archaeologici*).

Magyar Országos Levéltár (*Hungarian National Archives*): 1250 Budapest, I., Bécsikapu-tér 4; f. 1756; 33,000 metres of shelving; records dating from the 12th century to 1944; Gen. Dir. Dr. JÁNOS VARGA; Dir. JÁNOS BUZÁSI; publ. *Levéltári Közlemények* (Journal of the Hungarian National Archives).

Magyar Szinházi Intézet Könyvtára (*Library of the Hungarian Theatre Institute*): 1016 Budapest, Krisztina körut 57; f. 1957; Hungarian and universal theatre and drama theory and history; 50,000 vols.; collection includes periodicals, microfilms; Dir. Miss ERZSÉBET ANGYAL.

Magyar Testnevelési Főiskola Könyvtára (*Library of the Hungarian College of Physical Education*): 1123 Budapest, Alkotás utca 44; f. 1925; collection covers physical education, sport and allied domains, also literature by Hungarian and foreign authors; 64,000 vols.; 142 domestic and 195 foreign trade papers; Dir. FERENC KRASOVEC; publs. *List of New Accessions* (quarterly), *Bibliography of Hungarian Literature on Physical Education and Sport* (annually), *Bulletin of Foreign Sport Literature* (every 2 weeks), *Selected Articles on World Sport* (3 vols. a year, etc.).

Magyar Tudományos Akadémia Földrajztudományi Kutató Intézet Könyvtára (*Library of the Geographical Research Institute of the Hungarian Academy of Sciences*): 1388 Budapest, VI, Népköztársaság u. 62 (Budapest 62, P.O.B. 64); f. 1952; 58,168 vols., 16,527 maps, 7,252 MSS.; Librarian JUDIT SIMONFAI; publs. *Földrajzi Dokumentáció*†, *Területi Kutatások*†, *Abstracts*†.

Magyar Tudományos Akadémia Könyvtára (*Library of the Hungarian Academy of Sciences*): 1361 Budapest, V, Akadémia u. 2, pf. 7; f. 1826; 850,000 vols., 227,000 periodicals, 423,000 MSS.; collection includes Oriental manuscripts, old prints and incunabula; centre for exchange of publications between Hungarian Academy of Sciences and other countries; depository library for dissertations; Academy's archives; centre for interdisciplinary computerized database; reprography service (microfilm, xerox); Dir.-Gen. Dr. GYÖRGY RÓZSA; publs. *Publicationes Bibliothecae Academiae Scientiarum Hungaricae*†, *Tudományszervezési Tájékoztató*† (Bulletin of Science Organization) (every 2 months), *Catalogi Collectionis Manuscriptorum Bibliothecae Academiae Scientiarum Hungaricae*†, *Oriental Studies*†, *Budapest Oriental Reprints*†, *Bulletin of the Csoma de Kőrös Symposium*†, *Analecta Linguistica*†, *Scientometrics*†, *ECSSID Bulletin*†.

Marx Károly Közgazdaságtudományi Egyetem Központi Könyvtára (*Library of the Karl Marx University of Economic Science*): 1093 Budapest, IX, Dimitrov-tér 8; f. 1948; 509,516 vols.; Dir. Dr. GYULA WALLESHAUSEN; publs. *Hungarian Economic Literature*† (annually), *Information on Foreign Economic Literature*† (monthly), *Doctoral Theses*† (every 2 years), *Egyetemi Szemle*† (University Review, Essays, quarterly), and bibliographies†.

Mezőgazdasági és Élelmezésügyi Minisztérium Információs Központja (*Information Centre of the Ministry of Agriculture and Food*): 1012 Budapest, Attila u. 93; f. 1946; *c.* 350,000 vols.; Dir. Dr. SÁNDOR K. NAGY; publs. *Agrárirodalmi Szemle*† (Agricultural Review, monthly), *Mezőgazdasági Világirodalom*† (Agricultural World Literature, quarterly), *Magyar Agrárirodalmi Szemle*† (Hungarian Agricultural Review, quarterly in English, German and Russian), bulletins, etc. Administers:

Károlyi Mihály Országos Mezőgazdasági Könyvtár (*Mihály Károlyi National Agricultural Library*): 1012 Budapest, Attila u. 93; f. 1951; *c.* 350,000 vols.; Head ISTVÁNNÉ SZENTMIKLÓSI; publs. *Magyar Mezőgazdasági Bibliográfia*† (Hungarian Agricultural Bibliography, quarterly), leaflets, reprints, standards and patents in the *Agroinform* collection† (quarterly).

MSZMP KB Párttörténeti Intézetének Könyvtár és Dokumentációs Osztálya (*Library and Documentation Dept. of the Institute of the History of the Party*): Budapest, V, Alkotmány u. 2; f. 1948; 88,000 vols.; Dir. ROBERT VÉRTES; publs. *Párttörténeti Közlemények*.

Nehézipari Műszaki Egyetem Központi Könyvtára (*Central Library of the Technical University for Heavy Industry*): 3515 Miskolc, Egyetemváros; f. 1735; 351,000 vols., 74,000 periodicals; Dir. Dr. JÓZSEF ZSIDAI.

Országgyűlési Könyvtár (*Library of Parliament*): 1357 Budapest, Kossuth Lajos-tér 1-3; f. 1849; parliamentary papers (Hungarian and foreign), contemporary history, administrative and legal sciences, politics, UN depository library; 560,000 vols.; Dir. GÁBOR VÁLYI.

Országos Műszaki Könyvtár és Dokumentációs Központ (*Hungarian Central Technical Library and Documentation Centre*): 1428 Budapest, P.O.B. 12, Reviczky u. 6; f. 1883; 351,727 vols., 5,866 current periodicals, 527,228 translations; Dir.-Gen. Dr. PÉTER LÁZÁR; publs. *Hungarian Technical Abstracts*† (quarterly, in three languages), *Műszaki Lapszemle*† (monthly abstracts journal in 16 series), *Tudományos és Műszaki Tájékoztatás*† (monthly journal of scientific and technical information), *Műszaki Információ*† (monthly reviews in 12 series), *Műszaki-Gazdasági Információ*† (monthly reviews in 8 series), *Műszaki-Gazdasági Tájékoztató*† (monthly review and digest), *Technical Film Cards (International Selection)*† (quarterly, articles and reviews in three languages), *Audio-Vizuális Közlemények*† (every 2 months, review of audio visual techniques), etc.

Országos Orvostudományi Könyvtár és Dokumentációs Központ (*Hungarian Medical Library and Documentation Centre*): H-1372 Budapest, P.O.B. 452; centre for medical libraries and documentation; Hungarian and foreign medical and biological literature documented, and medical bibliographies and reviews compiled; library of 20,000 vols.; Dir. Dr. S. SZÉKELY; publs. *Hungarian Medical Bibliography* (bi-monthly, English edition yearly†), *Medical Librarian*† (quarterly).

Országos Pedagógiai Könyvtár és Múzeum (*Central Library and Museum of Education*): 1055 Budapest, V, Honvéd u. 19; f. 1877, reorganized 1958; methodological centre for educational and school libraries; documentation and information centre for education; pedagogical museum; 360,000 vols.; Dir. Dr. FERENC ARATÓ; publs. *Magyar Pedagógiai Információ*† (Hungarian Educational Information, 6 a year), *Külföldi Pedagógiai Információ*† (International Educational Bulletin, 6 a year), *Nemzetközi Oktatásügy*† (International Education), *Külföldi Pedagógiai Könyvek Országos Gyarapodási Jegyzéke*† (International Education Books Accession List, 2 a year), *Könyv és Nevelés*† (Book and Education), *Felsőoktatási Szakirodalmi Tájékoztató*† (Bulletin of Higher Education, 2 a year).

Országos Széchényi Könyvtár (*The National Széchényi Library*): 1827 Budapest, Múzeum-körut 14-16; f. 1802; 2,126,630 books and periodicals, 3,403,380 manuscripts, maps, prints, microfilms, etc.; Dir.-Gen. Dr. MAGDA JÓBORÚ; publs. include *Magyar Nemzeti Bibliográfia, Könyvek bibliográfiája* (Hungarian National Bibliography, Monographs) (fortnightly), *Magyar Nemzeti Bibliográfia: Időszaki kiadványok repertóriuma* (Hungarian National Bibliography, Repertory of Periodicals) (monthly), *Magyar Nemzeti Bibliográfia: Zeneművek bibliográfiája* (Hungarian National Bibliography, Musical Works, quarterly), *Az Országos Széchényi Könyvtár Évkönyve* (Yearbook); *Külföldi Társadalomtudományi Kézikönyvek* (current foreign acquisitions: reference books in social sciences, bi-annual), *Kurrens külföldi időszaki kiadványok a magyar konyvtárakban* (current foreign periodicals in Hungarian libraries, bi-annual), *Hungarika Irodalmi Szemle* (Selected Bibliography of Books and Articles concerning Hungary published abroad in foreign languages, quarterly), *Külföldi Magyar Nyelvü Kiadványok* (Selected Bibliography of Books and

Articles published Abroad in Hungarian, quarterly); the following libraries function under the organization of the Országos Széchényi Könyvtár:

Könyvtártudományi és Módszertani Központ (*Centre for Library Science and Methodology*): 1827 Budapest, Muzeum u. 3; f. 1959; research and development, promotion of inter-library co-operation, literature propaganda, public relations, training and library documentation services; library science library of 56,700 vols.; Dir. ISTVÁN PAPP; publs. *Könyvtári Figyelő*† (Library Bulletin), *A Magyar Könyvtári Szakirodalom Bibliográfiája*† (Hungarian Library Literature), *Könyvtári és Dokumentációs Szakirodalom. Referáló lap.*† (Foreign Library science and information abstracts), *Hungarian Library and Information Science Abstracts*† (in English and Russian), *Uj Könyvek* (New Books), Accessions guide, *Információ a könyvtári munka eszközeiről és berendezéseiről* (Information on library and reference equipment, in Hungarian, Russian and English).

Bajza József Library: 3200 Gyöngyös, Nemecz József tér 1; f. 15th century; 19,449 vols.

Reguly Antal Scientific Library: 8420 Zirc, Rákóczi-tér 1; f. 1720; 68,618 vols.

Pannonhalmi Szent-Benedek-Rend Központi Főkönyvtára (*Benedictine Abbey Library*): Pannonhalma, Győr vm.; f. 1802; collection of early records, MSS., codices, source material for the Magyar language; 280,000 vols.; Dir. Dr. DAVID SÖVEGES.

Pécsi Orvostudományi Egyetem Központi Könyvtára (*Central Library of the Pécs University of Medicine*): 7643 Pécs, Szigeti u. 12; f. 1961; collection covers medicine, chemistry, physics and biology; 154,000 vols.; Dir. Mrs. VERA RÚZSÁS, PH.D.; publ. *Bibliographia Publicationum Universitatis Scientiarum Medicarum Quinqueecclesiensis*† (irregular).

Pécsi Tudományegyetem Könyvtára (*Library of the University of Pécs*): H-7621 Pécs, Leonardo da Vinci u. 3; f. 1774; 500,000 vols.; Dir. MIKLÓS FÉNYES; publs. *Közlemények a Pécsi Egyetemi Könyvtárból*, *Studia iuridica auctoritate Universitatis Pécs publicata*†, *Dolgozatok az állam- és jogtudományok köréből*, *Dolgozatok a közgazdaságtudományok köréből*†.

Semmelweis Orvostudományi Egyetem Könyvtára (*Library of Semmelweis Medical University*): 1085 Budapest, VIII, Üllői u. 26; f. 1828; 390,688 vols.; Head Librarian Mrs. KATALIN VILMON (acting).

Somogyi-Könyvtár (*Somogyi Library*): 6720 Szeged, Roosevelt-tér 1-3; f. 1881; 580,000 vols.; Dir. BÉLA TÓTH; publs. *Somogyi-könyvtári Mühely* (Study of the Somogyi library), *Csongrád megyei Könyvtáros* (Librarian of the Csongrád district), *A Somogyi-könyvtár kiadványai* (Publications of the Somogyi library), etc.

Szegedi Orvostudományi Egyetem Központi Könyvtára (*Central Library of the Szeged University of Medicine*): 6701 Szeged, Lenin-krt. 109; f. 1926; 140,151 vols.; Dir. Dr. ANDOR ZALLÁR.

Tiszáninneni Református Egyházkerület Nagykönyvtára (*Library of the Reformed Church*): H-3950 Sárospatak, Rákóczy u. 1; f. 1531; 280,000 vols.; Dir. IMRE CZEGLE.

Tiszántuli Református Egyházkerület Nagykönyvtára (*Library of the Calvinist College*): Debrecen, Kálvin-tér 16; f. 1538; 551,000 vols.; Dir. Prof. Dr. LÁSZLÓ MAKKAI.

Uj Magyar Központi Levéltár (*New Central Archives of Hungary*): H-1014 Budapest, Hess András tér 4; f. 1970; shelf length 6,000 metres; records from after 1945 with country-wide reference; Dir. Dr. MIHÁLY KOROM.

Veszprémi Vegyipari Egyetem Központi Könyvtára (*Library of the Technical University of Chemical Engineering*): 8200 Veszprém, Schönherz Z. u. 10; f. 1949; 107,533 vols.; 32 staff members; Dir. Dr. ZOLTÁN KOVÁTS; publ. *Hungarian Journal of Industrial Chemistry*† (quarterly).

MUSEUMS

BUDAPEST

Budapesti Történeti Múzeum (*Historical Museum of Budapest*): Budapest, I, Szent György tér 2; f. 1887; relics of the thousand-year-old Hungarian capital and medieval royal palace; Dir.-Gen. Dr. MIKLÓS HORVÁTH; publs. *Budapest Régiségei* (Antiquities of Budapest), *Tanulmányok Budapest Múltjából* (Studies of the History of Budapest) (both irregular); administers:

Aquincumi Múzeum: Budapest, III, Szentendrei u. 139; relics of Roman camp, stone, mosaic, glass and jewellery; on the site of an old Roman colony.

Kiscelli Múzeum: Budapest, III, Kiscelli u. 108; modern history and art collection of Budapest.

Iparművészeti Múzeum (*Museum of Applied Arts*): Budapest, IX, Üllői u. 33; f. 1872; library: *see* Libraries; Dir.-in-Chief Dr. PÁL MIKLÓS; publs. catalogues, *Ars Decorativa*† (annual).

There are three component museums:

Hopp Ferenc Keletázsiai Művészeti Múzeum (*Hopp Museum of Eastern Asiatic Arts*): Budapest, VI, Népköztársasag u. 103; f. 1919; library; Dir. KÁROLY GOMBOS.

Kina Múzeum (*Chinese Museum*): Budapest, VI, Gorkij-fasor 12; f. 1955; Dir. KÁROLY GOMBOS.

Nagytétényi Kastélymúzeum (*Castle Museum of Nagytétény*): Budapest, XXII, Kastélymúzeum u. 9; f. 1948; European furniture of the 15th-17th centuries and Hungarian furniture of the 18th-19th centuries; exhibition of stove pottery, stoves, Roman castrum and stones.

Közlekedési Múzeum (*Transport Museum*): 1146 Budapest, XIV, Városligeti krt. 11; f. 1896; models of railway locomotives and rolling stock, old vehicles, nautical, aeronautic and urban transport collections, road- and bridge-building, etc.; four branch museums with open-air displays; library of 80,000 vols.; Dir. Dr. ÁKOS VASZKÓ; publs. *Yearbook*, scientific reviews (*c.* every 2 years).

Magyar Bélyegmúzeum: 1400 Budapest, VII, Hársfa u. 47; f. 1930; collections of *c.* 9 million Hungarian and foreign stamps; Curator SÁNDOR HUBAY.

Magyar Építészeti Múzeum (*Hungarian Museum of Architecture*): 1014 Budapest, Táncsics M.-u. 1; f. 1968; architecture and history of architecture; Curator LÁSZLÓ PUSZTAI.

Magyar Kereskedelmi és Vendéglátóipari Múzeum (*Hungarian Museum of Commerce and of the Catering Trade*): 1014 Budapest I, Fortuna-utca 4; f. 1966; collection covers the subjects of sales and services, particularly in tourism, hotels and hostelry, cuisine, coffee houses, confectionery, shop fittings; documents, photos, posters; Dir. Dr. JÓZSEF BORDA.

Magyar Mezőgazdasági Múzeum (*Hungarian Agricultural Museum*): 1367 Budapest, Vajdahunyadvár, Pf. 129; f. 1896; collects, exhibits and processes objects, documents, etc., relating to the development of Hungarian agriculture for scientific and educational purposes; 102 mems.; library of *c.* 30,000 vols., 30,000 periodicals; Dir.-Gen. Dr. LÓRÁND SZABÓ; publs. include *A Magyar Mezőgazdasági Múzeum Közleményei*† (Yearbook of the Museum), *Mezögazdaságtörténeti Tanulmányok*† (Studies in the History of Agriculture), *Bibliographia Historiae Rerum Rusticarum Internationalis*†.

Magyar Munkásmozgalmi Múzeum (*Museum of the Hungarian Labour Movement*): 1014 Budapest, Budavári Palota "A" épület (formerly called Legújabbkori Történeti Múzeum): f. 1949; history of the Hungarian labour movement from 1848 to the present day; library of 34,000 vols.; Dir. BÉLA ESTI; publs. *A Magyar Munkásmozgalmi Múzeum Évkönyve*† (Yearbook) and *A Magyar Munkásmozgalmi Múzeum Közleményei*† (Contemporary Museum Publications—3 a year).

Magyar Nemzeti Galéria (*Hungarian National Gallery*): 1250 Budapest, Budavári Palota, Pf. 31; f. 1957; collections include paintings, sculptures, drawings, engravings, panel paintings, Baroque art and medals from the 12th century onwards; Dir.-Gen.(vacant); publs. *A Magyar Nemzeti Galéria évkönyve*† (Annals), catalogues†.

Magyar Nemzeti Múzeum (*Hungarian National Museum*): Budapest, VIII, Múzeum-krt. 14-16; f. 1802; Dir.-Gen. Dr. FERENC FÜLEP; Depts.: Archaeological, Medieval, Modern, Numismatic, Historical Gallery, Documentation; library of 95,000 vols.; publs. *Folia Archaeologica*† (annually), *Folia Historica*† (annually), *Régészeti Füzetek* (*Fasciculi Archaeologici*)†.

Magyar Vizügyi Múzeum (*Hungarian Water Conservancy Museum*): 2500 Esztergom, Kölcsei-ut. 2; f. 1973; history of the industry; Curator GYULA FÁBIÁN.

Magyar Zenetörténeti Múzeum (*Hungarian Museum of History of Music*): 1014 Budapest I, Országház u. 9; f. 1969; collection of instruments, MSS., personal objects used by great musicians; Curator Dr. ZOLTÁN FALVY.

Mátyás Templom Egyháztörténeti Gyűjteménye (*Matthias Church History Collection*): 1014 Budapest I, Szentháromság tér 2; f. 1964; permanent collection of Roman Catholic religious objects in the crypt of Matthias Church; Curator Dr. JÁNOS FÁBIÁN.

Mücsarnok (*Art Gallery*): Budapest, XIV, Dózsa György u. 37; f. 1896; temporary exhibitions of Hungarian and foreign art; Dir. FERENC HIDVÉGI.

Néprajzi Múzeum (*Ethnographical Museum*): H-1055 Budapest, Kossuth Lajos tér 12; f. 1872; collections and research activities cover peasant and tribal folk cultures; Ethnographic Archive with 12,216 MSS. and 250,151 photographs; Ethnographic Library with 117,088 vols.; Folk Music Archive with 60,000 entries; Dir. Dr. TAMÁS HOFFMANN; publs. *Néprajzi Értesítő* (Yearbook), *Néprajzi Közlemények* (quarterly).

Öntődei Múzeum (*Foundry Museum*): 1027 Budapest, Bem József u. 20; f. 1969; world's only museum inside an actual foundry workshop, f. 1858 and used by Ábrahám Ganz and others until 1964; original foundry equipment; history of technological development of foundry trade, old mouldings; library of 1,354 vols.; Curator ZOLTÁN DÉVAY.

Országos Hadtörténeti Múzeum (*Military History Museum*): 1014 Budapest I, Tóth Arpád sétány 40; f. 1918; arms, medals, uniforms, documents, etc.; Dir. TIBOR HETÉS; publs. *Értesitője* (annals), papers†, catalogues†.

Országos Műszaki Múzeum (*National Museum of Science and Technology*): 1117 Budapest XI, Kaposvár-utca 13/15; f.: collection 1954, museum 1973; collection covers inventions and prototypes with reference to natural sciences and technology, historic exhibits from the early days of industry and its development to the present; library of 10,000 vols.; Dir. Dr. FERENC SZABADVÁRY; publ. *Technikatörténeti Szemle*† (Review of History of Technology).

Petőfi Irodalmi Múzeum (*Petőfi Museum of Hungarian Literature*): 1053 Budapest Pf. 71, V, Károlyi u. 16; f. 1954; 19th–20th-century literature; library of 96,000 vols.; Dir. SAROLTA RAFFAI; publs. *Évkönyve* (annually), *Irodalmi Múzeum* (2 a year), *Bibliográfiai Füzetei*† (6 a year).

Postamúzeum (*Postal Museum*): 1061 Budapest, Népköztársaság ut. 3; f. 1955; research and documentation institute and permanent exhibition of the history of post and telecommunications; library of 7,140 vols.; Curator GYÖRGY PRÁGAI; publ. *Posta-és Bélyegmúzeumi Szemle*† (three times yearly).

Semmelweis Orvostörténeti Múzeum, Könyvtár és Levéltár (*Semmelweis Medical Historical Museum, Library and Archives*): H-1013 Budapest, Apród. u. 1-3 (Museum and Archives); H-1023 Budapest, Török u. 12 (Library); f. 1965 (Museum), 1951 (Library), 1972 (Archives), now merged; 90,000 vols., 20,000 periodicals; Dir. Dr. JÓZSEF ANTALL; publ. *Orvostörténeti Közlemények*† (Communications, quarterly).

Szépművészeti Múzeum (*Museum of Fine Arts*): Budapest, XIV, Dózsa György u. 41; f. 1896; Dir. Dr. KLÁRA GARAS; collections and galleries include: Egyptian and Greco-Roman antiquities, foreign paintings, sculptures, drawings and engravings; library of 77,620 vols.; publs. *Közlemények* (Bulletin), catalogues.

Színháztörténeti Múzeum (*Historical Museum of the Theatre*): 1016 Budapest, Krisztina-krt. 57; f. 1952; under the control of Magyar Színházi Intézet (Hungarian Theatre Institute); Dir. Dr. ESZTER GYÖRGY; publ. *Színháztörténeti Füzerek*†.

Természettudományi Múzeum (*Hungarian Natural History Museum*): H-1088 Budapest, Baross u. 13; f. 1802; Depts.: Mineralogy, Petrography, Geology and Palaeontology, Botany, Zoology, Anthropology; library of 58,936 vols., 86,876 periodicals, 128,281 reprints; Chief Dir. Dr. Z. KASZAB; publs. *Annales Historico-Naturales Musei Nationalis Hungarici*†, *Folia Entomologica Hungarica*† (2 a year), *Anthropologica Hungarica*†, *Vertebrata Hungarica*†, *Studia Botanica*†, *Fragmenta Mineralogica et Palaeontologica*† (all annually).

Testnevelési és Sportmúzeum (*Museum of Physical Education and Sport*): 1143 Budapest, Dózsa György u. 3; f. 1963; Curator KÁROLY BAKONYI.

Textilipari Múzeum (*Museum of the Textile Industry*): 1113 Budapest, Rajk László u. 59; f. 1972.

Tüzoltó Múzeum (*Fire Brigade Museum*): 1105 Budapest, X, Martinovics tér 12; f. 1955; includes old fire-fighting equipment, pumps and hoses; universal and Hungarian history of fire protection, its means and organization; Curator JÁNOS MINÁROVICS.

Zsidó Vallási és Történeti Múzeum (*Museum of Jewish Religion and History*): 1077 Budapest VII, Dohány-u. 2; f. 1916; Jewish pieces of archaeology and art history, religious objects; Jewish works of art; Curator Dr. ILONA BENOSCHOFSKY.

PROVINCIAL MUSEUMS

Arany János Múzeum: 2750 Nagykőrös; f. 1928; Curator Dr. LÁSZLÓ NOVÁK.

Bakonyi Múzeum: H-8200 Veszprém, Lenin liget 5; f. 1902; natural history, ethnographic, archaeological and historical exhibits from the Bakony Mountains; library of 20,000 vols.; Dir. (vacant); publs. *Veszprém Megyei Múzeumok Közleményei*† (Bulletin of the

Museums of Veszprém Region), *A Bakony Természettudományi Kutatásának Eredményei*† (Results of Natural History Research in the Bakony Mountains).

Bakonyi Természettudományi Múzeum (*Bakony Mountains Natural History Museum*): 8420 Zirc; f. 1972; zoological, botanical and geological collections; library of 10,000 vols.; Curator Dr. SÁNDOR TÓTH; publ. *A Bakony természettudományi kutatásának eredményei*†.

Balassa Bálint Múzeum: 2501 Esztergom; f. 1894; history, archaeology, numismatics, applied arts; library of 5,000 vols.; Curator ISTVÁN HORVÁTH.

Balatoni Múzeum: Keszthely; f. 1898; prehistoric and historic collections relating to Lake Balaton; library of 15,000 vols.; Curator Dr. RÓBERT MÜLLER.

Balogh Ádám Múzeum: 7100 Szekszárd; f. 1895; collections of folk art and archaeology; Curator Dr. MIKLÓS SZILÁGYI.

Báthory István Múzeum: 4301 Nyirbátor; f. 1955; archaeology, local history and art; Curator BARNABÁS SZALONTAI.

Csontváry Múzeum: 7621 Pécs; f. 1973; art gallery comprising selected works by the expressionist painter Tivadar Csontváry Kosztka.

Damjanich János Múzeum: 5101 Szolnok; f. 1933; archaeology, palaeontology, applied art and local history collections; Dir. Dr. LÁSZLÓ SELMECZI.

Déri Múzeum: Debrecen, Déri tér 1; f. 1902; archaeological, ethnographic, fine and applied art, natural history and local history collections and exhibitions; Dir. Dr. IMRE DANKÓ; publs. *A Déri Múzeum Évkönyve* (Yearbook), *A Hajdu-Bihar Megyei Múzeumok Kiadványai* (Studies and Monographs), *Múzeumi Kurir* (Review).

Dobó István Vármúzeum: 3301 Eger, Vár 1; originally archiepiscopal picture gallery and museum; f. 1872; enlarged by Fort Eger excavation material 1949; local remains of archaeology, ethnography, history of literature and of arts, palaeontology; relics of the Turkish occupation; library of 16,000 vols.; Curator SANDOR BODÓ; publ. Yearbook.

Egry József Emlékmúzeum (*József Egry Memorial Museum*): 8260 Badacsony; f. 1973; art gallery of works by Lake Balaton landscape painter Egry.

Érc és Ásványbányászati Múzeum (*Museum of Mining of Metals and Minerals*): 3733 Rudabánya; f. 1956; history of the industry, exhibitions; Curator LÁSZLÓ MORVAY.

Erkel Ferenc Múzeum (*Ferenc Erkel Museum*): 5700 Gyula, Kossuth u. 15; f. 1865; archaeology, art, local history, musicological and ethnographic collections; Curator JÁNOS BENCSIK.

Ferenczy Múzeum: 2001 Szentendre, pf. 103, Marx-tér 6; f. 1951; archaeological, ethnographic and local history collections, paintings, drawings, sculptures and Gobelin tapestries; centre for the 29 museums in Pest County; library of 11,800 vols.; Dir. JÓZSEF BIHARI; publs. *Studia Comitatensia*† (yearbook of papers published by the Museums of Pest County), *Pest megyei Muzeumi Fuzetek*† (Pamphlets of the Museums of Pest County, irregular).

Göcseji Múzeum: 8900 Zalaegerszeg; f. 1950; collections of regional folk art, archaeology, ethnography, paintings and sculpture; library of 8,000 vols., open-air ethnographical museum, exhibition of sculpture by Zs. Kisfaludi-Strobl; Curator JÓZSEF NÉMETH.

Gorsium Szabadtéri Múzeum (*Gorsium Open-Air Museum*): 8121 Tác; f. 1963; excavations of a Roman city, the ruins showing original shape.

Győrffy István Nagykun Múzeum: 5301 Karcag; f. 1952; regional museum, ethnography; library of 2,000 vols.; Curator TIBOR BELLON.

Hajdúsági Múzeum: 4220 Hajdúböszörmény; f. 1924; Sections: Archaeology, Ethnography, History and Fine Arts; Curator MIKLÓS NYAKAS.

Hansági Múzeum: 9200 Mosonmagyaróvár; f. 1882; library of 7,216 vols.; Curator REZSŐ PUSZTAI.

Helytörténeti Múzeum (*Local History Museum*): 8500 Pápa; f. 1960; ethnographical, archaeological and industrial collections from the town and environment; library of 4,000 vols.; Dir. LÁSZLÓ HADNAGY.

Herman Ottó Múzeum: 3500 Miskolc, Felszabaditók ut. 28; f. 1899; collections of archaeology, regional ethnography, fine arts and applied arts; library 24,000 vols.; Curator JÓSZEF SZABADFALVY; publs. *A Herman Ottá Muzeum Evkonyve*† (Yearbook of the Herman Ottó Museum), *A Miskolci Herman Ottó Múzeum Közleményei*† (Communications of the Herman Ottó Museum), *Néprajzi Kiadványok*† (Ethnographical Studies), *Borsodi Kismonografiak*† (monographs), *Kiállitási Vezetök*† (Exhibition guides).

Intercisa Múzeum: 2400 Dunaujváros, Lenin tér 4; f. 1951; prehistoric, Roman and medieval collections; regional history, archaeology and ethnography; library of 4,800 vols.; Curator Mrs. LÁSZLÓ MATUSS.

István Király Múzeum: 8000 Székesfehérvár, Gagarin-tér 3; f. 1873; prehistoric, Roman and medieval collections, anthropological and zoological collections, regional ethnography, art gallery, musical collection, stones of the Basilica of King Stephen; library of 30,000 vols.; Dir. JENŐ FITZ; publs. *Bulletins of the István Király Museum, Alba Regia* (Scientific Almanac).

Janus Pannonius Múzeum: 7621 Pécs; f. 1904; natural sciences, archaeology, ethnography, modern Hungarian art, local history; library of 20,000 vols.; Dir. EVA HÁRS; publs. *Évkönyv* (Yearbook), *Dunántuli Dolgozatok* (Trans-Danubian Studies), *Füzetek* (Papers), booklets, art publications.

Jász Múzeum: 5101 Jászberény; f. 1873; collections from the later Stone, Copper, Bronze and Iron Ages; ethnography, local history; library 6,593 vols.; Curator JÁNOS TÓTH.

Jósa András Múzeum: 4401 Nyiregyháza Benczur tér 21, Pf. 57; f. 1868; collections of archaeology, ethnography and local history; library of 16,000 vols.; Dir. Dr. PÉTER NÉMETH; publ. *Museum Publications* (every 2 years).

Jurisics Miklós Múzeum: 9731 Kőszeg; f. 1932; collection of castle and town history; Dir. Dr. KORNÉL BAKAY.

Kanizsai Dorottya Múzeum: 7700 Mohács; f. 1923; ethnographical and folk art collections, ethnographical collection of the South-Slav minority; Curator GYÖRGY SAROSÁCZ.

Katona József Múzeum: 6001 Kecskemét, Bethlen város 75; f. 1894; archaeological, ethnographical, historical and fine art collections; Dir. PÁL BÁNSZKY.

Keresztény Múzeum (*Christian Museum*): 2501 Esztergom, Pf. 25, Berényi Zs. u. 2; f. 1875; ecclesiastical collection of Hungarian, Italian, Dutch, Austrian and French medieval panels and baroque pictures, tapestries, gold and silver artwork, porcelain, miniatures, etc.; library 4,500 vols.; Pres. PÁL CSÉFALVAY.

Kiskun Múzeum: 6100 Kiskunfélegyháza; f. 1902 ethnography; library of 20,000 vols.; Curator ISTVÁN FAZEKAS.

Kossuth Lajos Múzeum: 2700 Cegléd; f. 1917; relics of Lajos Kossuth; ethnography, archaeology, arts; library of 7,000 vols.; Dir. GYÚLA KOCSIS; publs. *Ceglédi Füzetek*† (annually).

Koszta József Múzeum: 6600 Szentes; f. 1894; archaeological and ethnographical collection and paintings by Koszta; Dirs. Dr. KATALIN HEGEDÜS, VERA NAGY (acting).

Központi Bányászati Múzeum (*Central Mining Museum*): 9400 Sopron, Templom u. 2; f. 1957; science and technology; history of mining in the Carpathian basin since prehistoric age; Dir. LÁSZLÓ MOLNAR.

Központi Kohászati Múzeum (*Central Foundry Museum*): 3517 Miskolc-Lillafüred; f. 1949; science and technology; archaeological foundry of the 9th-10th centuries; 18th-century foundry; Curator OSZKÁR SZINVAVÖLGYI.

Kubinyi Ferenc Múzeum: 3170 Szécsény; f. 1973; archaeology, numismatics and local history; Curator MIHÁLY PRAZNOVSZKY.

Kuny Domokos Múzeum: 2892 Tata; f. 1950; archaeological and applied art colections; Curator ENDRE BIRÓ.

Liszt Ferenc Múzeum: 9400 Sopron, Május 1. tér 1; f. 1867; relics of Liszt, archaeology, folk art and local Baroque art collections; library of 15,000 vols.; Dir. OTTÓ DOMONKOS.

Magyar Naiv Müvészek Múzeuma (*Museum of Hungarian Naive Art*): 6000 Kecskemét, Gáspár A. u. 11; f. 1974; exhibitions of works of Hungarian primitive painters and sculptors; Curator PÁL BÁNSZKY.

Magyar Olajipari Múzeum (*Oil Industry Museum*): 8901 Zalaegerszeg, Batthyány u. 2; f. 1969; exhibitions of the history of the professional and technical development of the oil industry; equipment, documents, photos, etc.; library of 4,500 vols.; Curator FERENC TÓTH.

Mátra Múzeum: 3200 Gyöngyös; f. 1957; natural history: zoology and botany of Mátra and Cserhát Mountains; history of hunting; library of 10,000 vols.; Curator JÓZSEF BERÉNYI.

Mátyás Király Múzeum (*King Matthias Museum*): managed by Magyar Nemzeti Múzeum of Budapest, 2025 Visegrád; f. 1933; archaeological and stonework remains of medieval and renaissance royal palace; Curator MIKLÓS HÉJJ.

Móra Ferenc Múzeum: 6720 Szeged, Roosevelt tér 1-3; f. 1883; archaeological, ethnographic and biological collections, history of arts and regional collections; Curator OTTÓ TROGMAYER; publ. *Móra Ferenc Múzeum Évkönyve*† (Yearbook).

Munkácsy Mihály Múzeum: 5601 Békéscsaba, Széchenyi u. 9; f. 1899; archaeological and regional ethnographic collections, modern Hungarian paintings, ornithology, natural science; library of 7,500 vols.; Curator LÁSZLÓ DÉR; publ. *A Békés Megyei Múzeumok Közleményei*† (Publications of Békés County Museums).

Munkásmozgalmi Múzeum (*Museum of Labour Movement*): 3100 Salgótarján; f. 1959; 19-20th century history of miners' revolutionary movements; library of 6,700 vols.; Dir. ISTVÁN HORVÁTH.

Nádasdy Ferenc Múzeum: 9600 Sárvár, Vár; f. 1951; late Renaissance and Baroque Hungarian milieu reconstructed in state rooms of 16th-century castle; Dir. ISTVÁN SÖPTEI.

Palóc Múzeum: 2661 Balassagyarmat, Palóc liget 1; f. 1891; Roman relics, ethnography, local folk art and shepherds' art; collections of Nógrád costumes, children's toys and folk instruments; library of 5,422 vols.; Dir. JÓZSEF ZÓLYOMI; publ. *Yearbook*†.

Pannonhalmi Főapátság Gyüjteménye (*Abbey of Pannonhalma Collection*): 9090 Pannonhalma, Vár-utca 1; f. 1803; paintings, sculptures, applied arts in the building of an ancient Benedictine Abbey.

Porcelán Múzeum: 8200 Herend; f. 1964; exhibits from the famous china factory, est. 1826.

Rákóczi Múzeum: 3950 Sárospatak; f. 1950; housed in the Castle of Sárospatak; historical, ethnographic and applied art collections; Curator Dr. ÁKOS JANÓ.

Rippl-Rónai Múzeum: 7400 Kaposvár, Rippl-Rónai tér 1; f. 1909; archaeological and ethnographic collections, contemporary history, fine arts; library of 15,000 vols.; Dir. JÁNOS HORVÁTH; publs. *Somogyi Múzeumok Közleményei, Somogyi Múzeumi Füzetek, Somogy Néprajza.*

Savaria Múzeum: Szombathely, Kisfaludy Sándor u. 9; f. 1872; natural history, minerals, archaeology, Roman finds, medieval stonework, ethnography, modern and applied arts; Dir. GÁBOR BÁNDI.

Szabadtéri Néprajzi Múzeum (*Open Air Ethnographical Museum*): 2000 Szentendre; f. 1972; collections indoors (at the Néprajzi Muzeum, Budapest) and outdoors, with an archive of 14,757 photographs, documents, films, etc.; Dir. Dr. ALBERT KURUCZ.

Szatmári Múzeum: 4700 Mátészalka; f. 1972; local history and ethnographic collections; Curator Dr. JÓZSEF FARKAS.

Széchenyi István Emlékmúzeum (*Széchenyi Memorial Museum*): 9485 Nagycenk, Kiscenki-utca 3; f. 1973; history of the Széchenyi family and life of 19th-century statesman Count István Széchenyi; library of 1,000 vols.; Curator ATTILA KÖRNYEI.

Tessedik Sámuel Múzeum: 5540 Szarvas, Vajda P. u. 1; f. 1951; archaeology, ethnography and local history collections; Dir. Dr. JÓZSEF PALOV.

Thorma János Múzeum: 6400 Kiskunhalas; f. 1874; ethnography and archaeology; Curator ERIKA WICKER.

Thury György Múzeum: 8800 Nagykanizsa, Szabadság ter 11; f. 1919; archaeological and ethnographical collections, local history displays, numismatics; Curator Dr. E. KERECSÉNYI.

Tihanyi Múzeum: 8237 Tihany; f. 1955; Lake Balaton in literature; Roman and medieval lapidarium; fine arts.

Tornyai János Múzeum: 6801 Hódmezővásárhely; f. 1905; archaeological, ethnographic and folk-art collections, Tornyai paintings and Medgyessy sculptures; pottery and farm-museum; Curator JÁNOS DÖMÖTÖR.

Türr István Múzeum: 6501 Baja, Deák Ferenc u. 1; f. 1935; archaeological and ethnographic collections, modern Hungarian painters; library of 10,000 vols.; Dir. Dr. EDE SOLYMOS; publs. *Türr István Múzeum Kiadványai, Bajai Dolgozatok.*

Vak Bottyán Múzeum: 2600 Vác; f. 1895; local history and fine arts exhibits; library of 7,000 vols.; Dir. EMIL RÁDULY.

Vármúzeum: Esztergom, Szt. István tér 1; f. 1967; excavated and reconstructed royal palace from the times of the Hungarian House of the Árpáds; municipal history of Esztergom as royal seat in the Middle Ages; Curator BÉLA HORVATH.

Vasarely Múzeum: 7621 Pécs; f. 1976; art gallery comprising works by Hungarian-born French artist Victor Vasarely.

Vegyészeti Múzeum (*Chemical Museum*): 8100 Várpalota; f. 1963; history of the chemical industry; library of 10,000 vols.; Dir. SÁNDOR P. NAGY.

Vértesszőllősi Östelep: 2837 Vértesszőllős; f. 1968; permanent open-air exhibition; dwelling-place and remains of early man.

Viski Károly Múzeum: 6300 Kalocsa; f. 1936; regional museum, folk art; Curator Dr. JÁNOS BÁRTH.

Xántus János Múzeum: 9022 Győr, Széchenyi tér 5; f. 1854; archaeological collection containing relics of the ancient town of Arrabona (now Győr); history, art, anthropology, natural science, Roman lapidarium; picture gallery; library of 20,000 vols.; Curator LAJOS DAVID; publ. *Arrabona* (annual).

Zrínyi Miklós Múzeum: 7900 Szigetvár; f. 1971; local history collection, relating particularly to the period of Turkish occupation (16th-17th centuries).

UNIVERSITIES

EÖTVÖS LORÁND TUDOMÁNYEGYETEM
(Eötvös Loránd University)

1364 BUDAPEST, V,
EGYETEM-TÉR 1-3, P.O.B. 109
Telephone: 180-820.
Founded 1635.

Academic year: September to June (two terms).

Rector: GYULA EŐRSI.
Pro-Rectors: KÁLMÁN MEDZIHRADSZKY, KÁLMÁN SZABÓ, GYŐRGY SZÉKELY.
Secretary-General: GYULA VARGA.

Library: *see* Libraries.

Number of teaching staff: 1,155 full-time, 112 part-time.

Number of students: 8,829.

Publications: *Annales*†, *Egyetemi Ertesitő*†, *Acta Facultatis Politico-Iuridicae*†, *Dissertationes Archaeologicae*†, *Opuscula Zoologica*†, *Az Egyetemi Könyvtár Értesitői*† (all annually).

DEANS:

Faculty of Political Science and Jurisprudence: PETER SCHMIDT.
Faculty of Science: I. KUBOVICS.
Faculty of Arts: I. DIÓSZEGI.

PROFESSORS:

Faculty of Political Science and Jurisprudence:

Institute of the Theory and History of State and Law:

BRÓSZ, R., Roman Law
HORVÁTH, P., Legal History.
KOVÁCS, K., Legal History of Hungary
SAMU, M., General Theory of State and Law (Director)

Institute of Civil Law:

EORSI, G., Civil Law (Director)
HAGELMAYER, Mrs., I. Labour Law
NÉVAI, L., Civil Procedure
SERES, I., Agricultural Law
VÉKÁS, L., Civil Law

Institute of Criminal Sciences:

KIRÁLY, T., Criminal Sciences (Director)
PINTÉR, J., Penal Law
SZABÓ-NAGY, Mrs. T., Criminal Procedure
VIGH, J., Criminology

Institute of Political Sciences and Administration:

BERÉNYI, S., Law of Administration
FÖLDESI, T., Philosophy
HARASZTI, G., International Law
KOVACSICS, J., Statistics
KOZMA, P., Political Economy
MAGYAR, G., Scientific Socialism
NAGY, T., Financial Law
TAKÁCS, I., Hungarian Constitutional Law (Director)

Faculty of Science (Budapest, VIII, Muzeum krt 6-8):

ÁDÁM, G., Physiology
ANTAL, Z., Economic Geography
BALÁZS, B., Astronomy
BÁLDI, T., Geology
BALOGH, J., Zootaxy
BARTA, GY., Geophysics
BIRÓ, E., Biochemistry
BÖRÖCZKY, K., Geometry
CSÁKVÁRI, B., General and Inorganic Chemistry
CSÁSZÁR, A., Mathematical Analysis
DOBOSI, Z., Meteorology
EIBEN, O., Anthropology
FRIDVALSZKY, L., Botany
GÉCZY, B., Palaeontology
HORVÁTH, J., Projective and Descriptive Geometry
KATAI, I., Data Processing and Numerical Mathematics
KERTÉSZ, L., Solid State Physics
KIRSCHNER, J., Theoretical Physics
KISS, J., Mineralogy
KISS, L., Physical Chemistry
KÓSA, A., Applied Mathematical Analysis
KOVÁCS, I., General Physics
KOVÁCS, J., Zootomy
KUBOVICS, I., Geochemistry and Petrology
KUCSMAN, Á., Organic Chemistry
LÁNG, F., Plant Biology
LIPTAI, E., Scientific Socialism
MARX, GY., Nuclear Physics
MOGYORÓDI, J., Probability Calculus
NAGY, K., Theoretical Physics
SÁRFALVI, B., Regional Geography
SIMON, T., Botanical Taxonomy and Botanical Geography
STEGENA, L., Topography
SURÁNYI, J., Algebra and Theory of Numbers
SZABÓ, Z., Inorganic and Analytical Chemistry
SZÉKELY, A., Geography
SZÜCS, E., General Technology
TÓRÁK, T., Inorganic and Analytical Chemistry
TÜDŐS, F., Chemical Technology
VARRÓ, T., Political Economy
VÉGH, Mrs. S., Applied Geology
VIDA, G., Genetics
WOLFRAM, E., Colloid Chemistry and Colloid Technology

Faculty of Arts:

ALMÁSI, M., Aesthetics
ANCSEL, Miss É., Philosophy
BABICZKY, B., Librarianship
BALECZKY, E., Russian Philology
BARKÓCZY, Miss I., General Psychology
BENKŐ, L., Hungarian Philology
BERECZKI, G., Finno-Hungarian Linguistics
BORZSÁK, I. Latin Philology
CSONGOR, B., Chinese and Far Eastern Languages
CZEGLÉDY, K., Arabic Literature and Semitic Philology
DIÓSZEGI, I., Modern History
ÉDER, Z., Hungarian Language
EGRI, P., English Language and Literature
ELEKES, L., Medieval Hungarian History
ERDEI, L., Logic
FALUS, R., Greek Philology
HAHN, I., Ancient History
HARMATTA, J., Indo-European Linguistics
HERMANN, I., History of Philosophy
HORÁNYI, M., Spanish Language
HORVÁTH, I., Foreign Languages
HUSZÁR, T., Sociology
KAKUK, Miss Zs., Turkish Language and Literature
KÁKOSSY, L., Ancient Oriental History
KÁLLAY, I., History
KARA, GY., Inner-Asian Languages
KARDOS, P., History of Hungarian Literature
KIRÁLY, I., History of Hungarian Literature
KIRÁLY, P., Slavonic Philology
MÁDL, A., German Language and Literature
MANHERCZ, K., German and Romance Languages
MEZEI, J., History of Hungarian Literature
MÓCSY, A., Archaeology
MOLNÁR, J., Phonetics
NAGY, B., Romanian Philology
NAGY, P., General Literature
NAGY, S., Education
NÉMET, L., History of Art
PERÉNYI, J., East European History
PÖLÖSKEI, F., Modern Hungarian History
SALAMON, J., Psychology
SALLAY, G., Italian Language and Literature
SIMON, P., Scientific Socialism
SIPOS, I., Polish Philology
SÜPEK, O., French Language and Literature
SZAKÁCS, K., Scientific Socialism
SZATHMÁRI, I., Hungarian Philology
SZÉKELY, G., Medieval History
SZIGETI, J., Philosophy
TÁLASI, I., Ethnography
TARNAY, A., History of Hungarian Literature
VILMOS, J., Political Economy
VOIGT, V., Folklore
ZSILKA, J., Linguistics

ATTACHED INSTITUTES:

Biological Experimentation Plant: 2131 Göd, Jávorka u.14; Dir. J. GERGELY.

Postgraduate Institute of Law and Political Science: 1364 Budapest, Egyetem tér 1–3; Dir. IMRE SÁRÁNDI.

Postgraduate College of Foreign Languages: 1085 Budapest, Rigó u.16; Dir. GYŐZŐ SIPŐCZY.

SEMMELWEIS ORVOSTUDOMÁNYI EGYETEM
(Semmelweis University of Medicine)

1085 BUDAPEST VIII,
ÜLLŐI UT 26
Telephone: 134-610.

Founded 1769 as Medical Faculty of the University of Pest; independent 1951; State control (Ministry of Health); Language of instruction: Hungarian; Academic year: September to May.

Rector: Prof. Dr. A. SZÉCSÉNY.
Vice-Rectors: Dr. T. TÖMBÖL, Dr. E. SOMOGYI, Prof. Dr. S. CSÖMÖR.
Registrar: Dr. P. ÁLMOSDI.
Librarian: K. VILMON.

Number of teaching staff: 1,155.
Number of students: 3,698.

DEANS:

Faculty of Medicine: Dr. Z. SZABÓ.
Faculty of Dentistry: Dr. T. ZELLES.
Faculty of Pharmacy: Dr. GY. SZÁSZ.

PROFESSORS:

Faculty of Medicine:

ACZÉL, GY., Social Medicine

Antoni, F., Biochemistry
Bálint, P., Physiology
Balogh, F., Urology
Csaba, Gy., Biology
Csanda, E., Neurology
Csömör, S., Obstetrics and Gynaecology
Gerlóczy, F., Paediatrics
Glauber, A., Orthopaedics
Gráf, F., Internal Medicine
Halász, B., Anatomy, Histology and Embryology
Halay, T., Marxism-Leninism
Hársing, L., Pathophysiology
Horváth, I., Biochemistry
Jellinek, H., Pathological Anatomy
Juhász, P., Psychiatry
Knoll, J., Pharmacology
Kovách, A., Physiology and Experimental Laboratory for Clinical Research
Lapis, K., Pathological Anatomy
Magyar, I., Internal Medecine
Marton, T., Surgery
Miskovits, G., Pneumology
Nász, I., Microbiology
Németh, B., Ophthalmology
Petrányi, G., Internal Medicine
Rácz, I., Dermatology and Venereology
Radnót, Magda, Ophthalmology
Révész, Gy., Oto-Rhino-Laryngology
Schuler, D., Paediatrics
Soltész, L., Vascular Surgery
Somogyi, E., Forensic Medicine
Stefanics, J., Surgery
Szécsény, A., Surgery
Tarján, I., Biophysics
Tömböl, T., Anatomy, Histology and Embryology
Török, I., Radiology
Vedres, I., Public Health and Epidemiology
Zsolnay, B., Obstetrics and Gynaecology

Faculty of Dentistry:

Bánóczy, Mrs. J., Preservation Dentistry
Fabián, T., Prosthetic Dentistry
Tóth, P., Dentistry for Children and Orthodontics

Faculty of Pharmacy:

Gyarmati, L., Pharmaceutics
Magyar, K., Pharmacodynamics
Petri, G., Pharmacognosy
Szabó, L., Pharmaceutical Organic Chemistry
Szász, Gy., Pharmaceutical Chemistry

MARX KÁROLY KÖZGAZDASÁGTUDOMÁNYI EGYETEM
(Karl Marx University of Economic Sciences)

1828 BUDAPEST IX,
DIMITROV-TÉR 8
Telephone: 186-855.

Founded 1948.

State control; Language of instruction Hungarian.

Rector: E. Csizmadia.
Vice-Rectors: T. Palánkai, M. Szuhay, I. Dobrovics.
Registrar: I. Vadász.
Librarian: Gy. Walleshausen.

Number of teaching staff: 367, including 41 professors.
Number of students: 3,952.
Publications: digests, bibliographies.

Deans:

Faculty of Industrial Economics: Cs. Csáki.
Faculty of Trade Economics: A. Kollarik.
Faculty of General Economics: A. Páliné.

Professors:

Barla, S., Political Economy
Barna, Gy., Transport Economics
Berend, I., Economic History
Bernáth, T., Economic Geography
Csanádi, Gy., Civil Law
Csizmadia, E., Agricultural Economics
Erdei, G., Political Economy
Erdős, T., Political Economy
Falus, Mrs. K., Political Economy
Fekete, F., Political Economy
Forgács, T., Economics of Home Trade
Fülei, Sz. E., Foreign Languages
Gazsó, F., Sociology
Hegedüs, J., Foreign Languages
Kiss, A., Philosophy
Kovács, F., Languages
Kovács, G., Planning of National Economy
Köves, P., Statistics
Kövér, K., Foreign Trade Economics
Krekó, B., Mathematics
Kreskay, F., Civil Law
László, A. Finance
László, J., Planning of National Economy
Máriás, A., Economics of Industry
Marton, I., Philosophy
Mátyás, A., History of Economic Thought
Megyeri, E., Economics of Industry
Neményi, I., Finance
Nyilas, J., International Economy
Ollé, L., Statistics
Párniczky, G., Statistics
Riesz, M., Finance
Stark, A., Planning of National Economy
Szabó, K., Political Economy
Szamarasz, O., Political Economy
Szentes, T., International Economy
Szép, J., Mathematics
Szuhay, M., Economic History
Timár, J., Labour Economics
Vági, F., Agriculture
Zelkó, L., Political Economy

KOSSUTH LAJOS TUDOMÁNYEGYETEM
(Lajos Kossuth University)

4010 DEBRECEN
Telephone: 16-666.

Founded 1912.

Rector: Dr. I. Kónya.
Vice-Rectors: Dr. G. J. Csikai, Dr. A. Fehér, Dr. I. Szendrey.
Registrar: Dr. L. Papp.
Librarian: Dr. I. Csüry.

Number of teaching staff: 420.
Number of students: *c.* 1,850.
Publication: *Évkönyv* (Yearbook).

Deans:

Faculty of Arts: Dr. I. Orosz.
Faculty of Science: Dr. Z. Daróczy.

Professors:

Faculty of Arts:

Darai, J., Political Economics
Dezső, L., General Linguistics
Durkó, M., Adult and Public Education
Farkas, D., Scientific Socialism
Fehér, A., Modern and Contemporary Hungarian History
Gorilovics, T., French
Havas, L., Classical Philology
Iglói, E., Slavic Literature
Julow, V., Hungarian Literature
Kálmán, B., Finno-Ugrian Linguistics
Kelemen, L., Psychology
Kónya, I., Philosophy
Kovács, K., Hungarian Literature
Némedi, L., German
Orosz, I., History
Pálffy, I., English
Papp, F., Slavic Linguistics
Petrikás, Á., Pedagogy
Sarkady, J., Ancient History
Sebestyen, Á., Hungarian Linguistics
Szendrey, I. Medieval Hungarian History
Tamás, A., Hungarian Literature
Ujvary, Z., Ethnology

Faculty of Science:

Beck, M. T., Physical Chemistry
Borsy, Z., Physical Geography
Brücher, E., Inorganic and Analytical Chemistry
Buzási, K., Algebra
Csikai, G. J., Experimental Physics
Daróczy, Z., Analysis
Fux, V., Mineralogy and Geology
Gáspár, R., Theoretical Physics
Jakucs, P., Ecology
Gesztelyi, E., Computing Science
Jakucs, P., Botany
Jékel, P., Computing
Justyák, J., Meteorology
Kedves, F., Applied Physics
Mády, I., Isotopes
Makleit, S., Organic Chemistry
Nánási, P., Biochemistry
Pinczés, Z., Economic and Regional Geography
Précsényi, I., Botany
Szabó, J., Zoology
Szabó, V., Applied Chemistry
Tamássy, L., Geometry
Tomkó, J., Applied Mathematics and Probability

ORVOSTOVÁBBKÉPZO INTÉZET
(Postgraduate Medical School)

1135 BUDAPEST XIII,
SZABOLCS-UTCA 35
Telephone: 408-900.

Founded 1910 as Central Commission for Medical Post-Graduate Training; re-established 1956 as autonomous institute; university standing 1974.

Rector: Prof. Dr. E. Endrőczi.
Vice-Rectors: Prof. Dr. I. Gáti, J. Sugár.

Number of teaching staff: 250.

Professors:

Antalóczy, Z., Internal Medicine
Bayer, I., Pharmaceutics
Bozsóky, S., Rheumatology and Physiotherapy
Böszörményi, M., Pulmonology
Csákány, Gy., Radiology
Eckhardt, S., Oncology
Endrőczi, E., Clinical and Experimental Medical Laboratory
Frank, K., Paediatrics
Gáti, I., Obstetrics and Gynaecology
Hollán, Zs., Haematology

JAKAB, T., Anaesthesiology and Intensive Therapy
JUHÁSZ, J., Pathological Anatomy
KÁDÁR, T., Organization of Health Service
KULKA, F., Thoracic Surgery
KUN, M., Surgery
LÁSZLÓ, J., Obstetrics and Gynaecology
LITTMANN, I., Surgery
MAGASI, P., Urology
MANNINGER, J., Traumatology
MOUSSONG, Mme. KOVÁCS E., Psychiatry
ORSÓS, S., Stomatology
PÁLOS, Á. L., Internal Medicine
PÁSZTOR, E., Neurosurgery
RISKÓ, T., Orthopaedics
RUDNAI, O., Public Health
SÁRKÁNY, J., Paediatrics
SUGÁR, J., Oncopathology
SURJÁN, L., Oto-Rhino-Laryngology
SZILÁGYI, G., Internal Medicine
TARISKA, I., Neurology and Psychiatry
TIMÁR, M., Labour Hygiene
VÁRNAI, F., Tropical Health

ATTACHED INSTITUTE:

Health College: Budapest IV, Erkel Ferenc-u. 26; for the training of specialists in hygienic gymnastics, dietetics, public health and epidemic control officers, nurses and head-nurses, ambulance officers; Dir. GY. KÁROLYI.

DEBRECENI ORVOSTUDOMÁNYI EGYETEM
(Debrecen University of Medicine)

4012 DEBRECEN,
NAGYERDEI KRT. 98
Telephone: 11-600.

Founded 1918 as the Faculty of Medicine of Lajos Kossuth University; independent 1951.

Rector: Dr. L. KARMAZSIN.
Vice-Rectors: Dr. GY. SZEGEDI, Dr. I. LAMPÉ, Dr. GY. SZÉKELY.
Registrar: A. BOLODÁR.

Number of teaching staff: 593.
Number of students: 1,342.

PROFESSORS:

ALBERTH, B., Ophthalmology
BALÁZS, GY., Surgery
BALOGH, E., Dermatology and Venereology
BORNEMISZA, G., Operative Surgery
BOT, G., Medical Chemistry
CSABA, B., Pathophysiology
CSORBA, S., Paediatrics
DAMJANOVICH, S., Biophysics
ELŐDI, P., Biochemistry
FACHET, J., Pathophysiology
FÖLDES, I., Anatomy, Histology, Embryology
FÜLÖP, T., Health Organization
GOMBA, S., Pathology
GÖMÖRY, A., Cardiosurgery
HADHAZY, CS., Anatomy, Histology, Embryology
HERNÁDI, F., Pharmacology
HULLAY, J., Neurosurgery
KARMAZSIN, L., Paediatrics
KELENTEY, B., Pharmacology
KERTAI, P., Hygiene and Epidemiology
KOVÁCS, L., Marxism-Leninism
KÖVÉR, A., Central Research Laboratory
KULCSÁR, A., Internal Medicine
LAMPÉ, I., Oto-Rhino-Laryngology
LAMPÉ, L., Obstetrics and Gynaecology
LEÖVEY, A., Internal Medicine
MAGYARÓDI, S., Marxism-Leninism
MIHÜCZI, L., Pulmonary Therapy
MOLNÁR, L., Neurology and Psychiatry
MUSZBEK, L., Diagnostic Laboratory
NAGY, E., Dermatology and Venereology
NAGY, J., Forensic Medicine
PAP, K., Orthopaedics
PINTÉR, J., Urology
RÁK, K., Internal Medicine
SCHNITZLER, J., Surgery
SZABÓ, G., Medical Biology
SZEGEDI, GY., Internal Medicine
SZEGI, J., Pharmacology
SZÉKELY, GY., Anatomy, Histology, Embryology
SZENTPÉTER, J., Stomatology
SZEPESI, K., Orthopaedics
SZILÁGYI, T., Patho-physiology
TAKÁCS, I., Obstetrics and Gynaecology
VARGA, E., Physiology
VARGHA, GY., Radiology
VÁCZI, L., Medical Microbiology

PÉCSI TUDOMÁNYEGYETEM
(University of Pécs)

7622 PÉCS, RÁKÓCZI UT. 80
Telephone: 12-902.

First founded in 1367, newly founded in 1922.

Rector: Dr. J. FOLDVÁRI.
Librarian: Dr. M. FÉNYES.

Number of teaching staff: 127.
Number of students: 1,400, including external students.
Publication: *Acta Universitatis Quinqueecclesiensis.*

DEANS:

Faculty of Law and Political Science: Dr. F. BENEDEK.
Faculty of Economics: Dr. B. TAKÁCS.

PROFESSORS:

Faculty of Law and Political Science (7622 Pécs, 48-as tér 1):
ÁDÁM, A., Public Law
BENEDEK, F., Roman Law
BIHARI, O., Public Law
BRUHÁCS, J., International Law
CSIZMADIA, A., History of Law
ERDÖSY, E., Criminal Law and Criminology
FARKAS, J. Civil Procedural Law
FÖLDES, I., Agricultural Law
FÖLDVÁRI, J., Criminal Law and Criminology
HERCZEGH, G., International Law
IVANCSICS, I., Administrative Law
JÓRI, J., Philosophy
JUDI, I., Philosophy
PÁLL, J., Civil Law
ROMÁN, L., Labour Law
SZAMEL, L., Administrative Law
SZITA, J., History of Law
SZOTÁCZKI, M., Theory of Law and State
TAMÁS, L., Civil Law
VARGHA, L., Criminal Procedural Law

Faculty of Economics:
BARAKONYI, K., Business Economics and Management
DANYI, P., Mathematics and Computation
GERTIG, B., Economic Geography
HOÓZ, I., Demography
KOMJÁTI, Z., Business Economics and Management
PAPP, L., Methodology
RUZSÁS, L., Historiography
SZÜCS, P., Business Economics and Management
TAKÁCS, B., Political Economy
TALLÓS, G., Finance
VÁRSZEGI, K., Accountancy
ZELLER, GY., Marketing
ZINHÓBER, F., Political Economy

PÉCSI ORVOSTUDOMÁNYI EGYETEM
(Medical University of Pécs)

PÉCS, SZIGETI U. 12
Telephone: 14-086.

Founded 1923 as the Faculty of Medicine of the University of Pécs; independent 1951.

Language of instruction: Hungarian; Academic year: September to May.

Rector: Prof. Dr. B. FLERKÓ.
Vice-Rectors: D. FRANG, O. BARTA, B. TÖRÖK.
Registrar: Dr. J. HAJNAL.
Librarian: Mrs. VERA RÚZSÁS.

Number of teachers: 440, including 30 professors.
Number of students: 1,382.
Publication: *A Pécsi Orvostudományi Egyetem Évkönyve* (Yearbook).

PROFESSORS:

ALKONYI, I., Biochemistry
BARTA, O., Orthopaedics
BAUER, M., Oto-Rhino-Laryngology
BELÁGYI, J., Central Laboratory
BIRÓ GY., Public Health
BURGER, T., Internal Medicine
CSABA, I., Obstetrics and Gynaecology
CSER, L., Foreign Languages Department
DÁVID, F., Pharmacy
FLERKÓ, B., Anatomy and Histology
FORGON, M., Surgery
FRANG, D., Urology
GRASTYÁN, E., Physiology
GRÓF, P., Dermatology
HARSÁNYI, L., Forensic Medicine
JÁVOR, T., Internal Medicine
JOBST, K., Clinical Laboratory
KELÉNYI, G., Pathological Anatomy
KÉTYI, I., Microbiology
KISS, T., Surgery
KUHN, E., Radiology
MESS, B., Anatomy and Histology
NIEDETZKY, A., Biophysics
PÁLFFY, GY., Mental Diseases
SZABÓ, D., Chemistry
SZABÓ, I., Stomatology
TAKÁTS, I., Ophthalmology
TEKERES, M., Intensive Therapy and Anaesthesia
TÉNYI, J., Social Medicine
TIGYI, A., Biology
TIGYI, J., Biophysics
TÖRÖK, B., Experimental Surgery
VARGA, F., Pharmacology

JÓZSEF ATTILA TUDOMÁNYEGYETEM
(Attila József University)

H-6701 SZEGED,
DUGONICS-TÉR 13
Telephone: 11-251.

Founded 1872, refounded 1921.
Academic year: September to June.
Rector: Prof. Dr. GYÖRGY ANTALFFY.

Pro-Rectors: Prof. Dr. GYULA KRAJKÓ (Academic Affairs), Prof Dr. GYULA KRISTÓ (Undergraduate Studies).
Head of the Rector's Office: B. DEÁK.
Librarian: Dr. BÉLA KARÁCSONYI.

Number of teachers: 489, including 52 professors.

Number of students: 3,702.

Publication: *Acta Universitatis Szegediensis de Attila József Nominatae*†.

DEANS:

Faculty of Law and Political Science: Prof. Dr. JÓZSEF VERESS.
Faculty of Arts: Prof. Dr. ISTVÁN CSUKÁS.
Faculty of Science: Prof. Dr. KÁROLY TANDORI.

PROFESSORS:

Faculty of Law and Political Science:
ANTALFFY, G., Theory of State and Law
BOTH, Ö., Legal History
FONYÓ, A., Criminal Law
HORVÁTH, R., Statistics
KEMENES, B., Civil Law
KOVÁCS, I., Constitutional Law
MARTONYI, J., Administrative and Financial Law
NAGY, K., International Law
NAGY, L., Political Economy
PÓLAY, E., Roman Law
VERESS, J., Agricultural and Labour Law

Faculty of Arts:
ÁGOSTON, G., Education
CSATÁRI, D., Modern History
CSUKÁS, I., Hungarian Literature
DEME, L., General Linguistics
DURÓ, L., Psychology
FEJÉR, Á., Russian Language and Literature
FERENCZI, I., Ethnography
FOGARASSY, M., Italian Language and Literature
GYIMESI, S., Medieval History and History of Latin America
HALÁSZ, E., German Language and Literature
HALÁSZ, Mrs. E., English Language and Literature
HORUCZI, L., Philosophy
KESERÜ, B., Hungarian Literature
KRISTÓ, G., Auxiliaries to the Study of History
MARÓTI, E., Ancient History and Archaeology
MÉREI, G., Modern Hungarian History
MIKOLA, T., Finno-Ugrian Linguistics
NAGY, G., French Language and Literature
RÁCZ, J., Scientific Socialism
RÓNA-TAS, A., Altaic Studies
SZÁDECZKY-KARDOSS, S., Classical Philology
SZÁNTÓ, I., Medieval Hungarian History
VAJDA, G. M., Comparative Literature

Faculty of Science:
BARTÓK, M., Organic Chemistry
BOROS, L., Biochemistry
CSÁKÁNY, B., Algebra and Theory of Numbers
CSÁSZÁR, J., General and Physical Chemistry
FEHÉR, O., Comparative Physiology
FEJES, P., Applied and Radiation Chemistry
FERENCZY, L., Microbiology
GÉCSEG, F., Principles of Mathematics and Cybernetics
GILDE, F., Theoretical Physics
GRASSELLY, G., Petrology, Geochemistry and Mineralogy
HORVÁTH, I., Plant Taxonomy
HUHN, P., Inorganic and Analytical Chemistry
JAKUCS, L., Geography
KOZMA, L., Experimental Physics
KRAJKÓ, G., Economic Geography
LEINDLER, L., Theory of Sets and Mathematical Logic
LIPTÁK, P., Anthropology
LOVÁSZ, L., Geometry
MÓCZÁR, L., Comparative Anatomy and Systematic Zoology
MOLNÁR, B., Geology and Palaeontology
OROSZ, L., Genetics
PÉCZELY, G., Climatology
SIROKMÁN, E., Plant Physiology
SZALAY, L., Biophysics
SZÁNTHÓ, F., Colloid Chemistry
SZŐKEFALVI-NAGY, B., Mathematical Analysis
TANDORI, K., Applied Mathematical Analysis

SZEGEDI ORVOSTUDOMÁNYI EGYETEM
(Szeged University of Medicine)

H-6720 SZEGED,
DUGONICS-TÉR 13
Telephone: 12-729.

Founded 1872, refounded 1921 as the Medical Faculty of Szeged University; independent 1951.

State control (Ministry of Health); Language of instruction: Hungarian; Academic year: September to June.

Rector: Prof. Dr. G. PETRI.
Vice-Rectors: Prof. I. CSERHÁTI, Prof. Dr. F. GUBA, Prof. Dr. J. SZILÁRD.
Administrative Director: Dr. Z. VASS.
Librarian: Dr. A. ZALLÁR.

Number of teaching staff: 519, including 28 full professors.

Number of students: 1,761.

Publications: *Studia Medica Szegedinensia, Évkönyv.*

DEANS:

Faculty of General Medicine: Prof. Dr. V. FÖLDES.
Faculty of Pharmacy: Prof. Dr. E. MINKER.

PROFESSORS:

Faculty of Medicine:
BÉLADI, I., Microbiology
BERENCSI, G., Public Health
BODA, D., Paediatrics
CSERHÁTI, I., Internal Medicine
CSILLIK, B., Anatomy and Histology
FÉNYES, GY., Surgery and Neuro-surgery
FÖLDES, V., Forensic Medicine
GUBA, F., Biochemistry
KAHÁN, A., Ophthalmology
KELEMEN, J., Radiology
KRÁMLI, A., Medical Chemistry
MOLNÁR, J., Biology
OBÁL, F., Physiology
ORMOS, J., Pathological Anatomy
PETRI, G., Clinical Surgery and Surgical Anatomy
RIBÁRI, O., Oto-Rhino-Laryngology
SAS, M., Obstetrics and Gynaecology
SIMON, M., Dermatology and Venereal Diseases
SZEKERES. L., Pharmacology
SZILÁRD, J., Neuro-psychopathology
TELEGDY, GY., Pathophysiology
TÓTH, K., Dentistry and Oral Surgery
VARRÓ, V., Internal Medicine
ZALÁNYI, S., Organization of Health Service

Faculty of Pharmacy:
BERNATH, G., Pharmaceutical Chemistry.
KEDVESSY, G., Pharmaceutical Technology
MINKER, E., Pharmacodynamics
SZENDREY, K., Pharmacognosy

TECHNICAL UNIVERSITIES

AGRÁRTUDOMÁNYI EGYETEM
(University of Agricultural Sciences)

GÖDÖLLŐ,
PÁTER KÁROLY U. 1
Telephone: Gödöllő 1.
Telex: 22 4892.
Founded 1945.

Controlled by the Ministry of Agriculture and Food; Language of instruction: Hungarian; Academic year: September to May.

Rector: Dr. LÁSZLÓ CSELŐTEI.
Pro-Rectors: Dr. KÁROLY KOCSIS, Dr. LÁSZLÓ LŐKÖS, Dr. LÁSZLÓ UDVARI.
Secretary-General: Dr. ELEMÉR RAÁTZ.
Librarian: Dr. GYULA LŐRINCZ.

Number of teaching staff (including professors): 353.

Number of students: 2,913.

Publications: *Annual Report,* scientific publications, Faculty publications, etc.

DEANS:

Faculty of Agricultural Sciences: Dr. JÓZSEF LŐRINCZ.
Faculty of Agricultural Engineering: Dr. ISTVÁN HUSZÁR.
Central Institute and Organization of Departments: Dr. JÓZSEF HECKENAST.

PROFESSORS:

Faculty of Agricultural Sciences:
ANTAL, J., Plant Cultivation
BÁLINT, A., Plant Improvement
BURJÁN, A., Agricultural Management
CSELŐTEI, L., Horticulture
DEBRECZENI, B., Agrochemistry
DOBOS, K., Agricultural Management
FEKETE, L., Animal Husbandry

HORTOBÁGYI, T., Botany and Plant Physiology
LŐKÖS, L., Agricultural Economics
LŐRINCZ, J., Plant Cultivation
MAGYARI, A., Animal Husbandry
NAGY, E., Zoology
NAGY, N., Animal Husbandry
PECZNIK, J., Chemistry
PETRASOVITS, I., Irrigated Farming
PETRÓCZI, I., Plant Protection
SIPOS, S., Tillage
STEFANOVITS, P., Pedology
SZÉP, I., Animal Physiology and Hygiene
SZEMES, L., Agricultural Management
TÓTH, B., Zoobiology
TÓTH, M., Agricultural Management
UDVARI, L., Agricultural Organization

Faculty of Agricultural Engineering:
BÁNHÁZI, J., Agricultural Machinery
BEER, GY., Agricultural Machinery
CZAKÓ, J., Behaviour of Farm Animals
GÖNCZI, I., Economics of Mechanization
HUSZÁR, I., Mechanics
JANIK, J., Agricultural Machinery
JESZENSZKY, Z., Operating of Agricultural Machines
KIRÁLY, L., Agricultural Machinery
KOCSIS, K., Agricultural Electrification
KOMÁNDI, GY., Dynamics of Tractors and Theory of Cross-country Capacity
LEHOCZKY, L., Agricultural Machinery
MIKECZ, I., Agricultural Electrification and Machines of Animal Husbandry
NAGY, A., Physics
SOÓS, P., Harvesters
TIBOLD, V., Operating of Agricultural Machines
VÁRADI, J., Tractors and Motor Vehicles, Theory of Machine Design

Central Institutes and Organization of Departments:
HECKENAST, J., History of Education
NAGY, GY., Agricultural Education
NAGY, L., Agricultural Law
PETHŐ, GY., Political Economy
POZSONYI, T., History of Education
VENDÉGH, S., Agricultural Education

AGRÁRTUDOMÁNYI EGYETEM KESZTHELY
(Keszthely Agricultural University)

8361 KESZTHELY,
DEÁK FERENC U. 16
Telephone: 123-30.
Founded 1797.

State control; Language of instruction: Hungarian; Academic year: September to June.

Rector: Prof. J. VARGA.
Vice-Rectors: Dr. Z. TÓTH, Dr. L. VINCZE, Dr. K. KÓTUN.
Secretary: F. AMBRUS.

Number of teaching staff: 210.
Number of students: 1,800.

Publications: Proceedings of the Faculties.

DEANS:

Keszthely Faculty of Agricultural Sciences: Dr. Z. KARDOS.
Mosonmagyaróvár Faculty of Agricultural Sciences: Dr. J. SCHMIDT.

PROFESSORS:

Keszthely Faculty of Agricultural Sciences:
BARTOS, A., Mathematics and Physics
BOZAI, J., Plant Protection
BUZÁS, GY., Business Management
FELLEG, J., Applied Business Management
GYŐRI, D., Soil Science
JÁRÁNYI, G., Soil Amelioration and Water Management
KARDOS, Z., Marxism-Leninism
KÁRPÁTI, I., Botany and Plant Physiology
KÖLÜS, G., Zoology
KOTUN, Mrs. K., Horticulture
KOVÁCS, J., Animal Husbandry
LÁNG, G., Plant Cultivation
POTSUBAY, J., Animal Physiology and Hygiene
TÓSZEGI, P., Agricultural Mechanization
VÁRI, A., Modern Languages
VÉGH, G., Chemistry

Mosonmagyarovar Faculty of Agricultural Sciences:
ENESE, L., Business Management
KUROLI, G., Plant Protection
LAKATOS, J., Mechanization and Electrification
MÁRTON, G., Botany and Plant Physiology
NAGY, GY., Horticulture
NAGY, L. V., Rural Economy
NÉMETH, D., Applied Business Management
NOSTICZIUS, Á., Chemistry-Soil Science
PATAKI, J., Marxism-Leninism
POHOLA, T., Modern Languages
SZABÓ, I., Animal Physiology and Veterinary Hygiene
SZAJKÓ, L., Animal Husbandry
SZŐLLŐSSY, L., Mathematics and Physics
TÓTH, Z., Zoology
VARGA, J., Plant Cultivation
ZUKÁL, E., Dairy Farming-Microbiology

ÁLLATORVOSTUDOMÁNYI EGYETEM
(University of Veterinary Science)

1078 BUDAPEST, VII,
LANDLER JENŐ U. 2
Telephone: 222-660.
Telex: 224439.
Founded 1787.

State control; Academic year: September to June.

Rector: Prof. Dr. L. VÁRNAGY.
Pro-Rectors: Prof. Dr. A. KARDEVÁN, Prof. Dr. F. KARSAI, Prof. Dr. F. KOVÁCS.
Secretary: Dr. L. M. KOVÁCS.
Librarian: Mrs. ILONA BAKONYI.

Library of 100,000 vols.
Number of teachers: 102.
Number of students: 517.

Publications: *Évkönyve*† (Yearbook), *Bibliography of Hungarian Veterinary Science.*

PROFESSORS:

BIRÓ, G., Food Hygiene
BOKORI, J., Animal Nutrition
DOHY, J., Animal Husbandry.
FEHÉR, GY., Anatomy and Histology
FELKAI, F., Ambulatory Clinic
HARASZTI, E., Botany
HARASZTI, J., Obstetrics and Gynaecology
HORVÁTH, G., Obstetrics
HORVÁTH, Z., Internal Medicine
KARDEVÁN, A., Pathological Anatomy
KARSAI, F., Pathophysiology
KASSAI, T., Parasitology
KOBULEJ, T., Parasitology
KOVÁCS, A. B., Surgery and Ophthalmology
KOVÁCS, F., Animal Hygiene
LAMI, GY., Postgraduate Veterinary Science
NÁDOR, K., Chemistry
PETHES, GY., Physiology
SIMON, F., Pharmacology
SZENT-IVÁNYI, T., Epidemiology
VÁRNAGY, L., Veterinary Administration
ZSARNÓCZAI, S., Marxism-Leninism

ASSOCIATED INSTITUTE:

Állategészségügyi Főiskolai Kar (*Higher Institute of Veterinary Medicine*): 6800 Hódmezővásárhely, Lenin u.15; f. 1970; 44 teachers, 229 students; Dir. Dr. F. KORELL.

BUDAPESTI MÜSZAKI EGYETEM
(Technical University of Budapest)

H-1521 BUDAPEST,
MÜEGYETEM-RKP. 3
Telephone: 664-011.

Founded in 1782 as Institutum Geometrico-Hydrotechnicum and reorganized as Hungarian Palatine Joseph Technical University in 1871. Építőipari és Közlekedési Müszaki Egyetem (Technical University of Building and Transport Engineering) was incorporated with the university in 1967.

Rector: Prof. Dr. J. MEISEL.
Pro-Rectors: Prof. Dr. G. BIRÓ, Prof. Dr. A. FRIGYES, Prof. Dr. I. SZABÓ.
Registrar: P. PÁLFAI.
Librarian: Dr. Eng. K. HÉBERGER.

Number of teachers: 2,328.
Number of students: 11,930.

Publications: *Periodica Polytechnica*†, *Chemical, Electrical, Mechanical, Architectural, Civil and Transport Engineering Series* (quarterly), *A Budapesti Müszaki Egyetem Évkönyve.*

DEANS:

Faculty of Civil Engineering: Dr. E. KERKÁPOLY.
Faculty of Mechanical Engineering: Dr. GY. BÉDA.
Faculty of Architecture: Dr. O. LÁSZLÓ.
Faculty of Chemical Engineering: Dr. E. PUNGOR.
Faculty of Electrical Engineering: Dr. I. VÁGÓ.
Faculty of Transport Engineering: Dr. Z. LÉVAI.

PROFESSORS:

Faculty of Civil Engineering:
BALÁZS, GY., Building Materials
BIRÓ, P., Geodesy
DETREKŐI, A., Photogrammetry
DOBOS, A., Water Management
HALÁSZ, O., Steel Structures
HASZPRA, O., Hydraulic Engineering
HOMORÓDI. L., Photogrammetry
KALISZKY, S., Mechanics
KARÁCSON, S., Building Construction
KERKÁPOLY, E., Railway Construction
KÉZDI, Á., Soil Mechanics
KOZÁK, M., Hydraulic Engineering
MEGYERI, J., Railway Construction
MEISEL, J. Geology and Mineralogy
MIKOLÁS, M., Mathematics

v. NAGY, I., Water Resources
NEMESDY, E., Road Construction
OROSZ, Á., Reinforced Concrete Structures
ÖLLŐS, G., Water Supply and Canalization
PETRASOVITS, G., Soil Mechanics
PLATTHY, P., Steel Structures
REIMANN, J., Mathematics
SÁRKÖZY, F., Surveying
SZABÓ, J., Statics
SZALAY, K., Reinforced Concrete Structures
TASSI, G., Reinforced Concrete Structures

Faculty of Mechanical Engineering:
ARTINGER, A., Mechanical Technology
BASSA, G., Heat Engines
BÉDA, GY., Technical Mechanics
BAKONDI, K., Machine Production
FARKAS, M., Mathematics
FEHÉR, J., Textile Machines
FÜZY, O., Hydraulic Machines
HARSÁNYI, I., Industrial Business Management
HORVÁTH, M., Machine Production
JEDERÁN, M., Textile Machines
KALÁSZI, J., Machine Production
KONKOLY, T., Mechanical Technology
LADÓ, L., Industrial Business Management
MAGYAR, J., Machine Parts
MENYHÁRT, J., Sanitary Engineering
NAGY, I., Electrotechnics
PÁPAI, L., Hydraulic Machines
PETRIK, O., Precision Mechanics-Optics
PRÉKOPA, A., Mathematics
PROHÁSZKA, J., Electrical Materials Technology
STROMMER, GY., Geometry
SZABÓ, I., Mechanical and Process Engineering
SZENTHE, J., Geometry
SZENTGYÖRGYI, S., Chemical and Food Engineering
SZENTMÁRTONY, T., Fluid Mechanics
THERNESZ, V., Agricultural Machines
TURI, Z., Precision Mechanics and Optics
VARGA, L., Machine Elements
ZALKA, A., Agricultural Machinery

Faculty of Architecture:
BALOGH, I., Drawing, Moulding
BONTA, J., Theory and History of Architecture
DEÁK, GY., Strength of Materials
FARAGÓ, K., Town Planning
FEKETE, I., Sanitary Engineering
GÁBOR, L., Building Construction
GÁDOROS, L., Design of Public Buildings
HAJNÓCZY, GY., History of Architecture
HARASTA, M., Industrial and Agricultural Architecture
HOFER, M., Design of Public Buildings
JÁNDY, G., Building Operations
KÜRTI, I., Building Management and Organization
LÁSZLÓ, O., Building Construction
MERÉNYI, F., History of Architecture
OLASZ, L., House Design
PERÉNYI, I., Town Planning
PETRICH, G., Descriptive Geometry
PETRÓ, B., Building Constructions
SEBESTYÉN, GY., Building Operations
VAJDA, Z., Construction
ZÁDOR, M., Preservation of Monuments

Faculty of Chemical Engineering:
FODOR, L., Agricultural Chemistry
FÖLDES, P., Chemical Unit Operations
HARDY, GY., Plastic and Rubber
HOLLÓ, J., Agricultural Chemistry
KORÁNYI, GY., Applied Chemistry
KRÁLIK, D., Mathematics
LÁSZTITY, R., Biochemistry and Food Technology
LEMPERT, K., Organic Chemistry
MÓSER, M., Chemical Engineering
NAGY, J., Inorganic Chemistry
NAGY, GY. L., Applied Chemistry
PETRÓ, J., Organic Chemistry
PUNGOR, E., General and Analytical Chemistry
RUSZNÁK, I., Technology of Organic Chemistry
SZABADVÁRY, F., General and Analytical Chemistry
SZÁNTAY, CS., Organic Chemistry
SZEBÉNYI, I., Technology of Chemistry
TŐKE, L., Technology of Organic Chemistry
VARSÁNYI, GY., Physical Chemistry
VERBA, A., Chemical Equipment

Faculty of Electrical Engineering:
AMBRÓZY, A., Communication and Instruments
BOSZNAY, Á., Technical Mechanics
CSIBI, S., Communication Electronics
FENYŐ, I., Mathematics
FERENCZY, P., Communication Electronics
FODOR, GY., Theory of Electricity
FRIGYES, A., Process Control
GESZTI, P. O., Electric Power Transmission and Distribution
GÉHER, K., Communication Electronics
HORVÁTH, T., High Voltage Equipment
KISS, O., Mathematics
PÁSZTORNICZKY, L., Microwave Communication
RÁCZ, J., Electric Machines
RETTER, I., Electric Machines
RÓZSA, P., Mathematics
SCHNELL, L., Instruments and Metrology
SIMONYI, K., Communication Electonics
TARNAY, K., Electronics Devices
TUSCHÁK, R., Automation
VALKÓ, I., Electron Tubes and Semiconductors
VÁGÓ, I., Theoretical Electricity

Faculty of Transport Engineering:
FELFÖLDI, L., Transport
HORVÁTH, K., Railways
ILOSVAI, L., Motor Vehicles
KELEMEN, T., Transport Automatics
LETTNER, F., Machine Production Technology
LÉVAI, Z., Motor Vehicles
MICHELBERGER, P., Mechanics
OROSZ, J., Transport Engineering and Organization
PÁSZTOR, E., Aero- and Thermo-Engineering
PRISTYÁK, A., Building and Transport Equipment
SVÁB, J., Building Machinery
SZÁSZ, G., Mathematics
TURÁNYI, J., Transport
VARGA, S., Transport

Central Departments:
ÁCHEL, GY., Physical Education
ADÁM, A., Atomic Physics
ANTAL, J., Physics
BAKOS, J., Experimental Physics
BARTA, L., Pedagogy
BENKE, I., Political Economy
BIRÓ, G., Experimental Physics
BORSI, Mrs. M., Scientific Socialism
DENKE, G., Political Economy
ERDŐS, P., Political Economy
FEKETE, J., Pedagogy
GIBER, J., Physics
HÁRSING, L., Philosophy
HOLLÓS, E., Scientific Socialism
KÓNYA, A., Physics
KOVÁCS, I., Atomic Physics
LÁNG, L., Physics

Institute of Foreign Languages:
FAZEKAS, Mrs. P.
FEHÉR, GY.
FENICZY, GY.
FÜVES, Ö.
HÁRS, Mrs. E.
SÓS, Mrs. P.
TÓTH, Mrs. M.

DEBRECENI AGRÁRTUDOMÁNYI EGYETEM

(Debrecen University of Agrarian Sciences)

H-4001 DEBRECEN,
P.O.B. 58
Telephone: 17-888.
Founded 1868.

State control; Language of instruction: Hungarian; Academic year: September to June.

Rector: Dr. J. TÓTH.
Pro-Rectors: Dr. B. KÁDÁR, Dr. GY. KURUCZ.
Registrar: Dr. L. GULÁCSI.
Librarian: L. BILINCSI.

Library of 92,000 vols.
Number of teachers: 260.
Number of students: 1,741.
Publication: *A Debreceni Agrártudományi Egyetem Tudományos Közleményei* (annual).

DEANS:

Faculty of Agricultural Sciences: Dr. F. LOCH.
Higher Institute of Irrigation and Reclamation, Szarvas: Dr. A. SZÁNTÓSI (Director).
Higher Institute of Agricultural Mechanization: Dr. I. PATKÓS (Director).

PROFESSORS:

Faculty of Agricultural Sciences:
BOCZ, E., Plant Production
BODNÁR, M., Agricultural Economics
HELMECZI, B., Soil Science and Microbiology
KÁDÁR, B., Farm Management
KECSKEMÉTI, J., Physical Education
KISS, I., Animal Husbandry
KURUCZ, G., Applied Farm Management
LOCH, J., Chemistry
MUNKÁCSI, F., Animal Physiology and Hygiene
NAGY, J., Mathematics and Physics
PETHŐ, F., Plant Physiology
PETHŐ, M., Plant Physiology
PETRIKÁS, A., Foreign Languages
POÓR, J., Marxism-Leninism
SZÁSZ, G., Agrometeorology
SZEPESSY, I., Plant Protection
SZIKI, G., Civil Engineering
TÓTH, J., Economic Mathematics, Statistics and Computing
VADÁSZ, L., Farm Management
VARGA, F., Agricultural Machinery
VINCZEFFY, I., Grass Production

ATTACHED INSTITUTES:

A Debreceni Agrártudományi Egyetem Kutató Intézete (*Research Institute*): 5300 Karcag, P.O.B. 11; Dir. Dr. F. BORSOS.

Termelésfejlesztési Intézet (*Institute for Production Development*): 4001 Debrecen, P.O.B. 58; Dir. Dr. J. ECSEDI.

ERDÉSZETI ÉS FAIPARI EGYETEM
(University of Forestry and Timber Industry)

9400 SOPRON,
BAJCSY-ZSILINSZKY U. 4
Telephone: Sopron 11-100.
Founded 1808.

Rector: Dr. S. KECSKÉS.
Pro-Rectors: Dr. J. KÁLDY, Dr. M. KUBINSZKY, Dr. E. SOMKUTI.
Head Official of Rectorate: Dr. S. MOLNÁR.
Librarian: Dr. I. HILLER

Number of teachers: 142.
Number of students: 794 undergraduate, 333 postgraduate.
Publication: *Erdészeti és Faipari Egyetem Tudományos Közleményei.*

DEANS:

Faculty of Forestry: Dr. I. HERPAY.
Faculty of Timber Industry: Dr. F. BÉLDI.
College of Surveying and Country Planning (in Székesfehérvár): Dr. B. KOVÁCS.

PROFESSORS:

BÁCSATYAY, L., Forestry Surveying and Mapping
BÉLDI, F., Physics—Electrical Engineering
CZAGÁNY, L., Furniture Manufacturing
CZIRÁKI, J., Panel Manufacturing
EPERJESI, B., Physical Education
GÁL, J., Afforestation
GENCSI, L., Botany and Soil Science
GUNDA, M., Descriptive Geometry
HERPAY, I., Forest Utilization
IGMÁNDY, Z., Forest Protection
KÁLDY, J., Forestry Mechanics
KECSKÉS, S., Forestry Transport
KIRÁLY, L., Forestry Management
KŐHALMY, T., Wildlife Management
KOVÁCS, B., Photogrammetry and Topography
KOVÁCS, I., Timber Technology
KRISCH, I., Foreign Languages
KUBINSZKY, M., Forestry Architecture
MAJER, A., Sylviculture
MOÓR, A., Mathematics
NAGY, J., Foundation Subjects
NAGY, L., Geodesy
RÓNAI, F., Mechanics
SOMKUTI, E., Forestry Economics
SZABÓ, J., Marxism-Leninism
SZENDREY, I., Chemistry
VÁRHELYI, I., Marxism-Leninism

ATTACHED INSTITUTE:

Erdészeti Talajmikrobiológiai Kutatócsoport (*Research Section for Soil Microbiology*): f. 1960; Dir. Dr. GYÖRGY PÁNTOS.

KERTÉSZETI EGYETEM
(University of Horticulture)

1118 BUDAPEST, XI,
VILLÁNYI U. 35-43
Telephone: 850–666.
Founded 1853.

Under the direction of the Ministry of Agriculture and Food.

Rector: Prof. Dr. I. DIMÉNY.
Pro-Rectors: Prof. Dr. P. KOZMA, Prof. Dr. P. PILLIS, Docent Dr. E. ERDÉLYI.
Registrar: Mrs. MÁRIA LONTI.
Librarian: Dr. GUSZTÁV GEDAY.

Library of 220,000 vols.
Number of teachers: 246.
Number of students: 1,414.
Publication: *Kertészeti Egyetem Közleményei*† (annually).

DEANS:

Faculty of Cultivation: Dr. JÁNOS KARAI.
Faculty of Preserving Industry: Dr. KÁLMÁN GASZTONYI.
Faculty of Cultivation, Kecskemét: Dr. ISTVÁN FILIUS.

PROFESSORS:

ALMÁSI, E., Food Technology and Microbiology
BOGNÁR, S., Plant Protection
BURGER, Mrs., Agricultural Economy
CSEPREGI, P., Viticulture
DIMÉNY, I., Economics
GASZTONYI, K., Food Chemistry
GOMBKÖTŐ, G., Chemistry
GYURÓ, F., Fruit Growing
HARGITAI, L., Pedology
KÁDÁR, GY., Oenology
KARAI, J., Mechanization
KOLEDA, I., Plant Genetics and Selection
KOZMA, P., Viticulture
KÓRÓDI, L., Vegetable Cultivation
NAGY, B., Ornamental Plant Growing
PAIS, I., Chemistry
PILLIS, P., Economics
PROBOCSKAY, E., Nursery Gardening
RÉDAI, I., Economics
SÁRKÖZY, P., Postgraduate Training
SOMOS, A., Vegetable Cultivation
SZABÓ, Z., Mechanization
TAMÁS, L., Agricultural History
TAMÁSSY, I., Plant Genetics and Selection
TERPÓ, A., Botany
VUKOV, K., Conservation Technology

ATTACHED INSTITUTE:

Kertészeti Egyetemi Tangazdaság (*University of Horticulture Research and Experimental Station*): Budapest-Soroksár.

NEHÉZIPARI MŰSZAKI EGYETEM
(Technical University of Heavy Industry)

3515 MISKOLC-EGYETEMVÁROS
Telephone: 13-691.
Founded 1770 in Selmecbánya; moved 1919 to Sopron: reorganized 1949 in Miskolc.

Academic year: September to June.

Rector: Dr. T. CZIBERE.
Vice-Rectors: Dr. J. CZEKKEL, Dr. I. KOZÁK, Dr. F. KOVÁCS.
Chief Administrative Officer: Dr. G. CZEPPER.
Librarian: Dr. J. ZSIDAI.

Number of teachers: 415.
Number of students: 2,640.
Publications: *Nehézipari Müszaki Egyetem Közleményei*† (papers in Hungarian, irregular), *Publications of the Technical University of Heavy Industry*† (papers in German, English, Russian and French, irregular), *Évkönyv*† (yearbook).

DEANS:

Faculty of Mechanical Engineering: Dr. I. LÉVAI.
Faculty of Metallurgical Engineering: Dr. B. VORSATZ.
Faculty of Mining Engineering: Dr. E. TAKÁCS.

PROFESSORS:

Faculty of Mechanical Engineering:

CSÓTAI, J., Physical Education
CZIBERE, T., Fluid and Thermal Engineering
DRAHOS, I., Descriptive Geometry
DROBNI, J., Mechanics
FÁBRY, GY., Chemical Machinery
FARKAS, J., Transport Equipment
FEJES, G., Chemical Machinery
GRIBOVSZKY, L., Machine Building Technology
KLAVSZKY, E. Mathematics
KOZÁK, I., Mechanics
LÉVAI, I., Transport Equipment
ROMVÁRI, P., Mechanical Technology
SÁLYI, I., Jr., Mechanics
SUSÁNSZKY, J., Industrial Economics
SZABÓ, J., Physics
SZALADNYA, S., Transport Equipment
SZARKA, T., Electrotechnics
SZENTIRMAI, L., Electrotechnics
SZÓTÉR, L., Physics
TAJNAFŐI, J., Machine Tools Design
TERPLÁN, Z., Machine Elements
VINCZE, E., Mathematics

Faculty of Metallurgical Engineering:

BERECZ, E., General and Physical Chemistry
CSABALIK, GY., Ferrous Metallurgy
FARKAS, O., Fuel Engineering
FARKAS, O., Metallurgy of Ferrous Metals
GÁRDUS, J., Foreign Languages
HORVÁTH, Z., Metallurgy of Non-Ferrous Metals
KÁLDOR, M., Physical Metallurgy
KISS, E., Hot Metal Working and Plastic Deformation
NÁNDORI, GY., Foundry Technology
SIMON, S., Metallurgy of Ferrous Metals
SULCZ, F., Automation
VORSATZ, B., Inorganic and Analytical Chemistry

Faculty of Mining Engineering:

ALLIQUANDER, Ö., Oil Production
BOCSÁNCZY, J., Mining Machinery
CSÓKÁS, J., Geophysics
HÁMOR, G., Geology and Mineral Deposits
JUHÁSZ, J., Engineering Geology, Hydrogeology
KOLZSVÁRI, G., Geodesy and Mine Surveying
KOVÁCS, F., Mining Exploitation
KUN, L., Marxism and Leninism
NÉMEDI VARGA, Z., Geology and Mineral Deposits
PATVAROS, J., Mining Exploitation
PETHŐ, SZ., Mineral Processing
POJJÁK, T., Mineralogy and Petrography
STEINER, F., Geophysics
SZILAS, A. P., Oil Production
TAKÁCS, E., Geophysics
TARJÁN, I., Mining Machinery
ZAMBÓ, J., Mining Exploitation

ASSOCIATE INSTITUTES:

Kohó- és Fémipari Főiskolai Kar (*Higher Institute of Metallurgical Technology*): 2400 Dunaujváros, Táncscics M. u. 1; f. 1962; became a Higher Institute in 1969; 95 teachers, 1,324 students; Dir. L. MOLNÁR.

Vegyipari Automatizálási Főiskolai Kar (*Higher Institute of Digital Control for Chemical Engineering*): 3700 Kazincbarcika, Lenin u. 1; f. 1962; became a Higher Institute in 1970; 41 teachers, 390 students; Dir. M. CSERVENKA.

VESZPRÉMI VEGYIPARI EGYETEM

(Veszprém University of Chemical Engineering)

H-8201 VESZPRÉM,
SCHÖNHERZ Z. U. 10
Telephone: 125-50.
Telex: 32 397 vegye h.
Founded 1949.

State controlled; Language of instruction: Hungarian; Academic year: September to June.

Rector: Dr. J. INCZÉDY.
Pro-Rectors: Dr. B. HEIL, Dr. S. PAPP.
General Secretary: Dr. Z. CSAPÓ.
Librarian: Dr. Z. KOVÁTS.

Library of 108,793 vols.

Number of teachers: 208.

Number of students: 938, including 241 on correspondence course and 76 postgraduate.

Publications: *Hungarian Journal of Industrial Chemistry*, joint publication of four scientific institutions of the chemical industry in Veszprém (quarterly), *Yearbook*.

PROFESSORS:

BAKOS, M., Chemical Process Engineering
BENE, L., Industrial Engineering and Management
BENKŐ, I., Radiochemistry
BODOR, E., Inorganic Chemistry
DÉRI, M., Silicate Chemistry
FÜLÖP, G., Political Economy
HALÁSZ, A., Mechanical Engineering
HÁZI, E., Radiochemistry
HEIL, B., Organic Chemistry
INCZÉDY, J., Analytical Chemistry
KÁLDI, P., Chemical Technology
LÁSZLÓ, A., Chemical Process Engineering
LENGYEL, T., Radiochemistry
MARKÓ, L., Organic Chemistry
MOHAI, B., Inorganic Chemistry
NEMECZ, E., Mineralogy
PÉCHY, L., Hydrocarbon and Coal Processing
POLINSZKY, K., Chemical Technology
STRAUB, GY., Radiochemistry
SZOLCSÁNYI, P., Chemical Process Engineering

ATTACHED INSTITUTES:

The Hungarian Academy of Sciences research groups for Petrochemistry and Analytical Chemistry and the Ministry of Education research group for Silicate Chemistry.

COLLEGES OF UNIVERSITY STANDING

Liszt Ferenc Zeneművészeti Főiskola (*Franz Liszt Academy of Music*): 1391 Budapest, Liszt Ferenc-tér 8; f. 1875; Rector J. UJFALUSSY; Librarian Dr. J. KÁRPÁTI; library of 138,000 vols.; 205 teachers, 466 students.

Magyar Iparművészeti Főiskola (*Hungarian College of Applied Arts*): 1121 Budapest, XII, Zugligeti u. 11-25; f. 1880, present status 1971; 58 teachers, 306 students; library of 25,000 vols.; Rector ENDRE GÁDOR.

Magyar Képzőművészeti Főiskola (*Hungarian Academy of Fine Arts*): Budapest, VI, Népköztársaság u. 71; f. 1871; courses in painting, sculpture, graphic art, advertising graphics and restoration; Dir. F. SOMOGYI; Librarian I. KOVANECZ; library of 45,000 vols.; 40 teachers; 135 students.

Magyar Szocialista Munkáspárt Politikai Főiskolája (*Political Academy of the Hungarian Socialist Workers Party*): 1146 Budapest XIV, Ajtósi Dürer sor 19/21; f. 1968; 13 departments; 800 students; library of 150,000 vols.; Rector Dr. JÓZSEF SZABÓ; Vice-Rectors Dr. ALADÁR SIPOS, Dr. BÉLA VÉSZI, JÁNOS MOLNÁR; publ. *A Politikai Főiskola Közleményei* (quarterly).

Magyar Testnevelési Főiskola (*Hungarian College for Physical Education*): 1123 Budapest, Alkotás u. 44; f. 1925; three departments for the education of teachers, coaches and sports organizers; 85 teachers, 1,150 students; library of 64,000 vols.; sponsors a research institute and a postgraduate institute; Rector ANDRÁS ZALKA; Pro-Rectors Dr. CSABA ISTVÁNFI, Dr. LÁSZLÓ NÁDORI; publs. *Testnevelési Főiskola Évkönyve* (Yearbook).

Szinház- és Filmművészeti Főiskola (*Academy of Dramatic and Cinematic Art*): Budapest, VIII, Vas u. 2/c.; f. 1865; Rector Dr. JENŐ SIMÓ; Gen. Sec. L. VADÁSZ; 68 teachers, 28; students.

OTHER COLLEGES

ARCHITECTURE

Ybl Miklós Építőipari Műszaki Főiskola (*College of Architecture*): Budapest, XIV, Thököly u. 74; f. 1972; 162 teachers, 2,060 students; Dir. LAJOS KISS.

BUSINESS AND COMMERCE

Kereskedelmi és Vendéglátóipari Főiskola (*College of Commerce and Catering*): Budapest, V, Alkotmány u. 9/11; f. 1969; 106 teachers, 1,824 students; Dir. K. SOLYMÁR.

Külkereskedelmi Főiskola (*College for Foreign Trade*): 1476 Budapest, Pf. 3; f. 1962; 150 teachers, 1,200 students; Dir. J. GULYÁS.

Pénzügyi és Számviteli Főiskola (*College of Finance and Accountancy*): 1426 Budapest, Buzogány u. 10; f. 1962; 149 teachers, 3,200 students; library of 98,500 vols.; Dir. Z. TÉTÉNYI.

TECHNOLOGY

Bánki Donát Gépipari Műszaki Főiskola (*Bánki Donát Mechanical Engineering College*): Budapest, VIII, Népszínház u. 8; f. 1969; 109 teachers, 1,769 students; library of 26,000 vols.; Dir. B. ANGYAL; publ. *Production Engineer*.

Budapesti Felsőfokú Élelmiszeripari Technikum (*Budapest College of Food Technology*): Budapest, VI, Izabella u. 46; f. 1961; library of 21,000 vols.; 60 teachers; 400 students; Rector Dr. G. FÁBRI; Librarian Mrs. L. POÓS.

Felsőfokú Epitőgépészeti Technikum (*College of Building Engineering*): Debrecen, Landler Jenő u. 4; f. 1962; 44 teachers, 449 students; library of 10,000 vols.; Dir. MIHÁLY BARÓCZI.

Felsőfokú Gépjárműközlekedési Technikum (*College of Motor Engineering*): Budapest, X, Újhegyi u. 14; f. 1962; 24 teachers, 418 students; library of 1,490 vols.; Dir. Ing. T. KÁZMÉR.

Felsőfokú Távközlési Technikum (*College of Telecommunications*): Budapest, IX, Gyáli u. 22; f. 1962; 20 teachers, 356 students; Dir. J. RÁCZ.

Felsőfokú Vasútforgalmi Technikum (*College of Railway Engineering*): Szeged, Marx tér 14; f. 1962; 32 teachers, 289 students; Dir. M. KÁLMÁN.

Felsőfokú Vegyipari Gépészeti Technikum (*College of Chemical Engineering*): Esztergom-Kenyérmező, Wesselényi u. 1; f. 1962; 120 students; library of 12,000 vols.; Dir. LAJOS KARAKAS; Pro-Dir. ZOLTÁN SASVÁRY.

Gépipari és Automatizálási Műszaki Főiskola (*Institute of Engineering and Automation*): 6001 Kecskemét, Izsáki u. 10; f. 1964; 86 teachers, 647 students; library of 38,000 vols.; Dir. S. KAPITÁNY.

Kandó Kálmán Villamosipari Műszaki Főiskola (*Kálmán Kandó Institute of Electrical Engineering*): Budapest III, Nagyszombat u. 19; f. 1969; 222 teachers, 3,193 students; library of 33,000 vols.; Dir. Prof. Dr. SÁNDOR DOMONKOS; publ. *Scientific Papers*†.

Könnyűipari Műszaki Főiskola (*College of Technology for Light Industry*): 1034 Budapest, Doberdó u. 6; f. 1972; training and research in the textile, clothing, leather, paper and printing industries; 80 teachers, 1,200 students; Gen. Dir. G. VÁMOS.

Közlekedési és Távközlési Műszaki Főiskola (*College of Transport and Telecommunications*): 9026 Győr, Ságvári Endre u. 3; f. 1962, reorganized 1971; departments of vehicle construction, traffic engineering, traffic and postal management, telecommunications and automation, training of technical teachers; 250 teachers, 2,500 students; Dir.-Gen. L. KISCELLI.

Szegedi Élelmiszeripari Főiskola (*Szeged College of Food Technology*): 6701 Szeged, Marx-tér 7 (Faculty of Animal Husbandry in Hódmezővásárhely); f. 1970; applied protein research; library of 27,000 vols.; 60 teachers, 500 students; Rector Dr. ELISABETH GÁBOR; Registrar Dr. JÓZSEF FARAGÓ; publ. *Scientific News*† (annual).

ICELAND

Population 223,900

LEARNED SOCIETIES AND RESEARCH INSTITUTES

Agriculture

Búnadarfélag Íslands (*Agricultural Society of Iceland*): Baendahöllinni, P.O.B. 7080, Reykjavík; f. 1899; carries out advisory services, administrative duties, promotion of the agricultural industry and research; publs. on agriculture and statistics; 4,000 mems.; Dir. Jónas Jónsson; Board of Directors: Asgeir Bjarnason (Chair.), Steindór Gestsson, Hjörtur E. Thórarinsson; publs. *Freyr*† (fortnightly), *Búnadarrit*† (bi-annual), *Handbók Baenda*† (annual).

Archaeology

Islenzka fornleifafélag, Hid (*Icelandic Archaeological Society*): Reykjavík; f. 1879; Pres. Dr. Kristian Eldjárn; Sec. Thorhallur Vilmundarson; 700 mems.; publ. *Árbók* (Year Book).

The Arts

Bandalag Íslenzkra Listamanna (*Union of Icelandic Artists*): P.O.B. 1251, Reykjavík; Pres. Thor Vilhjálmsson; 573 mems.; organized in the following divisions:

Arkitektafélag Íslands (*Icelandic Architects' Association*): Chair. Hilmar Olafsson; 100 mems.

Félag Íslenzkra Leikara (*Icelandic Actors' Association*): Chair. Gísli Alfredsson; 130 mems.

Félag Íslenzkra Listdansara (*Association of Icelandic Dance Artists*): Chair. Kristín Björnsdóttir; 30 mems.

Félag Íslenzkra Myndlistarmanna (*Icelandic Association of Pictorial Artists*): Chair. Hjörleifur Sigurdsson; 70 mems.

Félag Íslenzkra Tónlistarmanna (*Icelandic Musicians' Association*): Chair. Rögnvaldur Sigurjónsson; 40 mems.

Rithöfundasamband Íslands (*Icelandic Writers' Association*): Chair. Sigurdur A. Magnusson; 183 mems.

Tónskáldafélag Íslands (*Icelandic Composers' Society*): Chair. Atli Heimir Sveinsson; 20 mems.

Félag Íslenzkra Kvikmyndagerdarmanna (*Icelandic Film-Makers' Association*): Chair. Sigurdur Sverrir Pálsson; 20 mems.

Menntamálaráð (*Arts Council*) (includes **Menningarsjodur** (*Cultural Fund*)): P.O.B. 1398, Reykjavík; f. 1928; publishes Icelandic literature, translations of world literature, etc.; issues grants to artists; Chair. Einar Laxness; Man. Dir. Hrólfur Halldórsson; publs. *Andvari, Almanak, Studia Islandica.*

International Cultural Societies

Alliance Française: P.O.B. 1303, Kvisthaga 12, Reykjavík; f. 1911; 300 mems.; Chair. M. Albert Gudmundsson; Sec. Magnús G. Jónsson; publ. *Islande-France* (annually).

Anglia (*Anglo-Icelandic Society*): P.O.B. 154, Reykjavík; f. 1921; 250 mems.; library contains 2,000 vols.; Chair. Hilmar Foss; Sec. Kristin Hallsson.

Danske Selskab i Reykjavík (*Danish Society*): Reykjavík; f. 1923; Chair. H. Fenger; Librarian and Administrator K. Bruun, P.O.B. 222, Reykjavík.

Kvenfélagasamband Íslands (*Union of Women's Societies*): Hallveigarstöðum, Túngötu 14, Reykjavík; f. 1930; 25,000 mems.; Chair. Mrs. Maria Pétursdóttir; publ. *Húsfreyjan*.

Menningarstofnun Bandaríkjanna (*U.S. International Communication Agency*): Neshaga 16, Reykjavík.

Neytendasamtökin (*Consumers' Union of Iceland*): P.O.B. 1096, Reykjavík; f. 1953; 4,000 mems.; Pres. Reynir Ármannsson; publ. *Neytendabladid*.

Norraena Félagid (*Nordic Society*): P.O.B. 912, Reykjavík; f. 1922; 2,000 mems.; Pres. Sigurdur Bjarnason; Dir. Einar Pálsson; publ. *Norraen tídindi.*

General Science

Iceland Glaciological Society: P.O.B. 5194, Reykjavík; f. 1951; 400 mems.; Pres. Sigurdur Thorarinsson; Sec. Sigurjon Rist; publ. *Jökull*†.

Rannsóknaráð Ríkisins (*National Research Council*): Laugaveg 13, Reykjavík; f. 1965; aims to strengthen and co-ordinate science policy, initiate studies of the country's natural resources, advise the Government on scientific matters, procure funds for the promotion of science, promote international co-operation in science; a government institution subordinate to the Ministry of Culture and Education; Chair. Ingvar Gíslason (Minister of Culture and Education); Dir. Vilhjálmur Lúdvíksson.

Hafrannsóknastofnunin (*Marine Research Institute*): research into marine biological and oceanographic sciences; special divisions for pelagic fish, demersal fish, flat-fish, technology and fishing gear, hydrography, phytoplankton, zooplankton and benthos; Government institution subordinate to the Ministry of Fisheries; Chair. Jón Arnalds; Dir. Jón Jónsson.

Idntæknistofnun Íslands (*Technological Institute of Iceland*): research and service institution for industry; research on raw materials, machinery and end products to improve quality and competitiveness of Icelandic industrial production; special divisions for training and information, industrial development, technical services and for research; Government institution subordinate to the Ministry of Industry; Chair. Gudrún Hallgríms-Dóttir; Dir. Sveinn Björnsson.

Rannsóknastofnun landbúnaðarins (*Agricultural Research Institute*): government-financed research and experimental development in agriculture; special divisions for animal-breeding, ecology and cultivation and farming technology; Government institution subordinate to the Ministry of Agriculture; Chair. Bjarni Arason; Dir. Dr. Björn Sigurbjörnsson.

Rannsóknastofnun fiskidnaðarins (*Fish Industrial Research Institute*): research and services for the fish industry, quality control, etc.; divisions for chemistry, bacteriology and technology; Government institution subordinate to the Ministry of Fisheries; Chair. JÓN ARNALDS; Dir. Dr. BJÖRN DAGBJARTSSON.

Rannsóknastofnun byggingaidnadarins (*Building Research Institute*): f. 1965; scientific research and services for the construction and building industries; Government institution subordinate to the Ministry of Industry; Chair. GUDMUNDUR MAGNÚSSON; Dir. HARALDUR ASGEIRSSON.

Surtseyjarfélagid (*Surtsey Research Society*): P.O.B. 352, Reykjavík; f. 1965; to promote and co-ordinate scientific work in geo- and biological sciences especially on the island of Surtsey; 65 mems.; Chair. STEINGRIMUR HERMANNSSON; Sec. SVEINN JAKOBSSON; publ. *The Surtsey Progress Reports.*

Verkfrædingafélag Íslands (*Association of Chartered Engineers in Iceland*): P.O.B. 645, Reykjavík; f. 1912; *c.* 750 mems.; Pres. RAGNAR S. HALLDÓRSSON; Sec. HINRIK GUDMUNDSSON; publs. *Tímarit Verkfrædingafélags Islands* (6 a year), *Fréttabréf* (2 a month).

Visindafélag Islendinga (*Icelandic Scientific Society*): University of Iceland, Reykjavík; f. 1918; 95 mems.; Pres. JONAS KRISTJANSSON; publs. *Árbók*† (annually), *Rit*†, *Greinar*† (irregular).

HISTORY

Sögufélagid (*The Icelandic Historical Society*): c/o Isafold, Reykjavík; f. 1902; Pres. BJÖRN THORSTEINSSON.

LITERATURE

Íslenzka bókmenntafélag, Hid (*The Icelandic Literary Society*): Reykjavík; f. 1816; 1,450 mems.; Pres. SIGURDUR LÍNDAL; Sec. ÓSKAR HALLDÓRSSON; publs. *Annual Journal, Skírnir.*

METEOROLOGY

Vedurstofa Íslands (*Meteorological Institute*): Reykjavík; f. 1920; weather forecasts, climatology, aerology, seismology; Dir. H. SIGTRYGGSSON; staff of about 60; library of 7,000 vols.; publs. *Seismological Bulletin* (annual), *Vedráttan*† (monthly).

MUSIC

Tónlistarfélagid (*Music Society*): Reykjavík; f. 1930; operates a College of Music; affiliated societies in major towns; Chair. RAGNAR JÓNSSON; Man. HAUKUR H. GRÖNDAL; Headmaster of College JÓN NORDAL.

NATURAL HISTORY

Íslenzka náttúrúfrædifélag, Hid (*The Icelandic Natural History Society*): P.O.B. 846, 121 Reykjavík; f. 1889; Pres. KRISTJAN SAEMUNDSSON; Sec. ERLING ÓLAFSSON; 1,900 mems.; publ. *Náttúrufrædingurinn*† (quarterly journal of natural history).

PATHOLOGY

Rannsóknastofa Háskólans (*University Institute of Pathology and Bacteriology*): P.O.B. 150, Reykjavík; f. 1934; Dir. Prof. JONAS HALGRIMSSON.

Tilraunastöd Háskólans í meinafraedi á Keldum (*Institute for Experimental Pathology, University of Iceland*): P.O.B. 110, Reykjavík; f. 1948; affiliated to University Medical School; Dir. GUDMUNDUR PÉTURSSON.

STATISTICS

Hagstofa Íslands (*Statistical Bureau of Iceland*) :Reykjavík; f. 1914; Dir. KLEMENS TRYGGVASON; publs. *Hagtídindi* (monthly), *Hagskýrslur Islands* (statistical reports).

LIBRARIES

Borgarbókasafn Reykjavíkur (*City Library of Reykjavík*): Thingholtsstraeti 29A, Reykjavík; f. 1923; 255,230 vols.; Dir. ELFA BJÖRK GUNNARSDÓTTIR; publ. *Bókalisti* (book list) (3 a year).

Háskólabókasafn (*University Library*): Reykjavík; f. 1940; 204,000 vols.; Dir. EINAR SIGURDSSON.

Landsbókasafn Íslands (*National Library of Iceland*): Reykjavík; f. 1818; Dir. FINNBOGI GUDMUNDSSON, DR. PHIL.; 340,000 printed vols., 13,000 MSS.; open to the public; publs. *Islenzk bókaskrá* (The Icelandic National Bibliography); *Árbók* (Year Book).

Thjodskjalasafn (*National Archives*): Safnahús, Reykjavík; f. 1882; Dir. BJORNI-VILKJALMSSON.

MUSEUMS

Listasafn Einars Jónssonar (*National Einar Jónsson Art Gallery*): P.O.B. 1051, Reykjavík; f. 1920; sculpture and paintings by Einar Jónsson; Dir. FIL. KAND. ÓLAFUR KVARAN; publ. catalogue†.

Náttúrufraedistofnun Íslands (*Museum of Natural History*): P.O.B. 5320, Reykjavík; f. 1889 by Hid Íslenzka Náttúrufraedifélag (*The Icelandic Natural History Society*) and maintained by this Society until 1946; taken over by the State 1947; Dir., and Head Curator, Dept. of Botany, EYTHÓR EINARSSON, M.SC.; Dept. of Geology and Geography, Head Curator SVEINN JAKOBSSON, M.SC.; Dept. of Zoology, Head Curator AEVAR PETERSEN, PH.D.; publs. *Acta Naturalia Islandica*† abd *Reprint Series*†.

Thjódminjasafn (*National Museum*): P.O.B. 1739, Sudurgata 71, Reykjavík; f. 1863; the main collection is of Icelandic antiquities; collection of art and coins; Dir. THÓR MAGNÚSSON, State Antiquary; publs. *Skýrsla um Forngripasafn Islands, Thjódminjasafn Islands, Leidarvisir, Árbók hins islenzka fornleifafélags, Summary Guide.*

UNIVERSITY

HÁSKÓLI ÍSLANDS
(University of Iceland)

SUDURGATA, REYKJAVÍK

Telephone: 25088.

Founded 1911.

State control; Academic year: September to June.

Rector: Prof. GUDMUNDUR K. MAGNÚSSON.

Pro-Rector: Prof. VÍKINGUR H. ARNÓRSSON.

Vice-President for Financial Affairs: STEFÁN SÖRENSSON, CAND. JUR.

Vice-President for Academic Affairs: HALLDÓR GUDJÓNSSON, PH.D.

Librarian: EINAR SIGURDSSON.

Library: *see* Libraries.

Number of teachers: 350, including 75 professors.

Number of students: 3,000.

Publication: *Árbók Háskóla Islands.*

DEANS:

Faculty of Theology: Prof. BJÖRN BJÖRNSSON.

Faculty of Medicine: Prof. VÍKINGUR H. ARNÓRSSON.

Faculty of Law: Prof. GUNNAR G. SCHRAM.

Faculty of Economics: Prof. GYLFI TH. GÍSLASON.

Faculty of Philosophy: Prof. ALAN BOUCHER.
Faculty of Engineering and Science: Prof. RAGNAR INGIMARSSON.
Faculty of Dentistry: Prof. ÖRN BJARTMARS PÉTURSSON.
Faculty of Social Science: Prof. ANDRI ÍSAKSSON.

ATTACHED INSTITUTES:

Science Institute: Dunhaga 3, Reykjavík.
Institute of Experimental Pathology: Keldum, Mosfellssveit.

COLLEGES

Búnadarskólinn á Hólum i Hjaltadal (*Agricultural School*): Hólum i Hjaltadal; f. 1882.
Director: HAUKUR JØRUNDARSON.
The library contains 6,000 vols.
Number of teachers: 4 professors.
Number of students (men and women): 50.

Bændaskólinn á Hvanneyri (*Agricultural College*): Hvanneyri, pr. Borgarnes; f. 1889.
President: MINISTER OF AGRICULTURE.
Principal: MAGNUS B. JÓNSSON.
Number of teachers: 15.
Number of students: 80.
Number of books in library: 6,500.
Publications: *Skýrsla um tilraunir*†, *Skýrsla Baendaskólans á Hvanneyri.*

Reykjavik Tónlistarskólinn (*College of Music*): Skipholt 33, Reykjavík; f. 1930; teaching in piano, organ and orchestral music, singing, theory, composition, music history, including training for music teachers; Dir. JÓN NORDAL; 280 students.

Taekniskóli Íslands (*Technical College of Iceland*): Höfdabakka 9, Reykjavík; f. 1964; teaching staff of 22; 250 students; library of 5,000 vols.; Principal BJARNI KRISTJÁNSSON.

INDIA

Population 650,000,000

ACADEMIES

Academy of Zoology: Khandari Rd., Agra; f. 1954; 1,200 mems.; library of 80,000 vols., exchange service with other zoological institutions; international organization and forum for the advancement of zoology; Pres. Prof. B. C. MAHENDRA; Sec. Dr. D. P. S. BHATI; publs. *The Annals of Zoology*†.

Indian Academy of Sciences: P.O.B. 8005, Bangalore 560080; f. 1934; 450 Fellows, 46 Hon. Fellows; Pres. Dr. S. VARADARAJAN; publs. *Proceedings* (27 issues a year), *Pramana* (journal of physics, monthly), *Journal of Biosciences* (quarterly), *Journal of Astrophysics and Astronomy* (quarterly), *Bulletin of Materials Science* (quarterly).

Indian National Science Academy (formerly *National Institute of Sciences of India*): Bahadur Shah Zafar Marg, New Delhi 110002; f. 1935 to promote scientific knowledge, co-ordination between scientific bodies, and safeguard the interests of scientists in India; adhering organization of ICSU; 445 Fellows, 61 Foreign Fellows; library of 19,000 vols.; Pres. Dr. V. RAMALINGASWAMI; Secs. Dr. M. G. DEO, Dr. A. P. MITRA; publs. *Proceedings, Monographs, Bulletin, Progress of Science in India, Indian Journal of History of Sciences, Year Book, Indian Journal of Pure and Applied Mathematics, Biographical Memoirs.*

Jammu and Kashmir Academy of Art, Culture and Languages: Srinagar, Kashmir; f. 1958; to promote arts and languages of the State; library of 7,645 vols., 432 rare MSS.; Patron Governor Shri L. K. JHA; Pres. SHEIKH MOHAMMAD ABDULLAH; Sec. M. Y. TAING; publ. *Sheeraza*† (monthly in Urdu, every 2 months in Kashmiri, Dogri, Punjabi and Hindi, and in Ladakhi, Pahari and Gojri).

National Academy of Art (Lalit Kala Akademi): Rabindra Bhavan, New Delhi 110001; f. 1954; autonomous, government-financed; sponsors national and international exhibitions, such as the National Exhibition of Art (annual) and Triennale-India; arranges seminars, lectures, films, etc.; Chair. (vacant); Sec. R. L. BARTHOLOMEW; publs. art books, brochures and prints; *Lalit Kala* (annual ancient art journal), *Lalit Kala Contemporary* (2 a year).

National Academy of Letters (Sahitya Akademi): Rabindra Bhavan, 35 Ferozeshah Rd., New Delhi 110001; f. 1954 for the development of Indian literature, the co-ordination of literary activities in the Indian languages and research in Indian languages and literature; publication of literary works; promotion of cultural exchanges with other countries; Gen. Council consists of eminent persons in the field of letters, nominees of the Central and State Governments, representatives of the universities and one representative of each of the 22 languages of India recognized by the Academy; awards annual prizes in 22 Indian languages; library of 52,000 vols.; Pres. UMASHANKAR JOSHI; Sec. Dr. R. S. KELKAR; publs. *Indian Literature* (English, every 2 months), *Sanskrita Pratibha* (Sanskrit, annually), *Samakalin Bharatiya Sahitya* (Hindi, quarterly), books and translations into Indian languages.

National Academy of Sciences: 5 Lajpatrai Rd., Allahabad 211002, U.P.; f. 1930 for the cultivation and promotion of science in all its branches; 730 mems. including 169 fellows and 31 honorary fellows; Pres. Prof. A. C. CHATTERJI; Vice-Pres. Prof. N. R. DHAR, Prof. R. S. MISHRA; Secs. Prof. S. P. TANDON, Prof. V. PURI; Foreign Sec. Prof. P. L. SRIVASTRA; publs. *Proceedings* in two sections—*Section A: Physical Sciences, Section B: Biological Sciences* (quarterly).

Rajasthan Academy of Science: Birla College, Pilani 333031; f. 1951; Pres. Prof. V. L. NARAYANAN; Hon. Sec. Dr. H. L. KUNDU, PH.D.; Librarian P. K. RAMAN; publ. *Proceedings.*

Sangeet Natak Akademi (*National Academy of Music, Dance and Drama*): Rabindra Bhavan, Ferozeshah Rd., New Delhi 110001; f. 1953 for the development of dancing and drama and music; governed by a General Council; documents the performing arts through films, tapes and photographs; maintains a museum of musical instruments and a museum of costumes, masks and puppets; offers financial assistance to music, dance and drama institutions; maintains the Jawaharlal Nehru Manipuri Dance College, Imphal, and the Kathak Kendra Institute, Delhi; conducts festivals, seminars; gives awards and fellowships for outstanding work; Chair. KAMALADEVI CHATTOPADHYAYA (acting); Sec. Prof. MOHAN KHOKAR; publs. *Sangeet Natak* (quarterly), and a bi-monthly news bulletin.

LEARNED SOCIETIES

AGRICULTURE AND VETERINARY SCIENCE

Agr-Horticultural Society of India: Alipur Rd., Calcutta 700027; f. 1820; 1,200 mems.; library of 3,000 vols.; Pres. U. MUKHARJI; Sec. Dr. D. MUKHERJEE; publs. *Monthly Garden News Sheet, Horticultural Bulletin* (quarterly).

Agri-Horticultural Society of Madras: Cathedral P.O., Madras 600086; f. 1835; 3,211 mems.; Patron H.E. The GOVERNOR OF TAMIL NADU; Chair. R. SADASIVAM, B.A.M.L.; Hon. Sec. Prof. J. RAMCHANDRAN.

Indian Dairy Association: Idsa House, Sector 4, R. K. Puram, New Delhi 110022; 1,500 mems.; library of 2,800 vols.; Pres. P. H. BHATT; Sec.-Treas. F. C. PAHWA; publs. *Indian Journal of Dairy Science* (quarterly), *Indian Dairyman* (monthly).

Indian Society of Agricultural Economics: 46-48 Esplanade Mansions, Mahatma Gandhi Rd., Fort, Bombay 400023; f. 1939; 1,800 mems. and subscribers; library of 14,000 vols.; Pres. Prof. M. L. DANTWALA; Hon. Sec. Dr. J. N. BARMEDA; publ. *The Indian Journal of Agricultural Economics* (quarterly).

THE ARTS

General

The Crafts Council of Western India: 59 L. Jagmohandas Marg, Bombay 400006; f. 1972; asscn. of craftsmen, designers and artists formed to encourage the development of the handicrafts of India; 155 mems.; Chair. ROSHAN KALAPESI; Joint Secs. JANE VERMA, JAMINI AHLUWALIA; publ. *Crafts Bulletin*† (quarterly).

Indian Ceramic Society: Dept. of Ceramics, Banaras Hindu University, Varanasi 221005, U.P.; f. 1929; Sec. Prof. H. N. Roy; publ. *Transactions* (quarterly).

International Culture Centre: M-1, Kanjan Junga Bldg., Barakhamba Rd., New Delhi 110001; Akash Ganga, 89 Bhwabhai Desai Rd., Bombay 36; f. 1957; Chair. Shri Soli Godrej; Sec. Mrs. Madhuri Dayal; publs. *Folk Paintings of India, Balasaraswati and Tagore on Art and Aesthetics*, cultural profiles.

Fine Arts

All India Fine Arts and Crafts Society: Old Mill Rd., (Rafi Marg), New Delhi; f. 1928; holds art exhibitions including the All India Annual Art Exhibition, exhibitions of Indian art abroad and exhibitions of arts and crafts from foreign countries in India, talks and film shows on art; 510 mems.; library of 2,500 vols.; Pres. Dr. M. S. Randhawa; Sec. S. S. Bhagat; publs. *Roopa Lekha* (2 a year), *Arts News* (monthly).

Art Society of India: 524 Sandhurst House, Sandhurst Rd., Bombay 400004; f. 1918; 400 mems.; library of 2,000 vols.; Pres. Homi N. Dallas; Joint Hon. Secs. Jal K. J. Mehta, B. S. A. Nadkarni.

Bombay Art Society: Jehangir Art Gallery, Bombay 400023; f. 1888; Pres. V. B. Pathare; Hon. Sec. H. Raut; publ. *Art Journal*, illustrated catalogues of exhibitions.

Indian Society of Oriental Art (Calcutta): 17 Park St., Calcutta 700016; f. 1907; 350 mems.; to promote and research all aspects of ancient and contemporary Indian art; Hon. Sec. Miss Sarojini Hutheesing; publ. *Journal* (annual).

South India Society of Painters: No. 13, 111 Trust Cross, Madras 600028.

Bibliography, Library Science and Museology

Indian Association of Special Libraries and Information Centre (IASLIC): P.291, CIT Scheme No. 6M, Kankurgachi, Calcutta 700054; f. 1955 to promote study and research into Special Librarianship and Information Science; to hold conferences and co-ordinate activities among special libraries; publishes seminar and conference papers and books on information and library science; translation and reprographic service; Hon. Pres. Prof. B. K. Bachhawat; Hon. Gen. Sec. S. M. Ganguly; publs. *IASLIC Bulletin, Indian Library Science Abstracts, IASLIC Newsletter*, etc.

Indian Library Association: c/o Delhi Public Library, S.P. Mukerji Marg, Delhi 110006; f. 1933; 2,064 mems.; library of 5,000 vols.; Pres. B. L. Bharadwaja; Sec. O. P. Trikha; publ. *Bulletin* (quarterly).

Museums Association of India: National Museum of Natural History, Barakhamba Rd., New Delhi 110001; f. 1944; professional discussions, seminars, conferences, exhibitions, etc.; *c.* 500 individual and institutional mems.; Pres. Dr. N. R. Banerjee; Sec. P. G. Gupte; publs. *Journal of Indian Museums*†, *Museums Newsletter, Proceedings of All-India Museums Conferences* (annually), monographs.

National Book Trust, India: A-5, Green Park, New Delhi 110016; f. 1957; an autonomous body set up by the Government; activities include organization of Exhibitions and Book Fairs at home and abroad including a World Book Fair every 2 years, arranging Seminars and Workshops on problems connected with the writing, translation, publication and distribution of books; encourages the publishing of good books at moderate prices; publishes books in several series including *India—the Land and the People, National Biography, Nehru Library of Children's Literature, Young India Library, Folklore of India, Popular Science*, in English and various Indian languages; Chair. A. L. Dias; Dir. U. K. Mallya.

Economics, Law and Politics

Bar Association of India: Chamber 93, Supreme Court Bldg., New Delhi 110001; publ. *The Indian Advocate* (quarterly).

Indian Council of World Affairs: Sapru House, Barakhamba Rd., New Delhi 110001; f. 1943; non-governmental institution for the study of Indian and International questions; 1,506 mems.; library of 102,075 vols., 1,000 periodicals, 150,000 documents and all UN publs.; Pres. Sardar Swaran Singh; Sec.-Gen. (vacant); publs. *India Quarterly Foreign Affairs Reports* (monthly).

Indian Economic Association: Delhi School of Economics, Delhi 110009; f. 1918; Pres. Prof. V. M. Dandekar; Hon. Sec. Prof. K. A. Naqvi; publ. *Indian Economic Journal*.

Indian Law Institute: Opp. Supreme Court, New Delhi; f. 1956; purpose of the Institute is to promote advanced studies and research in law and reform of administration of law and justice; library of 40,000 vols.; Pres. Chief Justice of India; Dir. Dr. S. N. Jain; publs. *Journal of the Indian Law Institute* (quarterly), *Index to Indian Legal Periodicals* (half-yearly), *Annual Survey of Indian Law*, and research publications.

Institute of Chartered Accountants of India: Indraprastha Marg, New Delhi 110002; f. 1949; 20,000 mems.; library of 16,000 vols.; Pres. B. L. Kabra; Sec. P. S. Gopalakrishnan; publs. *The Chartered Accountant* (monthly), *CICA Newsletter* (monthly).

Education

Association of Indian Universities: Dyal Singh Library Bldg., Deendayal Upadhyaya Marg, New Delhi 110002; f. 1925; mems.: 99 universities; library of 6,938 vols., 95 periodicals; Chair. Dr. R. Mukherji; Sec. Dr. A. Singh; publs. *Universities Handbook* (every 2 years), University News (fortnightly).

Bal Bhavan Society: Kotla Rd., New Delhi 110001; f. 1958; a project of the Ministry of Education; comprises "Bal Bhavan and National Children's Museum"; provides planned environment and creative activities based on Arts and Science to children between the ages of 5 and 16; provides leadership and guidance to teachers towards fostering a creative approach in teaching of art and science, organizes orientation courses for teachers and parents, runs a repertory theatre for children; children's library of about 13,000 vols. and a reference library of 4,358 vols.; Chair. Mrs. R. D. Barakataki; Sec.-Gen. Km. Shanta Gandhi.

Hyderabad Educational Conference: 19 Bachelors' Quarters, Jawaharlal Nehru Rd., Hyderabad, Deccan; f. 1913; to promote academic research, assist needy students and further education in Andhra Pradesh; library of over 9,500 vols.; Pres. Ruknuddin Ahmed; Vice-Pres. Syed Ali Akbar; Sec. Burmanuddin Hussain; publs. (in Urdu) *Proceedings of Public Sessions, Educational Annual, Ruh-e-tarraqui*.

Indian Adult Education Association: 17B Indraprastha Marg, New Delhi 110002; f. 1939; recognized by national govt.; 800 mems.; library of 10,000 vols.; Pres. Dr. Malcolm S. Adiseshiah; Sec. V. S. Mathur; publs. *Indian Journal of Adult Education* (monthly), *Proudh Shiksha* (Hindi monthly), *IAEA Newsletter* (monthly).

J. N. Petit Institute: 312 Dr. Dadabhoy Naoroji Rd., Fort, Bombay 400001; f. 1856; organizes lectures and makes accessible literary, scientific and philosophic works;

4,300 mems.; library of 105,000 vols.; Pres. N. B. JEEJEEBHOY, M.A.; Hon. Sec. D. V. M. PATEL, LL.B.

University Grants Commission: Bahadur Shah Zafar Marg, New Delhi 110002; f. 1953 to promote and co-ordinate university education; to determine and maintain the standards of teaching, examination and research in universities; may allocate grants to universities and colleges for these purposes; library of 28,500 vols., receives 400 journals; Chair. Prof. SATISH CHANDRA; Sec. Shri R. K. CHHABRA; publs. *Annual Report, University Development in India* (annual statistical review), *Journal of Higher Education, Bulletin of Higher Education*, reports.

HISTORY, GEOGRAPHY AND ARCHAEOLOGY

Bharata Itihasa Samshodhaka Mandala: 1321 Sadashiva Peth, Poona, 411030; f. 1910 for collecting, conserving and publishing historical materials; collection of 5,200 coins; 28,000 Persian, Sanskrit and Marathi MSS.; 1,500,000 documents, about 1,200 old Indian paintings; 1,000 copperplates, sculptures and other antiquarian objects; 780 mems.; library of *c.* 20,000 vols.; Pres. THE RAJA SAHEB OF PHALTAN; Chair. Prof. G. H. KHARE; Sec. Dr. C. N. PARCHURE; publs. *Journal* (quarterly), *Sviya Granthamala Series* (109 issued), *Puraskrita Granthamala* (59 issued).

Geographical Society of India: c/o Dept. of Geography, Calcutta University, 35 Ballygunge Circular Rd., Calcutta 700019; f. 1933; 650 mems.; library of 13,363 vols., 5,617 journals; geographical lectures, seminars and exhibitions; encouragement of geographical research and training; Pres. Prof. K. G. BAGCHI; Sec. M. MAITY; Editor Dr. S. CHAKRABORTY; publ. *Geographical Review of India* (quarterly).

INTERNATIONAL CULTURAL INSTITUTES

Alliance Française de Delhi: D-6, New Delhi South Extension Part II, New Delhi 110049; f. 1956 to advance knowledge of French thought, culture and language and promote Indo-French cultural relations; provides lectures, teaching facilities, exchange-visit opportunities, social programmes, aid and support to educational institutions teaching French language and literature; brs. in Bangalore, Bombay, Calcutta, Karikal, Madras, Pondichery, Pune; 735 mems.; library of 15,510 vols.; Pres. S. BHOOTHALINGAM; Hon. Sec. RÉMY DURAND.

British Council: headquarters: 21 Jor Bagh, New Delhi 110003; Rep. J. M. URE, O.B.E.; regional offices: French Bank Bldg., Homji St., Bombay 400001, Reg. Rep. Dr. V. A. ATKINSON; 5 Shakespeare Sarani, Calcutta 700071, Reg. Rep. R. TWITE; 150A Anna Salai Madras 600002, Reg. Rep. Dr. R. E. WRIGHT; libraries: *see* Libraries.

Goethe-Institut: (*see* below, Max Mueller Bhavan).

India International Centre: 40 Lodi Estate, New Delhi 110003; f. 1958; international cultural organization for promotion of amity and understanding between the different communities in the world; programme of lectures, discussions, film evenings, etc.; mems.: 1,800 individuals, 109 corporate (including 30 univs.); library of 20,000 vols., also houses the India Collection of 3,500 rare documents on British India and the Himalayan Club Library of 900 vols.; Pres. Dr. C. D. DESHMUKH; Dir. U. S. BAJPAI; Sec. N. H. RAMACHANDRAN; publs. *IIC Quarterly*†.

Attached institute:

Council for Cultural Studies: f. 1961 as Research Council for Cultural Studies, present title 1971; to maintain contact and exchange information with similar organizations throughout the world; study courses, conferences, etc.; bibliographical projects and information service; research; Chair. Dr. C. D. DESHMUKH.

Indian Council for Cultural Relations: Azad Bhavan, Indraprastha Estate, New Delhi 110002; f. 1950 to establish and strengthen cultural relations between India and other countries; branch offices in Bombay, Calcutta, Madras, Bangalore and Varanasi; cultural centres in Suva (Fiji), Georgetown (Guyana) and Paramaribo (Surinam); activities include exchange visits between scholars, artists and men of eminence in the field of art and culture; exchange of exhibitions; international conferences and seminars, lectures by renowned scholars including Azad Memorial Lectures; establishment of chairs and centres of Indian studies abroad and welfare of overseas students in India; administration of Jawaharlal Nehru Award for International Understanding; presentation of books and Indian art objects to universities, libraries and museums in other countries; library of over 55,000 vols. on India and other countries; Pres. (vacant); Sec. J. N. DIXIT; publs. interpretations of Indian Art and Culture and translations of Indian works into foreign languages; periodicals: *Indian Horizons* (in English, quarterly), *Cultural News from India* (in English, quarterly), *Thaqafatul-Hind* (in Arabic, quarterly), *Papeles de la India* (in Spanish, quarterly), *Rencontre avec l'Inde* (in French, quarterly), *ICCR Newsletter* (English quarterly for foreign students), *Africa Quarterly, Gaganaanchal* (Hindi, quarterly).

Indian Institute of World Culture: P.O.B. 402, 6 Shri B.P. Wadia Rd., Basavangudi, Bangalore 560004; f. 1945; Bombay Office: Theosophy Hall, 40 New Marine Lines, Bombay 400020; London Office: 62 Queen's Gardens, W2 3AH; 970 mems.; library of 38,000 vols., 400 periodicals; objects: to provide opportunities for cultural and intellectual development, to promote exchange of thought between India and other countries and to raise the consideration of national and world problems to the plane of moral and spiritual values and to foster a sense of universal brotherhood; Pres. Mme. SOPHIA WADIA; Hon. Sec. ANAND R. KUNDAJI; publs. *Annual Reports, Transactions and Reprints*†, etc.

Iran League: Navsari Bldg., Dr. Dadabhoy Navroji Rd., Fort, Bombay 400001; f. 1922; 500 mems.; Pres. Sir JAMSETJEE JEJEEBHOY; Sec. D. C. LELINWALLA; publ. *Quarterly Newsletter*.

Iran Society: 12 Dr. M. Ishaque Rd., Calcutta 700016; f. 1944; promotes Iranian studies and Indo-Iranian cultural relations; 190 mems.; 6,897 vols.; Pres. Dr. A. K. BURKE, M.A., D.LITT.; Gen. Sec. M. A. MAJID, M.A.; publs. *Indo-Iranica* (quarterly) and many monographs and research works.

Max Mueller Bhavan (*Indo-German Cultural Centre*): 3 Kasturba Gandhi Marg, New Delhi; also at Bangalore, Bombay, Calcutta, Hyderabad, Madras, Poona, Rourkela; brs. of the Goethe-Institut; f. 1957; arranges German language classes and organizes cultural activities such as concerts, exhibitions, symposia; library in Delhi of 15,000 vols., also br. libraries; Dir. Delhi and Regional Rep. Dr. WALTER BREUER; publ. *Dialogue* (annual).

LANGUAGE AND LITERATURE

International Tamil League: c/o "Thenmozhi", Cuddalore 1, S.A.Dt., Tamil Nadu; f. 1968; research and development of Tamil language, literature and cultural history; 5,100 mems.; library of 8,300 vols.; Pres. G. DEVANEY APPAVANAR, M.A.; Gen. Sec. PERUNCHITHIRANAR; publ. *Thenmozhi* (bi-monthly).

Linguistic Society of India: c/o Deccan College, Poona 411006; f. 1928; holds annual conferences of Linguists;

691 mems.; library of 3,000 vols.; Pres. Dr. A. R. KELKAR; Sec. Dr. A. S. ACHARYA; publs. *Indian Linguistics*† (quarterly), *Bibliography of South Asian Linguistics* (annual), *Proceedings*, etc.

Madras Literary Society and Auxiliary of the Royal Asiatic Society: College Rd., Madras 600006; Pres. Hon. Justice S. SURYAMURTHY; Hon. Sec. S. V. B. Row.

Mythic Society: 2 Nripathunga Rd., Bangalore 560002; f. 1909; Pres. K. BALASUBRAMANYAM; Sec. J. RAJPUROHIT; publ. *Journal* (quarterly).

PEN All-India Centre: Theosophy Hall, 40 New Marine Lines, Bombay 400020; f. 1933; over 700 mems.; Founder-Organizer SOPHIA WADIA; Pres. MASTI VENKATESA IYENGAR; Sec.-Treas. S. M. Y. SASTRY; publs. *The Indian PEN* (6 a year), PEN series on Indian literatures, *PEN Conference Proceedings*.

Sanskrit Academy: Sanskrit College Buildings, Mylapore, Madras 600004.

Tamil Association: Kazanthai Tamil Sangam, Thanjavur 2, Tamil Nadu; f. 1911; conducts literary research and maintains schools for general education as well as a college for Tamil studies; 700 mems.; library of 10,300 vols.; Pres. Thiru S. BETHANNAN; Sec. Thiru V. SUBRAMANIAM, B.A.; publ. *Tamil Pozhil* (monthly).

Tamil Nadu Tamil Development and Research Council: Fort St. George, Madras 600009; f. 1959; development of Tamil in all its aspects, especially as a modern language; Chair. Chief Minister; Vice-Chair. Minister for Education; Sec. Director of Tamil Development; publ. *Tamil Nadu Tamil Bibliography*.

MEDICINE

Association of Surgeons of India: 18 Adams Rd., Chepauk. Madras 600005; f. 1939; 3,200 mems.; library of *c.* 10,000 vols.; Pres. Dr. M. S. RAMAKRISHNAN; Hon. Sec, Dr. M. NATARAJAN; publ. *Indian Journal of Surgery*† (monthly).

Bombay Medical Union: Blavatsky Lodge Bldg., Chowpatty, Bombay 400007; f. 1883; 237 mems.; Pres. Dr. U. N. BASTODKAR; Sec. Dr. Smt. M. K. THACKER.

Indian Cancer Society: Dr. E. Borges Marg, Parel, Bombay 400012, and Eucharistic Bldg., 5 Convent St., Bombay 400001; Charitable Trust subsisting on donations; objects: to support cancer research, to aid sufferers from cancer, to improve facilities for diagnosis, treatment and rehabilitation, to educate the public and the profession and to organize national conferences; Chair. N. H. TATA; Vice-Chair. P. A. NARIELWALA; Hon. Sec. Dr. D. J. JUSSAWALLA; publs. *Indian Journal of Cancer* (quarterly), *Newsletter*.

Indian Medical Association, The: I.M.A. House, Indraprastha Marg, New Delhi 110002; f. 1928; 45,000 mems.; Pres. Dr. R. K. MANDA; Hon. Gen. Sec. Dr. M. G. GARG; publs. *Journal* (fortnightly), *Your Health* (monthly), *I.M.A. News* (monthly); affiliated with the British Medical Association and the Nepal Medical Association; mem. of the World Medical Asscn.

Indian Pharmaceutical Association: Kalina, Santacruz East, Bombay 400098; 4,010 mems.; Pres. Dr. V. A. PADVAL; Hon. Gen. Sec. B. N. THAKORE; publs. *Indian Journal of Pharmaceutical Sciences*, *Pharma Times*.

Medical Council of India: P.O.B. 337, Temple Lane, Kotla Rd., New Delhi; 110002 f. 1934, reconstituted under the Indian Medical Council Acts 1956; maintenance of uniform standard of medical education, reciprocity in mutual recognition of medical qualifications with other countries, maintenance of Indian Medical Registrar; Pres. Hon. Brig. Dr. B. N. SINHA; Sec. Dr. U. B. KRISHNAN; publ. *Indian Medical Register*.

Pharmacy Council of India: 2nd Floor, Combined Councils, Building, Temple Lane, Kotla Rd., P.O.B. 7020, New Delhi 110002; f. 1949 to set and maintain educational standards for qualification and registration in pharmacy and to co-ordinate the practice thereof; Pres. Dr. P. C. DANDIYA; Asst. Sec. Sri DEVINDER K. JAIN.

NATURAL SCIENCES

General

Indian Science Congress Association: 14 Dr. B. Guha St., Calcutta 700017; f. 1914; 7,000 mems.; Pres. Prof. A. K. SHARMA; Gen. Secs. Dr. D. BASU, Prof. B. RAMACHANDRA RAO; publs. *Proceedings*† (annual, in 4 parts), *Progress of Science in India*, *Reviews* (occasional), *Everyman's Science*† (bi-monthly).

Bengal Natural History Society: Natural History Museum, Darjeeling, West Bengal; f. 1923; 100 mems.; library of 3,000 vols. and 50 periodicals; Chair. T. S. BROCA, I.A.S.; Sec. Shri N. PAL, I.F.S.; publ. *Journal of the Bengal Natural History Society* (2 a year).

Bombay Natural History Society: Hornbill House, Shahid Bhagat Singh Rd., Bombay 400023; f. 1883; 1,200 mems.; 9,000 vols.; Pres. Dr. SALIM ALI, D.SC., F.N.A.; Hon. Sec. Dr. A. N. D. NANAVATI, M.D.; publ. *Journal*.

Biological Sciences

Indian Biophysical Society: Saha Institute of Nuclear Physics, 92 Acharya Prafulla Chandra Rd., Calcutta 700009; f. 1965; *c.* 180 mems.; Pres. Prof. B. D. NAG CHAUDHURI; Gen. Sec. Prof. N. N. SAHA; publ. *Proceedings* (annually).

Indian Botanical Society: Dept. of Botany, Vikram University, Ujjain, M.P.; Pres. K. S. THIND; Sec. Prof. K. S. BHARGAVA; publ. *Journal*.

Indian Phytopathological Society: Indian Agricultural Research Institute, New Delhi 110012; f. 1947; 1,150 mems.; mycology and plant pathology; holds seminars, symposia, etc.; Pres. Dr. G. RANGASWAMI; Sec. Dr. M. S. CHATRATH; publ. *Indian Phytopathology* (quarterly).

Indian Society of Genetics and Plant Breeding: Indian Agricultural Research Institute, New Delhi 110012; f. 1941; plant breeding and genetical research; 950 mems.; Pres. Dr. DHARAMPAL SINGH; Sec. Dr. H. K. JAIN; publ. *Journal*.

Palynological Society of India: National Botanic Gdns., Lucknow; f. 1965; conducts symposia, seminars and annual lectures; 126 Indian, 79 foreign mems.; Pres. Prof. T. S. MAHABALE; Vice-Pres. Prof. P. N. MEHRA; Gen. Sec. Dr. P. K. K. NAIR; publ. *Journal of Palynology*.

Society of Biological Chemists, India: Indian Institute of Science, Bangalore 560012; f. 1930; 1,000 mems.; Pres. Dr. H. R. CAMA; publs. *Biochemical Reviews* (annual), *Proceedings* (annual), *News Letter* (quarterly).

Zoological Society of India: c/o Zoological Survey of India, 34 Chittaran Ave., Calcutta 700012; f. 1916; library of 37,100 vols., 875 periodicals.

Mathematics

Allahabad Mathematical Society: 5 C. Y. Chintamani Rd., Allahabad 211002; f. 1958; to further the cause of advanced study and research in various branches of mathematics, including theoretical physics; 160 mems.; library of 3,150 vols.; Pres. Prof. U. N. SINGH; Sec. Dr. S. R. SINHA; Librarian Dr. VIKRAMADITYA SINGH; publ. *Indian Journal of Mathematics*†.

Bharata Ganita Parisad (formerly Benares Mathematical Society): Dept. of Mathematics and Astronomy, University, Lucknow; f. 1950; 102 mems.; library of 2,000 vols.; Pres. Dr. D. N. MISRA; Sec. Dr. A. N.

MEHRA; publs. *Ganita*†, *Proceedings of the Benares Mathematical Society*.

Calcutta Mathematical Society: 92 Acharya Prafulla Chandra Rd., Calcutta 700009; f. 1908; special lectures, seminars and symposia in mathematical sciences; 600 mems.; 7,500 vols.; Pres. Prof. S. DUTTA MAJUMDER; Sec. Prof. M. DUTTA; publ. *Bulletin* (6 a year).

Indian Mathematical Society: Indian Institute of Technology, Kanpur 208016; f. 1907; 790 mems.; 2,500 vols.; Pres. Prof. U. N. SINGH; Sec. Prof. R. S. L. SRIVASTAVA; Editors Prof. K. G. RAMANATHAN and Prof. I. S. LUTHAR; publs. *Journal*†, *Mathematics Student*† (quarterly).

Physical Sciences

Astronomical Society of India: Dept. of Astronomy, Osmania University, Hyderabad 500007; f. 1973; 300 mems.; Pres. Prof. K. D. ABHYANKAR; Sec. Dr. N. B. SANWAL; publs. *Bulletin* (quarterly), *Memoirs* (occasional).

Electrochemical Society of India, The: Indian Institute of Science, Bangalore 560012; f. 1964 to promote the science and technology of electrochemistry, electrodeposition and plating, corrosion including high-temperature oxidation, electrometallurgy and metal finishing, semi-conductors and electronics, batteries, solid electrolytes, solid state electrochemistry, and protection of metals and materials against environmental attack; 140 mems.; library of 600 vols.; Pres. Dr. S. KRISHNAMURTHY; Sec. Dr. R. P. DAMBAL; publ. *Journal* (quarterly).

Indian Chemical Society: University Science College Bldgs., 92 Upper Circular Rd., Calcutta 700009; f. 1924; 1,584 mems.; library of 5,500 vols.; Pres. Dr. SUKHDEO; Hon. Sec. Prof. D. P. CHAKRABORTY; publ. *Journal* (monthly).

Optical Society of India, The: Applied Physics Dept., Calcutta Univ., 92 Acharya Prafulla Chandra Rd., Calcutta 700009; f. 1965 to promote and diffuse the knowledge of optics in all its branches, pure and applied; 237 mems.; Pres. Dr. D. SEN; Vice-Pres. Prof. A. K. GHATAK; publ. *Journal of Optics*† (quarterly).

RELIGION, SOCIOLOGY AND ANTHROPOLOGY

Anthropological Society of Bombay: 209 Dr. Dadabhai Naoroji Rd., Fort, Bombay 400001; f. 1886; Pres. Dr. J. F. BULSARA, M.A., LL.B., PH.D.; Hon. Sec. SAPUR F. DESAI, B.SC.

Asiatic Society of Bengal, The: 1 Park St., Calcutta 700016; f. 1784; 710 mems.; Pres. Dr. D. BOSE, M.A., F.A.S.; Gen. Sec. Dr. AMLENDDE; publs. *Journal*, *Year Book*, *Bibliotheca Indica*, *Monographs*, etc.

Asiatic Society of Bombay: Town Hall, Bombay 400023; f. 1804 as Bombay Literary Society; to investigate and encourage Sciences, Arts and Literature in relation to Asia and India in particular; to promote research and publish research works; in 1973 established Dr. P. V. Kane Research Institute for Oriental Studies; 1,512 mems.; maintains the Central Library for the State of Maharashtra (depository library); 206,515 vols. (478,384 in Central Library), 2,300 MSS., 5,000 old coins; Pres. SOLI J. SORABJEE; Hon. Sec. Mrs. BANSARI K. SHETH; publs. critical texts, journals, reports.

Indian Anthropological Association: Department of Anthropology, University of Delhi, Delhi 110007; f. 1964; *c.* 300 mems.; Pres. Prof. Dr. L. P. VIDYARTH; Sec.-Treas. Dr. P. K. DATTA; publs. *Indian Anthropologist* (2 a year), *News Bulletin* (annual), *Anthropologists in India* (every 2–3 years).

Theosophical Society, The: International Headquarters, Adyar, Madras 600020; f. in New York 1875; 35,000 mems. throughout the world; library of 150,000 vols. and 18,000 palm-leaf and paper MSS; aims: to form a nucleus of the Universal Brotherhood of Humanity without distinction of race, creed, sex, caste or colour, to encourage the study of comparative religion, philosophy and science, and to investigate unexplained laws of nature and the powers latent in man; Pres. JOHN B. S. COATS; Vice-Pres. SURENDRA NARAYAN; Sec. Dr. JEAN RAYMOND; publs. *The Theosophist* (monthly), *Adyar Library Bulletin*† (quarterly), *Adyar Newsletter* (quarterly).

TECHNOLOGY

Geological, Mining and Metallurgical Society of India: c/o Geology Dept., University College of Science and Technology, 35 B.C. Rd., Calcutta 700019; f. 1924; 865 fellows, 69 associates; Pres. Prof. S. SEN; Joint Secs. Dr. S. K. RAYCHAUDHURI, Dr. S. P. DAS GUPTA; publs. *Journal* (quarterly), *Bulletin*†.

Indian Association of Geohydrologists: c/o Geological Survey of India, 4 Chowringhee Lane, Calcutta 700016; f. 1964; 440 mems.; Pres. V. SUBRAMANYAM; Hon. Sec. A. K. ROY; publ. *Indian Geohydrology*.

Indian Institute of Metals: 2 Sambhunath Pandit St., Calcutta 700020; f. 1946; 4,000 mems.; Pres. E. G. RAMACHANDRAN; Hon. Sec. Dr. L. R. VAIDYANATH; publs. *Transactions* (every 2 months), *Metal News* (quarterly).

India Society of Engineers: 12-B Netaji Subhas Rd., Calcutta 1; f. 1934; library of 12,000 vols.; 6,000 mems.; Pres. S. SAMADDAR; Gen. Sec. P. K. CHAUDHURI; publ. *Science and Engineering*† (monthly in English).

Indian Standards Institution (ISI): 9 Bahadur Shah Zafar Marg, New Delhi 110002; f. 1947; library of 90,700 standards and technical publications and 600 periodicals; Dir.-Gen. Dr. A. K. GUPTA; Deputy Dir. (Library) Sh. VED P. VIJ; publs. *Current Published Information on Standardization, Additions to Library—Overseas Standards Part I, Additions to Library—Part II*.

Institution of Engineers (India): 8 Gokhale Rd., Calcutta 700020; f. 1920; incorp. by Royal Charter 1935; 103,300 mems.; 60 libraries; Pres. S. G. RAMACHANDRA; Sec. and Dir.-Gen. Col. B. T. NAGRANI; publs. *Journal*, *Bulletin*.

Mineralogical Society of India: Manasa Gangotri, Mysore 6; f. 1959; objects: to advance knowledge of crystallography, mineralogy, petrology, etc. by means of research and the holding of conferences, meetings and discussions; 400 mems.; library of 1,500 vols.; Pres. Dr. M. G. CHAKRAPANAI NAIDU; Sec. C. RAJAGOPLAN; publ. *The Indian Mineralogist*.

RESEARCH INSTITUTES

(*see* also under Universities)

COUNCIL OF SCIENTIFIC AND INDUSTRIAL RESEARCH

RAFI MARG, NEW DELHI

Founded 1942.

The national research laboratories described below have been established under the Council, which is itself responsible to the Department of Science and Technology, Ministry of Industrial Development (Government of India).

President: Smt. INDIRA GANDHI.

Vice-President: Prof. S. NURUL HASAN.

Director-General: Prof. M. G. K. MENON, F.R.S.

Chief Administrator: Shri K. C. SUNDRACHARI.

Publications: *Science Reporter and Technical Manpower Bulletin* (monthly).

Central Drug Research Institute: Chattar Manzil Palace, P.B. 173, Lucknow; f. 1951; biochemical, pharmacological, chemical, microbiological, endocrinological, biophysical and medical research; library of 20,000 vols.; Dir. Dr. NITYA NAND; publ. *Classified List of Current Scientific Literature* (monthly).

Central Electrochemical Research Institute: Karaikudi, Madras 623006; f. 1953; electrochemical and allied research; library of 25,600 vols.; Dir. Dr. H. V. K. UDUPA, M.A., M.SC., A.M., PH.D., A.R.I.C., F.I.C.

Central Electronics Engineering Research Institute: Pilani, Rajasthan; f. 1953; design and construction of electronic equipment, components and test equipment; Dir. Dr. AMARJIT SINGH, M.SC., M.ES., PH.D.; publ. *CEERI Newsletter* (quarterly).

Central Food Technological Research Institute: Cheluvamba Mansion, V. V. Mohalla P.O., Mysore 570013; f. 1950; library of 27,500 vols.; food processing; food conservation and preservation; nutritional, dietetic, technological and biochemical studies; microbiology, packaging, quality control and engineering aspects of food technology; information, statistics and extension services; Dir. C. P. NATARAJAN (acting); publs. *Ahara Vijnana* (Kannada (quarterly), *Khadya Vigyan* (Hindi quarterly), and others.

Central Glass and Ceramic Research Institute: Jadavpur, University P.O., Calcutta 700032; f. 1950; fundamental and applied research on glass, ceramics, vitreous enamels, refractories and mica; technical assistance to the industry, testing and standardization; library of 25,000 vols.; Dir. K. D. SHARMA; publ. *C.G.C.R.I. Bulletin.*

Central Institute of Medicinal and Aromatic Plants: Botanical Research Institute Compound, Lucknow; f. 1959; co-ordination of activities in the development of cultivation and utilization of medicinal and aromatic plants on organized basis; library of 2,688 vols.; Dir. Dr. A. HUSSAIN; publ. *Bulletin* (quarterly).

Central Leather Research Institute: Adyar, Madras 600020; f. 1953; all aspects of leather research; library of 16,050 vols.; Dir. Dr. N. RAMANATHAN (acting); publs. *Leather Science* (monthly), *Thol Vigyanam* (Tamil, quarterly), *Current Leather Literature* (monthly), *Leather Titles Service* (trimonthly), *Charma Vigyan* (Marathi, quarterly).

Central Mechanical Engineering Research Institute: Mahatma Gandhi Ave., Durgapur 9; f. 1958; materials, mechanisms and machines; heat engines and heat transfer; designs and production; library of 15,139 vols.; Dir. Dr. S. K. BASU.

Central Mining Research Station: Barwa Rd., Dhanbad, Bihar 826001; f. 1956; research on safety, health and efficiency in mining; library of 16,112 vols.; Dir. Dr. B. SINGH (acting).

Central Salt and Marine Chemicals Research Institute: Waghawadi Rd., Bhavnagar 364002; f. 1954; preparation of salt, potassium fertilizers, magnesium compounds, bromine and bromides, industrial trace metals; survey and cultivation of marine algae, water desalination by solar distillation, electrodialysis, ion-exchange and reverse osmosis techniques; library of 27,967 vols.; Dir. Dr. D. J. MEHTA; publs. *Salt Research and Industry* (2 a year), *Desalination News* (quarterly), *Annual Report.*

Central Scientific Instruments Organization: Sector 30, Chandigarh 20; f. 1959; 13,290 vols.; 240 periodicals; promotion and development of indigenous manufacture of scientific instruments for teaching, research, industry and essential services; Dir. Dr. HARSH VARDHAN; publ. *Instrument News* (quarterly).

Indian Institute of Experimental Medicine: 4 Raja S.C. Mullick Rd., Jadavpur, Calcutta 700032; f. 1956; solution of medical problems through fundamental and applied research in the basic biological sciences, with emphasis on projects bearing directly on the country's current biological and medical needs; library of 30,000 vols.; Dir. Prof. B. K. BACHHAWAT.

National Aeronautical Laboratory: P.B. 1779, Kodihalli, Bangalore 560017; f. 1959; scientific investigations of the problems of flight with a view to their practical application to the design, construction and operation of aircraft in India; library of 58,000 vols.; Dir. Dr. S. R. VALLURI; publs. *Newsletter* (monthly), *Annual Report.*

National Botanical Research Institute: Rana Pratap Marg, Lucknow 226001; f. 1953; undertakes research into economic botany and collection, introduction, propagation and improvement of ornamental and economic plants; 300 mems.; library of 28,600 vols.; Dir. Dr. T. N. KHOSHOO; publ. *Annual Report.*

National Chemical Laboratory of India: Pashan, Poona 8; f. 1950; physical, inorganic, organic synthesis, polymer chemistries; biochemistry; chemical engineering and process development; houses the National Collection of Industrial Micro-organisms; library of 75,000 vols.; Dir. Dr. L. K. DORAISWAMY; publs. *Annual Report, Agro-Chemicals and Pesticides* (monthly).

National Environmental Engineering Research Institute: Nagpur, Maharashtra; f. 1958; chemical, biological and microbiological research; instrumentation and field investigations; water, sewage, industrial waste, air pollution, industrial hygiene, rural sanitation; library of 20,000 vols.; Dir. Dr. B. B. SUNDARESAN; publs. *Indian Journal of Environmental Health, Technical Digest* (quarterly).

National Geophysical Research Institute: Hyderabad 7; f. 1961; basic and applied research into mineral exploration and investigation of the earth's interior through seismic, geomagnetic, electric, geochemical

(*C.S.I.R. contd.*)

and paleogeophysical studies; library of 20,000 vols.; Dir. Dr. S. BALAKRISHNAN (acting); publs. *Bulletin, Observatories Data* (quarterly), *Progress in Geophysics* (annually).

National Institute of Oceanography: Miramar, Panaji, Goa 403004; f. 1966; investigates physical, chemical, geological and biological oceanography, also functions as the National Oceanographic Data Centre; research on marine geophysics and instrumentation; maintenance of data pertaining to the Indian Ocean at Planning and Data Division; library of 7,000 vols.; Dir. Dr. S. Z. QASIM; publs. *Mahasagar* (quarterly), *Annual Report.*

National Metallurgical Laboratory: Jamshedpur 831007, Singhbhum District, Bihar; f. 1950; ore dressing, production, physical and chemical metallurgy; library of 35,000 vols.; Dir. Dr. V. A. ALTEKAR; publ. *NML Technical Journal.*

National Physical Laboratory of India: Hillside Rd., New Delhi 110012; f. 1950; fundamental and applied research in physics; maintenance of standards; testing; library of 80,000 vols.; Dir. Dr. A. R VERMA, M.SC., PH.D.; publ. *Technical Bulletin* (quarterly).

National Research Development Corporation of India: 20 Ring Rd., Lajpat Nagar III, New Delhi 110024; f. 1953 to develop inventions of government departments, commodity research committees, academic bodies or individuals; to enter into reciprocal agreements to exploit Indian inventions abroad and foreign inventions in India and to ensure production and sale of the produce of such inventions; to offer advice and assistance in respect of patents; library of 7,000 vols.; Chair. R. S. BHATT; publs. *Annual Report*, Preliminary Technical Notes, *Invention Intelligence* (monthly), *Awishkar* (monthly).

Publication and Information Directorate: Hillside Rd., New Delhi; f. 1951; collection and dissemination of scientific information; library of 20,100 vols.; Chief Editor Y. R. CHADHA; publs. *Wealth of India, Journal of Scientific and Industrial Research, Indian Journal of Chemistry, Indian Journal of Pure and Applied Physics, Indian Journal of Technology* (monthly), *Research and Industry, Indian Journal of Experimental Biology, Indian Journal of Biochemistry* (quarterly), *C.S.I.R. News* (fortnightly), Monographs, Symposia Proceedings, Annual Reports, etc.

Regional Research Laboratory: Bhubaneswar 4, Orissa; f. 1964; research in problems relating to the industry and raw materials of the region; Dir. Prof. P. K. JENA, M.SC., PH.D.

Regional Research Laboratory: Hyderabad 9; f. 1944; the first regional laboratory under the Council of Scientific and Industrial Research; research on utilization of regional raw materials and development of industries; physical, analytical, inorganic and organic chemistry; biochemistry; chemical engineering; coal; heavy chemicals and fertilizers; ceramics; essential oils; X-ray crystallography; entomology; library of 32,000 vols.; Dir. Dr. G. S. SIDHU; publs. *Annual Report, Industrial Development News, Seen in the Literature* (monthly).

Regional Research Laboratory: Canal Rd., Jammu-Tawi, Jammu & Kashmir; f. 1957; drug and medical plants; introduction of exotic plants, particularly from temperate zones; plant chemistry, extraction and processing of drugs; library of 18,317 vols.; Dir. Dr. C. K. ATAL; publ. *Newsletter* (6 a year).

Regional Research Laboratory: Jorhat, Assam; f. 1959; national laboratory, conducting research into such areas as coal, petroleum, pulp and paper, cement, drugs and pharmaceuticals, essential oil and medicinal plants, general and earthquake engineering; Dir. Dr. S. THYAGARAJAN.

Structural Engineering Research Centre: Roorkee, U.P.; f. 1965; research in specialized design and development work in structural problems connected with buildings, bridges and other structures; library of 6,998 vols.; Dir. Dr. M. RAMAIAH (acting); publ. *Journal* (quarterly).

AGRICULTURE AND VETERINARY SCIENCE

Agro-Economic Research Centre: Visva-Bharati University, Santiniketan, West Bengal; f. 1954; conducts research in agricultural economics; library of 5,300 vols.; Dir. S. C. SENGUPTA.

Central Arid Zone Research Institute: Jodhpur; f. 1959; eight divisions: Basic Resources Studies, Plant Studies, Wind Power and Solar Energy Utilization Studies, Economics and Extension, Animal Studies, Soil-Water-Plant Relationship Studies, Human Factor Studies, Extension and Training, Agricultural Economics; two national centres: Co-ordinating and Monitoring Centre for Rodent Research and Training, National Research Centre for Alternative Energy Sources; centre for seven All-India Co-ordinated Research Projects: rodent control, dryland farming, millet improvement, DPAP economic research, DPAP pasture development, arid zone horticulture, soil salinity research; library of 12,500 vols.; Dir. Dr. H. S. MANN; publ. *Annals of Arid Zone* (quarterly).

Central Inland Fisheries Research Institute: P.O. Barrackpore 743101, West Bengal; f. 1947; research into freshwater and brackish water aquaculture, estuarine, riverine and lacustrine capture fisheries, brackish water fin and shellfish culture, frog farming, weed control, and water pollution studies; economic and statistical evaluation of inland fisheries practices, fish farm engineering and fisheries extension; Dir. Dr. A. V. NATARAJAN.

Central Rice Research Institute: Cuttack, Orissa 753006; f. 1946; research on basic and applied aspects of all disciplines of rice culture; 300 mems.; library of 10,000 vols., 5,000 periodicals; Dir. Dr. H. K. PANDE; publs. *Annual Report*†, *Oryza*† (2 a year).

Central Tobacco Research Institute: Rajahmundry, Andhra Pradesh, S.C. Rly.; f. 1947; 490 staff; library of 8,600 vols., 292 periodicals; under the Indian Council of Agric. Research (Ministry of Food and Agriculture, Govt. of India); applied and fundamental research on all types of tobacco grown in India; regional stations at Guntur, Vedasandur, Pusa, Hunsur and Dinhata; Dir. Dr. N. C. GOPALACHARI; publs. *Research Reports* (annual), Leaflets (irregular), Documentation lists (irregular).

Forest Research Institute and Colleges: P.O. New Forest, Dehra Dun; f. 1906; library of 94,000 vols., 600 periodicals; Pres. Shri. J. C. VARMAH; Dirs. M. P. DAS (Forestry Education), R. C. GHOSH (Forestry Research), S. KEDARNATH (Biological Research), S. R. D. GUHA (Forest Products), V. B. SAHARIA (Wildlife Research Education); publs. *Indian Forest Records, Bulletins, Annual Report, F.R.I. Quarterly News Letter*, etc.

Indian Council of Agricultural Research: Krishi Bhavan, Dr. Rajendra Prasad Rd., New Delhi; f. 1929 to promote agricultural and animal husbandry research in conjunction with State Governments, Central and State Research Institutions, etc.; reconstituted 1966 to develop and administer a national programme of agricultural and food research; Pres. JAGJIVAN RAM; Dir.-Gen. Dr. M. S. SWAMINATHAN, F.R.S.; Sec. K. P. SINGH.

Indian Veterinary Research Institute: P.O. Izatnagar 243122 (U.P.); f. 1889 to undertake research, teaching and extension activities in all aspects of veterinary science and animal husbandry; 1,180 mems.; libraries at Izatnagar and Mukteswar provide 26,300 vols. and 766 periodicals; Dir. Dr. C. M. SINGH, M.S., PH.D.; publs. *Annual Report*, annual scientific reports, bibliographies, catalogues, etc.

Marine Biological Association of India: Cochin, Kerala (South India); f. 1958; Pres. Dr. E. G. SILAS; Vice-Pres. Dr. R. R. PRASAD, Dr. R. NATARAJAN; publs. *Journal of the Marine Biological Association of India* (twice a year), *Memoirs of the Marine Biological Association of India* (irregular), Proceedings of symposia (irregular).

National Dairy Research Institute: Karnal, Haryana; f. 1923; training and research; Regional Stations at Bangalore, Bombay and Kalyani; library of over 40,000 vols. and 650 periodicals; Dir. Dr. D. SUNDARESAN, PH.D.; publs. *N.D.R.I. News* (quarterly), *Reports* (annually), occasional publications.

National Sugar Institute: Kalimpur, Kanpur 208001, U.P.; f. 1923; library of 5,783 vols.; Dir. Dr. N. A. RAMAIAH; publ. *Sharkara*.

Rubber Board and Rubber Research Institute of India, The: Kottayam 686001, Kerala State; f. 1955 to promote the development of the industry; scientific, technological and economic research in improved methods of planting, cultivation, processing and consumption of natural rubber; 25 mems.; library of 15,000 vols.; Chair. S. G. SUNDARAM; Sec. V. B. PILLAY; Commr. for Production P. M. MENON; Dir. of Research V. K. B. NAIR; publs. *Rubber Board Bulletin*†, *Rubber, Indian Rubber Statistics*†, *Rubber Growers' Companion*, *Rubber Statistical News*.

THE ARTS

National Institute of Design: Paldi, Ahmedabad 380007; f. 1961; established by the Government of India as a research, training and service organization in industrial design, visual communication and environmental design; Diploma in Design after 5½ years' training, in Textile Design after 3½ years; short-term courses of in-service training in various disciplines; library of 18,860 vols., 105 current periodicals, 40,000 slides, 1,750 tapes and records, 1,200 other audio-visual aids and 600 well-designed objects for reference; Exec. Dir. ASHOKE CHATTERJEE.

BIBLIOGRAPHY AND LIBRARY SCIENCE

Documentation Research and Training Centre (*Indian Statistical Institute*): 31 Church St., Bangalore 560001; f. 1962; conducts research in the fields of library science, documentation and information science; trains documentalists, provides an advisory service to industry, academic and research institutions; library of 6,000 vols.; Head Prof. G. BHATTACHARYYA; publs. *D.R.T.C. Annual Seminar, D.R.T.C. Refresher Seminar, Library science with a slant to documentation* (quarterly).

ECONOMICS, LAW AND POLITICS

Gokhale Institute of Politics and Economics: Poona 411004; f. 1930; study and research concerning economic problems, training of research workers; 81 teaching and research staff; library of 183,645 vols., 850 periodicals; Joint Dirs. Prof. V. M. DANDEKAR, Prof. N. RATH; Registrar D. P. APTE; publs. *Artha Vijnana*† (quarterly), etc.

Indian Institute of Public Administration, The: Indraprastha Estate, Ring Rd. East, New Delhi 110002; f. 1954 to promote the study of public administration; research, training, consultancy; library; Dir. T. N. CHATURVEDI; publs. on Indian administration, *The Indian Journal of Public Administration* (quarterly).

Institute for Defence Studies and Analyses, The: Sapru House Annexe, Barakhamba Rd., New Delhi 110001; f. 1965; research on National Security, undertakes study on methods of warfare, strategy, disarmament and international relations; 1,564 mems.; library of 18,883 vols.; publs. *Journal* (quarterly), *Strategic Digest* (monthly), *Strategic Analysis* (monthly), *News Reviews* (monthly).

Madras Institute of Development Studies: 79 Second Main Rd., Gandhinagar, Adyar, Madras 600020; f. 1970; aims to contribute to the economic and social development of Tamil Nadu State and India; undertakes studies and research in micro-development problems; aims at upgrading economic research in the South Indian universities through research methodology courses and studies; recognized by Univ. of Madras for Ph.D. courses; library of 15,000 vols.; Chair. Dr. M. S. ADISESHIAH; Dir. Dr. C. T. KURIEN; publs. *Bulletin* (monthly), *Madras Development Seminar Series*.

National Council of Applied Economic Research: Parisila Bhavan, 11 Indraprastha Estate, New Delhi 110002; f. 1956; 48,000 vols.; 800 periodicals; independent research organization to study economic problems for government, international organizations and private business; Dir.-Gen. P. L. TANDON; Registrar S. R. CHAWLA; publ. *Margin* (quarterly).

National Productivity Council: 5-6 Institutional Area, Lodi Rd., New Delhi 110003; f. 1958 by the Government of India to help increase productivity in every sector of the national economy; nine regional directorates (Kanpur, Chandigarh, Calcutta, Madras, Bangalore, Gauhati, Bombay, Ahmedabad, Delhi); library of 12,000 vols.; Exec. Dir. G. R. DALVI; publs. *Productivity* (quarterly), *Productivity News* (monthly), *Utapadakata* (Hindi, monthly).

EDUCATION

Indian Institute of Advanced Study: Rashtrapati Nivas, Simla 171005; f. 1965 to undertake post-doctoral research, especially in the humanities and social sciences; library of 70,000 vols. and 900 periodicals; Dir. Prof. B. B. LAL; publs. *Bulletin*†, *Transactions*†, monographs†.

Indian Psychometric and Educational Research Association: Dept. of Education, Patna Training College Compound, Patna 800004; f. 1969 to promote and develop the study of, and undertake research into, psychology, education, statistics, etc.; 300 mems.; library of 3,050 vols.; Pres. Dr. A. K. P. SINHA; Vice-Pres. Dr. S. K. MITRA, Dr. V. S. MISHRA; Sec. Dr. R. P. SINGH; publ. *Indian Journal of Psychometry and Education*.

National Council of Educational Research and Training: Sri Aurobindo Marg, New Delhi 110016; f. 1961 with the aim of improving school education; academic adviser to the Ministry of Education and Social Welfare; co-ordinates research in all branches of education; organizes pre- and in-service training; six constituent units: National Institute of Education (research and training, publishing), Centre for Educational Technology, and 4 regional Colleges of Education in Ajmer, Bhopal, Bhubaneswar and Mysore; Pres. The Union Minister of Education; Dir. Prof. SHIB K. MITRA; publs. *Indian Educational Review* (2 a year), *NIE Journal* (2 a month), *School Science* (quarterly), *NCERT Newsletter* (monthly), *Primary Teacher* (quarterly).

National Institute of Basic Education: 41A, 43 and 55 Friends Colony, New Delhi 110014; f. 1956; carries out research, training of high-level personnel, production of literature and organization of programmes, etc.; functions as a clearing-house for information on basic education in India and provides guidance on research; Dir. J. K. SHUKLA; publs. *Basic Education Abstracts* (bi-annual), *Buniyadi Talim* (bi-lingual quarterly) and occasional pamphlets, research monographs, etc.

HISTORY, GEOGRAPHY AND ARCHAEOLOGY

Archaeological Survey of India: Government of India, New Delhi 110011; f. 1902; library of 80,000 vols.; Dir.-Gen. B. K. THAPAR; publs. articles on Indian history, archaeology and epigraphy, *Indian Archaeology* (annually), *Ajanta Murals.*

Bihar Research Society: Museum Bldgs., Patna 800001, Bihar; f. 1915; 180 mems.; library of 30,000 vols.; Pres. Dr. J. C. JHA; Sec. M. S. PANDEY; publ. *Journal.*

Indian Council of Historical Research: 35 Ferozeshah Rd., New Delhi 110001; gives grants for doctoral theses, research projects, historical journals, and for bibliographical and documentation works; Dir. B. R. GROVER; publ. *The Indian Historical Review* (2 a year).

K. P. Jayaswal Research Institute: Patna 800001; f. 1904 to promote historical research; library of 30,000 vols.; Dir. Dr. JATA SHANKAR JHA.

Kamarupa Anusandhan Samiti (*Assam Research Society*): Gauhati, Assam; f. 1912: historical and archaeological research; 200 mems.; Pres. BISWANARAYAN SHASTRI, M.A.; Joint Secs. Dr. DHARMESWAR CHUTIA, Dr. R. D. CHOUDHURY; publ. *Journal of Assam Research Society*† (annually).

Karnatak Historical Research Society: Diwan Bahadur Rodda Rd., Dharwad 1, Karnatak State; f. 1914; to promote historical research in the Karnatak; to popularize the study of history and culture by lectures, slides, exhibitions, celebrations of historical events, excursions, etc.; sections for research in language, culture and Vedic literature, socio-economic problems; 150 mems.; library of 3,000 vols.; Pres. Sri NITTOOR SRINIVAS RAO; Chair. VIDYARATNA R. S. PANCHAMUKHI; Secs. U. B. BIDI and Dr. P. R. PANCHAMUKHI; publs. *Karnatak Historical Review* (twice yearly in English and Kannada), and research publications.

National Atlas Organisation: 50A Gariahat Rd., Calcutta 700019; f. 1956; engaged in cartographical research and preparation of maps; library of 15,000 vols., 70,000 maps, 250 atlases; Dir. Dr. S. P. DAS GUPTA; publs. *National Atlas of India* (English and Hindi editions), *Irrigation Atlas of India* (in English), *Tourist Atlas of India* (in English), *Atlas of Forest Resources* (in English).

Survey of India: Map Record and Issue Office, Hathibarkala, Dehra Dun, U.P.; engaged in topographical, geographical and geodetic preparation of large scale development project maps.

LANGUAGE AND LITERATURE

Abul Kalam Azad Oriental Research Institute: Public Gardens, Hyderabad 500004, A.P.; f. 1959; research in history, philosophy, culture and languages, compilation of Urdu encyclopaedia; library of 15,000 vols.; Pres. Dr. N. M. AKBAR ALI KHAN; Chair. M. A. ABBASI; Hon. Gen. Sec. and Dir. KHWAJA MUHAMMAD AHMAD; publs. various.

All-India Oriental Conference: Bhandarkar Oriental Research Institute, Poona 411004; f. 1919; 1,200 mems.; mem. International Union for Oriental and Asian Studies; academic sessions every two years; Pres. Prof. K. A. SUBRAMANIA IYER; Sec. Prof. R. N. DANDEKAR; publs. Proceedings of Sessions, *Index of Papers* (in 3 vols.).

Anjuman-i-Islam Urdu Research Institute: 92 Dr. Dadabhoy Nawroji Rd., Bombay 400001; f. 1947; postgraduate teaching and research in Urdu language and literature, guidance to Ph.D. scholars and organization of lectures and symposia in Urdu; library of 20,000 vols.; Dir. Dr. N. S. GOREKAR; publs. *Nawa-e-Adab* (2 a year) and research books (in Urdu).

Bhandarkar Oriental Research Institute: Poona 411004; f. 1917; Sec. Dr. R. N. DANDEKAR, M.A., PH.D.; Dir. Dr. T. G. MAINKAR, M.A., PH.D., D.LITT.; 625 mems.; library of 42,000 vols., 20,000 MSS.; publ. *Annals* (annually).

K. R. Cama Oriental Institute and Library: 136 Bombay Samachar Marg, Fort, Bombay 400023; f. 1916; 150 mems.; 20,000 vols., 1,500 MSS., 4,150 journals; Pres. ADI N. CHINOY; Secs. N. D. MINOCHEHR-HOMJI, M.A., K. M. JAMASPASA, M.A., PH.D., H. E. EDULJEE, PH.D.; Librarian Miss H. B. TARAPOREVALA, B.A.; publ. *Journal* (annually).

Deccan College Postgraduate and Research Institute: Yeravda, Poona 411006; f. 1939; postgraduate research in linguistics, archaeology, history and sociology, anthropology; library of 11,000 vols.; Dirs. Dr. S. B. DEO, Dr. R. V. JOSHI; Curator of Archaeological Museum Dr. Z. D. ANSARI; Curator of Maratha History Museum M. R. KANTAK; Registrar R. S. BHAVE; Librarian V. B. BELSARE; publ. *Quarterly Bulletin.*

Ganganatha Jha Kendriya Sanskrit Vidyapeetha: Allahabad 211002, U.P.; f. 1943; research into Sanskrit and other Indological subjects; library of 30,000 vols., 25,000 MSS.; Principal Dr. G. C. TRIPATHI; publs. Quarterly Research Journal†, catalogues, bibliographies, Sanskrit texts and studies.

Gujarat Research Society: Samshodhan Sadan, Ramkrishna Mission Marg, Khar, Bombay 400052; f. 1936 to organize and co-ordinate research in social and cultural activities; teacher-training; library of 8,600 vols.; Pres. Dr. M. R. SHAH; publ. *Journal* (quarterly).

International Academy of Indian Culture: J 22 Hauz Khas Enclave, New Delhi 110016; f. 1935 to study India's artistic, literary and historic relations with other Asian countries; library of 25,000 vols., 40,000 MSS.; Hon. Dir. Dr. LOKESH CHANDRA; Hon. Sec. Dr. SHARADA RANI; publ. *Satapitaka Series* (irregular).

Kuppuswami Sastri Research Institute, The: Sanskrit College, Madras 600004; f. 1944; promotion of Oriental learning; 300 mems.; library of 20,000 vols. (including palm-leaf manuscripts); Pres. T. Y. VISWANATHANAIYAR; Sec. and Dir. Dr. V. RAGHAVAN; publs. *Journal of Oriental Research* and numerous research publs.

Mumbai Marathi Granth Sangrahalaya: Dadar, Bombay 400014; f. 1898; research in Marathi language and literature; library of 185,020 vols.; Pres. S. K. PATIL.

Nava Nalanda Pali Mahavihara (*Nalanda Institute of Buddhist Studies and Pali*): P.O. Nalanda, Bihar 803111; f. 1951; studies and research in Pali, ancient Indian and Asian studies; library of 32,000 vols.; Dir. Dr. C. S. UPASAK.

Oriental Institute: Lokmanya Tilak Rd., Baroda; f. 1915; library of 39,382 vols. on Indology and Sanskrit, MSS. library of 26,222 MSS.; 19 mems.; publication office of the famous *Gaekwad's Oriental Series*, of which 168 have been published; General Editor and Dir. Prof. Dr. A. N. JANI; Deputy Dir. J. P. THAKER; publs. *M.S. Lecture Series, M.S. University Oriental Series, Critical and Illustrated Edition of Valmiki Ramayana, Svadhtyaya* (Gujarati, quarterly), *Journal of the Oriental Institute* (quarterly).

Oriental Institute of Indian Languages: 32 Khorsheed Bldgs., P. M. Rd., Bombay 400001; founded to promote inter-regional and inter-continental understanding through the study of languages; Secs. A. RAHIM, A. A. ABEDI.

Oriental Research Institute: Mysore; library of 25,000 vols.; collection of 60,000 ancient MSS.; Dir. G. MARULASIDDAIAH, M.A., PH.D.

Sri Venkateswara University Oriental Research Institute: Tirupati, Andhra Pradesh 517502; f. 1939; given by T. T. DEVASTHANAMS to the University in 1956; research in language and literature, philosophy and religion, art and archaeology, history and social sciences; publs. *Institute Journal*, and other treatises.

Vishveshvaranand Vedic Research Institute: Sadhu Ashram P.O., Hoshiarpur 146021; f. 1903; 3,384 mems.; academic and cultural studies on Indian literatures and religion; Pres. DIWAN ANAND KUMAR; Dir. VEDA PRAKASHA; publs. *Vishva Jyoti* (cultural, Hindi monthly), *Vishva Samskritam* (cultural research, Sanskrit quarterly), *Vishveshvaranand Indological Series*, etc.

Vishveshvaranand Vishva Bandhu Institute of Sanskrit and Indological Studies: Hoshiarpur; f. 1965; postgraduate teaching, research and study in Indology; library of 71,328 vols., 10,000 ancient MSS.; Dir. S. BHASKARAN NAIR (acting); publs. *Vishveshvaranand Indological Journal* (research, English, 2 a year), *Panjab University Indological Series.*

MEDICINE

All-India Institute of Hygiene and Public Health: 110 Chittaranjan Ave., Calcutta 700073; f. 1932; specialist training in health sciences; research in community health, applied health sciences and administration; library of 42,000 vols.; Dir. Dr. N. S. DEODHAR.

B.M. Institute of Mental Health: Ashram Rd., Navrangpura, Ahmedabad 380009; f. 1951; comprehensive mental health services, teaching, and research; psychiatric clinic for the emotionally disturbed; clinic for children with learning difficulties; occupational therapy and rehabilitation services; speech and audiology clinic; experimental elementary school for normal children; postgraduate training in psychotherapy, psychiatric social work, psychiatric occupational therapy, speech and audiology, medical and social psychology; applied research; 130 mems.; library of 5,724 vols.; Dir. Mrs. KAMALINI SARABHAI.

Cancer Research Institute: Parel, Bombay 400012; Research Dir. Dr. M. G. DEO, M.D., PH.D., FAMS, F.N.A.

Central Jalma Institute for Leprosy: Taj Ganj, Agra 1, U.P.; f. 1966; part of Indian Council of Medical Research; treatment, research and training; 33 staff; Dir. Dr. K. V. DESIKAN.

Central Leprosy Teaching and Research Institute: P.O.B. 1, Chingleput, Tamil Nadu 603001; f. 1967; library of 3,000 vols.; Dir. Dr. H. SRINIVASAN; publ. *Annual Report.*

Central Public Health Research Institute: Alipur Rd., New Delhi 110006; Asst. Dir. D. D. PURI.

Central Research Institute: Kasauli, Himachal Pradesh; f. 1905; medical research, graduate and postgraduate training, manufacture of biological products; Institute of the Govt. of India; library of 20,000 vols.; Dir. Dr. S. N. SAXENA; publ. *Annual Scientific Report.*

Haffkine Institute: Parel, Bombay 400012; f. 1896; principal centre of research in medical and allied sciences in India; library of 8,000 vols.; Depts.: Bacteriology, Biochemistry, Chemotherapy, Clinical Pathology, Immunohaematology, Immunology, Pharmacology, Radiation Biology Unit, Toxicology and Human Pharmacology, Virology, and Zoonosis, each with its staff of scientists; Dir. Dr. K. D. SHARMA; publs. *Annual Report*†, *Bulletin of the Haffkine Institute*†.

Helminthological Society of India: Dept. of Parasitology, U.P. College of Veterinary Science and Animal Husbandry, Mathura; Pres. Prof. S. N. SINGH; Treas.-Sec. Prof. B. P. PANDE; publ. *Indian Journal of Helminthology* (bi-annual).

Indian Association of Parasitologists: 110 Chittaranjan Ave., Calcutta 700012; Pres. Dr. H. N. RAY; Sec. Dr. A. B. CHAUDHURY.

Indian Brain Research Association: Dept. of Biochemistry (Calcutta University), 35 Ballygunge Circular Rd., Calcutta 700019; f. 1964; 210 mems.; library of 1,000 vols.; Pres. Dr. B. MUKERJI; Ed. Sec. Prof. J. J. GHOSH; Exec. Sec. Dr. A. K. BHATTACHARYYA; publ. *Brain News*† (2 a year).

Indian Council of Medical Research: Medical Enclave, Ansari Nagar, P.B. 4508, New Delhi 110016; f. 1911; assists in financing medical research; maintains the National Institute of Nutrition (Hyderabad), Virus Research Centre (Poona), Tuberculosis Chemotherapy Centre (Madras), Cholera Research Centre (Calcutta), Indian Registry of Pathology (New Delhi), National Institute of Occupational Health (Ahmedabad), Blood Group Reference Centre (Bombay), Institute for Research in Reproduction (Bombay), Entero Virus Research Unit (Bombay), Laboratory Animals Information Service (Bombay), I.C.M.R. Research Unit, Pasteur Institute (Coonor), Toxoplasma Research Centre (New Delhi); library of 5,000 vols.; Pres. RAJ NARAIN; Dir.-Gen. Dr. C. GOPALAN, M.D., PH.D., D.SC., F.R.C.P.(E.); publs. *Indian Journal of Medical Research, ICMR Bulletin*, Annual Reports of the Council, Special Reports.

Institute of Child Health: 11 Dr. Biresh Guha St., Calcutta 700017; f. 1953; affiliated to College for Child Health, Calcutta University; Dir. Dr. SISIR KUMAR BOSE; departments of Clinical Paediatrics, Paediatric Surgery, Biochemistry, Radiology, Pathology, Preventive Paediatrics, Physiotherapy, Psychiatry, Dermatology, Ophthalmology and Oto-rhino-laryngology.

Institute of History of Medicine & Medical Research: Tughlaqabad, P. O. Madangir, New Delhi 110062; f. 1962 to promote medical education and research and the study of medical history and to make full scientific appraisal of the principles and practices of medicine; library of 55,000 vols.; Pres. HAKIM ABDUL HAMEED; publs. *Studies in History of Medicine* (quarterly), etc.

King Institute of Preventive Medicine: Guindy, Madras 600032; f. 1899; library of 20,137 vols.; Dir. Dr. K. V. MURTHY, M.D.; publ. *Annual Report.*

National Institute of Communicable Diseases: 22 Sham Nath Marg, Delhi 110054; f. 1963; formerly Malaria Institute of India, f. 1927; Research and Training Centre in field of communicable and vector-borne diseases; brs. at Calicut (Kerala), Rajamundry (Andhra Pradesh) and Varanasi (Uttar Pradesh) (all for research and training on filariasis); Southern Indian br. at Coonoor (Tamil Nadu); field practice unit at Alwar (Rajasthan), epidemiological unit at Varanasi; Kala-azar unit at Patna (Bihar), plague surveillance unit at Bangalore (Karnataka); Dir. Dr. SHARAD KUMAR; publs. *Annual Report*, health bulletins.

National Malaria Eradication Programme: 22 Shamnath Marg, Delhi 110054; co-ordination, technical guidance and planning of a nation-wide eradication programme; f. 1958; Dir. Dr. S. PATTANAYAK.

National Institute of Nutrition: Indian Council of Medical Research, Jamia-Osmania, Hyderabad 500007, Andhra Pradesh; f. 1918; principal research and training centre for South and South-East Asia; includes centres for Food and Drug Toxicology Research and Laboratory Animal Information Services; 125 mems.; library of 20,000 vols.; Dir. Dr. P. J. TULPULE, M.SC., PH.D. (acting); publs. *Annual Report, Nutrition* (quarterly), *Diet Atlas of India, Nutrition Atlas of India, Nutritive Value of Indian Foods*, etc.

National Tuberculosis Institute: Govt. of India, "Avalon", 8 Bellary Rd., Bangalore 560003; f. 1959; 240 mems.; research in epidemiology, applied tuberculosis bacteriology, sociological aspects and systems research with regard to tuberculosis control; training and control programme; Dir. D. R. NAGPAUL, M.B.B.S., T.D.D.

Pasteur Institute and Medical Research Institute: Shillong, Assam; f. 1915; library of 7,311 vols.; Dir. Dr. N. G. BANERJEE.

Pasteur Institute of India: Coonoor 643103 (Nilgiris); f. 1907; 12,500 vols.; work on virus diseases incl. rabies, influenza, adenoviruses, pox group of viruses and general bacteriology; Dir. Dr. V. R. KALYANARAM; publ. *Annual Report.*

Vallabhbhai Patel Chest Institute: Delhi; post-graduate teaching and research in tuberculosis, pulmonary diseases and related basic sciences.

NATURAL SCIENCES

General

Bose Institute: 93/1 Acharya Prafulla Chandra Rd., Calcutta 700009; f. 1917; research in biology, cytogenetics, mutation, physiological genetics, antibiotics, biochemistry, chemistry of plant products, physical chemistry, radiation and nuclear physics, solid state physics; experimental stations at Falta and Shamnagar; library of 5,510 vols.; Dir. Dr. S. C. BHATTACHARYA; publs. *Transactions, Annual Reports.*

Indian Association for the Cultivation of Science (I.A.C.S): Jadavpur, Calcutta 700032; f. 1876; research in theoretical physics, optics and spectroscopy, gen-physics and X-ray, magnetism, polymers, organic, inorganic, physical and macromolecular chemistry; 1,250 mems.; library of 36,300 vols.; Pres. Dr. B. K. BACHHAWAT; publs. *Indian Journal of Physics*†, *Bulletin of the I.A.C.S.* and special publications.

Raman Research Institute: Bangalore 560006; f. 1948; liquid crystals, cosmic physics, theoretical physics, electronics; 130 mems.; library of 10,396 vols. and 14,250 periodicals; Dir. Prof. V. RADHAKRISHNAN.

Tata Institute of Fundamental Research: Homi Bhabha Rd., Bombay 400005; f. 1945; fundamental research in pure and applied mathematics, theoretical physics, (particle physics, nuclear physics, solid state theory, astrophysics), chemical physics, hydrology, cosmic rays and high-energy physics, computer science and technology, molecular biology, virology, radioastronomy, solid state electronics, microwave engineering; national government research centre; Dir. Prof. B. V. SREEKANTAN.

Biological Sciences

Birbal Sahni Institute of Palaeobotany: 53 University Rd., Lucknow 226007; f. 1946; research on fossil plants in its purely scientific aspects and its application to problems of economic geology; coal and petroleum prospecting; library of *c.* 3,500 vols., 7,000 journals, 25,000 reprints and 225 microfilms, etc.; Dir. Dr. K. R. SURANGE; publs. *Sir Albert C. Seward Memorial Lectures, Birbal Sahni Memorial Lectures, Silver Jubilee Commemoration Lectures, The Palaeobotanist.*

Botanical Survey of India: P.O. Botanic Garden, Howrah 711103; f. 1890; botanical surveys and research; Headquarters: Central National Herbarium and Indian Botanic Garden at Howrah; Industrial Section, Indian Museum at Calcutta; regional circles at Allahabad, Poona, Coimbatore, Jodhpur, Port Blair, Shillong, Dehra Dun and Itanagar; library of 75,000 vols.; 240 scientific staff; Dir. Dr. S. K. JAIN; publs. *Bulletin*† (quarterly), *Records and Reports*† (annually), *Indian Floras*, etc.

Indian Association of Biological Sciences: Life Science Centre, Calcutta University, Calcutta 700019; Pres. Prof. B. M. JOHRI; Sec. Prof. A. B. DAS.

Indian Association of Systematic Zoologists: c/o Zoological Survey of India, 34 Chittaranjan Ave., Calcutta 700012; f. 1947; Pres. Dr. A. P. KAPUR.

Institute of Plant Industry: Indore, Madhya Pradesh; f. 1924; research in cotton genetics, and in crop improvement of cotton and rotation crops; Dir. RAI BAHADUR R. L. SETHI, I.A.S., M.SC., B.SC.

International Society for Tropical Ecology: *see* under International.

Tropical Botanic Garden and Research Institute: Navaranga Rd., Trivandrum 695 011; f. 1979 to promote and establish modern scientific research and development studies relating to plants of importance to India, and Kerala in particular; to establish a botanical garden, an arboretum and laboratories for botanical, horticultural and chemical research; Dir. Prof. A. ABRAHAM.

Zoological Survey of India: 34 Chittaranjan Ave., Calcutta 700012; f. 1916; activities include maintenance of National Zoological Collections of India, conduct of faunistic surveys and research on systematic zoology; regional stations at Dehra Dun, Jabalpur, Jodhpur, Madras, Patna, Poona, Shillong, Solan, Port Blair, Hyderabad, Kakdwip; library of about 46,000 vols., 866 periodicals; Dir. Dr. T. N. ANANTHAKRISHAN; publs. *Records* (quarterly), *Memoirs, Annual Reports, Fauna of India*, and a series of monographs.

Mathematics

Indian Statistical Institute: 203 Barrackpore Trunk Rd., Calcutta, 700035; f. 1931 to promote knowledge of and research on statistics and other subjects relating to national development and social welfare and to provide for, and undertake, the collection of information, investigations, projects and operational research for planning and the improvement of the efficiency of management and production; maintains research units, laboratories, and a Research and Training School that conducts courses leading to the Bachelor's, Master's and doctorate degrees; also courses in applied statistics, computer science and statistical quality control; specialized library of over 206,000 vols. and 2,202 current periodicals; Chair. Sri P. N. HAKSAR; Dir. Dr. B. P. ADHIKARI; publ. *Sankyā: The Indian Journal of Statistics, Technical Reports, Memoranda.*

Institute of Mathematical Sciences (Matscience): Adyar, Madras 600020; f. 1962; research in pure and applied mathematics, theoretical physics, and astrophysics; library of 16,662 vols. and periodicals; Dir. Prof. A. RAMAKRISHNAN; Librarian K. S. SANTHANAGOPALAN; publs. *Matscience Reports*†, *Seminar in Analysis*†, etc.

Physical Sciences

Alipore Observatory and Meteorological Office: Calcutta; f. 1877; publ. *The India Meteorological Department.*

Astronomical Observatory: Presidency College, Calcutta; f. 1898; Dir. Dr. P. CHOUDHURY.

Astronomical Observatory of St. Xavier's College: 30 Park St., Calcutta 700016; f. 1875; Dir. Rev. F. GOREUX, S.J.

Bhabha Atomic Research Centre (B.A.R.C.): Trombay, Bombay 400 085, Maharashtra; f. 1957; national centre for research in and development of nuclear energy for peaceful purposes; Facilities include: one 40 MW research reactor, CIRUS; one MW research reactor, APSARA; a zero energy reactor, ZERLINA; an experimental zero energy fast reactor, PURNIMA; Thorium Plant; Fuel Fabrication Plant; Plutonium Plant; 5 MeV Van de Graaff accelerator; Isotope Production Unit; central workshops; pilot plants for production of heavy water, zirconium, titanium, etc.; Uranium metal plant; Food Irradiation and Processing Laboratory;

3,317 scientific and 5,405 technical staff; 108,000 vols., 1,430 technical journals, 500,000 technical reports; Dir. (vacant); publ. *Nuclear India* (monthly).

Central Seismological Observatory: Shillong; headquarters at New Delhi.

Geodetic and Research Branch, Survey of India: P.O.B. 77, Dehra Dun 248001; f. 1800; geodetic and allied geophysical activities, including development and research of instrumentation; library of 55,000 vols.; Dir. Dr. M. G. Arur; publs. reports and technical publications.

Geological Survey of India: 27 Jawaharlal Nehru Rd. Calcutta 13; f. 1851; devoted to study of geology geophysics, engineering geology, mineral resources, exploration and research; library of 412,060 vols.; Dir.-Gen. V. S. Krishnaswamy; publs. *Records, Memoirs, Bulletins, Indian Minerals, Palaeontologia Indica, Miscellaneous Publications, Geological Survey of India News.*

India Meteorological Department: Lodi Rd., New Delhi 110003; f. 1875; five regional offices at New Delhi, Bombay, Calcutta, Madras and Nagpur; 11 State meteorological centres at Trivandrum, Bangalore, Hyderabad, Bhubaneshwar, Gauhati, Lucknow, Jaipur, Srinagar, Ahmedabad, Patna, and Bhopal; scientific activities cover research in all branches of meteorology, including agricultural and hydrometeorology, radio-meteorology and satellite meteorology, atmospheric electricity, seismology; New Delhi is Regional Telecommunication Hub and Regional Meteorological Centre under WMO World Weather Watch; Dir.-Gen. Dr. P. K. Das; publs. *Indian Astronomical Ephemeris* (annually), *Air Almanac* (2 a year), *Aerological Data of India* (monthly), *Mausam* (quarterly), *Indian Weather Review, Regional/State Daily Weather Reports, Memoirs, Monographs, Reviews* (occasional).

Indian Bureau of Mines: New Secretariat Bldg., Nagpur 440001; f. 1948; Government dept. responsible for the conservation and development of mineral resources; aid in mine and mineral development, technical consultancy in mining and mineral processing, collection and dissemination of mineral statistics and information, research on beneficiation of low grade ores and special mining problems; regional offices at Ajmer, Bangalore, Calcutta, Hyderabad, Hazaribagh, Dehradun, Goa, Jabalpur, Nagpur, Nellore, Udaipur; library of 50,000 vols.; Controller D. N. Bhargava; Controllers of Mines D. M. Sen, S. C. Singhal, S. Balagopal; publs. *Indian Minerals Yearbook*†, *Mineral Statistics of India*† (2 a year), *Quick Release to the Mineral Statistics of India*† (monthly), *Bulletin of Mineral Statistics and Information*† (every 2 months), *Foreign Trade in Minerals and Metals*† (annual), *Mineral Stocks*† (quarterly), *Mineral Industry at a Glance*† (annually), *Bulletin on Consumption of Non-ferrous Metals in India*† (quarterly), minerals, bulletins covering specific aspects of mining.

Indian Institute of Astrophytics: Bangalore 560034; f. 1792; specializes in the study of solar physics, stellar physics and radio-astronomy; library of 23,000 vols.; 136 staff; field stations at Kavalur, Kodaikanal and Gauri Bidanur; Dir. Dr. M. K. Vainu Bappu, a.m., m.sc., ph.d., f.r.a.s., f.a.s.c., f.n.a.; publs. *Bulletins, Annual Reports, Reprints.*

Indian Institute of Geomagnetism: Colaba, Bombay 400005; observatories in Alibag, Annamalainagar, Trivandrum, Jaipur, Ujjain, Gulmarg, Shillong; geomagnetism, solar terrestrial physics and geomagnetic induction; Dir. B. N. Bhargava.

Indian Institute of Radio Physics and Electronics: Calcutta; engaged in research in the field of radio physics and electronics.

Indian Space Research Organization (ISRO): F Block, Cauvery Bhavan, District Office Rd., Bangalore 560009; f. 1969; development of rockets, launchers and satellites; operates Thumba Equatorial Rocket Launching Station (TERLS); includes Vikram Sarabhai Space Centre, Space Applications Centre, ISRO Satellite Centre, SHAR Centre; library of 5,000 vols.; Chair. Prof. S. Dhawan; Assistant Scientific Sec. Y. S. Rajan.

Mineral Information Bureau: Delhi; aid in prospecting and exploitation of minerals.

Mining, Geological and Metallurgical Institute of India: 29 Jawaharlal Nehru Rd., Calcutta 700016; f. 1906; 1,500 mems.; library of *c.* 350,000 vols.; Pres. G. S. Marwaha; Hon. Sec. J. P. Goenka; publs. *Transactions* (2 a year), *Newsletter* (2 a month).

Nizamiah and Japal-Rangapur Observatories and Centre of Advanced Study in Astronomy: Osmania University, Hyderabad 500007; f. 1908, transferred to control of Osmania Univ. 1919; library of 19,830 vols., 2,390 periodicals; Dir. Prof. K. D. Abhyankar, m.sc., ph.d., f.r.a.s., f.a.sc.; publ. *Astronomical.*

Physical Research Laboratory: Ahmedabad 380009; f. 1947; 600 mems.; library of 16,800 vols.; centre for space research and postgraduate studies leading to Ph.D. degree; research into atomic physics, radio astronomy, aeronomy, nuclear physics, plasma theory and experiment, archaeology, hydrology, infra-red astronomy geocosmophysics, climate research; Dir. Prof. Devendra Lal, m.sc., ph.d., f.a.sc.

Saha Institute of Nuclear Physics: 92 A. P. Chandra Rd., Calcutta 700009; f. 1951; mems.: 136 research, 138 technical, 47 admin., 82 auxiliary/maintenance; library of 26,117 books and journals and 16,683 reports; research and teaching in nuclear and allied sciences; Dir. Prof. D. N. Kundu.

Philosophy and Psychology

Indian Institute of Philosophy: Amalner, Dt. Jalgaon, Maharashtra (E. Khandesh); f. 1916; comparative study of Indian and European philosophy; 12 mems.; library of 6,000 vols.; 6 fellowships awarded yearly for research.

Yoga Institute, The: Santa Cruz, Bombay 400055; f. 1918 to promote self-education, physical, mental, moral and psychic, aided by the science of Yoga; to conduct academic and scientific research in Yoga culture and technique; conducts teacher training Institute of Yoga and a Clinical and Psychosomatic Hospital based on Yoga; Pres. Yogendraji; publs. *Yoga Studies, Yoga: Journal of the Yoga Institute* (monthly), and other literature.

Religion, Sociology and Anthropology

Anthropological Survey of India: c/o The Indian Museum, 27 J. Nehru Rd., Calcutta 700013; f. 1945; field work and research; library of 29,783 vols.; Dir. Dr. D. P. Mukherjee; publs. *Bulletin, Memoir, Anthropology in India*, etc.

Ethnographic and Folk Culture Society: P.O.B. 209, C-861 Sector C, Mahanagar, Lucknow 226006; f. 1945; research in anthropological and ethnological sciences; museum of Folk Life and Culture; library; 354 mems.; Pres. B. D. Sanwal; Hon. Gen. Sec. Dr. B. R. K. Shukla, m.a., ph.d.; publs. *The Eastern Anthropologist*† (quarterly), *Manav*† (Hindi, quarterly), *Indian Journal of Physical Anthropology and Human Genetics* (2 a year), Monographs, Folk Culture Series, Rural Profiles, Human Genetics, Man and Society, etc.

Indian Council of Social Science Research: IIPA Hostel, Indraprastha Estate, Ring Rd., New Delhi 110002; regional centres in Bombay, Calcutta, Hyderabad, Chandigarh, Delhi and Shillong; f. 1969; sponsors research in social science, provides technical assistance for research programmes, awards fellowships and grants; conferences and publications; Documentation Centre; Data Archives; library of 13,000 vols., 50,000 periodicals; Chair. G. PARTHASARATHI; Sec. Prof. T. N. MADAN; publs. *Newsletter*† (quarterly), *ICSSR Research Abstracts* (quarterly), *Indian Dissertation Abstracts*†, *Indian Psychological Abstracts*†, *ICSSR Journal of Abstracts and Reviews*† (*Economics, Geography, Sociology and Social Anthropology*).

Indian Institute for Population Studies: Gandhinagar, Madras 600020; Dir. Dr. S. CHANDRASEKHAR; publ. *Population Review* (2 a year).

National Labour Institute: AB-6, Safdarjang Enclave, New Delhi 110016; f. 1964 as Indian Inst. of Labour Studies; research, training and consultancy; library of 16,000 vols.; Dir. Dr. PRAYAG MEHTA; publs. *Bulletin*†, *Awards Digest*† (monthly).

Institute of Applied Manpower Research: Indraprastha Estate, Ring Rd., New Delhi 110002; f. 1962; government-sponsored; it aims to promote the establishment of a skilled labour force which will be effectively deployed in the economic interests of the country; organizes short courses in manpower planning; library of 15,000 vols. and journals; Pres. Prof. D. T. LAKDAWALA; Dir. Prof. MALATHI BOLAR; publs. *Manpower Journal*†, *Manpower Documentation*† (quarterly).

Institute of Economic Growth, Research Centre on Social and Economic Development in Asia: University Enclave, Delhi 110007; f. 1967 to bring the resources of social science to bear on the solution of problems connected with social and economic development of South and South East Asia; specialized library and documentation service; Dir. of Institute Prof. C. H. HANUMANTHA RAO; Head of Centre Dr. T. N. MADAN; publs. *Asian Social Science Bibliography*, *Contributions to Indian Sociology: New Series* (annually), *Studies in Asian Social Development* (occasionally).

Islamic Research Association: Anjuman-i-Islam, D. N. Rd., Bombay; f. 1933; Pres. Prof. S. S. DESNAVI; publs. 12 vols. of research work on *Islamic Studies*.

Sikkim Research Institute of Tibetology: Gangtok, Sikkim; f. 1958; research centre for study of Mahayana (Northern Buddhism); library of Tibetan literature (canonical of all sects and secular) in MSS. and xylographs; museum of icons and art objects; Dir. Prof. NIRMAL C. SINHA; publs. in Tibetan, Sanskrit and English, including *Bulletin of Tibetology* (3 a year).

A. N. Sinha Institute of Social Studies: Patna 800001, Bihar; f. 1964 to undertake teaching and research in the Social Sciences, especially economics, sociology and social psychology; library of 22,578 vols.; Dir. Dr. SACHCHIDANAND; Sec. Shri B. PRASAD; publs. *Social Studies* (annually), reports on study projects.

Sri Aurobindo Centre: Adhchini, Junction of Sri Aurobindo Marg and Qutab Hotel Rd., New Delhi 110017; multidisciplinary research and training in the integral study of Man; research in comparative religions, Indian cultural values; undergraduate and postgraduate courses and orientation courses for foreign students; lectures, seminars, study groups, summer programmes; library; Chair. Dr. KARAN SINGH; Hon. Sec. S. K. SANYAL.

TECHNOLOGY

Birla Research Institute for Applied Sciences: Birlagram, Nagda (M.P.); f. 1965; registered society to help national industrial growth; Pres. D. P. MANDELIA; publ. *Annual Report*.

Central Water and Power Research Station: P.O. Khadakwasla Research Station, Poona 411024; f. 1916; 41 divisions: Flood Control, Bridge Engineering, Central Cell for Stable Channels, Rivers and Canals, High Head Structure, Gates and Valves, Calibration, Cavitation, Hydraulic Analysis and Prototype Testing, Ports and Harbours, Maritime Structures, Tidal Hydraulics, Coastal Engineering, Ship Hydrodynamics, Rating Tank, Instrumentation, Photoelasticity, Model Engineering, Soil and Concrete, Rock Mechanics, Computer, Mathematics, Chemistry, Statistics, Earthquake Engineering Research, Geophysics, Physics, Watershed Studies; 244 engineers and 114 scientists with supporting staff; library of 59,000 vols.; Dir. P. C. SAXENA; publs. *Annual Research Memoirs*†, Technical Memoranda†.

Cotton Technological Research Laboratory (I.C.A.R.): Adenwala Rd., Matunga, Bombay 400019; f. 1924; library of 7,300 vols.; Dir. Dr. V. SUNDARAM, M.SC., PH.D., A.R.I.C., F.T.I.; publs. *Technological Reports*, *C.T.R.L. Publications*, *Handbook of Methods of Tests for Cotton Fibres, Yarns and Fabrics* (revised), *Annual Reports*, *Fifty Years of Research*.

Directorate of Public Instruction: West Bengal; maintains the following Research Institutes:

Bengal Ceramic Institute: Calcutta 10; f. 1941.
Bengal Tanning Institute: Calcutta; f. 1919.
Bengal Textile Institute: Serampore; f. 1904.
Berhampore Textile Institute: Berhampore; f. 1925.

Indian Lac Research Institute: Namkum, Ranchi 834010, Bihar; f. 1924; Chemistry, Entomology, Agronomy, Technology and Extension Divisions: 290 mems. including Dir. and 67 research workers; about 24,000 vols.; Dir. Dr. T. P. S. TEOTIA; publs. *Research Bulletins*, *Technical Notes*, *Research Notes*, *Annual Reports*, books, etc.

Institute of Hydraulics and Hydrology: Poondi 602023, (Via) Trivellore, Chingleput District, Tamil Nadu; f. 1945; library of 8,000 vols. and 5,870 journals; Dir. T. S. SIVARAMAN; publ. *Annual Report*.

Irrigation and Power Research Station: Amritsar; conducts research in fields of irrigation and hydraulic engineering; Dir. Shri J. NATH.

Research Designs and Standards Organization: Ministry of Railways, Government of India, Manak Nagar, Lucknow-226011; f. 1957; conducts tests and trials of new railway stock and other assets and research into economic and effective maintenance of operating practices; library of 65,000 vols.; Dir.-Gen. R. M. SAMBAMOORTHI; publs. *Annual Report*, *Documentation Notes*, *Indian Railway Technical Bulletin*, Research Reports, Technical Papers, etc.

Telecommunications Research Centre: c/o Indian Posts and Telegraphs Dept., New Delhi 110050; f. 1956; library of 30,300 vols.; Dir. Shri H. J. MIRCHANDANI.

LIBRARIES AND ARCHIVES

Acharya Narendra Dev Pustakalaya: Moti Mahal, Lucknow; f. 1959; public library, with special emphasis on social sciences; 60,251 vols.; Librarian B. N. SINGH.

Adyar Library and Research Centre: The Theosophical Society, Adyar, Madras 600020; f. 1886; library and research facilities for the study of Indology; 17,300 MSS., 150,000 vols.; Librarian Dr. PRAN NATH; publ. *Brahmavidya* (annually).

Allahabad Public Library: Allahabad; f. 1864; 65,500 vols.; Librarian (vacant).

American Center Libraries (U.S. International Communication Agency): 24 Kasturba Gandhi Marg, New Delhi; also at 4 New Marine Lines, Bombay, 7 Jawaharlal Nehru Rd., Calcutta, Gemini Circle, Madras; American University Center, 1 Bidhan Sarani, Calcutta; collections include current books, pamphlets, periodicals, microforms and VTRs.

Bangalore State Central Library: Cubbon Park, Bangalore 1, Karnataka; f. 1914; 140,000 vols.; State Librarian and Head of Public Libraries Sri N. D. BAGERI.

British Council Libraries: *North India:* Aifacs Bldg., Rafi Marg, New Delhi 110001; f. 1956; 72,865 vols., 229 periodicals; Asst. Rep. (Libraries) I. W. KEMP, M.B.E., F.L.A.; *South India:* 150A Anna Salai, Madras 600002; f. 1949; 94,407 vols., 238 periodicals; Librarian (vacant); *East India:* 5 Shakespeare Sarani, Calcutta 700016; f. 1950; 111,408 vols., 188 periodicals; Librarian Miss R. MAJUMDAR, M.A., A.L.A.; *West and Central India:* 178 Backbay Reclamation, Bombay 400020; f. 1963; 101,500 vols., 255 periodicals; Librarian D. K. DEVNALLY.

Central Hindi Directorate Library: West Block No. 7, Ramakrishna Puram, New Delhi 110022; f. 1960; 65,000 vols.; development and propagation of Hindi, especially in non-Hindi speaking areas; publs. *Hindi-English Dictionary*, *English-Hindi consolidated Glossary*, 21 English-Hindi Glossaries, *Bhasha* (quarterly).

Central Library: Baroda, Gujarat; f. 1910; 180,000 vols.; State Librarian P. P. PAWAN.

Central Secretariat Library: G Block, Shastri Bhavan, New Delhi; f. 1890; 11 divisions: Acquisition and Processing, Reference and Circulation, Education, Rare Books, Indian Official Documents, Foreign Official Documents, Serials, Bibliography, Documentation, Book Preservation, Gift Exchange; 430,000 vols.; 80 staff; Dir. Mrs. S. NARASIMHAN (acting).

Connemara (State Central) Public Library: Egmore, Madras 600008; f. 1896; deposit library from 1954 for all Indian publications; also for publications of UN and UNESCO; 320,000 vols.; Librarian A. M. SUNDARARAJAN, M.A., B.LIB.SC.

Delhi Public Library: S. P. Mukerjee Marg, Delhi 110006; f. 1951 in association with UNESCO; established as a model for public library development in south-east Asia; central library has an adult lending and reference department, a children's department, a social education department and an extension services department serving 55 areas through mobile vans and 12 deposit stations; 3 hospital libraries, one prison library, and a Braille dept.; 4 brs. and 20 sub-brs.; 627,349 vols. in Hindi, English, Urdu, Punjabi, Sindhi, Bengali and Braille; Dir. J. C. MEHTA.

Gowthami Library: Rajahmundry 533104, Andhra Pradesh; f. 1898; management transferred to Andhra Pradesh Government, 1979; research library of 40,000 vols., 405 palm leaf MSS.; Dir. P. N. DEVA DAS, M.A., D.L.SC.

Gujarat Vidyapith Granthalaya: Ahmedabad 380014; f. 1920; University, State, Central and Public Library combined; depository collection; documentation services; 273,821 vols.; Librarian K. L. SHAH, M.A., B.LIB.SC.

Indian Council of World Affairs Library: Sapru House, Barakhamba Rd., New Delhi 110001; f. 1950; research collections on social sciences with special reference to international relations, international law and international economics; 102,075 vols., 1,000 periodicals, 125,000 documents; Press library; departments of maps, microfilms, documents and United Nations; Librarian NARINDER DATTA (acting); publ. *Documentation on Asia* (annual).

Indian Institute of Technology Central Library: Madras 600 036; f. 1959; includes collection of German scientific books; partial archive of scientific films; S.D.I. service; 166,062 vols. and periodicals, 325 films, 1,343 microfilms and microfiches; Librarian V. S. NAZIR AHMED; publs. *Technical Communications*†, *Library Information Bulletin*†, *Library Documentation Notes*.

Indian National Scientific Documentation Centre (INSDOC): Hillside Rd., Delhi 110012; f. 1952; national depository for scientific reports and periodicals; 72,700 vols., 4,000 current periodicals; supplies information to scientists and engineers on request; compiles bibliographies; supplies photocopies or translations of articles, etc.; trainee department; makes national scientific work known and available throughout the world; National Catalogue of Scientific Serials being compiled; Dir. S. PARTHASARATHY; 211 scientific staff; publs. *Annals of Library Science and Documentation* (quarterly), *Indian Science Abstracts* (monthly), *Russian Scientific and Technical Publications—An Accession List* (every 2 months), *Contents List of Soviet Scientific Periodicals* (monthly); Regional Centre at Indian Institute of Science, Bangalore 560012.

Jamsetjee Nesserwanjee Petit Institute Library: 312, Dr. Dadabhoy Naoroji Rd., Fort, Bombay 400001; f. 1856; as "Fort Improvement Library"; moved 1898 to own building; 105,000 vols.; Deputy Librarian A. J. KHAMBATTA.

Karvir Nagar Wachan Mandir Library: Kohlapur, Madras State; f. 1850; 37,000 vols.; children's library.

Khuda Bakhsh Oriental Public Library: Patna 800004, Bihar; f. 1891; contains over 14,000 MSS. and 65,000 vols. including rare MSS. in Arabic, Urdu and Persian, many illuminated; 20,000 periodicals; Dir. ABID RAZA BEDAR.

Madras Literary Society Library: Madras 600006; f. 1812, 104,940 vols.; Man. P. N. BALASUNDARAM; Hon. Sec. S. V. B. ROW.

National Archives of India: Janpath, New Delhi; f. 1891; valuable collections of public records, maps and private papers covering 25 km. of shelf space; 200,000 vols.; Dir. Dr. S. A. I. TIRMIZI; Librarian J. C. SRIVASTAVA. M.A.; publs. *Indian Archives* (2 a year), *Annual Report*.

National Library: Belvedere, Calcutta 700027; f. 1902 by the amalgamation of the Calcutta Public Library and the Imperial Library; depository and research library; 1,700,000 vols., 72,075 maps, 3,001 MSS. (approx.); 1,500 microfilms; Dir. Prof. R. K. DAS GUPTA, M.A., PH.D., D.PHIL.; publs. *India's National Library, General Collection Author and Subject Catalogues*, *Annual Reports*, etc.

Nehru Memorial Museum and Library: Teen Murti House, New Delhi 110011; research collections on modern Indian history with emphasis on Indian nationalism; f. 1964; 75,549 vols.; large collection of newspapers, microfilms, private papers, institutional records, photographs and oral history recordings; Dir. RAVINDER KUMAR.

Punjab University Extension Library: Civil Lines, Ludhiana, Punjab; f. 1960; serves educational institutions within a radius of 60 km.; 95,000 vols.; Librarian S. S. LAL; publs. *Indian News Index, Indian Biographical Literature.*

Secretariat Library: Patna 800015; f. 1910; 44,000 vols.; Librarian P. N. DOSHI.

Sheth Maheklal Jethabhai Pustakalaya (*Free Public Library*): Ellis Bridge, Ahmedabad, Gujarat State; f. 1933; 25,012 mems.; 178,317 vols.; UNESCO programmes for Children's Libraries; Librarian M. M. PATEL, M.A., DIP.LIB.SC.

Shrimati Radhika Sinha Institute and Sachchidananda Sinha Library (*State Central Library, Bihar*): P.O.B. 62, Patna; f. 1924; 109,989 vols.; Librarian Dr. R. S. P. SINGH, M.A., PH.D., D.L.SC.

Social Science Documentation Centre (*Indian Council of Social Science Research*): 35 Ferozshah Rd., New Delhi 110001; f. 1970; provides reference and documentation service in social sciences, an Inter-Library Resources Centre, Union Catalogue of Social Science Serials (32 vols.), Retrospective Index of Indian Social Science Periodicals, Area Studies Bibliographies of States and Union Territories of India, Social Science Research Bibliographies in all major Indian languages, reprographic services; library of 3,000 periodicals, 33,000 vols. of serials and monographs; Dir. S. P. AGRAWAL; publs. *Union Catalogues*†, *Gandhi Bibliography, Indian Dissertation Abstracts*†, ICSSR Journals of Abstracts and Reviews†, etc.

State Central Library: Hyderabad 12, A.P.; f. 1891; 160,000 vols.; 16,995 manuscripts; Librarian T. VENKATA RAMANAYYA, M.A., LL.B., DIP.L.SC.

Tamil Nadu Government Oriental Manuscripts Library: Chepauk, Madras 600005; f. 1928; acquistion, preservation and publication of rare and important collection of MSS. in Sanskrit, Islamic and South Indian languages; 20,966 vols., 66,000 MSS.; Curator R. BASKARAN; publs. *Bulletin*, catalogues, etc.

Trivandrum Public Library: Trivandrum, Kerala State; f. 1847; 172,000 vols.; Librarian P. V. VARGHESE.

MUSEUMS AND ART GALLERIES

Andhra Pradesh State Museum: Hyderabad 500034; f. 1930; sculpture, epigraphy, arms and weapons, Bidriware, bronze objects, miniatures and paintings, MSS, numismatics, European paintings (prints), decorative and modern arts, textiles; excavations at Yeleswaram Pochampai, Peddabankur; Dir. Dr. N. RAMESAN; publs. various on numismatics.

Archaeological Museum: Bodh Gaya, Bihar State; stone and bronze sculpture, etc.; Curator S. SINGH.

Archaeological Museum: Dampier Park, Mathura 281001, U.P.; f. 1874; approx. 1,000 exhibits, Indian art, culture, archaeology of the Mathura school, Kushana sculptures; library of 10,000 vols.; Curator R. C. SHARMA; publs. *Museum Catalogue, Museum Handbook, Mathura, Archaeology in U.P.*

Archaeological Museum: Nagarjunakonda, Guntur, Andhra Pradesh; f. 1966; pre-historic and historical antiquities, mainly sculptures, Buddhist and Hindu; Curator K. VEERABHADRA RAO.

Archaeological Museum: Nalanda, Bihar State; f. 1958; collections of antiquities, specializing in Buddhist sculptures; Curator S. K. SHARMA.

Assam State Museum: Gauhati 781001, Assam; f. 1940; Dir. G. N. BHUYAN, M.A.; publ. *Bulletin.*

Baroda Museum and Picture Gallery: Baroda 390005, Gujarat; f. museum 1894 and picture gallery 1920; Indian archaeology; prehistoric and historic; Indian art: ancient, medieval and modern; numismatic collections; modern Indian paintings; industrial art; Asiatic and Egyptian collections; Greek, Roman, European civilizations and art; European paintings; ethnology, zoology, geology, economic botany; library of 19,000 vols.; Dir. S. K. BHOWMIK; Keepers: M. N. GANDHI (Art and Archaeology Sections), R. I. PATEL (Natural History Sections); publ. *Bulletin.*

Birla Industrial and Technological Museum: 19A Gurusaday Rd., Calcutta 700019; f. 1959; administered by the National Council of Science Museums; portrays the history of science and technology; two regional science centres and three mobile science exhibition buses in rural areas; educational programmes for students and teachers; Senior Curator S. K. GHOSE, M.S., PH.D., M.I.E.E.E.

Central Museum: Nagpur 440001, Maharashtra; f. 1863; miscellaneous collection of objects relating to archaeology, art, ethnology, cottage industry, megalithic sites, copper implements, Buddhist sculptures, aboriginal tribal remains.

Crafts Museum: All India Handicrafts Board, Pragati Maidan, Bhairon Rd., New Delhi 110001; f. 1952; collections of Indian traditional crafts and folk and tribal arts; Folk Crafts section; library of 3,000 vols.; Dir. Mrs. S. J. BAXI.

Delhi Fort Museum: Mumtaz Mahal, Red Fort; f. 1909; 420 vols.; historical collections of the Mughal period; old arms, seals and signets, coins, miniatures, Mughal dresses and relics of India's War of Independence; Curator A. R. SIDDIQUI.

Dr. Bhau Daji Lad Museum: 91A Dr. B. Ambedkar Rd., Byculla, Bombay 400027; f. 1855; reference library on Indian and foreign art, archaeology, ethnology, geology, history, numismatics and museology; exhibits of agriculture and village life, armoury, cottage industries, ethnology, fine arts, fossils, Indian coins, minerals, miscellaneous collection, Old Bombay collection; Curator V. N. BARVE; publs. catalogues, etc.

Fort Museum: Fort St. George, Madras 600001; exhibits belong mainly to the days of the East India Co.; Dir. C. T. M. KOTRIAH.

Gandhi National Museum and Library: Rajghat, New Delhi 110001; f. 1948 by the Gandhi Memorial Museum Society to collect and display Gandhi's records and mementos and to promote the study of his life and work; library of 30,000 vols., 50,000 documents and 100 periodicals; 130 films and recordings; large picture gallery; Chair. SADIQ ALI; Sec. RANVIR PURI.

Government Museum: Kasturba Rd., Bangalore 560001. Karnataka; f. 1866; art, archaeology, industrial art and natural history; library of 2,000 vols.; Curator (vacant); publ. *Annual Report.*

Government Museum: Bikaner 334001, Rajasthan; f. 1937; collection of terracottas, sculptures, bronzes, coins, inscriptions, Rajasthani paintings, documents, arms and costumes, specimens of folk-culture; Curator P. C. BHARGAVA.

Government Museum and National Art Gallery: Pantheon Rd., Egmore, Madras 600008; f. 1851 (art gallery 1951); archaeology, ancient and modern Indian art, South Indian bronzes, Buddhist sculptures, numismatics, philately, anthropology, botany, zoology, geology, chemical conservation; Dir. N. HARINARAYANA, M.A., B.SC.; publs. *Annual Report*, guide books, *Madras Museum Bulletins*, *Newsletter* (2 a year).

Indian Museum: 27 Jawaharlal Nehru Rd., Calcutta 700016; f. 1814; collections of archaeology, art, coins, anthropology, geology, botany, zoology; Dir. Dr. S. C. RAY; publs. *Indian Museum Bulletin* (every 6 months), monographs, etc.

The International Doll Museum: Nehru House, 4 Bahadur Shah Zafar Marg, New Delhi 110001; f. 1965; 4,200 exhibits from all over the world; Curator Miss L. SHANKAR.

Kerala State Museums, Zoos and Government Gardens: include: (1) State Museum and Zoo, Trichur, f. 1885; (2) Govt. Museum and Zoological and Botanical Gardens, Trivandrum, f. 1857; natural history collections, Indian arts and crafts; (3) Art Gallery and Krishna-Menon Museum, Calicut; f. 1975; Dir. S. P. POTTI.

Maharaja Sawai Man Singh II Museum: City Palace, Jaipur 302002, Rajasthan; f. 1959; textiles and costumes, armoury, Mughal and Rajasthani miniature paintings, Persian and Mughal carpets, transport accessories, regalia, manuscript library of 18,000 Sanskrit, Persian, Hindi and Rajasthani MSS; Dir. Dr. ASOK KUMAR DAS; publs. catalogues†, etc.

Manipur State Museum: Polo-ground, Imphal, Manipur; general collection.

National Gallery of Modern Art: Jaipur House, New Delhi 110003; f. 1954; contemporary art (paintings, sculpture, drawings, graphics, architecture, industrial design, photography, prints and minor arts); Dir. Dr. L. P. SIHARE.

National Museum of India: Janpath, New Delhi 110011; f. 1949; Departments of Art, Archaeology, Anthropology, Modelling, Presentation, Preservation, Publication, Library and Photography; Indian prehistoric tools, protohistoric remains from Harappa, Mohenjodaro, etc., representative collections of sculptures, terracottas, stuccos and bronzes from 2nd century B.C. to 18th century A.D.; illustrated MSS. and miniatures; Stein Collection of Central Asian murals and other antiquities; decorative arts; textiles, coins and illuminated epigraphical charts; armour; copper-plate etchings; woodwork; library of 30,000 vols.; Dir. N. R. BANNERJEE; publs. *Bulletin*† (annually), special publs. on art and archaeology.

National Museum of Natural History: FICCI Museum Bldg., Barakhamba Rd., New Delhi 110001; f. 1978; ref. library of 2,500 vols.; public lectures, Discovery Room for children, Exhibit Bank of school loan kits, etc.; Dir. Dr. S. M. NAIR.

Orissa State Museum: Bhubaneswar 751006, Orissa; f. 1932; archaeology, epigraphy, numismatics, armoury, arts and crafts, anthropology, palmleaf MSS, natural history; library of 22,000 vols., 2,000 periodicals; Dir. Dr. H. C. DAS; publ. *Orissa Historical Research Journal*.

Patna Museum: Patna-Gaya Rd., Buddha Marg, Patna 800001, Bihar; f. 1917; archaeology, ethnology, geology and natural history; also rich collection of Tibetan paintings; coins; Curator Dr. H. K. PRASAD.

Prince of Wales Museum of Western India: Mahatma Gandhi Rd., Fort, Bombay 400023; f. 1905; sections: Art, Painting, Archaeology, Natural History; library of 11,000 vols.; Dir. S. V. GORAKSHKAR; publ. *Bulletin*, catalogues.

Rabindra Bhavan Art Gallery: 35 Ferozeshah Rd., New Delhi; f. 1955; permanent gallery of the Lalit Kala Akademi (National Academy of Art), and venue of the National Exhibition of Art and Triennale-India (international art); Chair. Shri RAM NIWAS MIRDHA; publs. *Lalit Kala* (annually), *Lalit Kala Contemporary* (2 a year).

Rabindra Bhavana (*Tagore Museum*): Visva-Bharati, P.O. Santiniketan, Pin. 731235; f. 1942; collection of MSS., letters, newspaper clippings, gramophone records, photographs, cine-film, books, paintings by Tagore and tape recordings of Rabindranath's voice, etc.; located at the Vichitra inside the Uttarayana Campus where the poet spent the last days of his life; Curator S. K. BAGCHI; publ. *Rabindra Jijnasa* (2 vols.).

Rajputana Museum: Ajmer 305001, Rajasthan; f. 1908; archaeology; rare sculptures, architectural carvings, old coins, epigraphs, Rajput paintings, arms and armour of Rajasthan; Curator R. D. SHARMA.

Salarjung Museum: Hyderabad 500002, A.P.; f. 1951; paintings, textiles, porcelain, jade, carpets, MSS., antiques, ivory, glass, silver- and bronze-ware; children's section; library of 50,000 vols. incl. Persian, Arabic and Urdu MSS.; Dir. Dr. M. L. NIGAM; publs. *Research Bulletin*† (2 a year), *Guide Book*.

Sarnath Museum: Varanasi 221001, U.P.; archaeological site museum four miles north of Benares; f. 1904; Buddhist collection from 3rd century B.C. to 12th century A.D.; Curator B. V. RAO.

Sri Chitra Art Gallery, Gallery of Asian Paintings: Trivandrum 695001, Kerala; f. 1935; sections: Pure Indian Art, Rajput, Mughal and Persian, Tanjore, Tibetan, Chinese, Japanese, Balinese, Indo-European (water and oil), etchings and woodcuts; Modern Indian Contemporary Art and Murals; library of 1,110 vols.; Dir. S. P. POTTI; publ. *Administration Report*.

Sri Pratap Singh Museum: Lalmandi, Srinagar 190001, Jammu and Kashmir; general collection; Curator M. H. MAKHDOOMI.

Sri Rallabandi Subba Rao Government Museum (formerly the *Andhra Historical Research Society*): Godavari Bund Rd., Rajahmundry, East Godavari District, Andhra Pradesh 533101; f. 1967; art, archaeology, epigraphy, history and numismatics; collection of coins, sculpture, pottery, terra cotta, palm-leaf MSS., inscriptions, etc.; Dir. Dr. N. RAMESAN, M.A., PH.D., I.A.S., F.R.A.S.; publ. *Journal of the A.H.R.S.*†

Uttar Pradesh State Museum: Banarasibagh, Lucknow, U.P.; f. 1863; Dir. Dr. N. P. JOSHI; Numismatic Officer Dr. A. K. SRIVASTAVA; publs. *Bulletins* (2 a year), *Catalogue of Indo-Greek Coins*, *Catalogue of Gandhara Sculptures*, *Catalogue of Brahmanical Sculptures*.

Victoria Memorial Hall: 1 Queens Way, Calcutta 700016; f. 1906; modern Indian historical museum; wide collection of art and historical pieces, mainly illustrating Indian history of the last three centuries; Sec. and Curator N. R. RAY, M.A.; publs. *Bulletin of the Victoria Memorial* (annual), *Selected Documents*, *Guidebook*.

Visvesvaraya Industrial and Technological Museum: Kasturba Rd., Bangalore 560001, Karnataka; f. 1962; aims to stimulate interest in science and education, thereby attracting children to research and engineering, and to portray the application of technology in industry and human welfare.

UNIVERSITIES

There are in India three types of university: Affiliating and Teaching (most teaching done in colleges affiliated to the university, but some teaching, mostly postgraduate, undertaken by the university); Residential and Teaching (all teaching done on one campus); Federal (a number of university or constituent colleges are closely associated with the university's work). It is not possible, for reasons of space, to give details of affiliated colleges.

AGRA UNIVERSITY

PALIWAL PARK, AGRA 280004, UTTAR PRADESH

Telephone: 64164.

Founded 1927; Affiliating and Teaching.

Languages of instruction: English and Hindi; Academic year: July to April (one term).

Chancellor: H.E. The GOVERNOR OF UTTAR PRADESH.

Vice-Chancellor: Dr. S. N. MEHROTRA.

Registrar: B. N. SINGH.

Hon. Librarian: Dr. D. D. JOSHI.

Library of 125,000 vols.

Number of students: 110,000.

DEANS:

Faculty of Arts: Dr. V. N. MISRA.

Faculty of Science: UMA NAG.

Faculty of Law: R. P. KAMAL.

Faculty of Commerce: H. C. MEHROTRA.

Faculty of Agriculture: Dr. O. P. S. SENGAR.

Faculty of Medicine: Dr. B. B. SHARMA.

Faculty of Engineering: V. G. SHASTRI.

CONSTITUENT INSTITUTES:

Institute of Social Sciences.
Director: Dr. D. D. JOSHI.
Number of teachers: 14.

K.M. Institute of Hindi Studies and Linguistics.
Director: Dr. V. N. MISRA.
Number of teachers: 15.

Institute of Household Art and Home Science.
Director: Miss U. NAG, M.SC., M.ED., PH.D.
Number of teachers: 10.

There are 39 affiliated colleges.

UNIVERSITY OF AGRICULTURAL SCIENCES

G.K.V.K., BANGALORE 560065, KARNATAKA

Telephone: 366753.

Founded 1964; Residential.

Language of instruction: English; State control; Academic year: July to June (three terms).

Chancellor: H.E. THE GOVERNOR OF KARNATAKA.

Pro-Chancellor: THE MINISTER OF AGRICULTURE, Karnataka.

Vice-Chancellor: Dr. R. DWARAKINATH.

Registrar: **R. KRISHNAPPA.**

Administrative Officer: B. J. NANJUNDAPPA.

Librarian: H. R. RAMCHANDRA.

Libraries of 186,000 vols.

Number of teachers: 603.
Number of students: 3,621.

Publications: *Diary* (monthly), *Annual Report, Calendar, Mysore Journal of Agricultural Sciences* (quarterly), *Current Research* (monthly), *Krishi Vijnana* (quarterly in Kannada), Technical Series, Extension Series, Research Series, Miscellaneous Series (irregular).

PROFESSORS:

BHOJAPPA, Dr. K. M., Horticulture
CHANNABASAVANNA, Dr. G. P., Entomology
DESHPANDE, Dr. P. B., Soil Science
DIXIT, Dr. L. A., Crop Production
GOUD, Dr. J. V., Agricultural Botany
HEGDE, Dr. R. K., Plant Pathology
HIREMATH, Dr. K. C., Agricultural Economics
HITTALMANI, V. C., Kannada Studies
KAMALAPUR, Dr. P. N., Veterinary Medicine
KESHAVAMURTHY, Dr. B. S., Veterinary Microbiology and Public Health
KRISHNAMURTHY, Dr. A. N., Agricultural Marketing
KRISHNA SASTRY, Dr. K. S., Crop Production
KULKARNI, Dr. G. N., Seed Technology
MUDDAPPA GOWDA, Dr. P. M., Horticulture
PATIL, Dr. R. V., Gynaecology and Obstetrics
RAI, Dr. A. V., Animal Genetics and Breeding
RAMAIAH, R., Agricultural Engineering
RAMANNA, Dr. R., Agricultural Economics
REDDY, Dr. H. RAMACHANDRA, Plant Pathology
REDDY, Dr. T. K. RAMACHANDRA, Agricultural Microbiology
RUDRA SETTY, Dr., Fish Culture
SALIAN, P. K., Fishery Engineering
SESHADRI, S. J., Veterinary Pathology
SESHAGIRI RAO, Dr. T., Soil Science
SETHU RAO, Dr. M. K., Extension Education
SETTY, Dr. K. G. H., Nematology
SETTY, Dr. S. V. S., Animal Nutrition Management and Products Technology
SHIVASHANKAR, Dr. G., Agricultural Botany
SRIHNIVASAMURTHY, J., Extension Education
SULLADMATH, Dr. U. V., Horticulture
SUNDERAJ, Dr. N., Statistics
THIMMAIAH, Dr. K., Veterinary Physiology
THIPPAIAH REDDY, Dr. P. H., Veterinary Surgery
THONTADARYA, Dr. T. S., Agricultural Entomology
TRIVIKRAMA RAO, Dr. K., Veterinary Anatomy
VARGHESE, T. G., Aquaculture
VEERARAYANA GOWDA, Dr. T. K., Veterinary Pharmacology
VEERESH, Dr. G. K., Entomology
VENKATARAM, Dr. J. V., Agricultural Finance and Co-operation
VIRUPAKSHA, Dr. T. K., Biochemistry

CONSTITUENT COLLEGES:

Agricultural Engineering Institute: Raichur; f. 1969.
Principal: N. L. MAURYA.

College of Agriculture: Hebbal, Bangalore; f. 1946.
Director: N. G. PERUR.

College of Agriculture: Dharwar; f. 1947.
Director: Dr. R. B. PATIL.

Veterinary College: Hebbal, Bangalore; f. 1957.
Director: (vacant).

College of Basic Sciences and Humanities: f. 1967.
Director: Dr. R. NARAYANA.

College of Post-Graduate Education: f. 1967.
Director: Dr. S. V. PATIL.

Fisheries College, Mangalore: f. 1970.
Director: H. P. C. SHETTY.

Home Science College: Dharwar; f. 1975.
Director: Dr. LEELA PHADNIS.

ALIGARH MUSLIM UNIVERSITY

ALIGARH, U.P. 202001

Telephone: 3020.

Founded as Anglo-Mohamedan Oriental College, 1875; raised to university status, 1921; Residential and Teaching; **Language of instruction: English; State control; Academic year: July to April (three terms).**

Chancellor: Nawab HAFIZ AHMAD SAID KHAN, Sahib of Chhtari, LL.D.

Vice-Chancellor: Dr. A. M. KHUSRO.

Pro-Vice Chancellor: Prof. M. SHAFI.

Registrar: J. RAHMAN.

Librarian: M. H. RAZVI.

The library contains 519,433 vols.; 13,281 MSS. in Arabic, Persian, Urdu and Hindi.

Number of teachers: 872.
Number of students: 14,048.

Publications: *Muslim University Gazette, Aligarh Magazine, Fikr-O-Nazar.*

DEANS:

Faculty of Arts: Dr. R. S. TRIPATHI.

Faculty of Engineering and Technology: Prof. J. A. MUNIR.

Faculty of Law: Prof. RASHEEDUZZAFAR.

Faculty of Science: Dr. Z. R. KHAN.

Faculty of Theology: O. M. A. BILGRAMI.

Faculty of Medicine: J. N. PRASAD.
Faculty of Commerce: M. HAFIZUDDIN.
Faculty of Social Sciences: Prof. A. ANSARI.

CONSTITUENT COLLEGES AND INSTITUTES:

Women's College: Aligarh; f. 1937.
Principal: Mrs. R. KHAN.

College of Engineering and Technology: Aligarh; f. 1944.
Principal: Dr. Y. ANSARI.

University Polytechnic: Aligarh; f. 1950.
Principal: S. A. ABBAS.

Ajmal Khan Tibbija College: Aligarh f. 1927.
Principal: Dr. TAIYAB.

Institute of Ophthalmology: Aligarh; f. 1952.

J.N. Medical College: Aligarh; f. 1962.

UNIVERSITY OF ALLAHABAD

ALLAHABAD 211002,
UTTAR PRADESH
Telephone: 50668.
Founded 1887; Residential and Teaching.

Languages of instruction: English and Hindi; Academic year: July to April.

Chancellor: H.E. THE GOVERNOR OF UTTAR PRADESH.
Vice-Chancellor: Dr. P. D. HAJELA.
Registrar: Dr. B. M. SINGH.
Librarian: Prof. S. S. ROY.

Library of 334,000 vols.

Number of students: 26,123.

DEANS:

Faculty of Arts: Prof. A. P. MISRA.
Faculty of Commerce: Prof. B. N. ASTHANA.
Faculty of Engineering: Prin. JAGDISH LAL.
Faculty of Law: (vacant).
Faculty of Medicine: Prin. T. N. MEHROTRA.
Faculty of Science: Dr. D. D. PANT.

UNIVERSITY COLLEGES:

Kali Prasad University College: Principal L. SHANKAR, M.A.

Madan Mohan Malaviya College: Principal R. P. ARGAL.

William Holland University College: Principal S. L. PARMAR, M.A., D.PHIL.

ASSOCIATED COLLEGES:

Allahabad Degree College: f. 1956; Principal P. THAKUR.

Allahabad Agricultural Institute: Naini; f. 1932; Principal J. B. CHITAMBER.

Ch. Mahadeo Prasad Degree College: f. 1950; Principal J. P. SRIVASTAVA.

Ewing Christian College: f. 1902; Principal (vacant).

Moti Lal Nehru Regional Engineering College: f. 1961; Principal JAGDISH LAL.

CONSTITUENT COLLEGE:

Moti Lal Nehru Medical College: f. 1961; Principal Prof. T. N. MEHROTRA.

ANDHRA UNIVERSITY

WALTAIR 530003, ANDHRA PRADESH
Telephone: 4871.
Founded 1926; Teaching and Affiliating.

Languages of instruction: English and Telugu; Academic year: July to June.

Chancellor: THE GOVERNOR OF ANDHRA PRADESH.
Vice-Chancellor: Sri M. R. APPA ROW, M.A.
Registrar: Sri M. G. K. REDDY, M.A.
Librarian: Sri K. VENKATARATNAM, M.A., M.S. IN L.S.

The library contains 274,000 vols.
Number of teachers: 677.
Number of students: 50,867.

Publications: *Annual Report, Handbook.*

DEANS:

Faculty of Arts: Prof. B. PRASADA RAO, M.A., PH.D.
Faculty of Science: Prof. T. V. AVADHANI, M.A., PH.D.
Faculty of Medicine: Prof. K. SANJEEVA RAO, M.S.
Faculty of Commerce: Prof. K. V. SIVVAYA, B.COM., M.B.A., PH.D.
Faculty of Education: Dr. S. CHANDRA SEKHARA SARMA, M.A., M.ED., PH.D.
Faculty of Law: Prof. B. S. MURTY, M.L., LL.M., J.S.D.
Faculty of Oriental Learning: Prof. S. V. JOGA RAO, M.A., PH.D.
Faculty of Fine Arts: (vacant).
Faculty of Engineering: Prof. M. S. RAJU, M.S.E.E., M.I.E.E.E.
Faculty of Pharmaceutical Sciences: Prof. N. VISWANADHAM, D.SC.
Faculty of Chemical Engineering and Technology: Prof. C. CHIRANJEEVI, D.SC., M.I.I.CH.E.

CONSTITUENT COLLEGES:

Erskine College of Natural Sciences: Waltair; f. 1941.

J.V.D. College of Science and Technology: Waltair; f. 1932.

University College of Arts and Commerce: Waltair; f. 1931; Principal Prof. N. V. SUBRAHMANYAM, PH.D.

University College of Engineering: Waltair; f. 1955; Principal Prof. M. S. RAJU, M.S.E.E., M.I.E.E.E.

University College of Law: Waltair; f. 1945; Principal (vacant).

There are 84 affiliated colleges. The University also runs postgraduate courses at Nuzvid, Srikakulam and Kakinada.

ANDHRA PRADESH AGRICULTURAL UNIVERSITY

RAJENDRANAGAR,
HYDERABAD-500030
ANDHRA PRADESH
Telephone: 48161, 48011.
Founded 1964.

Language of instruction: English; Academic year: July to June.

Chancellor: H.E. THE GOVERNOR OF ANDHRA PRADESH.
Vice-Chancellor: Sri J. RAGHOTHAM REDDY.
Registrar: Sri T. NARAYAN REDDY, I.A.S.
Librarian: Sri D. B. ESWARA REDDY, M.A.
Director of Agricultural Experimental Stations: Dr. A. APPA RAO, PH.D.
Director of Extension: Dr. A. ADIVI REDDY, PH.D.

Number of teachers: 438.
Number of students: 2,532.

Publication: *Research Journal* (English, quarterly).

DEANS:

Faculty of Agriculture: Dr. MIR HAMID ALI, M.SC., PH.D.
Faculty of Veterinary Science: Dr. C. V. REDDY, M.SC., PH.D.
Faculty of Home Science: Dr. P. PUSHPAMMA, M.SC., PH.D.
Faculty of Postgraduate Studies: Dr. K. V. RAMAN.

CONSTITUENT COLLEGES:

College of Agriculture: Bapatla; Principal: Dr. T. D. J. NAGABHUSHANAM.

College of Agriculture: Rajendranagar; Principal: Dr. B. H. KRISHNA MURTY.

Sri Venkateswara Agricultural College: Tirupati; Principal: Prof. SHANKAR REDDY.

College of Veterinary Science: Tirupati; Principal Sri K. SATYANARAYANA RAO.

College of Veterinary Science: Rajendranagar; Principal: Dr. D. VENKAYA.

College of Home Science: Hyderabad; Principal: Dr. P. PUSHPAMMA.

ANNAMALAI UNIVERSITY

ANNAMALAINAGAR P.O.,
TAMIL NADU 608101
Telephone: 249.
Founded 1929; Residential and Teaching.

Chancellor: H.E. THE GOVERNOR OF MADRAS.
Pro-Chancellor: Rajah Sir M. A. MUTHIAH CHETTIAR OF CHETTINAD, Kt., B.A., D.LITT., M.L.C.

Vice-Chancellor: Dr. Justice B. S. SOMASUNDARAM.
Registrar: M. GOWRISHANKAR.
Librarian: V. DURAIRAJAN.

The library contains 260,538 vols.
Number of teachers: 438.
Number of students: 7,220.

Publications: *Annamalai University Research Journal, Annamalai University Magazine.*

DEANS:

Faculty of Arts: Prof. M. O. MATHEW, PH.D.
Faculty of Science: Dr. P. GOVINDAN, M.A., PH.D.
Faculty of Engineering and Technology: Dr. S. M. LAKSHMANAN, M.SC., PH.D., D.I.C., A.M.INST.F., M.I.I.CHEM.E., A.M.A I.CH.E.
Faculty of Education: K. K. PILLAI.
Faculty of Indian Languages: K. VELLAIVARANAN.
Faculty of Fine Arts: M. S. SOMASUNDRAM.
Faculty of Agriculture: Dr. C. N. SAMBANDAM, B.SC.(AG.), M.SC., M.S., PH.D.
Faculty of Law: M. E. DAVID.

ASSAM AGRICULTURAL UNIVERSITY

JORHAT 785013, ASSAM
Telephone: 89.
Founded 1969.

Teaching, research and extension at undergraduate and postgraduate levels in agriculture and veterinary science (Khanapara campus) and teaching, research and extension in home science.

Chancellor: H.E. THE GOVERNOR OF ASSAM.
Vice-Chancellor: Dr. D. N. BORTHAKUR.
Registrar: Shri M. N. BHATTACHARYYA.
Librarian: R. C. PHOOKAN.

The library contains 34,300 vols.
Number of teachers: 137.
Number of students: 1,080.

DEANS:

Faculty of Agriculture: Dr. M. N. BORAL.
Faculty of Veterinary Science: Dr. P. K. SHARMA.
Faculty of Home Science: Dr. P. C. BORA (acting).

AWADHESH PRATAP SINGH UNIVERSITY

REWA 486003, MADHYA PRADESH
Telephone: 277.

Founded 1968; affiliating and teaching.

Languages of instruction: Hindi and English; autonomous control; Academic year: July to March.

Chancellor: H.E. THE GOVERNOR OF MADHYA PRADESH.
Vice-Chancellor: Dr. S. K. R. BHANDARI.
Registrar: Dr. S. C. MAJUMDAR.
Librarian: N. GUPTA (acting).

The library contains 31,536 vols.

Number of students: 27,729.

Publication: *Vindhya Bharati* (quarterly).

DEANS:

Faculty of Life Science: Dr. J. S. RATHAUR.
Faculty of Social Science: Dr. R. P. PANDEY.
Faculty of Arts: Dr. S. K. GUPTA.
Faculty of Law: S. C. JOSHI.
Faculty of Medicine: Dr. I. P. AGRAWAL.
Faculty of Engineering: Dr. O. N. KAUL.
Faculty of Education: Dr. S. S. MISHRA.
Faculty of Commerce: Dr. S. P. SHARMA.
Faculty of Science: Dr. V. S. JAULI.
Faculty of Ayurvedic: Dr. S. SHASTRI.

There are 11 constituent colleges and 43 affiliated colleges.

BANARAS HINDU UNIVERSITY

VARANASI 221005, U.P.
Telephone: 54291.

Founded 1916; Residential and Teaching.

Languages of instruction: Hindi and English; State control; Academic year: July to April (three terms).

Visitor: PRESIDENT OF THE REPUBLIC OF INDIA.
Chancellor: KASHI NARESH H.H. Maharaja VIBHUTI NARAIN SINGH.
Vice-Chancellor: Dr. HARI NARAIN.
Registrar: R. C. P. SINHA (acting).
Librarian: H. D. SHARMA.

Number of teachers: 1,400.
Number of students: 20,292.

Publications: *B.H.U. Journal, Prajana, B.H.U. News.*

DEANS:

Faculty of Arts: Prof. P. N. KAULA.
Faculty of Science: Prof. S. N. SINGH.
Faculty of Commerce and Business Management: Prof. S. K. R. BHANDARI.
Faculty of Oriental Learning and Theology: Prof. P. DWIVEDI.
Faculty of Agriculture: Prof. R. B. SINGH.
Faculty of Law: Prof. R. P. DHOKALIA.
Faculty of Indian Medicine: Prof. P. V. SHARMA.
Faculty of Medicine: Prof. J. NAGCHOUDHURY.
Faculty of Education: Dr. S. N. SINGH (acting).
Faculty of Performing Arts: Prof. LALMANI MISRA.
Faculty of Visual Arts: Dr. P. B. LALL.
Faculty of Social Sciences: Prof. MANORANJAN JHA.
Faculty of Engineering and Technology: Prof. S. L. MALHOTRA.

CONSTITUENT COLLEGES:

Evening College: Kamachha, Varanasi.

Women's College: Varanasi; f. 1929.

There are 4 affiliated colleges.

BANGALORE UNIVERSITY

JNANA BHARATHI,
BANGALORE 560056,
KARNATAKA STATE
Telephone: 601241.
Telegraphic Address: Unibangalore.

Founded 1964; affiliating.

Chancellor: H.E. THE GOVERNOR OF KARNATAKA.
Vice-Chancellor: T. R. JAYARAMAN.
Registrar: S. D. SYIEM.

Central Library of 138,600 vols.
Number of teachers: 3,556.
Number of students: 56,660.

DEANS:

Faculty of Arts: Dr. K. VENKATAGIRI GOWDA.
Faculty of Commerce: Dr. O. R. KRISHNASWAMI.
Faculty of Education: N. C. PARAPPA.
Faculty of Engineering: G. PARAMESWARAPPA.
Faculty of Law: M. BASEER HUSAIN.
Faculty of Medicine: Dr. C. V. JAYAKEERTHY.
Faculty of Science: T. RAMESAN.
Faculty of Technology: B. BASAVARAJ.
Faculty of Mental Health and Neurosciences: Dr. R. M. VARMA.
Faculty of Communication: Dr. H. S. ESWARA.

PROFESSORS:

BHARATHRAJ SINGH, M. E., M.A., English
BASHEER HUSSAIN, M., M.A., LL.M., A.M., Law
CHELUVARAJU, K. H., M.A., PH.D., Political Science
CHIDANANDAMURTHY, M., M.A., PH.D., Kannada
CHOWDAIAH, M. P., M.E., M.S., Mechanical Engineering
ESWARA, H. S., Communication
JERE, V. N., M.SC., Mathematics
JUSTO, C. E. G., M.E., PH.D., Civil Engineering
KRISHNASWAMI, O. R., M.A., M.COM., PH.D., Commerce
KUCHELA, K. N., M.SC., PH.D., Physics
LAKSHAMAN, T. K., M.A., PH.D., Economics
LAKSHAMANA REDDY, S., M.SC.(ENG.), Electrical Engineering
LINGAIAH, K., M.TECH., PH.D., Mechanical Engineering
MADAIAH, N., M.SC., PH.D., Physics
MOTHI RAO, J. K., B.A., B.COM., LL.M., Law
NAGANNA, C., D.SC., Geology
NAGARAJ, M., M.S., PH.D., Botany
NARASAIAH, K., M.A., PH.D., History
NARAYANA REDDY, G. K., M.SC., PH.D., Chemistry
NARAYANA REDDY, G. K., M.SC., PH.D. Electrical Engineering

PARAMASHIVAIAH, P., M.A., M.S., PH.D., Physics
PARAMESWARAPPA, G., M.S., Electrical Engineering
PARAPPA, N. C., M.S., Physical Education
RADHAKRISHNA, G. N., M.S., PH.D., Civil Engineering
RAJAGOPALAN, C., PH.D.
RAJANNA, B. C., M.S., Civil Engineering
RAMESAN, T., M.SC., Mathematics
RANGANATH, H. K., M.A., PH.D., Dance, Drama and Music
RUDRAIAH, N., M.SC., PH.D., Mathematics
SAMBEGOWDA, S., M.SC., D.PHIL., Geology
SARAGU KRISHNAMURTHY, PH.D., Hindi
SASTRY, M. K. L. N., PH.D., Civil Engineering
SHERIFF, A., M.SC., PH.D., Botany
SHIVAKUMARA SWAMY, M., PH.D., Sanskrit
SHIVANANDAIAH, K. M., M.SC., PH.D., Chemistry
SHIVARUDRAPPA, G. S., M.A., PH.D., Kannada
VENKATAGIRI GOWDA, K., M.A., PH.D., Economics
VENKATASWAMY SETTY, P. S., M.SC., PH.D., Physics

UNIVERSITY COLLEGES:

Central College: Principal M. SHADAKSHARASWAMY.

University College of Physical Education: Principal Prof. N. C. PARAPPA.

University Law College: Principal M. BASHEER HUSSAIN.

University Visvesaraya College of Engineering: Principal Prof. B. K. RAMAIAH.

There are 94 affiliated colleges.

THE MAHARAJA SAYAJIRAO UNIVERSITY OF BARODA

BARODA 390002, GUJARAT

Telephone: 64721, 64238.

Founded 1949; Residential and Teaching.

Language of instruction: English; Academic year: June to April (two terms).

Chancellor: Shri FATEHSINHRAO GAEKWAR OF BARODA (ex-officio).
Vice-Chancellor: Prof. P. J. MADAN, D.I.C., M.SC., F.I.E.
Pro-Vice-Chancellor: Prof. S. M. SETHNA, M.SC., PH.D.
Registrar: Shri K. A. AMIN, M.COM.
Librarian: L. M. PADHYA, M.A., PH.D., M.ED.

The library contains 44,154 vols.
Number of teachers: 882.
Number of students: 19,247.

Publications: *Handbook, Annual Report, Journal of Oriental Institute, Journal of Education and Psychology, Journal of Animal Morphology and Physiology, Journal of Education and Psychology, Swadhyaya, Pavo, Journal of Technology and Engineering* (annual).

DEANS:

Faculty of Arts: Prof. BIRJE PATIL, PH.D.ENG.
Faculty of Science: Prof. S. S. MERH, M.SC., PH.D.
Faculty of Commerce: Dr. H. P. CHOKSHI, M.A., PH.D.
Faculty of Education and Psychology: Prof. D. B. DESAI.
Faculty of Medicine: Dr. P. T. ACHARYA, M.B.B.S.
Faculty of Technology and Engineering: Dr. S. M. SEN, M.SC., PH.D.
Faculty of Fine Arts: Dr. RATAN PARIMOO, M.A., PH.D.
Faculty of Home Science: Prof. (Mrs.) A. B. VERMA.
Faculty of Social Work: Shri S. R. YARDI, M.A., LL.B.
Faculty of Law: Shri H. C. DHOLAKIA, M.A., LL.M.

PROFESSORS:

Faculty of Arts:

BIRJE, PATIL, J. D., M.A., PH.D., English
CHAVDA, V. K., PH.D., History
GUPTA, M. G., PH.D., Hindi
JANI, A. N., M.A., PH.D., Sanskrit
JAVADEKAR, A. G., M.A., PH.D., Philosophy
JOSHI, S. H., PH.D., Gujarati
KOTHARI, V. N., M.A., PH.D., Economics
MEHTA, R. N., M.A., PH.D., Archaeology
MEHTA, R. N., M.A., LL.B., English
MISRA, S. C., M.A., PH.D., History
RANA, A. P., M.A., LL.B., Political Science

Faculty of Science:

HASIM, S. R., PH.D., Economics
MEHTA, A. R., PH.D., Botany
MERH, S. S., M.SC., PH.D., Geology
MODI, V. V., M.SC., PH.D., Microbiology
PATEL, M. M., M.SC., PH.D., Physics
PATHAK, C. H., M.SC., PH.D., Botany
PHATAK, A. G., PH.D., Statistics
RAMKRISHNAN, C. V., M.SC., PH.D., Biochemistry
SHAH, R. V., M.SC., PH.D., Zoology
SHAH, V. M., M.SC., Mathematics
SREEHARI, M., PH.D., Statistics
SUBNIS, S. D., PH.D., Botany
TRIVEDI, K. N., M.SC., PH.D., Chemistry

Faculty of Medicine:

ACHARYA, P. T., M.B.B.S., PH.D., Biochemistry
BHATT, R. V., M.B.B.S., M.D., Obstetrics and Gynaecology
DESAI, C. A., M.B.B.S., M.SC., Physiology
GULATI, O. D., M.D., M.S., Pharmacology
GUPTE, P. S., M.B.B.S., M.SC., Anatomy
HAJRA, Miss M. N., M.D., Obstetrics and Gynaecology
JALIHAL, S. V., M.B.B.S., M.D., Pathology
KHURANA, A. B., M.D., D.P.M., Psychiatry
MATHUR, B. B. L., M.D., M.R.C., Pathology
MODI, Miss U. J., M.D., D.PED., Paediatrics
NAGPAL, P. S., M.S., Orthopaedics
PANDE, R. S., M.D., Medicine
PATRA, B. S., M.S., M.C.S., Surgery
PRABHUNE, P. V., Microbiology
SABNIS, S. S., M.D., Anaesthesiology
SHAH, A. R., M.D., D.PED., Paediatrics
SHAH, C. P., M.D., Medicine
SHAH, D. S., M.B.B.S., M.SC., Pharmacology
SHARMA, S. N., M.S., M.O.H., Plastic Surgery
SHETH, K. T., M.D., Ophthalmology
SRINIVASAN, S., M.SC., PH.D., Biochemistry
SRIVASTAVA, H. C., M.B.B.S., M.S., Anatomy
THAKKAR, A. M., F.R.C.S., F.R.G.S., Surgery
THAKORE, A. B., M.S., Surgery
TRIVEDI, D. H., M.D., Preventive and Scientific Medicine
TRIVEDI, P. M., M.B.B.S., M.S., Surgery
UDWADLA, R. B., M.S.
VAISHNAV, V. P., M.B.B.S., M.D., Pathology

Faculty of Technology and Engineering:

AGARWAL, A. K., M.E., Electrical Engineering
BANERJEE, S. K., M.PHARM., Pharmacy
DAMALE, S. K., M.S., A.M.S.C.E., Applied Mechanics
DERASARI, J. R., M.S., A.M.A.I.E.E.
DESAI, R. C., M.E.(ELECT)., PH.D., Electrical Engineering
DE, D. K., PH.D., Textile Engineering
GADGEEL, V. L., M.E., Metallurgical Engineering
HUMBOLDT, R., Pharmacy
JOSHI, R. V., M.SC., PH.D., Applied Physics
KARDILE, Y. K., Central Instrumentation
KOTHARI, G. C., M.E., PH.D., Electrical Engineering
MODI, P. M., M.E., A.M.I.E., Civil Engineering
PANCHAL, M. R., B.E., Electrical Engineering
PANDYA, S. B., M.SC.(TEXT.), DR.ING., Chemical Engineering
PARIKH, P. V., M.SC., A.M.I.E., Applied Mechanics
PATEL, O. H., M.S., F.I.E., Civil Engineering
PATEL, R. C., B.E.(ELECT. & MECH.), A.R.C.S.T.(MECH.), Mechanical Engineering
RUMY MISTRI, B.SC., B.TEXT., Textile Engineering
SEN, S. M., M.SC., D.I.I.SC., PH.D., M.I.R.E., Electrical Engineering
SESHADRI, V., M.E., DR.ING., M.SC., Metallurgy
SHAH, C. C., M.SC., Mathematics
SHAH, S. G., M.E., Electrical Engineering
SOMPURA, G. B., M.S., Civil Engineering
TALATI, A. M., M.SC., PH.D., Applied Chemistry
THATTE, V. S., M.E., PH.D., Applied Mechanics

Faculty of Education and Psychology:

DESAI, D. B., M.ED., PH.D., Education
DONGARE, P. K., Educational Administration
YADAV, M. S., PH.D., Education

Faculty of Commerce:

BEARI, G. C., PH.D.
CHOKSHI, H. P., M.A., PH.D., Business Economics
GUPTA, G. P., PH.D.
MEHTA, K. C., LL.B., Accounts
SHARMA, M. D., PH.D.

Faculty of Fine Arts:

PARIMOO, R., PH.D.
PATEL, J. D.

Faculty of Home Science:

GOPALDAS, Mrs. T., PH.D.
VERMA, Mrs. A. B., PH.D., M.A., Child Development

Faculty of Social Work:

PATEL, Miss I. M., B.A., M.S.W., Social Work

Faculty of Law:

DHOLAKIA, H. C., M.A., LL.B., LL.M., Law

CONSTITUENT COLLEGES:

Baroda Sanskrit Mahavidyalaya: Baroda; f. 1915; Dir. Prof. P. K. DONGARE.

College of Indian Music, Dance and Dramatics: Baroda; f. 1886; Principal M. J. BHATT.

Medical College: Baroda; Dean Dr. P. T. ACHARYA.

M. K. Amin Arts and Science College and College of Commerce: Padra; f. 1965; Principal: Shri I. A. DAVE.

Oriental Institute: Baroda; f. 1927; Dir. A. N. JANI.

Polytechnic: Baroda; f. 1957; Principal V. H. SHAH.

BERHAMPUR UNIVERSITY

BERHAMPUR 760007,
GANJAM, ORISSA
Telephone: 436.

Founded 1967; Teaching and Affiliating.

Language of instruction: English; Academic year: June to May.

Chancellor: THE GOVERNOR OF ORISSA.
Vice-Chancellor: Prof. T. RATHO.
Registrar: M. MAHAPATRA.

The library contains 27,996 vols.
Number of teachers: 140.
Number of students: 14,600.

DEANS:

Faculty of Arts: Prof. B. DAS.
Faculty of Science: Prof. A. S. MITRA.
Faculty of Commerce: Prof. G. P. PANDA.
Faculty of Law: S. MAHAPATRA.
Faculty of Education: R. R. DAS.
Faculty of Medicine: Prof. B. RAJGURU.

There are 22 affiliated colleges.

BHAGALPUR UNIVERSITY

BHAGALPUR, BIHAR 812007
Telephone: 302, 354.

Founded 1960; Teaching and Affiliating.

Chancellor: H.E. THE GOVERNOR OF BIHAR.
Vice-Chancellor: Dr. N. Q. TOHID.
Registrar: Dr. R. S. SINGH.
Librarian: P. N. GAUR.

Library of 64,263 vols.
Number of teachers: 900.
Number of students: 25,840.

DEANS:

Faculty of Arts: Prof. S. N. PRASAD.
Faculty of Science: Prof. K. P. SHARMA.
Faculty of Commerce: V. L. SRIVASTAVA.
Faculty of Law: R. N. PRASAD.
Faculty of Engineering: Prin. S. N. SINHA.
Faculty of Education: Prin. G. K. PRASAD.
Faculty of Medicine: Prin. B. K. SRIVASTAVA.

There are 19 constituent colleges and 24 affiliated colleges.

BHAVNAGAR UNIVERSITY

GIJUBHAI BADHEKA MARG,
BHAVNAGAR 364002,
GUJARAT STATE
Telephone: 5206/7.
Founded 1979.

Vice-Chancellor: R. S. TRIVEDI, M.A., M.ED.
Registrar: L. G. BHATT, B.SC., LL.B.

Library of 32,514 vols.
Number of teachers: 200.
Number of students: 3,744.

DEANS:

Faculty of Arts: S. S. MAJITHIA.
Faculty of Science: L. D. DAVE.
Faculty of Commerce: J. M. VACHHRAJANI.
Faculty of Education: R. S. SHAH.
Faculty of Law: C. D. SWAMINARAYAN.

ATTACHED INSTITUTE:

Central Salt and Marine Chemicals Research Institute: Dir. Dr. D. J. MEHTA.

BHOPAL UNIVERSITY

BHOPAL 462026, M.P.
Telephone: 62103/61465.

Founded 1970; Teaching and Affiliating.

Languages of instruction: Hindi and English.

Chancellor: THE GOVERNOR OF MADHYA PRADESH.
Vice-Chancellor: Dr. R. PRAKASH.
Registrar: Dr. M. G. PAITHANKAR.

The library contains 20,265 vols.
Number of teachers: 762.
Number of students: 28,840 (including Affiliated Colleges).

DEANS:

Faculty of Arts: Dr. ABU MOHD. SAHAR.
Faculty of Commerce: Prof. Dr. S. KHAN.
Faculty of Education: Dr. B. P. ARGAL.
Faculty of Engineering: (vacant).
Faculty of Home Science: Mrs. MADHU MISRA.
Faculty of Law: Dr. N. V. PARANJAPE.
Faculty of Medicine: Dr. P. L. TONDON.
Faculty of Science: Dr. R. C. DEO.
Faculty of Social Sciences: Dr A. C. MINOCHA.
Faculty of Life Science: Dr. D. K. BELSARE.

There are 26 affiliated colleges.

BIDHAN CHANDRA KRISHI VISWA VIDYALAYA

HARINGHATA, P.O. MOHANPUR
741246, DIST. NADIA, WEST
BENGAL
Founded 1975.

Vice-Chancellor: Dr. M. M. CHAKRABARTY.
Registrar: A. K. MITRA.

UNIVERSITY OF BIHAR

MUZAFFARPUR, BIHAR
Telephone: 3507.

Founded 1952, re-established 1960; Teaching and Affiliating.

Languages of instruction: English and Hindi; Academic year: June to May (three terms).

Chancellor: H.E. THE GOVERNOR OF BIHAR.
Vice-Chancellor: Dr. SHAKEELUR REHMAN.
Registrar: R. S. P. SINHA.
Librarian: R. ROY (acting).

Number of students: 38,300.
Publications: *Calendar, Journal.*

DEANS:

Faculty of Arts: Dr. J. MISHRA.
Faculty of Commerce: (vacant).
Faculty of Education: Dr. S. K. SINHA.
Faculty of Engineering: I. C. NAIK.
Faculty of Law: (vacant).
Faculty of Medicine: Dr. B. P. MISHRA.
Faculty of Science: Dr. B. R. SINGH.

There are 20 constituent colleges, two government colleges and 38 affiliated colleges.

BIRLA INSTITUTE OF TECHNOLOGY AND SCIENCE

PILANI, RAJASTHAN 333031
Telephone: Pilani 90, 92.
Founded 1964.

Private control; Language of instruction: English; Academic year: July to May (two semesters).

Chairman: G. D. BIRLA.
Director: Dr. C. R. MITRA.
Registrar: A. N. BHARGAVA.
Librarian: H. C. MEHTA.

Library of 165,700 vols.
Number of teachers: 223.
Number of students: 2,240.

Publications: *Academic Regulations, Bulletin.*

HEADS OF DEPARTMENTS:

Biological Sciences: Dr. M. C. JOSHI.
Chemical Engineering: Dr. R. K. SAKSENA.
Chemistry: Dr. J. N. JAITLEY.
Civil Engineering: Prof. K. M. DHOLAKIA.
Electrical and Electronics Engineering: S. C. RASTOGI.
Economics: Dr. G. P. AVASTHI.
Humanities: Dr. V. P. GAUR.
Languages: Dr. P. D. CHATURVEDI.
Management: Dr. S. K. PORWAL.
Mathematics: Dr. V. P. MAINRA.
Mechanical Engineering: Dr. M. P. KAKAR.
Museum Studies: Mrs. PARIMAL MANDKE.

Pharmacy: Dr. S. S. MATHUR.
Physics: T. N. R. K. KURUP.
Science and Technology Development: H. C. MEHTA.

UNIVERSITY OF BOMBAY

UNIVERSITY RD., FORT,
BOMBAY 400032
Telephone: 256038.

Founded 1857; Teaching and Federal.

Language of instruction: English; Academic year: June to April (two terms).

Chancellor: H.E. THE GOVERNOR OF MAHARASHTRA.
Vice-Chancellor: Prof. RAM JOSHI.
Registrar: P. S. SAWANT (acting).
Librarian: B. ANDERSON, M.A., PH.D.

The library contains 417,000 vols.
Number of students: 143,191.

Publications: *Journal of the University of Bombay, University Handbook Parts I-IV, University Series in Monetary and International Economics, University Economics Series, University Sociology Series, University of Bombay Studies, Sanskrit, Prakrit and Pali.* The university Publications Section publishes textbooks and research works done by students and teachers of the university.

DEANS:

Faculty of Arts: Dr. A. V. TORASKAR.
Faculty of Science: J. V. DESHPANDE.
Faculty of Technology: J. G. BODHE.
Faculty of Law: Prof. R. S. BONSALE.
Faculty of Medicine: Dr. C. K. DESHPANDE.
Faculty of Commerce: S. D. BAL.
Faculty of Dentistry: Dr. F. D. MIRZA.

PROFESSORS:

Faculty of Arts:
ANDERSON, B., PH.D., Library Science
BASU, K. S., M.B.B.S., Business Management
BHARADWAJ, M. A., PH.D., Economics
BRAHAMANAND, P. R., PH.D., Monetary Economics
DANTWALA, M. L., M.A., Agricultural Economics
DASTUR, Miss A. J., M.A., PH.D., Politics
DESAI, A. R., LL.B., PH.D., Sociology
DESHPANDE, C. O., M.A., D.LITT., Geography
GAJENDRAGADKAR, S. N., M.A., PH.D., Linguistics
KALE, S. V., M.A., PH.D., A.M., Applied Psychology
LAKDAWALA, D. T., M.A., PH.D., Economics
MAINKAR, T. G., M.A., PH.D., D.LITT., Sanskrit
MEHTA, Miss USHA H., PH.D., Politics
MURTY, V. S. R., M.B.A., M.COM., Business Management
PARANJPE, R. V., M.A., D.PHIL., German
RANADIVE, Miss K. R., M.A., Planning and Development
RAGHAVAN, S., PH.D., Mathematics
RANGACHARI, S. S., M.A., PH.D., Mathematics
SATHE, Y. S., M.SC., PH.D., Statistics
SHRIKHANDE, S. S., PH.D., Mathematics
SHUKLA, U., M.SC., Mathematics
WOOD, K., M.A., English

Faculty of Science:
JOSHI, M. C., M.SC., PH.D., Physics
KULKARNI, A. B., D.SC., Chemistry

Faculty of Law:
IRANI, P. K., M.A., LL.M., Law

Faculty of Technology:
ACHWAL, W. B., DR. RER NAT., PH.D., Fibre Science
ALTEKAR, V. A., M.S., D.SC.MET., Metallurgical Engineering
CHAKRABORTY, B. B., M.SC., PH.D., Mathematics
DARUWALA, E. H., M.SC., PH.D., F.R.I.C., Textile Chemistry
IYER, S. R. S., M.SC., PH.D., Physical Chemistry
JOSHI, M. V., B.SC., B.E., Engineering
KANE, J. G., M.SC., PH.D., Oil Technology
PADHYE, M. R., M.SC., PH.D., Applied Physics
POTNIS, S. P., M.SC., PH.D., Polymer Technology
PRADHAN, S. K., M.SC., PH.D., Chemical Technology
REBELLO, D., PH.D., Oil Chemistry
REGE, D. V., PH.D., Food Technology
SHARMA, M. M., M.SC., PH.D., Chemical Engineering
SUNTHANKAR, S. V., PH.D., Dyestuff Technology

There are 119 constituent colleges.

RECOGNIZED POSTGRADUATE INSTITUTIONS:

Anjuman-i-Islam Urdu Research Institute: 92 Dr. Dadabhoy Nowroji Road, Bombay; f. 1946.

Bhabha Atomic Research Centre.

Bharatiya Vidya Bhavan: Chowpatty, Bombay 7; f. 1938.

Bombay Labour Institute: Parel, Bombay 12.

Bombay Natural History Society: Hornbill House, Apollo Street, Bombay 1.

Cotton Technological Research Laboratory (I.C.A.R.): Bombay 19.

Demographic and Training Research Centre: Chembur, Bombay 71.

Haffkine Institute: Parel, Bombay 12; f. 1896.

Indian Cancer Research Centre: Parel, Bombay 12; f. 1950.

Marathi Sanshodhan Mandal: Mumba, Marathi Granth Sangrahalayai Dadar, Bombay 14; f. 1948.

Prince of Wales Museum of Western India: Bombay 1.

School of Social Work—Institute of of Social Service: Nirmala Niketan, 38 New Marine Lines, Bombay 1.

Taraporewala Marine Biological Research Station: Bombay 2; f. 1945.

Tata Institute of Fundamental Research: Colaba, Bombay 5; f. 1945.

Textile Research Institute: Bombay Textile Research Association, Ghatkopar, Bombay 77.

UNIVERSITY OF BURDWAN

BURDWAN 713104,
WEST BENGAL
Telephone: Burdwan 2371/2/3.

Founded 1960; Teaching and Affiliating.

Languages of instruction: English and Bengali; Academic year: June to May.

Chancellor: H.E. GOVERNOR OF WEST BENGAL.
Vice-Chancellor: Dr. RAMARANJAN MUKHERJI.
Registrar: A. K. CHAUDHURI.
Librarian: S. K. CHAUDHURI.

The library contains 125,000 vols.
Number of teachers: 2,467.
Number of students: 58,712.

PROFESSORS:

BANERJEE, A. K., Botany
BARUA, D. K., English
BHADRA, M. K., Philosophy
BHATTACHARYYA, S. J., Philosophy
BHATTACHARYYA, S. L., English
CHAKRABORTY, R. R., Political Science
CHAKRABORTY, S. C., Physics
CHAKRABORTY, S. K., Mathematics
CHANDRA, M. C., Law
CHATTERJEE, P. K., History
CHATTERJEE, S. S., Commerce
CHATTOPADHYAY, S., Sanskrit
CHAUDHURI, D. K., Zoology
CHAUDHURI, M., Geography
DUTTA, J. G., Chemistry
DUTTA, R. L., Chemistry
GHOSE, D. K., History
MAZUMDAR, G., Zoology
MOITRA, S. K., Zoology
MUKHOPADHYAY, G. G., Sanskrit
NANDI, B., Botany
NEOGI, D., Physics
RAKSHIT, S. C., Chemistry
ROY, H. N., Economics
ROY CHOUDHURY, K. C., Economics
SEN, D. P., Philosophy
SEN, H., Mathematics
SIDHANTA, S. K., Chemistry
SINHA ROY, J. B., Bengali
VYAKARANACHARYYA, A., Sanskrit

There are 57 affiliated colleges.

UNIVERSITY OF CALCUTTA

COLLEGE ST., CALCUTTA,
WEST BENGAL 700073
Telephone: 34-3014-19.

Founded 1857; Teaching and Affiliating.

Language of instruction: English.

Chancellor: H.E. THE GOVERNOR OF WEST BENGAL (*ex officio*).
Vice-Chancellor: Dr. R. K. PODDAR.
Registrar: Dr. S. P. BANERJEE.
Librarian: S. SENGUPTA, M.A., DIP.LIB.

The library contains 472,300 vols.
Number of professors: 62.
Number of students: 234,661.

Publications: *Calendar, Review, Journal, Bulletin.*

DEANS:

Faculty of Agriculture: Prof. B. B. ROY, M.SC., PH.D.
Faculty of Arts: Prof. S. K. BHATTACHARYA, M.A., PH.D.
Faculty of Commerce: Prof. K. M. MUKHERJEE, M.A., D.PHIL.
Faculty of Dental Science: Sri S. K. SARKAR, M.B.B.S., PH.D.
Faculty of Education: Dr. G. B. KAPAT.
Faculty of Engineering: (vacant).
Faculty of Fine Arts and Music: Prof. A. K. BANERJEE, M.A., D.PHIL.
Faculty of Home Science: Sm. M. ADHIKARI, M.A.
Faculty of Journalism: Sri S. BASU, M.A.
Faculty of Law: Prof. A. TRIPATHI.
Faculty of Library Science: S. SAMANT.
Faculty of Medicine: Sri A. K. BASU, M.S., F.R.C.S., F.A.C.S.
Faculty of Science: Prof. Mrs. A. CHATTERJEE, D.SC., F.N.I.
Faculty of Social Welfare and Business Management: Prof. S. ROY, M.SC., PH.D.
Faculty of Technology: Prof. N. K. BOSE, M.SC.
Faculty of Veterinary Science: Dr. P. KAR.

PROFESSORS:

ADITYA, S., M.A., PH.D., Applied Chemistry
BAGCHI, K. G., M.SC., Geography
BANERJEE, A. K., M.A., PH.D., Bengali
BANERJEE, D., PH.D., D.SC., Chemistry
BANERJEE, P. K., M.SC., M.B.B.S., D.PHIL., Physiology
BASU, M. S., M.SC., PH.D., Radiophysics and Electronics
BASU, N. K., SC.D., Applied Chemistry
BASU, S., D.SC., Pure Chemistry
BHATTACHARYA, D. C., M.A., Economics
BHATTACHARYA, D. L., M.SC., PH.D., Pure Physics
BHATTACHARYYA, P. C., D.SC., Pure Physics
BHATTACHARYYA, S. K., M.A., PH.D., Economics
BHATTACHARYA, S. P., M.SC., PH.D., Applied Physics
BOSE, A., M.B.B.S., F.F.A.R.C. & S., F.A.A., Anaesthesiology
BOSE, K. S., M.S., F.I.C.S., F.A.M.S., Orthopaedics
BOSE, S. B., F.F.R., D.M.R.D., R.C.S.I., F.A.M.S., Radio-Diagnosis
BOSE, S. K., M.SC., PH.D., Biochemistry
CHAKI, M. C., M.A., PH.D., Pure Mathematics
CHAKRABARTI, M. M., M.SC., F.R.I.C., Applied Chemistry
CHATTERJEE, Mrs. A., D.SC., F.N.I., Pure Chemistry
CHATTERJEE, P. B., M.A., L.L.B., PH.D., Philosophy
CHAUDHURI, A. K., M.SC., D.PHIL., Radio Physics and Chemistry
CHAUDHURI, P. K., M.SC., D.PHIL., Plastics and Rubber Technology
DAS, K., M.A., DR.LITT., Bengali
DAS, T. M., M.SC., PH.D., D.I.C., Agriculture
DASGUPTA, M. K., M.SC., PH.D., Radio Physics and Electronics
DATTA, M., M.SC., PH.D., Applied Mathematics
DAW, A. N., M.SC., PH.D., Radiophysics and Electronics
DE, M. R., M.SC., D.I.C., PH.D., Applied Physics
DEB, C. C., M.SC., PH.D., Physiology
GANGULI, D. N., M.SC., PH.D., F.Z.S.I., F.N.A.SC., Zoology
GANGULI, H. C., D.SC., Botany
GANGULI, K. K., M.A., PH.D., Ancient Indian History and Culture
GHOSH, A., M.SC., PH.D., Zoology
GHOSH, A., M.A., Economics
GHOSH, J. J., D.SC., D.PHIL., Biochemistry
GHOSH, P. K., M.SC., Applied Mathematics
GHOSH, S. N., D.SC., F.N.A., Applied Physics
LODHA, K. M., M.A., Hindi
MAJUMDAR, C. K., M.SC., PH.D., Pure Physics
MITTER, M., M.B.B.S., D.M.R.T., R.C.P. & S., Radiotherapeutics
MITRA, H. P., M.A., PH.D., Bengali
MUKHERJEE, B. N., M.A., PH.D., F.S.A., Ancient Indian History and Culture
MUKHERJEE, K. M., M.A., D.PHIL., Commerce
MUKHERJEE, S., D.SC., Applied Chemistry
MUKHERJEE, S. K., D.SC., Agriculture
MUCKHERJEE, S. K., M.A., D.LITT., Political Science
NAG, B. R., M.SC.(TECH.), M.S., D.PHIL., Radio Physics
NANDY, H. K., M.SC., Statistics
PODDAR, R. K., M.SC., PH.D., Pure Physics
RAY, B. B., M.SC., PH.D., Agriculture
RAY, P. R., M.B.B.S., PH.D., Anatomy
RAY, S. N., M.SC., PH.D., Applied Psychology
SEN, S. N., D.SC., Geology
SHARMA, A. K., D.SC., Botany
SINHA, N. C., M.A., PH.D., History
TALAPATRA, S. K., M.SC., PH.D., Chemistry
TRIPATHY, A., M.A., A.M., PH.D., History

UNIVERSITY COLLEGES:

University College of Arts: f. 1954.
Secretary: Dr. A. RAY, M.A., PH.D.

University College of Commerce: f. 1954.
Secretary: Dr. A. RAY, M.A., PH.D.

University College of Law: f. 1909.
Principal: M. L. UPADHYAY, PH.D.

University College of Medicine: f. 1957.
Secretary: Dr. A. K. DATTA.

University College of Science: f. 1954.
Secretary: Dr. SAKTI PRASAD SARKAR.

University College of Technology: f. 1954.
Secretary: Dr. SAKTI PRASAD SARKAR, D.SC.

CONSTITUENT COLLEGES:

All India Institute of Hygiene and Public Health: 110 Chitaranjan Ave., Calcutta; f. 1932.
Director: B. GHOSH RAY, PH.D.

Bengal Engineering College: Botanic Gardens, Shibpur Howrah; f. 1856.
Principal: Dr. D. BANERJEE.

David Hare Training College: 25/3 Ballygunge Circular Rd., Calcutta; f. 1908.
Principal: R. C. DAS, M.A., PH.D.

Medical College: 88 College St., Calcutta; f. 1835.
Principal: B. K. CHAKRABARTI.

Presidency College: 86/1 College St., Calcutta; f. 1817.
Principal: Dr. P. C. MUKHERJEE.

R. G. Kar Medical College: 1 Balgachia Rd., Calcutta; f. 1916.
Principal: D. N. BANERJEE.

Sanskrit College: Bankim Chatterjee St., Calcutta; f. 1824.
Principal: B. P. BHATTACHARYYA.

There are 211 affiliated colleges.

UNIVERSITY OF CALICUT

P.O. CALICUT UNIVERSITY,
THENHIPALAM 673635, KERALA
Telephone: 8361/3.

Founded 1968; Teaching and Affiliating.

State control; Languages of instruction: English and Malayaam; Academic year: July to March.

Chancellor: Mrs. JYOTI VENKITACHALLEM, GOVERNOR OF KERALA.
Vice-Chancellor: Prof. K. A. JALEEL.
Pro-Vice Chancellor: Prof. N. PURUSHOTHAMAN.
Registrar: Prof. I. G. MENON (acting).
Librarian: M. BAVAKUTTY (acting).

Number of teachers: 129 (University Depts.), 3,822 (Affiliated Colleges).

Number of students: 718 (University Depts.), 80,851 (Affiliated Colleges).

Publication: *University News*† (quarterly).

DEANS:

Faculty of Science: Prof. I. G. BHASKARA PANICKER.
Faculty of Engineering: Prof. R. G. MENON.
Faculty of Commerce: Prof. K. P. R. MENON.
Faculty of Medicine: Dr. OMMANA MATHEW.
Faculty of Education: (vacant).
Faculty of Humanities, including Philosophy: Dr. M. A. FAROQUI.
Faculty of Ayurveda: Dr. P. A. RAVINDRAN.
Faculty of Law: Dr. R. PRASANNAN.
Faculty of Journalism: Dr. NADIG KRISHNA MURTHI.
Faculty of Fine Arts: Dr. C. K. REVAMMA.
Faculty of Languages and Literature: Prof. SUKUMAR AZHIKODE.

HEADS OF DEPARTMENTS:

ADIYODI, K. G., Zoology (acting)
AHAMED, S. A., Journalism
AZHICODE, S., Malayalam
FAROQI, M. A., Psychology
KUTTY, Mathematics (acting)
MENON, M. S., Sanskrit
MOHAMMED, M., Hindi
MOOSATH, S. S., Chemistry
NADAVI, S. E. A., Arabic
NAIR, A. S., Education
NAIR, B. K., Botany
NAIR, C. N. PURUSHOTHAMAN, Commerce
NAIR, Mrs. S. B., Adult Education
NARAYANAN, M. G. S., History
NIRMALA, S., Russian
OOMMEN, M. A., Economics
PALATHINGAL, J. C., Physics
PILLAI, G. S., Drama and Fine Arts
RAMAKRISHNA, T., Life Science
VARIER, I., Philosophy
VELAYADHAN, English

There are 72 affiliated colleges.

UNIVERSITY OF COCHIN

HILL PALACE P.O.,
TRIPUNITHURA,
KERALA STATE 682 301
Telephone: 7450.

Founded 1971; Federal.

State control; Language of instruction: English; Academic year: July to April.

Chancellor: H.E. THE GOVERNOR OF KERALA.
Pro-Chancellor: THE MINISTER FOR EDUCATION, KERALA STATE.
Vice-Chancellor: Prof. M. V. PYLEE.
Pro-Vice-Chancellor: Dr. K. I. VASU.
Registrar: Dr. C. N. SATYAPALAN.
Librarian: (vacant).

Number of teachers: 121.
Number of students: 874.

Publications: *Law Review*†, *Marine Science Bulletin*†, *Indian Manager, Management Information Service, Sociological Aspects of Legal Education.*

DEANS:

Faculty of Law: Hon. Justice Dr. T. K. KOCHUTHOMMAN.
Faculty of Social Sciences: Dr. N. PARAMESWARAN NAIR.
Faculty of Science: Dr. K. SATHIANANDAN.
Faculty of Marine Science: Dr. C. T. SAMUEL.
Faculty of Humanities: Dr. N. RAMAN NAIR.
Faculty of Technology: Dr. C. P. KURIAKOSE.
Faculty of Engineering: Dr. S. VASUDEV.

PROFESSORS:

ABDI, W. H., Mathematics
DORA, Y. L., Marine Sciences
FRANCIS, J., Polymer Science
GEORGE, J., Physics
GOPALAKRISHNAN NAIR, K., Electronics
KRISHNA PILLAI, M. G., Physics
LEELAKRISHNAN, P., Law
PARAMESWARAN NAIR, N., Management Studies
RAJENDRA PRASAD, P. N., Management Studies
RAMACHANDRA PODUVAL, P., Management Studies
RAMAN NAIR, N., Hindi
RENGANATHAN, N., Management Studies
SAMUEL, C. T., Industrial Fisheries
SATHIANANDAN, K., Physics
SARMA, G. S., Marine Sciences
VATAKENCHERRY, P. A., Applied Chemistry
VISWANATHA IYER, N. E., Hindi

UNIVERSITY OF DELHI

DELHI 110007
Telephone: 221421.
Founded 1922: Teaching and Affiliating.

Languages of instruction: English and Hindi; Academic year: July to April (three terms).

Chancellor: VICE-PRESIDENT OF INDIA.
Pro-Chancellor: CHIEF JUSTICE OF INDIA.
Vice-Chancellor: Prof. R. GURUBAKHSH SINGH.
Registrar: K. N. THUSU.
Librarian: Prof. A. P. SRIVASTAVA.

The library contains 679,600 vols.
Number of professors: 100.
Number of students: 150,300.

DEANS:

Faculty of Arts: Prof. A. N. KAUL.
Faculty of Science: Prof. V. K. VERMA.
Faculty of Law: Prof. D. K. SINGH.
Faculty of Medical Sciences: Dr. Mrs. SANTOSH CHAWLA.
Faculty of Education: Dr. SUNITI DUTT.
Faculty of Social Sciences: Prof. DALEEP SINGH.
Faculty of Technology: Prof. U. N. SINGH.
Faculty of Music and Fine Arts: Prof. S. MUTATKAR.
Faculty of Mathematics: Dr. S. M. SINHA.
Faculty of Mathematics: Prof. N. R. CHATTERJEE.

PRIVATE TRUST COLLEGES:

Atma Ram Sanatan Dharam College: New Delhi; f. 1959.
Daulat Ram College: Delhi 7; f. 1960.
Gyan Devi Salwan College: New Delhi; f. 1970.
Hamdard College of Pharmacy: New Delhi; f. 1973.
Hamdard Tibbi College: Delhi; f. 1977.
Hans Raj College: Delhi; f. 1948.
Hindu College: Delhi; f. 1922.
Indraprastha College for Women: Delhi; f. 1924.
Institute of Home Economics: Delhi; f. 1969.
Janki Devi Mahavidyalaya: New Delhi; f. 1959.
Jesus and Mary College: New Delhi; f. 1968.
Kirori Mal College: Delhi; f. 1954.
Lady Irwin College: New Delhi; f. 1932.
Lady Shri Ram College for Women: New Delhi; f. 1956.
Mata Sundri College: New Delhi; f. 1967.
P.G.D.A.V. College: New Delhi; f. 1957.
Ramjas College: Delhi; f. 1917.
Rao Tula Ram College: New Delhi; f. 1970.
Shri Guru Teg Bahadur Khalsa College: Karol Bagh, Delhi; f. 1951 (evening college f. 1973).
Shri Ram College of Commerce: Delhi; f. 1926.
Shyam Lal College: Delhi; f. 1964.
Sri Venkateswara College: New Delhi; f. 1961.
St. Stephen's College: Delhi; f. 1881.
Zakir Hussain College: Delhi; f. 1924.

DELHI ADMINISTRATION COLLEGES:

Bhagat Singh College: New Delhi; f. 1967.
Bharati Mahila College: New Delhi; f. 1971.
Gargi College: New Delhi; f. 1957.
Kalindi College: New Delhi; f. 1967.
Kamla Nehru College: New Delhi; f. 1964.
Lakshmibai College: Delhi; f. 1965.
Maitreyi College: New Delhi; f. 1967.
Moti Lal Nehru College: New Delhi; f. 1964.
Rajdhani College: New Delhi; f. 1964.
Satyawati Co-educational College: Delhi f. 1972.
Shivaji College: New Delhi; f. 1961.
Shri Aurobindo College: New Delhi; f. 1972.
Shyama Prasad Mukherjee College: New Delhi; f. 1969.
Swami Shardhanand College: Delhi; f. 1967.
Vivekanand Mahila College: Delhi; f. 1970.

UNIVERSITY MAINTAINED COLLEGES:

Central Institute of Education: Delhi; f. 1948.
Delhi School of Social Work: f. 1948.
Deshbandhu College: Kalkaji, New Delhi; f. 1952.
Dyal Singh College: New Delhi; f. 1959.
Miranda House for Women: Delhi; f. 1948.
School of Correspondence Courses and Continuing Education: Delhi; f. 1962.
University College of Medical Sciences: Delhi; f. 1971.
Vallabhbhai Patel Chest Institute: Delhi; f. 1955.
College of Vocational Studies: New Delhi; f. 1972.
Ram Lal Anand College: New Delhi; f. 1964.

GOVERNMENT COLLEGES:

Ayurvedic and Unani Tabbia College: New Delhi; f. 1973.
College of Art: New Delhi; f. 1972.
College of Nursing: New Delhi; f. 1948.
College of Pharmacy: New Delhi; f. 1971.
Delhi College of Engineering: Kashmeri Gate, Delhi 6; f. 1959.
Lady Hardinge Medical College: New Delhi; f. 1916.
Maulana Azad Medical College: New Delhi; f. 1958.
School of Planning and Architecture: New Delhi; f. 1959.

DIBRUGARH UNIVERSITY

RAJABHETA, DIBRUGARH 786004, ASSAM

Telephone: Dibrugarh 630.

Founded 1965; Affiliating and Teaching.

State control; Languages of instruction: Assamese and English; Academic year: August to June.

Chancellor: H.E. THE GOVERNOR OF ASSAM.

Vice-Chancellor: Dr. S. D. GOGOI.

Registrar: D. PATHAK, M.SC., B.L.

Librarian: A. K. TALUKDAR, M.A., M.L.I.SC.

The library contains 97,360 vols.

Number of teachers: 110 (University Depts.).

Number of students: 800 (University Depts.).

Publications: *The North Eastern Research Bulletin* (irregular), *Assam Economic Journal, Bulletin of the Department of Anthropology, Journal of the Department of Assamese.*

PROFESSORS:

BARUA, K. C., Physics
BHAGAWATI, A. C., Anthropology
BORA, M. N., Assamese
BOSE, T. C., Political Science
CHOUDHURY, R. C., Life Sciences
DATTA, A., English
DUBEY, S. M., Sociology
FULORIA, R. C., Applied Geology
HAQUE, I., Chemistry
MEHROTRA, R., Economics
SAXENA, R. C., Commerce
SRIVASTAVA, A. C., Mathematics

There are 50 affiliated colleges.

GARHWAL UNIVERSITY

SRINAGAR, GARHWAL DIST., U.P. 246174.

Telephone: 67.

Founded 1973; Teaching and Affiliating.
Languages of instruction: Hindi and English; Academic year: July to June.

Chancellor: H.E. THE GOVERNOR OF UTTAR PRADESH.

Vice-Chancellor: U. C. GHILDYAL.

Registrar: P. L. CHHABRA.

Library of 10,000 vols.

Number of teachers: 600.

Number of students: 15,000.

DEANS:

Faculty of Arts: Prof. T. G. PRASAD.

Faculty of Science: Prof. I. P. VARSHNEY.

Faculty of Commerce: Dr. S. C. SAXENA.

Faculty of Education: (vacant).

Faculty of Law: R. P. DHOBAL.

There are 3 constituent and 16 affiliated colleges.

GAUHATI UNIVERSITY

GAUHATI 781014, ASSAM

Telephone: 88412, 88415.

Founded 1948; Teaching, Residential and Affiliating.

Language of instruction: English; Academic year: July to June (three terms).

Chancellor: H.E. THE GOVERNOR OF ASSAM.

Vice-Chancellor: Dr. J. M. CHOUDHURY.

Registrar: M. C. BHUYAN.

Librarian: J. SHARMA, M.A., DIP. IN LIB. SC.

The library contains 148,257 vols.

Number of students: 90,779.

DEANS:

Faculty of Arts: Dr. V. B. MISHRA.
Faculty of Commerce: Dr. A. K. SARMA.
Faculty of Science: Dr. N. N. S. SIDDHANTA.
Faculty of Medicine: Dr. J. C. MAHANTA.
Faculty of Law: K. N. SARMA.
Faculty of Engineering: D. GOSWAMI.

HEADS OF DEPARTMENTS:

BAROOAH, D. P., Political Science
BORA, K. P., Education
CHOUDHURY, B., Physics
DAS, B. M., Anthropology
GOSWAMI, P. D., Folklore Research
KAGTI, L. C., Botany
MEDHI, J. P., Statistics
MISHRA, V. B., History
SARMA, M. M., Sanskrit
SIDDHANTA, N. N. S., Chemistry

CONSTITUENT COLLEGE:

University Law College.
Principal: A. HUSSAIN, LL.M.

There are 128 affiliated colleges.

GORAKHPUR UNIVERSITY

GORAKHPUR, U.P. 273001

Telephone: 201.

Founded 1957; Teaching and Affiliating.

Languages of instruction: Hindi and English; Academic year: July to April (two terms).

Chancellor: H.E. THE GOVERNOR OF UTTAR PRADESH.

Vice-Chancellor: Prof. H. S. CHAUDHARY.

Registrar: CHANDER BHAN.

Librarian: R. S. GOYAL.

The library contains 152,000 vols.

Number of teachers: *c.* 200, including 10 professors.

Number of students: 115,000, including students of the colleges.

DEANS:

Faculty of Agriculture: Prof. K. S. BHARGAVA.
Faculty of Arts: Prof. V. S. PATHAK.
Faculty of Science: Prof. R. P. RASTOGI.
Faculty of Commerce: Dr. R. L. AGRAWAL.
Faculty of Law: Prof. U. R. RAI.
Faculty of Engineering: Dr. M. S. MURTHY.

There are 1 constituent college and 91 affiliated colleges.

GOVIND BALLABH PANT UNIVERSITY OF AGRICULTURE AND TECHNOLOGY

PANTNAGAR, NAINITAL, 263145 UTTAR PRADESH

Founded 1960.

Telephone: Rudrapur 1/30.

Languages of instruction: English and Hindi; State control; Academic year: July to June (three terms).

Chancellor: H.E. THE GOVERNOR OF UTTAR PRADESH.

Vice-Chancellor: Sri N. S. MATHUR, I.A.S.

Registrar: O. S. MISRA.

Librarian: R. TIRTH, M.SC., M.LIB.SC.

Library of 193,000 vols.

Number of teachers: 345.

Number of students: 2,500.

Publications: *G. B. Pant University of Agriculture and Technology* (fortnightly), *Pantnagar Patrika, Indian Farmers Digest, Kisan BHARTI.*

DEANS:

Faculty of Agriculture: Dr. R. P. CHAUDHRY.
Faculty of Basic Sciences and Humanities: Dr. K. G. GOLLAKOTA.
Faculty of Veterinary Medicine: Dr. I. P. SINGH.
Faculty of Technology: Dr. M. CHOUDHRY.
Faculty of Home Science: Mrs. S. SHINDE.
Faculty of Postgraduate Studies: Dr. K. G. GOLLAKOTA.

There are 6 constituent colleges and 29 teaching departments.

GUJARAT UNIVERSITY

NAVRANGPURA, AHMEDABAD 380009, GUJARAT STATE

Telephone: 40341.

Founded 1950; Teaching and Affiliating.

Languages of instruction: Gujarati, Hindi and English; Academic year: June to March (two terms).

Chancellor: H.E. THE GOVERNOR OF GUJARAT.

Vice-Chancellor: Dr. P. C. VAIDYA.

Registrar: Shri K. C. PARIKH, M.A., LL.B.

Librarian: Shri P. F. PATEL, M.A., M.LIB.SC.

The library contains 236,000 vols.

Number of students in affiliated colleges: 120,400.

DEANS:

Faculty of Arts, including Education: Shri AMBUBHAI T. DESAI.
Faculty of Commerce: Prin. B. M. PEERZADA.
Faculty of Dental Surgery: Dr. K. BHARGAV.
Faculty of Law: Prin. P. R. DESAI.
Faculty of Medicine: Dr. C. I. JHALA.
Faculty of Pharmacy: G. M. CHAUHAN.
Faculty of Science: Dr. M. N. DESAI.
Faculty of Technology, including Engineering: Prin. K. J. BHATT.

There are 147 affiliated colleges.

RECOGNIZED INSTITUTIONS:

Ahmedabad Textile Industry's Research Association: Ahmedabad 15; f. 1953.

Physical Research Laboratory: Navrangpura, Ahmedabad 9; f. 1948.

Sardar Patel Institute of Economics and Social Research: Thaltej, Ahmedabad 15; f. 1971.

Seth Kanaiyalal Motilal School of Postgraduate Medicine and Research: Ellis Bridge, Ahmedabad 6; f. 1931.

Shri Lalbhai Dalpathbhai Bharatiya Shanskriti Vidya Mandir: Navrangpura, Ahmedabad 9; f. 1963.

Sheth Bholabhai Jesingbhai Institute of Learning and Research: R.C. Rd., Ahmedabad 9; f. 1939.

B. M. Institute: Near Nehru Bridge, Ahmedabad 9; f. 1972.

National Institute of Occupational Health: opp. New Mental Hospital, Meghaninagar, Asarwa, Ahmedabad 16; f. 1973.

GUJARAT AGRICULTURAL UNIVERSITY

SARDARKRISHINAGAR 385506, DANTIWADA, DIST. BANASKANTHA, GUJARAT.

Telephone: 65588.

Founded 1969.

Chancellor: H.E. THE GOVERNOR OF GUJARAT.
Vice-Chancellor: I. J. PATEL.
Registrar: M. P. VAISHNAV.

Library of 2,000 vols.

Number of students: 1,800.

DEANS:

Faculty of Agriculture: Dr. H. C. MEHTA.
Faculty of Sciences and Humanities: Prof. P. D. MISTRY.
Faculty of Veterinary Science: Prof. A. D. DAVE.
Faculty of Dairy Science: Dr. J. R. PATEL.
Post-Graduate Research: Dr. D. R. MUDHOLKER.

CONSTITUENT COLLEGES:

Agricultural College: Junagadh; Principal M. V. KANZARIA.

Bansilal Amritlal College of Agriculture: Anand; Principal A. M. MAJDUMAR.

Dairy Science College: Principal J. R. PATEL.

Gujarat College of Veterinary Science and Animal Husbandry: Anand; Principal D. R. MUDHOLKER.

Shri Navinchandra Mafatlal College of Agriculture: Navsari; Principal H. C. MEHTA.

GUJARAT AYURVED UNIVERSITY

JAMNAGAR, GUJARAT

Telephone: 2038.

Founded 1966; Affiliating and Teaching.

Languages of instruction: Gujarati, Hindi, English and Sanskrit; Academic year: June to April (two terms).

Chancellor: H. E. THE GOVERNOR OF GUJARAT.
Vice-Chancellor: RAJUAIDYA RASIKLAL J. PARIKH.
Registrar: D. M. JOSHI.
Director of Pharmacy: D. PANDEY.
Dean of Faculty: V. J. THAKAR.

Library of 19,128 vols.

Number of students: 1,461.

There are 1 constituent college, 1 University department, and 9 affiliated colleges.

GUJARAT VIDYAPITH

AHMEDABAD 380014, GUJARAT

Telephone: 446148, 446349, 446547.

Founded 1920; University status 1963.

Language of instruction: Gujarati.

Vice-Chancellor: DAHYABHAI NAIK.
Registrar: V. R. TRIPATHI.
Librarian: KANUBHAI SHAH.

Number of teachers: 58.

Number of students: 389.

Publication: *Vidyapith* (every 2 months).

Faculties of Education and Social Sciences.

GURU NANAK DEV UNIVERSITY

AMRITSAR

Telephone: 4-8757/8.

Founded 1969; Affiliating and Teaching.

Languages of Instruction: Punjabi, Hindi and English.

Chancellor: THE GOVERNOR OF PUNJAB.
Vice-Chancellor: S. KARAM SINGH GILL.
Registrar: S. JAGJIT SINGH KHANNA.
Librarian: S. KIRPAL SINGH.

The library contains 171,000 vols.

Number of teachers: 2,177.

Number of students: 53,581.

Publications: *University Samachar*† (6 a year), *Khoj Darpan* (2 a year), *Journal of Sikh Studies* (English, 2 a year), *Journal of Chemical Sciences* (English, 2 a year), *Law Journal* (English, quarterly), *Economic Analyst* (English, 2 a year), *Punjab Journal of Politics, Calendar* (annually), *Annual Report.*

DEANS:

Faculty of Education: Mrs. L. B. NATH.
Faculty of Medical Sciences: Dr. C. PHILLIPS.
Faculty of Dental Sciences: Dr. ISHAS SINGH AHLUWALIA.
Faculty of Languages: Dr. HARSHARAN SINGH.
Faculty of Agriculture and Forestry: Dr. SUKHEV SINGH.
Faculty of Fine Arts and Architecture: Dr. SHANKAR LAL MISRA.
Faculty of Arts and Social Sciences: Dr. R. S. JOHAR.
Faculty of Sciences: Dr. S. S. SANDHU.
Faculty of Humanities and Religious Studies: Prof. PRITAM SINGH.
Faculty of Physical Planning: Dr. P. C. KHANNA.
Faculty of Ayurvedic Medicine: R. D. SHARMA.
Faculty of Business Administration and Commerce: Dr. R. S. JOHAR.
Faculty of Law: S. S. SANDHAWALIA.

HEADS OF DEPARTMENTS:

Biology: Dr. RAJINDER SINGH SANDHU.
Chemistry: Dr. S. S. SANDHU.
Mathematics: Dr. SURJIT SINGH.
Psychology: Dr. P. S. HUNDAL.
History: Dr. J. S. GREWAL.
Political Science: Dr. K. C. MARKANDAN.
Library Science: S. KIRPAL SINGH.
Punjab School of Economics: Dr. R. S. JOHAR.
Sociology: Dr. JASPAL SINGH.
English: Dr. HARSHARAN SINGH.
Hindi: Dr. R. K. MEGH.
Punjabi, Urdu and Persian: Dr. DEWAN SINGH.
Punjabi Language, Literature and Culture: Dr. KARNAIL SINGH THIND.
Law: Dr. KIRPAL SINGH.
Guru Nanak Studies: SARDAR PRITAL SINGH.
Guru Ram Dass Postgraduate School of Planning: Shri P. C. KHANNA.

There are 75 affiliated colleges.

HARYANA AGRICULTURAL UNIVERSITY

HISSAR-125004, HARYANA STATE

Telephone: 2294.

Founded 1970.

State control; Language of instruction: English; Academic year: July to June.

Chancellor: H.E. THE GOVERNOR OF HARYANA.

Vice-Chancellor: Dr. P. S. LAMBA.

Registrar: V. KUMAR.

Number of teachers: 285.

Number of students: 2,019.

Library of 138,686 vols.

Publications: *Journal of Research*†, *Thesis Abstracts*† (quarterly), *Haryana Kheti* (monthly), *Haryana Farming* (every 2 months).

DEANS:

College of Agriculture: Dr. D. S. GUPTA.
College of Agriculture, Kaul: O. P. SINGH.
College of Animal Sciences: Dr. K. PRADHAN.
College of Basic Sciences and Humanities: Dr. S. N. KAKAR.
College of Home Science: Dr. R. N. PAL.
College of Veterinary Science: Dr. L. D. DHINGRA.
Postgraduate Studies: Dr. R. P. S. TYAGI.
Sports College: Dr. S. SRINIVASAN.

PROFESSORS

College of Agriculture:

ARORA, N. D., Plant Breeding
BHATTI, D. S., Nematology
CHAND, J. N., Plant Pathology
GROVER, R. K., General Plant Pathology
GUPTA, D. S., Economic Entomology and Taxology
SHUKLA, U. C., Soil Fertility and Chemistry
SINGH, KIRTI, Olericulture
SINGH, Y. P., Communication and Research Methods

College of Veterinary Sciences:

AHMED, A., Pharmacology and Toxicology
DHINGRA, L. D., Anatomy
DUTT, S. C., Surgery
GAUTAM, O. P., Medicine
GUPTA, R. C., Veterinary Gynaecology
KALRA, D. S., Pathology, Public Health and Epidemiology
MALIK, P. D., Parasitology, Helminthology
NIGAM, J. M., Surgery, Anaesthesiology
SHARMA, V. K., Bacteriology

College of Animal Sciences:

PAL, R. N., Dairy Science and Technology
PANDA, P. C., Food Technology
PRADHAN, K., Nutrition
RAZDAN, M. N., Environmental Physiology, Dairy Cattle Physiology and Nutrition
SINGH BALAINE, DAYA, Genetics and Breeding

College of Basic Sciences and Humanities:

CHAUDHRY, J. B., Cytogenetics
GARG, O. P., Plant Physiology
KAPIL, R. P., Zoology, Entomology, Applied Biology (Radiation Biology)
SINGH, I. J., Production Economics, Farm Management, Agricultural Policy
SRIVASTAVA, O. P., Statistics
TAURO, P., Molecular Biology
WAGLE, D. S., Enzymology, Nutritional Biochemistry, Lipid Metabolism, Amino Acids, Novel Proteins

HIMACHAL PRADESH KRISHI VISHVA VIDYALAYA (H.P. Agricultural University)

PALAMPUR 176062, KANGRA

Telephone: 177.

Founded 1978; formerly Faculty of Agriculture of Himachal Pradesh University.

Vice-Chancellor: Dr. H. R. KALIA.

Registrar: A. S. BAJWA.

Librarian: C. D. HANDA.

Library of 18,568 vols., 6,951 periodidicals.

Number of teachers: 291.

Number of students: 786.

DEANS:

Postgraduate Studies (Solan Campus): Dr. D. R. THAKUR.
College of Agriculture (Solan Campus): Dr. O. P. AWASTHI.
College of Agriculture (Palampur Campus): Dr. B. R. TRIPATHI.
Director of Research: Dr. R. S. KANWAR.
Agricultural Extension Education: Dr. J. R. BHAMBOTA.

HIMACHAL PRADESH UNIVERSITY

SUMMER HILL, SIMLA 171005

Telephone: 3916, 5138, 3673.

Founded 1970; Affiliating and Teaching.

State control; Languages of inscruction: English and Hindi; Academic year: July to May.

Chancellor: H.E. THE GOVERNOR OF HIMACHAL PRADESH.

Vice-Chancellor: B. C. NEGI, I.A.S.

Registrar: Dr. K. D. GUPTA.

Librarian: Dr. R. L. MITTAL.

Number of teachers: 106.

Number of students: 1,334.

DEANS:

Faculty of Science: Dr. S. N. DUBE.
Faculty of Law: Dr. B. R. CHAUHAN.
Faculty of Arts: Dr. SOM P. SHARMA.
Faculty of Education: Dr. K. P. PANDEY.
Faculty of Commerce and Business Management: Dr. R. N. SINGH.
Faculty of Medicine: Dr. A. N. MEHROTRA.

There are 24 affiliated colleges and eight Sanskrit associated colleges.

UNIVERSITY OF HYDERABAD

CENTRAL UNIVERSITY P.O., HYDERABAD, ANDHRA PRADESH 500134

Telephone: 31275.

Founded 1974; Teaching.

State control; Language of instruction: English.

Chancellor: (vacant).

Vice-Chancellor: (vacant).

Registrar: P. V. GEORGE.

Librarian: (vacant).

Number of teachers: *c.* 100.

Number of students: *c.* 500.

PROFESSORS:

AGARWAL, G. S., Physics
BALASUBRAMANIAN, D., Chemistry
BHATNAGAR, A. K., Physics
CHANDRASEKHARA RAO, R. V. R., Political Science
GANDHI, R. C., Philosophy
JAIN, G. C., Urdu
KUMAR, S. K., English
LAL, K. S., History
MASALDAN, P. N., Political Science
MEHTA, G., Chemistry
NAGARAJAN, S., English
RADHAKRISHNA, R., Economics
RADHAKRISHNAN, A. N., Biochemistry
RAMA DAS, V. S., Plant Sciences
RAMAMURTHY, P. S., Animal Sciences
RAWAT, C. B., Hindi
REDDY, A. R., Mathematics
SINGH, H. N., Plant Sciences
SUBBA RAO, K., Animal Sciences
VEERABHADRA RAO, K., Telugu
VENKATRAMAN, M., Mathematics

INDIRA KALA SANGIT UNIVERSITY

KHAIRAGARH 491881, MADHYA PRADESH

Telephone: 32 and 34.

Founded 1956; Teaching and Affiliating.

Languages of instruction: Hindi and English; Academic year: July to June (two terms).

Chancellor: H.E. THE GOVERNOR OF MADHYA PRADESH.

Vice-Chancellor: Dr. A. K. SEN.

Registrar: D. K. GHOSH.

Deputy Librarian: K. B. SUNDARESAN.

Number of teachers: 350.

Number of students: 6,230.

Publications: *Shiv Mangalam, Bharat Bhashyam, Bhathkhande Smriti Granth, Kala Sauabh.*

DEANS:

Faculty of Music: V. K. JOSHI.
Faculty of Dance: Mrs. RASHMI BAJPAI.
Faculty of Fine Arts and Arts: Mrs. MADHURIMA SEKHAR.
Faculty of Painting: R. M. SINHA.

There are 29 affiliated colleges.

UNIVERSITY OF INDORE

UNIVERSITY HOUSE, INDORE 452-001, MADHYA PRADESH

Telephone: 5615 (Old Campus), 4688 (New Campus).

Founded 1964; Teaching and Affiliating.

Languages of instruction: Hindi and English; Private control; Academic year: July to April (three terms).

Chancellor: H.E. THE GOVERNOR OF MADHYA PRADESH.

Vice-Chancellor: Dr. D. SHARMA.

Registrar: M. L. TIWARI (acting).

Librarian: A. L. WADIKAR.

Library of 96,772 vols.

Number of teachers: 886.

Number of students: 20,770.

Publications: *Research Journal—Humanities and Social Sciences*†, *Research Journal—Science*† (2 a year).

DEANS:

Faculty of Arts: Dr. H. R. DHOLKIA.
Faculty of Ayurved: Dr. B. VERMA.
Faculty of Science: Dr. BHAGWANDAS.
Faculty of Technology: Dr. BHAGWANDAS.
Faculty of Law: A. K. SHARDA.
Faculty of Education: Dr. B. K. PASSI.
Faculty of Engineering: S. S. NIYOGI.
Faculty of Commerce: Dr. R. D. AGRAWAL.
Faculty of Home Science: Dr. M. M. LALORAYA.
Faculty of Social Sciences: Dr. V. D. NAGAR.
Faculty of Medicine: Dr. B. B. L. MATHUR.
Faculty of Life Sciences: Dr. M. M. LALORAYA.

There are 21 constituent and affiliated colleges.

JABALPUR UNIVERSITY

SARASWATI VIHAR,
JABALPUR, M.P. 482001

Telephone: 23567, 23568, 23569

Founded 1957; Teaching and Affiliating.

Languages of instruction: Hindi and English; Academic year: July to April (three terms).

Chancellor: H.E. THE GOVERNOR OF MADHYA PRADESH (*ex officio*).

Vice-Chancellor: K. CHAUDHURI.

Registrar: R. N. TRIPATHI.

Library of 12,3737 vols.

Number of teachers: 936.

Number of students: 17,590.

DEANS:

Faculty of Arts: Dr. TRILOCHAN PANDEY.
Faculty of Science: Dr. T. S. MURTY.
Faculty of Commerce: Dr. S. C. DIWAKAR.
Faculty of Education: Shri K. D. PANDEY.
Faculty of Law: Dr. P. L. SHRIVASTVA.
Faculty of Engineering: Prof. N. L. JAIN.
Faculty of Ayurveda: Dr. M. P. PANDEY.
Faculty of Home Science: M. MUDHOLKER.
Faculty of Medicine: Dr. S. L. AGRAWAL.
Faculty of Life Science: Dr. G. P. AGRAWAL.
Faculty of Social Sciences: Dr. P. CHANDRA.

There are 27 affiliated Colleges.

JADAVPUR UNIVERSITY

CALCUTTA 700032

Telephone: 72-4043.

Founded 1955; Residential and Teaching.

Language of instruction: English; Academic year: July to June (two terms).

Chancellor: H.E. THE GOVERNOR OF WEST BENGAL.

Vice-Chancellor: Prof. M. M. CHAKRABARTHY.

Registrar: A. K. GUPTA.

Finance Office: T. BHATTACHARYYA.

Chief Librarian: A. K. OHDEDAR.

Library: 292,917 vols.

Number of teachers: 506.

Number of students: 5,000.

DEANS:

Faculty of Engineering and Technology: Prof. J. K. CHAUDHURI.

Faculty of Science: Prof. R. N. BHATTACHARYA.

Faculty of Arts: Prof. A. GHOSH.

HEADS OF DEPARTMENTS:

BANERJEE, A. K., Architecture
BANERJEE, K. K., Philosophy
BHATTACHARYA, Dr. D., Bengali
BHATTACHARYA, Dr. R. N., Mathematics
CHATTERJEE, Dr. J. S., Instrumentation and Electronics Engineering
CHOWDHURY, Dr. A., Physics
DAS, Dr. M. N., Chemistry
DASGUPTA, Dr. J. B., International Relations
DUTT, D. K., Chemical Engineering
DUTTA, Dr. K. S., English
GOSWAMI, Dr. S., Sanskrit
GUHA, Dr. N., Literature
GUPTA, B. K., Pharmacy
MAJUMDER, Dr. S. K., Food Technology
MUKHERJEA, Dr. A., History
MUKHERJEE, Dr. B., Geological Sciences
MUKHERJEE, Dr. B. C., Mechanical Engineering
PATRA, Dr. S. P., Electrical Engineering
ROY, S., Metallurgical Engineering
SOM, P. K., Civil Engineering

JAMIA MILLIA ISLAMIA

JAMIA NAGAR,
NEW DELHI 110025

Telephone: 631717, 630490.

Founded 1920.

Autonomous control (government financed); Languages of instruction: Urdu, Hindi and English; Academic year: July to April.

Chancellor: Mr. Justice M. HIDAYATULLAH.

Vice-Chancellor: Shri ANWAR JAMAL KIDWAI.

Registrar: Shri SHARIFUL HASAN NAQVI.

Librarian: Shri SHAHABUDDIN ANSARI.

Library of 139,399 vols.

Number of teachers: 234.

Number of students: 3,138.

Publications: *Jamia Monthly* (in Urdu), *Islam and the Modern Age* (quarterly, English), *Islam Aur Asr-i-Jadeed* (quarterly, Urdu), Student magazines (in Urdu, Hindi, English).

DEANS:

Faculty of Education: ABDUL HAQ KHAN.

Faculty of Humanities and Sciences: ZIYA-UL-HASAN FARUQI.

HEADS OF DEPARTMENTS:

Faculty of Humanities and Sciences:
Urdu: Prof. GOPI CHAND NARANG.
Islamic and Arab-Iranian Studies: Prof. MUSHIRUL HAQ.
Social Work and Applied Social Sciences: Prof. SHAMSUR RAHMAN MOHSINI.
Economics: Prof. M. RAHMET ALI.
Political Science: Prof. ALI ASHRAF.
History and Culture: Dr. MURHIRUL HASAN.
Hindi: Shri MUJEEB HUSAIN RIZVI.
English: Shri ANWAR AHMAD SIDDIQI.
Physics: Dr. ZAHID HUSAIN ZAIDI.
Chemistry: Dr. S. IFTIKHAR ALI.
Mathematics: Dr. ARUNA KAPUR.
Geography: Dr. QAZI MOHAMMAD AHMAD.
Technology: Shri JALALUDDIN.

Faculty of Education:
Foundations of Education: Dr. M. ABU BAKER.
Teacher Training and Non-Formal Education: Dr. S. P. RUHELA.
Fine Arts and Crafts: Shri A. RAMACHANDRAN NAIR.

ATTACHED INSTITUTE:

Zakir Husain Institute of Islamic Studies: Dir. Shri ZIHA-UL-HASAN FARUQI.

UNIVERSITY OF JAMMU

CANAL RD., JAMMU (TAWI) 180001

Telephone: 7157, 7164.

Founded 1969; Affiliating and Teaching.

Language of instruction: English; Academic year: January to December (two terms).

Chancellor: L. K. JHA, H.E. THE GOVERNOR OF JAMMU AND KASHMIR.

Vice-Chancellor: Prof. S. C. DUBE.

Registrar: J. R. RATHORE.

Library of 148,556 vols.

Number of teachers: 210.
Number of students: 7,188.

DEANS:

Faculty of Arts: Dr. S. CHANDRA.
Faculty of Commerce: Dr. N. S. GUPTA.
Faculty of Education: Prof. V. R. TANEJA.
Faculty of Law: S. G. SINGH.
Faculty of Oriental Learning: Dr. V. GAHI.
Faculty of Science: Dr. T. R. SHARMA.
Faculty of Social Sciences: Prof. INDERJIT SINGH.
Faculty of Ayurvedic Medicine: Dr. S. N. TULI.
Faculty of Music and Fine Arts: Shri TK JALALI.
Faculty of Medicine: Dr. N. S. PATHANIA.
Student Welfare: Dr. V. N. GUPTA.

CONSTITUENT COLLEGES:

Govt. Ayurvedic College: Jammu; f. 1960.
Principal: Dr. S. N. TULI.

Govt. Medical College: Jammu; f. 1972.
Principal: Dr. N. S. PATHANIA.

Teachers' Training College: Jammu; f. 1954.
Principal: Shri O. P. BARU.

There are 10 affiliated colleges.

JAWAHARLAL NEHRU KRISHI VISHWA VIDYALALA
(Jawaharlal Nehru Agricultural University)

P.B. 80, KRISHNAGAR, JABALPUR 482004 (M.P.)
Telephone: 23771, 23772, 23773, 23608, 25221.
Founded 1964.

Languages of instruction: Hindi and English; Academic year: July to June (two terms).

Chancellor: H.E. THE GOVERNOR OF MADHYA PRADESH.
Vice-Chancellor: Dr. SUKHDEV SINGH.
Registrar: A. B. SHARMA.
Librarian: (vacant).

Library of 118,216 vols.
Number of students: 2,102.
Publications: *JNKVV News*† (quarterly), *JNKVV Research Journal*† (quarterly), *Krishi Vishwa*† (monthly).

DEANS:

Agriculture: Shri M. P. SINGH.
Veterinary Science and Animal Husbandry: Dr. B. S. MALIK.
Agricultural Engineering: Shri S. V. ARYA.

FACULTY OF AGRICULTURE

DEANS OF COLLEGES:

Jabalpur Agricultural College: Shri M. P. SINGH.
Gwalior Agriculture College: Dr. B. P. TIWARI.
Rewa Agriculture College: S. K. SINGH GOUR.
Sehore Agriculture College: Dr. S. N. DUBE.
Raipur Agriculture College: Dr. V. P. SHUKLA.
Indore Agricultural College: Dr. L. K. JOSHI.

HEADS OF DEPARTMENTS:

CHOUBEY, Dr. S. D., Agronomy
JAIN, A. C. Plant Pathology
MISHRA, R. S., Agricultural Economics and Farm Management
NAIR, P. K. R., Horticulture
RAWAT, R. R., Entomology
SINGH, S. P., Plant Breeding
SINHA, S. B., Soil Science and Agricultural Chemistry
VARMA, A. K., Extension Education

FACULTY OF VETERINARY SCIENCE AND ANIMAL HUSBANDRY

DEANS OF COLLEGES:

Jabalpur Veterinary College: Dr. B. S. MALIK.
Mhow Veterinary College: Dr. Y. B. RANGNEKAR.

HEADS OF DEPARTMENTS:

JOHAR, K. S., Animal Breeding and Genetics
MEHTA, M. L., Medicine
MEHTA, R. K., Pharmacology
NETKE, S. P., Animal Nutrition
PATEL, M. R., Surgery, Obstetrics and Gynaecology
RANGNEKAR, Y. B., Biochemistry
SAXENA, S. P., Microbiology
SEXENA, S. K., Physiology
SHAH, H. L., Parasitology
VEGAD, J. L., Veterinary Pathology

FACULTY OF AGRICULTURAL ENGINEERING

College of Agricultural Engineering: Dean Shri S. V. ARYA.

HEAD OF DEPARTMENT:

SHRIVASTAVA, R., Soil and Water Engineering.

JAWAHARLAL NEHRU UNIVERSITY

NEW MEHRAULI RD., NEW DELHI 110067
Telephone: 652282.
Founded 1969.

Chancellor: (vacant).
Vice-Chancellor: K. R. NARAYANAN.
Registrar: P. N. SHARMA.
Finance Officer: GOPAL SINGH.
Librarian: Shri GIRJA KUMAR.

The library contains 250,000 vols.
Number of teachers: 349.
Number of students: 3,217.

DEANS:

School of International Studies: Prof. K. P. MISRA.
School of Languages: Prof. NAMWAR SINGH.
School of Social Sciences: Prof. BIPAN CHANDRA.
School of Life Sciences: Prof. P. C. KESAVAN.
School of Environmental Sciences: J. M. DAVE.
Centre of Post-Graduate Studies, Imphal: H. RANBIR SINGH (Director).
School of Computer and Systems Sciences: Prof. D. K. BANERJEE.

HEADS OF CENTRES:

School of International Studies:

Centre for West Asian and African Studies: Prof. M. S. AGWANI, M.A., M.SS., PH.D.
Centre for Studies in Diplomacy, International Law and Economics: Prof. RAHWATULLA KHAN, LL.M., PH.D.
Centre for East Asian Studies: Prof. P. A. N. MURTHY, M.A., PH.D.
Centre for International Politics and Organization: Prof. K. P. SAKSENA, M.A., PH.D.
Centre for Soviet and East European Studies: Dr. R. R. SHARMA, M.A., PH.D.
Centre for South, South-East and Central Asian Studies: Prof. L. S. BARAL, M.A., PH.D.

School of Languages:

Centre of African and Asian Languages: Shri A. W. AZHAR, M.A., D.LITT.
Centre of French Studies: Dr. (Mrs.) A. KURTI, M.A. PH.D.
Centre of German Studies: R. P. JAIN, M.A., PH.D.
Centre for Indian Language: Dr. M. HASAN, M.A., PH.D.
Centre of Russian Studies: Prof. R. S. BAGGA, PH.D.
Centre of Spanish Studies: VASANT G. GACHE, M.A.
Centre of Linguistics and English: D. S. DIWEDI, M.LITT., PH.D.

School of Social Sciences:

Centre for Political Studies: Prof. RASHEEDUDDIN KHAN, M.A., PH.D.
Centre for the Study of Regional Development: Prof. MOONIS RAZA, M.A.
Centre of Social Medicine and Community Health: Dr. Mrs. P. RAMALINGASWAMI, M.A., PH.D.
Centre for the Study of Social Systems: Prof. R. K. JAIN, M.A., PH.D.
Centre for Historical Studies: Prof. S. BHATTACHARYA, M.A., D.PHIL.
Zakir Husain Centre of Educational Studies: Prof. YOGINDRA SINGH, M.A., PH.D.
Centre for Economic Studies and Planning: Dr. ANJAN MUKHERJI, M.A., PH.D.
University Instrumentation Centre: Prof. B. R. NAGAR.

JAWAHARLAL NEHRU TECHNOLOGICAL UNIVERSITY

HUMAYUN NAGAR,
HYDERABAD 500028
Telephone: 31745/31748.

Founded 1972.

Chancellor: H.E. THE GOVERNOR OF ANDHRA PRADESH.
Vice-Chancellor: Dr. N. S. RAO.
Registrar: Prof. T. V. REDDY.

The University has 4 constituent colleges: Engineering College, Anantapur; Engineering College, Kakinada; Nagarjunasagar Engineering College, Hyderabad; College of Fine Arts and Architecture, Hyderabad.

JIWAJI UNIVERSITY

VIDYA VIHAR,
GWALIOR 474002,
MADHYA PRADESH
Telephone: 20095.

Founded 1964; Teaching and Affiliating.

Languages of instruction: Hindi and English; Academic year: July to June.

Chancellor: H.E. THE GOVERNOR OF MADHYA PRADESH.
Vice-Chancellor: Dr. H. SWARUP.
Registrar: **Shri A. K. BHATTACHARYA.**
Librarian: Shri P. K. BANERJEA.

Library of 52,000 vols.

Number of students: 34,121.

Publications: ***Humanities, Science*** (2 a year).

DEANS:

Faculty of Arts: (vacant).
Faculty of Social Sciences: Dr. J. P. SAXENA.
Faculty of Science: Dr. K. G. BANSIGIR.
Faculty of Law: B. K. GOSWAMI.
Faculty of Education: (vacant).
Faculty of Engineering: Shri D. P. CHAKRAVARTI.
Faculty of Medicine: Dr. AJAI SHANKAR.
Faculty of Ayurved: G. L. SHARMA.
Faculty of Commerce: V. P. JOGLEKAR.
Faculty of Physical Education: **Shri** Dr. M. ROBSON.
Faculty of Home Science: Dr. K. G. BANSIGIR.

There are 39 affiliated colleges.

UNIVERSITY OF JODHPUR

JODHPUR, RAJASTHAN
Telephone: 23696.

Founded 1962.

Languages of instruction: English and Hindi.

Chancellor: THE GOVERNOR OF RAJASTHAN (*ex officio*).
Vice-Chancellor: Mr. Justice KAN SINGH.
Registrar: S. N. JODHAWAT.
Librarian: Dr. S. N. SAHAI, M.A., PH.D., D.L.SC.

The library contains 130,300 vols.

Number of teachers: 585.
Number of students: 10,192.

Publications: ***Jodhpur University Gazette and News Bulletin, The Beacons*** **(Engineering),** ***Annals of Economics, The University Times*** **(Students' Union).**

DEANS:

Faculty of Arts, Social Sciences and Education: Dr. M. C. JOSHI, M.A., PH.D.
Faculty of Commerce: **Prof. D. N.** ELHANCE, M.COM.
Faculty of Engineering: Prof. S. DIVAKARAN.
Faculty of Law: Dr. D. C. JAIN.
Faculty of Science: Prof. R. C. KAPOOR.
K. Nehru College for Women: Mrs. KAMINI DINESH.

PROFESSORS:

BANSAL, V. S., PH.D., Electrical Engineering
BHADADA, R., M.SC.C., A.I.S.M., F.C.C., Mining Engineering
CHARI, K. N., M.E., Civil Engineering
DIVAKARAN, S., M.ENG., PH.D., F.I.E., F.I.STRUCT.E., Structural Engineering
ELHANCE, D. N., M.COM., Commerce
GUPTA, K. S., PH.D., M.I.E., Mechanical Engineering
JOSHI, M. C., PH.D., Psychology
KUSHWAHA, R. S., M.SC., D.PHIL., PH.D., Mathematics
KAPOOR, R. C., M.SC., D.PHIL., D.SC., Chemistry
LAL, K. S., M.A., PH.D., History
MATHUR, M. L., F.I.E., M.C.I., PH.D., Mechanical Engineering
MISHRA, S. D., M.SC., PH.D., F.E.S.I., F.R.E.S., Zoology
MURTHY, S. K., M.E., PH.D., Electrical Engineering
NIGAM, A. N., M.SC., PH.D., Physics
RATHORE, L. S., M.A., PH.D., Political Science
SARAN, A. K., M.A., Sociology
SINGH, A., PH.D. (HON.), M.I.E., Civil Engineering

KALYANI UNIVERSITY

KALYANI 741235, NADIA.
WEST BENGAL
Telephone: Kly 220.

Founded 1960; Residential.

Language of instruction: English; Academic year: June to May.

Chancellor: THE GOVERNOR OF WEST BENGAL.
Vice-Chancellor: Prof. SUBIMAL K. MUKHERJEE.
Registrar: Dr. C. P. DUTTA.
Librarian: Shri K. SINHA.

Library of 76,000 vols.

Number of teachers: 197.
Number of students: 4,000.

DEANS:

Faculty of Science: Prof. P. SEN GUPTA.
Faculty of Arts: Prof. S. R. DUTTA GUPTA.
Faculty of Education: (vacant).

PROFESSORS:

BHATTACHARYYA, A., Sociology
BOSE, A. K., Zoology
CHATTERJEE, I. K., Commerce
DAS GUPTA, P., Physics
DUTTA GUPTA, S. R., Economics
GHOSH, J., Bengali
GUPTA, M. K., Statistics
LAHIRI, B. K., Pure Mathematics
MANNA, G. K., Zoology
MUKHERJEE, N., History
SAMADDAR, K. R., Botany
SARKAR, D. C., Physics
SEN, D. K., English
SEN, S. P., Botany
SEN GUPTA, A., Inorganic Chemistry
SEN GUPTA, P., Organic Chemistry
SEN GUPTA, P. R., Applied Mathematics
SEN GUPTA, R., Physical Chemistry

KAMARAJ UNIVERSITY

PALKALAI NAGAR.
MADURAI 625021,
TAMIL NADU STATE
Telephone: 33171-8.

Founded 1966; Teaching and Affiliating.

Languages of instruction: English and Tamil; **Academic year: July to April.**

Chancellor: H.E. PRABUDAS BHATWARI, GOVERNOR OF TAMIL NADU STATE.
Vice-Chancellor: Dr. V. C. KULANDAISAMY.
Registrar: B. MURUGAN, M.A.
Librarian: S. GNANAMUTTU, M.A., M.LIB.SC.

The library contains 132,900 vols.

Number of teachers: 279.
Number of students: 110,000.

Publications: *Newsletter* (quarterly), *Journal of Madurai University* (quarterly), *Peninsular Review of Politics* (quarterly).

DEANS:

Faculty of Arts: (vacant).
Faculty of Commerce: (vacant).
Faculty of Engineering: (vacant).
Faculty of Indian Medicine: (vacant).
Faculty of Science: Dr. M. A. THANGARAJ, M.A., PH.D.
Faculty of Teaching: (vacant).
Faculty of Business Administration: (vacant).

PROFESSORS:

ARUMUGAM, N., Physical, Organic and Inorganic Chemistry
BALASUBRAMANIAN, S., Theoretical Physics
CHANDRASEKARAN, K. S., Physics
FATEHALLY, R., Physics
GNANAM, A., Plant Physiology
IRAWATHY, **Miss A. R., Geography**
JAYARAMAN, J., Biochemistry
JOB, S. V., Animal Physiology
JOHN, D. K. SUNDER SINGH, Economics
KOTHANDA RAMIAH, T., Telugu
KOTHAI PILLAI, J. K., Education

KRISHNASWAMY, S., Environmental Biology
LAKSHMANAN, M., Microbiology
MUTHUKARUAPAN, V. R., Immunology
NAGARAJAN, K. R., Applied Mathematics
NEELAKANTAN, S., Natural Products and Physical Chemistry
PANDIAN, T. J., Environmental Physiology
RAAJYYAN, K., Modern History
SACHITANANDAN, V., English
SHUNMUGAM PILLAI, M., Tamil Studies
SRINIVASA RAGHAVN, N., Econometrics
SUBBARATNAM, N. R., Physical Chemistry
SUBRAMANIAN, S., Political Science
VENKATARATNAM, R., Sociology

There are 104 affiliated colleges.

KAMESHWAR SINGH DARBHANGA SANSKRIT UNIVERSITY

DARBHANGA, BIHAR 846004

Telephone: 2178.

Founded 1961; Teaching and Affiliating.

Chancellor: H.E. THE GOVERNOR OF BIHAR.
Vice-Chancellor: JAIKANT MISHRA.
Registrar: Dr. M. THAKUR.
Librarian: J. MAHTO.

Library of 18,000 vols.
Number of students: 23,100.

DEANS:

Faculty of Darshan: K. MISHRA.
Faculty of Jyotish: Pt. R. SHARMA.
Faculty of Samaj sastra: Pt. S. J. JHA.
Faculty of Vyakaran: B. MISHRA.
Faculty of Puran: G. SHARMA.
Faculty of Veda: Pt. M. M. JHA.
Faculty of Ayurved: Pt. R. N. JHA.

There are 4 government Sanskrit colleges and 3 research institutes affiliated to the University and 46 private affiliated Sanskrit colleges.

KANPUR UNIVERSITY

KALYANPUR, KANPUR 208024, U.P.

Telephone: 43301.

Founded 1966; Affiliating.

State control; Languages of instruction: English and Hindi; Academic year: July to June.

Chancellor: H.E. THE GOVERNOR OF UTTAR PRADESH.
Vice-Chancellor: Dr. HEMLATA SWARUP.
Registrar: Dr. D. R. TRIPATHI.
Librarian: N. ABRAHAM.

Library of 35,000. vols.
Number of students: 180,000.

DEANS:

Faculty of Arts: Dr. V. N. SRIVASTAVA.
Faculty of Science: Prof. S. P. NAGAM.
Faculty of Commerce: Dr. R. K. NIGAM.
Faculty of Agriculture: Dr. I. L. SRIVASTAVA.
Faculty of Law: Prof. S. K. KAPOOR.
Faculty of Education: Dr. I. B. SINGH.
Faculty of Medicine: Dr. TARA CHANDRA.
Faculty of Engineering and Technology: Dr. S. D. SHUKLA.
Faculty of Ayurvedic and Unani Medicines: Dr. J. P. SHARMA.
Faculty of Homeopathy: Dr. G. S. CHAUDHURY.

There are 1 constituent college and 74 affiliated colleges.

KARNATAK UNIVERSITY

DHARWAD, KARNATAKA 580003

Telephone: Dharwad 8194.

Founded 1949, incorporated 1950; Teaching and Affiliating.

Language of instruction: English; Academic year: June to March.

Chancellor: H.E. Shri GOVIND NARAIN, I.A.S., Governor of Karnataka.
Vice-Chancellor: S. S. WODEYAR, M.A., LL.B.
Registrar: Shri BRAHM DUTT.
Controller of Examinations: Shri S. R. HIREMATH.
Librarian: Shri K. S. DESHPANDE, M.A., DIP.LIB.SC.

Library of 232,596 vols.

Number of students: 4,128 (postgraduate).

Number of students in affiliated and constituent colleges: 52,255.

Number of postgraduate teachers: 394.

Number of college teachers: 3,913.

Publications: *Journal of the Karnataka University—Science, Humanities, Social Sciences; Karnatak Bharti* (quarterly), *Vijnana Bharati, Manavik Bharati* (2 a year), *Vidyarthi Bharati* (quarterly).

DEANS:

Faculty of Arts: Dr. K. KRISHNAMURTHY, M.A., PH.D.
Faculty of Commerce: Dr. C. C. PATTANASHETTI, M.A., PH.D.
Faculty of Education: Dr. G. SHIVARADRAPPA, M.A., M.ED., PH.D.
Faculty of Engineering: Prin. S. V. MALLAPUR, M.S.
Faculty of Medicine: Dr. S. G. DESAI, M.B.B.S., M.D., D.C.H.
Faculty of Law: Prin. G. V. AJJAPPA, B.A., LL.M.
Faculty of Science and Technology: Dr. M. S. CHANNAVEERAIAH, PH.D., D.SC.
Faculty of Social Sciences: Prof. K. J. SHAH, M.A.

POSTGRADUATE DEPARTMENTS:

Institute of Kannada Studies: Dr. M. S. SUNKAPUR, M.A., PH.D.
Department of Statistics: Dr. M. S. CHIKKAGOUDAR, M.A., PH.D.
Department of Chemistry: Dr. E. S. JAYADEVAPPA, M.SC., PH.D.
Department of Physics: Dr. K. SURYANARAYANARAO, D.SC.
Department of Geology: **Dr. M. S. SADASHIVAIAH, M.SC., PH.D., D.I.C., F.G.S., F.M.S., F.G.S. (INDIA).**
Department of History and Archaeology: Dr. S. SETTAR, M.A., PH.D.
Department of Political Science: Dr. A. M. RAJASEKHARIAH, M.A., PH.D.
Department of Economics: Dr. T. K. METI, M.A., PH.D.
Department of Sociology: Dr. K. CHANDRASEKHARIAH, M.A., D.PHIL.
Department of Anthropology: Dr. GOPALA SARANA, M.A., PH.D.
Department of Mathematics: Dr. K. S. AMUR, M.SC., PH.D.
Department of Sanskrit: Dr. K. KRISHNAMOORTHY, M.A., PH.D., B.T.
Department of Geography: Dr. N. C. VIJAYARAJ, M.A., PH.D.
Department of Philosophy, Criminology and Forensic Science: Shri K. J. SHAH, M.A.
Department of Botany: **Dr. M. S. CHENNAVEERAIAH, M.SC., PH.D., D.SC.**
Department of Zoology: **Dr. M. APPASWAMY RAO, M.SC., PH.D., M.S., F.A.A.Z.**
Department of Commerce: **Dr. C. C. PATTANSHETTI, M.A., PH.D.**
Department of Education: Dr. G. SHIVARUDRAPPA, M.ED., PH.D.
Department of Law: **Shri G. V. AJJAPPA, B.A., LL.M.**
Department of Foreign Languages: Dr. S. B. SHROTRI, M.A., PH.D.
Department of English: Shri T. R. RAJASEKHARIAH, M.A.
Department of Ancient Indian History and Epigraphy: Dr. S. H. RITTI, M.A., PH.D.
Department of Hindi: R. K. MUDALIAR, M.A.
Department of Library Science: M. R. KUMBAR, B.A., M.LIB.SC.
Department of Psychology: Shri K. R. MALLAPA, M.A.
Department of Social Work: Shri B. S. BIDARAKOPPA, M.A.
Kannada Research Institute: Dr. B. S KULKARNI, M.A., PH.D.
Kousali Institute of Management Studies: Sbri C. B. TIGADI, B.SC.

CONSTITUENT COLLEGES:

Karnatak Arts College: Dharwad; f. 1917.
Principal: Shri B. B. KANAVI, M.A., B.COM., LL.B.

Karnatak Science College: Dharwad; f. 1917.
Principal: Shri H. R. LADWA, M.SC.

University College of Education: Dharwad; f. 1962.
Principal: Shri B. C. PATIL, M.SC., M.ED.

University College of Law: Dharwad; f. 1962.
Principal: G. V. AJJAPPA, B.A., LL.M.

College of Geology and Mineral Processing: Nandihalli; f. 1975.
Principal: Dr. B. SOMASEKHAR, M.SC., PH.D.

University College of Music: Dharwad; f. 1975.

Principal: Smt. SHARADA HANAGAL, M.A.

There are 142 affiliated colleges.

UNIVERSITY OF KASHMIR

HAZRATBAL, SRINAGAR 190006, JAMMU AND KASHMIR

Telephone: Hazratbal 2231-33, 2333, 2342, 2745, 3541.

Founded 1969; Teaching and Affiliating.

Vice-Chancellor: Dr. RAIS AHMED.

Registrar: Prof. JAN MOHAMMAD.

Librarian: J. A. WAJID.

Library of 141,338 vols.

Number of teachers: 1,092.
Number of students: 14,004.

DEANS:

Faculty of Arts: Prof. R. K. SHARMA, D.LITT., PH.D.
Faculty of Science: D. N. FOTEDAR, M.SC., PH.D.
Faculty of Social Science: Dr. B. D. SHARMA, M.A., PH.D.
Faculty of Education: Dr. SALAMATULLAH, M.SC., PH.D.
Faculty of Medicine: S. N. AHMAD SHAH, M.B., M.R.C.P.
Faculty of Engineering: Dr. O. N. WAKHLOO, PH.D.
Faculty of Agriculture: HAKIM MOHAMAD TAHIR.
Faculty of Oriental Learning: Prof. SHAMAS-UD-DIN AHMAD, M.A., D.LITT., PH.D.
Faculty of Commerce: HABIB UR RAHMAN, PH.D.
Faculty of Music and Fine Arts: Shri VACHASPATI SHARMA.
Student Welfare: Shri G. N. SIDDIQI, M.A.

PROFESSORS:

AHMAD, S., Persian
ASIF-U-ZAMAN, Chemistry
BOMBWALL, K. R., Political Science
FOTEDAR, Dr. D. N., Zoology
HABIB-UR-REHMAN, Commerce
HAMIDI, Dr. H. U., Urdu
JAGDISH SHANKER, Research for Development
JAYA, RAMAN, T., English
KACHROO, Dr. P., Botany
KHERA, Dr. M. K., Physics
MAQBOOL, AHMAD, Central Asian Studies
NASEER-UD-DIN, Geography
SALAMATULLAH, Education
SAROOR, ALE AHMAD, Iqbal Institute
SHARMA, Dr. B. D., Economics
SHARMA, Dr. R. K., Hindi
SIDDIQI, Dr. Z. M. SHAHID, Law
SINGH, Dr. Y., Physics

UNIVERSITY OF KERALA

TRIVANDRUM 695001, KERALA STATE

Telephone: 60594.

Established 1937; Teaching and Affiliating.

Language of instruction: English; Academic year: June to March.

Chancellor: H.E. THE GOVERNOR OF KERALA.

Pro-Chancellor: THE MINISTER FOR EDUCATION OF KERALA.

Vice-Chancellor: Dr. V. K. SUKUMARAN NAYAR.

Pro-Vice-Chancellor: Dr. N. A. KARIM.

Registrar: C. K. DEVASSY.

Library of 187,829 vols.

Number of students: 143,091.

DEANS:

Faculty of Arts: Dr. K. E. EAPEN.
Faculty of Education: Dr. N. VEDAMONY MANUEL.
Faculty of Engineering Technology: Dr. S. VASUDEV.
Faculty of Law: Prof. R. SANKARADASAN THAMPI.
Faculty of Oriental Studies: Dr. K. RAGHAVAN PILLAI.
Faculty of Science: Dr. C. A. NINAN.
Faculty of Social Sciences: Dr. E. T. MATHEW.
Faculty of Commerce: K. J. JACOB.
Faculty of Medicine: Dr. M. BALARAMAN NAIR.
Faculty of Ayurveda: Dr. M. P. SREEDMARAN NAIR.
Faculty of Fine Arts: Mrs. K. SAROJINI AMMA.

PROFESSORS:

ALEXANDER, K. M., M.SC., PH.D., Zoology
ANANTHARAMAN, R., PH.D., Chemistry
ARULDAS, G., M.SC., PH.D., Physics
EAPEN, K. E., B.A., LL.B., M.S., PH.D., Journalism
ELAYAPERUMAL, M., M.A., M.LITT., PH.D., Tamil
GEORGE, E. I., M.A., PH.D., Psychology
ISSAC, K. A., B.SC., M.LIB.SC., Library Science
JOHN, P. A., PH.D., Aquatic Biology and Fisheries
JOSHUA, C. P., M.SC., PH.D., Chemistry
KURUP, P. A., M.SC., PH.D., Bio-chemistry
MANUEL, M., M.A., PH.D., English
MANUEL, N., VEDAMANI, M.A., M.ED., PH.D., Education
MATHEW, E. T., M.A., PH.D., Economics
MENON, DEVADAS K., M.A., PH.D., Psychology
NAIR, C. G. RAMACHANDRAN, M.SC., PH.D., Chemistry
NAIR, K. RAMACHANDRAN, M.A., PH.D., Malayalam
NAIR, N. BALAKRISHNAN, B.SC., M.A., PH.D., D.SC., Aquatic Biology and Fisheries
NAIR, P. K. B., M.A., PH.D., Sociology
NAIR, PRABODHACHANDRAN V. P., M.A., PH.D., Linguistics
NAIR, RAJENDRAN P. K., M.SC., A.I.S.M., PH.D., Geology
NAIR, R. RAMAKRISHNAN, M.A., PH.D., Politics
NAIR, V. K. SUKUMARAN, M.A., PH.D., Politics
NAMBOODIRI, A. N., M.SC., PH.D., Botany
NINAN, C. A., M.SC., PH.D., Botany
PHILIP, RAJU, M.SC., PH.D., Geology
PILLAI, K. RAMAN, M.A., PH.D., Politics
PILLAI, N. KRISHNA, M.SC., PH.D., Aquatic Biology and Fisheries
PILLAI, P. GOPALA, M.A., PH.D., Psychology
PILLAI, P. RAMACHANDRAN, M.A., PH.D., Malayam
PILLAI, R. KRISHNA, M.SC., M.A., M.S., PH.D., Statistics
PILLAI, K. RAGHAVAN, M.A., PH.D., Sanskrit
PRABHU, V. K. K., M.SC., PH.D., Zoology
RAMACHANDRA RAJ, G., M.A., PH.D., Sociology
RAMAKUMAR, R., M.SC., M.S., SC.D., Demography
RAVINDRAN, T. K., M.A., LL.B., PH.D., History
RAO, P. BALARAMA, M.SC., PH.D., Physics
SITARAMAN, Y., M.A., M.SC., PH.D., Mathematics
SUBRAMONIAM, V. I., M.A., PH.D., Linguistics
UNNI, PARAMESWARAN N., M.A., PH.D., Sanskrit
VISALAKSHY, N. R., M.A., M.LITT., PH.D., Politics
VISWANATHAN, K. S., M.A., PH.D., Physics

There are 104 affiliated colleges.

KERALA AGRICULTURAL UNIVERSITY

MANNUTHY 680651, TRICHUR, KERALA STATE

Telephone: 23432.

Founded 1972.

Chancellor: H.E. THE GOVERNOR OF KERALA.

Pro-Chancellor: THE MINISTER FOR AGRICULTURE, KERALA.

Vice-Chancellor: Shri N. KALEESWARAN, I.A.S.

Registrar: Shri E. DAMODARA MARAR.

Number of teachers: 575.
Number of students: 1,298.

CONSTITUENT COLLEGES:

College of Agriculture: Vellayani (formerly affiliated to University of Kerala); Dean Dr. N. SADANANDAN.

College of Fisheries: Mannuthy; f. 1979; Dean Dr. M. J. SEBASTIAN.

College of Horticulture: Vellanikkara; f. 1972; Dean Dr. P. C. SIVARAMAN NAIR.

College of Veterinary and Animal Sciences: Mannuthy (formerly affiliated to University of Calicut); Dean Dr. A. VENUGOPALAN (acting).

KONKAN AGRICULTURAL UNIVERSITY

DAPOLI 415712, RATNAGIRI, MAHARASHTRA

Telephone: 25,97.

Founded 1972.

State control; Language of instruction: English.

Chancellor: H.E. THE GOVERNOR OF MAHARASHTRA.

Vice-Chancellor: P. V. SALVI, M.S., PH.D.

Registrar: B. B. RANE, M.A., LL.M.

Number of teachers: 162.

Number of students: 595.

Publications: *Journal*†, Newsletter.

DEANS:

Faculty of Agriculture: (vacant).
Faculty of Veterinary Science: Dr. S. M. AJINKYA.
Faculty of Fisheries: Dr. M. R. RANADE.

CONSTITUENT COLLEGES:

College of Agriculture: Dapoli; Principal Dr. S. B. KADREKAR.

Veterinary College: Bombay; Principal Dr. S. M. AJINKYA.

KUMAUN UNIVERSITY

NAINITAL,
UTTAR PRADESH
Telephone: 343.

Founded 1973; Teaching and Affiliating.

Academic year: July to December, February to June (two terms).

Chancellor: H.E. THE GOVERNOR OF UTTAR PRADESH.
Vice-Chancellor: Dr. D. D. PANT.
Registrar: Dr. D. N. AGRAWAL.

Number of students: 11,364.

There are 10 affiliated colleges.

KURUKSHETRA UNIVERSITY

KURUKSHETRA 132119,
HARYANA, PUNJAB
Telephone: 26.

Founded 1956; Teaching and Affiliating.

Languages of instruction: English and Hindi; Academic year: July to May.

Chancellor: H.E. THE GOVERNOR OF HARYANA.
Vice-Chancellor: Dr. VIKAS MISHRA, M.COM., M.A., PH.D.
Pro-Vice-Chancellor: R. D. SHARMA, M.A.
Registrar: Dr. R. P. HOODA, M.A., PH.D.
Librarian: Shri K. S. DALAL, M.A., LL.B., M.LIB.SC.

Library of 165,256 vols. and 4,851 MSS.

Number of teachers: 2,101.
Number of students: 43,725.

Publications: *Annual Report, Handbook of Information, Digest of Indological Studies, Research Journal for Arts and Humanities, Sambhawana* (Hindi), *Calendar, Prospectus, Kurukshetra Law Journal.*

DEANS:

Faculty of Science: Dr. A. K. DATTA GUPTA, M.SC., PH.D.
Faculty of Arts and Languages: Dr. B. K. KALIA, M.A., PH.D.
Faculty of Social Sciences: Dr. V. S. BUDHRAJ, M.A., PH.D.
Faculty of Education: Dr. C. L. KUNDU, M.A., M.ED., PH.D.
Faculty of Indic Studies: Dr. GOPIKAMOHAN BATTHACHARYA, M.A., D.PHIL.
Faculty of Engineering and Technology: Prof. B. K. KAUL, M.SC., M.S., A.M.A.S.C.E., M.I.S.S.F.E., M.I.S.S.
Faculty of Law: Dr. SURYA P. SHARMA, LL.M., J.S.D.
Faculty of Commerce and Management: Dr. DOOL SINGH, M.COM., PH.D., I.T.P.
Faculty of Dairying, Animal Husbandry and Agriculture: Dr. D. SUNDARESEN, M.SC., PH.D.

PROFESSORS:

BHATNAGAR, H. L., M.SC., PH.D., Chemistry
BHATTACHARYA, G., M.A., D.PHIL., Sanskrit
BUDHRAJ, V. S., M.A., PH.D., Political Science
DATTA GUPTA, A. K., M.SC., PH.D., Zoology
DATTA, V. N., M.A., M.LITT., History
JAIN, P. C., M.A., PH.D., Economics
KALIA, B. K., M.A., PH.D., English
KUNDU, C. L., M.A., M.ED., PH.D., Education
MAHROTRA, R. S., M.SC., PH.D., Botany
MOHAN, C., M.SC., PH.D., F.S.S., F.N.A.SC., Mathematics
MUKHERJI, S. M., D.SC., PH.D., D.SC., F.N.I., Chemistry
NAGPAUL, K. K., M.SC., PH.D., Physics
NATH, N., M.SC., PH.D., Physics
PUJARI, H. K., M.SC., PH.D., F.I.C., J.S.D., Chemistry
SHARMA, S. P., LL.M., J.S.D., Law
SHASTRI, S. N., M.A., PH.D., Sanskrit
SINGH, D., M.COM., PH.D., Management
SINGH, J., M.A., PH.D., I.T.P., Geography
SINGH, UDAI VIR, M.A., PH.D., Ancient Indian History, Culture and Archaeology
SINHA, A. K., M.A., PH.D., Philosophy
TANDON, B. C., M.COM., D.LITT., Commerce
YATIRAJAM, V., M.SC., DR.RER.NAT., Chemistry

There are 59 affiliated colleges and 2 maintained colleges.

UNIVERSITY OF LUCKNOW

BADSHAH BAGH,
LUCKNOW, 226007 U.P.
Telephone: 22270/23138.

Founded 1921; Residential and Teaching.

Languages of instruction: English and Hindi; Academic year: July to April.

Chancellor: H.E. THE GOVERNOR OF UTTAR PRADESH.
Vice-Chancellor: Dr. R. V. SINGH.
Registrar: B. N. SINGH.

Number of teachers: *c.* 600.

Number of students: 39,261.

DEANS:

Faculty of Arts: Dr. K. N. SHUKLA.
Faculty of Science: Dr. P. S. KRISHNAN.
Faculty of Medicine: R. V. SINGH, M.B., M.S.
Faculty of Law: Mrs. S. KUMARI.
Faculty of Commerce: Dr. I. B. SINHA.
Faculty of Ayurveda: V. K. SHARMA.

CONSTITUENT COLLEGES:

King George's Medical College: Lucknow; f. 1911; 4-year postgraduate medical courses have been established.
Principal: Prof. R. V. SINGH.

State College of Ayurveda: Lucknow; f. 1954.
Principal: V. K. SHARMA.

There are 20 associated colleges.

UNIVERSITY OF MADRAS

CHEPAUK, TRIPLICANE P.O.,
MADRAS 600005, TAMIL NADU
Telephone: 86432-6.

Founded 1857; Teaching and Affiliating.

Languages of instruction: English and Tamil; Academic year: June to March (three terms).

Chancellor: H.E. THE GOVERNOR OF TAMIL NADU.
Vice-Chancellor: Prof. G. R. DAMODARAN.
Registrar: C. K. KUMARASWAMY.
Librarian: P. A. MOHANRAJ.

Library of 370,000 vols. and 2,261 maps.

Number of students: 162,000.

Publications: *University Calendar, University Journals, Annals of Oriental Research.*

FACULTY PRESIDENTS:

Faculty of Science: Prof. P. K. CHIDAMBARAM.
Faculty of Law: C. RAJARAMAN.
Faculty of Teaching: Dr. E. G. VEDANAYAGAM.
Faculty of Medicine: Dr. A. VENUGOPAL.
Faculty of Engineering: Dr. V. C. JULANDAISWAMY.
Faculty of Management Science: (vacant).
Faculty of Oriental Learning: M. VARADARAJAN, PH.D.
Faculty of Fine Arts: (vacant).
Faculty of Technology: Sri G. S. LADDHA, B.SC.(TECH.), M.S.CH.E., PH.D., A.M.I.CHEM.E.
Faculty of Commerce: Prin. V. V. RAMAN.
Faculty of Arts: K. S. NAGARAJAN.

There are 150 affiliated colleges.

MAGADH UNIVERSITY

BODHGAYA 824234,
BIHAR STATE
Telephone: 835.

Founded 1962; Teaching and Affiliating.

Languages of instruction: English and Hindi; Academic year: June to May.

Chancellor: H.E. THE GOVERNOR OF BIHAR.

Vice-Chancellor: Dr. K. K. MANDAL.
Registrar: S. N. MISHRA.
Librarian: N. SINGH.

The library contains 94,000 vols.
Number of students: 58,900.

DEANS:

Faculty of Arts: Dr. U. THAKUR.
Faculty of Science: Dr. G. P. SINGH.
Faculty of Commerce: Dr. N. C. AGRAWAL.
Faculty of Law: Shri ASGARAH.
Faculty of Medicine: Dr. HARI PRASAD

PROFESSORS:

GANGULY, S., M.A., PH.D., Economics
LAL, B. K., M.A., PH.D., Philosophy
PRASAD, B. N., M.A., D.LITT., Hindi
PRASAD, R. C., M.A., PH.D., Political Science
PRASAD, S. K., M.A., PH.D., English
SINGH, G. P., M.SC., PH.D., Physics
SINGH, H., M.A., PH.D., Economics
SINGH, R P., M.A., PH.D., Geography
SINGH, S., M.A., PH.D., Mathematics
SINGH, S. B., M.A., PH.D., History
SINGH, S. B., M.SC., PH.D., Zoology
THAKUR, U., M.A., PH.D., Ancient Indian History and Asian Studies
YADAV, A. S., M.SC., PH.D., Botany

There are 27 constituent colleges and 30 affiliated colleges.

MAHATMA PHULE KRISHI VIDYAPEETH

RAHURI,
AHMEDANAGAR DISTRICT,
MAHARASHTRA STATE

Telephone: 65.
Founded 1968.

Academic year: July to May.

Chancellor: H.E. THE GOVERNOR OF MAHARASHTRA.
Pro-Chancellor: THE MINISTER FOR AGRICULTURE.
Vice-Chancellor: Dr. A. B. JOSHI, M.SC. AGR., PH.D.
Registrar: V. K. MAHAJAN, M.SC.
Librarian: Shri A. G. KARANDE, M.COM., B.LIB.SC.

The library contains 33,445 vols.
Number of students: 2,100.

HEADS OF DEPARTMENTS:

CHAVAN, I. G., Animal Husbandry and Dairy Science
GHARAT, G. K., M.SC., Agricultural Engineering
KADAM, M. V., M.SC., PH.D., Agricultural Entomology
MORE, B. B., M.SC., Plant Pathology
PATIL, A. V., M.SC., PH.D., Horticulture
PATIL, B. B., M.SC., PH.D., Agronomy
PATIL, R. G., M.SC., PH.D., Agricultural Economics
SANGHAVE, R. A., M.SC., PH.D., Agricultural Botany
THORAT, S. S., M.SC., PH.D., Agricultural Extension
ZENDE, G. K., M.SC., PH.D., Agricultural Chemistry

CONSTITUENT COLLEGES:

Agricultural College: Dhulia; f. 1960; Dean Dr. B. D. KHOT.

Agricultural College: Kolhapur; f. 1963; Dean Shri P. S. DUDUSKAR.

Agricultural College: Poona; f. 1906; Dean Dr. K. S. PHARANDE.

College of Agricultural Engineering: Rahuri; f. 1969; Dean Shri G. K. GHARAT.

Postgraduate School: Rahuri; f. 1972; Dean Dr. T. K. T. ACHARYA.

MAHARSHI DAYANAND UNIVERSITY ROHTAK

ROHTAK 124001,
HARYANA

Telephone: 2119, 2639.
Founded 1976; Affiliating.

Vice-Chancellor: HARDWARI LAL.
Registrar: S. N. RAO.
Librarian: P. N. SHARMA (acting).

Library of 72,455 vols., 750 periodicals.

Number of teachers: 115.
Number of students: 37,639.

DEANS:

School of Commerce and Business Management: Dr. B. R. AGGARWAL.
School of Arts and Languages: Dr. O. P. GREWAL.
School of Physical Sciences: Dr. S. SINGH.
School of Social Sciences: Dr. R. D. GUPTA.
School of Para-Clinical Studies: Dr. A. H. KAUR.
School of Surgery and Allied Sciences: Dr. P. S. MAINI.
School of Pre-Clinical Studies: Dr. B. K. MAINI.
School of Textile Technology: Dr. R. C. D. KAUSHIK.
School of Medicine and Allied Sciences: Dr. K. C. VERMA.
School of Ayurvedic and Unani System of Medicine: Dr. R. P. SINGHAL.
School of Community Medicine: Dr. U. VERMA.
School of Education: (vacant).

ATTACHED INSTITUTE:

Technological Institute of Textiles: Bhiwani; Dir. Prof. R. C. D. KAUSHIK.

There are 61 affiliated colleges.

MARATHWADA UNIVERSITY

AURANGABAD (DECCAN),
MAHARASHTRA 431001

Telephone: 4431-37.

Founded 1958; Teaching and Affiliating.

Languages of instruction: English and Marathi; Academic year: June to April (two terms).

Chancellor: H.E. THE GOVERNOR OF MAHARASHTRA.
Vice-Chancellor: B. R. BHONSLE, M.SC., PH.D., D.SC., F.N.A.SC., F.A.M.S.
Registrar: B. H. RAJURKAR, M.A., PH.D.
Librarian: Shri. R. G. JOGDEO, M.A.

Library of 200,810 vols.

Number of teachers (incl. constituent colleges): 2,443.

Number of students: 23,863.

Publications: *Annual Report, University Journal, University Handbook, Rabindranath Tagore Lecture Series.*

DEANS:

Faculty of Arts: Y. M. PAITHAN, M.A., PH.D.
Faculty of Science: D. S. DESHPANDE, M.SC., PH.D.
Faculty of Law: S. K. SHELKE, LL.M.
Faculty of Medicine: A. M. VARE, M.B.B.S., M.SC.
Faculty of Commerce: V. D. CHAVAN, M.COM.
Faculty of Education: D. A. PATHRIKAR, M.A., B.P.ED.
Faculty of Engineering: D. B. GADVE, B.E.
Faculty of Ayurveda: M. Y. LELE, D.A.S.F.
Faculty of Social Sciences: B. M. PATODEKAR, M.A., PH.D.

FULL PROFESSORS:

AMUR, G. S., M.A., PH.D., English
BAPAT, N. G., Commerce
BORKAR, V. V., M.A., PH.D., Economics
ITAGI, V. V., M.SC., PH.D., Physics
KULKARNI, M. G., M.A., PH.D., Sociology
NAGABHUSHANAM, R., M.SC., PH.D., Zoology
PACHPATTE, B. G., M.SC., PH.D., Mathematics and Statistics
PAI, R. M., M.SC., PH.D., Botany
PATHAN, Y. M., M.A., B.T., PH.D., Marathi Language and Literature
PAWAR, S. S., M.SC., PH.D., Biochemistry
RAJURKAR, B. H., M.A., PH.D., Hindi
RAO, S. N., Zoology
SARMA, G. N., M.A., PH.D., Political Science
THAKAR, K. A., M.SC., PH.D., Chemistry

AFFILIATED COLLEGES:

There are 83 affiliated colleges, including two medical colleges, five law colleges, six teachers' training colleges. an Ayurvedic college, a science institute and an engineering college.

MARATHWADA AGRICULTURAL UNIVERSITY

PARBHANI 431402,
MAHARASHTRA STATE

Telephone: 301 PBX
Founded 1972.

State control; Language of instruction: English; Academic Year: June to May.

Chancellor: H.E. THE GOVERNOR OF MAHARASHTRA.
Vice-Chancellor and Dean of the Faculty of Agriculture: Dr. V. S. KHUSPE.

Registrar: Shri S. T. KACHWE.
Librarian: Shri R. SUBBAIAH.

Number of teachers: 163.
Number of students: 1,245.

Publications: *News Letter*† (English and Marathi, monthly), *Sheti Bhati* (Marathi, monthly), *Research Bulletin* (English, monthly).

PROFESSORS:

Faculty of Agriculture:
BONDE, H. S., Animal Husbandry and Dairy Farming
BORULKAR, D. N., Agronomy
MALI, Dr. V. R., Plant Pathology
NERKAR, Dr. Y. S., Botany
RAJMANE, Dr. K. D., Economics
RAODEO, Dr. A. K., Entomology
RAPTE, S. L., Agricultural Engineering
VARADE, Dr. S. B., Chemistry
SANGLE, Dr. G. K., Extension Studies
WARKE, D. C., Horticulture

Faculty of Agricultural Technology:
GUNJAL, B. B., Food Engineering
KADAM, Dr. S. S., Biochemistry
KULKARNI, D. N., Food Science and Agricultural Products
RATHI, S. D., Microbiology

Faculty of Home Science:
DEVI, Mrs. ROHINI, Food and Nutrition
HARODE, Miss SHYAMALA, Home Management
SHANTI, Miss V., Textiles and Clothing

Faculty of Veterinary and Animal Sciences:
KULKARNI, Dr. M. N., Microbiology
PARGAONKAR, Dr. D. R., Gynaecology
SAKHARE, P. G., Animal Management
SAWANTH, M. K., Surgery
WAG, K. R., Pharmacology

CONSTITUENT COLLEGES:

College of Agriculture: Parbhani.
Principal: Dr. K. R. PAWAR.

College of Agricultural Technology: Parbhani.
Principal: Dr. U. M. INGLE.

College of Home Science: Parbhani.
Principal: Dr. C. P. GHONSIKAR.

College of Veterinary and Animal Sciences: Parbhani.
Principal: Dr. M. A. GHAFOOR.

There are 16 affiliated research stations.

MEERUT UNIVERSITY

MEERUT, 250001 UTTAR PRADESH
Telephone: 75021-3.
Founded 1966; Affiliating and Teaching.

Languages of instruction: Hindi and English.

Chancellor: H.E. THE GOVERNOR OF UTTAR PRADESH.
Vice-Chancellor: Dr. D. C. SHARMA.
Registrar: Sri V. B. BANSAL.

The library contains 45,310 vols.
Number of students: 27,731.

DEANS:

Faculty of Arts: Dr. S. D. SINGH.
Faculty of Science: Dr. Y. S. MURTY.
Faculty of Commerce: Sri R. C. MITTAL.
Faculty of Education: Dr. R. P. BHATNAGAR.
Faculty of Agriculture: Dr. P. K. GUPTA.
Faculty of Law: Sri T. S. TYAGI.
Faculty of Medicine: Dr. KEDAR NATH.

There are 1 constituent college and 52 affiliated colleges.

MITHILA UNIVERSITY

KAMESHWARNAGAR, P.O.B. 13, DARBHANGA 846004, BIHAR
Telephone: 2166.
Founded 1972; Teaching and Affiliating.

Languages of instruction: Hindi and English; Academic year: June to May.

Chancellor: H.E. THE GOVERNOR OF BIHAR.
Vice-Chancellor: Dr. S. SINGH.
Registrar: D. P. VARMA.
Librarian: R. N. JHA.

Library of 128,300 vols.
Number of teachers: 1,251.
Number of students: 53,000.

DEANS:

Faculty of Arts: Dr. BACHASPATI THAKUR.
Faculty of Commerce: Dr. GOPAL LAL.
Faculty of Education: Shri K. N. SHARMA.
Faculty of Law: Dr. D. K. JHA.
Faculty of Medicine: Dr. T. N. JHA.
Faculty of Science: Dr. BABUNAND JHA.

PROFESSORS:

JHA, B. N., Mathematics
JHA, SHAILENDRA MOHAN, Maithili
JHA, U., English
LALL, G., Commerce
PATHAK, R. K., English
THAKUR, BACHASPATI, Economics
THAKUR, RUDRA NATH, Political Science

UNIVERSITY OF MYSORE

P.O.B. 14, MYSORE 570005, KARNATAKA STATE
Telephone: 20677.
Founded 1916; Teaching and Affiliating.

Language of instruction: English; Academic year: June to March (two terms).

Chancellor: H.E. THE GOVERNOR OF KARNATAK.
Vice-Chancellor: Prof. K. S. HEGDE.
Registrar: P. S. RAMANUJAM.
Librarian: P. K. PATIL, M.A., LL.B.

The library contains 375,000 vols. and 13,378 MSS.

Number of students: 99,130.

DEANS:

Faculty of Arts: Prof. H. M. NAYAK.
Faculty of Science: Dr. M. N. VISVANATHAIAH, M.SC., PH.D.
Faculty of Engineering: (vacant).
Faculty of Medicine: Dr. A. K. RAO.
Faculty of Education: J. N. RAMACHANDRAN.
Faculty of Law: G. D. DESHPANDY.
Faculty of Commerce: Prof. T. KRISHNA RAO.

UNIVERSITY COLLEGES:

Maharaja's College, Mysore; Yuvaraja's College, Mysore; Maharani's College for Women, Mysore; University Evening College, Mysore; College of Music and Dance, Mysore.

There are 118 affiliated colleges and 17 evening colleges.

NAGARJUNA UNIVERSITY

NAGARJUNANAGAR 522 510, ANDHRA PRADESH
Telephone: 23225.
Founded 1976.

Vice-Chancellor: Prof. B. SARVESWARA RAO, M.A., PH.D.
Registrar: D. MURALIKRISHNA, I.A.S.
Deputy Librarian: S. KOTESWARA RAO, M.A.

Library of *c.* 20,000 vols.
Number of teachers: 86.
Number of students: *c.* 850.
There are 29 affiliated colleges.

UNIVERSITY OF NAGPUR

RABINDRANATH TAGORE MARG, NAGPUR 440001, MAHARASHTRA
Telephone: 22417.
Founded 1923; Teaching and Affiliating.

Languages of instruction: English, Hindi and Marathi; Academic year: June to March (two terms).

Chancellor: H.E. THE GOVERNOR OF MAHARASHTRA.
Vice-Chancellor: Shri W. M. KALMEGH, M.SC., M.TECH.
Registrar: Shri B. Y. AHER, M.A., D.B.M.
Librarian: Dr. V. V. KULKARNI, M.A., M.LIB.SC., PH.D.

The library contains 278,511 vols., including 14,214 MSS.

Number of teachers: 4,009.
Number of students: 48,045.

DEANS:

Faculty of Arts (including Fine Art): B. R. ASHTIKAR, M.A., PH.D.
Faculty of Law: Shri R. V. PATIL, B.SC., LL.M.

Faculty of Medicine (including Ayurvedic Medicine): Dr. B. J. SUBHEDAR, M.D.
Faculty of Science: Prof. O. B. THAKRE, M.SC.
Faculty of Education: Shri P. A. VAIDYA, M.ED.
Faculty of Commerce: R. G. TATTE, M.COM.
Faculty of Engineering (including Technology): (vacant).
Faculty of Social Sciences: B. T. DESHMUKH, M,A.
Faculty of Home Science: R. D. KOLAPKAR, M.SC.,

CHAIRMEN OF BOARDS OF STUDIES:

Faculty of Arts (including Fine Art):
ASHTIKAR, B. R., M.A., PH.D., Sanskrit
DEO, PROMOD R., M.A., Other Foreign Languages
HAMID, K. M., M.A., PH.D., Urdu
JAIN, BHAGCHANDRA, M.A., PH.D., Pali and Prakrit
KASHIKAR, M. B., M.A., Music
KULKARNI, S. B., M.A., PH.D., Linguistics
MANDEOKAR, B. M., M.A., PH.D., Marathi
PARANJPE, J. B., M.A., PH.D., English
PATNAIK, S. C., M.A., PH.D., Hindi
RAB, ABDUL, M.A., Persian and Arabic
VAIDYA, H. R., Fine Art
VYAS, B. C., M.A., PH.D., Other Indian Languages

Faculty of Science:
BARHATE, A. V., M.SC., Physics
CHAKRABORTI, C. H., M.SC., PH.D., Biochemistry
DHANAGARE, P. N., M.A., Languages
GHURDE, V. R., M.SC., PH.D., Botany
JAJURLEY, D. S., M.SC., Zoology
JOHARAPURKAR, V. K., Statistics
JOSHI, M. G., M.SC., Mathematics
MUNSHI, K. N., M.SC., PH.D., Chemistry

Faculty of Law:
LAHORIA, S. C., B.A., LL.B.

Faculty of Education:
SARAL, Smt. DANI, M.A., M.ED., Education
VAIDYA, P. A., M.ED., Physical Education

Faculty of Commerce:
DESHMUKH, P. J., M.COM., PH.D., Business Management and Administration
DHOTEY, M. G., M.COM., LL.B., Commerce
KASAT, S. P., M.COM., Accounts and Statistics
KULKARNI, V. S., M.A., Business Economics
PARASKAR, M. G., M.A., M.ED., Languages

Faculty of Engineering and Technology:
DABHADE, S. B., M.TECH., PH.D., Oil Technology
DEODHAR, M. G., B.E., M.SC., Civil Engineering
DESHPANDE, S. A., G.D.ARCH., Architecture
GURTU, M.SC., D.PHIL., General Engineering, Applied Science and Humanities
KHER, M. G., M.SC., Chemical Engineering
PATIL, S. A., M.E., Mechanical Engineering
PINGLE, S. S., B.E., M.I.E., Electrical Engineering
TUPKARI, R. H., M.E., PH.D., Metallurgical Engineering
VENKATACHALAN, K. G., M.SC., PH.D., Chemical Technology

Faculty of Medicine (including Ayurvedic Medicine):
CHOUBEY, B. S., M.D., Medicine
DESHMUKH, V. K., M.PHARM., PH.D., Pharmaceutical Sciences
SATHYE, S. M., Ayurvedic Medicine

Faculty of Home Science:
KOLAPKAR, R. D., M.SC., Home Science

Faculty of Social Sciences:
BHANDARKAR, P. L., M.A., PH.D., Sociology
BUIT, KU. S. S., M.A., PH.D., Philosophy
CHINCHAMALATPURE, S. B., M.A., Geography
DEB, S., M.SC., PH.D., Home Science
DESHMUKH, M. K., Public Administration
KANE, P. S., M.A., Political Science
KASARE, M. L., M.A., Economics
KAUL, H. M., M.A., History
KUMAR, P. S. G., M.LIB.SC., Library Science
PADOLE, D. S., M.A., Rural Services
PANDHARIPANDE, P. S., M.A., PH.D., Psychology
SHASTRI, A. M., M.A., PH.D., Ancient Indian History, Culture and Archaeology
TAYAL, KU. S., M.A., M.S.W., Social Work

CONSTITUENT COLLEGES:

Laxminarayan Institute of Technology: f. 1942; number of teachers 51, students 520.
Director: M. G. KHER, M.SC., DR.ING.

University College of Law: f. 1925; number of teachers 54, students 1,194.
Principal: D. R. MEGHE, LL.M.

University College of Education: f. 1945; number of teachers 23, students 250.
Principal: Smt. PRAMILA DABIR, M.A., M.ED., LL.B.

There are 139 affiliated colleges.

UNIVERSITY OF NORTH BENGAL

P.O. NORTH BENGAL UNIVERSITY, RAJA RAMMOHUNPUR, DARJEELING DISTRICT, WEST BENGAL 734430
Telephone: S.L.G. 21455, 21035.
Founded 1962; Teaching and Affiliating.

Chancellor: H.E. THE GOVERNOR OF WEST BENGAL.
Vice-Chancellor: Dr. P. K. GHOSH.
Registrar: B. K. BAJPAIE, M.A., M.SC

The library contains 46,360 vols.
Number of students: 21,229.

DEANS:

Faculty of Arts: Prof. S. P. SENGUPTA, M.A., PH.D.
Faculty of Engineering and Technology: Prof. B. SEN, M.S., PH.D.
Faculty of Medicine and Pharmacy: Prof. L. K. GANGULY, B.SC., M.D., M.R.C.P., F.C.C.P.
Faculty of Science: Prof. S. N. SEN, M.SC., D.PHIL.

There are 2 constituent colleges, 4 university colleges, and 28 affiliated colleges.

NORTH-EASTERN HILL UNIVERSITY

SHILLONG, MEGHALAYA STATE 793001
Telephone: 3222.
Founded 1973; Teaching and Affiliating.

Language of instruction: English; Academic year: August to June.

Chancellor: THE PRIME MINISTER OF INDIA.
Vice-Chancellor: Dr. ANUJ KUMAR DHAN.
Registrar: Mrs. MARGARET ROSE MAWLONG.
Librarian: J. C. BINWAL.

Library of 100,000 vols.
Number of teachers: 120.
Number of students: 15,785.
Publication: *Drumbeats* (monthly).

DEANS:

School of Languages: Prof. A. G. GEORGE.
School of Life Sciences: Prof. P. S. RAMAKRISHNAN.
School of Social Sciences: Prof. G. S. ARORA.
School of Physical Sciences: Prof. K. K. GUPTA.
School of Environmental Sciences: (vacant).
School of Education: Prof. C. L. ANANO.

There are 28 affiliated colleges and 2 University Colleges.

ORISSA UNIVERSITY OF AGRICULTURE AND TECHNOLOGY

BHUBANESWAR 751003, DISTRICT PURI, ORISSA STATE
Telephone: 51424.
Founded 1962; Teaching and Research.

Chancellor: THE GOVERNOR OF ORISSA.
Vice-Chancellor: Dr. K. KANUNGO.
Registrar: Sri P. K. MISRA.
Librarian: Sri R. N. SENAPATY.

The library contains 101,842 vols.
Number of teachers: 135.
Number of students: 1,267.

DEANS:

Faculty of Agriculture: Dr. S. K. SINHA.
Faculty of Veterinary Science and Animal Husbandry: Dr. S. N. PANI.
College of Basic Science and Humanities: Dr. P. D. DAS.
Faculty of Agricultural Engineering and Technology: Dr. R. LAL.

OSMANIA UNIVERSITY

HYDERABAD, 500007,
ANDHRA PRADESH

Telephone: 71951.

Founded 1918; Teaching, Residential and Affiliating.

Languages of instruction: English. Hindi, Telugu, Urdu and Marathi; Academic year: June to April (two terms).

Chancellor: THE GOVERNOR OF ANDHRA PRADESH.

Vice-Chancellor: Prof. G. RAM REDDI.

Registrar: B. RAMCHANDRA REDDY.

Librarian: B. INAMDAR.

The library contains 341,801 vols.

Number of students: 41,929.

Publications: *Journal of Osmania University, Syllabuses, University Act, University Diary, List of Recognised Examinations of Other Universities, University Hand Book, Osmania Journal of English Studies, Research Bulletin of Department of Psychology,* etc.

DEANS:

Faculty of Arts: Prof. B. RAMA RAJU.
Faculty of Science: Prof. K. D. ABHAYANKAR.
Faculty of Social Sciences: Prof. SHAH MANZOOR ALAM.
Faculty of Commerce: Prof. C. LAXMINARAIN.
Faculty of Engineering: Prof. B. N. GARUDACHAR.
Faculty of Education: Prof. V. E. REDDY.
Faculty of Law: Sri MURTHZA ALI.
Faculty of Medicine: Dr. Y. R. REDDY.
Faculty of Technology: Prof. S. N. RAO.
Faculty of Ayurvedha and Unani: HAKEEM ZAHURUL HASAN.

UNIVERSITY COLLEGES:

University College of Arts: Hyderabad; f. 1918.
Principal: Prof. K. S. UPADHYAYA.

University College of Commerce and Business Management: Hyderabad; f. 1975.
Principal: Prof. J. SATYANARAYANA.

University College of Education: Hyderabad; f. 1928.
Principal: Dr. V. RUKMA RAO.

University College of Engineering: Hyderabad; f. 1929.
Principal: Prof. ALLADI PRABHAKAR.

University College of Law: Hyderabad; f. 1960.
Principal: Shri L. R. PENNA.

University College of Science: Hyderabad; f. 1918.
Principal: Dr. V. R. SRINIVASAN.

University College of Technology: Hyderabad 7; f. 1969.
Principal: Prof. P. S. RAMACHANDRAN.

CONSTITUENT COLLEGES:

College of Law: (Evening Session) Hyderabad; f. 1951.
Principal: T. S. A. NARAYANAN.

Evening College of Arts and Commerce: Secunderabad; f. 1949.
Principal: Shri MUSTAFA HUSSAIN.

Nizam College: Hyderabad; f. 1887.
Principal: Prof. M. L. N. REDDY.

Postgraduate College: Hyderabad; f. 1949.
Principal: S. SIRAJUDDIN.

Post-Graduate Centres: Bhiknoor, Nizambad district; Godavarikhani, Karimnagar district; Kothagudem, Khanmar district; f. 1976.
Principal: Dr. K. KONDAL REDDY.

Kothagudem School of Mines: Kothagudem 507101.
Principal: Prof. K. R. M. RAO.

Postgraduate Centre: Godavari Khani; f. 1976.
Principal: Dr. V. HYDERKHAN.

Postgraduate Centre in Geology: Kothagudem; f. 1976.
Principal: Prof. N. RAMANA RAO.

Saifabad Science College: Hyderabad; f. 1951.
Principal: V. D. THATTE.

Secunderabad Arts and Science College: Secunderabad; f. 1947.
Principal: Sri MANOHAR ANDRAIAH.

University College for Women: Hyderabad; f. 1924.
Principal: Prof. VANAJA IYENGAR.

There are 96 affiliated colleges.

PANJAB UNIVERSITY

CHANDIGARH 160014,
UNION TERRITORY

Telephone: 23324.

Founded 1947; Teaching and Affiliating.

Languages of instruction: English, Punjabi, Urdu and Hindi; Academic year: July to April (three terms).

Chancellor: THE VICE-PRESIDENT OF INDIA.

Vice-Chancellor: Prof. R. C. PAUL.

Registrar: D. P. VERMA.

Librarian: J. S. SHARMA, PH.D., M.A.

Libraries of 436,000 vols.

Number of students: 79,980.

Publications: *University News, Research Bulletin* (Arts), *Journal of Science, Parakh, Parishodh, Social Science Research Journal, Journal of Medieval Literature.*

DEANS:

Faculty of Arts: Prof. SHANTI SWARUP.
Faculty of Languages: Dr. JAGDISH CHANDER.
Faculty of Science: Prof. M. L. LAKHANPAL.
Faculty of Engineering and Technology: Prof. B. GHOSH.
Faculty of Education: A. S. SHANTE.
Faculty of Business Management and Commerce: Dr. T. N. KAPOOR.
Faculty of Law: Dr. G. S. DHILLON.
Faculty of Medicine: Dr. P. N. CHHUTTANI.
Faculty of Dairying, Animal Husbandry and Agriculture: Dr. D. SUNDARESAN.
Faculty of Design and Fine Arts: Dr. B. N. GOSWAMY.

There are 86 affiliated colleges.

UNIVERSITY OF PATNA

PATNA 800005, BIHAR STATE

Telephone: 52500.

Founded 1917: re-founded 1952; Residential and Teaching.

Languages of instruction: Hindi and English; Academic year: June to May (three terms).

Chancellor: H.E. THE GOVERNOR OF BIHAR.

Vice-Chancellor: K. N. PRASAD.

Registrar: P. S.K. SHARMA.

Library of 205,000 vols.

Librarian: B. P. MISHRA, M.A., DIP. IN L.SC.

The library contains 207,000 vols.

Number of students: 15,840.

Publications: *University of Patna Journal, Patna University News Bulletin* (monthly).

DEANS:

Faculty of Arts: Prof. Q. HUSSAIN.
Faculty of Education: R. R. SINGH.
Faculty of Engineering: R. K. VERMA.
Faculty of Law: Dr. R. C. HINGORANI.
Faculty of Medicine: Dr. A. K. SINHA, M.S., F.R.C.S.
Faculty of Commerce: Dr. N. L. NADDA.
Faculty of Science: Prof. D. MISHRA.

PROFESSORS:

AHMAD, Z., Sociology
GHOSH, S. P., Chemistry
HASAN, S. S., Persian
HINGORANI, R. C., Law
JHA, A., Philosophy
JHA, B., Sanskrit
JHA, C., Political Science
JHA, D., Economics
JHA, J. C., History
KARIMI, S. M., Geography
LAL, D. N., Statistics
MAZUMDAR, B. P., History
MOHSIN, S. M., Psychology
NADDA, N. L., Commerce
NARAIN, V. A., History
RAHMAN, M., Urdu
ROY, R. P., Botany
SHARAN, R. K., Zoology
SINGH, L. S., Physics
SINGH, R. P. K., Mathematics
SINGH, T. N., Hindi
SINHA, B. P., Ancient Indian History and Archaeology
SINHA, G. P., Labour and Social Welfare
SINHA, R. C., Geology
SINHA, R. K., English
SRIVASTAVA, B. N., Law
VARMA, V. P., Political Science

The university maintains 12 constituent colleges and forty postgraduate departments.

CONSTITUENT COLLEGES:

Arts and Crafts College: Patna 1; f. 1938.
Principal: P. S. NATHSINHA.
Number of teachers: 14.
Number of students: 100.

Bihar College of Engineering: Mahendru, Patna; f. 1924; 4-year course.
Principal: B. B. CHAKRAVARTY.
Number of teachers: 51.
Number of students: 450.

Bihar National College: Bankipur, Patna 4; f. 1917.
Principal: S. K. BOSE.
Number of teachers: 89.
Number of students: 2,500.

Commerce College: Patna 4; f. 1953.
Principal: Dr. P. N. SHARMA.
Number of teachers: 26.
Number of students: 1,300.

Magadh Mahila College: Patna; f. 1946.
Principal: Q. HUSSAIN.
Number of teachers: 52.
Number of students: 1,000.

Patna College: P.O. Bankipur, Patna, Bihar; f. 1863; the oldest college in the province, and the parent institution of three other colleges.
Principal: Dr. C. JHA.
Number of teachers: 105.
Number of students: 1,583.

Patna Law College: P.O. Mahendru, Patna, Bihar; f. 1906.
Principal: B. N. SRIVASTAVA, LL.M.
Number of teachers: 29.
Number of students: 1,400.

Patna Training College: Patna; f. 1908.
Principal: R. R. SINGH.
Number of teachers: 8.
Number of students: 264.

Patna Women's College: Patna; f. 1940.
Principal: Sister M. LUCILE, A.C., M.A.
Number of teachers: 55.
Number of students: 950.

Prince of Wales' Medical College: Bankipur, Patna; f. 1925.
Principal: Dr. M. SINGH.
Number of teachers: 60.
Number of students: 900.

Science College: Bankipur, Patna; f. 1927.
Principal: Dr. S. N. DAS.
Number of teachers: 104.
Number of students: 1,541.

Women's Training College: Patna; f. 1951.
Principal: Mrs. UMA BASU, M.A., DIP. IN ED.
Number of teachers: 8.
Number of students: 420.

PERARIGNAR ANNA UNIVERSITY OF TECHNOLOGY

SARDAR PATEL ROAD,
GUINDY, MADRAS 600025
Telephone: 414545, 415161.
Founded 1978.

Vice-Chancellor: P. SIVALINGAM, M.S.
Registrar: Dr. V. ANANDA RAO.
Librarian: C. RAMACHANDRAN.

Library of 109,186 vols.
Number of teachers: 444.
Number of students: 3,677.

DIRECTORS:

College of Engineering: Prof. W. P. VIJAYARAGHAVAN.
Alagappa Chettiar College of Technology: Dr. G. S. LADDHA.
School of Architecture and Planning: Prof. F. B. PITHAVADIAN.
Madras Institute of Technology (Chrompet Campus): Dr. S. SATHIKH.

UNIVERSITY OF POONA

GANESHKHIND, POONA 411007,
MAHARASHTRA
Telephone: 56061/9.
Founded 1949: Teaching and Affiliating.

Languages of instruction: English and (optional) Marathi; Academic year: June to March (two terms).

Chancellor: H.E. THE GOVERNOR OF MAHARASHTRA.
Vice-Chancellor: R. G. TAKWALE, M.SC., PH.D.
Registrar: G. J. ABHYANKAR, B.A.
Librarian: M. P. PETHE, M.A., PH.D.

The library contains 222,000 vols.

Number of students 96,000 (including affiliated colleges).

DEANS:

Faculty of Arts: Dr. P. A. TAKAWALE.
Faculty of Law: Dr. S. K. AGRAWALA.
Faculty of Medicine: Surg. Capt. J. K. SUAHDEVA.
Faculty of Science: Prin. S. D. PATIL.
Faculty of Engineering: Prof. A. G. PATWARDHAN.
Faculty of Mental, Moral and Social Science: Dr. N. R. INAMDAR.
Faculty of Ayurvedic Medicine: Vaidya M. D. RAJPATHAK.
Faculty of Commerce: Dr. M. L. ABHYANKAR.
Faculty of Education: Prin. G. S. DONGARE.

HEADS OF DEPARTMENTS:

Chemistry: Dr. V. K. PHANSALKAR.
Physics: Dr. M. R. BHIDAY.
Mathematics: Dr. S. S. ABHYANKAR.
Botany: Dr. S. B. DAVID.
Zoology: Dr. G. I. TONAPI.
Geography: Dr. K. R. DIKSHIT.
Sanskrit and Prakkrit Languages: Dr. S. D. JOSHI.
Marathi: Dr. M. S. KANADE.
Experimental Psychology: Dr. M. N. PALSANE.
Politics: Prof. V. M. SIRSIKAR.
Geology: Dr. K. B. POWAR.
Sociology: Dr. Y. B. DAMLE.
Modern European Languages: Prof. B. B. KULKARNI.
English: M. L. RAINA.
Hindi: Dr. A. P. DIKSHIT.
Archaeology: Dr. V. N. MISRA.
Linguistics: Dr. D. M. JOSHI.
Philosophy: Dr. S. S. BARLINGAY.
History: Dr. A. R. KULKARNI.
Journalism: Shri L. N. GOKHALE.
Defence Studies: Brig. K. G. PITRE.
Law: Dr. S. K. AGRAWALA.
Anthropology: Prof. R. K. MUTATKAR.
Statistics: Dr. S. K. ADKE.

PROFESSORS:

BAPAT, B. V., Education
DANDEKAR, V. M., Economics
GODBOLE, S. H., Microbiology
SHAIKH, A. N., Persian and Urdu
SHEJWALKAR, V. M., Commerce
TAKWALE, R. G., Physics

CONSTITUENT COLLEGES:

Adarsha College of Education: Erandawana, Karve Rd., Poona 4; f. 1970.

Adhyapak Mahavidyalaya College of Education: Aranyeshwar, Poona 9; f. 1970.

Armed Forces Medical College: Poona 1; f. 1948.

Arts and Commerce College: Hadapsar, Poona 28; f. 1971.

B.J. Medical College: Poona 1; f. 1946.

B.M. College of Commerce: Poona 4; f. 1943.

College of Engineering: Poona 5; f. 1854.

Fergusson College: Poona 4; f. 1885.

Jain College of Arts and Commerce: Chinchwad, Poona 19; f. 1971

Law College: Poona 4, f. 1924.

Loyola College: Poona 8; f. 1970.

M.E. Society's Abasaheb Garware College of Commerce: Poona 4; f. 1967.

M.E. Society's Abasaheb Garware College of Arts and Sciences: Poona 4; f. 1945.

Modern College of Arts, Science and Commerce: Shivajinagar, Poona 5.

Ness Wadia College of Commerce: Poona 1; f. 1969.

Nowrosjee Wadia College: 19 Bund Road, Poona 1; f. 1932.

Poona College of Arts, Science and Commerce: Compound of Anglo-Urdu High School, Shankarsheth Rd., Poona 1; f. 1970.

St. Mira's College for Girls: Poona 1; f. 1962.

Shahu Mandir Mahavidyalaya: Poona 9; f. 1960.

Sir Parashurambhau College: Poona 30; f. 1916.

St. Vincent College: 2004 St. Vincent St., Poona 1; f. 1970.

Symbiosis Institute of Management: Senapati Bapat Marg, Poona 411004.

Tilak College of Education: Poona 30; f. 1941.

Tilak Ayurveda Mahavidyalaya: 583/2 Rasta Peth, Poona 11; f. 1933.

There are 81 affiliated colleges.

PUNJAB AGRICULTURAL UNIVERSITY

LUDHIANA, 141004 PUNJAB

Telephone: 22960, 24955.

Founded 1962; Teaching, Research and Extension.

Autonomous control; Language of instruction: English; Academic year: August to July (four terms).

Chancellor: H.E. THE GOVERNOR OF PUNJAB.

Vice-Chancellor: Dr. AMRIK SINGH CHEEMA.

Registrar: Shri S. P. KARKARA.

Librarian: SARBJIT SINGH SANDHU, M.SC., M.S., M.L.S.

Library of 186,774 vols.

Number of teachers: 1,076.
Number of students: 2,881.

Publications: *Journal of Research* (monthly, in English), *Progressive Farming* (monthly, in English), *Changi Kheti* (monthly, in Punjabi), *PAU News* (monthly, in English).

DEANS:

College of Agriculture: Dr. KHEM SINGH GILL.
College of Agricultural Engineering: Dr. A. P. BHATNAGAR.
College of Veterinary Science: Dr. B. S. GILL.
College of Postgraduate Studies, Hissar: Dr. A. S. ATWAL.
College of Basic Science and Humanities: Dr. K. S. GILL.
College of Home Science: Dr. (Mrs). K. K. SHARMA.

PROFESSORS:

College of Agriculture:

BAINS, Dr. D. S., M.SC., PH.D., Agronomy
BAINS, G. S., M.SC., Science and Technology
BAJWA, M. S., Soils
BEDI, Dr. P. S., PH.D., Plant Pathology
BHATIA, B. S., Food Science and Technology
CHALAL, B. S., PH.D., Entomology
DEV, G., M.SC., PH.D., Soils
DHILLON, B. S., M.SC., PH.D., Horticulture
GANGWAR, P. C., M.SC., PH.D., Animal Science
GILL, Dr. G. S., PH.D., Animal Science
GILL, Dr. H. S., PH.D., Agronomy
GILL, S. S., PH.D., Animal Science
HUNDAL, L. S., M.SC., PH.D., Animal Science
ICHHOPONANI, J. S., M.SC., PH.D., Animal Science
JAIN, S. C., M.SC., PH.D., Science and Technology
JAWANDA, J. S., PH.D., Horticulture
JHOTTY, J. S., M.SC., Plant Pathology
KANWAR, R. S., M.SC., PH.D., Sugar Cane Agronomy
KHERA, A. S., M.SC., PH.D., Maize Breeding
LOBANA, K. S., M.SC., PH.D., Oilseed Breeding
MAVI, H. S., M.SC., PH.D., Agrometeorology
MEELU, O. P., P.D., Science
NANDPURI, Dr. K. S., M.SC., PH.D., Vegetation, Landscaping and Floriculture
NIJJAR, Dr. G. S., M.SC., PH.D., Horticulture
PAWAR, Dr. S. S., PH.D., Extension Education
PRIHAR, S. S., M.SC., PH.D., Soil Physics
RANDHAWA, K. S., M.SC., PH.D., Olericulture
SAINI, S. S., M.SC., PH.D., Crop Breeding
SANDHU, A. S., M.SC., PH.D., Training Programming
SEKHON, G. S., M.SC., PH.D., Soils
SIDHU, A. S., PH.D., Entomology
SINGH, DALBIR, M.SC., PH.D., Animal Science
SINGH, HARCHARAN, PH.D., Entomology
SINGH MEHAR, M.SC., PH.D., Animal Science
SINGH, N. T., M.SC., PH.D., Soil Physics
SINGH, RAGHBIR, M.SC., PH.D., Extension Education
SINGH, SAWAI, PH.D., Entomology
SINGH, T. H., M.SC, PH.D., Plant Breeding
SINHA, M. K., M.SC., PH.D., Soil Fertilization and Plant Nutrition
TAKKAR, P. N., M.SC., PH.D., Soil Science
TIWANA, M. S., PH.D., Animal Genetics

College of Agricultural Engineering:

CHEEMA, L. S., PH.D., Mechanical Engineering
ENGIRA, R. M., M.SC., PH.D., Electrical Engineering
KHEPAR, Shri S. D., M.E., Soil and Water Engineering
MANNAN, K. D., M.E., PH.D., Mechanical Engineering
MURTY, V. V. N., M.TECH., Soil and Water Engineering
SALARIYA, Dr. K. S, PH.D., Electrical Engineering
SINGH, C. P., PH.D., Farm Power and Machinery
SINGH, S. R., PH.D., Research Engineering
SRIVASTAVA, Dr. R. K., PH.D., Processing and Agricultural Structures
VARSHNEY, R. K., M.SC., PH.D., Electrical Engineering
VERMA, S. R., PH.D., Farm Power and Machinery
VYAS, Dr. K. S., PH.D., Civil Engineering

College of Basic Sciences and Humanities:

BAL, Dr. S. S., M.A., PH.D., Languages, Culture and History
BHATIA, B. S., Food Technology
BHATIA, Dr. I. S., M.SC., PH.D., Biochemistry
DEB, P. C., M.A., PH.D., Economics and Sociology
GILL, K. S., M.SC., PH.D., Genetics
GREWAL, G. S., PH.D., Chemistry
GREWAL, S. S., M.A., PH.D., Economics and Sociology
GUPTA, Dr. V. P., PH.D., Genetics
GURAYA, Dr. S. S., M.SC., D.SC., PH.D., Zoology
KALRA, Dr. M. S., PH.D., Microbiology
KALSI, P. S., M.SC., PH.D., Chemistry
MALIK, Dr. C. P., M.SC., PH.D., Botany
MINOCHA, J. L., PH.D., Genetics
RAJ, Dr. DEO, Physics
RAMASUBHAN, T. A., PH.D., Mathematics and Statistics
SIDHU, Dr. D. S., M.SC., PH.D., Economics and Sociology
SINGH, BACHAN, PH.D., Forestry and Natural Resources
SINGH, D. R., M.COM., PH.D., Business Management
SINGH, Dr. RATTAN, M.SC., PH.D., Research
TOOR, H. S., M.SC., PH.D., Zoology
VERMA, H. K., PH.D., Mathematics and Statistics
ZAHIR, Dr. M. A., PH.D., Business Management

College of Home Science:

BAJAJ, Mrs. S., M.SC., PH.D., Foods and Nutrition
CHOPRA, A. K., PH.D., Nutritional Research
DHESI, Dr. Mrs. J. K., M.A., PH.D., Home Management
ROY, Dr. S., PH.D., Home Science Education and Extension
SINGH, Dr. M. B., PH.D., Child Development
SRIVASTAVA, Mrs. P. L., M.SC., Education and Extension

College of Veterinary Science:

BAXI, Dr. K. K., M.SC., PH.D., Bacteriology and Virology
CHAUHAN, J. S., PH.D., Int. Director, Plant Disease Clinic
DASS, Dr. L. N., PH.D., Anatomy and Histology
DHILLON, S. S., M.V.SC., Veterinary Pathology
DUTT, S. C., M.SC., PH.D., Parasitology
GUPTA, Dr. P. P., PH.D., Veterinary Pathology
KALRA, R. K., PH.D., Insect Toxology
KOHLI, R. N., M.V.SC., D.SC., Surgery and Radiology
KWATRA, Dr. M. S., M.V.SC., PH.D., Snr. Investigations Officer
MISRA, Dr. S. K., PH.D., Veterinary Medicine
NANDA, B. S., M.V.SC., PH.D., Anatomy and Histology
PAUL, Dr. B. S., M.V.SC., PH.D., Veterinary Pharmacology
RATHOR, S. S., M.SC., PH.D., Clinics
SHARMA, Dr. R. D., PH.D., Obstetrics and Gynaecology
SHARMA, S. N., Virology
VERMAN, Dr. P. N., M.SC., PH.D., Veterinary Physiology

PUNJABI UNIVERSITY

PATIALA 147002, PUNJAB

Founded 1962.

Languages of instruction: Punjabi and English; State control; Academic year: July to June (three terms).

Chancellor: H.E. THE GOVERNOR OF PUNJAB.

Vice-Chancellor: Dr. BHAGAT SINGH.

Registrar: SARDAR GURBACHAN SINGH.

Librarian: Dr. R. L. MITTAL.

Library of 205,000 vols.

Number of students: 36,215.

Publications: *Punjabi University Bulletin, Journal of Religious Studies* (quarterly).

DEANS:

Faculty of Arts and Social Sciences: Dr. S. S. BAL.
Faculty of Life Sciences: Dr. S. S. BIR.
Faculty of Physical Sciences: Dr. B. S. MANHAS.
Faculty of Engineering and Technology: Prin. M. L. JAIN.
Faculty of Medicine: Dr. (Mrs.) LIELA R. KUMAR.
Faculty of Business Administration and Commerce: Dr. B. S. BHATIA.
Faculty of Languages: Dr. MANMOHAN SEHGAL.
Faculty of Law: Shri AJIT SINGH.
Faculty of Education: Dr. T. R. SHARMA.
Faculty of Humanities and Religious Studies: Prof. AVTAR SINGH.
Faculty of Ayurveda: V. KUMAR.
Faculty of Vocational Courses: Dr. C. S. KHURANA.

There are 50 affiliated colleges.

PUNJABRAO AGRICULTURE UNIVERSITY

KRISHINAGAR, AKOLA 444001, MAHARASHTRA

Telephone: 2372.

Founded 1969.

Chancellor: H.E. THE GOVERNOR OF MAHARASHTRA.

Pro-Chancellor: THE MINISTER FOR AGRICULTURE, MAHARASHTRA.

Vice-Chancellor: Dr. B. A. CHAUGULE.

Registrar: M. S. SAPKAL.

Librarian: P. P. DESHMUKH.

Library of 80,000 vols.
Number of students: 3,300.

The University maintains 5 constituent and 2 affiliated colleges and 40 research stations.

CONSTITUENT COLLEGES:

College of Agriculture: Akola; f. 1955; Principal Dr. B. G. BATHKAL.

College of Agriculture: Nagpur; f. 1906; Principal V. T. RAHATE.

College of Agricultural Engineering: Akola; f. 1970; Principal S. S. WANJARI.

Nagpur Veterinary College: Nagpur; f. 1958; Principal Dr. R. N. DEB.

Post Graduate Institute: Akola; f. 1970; Principal Dr. V. N. SHUKLA.

RABINDRA BHARATI UNIVERSITY

56A BARRACKPORE TRUNK RD., CALCUTTA 700050

Telephone: 56-2014/5, 56-2068, 56-2142.

Founded 1962.

Languages of instruction: Bengali and English; State control; Academic year: June to May (three terms).

Chancellor: H.E. THE GOVERNOR OF WEST BENGAL.

Vice-Chancellor: Dr. DEVIPADA BHATTACHARYA, M.A., PH.D.

Registrar: Prof. DILIP COOMER GHOSE, M.A., LL.B.

Librarian: Shri S. M. GANGULY, M.COM., DIP.LIB.

Number of teachers: 317.
Number of students: 2,835.

Publication: *Rabindra Bharati Journal* (English, annually), *Rabindra Bharati University Patrika* (Bengali, annually).

Departments of Bengali, English, Sanskrit, Philosophy, History, Economics, Political Science, Dance, Drama, Vocal Music, Instrumental Music, Rabindra Sangeet, Painting.

There are 56 associated colleges.

UNIVERSITY OF RAJASTHAN

GANDHI NAGAR, JAIPUR 302004

Telephone: 63211

Founded 1947: Teaching and Affiliating.

Languages of instruction: English and Hindi; Academic year: July to May (three terms); Independent control.

Chancellor: H.E. THE GOVERNOR OF RAJASTHAN.

Vice-Chancellor: Dr. IQBAL NARAIN.

Registrar: V. D. QAMRA.

Librarian: N. N. GIDWANI.

The library contains 229,255 vols.
Number of university teachers: 509.
Number of students: 112,474.

DEANS:

Faculty of Arts: Dr. D. KRISHNA.
Faculty of Science: Dr. R. C. MEHROTA.
Faculty of Commerce: N. M. KOTHARI.
Faculty of Law: Dr. G. S. SHARMA.
Faculty of Medicine: Dr. K. D. GUPTA.
Faculty of Education: Dr. L. K. OAD.
Faculty of Engineering: R. M. ADVANI.
Faculty of Social Sciences: Dr. G. C. PATNI.
Faculty of Ayurveda: P. D. SHARMA.
Faculty of Sanskrit: Dr. K. N. MISHRA.

PROFESSORS:

BHARGAVA, P. L., Sanskrit
CHAUDHERY, M. W., Geology
DAYA KRISHNA, Philosophy
GAUR, J. N., Chemistry
GUPTA, S. S., History
JOSHI, J. M., Economics
JOSHI, K. C., Chemistry
KAPOOR, A. S., Zoology
KAUL, R. K., English
LOKNATHAN, S., Physics
MEHROTRA, R. C., Chemistry
MATHUR, K. S., Accountancy and Business Statistics
OMPRAKASH, Economic Administration and Financial Management
PANDE, G. C., History and Indian Culture
PATNI, G. C., Mathematics
RAJ KRISHNA, Economics
SARAF, B. L., Physics
SARIN, R. G., Business Administration
SHARMA, G. N., History
SHARMA, G. S., Law
SHARMA, S. S., Hindi
SINHA, S. N., Psychology
SRIVASTAVA, P. N., Zoology
SUNDARAM, P. S., English
TIAGI, B., Botany
TIKKIWAL, B. D., Statistics
UNNITHAN, T. K. N., Sociology
VARMA, S. P., Political Science
ZIAUDDIN KHAN, Public Administration

UNIVERSITY COLLEGES:

Commerce College: Jaipur; f. 1956.

Maharaja's College: Jaipur; f. 1813.

Maharani's College: Jaipur; f. 1944.

Rajasthan College: Jaipur; f. 1962.

There are 160 affiliated colleges.

RAJENDRA AGRICULTURAL UNIVERSITY

PUSA, SAMASTIPUR, BIHAR STATE

Founded 1971.

Chancellor: H.E. THE GOVERNOR OF BIHAR.

Vice-Chancellor: Dr. S. K. MUKHERJEE.

Registrar: Dr. D. P. SINGH.

The University consists of all the agricultural and veterinary colleges previously affiliated to Bhagalpur, Bihar, Magadh, Mithila and Ranchi Universities.

RANCHI UNIVERSITY

RANCHI 834008, BIHAR

Telephone: 22553.

Founded 1960; Teaching and Affiliating.

Chancellor: H.E. THE GOVERNOR OF BIHAR.

Vice-Chancellor: Dr. A. K. DHAN.

Registrar: Dr. A. PRASAD.

Library of 71,300 vols.

Number of teachers: 1,590.
Number of students: 60,429.

Publications: *The University Journal, Journal of Social Research, The Geographical Outlook, Journal of Historical Research, Research Journal of Philosophy, Political Scientist, Journal of Agricultural Science.*

DEANS:

Faculty of Arts: Dr. P. N. OJHA.
Faculty of Science: Dr. K. C. BOSE.
Faculty of Commerce: M. R. CHURASIA.
Faculty of Law: Prin. H. K. LAL.
Faculty of Engineering: Dr. K. P. GUPTA.

Faculty of Education: Dr. R. SINGH.
Faculty of Medicine: Dr. B. B. P. ROY.

The University has 4 Constituent Colleges and 60 affiliated colleges.

RAVISHANKAR UNIVERSITY

RAIPUR, MADHYA PRADESH
492002
Telephone: 23957.

Founded 1963; Teaching and Affiliating.

Languages of instruction: Hindi and English; Private control; Academic year: July to June (two terms).

Chancellor: H.E. THE GOVERNOR OF MADHYA PRADESH.
Vice-Chancellor: K. P. CHOUBE.
Registrar: Dr. H. N. SHUKLA.
Librarian: R. SINGH.

Library of 46,842 vols.
Number of students: 35,900.

DEANS AND PRINCIPALS:

Faculty of Arts: C. S. TRIVEDI.
Faculty of Science: Dr. SURESH CHANDRA.
Faculty of Law: Prin. R. K. CHANDORKAR.
Faculty of Education: Smt. R. B. VERMA.
Faculty of Medicine: Dr. G. C. SIPAHA.
Faculty of Ayurved: (vacant).
Faculty of Commerce: Prin. N. L. SHARMA.
Faculty of Social Sciences: Dr. A. K. P. SINHA.
Faculty of Engineering: Dr. P. K. KARMALKAR.
Faculty of Life Science: Dr. S. M. AGRAWAL.
Faculty of Home Science: G. BAJPAI.

There are 62 affiliated colleges.

ROHILKHAND UNIVERSITY

204-B CIVIL LINES,
BAREILLY, U.P. 243001
Telephone: 3541, 3664.

Founded 1975; Affiliating.

State control; Languages of instruction: Hindi and English; Academic Year: July to June.

Chancellor: H.E. THE GOVERNOR OF UTTAR PRADESH.
Vice-Chancellor: Dr. RAMJI LAL SAHAYAK.
Registrar: Dr. J. N. SINGHAL.

Number of teachers: 902.
Number of students: 34,848.

DEANS:

Faculty of Agriculture: Dr. J. P. SINGH.
Faculty of Arts: Dr. G. S. TRIGUNAYAT.
Faculty of Commerce: Dr. R. C. AGARWAL.

UNIVERSITY OF ROORKEE

ROORKEE, U.P. 247667
Telephone: 405.

Founded in 1847 as Thomason College; inaugurated as a university 1949; Residential and Teaching; specializes in all branches of engineering.

Language of instruction: English; Academic year: July to May (two terms).

Chancellor: H.E. THE GOVERNOR OF UTTAR PRADESH.
Vice-Chancellor: Dr. J. NARAIN.
Registrar: O. N. CHATURVEDI.
Librarian: Sri R. S. SAXENA.

The library contains 143,000 vols.
Number of teachers: 301.
Number of students: 2,280.

SAMBALPUR UNIVERSITY

JYOTI VIHAR,
BURLA, SAMBALPUR 768017,
ORISSA
Telephone: 116, 137.

Founded 1967; Teaching and Affiliating.

Language of instruction: English; Academic year: June to May.

Chancellor: THE GOVERNOR OF ORISSA.
Vice-Chancellor: Dr. D. C. MISRA, M.A., PH.D.
Registrar: G. P. GURU, M.A.
Librarian: B. P. MAHAPATRA, M.A.

The library contains 42,000 vols.
Number of teachers: 1,260.
Number of students: 21,000.

Publications: *Saptarshi* (monthly), *Journal* (Science, annually), *Journal* (Humanities, annually).

DEANS:

Faculty of Arts: D. C. MISRA, M.A., PH.D.
Faculty of Science: K. S. R. MURTY, M.SC., PH.D.
Faculty of Commerce: Prof. B. K. MOHANTY, M.COM.
Faculty of Education: K. C. PATI, M.ED.
Faculty of Law: Y. MISHRA, B.A., B.L.
Faculty of Medicine: Prof. V. C. NAIK, M.D.
Faculty of Engineering: Prof. B. MOHAPATRA, B.E., M.SC., M.I.E.

PROFESSORS:

DAS, G., M.A., PH.D., D.SC., Mathematics
DAS, M. C., M.SC., PH.D., Biological Science
GUPTA, S. P., M.A., M.SC., LL.B., D.PHIL., Economics
MISHRA, G. C., M.A., D.LITT., Oriya
PADHI, A. P., M.A., PH.D., Political Science
PANI, S., M.SC., PH.D., Chemistry
PATI, P. K., M.A., PH.D., English
SAHU, N. K., M.A., PH.D., D.LITT., History
SATPATHY, R. K., M.SC., PH.D., Physics

There are 29 affiliated colleges and 2 constituent colleges.

SAMPURNANAND SANSKRIT UNIVERSITY

VARANASI 221002, U.P.
Telephone: 65947.

Founded 1958, Teaching and Affiliating.

Chancellor: THE GOVERNOR OF UTTAR PRADESH.
Vice-Chancellor: B. N. SHUKLA.
Registrar: V. N. TRIPATHI.
Librarian: L. N. TIWARI.

Library of 262,000 vols.
Number of students: 33,000.

There are 2 affiliated colleges on-campus, and 686 off-campus.

SARDAR PATEL UNIVERSITY

VALLABH VIDYANAGAR 388120,
KAIRA, GUJARAT
Telephone: 7008, 7073.

Founded 1955; Teaching and Affiliating.

Languages of instruction: Hindi, English or Gujarati; Academic year: June to April (two terms).

Chancellor: H.E. THE GOVERNOR OF GUJARAT.
Vice-Chancellor: R. M. PATEL, M.S., PH.D.
Registrar: R. C. THAKKAR, M.A.
Librarian: S. M. CHARAN, PH.D.

Number of teachers: 452, including 113 postgraduate.

Number of students: 8,309, including 1,126 postgraduate.

Publications: *Journal of Education and Psychology*, *Arth-Vikas* (Economics Journal).

DEANS:

Faculty of Arts: Prof. R. A. DAVE, M.A.
Faculty of Science: Prin. I. A. PATEL, M.SC., PH.D.
Faculty of Engineering and Technology: Prin. R. M. DAVE, M.S., PH.D.
Faculty of Home Science: Prin. (Smt.) G. SUBBULAKSHMI, M.SC.I., PH.D. (Home Sc.).
Faculty of Commerce: Prin. M. D. PATEL, M.COM.
Faculty of Law: Prin. B. I. PATEL, B.SC., LL.B.
Faculty of Education: Dr. C. B. PATYAL, M.ED., PH.D.

POSTGRADUATE DEPARTMENTS:
PROFESSORS:

ADHVARYU, J. H., M.A., PH.D., Economics
AGRAWAL, M. K., PH.D., Physics
DAVE, R. A., M.A., English
JOSHI, M. S., PH.D., Physics
JOSHI, V. R., M.COM., PH.D., Commerce
MISHRA, S. K., PH.D., D.LITT., Hindi
PATEL, J. M., M.A., Gujarati
PATEL, C. K., M.SC., PH.D., Chemistry
PATEL, K. C., M.SC., PH.D., Chemistry

PATEL, S. M., PH.D., Physics
PATEL, S. R., M.SC., PH.D., Chemistry
PATHAK, M. T., M.A., PH.D., Economics
SHAH, B. V., M.A., PH.D., Sociology
SHAH, J. J., M.SC., PH.D., Bio-Sciences
SHAH, M. M., M.COM., M.SC., Commerce
SHAH, S. M., M.SC., PH.D., Statistics
VASAVADA, M. H., M.SC., PH.D., Mathematics

There are 13 affiliated colleges.

UNIVERSITY OF SAUGAR

GOUR NAGAR, SAGAR,
MADHYA PRADESH 470003
Telephone: 2263.
Founded 1946; Teaching, Affiliating and Residential

Languages of instruction: Hindi and English; Private control; Academic year: July to April (two terms).

Chancellor: H.E. THE GOVERNOR OF MADHYA PRADESH.

Vice-Chancellor: Dr. D.. P. JATAR.

Registrar: R. N. DHARWAN (acting).

Librarian: Dr. H. S. SENGAR.

The library contains 165,000 vols.

Number of students: 27,600.

Publications: *Madhya Bharati—Research Journal* (annual, Hindi and English).

DEANS:

Faculty of Arts: Dr. PREM SHANKAR.
Faculty of Science: Dr. S. S. NIGAM.
Faculty of Law: G. S. SRIVASTAVA.
Faculty of Education: Prof. S. P. AHLUWALIA.,
Faculty of Life Sciences: Dr. R. S. SAINI.
Faculty of Social Sciences: Dr. B. N. SHARMA.
Faculty of Commerce: Prof. R. P. ROY.
Faculty of Technology: Dr. K. C. VERMA,
Faculty of Ayurved: Dr. V. S. PANDEY.

There are 50 affiliated colleges.

SAURASHTRA UNIVERSITY

UNIVERSITY CAMPUS,
KALAWAD RD., RAJKOT 360005,
GUJARAT STATE
Telephone: PBX 27601-4.
Founded 1967; Teaching and Affiliating.

State control; Languages of instruction: Gujarati, Hindi and English; Academic Year: June to March/April (two terms).

Chancellor: H.E. THE GOVERNOR OF GUJARAT STATE.

Vice-Chancellor: Prof. D. N. PATHAK.

Registrar: Shri V. M. DESAI, M.A., LL.B.

Librarian: Shri N. H. BARODIA.

Library of 70,000 vols.

Number of teachers: 1,296 (inc. affiliated colleges).

Number of students: 38,245 (inc. affiliated colleges).

Publications: *Annual Report, Annual Budget, Vak.*

DEANS:

Faculty of Arts: Prin. D. L. MUNIM.
Faculty of Science: Dr. V. M. THAKOR.
Faculty of Commerce: Prin. C. K. DHAMSANIA.
Faculty of Education: Dr. H. G. DESAI.
Faculty of Law: Prof. Y. S. MEHTA.
Faculty of Technology and Engineering: Prin. B. V. CHAR.
Faculty of Medicine: Dr. M. N. JINDAL.
Faculty of Rural Studies: Shri. K. D. THAKER.

HEADS OF DEPARTMENTS:

Biosciences: Dr. S. C. PANDEYA.
Chemistry: Dr. V. M. THAKOR.
Physics: Prof. R. G. KULKARNI.
Mathematics: Prof. P. B. RAMANUJAN.
Sociology: Dr. P. S. JETHWA.
Education: Dr. H. G. DESAI.
Economics: Dr. V. H. JOSHI.
History: Dr. R. G. PARIKH.
Gujarati: Dr. I. R. DAVE.

There are 55 affiliated colleges.

SHIVAJI UNIVERSITY

VIDYANAGAR, KOLHAPUR,
416004 MAHARASHTRA
Telephone: 4271.
Founded 1962; Teaching and Affiliating.

Languages of instruction: English and Marathi; Academic year: June to March (two terms).

Chancellor: H.E. THE GOVERNOR OF MAHARASHTRA.

Vice-Chancellor: K. BHOGISHA-YANA, M.A. (acting).

Registrar: U. G. ITHAPE, M.A., PH.D.

Librarian: B. C. JAKATI, M.A., M.LIB.SC.

Library of 125,000 vols.

Number of teachers: 2,698.

Number of students: 44,146 (inc. affiliated colleges).

Publication: *University Journal* (Humanities and Social Sciences Sections).

DEANS:

Faculty of Arts: K. BHOGISHAYANA.
Faculty of Social Sciences: Prin. R. D. GAIKWAD.
Faculty of Science: Prin. R. M. RAVERKAR.
Faculty of Commerce: A. D. SHINDE.
Faculty of Education: Prin. R. S. PATIL.
Faculty of Engineering: Prof. V. T. IDATE.
Faculty of Law: Prof. M. B. KARMARKAR.
Faculty of Medicine: Dr. P. N. DUBEY.

There are 82 affiliated colleges.

SHREEMATI NATHIBAI DAMODAR THACKERSEY WOMEN'S UNIVERSITY

1 NATHIBAI THACKERSEY RD.,
BOMBAY 400020 (BR)
Telephone: 291879.
Telegraphic Address: Uniwomen.
Founded 1916: Teaching and Affiliating.

State control; Languages of instruction: English, Gujarati, Marathi and Hindi; Academic year: June to March (two terms).

Chancellor: H.E. THE GOVERNOR OF MAHARASHTRA.

Vice-Chancellor: Dr. MADHURI R. SHAH, M.A., PH.D.

***Registrar:* Mrs. KAMALINI H. BHANSALI, B.A., M.ED.**

***Librarian:* Miss VIDYUT KHANDWALA, B.A., DIP.LIB.**

The library contains 161,316 vols.

Number of teachers: 715.

Number of students: 19,739, including 6,274 private students.

Publications: *University Research Journal*† (every 2 years), Prospectuses of Courses (occasional), Educational Textbooks, etc.

DEANS:

Faculty of Arts: Prof. J. G. TRIVEDI.
***Faculty of Education:* Miss S. MEHTA, M.S.**
Faculty of Fine Arts: Prof. V. R. ATHAVALE.
Faculty of Home Science: Mrs. KUMUD A. PATWA.
Faculty of Library Science: Miss VIDYUT KHANDWALA.
Faculty of Nursing: Dr. Mrs. JYOTI TRIVEDI.
Faculty of Social Science: Dr. NEERA DESAI.
Dean of Students: Miss BAKULA SHAH, M.ED.

PROFESSORS:

ASHAR, RAJANI R., Audio Visual
ATHAVALE, V. R., Music
DABHOLKAR, Miss AMBU A., Language Laboratory
DAFTARY, Miss BINDU, Textiles and Clothing
DALAL, S. P., Gujarati
DAVE, J. H., Sanskrit
DESAI, Mrs. NEERA A., Sociology
GANGAL, R. M., Extension Studies
INAMDAR, Dr. H. V., Marathi
KHANDWALA, Miss VIDYUT, Library Science
KELKAR, Dr. K. S., Hindi
KUDEHEDKAR, K. L., English
LAKDAWALA, Miss URMILA, Education
MALSHE, S. G., Marathi
MEHTA, Miss SHAKUNTALA, Education
MEHTA, VINAYBALA B., Education
MEHTA, YASHUMATI M., Special Education
OAK, A. W., Education
PATWA, Mrs. KUMUD A., Foods and Nutrition

PUNEKAR, B. D., Food and Nutrition
RANADE, G. S., Drawing
RANDERI, KALINDI, Polytechnic Courses
SHAH, BHANU C., Guidance and Counselling
SIGAMANY, Mrs. G., Nursing
SURTI, Mrs. URVASHI, Hindi
TARAPORE, Mrs. FRENY, Child Development
TRIVEDI, Mrs. ANASUYA, Gujarati

CONSTITUENT COLLEGES:

Sir Vithaldas Thackersey College of Home Science: Sir Vithaldas Vidyavihar, Juhu Rd., Bombay 400054; f. 1962.
Principal: Mrs. K. PATWA.

Leelabai Thackersey College of Nursing: Nathibai Thackersey Rd., Bombay 400020; f. 1964.
Principal: Mrs. G. SINGAMAY.

Premkunverbai Vithaldas Damodar Thackersey College of Education for Women: Nathibai Thackersey Rd., Bombay 400020; f. 1959.
Principal: Miss S. K. MEHTA.

Shree Hansraj Pragji Thackersey School of Library Science: 1 Nathibai Thackersey Rd., Bombay 400020; f. 1961.
Principal: Miss V. K. KHANDWALA.

Shree Hansraj Pragji Thackersey College of Science: 1 Nathibai Thackersey Rd., Bombay 400020; f. 1978.
Principal: Prof. A. N. KOTHARE.

Shreemati Nathibai Damodar Thackersey College of Arts and Commerce for Women: Karve Rd., Erandvana, Poona 4; f. 1916.
Principal: K. S. KELKAR.

Shreemati Nathibai Damodar Thackersey College of Arts and Commerce for Women: 1 Nathibai Thackersey Rd., Bombay 400020; f. 1931.
Principal: Dr. A. B. TRIVEDI.

Shreemati Nathibai Damodar Thackersey College of Education for Women: Karve Rd., Erandavana, Poona 411004; f. 1964.
Principal: Miss VINAYBALA B. MEHTA, M.SC., M.ED., PH.D.

S.N.D.T. College of Home Science: Yerandavana; Karve Rd., Poona 411004; f. 1968.
Principal: Mrs. F. Z. TARAPORE.

Premlila Vithaldas Polytechnic: Sir V. Vidhyarihar Juhu Rd., Bombay 400054; f. 1976.
Principal: Dr. KALINDI RANDERI.

There are 14 affiliated colleges.

SOUTH GUJARAT UNIVERSITY

P.B. 49, SURAT 395007, GUJARAT
Telephone: 87604-8.

Founded 1967; Teaching and Affiliating.

State control; Language of instruction: Gujarati; Academic year: June to March (two terms).

Chancellor: H.E. THE GOVERNOR OF GUJARAT.
Vice-Chancellor: Shri A. R. DESAI.
Registrar: Shri G. A. DESAI.
Librarian: M. J. DALAL.

Library of 62,000 vols.
Number of teachers: 995.
Number of students: 30,600.

Publication: *University Journal.*

DEANS:

Faculty of Arts: K. C. MEHTA.
Faculty of Science: Dr. B. G. NAIK.
Faculty of Commerce: Prin. T. M. VAKIL.
Faculty of Education: Dr. K. C. BHATT.
Faculty of Law: Prin. A. A. MANJI.
Faculty of Medicine: Dr. V. M. SHAH.
Faculty of Rural Studies: Dr. S. C. JAIN.
Faculty of Engineering and Technology: Prin. Y. V. N. RAO.

PROFESSORS:

Faculty of Arts:
DESAI, R. B., History
DOSHI, H. C., Sociology
MEHTA, B. V., Economics
PANDYA, H. J., Political Science
PARIKH, B. A., Psychology
PATEL, D. P., Sanskrit
PATEL, H. N., Home Science
SHUKLA, R. L., Hindi
TRIVEDI, H. C., English

Faculty of Commerce:
BHATT, R. N., Co-operation
GAMI, N. D., Commerce
GUPTA, O. S., Business and Industrial Management
SOPARIWALA, C. V., Accounting and Costing

Faculty of Education:
BHATT, K. C.
JOSHI, H. R.
SHAH, G. B.

Faculty of Engineering:
CHAUDHARI, J. R., Electrical Engineering
DESAI, M. B., Applied Mechanics and Structural Engineering
SHELAT, R. N., Civil Engineering

Faculty of Law:
NAIK, D. B., Law of Property
WADIWALA, R. D., Jurisprudence

Faculty of Medicine:
MEHTA, NIRANJAN R., Clinical
NATUBHAI, R., MEHTA, Para-Clinical
TAHAMANKER, B. P., Pre-Clinical

Faculty of Science:
ADVANI, S. R., Microbiology
JOGLEKAR, N. J., Zoology
NAIK, B. G., Chemistry
PARABIA, M. H., Botany
PATEL, G. C., Statistics
UPADHYAY, V. N., Physics
VERMA, A. P., Mathematics

There are 35 affiliated colleges.

SRI VENKATESWARA UNIVERSITY

TIRUPATI,
DISTRICT CHITTOOR,
ANDHRA PRADESH 517502
Telephone: Tirupati 2781.

Founded 1954 as Residential and Teaching; Affiliating since 1956.

Languages of instruction: English and Telugu; Academic year: June to April (three terms).

Chancellor: H.E. THE GOVERNOR OF ANDHRA PRADESH.
Vice-Chancellor: Prof. M. SANTHAPPA.
Registrar: Prof. K. SITARAM.
Librarian: Sri R. SREEPATHI NAIDU, M.A., M.LIB.SC.

Library of 224,877 vols.
Number of teachers: 2,557.
Number of students: 28,246.

Publications: *Annual Report, College Magazine, S.V. University Central Journal, Research Bulletin,* etc.

DEANS:

Faculty of Arts: Prof. V. M. REDDY.
Faculty of Science: Prof. K. SITARAM.
Faculty of Commerce: Dr. N. KAMARAJU PANTHULU.
Faculty of Engineering: Prof. K. GOPICHAND.
Faculty of Teaching: Prof. R. SRINIVASA RAO.
Faculty of Medicine: Dr. K. B. KRISHNA MOHAN.
Faculty of Oriental Learning: Prof. S. T. NARASIMHACHARI.
Faculty of Law: Prof. P. KOTESWARA RAO.

HEADS OF DEPARTMENTS:

Zoology: Prof. K. S. SWAMY.
Physics: Prof. P. JARARAMA REDDY.
Chemistry: Prof. V. R. KRISHNAN.
Botany: Prof. V. S. R. DAS.
Geology: Prof. K. V. SURYANARAYANA.
Mathematics: Prof. K. SITARAM.
Philosophy: Dr. G. S. HERBERT.
Economics: Prof. D. L. NARAYANA.
Commerce: Dr. N. KAMARAJU PANTHULU.
Psychology: Prof. S. NARAYANA RAO.
Statistics: Prof. M. PERAYYA SASTRY.
Home Science: Prof. PHILOMENA ROYAPPA REDDY.
History: Prof. V. M. REDDY.
English: Prof. M. V. R. SARMA.
Telugu: Prof. G. N. REDDY.
Hindi: Prof. S. T. NARASIMHACHARI.
Law: P. KOTESWARA RAO.
Library and Information Science: R. SREEPATHY NAIDU.
Politics: Prof. K. KAMALANATHAN.
Sanskrit: Prof. E. R. SRIKRISHNA SARMA.
Arabic, Persian and Urdu: Prof. RAZIUDDIN AHMED.
Tamil: Dr. G. DAMODARAM.
Mechanical Engineering: Prof. G. RAMAKRISHNAN.
Civil Engineering: Prof. B. M. RAO.
Electrical Engineering: Prof. K. GOPICHAND.
Mathematics: Prof. P. S. RAP.

Physics: Prof. K. SREERAMAMURTHY.
Chemistry: Prof. P. R. NAIDU.
Education: Prof. R. SRINIVASA RAO.
Adult Education: Dr. V. L. N. REDDY (Director).
Sociology: Dr. A. SATYANARAYANA MOORTHY.
Physical Anthropology: Dr. V. RAMI REDDY.
Social Anthropology: Dr. A. M. REDDY.
Geography: Prof. N. BALAKRISHNA REDDY.
Population Studies Centre: Sri SOHANLAL NAGDA (Director).
Institute of Correspondence Courses: Sri K. V. SAMBASIVA RAO (Director).
Electronics and Communications Engineering: Dr. C. RAJA RAO.

There are 5 university colleges, 6 oriental colleges and 43 affiliated colleges.

TAMIL NADU AGRICULTURAL UNIVERSITY

P.O. COIMBATORE 641003, TAMIL NADU

Telephone: 35461.

Founded 1971; Federal.

State control; Language of instruction: English; Academic year: July to April (three terms).

Chancellor: H.E. THE GOVERNOR OF TAMIL NADU.
Pro-Chancellor: THE MINISTER OF AGRICULTURE, TAMIL NADU.
Vice-Chancellor: T. A. VENKATARAMAN.
Registrar: Dr. D. RAJ.
Librarian: THIRU K. BALASUBRAMANIAN.

Library of 101,659 vols.

Publications: *TNAU News Letter* (monthly), *Valarum Velanmai* (Tamil, monthly), *Annual Report.*

Number of students: 2,633.

DEANS:

Agricultural College and Research Institute, Coimbatore: Dr. V. N. MADHAVA RAO.
Agricultural College and Research Institute, Madurai: Dr. K. K. KRISHNAMOORTHY.
College of Agricultural Engineering, Coimbatore: Thiru R. K. SIVANAPPAN.
Faculty of Basic Sciences and Humanities, Coimbatore: Dr. S. R. SREE RANGASAMY.
Faculty of Horticulture, Coimbatore: Dr. C. R. MUTUKRISHNAN.
Fisheries College, Tuticorin: Dr. M. N. KUTTY.
Madras Veterinary College: Dr. V. M. RAMASWAMY.
Postgraduate Studies: Dr. P. CHANDRASEKARAN.

UNIVERSITY OF UDAIPUR

PRATAP NAGAR, UDAIPUR 313001, RAJASTHAN

Founded 1962 as Rajasthan Agricultural University; Teaching and Affiliating.

Telephone: Udaipur 4035.

Autonomous control; Languages of instruction: English and Hindi; Academic year: July to June.

Chancellor: H.E. THE GOVERNOR OF RAJASTHAN.
Vice-Chancellor: Dr. RAJ NATH SINGH.
Registrar: G. S. SHARMA, B.A.
Librarian: Dr. G. V. BAKORE.

The library contains 301,211 vols.

Number of teachers: 498.
Number of students: 10,940.

Publications: *Information Bulletin* (annually), *University of Udaipur Research Studies, Annual Report.*

DEANS:

Faculty of Agriculture: R. S. RAWAT.
Faculty of Commerce: Shri K. K. MEHRISHI.
Faculty of Education: Shri K. N. SHRIVASTAVA.
Faculty of Law: D. D. SHARMA.
Faculty of Science: Dr. Y. D. TIAGI.
Faculty of Veterinary and Animal Science: Dr. MOHAN SINGH.
Faculty of Agricultural Engineering and Technology: Dr. K. N. NAG.
Faculty of Home Science: Dr. K. N. CHANDRASEKHARAN.
Faculty of Humanities: Dr. B. S. MATHUR.
Faculty of Social Sciences: Dr. O. P. SHARMA.

PROFESSORS:

Faculty of Science:
BAKORE, G. V., Chemistry
TEWARI, H. B., Zoology
TIAGI, Y. D., Botany
VERMA, J., Physics

Faculty of Humanities:
JOSHI, N. N., Hindi
MATHUR, B. S., History
SHARMA, K. L., English
SHARMA, R. G., 'Dinesh', Hindi

Faculty of Social Sciences:
RAI, G. C., Psychology
SHARMA, O. P., Sociology

Faculty of Agriculture:
CHAKARVARTI, B. P., Plant Pathology
GANDHI, S. M., Plant Breeding
KUSHWAHA, K. S., Zoology and Entomology
MANOHAR, M. S., Horticulture
MEHTA, R. C., Extension Education
RATHORE, B. S., Agricultural Economics
RAWAT, R. S., Dairy Science
SAXENA, S. N., Agricultural Chemistry and Soil Science
SHARMA, V. V., Animal Husbandry
SINGH, H. G., Agronomy
SINGH, K. S., Agricultural Chemistry and Soil Science
SUDHIR KUMAR, Agricultural Botany
VYAS, K. K., Agricultural Chemistry and Soil Science

Faculty of Veterinary and Animal Science:
ARYA, P. L., Veterinary Pathology
CHAUDHARY, A. L., Animal Breeding and Genetics
LODHA, K. R., Parasitology
MATHUR, C. S., Animal Nutrition
MEHROTRA, P. N., Veterinary Microbiology

CONSTITUENT COLLEGES:

College of Home Science: Udaipur; K. N. CHANDRASEKHARAN.

College of Law: Udaipur; Dean D. D. SHARMA.

College of Technology and Agricultural Engineering: Udaipur; Dean Dr. K. N. NAG.

College of Veterinary and Animal Science: Bikaner; Dean Dr. MOHAN SINGH.

Rajasthan College of Agriculture: Udaipur; Dean Dr. R. S. RAWAT.

S.K.N. College of Agriculture: Jobner; Associate Dean Dr. S. N. SAXENA.

School of Basic Sciences and Humanities: Udaipur; Dir. Shri K. K. MEHRISHI.

Agricultural Experiment Station: Udaipur; Dir. Dr. R. M. SINGH.

Directorate of Extension Education: Udaipur; Dir. Dr. H. N. MEHROTRA.

There are 7 affiliated colleges.

UTKAL UNIVERSITY

P.O. VANI VIHAR, BHUBANESWAR 751004, ORISSA STATE

Telephone: Bhubaneswar 52520.

Founded 1943: Teaching and Affiliating.

Language of instruction: English; Academic year: July to April (two terms).

Chancellor: H.E. THE GOVERNOR OF ORISSA.
Vice-Chancellor: Dr. B. MISRA.
Registrar: Dr. S. K. PANDA.
Librarian: A. K. DEB.

Library of 167,000 vols.

Number of teachers: 2,953.
Number of students: 62,553.

Publications: *University Calendar, Minutes, Syllabus and Courses,* textbooks and journals.

DEANS:

Faculty of Arts: Prof. B. DAS.
Faculty of Education: Dr. G. B. KANUNGO.
Faculty of Law: B. M. PATTNAIK.
Faculty of Science: M. K. ROUT.
Faculty of Commerce: Dr. S. K. DAS.
Faculty of Medicine: Dr. M. S. KHADANGA.
Faculty of Engineering: K. T. SUBUDHI.

PROFESSORS:

ACHARYA, Dr. S. N., Geology
BEHURA, Dr. B. K., Zoology
DAS, Dr. G., Mathematics
DAS, Dr. G. C., Paediatrics
DAS, Dr. H., Diseases of the Chest
DAS, Dr. M. N., History
DAS, Dr. S. K., Commerce
DEO, Dr. B. B., Physics
GAURO, K. D., Law
GHOSAL, Dr., A. K. Radiology
HAZARI, S. B., Anatomy
MAHAPATRA, Dr. L. K., Anthropology
MISHRA, Dr. B., Applied Economics
MITRA, Dr. A. S., Obstetrics and Gynaecology
MOHANTY, Dr. B., Oriya
MOHANTY, Dr. H. C., Dermatology and Venereal Diseases
MOHANTY, Dr. N. K., Forensic Medicine and Toxicology
MOHANTY, Dr. R. C., Orthopaedics
MOHANTY, Dr. S. R., Chemistry
NANDA, N. C., Plastic Surgery
NAYAK, Dr. B. N., Anaesthetics
NAYAK, Dr., G. C., Philosophy
NAYAK, Dr. U. P., Pathology
PADHI, Dr. B., Botany
PANDA, Dr. S., Obstetrics and Gynaecology
PARIDA, Dr. R. K., Medicine
PATI, Dr. I. M., Pharmacology
PATNAIK, Dr. B. K., Thoracic Surgery
PATNAIK, Dr. K. M., Economics
PATNAIK, Dr. N., Surgery
PATRO, Dr. A. P., Biochemistry
PRADHAN, Dr. N., Radiotherapy
RAJGURU, Dr. B., Ophthalmology
RATH, Dr. R., Psychology
RATH, Dr. S., Neurosurgery
RATH, Dr. S. N., Political Science
SARANGI, Dr. A., Medicine
SEN, Dr. S. K., Paediatrics
SINHA, Dr. B., Geography
SRIVASTAV, R. N., Sociology
SWAIN, Dr. A., Sanskrit
SWAIN, Dr. S., Social and Preventive Medicine

CONSTITUENT COLLEGES:

Madhu Sudan Law College: Cuttack; f. 1949; Prin. D. P. KAR.

University Law College: Vani Vihar, Bhubaneswar; f. 1975; Prin. K. MOHANTY.

There are 83 affiliated colleges.

VIKRAM UNIVERSITY

UNIVERSITY RD.,
UJJAIN, 456010 MADHYA PRADESH

Telephone: 229-30.

Founded 1957: Teaching and Affiliating.

Languages of instruction: English and Hindi; Academic year: July to June.

Chancellor: H.E. THE GOVERNOR OF MADHYA PRADESH.
Vice-Chancellor: Dr. P. N. KAWATHEKAR.
Registrar: Shri S. S. JHANWAR.
Librarian: Shri N. K. TRIVEDI.

Library of 93,376 vols.
Number of students: 25,040.

DEANS:

Faculty of Arts: Dr. R. M. TRIPATHI.
Faculty of Science: Dr. JOKHAN SINGH.
Faculty of Life Science: Dr. G. N. JOHRI.
Faculty of Commerce: (vacant).
Faculty of Law: Shri U. L. JAROLI.
Faculty of Engineering: Shri M. P. CHAURASIA.
Faculty of Education: Shri L. N. DIXIT.
Faculty of Social Sciences: Dr. R. K. AWASTHI.
Faculty of Ayurveda: Dr. K. C. PINDAWALLA.

PROFESSORS:

AWASTHI, R. K., M.A., PH.D., Political Science
BHARGAVA, G. D., M.A., M.LIB.SC., PH.D., Library Science
BOKADIA, M. M., D.PHIL., Chemistry
MALL, L. P., M.SC., PH.D., Botany
SINGH, B. D., M.A., PH.D., D. ÈS.SC., Mathematics
SINGH, J., PH.D., Statistics
SINGH, K. K., M.SC., PH.D., Geology
SINHA, B. M., PH.D., Zoology
TRIPATHUI, R. M., M.A., PH.D., D.LITT., Hindi
VENKATACHALAM, V., M.A., Sanskrit

CONSTITUENT COLLEGES:

Shri Nehru College: Agar; f 1966.
Principal: T. S. NIGAM.

Jawaharlal Nehru Mahavidyalaya: Barwaha; f. 1964.
Principal: Dr. K. N. VERMA.

Government College: Barwani; f. 1957.
Principal: Y. C. CHATURVEDI.

K.P. Government College: Dewas; f. 1958.
Principal: (vacant).

Government College: Dhar; f. 1957.
Principal: Dr. D. S. JOSHI.

Government College: Jaora; f. 1961.
Principal: Dr. R. V. RAO.

Government College: Jhabua; f. 1960.
Principal: Dr. K. T. MANDLOI.

Government College: Khargone; f. 1958.
Principal: Dr. K. C. BHANDARI.

Government College: Mandsaur; f. 1957.
Principal: I. A. KHAN.

Government College: Neemuch; f. 1958.
Principal: S. S. HASURKAR.

Government College: Narsinghgarh; f. 1962.
Principal: (vacant).

Government College: Ratlam; f. 1956.
Principal: M. K. SHINDE.

Government College: Rampura; f. 1958.
Principal: P. N. BHIWANI.

Government College: Rajgarh: f. 1958.
Principal: B. R. SADH.

Government College: Shajapur; f. 1958.
Principal: Dr. R. N. JAIN.

J.N.S. Government College: Shujalpur; f. 1958.
Principal: B. K. NILOSE.

Government College of Education: Ujjain; f. 1957.
Principal: B. K. DIXIT.

Government Girls' College: Ujjain; f. 1959.
Principal: Mrs. M. DATTA.

Madhav College: Ujjain; f. 1892.
Principal: (vacant).

Madhav Science College: Ujjain; f. 1969.
Principal: Dr. H. N. SHARMA.

Sandipani College: Ujjain; f. 1966.
Principal: (vacant).

There are 22 affiliated colleges and 14 university schools of studies.

VISVA-BHARATI

P.O. SANTINIKETAN,
BIRBHUM, W. BENGAL 731235

Telephone: Bolpur 451 to 456.

Founded 1951 (previously 1921); Teaching and Residential.

Private control; Languages of instruction: English and Bengali; Academic year: July to April (three terms).

Rector: H.E. THE GOVERNOR OF WEST BENGAL.
Vice-Chancellor: SURAJIT CHANDRA SINHA, M.A., PH.D.
Registrar: P. K. DAS GUPTA.
Librarian: B. K. DATTA.

Library of 440,000 vols.
Number of teachers: 355.
Number of students: 3,039.

HEADS OF DEPARTMENTS:

English and Other Modern European Languages: S. K. GHOSH.
Sanskrit, Pali and Prakrit: BISWANATH BANERJEE.
Bengali: B. CHOWDHURY.
Hindi: RAM SINGH TOMAR.
Oriya: KHAGESWAR MOHAPATRA.
Chinese: WEI KWEI SHUN.
Japanese: S. MAKINO.
Indo-Tibetan Studies: Sri C. R. LAMA.
Arabic, Persian and Islamic Studies: H. M. TAMERALI.
Philosophy and Religion: P. K. SENGUPTA.
History: ASHIN DASGUPTA.
Geography: SEKHAR MUKHERJEE.
Ancient Indian History and Culture: B. D. CHATTOPADHYAY.
Economics and Politics: ASHOK RUDRA.
Mathematics: RABINDRANATH CHATTERJEE.
Chemistry: K. C. RAY.
Physics: D. CHATARJI.
Zoology: A. B. DAS.
Botany: S. DUTTA.
Education: SRINIVAS BHATTACHARYA.
Paintings: Sri SUKHAMAY MITRA.

Sculpture: Sri A. CHAKRAVARTI.
Graphic Art: S. HORE.
History of Art: J. CHAKRAVARTY.
Rabindra Music and Dance: Mrs. KANIKA BANERJEA.
Classical Music: NIMAICHAND BURAL.
Social Work: K. L. BOSE.
Agriculture: S. K. MUKHOPADHAY.
Palli Charcha Kendra: Dr. B. K. ROY BURMAN.

CONSTITUENT COLLEGES:

Kala-Bhavana: f. 1919.
Principal: Prof. SOMNATH HORE.

Palli Siksha Sadana: f. 1963.
Principal: Prof. S. K. MUKHOPADHAY.

Rabindra-Bhavana: f. 1962.
Principal: Prof. BHABATOSH DATTA.

Sangit-Bhavana: f. 1934.
Principal: N. C. BARAL.

Siksha-Bhavana: f. 1921.
Principal: Prof. P. K. GHOSH.

Vidya-Bhavana: f. 1918.
Principal: Prof. BISWANATH BANERJEA.

Vinaya-Bhavana: f. 1948.
Principal: Prof. SRINIVAS BHATTACHARYA.

INSTITUTES WITH UNIVERSITY STATUS

Central Institute of English and Foreign Languages: Hyderabad, A.P. 500007; f. 1958; postgraduate degrees, diplomas, certificates; correspondence course; library of 50,000 vols.; *c.* 90 full-time students; Dir. Dr. R. MOHAN.

Indian Agricultural Research Institute: New Delhi 110012; f. 1905; postgraduate courses in all major branches of agriculture; library of 270,000 vols.; 566 students; Dir. H. K. JAIN, PH.D.; Registrar A. S. TANEJA; publ. *Scientific Report* (annually).

Indian Institute of Science: Bangalore, Karnataka 560012; f. 1909; library of 166,000 vols.; *c.* 380 postgraduate students; Dir. Dr. S. DHAWAN; Registrar T. NANJUNDA RAO; publ. *Journal.*

Indian Institute of Technology, Bombay: Powai, Bombay 400076, Maharashtra State; Tel. 581421; f. 1958; residential.

Director: Prof. A. K. DE, PH.D.
Registrar: K. JANARDHANAN.
Librarian: V. N. MISRA.

Library of 173,000 vols.
Number of teachers: 324.
Number of students: 2,394.

HEADS OF DEPARTMENTS:

Chemical Engineering: Dr. S. K. RAMAN.
Civil Engineering: Dr. S. H. NAGARAJA.
Electrical Engineering: Dr. M. V. HARIHARAN.
Mechanical Engineering: Dr. A. JAGAN MOHAN.
Metallurgical Engineering: Dr. P. R. MENON.
Aeronautical Engineering: Dr. M. M. KULKARNI.
Chemistry: Dr. R. N. MUKHERJEE.
Humanities: Dr. B. D. MISRA.
Mathematics: Dr. M. P. RANGA RAO.
Physics: Dr. G. THYAGARAJAN.
Computer Centre: Prof. J. R. ISAAC.
Industrial Design Centre: Prof. S. NADKARNI.

Indian Institute of Technology, Delhi: Hauz Khas, New Delhi 110016; Tel. 666979; f. 1961.

First degree courses in Civil, Mechanical, Electrical, Chemical Engineering, Textile Technology, Chemistry and Physics; Postgraduate courses in Physics, Chemistry, Mathematics, Textile Technology, Electrical, Mechanical, Chemical and Civil Engineering, Humanities and Social Sciences, Applied Mechanics, etc.

Offers research facilities and registration for Ph.D. in various engineering and science departments.

Library of 174,000 vols.

Director: Prof. O. P. JAIN.
Registrar: A. SINGH.

Number of students: 2,000.

DEANS:

Industrial Liaison and Development: Prof. M. C. CHATURVEDI.
Postgraduate Studies and Research: Prof. A. K. BASU.
Undergraduate Studies: Prof. P. S. SATSANG.
Students: Prof. S. K. GULHATI.

Indian Institute of Technology, Kanpur: I.I.T.P.O., Kanpur 208016, U.P.; f. 1960; State control; Language of instruction: English; Departments of Aeronautical Engineering, Chemistry, Chemical, Civil, Electrical, Mechanical and Metallurgical Engineering, Mathematics and Physics, Humanities and Social Sciences.

Chairman: Dr. M. L. DHAR.
Director: Dr. A. BHATTACHARYYA.
Registrar: G. KISHORE.
Librarian: (vacant).

Number of teachers: 270.
Number of students: 2,000.

Publications: *Courses of Study* (annual), *Research, Design and Development Capabilities* (annual), *Research Reports.*

DEANS:

Faculty: Dr. V. K. DESHPANDE.
Research and Development: Dr. N. C. NIGAM.
Students: Dr. A. P. KUDCHADKER.

Indian Institute of Technology, Kharagpur: Kharagpur 721302, Dist. Midnapore (W.B.); f. 1950.

Telephone Khang 221-224.

Director: Prof. SHANKAR LAL.
Registrar: A. K. SUR, M.A., F.C.A.
Librarian: A. K. MUKHERJEE, M.A., M.SC., DIP.LIB.

The library contains 145,000 vols.
Number of students: 2,680.

HEADS OF DEPARTMENTS:

Architecture and Regional Planning: Prof. R. M. CHAKRABORTY.
Chemistry: Prof. D. SEN.
Electronics and Electrical Communication Engineering: Dr. J. DAS.
Aeronautical Engineering: C. N. LAXINARAYAN.
Agricultural Engineering: Dr. T. P. OJHA.
Chemical Engineering: Dr. A. N. ROY.
Civil Engineering: Dr. S. K. MALLICK.
Electrical Engineering: Prof. N. KESAVAMURTHY.
Mechanical Engineering: Prof. S. G. MUKHERJEE.
Metallurgical Engineering: Prof. P. BANERJEE.
Mining Engineering: Prof. M. A. RAMLU.
Geology and Geophysics: Dr. D. K. GANGULY.
Humanities and Social Sciences: S. K. SEN.
Mathematics: Dr. A. S. GUPTA.
Naval Architecture and Marine Engineering: Prof. J. P. GHOSH.
Physics and Meteorology: Prof. H. N. BOSE.
Material Science Centre: Prof. J. K. MUKHERJEE.
Rice Process Engineering Centre: Prof. T. P. OJHA.
Radar Communication Centre: Prof. G. S. SANAYAL.
Industrial Management Centre: Prof. K. C. SAHU.

Indian Institute of Technology, Madras: Madras 600036; Tel. 415342; f. 1959; State control; Language of Instruction: English; Academic year: July to April.

Courses in Aeronautical Engineering, Applied Mechanics, Chemistry, Chemical, Civil, Electrical and Mechanical Engineering, Computer Science, Humanities and Social Sciences, Mathematics, Metallurgy, Ocean Engineering and Physics.

Director: Prof. P. V. INDIRESAN.
Registrar: S. VIRMANI.
Librarian: V. S. NAZIR AHMED, B.A., LL.B., D.L.SC.

Library: *see* Libraries.
Number of teachers: 380.
Number of students: 2,391.

Publications: *IIT at a Glance*, *Annual Report*†, *Academic Calendar*†, *Technical Communications*† (annual), *Journal of Mathematical and Physical Sciences*† (6 a year).

HEADS OF DEPARTMENTS:

ACHUTHAN, M. K., Electrical Engineering
BOSE, T. K., Aeronautical Engineering
GUPTA, R. K., Humanities and Social Sciences
MUTHUKRISHNAN, C. R. Computer Centre
RAMAMURTHY, V., Applied Mechanics
RAMASASTRI, C., Physics
RAO, P. S., Civil Engineering
ROSHAN, H., Metallurgy
RAYUDU, G. V. N., Mechanical Engineering
SARMA, L. V. K., Mathematics
SRINIVASAN, V., Chemistry
VARMA, Y. B. G., Mechanical Engineering

Indian School of Mines: Dhanbad 826004, Bihar; Tel. 2866, 2403, 2840; f. 1926; Residential; Language of Instruction: English; Academic year: July to June.

Degree and postgraduate courses in mining engineering, petroleum engineering, applied geophysics, applied geology, engineering and mining machinery, industrial engineering and management, chemistry, fuel and metallurgy, electronics and instrumentation, physics and mathematics, and humanities and social sciences.

Chairman of General Council: Sri J. G. KUMARMANGALAM.
Director: Prof. G. S. MARWAHA.
Registrar: Major S. P. VARMA.
Librarian: Miss SUJATA SEN.

Number of teachers: 109.
Number of students: 589.

Publications: *Inside I.S.M.* (6 a year).

HEADS OF DEPARTMENTS:

CHANDRA, Shri DINESH, Electronics and Instrumentation
CHATTERJEE, Shri A. K., Workshop Superintendent
CHUGH, C. P., Engineering and Mining Machinery
JHA, D. P., Humanities and Social Sciences
NAG, K. R., Physics and Mathematics
RAO, T. C., Chemistry, Fuel and Metallurgy
SARKAR, S. N., Applied Geology
SINGH, R. D., Mining Engineering
SINGH, VIJAY P., Continuing Education
SINHA, D. K., Industrial Engineering and Management
SRINI-VASAN, S., Petroleum Engineering
SUBRAHMANYAM, N. V. R., Dean, Student Affairs
VERMA, R. K., Applied Geophysics

Tata Institute of Social Sciences: Sion-Trombay Rd., Deonar, Bombay, Maharashtra 400088; f. 1936; postgraduate courses and professional training in the social sciences; research; library of 49,000 vols.; 237 students; Dir. Dr. M. S. GORE; Registrar N. KRISHNAMOORTHY; publs. *Indian Journal of Social Work*, *Research Abstracts*, *Sociology of Education Papers*.

COLLEGES

BUSINESS:

Administrative Staff College of India: Bella Vista, Hyderabad 500475; f. 1957; conducts post-experience management development programmes in general management and in specific fields; offers management and computer consultancy service to industry and conducts research into management techniques; library of 43,975 vols. and 11,235 bound vols. of periodicals; Principal J. B. D'SOUZA; Librarian A. K. DAS GUPTA; publs. *ASCI Journal of Management* (2 a year), *Current Management Literature*† (monthly).

Indian Institute of Management (1): Vastrapur, Ahmedabad 380015; f. 1962; 2-year postgraduate, 3-year doctoral programme in management; general and functional management programmes for practising managers, and special programmes for government officials, university teachers, trade union leaders and sectors such as agriculture, public systems; undertakes project research and consulting in the field of management; approx. 85 faculty members, 400 postgraduate programme students; library of 92,412 vols.; Dir. Dr. V. S. VYAS.

Indian Institute of Management, Calcutta: Diamond Harbour Rd., Joka, P.O.B. 16757, P.O. Alipore, Calcutta 700027; f. 1961 to promote improvement in management through education, research and consultation; two-year postgraduate course in management; fellowship and extension courses; executive development; faculty development through research and consulting services; B. C. Roy Memorial library 70,000 vols.; Dir. H. BHAYA.

ECONOMICS, SOCIOLOGY

National Institute of Rural Development: Rajendranagar, Hyderabad; f. 1958; training and research in social change in rural India; government-financed; 45 general and specialized courses; consultancy services offered to State governments, national and international organizations; 41 faculty mems.; library of 29,250 vols.; Dir. Gen. Dr. S. K. RAU; publs. *Behavioural Sciences and Rural Development* (2 a year), *Rural Development Digest* (quarterly).

EDUCATION

National Staff College for Educational Planners and Administrators: 17-B Sri Aurobindo Marg, New Delhi 110016; f. 1970; succeeds the Asian Institute of Educational Planning and Administration; pre-service and in-service training courses; research in all aspects of education; consultancy service for State govts.; collaboration with other institutions in India and abroad; offers fellowships and scholarships; library of 17,000 vols.; Dir. Prof. M. V. MATHUR.

LANGUAGES:

Central Institute of Indian Languages: Ministry of Education and Culture, Mysore 570006; f. 1969; research in language analysis, teaching, technology and use, with a bias towards problem solving and national integration; collaborates with language institutes and universities; 103 teachers, researchers and technicians; 5 Regional Language Centres in Mysore (languages: Kannada, Telugu, Malayalam, Tamil), Bhubaneswar (languages: Assamese, Bengali, Oriya), Poona (languages: Marathi, Gujarati, Sindhi), Patiala (languages: Urdu, Punjabi, Kashmiri) and Solon (Urdu); library of 39,000 vols. and 235 periodicals in 52 Indian and 25 foreign languages; Dir. D. P. PATTANAYAK; publ. *Vartavaha* (irregular).

LAW:

Indian Academy of International Law and Diplomacy: 7-8 Scindia House, Kasturba Gandhi Marg, New Delhi 110001; f. 1964; part of the Indian Society of International Law; includes a research institute.

MEDICINE:

All-India Institute of Medical Sciences: Ansari Nagar, New Delhi 100016; f. 1956; undergraduate and postgraduate training; research in all brs. of medicine; library of 70,000 vols.; Dir. Dr. L. P. AGARWAL; publ. *Journal* (quarterly).

National Institute of Health and Family Welfare (NIHFW): Nr. Munirka, New Delhi 110067; f. 1964; in-service training, M.D. course in health administration, research and consultancy in health and family welfare; specialized library of 30,000 vols.; Dir. R. K. SANYAL; publs. *Health and Population—Perspectives and Issues* (quarterly, in English) and Technical Report series.

TECHNOLOGY:

Institute of Radiophysics and Electronics: 92 Acharya Prafulla Chandra Rd., Calcutta 700009; f. 1949; houses postgraduate teaching and research dept. of Univ. of Calcutta, Faculty of Technology; 3-year course leading to B.Tech. degree followed by 2-year postgraduate course leading to M.Tech. degree in radiophysics and electronics; also 1-year postgraduate diploma course in computer and control engineering; research facilities in ionospherics, radio wave propagation, radio astronomy, solid state and microwave electronics, solid state devices, plasma and quantum electronics, control systems and computers, communication theory and systems; maintains ionosphere field station at Haringhata; 35 teachers; library of 10,000 vols.; Dir. Prof. M. K. DASGUPTA; publ. Annual Research Reports.

Seshasayee Institute of Technology: Industrial Colony Post, Tiruchirapalli 620010, Tamilnadu; f. 1952; training to diploma level in civil, mechanical and electrical engineering; there is also a course leading to the Technical High School Certificate; 49 teachers, 860 students; library of 6,550 vols.; Pres. H. K. RAMASWAMI; Principal ANANTHNANARAS IMHACHAR; publ. *SITMAG*

SCHOOLS OF ART AND MUSIC

Academy of Architecture: Plot No. 278, Shankar Ghanekar Marg, next to Tyresoles, Prabhadevi, Bombay 400025; f. 1955; five-year courses in Architecture; library of 3,800 vols. and 1,390 slides; Principal C. K. GUMASTE.

Bharatiya Vidya Bhavan: Kulapati Munshi Rd., Bombay 400007; f. 1938; aims to revitalize ancient Indian values to suit modern needs; postgraduate courses in Indology; colleges of arts, science, commerce and engineering; runs schools, Academy of Foreign Languages, College of Sanskrit; dept. of Ancient Insights and Modern Discoveries; Institute of Mass Communication and Management Studies; schools of music, dancing, dramatic art; library of 70,000 vols.; Pres. DHARAMSEY M. KHATAU; Hon. Dir. Prof. J. H. DAVE, M.A., LL.B.; Joint Dir. and Exec. Sec. S. RAMAKRISHNAN; publs. *Bharatiya Vidya* (quarterly), *Samvid* (Sanskrit quarterly), *Bhavan's Journal* (fortnightly), *Samarpan* (Gujarati fortnightly), 11 vols. of the *History and Culture of the Indian People*, and various series.

Kalakshetra: Tiruvanmiyur, Madras 41; f. 1936; centre for education in classical music, dancing, theatrical art, painting and handicraft; maintains a weaving-centre for the production of silk and cotton costumes in traditional design and a Kalamkari Unit for dyeing and hand-block printing with vegetable dyes; photographic division with photostat and microfilm sections; Vario Klischograph section making black-and-white and colour blocks; Dr. U. V. Swaminatha Aiyar library noted for classical MSS. and literature in Tamil; Pres. SRIMATHI RUKMINI DEVI; Joint Dir. K. SANKARA MENON; Sec. A. Y. SUNDARAM; publ. *Kalakshetra* (quarterly).

Music Academy: 306 Mowbray's Rd., Royapettah, Madras 14; f. 1927; research and study of Indian music; directs the Teachers' College of Music; Pres. K. R. S. IYER; Secs. T. S. RANGARAJAN, R. RANGANATHAN, T. S. PARTHASARATHY, S. NATARAJAN; publs. *Journal* and books.

National School of Drama: Bahawalpur House, Bhagwandas Rd., New Delhi 110001; f. 1959; three-year courses for a maximum of 30 students a year; library of 15,000 vols.; Dir. B. V. KARANTH; publ. *Theatre Impact* (biannual).

Sri Varalakshmi Academies of Fine Arts: Ramvilas, Kashipathy Agarahar, Chamaraja Double Rd., Mysore 4; f. 1945; educational and cultural research institution, gives advanced courses of study in Indian music; library of 4,620 vols.; Pres. Prof. T. S. SHAMA RAO, M.A.; Head Research Dept. Prof. R. SATHYANARAYANA, M.SC.

REPUBLIC OF INDONESIA

Population 141,000,000

LEARNED SOCIETIES

General

Lembaga Ilmu Pengetahuan Indonesia (*Indonesian Institute of Sciences*): Jalan Tenku Tjhik Ditiro 43, Jakarta; f. 1967; government agency to promote the development of science and technology, to serve as the national centre for regional and international scientific co-operation, to organize national research institutes; Chair. Prof. Dr. H. Tb. Bachtiar Rifai; Exec. Sec. Prof. Didin S. Sastrapraja; publs. *Berita LIPI* (quarterly), *Indonesian Abstracts* (quarterly), *Bulletin LIPI* (annually), *Annales Bogorienses* (irregular), *Reinwardtia, Treubia, Marine Research in Indonesia* (all irregular), *Bulletin of the National Institute of Geology and Mining* (quarterly), *Bulletin Kebun Raya* (3 a year), *Masyarakat Indonesia* (2 a year).

Affiliated Institutes:

National Biological Institute.

National Institute of Geology and Mining.

National Institute of Oceanology.

National Chemical Institute.

National Physical Institute.

National Institute of Metallurgy.

National Electrotechnical Institute.

National Institute for Instrumentation.

Pusat Dokumentasi Ilmiah Nasional (*National Scientific Documentation Centre*): *see* under Libraries.

National Economic and Social Research Institute.

National Institute for Cultural Studies.

The Arts

Jajasan Kerja-Sama Kebudajaan (*Foundation for Cultural Co-operation*): Jalan Gajah Mada 13, Bandung; to promote co-operation and mutual understanding between the countries of Western Europe and Indonesia; Rep. for Indonesia A. Koolhaas.

History, Geography and Archaeology

Lembaga Purbakala dan Peninggalan Nasional (*The National Archaeological Institute of Indonesia*): Jalan Kimia 12, P.O.B. 2533, Jakarta; Dir. R. Soekmono; publs. *Laporan Tahunan* (annual), *Berita Dinas Purbakala* (Nos. 1–4), *Berita Lembaga Purbakala dan Peninggalan Nasional* (No. 5 onwards), *Amerta*. brs. Prambanan, Jogjakarta; Gianjar, Bali; Mojokerto, E. Java.

International Cultural Institutes

Asia Foundation, The: Jalan Darmawangsa 50, Kebayoran Baru, Jakarta; one of 14 branches of the main organization in the U.S.A. (*q.v.*); Rep. Russell H. Betts.

British Council: S. Widjojo Centre, Jl. Jendral Sudirman 57, Jakarta; Rep. J. A. B. Smith; library: *see* Libraries.

Centre Culturel Français: 25 Jl. Salemba Raya, Jakarta Pusat; f. 1955 to promote Franco-Indonesian relations and acquaintance with French civilization and language; holds exhibitions of many art forms and offers language courses at all levels; *c.* 2,500 mems.; library of 8,500 vols., also films, video-cassettes, audio-visual equipment; Dir. C. Kieffer; publ. *Programme d'activités* (monthly).

U.S. International Communication Agency: Jalan Merdeka Selatan 4, Jakarta; also at Medan and Surabaya.

Medicine

Ikatan Dokter Indonesia (*Indonesian Medical Association*): Jalan Dr. Sam Ratulangi 29, Jakarta; f. 1950; 7,500 mems.; Pres. Dr. Utojo Sukaton; Sec. Dr. T. Sibarani; publ. *Majalah Kedokteran Indonesia* (monthly).

Natural Sciences

Astronomical Association of Indonesia: Jalan Lembong 14, Bandung; f. 1920; to promote the advancement of astronomical science; Pres. Prof. H. Th. M. Leeman; Dir. Astronomical Observatory Prof. Dr. G. B. van Albada; Sec. and Treas. H. Th. Mulié.

Balai Pengetahuan Umum Bandung (*Popular Science Society*: Universitas Bandung, Jl. Merdeka 27, Bandung; f. 1946; to promote the cultural development of Indonesia; Pres. Prof. Dr. L. van der Pijl; Vice-Pres. Prof. Dr. C. O. Schaeffer; Sec. F. J. Suyderhoud.

Technology

Persatuan Insinjur Indonesia (*Indonesian Society of Engineers*): Taman Jatibaru 1, Jakarta; Chair. Ir. R. H. Juanda; Sec. Ir. R. S. Danunagoro.

RESEARCH INSTITUTES

Agriculture and Veterinary Science

Balai Penelitian Perkebunan Bogor (*Research Institute for Estate Crops*): Jl. Taman Kencana 1, P.O.B. 81, Bogor; f. 1969; research in agronomy, plant protection, plant breeding, selection, soil and fertilizers, technology, economics and statistics of plantation crops (rubber, coffee and cacao); 165 staff; library of 7,232 vols., 854 periodicals; Dir. Ir. Sadikin Sumintawikarta; publs. *Menara Perkebunan*† (every 2 months, with English summary), *Annual Reports, Statistics of Crops.*

Balai Penelitian Perkebunan Medan (*Research Institute for Estate Crops*): P.O.B. 104, Medan; f. 1916; to promote agricultural improvement on the member estates; 320 mems.; 8,000 vols. plus 12,500 periodicals; Dir. Sadikin Sumintawikarta; publ. *Bulletin*† (quarterly, in Indonesian with English summaries).

Balai Penyelidikan Perusahaan Perkebunan Gula (*Indonesian Sugar Research Centre*): Jalan Pahlawan 25, Pasuruan; f. 1887; library of 15,000 vols.; Dir. Dr. Ir. Abdul Bari; publs. *Warta Bulanan*† (monthly report), *Majalah Perusahaan Gula*† (Sugar Journal, quarterly), *Berita*† (Communications), *Laporan Tahunan*† (Annual Report), etc.

Forest Research Institute: P.O.B. 66, Bogor; f. 1913; silviculture, forest botany, forest influences, forest mensuration, forest protection, sericulture; library of 20,000 vols.; Dir. R. Soerjono.

Lembaga Penelitian Hortikultura (*Institute of Horticulture, Ministry of Agriculture*): Pasarminggu, Jakarta Selatan; f. 1961; research on vegetables, fruit and ornamental plants; library of 3,500 vols.; Dir. SUBIYANTO; publ. *Buletin Penelitian Hortikultura* (quarterly).

Lembaga Penelitian Penyakit Hewan (*Animal Disease Research Institute, Agency of Agricultural Research and Development, Ministry of Agriculture*): Jl. Laks. Laut R.E. Martadinata 32, Bogor; f. 1908; depts. of bacteriology, diagnostics and serology, pathology, parasitology, mycology, biological products, virology; library of 8,914 vols. and periodicals; Dir. Dr. JAN NARI; Sec. SOEJOED, B.SC.; publ. *Bulletin LPPH*.

Lembaga Penelitian Peternakan (*Research Institute of Animal Husbandry*): Jalan Gunung Gede, Bogor; f. 1950; depts. of dairying, animal nutrition, poultry husbandry, meat production, manufacture of animal products, social economics of animal husbandry; Dir. Drh. R. RUSTANDI DANUMIHARDJA.

Lembaga Penelitian Tanah (*Institute of Soil Research, Ministry of Agriculture*): Jl. Ir. H. Juanda 98, Bogor; f. 1905; library of 3,500 vols.; Dir. M. SOEPRAPTOHARDJO.

Lembaga Penjelidikan Teknologi Makanan (*Food Technology Research Institute*): Pasarminggu, Jakarta; re-organized 1966; library of 4,000 vols.; Dir. Ir. MASMAN BEKTI; publs. *Bulletin Penelitian Hortikultura; Hortikultura, Majalah Ilmiah Populer; Informasi.*

Lembaga Pusat Penelitian Pertanian (*Central Research Institute for Agriculture*): Jalan Merdeka 99, Bogor; f. 1918; library of 10,876 vols.; Dir. Dr. RUSLI HAKIM; publs. several periodicals.

Lembaga Penelitian Pertanian Makassar (*Research Institute for Agriculture, Makassar*): Jalan Dr. Ratulangi 47, Ujungpandang; f. 1947; Dir. Dr. IBRAHIM MANWAN.

Lembaga Penelitian Pertanian Yogyakarta (*Research Institute for Agriculture, Yogyakarta*); Jalan Mrican Baru 1, Yogyakarta; Dir. SOETANTYO.

Lembaga Penelitian Pertanian Banjarmasin (*Research Institute for Agriculture, Banjarmasin*): Jalan Maj. Gen. D. I. Panjaitan 9a, Banjarmasin; Dir. NOORSJAMSI, B.SC.

Lembaga Penelitian Pertanian Malang (*Research Institute for Agriculture, Malang*): Industri Timur 36, Malang; Dir. ABDULLAH PRAWIROSAMUDRO, B.SC.

Lembaga Penelitian Pertanian Padang (*Research Institute for Agriculture, Padang*): Jalan Padang Baru Barat V/12, Padang; Dir. Ir. DARWIS.

Architecture and Town Planning

Direktorat Penyelidikan Masalah Bangunan-U.N. Regional Centre for Research on Human Settlements: Jalan Tamansari 84, Bandung; f. 1955; library of 20,000 vols.; Dir. Ir. KARMAN SOMAWIDJAJA; publ. *Masalah Bangunan* (quarterly, in English).

Economics, Law and Politics

Biro Pusat Statistik (*Central Bureau of Statistics*): Jalan Dr. Sutomo 8, Jakarta; f. 1925; library of 40,000 vols. and 1,700 periodicals; Dir. M. ABDULMADJID.

Indonesian Institute of World Affairs: c/o University of Indonesia, Jakarta; Chair. Prof. SUPOMO; Sec. Mr. SUDJATMOKO.

Lembaga Administrasi Negara (*National Institute of Public Administration*): Jalan Veteran 10, Jakarta; f. 1958; library of 16,000 vols.; Chair. Dr. SONDANG P. SIAGIAN; publ. *Majalah Administrasi Negara* (quarterly).

Lembaga Pers Dan Pendapat Umum (*Press and Public Opinion Institute, Ministry of Information*): Pegangsaan Timur 19 B, Jakarta; f. 1953; audience research of press, film and radio; library of approx. 4,500 vols.; Dir. Dr. MARBANGUN.

History, Geography and Archaeology

Dinas Intelijen Medan & Geografi Jawatan Topografi T.N.I.-A.D. (*Geographical Institute*): Jalan Dr. Wahidin 1/11, Jakarta; Dir. Capt. ASMARUL AMRI.

Linguistics

Pusat Pembinaan Dan Pengembangan Bahasa (*National Centre for Language Development*): Jalan Diponegoro 82, P.O.B. 2625, Jakarta; f. 1975; attached to the Ministry of Education and Culture; scientific research on languages and foreign language teaching; library of about 35,000 vols.; Dir. Prof. Dr. AMRAN HALIM; Librarian IPON PURAWIJAYA; publ. *Bahasa dan Sastra, Pengajaran Bahasa dan Sastra, Informasi Mutakhir* (2 a month).

Medicine

Central Institute for Leprosy Research: Jalan Kimia 17, Jakarta; f. 1935; Institute includes a clinic and laboratory; Dir. MOH. ARIF.

Laboratorium Kesehatan Daerah (*Pathological Laboratory Ministry of Health*): Jalan Laboratorium 5, Medan; f. 1906; investigation and control of contagious and endemic diseases in Sumatra; approx. 3,000 vols.; Dir. Dr. ISKAK KOIMAN.

Laboratorium Kesehatan Pusat Lembaga Eijkman (*Eijkman Institute*): Jalan Diponegoro 69, Jakarta; f. 1888; Head Dr. HENDRO JOEWONO; bacteriological-serological department, chemical department and virus division; publs. Reports, Papers.

Lembaga Farmasi Nasional (*National Institute of Pharmacy, Ministry of Health*): Jalan Pertjetakan Negara 1, Jakarta; f. 1963; special research in Indonesian medicinal plants, controlling of drugs, food and cosmetics; Dir. Dr. POERNOMOSINGGIH.

Lembaga Malaria (*Malaria Institute, Ministry of Health*): Jalan Kwini No. 7, Jakarta; f. 1920; Dir. Dr. H. T. SOEPARMO.

Perusahaan Negara Bio-Farma (*Pasteur Institute*): Jalan Pasteur 9, P.O.B. 47, Bandung; Dir. M. S. NASUTION.

Pusat Penelitian dan Pengembangan Pelayanan Kesehatan (*Health Services Research and Development Centre, Ministry of Health*): Jalan Indrapura 17, Surabaya; f. 1975; library of 2,167 vols., and 64 journals; research and development for strengthening of health services in Indonesia; 40 research scientists in public health management, operational research, sociology, behavioural science, demography, anthropology, economics; library; Head M. H. W. SOETOPO, M.D., D.P.H.; publ. *Research Reports* (occasional series).

Unit Diponegoro (*Nutrition Institute*): c/o Nutrition Centre, Seameo Tropmed–U.I., Campus University of Indonesia, Salemba 4, Jakarta; f. 1937; Dir. Dradjat D. PRAWIRANEGARA, M.D., M.P.H.

Natural Sciences

Biological Sciences

Lembaga Biologi Nasional (*National Biological Institute*): Jl. Raya Juanda 18, P.O.B. 110, Bogor; f. 1817; research in biology; 99 mems.; library of 9,120 vols., 1,870 periodicals, 22,445 reprints; Dir. Dr. SETIJATI SASTRAPRADJA; publs. *Alam Kita, Berita Biologi, BioIndonesia*† (irregular), *Indeks Beranotasi Sumber Daya Biologi* (every 2 months), *Pewarta* (monthly), various pamphlets.

Kebun Raya Indonesia (*Bogor Botanical Gardens*): Kebun Raya, Bogor; f. 1817; Head Dr. DIDIN S. SASTRAPRADJA; publs. *Buletin Kebun Raya*† (quarterly), *Alphabetical List of Plant Species*† (irregular), *Index Seminum*† (annually), various pamphlets.

Kebun Pegunungan Cibodas (*Cibodas Mountain Botanic Gardens*): Cibodas, Sindanglaya, Cianjur;

f. 1862; Head Dr. DIDIN S. SASTRAPRADJA; publ. *Alphabetical List of Plant Species*† (irregular).

Kebun Iklim Kering Purwodadi (*Purwodadi Botanical Gardens for Drought Resistant Plants*): Purwodadi, Pasuran; f. 1941; Head R. BIMANTORO.

Kebun Raya Eka Karya Bali (*Bali Eka Karya Botanical Gardens*): Bedugul, Candikuning, Tabanan, Bali; f. 1959; Head Dr. SUKENDAR (acting).

Pusat Penelitian Botani (*Treub Laboratory*): c/o Kebun Raya/Indonesia, Bogor; f. 1884; Head Dr. SUSONO SAONO; publ. *Annales Bogorienses*† (irregular).

Herbarium Bogoriense: Jl. Raya Juanda 22–24, Bogor; f. 1884; Head Dr. KUSWATA KARTAWINATA; publ. *Reinwardtia*† (irregularly).

Museum Zoologicum Bogoriense: *see* under Museums.

Lembaga Oseanologi Nasional (*National Institute of Oceanology*): Jl. Akuarium, Pasar Ikan, P.O.B. 580. Jakarta Barat; f. 1904; library of 2,000 vols.; Dir. Dr. APRILANI SOEGIARTO; publs. *Marine Research in Indonesia* (irregular), *Oseanologi Di Indonesia* (quarterly), *Oseana* (monthly), *Oceanographical Cruise Report.*

Physical Sciences

Balai Penelitian Kimia (*Institute of Chemical Research*): Jalan Ir. H. Juanda 5-9, Bogor; f. 1909; approx. 10,000 books, 12,000 periodicals; research on agricultural products, waste materials and new methods of analysis; tests import-export products and issues certificate of quality; Dir. DARDJO SOMAATMADJA.

Dinas Geodesi, Jawatan Topografi T.N.I.-A.D. (*Geodetic Section, Army Topographic Service*): Jalan Bangka 1, Bandung; f. 1855; approx. 2,000 vols.; 2,500 periodicals; Dir. Ir. MOH TAWIL.

Direktorat Geologi (*Geological Survey of Indonesia*): Jalan Diponegoro 57, Bandung; f. 1850; Dir. SALMAN PADMANAGARA; publs. *Publikasi Teknik*† (Technical Papers: General Geology, Economic Geology, Geophysics, Hydrogeology, Palaeontology Series), *Publikasi Khusus*† (Special Publication Bulletin), Maps†, *Bulletin.*

Direktorat Meteorologi dan Geofisik (*Meteorological and Geophysical Service*): Jalan Gereja Inggris 3, Jakarta; Dir. M. SUKANTO; publs. various papers.

Nuclear Research Centre: Bandung; f. 1964; houses an atomic reactor.

Observatorium Bosscha (*Bosscha Observatory*): Lembang; f. 1925; since 1958 the observatory has been part of the Bandung Institute of Technology, Bandung; Dir. Dr. BAMBANG HIDAJAT; publs. *Annals of the Bosscha Observatory* (irregular), *Contributions from the Bosscha Observatory* (irregular), *Annual Report of the Bosscha Observatory.*

Pusat Meteorologi dan Geofisika (*Meteorological and Geophysical Institute*): Jalan Arief Rakhman Hakim 3, Jakarta.

Technology

Akademi Teknologi Kulit (*Academy of Leather Technology, Ministry of Labour*): Jl. Diponegoro 101, Yogyakarta; Dir. P. SUKARBOWO.

Balai Fotogrametri (*Institute of Photogrammetry, Ministry of Defence*): Jalan Gunung Sahar 90, Jakarta; f. 1937; research on problems relative to photogrammetry, aerotriangulization, topographical maps, etc.; library of approx. 1,500 books and periodicals; Head, Major R. E. BEAUPAIN.

Balai Penelitian Industri (*Industrial Research Institute*): Jalan Karanganjar 55, Jakarta; Dir. Ir. K. SOEBIJARSO.

Balai Penjelidikan Bahan-Bahan (*Materials Testing Institute*): Jalan Ganeca 10, Bandung; f. 1912; library; Dir. SUMANTRI.

Balai Penelitian Batik & Kerajinan (*Batik and Handicraft Research Institute, Department of Industry*): Jl. Kusumanegara 2, Yogyakarta; f. 1951; research, testing, and training courses; 108 mems.; library of 1,792 vols.; Dir. Ir. Sri SOEDEWI SANISI.

Balai Penelitian Kulit (*Leather Research Institute, Ministry of Industry*): Jl. Sokonandi 3, Yogyakarta; f. 1954; 200 mems.; 2,258 books; Dir. Ir. P. SOEKARBOWO.

Institut Teknologi Tekstil (*Institute of Textile Technology*): Jl. Jond. A. Yani 318, Bandung; f. 1922; Dir. Maj. Jon SEORJOSEOJARSO.

Direktorat Penyelidikan Masalah Air (*Institute of Hydraulic Engineering*): attached to Ministry of Public Works; 193 Jalan Ir. H. Juanda, Bandung; f. 1966; survey, investigation and research in the field of water resources development; Dir. R. TIRTOTJONDRO.

Jajasan Dana Normalisasi Indonesia (*Indonesian Standards Institution*): Jl. Braga 38, (Atas) Bandung; f. 1920; Chair. Prof. Ir. R. SOEMONO; Sec. GANDI, M.SC.

Jawatan Hidro-Oseanografi (*Naval Hydrographic Service*): Jalan Gunung Sahari 87, Jakarta; f. 1947; hydrographical survey of Indonesia; staff of 600; Dir. D. U. MARTOJO; publs. Tide Tables, etc.

Jawatan Pertambangan (*Institute of Mining*): 8 Jalan Gajah Mada 8, Jakarta; f. 1850; Dir. Ir. SOEROJO RANOEKOESOEMO; Vice-Dir. S. M. SAIR.

Lembaga Research dan Pengujian Materiil Angkatan Darat (*Military Laboratory for Research and Testing Material, Ministry of Defence*): Jalan Ternate 6-8, Bandung; f. 1865; library of 1,500 vols.; Dir. Brig.-Gen. N. A. KUSOMO.

Panitya Induk untuk Meter dan Kilogram (*Institute of Standards*): Jalan Pasteur 27, Bandung; Sec. G. M. PUTERA.

LIBRARIES AND ARCHIVES

Bandung

British Council Library: Jl. Cipaganti 123; f. 1971; 20,343 vols., 115 periodicals; Librarian Miss POPPY SENDJAJA.

Perpustakaan Balai Penjelidikan Bahan-Bahan (*Library of Materials Testing Institute*): Jalan Ganeca 10; f. 1912; 3,000 vols.; Librarian Mrs. UNEPUTY COEN.

Perpustakaan Deirktorat Geologi (*Library of Geological Research and Development Centre*): Jalan Diponegoro 57; 7,000 vols., 580 periodicals, 6,000 maps, 8,000 unpublished reports, 6,000 reprints; Librarian Mrs. YOHANNA NOYA-SINAY.

Perpustakaan Pusat Institut Teknologi Bandung (*Central Library, Bandung Institute of Technology*): Jalan Ganesya 10, Bandung; 145,000 vols., 500 current periodicals, 30,000 bound vols.; rare books, pamphlets and reports on Indonesia, collection on fine arts; Librarian Drs. ADJAT SAKRI; publ. *ITB Proceedings*†.

Pusat Perpustakaan Angkatan Darat (*Central Military Library*): Jalan Kalimantan 6; 36,000 vols. in Central Library, and about 20,000 vols. in departmental, territorial and college and office libraries; Dir. Brig.-Gen. SOESATYO.

Bogor

Bibliotheca Bogoriensis (*Central Library for Biological Sciences and Agriculture*): Jalan Ir. Haji Juanda 20; f. 1842; 350,000 vols.; Dir. Dr. PRABOWO TJITROPRANOTO,

M.SC.; publs. *Serie Bibliografi*†, *Daftar Tesis*†, *Daftar Antikuariat*† (irregular), *Indeks Biologi Pertanian dan Ekonomi Pertanian*† (2 a month), *Indeks Berita Surat Kabar* (monthly).

Perpustakaan Institut Pertanian Bogor (*Bogor Agricultural University Library*): Jalan Gunung Gede; f. 1963; 32,000 vols.; 550 periodicals; Librarian Miss S. JUHROH IDRIS.

Jakarta

Arsip Nasional Republik Indonesia (*National Archives*): Jalan Ampera Raya, Cilandak 111; f. 1892; Dir. Dra SOEMARTINI; 5,000 vols.; publ. *Penerbitan Sumber Arsip Nasional Republik Indonesia*† (irregular).

British Council Library: S. Widjojo Centre, Jl. Jendral Sudirman 57; f. 1970; 21,739 vols., 244 periodicals; Chief Librarian, Indonesia, P .H. Cox.

Central Documentation and Library of the Ministry of Information: Medan Merdeka Barat 9; f. 1945; specializes in mass communication, social and political subjects, and supplies regional branch offices; press-cutting service from Indonesian newspapers since 1950; temporarily acting as Exchange Centre for government publications and official documents; 10,000 vols.; Head Drs. P. DALIMUNTHE; Librarian Mrs. SAMPOERNO.

Library of Political and Social History: Medan Merdeka Seletan 11; f. 1952; 65,000 vols.; includes the National Bibliographic Centre (*Kantor Bibliografi Nasional*) deposit library; Librarian Drs. SOEKARMAN; publs. *Berita Bulanan* (Monthly Bulletin), *Regional Bibliography of Social Sciences, Publications—Indonesia, Checklist of Serials in the Libraries of Indonesia*.

Perpustakaan Bagian Pathologi Klinik R. S. Dr. Tjipto Mangunkusumo (*Dr. Tjipto Mangunkusumo Hospital Library*): Jalan Diponegoro 69; 3,000 vols.; Dir. Prof. Dr. R. GANDASOEBRATA; medicine, public health.

Perpustakaan Biro Pusat Statistik (*Library of Central Bureau of Statistics*): Jalan Dr. Sutomo 8; 45,000 vols.; Librarian ALI UMAR.

Perpustakaan Dewan Perwakilan Rakjat Gotong Rojong (*Library of Indonesian Parliament*): Senajan Pintu 8; 200,000 vols.; Librarian Mrs. NURLAILA PAKUSADEWA.

Perpustakaan Kementerian Perekonomian (*Library of the Ministry of Economic Affairs*): Jalan Gajah Mada 1; Librarian J. M. SPIER.

Perpustakaan Museum Pusat, Direktorat Jenderal Kebudajaan, Dept. Pendidikan & Kebudajaan (*Library of the Central Museum, Ministry of Education and Culture*): Medan Merdeka Barat 12; f. 1778; 402,560 vols., 4,500 MSS.; Dir. Drs. BAMBANG SUMADIO; publ. subject catalogues.

Pusat Dokumentasi Ilmiah Nasional—Lembaga Ilmu Pengetahuan Indonesia (*National Scientific Documentation Centre—Indonesian Institute of Sciences*): Jalan Jendral Gatot Subroto, P.O.B. 3065/Jkt; f. 1965; 51,026 vols.; Dir. LUWARSIH PRINGGOADISURJO, M.A.; publs. *Index of Indonesian learned periodicals* † (annual), *Baca*† (Read, every 2 months), *Accessions List*† (quarterly), *Annual Report*†.

Tman Batjaan dan Perpustakaan Umum (*Public Library, Jakarta*): J. Budi Kemuliaan 3; 42,300 vols.; Librarian Miss A. J. MOERKERCKEN VAN DER MEULEN; seven branches.

Makassar (Ujungpandang)

Library of Hasanuddin University: Kampus UNHAS Baraya, Ph. 3029, Jalan Sunu; f. 1956; specializes in marine sciences and Lontara studies (ancient local MSS.); organizes book talks, lectures, library courses, films, etc.; 50,000 vols.; Dir. A. RAHMAN RAHIM; publ. *Warta Pustaka* (irregular).

Perpustakaan Umum Makassar (*Makassar Public Library*): Jl. Kajaolaliddo 16, P.O.B. 16; f. 1969; organizes lending library services in brs. throughout South Sulawesi Province; film and music programmes; foreign language courses; children's library services; exhibitions and talks; 17,000 vols.; Dir. A. RAHMAN RAHIM; publ. *Jurnal Perpustakaan*† (Library Journal).

Medan

British Council Library: Jl. Imam Bonjol 18; f. 1971; 6,069 cols., 5 periodicals; Librarian Miss L. CHEU.

Yogyakarta

Perpustakaan Islam (*Islamic Library*): Jalan P. Mangkubumi 38; f. 1942; under the Ministry of Religion; 40,000 vols.; MSS. and periodicals; Dir. Prof. H. FARID MA'RUF; Librarian H. MOHAMMAD MUQODDAS SJUHADA.

Perpustakaan Jajasan Hatta (*Hatta Foundation Library*): Malioboro 85; 43,000 vols.; Librarian R. SOEDJATMIKO.

Perpustakaan Negara (*State Library*): Malioboro 175; f. 1949; 65,000 vols.; Librarian JAJOESMAN.

MUSEUMS

Museum Bali: Jl. Letnan Kolonel Wisnu 1, Denpasar, Bali; f. 1932; exhibits of Bali culture; library of 1,970 vols., 1,605 magazines, 1,023 transcriptions of lontars (palm leaves); Dir. Drs. PUTU BUDIASTRA; publs. *Majalah Saraswati, Karya Widia tak berkala*, reports, etc.

Museum Pusat (*Museum of Indonesian Culture*): Jalan Merdeka Barat 12, Jakarta; f. 1778, formerly Lembaga Kebudayaan Indonesia; library of 360,000 vols.; departments of ceramics, ethnography, pre-history, classical archaeology, anthropology, manuscripts and education; Dir. Drs. BAMBANG SUMADIO; publs. subject catalogues.

Museum Zoologicum Bogoriense (*Bogor Zoological Museum*): Lembaga Biologi Nasional, Jl. Juanda 3, Bogor; f. 1894; co-ordinated by Indonesian Inst. of Sciences; tropical fauna, particularly S.E. Asia; research on utilization of animal resources; departments of animal biosystematics, economic zoology, environmental zoology and animal natural history; library of 2,000 vols.; Dir. SOENARTONO ADISOEMARTO; publ. *Treubia* (Journal on zoology of Indo-Australian archipelago) (irregular).

UNIVERSITAS AIRLANGGA
(Airlangga University)

JL. RAYA DR. SUTOMO 61, SURABAYA

Telephone: 66625, 66574.

Telex: 31138 Unair SB.

Founded 1954.

Language of instruction: Indonesian; Academic year: July to June.

Rector: Prof. ABDOEL GANI, S.H., M.S.

Vice-Rectors: Prof. MARSETIO DONOSEPOETRO, M.D. (Academic Affairs and Research), Prof. R. K. TAMIN RADJAMIN, M.D. (Administration), R. SOEDARSO DJOJONEGORO, M.D. (Student Affairs and Public Service).

Secretary: R. SOEDARSO DJOJONEGORO, M.D.

Librarian: Drs. PARLINAH MOEDJONO, M.A.

Number of teachers: 906.
Number of students: 5,031.

Publications: *Justicia, Veterinary, Majalah Kedokteran Gigi* (Dentistry), *Majalah Kedokteran Surabaya* (Medicine).

DEANS:

Faculty of Medicine: Prof. R. RACHMAT SANTOSO, M.D.

Faculty of Dentistry: Drg. SOEMARSIH SOENTORO.

Faculty of Law: Dr. J. E. SAHETAPY.

Faculty of Economics: Drs. Ec. MIENDROWO PRAWIRODJOEMENO.

Faculty of Pharmacy: Drs. SOETARJADI.

Faculty of Veterinary Medicine: Drh. I. G. B. AMITABA.

Faculty of Social Sciences: SOETANDYO WIGNJOSOEBROTO, M.P.A.

UNIVERSITAS ANDALAS
(Andalas University)

JL. PERINTIS KEMERDEKAAN 77 PADANG, WEST SUMATRA

Telephone: 21535, 21565.

Founded 1956.

Language of instruction: Indonesian; Academic year: August to July.

Rector: Drs. MAWARDI YUNUS.

Vice-Rector for Academic Affairs: Dr. Ir. NITZA ARBI.

Vice-Rector for Administration and Finance: Drs. RUSTIAN KAMALUDDIN.

Vice-Rector for Student Affairs: Dr. SABARUDDIN ABBAS.

Librarian: SYAMSUL BAHRI.

Number of teachers: 518.
Number of students: 3,248.

Publication: *Majalah Universitas Andalas* (Bulletin).

STATE UNIVERSITIES

DEANS:

Faculty of Law and Social Science: M. ZEN JAMIL.

Faculty of Medicine: Dr. DARWIN ARSYAD.

Faculty of Mathematics and Natural Sciences: Drs. MARLIS RAHMAN.

Faculty of Agriculture: Ir. FACHRI AHMAD.

Faculty of Animal Husbandry: Ir. MEILUS RIVA'I.

Faculty of Economics: Dr. ALFIAN LAINS.

PROFESSORS:

ALRASYID, S. H., Comparative Constitutional Law
BATUAH, I. DT., M.D., Pulmonology
DJAFARUDDIN, Phytopathology
HAKIM, W., M.D., Pathology
HANIF, M. D., Internal Medicine
JURNALIS, K., Horticulture
MUDANTON, M., Physiology
SIHOMBING, H., Public Law Administration

ATTACHED INSTITUTES:

Institute for Regional Economic Research: Dir. HENDRA ESMARA.

Institute for Management: Dir. CHAIDIR ANWAR.

Institute for Demography: Dir. Dra. ROSDIWATI.

INSTITUT TEKNOLOGI BANDUNG
(Bandung Institute of Technology)

JALAN TAMANSARI 64, BANDUNG

Telephone: 83047, 83048.

Founded 1959 as a merger of the Technical and Science Faculties of the University of Indonesia.

Language of instruction: Indonesian; Academic year: August to July.

Rector: (vacant).

Secretary for Academic Affairs: Prof. Dr. Ir. SOSROWINARSO.

Secretary for Administration: Dr. MATTHIAS AROEF.

Secretary for Student Affairs: Dr. Ir. HARSONO TARUPRATJEKA.

Secretary for Communication and Cultural Affairs: Drs. BUT MUCHTAR.

Secretary for Research and Development: Dr. Ir. FILINO HARAHAP.

Librarian: Drs. ADJAT SAKRI.

Number of teachers: 718.
Number of students: 7,980.

Publications: *Proceedings Institut Teknologi Bandung*† (quarterly).

DEANS:

Faculty of Civil Engineering and Design: Ir. DJUANDA SURAATMADJA.

Faculty of Industrial Technology: Ir. WARJONO SUMODINOTO.

Faculty of Mathematics and Natural Science: Prof. HARIADI SOEPANGKAT.

PROFESSORS:

ACHMAD, S. A., Chemistry
ALISJAHBANA, I., Electrical Engineering
AMIRUDDIN, A., Chemistry
ARISMUNANDAR, W., Mechanical Engineering
AROEF, M., Industrial Engineering
ASIKIN, S., Geology
ATMOSUTJIPTO, G., Architecture
BARMAWI, M., Physics
DANUNINGRAT, A., Civil Engineering
DANUSUGHONDO, I., Engineering Physics
DIRAN, O., M.S.A.E., Mechanical Engineering
GOENARSO, Mathematics
HABIBIE, B. J., Mechanical Engineering
HANDOJO, Mechanical Engineering
HARDJOSUPARTO, S., Chemical Engineering
HIDAYAT, B., Astronomy
KARTASUBARNA, E., Fine Arts
KATILI, J. A., Geology
KARSA, K., Electrical Engineering
MOEDOMO, Mathematics
NOERDIN, I., Chemistry
NOERHADI, E., Biology
OEI BAN LIANG, Chemistry
POERBOHADIWIDJOJO, H., Architecture
PRAMUTADI, S., Chemistry
PRAWIROWARDOJO, S., Meteorology and Geophysics
RAIS, J., Geodesy
REKSOWARDOJO, S., Chemistry
SADALI, A., Fine Arts
SAMADIKUN, S., Electrical Engineering
SAMUDRO Mechanical Engineering
SARTONO, Geology
SATIADARMA, K., Pharmacy
SEMAWI, A. M., Civil Engineering
SOEBIANTO, Civil Engineering
SOEDIGDO, P., Chemistry
SOEDIGDO, S., Chemistry
SOELAIMAN, T. M., Electrical Engineering
SOEMONO, Civil Engineering
SOETEDJO, Civil Engineering
SOEPANGKAT, H., Physics
SOSROWINARSO, Civil Engineering
SUDARWATI, S., Biology
SUDJONO, H. D., Architecture
SURIAATMADJA, R., Geology
TISNA AMIDJAJA, D. A., Biology
WAWORUNTOE, W. J., City Planning
WIRADIKARTA, D., Pharmacy
WIRJOSOEMARTO, H., Mechanical Engineering
WONGSOTJITRO, S., Geodesy
ZEN, M. T., Geology

INSTITUT PERTANIAN BOGOR
(Bogor Agricultural University)

JALAN RAYA PAJAJARAN, BOGOR

Telephone: (0251) 23081, 23082.

Founded 1963.

Languages of instruction: Indonesian and English for foreign visiting professors. Academic year: September to June (two semesters).

Rector: Ir. A. H. NASOETION, PH.D.

Registrar: Ir. DARWIS, S.G., PH.D.

Librarian: Drs. FAHIDIN, B.SC.

Number of teachers: 552.
Number of students: 3,789.

Publications: *Forum Graduate School, Media Veteriner, Bulletin Makanan Ternak, Bulletin Hama dan Penyakit Tumbuhan, Bulletin Agronomi.*

DEANS:

Faculty of Agriculture: Ir. GOESWONO SOEPARDI, PH.D.
Faculty of Veterinary Medicine: SOEWONDO DJOJOSOEBAGIO, PH.D.
Faculty of Animal Husbandry: HARIMURTI MARTOJO, PH.D.
Faculty of Forestry: Ir. SADAN WIDARMANA, PH.D.
Faculty of Fisheries: Ir. HASRIL HAMID JASIN, M.SC.
Faculty of Mechanization and Product Technology: Ir. SOESARSONO WIJANDI, M.SC.

PROFESSORS:

ANGGORODI, R., Poultry Nutrition
ARSYAD, S., Soil and Water Conservation
ATMAKUSUMA, A., Pharmacology
ATMAWIDJAYA, R., Forest Inventory, Remote Sensing
DJOJOSOEBAGIO, S., Endocrinology and Radiobiology
GO BAN HONG, Soil Sciences
HUTASOIT, J. H., Nutrition
KOSWARA, O., Soil Fertility
MARTOJO, H., Animal Breeding
NASOETION, A. H., Agricultural Experimental Statistics
PARTOATMODJO, S., Bacteriology
SAJOGYO, Rural Sociology
SASTRADIPRADJA, D. K., Physiology and Radiobiology
SASTRAKUSUMAH, S., Marine Biology and Physiology
SASTROHADINOTO, S., Histology
SATARI, A. M., Soil Science
SOEDARMO, D., Basic Biochemistry
SOEHARJO, A., Farm Management
SOESENO, H., Plant Physiology
SOEPARDJO, S., Agricultural Engineering
SOSROMARSONO, S., Agricultural Entomology
SUDJANADI, F., Agricultural Development
SUKRA, J., Embryology
SURIANEGARA, I., Forest Ecology and Natural Resources Management
TANUDIMADJA, K., Anatomy
TARUMINGKENG, R. CH., Forest Product Entomology
TEKEN, I. B., Agricultural Economics
TITUS, I., Veterinary Surgery
WAHJU, J., Poultry Nutrition

UNIVERSITAS BRAWIJAYA
(Brawijaya University)

MAYOR JENDRAL HARYONO 169, MALANG, EAST JAVA

Telephone: 7376.

Founded 1963.

Language of instruction: Indonesian, Academic year: August to July.

Rector: Drs. HARSONO.
Vice-Rector (Academic Affairs): Ir. BASKORO WINARNO.
Vice-Rector (Finance and Administration): Drs. Z. A. ACHMADY, M.P.A.
Vice-Rector (Student Affairs and Alumni): MASYHUR EFFENDY, S.H.
Librarian: Prof. F. PATTY, M.A.

Number of teachers: 383.
Number of students: 7,055.
Publications: *Mimbar Universitas Brawijaja*† (2 a month), *Siaran Universitas Brawijawa*† (weekly), *Publico*† (quarterly), *Febra*† (monthly), *Administrator*† (monthly), *Agrivita* (monthly).

DEANS:

Faculty of Law and Social Sciences: Moh. IDRIS, S.H.
Faculty of Economics: Drs. O. S. HASTOETI HARSONO.
Faculty of Business and Public Administration: Drs. TAHER ALHABSYI.
Faculty of Engineering: Prof. Ir. SOERJONO.
Faculty of Agriculture: Prof. Dr. H. SOETONO, M.AGR.
Faculty of Fishery and Animal Husbandry: Ir. IMAN SOETRISNO.
Faculty of Medicine: Dr. WAHJOETOMO.

UNIVERSITAS CENDERAWASIH

ABEPURA, JAYAPURA, IRIAN JAYA

Telephone: Abe—151

Founded 1962.

Language of instruction: Indonesian.

Rector: Prof. Dr. Ir. RUBINI ATMAWIDJAJA.
Vice-Rectors: Drs. MASMAN ANDARA, Drs. A. ISMANOE, Drs. TJIPTO DRADJATI.
Chief Administrative Officer: M. HATTU.
Librarian: Dra. NY. ENDANG T. SURYADI.

Library of 40,000 vols.
Number of teachers: 75.
Number of students: 1,500.
Publication: *Majalah Universitas Cenderawasih*† (quarterly), *Bulletin of Irian* (monthly).

DEANS:

Faculty of Law, Economics and Social Sciences: Drs. M. ARIFANDI.
Faculty of Teacher-Training: Drs. J. CH. SUJANTO.
Faculty of Agriculture, Forestry and Veterinary Science: Ir. H. MACKBON.
Faculty of Education: Drs. SUDARTO.

DIRECTORS:

Institute of Anthropology: Dr. I SUHARNO.
Institute of Agricultural Research: Dr. M. ANGSAR (acting).

UNIVERSITAS DIPONEGORO

JALAN IMAM BARJO, SH. 1-3, P.O.B. 270, SEMARANG

Telephone: 311520.

Telex: 22315 UNDIP SM.

Founded 1960.

Language of instruction: Indonesian. Academic year: July to June.

Rector: Prof. SUDARTO, S.H.
Vice-Rector (Academic Affairs): Prof. SIGIT MURYONO, M.D.
Vice-Rector (Administration and Finance): Drs. SOEHARDJO.
Vice-Rector (Research and Development): Drs. SOEHARDI.
Vice-Rector (Student Affairs): Dr. HERRY SOEPARDJO.
University Librarian: SLAMET RAHARDJO, M.A.

Number of books in library: 15,000.
Number of teachers: 491.
Number of students: 7,174.

Publications: *Bulletin Universitas, Gema Keadilan, Edent, Reator, Majalah Kedokteran, Bulletin Fakultas Peternakan & Perikanan, Lembaran Ilmu Sastra Budaya, Forum, Warta Perpustakaan, Bulletin Dharma Wanita—UNDIP.*

DEANS:

Faculty of Law: Dr. SATJIPTO RAHARDJO, S.H.
Faculty of Engineering: Ir. YUTATA HADIHARDOYO.
Faculty of Medicine: Dr. R.R.J. Sri DJOKOMULJANTO, M.D.
Faculty of Economics: Drs. R. B. SUNARDI.
Faculty of Animal Husbandry and Fisheries: Drh. SUTOPO ANDAR.
Faculty of Arts and Letters: Drs. SOEDJARWO.
Faculty of Social and Political Sciences: Drs. R. SOEMENDAR SOEROJOSOEDARMO.

PROFESSORS:

BOEDHI, DARMOJO R., Internal Medicine
DJANUAR, R., Reproduction
DJOEMANTORO, Biochemistry
HEYDER BIN HEYDER, Surgery
HOEDIONO, Oto-rhino-laryngology
ISMAIL JAKOEP, Islamic Law
KO TJAY SING, Private Law
LUBIS, D. A., Animal Nutrition
MOELJONO S. TRASTUTENOJO, Child Health
SAPARDI BRODJOHOEDOJO, Microbiology
SARDJONO DHANOEDIBROTO, R., Gynaecology
SIGIT MURYONO, Anatomy
SOEKANDAR, M., Dermatology
SOEKISNO HADIKOEMORO, Mechanical Engineering
SOEMARDI SASTRAKOESOEMAH, Marine Biology
SUDIRO, Civil Engineering
WIDAGDO, Ophthalmology
WINOTO, Food Technology

ATTACHED INSTITUTE:

Pusat Risat dan Pengembangan (*Research and Development Centre*): Jalan Imam Barjo S.H. 1-3, Semarang; Dir. Drs. SOEHARDI.

UNIVERSITAS GADJAH MADA
(Gadjah Mada University)

BULAKSUMUR, YOGYAKARTA

Telephone: 88688.

Telex: 2535 UGM YOGYA.

Founded 1949.

Language of instruction: Indonesian; Academic year: July to June.

Rector: Prof. Dr. SUKADJI RANUWIHARDJO.
Vice-Rector for Academic Affairs: Prof. Dr. MASRUN.

Vice-Rector for Administration and Financial Affairs: Drs. SUKAMTO, M.SC.
Vice-Rector for Students and Alumni: R. SOEPONO, M.SC.
Vice-Rector for Research and Foreign Relations: Drh. BUSONO, M.SC.
Librarian: Dra. SAWITTRI SUHARTO, M.A.

Number of teachers (full-time): 1,296.
Number of students: 17,274.

DEANS:

Faculty of Biology: Prof. Ir. MOESO SOERJOWINOTO.
Faculty of Economics: Dr. SUTATWO HADIWIGENO.
Faculty of Philosophy: R. SOEJADI, S.H.
Faculty of Pharmacy: Drs. SOERAIS SOEDIROMARGOSO.
Faculty of Geography: Drs. R. SOERASTOPO HADISOEMARNO.
Faculty of Law: Prof. Dr. R. M. SOEDIKNO MERTOKUSOMO, S.H.
Faculty of Science and Mathematics: Ir. PRIYANA, M.SC.
Faculty of Medicine: Dr. R. SOEPRONO.
Faculty of Dentistry: Prof. Drg. SUTATMI SURYO.
Faculty of Veterinary Medicine: Drh. M. P. EDDY MOELJONO, M.S.A., PH.D.
Faculty of Forestry: Dr. Ir. ACHMAD SUMITRO.
Faculty of Agriculture: Dr. Ir. JOEDORO SOEDARSONO.
Faculty of Animal Husbandry: Drh. SOEDOMO REKSOHADIPRODJO, M.SC.
Faculty of Psychology: Prof. Dr. SUMADI SURYOBROTO, M.A., ED.S.
Faculty of Letters and Culture: Dr. SULASTIN SUTRISNO.
Faculty of Social and Political Science: Drs. SUBAROTO.
Faculty of Engineering: Ir. BAMBANG SUHENDRO, M.SC., D.E.SC.
Faculty of Agricultural Technology: Ir. MOCHAMAD ROESDI.

UNIVERSITAS HASANUDDIN
(Hasanuddin University)

JALAN MESJID RAYA,
UJUNG PANDANG

Telephone: 5335, 6343.
Telegraphic Address: UNHAS.
Founded 1956.

Rector: Prof. Dr. A. AMIRUDDIN.
Registrar: TJIPTASURASA.
Librarian: RAHMAN RAHIM.

Number of teachers: 688.
Number of students: 7,907.

Publication: *Majalah Universitas Hasanuddin.*

DEANS:

Faculty of Law: ANDI MANSJUR DJUANA.
Faculty of Medical Sciences: SOLIHIN WIRASUGENA.
Faculty of Agricultural Sciences: Mrs. S. S. HARTONO.
Faculty of Science and Technology: MUH. RAMLI.
Faculty of Culture and Social Sciences: LATANRO.

DEANS OF POSTGRADUATE STUDIES:

Science and Technology: NUR ABDURRAHMAN.
Health Sciences: SOEROSO WIRJOWIDAGDO.
Agricultural Sciences: SOEMARMO.
Social Sciences and Letters: SJUKUR ABDULLAH.
Centre for Law and Economics: BURHAMZAH.

UNIVERSITAS INDONESIA

SALEMBA RAYA 4, JAKARTA

Telephone: 882955, 882992.
Founded 1950.

Language of instruction: Indonesian; Academic year: July to June (two semesters).

Rector: Prof. Dr. MAHAR MARDJONO.
Deputy Rector for Academic Affairs: Prof. Dr. SUJUDI.
Deputy Rector for Finance and Administration: SOEDARSONO, S.E.
Deputy Rector for Students: Dr. Sri EDI SWASONO.
Director for Community Services: R. M. GIRINDRO PRINGGODIGDO, S.H.
Director of Research: DOES SAMPOERNO, M.D., M.P.H.
Registrar: SANJOTO SOEBEKTI, S.E.
Librarian: URIP SUTONO, S.S.

Number of teachers: 2,209.
Number of students: 10,512.

Publications: *Media Academica* (monthly), *Media Aesculapius* (newspaper), *Salemba*† (every 2 weeks, newspaper), and various faculty bulletins.

DEANS:

Faculty of Medicine: Prof. R. GANDASOEBRATA.
Faculty of Dental Medicine: Drg. ALI DAHLAN.
Faculty of Mathematics and Natural Sciences: Prof. Dr. S. SOMADIKARTA.
Faculty of Technology: Ir. F. B. MEWENGKANG.
Faculty of Law: Mrs. S. J. HANIFAH WIGNJOSASTRO, S.H.
Faculty of Economics: Dr. DJUNAEDI HADISUMARTO.
Faculty of Letters: Prof. Dr. HARJATI SUBARDIO.
Faculty of Psychology: Dr. SAPARINAH SADLI.
Faculty of Social Sciences: Prof. MIRIAM BUDIARDJO.
Faculty of Public Health: FAHMI DJAFAR SAIFUDDIN, M.D., M.P.H.

AFFILIATED COLLEGES AND INSTITUTES:

Lembaga Demografi (*Institute of Demography*): Salemba 4, Jakarta; Dir. KARTOMO WIROSUHARDJO, S.E., M.A.

Lembaga Ekonomi dan Penelitian Masjarakat (*Institute of Economic and Social Research*): Dir. MOH. ARSJAD, S.E., M.B.A.

Lembaga Kriminologi (*Institute of Criminology*): Salemba 4, Jakarta; Dir. BOY MARDJONO REKSODIPUTRO, S.H., M.A.

Lembaga Management (*Institute of Management*): Salemba 4, Jakarta; Dir. Dr. DJUNAEDI HADISUMARTO.

Lembaga Penelitian Masyarakat (*Institute for Social Research*): Kompleks U.I. Rawamangun, Jakarta; Coordinator Dr. IHROMI SIMATUPANG.

Lembaga Konsultasi Hukum dan Bantuan Hukum (*Legal Consultation and Legal Aid Department*): Kompleks U.I. Rawamangun, Jakarta; Dir. HASNIL HARUN, S.H.

Pusat Dokumentasi Hukum (*Legal Documentation Centre*): Jl. Cirebon 5, Jakarta; Dir. BOY MARDJONO REKSODIPUTRO, S.H., M.A.

Lembaga Psychologi (*Institute of Psychology*): Kompleks U.I. Rawamangun, Jakarta; Dir. E. JOESOEF NOERSJIWAN, DRA.

Lembaga Teknologi (*Institute of Technology*): Salemba 4, Jakarta; Dir. Prof. Dr. ROOSENO.

Lembaga Antropologi (*Institute of Anthropology*): Kompleks U.I. Rawamangun, Jakarta; Dir. Prof. Dr. KUNTJARANINGRAT.

Lembaga Archeologi (*Institute of Archaeology*): Kompleks U.I. Rawamangun, Jakarta; Dir. BOECHARI, S.S.

Lembaga Sejarah (*Institute of History*): Kompleks U.I. Rawamangun, Jakarta; Chair. R. MOELA MARBUN, S.S.

Lembaga Literatur (*Institute of Literary Studies*): Kompleks U.I. Rawamangun, Jakarta; Chair. Dr. BOEN S. OEMARJATI.

Lembaga Penelitian Masyarakat dan Lembaga Hubungan Masyarakat (*Institute for Social Research and Institute of Mass Communications*): Kompleks U.I. Rawamangun, Jakarta; Dir. Prof. MIRIAM BUDIARDJO.

Pusat Bahasa (*Linguistics Centre*): Kompleks U.I. Rawamangun, Jakarta; Chair. DJOKO KENTJONO, M.A.

Pusat Ilmu Komputer (*Computer Science Centre*): Jl. Salemba 4, Jakarta; Dir. Dr. INDRO SUWANDI.

UNIVERSITAS NEGERI JAMBI
(Jambi State University)

JALAN DIPONEGORO 16, JAMBI,
TELANAIPURA

Telephone: 23178.
Founded 1963.

Language of instruction: Indonesian; Academic year: July to June.

Rector: Drs. KEMAS MOHAMAD SALEH.
Vice-Rector (Academic Affairs): Z. ANSORI AHMAD, S.H.
Vice-Rector (Administration): Ir. S. B. SAMAD.
Vice-Rector (Student Affairs): Drs. RAMLI.
Librarian: Drs. SYAHRIL ZAWIR.

Library of 16,243 vols.

Number of teachers: 74 full-time, 153 part-time.

Number of students: 883.

DEANS:

Faculty of Law: IDRIS JARFAR, S.H.
Faculty of Economics: Drs. AZWAR DURIN.
Faculty of Agriculture: Ir. DANIEL SAALUDDIN.
Faculty of Animal Husbandry: Drh. MD. TOHA.

UNIVERSITAS NEGERI JEMBER
(Jember State University)

JALAN VETERAN 3, GEDUNG TRI UBAYA SAKTI, JEMBER, JAVA

Telephone: 119-1089.

Founded 1957.

Rector: SOETARDJO, S.H.
Vice-Rector (Academic Affairs): Drs. S. WIDYOPRAKOSO.
Vice-Rector (Administration and Finance): A. M. M. SOSROKUSUMO, S.H.
Vice-Rector (Student Affairs): Drs. T. PRAWIROSUDIRDJO.
Librarian: Drs. K. ISKANDAR ZULKARNAIN.

The library contains 21,586 vols.

Number of teachers: 525 (266 full-time).

Number of students: 3,094.

Publications: *Gema Universitas, Argapura, Bulletin Fakultas Sastra.*

DEANS:

Faculty of Law: SOEHARSONO, S.H.
Faculty of Social and Political Sciences: Drs. A. KHUSYAIRI.
Faculty of Agriculture: Ir. RIYANTO.
Faculty of Economics: Drs. MURDIYANTO PURBANGKORO.
Faculty of Education: Drs. MULJONO HENDROSISWOJO.

PROFESSORS:

SOERIPTO, R. M., Law
SOEDARTO, Law
HARYONO DANUSASTRA, Agronomy
SOEDARSONO HADISAPUTRA, Business Economics, Agriculture
SOENYOTO SOEMODIHARDJO, Agricultural Engineering
SOEMPOMO DJOJOWARDONO, Personnel Management
SOEHARDI, R., S.H.
MOESO SOERJOWINOTO, Biology

UNIVERSITAS JENDERAL SOEDIRMAN
(General Soedirman University)

KAMPUS UNSOED GRENDENG, P.O.B. 15, PURWOKERTO, CENTRAL JAVA

Telephone: 292, 804, 805

Founded 1963.

Language of instruction: Indonesian; Academic year: March to March (two semesters).

Rector: Drs. SOEDAMAN HADISOETJIPTO.
Vice-Rector (Academic Affairs): Drs. SOETJIPTO MERTODIPOETRO.
Vice-Rector (Administration Affairs): Drs. ROEDHIRO.
Vice-Rector (Student Affairs): Drh. SOEDITO ADJISOEDARMO.
Chief Administrative Officer: S. H. ISWANTO.
Librarian: Dra. HARTATI, P.R.

Number of teachers: 293.

Number of students: 2,153.

Publications: *Berita UNSOED* (monthly), *Bulletin UNSOED.*

DEANS:

Faculty of Agriculture: Ir. DARYONO WATIMAN.
Faculty of Biology: Drs. RUBIYANTO MISMAN.
Faculty of Animal Husbandry: Drh. SOETRISNO.
Faculty of Economics: Drs. SOEJITNO.

UNIVERSITAS LAMBUNG MANGKURAT*

JALAN LAMBUNG MANKURAT 31, BANJARMASIN

Founded 1960.

Faculties of Law, Economics, Agriculture, Education, Political Science, Fisheries, Forestry, Teacher Training.

* No reply received to our questionnaire this year.

UNIVERSITAS LAMPUNG
(Lampung University)

JL. HASANUDIN 34, TELUKBETUNG

Telephone: 41286, 42550.

Founded 1965.

State control; Languages of instruction: Indonesian and English; Academic year: February to December (two terms).

Rector: Prof. Dr. Ir. SITANALA ARSYAD.
Vice-Rector (Academic Affairs): ALHUSNIDUKI HAMIM, S.E., M.SC.
Vice-Rector (Finance and Administration): RASJID MACHSUS AKRABI, S.H.
Vice-Rector (Student Affairs): ARIES PANUJU, S.E.
Vice-Rector (Planning and Development): SYAMSOEDIN, T.A., S.E.
Registrar: AZHAR, S.H.

Number of teachers: 160.

Number of students: 2,757.

Publications: *Buletin Penelitian†, Varia Universitas Lampung.*

DEANS:

Faculty of Law: KADRI HUSIN, S.H.
Faculty of Economics: ACHMAD ISMAIL, S.E.
Faculty of Education: Drs. A. KANTAN ABDULLAH.
Faculty of Teacher Training: Drs. FACHRUDIN ARFAN.
Faculty of Civil Engineering: Ir. SIGIT RAHARDJO.

DIRECTORS:

Bureau for Law Consultation and Aid: KADRI HUSIN.
Central Library: MUCHSIN BADAR, S.E.
Institute of Research and Public Service: RIZANI PUSPAWIDJAJA, S.H.
Institute of Management: NAWAWI MUNAF, S.E.
Institute of Language: ABDULKADIR MUHAMMAD, S.E.

UNIVERSITAS NEGERI MATARAM
(Mataram State University)

JL. LEMURU BARU, KOTAK POS 200 AMPENAN, LOMBOK, N.T.B.

Founded 1963.

President: M. JUSUF ABUBAKAR.
Registrar: H. M. ANWAR ABIDIN.
Librarian: MUSTRUDIN DJAJADY.

Library of 2,814 vols.

Number of teachers: 68.

Number of students: 785.

Faculties of Agriculture, Animal Husbandry, Economics and Law.

UNIVERSITAS MULAWARMAN

JL. P. FLORES 1, SAMARINDA, EAST KALIMANTAN

Telephone: 326.

Founded 1962.

Rector: Ir. R. S. WIRAKUSUMAH.

Number of teachers: 150 (full-time).

Publications: *Berita Unmul* (monthly), *Frontir†* (2 a year).

Faculties of agriculture, forestry, social and political sciences, economics.

UNIVERSITAS NUSA CENDANA

JL. SAM RATULANGI 72, KUPANG, TIMOR

Founded 1962.

Faculties of Veterinary Medicine and Animal Husbandry; Public Administration and Management; Education; and Teaching and Teacher Training.

UNIVERSITAS NEGERI PADJADJARAN
(Pajajaran State University)

JALAN DIPATI UKUR 35, BANDUNG, JAVA

Telephone: 83271/8.

Founded 1957.

Rector: Prof. Drs. HINDERSAH WIRATMADJA.
Librarian: Ir. SOEDARMINTO MARTODIREDJO.

Library of 110,000 vols.
Number of teachers: 1,180.
Number of students: 10,738.
Publications: *Sastra dan Budaja* (irregular), *Agriculture* (quarterly), *Economica, Publistica* (irregular), and others.

DEANS:

Faculty of Law: R. A. SALEH ADIWINATA, S.H.
Faculty of Social and Political Sciences: KOSASIH PURAWISASTRA.
Faculty of Economics: YUYUN WIRASASMITA, M.SC..
Faculty of Medicine: Prof. Dr. TOPO HARSONO.
Faculty of Dentistry: Drg. Mrs. SOERTINI E. LAMBRI, M.S.
Faculty of Literature: Dr. J. S. BADUDU.
Faculty of Agriculture: Dr. Ir. ACHMAD BAIHAKI, M.SC.
Faculty of Animal Husbandry: Prof. Dr. DIDI ATMADILAGA.
Faculty of Psychology: Prof. Dr. MAR'AT.
Faculty of Mathematics and Natural Sciences: Dr. ACHMAD YOENOES.
Faculty of Publicity and Journalism: Drs. ONONG UHYANA EFFENDI, M.A.

UNIVERSITAS NEGERI DI PALANGKA RAYA

KOMPLEX PELAJAR, PALANGKA RAYA

Founded 1963.

Chairman of the Presidium: Ir. R. SYLVANUS.

Library of 6,925 vols.
Number of teachers: 17 full-time, 154 part-time.
Number of students: 877.
Faculties of Teacher Training, Education, Economics.

UNIVERSITAS PATTIMURA AMBON

P.O.B. 95, JL. JENDERAL ACHMAD YANI, AMBON

Founded 1956; university status 1962.

Telephone: 2189, 2551, 3053.

Founded 1956, became university 1962.
State control; Language of instruction: Indonesian; Academic year: August to July.

Rector: MUHAMMAD R. L. LESTALUHU.
Assistant for Academic Affairs: PAUL J. SIWABESSY.
Assistant for Administration and Finance: A. K. P. VIGELEYN NIKIJULUW.
Assistant for Public Relations: R. SUYATNO.
Assistant for Student Affairs: C. M. PATTIRUHU.
Registrar: Z. J. LATUPAPUA.
Librarian: ALI SAWAWI.

Number of teachers: 447.
Number of students: 3,693.
Publication: *Bulletin Unpatti* (monthly).

DEANS:

Faculty of Law: M. A. H. TAHAPARY.
Faculty of Social Sciences: ASGAR BIXBY.
Faculty of Agriculture and Forestry: J. J. FRANSZ.
Faculty of Economics: MARTONO.
Faculty of Teacher Training: Mrs. E. VIGELEYN NIKIJULUW.
Faculty of Educational Sciences: W. LUSIKOOY.
Faculty of Animal Husbandry and Fishery: S. P. TELUSSA.
Faculty of Technology: M. WATTIMURY.

DIRECTORS:

Institute of Research and Public Service: R. SUYATNO.
Institute of Demography: A. G. SALAMPESSY.
Institute of Educational Studies: J. E. SITANALA.
Institute of Anthropology and Language: J. TH. F. PATTISELANNO.
Institute of Management: ISMAIL TAHIR.

UNIVERSITAS RIAU

JL. RONGGOWARSITO, PEKANBARU, SUMATRA

Founded 1962.

Rector: Drs. H. FARID KASMY.
Vice-Rectors: Drs. R. KAILANI HASAN, Drs. H. J. SIAGIAN, Drs. MOHAMMAD SAAD, Drs. SYAFRIL ANWAR.

Number of teachers: 474.
Number of students: 1,098.

DEANS:

Faculty of Politics and Social Science: Drs. ALFIAN.
Faculty of Economics: Drs. RUSYDI ILYAS.
Faculty of Physics and Mathematics: Ir. HARTONO.
Faculty of Fishery: Ir. FACHRUDIN.
Faculty of Teacher's Training: Drs. ANWAR SYAIR.
Faculty of Education: Drs. ZAINAL ZEN.

UNIVERSITAS SAM RATULANGI

JL. WOLTER MONGINSIDE, MANADO

Telephone: 3586-7.

Founded 1961.

Academic year: January to December (two semesters).

Rector: Prof. Dr. HENRICUS KANDOU.
Vice-Rector: Drs. KAREL WILLEM TIMBOELENG.
Registrar/Chief Administrative Officer: Drs. JACOB MONINGKA.
University Librarian: Mrs. M. PIRI KAUNANG (acting).

Number of teachers: 309 (full-time), 637 (part-time).
Number of students: 2,931.
Publication: *Kalawarta Unsrat.*

DEANS:

Faculty of Medicine: Dr. P. E. A. PANGALILA.
Faculty of Agriculture: Ir. Mrs. J. P. LANTANG POLITON.
Faculty of Animal Husbandry: Drh. J. S. W. D. SOEBROTO.
Faculty of Law: F. X. J. KALANGI, S.H.
Faculty of Economics: Drs. A. NIODE.
Faculty of Social and Political Science: Drs. S. A. ROLOS.
Faculty of Engineering: Drs. K. W. TIMBOELENG.
Faculty of Letters: Drs. A. MALUEGHA.
Faculty of Fishery: Ir. ALAMSJAH.

UNIVERSITAS SRIWIJAYA

BUMI SRIWIJAYA, PALEMBANG, SOUTH SUMATRA

Telephone: 26004, 26388, 23155.

Founded 1960.

State control; Language of Instruction: Indonesian; Academic year: July to June.

Chancellor: H.E. THE GOVERNOR OF SOUTH SUMATRA.
Vice-Chancellor and Rector: Drs. SJAFRAN SJAMSUDDIN.
Librarian: Drs. CHUZAIMAH DIEM, M.L.S.

Number of teachers: 504 full-time, 981 part-time.
Number of students: 8,054.
Publications: *Majalah Universitas Sriwijaya* (3 a year), and faculty bulletins.

DEANS:

Faculty of Economics: Drs. AMIRUDDIN.
Faculty of Law: TOTO KASIHAN, S.H.
Faculty of Engineering: Ir. MACHMUD HASJIM, M.M.E.
Faculty of Agriculture: Ir. A. RASYID HANAFIAH.
Faculty of Medicine: Dr. AZWAR AGOES.
Faculty of Teacher Training: Drs. ZAINAL ABIDIN GAFFAR.
Faculty of Education: Drs. ICHTIAR, H.K., M.ED.

PROFESSORS:

HALIM, A., Linguistics
HARDJOWIJONO, Dr. G., Paediatrics
MUKTI, H. D., Advance Management
MUSLIMIN, A., S.H., Administrative Law
SOELAIMAN, M., Adat Law

ATTACHED INSTITUTES:

Institute of Research and Community Service: Dir. Ir. BUCHORI RAHMAN, M.SC.

Language Teaching and Research Institute: Dir. Drs. ZULKARNAIN MUSTOFA.

University Planning Board: Chair. Dr. A. BAGHOWI BACHAR.

UNIVERSITAS SYIAH KUALA*

JALAN DARUSALAM,
BANDA ACEH

Founded 1961.

Faculties of Economics, Law, Veterinary Medicine, Civil Engineering, Agriculture and Education.

* No reply received to our questionnaire this year.

UNIVERSITAS SUMATERA UTARA
(University of North Sumatra)

JALAN UNIVERSITAS 22,
TELADAN, MEDAN

Founded 1952.

Chancellor: Brig. Gen. HAJI A. M. LUBIS.
Rector: HARRY SUWONDO.

Faculties of Law, Medicine, Agriculture, Engineering, Dentistry, Mathematics, Letters, Veterinary Medicine.

Number of teachers: 740.
Number of students: 7,500.

UNIVERSITAS TANJUNGPURA*

JALAN RAYA 17,
PONTIANAK

Founded 1963.

Faculties of Agriculture, Economics, Education, Engineering, Law, Social and Political Sciences.

* No reply received to our questionnaire this year.

INSTITUT TEKNOLOGI 10 NOPEMBER SURABAYA
(Surabaya Institute of Technology)

JL. COKROAMINOTO 12A,
SURABAYA

Telephone: 60652.
Telex: 31224 INTEKS SB.

Founded 1960.

Rector: MAHMUD ZAKI, M.SC.
Vice-Rector for Academic Affairs: OEDJOE DJOERIAMAN, M.SC., PH.D.
Vice-Rector for Administration: Ir. HARWIJONO DIRDJOSOEKARTO.
Vice-Rector for Students' Affairs: SUSANTO, M.SC.
Vice-Rector for Development: Ir. RACHMAT PURWONO.
Librarian: Dra. NARKANTI WIJADI.

Library of 36,586 vols.

Number of teachers: 277.
Number of students: 3,800.

DEANS:

Faculty of Civil Engineering: Ir. BAMBANG SUJADI.
Faculty of Mechanical Engineering: Ir. MOCH BACHRIE.
Faculty of Electrical Engineering: Ir. ADI SURJANTO.
Faculty of Chemical Engineering: OEDJOE DJOERIAMAN, PH.D.
Faculty of Shipbuilding Engineering: Ir. SOEGIONO.
Faculty of Architecture: Ir. HARYONO SIGIT.

Faculty of Sciences: ABDUL SALAM HUSIN, M.SC.

UNIVERSITAS UDAYANA

JALAN JENDRAL SUDIRMAN,
P.O.B. 105, DENPASAR, BALI

Telephone: 2793.

Founded 1962.

Rector: Prof. Dr. I. GOESTI NGOERAH GDE NGOERAH.
Assistants to the Rector: Dr. I. G. A. G. PUTHRA, Drs. PUTU KUNA WINAYA, Drs. Ng. RAI MIRSHA, PUTU DJAJA NEGARA, S.H., Drs. I. WAYAN RENDHA.

DEANS:

Faculty of Letters: Drs. I. GUSTI GDE ARDANA.
Faculty of Medicine: Dr. IDA BAGUS OKA.
Faculty of Veterinary Science and Animal Husbandry: Dr. I. MADE NITIS, M.RUR.SC.
Faculty of Law and Social Sciences: TJOKORDE RAKA DHERANA, S.H.
Faculty of Technical Sciences: Ir. TJOKORDE GDE MAYUN.
Faculty of Economics: Drs. I. GDE BUNGAYA.
Faculty of Agriculture: Ir. I. MADE SWARA.
Teachers Training College: Drs. NYOMAN TIRTA.
Faculty of Education: Drs. IDA BAGUS NETRA.

PRIVATE UNIVERSITIES

UNIVERSITAS 17 AGUSTUS 1945

46 JALAN TEUKU CIK DITIRO,
JAKARTA

Telephone: 45610.

Founded 1952.

Private control; Language of instruction: Indonesian.

Chancellor: Prof. Dr. PRAYUDHI ATMOSUDIRDJO, S.H.
Rector: WIRJONO KOESOEMO, S.H.
Secretary-General: Drs. S. SUPIT, PH.D.

Number of teachers: 166.
Number of students: 860.

Publication: *Untag Induk Bulletin*.

DEANS:

Faculty of Business and Public Administration: Prof. Dr. PRAYUDHI ATMOSUDIRDJO, S.H.
Faculty of Law: WIRJONO KOESOEMO, S.H.
Faculty of Political and Social Sciences: Prof. Dr. R. T. SOEBEKTI, M.P.A.
Faculty of Technology: Prof. Ir. P. C. HARJASUDIRDJA.
Faculty of Pharmacy: Drs. MULJONO.

UNIVERSITAS KRISTEN INDONESIA
(Christian University of Indonesia)

JALAN DIPONEGORO 86,
TROMOLPOS 2, JAKARTA

Telephone: 81493.

Founded 1953.

Chancellor: Dr. T. B. SIMATUPANG.
Vice-Chancellor: YAP THIAM HIEN, S.H.
Rector: R. S. MANGASTOWO.
Deputy Rectors: Drs. A. W. J. TUPANNO, Drs. W. LALISANG.
Registrar: ANTON REINHART, S.H.
Librarian: T. L. TOBING, S.H.

Number of teachers: 443.
Number of students: 2,556.

Publications: *UKI Bulletin, Bulletin Research Ekonomi* (Economic Review, quarterly), *Bulletin Lembaga Research dan Bantuan Hukum* (Law Review, quarterly), *Bulletin Research Pendidikan* (Educational Review, quarterly).

DEANS:

Faculty of Education: Drs. F. L. TOBING.
Faculty of English Language and Literature: Dra. RIA SIAGIAN.
Faculty of Economics: Dra. WANDA MULIA.
Faculty of Law: D. TAHITOE, S.H.
Faculty of Medicine: S. C. NAINGGOLAN, M.D., M.P.H.
Faculty of Technology: Dr. Ing. K. T. SIRAIT.

ATTACHED INSTITUTES:

Lembaga Research Ekonomi (*Institute of Economic Research*).

Lembaga Research dan Bantuan Hukum (*Institute of Law Research and Legal Aid*).

Lembaga Penelitian Pendidikan (*Institute of Educational Research*).

UNIVERSITAS BOGOR*

JL. BIOSKOP 31, BOGOR

Telephone: 505.

Founded 1958.

Rector: R. TADIWINATA.
Secretary: R. H. NATANEGARA.

Number of teachers: *c.* 60.
Number of students: *c.* 350.

Faculties of Law, Economics, Literature and Education.

* No reply received to our questionnaire this year.

UNIVERSITAS JAJABAJA

JL. SALEMBA RAYA 12, JAKARTA

Founded 1958.

Faculties of Law, Economics, Sociology and Business Management.

UNIVERSITAS IBNU CHALDUN, BOGOR

JL. PAPANDAJAN 25, BOGOR

Founded 1958.

Faculties of Economics, Law, Education and Letters.

UNIVERSITAS IBNU CHALDUN

SENEN RAYA 45-47, JAKARTA

Languages of instruction: Indonesian, English and Arabic.

Founded 1956.

Rector: Prof. Dr. BAHDER DJOHAN.
Vice-Rector: Drs. SJARIF USMAN.

Number of teachers: 80.
Number of students: 1,000.

Publication: *Berita U.I.C.*

DEANS:

Faculty of Journalism: Drs. H. AMURA.
Faculty of Social and Political Science: Drs. IHSAHUDDIN ILJAS.
Faculty of Law: Dr. ANWAR HARJONO, S.H
Faculty of Economics: Drs. RACHMAD RASJAD.
Faculty of Theology: Dr. H. A. ATJEH.
Faculty of Medicine: Prof. Dr. BAHDER DJOHAN.
Head of Foreign Relations: Drs. H. AMORA.

UNIVERSITAS ISLAM JAKARTA

JALAN PROF. MUH. YAMIN 57, JAKARTA

Telephone: 45286.

Founded 1951.

President: Prof. Dr. SOEMEDI.
Rector: SOEDJONO HARDJOSOEDIRO, S.H.
Registrar: RASJIDI OESMAN.
Librarian: ZAINAL ABIDIN.

Number of teachers: 34.
Number of students: 309.

DEANS:

Faculty of Law and Social Sciences: H. Drs. NAZARUDIN, S.H.
Faculty of Economics: TAHER IBRAHIM.
Faculty of Education: H. M. NUR ASJIK, M.A.

UNIVERSITAS ISLAM INDONESIA
(Islamic University of Indonesia)

JALAN CIK DI TIRO (TERBAN TAMAN) No. 1, YOGYAKARTA, JAVA

Telephone: 3091, 3704.

Founded 1945.

An independent and private Islamic university.

Rector: H. BPH. PRABUNINGRAT.
Vice-Rector, Scientific Affairs: Drs. S. MAHYUDDIN.
Vice-Rector, Religious and Financial Affairs: Ir. A. SAHIRUL ALIM, M.SC.
Secretary: S. WIRATMO, S.H.
Librarian: A. KHOTIB, B.SC.

Library of 18,500 vols.
Number of teachers: 181.
Number of students: 4,050.

UNIVERSITAS ISLAM INDONESIA CIREBON
(Islamic University of Indonesia in Cirebon)

31 JALAN KAPTEN SAMADIKUN, CIREBON

President: SA'DILLAH FATHONI, S.H.
Secretary: M. Z. ABIDIEN.

DEANS:

Faculty of Law: S. PRAWIRO, S.H.
Faculty of Economics: Drs. ROSYADI.
Faculty of Theology: H. MAS'OED.

UNIVERSITAS ISLAM NUSANTARA

JALAN TERUSAN HALIMUN 37, BANDUNG

Telephone: 56556.

Founded 1959 as Universitas Nahdlatul Ulama, present name 1976.

Rector: M. NAWAWI ACHMAD RUSTANDI.
Registrar: Drs. ABIN SYAMSUDDIN MAKMUN.
Administrative Officer: Drs. DJUDJU SUDJANA.
Librarian: Drs. ASE SUHERLAN MUHYIDDIN.

Library of 10,000 vols.
Number of teachers: 275.
Number of students: 5,000.

DEANS:

Faculty of Law: SAHIRI HERMAWAN.
Faculty of Economics: Drs. LILI ASDJUDIREDJA.
Faculty of Education: R. IYENG WIRAPUTRA.

DIRECTORS:

Research and Development and Community Services Centre: Prof. Dr. ACHMAD SANUSI, Drs. ACHMAD SURYADI.
Educational Research Centre: Drs. SUTARYAT TRISNAMANSYAH.
Social Studies and Curriculum Research and Development Centre: Drs. UDIN SARIPUDIN WINATAPUTRA.
Religious Services and Education Centre: K. H. MUHSIN.
Legal Services Centre: Drs. HUSNI THAMRIN.
Economic and Management Services Centre: Drs. SPM. HASIBUAN.

UNIVERSITAS ISLAM SUMATERA UTARA
(Islamic University of North Sumatra)

JALAN SINGAMANGARAJA, TELADAN, MEDAN, SUMATRA

Telephone: 20506.

Founded 1952.

Private control; Language of instruction: Indonesian; Academic year: February to January.

Chancellor: Brig.-Gen. A. MANAF LUBIS.
Vice-Chancellor: Major ARIFIN JONAIN HARAHAP.
Rector: M. YUSUF RANGKUTI, S.H.
Vice-Rectors: Dr. MUSTAFA MAJNU, M.SC., PH.D. (Academic Affairs), Drs. MOHD. ARDYAN TARIGAN (Administration and Finance), H. MAHMUD AZIZ SIREGAR, M.A. (Student and Alumni Affairs).
Registrar: Dra. HASNI RANGKUTI.
Librarian: M. YAHYA ROWTER, M.A.

Number of teachers: 330.
Number of students: 2,289.

Publication: *Alma Mater.*

DEANS:

Faculty of Law: AHMAD DAHLAN, S.H.
Faculty of Islamic Law: HAJI ZAINAL ARIFIN ABBAS.
Faculty of Economics: Drs. H. M. KASMAINI NASUTION.
Faculty of Education: Drs. M. YAMIN LUBIS.
Faculty of English Literature: M. YAHYA ROWTER, M.A.

Faculty of Teaching: Drs. MOHD. ARDYAN TARIGAN.
Faculty of Comparative Religions: Drs. JUNEID PARINDURI.
Faculty of Islamic Education: HAJI MAHMUD AZIZ SIREGAR, M.A.
Faculty of Political Science: HAJI BAHRUM JAMIL, S.H.
Faculty of Agriculture: Dr. MUSTAFA MAJNU.
Faculty of Medicine: Dr. H. GADING HAKIM.
Faculty of Engineering: Ir. M. ICHWAN NASUTION.

UNIVERSITAS KATOLIK INDONESIA ATMA JAYA

P.O.B. 2639 DAK,
JL. JENDRAL SUDIRMAN
PERC. 49A, SEMANGGI,
JAKARTA
Telephone: 582484.
Founded 1960.

Language of instruction: Indonesian.

Chairman of Board: Drs. F. X. SEDA.
Rector: Dr. K. S. GANI, D.P.H.
Deputy Rector for Academic Affairs: Drs. GORYS KERAF.
Librarian: Drs. W. A. G. LOMBOGIA, M.SC.

Library contains 15,000 vols.
Number of teachers: 328.
Number of students: 1,950.

DEANS:

Faculty of Economics: J. SUPRANTO, M.SC.
Faculty of Social and Political Sciences: Drs. J. SOEDJADI, M.A.
Faculty of Education: Drs. J. SOEITOE.
Faculty of Technology: Drs. SANTOSO MOERWANI.
Faculty of Law: T. G. NAPITUPULU, S.H.
Faculty of Medicine: Dr. A. H. TJAHJADI.

UNIVERSITAS KATOLIK PARAHYANGAN

JALAN MERDEKA 32, BANDUNG
Telephone: 52090.
Founded 1955.

Chancellor: Mgr. P. M. ARNTZ, O.S.C.
Rector: Dr. A. KOESDARMINTA.
Vice-Rector: Prof. Mgr. N. J. C. GEISE, O.F.M.
Vice-Rector (Academic Affairs): Drs. A. KOESDARMINTA.
Vice-Rector (Organization and Students' Affairs): Drs. F. VERMEULEN, O.S.C.
Vice-Rector (Financial Affairs): Drs. TAN DJIE LIAT.
Registrar: SUTAN MAKMUR.

Number of teachers: 273.
Number of students: 5,450.

DEANS:

Faculty of Economics: Drs. HASAN SIDIK.
Faculty of Law: Prof. R. SUBEKTI.
Faculty of Technology: Prof. Ir. HERMAN D. SOEDJONO, M. ARCH.
Faculty of Social and Political Sciences: Dr. WINARDI.

ATTACHED INSTITUTE:

Lembaga Penjelidikan Ilmiah (*Institute for Scientific Research*): Head Dr. W. HOFSTEEDE, O.F.M.

UNIVERSITAS KRISNADWIPAJANA

JALAN TEGAL 10, JAKARTA
Telephone: 51249.
Founded 1952.

Language of instruction: Indonesian; Academic year: February to December.

Chancellor: Prof. R. S. KARTANEGARA, LL.M.
Vice-Chancellor: Brig.-Gen. MOEHONO, LL.M.
Rector: Prof. R. SOEBEKTI, LL.M.
Secretary: S. WIRONEGORO, LL.M.
Registrar: E. DIMONTI, LL.M.
Librarian. Dr. DASPAN.

Number of teachers: 128.
Number of students: 2,000.

UNIVERSITAS MUHAMMADIJAH

JL. LIMAU 1,
KEB. BARU, JAKARTA

Faculties of Education, Law, Literature, Sociology.

UNIVERSITAS NASIONAL (National University)

JL. KALILIO 17-19, JAKARTA
Founded 1949.

Formerly the National Academy. The University comprises the Faculties of Social Science, Political Economics, Biology, Science, Indonesian and English Literature and Pharmacy.

President: Prof. SUKIRNA.

UNIVERSITAS H.K.B.P. NOMENSEN

JL. ASAHAN 4A,
PEMATANG SIANTAR

Faculties of Economics, Business Management and Administration, Education, and English Literature.

UNIVERSITAS KRISTEN SATYA WACANA (Satya Wacana Christian University)

JALAN DIPONEGORO 54-58,
SALATIGA,
CENTRAL JAVA
Telephone: (0298) 81362/3/4.
Founded 1956.

Academic year: August to June.

Rector: Rev. Dr. SUTARNO.
Deputy Rector for Academic Affairs: Dr. R. P. LOPULISA.
Deputy Rector for Finance and Administration: Drs. SUPARDAN.
Deputy Rector for Student Affairs: Drs. RICHARD M. GULTOM.
Deputy Rector for Planning, Development and Relations: Dr. W. TOISUTA.
Registrar: Drs. SUDARGO.
Librarian: Drs. TOWA P. HAMAKONDA, M.L.SC.

Number of teachers: 143 (full-time).
Number of students: 2,780.

Publications: *Bulletin Satya Wacana*† (weekly), *Warta Satya Wacana*, *Gita Mahasiwa*, *Dian Ekonomi*, *PIPAM* (monthly), *Kulumatra*†, *Cakrawala*†, *Gema Bimbingan*†, *Elektrika* (every 2 months), *Desa dan Desa* (quarterly), *Annual Report*, *Journal of Satya Wacana*.

DEANS:

Faculty of Law: SUWANDI, S.H.
Faculty of Economics: Dr. J. J. O. I. IHALAUW.
Faculty of Biology: Drs. F. X. SOEYONO.
Faculty of Agricultural Science: Ir. NURHADI ADAM.
Faculty of Electronics: SUDIGNO, M.SC.
Faculty of Theology: Dr. VICTOR TANYA.
Faculty of Teaching and Education: Drs. R. SOEBAGIJO.

ATTACHED RESEARCH INSTITUTE:

Lembaga Penelitian Ilmu-Ilmu Sosial (L.P.I.S.) (*Research Institute for Social Sciences*): Dir. Ir. KUTUT SUWONDO.

UNIVERSITAS PANCASILA

7 JALAN BOROBUDUR,
JAKARTA
Telephone: 322267.
Founded 1966.

Rector: SUNARTO PRAWIROSUJANTO.
Registrar: SOEJONO GAGAKSOEGONDO.
Librarian: R. KISMONO.

Library of 6,150 vols.

Number of teachers: 238.
Number of students: 1,628.

DEANS:

Faculty of Pharmacy: RESPATI B. SUTRISNO.
Faculty of Technology: MUSO C. SOENHADJI.
Faculty of Economics: SUTANTO.
Faculty of Law: SUTARSO.

PETRA CHRISTIAN UNIVERSITY

JALAN SIWALANKERTO 1,
TROMOLPOS 5304, SURABAYA
Telephone: 813040.
Founded 1965.

Rector: O. F. PATTY.

Registrar: Miss TJITRA CHANDRA.
Director of Academic Affairs and Development: M. OETAMA HARDJA.
Director of Finance and Administration: T. PRASADJA.
Director of Student Affairs: BENJAMIN L.
Director of Research: J. A. SOESILO.
Librarian: Miss ARLINAH I. R.

Library of 13,000 vols.

Number of teachers: 50 full-time, 68 part-time.

Number of students: 1,557.

DEANS:

Faculty of Letters: Mrs. ELIZABETH OETAMA HARDJA.
Faculty of Civil Engineering: Mr. OENTOENG.
Faculty of Architecture: Mr. KRISDIANTO.

UNIVERSITAS TARUMANEGARA

JALAN LET. JEN S. PARMAN, JAKARTA

Telephone: 591747.

Founded 1959.

Chancellor: P. K. OYONG, S.H.
Vice-Chancellor: Ir. CIPUTRA.
Rector: Prof. Drs. HARSOJO.
Vice-Rector and Registrar: D. KHUMARGA, S.H.

Number of teachers: 347.
Number of students: 2,975.

DEANS:

Faculty of Economics: Prof. Drs. HARSOJO.
Faculty of Law: D. KHUMARGA, S.H.
Faculty of Engineering: Ir. W. PRAGANTHA.
Faculty of Medicine: Dr. R. SOEWARNO.

UNIVERSITAS TJOKROAMINOTO SURAKARTA*

JALAN KUSUMOJUDAN, SURAKARTA

Telephone: 4035.

Founded 1955.

Rector: Drs. MALADI PRAWIRONAGORO.

First Assistant to the Rector: Kyai H. RUHANI A. HAKIM.

Second Assistant to the Rector: Drs. I. MUCHTAR.

Third Assistant to the Rector: EL U. I. BANDUNG.

Chairman of the Foundation: Dr. S. PRAWIRONOTO.

Number of teachers: 100.

Number of students: (at Surakarta and 6 branches): 4,000.

* No reply received to our questionnaire this year.

UNIVERSITAS TRISAKTI

JL. KIAI TAPA, GROGOL, JAKARTA

Telephone: 592461, 591960.

Founded 1965.

Language of instruction: Indonesian; Academic year: March to December.

Rector: Drs. SISWADJI, M.A.

Assistant Rectors: Ir. KARTOMO BROTOATMODJO, M.SC. (Academic Affairs), Drs. F. AMELN, S.H. (Administration and Finance), EKO PURWOTO, M.A. (Student Affairs).

University Librarian: Mrs. TITIEK POLIN.

Number of teachers: 803.
Number of students: 7,765.

Publication: *Bulletin Universitas Trisakti*† (monthly).

DEANS:

Faculty of Engineering: Ir. POEDJONO HARDJO PRAKOSO.

Faculty of Medicine: Prof. Dr. OETAMA.

Faculty of Dentistry: Drg. Mrs. YETTI RIZALI NOOR.

Faculty of Law and Social Sciences: BOEDIHARSONO, S.H.

Faculty of Economics: Drs. MULYATNO.

ATTACHED INSTITUTES:

Lembaga Administrasi Perusahaan (*Institute of Business Administration*): Dir. Drs. S. MULYATNO.

Sekolah Tinggi Arsitektur Pertamanan Trisakti (*Institute of Landscape Architecture*): Dir. Ir. KASLAN TOHIR.

Lembaga Pendidikan Perhotelan dan Katering (*Institute of Hotel, Tourism and Catering*): Dir. Drs. S. MULYATNO.

Akademi Angkutan Udara Niaga Trisakti (*Institute of Airline Travel and Air Cargo*): Dir. Drs. BAMBANG SUMARSONO.

Lembaga Konsultasi Hukum (*Bureau for Law Consultants*): Dir. BOEDIHARSONO, S.H.

Akademi Akunting Trisakti (*Trisakti Accountancy Institute*): Dir. Drs. SAROSO.

UNIVERSITAS VETERAN REPUBLIK INDONESIA

JL. SUPRATMAN 1, UJUNGPANDANG

Faculties of History, Law and Education.

IRAN

Population 36,800,000

LEARNED SOCIETIES

Ancient Iran Cultural Society, The: Jomhorie Eslamie Ave., Shahrokh St., P.O.B. 314-1262, Teheran; f. 1961; Man. Dir. A. Quoreshi.

Asian Cultural Documentation Centre for UNESCO: P.O.B. 41/2786, Teheran; f. 1975 to promote research into Asian culture and understanding between Asian peoples; 40 staff; library of 6,000 vols. (5,000 western, 1,000 Persian); Sec. Gen. Hossein Daneshi.

British Institute of Persian Studies: Khiaban Dr. Ali Shariati, Kucheh Alvand, Gholhak, P.O.B. 2617, Teheran 15; f. 1961; cultural institute, with special emphasis on history and archaeology; library of over 9,000 books and MSS.; 800 mems.; Hon. Sec. S. J. Whitwell; Dir. in Iran David Stronach, O.B.E.; publ. *Iran.*

Goethe-Institut: P.O.B. 1895, Teheran; f. 1958; library of 11,500 vols.; cultural programme; German language classes; Dir. Dr. Heinz Becker.

Institut Français de Téhéran: 58 Ave. Azarbayédjan, P.O.B. 11-1968, Teheran; f. 1946; teaching of French, cinema, theatre, exhibitions and conferences; 3,200 mems.; library of 30,000 vols.; regional centres at Shiraz, Isfahan, Tabriz; Dirs. Jean Roquemaurel, Guy Poittevin.

Département d'Iranologie: f. 1949; research and studies in Iranology; library of 9,000 vols.; Dir. Charles-Henri de Fouchécour; publ. *Abstracta Iranica.*

Iranian Academy, The (*Farhangistan*): c/o The Ministry of Education, Teheran; f. 1935; Pres. The Minister of Education.

Iranian Centre for Archaeological Research: Xiaban-e Prof. Rollin, Teheran; f. 1972 to replace General Direction of Archaeology and Anthropology; excavations, surveys, archaeological and cultural research, lectures, temporary exhibitions, annual symposium on archaeological research in Iran; library of 13,312 vols. under joint administration of Iran Bastan Museum; Dir.-Gen. Dr. Firouz Bagherzadeh.

Iranian Culture Foundation (*Bonyād-e Farhang-e Irān*): P.O.B. 3247, Teheran; f. 1964 by Imperial charter to study and safeguard the cultural heritage of Iran; studies in linguistics, preparation of a historical grammar and dictionary of modern Persian, study of Persian scientific and technical terminology, critical edition of unpublished Persian MSS.; research library of 15,700 vols.; Gen. Sec. Prof. Dr. Parviz N. Khanlari; publs. various, *Bulletin* (irregular), catalogue†.

Iranian Documentation Centre: P.O.B. 11-1387, Teheran; f. 1968; to serve as a national science and social science documentation centre; to advise and assist in the establishment of specialized information centres and to act as the national reference centre; part of the Institute for Research and Planning in Science and Education; Dir. Dr. S. A. Mirzadeh.

Iranian Library Association: P.O.B. 11-1391, Teheran; f. 1966 to promote the adoption of more effective systems of library service; to encourage the development of librarianship as a profession; 750 mems.; Pres. Ali Sinai; Sec. Mehrdad Niknam Vazifeh; publs. *Akhbar-e Mahaneh* (monthly), *Name-ye Anjoman-e Ketabdaran-e Iran* (quarterly).

Iranian Society of Microbiology: Department of Microbiology and Immunology, Faculty of Medicine, University of Teheran; f. 1940; 185 mems.; Gen. Sec. G. H. Nazari, M.D.

Iranian Society for Cultural Relations with the USSR: Vassal Shirazi Ave., Teheran; f. 1943; provides Russian language tuition, lectures and cultural activities, and arranges cultural visits between Iran and the U.S.S.R.; Pres. Abdol-Hossein Massud-Ansari; Sec. Gen. Ziaollah Forushani; publ. *Payam-e-Nowwin.*

Istituto Italiano di Cultura: Ave. Hafez, Kuche Hatef 5, Teheran; Dir. Prof. Gianclaudio Macchiarella.

National Association for Cultural Relations: Ministry of Culture and Arts, Bldg. No. 3, Taleghani Ave., Teheran; f. 1966 to create facilities in the field of cultural and artistic relations and exchanges; Sec.-Gen. Dr. Z. Hacobian.

National Cartographic Centre: P.O.B. 1844, Azadi Sq., Teheran.

Österreichisches Kulturinstitut: P.O.B. 876, ave. Villa 248, Teheran; f. 1958; scientific research, lectures, concerts, exhibitions, student exchange; library of 5,000 vols.; Dir. Prof. Dr. Helmut Slaby; publ. monthly programme.

P.E.N. Club of Iran: 34 Ave. Mirabad, St. 9, Teheran 16; Founder and Gen. Sec. Z. Rahnama.

Philosophy and Humanities Society of Iran: Faculty of Arts, University of Teheran; Pres. Prof. A. A. Siassi.

Society of Iranian Clinicians: Faculty of Medicine, University of Teheran; Pres. Prof. Y. Adle.

RESEARCH INSTITUTES

Centre for Iranian Anthropology—Ministry of Culture and Arts: Bldg. 3, Taleghani Ave., 1 Bandar-Mirabad St., Teheran 15; f. 1958; anthropological research; 110 mems.; library of 6,882 vols.; Dir. Dr. M. Khaligi; publ. *Mardom shenasi va Farhang-e-Amme Iran* (Anthropology and Folk Culture in Iran).

Institut Pasteur: Teheran; f. 1921; vaccine production, research in microbiology, biochemistry, virology, medicine and epidemiology, teaching and postgraduate training; Dir. S. Farman Farmaian.

Institute for Research and Planning in Science and Education: P.O.B. 11-1387, 46 Ave. Enghelab, Teheran; f. 1969; Dir. Dr. A. Naraghi; publs. *Abstract Bulletin on Science and Social Science Journals*, various directories, publications on educational planning; consists of four centres.

Centre for Scientific and Educational Planning: Dir. F. Darvish.

Iranian Documentation Centre: *see* above.

Teheran Book Processing Centre: P.O.B. 11-1126; Dir. Miss M. TAFAZZOLI.

Centre for Science and Research Policy.

International Scientific Research Institute: P.O.B. 377, Teheran; f. 1955; Dir. MOUSSA HEKMAT, K.T.K.C.G., M.D., F.R.S.M.; publs. *World Science Review* (quarterly, in Persian, Arabic, English), *Papers*.

Iranian Culture Research Institute (*Pažuheškade-ye Farhang-e Irān*): P.O.B. 14155 41/2346, Teheran; f. 1971 to train researchers in the fields of Iranian linguistics and history, Persian literature; M.A. and Ph.D. degree courses; Dir. Prof. Dr. M. ABOL-GHASSEMI.

National Organization for the Protection of Historical Monuments: Ave. Ostad Motahari, Ave. Larestan 60, Teheran; f. 1965; Sec.-Gen. Dr. MEHRAN.

Research and Study Centre for the Protection of Historical Monuments: Dir. Dr. P. VARDJAVAND.

Plant Pests and Diseases Research Institute: P.O.B. 3178 Teheran; f. 1961; research on pests and diseases of agricultural crops; botany, entomology and agricultural zoology; 141 research workers; library of *c.* 7,500 vols.; Dir. Dr. D. ERSHAD; publs. *Entomologie et Phytopathologie Appliquées* (2 a year).

Razi State Institute: P.O.B. 656, Teheran; f. 1930; epizootological and ecological studies of animal diseases and human and animal biology; preparation of all veterinary vaccines, some human vaccines and therapeutical sera; Gen. Dir. Prof. M. KAVEH; publ. *Archives of the Razi Institute*† (annually in English and French).

LIBRARIES

Astaneh Razavy Library: Mashhad; dates from *c.* 15th century; 54,850 vols. and 9,911 MSS.; Librarian Mr. MAKASSEBI.

Bibliothèque de l'Institut Français de Téhéran: P.O.B. 11-1968, Teheran; f. 1947; general library; 30,000 vols.; Dir. RAYMOND BERARD.

Central Library and Documentation Centre of Teheran University: Enghelab Ave., Teheran; f. 1949, re-housed 1970; 159,466 vols., 4,770 microfilms, 12,594 MSS., 7,043 vols. photographical reprint MSS., 26,572 pictures and 4,800 periodicals; Dir. IRAJ AFSHAR; various publs.

Central Library and Documentation Centre, University of Azarabadegan: Tabriz; f. 1945; 70,000 vols.; Librarian Dr. H. SARHANGIAN.

General Department of Audio-Visual Aids, Ministry of Culture and Arts: P.O.B. 519, Teheran; f. 1964 to help spread general scientific knowledge, and encourage educational and cultural activities; library of 2,000 vols.; Gen. Dir. ABBAS HONARVAR; publs. *Animator, Cultural Guide* (monthly).

Library of the Bank Markazi Iran (*Central Bank of Iran*): Ferdowsi Ave., Teheran; 37,000 vols.; Librarian A. POUR-AZAR.

Library of the Iran Bastan Museum: Xiaban-e Prof. Rollin, Teheran; f. 1946; 13,312 vols.; Librarian FATH RAZI.

Mahbubeh Motahedin University Libraries: Shiraz; f. 1946; 205,000 vols.; Dir. Dr. A. GHAVAMI.

Malek Library: Ave. Boozarjomehri, Bazar-e-Beinolharamein, Teheran; 25,000 vols.; Dir. ALI-REZA PAHLAWANI.

Mashhad University Central Library and Documentation Centre: P.O.B. 331, Mashhad; 200,000 vols.; Gen. Dir. A. J. DARBANDI.

Municipal Library: Isfahan; 29,000 vols.

National Library: See Tir Ave., Teheran; f. 1935; 100,000 vols.; rare Persian and Arabic MSS.; international book exchange service; Dir. NASSER MAZAHERI; publ. *National Bibliography*.

Parliament Library: Ketabkhaneh Majles Showraie Melli, Teheran; f. 1924; 120,000 vols.; Dir. Mrs. RASTKAR.

Senate Library (*Ketabkhaneh Majles Sena*): Teheran; f. 1950; 30,840 vols.; legal, reference material, MSS., Iranology, Islamology; Dir. KAYKAVOOS JAHANDARI.

Tabriz Public Library (*Ketabkhaneh Melli Tabriz*): Tabriz; 12,816 vols.; Dir. MAJID FARHANG.

Tarbiat Library: Ave. Atesh Neshani, Tabriz; 18,972 vols.; Dir. ABDOLLAH ABDOLELAHI FARD.

University of Isfahan Library: Isfahan; 112,150 vols., half in Persian and Arabic, the remainder in European languages; Persian MSS. and incunabula; Dir. Dr. DOOSTKHAN.

MUSEUMS

All Saviours' Cathedral Museum: Julfa, Isfahan; f. 1905; rehoused 1971 with additions; under the supervision of the Diocesan Council of the Armenians in Iran and India; Dir. The Diocesan Bishop.

Chehel Sotun Museum: Isfahan; Dir. KARIM NIKZAD.

Iran Bastan Museum: Meydan-e Muzeh, Teheran; f. 1918; part of Iranian Centre for Archaeological Research (*see* above); excavations, archaeological and cultural research, lectures, exhibitions on discoveries in Iran; five departments; library of 10,000 vols.; Dir. F. BAGHERZADEH.

Muzeye Mardomchenassi (*Ethnographical Museum*): Khiaean Sepah Nidanmuze, Teheran; f. 1938; Dir. Y. ZOKA.

Golestan Palace Museum: Maidan Ark, Golestan; f. 1894; Dir. H. GH. BASSIRI.

Mashhad Musuem: Mashhad; f. 1945; under the supervision of the Sanctuary of Mashhad.

Negarestan Museum: Palestine Ave. intersection, Teheran; f. 1975; 18th- and 19th-century Iranian art; organizes conferences and educational programmes; library in process of formation (1,000 vols. at present); Pres. Mrs. LAYLA SOUDAVAR DIBA; publs. catalogues.

Pars Museum: Shiraz; f. 1938; exhibits include manuscripts, earthenware, ancient coins; Dir. MOHAMMED HOSSEIN ESTAKHR; Curator HASRAT ZADEH SORUDE.

Qom Museum: Qom; f. 1936; under the supervision of the Archaeological Service; Dir. M. FATEMI.

Teheran Museum of Modern Art: Karegar Ave., Laleh Park, Teheran; f. 1977; library of 20,000 vols. in formation; Dir. KAMRAN DIBA.

UNIVERSITIES

(At the time of going to press, information received is that most universities are closed).

ARYA MEHR UNIVERSITY OF TECHNOLOGY

P.O.B. 3406, TEHERAN

Telephone: 972001-9.

Founded 1966.

Private control; Language of instruction: Persian.

Departments of Mechanical, Electrical, Chemical, Metallurgical, Structural and Industrial Engineering, Physics, Chemistry, Mathematics and Computer Science.

Isfahan Campus

P.O.B. 69-34, ANOSHIRAVAN ST., ARYA MEHR BLVD., ISFAHAN

Telephone: 32011, 38079.

Founded 1974.

Divisions of energy, information, materials, science, food and agriculture, human technological and societal systems.

UNIVERSITY OF AZARABADEGAN

TABRIZ

Telephone: 30081-9.

Founded 1949, formerly University of Tabriz.

Faculties of Agriculture, Arts, Education, Engineering, Medicine, Pharmacy, Science, Technology.

BALUCHISTAN UNIVERSITY

ZAHEDAN

Founded 1974.

Faculties of Civil, Mechanical and Electrical Engineering.

BU-ALI SINA UNIVERSITY

P.O.B. 211, HAMADAN

Telephone: (0261) 6041/5.

Languages of instruction: Persian, French and some English; Academic year: September to August.

Founded 1973.

Faculties of Health and Medical Sciences, Environmental Sciences and Natural Resources.

FARABI UNIVERSITY

85 PARK ST. AND 9TH AVE., TEHERAN

Telephone: 623721.

Founded 1975.

Chancellor: FARHAD NAZERZADEH KERMANI, PH.D.

Vice-Chancellors: REZA BASSIRY, PH.D., NASSRIN HAKAMI.

Administrative Officer: HADI KASHANINEJAD.

Librarian: Mrs. GOLROUKH EMAMI.

Number of teachers: 43.

Number of students: 250.

DEANS:

Faculty of Science and Culture: GHOLAMALI HATAM.

Faculty of Architecture and Environmental Planning: FARHAD ABOZIA.

Faculty of Music and Dramatic Arts: GHOLAMALI HATAM.

Faculty of Applied and Visual Arts: KAMBOZIA HASHEMI.

Faculty of Graduate Studies: RAHIM NAJFAR.

(Graduate) Faculty of Restoration of Historic Buildings: M. ASHOURI.

(Graduate) Faculty of Cultural Affairs: M. ALLAVI.

(Graduate) Faculty of Environmental Planning and Design: ALIREZA RABIE.

FREE UNIVERSITY OF IRAN

P.O.B. 11-1962, ABAN SHOMALI ST., KARIM KHAN BLVD., TEHERAN 15

Telephone: 891521-5.

Founded 1973.

State control; Academic year: Sep. to May (two semesters); Courses mainly in Farsi (Persian).

The university teaching system is an open one, based on correspondence courses, regional study centres, and radio and TV programmes.

GILAN UNIVERSITY

P.O.B. 401, RASHT

Telephone: (0231) 25928, 26074.

Founded 1977 by agreement between Iran and Federal Republic of Germany. State control; Languages of instruction: Farsi and German; Academic year: September to June (two semesters).

Faculties of Science, Agriculture, Technology, Humanities, Medicine.

UNIVERSITY OF ISFAHAN

ISFAHAN

Telephone: 22127.

Founded 1958.

Chancellor: Dr. GHOLAM ABBAS TAVASSOLI.

Vice-Chancellor for Finance and Administration: AHMAD KALBASSI.

Vice-Chancellor for Research and Academic Affairs: Dr. MOHAMAD SOUZANGAR.

Vice-Chancellor for Student Affairs: ALI NILFOROUSHAN.

Administrative Officer: HASSAN KIANPOUR.

Librarian: Mrs. FARANAK BAHMANYAR.

Number of teachers: 544.

Number of students: 8,019.

DEANS:

Faculty of Pharmacy and Pharmaceutical Sciences: Dr. FARIBORZ MOATTAR.

Faculty of Dentistry: Dr. AHMAD ROSTAMI.

Faculty of Foreign Languages: JAHANGIR FEKERI ERSHAD.

Faculty of Medicine: Dr. HOSSEIN BADRI.

Faculty of Sciences: MOHD. ALI SHAH ZAMANIAN.

Faculty of Letters and Humanities: MOHD. REZA KAVIANI.

Faculty of Education: YAHYA ASSADI.

Faculty of Animal Husbandry: YAHYA REZAI NEJAD.

Faculty of Economics and Administration: HOUSHANG SHAJARI.

Institute of Horticulture: HASSAN MOJTAHEDI.

JUNDI SHAPUR UNIVERSITY

AHWAZ, KHUZESTAN

Telephone: 30012-19.

Founded 1955.

State control; Language of instruction: Persian. Campuses in Lorestan and Persian Gulf.

Chancellor: Dr. A. JAMEI.

Vice-Chancellor: H. GHOTB.

Number of teachers: *c.* 400.

Number of students: *c.* 4,000.

Faculties of sciences, medicine, agriculture, architecture and civil engineering, veterinary science, education, modern languages, literature and humanities, economics and politics.

UNIVERSITY OF KERMAN

P.O.B. 333, KERMAN

Telephone: 0341-99511.

State control; Languages of instruction: Persian and English; Academic year: September to June.

Founded 1974; courses began 1976.

Departments of Sciences, Foreign Languages; Research Centre for Arid Regions.

MAHBUBEH MOTAHEDIN UNIVERSITY

VANAK, TEHERAN

Founded 1975 as Farah Pahlavi University, name changed 1980.

Faculties of Arts and Science, Education, Psychology.

MASHHAD UNIVERSITY

MASHHAD

Founded 1956, name changed to Ferdowsi University 1973–80.

Faculties of Arts, Science, Theology, Dentistry, Pharmacy, Engineering, Agriculture, Education, Ophthalmology.

MAZANDARAN UNIVERSITY

MAZANDARAN

Founded 1975 as Reza Shah Kabir University, name changed 1980.

The university offers postgraduate courses only and focuses on education and training of scientists to staff the universities and research institutes.

NATIONAL UNIVERSITY OF IRAN

EVEEN, TEHERAN

Telephone: 21411.

Founded 1960.

State control; Language of instruction: Farsi; Academic year: September to June.

President: Dr. ABDOULSAMAD TAGHIZADEH.

Vice-President for Academic Affairs: Dr. MANSOUR DOOSTKAM.

Vice-President for Student Affairs: Dr. MOHAMMAD SEPEHRI RAD.

Vice-President for Administrative and Financial Affairs: Dr. MOHAMAD HASSN AHMADI.

Librarian: Dr. MOHAMMAD MIRZAEE.

Library of 118,376 vols.

Number of teachers: 980.

Number of students: 9,800.

Publications: *Journal of the Faculty of Dentistry, Journal of the Faculty of Medicine, Journal of the Faculty of Architecture.*

DEANS:

School of Letters and Humanities: Dr. ALI MARZBAN.

Faculty of Medicine: Dr. BIZHAN ROOSTA.

Faculty of Dentistry: Dr. ABDOULRAZZAH MORVARID.

Faculty of Law: Dr. GOODARZ EFTEKHAR.

Faculty of Sciences: (vacant).

Faculty of Economics and Political Science: Dr. MOHSEN BOLOORFOROOSH.

Faculty of Architecture: Dr. HADI NADIMI.

Faculty of Education: Dr. MOHAMMAD HASSAN AHMADI.

Faculty of Earth Science: Dr. MANSOOR VOSOOGHI.

Faculty of Computer Science and Management: Dr. FARHAD SAHEBAN.

RAZI UNIVERSITY

P.O.B. 262, KERMANSHAH

Telephone: 28046.

Founded 1974.

Chancellor: Dr. MUDHAFFAR ASSADI, PH.D.

Vice-Chancellor: HOSSAIN ALI HOHESTANEE.

Administrative Officer: MALEK HUSSAINI.

Librarians: H. MOJABY (Persian section), SHERYL ASGABI (English section).

Number of teachers: 115.

Number of students: 1,974.

Colleges of Medicine and Science in Kermanshah, College of Education in Sanandaj, College of Animal Husbandry in Ilam.

UNIVERSITY OF SHIRAZ

SHIRAZ

Telephone: 32111-2, 32084 and 37596.

Founded 1945 as Pahlavi University, present name 1979.

Languages of instruction: Persian and English; Controlled by Board of Trustees; Academic year: September to June (two semesters).

Faculties of Medicine, Arts and Sciences, Engineering, Agriculture, Veterinary Medicine, Dentistry.

UNIVERSITY OF TEHERAN

(State University)

ENGHELAB AVENUE, TEHÉRAN

Telephone: 40021-5.

Founded 1934.

Supervisor: Dr. HASSAN AREFI.

Faculties of Arts, Sciences, Agriculture, Law, Medicine, Engineering, Islamic Theology, Education, Economics, Social Sciences.

COLLEGES

(There are *c.* 50 colleges of higher education in Iran, and *c.* 40 technological institutes, of which the following are a selection only.)

Abadan Institute of Technology: Abadan; f. 1939; reorganized 1971; courses: B.Sc. in Chemical, Electrical, Gas, Industrial, Mechanical, Petroleum and Petrochemical Engineering; library of 29,000 vols.; 450 students, 45 teachers; Pres. K. KORMI, PH.D.; Vice-Pres. R. BABAYAN, PH.D.

College of Economics and Social Science: Babolsar; f. 1970; economics, accounting and business studies, labour law, social economics.

Forestry and Range College: Gorgan; f. 1957 to provide trained staff for the scientific management and development of forest, range and soil; Dir. M. KHAVARI; 28 teachers, 250 students.

Higher Institute of Telecommunications Training—Ministry of Posts, Telegraphs and Telephones: Ave. Dr. Ali Shariati, Teheran; new-entrant and in-service training; f. 1939; Dir-Gen. MOHAMMED HOVEYDA.

Iran College of Science and Technology: P.O.B. 64/151, Teheran-Narmak; f. 1928; awards 1st degree in engineering; library of 30,000 vols.; 285 teachers, 5,000 students; civil, mechanical, chemical and industrial engineering, architecture, metallurgy, teacher training; Rector Prof. Dr. Ing. H. KHAKZAR.

Military Academy: Sepah Ave., Teheran; Departments of Military History, Military Science and Tactics, International Relations and Treaties, General Engineering Science, Physics and Electronics, Military Armaments, Nuclear Warfare.

National Conservatory of Music: South Palestine Ave., Teheran; f. 1949; composition and study of musical instruments.

Nafisi Technicom Institute: Baharestan St., Teheran; f. 1971; building, civil engineering, electronics, industrial engineering, mathematics.

College of Surveying: P.O.B. 1844, Azadi Sq., Teheran; f. 1965; national training centre for surveyors; 210 students; affiliated to National Geographic Organization; Dir. Col. (retd.) BABA MODAGHAM.

Teheran Polytechnic: Hafez St., Teheran; f. 1958; seven institutes for degree courses in Chemical, Petrochemical, Mechanical, Civil Electronics, Electrical and Textile Engineering.

Chancellor: HOSSAIN MAHBAN, PH.D.

Number of students: 3,000.

IRAQ

Population 12,029,000

LEARNED SOCIETIES AND RESEARCH INSTITUTES

(*See* also under Universities)

Arab Regional Branch of the International Council on Archives (ARBICA): P.O.B. 594, National Library Bldg., 2nd Floor, Bab-Al-Muadam, Baghdad; f. 1973; close collaboration with ICA, UNESCO and other international organizations; mems.: 18 Arab countries; Pres. Dr. AHMAD SHARKAS (Jordan); Sec.-Gen. SALIM AL-ALOUSI (Iraq); publ. *Arab Archives*† (annual).

British Council: P.O.B. 298, 7/2/9 Waziriya, Baghdad; Rep. R. A. JARVIS; library re-opened 1969; 15,233 vols., 183 periodicals.

British School of Archaeology in Iraq (Gertrude Bell Memorial): 31–34 Gordon Square, London, WC1H 0PY; f. 1932; Pres. Prof. SETON LLOYD, C.B.E.; Chair. Prof. D. J. WISEMAN, O.B.E., M.A., D.LIT., F.B.A., F.S.A.; publ. *Iraq* (2 a year).

Centre for Educational and Psychological Research: University of Baghdad, Waziriyah, Baghdad; f. 1966; educational and psychological research studies to make education an effective power for the acceleration of economic and social development; library of *c.* 6,000 vols.; Dir. Dr. MOHAMMED ALI KHALAF; publ. *Journal of Educational Psychological Research*† (2 a year).

Centre Culturel Français: 121 Abu-Nawas St., Baghdad; f. 1950; cultural activities and French language teaching; library of 13,000 vols.

Department of Scientific and Industrial Research: Directorate-General of Industry, Baghdad; f. 1935; staff 42; Dir.-Gen. of Industry SHEETH NA'AMANN; publs. *Technical Bulletin, Annual Report.*

Economic and Administrative Research Centre: Baghdad.

Foundation for Scientific Research: Jadiriyah, Baghdad; f. 1963; Pres. Dr. HATIF H. AL-JALIL; Sec.-Gen. Dr. JAMAL DOUGRAMEJI; the following are attached to the foundation:

Institute for Applied Research on Natural Resources: Jadiriyah; Dir. Dr. J. Z. AL-RAWI.

Petroleum Research Institute: Jadiriyah; Dir. Dr. FAIZ A. JAMIL.

Building Research Centre: Jadiriyah; Dir. Dr. ADNAN AL-ADEEB.

Biological Research Centre: Adhamiya; Dir. Dr. AZWAR NAAMAN.

Agricultural Research Centre: Fudhailiyah; Dir. Dr. R. AL-BADRAWI.

Dates and Date Palm Research Centre: Karadah; Dir. Dr. H. SHABANA.

Scientific Documentation Centre: Jadiriyah; Dir. AZZUDEEN AL-SAID. (*See* also under Libraries.)

Environmental Pollution Research Centre: Jadiriyah; Dir. Dr. AZWAR NAAMAN (acting).

Transfer of Technology Centre: Jadiriyah; Dir. Dr. H. H. AL-JALIL.

Pharmacognosy Research Centre: Fudhailiyah; Dir. Dr. ALI A. R. AL-ASKARI.

Instituto Hispano-Arabe de Cultura (*Hispano-Arabic Cultural Institute*): Saadun Park, P.O.B. 2256, Alwiyya, Baghdad; f. 1958; library of 6,400 vols.; promotion of Spanish language and culture in Iraq; Dir. RAFAEL VALENCIA.

Iraqi Academy: Waziriyah, Baghdad; f. 1947 with the aims of maintaining the Arabic language and heritage, undertaking research in Arabic and Muslim history, the history of Iraq and Arabic language and heritage; the Academy has Active Members, Associate Members and Honorary Members; the last two categories including Iraqi and other nationalities; Pres. Dr. SALEH A. AL-ALI; Sec.-Gen. Dr. NOORI H. AL-QISSI; publs. *Arabs before Islam* (8 vols.), *Majallat al Majima' al Ilmi al Iraqi* (literary quarterly).

Iraqi Medical Society: Maari St., Al Mansoor, Baghdad; f. 1920; 871 mems.; Pres. F. H. GHALI, F.R.C.S.(Ed.); Sec. A. K. AL KHATEEB, F.R.C.S.(Ed.).

Nuclear Research Institute (*Iraq Atomic Energy Commission*): Tuwaitha, Baghdad; f. 1967; includes nuclear research reactor, radioisotope production facilities; research in nuclear and solid state physics, analytical and radio-chemistry, biology and agriculture, health physics and geology.

Society of Iraqi Artists: Damascus St., Baghdad; f. 1956; exhibitions and occasional publs.; Pres. NOORI AL RAWI; Sec. AMER ALUBIDI.

Soviet Cultural Centre: Baghdad; f. 1962; library.

LIBRARIES

Al-Awqaf Central Library (*Library of Waqfs*): P.O.B. 14146, Baghdad; f. 1928; emphasis on Islamic religion and Islamic–Arabic history and literature; 30,000 vols., 50 periodicals, 7,000 original MSS., 1,000 microfilms and copies of MSS.; Dir. JASSIM M. AL-JUBOORY; publ. *Al-Rissala-Al-Islamiya.*

Al-Mustansiriyah University Library: Waziriyah, Baghdad; f. 1964; 114,000 vols. (12,000 vols. of periodicals, 300 rolls of film, 1,000 current periodicals; Dir. Mrs. ILHAM B. ALLOS.

Central Library, University of Baghdad: Safi Al-Din Al-Hilli St., P.O.B. 12, Baghdad; f. 1960; national and UN depository library; acts as Exchange and National Bibliographical Centre; 210,000 vols., 1,950 current periodicals, 10,190 maps, 1,420 Arabic MSS. on microfilm; indexes issued on various subjects; Librarian

ZAHIDA IBRAHIM, M.L.S.; publs. *Iraqi Publications Bulletin*† (irregular).

Educational Documentation Library: Ministry of Education, Baghdad; f. 1921; 43,000 vols., 94 periodicals; Librarian LAYLA QADOORI.

Iraqi Academy Library: Waziriyah, Baghdad; f. 1947; 48,480 vols., 32 original MSS., 1,147 copied MSS., 500 microfilms; Librarian SABAH M. NOAH.

Library of the Iraq Museum: Baghdad; f. 1934; 120,000 vols.; 32,000 MSS.; Librarian HIKMAT TOMASHI.

National Centre of Archives: National Library Building, 2nd Floor, Bab-Al-Muaddam, Baghdad; f. 1964; attached to the Ministry of Information; divisions of research and statistics, technical photography, palaeography and sigillography; library of 5,333 vols.; Dir.-Gen. SALIM AL-ALOUSI.

National Library: Al-Jumhuriya St., Baghdad; f. 1961; legal deposit centre and national bibliographic centre; 125,000 vols., 500 current periodicals, 3,000 rare books; Dir. FOUAD Y. M. QAZANCHI; publs. *Iraqi National Bibliography*† (quarterly), *Accumulation List*† (annually).

Scientific Documentation Centre: Abu Nuas Rd., P.O.B. 2441, Baghdad; f. 1972; scientific information services to researchers at the institutes/centres of the Foundation of Scientific Research (*q.v.*), and to others working in Iraqi laboratories, including UNDP experts; seven libraries are being developed, each attached to a research centre of the Foundation, including the Central Science Library; in-service training for students of Library Science and Documentation and librarians; 20 staff mems.; Dir. AZZUDEEN AL-SAID.

Technical Atomic Energy Library: Nuclear Research Institute, Tuwaitha, Baghdad; up-to-date references, reports, pamphlets, microcards, magazines and film reels; Librarian WADIA AL-HILLALI.

University of Basrah Central Library: Basrah; f. 1964; 100,000 vols., 200 MSS, 800 current periodicals; Librarian ABDUL-JABBAR ABDUL-RAHMAN; publ. catalogue (irregular).

University of Mosul Central Library: Mosul; f. 1965; 147,903 vols., 1,165 periodicals, depository of UN and Iraqi Govt. publications; Dir. AHMAD AL-HASSO, PH.D.; publs. *Adab Al-Rafidayn* (irregular), *Al-Jamia* (monthly), *Research Work of University Faculty Members* (annually), *Catalogue* (annually), etc.

University of Sulaimaniyah Central Library: Sulaimaniyah; f. 1968; 100,000 vols., 300 current periodicals; Dir. Dr. MOHAMED F. KAFTAN.

There are 7,070 school libraries, 134 public libraries, 33 Awqaf libraries, 81 special libraries, 51 academic libraries, 10 museum libraries, one national library.

MUSEUMS

The following museums, with the exception of the Natural History Research Centre and the National Museum of Modern Art, are under the control of the Department of the Directorate-General of Antiquities in Baghdad, a government body headed by Dr. ISA SALMAN. The Directorate-General of Antiquities organizes all museum exhibitions, conducts archaeological excavations and supervises excavations by foreign expeditions, issues archaeological reports and maps; publs. *Sumer* and *Al-Maskukat*.

Abbasid Palace Museum, The: Baghdad; a restored Palace (at present under reconstruction) dating back to the last Caliphs of the Abbasid dynasty (13th century A.D.); an exhibition of Arab antiquities and scale models of important Islamic monumental buildings in Iraq. Opened as a Museum in 1935.

Arbil Museum: Arbil; objects from Iraqi history up to Arabic-Islamic period.

Babylon Museum: f. 1949; contains models, pictures, and paintings of the remains at Babylon; the Museum is situated amongst the ruins.

Baghdad Museum: Bab-al-Shargi, Baghdad; f. 1970; museum of folklore and costumes, natural history; on the same premises is the Memorial Exhibition, containing the royal relics of King Faisal I; there is also a picture gallery.

Iraq Military Museum: A'dhamiya, Baghdad; f. 1974 combining Arms Museum (f. 1940) and Museum of War (f. 1966); contains old Arabian weapons, Othmanic firearms and contemporary Iraqi weapons.

Iraqi Museum, The: Salhiya quarter, Baghdad West; f. 1960, opened 1966; contains antiquities dating from the early Stone Age to the beginning of the 17th century A.D., including Islamic objects in almost uninterrupted sequence; more than 9,000 exhibits, 93,000 objects catalogued and thousands with excavation numbers only in its store rooms; 40,000 coins; Al-Sarraf gallery, containing only Islamic coins; library: *see* Libraries; Dir. ABDUL KADIR AL-TIKRITI; publs. *Sumer* (annually), *Al-Maskukat* (2 a year), *Iraq Museum Guide*, *Treasures of the Iraq Museum*.

Iraq Natural History Research Centre and Museum: Bab Al-Muadham, Baghdad; f. 1946; attached to the University of Baghdad; includes sections on zoology, botany and geology; research work in Natural History; exhibitions of animals, plants, rocks and minerals pertaining to Iraq; organizes cultural, educational and scientific training programmes; library of 27,000 vols., 700 periodicals; publs. scientific papers in English dealing with the natural history of Iraq and neighbouring countries in the series *Iraq Natural History Research Centre Publications*†, *Bulletin of the Iraq Natural History Research Centre*† and *Annual Report*†; Dir. MUNIR K. BUNNI, D.SC.

Mosul Museum: Dawassa, Mosul; f. 1951; collections Assyrian antiquities of the 9th and 8th centuries B.C. found at Nimrud, objects uncovered in the ruins of Hatra dating back to the 2nd century B.C. and 2nd century A.D., agricultural tools and pottery vessels from the 5th and 4th millennia B.C., photographs of excavated buildings at Tepe Gawra, maps of the Assyrian Empire, Nimrud and Hatra; Prehistoric and Islamic exhibits; assists in discovery and maintenance of several archaeological sites; library of *c.* 2,000 vols.; Dir. HAZIM A. AL HAMEED.

Museum of Arab Antiquities: Samawal St., Baghdad; it is a restored building of the 14th century A.D., which was opened as a Museum in 1937; collections of Arab antiquities illustrating different Islamic cultural periods in Iraq; exhibits mainly from Wasit, Samaria and Kufa.

Nasiryah Museum: Nasiryah; Sumerian and other archaeological objects.

National Museum of Modern Art: Al-Nafoura Square, Bal Al-Sharqi, Baghdad; f. 1962; Supervisor AMER AL-UBAIDI.

Natural History Museum of the University of Basrah: Cornish St., Basrah; f. 1971; study of flora and fauna of the marshes of South Iraq and the Arabian Gulf; sections on mammals, birds, reptiles and amphibia, and fishes; scientific collections in all sections accessible to specialists and exhibits open to public; Dir. Dr. KHALAF AL-ROBAAE; publ. *Bulletin*†.

Samarra Museum: Samarra; f. 1936; it is housed in one of the old city gates, and contains objects excavated in the ruins of ancient Samarra.

UNIVERSITIES

AL-MUSTANSIRIYAH UNIVERSITY

WAZIRIYAH, BAGHDAD

Telephone: 8828551.

Founded 1963.

State control; Languages of instruction: Arabic and English; Academic year: September to June.

President: Dr. HASHIM JABIR HASSAN.

Assistant to the President for Scientific Affairs: Dr. MOHIE AL-DEEN ABBAS.

Assistant to the President for Administrative and Student Affairs: Dr. HAYTHEM JASSAM MOHAMMED.

Registrar: YOUSIF RABIE YOUSIF.

Library: *see* Libraries.

Number of teachers: 328.

Number of students: 11,000.

Publications: *Al-Mustansiriyah University Magazine, Science College Magazine, Medical Science Magazine, Library Magazine, Administration and Economics Magazine.*

DEANS

College of Science: Dr. SABRI R. DAOUD.

College of Arts: HAMEED M. AHMED.

College of Administration and Economics: Dr. MUTHANA T. AL-HOURI.

College of Medicine: Dr. QAIS A. HAMEED KUBA.

College of Education: Dr. SAAD A. AZIZ ALI.

College of Medicine (Kufa): Dr. IHSANN IBRAHIM.

Institute for National and Social Studies: Dr. NAZAR ABDUL-LATIF (Dir.).

Institute for Teaching Arabic to Non-native Speakers: Dr. SALMAN D. SALMAN (Dir.).

UNIVERSITY OF BAGHDAD*

JADYRYA, BAGHDAD

Telephone: 93091.

Founded 1957.

State control; Languages of instruction: Arabic and English.

All the Institutes and Colleges listed below have been incorporated in the University. Each has its own library of Arabic and foreign books.

President: T. I. AL-ABDULLAH.

Registrar: Mrs. TUMADHR ABDULLAH.

Librarian: ZAHIDA IBRAHIM, M.L.S.

Library: *see* Libraries.

Number of teachers: *c.* 1,500.

Number of students: *c.* 19,300.

Publications: *Statistical Bulletin* (annual), *General Catalogue.*

INCORPORATED COLLEGES:

College of Administration and Economics: f. 1969; Dean HADI ABBAS HAMID AL-TAMIMI.

College of Agriculture: f. 1952; Dean Dr. ABDUL MEHDI ALAWI AL JANABI.

College of Arts: f. 1949; Dean Dr. NOORI HAMMOUDI.

College of Dentistry: f. 1953; Dean Dr. ALA'HDIN ABDULLAH MUSA.

College of Education: f. 1971; Dean Dr. KHASHI AYADAH MA'ADHIDI.

College of Engineering: f. 1942; Dean Dr. NAZAR KHALIL WAFI.

College of Law and Political Science: f. 1908; Dean Dr. RIYADH AZIZ HADI.

College of Medicine: f. 1927; Dean Dr. MUHAMMAD ALI AL-KHALIL.

College of Nursing: f. 1962; Dean Miss WADEAA AL-DAGHESTANI.

College of Pharmacy: f. 1936; Dean Dr. HATIF H. JALIL.

College of Physical Education: f. 1955; Dean N. D. AL-SEHREWERDI.

College of Sciences: f. 1949; Dean Dr. JALAL M. SALEH.

College of Veterinary Medicine: f. 1955; Dean MODAR M. ALI AL-FALWJI.

Academy of Fine Arts: f. 1967; Dean H. AL-DROBI.

AFFILIATED RESEARCH CENTRES:

Centre for Educational and Psychological Research: Dir. Dr. MOAFAK AL-HAMDANI.

Centre for Economic and Administrative Research: Dir. ABDUL LATIF AL-KASIR.

Centre for Palestinian Studies Research: Dir. Dr. GASSAN R. ATIYYAH.

Centre for Urban and Regional Planning (Graduate Studies): Dir. Dr. NUMAN AL-JALILI.

Psychology Clinic: Dir. Dr. ALI KAMAL.

Centre for Medical Research: Dir. Dr AHMAD AL-HALWANI.

* No reply received to our questionnaire this year.

UNIVERSITY OF TECHNOLOGY

BAGHDAD

Founded 1974; formerly the College of Engineering Technology of the University of Baghdad.

Languages of instruction: Arabic and English.

President: Dr. TAHA T. AL-NAIMI.

Assistant Presidents: Dr. K. N. FATTAH, Dr. S. A. AL-NASSRI.

Registrar: MOHAMMED AL-KAMACHI.

Librarian: KAMILA ABDUL MAJID.

Number of teachers: 150 full-time, 150 part-time.

Number of students: 6,042.

HEADS OF DEPARTMENTS:

Mechanical Engineering: J. M. SALIM.

Electrical Engineering: MAZIN A. H. KADHIM.

Building and Construction: K. N. FATTAH.

Production and Metallurgy: HASHIM M. ALI.

Control and Systems: MUNDHER N. B. AL-TIKRITI.

Chemical Engineering: ALI M. A. AL-ALLAK.

Education Technology: MAZIN M. A. JUMAH.

Architecture: RIYADH R. TAPPUNI.

Applied Sciences: A. A. AL-NAIMI.

UNIVERSITY OF BASRAH

BASRAH

Telephone: 217000-7.

Founded 1964.

State control; Languages of instruction: Arabic and English; Academic year: September to June.

President: Dr. ABDUL-ILAH Y. AL-KHASHAB.

Assistant to the President for Academic Affairs: Dr. D. H. JEREW.

Assistant to the President for Administrative Affairs: Dr. S. S. UMER.

Assistant to the President for Students' Affairs: Dr. A. J. SALEH.

Assistant to the President for Projects: Dr. HAZIM SH. AL-SALMAN.

Registrar: Dr. EDMOND M. HANNA.

Librarian: ABDUL-JABBAR ABDUL RAHMAN.

Number of teachers: 517.

Number of students: 10,278.

Publications: various college bulletins†.

DEANS:

College of Medicine: Dr. T. S. AL-CHALABI.

College of Engineering: Dr. ADNAN M. AL-NAJAFI.

College of Sciences: Dr. KAMAL A. AL-ANI.

College of Arts: Dr. K. S. AL-NASIRI.

College of Administration and Economics: Dr. WAJEEH A. AL-ALI.

College of Agriculture: Dr. MUHAMMAD A. AL-NAJIM.

College of Education: Dr. B. K. ABDUL-LATEEF.

DIRECTORS:

Centre for Arab Gulf Studies: Dr. M. A. K. AL-NAJJAR.

Cultural Centre: Dr. Z. A. AL-AZI.

Medical Centre: Dr. M. S. AL-ADNANI.

Centre for Marine Sciences: Dr. S. A. DARMORIAN.

Computer Centre: Dr. H. A. ALI.

Natural History Museum: Dr. A. H. Y. AL-ADHAB.

UNIVERSITY OF MOSUL

MOSUL

Telephone: 3231.

Founded 1967 as a separate university; the Faculties were formerly part of the University of Baghdad. Some Faculties are situated near Nineveh and others at Hamam al Alill.

State control; Languages of instruction: Arabic and English; Academic year: September to May (two terms).

President: MOHAMED MAJEED AL-SA'EED.

Assistant to the President for Administrative and Cultural Affairs: KHIDHIR JASSIM MOHAMMED.

Assistant to the President for Postgraduate Studies: RIADH H. AL-DABBAGH.

Assistant to the President for Scientific Affairs: Z. M. AL-SHAROOK, PH.D.

Registrar: Z. M. Z. GURGIA, PH.D.

Librarian: AHMED ABDULLAH AL-HASSO, PH.D.

Number of teachers: 875.

Number of students: 12,638.

Publications: *Al-Jamia* (monthly), *Mesopotamia Agriculture, Adab al Rafidain, Annals of the Medical College, Rafidain Journal of Science, Rafidain Engineering* (quarterly).

DEANS:

College of Agriculture and Forestry: BADIR JASSIM ALAWI.

College of Arts: TAWFIQ SULTAN AL-YUZBAKI.

College of Engineering: M. A. AL-LAILA, PH.D.

College of Medicine: RAJA MUSTAFFA HASAN.

College of Science: HISHAM YAHYA DHANNOUN.

College of Administration and Economics: KUBAIS SA'EED FAHADY.

College of Education: M.-E. TAWFIC, PH.D.

College of Veterinary Medicine: ZUHAIR G. HAYATIE.

College of Physical Education: NIZAR M. AL-TALIB.

DIRECTORS:

Research Centre of Management and Economics: SA'AD AL-NOORI.

Centre for Applied Agricultural Research: NAJEEB T. KAZZAL.

Centre for Applied Scientific Research: L. HAMEED ALI.

Centre for Archaeological and Cultural Research: AMIR SULAIMAN IBRAHIM.

UNIVERSITY OF SULAIMANIYAH

SULAIMANIYAH

Telephone: 23441/2.

Telex: 8912.

Founded 1968.

State control.

Languages of instruction: Arabic, English, Kurdish; Academic year: September to June (two terms).

President: Dr. TARIQ RASHEED ABDULLAH.

Assistant President for Scientific Affairs and Postgraduate Studies: Dr. SALAH AL-DIN M. A. MERANI.

Library: *see* Libraries.

Number of teachers: 404.

Number of students: 6,300.

Publications: *University News* (monthly, Arabic), *Statistical Abstract* (annually), *Zanco* (scientific journal, Arabic and English).

DEANS:

College of Engineering: Dr. KADER SALEH M. AMEEN.

College of Agriculture: Dr. KHUSROW G. SHALI.

College of Science: Dr. KHALEDMAGED HAMID.

College of Arts: Dr. KAMEL H. A. EL BASSIER.

College of Administration: Dr. SADEK BAKER SHAMSA.

College of Education: Dr. ALI HASSAN JASIM.

College of Medicine: Dr. NAWZAD A. EL-ATTAR.

COLLEGES

Al-Imam Al-A'dham College: Baghdad; f. 1967, affiliated to Baghdad University 1978; degree course in Islamic studies; 34 teachers, 516 students; Dean Dr. SUBHI MOHAMMAD JAMIL AL-KHAYYAT.

Foundation for Technical Institutes: Baghdad; f. 1972; attached to the Ministry of Higher Education and Scientific Research; groups all the institutes of technology; Pres. H. M. S. ABDUL WAHAB, PH.D. Incorporated institutes:

Institute of Technology: Baghdad; f. 1969; Dean N. S. MUSTAFA, PH.D.

Technical Institute, Basrah: f. 1973; technology and administration; Dean H. I. MOHAMMED.

Technical Institute of Agriculture: Abu-Ghraib (Baghdad); f. 1964; Dean S. A. HASSAN, PH.D.

Technical Institute of Medicine: (Baghdad); f. 1964; Dean A. S. AL-MASHAT.

Technical Institute in Sulaimania: f. 1973; medical technology and administration; Dean R. M. ABDULLAH, PH.D.

Institute of Administration: Rissafa (Baghdad); f. 1964; Dean A. S. AL-MASHAT.

Institute of Applied Arts: Baghdad; f. 1969; Dean A. NOOR-EDDIN, M.A.

Technical Institute in Mosul: f. 1976; technology and administration; Dean M. S. SAFFO, B.SC.

Technical Institute in Kirkuk: f. 1976; technology and administration; Dean M. ABDUL RAHMAN.

Technical Institute of Agriculture: Aski-Kalak (Arbil); f. 1976; Dean M. S. ABBASS.

Technical Institute of Agriculture: Kumait (Missan); f. 1976; Dean H. L. SADIK.

Technical Institute in Hilla: f. 1976; technology and administration; Dean S. B. DERWISH.

Institute of Administration in Karkh (Baghdad): f. 1976; Dean T. SHAKER.

Technical Institute in Ramadi: f. 1977; technology and administration; Dean J. M. AMIN.

Technical Institute in Najaf: f. 1978; technology and administration; Dean M. A. JASSIM.

Technical Institute in Arbil: f. 1978; technology and administration; Dean H. M. ABID.

Technical Institute in Missan: f. 1979; technology and administration.

Technical Institute of Agriculture: Mussaib-Babylon; f. 1979.

Technical Institute of Agriculture: Shatra-Thi Qar; f. 1979.

REPUBLIC OF IRELAND

Population 3,364,000

ACADEMIES

IRISH ACADEMY OF LETTERS

"ELSTOW", KHAPTON RD.,
DUN LAOGHAIRE, CO. DUBLIN

Founded by W. B. Yeats and G. B. Shaw in 1932

President: MERVYN WALL.
Vice-President: CONSTANTINE FITZGIBBON.
Hon. Secretary and Treasurer: JOHN RYAN.

ACADEMICIANS:

BOYLE, PATRICK (short story writer).
BRODERICK, JOHN (novelist).
FITZGIBBON, CONSTANTINE (novelist and historian).
GIBBON, W. MONK (essayist and poet).
GRAVES, ROBERT (poet, novelist, essayist).
GUINNESS, BRYAN (poet).
HANLY, GERARD (novelist).
HEWITT, JOHN (poet).
JOHNSTON, DENIS (dramatist).
KIELY, BENEDICT (short story writer, playwright, critic and novelist).
KILROY, THOMAS (short story writer, critic, playwright and novelist).
KINSELLA, THOMAS (poet).
LAVIN, MARY (novelist and short story writer).
LONGFORD, CHRISTINE (dramatist and novelist).
MAC MAHON, BRYAN (novelist, playwright and short story writer).
MCLAVERTY, MICHAEL (novelist and short story writer).
MONTAGUE, JOHN (poet).
MURDOCH, IRIS (novelist).
O'DIREÁIN, MAIRTÍN (poet).
O'DONNELL, PEADAR (novelist).
O'FARACHÁIN, ROIBEÁRD (poet).
O'FLAHERTY, LIAM (novelist).
PLUNKETT KELLY, JAMES (novelist and short story writer).
STARKIE, WALTER (literary historian).
STUART, FRANCIS (novelist).
TREVOR, WILLIAM (novelist).
USSHER, ARLAND (essayist and philosopher).
WALL, MERVYN (novelist and dramatist).
WHITE, TERENCE DE VERE (novelist).

ROYAL HIBERNIAN ACADEMY OF PAINTING, SCULPTURE AND ARCHITECTURE

STUDIO, WOODTOWN, RATHFARNHAM,
CO. DUBLIN 16

Founded 1823

President: DAVID HONE, R.H.A. (painter).
Secretary: DESMOND CARRICK, R.H.A. (painter).
Treasurer: HENRY HEALY, R.H.A. (painter).
Keeper: JAMES NOLAN, R.H.A. (painter).
Trustees: DAVID HONE, P.R.H.A., DESMOND CARRICK, R.H.A., JAMES NOLAN, R.H.A.

Number of members: 22 Academicians, 18 Hon. mems., 10 Assoc. mems.

ROYAL IRISH ACADEMY

19 DAWSON STREET, DUBLIN 2

Incorporated by Royal Charter 1786

President: P. MACCANA, M.A., PH.D.
Vice-Presidents: E. M. PHILBIN, D.SC., P. F. FOTTRELL, D.SC., J. P. HAUGHTON, M.SC., K. B. NOWLAN, PH.D.
Treasurer: T. D. SPEARMAN, PH.D., F.T.C.D.
Secretary: J. C. I. DOOGE, M.SC.
Secretary of the Science Committee: W. A. WATTS, SC.D., F.T.C.D.
Secretary of the Polite Literature and Antiquities Committee: G. L. HUXLEY, M.A.

Number of members: *c.* 240, plus 60 Honorary Members.

Library of 30,000 vols., 30,000 pamphlets, 1,700 current sets of periodicals and 2,500 MSS.

Publications: *Proceedings, Section A*† (Mathematical and Physical Sciences), *Section B*† (Biological, Geological and Chemical Sciences), *Section C*† (Archaeology, Celtic Studies, History, Linguistics and Literature).

COMMITTEE OF SCIENCE:

CUNNINGHAM, E. P., PH.D.
DOOGE, J. C. I., M.SC.
FOTTRELL, P. F., PH.D.
KERNAN, R. P., D.SC.
MCELHINNEY, R. S., PH.D.
PHILBIN, E. M., D.SC.
PORTER, N. A., D.SC.
RYAN, P., PH.D.
SCANLAN, J. O., D.SC.
SPEARMAN, T. D., PH.D., F.T.C.D.
WATTS, W. A., SC.D.

COMMITTEE OF POLITE LITERATURE AND ANTIQUITIES:

EOGAN, G., PH.D.
GIBSON, N. J., PH.D.
HARBISON, P., DR.PHIL.
HARMON, M., PH.D.
HAUGHTON, J. P., M.SC.
HERRIES DAVIES, G., PH.D.
HUXLEY, G. L., M.A.
LYNCH, P., M.A.
NOWLAN, K. B., PH.D.
TIERNEY, J. J., M.A.

LEARNED SOCIETIES AND RESEARCH INSTITUTES

AGRICULTURE AND VETERINARY SCIENCE

National Development Association: 3 St. Stephen's Green N., Dublin, 2; f. 1967 incorporating Nat. Agricultural Development Asscn. and Nat. Buy Irish Campaign; 100 mems.; Dir.-Gen. JOHN C. MCMAHON.

Royal Dublin Society: Ballsbridge, Dublin 4; f. 1731 for the advancement of agriculture, industry, science and art; this Society is responsible for the annual Dublin Horse Show; 15,000 mems.; the Society contains a scientific library; Pres. Prof. JOHN CARROLL; Registrar D. ALLAN; publs. *Journal of Earth Sciences, Journal of Life Sciences, Kerry Cattle Herd Book;* library: *see* Libraries.

Royal Horticultural Society of Ireland: Thomas Prior House, Merrion Rd., Dublin 4; f. 1830; 1,100 mems.; Pres. S. MASKELL; Sec. Mrs. MONICA NOLAN.

Veterinary Council: 53 Lansdowne Rd., Dublin 4; f. 1931; 1,531 registered names; Registrar T. Ó NUALLÁIN.

Architecture and Town Planning

Architectural Association of Ireland: 8 Merrion Square, Dublin; 250 mems.; Hon. Secs. JAMES COADY, TOAL Ó'MUIRÉ; publ. *The Green Book* (annual).

Royal Institution of Chartered Surveyors (*Republic of Ireland Branch*): 5 Wilton Place, Dublin 2; f. 1868; Administrator Capt. W. J. BREWER.

Royal Institute of the Architects of Ireland: 8 Merrion Square, Dublin 2; f. 1839; 820 mems.; Pres. JOHN E. O'REILLY; Hon. Sec. C. A. MANAHAN, M.R.I.A.I.; Gen. Sec. SEAMUS WARD; publ. *R.I.A.I. Year Book.*

The Arts

The Arts Council: 70 Merrion Square, Dublin 2; f. 1951; the statutory body appointed by the Taoiseach (Prime Minister) to promote and assist the arts; in addition to organizing and promoting exhibitions and other activities itself, the Council gives grant-aid to many organizations including the theatre, opera, arts centres, arts festivals, exhibitions and publishers; also awards bursaries and scholarships to individual artists; State Grant (1980) £2.70 million; Dir. COLM Ó BRIAIN.

Friends of the National Collections of Ireland, The: 32 Lower Baggot St., Dublin 2; estab. 1924; Pres. THE EARL OF ROSSE; Hon. Sec. JOHN GILMARTIN.

Irish Society for Design and Craftwork, The: f. 1894; Pres. Prof. DESMOND FITZGERALD, B.ARCH., F.R.I.A.I., A.R.I.B.A., A.M.T.P.I.; Chair. Prof. DOMHNALL O MURCHADHA; Hon. Sec. Miss ANGELA O'BRIEN, 112 Ranelagh, Dublin 6.

Irish Society of Arts and Commerce: f. 1911; Pres. Rt. Rev. Mgr. EDWARD KISSANE, D.D., D.LITT., L.S.S.; Sec. Miss A. VON MUNTZ, 55 Fairview Strand, Dublin.

Music Association of Ireland Ltd., The: 11 Suffolk St., Dublin 2; f. 1948; 650 mems.; Chair. P. O'KELLY; Hon. Sec. Miss JOAN COWLE; Organizer EOIN GARRETT; publs. *Counterpoint* (monthly), *Annual Report.*

Photographic Society of Ireland: P.O.B. 830, Dublin; f. 1854; 400 mems.; Pres. J. G. KENNA; Hon. Sec. P. SLATTERY, L.R.P.S.; publ. *The Lens* (quarterly).

Bibliography and Library Science

Library Association of Ireland (*Cumann Leabharlann na hÉireann*): Thomas Prior House, Merrion Rd., Dublin 4; f. 1928, incorporated 1952; Pres. S. BOHAN, B.A.; Hon. Sec. Miss N. HARDIMAN, F.L.A.I.; publ. *An Leabharlann, The Irish Library* (quarterly, jointly with Northern Ireland Branch of the Library Association).

Economics, Law and Politics

Economic and Social Research Institute: 4 Burlington Rd., Dublin 4; f. 1960; 234 individual mems. and 191 corporate mems.; library of 31,680 vols.; Pres. T. K. WHITAKER, D.ECON.SC., LL.D.; Dir. K. A. KENNEDY, B. COMM., B.PHIL., M.ECON.SC., PH.D.; Sec. J. ROUGHAN, B.COMM., B.A.; numerous publications.

Honourable Society of King's Inns: Henrietta St., Dublin; f. 1542, 45 brs.; all students and barristers are members of the Inns; library of over 110,000 vols.; Librarian Miss M. NEYLON.

Incorporated Law Society of Ireland: Blackhall Place, Dublin 7; f. 1841; 23,000 mems.; library of 10,000 vols.; Dir.-Gen. JAMES J. IVERS; Librarian MARGARET BYRNE; publs. *Law Directory* (annual), *Handbook, Gazette* (monthly).

Institute of Chartered Accountants in Ireland: Offices and Library: 7 Fitzwilliam Place, Dublin 2; Belfast Office: 11 Donegall Square South, Belfast, BT1 5JE; inc. by Royal Charter 1888; 3,601 mems.; Dir. R. F. HUSSEY, B.E.; Sec. R. L. DONOVAN, B.A., B.COM., F.C.A.

Statistical and Social Inquiry Society of Ireland: c/o Central Statistics Office, Ardee Rd., Rathmines, Dublin 6; f. 1847 to promote the study of social and economic developments; *c.* 500 mems.; Pres. R. O'CONNOR, M.AGR.SC., PH.D., D.ECON.SC.; Hon. Secs. MICHAEL A. McGURNAGHAN, B.SC(ECON), W. J. L. RYAN, M.A., PH.D., and W. KEATING B.SC.; publ. *Journal* (annually).

Education

Church Education Society: 28 Bachelor's Walk, Dublin 1; f. 1839; Hon. Sec. Rev. G. D. HOBSON, M.A.; Asst. Sec. and Inspector of Schools Rev. W. B. HENEY; publ. *Annual Report.*

History, Geography and Archaeology

Cork Historical and Archaeological Society: c/o Ballysheehy Lodge, Clogheen, Cork; f. 1891; 450 mems.; Pres. Very Rev. DEAN CAREY; Hon. Sec. PATRICK HOLOHAN, M.A.; publ. *Journal* (2 a year).

Folklore of Ireland Society: University College, Belfield, Dublin 4; f. 1926; Pres. AINDRIAS Ó MUIMHNEACHÁIN; Sec. CATHAL GOAN; Registrar SEÁN Ó SUILLEABHÁIN; Editor PÁDRAIG Ó HÉALAÍ; publ. *Béaloideas* (irregular).

Genealogical Office (formerly Office of Arms): Dublin Castle; estab. 1552; Chief Herald and Genealogical Officer GERARD SLEVIN, M.A.

Irish Manuscripts Commission: 73 Merrion Square, Dublin 2; estab. 1928; 18 mems.; Chair. Rev. Dr. DONAL F. CREGAN; Research Officer Dr. MICHAEL J. HAREN; Sec. Miss E. MORRISSEY; 145 published vols. of historical interest.

Military History Society of Ireland: University College, Newman House, 86 St. Stephen's Green, Dublin 2; f. 1949; 900 mems.; Hon. Secs. Lt.-Col. D. O'CARROLL, B.A. (Correspondence), Lt.-Col. B. D. H. CLARK, M.C., G.M. (Membership); publ. *The Irish Sword* (2 a year).

Old Dublin Society: Civic Museum, City Assembly House, 58 South William Street, Dublin 2; f. 1934; 1,000 mems.; Pres. TIMOTHY DAWSON; Hon. Secs. BRIAN SIGGINS, Mrs. MURIEL McCARTHY; publ. *Dublin Historical Record* (quarterly).

Royal Society of Antiquaries of Ireland: 63 Merrion Square, Dublin 2; f. 1849; *c.* 800 mems.; 13,000 vols. in library; Hon. Gen. Sec. C. N. SHEEHAN; publ. *Journal* (annually).

International Cultural Institutes

Alliance Française de Dublin: 1 Kildare St., Dublin 2; f. 1961; 350 mems.; 2,300 students; courses in French at all levels, cultural activities; library of 5,000 vols.; Dir. DAVID WECKSELMANN; publ. *Contacts* (in French, 2 a year).

Goethe Institut: 37 Merrion Square, Dublin 2; f. 1961; cultural events; language courses; reading room; public library of 12,000 vols.; Dir. Dr. D. KREPLIN; publs. programmes (bi-monthly) and yearly course syllabus.

Istituto Italiano di Cultura: 11 Fitzwilliam Square, Dublin; Dir. Prof. ANDREA TOSSI.

Language and Literature

Conradh na Gaeilge (*Gaelic League*): 6 Sráid Fhearchair, Baile Átha Cliath 2, Dublin 2; f. 1893; 250 brs.; Pres. ALBERT FRY; Gen. Sec. SEÁN MAC MATHÚNA; publs. *Feasta, Rosc. An tUltach* (monthlies), pamphlets.

Irish PEN: Chilham House, Rathfarnham Village, Dublin 14; f. 1928; 50 mems.; Pres. Dr. CHARLES E. KELLY; Hon. Sec. BARBARA WALSH.

MEDICINE

Apothecaries' Hall: 95 Merrion Square, Dublin 2; f. 1791; Gov. Dr. F. J. O'DONNELL, F.R.C.P.I., L.A.H.; Registrar and Clerk of Court Miss FRANCES COOLICAN (acting).

Dental Board: 57 Merrion Square, Dublin 2; Pres. Dr. VINCENT B. MORRIS; Registrar DONAL MURPHY.

Irish Medical Association: 10 Fitzwilliam Place, Dublin; f. 1936; Gen. Sec. Dr. NOEL REILLY; 2,000 mems.; publ. *Journal* (twice monthly).

Medical Registration Council: 6 Kildare St., Dublin; f. 1927; Pres. ANTHONY BURTON CLERY; Registrar MARY CAGNEY.

Medical Research Council of Ireland: 9 Clyde Rd., Dublin 4; f. 1937; 9 mems.; Chair. Prof. D. K. O'DONOVAN, M.D., PH.D., F.R.C.P.; Hon. Sec. Prof. J. SCOTT, M.A., PH.D.; publ. *Annual Report*†.

Pharmaceutical Society of Ireland: 37 Northumberland Rd., Dublin 4; f. 1875; Pres. MICHAEL SHANNON, M.P.S.I.; Registrar and Sec. MICHAEL J. CAHILL, B.L., F.P.S.I.; publ. *Calendar*.

Royal Academy of Medicine: 6 Kildare St., Dublin 2; f. 1882; 1,200 Fellows; Pres. M I. DRURY; Gen. Sec. and Treas. M. POWELL; publ. *Irish Journal of Medical Science* (monthly).

Royal College of Physicians of Ireland: 6 Kildare St., Dublin 2; inc. 1667, re-inc. 1692; 371 Fellows; Pres. A. GRANT, M.D., F.R.C.P.I.; Sec. D. A. LARMOUR.

NATURAL SCIENCE

Dublin University Biological Association: Trinity College, Dublin; f. 1874; 400 mems.; Pres. J. S. MCCORMICK; Hon. Sec. D. F. LARKIN.

Institute of Chemistry of Ireland, The: c/o Royal Dublin Society, Ballsbridge, Dublin 4; f. 1950; 281 mems.; Pres. Prof. D. C. PEPPER, M.A., PH.D., F.T.C.D., M.R.I.A., F.I.C.I.; Hon. Sec. Miss A. GRATHAN ESMONDE, B.SC., M.I.C.I.; publ. *Orbital* (twice yearly).

Irish Astronomical Society: c/o Armagh Observatory, Armagh BT61 9DG, N. Ireland; f. 1937; 200 mems.; Pres. J. O'CONNOR; Sec. P. B. BRYNE; publ. *Orbit* (6 a year).

Royal Zoological Society of Ireland: Phoenix Park, Dublin 8; f. 1830; 6,877 mems.; Pres. V. CRAIGIE; Hon. Secs. A. G. MASON, P. WILSON; Dir. E. T. MURPHY; publ. *Annual Report*.

PHILOSOPHY AND PSYCHOLOGY

Psychological Society of Ireland: 4-5 Eustace St., Dublin 2; f. 1970 to advance psychological knowledge and research in Ireland, to ensure maintenance of high standards of professional training and practice, to seek the development of psychological services; 345 mems.; Pres. STEPHEN KEALY; Hon. Sec. Dr. HOWARD SMITH; publ. *The Irish Journal of Psychology*, *The Irish Psychologist*.

Theosophical Society in Ireland: 31 Pembroke Rd., Dublin 4; f. 1919; Gen. Sec. Miss DOROTHY M. EMERSON.

University Philosophical Society: Trinity College, Dublin 2; f. 1684; "Major Society" for composition, reading and discussion of papers on literary, political, philosophical and scientific subjects; 900 mems.; Pres. JOHN W. JACKSON; Hon. Sec. BRIAN J. GOGGIN; publs. *Laws* (occasional), *UPS Bulletin* (termly).

TECHNOLOGY

Engineering and Scientific Association of Ireland: Green Hills, 13 Mather Rd. South, Mount Merrion, Co. Dublin; f. 1903; 100 mems.; Pres. T. A. MCINERNEY; Hon. Sec. and Treas. M. J. HIGGINS, B.E., B.COMM.; publ. *Annual Report*.

Institute for Industrial Research and Standards: Ballymun Rd., Dublin 9; f. 1946, reconstituted 1961; independent state-sponsored organization to promote the application of science and technology in Irish industry; library of 20,000 vols.; Dir.-Gen. M. J. CRANLEY, M.SC., F.R.I.C., F.I.C.I.; publs. *Technology Ireland*† (monthly), *Building Progress*†, *Engineering Progress*†, *Food Progress*† (6 a year).

Institution of Electrical Engineers, The (*Irish Branch*): Chair. B. K. P. SCAIFE, D.SC., PH.D., C.ENG., F.I.E.E.; Hon. Sec. P. D. MOLUMBY, 28 Stillorgan Grove, Blackrock, Co. Dublin.

Institution of Engineers of Ireland, The: 22 Clyde Rd., Ballsbridge, Dublin 4; f. 1835; 3,500 mems.; Pres. L. M. O'BRIEN, B.E., C.ENG., F.I.E.I.; Dir. P. F. CALLAGHAN, B.E., C.ENG., F.I.E.I.; Sec. M. B. O'DONOVAN, B.E., C.ENG., M.I.E.I.; publs. *Transactions*, *Monthly Journal*.

LIBRARIES AND ARCHIVES

Central Catholic Library: 74 Merrion Square, Dublin 2; controlled by the Central Catholic Library Association; open to the public; nearly 80,000 vols., incl. special collection of 2,000 vols. on Christian art; Hon. Librarian Dr. M. B. CROWE.

Chester Beatty Library and Gallery of Oriental Art: Shrewsbury Rd., Dublin; donated to the Irish nation by Sir Chester Beatty in 1968; contains one of the world's leading collections of Islamic and Far Eastern art, and important Western and Biblical MSS. and miniatures; Librarian P. HENCHY, LL.D.

Dublin Public Libraries: Pearse St.; 1.5 million vols.; special collections include early Dublin printing and fine binding, incunabula, 140 vols. on Swift, political pamphlets and cartoons, Dublin periodicals and 18th-century plays, Abbey Theatre material, Yeats material; extensive local history collection in books and pictures; representative holdings of modern Dublin presses; information service to Commerce and Technology; music and gramophone record library; City and County Librarian MÁIRÍN O'BYRNE, DIP.LIB., F.L.A.I.

Irish Central Library for Students: 53 Upper Mount St., Dublin; estab. in 1923 by Carnegie United Kingdom Trust to supplement the resources of public libraries and of the libraries of scientific and cultural organizations, by supplying on loan specialized books of an educational nature; in 1948 the library was presented by the Carnegie United Kingdom Trust as a gift to the nation, and is now under the control of An Chomhairle Leabharlanna (Library Council), a government-appointed body which advises local authorities on the improvement of their library services; approx. 50,000 vols.; Dir. THOMAS ARMITAGE, B.A., D.L.T., F.L.A.I.; publ. *Annual Report*.

Law Library: Four Courts, Dublin 7; controlled by the General Council of the Bar of Ireland; open to mems. of the Irish Bar only; 30,000 vols.; Librarian Group Capt. W. M. M. HURLEY, B.A., LL.B., BAR.-AT-LAW.

Marsh's Library: St. Patrick's Close, Dublin 8; f. 1707; 25,000 vols. and 300 MSS.; Keeper Canon J. S. BROWN, M.A., B.D.; publs. catalogues of the MSS, and of early French books, and *An Account of Marsh's Library*.

National Library of Ireland: Kildare St., Dublin; f. 1877; approx. 500,000 vols.; dept. of prints and drawings, MSS. dept., genealogical office, photocopying service;

serves as a national bibliographical centre; Dir. ALF MACLOCHLAINN.

Oireachtas Library: Leinster House, Dublin; selective works of parliamentary interest, the nucleus of which was the Chief Secretary's Office, Dublin Castle; Librarian LIAM Ó CAIRBRE.

Public Record Office of Ireland: Four Courts, Dublin 7; f. 1867 to preserve and make accessible the records of government offices, courts, probate registries and private donors; Deputy Keeper BREANDÁN MAC GIOLLA CHOILLE, M.A.; publ. Reports of Deputy Keeper.

State Paper Office: Dublin 2; f. 1702 to preserve and make accessible government records 1790–1922, Cabinet records 1919–1948; Keeper BREANDÁN MAC GIOLLA CHOILLE.

Representative Church Body Library: Braemor Park, Rathgar, Dublin 14; f. 1932; theological library controlled by the Representative Body of the Church of Ireland; 23,000 vols.: historical MSS. of Church of Ireland, including succession of all clergy from the Celtic period to date, Watson collection of Prayer Books, Welply collection of genealogical notes; Librarian GERALDINE WILLIS, A.L.A.

Royal College of Surgeons in Ireland Library: St. Stephen's Green, Dublin 2; f. 1784; 30,000 vols.; general medicine, surgery, obstetrics and related subjects; special collection: Arthur Jacob Library, general surgery and medicine; extensive collection of medical pamphlets from 17th century; Librarian and College Historian Dr. J. B. LYONS, F.R.C.P.I.; Exec. Librarian Mrs. K. M. BISHOP, B.A.; publ. *Journal of the Irish Colleges of Physicians and Surgeons* (quarterly).

Royal Dublin Society Library: Ballsbridge, Dublin 4; f. 1731; scientific collection of 100,000 vols., general collection of 104,000 vols., and an agricultural collection of 10,000 vols. and pamphlets; Librarian ALAN R. EAGER, F.L.A., F.L.A.I.

St. Patrick's College Library: Maynooth, Co. Kildare; 200,000 vols.; Librarian ALBERT HARRISON, M.A., F.L.A.

Trinity College Library: College St., Dublin 2; f. 1591; University and British/Irish copyright library; two million printed books, 5,000 MSS., including the Book of Kells and an extensive collection of music scores and maps; enjoys copyright privilege; Librarian PETER BROWN, M.A.

University College Cork Library: University College, Cork; f. 1849; 260,000 vols., including Bax Memorial (Music), Sexton (Anglo-Indian), and Gulbenkian Foundation (Music and Records) collections, and various MSS.; Librarian PATRICK QUIGG, B.SC.(ECON.), A.L.A.

University College Dublin Library: Main building at Belfield, Dublin 4; f. 1908; 600,000 vols., including Baron Palles (Law) Library of 2,500 vols., Zimmer (Celtic) Library of 2,000 vols.; Librarian SEAN PHILLIPS.

University College Galway Library: Galway; f. 1849; 180,000 vols.; extensive collection of books in Irish published since 1890; E.E.C. Documentation Centre; enjoys Irish copyright privilege; Librarian CHRISTOPHER J. TOWNLEY, B.A., B.COMM.

MUSEUMS AND ART GALLERIES

Civic Museum: 58 South William St., Dublin; f. 1953; original exhibits of antiquarian and historical interest pertaining to Dublin; pictures, tapestries, theatre bills, glass and silverwork, coins, newspapers.

Cork Public Museum: Fitzgerald Park, Cork; f. 1945; sections on archaeology, recent Irish history and City of Cork; Cork silver, glass and lace; the C. J. Carroll Collection of Birds; copies of the Book of Durrow, the Book of Kells, Book of Lindisfarne and St. Gall Miniatures; Curator SEAMUS O'COIGLIGH.

Hugh Lane Municipal Gallery of Modern Art: Parnell Square, Dublin; works of Irish, English and Continental artists; pictures from the Sir Hugh Lane collection; sculptures; Curator ETHNA M. WALDRON.

James Joyce Museum: Martello Tower, Sandycove, Co. Dublin; f. 1962; relics of the writer and critical works on him; Curator ROBERT NICHOLSON.

National Gallery of Ireland: Merrion Square, Dublin 2; f. 1864; national, historical and portrait galleries; continental European, American, British and Irish masters since 1250; 2,350 oil paintings, 3,750 drawings, sculpture, engravings, etc.; fine art library of 20,000 vols. open to the public; Dir. HOMAN POTTERTON; commemorative exhibitions held annually for which catalogues of artistic, literary and historical interest are available; publs. various.

National Museum of Ireland: Kildare Street, Dublin 2; f. 1731 by Royal Dublin Society; admin. under Dept. of Education; includes (1) Irish Antiquities Division (Keeper MICHAEL F. RYAN, M.A.); (2) Art and Industrial Division (Keeper JOHN TEAHAN, M.A.; (3) Irish Folklore Division (Keeper JOHN C. O'SULLIVAN, B.COMM., M.A.); (4) Natural History Division, which includes zoological and geological sections (Keeper C. E. O'RIORDAN, M.SC., PH.D.); Dir. A. B. O'RIORDAIN, M.A., M.R.I.A.

Royal College of Surgeons in Ireland Museum: St. Stephen's Green, Dublin 2; f. 1820; Curator P. D. J. HOLLAND.

University College Zoological Museum: Cork; Curator Prof. F. J. O'ROURKE.

UNIVERSITIES AND COLLEGES

UNIVERSITY OF DUBLIN TRINITY COLLEGE

DUBLIN 2

Telephone: Dublin 772941.

Founded 1592.

Chancellor: F. H. BOLAND, B.A., LL.D.

Pro-Chancellors: D. C. CRUISE-O'BRIEN, PH.D., LITT.D., W. B. STANFORD, M.A., LITT.D., MÁNÍN UÍ DHÁLAIGH, M.A., D.LITT. CELT., LITT.D.

Provost: F. S. L. LYONS, M.A., PH.D., LITT.D., F.R.HIST.S., F.B.A., F.R.S.L.

Vice-Provost: D. I. D. HOWIE, M.A., PH.D.

Bursar: A. CLARKE, M.A., PH.D.

Registrar: T. P. MCC. BROWN, M.A., PH.D.

Librarian: P. BROWN, M.A.

Library: *see* Libraries.

Teaching staff: 430 (including part-time).

Number of students: 6,184 (including postgraduate).

Publications: *Hermathena, Trinity News, T.C.D., Icarus, Liaison.*

DEANS:

Faculty of Arts (Humanities): A. K. ASMAL, M.A., LL.M.

Faculty of Arts (Letters): K. W. J. ADAMS, M.A.

Faculty of Mathematical and Engineering Sciences: F. G. FOSTER, M.A., D.PHIL.

Faculty of Medical and Dental Sciences: D. O'B. HOURIHANE, M.D., F.R.C.P.I., F.R.C.PATH.

Faculty of Science: C. H. HOLLAND, B.SC., M.A., PH.D.

Faculty of Economic and Social Studies: J. A. JACKSON, M.A.

Graduate Studies: C. J. STILLMAN, M.A., PH.D.

Visiting Students: EDA SAGARRA, M.A., DR.PHIL.

PROFESSORS:

Faculty of Arts (Humanities):

BOYDELL, B. P., Music
CLARKE, A., Modern History
CROOKSHANK, ANNE O., History of Art
CULLEN, L. M., Modern History
DAVIES, K. G., Modern History
FINDLAY, M. J., Law
FORREST, D. W., Psychology
FREYNE, S. V., Theology
FURLONG, E. J. J., Moral Philosophy
HARTIN, Rev. J., Pastoral Theology
HEYWOOD, J., Teacher Education
HUESTON, R. F. V., Law
LYDON, J. F. M., Medieval History
MCDOWELL, R. B., Modern History
OSBOROUGH, W. N., Law
RICE, J. V., Education
SLOTE, M. A., Philosophy
WOODHOUSE, Rev. H. F., Divinity

Faculty of Arts (Letters):

ADAMS, K. W. J., Spanish
DILLON, J. M., Greek
DIXON, V. F., Spanish
KENNELLY, T. B., Modern Literature
LITTLE, J. R. G., French
LUCE, J. V., Classics
MAYES, A. D. H., Hebrew
MITCHELL, T. N., Latin
Ó MURCHÚ, M., Irish
SAGARRA, EDA, German
SCATTERGOOD, V. J., Medieval and Renaissance Literature
WALTON, J. K., English Literature
WRIGHT, BARBARA, French Literature

Faculty of Mathematical and Engineering Sciences:

BYRNE, J. G., Computer Science
FOSTER, F. G., Statistics
KIRWAN, R. W., Engineering Science
SCAIFE, B. K. P., Engineering Science
SCAIFE, W. G. S., Engineering Science
WALLACE, P. W., Mechanical and Industrial Engineering Science.
WHELAN, M. V., Electrical and Electronic Engineering Science
WRIGHT, W., Engineering

Faculty of Medical and Dental Sciences:

BONNAR, J., Obstetrics and Gynaecology
BUTLER, N. P., Conservative Dentistry
DALRYMPLE, I. J., Clinical Obstetrics and Gynaecology
DOCKRELL, R. B., Orthodontics
ERSKINE, C. A., Human Anatomy and Embryology
FEGAN, W. G., Surgery
FINDLAY, I. A., Oral Surgery
HENNESSY, T. P. J., Surgery
HOURIHANE, D. O'B., Histopathology and Morbid Anatomy
KEANE, C. T., Clinical Microbiology
KEVANY, J. J., Community Health
LAWSON, W. A., Prosthetic Dentistry
MCCOLLUM, S. T., Surgery
MCCORMICK, J. S., Community Health
MCLOUGHLIN, J. V., Comparative Physiology
MEEHAN, P. J., Clinical Psychiatry
MOORE, R. E., Physiology
O'HALLORAN, M. J., Clinical Oncology
TEMPERLEY, I. J., Haematology
TUOHY, O., Oral Medicine and Pathology
WEBB, M. G. T., Psychiatry
WEIR, D. G., Medicine

Faculty of Science:

ANDREWS, J. H., Geography
ARBUTHNOTT, J. P., Microbiology
BRADLEY, D. J., Optical Electronics
CUNNINGHAM, E. P., Animal Genetics
CRANE, L. J., Applied Mathematics
DAWSON, G. W. P., Genetics
DELANEY, C. F. G., Experimental Physics
FLORIDES, P. S., Applied Mathematics
GRAINGER, J. N. R., Zoology and Comparative Anatomy
HAUGHTON, J. P., Geography
HENDERSON, B., Physics
HERRIES DAVIES, G. L., Geography
HOLLAND, C. H., Geology and Mineralogy
HOWIE, D. I. D., Zoology
KEANE, C. T., Clinical Microbiology
LLOYD, D. R., General Chemistry
MCBRIERTY, V. J., Polymer Physics
MCMURRY, T. B. H., Organic Chemistry
MILLER, J. J. H., Pure Mathematics
MURDOCH, B. H., Pure Mathematics
PEPPER, D. C., Physical Chemistry
SCOTT, J. M., Experimental Nutrition
SHAW, G. G., Pharmacology
SIMMS, D. J., Pure Mathematics
SPEARMAN, T. D., Applied Mathematics
TIMONEY, R. F., Pharmaceutical Chemistry
TIPTON, K. F., Biochemistry
WATTS, W. A., Quarternary Ecology
WEBB, D. A., Systematic Botany
WEST, T. T., Pure Mathematics
WINDER, F. G. A., Biochemistry

Faculty of Economic and Social Studies:

BRISTOW, J. A., Economics
CHUBB, F. B., Political Science
JACKSON, J. A., Sociology
KEATINGE, N. P., Political Science
KENNY, I. E., Political Economy
MCALEESE, D. F., Political Economy
MCCARTHY, C., Industrial Relations
O'DONOGHUE, M. J., Economics
RICHARDSON, D. H. S., Botany
RYAN, W. J. L., Political Economy

HEADS OF DEPARTMENTS (Non-Professorial):

Italian: CORINNA S. LONERGAN.
Remedial Linguistics: Sr. MARIE DE MONTFORT SUPPLE.
Russian: WINIFRED H. B. GREENWOOD.

NATIONAL UNIVERSITY OF IRELAND

49 MERRION SQUARE, DUBLIN
Telephone: 767246-7.
Telegraphic Address: Natuniv, Dublin
Founded 1909.

Chancellor: T. K. WHITAKER, D.ECON.SC.
Vice-Chancellor: COLM Ó HEOCHA, M.SC., PH.D.
Registrar: M. GILHEANY, M.ECON.SC.

The University has three constituent Colleges—the University Colleges of Dublin, Cork and Galway—and six Recognized Colleges—St. Patrick's, Maynooth; St. Patrick's College, Drumcondra, Dublin; Our Lady of Mercy College, Carysfort, Blackrock, Co. Dublin; Mary Immaculate College of Education, Limerick; Royal College of Surgeons in Ireland; St. Angela's College, Sligo.

Publications: *Calendar, Graduate Lists.*

University College

BELFIELD, DUBLIN 4
Telephone: 693244.
Founded 1909.

President: THOMAS MURPHY, M.D., F.R.C.P.I., F.R.C.S.I., M.R.I.A.
Secretary and Bursar: J. P. MACHALE, M.COMM., A.C.A., M.MANGT. SOC.
Registrar: MAURICE KENNEDY, M.SC., PH.D.
Librarian: SEAN PHILLIPS, B.A.

Library: *see* Libraries.
Number of teachers: *c.* 627.
Number of students: 9,559.

Publications: *President's Report, Calendar, University College Dublin The Past The Present The Plans.*

DEANS:

Faculty of Arts: Prof. DONAL MCCARTNEY, M.A., PH.D.
Faculty of Philosophy: Prof. PATRICK MASTERSON, M.A., PH.D.
Faculty of Celtic Studies: Prof. CONH O'CLEIRIGH, M.A.
Faculty of Science: GEORGE A. BAIRD, M.SC., PH.D.
Faculty of Law: Prof. JAMES C. BRADY, PH.D.
Faculty of Medicine: Prof. P. MEENAN, M.D., D.C.P., F.C.PATH., BAR.-AT-LAW.
Faculty of Commerce: Prof. EMDA HESSION, M.B.A., PH.D.
Faculty of Engineering and Architecture: JOHN J. KELLY, PH.D.
Faculty of General Agriculture: Prof. EAMONN J. GALLAGHER, M.AGR.SC., PH.D.
Faculty of Veterinary Science: SEOSAMH HANLY, M.SC., M.R.C.V.S.

PROFESSORS:

(*Most professors also have responsibilities in other faculties*)

Faculty of Arts:

BLISS, A. T., M.A., B.LITT., M.R.I.A., Old and Middle English
CALDICOTT, C. E., M.A., PH.D., French
CATHCART, K., M.A., Semitic Languages
DEAN, J. E., M.A. A.L.A., A.L.A.A., Library and Information Studies
DINEEN, S., D.SC., PH.D., Mathematics
EOGAN, G., PH.D., M.R.I.A., Archaeology
GALLAGHER, P., M.A., PH.D., Spanish
HUGHES, A. G., D.MUS., L.R.I.A.M., Music
HUGHES, T. S., M.A., Geography
MCCARTNEY, D., M.A., PH.D., History
MCQUILIAN, D., M.SC., PH.D., Mathematics
MARTIN, Rev. F. X., O.S.A., L.PH., M.A., PH.D., Medieval History
MARTIN, T. A., M.A., PH.D., Anglo-Irish Literature and Drama
NOLAN, D., M.A., PH.D., Italian
Ó BUACHALLA, B., M.A., PH.D., Modern Irish Language and Literature
Ó CONCHEANAINN, T. M. A., Classical Irish
O'MEARA, J. J., M.A., D.PHIL., Latin
RICHMOND, J., PH.D., Greek
RIDLEY, H. M., M.A., PH.D., German
ROWAN, A., PH.D., History of Art
SHEEHY, M. P., PH.D., D.LITT., Palaeography and Late Latin
SWAN, T. D., M.A., PH.D., Education
TIERNEY, J. J., M.A., M.R.I.A., Greek
WILLIAMS, T. D., M.A., Modern History

Faculty of Philosophy and Sociology:
CONNELL, Rev. D., M.A., PH.D., General Metaphysics
MARTIN, Rev. C. J., M.A., D.PHIL., Ethics and Politics
MASTERSON, P., M.A., PH.D., Special Metaphysics
O'DOHERTY, Rev. E. F., M.A., PH.D., Logic and Psychology
WARD, Rev. C. K., S.T.L., PH.D., Social Science

Faculty of Celtic Studies:
ALMQVIST, Bo, FIL.DR., Irish Folklore
BYRNE, F., M.A., Early and Medieval Irish History
DE BHALDRAITHE, T., M.A., PH.D., D.LITT., Irish Dialectology
MACCANA, P., M.A., PH.D., Early and Medieval Irish Language and Literature
Ó CLÉIRIGH, C., M.A., Linguistics

Faculty of Science:
BROWN, D. A., PH.D., D.SC., Inorganic Chemistry
CANNON, P. J., M.B., M.SC., M.R.I.A., Pharmacology
CARROLL, P. K., PH.D., D.SC., Optical Physics
DUKE, E., PH.D., D.SC., Zoology
FEAKINS, D., PH.D., D.SC., Physical Chemistry
GEOGHEGAN, M. J., M.AGR.SC., PH.D., Industrial Microbiology
HARRINGTON, M. G., PH.D., Biochemistry
HAYES, M., M.SC., PH.D., Mathematical Physics
HEGARTY, A. F., PH.D., D.SC., F.R.I.C., Organic Chemistry
KENNEDY, M. J., M.A., PH.D., Geology
MOORE, Rev. J. J., D.SC., Botany
PORTER, N. A., PH.D., D.SC., Electronic Physics
TIMONEY, R. F., M.SC., PH.D., F.R.S.I., Pharmacy
VAN RIJSBERGEN, C., PH.D., Computer Science

Faculty of Law:
BRADY, J. C., PH.D., Law of Prosperity and Equity
CASEY, J. P., PH.D., Law
KELLY, J., M.A., DR.JUR., BAR.-AT-LAW, Roman Law, Jurisprudence

Faculty of Medicine:
BOURKE, G. J., M.D., M.A., D.PH., D.I.H., Community Medicine and Epidemiology
BROWNE, I. W., F.R.C.P.I., M.SC., D.P.M., Psychiatry
COAKLEY, J. B., M.D., M.SC., Anatomy
COUNIHAN, T. B., M.D., M.R.C.P., Medicine
DE VALÉRA, E., M.D., M.A.O., B.SC., D.P.A., L.M., Midwifery and Gynaecology
DWYER-JOYCE, P. D., M.CH., D.O.M.S., Ophthalmology
FITZGERALD, M. X., M.B., B.CH., B.A.O., F.R.C.P.I., M.R.C.P., Medicine
FITZGERALD, O., M.D., M.SC., Therapeutics
GUINEY, E. J., M.B., B.CH., B.A.O., F.P.C.S.I., Paediatric Research
HARMAN, J. W., M.D., M.SC., F.C.A.P., Pathology
HICKEY, M. D., M.D., M.SC., D.PH., F.R.C.P.I., Forensic Medicine
MALONE, J. P., M.D., F.R.C.P.I., D.P.M., F.R.C.PSYCH., Psychiatry.
MASTERSON, J. G., M.D., B.CH., B.A.O., M.SC., M.R.C.P.I., M.R.C.PATH., Medical Genetics
MEENAN, P. N., M.D., BARRISTER-AT-LAW, Microbiology as applied to Medicine
MULDOWNEY, F. P., M.D., M.R.C.P.EDIN., M.R.C.P.I., Medicine (Research Professorship)
MURNAGHAN, M., M.D., M.SC., Physiology and Histology
O'DRISCOLL, K., M.D., M.A.O., F.R.C.P.I., F.R.C.O.G., Obstetrics and Gynaecology
O'HIGGINS, N. J., M.B., M.CH., B.A.O., B.SC., F.R.C.S.I., F.R.C.S., Surgery
O'MALLEY, E., M.CH., F.R.C.S.I., Surgery
WALSH, N., M.B., B.CH., B.A.O., D.P.M., F.R.C.P.(C.), Psychiatry
WARD, O. C., M.D., F.R.C.P.I., D.C.H., Paediatrics

Faculty of Commerce:
CUNNINGHAM, A. C., M.ECON.SC., PH.D., Marketing
HALLY, D. L., PH.D., F.C.A., A.C.A., Accountancy
HARRISON, H., M.A., PH.D., Management Information Systems
HESSION, E., M.B.A., PH.D., Corporate Planning
HILLERY, B. J., M.B.A., PH.D., Industrial Relations
MAC CORMAC, M. J., M.A., M.COMM., F.A.C.C.A., Business Administration
MORAH, B., M.B.A., PH.D., Business Administration
NEARY, J. P., M.A., D.PHIL., Political Economy
WALSH, B., M.A., PH.D., National Economics of Ireland and Applied Economics

Faculty of Engineering and Architecture:
DOOGE, J. C. I., M.E., M.SC., F.I.E.I., F.I.C.E., F.A.S.C.E., Civil Engineering
FEHILY, J. A., B.ARCH., Regional and Urban Planning
LEAHY, P., M.E., PH.D., F.I.MECH.E., F.I.E.I., Mechanical Engineering
MCNULTY, P. B., M.S., PH.D., Agricultural Engineering
O'DONNELL, J. P., M.E., B.SC., M.I.CHEM.E., F.I.MEC.E., M.I.E.I., Chemical Engineering
O'NEILL, C., M.ARCH., M.R.I.A.I., A.R.I.B.A., Architecture
POWER, H. M., M.SC., PH.D., D.SC., Electrical Engineering
SCANLAN, J. O., M.E., PH.D., Electronic Engineering

Faculty of General Agriculture:
CLEAR, T., M.AGR.SC., Forestry
EVANS, G. O., F.L.S., PH.D., D.SC., Agricultural Zoology
GALLAGHER, E. J., M.AGR.SC., PH.D., Crop Husbandry
GORDON, I., M.A., PH.D., Animal Husbandry
KAVANAGH, J. A., PH.D., D.I.C., Plant Pathology
MCALEESE, D. M., M.A., PH.D., M.AGR.SC., F.R.I.C., Agricultural Chemistry
MORGAN, J. V., M.S., PH.D., Horticulture
SHEEHY, S. J., PH.D., Applied Agricultural Economics

Faculty of Veterinary Medicine:
CUNNINGHAM, B., PH.D., M.R.C.V.S., Veterinary Pathology and Microbiology
HANNAN, J., M.V.B., M.A., M.S., PH.D., M.R.C.V.S., Veterinary Preventive Medicine and Food Hygiene
KEALY, J. K., M.V.M., M.R.C.V.S., D.V.R., Veterinary Surgery Obstetrics and Infertility
KELLY, W. R., M.A., M.V.M., M.R.C.V.S., Veterinary Medicine and Pharmacology
LEE, R. P., M.A., PH.D., M.R.C.V.S., Veterinary Parasitology
LEEK, B. F., B.V.M. & S., PH.D., M.R.C.V.S., Veterinary Physiology and Biochemistry

University College CORK

Telephone: Cork 021-26871.
Founded 1845 as Queen's College, Cork. Changed to above in 1908.

Academic year: October to September.
President: T. Ó CIARDHA, M.A., PH.D.
Vice-President: Prof. T. F. RAFTERY, M.AGR.SC.
Registrar: Prof. M. P. MORTELL, PH.D.
Finance Officer and Secretary: MICHAEL F. KELLEHER, B.A., F.C.C.A., F.C.I.S., M.C.I.T.
Librarian: PATRICK QUIGG, B.SC. (ECON.), A.L.A.

Number of teachers: 260.
Number of students: 4,347 full-time.
Publications: Many and various through the Cork University Press.

DEANS:

Faculty of Arts: Prof. J. J. LEE, M.A.
Faculty of Celtic Studies: Prof. P. S. Ó RIAIN, M.A., PH.D.
Faculty of Commerce: Prof. D. P. O'MAHONY, M.A., PH.D., B.L.
Faculty of Law: Prof. E. F. RYAN, M.A., B.L.
Faculty of Science: M. F. MULCAHY, M.SC., PH.D.
Faculty of Dairy Science: J. J. CONDON, M.SC. (DAIRYING), PH.D.
Faculty of Engineering: Prof. M. C. SEXTON, M.SC., PH.D., D.SC., C.ENG., M.I.E.E., F.INST.P., M.R.I.A.
Faculty of Medicine: Prof. J. D. SHEEHAN, B.SC., M.D., F.R.C.P.

PROFESSORS AND HEADS OF DEPARTMENTS:

(*Some professors also have responsibilities in other faculties.*)

Faculties of Arts and Celtic Studies:
BARRY, J. G., M.A., PH.D., Medieval History
BREATNACH, R. A., M.A., M.R.I.A., Irish Language and Literature
CALI, P., M.A., D. IN L. Italian
DEMPSEY, Rev. P. S. R., M.A., PH.D., D.D., L.S.S., F.B.PS.S., Applied Psychology
FLEISCHMANN, A. G., M.A., D.MUS., MUS.D., M.R.I.A., Music
FOGARTY, J. P., M.A., PH.D., Ancient Classics
FOLLEY, T. T., M.A., PH.D., Spanish
LEE, J. J., M.A., Modern History
LUCY, J. F., M.A., Modern English
MAGUIRE, J. M., M.A., D.PHIL., Social Theory and Institutions
MULCAHY, D. G., M.A., M.ED., PH.D., Education
MURPHY, J. A., M.A., Irish History
NEVILL, W. E., PH.D., Geology
Ó'CARRAGÁIN, E., M.A., A.T.O., PH.D., Old and Middle English
O'FLAHERTY, K. M. J., M.A., PH.D., French
O'KELLY, M. J., M.A., D.LITT., M.R.I.A., Archaeology
O'MAHONY, Very Rev. B. E., M.A., S.T.L., PH.D., Philosophy
ÓRIAIN, P. S., M.A., PH.D., Early Irish Language and Literature

Ó TUAMA, S., M.A., PH.D., Modern Irish Literature
ROCHE, K. F., M.A., History of Political Ideas
SCHÄUBLIN, P., D.PHIL., German
SMYTH, W. J., PH.D., Geography

Faculty of Commerce:
O'MAHONY, D. P., M.A., PH.D., Economics

Faculty of Law:
McMAHON, B. M. E., LL.M., PH.D., Law
MURPHY, B. J., B.A., LL.B., Jurisprudence
RYAN, E. F., M.A., B.L., Common Law

Faculty of Science:
BARRY, P. D., M.SC., PH.D., D.I.C., Mathematics
BRÜCK, P. M., M.SC., PH.D., Geology
CASSELLS, A. C., M.SC., PH.D., Botany
CUNNINGHAM, J., D.SC., PH.D., Physical Chemistry
DOONAN, S., PH.D., Biochemistry
FAHY, E. F., M.SC., PH.D., Experimental Physics
HATHAWAY, B. J., PH.D., Inorganic Chemistry
McKERVEY, M. A., PH.D., D.SC., Organic Chemistry
MORAN, M. A., M.SC., PH.D., F.I.M.A., Statistics
O'DONOVAN, D. G., M.SC., PH.D., M.R.I.A., F.R.I.C., Chemistry
O'REGAN, P. G., M.S., PH.D., Computer Science
O'ROURKE, F. J. F., M.B., M.SC., PH.D., M.R.I.A., Zoology
QUINLAN, P. M., D.SC., M.S., PH.D., F.I.E.I., Mathematical Physics
TEEGAN, J. P., M.SC., PH.D., F.R.I.C., M.R.I.A., Chemical Spectroscopy

Faculty of Dairy Science:
FOLEY, J., M.SC., PH.D., Dairy and Food Technology
FOX, P. F., PH.D., Dairy and Food Chemistry
LUCEY, D. I. F., M.SC., PH.D., Dairy and Food Economics
O'MULLANE, T., M.SC., Dairy and Food Microbiology
RAFTERY, T. F., M.AGR.SC., Agriculture
SYNNOTT, E. C., M.ENG.SC., PH.D., C.ENG., F.I.E.I., F.I.F.S.T., Dairy and Food Engineering

Faculty of Engineering:
DILLON, E. C., M.E., PH.D., Civil Engineering
SEXTON, M. C., PH.D., D.SC., C.ENG., F.I.E.E., M.I.E.E.E., F.INST.P., M.R.I.A., Electrical Engineering

Faculty of Medicine:
BARRETT, B. E., M.A., M.B., B.DENT.SC., F.D.S.R.C.S., F.F.D.R.C.S.I., Conservative Dentistry
BRADY, M. P., M.CH., F.R.C.S.I., F.A.C.S., Surgery
CORRIDAN, J. P., M.D., D.P.H., D.I.H., Social Medicine
CUSSEN, G. H., M.B., F.R.C.P.(C.), F.R.C.P.I., Paediatrics
DALY, R. J., M.A., M.D., D.P.M., M.R.C. PSYCH., M.R.C.P., Psychiatry
FRAHER, J. P., B.SC., M.B., PH.D., Anatomy
HALL, W. J., M.D., M.SC., PH.D., Physiology
HEGARTY, Mrs. MARY, B.D.S., F.D.S.R.C.S., F.F.D.R.C.S.I., D.ORTH., Orthodontics
JENKINS, D. M., M.B., M.D., M.R.C.O.G., Obstetrics and Gynaecology
MACCULLOCH, W. T., B.D.S., M.SC., PH.D., F.F.D.R.C.S.I., M.I.M., Dental Prosthetics
MAGEEAN, J. F., L.D.S., PH.D., F.R.S.H., Preventive Dentistry
O'MAHONY, D. P. J., M.D., B.SC., Pharmacology
O'SULLIVAN, D. J., M.D., F.R.C.P., F.R.C.P.I., F.R.C.P.A., Medicine
RUSSELL, J. G., M.B., B.D.S., F.D.S.R.C.S., F.F.D.R.C.S.I., Dental Surgery
SHEEHAN, J. D., B.SC., M.D., F.R.C.P., Physiology

University College GALWAY

Telephone: 7611.

Founded 1845 as Queen's College, Galway. Changed to above in 1908.

President: C. Ó hEOCHA, M.SC., PH.D., F.R.I.C.
Registrar: Prof. D. O CAOIMH, PH.D.
Secretary and Bursar: D. Ó COIRBHÍN, B.SC.(ECON.), A.C.A.
Academic Secretary: S. Ó CATHAIL, M.A., H.DIP.ED.
Librarian: C. TOWNLEY, B.A., B.COMM.

Library: *see* Libraries.
Number of teachers: 243.
Number of students: 4,000.

DEANS:

Faculty of Arts: K. WOODMAN, M.A.
Faculty of Celtic Studies: TOMÁS P. O. NEILL, M.A.
Faculty of Science: Prof. M. McCARTHY, D.SC., PH.D.
Faculty of Law: Prof. C. K. BOYLE, LL.B., BAR.-AT-LAW.
Faculty of Medicine: Prof. C. F. McCARTHY, M.D., F.R.C.P.I., F.R.C.P.
Faculty of Engineering: Prof. D. Ó. CAOIMH, PH.D.
Faculty of Commerce: J. L. PRATSCHKE, M.ECON.SC., PH.D.

PROFESSORS:

Faculty of Arts and Celtic Studies:
CANNY, N. P., M.A., PH.D., History
CASEY, T. J., M.A., D.PHIL., German
DOUGAN, Rev. Fr. E., O.F.M., B.A., LIC.SOC. ET POL.SCS., Political Science and Sociology
HARRIS, D., PH.D., Spanish
HENRY, P., M.ECON.SC., DR.PHIL., Old and Medieval English
KILLEEN, J. F., M.A., Ancient Classics
KILROY, T., M.A., Modern English
MACAODHA, B. S., M.A., Geography
MACAODHA, M. F., B.A., A.P.S.I., Psychology
MACEOIN, G. S., M.A., D.PHIL., Old and Middle Irish and Celtic Philology
MAC GIOLLARNÁTH, P., M.A., BARR.-AT-LAW, Romance Languages
Ó MADAGÁIN, B., PH.D., Modern Irish
Ó HEIDÉAIN, Rev. Fr. E., O.P., D.PHIL., H.DIP.ED., Education
RABBITTE, Rev. Fr. E., O.F.M., D.D., PH.D., Philosophy
RYNNE, E., M.A., Celtic Archaeology

Faculty of Science:
BARY, B. McK., PH.D., M.SC., Oceanography
BROCK, A., M.A., PH.D., Applied Geophysics
BUTLER, R., D.SC., PH.D., Chemistry
DUNICAN, L. K., PH.D., M.S., M.AGR.SC., Microbiology
FLAVIN, J. N., M.SC., PH.D., Mathematical Physics
FOTTRELL, P. F., M.SC., PH.D., Biochemistry
IMBUSCH, G. F., PH.D., D.SC., Experimental Physics
LARKIN, D. M., M.SC., PH.D., Electron Physics
LEE, E., M.SC., PH.D., Chemistry
MITCHELL, M., B.SC., D.UNIV., Botany
McCARTHY, M. F., PH.D., D.SC., Mathematical Physics
NEWELL, M. L., D.PHIL., D.SC., Mathematics
Ó CINNÉIDE, S., D.SC., Inorganic Chemistry
O'COLLA, P., D.SC., PH.D., Chemistry
TÓIBÍN, S. S., M.SC., PH.D., Mathematics
WALTON, P. W., PH.D., Applied Physics
WILKINS, N., B.SC., Zoology

Faculty of Law:
BOYLE, C. K., LL.B., BARR.-AT-LAW

Faculty of Medicine:
BURNS, J. K., PH.D., Physiology
FAHY, T. J., M.D., D.P.M., M.R.C.PSYCH., Psychiatry
FITZGERALD, J. T., M.D., PH.D., Anatomy
FLYNN, J., M.SC., PH.D., M.R.C., Bacteriology
KENNEDY, J. D., M.D., M.SC., M.R.C.P.I., Pathology
LAVELLE, J. M., M.D., Experimental Medicine and Practical Pharmacology
LEONARD, B. E., PH.D., D.SC., Pharmacology
McCARTHY, C. P., M.D., F.R.C.P.I., M.R.C.P., Medicine
McNICHOLL, B., M.D., M.R.C.P., D.C.H., Paediatrics
MURRAY, J. P., M.D., B.CH., B.A.O., F.F.R., D.M.R., Radiology
Ó CÉIDIGH, P., M.SC., PH.D., Zoology
O'DONOVAN, D. J., M.S., PH.D., Physiology
O'DWYER, E. M., M.B., M.A.O., M.A.C.O.G., Gynaecology and Obstetrics

Faculty of Commerce:
DOOLAN, J., M.B.A., B.A., F.C.A., Business Studies
Ó NUALLÁIN, L., B.A., D.ECON.SC., Economics, Commerce and Accountancy

Faculty of Engineering:
NASH, J. E., M.E., D.SC., Hydrology
O'KEEFFE, D., PH.D., Civil Engineering
O'KELLY, M., M.S., M.E., PH.D., Industrial Engineering
O'LOCHLÁINN, P., B.E., M.SC., Civil Engineering

DUBLIN INSTITUTE FOR ADVANCED STUDIES

10 BURLINGTON ROAD, DUBLIN 4
Telephone: (01) 680748.
Telex: 31687 DIAS EI.

Founded 1940.

Chairman of Council: Dr. T. K. WHITAKER, D.ECON.SC.
Registrar: Lt. Col. J. P. DUGGAN, M.LITT.

Comprising:

School of Celtic Studies.

Chairman: Prof. PROINSIAS MAC CANA, M.A., PH.D.

SENIOR PROFESSORS:

GREENE, D., M.A., D.LITT.
Ó CUÍV, B., M.A., D.LITT.
CARNEY, JAMES P., FIL.DR., D.LITT.

School of Theoretical Physics.
Chairman: Dr. A. J. McCONNELL, M.A., M.SC., SC.D., DOTT. D'UNIV. (ROME).

SENIOR PROFESSORS:

McCONNELL, Rev. J. R., M.A., D.SC.
Ó RAIFEARTAIGH, L. S., M.SC., PH.D.
LEWIS, J. T., PH.D.

School of Cosmic Physics.
Chairman: Prof. E. F. FAHY, M.SC., PH.D.

SENIOR PROFESSORS:

Ó CEALLAIGH, C., PH.D.
MURPHY, T., D.SC.
WAYMAN, P. A., PH.D.

NATIONAL INSTITUTE FOR HIGHER EDUCATION DUBLIN

GLASNEVIN, DUBLIN 9

Founded 1975; in process of formation.

Director: DANIEL P. O'HARE, PH.D.
Registrar: DONAL T. CLARKE.
Librarian: BRIAN NETTLEFOLD.

Number of teachers: 40.
Number of students: 300.

NATIONAL INSTITUTE FOR HIGHER EDUCATION

LIMERICK

Founded 1970.

Director: EDWARD M. WALSH, M.SC., PH.D., C.ENG., M.I.E.E., M.I.E.E.E., M.A.N.S.
Registrar: P. LEO COLGAN, D.P.A., B.COMM., B.A., M.B.A.
Director of Library Services Division: PATRICK J. KELLY, A.L.A.

Library of 80,000 vols.
Number of teachers: 182.
Number of students: 1,460.
Publication: *NIHE Bulletin* (quarterly).

DEANS:

College of Business: ROY HAYHURST, B.A.
College of Humanities: PATRICK F. DORAN, PH.D.
College of Engineering and Science: EVAN R. PETTY, PH.D., F.I.M.

ROYAL COLLEGE OF SURGEONS IN IRELAND

123 ST. STEPHEN'S GREEN, DUBLIN 2

Telephone: 780200.

Founded 1784.

President: K. SHAW.
Vice-President: J. A. O'CONNELL.
Hon. Secretary: F. A. DUFF.
Librarian: Dr. J. B. LYONS.
Registrar: Dr. H. O'FLANAGAN.
Academic Secretary: J. G. GRACE.

Library: *see* Libraries.
Number of teachers: 85.
Number of students: 750.
Publication: *Journal* (quarterly).

DEANS OF POSTGRADUATE FACULTIES:

Faculty of Anaesthetists: Dr. H. LOVE.
Faculty of Dentistry: Prof. I. FINDLAY.
Faculty of Radiologists: Dr. J. O. Y. COLE.
Faculty of Nursing: Miss M. F. CROWLEY.

PROFESSORS:

BOFIN, P. J., F.R.C.P.I., F.R.C.PATH, Forensic Medicine and Toxicology
BROWNE, A., M.D., F.R.C.P.I., F.R.C.O.G., Obstetrics and Gynaecology
CAHILL, K. M., M.D., Tropical Medicine
COLLINS, P. G., M.CH., F.R.C.S.I., F.R.C.S.(E.), Clinical Surgery
CONROY, R. T. W. L., L.R.C.P. & S.I., M.SC., PH.D., Physiology
DOYLE, J. S., M.B., B.CH., B.A.O., F.R.C.P.I., D.P.H., D.C.H., L.M., Medicine
DUNDON, S., M.D., F.R.C.P.I., D.C.H., Paediatrics
GAFFNEY, EITHNE, M.SC., PH.D., Chemistry and Physics
HOLLAND, P. D. J., F.R.C.P.I., F.R.C.PATH., Pathology
LYNCH, T., F.R.C.P.I., D.P.M., Psychiatry
LYONS, J. B., F.R.C.P.I., History of Medicine
McKENNA, J., M.A., M.ED., PH.D., Psychology
MOOREHOUSE, ELLEN, D.P.H., F.R.C.PATH., Microbiology
O'DONNELL, B., M.D., D.P.H., F.F.C.M.I., Social and Preventive Medicine
O'DWYER, W. F., M.D., F.R.C.P.I., Medicine
O'MALLEY, K., M.D., PH.D., M.R.C.P.I., M.R.C.P.(E.), Clinical Pharmacology
ROONEY, B., F.R.C.S.ED., Anatomy
THORNES, R. D., M.D., PH.D., M.A., Experimental Medicine

AFFILIATED INSTITUTE:

Institute of Clinical Science and Research: Dir. Prof. R. D. THORNES.

ST. PATRICK'S COLLEGE

MAYNOOTH, CO. KILDARE

Telephone: Celbridge 286261.

Founded 1795.

Languages of instruction: Irish and English.

Recognized College of the National University. A major seminary for the education of priests, with facilities in all departments open to all students, including non-Catholics.

Chancellor: Most Rev. TOMÁS Ó FIAICH, Primate of All Ireland.
President: Rt. Rev. MICHAEL G. OLDEN, D.HIST.ECCL.
Vice-Presidents: Rev. DENIS O'CALLAGHAN, B.A., D.D., D.C.L., Rev. BRENDAN DEVLIN, M.A., D.D.
Registrar (NUI Courses): Rev. Prof. G. McGREEVY, B.D., PH.D.
Registrar (Theology): Rev. MÍCHEÁL LEDWITH, D.D.
Librarian: ALBERT HARRISON, M.A., A.L.A.

Number of teachers: 99.
Number of students: 1,588.

Publications: *Social Studies* (a quarterly journal of sociology), *Irish Theological Quarterly*†, *The Furrow* (monthly), *Archivium Hibernicum* (annual), *An Sagart* (quarterly in Irish), *Irisleabhar Mhá Nuad* (annual in Irish), *Maynooth Review.*

DEANS:

Faculty of Arts: Rev. PETER CONNOLLY, B.D., M.A.
Faculty of Philosophy: Rev. Prof. M. O'DONNELL, M.A., B.D., PH.D.
Faculty of Science: Prof. MARTIN DOWNES, M.AGR.SC., PH.D.
Faculty of Theology: Rev. Prof. DENIS O'CALLAGHAN, B.A., D.D., D.C.L.
Faculty of Canon Law: Rev. Prof. P. F. CREMIN, J.U.D.

AFFILIATED INSTITUTE:

The Dunboyne Institute: postgraduate studies in Theology, Canon Law, Philosophy and Education; Coordinator Rev. THOMAS MARSH, B.A., D.D.

THE VETERINARY COLLEGE OF IRELAND

UNIVERSITY COLLEGE, DUBLIN 4

Founded 1895.

The College premises are the property of the State and are leased to University College, Dublin, for the Faculty of Veterinary Medicine.

Administrator: G. WRIGHT, M.ECON.SC., PH.D.

SCHOOLS OF ART AND MUSIC

NATIONAL COLLEGE OF ART AND DESIGN

KILDARE ST., DUBLIN 2

Founded 1746, reconstituted as an autonomous semi-state body 1971.

Courses in Fine Art, Communications, Fashion and Textiles Design, Industrial Design, Three-Dimension Design, Principles of Teaching, Design and Education; evening courses.

Director: (vacant).
Deputy Director: DAVID SHERLOCK, M.PHIL., M.S.D.I., F.R.S.A.
Secretary/Registrar: MEALLA C. GIBBONS, B.A.

HEADS OF FACULTIES:

Design: Prof. M. J. OSMIN.
Education and Extra-Mural Studies: Prof. J. BULLOWS.
Fine Art: Prof. CAMPBELL BRUCE.
History of Art and Design and Complementary Studies: Dr. JOHN TURPIN.

ROYAL IRISH ACADEMY OF MUSIC

36 WESTLAND ROW, DUBLIN 2

Founded 1856, incorporated 1889.

Chairman of Board of Studies: RHONA MARSHALL, F.R.I.A.M., L.R.A.M.
Secretary: J. CALLERY.

Number of teachers: 60.
Number of students: 3,000.

ISRAEL

Population 3,799,000

ACADEMY

ISRAEL ACADEMY OF SCIENCES AND HUMANITIES

P.O.B. 4040, JERUSALEM

Founded 1961.

The Academy promotes work in the sciences and humanities, advises the Government on scientific problems and maintains international contacts.

President: EFFRAYIM E. URBACH.

Vice-President: JOSHUA JORTNER.

Publications: *Proceedings* and occasional publications.

CHAIRMEN OF SECTIONS:

Humanities: DAN PATINKIN.

Sciences: SHIMSHON AMITSUR.

MEMBERS:

Humanities:

ABRAMSON, SHRAGA
AYALON, DAVID
BACHI, ROBERTO
BARAK, AHARON
BEN-HAYIM, ZEEV
BLAU, JOSHUA
BRUNO, MICHAEL
EISENSTADT, SHMUEL N.
FLUSSER, DAVID
GUTTMAN, LOUIS ELIAHU
KISTER, MEIR
KROOK-GILEAD, DOROTHEA
LIBERMAN, SHAUL
MAZAR, BENYAMIN
PATINKIN DAN
PINES, SHLOMO
POLOTZKY, JACOB
PRAWER, JOSHUA
ROTENSTREICH, NATHAN
SADAN, DOV
SAMBURSKY, SHMUEL
SCHOLEM, GERSHOM
SHIRMAN, HAYIM
STERN, MENAHEM
TEDESCHI, GAD
URBACH, EFRAYIM E.
YADIN, YIGAEL

Sciences:

AGMON, SAMUEL
AMITSUR, SHIMSHON
BERENBLUM, ISAAC
BERGMANN, FELIX
BLOCH, MOSHE RUDOLF
COHEN, SOLLY GABRIEL
DVORETZKY, ARYEH
FELDMAN, MICHAEL
FURSTENBERG, HARRY
GINSBURG, DAVID
HAAS, GEORG
HARARI, HAIM
JORTNER, JOSHUA
KATZIR (KATCHALSKY), EFRAIM
KOGAN, ABRAHAM
LINDNER, HANS R.
LIPKIN, ZVI HARRY
MICHAELSON, ISAAC CHESAR
NE'EMAN, YUVAL
OLLENDORFF, FRANZ
PEKERIS, CHAIM LEIB
PIATETSKI-SHAPIRO, ILYA
PICARD, YEHUDA LEO
ROSEN, NATHAN
SACHS, LEO
SELA, MICHAEL
STEIN, YECHESKIEL
TALMI, YIGAL
ZOHARY, MICHAEL

LEARNED SOCIETIES

ARCHITECTURE AND TOWN PLANNING

Architectural Association of Israel: P.O.B. 2425, Tel-Aviv; f. 1952; aims to secure and define the legal and professional status of architects and to promote planning education; offers its members an information service on all planning matters; Pres. Arch. JOSEPH HURVITZ; Sec. S. D. H. KRISS.

ARTS

ACUM Ltd. (Authors', Composers' and Music Publishers' Society): ACUM House, 118 Rothschild Blvd., Tel-Aviv (P.O.B. 11201); f. 1934; 1,100 mems.; Dir.-Gen. RAN KEDAR.

Israel Music Institute: P.O.B. 11253, Tel-Aviv; f. 1961; publishes and promotes Israeli music and musicological works throughout the world; since 1969 member of the International Music Information Centre; Chair. Prof. HERZL SHMUELI; Man. Dir. and Editor-in-Chief WILLIAM ELIAS.

Wilfrid Israel House for Oriental Art and Studies: Kibbutz Hazorea, Post Hazorea 30060; f. 1947; opened 1951 in memory of the late Wilfrid Israel; a cultural centre for study and art exhibitions; houses the Wilfrid Israel collection of Near and Far Eastern art and cultural materials; local archaeological exhibits from neolithic to Byzantine times; art library; Dir. Dr. M. MERON.

BIBLIOGRAPHY AND LIBRARY SCIENCE

Centre for Public Libraries: P.O.B. 242, Jerusalem 91000; established in 1965 by the Israel Library Asscn., Ministry of Education and Culture and Graduate Library School of the Hebrew University; provides centralized processing and other services for public libraries; organizes non-academic librarianship courses; Chair. Dr. J. MICHMAN-MELKMAN; Admin. Dir. G. ROSENBLATT; publs. *Leket* (on New Books) (2 a month), *Yad Lakore* (Journal) (quarterly), monographs.

Israel Library Association: P.O.B. 303, Tel Aviv; f. 1952; general organization of librarians, archivists and information specialists; promotes the interests and advances the professional standards of librarians; professional and examining body; 1,875 mems.; Chair. URY BLOCH; Vice-Chair. AMIKAM MARBACH; Sec. Mrs. RUTH PORATH; publ. *Yad-La-Kore* (Libraries and Archives Magazine).

Israel Society of Special Libraries and Information Centers (ISLIC): P.O.B. 20125, Tel-Aviv; f. 1966 to promote the utilization of recorded knowledge by disseminating information in the fields of science and technology, and to facilitate written and oral communication; 350 mems.; Chair. Mrs. LYDIA VILENTCHUK; publs. *Bulletin* (3 a year), contributions to *Information Science* (irregular).

ECONOMICS, LAW AND POLITICS

Israel Bar Association: 95 Eben Gvirol St., Tel-Aviv; 7,000 mems.; Pres. Dr. A. GOLDENBERG; Sec.-Gen. Z. MEITAR; Exec. Dir. M. YINON; publs. *Hapraklit*, *Orech-Hadin* (quarterly).

Israel Institute of Productivity: 4 Henrietta Szold St., P.O.B. 33010, Tel-Aviv; publ. *Hamif'al*.

Israel Political Science Association: c/o Dept. of Political Science, Tel-Aviv University, Tel-Aviv; research and discussions on political and economic problems; Chair. Prof. ASHER ARIAN; Hon. Sec. GIORA GOLDBERG.

Israel Society of Criminology: P.O.B. 1260, Jerusalem; 350 mems.; Pres. Justice HAIM COHEN; Sec. Dr. M. HOROWITZ.

HISTORY, GEOGRAPHY AND ARCHAEOLOGY

Historical Society of Israel, The: P.O.B. 4179, Jerusalem; f. 1925 to promote the study of Jewish history and general history; 1,000 mems.; Pres. Prof. S. ETTINGER; Sec. ZVI YEKUTIEL; publ. *Zion*† (quarterly), containing summaries in English.

Israel Association of Archaeologists: P.O.B. 586, Jerusalem; f. 1955; a professional organization; Sec. Dr. M. W. PRAUSNITZ.

Israel Geographical Society: c/o Dept. of Geography, Tel-Aviv University, Tel-Aviv; f. 1961; 520 mems.; Pres. Prof. MOSHE BRAWER; Sec. G. HOROWITZ; publ. *Merhavim.*

Orientalisches Institut der Görres-Gesellschaft (*Oriental Institute of the Görres Society*): Schmidt-Schule, Jerusalem; historical and archaeological studies.

INTERNATIONAL CULTURAL INSTITUTES

British Council: 140 Hayarkon St., P.O.B. 3302, Tel-Aviv; Rep. C. N. HORTON; libraries: *see* Libraries.

Central Institute for Cultural Relations between Israel, Ibero-America, Spain and Portugal: 6 Sokolow St., Jerusalem; f. 1955; to promote Israeli culture in Latin America and Latin American culture in Israel; 18 affiliated institutes in Latin America; 760 mems. in Israel, 4,500 mems. in Latin America; library of 6,750 vols.; Pres. YAACOV TSUR; Dir. NISSIM ITZHAK; publs. *Carta de Jerusalén*† (monthly), *Visión Cultural "Mabat"* (every 2 months), *Cuadernos de Jerusalén*† (annually).

Goethe Institut/German Cultural Centre: Asia House, 4 Weizmann St., Tel-Aviv.

Institut Français: 111 Hayarkon St., Tel-Aviv; f. 1966; library of 17,900 vols.; Dir. CLAUDE TROCHU.

Israeli Centre of the World Union of Jewish Students: 3 Reyness St., Kiryat Moshe, Jerusalem; brs. at the International Graduate Institute for Hebrew and Jewish studies in Arad and the cultural and educational centre of the W.U.J.S.; Sec. AMNON DANAN; Chief Officer NATAN AMMAR; publ. *Ellul.*

Istituto Italiano di Cultura: 4 Marmorek St., Tel-Aviv; Dir. Prof. MAURO CURRADI.

U.S. Cultural Center: 19 Keren Hayesod St., P.O.B. 920, Jerusalem.

LANGUAGE AND LITERATURE

Academy of the Hebrew Language: P.O.B. 3449, Jerusalem, and P.O.B. 7105, Tel-Aviv; f. 1953; studies the vocabulary, structure and history of the Hebrew language and is the official authority for its development; is compiling an historical dictionary of the Hebrew language; Pres. Prof. Z. BEN-HAYYIM; Vice-Pres. Prof. S. ABRAMSON; publs. *Zikhronot, Leshonenu* (quarterly), *Leshonenu La'am*, studies, dictionaries.

Association of Religious Writers: P.O.B. 7440, Jerusalem; Chair. JACOB EUEN CHEN; publ. *Mabua.*

Hebrew Writers Association in Israel: P.O.B 7111, Tel-Aviv; Sec.-Gen. MORDECHY OT-YAKAR; publ. *Moznayim* (monthly).

Mekise Nirdamin Society: 22 Hatibonim St., Jerusalem; f. 1863; the society publishes Hebrew works of the older classical Jewish literature; 600 mems.; Pres. S. J. AGNON; Sec. Prof. E. E. URBACH.

MEDICINE

Israel Gerontological Society: P.O.B. 11243, Tel-Aviv; f. 1956; 450 mems.; Chair. Dr. H. HAR-PAZ; Vice-Chair. Dr. M. RABINOWITCH; publ. *Gerontology* (quarterly).

Israel Medical Association: Central Committee, Hadar Dafna Building, 39 Shaul Hamelech, Tel-Aviv; f. 1912; 18 brs. in Israel; 5,700 mems. in Israel, 10,000 mems. abroad; Pres. Dr. R. ISHAY; publs. *Harefuha, Mikhtav Lekhaver* (fortnightly in Hebrew), *Quarterly Review* (English), *Bulletin de L'A.M.I.* (French), *Israel Journal of Medical Science* (bi-monthly in English).

Israel Society of Allergology: 23 Balfour St., Tel-Aviv; f. 1949; about 30 mems.; Pres. Dr. N. LASS.

MUSEOLOGY

Department of Antiquities and Museums (Ministry of Education and Culture): P.O.B. 586, Jerusalem; Offices: Rockefeller Bldg., Israel Museum Compound; Store Rooms: 25 Shelomo Hamelekh St., Jerusalem; f. 1948; engages in archaeological excavations and surveys, inspection and preservation of antiquities and ancient sites, scientific publications. *See also* Israel Museum, Rockefeller Museum, Research Archives and Library of the Dept. of Antiquities; Dir. of Antiquities A. EITAN; publs. *Atiqot*† (English and Hebrew series), *Newsletter*†.

Museums Association of Israel: P.O.B. 1299, Jerusalem; f. 1966; 55 member museums; Pres. MAGEN BROSHI; publ. list of museums (English and Hebrew).

NATURAL SCIENCES

General

Academic Circle of Tel-Aviv: P.O.B. 2425, Tel-Aviv; f. 1956 to encourage all branches of scientific research and to promote co-operation between scientists in Israel and abroad; Pres. MOSHE T. HURVITZ.

Association for the Advancement of Science in Israel: P.O.B. 7266, Jerusalem; f. 1953; 4,000 mems.; Chair. Prof. M. YAMER; Sec. Prof. M. ALBECK; publ. *Proceedings of Congress of Scientific Societies.*

Biological Sciences

Biochemical Society of Israel: c/o Biochemistry Dept., Tel Aviv University, Tel Aviv; f. 1958; 350 mems.; Pres. A. TIETZ-DVIR, PH.D.; Sec. G. FEINSTEIN, PH.D.

Botanical Society of Israel: c/o The Volcani Centre, Institute of Horticulture, P.O.B. 6, Bet Dagan; aims to promote the advancement of the fundamental and applied branches of botanical science; conducts research, organizes lectures and field work; Pres. E. SALOMON; Sec. B. STEINITZ.

Zoological Society of Israel: c/o Dept. of Zoology, Tel-Aviv University, Tel-Aviv; f. 1940; 300 mems.; Chair. Dr. Y. LOYA.

Mathematics

Israel Mathematical Union: Inst. of Mathematics, Hebrew University, Jerusalem; f. 1953; 200 mems.; Chair. Prof. Y. KATZENELSON; Sec. Prof. A. ZABRODSKY.

Physical Sciences

Israel Chemical Society: 30 Yehuda Halevy St., Tel-Aviv; a scientific and professional association; holds two conventions each year and organizes lectures and symposia in various parts of Israel; the society represents Israel in the International Union of Pure and Applied Chemistry; Chair. Exec. Council Dr. HERBERT BERNSTEIN; Gen. Sec. Dr. I. BLANK.

Israel Geological Society: P.O.B. 1239, Jerusalem; f. 1954; 250 mems.; Pres. G. GVIRTZMAN; Sec. A. SNEH; publ. *Bulletin.*

Israel Physical Society: c/o Physics Dept., Bar-Ilan University, Ramat-Gan; f. 1954; 250 mems.; Pres. Prof. MARSHALL LUBAN; Sec. Dr. Y. SCHLESINGER; publs. *I.P.S. Bulletin* (annually), *IPS Annals.*

PHILOSOPHY AND PSYCHOLOGY

Israel Psychological Association: 60 Bar-Kochba St., Tel-Aviv; f. 1958; 1,500 mems.; Pres. Prof. Dr. MORDECHAI ERAN; Correspondent Dr. AMOS NIR.

RELIGION, SOCIOLOGY AND ANTHROPOLOGY

Hechal Shlomo (Seat of Chief Rabbinate): King George St., Jerusalem; f. 1958; centre for Rabbinic Research and religious information; contains Central Rabbinical Library of Israel, museum and Rabbinical Law Courts; Hechal Shlomo is governed by a Committee which includes Rabbi SHLOMO GOREN and Rabbi OVADYA YOSEPH, the Chief Rabbis of Israel; Dir. M. A. JAFFE, LL.B.

Herzog World Academy of Jewish Studies: P.O.B. 5199, Jerusalem.

Israel Oriental Society, The: The Hebrew University, Jerusalem; f. 1949; aims to promote interest in and knowledge of history, politics, economics, culture and life in the Middle East, Asia and Africa; arranges lectures and symposia to study all aspects of contemporary Middle Eastern, Asian and African affairs; Pres. A. EBAN; publs. *Hamizrah Hehadash* (*The New East*) (quarterly), *Asian and African Studies* (3 a year).

TECHNOLOGY

Association of Engineers and Architects in Israel: 200 Dizengoff Rd., Tel-Aviv; f. 1922; brs. Jerusalem, Haifa, Nathanya, Beersheba, Safed; 10,000 mems.; Chair. URIEL STOCK, C.E.; library: *see* Libraries; publs. *Journal* (monthly), *Bulletin* (monthly), in Hebrew and English), *I.T.C.C. Review* (quarterly), *Technical Progress in Israel* (monthly overseas newsletter in Hebrew and English).

Israel Society of Aeronautics and Astronautics: P.O.B. 2956, Tel-Aviv 61000; f. 1951 as Israel Society of Aeronautical Sciences, merged 1968 with Israel Astronautical Society; lectures and conferences to foster the growth of aerospace science; *c.* 400 mems.; Chair. Prof. JOSEPH SINGER; Sec. N. KLETSHEVSKY; publ. *Proceedings*.

Society of Municipal Engineers of Israel: 200 Dizengoff St., Tel-Aviv; f. 1937; 120 mems.; Pres. Ing. J. KOEN, M.A.E.A.I.; Sec. Ing. J. KORNBLUM, M.A.E.A.I.

RESEARCH INSTITUTES

GENERAL

National Council for Research and Development: Building No. 3 Hakirya, Jerusalem 91000; f. 1950; attached to the Ministry of Energy and Infrastructure; advises the Government on national policy for applied research and technological development, evaluates research needs, their national importance and industrial applicability; initiates and promotes research in special subjects when these are not under the direct responsibility of another Government Ministry (environmental quality research, water desalination, etc.); fosters scientific relations with other countries at the governmental level in co-operation with the Ministry for Foreign Affairs; operates special library on Science Policy (organization and administration, R & D, economics, statistics, scientific manpower) and special subjects (water desalination, etc.); Dir. Prof. G. HETSRONI; publs. *Israel Journal of Chemistry, Zoology, Technology, Botany, Mathematics, Earth Sciences, Medical Sciences, Current R & D Projects in Israel* (every 2 years), *Journal d'Analyse Mathématique, Scientific Research in Israel* (every 2 years).

National Centre of Scientific and Technological Information: 84 Hachashmonaim St., P.O.B. 20125, Tel-Aviv; f. 1960; aims to advance and co-ordinate scientific and technological information activities; training professional manpower in information science; to provide international contacts in the fields of information; Dir. C. KEREN; publs. *Guides to Sources of Information* (series), *Calendar to Forthcoming Scientific and Technological Meetings in Israel* (2 a year), *Desalination Abstracts* (quarterly), *Artificial Rain*, and *Contents Pages in Electricity and Electronics*.

Technion Research and Development Foundation Ltd.: Senate House, Technion City, Haifa 32000; f. 1952; operates Industrial Testing Laboratories (building materials, geodetic research, soils and roads, etc.); administers sponsored research at Technion—Israel Institute of Technology at centres for mining, energy, chemical, agricultural and bio-medical engineering, fertilizer development, environmental engineering and water resources, urban and regional studies, etc.; academic departments for chemistry, biology, physics, medicine, electrical, aeronautical and nuclear engineering, etc.; Dir. Prof. E. LENZ; publs. *Research Reports, In the Field of Building, Hamatechet*.

AGRICULTURE

Agricultural Research Organization: The Volcani Centre, P.O.B. 6, Bet-Dagan; f. 1921; fundamental and applied research in agriculture; numerous scientific projects at 5 experiment stations; part of the Min. of Agriculture; Dir. Dr. YOASH VAADIA; publs. *Phytoparasitica* (3 a year), bulletins, special publications, preliminary reports (40–50 a year), research institute reports.

Beth Gordon Agriculture and Nature Study Institute: Deganya A 15 120, Emeq Ha-Yarden; f. 1935; inaugurated 1941; regional and research centre and museum of natural history and agriculture and history of the Kinneret (Lake of Galilee) Region; Dir. and Curator of Natural History S. LULAV; Curator of Archaeology Z. VINOGRADOV (*see* library).

EDUCATION

Henrietta Szold Institute—The National Institute for Research in the Behavioural Sciences: Ruth Bressler Center for Research in Education, 9 Colombia St., Kiryat Menachem, Jerusalem; f. 1941; non-profit organization to undertake research on human behaviour, with special emphasis on children and youth; Dir. CHANAN RAPAPORT, PH.D.; publs. research reports, *Megamot* (quarterly), *Be'ad Ve-Neged* (Pro and Con) pamphlet series for teachers and youth leaders, *Mechkar Shotef BeMadaei HaHitnahagut* (Current Research in Behavioural Sciences, quarterly).

HISTORY, GEOGRAPHY AND ARCHAEOLOGY

Centre for Pre-historic Research in Israel: P.O.B. 1502, Jerusalem; f. 1958; Sec. Dr. M. W. PRAUSNITZ.

Israel Exploration Society: 3 Shemuel ha- Nagid St., P.O.B. 7041, Jerusalem; f. 1913; aims: (*a*) to engage in excavations and allied research into the history and geography of Israel; (*b*) to publish the results of such research; (*c*) to educate the public in these matters by means of congresses, general meetings, etc.; 4,000 mems.; Chair. of Exec. Cttee. Prof. A. BIRAN; Hon. Pres. Prof. B. MAZAR; Hon. Sec. J. AVIRAM; publs. *Eretz-Israel* (Hebrew annual), *Qadmoniot* (Hebrew quarterly), *Israel Exploration Journal* (English quarterly).

William Foxwell Albright Institute of Archaeological Research in Jerusalem: 26 Salah ed-Din St., Jerusalem, P.O.B. 19096; f. 1900; 2,000 mems.; library of 15,000 vols.; research projects in Semitic languages, literatures, and history; archaeological surveys and excavations; Pres. ERNEST FRERICHS; Dir. ALBERT E. GLOCK; publs. *Annual*, *Bulletin*† (quarterly), *Biblical Archaeologist*† (quarterly), *Journal of Cuneiform Studies* (quarterly), *Newsletter*† (monthly).

MEDICINE

Rogoff-Wellcome Medical Research Institute: Beilinson Medical Center, Petah-Tikva; f. 1955; attached to Tel-Aviv University; Dir. Prof. A. NOVOGRODSKY, M.D., PH.D.

NATURAL SCIENCES

General

The Natural Resources Research Organisation: 38 Keren Hayesod St., Jerusalem; attached to the Ministry of Commerce and Industry; defines R & D needs in natural resources; plans and directs the research institutes under its jurisdiction; Chief Scientist Prof. A. HERMONI. Directs the following institutions:

Institute for Petroleum Research and Geophysics: 1 Hamashbir St., Holon; f. 1957; activities devoted chiefly to the exploration of petroleum, water and mineral resources and to engineering studies in Israel and abroad; documentation unit; data processing centre; Dir. Z. BEN-ARI.

Geological Institute of Israel: 30 Malkhei Israel St., Jerusalem; f. 1949; geological mapping, research and exploration of mineral deposits; Dir. E. ZOHAR.

Israel Mining Industries: Haifa Bay, P.O.B. 303, Haifa 31000; R & D in natural resources, particularly the development of petrochemical industries; Dir. M. REIS.

Israel Oceanographic and Limnological Research Company: P.O.B. 1793, Haifa 31000; f. 1967; amalgamated with Sea Fisheries Research Station in 1972; Dir. Y. BIN NUN.

Israel Desalination Engineering (Zarchin Process) Ltd.: P.O.B. 18041, Tel-Aviv; f. 1961; to develop water desalination technology; Dir. N. BERKMAN.

The Industrial Research Organization: 13 Ben Yehuda St., Jerusalem; attached to the Ministry of Commerce and Industry; f. 1970; initiates and promotes industrial research; allocates funds; plans and directs the research institutes under its jurisdiction; Chief Scientist Prof. YITZHAK YAAKOV. Directs the following:

The Fermentation Unit: Ein Karem Campus of the Hebrew University, P.O.B. 1172, Jerusalem; f. 1960; development of processes for the production of research chemicals and enzymes; Dir. Dr. ZVI ER'EL.

The Institute for Fibres and Forest Products: 3 Emek Refaim St., P.O.B. 8001, Jerusalem; f. 1953 to advance the textile, timber, pulp, paper and leather industries; Dir. Prof. M. LEWIN.

The Center for Industrial Research: Technion City, Haifa; f. 1960 to accelerate industrial development by the application of basic-research results to production, e.g. food technology, plastics, textile and fibres, minerals and industrial chemistry; Dir. Prof. Z. RESNICK.

Israel Wine Institute: P.O.B. 529, Rehovot; f. 1957 to improve the country's wines and promote their export; Dir. CHARLES LOUANGER.

The National Physical Laboratory: Hebrew University, Givat Ram Campus, Jerusalem; f. 1950; basic physical standards and applied research in the physical sciences; special interest in energy conversion such as harnessing of solar energy; Dir. A. KALISKY.

Rubber Research Association Ltd.: Technion City, Haifa; f. 1960; the advancement of the rubber industry in Israel; Dir. D. ZIMMERMAN.

The Paint Research Association Ltd.: Technion City, Haifa; f. 1960 to improve the quality of local raw materials for the Israeli paint industry; Dir. J. Z. WHITE.

Applied Research Institute, Research and Development Authority, Ben-Gurion University of the Negev: P.O.B. 1025, Beersheva; f. 1956; engages in applied research in chemistry and chemical technology, ceramics, membrane and ion-exchange technology, process engineering, desert agriculture, natural products and development of mechanical and electromechanical products; 180 staff; library of 11,300 vols.; Dir. J. SCHECHTER; publ. *Scientific Activities*° (annually).

Biological Sciences

Israel Institute for Biological Research: P.O.B. 19, Ness-Ziona; f. 1952; both basic and applied research in fields dealing with bacterial, rickettsial, viral and mycotic diseases; oncology, air pollution, polymer science, insecticides, development and screening of new drugs; 100 scientific staff; library of 50,000 vols. and 800 periodicals; affiliated to Tel-Aviv University; 13 departments and 350 employees; Dir. I. HERTMAN, PH.D.; publ. *OHOLO Annual Biology Conference*.

Israel Center for Psychobiology: Hebrew University Hadassah Medical School, Jerusalem; f. 1971 with funds from the Charles E. Smith Family Foundation, to create a network of scientists engaged in research in psychobiology, to further co-operative programmes between existing institutions, and to train personnel in the field of psychobiology; operates through the Research and Development Authority of the Hebrew University; Dir. AMIRAM CARMON; Sec. HADASSAH SHARON.

Physical Sciences

Israel Meteorological Service: P.O.B. 25, Bet Dagan; f. 1936; provides general service to public and detailed service to various orgs.; library; various publications; Dir. Y. L. TOKATLY.

RELIGION, SOCIOLOGY AND ANTHROPOLOGY

The Harry Fischel Institute for Research in Talmud and Jewish Law: 5 Hapisgah St., P.O.B. 16002, Jerusalem; f. 1932; seminary for Rabbis and Rabbinical Judges; legislation and research publications; codification of Jewish law; Jewish adult education centre; 80 mems.; affiliated with Ariel-United Israel Institutes; Chancellor Chief Rabbi SHEAR-YASHUV COHEN, M.JUR.ADV.

Israel Association for Asian Studies: c/o Institute of Asian and African Studies, Hebrew University of Jerusalem; f. 1972 to promote teaching and research on the cultures and societies of Asia and to foster understanding of Asian affairs; Pres. Prof. HAROLD Z. SCHIFFRIN; Sec. Dr. MARTIN RUDNER.

Israel Institute of Applied Social Research: 19 George Washington St., P.O.B. 7150, Jerusalem; f. 1948; conducts research in sociology, psychology, management, communications and related fields; 50 mems.; library of 2,500 vols.: Scientific Dir. LOUIS GUTTMAN; publs. *Yedion* (Hebrew quarterly), biennial research report in English.

Israel Society for Biblical Research: 18 Rehov Abarbanel, Jerusalem; affiliated with the World Jewish Bible Society; aims to disseminate a knowledge of the scriptures by organizing lectures and meetings; brs. throughout the world, each with its own study circle of Bible scholars and research workers; Chair. (World Society) Prof. HAIM GEVARYAHU; publs. *Beth*

Mikra (Hebrew, quarterly), *Dor Le-dor* (English, quarterly), *Lemor-Decir* (Spanish, quarterly).

Yad Izhak Ben-Zvi: P.O.B. 7660, Jerusalem; f. 1964 as a non-profit foundation by the Government to honour the memory of Israel's second President; aims to foster research into the history of the Jewish community in Israel and into that of Jerusalem, to promote the study of the Jewish communities of the Middle Eastern countries, to reflect the involvement of Izhak Ben-Zvi in the Jewish community, and the Zionist and Labour Movements of Israel; Dir. Y. BEN-PORATH; publ. *Cathedra* (quarterly). Administers the following:

Institute for Research of Eretz-Israel: studies on history and culture of the Jewish people in Israel from the destruction of the Second Temple to the establishment of the State of Israel; research and studies based on the work of scientists at the main universities.

Ben-Zvi Institute for the Study of Jewish Communities in the East: P.O.B. 7504, Jerusalem; f. 1945; sponsors research in the history and culture of Jewish communities in Muslim countries from the seventh century to the present day; operates Centre for the Study of North African Jewry in co-operation with the World Organization of North African Jews; maintains a large collection of MSS, and other historical documents and photographic reproductions from the archives of libraries all over the world; Dir. Dr. Prof. AMNON COHEN; publs. *Sefunot*† (annually), *Pe'amim*† (quarterly), numerous books and documents.

There are also a Cultural and Educational Department (lectures, conferences, etc.), a Center for the Study of Jerusalem (for young people), the Library of the History of the Land of Israel and its Jewish Communities (public library based on the collection of the late Izhak and Rachel Ben Zvi), and the Historical Archives.

TECHNOLOGY

Atomic Energy Commission: 26 Rh. Hauniversita, Ramat Aviv, P.O.B. 17120, Tel-Aviv; f. 1952; advises the Government on long-term policies, priorities and the advancement of nuclear research and development; supervises the implementation of approved policies; represents Israel in relations with scientific institutions and organizations abroad; Chair. The PRIME MINISTER; Dir.-Gen. UZI EILAM.

There are two research establishments, Soreq and Negev Nuclear Research Centres.

Israel Ceramic and Silicate Institute: Technion City, Haifa; f. 1962 to broaden the scope of technical assistance to the local ceramic industry; research with special emphasis on developing the use of Israel's own raw materials; Dir. Dr. M. ISH-SHALOM.

Standards Institution of Israel: 42 University St., Ramat Aviv, Tel-Aviv; f. 1923; tests the compliance of commodities with the requirements of standard specifications; grants standard marks; conducts technological research; publishes the National Standards Specifications and Codes; library of 200,000 standards; Dir. AHARON GILAT, MECH.E.; publ. *Mati*† (quarterly).

LIBRARIES AND ARCHIVES

A.M.L.I. Central Library for Music and Dance: 26 Bialik St., Tel-Aviv (P.O.B. 4882); f. 1950; 58,400 vols., 10,800 records, Bronislav Huberman archive, Menashe Ravina archive; Librarian YAACOV SNIR.

Awkaf Supreme Council Library: The Haram Area, Jerusalem; f. 1931; contains Arabic and Islamic MSS.

Bar-Ilan University Library: Ramat-Gan; f. 1955; 200,000 bibliographical items (in 300,000 vols.) and 3,000 current journals; special collections include the Mordecai Margulies collection of rare 16th- and 17th-century Hebrew books and 800 Hebrew Oriental MSS., rare Latin and German edns. of books on Jewish studies, Old Testament criticism, material on the Dead Sea Scrolls and the Samaritans; a collection of material on the development of Religious Zionism; collection of Responsa and Jewish studies; Dir. Dr. D. KOLIEB.

Ben-Gurion University of the Negev Library: P.O.B. 653, Beersheva; f. 1966; 45,000 vols. and journals, 1,300 microfilms, 15,000 microfiche; Dir. Prof. D. MEYERSTEIN.

Bibliothèque de l'Ecole Biblique et Archéologique Française: P.O.B. 19053, 91019, Jerusalem; f. 1890; 60,000 vols.; Librarians M. SIGRIST, J. ROUSÉE.

Borochov Library: c/o Haifa Labour Council, P.O.B. 5226, Haifa; f. 1921; number of vols., 40,000 in central library, 60,000 in 24 brs.; Chief Librarian EZECHIEL OREN.

British Council Libraries: P.O.B. 3302, Tel-Aviv; f. 1950; 21,884 vols., 215 periodicals; Librarian Mrs. G. MARX; P.O.B. 7437, Jerusalem; f. 1961; 13,485 vols., 85 periodicals.

Central Agricultural Library: 25 Lilienblum St., P.O.B. 1575, Tel-Aviv; f. 1938; 32,000 books and 40,000 booklets, in Hebrew, English, Russian, German and French; Librarian ISRAEL BEN-SHEM.

Central Archives for the History of the Jewish People, The: (formerly Jewish Historical General Archives); P.O.B. 1149, Jerusalem; f. 1969; Dir. Dr. D. J. COHEN, PH.D.; this institution is intended to serve as the central archives of Jewish history; publ. *Newsletter-Ginzei Am Olam*.

Central Library of Agricultural Science: P.O.B. 12, Rehovot 76100; f. 1960; National Agricultural Library, operated jointly by the Volcani Centre of the Ministry of Agriculture's Agricultural Research Organization and the Hebrew University's Faculty of Agriculture; maintains exchange relations all over the world; 215,000 vols., 3,100 current periodicals and serials, 140,000 documents; regional libraries at Gilath, Ilanoth, Dor and N've Ya'ar; Dir. N. CZARNY.

Central Rabbinical Library of Israel: Heichal Shlomo, Jerusalem; f. 1953; 50,000 vols. on Rabbinica and Judaica; Dir. and Chief Librarian Rabbi Dr. ZVI HARKAVY; publ. *Hasefer* (The Book, annual).

Central Zionist Archives, The: P.O.B. 92, Jerusalem; f. 1919; number of volumes 83,000, 4,500 m. of files; 4,700 newspapers, 400,000 pictures, 354 private archives and collections; 250 magnetic tapes; 165,000 items of small printed matter; Dir. Dr. M. HEYMANN; Librarian Mrs. H. ABRAHAMI; publs. complete Hebrew edn. of Theodor Herzl's writings; guides to the collections; selected documents; *Zionist Literature* (bibliographic bulletin, 6 a year).

"Dvir Bialik" Municipal Central Public Library: Hibat-Zion St. 14, Ramat-Gan; f. 1945; 200,000 vols., including special Rabbinic literature and Social Sciences collection; maintains ten branches; Chief Librarian JERACHMIEL SLUZKY.

General Archives of the City of Tel-Aviv-Yafo: Municipality Building, Kikar Malkhei Israel, Tel-Aviv; Chief Registrar PINCHAS RASSIS; Archivist Dr. ARYEH YODFAT.

Gulbenkian Library (Donated by the late Mr. Calouste Gulbenkian): Armenian Patriarchate, P.O.B. 14106, Old City, Jerusalem; f. 1929; the library is one of the three great Armenian libraries in the diaspora, the others being the Mekhitarist Fathers' Library in Venice and another in Vienna; public library circa 75,000 vols. of which 30,000 are Armenian and 45,000 in French and English with a few in other languages; Sec. and Librarian Sahag Kalaydjian; receives over 360 newspapers, magazines, periodicals (of which more than half are Armenian) from foreign countries; complete collections of newspapers and magazines dating from the 1850s, and a copy of the first Armenian newspaper, *Aztarar*, published in Madras in 1794; a copy of the first printed Armenian Bible (1666), and a copy of the first printed Armenian map of the world (1695); library of 3,800 Armenian MSS. (Manuscripts Librarian Bishop Norayr Bogharian); publ. *Sion* (monthly, official organ of the Armenian Patriarchate).

Israel State Archives: Prime Minister's Office, Jerusalem; f. 1949; comprises six sections: Department of Files and Manuscripts, Library Department, Records Management, Supervision Department of Public and Private Archives, Services to the Public, Technical Services Department and Publication of State Papers; holdings include files occupying 20 kilometres of shelving, 150,000 printed items and 25,000 books; administrative records are accessible after 20 years, records on foreign relations after 30 years and on defence after 50 years; to be re-housed in a central Archives Building to be erected opposite the Knesset, together with the Central Archives of the Jewish People, the Central Zionist Archives of the Jewish Agency; State Archivist P. A. Alsberg, ph.d.; various publs.

Jerusalem City (Public) Library: Beth Ha'am, Jerusalem; f. 1961; 750,000 vols.; 25 brs. and 3 Bookmobiles; Dir. Abraham Vilner.

Jewish National and University Library: P.O.B. 503, Jerusalem 91000; f. 1892; number of volumes: two million, including those in departmental libraries; over 10,000 MSS.; 200 incunabula (120 Hebrew and 80 in other languages); large medical department with 160,000 bound vols. of periodicals, and 45,000 books; 17,000 current periodicals; laboratory for preservation and restoration of books and MSS.; special collections include the Dr. Abraham Schwadron Collection of Jewish Autographs and Portraits, Yahuda Collection, Dr. Israel Mehlman Collection of Hebraica, the Dr. Harry Friedenwald Collection on the History of Medicine, the Prof. M. Buber archives, the National Sound Archives and the Jacob Michael Collection of Jewish Music; Dir. Prof. Malachi Beit-Arié; Head Librarian Prof. Peretz Tishby; Head Technical Services Dr. Jonathan Joel; publs. *Kirjath Sepher* (bibliography, quarterly), *Index of Articles on Jewish Studies* (annually).

Kfar Giladi Library: Kfar Giladi, Upper Galilee; f. 1934; number of volumes 35,000, 110 periodicals; maintains reading-room for members of the Kfar Giladi settlement; organizes concerts and exhibitions of paintings; collection of classical music records; Librarian M. O. Mayer.

Library of Life Sciences and Medicine, Tel-Aviv University: P.O.B. 39345, Ramat-Aviv, Tel-Aviv; f. 1964; 150,000 vols., 1,700 periodicals and serials; inc. the Morris and Ida Leikind Medical History Collection; Dir. Ilana Peled.

Library of the Beth Gordon Institute of Agriculture and Nature Study: Deganya A 15 120, Emeq Ha Yarden; 55,000 vols. of which 17,000 in Hebrew; also periodicals; Librarian T. Loewenkopf.

Library of the Association of Engineers and Architects in Israel: 200 Dizgenoff Rd., Tel-Aviv; f. 1939; covers all branches of engineering and chemical technology; open to the general public; 20,000 vols., 300 current periodicals; Librarian Mrs. M. Gillam.

Library of the Central Bureau of Statistics: P.O.B. 13015, Hakirya 91-130, Jerusalem; f. 1948; *c.* 25,000 vols.; Dir. D. Neumann; Librarian Mrs. M. Helfgott; all publs. available for exchange.

Library of the Israel Department of Antiquities and Museums (Ministry of Education and Culture): Rockefeller Bldg., P.O.B. 586, Jerusalem; collections mainly on the archaeology, ancient history and civilizations of Israel and the ancient Near East; *c.* 50,000 vols.; Librarian Wanda Aftergood.

Library of the Knesset: Knesset, Jerusalem; f. 1949; principally for members' use; 150,000 vols., including books, bound periodicals and collection of all Israeli Government publications, UN publications and foreign parliamentary papers; Librarian Dr. Erika Yeshaiahu.

Library of the Ministry of Foreign Affairs: Jerusalem; f. 1948; 38,000 vols., 300 periodicals.

Library of the Ministry of Justice: P.O.B. 1087, 29 Saladin Rd., Jerusalem; f. 1922; including 19 branch libraries, 49,000 vols.; Chief Librarian Dr. A. Silberfeld.

Library of the Seminar Hakibbutzim: Tel-Aviv; 54,000 vols.; Librarian Rachel Shachar.

Library of the Studium Biblicum Franciscanum: P.O.B. 19424, Monastery of the Flagellation, via Dolorosa, Jerusalem; f. 1924; 15,000 vols.; chiefly on archaeology, judaeo-christianism, biblical and patristic studies; 20 mems.; Librarian A. Donneschi; publs. *Liber Annuus*† (annually), *Collectio Maior*† *Collectio Minor*†, *Analecta*†, *S.B.F. Museum*†.

Library of the Supreme Court: Jerusalem; f. 1949; 40,000 vols.; Librarian J. Hai Isac.

Library of Tel-Hai Regional College: Upper Galilee, nr. Kiryat Shmona 12210; 20,000 vols., 260 periodicals; includes the Calvary Collection; audiovisual department and pedagogic centre; Library Dir. Carol Hoffman.

Municipal Library in Memory of William and Chia Boorstein: Nahariva; f. 1946; under the supervision of the Ministry of Education and Culture, Jerusalem; number of volumes, 65,000; Chief Librarian Ruth Segal.

Pevsner Public Library: 54 Pevsner St., P.O.B. 5345, Haifa; f. 1934; 200,000 vols. covering all fields of literature and science, in Hebrew, English and German; 11 brs.; Chief Librarian Dr. S. Back.

Rambam Library: 25 King Saul Blvd., Tel-Aviv; f. 1935; 60,000 vols.; specializes in Judaica; Librarian Rabbi R. Elitzur.

Research Archives of the Israel Department of Antiquities and Museums (Ministry of Education): P.O.B. 586, Jerusalem; f. 1948; written records, photographic records, maps and plans; Dir. of Antiquities A. Eitan; Archivist R. Reich.

Schocken Library: Rehavia, Jerusalem; f. 1900; number of vols. 55,000, MSS. 200, photostats (Hebrew Liturgy and Poetry) 20,000; Librarian H. J. Katzenstein.

Sourasky Central Library, Tel-Aviv University: P.O.B. 39038, Ramat-Aviv, Tel-Aviv; f. 1954; 500,000 vols. and 5,000 current periodicals; includes the Pevsner Collection of Hebrew Press, the Faitlovitch collection, the Collection of Yiddish Literature and Culture in memory of Benzion and Pearl Margulies; Dir. Dr. Dan Simon.

Technion—Israel Institute of Technology, Library System: Technion City, Haifa 32000; f. 1925; oldest and largest centre for scientific and technical information in Israel; open to the public; Elyacher (Central) Library, 22 departmental libraries; 350,000 vols., 200,000 bound periodicals, 4,000 current periodicals; Dir. NURIT ROITBERG.

Tel-Aviv Central Public Library "Shaar Zion": 25 King Saul Blvd., P.O.B. 33235, Tel-Aviv; f. 1891; 500,000 vols. (in 20 branches); General Library in 8 languages; Dir. ISRAEL SHAPIRO.

University of Haifa Library: Mount Carmel, Haifa; f. 1963; 500,000 vols., 9,000 periodicals; special collections include Abba Houshi Archives, rare books, area studies, media centre, 60,000 art slides; Dir. SHMUEL SEVER, PH.D.; publ. *Index to Hebrew Periodicals* (annually).

Weizmann Archives: Neveh Weizmann, Rehovoth; f. 1950; contains assembled letters, papers, and other documents relating to political and scientific activities of late First President of Israel; approx. 100,000 items; Weizmann Exhibition gives graphic depiction of late President's life; Curator Archives NEHAMA A. CHALOM.

Weizmann Institute of Science Libraries: Rehovot; f. 1934; Wix Central Library and five regional libraries; number of vols.: 125,430; Librarian Mrs. A. ROSENHECK; publs. *Weizmann Institute of Science, Scientific Activities*†.

Workers' Library: New Histadrut Building, Jerusalem; f. 1950; 95,000 vols., including children's books, fiction and popular science; special emphasis on Hebrew literature, Jewish history and social sciences; three branch libraries; Chief Librarian SHALOM YOELI.

Y.M.C.A. Library: P.O. Box 294, David Hamelech St., Jerusalem; f. 1933; number of vols. *c.* 25,000; Librarian ARDAVAST OHANESSIAN.

MUSEUMS

Akko Municipal Museum: Akko, Old City; f. 1954; housed in an old Turkish bathhouse; collections of local antiquities; medieval and modern Arab and Druze folklore; arms and oriental jewellery section; Crusader excavations including the once famous quarter of the Knights of St. John (Hospitalers), the Knights' Halls, the Grand Maneir, the Refectory (Crypt), the Tunnel and the Domus Infirmorum; Dir. M. YEHIELI.

Archaeological (Rockefeller) Museum: Rockefeller Bldg., East Jerusalem; f. 1938; formerly Palestine Archaeological Museum; archaeology of Israel from earliest times up until end of Islamic period; largely material found in excavations before 1948; Curator MICHAL DAYAGI.

Beit Chaim Sturman House: Museum and regional centre for science and education in Gilboa-Beth-Shean Region; District Council Gilboa, M.P. Gilboa; f. 1941; depts. of archaeology, history, economy, natural history and defence; Dir. ABRAHAM LOEWY.

Beit Ha'Omanim (*Jerusalem Artists' House*): 12 Shmuel Hanagid St., Jerusalem; David Hamelech St., Jerusalem; exhibitions and permanent gallery of works by Jerusalem artists.

Caesarea Museum: Kibbutz Sedot Yam; f. 1950; collection of antiquities from the region of ancient Caesarea; Dir. A. WEGMAN.

Ethnological Museum and Folklore Archives: 19 Arlosoroff St., Haifa; f. 1956; ethnographical material from all countries, with special emphasis on Israel and Jewish objects; collection of folk tales from Israel; Hebrew publications including English summaries of Jewish folk-literature; Dir. Prof. Dr. DOV NOY; publs. exhibition catalogues† (bilingual Hebrew and English).

Glicenstein Museum: Safad; f. 1953; paintings and sculptures of the late Hanoch Glicenstein; Bernard Shapiro collection; exhibitions of various artists; Dir. ISAAC LICHTENSTEIN.

Haaretz Museum: Ramat Aviv, Tel-Aviv, P.O.B. 17068; comprises museums and excavations listed below; library of approx. 7,000 vols.; Dir.-Gen. J. CALEFF.

Alphabet Museum: f. 1965; documentary exhibition on the development of the alphabets; Dir. Mrs. Z. SUCHOWOLSKI.

Ceramics Museum: f. 1966; exhibition showing pottery in service of men and demonstrating the significance of pottery in the study of human history; Curator Mrs. UZZA ZEVULUN.

Glass Museum: f. 1959; contains ancient glass from about 1500 B.C.; Curator GUSTA LEHRER.

Historical Museum of Tel-Aviv-Yafo: 27 Bialik St., Tel-Aviv-Yafo; f. 1959; documents, letters, notes and photographs relating to the City's foundation; Dir. Mrs. A. KAPLAN.

Independence Hall: f. 1978; exhibition of the events of the three days that preceded the founding of the State of Israel.

Israel Theater Museum: f. 1975; documentary material on the Jewish theatre from its origin; Dir. J. GABBAY.

Kadman Numismatic Museum: f. 1962; history of coinage from beginnings to present day; Dir. A. KINDLER.

Lasky Planetarium: f. 1966; Dir. Mrs. B. NEVO.

Man and His Work Museum: f. 1980; exhibition of the history of work implements, production installations and processes in Eretz-Israel; Dir. Prof. S. AVITZUR.

Museum of Antiquities of Tel-Aviv-Yafo: f. 1961; exhibition of archaeological findings excavated in the Yafo-Tel-Aviv area, ranging from Neolithic to Byzantine Period; Dir. Dr. J. KAPLAN.

Museum of Ethnography and Folklore: f. 1963; exhibition of Jewish popular art and costumes; Dir. Ing. D. DAVIDOWITZ.

Museum of Science and Technology: f. 1964; exhibition of applied mathematics, physics, aeronautics, energy; Dir. Mrs. R. DANOR.

Tel-Quasila Excavations: f. 1948; findings from excavations of Israelite city, ranging from Period of Monarchy to Islamic Period.

Nechustan Pavilion—Timna Excavations: f. 1968; finds from the Timna excavations; Curator Dr. B. ROTHENBERG.

Young Persons' Institute for the Promotion of Art and Science: f. 1968; guided tours and lectures for children and adults; workshops and summer camps; special department for gifted children; Dir. Dr. E. LANDAU.

Haifa Museum of Modern Art: 26 Shabbetai Levi St., Haifa; f. 1951; collections of Israeli and world contemporary art, prints, art posters, paintings and sculptures; library of 10,000 vols.; Dir. GABRIEL TADMOR.

Israel Museum: Jerusalem; f. 1965; Dir. YORAM RAVIN; publ. *Israel Museum News* (annually). Comprises the following collections:

"Bezalel" National Art Museum: f. 1906; large collection of Jewish ceremonial art, ethnological objects, paintings, sculptures, drawings and prints; temporary exhibitions; lending library of reproductions and slides; Chief Curator Dr. MARTIN WEYL.

Billy Rose Art Garden: designed by Isamo Noguchi; contains collection of modern European, American and Israeli sculpture and Reuven Lipchitz collection of Jacques Lipchitz's bronze sketches; Curator Dr. MARTIN WEYL.

Bronfman Biblical and Archaeological Museum: f. 1965; very large collection of archaeology of Israel from earliest times to Islamic and Crusader periods; material found in excavations since 1948; neighbouring cultures (from Iran to Italy); Chief Curator Mrs. MIRIAM TADMOR.

Ruth Youth Wing: permanent and travelling educational exhibitions; 55 classes in painting, sculpture, drama, movement, etc.; Chief Curator Mrs. AYALA GORDON.

Shrine of the Book: D. Samuel and Jeanne H. Gottesman Center for Biblical MSS.; houses the Dead Sea Scrolls (discovered in Qumran) and manuscripts from adjacent sites on western shore of the Dead Sea, Masada and Nahal Hever; Curator MAGEN BROSHI.

Library: 65,000 vols. and catalogues; Librarian ELISHEVA RECHTMAN.

Jabotinsky Institute in Israel: 38 King George St., P.O.B. 23110, Tel Aviv 63298.

Ma'ayan Baruch Prehistoric Museum of the Huleh Valley: Ma'ayan Baruch, Upper Galilee; f. 1952; regional antiquities including implements from all prehistoric periods and exhibits from Middle Bronze Age tombs and from Roman and Byzantine periods; Dir. A. ASSAF.

Municipal Museum: Beit Shean; f. 1949; housed in a 15th-century mosque; prehistoric flint, pottery, bronze, etc.; finds from all periods particularly Canaanite, Israelite, Roman and Byzantine, including a 6th-century monastery and several new excavations; Roman villa mosaics and funerary busts, artefacts and floor mosaics from secular and religious structures of the Jewish and Christian communities in Scythopolis—Beit Shean of the Byzantine period; outstanding selection of Roman and Byzantine decorated capitals in museum garden; library of 450 vols.; Dir. ARIE EIZENBERG.

Municipal Museum of Antiquities: Lake Front, Tiberias; f. 1953; collection of antiquities from Tiberias and region, mainly of the Roman, Byzantine and Arab periods; Dir. ELISHEVA BALLHORN.

Museum of Ancient Art: 26 Shabatai Levi St., Haifa; f. 1948; Cypriot, Greek and Roman sculpture and terracottas; archaeological findings from Shikmona (Haifa) from the Bronze Age to the Byzantine period; decorated vases; Curator ZEMER AVSHALOM.

Museum of Japanese Art: 89 Hanassi Ave., Haifa; f. 1960; 6,500 items; paintings, prints, drawings, textiles, netsuke, lacquer work, ceramics, metalwork, collection of Mingei (folk art); library of 2,500 vols.; Dir ELI LANCMAN; publs. catalogues†.

Museum of Prehistory: Sha'ar Ha-golan, Jordan Valley; f. 1950; large number of exhibits from the neolithic Yarmukian culture excavated in the region; Dir. Y. ROTH.

Museum of Prehistory of the Institute of Archaeology in the Hebrew University: Mt. Scopus Campus, Jerusalem; f. 1955; large collection of objects from prehistoric sites in Israel; library.

Museum of the Studium Biblicum Franciscanum: P.O.B. 19424, Monastery of the Flagellation, Via Dolorosa, Jerusalem; f. 1923; Palestinian archaeology: city coins of Palestine, Roman-Byzantine-Crusader pottery and objects; Curator M. PICCIRILLO; publ. *S.B.F. Museum*†.

National Maritime Museum: 198 Allenby Rd., Haifa; f. 1954; large collection of ship models illustrating 5,000 years of navigation and shipbuilding, old maps, undersea archaeology, and ancient coins connected with seafaring and maritime symbols; civilizations of ancient peoples and marine ethnology; scientific instruments; Dir. Lt.-Cdr. A. BEN-ELI; publs. *Sefunim*†, *Bulletin* (irregular).

Negev Museum: Beersheva; f. 1954; exhibits from regional excavations, mainly from the Chalcolithic, Israelite, Roman and Byzantine periods; Bedouin Folklore collection; history of Beersheva; Curator JOSEPH DUBI.

Shephela Museum: Kibbutz Kefar-Menahem 79875, Post Kefar-Menahem; f. 1949; educational museum for creative activity and instructive exhibitions; collections of regional antiquities, fine arts and children's art; Dir. M. ISRAEL; publs. *Museum News, Chronicle*† (6–10 a year) (in Hebrew), *For the Young Visitor*† (in Hebrew), catalogues, guides†.

Tel-Aviv Museum: 27-29 Shaul Hameleh Blvd.; also at Helena Rubinstein Pavilion, 6 Tarsat St., Tel-Aviv; f. 1931; art collection consisting of works from the 17th century to the present day; collection of Israeli art; temporary exhibitions of fine arts, design, photography; art library containing over 30,000 vols.; concerts, lectures and films on art; workshops, educational activities and circulating exhibitions service Dir. MARC SCHEPS.

Tel Hai Museum: Upper Galilee, nr. Kiryat Shmona, 12210; reconstruction of a Jewish settlement from the beginning of the 20th century; documents of Joseph Trumpeldor and his defence of the region in 1920.

Terra Sancta Museum: Terra Sancta Monastery, P.O.B. 23, Nazareth; f. 1920; Byzantine (and later) remains, coins, Roman and Byzantine glass; collection of antiquities from excavations made in the monastery compound; Vicar of Monastery Rev. P. JOSÉ MONTALVERNE DE LANCASTRE, O.F.M.

Y.M.C.A. "Herbert E. Clark" Collection of Near Eastern Antiquities: Y.M.C.A. Building, King David St., Jerusalem; f. 1933; flint implements, pottery, glass, jewellery, cylinder seals, cuneiform tablets, scarabs, terracotta and bronze figurines.

UNIVERSITIES

BAR-ILAN UNIVERSITY

RAMAT-GAN

Telephone: 718111.

Founded 1953; inaugurated 1955.

Private control; Language of instruction: Hebrew; Academic year: October to June.

President: Prof. E. RACKMAN, PH.D.
Rector: Prof. S. ECKSTEIN, PH.D.
Director-General: S. MAYEVSKY (acting).
Registrar: A. POMERANTZ, M.JUR.
Librarian: J. MOLAD.

Library: *see* Libraries.

Number of teaching staff: 1,100.
Number of students: 10,000.

Publications: *Bar-Ilan Annual*† (Judaica), *Bar-Ilan Volume*† (Humanities and Social Studies), Research Monographs†, Annual Catalogue†, *Criticism and Interpretation*† (quarterly review), *Archive of the New Rabbinical Hebrew Dictionary*†, *Philosophia*† (quarterly).

DEANS:

Faculty of Jewish Studies: Dr. MENACHEM COHEN.
Faculty of Humanities: Prof. DAVID SOHLBERG.
Faculty of Social Sciences: Prof. YAAKOV RAND.
Faculty of Natural Sciences: Prof. SHLOMO GROSSMAN.
Faculty of Law: Prof. HERBERT SCHREIBER

PROFESSORS:

Faculty of Jewish Studies:
ARTZI, P., PH.D., Hebrew Language and History
BARZEL, H., PH.D., Hebrew Literature
BEER, M., PH.D., Jewish History
ELIAV, M., PH.D. Jewish History
GILAT, Y., PH.D., Talmud
GOSHEN-GOTTSTEIN, M., PH.D., Bible and Semitic Philology
KADDARI, M. Z., Hebrew and Semitic Languages
KATZBURG, N., PH.D., Jewish History
RATZHABI, Y., PH.D. Hebrew Literature
RUBENSTEIN, A., PH.D., Jewish History
SALTMAN, A., PH.D., History
SCHARF, A., PH.D., History
SCHWARZFUCHS, S., PH.D., Jewish History
SPERBER, D., PH.D., Talmud

Faculty of Humanities:
AMADO LEVY-VALENSI, E., PH.D., Philosophy
CHURGIN, B., PH.D., Musicology
FISCH, H., B.LITT., English
ROSTON, M., PH.D., English
SHA'ANAN, A., PH.D., World Literature

Faculty of Social Sciences:
AMIR, Y., PH.D., Psychology
DESHEN, S., PH.D., Sociology and Anthropology
DON, Y., PH.D., Economics
ECKSTEIN, S., PH.D., Economics
ELAZAR, D., PH.D., Political Studies
GLANZ, J., PH.D., Education
KRAUSZ, E., PH.D., Sociology
LAPPIN, B., D.S.W., School of Social Work
LAZAROVITCH, B., PH.D., Sociology
LIEBMAN, Y., PH.D., Political Sciences
LOWENBERG, F., PH.D., School of Social Work
PARUSH, Y., PH.D., Economics
WELLER, L., PH.D., Sociology

Faculty of Natural Sciences and Mathematics:
ALBECK, M., PH.D., Chemistry
AVIEZER, N., PH.D., Physics
BASCH, H., PH.D., Chemistry
FELIKS, Y., PH.D., Botany
FREUND, Y., PH.D., Physics
GABAI, D., PH.D., Mathematics
GREENFIELD, J., PH.D., Physics
JAMMER, M., PH.D., Physics
KANTOROVITZ, S., PH.D., Mathematics
LESHEM, Y., PH.D., Life Sciences
LUBAN, M., PH.D., Physics
PINSKY, E., PH.D., Biology
SIMPSON, S., PH.D., Life Sciences
SOMPOLINSKY, D., M.D., PH.D., Microbiology
SPRECHER, M., PH.D., Chemistry

Faculty of Law:
ALBECK, S., PH.D.
BARIS, P., LL.D.
ENKER, A., LL.B.

AFFILIATED SCHOOLS AND INSTITUTES:

School of Education.
Director: J. GLANTZ, PH.D.

School of Social Work.
Director: Mrs. F. MITTWOCH.

Institute for the Study of Jews in Islamic Lands: incorporates the Rivlin Institute for the study of the Old Yishuv.
Director: Prof. S. SCHWARTSFUCHS.

Institute for the Study of Jews in Diaspora.
Director: Prof. E. STERN.

Institute of Local Government.
Director: Dr. KALCHAN.

Institute for Advanced Torah Studies.
Director: (vacant).

Institute for Research into Religious Zionism.
Director: Prof. N. KATZBURG, PH.D.

Institute for Accountancy Research.
Director: Prof. S. FLINK, PH.D.

Institute for Data Retrieval.
Director: Y. CHOUEKA, PH.D.

Centre for Lexicography.
Directors: Prof. M. GOSHEN-GOTTSTEIN, PH.D., Prof. M. Z. KADDARI, PH.D.

EVERYMAN'S UNIVERSITY

16 KLAUSNER ST., RAMAT AVIV, P.O.B. 39328, TEL AVIV

Telephone: (03) 422511.

Founded 1974; first courses 1976. Sponsored by Government and Rothschild Foundation. Aims to provide in-service teacher education, degree courses for disadvantaged students, vocational and pre-academic courses and adult education; Language of instruction: Hebrew.

President: Prof. AVRAHAM GINZBURG.
Registrar: SARA JOLLES.
Librarian: Mrs. LEONORE COHEN.

Library of 4,500 vols. and audio-visual material.

Number of students: 9,000.

HEADS OF DEPARTMENTS:

Natural Sciences: Prof. A. ADAM.
Mathematics: Prof. A. GINZBURG.
Liberal Arts: Prof. M. ROSTON.
Jewish Studies: Prof. S. FRIEDLANDER.

HAIFA UNIVERSITY

MOUNT CARMEL, HAIFA

Telephone: 240111.

Founded 1963.

Language of instruction: Hebrew; Academic year: October to June.

President: GERSHON AVNER.
Rector: Prof. E. O. SCHILD.
Librarian: Prof. SHMUEL SEVER.

Number of teachers: 350.
Number of students: 6,200.

DEANS:

Graduate School: Prof. A. RAPPAPORT.
Humanities: Prof. Y. MANSOUR.
Social and Mathematical Sciences: Prof. M. LANSBERG.

HEADS OF DEPARTMENTS:

Humanities:
Arabic Language and Literature: ISRAEL SCHEIN.
Biblical Studies: Dr. Z. WEISSMANN.
Creative Art: A. OFEK.
English Language and Literature: Dr. L. PRAGER.
Eretz Israel Studies: Prof. AVRAHAM RONEN.
Foreign Language Studies: Dr. DONALD SIM.
French Language and Literature: Dr. JACQUELINE MICHEL.
General History: Dr. DAVID GOLAN.
General Literature: Dr. CHARLOTTE YARDI.
Hebrew Language: Dr. MOSHE AZAR.
Hebrew Literature: Dr. ALIZA SHEN HAR.
History of Art: Dr. J. HOFFMAN.
History of the Jewish People: Dr. D. GOLDBLATT.
History of the Maritime Civilizations: Dr. A. LINDER.
History of the Middle East: Dr. D. GILBAR.
Jewish Thought: Prof. SARAH HELER WILENSKI.
Librarianship: Prof. S. SEVER.

Philosophy: Prof. ABRAHAM KAPLAN.
Social and Mathematical Sciences:
Computer Studies: Prof. LUBA BREZINIA.
Economics: Prof. A. MELNICK.
Geography: Dr. B. KIPNIS.
Kibbutz and Co-operative Movement: M. ROSNER.
Mathematics: Prof. JONATHAN GOLAN.
Political Science: Dr. A. BRICHTA.
Psychology: Dr. B. NEVO.
School of Social Work: Prof. NAOMI GOLAN.
Sociology and Anthropology: Dr. O. SHAPIRO.
Statistics: Dr. B. LEWIKSON.
School of Education: Dr. ADIR COHEN.
Department of Education: Dr. LEA KRAMER.
The A. Biram Department of High School Training: Dr. MIRIAM BEN PERERETZ.
Evolutionary Biology: Prof. A. NEVO.

THE HEBREW UNIVERSITY OF JERUSALEM

MOUNT SCOPUS, JERUSALEM
Telephone: 02-882111.
Telex: 26458 SCOPM IL.
Founded 1918; inaugurated 1925.

Private control, partially supported by the Government; Academic year: October to June; Language of instruction: Hebrew.

Chairman, Board of Governors: SAMUEL ROTHBERG.
President: AVRAHAM HARMAN.
Rector: Prof. RAPHAEL MECHOULAM.
Vice-Presidents: BERNARD CHERRICK, SIMCHA DINITZ, Prof. ALEXANDER KEYNAN, Prof. MICHAEL SCHLESINGER, Prof. JOASH VAADIA.
Academic Secretary: SHLOMO BIRNBAUM.
Director, Department of Information and Public Affairs: ELIGAHU HONIG.
Library Director: Prof. MALACHI BEIT-ARIE.

Libraries: *see* Libraries.

Number of teachers: 2,235.

Number of students: *c.* 15,000.

Publications include: *Scopus* (annually in English), *Ha-Universita* (annually in Hebrew), *News from the Hebrew University* (quarterly in English, 2 a year in Spanish, French and German), faculty handbooks, etc.

DEANS AND DIRECTORS:

Faculty of Humanities: Prof. NEHEMIA LEVTZION.
Faculty of Science: Prof. SHLOMO ALEXANDER.
Faculty of Medicine: Prof. SHAUL FELDMAN.
Faculty of Law: Prof. CLAUDE KLEIN.
Faculty of Agriculture: Prof. AMRAM ASHRI.
Faculty of Social Science: Prof. JOSEPH YAHAR.
Faculty of Dental Medicine: Prof. YAIR SHARAV.
School of Education: Prof. SEYMOUR FOX.
Paul Baerwald School of Social Work: Prof. ABRAHAM DORON.
Graduate School of Library and Archive Studies: Dr. DOV SHIDORSKY.
School of Applied Science and Technology: Prof. DOV FROHMAN-BENTCHKOWSKY.
School of Nutritional and Domestic Sciences: Dr. NAOMI TROSTLER.
School of Business Administration: Dr. YORAM PELES.
School for Overseas Students: Dr. ZEEV KLEIN.
Dean of Students: Prof. LINA BEN-DOR.

PROFESSORS:

Faculty of Humanities:
(including the Institutes of: Jewish Studies; Contemporary Jewry; Asian and African Studies; Archaeology, Philosophy and History; Languages, Literatures and Art; School of Education; Sir Isaac Wolfson Center for Talmudic Studies.)

ABRAMSON, S., D.H.L., Talmud
ADAR, Z., PH.D., Secondary Education
ADLER, I., DR. 3E CYCLE, Musicology
AMIT, M., PH.D., Ancient History
ARIELI, Y., PH.D., American History
ASHERI, D., PH.D., History
AYALON, D., PH.D., History of the Muslim Countries
BARASCH, M., Architecture and Fine Arts
BAER, G., PH.D., History of the Muslim Countries
BAUER, Y., PH.D., Holocaust Studies
BEINART, H., PH.D., History of the Jewish People
BLANC, H., PH.D., Arabic Linguistics
BLAU, J., PH.D., Islamic Studies
BRANDWAJN, R., PH.D., French Language and Literature
BREGEL, Y., PH.D., History of Muslim Countries
DALESKI, H., PH.D., English Literature
DAN, J., PH.D., Jewish Thought
DAVIS, M., PH.D., American Jewish History and Institutions
ETTINGER, S., PH.D., Jewish History
FLEISCHER, E., PH.D., Hebrew Literature
FLUSSER, D., PH.D., Comparative Religion
FRIEDLANDER, D., PH.D., Demography
GOLDBERG, A., PH.D., Talmud
GOSHEN-GOTTSTEIN, M., PH.D., Semitic Linguistics and Biblical Philology
GREENBERG, M., PH.D., Bible
GREENFIELD, J. C., PH.D., Ancient Semitic Languages
GROLL, S., PH.D., Egyptology
HARAN, M., PH.D., Bible
HARRAN, D., PH.D., Musicology
HARKABI, Y., PH.D., International Relations and Middle East Affairs
JACOBY, D., DR., History
KARMON, Y., PH.D., Geography
KISTER, M., PH.D., Arabic Language and Literature
LEVTZION, N., PH.D., African and Islamic History.
LORIAN, A., DR., French Civilization
MALAMAT, A., PH.D., Jewish History (Biblical Period)
MIRON, D., PH.D., Hebrew Literature
MIRSKY, A., PH.D., Hebrew Literature
MORAG, S., PH.D., Hebrew Linguistics
MUSSA, G., PH.D., German History
NEVO, R., PH.D., English Language and Literature
PAGIS, D., PH.D., Hebrew Literature
PERLMAN, I., PH.D., Archeometrical Chemistry (Archaeology)
PRAWER, J., PH.D., Medieval History
RABIN, CH., PH.D., DR.PHIL., Hebrew Language
ROSEN, H., PH.D., General and Indo-European Linguistics
ROTENSTREICH, N., PH.D., Philosophy
SAFRAI, S., PH.D., Jewish History
SEGAL, D., PH.D., Russian and Slavic Studies and Comparative Literature
SERMONETA, J., PH.D., Jewish Thought, Romance Studies and Philosophy.
SHAKED, G., PH.D., Hebrew Literature
SHAKED, S., PH.D., Iranian Studies and Comparative Religion
SHILOAH, A., PH.D., Musicology
SHINAR, P., PH.D., Islamic Civilization
SHMERUK, CH., PH.D., Yiddish Literature
SIVAN, D., DR., History
STERN, M., PH.D., History of the Second Temple
TADMOR, H., PH.D., Assyriology
TAL, J., Musicology
TALMON, S., PH.D., Bible
URBACH, E., DOTT. in LETT., Talmud
WASSERSTEIN, A., PH.D., Greek
WEINFELD, M., PH.D., Bible
WERBLOWSKY, Z., D. ÈS L., Comparative Religion and History of Jewish Thought
WERSES, S., Hebrew Literature
YADIN, Y., PH.D., Archaeology
ZAND, M., Persian and Tajik Literature

Faculty of Social Sciences:
(the Eliezer Kaplan School of Economics and Social Sciences; includes the Jerusalem School of Business Administration)

AMIRAN, D., DR.PHIL.NAT., Geography
AVINERI, S., PH.D., Political Science
BARKAI, H., PH.D., Economics
BEN-DAVID, J., PH.D., Sociology
BEN-PORATH, Y., PH.D., Economics
BRUNO, M., PH.D., Economics
DROR, Y., S.J.D., Public Administration
EISENSTADT, S. N., PH.D., Sociology
GUTTMAN, E. L., PH.D., Social and Psychological Measurement
HANOCH, G., PH.D., Economics
INBAR, M., PH.D., Sociology
KAGAN, A., PH.D., Statistics
KAHNEMAN, D., PH.D., Psychology
KATZ, E., PH.D., Sociology and Communications
KLEIMAN, E., PH.D., Economics
KUGELMASS, S., PH.D., Psychology
LANDAU, J., PH.D., Political Science
LEVHARI, D., PH.D., Economics
LEVY, H., PH.D., Business Administration
LISSAK, M., PH.D., Sociology
LIVIATAN, N., PH.D., Economics
MICHAELY, M., PH.D., International Trade
MUHSAM, H., D. ÈS SC., Demography and Statistics
NIR, D., PH.D., Geography
PATINKIN, D., PH.D., Economics
SAMUEL-CAHN, E., PH.D., Statistics
SARNAT, M., PH.D., Business Administration
SCHICK, A. P., PH.D., Geography
SCHLESINGER, I., PH.D., Psychology
SELIGER, M., PH.D., Political Science
SHARKANSKY, I., PH.D., Political Science
SHESHINSKI, E., PH.D., Public Finance
TVERSKY, A., PH.D., Psychology

YAARI, M., PH.D., Mathematical Economics
YAHAR, J., PH.D., Statistics

Faculty of Law:

(including the Institute of Criminology, the Harry Sacher Institute for Legislative Research and Comparative Law, the Israel Matz Institute for Research in Jewish Law.)

BARAK, A., DR.JUR., Commercial Law
ELON, M., DR.JUR., Jewish Law
ENGLARD, I., D.U. Law of Obligations
FELLER, S. Z., LL.M., Criminal Law
GOLDSTEIN, S., J.D., Civil Procedure
LEVONTIN, A., S.J.D., International and Interreligious Law
WEISMAN, J., DR.JUR., Law
YARON, R., M.JUR., D.PHIL., Roman Law and Ancient Near Eastern Law
ZAMIR, I., M.JUR., PH.D., Labour Law

Faculty of Science:

(including the Einstein Institute of Mathematics; Racah Institute of Physics; Institute of Chemistry; Alexander Silberman Institute of Life Sciences; Institute of Earth Sciences; Heinz Steinitz Marine Biological Laboratory (at Elat); School of Applied Science and Technology)

AGMON, S., D.ÈS SC., Mathematics
AGRANAT, I., PH.D., Organic Chemistry
ALEXANDER, S., PH.D., Theoretical Physics
AMIT, D., PH.D., Theoretical Physics
AMITSUR, S. A., PH.D., Mathematics
ARDON, M., PH.D., Inorganic and Analytical Chemistry
AUMANN, R. J., PH.D., Mathematics
BEN-NAIM, A., PH.D., Physical Chemistry
BENTOR, Y., PH.D., D. ÈS SC., Geology
BENZIMAN, B., PH.D., Biological Chemistry
BLAUER, G., PH.D., Biological Chemistry
BLUM, J., PH.D., Organic Chemistry
CEVIDALLI, G., PH.D., Applied Chemistry
COHEN, D., PH.D., Botany
COHEN, M., D.PHIL., Theoretical Chemistry
COHEN, S. G., PH.D., Nuclear Physics
CZAPSKI, G., PH.D., Physical Chemistry
DE GROOT, N. H., PH.D., Biological Chemistry
DVORETZKY, A., PH.D., Science and Mathematics
ECKSTEIN, B., PH.D., Zoology
ESKIN, G., PH.D., Mathematics
ESTHERSON, G., PH.D., Applied Chemistry
FAHN, A., PH.D., Botany
FALK, R., PH.D., Genetics
FARKAS, H., PH.D., Mathematics
FEITELSON, J., PH.D., Physical Chemistry
FOGUEL, S., PH.D., Mathematics
FRAENKEL, B. Z., PH.D., Experimental Physics
FRIEDMAN, E., PH.D., Experimental Physics
FURSTENBERG, H., PH.D., Mathematics
GAIFMAN, H., PH.D., History and Philosophy of Science
GAL, A., PH.D., Theoretical Physics
GALLILY, I., PH.D., Atmospheric Sciences
GALUN, R., PH.D., Zoology
GLASNER, A., PH.D., Inorganic and Analytical Chemistry
GOLDENFELD, I. V., PH.D., Theoretical Physics
GUTFREUND, H., PH.D., Theoretical Physics
HALPERIN, A., PH.D., Physics
HAYMAN, Z., PH.D., Physical Chemistry
HEYN-BLAU, C. C., PH.D., Botany
HIRSCHFELD, J., PH.D., Physics
JOFFE, A., DR.PHIL., Botany
KAGEN, MU., PH.D., Physics
KALLAI-HELLER, L., PH.D., Geology
KATZNELSON, Y., D. ÈS SC., Mathematics
KERTES, A. S., PH.D., Inorganic and Analytical Chemistry
KLEIN, J., D. ÈS SC., Organic Chemistry
KLEIN, S., PH.D., Botany
KULKA, R., PH.D., Biological Chemistry
LAPIDOT, Y., PH.D., Biological Chemistry
LEVINE, R., PH.D., D.PHIL., Theoretical Chemistry
LEVITSKI, A., PH.D., Biological Chemistry
LEVY, A., PH.D., Mathematics
LIFSCHITZ, A., PH.D., Physical Chemistry
LIFSHITZ, C., PH.D., Physical Chemistry
LINDENSTRAUSS, J., PH.D., Mathematics
LOW, W. Z., PH.D., Physics
LOYTER, A., PH.D., Biological Chemistry
MANY, A., PH.D., Physics
MARCUS, Y., PH.D., Inorganic and Analytical Chemistry
MASCHLER, M., PH.D., Mathematics
MAYER, A. M., PH.D., Botany
MEJZLER, D., PH.D., Mathematics and Statistics
MENDOZA, E., PH.D., Science Teaching
MOAV, R., PH.D., Genetics
NEUMANN, J., M.SC., Atmospheric Sciences
NOWIK, I., PH.D., Experimental Physics
NOY-MEIR, I., PH.D., Botany
OFER, S., PH.D., Experimental Physics
OHAD, I., PH.D., Biological Chemistry
ORSHAN, G., PH.D., Botany
OTTOLENGHI, M., PH.D., Physical Chemistry
PARNAS, I., PH.D., Neurobiology
PATAI, S., PH.D., Organic Chemistry
PAZY, A., PH.D., Mathematics
PELEG, B., PH.D., Mathematics
PERAKH, M., DR.SCI., Applied Science
PERLMUTTER-HAYMAN, B., PH.D., Physical Chemistry
POLJAKOFF-MAYBER, A., PH.D., Botany
POR, D., PH.D., Zoology
RABANI, J., PH.D., Physical Chemistry
RABIN, M., PH.D., Mathematics
RABINOVITZ, M., Organic Chemistry
RAKAVY, G., PH.D., Theoretical Physics
RAPPAPORT, Z., PH.D., Organic Chemistry
REINHOLD, L., PH.D., DR.PHIL., Botany
REISFELD, R., PH.D., Inorganic and Analytical Chemistry
REISS, Z., PH.D., Paleontology
RUBINSTEIN, L., PH.D., Applied Mathematics
SCHIEBER, M., PH.D., Materials Science
SCHRAMM, M., PH.D., Biological Chemistry
SELIG, H., PH.D., Inorganic and Analytical Chemistry
SELINGER, Z., M.D., Biological Chemistry
SHAHAM, J., PH.D., Physics
SHAMIR, E., PH.D., Mathematics
SHAMIR, J., PH.D., Inorganic and Analytical Chemistry
SHELAH, S., PH.D., Mathematics
SHILO, M., PH.D., Molecular and Microbiological Ecology
SIMCHEN, G., PH.D., Genetics
SOLLER, M., PH.D., Genetics
STEIN, W. Z., PH.D., Botany (Biophysics)
STEINBERGER, I. T., PH.D., Experimental Physics
TREININ, A., PH.D., Physical Chemistry
TZAFRIRI, L., PH.D., Mathematics
WAHRMAN, J., PH.D., Genetics
WEGER, M., PH.D., Physics
WEINRER, A., PH.D., Experimental Physics
WEISS, B., PH.D., Mathematics
WERMAN, R., M.D., Neurophysiology
WERNER, Y., PH.D., Zoology
YAALON, D., PH.D., Pedology
YATSIV, S., PH.D., Experimental Physics
ZABRODSKY, A., PH.D., Mathematics
ZELDES, N., PH.D., Theoretical Physics
ZILKHA, A., PH.D., Organic Chemistry
ZOHARY, D., PH.D., Genetics

Faculty of Agriculture:

(the Levi Eshkol School of Agriculture, including the School of Nutritional and Domestic Sciences)

APPLEBAUM, S. W., PH.D., Entomology
ASHRI, A., PH.D., Field and Vegetable Crops (Genetics)
BANIN, A., PH.D., Soil and Water Sciences
BERMAN, A., PH.D., Animal Sciences
BIRK, Y., PH.D., Agricultural Biochemistry
BUDOWSKI, P., PH.D., Agricultural Biochemistry
GOLDBERG, D., PH.D., Soil and Water Sciences
GOREN, R., PH.D., Horticulture
HALEVY, A., PH.D., Agricultural Biochemistry
HARPAZ, I., PH.D., Entomology
HENIS, Y., PH.D., Bacteriology
HILLEL, D., PH.D., Soil Physics
HILLMAN, P., PH.D., Neurobiology
HORWITZ, G., PH.D., Theoretical Physics
HURWITZ, S., PH.D., Animal Husbandry
JACOBY, B., PH.D., Agricultural Botany and Plant Physiology
KATAN, Y., PH.D., Plant Pathology
KEDAR, N., PH.D., Agricultural Botany
KOLLER, D., PH.D., Agricultural Botany
LASHAV, N., PH.D., Soil and Water Sciences
LAVEE, S., PH.D., Horticulture
MANDEL, S., PH.D., Soil and Water Sciences
MONSELISE, S. P., PH.D., Horticulture
MUNDLAK, Y., PH.D., Agricultural Economics
NIR, I., PH.D., Animal Sciences
PERK, K., DR.MED.VET., Animal Anatomy and Physiology
ROSEN, D., PH.D., Entomology
SACHS, T., PH.D., Botany
SNAPIR, N., PH.D., Animal Sciences
VOLCANI, R., PH.D., Animal Husbandry

Faculty of Medicine:

(the Hebrew University-Hadassah Medical School, including the School of Pharmacy and the Hadassah-Henrietta Szold School of Nursing)

ABRAMSON, H. A., M.B., CH.B., Social Medicine
AUERBACH, E., DR. EN MED., Ophthalmological Research
BACHRACH, U., PH.D., Microbiology
BECKER, Y., PH.D., Virology
BEHAR, A., DR.MED., Pathology
BEKIERKUNST, A., PH.D., Bacteriology
BEN-HUR, N., M.D., Plastic Surgery
BERMAN, E. R., PH.D., Ophthalmology/Medical Biochemistry
BLEYER, E., M.D., Surgery
BLONDHEIM, H. S., M.D., Medicine
BORMAN, J. B., CH.B., F.R.C.S., Surgery
CAINE, M., M.B., M.S., F.R.C.S., Urology
CERASI, E., M.D., Chemical Endocrinology
CITRI, N., PH.D., Bacteriology
COHEN, A. M., M.D., Medicine
COHEN, M., PH.D., Human Genetics
CZACZKES, W., PH.D., M.D., Nephrology
CZERNOBILSKY, B., M.D., Pathology
DAVIDSON, J. T., L.R.C.P.S., F.F.A.R.C.S., Anaesthesiology
DAVIES, A. M., M.D., M.R.C.S., L.R.C.P., Medical Ecology

EFRATI, P., DR.MED., Medicine
EHRENFELD, E. N., DR.MED., Medicine
ELIAKIM, M., M.D., Medicine
EYAL, Z., M.D., Surgery
FEINMESSER, M., DOTT. IN MED., Otorhinolaryngology
FELDMAN, S., M.D., Neurology
FELDMAN-MUHSAM, B., PH.D., Medical Entomology
FINKELSTEIN, M., PH.D., Endocrinology
FUKS, Z., M.D., Oncology
GATT, S., PH.D., Biochemistry
GODFREY, S., M.D., PH.D., F.R.C.P., Paediatrics
GOLDBLUM, N., PH.D., Virology
GOTSMAN, M., M.B., CH.B., D.T.M.H., M.R.C.P., Medicine
GREENBLATT, C., M.D., Parasitology
GROSS, J., M.D., C.M., PH.D., Experimental Medicine and Cancer Research
GROSSOWICZ, N., PH.D., Bacteriology and Hygiene
GUNDERS, A., M.D., D.T.M.&H., PH.D., Medical Ecology
GUTMAN, Y., M.D., Pharmacology
HALPERN, Y., PH.D., Bacteriology
HERSHKO, CH., M.D., Haematology
KAEMPFER, R., PH.D., Molecular Virology
KENNETH, R., PH.D., Plant Pathology and Microbiology
LAUFER, A., DR.MED., Pathology
LAVY, S., M.D., Neurology
LEVIJ, I., M.D., Pathology
LEVIN, S., CH.B., Paediatrics
MAGORA, A., M.D., Physical Medicine and Rehabilitation
MAKIN, M., M.B., CH.B., F.A.C.S., F.R.C.S., Orthopaedic Surgery
MATELES, R., SC.D., Applied Microbiology
MECHOULAM, R., PH.D., Medicinal Chemistry (Natural Products and Pharmacognosy)
MENCZEL, J., M.D., Medicine
NELKEN, D., M.D., Immunology
NIR, I., PH.D., Applied Pharmacology
PFAU, A., DR.MED., Urology
POLLIAK, A., M.D., Haematology
POPOWITZER, M., M.D., Nephrology
RAHAMIMOFF, R., M.D., Physiology
RAZIN, S., PH.D., Clinical Microbiology
ROBIN, G., M.B., CH.B., F.R.C.S., Orthopaedic Surgery
ROGEL, S., M.D., Medicine
ROMANOFF, H., M.D., Surgery
ROSENBAUM, M., M.D., Psychiatry
ROSENBERGER, R. F., PH.D., Microbiological Chemistry
ROSENMANN, E., M.D., Pathology
RUSSELL, A., M.B., D.P.H., M.R.C.P., Paediatrics
SACKS, T. G., M.B., CH.B., M.MED., F.R.C.P., Clinical Microbiology
SADOVSKY, E., M.D., Gynaecology and Obstetrics
SALTZ, N., M.D., Surgery
SAMUELOFF, S., M.D., Physiology
SAREL, S., PH.D., Pharmaceutical Chemistry
SCHILLER, M. M.D., Paediatric Surgery
SCHLESINGER, M., M.D., Experimental Medicine and Cancer Research
SCHWARTZ, A., DR.MED., Diagnostic Roentgenology
SHAFRIR, E., PH.D., Clinical Biochemistry
SHAPIRO, B., PH.D., Human Biochemistry
SHUVAL, H., C.E., M.P.H., Environmental Health
STEIN, O., M.D., Experimental Medicine and Cancer Research
STEIN, Y., M.D., Medicine
STERN, S., M.D., Medicine
SULITZEANU, D., PH.D., Immunology
WASSERMAN, M., DR.MED., Occupational Health
WEISS, D., PH.D., DR.PHIL., Immunology
ZAUBERMAN, H., M.D., Ophthalmology
ZLOTNICK, A., DR.MED., Medicine

Faculty of Dental Medicine:
(the Hebrew University-Hadassah School of Dental Medicine)

GEDALIA, I., PH.D., Preventive Dentistry
GINSBURG, I., PH.D., Microbiology
LEWIN-EPSTEIN, J., D.D.S., Oral Surgery
SHARAV, Y., D.M.D., Oral Medicine
ULMANSKY, M., DR.ODONT., Pathology and Oral Pathology

RESEARCH CENTERS:

Institute for Advanced Studies: Dir. Prof. ARYEH DVORETZKY.

Harry S. Truman Research Institute for the Advancement of Peace: Dir. Prof. HAROLD ZVI SCHIFFRIN.

Institute for Jerusalem Studies: Dir. Prof. DAVID AMIRAN.

S. H. Bergman Center for Philosophical Studies: Dir. Prof. YIRMIAHU YOVEL.

Queen Elisabeth of the Belgians Institute of Archaeology: Dir. JOSEPH AVIRAM.

Slavic Languages and Literatures Research Center: Chair. Prof. DMITRI SEGAL.

Center for Jewish Art: Dir. Prof. BEZALEL NARKISS.

Jewish Music Research Center: Chair. Prof. ISRAEL ADLER.

Folklore Research Center: Dir. Prof. DOV NOY.

Center for Research and Documentation of East European Jewry: Chair. Prof. SHMUEL ETTINGER.

Ben-Zion Dinur Institute for Research on the History of the Jewish People: Chair. Prof. SHMUEL ETTINGER.

Center for Research on Dutch Jewry: Dir. Dr. YOSEF MICHMAN.

Center for Research on Romanian Jewry: Dir. Dr. THEODORE LAVY.

Center for the Study of the History of Eretz Yisrael and the Yishuv: Chair. Prof. YEHOSHUAH BEN-ARIEH.

Ben-Zvi Institute for the Study of Jewish Communities in the Middle East: *see* Research Institutes.

Misgav Yerushalayim—Institute for Study and Research on the Sephardi and Oriental Jewish Heritage: Dir. Dr. ISSACHAR BEN-AMI.

Hebrew University Bible Project: Chair. Prof. MOSHE GOSHEN-GOTTSTEIN.

Maurice Falk Institute for Economic Research in Israel: Dir. Prof. YORAM BEN-PORATH.

Leonard Davis Institute for International Relations: Dir. Prof. DAN HOROWITZ.

Levi Eshkol Institute for Economic, Social and Political Research: Dir. Prof. DOV FRIEDLANDER.

Center for Soviet and East European Research: Dir. Dr. AMNON SELLA.

Franz Suchan Center for European Studies: Dir. Dr. EMANUEL GUTMANN.

Pinhas Lavon Labor History Research Institute: Dir. Prof. SHLOMO AVINERI.

Work and Welfare Research Institute: Dir. Prof. MOSHE LISSAK.

Center for Human Development: Dir. Dr. AMIA LIEBLICH.

Scheinfeld Center for Human Genetics in the Social Sciences: Dir. Prof. RUTH GUTTMAN.

Institute for Urban and Regional Studies: Dir. Prof. ARIE SHACHAR.

Israel Matz Institute for Research in Jewish Law: Dir. Dr. SHMUEL SHILO.

Harry Sacher Institute for Legislative Research and Comparative Law: Dir. Dr. AARON YORAN.

Institute of Criminology: Dir. Dr. MENACHEM AMIR.

Center for Research in Mathematical Economics and Game Theory: Dir. Prof. ROBERT J. AUMANN.

Energy Research Center: Dir. Prof. JOSEPH RABANI.

Swiss Friends' Center for Groundwater Research: Dir. Prof. SAMUEL MANDEL.

Casali Institute of Applied Chemistry: Dir. Prof. HANS FEILCHENFELD.

Amos de Shalit Science Teaching Center: Dir. Prof. ALEXANDRA POLJAKOFF-MAYBER.

Marine Sciences Center: Chair. Prof. MOSHE SHILO.

Heinz Steinitz Marine Biology Laboratory at Elat: Dir. Dr. YEHUDA COHEN.

Drug Research Center: Chair. Prof. RAPHAEL MECHOULAM.

Laser Research Center: Chair. Prof. SHAUL YATSIV.

Integrated Pest Control Research Center: Dir. Prof. ISAAC HARPAZ.

Center for Agricultural Economics: Dir. Prof. YAIR MUNDLAK.

Triwaks Bee Research Center: Dir. Prof. YAACOV LENSKY.

Sanford F. Kurvin Center for the Study of Infectious and Tropical Diseases: Dir. Prof. CHARLES GREENBLATT.

Alexander Silberman Institute of Life Sciences: Chair. Prof. DANIEL ZOHARY.

Lautenberg Center for General and Tumour Immunology: Dir. Prof. DAVID WEISS.

Chanock Center for Virology: Dir. Prof. NATAN GOLDBLUM.

Institute of Microbiology: Dir. Prof. DAN SHAPRA.

Hubert H. Humphrey Center for Experimental Medicine and Cancer Research: Dir. Prof. JACK GROSS.

Fermentation Unit: see Research Institutes.

National Council of Jewish Women Research Institute for Innovation in Education: Dir. Prof. CHAIM ADLER.

Samuel Mendel Melton Center for Jewish Education in the Diaspora: Dir. Prof. SEYMOUR FOX (acting).

Research Center for Human Sciences: Dir. Prof. JONAH ROSENFELD.

Joseph J. Schwartz Graduate Program for Training Community Center Directors and Senior Personnel: Dir. Dr. BENJAMIN GIDRON.

Martin Buber Adult Education Center: Dir. KALMAN YARON.

Board for Jerusalem Examination in Proficiency in Hebrew: Dir. Prof. DAVID TENE.

University Institute for Post-graduate Medical Training: Dir. Prof. SHLOMO ROGEL.

Center for Applied Linguistics: Dir. Dr. ANDREW COHEN.

Robert Szold Institute for Applied Research Projects: Chair. SIDNEY BECKER.

YISSUM Research Development Company: Chair. Board of Directors GIDEON LAHAV.

Authority for Research and Development: Chair. Prof. MICHAEL SCHLESINGER.

BEN GURION UNIVERSITY OF THE NEGEV

P.O.B. 653, BEERSHEVA 84120

Telephone: 057-61111.

Founded 1965.

Language of instruction: Hebrew; Academic year: October to June.

President: YOSEF TEKOAH.

Rector: Prof. DAVID WOLF.

Academic Secretary: YAIR MAGEN.

Librarian: Prof. DAN MEYERSTEIN.

Library: *see* Libraries.

Number of teachers: 960.
Number of students: 4,800.

DEANS:

Technology: Prof. JAIME WISHNIAK.

Natural Sciences: Prof. JESSE M. SHAPIRO.

Humanities and Social Sciences: Prof. SELWYN TROEN.

Health Sciences: Prof. MOSHE PRYWES.

PROFESSORS:

Faculty of Technology:

BRANOVER, H., Mechanical Engineering
DARIEL, M., Materials Engineering
ELATA, H., Mechanical Engineering
ELPERIN, I., Chemical Engineering
HADARI, Z., Nuclear Engineering
LANG, S. B., Chemical Engineering
LOEV, S., Chemical Engineering
PELEG, J., Materials Engineering
ROSEN, M., Materials Engineering
RUBENSTEIN, S., Mechanical Engineering
SHILKRUT, D., Mechanical Engineering
TABAK, D., Electrical Engineering
TAMIR, A., Chemical Engineering
WISHNIAK, J., Chemical Engineering
WOLF, D., Chemical Engineering
ZAYEZDNY, A., Electrical Engineering

Faculty of Natural Sciences:

BEKENSTEIN, J., Physics
CARMELI, M., Physics
EILAM, G., Statistics
GUREVICHY, Mathematics
LIVNE, A., Biology
LIVSHITZ, M., Mathematics
MEYERSTEIN, D., Chemistry
MOREH, R., Physics
PELAH, Z., Chemistry
RICHMOND, A., Biology
SHAKED, H., Physics
SHAPIRO, J. N., Mathematics
SHAVIT, N., Biology
THIBERGER, R., Physics
WEISS, S., Chemistry

Faculty of Humanities and Social Sciences:

ACKERMAN, W., Education
ALLONY, N., Hebrew Language and Literature
APPELEFELD, A., Hebrew Language and Literature
WEINGROD, A., Behavioural Sciences

Faculty of Health Sciences:

ANTONOVSKY, A., Medical Sociology
BERLYNE, G. M., Nephrology
COHEN, D., Comparative Medicine
GLICK, S., Internal Medicine
GOLDSMITH, J., Epidemiology
MOSES, S. W., Paediatrics
PRYWES, M., Medical Education
SACHS, M., Pathology

Institute for Desert Research:

BERKOFSDY, L.
GIVONI, B.
RICHMOND, A.

TEL-AVIV UNIVERSITY

RAMAT-AVIV, TEL-AVIV

Telephone: (03) 420111.

Founded 1953; inaugurated 1956.

Language of instruction: Hebrew; Academic year: October to June (two terms).

Chancellor: Prof. G. S. WISE.

President: Prof. H. BEN-SHAHAR.

Rector: Prof. R. DINSTEIN.

Vice-Rector: Prof. D. HORN.

Vice-President (Foreign Relations): Y. BEN-ZVI.

Vice-President (Research and Development): Prof. M. SOKOLOVSKY.

Vice-President and Director-General: A. GOLAN.

Academic Secretary: Mrs. H. BEN-SHEFFER.

Library: *see* Libraries.

Number of teachers: 1,426.
Number of students: 18,000.

Publications: *Hasifrut* (quarterly), *Middle East Record, Middle East Contemporary Survey, Israel Studies in Criminology* (annually), *Iunei Mishpat* (monthly).

DEANS:

Faculty of Humanities: Prof. M. BRAWER.

Faculty of Social Sciences: Prof. A. ARIAN.

Faculty of Management: Prof. B. LEV.

Faculty of Law: Prof. A. SHAPIRA.

Faculty of Life Sciences: Prof. I. WITZ.

Faculty of Exact Sciences: Prof. E. GILEADI.

Faculty of Engineering: Prof. E. MAROM.

Sackler School of Medicine: Prof. T. WIZNITZER.

Faculty of Visual and Performing Arts: Prof. A. RONEN.

School of Social Work: Dr. U. AVIRAM.

PROFESSORS:

ABARBANEL, S., Applied Mathematics
ABOUDI, J., Engineering
AGASSI, J., Philosophy
AHARONI, Y., Business Administration
AHARONOV, Y., Physics
AHARONY, A., Physics
ALEXANDER, G., Physics
ANKORI, Z., Jewish History
ARIAN, A., Political Sciences
ARZEE, T., Botany
ATZMON, A., Medicine
AUERBACH, N., Physics
AZBEL, M., Physics
BAHCALL, J., Physics
BANITT, M., French Linguistics
BAUM, G., Medicine
BEHAR, A., Pathology
BEJA, A., Business Administration
BEN-EFRAIM, S., Human Microbiology
BEN-REUVEN, A., Chemistry
BEN-SHAHAR, H., Economics
BEN-SHAUL, Y., Botany
BENTWICH, M., Mechanics
BERAN, M. J., Engineering Sciences
BERGLAS, E., Economics
BERGMAN, M., Communication Disorders
BILEN, M., French Language and Literature
BLAU, J., Hebrew Linguistics
BLOCH, C. J., Modern History of Western Europe
BOIM, L., Political Sciences
BRAWER, M., Geography
BRUDERMAN, I., Internal Medicine
BRULL, M., Applied Mechanics
CARPI, D., Jewish History
COHEN, S., Pharmacology
CONFINO, M., History
CUPERMAN, S., Physics
DAGAN, G., Fluid Mechanics and Heat Transfer
DANIEL, E., Biochemistry
DEUTSCH, U., Diagnostic Radiology
DEUTSCHER, G., Physics
DE VRIES, A., Medicine
DINSTEIN, Y., International Law
DJALDETTI, M., Medicine
DOTAN, A., Hebrew Linguistics
EDERY, H., Pharmacology
EISENBERG, J., Physics
EVEN-ZOHAR, I., Poetics and Comparative Literature
FAIN, B., Chemistry
FEUERMAN, E., Dermatology
FINEMAN, D. A., English
FISHBEIN, E., Educational Psychology
FISHELSON, L., Zoology
FLEISCHMANN, J. E., Philosophy
FRIEDLAND, S., Applied Physics
FRIEDLANDER, S., History
FRIEDMAN, D., Law
FUNKENSTEIN, A., History
GAFNI, J., Medicine
GALIL, J., Botany
GALON, M., Botany
GARTNER, L. P., Jewish History
GILAT, T., Internal Medicine

GILEADI, E., Chemistry
GITTER, SH., Pharmacology
GOCHBERG, I., Applied Mathematics
GOODMAN, R. N., Human Genetics
GOTESMAN, A., Physics
GRAB, W., Modern History
GREENBERG, H., Statistics
GROSS, J., Commercial Law
HESHIN, Z., Applied Mechanics
HERSCHLAG, Z. Y., Economic History and Economy of Developing Countries
HIRSCH, Z., Business Administration
HORN, D., Physics
HORWITZ, L. P., Physics
HRUSHOVSKI, B., Poetry and Comparative Literature
IMRY, Y., Physics
JAKIMOVSKI, A., Mathematics
JORTNER, J., Physical Chemistry
KALIR, A., Physiology
KAPLAN, I., Surgery
KASHER, A., Philosophy
KATZIR, E., Biophysics
KELSON, I., Physics
KLEINBERGER, A. F., Education
KLIBANSKY, CH., Chemical Pathology
KOCHVA, E., Zoology
KOHN, A., Virology
KOLTIN, Y., Microbiology
KONIJN, H., Statistics
KOSOWER, E. M., Chemistry
KOVETZ, A., Geophysics
KRAICER, P., Zoology
KREITLER, H., Psychology
KROOK-GILEAD, D., English
KUGLER, J., Zoology
LAQUER, W., History
LARON, Z., Paediatric Endocrinology
LEES, R., Linguistics
LEV, B., Business Administration
LEVIATAN, D., Mathematics
LEVY, M., Surgery
LEVICH, B. G., Chemistry
LEWIN, L., Chemical Pathology
LEWIN, Y., Hebrew Literature
LIBAN, E., Pathology
LICHT, J., Bible
LOEBENSTEIN, G., Botany
MAROM, E., Electronics
MARX, E., Sociology and Anthropology
MATOTH, Y., Paediatrics
MEDALIE, J., Family Medicine
MENDELSSOHN, H., Zoology
MILGRAM, N. A., Psychology
MILMAN, D., Mathematics
MODAN, B., Preventive and Social Medicine
MYSLOBOTSKY, M., Psychology
NA'AMAN, S., History
NAVON, G., Chemistry
NEBEL, L., Embryology
NE'EMAN, Y., Physics
NEUFELD, H., Medicine
NEUMAN, J., Botany
NITZAN, M., Paediatrics
NUSSINOV, S., Physics
ORGLER, Y., Business Administration
PERLMAN, S., Greek History
PERRY, A., Entomology
PIATESKII-SHAPIRO, Mathematics
PINKHAS, J., Medicine
PROCACCIA, G., Commercial Law
RAMOT, B., Haematology
RAZIN, A., Economics
ROSEN, H., Classical Studies
ROSENBERG, E., Remote Sensing
ROSENBERG, N., Electronics
RUBINSTEIN, A., Law
RUBINSTEIN, M., Oto-Rhino-Laryngology
SADE, J., Oto-rhino-laryngology
SAIDMAN, A., Engineering
SANDBANK, U., Pathology
SCHARFSTEIN, B. A., Philosophy
SCHEJTER, A. S., Biochemistry
SCHMEIDLER, D., Statistics and Economics
SCHORR, S., Diagnostic Radiology
SEGAL, E., Theatre Arts and Classical Studies
SERR, D., Obstetrics and Gynaecology
SHAMIR, S., History of the Middle East and Africa
SHAPIRO, Y., Sociology
SHAVIV, G., Physics
SHKOLNIK, A., Zoology
SHOHAM, S., Criminology
SIMONSOHN, S., Jewish History
SMORODINSKY, M., Statistics
SOHAR, E., Medicine
SOKOLOVSKY, M., Biochemistry
SOMEK, S., Arabic Language and Literature
SPERLING, O., Chemical Pathology
SUSSKIND, L., Physics
SZEINBERG, A., Chemical Pathology
TAITEL, Y., Engineering
TAL, U., Jewish History
TAUBER, G., Mathematical Physics
TIETZ-DEVIR, A., Biochemistry
TOURY, J., Jewish History
TSINOBER, A., Mechanical and Transport Engineering
UFFENHEIMER, B., Bible
VITAL, D., Political Science
VORONEL, A., Physics
WAHL, I., Botany
WAISEL, Y., Botany
WALLACH, J. L., History
WEINREB, M. M., Dental Histology
WEISS, Y., Economics
WITZ, I., Microbiology
WIZNITZER, T., Surgery
WOLMAN, M., Pathology
WYGNANSKY, I., Aerodynamics
YAVETZ, Z., Ancient History
YAVIN, A., Physics
YOELI, P., Geography

ATTACHED RESEARCH INSTITUTES:

Chaim Weizmann Zionist Research Institute.
Diaspora Research Institute.
Benzion Katz Institute for Research in Hebrew Literature.
Institute for Archaeological Research.
Shiloah Center for Middle Eastern and African Studies.
Institute for Soviet and East European Studies.
Institute for German History.
Israeli Institute for Poetics and Semiotics.
Center for Technological Education.
Center for Urban and Regional Studies.
Institute for Labour and Social Studies.
Foerder Institute for Economic Research.
Institute for Social Research.
David Horowitz Research Institute for Developing Countries.
Institute of Criminology and Criminal Law.
Israel Institute of Business Research.
Foreign Trade Institute.
Business History Documentation Center.
Operations Research Center.
Case Center.
Institute of Space and Planetary Science.
Florence and George S. Wise Observatory.
Institute for the History and Philosophy of Sciences.
Institute for Nature Preservation Research.
Institute for Cereal Crops Improvement.
Rogoff-Wellcome Medical Research Institute: *see* under Research Institutes.
Institute of Physiological Hygiene.
Research Institute for Environmental Health.
B. Gattegno Research Institute of Human Reproduction and Fetal Development.
Center for Advanced Studies.
Center for Bio-Technology.
Center for Nuclear Research, Nahal Soreq.
Center for Research in the Biology of Cancer.
Center for Strategic Studies.
Institute of Mathematical Sciences.
Institute for Petroleum Research and Geophysics: *see* Research Institutes.
Israel Institute for Biological Research.
Interdisciplinary Center for Technological Analysis and Forecasting.
Kimron Veterinary Institute.
Pinchas Sapir International Center for Development.
University Institute of Petroleum and Energy Studies.
Center of Occupational Therapy, Hygiene and Health.
Center for the Study of Polish Jewry.

TECHNION—ISRAEL INSTITUTE OF TECHNOLOGY

HAIFA

Telephone: 04-292111/225111.
Telex: 46406 TECON IL.
Telegraphic Address: Technion, Haifa.

Founded 1912; inaugurated 1924.

Language of instruction: Hebrew.

Academic year: October to July.

Chairman of Board of Governors: UZIA GALIL.
President: AMOS HOREV, M.SC.MECH.E.
Vice-President for Development: Prof. P. SINGER.
Vice-President for Academic Affairs: Prof. J. ZIV.
Vice-President for Research: Prof. E. LENZ.
Vice-President for Finance and Administration: I. NISSAN.
Dean of Undergraduate Students: Prof. BRIAN SILVER.
Dean of Graduate School: Prof. A. SOLAN.
Dean of Students: Prof. RAPHAEL SIVAN.

Library: *see* Libraries.

Number of teachers: 1,100.

Number of students: 5,600 undergraduates, 1,900 graduates.

Publications: *The Joseph Wunsch Lectures* (annual), *Shlomo Kaplansky Memorial Series* (incorporated in *Israel Journal of Technology*), *Synopses of D.Sc. and M.Sc. Theses* (annual), *Catalogue* (annual), *Research Report* (annual), *Technion* (quarterly), *Bulletin* (weekly).

DEANS:

Faculty of Civil Engineering (including Mineral Engineering): Prof. M. LIVNEH.
Faculty of Architecture and Town Planning: Prof. YOHANAN ELON.
Faculty of Mechanical Engineering: Assoc. Prof. H. GUTFINGER.
Department of Materials Engineering: Prof. DOV KATZ.
Faculty of Electrical Engineering: Prof. ZVI KOHAVI.
Faculty of Chemical Engineering: Prof. E. RUBIN.
Department of Food Engineering and Biotechnology: Assoc. Prof. S. MIZRAHI.
The Walter C. Lowdermilk Faculty of Agricultural Engineering: Assoc. Prof. I. RAVINA.
Faculty of Aeronautical Engineering: Prof. E NISSIM.
Faculty of Industrial and Management Engineering: Prof. MICHAEL RUBINOVITCH.
Faculty of Mathematics: Prof. Z. ZIEGLER.
Faculty of Physics: Prof. A. RON.
Faculty of Chemistry: Prof. MAGDA ARIEL.
Department of Biology: Assoc. Prof. Y. SHALITIN.
Department of Nuclear Science: Assoc. Prof. AMOS NOTEA.
Department of General Studies: Prof. Y. RADDAY.
Department of Teacher Training: Prof. A. EVIATAR.
Department of Computer Science: Prof. S. EVAN.
Faculty of Medicine: Prof. D. BARZILAI.
Inter-Disciplinary Unit of Medical Engineering: Prof. SHMUEL SIDEMAN.

PROFESSORS:

Faculty of Civil Engineering:
ALPAN, J., Foundation Engineering
BEAR, J., Hydraulic Engineering
DISKIN, M., Hydrotechnics
GLÜCKLICH, J., Mechanical Behaviour of Materials
KARNI, J., Building Materials
KOMORNIK, A., Soil Engineering
KOTT, YEHUDA, Environmental Engineering
LIVNEH, M., Transportation Engineering
METZER, A., Mineral Engineering
POREH, M., Fluid Mechanics
REBHUN, M., Environmental Engineering
REISS, M., Structural Engineering
SHAMIR, U., Water Resources Systems
SHELEF, G., Waste Water Treatment and Reclamation
SHMUTTER, B., Geodesy-Photogrammetry
SOROKA, I., Building Materials
WACHS, A., Environmental Engineering
WINOKUR, A., Structural Engineering
WISEMAN, G., Foundation Engineering and Rock Mechanics
ZEITLEN, J. G., Soil Engineering

Faculty of Architecture and Town Planning:
ELON, Y., Town Planning
HERBERT, G., Town and Regional Planning
HILL, M., Urban and Regional Planning
KASHTAN, A., Theory of Architecture

Faculty of Mechanical Engineering:
BODNER, S., Materials Science
GUTFINGER, E. H., Fluid Mechanics
HETSRONI, G., Two Phase Flow, Transport Dynamics
ISHAI, O., Mechanics of Structural Materials
LENZ, E., Machine Tools
PNUELI, D., Thermodynamics
SOLAN, A., Fluid Mechanics, Desalination
WEIL, R., Machine Design
WOLBERG, J., Radiology, Desalination and Reactor Physics

Department of Material Engineering:
BLECH, I., Microelectronics
BRANDON, D., Metallurgy
KATZ, D., Composite and Polymer Materials
MINKOFF, J., Metallurgy-Crystallography
ROSEANOU, L., Lubrication, Friction, Wear
ROSEN, A., Aluminium Alloys
WEISS, B. Z., Mechanical Metallurgy
YAHALOM, J., Metallic Corrosion

Faculty of Electrical Engineering:
BAR-DAVID, J., Statistical Theory of Communication, Detection and Estimation
BAR-LEV, A., Semiconductors
ERLICKI, M., Energy Conversion
HEYMANN, M., Optimization, Control
KATZENELSON, J., Circuits and Systems
KIDRON, I., Electronics
KLEIN, N., Solid State Electronics
KOHAVI, Z., Computational Model Switching and Automata Theory
LEMPEL, A., Communication
OLLENDORFF, F., Electronics and Telecommunication
NAVOT, I., Network Synthesis
RAZ, SH., Sonar and Communication System
SCHIEBER, D., Energy Conversion
SIVAN, R., Automatic Control
WEISER, K., Solid State Physics
ZAKAY, M., Telecommunication
ZIV, J., Statistical Communication. Information Theory

Faculty of Chemical Engineering:
HASSON, D., Chemical Engineering
KEHAT, E., Chemical Engineering
PISMAN, L., Chemical Engineering
RAM, A., Plastic Materials
RESNICK, W., Chemical Engineering
RIGBI, Z., Rubber Engineering
RUBIN, E., Mass Transfer
SIDEMAN, S., Chemical Engineering, Transport
TADMOR, Z., Polymer Engineering

Department of Food Engineering and Biotechnology:
BERK, Z., Food Process Development
MANNHEIM, H., Food Technology

Faculty of Aeronautical Engineering:
BARUCH, M., Dynamics of Structures
GAL-OR, B., Fluid Dynamics
HANIN, M., Aerodynamics
KOGAN, A., Fluid Dynamics
LIBAI, A., Aeronautical Structures
MERHAV, S., Control Systems Engineering
NISSIM, E., Aeroelasticity, Aerodynamics
ROM, J., Aerodynamics
SINGER, J., Aircraft Structures
STAVSKY, Y., Mechanics of Structures
TIMNAT, Y., Propulsion and Combustion

Faculty of Agricultural Engineering:
BURAS, N., Soil and Water Development
HAGIN, J., Soil Science
KORNECKI, A., Strength of Materials
SEGINER, I., Agricultural Micrometeorology
ZASLAVSKY, D., Soil Physics

Faculty of Industrial and Management Engineering:
AVI-ITZHAK, B., Operations Research
AVRIEL, M., Mathematical Programming, Energy Policy
DAR-EL, E., Production Planning, Human Factors and Safety Research
EPSTEIN, B., Operations Research and Statistics
MANNHEIM, B., Industrial Sociology
PASSY, U., Mathematical Programming
SHLIFER, EL., Operations Research of Logistic Systems
YADIN, M., Operations Research, Statistics

Faculty of Mathematics:
AHARONOV, D., Theory of Functions
EVYATAR, A., Topology, Algebra
FINZI, A., Mathematical Astrophysics
LEWIN, M., Combinatorics
MARCUS, M., Functional Analysis
NETHANYAHU, E., Mathematics
RECHAW, M., Topology and Functional Analysis
SAPHAR, P., Functional Analysis
SCHWARTZ, B., Mathematics
ZAKS, A., Semi-Primary Rings
ZIEGLER, Z., Theory of Approximation

Faculty of Physics:
DAR, A., Nuclear Physics
ECKSTEIN, Y., Solid State Physics
GILAT, G., Raman Scattering in Solids
HIRSCH, A. A., Applied Physics
KALISH, R., Ion-Implantation—Hyperfine Interactions
KUPER, C. G., Theoretical Physics
OPHER, R., Astrophysics, Solid State
PERES, A., Fundamental Particle Physics
REVZEN, M., Solid State Physics
RON, A., Theoretical Solid State Physics
ROSNER, B., Nuclear Physics
RUDMAN, P., Solid State Physics
SCHULMAN, L. S., Statistical Mechanics
SINGER, P., Elementary Particles Physics
TANNHAUSER, D. S., Solid State Physics
ZAK, J., Solid State Physics

Faculty of Chemistry:
ARIEL, M., Analytical Chemistry
BEN-ISHAI, D., Nitrogen Heterocycles and Amino Acids
CAIS, M., Organo-metallic Chemistry
DORI, Z., Bio-inorganic Chemistry
FOLMAN, M., Physical Chemistry
GINSBURG, D., Organic Chemistry
HALEVI, A., Physical Chemistry
HERBSTEIN, F., Inorganic Chemistry
KIMMEL, S., Isotope Non-Linear Optics
LOEWENSTEIN, A., NMR and ESR
LOEWENTHAL, H. E., Organic Chemistry
PAUNCZ, R., Physical Chemistry
RUBIN, M., Organic Chemistry
SILVER, B., Inorganic Chemistry

Department of Biology:
AVI-DOR, J., Biochemistry
BEN-ISHAI, R., Molecular Biology
GERSHON, D., Gerontology
WARBURG, H., Physiological Ecology of Animals

Faculty of Medicine:
BARZILAI, D., Internal Medicine, Endocrinology
BETTER, O., Nephrology and Internal Medicine
GELLEI, B., Pathology
HAIM, S., Dermatology

HERSHKO, A., Biochemical Mechanisms of intracellular protein degradation
PALTI, Y., Physiology
PEISER, E., Neurosurgery
ROBINSOHN, E., Oncology
VALERO, A., Internal Medicine
WINTER, S., Paediatrics
YOUDIM, M., Psychopharmacology and Neochemistry

Department of Computer Science:
EVEN, S., Automata Theory and Graph Theory
GINSBURG, A., Automation Theory
PAZ, A., Automata Theory
YOELI, M., Switching Theory

Department of General Studies:
RADDAY, Y., The Narrative Technique of the Bible

Department of Nuclear Engineering:
ROTHENSTEIN, W., Nuclear Reactor Theory
SHAFRIR, N. H., Nuclear Chemistry

Department of Education:
AVITAL, SH., Problems in Mathematics Teaching and Learning
EVIATAR, A., Education in Mathematics

Samuel Neaman Institute for Advanced Studies in Science and Technology: Dir. Prof. J. BEAR.

AFFILIATED INSTITUTES

Technion Research and Development Foundation Ltd.:
The Michel Pollak Building Research Station.
Centre for Research in Environmental and Water Resources Engineering.
Mineral Engineering Research Centre.
Energy Engineering Centre, Dept. of Mechanical Engineering.
Microelectronics Research Centre.
Bruner Institute of Transportation.
Centre for Urban and Regional Studies.
Stone Technology Centre.
Food Industries Research and Development Centre.
Solid State Institute.
Centre for Applied Computer Research.
Materials Engineering Research Centre.
Material Processing and Machine Tool Centre.
Chemical Engineering Research Centre.
Agricultural Engineering Research Centre: Agricultural Machinery Division, Fertilizer and Soil Division, Irrigation Division.
Aeronautical Research Centre.
Centre for Research in Management Sciences.
Research Centre for Work Safety and Human Engineering.
Centre for Study of Man at Work.
J. Silver Institute of Bio-Medical Engineering Sciences.
Centre for R & D in Technology and Science Education and Vocational Training.

Israel Institute of Metals.

THE WEIZMANN INSTITUTE OF SCIENCE

P.O.B. 26, REHOVOT
Telephone: (054) 82111.
Telex: 31900.

Founded 1949; includes the Daniel Sieff Research Institute (f. 1934).

The Institute is a private non-profit corporation for fundamental and applied research in the Natural Sciences. The Feinberg Graduate School offers courses towards the M.Sc. and Ph.D. degrees.

Chairman, Board of Governors: Lord SIEFF OF BRIMPTON.
President: Prof. MICHAEL SELA.
Chairman, Scientific Council: Prof. U. Z. LITTAUER.
Vice-President, Finance and Administration: TANCHUM GRIZIM.
Academic Secretary: Dr. A. NISSENBAUM.
Chief Librarian: Mrs. ALMA ROSENHECK.

Library of 150,000 vols. and periodicals.

Number of teachers: 300.
Number of graduate students: 480.
Publications: *Annual Report of Scientific Activities*†, *Rehovot Magazine*†, *Interface*†, *Research*†.

DEANS AND HEADS OF DEPARTMENTS

Faculty of Mathematical Sciences: L. A. SEGEL.
Department of Applied Mathematics: A. BRANDT.
Department of Theoretical Mathematics: H. DYM.

Faculty of Physics: I. TALMI.
Department of Electronics: D. TREVES.
Department of Nuclear Physics: Z. FRAENKEL.

Faculty of Chemistry: Z. LUZ.
Department of Chemical Physics: M. SHAPIRO.
Department of Isotope Research: J. R. GAT.
Department of Organic Chemistry: Y. MAZUR.
Department of Plastics Research: M. LEVY.
Department of Structural Chemistry: M. COHEN.

Faculty of Biophysics-Biochemistry: M. AVRON.
Department of Biochemistry: V. DANIEL.
Department of Biophysics: N. SHARON.
Department of Membrane Research: C. GITLER.
Department of Neurobiology: U. Z. LITTAUER.
Department of Polymer Research: A. SILBERBERG.

Faculty of Biology: H. LINDNER.
Department of Cell Biology: M. FELDMAN.
Department of Chemical Immunology: D. GIVOL.
Unit of Experimental Biology: I. BERENBLUM.
Department of Genetics: L. SACHS.
Department of Hormone Research: H. LINDNER.
Department of Plant Genetics: E. GALUN.
Department of Virology: E. WINOCOUR.

Feinberg Graduate School: S. SHALTIEL.
Department of Science Teaching: M. BRUCKHEIMER.
Center for Biology of Ageing: D. DANON.
Center for Energy Research: I. DOSTROVSKY.
Center for Industrial Research: D. VOFSI.
Center for Neurosciences and Behavioral Research: D. SAMUEL.

COLLEGES AND HIGHER INSTITUTES

The American College in Jerusalem: 2 Hameiri Blvd., Kiryat Moshe, Jerusalem; f. 1967; 40 teachers, 300 students; library of 15,000 vols.; Pres. Dr. NORMAN GREENWALD.

Bezalel Academy of Arts and Design: 10 Shmuel Hanagid St., Jerusalem; f. 1906; 4-year degree course in fine arts, graphic design, gold- and silver-smithing, environmental and industrial design, ceramics; library of 10,000 vols.; 130 lecturers, 550 students; Dir. RAN SHECHORI.

British School of Archaeology in Jerusalem: P.O.B. 19283, Jerusalem; f. 1920; conducts archaeological excavation, survey and research; library of 6,000 vols.; Pres. The Rev. Prof. HENRY CHADWICK; Chair. The Rev. Prof. P. R. ACKROYD; Dir. The Rev. JOHN WILKINSON; publ. *Levant*† (annually).

Conservatory of Music: 7 Bilu St., Holon; f. 1942 by the late Prof. David Shor; general musical and instrumental training provided; public concerts organized for charity; mem. of ISME (Int. Soc. for Music Educ.) and approved by the Ministry of Education and Culture; 25 teachers, 300 students; library of nearly 1,400 vols.; Dir. Mrs. NADIVA SHOR.

Ecole Biblique et Ecole Archéologique Française: P.O.B. 19053, Jerusalem; f. 1890; Research, Biblical and Oriental studies, exploration and excavation in Palestine; 15 professors; Dir. R. TOURNAY, O.P.; library of 80,000 vols.; publs. *Revue Biblique*† (quarterly), *Etudes Bibliques, Etudes Palestiniennes et Orientales, Cahiers de la Revue Biblique.*

Etz Hayim, General Talmud Torah and Grand Teshivah: P.O.B. 300, Jerusalem; f. 1841; 1,400 students; library of 10,000 vols.; Pres. Rabbi I. Z. MELTZER.

Graduate School of Surveying: Holon; under the Survey Dept. of the Ministry of Labour; three-year course for land surveyors.

Hebrew Union College—Jewish Institute of Religion, Jerusalem School: 13 King David St., Jerusalem; f. 1963; branch of the same institution in the United States of America; the first year of graduate rabbinic studies and a research programme in biblical archaeology; undergraduate one-year study programme on a Kibbutz; library of 20,000 vols.; microfilm collection from American Jewish Archives; Pres. ALFRED GOTTSCHALK; Dean MICHAEL L. KLEIN (acting).

Institute of Holy Land Studies: Mount Zion, Jerusalem, P.O.B. 1276; f. 1959; independent educational corporation controlled by private board of directors in U.S.A.; Pres. GEORGE GIACUMAKIS.

International Institute for Development, Co-operation and Labour Studies: Neharde'a St. 7, P.O.B. 16201, Tel-Aviv 69235; f. 1958 to train labour and co-operative movement leadership in Asia, Africa and Caribbean; candidates nominated by trade unions, co-operatives, universities, international labour organizations, etc.; annual courses on "Labour and Co-operation in the Service of Development"; English-speaking course April-July, August-November, French-speaking course January-March; library of 11,500 vols. and over 150 periodicals; 10,500 graduates from 109 countries; Chair. M. BAR-TAL; Dir. and Principal Dr. YEHUDAH PAZ; publs. *Bulletin*† (2 a year), study and background material for courses.

Mosad Harav Kook: P.O.B. 642, Jerusalem; f. 1937 to educate and train young men for research in the field of Torah Literature and to infuse the original Hebrew culture in all classes of the people; Dir. YITZCHAK RAPHAEL; publs. Torah-Science books, including the printing of MSS. of previously unpublished *Rishonim* works that are still retained in Genizah form.

Pontifical Biblical Institute: King David and Botta Streets, Jerusalem, P.O.B. 497; f. 1927 as a branch of the Pontifical Biblical Institute of Rome; fosters the study of Biblical geography and archaeology; organizes student tours with topographical lectures; Prehistorical Museum containing discoveries of Teleilat Ghassul, a chalcolithic site in the Jordan valley, excavated by the Institute; Dir. Rev. FRANCIS FURLONG, S.J.; publs. *Biblica, Orientalia.*

Rubin Academy of Music, Jerusalem: 7 Smolenskin St., Jerusalem; f. 1947; courses leading to B.Mus., B.A. Mus., in co-operation with the Hebrew University; Masters Degree in co-operation with New York University; Teacher Training College; 160 teachers, 1,500 students; library of 30,000 vols.; museum of musical instruments; Dir. Mrs. Y. KOPERNIK-DOSTROVSKY; publ. *Calendar of Events* (monthly).

Studium Biblicum Franciscanum: P.O.B. 19424, Monastery of the Flagellation, Jerusalem (Old City); f. 1927; centre of archaeological research directed by the Franciscan Custody of the Holy Land, biblical section of the *Pontificium Athenaeum Antonianum*, Rome, for degrees of Licentiate and Doctorate in Biblical Theology, and diploma in biblico-oriental sciences; 30 mems.; Dir. S. LOFFREDA; publs. *Liber Annuus*†, *Collectio Maior*†, *Collectio Minor*†, *Analecta*†, *S.B.F. Museum*†.

Swedish Theological Institute: 58 Rehov Hanevi'im, P.O.B. 37, Jerusalem; f. 1951; biblical, Semitic and Jewish Studies; Dir. Dr. GÖRAN LARSSON; publ. *Annual.*

Tel Hai Regional College: Upper Galilee, nr. Kiryat Shmona, 12210; f. 1960; university and adult education courses in agriculture, humanities, social sciences, languages, mathematics, engineering, arts and crafts, industrial and labour problems; studies in Arabic for Druse students; library, *see* Libraries; 2,000 students; Dir. MILIA SPACHNER.

ITALY

Population 56,828,000

ACADEMIES

ACCADEMIA NAZIONALE DEI LINCEI

PALAZZO CORSINI, VIA DELLA LUNGARA 10, 00165 ROME

Telephone: 650831

Founded 1603.

President: Prof. ANTONIO CARRELLI.

Vice-President: Amb. ENRICO CERULLI.

Administrator: Prof. SANTORO FRANCESCO PASSARELLI.

It is divided into two classes: (1) Physics, Mathematics, and Natural Sciences, with seventy-two national associates; and (2) Philosophy, History, and Philology, with seventy-two national associates.

Library: *see* libraries.

Publications: *Rendiconti della Classe di Scienze Fisiche, Matematiche e Naturali; Rendiconti della Classe di Scienze Morali, Storiche e Filologiche; Memorie della Classe di Scienze Fisiche, Matematiche e Naturali; Memorie della Classe di Scienze Morali, Storiche e Filologiche; Monumenti Antichi; Notizie degli Scavi; Quaderni; Annuario.*

MATHEMATICS AND MECHANICS

A. Mathematics	*B. Mechanics*
MARTINELLI, E.	AGOSTINELLI, C.
MIRANDA, C.	CICALA, P.
SANSONE, G.	CATTANEO, C.
SCORZA DRAGONI, G.	CROCCO, L.
TRICOMI, F. G.	EVANGELISTI, G.
ZAPPA, G.	FERRARI, C.
	GRAFFI, D.
	SUPINO, G.

ASTRONOMY, GEODESY AND GEOPHYSICS

A. Astronomy	*B. Geodesy and Geophysics*
ABETTI, G.	CALOI, P.
DALLAPORTA, N.	MARUSSI, A.
GRATTON, L.	SOLAINI, L.
RIGHINI, G.	
ROSINO, L.	

PHYSICS AND CHEMISTRY

A. Physics	*B. Chemistry*
AMALDI, E.	BONINO, G. B.
BERNARDINI, G.	CAGLIOTI, V.
CARRELLI, A.	NATTA, G.
CONVERSI, M.	PANIZZI, L.
FERRETTI, B.	QUILICO, A.
OCCHIALINI, G. P. S.	SARTORI, G.
RASETTI, F.	SEMERANO, G.
ROSTAGNI, A.	SIMONETTA, M.
SALVINI, G.	
WATAGHIN, G.	

GEOLOGY, PALAEONTOLOGY AND MINERALOGY

A. Geology and Palaeontology	*B. Mineralogy*
DAL PIAZ, G. B.	CAROBBI, G.
DESIO, A.	GALLITELLI, P.
LEONARDI, P.	SCHERILLO, A.
MERLA, G.	SCHIAVINATO, G.
TREVISAN, L.	

BIOLOGICAL SCIENCES

A. Botany	*B. Zoology*
CAPPELLETTI, C.	AMPRINO, R.
FRANCINI CORTI, E.	BARIGOZZI, C.
LONA, F.	BENAZZI, M.
TONZIG, S.	MONTALENTI, G.
	OLIVO, O. M.
	RANZI, S.
	STEFANELLI, A.

C. Physiology	*D. Pathology*
BOVET, D.	ALOISI, M.
ERSPAMER, V.	CIARANFI, E.
MARGARIA, R.	FAVILLI, G.
MORUZZI, G.	GIORDANO, A.
ROSSI-FANELLI, A.	MOTTURA, G.
STELLA, G.	

PHILOLOGY AND LINGUISTICS

BONFANTE, G.	LAVAGNINI, B.
BOSCO, U.	LO GATTO, E.
CERULLI, E.	MALCOVATI, E.
CONTINI, G.	MERIGGI, P.
FRANCESCHINI, E.	MOSCATI, S.
GABRIELI, F.	PARATORE, E.
GALLAVOTTI, C.	PRAZ, M.

ARCHAEOLOGY

ADRIANI, A.	LEVI, D.
CAPUTO, G.	PALLOTTINO, M.
FERRI, S.	ROMANELLI, P.
GUARDUCCI, M.	ZANCANI MONTUORO, P

ART, POETRY AND CRITICISM

BACCHELLI, R.	PALLUCCHINI, R.
BINNI, W.	RONGA, L.
BRIZIO, A. M.	SALMI, M.
GNUDI, C.	SAPEGNO, N.

HISTORY AND ANTHROPOLOGY

COGNASSO, F.	PONTIERI, E.
GHISALBERTI, A. M.	RICCARDI, R.
MAZZARINO, S.	RIDOLFI, R.
MOMIGLIANO, A.	SESTAN, E.
MORGHEN, R.	SESTINI, A.

PHILOSOPHICAL SCIENCES

ABBAGNANO, N.	GUZZO, A.
CALOGERO, G.	SPIRITO, U.
CILENTO, V.	

JURIDICAL SCIENCES

BOBBIO, N.	MORELLI, G.
BRANCA, G.	MORTATI, C.
GORLA, L.	OPPO, G.
JEMOLO, C. A.	PARADISI, B.
LUZZATTO, G. I.	SANTORO PASSARELLI, F.
MENGONI, L.	VOLTERRA, E.

SOCIAL AND POLITICAL SCIENCES

BAFFI, P.	LUZZATTO FEGIZ, P.
CORBINO, E.	MILONE, F.
DEMARIA, G.	PAPI, G. U.
DI NARDI, G.	RÉPACI, F. A.
DOMINEDÒ, V.	SRAFFA, P.
LENTI, L.	TRAVAGLINI, V.

ACCADEMIA NAZIONALE DI SAN LUCA

PIAZZA DELL'ACCADEMIA DI SAN LUCA 77, ROME

Founded in the fourteenth century.

President: VENANZO CROCETTI.

Secretary-General: GAETANA SCANO.

It is divided into three main classes with 18 national mems., 30 corresponding mems. and 10 foreign mems. in each class: Painters, Sculptors and Architects: in addition there are an unspecified number of cultural and honorary mems. totalling 55 at present.

The main library "Romana Biblioteca Sarti" contains over 40,000 vols.

Publication: *Annuario.*

Istituto Lombardo Accademia di Scienze e Lettere: Via Brera 28, 20121 Milan; f. 1803; Pres. Prof. ALFONSO GIORDANO; it is divided into two classes: Mathematics and Natural Sciences (Sec. Prof. SILVIO CINQUINI; 42 mems., 82 corresponding associates, 20 foreign mems.); Moral Sciences (Sec. Prof. ENRICA MALCOVATI; 40 mems., 80 corresponding associates, 20 foreign mems.); library of 190,000 vols., 330 Italian periodicals, 600 foreign periodicals; publs. *Rendiconti della Sezione di Scienze Matematiche e Naturali, Rendiconti della Sezione di Scienze Biologiche e Mediche, Rendiconti della Classe di Scienze Morali, Memorie della Classe di Scienze Matematiche e Naturali, Memorie della Classe di Scienze Morali,* Proceedings of Symposiums.

Accademia dei Filedoni: Piazza Italia 2, Perugia; f. 1816; Pres. T. ANSIDEI DI CATRANO.

Accademia della Crusca: Villa medicea di Castello, via di Castello 46, Florence; f. 1582; Pres. Prof. GIOVANNI NENCIONI; Dir. of Philological Studies DOMENICO DE ROBERTIS; Dir. of Lexicographical Studies D'ARCO SILVIO AVALLE; Dir. of Grammatical Studies GIOVANNI NENCIONI; Sec. PIERO FIORELLI; publs. *Vocabolario degli Accademici della Crusca, Autori classici e documenti di lingua, Vocabolari e Glossari, Studi di filologia italiana, Studi di Grammatica Italiana, Studi di Lessicografia Italiana.*

Accademia delle Scienze dell'Istituto di Bologna: Via Zamboni 31, Bologna; f. 1711; 60 mems., 200 corresponding mems.; Pres. Prof. ENRICO VANNINI; Sec. Prof. OLIVIERO M. OLIVO.

Accademia delle Scienze di Ferrara: Via Scienze 17, 44100 Ferrara; f. 1823; 210 mems.; library of 3,000 vols.; Pres. Prof. CARLO CANELLA; Sec. AVV. GIORGIO FRANCESCHINI; publ. *Atti della Accademia della Scienze di Ferrara*†.

Accademia delle Scienze di Torino (*Turin Academy of Sciences*): Via Accademia delle Scienze 6, and Via Maria Vittoria 3, 10123 Turin; f. 1757; 240 mems.; all fields of learning: publications, congresses and lectures; library: see Libraries; Pres. Prof. CATALDO AGOSTINELLI; publs. *Memorie*†, *Atti*† (annually).

Accademia delle Scienze Mediche di Palermo: Policlinico, via Liborio Giuffrè, Palermo; f. 1621; Pres. Prof. P. LI VOTI.

Accademia di Agricoltura di Torino (*Academy of Agriculture of Turin*): Via Andrea Doria 10, Turin; f. 1785; library of 14,300 vols.; Dir. Dott. Prof. EMANUELE BATTISTELLI.

Accademia di Medicina di Torino (*Academy of Medicine*): Via Po 18, Turin; f. 1946; Pres. Prof. ACHILLE DOGLIOTTI; Sec.-Gen. Prof. A. BERETTA-ANGUISOSSOLA.

Accademia di Scienze, Lettere ed Arti (*Academy of Sciences, Letters and Arts*): Piazza Indipendenza 17, 90129 Palermo; library of 14,000 vols.; Pres. Prof. BENEDETTO PETTINEO; Gen. Sec. Prof. ROMUALDO GIUFFRIDA.

Accademia di Scienze, Lettere, Arti: Via Marazzani 12, 20132 Milan; f. 1919; 200 mems.; library of 12,000 vols.; Pres. Prof. MARIO POCOBELLI; publ. *Conferenze* (monthly).

Accademia Economico-Agraria dei Georgofili (*Academy of Agrarian Economics*): Loggiato degli Uffizi, Florence; f. 1753; library of approx. 34,000 vols.; Pres. Prof. G. STEFANELLI; Librarian Prof. SERGIO ORSI.

Accademia Etrusca: Palazzo Casali, Piazza Signorelli, Cortona-Arezzo; Pres. Dott. Prof. P. ROMANELLI.

Accademia Filarmonica Romana (*Rome Philharmonic Academy*): Via Flaminia 118, Rome; f. 1821; library of 1,500 vols.; Pres. ADRIANA PANNI; Vice-Pres. MARIO PERAGALLO, GOFFREDO PETRASSI.

Accademia Gioenia di Scienze Naturali: Corso Italia 55, 95129 Catania; f. 1824; 136 mems.; library of 20,000 vols., 400 periodicals; Pres. Prof. B. FORESTI; Gen. Sec. Prof. G. DI MAGGIO; publs. *Bollettino delle Sedute della Accademia Gioenia di Scienze Naturali in Catania, Atti della Accademia Gioenia di Scienze Naturali in Catania.*

Accademia Italiana di Scienze Forestali: Piazza Edison 11, 50133 Florence; f. 1952; Pres. Prof. G. PATRONE.

Accademia Ligure di Scienze e Lettere (*Academy of Sciences and Letters*): Via Balbi 10, 16126 Genoa; f. 1890; library of 34,000 vols.; Dir. Prof. A. OBERTELLO; Sec.-Gen. P. SCOTTI.

Accademia Medica di Roma: Policlinico Umberto I, Rome; f. 1876; library of 20,000 vols.; *c.* 400 mems.; Pres. Prof. GIUSEPPE GIUNCHI; Sec. Prof. L. TRAVIA; publ. *Bollettino ed Atti* (annually).

Accademia Musicale Chigiana: via di Città 89, 53100 Siena; f. 1932 to support the training of young artists; master classes in music, lectures, conferences, concerts; Pres. AVV. DANILO VERZILI.

Accademia Nazionale dei Sartori: via Due Macelli 73, Rome; Pres. CIRO GIULIANO.

Accademia Nazionale delle Scienze, detta dei XL (*National Academy of Sciences, known as the Forty*): Palazzo Civiltà del Lavoro, EUR, Rome; f. 1782 as the Italian Society of Sciences; 40 Italian, 12 foreign mems.; Pres. Prof. PIETRO DI MATTEI; Sec. Prof. G. B. MARINI BETTOLO; publ. *Rendiconti*† (annually).

Accademia Nazionale di Agricoltura: Via Farini 14, Bologna; f. 1807; 71 mems. and 140 corresponding mems.; library of 10,000 vols. and 14,000 pamphlets; Pres. Prof. GIUSEPPE MEDICI; Sec. Prof. GIAN FRANCO BALDINI; publ. *Annali* (quarterly).

Accademia Nazionale di Marina Mercantile: Via Garibaldi 4, Genoa; f. 1945; 50 national mems.; Pres. Prof. C. PERSICO; Sec. Dr. M. RAVEDATI.

Centro Italiano Studi Containers: Via Garibaldi 4, Genoa; f. 1967; 65 mems.; Pres. J. CLERICI; Sec. M. RAVEDATI.

Accademia Nazionale di Santa Cecilia: Via Vittoria 6, Rome; f. 1566; 70 national mems. and 30 foreign mems.; Pres. MARIO ZAFRED (acting).

Accademia Nazionale di Scienze, Lettere ed Arti: Palazzo Coccapani, Corso Vittorio Emanuele II 59, Modena; f. 1680; 40 mems., 60 corresponding mems., 30 honorary mems.; library of 104,000 vols.; Pres. Prof. ANTONIO PIGNEDOLI; publ. *Atti e Memorie.*

Accademia Petrarca di Lettere, Arti e Scienze (*Petrarch Academy of Letters, Arts and Science*): Via dell' Orto, Arezzo; f. 1810; 413 mems.; library of 16,000 vols.; Pres. Prof. MARIO SALMI; Sec. Dr. GUIDO GOTI; publs. *Atti e Memorie, Studi Petrarcheschi.*

Accademia Spoletina: Palazzo Mauri, Via Brignone, Spoleto; f. 1477; 10 honorary mems., 40 mems., and 150 corresponding mems.; library of 10,000 vols.; Pres. Dott. FABRIZIO ANTOLINI; publs. *Spoletium, Rivista di Arte Storia Cultura* (2 a year).

Accademia Tiberina: Via del Vantaggio 22, 00186 Rome; f. 1813; 200 mems. and 2,000 assoc., corresp., resident and hon. mems.; applied sciences, psychology, arts, hygiene and health, anthropology, Yoga-Vedanta centre; library of 10,000 vols.; Pres. Prof. Dott. IGOR ISTÓMIN-DURANTI; Sec. SILVIA RAMINI.

Accademia Toscana di Scienze e Lettere la Colombaria (*La Colombaria Tuscan Academy of Science and Letters*): Via S. Egidio 21, Florence; f. 1735; library of 7,000 vols.; Pres. Prof. GIACOMO DEVOTO; Gen. Sec. Prof. FRANCESCO ADORNO.

Accademia Virgiliana di Scienze, Lettere ed Arti di Mantova: Via Accademia 47, Mantua; f. 1562, present name 1797; 77 mems.; 13 hon. mems.; library: *see* Libraries; Pres. Prof. E. BENEDINI; Sec. Comm. G. AMADEI; periodical publs. *Atti e Memorie N.S.* (annual).

Accademie di Belle Arti, *see* Colleges of Art and Music at the end of the chapter.

LEARNED SOCIETIES

AGRICULTURE AND VETERINARY SCIENCE

Associazione Forestale Italiana: Via Salaria 30, Rome; Pres. Dott. G. TRIPODO.

Istituto Agronomico per l'Oltremare (*Agronomic Institute for Overseas*): Via Antonio Cocchi 4, 50131 Florence; f. 1904; 50 mems.; library of 108,091 vols.; Gen. Dir. Prof. VINCENZO FAENZA; publ. *Rivista di Agricoltura Subtropicale e Tropicale* (quarterly).

Società Italiana delle Scienze Veterinarie: Via A. Bianchi 1, 25100 Brescia; f. 1947; 1,050 mems.; Pres. Prof. REMO FAUSTINI; publs. *Atti*†.

Società Italiana di Economia Agraria: Istituto di Economia e Politica Agraria, Piazzale Cascine 18, Florence; f. 1862; 130 mems.; Pres. Prof. M. TOFANI; publ. *Atti* (annual).

ARCHITECTURE AND TOWN PLANNING

Centro Internazionale di Studi di Architettura "Andrea Palladio": Domus Comestabilis–Basilica Palladiana, C.P. 593, 36100 Vicenza; f. 1959 to make known the work of Andrea Palladio, b. Padua 1508, and to encourage the study of Palladianism and of Venetian architecture of all ages; Pres. Avv. G. CAPPELLETTI; publ. *Bollettino* (annually).

Istituto Nazionale di Architettura (IN-ARCH): Palazzo Taverna, Via di Monte Giordano 36, Rome; f. 1959; 1,500 mems.; Pres. Sen. Dott. Ing. E. BATTISTA.

Istituto Nazionale di Urbanistica (INU): Via S. Caterina da Siena 46, Rome; f. 1930; 657 mems.; 1,831 assoc. mems.; Pres. C. RIPAMONTI; Sec. Prof. Arch. B. ZEVI; publ. *Urbanistica* (quarterly).

Italia Nostra—Associazione Nazionale per la Tutela del Patrimonio Storico Artistico e Naturale della Nazione (*Italia Nostra—National Association for the Preservation of the Historical, Artistic and Natural Heritage of the Nation*): Corso Vittorio Emanuele 287, Rome; f. 1955; library of 1,000 vols.; 20,000 mems.; Pres. GIORGIO LUCIANI; Sec.-Gen. SERENA MADONNA; publ. *Italia Nostra* (bi-monthly).

THE ARTS

Academia Española de Bellas Artes en Roma (*Spanish Fine Arts Academy in Rome*): Piazza San Pietro in Montorio 3 (Gianicolo), 00153 Rome; f. 1873; Dir. Prof. FEDERICO SOPEÑA IBÁÑEZ.

Associazione Filatelica Italiana: Via Vittoria Colonna 11, 00193 Rome; f. 1914; 700 mems.; library of 500 vols.; Pres. Dott. A. DIENA; Sec. MARIO COLONNELLI.

Centro Internazionale delle Arti e del Costume (*International Centre of Arts and Costume*): Palazzo Grassi, Venice and 27 via Montebello, Milan; f. 1951; research and documentation of History of Costume and recent expressions of contemporary art; Pres. Dott. P. MARINOTTI.

Consiglio Nazionale per i Beni Culturali e Ambientali (*National Council for Culture and the Environment*): Ministry of Culture and the Environment, Via del Collegio Romano 27, Rome; five committees: environment and architecture (Pres. G. DE ANGELIS D'OSSAT); archaeology (Pres. Prof G. MAETZKE); history of art (Pres. Prof. C. BRANDI); archives (Prof. G. I. CASSANDRO), books and cultural institutes (Pres. Prof. A. M. VINAY); Pres. of the Council, Minister for Culture and the Environment; Vice-Pres. Prof. C. GNUDI; Sec. Prof. V. GALLINARI.

Istituto di Studi Verdiani (*Institute of Verdi Studies*): Strada della Repubblica 57, 43100 Parma; f. 1960 under the patronage of the International Music Council and the Italian Ministry of Education; to study the life and works of Giuseppe Verdi; public body from 1963; library of 5,000 vols., archives of 7,500 documents; Pres. BRUNO MOLAJOLI; Dir. PIERLUIGI PETROBELLI; publs. *Verdi Bulletin, Quaderni, Proceedings of Congresses, Studi Verdiani.*

Istituto Italiano di Arti Grafiche S. p. A. (*Italian Institute of Graphic Art*): Via Zanica 92, 24100 Bergamo; library of 15,000 vols.; Dir. ROMANO MONTANARI.

Istituto Italiano per la Storia della Musica (*Italian Institute for the History of Music*): c/o Accademia di Santa Cecilia, Via Vittoria 6, 00187 Rome; Pres. Prof. L. RONGA; publ. *Bollettino.*

Istituto Universitario Olandese di Storia dell'Arte (*Dutch University Institute for the History of Art*): Viale Torricelli 5, 50125 Florence; f. 1955; library of 20,000 vols.; Dir. B. W. MEIJER.

Kunsthistorisches Institut (*Institute for the Study of the History of Art*): Via Giuseppe Giusti 44, Florence; f. 1897; library of 120,000 vols. and 320,000 reproductions; Dir. Prof. Dr. HERBERT KEUTNER.

Società Incoraggiamento Arti e Mestieri (*Society for the Encouragement of Arts and Crafts*): Via S. Marta 18, Milan; f. 1838.

Società Italiana di Musicologia: c/o Teatro Regio, Piazza Castello 215, 10124 Turin; f. 1964; 500 mems.; Pres. ALBERTO BASSO; publs. *Rivista Italiana di Musicologia, Quaderni della Rivista Italiana di Musicologia, Monumenti Musicali Italiani.*

Società Italiana Musica Contemporanea: Via Arno 47, Rome; Pres. M. PERAGALLO; Sec. V. FELLEGARA.

BIBLIOGRAPHY, LIBRARY SCIENCE AND MUSEOLOGY

Associazione Italiana Biblioteche: Via Milano 76, c/o Istituto di patologia del libro, 00184 Rome; f. 1930; 1,500 mems.; Pres. Dr. A. VINAY; Sec. Dr. A. M. CAPRONI; publ. *Bollettino d'informazioni*† (quarterly).

Associazione Nazionale dei Musei Italiani: Piazza San Marco 49, Rome; Pres. Prof. P. ROMANELLI; Sec. Prof. D. BERNINI; publ. *Musei e Gallerie d'Italia.*

Centro Di (*International Documentation Centre*): Piazza de'Mozzi Ir, 50125 Florence; f. 1968; documentation, distribution of books and catalogues in the field of art, architecture, visual communication; library of 8,000 vols.; Dir. F. MARCHI; publs. bulletin of catalogues, indexes.

Istituto Centrale di Patologia del Libro (*Central Institute of Book Pathology*): Via Milano 76, 00184 Rome; f. 1938; book restoration and preservation; library of 12,000 vols.; Dir. Prof. Dott. MARIA DI FRANCO; publ. *Bollettino*† (annually).

Economics, Law and Politics

Associazione Italiana di Diritto Marittimo (*Italian Maritime Law Association*): Via Po 1, Palazzo Assitalia, Rome; Sec.-Gen. Camilla Dagna.

Cenacolo Triestino: Palazzo della Camera di Commercio, Trieste; academy of economic and social studies; Piazzo della Borsa 14, Trieste; academy of economic and social studies; publs. *Bollettino*, and *Observatore Economico e Sociale*.

Istituto di Diritto Romano e dei Diritti dell' Oriente Mediterraneo: Facoltà di Giurisprudenza, Città Universitaria, Rome; f. 1937; library of 40,000 vols.; Dir. Prof. Giuseppe Branca.

Istituto di Economia Politica: Palazzo Universitario, L'Aquila; Dir. Prof. F. Pitigliani; Sec. Prof. M. Cremonese.

Istituto di Studi sul Lavoro: Palazzo della Civiltà del Lavoro, Quadrato della Concordia, Rome, EUR; f. 1926, re-organized 1947; library of 15,000 vols.; Pres. Avv. Guiliano Santoro; Sec.-Gen. Dr. Mario Telleschi; publs. *Studi sul Lavoro* (quarterly), *Corriere dei Congressi* (monthly), *Bollettino bibliografico ISL* (fortnightly), *Settimanale di diritto e legislazione del lavoro* (weekly), *C.N.I.O.S.*

Istituto Italiano di Diritto Spaziale: Via Giulia 251, Rome; f. 1962; Pres. Avv. Prof. P. Magno; 120 mems.; library of 2,600 vols.; Sec.-Gen. Dott. E. Scifoni.

Istituto per gli Studi di Politica Internazionale: Via Clerici 5, Milan; f. 1934 for the promotion of the study and knowledge of all problems concerning international relations; seminars at postgraduate level; library of 40,000 vols.; Pres. Enrico Aillaud; Gen. Dir. Giovanni Lovisetti; publs. *Relazioni Internazionali* (weekly), *ISPI Economia* (monthly), *Annuario di Politica Internazionale* (yearly).

Istituto per il Rinnovamento Economico (I.R.E.): Via Firenze 38, 00184 Rome; f. 1924; promotes international economic and monetary reform; Pres. G. di Domenico.

Istituto per l'Economia Europea: Via C. Colombo 70, 00147 Rome; f. 1960; 62 mems.; library of 1,500 vols.; Pres. Sen. Prof. Gaetano Stammati; Sec.-Gen. Dr. Angelo Bormioli; publs. *Europa: Fatti e Idee*†, *Europa Selezione*† (quarterly).

Società Italiana degli Economisti: Via Garibaldi 4, 16124 Genoa; f. 1950; 195 mems.; Pres. Prof. Steve; Sec-Gen. Prof. D'Alauro; publ. *Bollettino*.

Società Italiana di Economia Demografia e Statistica: Via F. Nicolai 49, 00136 Rome; Pres. Prof. Vittorio Castellano; Sec.-Gen. Prof. Stefano Somogyi.

Società Italiana per l'Organizzazione Internazionale (S.I.O.I.) (*UN Asscn. for Italy*): Via S. Marco 3, Palazzetto di Venezia, 00186 Rome; f. 1944; sections in Florence, Genoa, Milan, Naples, Turin; library *see* libraries; Pres. Prof. Roberto Ago; Sec.-Gen. Prof. Riccardo Monaco; publ. *La Comunità Internazionale* (quarterly).

Education

Centro Didattico Nazionale di Studi e Documentazione: Via Buonarroti 10, 50122 Florence, c/c Postale 5/11802; f. 1942; pedagogy, psychology, didactics, visual aids; library of 50,000 vols.; Dir. Prof. Enzo Petrini; publs. *Servizio d'Informazione e Documentazione Pedagogica*† (monthly), *Schedario*† (2 a month), *Archivio Didattico*†, *Quaderni dell'aggiornamento*†.

Istituto per la Cooperazione Universitaria: Viale Rossini 26, 00198 Rome; f. 1967; to promote cultural relations between different countries, chiefly through university co-operation, international meetings and study groups; international technical co-operation by sending volunteers and experts to developing countries; Pres. Prof. Raffaello Cortesini; Sec.-Gen. Dott. Umberto Farri; publs. *Co-operation in Education*† (quarterly in English), *SIPE—International Student Press Service*† (monthly in Italian), *Educazione e Sviluppo*† (quarterly).

History, Geography and Archaeology

Associazione Archeologica Romana (*Roman Archaeological Society*): Vicolo del Governo Vecchio 8, 00186 Rome; f. 1902; 500 mems.; library of 5,000 vols.; Pres. Prof. Pietro Romanelli; Sec. Avv. Mario Rist; publ. *Romana Gens* (monthly).

Deutsches Archäologisches Institut (*German Archaeological Institute*): Via Sardegna 79, 00187 Rome; f. 1829; 120,000 vols.; Dir. Prof. Dr. Theodor Kraus; Librarian Dr. Horst Blanck; publ. *Römische Mitteilungen*.

Ecole Française de Rome (Scuola Francese di Roma): Piazza Farnese 67, Rome; f. 1873; French school of archaeology and history; library of 98,000 vols., 1,400 periodicals and 13,000 off-prints; Dir. Georges Vallet; Dirs. of Studies Michel Gras, Jean-Claude Maire-Vigueur, Philippe Levillain; Librarian Noëlle Poinçon de la Blanchardière; publs. *Mélanges d'Archéologie et d'Histoire*, series *Antiquité* and *Moyen Age—Temps Modernes* (2 a year), *Suppléments aux Mélanges, Collection, Bibliothèque des Ecoles françaises d'Athènes et de Rome, Registres des Papes, Acta Nuntiaturae Gallicae*.

Fondazione Giangiacomo Feltrinelli: Via Romagnosi 3, 20121 Milan; f. 1949; history of international socialism, communism and labour movement; Dir. Giuseppe Del Bo; library of 400,000 vols., 20,000 periodicals; publs. *Annali, Quaderni, Papers*.

Istituto di Norvegia in Roma di Archaeologia e Storia dell'Arte: Viale XXX Aprile 33, Rome; f. 1962; library of 13,700 vols.; Dir. Prof. Hjalmar Torp; publ. *Acta ad Archaeologiam et Artium Historiam Pertinentia* (alternate years).

Istituto di Studi Etruschi ed Italici (*Institute for Etruscan and Italic Studies*): Via della Pergola 65, Florence; f. 1926; 190 mems.; library of 11,700 vols.; Pres. Prof. Massimo Pallottino; Sec. Dott. Guglielmo Maetzke; publs. *Studi etruschi*† (annual) and four series of books.

Istituto Ellenico di Studi Bizantini e Postbizantini di Venezia (*Hellenic Institute of Byzantine and Post-Byzantine Studies of Venice*): Castello 3412, 30122 Venice; f. 1951; library of 8,000 vols., and archives containing 200,000 documents of 16th to 19th centuries relating to the Ancient Community of Greek Orthodox Church; Dir. Prof. Manoussos Manoussacas; Sec.-Gen. Dr. Sotirios Messinis; publ. *Thesaurismata* (annual).

Istituto Geografico Militare: Via C. Battisti 10, Florence; f. 1872; geodetic and topographical surveying; official cartography; library of 110,000 vols.; Dir.-Gen. Br. Celestino Revelli; publ. *L'Universo* (2 a month).

Istituto Italiano di Numismatica: Palazzo Barberini, Via Quattro Fontane 13, Rome; f. 1936; Pres. Prof. Laura Breglia; publ. *Annali*.

Istituto Italiano di Paleontologia Umana: Piazza Mincio 2, 00198 Rome; f. 1913; quaternary environment, geology, palaeontology, palaeoanthropology, archaeology; 235 mems.; library of 5,000 vols., 50 periodicals; Pres. Prof. Dr. A. Ascenzi; Sec.-Gen. Prof. E. Segre-Naldini; publ. *Memorie*† (irregular).

Istituto Italiano per la Storia Antica: Via Milano 76, Rome; f. 1935; library of 15,000 vols.; Pres. Prof. S. Accame; publ. *Miscellanea Greca e Romana*†.

Istituto Nazionale di Archeologia e Storia dell'Arte: Piazza San Marco 49, Rome; f. 1922; library of 500,000 vols.; Commissioner Prof. M. Cagiano de Azevedo; publ. *Rivista*† (annually).

Istituto Nazionale di Studi sul Rinascimento: Palazzo Strozzi, 50123 Firenze; f. 1937; renaissance literature, history and philosophy, history of art; library of 20,000 vols.; 300 periodicals, 50,000 photographs; Pres. EUGENIO GARIN; Librarian CESARE VASOLI; publs. *Rinascimento* (annually), *Studi e Testi*.

Istituto Olandese a Roma (*Netherlands Institute*): Via Omero 10-12, 00197 Rome; f. 1904; classical archaeology, modern history, history of art; library of 40,000 vols.; Dir. (vacant); publs. *Mededelingen*†, *Studiën*†, *Scripta Minora*†.

Istituto Papirologico "Girolamo Vitelli": Università degli Studi, Via degli Alfani 46/48, Florence; f. 1908; study of Greek and Latin papyri; library of 9,000 vols.; Dir. Prof. MANFREDO MANFREDI; Curator Dr. GABRIELLA MESSERI SAVORELLI; publs. *Papiri Greci e Latini della Società Italiana* (*P.S.I.*), *Studi e Testi di Papirologia*.

Istituto per la Storia del Risorgimento Italiano (*Institute for the History of the Italian Risorgimento*): Vittoriano, Rome; f. 1935; 3,400 mems.; Pres. Prof. A. M. GHISALBERTI; Sec.-Gen. Prof. E. MORELLI; publs. *Rassegna storica del Risorgimento*, *Biblioteca Scientifica* (3 series).

Istituto Storico Germanico (*German Historical Institute*): Via Aurelia Antica 391, 00165 Rome; f. 1888; medieval and modern history; library of 100,000 vols.; Dir. Prof. R. ELZE; publ. *Quellen und Forschungen aus Italienischen Archiven und Bibliotheken*†.

Istituto Storico Italiano per il Medio Evo (*Italian Institute of Medieval History*): Piazza dell' Orologio 4, 00186 Rome; f. 1883; library of 100,000 vols.; Pres. Prof. RAFFAELLO MORGHEN; publs. *Bullettino*†, *Fonti per la Storia d'Italia*, *Regesta Chartarum Italiae*, *Studi Storici*, *Repertorium Fontium Historiae Medii Aevi*.

Istituto Storico Italiano per l'Età Moderna e Contemporanea: Via Michelangelo Caetani 32, Rome; Pres. ARMANDO SAITTA; Sec. Dott. C. LAMARO.

Istituto Svedese di Studi Classici (*Swedish Institute of Classical Studies*): Via Omero 14—Valle Giulia, 00197 Rome; f. 1926; 30 mems.; research in ancient history, archaeology, history of art and architecture, and to promote Swedish artistic activities in Italy; library of 38,500 vols.; Dir. CARL NYLANDER; publ. *Acta Instituti Romani Sveciae*†.

Scuola Spagnola di Storia e Archaeologia in Roma: Via di Villa Albani 16, Rome; f. 1910; library of 8,200 vols.; Dir. Prof. MARTIN ALMAGRO-GORBEA; publs. *Cuadernos de trabajos de la Escuela*†, *Biblioteca de la Escuela*†, *Monumentos de la Música Española*.

Società di Minerva: Piazza Hortis 4, Trieste; f. 1810 for the study of the history, art and culture of Trieste, Istria and Gorizia; 150 mems.; Pres. DOMENICO Conte ROSSETTI DE SCANDER; Sec. A. SERI; publ. *Archeografo Triestino* (annually).

Società di Studi Geografici (*Society for Geographical Studies*): Via Laura 48, Florence; f. 1895; 600 mems.; library of 18,000 vols.; Pres. Prof. PIERO INNOCENTI; Sec. Prof. PAOLO MARCACCINI; publ. *Rivista Geografica Italiana*† (quarterly).

Società Geografica Italiana: Villa Celimontana, Via della Navicella 12, Rome; f. 1867; library: *see* Libraries; Pres. Prof. ERNESTO MASSI; publs. *Bollettino*, *Memorie*.

Società Napoletana di Storia Patria (*Neapolitan Society of Italian History*): Piazza Municipio Maschio Angioino, Naples; f. 1876; 650 mems.; Pres. Prof. GUISEPPE GALASSO; Sec. Prof. ALBERTO VARVARO; publ. *Archivio Storico per le Province Napoletane*.

Società Romana di Storia Patria: Biblioteca Vallicelliana, Piazza della Chiesa Nuova 18, 00186 Rome; f. 1876; *c.* 100 mems.; Pres. Prof. GIULIO BATTELI; Sec. Prof. RENATO LEFEVRE; publs. *Archivio della Società* (annual), *Miscellanea della Società* (irregular).

Società Storica Lombarda: Via Morone 1, 20121 Milan; f. 1874; 450 mems.; library of 40,000 vols.; Pres. Marchese Dr. A. B. SFORZA; Sec. Conte Dr. F. ARESE; publ. *Archivio Storico Lombardo*†.

INTERNATIONAL CULTURAL INSTITUTES

(*See also* under Archaeology, Art, Law, History and Literature, Libraries).

Accademia Americana (*American Academy in Rome*): Via Angelo Masina 5, Rome; f. 1894; library of 92,000 vols.; Dir. SOPHIE CONSAGRA; Librarian ROGERS V. SCUDDER.

Academia Belgica: Via Omero 8, Rome; f. 1939; library of 89,000 vols.; research centre and residence; Dir. Prof. J. A. VAN HOUTTE; publ. *Bulletin de l'Institut Historique Belge de Rome*.

Accademia di Danimarca (*Danish Institute of Science and Art in Rome*): Via Omero 18, Rome; f. 1956; archaeology, philology, art, history of art, history of music, literature; library of *c.* 12,000; Dir. Prof. SØREN SKOVGAARD JENSEN; Sec. and Librarian Dr. KAREN ASCANI; publ. *Analecta Romana Instituti Danici*.

Accademia di Francia: Villa Medici, Viale Trinità dei Monti 1, 00187 Rome; f. 1666; library of 15,000 vols.; Dir. JEAN LEYMARIE.

Accademia Tedesca (*German Academy in Rome*): Villa Massimo, Largo di Villa Massimo 1-2, Rome; Dir. Dott. ELISABETH WOLKEN.

British Council: Palazzo del Drago, Via Quattro Fontane 20, 00184 Rome; f. 1945; libraries: *see* Libraries; Rep. M. J. WARD.

British Council Regional Directorate: via Manzoni 38, 20121 Milan; Reg. Dir. H. A. C. MEYRIC HUGHES.

British Institute: Palazzo Lanfredini, 9 Lungarno Guicciardini, Florence; f. 1917; courses in language, literature, history, etc.; cultural activities; 2,600 students; library of 60,000 vols.; Chair. Sir RONALD ARCULUS, K.C.M.G.; Dir. IAN GREENLEES, O.B.E.

British Institute: Via Quattro Fontane 109, Rome; 1,450 students; Dir. PATRICK CLARE, M.A.

British School at Rome: Via Gramsci 61, 00197 Rome; f. 1901, inc. by Royal Charter 1912; prehistoric archaeology, classical studies, medieval and later archaeology, history and art history, architecture, fine arts; library of *c.* 50,000 vols.; Dir. D. B. WHITEHOUSE, M.A., PH.D., F.S.A., F.R.G.S.; publs. *Papers* (annual), *Supplementary Publications* (occasional).

Canadian Cultural Institute in Rome: c/o Canadian Embassy, Via G.B. de Rossi 27, 00161 Rome; f. 1966; to foster and promote the cultural ties between Canada and Italy by organizing various cultural events in the performing and visual arts, and by promoting academic exchanges; Pres. J. E. G. HARDY, Canadian Amb. to Italy; Sec. Dr. DAVID G. H. ANIDO, Cultural Attaché.

Casa de Cervantes: Via del Collegio di Spagna 4A, 40123 Bologna; f. 1955 by Colegio de España; Spanish cultural centre; lectures, concerts, exhibitions; library of 20,000 vols.; Dir. Prof. EVELIO VERDERA Y TUELLS.

Centre Culturel Français: Via Bigli 2, Milan; f. 1950; library of 50,000 vols.; Dir. (vacant); Sec.-Gen. CLAUDE MATHIS.

Centre Culturel Français: Via Quintino Sella 76, Palermo; f. 1952; 500 mems.; library of 14,000 vols.; Dir. M. A. H. CHEREL; Sec.-Gen. Mme ANGELE MARANZANO.

Centre Culturel Français: Piazza Campitelli 3, Rome; Dir. ETIENNE GUELAUD; Sec.-Gen. JACQUES BREANT.

Centre Culturel Franco-Italien Galliera (*Franco-Italian Cultural Centre*): Via Garibaldi 20, 16124 Genoa; f. 1959; 1,500 mems.; library of 16,000 vols.; Dir. R. MORLET.

Centro Culturale Tedesco—Goethe Institut: Via Vaccarini 1, Palermo; f. 1963; Dir. Dr. HANS STIEBER.

Deutsches Kulturinstitut: Via Coroneo 15, Trieste; f. 1961; library of 7,500 vols.; Dir. HANS-OTTO BROECKER.

Deutsches Kulturinstitut: Riviera de Chiaia 202, 80121 Naples; f. 1970; concerts, films, exhibitions; Dir. (vacant).

Goethe Institut: Salita S. Caterina 4, 16123 Genoa; f. 1959; Dir. Dott. BERNHARD WITTEK.

Goethe Institut Mailand: Via dei Bossi 4, 20121 Milan; f. 1958; cultural activities, language courses; library of 22,000 vols.; Dir. Dr. RENATE ALBRECHT.

Goethe-Institut Rom: Via del Corso 262-67, 00186 Rome; f. 1956; library of 30,000 vols.; Dir. Dr. CH. SCHMITT.

Instituto Español de Santiago (*Spanish Institute*): Via d, San Giacomo 40, 80133 Naples; f. 1951; Dir. Prof. P. J. CABELLO.

Institutum Romanum Finlandiae: Villa Lante, Passeggiata del Gianicolo 10, Rome; f. 1938; Classical and Italian studies; library of 8,600 vols.; Dir. Prof. EVA MARGARETA STEINBY; publ. *Acta Instituti Romani Finlandiae*†.

Istituto Austriaco di Cultura in Roma (*Austrian Institute of Culture in Rome*): Viale Bruno Buozzi 113, Rome; f. 1881; library of 30,000 vols.; Dir. Prof. Dr. HEINRICH SCHMIDINGER; publs. *Römische Historische Mitteilungen*†, *Publikationen des Österreichischen Kultur-Institutes in Rom*†.

Istituto Culturale Italo-Braziliano: Palazzo Doria Pamphili, Piazza Navona 14, Rome; Dir. Prof. M. MENDES.

Istituto Danese di Cultura (*The Danish Institute*): Via Dogana 2, 20123 Milan; f. 1948; library contains 3,000 vols.; publ. *Relazione con la Danimarca* (2 a year).

Istituto Giapponese di Cultura: Via Antonio Gramsci 74, 00197 Rome; f. 1962; library of 16,000 vols.; Dir. MORIHIKO OKATSU; Librarian MASAHARU YAMADA; publs. *Annuario*†, *Notiziario*†.

Istituto Italiano di Studi Germanici (*Italian Institute for Germanic Studies*): Via Calandrelli 25, Rome; f. 1932; library of 60,000 vols.; Dir. Prof. PAOLO CHIARINI; publ. *Studi Germanici*†.

Istituto Italo-Africano: Via Ulisse Aldrovandi 16, 00197 Rome; Pres. Prof. PARIDE STEFANINI; Sec.-Gen. Amb. LUIGI GASBARRI; publs. *Africa* (quarterly), *La Voce dell' Africa* (monthly).

Istituto Italo-Latino Americano: Piazza Guglielmo Marconi 00144 Rome; f. 1966; library: *see* Libraries; Sec.-Gen. CARLO PERRONE CAPANO; publs. *Bollettino Mensile*, etc.

Istituto Svizzero di Roma: Via Ludovisi 48, 00187 Rome; Dir. Prof. Dr. C. KRAUSE.

Polska Akademia Nauk (*Polish Academy of Sciences*): Vicolo Doria 2, Rome; f. 1886; library of 30,000 vols.; 60,000 photographs; Dir. Prof. Dr. BRONISŁAW BILIŃSKI; Librarian Dott. MARIA RECZEK.

Real Colegio de San Clemente de los Españoles (*Royal College of St. Clements'*): Via del Collegio di Spagna 4, 40123 Bologna; f. 1364 under Will of Cardinal don Gil de Albornoz; study centre for 20 Spanish postgraduates; library of 12,000 vols.; Rector Prof. Dr. EVELIO VERDERA Y TUELLS; publ. *Studia Albornotiana* (irregular).

Svenska Institutet i Rom (*Swedish Institute in Rome*): Via Omero 14, 00197 Rome; f. 1926; library of 37,000 vols.; Dir. Prof. CARL NYLANDER; courses for students of classical archaeology and history of art; fellowships in classical philology, archaeology and architecture; excavations at San Giovenale and Acquarossa; publ. *Acta Instituti Romani Regni Sueciae*†, including *Opuscula Romana*†.

U.S. Information Service: Via Boncompagni 2, Rome; also in Milan and Naples; libraries in Rome, Milan and Naples.

LANGUAGE AND LITERATURE

Keats-Shelley Memorial Association: Piazza di Spagna 26, Rome; f. 1909; library of 7,800 vols.; Dir. Sir JOSEPH CHEYNE, publs. *Bulletin*, *Journal*.

P.E.N. International Centre: via M. Clementi 64, Rome; Pres. MARIA BELLONCI; Sec.-Gen. ROSARIO ASSUNTO.

Società Dante Alighieri: Palazzo di Firenze, Piazza Firenze 27, Rome; f. 1889; Sec.-Gen. GIUSEPPE COTA.

Società Dantesca Italiana (*Italian Dante Society*): Via dell'Arte della Lana 1, 50123 Florence; f. 1888; library of 15,000 vols., 1,500 microfilms; Pres. Prof. FRANCESCO MAZZONI; publs. *Studi Danteschi*, *Quaderni degli "Studi Danteschi"*, *Edizione Nazionale delle Opere di Dante Alighieri*.

Società Filologica Romana: Città Universitaria, Rome; f. 1901; library of 8,000 vols.; Pres. AURELIO RONCAGLIA; publ. *Studi Romanzi*.

Società Letteraria (*Literary Society*): Piazzetta Scalette Rubiani 1, Verona; f. 1808; library of 107,000 vols.; Dir. Avvocato ALFONSO BALIS CREMA; publ. *Bollettino* (annually).

MEDICINE

Associazione Italiana di Dietetica e Nutrizione Clinica (ADI): Via dei Penitenzieri 13, 00193 Rome; Pres. Prof. P. MONTENERO.

Associazione Italiana di Medicina Aeronautica e Spaziale: Via Piero Gobetti 2-A, Rome; Sec.-Gen. Prof. ARISTIDE SCANO.

Associazione Italiana di Radiologia Medica e Medicina Nucleare (S.I.R.M.N.): Istituto di Radiologia dell'Università, Policlinico San Matteo, 27100 Pavia; Pres. Prof. L. DI GUGLIELMO; Sec. Prof. C. MONTEMARTINI.

Centro di Studi e Ricerche di Medicina Aeronautica e Spaziale dell'Aeronautica Militare: Via Piero Gobetti 2A, 00185 Rome; f. 1951; library of 4,000 vols.; Dir. Col. GIORGIO MEINERI.

Fondazione "Centro di Studi di Patologia Molecolare Applicata alla Clinica": Via Pace 15, 20122 Milan; f. 1969; research in molecular biology; library of 4,000 vols.; Pres. Dir. Prof. LUIGI VILLA; Sec.-Librarian Dr. OLGA MOSCA.

Istituto Sieroterapico Milanese (*Milan Serum Institute*): Via Darwin 20, Milan; f. 1896; library of 32,487 vols.; Dir. Prof. A. DE BARBIERI.

Società Italiana di Anestesiologia e Rianimazione: Corso Bramante 83, Turin; Pres. Prof. A. D. CATTANEO; Sec.-Gen. Dott. L. SEMINO.

Società Italiana di Cancerologia: Istituto di Anatomia, Università di Napoli, Via L. Armanni 5, Naples; Pres. Prof. P. VERGA; Sec. Prof. P. BUCALOSSI.

Società Italiana di Chirurgia: Clinica Chirurgica Umberto 1, Policlinico, 00161 Rome; Pres. Prof. GIUSEPPE ZANNINI.

Società Italiana di Epatologia: Via Crescenzio 48, 00193 Rome; Pres. Prof. L. CONDORELLI; Sec. Prof. P. VALORI.

Società Italiana di Medicina del Traffico: Istituto di Clinica Ortopedica e Traumatologica dell'Università Piazzale delle Scienze, Rome; f. 1958; 688 mems.; Pres. Prof. GIORGIO MONTICELLI; Vice-Pres. Prof. FERDINANDO NICOLETTI, FERDINANDO ANTONIOTTI; Gen. Sec. Prof. LAMBERTO PERUGIA.

Società Italiana di Medicina del Lavoro: Via S. Barnaba 8. 20122 Milan; f. 1906; 900 mems.; Pres. Prof. DUILIO CASULA.

Società Italiana di Medicina Interna: Corso Francia 197, 00191 Rome; Pres. Prof. ALESSANDRO BERETTA ANGUISSOLA; Sec. Prof. ANDREA SCIACCA.

Società Italiana di Medicina Legale e delle Assicurazioni: Via Falloppio 50, Padua; Pres. Prof. FRANCESCO INTRONA; Sec. SILVIO MERLY.

Società Italiana di Neuroradiologia: Via Gen. Orsini 40, Naples; Sec. Prof. ENZO VALENTINO.

Società Italiana di Odontostomatologia e Chirurgia Maxillo-Facciale: Clinica Odontoiatrica, Viale Regina Elena 287, Rome; f. 1957; 380 mems.; Pres. Prof. LUIGI CAPOZZI; Sec. Prof. GIORGIO RE; publ. *Minerva Stomatologica* (every two months).

Società Italiana di Ortopedia e Traumatologia: presso Clinica Ortopedica, Università, Piazzale delle Scienze 5, Rome; f. 1906; 1,199 mems.; Pres. Prof. LUIGI BOECH; Sec. Prof. MARCELLO PIZZETTI; publ. *Atti e Relazioni del Congresso* (annual).

Società Italiana di Ostetricia e Ginecologia: Policlinico Umberto 1, 00161 Rome; f. 1892; 1,050 mems.; Pres. Prof. FRANCO CRAINZ; publs. *Atti, Bollettino.*

Società Italiana di Reumatologia: Istituto di Reumatologia, Policlinico Umberto 1, Rome; Pres. Prof. DOMENICO GIGANTE; Sec.-Gen. Prof. V. PIPITONE.

Società Italiana di Scienze Farmaceutiche: Via Giorgio Jan 18, 20129 Milan; f. 1953; 550 mems.; Pres. Prof. PIERO SENSI; Exec. Sec. Prof. FRANCO BONATI; publ. *Cronache Farmaceutiche* (bi-monthly).

Società Medica Chirurgica di Bologna (*Society of Medicine and Surgery*): Piazza Galvani 1, 40124 Bologna; 330 mems.; library of 15,000 vols.; Sec. Prof. MICHELE FIORENTINO; publ. *Bullettino delle Scienze Mediche*†.

NATURAL SCIENCES

General

Gruppo Italiano di Storia della Scienza (*Italian History of Science Group*): Largo E. Fermi 6, Florence; Pres. Prof. V. RONCHI.

Istituto di Studi Adriatici (*Institute of Adriatic Studies*): 1364-A Riva 7 Martiri, 30122 Venice; f. 1946; Pres. Prof. G. FERRO; publ. *Memorie di Biogeografia Adriatica.*

Istituto di Studi e Ricerche Carlo Cattaneo: Via Santo Stefano 6, 40100 Bologna; f. 1956; study and research in the field of social science with particular regard to education, politics, religion and family; 5 full-time researchers, 12 part-time; library of 9,000 vols. in sociology and political science; 1,120 specialized journals; Pres. Prof. ARTURO PARISI; Sec. Dr. GIUSEPPE LOVATO.

Società Adriatica di Scienze (*Adriatic Society of Sciences*): Piazza G. Verdi 1, 34121 Trieste; f. 1874; 200 mems.; library of 27,000 vols.; Pres. Prof. EDMONDO HONSELL; Vice-Pres. Prof. DUILIO LAUSI; Sec. Dr. FRANCO STRAVISI; publ. *Bollettino*† (annually).

Società Italiana di Scienze Naturali (*Italian Society of Natural Sciences*): presso il Civico Museo di Storia Naturale, Corso Venezia 55, 20121 Milan; f. 1857; library of 1,200 periodicals; Sec. E. BANFI; publs. *Atti*†, *Natura*†, *Memorie*†.

Società Italiana per Il Progresso delle Scienze: Viale di Porta Tiburtina 36, 00185 Rome; f. 1839; library of 30,000 vols.; Pres. Prof. ANTONIO CARRELLI; Sec.-Gen. Prof. VALERIO GIACOMINI; publ. *Atti delle Riunioni della SIPS, Scienza e Tecnica* (monthly).

Società Toscana di Scienze Naturali (*Tuscan Society of Natural Sciences*): Via S. Maria 53, 56100 Pisa; f. 1847; 400 mems.; library of 50,000 vols.; Sec.-Gen. Prof. CARLO TOZZI; publ. *Atti* (2 a year).

Biological Sciences

Herbarium Universitatis Florentinae (Museo Botanico): Via La Pira 4, 50121 Florence; f. 1842; systematic botany, plant geography; Dir. Prof. GUIDO MOGGI; publ. *Webbia*† (bi-annually).

Istituto Nazionale di Entomologia (*National Institute of Entomology*): Via Catone 34, 00192 Rome; f. 1940; Pres. (vacant); publ. *Fragmenta Entomologica.*

Società Botanica Italiana (*Italian Botanical Society*): Via Giorgio La Pira 4, 50121 Florence; f. 1888; 900 mems.; library of 9,000 vols.; Pres. Prof. RUGGERO TOMASELLI; Sec. Prof. EDMONDO HONSELL; publs. *Giornale Botanico Italiano*†, *Informatore Botanico Italiano*†.

Società Entomologica Italiana (*Italian Entomological Society*): Museo Civico di Storia Naturale, via Brigata Liguria 9, 16121 Genoa; f. 1869.

Mathematics

Istituto Centrale di Statistica (*Central Institute of Statistics*): Via Cesare Balbo 16, Rome; f. 1926; library of 100,000 vols.; Dirs.-Gen. S. MARINO and L. PINTO; publs. *Annuario, Compendio* (yearly), *Bollettino* (monthly), Yearbooks on main statistics, etc.

Istituto Nazionale di Alta Matematica Francesco Severi: Città Universitaria, Rome; f. 1939; Pres. Prof. EDOARDO VESENTINI; publs. *Rendiconti di Matematica, Symposia Mathematica.*

Società Italiana di Statistica: c/o Facoltà di Scienze Statistiche dell' Università, Via Nomentana 41, 00161 Rome; f. 1939; 520 mems.; Pres. Prof. GUISEPPE LETI; Gen. Sec. Prof. LUCIANO CIUCCI; publ. Proceedings of the Scientific Meeting.

Physical Sciences

Associazione Geofisica Italiana: c/o Istituto Fisica Atmosfera, Piazzale Luigi Sturzo 31, 00144 Rome; f. 1942; 300 mems.; library of 1,500 vols.; Pres. Prof. GIORGIO FEA; Sec. Dr. FRANCO VIVONA; publs. *Rivista Italiana di Geofisica, Bollettino Geofisico.*

Istituto Biochimico Italiano (*Italian Biochemical Institute*): Via Brembo 59, Milan; f. 1918; library of 12,000 vols.

Istituto Idrografico dell Marina (*Naval Institute of Hydrography*): Passo Osservatorio 4, 16134 Genoa; f. 1872; library of 36,000 vols.; Library Dir. Mrs. P. PRESCIUTTINI BELLEZZA.

Istituto Italiano di Idrobiologia "Marco de Marchi" (*Italian Hydrobiological Institute*): Verbania Pallanza; f. 1938; ecological research into inland waters, physiographical studies on drainage basins and chemical, physical and biological characterization of rivers and lakes; library of 4,280 vols., 35,600 reprints and 656 periodicals; Pres. Dr. EMILIANO BERTONE; Dir. Prof. Dott. LIVIA TONOLLI; publ. *Memorie dell'Istituto Italiano di Idrobiologia* (1–2 per year).

Istituto Italiano di Storia della Chimica: Via G. B. Morgagni 32, Rome; Pres. Prof. M. TALENTI; Sec.-Gen. Prof. A. VITOLO.

Istituto Nazionale di Geofisica (*National Institute of Geophysics*): Città Universitaria, Rome; Dir. Prof. E. MEDI.

Istituto Nazionale di Ottica (*National Institute of Optics*). Largo Enrico Fermi 6, 50125 Florence; f. 1927; quantum, instrumental and physiological optics; 25 mems.; library of 2,000 vols.; Pres. and Dir. Prof. F. TITO ARECCHI.

Servizio Geologico d'Italia (*Italian Geological Survey*): Largo Santa Susanna, n. 13, Rome; f. 1873; study of earth sciences; library of 100,000 vols.; Dir. ALFREDO JACOBACCI; publs. *Bollettino*† (yearly), *Memorie per servire alla descrizione della Carta geologica d'Italia*† (irregular), *Memorie descrittive della Carta geologica d'Italia*† (irregular), *Carta geologica d'Italia 1: 100,000*†, maps on various scales.

Società Astronomica Italiana (*Italian Astronomical Society*): Via Brera 28, 20121 Milan; f. 1920; 560 mems.; Pres. Prof. MARIO RIGUTTI; Sec. Prof. GIUSEPPE TAGLIAFERRI; publs. *Memorie* (quarterly), *Giornale di Astronomia* (quarterly).

Società Chimica Italiana: Viale Liegi 48, Rome; f. 1919; Pres. Prof. LAMBERTO MALATESTA; Sec. Dott. M. ANTONIETTA BERARDI; publs. *Gazzetta Chimica Italiana, Annali di Chimica, La Chimica e l'Industria.*

Società Geologica Italiana: c/o Istituto di Geologia, Città Universitaria, Rome; f. 1881; 1,550 mems.; Sec. Dott. ACHILLE ZUCCARI; publs. *Bollettino*† (quarterly), *Memorie*† (quarterly).

Società Italiana di Fisica (*Italian Physics Society*): Via L. degli Andalò 2, 40124 Bologna; 1,391 mems.; library of 6,500 vols.; Pres. Prof. C. CASTAGNOLI; Sec.-Gen. Dr. G. A. WOLZAK; publs. *Il Nuovo Cimento* (3 a month), *Lettere al Nuovo Cimento* (weekly), *Rivista del Nuovo Cimento* (quarterly), *Bollettino* (irregular), *Giornale di Fisica, Fisica e Tecnologia* (quarterly).

Ufficio Centrale di Ecologia Agraria e difesa delle Piante coltivate dalle Avversità Meteoriche (*Meteorological and Ecological Centre*): Ministero di Agricoltura, Via del Caravita 7A, Rome; controls the following observatories: Catania, Monte Rosa, Sperimentale di Verona; Dir. Prof. EZIO ROSINI.

PHILOSOPHY AND PSYCHOLOGY

Associazione Internazionale Filosofia, Arti e Scienze: Via Oberdan 15, 40126 Bologna; f. 1957; Pres. Prof. F. FLARER; Sec.-Gen. Prof. C. GENOVESE; publ. *Quaderni FAS.*

Istituto Veneto di Scienze, Lettere ed Arti (*Venetian Institute of Science, Letters and Arts*): Campo S. Stefano 2945, Venice; f. 1838; library of 184,000 vols.; Pres. Prof. VITTORE BRANCA; publs. *Atti, Memorie.*

Società di Letture e Conversazioni Scientifiche (*Scientific Society*): Piazza Fontane Marose 6, Genoa; f. 1866; library of 15,310 vols.; Dir. P. BOZZO-COSTA.

Società Italiana di Parapsicologia: Via Filippo Nicolai 49, 00136 Rome; f. 1937; 300 mems.; Pres. Prof. STEFANO SOMOGYI; Vice-Pres. Prof. GUISEPPE LETI, SYLVIO VIANELLI; publs. *Rassegna Italiana di Ricerca Psichica* (3 times a year), *Studi e Problemi di Parapsicologia* (periodically).

Società Italiana per gli Studi Filosofici e Religiosi: presso l'Università Cattolica del Sacro Cuore, Piazza S. Ambrogio 9, Milan; library of 25,618 vols.; Pres. Prof. GUSTAVO BONTADINI; Librarian Dott. VALENTINO FOFFANO.

Società Nazionale di Scienze, Lettere ed Arti—Ex-Società Reale (*National Society of Science, Arts and Letters*): Via Mezzocannone 8, Naples; library of 9,875 vols.; Pres. Prof. E. PONTIERI; Sec.-Gen. Prot. A. SCHERILLO.

RELIGION, SOCIOLOGY AND ANTHROPOLOGY

Comitato Italiano per lo Studio dei Problemi della Popolazione (*Italian Committee for the Study of Population Problems*): Via Nomentana 41, 00161 Rome; f. 1928; library of 8,000 vols.; Pres. Prof. N. FEDERICI; Sec-Gen. Dott. E. BRIGHENTI; publ. *Genus* (2 a year).

Fondazione Internazionale Premio E. Balzan: Secretariat: Via A. Manzoni 38, Milan; also Claridenstr. 35, Zürich, Switzerland; f. 1957; prizes and funds used as a contribution towards peace and a better understanding of the arts and sciences; Pres. G. COLLI; Sec. N. MERZAGORA.

Fondazione Marco Besso (*Marco Besso Foundation*): Largo di Torre Argentina 11, Rome; promotes development of Italian economy; library of more than 80,000 vols.; Pres. Prof. ALBERTO MARIA GHISALBERTI.

Istituto Italiano di Antropologia (*Italian Institute of Anthropology*) **(formerly Società Romana di Antropologia):** Città Universitaria, Rome; f. 1893; Pres. Prof. G. D. BOVET; Technical Dir. and Sec. Prof. V. CORRENTI; publ. *Rivista di Antropologia* (annual).

Istituto Italiano per il Medio e l'Estremo Oriente (I.S.M.E.O.) (*Italian Institute for the Middle and Far East*): Palazzo Brancaccio, via Merulana 248, Rome; f. 1933; Pres. Prof. GHERARDO GNOLI; a library and museum of oriental art are attached to the Institute; publs. *East and West* (quarterly), *Rome Oriental Series, Nuovo Ramusio, Archaeological reports, Cina, Il Giappone* (annually).

Istituto Superiore di Scienze e Tecniche dell' Opinione Pubblica (*Institute of the Science of Public Opinion*): Viale Pola 12, 00198 Rome; f. 1944; branches in Milan and Turin; Pres. F. A. MORLION, Co-Pres. Prof. V. ROVIGATTI.

Società di Etnografia Italiana: Via Tacito 50, 00193 Rome; f. 1911 to investigate the folklore of Italy; library of 4,000 vols.; 170 mems.; Pres. Prof. PADLO TOSCHI; publ. *Lares* (quarterly).

Società Italiana di Sociologia: Istituto di Statistica e Ricerca Sociale "C-Gini", Piazza delle Scienze 5, 00185 Rome; f. 1937.

TECHNOLOGY

Associazione Elettrotecnica ed Elettronica Italiana (AEI) (*Italian Electrical Engineering and Electronics Association*): Viale Monza 259, 20126 Milan; f. 1896; Pres. G. DAL MONTE; publs. *L'Elettrotecnica, L'Energia Elettrica* (monthly), *Alta Frequenza* (2 a month).

Associazione Italiana per le Scienze Astronautiche: Via. Borghesano Lucchese 24, Rome; f. 1952; Pres. Prof. V. RONCHI.

Associazione Nazionale di Ingegneria Nucleare: Piazza Sallustio 24, Rome; Sec.-Gen. ARTURO CALORI.

Comitato Elettrotecnico Italiano (C.E.I.) (*Italian Electrotechnical Committee*): Viale Monza 259, 20126 Milan; Pres. Prof. CORRADO GENESIO.

Comitato Termotecnico Italiano (C.T.I.) (*Italian Thermotechnical Committee*): c/o Istituto di Fisica Tecnica, Politecnico, Turin; f. 1950; Pres. Prof. CAMILLO ZANCHI; Gen. Sec. Prof. VINCENZO FERRO.

Ente Nazionale Italiano di Unificazione (UNI) (*Italian National Standards Association*): Piazza Diaz 2, 20123 Milan; f. 1921; Pres. PIERO GIUSTINIANI; Vice-Pres. and Dir.-Gen. FRANCO BECCALLI; publ. *Unificazione* (quarterly).

Istituto di Studi Nucleari per l'Agricoltura (I.S.N.A.): Via IV Novembre 152, 00187 Rome; f. 1959; Pres. Avv. G. GESUALDI; Sec.-Gen. Prof. M. L. SCARSELLI; publs. *Agricoltura d'Italia* (monthly), *Il Corriere di Roma, Terra e macchine, Quaderni I.S.N.A.*

Istituto Elettrotecnico Nazionale 'Galileo Ferraris' (*The Galileo Ferraris National Electrotechnical Institute*): Corso Massimo d'Azeglio 42, Turin; f. 1935; 200 mems.; Pres. Prof. Dott. MARIO REY; publ. *Pubblicazioni IEN*† (*c.* 75 a year).

Istituto Italiano del Marchio di Qualità (*Italian Institute of the Quality Mark*): Via dei Pestagalli 1, 20138 Milan; f. 1951; Pres. FRANCO BIANCHI DI CASTELBIANCO; publs. *Elenco dei materiali ed apparecchi ammessi al Marchio.*

Istituto Italiano della Saldatura (*Italian Welding Institute*): Viale Sauli 39/5, 16121 Genoa; f. 1948; 800 mems.; Pres. F. CATTANEI; publ. *Rivista Italiana della Saldatura*†.

RESEARCH INSTITUTES

(*see* also under Universities)

CONSIGLIO NAZIONALE DELLE RICERCHE (C.N.R.)

(National Research Council of Italy)

PIAZZALE DELLE SCIENZE 7, ROME

Founded 1923

Objects: (1) to promote and co-ordinate scientific research in the field of mathematical, physical and natural sciences, both pure and applied (inclusive of engineering, medicine and agriculture, and exclusive of nuclear research); (2) to make grants-in-aid to scientific institutes or to individual research workers; (3) to advise the various ministries on scientific and technical matters.

President: Prof. ALESSANDRO FAEDO.

Secretary-General: Dott. ERNESTO MANGO.

Presidential Council (Consiglio di Presidenza): 14 mems.: the President, the 11 Chairmen of the National Consultative Committees, the Governor of the Bank of Italy, Secretary-General of the Plan and the Secretary-General of the C.N.R.; the Presidential Council is responsible for scientific and technical administration.

Administrative Board (Giunta Amministrativa): 5 mems.: the President, the Chairmen of 2 National Consultative Committees, the Governor of the Bank of Italy and the Secretary-General of the C.N.R.; the Board is responsible for the economic and financial administration of the C.N.R.

National Consultative Committees (Comitati Nazionali di Consulenza): The field of activities of the C.N.R. includes 11 divisions (Mathematics; Physics; Chemistry; Biology and Medicine; Geology and Mining; Agriculture; Engineering and Architecture; History, Philosophy and Philology; Juridical and Political Sciences; Economics, Sociology and Statistics; Technological Research) with 140 members.

Study Commissions: at present 50; appointed by the President to deal with certain problems.

Institutes: (21 in own premises) and

Research Centres and Laboratories: 191, mostly attached to universities.

CNR INSTITUTES AND RESEARCH CENTRES:

Mathematical Sciences

Istituto Applicazione Calcolo "Mauro Picone": Viale del Policlinico 137, 00010 Rome; Dir. Prof. I. GALLIGANI.

Five laboratories and research centres.

Physical Sciences

Istituto di Acustica "O. M. Corbino": via Cassia 1216, 00189 Rome; Dir. Prof. A. BARONE.

Istituto di Elaborazione della Informazione: via S. Maria 46, 56100 Pisa; f. 1968; applied mathematics and numerical analysis, programming systems, biomedical engineering, information processing systems, non-numerical information processing; library of 4,000 vols.; Dir. Prof. G. CAPRIZ; publ. *Calcolo* (quarterly).

Istituto per la Fisica dell'Atmosfera: piazzale Luigi Sturzo 31, 00144 Rome; f. 1961; meteorology, atmospheric physics, geophysics, oceanography; library of 3,000 vols.; Dir. Prof. G. FEA.

Istituto di Ricerca sulle Onde Elettromagnetiche: via Panciatichi 56, 50127 Florence; Dir. Prof. G. TORALDO DI FRANCIA.

Twenty-one laboratories and research centres.

Chemical Sciences

Istituto di Chimica delle Macromolecole: via A. Corti 12, Milan; f. 1970; research in the field of chemistry, physical chemistry and physics of synthetic and natural macromolecules and of their molecular models; Dir. Prof. G. ZERBI.

Forty-six laboratories and research centres.

Engineering and Architectural Sciences

Istituto Motori: Piazza Barsanti e Matteucci I, 80125 Naples; f. 1940; theoretical and experimental research on i.c. engines and accessories; library of 2,000 vols.; Dir. Prof. C. CAPUTO.

Istituto "CNUCE": via S. Maria 36, 56100 Pisa; Dir. Prof. G. TORRIGIANI.

Twenty-three laboratories and research centres.

Biological and Medical Sciences

Istituto di Biologia del Mare: Riva 7 Martiri 1364/A, 30122 Venice; Dir. Prof. B. BATTAGLIA.

Istituto Internazionale di Genetica e Biofisica: via Marconi 10, 80125 Naples; f. 1962; basic and molecular biology, genetics and biochemistry of viruses and cells, biophysics, neurochemistry, human genetics; library of *c.* 8,000 books and periodicals; Dir. LUCIO LUZZATTO.

Istituto di Psicologia: via dei Monti Tiburtini 509, 00157 Rome; Dir. Prof. R. MISITI.

Twenty-eight laboratories and research centres.

Agricultural Sciences

Thirty laboratories and research centres.

Geological and Mineralogical Sciences

Istituto di Ricerca per la Protezione Idrogeologica nell'Italia Meridionale ed Insulare: 87033 Castiglione Cosentino Scalo (Cosenza); Dir. Prof. C. RODA.

Istituto Internazionale per le Ricerche Geotermiche: Lungarno Pacinotti 55, 56100 Pisa; Dir. Prof. E. TONGIORGI.

Istituto Internazionale di Vulcanologia: viale Regina Margherita 6, Catania; Dir. Prof. G. MARINELLI.

Twenty-two laboratories and research centres.

Historical, Philosophical and Philological Sciences

Istituto per gli Studi Micenei e Egeo-anatolici: via Monzambano 9, Rome; Dir. Prof. C. GALLAVOTTI.

Eleven research centres.

Juridical and Political Sciences

Istituto per la Documentazione Giuridica: via Panciatichi 56/16, Florence; Dir. Prof. L. LOMBARDI-VALLAURI.

Istituto di Studi Sulle Regioni: Piazza Cavour 19, 00193 Rome; Dir. Prof. A. LA PERGOLA.

Economic, Sociological and Statistical Sciences

One research centre.

Technological Sciences

Istituto Centrale per l'Industrializzazione e la Tecnologia Edilizia: via del Vecchio Politecnico 3, Milan; Dir. M. MANFREDI.

Istituto del Legno: piazza Edison 11, Florence; f. 1954; library of 3,500 vols.; Dir. Prof. G. GIORDANO; publs. *Contributi Scientifico-Pratici per una Migliore Conoscenza ed Utilizzazione del Legno*† (twice yearly).

Istituto di Metrologia "Gustavo Colonetti": Strada delle Cacce 73, Turin; Dir. Prof. A. BRAY.

Istituto di Ricerca sulle Acque: via Reno 1, 00198 Rome; Dir. Prof. R. PASSINO.

Thirteen laboratories and research centres.

AGRICULTURE AND VETERINARY SCIENCE

Istituto Sperimentale per la Cerealicoltura: Via Cassia 176, 00191 Rome; f. 1919; cereal crops improvement; 40 scientific staff; library of 15,000 vols.; Pres. D. BIANCHI; Dir. Prof. A. BIANCHI; publs. *Annali*†, *Genetica agraria*, *Maydica* (quarterly).

Istituto Sperimentale per la Zoologia Agraria (*Experimental Institute of Agricultural Zoology*): Via Lanciola-Cascine del Riccio, 50125 Florence; f. 1875; library of 42,000 vols.; Dir. R. ZOCCHI; publ. *Redia* (yearly).

THE ARTS

Centro Italiano di Ricerche Teatrali (*Centre of Theatre Research*): Piazza San Marco 47, Rome; Pres. Prof. Dott. PAOLO TOSCHI; Sec. Dott. A. D'AMICO.

Centro Sperimentale di Cinematografia: Via Tuscolana 1524, Rome; f. 1935; includes the National Film Theatre; Dir. Dott. L. FIORAVANTI.

ECONOMICS, LAW AND POLITICS

Istituto Affari Internazionali: Viale Mazzini 88, 00195 Rome; f. 1966; library of 8,000 vols.; Pres. CESARE MERLINI; Dir. ROBERTO ALIBONI; publs. *Lo Spettatore Internazionale*† (quarterly in English), *L'Italia nella Politica Internazionale* (annually), *Collana dello spettatore internazionale* (quarterly).

Istituto di Studi Europei "Alcide De Gasperi": Via Poli 29, 00187 Rome; f. 1955; Pres. Prof. Dr. EDOARDO MARTINO; Sec.-Gen. MICHELE FORMICA.

Istituto Italiano di Studi Legislativi: Via Bertoloni 8, Rome; f. 1925 to promote the scientific and technical studies of legislation; Pres. Prof. G. PIERO ORSELLO; Gen. Sec. Prof. G. PENNISI; publ. *Yearbook of Comparative Law and Legislative Studies*.

EDUCATION

Centro Europeo dell'Educazione: Villa Falconieri, Frascati; f. 1960; library of 4,000 vols.; Dir. Prof. ALDO M. MUSU.

HISTORY, GEOGRAPHY AND ARCHAEOLOGY

Centro Camuno di Studi Preistorici: 25044 Capo di Ponte Valcamonica; f. 1964; archaeological research, prehistoric art, primitive religions, anthropology and ethnology; specialized library; central archives on prehistoric art; summer seminars; international symposia; provides advisers and consultants on conservation, exhibition and evaluation of prehistoric and primitive art; Dir. Prof. EMMANUEL ANATI; publs. *Bollettino* (twice yearly), Monograph series, occasional vols.

Istituto di Studi Romani: Piazza dei Cavalieri di Malta 2, 00153 Rome; f. 1925; promotes the study of Rome and Latin; 90 mems.; library of 10,000 vols.; Pres. Prof. GIORGIO PETROCCHI; Vice-Pres. Prof. PAOLO BREZZI; Dir. Dott. FERNANDA ROSCETTI; publs. *Studi Romani* (quarterly), *Rassegna d'Informazioni* (fortnightly).

Istituto Siciliano di Studi Bizantini e Neoellenici: Via Noto 34, Palermo; f. 1952; 40 ordinary mems.; 40 corresponding mems.; library of 6,000 vols.; Pres. Prof. BRUNO LAVAGNINI; Sec.-Gen. Prof. GIROLAMO CARACAUSI.

MEDICINE

Associazione Italiana di Ricerca Operativa: Via Cesare Balbo 16, Rome; f. 1961; 225 mems.; Pres. Prof. B. BARBERI; publs. *Quaderni di RO* (annual), *Notiziario RO* (quarterly).

Centro Ricerche sulle Attività Umane Superiori: Istituto Fisica, Università di Ferrara, Ferrara; f. 1964; research on normal, mental and pathological phenomena concerned in experiences of graphic activity; Pres. Prof. A. DRIGO; Dir. Prof. F. FLARER; Sec. Dott. C. GENOVESE.

NATURAL SCIENCES

Centro Siciliano di Fisica Nucleare e di Struttura della Materia (C.S.F.Ne.S.M.) (*Sicilian Centre of Nuclear Physics and of Structure of Matter*): Corso Italia 57, 95129 Catania; f. 1955; to develop studies of nuclear physics and of structure of matter in collaboration with Universities of Palermo, Messina and Catania; Pres. Prof. A. AGODI; Vice-Pres. Prof. E. TURRISI.

Comitato Glaciologico Italiano (*Italian Glaciological Committee*): Via Accademia delle Scienze 5, 10123 Turin; f. 1913; *c.* 40 mems.; library of 550 books; Pres. Prof. R. MALARODA; publ. *Geografia Fisica e Dinamica quaternaria* (2 a year).

Istituto di Ingegneria Nucleare, Centro di Studi Nucleari Enrico Fermi (CESNEF) (*E. Fermi Centre for Nuclear Studies*): Via Ponzio 34/3, 1 20133 Milan; part of Politecnico di Milano; trains technical personnel in the fields of nuclear energy, physics of materials, and electronics.

Istituto Italiano di Speleologia: Castellana-Grotte, 70013 Bari; f. 1929; exploration and scientific research in natural caves; 5 mems.; library of 1,250 vols.; Chief Officers Prof. RAIMONDO SELLI, FRANCO OROFINO; publ. *Le Grotte d'Italia* (2 issues a year).

Istituto Nazionale di Fisica Nucleare (I.N.F.N.) (*National Institute of Nuclear Physics*): Casella Postale 56, 00044 Frascati, Rome; f. 1951; promotes and undertakes research in fundamental nuclear physics; consists of: Central Administration (Frascati), 14 sections, 2 groups, 3 National Laboratories (Frascati, Legnaro and Catania) and a National Centre for Photogram Analysis (CNAF Bologna); the sections are at the Institutes of Physics at the Universities of Turin, Milan, Padua, Genoa, Trieste, Bologna, Pisa, Pavia, Florence, Rome, Naples, Bari, Catania, and at the Istituto Superiore di Sanità in Rome; the groups are at the Politecnico, Turin, and the Scuola Normale Superiore, Pisa; Pres. Prof. ANTONINO ZICHICHI.

Osservatorio Astronomico: Padua; f. 1767; library of 10,000 vols.; Dir. Prof. LEONIDA ROSINO; publs. various papers.

Osservatorio Astronomico: Via Tiepolo 11, Trieste; f. 1898; research in astrophysics; 45 mems.; library of 9,000 vols.; Dir. Prof. MARGHERITA HACK; publ. *Pubblicazioni*.

Osservatorio Astronomico di Capodimonte: Via Moiariello 16, 80131 Naples; f. 1819; 12 astronomers; library of 17,000 vols.; Dir. Prof. MARIO RIGUTTI; publs. *Memorie Astronomiche, Contributi*.

Osservatorio Astronomico di Roma: Via del Parco Mellini 84, 00136 Rome; f. 1827; faculty of science attached to the Observatory; library of 25,000 vols., 400 astronomical reviews; astronomical museum and attached astronomical stations on the Grande Sasso and Monte Porzio; Dir. Prof. PIETRO GIANNONE; publ. *Solar Phenomena*† (monthly).

Osservatorio Geofisico Sperimentale (*Experimental Geophysics Observatory*): P.O.B. 2011, 36016 Trieste; Pres. Prof. ANTONIO BRAMBATI; Dir. Prof. FRANCESCO GIORGETTI.

Osservatorio Vesuviano: Ercolano, Naples; f. 1841; chiefly concerned with research on geophysical warning of Vesuvius and other volcanoes; Dir. Prof. PAOLO GASPARINI; publs. annual report and various papers in specialized journals.

Società Italiana per lo Studio delle Sostanze Grasse: Via Lauro 3, Milan; Pres. Prof. UMBERTO PALLOTTA; Sec. Prof. GIOVANNI JACINI.

Stazione Zoologica di Napoli (*Zoological Station of Naples*): Villa Comunale, 80121 Naples; f. 1873 to promote experimental biology on marine life and making available equipped laboratories and technical staff to any qualified research worker; has permanent rental arrangements with learned societies from many countries; library of over 1,000 current biological periodicals and 80,000 vols.; Dir. Prof. A. MONROY; publs. *History and Philosophy of Life Sciences*, *Marine Ecology*.

Philosophy and Psychology

Centro Superiore di Logica e Scienze Comparate: Via Belmeloro 3, Bologna; f. 1969; promotes the study of Logic and contributes to research in this field; 1,250 mems.; library and archives; Pres. Prof. F. Spisani; Research Dirs. Profs. I. M. Copi, C. G. Hempel, A. Martinet, E. Nagel, K. Popper, P. Ricoeur, P. Suppes; publ. *International Logic Review—Rassegna Internazionale di Logica* (2 a year).

Istituto di Studi Filosofici: Università, Rome; f. 1939; Pres. Sen. E. Bertola; Dir. Prof. E. Castelli Gattinara di Zubiena; publs. *Edizione Naz. dei Classici del pensiero italiano, Settimana di studi filosofici internazionali* (annually), *Archivio di Filosofia* (quarterly), *Bibliografia Filosofica Italiana, Edizione Naz A. Rosmini, Edizione Naz. V. Gioberti, Studi Filosofici e Religiosi.*

Istituto Luigi Sturzo: Via delle Coppelle 35, 00186 Rome; f. 1951; sociological research; library of 30,000 vols.; Pres. Prof. Gabriele De Rosa; Sec.-Gen. Prof. Ignazio Ughi; publ. *Sociologia* (3 a year).

Religion, Sociology and Anthropology

Istituto per l'Oriente: Via Alberto Caroncini 19, Rome; f. 1921; research on modern and ancient Near East; library of 30,000 vols.; Pres. Prof. L. Santa Maria; Scientific Dir. Prof. R. Rubinacci; publs. *Oriente Moderno*† (monthly), *Rassegna di Studi Etiopici*†, *Oriens Antiquus.*

Scuola di Perfezionamento in Studi Europei: Piazza Cairoli 3, Rome; Dir. Prof. G. Bosco; Sec.-Gen. Prof. Maria L. Cremona.

Technology

Direzione delle Attività del Comitato Nazionale per l'Energia Nucleare a Ispra (*Centre for Nuclear Studies at Ispra*): head office, CNEN, Viale Regina Margherita 125, Rome; research in physics of materials by slow neutron spectrometry; Dir. (vacant); reports included in *Serie di Rapporti* published by CNEN.

Centro Fusione e Applicazioni Laser (*Fusion and Laser Applications Laboratories*): CP 65, 00044 Frascati, Rome; established by C.N.E.N. for experimental and theoretical research on plasma physics and application of laser to fusion and isotope separation; library of 10,000 vols.; Dir. Prof. Romano Toschi; publ. laboratory reports†.

Centro Informazioni Studi Esperienze (C.I.S.E.) (*Centre of Information, Studies and Experiments*): C.P. 12081, 20100 Milan; f. 1946; fields of activity: nuclear energy (thermal-hydraulic experimentation, development of neutronic and thermal-hydraulic codes for HWR and LWR plant design, operation, safety analysis); solar energy (photovoltaic conversion); energy savings behaviour; environmental pollution surveillance; and diagnostics; research on industrial material behaviour; environmental pollution surveillance; development and application of laser sources; developments of electronic components and instrumentation; development of data acquisition and elaboration systems, etc.; library of 20,000 vols.; Pres. Dr. Eng. Massimo Moretti; Man. Dir. Dr. Eng. Francesco Orsenigo.

Centro Radioelettrico Sperimentale 'Guglielmo Marconi' (*Marconi Experimental Radio-electric Centre*): Viale Trastevere 189, 00100 Rome; f. 1937; attached to the Istituto Superiore delle Poste e Telecommunicazioni; experimental research on propagation of radio waves; Pres. Dr. A. Laghi; Dir. Prof. Ivo Ranzi.

Centro per lo Sviluppo dei Trasporti Aerei: (*Air Transport Development Centre*): Via Sardegna 38, 00187 Rome; f. 1951; 400 mems.; promotes the publication and distribution of research works, reports, information and news about the development of commercial aviation in the various countries of the world; specialized library of over 6,000 books, documents etc.; Pres. Dott. E. Carenini; series of more than 100 publications, including *Trasporti Aerei* (monthly), *Aviazione Civile* (weekly).

Centro Sperimentale Metallurgico S.p.A.: Via di Castel Romano, 00129 Rome; f. 1963; library of over 25,500 vols.; Chair. F. Savioli; Chief Exec. Officer G. Odone.

Comitato Nazionale per l'Energia Nucleare (C.N.E.N.) (*National Committee for Nuclear Energy*): Viale Regina Margherita 125, 00198 Rome; f. 1960; conducts studies, research and experiments in nuclear field; promotes development of industrial applications of nuclear energy; takes part in international collaboration in the nuclear field; maintains the control and technical supervision of the construction and operation of nuclear plants; mem. of Eurochemic, Halden, Eurodif, Coredif, Esarda, Inter-ramp, Over-ramp, and participates in the activities of Euratom, NEA, IAEA, etc.; library of 250,000 vols.; Pres. Umberto Colombo; Vice-Pres. Carlo Salvetti; staff of about 3,600; chief publs. *Notiziario* (monthly, nuclear news), technical reports in the field of nuclear engineering, physics, chemistry, biology, medicine and geology.

Istituto Nazionale per Studi ed Esperienze di Architettura Navale (*National Institute of Naval Architecture Studies and Experiments*): via Corrado Segre 60, 00146 Rome; f. 1927; library of 1,200 vols.; Pres. Ing. A. Ferrauto; publ. *Quaderni* (annual).

Laboratori Nazionali di Frascati dell'INFN (Istituto Nazionale di Fisica Nucleare) (*National Laboratories of INFN, Frascati*): CP 13, 00044 Frascati, Rome; f. 1953; 450 MeV Linear accelerator for electrons and positrons, 1.5 GeV electron positron storage ring; theoretical research group, high energy and nuclear physics research, electronics and radio-frequency laboratory, laboratory of technology and vacuum; Dir. Prof. Renato Scrimaglio.

SORIN Biomedica S.p.A.: 13040 Saluggia, Vercelli; f. 1956; owned by FIAT; applied research; radio-chemistry; production and development of radioisotopes, labelled compounds and radio-immunoassay kits; production and development in bio-engineering (pace-makers, artificial kidneys, etc.); Pres. Dott. Ubaldo Scassellati.

LIBRARIES

Istituto Centrale per il Catalogo Unico delle Biblioteche Italiane e per le Informazioni Bibliografiche (*Central Institute of the Union Catalogue of Italian Libraries and Bibliographical Information*): viale del Castro Pretorio, Rome; f. 1951; Dir. Dr. ANGELA VINAY; publs. *Primo Catalogo collettivo della Biblioteche Italiane a cura dell'Ufficio esecutivo, Catalogo Cumulativo 1886–1957 del Bollettino di Firenze a cura dell'Ufficio Esecutivo, Bibliografia Nazionale Italiana a cura della Biblioteca Nazionale Centrale di Firenze, Scheda a stampa a cura della Biblioteca Nazionale Centrale di Firenze, Soggettario* (Subject Headings) *a cura della Biblioteca Nazionale Centrale di Firenze, Manuale del catalogatore, Bibliografia Nazionale Italiana: Periodici.*

Alessandria

Biblioteca Civica: Via Tripoli 16; f. 1806; 107,953 vols.; Dir. Dr. A. PANIZZA.

Ancona

Biblioteca Comunale Luciano Benincasa: Via Ascoli Piceno 10; f. 1669; 105,673 vols.; Dir. Dr. MARIA TONNARELLI.

Arezzo

Biblioteca della Città di Arezzo: Via dei Pileati-Palazzo Pretorio; f. 1603; 120,000 vols. and 658 MSS. and incunabula.

Ascoli Piceno

Biblioteca Comunale: presso il Palazzo Comunale; f. 1773; 72,821 vols.; Dir. Dott. VITTORI EMIDIO.

Avellino

Biblioteca Provinciale Scipione e Giulio Capone: Corso Europa; f. 1885; 101,500 vols.; Dir. Dott. MARIO SARRO.

Bari

Biblioteca Nazionale 'Sagarriga-Visconti-Volpi': Palazzo Ateneo, Piazza Umberto; f. 1865; 250,000 vols.; Dir. Dssa. MARIA CECARO.

Bergamo

Biblioteca Civica A. Mai: Piazza Vecchia 15; f. 1760; 570,000 vols.. 9,380 MSS., 37,478 documents, 1,640 incunabula; Dir. GIANNI BARACHETTI.

Bologna

Biblioteca Carducci: Piazza Carducci 5; given to the commune of Bologna in 1907 by Marguerite of Savoy, inaugurated in 1921; the library preserves the surroundings of the poet Giosue Carducci and contains his collected works, as well as many rare editions of other works; 55,000 vols.; Dir. Dott. GINO NENZIONI.

Biblioteca Comunale dell'Archiginnasio: Piazza Galvani 1; f. 1801; contains 700,000 vols., including 2,500 incunabula and 15,000 rare editions of the 16th century; 12,000 MSS., 500,000 letters and documents; Dir. Dott. GINO NENZIONI; publs. *L'Archiginnasio, Bollettino della Biblioteca Comunale di Bologna.*

Biblioteca dell'Istituto Giuridico 'Antonio Cicu': Via Zamboni 27-29; f. 1927; 195,000 vols.; Dir. Prof. ROBERTO BONINI; publ. *Pubblicazioni del Seminario Giuridico della Università di Bologna*† (3-4 a year).

Biblioteca della Cassa di Risparmio: Via Farini 22; f. 1837; 48,000 vols.; Dir. Dott. GINO TROMBI.

Biblioteca 'Studium' S. Domenico: Convento San Domenico; f. 1218; 78,000 vols., incunabula and MSS.; special collection philosophy and theology; Dir. P. LEANDRO BERNARDINI, O.P.

Biblioteca Universitaria: Via Zamboni 35; f. 1712; *c.* 800,000 vols., 7,500 MSS., 1,000 incunabula; Dir. Dott. CARLA BONANNI GUIDUCCI.

Brescia

Biblioteca Civica Queriniana: Via Mazzini 1; f. 1747; 410,000 vols.; Dir. Dott. ORNELLO VALETTI.

Cagliari

Biblioteca Universitaria: Via Università 32-A; f. 1792; 460,470 vols.; 1,033 MSS., 5,469 letters and documents, 241 incunabula, 2,784 magazines; Gabinetto delle Stampe "Anna Marongiu Pernis" contains 4,541 etchings; Dir. Dott. GRAZIELLA SEDDA DELITALA.

Catania

Biblioteca Universitaria: Piazza dell'Università 2; f. 1755; 227,000 vols., 127 incunabula, 390 MSS.; Dir. SALVATORE MIRONE (acting).

Cesena (Forlì)

Biblioteca Comunale Malatestiana: Piazza Bufalini 1; f. 1452; 200,000 vols.; Dir. Dr. ANTONIO BRASINI.

Como

Biblioteca Comunale: Via Cesare Cantù 15; f. 17th century; approx. 180,000 vols. in library; Dir. A. BORTONE.

Cremona

Biblioteca del Seminario Vescovile: Via Milano 5; f. 1592; 89,793 vols.; Dir. don GIUSEPPE GALLINA.

Biblioteca Statale e Libreria Civica: Via Ugolani Dati 4; f. *c* 1600; 500,000 vols., 1,313 MSS, 10,456 letters and documents, 2,640 parchments, 366 incunabula, *c.* 6,000 16th-century editions; Dir. Dott. RITA BARBISOTTI; publs. *Annali*†, *Mostre*†, *Fonti e Sussidi*†.

Fermo (Ascoli Piceno)

Biblioteca Comunale: Piazza del Popolo 63; f. 1688; 350,000 vols.; Dir. Dott. Prof. MARIO SANTORO.

Ferrara

Biblioteca Comunale Ariostea: Via Scienze 17; f. 1753; 140,000 vols.; Dir. Dott. L. CAPRA.

Florence

Biblioteca del Gabinetto Scientifico Letterario G. P. Vieusseux: Palazzo Strozzi, Piazza Strozzi; f. 1819; 450,000 vols.; Dir. Prof. ALESSANDRO BONSANTI.

Biblioteca della Facoltà di Lettere e Filosofia dell' Università: Piazza Brunelleschi, 50121; f. 1859; 1,537,000 vols.; Dir. Dott. TOMASO URSO.

Biblioteca della Galleria degli Uffizi: Via della Ninna 5; f. 1770; 40,000 vols.; Dir. Dssa A. M. PETRIOLI TOFANI.

Biblioteca Marucelliana: Via Cavour 43; f. 1752; 498,500 vols.; 2,130 MSS., 484 incunabula, 2,000 drawings, 20,000 prints, 7,986 16th century editions, 12,000 letters; Dir. Dott. CLEMENTINA ROTONDI.

Biblioteca Medicea-Laurenziana: Piazza S. Lorenzo 9; f. 1571; contains the private Medici Library, collections of MSS. from the Grand Dukes of Lorena, S. Croce, S. Marco, Badia Fiesolana, cathedral of Florence, and private family collections; 15th- and 16th-century first editions; 10,506 MSS. of the 5th–19th century; 1,570 papyri, 45 ostraca, 74,000 vols.; Dir. Dott. ANTONIETTA MORANDINI.

Biblioteca Moreniana: Via dei Ginori 10; f. 1869; 34,000 vols., about 2,000 MSS; Dir. Dott. MARIA JOLE MINICUCCI.

Biblioteca Nazionale Centrale: Piazza dei Cavalleggeri 1A; f. 1747; 4,000,000 vols., pamphlets, 24,000 MSS., 4,000 incunabula; Dir. Dr. ANNA LENZUNI; publs. *Bibliografia nazionale italiana*† (monthly, annual accumulations, printed cards).

Biblioteca Nazionale Pedagogica: Via Buonarroti 10; f. 1942; 52,000 vols.; 640 periodicals; Dir. Prof. ENZO PETRINI; publs. *Collana Scritti Inediti e Rari*.

Biblioteca Riccardiana: Via dei Ginori 10; f. 1815; 70,000 vols. and about 6,000 MSS.; Dir. Dott. MARIA JOLE MINICUCCI.

Forlì

Biblioteca Comunale "A. Saffi": Corso della Repubblica 72; 250,000 vols.; Dir. Dott. WALTER VICHI.

Genoa

Biblioteca Durazzo Giustiniani: Via Balbi 1; f. 1806; 100,000 vols.

Biblioteca Universitaria: Via Balbi 3; f. 17th century; 368,088 vols., 1,036 incunabula, 1,854 MSS., 12,975 letters and documents; Dir. Reg. Dssa. ANNA MARIA BELLEZZA.

Imola (Bologna)

Biblioteca Comunale: Via Emilia 80—Ex-Convento di S. Francesco; f. 1608; 250,000 vols., 138 incunabula, 1,349 MSS.; Dir. Dott. GRAZIA V. GURRIERI.

L'Aquila

Biblioteca Provinciale 'Salvatore Tommasi': Piazza Palazzo 30; f. 1848; 141,000 vols.; 123 incunabula, 845 MSS., 3,207 *cinquecentine* (rare 16th-century editions); Dir. Dott. WALTER CAPEZZALI.

Leghorn

Biblioteca Comunale 'Labronica' Francesco Domenico Guerrazzi: Villa Fabbricotti, Viale della Libertà 30, 57100 Livorno; f. 1816; 320,000 vols. including 3,000 15th-century editions, various MSS. and 56,000 letters and documents; Dir. Dott. LUCA BADALONI; publ. *Quaderni della Labronica*† (quarterly).

Lucca

Biblioteca del Giardino Botanico: contains very rare books on natural sciences.

Biblioteca Statale di Lucca: Via S. Maria Corteorlandini 12; f. 18th century; 387,699 vols., 867 incunabula, 4,210 MSS.; musical collection of 67 MSS. and *c.* 500 scores; Dir. Dott. ALBERTO TINTO.

Macerata

Biblioteca Comunale Mozzi-Borgetti: Piazza Vittorio Veneto 2, 62100; f. 1773; 212,000 vols.; Dir. Dott. ALDO ADVERSI.

Mantua

Biblioteca Comunale: Via Roberto Ardigò 13; f. 1780; 244,000 vols., 1,338 MSS., 1,495 incunabula; Dir. Dr. GIANCARLO SCHIZZEROTTO.

Biblioteca dell' Accademia Virgiliana: Via dell' Accademia 47, 46100; f. 1768; 63,500 vols.; Librarian Mons. LUIGI BOSIO; publs. *Atti e Memorie, Nuova Serie* (annual).

Messina

Biblioteca Universitaria: Via dei Verdi 71; f. 1548; 170,000 vols., 1,255 MSS,. 418 incunabula; Dir. Dott. MARIA LUISA GARVIONI.

Milan

Biblioteca Ambrosiana: Piazza Pio XI 2; f. 1609; 850,000 vols. and rare prints, 35,000 MSS. mostly Latin, Greek, and Oriental, 2,100 incunabula, 12,000 parchments, 19,800 prints, 5,000 drawings; Dirs. Dott. A. PAREDI, E. GALBIATI, C. MARCORA.

Biblioteca Centrale del Politecnico di Milano: Piazza Leonardo da Vinci 32; 118,144 vols.; 43 MSS., 2,600 periodicals.

Biblioteca Civica: Palazzo Sormani, Corso di Porta Vittoria 6; f. 1890; 929,952 vols.; Dir. RENATO PAGETTI.

Biblioteca d'Arte: Castello Sforzesco; f. 1930; art library and Leonardo da Vinci Collection; Librarian Dott. LIA GANDOLFI.

Biblioteca degli Istituti Ospedalieri: Piazza Ospedale Maggiore 3; f. 1842; 90,000 vols.; Dir. Dott. GIULIO BRUNETTI.

Biblioteca del Centro Nazionale di Studi Manzoniani: Via Morone 1; f. 1937; 15,000 vols.; Pres. Prof. Dott. CLAUDIO CESARE SECCHI; publs. *Annali*†, *Edizione Nazionale Opere di A. Manzoni*.

Biblioteca del Conservatorio di Musica G. Verdi: Via del Conservatorio 12; f. 1808; 350,000 vols.; books on music, scores and MSS. of 16–20th centuries; Dir. Dott. AGOSTINA ZECCA LATERZA; publ. *Annuario*†.

Biblioteca della Facoltà di Agraria: Via G. Celoria 2; *c.* 43,500 vols.; Dir. Prof. R. LOCCI; Librarian ISIDE MARENGHI MARCHETTI.

Biblioteca delle Facoltà di Giurisprudenza e di Lettere e Filosofia dell'Università: Via Festa del Perdono 7; f. 1923; 560,000 vols.; Dir. Dott. GIULIANA SAPORI.

Biblioteca dell' Istituto Lombardo Accademia di Scienze e Lettere: Via Borgonuovo 25; f. 1803; 190,000 vols.

Biblioteca dell' Università Cattolica del S. Cuore: Largo Gemelli 1; f. 1921; 880,870 vols. and pamphlets, 2,530 publication in series, 8,520 periodicals; Dir. Dott. TINO FOFFANO.

Biblioteca dell' Università Commerciale Luigi Bocconi: Via Sarfatti 25; f. 1902; 370,000 vols. and 5,666 periodical publs.; Librarian Dr. A. BACIGALUPO.

Biblioteca e Archivio, Raccolte Storiche del Comune di Milano, dei Musei del Risorgimento e Storia Contemporanea: Palazzo De Marchi, Via Borgonuovo 23; f. 1884; 445,000 vols., newspapers and pamphlets, 3,825 files of documents of the period 1750 to the present day; Dir. Dott. GIULIA BOLOGNA.

Biblioteca Nazionale Braidense: Via Brera 28; f. 1763; 823,207 vols., 13,355 periodicals, 21,721 autographs, 2,081 MSS.; Dir. Dssa. LETIZIA PECORELLA VERGNANO.

Biblioteca Trivulziana: Castello Sforzesco; f. 18th century; 35,000 vols., 1,300 codices, including MSS. from the 8th century, parchment books from the 11th century, 1,050 incunabula, and rare editions of works on history and literature; Dir. Prof. GIULIA BOLOGNA.

Biblioteca Morando: Castello Sforzesco; f. 19th century; 4,100 vols., 41 rare incunabula; specializes in astrology and chiromancy.

Biblioteca Weil-Weiss: Castello Sforzesco; f. 19th century; 7,000 vols., 19th–20th-century *de luxe* and illustrated editions.

Laboratorio di Restauro di Documenti Libri e Legature: Piazza Castello 3.

British Council Library: Via Manzoni 38; f. 1946; 13,486 vols., 105 periodicals; Librarian G. MCMULLAN.

Modena

Biblioteca Estense: Palazzo dei Musei, Piazza S. Agostino 337; f. 15th century; 600,000 vols., 13,500 MSS.,1,642 incunabula, 165,000 autographs; Dir. Dott. SILVANA VERDINI.

Biblioteca Universitaria: Palazzo dei Musei, Piazza S. Agostino 337; f. 1772; 120,000 vols., 65 MSS., 5 incunabula; Dir. Dott. ERNESTO MILANO.

Naples

Biblioteca Arcivescovile: Viale Colli Aminei 1, Capodimonte; f. 1851; 100,000 vols.; Dir. RUSSO FRANCESCO.

Biblioteca del Conservatorio di Musica S. Pietro a Maiella: Via S. Pietro a Maiella, n. 35; f. 1791; 300,000 vols., 4 incunabula; Dir. FRANCESCO MELISI.

Biblioteca della Facoltà di Scienze Agrarie dell' Università di Napoli: Via dell' Università 100, Portici; f. 1872; 20,000 vols., 2,400 periodicals; Dir. Prof. E. TREMBLAY.

Biblioteca della Società Napoletana di Storia Patria: Piazza Municipio, Maschio Angiono; f. 1876; 270,000 vols., 3,000 MSS., 5,000 periodicals, 15,000 pamphlets; Dir. Prof. ALFREDO PARENTE; Librarian Dr. GIUSEPPE DE NITTO.

Biblioteca di Castelcapuano: Piazza dei Tribunali, Palazzo di Giustizia; f. 1848; 40,000 vols.; Dir. Dott. ROSSI BUSSOLA RAFFAELLO.

Biblioteca Nazionale 'Vittorio Emanuele III': Palazzo Reale; f. 1804; 1,531,936 vols., 30,142 MSS. and documents, 4,546 incunabula, 1,786 papyri from Herculaneum; Dir. Dott. ALBERTO GUARINO.

Biblioteca Oratoriana del Monumento Nazionale dei Girolamini: Via Duomo 142; f. 1586; 135,000 vols., 105 incunabula, 482 MSS.; Dir. P. GIOVANNI FERRARA, d.O.

Biblioteca Universitaria di Napoli: Via G. Paladino 39; f. 1615; 750,000 vols.; open to the public; Dir. Prof. Dr. NICOLA SCAFATI.

British Council Library: Riviera di Chiaia 185; f. 1958; 16,525 vols., 89 periodicals; Librarian (vacant).

Novara

Biblioteche Riunite "Civica" e "Negroni": Corso Felice Cavallotti 4; f. 1847 and 1898 respectively; 196,396 vols., 519 periodicals, 4,084 records, 130 incunabula, 420 MSS., maps, etc.; Dir. CARLA BERTONA.

Padua

Biblioteca Antoniana: Basilica del Santo; f. 1352; 75,000 vols., 800 MSS.; Dir. Prof. GIOVANNI M. LUISETTO.

Biblioteca Civica: Piazza del Santo 10; f. 1839; 308,244 vols.; Dir. Dott. ALESSANDRO PROSDOCIMI.

Biblioteca del Seminario Vescovile: Via Seminario 29; f. 1671; 300,000 vols., 1,135 MSS., 417 incunabula; Dir. PIERANTONIO GIOS.

Biblioteca Universitaria: Via S. Biagio 7; f. 1629; 607,532 vols., 2,600 MSS., 1,633 incunabula, 4,882 reviews, 1,225 maps, and 4,000 engravings; Dir. Dott. E. GOVI.

Palermo

Biblioteca Centrale della Regione Siciliana: Corso Vittorio Emanuele 429–431; f. 1782; 455,404 vols.; 14,887 MSS. and 1,041 incunabula; Dir. Dssa. CARMELA PERRETTA.

Biblioteca Comunale: Piazza Brunaccini; f. 1760; 350,000 vols.; Dir. Dott. EMMA ALAIMO.

Biblioteca dell' Università: via Maqueda; 120,000 vols.; Dir. Prof. EUGENIO DI CARLO.

Parma

Biblioteca Palatina: Palazzo della Pilotta; f. 1769; 600,000 vols., 5,000 MSS.; 3,000 incunabula; Dir. Regg. Dr. GIOVANNI PETTENATI; musical section: via Conservatorio 27; 80,000 vols.; 1,000 MSS.; Librarian MARCELLO PAVARANI.

Biblioteca Palatina-Sezione Musicale Presso Il Conservatorio di Musica 'A. Boito': Via del Conservatorio 27; f. 1889; 79,000 vols.; Dir. Dott. SERENELLA BALDELLI CHERUBINI.

Pavia

Biblioteca Civica: Piazza Petrarca 2; Dir. Dott. FELICE MILANI.

Biblioteca Universitaria: Palazzo dell' Università; f. 1763; 399,903 vols., 1,829 MSS., 668 incunabula, 743 periodicals; Librarian Dotta. MARIA GOLE MINICUCCI.

Perugia

Biblioteca Augusta: Palazzo Conestabile, Via delle Prome 15; f. 1615; 230,000 vols.; Dir. Dott. MARIO RONCETTI.

Pesaro

Biblioteca e Musei Oliveriani: Via Mazza 97; f. 1793; 150,000 vols. on general culture and local history; Librarian Prof. Dott. ANTONIO BRANCATI; publ. *Studia Oliveriana* (annual).

Piacenza

Biblioteca Cardinale Giulio Alberoni: Collegio Alberoni—Frazione S. Lazzaro Alberoni, Via Emilia Parmense 77; f. 1751; 150,000 vols.; Dir. Dott. LUIGI MEZZADRI; publs. *Divus Thomas* (quarterly), *Monografie del Collegio Alberoni*.

Biblioteca Comunale Passerini Landi: Via G. Carducci 18; f. 1774; 200,000 vols.; Dir. Dott. CARLO EMANUELE MANFREDI.

Pisa

Biblioteca Universitaria: Via Curtatone Montanara 15; f. 1742; 367,800 vols., 1,046 MSS., 2,161 documents, 155 incunabula, 707 current periodicals; Dir. Dott. LILIA PARADISI D'ELIA.

Pistoia

Biblioteca Comunale Forteguerriana: Piazza della Sapienza 1; f. 1473; 260,000 vols.; Dir. Prof. GIANCARLO SAVINO.

Portici (Naples)

Biblioteca dell'Istituto di Entomologia Agraria dell' Università di Napoli: Via Università 100, 80055 Portici; f. 1872; applied entomology and biological control; 50,000 vols.; Dirs. Prof. E. TREMBLAY, Prof. G. VIGGIANI; publs. *Bollettino, Note divulgative* (annually).

Ravenna

Biblioteca Comunale Classense: f. 1707–1711; 250,000 vols.; Dir. Dott. NERVIO ZORZETTI; publ. *Letture Classensi*.

Reggio Emilia

Biblioteca Municipale 'A Panizzi': Via Farini 3; f. 1796; 300,000 vols., 10,000 MSS.; Dir. Dr. MAURIZIO FESTANTI.

Rimini

Biblioteca Civica Gambalunga: Via Gambalunga 27; f. 1619; 149,024 vols., 384 incunabula, 1,295 MSS.; Dir. Prof. PIERO MELDINI.

Rome

Archivio Centrale dello Stato: Piazzale degli Archivi, EUR; f. 1871; 120,000 vols.; political, administrative, cultural and judicial archives of The Kingdom of Italy and Italian Republic; Dir. Prof. R. GRISPO.

Biblioteca Angelica: Piazza S. Agostino 8, 00186; f. 1605; 182,000 vols, 2,667 MSS., 1,125 incunabula; 16–18th-century literature; Augustinian, Jansenist, Reformation and Counter-reformation collections; Dir. Dott. CANDIDA VISCO ROMITI.

Biblioteca Casanatense: Via S. Ignazio 52; f. 1700; 352,000 vols., 6,456 MSS., 2,187 incunabula; Dir. Dott. FRANCESCA DI CESARE.

Biblioteca Centrale del Consiglio Nazionale delle Ricerche (*Central Library of National Research Council*): Piazzale delle Scienze 7; f. 1927; 400,000 vols., 10,000 periodicals; scientific and technical subjects; Dir. Dott. MARIA CALIFANO TENTORI.

Biblioteca Centrale Giuridica presso il Ministero di Grazia e Giustizia: Via Arenula; f. 1866; 500,000 vols.; Dir. Dr. UMBERTO PETTINARI.

Biblioteca dell' Accademia Nazionale dei Lincei e Corsiniana: via della Lungara 10; f. 1730; 462,974 vols., 4,000 MSS. 2,293 incunabula; Dir. Dr. AMELIA COSATTI.

Biblioteca dell'Istituto Italo-Latino Americano: Piazza Guglielmo Marconi, EUR; specializes in contemporary Latin-American life; 47,500 vols., 1,800 periodicals; 4,900 items in music collections; services; offsets of any item in library, in-service library loans, information service; Librarian Dr. TERESA IMPARATO; publs. annotated bibliographical catalogues†, lists of book exhibits†.

Biblioteca dell' Istituto Nazionale d'Archeologia e Storia dell'Arte: Piazza Venezia 3, 00186; f. 1922; *c.* 220,000 vols., 15,000 prints; Dir. Dott. NEDA JANNI; publ. *Annuario Bibliografico di Storia dell'Arte.*

Biblioteca della Camera dei Deputati: Palazzo di Montecitorio, Via della Missione 8; f. 1848 in Turin; 450,000 vols.; open to Members of Parliament; Dir. Dott. S. FURLANI; publs. *Catalogo, Bollettino.*

Biblioteca della Fondazione Marco Besso: Largo di Torre Argentina 11; more than 75,000 vols.; special collections: Rome, Dante Alighieri, Tuscia; Cur. ANNA MARIA BURATTINI.

Biblioteca della Galleria Nazionale d'Arte Moderna: Valle Giulia; f. 1945; 40,000 vols. on 19th- and 20th-century art; historical and biographical archives; Dir. PALMA BUCARELLI.

Biblioteca della Società Geografica Italiana: Villa Celimontana, via della Navicella 12; f. 1867; 200,000 vols.; Library Counsellor Prof. ERNESTO MASSI.

Biblioteca della Società Italiana per l'Organizzazione Internazionale (S.I.O.I.): Via di S. Marco 3, Palazzetto di Venezia; f. 1945; 290,000 UN documents; 70,000 vols., 750 periodicals; Librarian MARIA GRAZIA GIOVANNINI.

Biblioteca del Ministero degli Affari Esteri: Farnesina; f. 1850; 200,000 vols.; Dir. Dott. RAFFAELLA MAINIERI.

Biblioteca del Ministero dell'Agricoltura e delle Foreste: Via XX Settembre 20; f. 1860; 800,000 vols.; Dir. Prof. PAOLO SYLOS LABINI.

Biblioteca del Ministero delle Finanze e del Tesoro: Palazzo del Ministero delle Finanze, via XX Settembre; f. 1857; 160,000 vols.; Dir. Prof. WALTER D'AVANZO.

Biblioteca del Ministero dell'Interno: Palazzo del Viminale, Via Agostino Depretis; f. 1872; 170,000 vols., Dir. ARTURO LETIZIA.

Biblioteca del Senato: Palazzo Madama, Via Dogana Vecchia 27; f. 1848; 500,000 vols.; chiefly works on law, history and politics; medieval statutes; Dir. Dott. CARLO CHIMENTI.

Biblioteca di Storia Moderna e Contemporanea: Via M. Caetani 32; f. 1917; 250,000 vols.; Dir. Dott. GIOVANNELLA MORGHEN GOLISANO.

Bibliotheca Hertziana (Max-Planck-Institut): Via Gregoriana 28; f. 1913; 125,000 vols. on the history of Italian art; 300,000 photographs of Italian art; Dirs. Prof. Dott. CHRISTOPH LUITPOLD FROMMEL, Prof. Dr. MATTHIAS WINNER; Librarian Dr. ERNST GULDAN.

Biblioteca Lancisiana: Borgo S. Spirito 3; f. 1711; 17,932 vols.; Dir. Dott. PIETRO DE ANGELIS.

Biblioteca Musicale S. Cecilia: Via dei Greci 18; f. 1584; 145,367 MSS. and printed works; Dir. Dott. EMILIA ZANETTI.

Biblioteca Nazionale Centrale Vittorio Emanuele II: Viale Castro Pretorio; f. 1876; 2,710,000 vols.; 6,511 MSS; Dir. Dott. LUCIANA MANCUSI CRISARI; publ. *Bollettino delle opere moderne straniere acquistate dalle Biblioteche pubbliche governative italiane* (annual).

Biblioteca Romana A. Sarti: Piazza dell'Accademia di S. Luca; f. 1877; 40,000 vols. on architecture and modern decorative art, with particular regard to Rome; Librarian Dott. GAETANA SCANO.

Biblioteca Universitaria Alessandrina: Città Universitaria; f. 1661; 1,062,000 vols.; Dir. ALFREDO SERRAI.

Biblioteca Vallicelliana: Piazza della Chiesa Nuova 18; f. 1581; 82,000 vols., 3,061 MSS., 500 incunabula; also contains library of "Società Romana di Storia Patria", 50,000 vols.; Dir. Dr. SERGIO MOTTIRONI.

British Council Library: Palazzo del Drago, Via IV Fontane 20; f. 1946; 28,653 vols., 170 periodicals; Librarian D. SPIBY, F.L.A.

Discoteca di Stato (*State Gramophone Record Library*): Via dei Funari 31, Rome; Dir. Dott. GIUSEPPE DE CILLIS.

Library of the Food and Agriculture Organization of the United Nations (David Lubin Memorial Library): Via delle Terme di Caracalla; f. 1946; 1,000,000 vols., 12,000 serials, documents of UN and Specialized Agencies; collection of former International Institute of Agriculture; Librarian K. HARADA.

Rovigo

Biblioteca dell' Accademia dei Concordi: Piazza V. Emanuele II 14; f. 1580; 110,00 vols.

Sassari

Biblioteca Universitaria: f. about 1550; 200,000 vols.; Dir. Dr. MARIA CARLA SOTGIU CAVAGNIS.

Siena

Biblioteca Comunale degli Intronati: Via della Sapienza 5; f. 1758; 350,000 vols.; Dir. Dott. GINO GAROSI.

Teramo

Biblioteca Provinciale Melchiorre Delfico: Convitto Nazionale, Via del Nardo; f. 1816; 130,906 vols.: Dir. M. MUZII.

Trento

Biblioteca Comunale: Via Roma 51; f. 1856; 188,600 vols.; Dir. Dott. ANNAMARIA PAISSAN SCHLECHTER.

Treviso

Biblioteca Comunale: Borgo Cavour 18; f. 1770; 350,000 vols.; Dir. LUCIO PUTTIN; publ. *Studi Trevisani*†

Trieste

Biblioteca Civica: Piazza Attilio Hortis 4; f. 1793; 390,000 vols., includes Petrarch-Piccolomini and Svevo sections and historical archives.

Biblioteca del Popolo: via del Teatro Romano 17; f. 1956; 134,000 vols.; Dir. GIOVANNI PALLADINI.

Narodna in Študijska Knjižnica v Trstu (*Slovene National Study Library*): Via Geppa 9.

Turin

Biblioteca del Politecnico di Torino: Castello del Valentino; 15,000 vols.; Librarian GIACOMO TRIVERO.

Biblioteca dell' Accademia delle Scienze di Torino: Via Maria Vittoria 3, 10123 Turin; f. 1757; all fields of learning; *c.* 200,000 vols.

Biblioteca Matematica dell' Università di Torino: Via Carlo Alberto 10; f. 1883; 35,000 vols.; Dir. Prof. M. ZEULI.

Biblioteca Nazionale Universitaria: Piazza Carlo Alberto 3; f. 1723; 850,000 vols., 12,000 periodicals, 3,700 MSS., 1,600 incunabula, 15,000 drawings and engravings, 5,000 maps; Dir. GIUSEPPE DONDI.

Biblioteca Reale: Piazza Castello 191; f. 1837; 150,000 vols.; 4,000 MSS.; Dir. Dott. G. DONDI.

Biblioteche Civiche e Raccolte Storiche: Via Cittadella 5; f. 1869; 350,000 vols.; Dir. Prof. ENZO BOTTASSO.

Udine

Biblioteca Comunale Joppi: Piazza Marconi 8; f. 1864; 370,000 vols.; Dir. Dott. LELIA SERENI; publ. *Udine, Bollettino delle Civiche Istituzioni Culturali.*

Urbino (Pesaro)

Biblioteca Universitaria: Via Aurelio Saffi 2; f. 1720; 136,491 vols.; Dir. LUIGI MORANTI.

Venice

Biblioteca del Civico Museo Correr: Piazza S. Marco 52, Procuratie Nuove; f. 1830; specializes in history of art and Venetian history; 97,000 vols., 300 periodicals; Dir. GIANDOMENICO ROMANELLI.

Biblioteca della Congregazione dei Mechitaristi: Isola S. Lazzaro; f. 1701; 100,000 vols.; Dir. Dr. GIACOMO CIANTAYAN.

Biblioteca Nazionale Marciana: Palazzi della Libreria Vecchia e della Zecca, San Marco 7; f. 1468; 800,000 vols.; 13,000 MSS.; Dir. Dott. GIAN ALBINO RAVALLI MODONI.

Fondazione Querini-Stampalia: S. Zaccaria 4778; f. 1869; 250,000 vols.; Pres. Prof. Don GERMANO PATTARO; Dir. Prof. UGO RUGGERI.

Verona

Biblioteca Civica: Via Cappello 43; f. 1792; 525,402 vols.; 1,189 incunabula; 3,309 MSS.; Dir. Dott. MARIO CARRARA.

Vicenza

Biblioteca Civica Bertoliana: f. 1696; 362,600 vols., 955 incunabula, 3,972 MSS.; Librarian L. OLIVA.

MUSEUMS AND ART GALLERIES

Ancona

Museo Nazionale: Palazzo Ferretti, Via Ferretti 6; f. 1871; Italian, Greek and Roman archaeology; large collection of pre-Roman archaeology; Dir. Dr. ROBERTO VIGHI.

Aquileia

Museo Archeologico: Via Roma 1; f. 1882; collection of Roman architecture, sculpture, inscriptions, mosaics, etc. from excavations in the town; library of 7,000 vols.; Dir. Prof. LUISA BERTACCHI; publ. *Aquileia Nostra*† (annual).

Museo Paleocristiano: Piazza Monastero; f. 1961; mosaics and inscriptions from the palaeo-Christian era.

Ardea

Museo Giacomo Manzù: f. 1969; paintings and sculptures by Manzù (b. 1908 in Bergamo).

Arezzo

Galleria e Museo Medioevale e Moderno: Palazzo di Giulio III, Via San Lorentino; f. 1957; Italian paintings from 13th century to 19th century, Majolica ware glass, ivories, seals and coins; Curator Dott. ANNA MARIA MAETZKE.

Museo Archeologico: Via Margaritone; f. 1832; Etruscan, Greek and Roman antiquities, Coralline vases of Augustan period, sarcophagi, mosaics, coins and bronzes; Management: Superintendent of Antiquities, Florence.

Assisi

Museo-Tesoro della Basilica di S. Francesco: 06082 Assisi (PG) 1; history of Saint Francis; library of 15,000 vols.; Curator Fr. LUDOVICO BERTAZZO.

Bari

Museo Archeologico: Palazzo dell'Ateneo; f. 1882; library of 2,500 vols.; Dir. Dott. ETTORE DE JULIIS.

Pinacoteca Provinciale: Palazzo della Provincia; f. 1928; Apulian, Venetian and Neapolitan paintings and sculpture from 11th century to 19th century; Dir. Dott. PINA BELLI D'ELIA.

Bergamo

Galleria dell' Accademia Carrara: Piazza Giacomo Carrara 82/A; collection includes paintings by Bellini, Raffaello, Pisanello, Mantegna, Botticelli, Beato Angelico, Previtali, Tiepolo, Dürer, Brueghel, Van Dyck, etc.; Pres. Ing. CARLO PESENTI; Dir. Dr. F. ROSSI.

Bologna

Pinacoteca Nazionale: via Belle Arti 56; f. 1808; Bolognese painting 14-18th century, and other Italian schools; German and Italian engravings; Dir. Prof. ANDREA EMILIANI.

Museo Civico Archeologico: Via Archiginnasio 2; f. 1881; prehistoric Egyptian, Greek, Roman, Villanovan, Etruscan, Celtic antiquities; library of 8,060 vols.; Dir. Dott. CRISTIANA MORIGI GOVI.

Museo Etrusco: Marzabotto; f. 1950; Dir. Prof. GINO VINICIO GENTILI.

Bolzano

Museo Civico di Bolzano: Via Cassa di Risparmio 14; Dir. Prof. Dott. NICOLÒ RASMO.

Brescia

Direzione Civici Musei d'Arte e Storia: Via Martinengo da Barco 1; Dir. Prof. BRUNO PASSAMANI:

Pinacoteca Tosio Martinengo: Via Martinengo da Barco 1; f. 1906; art of the 13th to 18th centuries; Dir. Dr. BRUNO PASSAMANI.

Museo Romano: Via Musei 57/A; f. 1830; prehistoric, pre-Roman and Roman remains.

Museo dell'Età Cristiana: Via Piamarta 4; f. 1882; collections of the palaeochristian to the neoclassic eras.

Galleria d'Arte Moderna: Via Musei 81; f. 1964; art from end of 18th century to modern times.

Museo del Risorgimento: Castello; f. 1959; 19th century historical exhibits.

Museo delle Armi Antiche: Castello.

Museo Civico di Storia Naturale: Via Gualla 3; f. 1949; zoological, ornithological, entomological, geological, and mineralogical collections; Dir. PIERFRANCO BLESIO.

Museo Diocesano d'Arte Sacra: Via Gasparo da Salò; f. 1978; Dir. Prof. GIOVANNI VEZZOLI.

Cagliari

Museo Archeologico Nazionale: Piazza Indipendenza; f. 1806; Sardinian antiquities (prehistorical, Punic, Roman periods) and folklore, picture gallery, library of 5,262 vols.; Dir. Prof. FERRUCCIO BARRECA.

Capua

Museo Provinciale Campano: Dir. LUIGI GAROFANO VENOSTA.

Chieti

Museo Nazionale: Villa Comunale; Dir. Dott. VALERIO CIANFARANI.

Cividale

Museo Archeologico Nazionale: f. 1820; prehistoric, Roman and medieval archaeology, jewellery and miniatures;

library of 12,000 vols. and archives; publishes various monographs; Dir. MARIO BROZZI.

Faenza

Museo Internazionale delle Ceramiche: Piazza Gen. Pasi; 48018; f. 1908; history, art and techniques of ceramics, library of 30,200 vols.; Dir. Prof. GIUSEPPE LIVERANI; publ. *Faenza* (6 a year).

Ferrara

Museo Archeologico Nazionale di Spina: Via XX Settembre 124 (Palazzo di Ludovico il Moro); f. 1935; Greco-Etruscan vases, statuettes, bronzes and gold ornaments from the graves of Spina; Dir. Dr. FEDE BERTI.

Musei Civici: Palazzo dei Diamanti, corso Ercole I d'Este.

Pinacoteca Nazionale: Dir. Dott. JADRANKA BENTINI.

Direzione Musei Civici d'Arte Moderna: Museo Boldini, Galleria Civica d'Arte Moderna, Centro Attività Visive, Sala d'Arte Benvenuto Tisi, Padiglione d'Arte Contemporanea; Dir. FRANCO FARINA.

Florence

Appartamenti Monumentali: Palazzo Pitti; furniture of the 18th and 19th centuries; Dir. Dr. MARCO CHIARINI.

Gabinetto Disegni e Stampe: Galleria degli Uffizi; Dir. Dott. ANNA FORLANI-TEMPESTI; Vice-Dir. Dott. ANNA MARIA PETRIOLI-TOFANI.

Galleria d'Arte Moderna: Palazzo Pitti, Piazza Pitti; f. 1860; contains paintings and sculptures of the 19th and 20th centuries; Dir. Dr. SANDRA PINTO.

Galleria degli Uffizi: Piazzale degli Uffizi; f. 16th painting the finest collection of Florentine Renaissance century; in the world; Dir. Prof. L. BERTI.

Galleria dell' Accademia: Via Ricasoli 60; f. 1784; contains the most complete collection of Michelangelo's statues in Florence and paintings of 13th-16th-century masters, mostly Tuscan; Dir. Dott. LUCIANO BELLOSI.

Galleria Palatina: Palazzo Pitti, Piazza Pitti; f. 17th century; contains a fine collection of paintings of 16th and 17th centuries; Dir. Dott. MARCO CHIARINI.

Museo Archeologico: Via della Colonna 38; f. 1870; Egyptian, Etruscan and Greco-Roman archaeology; Dir. Dott. GUGLIEMO MAETZKE.

Museo Bardini: Piazza dei Mozzi 1; f. 1925; collection of muscial instruments 16th-19th centuries, altar pieces, madonnas, sculpture, tapestries, furniture, paintings from 14th to 17th centuries.

Museo degli Argenti: Palazzo Pitti; summer state apartments of the Medici Grand Dukes; collections of gold, silver, enamel, *objets d'art*, hardstones, ivory, amber, cameos and jewels, principally from the 15th to the 18th centuries; Dir. Dr. KIRSTEN ASCHENGREEN PIACENTI.

Museo della Casa Buonarroti: Via Ghibellina 70; f. 1858; works by Michelangelo and others; Dir. Prof. CHARLES DE TOLNAY.

Museo dell' Opera del Duomo: Piazza del Duomo 9; f. 1891; Dir. ENZO SETTESOLDI.

Museo delle Porcellane: Boboli Gardens; collection of European porcelain from *c.* 1720 to 1850; Dir. Dr. KIRSTEN ASCHENGREEN PIACENTI.

Museo di S. Marco o dell' Angelico: Piazza San Marco; f. 1869; contains the largest existing collection of paintings by Fra Angelico; Dir. Dott. G. BONSANTI.

Museo di Storia della Scienza a Firenze: Piazza dei Giudici 1. 50122; f. 1927; libraries of 15,000 vols.; Dir. Prof. MARIA LUISA RIGHINI BONELLI; publs. *Physis* (quarterly), *Annali* (2 a year).

Museo Horne: Fondazione Horne, Via dei Benci; furniture and works of art of the 14th, 15th and 16th centuries; Pres. Dr. UGO PROCACCI.

Museo Mediceo: Palazzo Medici-Riccardi, Via Cavour 1; chapel built by Michelozzo and frescoed by Benozzo Gozzoli (1459); gallery with frescoes by Luca Giordano (1680).

Museo Nazionale (Bargello): Via del Proconsolo 4; f. 1859; mediaeval and modern sculpture and objets d'art; Dir. Dr. EMMA MICHELETTI.

Museo Nazionale della Scuola: c/o Centro Didattico Nazionale di Studi e Documentazione, Via Buonarroti 10; f. 1928; rare books, relics, facsimiles, manuscripts, drawings, audio-visual aids; Dir. Prof. E. PETRINI.

Museo Stibbert: Via F. Stibbert 26, 50134; f. 1908; Etruscan, Roman and medieval arms and armour; 15th–19th-century European and Oriental arms and engravings; holy objects and vestments; 18th and 19th-century European and Oriental costumes, etc.; 15th--17th-century Flemish tapestries; 14th–19th-century Italian and foreign murals; library of 3,500 vols.; Dir. Prof. Dott. Arch. LIONELLO G. BOCCIA.

Palazzo Davanzati—Museo della Casa Fiorentina Antica: Via Porta Rossa 13; Dir. Dssa. MARIA FOSSI TODOROW.

Palazzo Vecchio: Piazza della Signoria; paintings, furnishings; Halls of the *Cinquecento* and the *Duecento*, Francis I's studio; Bronzino frescoes; frescoes by Vasari and pupils.

Forlì

Istituti Culturali ed Artistici: Corso della Repubblica 72; comprises a picture gallery, collection of prints and engravings, archaeological and ethnographical museums, ceramics, sculpture and local history; Piancastelil collection of paintings, medals and coins; Dir. Dott. WALTER VICHI.

Pinacoteca e Musei Comunali: Dir. Dott. WALTER VICHI.

Genoa

Direzione Belle Arti e Storia: Via Garibaldi 18; f. 1908; Dir. Dr. arch. VINCENZO ODDI; museums and galleries under its control:

Museo di Palazzo Rosso: Via Garibaldi 18; paintings and sculpture, frescoes and stuccoes, prints and drawings, nativity models, coins, weights and measures, Ligurian ceramics; library of 35,000 vols.

Galleria di Palazzo Bianco: Via Garibaldi 11; paintings by Genoese and Flemish masters and other schools.

Museo Navale: Villa Doria, Piazza Bonavino, Genoa-Pegli; models of ships, nautical instruments, navigation maps, prints.

Galleria di Arte Moderna: Villa Serra, Via Capolungo, Nervi; 19th and 20th century paintings.

Museo Giannettino Luxoro: Via Aurelia, Nervi; Flemish and Genoese paintings of the 17th and 18th centuries, furniture, ceramics.

Museo del Tesoro di San Lorenzo: Cattedrale di San Lorenzo; relics, copes and goldsmiths' work.

Museo del Risorgimento e Istituto Mazziniano: Casa di Mazzini, via Lomellini 11; exhibits illustrating life and work of Mazzini, 19th century documents and arms, specialized library containing works from the 18th to the 20th century.

Museo di Architettura e Scultura Ligure: Piazza R. Negri; sculpture from 9th to 18th century (closed for complete renovation).

Museo Etnografico del Castello d'Albertis: Corso Dogali 18; American ethnographical collections (closed for complete renovation).

Museo d'Arte Orientale 'Edoardo Chiossone': Villetta di Negro; f. 1905; paintings from 11th to 19th century; Chinese and Japanese works of art.

Museo Civico di Archeologia Ligure: Villa Durazzo-Pallavicini; f. 1892; Ligurian archaeology of the periods up to the Roman era; collection of Greek vases.

Archivi Istorici della Città di Genoa: Via Garibaldi 9; documents from 15th to 19th centuries.

Raccolte di Palazzo Tursi: Via Garibaldi 9; treasures include Paganini's violin and the letters of Columbus.

Galleria di Palazzo Spinola: Dir. Prof. GIAN VITTORIO CASTELNOVI.

Museo Civico di Storia Naturale 'G. Doria': Via Brigata Liguria 9, 16121; f. 1867; research in natural history; zoological, mineralogical, geological and botanical collections; library of 20,000 vols.; Dir. Dr. LILIA CAPOCACCIA; publs. *Annali*† (yearly), *Doriana*†.

Soprintendenza Archeologica della Liguria: Palazzo Reale, Via Balbi 10; f. 1939; preservation of monuments and excavations of Liguria (prehistoric and Roman) and ancient city of Luni and prehistoric caves of Balzi Rossi; Dir. Dott. Prof. GIOVANNA BERMOND MONTANARI.

Grosseto

Museo Archeologico e d'Arte della Maremma: Piazza Baccarini; f. 1865; medieval archaeological findings from the Maremma; 3,000 vols.; Dir. Prof. ALDO MAZZOLAI.

L'Aquila

Museo Nazionale d'Abruzzo: f. 1949; art from the early Middle Ages to contemporary times; Dir. Dott. Arch. MARGHERITA ASSO.

Lecce

Museo Archeologico Provinciale Sigismondo Castromediano: Collegio Argento Viale Gallipoli 1; f. 1868; archaeology; 1,000 vols., 1,436 pamphlets and off-prints; Dir. GIOVANNA DELLI PONTI.

Lucca

Museo di Villa Guinigi: Villa Guinigi, Via della Quarquonia; collection of Roman and late Roman sculptures and mosaics; Romanesque, Gothic, Renaissance and Neoclassical sculpture; paintings from 12th to 18th century including Fra Bartolomeo and Vasari; wood inlays, textiles, medieval goldsmiths' art; Dir. Dr. CLARA BARACCHINI.

Museo e Pinacoteca Nazionale di Palazzo Mansi: Via Galli Tassi 43; f. 1868; paintings by Titian, Tintoretto, etc., and Tuscan, Venetian, French and Flemish Schools; Dir. Dott. CLARA BARACCHINI.

Mantua

Galleria e Museo di Palazzo Ducale: Piazza Sordello; contains collections of Museo Statuario d'Arte Greca e Romana, f. 1773; Museo Egiziano, f. 1877; Museo Civico, f. 1852; and Galleria di Pittura, f. 1915; Dir. Dr. ILARIA TOESCA BERTELLI; publ. *Catalogue* (fully illustrated).

Matera

Museo Nazionale D. Ridola: Via D. Ridola 24; Dir. Dr. ELENA LATTANZI.

Messina

Museo Nazionale: Via della Libertà 465; f. 1953; Dir. Dssa. FRANCESCA CICALA CAMPAGNA.

Milan

Gabinetto Numismatico di Brera e Civiche Raccolte Numismatiche: Castello Sforzesco; f. 1807; coins and medals of all periods, specializing in Roman and Milanese coins; Dir. Dr. ERMANNO A. ARSLAN.

Galleria d'Arte Moderna e Padiglione d'Arte Contemporanea: Villa Reale, Via Palestro 16; painting and sculpture from Neo-Classical period to present day; includes the Grassi collection and Museo Marino Marini (*c.* 200 sculptures, portraits, paintings, drawings and etchings by Marini); Dir. Dott. MERCEDES GARBERI.

Museo Archeologico: Corso Magenta 15; f. 1807; Greek and Italic vases, Roman sculpture and mosaics, Roman glass including famous "Tazza diatreta", Etruscan art; Dir. Dr. ERMANNO A. ARSLAN.

Castello Sforzesco (Dungeon of "Rocchetta"): prehistoric collections, Egyptian dept.

Museo d'Arte Antica: Castello Sforzesco; f. 1893; sculpture from Middle Ages to 17th century, including the *Pietà* of Michelangelo; drawings, paintings, including works by Mantegna, Foppa, Lippi, Bellini, Lotto, Tintoretto, Tiepolo, Guardi, etc.; furniture, silver, bronzes, ivories, ceramics, musical instruments, tapestries by Bramantino, Bertarelli stamp collection; library of 41,000 vols.; Dir. Dr. MERCEDES PRECERUTTI-GARBERI, Dr. CLELIA ALBERICI.

Museo del Risorgimento e Raccolte Storiche del Comune di Milano: Palazzo De Marchi, Via Borgonuovo 23; museum f. 1884; documents, relics, etc., of the period 1750 to the present day; Dir. Prof. Dott. GIULIA BOLOGNA.

Museo Nazionale della Scienza e della Tecnica "Leonardo da Vinci": Via San Vittore 21, 20123; f. 1953; scientific and technical activities, displaying relics, models and designs, with particular emphasis on Leonardo's work; Pres. Prof. FRANCESCO OGLIARI; Tech. Dir. ing. ORAZIO CURTI; publ. *Museoscienza* (6 a year).

Museo Poldi Pezzoli: Via A. Manzoni 12; f. 1881; paintings from 14th-18th centuries; armour, tapestries, rugs, jewellery, porcelain, glass, textiles, furniture, clocks and watches, etc.; library of 5,500 vols.; Dir. Dott. ALESSANDRA MOTTOLA MOLFINO.

Pinacoteca Ambrosiana: Piazza Pio XI 2; f. 1618; paintings by Raphael, Botticelli, Titian, Bramante, Luini, etc.; drawings by Leonardo, Dürer, Rubens, etc.; miniatures, enamels, ceramics and medallions; Dir. Dott. ANGELO PAREDI.

Pinacoteca di Brera: Via Brera 28; f. 1809; pictures of all schools, especially Lombard and Venetian; paintings by Mantegna, Bellini, Crivelli, Lotto, Titian, Veronese, Tintoretto, Tiepolo, Foppa, Bergognone, Luini, Piero della Francesca, Bramante, Raphael, Caravaggio, Rembrandt, Van Dyck, Rubens; also 20th-century works, mostly Italian; Dir. Prof. CARLO BERTELLI.

Modena

Galleria, Museo e Medagliere Estense: Palazzo dei Musei, Piazza S. Agostino 109; f. 15th century in Ferrara, transferred to Palazzo Ducale, Modena, 1598, to Palazzo di Musei 1894; collections include about 2,000 paintings and drawings of 14th to 18th centuries, sculpture, engravings, medals, etc.; library of 5,000 vols.; Dir. Dr. GIORGIO BONSANTI.

Museo Civico: Piazza S. Agostino 109; f. 1871; Dir. Prehistoric and Archaeological Section Dr. BENEDETTI BENEDETTO; Dir. Medieval and Modern Section Dott. GABRIELLA GUANDALINI; publs. *Emilia Preromana*, *Bollettino del Museo Civico*.

Museo Lapidario Estense: Largo Porta S. Agostino 48; f. 1808; Roman and medieval archaeological collections; Dir. Dr. GIORGIO BONSANTI.

Naples

Museo Archeologico Nazionale: Via Museo 18; f. 18th century; Greek, Roman, Italian and Egyptian antiquities; Curator Prof. FAUSTO ZEVI.

Museo Civico "Gaetano Filangieri": Via Duomo 288; f. 1888; paintings, furniture, archives, photographs, library of 15,000 vols., and coin collection of Neapolitan history; Dir. FRANCESCO ACTON DI LEPORANO.

Museo "Duca di Martina" alla Floridiana: Via Cimarosa 77; ceramics; Dir. Dott. NICOLA SPINOSA.

Museo e Gallerie Nazionali di Capodimonte: f. 1738; paintings from 13th to 18th centuries; paintings and sculptures of 19th century; collection of arms and armour; medals and bronzes of the Renaissance; porcelain; library of 8,355 vols.; Dir. Prof. RAFFAELLO CAUSA.

Museo Nazionale di S. Martino: f. 1872; ancient church of S. Martino with 17th century pictures, 17th century paintings, 13th to 17th century sculpture, majolicas and porcelains, Neapolitan historical records and topographical collection, naval collection, arms and military costumes, opaline glass, section of modern painting, prints and engravings; Dir. Dott. T. FITTIPALDI.

Scavi di Pompei e di Ercolano: 80056 Resina; f. 1738-48; excavated cities Pompeii and Herculaneum; Dir. Prof. ALFONSO DE FRANCISCIS.

Padua

Cappella degli Scrovegni: Piazza Eremitani; Giotto frescoes.

Museo Civico: Piazza del Santo; f. 1825; Art Gallery (painting, sculpture, bronzes, ceramics, industrial arts), Archaeological Museum, Renaissance Museum, Museo Bottacin (Greco-Roman, Paduan, Venetian, Italian, Napoleonic coins and medals); library: Dir. ALESSANDRO PROSDOCIMI.

Palermo

Museo Regionale Archeologico: Piazza Olivella; f. 1868; prehistoric, Greek, Punic, Roman and Etruscan antiquities; library of 5,847 vols.; Dir. Prof. VINCENZO TUSA.

Parma

Galleria Nazionale: Palazzo della Pilotta; f. 1752, later reconstructed and added to; paintings from 13th to 19th centuries, including works by Correggio, Parmigianino, Cima, Greco, Piazzetta, Tiepolo, Holbein, Van Dyck, Mor, Nattier, and several painters of the school of Parma; also a modern art section; Superintendent Prof. EUGENIO RICCOMINI.

Museo Archeologico Nazionale: Via della Pilotta 4; f. 1760; archaeological collection of sculptures and other monuments from Veleia; Pre-Roman and Roman monuments from Parmesan; Egyptian, Greek, Etruscan and Roman art documents; Dir. Dr. MIRELLA CALVANI MARINI.

Museo Bodoniano: f. 1963; one of the richest museums of the art of printing: punches, original matrices and moulds (*c.* 80,000) from Bodoni's printing works; rare editions, technical manuals, press and tools of "the prince of printers"; Pres.-Dir. Dott. ANGELO CIAVARELLA; publ. *Bollettino*.

Pavia

Civici Musei—Castello Visconteo: Castello; f. 1838; Curator Dott. DONATA VICINI.

Perugia

Galleria Nazionale dell' Umbria: Palazzo dei Priori, Corso Vannucci; f. 1863; paintings of Umbrian school, 13th-18th centuries; also sculptures and jewellery; Dir. Dott. FRANCESCO SANTI.

Museo Archeologico Nazionale dell'Umbria: Piazza Giordano Bruno 10; Dir. A. E. FERUGLIO.

Pesaro

Museo Civico: Piazza Mosca 29; f. 1936; Dir. Dott. MARIA MANCINI.

Pisa

Museo Nazionale di S. Matteo: Convento di S. Matteo, Lungarno Mediceo; sculptures by the Pisanos and their school; important collection of the Pisan school of the 13th and 14th centuries, and paintings of the 15th, 16th and 17th centuries, ceramics, important collection of coins and medals, etc.; Dir. Dott. ANTONINO CALECA.

Portoferraio, Elba

Museo Napoleonico di S. Martino.

Ravenna

Museo Nazionale di Ravenna: Via S. Vitale 17; State property since 1887; Dir. GIOVANNA BERMOND MONTANARI.

Reggio Calabria

Museo Nazionale: Piazza De Nava 26; f. 1958; archaeological objects from Calabria from prehistoric era to Roman times; also *Antiquarium di Locri* (Locri), *Museo Archaeologico* (Vibo Valentia), *Museo Archaeologico* (Crotone), *Museo della Sibaritide* (Sibari); library of 7,000 vols.; Dir. Prof. GIUSEPPE FOTI; publ. *Klearchos.*

Rome

(*For the Vatican Museums*, see *the Vatican Chapter*.)

Galleria Borghese: Villa Borghese, 00197 Rome; f. 1616 (*circa*); picture gallery, collections of classical and Baroque sculpture; Dir. Dssa. SARA STACCIOLI.

Galleria Nazionale d'Arte Antica: Palazzo Barberini, Via Quattro Fontane 13; Palazzo Corsini, via della Lungara 10; 12th–18th-century Italian and European paintings, Baroque architecture; Dir. Dr. G. MAGNANIMI.

Galleria Nazionale d'Arte Moderna—Arte Contemporanea: Viale delle Belle Arti 131, 00197; f. 1883; art of 19th and 20th centuries; Dir. Dott. PALMA BUCARELLI.

Istituto Nazionale per la Grafica—Gabinetto Nazionale delle Stampe: Farnesina, Via della Lungara 230; f. 1895; Italian and foreign prints and drawings from 14th century to present time; Dir. Dott. MARIA CATELLI ISOLA.

Museo Barracco: Corso Vittorio Emanuele 168; f. 1905; evolution of sculpture from Egyptian to Roman styles; Dir. ETTORE DE JULIIS.

Musei Capitolini: Piazza del Campidoglio 1471; Dir. Prof. CARLO PIETRANGELI.

Museo della Civiltà Romana: Piazza G. Agnelli 15, Rome, EUR 00144; f. 1952; Curator Dssa. G. PISANI SARTORIO.

Museo di Palazzo di Venezia: Piazza Venezia 1; Dir. FILIPPA M. ALIBERTI GAUDIOSO.

Museo di Roma: Piazza S. Pantaleo; Dir. Prof. GEMMA DI DOMENICO CORTESE.

Museo Nazionale d'Arte Orientale: Palazzo Brancaccio, via Merulana 248; f. 1958; Dir. Dott. DONATELLA MAZZEO; library of 4,255 vols.

Museo Nazionale delle Arti e Tradizioni Popolari: Piazza Marconi 8, 00144; f. 1923; library of 8,500 vols.; archives of musical, spoken and photo-cinematographic material; Dir. Prof. Dssa. ANNABELLA ROSSI; Curator Prof. GAETANO RECUPERO.

Museo Nazionale di Castel Sant'Angelo: Lungotevere Castello 1; f. 1925; ancient and modern armoury, military costumes of Italian State and Nat. Army since 1940; architectural and monumental remains, frescoes, pictures and period furniture; library of 5,400 vols.; publishes monographs and guide books; Dir.-Gen. C.D'A. ANTONIO SEVERONI.

Museo Nazionale di Villa Giulia: Piazzale di Villa Giulia 9; f. 1889; Etruscan and Italian antiquities; Dir. Dr. PAOLA PELGATTI.

Museo Nazionale Preistorico ed Etnografico Luigi Pigorini: Piazzale G. Marconi 1, via A. Lincoln 1; new building: viale A. Lincoln 1, EUR; f. 1875; Superintendent Prof. CLELIA LAVIOSA; publ. *Bullettino di Paletnologia Italiana* (annual).

Museo Nazionale Romano: Piazza dei Cinquecento 79; f. 1889; Greek, Hellenistic and Roman sculpture and bronzes, pictures and mosaics, numismatics; archaeological collection; Dir. Prof. A. LA REGINA.

Scavi di Ostia: Roman antiquities, monuments, paintings, sculpture, mosaics, etc.; Curator Dotta. VALNEA SANTAMARIA SCRINARI.

Soprintendenza Archeologica di Roma: Piazza S. Maria Nova 53; Superintendent Prof. ADRIANO LA REGINA.

Villa della Farnesina: via della Lungara 230; now the property of the Accademia Nazionale dei Lincei; built 1509 by Peruzzi; decorated by Raphael, Peruzzi and others.

Sarsina (Forli)

Museo Archeologico: f. 1938; closed for restoration purposes; Dir. Prof. NINO FINAMORE.

Sassari

Museo Nazionale G. A. Sanna: f. 1932; archaeology, medieval and modern art, ethnography; Dir. Dott. F. NICOSIA.

Siena

Museo Archeologico: Via della Sapienza; Dir. ELISABETTA MANGANI.

Museo Aurelio Castelli: Via dell'Osservanza 7.

Pinacoteca Nazionale: Via S. Pietro; f. 1930; 650 paintings exhibited; Dir. Prof. PIERO TORRITI.

Syracuse

Museo Archeologico Regionale: Piazza del Duomo 14; f. 1886; prehistory, statuary, coins and antiques from the excavations of the Greco-Roman city and from Eastern Sicily; Dir. GIUSEPPE VOZA.

Taranto

Museo Nazionale: Corso Umberto 41; Dir. Dott. ETTORE MARIA DE JULIIS.

Tarquinia

Museo Nazionale Tarquiniense: Palazzo Vitelleschi; f. 1924; Etruscan Sarcophagi 4th and 3rd centuries B.C., Etruscan and Greek vases, bronzes, ornaments; small art gallery, works by Lippi, Batoni and Camuccini; Dir. Dott. MARIO MORETTO.

Trento

Museo Provinciale d'Arte: Castello del Buonconsiglio, via B. Clesio 5, 38100; Dir. Arch. MICHELANGELO LUPO.

Trieste

Musei Civici di Storia ed Arte di Trieste: Piazza Cattedrale 1 e Via Cattedrale 15; Dir. Dott. LAURA RUARO LOSERI; Curators Dott. GRAZIA BRAVAR, Dott. BIANCA MARIA FAVETTA. Comprises:

Civico Museo di Storia ed Arte e Orto Lapidario.

Civico Museo del Castello di San Giusto: piazza Cattedrale 3.

Civico Museo Sartorio: Largo Papa Giovanni XXIII 1.

Civico Museo di Storia Patria—Museo Morpurgo de Nilma—Collezioni artistiche Stavropulos: via Imbriani 5.

Civico Museo del Risorgimento e Sacrario Oberdan: via XXIV Maggio 4.

Civico Museo Teatrale di Fondazione Carlo Schmidl: piazza Verdi 1.

Civico Museo della Risiera di S. Sabba: Ratto della Pileria 1.

Turin

Armeria Reale: Piazza Castello 191; f. 1837; considered as one of the best collections of arms in Europe; includes the famous equestrian armour of Otto Heinrich and works by G. Paolo Negroli, Lucio Piccinino and the famous engravers of the Monaco di Baviera school, Emanuele Sadeler, Daniel Sadeler and Kaspar Spät; Dir. Prof. FRANCO MAZZINI; Curator Cav. RAFFAELE NATTA-SOLERI.

Museo Civico di Torino: Via Magenta 31; Dir. Dott. ANNA SERENA FAVA (acting); Curator for Coins Dott. ANNA SERENA FAVA; Curator for the artistic collections Dott. SILVANA PETTENATI, ROSANNA MAGGIO SERRA; comprises:

Museo Civico d'Arte Antica: Palazzo Madama.

Medagliere: Palazzo Madama.

Galleria Civica d'Arte Moderna: via Magenta 31.

Borgo e Castello Medioevali: Parco del Valentino.

Museo Pietro Micca: via Guicciardini, 7.

Museo di Antichità: via Accademia delle Scienze 6; Dir. Prof. LILIANA MERCANDO.

Museo Egizio: via Accademia delle Scienze, 6; f. 1824; sarcophagi, mummies, stele, statues, papyri, Ptolemaic and Coptic antiquities; entire furnishings of the tomb of architect Kha and his wife, reconstructed Nile temple of 18th dynasty, presented by the Egyptian Government; Dir. SILVIO CURTO.

Galleria Sabauda: via Accademia delle Scienze 6; f. 1832; one of principal Flemish and Dutch collections, and early Italian, also Bronzino, Veronese, Tiepolo and Lombard and Piedmontese schools, furniture, sculpture and jewellery; Dir. Dott. GIOVANNI ROMANO.

Udine

Civici Musei e Gallerie di Storia ed Arte: Via Ampezzo 2, 33100 Udine; f. 1866; Dir. Dott. ALDO RIZZI; publ. *Bollettino delle Civiche Istituzioni Culturali* (annually).

Urbino

Galleria Nazionale delle Marche (Palazzo Ducale): f. 1912; medieval and Renaissance works of art originating in the town of Urbino and the provinces of Marche; Dir. Prof. DANTE BERNINI.

Venice

Civici Musei Veneziani d'Arte e di Storia: S. Marco 52; Dir. Prof. GIANDOMENICO ROMANELLI.

Museo Correr: f. 1830 by Todoro Correr who bequeathed his collections to the City; Venetian art and history of the Serenissima; publ. *Bollettino* (quarterly).

Ca' Rezzonico: S. Barnabe-Fondamenta Rezzonico, Canal Grande; f. 1935; Venetian Settecento.

Museo Vetrario di Murano: Fondamenta Giustiniani 8, 30121 Murano; f. 1861; Venetian glass from middle ages to the present; also collections of 1st-century Roman glass, Spanish, Bohemian and English collections; archives and photographic collection; special exhibitions and educational projects.

Museo del Risorgimento: S. Marco 52; history of Venice from 1797 to First World War.

Palazzo Mocenigo: palace of the noble Venetian family which provided several of the doges.

Gabinetto delle Stampe e Disegni.

Casa Goldoni: house of the comedy writer (1707–93).

Biennale di Venezia: S. Marco, Ca' Giustinian; f. 1895; an autonomous body; organizes artistic and cultural events throughout the year: visual arts, architecture, cinema, theatre, music, special projects, etc.; the Biennale owns historical archives of contemporary art (library of 100,000 vols. and catalogues, photographs, etc.); Pres. GIUSEPPE GALASSO; publ. *La Biennale di Venezia, Annuario-Eventi.*

Galleria "G. Franchetti" alla Ca' d'Oro: f. 1927; sculpture and paintings.

Gallerie dell'Accademia: Campo della Carità 1059A; f. 1807; Venetian painting, 1330–1700; Dir. Dott. GIOVANNA SCIRÈNEPI.

Galleria Querini-Stampalia: Palazzo Querini-Stampalia, San Zaccaria 4778; f. 1869; 14th–19th-century Italian paintings.

Museo Archeologico: Palazzo già Reale in Piazzetta S. Marco; f. 1523, reorganised 1923-26 and again after 1945; Greek and Roman sculpture, jewels and coins, mosaics and sculptures from the 5th century B.C. to the 11th A.D.; Dir. Dott. GIULIA FOGOLARI.

Museo Civico di Storia Naturale: Fontego dei Turchi 1737; f. 1921; marine fauna of the Adriatic, ornithology, entomology; collections of plants and algae of the world; Dir. Prof. A. GIORDANI SOIKA; publ. *Bollettino*† (annually).

Museo d'Arte Moderna: Ca' Pesaro, Canal Grande; f. 1897; 19th- and 20th-century works of art; Dir. Prof. GUIDO PEROCCO.

Museo d'Arte Orientale: Ca' Pesaro, Canal Grande; 17th-19th-century decorative arts from the Far East; Dir. Dott. ADRIANA RUGGERI.

Museo Storico Navale: Riva degli Schiavoni 2148; f. 1923; library of 3,000 vols.; Dir. CARLO GOTTARDI.

Palazzo Ducale: Piazza S. Marco; Dir. Prof. Arch. UMBERTO FRANZOI.

Peggy Guggenheim Collection of the Solomon R. Guggenheim Foundation (New York): Palazzo Venier dei Leoni, 701 Dorsoduro; f. 1980; art from 1910 to the present day; Admin. PHILIP RYLANDS.

Pinacoteca Manfrediniana: Campo della Salute; f. 1827; paintings and sculpture of the Roman, Gothic, Renaissance, Neo-classical periods; Dir. A. NIERO.

Verona

Musei Civici di Verona: Castelvecchio 2; Dir. Dott. LISISCO MAGAGNATO; includes:

Museo Archaeologico al Teatro Romano.

Museo di Castelvecchio.

Museo Maffeiano.

Vicenza

Museo Civico: Palazzo Chiericati; Curator Dott. GINO BARIOLI.

Viterbo

Museo Civico: Dir. Dott. MARIO MORETTI.

Volterra

Museo Diocesano d'Arte Sacra: Palazzo Vescovile; sculpture, paintings, costumes, ornaments, etc.

Museo Etrusco: Via Don Minzoni 15; f. 1761; Roman and Etruscan coins, urns, bronzes, etc.; Dir. Prof. ENRICO FIUMI.

STATE UNIVERSITIES

UNIVERSITÀ DEGLI STUDI DI ANCONA

PIAZZA ROMA 22,
60100 ANCONA
Telephone: (071) 28212-6
Founded 1969.

Academic year: November to October.

Rector: Prof. FELICE SANTAGATA.
Vice-Rector: Prof. GIANMARIO MARIUZZI.
Director: Dott. FRANCESCO RICCI.
Librarian: Dessa. SILVIA SOTTILI.

Library of 11,455 vols.
Number of teachers: 140.
Number of students: 3,455.

DEANS:

Faculty of Engineering: Prof. PIETRO DI FILIPPO.
Faculty of Medicine and Surgery: SALVATORE OCCHIPINTI.

UNIVERSITÀ DEGLI STUDI

PIAZZA UMBERTO 1, 70100 BARI
Telephone: 080-369100.
Founded 1924.

Rector: Prof. LUIGI AMBROSI.
Vice-Rector: Prof. CLAUDIO MALAGUZZI VALERI.
Registrar: Dott. M. NATALE.

Number of teachers: 700.
Number of students: 42,439.

DEANS:

Faculty of Economics and Commerce: Prof. G. CHIASSINO.
Faculty of Medicine: Prof. A. DELL'ERBA.
Faculty of Pharmacology: Prof. V. TORTORELLA.
Faculty of Jurisprudence: Prof. V. STARACE.
Faculty of Agriculture: Prof. O. MONTEMURRO.
Faculty of Letters and Philosophy: Prof. F. TATEO.
Faculty of Science: Prof. A. COSSU.
Faculty of Engineering: Prof. V. COTECCHIA.
Faculty of Education: Prof. L. GAMBERALE.
Faculty of Foreign Languages: Prof. V. MASIELLO.
Faculty of Veterinary Medicine: Prof. G. O. MARCOTRIGIANO.

PROFESSORS:

Faculty of Economics and Commerce:

ALBANO, L., Mathematics
BARBIERA, L., Private Law
BELVISO, U., Private Law
BISSANTI, A. A., Economic Geography
CHIASSINO, G., Mathematics of Finance
DELVECCHIO, F., Social Statistics
GAROFALO, S., Agrarian Economics and Politics
GIRONE, G., Statistics
NEBBIA, G., Commerce
PIZZOLI, E. M., Commerce
PUGLIESE, F., Administrative Law
SALVEMINI RISTUCCIA, M. T., Political Economy
STASOLLA, V., Techniques of Banking, Industry and Commerce
ZALIN, G., Economic History

Faculty of Medicine and Surgery:

ADAMO, M., Forensic and Insurance Medicine
ALBANO, O., Medical Semeiology
AMBROSI, L., Industrial Medicine
AMPRINO, R., Human Anatomy
BARBERA, V., Anatomy and Histology
BETTOCCHI, S., Obstetrics and Gynaecology
BONOMO, L., Clinical Medicine
CAGNAZZO, G., Obstetrics and Gynaecology
CERVELLERA, G., Oto-Rhino-Laryngology
DE BLASI, A., Anaesthetics and Reanimation
DE GIACOMO, P., Psychiatry
DELL'ERBA, A., Forensic Medicine and Insurance Medicine
DIOMEDE FRESA, V., General Pathology
FERRARI, E., Nervous and Mental Diseases
FERSINI, M. C., Accident and Emergency Surgery
FUMAROLA, D., Microbiology
GIORDANO, D., General Pathology
GROSSO, E., Hygiene
IURATO, S., Bioacoustics
LAFORGIA, P., Odontology
LEGGIO, A., Paediatric Surgery
MACARINI, N., Radiology
MALAGUZZI VALERI, C., Clinical Medicine
MARINO, A., Pharmacology
MENEGHINI, C., Dermatosyphilopathy
MITOLO, V., Human Anatomy
PAPA, S., Bio-Chemistry
PEROSA, L., Specialised Pathology
PIPINO, F., Orthopaedics
PIPITONE, V., Rheumatology
RUBINO, M., Special Surgical Pathology
SCHETTINI, F., Child Welfare
SCHIRALDI, O., Infectious Diseases
TESTINI, A., Heart Surgery
TURSI, I., Immunology
VECCHIO, F., Paediatrics
ZAMBONI, P., Pharmacology

Faculty of Pharmacology:

BARBUTI, S., Hygiene
CASINI, G., Pharmaceutical and Toxicological Chemistry
TORTORELLA, V., Physical Methods of Organic Chemistry

Faculty of Jurisprudence:

BACCARI, R., Ecclesiastical Law
BRETONE, M., Sources of Roman Law
BUTTARO, L., Commercial Law
CAMPANALE, D., Philosophy of Politics

COLOMBO, G., Agrarian Economics and Politics
CONTENTO, G., Penal Law
COSTANTINO, M., Private Law
D'AMATI, N., Finance
DE ROBERTIS, F. M., Fundamentals of Roman Law
DELL'ANDRO, R., Penal Law
DEL PRETE, P., Administrative Law
DI COMITE, L., Demography
GRELLE, F., History of Roman Law
MOSCO, L., Private Law
PATRONI GRIFFI, A., Commercial Law
PICONE, P., International Law
ROSITI, F., Sociology
SPINELLI, M., Private Law
STARACE, V., International Law
TUCCI, G., Private Law
VACCA, G., History of Political Doctrines
VENETO, G., Labour Law
VENEZIANI, B., Labour Law

Faculty of Agriculture:
AMIRANTE, P., Machinery and Plant
BELLITTI, E., Zoognostics
BIANCHI, A., Agricultural Engineering
BIANCO, V. V., Horticulture
CALIANDRO, A., General Agriculture and Herbaceous cultivation
CIANCI, D., Domestic Animals
CICCARONE, A., Plant Pathology
DI PAOLA, G., Agrarian Mechanics and Applied Drawing
ERCOLANI, G. L., Microbiology
GIANNINI, F., Forestry
GIORDANO, E., Silviculture
LISANTI, L., Agrarian Chemistry
MARZI, V., Agronomy and Cultivation
MONTEMURRO, O., Special Zootechnics
PUGLISI, S., Hydraulic Systems
ROBERTI, D., Agrarian Entomology
SALERNO, M., Physiopathology
SCARASCIA MUGNOZZA, G. T., Plant Genetics
SOLINAS, M., Entomology
VITAGLIANO, M., Agrarian Industry

Faculty of Letters and Philosophy:
BIANCOFIORE, F., Pre-classical Civilisation
BRONZINI, G., History of Popular Traditions
CANCIANI, F., Archaeology and History of Greek and Roman Art
CANFORA, L., Greek and Roman History
CIVES, G., Pedagogics
CORVINO, F., History of Medieval Philosophy
DE RITA, L., Psychology
FANIZZA, F., Aesthetics
FARESE, G., German
FEDELI, P., Classical Philology
FUIANO, M., Medieval History
LABUA, V., Greek History
LAMACCIA, A., History of Philosophy
LAURENTI, R., History of Ancient Philosophy
LEONE DE CASTRIS, A., Modern Philology
MELILLO, M., Italian Dialectology
PEZZELLA, S., History of Christianity
RUSSO, C. F., Greek Literature
TATEO, F., History of Science

Faculty of Mathematics, Physics and Natural Science:
AQUARO, G., Higher Analysis
ARMENISE, N., Physics
ARNESE, G., Mathematical Analysis
ARRIGONI, O., Botany
AVANTAGGIATI, A., Mathematical Analysis
CINGOLANI, A., Physics
COSSU, A., Geometry
CRAMAROSSA, F., Chemistry
CREMASCHI, D., Physiology
CURCI, R., Organic Chemistry
DELL'ANNA, L., Mineralogy
FRONSDAL, C., Physics
GARAVELLI, C., Mineralogy
GIACOVAZZO, C., Mineralogy
GIANTURCO, F. A., Physical Chemistry
GRIGOLO, A., Zoology
GRILLI, M., General Physics
LIPPE, C., General Physiology
MASTROGIACOMO, P., Geometry
MUNI, G., Mathematical Analysis
NASO, F., Organic Chemistry
NATALI, S., Experimental Physics
PLANTAMURA VITO, L., Numerical and Analogical Techniques
PREPARATA, G., Theoretical Physics
QUAGLIARIELLO SACCONE, C., Biological Chemistry
RADINA, B., Geology
RITOSSA, F., Genetics
ROMANO, A., Physics
SACCO, A., General Chemistry
VALDUGA, A., Geology
ZAMBONIN, P. G., Analytical Chemistry

Faculty of Engineering:
ABBRESCIA, G., Roads, Railways and Airport Construction
BONDI, P., Technical Physics
COTECCHIA, V., Road and Railway Construction
DADONE, A., Machine Parts
DAMIANI, A., Hydraulics and Hydraulic Constructions
DE LEO, R., Microwaves
DI LECCE, F., Electro-technics
FASANO, A., Rational Mechanics
FOTI, C., Construction
GRISOTTI, M., Architecture and Town Planning
GUERRIERO, L., Physics
INFANTINO, R., Mathematical Analysis
IOVANE, F., Technology
MAIONE, B., Electrical Engineering
MARGARITA, E., Electrical Plant
MELIDORO, G., Rock Mechanics
RUGGIERO, U., Technical Physics
SOLLAZZO, A., Construction Engineering
TRENTADUE, A., Machine Construction

Faculty of Education:
BOSIO, G., Theoretical Philosophy
CHIARELLI, R., Public Law and Educational Law
CONIGLIO, G., History and Political Science
DELL'AQUILA, M., Italian Language and Literature
GAMBERALE, L., Latin Language and Literature
LAMACCHIA, R., Latin Grammar
LOMIENTO, G., Ancient Christian Literature
PALAGIANO, C., Geography
RECCHIA, V., Medieval Latin
SANTELLI BECCEGATO, L., Pedagogics
SIRAGO, V., Roman History

Faculty of Foreign Languages:
CAROFIGLIO, V., French Language and Literature
DE MICHELIS, C., Russian Language and Literature
DI SARRA, D. D., Serbo-Croat
DURANTE, E., German Philology
FORTE, L., German Language and Literature
LAPICCIRELLA ROSSI, R., Spanish Language and Literature
MASIELLO, V., Italian Language and Literature
MIRIZZI, P., English
PANUNZIO, S., Romance Philology
RENDI, A., German
SABBADINI, S., English Language and Literature

Faculty of Veterinary Medicine:
BUONACCORSI, A., Clinical Medicine
CIRUZZI, B., Alimentation and Nutrition
COMPAGNUCCI, M., Pathology of Infectious Diseases
FEDRIGO, M., Veterinary Surgery
MARCOTRIGIANO, O., Chemistry
MASTRONARDI, M., Clinical Surgery
PASSANTINO, G. F. G., Comparative Anatomy
TIECCO, G., Alimentation

UNIVERSITÀ DEGLI STUDI

VIA ZAMBONI 33, 40126 BOLOGNA
Telephone: 272933.
Telex: 511650 UNIVBO I.
Founded 11th Century.

Rector: Prof. C. RIZZOLI.
General Secretary: Dott. A. FANTAZZINI.
Number of teachers: 2,500.
Number of students: 60,047.

DEANS:

Faculty of Jurisprudence: Prof. R. NARDI.
Faculty of Political Science: Prof. U. ROMAGNOLI.
Faculty of Economics and Commerce: Prof. G. GHETTI.
Faculty of Arts and Philosophy: Prof. G. SUSINI.
Faculty of Education: Prof. M. PAZZAGLIA.
Faculty of Medicine: Prof. L. SPERTI.
Faculty of Mathematics, Physics and Natural Sciences: Prof. C. CONCILIO.
Faculty of Industrial Chemistry: Prof. C. ZAULI.
Faculty of Pharmacy: Prof. C. A. ROSSI.
Faculty of Engineering: Prof. G. FOLLONI.
Faculty of Agriculture: Prof. G. GOIDANICH.
Faculty of Veterinary Medicine: Prof. G. GENTILE.

UNIVERSITÀ DI CAGLIARI*

VIA UNIVERSITÀ 40,
09100 CAGLIARI, SARDINIA
Telephone: 66-79-41.
Founded 1606 by Pope Paolo V.

Rector: Prof. DUILIO CASULA.
Administrative Director: Dott. S. CALABRESE.
Librarian: Dott. GRAZIELLA SEDDA DELITALA.

Number of teachers: *c.* 1,000.
Number of students: *c.* 18,000.

Publications: *Studi economico-giuridici* and publications from each Faculty.

Faculties of Economics, Education, Engineering, Law, Medicine, Philosophy and Letters, Politics, Pharmacy, Sciences.

* No reply received to our questionnaire this year.

UNIVERSITÀ DI CALABRIA

CONTRADA ARCAVATA,
87036 RENDE
Founded 1972.

Rector: Prof. PIETRO BUCCI.

Faculties of Economics, Engineering, Letters, Sciences.

UNIVERSITÀ DI CAMERINO

PIAZZA CAVOUR,
62032 CAMERINO
Telephone: 36141.

Founded 1336; University status 1727.
Academic year: November to October.

Rector: Prof. ROMANO CIPOLLINI.
Administrative Director: Dr. ANTONIO SCARPERIA.

Number of teachers: 400.
Number of students: 2,900.

Publications: *Annuario, Notiziario, Studi geologici camerti, Index—International Survey of Roman Law.*

DEANS:

Faculty of Jurisprudence: Prof. LUIGI FERRAJOLI.
Faculty of Science: Prof. FULVIO GUALTIERI.
Faculty of Pharmacy: Prof. GUIDO GIACOMO TEDESCHI.

ATTACHED INSTITUTES:

School of Postgraduate Studies in Civil Law: Dir. Prof. PIETRO PERLINGIERI.
School of Clinical-Chemical Research: Dir. Prof. GUIDO GIACOMO TEDESCHI.

UNIVERSITÀ DI CATANIA

PIAZZA DELL' UNIVERSITÀ,
95129 CATANIA
Telephone: 220355.
Founded 1434.

Rector: Prof. GASPARE RODOLICO.
Administrative Director: Dott. ANGELO LA SETA.

Number of teachers: 856.
Number of students: 32,380.

DEANS:

Faculty of Jurisprudence: Prof. C. COSENTINI.
Faculty of Political Science: Prof. FRANCESCO LEONARDI.
Faculty of Economics and Commerce: Prof. EMILIO GIARDINA.
Faculty of Letters and Philosophy: **Prof.** G. GIARRIZZO.
Faculty of Medicine: Prof. ATTILIO BASILE.
Faculty of Mathematics, Physics, Chemistry and Natural Sciences: Prof. ATTILIO AGODI.
Faculty of Pharmacy: Prof. GIOVANNI PAPPALARDO.
Faculty of Agriculture: Prof. PATRIZIO DAMIGELLA.
Faculty of Engineering: Prof. ENRICO OLIVERI.

UNIVERSITÀ DEGLI STUDI

VIA SAVONAROLA 9,
44100 FERRARA
Telephone: 39-181.
Founded 1391.

Rector: Prof. ANTONIO ROSSI.
Pro-Rector: Prof. G. TRABANELLI.
Administrative Director: Dott. L. LIVATINO.

Number of teachers: 352, including 85 professors.
Number of students: 6,247.

Publications: *Annali dell' Università, Annuario.*

DEANS:

Faculty of Jurisprudence: Prof. V. CAVALLARI.
Faculty of Education: Prof. A. BASSI.
Faculty of Medicine: Prof. R. PANSINI.
Faculty of Mathematical, Physical and Natural Sciences: Prof. L. BIASINI.
Faculty of Pharmacy: Prof. L. BRIGHENTI.

PROFESSORS:

Faculty of Jurisprudence:
BATTAGLINI, G., International Law
BORGHESI, D., Civil Precedural Law
CARLASSARE, L., Constitutional Law
CATTANEO, M. A., Philosophy of Law
CAVALLARI, V., Criminal Procedure
CIAN, G., Civil Law
COLORNI, V., History of Italian Law
FERRABOSCHI, M., Ecclesiastical Law
FUMAGALLI CARULLI, O. B., Canon Law
GALLO, E., Penal Law Institutions
MAFFEI ALBERTI, A., Commercial Law
MOSCHELLA, A., Commercial Law
STEFANI, G., Financial Law
ZAMORANI, P., Institutions of Roman Law

Faculty of Education:
DUSE, U., History of Music
MAGRI, P., Physiology
MIEGGE, M., Philosophy
MORETTI, W., Italian Language and Literature
ROCHAT, G., Contemporary History

Faculty of Medicine:
BALLERINI, G., Medical Pathology
BATTAGLIA, G., Human Anatomy
BEANI, L., Pharmacology
BENASSI, G., Pathology
BOREA, G., Clinical Odontology
CALEARO, C. V., Oto-Rhino-Laryngology
CALIFANO, A., Dermo-syphilopathic Clinic
CARINCI, P., Histology and General Embryology
CARRERAS, M., Clinical Neurology
CONCONI, F., Bio-chemistry
CORAZZA, B., Human Physiology
DONINI, G. I., Surgery
FERSINI, C., Systematic Medical Therapy
GRAZI, E., Biological Chemistry
GUERRIERI, S., Anaesthesiology and Reanimation
LANZA, G., Anatomy and Pathological Histology
MATTIUZ, P. L., Medical Genetics
MENGHI, G., Paediatrics
MIGLIORE, A., Neurosurgery
NAPPI, R., Obstetrics and Gynaecology
PANSINI, R., Clinical Medicine
PERRI, V., Human Physiology
REMELLI, L., Surgical Semeiology
RIPPA, M., Chemistry
ROSSI, A., Ophthalmology
ROSSOTTO, P., Special Surgical Pathology
TEATINI, G., Audiology
TORTORA, M., Obstetrics and Gynaecology
TOTI, A., Radiology
TREVISI, M., Human Anatomy
VOLPATO, S., Paediatrics

Faculty of Mathematical, Physical and Natural Sciences:
AMBROSETTI, M., Mathematical Analysis
ANCONA, V., Geometry
BANFI, C., Rational Mechanics
BASSI BERNELLI, Z. M., Botany
BARRAI, I., Genetics
BIASINI, L., Numerical Analysis
BIGHI, C., Analytical Chemistry
BOSELLINI, A., Sedimentology
BROGLIO, A., Human Palaeontology
CARASSITI, V., General and Inorganic Chemistry
COLOMBO, G., Zoology
D'ANGELI, F., Organic Chemistry
DONDONI, A., Organic Chemistry
FABRIZIO, M., Mathematical Physics
FIORENTINI, M., Higher Geometry
GILLI, G., Chemistry
LOVITCH, L., Nuclear Physics
MAGON, L., Nuclear Chemistry
MANTOVANI, G., Industrial Chemistry
MARZIANI, M., Rational Mechanics
MUTTI, E., Geology
OGNIBEN, G., Mineralogy
ORTALLI, I., Physics
PEPE, L., Mathematical Analysis
PERRI, V., General Physiology
PINELLI, T., General Physics
RAUNICH, L., Comparative Anatomy
REATTO, L., Structure of Matter
RIMONDI, O., Health Physics
RIPPA, M., Chemistry and Biochemistry
RIVALENTI, G., Petrography
SACCHI, O., General Physiology
SALVATORELLI, G., Histology and Embryology
SCHIFFER, G., Theoretical Physics
TOGNOLI, A., Algebra
TRABANELLI, G., Theory and Practice of Phenomena of Corrosion

Faculty of Pharmacy:
BEANI, L., Pharmacology and Pharmacognosy
BRIGHENTI, L., General Physiology
DALL'OLIO, G., Pharmaceutical Botany
D'ANGELI, F., Organic Chemistry
GUARNERI, M., Pharmaceutical Chemistry and Toxicology
TRANIELLO, M. S., Biological Chemistry

UNIVERSITÀ DEGLI STUDI

PIAZZA SAN MARCO 4,
50121 FLORENCE
Telephone: 26-23-51.
Founded 1321.

Rector: Prof. FRANCO SCARAMUZZI.
Registrar: Dott. M. SACCO.
Librarian: Dott. T. URSO.

Number of professors: 378.
Number of students: 44,331.

DEANS:

Faculty of Jurisprudence: Prof. F. ROMANO.

Faculty of Political Sciences: Prof. L. LOTTI.
Faculty of Economics and Commerce: G. STANCANELLI.
Faculty of Letters and Philosophy: Prof. E. CASARI.
Faculty of Education: Prof. M. MONTINARI.
Faculty of Medicine and Surgery: A. GIACHETTI.
Faculty of Science: Prof. F. FABRI.
Faculty of Pharmacology: Prof. P. PAPINI.
Faculty of Architecture: Prof. D. CARDINI.
Faculty of Agriculture and Forestry: Prof. U. SORBI.
Faculty of Engineering: Prof. D. QUILGHINI.

PROFESSORS:

Faculty of Jurisprudence:

AMODIO, E., Penal Procedure
ARANGUREN, A., Labour Law
ARCHI, G., Roman Law
BARILE, P., Constitutional Law
BASSANINI, F., Constitutional Law
BELLINI, P., Canon Law
BENEDETTI, G., Fundamentals of Private Law
BERTI, G., Fundamentals of Public Law
BRETONE, M., History of Roman Law
CALVI, A. A., Penal Law
CAPACCIOLI, E., Administrative Law
CAPPELLETTI, M., Civil Procedural Law
CARRESI, Civil Law
CHELI, E., Fundamentals of Public Law
CONDORELLI, L., International Law
FIORELLI, P., History of Italian Law
FREZZA, P., History of Roman Law
GAJA, G., International Law
GALLI, R., Political Economy
GROSSI, P., History of Italian Law
LIBONATI, B., Commercial Law
LOMBARDI VALLAURI, L., Philosophy of Law
MANTOVANI, F., Penal Law
MAZZONI, G., Labour Legislation
MIELE, G., Administrative Law
ONIDA, F., Ecclesiastical Law
PACE, A., Fundamentals of Public Law
PROTO PISANI, Civil Law Procedure
PUCCINI, L., Fundamentals of Private Law
ROMAGNOLI, E., Comparative Agrarian Law
ROMANO, F., Civil Law
SANTALUCIA, B., Fundamentals of Roman Law
VITALE, P., Fundamentals of Private Law
ZILLETTI, U., Roman Law

Faculty of Political Sciences:

ANDRÉ, G., History of International Relations
ARFÉ, G., History of Italian Unification
CALVI, G., International Organizations
CAVALLI, L., Sociology
CECIONI, C. G., English Language
CURATOLO, R., Statistics
DURANTE, F., International Law
FISICHELLA, D., State Doctrine
GORI, U., International Relations
LOTTI, L., Modern History
MARGIOTTA BROGLIO MASSUCCI, F., History of Religious Institutions
MOSCA, R., History of International Relations
PASSIGLI, S., Administrative Science
PREDIERI, A., Fundamentals of Public Law
RAVA, R., Labour Law
RUSSO, P., Financial Law
SARTORI, G , Political Science
SPADOLINI, G., Contemporary History
TAGLIACOZZO, E., History of Political Parties and Ideologies
TARANTELLI, E., Economic and Financial Politics
TOSI, S., Italian Constitutional and Comparative Law
TREZZA, B., Economic and Financial Politics
TULLIO ALTAN, C., Cultural Anthropology
VICARELLI, F., Political Economics
ZANFARINO, A., History of Political Doctrines

Faculty of Economics and Commerce:

BANDETTINI, A., General and Applied Accountancy
BARETTONI ARLERI, A., Public Accounts
BARUCCI, P., History of Economics
BECATTINI, G., Political Economy
CIANFERONI, R., Agrarian Economics and Politics
CORSI, F., Commercial Law
CORSINI, C., Historical Demography
DI LAZZARO, M., Mathematics of Finance
FAZZI, R., Industrial and Commercial Techniques
FRANCHINI STAPPO, A., Political and Financial Economics
INNOCENTI, P., Economic Geography
LEONI, R., Statistics of Economics
LIVI BACCI, M., Demography
MESSINETTI, D., Private Law
MORI, G., Economic History
NICE, B., Economic Geography
PARENTI, G., Statistics
PARRINELLO, S., Political Economy
RASTELLO, L., Tributary Law
STANCANELLI, G., Public Law
TERZANI, S., General and Applied Accountancy
VOLPI, F., Finance

Faculty of Letters and Philosophy:

ADORNO, F., History of Ancient Philosophy
ARAGONE TERNI, E., Spanish Language and Literature
AVALLE D'ARCO, S., Romance Philology
BALDI, S., English Language and Literature
BARBIERI, G., Geography
BARIGAZZI, A., Greek Literature
BETTARINI BIGAZZI, R., Italian Philology
BEVILACQUA, G., German Language and Literature
BOSTICCO, S., Egyptology
CAMPOREALE, G. A., Etruscology and Italian Archaeology
CARETTI, L., Italian Literature
CASAMASSIMA, E., Palaeography and Diplomacy
CASARI, E., Philosophy of Science
CASTELLANI, E., History of Italian Language
CLEMENTE, G., Roman History
CONTI, E., Medieval History
DALLA CHIARA SCABIA, M. L., Logic
DANTI, A., Slav Philology
DE ROBERTIS, D., Italian Literature
FRONZAROLI, P., Hebrew Philology
GARAVINI, F., French Language and Literature
GHINASSI, G., History of Italian Language
GREGORI, G., History of Medieval and Modern Art
IMPARATI, F., Ancient History
INAMORATI, G., Italian Literature
LANDUCCI, S., Moral Philosophy
LA PENNA, A., Latin Literature
LEONARDO, C., History of Medieval Latin Literature
LUPORINI, C., Moral Philosophy
LUTI, G., Italian Literature
MASTRELLI, C. A., Glottology
MAZZONI, F., Dantesque Philology
PARIBENI, E., Archaeology and History of Classical Art
PASCUCCI, G., Greek and Latin Grammar
PELLEGRINI, C., English
PEROSA, A., Medieval Philology and Humanism
PIZZORUSSO, A., French Language and Literature
PROCACCI, G., Modern History
RANCHETTI, M., Church History
RONCONI, A., Latin Literature
ROSSI MONTI, P., History of Philosophy
SALVESTRINI, A., History of Italian Unification
SALVINI, R., History of Medieval and Modern Art
SCARDIGLI, P., German Philology
SESTINI, A., Geography
VASA, A., Theoretical Philosophy
VASOLI, E., History of Philosophy
VILLARI, R., Modern History
VIVARELLI, R., Contemporary History
ZAMBELLI, P. R., History of Philosophy
ZANARDO, A., Moral Philosophy

Faculty of Education:

BALDACCI, L., Italian Language and Literature
BIGONGIARI, P., History of Modern and Contemporary Italian Literature
BORGHI, L., Pedagogy
BOSCHERINI, S., Latin Language and Literature
CAPONETTO, S., Modern History
CARAMASCHI, V., French Language and Literature
CARBONARO, A., Sociology
CARDINI, R., History of Medieval Latin and Humanist Literature
CERRITO, B., Contemporary History
CHIARINI, G., Romance Philology
CORDIE, C., French Language and Literature
FACCIOLI, E., Italian Language and Literature
FALORNI, M. L., Psychology of the Evolutionary Era
FRANCOVICH, C., History of the Risorgimento
GALLINARO LUPORINI, M. B., Russian Language and Literature
JANNACO, C., Italian Language and Literature
MACRI, O., Spanish Language and Literature
MARZI, A., Psychology
MASTELLONE, S., History
MONTINARI, M., German Language and Literature
MORAVIA, S., History of Philosophy
PAGNINI, M., English Language and Literature
PAOLI, R., Spanish-American Language and Literature
PERUZZI, E., Linguistics
POLLIDORI CASTELLANI, O., History of Italian Grammar
PORRU MAZZUOLI, G., Germanic Philology
ROMAGNOLI, S., Italian Language and Literature
SANTONI RUGI, A., Pedagogy
SERPIERI, A., English Language and Literature
SPINI, G., History
VARESE, C., Italian Language and Literature
VENTURA TOMASI, A., Pedagogy
VICCHI NOFERI, A., Italian Language and Literature

Faculty of Medicine and Surgery:

Alajmo, E., Clinical Oto-Rhino-Laryngology
Alfieri, G., Physio-Pathological Optics
Allara, E., Histology and General Embryology
Allegra, G., Surgical and Propaedeutic Pathology
Amaducci, L., Clinical Neurology
Antonini, F. M., Gerontology and Geriatrics
Arcangeli, P., Medical Pathology and Clinical Methodology
Baccari, V., Biochemistry
Balboni, G., Human Anatomy
Bertini, D., Vascular Surgery
Bigozzi, U., Medical Genetics
Brizzi, E., Human Anatomy
Cagnoni, M., Semeiological Medicine
Chiodi, V., Forensic Medicine
Corda, M., Human Physiology
Cortesini, C., Experimental Surgery
Costa, A., Anatomy and Histopathology
Costantini, A., Urology
D'Alessandro, A., Gerontology
Davoli, R., Microbiology
De Giuli, G., Radiology
Del Federico de Dominicis, R., Radiology
Della Corte, M., Physics
Di Guglielmo, R., General Clinical and Therapeutic Medicine
Fazzari, C., Forensic Medicine
Focosi, M., Ophthalmology
Fonnesu, A., General Pathology
Galletti, R., Special Medical Pathology and Clinical Methodology
Gargani, G., Microbiology
Gasparri, F., Obstetrics and Gynaecology
Gentilini, P., Special Medical Pathology and Clinical Methodology
Giaccai, F., Otology
Giachetti, A., Human Physiology
Giotti, A., Pharmacology
Giusti, G., Constitutional and Endocrinological Medicine
Grandocini, F., Nuclear Medicine
Loddi, L., Special Medical Pathology
Maleci, O., Clinical Neurology
Mannaioni, P. F., Toxicology
Marsilii, G., General Pathology
Morandi, G., Rheumatology
Morelli, A., Industrial Medicine
Nassi, L., Child Welfare
Nocentini, L., Special Surgical and Propedeutical Pathology
Novelli, G. P., Anaesthetics
Orlandi, G., Normal Anatomy
Panconesi, E., Dermatology and Syphilology
Pansini, A., Neurosurgery
Pepeu, G., Pharmacology
Periti, P., Chemotherapy
Peruzzi, P., Physiology
Ragazzini, F., Paediatrics
Ramponi, G., Biochemistry
Rapi, G., Chemistry
Renzi, R., Physics
Scaglietti, O., Orthopaedics
Sicuteri, F., Clinical Pharmacology
Signorini, L., Hygiene
Simonetta Bono, Oto-Rhino-Laryngology
Stringa, G., Orthopaedics
Stigliani, R., Pathological Anatomy and Histology
Teodori, U., General Clinical Medicine
Tonelli, L., General Clinical and Therapeutic Surgery
Vichi, F., Odontology
Zampi, G., Histopathology
Zappoli Thjrion, R., Neuropathology
Zilletti, L., Pharmacology

Faculty of Science:

Abbate, E., Stratigraphy
Ademollo, M., Theoretical Physics
Arrigoni, P. V., Geography
Azzaroli, A., Paleontology
Bertolotti, V., Geology
Bizzeti, P., Nuclear Physics
Bonetti, A., Space Physics
Bosco, B., Theoretical Physics
Califano, S., Physical Chemistry
Campedelli, L., Geometry
Ciampolini, M., General and Inorganic Chemistry
Cini, R., Technical Physical Chemistry
Cipriani, C., Mineralogy
Conti, R., Mathematical Analysis
Coradossi, N., Geochemistry
Corti Francini, E., Botany
Cozzi, D., Analytical Chemistry
Desideri, P. G., Analytical Chemistry
Di Caponialco, G., Physics
Fabbri, F., Cytology and Vegetal Embryology
Fazzini, T., Experimental Physics
Ferroni, E., Physical Chemistry
Franchetti, S., General Physics
Furieri, P., Comparative Anatomy
Gherardelli, F., Geometry
Godoli, G., Solar Physics
Graziosi, P., Anthropology
Guidelli, R., Electrochemistry
Innamorati, M., Vegetal Ecology
Lanza, B., General Biology
Longhi, G., Fundamentals of Theoretical Physics
Malesani, P., Petrography
Mando, M., General Physics
Mangani, P., Algebraic Structures
Martelli, M., Fundamental Mathematics
Maugini, E., Botany
Merla, G., Geology
Messeri, P., Human Palaeontology
Moggi, G., Botany
Pacini, F., Astrophysics
Padoa, E., Comparative Anatomy
Pantani, F., Analytical Chemistry
Paoletti, P., General and Inorganic Chemistry
Pardi, L., Zoology
Parrini, V., Chemical Dyes
Pasquali, A., Numerical Analysis
Piacenti, F., Organic Industrial Chemistry
Polsinelli, M., Genetics
Primicerio, M., Mechanics
Pucci, C., Higher Analysis
Querzoli, R., General Physics
Ricci, A., Organic Chemistry
Righini, G., Astronomy
Rosati, L. A., Geometry
Sacconi, L., General and Inorganic Chemistry
Schettino, V., Molecular Spectroscopy
Sestini, G., Rational Mechanics (for Engineers)
Speroni, G., Organic Chemistry
Tagliaferri, G., Cosmology
Talenti, G., Mathematical Analysis
Tomassini, G., Geometry
Toraldo di Francia, G., Higher Physics
Torre, D., Palaeontology
Vacca, A., Chemistry
Vergnano Gambi, O., Vegetal Physiology
Zappa, G., Algebra

Faculty of Pharmacology:

Bertini, I., General and Inorganic Chemistry
Buffoni, F., Molecular Pharmacology
Colosi, G., Human Anatomy
Marzocchi, M. P., Physics of Chemistry
Papini, P., Pharmaceutical Techniques and Legislation
Ridi, M., Pharmaceutical and Toxicological Chemistry

Faculty of Architecture:

Bardazzi, S., Town Planning
Borsi, G., History of Architecture
Cardini, D., Architectural Composition
Cetica, P. A., Architectural Technology
Cimboli Spagnesi, G., History of Architecture
Cusmano, M., Town Planning
De Blasi, F. S., Analytical Mathematics and Geometry
De Luigi, L., Town Planning
Detti, E., Town Planning
Di Pasquale, S., Building Science
Fagioli, M., Style and Structure of Monuments
Fatinnanzi, E., Valuations in Professional Practice
Franchetti Pardo, V., History of Architecture
Gamberini, I., Architectural Composition
Ghio, M., Town Planning
Koenig, G. K., History of Architecture
Ricci, L., Town Planning
Rocchi, G. Restoration of Monuments
Rodolico, F., Mineralogy and Geology
Sanpaolesi, P., Restoration of Monuments
Savioli, L., Furnishing
Spadolini, P. L., Industrial Planning
Turchini, G., Building Assembly and Prefabrication
Vagnetti, L., Architectural Composition
Zaffagnini, M., Technology of Architecture

Faculty of Agriculture and Forestry:

Bellucci, V., Forest Valuation and Economics
Bernetti, G., Dendrometry
Borgioli, E., General Zootechnics
Cantiani, M., Planned Forestry
Casini, E., Fruit Culture
Cecconi, S., Agrarian Chemistry
Ciampi, C., Systematic Botany
Corti, R., General Botany
Dallari, F. A., Agrarian Mechanics and Mechanical Design
De Philippis, A., Silviculture I
Florenzano, G., Agrarian Microbiology
Geri, G., Special Zootechnics
Giorgi, E., Agrarian Economy and Policy II
Grasso, V., Plant Pathology
Grazi, S., Hydraulic and Forest Systems
Hippoliti, G., Forest Technology
Landi, R., General Agronomy and Arboriculture
Magini, E., Silviculture II
Malquori, A., Forest Chemistry
Mancini, F., Applied Geology
Meregalli, A., Zoognostics
Orsi, S., General Agronomy
Scaramuzzi, F., Arboreal Culture
Sorbi, U., Rural Valuation
Stella, C., Agrarian Industries
Talamucci, P., Alpine Culture

Faculty of Engineering:

Augusti, G., Science of Structures
Barbuti, U., Mathematical Analysis
Belleni, A. M., Theoretical Mechanics
Calamia, M., Electromagnetic Fields and Circuits
Cappelini, V., Telecommunications
Del Puglia, A., Machine Construction
Fondelli, M., Topography
Francini, G., Applied Electronics
Furi, M., Analytical Mathematics

LIBERATORE, A., Theory of Electrical Circuits
LISINI, G. G., Applied Mechanics
MASOTTI, L., General Electronics
MOSCA, E., Systems Theory
NERLI, G., Machine Construction
QUILGHINI, D., Theoretical Mechanics
RASPOLINI, R., Architecture and Architectural Construction
SANTORO, P., Mathematical Analysis
VILLARI, G., Mathematical Analysis
ZANINI, A., Electronic Gauges

ATTACHED INSTITUTE:

Scuola di Perfezionamento in Studi Politici Internazionali (*Postgraduate School of International Affairs*): f. 1979; attached to the Faculty of Political Sciences; 2-year course open to foreign graduates; Dir. ANTONIO CASSESE.

UNIVERSITA DEGLI STUDI DI GENOVA

VIA BALBI 5,
16126 GENOA
Telephone: 284151.
Founded 1471.

Academic year: November-October.

***Rector:* Prof. C. A. ROMANZI.**

Administrative Director: Dott. A. PAPAGNA.

Number of teachers: 1,092, including **292 professors.**

Number of students: 33,653.

DEANS:

Faculty of Jurisprudence: Prof. L. ACQUARONE.
Faculty of Political Science: Prof. F. CUOCOLO.
***Faculty of Economics and Commerce:* Prof. A. SCOTTO.**
***Faculty of Letters and Philosophy:* Prof.** C. MARLTESE.
Faculty of Education: Prof. G. FERRO.
Faculty of Medicine: Prof. A. FRANCHINI.
***Faculty of Mathematics, Physics and** Natural Science:* Prof. R. FERRO.
Faculty of Pharmacy: Prof. F. SPARATORE.
Faculty of Engineering: Prof. R. BALDACCI.
Faculty of Architecture: Prof. L. N. CARBONERI.

DIRECTORS:

Faculty of Jurisprudence:
ACQUARONE, L., Administrative Law
AMELOTTI, M., Roman Law
BESSONE, M., Italian Private and Comparative Law
CANDIAN, A., Penal Procedure
FERRARINI ,S., Navigation Law
GOMEZ DEAYALA, A., Ecclesiastical Law
LUCIFREDI, P. G., Constitutional Law
LUCIFREDI, R., Administrative Law
MANDRIOLI, C., Civil Law Procedure
PIERGIOVANNI, V., History of Law
SCERNI, M., International Law
SOMMA, E., Penal Law
TARELLO, G., Philosophy of Law
UCKMAR, V., Financial Law
VERRUCOLI, P., Commercial Law

Faculty of Political Science:
CUOCOLO, F., Elements of Public Law
DE BERNARDIS, L. M., Ecclesiastical Law and Politics
SIROTTI, V., Economics
VIDAL, E., History of Political Theory

Faculty of Economics and Commerce:
BERLINGIERI, F., Navigation Law
BIONDA, G., Study of Commodities
BRUSA, A., Economic Geography
CACACE, L., Mathematics of Finance
D'ALAURO, O., Political Economy and Finance
DE DOMINICIS, U., General and Applied Accountancy
FELLONI, G., Economic History
FROSINI, B., Statistics
SCOTTO, A., Financial Science and Financial Law
SIROTTI, V., Political Economy
VACCÀ, S., Industrial and Commercial Methods

Faculty of Letters and Philosophy:
AGAZZI, E., Philosophy of Science
BORMANN, F., Greek
BRIAN, L., Anthropology
BULFERETTI, L., Modern History
CERESA GASTALDO, A., Classical and Medieval Philology
CERULLI, E., Ethnology
CORSANI, M., English and Anglo-American
CROCE BERMONDI, F., Italian Literature
DELLA CORTE, F., Latin Literature
FOSSATI, G., History of Medieval and Modern Art
PASERO, N., Romance Philology
PICCIRILLI, L., Ancient History
PISTÁRINO, G., Palaeography and Diplomacy
RUOCCO, D., Geography
SICHEL, G., German Language and Literature
TINE SANTE, Archaeology

Faculty of Education:
ARATA, C., Philosophy
BELVEDERI, R., History
BOZZO, T., Education
CALDERA, E., Foreign Languages and Literatures
MONTANARI, F., Italian Language and Literature
PUCCIONI DELLA CASA, A., Latin Grammar
PUPPO, M., Italian Language and Literature
RASCHINI, M. A., History of Philosophy
SCHIAVONE, M., Moral Philosophy
SCIACCA, M. F., Philosophy
VALLEGA, A., Geography
ZOLLA, V. E., Anglo-American Literature

Faculty of Medicine:
AGNESE G., Medica Statistics and Biometrics
AGRIFOGLIO, E., Orthopaedics
ARRIGO, L., Physiology
BATTEZZATI, M., General Surgery
BONSIGNORE, A., Biochemistry
BRAMBILLA, G., Pharmacology
BULGARELLI, R., Paediatrics
CANEPA, G., Criminal Anthropology
CAPURRO, S., Histology and General Embryology
CATTANEO ,A. D., Anaesthesiology
DAVINI, V., Neurosurgery
DE TONI, E., Child Welfare
FILIPPI, P., Oto-Rhino-Laryngology
FRANCHINI, A., Forensic and Insurance Medicine
GIAMPALMO, A., Anatomy and Pathological History
GIBERTI, F., Psychiatry
GIULIANI, L., Urology
LOEB, W. C., Nervous and Mental Diseases
MORETTI, G., Dermato-syphilology
NOVELLI, A., General Pathology
OLIVA, L., Radiology
PESCETTO, G., Obstetrics and Gynaecology
PETRILLI, F. L., Hygiene
PRIOR, C., Surgical Anatomy
ROMANZI, C., Microbiology
RUFFO, A., Specialized Pathological Surgery
SALUIDIO, E., General Medicine
SANTI, L., Oncology
SCOPINARO, D., Specialized Pathology and Clinical Methodology
SILVESTRINI-BIAVATI, M., Dentistry
TOLENTINO, P., Infectious Diseases
TOSATTI, E., General Surgery
VALENTI, S., Tubercular Diseases
ZACCHEO, D., Normal Anatomy
ZECCA, G., Psychology
ZINGRIAN, M., Ophthalmology

Faculty of Mathematics, Physics and Natural Science:
BELLINI, A., Geology
ELENA, A., Geophysics and Geodetics
FERRO, R., General and Inorganic Chemistry
FRISANI, A., Numerical Calculus
GALLI, M., Petrography
GENTILE, S., Botany
IANDELLI, A., Physical Chemistry
ISETTI, G., Mineralogy
LEANDRI, G., Organic Chemistry
MARTINI, V., General Physiology
MINGANTI, A., Comparative Anatomy
MUNARI, S., Industrial Chemistry
PONTIGGIA, C., Physics
RIZZUTO PRIORI, A. M., Numerical Calculus
SALMON, P., Algebra
SARÀ, M., Zoology
TRECCANI, G., Mathematics

Faculty of Pharmacy:
BIGNARDI, G., Pharmaceutics
CUGARRA, F., Pharmacology and Pharmacognosy
ERMILI, A., Applied Chemical Pharmaceutics
FORINA, M., Analytical Chemistry
GANDINI, A., Pharmaceutical Chemistry and Toxicology

Faculty of Engineering:
ACTON, O., Machines
BALDACCI, R., Strength of Materials and Theory of Construction
BIANCHEDI, R., Techniques and Economy of Transports
BIORCI, G., Electrotechnics
CHIESORIN, P., Mechanical Technology
CHIGLIAZZA, R., Applied Mechanics
FERRAIOLO, G., Chemical Installations
FUSELLI, E., Town Planning
LORENZELLI, V., Chemistry
MAGRINI, U., Technical Physics
MARCHI, E., Hydraulics
MARSICH, S., Merchant Ship Construction

Faculty of Architecture:
CARBONERI, L., History of Architecture
DE FIORE, G., Drawing and Relief
GALLARATI, D., Technical Discipline
MARETTO, P., Architectural Projections
ZANDERI, G., History of Architecture

UNIVERSITÀ DEGLI STUDI DI LECCE

PIAZZA ARCO DI TRIONFO, 73100 LECCE

Telephone: 4711.

Founded 1956.

Academic year: November October.

Rector: Prof. MARIO MARTI.

Administrative Director: Dott. M. BRIENZA.

Librarian: Dott. M. G. D'ALOISIO.

The library contains 80,000 vols.

Number of teachers: 184.

Number of students: *c.* 7,000.

Publications: *Annuario Accademico*†, *Quaderni della Biblioteca Centrale.*

Faculties of Education, Letters, Sciences.

UNIVERSITÀ DEGLI STUDI DI MACERATA

PIAZZA DELLA LIBERTÀ, 62100 MACERATA

Telephone: 45082.

Founded 1290.

Rector: Prof ATTILIO MORONI.

Secretary: Dott. MARIO DI CESARE.

Librarian: Prof. V. S. VIGORITA.

Number of teachers: *c.* 180.
Number of students: *c.* 5,500.
Publication: *Annali.*

Faculties of Law, Letters, Philosophy.

UNIVERSITA DEGLI STUDI*

VIA TOMMASO CANNIZZARO, 98100 MESSINA

Telephone 218846-8.

Founded 1548.

Rector: Prof. GAETANO LIVREA.

Administrative Director: ANTONINO CASELLA.

Number of teachers: *c.* 150.
Number of students: *c.* 15,000.

DEANS:

Faculty of Jurisprudence: Prof. A. FALZEA.

Faculty of Letters and Philosophy: Prof. G. RESTA.

Faculty of Medicine: Prof. S. BARBERI.

Faculty of Science and Mathematics: Prof. G. STAGNO D'ALEONTRES.

Faculty of Pharmacy: Prof. A. INEBESI.

* No reply received to our questionnaire this year.

UNIVERSITÀ DEGLI STUDI

VIA FESTA DEL PERDONO 7, 20122 MILAN

Telephone: 8846.

Founded 1923.

Academic year: November to October.

Rector: Prof. G. SCHIAVINATO.

Administrative Director: Dott. M. LUZI.

Librarian: Dott. GIULIANA SAPORI.

Number of teachers: 1,038.
Number of students: 62,187.
Publications: *Statuto dell' Università, Annuario* (annual), *Guida dello Studente* (annual), and various faculty publications.

DEANS:

Faculty of Law: Prof. A. AMORTH.

Faculty of Political Sciences: Prof. A. MIGLIAZZA.

Faculty of Letters and Philosophy: Prof. E. EVANGELISTI.

Faculty of Medicine: Prof. P. MANTEGAZZA.

Faculty of Sciences: Prof. M. CUGIANI.

Faculty of Pharmacy: Prof. P. PRATESI.

Faculty of Agriculture: Prof. V. TRECCANI DEGLI ALFIERI.

Faculty of Veterinary Medicine: Prof. G. AURELI.

PROFESSORS:

Faculty of Law:
ALLORIO, E., Civil Procedural Law
ANDREOLI, G., Elements of Private Law
BISCARDI, A., Roman Law
BISCARETTI DI RUFFIA, P., Constitutional Law
CANDIAN, A., Procedural Penal Law
CATTANEO, G., Agricultural Law
GALEOTTI, S., Constitutional Law
GIULIANO, M., International Law
GRASSETTI, C., Civil Law
JAEGER, A., Commercial Law
LANCELLOTTI, E., Financial Science and Law
LOMBARDI, G., History of Roman Law
NUVOLONE, P., Penal Law
PASTORI, F., Roman Law II
PEDRAZZI, C., Penal Law
PELOSI, A. C., Agricultural Law
PISAPIA, D., Procedural Penal Law
POTOTSCHBIG, U., Administrative Law
SCARPELLI, U., Philosophy of Law
SENA, G., Commercial Law
TALAMONA, M., Political Economy
TARZIA, G., Civil Procedural Law
TREVES, R. S., Sociology of Law
TRIMARCHI, P., Elements of Private Law
VISMARA, G., History of Italian Law
ZICCARDI, P., International Law

Faculty of Political Sciences:
ALBERONI, F., Sociology
ANNONI, A., Modern History
AVONDO BODINO, G., Mathematics
BAGIOTTI, T., Political Economy
BRUNI ROCCIA, G., Political Science
DE GIOVANNI PIZZORNO, A., Sociology
GARAVELLO, O., Financial Economic Politics
ITALIA, V., Public Law
LANDENNA, G., Statistics
MAURI, A., Business Economy
MIGLIAZZA, A., European Community Law
POCAR, F., International Law
RAINERO, R., Contemporary History
SMURAGLIA, C., Labour Law
SPRANZI, A., Industrial Political Economy
VITALI, E. G., Ecclesiastical Law

Faculty of Letters and Philosophy:
ARENA, R., Greek and Latin Grammar
BALMAS, E., French
BARBIERI, F., Medieval History
BAZZARELLI, E., Russian Language and Literature
BIGI, E., Italian Literature I
BOSCOLO, A., Medieval History
CORNA PELLEGRINI SPANDRE, G., Geography
COSTAMAGNA, G., Palaeography and Diplomatics
D'AGOSTINO, N., English Language and Literature
DAL PRA, M., History of Philosophy
DECLEVA, E., Contemporary History
DEL CORNO, D., Greek Literature
DELLA CASA, C., Sanskrit
DELLA PERUTA, F., History of the Risorgimento
DOLFINI, G., Germanic Philology
EVANGELISTI, E., Linguistics
FERMEGLIA, G., Slavonic Philology
FORNARI, F., Psychology
GATTI, C., Roman History
GRILLI, A., Latin Literature II
GIORELLO, G., Philosophy of Science
GUALANDRI, I., Latin Literature
LIMENTANI CALABI, I., Greek and Roman Antiquity
MANGIONE, C., Logic
MASTRANGELO CREMONESI, C., Romance Philology
NATALE, A. R., Archivistics
ORLANDI, G., Latin Medieval Literature
ORLANDINI, P., Archaeology and History of Greek and Roman Art
PACCHI, A., History of Philosophy
RUMI, G., Contemporary History
SICHIROLLO, L., Moral Philosophy
SINI, C., Theoretical Philosophy
SPINAZZOLA, V., History of Modern Italian Literature
VIGEZZI, B., Modern History
VITALE, M., History of the Italian Language

Faculty of Medicine:
AGOSTINI, A., Special Medical Pathology and Clinical Methodology
AGOSTONI, E., Human Physiology
AGRIFOGLIO, G., Vascular Surgery
ALBANO, A., Hygiene
BAIRATI, A., Human Anatomy
BALLABIO, B., Rheumatology
BARTORELLI, C., General Medicine
BASILE, L., Forensic and Insurance Medicine
BELLONI, L., History of Medicine
BERGAMINI, F., Virology
BERNELLI ZARRERA, A., General Pathology
BOCCA, E., Oto-Rhino-Laryngology
BOELLA, G., Physics
CACCIALANZA-MIGLIO, P., Dermo-Syphilopathic Medicine
CANDIANI, G. B., Obstetrics and Gynaecology
CAREDDU, P., Child Welfare
CASSANI, G., Biology
CAVAGNA, G., Human Physiology
CAZZULLO, C. L., Clinical Psychiatry
CAZZULLO GUARESCHI, A., Child Neuropsychiatry
CERRETELLI, P., Human Physiology
CESA BIANCHI, M., Psychology
CHIUMELLO, G., Paediatrics
CLEMENTI, F., Pharmacology
CLERICI, E., Immunology
COCUZZA, G., Microbiology
COGGI, G., Pathological Anatomy and Histology
CROSIGUARNI, P. G., Obstetrics and Gynaecology
DAMIA, G., Anaesthesiology
DEL BO, M., Audiology

Del Monte, U., General Pathology
Deotto, R., Microbiology
Dioguardi, N., General Medicine
Fara, G., Hygiene
Fasoli, A., Medical Therapy
Fiecchi, A., Chemistry
Folli, G., Pathology
Fraschini, F., Chemotherapy
Fumigalli, G., Respiratory Physio therapy
Fuhrman Conti, A. M., Biology
Gaja, G., General Pathology
Gallone, L., General Surgery and Therapeutic Surgery
Gastaldi, A., Obstetrics and Gynaecology
Genovese, E., Pharmacology
Gianni, E. A., Odontology
Gianotti, F., Child Dermatology
Giordano, A., Pathological Anatomy and Histology
Gualtierotti, T., Human Physiology
Lasio, E., Urology
Libretti, A., Special Pathology
Longo, T., Semiotics
Luvoni, R., Forensic Medicine and Insurance
Maderna, A. M., Psychology
Mancia, M., Human Physiology
Mantegazza, P., Pharmacology
Marossero, F., Neuro-Surgery
Marubini, E., Medical Statistics
Matturri, L., Pathological Anatomy and Histology
Miani, A., Normal Anatomy
Miglior, M., Ophthalmology
Montorsi, W., General and Therapeutic Surgery
Morganti, G., Human Genetics
Mosca, L., Pathology, Anatomy and Histology
Mujesan, G., General Medicine
Ottaviani, A., Oto-Rhino-Laryngology
Pannese, E., Neurocytology
Parrini, L., Orthopaedics
Pazardjiklian, M., Phthisiology
Pecile, A., Pharmacology
Pellegrini, G., General and Therapeutic Surgery
Perussia, A., Radiology
Pietrogrande, V., Orthopaedics
Pini, C. E., Maxillo-Facial Surgery
Polli, E., General Medicine
Polvani, F., Obstetrics and Gynaecology
Ponti, G., Criminal Anthropology
Pozza, G., Special Medical Pathology
Pozzato, R., Forensic and Insurance Medicine
Puccinelli, V., Dermosyphilology
Remotti, G., Obstetrics and Gynaecology
Rossi, R., Special Surgical Pathology
Rossini, R., Clinical Neurology
Ruberti, U., Special Surgical Pathology
Scala, A. E., Chemistry
Sereni, F., Paediatrics
Staudacher, V., General Surgery
Tettamanti, G., Biological Chemistry
Tiberio, G., Surgical Semiotics
Tiengo, M., Anaesthesia and Reanimation
Toselli, C., Ophthalmology
Trazzi, R., Anaesthesia and Reanimation
Vincre, G., Thoracic Surgery
Zanchetti, A., Special Medical Pathology
Zanussi, C., Special Medical Pathology and Clinical Methodology

Faculty of Sciences:

Alberghina, L. A. M., Comparative Biochemistry
Bairati, A., Histology and Embryology
Baldini, G., Solid State Physics
Balsotti Camatini, M., Comparative Anatomy
Bellobono, I. R., Chemistry
Bellini, G., Physics
Bellon, P., General and Inorganic Chemistry
Belloni, S., Physical Geography
Beltrame, P., Industrial Chemical Plants
Bianchetti, R., Plant Physiology
Bianchi, G., Electrical Chemistry
Boriani, A., Petrography
Caldirola, P., Physics
Canonica, L., Organic Chemistry
Capraro, V., General Physiology
Cassinis, R., Terrestrial Physics
Cenini, S., General and Inorganic Chemistry
Ceresa Castellani, L., Cytology
Chini, P., General and Inorganic Chemistry
Cinquini, M., Organic Chemistry
Cirelli, R., Mathematical Methods of Physics
Cugiani, M., Numerical and Graphical Calculus
Curti, B., Biological Chemistry
Dedo, M., Geometry
Degli Antoni, G., Cybernetics and Theory of Information
Di Corato, M., Atomic Physics
Esposito, G. C., General Physiology
Facchini, U., General Physics
Farina, M., Macromolecular Chemistry
Favini, G., Molecular Spectroscopy
Ferroni, A., General Physiology
Fiorini, E., Experimental Physics
Fontanesi, M., Physics
Forti, G., Plant Physiology
Fusco, R., Industrial Chemistry
Gelati, R., Geology
Gerola, F., Botany
Gianinetti, E., Quantistic Chemistry
Gnaccolini, M., Sedimentology
Gori, E., Pharmacology
Gregnanin, A., Applied Petrography
Guerritore, A., Biological Chemistry
Iori, I., General Physics
Jommi, G., Organic Chemistry
Kranjc, A., Astronomy
Lanzavecchia, G., Zoology
Leonardi Cigada, M., Zoology
Leone, V. G., Zoology
Loinger, A., Theoretical Physics
Longo, C., Botany
Lunelli, M., Computing
Magni, G., Genetics
Maiorana, S., Organic Chemistry
Malatesta, L., General and Inorganic Chemistry
Manara, C. F., Institutions of Higher Geometry
Manitto, P. M., Organic Chemistry
Marchetti, R., Ecology
Marchionna, E., Geometry
Marchionna Tibiletti, C., Algebra
Marrè, E., Plant Physiology
Martinis, B., Geology
Mazza, F., Corrosion and Protection of Metals
Milazzo Colli, L., Nuclear Physcis
Milla, E., General Physiology
Montaldi, E., Thermodynamics
Montanari, F., Organic Chemistry
Mussini, T., Organic Electrochemistry
Nardelli, G., General Physics
Nicola, P. C., Mathematical Economics
Occhialini Dilworth, C., Radioactivity
Ottaviano, E., Genetics
Paganoni, L., Mathematical Analysis
Pasquare, G., Regional Geology
Peyronel Pagliani, G., Petrography
Pignanelli, M., Experimental Physics
Pini De Socio, M. L., Rational Mechanics
Pozzi, R., Applied Geology
Prosperi, G. M., Theoretical Physics
Pullia, A., General Physics
Resmini, F., General Physics
Ronchetti Rossi, C., Palaeontology
Roux, D., Mathematical Analysis
Russo, G., Organic Chemistry
Salvetti, C., General Physics
Scatturin, V., General and Inorganic Chemistry
Schiavinato, G., Mineralogy
Sestini Fantini, N., Palaeontology
Simonetta, M., Physical Chemistry
Sironi Cita, M. B., Geology
Sironi, G., Micro-organism Genetics
Soardi, P. M., Mathematical Analysis
Sparvoli, E., Botany
Spinolo, G., Experimental Physics
Succi, C., General Physics
Tagliaferri, G., Structure of Matter
Torelli, G., General Physiology
Trezzi, F., Botany
Udeschini, P., Rational Mechanics
Ugo, R., Analytical Chemistry
Zambelli, V., Algebra
Zuffardi, P., Mining deposits

Faculty of Pharmacy:

Berti, F., Pharmaceutic Tests
Bianchetti, G., Organic Chemistry
Martini, L., Endocrinology
Paoletti, R., Pharmacology and Pharmacognosy
Villa, L., Toxicological Chemistry

Faculty of Agriculture:

Albonico, F., Milk Chemistry and Technology
Amadei, G., Agrarian Economics, Politics
Baldacci, E., Plant Pathology
Baldissera Nordio, C., Anatomy and Physiology of Domestic Animals
Betto, E., Vegetal Physiopathology
Cagnasso Ravazzoni, C., Organic Chemistry
Cantarelli, C., Food Industry
Cerletti, P., General Biochemistry
Cerutti, G., Alimentary Products
Cocucci, S., Vegetal Physiology
Craveri, R., Industrial Microbiology
Curto, G. M., General Zootechnics
Gasparetto, E., Agricultural Mechanization
Ghisleni, L., Plant Breeding
Giura, R., Drainage
Goldberg Federico, L., Agricultural Chemistry
Lalatta, F., Arboreal Cultivation
Lechi, F., Rural Evaluation
Locci, R., Mycology
Martelli, M., Agricultural Entomology
Merlini, L., Organic Chemistry
Ottogalli, G., Dairy Microbiology
Pellizzi, G., Agricultural Mechanics
Peri, C., Food Industry
Poma Treccani, C., Industrial Fruit-growing
Resmini, P., Agricultural Industry
Romita, P. L., Agricultural Hydraulics
Treccani Degli Alfieri, V., Soil Microbiology

Faculty of Veterinary Medicine:

Agnes Rizotti, M., General and Special Histology
Aguggini, G., Animal Physiology
Aureli, G., Anatomy of Domestic Animals, Histology, Embryology
Bagedda, G., Obstetrics and Gynaecology
Baglioni, T., Physiopathology
Beretta, C., Veterinary Toxicology
Boccadoro, B., Radiology
Cantoni, C. A., Animal Foodstuffs Control

CANZIANI, P. L., Forensic Veterinary Medicine
CHELI, R., Special Pathology and Surgery
CORSICO, G., Animal Foodstuffs Technical Preservation
FAUSTINI, R., Pharmacology
LEONARDI, L., Radiology
LOCATELLI, A., General Comparative Pathology
MANDELLI, G., General Veterinary Pathology
OLIVA, O., Obstetrics and Gynaecology
POLIDORI, F., Animal Feeding
REDAELLI, G. L., Infectious Diseases, Prophylaxis, Veterinary Regulations
ROGNONI, G. General Zootechnics
VACIRCA, G., Medical Seminology

UNIVERSITÀ DEGLI STUDI

VIA UNIVERSITÀ 4,
41100 MODENA
Telephone: 239096-7-8.
Founded 1175.

Rector: Prof. F. TADDEI.
Pro-Rector: Prof. G. MAROTTI.
Administrator: Dott. F. PIERPAOLI.

Number of teachers: 201 professors.
Number of students: 8,653.

Publications: *Annuario, Notiziario.*

DEANS:

Faculty of Jurisprudence: Prof. F. LANCELLOTTI.
Faculty of Economics and Commerce: Prof. F. CAVAZZUTI.
Faculty of Medicine: U. MUSEATELLO.
Faculty of Mathematics, Physics and Natural Sciences: Prof. P. FAZZINI.
Faculty of Pharmacy: Prof. L. RAFFA.

PROFESSORS:

Faculty of Jurisprudence:

AMBROSETTI, G., Philosophy of Law
BAROSIO, V., Penal Procedure
BIONE, M., Commercial Law
BUSSI, E., History of Italian Law
DELL'ORO, A., Civil Law
GHIDINI, G., Industrial Law
GIANOLIO, R. C., Administrative Law
LAMBERTI ZANARDI, P., International Law
LANCELLOTTI, F., Civil Procedure
MARANI, F., Private Law
ONIDA, F., Political Economy
RICCI, E. F., Civil Procedure
SANTARELLI, U., History of Italian Law

Faculty of Economics and Commerce:

BIASCO, S., International Economics
CATALANO, F., Contemporary Social History
CAVAZZUTI, F., Commercial Law
COLOMBO, G. E., Commercial Law
ONADO, M., Professional and Banking Procedure
PIVETTI, M., Political Economy
RESCIGNO, G. U., Public Law
SALVATI, M., Industrial Economy

Faculty of Medicine and Surgery:

ACANFORA, G., Infectious and Tropical Diseases
BAGOLINI, B., Ophthalmology
BARBIROLI, B., Biochemistry
BATTAGLIA, S., Anatomy and Pathological Histology
BERTOLINI, A., Pharmacology
BONATI, B., Special Pathology
BONCINELLI, U., Dermosyphilology
BUFFA, P., General Pathology
CAVAZUTTI, G. B., Neonatal Pathology
CHELI, E., Paediatrics
CENNAMO, C., Medical Chemistry
COPPO, M., Clinical Medicine
DE FAZIO, F. A., Forensic Medicine
DE RENZI, E., Neurology
FABIO, U., Microbiology
FERRARI, W., Pharmacology
GALLI, G., Normal Human Anatomy
GIBERTINI, G., General Clinical Surgery
GUARALDI, G., Infantile Neuropsychiatry
LENZI, M., Radiology
LODI, R., Surgical Semiotics
MACCIOTTA, M., Obstetrics and Gynaecology
MARRAMA, P., Endocrinology
MAROTTI, G., Normal Anatomy
MATTIOLI, G., Cardio-vascular Diseases
MAURI, C., Clinical Medicine
MUSCATELLO, U., Pathology
OLIVI, O., Paediatrics
OLIVO, R., Hygiene
PESERICO, L., Neurosurgery
REMAGGI, P. L., Oto-Rhino-Laryngology
SAVIANO, M., Human Physiology
STERNIERI, E., Clinical Pharmacology
TORELLI, U., Haematology
VECCHI, G. P., Gerontology
VIVOLI ,G., Hygiene

Faculty of Mathematics, Physics and Natural Sciences:

ALBERIGI DEI CONTI QUARANTA, A., Electronics
ALIETTI, A., Mineralogy
BAFFONI, G., Comparative Anatomy
BAIADA, E., Mathematical Analysis
BERTOLANI, M., Petrography
BONI, M., Mathematical Analysis
COGNETTI, G., Zoology
DIECI, G., Micropalaeontology
FABBRI, G., Physical Chemistry
FANTIN, BOLOGNANI, A. M., Histology and Embryology
FAZZINI, P., Geology
FERRARI, I., Mathematical Physics
GEMIGNANI, G., Algebra
GOTTARDI, G., Mineralogy
GRAFFI, S., Mathematical Physics
LAUDI, G., Botany
LEVONI, S., Mathematical Physics
LORIA, G., Preparation of Experiments
LOSACCO, U., Geology
MANNINO, G., Numerical Analysis
MINGUZZI, A., Theoretical Physics
MIRONE, P., Physical Chemistry
MOMICCHIOLI, F., Physical Chemistry
MONTANARO GALLITELLI, E., Palaeontology
OTTAVIANI, G., Structure of Materials
PAREA, G. C., Sedimentology
PEYRONEL, G., General and Inorganic Chemistry
PEZZANA, M., Geometry
QUATROCCHI, P., Elementary Mathematics
SANTANGELO, R., Nuclear Physics
SERPAGLI, E., Palaeontology
TADDEI, F., Higher Organic Chemistry
TONGIORGI, P., Zoology
TRAVE, R., Organic Chemistry
VAONA, G., Analytical Geometry
VIVARELLI, P., Chemistry of Dyes

Faculty of Pharmacy:

CAMERONI, R., Applied Pharmaceutical Chemistry
COPPINI, D., Food Chemistry
DI BELLA, M., Pharmaceutical and Toxicological Training
RAFFA, L., Pharmaceutical and Toxicological Chemistry

UNIVERSITÀ DEGLI STUDI

CORSO UMBERTO 1,
80100 NAPLES
Telephone: 325060.
Founded 1224.

Rector: Prof. G. CUOMO.
Administrative Director: Dott. R. CAPUNZO.

Number of teachers: *c.* 2,500.
Number of students: *c.* 80,000.

DEANS:

Agriculture: C. NOVIELLO.
Architecture: A. VENDITTI.
Economics: G. MINERVINI.
Pharmacy: M. COVELLO.
Law: L. CARIOTA FERRARA.
Political Science: U. LEANZA.
Engineering: L. MASSIMILLA.
Letters and Philosophy: G. GALASSO.
Medicine: G. HURANO.
Medicine II: G. ZANNINI.
Mathematics and Natural Sciences: C. CILIBERTO.
Veterinary Medicine: A. DI GIROLAMO.

UNIVERSITÀ DEGLI STUDI

VIA 8 FEBBRAIO 2,
35100 PADUA
Telephone: 651400.

Founded 1222; the faculties of Economics and Commerce, Foreign Languages, Letters and Medicine are situated in Verona.

Rector: Prof. L. MERIGLIANO.
Secretary: Dott. M. MIOLA.

Number of teachers: 2,883.
Number of students: 52,792.

Publications: *Annuario, Bollettino-Notiziario* (annually).

DEANS:

Faculty of Jurisprudence: Prof. A. TRABUCCHI.
Faculty of Political Science: Prof. S. STERPI.
Faculty of Economics and Commerce: Prof. G. BARBIERI.
Faculty of Statistical Sciences, Demography and Actuarial Science: Prof. P. DE SANDRE.
Faculty of Letters and Philosophy: Prof. O. LONGO.
Faculty of Education: Prof. L. BRIGUGLIO.
Faculty of Medicine and Surgery: Prof. G. PATRASSI.
Faculty of Mathematics, Physics, and Natural Sciences: Prof. G. GIACOMETTI.
Faculty of Pharmacy: Prof. G. RODIGHIERO.
Faculty of Engineering: Prof. B. DALL'AGLIO.
Faculty of Agriculture: Prof. M. RIONO VOLPATO.

UNIVERSITÀ DEGLI STUDI*

175 VIA MAQUEDA,
90134 PALERMO

Telephone: 23-56-51.

Founded 1777.

Rector: Prof. G. La Grutta.

Administrative Director: Dott. F. Catalano.

Number of teachers: *c.* 1,200.
Number of students: *c.* 19,000.

Publications: ***Annali del Seminario Giuridico, Circolo Giuridico L. Sampolo, Annali della Facoltà di Economia e Commercio.***

Deans:

Agriculture: C. Schifano.
Architecture: U. Fuxa.
Economics: S. Vianelli.
Pharmacy: G. Caronna.
Law: S. Orlando.
Engineering: G. Benfratello.
Letters and Philosophy: B. Lavagnini.
Education: I. Peri
Medicine: P. Benigno.
Mathematics: (vacant).

* No reply received to our questionnaire this year.

UNIVERSITÀ DEGLI STUDI

VIA UNIVERSITA 12,
43100 PARMA

Telephone: 68151.

Founded 1064.

Rector: Prof. E. Zanella.

Administrative Director: Dott. G. P. Usberti.

Number of teachers: 950.
Number of students: 18,981.

Deans:

Faculty of Jurisprudence: Prof. C. Pecorella.
Faculty of Medicine: Prof. A. Borghetti.
Faculty of Pharmacy: Prof. T. Vitali.
Faculty of Physical, Mathematical and Natural Sciences: Prof. M. de Riu.
Faculty of Veterinary Medicine: Prof. D. Artioli.
Faculty of Economics and Commerce: Prof. L. Frey.
Faculty of Education: Prof. D. Pesce.

Professors:

Faculty of Jurisprudence:
Bassi, F., Administrative Law
Bonsignori, A., Law of Bankruptcy
Boscarelli, M., Penal Law
Cerino Canova, A., Civil Procedural Law
Colliva, P., History of Italian Law
Dominioni, O., Penal Procedure
Feliciani, G., Ecclesiastical Law
Gallo, F., Law of Debts
Ghidini, M., Commercial Law
Guarneri, G., Penal Law
Mirabelli, C., Ecclesiastical Law
Pecorella, C., Common Law
Ravazzoni, A., Civil Law
Reggi, R., Interpretation of Roman Law
Ubertazzi, G. M., International Organization
Venturini, G., International Law

Faculty of Medicine:
Allegra, F., Dermato-Syphilopathy
Arduini, A., Human Physiology
Azzali, G., Human Anatomy
Azzolini, A., Plastic Surgery
Bellelli, E., Hygiene
Bertaccini, G., Pharmacology
Bianchi, C., Medicine I
Bocchi, L., Orthopaedics
Borghetti, A., Medical Semeiotics I
Braibanti, T., Radiology
Brizzi, R., Neuro-surgery
Butturini, U., Specialised Pathology and Methodology
De Risio, C., Psychiatry
Faienza, C., Child Neuropsychiatry
Giovannelli, G., Paediatrics
Gnudi, A., Endocrinology
Goffrini, P., Surgery I
Guareschi, G., Forensic Medicine
Guidotti, G., General Pathology
Lechi, A., Nervous and Mental Diseases II
Maffei, G., Oto-Rhino-Laryngology I
Mainardi, D., Biology and Zoology
Maione, M., Ophthalmology I
Maraini, G., Ophthalmology I
Masotti, L., Biochemistry
Migone, L., Medicine II
Moretti, M., Paediatrics
Parma, M., Nervous and Mental Diseases I
Passeri, M., Gerontology and Geriatrics
Peracchia, A., Surgical Pathology II
Rizzolatti, G., Human Physiology II
Rusconi, L., Odontology
Salvadori, B., Obstetrics and Gynaecology
Schito, G. C., Microbiology
Starcich, R., Pathology II
Tardini, A., Anatomy and Pathological Histology
Turano, A., Microbiology
Vidoni, G., Forensic Medicine
Visioli, O., Cardiovascular Illnesses
Zanella, E., Clinical Surgery II
Zini, C., Oto-Rhino-Laryngology

Faculty of Pharmacy:
Amoretti, L., Applied Pharmaceutical and Toxicological Chemistry
Bellotti, A., Applied Pharmaceutical and Toxicological Chemistry
Braibanti, A., Physical Methods in Organic Chemistry
Impicciatore, M., Pharmacological Samples and Doses
Mossini, F., Pharmaceutical Analysis
Vitali, T., Pharmaceutical and Toxicological Chemistry

Faculty of Physical, Mathematical and Natural Sciences:
Albanesi, G., Industrial Chemistry
Andreetti, G. D., Organic Crystalline Chemistry
Bassotti Rizza, L., Numerical and Graphic Calculus
Bretolini, F., Mathematical Analysis
Bucci, C., Solid State Physics
Casnati, G., Organic Chemistry
Cavalca, L., Chemical Structures
Conterio, F., Genetics
Chiusoli, G., Applied Organic Chemistry
Dascola, G., Physics
Deriu, M., Petrography
Duimio, F., Theoretical Physics
Emiliani Zauli Naldi, F., Mineralogy
Fava Gasparri, G., General and Inorganic Chemistry
Ferrero, G., Algebra
Fieschi, R., Structure of Matter
Lona, F., Botany
Manfredi, B., Mechanics
Mezzadri, G., Petrography
Moroni, A., Ecology
Nardelli, M., Structural Chemistry
Oleari, L., Physical Chemistry
Orzalesi, C., Theoretical Physics
Parisi, V., Zoology
Pauri, M., Relativity
Pelosio, G., Palaeontology
Puglisi, P. P., Genetics of Micro-Organisms
Rizza, G., Analytical Geometry
Schreiber, B., Zoology
Scotti, A., Theory of Nuclear Forces
Servi, M., Mathematical Logic
Speranza, F., Mathematics
Taccardi, B., General Physiology
Tanzi Cattabianchi, L., Mathematical Analysis
Vanzo, S., Geology
Zanzucchi, G., Geology

Faculty of Veterinary Medicine:
Artioli, D., Inspection of Foodstuffs of Animal Origin
Ballarini, G., Veterinary Medicine
Bonomi, A., Nutrition and Feeding
Buiatti, P. G., Zootechnics
Culzoni, V., Veterinary Anatomy
Flammini, C., Pathology and Prophylaxis of Infectious Diseases
Gianelli, F., Microbiology and Immunology
Maggi, E., Inspection of Foodstuffs
Pezzoli, G., Special Pathology
Scaccini, A., Anatomy of Domestic Animals
Scatozza, F., Infectious Diseases, Prophylaxis and Veterinary Regulations

Faculty of Economics and Commerce:
Azzini, L., General and Applied Accountancy
Baglioni, G., Economic Sociology
Feroldi, F., Political Economy
Frey, L., Political Economy
Garavella, O., Political Economy
Mottura, P., Banking Procedure
Predetti, A., Economic Statistics
Trovato, M., Mathematics
Valiani, R., Finance

Faculty of Education:
Ageno Brambilla, F., Italian Language and Literature
Andreotti, R., History
Ara, A., Contemporary History
Balsamo, L., Library Science
Gallico, G., History of Music
Lumbelli, L., Education
Pesce, D., History of Philosophy
Raponi, N., History of the Risorgimento
Richter, M., French Language and Literature
Scarpat, G., Latin Language and Literature
Scivoletto, A., Sociology
Tampieri, P., Psychology
Zucchelli, B., Latin Grammar

UNIVERSITÀ DEGLI STUDI

CORSO STRADA NUOVA 65,
27100 PAVIA

Telephone: 35491.

Founded 1361 by Emperor Charles IV.

Rector: Prof. A. G. Berzolari.

Administrative Director: Dr. Gesuino Piga.

Curator of the Museum of University History: Prof. B. Zanobio.

Number of teachers: 370, including 120 professors.

Number of students: 8,872 men, 2,688 women, total 11,560.

Publications: *Haematologica, Atti dell'Istituto Botanico e Laboratorio Crittogamico della Universita, Athenaeum, Studi nelle Scienze giuridiche sociali, Rivista di Diritto finanziario e Scienza delle Finanze, Il Politico, Scienzia genetica, Genetica agraria, Atti dell' Instituto Geologico, Annuario, Guida dello Studente.*

DEANS:

Faculty of Jurisprudence: Prof. U. POTOTSCHNIG.
Faculty of Political Sciences: Prof. C. CIGLIO.
Faculty of Economics and Commerce: Prof. R. ARGENZIANO.
Faculty of Letters and Philosophy: Prof. F. ALESSIO.
Faculty of Medicine: Prof. M. CHERUBINO.
Faculty of Science: Prof. A. G. BERZOLARI.
Faculty of Pharmacy: Prof. A. LA MANNA.
Faculty of Engineering: Prof. U. MAIONE.

UNIVERSITÀ DEGLI STUDI

PIAZZA DELL' UNIVERSITÀ,
06100 PERUGIA

Telephone: 45241.
Founded 1200.

Rector: G. DOZZA.
Administrative Director: Dott. C. SAETTA.
Librarian: **Dott. L. SCARAMUCCI.**

Number of professors: 157.
Number of students: 19,606.

DEANS:

Faculty of Jurisprudence: Prof. F. COPPI.
Faculty of Political Science: Prof. F. D'AMOYA.
Faculty of Economic Science: **Prof. G. MANNELLI.**
Faculty of Letters and Philosophy: **Prof. A. PIERETTI.**
Faculty of Education: **Prof. A. SCIVOLETTO.**
Faculty of Medicine: Prof. M. BINAZZI.
Faculty of Mathematical, Physical and Natural Sciences: Prof. G. MARINO.
Faculty of Pharmacy: Prof. G. PORCELLATI.
Faculty of Agrarian Science: Prof. G. MONTEDORO.
Faculty of Veterinary Medicine: **Prof. B. BALDELLI.**

PROFESSORS:

Faculty of Jurisprudence:
BADIALI, G., International Law
BALDASSARE, A., Constitutional Law
CANCELLI, F., History of Roman Law
CAPRIOLI, S., History of Italian Law
COPPI, F. C., Penal Law
GIALDINO, A. C., International Law
GIULIANI, A., Philosophy of Law
LARICCIA, S., Canon Law
LAVAGGI, G., Foundations of Roman Law
LENER, A., Foundations of Private Law
MOSCHELLA, R., Foundations of Private Law II
PANUNZIO, S., Constitutional Law I
PERRONE, L., Tax Law
RUSSO, E., Civil Law
SATTA, F., Administrative Law
VOLPE-PUTZOLU, G., Commercial Law

Faculty of Letters:
BABOLIN, A., Philosophy of Religion
BARTOCCINI, F., History of the Risorgimento
CARACCIOLO, A. M., Modern History
CIMMINO, N. F. Modern Philology
COLONNA, A., Classical Philology
FABRO, C., Theoretical Philosophy
MARABOTTINI, A. M., History of Medieval and Modern Art
NALDINI, M., Ancient Christian Literature
PIERETTI, A., Philosophy of Language
PIZZANI, U., Latin Literature
SANTACHIARA, U., Church History
SECCI, E., German Language and Literature
TORELLI, M., Archaeology and History of Greek and Roman Art
UGOLINI, F., Romance Philology

Faculty of Political Science:
BERTELLI, S., Modern History
BONO, S., History and Institutions of Afro-Asian Countries
CERVATI, A., Italian and Comparative Constitutional Law
COMPARATO, V. I., History of Political Doctrine
CRESPI, F., Sociology
D'AMOJA, F., History of International Relations
FLICK, G. M., Foundations of Law and Penal Procedure
FLORIDIA, E., Political and Economic Geography
GRASSELLI, P., Political Economy and Finance
LUPOI, M., Comparative Private Law
MELOGRANI, P., Modern History
TRAMONTANA, A., Finance

Faculty of Economics and Commerce:
CARAVALE, G., Political Economy
CORRALLINI, S., Professional Banking
FERRO-LUZZI, P., Commercial Law I
LORENZINI, G., Industry and Commerce
MANNELLI, G., Commerce
NARDUZZI, N., Economic and Financial Policies
PESCATORE, S., Commercial Law II
SANTOBONI, L., Statistics
STOLFI, C., Industrial Law

Faculty of Medicine and Surgery:
BIANCIFIORI, C., Pathological Anatomy and Histology
BONMASSAR, E., Pharmacology
BO, G., Hygiene
BINAZZI, M., Skin and Venereal Diseases
CAPRINO, G., Radiology
CIUFFINI, F., General Surgery and Surgical Therapy
DE BIASE, S., Dentistry
DELOGU, A., Ophthalmology
FURBETTA, D., Industrial Medicine
GERLI, M., Obstetrics and Gynaecology
LARIZZA, P., General Clinical Medicine and Medical Therapy
LIOTTI, F. S., Biology, Zoology and Genetics
LUCHERONI, A., Normal Human Anatomy
MAGNI, F., Human Physiology
MAURIZI, M., Clinical Oto-Rhino-Laryngology
PAULUZZI, S., Infectious Diseases
PITZURRA, M., Microbiology
RICCI, A., Chemistry
VENTURA, A., Gerontology
VIOLA MAGNI, M. P., Pathology

Faculty of Pharmacy:
CAGNOLI, N., Organic Chemistry
CORSANO LEOPIZZI, S., Chemistry
FIDANZA, F., Nutrition
PORCELLATI, G., Biological Chemistry
SCASSELLATI SFORZOLINI, G., Hygiene
TIECCO, M., Physics in Organic Chemistry

Faculty of Agrarian Science:
BALTADORI, A., Ecology
BATTAGLINI, M., Zooculture
BONCIARELLI, F., General Agronomy and Control of Weeds
DE CAPITE, L., General Botany
FIORI, G., Agrarian Entomology
FRATTEGGIANI BIANCHI, R., Zoognostics
GIOVAGNOTTI, C., Geopedology
GUERRIERI, G., Agrarian Economics and Politics
JACOBONI, N., Silviculture
LIPPI BONCAMBI, C., Applied Geology
LORENZETTI, F., Agarian Genetics
MONTEDORO, G., Industrial Agriculture
PANELLA, A., General Agronomy and Grass Crops
RAGGI, V., Plant Pathology
RIBALDI, M., Mycology
ROSSI, A. C., Agrarian Economics and Politics
ROSSI, J., Dairy Research
TAFURI, F., Agrarian Chemistry
TOMBESI, A., Industrial Fruit-Growing

Faculty of Veterinary Medicine:
ASDRUBALI, G. P., Pathology of Birds
AVELLINI, G., Pathology of Domestic Animals
BALDELLI, B., Parasitology
BEGHELLI, V., Physiology
CALISTI, V., Obstetrics and Gynaecology
CASTRUCCI, G., Infectious Diseases
DOZZA, G., Special Pathology and Veterinary Surgery
MANOCCHIO, I., Pathological Anatomy
MORETTI, B., Pathology and Clinical Medicine
MORICONI, A., Topographical Veterinary Anatomy
PEDINI, B., Medical Seminology, Veterinary Methodology
ROMANELLI, V., Technical Autopsy
VALFRE, F., Animal Nutrition

Faculty of Mathematical, Physical and Natural Sciences:
ALBERTI, G., General and Inorganic Chemistry II
ALIPPI, A., Physics
AMBROSETTI, P. L., Palaeontology
AVERNA, A., Mathematical Analysis
BACIOCCHI, E., Organic Chemistry
BARTOCCI, U., Geometry
BASSANINI, P., Rational Mechanics
BONDI, C., Comparative Anatomy
CANDELI. A., Hygiene
COCCO, G., Mineralogy
COLACICCHI, R., Geology
DI GIOVANNI, M. V., Zoology
FARAONE, D., Mineralogy
FRINGUELLI, F., Organic Chemistry
GIANOTTI, F. S., Zoology
GUAZZONE, S., Algebra
LEVI, F., Physics
MARINO, G., Organic Chemistry
MAZZUCATO, U., Physical Chemistry
MORETTI, G. P., Zoology

Pichi Sermolli, R., Botany
Renzini, G., Microbiology
Sermonti, G., Histology and Embryology
Sgamellotti, A., Inorganic Chemistry
Tarantelli, T., General, Inorganic and Analytical Chemistry
Verdini, L., Experimental Physics
Vinti, C., Mathematics
Volpi, G., General and Inorganic Chemistry
Zanazzi, P. F., Crystallography

Faculty of Education:
De Marco, M., Medieval Latin Literature
Forni, G., Roman History
Mancini, F., Italian Language and Literature
Mirri, E., Philosophy
Nava, G., History of Italian Literature
Negri, A., History of Philosophy
Pepe, L., Latin Language and Literature
Quatrrocchi, L., German Language and Literature
Scivoletto, A., Latin Language and Literature
Setaioli, A., Latin Grammar
Spaziani, M., French Language and Literature
Stella, P., Modern History
Valeriani, A., Pedagogic Discipline

UNIVERSITÀ DEGLI STUDI

LUNGARNO PACINOTTI 43,
56100 PISA
Telephone: 590-000.
Founded 1343.

Rector: Prof. R. Favilli.
Director: Dr. M. Nencetti.

Number of teachers: *c.* 300.
Number of students: 28,000.

Deans:

Faculty of Law: Prof. V. Palazzolo.
Faculty of Economics and Commerce: Prof. U. Bertini.
Faculty of Political Science: Prof. A. Palazzo.
Faculty of Letters and Philosophy: Prof. S. Settis.
Faculty of Foreign Languages and Literature: Prof. G. Mancini.
Faculty of Medicine: Prof. C. Pellegrino.
Faculty of Mathematical, Physical and Natural Sciences: Prof. P. Meletti.
Faculty of Pharmacy: Prof. S. Carboni.
Faculty of Engineering: L. Lazzarino.
Faculty of Agrarian Science: A. Panattoni.
Faculty of Veterinary Medicine: Prof. R. Farina.

Professors:

Faculty of Law:
Barrilaro, D., General Public Law
Breccia, U., Institutions of Private Law
Busnelli, F. D., Private Law
Carrozza, A., Agrarian Law
Corradini, D., Philosophy of Law
Gaeta, D., Navigation Law
Merusi, F., General Public Law
Natoli, U., Civil Law
Palazzolo, V., Philosophy of Law
Pera, G., Industrial Law
Petronio, U., History of Italian Law
Piras, A., Commercial Law
Pizzorusso, A., Constitutional Law
Ripepe, E., General Theory of Law
Volpe, G., General Public Law

Faculty of Political Sciences:
Are, G., Modern History
Corsi, M., History of Political Thought
Costanzo Beccaria, G., Social Anthropology
Elia, G., Urban Sociology
Filippone Thaulero, G., History of International Relations
Flammia, R., Labour Law
Marini, G., Philosophy of Politics
Marrara, D., History of Political Institutions
Palazzo, A., Sociology

Faculty of Letters and Philosophy:
Anzilotti, G. R., Anglo-American Literature
Arrighetti, G., Greek Literature
Arias, P. E., Archaeology and History of Greco-Roman Art
Badaloni, N., History of Philosophy
Banti, O., Palaeography and Diplomacy
Barone, F., Theoretical Philosophy
Beschi, L., Mathematical Linguistics
Blassucci, L., Italian Literature
Bolelli, T., Linguistics
Bresciani, E., Egyptology
Campanile, E., Linguistics
Candeloro, G., History of Italian Unification
Carlini, A., Greek and Latin Philology
Carpi, U., Italian Literature
Conte, G. B., Latin Literature
Cori, B., Geography
Cristiani, E., Medieval History
Di Benedetto, V., Greek and Latin Philology
Gargani, A., History of Modern and Contemporary Philosophy
Laffi, U., Roman History
Lazzeroni. R., Linguistics
Luporini, E., History of Medieval and Modern Art
Madrignani, C. A., Italian Literature
Marcucci, S., Theoretical Philosophy
Marianelli, M., German Language and Literature
Martinengo, A., Spanish
Massa, E., Medieval Latin
Matucci, M., French Language and Literature
Mirri, M., Modern History
Mori, A., Geography
Pizzorusso Bertolucci, V., Romance Philology
Raggiunti, R., Theoretical Philosophy
Rosa, M., Modern History
Rossetti, G., Medieval Institutions
Russi, A., Aesthetics
Sainati, V., Moral Philosophy
Settis, S., Archaeology and History of Greek and Roman Art
Stussi, A., Italian Philology
Violante, C., Medieval History
Zampolli, A., Mathematical Linguistics

Faculty of Foreign Languages and Literature:
Ambrosini, R., Linguistics
Arcamone, M. G., German Philogy
Bini, F., English
Braccini, M., Romance Philology
Brugnoli, G., Latin
Canali, L., Latin
Cecchini, A., Education
Crinó, A. M., English
Dell'Agata, G., Russian
Di Stefano, G., Spanish
Fasano, G., French
Freer, A. J., French
Mancini, G., Spanish
Pasi, C., French
Pedreschi, L., Geography
Varanini, G., French

Faculty of Medicine:
Bandettini, R., Clinical Dentistry
Baschieri, L., Medical Pathology and Clinical Methodology
Bendinelli, M., Microbiology
Berlucchi, G., Human Physiology
Bertelli, A., Pharmacology
Bianchi, R., Clinical and Therapeutic Medicine
Bottone, E., Paediatrics
Colizzi, C., Clinical Pathology
Donato, L., Medical Pathology and Clinical Methodology
Ermini, M., Special Surgical Pathology and Clinical Propadeutics
Falcone, G., Microbiology
Fioretti, P., Clinical Obstetrics and Gynaecology
Franchi, M., Radiology
Gigli, G., General Clinical and Therapeutic Medicine
Giovannetti, S., Semeiotic Medicine
Gomirato, G., Nervous and Mental Diseases
Grassi, B., Clinical Pathology
Marchetti, P. G., Orthopaedics
Massart, C., Human Anatomy
Mazzanti, L., Pharmacology
Mian, E., Dermo-syphilology
Michelucci, S., General Histology and Embryology
Moruzzi, G., Physiology
Muratorio, A., Nervous and Mental Disease
Parvis, D., Hygiene
Pasero, G., Clinical Pathology
Pellegrino, C., General Pathology
Pera, L., Anatomy
Pfaner, P., Infantile Neuropsychiatry
Pompeiano, O., Physiology
Ronca, G., Biological Chemistry
Sarteschi, P., Psychiatry
Scalori, G., Oto-Rhino-Laryngology
Selli, M., General and Therapeutic Surgery
Spoto, P., Clincial Obstetrics and Gynaecology
Squartini, F., Anatomy and Pathological Histology
Toniolo, G., Radiology
Tronchetti, F., General Clinical and Therapeutic Medicine
Tusini, G., Neurosurgery
Wirth, A. M., Ophthalmology

Faculty of Mathematical, Physical and Natural Science:
Alzetta, G., Spectroscopy and Radio Frequency
Arrighini, G. P., Physical Chemistry
Avanzi, S., Plant Cytology and Embryology
Barberi, F., Vulcanology
Battaglia, A., Physics
Bemporad, C., Higher Physics
Bertanza, L., Physics
Bovet, D. P., Information Systems
Cabani, S., Physical Chemistry
Calderazzo, F., General and Inorganic Chemistry
Campanato, S., Analytical Mathematics
Capriz, G., Mechanics
Checcucci, V., Didactics of Mathematics
Cognetti, G., Marine Biology
Crespi, G., Lexicography
Dessau, G., Ore Deposits
Di Giacomo, A., Quantum Mechanics
Di Jorio, M., Optics
Elter, P., Geology
Fabri, E., Theoretical Physics

Felicioli, R., Biological Chemistry
Floris, C., Vegetal Physiology
Franzini, M., Mineralogy
Gerace, G. B., Information Systems
Germano, G., Theory of Algorithms and Calculation
Gestri, G., Theory and Application of Computers
Giannessi, F., Mathematics of Finance
Giusti, E., Mathematical Analysis
Gozzini, A., Structure of Materials
Innocenti, F., Petrography
Ipata, P. L., Biochemistry
Lardicci, L., Organic Chemistry
Lazzeri, F., Geometry
Letta, G., Probability Theory
Loprieno, N., Genetics
Luccio, F., Information Systems
Mancino, G., Histology and Embryology
Mannelli, I., Physics of Elementary Particles
Marinelli, G., Petrography
Marino, A., Mathematical Analysis
Meletti, P., Botany
Merlino, S., Crystallography
Moccia, R., Theoretical Chemistry
Montanari, U., Information Handling Methods
Nardi, R., Geological Relief
Nobili, R., Zoology
Papi, F., Zoology
Papoff, P., Analytical Chemistry
Polacco, E., Physics
Prodi, G., Mathematical Analysis
Radmilli, A., Human Palaeontology
Raspi, G., Analytical Chemistry
Rosati, S., Nuclear Physics
Salvetti, O., Physical Chemistry
Scandone, P., Marine Geology
Spagnolo, S., Analytical Mathematics
Stoppini, G., General Physics
Tongiorgi, E., Nuclear Geology
Tongiorgio, M., Regional Geology
Torelli, G., General Physics
Traverso, C., Geometry
Trevisan, L., Geology
Villani, V., Geometry

Faculty of Pharmacy:

Baccaredda Boy, M., Industrial Chemistry
Berti, G., Organic Chemistry
Bottari, F., Technical and Legal Pharmacology
Carboni, S., Pharmaceutical Chemistry and Toxicology
Da Settimo Passetti, A., Pharmaceutical Chemistry and Toxicology
Macchia, B., Pharmaceutical Chemical Analysis
Marsili, A., Organic Chemistry

Faculty of Engineering:

Bassani, R., Mechanics Applied to Machines
Battistini, G., Electrotechnics
Butta, E., Chemistry
Caligo, D., Mathematical Analysis
Carmignani, C., Chemical Apparatus Construction
Caroti, L., Construction of Roads, Railways and Airports
De Carli, A., Automatic Controls .
Di Gangi, I., Machinery
Dini, D., Engines
Dini, E., Automobile Construction
Faedo, A., Mathematical Analysis
Faggiani, S., Technical Physics
Frosini, V., Materials Technology and Applied Chemistry
Ghelardoni, G., Chair of Mathematical Analysis
Giusti, F., Mechanical Technology
Giusti, P., Chemistry
Guerrini, B., Nuclear Installations
Lazzarino, L., Mechanical Construction
Magagnini, P. L., Physical Properties and Technology of Higher Polymers
Manacorda, T., Rational Mechanics
Mancianti, M., Telecommunications
Mancino, O. G., Mathematical Analysis
Marini, M., Applied Mechanics
Mariotti, G., Electric Machines
Marzulli, P., Numerical Calculus
Mattei, G., Rational Mechanics
Mengali, U., Statistical Theories of Communications
Montagnini, B., Physics of Nuclear Reactors
Mozzi, G., Mechanics
Nardini, G., Chemical Installations
Nencetti, G., Principles of Chemical Engineering
Nencioni, F., Electrical Engineering
Nuti, G., Architecture and Architectural Composition
Paganini, L., Special Nuclear Materials
Pellegrini, B., Applied Electronics
Podio, G. P., Construction
Poletti, M., Geometry
Poli, G., Science of Metals
Raymondi, C., Science of Building
Salvetti, A., Aeronautical Construction
Sampaolesi De Falena, L., Construction Techniques
Sassoli, F., Hydraulics
Tartarelli, R., Complements of Chemical Engineering
Teani, R., Business Management
Torrigiani, G., Mathematics
Trombetti, C., Topography
Vallini, A., Electrotechnics
Villaggio, R., Science of Construction
Zanelli, S., Transfer Processes and Apparatus

Faculty of Agrarian Science:

Basso, M., Industrial Fruit-Culture
Benvenuti, A., General Agronomy
Campus, F., Agrarian Economics and Estimates
Carloni, L., Agrarian Chemistry
Crovetti, A., Agrarian Entomology
D'Amato, F., Genetics
Favilli, R., General Agronomy and Grass Crops
Galoppini, C., Agricultural Industry
Gambogi, P., Mycology
Loreti, F., Tree Cultivation
Lotti, G., Agrarian Chemistry
Massantani, F., Ecology
Moschini, E., Horticulture and Floriculture
Onnis, A., Systematic Botany
Panattoni, A., Agrarian Economy and Politics
Pellegrini, S., Anatomy and Physiology of Domestic Animals
Picci, G., Agrarian and Technical Microbiology
Scaramuzzi, G., Vegetable Pathology
Tognoni, F., Technology of Protected Crops
Trimarchi, G., Special Zootechnics

Faculty of Veterinary Medicine:

Buonaccorsi, A., Pathology of Domestic Animals
Casarosa, L., Parasitology
Cenni, B., General Zootechnics
Del Bono, G., Comparative General Pathology
Farina, R., Infectious Diseases, Veterinary Prophylaxis and Policy
Fedeli, C., Zooculture
Frateschi, T. L., General Physiology of Domestic Animals and Biochemistry
Janella, G. G., Animal Genetics and General Animal Husbandry
Pellegrini, N., General and Special Veterinary Pathological Anatomy
Puntoni, P., Veterinary Operative Medicine
Romagnoli, A., Special Pathology and Medicine
Romboli, B., General Pathology, Pathological Anatomy
Salerno, G., Veterinary Surgery
Salutini, E., Special Pathology and Veterinary Medicine
Spisni, D., Physiology of Animals and Biochemistry

Faculty of Economics and Commerce:

Bertini, U., General and Applied Accountancy
Bruno, V., Statistics
Caparvi, R., Banking and Professional Methods
Caramiello, C., General and Applied Accountancy
Corticelli, R., General and Applied Accountancy
D'Albergo, S., Administrative Law
Giannessi, E., General and Applied Accountancy
Manca, P., Financial Mathematics
Padroni, G., Business Organizations
Pinna, M., Economic Geography
Ricci, R., Banking and Professional Methods
Varaldo, R., Industrial and Commercial Methods

UNIVERSITÀ DEGLI STUDI

CITTÀ UNIVERSITARIA,
00100 ROME
Telephone: 4991.

Founded 1303 by Pope Boniface VIII, with the Papal Bull "In Supremae praeminentia dignitatis".

Rector: Prof. A. Ruberti.
Director: G. Falconi.
Librarian: A. Serrai.

Number of teachers: 813 professors.
Number of students: 150,000.

Deans:

Faculty of Jurisprudence: Prof. R. Nicolò.
Faculty of Political Science: R. Monaco.
Faculty of Economics and Commerce: Prof. R. Cacciafesta.
Faculty of Statistics, Demography and Actuarial Science: Prof. V. Castellano.
Faculty of Letters and Philosophy: Prof. L. de Nardis.
Faculty of Education: Prof. E. de Grada.
Faculty of Medicine: Prof. A. Cimmino.
Faculty of Mathematics, Physics and Natural Science: Prof. G. Tecce.
Faculty of Pharmacy: Prof. A. Romeo.
Faculty of Engineering: Prof. M. Murgo.
School of Aerospace Engineering: Prof. L. Broglio.
Faculty of Architecture: Prof. C. Cicconcelli.
School of Librarianship and Archivists: Prof. L. Sandri.

Professors:

Faculty of Jurisprudence:

Antonini, E., Debtors' Law
Arango-Ruiz, G., International Law
Barile, G., International Law

BIANCA, C. M., Civil Law
BONIFACIO, F. P., General Public Law
BRUTTI, M., Roman Law
CAMPA, G., Finance and Financial Law
CANNADA BARTOLI, E., Administrative Justice
CAPOGROSSI COLOGNESI, L., History of Roman Law
CASSANDRO, G., History of Italian Law
CATALANO, P., Roman Law
CATAUDELLA, A., Private Law
CORDERO, F., Penal Procedure
COTTA, S., Philosophy of Law
CRISAFULLI, V., Constitutional Law
DE LUCA, G., Penal Procedure
DE LUCA, L., Ecclesiastical Law
DE MARTINI, A., Commercial Law
DI MAJO GIAQUINTO, A., Civil Law
DI NARDI, G., Political Economy
FAZZALARI, E., Civil Procedure
FEDELE, P., Canon Law
FERRARA, G., General Public Law
FERRARI, G., General Public Law
FERRI, G., Commercial Law
FINOCCHIARO, F., Ecclesiastical Law
FOIS, S., Constitutional Law
FRANCESCHELLI, R., Commercial Law
FROSINI, V., Philosophy of Law
GALLO, I. M., Penal Law
GAMBINO, A., Bankruptcy Law
GIANNINI, M. A., Administrative Law
GIORGANNI, M., Civil Law
GISMONDI, P., Ecclesiastical Law
GIUGNI, L., Labour Law
GUARINO, G., Administrative Law
IRTI, N., Private Law
LATAGLIATA, A. R., Penal Law
LIPARI, N., Private Law
MAFFEI, D., History of Italian Law
MALINTOPPI, A., European Community Law
MAZZIOTTI, M., Constitutional Law
MICHELI, G. A., Debtors' Law
MINERVINI, G., Commercial Law
MONTESANO, L., Procedural Law
MOTZO, G., General Public Law
NICOLO, R., Civil Law
NIGRO, M., Administrative Law
OPPO, G., Commercial Law
PACE, C., Political Economy
PEDONE, A., Finance and Financial Law
PERSIANI, M., Labour Law
PIANO MORTARI, V., History of Italian Law
PIRAS, A., Administrative Law
PUGLIESE, G., History of Roman Law
PUNZI, C., Civil Procedure
RAVA, T., Industrial Law
RESCIGNO, P., Private Law
RODOTÁ, S., Civil Law
ROMANI, F., Political Economy
SANDULLI, A., Constitutional Law
SCOGNAMIGLIO, R., Labour Law
SERRAO, F., Fundamentals of Roman Law
SIRACUSANO, D., Penal Procecdure
SPASARI, M., Penal Law
SPINELLI, L., Canon Law
TALAMANCA, M., History of Roman Law
VASSALLI, G., Penal Law

Faculty of Political Science:
AMATO, G., Italian and Comparative Constitutional History
ANDRE, G., History of North America
ARMANI, P., Political Economy and Finance
BASSANINI, F., Regional Law
BATTISTA, A. M., History of Political Doctrines
BRANCA, G., Labour Law
CACCAMO, D., East European History
CAPOTORTI, F., Private International Law
CARAVALE, G., Political Economy
CARAVALE, M., History of Political Institutions
CIPROTTI, P., Italian and Comparative Ecclesiastical Law
COSENZA, C., History of Political Thought
D'ADDIO, M., History of Politics
D'AMATO, L., Political Sociology
DE CUPIS, A., Private Law
DEL NOCE, A., Philosophy of Politics
DEL PUNTA, V., Economic Planning
DEL VISCOVO, M., Economics and Politics of Transport
DE ROSA, G., Contemporary History
DURANTE, F., International Organizations
FERRARI BRAVO, L., European Community Law
FRANCHINI, F., Administrative Law
GALIZIA, M., Italian and Comparative Constitutional Law
GIUSTI, F., Economic Statistics
GUERRIERI, G., Statistics
LAVAGNA, C., Public Law
MALGERI, F., History of State and Church Relations.
MANCINI, F., Labour Law and Social Legislation
MARTINO, A., Monetary History and Politics
MARZANO, A., Political Economy and Finance
MODUGNO, F., Public Law
MONTICONE, A., Modern History
MORI, R., Contemporary History
PASTORELLI, P., History of Treaties and International Politics
SAITTA, A., Modern History
SOMOGYI, G., Economic Planning
SPERDUTI, G., International Organizations
TOSATO, G., Private International Law
VEDOVATO, G., History of Treaties and International Politics
VITALI, O., Economic Statistics

Faculty of Economics and Commerce:
ARCELLI, M., Political Economy
BARETTONI ARLERI, A., State Accounting.
CACCIAFESTA, R., Financial Mathematics
CAFFÉ, F., Political Economy and Finance
CAPALDO, P., General and Applied Accountancy
CAROSELLI, M. R., Economic History
CASSANDRO, P. E., General and Applied Accountancy
CHIACCHIERINI, E., Marketing
D'ALESSANDRO, F., Law of Bankruptcy
D'ALESSANDRO, L., Public Service Administration
DE BENEDICTIS, M., Agrarian Ecomonics and Politics
FANFANI, A., Economic History
FANTOZZI, A., Tax Law
FORTUNA, F., Industrial and Commercial Methods
FÜRST, D., General Mathematics
GALATERIA, L., Administrative Law
GANDOLFO, G., International Economics
GAREGNANI, P., Political Economy
GASPERONI, N., Industrial Law
LEDDA, F., Institutions of Public Law
LO MONACO, M., Economic Geography
MARRAMA, V., Political Economy
MERLANI, C., Industrial and Commercial Techniques
MIELE, M., International Law
MIRA, G., Economic History
ORLANDO, G., Agrarian Economics and Politics
OTTAVIANI, G., Financial Mathematics
PARRAVICINI, G., Money and Credit Economics
PARRILLO, F., Techniques of Banking
PICARDI, N., Civil Procedure
PINO, A., Private Law
RENZI, A., Research Techniques in Commerce
STEVE, S., Science of Finance and Financial Law
TREZZA, B., Political Economy
ZANDANO, G., Political Economy

Faculty of Statistics, Demography and Actuarial Science:
AMMASSARI, P., Methodology and Techniques of Social Research
BALDESSARI, B. A., Probability Calculus
BENEDETTI, C., Statistics
BERTINO, S., Contingency and Theory of Expectation
BRUNO, S., Finance
COPPINI, M. A., Social Insurance
DALL'AGLIO, G., Probability Calculus
DE LUCIA, L., Methodology, Statistics
D'IPPOLITO, G., Applied Calculus
DONATI, A., Insurance Law
EMANUELI, F., Financial and Actuarial Mathematics
FEDERICI, N., Demography
GIANNONE, A., Economic Statistics
GOLINI, A., Demography
GRAZIA RESI, B., Social Statistics
GUARINI, R., Economic Statistics
HERZEL, A., Methodology and Statistics of Experimental Research
IZZO, L., Political Economy
LETI, G., Statistics
MARBACH, G., Commercial Analysis
MAROTTA, M., General Sociology
MINISOLA, F., Actuarial Techniques of Insurance against Damages
OTTAVIANI, R., Actuarial Techniques of Life Assurance
PERUZY, A. D., Health Statistics
PETRILLI, G., Economics and Finance of Insurance Companies
PICCINATO, L., Theory of Speculation and Decisions
RIZZI, A., Statistics
SAGGESE PASSAQUINDICI, M., Applied Mechanics and Electronics
SPAVENTA, L., Political Economy
SYLOS LABINI, P., Political Economy
VIANELLO, G., Labour Sociology and Economics
ZAGHINI, E., Econometrics

Faculty of Letters and Philosophy:
ACCAME, S., Greek History
AQUARONE, A., History of the Risorgimento
ARNALDI, G., Medieval History
ASOR ROSA, A., Italian Literature
AVESANI, R., Medieval and Modern Philology
BALDACCI, O., Geography
BALDELLI, I., History of Italian Language
BAUSANI, A., Islamic Studies
BEDESCHI, G., Moral Philosophy
BELARDI, W., Glottology
BIANCHI, U., History of Religions
BINNI, W., Italian Literature
BONICATTI, M., History of Art
BORSELLINO, A., Italian Literature
BREGLIA, L., Greek and Roman Numismatics
BREZZI, P., Medieval History
BUSSAGLI, M., History of Indian and Central Asian Art
CALABRÓ, G., Moral Philosophy
CALVESI, M., History of Modern Art
CARPITELLA, D., Ethnomusicology
CASINI, P., History of Modern and Contemporary Philosophy
CASTAGNOLI, F., Topography of Rome
CAVALLO, G., Greek Palaeography
CELLUCCI, C., Logic

CHIARINI, P., German Language and Literature
CIASCA, A., Antiquities
CIRESE, A. M., Cultural Anthropology
CIVES, G., History of Education
COLESANTI, M., French Language and Literature
COLLETTI, L., Theoretical Philosophy
COLOMBO SMITH, R. M., English Language and Literature
COSTA CORDA, M., Education
COLUCCI, M., Russian
COSTANZO BECCARIA, M., History of Literary Criticism
CREMANTE CARETTI, L., English Language and Literature
DAFFINA, P., History of Central Asia
D'AMICO, F., History of Music
D'ANNA, G., Latin Literature
D'AVINO, R., Glottology
DE'MAFFEI, F., History of Byzantine Art
DE MAURO, T., Philosophy of Language
DE NARDIS, L., French Language and Literature
DONADONI, F., Egyptology
DURANTE, M., Glottology
FOLLIERI, E., Philology and Byzantine History
GAETA, F., Modern History
GARRONI, E., Aesthetics
GHISALBERTI, C., History of Italian Law
GIANNANTONI, G., History of Ancient Philosophy
GIULIANO, A., Archaeology and Art History of Greece and Rome
GNOLI, R., Indology
GRACIOTTI, S., Slavic Philology
GREGORY, T., History of Philosophy
GROTTANELLI, V. L., Ethnology
GUERRA, A., Moral Philosophy
GUERRINI, L., Archaeology and Art History of Greece and Rome
LIVERANI, M., History of the Near East
LOMBARDO, A., English Language and Literature
LUISELLI, B., Latin Literature
MACCHI, G., Portuguese Language and Literature
MACCHIA, G., French Language and Literature
MAIERÚ, A., History of Medieval Philosophy
MALTESE, C., History of Modern Art
MANACORDA, M. A., History of Education
MANSELLI, R., Medieval History
MARA, M. G., History of Christianity
MARIOTTI, S., Classical Philology
MARTINELLI, V., History of Modern Art
MASARACCHIA, A., Greek Literature
MATTHIAE, P., Ancient Near East Archaeology and History of Art
MAZZARINO, S., Roman History and Epigraphy
MERKER, N., History of Modern and Contemporary Philosophy
MESCHIERI, L., Psychology
MORELLI, EMILIA, History of the Risorgimento
MORELLI, G., History of Latin Language
MORETTI, L., Epigraphy of Ancient Greece
MOSCATI, R., Modern History
MUSCETTA, C., Italian Literature
OLIVETTI, M. M., Philosophy of Religion
ORLANDI, T., Coptic Language and Literature
PALAGIANO, C., Geography
PALLOTTINO, M., Archaeology and Etruscology
PALMIERI, A., Prehistory of the Near and Middle East
PANCIERA, S., Roman Epigraphy and Antiquities
PARENTE ISNARDI, M., History of Political Doctrine
PAROLI, T., Germanic Philology
PENSA, C., Religions and Philosophies of India and the Far East
PERICOLI RIDOLFINI, F. S., History of Eastern Christianity
PERONI, R., Ancient European History
PETECH, L., History of Eastern Asia
PETRUCCI, A., Palaeography and Diplomatics
PETRUCCIANI, M., History of Modern and Contemporary Italian Literature
PETTINATO, G., Assyriology
PICCALUGA, G., Religions of the Classical World
PIEMONTESE, A. M., Persian Language and Literature
PONENTE, A., History of Contemporary Art
PUCCINI, D., Hispano-American Literature
PUGLISI, S., Palaeo-ethnology
QUONDAM, A., Italian Literature
RESSULI, N., Albanian Language and Literature
ROMANINI, A. M., History of Medieval Art
ROMEO, ROSARIO, Modern History
RONCAGLIA, A., Romance Philology
SABBATUCCI, D., History of Religion
SACCONI, A., Mycenean Philology
SAMONÀ, C., Spanish Language and Literature
SASSO, G., History of Philosophy
SAVARESE, G., Italian Literature
SCARCIA AMORETTI, B. M., Islamic Studies
SCERRATO, U., Muslim and Coptic Art History
SCOLES, E., Spanish Language and Literature
SCRIVANO, R., Italian Literature
SIMONETTI, M., History of Christianity
SINISCALO, P., Ancient Christian Greek and Latin Literature
SOMENZI, V., Philosophy of Science
SOMMELLA, P., Topography and Town Planning of the Classical World
SOMENZI, V., Philosophy of Science
SQUARCIAPINO FLORIANI, M., Archaeology of Roman Provinces
STEGAGNO PICCHIO, L., Portuguese Language and Literature
STUCCHI, A., Archaeology and History of Greek and Roman Art
TAMBORRA, A., History of Eastern Europe
TANDOI, V., Latin Literature
TAVANI, G., Romance Philology
TESTINI, P., Christian Archaeology
VALENTINI, F., Theoretical Philosophy
VILLARI, R., Modern History
VINAY, G., Medieval Latin Literature
VISALBERGHI, A., Education
VITUCCI, G., Roman History and Epigraphy

Faculty of Education:

ACCAME BOBBIO, A., Italian Language and Literature
AMBROGIO, I., Russian Language and Literature
AURIGEMMA, M., Italian Language and Literature
BAFFIONI, G., Latin Grammar
BANISSONI, M., Social Psychology
BARBERO, G., Economic Sociology
BARIDON, S., French Language and Literature
BERTINI, M., Physiological Psychology and Biology of Mental Processes
BIANCO, F., Modern and Contemporary Philosophy
BONAIUTO, P., General Psychology
BORTOLOTTO, M., History of Music
BOTTASSO, V., Bibliography and Library Science
BROCCOLI, A., History of Education
BUSNELLI, C., Development Psychology
CAPIZZI, C., Byzantine History
CARLI, R., Psychology
CERRONI, U., Political Science
CHINOL, E., English Language and Literature
DARDANO, M., History of Italian Grammar and Language
DE GRADA, E., Social Psychology
DEL BONO, F., German Philology
FERRAROTTI, F., Sociology
FONZI, F., Contemporary History
GABRIELI, V., English Language and Literature
GENTILE, M. T., Education
GIORCELLI, M. C., Anglo-American Literature
GRASSI, L., History of Modern Art
GRASSO, P. G., Social Psychology
GRECO, A. L., Italian Language and Literature
IACOBELLI ISOLDI, A. M., Moral Philosophy
IZZO, A., History of Sociology
JANNINI, P., French Language and Literature
LAENG, M., Education
LANTERNARI, V., Ethnology
LA PORTA, R., Education
LUGARINI, L., History of Ancient Philosophy
MARIANI, G., History of Modern Italian Literature
MELCHIORI ARNETT, B., English Language and Literature
MELCHIORI, G., English Language and Literature
NERI, R., Education
OSSICINI, A., Psychology
PASQUAZI, S., Italian Language and Literature
PAVAN, M., Roman History
PETROCCHI, G., Italian Language and Literature
PETROCCHI, M., Modern History
PICCO, I., Pedagogic Disciplines
PIZZAMIGLIO, L., Psycholinguistics
PONTECORVO PIPERNO, C., Educational Institutions
PONZO, E., Development Psychology
PRINI, P., History of Philosophy
PRODI, P., Modern History
QUACQUARELLI, A., Ancient Christian Literature
RAVAGLIOLI, F., History of Education
RIGOBELLO, A., History of Philosophy
ROSSI LAPICCIRELLA, R., Spanish
SABA, G., History of French Language
SABATINI, F., History of Italian Grammar and Language
SAITO, G., German Language and Literature
SANSONE, G., Romance Philology
SANTACROCE RISSET, J., French Language and Literature
SCOPPOLA, P., Contemporary History
SCOTTI, M., Italian Language and Literature
SOCRATE GENTILI, V. M., English Language and Literature
SOCRATE, M., Spanish Language and Literature
SPANO, B., Geography
STATERA, G., Methodology and Techniques of Social Research
TALAMO, G., History of the Risorgimento
TEDESCHINI LALLI, B. M., Anglo-American Literature
TENTORI, T., Cultural Anthropology
TITONE, R., Psycho-education

Ulivi, F., Italian Language and Literature
Ussani, V., Latin Language and Literature
Venturini, R., Physiological Psychology
Verdone, M., History and Criticism of Film
Verra, V., History of Philosophy
Volpi Orlandini, M., Sociology of Art
Zavalloni, A., Special Education
Zolla, V. E., Anglo-American Literature

Faculty of Medicine:

Alescio, T., General Biology and Zoology
Andreani, D., Constitutional Medicine and Endocrinology
Angelucci, L., Pharmacology
Antonini, E., Chemistry
Antoniotti, F., Social Medicine
Ascenzi, A., Anatomy and Pathological Histology
Ballesio, P. L., Physics
Balsano, F., Semeiology
Becelli, S., Surgery
Benedetti, P., Infant Neuropsychiatry
Beretta Anguissola, A., General Medicine
Biagini, C., Radiology
Biocca, E., Parasitology
Biocca, P., General Clinical and Therapeutic Medicine
Bollea, G., Child Neuropsychiatry
Bologna, U., Obstetric and Gynaecological Pathology
Bompiani, C., Radiology
Bracci, U., Urology
Brancati, A., Physiology
Brunori, M., Chemistry
Bucci, G., Child Welfare
Cantore, G., Neurotraumatology
Capozzi, L., Clinical Dentistry
Caramia, F. G., General Pathology
Carenza, L., Obstetrics and Gynaecology
Casciani, C. U., Pathology
Castrini, G., General Clinical and Therapeutic Surgery
Cavallini, D., Biochemistry
Cerquiglini, S., Human Physiology
Chiaroni, T., Special Medical Pathology
Ciani, N., Psychiatry
Cirenei, A., Emergency Surgery
Conti, C., Special Medical Pathology and Clinical Methodology
Corsi, Semeiology
Cortesini, R., Experimental Surgery
Crainz, F., Obstetrics and Gynaecology
Crifo, S., Audiology
Curatolo, A., Human Physiology
Dagianti, A., Cardio-vascular Diseases
D'Arca, S. U., Hygiene
De Marco, C., Biochemistry
De Vincentiis, I., Clinical Oto-Rhino-Laryngology
Di Matteo, G., Surgical Pathology and Clinical Propaedeutics
Farulla, A., Industrial Medicine
Fasella, P. M., Biological Chemistry
Fazio, C., Nervous and Mental Diseases
Fegiz, G., Special Surgical Pathology and Clinical Propaedeutics
Ferracuti, F., Forensic Medicine
Fieschi, C., Nervous and Mental Diseases
Filadoro, F., Microbiology
Fiorani, P., Vascular Surgery
Floris, V., Nervous and Mental Diseases
Fortuna, A., Neurosurgery
Franconi, C., Physics
Fumagalli, Z., Human Anatomy
Gandini, E., Genetics
Garaci, E., Microbiology
Gasparetto, A., Anaesthetics
Gigante, D., Rheumatology
Giunchi, G., General Clinical and Therapeutic Medicine
Granati, A., Industrial Medicine
Grippaudo, G., Dental Surgery
Guidetti, B., Neurosurgery
Imperato, C., Clinical Paediatrics
Lazzari, R., Psychology
Lentini, S., Systematic Medicine
Lucchesi, M., Phthisiology
Maggioni, G., Paediatrics
Malaguzzi Valeri, O., Child Welfare
Mandelli, F., Haematology
Marcozzi, G., General and Therapeutic Surgery
Marino, B., Heart Surgery
Marinozzi, G., Human Anatomy
Marinozzi, V., Pathological Histology and Anatomy
Martinelli, V., Geriatric Surgery
Marullo, T., Oto-Rhino-Laryngology
Melchiorri, P., Pharmacology
Merli, S., Forensic and Insurance Medicine
Merlini, D., General Pathology
Messinetti, S., Surgical Semeiology
Molinaro, M., Histology and Embryology
Monesi, V., Histology and General Embryology
Monteleone, M., Clinical Orthopaedics
Monticelli, G., Clinical Orthopaedics
Morocutti, C., Clinical Neurology
Motta, P., Human Anatomy
Nicoletti, B., Biology and General Zoology
Orsi, N., Microbiology
Ottaviani, P., Special Medical Pathology and Methodology
Palazzetti, P., Obstetric and Gynaecological Pathology
Pannarale, R., Physiopathological Optics
Paroli, E., Pharmacology
Perugia, L., Clinical Orthopaedics
Piat, G., Experimental Surgery
Pontieri, G., General Pathology
Provenzale, L., Cardiovascular Surgery
Reale, A., Cardiovascular Diseases
Reda, G., Clinical Psychiatry
Rezza, E., Clinical Paediatrics
Ribuffo, A., Clinical Syphilology
Ribotta, G., Surgical Anatomy
Ricci, C., Thoracic Surgery
Ricci, G., Infectious Diseases
Ricci, G. F., Neuropsychiatry
Sangiorgi, M., Semeiology
Scavo, D., Medical Semeiology
Sciacca, A., Medical Semeiology
Scuderi, G., Ophthalmology
Sebastiani, A., Tropical and Infectious Diseases
Semerari, A., Criminological Medicine and Forensic Psychiatry
Serafini, U., Surgical Pathology and Clinical Methodolgy
Sorice, F., Tropical and Infectious Diseases
Speranza, V., Special Surgical Pathology and Clinical Propaedeutics
Stefanini, M., Histology and Embryology
Stipa, S., Surgical Semeiology
Strom, R., Applied Biochemistry
Stroppiani, L., History of Medicine
Tacciuoli, M., Clinical Urology
Torsoli, A., Gastroenterology
Vella, G., Clinical Psychiatry

Faculty of Mathematics, Physics and Natural Science:

Accascina, F., Electrochemistry
Accordi, B., Geology
Ageno, M., Biophysics
Angelucci, A., Sedimentology
Aparo, E. L., Mathematical Institutions
Azzarri Cervone, E., General and Inorganic Chemistry
Ballio, A., Biochemistry
Ballario, C., Physics
Baroni, G., General Physics
Bassani, G. F., Solid State Physics
Battaglia, E., Cytology and Vegetal Embryology
Bella, F., Experimental Physics
Beneventano, M., Elementary Particle Physics
Berlinguer, G., Industrial Hygiene and Physiology
Bernardini, C., Nuclear Physics
Bizarri, R., General Physics
Bohm, C., Computer Programming
Bossa, F., Biological Chemistry
Bovet, D. P., Programming
Brufani, M., Pharmaceutical Chemistry
Bullini, L., Ecology and Animal Etiology
Cabibbo, N., Theoretical Physics
Calef, E., Genetics
Calogero, F., Theoretical Physics
Capanna, E., Zoology of Vertebrates
Caputo, M., Seismology
Careri, G., Structure of Materials
Caricato, G., Rational Mechanics
Cartoni, G., Chemical Analysis
Carunchio, V., Qualitative Chemical Analysis
Castellani Rizzonelli, P. A., Mathematical Analysis
Cavalieri, A., Astrophysics
Ceccherini, P. V., Geometry
Chiarotti, G., General Physics
Cimino, A., General Chemistry
Cini, M., Theoretical Physics
Consiglio, C., Zoology
Conti, F., Spectroscopy and Radio Frequency
Conti, L., Regional Petrography
Conversi, M., Higher Physics
Cortesi, C., Mineralogy
Cortini, G., Physics
Crescenzi, V., Physical Chemistry
Cresta, M., Human Ecology
Cunsolo, S., Structure of Materials
De Angelis, G., Analytical Chemistry
Dell'Antonio, G., Rational Mechanics
De Maria, G., Physical Chemistry
De Martini, F., Optics
De Santis, P., Physical Chemistry
De Stefano, G., Anthropometry
De Vito, L., Numerical Analysis
De Voto, G., Regional Geology
Di Castro, C., Physics of Liquids
Di Maio, G., Organic Stereochemistry
Doplicher, S., Quantum Mechanics
Farinacci, A., Micropalaeontology
Federico Santonocito, M., Mineralogy
Ferrarese, G., Rational Mechanics
Ferrari, E., Theoretical Physics
Fichera, G., Mathematical Analysis
Figa' Talamanca, A., Mathematical Analysis
Fiocco, G., Terrestrial Physics
Fontana, M., Algebra
Fornaseri, M., Geochemistry
Frova, A., Electronics
Furlani, C., General and Inorganic Chemistry
Furlani Donda, A., General Chemistry
Gallavotti, G., Rational Mechanics
Giacomini, V., Botany
Giannone, P., Astronomy
Gianturco, F. A., Quantitative Chemistry
Giglio, E., Physical Chemistry
Gratton, L., Astrophysics
Graziosi, F., Microbiology
Grilli, M., General Physics
Gross, W., Numerical Analysis
Guerra, F., Statistical Mechanics

Illuminati, G., Organic Chemistry
Ippolito, F., Geology
Jona-Lasinio, G., Mathematical Methods of Physics
Kock, G., Probability Calculus
Liberti, A., Analytical Chemistry
Liquori, A. M., Physical Chemistry
Lombardo Radice, L., Mathematics
Ludovici Sneider, M. A., Numerical Analysis
Maccagno, A. M., Palaeontology
Maiani, L., Theoretical Physics
Manelli, E., Zoology
Manfredini, A., Physics
Mariani, F., Geomagnetism
Marini Bettolo Marconi, G. B., General and Inorganic Chemistry
Martinelli, E., Geometry
Mele, A., Chemistry
Miragliulo Scarpati, M. L., Organic Chemistry
Modena, I., Experimental Chemistry
Modiano, G., Human Genetics
Molinari, E., General and Inorganic Chemistry
Morbidelli, L., Petrography
Morpurgo, G. P., Plant Physiology
Mosco, U., Mathematical Analysis
Mottana, A., Mineralogy
Negretti, G., Petrography
Nicoletti, R., Organic Chemistry
Oliverio, A., Phytobiology
Olivieri, G., Genetics
Ortaggi, G., Organic Chemistry
Paparo Frontali, L., Fermentation Chemistry and Industrial Bacteriology
Passino, R., Industrial Chemical Plants
Piacente, V., Physical Chemistry
Pizzella, G., Physics Laboratory Work
Platone Garroni, M. G., Mathematical Analysis
Porta, P., General and Inorganic Chemistry
Procesi, C., Algebra
Rambelli, A., Mycology
Ricci, F. P., Materials Structures
Ricci, I., Botany
Rossi, A., Comparative Anatomy
Rotilio, G., Biochemistry
Ruffini, R., Theoretical Physics
Russo-Caia, S., Histology and Embryology
Salvetti, F., Inorganic and General Chemistry
Salvini, G., General Physics
Scarano, E., Applied Chemical Analysis
Scarpini, F., Mathematical Analysis
Schaerf, C., Physics
Sgarlata, F., Crystallography
Silvestri, L., Microbiology
Sirna, G., Palaeontology
Succi, F., Geometry
Tadini Vitagliano, G., Ecology
Taddeucci, A., Applied Geochemistry
Tallini, G., Geometry
Tallini Scafati, M., Algebra
Tecce, G., Molecular Biology
Toschi, G., General Physiology
Urbani, E., Histology and Embryology
Vaciago, A., Structural Chemistry
Vicedomini, M., Instrumental Chemical Analysis and Electrochemical Methods

Faculty of Pharmacy:
Anzalone, B., Pharmaceutical Botany
Bottrè, C., Physical Chemistry
Cacace, F., Inorganic and General Chemistry
Caglioti, L., Organic Chemistry
Carelli, V., Applied Pharmaceutical Chemistry
Fidanza, A., General Physiology
Finazzi Agro, A., Biological Chemistry
Giuliano, R., Pharmaceutics and Toxicology
Liberatore, F., Food Chemistry
Lucente, G., Chemico-pharmaceutical Analyses
Misiti, D., Organic Chemistry
Mondovi, B., Applied Biochemistry
Piccinelli, D., Pharmacology and Pharmacognosis
Riccieri, F., Pharmaceutics
Romeo, A., Pharmaceutics and Toxicology
Simonetti, N., Microbiology
Stein, M. L., Pharmaceutical and Toxicological Chemistry
Turano, C., Biochemistry

Faculty of Engineering:
Astuni, E., Electrotechnics
Avantaggiati, A., Mathematical Analysis
Barducci, I., Technical Physics
Barzilai, G., Applied Electronics
Benini, A., Construction of Roads, Railways and Airports
Benvenuti, P., Rational Mechanics
Bernabini, M., Mineral Geophysics
Bernardi, P., Measurement and Hyperfrequency
Bertolotti, M., Physics
Birardi, G., Topography
Bordoni, P. G., Rational Mechanics
Borgia, E., Air and Naval Transport
Branca, P. F., Mechanical Measurement
Bruni, C., Automatic Control
Brutti, C., Machine Building
Calabresi, G., Building Foundations Technology
Cappuccino, F., Applied Electronics
Caputo, C., Machinery
Carrara, G., Technology of Industrial Construction
Cattaneo Gasparini, I., Geometry and Algebra
Ceradini, G., Building Science
Colombo, G. M., Electrical Applications
Cumo, M., Nuclear Installations
D'Auria, G., Antennae and Broadcasting
De Feo, V., Architecture and Architectural Composition
Del Bufalo, L., Programming and Costing
Del Pasqua, D., Mathematical Analysis
Di Blasio, G., Statistical Theories of Telecommunications
Di Cave, S., Chemical Installations
Di Cuonzo, V., Geometry
Ercoli, P., Electronic Calculations
Esu, F., Geotechnics applied to Hydraulics
Fantini, A., Thermotechnical Installations
Fontana, D. M., Technical Physics
Fumasoni, S., Organic Chemistry
Gaddini, B., Hydraulics
Gavarini, C., Structural Dynamics
Gerosa, G., Microwaves
Giacomelli, L., Theory of Non-linear Networks
Giannini, F., Road Networks
Giannini, M., Nuclear Measurement
Giona, A. R., Principles of Chemical Engineering
Gorio, F., Urban Studies
Gravina, P., Building Science
Guzzanti, C., Methods and Economics of Transport
Iliceto, F., Electrical Installations
Isidori, A., Automatic Controls
Mandarini, P., Theory of Information and Codes
Mandolesi, E., Technical Architecture
Manfredini, M., Geology
Mariani, E., Industrial Chemistry
Martinelli, G., Technical Electronics
Massacci, P., Special Mineral Technology
Maura, G., Materials Technology and Applied Chemistry
Mencuccini, C., Physics
Mongiardini, V., Hydraulics
Murgo, M., Automatic Controls
Nicoló, F., Servo Control
Nicosia, S., Automatic Controls
Ossicini, A., Mathematics
Ottavi, C. M., Applied Electronics
Paoletti, A., Physics
Papa, T., Physics
Paribeni, M., Technical Physics
Parolini, G., Energy
Parrinello, S., Mathematical Economics applied to Engineering
Pavesi, O., Transport Planning
Peroni, B., Telecommunications
Petternella, M., Automatic Measurement and Instrumentation
Picardi, G., Systems of Surveying and Identification
Piga, P., Mineral Arts
Rallo, F., Chemistry
Ratti, U., Electrotechnics
Rebecchini, M., Building Construction
Rio, A., High Polymer Technology
Roghi, G., Numerical Analysis and Programming
Roma, C., Nuclear Machinery
Rosati, F., Mathematical Analysis
Roveri, A., Telegraphic and Telephonic Communications
Ruberti, A., Telegraphic and Telephonic Communications
Schiaffino, P., Telegraphic and Telephonic Technology
Sciuti, S., Nuclear Physics
Scozzafava, R., Probability Calculus
Sebastiani, E., Chemical Plant
Sette, D., Physics
Signorelli, G., Metallurgy and Metallography
Silvestroni, P., Chemistry
Turriziani, R., Applied Chemistry
Vaccaro, G., Geometry
Ventriglia, U., Applied Geology
Violi, G., Metallurgy

School of Aerospace Engineering:
Arduini, C., Space Systems
Broglio, L., Aeronautical Construction
Buongiorno, C., Experimental Gas Dynamics
Cunsolo, D., Gas Dynamics
Ponzi, U., Aerospace Installations
Santini, P., Elements of Aircraft Construction
Sirinian Dicran, M., Mechanics and Stability of Aerodynes

Faculty of Architecture:
Anversa Ferretti, L., Architectural Composition
Benedetti, S., History of Architecture
Boaga, G., Technology of Architecture
Bonelli, R., History of Architecture
Bruschi, A., History of Architecture
Calzolari, M. V., Town Planning
Carbonara, P., Architectural Composition
Cicconcelli, C., Social Architecture
Coppa, M., Town Planning
D'Alessandro, M., Technology of Architecture
Dall'olio, C., Architectural Composition
Dardi, C., Architectural Composition
Dierna, S., Architectural Composition
Fiorentini, M., Architectural Composition
Gatti De Sanctis, D., Architectural Composition
Giuffré, A., Techniques of Construction
Lenci, S., Architectural Composition

LUGLI, P. M., Town Planning
MALUSARDI, F., Urban Planning
MELE, M., Bridges and Large Structures
MELOGRANI, C., Architectural Composition
MUSCARA, C., Urban Geography
PELLEGRIN, L., Architectural Composition
PERUGINI, G., Architectural Composition
PINTO, P. E., Earthquake-Resistant Constructions
QUARONI, L., Architectural Composition
RAU, S., History of Architecture
RENZULLI, T., Construction
SACRIPANTI, M., Architectural Composition
SCIMEMI, G., Town Planning
TIBERI, C., History of Architecture
VITTORIA, E., Artistic Design for Industry

School of Librarianship and Archivists:
CORTESE, E., Medieval and Modern Juridical Institutions
D'ADDARIO, A., General Archives, History of Archives
PRATESI, A., Diplomatics
SCALIA, G., History of Archivistics

UNIVERSITÀ DEGLI STUDI DI SALERNO

VIA URBANO II,
84100 SALERNO
Telephone: (39-89) 225488.
Founded 1970.

Rector: Prof. LUIGI AMIRANTE.
Administrative Director: TOMMASO PELOSI.

Faculties of law, economics, letters, sciences.

UNIVERSITÀ DEGLI STUDI

PIAZZA UNIVERSITÀ,
07100 SASSARI, SARDINIA
Telephone: 219111.
Founded 1562.

Rector: Prof. A. MILELLA.
Administrative Director and Secretary: Dott. ORAZIO NICOTRA.

Number of teachers: *c.* 300.
Number of students: *c.* 7,500.
Publications: *Annuario, Studi.*

DEANS:

Faculty of Law: Prof. F. CHIOMENTI.
Faculty of Medicine and Surgery: Prof. S. CAMPUS.
Faculty of Pharmacy: Prof. G. CIGNARELLA.
Faculty of Veterinary Medicine: Prof. G. MANUNTA.
Faculty of Agronomy: Prof. G. RIVOIRA.
Faculty of Mathematics, Physics and Natural Sciences: Prof. A. GAMBA.
Faculty of Education: Prof. E. CONTU.

UNIVERSITÀ DEGLI STUDI

BANCHI DI SOTTO 55,
53100 SIENA
Telephone: 44.191.
Founded 1240.

Rector: Prof. ADALBERTO GROSSI.
Director: Dr. J. SEMPLICI.
Librarian: M. CANTUCCI.

Number of professors: 456.
Number of students: 11,000.

Publications: *Studi Senesi* (Law, Political and Social Science), *Albi della Facoltà Medica Senese* (Medical School), *Annuario Accademico.*

DEANS AND DIRECTORS:

Faculty of Jurisprudence: R. MARTINI.
School for Social Assistance: M. CANTUCCI.
M. Bracci College: R. MARTINI.

Faculty of Medicine: C. RICCI.
Advanced School of Clinical Obstetrics and Gynaecology: Prof. N. D'ANTONA.
Advanced School of Clinical Ophthalmology: R. FREZZOTTI.
Advanced School of Clinical Pediatrics: A. FOIS.
Advanced School of Urology: Prof. S. ARMENIO.
Advanced School of Cardiovascular and Rheumatic Diseases: A. CANIGGIA.
Advanced School of Anaesthesiology: Prof. G. BELLUCCI.
Advanced School of Neurology: G. GUAZZI.
Advanced School of Orthopaedics and Traumatology: Prof. L. BOCCHI.
Advanced School of Radiology: Prof. C. STUART.
School of Forensic Medicine and Insurance: Prof. M. BARNI.
Advanced School of Oto-Rhino-Laryngology and Cervico-Facial Pathology: Prof. C. PIERANGELI.
Advanced School of Infectious Diseases: Prof. A. ROSSOLINI.
Advanced School of Hygiene and Preventive Medicine: Prof. G. BOSCO.
Advanced School of Clinical Dermosyphilopathy: Prof. F. OTTOLENGHI.
Medico-Biological Institutes: Prof. G. WEBER.
Advanced School of Psychology: Prof. V. LAZZERONI.
Advanced School of Psychiatry: Prof. N. BATTISTINI.
Advanced School of Tubercular Medicine: Prof. C. PANA.
School of Audiometry: Prof. C. PIERANGELI.
School of Rehabilitation Therapy: Prof. A. FOIS.
School of Odonto-stomatology: P. MASI.
School of Thoracic Surgery: A. GROSSI.
School of Emergency Surgery: B. ROCCO.
School of Sports Medicine: G. CARLI.
Faculty of Mathematics, Physics and Natural Sciences: B. BACCETTI.
Faculty of Pharmacy: G. FRANCHI.
Faculty of Economics and Banking: E. MONTANARO.
Faculty of Education: G. RAUSA.
Faculty of Letters and Philosophy: M. CRISTOFANI.

UNIVERSITÀ DEGLI STUDI DI TORINO

VIA PO 17,
10124 TURIN
Telephone: 543397.
Founded 1404.

Rector: Prof. GIORGIO CAVALLO.
Vice-Rector: Prof. SILVIO ROMANO.
Registrar: (vacant).

Number of teachers: 1,100.
Number of students: 42,101.

DEANS:

Agriculture: A. BOSTICCO.
Economics: O. CASTELLINO.
Pharmacy: G. TAPPI.
Law: E. CASETTA.
Letters and Philosophy: G. VATTIMO.
Education: G. QUAZZA.
Medicine: M. U. DIANZANI.
Veterinary Medicine: F. MONTI.
Mathematics and Natural Sciences: E. BORELLO.
Political Sciences: G. MARTINOTTI.

ATTACHED INSTITUTE:

Centro di Giuscibernetica: via Sant' Ottavio 20, 10124 Turin; Dir. M. G. LOSANO; publ. *Systema* (quarterly in English, French and Italian).

UNIVERSITÀ DEGLI STUDI DI TRIESTE

PIAZZALE EUROPA 1,
34100 TRIESTE
Telephone: 57 11 21.
Founded 1938.

Rector: G. DE FERRA.
Vice-Rector: O. RONDINI.
Administrative Director: M. DOBRAN.
Librarian: C. POLDRUGO.

Number of teachers: 618.
Number of students: *c.* 13,000.

DEANS:

Faculty of Jurisprudence: F. A. QUERCI.
Faculty of Political Science: G. RINALDI.
Faculty of Commerce and Economics: C. CALZOLARI.
Faculty of Letters and Philosophy: G. PETRONIO.
Faculty of Education: R. F. ROSSI.
Faculty of Medicine: F. S. FERUGLIO.
Faculty of Mathematics, Physics and Natural Sciences: G. COSTA.
Faculty of Pharmacy: C. RUNTI.
Faculty of Engineering: A. COCCO.

PROFESSORS:

Faculty of Jurisprudence:
ADAMI, F. E., Canon Law
ASSANTI, C., Labour Law
CERVENCA, G., History of Roman Law
CROSARA, F., History of Italian Law
DECLEVA, M., International Law
DE FERRA, G., Commercial Law
GABRIELLI, G., Institutions of Private Law

GIACOMAZZO, G. R., Canon Law
GREGORI, G., Criminal Law
IMPALLOMENI, G. B., Roman Law
NOCILLA, D., Constitutional Law
QUERCI, F., Maritime Law
SANTA MARIA, A., International Law
VERBARI, G. B., Administrative Law

Faculty of Political Science:
BARBO, F., Philosophy
BIANCHI, G., History of Treaties and International Politics
CARON, P. G., History of Relations between State and Church
CRESPI, P., Sociology
GIORGIANNI, V., Political Science
GUASTINI, R., State Doctrine
OLIVETTI, M. M., Moral Philosophy

Faculty of Commerce and Economics:
BONETTI, E., Economic Geography
CALZOLARI, C., Science of the Properties and Quality of Commercial Products
CASELLI, C., General Law
CERMA, E., Technologies of Productive Cycles
CRISMA, L., Financial Mathematics
DABONI, L., Financial Mathematics
DE FERRA, C., General Mathematics
DEPOLLO, A., Economics
FANNI, M., Accountancy
FAVRETTO, L., Science of the Properties and Quality of Commercial Products
LINDA RONDINI, L., Statistics
PRESTAMBURGO, M., Agrarian Economy and Politics
RONDINI, O., Industrial and Commercial Techniques
SARTORATI, G., Science of Finance and Financial Law
TAGLIAFERRI, A., Economic History
VALUSSI, G., Applied Geography
WEDLIN, A., Econometrics

Faculty of Letters and Philosophy:
AGNELLI, A., History of Political Teachings
BOZZI, P., Methodology of Sciences of Behaviour
CANCIANI, F., Archaeology of Roman Provinces
CASSOLA, F., Roman History
CORBATO, C., Greek Literature
DORFLES, A., Aesthetics
DORIA, M., Glottology
FRANCESCATO, G., Linguistics
GIOSEFFI, D., History of Medieval and Modern Art
KANIZSA, G., Psychology
LEGRENZI, P., Psychology
LUCCIO, R., Applied Psychology
MAGRIS, C., German Language and Literature
MICCOLI, G., Medieval and Modern History
MIRABELLA ROBERTI, M., Christian Archaeology
NEGRELLI, G., History of Political Doctrines
ROSSI-LANDI, F., Theoretical Philosophy
TULLIO-ALTAN, C., Cultural Anthropology
PETRONIO, G., Italian Literature

Faculty of Education:
CUCAGNA, A., Geography
D'ARONCO, G., History of Popular Tradition
DEROSSI, G., Philosophy
MAIER, B., Modern Philology and Italian Literature
PETRINI, F., Education
ROSELLINI, A., French Language and Literature
ROSSI, R., Roman History
TAMPIERI, G., Psychology
TREMOLI, P., Latin Literature
VERGA, L., Moral Philosophy
PETTOELLO MANTOVANI, L., Criminal Law

Faculty of Medicine:
BONIFACIO, A., Forensic Medicine and Insurance
BOSATRA, A., Oto-Rhino-Laryngology
BRANCATO, R., Ophthalmology
CAMPAILLA, G., Psychiatry
CAMPANACCI, L., Special Medical Pathology
CAZZATO, G., Mental and Nervous Diseases
DALLA PALMA, L., Radiology
DE BERNARD, Biological Chemistry
FERUGLIO, F. S., General Medicine
FILIPPI, G., Medical Genetics
FUSAROLI, P., Human Anatomy
GIARELLI, L., Pathological Anatomy and Histology
GOBBATO, F., Industrial Medicine
LEGGERI, A., Special Surgical Pathology
MAJORI, L., Hygiene
MOCAVERO, G., Anaesthesiology
MONTI, G., General Clinical Surgery
MONTI BRAGADIN, C., Microbiology
NORDIO, S., Puericulture
PANIZON, F., Paediatrics
PIETRI, P., Surgical Semiotics
ROCCA ROSSETTI, S., Urology
ROSSI, F., General Pathology
SCARPA, C., Dermatology and Skin Diseases
SILLA, M. A., Dentistry
SPANIO, P., Obstetrics and Gynaecology
VIGLIANI, F., Orthopaedics

Faculty of Mathematics, Physics and Natural Sciences:
BARBON, R., Astronomy
BERTOCCHI, L., Quantum Mechanics
BRAMBATI, A., Sedimentology
BRESADOLA, S., General and Inorganic Chemistry
BUDINI, P., Theoretical Physics
CERNIGOI, C., General Physics
COLAUTTI, M. P., Mathematical Analysis
COSTA, G., Physical Chemistry
DE ALTI, G., Physical Chemistry
FIDECARO, G., Experimental Elementary Particle Physics
FINETTI, I., Applied Geophysics
FOA, L., General Physics
FONDA, L., Theoretical Physics
FURLAN, G., Elementary Particle Physics
GHIRARDELLI, E., Zoology
GHIRARDI, G., Theoretical Physics
GRAZIANI, M., General and Inorganic Chemistry
HACK DE ROSA, M., Astronomy
HONSELL, E., Plant Physiology
IENGO, R., Theoretical Physics
LAUSI, D., Botany
MOSETTI, F., Oceanographical Measurements
PERMUTTI, R., Algebra
PIGNATTI, A., Botany
POIANI, G., Higher Physics
POLDINI, L., Botany
PREDONZAN, A., Analytical Geometry
RANZOLI, F., Comparative Anatomy
RISALITI, A., Organic Chemistry
STOLFA, D., Mineralogy
TOSI, M., Materials Structure
VENZO, G. A., Geology and Palaeontology
VIDOSSICH, G., Phytogeography
WIKUS PIGNATTI, E., Spectroscopy
ZADRO BOZZI, M., Terrestrial Physics
ZERBI, G., Spectroscopy

Faculty of Pharmacy:
BALDINI, L., Pharmacology and Pharmacognosy
RUNTI, C., Applied Pharmaceutical Chemistry
SCIORTINO, T., Pharmaceutical Technology
SOTTOCASA, G. L., Biological Chemistry
VERTUA, R., Pharmacology and Pharmacognosis

Faculty of Engineering:
AMODEO, A., Road, Railway, Airport Construction
ANTONINI, A., Machinery
BATTI, P., Technology of Materials and Applied Chemistry
BENCO, C., Electrical Engineering
CAROZZO, M. T., Mineral Geophysics
COCCO, A., Applied Chemistry
COMINI, G., Technical Physics
CORZIANI, T., Microwaves
COSTA, R., Technical Architecture
DELCARO, L., Applied Electronics
D. MARINO, F., Applied Mechanics
DOLCHER, M., Mathematical Analysis
FERRARA, G., Mineral Arts
FINZI CONTINI, B., Technical Physics
FRATEILI, E., Planning
GUACCI, A., Design
LONGO, G., Informatica
LONGO, V., Technology Materials
MACHNE, G., Complements of Hydraulics
MARZOLLO, A., Complements of Automatics
MATERNINI, M., Technique and Economy of Transport
MAURO, A., Constructions in Wood, Iron and Reinforced Concrete
MILO, S., Control System Technology
MORELLI, C., Applied Geophysics
PELLIS, P., Traffic Organization
POLICASTRO, M., Automation and Control
TONTI, E., Rational Mechanics
VOLCIC, A., Mathematical Analysis

UNIVERSITÀ DEGLI STUDI DI UDINE

VIA ANTONINI 8, UDINE

Telephone: 0432 27105.

Founded 1977.

Rector: Prof. ANTONIO SERVADEI.
Librarian: Dr. CARLO BATTISTI.

Library of 45,000 vols.
Number of teachers: 65.
Number of students: 1,700.

DEANS:

Faculty of Modern Languages: R. GUSMANI.
Faculty of Engineering: G. GRANDORI.
Faculty of Science: B. MARTINIS.
Faculty of Literature: L. PROSDOCIMI.
Faculty of Agriculture: M. BONSEMBIANTI.

UNIVERSITÀ DEGLI STUDI DI VENEZIA

PALAZZI FOSCARI E GIUSTINIAN DEI VESCOVI, VENICE

Telephone: 85-420.

Founded 1868, formerly Istituto Universitario di Economia e Commercio e di Lingue e Letterature Straniere.

Rector: Prof. F. BENVENUTI.
Administrative Director: Dott. F. STUMPO.

Librarian: Dott. S. CORRADINI.

Number of students: 9,898.

DEANS:

Faculty of Economics and Commerce: Prof. G. CASTELLINI.

Faculty of Foreign Languages and Literature: Prof. M. BARATTO.

Faculty of Letters and Philosophy: Prof. G. MAZZARIOL.

Faculty of Industrial Chemistry: Prof. L. CATTALINI.

PROFESSORS:

Faculty of Economics and Commerce:
- BENVENUTI, F., Public Law
- BERTONI, A., Banking and Professional Techniques
- CASTELLANI, G., Financial Mathematics
- FOIS, C., Commercial Law
- FRANCHI, G., Private Law
- FRANCO, G., Economic and Financial Politics
- GUARINI, A., General and Applied Accountancy
- LANDO, F., Economic Geography
- MEOLI, U., History of Economic Thought
- ROSSI, F. P., Labour Law
- ZANARDI, G., Statistics

Faculty of Foreign Languages and Literature:
- MEO ZILIO, G., History of Iberian Languages
- MEREGALLI, F., Spanish Language and Literature
- NICOLETTI, G., French Language and Literature
- PEROSA, S., Anglo-American Language and Literature
- ROMERO MUNOZ, C., Spanish Language and Literature
- SABATTINI, M., Chinese Language and Literature
- SCARCIA, G., Iranian Language and Literature
- STRADA, V., Russian Language and Literature
- ZANETTO, G., Geography

Faculty of Letters and Philosophy:
- BERENGO, M., History of Political and Social Institutions
- COZZI, G., Modern History
- MAZZARIOL, G., History of Contemporary Art
- MICHELINI TOCCI, F., History of Religion
- ORLANDO, F., French Language and Literature
- PADOAN, G., Humanist and Italian Literature
- SEVERINO, E., Theoretical Philosophy
- TRAVERSARI, G., Archaeology and History of Greek and Roman Art
- TREVES, P., Greek History

Faculty of Industrial Chemistry:
- CATTALINI, L., General and Inorganic Chemistry
- CESCON, P., Analytic Chemistry
- DEJAK, C., Physical Chemistry
- GHERSETTI, S., Organic Chemistry
- MERLIN, M., Experimental Physics
- MERLIN HIEKE, O., Mineralogy
- ORIO, A. A., General and Inorganic Chemistry
- PASSERINI, R., Industrial Chemistry
- PUPPI, G., Experimental Physics

POLITECNICO DI MILANO

PIAZZA LEONARDO DA VINCI 32, 20133 MILAN

Telephone: 292101.

Founded 1863.

Academic year: November to October.

Rector: Prof. Dott. Ing. LUIGI DADDA.

Administrative Director: Dott. PIETRO ORSOLINI.

Librarian: **Dott. Ing. LORENZO LUNELLI.**

Number of students: 20,441.

DEANS:

Faculty of Engineering: Prof. Dott. CESARE CARDANI.

Faculty of Architecture: Prof. BERNARDO SECCHI.

POLITECNICO DI TORINO

CORSO DUCA DEGLI ABRUZZI 24, 10128 TURIN

Telephone: 55.16.16.

Founded 1859.

Higher Institute of Engineering and Architecture.

Academic year: November to October.

Rector: Prof. R. RIGAMONTI.

Vice-Rector: Prof. G. MICHELETTI.

Administrative Director: Dott. D. GUELFO.

Librarians: Ing. G. TRIVERO (Faculty of Engineering), Prof. R. GABETTI (Faculty of Architecture).

Library of 18,000 vols.

Number of teachers: 626.

Number of students: 12,000.

DEANS:

Faculty of Architecture: Prof. M. ROGGERO.

Faculty of Engineering: Prof. A. BURDESE.

School of Aerospace Engineering: Prof. E. ANTONA.

School of Graphic Art and Science: Prof. C. GORIA.

HEADS OF DEPARTMENT:

Faculty of Engineering:
- *Technical Architecture:* M. OREGLIA.
- *Mining:* L. STRAGIOTTI.
- *General and Applied Chemistry and Metallurgy:* V. CIRILLI.
- *Industrial Chemistry:* U. FASOLI.
- *Machine Design:* R. GIOVANNOZZI.
- *Electronics and Telecommunications:* G. ZITO.
- *General Electrotechnics:* G. FIORIO BELLETTI.
- *Experimental Physics:* F. DEMICHELIS.
- *Technical Physics and Nuclear Plants:* V. FERRO.
- *Economic and Applied Geology:* S. ZUCCHETTI.
- *Electrical Engines:* F. DONATI.
- *Aircraft Machines and Engines:* M. ANDRIANO.
- *Mathematics:* P. P. CIVALLERI.
- *Applied Mechanics, Aerodynamics and Gas Dynamics:* A. ROMITI.
- *Rational Mechanics:* S. NOCILLA.
- *Automotive Engineering:* P. CALDERALE.
- *Aircraft Design:* E. ANTONA.
- *Structural Mechanics and Strength of Materials:* F. LEVI.
- *Constructions:* G. OBERTI.
- *Mechanical Technology:* G. F. MICHELETTI.
- *Topography:* B. ASTORI.
- *Transport and Industrial Management:* A. RUSSO FRATTASI.

Faculty of Architecture:
- *General and Applied Chemistry:* C. GORIA.
- *Technology of the Built Environment:* G. CIRIBINI.
- *Architectural Criticism and Design:* C. OLMO.
- *Architectural and Programming Systems Science:* G. DONATO.
- *Architectural Methodology and Design:* G. VARALDO.
- *Town and Country Planning and Design:* G. P. ZUCCOTTI.
- *Structural Mechanics and Strength of Materials:* G. PIZZETTI.
- *History of Architecture:* D. DE BERNARDI.

OTHER UNIVERSITIES, COLLEGES AND INSTITUTES

UNIVERSITÀ DEGLI STUDI

PIAZZA DELL'ANNUNZIATA 1, 67100 L'AQUILA

Telephone: 27547.

Telex: 600213.

Founded 1952.

Private control; state recognition 1977

Rector: Prof. GIULIANO SORANI.

Registrar: **Dr. LAURA PAONI.**

Library of 85,000 vols.

Number of teachers: 132.

Number of students: 5,250.

DEANS:

Faculty of Sciences: Prof. ADALBERTO BALZAROTTI.

Faculty of Engineering: Prof. GIOVANNI SCHIPPA.

Faculty of Education: Prof. GIUSEPPE PROFETA.

PROFESSORS:

- ADORISIO, I., Techniques and Economics of Transport
- BALZAROTTI, A., Physics
- BISCOGLI, L., Architecture
- BRIGNOLI, P., Zoology
- DI CASTRO, C., Physics
- GAUDIANO, G., Chemistry
- GIACHERY, E., Education
- MARTINELLI, L., Education
- MESSINA, U., Hydraulics
- PETRUCCI, D., Biology
- PROFETA, G., Education
- REA, C., Geometry
- SCHIPPA, G., Applied and Industrial Chemistry
- SORANI, G., Geometry
- VACCARO, M., Geometry

EUROPEAN UNIVERSITY INSTITUTE

VIA DEI ROCCETTINI 5,
50016 FIESOLE, FLORENCE
Telephone: (055) 477-931.

Founded 1972 by the European Economic Community.

Academic year: September to June; official Institute languages: German, French, Italian, English, Dutch, Danish.

President: Max Kohnstamm.
Secretary: Marcello Buzzonetti.
Librarian: K. W. Humphreys.

Library of 150,000 vols.

Number of teachers (full-time): 25.
Number of students: *c.* 110.

PROFESSORS:

Department of History and Civilization:
Cipolla, C.
Ludlow, P.
Riis, T.
Wilson, C.

Department of Economics:
De Cecco, M.
Duquesne de la Vinelle, L.
Fitoussi, J.-P.
Shonfield, Sir Andrew
Streit, M. E.
Willke, G. P

Department of Law:
Cappelletti, M.
Hand, G.
Hopt, K.
Meny, Y.

Department of Political and Social Sciences:
Cranston, M.
Flora, P.
Georgel, J.
Moulakis, A.
Wildenmann, R.

UNIVERSITÀ CATTOLICA DEL SACRO CUORE

(Catholic University of the Sacred Heart)

LARGO A. GEMELLI 1,
20123 MILAN
Telephone: 8856.

Founded 1920; recognised by the Government 1924.

Rector: Prof. G. Lazzati.
Administrative Officer: Dott. D. Lofrese.
Librarian: Dott. V. Foffano.

Number of teachers: 452 professors.
Number of students: 20,109.

Publications: various, published by individual Faculties.

DEANS:

Faculty of Law: Prof. A. Crespi.
Faculty of Political Sciences: Prof. G. Miglio.
Faculty of Economics and Commerce: Prof. A. Confalonieri.
Faculty of Letters and Philosophy: Prof. A. Bausola.
Faculty of Higher Education: Prof. S. Cigada.
Faculty of Agrarian Sciences: Prof. G. Piana.
Faculty of Medicine: Prof. A. Sanna.
Faculty of Mathematical, Physical and Natural Sciences: Prof. G. Melzi.
Department of Religious Sciences: Prof. Luigi Pizzolato.

UNIVERSITÀ COMMERCIALE LUIGI BOCCONI

VIA R. SARFATTI 23,
20136 MILAN
Telephone: 8384-1.
Founded 1902.

President: Sen. Prof. G. Spadolini.
Rector: Prof. I. Gasparini.
Administrative Director: Dott. E. Resti.
Librarian: Dott. Anna Bacigalupo.

Number of teachers: 340.
Number of students: 5,277.

Publications: *Giornale degli Economisti e Annali di Economia, Economia delle fonti di energia.*

DEANS:

Department of Economics: Prof. I. Gasparini.
Department of Business Administration: Prof. R. Ruozi.

DIRECTORS:

Department of Economics:
Institute of Political Economics: Prof. I. Gasparini.
Institute of Quantitative Methods: Prof. F. Brambilla.
Institute of Economic History: Prof. A. de Maddalena.
Institute of Comparative Law: Prof. Ariberto Mignoli.
Computer Centre: Prof. G. Faini.
Centre for Economic and Social Studies for East Asia: Prof. I. Gasparini.
Centre for Studies in Economics of Labour: Prof. A. Predetti.
Centre for Studies and Research in Comparative Politics: Prof. G. Urbani.
Centre for Management Studies: Prof. I. Gasparini.
Institute of Latin-American Studies: (vacant).
Research Centre for Public Sector Economics: Prof. E. Gerelli.

Department of Business Administration:
Institute of Business Administration: (vacant).
Institute of Economics of Industrial and Commercial Companies: Prof. G. Pivato.
Institute for Studies of the Stock Exchange: Prof. G. Pivato.
Institute of Energy Economics: Prof. S. Vacca.
Research Centre on Distributive Trade: Prof. A. Spranzi.
Research Centre for Health Care Management: Dr. E. Borgonovi.
Research Centre for Organizational Behaviour: Prof. A. Rugiadini.
Centre for Economic and Business Research: Prof. A. Bertoni.
School of Business Administration: Prof. T. Bianchi.

PROFESSORS:

Bianchi, T., Banking
Brambilla, F., Statistics
Coda, V., Business Administration
De Maddalena, A., Economic History
Gasparini, I., Political Economics
Guatri, L., Marketing
Masini, C., Business Administration
Mignoli, A., Commercial Law
Monti, M., Monetary Theory and Policy
Pivato, G., Industrial Economics
Predetti, A., Economic and Financial Policy
Ruozi, R., Banking
Scalfi, G., Private Law, Public Law

UNIVERSITÀ DEGLI STUDI DI URBINO

VIA SAFFI 2, 61029 URBINO
Telephone: (0722) 31-41

Founded 1506; Private control; state recognition 1977.

Rector: Prof. Dott. C. Bo.
Administrative Director: Dott. G. Rossi.
Librarian: (vacant).

Number of teachers: 625, including 450 professors.
Number of students: 13,495.

Publications: *Studi Urbinati—A* (Law and Economics), *Studi Urbinati—B* (History, Philosophy and Literature), *Studi Urbinati—C* (Pharmacy), *Notizie da Palazzo Albani* (Art Review), *Annuario, L'Università Urbinate* (monthly).

DEANS:

Faculty of Jurisprudence: G. Gualandi.
Faculty of Economics and Commerce: P. Pettenati.
***Faculty of Letters and Philosophy:* B. Gentili.**
Faculty of Education: P. Salvucci.
***Faculty of Pharmacy:* G. Fornaini.**
Faculty of Mathematics, Physics and Natural Sciences: C. Bo.

PROFESSORS:

Faculty of Jurisprudence:
Antonelli, S., Institutions of Public Law and Constitutional Law
Ballarino, T., State Doctrine
Barettoni Arleri, A., National Accountancy and Administration
Beduschi, C., History of Roman Law
Bo, C., Spanish and French
Braghin, P., Sociology
Cagnazzo, O., Commercial Law
Cignoli, P., Statistics
Coscia, G., International Private Law
De Francesco, G. V., Penal Commercial Law
De Lorenzi, V., Private Law
Del Vecchio, A. M., International Organizations
Fabroni, F., Forensic and Insurance Medicine and Criminal Anthropology
Ferrari Bravo, D., Russian
Ferri, C., Civil Procedural Law
Granelli, A. E., Financial and Tax Law

GUALANDI, G., Roman Law and San Marino Law
GUALTIERI, P., Legal Constitutions
MAGRI, P., Afro-Asian Institutions
MANCINI, I., Philosophy of Law
MANTOVANI, S., Political Economics
MARI, L., History of Treaties and International Politics
MOLTENI, G., Ecclesiastical and Economic Law
NEGRI, G., Institutions of Roman Law
PALEARI, E., Comparative Private Law
PANSINI, G., Penal Prodecure
PANSOLLI, L., History of Italian Law
PARLATO, V., Canon Law
PENT FORNENGO, G., Political Economy
PEREGO, E., Civil Law
PERUZZI, P., Common Law
PERSI, P., Political and Economic Geography
POLITI, M., International Law
REY, M., Financial Science
RIZZARDI, A., English Language
RUDAN, MARINA, Labour Law
STENDARDI, G., Administrative Law
STILE, A. M., Penal Law and Criminology
TANTURRI DE HORATIO, R., History of Political Doctrine
TARQUINIO, O., Finance and Financial Law
TORTORANO, F., Industrial Law
ZECCHINO, O., Legal Institutions and Penal Procedure
ZENOBI, B. G., Modern History

Faculty of Letters and Philosophy:

ANGELINI, W., History of the Risorgimento and Modern History
ASSUNTO, R., Aesthetics
BALDUCCI, S., History of the Italian Language
BARATTA, G., Logic
BARBUTO, A., Sociology of Literature
BELPASSI, P., Pedagogics
BERNARDINI, P., Greek and Roman Antiquities
BISI, A. M., Near Eastern Archaeology
BOGLIOLO, G., French
BONIFAZI, N., Italian
BRESCHI, G., Romance Philology
BROGI, G., Slavic Philology
BRUSCIA, M., Critical History
CAGLI, B., History of Theatre
CECCHINI, F. M., Contemporary History
CIARLETTA, NICOLA, Moral Philosophy
COMBA JERVIS, L., Psychology
COMOTTI, G., History of Greek and Roman Theatre
CONSIGLIO, F., Philosophy of Law
DEAN, M., Geography
DONDOLI, L., History of Historiography
FERRARI BRAVO, D., Russian
FERRERO, M. C., Japanese
FORSTER SCARDIGLI, B., Roman History
FRANCESCHI, T., Dialectology
FRANCHI DE BELLIS, A., General Linguistics
GALLI, F., Latin Epigraphy
GASPARRI, C., Archaeology, History of Greek and Roman Art
GATTUCCI, A., History of Christianity and Medieval History
GENTILI, B., Greek Literature and Greek and Latin Metric Verse
GIANCOTTI, E., History of Modern Philosophy
GIANNINI, P., Greek Dialectology
HAMILTON, A., English
ILLUMINATI, A., Sociology
KAMMERER, P., History of Economic Doctrines
KRIPPENDORF, E., Philosophy of History
LACORTE, C., Theoretical Philosophy
LUNI, M., Ancient Topography
LUZI, A., History of Modern Literature
MANACORDA, G., German Language and Literature
MANCINI, A., Glottology
MANIERI, F., Methodology and Practice of Social Research
MASSENZIO, M., History of Religion
MASTROMATTEI, R., Anthropology
MAZZINI, I., Greek and Latin Grammar
MOGGI, M., Greek History
PASTORINO, A., Early Christian Literature
PEDROCCO, G., History of Science
PERUSINO, F., Greek and Latin Philology
PIRONTI, A., History of Music
PRETAGOSTINI, R., Greek Grammar
QUESTA, C., Latin Literature
SAVOIA, L. M., General Linguistics
VECCHIOTTI, I., History of Philosophy and Oriental Religions
VENTURELLI, G., History of Popular Traditions
VITALI, R., History of Ancient Philosophy
VYHNANKOVA, V., Czechoslovakian
ZAMPETTI, P., History of Art
ZUFFA, M., Archaeology, Etruscology and Palaeontology

Faculty of Education:

ABBATECOLA, G., Industrial Sociology
ANSELMI, S., Economic History
ARBIZZONI, G., Humanistic Literature
BAJARDI CERBONI, G., Italian Language
BEDESCHI, L., History of Political Parties and Movements
BERTONINI, A., Children's Literature
BO, C., French and Spanish Language and Literature
BOLDRINI, S., History of Latin Language
BONIFAZI, N., Italian Language and Literature
BRAGHIN, P., Sociology
BRANCATI, A., Roman History
BRUSCIOTTI, B., Social Legislation
BUTTIGLIONE, R., Political Philosophy
CAPPELLO GUARINO, F., Sociology of Labour
CARUGATI, F., Social Psychology
CATOLFI, C., Geography
CECCHINI, E., Medieval Latin Literature
CERRATO, R., Modern History
CIACCI, M., Sociology
CODIGNOLA, L., History of the Theatre
CUCCU, R., History of the Cinema
DEI, M., Sociology of Education
DE SANCTIS, N., Logic
DEL NINNO, M., General Linguistics
ERCOLANI, P., History of Economic Doctrines
FABBRI, P., Socio-linguistics
FABI, A., Pedagogics
FILOGRASSO, N., Pedagogy and History of Education
FONTANA, W., Medieval and Modern Art
GARULLI, E., History of Modern Philosophy, Philosophy of Science
GASPARI, A., History of Pedagogy
GRASSI, P., Sociology of Religion
GRAZIOSI, B., Sociology of Law
LABBROZZI, E., Methodology and Didactics
LOSURDO, D., Philosophy of History
LUZI, M., Comparative Literature
MAGGIONO, G., History of Sociology
MANCINI, I., Philosophy
MARZOCCHI, S., Cultural Anthropology
MASSI, M., Philosophy of Law
MASCILLI MIGLIORINI, E., Sociology of Communication
MAZZONI, R., Social Research
MOLINELLI, R., Medieval and Modern History
NISI, C., Social Education
ORSELLO, G., International Organization
PAIONI, G., Romance Philology
PALA, L., History of Political Doctrines
PALMA, B., Institutions of Public Law
PERSI, P., Geography
PIERSANTI, U., Sociology of Art and Literature
POGGIALI, A., Sociology of Learning
POLIDORI, G., Political Economy
QUESTA, C., Latin Literature
RIPANTI, G., Philosophy of Religion
RIZZARDI, A., English and American Language and Literature
ROCCHEGGIANI, A., Statistics
ROSSI, S., Educational Psychology
ROZZI, R., Social Psychology
SALVUCCI, P., History of Philosophy and Moral Philosophy
SANTARELLI, E., Modern History
SCODITTI, G., Ethnology
SCRIBONI, G., Literary Criticism
SPADONI, A., Latin Grammar
TABONI, P., Political Sociology
TOMMASOLI, W., Medieval History
TRAPANESE, E. V., Sociology of Groups
VENTURI, G. A., Italian Language and Literature
VOGT, U., German Philology, Language and Literature
ZEPPIERI, C., French Language and Literature

Faculty of Pharmacy:

ACCORSI, A., Immunochemistry
ALBANO, A., Hygiene
BONSIGNORE, A., Industrial Toxicology
BORGOGELLI, E., Physics
BOSSÛ, M., Clinical Chemistry and Alimentation
CAPPELLINI, O., Human Anatomy
CARPI, P., Applied Pharmacology
DACHA, M., Applied Biochemistry
DIONIGI, C., Bromatological Chemistry
DURANTI, E., Organic and Applied Pharmaceutical Chemistry
FORNAINI, G., Biological Chemistry
GHIANDONI, G., Higher Mathematics
GIANOTTI, M., Experimental Chemistry
MAGNANI, M., Molecular Biology
MARRAS, O., Industrial Toxicology
MAZZOLI, G., Pharmaceutical Technology
MICHELI, M., Analytical Chemistry
MONTANARI, L., Natural Physiology
PENNA, M., Microchemistry
PETRUCCIANI, P., General Pathology
PIACENTINI, G., Laboratory Histology
PIATTI, E., Alimentation
RAULLI SCOCCIANTI, **MARIA, Mineralogy**
ROSSI, W., Pharmaceutical Chemistry and Toxicology
SALVATORI, A., Experimental Chemistry
SAMMARTINO, V., Hydrology
SCARAMELLA, P., Pharmaceutical Botany
SCARINCI, V., Pharmacology and Pharmacognosy
STACCIOLI, L., Experimental Chemistry
STRANO QUAGLIA, M. G., Pharmaceutical Plant and Machinery
TESTA, G., General and Inorganic Chemistry

Faculty of Economics and Commerce:

ALESSANDRINI, P., Financial Economics
ALLEVA, P., Labour Law
ANSELMI, S., History of Economics
BACCHIELLI, R., English Language
BALLONI, V., Industrial Economics and Politics
BARTOLA, A., Economics and Agrarian Politics
BECCHI COLIDA, A., Economic Geography
CALZA BINI, P., Sociology
CARINCI, F., Labour Law
CERRAI, A., Commercial Law
CIANI, A., Finance and Financial Law
CONTI, G., International Economics

CRIVELLINI, M., Political Economy
CUOMO, G., Industrial and Commercial Techniques
D'ALBERTI, M., Public Law of Economics
EMINENTE, G., Industrial and Commercial Practice, International Commerce
FUA, G., Political Economy and Finance
LIZZA, F., General and Applied Accountancy
LOKAR, A., Commerce
LUCIANETTI, C., General and Applied Accountancy
MANNA, D., Economic Statistics
MARIUCCI, L., Industrial Law
MARCHINI, I., General and Applied Accountancy
MASSERA, A., Public Law of Economy
MATTIOLI, E., Demography
MERLI SCALCETTI, V., German Language
MERLINI, A., Statistics
MURA, F., Institutions of Public Law
PACI, M., Economic Sociology
PAOLINELLI, Financial Mathematics
PESCIARELLI, E., History of Economic Doctrines
PETTENATI, Political Economy
PIACESI, S., French Language
POLIDORI, G., Transport Economics
RAGGETTI, G., Banking
REY, G., Political Economics
ROBERTI, P., Economic and Financial Policy, Economic Geography
ROBOTTI, L., Finance and Financial Law
ROPPO, V., Private Law
ROSINI, E., Tax Law
SANTEUSANIO, A., Statistics
SAURIN, M. R., Spanish Language
SERRANI ,D., Institutions of Public Law
SORI, E., Economic History
VACIAGO, G., Political Economics
VINCENZI, D., Private Law
VIOLA, CLARA, Financial and General Mathematics
VISANI, L., Mathematics

Faculty of Mathematics, Physics and Natural Sciences:

ATTANASI, O. A., Organic Chemistry
AUREGGI, A., Pathological Histology
BARTOLE, R., Terrestrial Physics
BELBUSTI, F., Human Biology
BERETTA, E., Biophysics
BISCHI, A., General and Inorganic Chemistry
BONI, E., General Chemistry
BORGIA, G. C., Geophysics
BRUNER, F., Analytical Chemistry
BRUNO, C., General Physiology
BRUSCOLINI, F., Microbiology
BUCCIARELLI, E., Normal Human Anatomy
CANESRARI, F., Cellular Biochemistry
CIABATTI, M., Physical Geography
COMATO, V., Micropalaeontology
CRESCENTINI, G., Physical Chemistry
DACHA, U., Comparative Biochemistry
DALLAPICCOLA, B., Genetics
DE DONATO, S., Microbiology
DEL GRANDE, P., Comparative Anatomy
DE RENZI, G., Ecology
DIDERO, M., Hydrogeology
DITONDO, U., Histology and Embryology
ELMI, C., Applied Geology
FARONI, D. G., Anthropology
FAZI, A., Enzymology
FERRARI, A., Palaeontology
FORNAINI, G., Biological Chemistry
GARGANO, M., General Biology
GAZZANELLI, G., Zoology
GIOMARO, G. M., Botany
GORI, U., Geotechnics
GRIANTI, F., Physics
GUERRERA, F., Topography and Cartography
MAGNANI, M., Molecular Biology
MANGINI, C., Cytogenetics and General Pathology
MARTELLI, G., Regional Geology
MASI, U., Geochemistry
NAPPI, G., Vulcanology
NORI BUFALINI G., Radiobiology
ODONE, L., Psychology
PEDEMONTE, G. M., Petrography
PERSI, P., Geography
PERUZZI, G., Comparative Endocrinology and Pharmacology
PETRI SCARAMELLA, P., Botany
PIATTI, E., Alimentation
RICCI, D., Plant Pathology
ROCCHEGGIANI, A., Statistics
SALVAGGIO, L., Hygiene
SOLIMANO, F., Mathematical Institutions
STELLA, F., Cytology
TOMADIN, L., Mineralogy
TROCCOLI, R., Biological and Laboratory Analysis, Human Anatomy
VETRANO, F., Experimental Physics
WEZEL-FORESE, C., Anatomy and Oceanography

UNIVERSITÀ ITALIANA PER STRANIERI

PALAZZO GALLENGA
06100, PERUGIA
Telephone: 64344.
Founded 1925.

Academic year: January to December.
Founded for the diffusion abroad of Italian language and culture; courses in Italian language and civilization to foreigners of all nationalities. There are courses in Advanced Culture on Italian institutions, literature, pedagogy, history of art, the geography of Italy, Italian history, and Italian thought throughout the centuries; also courses in Italian Language and Culture, divided into three sections: Preparatory, Intermediate, Advanced; there is also in the summer term a special course in Etruscology and a course for teachers of Italian abroad. Lectures and classes are given by Professors of Italian Universities, leading members of Academies, etc.

Rector: Prof. SALVATORE VALITUTTI.
Administrator: Dr. CARLO VIDONI GUIDONI.
Librarian: Mrs. LIANA LISCIO PELLICCIA.

Library of 58,000 vols.
Number of teachers: *c.* 105.
Number of students: 7,000.
Publication: *Vita dell'Università.*

ISTITUTO UNIVERSITARIO DI LINGUE E LETTERATURE STRANIERE

VIA SALVECCHIO 19,
24100 BERGAMO
Telephone: 21-71-95.
Founded 1968.

President: Prof. G. P. GALIZZI.
Registrar: Prof. G. SZEGÖ.
Librarian: Dr. C. PEDROLI.

Library of 38,000 vols.
Number of teachers: 161.
Number of students: 1,975.

ISTITUTO UNIVERSITARIO STATALE DI ARCHITETTURA

VIA CIMINO 2,
89100 REGGIO CALABRIA
Telephone: 90148.
Founded 1967.

Director: Prof. A. QUISTELLI.

Library of 8,000 vols.
Number of teachers: *c.* 50.
Number of students: *c.* 1,000.

INSTITUT UNIVERSITAIRE D'ÉTUDES EUROPÉENNES

CORSO VITTORIO EMANUELE 83,
10128 TURIN
Telephone: 553269–544193.
Founded 1952.

President: Prof. ANDREA COMBA.

ISTITUTO UNIVERSITARIO DI ARCHITETTURA

CAMPAZZO DEI TOLENTINI 191,
30125 VENICE
Telephone: 703377.
Founded 1926.

State control; Academic year: November to October.

Director: Prof. C. AYMONINO.
Administrative Director: Dott. P. POSSAMAI.
Librarian: MARIA LUISA BONALDI.

The library contains 10,000 vols.
Number of teachers: *c.* 60.
Number of students: 2,500.

ISTITUTO UNIVERSITARIO NAVALE

VIA AMMIRAGLIO ACTON 38,
80134 NAPLES

Telephone: 313.972, 313.975, 320.327.
Founded 1920.

Rector: Prof. GIANFRANCO PALERMO.
Secretary: Dott. M. VITO-COLONNA.

The library contains 47,500 vols.
Number of teachers: *c.* 60.
Number of students: *c.* 2,600.
Publication: *Annali.*

Faculties of nautical science and maritime economy.

ISTITUTO UNIVERSITARIO ORIENTALE

PIAZZA S. GIOVANNI
MAGGIORE 30, 80134 NAPLES
Founded 1732.

Director: Prof. G. GNOLI.

Administrative Director: Dott. C. GHEDUZZI.
Dean: Prof. Dott. L. PACINI.

LIBERA UNIVERSITÀ ABRUZZESE DEGLI STUDI G. D'ANNUNZIO

CITTÀ UNIVERSITARIA, VIA DEI VESTINI, COLLE DELL'ARA, 66100 CHIETI

Telephone: 56141.

Founded 1965; state recognition 1977.

President: Prof. BRUNO CAVALLO.
Registrar: Avv. ANTONIO CATALANO.

The library contains 180,000 vols.
Number of teachers: 600.
Number of students: 16,000.

LIBERA UNIVERSITÀ INTERNAZIONALE DEGLI STUDI SOCIALI IN ROMA
(Independent International University of Social Studies in Rome)

VIALE POLA 12, 00198 ROME

Telephone: 84.10.51.

Founded 1945, recognized by the Government 1966.

President: Dr. GUIDO CARLI.
Rector: Prof. ROSARIO ROMEO.
Registrar: Dr. GIOVANNI NOCCO.

Library of 41,300 vols. and 1,200 periodicals.

Number of teachers: 101.
Number of students: 1,072.

DEANS:

Faculty of Political Science: Prof. N. IRTI.
Faculty of Economics: Prof. M. DI LAZZARO.

LIBERA UNIVERSITÀ DEGLI STUDI DI TRENTO

VIA BELENZANI 12, 38100 TRENTO

Telephone: 81136.

Founded 1967.

Control: Province of Trento; Academic year: November to October.

President: Dott. Avv. BRUNO KESSLER.
Rector: Prof. F. FERRARI.
Administrative Director: Dott. T. ANDREOLLI.
Librarian: M. ZENATTI.

Library of 66,000 vols. and 2,200 periodicals.

Number of teachers: *c.* 114.
Number of students: 3,300.
Publications: various.

DEANS:

Faculty of Sociology: Prof. MARINO LIVOLSI.
Faculty of Mathematics, Physics and Natural Sciences: Prof. MARCO TOLLER.
Faculty of Economics: Prof. SERGIO ZANINELLI.

THE BOLOGNA CENTER SCHOOL OF ADVANCED INTERNATIONAL STUDIES OF THE JOHNS HOPKINS UNIVERSITY

VIA BELMELORO 11, 40126 BOLOGNA

Telephone: 232.185.

Telegraphic Address: Centro-JHU.

Founded 1955.

Academic year: September to May.

Objective: graduate work in international affairs.

Director: RONALD S. TIERSKY.
Registrar: KAY F. BUTLER.
Librarian: ALDO ROSSI.

Teachers from U.S.A., Italy, France, Great Britain, Germany, Turkey, Yugoslavia: 23.

Students from U.S.A., Italy, France, Austria, Germany, Great Britain, Benelux, Scandinavia, Greece, Spain, African, Asian and Latin American countries: 120.

Library of 70,000 vols.

Publications: *Bologna Center Catalogue, Discussion Paper Series.*

SCUOLA NORMALE SUPERIORE DI PISA

PIAZZA DEI CAVALIERI 7, 56100 PISA

Telephone: 43554.

Founded 1813.

Director: Prof. EDOARDO VESENTINI.
Librarian: Dssa. S. DI MAIO.

The library contains 280,000 vols.
Number of teachers: 45.
Number of students: 232.

Publications: *Annali* (Arts series, Science series), *Studi e Testi, Studi Linguistici e Filologici, Quaderni di Matematica, Testi umanistici inediti o rari, Italia dialettale.*

SCUOLA SUPERIORE ENRICO MATTEI E.N.I.

SAN DONATO MILANESE, MILAN, C.A.P. 20097

Telephone: 53533960.

Founded 1957.

President: Prof. F. FORTE.

Economic and management studies.

The library contains 15,000 vols.

Number of teachers: 25.

Number of students: annual intake of 40-50.

SCHOOLS OF MUSIC AND ART

MUSIC

Conservatorio di Musica, Santa Cecilia": via dei Greci 18, Rome.
Director: Maestro J. NAPOLI.

Conservatorio Statale di Musica G. B. Martini: Piazza Rossini 2, Bologna; f. 1804.
Director: A. ZECCHI.

Conservatorio di Musica G. Verdi: via del Conservatorio 12, Milan; f. 1808; library of 350,000 vols.
Director: MARCELLO ABBADO.
Librarian: Prof. AGOSTINA ZECCA LATERZA.

Conservatorio di Musica "Gioacchino Rossini": Piazza Olivieri 5, 61100 Pesaro; f. 1882; library of *c.* 25,000 vols.
Director: GHERARDO MACARINI CARMIGNANI.

Conservatorio Statale di Musica "Giuseppe Verdi": via Mazzini 11, Turin; f. 1867.
Director: Mo. S. FUGA.

Conservatorio Nazionale di Musica "Benedetto Marcello": Campo S. Stefano, Venice; f. 1877, reorganized 1940.
Director: Maestro G. BIANCHI.

Conservatorio di Musica Niccolò Piccinni: via Brigata Bari 26, Bari 70124; f. 1959; library of 11,000 vols.
Director: G. ROTA.
Secretary: Dr. V. A. DELLEGRAZIE.

Conservatorio Statale di Musica "C. Monteverdi": Piazza Domenicani 19, 39100 Bolzano; f. 1940; library of 8,700 vols.
Director: G. CAMBISSA.
Director of Secretariat: G. MATTIVI.
International Busoni Piano Competition held yearly.

Conservatorio Statale di Musica "G. Pierluigi da Palestrina": Via Bacaredda, Cagliari; f. 1939.
Director: NINO BONAVOLONTÁ.

Conservatorio di Musica "L. Cherubini": Piazzetta delle Belle Arti 2, Florence; f. 1861.
Director: Maestro F. SIFONIA.
Secretary: Dott. V. RUSSO.

Conservatorio di Musica "S. Pietro a Maiella": via S. Pietro a Maiella 35, Naples.
Director: Maestro B. MAZZOTTA.

Conservatorio di Musica "V. Bellini": via Squarcialupo 45, Palermo.
Director: V. MANNINO.

Conservatorio di Musica "A. Boito": via Conservatorio 27, Parma; f. 1825; library of 70,000 vols.
Director: P. GUARINO.

Conservatorio di Musica Giuseppe Tartini: via Carlo Ghega 12, Trieste.

ART

Accademia Albertina di Belle Arti: via Accademia Albertina 6, Turin; f. 1652; Pres. Prof. P. DELLE RONCOLE; Dir. Prof. S. SARONI; Sec. Dott. G. SIMONETTI.

Accademia di Belle Arti (*Academy of Fine Arts*): via Ricasoli 66, 50122 Florence; f. 1801; library of 22,000 vols.

Accademia di Belle Arti (*Academy of Fine Arts*): Palazzo di Brera, via Brera 28, 20121 Milan; f. 1776; library of 20,000 vols.; Pres. Dott. A. DE MICHELI; Dir. Arch. Prof. T VARISCO.

Accademia di Belle Arti (*Academy of Fine Arts*): Piazza S. Francesco 5, Perugia; f. 1546; 765 Academicians, 729 Hon. Academicians; collections of paintings, engravings, drawings, etc.; Summer Academy of Fine Arts (painting, sculpture, engraving) for foreigners; Pres. Ing. MARIO SERRA; Dir. Prof. GIORGIO ASCANI NUVOLO; Co-ordinator Prof. G. F. BISSIETTA.

Accademia di Belle Arti (*Academy of Fine Arts*): via di Roma 13, Ravenna; f. 1827; library of 5,000 vols.; Dir. Prof. C. SPADONI; Sec.-Gen. Rag. G. BUSTACCHINI.

Accademia di Belle Arti e Liceo Artistico (*Academy of Fine Arts*): via Belle Arti 54, 40126 Bologna; library of 15,000 vols.; Dir. Prof. E. PASQUALINI; Librarian S. ZAMBONI.

Accademia di Belle Arti e Liceo Artistico (*Academy of Fine Arts*): Palazzo Malaspina, Piazza dell'Accademia, 54033 Carrara; courses in painting, sculpture and scene-painting.

Accademia di Belle Arti e Liceo Artistico (*Academy of Fine Arts*): via Lombardia 7, 73100 Lecce; Dir. Dott. Prof. SPIZZICO.

Accademia di Belle Arti e Liceo Artistico (*Academy of Fine Arts*): via Bellini 36, Naples; f. 1838; library of 7,000 vols.; Dir. Prof. C. LORENZETTI.

Accademia di Belle Arti (*Academy of Fine Arts*): via Papireto 20, Palermo.

Accademia di Belle Arti e Liceo Artistico (*Academy of Fine Arts*): via Ripetta 222, 00186 Rome; Dir. Prof. MARCELLO AVENALI.

Accademia di Belle Arti (*Academy of Fine Arts*): Dorsoduro 1050, Venice; f. 1750; Dir. Prof. NEDO FIORENTIN.

Accademia Nazionale di Arte Drammatica "Silvio d'Amico": Lungotevere Mellini 10, 00193 Rome; f. 1935; Dir. Prof. RUGGERO JACOBBI.

Accademia Nazionale di Danza: Largo Arrigo VII 5, Castello dei Cesari (Aventino), 00153 Rome; f. 1948; Pres. CARLO SCARASCIA MUGNOZZA; Dir. GIULIANA PENZI.

Istituto Centrale del Restauro (*Central Institute for the Restoration of Works of Art*): Piazza S. Francesco di Paola 9, Rome.

Istituto d'Arte: Piazza Armi 16, Sassari; woodwork, metal work, weaving, painting, ceramics and architecture.

Istituto Statale d'Arte per la Ceramica: Corso Baccarini 17, Faenza; normal courses in Ceramic Technology; Higher courses of Industrial Design and Ceramic Technology, special courses for foreigners.

Istituto Statale d'Arte 'Enrico e Umberto Nordio': Via di Calvola, 34100 Trieste; f. 1955; furnishing and interior decorating; library of 5,112 vols.; Dir. Prof. REMO STASI.

Istituto Statale d'Arte: Piazza Duca Federico 1, Urbino; f. 1865; engraving, page-setting, lithography, bookbinding, photo-engraving (animated cartoons), ceramics; Pres. Prof. NICOLÓ NICOSIA.

Liceo Artistico Statale "Mattia Preti": Via Domenico Romeo 2, Reggio Calabria: Dir. Dott. Ing. G. PANI.

IVORY COAST

Population 7,613,000

RESEARCH INSTITUTES

(*see* also under University)

Bureau de Recherches Géologiques et Minières (BRGM): B.P. 1335, Abidjan; gold-mining stations at Ity, Aboisso, Toumodi, Toulepleu.

Centre des Sciences Humaines: B.P. 1600, Abidjan; f. 1960; ethnological and sociological research, especially in the cultural and religious field; museology, conservation, exhibitions; Dir. Dr. B. Holas; *see* also Musée de la Côte d'Ivoire.

Centre de Recherches Zootechniques: B.P. 449, Bouaké; Dir. M. Bouvier.

Centre National de Recherches Océanographiques: B.P. V18, Abidjan; biological oceanography, physics and chemistry, hydrobiology; aided and managed by ORSTOM (*see* under France).

Centre Technique Forestier Tropical: B.P. 8033, Abidjan; f. 1962; research in silviculture, wood technology and pisciculture; library of 1,800 vols.; Dir. Pierre Barbaud.

Direction de la Géologie et de la Prospection Minière: B.P. 1368, Abidjan; Dir. M. Bardet.

Institut Africain pour le Développement Economique et Social (INADES): 08 B.P. 8, Abidjan 08; f. 1962 by the Society of Jesus to promote the development of newly-independent countries; research in development planning, economics, sociology, ethnology; library of 35,000 vols., 400 periodicals; 18 staff; Dir. Eric de Rosny; publ. *Fichier-Afrique* (fortnightly).

INADES-Formation: f. 1972 to take over the training and advisory services of INADES; runs training sessions, correspondence courses and advisory service for rural areas; offices in 10 countries: Burundi, Cameroon, Chad, Ethiopia, Ivory Coast, Kenya, Rwanda, Togo, Upper Volta, Zaire; 140 staff; Dir. Gen. Philippe Dubin; publ. *Agripromo*† (quarterly).

Institut d'Elevage et de Médecine Vétérinaire des Pays Tropicaux: B.P. 449, Bouaké; Dir. M. Coulomb.

Institut d'Hygiène: Abidjan.

Institut des Savanes—Département des Cultures Vivrières (IRAT): B.P. 635, Bouaké; f. 1968; rice and maize breeding, rice pathology, entomology, agronomy and physiology; 25 mems.; library of 2,400 vols.; stations at Bouaké, Ferkessedougou, Gagnoa; Man. Dir. M. Poulain.

Institut de Recherches du Coton et des Textiles Exotiques (IRCT) (*Research Institute on Cotton and Tropical Textiles*): B.P. 604, Bouaké; f. 1946; 12 mems.; Dir. A. Angelini; publ. *Bulletin* (3 times a year).

Institut de Recherches pour les Huiles et Oléagineux (IRHO) (*Research Institute for Oils and Oily Substances*): B.P. 13, Bingerville; f. 1923; oil palm research (breeding, agronomy, pathology); coconut oil research station at Port Bouet.

Institut de Recherches sur le Caoutchouc (IRCA) (*Institute of Rubber Research*): 01 B.P. 1536, Abidjan 01; f. 1956; agronomy, physiology and technology; 12 staff; library of 800 vols.; Dir. P. Boyer; publ. *Revue Générale des Caoutchoucs et Plastiques*†.

Institut de Recherches sur les Fruits et Agrumes (I.R.F.A.): B.P. 1740, Abidjan.

Institut Français du Café et du Cacao (IFCC) (*Cocoa and Coffee Research Station*): B.P. 1827, Abidjan; f. 1958; library of 3,000 vols.; Dir. J. Capot; publ. *Café, Cacao, Thé*† (quarterly).

Station Centrale: Divo.

Bureaux et Laboratoires: Bingerville.

Station Régionale: Abengourou.

Centres d'essais multilocaux: San Pedro, Zagne.

Institut Pasteur de Côte d'Ivoire: 01 B.P. 490, Abidjan 01; f. 1972; research laboratories for the study of viral diseases, such as yellow fever, poliomyelitis, rabies, influenza, Burkitt lymphoma, lassa fever, etc.; clinical analysis laboratories used by the Centre Hospitalier Universitaire, Cocody; staff of 9 scientists, 14 technicians and 80 other employees; small library in process of formation; Dir. Dr. A. Chippaux.

Ministère de la Recherche Scientifique: Abidjan; f. 1971; scientific and financial programme co-ordinating research in the Ivory Coast in institutes and the university; Minister Prof. J. G. Lorougnon Guede; Dirs. C. J. du Plessix, M. Benon, M. Anibié.

Office de la Recherche Scientifique et Technique Outre-Mer (ORSTOM): B.P. 2002, Abidjan 08; f. 1946; Dir. B. Pouyaud. (*See* main entry under France).

Centre d'Adiopodoumé: B.P. V51, Abidjan; geology, pedology, hydrology, bioclimatology, petrography, botany and vegetal biology, biology and amelioration of plants, soil biology, vegetal physiology, applied zoology, agronomy, phytopathology, mammalogy, primatology, geography, cartography, entomology, genetics, virology; laboratory for utilization of radio isotopes; experimental biological station; library; Dir. J. Collinet.

Mission de Bouaké: B.P. 604, Bouaké; entomology, agronomy, hydrobiology; Dir. C. Fillonneau.

Station de Man: B.P. 434, Man; genetics.

Centre de Petit Bassam: B.P. 293, Abidjan 04; psychosociology, economics, demography, psychology, sociology; Dir. Y. Mersadier.

Société pour le Développement Minier de la Côte d'Ivoire—SODEMI: B.P. 2816, Abidjan 01; f. 1962; carries out a programme of geological exploration and mineral prospecting; library of 5,518 vols., 57 current periodicals, 456 geological or prospecting reports; Dir.-Gen. J. N'zi; publ. *Rapport annuel*.

Station Géophysique de Lamto: 01 B.P. 398, Abidjan 01; f. 1965; seismological and climatological studies; Dir. J. L. Tournier.

LIBRARIES

Archives Nationales: B.P. V126, Abidjan; f. 1957; Dir. Tchriffo Dominique; publ. *Warbica*† (2 a year).

Bibliothèque Centrale de la Côte d'Ivoire: Abidjan-Treichville, B.P. 6243; f. 1963; a service of the Ministry of

National Education; public lecture service; library: 14,000 volumes; founded with the help of UNESCO; Librarian P. ZELLI ANY-GRAH.

Bibliothèque Centrale de l'Université Nationale de Côte d'Ivoire: 08 B.P. 859, Abidjan; f. 1963; 64,000 vols. and 1,650 periodicals; Librarian Mme F. N'GORAN.

Bibliothèque du Centre Culturel Américain: B.P. 1866; Abidjan.

Bibliothèque du Centre Culturel Français: 01 B.P. 3995, 01 Abidjan; 19,000 vols., and 1,500 vols. in African section; documentation centre; periodicals and reviews of Black Africa and Madagascar; Dir. ANNE CROS.

Bibliothèque du Service d'Information: B.P. 1879, Abidjan.

Bibliothèque Municipale: Platena, Abidjan; 50,000 vols.

Bibliothèque Nationale: B.P.V. 180, Abidjan; f. 1968; scientific library of 30,000 vols. and 800 current periodicals; part of the former centre of the Institut Français d'Afrique Noire in the Ivory Coast; Dir. SEYDOU GUEYE; publ. *Bibliographie de la Côte d'Ivoire* (annual).

MUSEUM

Musée de la Côte d'Ivoire: B.P. 1600, Abidjan; exhibits of ethnographical, sociological, artistic and scientific nature; attached to the Centre des Sciences Humaines; Dir. Dr. B. HOLAS.

UNIVERSITY

UNIVERSITÉ NATIONALE DE CÔTE D'IVOIRE

01 B.P. V 34, ABIDJAN 01
Telephone: 43-90-00.

Founded as the Centre d'Enseignement Supérieur d'Abidjan 1958; University 1964.

Language of instruction: French.

Rector: Prof. V. DIARRASSOUBA.
General Secretary: Mlle SANGARET.
Librarian: Mme F. N'GORAN.

Number of teachers: 580.
Number of students: 12,765.

Publications: *Annales de l'Université, Bulletin des Instituts de Recherche.*

DEANS:

Faculty of Law: D. VEAUX.
Faculty of Letters: LANCINE SYLLA.
Faculty of Medicine: YANGNI ANGATE.
Faculty of Sciences: TOURE BAKARY.
Faculty of Economic Sciences: AUGUSTE LOUIS ANTOINE.

DIRECTORS:

Institute of Ethnosociology: M. DIABATE.
Institute of Applied Linguistics: PASCAL KOKORA.
Institute of Tropical Geography: ASSEYPO HAUHOUOT.
Institute of Tropical Ecology: M. DOSSO.
Institute of Odonto-Stomatology: J. VILLASCO.
Institute of Criminology: MARCEL ETTE.
Institute of African History of Art and Archaeology: LAURENT GBAGBO.
Institute of African Literature and Aesthetics: M. DAILLY.
Institute of Mathematical Research: SALIOU TOURE.
School of Pharmacy: A. RAMBAUD.
University Centre for French Studies: PIERRE N'DA.
University Centre for Information: BOURRIQUEN.
Centre for Audio-visual Teaching and Research: ALANGBA.
Centre for Studies and Research in Applied Psychology: JOSEPH AKA KOUADIO.
Centre for Architectural and Urban Research: KOFFI VANGAH.
National Centre for Flora: AKE ASSI.
Centre for Study and Research in Law: Mme PAULETTE VEAUX.
Centre for Economic and Social Research: HIEY PEGA-TIENAN.

COLLEGES

Ecole de Statistique d'Abidjan: B.P. 8003, Abidjan, Cocody; f. 1961; 95 students; library of 1,300 books; Dir. FRANÇOIS YATTIEN-AMIGUET.

Ecole Nationale d'Administration: B.P. V-20, Abidjan; f. 1960; 450 students; library of 10,500 vols.; Dir. ABDRAMANE HAMZA.

Ecole Nationale des Postes et Télécommunications: Abidjan.

Ecole Nationale Supérieure Agronomique: B.P. 8035, Abidjan; f. 1965; 5-year course; 20 full-time and 14 part-time staff; Dir. M. HUGUES.

Ecole Nationale Supérieure des Travaux Publics: B.P. 2279, Abidjan; f. 1962; comprises l'Ecole d'Ingénieurs and l'Ecole de Techniciens; 5-year course; library of 3,000 vols.; 67 teachers, 115 students; Dir. J. MOUY.

Institut National Supérieur de l'Enseignement Technique: B.P. V79, Abidjan; f. 1975; 120 teachers, 710 students; consists of the following institutions:

Ecole Supérieure de Commerce d'Abidjan.
Ecole Nationale Supérieure d'Ingénieurs d'Abidjan: f. 1976.
Institut de Technologie Tertiaire.
Institut de Technologie Industrielle.
Institut Supérieur d'Informatique.

JAMAICA

Population 2,137,000

LEARNED SOCIETIES AND RESEARCH INSTITUTES

Alliance Française: 3 March Drive, off Garth Rd., Kingston 8; f. 1951; brs. in Montego Bay and Mandeville; teaches French language; 1,250 mems.; 750 students; cultural club; library of 4,500 vols.; Pres. PROBYN V. MARSH; Dir. ROLAND R. DRIVON; publ. monthly bulletin.

Caribbean Food and Nutrition Institute (CFNI): Jamaica Centre, P.O.B. 140, Mona, Kingston 7; f. 1967; conducts research and training courses and provides technical advisory services to governments of the English-speaking Caribbean on matters relating to food and nutrition; there is a centre at Trinidad; library of *c.* 3,000 vols.; Dir. Dr. J. M. GURNEY; publs. *Cajanus*†, *Nyam News*, *Nutrient-Cost Tables* (quarterly).

Institute of Jamaica: 12–16 East St., Kingston; f. 1879; comprises the National Library of over 30,000 vols. and 50,000 items (responsible for National Bibliography); the Cultural Training Centre (schools of art, dance, drama and music); four Junior Cultural Centres; Natural History Division; Arawak (Indian) Museum; Jamaica Folk Museum; Museum of Traditional African Art and Craft; Archaeological Museum; the National Gallery of Jamaica; the African-Caribbean Institute; Exec. Dir. NEVILLE DAWES, M.A.; publs. *Bulletin* (Science Series), *Sloanea* (occasional papers in natural history), *Jamaica Journal* (quarterly), *Jamaican National Bibliography* (annual), *African-Caribbean Monographs*.

Institute of Social and Economic Research: *see* under University of the West Indies below.

Jamaican Association of Sugar Technologists: c/o Sugar Industry Research Institute, Mandeville; f. 1937 by the Local Sugar Industry to conduct research and investigate technical problems of the Jamaican sugar industry; 333 mems.; uses library of Sugar Industry Research Institute; Pres. W. A. KENNEDY; Sec. T. FALLOON; publ. *J.A.S.T. Journal* (annually).

Jamaica National Trust Commission: P.O.B. 473, Hope Gardens, Kingston 6; f. 1959; restoration and preservation of monuments of national, historical and architectural importance; Chair. V. S. REID.

Medical Association of Jamaica: 19 Ruthven Rd., Kingston 10; f. 1966; for the promotion of medical and allied sciences and of the medical profession; 300 mems.; Pres. Dr. K. HAGLEY; Sec. Dr. D. ASHLEY; publ. *News Letter* (monthly).

Medical Research Council Laboratories: University of West Indies, Mona, Kingston 7; attached to Medical Research Council, London; Dir. G. R. SERJEANT, M.D., F.R.C.P.

National Planning Agency: Office of the Prime Minister, P.O.B. 634, Kingston; f. 1955; for social and economic development projects; publs. *Economic Survey of Jamaica* (annually), development plans and irregular publications.

P.E.N. International (Jamaica Centre): c/o Institute of Jamaica, 14 East St., Kingston; f. 1947; 50 mems.; Pres. Mrs. JEANNE WILSON; Sec. GEORGE CLOUGH; publ. *Jamaica P.E.N. Bulletin* (2 a year).

Scientific Research Council: P.O.B. 350, Kingston 6; f. 1960; undertakes, fosters and co-ordinates scientific research in the island; departments of Mineral Resources (Ceramics and Mineralogy), Agro-Industry (Exploratory Natural Products Chemistry; Process Development), Food Science and Nutrition and Industrial Development; Technical Information (library); Council of 16 mems.; Chair./Dir. Dr. A. K. VENTURA; publs. *Journal of the SRC*† (2 a year), *Topical Notes*† (every 2 months), *Technical Paper*† (occasional).

Sugar Industry Research Institute of the Sugar Industry Authority: Kendal Rd., Mandeville; f. 1973; formerly Sugar Research Dept., Sugar Manufacturers' Association (of Jamaica) Ltd.; research in sugar cane production; laboratories; staff of 65; library of 660 vols.; Dir. of Research M. E. A. SHAW; publs. *Annual Report*†, *Annual Sugar Cane Production Cost Survey*†, *Sugar Cane*† (every 3 months), various technical bulletins.

LIBRARIES AND MUSEUM

Institute of Jamaica Library: (*see* above).

Institute of Jamaica Museum: (*see* above).

Jamaica Archives: Spanish Town; f. 1659; national archives of Jamaica; special collection of ecclesiastical records; Archivist C. V. BLACK.

Jamaica Library Service: P.O.B. 58, 2 Tom Redcam Drive, Kingston 5; f. 1948; provides an island-wide network of 574 service points, including parish libraries; branch libraries, book centres, and fourteen bookmobiles; total bookstock 1,097,025 vols.; a Schools Library Service has been operated since 1952 to primary and secondary schools, with a bookstock of 1,036,684 vols.; Dir. Miss LEILA T. THOMAS.

University of the West Indies Library: Mona, Kingston 7; f. 1948; 274,780 vols. including 10,000 periodicals in the Main Library and two branch libraries for the Medical (22,910 vols.) and Scientific (52,800 vols.) Collections; Librarian K. E. N. INGRAM, B.A., M.PHIL., F.L.A. (*see* also Barbados and Trinidad and Tobago).

UNIVERSITY

UNIVERSITY OF THE WEST INDIES

MONA, KINGSTON 7

Telephone: 92-76661.

Founded 1948, University 1962.

Serves Jamaica, Trinidad and Tobago, Barbados, Grenada, Saint Vincent and the Grenadines, Saint Lucia, Dominica, the British Associated States and Colonies in the Caribbean, and the Bahamas. The Faculties of Arts and General Studies, Natural Sciences, Social Sciences and School of Education are located on all three campuses. The Faculty of Law is in Barbados, Medicine in Jamaica, Agriculture and Engineering in Trinidad.

Chancellor: Sir ALLEN MONTGOMERY LEWIS, Kt., Q.C., LL.B.

Vice-Chancellor: A. Z. PRESTON, J.P., LL.B., F.C.A., F.C.C.A., F.C.I.S., F.R. ECONS.

Pro-Vice-Chancellors: F. R. AUGIER, M.A., PH.D., L. R. B. ROBINSON, M.A. (Planning), S. L. MARTIN, M.SC., A.R.C.S., D.I.C., F.R.I.C. (Principal, Cave Hill), Prof. L. E. S. BRAITHWAITE, B.A. (Principal, St. Augustine), Prof. G. C. LALOR, PH.D.

Registrar: C. E. JACKMAN, M.A., DIP.ED.

Librarian: K. E. INGRAM, B.A., M.PHIL., F.L.A.

Number of teachers: 760.
Number of students: 8,041.

Publications: *Calendar*†, *Caribbean Quarterly*†, *Vice-Chancellor's Report*, *Departmental Reports*†, *Social and Economic Studies*†, *West Indian Medical Journal*†

DEANS AND VICE-DEANS AT MONA:

Faculty of Arts and General Studies: Dr. N. A. T. HALL.

School of Education: Dr. T. TURNER.

Faculty of Medicine: Dr. W. N. GIBBS (Clinical), Dr. E. V. ELLINGTON (Pre-Clinical).

Faculty of Natural Sciences: Dr. M. G. R. AUB.

Faculty of Social Sciences: G. E. EDMONDSON, M.A., PH.D.

PROFESSORS:

AHMAD, N., Agriculture—Soil Science
ALLEYNE, G. A. O., Medicine
ANNAMUNTHODO, Sir HARRY, Clinical Surgery
BAUGH, E., English
BECKFORD, G., Economics
BROOKS, S. E. H., Pathology
BUISSERET, D., History
COORE, H. G., Biochemistry
CROSS, J., Neurosurgery
FRANCIS, A. A. J., Applied Economics
CRAIG, D. R., Language Education
GOLDING, J. S. A., Tropical Orthopaedics and Rehabilitation
GOODBODY, I. M., Zoology
GOVEIA, ELSA V., West Indian History
HALL, D. G. H., History
HARLAND, P., Child Health
HOMI, J., Anaesthetics
KENT, G. S., Physics
LALOR, G. C., Chemistry
MELVILLE, G. N., Physiology
MILLS, G. E. M., Public Administration and Director of Training in Public Administration
NETTLEFORD, R. N., Extra-Mural Studies
NIEDERREITER, H., Mathematics
PERSAUD, V., Anatomical Pathology
PHILLIPS, A. S., Education
PICOU, D., Experimental Medicine
REID, L. H. E., Education
RICHARDS, R., Medicine
ROBERTS, G. W., Demography
ROBINSON, E., Geology
SIDRAK, G., Botany
STANDARD, K. L., Social and Preventive Medicine
TIK LIEN, Anatomy
WILLIAMS, R. L., Accounting
WYNTER, H. H., Obstetrics and Gynaecology

ATTACHED INSTITUTES:

Caribbean Agricultural Research and Development Institute: Dir. REGINALD PIERRE, M.SC., PH.D.

Department of Extra Mural Studies.
Director: R. M. NETTLEFORD, B.PHIL.

Creative Arts Centre: f. 1967; the Centre's programme includes: term-to-term activity in Painting, Sculpture, Dance, Theatre, Writing, Exhibitions, Readings, etc.; acting as the home for I.C.C. Week activities; the mounting of a small Caribbean Arts Festival.
Secretary: (vacant).

Institute of International Relations: Dir. BASIL A. INCE (acting).

Institute of Social and Economic Research.
Director: V. LEWIS, M.A., PH.D.

Trade Union Education Institute.
Director of Studies: R. M. NETTLEFORD, B.A., B.PHIL.

COLLEGES

COLLEGE OF ARTS, SCIENCE AND TECHNOLOGY

237 OLD HOPE RD., KINGSTON 6

Founded 1958.

Principal: Dr. A. W. SANGSTER, PH.D.
Registrar: P. C. CRAWFORD.

Number of teachers: 144 full-time, 106 part-time.

Number of students: 1,580 full-time, 1,100 part-time, 700 evening.

Library of 25,000 vols.

Full-time and part-time courses for Diplomas and Certificates in Mechanical, Electrical, and Construction Engineering, Land and Quantity Surveying, Banking, Computing, Business Administration, Institutional Management, Medical Technology, Instrument Technology, Pharmacy and Technical Teacher Training; other courses lead to professional recognition in various fields including accounting, banking, computing and marketing.

SCHOOL OF AGRICULTURE

TWICKENHAM PARK, SPANISH TOWN

Founded 1910.

Principal: Dr. W. E. NELSON.

Number of teachers: *c.* 30.
Number of students: 450.

Three-year courses in agricultural economics, agronomy, agricultural engineering, animal husbandry, botany, chemistry, English, extension education, geology, physics, soils, surveying, zoology, veterinary science, etc., leading to Diploma in Agriculture.

JAPAN

Population 115,174,000

ACADEMY

NIPPON GAKUSHIIN
(Japan Academy)

UENO PARK, TOKYO

Founded 1879.

The Japan Academy—which is a member of the International Union of Academies—is an honorary organization which affords membership and preferential treatment to those who have made outstanding contributions to the advancement of science and learning.

President: Dr. KIYOO WADATI.

Secretary-General: Prof. HIROMI ARISAWA.

Total number of members: 135.

Publications: *Proceedings: Series A, Series B* (10 a year), *Nippon Gakushiin Kiyo* (3 a year).

CHAIRMAN OF SECTIONS:

Section 1 (Social Sciences and Humanities): Prof. KISABURO YOKOTA.

Section 2 (Natural Sciences and their Application): Prof. CHUJI TSUBOI.

MEMBERS:

Section 1

ARISAWA, HIROMI (Economics and Statistics).
HATTORI, SHIRÔ (Linguistics).
HIKATA, RYUSHO (History of Indian Philosophy).
HORI, TSUNEO (History of Social and Economic Thought).
ICHIKO, TEIJI (Japanese Literature).
IMANAKA, TSUGIMARO (Political Science).
ISHII, RYÔSUKE (History of Japanese Law).
IWAO, SEIICHI (Japanese History).
KAMIKAWA, HIKOMATSU (International Politics and International Political History).
KANAKURA, YENSHO (Indian Philosophy).
KANDA, KIICHIRÔ (Sinology).
KANEKO, TAKEZO (Philosophy).
KATSUMOTO, MASAAKIRA (Civil Law, Copyright, Patent Law).
KATSURA, JUICHI (Philosophy).
KAWASHIMA, TAKEYOSHI (Civil Law and Sociology of Law).
KIKUI, TSUNAHIRO (Law of Civil Procedure).
KITAZAWA, SHINJIRO (Economics).
KIYOMIYA, SHIRO (Constitutional Law).
KOBATA, ATSUSHI (Japanese History).
MARUYAMA, MASAO (History of Japanese Political Ideas).
MIYAKE, GOICHI (Philosophy).
MIYAMOTO, MATAJI (Economic History of Japan and Business History of Japan).
MURAKAWA, KENTARÔ (History of European Civilization).
NAKAJIMA, FUMIO (English Linguistics).
NISHITANI, KEIJI (Philosophy).
OKA, YOSHITAKE (Political History).
OKAZAKI, YOSHIE (Japanese Literature).
OKOCHI, KAZUO (Labour and Industrial Relations, Economics).
ONO, SEIITIRO (Criminal Law and Criminal Procedure).
OSUMI, KEN'ICHIRO (Commercial and Economic Law).
ÔTSUKA, HISAO (Economic History).
SAITO, TAKESHI (English Literature).
SAKAMOTO, TARÔ (Japanese History).
SHIMMEI, MASAMICHI (Sociology).
SHIMOMURA, TORATARO (Philosophy).
SUENAGA, MASAO (Archaeology).
SUGI, TOSHIO (French Language and Literature).
SUYENOBU, SANJI (Anglo-American Law).
SUZUKI, TAKEO (Commercial Law and Securities Law).
TAKAGAKI, TORAJIRO (Economics).
TAKAGI, YASAKA (Political Science and Political History).
TAKAHASHI, SEIICHIRO (History of Economics).
TAKAMURA, SHOHEI (Western Economic History).
TAKAYANAGI, SHINZO (Legal History of Japan).
TAKÉUCHI, TOSHIO (Aesthetics).
TANAKA, JIRO (Administrative Law).
TANIGUCHI, TOMOHEI (Civil Law).
TAOKA, RYÔICHI (International Law).
TEZUKA, TOMIO (German Literature).
TÔBATA, SEIICHI, (Agricultural Economics).
TSUCHIYA, TAKAO (Japanese Economic History).
TSUJI, NAOSHIRÔ (Sanskrit Philology).
WAKIMURA, YOSHITARO (Economics).
YAMADA, MORITARO (Economics).
YAMADA, YUZO (Economics).
YAMAMOTO, TATSURO (Oriental History).
YANASE, YOSHIMOTO (Administrative Law).
YOKOTA, KISABURO (Public International Law).

Section 2

AKABORI, SHIRO (Organic Biochemistry).
AMEMIYA, IKUSAKU (Fishery and Marine Zoology).
AOKI, KUSUO (Civil Engineering).
BAN, SHIZUO (Architecture).
EBASHI, SETSURO (Pharmacology and Biophysics).
ESAKI, LEO (Physics).
FUJITA, YOSHIO (Astronomy).
FUKUSHI, TEIKICHI (Plant Pathology and Virology).
HAYAISHI, OSAMU (Biochemistry and Medical Chemistry).
HIDAKA, KOJI (Physical Oceanography).
HIRASAWA, KÔ (Anatomy)
HIRATSUKA, EIKITI (Sericulture and Agricultural Chemistry).
HIRATSUKA, NAOHIDE (Plant Pathology and Mycology).
HIRONAKA, HEISUKE (Mathematics).
ICHIKAWA, TOKUJI (Urology).
IMAI, YUNOSHIN (Steel Engineering).
ISEKI, SHOEI (Medical Law).
ITO, TEI-ICHI (Crystallography and Mineralogy).
IYANAGA, SHOKICHI (Mathematics).
KATSUKI, YASUJI (Physiology).
KAYA, SEIJI (Physics).
KIHARA, HITOSHI (Genetics).
KIMURA, KENJIRO (Analytical Chemistry).
KIMURA, REN (Microbiology).
KOBAYASHI, TEIICHI (Historical Geology and Palaeontology).
KODAIRA, KUNIHIKO (Mathematics).
KOGA, ISAAC (Electronics).
KOTANI, MASAO (Physics)
KUROKAWA, TOSHIO (Internal Medicine).
KUWADA, YOSHINARI (Plant Cytology).
MAKINO, SAJIRO (Cytogenetics).
MASUI, KIYOSHI (Animal Breeding and Genetics).
MASUMOTO, HAKARU (Physical Metallurgy).
MATSUMOTO, SHIN-ICHI (Dermatology and Syphilology).
MIZUSHIMA, SANICHIRO (Physical Chemistry).
MUTO, KIYOSHI (Aseismic Structural Engineering).
NAGAI, KENZO (Communication Engineering).
NAGAO, SEIJIN (Plant Breeding).
NITTA, ISAMU (Physical Chemistry).
NOZOE, TETSUO (Organic Chemistry).
NUMACHI, FUKUSABURO (Mechanical Engineering).
OGAWA, TEIZO (Anatomy, Neurology, Medical History).
OKADA, MASAHIRO (Pharmacology).
OKAMOTO, KOZO (Pathology).
OKINAKA, SHIGEO (Internal Medicine and Neurology).
OTSUKI, MASAO (Farm Management and Agricultural Accounting).
SAKAGUCHI, KINICHIRO (Fermentation).
SAKAMURA, TETSU (Plant Physiology).
SAKURADA, ICHIRO (Applied and Polymer Chemistry).
SAWAMURA, HIROSHI (Iron Metallurgy).
SHIBATA, YUJI (Inorganic Chemistry).

SOMIYA, TAKAYUKI (Applied Chemistry and Technical Analysis).
SUGASAWA, SHIGEHIKO (Organic Pharmaceutical Synthetics).
TAKAHARA, SHIGEO (Oto-Rhino-Laryngology).
TAKEI, SANKICHI (Agricultural Chemistry and Chemistry of Pesticides).
TAKEWAKI, KIYOSHI (Endocrinology).
TAMIYA, HIROSHI (Cellular Biochemistry).
TANI, ITIRO (Applied Physics and Fluid Dynamics).
TOMONAGA, SIN-ITIRO (Physics).
TORIYAMA, YOTSUO (Electrical Engineering).
TOYAMA, YOSHIYUKI (Applied and Fat Chemistry).
TSUBOI, CHUJI (Geophysics).
TSUBOI, SEITARÔ (Petrology).
TSUDA, KYOSUKE (Pharmaceutical Chemistry and Chemistry of Natural Products).
UCHIMURA, YÛSHI (Psychiatry and Neuropathology).
UMEZAWA, HAMAO (Microbial Chemistry).
WADATI, KIYOO (Geophysics).
WATANABE, TAKEO (Economic Geology, Mineral Deposits).
YAMAGATA, MASAO (Naval Architecture).
YAMAMOTO, GIICHI (Meteorology).
YAMANOUCHI, TAKAHIKO (Theoretical Physics).
YAMAOKA, KENJI (Internal Medicine).
YOSIDA, KÔSAKU (Mathematics).
YUKAWA, HIDEKI (Theoretical Physics).

HONORARY FELLOW

H.R.H. The Prince PHILIP, Duke of Edinburgh

HONORARY MEMBERS

BARDEEN, JOHN (Physics and Electrical Engineering).
BEADLE, GEORGE WELLS (Genetics).
BUTENANDT, ADOLF (Biochemistry).
CALVIN, MELVIN (Biochemistry and Biophysics).
CARTAN, HENRI (Mathematics).
HERZBERG, GERHARD (Spectroscopy).
MOTHES, KURT (Plant Physiology and Biochemistry).
PAL, BENJAMIN PEARY (Plant Breeding).
RABI, ISIDOR ISAAC (Physics).
REISCHAUER, EDWIN OLDFATHER (East Asian History).
TODD, ALEXANDER, R. (Organic Chemistry).
TUCCI, GIUSEPPE (Orientalism).

LEARNED SOCIETIES

NIHON GAKUJUTSU KAIGI
(Science Council of Japan) (J.S.C.)

22-34, ROPPONGI 7-CHOME, MINATO-KU, TOKYO 106

Founded on January 20th, 1949, as the governmental organization representative of all Japanese scientists. Its functions are to promote and reflect scientific development throughout national life, industry and administration, to co-ordinate scientific research and to link scientific organizations abroad.

President: KODI HUSIMI.

Vice-Presidents: KOSHIRO OKAKURA, REIJI NATORI.

Secretary-General: TADASHI OHAMA.

Libraries: *see* **Libraries.**

Number of members: 210.

Publications (English): ***Annual Report, Law and Politics, Bibliography of Economics, Recent Progress of Natural Sciences in Japan, Catalogues of Documents of Literature.***

CHAIRMEN OF SECTIONS:

Section 1 (Literature, Philosophy, Pedagogy, Psychology and Sociology, History): BOKURO EGUCHI.
Section 2 (Law and Political Science): YOZO WATANABE.
Section 3 (Economics, Commerce and Business Administration): JOUKICHI UCHIDA.
Section 4 (Pure Science): SHOHEI MIYAHARA.
Section 5 (Engineering): MASAMITSU KAWAKAMI.
Section 6 (Agriculture): SEIJIRO MOROHOSHI.
Section 7 (Medicine, Dentistry, Pharmacology): SHOICHI YAMAGATA.

The council sponsors committees on all branches of science. There are 58 national committees, ten special and six standing committees, a central returning committee and a management committee.

AGRICULTURE AND VETERINARY SCIENCE

Danchi-Nogaku Kenkyu-Kai (*Southern Agricultural Society*): Miyazaki University, Faculty of Agriculture, Funatsuka-cho 3-210, Miyazaki 880; f. 1947; 200 mems.; Pres. SHIGEO ASANO; publ. *Danchi-Nogaku.*

Engei Gakkai (*Japanese Society for Horticultural Science*): c/o Faculty of Agriculture, University of Tokyo, Bunkyo-ku, Tokyo; f. 1923; 2,200 mems.; Pres. TAKASHI TOMANA; Sec. RYOZO SAKIYAMA; publ. *Journal* (quarterly).

Gyogyo Keizai Gakkai (*The Fisheries Economic Society*): c/o Nippon Univ., Dept. of Economics, Chiyoda-ku, Tokyo; f. 1953; 375 mems.; Pres. SEIZO OKAMOTO; publ. *Journal* (quarterly).

Nihon Denpun Gakkai (*Japanese Society of Starch Science*): c/o National Food Research Institute, Ministry of Agriculture, Forestry and Fisheries, 2-1-2 Kannondai, Yatabe, Tsukuba, Ibaraki 305; f. 1952; 1,000 mems.; Pres. S. SUZUKI; publ. *Journal.*

Nihon Hakkokogaku-kai (*Japanese Society of Fermentation Technology*): c/o Faculty of Engineering, Osaka University, Yamada-kami, Suita-city, Osaka; f. 1923; 3,100 mems.; Pres. SABURO FUKUI; publ. *Journal of Fermentation Technology* (every 2 months, English), *Hakkokogaku-Kaishi* (every 2 months, Japanese).

Nihon Ju-i Gakkai (*Japanese Society of Veterinary Science*): Faculty of Agriculture, University of Tokyo; f. 1885; 3,300 mems.; Pres. SHUTARO YAMAMOTO; publ. *Journal*† (bi-monthly).

Nihon Ikushu Gakkai (*Japanese Society of Stockbreeding*): c/o Faculty of Agriculture, University of Tokyo, Bunkyo-ku, Tokyo 113; f. 1951; 1,200 mems.; Pres. RYUHEI TAKAHASHI; publ. *Japanese Journal of Breeding* (quarterly).

Nippon Mokuzai Gakkai (*The Japanese Wood Research Society*): 21-4-405, Hongo 6-chome, Bunkyo-ku, Tokyo 113; f. 1955; 1,396 mems.; Pres. Prof. Dr. MINORU SAWADA; publ. *Mokuzai Gakkaishi* (Journal of the Japan Wood Research Society).

Nippon Chikusan Gakkai (*The Japanese Society of Zootechnical Science*): 201 Nagatani Corporas, Ikenohata 2-9-4, Taito-ku, Tokyo 110; f. 1924; 2,000 mems.; Pres. TATSUO KATSUKI; publ. *The Japanese Journal of Zootechnical Science* (monthly).

Nippon Dojyo-Hiryo Gakkai (*The Society of the Science of Soil and Manure of Japan*): 26-10-202 Hongo, 6 chome, Bunkyo-ku, Tokyo; f. 1914; 2,127 mems.; Pres. KYOICHI KUMADA; publs. *Journal* (every 2 months), *Soil Science and Plant Nutrition* (quarterly).

Nippon Nogakkai (*Japanese Association of Agricultural Science Societies*): Toyo Bunko, Honkomagome, 2-chome 28-21, Bunkyo-ku, Tokyo 113; f. 1930; 26 mem. societies; Pres. YUICHI OCHI.

Nippon Nogei Kagaku Kai (*Agricultural Chemical Society of Japan*): 4-16 Yayoi 2-chome, Bunkyo-ku, Tokyo 113;

f. 1924; 7,853 mems.; Pres. KÔICHA YAMADA; publs. *Agricultural and Biological Chemistry* (in English, monthly), *Journal of the Agricultural Chemical Society of Japan* (in Japanese, monthly).

Nippon Nogyo Keizai Gakkai (*Agricultural Economic Society*): Faculty of Agriculture, University of Tokyo; f. 1924; 650 mems.; Pres. TOSHIO FURUSHIMA; publ. *Journal of Rural Economics* (quarterly).

Nippon Ringakukai (*The Japanese Forestry Society*): c/o Japan Forest Technical Asscn., Rokubancho 7, Chiyoda-ku, Tokyo; f. 1914; forestry research; 2,800 mems.; Pres. NOBUYOSHI HASHIMOTO; publ. *Journal* (monthly).

Nippon Sakumotsu Gakkai (*The Crop Science Society of Japan*): c/o Faculty of Agriculture, University of Tokyo; f. 1927; 1,800 mems.; Pres. TOMOSHIRO TAKEDA; Sec. ATSUHIKO KUMURA; publ. *Japanese Journal of Crop Science* (quarterly).

Nippon Sanshi Gakkai (*The Sericulture Society of Japan*): c/o The Sericultural Experiment Station, Suginami-ku, Tokyo; f. 1930; 1,393 mems.; Pres. T. FUKUDA; publ. *Journal* (bi-monthly).

Nippon Shokubutsu-Byori Gakkai (*The Phytopathological Society of Japan*): c/o Japan Plant Protection Association, 11-43-1-chome, Komagome, Toshima-ku, Tokyo 170; f. 1916 to promote research on plant diseases; 1,800 regular mems.; Pres. TAKUJI KOZAKA; publ. *Annals* (5 issues yearly).

Nippon Suisan Gakkai (*Japanese Society of Scientific Fisheries*): Tokyo University of Fisheries, 4-5-7 Konan Minato-ku, Tokyo; f. 1932; 2,936 mems.; Pres. Prof. Y. HIYAMA; publ. *Bulletin* (monthly).

Nogyokikai Gakkai (*The Society of Agricultural Machinery*): c/o Department of Agricultural Engineering, Faculty of Agriculture, University of Tokyo, Bunkyo-ku, Tokyo; f. 1937; 1,650 mems.; Pres. AKIRA HOSOKAWA; publ. *Journal* (quarterly).

Sapporo Norin Gakkai (*Sapporo Society of Agriculture and Fisheries*): Faculty of Agriculture, Hokkaido University; f. 1908; 700 mems.; Pres. MYODO HORICHI; publ. *Journal* (irregular).

Tottori Nogakkai (*Tottori Society of Agricultural Science*): Tottori University, Tottori; f. 1926; 1,200 mems.; Pres. TNETOMO HAVASHI; publ. *Bulletin*.

ARCHITECTURE AND TOWN PLANNING

Kansai Zosen Kyokai (*The Kansai Society of Naval Architects*): Osaka University, Yamada-kami, Suita, Osaka; f. 1912; 2,600 mems.; Pres. H. SASAJIMA; publ. *Journal* (quarterly).

Nihon Zoen Gakkai (*Japanese Institute of Landscape Architects*): c/o Faculty of Agriculture, The University of Tokyo; f. 1924; 1,800 mems.; Pres. AKIRA HOMMA; publ. *Journal of the Japanese Institute of Landscape Architects*.

Nihon Zosen Gakkai (*Society of Naval Architects of Japan*): Sempaku-Shinko Building, 15-16 Toranomon 1-chome, Minato-ku, Tokyo 105; f. 1897; 5,500 mems.; Pres. H. SHINTO; publs. *Journal* (twice yearly), *Bulletin* (monthly).

Nippon Kenchiku Gakkai (*Architectural Institute of Japan*): 2-19, Ginza 3-chome, Chuo-ku, Tokyo; f. 1886; 23,240 mems.; Pres. T. YOSIZAKA; publs. *Journal* (14 issues yearly), *Transactions* (monthly).

Nippon Toshi Keikaku Gakkai (*The City Planning Institute of Japan*): Toshi-Keikaku-Kaikan, 2-16-14 Hirakawa-cho, Chiyoda-ku, Tokyo; f. 1951; 2,882 mems.; Pres. TADASHI HIGASA; publ. *City Planning Review* (6 a year).

THE ARTS

Bijutsu-shi Gakkai (*The Japanese Art History Society*): c/o Tokyo National Research Institute of Cultural Properties, 13-27 Ueno Park, Taito-ku, Tokyo 110; f. 1949; 665 mems.; publ. *Journal* (quarterly).

Nippon Engeki Gakkai (*Japanese Society for Theatre Research*): Waseda University, 1 Totsuka-cho, Shinjuku-ku, Tokyo; f. 1949; Pres. K. SHUZUI; publ. *Kiyo* (annually).

Ongaku Gakkai (*Japanese Musicological Society*): Tokyo National University of Fine Arts and Music, Ueno Park, Taitô-ku, Tokyo; f. 1952; 1,100 mems.; Pres. K. HATTORI; publ. *Journal* (3 a year).

BIBLIOGRAPHY, LIBRARY SCIENCE AND MUSEOLOGY

Gakujutsu Bunken Fukyu-Kai (*Association for Science Documents Information*): c/o Tokyo Institute of Technology, 2-15-1 O-okayama, Meguro-ku, Tokyo; f. 1933; Pres. TAKU UEMURA; publs. *Union Catalog of Books on Japan in Western Languages* (English), *Reports on Progress in Polymer Physics in Japan* (English), *Directory of Japanese Scientific Periodicals* (English), *Aseismic Design and Testing of Nuclear Facilities* (English).

Joho Shori Gakkai (*Information Processing Society of Japan*): Kikai Shinko-Kai Building No. 3-5-8, Shiba-Koen, Minato-ku, Tokyo; f. 1960; 14,000 mems.; Pres. K. KOBAYASHI; publs. *Journal of Information Processing* (quarterly), *Joho Shori* (Japanese, monthly), *Transactions* (Japanese, every 2 months).

Nihon Hakubutsukan Kyokai (*Japanese Association of Museums*): c/o Uragami Tenshudo Bldg. 1-10-1, Kayabacho, Nihonbashi, Chuo-ku, Tokyo; publ. *Museum Studies*† (monthly).

Nihon Toshokan Kyokai (*Japan Library Association*): 1-10, 1-chome, Taishido, Setagaya-ku, Tokyo 154; f. 1892; all aspects of library development; 6,000 mems.; library of *c.* 3,000 vols.; Sec.-Gen. HITOSHI KURIHARA; publs. *Toshokan Zasshi*† (monthly), *Gendai no Toshokan* (quarterly), *Nihon no Sankotosho Shikiban* (quarterly), *Nihon no Toshokan* (annually).

Nippon Dokumentêsyon Kyôkai (*Japan Documentation Society*): Sasaki Bldg., 5-7 Koisikawa 2, Bunkyo-ku, Tokyo; f. 1950; 1,200 mems.; Pres. S. HAMADA; publ. *Documentation Study* (monthly).

Nippon Kagaku-Gijutsu Joho Sentah (*Japan Information Centre of Science and Technology—JICST*): P.O.B. 1478, Tokyo; f. 1957; preparation of abstracts, on-line and manual search services, translation and photo-duplication service, library service, computer processing; 338 mems.; Pres. T. OKA; publs. *Current Bibliography on Science and Technology* (Abstracts from about 9,600 journals; 11 series); *Foreign Patent News* (weekly), *Information and Documentation, Technical Highlights from Overseas, Manual of Public Research Institutes in Japan, Thesaurus, Guide to the Public Laboratories and Research Organizations in Japan.*

Nippon Kenchiku Bunken Sentah (*Japan Building Documentation Centre*): c/o Kenchiku-Setsubi-Sogo-Kyokai, Minakawa Bldg., Ginza 1-6, Chuo-ku, Tokyo; publ. *Building Technique Digest* (Japanese, quarterly).

Nippon Toshokan Gakkai (*Japan Society of Library Science*): National College of Library Science, 4-1 Shimouma, 1-chome, Setagaya-ku, Tokyo; f. 1953; 386 mems.; Pres. N. OKADA; publ. *Annals of the Society of Library Science* (quarterly).

Economics, Law and Politics

Ajia Seikei Gakkai (*Society for Asian Political and Economic Studies*): c/o Prof. S. Yamada, Institute of Oriental Culture, Univ. of Tokyo, 3-1 Hongo 7, Bunkyo, Tokyo; f. 1953; 550 mems.; Pres. S. Eto; publ. *Asiatic Studies* (quarterly).

Foreign Affairs Association of Japan: Togyo Kaikan, 7, 1-chome, Yuraku-cho, Chiyoda-ku, Tokyo; f. 1932; Rep. Helen M. Uno; publs. *Contemporary Japan* (quarterly), *Japan Year Book*.

Hikaku-ho Gakkai (*Japan Society of Comparative Law*): c/o Faculty of Law, Tokyo University, Hongo, Bunkyo-ku, Tokyo 113; f. 1950; 635 mems.; Pres. A. Yamada; publ. *Journal* (annual).

Hogaku Kyokai (*The Jurisprudence Association*): Faculty of Law, University of Tokyo; f. 1884; 600 mems.; Pres. Sueo Ikehara; publs. *Hogaku Kyokai Zasshi, Journal*.

Hosei-shi Gakkai (*Legal History Association*): University of Tokyo; f. 1949; 220 mems.; Pres. R. Ishii; publ. *Legal History Review* (annual).

Hosokai (*Lawyers' Association*): 1, 1-chome, Kasumigaseki, Chiyoda-ku, Tokyo; f. 1891; 20,000 mems.; library of 30,000 vols.; Pres. Kazuto Ishida; Dir. Kiyoshi Nagai; publ. *Hoso Jiho*.

Keizai Riron Gakkai (*Japan Society of Political Economy*): Faculty of Economics, Rikkyo University, 3 Ikebukuro, Toshima-ku, Tokyo; f. 1959; 865 mems.; Pres. H. Oouchi.

Keizai-ho Gakkai (*Association of Economic Jurisprudence*): Hitotsubashi University, Kunitachi, Tokyo; f. 1951; 280 mems.; publ. *Journal* (annual).

Keizaigaku-shi Gakkai (*Japan Society for the History of Social and Economic Thought*): Faculty of Economics, Kansai-Gakuin Univ., Nishinomiya City; f. 1949; 440 mems.; Pres. T. Hori; publ. *Annual Bulletin*.

Kinyu Gakkai (*Financial Science Association*): c/o Toyo Keizai, Motoishi 1-4 Nihonbashi, Chuo-ku, Tokyo; f. 1943; 459 mems.; Pres. T. Takagaku; publ. *Report* (2 issues yearly).

Kokusaiho Gakkai (*Association of International Law*): Faculty of Law, University of Tokyo; f. 1897; 420 mems.; Pres. Hidebumi Egawa; publs. *Kokusaiho Gaiko Zasshi, Journal of International Law and Diplomacy*.

Minji Soshoho Gakkai (*Japan Association of Civil Procedure*): Osaka University, Faculty of Law, 1-1 Machikaneyama, Toyonakashi, Osaka; f. 1949; 450 mems.; Pres. T. Nakano; publ. *Journal of Civil Procedure* (annually).

Nichibei Hogakkai/Japanese American Society for Legal Studies: c/o Faculty of Law, Rikkyo University, Nishi-Ikebukuro, Toshima, Tokyo 171; (American branch: c/o Asian Law Program, University of Washington School of Law, JB-20, Seattle, Wash. 98195, U.S.A.); f. 1964; promotion of comparative study of Japanese and American law and co-operation among the lawyers of both countries; 850 mems.; Rep. Dirs. B. J. George, H. Tanaka; publs. *Amerika Hō* (Law in the United States) (2 a year), *Law in Japan* (annual).

Nihon Koho Gakkai (*Japan Public Law Association*): University of Tokyo; f. 1948; 800 mems.; Pres. J. Tanaka; publ. *Koho-Kenkyu* (Public Law Review, annually).

Nihon Zaisei Gakkai (*Japanese Association of Fiscal Science*): Hitotsubashi University, Kunitachi, Tokyo; f. 1940; 195 mems.

Nippon Gyosei Gakkai (*Japanese Society for Public Administration*): University of Tokyo; f. 1945; 340 mems.; Pres. K. Tsuji; publ. *Annals* (annual).

Nippon Hoshakai Gakkai (*Japan Association of Sociology of Law*): University of Tokyo; f. 1947; 532 mems.; Pres. H. Suekawa; publ. *Sociology of Law* (annual).

Nippon Hotetsu-Gakkai (*The Japanese Association for Legal Philosophy*): Faculty of Law, Kyoto University, Sakyo-ku, Kyoto; f. 1948; 343 mems.; Pres. S. Kato; publ. *Annual*.

Nippon Kaiho Gakkai (*Maritime Law Association of Japan*): Chuo University, Surugadai 3-9 Kanda, Chiyoda-ku, Tokyo; f. 1950; 165 mems.; Pres. T. Ishii; publ. *Report*.

Nippon Keiei Gakkai (*Japan Society for the Study of Business Administration*): Hitotsubashi University, Kunitachi, Tokyo; f. 1926; 1,367 mems.; Pres. Y. Kobayashi.

Nippon Keiho Gakkai (*The Criminal Law Society of Japan*): University of Tokyo; f. 1949; 727 mems.; Pres. R. Hirano; publ. *Journal* (quarterly).

Nippon Keizai Seisaku Gakkai (*Japan Economic Policy Association*): Keio University, Mita, Minato-ku, Tokyo; f. 1940; 862 mems.; Pres. T. Yamanaka; publ. *Annals*.

Nippon Kokusai Seiji Gakkai (*The Japan Association of International Relations*): Hosei University, Fujimi-cho, Chiyoda-ku, Tokyo; f. 1956; 512 mems.; Pres. H. Kamikawa; publ. *International Relations* (quarterly).

Nippon Rodo-ho Gakkai (*Japanese Labour Law Association*): Keio University, Shiba Mita, Minato-ku, Tokyo; f. 1950; 370 mems.; Pres. H. Nomura; publ. *Journal* (2 issues yearly).

Nippon Seizi Gakkai (*Japanese Political Science Association*): Faculty of Law, Rikkyo University, 3-34-1, Nishi-Ikebukuro, Toshima-ku, Tokyo 171; 820 mems.; Pres. Jiro Kamishima.

Nippon Shiho Gakkai (*Japan Association of Private Law*): University of Tokyo; f. 1948; 688 mems.; Pres. T. Suzuki; publ. *Journal* (annual).

Nippon Shogyo Gakkai (*Japan Society of Commercial Sciences*): Meiji University, Surugadai Kanda, Chiyoda-ku, Tokyo; f. 1951; 429 mems.; Pres. K. Fukuda.

Nippon Tokei Gakkai (*Japan Statistical Society*): c/o The Institute of Statistical Mathematics, 4-7-6 Minamiazabu, Minato-ku, Tokyo; f. 1931; 560 mems.; Pres. J. Yamamoto; publ. *Journal of the Japan Statistical Society* (annual).

Nogyo-Ho Gakkai (*Japan Agricultural Law Association*): University of Tokyo; f. 1956; 233 mems.; Pres. B. Okura; publ. *Nogyo-ho Kenkyu* (annual).

Riron Keizai Gakkai (*Association of Theoretical Economics*): c/o Hitotsubashi University, Kunitachi, Tokyo; f. 1934; 147 mems.; Pres. Ichiro Nakayama, Isamu Yamada, Yukio Kitano.

Tokyo Daigaku Keizai Gakkai (*Society of Economics*): Faculty of Economics, University of Tokyo, Bunkyo-ku, Tokyo; f. 1922; 500 mems.; Pres. Ryutaro Komiya; publ. *Journal of Economics* (quarterly).

Education

Kyoiku Tetsugakkai (*Society of Educational Philosophy*): Jochi University, Kioi-cho, Chiyoda-ku, Tokyo; f. 1957; 341 mems.; Pres. E. Inatomi; publ. *Studies in the Philosophy of Education*.

Nihon Gakko-hoken Gakkai (*Japanese Society of School Health*): Faculty of Education, University of Tokyo; f. 1954; 1,000 mems.; Pres. Yoshio Ohba; publ. *Gakko-hoken Kenkyu* (monthly journal).

Nihon Hikaku Kyoiku Gakkai (*Japan Comparative Education Society*): c/o N.I.E.R., 6-5-22, Shimomeguro,

Meguro-ku, Tokyo 153; f. 1965; 400 mems.; Pres. M. HIRATSUKA; publ. *Research Bulletin.*

Nihon Kyoiku Gakkai (*The Japanese Society for the Study of Education*): Faculty of Education, University of Tokyo; f. 1941; 1,400 mems.; Pres. TOKIOMI KAIGO; publ. *The Japanese Journal of Educational Research* (quarterly).

Nihon Kyoiku-shakai Gakkai (*The Japan Society for the Study of Educational Sociology*): Faculty of Education, University of Tokyo; f. 1949; 520 mems.; Pres. YOSHIHIRO SHIMIZU; publ. *The Journal of Educational Sociology* (annual).

Nihon Kyoiku-shinri Gakkai (*The Japanese Association of Educational Psychology*): Faculty of Education, University of Tokyo; f. 1952; 2,800 mems.; Pres. TADASHI HIDANO; publs. *The Japanese Journal of Educational Psychology* (quarterly), *The Annual Report of Educational Psychology in Japan.*

Nippon Kagaku Kyoiku Gakukai (*Japan Society for Science Education*): National Institute for Educational Research, 6-5-22 Shimomeguro, Meguro-ku, Tokyo 153; f. 1977; science education and educational technology; 730 mems.; Pres. Dr. A. OOTUKA; publs. *Journal*† (quarterly), *Letter* (every 2 months).

Nippon Taiiku Gakkai (*Japanese Society of Physical Education*): c/o School of Education, University of Tokyo; f. 1950; 2,315 mems.; Pres. M. MATSUI; publs. *Research Journal* (quarterly), *Journal of Health and Physical Education* (monthly).

HISTORY, GEOGRAPHY AND ARCHAEOLOGY

Keizai Chiri Gakkai (*Association of Economic Geographers*): Institute of Economic Geography, Faculty of Economics, Hitotsubashi University, Naka 2-1, Kunitachi-shi, Tokyo; f. 1954; 640 mems.; Pres. T. KAWASHIMA; publ. *Annals* (quarterly).

Kokushi-Gakkai (*The Society of Japanese Historical Research*): Kokugakuin University, 10-28, Higashi 4-chome, Shibuya-ku, Tokyo; f. 1910; Sec. H. ROMIE TSUBAKI; publ. *Kokushigaku* (Journal of Japanese History).

Nihon Chiri Gakkai (*Association of Japanese Geographers*): c/o Building of Academic Societies Centre, 2-4-16 Yayoi, Bunkyo-ku, Tokyo, Japan 113; f. 1925; 3,000 mems.; Pres. S. YAMAMOTO; publ. *Geographical Review of Japan* (monthly).

Nihon Kokogakkai (*Archaeological Society of Japan*): c/o Tokyo National Museum, Ueno Park, Daito-ku, Tokyo; f. 1895; Pres. Dr. WADA GUN'ICHI; publ. *Kokogaku Zasshi* (quarterly).

Nippon Kokogaku Kyokai (*The Japanese Archaeologists Association*): Gakukai Center Building, 2-4-16 Yayoi, Bunkyo-ku, Tokyo 113; f. 1948; 750 mems.; Pres N. EGAMI; publ. *Archaeologia Japonica* (Annual Report).

Nippon Orient Gakkai (*The Society for Near Eastern Studies in Japan*): 9th Floor, Tokyo-Tenrikyokan 9, 1-chome, Kanda Nishiki-cho, Chiyoda-ku, Tokyo 101; f. 1954; 715 mems.; Pres. Dr. ATSUUJI ASHIKAGA; publs. *Orient* (2 a year in Japanese, annually in foreign languages).

Nippon Seibutsuchiri Gakkai (*Biogeographical Society of Japan*): c/o Science Museum of Tokyo University of Fisheries, 4-5-7 Konan, Minato-ku, Tokyo f. 1928; 300 mems.; Pres. YAICHIRO OKADA; publs. *Bulletin, Biogeographica, Fauna Japonica.*

Nippon Seiyoshi Gakkai (*The Japanese Society of Western History*): Osaka University, Toyonaka-shi, Osaka-fu; f. 1948; 800 mems.; Pres. Prof. M. UEMURA; publ. *Studies in Western History* (quarterly).

Shigaku-kai (*Historical Society of Japan*): University of Tokyo, Hongo; f. 1889; *c.* 2,300 mems.; Pres. MASAO MORI; publ. *Shigaku-Zasshi*† (Historical Journal of Japan).

Tokyo Chigaku Kyokai (*Tokyo Geographical Society*): 12 Nibancho, Chiyoda-ku, Tokyo; f. 1879; 596 mems.; Pres. MORITATSU HOSOKAWA; publ. *Journal of Geography* (bi-monthly).

Toyoshi Kenkyukai (*The Society of Oriental Research*): Kyoto University, Kyoto City; f. 1935; 1,350 mems.; Pres. I. MIYAZAKI; publ. *Journal of Oriental Research*† (quarterly).

INTERNATIONAL CULTURAL INSTITUTES

American Center in Japan: 11th Floor, ABC Kaikan, 6-3 Shibakoen 2-chome, Minato-ku, Tokyo 105; brs. in Fukuoka, Kyoto, Nagoya, Osaka, Sapporo.

Asia Foundation, The: 31 Kowa Bldg., 19-1 Shirokanedai 3-chome, Minato-ku, Tokyo 108; one of 12 branches of the main organization in the U.S.A. (*q.v.*); Rep. JAMES L. STEWART.

Asian Cultural Centre for Unesco (ACCU): 6 Fukuromachi, Shinjuku-ku, Tokyo 162; f. 1971; book development and other regional cultural activities; library of 9,000 vols.; Pres. TORAJIRO TAKAGAKI; Dir.-Gen. RYOJI ITO; publs. *Annual Report, ACCU News* (Japanese, monthly), *Asian Culture* (English, quarterly), *Asian Book Development* (English, quarterly).

Asian Students Cultural Association, The: 12-13 Honkomagome 2-chome, Bunkyo-ku, Tokyo 113; f. 1957; to establish good relations between Afro-Asian and Latin-American students; runs Asian Students Cultural House (Asia Bunka Kaikan), promotes mutual co-operation in cultural, economic and technical fields; 30 mems.; library of 2,000 vols.; Pres. HOZUMI GOICHI; Sec. TAI SHIGEHARU; publ. *Asia no Tomo.*

British Council: Iwanami Bldg., 1,2-chome Jimbo-cho, Kanda, Chiyoda-ku, Tokyo 101; Rep. R. P. MARTIN (77 Kitashirakawa-Nishimachi, Sakyo-ku, Kyoto 606); Regional Dir. S. J. McENALLY; library: *see* Libraries.

Deutsches Kulturinstitut: 7-5-56 Akasaka, Minato-ku, Tokyo 107; Tokyo Branch of Goethe-Institut, Munich; lectures, concerts, films, exhibitions; library of 18,000 vols.

Institut Franco-Japonais de Tokyo: 15 Funagawara-cho Ichigaya, Shinjuku-ku; f. 1951; Dir. C. MOUTOUT; Sec.-Gen. J. SILVESTRE.

Istituto Italiano di Cultura: Kudan Minami 2-1-30 Chiyoda-ku, Tokyo 102; f. 1959 to develop cultural exchange activities between Japan and Italy and promote Italian culture in Japan; operates courses on Italian language and culture and provides information on educational institutions in Italy; library of 9,000 vols. (8,000 in Italian, 1,000 in Japanese); Dir. Prof. PIERO CORRADINI; occasional publs.

LANGUAGE AND LITERATURE

Japan PEN Club: Room 265, Syuwa Residential Hotel, 9-1-7 Akasaka, Minato-ku, Tokyo; f. 1935; 632 mems.; library of 15,000 vols.; Pres. KENJI TAKAHASHI; Sec. YUZO TOKI; publ. *Japanese Literature Today* (annually).

Kokugogakkai (*Society for the Study of Japanese Language*): Faculty of Letters, University of Tokyo; f. 1944; 1,500 mems.; Pres. ETSUTARO IWABUCHI; publ. *Studies in the Japanese Language* (quarterly).

Manyo Gakkai (*Society for Manyo Studies*): Kansai University, Senriyama Suita-shi, Osaka; f. 1951; 810 mems.; publ. *The Manyo* (quarterly).

Nihon Dokubungakkai (*Japanese Society of German Literature*): c/o Ikubundo, Hongo 5-30-21, Bunkyo-ku, Tokyo 113; f. 1947; 2,000 mems.; Pres. Prof. EIJIRO IWASAKI; publ. *Doitsu Bungaku*† (German Literature) (2 a year).

Nihon Eibungakkai (*English Literary Society of Japan*): 18 Nakamachi, Shinjuku-ku, Tokyo 162; f. 1917; 2,900 mems.; Pres. YOSHIAKI FUHARA; publ. *Studies in English Literature* (3 a year).

Nihon Esperanto Gakkai (*Japanese Esperanto Institute*): Waseda-mati 12-3, Sinzyuku-ku, 162 Tokyo; f. 1919; 2,000 mems.; Pres. FUJIO EGAMI; Sec. OSIOKA MORITAKA; publ. *La Revuo Orienta* (monthly).

Nihon Furansu-go Furansu-bungaku-kai (*Japanese Society of French Language and Literature*): Nichi-futsu Kaikan (Maison Franco-Japonaise), Tokyo; f. 1946, reorganized 1962; 700 mems.; Pres. SHINTARO SUZUKI; publ. *Studies in French Language and Literature* (three times a year).

Nihon Gengogakkai (*Linguistic Society of Japan*): Taishukan Building, 3-26 Kandanishiki-cho, Chiyoda-ku, Tokyo 101; f. 1938; 950 mems.; Pres. HISANOSUKE IZUI; publ. *Gengo Kenkyu* (Journal of the Linguistic Society of Japan (2 a year).

Nippon Bungaku Kyokai (*Japanese Literature Association*): 2-17-10 Minami-otsuka, Toshima-ku, Tokyo; f. 1946; 1,500 mems.; library of 2,000 vols.; Pres. TAMOTU HIROSUE; publ. *Japanese Literature* (monthly).

Nippon Hikaku Bungakukai (*The Comparative Literature Society of Japan*): Aoyamagakuin University, Shibuya-ku, Tokyo; f. 1948; 400 mems.; Pres. K. NAKAJIMA; Gen. Sec. SABURO OTA; publs. *Journal* (annual), *Bulletin* (quarterly).

Nippon Onsei Gakkai (*The Phonetic Society of Japan*): 13, Daita-2, Setagaya-ku, Tokyo; f. 1926; 1,200 mems.; library of 30,000 vols.; Pres. MASAO ONISHI; publs. *Bulletin* (3 a year), *Study of Sounds* (every 2 years), *World Papers in Phonetics*.

Nippon Romazikai (*Japanese Society for Roman Letters*): Yosida Honmati 27, Kyoto; f. 1910; Pres. AKABORI SIRO; publ. *Romazi Sekai* (The World of Roman Letters).

Nippon Rosiya Bungakkai (*Russian Literary Society in Japan*): Faculty of Literature, Waseda University, Toyama-cho, Shinjuku-ku, Tokyo; 150 mems.; Pres. MASAO YONEKAWA; Sec.-Gen. General K. NAKANO; publ. *Bulletin*.

Nippon Seiyo Koten Gakkai (*The Classical Society of Japan*): Dept. of Classics, Faculty of Letters, Kyoto Univ., Kyoto; f. 1950; 500 mems.; Pres. CHIAKI MATSUDAIRA; publ. *Journal of Classical Studies*† (annual).

Tokyo Shina Gakkai (*Tokyo Sinological Society*): Faculty of Letters, The University of Tokyo, Bunkyo-ku, Tokyo; f. 1897; Pres. SEIICHI UNO; publ. *Tokyo Shinagaku-ho*.

MEDICINE

Nihon Ishi-Kai (*The Japan Medical Association*): Nihon Ishi Kaikan, 5 Kanda Surugadai 2- chome, Chiyoda-ku, Tokyo 101; f. 1916; 98,400 mems.: Pres. T. TAKEMI; publs. *Journal* (in Japanese, 24 a year), *Asian Medical Journal* (in English, monthly).

Nihon Koko Geka Gakkai (*Japanese Society of Oral Surgeons*): Tokyo Joshi Ika Daigaku, 10 Kawada-cho, Shinjuku-ku, Tokyo; f. 1952; 2,000 mems.; Gen. Sec. M. MURASE; publ. *Japanese Journal of Oral Surgery* (4 issues yearly).

Nihon Kakuigakukai (*Japanese Society of Nuclear Medicine*): c/o Japan Radioisotope Association, 28-45 Hon-Komagome 2-chome, Bunkyo-ku, Tokyo; f. 1963; 2,000 mems.; Pres. HIROTAKE KAKEHI; publ. *Japanese Journal of Nuclear Medicine* (bi-monthly).

Nihon Koku Eisei Gakkai (*Japanese Society for Dental Health*): c/o Koku Hoken Kyokai 38-6, Komagome 1-chome Toshima-ku, Tokyo 170; f. 1952; 2,000 mems.; Pres. Y. SAKAKIBARA; publ. *Journal* (quarterly).

Nihon Kokuka Gakkai (*Japanese Stomatological Society*): Department of Oral Surgery, School of Medicine, University of Tokyo; f. 1947; 2,200 mems.; Dir. HAJIME HAYASHI; publ. *Journal of the Japanese Stomatological Society* (quarterly).

Nihon Kyosei Shikagakkai (*Japan Orthodontic Society*): c/o Dept. of Orthodontics, School of Dentistry, Tokyo Medical and Dental University, 1-5-45 Yushima, Bunkyo-ku, Tokyo 113; f. 1926; 1,569 mems.; Pres. FUJIO MIURA; Vice-Pres. ZENNOSUKE KINOSHITA; publ. *Journal of the Japan Orthodontic Society* (4 a year).

Nihon Naika Gakkai (*Japanese Society of Internal Medicine*): Hongo Daiichi Building, 34-3, Hongo 3-chome, Bunkyo-ku, Tokyo 113; f. 1903; 20,700 mems.; Chief Dir. KIKU NAKAO; publs. *Journal of the Japanese Society of Internal Medicine* (monthly in Japanese), *Japanese Journal of Medicine* (quarterly in English).

Nihon Ronen Igakukai (*Japanese Geriatrics Society*): Department of Geriatrics, Faculty of Medicine, University of Tokyo; f. 1975; 3,400 mems.; Pres. TAKESHI NAKAMURA; Chair. Prof. M. YOSHIKAWA, M.D.; publ. *Journal* (quarterly).

Nihon Seishin Shinkei Gakkai (*Japanese Society of Neurology and Psychiatry*): Neuropsychiatric Clinic, Faculty of Medicine, University of Tokyo; 3,500 mems.; Pres. HARUO AKIMOTO; publs. *Seishin Shinkeigaku Zasshi* (Japanese—monthly), *Psychiatra et Neurologia Japonica* (English—quarterly).

Nihon Syoyakugakkai (*Japanese Society of Pharmacognosy*): Faculty of Pharmaceutical Sciences, Kyoto Univ., Sakyo-ku, Kyoto; f. 1946; 516 mems.; Pres. K. KIMURA; publ. *Japanese Journal of Pharmacognosy* (2 issues yearly).

Nippon Arerugi Gakkai (*Japanese Society of Allergology*): Department of Microbiology and Immunology, Nippon Medical School, 1-1-5 Sendagi, Bunkyo-ku, Tokyo; f. 1952; 2,890 mems.; Pres. YOSHITAMI KIMURA; publ. *Japanese Journal of Allergology* (monthly).

Nippon Bitamin Gakkai (*Japanese Vitamin Society*): Nippon Italy Kyoto-Kaikan 3rd floor, 04-Ushinomiya-cho, Yoshida, Sakyo-ku, Kyoto 606; f. 1974; 2,000 mems.; Pres. Dr. Y. NOSE; publs. *Journal of Nutritional Science and Vitaminology* (English, six times a year), *Vitamins* (Japanese, monthly).

Nippon Byorigakkai (*Japanese Pathological Society*): c/o Department of Pathology, Faculty of Medicine, University of Tokyo, Bunkyo-ku, Tokyo; f. 1911; 2,500 mems.; Sec.-Gen. TETSURO SHIMAMINE; publs. *Acta Pathologica Japonica* (bi-monthly in English), *Transactions* (Japanese), *Annual of Pathological Autopsy Cases in Japan* (Japanese).

Nippon Densenbyo Gakkai (*The Japanese Association for Infectious Diseases*): Myogi-saka Mansion 604, 20-12 Komagome 3-chome, Toshima-ku, Tokyo; f. 1926; 1,500 mems.; Pres. Y. MIKAMO; publ. *The Journal* (monthly).

Nippon Eisei Gakkai (*The Japanese Society for Hygiene*): Dept. of Public Health, Faculty of Medicine, Kyoto University, Yoshida, Sakyo-ku, Kyoto 606; f. 1929; publ. *Japanese Journal of Hygiene* (6 issues yearly).

Nippon Gan Gakkai (*Japanese Cancer Association*): c/o Cancer Institute, Kami-Ikebukuro 1-37-1, Toshima-ku, Tokyo 170; f. 1907; 6,900 mems.; Pres. SHICHIRO ISHIKAWA; publs. *GANN* (every 2 months), *GANN Monograph* (irregular).

Nippon Ganka Gakkai (*Japanese Ophthalmological Society*): Nippon Ishi Kaikan, 2-5 Kanda Surugadai, Chiyoda-ku, Tokyo; f. 1897; 3,638 mems.; Pres. SH. SHIKANO; publ. *Acta Societatis Ophthalmologicae Japonicae* (monthly).

Nippon Geka Gakkai (*Japan Surgical Society*): Nippon Ishi Kaikan, 2-5 Kanda Surugadai, Chiyoda-ku, Tokyo; f. 1899; 12,750 mems.; Pres. N. SHIMADA; publ. *Journal* (monthly).

Nippon Hifu-ka Gakkai (*Japanese Dermatological Assn.*): Taisei Bldg., 14-10 3-chome, Hongo, Bunkyo-ku, Tokyo; f. 1901; 4,335 mems.; Pres. A. KUKITA; publs. *Japanese Journal of Dermatology* (Japanese, 14 a year), *Journal of Dermatology*† (English, every 2 months).

Nippon Hinyoki-ka Gakkai (*Japanese Urological Association*): Taisei Bldg., Hongo 3-14-10, Bunkyo-ku, Tokyo; f. 1912; 2,800 mems.; Pres. TADAO NIIJIMA; publ. *The Japanese Journal of Urology* (monthly).

Nippon Hoi Gakkai (*Medico-Legal Society of Japan*): Department of Legal Medicine, Faculty of Medicine, University of Tokyo, 7-3-1 Hongo, Bunkyo-ku, Tokyo 113; f. 1914; 964 mems.; Pres. SUGURU AKAISHI; Sec. A. TAKATSU; publ. *Journal* (6 a year).

Nippon Hoshasen Eikyo Gakkai (*The Japan Radiation Research Society*): National Institute of Radiological Sciences, 9-1, Anagawa-4-chome, Chiba-shi; f. 1959; 750 mems.; Pres. T. KUMATORI; publ. *Journal of Radiation Research* (quarterly).

Nippon Hotetsu Shika Gakkai (*Japan Prosthodontic Society*): c/o Koku Hoken Kyokai, 1-38-6 Komagome, Toshima-ku, Tokyo; f. 1931; 2,900 mems.; Pres. TOMIO KOMORI; publ. *Journal of the Japan Prosthodontic Society* (4 issues yearly).

Nippon Igaku Hoshasen Gakkai (*Japanese Radiology Society*): Room 301 Akamon Habitation, 5-29-13 Hongo, Bunkyo-ku, Tokyo; f. 1923; 2,700 mems.; Pres. K. MISONOU; publ. *Nippon Acta Radiologica* (monthly).

Nippon Jibi-Inkoka Gakkai (*Oto-Rhino-Laryngological Society of Japan*): c/o Chateau-Takanawa 23-14, 3-chome Takanawa, Minato-ku, Tokyo; f. 1893; 5,900 mems.; Pres. KAORU YAMAMOTO; publ. *Journal of Otolaryngology of Japan* (monthly).

Nippon Junkan-ki Gakkai (*The Japanese Circulation Society*): Faculty of Medicine, Kyoto University, Sakyo-ku, Kyoto; f. 1935; 5,000 mems.; Pres. K. YAMADA; Dir.-in-Chief E. KIMURA; publ. *Japanese Circulation Journal* (monthly).

Nippon Kaibo Gakkai (*Japanese Anatomical Association*): Department of Anatomy, Faculty of Medicine, University of Tokyo; f. 1893; 1,850 mems.; Pres. MITSUI TADAO; publ. *Kaibogaku Zasshi*.

Nippon Kekkaku-byo Gakkai (*The Japanese Society for Tuberculosis*): 1-24, Matsuyama 3-chome, Kiyose-shi, Tokyo 180-04; f. 1923; 3,000 mems.; Pres. Prof. K. KONNO; Chair. Dr. K. SHIMAMURA; publ. *Kekkaku* (monthly).

Nippon Ketsueki Gakkai (*Japan Haematological Society*): Department of Internal Medicine, Faculty of Medicine, Kyoto University, Sakyo-ku, Kyoto; f. 1937; 2,200 mems.; Pres. G. WAKISAKA; publ. *Acta Haematologica Japonica* (6 issues yearly).

Nippon Kikan-Shokudo-ka Gakkai (*Japan Broncho-Esophagological Society*): School of Medicine, Keio University, 35 Shinano-machi, Shinjuku-ku, Tokyo; f. 1949; 2,000 mems.; Dir. Dr. I. HIROTO; publ. *Journal* (6 a year).

Nippon Kisei-chu Gakkai (*Japanese Society of Parasitology*): Keio University School of Medicine, Shinjuku-ku, Tokyo; f. 1926; 951 mems.; Sec.-Gen. K. ASAMI; publ. *Japanese Journal of Parasitology* (6 issues yearly).

Nippon Koshu-Eisei Kyokai (*Japanese Society of Public Health*): Koei Building, 78 Hanazono-cho, Shinjuku-ku, Tokyo; f. 1883; 3,000 mems.; Pres. UKICHI ISHIBASHI; publs. *Japanese Journal of Public Health* (monthly), *Public Health Information* (monthly), *Health Guide* (monthly).

Nippon Kyobe Shikkan Gakkai (*Japan Society of Chest Diseases*): Joyobunko, 2-28-21, Honkomagome, Bunkyo-ku, Tokyo; f. 1961; 2,996 mems.; publ. *The Japanese Journal of Thoracic Diseases* (monthly).

Nippon Masui Gakkai (*Japan Society of Anaesthesiology*): Faculty of Medicine, University of Tokyo, 3-1 Hongo 7-chome, Bunkyo-ku, Tokyo; f. 1954; 1,640 mems.; Pres. T. SATO; Secs. Y. ONJI and T. YONEZAWA; publ. *The Japanese Journal of Anaesthesiology* (monthly).

Nippon Naibumpigaku-Kai Tobu-bukai (*Eastern Branch of Japan Endocrinological Society*): c/o Department of Urology, School of Medicine, Gumma University, Maebashi; f. 1954; 1,300 mems.; Pres. K. SHIDA; publ. *Endocrinologia Japonica* (every two months in English, German, French).

Nippon No-Shinkei Gek Gakkai (*Japan Neurosurgical Society*): Dept. of Neurosurgery, Faculty of Medicine, University of Tokyo, 7 Hongo, Bunkyo-ku, Tokyo; f. 1948; 2,600 mems.; Sec. K. SANO; publs. *Neurologia Medico-Chirurgica* (Part I annually in English, Part II bi-monthly in Japanese).

Nippon Rai Gakkai (*Japanese Leprosy Association*): c/o Tofu Kyokai, Shinei Building, Uchisaiwaicho,Chiyoda, ku, Tokyo; f. 1927; 355 mems.; Pres. SHUNPEI YAMAMOTO; publ. *La Lepro* (bi-monthly).

Nippon Saikingakkai (*Japanese Society for Bacteriology*): Japanese Business Center for Academic Societies, 2-4-16 Yayoi, Bunkyo-ku, Tokyo; f. 1927; 3,000 mems.; Chief Dir. KENJI TAKEYA; publs. *Japanese Journal of Bacteriology, Microbiology and Immunology*.

Nippon Sanka-Fujinka Gakkai (*Japan Society of Obstetrics and Gynaecology*): c/o Hoken Kaikan Bldg., 1-1, Sadohara-cho, Ichigaya, Shinjuku-ku, Tokyo 162; f. 1949; 15,000 mems.; Pres. Prof. SHOSHICHI TAKEUCHI; publ. *Acta Obstetrica et Gynaecologica Japonica* (monthly).

Nippon Seikei Geka Gakkai (*Japanese Orthopaedic Association*): c/o Toyobunko, 2-28-21, Honkomagome, Bunkyo-ku, 113 Tokyo; f. 1926; 8,500 mems.; Pres. KOKICHI TSUCHIYA; publ. *Journal* (monthly).

Nippon Seiri Gakkai (*Physiological Society of Japan*): Toyobunko, 28-21, Honkomagome 2-chome, Bunkyo-ku, Tokyo; f. 1922; 2,994 mems.; Pres. M. ITO; publ. *Journal*.

Nippon Shika Hoshasen Gakkai (*Japanese Society of Dental Radiology*): Tokyo Dental College, 2-9-18, Misakicho, Chiyoda-ku, Tokyo; f. 1951; 319 mems.; Pres. S. ANDO; publ. *Dental Radiology* (annual).

Nippon Shika Hozon Gakkai (*The Japanese Society of Conservative Dentistry*): Tokyo Dental Univ., 1 Misakicho Kanda, Chiyoda-ku, Tokyo; f. 1955; 826 mems.; Pres. E. SEKINE; publ. *Journal* (2 a year).

Nippon Shika Igakkai (*Japanese Association for Dental Science*): c/o Japan Dental Association, 1-20 Kudankita 4-chome, Chiyoda-ku, Tokyo; f. 1960; 51,000 mems.; 14 mem. societies; Pres. M. SHIRASU; publ. *Dentistry in Japan* (annually).

Nippon Shikei Gakkai (*Japanese Society of Neurology*): Aoido Building 2-40-6 Hongo, Bunkyo-ku, Tokyo; f. 1960; 3,734 mems.; Pres. T. TSUBAKI; publ. *Clinical Neurology* (monthly).

Nippon Shinkeikagaku Kyokai (*Japan Neuroscience Society*): Dept. of Physiology, Faculty of Medicine, University of Tokyo, 7-3-1 Hongo, Bunkyo-ku, Tokyo; f. 1974; 454 mems.; Pres. Y. KATSUKI; publ. *News*.

Nippon Shokaki-byo Gakkai (*Japanese Society of Gastroenterology*): Gyosei Building, Ginza 7-4-12, Chuo-ku, Tokyo; f. 1899; 9,500 mems.; Pres. T. TAKAHASHI;

publs. *Nihon Shokaki-byo Gakkai Zasshi*† (Japanese, monthly), *Gastroenterologia Japonica*† (English, every 2 months).

Nippon Shonika Gakkai (*Japan Paediatric Society*): Nippon-Koshu-Eisei Kyokai Bldg., 1-29-8 Shinjuku, Shinjuku-ku, Tokyo; f. 1896; 7,200 mems.; Pres. Y. ICHIHASHI; publ. *Acta Paediatrica Japonica*—Overseas edn. (2 issues yearly).

Nippon Teiinoshujutsu Kenkyukai (*Japanese Society for Stereotactic Functional Neurosurgery*): Dept. of Neurosurgery, Nihon University, 30-1 Ohyaguchi Kami-machi, Itabashi-ku, Tokyo; f. 1963; 450 mems.; Sec.-Gen. Assoc. Prof. T. TSUBOKAWA; publ. *Neurologia Medico Chirurgica* (monthly).

Nippon Tonyo-byo Gakkai (*Japan Diabetic Society*): c/o Toyo-Bunko, 28-21, Honkomagome 2-chome, Bunkyo-ku, Tokyo 113; f. 1958; 2,600 mems.; Pres. NOBUSADA KUZUYA, M.D.; publ. *Journal* (6 a year).

Nippon Uirusu Gakkai (*The Society of Japanese Virologists*): Japanese Business Centre for Academic Societies, 4-16 Yayoi 2-chome, Bunkyo-ku, Tokyo; f. 1958; 2,141 mems.; Pres. Dr. N. ISHIDA; publs. *Virus* (Japanese text with English summary, 2 a year), *Microbiology and Immunology*.

Nippon Yakugaku-Kai (*Pharmaceutical Society of Japan*), 12-15-501, Shibuya 2-chome, Shibuya-ku, Tokyo. f. 1880; 16,579 mems.; Pres. D. MIZUNO; publs. *Chemical and Pharmaceutical Bulletin* (monthly,) *Yakugaku Zasshi* (journal—monthly), *The Journal of Hygienic Chemistry* (bi-monthly), *The Archives of Practical Pharmacy* (quarterly), *Farumashia* (monthly); *Journal of Pharmacobio-Dynamics* (monthly).

Nippon Yakuri Gakkai (*Japanese Pharmacological Society*): Faculty of Medicine, University of Tokyo, 7 Hongo, Bunkyo-ku, Tokyo; f. 1927; 1,021 mems.; Pres. H. YAMADA; publs. *Folia Pharmacologica Japonica* (bi-monthly in Japanese), *The Japanese Journal of Pharmacology* (quarterly in English).

Nippon Yuketsu Gakkai (*Japan Society of Blood Transfusion*): Nisseki Chuo-Ketsueki Center, 1-31 4 Hiroo, Shibuya-ku, Tokyo; f. 1954; 1,260 mems.; Pres. S. MURAKAMI; publ. *Journal* (6 issues yearly).

NATURAL SCIENCES

General

Nihon Gakujutsu Shinko-kai (*Japan Society for the Promotion of Science*): 5-3-1 Kojimachi, Chiyoda-ku, Tokyo f. 1967; supervised by Minister of Education; Pres. Dr. SHIRO MASUDA; publ. *Japanese Scientific Monthly*.

Nippon Kagakushi Gakkai (*The History of Science Society of Japan*): c/o Tokyo Institute of Technology, O-okayama, Meguro-ku, Tokyo; f. 1941; 800 mems.; Pres. M. YUASA; publs. *Kagakushi Kenkyu* (4 issues yearly), *Japanese Studies in the History of Science* (annual).

Biological Sciences

Hassei Seibutsu Gakkai (*Japanese Society of Developmental Biologists*): Department of Biology, Faculty of Science, Osaka City University; f. 1968; 500 mems.; Pres. M. SUGIYAMA; publs. *Journals* (quarterly, English).

Kokusai Saibo Gakkai (*International Society of Cytology*): Editorial and Business Office, Cytologia, c/o Tōyō Bunko, Honkomagome 2-28-21, Bunkyo-ku, Tokyo 113; f. 1929; 1,100 mems.; Pres. Y. SINOTÔ; publ. *Cytologia* (quarterly).

Nihon Dobutsu Gakkai (*Zoological Society of Japan*): Oriental Library, 2-28-21 Honkomagome, Bunkyo-ku, Tokyo 113; f. 1878; 2,000 mems.; Pres. NOBUO EGAMI; publs. *Zoological Magazine*, *Annotationes Zoologicae Japonenses* (quarterly).

Nippon Chô Gakkai (*Ornithological Society of Japan*): c/o Department of Zoology, National Science Museum, Hyakunin-cho 3-23-1, Shinjuku-ku, Tokyo 160; f. 1912; 600 mems.; library of *c.* 500 vols.; Pres. T. KOGA; publ. *Tori* (3 a year).

Nippon Eisei-Konchu Gakkai (*Japanese Society of Medical and Veterinary Entomology*): Research Institute of Natural Resources, 4 Hyakunin-cho, Shinjuku-ku, Tokyo; f. 1943; 150 mems.; Pres. TAKEO TAMIYA.

Nippon Iden Gakkai (*The Genetics Society of Japan*): National Institute of Genetics, Misima, 411; f. 1920; 1,548 mems.; Pres. C. OSHIMA; publ. *Japanese Journal of Genetics* (6 a year).

Nippon Jinrui Iden Gakkai (*The Japan Society of Human Genetics*): Tokyo Medical and Dental University; 1 Yushima, Bunkyo-ku, Tokyo; f. 1956; 800 mems.; Pres. E. INOUYE; publ. *Journal* (quarterly).

Nippon Kairui Gakkai (*The Malacological Society of Japan*): National Science Museum, 23-1, 3-chome, Hyakunin-cho, Shinjuku, Tokyo; f. 1928; 700 mems.; Pres. T. HABE; publs. *Venus* (quarterly), *Chiribotan* (in Japanese, quarterly).

Nippon Kin Gakkai (*Mycological Society of Japan*): National Science Museum, Ueno Park, Daito-ku, Tokyo; f. 1956; 450 mems.; Pres. Y. KOBAYASHI; publ. *Transactions* (3 issues yearly).

Nippon Kontyû Gakkai (*Entomological Society of Japan*): c/o Dept. of Zoology, National Science Museum (Natural History), 3-23-1 Hyakunin-chô, Shinjuku, Tokyo 160; f. 1917; 1,200 mems.; Pres. T. HIDAKA; publ. *Kontyû*† (quarterly).

Nippon Oyo-Dobutsu-Konchu Gakkai (*Japanese Society of Applied Entomology and Zoology*): c/o Japan Plant Protection Asscn., 11-43-1-chome, Komagome, Toshima-ku, Tokyo 170; f. 1957; 1,650 mems.; Pres. TETSUO SAITO; publs. *Applied Entomology and Zoology*† (in foreign languages, quarterly), *Japanese Journal of Applied Entomology and Zoology*† (Japanese with English synopsis, quarterly).

Nippon Rikusui Gakkai (*Japanese Society of Limnology*): Otsu Hydrobiological Station, Kyoto University, Shimosakamoto, Otsu, Shiga-ken 520-01; f. 1931; 1,000 mems.; Pres. Prof. Y. SAIJO; Sec. MASAMI NAKANISHI; publ. *Japanese Journal of Limnology*†.

Nippon Seibutsu Kankyo Chosetsu Kenkyukai (*Japanese Society of Environment Control in Biology*): Faculty of Agriculture, University of Tokyo; f. 1963; 467 mems.; Pres. M KANDATSU; publ. *Seibutsu Kankyo Chosetsu* (bi-annual).

Nippon Seikagakukai (*The Japanese Biochemical Society*): Japan Academic Societies Centre, Yayoi 2-4-16, Bunkyo-ku, Tokyo 113; f. 1923; 8,800 mems.; Pres. R. SATO; publs. *Journal of Biochemistry* (monthly in English, German and French); *Seikagaku* (monthly in Japanese.)

Nippon Seitai Gakkai (*The Ecological Society of Japan*): c/o Botanical Institute, Faculty of Science, Hiroshima University, Higashisenda-machi, Hiroshima 730; f. 1953; 2,400 mems.; Pres. T. KIRA; publ. *Japanese Journal of Ecology* (quarterly).

Nippon Shokubutsu Gakkai (*The Botanical Society of Japan*): c/o Toyobunko, 2 Chome 28-21 Honkomagome, Bunkyo-ku, Tokyo; f. 1882; 1,830 mems.; Pres. H. HARA; publs. *The Botanical Magazine, Tokyo*† (quarterly).

Nippon Shokubutsu Seiri Gakkai (*Japanese Society of Plant Physiologists*): Shimotachiuri Ogawa Higashi Kamikyoku, Kyoto 602; f. 1959; 2,674 mems.; Pres. Y. MASUDA; publ. *Plant and Cell Physiology* (8 a year).

Shokubutsu Bunrui Chiri Gakkai (*Phytogeographical Society*): Department of Botany, Faculty of Science, Kyoto University, Kyoto 606; f. 1932; 460 mems.; plant taxonomy and phytogeography; Pres. Siro Kitamura; publ. *Acta Phytotaxonomica et Geobotanica*† (annually).

Toa Kumo Gakkai (*Arachnological Society of East Asia*): c/o Biological Laboratory, Ohtemon-Gakuin University, 230, Ai, Ibaraki, Osaka 567; f. 1936; 330 mems.; Pres. Dr. T. Yaginuma; publ. *Acta Arachnologica* (biannual).

Mathematics

Nippon Sugaku Kai (*Mathematical Society of Japan*): c/o The Toyo Bunko, 28-21, Honkomagome 2-chome, Bunkyo-ku, Tokyo 113; f. 1877; 4,000 mems.; Pres. Kiyosi Ito; publs. *Journal*†, *Sugaku* (both quarterly), *Publications of the Mathematical Society of Japan* (irregular), *Japanese Journal of Mathematics* (2 a year).

Nippon Sugaku Kyoiku Gakkai (*Japan Society of Mathematical Education*): 1-3 Zoshigaya 2-chome, Toshima-ku, Tokyo 171; f. 1919; 4,732 mems.; Pres. Prof. T. Kawaguchi; publs. *Journal*† (monthly), *Supplementary issue, Report on Mathematical Education*† (2 a year).

Physical Sciences

Butsuri Tansa Gakkai (*Society of Exploration Geophysicists of Japan*): B 102 Takanawa Sky Heights, 4-19-11 Takanawa, Minato-ku Tokyo; f. 1948; 1,380 mems.; Pres. Dr. S. Omote; publ. *Butsuri Tanko* (Geophysical Exploration, 6 a year).

Chigaku Dantai Kenkyu-kai (*The Association for Geological Collaboration*): 2-32-12, Minami-Ikebukuro, Toshima-ku, Tokyo; f. 1947; study of geology, mineralogy, paleontology and related earth sciences; 3,000 mems.; Pres. Takao Tokuoka; Sec. Kumiko Yano; publs. *Geologj Demokratiaj* (monthly), *Earth Science* (twice monthly), *Earth Science Series Monograph* (irregular).

Ikomasan Tenmon Kyokai (*Ikomasan Astronomical Society*): Ikoma-Sanzyo, Ikoma-gun Nara Ken; f. 1942; 705 mems.; Pres. Joe Ueta; Sec. H. Hamane; publ. *Tenmon Kyositu* (Astronomical Class) (monthly).

Japan Weather Association: Research Institute, Kaiji Center Bldg., 5, 4-chome, Kojimachi, Chiyoda-ku, Tokyo; f. 1950; Pres. Naoshi Machida; publs. *Kisho, Daily Weather Maps, Journal of Meteorological Research* (all monthly), *Geophysical Magazine, Oceanographical Magazine* (quarterly).

Kaiyoo Kisho Gakkai (*Oceanographical and Meteorological Society*): 7-chome, Ikutaku, Kobe; f. 1921; 310 mems.; Pres. Takematsu Okada; publ. *Sea and Sky* (bimonthly).

Kobunshi Gakkai (*The Society of Polymer Science, Japan*): Honshu Bldg., 5-12-8 Ginza, Chuo-ku, Tokyo 104; f. 1951; 11,000 mems.; Pres. A. Nakajima; publs. *Kobunshi* (monthly), *Kobunshi Ronbunshu* (monthly), *Polymer Journal* (monthly in English).

Nihon Bunseki Kagaku-Kai (*Japan Society for Analytical Chemistry*): Gotanda Sanhaitsu, 26-2, Nishigotanda 1-chome, Shinagawa-ku, Tokyo 141; f. 1952; 8,073 mems.; Pres. T. Fujinaga; publs. *Bunseki Kagaku* (monthly), *Bunseki* (monthly).

Nihon Seppyo Gakkai (*Japanese Society of Snow and Ice*): Room 308, Bancho Heim, 1-2, Nibancho, Chiyoda-ku, Tokyo; f. 1939; 1,000 mems.; Pres. Dr. Zyungo Yosida; Sec. Kou Kusunoki; publs. *Seppyo* (Journal of Japanese Society of Snow and Ice, 4 a year, in Japanese), occasional papers and bibliography.

Nippon Bunko Gakkai (*Spectroscopical Society of Japan*): c/o Sanshiken Bldg., 3-25-2 Hyakunin-cho, Shinjuku-ku, Tokyo 160; f. 1951; 1,000 mems.; Pres. S. Minami; publ. *Journal*† (6 a year).

Nippon Butsuri Gakkai (*Physical Society of Japan*): Room No. 211, Kikai-Shinko Bldg. 3-5-8 Shiba-Koen, Minato-ku, Tokyo 105; f. 1946; 11,835 mems.; Pres. T. Oguchi; publs. *Butsuri* (monthly, in Japanese), *Journal* (monthly), *Japanese Journal of Applied Physics* (monthly), *Progress of Theoretical Physics* (monthly).

Nippon Butsuri-Kagaku Kenkyukai (*Physico-Chemical Society of Japan*): Faculty of Science, Kyoto University, Kyoto; f. 1926; 360 mems.; Pres. Wasaburo Jono; publ. *Review of Physical Chemistry of Japan*.

Nippon Chikyu Denki Ziki Gakkai (*Society of Terrestrial Magnetism and Electricity of Japan*): c/o Japan Academic Societies Business Centre, 2-4-16 Yayoi, Bunkyo-ku, Tokyo; f. 1947; 500 mems.; Dir. Prof. Susumu Kato; publ. *Journal of Geomagnetism and Geo-electricity* (monthly).

Nippon Chishitsu Gakkai (*Geological Society of Japan*); Maruishi Bldg., 10-4, Kajicho 1-chome, Chiyoda-ku, Tokyo 101; f. 1893; 4,321 mems.; Pres. Yutaka Ikebe; publ. *Journal* (monthly).

Nippon Dai-Yonki Gakkai (*Japan Association for Quaternary Research*): c/o Gakkai Center Bldg., Yayoi 2-4-16, Bunkyo-ku, Tokyo 113: f. 1956; 1,500 mems.; Pres. N. Watanabe; publ. *Quaternary Research* (quarterly).

Nippon Denshi Kenbikyo Gakkai (*Japanese Society of Electron Microscopy*): c/o Business Centre for Academic Societies, 4-16 Yayoi 2-chome, Bunkyo-ku, Tokyo; f. 1949; 2,500 mems.; Pres. T. Taoka; publ. *Journal* (quarterly).

Nippon Ganseki Kobutsu Kosho Gakkai (*Japanese Association of Mineralogists, Petrologists and Economic Geologists*): Faculty of Science, Tohoku University, Sendai; f. 1930; 1,000 mems.; library of 17,000 vols.; Pres. Yoshio Ueda; publ. *Journal* (monthly).

Nippon Kagakukai (*Chemical Society of Japan*): 5, 1-chome, Kanda-Surugadai, Chiyoda-ku, Tokyo; f. 1878; 32,000 mems.; Pres. Sumio Umezawa; Exec. Dir. Hiroshi Hamada; publs. *Kagaku to Kogyo, Nippon Kagaku Kaishi, Chemistry Letters, Bulletin* (monthly).

Nippon Kaisui Gakkai (*The Society of Sea Water Science, Japan*): c/o The Japan Salt Industry Association, 7-15-14, Roppongi, Minato-ku, Tokyo; f. 1950; 485 mems.; Pres. Takeo Yamabe.

Nippon Kaiyo Gakkai (*Oceanographical Society of Japan*): c/o Ocean Research Institute, University of Tokyo, 1 Minamidai, Nakano, Tokyo; f. 1941; 1,650 mems.; Pres. Toshio Nannichi; publ. *Journal* (every 2 months).

Nippon Kazan Gakkai (*Volcanological Society of Japan*): Earthquake Research Institute, University of Tokyo, 1 Yayoi-cho, Bunkyo-ku, Tokyo; f. 1932; 700 mems.; Pres. Y. Katsui; publs. *Bulletin* (quarterly), *Bulletin of Volcanic Eruptions* (annually).

Nippon Kessho Gakkai (*The Crystallographic Society of Japan*): Nihon Gakkai Jimu Centre, 2-4-16 Yayoi, Bunkyo-ku, Tokyo 113; f. 1950; 1,000 mems.; Pres. S. Hosoya; publ. *Journal* (6 a year).

Nippon Kisho Gakkai (*The Meteorological Society of Japan*): c/o Japan Meteorological Agency, Ote-machi, Chiyoda-ku, Tokyo; f. 1882; 4,000 mems.; Pres. K. Ganbo; publs. *Tenki* (monthly), *Journal* (6 a year), *Papers in Meteorology and Geophysics* (quarterly).

Nippon Kokai Gakkai (*Japan Institute of Navigation*): Tokyo University of Mercantile Marine, 2-1-6 Etchujima, Koto-ku, Tokyo; f. 1948; 930 mems.; Pres. Prof. H. Kikutani; publs. *Journal*† (2 a year), *Navigation* (quarterly).

Nippon Koseibutsu Gakkai (*Palaeontological Society of Japan*): c/o Business Centre for Academic Societies, Yayoi 2-4-16, Bunkyo-ku, Tokyo 113; f. 1935; 470

mems.; Pres. TATSURO MATSUMOTO; publs. *Transactions and Proceedings* (quarterly), *Fossils* (2 a year), special papers (occasional).

Nippon Nendo Gakkai (*The Clay Science Society of Japan*): c/o Kôshinsha, 3-20, Kanda Nishikicho, Chiyoda-ku, Tokyo; f. 1956; 500 mems.; Pres. A. ARIIZUMI; publs. *Journal* (quarterly), *Clay Science* (annually).

Nippon Nensho Kenkyu-kai (*Combustion Society of Japan*): Department of Reaction Chemistry, Faculty of Engineering, University of Tokyo, 7 Hongo, Bunkyo-ku, Tokyo; f. 1953; 430 mems.; Pres. H. TSUJI; publ. *Nensho Kenkyu* (3/4 issues yearly).

Nippon Nogyo-Kisho Gakkai (*Society of Agricultural Meteorology of Japan*): c/o Faculty of Horticulture, Chiba University, Matsudo, Chiba 271; f. 1942; 873 mems.; Pres. YASOJI TSUBOI; publ. *Nogyo-Kisho* (Journal of Agricultural Meteorology, quarterly).

Nippon Onkyo Gakkai (*The Acoustical Society of Japan*): 4th Floor, Ikeda Bldg. 7-7, Yoyogi 2 chome, Shibuya-ku, Tokyo; f. 1936; 2,600 mems.; Pres. T. NIMURA; publs. *Journal* (12 a year), *Reports of Spring and Autumn Meetings* (2 a year).

Nippon Sokuchi Gakkai (*The Geodetic Society of Japan*): Geographical Survey Institute, Higashiyama 3-24-13, Meguro-ku, Tokyo; f. 1954; studies Astronomy, Crustal activity, Earth tide, Geodesy, Geomagnetism, Gravity, etc.; 500 mems.; library of 5,000 vols.; Pres. K. IIDA; publ. *Journal* (quarterly).

Nippon Temmon Gakkai (*Astronomical Society of Japan*): Tokyo Astronomical Observatory, Osawa Mitaka, Tokyo; f. 1908; 2,028 mems.; Pres. I. TSUBOKAWA; publs. *Publications* (quarterly), *The Astronomical Herald* (monthly, in Japanese).

Nippon Yukagaku Kyokai (*Japan Oil Chemists' Society*): 7th Floor, Yushi Kogyo Kaikan, 13-11, Nihonbashi 3-chome, Chūo-ku, Tokyo 103; f. 1951; 2,500 mems.; Pres. TARO MATSUMOTO; publ. *Journal* (monthly).

Oyo-buturi Gakkai (*Japan Society of Applied Physics*): Kikai-Shinko Bldg., 3-5-8 Shiba-Koen, Minato-ku, Tokyo; f. 1932; 9,000 mems.; Pres. TOSHIHIRO OKADA; publs. *Oyo-buturi*, *JJAP* (monthly).

Sen-i Gakkai (*Society of Fibre Science and Technology, Japan*): 3-3-9-208 Kamiosaki, Shinagawa-ku, Tokyo 141; f. 1943; *c.* 3,000 mems.; Pres. HIROMICHI KAWAI; publ. *Journal* (monthly).

Shokubai Gakkai (*Catalysis Society of Japan*): Tokyo Institute of Technology, 2 Oo-okayama, Meguro-ku, Tokyo; f. 1958; 1,415 mems.; Pres. O. TOYAMA; publ. *Catalyst* (6 issues yearly).

Zisin Gakkai (*Seismological Society of Japan*): Earthquake Research Institute, The University of Tokyo, Yayoi 1-1-1 Bunkyo-ku, Tokyo; f. 1929; 1,130 mems.; Chair. RYOSUKE SATO; publs. *Zisin* (Journal, quarterly), *Journal of Physics of the Earth* (6 a year).

PHILOSOPHY AND PSYCHOLOGY

Bigaku-Kai (*Japanese Society for Aesthetics*): Department of Aesthetics, Faculty of Letters, The University of Tokyo, 7-3-1 Hongo, Bunkyo-ku, Tokyo; f. 1950; 800 mems.; Pres. TOSHIO TAKEUCHI; publ. *Bigaku*† (Aesthetics; quarterly).

Moralogy Kenkyusho (*Institute of Moralogy*): 1-1, 2-chome, Hikarigaoka, Kashiwa-shi, Chiba-ken; f. 1926; Pres. S. HIROIKE; publs. *Studies in Moralogy*†, monthly magazines.

Nihon Oyo Shinri-gakkai (*Japan Association of Applied Psychology*): Counselling center, Keio University, 2-15-45 Mita Minato-ku, Tokyo; f. 1931; Pres. ZUIICHIRŌ OTAGAKI; Sec. MITSUGI HASEGAWA.

Nihon Rinrigakukai (*Japanese Society for Ethics*): Department of Ethics, Faculty of Letters, The University of Tokyo, Bunkyo-ku, Tokyo 165; f. 1950; 700 mems.; Pres. TAKEZO KANEKO; publs. *Rinrigakunenpo*† (Annals), *Rinrigakukaironshu* (Transactions of annual meeting).

Nippon Dobutsu Shinri Gakkai (*The Japanese Society for Animal Psychology*): Faculty of Letters, University of Tokyo, 7 Hongo, Bunkyo-ku, Tokyo; f. 1933; 450 mems.; Pres. B. YAGI; publ. *Annual of Animal Psychology*† (2 a year).

Nippon Shakai Shinri Gakkai (*The Japanese Society of Social Psychology*): Department of Psychology, University of the Sacred Heart, Hirowo 4-3-1, Shibuya-ku, Tokyo 150; f. 1960; 600 mems.; Pres. H. MINAMI; publ. *The Annals of Social Psychology, Bulletin of the Japanese Society of Social Psychology* (quarterly).

Nippon Shinrigakkai (*Japanese Psychological Association*): 37-13-802, Hongo 4-chome, Bunkyo-ku, Tokyo 113; f. 1927; 3,000 mems.; Pres. GENICHI HAGINO; publs. *Japanese Journal of Psychology* (bi-monthly), *Japanese Psychological Research* (quarterly).

Tetsugaku-kai (*Philosophical Society*): Faculty of Letters, University of Tokyo, Hongo, Bunkyo-ku, Tokyo; f. 1884; 500 mems.; Pres. JUICHI KATSURA; publ. *Tetsugaku-zasshi* (annual).

RELIGION, SOCIOLOGY, ANTHROPOLOGY

(Toho Gakkai) Institute of Eastern Culture: 4-1, Nishi Kanda, 2 chome, Chiyoda-ku, Tokyo 101; f. 1947; 900 mems.; Pres. KŌJIRŌ YOSHIKAWA; Chair. Prof. TATSURO YAMAMOTO; publs. *Acta Asiatica*† (annually), *Tohogaku*† (every 2 years), *Transactions of the International Conference of Orientalists in Japan* (annually).

Japan Center for International Exchange: 9-17 Minami-Azabu 4-chome, Minato-ku, Tokyo; f. 1971 to promote dialogue between Japan and the rest of the world; international conferences and seminars, overseas programme planning, exchange of persons, liaison and representation, publications and translation; Dir. TADASHI YAMAMOTO; publ. *Education in World Perspective*.

Nihon-Indogaku-Bukkyôgakukai (*Japanese Association of Indian and Buddhist Studies*): c/o Dept. of Indian Philosophy and Sanskrit Philology, Faculty of Letters, The University of Tokyo, Bunkyo-ku, Tokyo; f. 1951; 2,023 mems.; Pres. SHOSON MIYAMOTO; publ. *Indogaku Bukkyôgaku Kenkyû* (Journal of Indian and Buddhist Studies).

Nihon Shukyo Gakkai (*Japanese Association for Religious Studies*): Department of Religious Studies, Faculty of Letters, University of Tokyo, 113 Bunkyo-ku, Tokyo 113; f. 1930; 1,200 mems.; Pres. ICHI OGUCHI; publ. *Journal of Religious Studies* (quarterly).

Nippon Dokyo Gakkai (*Japan Society of Taoistic Research*), Faculty of Letters, Rissho University, 4-2-16, Osaki: Shinagawa-ku, Tokyo; f. 1950; 400 mems.; Pres. T. SAKAI; publ. *The Journal of Eastern Religions* (2 issues yearly).

Nippon Jinruigaku Kai (*Anthropological Society of Japan*): Department of Anthropology, Faculty of Science, University of Tokyo, Bunkyo-ku, Tokyo; f. 1884; 689 mems.; Pres. NAOTUNE WATANABE; publ. *Journal* (quarterly).

Nippon Shakai Gakkai (*Japanese Sociological Society*): Department of Sociology, Faculty of Letters, The University of Tokyo, Bunkyo-ku, Tokyo; f. 1923; 1,180 mems.; Pres. TADASHI FUKUTAKE; publ. *Shakaigaku Hyôron* (Japanese Sociological Review; quarterly).

Nippon Shimbun Gakkai (*Japan Society for Journalism and Mass Communication*): Institute of Journalism, University of Tokyo, 7 Hongo, Bunkyo-ku, Tokyo; f. 1951; 492 mems.; Pres. K. Yoneyama; publ. *Japanese Journalism Review* (annual).

Okurayama Bunka Kagaku Kenkyujo (*Okurayama Research Institute for Cultural Science*): Okurayama, Futoo-machi, Kohoku-ku, Yokohama; f. 1923; Pres. Yasaburo Shimonaka.

K. Shibusawa Memorial Foundation for Ethnology: Higashicho 3-1-17, Hoya-shi, Tokyo; f. 1935; 900 mems.; library of 45,000 vols.; Dir. Furuno Kiyoto; publs. *Minzokugaku-Kenkyu* (Japanese Journal of Ethnology) (quarterly), *Ethnology in Japan* (Historical Review).

Technology

Denki Gakkai (*Institute of Electrical Engineers of Japan*): 1-12-1, Yurakucho, Chiyoda-ku, Tokyo 100; f. 1888; 20,000 mems.; 9 brs.; Pres. Chikasa Uenosono; publs. *Journal* (monthly), *Transactions* (every 2 months, English).

Denshi Tsushin Gakkai (*The Institute of Electronics and Communication Engineers of Japan*): Kikai Shinko Kaikan 5-8, Shibakoen 3-chome, Minato-ku, Tokyo 105; f. 1917; 27,000 mems.; Pres. B. Oguchi; publs. *Journal, Transactions* (monthly), *Original Contributions in English and Abstracts in English from the Transactions* (monthly).

Doboku-Gakkai (*Japan Society of Civil Engineers*): Yotsuya 1-chome, Shinjuku-ku, Tokyo; f. 1914; 27,754 mems.; library of 23,000 vols.; Pres. Kuniichiro Takahashi; Man. Dir. Tatsuo Kawagoe; publs. *Journal of the Japan Society of Civil Engineers, Transactions*†, *Civil Engineering in Japan*†, *Coastal Engineering in Japan* (in English, annual), *Proceedings* (monthly).

Doshitsu Kogakkai (*The Japanese Society of Soil Mechanics and Foundation Engineering*): Sugayama Bldg. 4F, Kanda Awaji-cho 2-23, Chiyoda-ku, Tokyo; f. 1949; 13,300 mems.; Pres. Gosaburo Miki; publs. *Soils and Foundations* (quarterly), *Tsuchi to Kiso* (monthly).

Keikinzoku Gakkai (*Japanese Institute of Light Metals*): Nihonbashi Asahiseimei Bldg., 1-3, Nihonbashi 2 chome, Chuo-ku, Tokyo 103; f. 1965; 1,790 mems.; Pres. Kikuo Yasuda; publ. *Journal of the Japanese Institute of Light Metals* (monthly in Japanese and English).

Keisoku Jidoseigyo Gakkai (*Society of Instrument and Control Engineers*): Kotohira Annex 39, Kotohira-cho Shiba, Minato-ku, Tokyo 105; f. 1962; 6,000 mems.; Pres. Yasutaka Saito; publs. *Journal* (monthly), *Transactions* (6 issues yearly).

Kogyo Kayaku Kyokai (*The Industrial Explosives Society of Japan*): Gunma Bldg., 2-3-21 Nihonbashi, Chuo-ku, Tokyo 103; f. 1939; 870 mems.; Pres. Tsutomu Hikita; publ. *Journal* (bi-monthly).

Kuki-Chowa Eisei Kogakkai (*The Society of Heating, Air-conditioning and Sanitary Engineers of Japan*): 8-1, 1-chome, Kitashinjuku, Shinjuku-ku, Tokyo; f. 1917; 18,000 mems.; library of 10,000 vols.; Pres. U. Inoue; publs. *Journal* (monthly), *Transactions* (3 a year).

Nihon Kasai Gakkai (*The Japanese Asscn. of Fire Science and Engineering*): Gakkai Centre Bldg., 2-chome 4-16 Yayoi, Bunkyo-ku, Tokyo; f. 1951; 1,800 mems.; Pres. Kunio Kawagoe; publs. *Kasai* (Fire, every 2 months), *Bulletin* (2 a year).

Nihon Kikai Gakkai (*Japan Society of Mechanical Engineers*): Sanshin Hokusei Bldg., 4-9 Yoyogi 2-chome, Shibuya-ku, Tokyo; f. 1897; 41,000 mems.; Pres. S. Fujii; publs. *Yearbook, Journal, Transactions* (monthly), *Bulletin* (in English, monthly).

Nippon Genshiryoku Gakkai (*Atomic Energy Society of Japan*): 1-5-4 Ohte-machi, Chiyoda-ku, Tokyo; f. 1959; 5,434 mems.; Pres. T. Ito; Sec.-Gen. M. Masamoto; publs. *Nihon-Genshiryoku-Gakkai Shi* (monthly), *Journal of Nuclear Science and Technology* (monthly).

Nippon Jidoseigyo Kyokai (*Japan Association of Automatic Control Engineers*): 14 Kawahara-cho, Yoshida, Sakyo-ku, Kyoto; f. 1957; 1,939 mems.; Pres. Toshio Ikezima; publ. *Systems and Control*† (monthly).

Nippon Junkatsu Gakkai (*Japan Society of Lubrication Engineers*): c/o Kikai Shinko Kaikan No. 407-2, 5-8, Shiba Koen 3-chome, Minato-ku, Tokyo 105; f. 1956; 2,500 mems.; Pres. F. Hirano; publ. *Journal* (monthly).

Nippon Kinzoku Gakkai (*Japan Institute of Metals*): Aoba Aramaki, Sendai 980; f. 1937; 11,000 mems.; Pres. Jin-ichi Takamura; publs. *Journal* (monthly), *Bulletin* (monthly), *Transactions* (monthly).

Nippon Kogakukai (*Japan Federation of Engineering Societies*): c/o The Society of Japanese Naval Architects, 35 Shiba Kotohira-cho, Minato-ku, Tokyo; f. 1879; publ. *Journal* (quarterly).

Nippon Kogyokai (*Mining and Metallurgical Institute of Japan*): 8-5-4 Ginza, Chuo-ku, Tokyo 104; f. 1885; 4,500 mems.; publ. *Journal* (12 a year, in Japanese and English).

Nippon Koku Gakkai (*Japan Society for Aeronautical and Space Science*): 18-1 Shinbashi 1-chome, Minato-ku, Tokyo; f. 1934; 1,800 mems.; Pres. Y. Matsuura; publs. *Journal* (monthly), *Transactions* (2 a year).

Nippon Shashin Gakkai (*The Society of Photographic Science and Technology of Japan*): Tokyo College of Photography, 2-9-5 Hon-cho, Nakano-ku, Tokyo; f. 1925; 1,550 mems.; Pres. E. Inoue; publs. *Journal* (6 a year).

Nippon Shashin Sokuryo Gakkai (*The Japan Society of Photogrammetry*): Daichi Honan Bldg. 601, 2-8-17 Minami Ikebukoro, Toshima-ku, Tokyo 171; f. 1962; 906 mems.; Pres. E. Inoue; publ. *Journal* (quarterly, overseas edn. annual).

Nippon Tekko Kyokai (*Iron and Steel Institute of Japan*): Keidanren Kaikan (3rd Floor) No. 9-4, Otemachi, 1-chome, Chiyoda-ku, Tokyo; f. 1915; 9,500 mems.; Pres. Toru Araki; publs. *Tetsu-to-Hagane* (Iron and Steel, monthly), *Transactions* (monthly).

Nogyo-Doboku Gakkai (*The Japanese Society of Irrigation, Drainage and Reclamation Engineering*): Nogyo Doboku-Kaikan, 34-4 Shinbashi 5-chome, Minato-ku, Tokyo 105; f. 1929; 12,000 mems.; Pres. Prof. Hiroyuki Ogata; publs. *Journal* (monthly), *Transactions* (bi-monthly).

Seisan Gijutsu Kenkyusho (*Institute of Industrial Science*): The University of Tokyo, 7-22-1 Roppongi, Minato-ku, Tokyo; f. 1949; Dir. Prof. Dr. Hisashi Tanaka; publ. *Report* (6–8 a year).

Shomei Gakkai (*Illuminating Engineering Institute of Japan*): 7-1 Yurakucho 1 chome, Chiyoda-ku, Tokyo 100; f. 1916; 4,782 mems.; Pres. K. Obara; publs. *Shomei Gakkai Zasshi* (Journal), *Journal of Light and Visual Environment.*

Yogyo Kyokai (*Ceramic Society of Japan*): 22-17, 2-chome, Hyakunicho, Shinjuku-ku, Tokyo 160; f. 1891; 5,024 mems.; Pres. Tsuneo Ohtomo; publs. *Yogyo-Kyokai-shi, Ceramics Japan, Japan Ceramics Statistical Monthly.*

Yosetsu Gakkai (*Japan Welding Society*): 1-11 Sakuma-cho, Kanda, Chiyoda-ku, Tokyo; f. 1925; 5,000 mems.; Pres. Dr. Prof. Dr. Isao Masumoto; publs. *Journal* (monthly), *Transactions* (2 a year).

RESEARCH INSTITUTES

(*See* also under Universities.)

Agriculture and Veterinary Science

(all institutes in this section are part of the Ministry of Agriculture, Forestry and Fisheries)

Central Agricultural Experiment Station: 1,227 Konosu, Konosu-shi, Saitama-Ken 365; f. 1923; 250 mems.; library of 50,000 vols.; Dir. Dr. K. Kishi; publ. *Journal* (2 issues a year in Japanese, with English summary).

Forest and Forest Products Research Institute: P.O.B. 2, Ushiku, Ibaraki 300-12; f. 1878; library of 150,000 vols. (including Br. Stations); Dir. Dr. Mitsuma Matsui; publ. *Bulletin* (8–10 a year).

Fruit Tree Research Station: 2-1 Fujimoto, Yatabe, Ibaraki (4 branches); f. 1921; research on fruit tree cultivation, breeding of fruit trees, and disease and pest control; 115 mems.; library of 40,000 vols.; Dir. Taro Suyama; publs. *Bulletin*†, *Series A, B, C, D and E* (annually).

National Food Research Institute: Yatabe, Tsukuba, Ibaraki 305; f. 1934; food processing, chemistry, technology, storage, engineering, distribution, nutrition; applied microbiology, analysis, radiation; 139 mems.; library of 30,000 vols.; Dir. H. Miura; publs. *Report*†, *Food, its Science and Technology*†, *A Series for Food Processing Technology*† (annually).

National Institute of Agricultural Sciences: 2-1-7 Nishigahara, Kita-ku, Tokyo; f. 1950; 449 mems.; library of 120,000 vols.; Dir. Isamu Baba; publs. *Bulletin, Series A, B, C, D, H* (1–2 a year of each).

National Institute of Animal Health: 1-1, Kannondai 3-chome, Yatabe-machi, Tsukuba-gun, Ibaraki-ken 305; f. 1910; 350 mems.; 5 branch laboratories; 1,600 serial titles in library; Dir. Dr. T. Shimizu; publs. *National Institute of Animal Health Quarterly*†, *Bulletin* (2 a year, in Japanese), *Annual Report*.

National Institute of Animal Industry: Tsukuba Norindanchi, P.O.B. 5, Ibaraki 305; 121 staff; library of 31,262 vols.; f. 1916; Dir. T. Abe; publs. *Bulletin* (irregular), *Summaries* (irregular, in English), *Annual Report*.

National Research Institute of Agricultural Economics: 2-2-1 Nishigahara, Kita-ku, Tokyo; f. 1946; library of 231,000 vols.; Dir. Y. Koyama; publ. *Quarterly Journal* (in Japanese).

National Research Institute of Agricultural Engineering: 2-1-2 Kannondai, Yatabe-machi, Tsukuba-gun, Ibaraki; f. 1961; tests, research, investigation, analysis, identification and training with regard to irrigation, drainage, reclamation, farm facilities, rural planning; 123 mems.; library of 21,000 vols.; Dir. T. Takasu; publs. *Bulletin*† (annual), and *Technical Report*† (irregular).

Sericultural Experiment Station: 1-2 Ohwashi Yatabe-cho, Tsukuba-gun, Ibaraki 305; f. 1911; Dir. N. Fukuda; publs. *Bulletin* (irregular), *Technical Bulletin* (irregular) and *Acta Sericologica* (quarterly).

Tea Research Station: 2769 Kanaya-cho, Haibara-gan, Shizuoka; f. 1919; Dir. K. Furuya; publs. *Bulletin* (annual) and *Study of Tea* (2 a year).

The Arts

Institute of Art Research: Ueno Park, Taito-ku, Tokyo; f. 1930; research in historical art; 19 mems.; library of 60,000 vols.; Dir. K. Kawakami; publs. *Bisutsu Kenkyu* (Journal of Art Studies) (6 a year), *The Year-Book of Japanese Art*.

Toyo Ongaku Gakkai (*The Society for Research in Asiatic Music*): c/o Tokyo National Research Institute of Cultural Properties, 13-27 Ueno Park, Taito-ku, Tokyo 110; f. 1936; aims to promote research in Asian music and ethno-musicology; 500 mems.; Pres. Prof. Hisao Tanabe; publ. *Journal* (quarterly).

Economics, Law and Politics

Ajia Keizai Kenkyusho (*Institute of Developing Economies*): 42 Ichigaya-Hommura-cho, Shinjuku-ku, Tokyo 162, Japan; f. 1960; 275 staff; Chair. Miyohei Shinohara; Pres. Hisatoshi Morisaki; Dirs. Yoshiyuki Hagiwara, Koji Fujitani, Tomijiro Negishi; library of 160,000 vols.; publs. *Ajia Keizai* (monthly), *The Developing Economies* (quarterly, in English), *Library Bulletin* (monthly), *Ajia Doko Nempo* (annually), Occasional Papers Series (irregular, in English), *IDE Special Papers* (irregular in English), *Union Catalogues*, etc.

Asia Pacific Association of Japan: Hotel New Japan, Annex 463, 2-13-8, Nagata-cho, Chiyoda-ku, Tokyo 100; f. 1966; research and study on international affairs and diplomatic problems; 67 mems.; library of *c.* 1,000 vols.; Pres. Shizuo Saito; Sec. Shoichi Kobayashi; publs. occasional reports.

China Research Institute: 4-1-34 Kudan-kita, Chiyoda-ku, Tokyo; f. 1946; Dir. T. Ito: publs. *China Research Monthly, Asia Economic Bulletin* (36 issues yearly) and *New China Year Book.*

Chuto Chosakai (*Middle East Institute of Japan*): 802, 15th Mori Bldg., 2-8-10, Toranomon, Minato-ku, Tokyo; f. 1956; government-aided; exchanges information with other countries; research activities in four areas: political and diplomatic affairs, industry, economy, natural resources; library in process of formation; Chair. Yoshihiro Nakayama; publs. *Chuto Tsuho* (Middle East News, every 2 months), *Chuto Kitaafurika Nenkan* (Yearbook of the Middle East and North Africa), *Chuto Seiji Keizai News* (Political and Economic News of the Middle East; 2 a month).

Institute of Local Government: 1-11-35, Nagata-cho, Chiyoda-ku, Tokyo; f. 1946; independent research institute which undertakes self-initiated and contractual projects in the fields of development of local government and improvement of welfare and democratic politics; 41 research staff; library of 5,000 vols.; Chair. Kokichi Yamano; Sec.-Gen. Kuniyoshi Mukai.

Institute of Politics and Economy: Ushigome Mansion, 198 Yamabuki-cho, Shinjuku-ku, Tokyo; f. 1946; Dir. H. Ichikawa; publ. *Seikei Kenkyu* (2 a year).

Institute of Population Problems (*Ministry of Health and Welfare*): 1-2-2 Kasumigaseki, Chiyoda-ku, Tokyo; f. 1939; 45 mems.; library of 16,000 vols.; Dir. Nobuo Shinozaki; publs. *The Journal* (quarterly), *Annual Reports* (several issues a year), *Research Series, English Pamphlet Series* (irregular), *Field Survey Report* (annual), *Selected Demographic Statistics* (half-yearly).

Kabushikikaisha Mitsubishi Sogo Kenkyusho (*Mitsubishi Research Institute, Inc.*): Time & Life Building, 3-6, Otemachi 2-chome, Chiyoda-ku, Tokyo 100; f. 1970; aims to meet new social, economic and industrial requirements in an age of rapid economic growth and internationalization; research on national and international scale to serve the needs of government agencies and industry in the fields of economic, political, industrial and management affairs, techno-economics, social engineering, technology and data processing; 467 mems.; library of 31,000 vols., 1,100 periodicals; Chair. Masaki Nakajima; Senior Man.

Dir. Shoichi Kamiya; publs. *Chart for Brighter Business*†, *Forecast of the Japanese Economy*† (2 a year), *Journal*† (annually), *MRI Newsletter*† (quarterly), *Top Management Service*† (every 2 months).

Kaiji Sangyo Kenkyusho (*Japan Maritime Research Institute*): Kaiun Bldg., 6-4, 2-chome, Hirakawa-cho, Chiyoda-ku, Tokyo; f. 1966; library of 14,000 vols.; Chair. Prof. Dr. Yoshitaro Wakimura; Dir. Masami Yasui; publ. *Bulletin*† (monthly).

Keidanren Kaikan (*Federation of Economic Organizations*): 9-4, Otemachi 1-chome, Chiyoda-ku, Tokyo 100; f. 1946; an independent body which aims to maintain contact with various economic sectors, to sound out opinions in business circles on economic problems, domestic and international, and to obtain practical solutions to these problems thereby promoting sound development of the national economy; carries out surveys, research, studies; gives assistance in the exchange of information, dissemination of materials, etc.; 985 mems.; library of 40,000 vols.; Chair. Yoshihiro Inayama; Dir.-Gen. Nihachiro Hanamura; publs. *Keidanren Review* (every 2 months, English), *Keidanren Geppo* (monthly), *Keidanren Shuho* (weekly).

Nihon Keizai Kenkyu Center (*Japan Economic Research Center*): Nikkei Bldg., 9-5, 1-chome, Otemachi, Chiyoda-ku, Tokyo 100; f. 1963; 280 institutional, 400 individual mems.; library of 22,000 vols, 690 periodicals; Pres. H. Kanamori; publs. *Keizai Kenkyu Center Kaiho*† (fortnightly), *Quarterly Forecast of Japan's Economy* (3 a year).

Nikko Research Center Ltd.: Kokusai Bldg., 1-1, Marunouchi 3-chome, Chiyoda-ku, Tokyo 100; f. 1970; provides investment information for Nikko Securities Ltd. and its clients; economic research on Japanese economy; business research on Japanese companies; investment advisory services to domestic and overseas investors, including advisory service to Japan fund; projects research sponsored by governments and corporations; 100 mems.; library of 20,000 vols.; Pres. Shogo Watanabe; Dir.-Gen. Toshio Shishido; publs. various monthly reports, *Nikko Quarterly Bulletin* (in English), *NRC Chartroom—A Graphic Survey of the Japanese Economy and Securities Market* (monthly, in English).

Nippon Research Center Ltd.: Daini-Nagaoka Bldg., 2-8-5 Hatchobori, Chuo-ku, Tokyo 104; f. 1960 by interdisciplinary researchers and business men to meet the needs of industrial and economic circles; marketing and public opinion research, marketing consultancy, public relations, economic forecasting and urban and regional development; 88 staff; library of *c.* 3,000 vols.; Chair. Kyoji Suzuki; Dir. of Research Kohji Niki; publ. *Bulletin of Marketing Research* (2 a year, in Japanese).

Rôdô Kagaku Kenkyusho (*Japanese Institute of Labour Science*): 1544, Sugao, Takatsu-ku, Kawasatu-shi, Kanagawa-ken; f. 1921; sections: physiology, biochemistry, pathology, hygiene, psychology, economics, agricultural economics; Chair. of Board of Dirs. Tatsuo Morito; Dir. of Research Hajime Saito, M.D.; publs. *Rôdô Kagaku* (Journal of Science of Labour, monthly), *Rôdô no Kagaku* (Digest of Science of Labour, monthly), *Reports and Monographs*.

Seisaku Kagaku Kenkyu Sho (*Institute for Policy Sciences*): Friend Bldg., 2-4-11, Nagata-cho, Chiyoda-ku, Tokyo; f. 1971; independent institute authorized by the Ministries of Finance and International Trade and Industry; undertakes its own and contractual research in the problems of advanced societies caused by technological innovation, industrialization, urbanization, etc.; research in the fields of regional development, land use, environment, energy and natural resources, international relations, economic and social problems, manpower development, etc.; Chair. and Exec. Dir. Tohata Seiichi; publs. research reports, *Policy-Gendai Seisaku Kagaku* (Contemporary Policy Science, quarterly).

Shakai Hosho Kenkyusho (*Social Development Research Institute*): Shakai-Jigyo-Kaikan, 3-3-4 Kasumigaseki, Chiyoda-ku, Tokyo; f. 1965; Dir. K. Baba; publ. *The Quarterly of Social Security Research.*

Shakai Keisai Kenkyujo (*Institute for Social and Economic Problems*): 505 Nukui, Koganei-machi, Kitatama-gun, Tokyo; Dir. Mitsugu Tanaka.

Social and Economic Affairs Research Institute: The Mitsui Bank, Ltd., Motimachi-shiten Bldg., 3-3 Nihombashi Motomachi, Chuo-ku, Tokyo; f. 1959; Dir. H. Matsuzumi; publ. *Kokumin Seikatsu Kenkyu* (monthly).

Education

National Institute for Educational Research: 6-5-22 Shimomeguro, Meguro-ku, Tokyo 153; f. 1949; library of 290,000 vols.; Dir.-Gen. Hiroshi Kida; publs. *Bulletin* (Japanese and English), *Koho* (Japanese, 3 a year), *Unesco-NIER Newsletter* (in English, 2 a year).

Consists of 6 departments:

i Department for Administrative Affairs; Dir. A. Okamoto.

ii History of Japanese Education, Philosophy of Education, Comparative Education, Historical Documents; Dir. T. Tezuka.

iii Educational Planning, Educational Systems, Educational Administration and Finance, Teacher Education, Education in Asia; Dir. S. Ichikawa.

iv Disposition and Abilities of Pupils, Evaluation and Measurement, Guidance, Counselling and Selection Methods, Infant Education; Dir. S. Nagano.

v Elementary and Secondary School Curriculum, Industrial Education, Social Education, Moral Education; Dir. K. Kihara.

vi Department for Planning, External Relations, Educational Co-operation in Asia; Dir. M. Shuhara.

Research Centre for Science Education: Dir. S. Kojima.

History, Geography and Archaeology

Geographical Survey Institute (*Ministry of Construction*): 24-13, 3-chome, Higashiyama, Meguro-ku, Tokyo; f. 1945; library of 12,000 vols.; Dir. N. Shigekane; publ. *Bulletin* (irregular).

Shiryo Hensanjo (*Historiographical Institute of the University of Tokyo*): 3-1, Hongo 7-chome, Bunkyo-ku, Tokyo 113; f. 1869, affiliated with the University in 1888; active in the study, compilation and publication of historical sources on Japan; 89 mems.; library of approx. 400,000 vols.; Dir. Prof. Yujiro Kikuchi; Sec. Shoichi Miyashige; publs. *Tokyo Daigaku Shiryo Hensanjo-ho* (Annual Report).

Language and Literature

Gengo Bunka Kenkyujo (*Research Institute for Linguistic Culture*): 16-26 Nampeidai-machi, Shibuya-ku, Tokyo; Pres. Morito Naganuma; publ. *Nippongo Kyoiku Kenkyo* (twice a year, Japanese).

Gogaku Kyoikû Kenkyujô (*Institute for Research in Language Teaching*): 108 Central Corporus, 15 Ageba-cho, Shinjuku-ku, Tokyo; f. 1922 as the Institute for Research in English Teaching; Dir. Rikutaro Fukuda.

Kokubungaku Kenkyu Siryokan (*National Institute of Japanese Literature*): 16-10 Yutaka-cho 1-chome, Sinagawa-ku, Tokyo 142; f. 1972 by the Ministry of Education, Science and Culture at the recommendation of the Japan Science Council and in response to requests for a centre for the preservation of Japanese classical literature; surveys, collects (largely in microfilm), studies, processes, preserves and provides access to MSS and old printed books relating to Japanese literature before 1868; also undertakes research in this field; provides scholarly community with facilities for consultation and reproduction of materials; historical documents division collects and preserves documents of *kinsei* (1600–1867); library: *see* Libraries; 76 staff; Dir.-Gen. Dr. TEIJI ICHIKO; publs. *Bulletin* (annually), *NIJL Technical Report* (2 a year), *NIJL Report* (2 a year), *Annual Bibliography of Current Research*.

Kokuritsu Kokugo Kenkyusho (*National Language Research Institute*): 3-9-14, Nisigaoka, Kita-ku, Tokyo 115; f. 1948; Dir. O. HAYASI; publs. *Annual Report, Report, Linguistic Atlas of Japan* (6 vols.).

MEDICINE

Cancer Institute, Japanese Foundation for Cancer Research: Kami-Ikebukuro, Toshima-ku, Tokyo, 170; f. 1908; departments of pathology, experimental pathology, cell biology, viral oncology, biochemistry, physics and cancer chemotherapy; 69 mems.; library of 5,000 vols., 10,000 periodicals; Cancer Institute Hospital and Cancer Chemotherapy Centre attached; Dir. H. SUGANO; publ. *GANN Journal* (6 issues a year)†.

Cardiovascular Institute: 8-1-22 Akasaka, Minato-ku, Tokyo; f. 1959; Dir. S. KOYAMA.

Chemotherapeutic Institute: 6-1-14 Kokufudai, Ichikawa-city, Chiba; f. 1939; Dir. M. KOJIMA; publ. *Studies from C.I. for Medical Research* (annual).

The Kohno Clinical Medicine Research Institute: 1-23-19 Kita-Shinagawa, Shinagawa-ku, Tokyo; f. 1951; Dir. M. KOHNO; publs. *Archives, Quarterlies*.

Institute of Brain and Blood Vessels: 6-23 Ootemachi, Isezaki-city, Gumma; f. 1964; Dir. H. MIHARA; publ. *No-Sotchu no Kenkyu* (Studies on apoplexy).

Institute of Public Health (*Ministry of Health and Welfare*): 4-6-1 Shirokanedai, Minato-ku, Tokyo; f. 1938; Post-graduate education and research in public health; 221 mems.; library of 42,597 vols., 695 periodicals; Dir. T. SODA; publ. *Bulletin* (quarterly).

Kekkaku Yobo Kai Kekkaku Kenkyujo (*Research Institute of Tuberculosis, Japan Anti-Tuberculosis Association*): 1-24 Matsuyama 3-chome, Kiyose-shi, Tokyo 180-04; f. 1939; health education campaign against TB, research, diagnosis and treatment, staff training; 56 mems.; library of 17,500 vols.; Dir. Dr. T. SHIMAO; publs. *Abstracts of the Current Literature on TB and Respiratory Disease* (monthly), *Reports on Medical Research Problems* (annually), *Red Double-Barred Cross* (6 a year), *Review of Tuberculosis for Public Health Nurses* (2 a year), Medical Conference series, etc.

Miyake Medical Institute: 1-3 Tenjin-mae, Takamatsu-city, Kagawa; f. 1949; Dir. T. MIYAKE.

National Cancer Centre (*Ministry of Health and Welfare*): 1-1 Tsukiji 5-chome, Chuo-ku, Tokyo 104; f. 1962; diagnosis, treatment and research of cancer and allied diseases; library of 22,000 vols., 8,500 monographs, 550 periodicals; Pres. S. ISHIKAWA; Dirs. S. SHIMADA (Administration), H. ICHIKAWA (Hospital) and T. SUGIMURA (Research Inst.); publs. (distributed free to libraries) *Collected Papers*† (in English, annual), *Annual Report*† (in Japanese), *Bone Tumor Registration in Japan*† (in Japanese and English, annual)†, *Clinical Staging of Lung Cancer*†, *Registration and Clinical Statistics of Stomach Cancer in Japan*†, *The Report of Hematologic Neoplasms Registration in Japan*† (in Japanese, annual), *Japanese Journal of Clinical Oncology*† (in English, 2 a year).

National Institute for Leprosy Research (*Ministry of Health and Welfare*): 4-1455 Aoba-cho, Higashi-murayama-city, Tokyo; f. 1955; Dir. Y. YOSHIE.

National Institute of Genetics (*Ministry of Education*): 1, 111 Yata, Mishima-city, Shizuoka; f. 1949; Dir. Y. TAZIMA; publ. *Annual Report*†.

National Institute of Health (*Ministry of Health and Welfare*): 10-35, Kamiosaki 2-chome Shinagawa-ku, Tokyo 141; f. 1947; 465 mems.; library of 23,000 vols.; Dir. RYOSUKE MURATA; publ. *The Japanese Journal of Medical Science and Biology* (6 issues a year).

National Institute of Hospital Administration (*Ministry of Health and Welfare*): 1 Toyama-cho, Shinjuku-ku, Tokyo 162; f. 1948; Dir. S. HASHIMOTO; publs. *Annual Report* and *Report in Research* (9 a year).

National Institute of Hygienic Sciences: 18-1 Kamiyoga, 1-chome, Setagaya-ku, Tokyo; f. 1874; Dir. T. SHIMOMURA; publ. *Bulletin* (annual).

National Institute of Industrial Health (*Ministry of Labour*): 21-1, Nagao 6-chome, Tama-ku, Kawasaki-city, Kanagawa; f. 1956; Dir. H. SAKABE; publ. *Industrial Health*† (quarterly).

National Institute of Mental Health (*Ministry of Health and Welfare*): 1-7-3 Kokufudai, Ichikawa-city, Chiba; f. 1952; Dir. T. MURAMATSU; publs. *Journal of Mental Health* (annual) and *Annual Report on Mental Health*.

Neuropsychiatric Research Institute: 91 Benten-cho, Shinjuku-ku, Tokyo; f. 1951; Dir. H. UCHIMURA.

Nukada Institute for Medical and Biological Research: 5-18 Inage-cho, Chiba-city, Chiba; f. 1939; Dir. H. NUKADA; publ. *The Report* (irregular).

Ogata Institute for Medical and Chemical Research: 2-3-5 Nihonbashi-Bakurocho, Chuo, Tokyo 103; f. 1962; library oi 7,500 vols.; Pres. TOMIO OGATA; publ. *Igaku to Seibutsugaku* (Medicine and Biology, monthly).

Pharmaceutical Research Institute: 2-7 Daigaku-cho, Takatsuki-city, Osaka; f. 1947; Dir. S. MATSUMOTO; publ. *Bulletin* (3 to 6 issues a year).

Research Institute of Medicinal Sources: 3-8-3, Nukui-Kitamachi, Koganei-city, Tokyo; f. 1946; Dir. T. FUJISAWA; publ. *Nempo* (annual).

NATURAL SCIENCES

Chemical Economy Research Institute: 13-7, 1-chome, Uchikanda, Chiyoda-ku, Tokyo 101; f. 1954; Dir. (Chair.) KANICHI NAKAYUSU; publs. *Kagaku-Keizai* (monthly), *Chemical Economy and Engineering Review* (monthly in English).

Fukada Geological Institute: 2-13-12 Hon-Komagome, Bunkyo-ku, Tokyo; f. 1954; Dir. I. TATEIWA; publs. *Doboku Chishitsu Shiryo* (annual) and *Buttan Gijutsu* (annual).

Geological Survey of Japan: Higashi 1-chome 1-3, Yatabe-machi, Tsukuba-gun, Ibaraki; f. 1882; part of Science and Technology Agency; 436 mems.; library of 16,000 vols.; Dir. S. SATO; publs. *Report*† (irregular), *Bulletin*† (monthly), Geological maps†.

Institute of Applied Electricity and Magnetism: 6-17-25 Hon-komagome, Bunkyo-ku, Tokyo; f. 1944; Dir. M KAWARADA.

The Institute of Statistical Mathematics (*Ministry of Education*): 4-6-7 Minami Azabu, Minato-ku, Tokyo; f. 1944; research in statistics; library of 20,617 vols.; Dir. C. HAYASHI; publs. *Annals*† (3 a year), *Proceedings*† (2 a year), *Computer Science Monographs* (*c.* 3 a year).

International Latitude Observatory of Mizusawa (*Ministry of Education*): 2-12 Hoshigaoka-machi, Mizusawa-city, Iwate; f. 1899; library of 41,751 vols.; Dir. T. OKUDA; publs. *Publications of the ILOM* (annual), *Annual Meteorological Report, Geophysical Report, Bulletins,*

Time Service of the Mizusawa Observatory (annual), *Proceedings* (annual, in Japanese), and others.

Japan Atomic Energy Research Institute: Fukoku-Seimei Bldg., 2-2-2 Uchigaiwai-cho, Chiyoda-ku, Tokyo; f. 1956; 2,370 mems.; library of 50,000 vols.; Pres. H. MURATA; Vice-Pres. K. YAMAMOTO; publs. *Nuclear Science Information of Japan*† (irregular), *JAERI Reports*† (irregular), *JAERI—M Reports*† (irregular).

Kihara Institute for Biological Research: 4-122-23 Mutsukawa, Yokohama-city 233; f. 1942; Dir. H. KIHARA; publ. *Seiken Ziho* (annual).

The Kitasato Institute: 5-9-1 Shirokane, Minato-ku, Tokyo 108; f. 1914; research on the cause, prevention and therapy of various diseases; 55 mems.; Dir. T. HATA; publ. *The Kitasato Archives of Experimental Medicine* (quarterly).

Kobayasi Institute of Physical Research: 3-20-41 Higashi-Motomachi, Kokubunji, Tokyo; f. 1940; Dir. J. IGARASHI; publ. *Bulletin* (annually).

Kokuritsu Kyokuchi Kenkyujyo (*National Institute of Polar Research*): 9-10, Kaga 1-chome, Itabashi-ku, Tokyo 173; f. 1973; replaces the frmr. Polar Research Centre of the National Science Museum; government-sponsored; implements programmes of the Japanese Antarctic Research Expeditions (JARE), organizes postgraduate courses in polar subjects, offers research facilities to national and foreign universities and individual researchers; library of *c.* 11,400 vols. and bound periodicals, 108 full-time staff; Dir. Prof. TAKESI NAGATA; publs. *Antarctic Record, Memoirs of the National Institute of Polar Research, JARE Data Reports, Antarctic Geological Map Series.*

Meteorological Research Institute: 35-8 Koenji-Kita 4-chome, Suginami-ku, Tokyo; f. 1946; Dir. K. SEKIHARA; publ. *Papers in Meteorology and Geophysics* (quarterly).

Mitsubishi-Kasei Institute of Life Sciences: 11 Minamiooya, Machida-shi, Tokyo 194; f. 1971; 122 research staff; Dir. FUJIO EGAMI.

National Aerospace Laboratory (*Science and Technological Agency*): 1880 Jindaiji, Chofu-city, Tokyo; f. 1955; 478 staff; library of 29,000 vols.; Dir. T. KAWASAKI; publ. *Technical Report*† (irregular).

National Institute for Research in Inorganic Materials (*Science and Technology Agency*): Kurakeke Sakura mure, Nirhari-gun, Ibaraki; f. 1966; synthesis of high purity inorganic materials and their physical analysis; 131 mems.; library of 2,000 vols.; Dir. S. YAMAUCHI.

National Institute of Nutrition (*Ministry of Health and Welfare*): 1 Toyama-cho, Shinjuku-ku, Tokyo; f. 1920; library of 30,000 vols.; Dir. T. FUKUI; publs. *Annual Report,* and *The Japanese Journal of Nutrition* (6 issues a year).

National Institute of Radiological Sciences (*Science and Technological Agency*): 9-1, Anagawa 4-chome, Chiba-shi, Chiba 260; f. 1957; official research organization; 417 mems.; library of 25,000 vols.; Dir.-Gen. T. KUMATORI; publs. *Annual Report, NIRS, Radioactivity Survey Data in Japan* (quarterly).

National Research Institute for Metals: 2-3-12 Nakameguro, Meguro-ku, Tokyo 153; Dir. T. ARAKI; publs. *Report of NRIM* (annually), *Research Activities in NRIM* (annually), *Kinzaigikem News* (monthly), *Transactions of NRIM* (quarterly), *Fatigue Data Sheets, CreepData Sheets* (irregular).

National Research Institute for Pollution and Resources (*Agency of Industrial Science and Technology*): 1-1 Kawaguchi 3-chome, Kawaguchi-shi, Saitama; f. 1952; Dir. Dr. S. ASHIDA; publs. *Annual Report, Pollution Control* (bi-monthly), *Report* (irregular), *NRIPR News* (monthly), *Bulletin of Inspection of Underground Articles Used in Mines* (bi-monthly), *Mining and Safety* (monthly), *Bulletin of National Research Institute for Pollution and Resources* (quarterly).

National Research Laboratory of Metrology (*Agency of Industrial Science and Technology*): 1-4, 1-chome, Umezono, Sakura-Mura, Niihari-gun, Ibaraki 305; f. 1903; 238 mems.; 20,000 vols.; Dir. M. KAWATA; publ. *Bulletin*† (2 issues a year), *Report*† (quarterly).

Nippon Institute for Biological Science: 3-28-19, Akebono cho, Tachikawa, Tokyo; f. 1947; 80 mems.; library of 900 books and 600 periodicals; Dir. K. ARAI; publ. *NIBS Bulletin* (annual), *Biological Research* (annual).

Research Institute for Chemobiodynamics: Chiba University, 1-8-1, Inohana, Chiba; f. 1946; Dir. TETSURO KUGA; publ. *Annual Report.*

Research Institute for Natural Resources: 4-400 Hyakunin-cho, Shinjuku-ku, Tokyo; f. 1941; Dir. K. AGI; publs. *Miscellaneous Reports* (2 a year), *Water Pollution Research* (annually).

Rikagaku Kenkyusho (*The Institute of Physical and Chemical Research*): Wakoshi, Saitama; f. 1917; 600 mems.; library of 100,000 vols.; Dir. T. HOSHINO; publs. *Scientific Papers*† (quarterly) and *Reports*† (bi-monthly).

Space Activities Commission: 2-2-1 Kasumigaseki, Chiyoda-ku, Tokyo 100; f. 1968; contributes to a comprehensive and streamlined execution of government programmes on space development, including organization of administrative agencies, planning of general policies and outlining training programmes for researchers and technicians; Chair. TSUYOSHI AMISHIMA; publ. *Monthly Report.*

Tokyo Astronomical Observatory: University of Tokyo, 2-21-1 Oosawa, Mitaka-city, Tokyo; f. 1878; Dir. Z. SUEMOTO; publs. *Annals* (2nd series; irregular), *Reprints* (irregular), *Bulletin* (2nd series; irregular), *Time and Latitude Bulletin* (quarterly), *Tokyo Tenmondaiho* (in Japanese, irregular), *Rekishonenpyo* (Japanese, (annually), *Kiso Information Bulletin* (irregular).

Tokyo Biochemical Research Institute: 41-8 Takada, 3-chome, Toshima-ku, Tokyo; f. 1950; Dir. M. OKADA; publ. *Report* (annual).

RELIGION, SOCIOLOGY, ANTHROPOLOGY

National Institute for Research Advancement: 37F Shinjuku Mitsui Bldg., 2-1-1, Nishi-Shinjuku, Shinjuku-ku, Tokyo 160; f. 1974 under Parliamentary legislation to promote and conduct inter-disciplinary research that focuses on the problems facing modern society and their alleviation; conducts its own research and also commissions and subsidizes research by other bodies; research results are made public through lectures, symposia or publication of reports; Chair. TADASHI SASAKI; Dirs. KYOICHIRO KOBAYASHI (Gen. Affairs), YUICHI MORIYA (Research and Planning).

Okura Institute for Spiritual Culture: 706 Futoo-cho, Kohoku-ku, Yokohama; f. 1929; Dir. K. OOKURA.

Toyo Bunka Kenkyusho (*Institute of Oriental Culture*): The University of Tokyo, Hongo, Bunkyo-ku, Tokyo; f. 1941; full-time research staff; fine collection of books; Dir. Dr. SHINJI FUKAI.

Zinbun Kagaku Kenkyusho (*Research Institute for Humanistic Studies*): 1 Ushinomiyacho, Yoshida, Sakyo-ku, Kyoto; f. 1939; 69 mems.; library of 348,731 vols.; attached to Kyoto University; Pres. MITSUJI FUKUNAGA; the Institute is divided into three sections, dealing with Japanese, Oriental and Western Culture; publs. *Zinbun Gakuho* (annually), *Toho Gakuho* (annually), *Annual Bibliography of Oriental Studies, Social Survey Reports* (annually), *Zinbun* (*annually*).

TECHNOLOGY

Applied Science Research Institute: 49 Naka-ooseki-cho, Sakyo-ku, Kyoto; f. 1916; Dir. R. TORIKAI.

Building Research Institute (*Ministry of Construction*): No. 8-28-3-chome, Hyakunin-cho, Shinjuku-ku, Tokyo; f. 1946; town planning, building materials, construction techniques, earthquake engineering; 181 mems.; 7,000 vols.; Dir. K. KAWAGOE; publs. *Annual Report*, *B.R.I. Research Papers*.

Civil Engineering Research Institute (*Hokkaido Development Agency*): Hiragishi, Sapporo-city; f. 1951; 254 mems.; 23,000 vols. in library; Dir. K. KAKUTA; publs. *Monthly Report* and *Report* (quarterly), *Annual Report*.

Doboku Kenkyujo (*Public Works Research Institute, Ministry of Construction*): Tsukuba Science City, Ibaraki-Pref. 305; f. 1921; has 11 divisions; 496 staff; library of 55,000 vols.; Dir. Y. SAKAGAMI; publs. *Journal of Research*† (in English), *Report*, *Technical Note*†, *Technical Memorandum*, *Civil Engineering Journal*, *Annual Research Report*, *Annual Report*, and others.

Engineering Research Institute: Faculty of Engineering, University of Tokyo, 11-16, Yayoi, 2 chome, Bunkyo-ku, Tokyo; f. 1939; 67 mems.; library of 6,747 vols.; Dir. SUMIJI FUJII; publ. *Annual Report*†.

Fermentation Research Institute (*Agency of Industrial Science and Technology*): 4-5-2 Inage Higashi, Chiba city, Chiba; f. 1940; 73 mems.; Dir. S. SHICHIJI; publ. *Report of Fermentation Research Institute* (2 issues a year).

Fire Research Institute (*Fire Defence Agency*): 14-1 Nakahara, 3-chome, Mitaka-city, Tokyo; f. 1948; library of 4,500 vols.; Dir. YOSHIRO YAHAZUNO; publs. *Report* (2 issues a year), *Special Report* (irregular), *Shoken Syuho* (2 a year), *Technical Memorandum* (irregular).

Fuyo Research Institute: 4-7-14 Akasaka, Minato-ku, Tokyo 107; f. 1970 by Fuyo Data Processing and Systems Development Ltd.; research in the fields of natural resources and energy; environmental conservation and pollution control; local administration and community problems; urban and regional planning; traffic, transport, physical distribution and tourism; economic analysis; corporate management and market research; statistical analysis; library of 20,000 vols.; Dir. SATORU SHIBUE; Sec. SETSUKO KINUKAWA.

Government Mechanical Laboratory: 12-1 Igusa, 4-chome, Suginami-ku, Tokyo; f. 1937; Dir. M. KUBOTA; publs. *Journal* (2 issues a year), *Report* (irregularly, Japanese), *Journal* (at least 2 issues annually).

Industrial Research Institute, Japan: 1-7, Shinkawa 2-chome, Chuo-ku, Tokyo 104; f. 1959; independent; innovative research and development on technology and socio-technology, including alternative energy sources, environmental problems and related innovative problems; 25 research staff; library of *c.* 1,000 vols.; Pres. KOJI KOBAYASHI; Sec.-Gen. MIKIO MUNAKATA; publ. *Proceedings on current technologies in Japanese industries* (monthly).

Institute for Fermentation: 17-85, Juso-honmachi 2-chome, Yodogawaku, Osaka 532; f. 1944; preservation and distribution of micro-organisms; 20 staff; library of 800 vols.; Dir. TEIJI IIJIMA; publs. *List of Cultures*, *I.F.O. Research Communications* (every two years).

Institute for Future Technology: 2-1, Kitanomaru-koen, Chiyoda-ku, Tokyo 102; f. 1971 as an independent institute under the auspices of the Science and Technology Agency; research in the fields of technology forecasting, technology assessment and other socio-economic research in future technologies (electronics, telecommunications, space and energy); 51 research staff; library of 15,000 vols.; Pres. KEN'ICHIRO HIROTA; Chief Sec. YOSHIO FUKUDA; publ. *Kenkyu Seika Gaiyo* (research results, annually).

Institute of Energy Economics: No. 10 Mori Bldg., 18-1 Toranomon 1-chome, Minato-ku, Tokyo; inc. 1966; co-ordinates information related to energy, its use, supply, conservation and economic aspects; provides material as basis for planning and policy formation by government and private business; 118 mems. incl. energy-related industries and research institutions; Chair. MASAO SAKISAKA; Pres. TOYOAKI IKUTA; Man. Dir. MASASADA OHMORI; publs. *Energy in Japan* (quarterly, in English), *Energy Economy* (monthly, in Japanese), *International Energy News Abstracts* (2 a week, in Japanese).

International Association of Traffic and Safety Sciences: 6-20, 2-chome, Yaesu, Chuo-ku, Tokyo 104; f. 1974; aims to contribute to the realization of a better traffic society through the practical application of research conducted in a variety of fields; research surveys on traffic and its safety; collection and retrieval of information on traffic-related sciences; sponsorship of domestic and international symposia and study meetings; provision of awards and grants-in-aid; 17 Counsellors, 29 mems.; Exec. Dir. KIYOTSUGU NISHIKAWA; publs. *IATSS Review* (quarterly), *IATSS Research* (annually, in English), *White Paper on Transportation Safety* (annually, in Japanese and English), *Statistics of Road Traffic Accidents in Japan* (annually, in English), reports, proceedings of symposia, etc.

Japan Construction Method and Machinery Research Institute: 3154 Oobuchi, Fuji-shi, Shizuoka; f. 1964; Dir. T. MITANI; publ. *NEMPO* (annual).

National Chemical Laboratory for Industry: Yatabe, Ibaraki 305; f. 1900 (formerly Government Chemical Industrial Research Institute); 300 research staff, 200 administrative staff; library of 60,000 vols.; Dir. Dr. JUN KATO; publs. *Journal*† (monthly), *Annual Report*.

National Research Center for Disaster Prevention: Tennodai 3-chome, Sakura-mura, Niihari-gun, Ibaraki-ken 300-32; f. 1963; 117 mems.; library of *c.* 28,000 vols.; Dir. NARUTO OHHIRA; publs. *Report of the N.R.C.D.P.*† (2 a year), *Review of Research for Disaster Prevention*† (irregular), *Strong-motion Earthquake Records in Japan*† (annual).

Branches of the Center:

Hiratsuka Branch: 9-2, Nijigahama, Hiratsuka-shi, Kanagawa-ken 254; study in coastal oceanology.

Institute of Snow and Ice Studies: 9628, Maeyama, Suyoshi-machi, Nagaoka-shi, Niigata-ken 940.

Shinjo Branch: 1400, Takadan, Toka-machi, Shinjo-shi, Yamagata-ken 996; study of the prevention of disasters caused by snow and ice.

Iwatsuki Crustal Activity Observatory: Makinoue, Sueta, Iwatsuki-shi, Saitama-ken 339.

National Research Institute of Brewing (*Tax Administration Agency*): 2-6-30 Takinogawa, Kita-ku, Tokyo; f. 1904; Dir. H. MURAKAMI; publ. *Report* (annual).

Noguchi Institute: 1-8-1 Kaga, Itabashi-ku, Tokyo; f. 1941; Dir. E. MUNEKATA; publ. *Annual Report*.

Port and Harbour Research Institute (*Ministry of Transport*): 1-1, 3-chome, Nagase, Yokosuka, Kanagawa; f. 1962; research on harbour and coastal hydraulic engineering; 197 mems.; library of 13,000 vols.; Dir. S. TURUTA; publs. *Report* (quarterly), *Technical Notes* (quarterly), *Annual Report*.

Radio Research Laboratories (*Ministry of Posts and Telecommunications*): 2-1 Nukuikitamachi 4-chome, Koganeishi, Tokyo 184; f. 1952; 471 staff; library of 140,000 vols.; Dir. K. TAO; publs. *Journal*† (in English; 3 a year), *Review*† (in Japanese; quarterly), *Ionospheric Data in Japan*† (in English, monthly), *Radio Propagation Prediction* (in Japanese; monthly), *Catalogue of Data in WDC C2 Centre for Ionosphere*† (in

English, annually), *Radio and Space Data* (annually), *Standard Frequency and Time Service Bulletin*† (monthly), *Ionospheric Data at Syowa Station*† (2 a year), *Data on Topside Ionosphere* (irregular).

Railway Technical Research Institute (*Japanese National Railways*): 2-8-28 Hikari-cho, Kokubunji-city, Tokyo; f. 1907; 770 staff; Dir. HIROSHI TOYOTA; publ. *Quarterly Report*†.

Research Institute for Polymers and Textiles (*Agency of Industrial Science and Technology*): 1-1-4 Yatabe-Higachi, Tsukuba, Ibaraki Pref. 300-21; f. 1918; research in polymer science and technology; 135 mems. (including 104 scientists); library of 19,213 vols.; Dir.-Gen. Dr. A. OKADA; publs. *Bulletin*† (quarterly), *News*† (every 2 months, in Japanese), *Annual Report*†, *Survey*† (annually).

Research Institute for Production Development: 15 Shimo Kamomori Honmachi, Sakyo-ku, Kyoto; f. 1947; Dir. A. OKUDA.

Research Institute of Printing Bureau (*Ministry of Finance*): 1-6-1 Ooji, Kita-ku, Tokyo; f. 1891; Dir. H. NONAKA; publ. *Research Bulletin* (2 a year).

Research Institute of Welding: 3-2 Kayaba-cho Nihombashi, Chuo-ku, Tokyo; f. 1944; Dir. Y. NAKAI.

Ship Research Institute (*Ministry of Transport*): 38-1, 6-chome, Shinkawa, Mitaka, Tokyo; f. 1916; shipbuilding and marine engineering; 289 mems.; 45,000 books in library; Dir. N. ANDO; publs. *Report*† (6 a year), *Papers*† (irregularly).

Tensor Society: c/o Kawaguchi Institute of Mathematical Sciences, Matsu-ga-oka 2-7-15, Chigasaki 253; f. 1937; undertakes original research in the field of Tensor Analysis and its applications; 550 mems. world-wide; library of 23,000 vols.; Pres. Prof. Dr. A. KAWAGUCHI; Secs. Prof. Dr. S. WATANABE, Prof. Dr. S. KAWAGUCHI, Prof. M. YOSHIDA, Prof. H. IZUMI; publ. *Tensor*† (3 a year).

Uchu Koku Kenkyusho (*Institute of Space and Aeronautical Science*): University of Tokyo, Komaba, Meguro-ku, Tokyo; f. 1964; advanced rocket and space research programmes; 420 mems.; library of 75,000 vols.; Dir. DAIKICHIRO MORI; publs. *Bulletin* (Japanese, quarterly), *Report* (English irregular).

LIBRARIES

TOKYO

British Council Library: Iwanami Bldg., 1-2-chome, Jimbo-cho, Kanda, Chiyoda-ku, Tokyo 101; f. 1953; 24,545 vols., 171 periodicals; Librarian A. D. BENTLEY.

Chuo University Library: 742 Higashinakano Hachiojishi; f. 1885; 836,642 vols. (340,391 in foreign languages), 4,646 periodicals; Librarian Prof. HARUYA SHIMAZAKI.

Communications Museum Library: Teishin Hakubutsukan, 3 Fujimi-cho 2-chome, Chiyoda-ku; 50,000 vols.

Hitotsubashi University Library: Naka 2-1, Kunitachi-city; f. 1887; 810,000 vols. (including Kodaira branch); Librarian M. KIMURA; houses branch library for Institute of Economic Research; f. 1940; 200,000 vols.; Dir. Y. KURABAYASHI.

Hosei University Library: Fujimi, Chiyoda-ku; 480,000 vols.; Librarian M. NODA.

Imperial Household Agency Library: Imperial Palace, Chiyoda-ku; f. 1948; 76,583 vols.; Librarian MAMADA.

International Christian University Library: 10 Osawa 3-chome, Mitaka-city; 237,459 vols. (including 115,633 foreign); Librarian AKIRA MIYAKE.

Japan Meteorological Agency Library: 1-3-4 Ote-machi, Chiyoda-ku; f. 1875; 29 mems.; 170,000 vols.; Chief Librarian KOICHI MAKI.

Keio University Engineering Library and Information Center (Matsishita Memorial Library): 3-14-1 Hiyoshi Kohoku-ku, Yokohama-shi; f. 1972; 109,267 vols. including 76,041 bound periodicals; Chief Officer Prof. ICHIRO ARIGA.

Keio University Library and Information Center at Mita: 2-15-45 Mita, Minato-ku 108; f. 1890; 907,915 vols. (including 401,711 foreign); Dir. Prof. MASAO TAKATORI.

Keio University Medical Library and Information Center (*Kitasato Memorial Medical Library*): 35 Shinanomachi, Shinjuku-ku; f. 1937; 139,000 vols. and 2,300 current medical journals; Dir. Dr. H. HOSAKI; publ. *Kitasato News* (monthly).

Keio University School of Library and Information Science Library: 2-15-45, Mita, Minato-ku; f. 1951; 15,093 vols.; Librarian KEIKO TAKEI (acting).

Kokugakuin University Library: 10-28 Higachi 4-chome, Shibuya; f. 1882; 478,230 vols.; Librarian Prof. HIROSHI MIZUTA; publ. *Nenji Hokoku* (Annual Report).

Kokuritsu Kobunshokan (*National Archives*): 3-2 Kitanomaru Park, Chiyoda-ku; f. 1971; attached to the Prime Minister's office; 47 mems.; library; the Cabinet Library (*see below*); Dir. NORIO IWAKURA; publs. *Annual Report*, *Journal*†.

Cabinet Library: 3-2 Kitanomaru-Park, Chiyoda-ku; f. 1884; 520,207 vols.; special collections: Momijiyama Library, established in Yedo Castle in 1602 by Iyeyasu Tokugawa (74,700 Japanese and Chinese books), and Shohei School Library, attached to the University of Tokugawa Shogunate and established 1630; Librarian YOSHIO HIRAI.

Kokuritsu Kyoiku Kenkyusho Toshokan (*National Institute for Educational Research Library*): 6-5-22 Shimomeguro, Meguro-ku; f. 1949; 291,000 vols.; Librarian T. YOKOWO; publ. *Education Index* (Kyoiku Sakuin, quarterly).

Meiji University Library: Kanda-Surugadai, Chiyoda-ku, Tokyo 101; f. 1903; 857,000 vols. (including 275,000 foreign); Librarian Y. KATO.

Ministry of Education Library: 3-2-2 Kasumigaseki, Chiyoda-ku; 120,000 vols.; Librarian A. OKAMOTO.

Ministry of Foreign Affairs Library: 2-2 Kasumigaseki, Chiyoda-ku; 82,040 vols. and 190 periodicals; Librarian M. KITAMURA.

Ministry of Justice Library: 1-1, 1-chome, Kasumigaseki, Chiyoda-ku; f. 1928; 220,000 vols.; Chief Librarian TOSHIAKI SASAKI.

National Diet Library: 10-1, 1-chome, Nagata-cho, Chiyoda-ku, Tokyo 100; f. 1948; deposit library for Japanese publs. and publs. of U.S. Government, UN, UNESCO, ILO, WHO, ICAO, GATT, etc.; international book exchange and information centre of Japan; is divided into one dept. and six divisions: Administrative, Research and Legislative Reference, Acquisitions and Processing, Serial Publications, Circulation, Reference and Bibliography and Inter-library Services; consists of the Central Library, Detached Library in the Diet and

Ueno Library (3,494,002 vols. and 31,366 periodicals), Toyo (Oriental) Library (604,082 vols.) and 33 branch libraries in the Executive and Judicial branches of the Government (3,087,289 vols.); Librarian MINORU KISHIDA; publs. *Japanese National Bibliography* (weekly and annually), *Japanese Periodicals Index* (quarterly), *National Diet Library Monthly Bulletin*, *Union Catalogue of Foreign Books* (annually), *General Index to the Debates* (each Diet Session), *Index to the Japanese Laws and Regulations in Force* (annual), *Reference* (monthly), *Annual Report of the National Diet Library*, *National Diet Library Newsletter* (in English), etc. Branch library:

National Institute of Japanese Literature Library: 16-10 Yutaka-cho 1-chome, Sinagawa-ku, Tokyo 142; f. 1972; microforms of woodcuts, old printed books and MSS; 9,255 reels microfilm, 9,750 sheets microfiche, 14,355 vols. paper copy; 41,000 vols. old and current books; 30,000 vols. serials; Archives for Japanese Historical Documents: 500,000 items (holdings), 8,000 items deposited, 1,349 reels microfilm, 5,000 articles of folk material; Dir. of Bibliographic and Reference Services Y. HONDA; Historical Documents Division S. ENOMOTO; publs. catalogues.

Norinsho Toshokan (*Ministry of Agriculture, Forestry and Fisheries Library*): 2-1, Kasumigaseki, 1-chome, Chiyoda-ku, Tokyo 100; f. 1948; 199,000 vols.; Librarian KYŌ BAN; publs. *Norin Tosho Shiryo Geppo*† (report of publs. on Agriculture, Forestry and Fisheries, monthly), *Norin Bunken Kaidai*† (bibliographical notes, annually).

Ochanomizu University Library: Otsuka 2-chome, Bunkyo-ku, Tokyo 112; 270,892 (including 79,000 foreign) vols.; Librarian JIRO OHTA.

Oriental Library (*Toyo Bunko*): Honkomagome 2-chome, 28-21, Bunkyo-ku, Tokyo 113; f. 1924; 512,168 vols.; Librarian NAOSHIRO TSUJI; publs. *Toyo Gakuho* (quarterly), *Memoirs of the Research Department*, Monographs Series A, Miscellaneous Series C (*see also* National Diet Library).

Patent Office Library: 1-1 Sannen-cho, Chiyoda-ku, Tokyo; 144,502 vols.; Librarian T. NAKASHIBA.

Prime Minister's Office, Statistics Bureau, Library: 95 Wakamatsu-cho, Shinjuku-ku, Tokyo; f. 1946; 300,520 vols.; Librarian KOICHO KUBODERA; publs. numerous reports and statistical handbooks.

Science Council of Japan, Secretariat, Library Section: 23-24, Roppongi 7-chome, Minato-ku, Tokyo 106; 43,200 vols.; Librarian T. HARADA.

Seikado Bunko Library: 912 Okamoto-cho, Setagaya-ku; 196,974 vols. of Chinese and Japanese classics.

Sophia (Jôchi) University Library: 7 Kioicho, Chiyoda-ku, f. 1913; 352,809 vols.; Librarian L. ARMBRUSTER.

Supreme Court Library: 4-2 Hayabusacho, Chiyoda-ku, Tokyo 102; f. 1949; 177,148 vols.; Librarian T. ABE.

Tokyo Geijutsu Daigaku Toshokan (*Tokyo National University of Fine Arts and Music Library*): Ueno Park, Daito-ku; over 175,108 vols., 1,747 microfilm reels; also music and gramophone record collections (83,168 scores, 18,421 records); Librarian T. NARUKAWA.

Tokyo Metropolitan Central Library: 5-7-13 Minami-Azabu, Minato-ku, Tokyo 106; f. 1972; research and reference centre, centre of library co-operation in Tokyo; 750,600 vols. and 5,761 periodicals; Yedo Collection, Kaga Collection (rare books of the Yedo Era), Morohashi Collection (Chinese classics), Sanetoh Collection (Chinese literature) and others; Dir. SADAMICHI OKUNO; publs. *Hibiya*† (2 a year), *Library Science Bulletin* (annually), *Annual Report*†.

Tokyo Metropolitan Hibiya Library: 1-4 Hibiya Park, Chiyoda-ku, Tokyo 100; f. 1908; lending, children's, and audio-visual services; 190,131 vols., 1,171 periodicals; Dir. KOICHI KAWANA.

Tokyo Metropolitan University Library: 1-1-1 Yakumo, Meguro-ku, Tokyo 152; f. 1950; 554,092 vols. (including 259,396 foreign); Librarian Prof. T. MATSUNAMI.

Tokyo University of Fisheries Library: Konan 4-5-7, Minato-ku, Tokyo 108; f. 1888; 150,431 vols. (including 36,982 foreign); Librarian Dr. M. KUBOTA; publs. *Journal* (bi-annually), *Report* (annually), *Transactions* (irregular).

Tokyo University of Foreign Studies Library: 4-51-21 Nishigahara, Kita-ku; f. 1897; 186,455 vols. (including 107,482 foreign); Dir. S. WAKURI.

University of Tokyo Library: Hongo 7-chome, Bunkyo-ku; f. 1887; general library and libraries of 10 faculties and 14 institutes; 4,500,000 vols.; Dir. Dr. Y. ANDO.

Waseda University Library: Nishiwaseda, Shinjuku-ku; f. 1882; 1,134,524 vols.; Librarian H. FURUKAWA; publs. *Acquisition Report* (monthly), *Bulletin* (annually).

PROVINCES

Akita Prefectural Library: 2-52 Senshumeitoku-cho, Akita; f. 1899; 337,632 vols.; Librarian A. MATAI.

British Council Library: 77 Kitashirakawa-Nishimachi, Sakyo-ku, Kyoto; f. 1954; 9,094 vols., 41 periodicals; Librarian Mrs. C. YAMAGUCHI.

Chiba Prefectural Central Library: 26 Ichiba-machi, Chiba City; 268,488 vols.; Librarian S. TATEISHI.

Hakodate City Library: 23 Aoyagi-cho, Hakodate City; 122,500 vols. (including branch library); Librarian I. FUKUDA.

Hiroshima Prefectural Library: 2-20 Kami-Nobori-machi, Hiroshima City; 100,460 vols.; Librarian K. KAWASHIMA.

Hokkaido University Library: Kita 8 Nishi 5, Kita-ku, Sapporo; f. 1876; 17 br. libraries; 1,920,000 vols. (including 796,400 foreign); special collections on Slavic studies and North Eurasian culture studies; Librarian Prof. Y. SHIOYA; publ. *Yuin* (quarterly).

Kagoshima Prefectural Library: 1-1 Shiroyama-machi, Kagoshima City; 222,357 vols.; Librarian H. KUBOTA.

Kanagawa Prefectural Library: 9-2 Momijigaoka, Nishi-ku, Yokohama City; f. 1954; 113 mems.; 474,570 vols.; Librarian E. TAKEDA; publ. *Kanagawa Bunka*† (every 2 months).

Kanazawa City Library: 65 Tono-machi, Kanazawa City; 156,769 vols.; Librarian T. NAKAJIMA.

Kansai University Library: 3-3-35 Yamate-cho, Suita-shi, Osaka; 750,000 vols. (including 230,000 foreign); Librarian Y. NAKAMURA.

Kobe City Library: 7-2 Kununoki-cho, Ikuta, Kobe; f. 1911; 240,000 vols.; Librarian S. AKAI.

Kobe University Library: Rokkodai-cho, Nadu-ku, Kobe; f. 1908; 7 branch libraries; 898,024 vols. (including 290,000 foreign); Librarian J. YAO.

Kochi Prefectural Library: 3 Marunouchi, Kochi City; 141,927 vols.; Librarian N. SHIMESHINO.

Kwansei Gakuin University Library: 155-1-1 Uegahara, Nishinomiya-shi, Hyogo-ken; f. 1889; 580,000 vols., nearly 40 per cent in foreign languages; branch libraries for 7 faculties and Industrial Research Institute; Niwa, Sato and Shibata collections; Librarian Prof. DAIZEN KAWAMURA; publ. *Tokeidai* (Bulletin, twice yearly).

Kyoto Prefectural Library: Okazaki Park, Kyoto Shi, Kyoto; f. 1909; 269,034 vols.

Kyoto University Library: Yoshida Hommachi, Sakyo-ku, Kyoto 606; f. 1899; general library and libraries of 10 faculties and 17 institutes; 3,836,409 vols.; Librarian RYOHEI HAYASHI.

Kyushu University Library: 3576 Hakozaki-machi, Fukuoka City, Fukuoka Prefecture; f. 1911; 1,670,000 vols. (including 733,700 foreign); Dir. R. MATUURA; publ. *Bulletin* (monthly).

Matsuyama University of Commerce Library: 4-2 Bunkyo-cho, Matsuyama 790; f. 1923; 120,000 vols.; collection of rare books, including first editions of eighteenth- and nineteenth-century works on political economics; Librarian Prof. T. IDE.

Mie Shinto Library: Kushimoto-Machi, Kanda, Ujiyamada, Mie Prefecture; 189,000 vols.; Librarian MASAATSU NOGAMI.

Nagano Prefectural Library: 1097 Nagato-machi, Nagano City; 174,253 vols.; Librarian K. MOMOSE.

Nagasaki Prefectural Library: 1 Nishiyama-cho, Nagasaki; f. 1912.

Nagoya University Library: Furo-cho, Chikusa-ku, Nagoya; f. 1942; 13 branch libraries; 1,446,497 vols.; Dir. Dr. E. YOKOGOSHI.

Naha Cultural Center Library: Naha, Okinawa; public library; 17,500 vols.

Nara Prefectural Library: 48 Nobori Ooji, Nara City; f. 1908; 29 mems.; 163,842 vols.; Librarian NOBUKAZU OOHIGASHI; publ. *Untei*.

Niigata Prefectural Library: 5977 Ichiban-bori, Niigata City; f. 1915; 219,313 vols.; Librarian T. HOMMA.

Niigata University Library: Ikarashi 2-Nocho, Niigata City; f. 1949; 703,794 vols., 13,050 periodicals; Librarian H. YAMADA.

Okayama University Library: Naka 3-chome 1-1, Tsushima, Okayama City; f. 1949; 5 br. libraries; 1,008,372 vols.; Dir. K. TAKAHASHI.

Okinawa University Library: Naha, Okinawa; f. 1961; 24,930 vols., mostly in Japanese.

Osaka Prefectural Nakanoshima Library: 1-2-10 Nakanoshima, Kita-ku, Osaka; f. 1903; 657,111 vols.; Head Librarian KATSUYA ASAMI.

Osaka Prefectural Yûhigaoka Library: Reijin-cho, Tennoji-ku, Osaka; f. 1974; 283,600 vols.; Head Librarian HIDEO MARUYAMA.

Osaka University Library: 1-1, Machikaneyama-cho, Toyonaka-shi, Osaka-fu; 1,258,922 vols.; 3 branch libraries; Dir. KAORU TAKADA; Librarian MASAYOSHI MIYATAKE.

Research Institute for Humanistic Studies Library: 1 Ushinomiyacho, Yoshida 606, Sakyo-ku, Kyoto; attached to Kyoto University; 348,731 vols., including a large collection of Chinese Classics; Dir. Prof. MITSUJI FUKUNAGA.

Ryukoku University Library: 67 Fukakusa tsukamoto-cho, Fushimi-ku, Kyoto; f. 1639; 613,435 vols. (including 146,391 foreign); Librarian KEEICHI MASUNAGA; publs. *Ryukoku Daigaku Ronshu*† (Journal of Ryukoku Univ.) and various univ. institute journals.

Ryukyu Islands Central Library: Central Library Building, Naha, Okinawa; f. 1950; 45,926 vols.; central deposit library.

Shikiya Memorial Library: University of the Ryukyus, Naha, Okinawa; f. 1950; 153,461 vols.; 1,011 periodicals; most of the books are in Japanese, but also a large collection in Ryukyuana.

Shizuoka Prefectural Library: 620 Yada, Shizuoka City; 192,555 vols.; Librarian TOMONOBU SO.

Tenri Central Library: Tenri City, Nara; f. 1930; Tenri University Library also open to the public; 1,244,233 vols. (including 290,410 foreign); Chief Librarian HIDETSUGU UEDA; special libraries: Yorozuyo Library on Christian Missions (including Jesuit mission printings in Japan), Kogido Library of Ito Jinsai on Confucian Studies, Wataya Library on Renga and Haikai Works (*c.* 20,000 items), Africana Collection (6,000 vols.); publ. *Biblia*† (3 times a year, Japanese).

Tochigi Prefectural Library: 357 Banda-cho, Utsunomiya City; 196,579 vols.; Librarian T. IZUMI.

Tohoku University Library: Kawauchi, Sendai City 980; f. 1911; 1,579,751 vols., including Kano Collection (108,000 vols.) in Japanese and Chinese, the Tibetan Buddhist Canons (6,652 vols.), Wundt Collection (15,800 vols.) and several other special collections; Dir. H. HARAFUJI; medical library at 1-1 Seiryo-cho, Sendai City 980; f. 1915; 252,101 vols.; Dir. T. YAMAMOTO; agricultural library at 1-1 Amamiya-cho, Sendai City 980; f. 1947; 95,349 vols.; Dir. H. TAKAHASHI; engineering library at Aoba, Aramaki, Sendai City 980; f. 1919; 196,902 vols.; Dir. H. SAITO.

Tsurumai (Nagoya) Central Library: 43 Tsurumai-cho, Showa-ku, Nagoya City; 201,519 vols.; Librarian M. WATANABE.

Yamaguchi Prefectural Library: 150-1 Matsue, Ushirogawa, Yamaguchi City; f. 1903; 389,104 vols.; Librarian TANAKA HIROSHI; publ. *Toshokan Yamaguchi*.

Yamaguchi University Library: Yoshida, Yamaguchi City 753; f. 1949; 2 br. libraries; 844,270 vols. (including 236,951 foreign); Librarian HIDEO IWAKI.

Yokahama National University Library: 156 Tokiwadai, Hodogayaku, Yokahama City; f. 1949; 541,889 vols.; Librarian S. NOMURA.

MUSEUMS AND ART GALLERIES

Museums in Japan, except for a few modern ones in the big cities, take the form of treasure halls, and are usually in the precincts of temples and shrines.

TOKYO CITY

Bridgestone Museum of Art: Kyobashi, Chuo-ku, Tokyo; f. 1952 by Shojiro Ishibashi; public museum of modern Japanese art and Western arts; Exec. Dir. YASUO KAMON.

Gotoh Art Museum: 9-25 3-chome Kaminoge, Setagaya-ku, Tokyo; f. 1960; about 1,000 exhibits, including the "Tales of Genji" scroll.

Inokashira Onshi Koen Shizen Bunkaen (*Natural Science Park in Inokashira Park*): 1-17-6 Gotenyama, Musashinoshi; zoo, botanical garden, research room, marine biology room.

Kokuritsu Kagaku Hakubutsukan (*National Science Museum*): Ueno Park 7-20, Daito-ku, Tokyo 110; f. 1877; exhibits of natural history, physical science and engineering; 168 mems.; library of 45,400 vols.; Dir. SHIGERU FUKADA; publs. *Bulletin* (in 4 parts, quarterly), *Memoirs, Newsletter* (3 a year), *Natural Science and Museums* (quarterly).

Kotsu Hakubutsukan (*Transport Museum*): 25 1-chome, Kanda-Suda-cho, Chiyoda-ku; f. 1921; 15,000 articles, including locomotives, electric equipment, motor-cars, aircraft, ships, etc.; Curator Y. FURUYA.

Meiji Jingu Homotsuden (*Meiji Shrine Treasure Museum*): Yoyogi, Shibuya-ku; f. 1921; 102 treasures and possessions of Emperor Meiji and 74 objects belonging to Empress Shoken; there is also a Memorial Picture Gallery.

National Museum of Modern Art, Tokyo: 3 Kitanomaru Koen, Chiyoda-ku, Tokyo 102; f. 1952; collection of Japanese-style paintings, oil paintings, prints, sculpture, drawings, watercolours and calligraphies; Dir. KENJI ADACHI; publ. *Gendai no Me* (monthly, Japanese).

National Museum of Western Art: Ueno Park, Taito-ku; f. 1959 (designed by Le Corbusier); 19th-century European paintings and sculptures collected by the late Kojiro Matsukata and new acquisitions of old masters; library of 5,000 vols.; Dir. TADASHI UCHIYAMA; publs. *Bulletin* (annually), catalogues of several special exhibitions and of the Museum's whole collection, album of selected masterpieces of the Museum's collection.

Nezu Art Museum: 6-5-36 Minami-aoyama, Minato-ku, Tokyo; f. 1940; private collection by Kaichiro Nezui of 7,195 paintings, calligraphy, sculpture, swords, ceramics, lacquer-ware, archaeological exhibits; 173 items designated as national treasures; Dir. KAICHIRO NEZU, Jr.; Assoc. Dir. HISAO SUGAHARA.

Nippon Mingei-Kan (*Japanese Folk Art Museum*): 861 Komaba-machi, Meguro-ku; 20,000 objects of folk-craft arts from all parts of the world; Curator S. HAMADA.

Okura Shukokan (*Okura Museum*): Akasaka-Aoicho, Minato-ku; f. 1917; 1,676 articles of fine arts; 35,560 vols. Chinese classics; Pres. SHINKICHI OSAKI; publ. *Shuko Meikau.*

Shodo Hakubutsukan (*Calligraphy Museum*): 125 Kami-negishi, Daito-ku; f. 1936; collection of the calligrapher, the late F. NAKAMURA; 1,000 rubbed copies of the stone tablets and "hōjō", ancient texts of calligraphy (10,000 articles).

Teishin Hakubutsukan (*Communications Museum*): 3 Fujimi-cho 2-chome, Chiyoda-ku; 12,774 exhibits; Curator TAKEO MIYAMOTO.

Tokyo Daigaku Rigakubu Fuzoku Shokubutsuen (*Botanical Gardens of the Faculty of Science, University of Tokyo*): 7-1, Hakusan 3, Bunkyo-ku; f. 1877; Nikko branch; f. 1902; 6,000 kinds of plants; 2,500 in Nikko; library of 1,490 vols.; Dir. Prof. Dr. M. FURUYA; publs. *Journal of Fac. Sci., Sect. III (Bot.), Index Seminum.*

Tokyo Kokuritsu Hakubutsukan (*Tokyo National Museum*): 13-9 Ueno Park, Daito-ku; f. 1871; largest art museum in Japan; 86,000 objects of Eastern fine arts, including paintings, calligraphy, sculpture, metal work, ceramic art, textiles, lacquer ware, archaeological exhibits, etc.; Dir. SEI SAITO; publ. *Museum* (monthly).

Tokyo National University of Fine Arts and Music Art Museum: Ueno Park, Daito-ku, Tokyo; 38,051 exhibits including paintings, sculptures and industrial art of Japan, China and Korea.

Tokyo-to Bijutsukan (*Tokyo Metropolitan Art Museum*): Ueno Park 8, Daito-ku; f. 1925; modern and contemporary art exhibition, educational service, art library of 7,500 vols. and gallery for group exhibitions; Dir. KAZUAKI KUDO; publs. *Bijutsukan News*† (monthly), *Bulletin*† (annually).

Waseda Daigaku Tsubouchi Hakase Kinen Engeki Hakubutsukan (*The Tsubouchi Memorial Theatre Museum, Waseda University*): 1-6-1 Nishi-Waseda; f. 1928; 78,888 (Japanese), 12,067 (foreign) books on drama and over 209,324 items including wood-block colour prints, programmes, pictures, costumes, properties, and other equipment used on the stage; Dir. TAKESHI KURAHASHI; publs. *News Bulletin, Catalogues, The Theatre Annual of Japan, Studies in Dramatic Art.*

KYOTO CITY

Bukkyo Jido Hakubutsukan (*Children's Buddhist Museum*): in Maruyama Park, Higashiyama-ku; 14,432 objects of interest in the study of Buddhism, history, geography, science, the fine arts, and old customs.

Chishakuin (*Treasure Hall of the Chishakuin Temple*): Higashi-Kawaramachi, Higashiyama-ku; Buddhist equipment and utensils, old documents, paintings, calligraphs, sutras, and books in Japanese and in Chinese.

Daigoji Reihoden (*Treasure Hall of the Daigoji Temple*): Daigo, Fushimi-ku; f. 1936; contains 1,500 old art objects and 120,000 historical documents relating chiefly to Buddhism.

Jishoji (popularly known as **Ginkakuji,** the Silver Temple): Ginkakuji-cho, Sakyo-ku, Kyoto; f. 1483 by Soami, a Shogun of Ashikaga, as twelve separate buildings in thegr ounds of his villa; only the Ginkaku or Silver Hall, and the Togudo are now left; Curator Rev. G. SUGA.

Kitano Temmangu Homotsuden (*Treasure Hall of Kitano-Temmangu shrine*): Kitano Bakuro-cho. Kamigyo-ku; shrine dedicated to Michizane Sugawara, statesman and great scholar of Heian period; exhibits of treasure hall include the "Kitano-Tenjin" history picture scrolls and an ancient copy of the "Nihon Shoki".

Koryūji Reihōden (*Treasure Museum of the Koryuji Temple*): Koryuji Temple, Uzumasa, Ukyo-ku; f. 1922; many Buddhist images and pictures, including the two images of "Miroku Bosatsu"; Curator EIKO KIYOTAKI.

Kyoto Daigaku Bungakubu Chinretsukan (*Museum of Faculty of Letters, Kyoto University*): Yoshida Honmachi, Sakyō-ku, Kyoto; f. 1911; 63,850 specimens of interest in the study of archaeology, history and geography of the Far East, including Japan, Korea and China; library of 93,000 vols.; Dir. Prof. TAKAYASU HIGUCHI; publ. *Archaeological Research Report.*

Kyoto Kokuritsu Hakubutsukan (*Kyoto National Museum*): 527 Chaya-machi, Higashiyama-ku; f. 1889 as Imperial Kyoto Museum; reorganized in 1952 as National Museum; 56 mems.; 23,515 books and 57,146 research photographs; 11,031 exhibits, including fine art and handicraft exhibits and historical materials of Asia, chiefly of Japan; Dir. TAKAAKI MATSUSHITA; Chief Curator HIROSHI SUZUKI; publs. *Reports of the Ueno Memorial Foundation for the Study of Buddhist Art.*

Kyoto-shi Bijutsukan (*Kyoto Municipal Museum of Art*): Okazaki Park, Sakyo-ku; f. 1933 for exhibitions of contemporary art; a collection of contemporary fine arts objects, including 514 Japanese pictures (of which 215 are oils), 39 Japanese sculptures, 86 decorative arts exhibits and 24 Japanese prints; Dir. T. FUJIKAWA; publs. *Annual Report News*, Exhibition Catalogues, *Museum Newspaper, The Arts of Kyoto* (series), etc.

Myōhōin (*Treasure House of the Myōhōin Temple*): Myohoin-maegawa-cho, Higashiyama-ku; possessions of Toyotomi-Hideyoshi and many other national treasures.

National Museum of Modern Art: Enshoji-cho, Okazaki, Sakyo-ku; f. 1963; modern handicrafts, paintings, sculptures; Dir. MICHIAKI KAWAKITA; Chief Curator TADAO OGURA.

Ninnaji Reihōden (*Treasure Hall of the Ninnaji Temple*): Ninnaji Temple, Omuro Daimon-cho, Ukyo-ku.

Rengeoin (Sanjusangendo) (*Treasure House of the Rengeoin Temple*): Mawari-cho, Higashiyama-ku; "One Thousand Images" and many other Buddhist images.

Rokuonji (*Treasures of the Rokuonji Temple*): Kinkakuji-cho, Kitaku, Kyoto; famed for its garden and gold pavilion.

Shoren-in (*Treasure House of the Shōren-in Temple*); Sanjōbō-machi, Awadaguchi, Higashiyama-ku; f. 1153:

Dir. JIKO HIGASHIFUSHIMI; library of 5,000 vols.; rare books, writings, paintings, etc.

Taiten Kinen Kyoto Shokubutsuen (*Kyoto Prefectural Museum Botanical Garden*): Hangi-machi, Shimogamo, Sakyô-ku; 70,000 plants and 5,500 botanical specimens.

Toyokuni Jinja Hómotsuden (*Treasure Hall of the Toyokuni Shrine*): Shomen Chaya-machi Yamato-Ooji, Higashiyama-ku; treasures and possessions of Toyotomi-Hideyoshi, including paintings, painted screens, swords, etc.

Yogen-In (*Treasure Hall of the Yōgen-In Temple*): Sanjusangendō-mae, Yamato-ōji Shichijō Higashi Iru, Higashiyama-ku.

Yūrinkan (*The Yurinkan Collection*): 44 Okazaki-Enshōji-machi, Sakyō-ku, Kyoto; f. 1926; some 30,000 exhibits of rare antique Chinese fine arts and curios, including bronze and jade ware, porcelain, seals, Buddhist images, pictures, and calligraphy; Curator S. FUJII. The collection is privately owned by the Fujii Foundation.

OSAKA CITY

Osaka Municipal Electricity Museum: 1-6 Kitadori, Nagahori, Nishi-ku, Osaka; f. 1937; Zeiss Planetarium, atomic power, electric wave and communication exhibits; Dir. T. URANO.

Osaka Municipal Museum of Fine Arts: Tennoji Park, Chausuyama, Tennoji-ku, Osaka; f. 1936; Chinese, Korean and Japanese fine art; library of *c.* 6,000 vols.; Dir. JOJI OKAZAKI.

Osaka Museum of Natural History: Nagai Park, Higashi-sumiyoshi-ku, Osaka 546; f. 1952; entomology, zoology, botany, geology and palaeontology; Dir. Dr. MANZO CHIJI; Head Curator ISAMU HIURA; publs. *Bulletin*†, *Occasional Papers*†, *Special Publications*†, *Annual Report, Nature Study*.

AICHI PREFECTURE

Nagoya Castle Gallery: 1 Hon-maru, Naka-ku, Nagoya; built in 1612 by Ieyasu Tokugawa; destroyed by fire 1945; restored to its original form 1959; exhibition rooms, galleries and observatory; 331 frescoes painted by Tan-yu Kano and his successors.

CHIBA PREFECTURE

Naritasan Museum (*Treasure Hall of the Naritasan-Shinshoji Temple*): Narita Park, Narita-City, Chiba Pref.; f. 1947; contains treasures dedicated to the shrine and archaeological pieces from the region, 12,113 MSS. and books, sculptures, botanical specimens; Curator MASAJI OHNO.

EHIME PREFECTURE

Oyamazumi Jinja Kokuhokan (*Treasure Hall of the Oyamazumi Shrine*): Oyamazumi Shrine, Omishima town, Ochigun; f. A.D. 1; 2,000 exhibits, including a large collection of ancient armour, swords, and the oldest mirrors in Japan; library of 20,000 vols.; Curator YASUHISA MISHIMA.

GIFU PREFECTURE

Ogawa Eiichi Collection: Oebi Ono-machi Ibi-gun; 10,000 old ceramics excavated in and around the region.

HIROSHIMA PREFECTURE

Itsukushima Jinja Homotsukan (*Treasure Hall of the Itsukushima Shinto Shrine*): Miyajima-cho, Saeki-gun; f. 1895; 2,500 exhibits of paintings, calligraphy, sutras, swords, and other ancient weapons; Curator and Chief Priest MOTOSADA NOZAKA.

HOKKAIDO PREFECTURE

Abashiri Kyodo Hakubutsukan (*Abashiri Municipal Museum*): Katsuragaoka Park, Abashiri; f. 1936; 600 local products, 10,000 articles of historical, geographical and archaeological interest, and 100 miscellaneous exhibits; Dir. T. YONEMURA.

Asahikawa Kyodo Hakubutsukan (*Asahikawa Folk Museum*): 2-chome Hanasaki-cho, Asahikawa City; f. 1952; cultural objects of Ainu race and many archaeological items.

Hakodate City Museum: Hakodate Park, 17-1 Aoyagi-cho, Hakodate City; f. 1879; oldest local museum in Japan; Dir. M. ISHIKAWA.

Kushiro-shi Kyodo Hakubutukan (*Kushiro Municipal Museum*): 1-10-35 Tsurugadai Park, Kushiro; f. 1936; 12,130 earthenware articles, many different kinds of birds and animals, plants, insects, minerals and objects of local interest; Curator HIROYUKI MASATOMI.

HYŌGO PREFECTURE

Hakutsuru Bijitsukan (*Hakutsuru Fine Art Museum*): 6-1-1 Sumiyoshitamate, Higashinada-ku, Kobe; f. 1934; 1,000 specimens of fine art, including noted Chinese ceramics and old bronze vases and silver ware; Dir. MASAHARU KANO.

Kobe Municipal Museum of Nanban Art: 1-chome Kumochi-cho, Fukiai-ku, Kobe; 4,000 exhibits depicting influence of first contact with western civilization late 16th century to Meji Restoration; Dir. YASUO ORIMO.

IWATE PREFECTURE

Chuson-ji Sanko-zo (*Chuson-ji Temple Sanko Repository*): Hiraizumi-machi, Nishi-Iwai-gun; f. 1955 to preserve treasures and possessions of the Fujiwara family who were important in the late period of Heian (801-1185).

KAGAWA PREFECTURE

Kotohira-gū Hakubutsukan (*Museum in the Kotohira Shrine*): Kotohira-gū Shrine, Kotohira-machi, Nakatadogun; 3,011 exhibits; Chair. MITSUSHIGE KOTOOKA; Sec. HAZIME HIRAO KOTOHIRA.

KANAGAWA PREFECTURE

Kamakura Kokuhokan (*Kamakura Museum*): 2-1-1 Yukinoshita, Kamakura City; f. 1928; Japanese art and history in the Middle Ages; 1,760 valuable specimens of Japanese fine arts; 12 mems.; library of 2,860 vols.; Dir. TATSUTO NUKI; publs. *Kokuhokan-zuroku, Kokuhokan-ronshu*.

Kanazawa Bunko Museum (*Museum and Library*): Shomyoji Temple, 217 Kanazawa-machi, Kanagawa-ku, Yokohama City; Temple f. 1275; 680 articles, including various specimens of Japanese fine arts, 20,000 old books and 5,000 documents; nine national treasures (images of Buddha, etc.); Curator ISAKICHI KUTSUKAKE.

Kyusei Hakone Art Museum: Gora, Kanagawa Pref.; f. 1952; private collection of Okada Mokichi (founder of the Church of World Messianity) of Japanese and Chinese ceramic works of art; Dir. YOJI YOSHIOKA.

Museum of Modern Art, Kamakura: 2-1-53 Yukinoshita, Kamakura 248; f. 1951; modern and contemporary art in Japan and Europe; Dir. TEIICHI HIJIKATA; publ. *Kanagawa Bijutsu Fudoki*.

KOCHI PREFECTURE

Kochi Koen Kaitokukan (*Museum in Kochi Park*): Marunouchi, Kochi City; 800 exhibits, including autographs and material of interest in Japanese historical research.

KUMAMOTO PREFECTURE

Kumamoto Museum: 7-17 Hanabata-machi, Kumamoto City; f. 1952; 10,000 books; 80,000 items of natural scientific interest (sea shells, minerals, rocks etc.) and 30,000 items of historical interest (folklore, archaeology etc.); Chief Officer KENICHI UEMURA; publ. *Kumamoto Museum Gazette*.

MIE PREFECTURE

Iga Bunka Sangyó Kyokai (*Iga Art and Industry Institute*): 6, 1-Marunouchi, Ueno, Ueno City; 3,000 articles.

Jingū Chókokan (*Jingu Historical Museum*): Kuratayama, Ise-city; 1,734 exhibits, including treasures of the Grand Shrine of Ise (Naiku Shrine and Geku Shrine) and many objects of historical interest; library of 1,082 vols., MSS. and pictures; Dir. and Chief of Cultural Section of the Grand Shrine of Ise YASUJI AKIOKA.

Jingu Nogyokan (*Agricultural Museum*): Kuratayama, Ise-city; f. 1905; 9,583 exhibits connected with agriculture, forestry, and fishing (including collection of over 40 species of shark); Dir. YASUJI AKIOKA.

MIYAZAKI PREFECTURE

Miyazakijingū Chókokan (*Historical Museum in the Miyazaki Shrine*): 360 Jingu-machi, Miyazaki City; 4,000 objects of historical and archaeological interest; Dir. H. YANAGI.

NAGANO PREFECTURE

Matsumoto Kinenkan (*Matsumoto Historical Museum*): 2 Marunouchi, Matsumoto City; 45,000 exhibits of geological, historical and archaeological interest; fine art.

NARA PREFECTURE

Hōryūji ((*Hōryūji Temple*): Aza Hōryūji, Ikaruga-cho, Ikoma-gun, Nara Prefecture; a large number of Buddhist images and paintings; the buildings date from the Asuka, Nara, Heian, Kamakura, Ashikaga, and Tokugawa periods.

Kasugataisha Homotsuden (*Treasure Hall of the Kasugataisha Shrine*): Kasugataisha Shrine, Kasugano-cho, Nara City; f. 1934; the ancient, curvilinear style of architecture is called "Kasuga Zukuri" after this shrine; Shrine Master SANEHARU SANJO; Man-nyo Botanical Garden and Library of 4,000 vols.; publ. *Sika* (The Deer).

Museum Yamato Bunkakan: 1-11-6 Gakuen-minami, Nara City; f. 1960; art objects of East Asia, chiefly Japan, China and Korea; library of 15,000 vols.; Dir. MASAO ISHIZAWA; publs. *Yamato Bunka* (2 a year), *Catalogues* (English).

Nara Art Museum: Isuien Park, 74 Suimon-cho, Nara City; f. 1939; ancient Chinese bronze mirrors, seals, etc., and Korean potteries.

Nara Kokuritsu Hakubutsukan (*Nara National Museum*): 50 Nobori-oji-cho, Nara-shi 630; f. 1895; Buddhist art and archaeology; Dir. BUNSAKU KURATA.

Tenri Sankokan Museum: 1 Furu, Tenri City; f. 1930; attached to Tenri University; ethnographic and archaeological items from all parts of the world.

Tódaiji (*Treasure Hall of the Tódaiji Temple*): 406 Zoshi-cho, Nara City; f. 752; 29 Buddhist priests, 76 staff; Daibutsuden: the world-famous Great Image of Buddha, Two Deva Kings, and many other treasures and ancient documents; attached buildings are the Hokkedo, Kaidan-in, Nigatudo, which contain many famous images of Buddha; Shosoin Treasure House (now belonging to the Japanese Emperor); 3,000 treasures and personal belongings of Emperor Shomu; Dir. K. SHIMIZU; library of 150,000 vols.; publ. *Nanto Bukkyo: Journal of the Nanto Society for Buddhist Studies* (twice yearly).

Yakushiji (*Yakushiji Temple*): Nishi-no-Kyō-machi, Nara City; famous bronze images of the Yakushi Trinity; a pagoda 1,300 years old.

OKAYAMA PREFECTURE

Ohara Bijitsukan (*Ohara Art Gallery*): 1-1-15 Chuo, Kurashiki-city; f. 1930; ceramics and sculptures from Egypt, Persia and Turkey; European paintings and sculpture of nineteenth and twentieth centuries; gallery of Japanese paintings; arts and crafts; Curator S. FUJITA.

SHIMANE PREFECTURE

Koizumi-Yakumo Kinenkan (*Lafcadio Hearn Memorial Hall*): 322-4 Okudani-machi, Matsue City; 49 possessions of Lafcadio Hearn, 530 books and pictures.

Shimane Prefectural Museum: 1 Tono-machi, Matsue City; f. 1959; unique collection of Gagaku instruments.

SHIZUOKA PREFECTURE

Kyusei Atami Art Museum: Atami; f. 1957; Oriental fine arts; Dir. YOJI YOSHIOKA; publ. *Meihin Zuroku*† (3 vols.).

TOTTORI PREFECTURE

San-in Rekishikan (*San-in Historical Museum*): Nishi-machi, Yonago City; f. 1940; 23,500 exhibits, including specimens and material of value in historical and archaeological research.

WAKAYAMA PREFECTURE

Kōyasan Reihōkan (*Museum of Buddhist Art on Mount Kōya*): Kōyasan, Kōya-cho, Ito-gun; f. 1926; 25,000 exhibits, including Buddhist paintings and images, sutras and old documents, some of them registered National Treasures and Important Cultural Properties; a centre of Buddhism in Japan; Curator CHIKYŌ YAMAMOTO, PH.D.

YAMANASHI PREFECTURE

Entomological Museum of Fujikyu: Fujikyu Highland, P.O.B. 12, Fujiyoshida, Yamanashiken; f. 1968; entomological research centre containing the largest collection of exotic Coleoptera in Japan; Dir. HIKARU NAKAMURA.

Minobusan Homotsukan (*Treasury of the Kuonji Temple*): Kuonji Temple, Minobu-machi, Minami-Koma-gun; 300 articles, examples of the fine arts, and materials connected with the history of the Nichiren Sect of Buddhism, the biography of Saint Nichiren.

NATIONAL UNIVERSITIES

AKITA UNIVERSITY

1-1 TEGATA GAKUENCHO,
AKITA CITY 010
Telephone: 0188-33-5261.
Founded 1949.

Academic year: April to March.

President: KATSUJI KUSHIMA, M.D.
Director of Administrative Bureau: SHIGEO KIMURA.
Dean of Student Administration: YASUO KUDO.
Librarian: YO ISHIKAWA.

Number of teachers: 464.
Number of students: 3,524.
Publication: *Bulletin*†.

DEANS:

College of Education: TATSUO ANAZAWA.
School of Medicine and Graduate School of Medicine: YOSHITANE WATABE, M.D.
Mining College and Graduate School of Mining: CHIKAI KIMURA, D.ENG.

ATTACHED INSTITUTES:

Research Institute of Underground Resources: Dir. CHIKAI KIMURA, D.ENG.

Mineral Industry Museum: Dir. CHIKAI KIMURA, D.ENG.

CHIBA UNIVERSITY

1-33 YAYOICHO, CHIBASHI
Telephone: (51) 1111.
Founded 1949.

President: H. KATSUKI.
Director-General of Administration Bureau: K. KOJIMA.
Dean of Student Bureau: S. KONDO.
Librarian: K. TAKEDA.

Number of full-time teachers: 1,020.
Number of students: 9,212.
Publications: Each faculty publishes a *Journal*† or *Bulletin*†.

DEANS:

Faculty of Humanities and Social Sciences: N. OGASAWARA.
Faculty of Education: H. INOUE.
Faculty of Science: M. NUMATA.
School of Medicine: G. IDE.
Faculty of Pharmaceutical Sciences: T. HINO.
School of Nursing: Y. ISHIGURO.
Faculty of Engineering: J. KOHARA.
Faculty of Horticulture: M. KOJIMA.
College of General Education: G. ABE.

DIRECTORS:

Institute of Chemobiodynamics: T. KUGA.
University Hospital: H. SATO.

PROFESSORS:

Faculty of Humanities and Social Sciences:

EMORI, I., Sociology of Law
HAKUTA, T., Ethics
HANAMURA, J., Law of Civil Procedure
HARADA, K., American Literature
HAYASHIDA, A., Japanese Linguistics
INOURA, Y., Japanese Literature
ITO, M., Economics Policy
IWANAGA, K., Administrative Theory
KOJIMA, S., German Literature
MAEDA, Y., Political Theory
NAGATA, I., Business Administration
NAKAGAWA, Y., Civil Law
NAKAMURA, H., Philosophy
NAKANO, T., Sociology and Social Research
OBUKI, Y., Constitutional Law
OGASAWARA, N., Japanese History
OYAMA, M., Oriental History
OYAMA, T., Experimental Psychology
SASAKI, Y., Economic History
SAWADA, T., Oriental Philosophy
SHIMADA, S., French Linguistics
SHIMIZUGAWA, S., Theoretical Economics
SHINOZAKI, F., German Linguistics
TAGUCHI, T., Statistics and Econometrics
TANAKA, H., Business Management
UNO, T., Japanese History

Faculty of Education:

AOYAGI, M., Mathematics Teaching
CHISAKA, T., Physical Geography
CHONAN, M., Design and Craft
CHUMA, T., Machinery
EBISAWA, I., Painting
FUKUO, T., Adult Education
HAYAKAWA, S., Machinery
HIWATASHI, M., English and American Literature
IGAMI, D., Science Teaching
IKEDA, T., Japanese Literature
IKEDA, Y., American and European History
INOUE, H., Education
ISHIGURO, I., Music Teaching
ISHIHARA, B., Physical Education
ITO, T., Sculpture
IWASAWA, F., Japanese Language Teaching
KATO, H., Science of Health Education
KATO, N., Japanese Language
KOIDE, S., Education of Handicapped Children
KURATA, T., English Teaching
MATSUOKA, A., Surgical Nursing
MATSUSHITA, S., Food Science
MINAGAWA, Y., Sociology
MIYAMA, M., Science Teaching
MIYAMOTO, S., Psychology of Handicapped Children
MIZUNO, S., Study of Curriculum for Young Children
MURATA, H., Instrumental Music
NAKAJIMA, T., Japanese Literature
SAKAMOTO, S., Education
SHIINA, M., History of Education
SHIMA, H., Economics
SHIMADA, R., Health and Physical Education Teaching
SHIMAMURA, T., Electricity
SHIMAZAKI, S., Physical Exercise
SHIMIZU, K., Geography
SHIMURA, K., Chinese Classics
SHINOMIYA, A., Developmental Psychology
SHIROMARU, A., Educational System
SUGIOKA, S., Mathematics Teaching
SUNADA, J., Physics
SUZUKI, K., Biology
SUZUKI, M., Theory and History of Physical Education
TAGO, A., Educational Psychology
TAKEDA, T., Basic Medical Science
TAKEFUTA, Y., English Linguistics
TAKEUCHI, K., Theory and History of Art
TAKEUCHI, T., Educational Psychology
TERAUCHI, A., Composition
TOMONARI, A., Chemistry
TSUCHIYA, N., Basic Science for Nursing
UCHIDA, M., Science Teaching
UEHARA, S., Clinical Medical Science and Nursing
USAMI, H., Education
UTSUMI, K., Basic Science for Nursing
YAMAMOTO, K., Vocal Music
YAMAMOTO, T., Music Teaching
YAMANAKA, T., Chemistry

Faculty of Science:

ASAI, A., Mathematical Statistics
HIRATA, K., Algebra and Geometry
HIROKAWA, H., Applied Mathematics
INOUE, K., Physical Chemistry
KANAZAWA, H., Theoretical Physics
KANEHIRA, K., Mineralogy
MAEDA, S., Geology
MARUYAMA, K., Physiology
MURAUCHI, S., Geophysics
NISHIDA, M., Phylogeny
NUMATA, M., Ecology
OYAGI, Y., Inorganic and Analytical Chemistry
TAKESHIMA, T., Organic Chemistry
TOBITA, T., Biochemistry
WATANABE, Y., Experimental Physics
YANAGIHARA, N., Analysis

School of Medicine:

ARIMIZU, N., Radiology
FURIYA, S., Laboratory Medicine
HAGIHARA, Y., Neuropharmacology
HAYASHI, Y., Pathology
HIRAYAMA, K., Neurology
HONDA, Y., Physiology
HONMA, S., Physiology
IDE, G., Pathology
INAGAKI, Y., Internal Medicine
INOUE, S., Orthopaedic Surgery
ISHIKAWA, K., Hygiene
ISHIKAWA, K., Ophthalmology
ITO, K., Surgery
KANAKUBO, Y., Pharmaceutical Services
KANEKO, T., Oto-Rhino-Laryngology
KIMURA, Y., Forensic Medicine
KONDO, Y. Pathology
KUMAGAI, A., Internal Medicine
KUWATA, T., Microbiology
MAKINO, H., Neurosurgery
MIURA, Y., Biochemistry
MURAYAMA, S., Pharmacology
NAGANO, T., Anatomy
NAKAJIMA, H., Paediatrics
OKAMOTO, S., Dermatology
OKUDA, K., Internal Medicine
OTANI, K., Anatomy
SATO, H., Surgery
SATO, I., Neuropsychiatry
SATO, K., Oral Surgery
SHIMADA, Y., Anatomy
SHIMAZAKI, J., Urology
TACHIBANA, M., Biochemistry
TADA, T., Immunology
TAKAMIZAWA, H., Obstetrics and Gynaecology
UCHIDA, A., Rural Medicine
WATANABE, S., Respiratory Medicine
YAMAGUCHI, Y., Chest Surgery
YOKOGAWA, M., Parasitology
YONEZAWA, T., Anaesthesiology
YOSHIDA, R., Public Health

Faculty of Pharmaceutical Sciences:

HAGINIWA, J., Pharmacognosy
HARADA, M., Medical Chemistry
HINO, T., Synthetic Organic Chemistry

HIROSE, S., Physiological Chemistry
HOSOYA, T., Pharmaceutical Physical Chemistry
IKEDA, J., Pharmaceutical Chemistry
IMANARI, T., Analytical Chemistry
KITAGAWA, H., Biochemical Pharmacology
NAKAI, Y., Pharmaceutical Technology
SAKAI, S., Pharmaceutical Chemistry
SUZUKI, T., Pharmaceutics
YAMAGISHI, S., Microbial Chemistry
YAMANE, Y., Hygienic Chemistry

School of Nursing:

HASHIZUME, S., Pathology and Microbiology
ISHIGURO, Y., Medical-Surgical Nursing II
ISHIKAWA, T., Physiology and Biochemistry
KOBAYASHI, F., Social Health Science
MITOH, T., Nursing Education
NOZAWA, E., Psychiatric Nursing
USUI, H., Nursing Principles and Practice
YAMAGUCHI, K., Medical Surgical Nursing I
YOSHITAKE, K., Paediatric Nursing

Faculty of Engineering:

AKANA, H., Plastic Arts
ARAI, J., Engineering of Plasticity
EMORI, Y., Institute of Natural Colour Technology
FUKUYO, H., Electric Power Systems
GENTA, H., Institute of Natural Colour Technology
HANAOKA, T., Manufacturing Technology
HASHIMOTO, H., Industrial Physica Chemistry
HISHIKI, Y., Applied Image Engineering of Plasticity
HONMA, H., Fluids Engineering
HORI, M., Mathematics for Engineering
IIDA, H., Synthetic Organic Chemistry
ISHIKAWA, T., Institute of Natural Colour Technology
ITO, M., Architectural Design and Planning
KANEKO, Y., Methodology of Design
KAWADA, K., Mechanical Engineering
KAWASE, T., Electric Power and Illumination Engineering
KIKUCHI, Y., Ergonomics
KINOSHITA, Y., Electrical Communications
KOGO, H., Electronic Circuits
KOHARA, J., Interior Design
KOIZUMI, S., Architectural History, and Residential Science
KOJIMA, K., Polymer Chemistry
KUBO, S., Visual Science
KURODA, R., Analytical Chemistry
MARUYASU, T., Institute of Natural Colour Technology
MASHIKO, Y., Chemical Measurements
MATSUMOTO, K., Printing Technology
MIZUSAWA, S., Photographic Engineering
MORIMOTO, M., Industrial Design
MORIYA, H., Planning and Design of Housing
MOURI, J., Industrial Inorganic Chemistry
MURAKAMI, M., Structural Engineering
NAGAKUBO, K., Synthetic Polymer Chemistry
NAKAGUCHI, H., Machine Design
NAKAMICHI, M., Electronic Control Engineering
NAKANO, Y., Mechanical Engineering for Production
NISHIMAKI, M., Fundamental Electronics
NOZAKI, F., Chemical Engineering
OHE, S., Photographic Technology
OKAMOTO, J., Machine Elements
OKAWA, N., Productive Process of Architecture
OKAWA, S., Applied Information Science
OZAKI, M., Disaster Prevention
OKI, H., Electric Materials and High Voltage Engineering
SAITO, H., Structural Design
SAKAGUCHI, T., Photo-sensitive Material Technology
SASAI, A., Photographic Chemistry, Applied Photography
SHIMO, C., Engineering for Precision Machinery
SUGA, K., Industrial Organic Chemistry
SUGIHARA, E., Electric Machinery
SUZUKI, S., Environmental Chemistry
SUZUKI, T., Design Materials
TAGA, Y., Information Processing
TAMURA, M., Applied Physics
TESHIROGI, N., Thermodynamics and Heat Engineering
TOTANI, T., Automatic Control
TSUNODA, T., Imaging Materials
UDOGUCHI, T., Elasticity and Plasticity
UEDA, S., Synthetic Inorganic Chemistry
WAKESHIMA, H., Imaging Technology
WATANABE, K., Graphic Engineering
YAMADA, K., Organic Material Chemistry
YAMAMOTO, H., Microwave Measurements
YOSHIE, K., Electromagnetism

Faculty of Horticulture:

AOBA, T., Vegetable Science
ASANO, J., Planting Design
AYANO, Y., Food and Nutritional Chemistry
FUKUTOMI, H., Landscape Planning and Design
HANYU, J., Agricultural Meteorology
HIROYASU, T., Biological Chemistry
HONDA, H., Botany for Landscaping
IGARISHI, K., Horticultural Farming and Economy
IIDA, W., Plant Pathology
IIZUKA, M., Field Work
ISHII, H., Theory and History of Landscape Planning
IWASA, R., Thremmatology
KOJIMA, M., Soil Science and Plant Nutrition
KOSUGI, K., Floriculture
MATSUO, M., Horticultural Machinery
MIHARA, Y., Horticultural Engineering
MIYAZAKI, M., Urban and Rural Planning
NODA, T., Pomology
NOMURA, K., Environmental Biology
OGURA, N., Food Chemistry and Technology
OIZUMI, H., Crop Production and Management
SEKIGUCHI, A., Landscape Engineering
SUZUKI, T., Horticultural Business and Economy
TAKAHASHI, K., Nature Conservation
YABUKI, M., Fermentation Technology and Applied Microbiology

College of General Education:

ABE, G., History
FUKAO, K., Chemistry
HASHIGUCHI, M., French
HAYASHI, M., Chemistry
HIDAKA, A., Physical Education
HIRAI, I., Mathematics
HORIKAWA, T., English
IWASHIGE, M., Politics
IWATSUKI, S., English
KAYA, T., Chemistry
KIUCHI, N., English
KOBAYASHI, S., Physical Education
KONDO, S., Earth Science
KUBO, K., German
MATSUZAKI, Y., French
MIYAMOTO, T., Physical Education
MORI, Y., English
MURAKAMI, M., Statistics
NAKAMORI, Y., Arts
NAKANO, Y., Sociology
OHSAWA, K., Regional Science
OHZEKI, N., Mathematics
OKAZAKI, K., German
SHIMADA, R., Japanese Literature
SHIMIZU, T., Mathematics
SHINBORI, M., Physical Education
SUZUKI, Y., Physics
TADA, A., Economics
TAKADA, Y., Physics
TAKAI, K., English
TAKEDA, K., Philosophy
TAMANOI, I., Biology
TANAKA, T., Economics
TANNO, Y., Mathematics
UNOKI, K., English
WAKABAYASHI, T., Physics
YAMADA, Y., Regional Science
YOKOTA, T., German
YOSHIDA, O., Biology

Research Institute for Chemobiodynamics:

ARAI, T., Antibiotics
HAYASHI, M., Enzymology
KUGA, T., Experimental Pharmacology
MIYAJI, H., Sanitary Bacteriology
TERAO, K., Toxicology and Experimental Pathology
UNEMOTO, T., Membrane Biochemistry
YAMAZAKI, M., Chemistry of Natural Products

ATTACHED INSTITUTES:

Institute of Epidemiology (attached to School of Medicine): Inohana, Chiba City.

Institute of Brain Research (attached to School of Medicine): Inohana, Chiba City.

Institute of Pulmonary Cancer Research (attached to School of Medicine): Inohana, Chiba City.

Institute of Natural Colour Technology (attached to Faculty of Engineering): Yayoi-cho, Chiba City.

EHIME UNIVERSITY

10–13 HIMATA-CHO, MATSUYAMA 790

Founded 1949.

President: H. NOMOTO.

Library of 529,883 vols.

Number of teachers: 800.

Faculties of law and literature, education, science, medicine, engineering, agriculture.

GIFU UNIVERSITY

NAKA MONZEN-CHO, KAKAMIGAHARA-SHI, GIFU-KEN

Telephone: 0583-82-1201.

Founded 1949.

President: M. TATI.
Secretary-General: Y. KOIKE.
Librarian: Y. TANIMURA.

Library of 502,197 vols., 8,800 periodicals.

Number of full-time teachers: 604.
Number of students: 4,256.
Publications: *Acta Scholae Medicinalis Universitatis in Gifu* (every 2 months), Research Bulletins and Reports from each faculty (annually).

DEANS:

Faculty of Education: H. HIROSE.
School of Medicine: S. SUZUKI.
Faculty of Engineering: H. WAKITA.
Faculty of Agriculture: Y. NAGATA.
Faculty of General Education: G. YAMAMOTO.

ATTACHED INSTITUTES:

Curriculum Research and Development Center: Dir. Prof. T. TAKANO.

Institute of Equilibrium Research: Dir. Prof. S. WATANABE.

Institute of Anaerobic Bacteriology: Dir. Prof. K. UENO.

Institute for the Development of Mountain Regions: Dir. Prof. T. ISHIKAWA.

GUMMA UNIVERSITY

1375 ARAMAKI-MACHI, MAEBASHI

Telephone: (32) 1611.

Founded 1949.

Academic year: April to March.

President: T. HATA.
Administrator: H. KANGAWA.
Librarian: T. MORITA.

Number of full-time teachers: 693.
Number of students: 4,703.
Publications: *Annual Reports, Science Reports, Journal of Liberal Arts and Science, Journal of Medical Science, Symposia on Endocrinology.*

DEANS:

Faculty of Education: Y. KIZAKI.
Faculty of Medicine: J. KAWAFUCHI.
Faculty of Technology: S. MACHIDA.
Faculty of General Study: S. HAYASHI.
Institute of Endocrinology: K. IWAI.
Junior Engineering College: T. HATA.
Medical and Technical Junior College: T. HATA.
Student Affairs: K. TOKUE.

PROFESSORS:

Faculty of Education:
ARAI, F., Geology
ARISUE, T., Geography
ASO, Y., Physics
ATSUMI, K., Mathematics
CHO, S., Chemistry
HAGIWARA, M., Pedagogy
HAGIWARA, Y., Physical Education
IGARASHI, S., Japanese Literature
INOKUMA, T., Mathematics
KANO, M., Fine Arts
KATSUMORI, S., Japanese History
KIMURA, S., Psychology
KITAGAWA, C., Pedagogy
KITAOKA, S., Japanese Education
KIZAKI, Y., Geology
KOGURE, M., Science Education
MASHIMO, Y., English Education
MATHIDA, Y., Fine Arts
MATSUKI, M., Physical Education
MIZUKAMI, S., Chinese Classics
MUKAI, H., Classification Morphology
MURAOKA, G., Agriculture
NISHI, K., American Literature
NISHIO, T., Japanese Language
NUNOKAWA, M., Mathematics
OOBAYASHI, Y., Physical Education
SHIBUYA, M., Music
SHIMAZU, T., Home Economics
SHIMIZU, T., Chemistry
SHIMIZU, Y., Pedagogy
SHIOTA, T., Psychology
SHINOHARA, H., Physics
SUGAWA, A., Geology
TAKAHASHI, K., Japanese Literature
TAKAHASHI, T., Technical Education
TANAKA, K., Ethics
TOKUE. K., Politics
TSUZUKI, Y., English Language
UEDA, M., Mechanics
WATANABE, O., Economics
YAMADA. K., Philosophy
YAMADA, Y., Biology
YAMAGUCHI, T., Pedagogy
YOSHIOKA, R., Electricity

Faculty of Medicine:
FUJITA, T., Anaesthesiology
FURUKAWA, K., Legal Medicine
HIRAI, S., Neurology
HIRAO, T., Physiology
IGARASHI, M., Gynaecology
ISHIDA, Y., Pathology
ISHII, H., Oto-Rhino-Laryngology
ISHIKAWA, H., Dermatology
IZUO, M., Surgery
KAWAFUCHI, J., Neuro-Surgery
KOBOYASHI, S., Internal Medicine
KUROUME, T., Paediatrics
MACHIYAMA, Y., Neuropsychiatry
MAEKAWA, T., Internal Medicine
MATSUDA, N., Dental Surgery
MITSUHASHI, S., Microbiology
MIURA, M., Physiology
MURATA, K., Internal Medicine
NAGAI, T., Radiology
NAKAMURA, T., Surgery
OBATA, K., Pharmacology
ONEDA, G., Pathology
SHIBASAKI, S., Anatomy
SHIDA. K.. Urology
SHIMIZU, K., Ophthalmology
SHIRAKURA, T., Internal Medicine
SUZUKI, M., Parasitology
TADOKORO, S., Analytic Chemistry
TAKAGI, S., Physiology
TAKIZAWA, A., Anatomy
TANAMI, F., Bacteriology
TSUJI, T., Public Health
UDAGAWA, E., Orthopaedics
WADA, O., Hygiene
YAMASHITA, T., Biochemistry

Faculty of Technology:
AKAIWA, H., Analytical Chemistry
AONUMA, T., Chemical Kinetics
EZAKI, K., Civil Engineering
HARUMI, K., Applied Mathematics
HIKAGE, T., Material Science and Metallurgy
HIRANO, K., Electronics
IEIRI, S., Information Processing
ISHII, Y., Dyeing Engineering
IWAYANAGI, S., Polymer Science
KAGA, H., Applied Mechanics
KAKIAGE, S., Textile Engineering
KATO, K., Chemical Reaction Engineering
KINOSHITA, S., Polymer Science
KURABAYASHI, T., Heat and Heat Engineering
KUWAHARA, N., Polymer Science
KUWAMURA, T., Organic Applied Chemistry
MACHIDA, S., Mechanics
MATSUDA S., Inorganic Chemistry
MATSUI, K., Organic Synthetic Chemistry
MICHIWAKI, Y., Applied Mathematics
MIGITA, T., Organic Chemistry
MINAMI, S., Applied Physics
MITSUISHI, T., Physics of Semi-conductors
MIYAZAKA, Y., Applied Thermal Engineering
MIYAZAKI, H., Applied Probability Statistics and Combinations
MIYAZAKI, K., Control Engineering
MORI, M., Construction and Measuring
MORINAGA, T., Electronics
MORITA, T., Physical Chemistry
NAGAI, T., Applied Physical Organic Chemistry
NAKAMURA, Y., Applied Physics
NISHIMURA, T., Electronics
OGIWARA, Y., Polymer Chemistry
OKUBO, M., Information Science
OSAWA, G., Textile Material and Machinery
OTANI, S., Inorganic Material Chemistry
SAKAI, T., Chemical Reaction Engineering
SHIMIZU, K., Computer Architecture
SUGAWARA, M., Basic Electricity
SUMIYOSHI, Y., Inorganic Industrial Chemistry
SUTO, T., Electric and Control Engineering
TAKAHASHI, A., Applied Physics
TAKIGUCHI, T., Organic Material Chemistry
UEDA, S., Polymer Engineering
YOKOYAMA, S., Fluid Mechanics
YUKAWA, H., Basic Engineering

Faculty of General Studies:
DOI, Y., Physical Education
FUKUSHI, N., Chemistry
HAYASHI, S., Physics
HITOTSUYANAGI, T., English
HOSOHARA, K., Chemistry
ICHIKAWA, K., German
IMAI, K., Biology
KATSUYAMA, K., Japanese Literature
KOBAYASHI, I., Mathematics
KOIKE, Z., Sociology
MASUDA, R., Philosophy
NAKAMURA, K., Law
NOMURA, S., Geology
SEKINO, S., English
SHUDO, S., English
TAKANO, Y., Physics
TAKIZAWA, T., Physics
TANAKA, T., German
TAZAKI, T., Psychology
UCHIDA, M., Physical Education
YABUKI, S., Physics
YOSHINO, K., Ethics

Institute of Endocrinology:
INOUE, S., Comparative Endocrinology
IWAI, K., Protein Chemistry
KUROSUMI, K., Morphology
SUZUKI, M., Physiology
TAKIKAWA, H., Pharmaceutical Chemistry
UI, N., Physical Biochemistry
WAKABAYASHI, K., Hormone Assay Center

HIROSAKI UNIVERSITY

1 BUNKYO-CHO, 036 HIROSAKI CITY

Telephone: 0172-36-2111.

Founded 1949.

State control; Academic year: April to March (two terms, three in Faculty of Medicine).

President: Y. OIKE.
Registrar: H. OCHI.
Librarian: K. TONOSAKI.
Director of the Hospital: Y. KATABIRA.

Number of teachers: 573.
Number of students: 4,578.

Publications: *School Outline* (annually), *Student Handbook* (annually), Faculty Bulletins.

DEANS:

Faculty of Humanities and Economics: Y. KUDO.
Faculty of Education: K. MAKINO.
Faculty of Science: K. TANAKA.
Faculty of Medicine: S. TONO.
Faculty of Agriculture: N. SASAKI.
College of Liberal Arts: M. AKASHI.

PROFESSORS:

Faculty of Humanities and Economics:
AKIZUKI, K., Oriental History
AZUMA, G., English Literature
FUJINO, M., Japanese History
ITO, Y., Ethics
KUDO, Y., Economic Theory
SATO, T., Law
OGASAWARA, S., German Literature
SEKIYA, K., Economic Policy
TAKAHASHI, F., Statistics
YOSHINAGA, Y., Business Economics

Faculty of Education:
AKIHA, F., Food Science
FUKUSHI, Y., Basic Medical Science
HANADA, T., Educational Sociology
HANAWA, J., Biology
HASHIMOTO, S., Education of Mentally Retarded Children
HIRATA, S., Natural Science Education
HORIGOME, S., Study of Material for Pre-school Education
ISHII, J., Analysis and Applied Mathematics
ISHIZAKI, N., Social Studies Education
IWAI, T., Earth Science
IWABUCHI, N., Physical Education
KASAI, M., Instrumental Music
KAWAKAMI, S., Medical Nursing
KAWAMURA, S., Painting
KON, M., Surgical Nursing
MAKINO, K., History of Education
MOGAMI, T., Pedagogy
MURAKOSHI, K., History
OBA, K., Physiology and Hygiene
OKUTA, M., Physics
OSADA, S., Japanese Literature
OSANAI, T., Japanese Literature
OUCHI, G., Educational Psychology
SATO, K., Chemistry
TAKAMATSU, M., Clinical Science, Science of Nursing
TAKEDA, J., Health Pedagogy
TAKEUCHI, T., Developmental Psychology
TOKUNAGA, J., English Language
TORAO, T., History
YOKOYAMA, H., Geography

Faculty of Science:
DOI, K., Organic Chemistry
FURUTA, T., Analysis
HATAKEYAMA, Y., Geometry
KATAGIRI, S., Physical Chemistry
MIDORIKAWA, B., Environmental Biology
MIYAZAWA, R., Solid State Physics
NABETANI, S., Geodynamics
ONUKI, H., Geology and Petrology
SAITO, K., Phylogeny and Morphology
SATO, H., Seismology
TAKAHASHI, K., Applied Mathematics
TANAKA, K., Cytology, Genetics and Physiological Chemistry
TESHIROGI, W., Physiology and Embryology
TONOSAKI, K., Analytical Chemistry
TSUCHIDA, K., Algebra
WATANABE, Z., Atomic Physics
YAMAMOTO, T., Quantum Physics
YUI, S., Geochemistry and Mineralogy

Faculty of Medicine:
FUKUDA, M., Rehabilitation Medicine
FUKUSHI, K., Bacteriology
FUNYU, T., Urology
HIYAMA, N., Biochemistry
HOZAWA, J., Oto-Rhino-Laryngology
IWABUCHI, T., Neurosurgery
IWAMI, S., Pharmacology
IZUMI, Y., Paediatrics
KASAI, T., Anatomy
KATABIRA, Y., Dermatology
KOIE, H., Surgery
KOYA, G., Pathology
MATSUYAMA, S., Ophthalmology
MIZUNO, S., Pathological Physiology
MURAKAMI, S., Legal Medicine
NAGAI, K., Pathology
OIKE, Y., Internal Medicine
ONODERA, K., Internal Medicine
OUCHI, K., Surgery
OYAMA, T., Anaesthesiology
OZAKI, T., Physiology
SASAKI, N., Hygiene
SATO, K., Biochemistry
SATO, T., Neuropsychiatry
SHINAGAWA, S., Obstetrics and Gynæcology
SHINOZAKI, T., Radiology
SUZUKI, T., Physiology
TAKEBE, K., Internal Medicine
TONO, S., Orthopædic Surgery
USUBUCHI, I., Pathology
USUTANI, S., Public Health
YAMADORI, T., Anatomy
YAMAGUCHI, T., Parasitology
YOSHIDA, Y , Internal Medicine

Faculty of Agriculture:
HANADA, S., Soil Science, Plant Nutrition and Manuring
HASEBE, J., Land Reclamation Engineering
KIKUCHI, T., Pomology
MASAKI, S., Applied Entomology
OKAMOTO, T., Utilization of Horticultural Products
OKUMURA, M., Vegetable Crops and Floricultural Science
OTSUKA, K., Agricultural Structures and Construction Engineering
SAITO, K., Plant Breeding
SAITO, Z., Utilization of Agricultural Products
SASANABE, S., Irrigation and Drainage Engineering
SASAKI, N., Crop Science
SAWAI, K., Biochemistry
SAWAMURA, K., Phytopathology
TAKEDA, T., Agricultural Power
TANABE, Y., Agricultural Marketing
TSUBOMATSU, K., Stockbreeding

College of Liberal Arts:
AKASHI, M., Physics
HASEGAWA, Y., Mathematics
IKEDA, Y., German Language
IMAI, T., Geography
KODAMA, M., Chemistry
MATSUEDA, S., Chemistry
MIYAGI, K., Earth Science
NARA, N., Biology
OTA, T., Health and Physical Education

HIROSHIMA UNIVERSITY

1-1-89 HIGASHI-SENDA-MACHI, NAKA-KU, HIROSHIMA 730
Telephone: (0822) 41-1221.

Founded 1949.

Academic year: April to March (two semesters).

President: H. TAKEYAMA, D.SC.
Chief Administrative Officer: N. OKABE.
Dean of Students: M. SEGAWA, D.SC.
Librarian: H. ISHIDA, D.LITT., PH.D.

The library contains 1,673,236 vols., including 645,958 in foreign languages.

Number of teachers: 1,470, including 423 professors.

Number of students: 12,029, including 1,169 graduates.

Publications: *Journal of Science of Hiroshima University: Hiroshima Mathematical Journal, Physics and Chemistry, Zoology, Botany, Geology and Mineralogy, Hiroshima University Studies—Faculty of Literature, Education in Japan, Hiroshima Journal of Medical Sciences, Memoirs of the Faculty of Engineering, Proceedings of the Research Institute for Nuclear Medicine and Biology, Scientific Report of the Laboratory for Amphibian Biology.*

DEANS AND DIRECTORS:

Faculty of Integrated Arts and Sciences: H. SHIKIBU, D.LITT.
Faculty of Letters: H. MATSUOKA, D.LITT.
Faculty of Education: M. SHIMBORI, D.LITT.
Faculty of Education at Fukuyama: S. FUJII, D.SC.
Faculty of Law: F. KANAZAWA.
Faculty of Economics: M. KOYAMA, D.ECON.
Faculty of Science: Y. YAMAMOTO, D.SC.
School of Medicine: H. NIHIRA, M.D.
University Hospital (Medical): M. MORIO, M.D. (*Director*).
School of Dentistry: I. IMANISHI, M.D.
University Hospital (Dental): K. YAMAUCHI, D.D.S. (*Director*).
Faculty of Engineering: M. YORIZANE, D.ENG.
Faculty of Applied Biological Science: Y. MURAKAMI, D.AGR.
Research Institute for Nuclear Medicine and Biology: T. OHKITA, D.SC. (*Director*).
Research Institute for Theoretical Physics: T. KIMURA, D.SC. (*Director*).

HITOTSUBASHI UNIVERSITY

KUNITACHI-CITY, TOKYO
Telephone: (0425) 72-1101.

Founded 1875.

President: K. TADENUMA.
Administrator: M. NEMOTO.
Dean of Students: A. KATSUTA.
Librarian: M. KIMURA.

Library: *see* Libraries.
Number of full-time teachers: 261.
Number of students: 4,034.

DEANS:

Faculty of Commerce: T. MIYAKAWA.
Faculty of Economics: S. TAMESE.
Faculty of Law: T. FUKUDA.
Faculty of Social Science: C. RACHI.

ATTACHED INSTITUTE:

Institute of Economic Research: f. 1940; 57 mems.; library of 269,914 vols.; Dir. Y. KURABAYASHI; publ. *Economic Research Series* (annually).

HOKKAIDO UNIVERSITY

NORTH 8, WEST 5, KITAKU, SAPPORO 060
Telephone: 711-2111.
Founded 1876.

President: S. IMAMURA, LL.D.
Director-General: K. MORI.
Dean of Students: T. SUGAWARA.
Librarian: M. TAKASHIMA.

Number of teachers: 1,893.
Number of students: 12,208.

DEANS:

Faculty of Literature: H. NAGAI.
Faculty of Education: M. KANOH.
Faculty of Law: T. FUKASE.
Faculty of Economics: Y. MATSUI.
Faculty of Science: K. TAJIME.
Faculty of Medicine: Y. OMMURA.
Faculty of Dentistry: J. ISHIKAWA.
Faculty of Pharmaceutical Sciences: Y. BAN.
Faculty of Engineering: M. ARIE.
Faculty of Agriculture: M. TAKAHASHI.
Faculty of Veterinary Medicine: Y. FUJIMOTO.
Faculty of Fisheries: M. AKIBA.
Department of General Education: Y. INOUE.
Graduate School of Environmental Science: E. TAKAKUWA.

PROFESSORS:

Faculty of Literature:
AIBA, S., Experimental Psychology
FUJII, T., German
FUJITA, K., Indian Philosophy
FUKUOKA, S., Russian Literature
HANADA, K., Western Literature
HONDA, K., Western Literature
IKEGAMI, J., Linguistics
IMAI, S., Psychology
INOUE, Y., Western History
IWATA, T., Western History
KANEDA, H., Sociology
KASAI, A., Philosophy
KIGOSHI, F., English
KITAICHI, Y., English
KIKUCHI, H., Oriental History
KONDO, J., Japanese Literature
KOUCHI, T., German
KUMAGAI, T. Western Philosophy
MIZUNO, H., Philosophy
NAGAI, H., Japanese History
NAGAI, Y., German
NAKAMURA, K., Western Philosophy
NIIZUMA, A., German
OHATA, J., Philosophy
OKANO, S., English
OKUYAMA, J., History of Social Thought
SATO, I., Chinese Philosophy
SAEKI, A., Japanese History
SHIBUYA, J., German
SHIOYA, Y., German Philology
SUZUKI, J., English
TAHARA, T., Japanese History
TAKAHATA, M., Oriental History
TAKAKU, S., English
TANAKA, A., Japanese History
TERAOKA, T., Behavioural Science
TODA, M., Behavioural Science
TORIYAMA, S., Western History
UNO, M., Philosophy of Religion
UTSUNOMIYA, Y., Ethics
WADA, K., Japanese Literature
YONEMURA, S., Sociology

Faculty of Education:
FUSE, T., Educational Sociology
KANO, M., Clinical Psychology
MICHIMATA, K., Vocational Education
MITORO, T., Adult Education
MIYAKE, K.. Developmental Psychology
MUROKI, Y., Practical Training of Physical Education
OHMIYA, H., Practical Training of Physical Education
SUZUKI, S., Teaching Methods

Faculty of Law:
ARAKI, T., Political Science
ENDO, H., Administrative Law
FUJIOKA, Y., Civil Law
FUKASE, T., Constitutional Law
HOBARA, K., Labour Law
IGARASHI, K., Comparative Law
ISHIKAWA, T., Legal History
ITO, D., Public Administration
KOGURE, T., Criminal Law
KONDO, K., Commercial Law
KOSUGE, T., History of Law
KOYAMA, N., Civil Procedural Law
MATSUZAWA, H., History of Political Ideas
MORIYA, M., Philosophy of Law
NAKAMURA, M., Constitutional Law
NOSE, H., Law of Criminal Procedure
OGAWA, K., History of Political Ideas
OKA, T., Political History
SANEKATA, K., Commercial Law
SHIMOI, T., Labour Law
SHOJI, K., Civil Law
SUGIHARA, T., International Law
SONO, K., Private International Law
TOMITA, Y., Political Science
UCHIDA, F., Criminal Law
YABU, S., Civil Law
YAMAHATA, M., Civil Law

Faculty of Economics:
ARAMATA, S., Social Policy
HAYAKAWA, Y., Principles of Economics
HAYASHI, Y., Hokkaido Economic History
ISHIGAKI, H., History of Economic Doctrines
ISHIZAKA, A., Western Economic History
KOBAYASHI, Y., Economic Policy
KORENAGA, S., Economic Statistics
MANO, O., Personnel Management
MATSUI, Y., Banking
MORI, T., Business Formation
NAGAOKA, S., Japanese Economic History
NAKAMURA, M., Security Market
OHYA, E., Theory of Industrial Location
SATO, S., Principles of Economics
SUGAWARA, H., Accounting
TOKORO, T., World Economics
TOMINOMORI, K., Industrial Policy

Faculty of Science:
AOTO, T., Biology
ARAKAWA, K., Physics
BANBA, T., Applied Geology
DOI, K., Number Theory
FUJIMOTO, M., Inorganic Chemistry
HARADA, I., Plant Morphogenesis and Genetics
HASHIMOTO, S., Geology
HIKICHI, K., Polymer Physics
HIKIME, S., Chemistry
HISADA, M., Animal Physiology
HORI, J., Mathematical Physics
ISHIGURO, K. Mathematics
ITOH, E., Biochemistry
IWATA, H. Biology
KAMBARA, T., Analytical Chemistry
KANAZAWA, A., Physics
KANEKO, M., Polymer Physics
KANO, Y., Marine Biology
KATSUI, Y., Petrology
KATSUI, N., Chemistry
KIMURA, M., Physical Chemistry
KITA, H., Chemistry
KOSHI, S., Functional Analysis
KURAMOCHI, Z., Theory of Complex Functions
KUROGI, M., Systematic Botany
KUROSAWA, E., Physics
MAGONO, C., Atmospheric Physics
MASAMUNE, T., Organic Chemistry
MASUBUCHI, N., Biology
MATSUMOTO, T., Organic Chemistry
MATSUNAGA, Y., Physical Chemistry of Matter
MATSUSHITA, S., Physical Chemistry
MINATO, M., Historical Geology
NAKAGAWA, T., Physical Chemistry of High Polymers
NAGAI, T., Differential Geometry
NAKAO, K., Physical Hydrology
NISHIDA, S., Organic Chemistry
OHNO, A., Physics
OHNO, K., Quantum Chemistry
OKADA, H., Geology
ONODERA, T., Mathematics
SAHO, T., Biology
SAKAI, S., Plant Physiology and Microbiology
SAKAI, Y., Algological Research
SAKASHITA, S., Physics
SASAKI, A., Biology
SASAKI, K., Biology
SASAKI, M., Cytogenetics
SAWAGUCHI, E., Electricity and Magnetism
SHIMOJI, M., Physical Chemistry
SHIROTA T., Theory of Functional Equations
SUGAI, S., Biopolymers
SUZUKI, H., Theory of Manifolds
TAGA, M., Chemistry
TANABE, K., Physical Chemistry
TANAI, T., Paleontology
TANAKA, H., Nuclear Physics
TANAKA, N., Differential Geometry
TAZIME, K., Applied Geophysics
TSUZUKU, T., Group Theory
UOZUMI, S., Geology
YAGI, K., Biochemistry
YAMADA, M., Plant Physiology
YAMAMOTO, T., Biology
YOKOKAWA, T., Inorganic Chemistry
YOKOYAMA, I., Solid Geophysics
YOSHIDA, H., Chemistry

School of Medicine:
AGISHI, Y., Balneology
AIZAWA, M., Pathology
FURUKAWA, K., Anaesthesiology
HIRAI, H., Biochemistry
HIROSHIGE, T., Physiology
ICHINOHE, K., Gynaecology and Obstetrics
IIDA, H., Bacteriology
IMAI, Y., Biochemistry
INOUE, Y., Anatomy
IRIE, G., Radiology
ISHII, K., Public Health
ITO, T., Anatomy
KANNO, M., Pharmacology
KASAI, Y., Surgery

KATO, M., Physiology
KOBAYASHI, H., Pathology
KODAMA, G., Anatomy
MAKITA, A., Biochemistry
MATSUDA, H., Ophthalmology
MATSUMOTO, S., Paediatrics
MATSUNO, S., Orthopaedics
MIURA, Y., Dermatology
MURAO, M., Internal Medicine
NAKAGAWA, S., Internal Medicine
OHSATO, T., Virology, Cancer Institute
OMMURA, Y., Pathology
SAITO, H., Pharmacology
SAITO, K., Hot-Springs Therapeutics
SHIRAISHI, T., Internal Medicine
SUGIE, S., Surgery
SUZUTANI, T., Legal Medicine
TAKAHASHI, K., Internal Medicine
TAKAKUWA, E., Hygiene and Preventive Medicine
TERAYAMA, Y., Oto-Rhino-Laryngology
TSUJI, I., Urology
TSURU, M., Neurosurgery
YAMADA, N., Paediatrics
YAMASHITA, I., Psychiatry and Neurology
YASUDA, H., Cardiovascular Medicine

School of Dentistry:

AMEMIYA, A., Oral Pathology
HOSHINO, T., Oral Anatomy II
IIDA, S., Dental Pharmacology
ISHIKAWA, J., Conservative Dentistry
KAMEDA, K., Oral Physiology
KATSURA, N., Preventive Dentistry
KAWAMURA, M., Oral Surgery
MIKI, K., Prosthetic Dentistry
NAKAMURA, S., Orthodontics
NAKANE, F., Oral Anatomy I
NISHIKAZE, O., Oral Biochemistry
OIKAWA, K., Pedodontics
OTA, M., Technical Dentistry
OKADA, S., Preventive Dentistry
OKADA, Y., Conservative Dentistry I
SUZUKI, T., Oral Microbiology
TOMITA, K., Oral Surgery
UCHIYAMA, Y., Prosthetic Dentistry
YAMAZAKI, M., Dental Radiology

Faculty of Pharmaceutical Sciences:

BAN, Y., Industrial and Pharmaceutical Chemistry
ISHII, S., Biological Chemistry
ISHIMOTO, M., Chemical Microbiology
KANAOKA, Y., Pharmaceutical Synthetic Chemistry
KIMURA, M., Analytical Chemistry
KOBATAKE, Y., Physical Chemistry
KOYAMA, J., Hygienic Chemistry
MITSUHASHI, H., Pharmacognosy
MIZUNO, Y., Pharmaceutical Chemistry
UEDA, T., Pharmaceutical Organic Chemistry
UI, M., Chemical Pharmacology
YONEMITSU, O., Plant Chemistry

Faculty of Engineering:

ABE, Y., Quantum Instrumentation and Solid-State Physics
ADACHI, F., Housing
AOKI, Y., Computer Science
AOMURA, K., Petroleum Chemistry
ARATANI, N., Environmental Engineering of Building
ARIE, M., Fluid Mechanics
DOBASHI, Y., Structural Mechanics
DOI, O., Machine Design
ENDO, K., Mixing and Transport Phenomena
FUJITA, Y., Concrete and Reinforced Concrete Engineering
FUJIWARA, H., Theory and Application of Electrical Machines
FUKAI, I., Electromagnetic Theory
FUKUOKA, J., Electromagnetics
HANZAWA, H., Strength of Materials
HASHIMOTO, K., Safety Engineering
HATA, K., Plasticity for Engineers
HAYASHI, J., High Polymer Chemistry
HIDESHIMA, T., Molecular Engineering
HIGASHI, A., Applied Crystal Physics
HOTTA, K., System Dynamics
IGARASHI, H., City and Transport Planning
INOUE, K., Neutron Sources
INOUE, R., Air Pollution Control
IRIE, T., Mechanics of Machinery
ISHII, T., Industrial Inorganic Chemistry
ISHIGURO, R., Reactor Heat Transfer and Nuclear Safety
ISHIKAWA, T., Corrosion Science and Electrometallurgy
ISOBE, T., Mining Engineering.
ITO, K., Microwave Engineering and Antennae
KAJI, I., System Engineering
KAKU, T., Traffic Engineering
KOYAMA, K., Solid Waste Disposal
KANAUCHI, T., Machine Tools
KASHIWAMURA, M., Applied Hydrodynamics
KATAYAMA, M., Radiation Chemistry
KAWAGUCHI, M., Differential Geometry
KINOSHITA, S., Mechanical Engineering for Resources Development
KISHI, T., Hydraulics, Hydrology and River Engineering
KITAGO, S., Soil Mechanics
KITAMURA, M., Mathematical Physics
KOBAYASHI, H., Chemical Reaction Engineering
KOBASHI, Y., Fluid Mechanics
KOH, E., Building Materials
KONDO, S., Metallurgy
KUGO, M., Chemical Engineering Unit Operations
KUROBE, T., Electronic Circuits
MAEDA, M., Physical Electronics
MATSUBARA, K., Welding of Metals, Mechanical Metallurgy
MATSUMOTO, T., Microwave Engineering and Antennae
MATSUSHITA, T., Structural Inorganic Chemistry
MIURA, R., Automatic Control
MOROZUMI, T., Reactor Chemistry
MURATA, K., Applied Optics
MURAYAMA, T., Heat and Mass Transfer
NAGAOKA, K., Engineering Materials
NAGATA, K., Electroacoustics
NAGAYAMA, M., Electrochemistry
NAITO, M., Electric Machinery
NAKAE, H., Engineering Material Physics
NASU, Y., Water Chemistry
NISHIDA, K., Diffusion in Solid Metals and High-Temperature Corrosion
NOMACHI, S., Structural Engineering
OCHIFUJI, K., Heating and Ventilating
ODAJIMA, A., Solid State Physics
OGAWA, Y., Nuclear Reactor Engineering
OHTA, M., Urban Design and Architectural Planning
OHTA, Y., Earthquake Engineering
OHTSUKA, Y., Engineering Mathematics
OKINO, N., Machine Design
OKITA, T., Air Pollution Control
OUCHI, K., Fuel Technology
OZAKI, A., Harbour Engineering
OZAWA, Y., Nuclear Engineering
SAITO, K., Precision Machining
SAKAMOTO, S., High Voltage Engineering
SAKUMA, T., Mathematical Physics
SAKURABA, I., Micro-wave Electron Devices and Quantum Electronics
SANADA, Y., Coal Chemistry
SATO, N., Physical Chemistry
SATO, S., X-ray Crystallography and Electron Physics
SATO, T., Precision Machining
SEKI, N., Heat and Mass Transfer
SHIBATA, T., Building Construction
SHINPO, M., Information Processing
SOHMA, J., Physical Chemistry
SUGAWARA, T., Highway Construction and Materials
SUZUKI, A., Petroleum Engineering
SUZUKI, M., Micro-wave Theory and **Techniques**
TAGASHIRA, H., Electrical Properties of Matter
TAGAWA, R., Control Engineering
TAKADA, Y., Polymer Chemistry
TAKAHASHI, T., Iron and Steel Materials
TAKAMORI, T., Mineral Processing
TAKEYAMA, T., Physical Metallurgy
TAKIZAWA, E., Engineering Physics
TAMBO, N., Water Works
TANAKA, TATSUO, Micromeritics
TANAKA, TOKIAKI, Non-ferrous Extractive Metallurgy
TANIGUCHI, H., Heat and Mass Transfer
TOKI, S., Railway Engineering and Soil Mechanics
TSUDA, T., Computer Science
USHIZAWA, N., Economic Geology
WATANABE, K., Non-ferrous metals and Physical Metallurgy
WATANABE, N., Bridge Engineering
WATANABE, Y., Mechanical Engineering for Resources Development
YAKUWA, I., Applied Physics
YAMAOKA, I., Applied Hydraulics and **Dam Engineering**
YAMASHINA, T., Vacuum Science and Surface Chemistry of Solids
YAMAZAKI, H., Plasma Physics
YOSHIDA, H., Physical Chemistry
YOSHIMURA, J., Structural Mechanics

Faculty of Agriculture:

ASAHIDA, Y., Feeding and Management of Livestock
ARIMA, S., Dairy Science
DOKOSHI, J., Agricultural Physics
EGUCHI, Y., Microbial Engineering and Technology
GOTOH, K., Food Crops
HACHINOHE, Y., Introduction to Animals
HIGASHI, S., Erosion Control Engineering
HIROSE, Y., Animal Nutrition
IIJIMA, G., Agricultural Co-operation
IKEUCHI, Y., Agricultural Electrification
ISHIDA, S., Wood Anatomy
IZAWA, M., Food and Nutrition Science
KATAOKA, T., Land Improvement
KAYAMA, T., Chemical Utilization of Forest Products
KOSEKI, T., Forest Management
MATSUI, K., Agricultural Power
MIZUTANI, J., Agricultural Organic Chemistry
MOMONO, S., Farm Management
MORI, H., Applied Zoology
MUTO, K., Silviculture and tree breeding
MYODO, H., Floriculture and Landscape Architecture
NAKASIMA, T., Entomology
OGANE, E., Business Economics in Forestry
OKAJIMA, H., Soil Science
OKAMURA, T., Agricultural Machinery
OKAZAWA, Y., Applied Plant Physiology
OSUGI, T., Chemistry and Technology of Leather Manufacture
SAKAKIBARA, A., Wood Chemistry
SAKAMURA, S., Food Technology of Agricultural Products
SAKIMOTO, Y., Chemistry and Technology of Leather Manufacture
SAKIURA, S., Agricultural Development
SASAKI, S., Soil Improvement
SAWADA, M., Wood Mechanics
SHIKATA, E., Plant Virology

TAKAHASHI, M., Plant Breeding
TAKAO, S., Applied Microbiology
TAKIZAWA, Y., Sericology
TAMURA, T., Pomology and Preservation of Horticultural Products
TANAKA, A., Plant Nutrition and Fertilizer
TSUDA, C., Industrial Crops
UI, T., Plant Pathology
YASUI, T., Science and Technology of Meat and Meat Products
YUZAWA, M., Agricultural Marketing

Faculty of Veterinary Medicine:
FUJIMOTO, Y., Comparative Pathology
HASHIMOTO, N., Public Health
ISHIKAWA, T., Veterinary Andrology
IZAWA, H., Epizootology
KANNO, T., Veterinary Physiology
KUBO, S., Veterinary Biochemistry
KUDO, N., Veterinary Anatomy
NAMIOKA, S., Internal Medicine and Clinics
OHBAYASHI, M., Parasitology
OHGA, A., Veterinary Pharmacology
SAKAI, T., Surgery and Clinics
YANAGAWA, R., Veterinary Hygiene and Microbiology
YOSHII, G., Experimental Radiobiology

Faculty of Fisheries:
AKIBA, M., Marine Food Technology
FUJI, A., Propagation of Marine Resources
FUKASE, S., Marine Chemistry
FUKUOKA, J., Oceanography
GOTO, K., Chemical Engineering
HAMADA, K., Animal Histology
HIRAIWA, T., Fishing Navigation
IGARASHI, T., Marine Zoology and Freshwater Fish Culture
ISHIDA, M., Fishery Electrical Engineering
ISHIHARA, Y., Polymer Chemistry of Marine Products
KAWAMURA, T., Planktology
KAWASHIMA, R., Nautical Dynamics
KIMURA, T., Mycology
KUBO, T., Fish Culture
KYUSHIN, K., Biology of Fish Population
MASAKI, T., Marine Botany
MIKI, M., Chemical Engineering
MINODA, T., Planktology
NISHIMURA, M., Analytical Chemistry
NISHIYAMA, S., Operation of Fishing Gear
SATO, O., Fishing Gear Engineering
TAKAGI, M., Food Hygiene
TAKAGI, T., Chemistry of Fats and Oils
TAKAHASHI, H., Freshwater Fish Culture
UENO, M., Fishing Grounds
YAMADA, J., Animal Physiology, Ecology
ZAMA, K., Food Chemistry

Graduate School of Environmental Science:
HOBARA, K., Labour Law
ITO, K., Biosystem Conservation
KADOMURA, H., Fundamental Research
KAMBARA, T., Analytical Chemistry
KITAGO, S., Soil Mechanics
KUROIWA, D., Physics
KUROGI, M., Systematic Botany
MAGONO, C., Atmospheric Physics
MYODO, H., Floriculture and Landscape
OHTA, M., Urban Design and Planning
SAITO, K., Environmental Medicine
SEKI, K., Regional Planning
SHIMOI, T., Labour Law
TAKAKUWA, E., Hygiene and Preventive Medicine
TAKASHIMA, M., Agricultural Policy
YAMADA, M., Invertebrate Zoology

ATTACHED INSTITUTES:

Research Institute for Catalysis: f. 1943; Dir. A. MATSUDA; publ. *Journal.*

Institute of Low Temperature Science: f. 1941; Dir. D. KUROIWA; publs. *Contributions from the ILTS, Series A and B* (irregular).

Research Institute of Immunological Science: f. 1950; Dir. K. MORIKAWA; publ. *Tuberculosis Research* (annually).

Research Institute of Applied Electricity: f. 1943; Dir. H. BABA; publ. *Monography Series* (annually).

IBARAKI UNIVERSITY

2-1-1, BUNKYO, MITO-SHI, IBARAKI-KEN
Telephone: 0292-(26)-1621.

Founded 1949.

President: S. ICHIMURA.
Administrator: D. IMURA.
Librarian: T. HIGASHI.

The library contains 349,711 vols.

Number of full-time teachers: 481.
Number of students: 5,346.

Publications (in Japanese): Bulletins and Journals of the faculties.

DEANS:

Student Affairs: K. OONISHI.
Faculty of Liberal Arts: A. SAKURAI.
Faculty of Education: K. AKIYAMA.
Faculty of Humanities: S. KIDOTA.
Faculty of Science: O. YODA.
Faculty of Engineering: 4-12-1, Nakanarusawa-cho, Hitachi-shi, Ibarakiken; G. MIYAMOTO.
Faculty of Agriculture: 3998 Amimachi, Inashiki-gun, Ibaraki-ken; M. SOEJIMA.

IWATE UNIVERSITY

3-18-8 UEDA, MORIOKA, IWATE
Telephone: Morioka 23-5171.
Founded 1949.
State control.

President: HISAYA KATŌ.
Chief Administrative Officer: T. TEROUCHI.
Librarian: S. OKAWA.

Library of *c.* 310,000 vols.
Number of teachers: *c.* 400.
Number of students: *c.* 4,400.

Publications: *Journal of the Faculty of Agriculture, Report on Technology of Iwate University, Annual Report of the Faculty of Education, Artes Liberales.*

DEANS:

Faculty of Agriculture: T. ISHIKAWA.
Faculty of Technology: K. NAKAZAWA.
Faculty of Education: H. TAKAHASHI.
College of Humanities and Social Sciences: S. KUSAMA.

KAGAWA UNIVERSITY

1-1 SAIWAI-CHO, TAKAMATSU-SHI 760
Telephone: 0878-61-4141.

Founded 1949.

President: SHIN-ICHI ENDOH.
Secretary-General: MASATOSHI FURUICHI.
Librarian: JUNZABURO NAKA.

Library of 339,647 vols.
Number of teachers: 262.
Number of students: 3,020.

DEANS:

Faculty of Agriculture: MINORU SAITO.
Faculty of Economics: HITOSHI KIMURA.
Faculty of Education: NORIO TSUKUDA.

KAGOSHIMA UNIVERSITY

21-24, 1-CHOME, KOURIMOTO, KAGOSHIMA-SHI 890
Telephone: (54) 7141.

Founded 1949.

President: MATSUO KANIE.
Secretary-General: SEIZO UCHINO.

Library of 721,820 vols.
Number of full-time teachers: 935.
Number of students: 7,838.

DEANS:

Faculty of Law and Literature: G. KAMIMURA.
Faculty of Education: T. NOZOE.
Faculty of Science: T. TSUYUKI.
Faculty of Medicine: H. AKITA.
Faculty of Dentistry: S. NAKAZAWA.
Faculty of Engineering: H. KUSAKABE.
Faculty of Agriculture: M. TAKETOMI.
Faculty of Fisheries: F. OTA.
College of Liberal Arts: H. SAISHOJI.

KANAZAWA UNIVERSITY

1-1 MARUNOUCHI, KANAZAWA CITY 920
Telephone: 0762-624281.

Founded 1949.

President: K. KANEKO.
Secretary-General: Y. HENMI.

The libraries contain 893,058 vols.

Number of full-time teachers: 941.
Number of students: 6,161.

Publications: Journals, Studies, Memoirs of the faculties.

DEANS:

Faculty of Letters: K. SUKUZI.
Faculty of Education: T. YAGASAKI.
Faculty of Law: Z. MIYOKAWA.
Faculty of Economics: K. YAMAMURA.
Faculty of Science: M. SIBATA.
Faculty of Medicine: R. HONZIN.
Faculty of Pharmacy: T. HUZII.
Faculty of Technology: G. YOSIMURA.

AFFILIATED INSTITUTES INCLUDE:

Marine Biological Laboratory (*Faculty of Science*): Dir. Prof. S. ISAKA, D.SC.

University Hospital (*School of Medicine*): Dir. Prof. T. YONEMURA.

Cancer Research Institute: Dir. Prof. S. KOSIMURA.

KOBE UNIVERSITY

ROKKODAI-CHO,
NADA-KU, KOBE

Telephone: Kobe (078) 881-1212.

Founded 1949.

Academic year: April to March.

President: I. SUDA.

Director of Administration: S. FUJIMORI.

Dean of Students' Affairs: M. TANGE.

Library Director: R. MATSUMOTO.

Library: *see* Libraries.

Number of full-time teachers: 995.
Number of students: 9,790.

Publications: *Outline of Kobe University* and various faculty publs.

DEANS:

Faculty of Literature: J. SUGINOHARA..
Faculty of Education: A. SUGIYAMA.
Faculty of Law: I. KAWAMOTO.
Faculty of Economics: H. SHIMBO.
Faculty of Business Administration: S. KAIDO.
Faculty of Science: Y. KATO.
Faculty of Medicine: S. IWAI.
Faculty of Engineering: Y. GYOTEN.
Faculty of Agriculture: M. KOMOTO.
College of Liberal Arts: Y. IZAWA.
Research Institute for Economics and Business Administration: M. FUJITA.

PROFESSORS:

Faculty of Literature:

FUJIOKA, T., Japanese Literature
HASEGAWA, Y., Theoretical Sociology
HASHIMOTO, M., Ethics
ICHIKAWA, S., Modern History of Europe and America
INOUE, S., History of European Philosophy
ITO, M., Ancient and Medieval History of Asia
ITO, M., Sinology
IWAMI, H., Modern History of Asia
IWAYAMA, S., Science of Art
KAKEI, H., English Philology
KANAZAWA, M., Theoretical Sociology
KIUCHI, T., French Language and Literature
KOBAYASHI, M., Philology
MIKI, M., German Language and Literature
MIYAZAKI, Y., English Language
MORIKIYO, Y., Psychology
MORI, H., History of Art
SAITO, M., Geography
SHIMIZU, M., European Philosophy
SOMA, T., Modern Japanese Literature
SUGINOHARA, J., Empirical Sociology
TAKAO, K., Modern History of Japan
TERADA, T., English and American Literature
TODA, Y., Ancient and Medieval Japanese History

Faculty of Education:

ASAI, H., Mechanical Engineering
ATSUTA, I., Method of Teaching Social Studies
HAMAGUCHI, T., Woodwork
HAYAKAWA, H., Chemistry
HIRAHARA, H., Educational System
ISHIDA, J., Music Teaching
ITO, R., Psychology of Exceptional Children
IWATA, A., Technical Training in Physical Education
KAMAE, M., Agriculture
KASAHARA, S., Analysis and Applied Mathematics
KAWABATA, M., Political Science
KOBAYASHI, T., Instrumental Music
KOSAWA, Y., Development Psychology
KURODA, K., Method of Teaching English
MAEDA, M., Japanese Philosophy
MATSUMOTO, H., Construction
MATSUSHIMA, T., English Philology
NAKAJIMA, W., Earth Science
NAKAMURA, S., Composition
NAKANISHI, S., Methods of Teaching Science
NAMBA, K., Methods of Teaching in Japanese Education
NEGORO, T., Methods of Teaching in Japanese Education
ODAN, K., Method of Teaching School Health and Physical Education
OHARA, H., Geography
OKATSU, K., Method of Teaching Fine Arts
ONDO, T., Method of Teaching Science
ONISHI, M., Algebra and Geometry
SAEKI, K., Physics
SAITO, K., History of Education
SEKI, S., Developmental Psychology
SUGIYAMA, A., History of Education
TAMURA, S., Method of Teaching Mathematics
TAKEYA, Y., Instrumental Music
TOMIMOTO, Y., Educational Psychology
TSUDAKA, M., Social Education
TSUJIMOTO, I., English and American Literature
YAMASHIRO, M., Health Care Education

Faculty of Law:

ABE, Y., Legal Theory
HAMADA, F., International Law
HANAWA, H., Western Legal History
INDO, K., Constitutional Law
ISHIDA, K., Civil Law
KANZAKI, K., Commercial Law
KAWAMOTO, I., Commercial Law
KIDO, S., International Relations
KUBO, K., Labour Law
KUBOTA, H., Maritime Law
MATSUSHITA., T., Comparative Law
MITSUI, M., Criminal Procedure
NEGISHI, A., Economic Law
NISHI, M., Private International Law
NISHIHARA, M., Sociology of Law
NISHIKAWA, T., Political Science
OTAKE, H., Legal History
SHIBAHARA, K., Criminal Law
SUZUKI, M., Civil Prodecure
TAKAGI, T., Civil Law
YAMADA, Y., Administrative Law

Faculty of Economics:

ADACHI, H., Theoretical Economics
DODO, K., Social Economics
FUJIMOTO, A., Foreign Economics (General)
IKEMOTO, K., International Economics
ISHIMITSU, T., Economic Geography
KAMIKI, T., Economic History
MIKITANI, R., Foreign Economics (Specialized)
MINAKATA, K., History of Economic Doctrines
MURAKAMI, A., Foreign Trade Policy
NAKAMURA, K., Public Finance
NIINO, K., National Economics
NOJIRI, T., Principles of Economic Policy
NORITAKE, Y., International Finance
OKISHIO, N., Mathematical Economics
ONO, K., Comparative Economic Studies
SAITO, M., Economic Statistics
SHIMBO, H., Japanese Economy
SHINJO, K., Industrial Policy
TANAKA, O., Agricultural Policy
TOYODA, T., Statistics
YAMASE, Z., Economic History (General)
YAO, J., Money and Banking

Faculty of Business Administration:

AKIYAMA, K., Transportation
AMANO, A., Foreign Trade
ARAKAWA, Y., Marketing
FUTATSUGI, Y., Securities Market
ICHIHARA, K., Business Administration
IGA, T., Business Mathematics
ISHII, T., Financial Institutions
KAIDO, S., Labour Management
KOBAYASHI, T., Cost Accounting
MATSUDA, K., Business Statistics
MIZOGUCHI, K., Management Accounting
MIZUSHIMA, K., Insurance
MORI, A., Business Finance
ONO, J., Securities
TAKAMURA, T., Theory of Shipping
TAKATA, M., Auditing
TAKEDA, R., Tax Accounting
TAMURA, M., Distribution System
TANIBATA, H., Principles of Accounting
URABE, K., Science of Business Management

Faculty of Science:

AIZAWA, S., Analysis
ASAYAMA, K., Radio Frequency Spectroscopy
FUJIOKA, G., High Energy Physics
FUKAZAWA, H., Cytology
HOSOKAWA, F., Geometry
IDA, M., Elementary Particle Physics
ISEKI, K., Algebra and Topology
ITO, K., Petrology and Mineralogy
KANEHISA, T., Microbial Biochemistry
KATO, Y., Structural Chemistry
KIRIYAMA, H., Inorganic Chemistry
MASUDA, A., Geochemistry
NAGAI, O., Solid State Physics
NISHIO, M., Applied Mathematics
SANTO, T., Geophysics
SEKIDO, E., Analytical Chemistry
SERA, A., Organic Chemistry
SUDA, S., Physiology
SUGIMURA, A., Geology
TOYODA, Y., Cosmic Ray Physics
URA, T., Analysis
YASUKAWA, K., Marine Geophysics

Faculty of Medicine:

BABA, S., Internal Medicine
FUJITA, T., Internal Medicine
FUJIWARA, Y., Radiation Biophysics
FUKUZAKI, H., Internal Medicine
HANAWA, I., Physiology
HATTORI, H., Oto-Rhino-Laryngology
HIROHATA, K., Orthopaedic Surgery
HOTTA, S., Microbiology
ISAYAMA, Y., Ophthalmology
ISHIGAMI, J., Urology
IWAI, S., Anaesthetics
KIMURA, S., Radiology
KOBATA, A., Biochemistry
KURODA, K., Biopharmacy
MATSUMURA, T., Medical Zoology
MATSUMOTO, S., Neurological Surgery
MATSUO, T., Paediatrics
MISHIMA, Y., Dermatology
MIZOGUCHI, F., Anatomy
MIZOI, Y., Legal Medicine

Murakami, H., Hygiene
Nakamura, K., Surgery
Nishizuka, Y., Biochemistry
Saito, Y., Surgery
Shimada, K., Oral Surgery
Sumino, K., Public Health
Takeda, H., Anatomy
Tanaka, C. Pharmacology
Tojyo, S., Obstetrics and Gynaecology
Urano, Y., Pathology
Yamaguchi, N., Laboratory Medicine

Faculty of Engineering:

Abe, K., Fundamental Electrical Engineering
Akagawa, K., Power Engineering
Ashida, M., Industrial Physical Chemistry
Bou, H., Semi-conductor Electronics
Edamura, T., Traffic Engineering
Gyoten, Y., Structural Dynamics and Earthquake Resistant Design
Hayakawa, K., Environmental and Community Facilities Planning
Hayashi, S., Diffusional Operation Engineering
Hirai, K., System Analysis
Hirano, K., Electric Circuit Engineering
Hojo, M., Synthetic Organic Chemistry
Iwata, K., Production Engineering
Kanatani, H., Applied Mechanics and Steel Structures
Kaneku, M., Electric Circuit and Information Engineering
Kawatani, T., Reclamation Engineering
Kimura, T., Fluid Mechanics and Hydraulic Machinery
Kuroda, K., Automatic Control
Maekawa, J., Physical Environmental Planning
Maekawa, S., Systems Information
Makita, T., High-Pressure Chemical Engineering
Maruhashi, T., Electrical Machines and Control Engineering
Matsumoto, H., Electronic Instrumentation
Matsumoto, M., Environmental Analysis
Matsumoto, R., Thermodynamics and Internal Combustion Engine
Matsumoto, T., Polymer Chemistry
Matsunashi, J., Sanitary Engineering
Mizuhata, K., Regional Planning and Disaster Prevention
Mugibayashi, N., Fundamental Electrical Engineering
Mukai, M., Architectural History
Murakami, H., Applied Mathematics
Nakagawa, T., Materials Research for Machinery
Nakanishi, E., Process Design and Control
Nishimura, A., Bridge Engineering and Engineering Materials
Sakaguchi, T., Thermo-Fluid Engineering
Sakurai, S., Structural Mechanics and Earthquake Engineering
Seguchi, Y., System Design
Shindo, A., Strength of Materials
Tanimoto, K., Soil Engineering
Tsunoda, Y., Electric Power Engineering
Wakabayashi, N., Applied Physics for Instrumentation
Yamada, M., Building Materials and Construction
Yano, M., Hydraulic Engineering
Yonemochi, M., Mechanical Instrumentation

Faculty of Agriculture:

Azuma, J., Soil Science
Fukushima, T., Animal Breeding
Ichii, T., Pomology
Igaki, C., Agricultural Power
Kanda, S., Animal Reproduction
Kimura, S., Animal Hygiene
Kira, H., Water Use Engineering
Komoto, M., Technology of Agricultural Products
Kondo, K., Chemistry and Technology of Animal Products
Miyamoto, Y., Plant Pathology
Matsubayashi, M., Plant Breeding
Matsunaka, S., Agricultural Chemicals
Mizuno, S., Preservation Technology
Mizuno, T., Animal Feeding
Nakamura, N., Floriculture and Olericulture
Natake, M., Food and Nutritional Chemistry
Nishimura, I., Farm Equipment and Machinery
Nishira, H., Fermentation Technology
Okamoto, S., Plant Nutrition
Okutani, T., Entomology
Ono, H., Genetics
Ozaki, E., Land Use Engineering
Shimoda, Y., Animal Management
Takayama, T., Farm Management
Tange, M., Crop Science
Ueda, S., Agricultural Processing Machinery
Ueyama, Y., Crop Science
Yamaguchi, T., Tropical Economic Botany
Yamamoto, O., Agricultural Economics
Yoshikawa, M., Biochemistry

College of Liberal Arts:

Aoki, N., English
Chiba, K., English
Goto, H., Physical Geography
Hasegawa, M., Chemistry
Honda, A., French
Iimori, T., English
Ikkai, T., Literature
Imazu, K., History of Natural Science
Ishimuro, A., Mathematics
Ito, M., Literature
Iyasu, T., Sociology
Izawa, Y., French
Izumi, H., English
Kajikawa, Y., Health and Physical Education
Kakehi, K., Chinese
Katsura, A., Historical Science
Kawabata, R., English
Kawaguchi, M., Informatics
Kimura, I., Mathematics
Kitadani, M., Chemistry
Kitamura, Y., Physical Geography
Kobayakawa, K., Physics
Kojima, T., Literature
Komatsubara, C., German
Konishi, M., Legal Science
Kugai, S., History of Social Thought
Kurasawa, Y., Science of Art
Kurematsu, Y., Philosophy
Maeno, S., English
Matsuda, M., English
Misaki, N., Health and Physical Education
Miura, T., English
Miyada, S., Biology
Miyagaki, M., Physics
Mizuno, K., Ethics
Mori, H., English
Motooka, I., Chemistry
Mukai, T., Economics
Nakamura, G., Political Science
Natsume, T., Economics
Noguchi, H., Legal Science
Odaka, S., Graphic Engineering and Descriptive Geometry
Okochi, R., German
Saito, A., Chemistry
Saito, Y., Physics
Suzuki, K., European Classical Languages
Taguchi, K., Philosophy
Takahashi, M., Mathematics
Takeuchi, Y. English
Takeyama, K., Graphic Engineering and Descriptive Geometry
Tanaka, S., Geography
Togami, H., Economics
Tsubo, Y., Biology
Tsuzuki, Y., Physics
Uchida, A., Biology
Ukegawa, T., Mathematics
Wada, M., Literature
Wakuda, Y., Health and Physical Education
Yutarai, S., Chemistry
Yagi, A., Historical Science
Yamanaka, Y., Health and Physical Education
Yamazaki, K., Literature
Yanagawa, T., Mathematics
Yoshimura, T., English
Yoshiyasu, M., German
Waki, S., Biology

Health Administration Centre:

Hashimoto, Y., Neurology and Psychiatry

Research Institute for Economics and Business Administration:

Fujita, M., International Finance
Inoue, T., International Management
Katano, H., International Trade
Nakano, I., Accounting
Nishimukai, Y., Latin American Economy
Nose, N., Business Statistics
Sasaki, A., Maritime Economics
Yamamoto, H., International Labour Relations

KUMAMOTO UNIVERSITY

39-1, Kurokami 2-Chome,
Kumamoto-Shi, 860
Telephone: 0963 (44) 2111.
Founded 1949.

Academic year; April to March (two terms.)

President: Prof. Fumio Takenaka.

Director of Administration Bureau: Tsutomu Ibe.

Librarian: Prof. Hisashi Ichibagase.

Number of teachers: 910.
Number of students: 7,962.
Publications: Faculty Journals† (annually or quarterly).

Deans:

Faculty of Letters: Prof. Yutaka Matsugaki.
Faculty of Law: Prof. Hiroshi Kamata.
Faculty of Medicine: Prof. Keiichi Ikegami.
Faculty of Engineering: Prof. Itsuro Tatsukawa.
Faculty of Education: Prof. Shinichi Kanamori.
Faculty of Science: Prof. Keisuke Kaminishi.
Faculty of Pharmaceutical Sciences: Prof. Yoshitoshi Kase.
Faculty of General Education: Prof. Torao Nishioka.

KYOTO UNIVERSITY

YOSHIDA-HONMACHI, SAKYO-KU, KYOTO

Telephone: 751-2111.

Founded 1897.

Academic year: April to March.

President: T. SAWADA.
Director-General: T. OHTSUKA.
Dean of Students: O. MIDORIKAWA.
Librarian: R. HAYASHI.

Number of professors: 645.
Number of students: 14,845.

Publications include ***Journal of Mathematics of Kyoto University, Publications of the Seto Marine Biological Laboratory, Bulletin of the Institute for*** *Chemical Research, Kyoto University Bulletin, Guide Book for Foreign Students,* etc.

DEANS:

Faculty of Letters: K. YOSHIOKA.
Faculty of Education: H. KAWAI.
Faculty of Law: N. KATAOKA.
Faculty of Economics: S. NAKAMURA.
Faculty of Science: M. KATO.
Faculty of Medicine: O. HAYAISHI.
Faculty of Pharmaceutical Sciences: H. TAKAGI.
Faculty of Engineering: Y. NISHIJIMA.
Faculty of Agriculture: K. SAKAMOTO.
College of Liberal Arts: T. INOUE.

PROFESSORS:

Faculty of Letters:

AOKI, T., American Literature
FUJINAWA, K., Occidental History
FUJISAWA, N., History of Western Philosophy
HAGIWARA, J., Oriental History
HATTORI, M., History of Indian Philosophy
HIGUCHI, T., Archaeology
HIRAI, T., German Language and Literature
HIRANO, T., Psychology
HONDA, M., History of South West-Asia
IMAZU, A., Contemporary History
KAJIYAMA, Y., Buddhism
KISHI, T., Japanese History
MORIGUCHI, M., Ethics
MOTOYOSHI, R., Psychology
NAKA, H., Sociology
NAKAGAWA, H., French Language and Literature
NISHIDA, T., Linguistics
OCHI, T., Occidental History
OJIHARA, Y., Sanskrit Language and Literature
OKA, M., Greek and Latin
OKA, T., English Language and Literature
SAKAI, O., History of Western Philosophy
SATAKE, A., Japanese Language and Literature
SHIMADA, K., Oriental History
SHIMIZU, J., Italian Language and Literature
SHIMIZU, S., Chinese Language and Literature
SUITSU, I., Geography
TANIGAWA, M., Oriental History
TSUJIMURA, K., History of Western Philosophy
UEDA, S., Science of Religion
YAMADA, A., Philosophy, History of Philosophy
YOSHIOKA, K., Aesthetics and History of Fine Arts
YUASA, Y., Chinese Philosophy

Faculty of Education:

HACHIYA, K., Educational Anthropology
HYODO, T., Educational Administration
INABA, H., Curriculum Development
KAWAI, H., Clinical Psychology
KOBAYASHI, T., Comparative Education
MORI, K., Library Science
MORIGUCHI, K., Adult Education
MOTOYAMA, Y., History of Education
UMEMOTO, T., Educational Psychology
WADA, S., Pedagogy
WATANABE, Y., Educational Sociology

Faculty of Law:

ABE, T., Constitutional Law
FUKUSHIMA, T., Political Science
HAYASHI, R., Civil Law
INUI, K., Soviet Law
KATAOKA, N., Labour Law
KATSUDA, K., History of Political Thought
KAWAMATA, Y., Commercial Law
KIMURA, M., Comparative Politics
KITAGAWA, Z., Civil Law
KIYONAGA, K., Law of Taxation
KOSAKA, M., International Politics
KOZAI, S., International Organizations
MAEDA, T., Civil Law
MICHIDA, S., Anglo-American Law
MURAMATSU, M., Public Administration
NAKATSUKASA, T., Law of Civil Procedure
NAKAZAWA, K., Japanese Legal History
NOGUCHI, N., Political History
OKUDA, M., Civil Law
SATO, K., General Legal Theory of State
SHIBATA, M., Roman Law
SUZUKI, S., Criminal Procedure
TAIJUDO, K., International Law
TAMEIKE, Y., Private International Law
TANAKA, S., Philosophy of Law
TANIGUCHI, Y., Law of Civil Procedure
TATSUTA, M., Commercial Law
UEYAMA, Y., Occidental Legal History
UEYANAGI, K., Commercial Law

Faculty of Economics:

FURIHATA, T., Business Administration
HASHIMOTO, I., Marketing
HIRAI, T., History of Social Thought
HIRATA, K., Principles of Economics
HISHIYAMA, I., History of Economic Theories
IKEGAMI, J., Public Finance
KIHARA, M., Statistics
MAEKAWA, K., Social Policy
NAKAMURA, S., Economic History
OHNO, E., Economic Policy
ONO, K., International Economics
TAKATERA, S., Accounting
WATASE, H., Business Policy
YAMADA, H., Transportation Economics

Faculty of Science:

ASAI, K., Dielectrics, High Polymer Physics
ENDO, H., Metal and Semiconductor Physics
FUJINAGA, T., Analytical Chemistry
HARADA, E., Invertebrate Zoology
HASEGAWA, H. Cosmic Ray Physics
HASHI, T., Magnetic Resonance and Quantum Electronics
HATANO, H., Radiation and Analytical Biochemistry
HAYASHI, C.. Nuclear Astrophysics
HIDAKA, T., Comparative Physiology
HIJIKATA, H., Number Theory
HIROTA, N., Solid State Chemical Physics
HORIE, S., Palaeolimnology
ICHINOHE, T. Geodesy and Solid Earth Physics
IKEBE, T., Mathematical Physics
IKEDA, J., Anthropology
IWATSUKI, K., Plant Taxonomy
KACHI, S., Solid State Chemistry
KAJI, A., Organic Chemistry
KAMEI, T., Historical Geology
KATO, MI., Radiation Biology
KATO, S., Astrophysics
KATSUKI, H., Biochemistry
KAWAGUCHI, I., Solar Physics
KAWANABE, H., Animal Ecology
KIKKAWA, K., Geophysics
KOBAYASHI, S., Experimental Nuclear Physics
KOGURE, T., General Astronomy
KUBOTERA, A., Volcanology
KUNISHI, H., Oceanography and Hydrology
KUROIWA, S., Plant Ecology
KUSUNOKI, Y., Theory of Functions of a Complex Variable
MACHIDA, S., Theory of Elementary Particles
MAEDA, H., Geomagnetism and Space Physics
MARUYAMA, K., Organic Chemistry
MATSUBARA, T., Statistical Mechanics, Solid State Physics
MIKI, H., Seismology
MINAGAWA, T., Microbial Physiology and Genetics
MIYAKE, K., Experimental Particle Physics
MIZOHATA, S., Differential Equations
MORIMOTO, N., Mineralogy and Crystallography
MUTO, J., Experimental Nuclear Physics
NAGATA, M., Algebra and Algebraic Geometry
NAKAI, Y., Solid State Spectroscopy
NAKAZAWA, K., Stratigraphy and Invertebrate Palaeontology
OHNISHI, S., Biophysical Chemistry
OKADA, T. S., Cell Differentiation Problems
ONCHI, M., Surface Sciences
OSUGI, J, Physical Chemistry
OZAWA, I., Applied Geophysics
OZEKI, H., Molecular Genetics
SAIKA, A., Structural Chemistry
SASAJIMA, S., Physical Geology
TAKEUCHI, I., Cell Biology
TAMAGAKI, R., Theoretical Nuclear Physics
TANAKA, S., Theory of Elementary Particles
TANAKA, S., Plasma Physics
TATSUMI, T., Applied Mathematics, Fluid Mechanics
TERAMOTO, E. Theoretical Biophysics
TEZUKA, Y., Freshwater Ecology
TODA, H., Algebraic Topology
TOMITA, K., Irreversible Process Theory, Statistical Mechanics, Solid State Theory
TSUJIKAWA, I., Spectroscopic and Magnetic Chemistry
TSUNETO, T., Low Temperature Physics
WATANABE, S., Probability Theory
YAMAGUCHI, M., Numerical Analysis, Differential Equations
YAMAMOTO, R., Meteorology and Atmospheric Physics
YAMAMOTO, T., Theoretical Chemistry
YANAGIDA, M., Molecular Biology
YONEDA, M., Developmental Biology
YOSHIZAWA, H., Functional Analysis
YOSHIZAWA, T., Photobiology

Faculty of Medicine:

ABE, M., Radiology
ARAKI, **T., Physiology**
FUJIWARA, M., Pharmacology
HAMASHIMA, Y., Pathology

HANDA, H., Neuro-Surgery
HAYAISHI, O., Medical Chemistry
HIKASA, Y., Surgery
HINOKI, M., Oto-Laryngology
HORI, R., Pharmacy
HOSHINO, K., Anatomy
IMAMURA, S., Dermatology and Syphilology
IMURA, H., Internal Medicine
ISSHIKI, N. Plastic Surgery
ITO, Y., Microbiology
ITOKAWA, Y., Hygiene
KAMEYAMA, M., Neurology
KAWAI, C., Internal Medicine
KUNO, M., Physiology
MIDORIKAWA, O., Pathology
MIKAWA, H., Paediatrics
MIZUNO, N., Anatomy
MORI, K., Anaesthesiology
MURACHI, T., Biochemistry
NISHIMURA, T., Gynaecology and Obstetrics
NISHIURA, M., Leprosy
NUMA, S., Medical Chemistry
OGAWA, K., Anatomy
OHASHI, H., Psychiatry
ONO, T., Stomatology
SANO, S., Public Health
SASAKI, K., Neurophysiology
SUGAHARA, T., Experimental Radiology
TAKAORI, S., Pharmacology
TOBE, T., Surgery
TORIZUKA, K., Nuclear Medicine
TUKAHARA, I., Ophthalmology
UCHINO, H., Internal Medicine
UEDA, M., Legal Medicine
YAMAMURO, T., Orthopaedic Surgery
YOSHIDA, O., Urology

Faculty of Pharmaceutical Sciences:

INOUYE, H., Phytochemistry
INUBUSHI, Y., Organic Chemistry
NAKAGAKI, M., Physical Chemistry
OKADA, J., Pharmaceutical Engineering
OSAKI, K., Inorganic Chemistry
SEZAKI, H., Pharmaceutics
TABATA, M., Pharmacognosy
TAKAGI, H., Pharmacology
TANAKA, H., Radiopharmaceutical Chemistry
TOMITA, K., Health Chemistry
UNO, T., Analytical Chemistry
YAJIMA, H., Pharmaceutical Manufacturing Chemistry
YAMASHINA, I., Biological Chemistry

Faculty of Engineering:

ADACHI, M., Structural Metallurgy
AKAI, K., Foundation Engineering
AKAMATSU, T., Fluid Mechanics
AKASHI, H., Systems Control Engineering
AMANO, K., Urban Transportation Engineering
ANDO, T., Industrial Analytical Chemistry
DOSHITA, S., Information Processing
ENDO, K., Engineering Materials
FUJINAKA, Y., Mining Machinery
FUKAWA, H., Engineering Mathematics
FUKUDA, K., Spectroscopy
FUKUI, K., Hydrocarbon Physical Chemistry
FUKUI, S., Industrial Biochemistry and Fermentation Chemistry
FURUKAWA, O., Building Construction
GOTO, H., Transport Structural Problems
HADA, H., Industrial Physical Chemistry
HAGIWARA, H., Computer Systems
HANAFUSA, H., Process Control Systems
HASEGAWA, T., Logical Systems
HASHIMOTO, K., Chemical Reaction Engineering
HATA, S., Construction Engineering
HAYASHI, M., Electric Power Generation, Transmission and Distribution
HIGASHIMURA, T., Polymer Synthesis
HIRAOKA, M., Environmental Process Engineering
HITOMI, K., Manufacturing Systems and Production Management
HOSHIKAZI, N., Nuclear Physics
HYODO, T., Nuclear Reactor Shielding
ICHIKAWA, K., Petrochemical Engineering
IHARA, C., Engineering Mechanics
IINOYA, K., Process Dynamics and Control, Powder Technology
IKEDA, M., Engineering Mathematics
IKEGAMI, F., Radio Communication Engineering
IKEGAMI, M., Power Engineering
IKENOUE, J., High-Frequency Engineering
IMANISHI, Y., Biofunctional Polymers
INOUE, Y., Radiological Health Engineering
ISE, N., Fundamental Polymer Chemistry
ITATANI, R., Plasma Physics
IWAGAKI, Y., Coastal Engineering
IWAI, S., Systems Engineering
IWASA, Y., River Engineering
JINNO, H., Industrial Solid-State Chemistry
KAGIYA, T., Catalyst Physics
KANETA, K., Theory of Steel Structures
KATO, S., Aeronomy and Space Physics
KAWABATA, A., Electronic Materials
KAWAI, H., Mechanical Properties of Polymers and Polymer Processing
KAWAKAMI, M., History of Architecture
KAWANISHI, M., Organic Chemistry of Natural Products
KIMURA, I., Radio Communication Engineering
KISHIMA, A., Electric Circuit Theory
KOBAYASHI, S., Design in Civil Engineering
KOBORI, T., Soil and Foundation Engineering
KOJIMA, T., General Analytical Chemistry
KOKADO, J., Mining and Metallurgical Machinery
KONDO, B., Automatic Control
KONDO, Y., Process Metallurgy and Quality Control
KUMADA, M., Organometallic Chemistry
KUNITOMO, T., Thermophysical Properties of Materials
KUWAHARA, M., Electronic Materials and Circuit Elements in Control Systems
MAEDA, H., Aeroplane Construction
MAJIMA, H., Electrometallurgy and Hydrometallurgy
MANNAMI, M., Solid State Physics
MATSUO, S., Soil Mechanics
MATSUURA, K., Architectural Environmental Control Engineering
MATSUURA, T., Free Radical Chemistry
MICHIYOSHI, I., Nuclear Reactor Engineering
MINATO, T., Economic Geology
MINE, H., Operations Research
MIURA, S., Crystal Plasticity
MIZUNO, M., Welding Engineering
MIZUSHINA, T., Transport Phenomena
MORI, H., Lubrication and Hydraulic Engineering
MORI, T., Pyrochemical Metallurgy
MORITA, S., Building Materials
MORIYAMA, J., Non-Ferrous Metallurgy and Thermochemistry
MUGURUMA, H., Reinforced Concrete Structures
MURAKAMI, Y., Science of Metallic Materials
NAGAO, M., Electrical Communication Engineering
NAGAO, Y., Terminal Facilities
NAKAGAWA, H., Hydraulics
NAKAJIMA, A., Molecular Properties of Polymers
NAKAMURA, T., Mechanics of Building
NAKAMURA, Y., Metal Physics
NISHIHARA, H., Nuclear Reactor Physics
NISHIJIMA, Y., Polymer Structure
NISHIKAWA, K., Planning for Urban Redevelopment and Conservation
NISHIKAWA, Y., Measurement, Instrumentation and Control
NIWA, Y., Structural Mechanics
NOZAKI, H., Chemistry of Organic Reactions
OGAWA, T., High Altitude Radio Engineering
OHNO, Y., Information Systems Engineering
OHYA, Y., Applied Mathematics
OISHI, J., Nuclear Chemical Engineering
OKADA, K., Construction Materials
OKADA, T., Electrical Machinery
OKAMOTO, K., Hydrocarbon Chemistry Fundamentals
OKAMURA, K., Automatic Machines
ONOGI, S., Polymer Physics
OYANE, M., Engineering Plasticity
SADA, E., Chemical Engineering Thermodynamics and Mass Transfer
SAEGUSA, T., Polymerization Chemistry
SAKAI, T., Information Science Fundamentals
SAKISAKA, M., Radiation Physics and Nuclear Instruments
SAKURAI, T., Gas Dynamics
SASAKI, A., Electronic Materials and Device Physics Engineering
SASAKI, T. Transport and Traffic Planning
SATO, S., Vibration Engineering
SATO, T., Heat Transfer
SHIRAISHI, H., Bridge Engineering
SHONO, T., Organic Synthesis
SOGA, N., Inorganic Structural Chemistry
SOMIYA, I., Water Quality Engineering
SONE, Y., Fluid Dynamics and Kinetic Theory of Gas Flow
SUMITOMO, H., Water Supply and Sewage Engineering
TABUSHI, I., Organic Catalytic Chemistry
TAKAGI, T., Electron Devices, Ion Beam Engineering
TAKAMATSU, T., Process Systems Engineering
TAKAMURA, J., Lattice Defects and Crystal Plasticity
TAKASAO, T., Hydraulic Systems Analysis
TAKEGAMI, Y., Petroleum Conversion and Catalyst Engineering
TAMARU, K., Digital Electronics
TAMURA, I., Science of Steels
TANAKA, K., Strength of Structures
TATSUMI, K., Architectural Planning
TERASHIMA, Y., Industrial Health Engineering
TOEI, R., Transport Phenomena in Dispersed System, Diffusional Unit Operation
TOKUMARU, H., Applied Systems Analysis
TOKUOKA, T., Theory of Vibration
TSUDA, T., Computer Software
UEDA, A., Applied Mechanics
UENOSONO, C., Power System Engineering
UMOTO, J., Electromagnetic Theory
WAKAMATSU, T., Mineral Processing
YABE, H., Machine Elements
YAJIMA, S., Logic Circuits and Automata
YAMADA, T. .Mechanics of Materials

YAMADA, Y., Structural Earthquake Engineering
YAMAMOTO, T., Environmental Hygiene
YONEZAWA, T., High Temperature Chemistry
YOSHIDA, Z., Physical Organic Chemistry
YOSHIKAWA, K., Regional Planning and Systems Analysis
YOSHIOKA, N., Mechanical Unit Operations
YOSHIZAWA, S., Industrial Electrochemistry
YOSHIZUMI, E., Geophysical Prospecting

Faculty of Agriculture:

ASAHIRA, T., Oleoriculture and Floriculture
CHIBA, H., Food Chemistry
FUKAMI, H., Chemical Literature in German
HANDA, R., Forest Management
HARADA, H., Wood Structure
HASEGAWA, T., Agricultural Structural Engineering
HIROMI, K., Enzyme Chemistry
IKEDA, S., Fishery Chemistry
IRITANI, A., Reproductive Physiology of Farm Animals
ISHIBASHI, T., Functional Anatomy of Farm Animals
IWAI, K., Nutrition Chemistry
IWAI, T., Aquatic Biology
IWAO, S., Entomology
KADOTA, H., Microbiology for Fishery
KAMIKUBO, T., Agricultural Products
KAWAI, H., Applied Physics in Fishing
KAWAMURA, N., Agricultural Equipment and Machinery
KAWANABE, S., Silviculture and Forest Yield Study
KAWASHIMA, R., Animal Nutrition
KIKUCHI, T., Economic Analysis and Farm Planning
KISHINE, T., Forest Policy
KOMANO, T., Biological Chemistry
KOSHIMIZU, K., Analysis of Agricultural Products
KURIHARA, H., Crop Science
KYUMA, K., Soil Science
MARUYAMA, T., Irrigation and Drainage
MINAMI, I., Agricultural Water Use Engineering
MIYOSHI, M., Agricultural History
MURAKAMI, K., Chemistry of Wood and Forest Products
NAKAJIMA, C., Agricultural Policy
NAKAJIMA, M., Pesticide Chemistry
NAKAMURA, M., Landscape Agriculture
NAKATO, K., Wood Technology
NAMIKAWA, K., Animal Breeding
NISHIGUCHI, T., Rural Planning
OKAMOTO, H., Chemical Processing of Wood
SAKAMOTO, K., Principles of Agricultural Sciences
SASAKI, I., Forestry Engineering
SENDA, M., Chemistry of Biopolymer
SHIGENAGA, S., Plant Cultivation
SUGIHARA, H., Woodworking Machinery
TAKAHASHI, E., Plant Nutrition
TAKEI, A., Erosion Control Engineering
TAKIMOTO, A., Applied Botany
TANAKA, M., Crop Genetics and Evolution
TANAKA, T., Agricultural Principles
TOCHIKURA, T., Industrial Microbiology
TOMANA, T., Pomology
TSUNEWAKI, K., Genetics
TSUTSUMI, T., Forest Ecology
UEKI, K., Principles of Weed Control
UEMURA, K., Farm Accounting
UEYAMA, A., Principles of Pesticidal Actions, Insect Physiology
WADA. S., Forest Mensuration
YAMADA, H., Physiology of Fermentation and Applied Microbiology
YAMAGATA, H., Plant Breeding
YAMAMOTO, M., Plant Pathology
YAMASHITA, R., Agricultural Process Engineering
YOKOTA, T., Materials for Wood Improvement
YORI, T., Farm Management Planning

College of Liberal Arts:

ANDO, S., English Language
AOKI, K., English Language
ASHIKAGA, S., Economics
ASHIZU, T., German Language
DEGUCHI, Y., Chemistry
DOHI, Y., German Language
FUJIIE, T., Mathematics
FUJINAWA, A., Psychology
HACHIYA, A., English Language
HAMADA, K., Japanese Language and Literature
HASEGAWA, T., English Language
HATANO, S., Physics
HAYAMI, J., Chemistry
HAYASHI, K., Mathematics
HIGASHI, S., Chemistry
INOKUCHI, S., German Language
INOUE, T., Physics
INUI, Y., Science of Arts
IWAHASHI, T., German Language
IWAI, N., Physical Training and Sports Medicine
KAWAI, R., Mathematics
KAWAI, T., Physics
KIHO, H., Physics
KINOSHITA, K., Chemistry
KINOSHITA, T., Psychology
KITA, H., Physics
KOJIMA, M., German Language
KOYAMA, R., Physics
KUMAMOTO, M., Sports Medicine, Physical Training
MAEDA, K., German Language
MAEKAWA, M., Descriptive Geometry and Drawing
MAN-I, M., Sports Medicine, Physical Training
MASUYAMA, S., English Language
MATSUMOTO, M., Mathematics
MATSUSHIMA, S., Earth Science
MATSUSHITA, S., English Language
MIYATAKE, Y., Physics
MIZOKAWA, K., Economics
MORI, TA, Jurisprudence
MORI, TSU, Mathematics
NAGANO, Y., English Language
NAKAJIMA, S., Psychology
NISHIMURA, H., Mathematics
NISHIMURA, S., Biology
NITTA, H., Art
NOMURA, O., German Language
OGATA, T., English Language
OHASHI, Y., French Language
OKUDA, M., Biology
OTSUKA, K., Mathematics
SAKAI, K., English Language
SAKAKURA, A., Japanese Language and Literature
SAKUDA, K., Sociology
SASABE, H., English Language
SHIGESAWA, K., Earth Science
SUZUKI, S., Mathematics
TAKAGI, H., German Language
TAKEYAMA, M., Physics
TAKEMORI, O., English Language
TAKIZAWA, S., Mathematics
TANDAI, K., Mathematics
TOITA, T., Pedagogy
TOKUBO, K., Chemistry
TOKUOKA, Z., Physics
TOMIOKA, J., Western History
TOYODA, Y., Jurisprudence
TSURU, H., Chinese Language
UEDA, M., Japanese History
UEDA, Y., Philosophy and Logic
UENO, S., Russian Language
UKITA, T., Human Geography
UWAYOKOTE, M., Japanese History
WATANABE, M., Japanese Language and Literature
YAGIU, T., Mathematics
YAMAMOTO, S., Religion, History of Western Social Thought
YAMAZAKI, K., Physics
YANAGISHIMA, S., Biology

ATTACHED INSTITUTES:

Centre for Archaeological Operations: Yoshida Honmachi, Sakyo-ku, Kyoto; f. 1977; Dir. Prof. Dr. T. HIGUCHI; publs. *Annual*, *Excavation Report* (irregular).

Centre for Southeast Asian Studies: Shimoadachi-cho46, Yoshida, Sakyo-ku, Kyoto; f. 1965; Dir. Prof. T. WATABE; publs. *Southeast Asian Studies* (quarterly), *Natural Science Series* (irregular), *Social Science Series* (irregular).

Chest Disease Research Institute: Kawara-cho, Shogoin, Sakyo-ku, Kyoto; f. 1941; Dir. Prof. N. MAEKAWA; publ. *Bulletin* (2 a year).

Data Processing Centre: Yoshida-Honmachi, Sakyo-ku, Kyoto; f. 1969; Dir. Prof. Y. NIWA; publ. *Bulletin* (every 2 months, in Japanese).

Disaster Prevention Research Institute: Gokasho, Uji City, Kyoto; Dir. Prof. M. WAKABAYASHI; publs. *Bulletin* (quarterly) and *Annuals*.

Educational Centre for Information Processing: Yoshida Honmachi, Sakyo-ku, Kyoto; f. 1978; Dir. Prof. Dr. Y. OHNO.

Environment Preservation Centre: Yoshida Honmachi, Sakyo-ku, Kyoto; f. 1977; Dir. Prof. S. ONOGI.

Institute of Atomic Energy: Gokasho, Uji City, Kyoto; f. 1941; Dir. Prof. Y. HATTORI; publs. *Technical Reports* (irregular), *Bulletin* (2 a year in Japanese), *Research Activities* (annually).

Institute for Chemical Research: Gokasho, Uji City, Kyoto; f. 1926; 157 mems.; library of 30,513 vols.; Dir. Prof. T. TAKADA; publ. *Bulletin* (6 a year).

Institute for Virus Research: Kawara-cho, Shogoin, Sakyo-ku, Kyoto; f. 1956; Dir. Prof. S. MATSUMOTO; publ. *Annual Report*.

Institute of Economic Research: Sakyo-ku, Kyoto; f. 1962; library of 39,446 vols.; Dir. Prof. Dr. Y. MIYAZAKI.

Plasma Physics Laboratory: Gokasho, Uji City, Kyoto; f. 1976; research and postgraduate training in plasma physics and controlled fusion; Dir. Prof. K. UO.

Primate Research Institute: Inuyama City, Aichi Prefecture; f. 1967; Dir. Prof. M. KAWAI.

Radiation Biology Centre: Yoshida Konoecho, Sakyo-ku, Kyoto; f. 1976; research and postgraduate training in radiation biology; Dir. Prof. K. TORIZUKA.

Radioisotope Research Centre: Yoshida Konoecho, Sakyo-ku, Kyoto; f. 1971; Dir. Prof. Dr. Z. KASAI.

Research Centre for Medical Polymers and Biomaterials: Shogoin Kawara-cho, Sakyo-ku, Kyoto; f. 1980; Dir. Prof. T. YAMAMURO.

Research Centre for Sports Science: Yoshida Honmachi, Sakyo-ku, Kyoto; f. 1972; Dir. Prof. M. MAN-I; publ. *Area Services* (Japanese).

Research Institute for Food Science: Gokasho, Uji City, Kyoto; f. 1946; research and postgraduate training in food science; Dir. Prof. Dr. Y. MORITA; publs. *Memoirs* (irregular), *Bulletin* (annual).

Research Institute for Fundamental Physics: Kitashirakawa, Sakyo-ku, Kyoto; f. 1953; Dir. Prof. Z. MAKI; publs. *Progress of Theoretical Physics* (monthly), *Supplement* (quarterly).

Research Institute for Humanistic Studies: Ushinomiyacho, Sakyo-ku, Kyoto; f. 1939; Dir. Prof. M. FUKUNAGA; publs. *Journal of Oriental Studies* (annual), *Journal of Humanistic Studies* (annual), *Social Survey Report* (annual), *Annual Bibliography of Oriental Studies*, *Memoirs* (annual).

Research Institute for Mathematical Sciences: Kitashirakawa, Sakyo-ku, Kyoto; f. 1963; research and postgraduate training in mathematical sciences; 34 mems.; library of 49,408 vols.; Dir. Prof. N. SHIMADA; publs. *Publications* (3 a year), *Seminar Reports "Kokyuroku"* (28 a year, in Japanese).

Research Reactor Institute: Kumatori-cho, Sennan-gun, Osaka; f. 1963; 213 mems.; library of 30,252 vols.; Dir. Prof. T. HAYASHI; publs. *Annual Reports* (in English), *Technical Reports* (in Japanese, irregular).

Wood Research Institute: Uji, Kyoto; f. 1944; Dir. Prof. T. HIGUCHI; publ. *Wood Research* (3 a year).

ATTACHED COLLEGE:

College of Medical Technology: 53 Shogoin Kawara-cho, Sakyo-ku, Kyoto; f. 1975; Dean Prof. S. TOMITA.

KYUSHU INSTITUTE OF TECHNOLOGY

KITAKYUSHU-SHI, TOBATA-KU, FUKUOKA-KEN 804

Telephone: (093) 871-1931.

Founded 1909.

President: TERUZO ASAHARA.
Registrar: HIROSHI HISANAGA.
Librarian: TETSUJI KATSUHARA.

Library of 215,219.

Number of full-time teachers: 197.
Number of students: 2,600.
Publications: *Bulletin, Memoirs.*

KYUSHU UNIVERSITY

HAKOZAKI, HIGASHI-KU, FUKUOKA-SHI

Telephone: Fukuoka (641) 1101.

Founded 1911.

Academic year: April to March.

President: Y. KANDA.
Administrator: T. MURAKAMI.
Librarian: H. TSUKAHARA.

Number of teachers: 2,131, including 558 professors.

Number of students: 11,204.

Publications: numerous faculty and institute journals and reports.

DEANS:

Faculty of Literature: T. FUNATSU.
Faculty of Education: K. TAKANO.
Faculty of Law: S. ARAKI.
Faculty of Economics: Y. OYA.
Faculty of Science: R. TAKAHASHI.
Faculty of Medicine: K. MATSUURA.
Faculty of Dentistry: M. YAMANE.
Faculty of Pharmaceutical Sciences: Y. UEDA.
Faculty of Engineering: K. YASUURA.
Faculty of Agriculture: T. MATSUMOTO.
College of General Education: K. KONO.

DIRECTORS:

Interdisciplinary Graduate School of Engineering Sciences: T. SEIYAMA.

Research Institute of Balneotherapeutics: J. OKABE.

Research Institute of Industrial Science: T YAMASAKI.

Research Institute for Applied Mechanics: J. OKABE.

Institute of Health Science: M. OGATA.

PROFESSORS:

Faculty of Literature:

ARAKI, K., Chinese Philosophy
FUJINO, T., Japanese History
FUNATSU, T., Psychology
HIRATA, Y., Aesthetics and History of Fine Arts
IHARA, S., Indian Philosophy
IMAI, G., Japanese Literature
INAGAKI, R., Occidental Philosophy
KAWAZOE, S., Japanese History
MASUNAGA, Y., Ethics
MATSUDA, I., Linguistics
MATSUNAGA, Y., Western Philosophy
MORI, H., Occidental History
NISHIDA, E., German Literature
NOMURA, N., Science of Religion
OCHI, S., Oriental History
OHYE, S., English Literature
OKAMURA, S., Chinese Literature
OKAZAKI, T., Archaeology
OKUMURA, M., Japanese Literature
TANAKA, E., French Literature
YOKOYAMA, K., Japanese History

Faculty of Education:

GONDO, Y., Comparative Education, Problem Approach
KOBAYASHI, H., Contemporary Philosophy of Education
NARUSE, G., Educational Psychology
TAKANO, K., School Administration and Management
TANAKA, I., Sociology of Educational Organization
YAMAUCHI, M., Educational Psychology

Faculty of Law:

ARAKI, S., Law of Social Insurance and Social Security
ARICHI, T., Civil Law
HARASHIMA, S., Civil Law
HASUI, Y., Commercial Law
HATA, M., Sociology of Law
HAYASHI, M., Social Law
IMAI, H., Commercial Law
INOUE, S., Judicial Process
INOUE, Y., Criminal Law
ISHIZUKA, H., Japanese Legal History
KONDO, S., Administrative Law
MISHIMA, Y., History of Legal Thought
MIZUNAMI, A., Comparative Theory of Constitution
SOMA, M., Political Science
TAKABAYISHI, H., International Law
TANIGAWA, Y., International Politics
TESHIMA, T., Constitutional Law
TOKUMOTO, M., Civil Law
UNABARA, B., Anglo-American Law
YOKOYAMA, K., Law of Criminal Procedure
YOSHIMURA, T., Law of Civil Procedure

Faculty of Economics:

ARAMAKI, M., History of Economic Thought
FUKAMACHI, I., Money and Finance
HARADA, M., Personnel Administration
HATTORI, S., Principles of Accounting; Principles of Book Keeping
HIDEMURA, S., Economic History of Japan
ICHIMURA, S., Management Engineering
IWAMOTO, K., Public Finance
KATAYAMA, G., Business Finance
KAWABATA, H., Business Administration
KINOSHITA, E., World Economy
KODAMA, Y., Economic Mathematics
NAKATATE, K., Industrial Planning
NOGUCHI, Y., Industrial Planning
OYA, Y., Statistics
TAKENO, H., Industrial Planning
TSUMORI, T., Cost Accounting
TSURU, D., Agricultural Policy
YAMASAKI, Y., Econometrics
YUMURA, T., Economic History

Faculty of Science:

ASANO, C., Information Processing
FURUKAWA, N., Mathematical Programming and Control
HIRONO, M., Geophysics
HIROWATARI, F., Economic Geology
HUZINO, S., Computational Mathematics
ISOYA, A., Experimental Nuclear Physics
IWANAGA, S., Protein Chemistry
IZUMIYA, N., Biochemistry
KAJIWARA, J., Analysis
KANMERA, K., Stratigraphy
KANO, S., Information Theory
KAWAI, M., Theoretical Nuclear Physics
KAWASAKI, K., Statistical Physics of Matter
KIDA S., Co-ordination Chemistry
KIKUCHI, T., Marine Biology
KIMIZUKA, H., Polymer Chemistry
KUDO, A., Mathematical Statistics
KUDO, T., Topology

KUROYANAGI, T., Experimental Nuclear Physics
MAKISUMI, S., Enzyme Chemistry
MASE, S., Physics of Magnetic Materials
MATSUDA, H., Theoretical Biology
MATUMURA, O., Semiconductor Physics
MATUURA, R., Physical Chemistry
MORI, H., Statistical Physics of Matter
MORITA, H., Physical Biology
MUKAI, T., Cytogenetics and Population Genetics
NISHIMURA, M., Plant Physiology
OHASHI, S., Analytical Chemistry
OKAZAKI, A., Low Temperature Physics
OMURA, T., Biochemistry
ONO, Y., Ecology
OTSUKI, S., Theory of Elementary Particles
SEKIGUCHI, M., Molecular Genetics
SHIMADA, R., Quantum Chemistry
SHIRATANI, K., Algebra
SHIROZU, H., Mineralogy
SHUTO, T., Palaeontology
TAKAHASHI, R., Coal Geology
TAKASHIMA, Y., Radiochemistry
TANEDA, S., Petrology
TARUTANI, T., Inorganic Chemistry
TOMITA, M., Functional Analysis
TSUNO, Y., Theoretical Chemistry
YAMAGUCHI, M., Synthetic Organic Chemistry
YAMANA, K., Developmental Biology
YOSHINO, T., Organic Chemistry

Faculty of Medicine:

BABA, T., Cancer Cell Biology
ENDO, H., Biochemical Oncology
ENJOJI, M., Pathology
GOTO, M., Physiology
GOYA, N., Paediatrics
HIROTO, I., Oto-Rhino-Laryngology
HORIOKA, M., Pharmacy
IBAYASHI, H., Internal Medicine
IKEDA, K., Paediatric Surgery
INOKUCHI, K., Surgery
ISHII, Y., Parasitology
ISHINISHI, N., Hygiene
KANASEKI, T., Anatomy
KIMURA, G., Viral Oncology
KITAMURA, K., Neurosurgery
KURATUNE, M., Public Health
KURIYAMA, H., Pharmacology
KUROIWA, Y., Neurology
MAKIZUMI, S., Legal Medicine
MATSUURA, K., Radiology
MINAKAMI, S., Biochemistry
MOMOSE, S., Urology
MORI, R., Virology
NAGAI, M., Anatomy
NAKAGAWA, T., Psychosomatic Medicine
NAKAMURA, M., Internal Medicine
NAKAO, H., Neuro-Psychiatry
NAKAYAMA, F., General and Pulmonary Surgery
NISHIO, A., Orthopaedic Surgery
NOMOTO, K., Immunobiology
OKOCHI, K., Clinical Serology
OMAE, T., Internal Medicine
OOMURA, Y., Physiology
OTSUKI, I., Clinical Pharmacology
TAKAGI, Y., Biochemistry
TAKEYA, K., Bacteriology
TAKI, I., Gynaecology and Obstetrics
TANAKA, K., Pathology
TANIGUCHI, Y., Ophthalmology
TATEISHI, J., Neuropathology
TOKUNAGA, K., Cardiac Surgery
URABE, H., Dermatology
YAMAMOTO, T., Anatomy
YANASE, T., Internal Medicine
YOSHITAKE, J., Anaesthesiology

Faculty of Dentistry:

AONO, M., Conservative Dentistry
HASEGAWA, K., General Anatomy
HASHIMOTO, N., Oral Pathology
HIRAYASU, R., Prosthetic Dentistry
KANDA, S., Dental Radiology
KATSUDA, N., Dental Pharmacology
KOGA, T., Oral Biochemistry
KURISU, K., Oral Anatomy and Histology
KURIYAMA, H., Oral Physiology
MORIOKA, T., Preventive Dentistry
NAGASAWA, H., Conservative Dentistry
NAKATA, M., Paediatric Dentistry
NAKAYAMA, H., Oral Microbiology
OHTA, M., Oral Physiology
OKA, M., Oral Surgery
SUETSUGU, T., Prosthetic Dentistry
TAKAHAMA, Y., Orthodontics
TASHIRO, H., Oral Surgery
YAMANE, M., Dental Engineering

Faculty of Pharmaceutical Sciences:

HAMANA, M., Pharmaceutical Chemistry
HORIUCHI, T., Chemistry of Microorganisms
IGUCHI, S., Pharmaceutics
IMOTO, T., Chemical Engineering and Technology
KANEMATSU, K., Pharmaceutical Synthetic Chemistry
KATO, K., Physiological Chemistry
KAWASAKI, T., Plant Chemistry
KOJIMA, M., Radio Pharmaceutical Chemistry
NISHIOKA, I., Pharmacognosy
OHKURA, Y., Analytical Chemistry
UEDA, Y., Physical Chemistry
UEKI, S., Pharmacology
YOSHIMURA, H., Hygienic and Forensic Chemistry

Faculty of Engineering:

AOKI, K., Computer Hardware and Communication Devices
AOKI, M., Architectural Planning
ASO, K., Mineral Processing
AWAYA, Y., Sewage Engineering
ECHIGO, R., Gas Thermodynamics
FUJITA, Y., Steam Engineering
FUKUDA, J., Design of Merchant Ships
FUKUMITSU, O., Electronic Elements in Computers and Communication Devices
FURUYA, H., Nuclear Fuel Technology
HARADA, K., Electronic Circuits
HASEGAWA, S., Nuclear Mechanical Engineering
HASHIMOTO, K., Solid State Electrophysics
HAYASHI, M., Aerodynamics
HIGASHI, K., Non-Ferrous Metallurgy
HIRAKAWA, K., Industrial Electronics
HIRANO, F., Machine Design
ICHIMARU, Precision Surface Finishing
IHARA, M., Mining Machinery
IKUI, T., Air Science
IJIMA, T., Coastal Engineering
INOUE, J., Mechanics of Machinery
INOUE, S., Hydrodynamics and Dynamics of Ships
IRIE, F., Electronic Measurement
ISHIBASHI, N., Instrumental Analysis
ISHIDA, M., Strength of Materials
ITO, T., Steam Power
IWASAKI, M., Aircraft Dynamics, Performance and Propulsion
KATASE, A., Radiation Measurement and Protection Engineering
KATO, A., Structural Inorganic Chemistry and High Temperature Chemistry
KATO, Y., Chemical Reaction Engineering
KAWAI, Y., Physical Chemistry of Melts
KIMURA, H., Aircraft Equipment, Control and Guidance
KITAJIMA, S., Science and Technology of Radiation Effects
KOGA, T., Computer and Communication Systems
KOTSUBO, S., Structures for Civil Engineering
KUMABE, I., Nuclear Apparatus and Instrumentation
KUNITA, H., Applied Mathematics
KUNITAKE, T., Synthetic Macro-Molecular Chemistry
KUSUNOKI, K., Chemical Reaction Process
MAKINO, M., Earthquake and Wind Engineering
MATSUDA, K., Technological Metallurgy
MATSUDA, K., Metallurgy
MATSUDA, T., Synthetic Chemistry of Low Molecular Compounds
MATSUI, C., Steel Structure; Structural Mechanics
MATSUO, T., Theoretical Organic Chemistry
MATSUYAMA, H., Process Control
MITSUISHI, N., Nuclear Chemical Engineering
MITSUYOSHI, K., Urban Design, City Planning
MIYAZOE, Y., Theory of Electromagnetics
MUKAIYAMA, H., Economic Geology
MUNAKATA, T., Design of Chemical Apparatus
MURAKAMI, T., Dynamics
MURAKAMI, Y., Chemistry of Enzyme and Catalysis
MURAKAMI, Y., Fluid Flow in Chemical Engineering
NAGATA, T., Control System and Artificial Intelligence
NAKAMURA, Y. Industrial Aerodynamics
NAKASHIO, F., Chemical Process Design and Control
NAMBA, M., Aircraft Propulsion Systems
NARITA, K., Electrical Measurement
NISHIKAWA, K., Heat Transfer
NISHINO, T., Applied Mathematics
NISHITANI, H., Strength of Materials
NONAKA, S., Electrical Machinery
NUMATA, M., Railway Engineering
OHIRA, H., Aircraft Structure, Materials and Design
OHTA, M., Reactor Engineering
OHTANI, N., Surface Chemistry of Metals
OISHI, Y., Science of Reactor Materials
ONO, S., Combustion
ONO, Y., Extractive Metallurgy of Iron and Steel
ONODERA, S., Exploration Geophysics
OONO, Y., Fundamentals of Information and Networks
OYAMA, T., Physical Chemistry
OZAKI, T., Metal Processing
SAGARA, S., System Control
SAJI, T., Building Materials: Construction Methods
SAKUMA, K., Tools and Machine Tools
SEKOGUCHI, K., Heat Transfer in Chemical Engineering
SHIMIZU, M., Technology of Metal Working
SUHARA, J., Technical Theory of Shipbuilding
SUMI, S., Aircraft Strength and Vibration
SUNAGA, T., Design and Planning for Production
TAKATA, M., Automatic Control
TAKAMATSU, Y., Fluid Machinery
TAKAYANAGI, M., Polymer Chemistry and Material Science of Polymers
TAKEMURA, T., Applied Physics
TAMURA, H., Dynamics of Machinery
TANIGUCHI, H., Industrial Organic Chemistry

TOKUMITSU, Y., Execution of Works and Concrete Engineering
TOKUNAGA, Y., Material Science of Iron and Steel
TOMII, M., Architectural Structure
TSUBAKI, T., Applied Hydraulics
TSUJI, M., Dynamics
TSUJI, I., Design of Welding
UCHIDA, I., Road Engineering
UEDA, T., Water Supply and Water Resources Engineering
UENO, K., Organic Analytical Chemistry
UENO, T., Machining
URANO, Y., Environmental Engineering in Architecture
USHIJIMA, K., Computer Software
WAKURI, Y., Internal Combustion Engines
WATANABE, H., Mathematical Analysis
YAMAFUJI, K., Solid State Electronics
YAMAKOSHI, M., Strength and Vibration of Ships
YAMANOUCHI, T., Soil Mechanics
YAMAZAKI, R., Resistance and propulsion of Ships
YANAGIMOTO, T., Mining
YASUURA, K., Wave Theory and Applications
YOSHIDA, S., Information Processing System
YOSHIDA, S., Thermodynamics
YOSHIKAWA, H., Applied Mathematics
YUHARA, K., Geothermics

Faculty of Agriculture:

AIZAWA, K., Insect Pathology
AOKI, T., Forest Growth and Yield
CHO, T., Irrigation and Water Utilization
CHUMA, Y., Agricultural Process Engineering
ETO, M., Pesticide Chemistry
FUJIKAWA, T., Land Improvement and Conservation
FUKAZAWA, T., Chemistry and Technology of Animal Products
GOTO, I., Forage Science and Animal Behaviour
FUNATSU, G., Biochemistry
HANADA, J., Agricultural Policy
HAYASHI, K., Sericultural Chemistry
HAYASHIDA, S., Applied Microbiology
HIRASHIMA, Y., Entomology
ISHIO, S., Fisheries Chemistry
ITAZAWA, Y., Marine Biology
KATOH, T., Landscape Architecture
KAWANAMI, G., Far Management
KOBAYASHI, K., Fisheries Environmental Science
KONDO, T., Wood Chemistry
KURODA, M., Forest Policy
MATSUI, T., Environment Control in Biology
MATSUMOTO, S., Crop Science
MATSUMOTO, T., Wood Science
MIYAJIMA, H., Silviculture
MORI, M., Wood Technology
MURANISHI, S., Technology of Agricultural Production
NISHIYAMA, H., Animal Breeding and Reproduction
NISHIZAWA, M., Forest Management
NOMURA, D., Food Technology
OMURA, H., Food Chemistry
OMURA, T., Plant Breeding
OSAJIMA, Y., Food Analysis
SAKAGUCHI, B., Sericulture
SAKAI, J., Agricultural Machinery
SAKANOUE, T., Agricultural Meteorology
SAKATA, I., Polymer Chemistry of Woody Materials
SUE, K., Erosion Control
SUGANO, M., Nutrition Chemistry
SUMIMOTO, M., Industrial Chemistry of Wood
TAKAHASHI, I., Agricultural Marketing
TAKEDA, T., Crop Husbandry
TANAKA, K., Drainage and Reclamation
TASHIRO, T., Agricultural Economics
TOMITA, G., Biophysics
TOYOMIZU, M., Fisheries Technology
TSUCHIYA, K., Quantitative Analysis of Agriculture
TSUKAHARA, H. Fisheries Biology
UCHIDA, T., Zoology
UEDA, S., Biochemical Engineering
UEMOTO, S., Horticulture
WADA, K., Soils
WAKIMOTO, S., Plant Pathology
WATANABE, T., Food Hygienic Chemistry
YAMADA, Y., Soil Fertility and Plant Nutrition
YONE, Y., Fish Nutriology

Interdisciplinary Graduate School of Engineering Sciences:

AKAZAKI, M., Fundamentals for Energy Conversion
ASANO, C., Information Retrieval Systems
EGUCHI, T., Quantum Theory of Matter
HASEGAWA, S., Thermal Energy and Its Conversion Systems
KANDA, Y., Fundamentals for Energy Conversion
KANO, S., Information Models
KOBAYASHI, H., Selectivity in Organic Reactions
MATOBA, M., Application of Nuclear Energy
MATSUO, K., Applied Gas Dynamics
MURAOKA, K., Advanced Plasma Dynamics
NISHIMURA, Y., Molecular Reaction Dynamics
OGAWA, T., Molecular Spectroscopy
OISHI, Y., Theory of Transport Phenomena
ONO, S., Fundamentals for Energy Conversion
OYAMA, T., Properties of Polymers
SAGARA, S., Energy Conversion Systems Control
SAITO, S., Organic Photoconductors
SEIYAMA, T., Theory of Crystal Growth
TAKESHITA, H., Chemical Reactions of Excited Molecules
TAKESHITA, K., Technology of Functional Molecules
TAMACHI, T., Information Recognition
TASHIRO, M., Chemistry of Reactive Species
TSUGE, O., Molecular Design
YANAGASE, T., Structure of Noncrystalline Materials
YASUURA, K., Information Transmission
YOSHIDA, S., Computational Linguistics
YOSHINAGA, H., Science of Structural Materials

College of General Education:

AKAMA, H., Physics
ANDO, N., Psychology
ANDO, T., Chemistry
ANNO, T., Chemistry
BABA, N., Occidental History
BABA, R., Geometry and Drawing
DEMURA, Y., Chemistry
FUKAYAMA, K. Law
FUNAKI, K., Statistics
GOTO, K., Physics
HAMA, F., French
HAMADA, T., Psychology
HARADA, H., Economics
HASHIGUCHI, Y., English
HASHIMOTO, I., Earth Science
HAYASHI, T., English
HIRATA, T., Chemistry
IDE, Y., Chemistry
IKI, H., Ethics
INADA, A., Biology
KAKITA, A., English
KAKU, S., Biology
KAMIMURA, H., German
KINUGASA, T., Political History
KODAMA, T., Mathematics
KOJIMA, T., Economic History
KONDO, S., Practical Geometry and Drawing
KONO, K., Mathematics
KUGA, T., German
MATSUBARA, A., Chemistry
MORI, S., Physics
MORIYAMA, T., Japanese Literature
MURASE, I., Chemistry
NAGAYA, D., German
NAKAMURA, M., Sociology
NAKAMURA, M., Chemistry
NAKANO, Y., English
NAKAYAMA, M., Physics
NASU, K., Chinese
NISHIMURA, H., Physics
NOGUCHI, K., English
NOGUCHI, K., Japanese History
O'HARA, J., Earth Science
OHARA, N., Law
OOHATA, K., Physics
OHMURA, T., Psychology
OHTSUKA, E., Biology
OKAYAMA, S., Biology
OKUDA, H., History of Social Systems
ONIIZUKA, K., English
ONO, A., Mathematics
ONO, K., Human Geography
OSAKA, O., English
OTANI, T., German
OWADA, H., Mathematics
SAIGUSA, T., Biology
SAITO, F., Constitutional Law of Japan
SAKAGUCHI, M., Chemistry
SAKUMA, A., Psychology
SHIGEMATSU, Y., Japanese Literature
SHIGYO, A., Sociology
SHIMIZU, T., European Literature
SHIROZU, T., Biology
SONODA, H., Physics
SORAI, G., German
TAKETA, H., Physics
TAKETATSU, T., Chemistry
TASHIRO, T., German
TATEDA, A., Chemistry
TOKUMOTO, M., Political Science
TSUDA, T., Mathematics
UEDA, I., Physics
UENO, S., Mathematics
URATA, H., Earth Science
YAKABE, I., Mathematics
YAMAGUCHI, M., Japanese History
YAMASAKI, T., French
YAMAUCHI, T., Physics

Research Institute of Balneotherapeutics:

KADOTA, T., Obstetrics and Gynaecology
KOGA, A., Chemistry and Physics
NAKAMIZO, Y., Dermatology and Urology
NOBUNAGA, M., Internal Medicine
TSUJI, H., Surgery
YANAGA, T., Bioclimatology

Research Institute of Industrial Science:

FUJII, T., Heat and Mass Transfer
KOBAYASHI, H., Chemistry of Organic Catalytic Reactions
MIYATAKE, O., Thermodynamics
NISHIDA, T., Ground Dynamics
NISHIMURA, Y., Unstable Species in Gaseous Reactions
SENOO, Y., Fluid Dynamics
TAKESHITA, H., Chemistry of Organic Resources
TAKESHITA, K., Coal Chemistry
TASHIRO, M., Unstable Organic Intermediate Chemistry

TSUGE, O., Organic Synthesis
YAMASAKI, T., Geothermal Geology

Research Institute for Applied Mechanics:
ITOH, S., Applied High-Energy Mechanics
KAWATAKE, K., Fluid Elasticity
KITAJIMA, K., Strength of Materials in High Energy Range
MITSUYASU, H., Near Shore Oceanography
NAKAMURA, Y., Industrial Aerodynamics
OKABE, J., Fluid Mechanics
SUHARA, T., Elasticity
TAKEMATSU, M., Ocean Hydrodynamics
TANEDA, S., Experimental Fluid Mechanics
TASAI, F., Seaworthiness of Marine Structures
YAJIMA, N., High Energy Fluid Mechanics

Institute of Health Sciences:
MATSUMOTO, J., Physical Education
OGATA, M., Physical Education
OKABE, H., Physical Education
TAKEYA, Y., Health Care

MIE UNIVERSITY

1515 KAMIHAMA-CHO, TSU-SHI, MIE 514

Telephone: 0592-32-1211

Founded 1949.

President: YOSHIKI MIKAMI.
Chief Administration Officer: TADASHI OHGUSHI.
Librarian: TAKASHI ITO.

Library of 383,855 vols.
Number of teachers: 584.
Number of students: 3,993.

DEANS:

Faculty of Education: TOSHIYUKI MIURA.
School of Medicine: TADSAU IZAWA.
Faculty of Engineering: TETSUO FUJIMOTO.
Faculty of Agriculture: HIROSHI ISHIZAKI.
Faculty of Fisheries: YOSHISHIGE HORIGUCHI.

MIYAZAKI UNIVERSITY

210 FUNATSUKA 3-CHOME, MIYAZAKI

Telephone: 27-0214.

Founded 1949.

President: Y. INOUE.
Registrar: K. TSUKUDA.
Librarian: I. NIKI.

Number of teachers: 349, including 95 professors.

Number of students: 2,741.

Publications: Bulletins† and memoirs of the faculties†.

DEANS:

Faculty of Agriculture: Y. NAKAMURA.
Faculty of Education: M. HAKADA.
Faculty of Engineering: H. FUJIMOTO.

MURORAN INSTITUTE OF TECHNOLOGY

MIZUMOTO-CHO 27, MURORAN 050, HOKKAIDO

Telephone: 0143-44-4181.

Founded 1949.

President: MASAO YOSHIDA.
Administrative Officer: MASUTO OHTA.
Chief Librarian: HISAO KANO.

Library of 162,806 vols.
Number of teachers: 175.
Number of students: 2,352.

Publications: *Memoirs: I Cultural Science, II Science and Engineering*†.

HEADS OF DEPARTMENT:

Humanities, Sociology, Languages, Gymnastics: YUTAKA TAKEUCHI.
Natural Science: NOBUO KOJIMA.
Electrical Engineering: TAIKICHI HATTORI.
Electronic Engineering: JIRO FUTATSUGI.
Industrial Chemistry: FUJIO KOMATSU.
Chemical Engineering: YOSHITERU JOMOTO.
Mineral Resources Engineering: RINPEI KAMADA.
Metallurgical Engineering: HIDEO SUGAWARA.
Civil Engineering: FUMIHIRO KONO.
Architecture and Building Engineering: TAKESHI YOSHIKAWA.
Mechanical Engineering: CHUJI MIZUNO.
Industrial Mechanical Engineering: HAKARU SAITO.
Applied Material Science: NOBORU NISHIDA.
Evening Course: KAZUYUKI KIKUCHI.

NAGASAKI UNIVERSITY

1-14 BUNKYO-MACHI, NAGASAKI

Telephone: 47-1111.

Founded 1949.

Academic year: April to March.

President: K. GUSIMA.
Secretary: M. SEKI.
***Librarian:* T. MATAKE.**

Library of 306,000 vols.

Number of full-time teachers: *c.* 620.
Number of students: *c.* 4,000.

Publications: Numerous faculty journals and bulletins.

DEANS:

Faculty of Education: T. KUMAGAI.
Faculty of Economics: H. KAWAMOTO.
School of Medicine: M. NOGITA.
Faculty of Pharmaceutical Science: M. YANAI.
Faculty of Engineering: T. MATAKE.
Faculty of Fisheries: M. OKA.
Faculty of Liberal Arts: K. TAKAHARI.

NAGOYA INSTITUTE OF TECHNOLOGY

GOKISO-CHO, SHOWA-KU, NAGOYA

Courses in all branches of Engineering.

Founded 1905.

Library of 20,000 vols.
Number of teachers: 311.
Number of students: *c.* 4,600.

NAGOYA UNIVERSITY

FURO-CHO, CHIKUSA-KU, NAGOYA

Telephone: 781-5111.

Founded 1939.

Academic year: April to March (two semesters).

President: N. ISHIZUKA.
Secretary: S. SETTA.
Director of the Library: E. YOKOGOSHI.

Library: *see* Libraries.

Number of full-time teachers: 1,626.
Number of students: 8,594.

Publications: Numerous faculty journals and bulletins.

DEANS:

School of Letters: K. IKEZI.
School of Education: K. MATUURA.
School of Law: T. INAKO.
School of Economics: K. TAKIZAWA.
School of Science: S. HAYAKAWA.
School of Medicine: S. IIJIMA.
School of Engineering: M. NAGASAWA.
School of Agriculture: K. KUMADA.
College of General Education: Y. HISAMURA.
Research Institute of Environmental Medicine: R. OSAKA.
Research Institute of Atmospherics: A. IWAI.
Water Research Institute: Y. KITANO.
Institute of Plasma Physics: H. KAKIHANA.

PROFESSORS:

School of Letters:
ARAKI, K., English Philology
GOTO, S., Japanese Literature
HASEGAWA, H., Western History
IMATAKA, M., Chinese Literature
ISHIMIZU, T., Geography
IZEKI, H., Human Geography
KAMIZAWA, E., French Literature
KAWASAKI, T., English Literature
KITAGAWA, R., Sociology
KITAMURA, T., European History
KUNIHARA, K., Classics
MAEDA, H., Psychology
MIYASAKA, Y., Indian Philosophy
MORI, M., Oriental History
NARASAKI, S., Archaeology
OSHIKA, K., History of European Philosophy
SATO, J., German Literature
TSUJI, S., Aesthetics and Art History
UCHIYAMA, M., Psychology
YAMAGUCHI, K., Japanese History
YAMASHITA, R., Chinese Philosophy

School of Education:

ETO, K., History of Education
ISHIGURO, K., Curriculum
KUZE, T., Educational Psychology
MARUI, F., Educational Psychology
MURAKAMI, E., Educational Psychology
OGAWA, T., Adult Education
OHASHI, M., Educational Psychology
SAIGUSA, T., Methods of Education
SUZUKI, E., Educational Administration and System
TAKAKUWA, Y., Educational Administration
TAURA, T., Philosophy of Education
UCHIDA, Y., Educational Investigation and Statistics
USHIOGI, M., Educational Sociology

School of Law:

FUKUTA, S., International Politics
HASEGAWA, M., Constitution
HIRAIDE, Y., Commercial Law
HIRAMATSU, Y., Japanese Legal History
HIRANO, T., Philosophy of Law
INAKO, T., Foreign Law
ITO, T., Civil Law
KITAZAWA, M., Commercial Law
MATSUI, Y., International Law
MATSUURA, K., Civil Procedure Law
MIYAKE, M., Civil Law, Labour Law
MORISHIMA, A., Civil Law
MUROI, T., Administrative Law
NAKAGI, Y., European Political History
OKUBO, Y., Western Legal History
OTSUKA, H., Criminal Law
TAGUCHI, F., Public Administration
YAMADA, K., History of Political Theory
YAMADA, R., International Private Law
YOKOGOSHI, E., Political Science

School of Economics:

FUJII, T., Principles of Economic Policy
FUJISE, H., History of Social Thought
HOSOI, T., Business Administration
IIDA, T., Economic Theory
JOJIMA, K., Agricultural Policy
KANISHIMA, T., Accounting and Auditing
KOIKE, K., General Business Economics
MIZUNO, M., Public Finance
MIZUTA, H., History of Social Thought
OGAWA, E., Production Management
OSHIMA, Y., Economic Theory
SAITO, T., Accounting
SHIOSAWA, K., Economic History
TAKIZAWA, K., Industrial Organization and Policy
YAMAZAKI, K., Finance

School of Science:

AOKI, H., Seismology
AOMOTO, K., Analytics
ASAKURA, A., Molecular Biology
EGUCHI, G., Molecular Biology
FUJITA, J., Inorganic Chemistry
FUKUI, S., Nuclear Physics
HATANO, S., Molecular Biology
HAYAKAWA, S., Infra-red Astronomy
HIDA, T., Analytics
IKEDA, S., Physical Chemistry
ISHIOKA, K., Petrology and Economic Geology
KAJIKAWA, R., Crystallography
KAWABATA, K., Astronomy
KUBOTA, T., Mathematics
MASUDA, Y., Statistical Physics
MATSUMURA, H., Algebra
MIZUTANI, S., Structural Geology
MORIKAWA, H., Geometry
MORIMOTO, A., Mathematical Logic
MORISHITA, A., Historical Geology
MURAKAMI, K., Cosmic Ray Physics
MURAYAMA, T., High Energy Astronomy
NAGASHIMA, K., Cosmic Ray Physics
NAKAI, N., Geochemistry
NAKAMURA, D., Physical Chemistry
NAKANO, E., Physiological Zoology
NIU, K., Nuclear Measurement
NOYORI, R., Organic Reaction Chemistry
OGAWA, S., Nuclear Theory
ONISHI, E., Chemical Embryology
OHNUKI, Y., Nuclear and Particle Physics
SATO, H., Marine Biological Laboratory
SHIKATA, Y., Mathematical Statistics
SHIMAZU, Y., Geophysics
SUZUKI, S., Organic Chemistry
TAKABAYASHI, T., Fundamental Physics
TAKEBE, I., Microbiology
TAKEMURA, A., Molecular Biology
TANAKA, J., Organic Chemistry
TANAKA, M., Analytical Chemistry
TANIUCHI, T., Nuclear Physics
USUI, T., Solid State Physics
YAMADA, K., Organic Chemistry
YAMADERA, H., Isotope Chemistry
YANAGISHIMA, N., Microbiology
YOMOSA, S., Biological Physics
YOSHIOKA, H., Atomic Measurement

School of Medicine:

AOKI, K., Preventive Medicine
HOSHINO, M., Pathology
ICHIAWA, H., Ophthalmology
IIJIMA, S., Pathology
INOUE, T., Hygiene
ITO, F., Physiology
IYOMASA, Y., Surgery
KAGEYAMA, N., Neurosurgery
KASAHARA, Y., Psychiatry
KATO, N., Bacteriology
KONDO, T., Surgery
KUMADA, N., Medical Zoology
KUZUYA, F., Geriatrics
MAENO, K., Microbiology
MITSUYA, H., Urology
MIYAKE, H., Oto-Rhino-Laryngology
NAKAGAWA, M., Orthopaedic Surgery
OHASHI, M., Dermatology
OKA, T., Oral Surgery
OZAWA, T., Biochemistry
SAKAI, H., Embryology
SAKAMOTO, N., Internal Medicine
SAKUMA, S., Radiology
SANO, M., Anatomy
SHIGEI, T., Pharmacology
SATAKE, T., Internal Medicine
SOBUE, I., Internal Medicine
SUZUKI, S., Paediatrics
TAKESHIMA, N., Anaesthesiology
TANAKA, K., Mycology
TOMIDA, T., Physiology
TOMODA, Y., Obstetrics and Gynaecology
YADA, S., Forensic Medicine
YAGI, K., Biochemistry
YAMADA, S., Public Health

School of Engineering:

ABE, R., Applied Physics
ADACHI, K., Solid State Physics
AKAO, Y., Electromagnetic Waves
AMANUMA, T., Reactor Materials
AMEMIYA, Y., General Electrical Engineering
ANDO, S., Flight Dynamics
ASHIDA, T., Organic Chemistry Materials
FUEKI, K., Synthetic Radiation Chemistry
FUKUMURA, T., Computer Language
FUKUMOTO, Y., Civil Engineering
HARADA, J., Industrial Solid State Physics
HASATANI, S., Combustion and Heat Transmission
HATTORI, S., High Frequency Engineering
HONDA, N., Basic Electronics
HORII, K., Applied Electronics
IEDA, M., Electrical Engineering
IIDA, K., Architecture
IKEBE, Y., Radiation Safety, Fusion Reactor Engineering
IKEGAYA, K., Electro-acoustics
IMURA, T., Physical Metallurgy
ISHIBASHI, Y., Crystal Physics
ISHII, D., Techno-analytical Chemistry
ITO, M., Automatic Control Engineering
ITO, N., Material Coordination Engineering
ITO, T., Dynamics of Machinery
IWAMA, Y., Device Materials Engineering
IWATA, K., Industrial Electronics
IZUMI, R., Internal Combustion Engines
IZUMI, Y., Petro-chemistry
JIMBO, G., Chemical Engineering
KANAGAWA, A., Nuclear Engineering
KATO, N., Crystal Growth Engineering
KATO, S., Workshop Technology
KATO, T., Nuclear Engineering
KATO, Y., Engineering Mathematics
KAWAI, N., Deformation Processes
KAWAKAMI, S., Civil Engineering Planning
KAWAMOTO, T., Civil Engineering
KIKUCHI, Y., Civil Engineering Planning
KIRIHARA, T., Reactor Engineering
KITO, Y., Electrical Engineering
KOMAI, M., Electronic Circuits
KOSAKA, Y., Architecture
KUWABARA, S., Engineering Mathematics
MARUSE, S., Electron Tubes
MASUMOTO, I., Welding and Working of Metals
MATSUBARA, S., Chemical Engineering
MATSUO, M., Civil Engineering
MATSUOKA, O., Building Construction
MIHAMA, K., Applied Physics
MIYAHARA, Y., Industrial Physical Chemistry
MIYACHI, I., Electrical Engineering
MIZUIKE, A., Analytical Chemistry
MORI, K., Metallurgical Engineering
MUCHI, I., Reaction Engineering
MURAKAMI, M., Fluid Mechanics
MURAKAMI, Y., Synthetic Chemistry
NAGASAWA, M., Physical Chemistry
NAITO, K., Nuclear Engineering
NAKA, S., Inorganic Chemistry
NAKAHARA, N., Architectural Engineering
NAKAMURA, I., Fluid Machinery
NAKAMURA, K., Automatic Control Engineering
NAKANO, F., Statistical Physics
NARUOKA, M., Civil Engineering
NINOMIYA, I., Information Science
NISHIMURA, T., Aircraft Structure
OGATA, Y., Applied Chemistry
OHASHI, Y., Strength of Materials
OKI, T., Non-Ferrous Metallurgy
OKUDA, T., Electronics
OTA, H., Automobile Engineering
OTSUKA, A., Strength of Metals
OTSUKA, S., Aeronautical Engineering
SAITO, H., Applied Inorganic Chemistry
SAKAMOTO, J., Steel Construction
SAKAO, H., Chemical Metallurgy
SASAKI, T., Industrial Organic Chemistry
SEIKA, M., Applied Mechanics
SHIMADA, S., Materials Engineering
SHIMIZU, M., Applied Physics
SHIRATO, M., Fluid Mechanics
SUGIE, N., Information Processing
SUGIURA, I., Aeronautical Engineering
TAKAGI, F., Hydraulics
TAKAHAMA, H., Mechanical Engineering
TAMAGAWA, H., Nuclear Instruments
TESHIMA, H., Chemical Engineering
TOYAMA, S., Transport Phenomena
TOZAWA, Y., Plastic Working of Metals
TSUKISHIMA, T., Electronic Control Engineering
UCHIDA, S., Aeronautical Engineering

UCHIYAMA, S., Theory of Electrical Engineering
UEDA, M., Electrical Machinery
UEDA, Y., Metallic Materials
UESHITA, K., Soil Mechanics
WATANABE, T., Nuclear Engineering
YAMAGUCHI, K., Machine Tools
YAMAMOTO, T., Dynamics and Design of Machinery
YAMASHITA, Y., Chemistry of Polymerisation
YANAGISAWA, M., Architecture
YASUHARA, M., Aeronautics
YOSHIHARA, K., Applied Physics

School of Agriculture:

AKAZAWA, T., Biochemistry
FUJIOKA, S., Comparative Anatomy
FUKUI, H., Wood Industrial Machinery
FUTSUHARA, Y., Plant Breeding
GOTO, T., Organic Chemistry
HORI, T., Forest Utilization
HOZUMI, K., Silviculture
IMAZEKI, H., Biochemical Regulation
IWAMURA, T., Biochemistry
KANEKO, Y., Microbiology
KATAOKA, J., Soil and Water Conservation
KAWASE, S., Sericultural Science
KAYAMA, R., University Farm
KOBAYASHI, Y., University Farm
KONDO, K., Animal Genetics
KUMADA, K., Soil Science
MATSUO, M., Farm Management and Agricultural Policy
MUNAKATA, K., Pesticides Chemistry
NAMIKI, M., Chemistry of Plant Products
NOGUCHI, H., Physical Chemistry
SAITO, T., Applied Entomology
SATO, K., Animal Physiology
SATO, Y., Chemistry of Animal Products
SHIMIZU, S., Bio-Reaction Technology
SUGIMOTO, E., Biochemical Regulation
SUMITOMO, H., Chemical Technology of Wood
SUZUKI, T., Forest Taxation
TAKEMURA, T., Wood Technology
TAMURA, T., Fish Biology
TASAKI, I., Animal Nutrition
TERAZAWA, S., Wood Physics
TERASHIMA, N., Chemistry of Forest Products
UDAKA, S., Fermentation Chemistry
URITANI, I., Biological Chemistry
YAMAMOTO, R., Crop Science
YAMAMOTO, S., Horticulture
YATAZAWA, M., Plant Nutrition
YOKOYAMA, A., Reproductive Physiology
YOSHIDA, A., Nutritional Biochemistry

College of General Education:

ARAKAWA, T., Physics
FUKANO, Y., Physics
HAYASHI, I., Mathematics
HIJIKATA, K., History of Social Thought
HIRABAYASHI, Y., Philosophy
HIRATA, H., Law
HISAMURA, Y., Oriental History
HORIKAWA, T., Geography
INAGE, M., Economics
KAINUMA, Y., Physics
KAMIYA, I., Chemistry
KANEOKA, T., Japanese Literature
KANO, Y., Physics
KASHIWAGI, H., Chemistry
KATO, H., Chemistry
KATO, Y., Geology
KAWARABAYASHI, Y., Chemistry
KISHI, M., Mathematics
KISHIDA, T., European History
KONDO, T., Social and Economic History
MASUDA, K., Mathematics
MATSUMOTO, K., Mathematics
MATSUOKA, K., Economics
MATSUURA, S., Chemistry
NAKATA, M., Sociology
NOMOTO, H., Mathematics
OI, Y., Biology
OKI, K., Biology
OHASHI, K., Philosophy
SAKAKI, T., Chemistry
SASAKI, T., Sociology
SHIRAIWA, K., Mathematics
SUGIYAMA, A., Physics
TAKAHASHI, C., Biology
TANAKA, T., Graphic Science
TOYODA, T., Physics
TSUGE, T., Mathematics
YAESHIMA, K., Psychology
YAMAGUCHI, T., Politics
YASUDA, M., Chemistry
YOKOI, H., Mathematics

ATTACHED INSTITUTES:

Research Institute of Environmental Medicine: f. 1946; Dir. R. OSAKA; publ. *Annual Report.*

Research Institute of Atmospherics: f. 1949; Dir. A. IWAI; publ. *Proceedings* (annual).

Water Research Institute: f. 1973; Dir. Y. KITANO; publ. *Collected Papers on Sciences of Atmosphere and Hydrosphere.*

Institute of Plasma Physics: f. 1961; Dir. K. H. KAKIHANA; publs. *Technical Report, Research Report, Annual Review.*

NARA WOMEN'S UNIVERSITY

KITA-UOYA-HIGASHI-MACHI,
NARA CITY 630

Founded 1908.

President: TORU KAWAMURA.
Secretary-General: M. YASUDA.

Library of 298,034 vols.
Number of teachers: 341.
Number of students: 1,683.

Publications: *Annual Report of Studies in Humanities and Social Sciences, Studies in Home Economic.*

DEANS:

Department of Literature: Prof. G. HONDA.
Department of Science: Prof. F. TAKEMURA.
Department of Home Economics: Prof. M. OHGIDA.

NIIGATA UNIVERSITY

IKARASHI 2-NOCHO,
NIIGATA 950-21

Founded 1949.

President: S. KITAMURA.
Chief Administrative Officer: T. TEROUCHI.
Librarian: H. YAMADA.

Library: *see* Libraries.

Number of teachers: 965.
Number of students: 6,760.

Publications: *Journal of Economics, Journal of Law and Politics, Educational Science Memoirs, Acta Medica et Biologica* (in English), *Study of Cultural Science, Science Reports* (in English), *Niigata Dental Journal, Research Reports of the Engineering Faculty, Faculty of Agriculture Bulletin,* etc.

DEANS:

Faculty of Humanities: M. KUMON.
Faculty of Education: S. KORESAWA.
Faculty of Science: T. SOTOBAYASHI.
Faculty of Medicine: G. WATANABE.
Faculty of Dentistry: K. ISHIOKA.
Faculty of Engineering: N. SAITO.
Faculty of Agriculture: T. YAMADA.
General Education Department: K. TAKENOUCHI.
Brain Research Institute: K. UEKI, M.D.

OBIHIRO UNIVERSITY OF AGRICULTURE AND VETERINARY MEDICINE

INADA-CHO, OBIHIRO,
HOKKAIDO 080

Telephone: (48) 5111.

Founded 1949.

President: Y. NISHIKAWA.
Administrator: S. OONEDA.
Librarian: S. NISHIMURA.

Library of 94,485 vols.
Number of teachers: 137.
Number of students: 1,211.

OCHANOMIZU UNIVERSITY

1-1, OTSUKA, 2-CHOME,
BUNKYO-KU, TOKYO 112

Telephone: 943-3151.

Founded 1874; reorganized 1949 as National University.

President: S. INOUE.
Administrator: K. IKEDA.

Number of teachers: 239.
Number of students: 1,698.

DEANS:

Faculty of Letters and Education: M. SHIKI.
Faculty of Science: T. TACHIBANA.
Faculty of Home Economics: M. THUMORI.

OKAYAMA UNIVERSITY

TSUSHIMA, OKAYAMA

Telephone: Okayama 0862 (52) 1111.

Founded 1949.
State control.

Academic year: April to March (April-October, October-March).

President: K. KOSAKA.
Chief Secretary: M. INAGAKI.

Library: *see* Libraries.

Number of full-time teachers: 1,071.
Number of students: 7,768.

Publications: Bulletins and Journals of the Faculties.

DEANS:

Students: K. NAGAHORI.
School of Literature: F. SUGI.
School of Law: M. YAMAMOTO.
School of Economics: I. TANAKA.
School of Education: Y. KATAYAMA.
School of Science: K. HENMI.

Medical School: T. Oofuji.
School of Pharmaceutical Science: Y. Tanaka.
School of Dentistry: K. Nishijima.
School of Engineering: T. Misaki.
School of Agriculture: M. Shiroishi.
Department of General Education: H. Ueno.

PROFESSORS:

School of Literature:

Akahane, M., Japanese Literature
Fujikawa, K., English Literature
Fujinaka, M., Philosophy
Fukuda, J., Chinese Language and Literature
Hosoya, S., History of Philosophy
Kodama, A., German Literature
Kondo, Y., Archaeology
Konishi, K., Ethics
Moritaki, K., Geography
Oba, S., Cognitive Psychology
Otomo, S., Japanese Linguistics
Saito, T., Aesthetics and History of Art
Sugi, F., French Linguistics
Takeuchi, K., Linguistics
Tanabe, T., French Literature
Tsuboi, K., American Literature
Yasuda, K., History of Europe
Yoshida, A., History of Japan
Yoshinami, T., History of Asia

School of Law:

Abe, K., Civil Law
Abe, T., Civil Law
Agui, K., Labor Law
Eguchi, S., Penal Law
Fujii, T., Commercial Law
Handa, T., Political Science
Harano, A., Administrative Law
Inada, Y., Constitutional Law
Iwama, K., History of Asian Political Ideas
Kamiyama, T., Penal Law
Kawano, M., Social Security Law
Maruoka, M., Private International Law
Nakamura, O., International Law
Niyama, U., Commercial Law
Uematsu, H., Philosophy of Law
Uemura, A., Law of Civil Engineering
Ueno, M., Civil Law
Yamamoto, M., Civil Law

School of Economics:

Awaji, K., International Economy
Fujimoto, T., Econometrics
Habu, Y., Public Finance
Hashimoto, H., International Economics
Hatori, T., History of Economic Theory
Kajimoto, Y., Management
Kandachi, H., Economic History of Japan
Kurushima, Y., Principles of Political Economy
Matsuo, N., Economic History
Makai, Y., Labor Economics
Noda, T., Macro-economic Theory
Sakamoto, T., Public Finance
Takagi, A., Economic Theory
Takeshita, S., Accounting
Tanaka, I., Money and Banking
Urata, M., Statistics

School of Education:

Akita, S., Japanese Linguistics
Akiyama, K., Infant Education
Andoh, J., Instrumental Music
Fujimura, K., Vocal Music
Fukada, S., Home Economics Education
Hayashi, S., Clinical Medicine and Science of Nursing
Hiruta, J., Sculpture
Hosoda, K., Educational Psychology
Imura, S., Educational Sociology
Ishibashi, T., Health and Physical Education
Izawa, S., Psychology of Mentally Retarded Children
Kanamitsu, T., Nutrition Research
Katayama, Y., English Linguistics
Kihara, T., Educational Social Service
Kishida Y., Biology
Kumamoto, T., Art and Craft Education
Kuwata, H., Chemistry
Matsui, T., Japanese Literature
Matsuura, M., English Linguistics
Matsuura, Y., Fundamental Music
Mimuro, K., Physical Education
Miura, M., Economics
Mohri, S., Education of Mentally Retarded Children
Monma, T., Algebra and Geometry
Nagata, H., Japanese Language
Nakashima, Y., School Management
Nanba, R., Fundamental Medicine
Numano, T., Earth Science
Ohshio, S., Mathematics Education
Ohshima, I., European Painting
Okuno, S., Developmental Psychology
Ono, K., Science of Food
Sahashi, K., Physics
Sakata, H., Analytics and Applied Mathematics
Shimizu, K., Cubic Structure
Takahashi, T., Geography
Takashige, S., Geography
Takatori, K., Biology
Usui, S., Pathology of Mentally Retarded Children
Yamasaki, T., Physical Education
Yoshida, S., Art and Craft Education
Yoshida, T., Natural Science Education
Yukiyasu, S., Ethics

School of Science:

Asano, S., Solid State Physics
Enomoto, M., Microbial Genetics
Haisa, M., High Polymer Chemistry
Henmi, K., Geochemistry
Huzisige, H., Plant Physiology
Inokawa, S., Organic Chemistry
Kawahara, A., Mineralogy
Kobayashi, Y., Animal Morphology
Koseki, K., Topology
Mitsuno, C., Geology
Morimoto, T., Inorganic Chemistry
Mannari, I., Theoretical Physics
Morosawa, S., Synthetic and Physical Organic Chemistry
Nagahara, T., Applied Mathematics
Nasu, Y., Geometry
Nishimura, N., Physical Chemistry
Okazaki, S., Semiconductors and Electronics
Sato, R. Analysis
Seya, K., Geophysics
Sibsta, H., Nuclear Physics
Takemaru, T., Plant Morphology
Toei, K., Analytical Chemistry
Tominaga, H., Algebra
Tomishima, Y., Mathematical Physics
Yamada, O., Magnetism
Yamaguchi, T., Animal Physiology
Yoshida, M., Marine Biology
Yoshimoto, H., Plasma Physics

School of Medicine:

Aoyama, H., Hygiene
Awai, M., Pathology
Hori, Y., Physiology
Inatomi, S., Parasitology
Kanemasa, Y., Bacteriology
Kimoto, H., Paediatrics
Kimura, I., Internal Medicine
Kosaka, F., Anaesthesiology
Mathuo, N., Ophthalmology
Mizuhara, S., Biochemistry
Mori, A., Chemistry of Brain Function
Nagashima, H., Internal Medicine
Nakayama, S., Physiology
Nanikawa, S., Forensic Medicine
Nii, S., Virology
Niimi, K., Anatomy
Nishimoto, A., Neurosurgery
Nohara, N., Dermatology
Oda, T., Cancer Research Centre
Ogata, M., Public Health
Ogawa, K., Pathology
Ogura, Y., Oto-Rhino-Laryngology
Oofuji, T., Internal Medicine
Oomori, H., Urology
Orita, K., Surgery
Otahara, S., Developmental Neuroscience and Child Neurology
Otsuka, N., Anatomy
Otsuki, S., Neuro-Psychiatry
Ouchi, H., Anatomy
Saeki, K., Pharmacology
Satô, J., Cancer Research
Sekiba, K., Obstetrics and Gynaecology
Shômori, T., Chemistry of Brain Function
Tanabe, G., Orthopaedic Surgery
Teramoto, S., Surgery
Yabe, Y., Cancer Research Centre
Yamamoto, M., Radiation Medicine

School of Dentistry:

Adachi, A., Oral Physiology
Kishi, K., Dental Radiology
Nagai, H., Oral Anatomy
Nakago, T., Orthodontics
Nishishima, K., Oral Surgery

School of Pharmaceutical Sciences:

Fujita, Y., Pharmaceutical Physical Chemistry
Futai, M., Microbiological Chemistry
Goto, S., Pharmaceutics
Hayakawa, S., Pharmaceutical Chemistry
Hayatsu, H., Medicinal Chemistry
Makita, M., Hygienic Chemistry
Okuda, T., Pharmacognosy
Omori, S., Physiological Chemistry
Shinoda, S., Environmental Hygienic Chemistry
Tanaka, Y., Pharmaceutical Analytical Chemistry
Tasaka, K., Pharmacology
Yamamoto, I., Medicinal Biochemistry
Yamato, M., Synthetic Medicinal Chemistry

School of Engineering:

Abe, T., Material Design
Fujita, K., Machine Design
Fukui, K., Electronic Circuit Engineering
Furutani, Y., Physical Electronics
Hamada, H., Instrument and Control Engineering
Hashimoto, F., Applied Physics
Himei, T., Electrical Machinery
Hirai, T., Synthetic Inorganic Chemistry
Hirose, K., Hydrodynamics
Honda, H., Thermal Engineering
Honda, K., Material Mechanics
Kanamaru, F., Research Institute for Non-Crystalline Materials
Kasaoka, S., Chemical Reactor Engineering
Kikuchi, S., Industrial Management
Kometani, E., Transport Facilities
Kono, I., Construction Engineering and Materials
Misaki, T., Communication Engineering
Monobe, K., Polymer Chemistry
Mori, T., Analysis and Design of Structures

MORIWAKE, T., Synthetic Polymer Chemistry
MYOJIN, S., Transport Faculties
NAGO, H., Sanitary Engineering
NAKAJIMA, T., Precision Machining
NAKATA, T., Power Apparatus and Systems
SAYAMA, H., Process Design and Control
SANO, H., Electronics Machinery
OTA, M., Metallurgy
SHIMAMOTO, Y., Applied Thermodynamics
TAKAHASHI, K., Industrial Inorganic Chemistry
TAKAHASHI, T., Physical Chemistry and Chemical Engineering
TAKEDA, A., Industrial Organic Chemistry
TORII, S., Industrial Organic Chemistry
WADA, T., Automation and Control Engineering
YAMAMOTO, K., Theoretical Dynamics
YAMAMOTO, T., Electromagnetic Theory

School of Agriculture:
ENDO, S., Agricultural Machinery
FUKUDA, M., Food Production and Management
HORIGOME, T., Animal Nutrition
IMAI, K., Zymology
INO, T., Animal Genetics and Breeding
INOUE, R., Agricultural Practice
IWASA, J., Chemical Technology of Agricultural Products
KONISHI, K., Floriculture
KUROYANAGI, S., Landscape Architecture
MURAMATU, M., Plant Breeding
MASUDA, T., Olericulture
MESE, M., Resource Management
NAGAHORI, K., Land Reclamation
NAKAE, T., Animal Products Technology
NAKAMURA, R., Horticulture
OGO, T., Crop Plantation
OKU, H., Plant Pathology
SHIMAMURA, K., Pomology
SIMOSE, N., Soil and Fertilizers
SHIROISHI, M., Biochemistry
TORIUMI, T., Animal Hygiene
WADA, H., Animal Reproduction
WATANABE, T., Construction Engineering
YOMODA, A., Irrigation and Drainage
YOSHIDA, T., Applied Entomology

Department of General Education:
FUKUI, E., Music
FUNAHASHI, H., Philosophy
HASHIZUME, M., Geophysics
HAYAMA, N., Chemistry
HAYAMI, T., Chemistry
HAYASE, T., Politics
HIRAMATSU, M., Physics
HORINO, T., English
ISHIDA, Y., History
ISHIHARA, T., Geography
IRIE, K., English
IWACHIDO, T., Chemistry
KITAYAMA, T., Mathematics
KITTAKA, T., Physics
KONDO, T., English
KOSAKA, S., Literature
MAKINO, M., German
MUROYA, Y., English
NAKANO, T., German
NARITA, H., German
NODA, R., Mathematics
NUREKI, T., Geology
OMORI, H., Mathematics
OKABE, T., French
SADAKANE, N., Ethics
SHIGETA, J., Physics
TAKATA, T., Health and Physical Education
TERAO, T., German
TOMOTSU, M., Health and Physical Education
TSUTSUMI, A., Mathematics
UENO, H., Law
UESUGI, J., English
WAKIMOTO, K., Mathematics
WATANABE, M., Economics
WATANABE, M., Biology
YAMANE, Y., Biology
YUIHAMA, S., Geography

ATTACHED INSTITUTES:

Institute for Agricultural and Biological Sciences: 2-20-1 Chuo, Kurashikishi, Okayama-ken; f. 1914; affiliated 1953; Dir. Prof. Dr. T. SEO.

Institute for Thermal Spring Research: Misasa-cho, Tohaku-gun, Tottori-ken; f. 1937; affiliated 1949; Dir. Prof. H. SAKAI.

OSAKA UNIVERSITY

YAMADAKAMI, SUITA-SHI, OSAKA

Telephone: 06 (877) 5111.

Founded 1931.

Academic year: April to March.

President: Dr. YUICHI YAMAMURA.
Director: SADAO NAKANISHI.
Librarian: Dr. NOBUO YAMADA.

Libraries: ***see*** **Libraries.**

Number of teachers: 2,107, including 482 professors.

Number of students: 11,797.

Publications include: *Osaka Journal of Mathematics, Medical Journal, Law Review, Osaka Economic Papers, Dental School Journal, Memoirs of the Faculty of Pharmaceutical Sciences, Science Reports, Technology Reports, Memoirs of the Institute of Scientific and Industrial Research, Studies in Language and Culture,* reprint series, discussion papers, etc.

DEANS:

Faculty of Letters: YUTAKA NIYAJI.
Faculty of Human Sciences: KAZUE KODA.
Faculty of Law: SATOSHI TAKADA.
Faculty of Economics: SUSUMU KOIZUMI.
Faculty of Science: KIYOTERU OTOZAI.
Faculty of Medicine: YOSHIYA IWAMA.
Faculty of Dentistry: SHOZO KOTANI.
Faculty of Pharmaceutical Sciences: HEITARO IWATA.
Faculty of Engineering: SHOICHI NAKAMURA.
Faculty of Engineering Sciences: SHICHIRO TERANISHI.
Faculty of Language and Culture: TSUTOMU NAKAGAWA.
College of General Education: SHOJI SATO.

PROFESSORS:

Faculty of Letters:
HARA, K., French Literature
HIHARA, T., Chinese Philosophy
ISHIDA, A., Aesthetics
KATAYAMA, R., German Literature
KIMURA, S., History of Art II
KISHIHATA, Y., Ethics
KURODA, T., History of Japanese Thought
MIWA, M., Philosophy, History of Philosophy I
MIYAJI, Y., Japanese Linguistics
OKABE, T., European History
SHIBA, Y., East Asian Studies
TAKAHASHI, S., Philosophy, History of Philosophy II
TAKEDA, T., History of Art I
TANAKA, Y., Japanese Literature
TANIMURA, K., Musicology
TOKUGAWA, M., Social Linguistics
TOZU, T., Science of Literature
UMETANI, N., Japanese History
UEMURA, M., Modern European History
YAMADA, N., History of Asian Peoples
YAMAGUCHI, E., Indian Philosophy
YAMAKAWA, K., English Literature
YAMAZAKI, M., History of Performing Arts and Theatre Science
YAMORI, K., Comparative Cultures
YUASA, Y., Japanese Culture

Faculty of Human Sciences:
AOKI, T., Cultural Anthropology
ASO, M., Theory of Educational Planning
HIGUCHI, S., Industrial Psychology
KANEKO, T., Educational Organization and Administration
KAWAGUCHI, I., Comparative and Developmental Psychology
KAYANO, Y., Philosophical Anthropology
KODA, K., Empirical Sociology and Methods of Social Research
MATANO, S., Biological and Ecological Anthropology
MISUMI, J., Social Psychology
MIYAMOTO, K., Behavioural Engineering
MORITA, T., Philosophy of Education
MOTOKI, K., Theory of Out-of-School Education
NINOSEKI, T., Sociology of Education
NISHIDA, H., Theory Communication
OGIYA, S., Educational Technology
SHIMOKOCHI, M., Behavioural Physiology
SHIOBARA, T., Theoretical Sociology and History of Sociological Thought
TANAKA, SEIGO, Educational Psychology
TANAKA, SEISUKE, Theory of Social Groups and Organizational Sociology
TOKUNAGA, M., Foundation of Human Sciences

Faculty of Law:
HAMAGAMI, N., International Transaction Law and Civil Law II
KAKUDO, T., Constitutional Law
KAWASHIMA, Y., International Law
KUKI, T., Civil Law III
KUMAGAI, K., Japanese Legal History
MATSUSHIMA, J., Local Government Law, Tax Law
NAKANISHI, M., Commercial Law II
NAKANO, T., Civil Procedure
OKUBO, M., Public Administration
SAKANO, M., Political Science
TAKADA, S., Administrative Law
TAKADA, T., Criminal Procedure
TANAKA, S., Civil Law I
YAMAGUCHI, K., Commercial Law I
YAMANAKA, E., European and American Legal History
YASAKI, M., Jurisprudence

Faculty of Economics:
FUJITA, S., Public Finance
FUKUBA, Y., Business
HARADA, T., Japanese Economic History
HATANAKA, M., Statistics
KITANO, T., Business Administration

Institute of Social and Economic Research: Suita Campus, Yamada Kami, Suita City; Dir. KEN-ICHI INADA.

Welding Research Institute: Suita Campus, Yamada Kami, Suita City; Dir. YOSHIAKI ARATA.

OSAKA UNIVERSITY OF FOREIGN STUDIES

2734 AOMADANI, MINOO CITY, OSAKA PREFECTURE

Telephone: 06-772-1271.

Founded 1949.

President: YOSHITSUGU IJICHI.
Librarian: Prof. YOSHIO YAMADA.

Library of 232,000 vols.
Number of teachers: 130.
Number of students: 1,754 day courses, 1,009 evening course.

There is also a Graduate School.

UNIVERSITY OF THE RYUKYUS

1, 3-CHOME, TONOKURA-CHO, SHURI, NAHA, OKINAWA

Telephone: (0988) 87-0101.

Founded 1950.

Academic year: April to March (2 semesters).

President: Prof. KEN MIYAGI.
Business Manager: CHOJUN MAESHIRO.
Business Manager: C. MAESHIRO.
Dean of Students: Prof. TAKEHIKO KITSUKAWA.
Librarian: Prof. SEIKEN KOCHI.

Number of teachers: 583.
Number of students: 5,015.
Library of 309,858 vols.

DEANS:

College of Law and Literature: Prof. KEISHO SUNAGAWA.
College of Education: Prof. ASAO YARA.
College of Sciences: Prof. KIYOSHI YAMAZATO.
College of Engineering: Dr. HOSEI UEHARA.
College of Agriculture: Prof. HIROMI IZUMI.
Medical School: Dr. MASAMITSU OTSURU.
College of Health Science: Dr. KANZEN TERUYA.
General Education Division: Prof. IWAO MORI.
Director, Junior College: Prof. KENKI HESHIKI.

PROFESSORS:

College of Law and Literature:
ADANIYA, Y., Education
AGARIYE, N., Psychology
GAKIYA, R., Sociology
ISHIMINE, K., Civil Procedural Law
IYE, T., Sociology
KAMEKAWA, S., English Literature
KINJO, H., Law
KINJO, S., History
KISHABA, K., History
KOCHI, S., Law
KOMESU, O., English Literature
MIURA, K., Business Administration
MIYAZATO, S., Law
NAKASONE, K., Management
NAKAYAMA, M., Geography
NISHI, K., Economics
OTA, M., Sociology
SHIMABUKURO, K., Political Science
SHIMABUKURO, T., Commercial Law
SHIMABUKURO, Y., English Literature
SHIMAMURA, J., Business Administration
SHINJO, T., Law
SUNAGAWA, K., Law
SUNAGAWA, KEISHO, Economics
TASATO, Y., Geography
TERUYA, Y., History
UEMURA, Y., Japanese Language
YABIKU, H., English
YAMASHIRO, S., Economics
YAMAZATO, S., Economics
YONEMORI, Y., Philosophy
WAKUGAMI, M., Japanese Literature

College of Education:
AGARIE, Y., Psychology
AHAGON, N., History of Education
ARAKAKI, H., Home Economics
ARAKAKI, T., Home Economics
ASHIMINE, K., Fine Arts
ASHITOMI, C., Fine Arts
FUMIZAWA, Y., Psychology
HIGA, I., Mathematics
HIGA, T., Physical Education
HIGA, Y., Chemistry
HOKAMA, S., Physical Education
HOKAMA, Y., Home Economics
ISHIMINE, C., Music
KINJO, M., Physical Education
KITSUKAWA, T., Abnormal Child Psychology
KOJIMA, Y., Japanese Literature
MIYAGI, K., Fine Arts
NAGAHAMA, K., Science Education
NAKAIMA, S., Japanese Education
NAKAMATSU, T., Japanese Literature
NASHIRO, S., Psychology
NIRO, Y., Biology
NOHARA, T., Earth Science
OSHIRO, K., English
OSHIRO, S., Dyeing
SAKIYAMA, S., Electrical Engineering
SENAHA, E., English
SHIMABUKURO, S., Educational Administration
SHIROMA, S., Music
SHO, H., Home Economics
SUNAGAWA, K., English
TAMAKI, M., Education
TAMAKI, T., Educational System
TAMANAHA, S., Fine Arts
TAMINATO, C., History
UEHARA, S., Electronics
YARA, A., Physics

College of Sciences:
FUJIYAMA, T., Marine Environment
FURUSAWA, S., Biology
HOKAMA, K., Chemistry
IKEHARA, N., Biology
IKEHARA, S., Biology
ISHIKAWA, H., Mathematics
KADENA, Y., Physics
KANESHIMA, K., Chemistry
KATSURA, K., Chemistry
KINJO, A., Chemistry
KIZAKI, K., Earth Science
MAEHARA, R., Mathematics
MARUYAMA, S., Analysis
MATAYOSHI, S., Physics
TOMIKI, T., Physics
UJIIE, H., Oceanography
YAMAZATO, K., Biology
YONAHA, M., Mathematics

College of Engineering:
AFUSO, C., Electronics
GUSHI, K., Civil Engineering
HESHIKI, K., Mechanical Engineering
INAMI, T., Electrical Engineering
KONO, F., Civil Engineering
KYAN, S., Electronics
MAKISHI, K., Mechanical Engineering
MORITA, D., Construction Engineering
OSHIRO, T., Construction Engineering
UEMA, K., Civil Engineering
UEHARA, H., Civil Engineering
YAMASHITA, T., Electrical Engineering
YAMAZATO, E., Mechanical Engineering

Medical School:
KOBARI, K., Internal Medicine
OTSURU, M., Parasitology
TANAKA, S., Anatomy

College of Health Sciences:
AKAMATSU, T., Adult Health
IIBUCHI, Y., Epidemiology
IMAMURA, T., Microbiology
ITO, E., Pathology
MATSUZAKI, Y., Toxicology
MIYAGI, I., Medical Zoology
MIYAGI, K., Clinical Pathology
NAKADA, F., Biochemistry
NISHIDA, T., Rehabilitation
NISHIYAMA, I., Human Ecology
NOHARA, T., Health Sociology
SAKURAI, T., Health Nutrition
SANO, H., Anatomy
SASAKI, Y., Mental Hygiene
SUGIURA, M., Physiology
TAKENAKA, S., Children and Maternal Health
TERUYA, K., Health Administration

College of Agriculture:
AZUMA, S., Insectology
HOCAMA, K., Agricultural Chemistry
IZUMI, H., Agricultural Engineering
KODA, Y., Agricultural Engineering
MIYAGI, E., Animal Husbandry
MIYAZATO, K., Agricultural Chemistry
MIYAZATO, K., Agriculture
MOROMIZATO, S., Forestry
NAKADA, S., Agricultural Engineering
NAKASONE, H., Forestry
ODA, R., Animal Husbandry
OGIMI, C., Forestry
OYA, K., Soil Science
SHINJO, C., Agriculture
SHIROMA, M., Agricultural Engineering
SUNAGAWA, S., Forestry
TAKAHASHI, H., Animal Husbandry
TAMORI, M., Agriculture
TOKASHIKI, S., Animal Husbandry
TOYAMA, S., Agricultural Chemistry
YOMO, H., Biochemistry

General Education Division:
FURUKAWA, H., Earth Science
HIGA, C., English
KAKINOHANA, H., Law
MIYAGI, I., Physical Education
MORI, I., Chemistry
NAKASONE, I., Economics
NAKAZA, G., English
OSHIRO, S., Mathematics
SHINZATO, S., Physical Education
SHIROMA, M., History
TOMA, S., Chemistry
YAGI, S., English

Junior College:
HIGA, M., Anthropology
HIGA, Y., Philosophy
ISHIJIMA, S., Physics
ITO, F., English
MAEDA, G., Mechanical Engineering
NAKAHARA, T., Commercial Law

Attached Hospital:
HOKAMA, S., Clinical Examination
MIMURA, G., Internal Medicine

NISHIDA, T., Scientific Remedy
SHO, Y., External Medicine
SUZUKI, K., Regional Medicine
TAKEUCHI, S., Obstetrics and Gynaecology

ATTACHED INSTITUTES:

College of Health Sciences Hospital: 585 Yogi, Naha City, Okinawa; Dir. Dr. GORO MIURA.

Sesoko Marine Laboratory: 3422 Sesoko, Motobu-cho, Okinawa; attached to College of Sciences; Dir. Dr. KIYOSHI YAMAZATO.

Tropical Agriculture Research Facilities: 870 Taketomi-cho-Uehara, Iriomote, Yaeyama, Okinawa; attached to College of Agriculture; Dir. Dr. SHUSAI MOROMIZATO.

SAGA UNIVERSITY

HONJO-MACHI 1,
SAGA CITY
Telephone: 0952-24-5191.
Founded 1949.

President: KAZUYOSHI IKEDA.
Administrative Officer: TADASHI YASUGOCHI.
Librarian: MITSUO MAJIMA.

Library of 272,784 vols.
Number of teachers: 338.
Number of students: 76 graduate, 3,365 undergraduate.

DEANS:

Faculty of Education: MASAKI INOUE.
Faculty of Economics: KOZO WANI.
Faculty of Engineering: MASARU YAGI.
Faculty of Agriculture: JOSHINORI FUJII.
Faculty of General Education: FUMIO YAMAMOTO.

SAITAMA UNIVERSITY

255 SHIMO-OKUBO,
URAWA CITY

President: S. OKAMOTO.
Director of Administration: K. KAMATA.
Director of Library: AKIRA MATSUMOTO.
Director of Student Personnel: T. SUMI.

Library of over 323,000 vols.
Number of teachers: 401 full-time, 446 part-time.
Number of students: 5,697.
Publications: *Science Reports.*

DEANS:

Faculty of Liberal Arts: H. KANEKATSU.
Faculty of Education: KOJIRO KAMITAKI.
Faculty of Economics: HIRONARI OYAMA.
Faculty of Science: M. TAKEUCHI.
Faculty of Engineering: TOSHIE OKUMURA.
College of Liberal Arts: IWAO NAGANO.
Junior College of Economics: Y. SAKAIBARA.

SHIGA UNIVERSITY

1-1-1 BANBA, HIKONE-SHI,
SHIGA-KEN 522
Telephone: 0749-22-5600.
Founded 1949.

Rector: HAJIME KAWASAKI.
Registrar: HISANAKA OHARA.
Librarian: SUEJIRO NAKAMURA.

Library of 303,611 vols.
Number of teachers: 177.
Number of students: 2,787.

DEANS:

Faculty of Education: IMAO OKAMOTO.
Faculty of Economics: KATSUMI SHINDO.

ATTACHED INSTITUTES:

Institute of Lake Sciences: OSAMU ITASAKA.
Archives Museum: ISAO DENDA.

SHIMANE UNIVERSITY

1060 NISHIKAWATSU-CHO
MATSUE-SHI, SHIMANE-KEN
Telephone: (21) 7100.
Founded 1949.

President: K. MITANI.
Registrar: S. YAOITA.
Librarian: S. NAITO.

Library of 423,380 vols.
Number of teachers: 310.
Number of students: 3,515.

DEANS:

Faculty of Law and Literature: T. TAKEUCHI.
Faculty of Education: Y. NOZU.
Faculty of Science: M. YAMADA.
Faculty of Agriculture: I. YAMADA.

SHINSHU UNIVERSITY

ASAHI 3-1-1, MATSUMOTO,
NAGANO-KEN.
Telephone: (0263) 35-4600.
Founded 1949.

President: SEIICHI KATO.
Administrator: MASAO MOGI.

Number of full-time teachers: 954.
Number of students: 6,690.

DEANS:

Faculty of Arts: K. NAGAI.
Faculty of Science: M. YOKOI.
Faculty of Education: J. OKAMIYA.
Faculty of Medicine: R. FURIHATA.
Faculty of Engineering: N. DAIMON.
Faculty of Agriculture: T. IIJIMA.
Faculty of Textiles: N. HOJO.
Faculty of Liberal Arts: H. MATSUZAKI

SHIZUOKA UNIVERSITY

OOYA 836, SHIZUOKA-SHI 422
Telephone: Shizuoka 37-1111.
Founded 1949.

President: K. MARUYAMA.
Head of Secretariat: K. KAWAGUCHI.

Number of full-time teachers: 596.
Number of students: 7,175.

DEANS:

Faculty of Humanities: N. UEHARA.
Faculty of Education: A. WAKABAYASHI.
Faculty of Science: T. ISHI.
Faculty of Engineering: T. ARAI.
Faculty of Agriculture: S. KIRU.
College of General Education: K. KATO.
Research Institute of Electronics: K. MITSUHASHI.

TOHOKU UNIVERSITY

1-1-2-CHOME, KATAHIRA,
SENDAI
Telephone: Sendai 27-6200.
Founded 1907.

President: SIRO MAEDA.
Chief Administrative Officer: JUN IGARASHI.
Director of University Library: HIROSHI HARAFUJI.

Library: *see* Libraries.
Number of teachers: 2,587.
Number of students: 9,539 undergraduate, 1,910 graduate.

Publications: *Science Reports, Ecological Review, Bulletin of the Marine Biological Station of Asamushi, Tohuku Journal of Experimental Medicine, Tohuku Journal of Agricultural Research, Science Reports of the Research Institutes, Technology Reports, Reports of the Research Institute for Strength and Fracture of Materials, Reports of the Institute of High Speed Mechanics, Reports of the Research Institute of Electrical Communications.*

DEANS:

Faculty of Science: SHO ITO.
Faculty of Medicine: TAIZO SUZUKI.
Faculty of Dentistry: MASATOMO SAHEKI.
Faculty of Pharmaceutical Sciences: TETSUZO KATO.
Faculty of Engineering: TADASHI YAMAGUCHI.
Faculty of Law: ROKUYA SUZUKI.
Faculty of Arts and Letters: YOSHIO SAITO.
Faculty of Economics: TAKASHI SHIMADA.
Faculty of Education: TETSUNDO TSUKAMOTO.
Faculty of Agriculture: KENSUKE SHIMURA.
College of General Education: HIDEAKI OUCHI.

PROFESSORS:

Faculty of Arts and Letters:
IESAKA, K., Sociology
INOUE, S., Comparative Study Section
IWATA, Y., History of European Philosophy I
KAMATA, H., French Literature

KAMEI, H., Ethics
KANAYA, O., Chinese Philosophy
KASIWABARA, K., Contemporary Philosophy
KIKUTA, S., Japanese Literature
KUSUNOKI, M., Science and History of Religion
KUWAHARA, T., English Linguistics
MARUYAMA, K., Psychology
MINAMOTO, R., Fundamental Section
NISIDA, H., Aesthetics and History of Fine Arts
OGURI, H., German Literature
SAITO, Y., Sociology
SATO, I., European History I
SATO, K., Oriental History I
SEKI, A., Japanese History I
SERIZAWA, T., Archaeology
SIMURA, R., Chinese Literature
TAKIURA, S., History of European Philosophy II
TERADA, T., Oriental History II
TUKAMOTO, K., History of Indian Buddhism
TUZI, N., History of Oriental and Japanese Fine Arts
WATANABE, N., Japanese History II
YOSIOKA, A., European History II

Faculty of Education:
ARAI, T., History of Education
HOSOYA, J., Psychology of Personality and Learning
IWASHITA, S., Educational Administration
KOBAYASHI, M., Philosophy of Education
MAEHARA, H., School Curriculum and Teaching Method
MATSUI, I., School Administration
MATSUNO, Y., Mental Retardation Research
MIYAKAWA, T., Psychology of Childhood and Adolescence
NAGAFUCHI, M., Audiology and Speech Sciences
SASAKI, T., Sociology of Education
TAHARA, O., Sociology of Higher Education
TUKAMOTO, T., Adult Education
YAMASHITA, E., Science for the Visually Retarded

Faculty of Law:
ABE, J., Criminology
AOI, H., Legal Philosophy
FUJITA, T., Administrative Law I
HARAFUJI, H., Japanese Legal History
HATTORI, E., Commercial Law I
HAYASHIYA, R., Bankruptcy Law and Execution Law
HIGUCHI, Y., Comparative Constitutional Law
HIRONAKA, T., Civil Law I
HOKAO, K., Labour Law and Social Legislation
IKEDA, K., Comparative Politics
IKUYO, T., Civil Law III
KOJIMA, K., Constitutional Law
KOYAMA, S., Occidental Legal History
MIYATA, M., History of Political Theory
MOCHIZUKI, R., Anglo-American Law
ODANAKA, S., Criminal Procedure
OTA, T., Civil Law III
SEKIGUCHI, E., Political Science
SHOJI, K., Criminal Law
SUGAWARA, K., Commercial Law II
SUZUKI, R., Civil Law II
YAMAMOTO, S., International Law

Faculty of Economics:
HAGA, H., Economic Theory
HARASAWA, Y., Organization and Management
HATTORI, H., History of Political Economy
KAMIMURA, H., Auditing
KANADA, S., Economy of Japan
KATO, K., General Management
KIKUCHI, K., Accounting
KOSE, D., Management Analysis
MURAOKA, S., Money and Banking
OTUKI, M., Economic Policy
SHIMADA, T., Economic History
SHINOZUKA, N., Business History
TAKEUCHI, K., Marketing
TANAKA, K., Theory of Political Economy
TOKUNAGA, S., Social Policy
TOYOSHIMA, Y., Management Accounting
WATANABE, H., Agricultural Economics
YOSHIDA, S., Public Finance

Faculty of Science:
AOKI, K., Science of Petroleum Deposits
HIRASAWA, T., Seismology
HIWATASHI, K., Developmental Biology and Genetics
IGARI, S., Real Analysis
IIZUMI, S., Plant Ecology
ISHIKAWA, Y., Neutron Scattering and Solid State Physics
ISHIMATSU, T., Applied Nuclear Physics
ITAKURA, K., Human Geography
ITO, M., Quantum Chemistry
ITO, S., Analytical Organic Chemistry
KAMIYAMA, H., Geomagnetism and Geoelectricity
KASUYA, T., Theoretical Solid State Physics Magnetism and Solid State Physics
KATO, J., Functional Analysis
KIKUCHI, S., Theoretical Astronomy
KITAGAKI, T., High Energy Physics
KITAMURA, N., Geology
KODAKA, T., Historical Geology
KOHIMA, T., Optical Properties of Solids and Solid State Spectroscopy
KONDO, J., Meteorology
KONISHI, K., Physiological Chemistry
KOTAKE, T., Numerical Analysis
KURIHARA, Y., Environmental Biology and Animal Ecology
KURODA, T., Complex Analysis
MORITA, A., Solid State Physics
MORITA, S., Nuclear Physics
MUKAI, T., Organic Chemistry I
MUTO, Y., Physics of Iron and Steel III
NAKAGAWA, I., Theoretical Chemistry
NAKAJIMA, T., Physical Chemistry
ODA, T., Algebra
OHASHI, H., Plant Taxonomy and Morphology
OOTSUKA, T., Low Temperature Physics
OOYA, H., Geomagnetism and Geoelectricity
OSANAI, K., Environmental Biology and Animal Ecology
SAGAWA, T., X-ray and VUV Spectroscopy and Photo-electron Spectroscopy
SAITO, K., Coordination Chemistry
SAKURAI, H., Organic Chemistry
SATO, I., Theoretical High Energy Physics
SHIBAOKA, T., Cell and Plant Physiology
SHITARA, H., Physical Geography
SHODA, K., Nuclear Physics
SUGAKI, A., Science of Metallic Deposits
SUNAGAWA, I., Mineralogy
SUZUKI, J., Seismology
SUZUKI, N., Analytical Chemistry
TACHIKI, M., Physics of Iron and Steel I
TAKAGE, A., Seismology
TAKAKUBO, K., Astrophysics
TAKASE, K., Synthetic Organic Chemistry
TAKAYANGI, Y., Palaeontology
TAKEDA, G., Theory of Elementary Particles
TAMIYA, N., Bio-organic Chemistry
TANAKA, M., Meteorology
TANAKA, N., Inorganic Chemistry
TOBA, Y., Physical Oceanography
TORIZUKA, M., Nuclear Physics
TSUCHIKURA, T., Mathematical Statistics
TUZUKI, T., Statistical Physics and Solid State Physics
UEDA, M., Optical Properties of Solids
UEDA, Y., Petrology
WATANABE, D., Diffraction Physics
YOSHIDA, S., Nuclear Structure Theory
YOSHIZAWA, T., Differential Equations

Faculty of Medicine:
AKAISHI, S., Forensic Medicine
AMAHA, K., Anaesthesiology
ENDO, M., Pharmacology I
FUJISAKU, S., Hospital Administration
GOTO, Y., Internal Medicine III
HORIUCHI, T., Thoracic Cardiovascular Surgery
HOSHINO, F., Radiology
IKEDA, M., Environmental Health
ISHIDA, N., Bacteriology
ISHII, T., Anatomy I
KASAI, M., Surgery II
KAWAMOTO, K., Oto-Rhino-Laryngology
KIKUCHI, G., Biochemistry I
KOGURE, K., Division of Clinical Neurology
KYOGOKU, M., Pathology I
MIZUNO, K., Ophthalmology
MORI, T., Anatomy III
NAKAHAMA, H., Division of Neurophysiology
NAKAMURA, R., Rehabilitation Medicine
OKUMA, T., Psychiatry and Neurology
ORIKASA, S., Urology
SAKKA, M., Radiation Research
SASANO, N., Pathology II
SATO, T., Surgery I
SEIJI, M., Dermatology
SUZUKI, J., Division of Osneurosurgery
SUZUKI, M., Obstetrics and Gynaecology
SUZUKI, T., Applied Physiology
TADA, K., Paediatrics
TAIRA, N., Pharmacology II
TAKISHIMA, T., Internal Medicine I
TASAKI, K., Physiology II
WAKAMATSU, E., Orthopaedic Surgery
YAMAMOTO, T., Anatomy II
YOSHINAGA, K., Internal Medicine II
YOSHIZAWA, Z., Biochemistry II

Faculty of Dentistry:
AOKI, T., Oral Physiology
HAYASHI, S., Oral Surgery I
HORIUCHI, H., Endodontics & Periodontics I
KAGAYAMA, M., Oral Anatomy II
KAMIYAMA, K., Pedondotics
KANUMA, A., Prosthetic Dentistry II
KAWAKAMI, M., Dental Material Science
KUMAGAI, K., Oral Microbiology
OGURA, Y., Dental Pharmacology
OKUDA, R., Endodontics & Periodontics II
SAHEKI, M., Oral Anatomy I
SAKAMOTO, T., Orthodontics
SANJO, D., Oral Diagnosis & Dental Radiology
SHIMADA, Y., Preventive Dentistry
TEJIMA, T., Oral Surgery II
YAMADA, T., Oral Biochemistry
YAMAMOTO, H., Oral Pathology
YOSHIDA, K., Prosthetic Dentistry I

Faculty of Pharmacy:
HASHIMOTO, Y., Hygienic Chemistry
HIKINO, H., Natural Products Chemistry
KAMETANI, T., Organic Chemistry
KATO, T., Pharmaceutical Chemistry
NAMBARA, T., Analytical Chemistry
NOZOE, S., Pharmacognosy
OSA, T., Physical Chemistry

TAKANO, S., Synthetic Organic Chemistry
TSURUFUJI, S., Biochemistry
YAMANAKA, H., Heterocyclic Chemistry

Faculty of Engineering:
ABE, H., Stress and Elasticity
ADACHI, S., Electromagnetic Theory
AITA, K., Basic Physical Chemistry
AMANO, A., Industrial Organic Chemistry III
ANAYAMA, T., Electrical Engineering Science
ATSUMI, A., Theory of Elasticity and Continuum Mechanics
AZAGAMI, T., Non-ferrous Extractive Metallurgy
BANYA, S., Chemical Metallurgy
CHIBA, S., Applied Mechanics
CHUBACHI, N., Electrical Measurement
EJIMA, T., Electrometallurgy
FUKUDA, T., Highway Engineering
GOTO, Y., Concrete Engineering
HAKOMORI, K., Automatic Control
HASEGAWA, F., Building Equipments
HASHIMOTO, H., Industrial Organic Chemistry II
HIGUCHI, T., Electronic Control
HIRAI, M., Applied Optics
HIRANO, K., Metal Physics
HIROIKE, K., Applied Mathematics
HOJO, H., Mechanical Control Engineering
HONMA, M., Special Materials
HORIE, C., Applied Solid State Physics I
HOSHIKO, Y., Information Device
IGAKI, K., Chemistry of Metals
IKAWA, K., Foundry Engineering
IKEDA, T., Applied Electrodynamics
IMAIZUMI, S., Applied Organic Chemistry
INOUE, Y., Nuclear Fuel Technology
ISHIHAMA, W., Exploitation Plant Engineering
ITO, T., Information Device
IWASAKI, T., Coastal Hydraulics
IZUMI, M., Building Mechanics
KAKEHI, K., Architectural Planning II
KARASHIMA, S., Strength of Metals
KATSURA, S., Applied Mathematical Physics
KAWASAKI, T., Theory of Machine and Design Analysis
KAWASHIMA, T., Exploitation Machinery
KAYABA, T., Materials and Mechanical Technology
KIMURA, M., System Engineering
KIYONO, S., Applied Radiation Technology
KOBAYASHI, R., Rock Mechanics
KURANISHI, S., Bridge Engineering
KUWANA, T., Welding Engineering
MAEKAWA, I., Institute for Strength and Fracture of Materials Division I
MASUDA, Y., Power Metallurgy
MATSUI, S., Precision Machining
MATSUO, M., Solid State Physics
MATSUMOTO, J., Pollution Control Engineering
MITO, S., Fundamentals of Machinework
MURAKAMI, K., Electrical Power Application
MUSHIAKE, Y., High Frequency
NAGAI, N., Measurement and Instrument Technology
NAGAO, S., Reactor Materials Engineering
NISHIYAMA, T., Fluid Mechanics
NISHIZAWA, T., Physical Metallurgy
OGINO, Y., High Temperature and High Pressure
OHARA, H., Mechanics of Plastic Solids
OKABE, T., Industrial Inorganic Chemistry
OSAKA, Y., Structural Engineering
OTANI, S., Chemical Engineering I
OTSUKA, Y., Internal Combustion Engine
SAITO, H., Dynamics of Machinery and Machine Design
SAITO, N., Circuit Theory
SAITO, S., Chemical Engineering Thermodynamics
SAKAI, T., Precision Machinery
SATAKE, M., Strength of Materials and Structural Mechanics
SATO, A., Water Engineering
SATO, N., Gaseous Electronics and Plasma Physics
SATO, R., Information Transmission
SATO, T., Architectural History and Design
SAWAYA, T., Process Control
SETO, K., Nuclear Chemical Engineering
SHIBATA, Y., Electron Devices
SHIGA, T., Building Construction
SHIGEI, Y., Computer Engineering
SHIMADA, H., Mechanical Metallurgy
SHIMIZU, H., Electroacoustics
SHIMOIIZAKA, J., Mineral Processing
SHUDO, N., Fluvial Hydraulics
SONE, T., Communication System
SUDA, H., Experimental Mechanics
SUDO, H., Structural Materials
SUETAKA, W., Interface Science of Metals
SUGIYAMA, K., Nuclear Measurements and Instrumentation
SUZUKI, M., Chemical Engineering II
TADAKI, T., Reaction Engineering
TAKAGI, T., Applied Electrical Measurement and Instrumentation
TAKAHASHI, H., Plastic Working of Metals
TAKAHASHI, M., Applied Solid State Physics II
TAKEDA, H., Control Theory
TAKEYAMA, T., Heat and Thermodynamics
TAKIMOTO, N., Engineering Mechanics
TOBE, T., Precision Machine Elements
TOSHIMA, S., Electrochemistry
TSUCHIKAWA, T., Materials for Precision Machinery
UCHIYAMA, K., Building Disaster Prevention
UMEYA, K., Silicate Chemistry
WAKIYAMA, T., Solid State Physics
YAMAGUCHI, T., Industrial Organic Chemistry I
YOKOBORI, T., Mechanical Behaviour of Materials
YOKOYAMA, H., Mineral Material Engineering
YOTSUYANAGI, T., Industrial Analytical Chemistry

Faculty of Agriculture:
ADACHI, S., Animal Products Technology
HATA, M., Fishery Chemistry
HAYASHI, K., Grass Land Utilization
HORI, Y., Horticulture
KANEDA, T., Food Chemistry, Food Science
KATSUNO, M., Animal Hygiene
KAWASAKI, T., Fishery Biology
KIKUMOTO, T., Farm Management
KIMURA, S., Chemistry of Nutrition
MASAKI, J., Animal Reproduction
MATSUDA, K., Chemurgy and Applied Biochemistry
MATSUMOTO, T., Animal Nutrition
MEGURO, H., Analytical Chemistry of Organic Compounds, Food Chemistry
MIZUMA, Y., Animal Breeding
NISHIZAWA, S., Oceanography
NOMURA, T., Propagation Biology
OHIRA, K., Plant Nutrition
SAKAI, H., Crop Science
SATO, K., Crop Science
SHIBASAKI, K., Food Preservation
SHIMURA, K., Biochemistry
SHOJI, S., Edaphology
TAKAHASHI, H., Applied Microbiology
TAMATE, H., Animal Morphology
TSUDA, T., Animal Physiology
TSUNODA, S., Plant Breeding
YAMANAKA, S., Plant Pathology
YAMASHITA, K., Pesticides Chemistry
YASUMOTO, T., Food Hygiene

College of General Education:
ABE, H., English
ABE, T., Chemistry
AMAKO, Y., Chemistry
ANO, F., English
ARAI, M., Chemistry
ASAO, T., Chemistry
ESASHI, Y., Biological Science
FUJITA, M., German
FUKUDA, Y., Physics
FURUTA, J., Philosophy
HARA, J., French
HOSOYA, T., Sociology
INOUE, N., Chemistry
IWATA, K., Mathematics
IWATA, T., Physics
IZUMIDA, T., French
KANISAWA, S., Earth Science
KANNO, K., Law
KATANO, T., Japanese Literature and Language
KATO, E., Law
KATO, T., Chemistry
KATO, T., Philosophy
KAWAKAMI, M., Geography
KITAMURA, J., Health and Physical Education
KOBAYASHI, I., Ethics
KONDO, I., Philosophy
KUSHIDA, T., German
MATSUNO, Y., Japanese Literature and Language
MISONOU, Y., Mathematics
MOCHIZUKI, N., Mathematics
MORI, H., Sociology
NAKAMURA, K., German
NEMOTO, Y., English
ODA, M., English
ODA, S., Ethics
OGAWA, A., English
OHASHI, T., German
OIDE, K., Earth Science
OKAWARA, J., German
OKI, T., French
ONUKI, Y., Physics
OTOMO, Y., English
OUCHI, H., Economics
SASAYA, T., German
SAITO, T., Mathematics
SATO, M., German
SATO, S., Japanese History
SATO, T., Psychology
SHIBATA, S., Chemistry
SHIRAI, T., English
SOUMA, K., Biological Science
SUGAHARA, K., English
SUGANO, S., Economics
SUZUKI, M., Physics
SUZUKI, Y., Mathematics
TAKAHASHI, T., Japanese History
TAKEMARU, K., English
TAKEUCHI, T., Biological Science
TSUSHIMA, S., Sociology
WADA, H., Mathematics
WATANABE, H., European and Oriental History
WATANABE, Y., Philosophy
YAGI, H., Economics
YAMAGUCHI, S., Chemistry
YAMAOKA, K., Earth Science
YOKOYAMA, I., English
YOSHIDA, K., Physics

ATTACHED INSTITUTES:

Chemical Research Institute of Non-Aqueous Solutions: f. 1944; Dir. YASUKATU TAMAI; publ. *HOKOKU* (yearly).

Institute for Agricultural Research: f. 1939; Dir. M. KANDA; publs. *Bulletin* (2 a year) and *Reports* (annual).

Institute of High Speed Mechanics: f. 1943; Dir. M. HONDA; publ. *Reports* (annual).

Research Institute for Iron, Steel and Other Metals: f. 1919; Dir. E. TANAKA; publ. *Science Report, Series A* (6 a year).

Research Institute for Scientific Measurements: 19 Sanjo-machi, Sendai City, Miyagi; f. 1943; Dir. K. KAMIYOSHI; publ. *Bulletin* (3 a year).

Research Institute of Electrical Communication: f. 1935; Dir. TADASHI TAKAHASHI; publs. *The Record* (quarterly), *The Report* (quarterly).

Research Institute of Mineral Dressing and Metallurgy: f. 1941; Dir. M. OTANI; publs. *Bulletin* (2 a year), *The Science Reports, Series A* (6 a year).

Research Institute for Tuberculosis and Cancer: Hirose-Machi, Sendai-City, Miyagi; f. 1941; Dir. H. SATO; publ. *Science Reports, Series C* (quarterly).

UNIVERSITY OF TOKUSHIMA

24 SHINKURA-CHO 2-CHOME,
TOKUSHIMA-SHI,
TOKUSHIMA-KEN
Telephone: (22) 5131.

Founded 1949.

State control; Academic year: April to March.

President: Y. OKA, M.D.
Bureau of Student Affairs: T. TANAKA, D.SC.
Registrar: T. ONO.
Librarian: S. TAKEJI, M.D.

Number of full-time teachers: 647.
Number of students: 4,140.

Publications: Scientific Papers, Faculty Journals.

DEANS:

Faculty of Education: T. HIRASHIMA.
School of Dentistry: Y. TAKEDA, M.D.
School of Medicine: N. KATUNUMA, M.D.
Faculty of Pharmaceutical Sciences: Y. ISHIDA, PH.D.
Faculty of Engineering: T. SOEDA, D.ENG.
College of General Education: M. HONKE, D.LITT.

PROFESSORS:

Faculty of Education:

BANDO, F., Sculpture
ETO, T., Composition
GOTO, S., PH.D., Economics
HAMAGUCHI, M., D.SC., Physics
HIRAKI, M., Educational Sociology
HIRASHIMA, T., Mathematics Education
HONDA, H., M.LITT., Japanese Literature
ICHIMIYA, S., M.ED., Education of Mentally Retarded Children
IKUTA, Y., Physiology and Hygiene
INUBUSHI, H., D.V.M., Science of Agriculture
ISHII, H., Instrumental Music
ITSUKI, M., Teaching of Physical and Health Education
IWASAKI, M., D.SC., Geology
KAWANO, K., D.ENG., Mechanics
KIMURA, A., M.D., Basic Medicine
KISHIDA, M., D.LITT., Educational Psychology
KIYOMURA, T., English Language Education
KONDO, T., Vocal Music
MAEHARA, T., Music Education
MATSUURA, Y., Development Psychology
MIYAMOTO, M., Social Science Education
MURAI, M., Pedagogy
MURATA, S., M.D., Fundamental Nursing
NAKAGAWA, T., D.SC., Geology
OKA, Y., M.D., Basic Medicine
OKAMOTO, T., Theory and History of Physical Education
OMURA, Y., Science of Clothing
ORITANI, K., English Philology
SATO, K., Industrial Arts Education
SHIMODA, I., D.SC., Analytics and Applied Mathematics
SHIMOIZUMI, M., D.SC., Biology
TAKAGI, H., Geography
TAKAHASHI, T., Course of Study for Kindergarten
TAKEJI, S., D.LITT., Chinese Classics
TAKEMURA, K., Pedagogy
TAMANO, K., Practice of Physical Education
TANAKA, A., D.ED., History of Education
TANIGUCHI, H., PH.D., Nursery Teachers Training
TSURUTA, S., History
UCHIWA, N., M.D., Adult Nursing
WAKI, T., D.SC., Chemistry
YOSHIMORI, A., Vocal Music
YOSHINARI, T., Nursing

School of Medicine:

AKI, K., M.D., Enzyme Regulation
DAIKOKU, S., M.D., Anatomy
HAGIHIRA, H., M.D., Clinico-Pathological Nutrition
HIZAWA, K., M.D., Pathology
ICHIHARA, A., M.D., Enzyme Pathology
IGATA, T., M.D., Orthopaedic Surgery
IKUTA, T., M.D., Psychiatry and Neurology
INOUE, G., M.D., Nutritional Physiology
INOUE, K., M.D., Surgery
KATUNUMA, N., M.D., Enzyme Chemistry
KAWAMURA, F., M.D., Radiology
KAWATA, T., M.D., Food Hygiene
KISHINO, Y., M.D., Applied Nutrition
KOMI, N., M.D., Surgery
KUROKAWA, K., M.D., Urology
MAEIWA, M., M.D., Forensic Medicine
MATSUMOTO, J., M.D., Physiology
MATSUMOTO, K., M.D., Neurosurgery
MIYAO, M., M.D., Paediatrics
MIYOSHI, T., M.D., Public Health
MORI, H., M.D., Internal Medicine
MOTOKAWA, Y., M.D., Enzyme Physiology
NATORI, Y., D.SC., Nutritional Chemistry
NIIYAMA, Y., M.D., Special Nutrition
NISHIYAMA, K., M.D., Hygiene
OKA, M., PH.D., Pharmacology
OSAKI, H., M.D., Parasitology
OUNISHI, Y., M.D., Bacteriology
OUSAKI, K., M.D., Oto-Rhino-Laryngology
OUTSUKA ,H., M.D., Pathology
SAITO, S., Laboratory Medicine
SAITO, T., M.D., Anaesthesiology
SASAOKA, K., D.AGR., Foods Science
TAKEDA, K., M.D., Dermatology
TSUBURA, E., M.D., Internal Medicine
UCHIDA, T., M.D., Virology
YAMADA, M., M.D., Anatomy
YAMAMOTO, S., M.D., Biochemistry

School of Dentistry:

BANDO, E., D.D., Fixed Prosthodontics
FUKUI, K., M.D., Microbiology
ISHIDA, H., D.D., Pharmacology
KATSURA, S., M.D., Oral Anatomy I
KAWATA, T., D.D., Orthodontics
KOMORI, A., D.D., Oral Pathology
KUWAYAMA, N., D.D., Dental Engineering
MATSUMOTO, N., D.D., Removable Prosthodontics
NAKAMURA, R., D.D., Preventive Dentistry
NISHINO, M., D.D., Operative Dentistry
SATO, M., M.D., Oral and Maxillofacial Surgery II
TAKADA, M., D.SC., Oral Physiology
TAKAGI, T., D.SC., Oral Anatomy II
TAKEDA, Y., M.D., Biochemistry
TSUTSUI, H., M.D., Oral and Maxillofacial Surgery I
UEMURA, S., M.D., Oral Radiology
WAKANO, Y., D.D., Periodontology and Endodontology

Faculty of Pharmaceutical Sciences:

AKITA, T., PH.D., Chemical and Pharmaceutical Technology
FUJITA, T., PH.D., Bio-organic Chemistry
ISHIDA, Y., PH.D., Chemical Pharmacology
KAMETANI, F., PH.D., Pharmaceutical Physical Chemistry
KAWATA, J., PH.D., Biochemistry
KOBAYASHI, S. PH.D., Pharmaceutical Chemistry
KUBOTA, S., PH.D., Synthetic Pharmaceutical Chemistry
MATSUURA, H., M.D., Pharmaceutics
SHIMOMURA, S., PH.D., Pharmaceutical Analytical Chemistry
TANI, I., M.D., Microbial Chemistry
TOMIMATSU, T., PH.D., Pharmacognosy
TSUKATANI, H., PH.D., Hygienic and Forensic Chemistry
YAMASHITA, T., D.SC., Pharmaceutical Engineering

Faculty of Engineering:

AKIZONO, K., D.ENG., Mechanical Behaviour of Materials
FUJIWARA, H., D.ENG., Precision Measurement
GOSYO, Y., D.ENG., Vacuum-tube and Gaseous Electronics
HISANO, T., D.SC., Inorganic Chemistry and Electrochemistry
INADA, S., D.ENG., Engineering Materials and Strength of Materials
KANDA, S., D.SC., Physical Chemistry
KASEI, S., D.ENG., Precision Machining
KINNO, H., D.ENG. Automatic Control
KOBAYASHI, K., D.ENG., Electronic Control Engineering
KOONO, K., D.ENG., Concrete Engineering
MASUMURA, M., D.SC., Organic Chemistry
MATSUI, K., D.ENG., Chemical Plants and Chemical Engineering Materials
MITSUI, H., D.ENG., Hydraulics and Water Works
MORIMOTO, S., D.SC., Chemical Reaction Engineering
ODA, E., D.ENG., Geotechnical Engineering
OKAZAKI, T., D.ENG., Unit Operation

OKITSU, H., D.ENG., Electrical Machines and Apparatus
SADAI, Y., D.ENG., City and Regional Planning
SATO, M., D.SC., Applied Physics
SAWADA, K., D.ENG., Highway and Railway Engineering
SHIMADA, R., D.ENG., Basic Information Science
SHINOHARA, Y., D.SC., Applied Mathematics
SOEDA, T., D.ENG., Dynamics of Machines and Design of Machine Elements
SUGIO, S., D.ENG., Disaster Prevention Engineering
SYOMAN, T., D.ENG., Planning and Programming Engineering
TADA, O., D.ENG., Solid-State Electronics
TAKAHASHI, Y., D.ENG., Applied Information Science
TANAKA, T., D.SC., Applied Mathematics
TOMITA, Y., D.ENG., Data Processing Engineering
URAKAWA, K., D.ENG., Heat Engineering
USHIDA, T., D.ENG., Communications Engineering
WATANABE, T., D.ENG., Fluid Mechanics
YOKOI, Y., D.ENG., Electric Power Engineering

College of General Education:
BABA, T., M.LITT., German
GOTO, K., German
GOTO, T., D.SC., Biology
HATTORI, T., D.SC., Physics
HAYASHI, K., M.LL., Law
HONKE, M., D.LITT., Philosophy
ICHIJO, Y., D.SC., Mathematics
IMADA, Y., Health and Physical Education
ISHII, T., D.SC., Biology
ISHIODORI, T., M.LITT., History
ITO, H., D.SC., Chemistry
ITO, M., D.LITT., Psychology
ITO, Y., M.SC., Mathematics
KANAYA, H., M.LITT., Sociology
KIMURA, A., M.LITT., German
KURODA, H., Health and Physical Education
MATSUMOTO, M., D.SC., Chemistry
MATSUSHITA, M., M.LITT., English
MOTOKI, Y., M.LITT., English
OKABE, T., Economics
OUNISHI, S., Geography
SETO, Y., English
SUYARI, K., D.SC., Earth Science
SUZUKI, T., M.LL., Politics
TAGA, S., Mathematics
TANIZAKI, T., M.LITT., English
TODA, H., M.LITT., Ethics
YAGI, S., D.SC., Biology
YAMAGUCHI, H., D.SC., Physics

THE UNIVERSITY OF TOKYO

HONGO, BUNKYO-KU, TOKYO

Central Telephone: 812-2111.

Telegraphic Address: Tokuniv.

Founded 1877.

President: T. MUKAIBO.
Administrator: T. MOCHIZUKI.
Librarian: S. FUJIWARA.

Library: *see* **Libraries.**

Number of teachers: 3,892, including 881 **professors.**

Number of students: 19,012.

DEANS:

College of General Education: H. ISODA.
Faculty of Law: N. ASHIBE.
Faculty of Economics: R. KOMIYA.
Faculty of Letters: M. SHIBATA.
Faculty of Education: M. SAJI.
Faculty of Engineering: Y. HISAMATSU.
Faculty of Science: K. NISHIJIMA.
Faculty of Agriculture: K. HEMMI.
Faculty of Medicine: T. ODA.
Faculty of Pharmaceutical Sciences: S. NOJIMA.

PROFESSORS:

College of General Education:
ABE, R., Physics
AOYAGI, K., English
ARAI, S., Classical Languages
ARAKI, S., French
EBARA, N., Chemistry
ETO, S., International Relations
FUJII, Y., Physics
FUJIMOTO, A., German
FUJIMOTO, F., Physics
FUJISAKI, G., Mathematics
FUKUI, Y., French
FURUTA, T., Japanese Literature
HAGA, T., Comparative Literature and French
HAMADA, T., Palaeontology
HARA, M., Graphics
HARA, N., Biology
HARADA, N., Law
HASIGUTI, M., English
HATTORI, A., Mathematics
HAYASHI, S. Statistics
HAYASHI, T., Biology
HIDAKA, H., English
HIRAKAWA, S., Comparative Literature and French
HIRANO, K., English
HIRATA, H., Physical Education
HIROTA, K., Physical Education
HONMA, N., English
INAOKA, K., Japanese Literature
INOUE, T., Greek Philosophy
ISO, K., Chemistry
ISODA, H., Graphics
ISOGAI, Y., Biology
ITO, K., Biology
ITO, K., Chinese
ITO, S., History and Philosophy of Science
ITO, T., Physics
IWAMOTO, F., Physics
IWAMURA, Y., German
IZUYAMA, T., Physics
KAJI, M., Economics
KATAYAMA, M., Chemistry
KATORI, H., Psychology
KAWAHARA, T., German
KIKUCHI, M., International Relations
KIMURA, S., European History
KOBAYASHI, Y., French
KOIDE, S., Physics
KOIKE, K., English
KOJIMA, S., Chinese History
KOMATSUBARA, S., English
KONDO, T., Mathematics
KOSHINA, Y., German
KOYAMA, H., Japanese Literature
KUBO, S., Chemistry
KUMON, S., International Relations
KURODA, S., Mathematics
KURODA, Y., Physical Education
MAEDA, K., German
MASUDA, S., Spanish, English
MASUMI, T., Physics
MATSUSHIMA, S., Sociology
MINATO, H., Mineralogy
MIZUNO, Y., Physics
MOHRI, H., Biology
MORIMOTO, K., French
MURAKAMI, Y., Statistics
NAGAI, Y., English
NAGAO, R., Law
NAKAMURA, J., Physics
NAKAMURA, T., Statistics
NAKAMURA, T., Mathematics
NAKANORI, K., English
NANBARA, M., German
NAONO, A., Russian
NIIRO, F., Mathematics
NISHI, Y., German
NISHIKAWA, O., Human Geography
NOMURA, Y., Chemistry
OBI, S., Astronomy
OCHI, H., Japanese Literature
ODAJIMA, Y., English
OGINO, K., Polymer Chemistry
OHBAYASI, T., Cultural Anthropology
OHMORI, S., History and Philosophy of Science
OHUCHI, A., Chemistry
OHZEKI, K., Biology
OIKAWA, K., Mathematics
ONODERA, K., German
SAEKI, S., English, Comparative Literature
SAITO, M. Mathematics
SATO, J., Russian
SATO, S., Political Science
SATO, T., Ethics
SEKI, K., German
SENGOKU, T., German
SHIGI, T., German
SHIMOMURA, S., English
SHIRAI, M., Chemistry
SHIROTSUKA, N., History of Social Thought
SUEKI, T., Philosophy
SUGIURA, M., Mathematics
SUGIYAMA, T., English
SUGIYAMA, Y., German
SUZUKI, H., Chemistry
TAKAHASI, Y., English
TAKEDA, A., Chinese Classics
TAKITA, F., French
TAKIZAWA, H., Physical Education
TAMAMUSHI, S., German
TANAKA, M., English
TERADA, K., Cultural Anthropology
TERASAWA, T., Physics
TERASAWA, Y., English
TODA, M., English
TORII, S., Psychology
TSUCHIYA, S., Physical Organic Chemistry
TSUESHITA, R., Philosophy
TSUJI, H., German
TSUKAMOTO, T., Economics
TSUTSUI, W., Law
UCHIDA, T., Economics
UCHIGAKI, K., German
UEHARA, T., Chinese History
UENO, T., Mathematics
WATANABE, A., International Relations
WATANABE, M., French
WATANABE, T., Physical Education
YAJIMA, K., History of Social Thought
YAMADA, M., Biology
YAMAMOTO, A., German
YAMASHITA, H., German
YAMAZAKI, K., Mathematics
YAMAZAKI, M., D.SC., Chemistry
YURA, K., English
YONEKAWA, T., Russian
YOSHIDA, T., Cultural Anthropology
YOSHIOKA, K., Chemistry
YUGE, T., Western History

Faculty of Law:
AOMI, J., Philosophy of Law
AOYAMA, Y., Civil Procedure
ASHIBE, N., Constitutional Law
FUKUDA, K., History of Political Theory
HIRAI, Y., Civil Law
HIRANO, R., Criminal Law
HOSHINO, E., Civil Law

ISHII, S., Japanese Legal History
KANEKO, H., Tax Law
KATAOKA, T., Roman Law
KATO, I., Civil Law
KOBAYASHI, N., Constitutional Law
KYOGOKU, J., Political Process
MATSUMOTO, S., History of Japanese Political Thought
MATSUO, K., Criminal Law
MIKAZUKI, A., Judicial Administration
MITANI, T., Japanese Political and Diplomatic History
MURAKAMI, J., German Law
NAITO, K., Criminology
NISHIO, M., Science of Public Administration
OGAWA, I., Administrative Law
OKA, Y., Political Science
OHTORI, T., Commercial Law
ROKUMOTO, K., Sociology
SAITO, M., American Political and Diplomatic History
SAKAMOTO, Y., International Politics
SASAKI, T., History of Political Theory
SHIGA, S., Oriental Legal History
SHINDO, K., Civil Procedure
SHINOHARA, H., European Political History
SHIONO, H., Administrative Law
TAKEUCHI, A., Commercial Law
TANAKA, H., Anglo-American Law
TANIUCHI, Y., Comparative Government
TERASAWA, H., International Law
UCHIDA, H., Law of International Organizations
YAMAGUCHI, T., French Law
YONEKURA, A., Civil Law

Faculty of Economics:

EMURA, M., Accounting
HAYASHI, T., Public Finance
HIZEN, E., German Economic History
HYODO, T., Labour Economics
ITOH, M., Economic Theory
KAIZUKA, K., Public Finance, Money and Banking
KATO, S., Japanese Economy
KOMIYA, R., International Trade
MOROI, K., Accounting and Financial Management
MORITA, K., International Economics
NAKAGAWA, K., Business History
NAKAMURA, M., Econometrics
NAKANISHI, Y., Industrial Relations
NEGISHI, T., Economic Theory
OISHI, Y., Economic Theory and Statistics
OKAMOTO, Y., Business Administration
OKANO, Y., Transportation Economics
ONO, E., Economic Policy
OUCHI, T., Agricultural Economics
SAEKI, N., Agricultural Economics
SATO, S., Public Finance
SEKIGUCHI, Y., Western Economic History
SUZUKI, Y., Mathematical Statistics
TACHI, R., Money and Finance
TAKAHASHI, A., Developing Economics and Asian Studies
TAKEUCHI, K., Statistics
TAKUMI, M., Economic Theory
TSUCHIYA, M., Business Administration
TSUMAGARI, N., Accounting
UZAWA, H., Economic Dynamics
YAMAGUCHI, S., Economic Theory

Faculty of Letters:

AKIYAMA, K., Ancient Japanese Literature
BITO, M., Japanese History
HAMAKAWA, S., German Language
HARA, M., Sanskrit Language and Literature
HASEGAWA, K., English Linguistics
HAYASHIMA, K., Buddhism
IMAMICHI, T., Aesthetics
ISII, S., Medieval Japanese History
ITO, S., Chinese Literature
KAZAMA, K., Indo-European Linguistics
KUBO, M., Classical Language and Literature
KURODA, W., Philosophy
MAENO, N., Chinese Literature
MIZUHARA, T., Sociology
MIYOSHI, Y., Modern Japanese Literature
MORI, M., North Asian History
NAGAZUMI, A., South East Asian History
NARUSE, O., Modern History of Europe
NINOMIYA, T., French Language and Literature
OGURA, Y., Ethics
OYAMA, T., Perception (Psychology)
SAGARA, T., Ethics
SHIBATA, M., Modern European History
SHONO, K., German Literature
TAKAHASHI, A., Studies into Public Opinion and Propaganda
TAKAMATSU, Y., English Literature
TAKASAKI, J., Indian Philosophy
TAKASHINA, S., History of Western Art
TAMURA, Y., Indian Philosophy
TANAKA, M., Chinese History
TOGAWA, Y., Chinese Philosophy
TOMINAGA, K., Economic and Industrial Sociology
TSUKISHIMA, H., Ancient Japanese Language
TUCHIDA, N., Japanese History
TUJIMURA, A., Sociology
UMEOKA, Y., Psychology
WAKIMOTO, T., Psychological Study of Religion
WATANABE, J., Philosophy
YAMADA, J., French Language and Literature
YAMAGUCHI, Z., Tibetan Language
YAMAMOTO, M., Philosophy
YAMANOI, Y., Chinese Philosophy
YANAGAWA, K., Sociology of Religion
YOSHIDA, T., Social Theories

Faculty of Education:

AZUMA, H., Methods of Education
EBASHI, S., Physical Education
HIDANO, T., Educational Psychology
HORIO, T., Science of Education
INAGAKI, T., Methods of Education
MATSUBARA, H., Educational Sociology
MIYASAKA, K., Adult Education and Youth Services
SAJI, M., Clinical Psychology
SIBA, S., Educational Measurement
SIBATA, Y., Curriculum
TERASAKI, M., History of Japanese Education
URATA, T., Library Science
USUI, M., Adult Education and Youth Services
YAMANOUCHI, T., Comparative Education

Faculty of Engineering:

ABE, H., Structure of Metals
AIHARA, Y., Aerodynamics
AKASHI, K., Electrometallurgy
AKITA, K., Combustion and Safety Engineering
AKIYAMA, M., Reactor Heat Transfer
AKIYAMA, M., Communication Systems Design and Switching Engineering
AN, S., Nuclear Reactor Engineering
ANDO, Y., Nuclear Propulsion and Structural Engineering
AOKI, M., Physical Electronics
AOKI, R., Powder Technology
AOYAMA, H., Reinforced Concrete Structure, Structural Dynamics
ASABA, T., Gas Phase Reaction Kinetics and High Temperature Chemical Physics
CHIJIIWA, K., Casting, Welding, Plastic Working
DOYAMA, M., Applied Solid State Physics
FUEKI, K., Solid State Chemistry
FUJII, S., Automatic Control and Mechanical Vibrations
FUJISAKI, H., Human Information Processing and Artificial Intelligence
FUJITA, K., Sanitary Engineering
FUJITA, T., Iron and Steel Materials
FUJITA, Y., Ship Welding and Construction
FUNAKUBO, H., Functional Materials and Elements, Bio-engineering
GOTO, S., Non-ferrous Extractive Metallurgy
HANAMURA, E., Solid State Physics
HARA, K., Precision Measurement, Fundamental Constants and Cryogenics
HASEGAWA, M., Solid State Organic Chemistry, Polymer Chemistry
HAYAMA, S., Gas Turbine and Flow-induced Vibrations
HIGASA, T., City Planning
HIGUCHI, Y., Construction Materials
HIRAI, H., Industrial Physical Chemistry, Polymer Chemistry
HIRAKAWA, S., Petroleum Reservoir Engineering
HISAMATSU, Y., Surface Technology
HIRATA, M., Marine Engineering and Heat Transfer
HOKAO, Z., Fire Jet Technology and Coal Mining
HONDA, K., Electrochemistry, Photochemistry
HONGO, K., Design of Machine Elements
HORI, Y., Machine Construction
HORIKAWA, K., Harbour and Coastal Engineering
HYODO, S., Mechanical Properties of Solids
IGATA, N., Strength of Materials
IGUCHI, M., Automobile and Railway Vehicle Engineering
IIDA, K., Strength of Ocean Structure
IINUMA, K., Combustion and Aero-engines
IMAIZUMI, T., Mineral Processing
INAGAKI, E., History of Architecture
INOSE, H., Electronic Systems
INOUE, H., Chemical Reaction Engineering
INOUE, S., Polymer Chemistry, Organometallic Chemistry
IRI, M., Mathematical Engineering
ISHIHARA, K., Soil Mechanics and Foundation Engineering
ISHII, T., System Engineering and Management Science
ISHII, Y., Exploration Geophysics
ITO, M., Bridge and Structural Engineering
JIMBO, Y., Precision Machinery and Vibration
KAJITANI, H., Ship Resistance and Propulsion
KAMIYA, Y., Hydrocarbon Chemistry and Catalytic Reaction
KANAZAWA, T., Strength of Materials
KANNO, M., Nuclear Reactor Materials
KATO, B., Welding, Steel Structure
KATO, H., High Speed Dynamics of Ships
KATO, K., Dynamics of Flight and Control Theory
KATTO, Y., Heat and Mass Transfer and Two-Phase Flow
KAWAKAMI, H., City Planning
KAWAZOE, K., Transport Phenomena and Absorption Engineering
KAYA, Y., Control and System Science
KIMURA, I., Aero-space Propulsion
KIMURA, Y., Metal Casting

KINOSHITA, N., Production of Precision Machinery and Electrical Machining
KISHITANI, K., Materials Engineering and Fire Science
KITAMORI, T., Measurement and Control Engineering
KIYOSE, R., Nuclear Chemical Engineering
KOBAYASHI, S., Dynamics of Aircraft and Spacecraft Structures
KODA, T., Solid State Physics
KOUNO, T., High Voltage Engineering
KOYAMA, T., Merchant Ship Design
KUME, H., Quality Control and Statistical Process Analysis
KUNII, D., Heat Transfer Operations, Fluidization Engineering
MAEDA, T., Precision Machinery and Plastic Working
MAKI, F., Architectural Design
MASUDA, S., Electrical Power Application and Applied Electrostatics
MATSUMOTO, J., Sanitary Engineering
MATSUMOTO, Y., Transportation and Railway Engineering
MATSUZAKI, K., Polymer, Fibre Chemistry
MISHIMA, Y., Nuclear Fuels and Metallurgy
MIURA, H., Mechanics and Dynamics of Machines
MIYAGAWA, M., Mechanical Metallurgy
MIYAKAWA, H., Information Theory
MIYAUCHI, T., Mass Transfer Operations
MORI, D., Astronautics, Structural Dynamics
MOTOOKA, T., Electronic Digital Computer, Digital Control
MOTORA, S., Dynamics of Ships
NAGAO, T., Materials and Machine Tool Processing
NAGUMO, J., Mathematical Engineering and Cybernetics
NAKAMURA, H., Surveying and Regional Planning
NIITANI, Y., Urban Transportation Planning
NIKI, E., Instrumental Analytical Chemistry, Inorganic Materials
NISHIMATSU, Y., Mining Machinery and Rock Mechanics
NISHIMURA, H., Environmental System Engineering
NISHINO, F., Applied Mechanics
NOMURA, T., Air Conditioning, Meteorology of Buildings
OHASHI, H., Fluids Engineering and Turbo-machinery
OHSAKI, Y., Soil Dynamics, Foundation Engineering
OKAMURA, H., Strength of Materials
OKANO, K., Physics of Polymers and Liquid Crystals
OKOSHI, T., Microwave and Optoelectronics
OKUNO, T., Applied Statistics, Multivariate Analysis
OSHIMA, K., Applied Radiation Chemistry, Nuclear Reactor Chemistry and Cryogenic Engineering
OSHIMA, N., Mathematical Engineering, Continuum Physics
OTANI, S., Urban Design
SAITO, T., Thermodynamics, Heat Engineering
SANO, N., Iron and Steelmaking
SATA, T., Material Processing and Manufacturing System Analysis
SEKIGUCHI, A., Nuclear Radiation Measurements
SEKIGUCHI, T., Theory and Application of Plasmas
SEKINE, Y., System Theory and Power Engineering
SHIMOFUSA, K., Housing
SHIOIRI, J., Aeroengines, Aircraft Materials
SOMA, T., Metallurgical Reaction Engineering
SOMEYA, T., Internal Combustion Engines
SUGANO, T., Semi-conductor Electronics
SUZUKI, H. Non-ferrous Metals and Alloys
SUZUKI, S., Architectural Planning and Design
TABATA, Y., Radiation and Nuclear Chemistry, and Polymer Chemistry
TAGORI, T., Control, Fluid Engineering and Propulsion
TAKAHASI, Y., River Engineering and Hydrology
TAKAMI, H., Hydrodynamics and Applied Mathematics
TAKANO, A., Aerodynamics
TAKANO, M., Dynamics of Mechanisms
TAKATA, H., Aeroengines
TAKEHANA, M., Special Ship Design
TAKENOUCHI, S., Mining Geology and Applied Mineralogy
TAMURA, T., Nuclear Reactor Engineering, Applied Radiation Chemistry
TANABE, Y., Solid State Physics
TANAKA, S., Solid State Physics and its Application
TANAKA, S., Applied Optics
TANAKA, S., Organic Analytical Chemistry
TOGO, Y., Nuclear Reactor Engineering
TOMINAGA, G., Vacuum Engineering
TOMINAGA, H., Reaction Kinetics and Petroleum Chemistry
TOYOTA, H., Measurement and Control in Industry, Remote Sensing
TSUDA, K., Internal Combustion Engines
UCHIDA, T., Nuclear Fusion Engineering
UCHIDA, Y., Building Construction
UCHIDA, Y., Organometallic Chemistry
UCHIO, T., Marine Geology and Marine Mineral Resources
UEDA, T., Steam Engineering, Two Phase Flow
UTSUNOMIYA, T., Electronic Circuit Applications
UYEMURA, T., Image Technology and High-Speed Photography
WADA, E., Software Engineering
WADA, Y., Polymer Physics, Physical Acoustics
WASHIZU, K., Dynamics of Flight and Aeroelasticity
YAMAGUCHI, U., Metal Mining and Rock Mechanics
YAMAMOTO, Y., Strength of Ships
YAMASAKI, H., Instruments and Control Engineering, Flow Measurement
YANAGIDA, H., Applied Mineral Chemistry
YANAI, H., Semiconductor Electronics
YONEDA, Y., Industrial Catalytic Chemistry
YOSHIDA, T., Chemistry of Hazardous Materials
YOSHIKAWA, H., General Design Theory
YOSHIKAWA, S., Coordination Chemistry, Organic Chemistry

Faculty of Science:

ANRAKU, Y., Membrane Biochemistry and Bioenergetics
ARIMA, A., Theoretical Physics
EBASHI, S., Biophysics
EGAMI, N., Radiation Biology
FUJII, T., High Energy Physics
FUJITA, H., Functional Analysis, Numerical Analysis
FUJIWARA, S., Analytical Chemistry
FUKUSHIMA, N., Geomagnetism
FURUYA, M., Developmental Biology and Photobiology
FUWA, K., Inorganic Chemistry
GAMBO, K., Meteorology
GOTO, E., Information Science
HANAI, T., Palaeontology
HANIHARA, K., Physical Anthropology
HASIMOTO, H., Physics of Fluids
HATTORI, A., Algebraic Topology
HIRAKAWA, H., Electromagnetism and Relativity
HORI, G., Celestial Mechanics
IHARA, Y., Number Theory
IIDA, S., Magnetism
IIJIMA, A., Sedimentary Petrology
IINO, T., Microbial Genetics and Molecular Biology
IIYAMA, T., Petrology, Mineralogy and Applied Geology
INAMOTO, N., Organic Chemistry
ITÔ, S., Functional Analysis, Probability
IWAHORI, N., Theory of Groups
KAMIMURA, H., Solid State Physics Theory
KIMURA, T., Historical and Structural Geology
KIMURA, T., Differential Equations
KINOSHITA, S., Cell Biology
KOMATSU, H., Functional Analysis, Differential Equations
KOSHIBA, M., High Energy Particle Physics
KUCHITSU, K., Physical Chemistry
KUNII, TOSIYASU L., Information Science
KURODA, H., Physical Chemistry
KUSHIRO, I., Petrology
KUWABARA, G., Optics
MIYAMOTO, K., Plasma Physics
MIYAZAWA, H., Quantum Mechanics
MIYAZAWA, T., Biophysical Chemistry
MIZUNO, T., Experimental Embryology
MUKAIYAMA, T., Organic Chemistry
NAGATA, Y., Physical Oceanography
NISHIJIMA, K., Theory of Elementary Particles
NODA, H., Biophysical Chemistry
OGUTI, T., Radiowave Geophysics
OKADA, Y., Molecular Biology
OKI, M., Organic Chemistry
OMOTO, K., Human Genetics
OZIMA, M., Geomagnetism and Geochronology
SADANAGA, R., Crystallography, Mineralogy
SAEKI, T., Plant Ecology
SAKAGUCHI, Y., Physical and Regional Geography
SAKAI, H., Cellular Biochemistry
SASAKI, W., Solid State Physics
SASAKI, Y., Inorganic Chemistry
SATO, R., Theory on Seismic Waves
SHIMODA, K., Experimental Physics
SUZUKI, HIDEJI, Solid State Physics
TAKAHASHI, K., Animal Physiology
TAKAHASHI, T., Organic Chemistry
TAKAKURA, T., Radio Astronomy
TAKEUCHI, H., Solid Geophysics
TAKÉUCHI, Y., X-ray Crystallography, Mineralogy
TAMAO, T., Space Plasma Physics
TAMARU, K., Physical Chemistry
TAMURA, I., Differential Topology
TASUMI, M., Physical Chemistry
TAZAWA, M., Plant Cell Physiology
TERAYAMA, H., Biochemistry, Developmental Biology, Cell Biology
TOMINAGA, T., Radiochemistry
UEDA, K., Behavioral Biology
UEMURA, Y., Solid State Physics
UNNO, W., Theoretical Astrophysics
WADA, A., Biophysics
WADA, Y., Solid State Physics
YAMADA, M. H., Information Science
YAMAGUCHI, Y., High Energy and Nuclear Physics
YAMAZAKI, T., Nuclear Physics
YAMAZAKI, T., Taxonomy

YONEDA, N., Information Science
YOSHIKAWA, T., Physical Geography, **Regional Geography**

Faculty of Agriculture:

ASANO, I., Wood Physics
BEPPU, T., Microbiology and Fermentation
DOI, J., Centre of Environment Regulation System for Agriculture
FUJIWARA, K., Veterinary Pathology
GOO, M., University Forests
HAMAYA, T., Forest Biology
HANYU, I., Fish Physiology
HASHIMOTO, K., Marine Biochemistry
HATANO, K., University Forests
HEMMI, K., Agricultural Economics
HIRANO, R., Fisheries Oceanography
HIRATA, T., Forest Management
HOMMA, K., Veterinary Physiology
HOSOKAWA, A., Agricultural Processing Machinery
IWATA, M., Horticulture
KADOYA, T., Pulp and Paper Science
KAMIIZAKA, M., Forest Utilization
KANAZAWA, N., Farm Management
KANO, Y., University Stock Farm
KATO, H., Food Chemistry
KATO, Y., Agricultural Finance
KITAMURA, F., Landscape Architecture
KITANI, O., Farm Power and Machinery
KONOSU, S., Marine Biochemistry
KUMAZAWA, K., Plant Nutrition and Fertilizers
MAEZAWA, K., Forest Management
MARUYAMA, Y., Biochemistry
MATSUMOTO, Y., Applied Entomology
MINODA, Y., Utilization of Microorganisms
MORI, K., Organic Chemistry
MOTIZUKI, K., Veterinary Anatomy
MURATA, Y., Crop Science
NAITO, H., Nutritional Chemistry and Animal Nutrition
NAKAJIMA, T., Plant Breeding and Genetics
NAKANO, J., Wood Chemistry
NOSE, Y., Fisheries Biology
OGATA, M. Veterinary Microbiology
OOTA, T., Enzymology
SAIO, K., Biometrics
SAKAMOTO, K., Agricultural Policy
SAWAZAKI, H., Animal Management and Hygiene
SHIINA, S., Agricultural History
SHIMIZU, C., Fisheries Laboratory
SHIMURA, H., Agricultural Hydrology
SHIRAI, K., Soil Physics and Soil Hydrology
SHODA, Y., Animal Breeding
SUGIYAMA, H., Wood-based Material
SZUUKI, A., Bio-organic Chemistry
TACHIBANA, K., Forest Zoology
TACHIBANA, K., Environment Control in Agriculture
TAKAHASI, N., Pesticide Chemistry
TAKAI, Y., Soil Science
TAKENAKA, H., Farm Land Reclamation and Conservation
TAMURA, G., Microbiology
TODA, S., Analytical Chemistry
TOMODA, I., Veterinary Medicine and Parasitology
TUNODA, K., Experimental Farms
TUTUI, M., Forest Policy
URAKAWA, N., Veterinary Pharmacology
USUI, K., Veterinary Medicine and Parasitology
WATANABE, A., University Forests
YAMAGUCHI, H., Radiation Genetics
YAMAGUCHI, I., Forest Hydrology and Erosion Control
YAMAUCHI, K., Chemistry and Technology of Animal Products
YAMAZAKI, K., Plant Ecology and Morphogenesis
YANO, K., Radiation Genetics
YANO, T., Food Engineering
YORA, K., Plant Pathology
YOSHIMOTO, T., Forest Chemistry
YOSHITAKE, N., Sericulture

Faculty of Medicine:

ATSUMI, K., Medical Electronics
EBASHI, S., Pharmacology
FUKUDA, O., Plastic Surgery
FURUKAWA, T., Medical Electronics
HARASAWA, M., Geriatrics
HIRAYAMA, M., Maternal and Child Health
HORIUCHI, Y., Physical Therapy
HOSHI, T., Physiology
HOSOYA, N., Nutrition
IMAHORI, K., Biochemistry
INADA, Y., Anaesthetics
ITO, M., Physiology
KANEMITSU, A., Neuroanatomy
KAZIRO, Y., Chemistry
KOBAYASHI, N., Paediatrics
KOIZUMI, A., Public Health
KONDŌ, Y., Surgery
KOSAKA, K., Medicine
KUKITA, A., Dermatology
KUROKAWA, M., Neurobiochemistry
KUSAMA, S., Surgery
MAEDA, K., Epidemiology, Hygiene and Preventive Medicine
MANO, Y., Nutrition
MIKI, T., Forensic Medicine
MISHIMA, S., Ophthalmology
MIYASAKA, T., Health Sociology
MORI, W., Pathology
MURAO, S., Medicine
NEGISHI, T., Adult Health
NIIJIMA, T., Urology
NOMURA, Y., Otolaryngology
ODA, T., Medicine
OGATA, E., Medicine
OHTANI, S., Medicine
OKADA, S., Radiation Biophysics, Cell **Biology**
OOE, T., Anatomy
SAIGUSA, M., Thoracic Surgery
SAITO, M., Medical Electronics
SAITO, S., Speech Therapy
SAKAI, F., Pharmacology
SAKAMOTO, S., Obstetrics and Gynaecology
SANO, K., Neurosurgery
SASAKI, S., Physical Therapy
SAWASHIMA, M., Logopaedics and Phoniatrics
SHIMAMINE, T., Pathology
SHIMAZU, H., Neurophysiology
SUZUKI, T., Human Ecology
TADA, T., Serology
TAMURA, Z., Pharmacology
TANAKA, T., Health Administration
TASAKA, A., Radiology
TOYOKURA, Y., Medicine
TSUMITA, T., Cell Chemistry
TSUYAMA, N., Orthopaedic Surgery
TSUZUKI, M., Surgery
WADA, T., Surgery
YAMADA, E., Anatomy
YAMAKAWA, T., Biochemistry
YAMAMOTO, S., Epidemiology, Hygiene and Preventive Medicine
YAMAMOTO, T., Neuropathology
YAMANAKA, M., Medicine
YAMAUCHI, A., Anatomy
YOSHIZAWA, Y., Radiology

Faculty of Pharmaceutical Sciences:

FUKUDA, H., Toxicology and Pharmacology
HANANO, M., Pharmaceutics
HIROBE, M., Bio-organic and Medicinal Chemistry
IITAKA, Y., Physico-Chemical Analysis
KASUYA, U., Chemical Pharmacology
KOGA, K., Pharmaceutical Technochemistry
NATORI, S., Microbial Chemistry
NOJIMA, S., Hygienic and Forensic Chemistry
OHNO, M., Pharmaceutical Synthetic Chemistry
OKAMOTO, T., Pharmaceutical Chemistry
OSAWA, T., Chemical Toxicology and Immunochemistry
SANKAWA, U., Pharmacognosy and Plant Chemistry
SHIMIZU, H., Physico-chemical Technology
TAMURA, Z., Pharmaceutical Analytical Chemistry
TSUBOI, M., Physical Chemistry
YAMADA, M., Physiological Chemistry

ATTACHED INSTITUTES:

Cosmic Ray Laboratory: 3-2-1, Midori-cho, Tanashi-shi, Tokyo; f. 1953; Dir. S. MIYAKE.

Earthquake Research Institute: 1-1-1 Yayoi, Bunkyo-ku, Tokyo; f. 1925; Dir. K. KASAHARA; publ. *Bulletin* (quarterly).

Historiographical Institute: *see* Learned Societies.

Institute for Nuclear Study: University of Tokyo, Midori-cho 3-chome, Tanashi, Yokyo; f. 1955; Dir. K. SUGIMOTO; publs. *Annual Report* and *INS-J* (irregularly).

Institute for Solid State Physics: 22-1 Roppongi 7-chome, Minato-ku, Tokyo; f. 1957; Dir. K. YOSIDA; publ. *Technical Report:* (60 a year).

Institute of Applied Microbiology: 1-1-1 Yayoi, Bunkyo-ku, Tokyo; f. 1953; Dir. S. KOGA; publs. *Reports* (annually) and *Journal of General and Applied Microbiology* (bi-monthly).

Institute of Industrial Science: 7-22-1 Roppongi, Minato-ku, Tokyo 106; f. 1949; Dir. H. TANAKA; publ. *Report* (6 to 8 a year).

Institute of Journalism: f. 1949; Dir. M. INABA; publ. *Bulletin* (annually).

Institute of Medical Science: Shirokanedai, Minato-ku, Tokyo-108; f. 1892; Dir. T. TSUMITA; publs. *The Japanese Journal of Experimental Medicine* (6 issues a year) and *The Japanese Journal of Tuberculosis and Chest Diseases* (2 a year).

Institute of Oriental Culture: f. 1941; Dir. C. NAKANE; publs. *Memoirs* (3 a year), *Asian Culture* (annually).

Institute of Social Science: f. 1946; Dir. I. FUJITA; publs. *Journal of Social Science* (6 issues a year), *Annals of the Institute of Social Science.*

Institute of Space and Aeronautical Science: 4-6-1 Komaba, Meguro-ku, Tokyo; f. 1964; Dir. T. NOMURA; publs. *Report* (irregularly) and *Bulletin* (quarterly).

Ocean Research Institute: 15-1, 1, chome, Minamidai, Nakano-ku-Tokyo; f. 1962; Dir. N. NASU; publs. *Bulletin* (irregularly), *Preliminary Cruise Report* (irregularly).

Tokyo Astronomical Observatory: *See* under Research Institutes.

TOKYO INSTITUTE OF TECHNOLOGY
(Tokyo Kogyo Daigaku)

12-1, 2-CHOME, O-OKAYAMA,
MEGURO-KU, TOKYO
Telephone: 03-726-1111.
Telex: 2466360 TITECH J.
Founded 1881.

President: S. SAITO.
Director-General: T. YOKOE.
Dean of Students: S. KOKUSHO.
Librarian: E. INOUE.

Library of 428,672 vols.
Number of full-time teachers: *c.* 970.
Number of students: *c.* 4,957.

Publication: *Tokyo Kogyo Daigaku Gakuho* (Bulletin including Reports from attached Research Laboratories; Resources Utilization, Precision Machinery and Electronics, Engineering Materials, Nuclear Power; annually).

DEANS:

Faculty of Science: T. OGUCHI.
Faculty of Engineering: T. SEKIGUCHI.
Graduate School at Nagatsuta: H. KOBAYASHI.

DIRECTORS:

Research Laboratory of Resources Utilization: M. OKAWARA.
Research Laboratory of Precision Machinery and Electronics: Y. IKEBE.
Research Laboratory of Engineering Materials: T. SATA.
Research Laboratory for Nuclear Reactors: Y. TAKASHIMA.
Research Laboratory of Resources Recycling Processes: H. KUBOTA.
Research Laboratory of Hydrothermal Synthesis: S. SOMIYA.

TOKYO MEDICAL AND DENTAL UNIVERSITY

5-45, YUSHIMA 1-CHOME
BUNKYO-KU, TOKYO 113
Telephone: 03-813-6111.
Founded 1946.
Academic year: April to March (two semesters).

President: H. YOSHIDA.
Chief Secretary: I. HEIMA.
Chief Librarian: H. MANNEN.

The library contains *c.* 133,200 vols.
Number of teachers: *c.* 624.
Number of students: *c.* 1,194.

Publications: *Bulletin, Bulletin of the Department of General Education, Reports of the Medical Research Institute, Reports of the Institute for Medical and Dental Engineering.*

DEANS:

Faculty of Medicine: R. KANO.
Faculty of Dentistry: G. ISHIKAWA.
Department of General Education: K. SHIMAO.

HEADS OF DEPARTMENTS:

Faculty of Medicine:
Anatomy 1: K. WAKE.
Anatomy 2: T. SATO.
Anatomy 3: H. MANNEN.
Physiology: T. FURUKAWA.
Biochemistry 1: M. NAKAO.
Biochemistry 2: S. HANDA.
Pharmacology: M. OTSUKA.
Pathology 1: S. HATAKEYAMA.
Pathology 2: T. KASUGA.
Microbiology: R. NAKAYA.
Hygiene: S. IMAMURA.
Public Health: H. MAEDA.
Medical Zoology: R. KANO.
Forensic Medicine: M. OKAJIMA.
Internal Medicine 1: H. MOMOI.
Internal Medicine 2: J. TAKEUCHI.
Internal Medicine 3: H. MAEZAWA.
Neurology: H. TSUKAGOSHI.
Neuropsychiatry: Y. SHIMAZONO.
Paediatrics: J. YATA.
Surgery 1: T. MURAKAMI.
Surgery 2: K. ASANO.
Neurosurgery: Y. INABA.
Orthopaedic Surgery: K. FURUYA.
Dermatology: S. KAGAWA.
Urology: M. YOKOKAWA.
Ophthalmology: T. TOKORO.
Oto-Rhino-Laryngology: I. WATANABE.
Radiology: S. SUZUKI.
Obstetrics and Gynaecology: M. SAITO.
Anaesthesiology: E. IKEZONO.

Faculty of Dentistry:
Oral Anatomy 1: T. KIRONI.
Oral Anatomy 2: T. ICHIJO.
Oral Physiology: M. ICHIOKA.
Biochemistry: S. SASAKI.
Oral Pathology: G. ISHIKAWA.
Oral Microbiology: T. HORIKAWA.
Dental Pharmacology: H. OGURA.
Dental Technology 1: S. NOMOTO.
Dental Technology 2: A. SATO.
Preventive Dentistry and Oral Hygiene: S. OKADA.
Conservative Dentistry 1: T. FUSAYAMA.
Conservative Dentistry 2: S. KINOSHITA.
Conservative Dentistry 3: I. SUNADA.
Oral Surgery 1: S. SHIODA.
Oral Surgery 2: H. ITO.
Prosthodontics 1: M. AI.
Prosthodontics 2: T. TABATA.
Prosthodontics 3: T. HAYASHI.
Orthodontics: F. MIURA.
Pedodontics: H. ONO.
Dental Radiology: T. NAKAMURA.
Anatomy: K. KUBOTA.
Dental Anaesthesiology: Y. KUBOTA.

ATTACHED INSTITUTES:

Institute for Medical and Dental Engineering: 3-10, Kandasurugadai 2-chome, Chiyoda-ku, Tokyo 101; Dir. A. MURAMATSU.

Medical Research Institute: 3-10, Kandasurugadai 2-chome, Chiyoda-ku, Tokyo 101; Dir. F. YANAGISAWA.

TOKYO NATIONAL UNIVERSITY OF FINE ARTS AND MUSIC

UENO PARK, TAITO-KU, TOKYO
Telephone: 03-828-6111.
Founded 1949.

President: N. FUKUI.

Library: *see* Libraries.
Number of full-time teachers: 183.
Number of students: 2,587.

TOKYO UNIVERSITY OF AGRICULTURE AND TECHNOLOGY

1-8 HARUMI-CHO, 3-CHOME,
FUCHU-SHI, TOKYO 183

Courses in Agriculture and Textile Engineering.

TOKYO UNIVERSITY OF FISHERIES

KONAN 4-5-7, MINATO-KU,
TOKYO 108
Telephone: 03 (471) 1251.
Founded 1888.

President: DR. T. SASAKI.
Director of Library: K. IWAMOTO.

Publications: *Journal of the T.U.F.* (bi-annually), *Report of the T.U.F.* (annually).

TOKYO UNIVERSITY OF FOREIGN STUDIES

4-51 NISHIGAHARA
4-CHOME KITA-KU, TOKYO 114
Telephone: 917-6111.
Founded 1899. Reorganized 1949.

President: K. SAKAMOTO.
Administrator: M. HIRAO.
Dean: Y. SUZUKI.

Library: *see* Libraries.
Number of full-time teachers: 108.
Number of students: 2,503.

Publication: *Area and Culture Studies* (annually).

ATTACHED INSTITUTE:

Institute for the Study of Languages and Cultures of Asia and Africa: f. 1964; 35 researchers, 32 administrators; 23,890 vols.; Dir. H. KITAMURA; publs. *Journal of Asian and African Studies* (annually), *Newsletter* (thrice yearly).

TOKYO UNIVERSITY OF MERCANTILE MARINE

2-1-6 ETCHUJIMA,
KOTO-KU, TOKYO
Telephone: (03) 641-1171.
Founded 1949.

President: H. TANI.

Director of Administration Bureau: A. HATAE.
Library Director: S. ANNAKA.

Number of full-time teachers: 99.
Number of students: 823.

Publication: *Journal.*

UNIVERSITY OF ELECTRO-COMMUNICATIONS

1-5-1 CHOFUGAOKA, CHOFU-SHI, TOKYO 182

Telephone: (0424) 83-2161.

Founded 1949.

President: M. HIRASHIMA.
Director of Secretariat: A. UCHIDA.
Library Director: M. ISHII.

Number of full-time teachers: 244.
Number of students: 3,440.

TOTTORI UNIVERSITY

1-1 KOYAMA-CHO, TOTTORI CITY

Telephone: 28-0321.

President: M. AYABE.
Administrator: N. MORINAGA.
Librarian: K. NAKAGAWA.

Number of full-time teachers: 606.
Number of students: 3,040.

DEANS:

Faculty of Education: M. IWANAGA.
Faculty of Liberal Arts: S. OSAKI.
Faculty of Medicine: T. HOTTA.
Faculty of Engineering: M. UMEZA.
Faculty of Agriculture: T. NAKAYAMA.

TOYAMA UNIVERSITY

3,190 GOFUKU TOYAMA CITY

Telephone: (41) 1271.

Founded 1949.

Academic year: April to March (two terms).

President: T. YANGITA.
Chief Administrative Officer: N. HASEGAWA.
Librarian: H. FUTAGAMI.

Number of full-time teachers: *c.* 395.
Number of students: 4,783.

DEANS:

College of Liberal Arts: R. UMEHARA.
Faculty of Humanities: H. HONDA.
Faculty of Education: K. OHSAWA.
Faculty of Economics: M. UEMURA.
Faculty of Science: T. TAKEUCHI.
Faculty of Engineering: S. OHI.

UNIVERSITY OF TSUKUBA

1-1-1 TENNODAI, SAKURA-MURA, NIIHARI-GUN, IBARAKI-KEN 305

Telephone: (0298) 53-2111.

Telex: 3652580 UNTUKU J.

Founded 1973.

State control; Language of instruction: Japanese; Academic year: April to March.

President: NOBUYUKI FUKUDA.
Vice-Presidents: ISAO MIURA (Educational Affairs), MASAMI ICHIKAWA (Research Affairs), KOICHI ANAN (Medical Affairs), ETSUYUKI MATSUURA (General Affairs), SUSUMU TAKAHASHI (Student Affairs).
Provosts: SEIICHI ANAN (1st group of colleges), HIROSHI NAGAI (2nd group of colleges), SEI HACHISU (3rd group of colleges), TATSUICHIRO HASHIMOTO (School of Medicine), YUZO KISHINO (School of Physical Education), RYOICHI HAYASHI (School of Art and Design).
Secretary-General: KOHEI SHINOZAWA.
Librarian: KEIJI OKAMOTO.

Library of 1,085,051 vols., 7,344 periodicals.

Number of teachers: 1,351.

Number of students: 8,226 (6,570 undergraduates, 1,656 postgraduates).

DEANS:

College of Humanities: TATSUO INOUE.
College of Natural Sciences: JINSAI HIDAKA.
College of Social Sciences: YOSHINAO CHUMA.
College of Agriculture and Forestry: SHINGO YAMAZAWA.
College of Biological Sciences: ARINOBU EBARRA.
College of Comparative Culture: NOBORU HAGA.
College of Human Sciences: YOSHIO SAITO.
College of Basic Technology: SHIGEO OKUDA.
College of Information Sciences: RYOICHI MORI.
College of Socio-Economic Planning: YOSHIRO KURATANI.
Master's Degree Programme: MIYAO MANO.
Doctor's Degree Programme: ISAMU MOGI.

CHAIRMEN OF INSTITUTES:

Philosophy and Thought: HIDEYO YAMADA.
History and Anthropology: SHINPEI KATO.
Literature and Linguistics: HIROSHI ITO.
Modern Languages and Modern Culture: TOSHIO GUNJI.
Education: HITOSHI MATSUSHIMA.
Psychology: TAKAO AIKAWA.
Special Education: YASUMASA SATO.
Social Sciences: (vacant).
Socio-Economic Planning: SHUNTARO SHISHIDO.
Biological Sciences: SHUNEI ICHIMURA.
Agriculture and Forestry: SHOJI SATO.
Agricultural and Forestry Engineering: TSUNEO AOYAMA.
Applied Biochemistry: TATSURO ITO.
Mathematics: MUTSUHIDE MATSUMURA.
Physics: MASATOSHI NAKAMURA.
Chemistry: KOZO NAGASHIMA.
Geosciences: SHOZO YAMAMOTO.
Scientific Technology: YOSHIMI SAKAYANAGI.
Materials Science: MAKOTO OKAZAKI.
Structural Engineering: HARUO TAHARA.
Electronics and Information Science: YASUHIKO IKEBE.
Health and Sport Science: TETSUZO TAKAHASHI.
Art and Design: SUMIO YOSHINO.
Medical Sciences: YOSHIKI SUGITA.
Clinical Medicine: SHIZUO TOJO.
Community Medicine: KIKUO FUJIWARA.

DIRECTORS OF RESEARCH INSTITUTES:

Foreign Language Center: AKIO SAWADA.
Physical Education and Sports Center: TAKAO ASADA.
Agricultural and Forestry Research Center: KANICHI MURAKAMI.
Educational Media Center: KATSUMI KURIYAMA.
Tandem Accelerator Center: TAKASHI MIKUMO.
Cryogenics Center: KAZUHIRO OTSUKA.
Scientific Information Processing Center: KAZUHIKO NAKAYAMA.
Isotope Center: NAGAO IKEDA.
Chemical Analysis Center: YOSHIMORI OMOTE.
Central Workshop: YOSHIHITO ABE.
Environmental Research Center: MASAO IGUCHI.
Center for Laboratory Animal Science: KAZUO YASURAOKA.
Plasma Research Center: SHOICHI MIYOSHI.
Shimoda Marine Research Center: HIROSHI WATANABE.
Sugadaira Montane Research Center: SHUNEI ICHIMURA.

UTSUNOMIYA UNIVERSITY

350 MINE-MACHI, UTSUNOMIYA-SHI

Telephone: (36) 1515.

Founded 1949.

President: MASAMI KONDO (acting).
Director-General of Administration: MOTOHARU TATEISHI.
Librarian: NOBUO TAKEDA.

Number of teachers: 713.

Number of students: 3,596 undergraduates, 145 graduates.

DEANS:

College of Education: KAZUHIKO MARUYAMA.
College of Engineering: KAZUO SUZUKI.
College of Agriculture: MASAMI KONDO.
College of General Education: JUN AKUTSU.

WAKAYAMA UNIVERSITY

NISHITAKAMATSU 1-7-1, WAKAYAMA-SHI

Telephone: (22) 6122.

Founded 1949.

Academic year: April to March.

President: N. TSUTSUI.

Chief Administrative Officer: Y. MIWA.
Librarian: Y. NAKASHIMA.

Library of 417,547 vols.

Number of teachers: 166.
Number of students: 2,965.

Publications: *Bulletin of the Faculty of Education, The Wakayama Economic Review.*

DEANS:

Faculty of Education: K. TAKAHASHI.
Faculty of Economics: R. MIKAMI.

YAMAGATA UNIVERSITY

4-12 KOJIRAKAWA-MACHI,
1-CHOME, YAMAGATA CITY 990

Telephone: 31-1421.

Founded 1949.

State control; Academic year: April to March (two semesters).

***President:* T. HIRONE.**
Secretary-General: MINORU ODANO.
Librarian: GIICHI NOJIMA.

Number of teachers: *c.* 673.
Number of students: *c.* 6,437.

DEANS:

Faculty of Literature and Social Sciences: TOSHIO GOTO.
Faculty of Education: KENZO MIZOGUCHI.
***Faculty of Sciences:* MAMORU KUSA.**
School of Medicine: MASAJI MOCHIZUKI.
Faculty of Engineering: MASASHI KONNO.
Faculty of Agriculture: IWAO HIURA.
Faculty of General Education: YOSHIZO MORI.
Technical Junior College, Yamagata University: TOKUTARO HIRONE.

YAMAGUCHI UNIVERSITY

1677-1 YOSHIDA, YAMAGUCHI

Telephone: (2) 6111.

Founded 1949.

State control; Academic year: April to March (two terms).

President: SHUNZO KONISHI.
Chief Administrative Officer: T. WAKANA.
Chief Librarian: K. YAGISHITA.

Library: *see* Libraries.

Number of teachers: 793, including 251 professors.
Number of students: 6,980.

Publications: Faculty and Student Society journals and bulletins.

DEANS:

Faculty of Humanities: S. WATANABE.
Faculty of Education: Y. OKAMURA.
Faculty of Economics: K. ABE.
Faculty of Science: Y. NAGATANI.
School of Medicine: K. AWAYA.
Faculty of Engineering: S. OHARA.
Faculty of Agriculture: M. TODA.
Faculty of Liberal Arts: T. KUBO.
University Hospital: H. FUJITA.
Yamaguchi Technical College: T. SHIMIZU.

YAMANASHI UNIVERSITY

TAKEDA 4-CHOME,
KOFU 400

Telephone: 0552-52-1111.

Founded 1949.

President: N. FURUYA.
Registrar: K. TSUKADA.
Librarian: K. SANO.

Library of 304,880 volumes.

Number of teachers: 584.
Number of students: 3,178.

Publications: *Memoirs of the Faculty of Liberal Arts and Education, Bulletin of the Faculty of Education, Reports of the Faculty of Engineering.*

DEANS:

Faculty of Education: S. ITO.
Faculty of Engineering: K. TANAKA.

ATTACHED INSTITUTES:

Research Institute of Fermentation (attached to the Faculty of Engineering).

Research Institute of Inorganic Synthesis (attached to the Faculty of Engineering).

Research Institute of Fuel Cells (attached to the Faculty of Engineering).

YOKOHAMA NATIONAL UNIVERSITY

156 TOKIWADI, HODOGAYA-KU,
YOKOHAMA

Telephone: 33-1451.

Founded 1949.

President: R. KUBOMURA.
Administrator: M. INAGAKI.
Librarian: S. NOMURA.

Library: *see* Libraries.

Number of full-time teachers: 462.
Number of students: 6,943.

Publications: *Journal, Bulletin.*

DEANS:

Faculty of Arts and Education: R. SEKI.
Faculty of Economics: S. NUITA.
Faculty of Technology: T. YOKOYAMA.
Faculty of Business Administration: M. OYAMA.

MUNICIPAL INSTITUTIONS

FUKUSHIMA MEDICAL COLLEGE

FUKUSHIMA CITY

Founded 1950.

Faculty of Medicine, postgraduate research institute, hospital and nurses' school.

President: Y. TSUJI, M.D.
Director of Library: S. KURODA.
Secretary: S. SATO.
Hospital Director: A. OKUAKI.

Library of 85,000 vols.

Number of teachers: 231.
Number of students: 602.

Publications: *Fukushima Igaku Zasshi* (Fukishima Medical Journal, every 2 months), *Fukushima Journal of Medical Science* (quarterly).

HIMEJI INSTITUTE OF TECHNOLOGY

SHOSHA, HIMEJI 671-22, HYOGO

Founded 1944 as Hyogo Prefectural Special College of Technology, 1949 under present name.

President: YOSHITAKE YAMAMOTO.

Library of *c.* 87,877 vols.

Number of teachers: *c.* 136.
Number of students: *c.* 1,330.

Publication: *Kenkyu Hokoku.*

Faculties of Electrical, Electronic, Chemical and Mechanical Engineering, Applied Chemistry, and Material Science.

KYOTO PREFECTURAL UNIVERSITY OF MEDICINE

465 KAJII-CHO, KAWARAMACHI,
HIROKOJI, KAMIKYO-KU,
KYOTO

Telephone: 075 (251) 5111.

Founded 1873.

President: O. MIZUKOSHI, M.D.
Librarian: T. KISHIDA, M.D.

Library of 177,295 vols.

Number of teachers: 256.

Number of students: 644 undergraduate, 224 postgraduate.

Publication: *Kyoto Furitsu Ikadaigaku Zasshi* (Journal).

NAGOYA CITY UNIVERSITY

1 KAWASUMI, MIZUHO-CHO,
MIZUHO-KU, NAGOYA

Telephone: 851-5511.

Founded 1950.

President: K. SHIBATA, M.D.
Secretary-General: S. MORITOU.
Library Director: M. TANAKA.

Library of 239,271 vols.

Number of teachers: 376.
Number of students: 1,924.

Publications: *Nagoya Medical Journal*† (quarterly, English), *Annual Report of the Faculty of Pharmaceutical Science, N.C.U.*† (Japanese), *Bulletin of the College of General Education, N.C.U.*† (annual, Japanese), *Oikonomika*† (quarterly, Japanese).

DEANS:

Medical School: Y. HACHISUKA.
Faculty of Pharmaceutical Sciences: I. ITO.
Faculty of Economics: T. USHIJIMA.
College of General Education: H. ISHIHARA.

NARA MEDICAL UNIVERSITY*

SHIJO-CHO,
KASHIHARA-SHI, NARA 634

Telephone: 07442-2-3051.

Founded 1945.

Academic year: April to March.

President: J. OGATA.
Chief Administrative Officer: T. OKAMOTO.
Librarian: Y. KUROGOCHI.

Number of teachers: *c.* 250.
Number of students: *c.* 430.

Publication: *Journal of the Nara Medical Association.*

* No reply received to our questionnaire this year.

OSAKA CITY UNIVERSITY

459, SUGIMOTO-CHO,
SUMIYOSHI-KU, OSAKA

Telephone: 692-1231.

Founded 1949.

President: E. KIMURA.
Administrator: T. TAMAN.
Dean of Students' Guidance Bureau: RYO IWASAKI.
Dean of Education Bureau: K. KONISHI.

Library of 1,191,982 vols.

Number of teachers: 845, including 236 professors.

Number of students: 6,526.

Publications: *University Bulletin, Business Review, Journal of Economics, Annals of Economics Research Series, Economic Review, Series of Law and Politics, Journal of Law and Politics, Studies in the Humanities, Journal of Mathematics, Journal of Geoscience, Memoirs of the Faculty of Engineering, Osaka City Medical Journal, Journal of the Osaka City Medical Centre, Reports of the Science of Living, Economic Studies and Surveys, Annual Report of the Institute for Economic Research, Survey Reports, Journal of Chinese Economy.*

DEANS:

Faculty of Business: T. YAMAGAMI.
Faculty of Economics: N. OKABE.
Faculty of Law: M. ISHIBE.
Faculty of Letters: S. SATO.
Faculty of Science: Y. SHIBAOKA.
Faculty of Engineering: M. MIWA.
Faculty of Science of Living: E. FUWA.
College of General Education: K. KAWAKUBO.
School of Medicine: K. OWADA.

ATTACHED INSTITUTES:

Institute of Economic Research: Dir. S. OKUMURA.
Research Institute of Atomic Energy: Dir. T. OSHIO.
University Hospital: Dir. S. NISHIMURA.

UNIVERSITY OF OSAKA PREFECTURE

804 MOZU-UMEMACHI 4-CHO,
SAKAI, OSAKA

Telephone: 0722-52-1161.

Founded 1949.

President: TETSUO INABA.
Administrative Officer: YOSHIO NAKAYA, LL.B.
Librarian: TOYOJI YAMAUCHI, D.AGR.

Library of 647,326 vols.

Number of teachers: 640.
Number of students: 4,438.

Publications: *Bulletin*—series A, B, C, D, *Mathematica Japonicae, Journal of Economic Studies, Studies in British and American Literature, Gakuho.*

DEANS:

College of Engineering: SHUSUKE IIDA.
College of Agriculture: TAKEHIKO WATANABE.
School of Economics: HIDEYO ICHIHASHI.
College of Integrated Arts and Sciences: ZENTARO INOUE.
Junior College of Engineering: TARO HAYASHI.

SAPPORO MEDICAL COLLEGE

NISHI 17-CHOME,
MINAMI 1-JO, CHUO-KU,
SAPPORO 060

Founded 1945 as Hokkaido Women's Medical College, name changed 1950.

President: S. WATANABE.

Library of 96,576 vols.

Number of teachers: 297.
Number of students: 565.

Publication: *Sapporo Igaku Zasshi* (Sapporo Medical Journal, with English summaries).

ATTACHED INSTITUTE:

Cancer Research Institute: f. 1952; Dir. I. URUSHIZAKI; publ. *Tumor Research* (2 issues yearly).

SHIZUOKA COLLEGE OF PHARMACY

2-2-1 OSHIKA, SHIZUOKA-SHI,
SHIZUOKA-KEN

Telephone: 0542-85-6186.

Founded 1953.

Municipal control; Academic year: April to March.

President: S. UYEO, PH.D.
Chief Administrative Officer: S. OSA.
Librarian: F. ENDO, PH.D.

Number of teachers: *c.* 100.
Number of students: *c.* 600.

TOKYO METROPOLITAN UNIVERSITY

1-1-1 YAGUMO, MEGURO-KU,
TOKYO

Telephone: 03 (717) 0111.

Founded 1949.

Municipal control; Academic year: April to March (two terms).

President: Dr. I. NUMATA.
Director of Administrative Bureau: T. SUZUKI.
Librarian: T. MATSUNAMI.

Library: *see* Libraries.

Number of teachers: 602.
Number of students: 4,405.

Publication: *Hongaku no Genkyo* (University Information).

DEANS:

Faculty of Social Sciences and Humanities: S. TOTSUKA.
Faculty of Law: E. SHIMOYAMA.
Faculty of Economics: K. JOZA.
Faculty of Science: T. SIRAO.
Faculty of Technology: T. MORITA.

PROFESSORS:

Faculty of Social Sciences and Humanities:

IMAI, S., Psychology
ISHIKAWA, E., Social Anthropology
ISHIZUKA, H., Modern Japanese History
ISONO, S., Urban Education, Further Education
KAWAMATA, K., French Linguistics
KAWAMURA, J., German Literature
KAWAMURA, N., Sociology
KOIKE, S., American Literature
KONISHI, S., Modern German Literature
KUDO, A., English Literature
KURASAWA, S., Metropolitan Sociology
MATSUI, H., Modern Chinese Literature
MATSUNAMI, T., English Linguistics
MIURA, T., Psychology
MIYOSHI, Y., Western History
MURAMATSU, K., Chinese Language and Literature

MURATAKE, S., Cultural and Social Anthropology
NATORI, S., French Literature
NOZAKI, T., American Literature
NOZAWA, Y., Asian History
OISHI, S., Japanese Language and Literature
OKUTSU, K., Japanese Linguistics
ONO, S., English Linguistics
OKURA, T., Educational Studies
OSHIMA, I., Japanese Linguistics
OTA, H., Western History
SHINODA, K., English Literature
SHIROYAMA, Y., German Language and Literature
SUZUKI, K., English Literature
TAJIMA, S., Philosophy
TAKAMOTO, K., German Language and Literature
TAKAMURA, S., Modern French Poetry
TAKUMA, T., Experimental Psychology
TERASAWA, T., Philosophy
TOCHIKAWA, K., Historical Methodology
TOTSUKA, H., Philosophy
WATANABE, A., French Literature
YANAGAWA, N., German Language and Literature
YOSHIZAWA, D., Ethics

Faculty of Law:

AKAGI, S., Public Administration
BAI, K., Family Law, Medical Law
CHIBA, M., Philosophy of Law and History of Legal Thought
ETO, Y., Civil Procedure
HANZAWA, T., History of European Political Thought
HARIU, S., Constitutional Law
ISHIMURA, Z., Sociology of Law, Method of Social Research, Law of Property and Contract
ISOBE, T., Civil Law, Creditor-Debtor Relations
KAMIKAWA, N., Western Political History
KANEKO, M., Administrative Law, Educational Law
MASUMI, J., Political Science
MATSUOKA, S., Corporation Law
MOMII, T., Labour Law and Social Security Law
NOMURA, Y., Law of Torts and Public Nuisance
OKABE, T., International Politics
SEKIGUCHI, A., Conflicts of Law
SHIBUYA, T., Criminal Law
SHIMIZU, M., General Theory of Law of Obligation, Mortgage Law
SHIMOYAMA, E., Administrative Law, English Law

Faculty of Economics:

FUTAMURA, T., Business Administration, Organization Theory
HAYAMI, Y., Economic Policy
JOZA, K., Economic Theory
KANEKO, H., Economic Theory, History of Economic Thought
MIZUNUMA, T., Economic History of Japan
OKUGUCHI, K., Mathematical Economics, Economic Theory
SAEGUSA, Y., Statistics
SHIRAKI, T., Personnel Management
TAKATA, S., Managerial Accounting and Financial Management
TAKEUCHI, M., Modern Economic History

Faculty of Science:

AKINO, M., Physiological Chemistry, Enzymology
ENDO, S., Mathematics
HANYA, T., Geochemistry
INOUE, M., Solid State Physics
ISHIDA, M., Mathematics
IWANO, M., Mathematics
KAIZUKA, S., Geomorphology and Quaternary Geography
KANEKO, Y., Atomic Collision Physics
KASAKI, H., Natural History
KITAMURA, H., Microbial Physiology and Chemistry
KOBAYASHI, M., Organic Chemistry
KOBAYASHI, T., High Energy Physics
KONDO, M., Radiation Chemistry
KUME, K., Solid State Physics, Nuclear Magnetic Resonance
KUSUKAWA, K., Fluid Mechanics
MAEJIMA, I., Climatology
MARUYAMA, Y., Microbial Physiology
MESHIZUKA, T., Physical Education
MIYASHITA, K., Animal Ecology
NAKAMURA, M., Physical Education
NAKANISHI, M., Physical Education
NAKANO, T., Environmental Studies, Cartography
OBATA, M., Mathematics
OHKASAKI, K., Developmental Biology
OKUYAMA, T., Biochemistry
OOKUBO, K., Mathematics
SANO, H., Inorganic Chemistry
SATO, T., Solid State Physics
SATO, T., Organic Chemistry
SETO, T., Polymer Physics
SIRAO, T., Mathematics
TOKUDA, T., Physical Chemistry
TOYA, H., Regional Geography
TSURUMI, S., Mathematics
WATANABE, Y., Human Geography
YAMAGATA, T., High Energy Physics
YAMAGUCHI, S., Solid State Physics, Spectroscopy
YANAGISAWA, T., Embryology, Biochemical Embryology
YANO, S., Mathematics
YONEMITSU, K., Electron Theory of Metals
YOSHIDA, S., Plant Physiology and Biochemistry

*Faculty of **Technology**:*

AWAKUNI, Y., Photoelectric Materials and their Application
BABA, H., Electrochemistry
FUSE, T., Electromagnetic Theory
HIDA, M., Synthetic Organic Chemistry
HIGASHI, Y., Structural Engineering Theory of Structure
HIRATA, M., Chemical Engineering
HIRAYAMA, N., Environmental Engineering, Aerodynamics, Turbomachinery
HORIGUCHI, T., Coastal Engineering, Harbour Engineering
INOUE, H., Traffic Engineering
ITOH, F., Bridge and Structural Engineering
ITOH, N., Environmental Engineering
KANAZAWA, T., Inorganic Phosphates and Inorganic Surface Chemistry
KASUYA, I., Radio Wave Propagation
KATO, H., Hydraulics, Applied Hydrodynamics, Hydraulic Machinery
KAWAGUCHI, S., Sanitary Engineering
KIRISHIKI, S., Architectural History
KOBAYASHI, Y., Physical Properties of Polymers
KOIZUMI, Y., Earthquake Engineering and Soil Mechanics
MAEDA, T., Thermodynamics, Aerodynamics, Turbomachinery
MIYAGAWA, O., Engineering Materials
MIYASHITA, M., Automatic Control, Control Engineering
MORITA, T., Power System Engineering
MURATA, J., Concrete Technology
NAGAKURA, Y., Architectural Design
OGASAWARA, N., Radio and Communication Engineering
SATO, H., Architectural Acoustics
SHIOYA, M., Electric Machinery and Power Electronics
SUZUKI, S., Industrial Analytical Chemistry
TAZIMA, S., Inorganic and Metal Chemistry
TERADA, S., Structural Engineering
WADA, H., Precision Measurements
YAMAMOTO, M., Applied Mechanics for Civil Engineering
YAMAZAKI, Y., Industrial Organic Chemistry

WAKAYAMA MEDICAL COLLEGE

9 KYUBAN-CHO,
WAKAYAMA CITY

Founded 1945.

President: Y. MIYANO.

Library of 30,620 vols.

Number of teachers: *c.* 260.
Number of students: *c.* 399.

Publications: *Wakayama Medical Reports* (in English, quarterly), *Wakayama Igaku* (in Japanese, quarterly).

YOKOHAMA CITY UNIVERSITY

22-2 SETO, KANAZAWA-KU,
YOKOHAMA 7236

Telephone: (781) 1311.

Founded 1949.

Academic year: April to March.

Chancellor and President: HEIJI KAWAI.

Chief Administrative Officer: YOSHIKAZU KATO.

Librarian: SHOJI TANAKA.

Library of 235,831 vols.

Number of teachers: *c.* 307.

Number of students: *c.* 2,703.

Publications: *Yokohama Shiritsu Daigaku Ronso*† (Bulletin, annually), *Yokohama Shiritsu Daigaku Kiyo*† (Journal, annually), *Keizai-to-Boeki*† (Industry and Trade, quarterly), *Yokohama Medical Bulletin*† (English, bimonthly), *Yokohama Igaku*† (Medical Journal, every 2 months).

DEANS:

Faculty of Economics and Business Administration: HIDEO UNAYAMA.

Faculty of Literature and Science: SEIICHI IMAI.

Department of General Education: MASAE ORIHARA.

School of Medicine: MASAZUMI KAWAKAMI.

ATTACHED INSTITUTE:

Economics Research Institute: Dir. GORO OSADA.

PRIVATE UNIVERSITIES AND COLLEGES

AOYAMAGAKUIN UNIVERSITY

4-4-25 SHIBUYA,
SHIBUYA-KU, TOKYO 150

Telephone: 03-409-8111.

Founded 1874.

Chancellor: Dr. K. OHKI.

President: E. HOSAKA.

Administrative Officer: S. MATSUDA.

Library Director: K. KASEGAWA.

Library of 480,000 vols.

Number of full-time teachers: 334.

Number of students: 17,356.

Publications: *Aoyama Journal of Business, Aoyama Journal of Economics, Aoyama Law Review* (all quarterly), *Aoyama Journal of General Education, Thought Currents in English Literature, Journal of Education Research, KIYO* (Journal of Literature), *Aoyama Gobun* (Journal of Japanese Literature), *Aoyama Shigaku* (Journal of History), *Aoyama Business Review* (all annual).

DEANS:

College of Literature: T. NUKI.
College of Economics: Dr. H. NISHIOKA.
College of Law: Dr. A. MORIIZUMI.
College of Business Administration: T. KITAMI.
College of Science and Engineering: Dr. K. OHTA.
General Education: S. NAITO.

CHAIRMEN:

College of Literature:
Department of Education: N. KINOSHITA.
Department of Education (night): S. YONEZAWA.
Department of English-American Literature: T. MAKINO.
Department of English-American Literature (night): Y. OZAKI.
Department of French Literature: T. HIROSHIMA.
Department of Japanese Literature: O. HAYASHI.
Department of History: S. YOSHIDA.

College of Economics:
Department of Economics: S. HYUGAJI.
Department of Economics (night): Dr. H. KANAMARU.

College of Law:
Department of Public Law: S. KONDO.
Department of Private Law: Dr. S. YUUKI.

College of Business Administration:
Department of Business Administration: M. UZAWA.
Department of Business Administration (night): Dr. M. SAKAI.

College of Science and Engineering:
Department of Physics: Dr. T. KOMODA.
Department of Chemistry: Dr. K. KIMURA.
Department of Mechanical Engineering: Dr. S. MIWA.
Department of Electronics and Electrical Engineering: Dr. A. KUNIOKA.
Department of Industrial and Systems Engineering: Dr. E. KOYANO.

ASIA UNIVERSITY

5-24-10 SAKAI, MUSASHINO-SHI,
TOKYO 180

Telephone: 0422-54-3111.

Founded 1941.

Academic year: April to March (two terms).

President: KOZO OTA.

Librarian: TETSUSHI FURUKAWA.

Library of 229,850 vols.

Number of teachers: 296.

Number of students: 9,017.

DEANS:

Graduate School of Business Administration: E. FURUKAWA.
Graduate School of Economics: Y. ITAGAKI.
Graduate School of Law: S. TANAKA.
Department of Business Administration: T. YAMAGUCHI.
Department of Economics: Y. NAKANO.
Department of Law: J. TAGAMI.
Department of General Education: M. YAKU.

ATTACHED INSTITUTES:

Institute for Asian Studies: f. 1973; Dir. N. KAJIMURA; publ. *Journal* (annually), *Bulletin* (quarterly).

Special Course for Foreign Students: f. 1953; Dir. T. IIJIMA.

AZABU VETERINARY COLLEGE

1-17-71 FUCHINOBE,
SAGAMIHARA CITY, KANAGAWA

Telephone: (0427) 54-7111.

Founded 1890.

President: Y. OCHI.
Registrar: F. FUJIOKA.
Librarian: H. ITAGAKI.

Library of 37,200 vols.

Number of teachers: 62.

Number of students: 1,000.

Publication: *Bulletin.*

BUKKYO UNIVERSITY

96 KITAHANANOBO-CHO,
MURASAKINO, KITA-KU,
KYOTO

Telephone: (075) 491-2141.

Founded 1903.

Academic year: April to March.

President: R. FUJIWARA.

Registrar: K. MIZUTANI.

Librarian: H. INOUE.

Library of 250,000 vols.

Number of teachers: 200.

Number of students: 4,100.

DEANS:

Faculty of Letters: S. TUBOI.

Faculty of Sociology: S. MIFUNE.

CHUBU INSTITUTE OF TECHNOLOGY

KASUGAI, NAGOYA-SHIGAI, 487

Founded 1964.

President: K. YAMADA.
Provost: R. ONISHI.

Library of 110,000.

Number of teachers: 224, including 76 professors.

Number of students: 5,459.

Publications: *Memoirs*† (annually).

Faculties of Architecture, Electrical, Civil, Mechanical and Electronic Engineering, Industrial Chemistry and Engineering Physics.

ATTACHED INSTITUTE:

Research Institute of Magnetosphere.

CHUO UNIVERSITY

742-1 HIGASHINAKANO,
HACHIOJI-CITY, TOKYO

Telephone: 0426-74-2111.

Founded 1885.

President: S. TODA.

Library: *see* Libraries.

Number of teachers: 1,325.

Number of students: 31,216.

Publications: *Chuo Law Review*†, *Journal of Economics*†, *Journal of Commerce*†, *Bulletin of the Faculty of Science and Engineering, Journal of the Faculty of Literature, English Language and Literature, Bulletin d'Etudes Françaises de l'Université Chuo, Jahresberichte der Gesellschaft für deutsche Kultur und Sprache an der Chuo-Universität, Research of Physical Education, Journal of Liberal Arts, Bulletin of Graduate Studies.*

DEANS:

Faculty of Law: G. TAMURA.
Faculty of Economics: K. IWANAMI.
Faculty of Commerce: Y. YAMASHITA.
Faculty of Engineering: H. CHIKUMA.
Faculty of Literature: J. SHIMADA.

DIRECTORS:

Institute of Comparative Law: YOSHIHIRO YOKOI.
Institute of Accounting Research: TOSHIO IINO.

Institute of Economic Research: GENTA KURIHARA.
Institute of Business Research: HIROZUMI IWAO.
Institute of Social Science: HARUO KOMATSU.
Institute of Cultural Science: MASATOSHI SERA.
Institute of Health and Physical Education: SAKIO TSUKUI.

DAITO BUNKA UNIVERSITY*

TAKASHIMADAIRA 1-CHOME, ITABASHI-KU, TOKYO 175
Telephone: 932-5151.
Founded 1923.

President: **U. SAEKI.**
Registrar: **N. KANEKO.**
Librarian: **C. TANAKA.**

Library of 94,000 vols.
Number of teachers: *c.* 150.

Faculties of Economics and Literature.

* No reply received to our questionnaire this year.

DOSHISHA UNIVERSITY

KARASUMA IMADEGAWA, KAMIKYO-KU, KYOTO 602
Telephone: Kyoto (075) 251-3223.
Founded 1875.

Chancellor: N. UENO.
President: Y. MATSUYAMA.
Dean of Academic Affairs: M. MOTOKI.
Administrative Officer: H. WATANABE.
Librarian: S. OGATA.

Library of *c.* 800,000 vols.
Number of full-time teachers: 408.
Number of students: 19,498.
University publications: *Studies in the Christian Religions, Studies in Humanities, Law Review, Economics Review, Business Review, Science and Engineering Review, Doshisha American Studies, The Social Sciences, The Humanities, The Study of Christianity and Social Problems.*

DEANS:

Faculty of Tehology: K. HIGUCHI.
Faculty of Letters: T. KIMURA.
Faculty of Law: R. TOMA.
Faculty of Economics: T. NOMA.
Faculty of Commerce: S. YASUOKA.
Faculty of Engineering: H. MIKI.

DIRECTORS:

Institute for the Study of Humanities and Social Sciences: M. TAKENAKA.
Center for American Studies: N. MATSUYAMA.
Science and Engineering Institute: T. HARA.
Computer Center: K. MORI.

DOSHISHA WOMEN'S UNIVERSITY

602 GENBU-CHO, TERAMACHI-NISHIIRU, IMADEGAWA-DORI, KAMIKYO-KU, KYOTO
Telephone: (251) 4112.
Founded 1876.

Academic year: April to March.

Chancellor: N. UENO.
President: H. OKANO.
Registrar: J. HAYASHI.
Librarian: K. UKITA.

Library of *c.* 120,000 vols.
Number of teachers: *c.* 200.
Number of students: *c.* 2,500.
Publications: *Annual Reports of Studies.*†

DEANS:

Liberal Arts: A. ISHIDA.
Home Economics: H. TAMAKI.

FUKUOKA UNIVERSITY

NANAKUMA, NISHI-KU, FUKUOKA 814
Founded 1934.

President: M. ITO.
Library of *c.* 560,000 vols.
Number of full-time teachers: 670.
Number of students: 22,671.
Publications: *Reviews, Bulletin, Reports.*

DEANS:

Faculty of Literature and Humanities: H. KANAGAKI.
Faculty of Law: K. TAKADA.
Faculty of Economics: M. MIZUTANI.
Faculty of Commercial Sciences: S. TAKEOKA.
Faculty of Science: K. YASUDA.
Faculty of Technology: O. MORI.
Faculty of Medicine: M. NISHIZONO.
Faculty of Pharmacy: S. TOKI.
Faculty of Physical Education: H. KAJIYAMA.

GAKUSHUIN UNIVERSITY

1-5-1 MEJIRO, TOSHIMA-KU, TOKYO
Telephone: 03-986-0221.
Founded 1949.

President: T. ISOBE.
Librarian: S. UNO.

Library of 521,900 vols.
Number of full-time teachers: 194.
Number of students: 6,445.
Publications: *Gakushuin Daigaku Hogaku-Bu Kenkyu Nenpo* (Review of Law and Politics, annually), *Gakushuin Daigaku Keizai Ronshu* (Economic Papers, 2 or 3 a year), *Gakushuin Daigaku Bungaku-Bu Kenkyu Nenpo* (annually), Series of Treatises.

ATTACHED INSTITUTE:

Gakushuin Toyo Bunka Kenkyu-Jo (*Gakushuin University Research Institute for Oriental Studies*): f. 1953; Dir. Y. IZAKA.

HIROSHIMA JOGAKUIN COLLEGE

13-1, HIGASHI 4-CHOME, USHITA, HIROSHIMA CITY
Telephone: (0822) 28-0386.
Founded 1886, as college 1949.

President: Prof. M. IMAISHI.
Registrar: H. TOKUNAGA.
Librarian: Prof. Y. KUWAHARA.

Library of 67,000 vols.
Number of teachers: 65.
Number of students: 900.
Publication: *Bulletin* (yearly).

HOKKAI GAKUEN UNIVERSITY

4-1-40, ASAHIMACHI, TOYOHIRAKU, SAPPORO, 062
Telephone: (011) 841-1166.
Founded 1950.

President: **S. TAKAKURA.**
Librarian: MIEKO SASAKI.

Library of 200,000 vols.
Number of full-time teachers: 91.
Number of students: 6,900.
Publications: *Keizai Ronshu* (Journal of Economics), *Hogaku Kenkyu* (Law Journal), *Gakuen Ronshu* (Gakuen Review: Journal of Humanities and Science), *Kogakubu Kenkyu Hokoku* (Bulletin of the Faculty of Engineering).

DEANS:

Faculty of Economics: O. TANAKA.
Faculty of Law: K. YAMASHITA.
Faculty of Engineering: T. SAKAUE.
Faculty of Commerce (in Kitami): R. OKAMOTO.
Department of General Education: S. NISHIZAWA.

ATTACHED INSTITUTE:

Development Research Institute: f. 1957; Dir. M. KAWAMURA; publ. *Kaihatsu Ronshu* (Journal of Development Research).

HOSEI UNIVERSITY

2-17-1 FUJIMI, CHIYODA-KU, TOKYO
Telephone: (03) 264-9662.
Founded 1880.

President: AKIRA NAKAMURA.
Registrar: KOJI SATO.
Librarian: MASAHO NODA.

Number of full-time teachers: 489.
Number of students: 28,298.
Publications: *Hogaku-Shirin* (Law and Political Sciences Review), *Hosei Daigaku Bungakubu Kiyo* (Bulletin of Faculty of Letters), *Keizai-Shirin*

(Economic Review), *Shakai Rodo Kenkyu* (Society and Labour), *Keiei Shirin* (Business Journal), *Hosei Daigaku Kogakubu Kenkyu Shuho* (College of Engineering Bulletin).

Faculties of Law, Humanities and Sciences, Economics, Social Sciences, Business Administration and Engineering.

ATTACHED INSTITUTES:

Nogami Memorial Noh Drama Research Institute: f. 1952; 4 mems.; library of 15,000 vols.; Pres. T. MURAKAMI; publ. *Catalogue Noh Drama Collections*.

Ohara Institute for Social Research: f. 1919; 15 mems.; library of 45,000 vols.; Dir. N. FUNABASHI; publs. *The Labour Yearbook of Japan* (annual), *Report* (monthly).

Institute for Study of Okinawan Culture: f. 1972; 6 mems.; library of 5,000 vols.; publs. *Bulletin*, *Report* (annual).

INTERNATIONAL CHRISTIAN UNIVERSITY

10-2, OSAWA 3-CHOME, MITAKA-SHI, TOKYO 181

Telephone: 0422-33-3131.

Founded 1949.

An ecumenical university, accepting students of high academic ability from all countries; the Japan International Christian University Foundation (Room 720, 475 Riverside Drive, New York, N.Y. 10115, U.S.A.) is a support organ and information agency for the University; Languages of instruction: Japanese and English; Academic year: April to March or September to June.

President: Dr. HIDEYASU NAKAGAWA.
Vice-President for Financial Affairs: MINORU TABUCHI.
Vice-President for Academic Affairs: Dr. H. NAKAGAWA.
Library Director: Dr. AKIRA MIYAKE.

Number of teachers: 123 (full-time).
Number of students: *c.* 2,000.

Publications: *Humanities*†, *Educational Studies*†, *Linguistics*†, *Asian Cultural Studies*†, *Social Science*†, also occasional books and monographs.

DEANS:

College of Liberal Arts: Dr. J. E. KIDDER.
Graduate School: Dr. TERUMI NAKANO.
Student Affairs: Prof. YOSHIO NIWA.

PROFESSORS:

AKUTSU, Dr. Y., Audio-Visual Education
AOYAGI, Dr. K., Social Anthropology
ARAKI, T., French Literature
BANNO, M., International Relations
BRANNEN, Dr. N. S., Linguistics
CHO, Dr. K., History of Thought
DOI, Dr. T., Psychology
DUKE, Dr. B. C., Comparative Education
EBISAWA, Dr. A., Japanese History
FUJITA, T., Business Administration
FURUYA, Dr. Y., Religion
HARA, Dr. KAZUO, Psychology
HARA, Dr. KIMI, Educational Sociology
HOSHINO, A., Psychology
ICHINOSE, Dr. T., Financial Administration
INOUE, Dr. K., Linguistics
ISHIKAWA, Dr. M., Physics
ISHIWATA, S., Economics
KAKIUCHI, Dr. I. Y., Physics
KATSUMI, Dr. M., Biology
KAWASE, K., Philosophy of Education
KIDDER, Dr. J. E., Fine Arts and Archaeology
KINUKAWA, Dr. M., Mathematics
KOBAYASHI, Dr. E., English Language
LINDE, Dr. R., English
MATTHEWS, Dr. R., English Literature
MINEMURA, Dr. F., Japanese Literature
MIYAKE, Dr. A., Physics
MURAKAMI, M., Economics
MURAKI, Dr. M., Linguistics
NAKAGAWA, Dr. H., Philosophy of Education
NAKAJIMA, Dr. S., Business Administration
NAKANO, Dr. T., Audio-Visual Education
NAKAUCHI, T., Economics
NIWA, Y., Physical Education
NOZAKI, A., Mathematics
OGUCHI, Dr. K., Mathematics
OMORI, M., Anthropology
PENG, Dr. F. C. C., Linguistics
SAITO, K., English Literature
SAITO, Dr. M., Communication
SANUKI, K., Philosophy of Education
TAKAGI, T., Biology
TANAKA, F., Art
TANAKA, Dr. M., Political Science
TSUJI, Dr. K., Political Science
TSURU, Dr. H., Education
UOZUMI, M., History
WATANABE, Y., Public Administration
WORTH, Dr. D. C., Physics
YAMAGUCHI, Dr. T., Biology
YAMAMOTO, Dr. T., History
YOKOTA, Dr. Y., Political Science

ATTACHED INSTITUTES:

Institute of Asian Cultural Studies: f. 1971, replacing Committee f. 1958; Dir. K. CHO; publs. *Asian Cultural Studies* (annual), *Studies in Comparative Modernization*, etc.

Institute of Educational Research and Service: f. 1953; Dir. A. MIYAKE; publs. *Educational Studies* (annual), *Proceedings of the Conference of Audio-Visual Education* (annual).

Institute for the Study of Christianity and Culture: f. 1963; Dir. R. MATTHEWS; publ. *Christianity and Culture* (annual).

Social Science Research Institute: f. 1958; Dir. K. AOYAGI; publ. *Journal of Social Science* (annual).

IWATE MEDICAL UNIVERSITY

19-1 UCHIMARU, MORIOKA 020, IWATE

Founded 1928, University 1952.

President: TOSHISADA MITA, D.M.SC.
Vice-President: KIJURO OBARA.

Library of 107,563 vols.

Number of teachers: 370 (including 52 professors).
Number of students: 1,597.

Publications: *Journal of the Iwate Medical Association, Annual Report, School of Liberal Arts and Sciences.*

DEANS:

School of Medicine: H. WAKO.
School of Dentistry: Y. FUZIOKA, D.M.SC.
Premedical Course: T. ICHINOHE.

JIKEI UNIVERSITY SCHOOL OF MEDICINE

3-25-8 NISHI SHINBASHI, MINATO-KU, TOKYO 105

Telephone: 433-1111.

Founded 1881.

President: R. NATORI, M.D.
Chairman of Board of Education: M. TOKUTOME, M.D.
***Director of Medical Museum:* F. YOSHIMURA, M.D.**
Director of University Hospital: M. ABE, M.D.
***Librarian:* T. MATSUMOTO, M.D.**

The library contains 126,712 vols.
Number of teachers: 851.
Number of students: 1,206.

Publications: *Tokyo Jikeikai Ika Daigaku Zasshi*† (bi-monthly in Japanese), *Jikeikai Medical Journal*† (quarterly in English).

KANSAI UNIVERSITY

3-35, YAMATE-CHO 3-CHOME, SUITA-SHI, OSAKA

Telephone: Osaka 388-1121.

Founded 1886.

President: A. ONISHI.
Chairman of the Board of Trustees: T. HISAI.
***Registrar:* Y. IMAI.**
Librarian: O. OBA.

Library: *see* **Libraries.**

Number of teachers: 512, **including** 287 **professors.**
Number of students: 21,117.

Publications: ***Bungaku Ronshu*** **(Literary Essays),** ***Hogaku Ronshu*** **(Law** Review), *Shakaigakubu Kiyo* (Journal of Sociological Research), ***Keizai Ronshu*** (Economic Review), ***Shogaku Ronshu*** (Business Review), ***Kogaku Kenkyu*** *Hokoku* (Technology Reports).

DEANS:

Graduate School: M. SHIMBO.
Faculty of Law: M. HISHIDA.
Faculty of Economics: S. TSURUSHIMA.
Faculty of Literature: H. FUGII.
Faculty of Commerce: S. OHASHI.
Faculty of Engineering: H. MAEDA.
Faculty of Sociology: Y. HONJO.

KEIO UNIVERSITY

MITA 2-CHOME, MINATO-KU, TOKYO 108

Telephone: 453-4511.

Founded 1858.

President: T. ISHIKAWA, D.LAW.
Secretary: T. SHIRAGAMI.
Registrar: I. ONO.
Director of Libraries: M. TAKATORI, D.LAW.

Library: *see* Libraries.

Number of full-time teachers: *c.* 1,240.

Number of students: *c.* 24,711.

Publications: *Mita Gakkai Zasshi* (Mita Journal of Economics), *Keio Economic Studies, Mita Shogaku Kenkyu* (Mita Business Review), *Keio Business Review, Hogaku Kenkyu* (Journal of Law, Politics and Sociology), *Keio Journal of Politics, Shigaku* (Historical Science), *Tetsugaku* (Philosophy), *Library and Information Science, Keio Igaku* (Keio Medical Journal), *Keio Journal of Medicine, Okajimais Folia Anatomica Japonica, Keio Engineering Reports, Geibun Kenkyu* (Journal of Arts and Letters).

DEANS:

Faculty of Letters: N. MIKUMO.
Faculty of Economics: Dr. I. OHKUMA.
Faculty of Law: Dr. M. IKUTA.
Faculty of Business and Commerce: Dr. I. ISHIZAKA.
Faculty of Engineering: Dr. H. FUJITA.
School of Medicine: K. ASAMI.

DIRECTORS:

Institute of Cultural and Linguistic Studies: Y. IKEDA.
Institute for Communication Research: M. IKUTA.
Institute for Management and Labour Studies: K. TSUJIMURA.
Institute of Physical Education: T. YUASA.
Institute of Oriental Culture: N. NAKAI.
Institute of Audio-Visual Language Education: M. NISHIGOORI.
Electron Microscope Laboratory: K. ASAMI.
Institute of Information Science: A. CHE.
Laboratory of Pharmaco-Chemical Research: K. ASAMI.
International Center: R. TAIRA.
Keio Business School: I. KATEOKA.

KINKI UNIVERSITY*

KOWAKAE 3-CHOME, HIGASHI, OSAKA

Founded 1925.

***President:* M. SEKŌ, M.D.**

Number of full-time teachers: *c.* 450.
Number of students: *c.* 24,000.

* No reply received to our questionnaire this year.

KOBE-GAKUIN UNIVERSITY

IGAWADANI TARUMI, KOBE 673

Telephone: 078-974-1551.

Founded 1966.

President: KAKUTARO YAMASHITA.
Chief Director: BUNMON NAKANO.
Administrative Officer: TERUZO TAKEUCHI.
Librarian: UTAKO OKAMOTO.

Library of 200,000 vols.
Number of teachers: 280.
Number of students: 6,877.

Publications: *Hogaku* (Law and Politics Review), *Economic Papers, Kobe Gakuin Research Institute of Pharmaceutical and Health Science Report, Annals.*

DEANS:

Faculty of Law: AKIRA ISHIHARA.
Faculty of Economics: KAKUTARO YAMASHITA.
Faculty of Nutrition: BUNSAKU SAKAKIBARA.
Faculty of Pharmacy: CHIKATARO KAWASAKI.
General Education Division: KUMEICHI KUROHASHI.

KOGAKUIN UNIVERSITY

1-24-2, NISHI-SHINJUKU, SHINJUKU-KU, TOKYO 160

Telephone: Tokyo 342-1211.

Founded 1887, university status 1949.

President: TEIJI ITOH.
Registrar: NORIKAZU HIRAKAWA.
Librarian: MICHIO SEKIYA.

Library of 146,000 vols.

Number of teachers: 214.

Number of students: 6,841 undergraduates (4,770 full-time, 2,071 evening), 61 graduates.

Publications: *Kogakuin Daigaku Kenkyu Hokoku*† (Research Reports, 2 a year), *Ronso*† (Journal).

Faculty and Graduate School of Engineering.

KOKUGAKUIN UNIVERSITY

10-28, HIGASHI 4-CHOME, SHIBUYA-KU, TOKYO

Telephone: 409-0111.

Founded 1882.

President: Y. YOSHIKAWA.
Registrar: N. TAKAFUJI.
Librarian: H. MIZUTA.

Library: *see* Libraries.

Number of teachers: 564.
Number of students: 12,937.

Publications: *Kokugakuin Zasshi* (The Journal of Kokugakuin University), *Kokugakuin Keizaigaku* (The Kokugakuin University Economic Review), *Kokugakuin Hogaku* (The Journal of the Faculty of Law and Politics). *Kokugakuin Daigaku Kiyo* (Transactions of Kokugakuin University).

DEANS:

Faculty of Literature: R. HAYASHI.
Faculty of Economics: M. MIWA.
Faculty of Law: T. SAWANOBORI.
Graduate School: T. SAKAMOTO.

KOMAZAWA UNIVERSITY

1-23-1 KOMAZAWA, SETAGAYA-KU, TOKYO 154

Telephone: 03 (418) 9111.

Founded 1882.

President: D. OKUBO.
Registrar: R. TANAKA.

Number of teachers: *c.* 305.
Number of students: *c.* 20,909.

KONAN UNIVERSITY

8-9-1, OKAMOTO, HIGASHINADA-KU, KOBE

President: J. ITOH.

Library of 421,709 vols.
Number of full-time teachers: 176.
Number of students: *c.* 6,996.

DEANS:

Faculty of Letters: K. MASUDA.
Faculty of Science: K. YUASA.
Faculty of Economics: M. TANAKA.
Faculty of Law: M. YAMAGUCHI.
Faculty of Business Administration: T. YAMADA.

KURUME UNIVERSITY

67 ASAHI-MACHI, KURUME 830

Telephone: 0942-35-3311.

Founded 1928.

Faculties of **Commerce and Medicine.**

President: NOBORU KIMURA.
Director of Administrative Office: HIROSHI MIZOGUCHI.

Library of 221,000 vols.
Number of teachers: 489.
Number of students: 4,101.

Publications: *The Kurume Medical Journal*† (quarterly), *The Journal of the Kurume Medical Association* (monthly), *The Journal for Studies on Industrial Economics* (quarterly).

KWANSEI GAKUIN UNIVERSITY

155-1-1 UEGAHARA, NISHINOMIYA, HYÔGO

Telephone: 0798-51-0912.

Founded 1889.

President: T. KODERA.
Library Director: J. SAKAMOTO.

Library: *see* Libraries.

Number of full-time teachers: 282.
Number of students: 13,880.

Publications: *Theological Studies*, *Humanities Review, Sociology Depart-*

ment Studies, Journal of Law and Politics, Journal of Economics, Journal of Business Administration, Law Reviews, Annual Studies, and others.

DEANS:

Faculty of Theology: S. Jôzaki.
Faculty of Humanities: S. Shiotani.
Faculty of Sociology: W. Kurata.
Faculty of Law: T. Hirooka.
Faculty of Economics: T. Hashimoto.
Faculty of Commerce: S. Wada.
Faculty of Science: S. Naya.

KYOTO COLLEGE OF PHARMACY

5-NAKAUCHI-CHO, MISASAGI
YAMASHINA-KU, KYOTO 607
Telephone: 075-581-3161.
Founded 1884.

President: Dr. S. Kimoto.
Registrar: Dr. E. Ibuki.
Librarian: Dr. H. Imahara.

Library of 45,819 vols.
Number of teachers: 47.
Number of students: 1,474.

MATSUYAMA UNIVERSITY OF COMMERCE

4-2 BUNKYO-CHO,
MATSUYAMA 790
Telephone: 0899-21-6181.
Founded 1923.

President: Prof. K. Yagi.
Registrar: H. Sumioka.
Librarian: Prof. T. Ide.

Library: *see* Libraries.
Number of teachers: 150.
Number of students: 4,136.

DEANS:

Faculty of College of Economics: Prof. S. Irie.
Faculty and College of Business Administration: Prof. K. Motoki.
Graduate School of Economics: Prof. A. Ote.
Junior College: Prof. K. Kohara.

MEIJI UNIVERSITY

1-1, KANDA-SURUGADAI,
CHIYODA-KU, TOKYO 101
Telephone: (03) 296-4545.
Founded 1881.

Chancellor: H. Aso.
President: M. Saito.
Chief Administrative Officer: S. Nakamura.
Librarian: Y. Kato.

Library of 820,000 vols.
Number of teachers: 1,308.
Number of students: 31,143 undergraduates, 718 graduates.

Publications: various faculty and institute bulletins, etc.

DEANS:

School of Law: Teishi Komazawa.
School of Commerce: Tomisaburo Mikami.
School of Political Science and Economics: Isshin Ikeda.
School of Literature: Motosuke Ishii.
School of Engineering: Hiroshi Yoshimoto.
School of Agriculture: Hiroaki Iwamoto.
School of Business Administration: S. Fujiyoshi.
Postgraduate School: Sakuzo Daigo.
Women's Junior College: Yamato Kawakami.

CHAIRMEN:

Graduate School of Law: Tatsuhiko Tateishi.
Graduate School of Commerce: Sadao Ishida.
Graduate School of Political Science and Economics: Tadashi Ooi.
Graduate School of Literature: Takeo Ikeda.
Graduate School of Engineering: Koichiro Ogura.
Graduate School of Agriculture: Koichi Sato.
Graduate School of Business Administration: Ko Takahashi.

ATTACHED INSTITUTES:

Institute of Cultural Sciences: Dir. Yuji Ejima.
Institute of Social Sciences: Dir. Kiyoshi Mizukoshi.
Institute of Sciences and Technology: Dir. Toshio Yahata.
Criminological Museum: Dir. Hajime Nabeta.
Archaeological Museum: Dir. Sosuke Sugihara.
Computation Centre: Dir. Toshiro Shimada.

MEIJI GAKUIN UNIVERSITY

SHIROKANEDAI 1-CHOME,
MINATO-KU, TOKYO 108
Telephone: 448-5111.
Founded 1877.

President: Dr. N. Hiraide.
Librarian: Prof. M. Onishi.

Library of 266,000 vols.
Number of teachers: 490.
Number of students: 11,000.

DEANS:

College of Economics: Prof. H. Tsuda.
College of Law: Prof. Dr. Y. Hirose.
College of Liberal Arts: Prof. M. Morii.
College of Social Work and Sociology: Prof. T. Fukuda.
General Education: Prof. T. Ono.
Dean of Students: Prof. N. Saito.

MEIJO UNIVERSITY*

TENPAKU-CHO,
SHOWA-KU, NAGOYA 467
Telephone: (832) 1151.
Founded 1948.

President: J. Migumo.
Dean: T. Murai.
Registrar: S. Watanabe.
Librarian: K. Ono.

Library of 100,000 vols.
Number of teachers: 470.
Number of students: 18,000.

* No reply received to our questionnaire this year.

MIYAGI GAKUIN WOMEN'S COLLEGE

1-6, CHUO 4-CHOME,
SENDAI CITY
Telephone: (0222) 21-6211.

Founded 1886; first degree courses.

Chancellor: R. Hayasaka.
President: K. Matsuzaki.
Librarian: Y. Endo.

Library of 105,802 vols.
Number of teachers: 133.
Number of students: 1,488.

DEANS:

Department of Music: T. Yamanouchi
Department of English Literature: T. Nosaka.
Department of Japanese Literature: T. Tanaka.
Department of Home Economics: T. Kozaki.

NANZAN UNIVERSITY

18 YAMAZATO-CHO,
SHOWA-KU, NAGOYA 466
Telephone: (052) 832-3111.
Founded 1949.

President: J. Hirschmeier.
Chief Administrative Officer: I. Yamamoto.
Librarian: T. Ishiguro.

Library of 242,219 vols.

Number of teachers: 179 full-time, 163 part-time.

Number of students: 5,377.

Publications: *Academia, Bulletin of the Anthropological Institute, Law Review, Theological Review* (Japanese), *Asian Folklore Studies, Review of American Studies* (English).

DEANS:

Faculty of Arts and Letters: R. Yamada.
Faculty of Foreign Studies: H. Nishiwaki.
Faculty of Economics: S. Mori.
Faculty of Business Administration: N. Kamata.
Faculty of Law: H. Yagi.

ATTACHED INSTITUTES:

Centre for Japanese Studies: a one-year programme for foreign students who wish to study all aspects of Japanese language and culture.

Institute of Anthropology: research in cultural anthropology, mainly in S.E. and East Asia; attached museum with collections from Japan and New Guinea.

Institute for Religion and Culture: a research institute (post-doctoral level) in the area of Asian religions and their cultural conditioning, with special reference to Christianity. Japanese and foreign scholars to co-operate in joint research.

Centre for American Studies: an institute for the study of contemporary American society and its relationship to Japan.

NIHON UNIVERSITY

6-16 NISHI-KANDA, 2-CHOME,
CHIYODA-KU, TOKYO 101
Telephone: 262-2271.

Founded as College 1889, University status 1903.

Chairman of Board: M. SUZUKI, D.M., D.D.
President: M. SUZUKI, D.M., D.D.
Librarian: M. AKASAKA.

Library of 2,184,000 vols.

Number of full-time teachers: 5,877.
Number of students: 85,715.

Publications include various periodicals from all departments.

DEANS:

College of Law: Y. UZAWA.
College of Humanities and Sciences: S. TSUMAKURA.
College of Economics: S. IDE.
College of Commerce: H. SONODA.
College of Science and Technology: W. KATO.
College of International Relations: M. TAKANASHI.
College of Industrial Technology: T. SAKAI.
College of Engineering: T. HIROKAWA.
School of Medicine: M. KOYABASHI.
School of Dentistry: M. SATO.
School of Dentistry, Matsudo: H. TAKIGUCHI.
College of Art: (vacant).
College of Agriculture and Veterinary Science: S. KOBORI.
Department of Correspondence Study: S. IDE.
Graduate School: M. SUZUKI.

NIPPON DENTAL UNIVERSITY

1-9-20 FUJIMI,
CHIYODA-KU, TOKYO
Telephone: (261) 8311.

Founded 1907.

President: M. NAKAHARA.
Chief Administrative Officer: T. KOMATSU.
Deans: SOH NAKAHARA (Tokyo Faculty), SEN NAKAHARA (Niigata Faculty).
Librarians: S. NAGAHAMA (Tokyo Faculty), S. HATADE (Niigata Faculty).

Library of 67,784 vols. (Tokyo Faculty), 48,801 vols. (Niigata Faculty).

Number of teachers: 478.
Number of students: 2,497.

Publication: *Odontology*† (bimonthly).

NOTRE DAME WOMEN'S COLLEGE

(Notre Dame Joshi Daigaku)

1-2 MINAMI NONOGAMI-CHO,
SHIMOGAMO, SAKYO-KU,
KYOTO 606
Telephone: 781-1173.

Founded 1961.

Private control; Language of instruction: Japanese; Academic year: April to March.

President: Sister MARY MICHAEL TASHIRO, S.S.N.D.
Secretary-General: Y. HONDA.
Registrar: K. SUMIDA.
Librarian: C. OGURA.

Library of 55,846 vols.

Number of teachers: 45 full-time, 45 **part-time.**

Number of students: 1,161.

Publications: *Kiyo*†, *Insight*† (annual).

Departments of English and Culture Living.

OKINAWA UNIVERSITY

KOKUBA, NAHA, OKINAWA
Telephone: 32-1768.

Founded 1956.

Language of instruction: Japanese; Private control; Academic year: April to March (two semesters); First-degree courses.

Chancellor: NOBORU KAKAZU.
President: K. TAKAMIYA.
Registrar: S. SAKUGAWA.

Number of teachers: 27.
Number of students: 2,835.
Publication: *Okidai Ronso.*

DEANS:

Department of English: H. NAKACHI.
Department of Law: T. KAMIYAMA.
Department of Economics: K. TAIRA.
Department of Business Administration: S. MIYAHIRA.

OSAKA MEDICAL COLLEGE

7-2 DAIGAKUMACHI,
TAKATSUKI CITY, OSAKA
Telephone: 0726-83-1221.

Founded 1927.

President: M. YAMANAKA.
Registrar: H. KITAMURA.
Librarian: H. MATSUMOTO.

Library of 93,955 vols.

Number of teachers: 265.
Number of students: 888.

Publications: *Journal*† (in Japanese), *Bulletin*† (in English).

RIKKYO UNIVERSITY

(St. Paul's University)

NISHI-IKEBUKURO,
TOSHIMA-KU, TOKYO
Telephone: 985-2204

Founded 1874.

President: N. OGATA.
Registrar: R. MIZUGUCHI.
Librarian: K. UKAWA.

Library of 550,000 vols.

Number of teachers: 786.
Number of students: 12,276.

Publications: ***Christian Studies, Rikkyo Review*** **(Arts and Letters),** ***The Shien*** **(Historical Journal),** ***Review of Japanese Literature, Commentarii Mathematici Universitatis Sancti Pauli, Journal of Applied Sociology, Economic Review, Rikkyo Hogaku*** **(Review of Law and Politics),** *Mouseion*, ***The Rikkyo Quarterly, Review of French Literature, Aspekt*** **(German Literature Journal),** ***Research Reports of Depts. of Natural Science and Civilization, JICE Tsushin*** (Japanese Institute of Christian Education publication) and other faculty publications.

DEANS:

Faculty of Arts: Y. HAMADA.
Faculty of Economics: T. KOBAYASHI.
Faculty of Science: I. MURAMATSU.
Faculty of Law and Politics: M. IKEDA.
Faculty of Social Relations: S. TAKEZAWA.
Faculty of General Education: T. TAKAHASHI.

RISSHO UNIVERSITY

OSAKI 4-CHOME,
SHINAGAWA-KU, TOKYO 141

Founded 1904.

Rector: H. SAKAMOTO.

Number of full-time teachers: 98.
Number of students: 3,536.

DEANS:

Faculty of Buddhism: **S. NOMURA.**
Faculty of Letters: **M. SASE.**
Faculty of Economics: **K. AGEI.**

RITSUMEIKAN UNIVERSITY

TOJIIN KITAMACHI, KITA-KU,
KYOTO 603
Telephone: 075-463-1131.

Founded 1900.

Academic year: April to March.

President: K. AMANO.

Chief Director: K. UENISHI.

Number of full-time teachers: 351.
Number of students: 21,186.

Undergraduate and graduate courses in law, economics, business administration, industrial sociology, letters, science and engineering.

RYUKOKU UNIVERSITY

TSUKAMOTO-CHO, FUKAKUSA, FUSHIMI-KU, KYOTO

Telephone: (075) 642-1111.

Founded 1639.

Academic year: April to March.

President: Dr. KENKO FUTABA.

Administrator: KEIZO GOTO.

Librarian: Prof. KEIICHI MASUNAGA.

Library of 589,935 vols.

Number of teachers: 539.
Number of students: 8,068.

Publications: *Bulletin of Buddhist Cultural Institute* (annually), *Annual Bulletin of Research Institute for Social Science* (annually), *Ryukoku Hogaku* (quarterly), *The Journal of Economic and Business Studies* (quarterly), *Ryudai Ronshu* (half-yearly), *Ryokoku Kiyo* (2 a year), etc.

DEANS:

Faculty of Literature: Prof. TSUTOMU MIMURA.
Faculty of Economics: Prof. MASAO MIYANAGA.
Faculty of Business Administration: Prof. KOZO IKEMOTO.
Faculty of Law: YUJIRO OBATA.

PROFESSORS:

Faculty of Literature:

AOYAMA, Y., German
ASAI, N., Shin Buddhism
ASANO, K., Shin Buddhism
CHIBA, J., Japanese History
FUGEN, K., Shin Buddhism
FUJIKI, H., English Literature
FUKUMA, K., Buddhist History
FUKUSHIMA, K., Japanese History
FUNAHASHI, K., Sociology
FUTABA, K., Buddhism History
GO, K., Physical Education
HAMADA, A., Japanese Literature
HAYASHI, S., Social Work
HIGASHINAKA, I., English Literature
HINO, A., Japanese History
HIRAMATSU, R., Japanese History
INOGUCHI, T., Buddhism
ISHIDA, Y., Philosophy
ISHIHARA, K., Japanese Literature
KASAHARA, S., Sociology
KATO, K., Mathematics
KATO, S., Pedagogy
KAWAMORI, K., Pedagogy
KAWASAKI, E., Sociology
KIMURA, K., English
KITABATAKE, N., Buddhism
KITAHARA, M., French
KITAMURA, H., Oriental History
KOJIMA, M., Pedagogy
KOJIMA, N., Japanese Literature
KUCHIBA, M., Sociology
MARUYAMA, T., Philosophy
MASUNAGA, K., English Literature
MATSUBARA, I., Social Work
MIKOGAMI, E., Buddhism
MIMURA, T., Philosophy
MINAMOTO, J., Shin Buddhism
MIYAMOTO, S., English
MUNEMASA, I., Japanese Literature
MURAKAMI, S., English Literature
MURAKAMI, S., Shin Buddhism
NAKAGAKI, M., Social Work
NAKAGAWA, H., Japanese Literature
NAKAYAMA, S., Buddhist History
NISHIDA, N., Social Work
NISHIYAMA, R., Mathematics
ODA, Y., Oriental History
OGUMA, S., Philosophy
OKA, R., Shin Buddhism
OKITA, H., English
ONISHI, K., Education
ONO, K., Oriental History
SATO, M., Philosophy
SATO, M., Pedagogy
SHIGARAKI, T., Shin Buddhism
TAJIRI, Y., Spanish
TAKEMURA, S., Buddhism
TAKEUCHI, S., Buddhism
TAKIGAWA, Y., Sociology
TERATANI, T., Japanese Literature
UCHIDA, G., Oriental History
UEYAMA, D., Buddhism
UMITANI, N., Pedagogy
WATANABE, K., Physical Education
WATANABE, T., Buddhism
YUKI, S., Philosophy
YAMADA, Y., English Literature
YAMATO, C., Social Work
YAMAZAKI, K., Buddhism

Faculty of Economics:

BAN, E., Japanese Literature
FUJII, K., Japanese Economy
FUJINAGA, Y., International Monetary Economy
HIGUCHI, M., Spanish
IGUCHI, T., Industrial Economy
IMAI, K., Psychology
KANEKO, H., Political Economy
KAWAMURA, T., German
KAWAMURA, Y., Agricultural Economy
KISHIDA, O., History of Economics
MATSUOKA, T., Political Economy
MISAKI, S., Political Economy
MIYAGAWA, C., French
MIYANAGA, M., Japanese Economy
MIZUHARA, S., Economic Theory
NAGATA, H., Case Study of Foreign Economic History (U.S.A.)
NAGAYA, M., Economic Statistics
NISHIBORI, F., Economic Theory
NISHINARITA, Y., Japanese Economic History
OKADA, M., International Economy
ONO, K., History of Natural Science
OTSU, S., Political Economy
OTSUKA, K., Economic Theory
SAIGUSA, T., Statistics
SHIMIZU, K., English
SODA, O., Economic Policy
TAIGUCHI, T., Theories of Physical Education
TAGUCHI, Y., Case Study of Foreign Economy
TAKEDA, R., Shin Buddhism
TANAKA, Y., Socialist Economy
TERADA, K., Public Finance
TOSHIOKA, S., Principles of Economics
TSUBOUCHI, R., Sociology
UEDA, S., Commercial Economy
YADA, B., Physics
YAMADA, T., English
YOSHIDA, S., History of Social Thought

Faculty of Business Administration:

ABE, D., Principles of Economics
ARITA, T., Chinese
FUKUDA, T., Geography
HAYASHI, A., Management Science
HAYASHI, K., Cost Accounting
HONDA, H., Financial Management
IIDA, S., Book Keeping
IKEMOTO, K., General Economic History
INOUE, H., Business Management
INOUE, K., Business Finance
INOUE, K., English
KANEKO, A., Commercial Science
KATAOKA, S., History of Business Doctrine
KAWAMURA, S., Portuguese
KITAMURA, S., Structure of Japanese Industry
KOBAYASHI, K., Business History
KOIKE, T., Information Processing Systems
KUME, N., Biology
MASAOKA, M., Managerial Accounting
MISHIMA, R., Industrial and Social Psychology
MITSUKAWA, T., Buddhism
MORIYA, H., Science of Merchandise
MOTOOKA, A., Marketing
MURAKAMI, J., Book Keeping
NAKAI, G., English
NAKAYAMA, J., German
OKABE, T., Accounting
ONISHI, K., Information Industry
OSUGI, M., Economic Policy
OTA, Y., Industrial Management
SAKAI, H., Business History of Japan
SHIMAMOTO, K., Religion
TAICHI, Y., Labour Management
TAKAYANAGI, K., Sociology of Statistics
TANO, T., Physical Education
TOYOSAKI, M., Principles of Economics
TSUNOKUNI, C., Book Keeping
YOKOYAMA, K., Sociology
YOSHIMOTO, A., English

Faculty of Law:

ASAI, K., Labour Law
HIGASHI, F., Physical Education
HIRANO, T., Constitutional Law
IKEDA, S., Politics
ISHIDA, T., Political Science
ISHII, K., Philosophy
KATSURA, F., English
KAWABATA, M., Politics
KAZAMA, T., Civil Law
KISAKA, Z., Political History
KUBOTA, M., Physical Education
MATSUBARA, H., History
MORI, K., Civil Law
NAGARA, K., Administrative Law
NAKAGAWA, H., English
NAKAGAWA, S., Criminal Law
NISHIMURA, N., Civil Law
OBATA, Y., Commercial Law
OSAKADANI, K., Commercial Law
OSAKI, T., Physics
SHIBAGAKI, Y., Chinese
SHIGETA, Z., Law of Criminal Procedure
SUGIMURA, T., Administrative Law
TAIRA, H., Chinese Literature
TAKAGI, K., Health Education
TAKASHIMA, G., Criminology
TAKEHISA, S., Commercial Law
TAKITA, R., International Politics
TSUJITA, J., Physics
UEDA, K., Constitutional Law
WAKAKI, Y., Shin Buddhism
WATARI, H., English
YAMAUCHI, S., German
YASUTAKE, T., Civil Law
YOROI, T., Labour Law

ATTACHED RESEARCH INSTITUTES:

Institute of Buddhist Culture: Dir. Prof. SHOKO TAKEUCHI.

Institute of Social Science: Dir. Prof. KESAJI KOBAYASHI.

SAGAMI INSTITUTE OF TECHNOLOGY

1-1 NISHIKAIGAN TSUJIDO, FUJISAWA CITY, KANAGAWA PRE., 251

Founded 1963.

Courses in Engineering and Science, with emphasis on research methods.

President: Dr. H. ROKKAKU.
Secretary: K. TASAKA.

Library of 31,000 vols.
Number of teachers: 200.
Number of students: 2,200.
Publication: *Memoirs.*

HEADS OF DEPARTMENTS:

Information Science: Dr. T. TANEMURA.
Electrical Engineering: Dr. K. OKUBO.
Mechanical Engineering: Dr. M. MASHIO.

UNIVERSITY OF THE SACRED HEART, TOKYO

HIROO 4 CHOME 3-1, SHIBUYA-KU, TOKYO
Telephone: 03-407-5811.
Founded 1948.

President: Prof. ICHI SAGARA
Business Chief: M. HATTORI..
Registrar: I. HORIGUCHI.
Librarian: Prof. Y. TANAKA.

Library of 200,000 vols.

Number of teachers: 244.
Number of students: 1,801.

DEANS:

Dean of Studies: T. UCHIYAMA.
Dean of Students: S. SATOMI.

Publication: *Seishin Studies* (bi-annually).

SAPPORO UNIVERSITY

3 JYO 7 CHIYOME, 243-2, NISHIOKA, TOYOHIRA-KU, SAPPORO
Telephone: 852-1181.
Founded 1967.

President: TSUTOMU TAKEDA.
Administrator: MOTOAKI MATSUBARA.
Librarian: MASAMI SHIONO.

Number of teachers: 96.
Number of students: 5,702.

Library of 130,000 vols.

Publications: *Culture and Language, Review of Economics and Business Administration, Journal of Faculty of General Education.*

DEANS:

Faculty of Foreign Languages: KEIICHI SUGANAMA.
Faculty of Economics: TERUKIYO HAYASHI.
Faculty of Business Administration: TSUGUO NARUSE.
Faculty of General Education: TAKAHIRO MIYARA.
Women's Junior College: IKUNOSUKE OMORI.

SEIJO UNIVERSITY

6-1-20 SEIJO, SETAGAYA-KU, TOKYO
Telephone: (482) 1181.

Founded 1950.

Faculties of Economics, Arts and Literature, Law.

Graduate School: Economics; Arts and Literature.

President: T. MITSUFUJI.
Registrar: K. OKADA.
Librarian: H. ISHIKAWA.

Library of 300,000 vols.

Number of teachers: 136 full-time, 183 part-time.

Number of students: 4,585.

SEISEN WOMEN'S COLLEGE

3-CHOME, 16 BAN 21 GO, HIGASHI-GOTANDA, SHINAGAWA-KU, TOKYO
Telephone: 447-1675.
Founded 1950.

Undergraduate faculties of Japanese and English Literature, Christian Culture and Spanish Language and Literature.

President: S. TOHYAMA.
Librarian: J. KOBAYASHI.

Library of 91,320 vols.
Number of teachers: 111.
Number of students: 1,374.

SENSHU UNIVERSITY

JIMBO-CHO 3-8, KANDA, CHIYODA-KU, TOKYO 101
Telephone: 03-265-6211.

Founded 1880.

Chancellor: K. SOMA.
President: C. TAKAHASHI.
Librarian: FURUSHIMA.

Library of 500,000 vols.

Number of full-time teachers: 303.
Number of students: 19,551.

Publications: *Senshu Shakai Kagaku Nenpo* (Annual Bulletin of Social Science), *Senshu Keizaigaku Ronshu* (Economic Bulletin), *Senshu Hogaku Ronshu* (Journal of Law and Political Science), *Senshu Keieigaku Ronshu* (Business Review), *Senshu Shogaku Ronshu* (Commercial Review), *Shenshu Jinbunkagaku Nenpo* (Annual Bulletin of the Humanities), *Senshu Shizenkagaku Kiyo* (Natural Science Bulletin).

DEANS:

Faculty of Commerce: A. SASAI.
Faculty of Law: T. SUNADA.
Faculty of Business Administration: M. DEUSHI.
Faculty of Economics: Y. YOSHIZAWA.
Faculty of Literature: M. FUJINO.

SOPHIA UNIVERSITY (Jôchi University)

CHIYODA-KU, KIOICHO 7, TOKYO
Telephone: 283-3111.
Founded 1913.

Languages of instruction: Japanese and English.

Chancellor: M. YANASE.
President: J. PITTAU.
Vice-Presidents: W. CURRIE, H. AKABAE, M. HASHIGUCHI.
Registrar: H. HITOMI.
Librarian: L. ARMBRUSTER.

Library: *see* Libraries.

Number of professors: 785.

Number of students: 9,649 in Japanese Language Programmes, 801 in English Programmes.

Publications: *Monumenta Nipponica* (quarterly in English), *Sophia* (quarterly in Japanese), *Sophia Economic Review, Sophia Law Review, Historical Studies, German Literature Review, Catholic Theology, Studies in English Literature, Studies in Japanese Literature, Bulletin of the Foreign Languages Faculty, Studies in French Literature* (all half-yearly in Japanese).

DEANS:

International College: P. P. DEL CAMPANA.
Faculty of Literature: Y. TSUCHIDA.
Faculty of Law: T. HANAMI.
Faculty of Economics: N. YOKENO.
Faculty of Foreign Languages: K. KANKI.
Faculty of Science and Engineering: K. ICHIKAWA.
Faculty of Theology: J. VIERHAUS.

DIRECTORS:

Institute of International Relations: T. KAWATA.
Socio-Economic Institute: R. BALLON.
Ibero-American Institute: G. ANDRADE.
Institute of Oriental Religions: T. IMOOS.
Institute of Christian Culture: P. NEMESHEGYI.

TAKUSHOKU UNIVERSITY

3-4-14 KOHINATA, BUNKYO-KU, TOKYO
Telephone: 03-947-2261
Founded 1900.
Campus at Hachioji.

President: J. TAKASE.
Vice-President: S. MORIGAKI.
Chairman of Board of Directors: J. TAKASE.
Librarian: H. EMURA.

Library of 300,000 vols.
Number of teachers: 133.
Number of students: 7,783.

DEANS:

Faculty of Commerce: T. OSAKAI.

Faculty of Political Science and Economics: D. HOSOGAI.
Faculty of Foreign Languages: R. URITANI.
Japanese Language Section for Foreign Students: J. KUSUMI.
Takushoku Junior College: S. ICHIKO.
Hokkaido Takushoku Junior College: K. TAGUCHI.
Graduate School: M. IZUMI.

TAMAGAWA UNIVERSITY

6-1-1 TAMAGAWA GAKUEN
MACHIDA-SHI, TOKYO 194
Telephone: 0427-32-9111.

Founded 1929.

Founder: Prof. Dr. K. OBARA.
President: Prof. Dr. T. OBARA.
Registrar: Dr. T. SAKAI.
Librarian: Dr. T. MATSUMURA.

Library of 483,127 vols.
Number of teachers: 578.
Number of students: 5,562 full-time and 15,163 correspondence.

DEANS:

Faculty of Agriculture: Dr. S. AOYAGI.
Faculties of Education: Dr. A. OKADA.
Faculties of Literature: Dr. M. HAMADA.
Faculty of Technology: Dr. T. AKAGI.

TOHOKU GAKUIN UNIVERSITY
(North Japan College)

3-1 TSUCHITOI-1-CHOME,
SENDAI 980

President: TADAO ODA.

Number of full-time teachers: 244.
Number of students: 12,768.

TOKAI UNIVERSITY

2-28 TOMIGAYA, SHIBUYA-KU,
TOKYO
Telephone: 03-467-2211.

Founded 1942.

Academic year: April to March.

President: S. MATSUMAE.
Chief Administrative Officer: T. MATSUMAE (Academic Affairs).
Librarian: HACHISHI SUZUKI.

Number of full-time teachers: 1,328.
Number of students: 31,474.

Publications: *Tokai Journal of Experimental and Clinical Medicine*, bulletins of the various schools.

DEANS:

School of Letters: KEITARO SHOJU.
School of Political Science and Economics: KEIZO YONEYAMA.
School of Science: MASARU INAGAKI.
School of Engineering: SANNI HAGI.
School of Marine Science and Technology: MINORU NISHIMURA.
School of Physical Education: SHIGEO KASAI.
School of Humanities and Culture: NORIO MATSUMAE.
School of Medicine: SHOGO SASAKI.

DIRECTORS:

Research Institute of Industrial Science: SADAICHI MORITA.
Research Institute of Civilization: KEITARO SHOJU.
Institute of Social and Behavioural Science: TADASHI YOSHIMURA.
Institute of Oceanic Research: MITSUO IWASHITA.
Research Institute of Visual Arts: S. MATSUMAE.
Institute of Educational Technology: SONOSUKE KATORI.
Research and Development Institute: TATSURO MATSUMAE.

TOKYO COLLEGE OF PHARMACY

1432-1 HORINOUCHI, HACHIOJI,
TOKYO 192-03
Telephone: (0426) 76-5111.

Founded 1880.

President: Dr. S. OHKI.
Librarian: Prof. K. ASAHINA.

Library of 50,000 vols.
Number of teachers: *c.* 200.
Number of students: *c.* 2,000.

Publication: *Annual Report.*

TOKYO ELECTRICAL ENGINEERING UNIVERSITY

KANDA-NISHIKI-CHO,
CHIYODA-KU, TOKYO
Telephone: 03-294-1551.

Founded 1907.

President: Dr. T. SAKAMOTO.
Librarian: Prof. J. KAWADA.

Library of 136,000 vols., 700 periodicals.

Number of teachers: *c.* 310 full-time, *c.* 260 part-time.

Number of students: *c.* 8,500 undergraduates (*c.* 5,500 day time, *c.* 3,000 evening), *c.* 50 graduates.

Publications: *Research Reports.*

DEANS:

Graduate School: S. OKAMURA.
Faculty of Engineering: T. KUBOTA.
Faculty of Science and Engineering: I. KOIZUMI.
Junior College: N. NAKAMURA.

DIRECTORS:

Institute of Electro-Motive-Power Application: S. MIYAIRI.
Institute of Information Science and Technology: M. NAKANO.

TOKYO KEIZAI UNIVERSITY

7 MINAMISHO 1-CHOME,
KOKUBUNJI, TOKYO 185
Telephone: 0423-21-1941.

Founded 1900 as Ohkura School of Commerce.

Faculties of Economics and Business Administration and Graduate School of Economics.

President T. WATANABE.
Registrar: SHIRO MASUDA.
Librarian: Y. YORIMITSU.

Library of 240,000 vols.
Number of teachers: 286.
Number of students: 7,780.

TOKYO SCIENCE UNIVERSITY

1-3 KAGURAZAKA,
SHINJUKU-KU, TOKYO
Telephone: (260) 4271.

Founded 1881.

President: MASAO KOTANI.
Librarian: M. TAKEDA.

Library of 252,096 vols.
Number of teachers: 604.
Number of students: 15,915.

TOKYO UNIVERSITY OF AGRICULTURE

1-1-1 SAKURAGAOKA,
SETAGAYA-KU, TOKYO
Telephone: 420-2131.

Founded 1891.

President: Dr. T. SUZUKI.
Dean: Dr. Y. KANAKI.
Registrar: S. ONO.
Librarian: Dr. K. OHASHI.

Library of 250,000 vols.
Number of teachers: 431.
Number of students: 9,104.

TOKYO WOMEN'S MEDICAL COLLEGE

ICHIGAYA KAWADA-CHO,
SHINJUKU-KU, TOKYO 162
Telephone: (353) 8111.

Founded 1900.

President: H. YOSHIOKA, M.D.
Registrar: I. NAGATA.
Librarian: T. ISHII, M.D.

Library of 71,500 vols.
Number of teachers: 441.
Number of students: 594.

TOYO UNIVERSITY

5-28-20 HAKUSAN,
BUNKYO-KU, TOKYO 112
Telephone: 03 (945) 7211.

Founded 1887.

President: H. HORI.

Library of 302,898 vols.
Number of full-time teachers: 393.
Number of students: 20,889.

DEANS:

Faculty of Letters: S. KANAOKA.
Faculty of Economics: F. OGAWA.

Faculty of Law: N. NAKANO.
Faculty of Sociology: F. NAITO.
Faculty of Technology: M. HONMA.
Faculty of Liberal Arts: K. MORIKAWA.
Faculty of Industrial Administration: K. MATSUMOTO.

TSUDA COLLEGE

2-1-1 TSUDA-MACHI,
KODAIRA-SHI, TOKYO 187

Founded 1900.

President: FUMIO NAKAJIMA.

Library of 130,000 vols., 845 periodicals.

Number of full-time teachers: 80.

Number of students: 2,400 (105 postgraduate).

Publications: *Tsuda Review, Journal of Tsuda College, International and Cultural Studies.*

Departments of English Literature and Language, Mathematics, International and Cultural Studies.

WASEDA UNIVERSITY

6-1 NISHIWASEDA 1-CHOME,
SHINJUKU-KU, TOKYO 160

Telephone: 203-4141.

Founded 1882.

Private control; Academic year: April to July, September to February.

President: T. SHIMIZU.

Librarian: H. FURUKAWA.

Library: *see* Libraries.

Number of teachers: 2,552.

Number of students: 40,773 undergraduates (34,502 day-time division, 6,271 evening division), 2,648 graduates.

Publications: *The Waseda Journal of Political Science and Economics* (bi-monthly), *The Waseda Law Review* (half-yearly), *The Journal for the Study of Japanese Literature* (half-yearly), *Shikan* (Historical Review) (twice a year), *Studies on Oriental Literature* (yearly), *Report of Waseda Architecture* (annually), *Waseda Business and Economic Studies* (annually), *Library News* (monthly), *Comparative Law Review* (half-yearly), *Journal of the System Science Institute* (half-yearly), etc.

DEANS:

Day-time Divisions:

School of Political Science and Economics: M. KOMATSU.
School of Law: T. UCHIDA.
School of Literature: Y. MIDSUNO.
School of Education: M. SAKURAI.
School of Commerce: R. ASAOKA.
School of Science and Engineering: H. MURAKAMI.

Evening Divisions:

School of Social Sciences: S. KOBAYASHI.
School of Literature: L. KOBAYASHI.

CHAIRMEN:

Graduate School of Political Science: S. FUKUDA.
Graduate School of Economics: Y. YAMAKAWA.
Graduate School of Law: H. TAKASHIMA.
Graduate School of Literature: K. ASAI.
Graduate School of Commerce: K. TOBA.
Graduate School of Science and Engineering: T. SAITO.

FULL PROFESSORS:

School of Political Science and Economics.

AKIYAMA, S., French
ANDO, H., Chinese Economy
ANDO, T., Social Policy
DATE, K., Economics
FUJII, A., English
FUJIWARA, Y., History of Political Thought
FUKUDA, K., Political Science
FUKUHARA, F., German
HIRATA, K., Public Finance
HORIE, T., Economics
HORIKE, B., Money and Banking
IIJIMA, M., Biology
ISHII, Y., French
IWAKURA, S., Journalism
KANECHIKA, T., Political History
KANEDA, M., English
KASHIWAZAKI, T., Economics
KATAOKA, H., Political Science
KOBAYASHI, K., Economics
KOBAYASHI, S., Political Science
KOGA, H., Social Policy
KOMATSU, M., Economic Policy
KURATA, K., Economic Mathematics
MASUDA, T., Economic History of Europe
MINAMI, E., English
NAKAMURA, S., French
NAKAMURA, T., German
NEGISHI, K., German
NISHIKAWA, J., Economics
NISHIO, I., English
OKAYAMA, T., International Economics
OUCHI, G., English
OWASE, T., Economics
SAKAZAKI, O., German
SATAKE, G., Economic Statistics
SATO, F., Mathematics
SATO, T., Law of Public Administration
SEKI, Y., History of Social Thought
SHIGA, K., English
SHIMAMURA, N., German
SHIMIZU, N., Political Science
SHIMIZU, T., Mathematics
SHODA, K., Economic History of Japan
SUWA, S., Economics
SUZUKI, H., English
SUZUKI, M., English
SUZUKI, T., English
TAKAGI, S., English
TAKEDA, K., English
TANAKA, K., Economics
TODO, A., Chinese
TSURUOKA, G., Money and Banking
TSUTSUMIGUCHI, Y., Law of Public Administration
UCHIDA, M., Political Science
UEHARA, K., Economics
WAKURI, S., Russian
YAMAKAWA, Y., Economics
YAMAMOTO, T., English
YASUDA, J., Statistics
YORIMOTO, K., Political Science
YOSHIMURA, K., International Politics

School of Law:

ANDO, M., French
ANZAI, C., French
ARAI, R., Public Law
DEGUCHI, S., German
DOI, T., International Private Law
HAMADA, T., French
HATA, M., Sociology of Law
HOSHINO, T., English
ICHIKAWA, S., English
IHARA, K., German
INOUE, Z., English
IWATA, J., English
KANAZAWA, O., Commercial Law
KAZUE, J., French
KIMURA, S., German
KISHI, Y., Chinese
KUROKI, S., Civil Law
KUROYANAGI, H., English
KUSUMOTO, H., Anglo-American Law
MACHIDA, T., French
MAKI, M., English
MATSUBARA, K., English
MIYASAKA, T., Commercial Law
NAGAHAMA, Y., Commercial Law
NAKAMURA, H., Law of Civil Procedure
NAKAMURA, K., Japanese Legal History
NAKAMURA, M., Commercial Law
NAKANO, T., Criminal Law
NAKAYAMA, K., Labour Law
NISHIHARA, H. ,Criminal Law
NOMURA, H., English
OHATA, T., History of Foreign Policy
OKADA, K., German
OKAMURA, M., English
OKOSO, Y., English
OKUSHIMA, T., Commercial Law
OKUYAMA, Y., English
OSUKA, A., Constitutional Law
SAITO, KAZUE, English
SAKAMAKI, T., Commercial Law
SAKURAI, K., Civil Law
SASAKI, H., Civil Law
SATO, A., Labour Law
SATO, H., Constitutional Law
SATO, T., Legal History
SAWAMURA, K., English
SHIMADA, N., Civil Law
SHIMAOKA, S., French
SHINOZUKA, S., Civil Law
SHIOYA, T., Philosophy
SUGIYAMA, H., Japanese Legal History
SUSATO, J., Spanish
SUSUKI, S., Criminal Law
SUSUKI, S., Criminal Law
SUZUKI, S., Law of Civil Procedure
TAKANO, T., Civil Law
TAKASHIMA, H. ,Civil Law
TAKAYAMA, A., Russian
TAYAMA, T., Civil Law
UCHIDA, I., Criminal Law
UCHIDA, T., Civil Procedure Law
UCHIYAMA, S., English
URATA, K., Constitutional Law
USHIYAMA, T., Civil Law
YAMADA, H., German
YAMAGATA, M., English
YASUI, Y., German
YATO, T., Anglo-American Law
YOKOKAWA, T., Criminal Procedure

School of Literature:

AKIMOTO, R., Sociology
AKINAGA, K., Japanese
ANDO, N., Drama
ANZAI, K., Occidental History
ARAI, S., German
ARAYA, K., Russian
ASAI, K., Psychology
ASHIDA, T., Chinese
BAN, H., Philosophy
EIDA, T., Occidental History
ENDO, H., Philosophy
FRIEND, D. B., English
FUJIHIRA, H., Japanese
FUJINUMA, T., Russian
FUKUI, F., Oriental Philosophy
FUKUI, S., Chinese History
FURUKAWA, H., Linguistics
GUNJI, M., Kabuki Drama

HAMAGUCHI, H., Sociology
HAMAYA, K., History of Occidental Fine Arts
HARADA, M., Chinese Philosophy
HARUKI, Y., Psychology
HASEGAWA, R., Chinese
HASHIMOTO, F., Japanese
HATTORI, H., Psychology
HAYASHI, A., English
HAYASHI, M., German
HAZAMA, H., Sociology
HIKICHI, M., English
HIMURO, M., English
HIRAKAWA, A., Indian Thought
HIRAOKA, T., French
HIRATA, Y., Occidental History
ICHIKAWA, S., French
INOUCHI, Y., English
INOUE, N., French
ISHIZEKI, K., Philosophy
ISONO, T. Philosophy
IWANAMI, T., Philosophy
IWASE, T., French
IWASHITA, T., Psychology
JIMBO, K., Japanese
KAI, M., English
KANEMOTO, G., Russian
KANO, M., Japanese History
KATO, N., French
KATO, T., French
KAWAHARA, E., Philosophy
KAWAMOTO, S., Linguistics
KAWATAKE, T., Drama
KIMURA, S., Russian
KITAMURA, N., Philosophy
KOBAYASHI, L., French
KOGA, N., Chinese History
KOIKE, N., English
KOJIMA, K., Psychology
KONNO, K., English
KOSUGI, K., History of Oriental Arts
KOYAMA, C., Philosophy
KUBOTA, H., French
KUME, M., Psychology
KUNISAKI, F., Japanese
KURAHASHI, T., English
KUSUYAMA, H., Oriental Philosophy
LENDON, K. H., English
MASAOKA, K., Sociology
MATSUBARA, T., English
MATSUMARA, K., Pedagogy
MATSUNAMI, S., Philosophy
MATSUURA, T., Chinese
MIDSUNO, Y., Japanese History
MISAKI, R., Oriental Philosophy
MITANI, T., English
MIURA, O., English
MORI, Y., German
MORIYA, T., English
MOTOAKI, H., Psychology
MURAKAMI, K., French Literature
MURATA, K., Pedagogy
MURAYAMA, Y., Chinese
MURO, J., French Literature
NAGASAWA, K., Oriental History
NAKAJIMA, H., Pedagogy
NAKAJIMA, K., Historical Geography
NAKAMURA, H., German Literature
NAKAYAMA, S., English
NATSUMEDA, M., German
NISHIKAWA, M., English
NOGUCHI, Y., Occidental History
NONAKA, R., English
NOZAKI, N., Occidental History
OI, K., English
OKADA, H., English
OKI, K., German
OKUBO, S., German
OMI, T., Sociology
ONUMA, H., English
OSHIMURA, N., Pedagogy
OTSUKI, T., Pedagogy
SAGAZA, H., Population Problems
SAKATA, K., German
SAKURAI, K., Archaeology
SASAKI, K., History of Oriental Fine Arts
SASAKI, M., Japanese
SATO, M., French
SATO, Y., Sociology
SAWADA, M., Chinese
SAWAYANAGI, D., Fine Arts
SHIBA, K., German Literature
SHIBATA, K., German
SHIGEHARA, A., German
SHIMIZU, S., French
SHIMIZU, S., Japanese
SHIMPO, S., English
SHINADA, M., French
SOMA, I., Psychology
SUGAHARA, S., Oriental Philosophy
SUGIMOTO, T., Chinese
SUGIMOTO, T., Japanese
SUZUKI, Y., English Literature
TAKAHASHI, E., History of Occidental Fine Arts
TAKAHASHI, N., Philosophy
TAKEMORI, T., Japanese
TAKIZAWA, T., Japanese History
TANIGUCHI, T., Philosophy
TOMITA, M., Psychology
TONOKI, N., Sociology
TORAIWA, M., English
TORIGOE, B., Kabuki Drama
TSUJIMURA, T., Japanese Language
UENO, O., Japanese
UESAKA, N., Japanese
USUI, Y., English
WASHIDA, T., French
YAMADA, H., German
YAMAMOTO, K., Drama
YAMAMOTO, T., Occidental History
YANAGI, T., Russian
YASUI, G., French Literature
YASUI, R., Russian
YOSHIMURA, M., History of Occidental Fine Arts
YUGE, M., French
YUI, M., Japanese History

School of Education:

ABE, K., Physical Education
AZUMA, K., Psychology
DEGUCHI, Y., English
ENOMOTO, T., Japanese
FURUSAWA, K., German
HAMAJI, K., Political Science
HASEGAWA, M., English
HASHIMOTO, H., English
HASHIMOTO, H., Psychology
HATTORI, K., Psychology
HIDAKA, Y., Social Education
HINOHARA, Y., Algebra
HOSHI, S., English
ICHIMURA, N., Pedagogy
INADA, S., French
ISHIGAKI, H., Analysis
ISHII, S., Zoology
ITO, H., Physiology
ITO, H., French
KAJIWARA, M., Japanese
KAKUYAMA, M., French
KANZAKI, I., German
KAWASAKI, T., Russian
KIKUYAMA, S., Biology
KOBAYASHI, K., English
KOJIMA, Y., English
KOMADA, S., Chinese Classics
KONO, T., Japanese
KUMAGAI, K., Japanese History
MAKINO, T., Psychology
MARIKO, T., Petrology
MARUYAMA, T., Business Administration
MATSUDA, K., Economics
MINAGAWA, T., Geometry
MINO, S., Chinese
MISHIMA, J., Psychology
MIYADERA, I., Functional Analysis
MORIKAWA, Y., Psychology
MURAOKA, A., Occidental History
MURATA, Y., Japanese History
NAKAJIMA, M., Human Geography
NAKAMURA, T., Mineralogy
NAKANO, K., Japanese
NAKAO, K., English
NIIJIMA, M., English Language
NISHIMURA, M., Archaeology
OBATA, A., French
OHARU, S., Algebra
OHSUGI, A., Petroleum Geology
OKITSU, K., Japanese
OKUBO, T., Geography
OSADA, M., Pedagogy
OSHIMA, Y., Botany
OTSUKI, H., History of Social Education
OYA, M., Geography
PETERSON, A. W., English
SAKA, Y., Structural Geology
SAKURAI, H., Botany
SAKURAI, M., Japanese
SATO, I., German
SHIBANUMA, T., Economics
SHIRAISH, D., Japanese Linguistics
SUZUKI, I., History
SUZUKI, S., English
SUZUKI, S., Pedagogy
SUZUKI, T., English
TAIRA, T., Zoology
TAKADA, K., English
TAKAHASHI, H., French
TAKAHASHI, T., Educational Engineering
TAKIGUCHI, H., Archaeology
TANABE, Y., English
TANGE, R., Sociology
TOMITA, T., Psychology
TOMURO, H., German
TORIGOE, S., Juvenile Literature
TOYA, T., Japanese
TSUKAWAKI, S., Physical Education
TSUTSUMI, S., Mineralogy
UEDA, M., English
UMEZAWA, N., Physical Education
WADA, J., Functional Analysis
YAJIMA, M., English
YAMAMOTO, J., Japanese Drama
YAMAOKA, K., Industrial Economics
YAMASHITA, T., History of Education
YASUMASU, I., Zoology

School of Commerce:

AOKI, S., Accounting
ARAI, K., Accounting
ARITA, J., Philosophy
ASAOKA, R., Trade Practices
FUJITA, Y., Accounting
FURUTA, M., Economic Statistics
FUTAGAMI, K., Business Administration
HARADA, T., Marketing
HAYASHI, F., Economic Statistics
HIROTA, N., English
HOMMA, T., Commercial Law
ICHIKAWA, T., Economic History
IIJIMA, Y., Merchandise Economics
ISHIZUKA, H., Accounting
ITO, K., Trade Practices
JINBO, H., English
KAKUMOTO, R., Traffic Economy
KAMEI, A., Advertising
KANZAWA, S., Philosophy
KOBAYASHI, F., English
KOBAYASHI, M., English
KOBAYASHI, S., Business Management
KOBAYASHI, T., Advertising
KONDO .H., French
KUDO, K., Japanese Economic History
KURIYAMA, S., English
KURUMADO, M., Business Administration
MACHIDA, M., International Trade
MATSUBARA, A., Industrial Economics
MINESHIMA, H., Philosophy
MITSUHASHI, S., Money and Banking
MIYASHITA, F., Economic Geography
MOCHIZUKI, S., Money and Banking
NAGAYAMA, T., Labour Problems

NAKANISHI, C., Traffic Economy
NINAGAWA, C., French
NISHIMIYA, T., Theory of Wages
NISHIZAWA, O., Accounting
OGAWA, K., Accounting
OKADA, J., Principles of Economics
OKADA, K., Commercial Law
OKETA, A., Securities
OTANI, K., Securities
OTSUKA, M., Accounting
ROKKAKU, T., Chinese
SAGUCHI, T., Social Policy
SAKAMOTO, K., Civil Law
SAKAMOTO, N., Physics
SHINODA, Y., English
SHINZAWA, Y., Econometrics
SHIOBARA, I., Accounting
SOMEYA, K., Accounting
SUSATO, S., Sociology
SUZUKI, H., Business Administration
SUZUKI, T., Insurance
SUZUKI, Y., French
TAKASE, R., Mathematics
TANAKA, K., International Trade
TANIZAKI, H., German
TOBA, K., Economic History
TOYA, T., English
UEDA, S., Philosophy
UNO, M., Marketing
YAJIMA, Y., Money and Banking
YAMAKAWA, H., Business Administration
YAMAMOTO, S., German
YAMANE, Y., Commercial English
YASUGI, R., Biology
YOKOYAMA, H., Chinese

School of Science and Engineering:
ADACHI, T., Mathematics
AKIZUKI, K., Electrical Circuits
ANDO, K., Architectural Planning
ARIMA, S. Algebraic Geometry
ASAI, H., Biophysics
CHIBA, A., Physics
ENDO, I., Sanitary Engineering
ENOMOTO, S., German
FUJISE, N., Electric Metallurgy
FUKUYAMA, M., Mathematics
FURUKAWA, H., Process Engineering and Control
FUSAMURA, N., Mine Safety
FUSHIMI, H., Dressing Engineering
GOTO, S., Soil Engineering
HAGIWARA, Y., Mine Developments
HARADA, T., Mineral Processing
HASEGAWA, H., Organic Chemistry
HASEGAWA, M., Ferrous Materials
HASHIMOTO, B., Safety Engineering
HAYAMA, F., Metal Finishing
HAYASHI, H., Mechanical Engineering
HAYASHI, I., Solid Dynamics
HIGASHIURA, Y., English
HIRASHIMA, M., Structural Engineering
HIRATA, A., Chemical Engineering
HIRAYAMA, H., Electrical Engineering
HIROSE, K., Mathematics
HIROSE, S., Plastics Engineering
HISAMURA, T., Measurement and Control Engineering
HORII, K., Structural Engineering
HORIUCHI, K., Electronics and Electrical Communications Engineering
HOZUMI, N., Architectural Planning
ICHINOKAWA, T., Theory of Matter
IGUCHI, K., Physical Chemistry
IGUCHI, N., Machine Materials
IINO, R., Functional Equations
IKEHARA, Y., Architectural Planning
IKEZAWA, T., Quality Control
IMAI, N., Geology
IMANISHI, M., English
INOUE, U., Building Equipment Engineering
IRIE, S., Theory of Functions
ISHIDATE, T., Plant Engineering
ISHII, H., English
ISHITSUKA, Y., Electric Circuits
ISHIWATA, T., Production Planning
ITO, K., Structural Chemistry
ITO, R., Quantum Chemistry
ITO, S., Linguistics
ITO, T., Electrical Communication
ITO, T., Acoustics
KADOKURA, T., Computers
KAKITA, T., Mathematics
KAMIYAMA, K., Functional Analysis
KASAI, H., Microwaves
KASAMA, K., Russian
KASUGAI, H., Operations Research
KATO, C., Applied Inorganic Chemistry
KATO, E., Physical Chemistry
KATO, I., Control Engineering
KATO, S., German
KATO, T., International Relations
KATO, T., Electrical Measurement
KATSUMURA, S., Politics
KAWAHARA, H., Political Science
KAWAI, S., Control Engineering
KAWAI, Y., Metallurgy
KAWASE, T., Fluid Engineering
KAYAMA, N., Foundry
KIKUCHI, E., Fuel Chemistry, Catalytic Chemistry
KIKKAWA, H., River Hydraulics
KIKUCHI, Y., Anthropology of South-east Asia
KIMATA. M, Electronic Engineering
KIMURA, K., Architectural Environmental Engineering
KINASE, W., Physics
KINOSHITA, M., Algebra
KOBAYASHI, H., Measurement Engineering
KOBAYASHI, J., Crystal Physics
KOBAYASHI, S., Electric Measurement and Control
KOIZUMI, M., Combustion Engineering
KOJIMA, J., Analysis
KON, K., Partial Differential
KOORI, T., Mathematics
KUSAKAWA, T., Metallurgy
KUSAMA, T., Mathematical Statistics
MATSUI, G., Reinforced Concrete Construction
MATSUMOTO, T., Circuit Theory
MATSUURA, Y., Plastics Engineering
MITA, Y., Electrical Engineering
MIYAHARA, F., Mechanics of Materials
MIYAZAKI, T., Physical Organic Chemistry
MORI, A., Highway Engineering
MORI, J., English
MORITA, H., Precision Machinery
MORITA, S., English
MORITA, T., Production Planning and Control
MORITA, Y., Catalytic Chemistry
MOTOMURA, M., Plasticity Processing
MURAKAMI, H., Applied Mechanics
MURAMATSU, R., Production Control
MUROYA, Y., Numerical Analysis
NAKAI, H., Metallurgy
NAKAI, S., Plant Planning
NAKAJIMA, K., Applied Mathematics
NAKAMURA, K., German Literature
NAKAMURA, K., Metrology
NAKANE, K., Welding Engineering
NAKATA, E., Metallurgical Mechanics
NAMIKI, M., Quantum Mechanics
NARITA, S., Electric Power Engineering
NITTA, M., Organic Chemistry
NOGUCHI, H., Topology
OBA, I., Physics
ODOMARI, I., Electronic Material Science
OHARA, H. Computing
OL, K., Physics
OJIMA, T., Building Engineering
OKUMURA, A., Applied Mechanics
ONUKI. T.. Electric Machinery
OTA, E., Fluid Mechanics
OTERU, S., Metrology
OTSUKA, R., Clay Minerals
OTSUKA, Z., City Planning
OTSUKI, T., Network Theory
OTSUKI, Y., Quantum Statistical Theory of Matter
OYA, S., Non-Ferrous Metals
OZAKI, H., ElectronicEngineering
OZEKI, M., Labour Management
OZU, H., Applied Optics
SAITO, N., Theory of Matter (Quantum)
SAITO, T., Thermodynamics
SAKAI, K., Chemical Engineering
SATO, T., Organic Chemistry
SEKINE, Y., High Polymer Chemistry
SENGA, M., Industrial Marketing
SHIMEMURA, E., Control Engineering
SHIMIZU, T., Electronic Materials
SHINOHARA, I., High Polymer Chemistry
SHIOZAWA, K., Production Planning and Control
SHIRABE, K., French
SHIRAI, K., Electric Circuits
SHIROTSUKA, T., Chemical Engineering
SOEJIMA, T., Electromagnetic Theory
SOGA, M., English
SOSHIRODA, S., Production Planning and Control
SUGIYAMA, S., Differential Equation
SUKEGAWA, N., River Engineering
SUKEHIRO, G., German
SUNOUCHI, H., Mathematical Analysis
SUZUKI, H., Industrial Chemistry
SUZUKI, H., Quantum Statistical Theory of Matter
TADA, M., Organic Chemistry
TAJIMA, K., Fluid Mechanics
TAKAGI, M., German
TAKAHASHI, H., Chemistry
TAKAHASHI, T., Automatic Control
TAKAMIYA, N., Fuel Chemistry
TAKANO, R., English
TAKEUCHI, M., Architecture
TAMURA, Y., Electric Power System Engineering
TAMURA, Y., Building Materials
TANAKA, C., Theory of Functions
TANAKA, Y., Architectural Structures
TANI, S., Architecture
TERADA, F., Theory of Numbers
TOMINAGA, H., Computer Sciences and Communication Engineering
TONUMA, K., Urban Design
TOYOKURA, K., Chemical Engineering
TSUBOUCHI, K., Human Engineering
TSUCHIDA, E., Polymer Chemistry
TSUCHIYA, K., Automatic Control
TSUTSUMI, M., Mathematical Physics
TSUTSUMI, N., Ferrous Steel Materials
UCHIYAMA, A., Pulse Engineering
UEDA. R., Solid State Physics
UEDA, S., Metallurgy
UEMATSU, K., Radio Engineering
USAMI, S.. Fermentation Chemistry
WADA, S., Machine Design
WADA, T., Economics
WATANABE, S., Industrial Engineering
WATANABE, Y., Architectural History
YAHAGI, K., High Voltage Engineering
YAMANE, M., Mechanics of Materials
YAMAZAKI, H., Electrical Engineering
YAMAZAKI, S., Petrology
YAMAZAKI, T., Petroleum Reservoir Engineering
YOKOMIZO, K., Work Study
YOSHIDA, T., Electrochemistry
YOSHIZAKA, T., Urban Design

School of Social Sciences:
FUKUYAMA, S., Legal Philosophy
HARADA, K., English
HASEGAWA, S., Accounting
HASEGAWA, Y., English
HAYAKAWA, J., German
HONDO, H., English

IKESHIMA, H., Commercial Law
KAKESHITA, E., Philosophy
KIMURA, T., Japanese History
KOBAYASHI, S., Agricultural Economics
MORI, K., French
MUKAWA, C., Literature
NAGAYASU, Y., Economics
NAKABAYASHI, Z., English
OHATA, H., International Politics
OHATA, Y., International Economy
OHIRA, K., Marketing
OKANO, M., Criminal Law
ONO, T., Economics
OTANI, S., Political Science
SATO, K., English
SHIMODA, M., Political Science
TAKAHASHI, E., English
TAKESHITA, H., Labour Law
TAMURA, S., Economics
TANAKA, Y., Marketing
TERUYA, Y., English
TOKIOKA, H., Constitutional History
YAMANOUCHI, T., Public Finance

ATTACHED INSTITUTES:

Casting Research Laboratory: Dir. T. KUSAKAWA.

Institute of Social Sciences: Dir. T. KIMURA.

Institute of Comparative Law: Dir. T. YATO.

Institute of Language Teaching: Dir. T. TSUJIMURA.

Electronic Computation Centre: Dir. B. HORIKE.

Science and Engineering Research Laboratory: Dir. C. KATO.

System Science Institute: Dir. T. HARADA.

Institute for Business Administration Research: Dir. T. NISHIMIYA.

Institute for Research in Contemporary Political and Economic Affairs: Dir. T. KANECHIKA.

SCHOOLS OF ART AND MUSIC

City Arts University of Kyoto: 50 Hiyoshi-cho, Imagumano, Higashiyama-ku, Kyoto; 125 students.

Elizabeth University of Music: 4-15 Noboricho, Naka-ku, Hiroshima; f. 1952.

President: J. I. TEJÓN, S.J.
General Secretary: M. MURAKAMI.

Library of 40,100 vols.
Number of students: 510.
Publication: *Ars et Mystica* (annually).

Kanazawa College of Fine and Industrial Arts: 11-1, Kodachino 5-chome, Kanazawa City 920; arts and crafts; f. 1950; 47 full-time staff, 550 students; gallery of ceramics and library of 150,000 vols.; Pres. MAMORU OSAWA; publ. *Bulletin*† (annual).

Kunitachi College of Music: 5-5-1 Kashiwa-cho, Tachikawa-shi, 190 Tokyo; f. 1950; 369 teachers; 4,000 students; library of 70,000 vols.; Pres. Prof. B. EBISAWA; publs. *Kenkyu Kiyo* (Memoirs), *Daigakuin Nempo* (annual publication of the post-graduate school).

Musashino College of Music: 1-13 Hazawa, Nerima-ku, Tokyo; f. 1929; 390 staff, 3,262 students: library of 60,000 vols.; Pres. N. FUKUI, Dean N. FUKUI; Librarian T. FURUSHO; publ. *Review of Studies* (in Japanese, yearly).

Osaka College of Music: 8-1-1, Saiwai-cho, Shonai, Toyonaka City, Osaka; 1,255 students; Pres. K. TANAKA.

Tama Art University: 3-15-34 Kaminoge, Setagaya-ku, Tokyo; paintings, sculpture, architecture, design; 188 teachers, 2,240 students; Pres. Y. NAITO.

Toho-Gakuen School of Music: 41-1, 1-chome, Wakaba-cho, Chofu-shi, Tokyo 182; f. 1961; 334 staff, 754 students; library of 55,000 vols.; Pres. A. MIYOSHI.

Tokyo College of Music: 3-4-5, Minami, Ikebukuro, Toshimaku, Tokyo; f. 1907; 2,217 students; library of 25,000 vols.; Pres. AKIRA IFUKUBE; Chief Dir. RYOHEI NOMOTO; publ. *Tokyo College of Music News* (2 a year).

Ueno Gakuen College (Music): 24-12, 4-chome, Higashi-Ueno, Taitoku, Tokyo; f. 1958; 202 teachers; 985 students; library of 76,969 vols.; Pres. Prof. Mrs. MASUE ISHIBASHI; Gen. Sec. S. YASUNO.

JORDAN

Population 2,779,000

LEARNED SOCIETIES AND RESEARCH INSTITUTES

British Council: Amman Centre, Jebel Amman, Amman; library (*see* below); Rep. C. W. R. LONG.

Department of Agricultural and Scientific Research and Extension: P.O.B. 226 and P.O.B. 2178, Amman; f. 1958; covers all branches of agricultural research, information and extension; staff of 52; library of 18,500 vols.; Dir. SAID GHEZAWI.

Department of Culture and Arts: Ministry of Culture and Information, P.O.B. 6140, Amman; aims to encourage talents and prepare specialists in all fields of culture and fine arts. Consists of 7 sections:

Culture Section: publishes books, issues the literary magazines *Afkar* and *Resalat al-Urdon*, arranges lectures, and collaborates with men of letters in the Kingdom.

Folkloric Arts Section: issues a quarterly journal covering all aspects of folkloric arts of various countries, carries out research and promotes the traditional customs of folkloric arts; organizes folklore festivals in different parts of the Kingdom.

Theatre Section: aims to train actors; produces plays and encourages playwrights.

Institute of Fine Arts: aims to encourage painting and sculpture and to offer all assistance to improve and widen talents in these fields; regular courses for students; arranges exhibitions.

Jordan Conservatory of Music: aims to develop musical talents on a sound and educational basis.

Folklore Dancing Troupe of Jordan: revives folk dancing in Jordan and organizes festivals in different parts of the world.

Public Relations Section.

Goethe Institut: Ibn Sina St., P.O.B. 1676, Amman; f. 1961; German cultural institute and library, language courses; Dir. Dr. RICHARD SCHMIED.

Jordan Library Association: P.O.B. 6289, Amman; f. 1963; 450 mems.; Pres. MAHMUD EL-AKHRAS; Sec. YOUSEF DANDIL; publs. *Rissalat al-Maktaba* (The Message of the Library)† (quarterly), *Palestinian-Jordanian Bibliography*†, *Directory of the Libraries in Jordan*†.

Jordan Research Council: P.O.B. 6070, Amman; f. 1964; to supervise the planning, organization, and co-ordination of research to raise the scientific, economic, social and health standards in the country; to encourage and support research, either governmental or private; 53 mems.; library of 1,767 vols.; Gen. Sec. ISSAM KHAIRY.

Royal Scientific Society: P.O.B. 6945, Amman, Jordan; f. 1970; industrial research and development centre; education, electrical and electronic engineering, computer systems, mechanical engineering, chemical industry, building materials research centre, economics; library of 40,000 vols., 1,500 periodicals, includes a Technical Information Centre; Pres. Dr. ALBERT BUTROS; publs. *Monthly Accessions List, Bibliography of Jordan, Curretn List of Periodicals Holdings.*

U.S. International Communication Agency—American Center: Jabal Amman, Third Circle, P.O.B. 676, Amman; f. 1952; offers media relations, cultural performances, academic exchange, lectures; library of 3,500 vols., 120 periodicals; Public Affairs Officer LARRY TAYLOR.

LIBRARIES

British Council Library: Amman Centre, Jebel Amman, Amman; f. 1950; 15,806 vols., 125 periodicals; Regional Librarian (based in Damascus) Miss V. TEAGUE.

Public Library: P.O.B. 132, Amman; f. 1960; 65,000 vols. in Arabic and English; 296 current periodicals; 2 children's sections, Deposit Library for UNESCO; Librarian FAROUK MO'AZ; 450 Jordanian publications available for exchange.

Public Library: P.O.B. 348, Irbid; f. 1957; 5,587 vols. in Arabic, 5,815 vols. in English, 178 vols. in other languages; Librarian HESHAM JOWHAR MAHDAWI.

Public Library: Nablus; f. 1960; 35,500 vols., mainly in Arabic and English; cultural activities; Librarian ABDEL-MUN'EM SALEH AL-FARRAN.

Public Library: Ramallah; f. 1962; 3,500 vols.; Librarian ADEL UWAIS.

University of Jordan Library: P.O.B. 1682, Amman; f. 1962; 220,000 vols., 2,000 current periodicals; legal deposit for UN, WHO, FAO, World Bank, UNESCO documents; Dir. Dr. K. ASALI; publs. *Library Guide* (annual), *Accession List: Natural Sciences and Humanities* (monthly), *Reader's Guide* (annually), *Bibliographical list and indexes* (irregular), *Bibliography of Jordan.*

MUSEUMS

Department of Antiquities: P.O.B. 88, Amman; f. 1923; attached to the Ministry of Tourism and Antiquities; organizes and supervises archaeological excavations; responsible for all government museums; co-operates with local Arab and foreign archaeological institutions; library of 3,527 vols.; Dir. Gen. Dir. ADNAN HADIDI; publ. *Annual*†.

Jordan Archaeological Museum: Amman; f. 1951; 10 staff; library of 3,560 vols.; Curator Miss SIHAM BALQAR.

Folklore Museum: Amman, housed by the Department of Culture and Arts; f. 1972; collection of national traditional costumes; Curator YACOUB OWEIS.

Popular Life Museum: Amman; f. 1973; local domestic history; brs. in Petra, Madaba and Karak; Curator Miss HADIA ABAZA.

Mosaic Gallery: Amman; f. 1972; pieces from the Byzantine era found in Jarash and Madaba.

National Memorial Museum: Military General Headquarters, Amman.

UNIVERSITIES

UNIVERSITY OF JORDAN

P.O.B. 1682, AMMAN

Telephone: 65111-65130, 6317-63180, 64101-64105.

Telex: 21629 UNIV JO.

Founded 1962.

Languages of instruction: Arabic and English; National and autonomous control; Academic year: October to June (two semesters and a summer session).

President: Dr. NASSER EL-DIN EL-ASSAD.
Vice-President for Academic Affairs: Dr. MAHMUD SAMRA.
Vice-President for Planning: Dr. ABD AL-KARIM GHARAIBEH.
Secretary-General: MOHAMMED SALEH ABD AL-ATI.
Registrar: GHAZI MUFTI.
Librarian: Dr. K. ASALI.

Number of teachers: 580.
Number of students: 8,970.

Publications: *Catalogue*† (annually), *Yearbook*, *Dirasat Journal*† (2 a year), *The University News-Letter* (monthly).

DEANS:

Faculty of Arts: Dr. FAHMY JADAAN.
Faculty of Economics and Commerce: Dr. WADIE SHARAYHA.
Faculty of Sciences: Dr. MARWAN KAMAL.
Faculty of Islamic Studies: Dr. ABD AL-AZIZ EL-KHAYAT.
Faculty of Medicine: Dr. ABD AL-WAHAB EL-BORLOSSY.
Faculty of Nursing: Dr. WARIFA SAAD.
Faculty of Agriculture: Dr. SUBHI QASEM.
Faculty of Education: Dr. HANI A. SALIH.
Faculty of Engineering: Dr. BASSAM ABU GHAZALEH (acting).
Faculty of Law: Dr. RASHID DAKR.
Dean of Research and Graduate Studies: Dr. HASHIM YAGHI.
Dean of Students: Dr. MOHAMMAD A. HAMDAN.
Faculty of Physical Training: Dr. MOHAMMAD A. HAMDAN.
University Hospital: Dr. IZZAT SANKARY.

BETHLEHEM UNIVERSITY

P.O.B. 9, BETHLEHEM,
WEST BANK, VIA ISRAEL

Telephone: 02-743276, 743282.

Founded 1973.

Private control; Languages of instruction: Arabic and English; Academic year: September to May.

Chancellor: Most Rev. WILLIAM A. CAREW, D.D.
President: Dr. JOSEPH B. LOEWENSTEIN, F.S.C.
Executive Vice-President: Dr. ANTON SANSOUR.
Registrar: Br. ROBERT JOHN DASZKIEWICZ, F.S.C.
Librarian: Miss CONCEPCION PACIA.

Library of 100,000 vols.
Number of teachers: 80.
Number of students: 850 (day and evening).

DEANS:

College of Arts and Sciences: Dr. THIAB AYYOUSH.
Business Administration: JIRIES ATRASH.
School of Nursing: Sr. MARGARET AHL.
Teachers College: Miss VIOLET FASHEH.
Institute of Hotel Management: A. WALID DAJANI.

BIRZEIT UNIVERSITY

P.O.B. 14, BIRZEIT, VIA ISRAEL

Telephone: 952428 Ramallah.

Founded 1924 as school, 1951 college, present status 1975. Private autonomous Arab institution; Academic year: October to July (two semesters), summer session July–August.

President: HANNA NASIR, PH.D.
Vice-President and Acting President: GABI BARAMKI, PH.D.
Vice-President for Academic Affairs: MOHAMMAD HALLAJ, PH.D.
Vice-President for Administrative and Financial Affairs: IZZAT GHURANI, PH.D.

DEANS:

Arts: KAMAL ABDEL-FATTAH, PH.D. (acting).
Science: RAMZI RIHAN.
Commerce and Economics: IZZAT GHURANI, PH.D. (acting)
Engineering: RAMI ABDEL-HADI, PH.D.

Library of 47,000 vols.
Number of teachers: 122.
Number of students: 1,390.

Publications: *Al Ghadeer*† (6 a year), university catalogues (annually).

Four-year first degree courses; graduate programme leading to M.A. in education.

YARMOUK UNIVERSITY

IRBID

(Amman Liaison Office: P.O.B. 20184, Amman.)

Telephone: 71100-71115.

Telex: 51533 YARMUK JO.

Founded 1976.

National and autonomous control; Languages of instruction: Arabic and English; Academic year: October to January, February to June (2 semesters), and summer session.

President: Dr. ADNAN BADRAN.
Registrar: ISMAIL BUHEIS (acting).
Librarian: Dr. TALAL AKASHEH (acting).

Library of 35,000 vols.
Number of teachers: 153.
Number of students: 3,263.

DEANS:

Faculty of Science and Arts: Dr. VICTOR BILLEH (acting).
Faculty of Engineering: Dr. ALI NAYFH.
Research and Graduate Studies: Dr. AHMED SALEM (acting).
Faculty of Medical Science: Dr. ADNAN BADRAN.

COLLEGES

AGRICULTURAL INSTITUTE

TULKARM, WEST BANK, VIA ISRAEL

Founded 1931.

Dean: Dr. S. A. NASHEF.

Library of 25,000 vols.
Number of teachers: 22.
Number of students: 279.

The Institute is a teacher-training institute preparing teachers of agriculture, science, mathematics, Arabic, Islamic and social studies, English and physical education.

Institute of Public Administration: P.O.B. 13055, Amman; f. 1968; a joint Ford Foundation and Government of Jordan project; library of 3,000 vols; Dir. Dr. ABDALLA R. ZOUBI.

Jordan Statistical Training Centre: Amman; f. 1964 for the training of government employees and other applicants in statistical methods; library of *c.* 700 vols.; Dir. SHUJA' EL ASAD; publs. *Annual Report, Students' Reports.*

KAMPUCHEA*

(CAMBODIA)

Population 6,000,000

LEARNED SOCIETIES

Association des Bouddhistes du Cambodge (*Buddhika samakum Kampuchea ratth*): Phnom-Penh; f. 1952; affiliated to the World Buddhist Association; publ. *La Lumière Bouddhique*.

Association des Ecrivains Khmers: Phnom-Penh; f. 1962 for the encouragement of writers and the development of literature in the Khmer language; library 4,525 vols.; Pres. TRINH HOANH; publ. monthly literary review.

Institut Bouddhique: Phnom-Penh; f. 1930; Buddhist studies and Khmer culture; publs. *Dictionnaire Cambodgien* and numerous bulletins; Dir. LEANG HAP AN.

Institut National de la Statistique et des Recherches Economiques: B.P. 105, Phnom-Penh; f. 1963; to promote and organize all statistical and economic research; to compile national and international statistical and economic documentation; trains personnel; documentation centre of 300 vols.; Dir.-Gen. SIM-THAI PHENG; publs. *Bulletin trimestriel de statistique, Annuaire statistique, Comptes économiques.*

Mission d'Entomologie Médicale auprès de l'Institut Pasteur de Khmer: B.P. 174, Phnom-Penh.

LIBRARIES

Archives et Bibliothèque Nationales: B.P. 4, Phnom-Penh; f. 1923; library of 31,000 vols.; national deposit library.

Bibliothèque de l'Institut Bouddhique: Phnom-Penh; f. 1923; books and MSS. in French, English, Thai, Burmese, Singhalese, Chinese, Tibetan, Mongolian, etc.; also documents in Khmer and Pali on Buddhism and Khmer folklore; 40,000 vols. and 16,200 MSS. on palm leaves; Librarian DIK KEAM.

Bibliothèque du Ministère de l'Information: Phnom-Penh.

MUSEUMS

Conservation d'Angkor: Siemreap-Angkor; f. 1907; national authority for the conservation and restoration of Angkor and Northern Cambodia monuments; central depository and restoration centre for Northern Cambodian art objects, archaeological artifacts and inscriptions; rubbings of Khmer inscriptions; archives of archaeological surveys and researches in Cambodia; photographic library with 18,000 photographs, plan-centre with 5,000 plans of Khmer monuments; 10 scientists, 150 technicians, 800 workers; Curator BERNARD P. GROSLIER.

Exposition Permanente des Réalisations du Sangkum Reastr Niyum: Phnom-Penh.

Musée de l'Armée: Phnom-Penh.

Musée de l'Institut Bouddhique: Phnom-Penh; f. 1923; a collection concerned with the manners and customs of Khmer; Chief of Bureau Mrs. PICH SAL.

Musée National de Phnom-Penh: 229 Vithei Pau Kambô, P.O.B. 763, Phnom-Penh; f. 1920; to be extended to the buildings of the former Palais Royal and Ecole de-Arts, which will house the Department of posts Angkorian Art and History and the Department of Ethnology respectively, the present museum retaining the Department of National Antiquities; main exhibits include prehistoric and protohistoric artefacts, many examples of art of the ancient Khmer civilization, Brahmin and Buddhist works in stone and bronze of 6th to 13th centuries, wooden sculpture of 16th to 19th centuries, ceramics collection; Curator L. Y. VOUONG.

UNIVERSITIES

UNIVERSITÉ DES BEAUX-ARTS

MOHA VITHEI DE L'URSS, PHNOM-PENH

Founded 1965.

Rector: HANG THUM HAK.

Manager: PROM NUON THOL.

Number of teachers: *c.* 120.

Number of students: *c.* 500.

Faculties of Choreography, Music, Architecture and Town Planning, Archaeology.

UNIVERSITÉ BOUDDHIQUE

B.P. 117, QUAI SISOWATH, PHNOM-PENH

Founded 1954, re-founded 1970.

Language of instruction: Khmer; Academic year: May to February.

Number of teachers: *c.* 20.
Number of students: *c.* 180 (men).

Faculties of Religion, Philosophy, Linguistics, Khmer Civilization, Classical Languages (Sanskrit and Pali), Modern Languages, History and Geography.

UNIVERSITÉ DE PHNOM-PENH

133 MOHA VIETHEI PREAH BAT NORODAM, PHNOM-PENH

Founded 1960.

State control; Languages of instruction: French and Khmer; Academic year: September to December, January to May.

Number of teachers: *c.* 340.

Number of students: *c.* 5,300.

Faculties of Law and Economics; Medicine, Pharmacy and Para-medical Sciences; Odonto-stomatology; Letters and Human Sciences; Sciences; Commercial Sciences.

UNIVERSITÉ DES SCIENCES AGRONOMIQUES

B.P. 172, PHNOM-PENH

Founded 1965.

Rector: TAN KIM HUON.
Registrar: SOR SAVAY.
Librarian: EK VAN.

Library of 5,000 vols.
Number of teachers: 46.
Number of students: 124.

Faculties of Agriculture, Veterinary Science, Agricultural Economics, Forestry, Fisheries.

UNIVERSITÉ TECHNIQUE

ANGLE VITHEI MOAT CHROUK ET HING PEN, PHNOM-PENH

Telephone: 2 2114

Founded 1965

Languages of instruction: Khmer and French.

Rector: IM SAROEUN.
Secretary-General: KAUV KEA HENG.
Librarian: KE HOC BIN.

Number of teachers: 234.
Number of students: 928.

Faculties of Electronics, Arts and Crafts, Civil Engineering; Higher Schools of Applied Chemistry, Civil Aeronautics; Higher Institute of Soviet-Khmer Friendship.

*No new information having been received this year, the chapter appears as in the previous edition.

KENYA

Population 15,322,000

LEARNED SOCIETIES

Agricultural Society of Kenya: P.O.B. 30176, Nairobi; f. 1901; encourages and assists agriculture in Kenya; holds 12 shows a year and holds farming competitions; 11,000 mems.; Chair. J. J. MAGERIA; Chief Exec. H. R. WERE; publ. *The Kenya Farmer* (monthly).

Association of Surgeons of East Africa: P.O.B. 30726, Nairobi; f. 1950 for the advancement of the science and art of surgery and the promotion of friendship and exchange of ideas among surgeons in East Africa; mem. of Int. Fed. of Surgical Colleges; annual conference held in Kampala, Nairobi, Dar es Salaam or Lusaka; 353 mems.; Chair. G. E. NEVILL; Hon. Sec. J. E. JELLIS; publ. *Proceedings*†.

British Council, The: P.O.B. 40751, Harry Thuku Rd., Nairobi; Rep. P. K. CAVAYE; Regional Offices: City House, Nyerere Ave., Mombasa; Dir. S. MOSS; Oginga Odinga Rd., Kisumu; Dir. J. R. DAY.

East African Wildlife Society: P.O.B. 20110, Nairobi; f. 1961; non-profit org.; maintains interest in wildlife and its conservation and preserves its habitat as a national and international resource; 10,000 mems.; publs. *Swara* (every 2 months), *African Journal of Ecology* (quarterly).

Goethe Institut: P.O.B. 49468, Nairobi; f. 1963; library of 8,000 vols. in German and English; German language classes, promotes cultural exchange; Dir. R. DINKELMEYER.

Historical Association of Kenya: P.O.B. 27028, Nairobi; f. 1966; Chair. Prof. BETHWELL A. OGOT; Sec. Dr. GODFREY MURIUKI; publ. *Kenya Historical Review* (2 a year).

Kenya Library Association: P.O.B. 46031, Nairobi; f. 1956 to promote, establish and improve libraries and book production; *c.* 200 mems.; Chair J. NDEGWA; Sec. N. NDEGWA; publ. *Maktaba* (quarterly).

Kenya National Academy for Advancement of Arts and Sciences: P.O.B. 47288, Nairobi; f. 1977; advancement of learning and research; 200 mems.; Chair. Prof. C. P. M. KHAMALA; Sec. Dr. F. J. WANG'ATI; publs. *Proceedings of Symposia*, *Newsletter*†, *Post Magazine*†.

Kenya Natural History Society: P.O.B. 44486, Nairobi; f. 1909; 700 mems.; Chair. J. S. KARMALI; publ. *Journal of the East African Natural History Society and the National Museum*†, *EANHS Bulletin*.

Mines and Geological Department: Machakos Rd., P.O.B. 30009, Nairobi; f. 1932; undertakes geological mapping and mineral exploration, and administers mining laws; 50 staff; library of 25,000 vols.; Commr. J. H. O. OMINO; publ. *Annual Report*.

Unesco Regional Office for Science and Technology for Africa: P.O.B. 30592, Nairobi; f. 1965 to promote and co-ordinate Unesco projects and activities in science and technology in 40 sub-Saharan African member states in East, Central and West Africa; library of 4,300 vols.; Dir. Chief OLU IBUKUN; publs. *Bulletin*† (quarterly, English and French), *Science and Technology Education Newsletter*† (2 a year, English and French), Reports.

RESEARCH INSTITUTES

(*See* also under University)

British Institute in Eastern Africa: P.O.B. 30710, Nairobi; f. 1960; library of 3,000 vols.; research into the history and archaeology of Eastern Africa, for which occasional studentships are offered; Pres. Sir LAURENCE KIRWAN, K.C.M.G.; Dir. NEVILLE CHITTICK; publs. *Azania*† (annually), *Memoirs*†.

Coffee Research Foundation: Coffee Research Station, P.O.B. 4, Ruiru; f. 1949; coffee berry disease research and new systems of coffee culture; Dir. A. M. KABAARA, PH.D.; publs. *Annual Report*†, *Kenya Coffee*†.

Cotton Research Station: P.O. Kibos, Nyanza Province; Dir. J. H. BRETTELL.

Desert Locust Control Organization for Eastern Africa: P.O.B. 30023, Nairobi; f. 1962; headquarters in Addis Ababa, P.O.B. 4255, Ethiopia; investigates methods of control of desert locust and other pests, incl. armyworm, quelea quelea and tsetse fly.

Grassland Research Station: P.O.B. 144, Molo; f. 1952; sub-station of the National Agricultural Research Station, Kitale; Officer-in-Charge I. J. PARTRIDGE.

Institute for Medical Research and Training: c/o Medical Research Laboratory, P.O.B. 30141, Nairobi; f. 1964 for research and medical training; *see* also Medical Training Centre, Medical School, under Colleges.

Interafrican Bureau for Animal Resources: Central Bank of Kenya, Haile Selassie Ave., P.O.B. 30786, Nairobi; f. 1953; veterinary and livestock health and production covering all 49 member states of the OAU in Africa; library of over 3,500 vols.; Dir. P. G. ATANG; publs. *Bulletin of Animal Health and Production in Africa* (quarterly), *IBAR Information Leaflets* (monthly).

International Centre of Insect Physiology and Ecology: P.O.B. 30772, Nairobi; f. 1970; advanced research in insect biology; provides training in research methods for pre- and post-doctoral research fellows; acts as an international forum for discussion and exchange of knowledge; seminars, symposia, conferences; 63 research staff; library of 1,000 vols., 120 periodicals; Dir. Prof. THOMAS R. ODHIAMBO; publs. *ICIPE Annual Report*†, *Dudu*† (quarterly news magazine).

Kenya Agricultural Research Institute: P.O.B. 30148, Nairobi; agricultural and forest research, plant science, soil science and animal industry; Dir. F. J. WANG'ATI.

Veterinary Research Department (Muguga): P.O.B. 32, Kikuyu; preparation and issue of biological products and research into animal health and animal diseases; Dir. Dr. W. N. MASIGA.

Kenya Industrial Research Organization: P.O.B. 30650, Nairobi; f. 1948; provides advice for established local industrial concerns and gives assistance in the establishment of new industries on the utilization of local materials; Dir. C. Tarimo; publ. *Annual Report.*

Kenya Leprosy Research Centre (*The John Lowe Memorial*): P.O.B. 3, Busia; Dir. Dr. Y. Otsyula; publ. *Annual Report.*

Kenya Tuberculosis Investigation Centre: P.O.B. 47855, Nairobi, Kenya; f. 1960; research on all aspects of tuberculosis, with special reference to (*a*) diagnostic and treatment procedures relevant to developing country situations and to (*b*) the epidemiology of the disease; operating in Kenya, Uganda, Tanzania and Zambia; Dir. Dr. J. A. Aluoch; publs. *Annual Report* and some 2 to 5 scientific publications each year.

Medical Research Laboratory (Medical Department, Kenya): P.O.B. 30141, Nairobi; all branches of medicine; library; Dir. M. G. Rogoff.

Ministry of Agriculture Division of Veterinary Services: P.O. Kabete; f. 1903; veterinary research; library of 21,500 vols.; Dir. I. E. Muriithi, B.V.M.S., M.R.C.V.S.; publ. *Annual Report*†.

National Agricultural Laboratories: Ministry of Agriculture; P.O.B. 30028, Nairobi; f. 1908; Dir. J. J. Njoroge, PH.D.

National Horticultural Research Station: P.O.B. 220, Thika; f. 1955; research into crop protection, seed production, and sericulture; breeds for multiple disease resistance to common bean diseases; Dir. S. K. Njuguna.

Plant Breeding Station: Ministry of Agriculture, P.O. Njoro; f. 1927; 20 professional staff; Officer-in-Charge Dr. R. C. McGinnis; improvement of wheat, barley and oats.

Pyrethrum Bureau: P.O.B. 420, Nakuru; f. 1960; technical information on pyrethrum as an insecticide; publ. *Pyrethrum Post*† (2 a year).

Tea Research Institute of East Africa: P.O.B. 91, Kericho; studies on the production of tea, with special emphasis on agronomic, botanical and chemical aspects; sub-stations in Tanzania and Uganda; library; Dir. (vacant).

LIBRARIES

American Cultural Center Library: P.O.B. 30143, Harambee Ave., Nairobi; foreign affairs, American history and society, business and management, communications and arts; 6,500 vols., 100 periodicals; Dir. Joseph J. Brennig.

British Council Library: P.O.B. 40751, Harry Thuku Rd., Nairobi; f. 1948; 12,478 vols., 98 periodicals; Librarian Miss C. R. McDonald; brs. at Mombasa (13,615 vols., 97 periodicals) and Kisumu (12,935 vols., 96 periodicals).

Central Government Archives: P.O.B. 30050, Nairobi.

Desai Memorial Library: P.O.B. 1253, Nairobi; f. 1942; public library and reading room; 31,800 vols.; books in Swahili, Gujarati, Hindi, Urdu, Gurumukhi and English; reference, newspaper and periodical sections; 1,151 mems.; Pres. A. M. Sadaruddin; Sec. Harshad Joshi.

High Court of Kenya Library: Law Courts, P.O.B. 30041, Nairobi; f. 1935; comprises High Court Library and Court of Appeal Library in Nairobi, and 4 major br. libraries at Mombasa, Kisumu, Nakuru and Nyeri; 40,000 vols., 55 periodicals on practitioner's law, with special emphasis on Kenyan and English law; Librarian J. N. Otike, DIP.LIB.SC.

Ismail Rahimtulla Trust Library: P.O.B. 333, Nairobi; 5,250 vols.; Librarian C. M. Patel.

Kenya Agricultural Research Institute Library: P.O.B. 30148, Nairobi; f. 1928; extends current scientific literature service to all research and academic centres and official depts. within East Africa; acts as Regional Centre for East Africa for AGINLET; 55,000 vols.; joint library with the East African Veterinary Research Organization; Research Librarian Daniel L. Njoroge; publs. *East African Agricultural and Forestry Journal* (quarterly), *Record of Research*† (annual report).

Kenya National Archives: P.O.B. 30520, Nairobi.

Kenya National Library Service: P.O.B. 30573, Nairobi; f. 1967; 100,000 vols., 200 periodicals; 8 brs.; mobile service for Nairobi area; Chief Librarian Francis Otieno Pala, M.A., B.LS.

McMillan Memorial Library: P.O.B. 40791, Nairobi; f. 1931; two branch libraries at Kaloleni and Eastlands; comprises Nairobi City Library Services; Africana collection; 160,000 vols., over 5,500 serial publs.; Chief Librarian R. G. Opondo.

Seif Bin Salim Public Library: P.O.B. 90283, Mombasa; f. 1903; 18,675 vols., general subjects, mainly in English and Gujarati; Librarian Mrs. M. D. Karkaria.

University of Nairobi Libraries: P.O.B. 30197, Nairobi; f. 1956; 270,000 vols., 3,300 periodicals; 7 brs.; acts as legal national depository and UN deposit library; Librarian J. Ndegwa, M.A., F.L.A.

MUSEUMS

Fort Jesus Museum: P.O.B. 82412, Mombasa; f. 1960; inside 16th-century Portuguese fortress overlooking Mombasa harbour; finds from various coastal Islamic sites, from Fort Jesus, and from a 17th-century Portuguese wreck show the history of the Kenya coast; library of 280 vols. and numerous offprints; Curator Omar Bwana.

National Museum of Western Kenya: Box 1219, Kitale; f. 1926; history and science, emphasis on education; library of *c.* 5,000 vols.; Curator Alfred C. Cherutich.

National Museums of Kenya: P.O.B. 40658, Nairobi; f. 1911; all branches of natural history, pre-history, and geology; controlled by Museum Trustees of Kenya; joint library with East Africa Natural History Society, 10,000 vols.; brs. at Lamu, Mombasa, Kitale and Meru; Dir. R. E. Leakey; publ. *Journal of The East Africa Natural History Society and National Museum.*

UNIVERSITY

UNIVERSITY OF NAIROBI

P.O.B. 30197, NAIROBI

Telephone: Nairobi 334244.

Telegraphic Address: Varsity, Nairobi.

Founded in 1956 as Royal Technical College of East Africa; present name 1970.

Language of instruction: English; Academic year: October to July.

Chancellor: H.E. Daniel Arap Moi.

Vice-Chancellor: Joseph M. Mungai, M.B., CH.B., PH.D.

Registrar: E. N. Gicuhi, B.A.

Librarian: J. Ndegwa, M.A., F.L.A.

Number of teachers: 673.

Number of students: 5,033.

Publication: *University of Nairobi News and Views.*

DEANS:

Faculty of Agriculture: C. N. KARUE.
Faculty of Architecture, Design and Development: H. S. WOOD.
Faculty of Arts: R. S. OGENDO.
Faculty of Commerce: N. O. NZOMO.
Faculty of Engineering: R. P. PATEL.
Faculty of Law: H. OKOTH-OGENDO.
Faculty of Medicine: K. THAIRU.
Faculty of Science: M. S. ALALA.
Faculty of Veterinary Medicine: G. M. O. MALOIY.

PROFESSORS:

Faculty of Agriculture:
AHN, P. M., Soil Science
MIAN, A. L., Crop Science
SCHENK, E. W., Agricultural Economics

Faculty of Architecture:
WOOD, H. S., Architecture

Faculty of Arts:
ABDULAZIZ, M. H., Linguistics and African Languages
DONDERS, J. G., Philosophy and Religious Studies
MAITHA, J. K., Economics
MBITHI, P. M., Sociology
WERE, G. S., History

Faculty of Commerce:
CHEDZEV, C. S. D., Management Science

Faculty of Engineering:
GITHINJI, P. M., Mechanical Engineering
ROSTOM, R. S., Surveying and Photogrammetry
SMITH, R. B. L., Civil Engineering

Faculty of Law:
MUTUNGI, O. K., Commercial Law
ZAFER, M. R., Public Law

Faculty of Medicine:
BENCIVENGA, A., Orthopaedic Surgery
BWIBO, N. O., Paediatrics
KUNGU, A., Medical Pathology
MATI, J. K. G., Obstetrics and Gynaecology
MUHANGI, J., Psychiatry
MUNGAI, J. M., Human Anatomy
OJIAMBO, H. P., Medicine
TALALAJ, S., Pharmacy
THAIRU, K., Medical Physiology
WASUNNA, A. E., Surgery
WHITTAKER, L. R., Diagnostic Radiology

Faculty of Science:
ALALA, M. S., Mathematics
ASNAN, G. C., Meteorology
HYDER, M., Zoology
IMBAMBA, S. K., Botany
LOUPEKINE, I. S., Geology
ODHIAMBO, D., Entomology
ROBINS, P. A., Chemistry

Faculty of Veterinary Medicine:
MALOIY, G. M. O., Veterinary Physiology
MUGERA, G. M., Pathology and Microbiology
MUSANGI, R. S., Animal Production

ATTACHED INSTITUTES:

Institute of Adult Studies: f. 1961; diploma course in adult education; Dir. P. E. KINYANVUI, M. A. (acting).

Institute for Development Studies: f. 1965; research in social science and problems of development in Kenya and East Africa; Dir. W. M. SENGA, M.A., PH.D.

Institute of African Studies: f. 1965; research in history, anthropology, linguistics, music, dance, literature, arts and crafts, religions; Dir. B. E. KIPKORIR, PH.D.

School of Journalism: P.O.B. 30179, Nairobi; f. 1970; 1-year postgraduate diploma course; Dir. W. H. MCATEER (acting).

CONSTITUENT COLLEGE:

Kenyatta University College: P.O.B. 43844, Nairobi; f. 1972; trains graduate teachers for secondary schools and teacher training colleges; library of 130,000 vols. and 1,200 periodicals.
Principal: J. K. KOINANGE.
Registrar: L. M. MUNGAI.
Librarian: J. M. NG'ANG'A, A.L.A.
Number of teachers: 173.
Number of students: 1,840.
Publications: *Annual Report, College Calendar, Directory of Research.*

DEANS:

Faculty of Education: Dr. M. K. MALECHE.
Faculty of Arts: Prof. R. MURUNGI.
Faculty of Science: Prof. J. MUTIO.

COLLEGES

Egerton College: P.O. Njoro; f. 1939; diplomas in agriculture, farm management, animal husbandry, range management, ranch management, dairy technology, soil and water engineering, farm mechanization, agricultural education, horticulture, agriculture and home economics, food science and technology, veterinary medicine; Principal Dr. P. T. OBWAKA, PH.D.; 800 students from 13 African countries; library of 27,000 vols.; publs. *Egertonian* (annually), *Annual Report, College Catalogue* (annually), *Students Magazine* (2 a month), *Agricultural Bulletin* (2 a year).

Kenya Conservatoire of Music: P.O.B. 41343, Nairobi, Kenya; f. 1944; Dir. NAT KOFSKY, O.B.E.

Kenya Institute of Administration: P.O. Lower Kabete; f. 1961; residential training for the Kenya Public Service in public administration, project development, local government, community development, public accountancy, social work, management, probation and allied fields; research department; library of 40,000 vols. and a fully equipped audio-visual aids centre and language laboratory; Principal H. J. NYAMU; 85 teachers, 500 students; publs. *Journal*†, *K.I.A. Occasional Papers*†.

Kenya Polytechnic: P.O.B. 52428 Nairobi; f. 1961 with UNDP aid; Depts. of Mechanical, Electrical and Electronic Engineering, Science, Building, Business Studies, Printing, Institutional Management, Library and Archive Studies, General Studies.
Principal: J. D. MAMBO, M.SC.
Librarian: S. K. NG'ANG'A.
Number of teachers: 207.
Number of students: 2,128.
Library of 17,000 vols. and 150 periodicals.

Kenya School of Law: P.O.B. 30369, Nairobi; f. 1963.
Principal: T. JACKSON.
Bursar: D. M. V. CASTELINO.
Librarian: Mrs. R. J. SUTTILL.
Library of 3,000 vols.
Number of students (postgraduate): 80.

Mombasa Polytechnic: P.O.B. 90420, Mombasa; f. 1948; full-time, sandwich, block-release and day-release courses.
Principal: P. G. KING'ORI.
Number of teachers: 90.
Number of students: 1,254 (830 full-time).

Strathmore College: P.O.B. 25095, Nairobi; f. 1960; 450 students; courses in science and accountancy; library of 15,000 vols.

KIRIBATI

Population 56,400

LIBRARY AND ARCHIVES

National Library and Archives: P.O.B. 6, Bairiki, Tarawa; f. 1979 (fmrly. Gilbert Islands National Archives); lending section of 20,000 vols.; 10,000 vols. in small library units throughout Kiribati; National Collection (housed in Archives) of 2,000 published items; archives records of 25,000 items; small philatelic, photograph, and sound recording collections; Librarian/Archivist RICHARD OVERY.

MUSEUM

National Museum: c/o Cultural Affairs Officer, P.O.B. 263, Bikenibeu, Tarawa; in process of formation; Cultural Affairs Officer BWERE ERITAIA.

COLLEGE

University of the South Pacific: Kiribati Extension Centre: P.O.B. 59, Bairiki, Tarawa; f. 1973; an external campus of the University of the South Pacific; part-time undergraduate and diploma courses; library of 5,000 vols.; 4 staff; *c.* 100 students; Dir. NOEL FINCH, M.A.

Atoll Research Unit: Tanaea, Tarawa; f. 1980 by Kiribati Government and U.S.P.; research in all aspects of atoll environment and ecology, including marine environment and ecology; Dir. GORDON W. GROVES, PH.D.

DEMOCRATIC PEOPLE'S REPUBLIC OF KOREA

Population 17,072,000

ACADEMIES

ACADEMY OF SCIENCES

SOSONG DISTRICT, PYONGYANG

Founded 1952.

President: GUAK DAI HONG.

Vice-Presidents: CHOI HWA CHUN, CHOI MAN HYUN, KIM DAL HYUN.

ATTACHED RESEARCH INSTITUTES:

Research Institute of Physics and Mathematics: Pyongsong, South Pyongan Province; Head HO GON.

Research Institute of Experimental Biology: Pyongsong, South Pyongan Province; Head JO IN JE.

Research Institute of Mining Engineering: Pyongsong, South Pyongan Province; Head SIN MUN GYU.

Astronomical Observatory: Daesong District, Pyongyang; Head KIM YONG HYOK.

Research Institute of Ferrous Metal: Daean, South Pyongan Province; Vice-Head CHOI SANG GYO.

Research Institute of Automation: Pyongsong, South Pyongan Province; Head HAN BYONG HI.

Research Institute of Fuel: Songrim, North Hwanghai Province; Head GO YONG JIN.

Research Institute of Geology and Geography: Pyongsong, South Pyongan Province; Head PAK SONG UK.

Research Institute of Machine Building Engineering: Pyongsong, South Pyongan Province; Head KIM UNG SAM.

Research Institute of Silicates: Daedong County, South Pyongan Province; Head KIM UNG SANG.

Research Institute of Heat Engineering: Pyongsong, South Pyongan Province; Head HAN DONG SIK.

Research Institute of Nonferrous Metal: Nampo, South Pyongan Province; Head KIM MYONG RIN.

Research Institute of Pure Metal: Hamhung, South Hamgyong Province; Head RI MAN HYOK.

Research Institute of Building Science: Sungho District, Pyongyang; Head AN HO RYON.

Research Institute of Building Material: Hamhung, South Hamgyong Province; Head KIM HI CHOL.

Research Institute of Irrigation Engineering: Sadong District, Pyongyang; Head CHOI TAI JIN.

Research Institute of Chemical Fibre: Siniju, North Pyongan Province; Head MA HYONG OK.

Research Institute of Electronics: Pyongsong, South Pyongan Province; Vice-Head RO JONG YON.

Research Institute of Electricity: Pyongsong, South Pyongan Province; Vice-Head RI JUN HO.

Research Institute of Botany: Daesong District, Pyongyang; Head GUAK JONG SONG.

Research Institute of Industrial Microbiology: Pyongsong, South Pyong Province; Head RI CHUN HO.

Research Institute of Zoology: Daesong District, Pyongyang; Head PAEK JONG HWAN.

HAMHUNG DIVISION OF ACADEMY
HAMHUNG, SOUTH HAMGYONG PROVINCE

Head: RI SEUNG GI.

Vice-Heads: JU SUNG SOP, SIN BYONG JONG.

Research Institute of Inorganic Chemistry: Head JO DONG GYU.

Research Institute of Organic Chemistry: Head HONG HA GYONG.

Research Institute of High Polymer Chemistry: Head LI SANG GYUN.

Research Institute of Chemical Engineering: Head LI JAE OP.

Research Institute of Analytical Chemistry: Head KIM GUN ON.

Research Institute of the Preservation of Revolutionary Relics: Head RYOM CHOL.

ACADEMY OF SOCIAL SCIENCES

CENTRAL DISTRICT, PYONGYANG

Founded 1952.

President: YANG HYONG SOP.

Vice-Presidents: HONG KIM MUN, JONG SONG CHOL.

ATTACHED INSTITUTES:

Institute of the Juche Idea.

Institute of Economics: Head KIM CHOL SIK.

Institute of Law: Head SIM HYONG IL.

Institute of History: Head KIM SOK HYONG.

Institute of Philosophy: Head KIM CHANG WON.

Institute of Linguistics: Head HA CHI ZIN.

Institute of Literature: Head KIM HA MYONG.

Institute of Archaeology: Head KIM YONG NAM.

Institute of National Classics.

ACADEMY OF MEDICAL SCIENCES

President: PAIK CHUN HYOP.

Vice-Presidents: RYU GYONG HUI, CHOI WON SOK, YUN HUI.

ATTACHED INSTITUTES:

Research Institute of Hygiene: Mangyongdae District, Pyongyang; Head JE HYONG DO.

Industrial Medicine Institute: Hamhung, South Hamgyong Province; Head KIM DAE IN.

Research Institute of Tonguihak Medicine: Tongdaewon District, Pyongyang; Vice-Head HAN BONG DU.

Research Institute of Hepatitis: Rakrang District, Pyongyang; Head MUN HUI SOON.

Clinical Medicine Institute: Woesong District, Pyongyang; Head HAN CHANG HWAL.

Research Institute of Clinical Oncology: Pyongchon District, Pyongyang; Head KIM CHUN WON.

Research Institute of Pharmacology: Songyo District, Pyongyang; Head CHOI JONG HWAL.

Research Institute of Medical Appliances: Songyo District, Pyongyang; Head KIM YUN TAIK.

Hamhung Clinical Medicine Institute: Hamhung, South Hamgyong Province; Vice-Head JU DU BYOK.

Research Institute of Tuberculosis: Hamhung, South Hamgyong Province; Head LI DONG SU.

Research Institute of Synthetic Pharmacy: Hamhung, South Hamgyong Province; Head LI GI SOP.

Research Institute of Antibiotics: Sunchon County, South Pyongan Province; Head KIM WON GYOM.

Research Institute of Microbiology: Jongju County, North Pyongan Province; Head HAN GIL PYONG.

Research Institute of Cultivation of Insam & Medicinal Herbs: Kaesong; Head KIM JONG HYON.

Research Institute of Blood Transfusion: Tongdaewon District, Pyongyang; Head KIM HAK KON.

ACADEMY OF AGRICULTURAL SCIENCE

RYONGSONG DISTRICT, PYONGYANG

Founded 1955.

President: RI YONG KYUN.

Vice-Presidents: KIM WON JIN, HONG SONG MAN.

ATTACHED RESEARCH INSTITUTES:

Seed Cultivation Research Institute: Sadong District, Pyongyang; Head RYOM DOK SU.

Soil Science Research Institute: Ryongsong District, Pyongyang; Vice-Head KANG BYONG HA.

Agricultural Chemicalization Research Institute: Ryongsong District, Pyongyang; Head KIM KI SONG.

Agricultural Mechanization Research Institute: Sadong District, Pyongyang; Head KANG SONG RYONG.

Fruit Cultivation Research Institute: Sukchon County, South Pyongan Province; Head CHANG HUI KUNG.

Sericulture Research Institute: Dongrim County, North Pyongan Province; Head KIM SUN JONG.

Zoology Research Institute: Pyongsong, South Pyongan Province; Vice-Head KIM GIL KON.

Poultry Science Research Institute: Hyongjaesan District, Pyongyang; Head BANG TAI HO.

Veterinary Science Research Institute: Ryongsong District, Pyongyang; Vice-Head LI YONG KON.

Vegetable Science Research Institute: Sadong District, Pyongyang; Head KIM HAK SON.

ACADEMY OF FORESTRY SCIENCE

TAISONG DISTRICT, PYONGYANG

Founded 1948.

President: IM ROK JAE.

ATTACHED RESEARCH INSTITUTES:

Fungus Research Institute: Taesong District, Pyongyang; Head CHOI YONG YYOP.

Forest Economics Research Institute: Taesong District, Pyongyang; Head CHON HAK GYU.

Forest Conservation Research Institute: Sunan District, Pyongyang; Head ON CHANG SON.

Forest Management Research Institute: Sunan District, Pyongyang; Head KIM SA RYUL (acting).

ACADEMY OF RAILWAY SCIENCES

HYONGJAESAN DISTRICT, PYONGYANG

Director: KIM HYON JU.

ATTACHED RESEARCH INSTITUTES:

Research Institute of Railway Carriages: Sosong District, Pyongyang; Head SOK KI HYON.

Research Institute of Transport Engineering: Sosong District, Pyongyang; Head CHANG CHUL.

Research Institute of Railway Electrification: Wonsan, Kangwon Province; Head HANG DOK GI.

Research Institute of Track Engineering: Sosong District, Pyongyang.

ACADEMY OF FISHERIES

WOESONG DISTRICT, PYONGYANG

Founded 1969.

Director: HAN UNG GYU.

ATTACHED INSTITUTES:

Donghae Institute of Fisheries: Wonsan, Kangwon Province; Head HAN UNG GOO.

Sohae Institute of Fisheries: Nampo, South Pyongan Province; Head TOGKO WON YONG.

Institute of Sea Culture: Munchon County, Kangwon Province; Head AN SAE HONG.

Institute of Sea Products Processing: Sinpo, South Hamgyong Province; Head KIM SI YUN.

Institute of Fisheries Machinery: Sinpo, South Hamgyong Province; Head LI JONG GIL.

ACADEMY OF LIGHT INDUSTRY SCIENCE

SONGYO DISTRICT, PYONGYANG

Founded 1954.

Director: KIM KYE SOK.

ATTACHED INSTITUTES:

Research Institute of Enzyme Technology: Waesong District, Pyongyang; Head LI RAN.

Research Institute of Basic Necessities Technology: Songyo District, Pyongyang; Head HWANG GOL.

Textile Institute: Songyo District, Pyongyang; Head RI GUON BYONG.

Research Institute of Foodstuffs Processing: Songyo District, Pyongyang; Head CHOI ZAE WON.

Research Institute of Maize Processing: Rakrang District, Pyongyang; Head CHONG JONG DOK.

Research Institute of Footwear Technology: Sadong District, Pyongyang; Head HYON HAN YONG.

State Committee for Atomic Energy: Sosong District, Pyongyang; f. 1952; Chair. CHOI HAK GUN.

Research Centre for Atomic Energy: Sosong District, Pyongyang; Pres. PAK GWAN O.

LIBRARIES

Central Library: Pyongyang; Chief Librarian HAM JIN SOOK.

Library of the Academy of Sciences: Pyongsong, South Pyongan Province; Chief Librarian KIM HAK JAE.

Fundamental Library of the Academy of Social Science: Central District, Pyongyang; Chief Librarian KIM SAE SONG.

North Hamgyong Provincial Library: Chongjin; Librarian CHOI MYONG OK.

South Hamgyong Provincial Library: Hamhung; Librarian KIM SOOK JONG.

North Pyongan Provincial Library: Shinuiju; Librarian LI YONG SIK.

South Hwanghae Provincial Library: Haeju; Librarian CHOI CHI DO.

North Hwanghae Provincial Library: Sariwon; Librarian KIM HYO DAL.

Kangwon Provincial Library: Wonsan; Librarian JI GYU HYOK.

Chagang Provincial Library: Kangge; Librarian SONG AAI GUN.

South Pyongan Provincial Library: Pyongsong; Librarian KIM DUK KWAN.

Ryanggang Provincial Library: Hesan; Librarian KIM CHOL WOO.

Kaesong City Library: Kaesong; Librarian HAN IL.

Chongjin City Library: Chongjin; Librarian KANG CHAE GUM.

Pyongyang Scientific Library: Central District, Pyongyang.

MUSEUMS

Korean Revolutionary Museum: Central District, Pyongyang; historical exhibits from second half of 19th century; Curator PAK YONG SUN.

Memorial Museum of the War of Liberation: Moranbong District, Pyongyang; historical materials from the latter half of the 19th century to the present day, including exhibits from the armed struggle against Japan in the 1930s and the Korea war; Dir. SONG JIN OK.

Korean Central Historical Museum: Central District, Pyongyang; exhibits date from the pre-historical period to the early 20th century (the end of the Li Dynasty); Curator KIM SIN SOOK.

Korean Ethnographic Museum: Central District, Pyongyang; Curator JON MOON JIN.

Korean Fine Arts Museum: Central District, Pyongyang.

Shinuiju Historical Museum: Shinuiju, North Pyongan Province; Curator PAK YONG GWAN.

Haeju Historical Museum: Haeju, South Hwanghae Province.

Wonsan Historical Museum: Wonsan, Kangwon Province; Curator JO GANG BAIK.

Hamhung Historical Museum: Hamhung, South Hamgyong Province; Curator KIM IK MYON.

Chongjin Historical Library: Chongjin; Curator EU JAI GYONG.

Kaesong Historical Library: Kaesong; Curator CHOI SAE YONG.

Mt. Myohyang-san Museum: Hyangsan County, North Pyongan Province; Curator CHOI HYONG MIN.

Shinchon Museum: Shinchon County, South Hwanghae Province; Curator PAK IN CHAIK.

UNIVERSITIES AND COLLEGES

KIM IL SUNG UNIVERSITY

DAESONG DISTRICT, PYONGYANG

Founded 1946.

President: HWANG JANG YOP.

Vice-Presidents: J. CHANG IK, RO SONG CHAN, PAI JAE UK.

Number of teachers: *c.* 900.

Number of students: *c.* 16,000 full and part-time.

Faculties: History, Philosophy, Political Economics, Law, Philology, Foreign Literature, Geography, Geology, Physics and Mathematics, Chemistry and Biology.

Kim Chaek Polytechnic Institute: Waesong District, Pyongyang; Rector CHOI TAI BOK; faculties of geology, mining, metallurgy, mechanical and electrical engineering, shipbuilding, electronics, nuclear technology.

Kim Hyong-chik Normal University: Pyongyang; faculties of revolutionary history, pedagogy, history and geography, language and literature, foreign languages, mathematics, physics, biology, music, fine arts, physical education; 4-year degree course, short-term courses for teachers, correspondence and post-graduate courses.

Pyongyang Medical Institute: Woesong District, Pyongyang; Rector LI JONG RYUL.

There are 82 colleges of higher and professional education (engineering, agriculture, fisheries, teacher training), situated in all the main towns; there are also *c.* 60 Factory (Engineering) Colleges.

REPUBLIC OF KOREA

Population 37,355,000

ACADEMIES

NATIONAL ACADEMY OF ARTS

1 SEJONGRO, CHONGNO-KU, SEOUL

Founded 1954.

Number of mems.: 50; number of books in library: 5,000 vols.; publs. *Journal of the National Academy of Arts, Korean Academy of Arts Bulletin, Survey of Korea Arts.*

President: CHONG-HWA PARK.
Vice-President: HANG-SEOK SEO.
Secretary: SUNG-SHIK SON.

HEADS OF SECTIONS:

Literature: YOUN-SOOK MOH.
Fine Arts: GYEONG-SEUNG KIM.
Music: SUNG-TAI KIM.
Theatre: HAE-RANG LEE.

NATIONAL ACADEMY OF SCIENCES

1 SEJONGRO, CHONGNO-KU, SEOUL

Founded 1954.

The Academy was set up in order to develop science, and to give help to scientists; provides advice to government; awards prizes; number of mems.: 100; library of 3,000 vols.; publs. *Bulletin*†, *Journal*†, *Bibliography*†.

President: Dr. BYONG-DO LEE.
Vice-Presidents: Dr. HI SEUNG LEE, Dr. DONG GIL PARK.
Secretary-General: DUG-JU PARK.

LEARNED SOCIETIES

Asia Foundation, The: Gwang Wha Moon P.O.B. 738, Seoul 110; f. 1954; one of 12 brs. of the main organization in the U.S.A. (*q.v.*); Rep. BENJAMIN J. KREMENAK.

British Council: c/o British Embassy, 1-122, 2-ka Shinmoon-ro, Jongro-gu, Seoul; library of 6,666 vols., 114 periodicals; Rep. Dr. W. A. BARR.

Goethe Institut: 118, 1-ka, Changchung-dong, Chung-ku, Seoul; f. 1968; German cultural centre providing language courses, concerts, plays, seminars, scholarships; library of 5,500 vols.; Dir. Dr. WALTER BREUER.

International Cultural Society of Korea (ICSK): P.O.B. 2147, 34-5, 3-ka, Namsan-dong, Chung-ku, Seoul 100; f. 1972 to promote mutual international understanding, friendship and peace; organizes cultural exchange programmes and presentation programmes of Korean culture; 114 staff; Pres. MYONG WHAI KIM; Vice-Pres. SHIN YUNG CHUL; publs. *Korea Newsreview*† (weekly, in English), *Asia Koron*† (monthly, in Japanese).

Korea Branch of the Royal Asiatic Society: C.P.O. Box 255, Seoul; f. 1900 to stimulate interest in, and promote study and dissemination of knowledge about the arts, history, literature and customs of Korea and the neighbouring countries; 1,200 mems.; reference library of 1,000 vols.; Pres. PAUL VAN WEDDINGEN; Corresponding Sec. MARY ALICE BALL; publ. *Transactions*†.

Korean Association of Sinology: c/o Asiatic Research Center, Korea University, Anam-dong, Seoul; f. 1955; 100 mems.; Chair. JUN-YOP KIM; publ. *Journal of Chinese Studies.*

Korean Chemical Society: 35, 5-ga, Anam-dong, Seongbuk-ku, Seoul; f. 1946; Pres. DONG IL KIM; Sec.-Gen. SANG UP CHOI.

Korean Economic Association: 62-41, Sindang-dong, Chung-ku, Seoul; f. 1952; theory, policy and history of economics and business administration; 300 mems.; library of 3,000 vols.; Pres. HOCHIN CHOI; Sec.-Gen. PIL WOO LEE; publ. *Korean Economic Review* (annually).

Korean Engineers' Association: 5-5, Myong-dong, 2, Choong-ku, Seoul; f. 1952; Sec.-Gen. TAE WOOK KIM.

Korean Forestry Association: c/o College of Agriculture, Seoul National University, Suweon 170; f. 1951 to foster the study of all aspects of forestry, to promote organic union among members; 500 mems.; Pres. Prof. YIM KYONG-BIN; Sec. Prof. WOO BO-MYEONG; publ. *Journal* (quarterly).

Korean Geographical Society: Dept. of Geography, Dongguk University, Chungku, Seoul 100; f. 1945 to promote mutual co-operation in academic work and international understanding; 450 mems.; Pres. KIE-JOO HYONG; Sec. BO-UNG CHANG; publ. *Chiri Hak.*

Korean Historical Association: 2-5, Myong-nyun-dong 3-ga, Chongno-ku, Seoul; f. 1952; research into Eastern and Western history; 400 mems.; Principal Officers W. S. LEE, H. S. CHA; publ. *Yoksa Hakbo* (The Korean Historical Review, quarterly).

Korean Library Association: 100-177, 1-Ka, Hoehyun-Dong, Choong-ku, Seoul; f. 1955; a social and academic institution comprising all the libraries and librarians in Korea; 530 institutional, 440 individual mems.; Pres. HYO-SOON SONG; Exec.-Dir. DAE-KWON PARK; publ. *KLA Bulletin* (monthly).

Korean Medical Association: I.P.O. Box 2062, Seoul; f. 1908; to develop the medical sciences and medical education by encouraging research and investigation; 10,500 mems.; library of 2,800 vols.; Pres. TONG SOO CHO, M.D.; Sec. PYO OH; publ. *Journal of the K.M.A.* (monthly).

Korean PEN Centre: 163 Ankuk-dong, Chongno-ku, Seoul 110; f. 1954; 200 mems.; library of 5,000 vols.; Pres. Dr. YOUN-SOOK MOH; Exec. Sec. Dr. JUNG-KEE LEE; publs. *The Korean PEN*†, *Asian Literature*†.

Korean Psychological Association: 1-2, 5-ga, Anam-dong, Seongbuk-ku, Seoul; f. 1946; 159 mems.; Pres. SUNG-TAE KIM; publs. *Korean Journal of Psychology* (twice yearly), *Korean Journal of Clinical Psychology* (twice yearly).

Korea Scientific and Technological Information Center (Korstic): 206-9, Cheongryangri-dong, Dongdaimun-ku, Seoul (P.O.B. 205, Seoul); f. 1962; central organizations in Korea; computer-based information retrieval service for foreign and Korean data bases; engaged in the acquisition and dissemination of scientific, technical, patent and medical information; trade catalogue centre for industrial organizations in Korea; library of 4,500 vols. and 6,500 periodical titles; Dir.-Gen. DOO-HONG KIM; Dir. Office of Planning and Co-ordination CHANG-KYO LEE; publs. *Korean Scientific Abstracts, Technological Information* (every 2 months), *Korean Medical Abstracts* (quarterly), 17 series of *Technical Information Bulletin by Type of Industry* (*TIB-BTI*), 10 series of secondary publications giving bibliographic descriptions of journal articles and patents.

Kyungje-Kwahak-Shimuihoeui (*President's Council of Economic and Scientific Advisers*): 77 Sejongro, Chongno-ku, Seoul; f. 1964; to advise the Government on questions of policy relating to the advancement of science and technology and the national economy; proposes research projects and awards grants to institutions and individuals; library of 20,000 vols.; Sec.-Gen. YOUN HWI-WOOH.

Music Association of Korea: Room No. 303, F.A.C.O. Bldg., 81-6, Sechon-Ro, Chongro-ku, Seoul; f. 1961; to develop Korean national music and to promote and protect Korean musicians; organizes concerts, encourages musical composition and nation-wide singing, is active in the international musical exchange and in music education; awards the Prize of Musical Culture; 700 mems.; small library; Pres. Dr. TAI JOON PARK; Sec. DAE YUP SOHN.

RESEARCH INSTITUTES

(*see* also under Universities)

Central Meteorological Office: 1 Songweol-dong, Seodaemun-gu, Seoul 120; under the control of the Ministry of Science and Technology; Dir.-Gen. Dr. I. K. YANG; publs. Monthly and Annual Meteorological Reports.

Defence Ministry's Science Research Institute: Seoul.

Korea Advanced Institute of Science: P.O.B. 150, Chongyangni, Seoul; f. 1971; research-oriented graduate school; training in applied sciences and engineering essential for development of Korean industry; 614 students; library of 30,000 vols.; Pres. Dr. SOON-TAHK CHOH; publs. *KAIS Bulletin* (monthly), *Collected reprints of KAIS Research* (annually), *Abstracts of Dissertations Presented for Degree at KAIS* (annually).

Korea Atomic Energy Research Institute: P.O.B. 7, Cheong Ryang, Seoul; f. 1959; library of 32,000 vols. and 920 periodicals; Pres. KYUNG HO HYUN; publs. *Journal of Nuclear Science, Technical Reports, KAERI Collected Reprints, Abstracts of KAERI Publications.*

Korea Institute of Science and Technology: P.O.B. 131, Dongdaemun, Seoul; f. 1966; chemical, environmental, electronics, mechanical and metallurgical engineering, polymer and material science, food, bio-, precision machinery and foundry technology, project, software, ocean and regional development, industrial economics, technology transfer, solar energy; *c.* 1,200 research staff; library of 50,000 vols., 1,700 journals, *c.* 5,000 technical papers; Pres. CHUN BYONG DOO; Vice-Pres. KWON TAI WAN (Research), PARK WON HEE (Technical Services), RHEE CHAN JUH (Administration), YUN YEO GYEONG (Management Planning); publs. *Newsletter*† (quarterly), *Annual Review*†, *Collected Reprints of KIST Research.*

Korea Research Institute of Geosciences and Mineral Resources: 219-5, Garibong-dong, Youngdeungpo gu, Seoul 150-06; f. 1976 to conduct research in geosciences and resources development; supported by Ministry of Energy and Resources; *c.* 300 mems.; library of 7,800 vols.; Pres. BYUNG KOO HYUN; publs. *Report on Geoscience and Mineral Resources* (2 a year), *Geological Maps, 1:50,000, Annual Report.*

Korean Educational Development Institute: 8-20 Yejang Dong, Chung-ku, Seoul; f. 1972; independent, government-aided research and development centre; undertakes educational reform for Korean schools; activities include: studies on educational ideals, curriculum, development of instructional materials and management systems, and an educational TV/radio station, in-service teacher-training courses; library of 15,000 vols.; Dir. Dr. YUNG DUG LEE; publs. *Korean Education*† (abstract in English), *Educational Development Newsletter*† (Korean), *Classroom Studies*† (Korean), *Yunbo*† (annual report, English), research reports† and bulletins† (abstracts in English).

Korean Institute for Research in the Behavioural Sciences: C.P.O.B. 3528, 163 Ankook-Dong, Chongno-Ku, Seoul; f. 1968; basic and applied research in five areas: social, child, learning, organization, and psychological testing; 70 researchers; library of 5,000 vols.; Dir. SUNG JIN LEE, PH.D.; publs. *Research Bulletin, Research Notes, Research Monograph.*

Korean Social Sciences Research Society: 90.1, Chungjungro I, Sudaemun-ku, Seoul; Pres. Dr. BYUNG DO LEE.

National Industrial Research Institute: 199 Dongsoong-dong, Chongno-ku, Seoul; f. 1883; Dir. LEE BOM SOON.

National Institute of Education: 25 Samcheong-dong, Jongro-gu, Seoul; f. 1974; government institute attached to Ministry of Education; research into educational theory and practice; in-service training courses; 40 branch institutes.

Office of Rural Development: Ministry of Agriculture and Fisheries, Suweon; f. 1906 to carry out agricultural research and guidance work; 9,373 mems.; library of 53,000 vols.; Dir.-Gen. Dr. IN HWAN KIM; publs. *Annual Research Report*† (Korean and English), *Agricultural Research Newsletter* (monthly), *Research and Guidance* (quarterly), *Agricultural Technical Bulletin* (monthly), *Monthly Bulletin of Agricultural Information.*

LIBRARIES

American Cultural Center Library: Uljiro 1-ka, Jung-ku, Seoul; also in Taegu, Pusan, Kwangju.

Busan National University Library: 30 Jangjeon-Dong, Dongnaeku, Busan; f. 1946; 140,637 vols. in Japanese, Chinese and Korean, 64,316 vols. in Western languages; Dir. Prof. TONG-WON CHOI.

Central National Library: 100-177, 1 Ga, Hoe-Hyeon-Dong, Jung-Gu, Seoul; f. 1925; 700,000 vols.; national and international exchange, research in library science, training; Dir. HEE SHIK SOHN; publs. *Korean National Bibliography, Bibliographic Index of Korea, Library, Literary Information* (monthly).

Chungang University Library: 221 Huksuk-dong, Dongjak-ku, Seoul; f. 1949; 246,990 vols.; Dir. HEE YOUNG WHANG.

Dongguk University Library: 263-KA, Pil-dong, Seoul; f. 1906; Buddhist and Oriental studies; 350,000 vols., 1,100 periodicals; Dir. JUNG-SIK HONG.

Ewha Women's University Library: 11-1, Daehyun-dong, Sudaemun-ku, Seoul; f. 1923; 283,602 vols.; Dir. BONG SOON LEE.

Korea University Library: 1 Anam-dong, Sungbuk-ku, Seoul; f. 1937; 400,132 vols.; Dir. CHI-GYU KIM.

Kyungpook National University Library: 1370 ,San-gyuck-dong, Bukgu, Daegu 635; f. 1952; 234,218 vols.; Dir. PARK BONG MOK.

Namdalmoon Library: Seoul; f. 1922; 68,110 vols.

National Assembly Library: Taepyong-Ro, Chung-ku, Seoul; f. 1952; library service for members of the National Assembly, the Legislative, the Executive, the Judiciary and for professors and scholars and legislative research activities; 170,000 vols.; international publications exchange; Chief Librarian CHU-CHIN KANG; Exchange Librarian PYOUNG-SOO RHEE; Dir. of Legislative Research Bureau SOON-YOUNG KIM; Dir. of Processing Reference Bureau CHONG-KO KIM; publs. *National Assembly Library Review, Legislative Research Monthly, Korean Periodicals Index, Government Publications in Korea*, etc.

Seoul National University Library: San 56-1, Sinlim-Dong, Seoul 151; f. 1926; 1,010,059 vols.; collections on the arts, sciences, law, education, music, medicine, engineering, economics and commerce; Dir. CHI-HOON CHOI; publs. *Bulletin, Catalogue of Occidental Books, Index of Foreign Periodicals in the libraries of S.N.U., S.N.U. Faculty Papers*†, *S.N.U. Journal*†, etc.

Transport Library: Seoul; f. 1920; 32,000 vols.; Dir. CHO WOO HYUN; Chief Librarian KIM DOO HO; publ. *Korean National Railroad Bulletin* (monthly).

United Nations Depository Library: Korea University, 1 An-Am-Dong, Sungbuk-ku, Seoul; f. 1957; 20,000 vols.; Dir. IL-CHUL SHIN; Librarian PARK HU-YONG.

Yonsei University Library: Yonsei University, 134 Sinchon-dong, Sudaemoon-ku, Seoul; f. 1915; 412,212 vols. including Korean archives; Dir. HAN YONG LEE; publs. *Dong Bang Hak Chi*† (Journal of Far Eastern Studies), *Inmun Kwahak*† (Journal of Humanistic Studies), *International Journal of Korean Studies, Journal of East and West Studies*†, *Kyo Yuk Non Jib*† (Journal of Education), *Yonsei Non-Chong*† (Journal of Graduate School), *Yonsei Social Science Review, Abstracts of Faculty Research Report*†, *News of Yonsei University Library* (monthly).

MUSEUMS

Busan National University Museum: Korean archaeology with special collection of historical remains of Kyong-sang-Namdo province, arts, ethnology, etc.; Dir. Prof. SUK-HEE KIM; publ. *Research Reports* (irregularly).

National Museum: Kyongbok Palace, Seoul; f. 1915; Korean culture and folklore; library of 11,150 vols.; Dir. CHOI SUNU; publs. *Report of Researches of Antiquities, Misul Charyo* (Materials in Art, 2 a year), *Museum News* (monthly). Five branch museums:

Kyongju National Museum.
Kwangju National Museum.
Puyo National Museum.
Kongju National Museum.
National Folklore Museum.

National Science Museum: 2 Waryong-dong, Chongno-ku, Seoul 110; f. 1926; holds National Science Fair, exhibitions, Science Classrooms, Film Service, etc.; library of 2,000 vols. on science and technology; Dir. CHI-EUN KIM; publ. *Bulletin.*

Gyungbok Art Gallery: Gyungbok Palace; national art exhibition held here annually.

Yonsei University Museum: Suhdaemoon-ku, Seoul; f. 1965; research and excavation of palaeolithic and neolithic sites; Dir. Prof. POW-KEY SOHN; publs. occasional papers, excavation reports†.

UNIVERSITIES

BUSAN NATIONAL UNIVERSITY

30 JANGJEON-DONG,
DONGNAE-KU, BUSAN

Telephone: 56-0171-9.

Founded 1946.

Academic year: March to February.

President: HONG-JOO MOON.
Dean of Academic Affairs: JAE-YEONG ROH.
Dean of Student Affairs: JANG-IL UM.
Administrative Officer: BYENG-YOUG PARK.
Directory of Library: TONG-WON CHOI.

Library: *see* Libraries.

Museum: *see* Museums.

Number of teachers: 410.
Number of students: 13,500.

Publications: *University Academic Journal* (Annual Collection of Theses), weekly newspaper, *College Academic Journal.*

DEANS:

Graduate School: SUK-HWAN KIM.
Graduate School of Business Administration: CHAN-GEUN CHUNG.
Graduate School of Public Administration: JU-SIL SUH.
Graduate School of Education: MOON-SEON CHA.
College of Engineering: KYU-NAM KIM.
College of Liberal Arts and Sciences: KYU-SHIK HWANG.
College of Law and Political Sciences: SOO-HYUN LEW.
College of Education: HYUN-KEE LEE.
College of Business: CHIN-HO KANG.
College of Pharmacy: SANG-ROK LEE.
College of Medicine: CHAN-HYUN KIM.
College of Home Economics: HYUN-KI LEE.

ATTACHED INSTITUTES:

Coastal Region Development Research Institute
Institute of Production Technology
Institute of Environmental Pollution
Institute of Urban Problems
Business Management Research Institute
Bolld Research Center
Korean Japanese Cultural Research Center
Institute of Legal Studies
Institute of Korean Reunification
Institute of Foreign Language Studies
Institute of Chinese Studies
Institute of American Studies
Population and Census Research Center
Electronic Computer Operation Center

NATIONAL FISHERIES UNIVERSITY OF BUSAN

599 DAEYONDONG,
BUSAN 601-01

Founded 1941 as Busan Fisheries College, attained university status 1980.

President: KWANG-OK KIM.
Dean of Graduate Studies: SING WON PARK.

Library of 40,000 vols.

Number of teachers: 92.
Number of students: 1,740.

Publications†: *Bulletin, Publication of Institute of Marine Science.*

CHONNAM NATIONAL UNIVERSITY

318 YANG-DONG, KWANGJU

Founded 1952.

President: MIN JUN-SHIK.
Registrar: JAE SOO LEE.
Librarian: CHONG-SOO KIM.

Number of teachers: 321.
Number of students: 5,800.

Publications: *Journal of the Institute of Honam Area Studies*†, *Rural Development Review*†, *Law Review*†, *Historical Review*†, *Chonnam Medical Journal*†,

Technological Review†, Theses Collection on Korean Literature and Language.

DEANS:

College of Engineering: KYUNG-RAM HUR.
College of Commerce: HAK-SHIN CHUNG.
College of Agriculture: CHONG-MAN PARK.
College of Law: SUNG-KYU SON.
College of Medicine: WON-SIK KIL.
College of Liberal Arts and Sciences: JOE HYUN CHOI.
Graduate School: KYU-CHAN CHO.

CHOSUN UNIVERSITY

375, SEOSUK-DONG, KWANGJU, CHOLLANAMDO 500

Founded 1946; private control.

Founder-President: CHYULL WOONG PARK, LL.D.
Dean of Academic Affairs: CHULIN JUNG.

Library of 370,917 vols.
Number of teachers: 453.
Number of students: 12,400.

Publications: various research journals†.

Colleges of liberal arts and sciences, law and political science, business administration, engineering, education, physical education, medicine, dentistry, pharmacy; Women's Industrial College, Evening College, Evening College Graduate School, Graduate School of Education.

ATTACHED INSTITUTES:

Humanities Research Institute.
Social Science Research Institute.
Natural Science Research Institute.
Production Technology Research Institute.
National Development Research Intitute.
Atomic Energy Research Institute.
Energy and Resources Research Institute.
Korean History Research Institute.
National Unification Research Institute.
Foreign Cultural Research Institute.
Educational Research Institute.
Medical Research Institute.
Dental-Biology Research Institute.
Pharmaceutical Research Institute.
Business Administration Research Institute.
Agricultural Research Institute.
Saemaul Research Institute.
Student Guidance Research Institute.

CHUNG-ANG UNIVERSITY

221 HUKSUK DONG, KWAN-AK-KU, SEOUL 151
Telephone: 829-5031/38.
Telex: CAUNIV K24763.

Founded 1918.

Private control; Academic year: March to February (two semesters).

President: CHURL SOON YIM.
Vice-President: BYUNG JUNE WHANG.
Dean of Faculties: BYUNG JIB MOON.
Director of Medical Centre: KWANG SE RHIM.
Director of Research and Librarian: MOON OK PARK.

Number of teachers: 606 (354 full-time).
Number of students: 8,992.

Publications: *Theses Collection*† (annual), College Journals (2 a year), *Korean Studies Journal* (monthly), *Journal of Chungang Pharmacy*, *Korean Journal of Comparative Law* (annual), *Korean Education Index:* (annual), *Journal of Economic Development*† (annual).

DEANS:

College of Liberal Arts and Sciences: SUP HEE RHEE.
College of Engineering: WON EUN CHOI.
College of Education: KI SUP YUH.
College of Law: KYU JUNG KIM.
College of Political Science and Economics: HAE DONG CHUNG.
College of Business Administration: WON KYUNG KIM.
College of Agriculture: DONG HYO CHUNG.
College of Pharmacy: IL HYUK KIM.
College of Medicine: SANG DON RHEE.
College of Arts: CHURL SOON YIM.
Graduate School: BYUNG JUNE WHANG.
Graduate School of Social Development: YOUNG WHAN HAHN.
Graduate School of International Management: YOUNG WHAN HAHN.
Evening College: WON EUN CHOI.
Cansung Campus: HYUNG NAM CHOI (acting).

CHAIRMEN OF DEPARTMENTS:

College of Liberal Arts and Sciences:
CHOO, JONG GIL, Biology
KIM, JONG KUN, English
KIM, YOUNG MO, Social Work
KOH, HOON WHA, Psychology
KWON, SUK BONG, History
LEE, SUK YONG, Mathematics
MOON, BYUNG YUL, Chemistry
PARK, JOON TAEK, Philosophy
SHIM, WOO JOON, Library Science
WHANG, HEE YOUNG, Korean Language and Literature
YOON, IL BYUNG, Physics

College of Engineering:
CHUNG, JAE GIL, Electrical Engineering
HAHN, JUNG SOO, Mechanical Engineering
KIM, CHUNG, GI, Electrical Engineering
KIM, DUK JE, Architecture
KIM, SUNG SOON, Civil Engineering
KIM, YOUNG CHAN, Computer Science
LEE, KUN BAE, Chemical Engineering

College of Education:
CHANG, NAM JOON, German Education
CHOI ,YOUNG DUCK, Physical Education
CHUNG, JAE CHULL, Education
LEE, KI YONG, English Education
LEE, WON YOUNG, Pre-School Education
YOON, SEO SUCK, Home Economics

College of Law:
KIM, EE YOL, Public Administration
LEE, BONG, Law

College of Political Science and Economics:
CHOI, JIN WOO, Journalism and Broadcasting
CHUNG, JO SUB, Economics
LEE, DAE RYONG, Public Relations
LEE, YOON JONG, Statistics
YOON, JUNG SUK, Political Science and Diplomacy

College of Business Administration:
HAHN, JU SUP, Foreign Trade
SHIM, JAE SUCK, Business Administration

College of Agriculture:
KIM, CHANG JU, Agricultural Management
KIM, CHANG KUN, Animal Husbandry
KIM, JOON PYUNG, Food Technology
SUL, BONG SHIK, Community Development

College of Arts:
CHE, RI SOOK, Music
CHUNG, YOUNG YOL, Painting
KANG, MYUNG GU, Architecture
KWAK, WON MO, Applied Art
LEE, CHUNG GEO, Drama and Cinema
SONG, CHUL KYO, Dancing
YOO, JU HYUN, Manuscript Writing
YOO, MAN YOUNG, Photography

College of Medicine:
BAE, DO WHAN, Obstetrics and Gynaecology
CHANG, JIN, YO, Dermatology
CHANG, SUN TAEK, Surgery
CHO, HYUNG SANG, Anaesthetics
CHUNG, KYU CHUL, Preventive Medicine
CHUNG, YEON TAE, Nursing
KANG, HONG GU, Dentistry
KIM, CHONG SOOH, Internal Medicine
KIM, CHOONG HWAN, Oto-Rhino-Laryngology
KIM, KI SOO, Urology
KOO, BON SOOL, Ophthalmology
LEE, KUN BAE, Biochemistry
LEE, KWANG SOO, Pharmacology
LEE, SOON HYUNG, Parasitology
LEE, SOON HYUNG, Pre-Medical
LEE, WON WOO, Reconstructive Surgery
MIN, BYUNG KUN, Neurology
MIN, DAE HONG, Plastic Surgery
NA, BONG JIN, Histology
NA, BON JIN, Medicine
PARK, SOO SUNG, Radiology
PARK, TAE SOO, Pathology
RHEE, SANG DON, Physiology
RHIM, KWANG SE, Neurosurgery
SHIM, TAE SUP, Paediatrics
YANG, KI MIN, Chest Surgery
YANG, YONG TAE, Microbiology

College of Pharmacy:
CHOI, SUK SANG, Manufacturing Pharmacy
HUH, IN HOI, Pharmacy

DIRECTORS:

Institute of Humanities: DONG GWON YIM.
Research Institute of Developing Countries: KYOUNG KUN HAR.
Research Institute for Korean Education: KI SUP YUH.
Institute of Laws: JU CHAN SONN.
Institute of Technology and Science: KYU HWAN LEE.
Institute of Community Development: BYUNG JIB MOON.
Institute of Oriental Medicine: DUG RYONG HAHN.

Research Institute of Medical Science of Korea: KWANG SE RHIM.
Research Institute of National Culture: DONG GWON YIM.
Korean Studies Institute: KUN SOO KIM.
Korean Institute of Advanced Executive Development: YOUNG WHAN HAHN.
Korean Economic Research Institute: IN KIE KIM.
Korean Research Institute of Comparative Law: CHAN JIN KIM.
Japanese Studies Institute: DONG GWON YIM.
Adolescent Problems Research Institute: BYUNG KUN MIN.
Student Problems Research Institute: CHAN KYE PARK.

CHUNGBUK NATIONAL UNIVERSITY

48 GAESIN-DONG,
CHEONGJU, CHUNGBUK 310

Founded 1951 as Agricultural College, university status 1978.

President: BOM MO CHUNG.
Director of General Affairs: JONG BOK KWON.

Library of 74,000 vols.

Number of teachers: 242.
Number of students: 6,251.

Publications: *Research Reports, Theses Collection of the Graduate School, Research Reports of the Tobacco Research Institute, Research Reports of the Student Guidance Centre.*

Courses in agriculture, education, engineering, humanities, natural sciences, pharmacy and social sciences.

CHUNGNAM NATIONAL UNIVERSITY

1 MOONHWWA-DONG, DAEJON,
CHUNGNAM 300-01
Telephone: 45-0081-92.

Founded 1952.

Chancellor: SUHR MYONG-WON.
Dean of Academic Affairs: KIM YOUNG-RAE.
Dean of Student Affairs: SHIN DAE-HYON.
Administrative Director: KIM CHAN-JAE.
Librarian: Dr. MIN DONG-KUN.

The library contains *c.* 47,000 vols., Medical College library contains *c.* 11,600 vols.

Number of teachers: 341.
Number of students: 11,395.

Publications† (all annually): *Medical Journal, Thesis Collection, Theses on Sae Maum, Journal of Law and Public Administration, Journal of American Studies, Journal of Management and Economics,* reports of research institutes.

Research institutes for agriculture, humanities, natural science, social science, local community medicine, national re-unification and Baekje dynasty.

DEANS:

College of Sciences: Dr. YOON WHA-JOONG.
College of Agriculture: Dr. CHOE CHUNG-YULL.
College of Liberal Arts: Dr. RHEE JUNG-BOK.
College of Law: Dr. KIM YOUNG-CHULL.
College of Business Administration: Dr. OH DUCK-KYUN.
College of Medicine: Dr. SHIM WOON-TACK.
College of Industrial Education: Dr. MANG KER-SUCK.
Graduate School: Dr. LEE CHANG-KAP.
Graduate School of Business Administration: Dr. KIM HONG-JOONG.
Graduate School of Education: Dr. OH HEE-PILL.

DAN KOOK UNIVERSITY

8 HANNAM-DONG,
YONGSAN-KU, SEOUL

Founded 1947, university status 1967; private control.

President: CHOONG SIK CHANG.

Library of 140,000 vols.

Publications: Reviews, *Dan Won.*

Colleges of Liberal Arts and Sciences, Law, Engineering, Commerce and Economics, Education; graduate school.

DONG-A UNIVERSITY

1, 3-KA DONGDAESHIN-DONG,
SEO-KU, BUSAN 600
Telephone: (43) 0011-0015.

Founded 1947.

Private control; Language of instruction: Korean; Academic year: March to February.

Chancellor: SOO-BONG CHUNG, LL.D.
Director, Academic Affairs: SOON-GI SHIN, LL.D.
Director, Student Affairs: HYON-SOO SON, D.AGR.
Director of Finance: JIN-SOOL SON.
University Librarian: MUN-TAEK HEO, LITT.D.

Library of 220,164 vols.

Number of professors: 202.
Number of students: 8,375.

Publications: *Bulletin* (weekly), *Dong-A Ronchong, Arts and Sciences Journal, Korean, Law and Economics Ronchong, Journal of Social Development Studies, Abstracts of Theses and Dissertations, College of Engineering Bulletin, Management Ronchong, Student Research, Graduate School Papers* (annually), *Law and Economic Times, General Culture Series* (2 a year).

DEANS:

Graduate School: BYONG-KYU KIM, LL.D.
Management Graduate School: CHEOL-SE PAE.
Graduate School of Education: JAE-IL JANG, D.SC.
College of Arts and Sciences: SUNG-IL KANG, LITT.D.
College of Law and Economics: WOO-HYON DO, D.ECON.
College of Agricultural Science: JEONG-KI KIM, D.AGR.
College of Engineering: HEE-JONG KIM, D.ENG.
College of Evening Courses: HO-YEONG CHUNG, LITT.D.

DIRECTORS:

Institute of Classical Literature: JUNG-HWAN CHUNG, LITT.D.
Institute of Folklore: SUNG-IL KANG, LITT.D.
Institute of Agricultural Technology: CHUNG-KI KIM, D.AGR.
Institute of Natural Resources Development: KOO-JE CHUN, M.ENG.
Institute of Public Hazard Research: HUI-JONG KIM, D.ENG.
Institute of Management Problems: BYONG-TAE CHO, D.ECON.
Institute for New Villages: HYON-SOO SON, D.AGR.
Institute of Social Development: KYU-SANG PARK, D.ECON.
Population Research Centre: JAE-YEONG PARK, M.ECON.
Student Guidance Centre: HAE-CHUN CHOL, LITT.D.

DONGGUK UNIVERSITY

26 3-KA PIL-DONG,
CHUNG-KU, SEOUL
Telephone: 267-8131-9.

Founded 1906, university status 1953; private control.

President: Dr. CHAI-KAK CHUNG.
Vice-President: (vacant).
Librarian: JUNG-SIK HONG.

Library: *see* Libraries.

Number of teachers: 450.
Number of students: 7,000.

Publications: *The Dongguk University Press* (weekly), *The Dongguk Post* (monthly), *Pulgyo Hakpo* (The Journal of Buddhist Studies).

Colleges of Buddhism, liberal arts and sciences, law and political science, economics and commerce, agriculture and forestry, engineering, education; school of general studies, graduate school, graduate school of public administration, graduate school of business administration, graduate school of education, college at Kyongju Campus.

Research Institutes: Buddhist culture, comparative literature, statistical science, law and political science, business management, agriculture and forestry, overseas development, national security, computer, Middle

Eastern and East European affairs, Korean studies, Saemaul research, landscape art, industrial technology, translation of Buddhist scriptures.

EWHA WOMEN'S UNIVERSITY

11-1 DAIHYUN-DONG,
SEODAIMOON KU, SEOUL
Telephone: (33) 0151-0180.
Founded 1886.

Language of instruction: Korean; Private control; Academic year: March to February (two semesters).

President: Dr. OKGILL KIM.
Dean of the Faculty: YONG JAI CHUNG.
Dean of Students: YOON-AI CHOI.
Director of Business Administration: SUK-KON LEE.
Director of Planning and Co-ordination: BONG-HO RYU.
Librarian: Miss BONG-SOON LEE.

Library of 309,367 vols.
Number of teachers: 447.
Number of students: 10,027.

Publications: *Ewha Voice*† (monthly, in English), *Ewha Hak Bo*† (weekly, in Korean), *Journal of Korean Cultural Research Institute*† (annually, in Korean, abstract in English), *Journal of Korean Research Institute for Better Living*† (annually, in Korean, abstract in English), *Bulletin*† (English and Korean).

DEANS:

Graduate School: KEUN-HO RHEE.
Graduate School of Education: SOOK NEY LEE.
College of Liberal Arts and Sciences: KWANG-SUN SUH.
College of Music: BO-HI YOON.
College of Fine Arts: JOON LEE.
College of Physical Education: JUNG-SOON SUNG.
College of Education: CHAI-SOON CHA.
College of Law and Political Science: HOO-JUNG YOON.
College of Medicine: KU-JA KIM.
College of Nursing: YOUNG-SOO HA.
College of Pharmacy: YOUNG-OK AHN.
College of Home Economics: IL-WHA PARK.

ATTACHED RESEARCH INSTITUTES:

Korean Cultural Research Institute.
Korean Research Institute for Better Living.
Audio-Visual Research Centre.
Student Guidance Centre.
Korean Rural Research Institute.
Asia Food and Nutrition Research Institute.
Environmental Research Institute.
Korean Women's Institute.
Research Institute for Human Development.
Management Research Centre.
Ewha Historical Research Centre.
Korean Language and Literature Research Institute.
Health and Physical Education Institute.
Ceramics Research Institute.
East West Education Research Institute.

HANKUK UNIVERSITY OF FOREIGN STUDIES

270 LY MOON DONG,
DONG DAE MOON KU, SEOUL
Telephone: 967-1811.
Founded 1954.
Private control.

President: Dr. WAN-BOK CHOI.
Dean of Academic Affairs: Prof. KYU-CHUE CHO.
Dean of Student Affairs: Prof. BYONG-MAN AHN.
Chief Administration Officer: YOO KEUN PARK.
Librarian: Dr. SE-WOOK HUH.

Library of 150,000 vols.
Number of teachers: 250.
Number of students: 4,200.

Publications: *Oe-Dae Hakbo* (3 a month, Korean), *Argus* (bi-monthly, English and other foreign languages).

DEANS:

Audio-Visual Education Institute: Dr. SOON-HAM PARK KIM.
Graduate School: Dr. SUNG-HIE KIM.
Graduate School of International Trade: Dr. SUNG-HIE KIM.

DIRECTORS:

Foreign Language Training and Research Centre: Dr. IN-SEOK YANG.
Foreign Trade Research Institute: Dr. BYUNG-HO PARK.
Institute for Research in Languages and Linguistics: Dr. SOON-HAM PARK KIM.
Chinese Studies Institute: Dr. SE-WOOK HUH.
Russian and East European Institute: Prof. KYU-WHA CHO.
Institute of Latin-American Studies: Prof. I-BAE KIM.
Institute of Middle East Studies: Dr. JEONG-YOLE REW.
Institute of African Studies: Dr. WON-TAK PARK.

HANYANG UNIVERSITY

8-2, HAENGDANG-DONG,
SUNGDONG-KU, SEOUL
Telephone: 52-4111, 54-3111.

Founded 1939 as Hanyang Institute of Technology; present status 1959.

Private control; Academic year: March to July, September to December.

President: Dr. LYUN JOON KIM.
Academic Dean: Dr. HAINAM LEE.

Library of 250,000 vols.
Number of teachers: *c.* 640.
Number of students: *c.* 9,200.
Publication: *Hanyang Nonmun Dzip.*

Colleges of Engineering (including Architectural Engineering), Liberal Arts and Sciences (including Journalism and the Cinema), Commerce and Economics, Law and Political Science, Music, Physical Education, Education, Medicine; Evening Engineering College; Graduate School, Graduate School of Industrial Management.

HONG-IK UNIVERSITY

72-1 SANGSU-DONG, MAPO-GU,
SEOUL 121
Telephone: 32-0150/6.
Founded 1948.

President: Prof. HANG-NYONG LEE.
Registrar: Prof. JAE-MAN SONG.
Librarian: Prof. CHEUL-HO KIM.

Library of 200,000 vols.
Number of teachers: 104.
Number of students: 3,572.

DEANS:

College of Engineering: Prof. BYUNG-JOO PARK.
College of Commerce and Economics: Prof. SUNG-SOON LEE.
College of Fine Arts: Prof. DO-RYONG HAN.
College of Education: Prof. KYUNG-CHUN MIN.
Evening College: Prof. CHANG-JIP KIM.

INHA UNIVERSITY

253 YONGHYEON-DONG,
NAM-KU, INCHEON.
Founded 1954; private control.

President: RHI JAE-CHUL.

Library of 102,046 vols.
Number of teachers: 224.
Number of students: 7,956.

Colleges of engineering, science, business administration, education; graduate school, evening division.

JEONBUG NATIONAL UNIVERSITY

664-14 DEOGJIN DONG 1-GA,
JEONJU, JEONBUG
Telephone: 3-0031.
Founded 1952.

State control; Academic year: March to February (two semesters).

President: CHONG SUPP SHIM, PH.D.
Librarian: JONG-KYU HWANG, PH.D.

Library of 115,396 vols.
Number of teachers: 377.
Number of students: 9,840.

Publications: annual bulletins of research institutes.

DEANS:

Academic Affairs: CHONG-EUI YANG.
Student Affairs: JUN-BAE KIM.

College of Engineering: DONG-GYU CHOI.
College of Agriculture: HWAN-SEUNG RYANG.
College of Humanities: UN-WHAN LEE.
College of Law and Political Science: HAK-SOO KIM.
College of Education: HO-GWAN HWANG.
College of Commerce: SUNG-KUN LIEW.
College of Science: YOUNG-KI KIM.
Medical School: TAI-YOU HA.
Graduate School of Education: CHEOL-SOON SHIN.
Graduate School: JONG-SOON LEE.
Graduate School of Business Administration: JHONG-ROCK RIE.

DIRECTORS:

Student Guidance and Counselling Centre: HYUN-SEOB SONG.
Saemaul Research Institute: BANG-HWAN LEE.
Language Research Institute: SOO-GON KIM.
Research Institute of Industrial Technology: HONG-MIN KIM.
Research Institute of Agricultural Development: BYUNG-KI LEE.
Social Science Research Institute: CHOO-WHANG PARK.
Research Institute for Basic Science: JAE-SOON HWANG.
Centre for Research in International Culture: YOUNG-BIN CHO.
Institute of Science Education: BYUNG-HOON LEE.
Research Institute of Industrial Development: SEON-WOONG CHO.
Institute for Medical Science: TAI-YOU HA.
Humanistic Research Institute: DAN-SUCK HAN.
Institute of Genetics: GEUM-YEONG LEE.
Bureau of Business Affairs: KUN-MYUNG LEE.

KEIMYUNG UNIVERSITY

2139 DAEMYUNG-DONG, NAM-KU, DAEGU 634
Telephone: 67-1321.
Founded 1954.

President: ILHI SYNN, PH.D.
Vice-President: MANDUK CHUNG, PH.D.
Dean of Graduate School: JONGKON HWANG, PH.D.
Dean of Faculty: HYONGDUK LEE, PH.D.
Dean of Students: CHONSOO LEE, PH.D.
Librarian: KOOHO YOON.

Library of 250,000 vols.
Number of teachers: 225.
Number of students: 6,218.

Faculties of English, Korean, history and philosophy, domestic science, business management, music, education, applied art.

KON-KUK UNIVERSITY

93-1 MOJIN-DONG, SUNGDONG-GU, SEOUL
Telephone: 45-0061-70.
Founded 1946, university 1959.

President: CHONG WON-KWAK, PH.D.
Registrar: KWON YUNG-CHAN, PH.D.
Librarian: HYUN DOO-IL, PH.D.

Library of 227,531 vols.
Number of teachers: 250.
Number of students: 8,000.

Faculties of liberal arts and sciences, law and economics, animal husbandry, agriculture and engineering, home economics, education. Graduate schools of arts and sciences, public administration.

KOREA UNIVERSITY

ANAM-DONG, SEOUL
Telephone: Seoul 92-2600/9.
Founded 1905, as Posung College.

Private control: financed by the Korea-Choongang Educational Foundation Inc.; Language of instruction: Korean; Academic year: March to February (two semesters).

President: SANG HYUP KIM.
Dean of General Affairs: HAE-CHUN KIM, DR.RER.POL.
Dean of Academic Affairs: KWON-HO KIM, M.A.
Dean of Students: WOO-KAP KIM, D.SC.
Librarian: IL-CHUL SHIN, D.PHIL.

Library: *see* Libraries.
Number of teachers: 425.
Number of students: 10,250.

Publications†: *Kodai Shinmoon*, (Korean, weekly), *The Granite Tower* (English, fortnightly), *Gyongyong Shinmoon* (Korean, weekly), *Gyo Yang* (Korean, annual), *Godae Moonwha* (Korean, annual), *Phoenix* (bilingual, annual), *The Journal of Asiatic Studies* (bilingual, bi-monthly), *Business Review* (Korean, monthly), *Korea University Bulletin* (bi-lingual, annual), and many other periodicals.

DEANS:

College of Education: HAN-SOOK CHUNG, B.A.
College of Law: CHIN-WOONG KIM, LL.B.
College of Business Administration: SE-HWAN YU, D.B.A.
College of Liberal Arts: CHI-GYU KIM, B.A.
College of Medicine: MAN-NYON SHIN, M.D., M.SC.
College of Agriculture: YONG-KYO KIM, D.AG.
College of Political Science and Economics: UHN-BONG PAIK, PH.D.
College of Science: BONG-WHAN LAU, D.SC.
College of Engineering: TONG-SOK YUN, D.ENG.
Graduate School: SE-CHANG YUN, J.S.D.
Graduate School of Business Administration: CHANG-HWAN SEONG, D.ECON.
Graduate School of Education: CHANG-WHAN KIM, D.SC.

AFFILIATED RESEARCH INSTITUTES:

Anglo-American Studies Institute. *Director:* Prof. HEE-YOP NOH.
Asiatic Research Center. *Director:* Prof. JOON-YUP KIM.
Basic Sciences Research Institute. *Director:* Prof. TAE-RIN KIM.
Behavioral Science Research Center. *Director:* Prof. KI-SUK KIM.
Business Management Research Center. *Director:* Prof. HI-JIP KIM.
Institute of Economic Development. *Director:* Prof. YUNG-CHUL PARK.
Institute of Education. *Director:* Prof. JONG-GYU HWANG.
Institute of Environmental Health. *Director:* Prof. CHUL-HWAN CHA.
German Studies Institute. *Director:* Prof. PONG-HEUM HAN.
Institute of Industrial Science and Technology. *Director:* Prof. HEE-YOUNG CHUN.
Institute of Law and Public Administration. *Director:* Prof. HYUNG-BAE KIM.
International Management Institute. *Director:* Prof. DONG-KI KIM.
Korea Research Institute of Agriculture. *Director:* Prof. KI-CHANG HONG.
Korean Cultural Research Center. *Director:* Prof. IL-SHIK HONG.
Korean Entomological Institute. *Director:* Dr. IL-BYONG YUN.
Labour Education and Research Institute. *Director:* KI JUN CHO.
Mass Communications Research Institute. *Director:* Prof. WOO-HYUN WON.
Institute of Tropical Endemic Diseases. *Director:* Prof. HAN-JONG LIM.
Institute of Viral Diseases. *Director:* Prof. HO-WANG LEE.
Institute of Medico-Legal Affairs. *Director:* Prof. KUK-CHIN MUN.
Institute of Statistics. *Director:* HAN-POONG SHIN.

KYUNG HEE UNIVERSITY

1 HOIKI DONG, DONGDAEMUN-KU, SEOUL 131
Telephone: 966-0061-5, 967-3901-5, 966-1244.
Founded 1950; renamed 1958.

Private control; Academic year: March to December (two terms).

President: Dr. YOUNG SEEK CHOUE.
Vice-President for Academic Affairs: KYONG CHOL CHOU.

Vice-President for Administrative Affairs: Chum Kon Kim.

Registrar: Dr. Tae Man Kim.

Librarian: Sang Chil Sim.

Library of 500,000 vols., separate medical library of 4,000 vols.

Number of teachers: 600.
Number of students: 14,000.

Publications: *University Life, Theses Collections, Reconstruction of Human Society, The Ko Hwang* (all annually), *Lux Mundi* (2 a year), annual research bulletins for each College.

DEANS:

College of Liberal Arts and Sciences: Jai Doo Park.
College of Law: Yon Ho Park.
College of Political Science and Economics: Chong Ill Rha.
College of Education: Duk Heeu Choi.
College of Medicine: Yang Won Park.
College of Dentistry: In Chul Kim.
College of Oriental Medicine: Jung Je Kim.
College of Pharmacy: In Suck Ko.
College of Engineering: Nam Chul Paik.
College of Industry: Kwang Rai Kim.
College of Music: Seong Sam Lee.
College of Physical Education: Young Kun Choi.
Graduate School: Suk Ryun Lee.
Graduate School of Business and Public Administration: Chum Kon Kim.
Graduate School of Education: Sun Ho Kim.

CHAIRMEN OF DEPARTMENTS:

College of Liberal Arts and Sciences:
Korean Language and Literature: Jung Bum Suh.
English Language and Literature: Byung Soo Park.
Ethics: Soon Yung Park.
History: Sung Bong Park.
Biology: Yoo Hong Shin.
Geography: Hak Hi Won.
Physics: Bok Keun Jung.
Chemistry: Kyu Chang Park.
Home Management: Jung Ok Chang.
Food and Nutrition: Hyun Shu Park.
Dress Design: Yoon Ja Nam.
College of Law:
Law: Yun Chang Koo.
Public Administration: Sae Duk Oh.
College of Political Science and Economics:
Politics and Diplomacy: Hong Woo Kim.
Mass Communication: Byung Ku Han.
Economics: Gi Ho Jun.
Business Administration: Jung Kyu Lee.
College of Education:
Foreign Languages: Ki Ban Park.
Fine Arts: Hee Yung Yoo.
College of Medicine:
Medicine: Kap Soo Hahn.
Nursing: Hi Ja Moon.
College of Dentistry:
Dentistry: Han Kuk Cho.
College of Oriental Medicine:
Oriental Medicine: Joon Jeon Moon.
College of Pharmacy:
Pharmacy: Sin Kyu Kim.
College of Engineering:
Mechanical Engineering: Whan Tae Sung.
Textile Engineering: Un Young Yoo.
Electronic Engineering: Dai Young Lee.
Chemical Engineering: Nam Chul Paik.
Civil Engineering: Chong Nam Lee.
Architectural Engineering: Chang Han Cho.
College of Industry:
Agriculture and Forestry: Sang Keun Jean.
Horticulture: Jung Myung Lee.
Food Processing: Je Shun Cho.
Ceramic Arts: Moon Ho Chang.
Beautification: Bong Won Ahn.
College of Music:
Musical Composition: Dong Jin Kim.
Vocal Music: Jung Hang Um.
Musical Instruments: Dukh Sung La.
College of Physical Education:
Physical Education: Chul Bin Park.
Dancing: Jae Seung Ahn.

AFFILIATED COLLEGES:

Kyung Hee University Su-Won Campus: 11-San, Seochon-ri, Giheung-myon, Yongin-kun, Kyonggi-do, 170-73; f. 1979; Dean Dr. Bong Kul Kim.

International School of Hotel Administration: Kyung Hee University Campus; f. 1975; Dean Prof. Byung Woon Kim.

College of Evening Programme: Kyung Hee University Campus; f. 1979; Dean Dr. Kyung Suk Choe.

Kyung Hee School of Nursing: Kyung Hee University Campus; f. 1966; Dean Sang Soon Choi.

ATTACHED INSTITUTES:

Centre for the Reconstruction of Human Society: f. 1976; Dir.-Gen. Dr. Kee Hyong Kim.

Korean Institute of Bright Society.

Research Centre for Land Development.

Research Institute of Educational Affairs.

Kyung Hee Language Institute.

Research Institute of Social Science.

Korean Institute of Plant Resources.

Research Institute of Medicine.

Korean Institute of Ornithological Studies.

Korean Research Institute of Physical Education.

Korean Institute of the History of Economics and Business Administration.

Institute of Industrial Management.

Institute of Legal Studies.

Marketing Survey Research Institute.

Tax Accounting Research Institute.

Institute of Architecture and Urban Studies.

Research Institute of Industrial Technology.

Korean Institute of National Security.

Kyung Hee Research Institute of Oriental Drugs.

Institute of Labor-Management Relations; f. 1974.

Communication Research Center; f. 1974.

Institute of Korean Culture.

Research Institute of Food Development: f. 1977.

Institute of Brazilian Studies: f. 1978.

Solar Energy Research Institute: f. 1978.

Institute of Folklore: f. 1978.

East-West Medical Research Institute.

Centre for International Peace Studies.

Global Co-operation Society International.

KYUNGPOOK NATIONAL UNIVERSITY

1370 SAN-GYUCK-DONG,
BUKGU, DAEGU 635.

Telephone: (92) 1071-1073, 1081-1085.

Founded 1946.

State control; Academic year: March to February (two semesters).

President: Suh Ton-kak.

Dean of Academic Affairs: Sohn Mun-Gu.

Dean of Student Affairs: Lee Chul-won.

Director of Business Affairs: Lee Won-bark.

Library: *see* Libraries.

Number of teachers: 483.
Number of students: 12,825.

Publications: *Theses Collection of Kyungpook University, Kyungpook University Press* (Korean and English edns.), etc.

DEANS:

Graduate School: Hong Suk-jae.
Graduate School of Education: Suh Byung-kook.
College of Law and Political Science: Kim Mun-dal.
College of Economics and Commerce: Kim Jae-jin.
College of Engineering: Lee Wu-il.
College of Liberal Arts and Science: Kim Ki-tae.
College of Agriculture: Je Sang-yull.
Teachers' College: Kim Young-ha.
School of Medicine: Hwang kee-suk.
Dental College: Lee yeoul-hi.
Division of General Education: Kang Young-ho.

MYONG JI UNIVERSITY

NAMGAJWA-DONG,
SEODAEMUN-KU, SEOUL

Telephone: 34-8401-3.

Founded 1948, present status 1963; private control.

President: Prof. IL KYUNG PARK, LL.D.
Dean of Academic Affairs: Prof. JUNG IN LEE.
Dean of Student Affairs: Prof. DAE YOUNG LEE.
Library Director: Prof. KWANG CHUN MOON.

Library of 80,000 vols.
Number of teachers: 180.
Number of students: 2,300.

DEANS:

Graduate School: Dr. TONG SUP PARK.
General Education: Dr. SANG BO LEE.
Teacher Education: Dr. DO YANG ROH.
Economics and Commerce: Dr. JONG SOON KIM.
Science and Engineering: Dr. YONG OCK LEE.

SEOUL NATIONAL UNIVERSITY

SINLIM-DONG GWANG-GU,
SEOUL 151

Telephone: 877-1601, 2891.

Founded 1946.

State control; Academic year: March to February.

President: Dr. E-HYOCK KWON.
Vice-President: Dr. LEE-HYUN JAE.
Registrar: HEE-KAP SUK.
Dean of Academic Affairs: Dr. CHONG-UN KIM.
Dean of Student Affairs: Dr. SONG-WA CHOI.

Library: *see* Libraries.
Number of teachers: 1,159.
Number of students: 18,236.

Publication: *University Gazette* (weekly).

DEANS:

College of Agriculture: Dr. UN-WOONG LEE.
College of Humanities: Dr. TOU-SHIK KANG.
College of Dentistry: Dr. HYUNG-KYU AHN.
College of Fine Arts: SE-WEON PARK.
College of Engineering: Dr. TAIK-SIK LEE.
College of Law: CHI-SUN KIM.
College of Natural Sciences: Dr. YOON-SUK KOH.
College of Music: MIN-JONG PARK.
College of Medicine: Dr. BUONG-SEOL SEO.
College of Pharmacy: Dr. SANG-SUP LEE.
College of Education: Dr. WON-SHIK CHUNG.
College of Home Economics: HEI-SOO RHEE.
College of Social Sciences: Dr. YOUNG-KOOK KIM.
College of Veterinary Science: Dr. YOUNG-SO LEE.
College of Business Administration: Dr. YONG-JOON LEE.
Graduate School: Dr. MAN-GAP LEE.
School of Public Administration: Dr. HOON YU.
School of Public Health: JONG HOII.
School of Environmental Studies: Dr. TAI-JOON KWON.

ATTACHED INSTITUTES:

Natural Products Research Institute: Dir. Dr. BYUNG-HOON HAN.
Language Research Institute: Dir. Dr. CHUNG-MIN LEE.
Institute of Social Sciences: Dir. Dr. KONG-KOO LEE.
Institute of Economic Research: Dir. Dr. JONG-HYUN KIM.
Law Research Institute: Dir. Dr. JAE-SHIK PAE.
Institute of Korean Culture: Dir. Dr. WOO-KEUN HAN.
Institute of American Studies: Dir. Dr. YOUNG-NOK KOO.
Institute of Sae-maul Studies: Dir. Dr. MAN-GAP LEE.

SOGANG UNIVERSITY

C.P.O. 1142, SEOUL

Telephone: 32-0141.

Founded 1960.

Private control; Languages of instruction: Korean, with some English; Academic year: March to December (two semesters).

President: M. DELMAR SKILLINGSTAD, S.J.
Academic Dean: JUESON MAENG.
Vice-President: KWANG RIN LEE.
Director of Library: JOHN P. DALY, S.J.

Number of teachers: 205.
Number of students: 3,827.

Publications: *Sogang Herald*† (every 2 months), *Sogang Times* (monthly), various monographs†, research reports†.

DEANS:

Graduate School: KO YONG PAK, S.J.
College of Liberal Arts: YONG KWON KIM.
College of Science and Engineering: NUNG MIN YOON.
College of Commerce: BYUNG GIL VAN.

PROFESSORS:

Liberal Arts:

BIERNATZKI, W. E., S.J., Sociology
HA SOON CHA, Western History
HAE JONG CHUN, Oriental History
YUN CHAN CHUNG, Korean Language
DALY, J. P., S.J., English
FARREN, E. J., S.J., Philosophy
HERBST, C. A., S.J., History
HYEON DEW KANG, Mass Communication
HYUN MO KEEL, Western History
KELLY, R. J., S.J., Theology
HAK DONG KIM, Korean Literature
IN ZA KIM, Education
KYU KIM, Mass Communication
KYU YOUNG KIM, Philosophy
SANG JOON KIM, Political Science
TAE OK KIM, English
TOBIAS TEGWAN KIM, S.J., Philosophy
YOL KYU KIM, Korean Literature
YONG KWON KIM, English Literature
KISTER, D. A., English Literature
IN CHUL KOH, Physical Education
BOK NOCK KWACK, German Literature
BO HYUNG LEE, Western History
DUCK HO LEE, German Linguistics
GUN SAM LEE, Dramatic Literature
JAE SON LEE, Korean Literature
KI-BAIK LEE, Korean History
KWANG-RIN LEE, Korean History
SUNG UK LEE, Korean Literature
YOO YUNG LEE, German Literature
MURDOCK, J. R., Western History
KIE PYUNG OH, Political Science
KO YONG PAK, S.J., Philosophy
CHUL HEE PARK, Korean Literature
KAP SUNG PARK, Philosophy
PRICE, B. M., S.J., Western History
SANG-WOO RHEE, Political Science
SKILLINGSTAD, M. D., S.J., Education
SONG, MARY Y., French
SPALATIN, C. A., Philosophy
CHUNG HO SUH, Law
TRACY, N. J., S.J., Education
JAE CHEON YU, Mass Communication

Science and Engineering:

IK SOO CHANG, Electronic Engineering
JIN CHANG, Biology
TAE GEUN CHO, Mathematics
SANG UP CHOI, Chemistry
KOO SOON CHUNG, Chemistry
FRANK, E. N., Electronic Engineering
KEE YONG KIM, Physics
TAIK YUNG KIM, Biochemistry
YONG DUK KIM, Physics
BYUNG HYUK LEE, Physics
HI MYUNG LEE, Biology
HUNG CHUN LEE, Mathematics
WON HONG LEE, Chemical Engineering
KYE CHIL OH, Botany
WOON-KIE PAIK, Chemistry
BYUNG SO PAK, Electronic Engineering
SEUNG AHN PARK, Mathematics
CHONGSUH PYUN, Chemistry
JAE CHUL RHO, Mathematics
TAE SOON YIM, Physics
BYUNG HO YOON, Mathematics
NUNG MIN YOON, Chemistry

Commerce:

YONG HEE CHEE, Trade
SUNG HWAN JO, Economics
CHONG IN KIM, Economics
DUK CHOONG KIM, Economics
JUNG SAE KIM, Economics
PYUNG JOO KIM, Economics
JUNG SUP KOH, Accounting
NEI HEI PARK, Business Administration
TAI WI PARK, Trade
YOUNG KI PARK, Business Administration
SANG RYONG SUH, Business Administration
BYUNG GIL VAN, Business Administration

ATTACHED RESEARCH INSTITUTES:

Advanced Institute of Accounting.
Research Institute of Economics and Business.
Research Institute of Humanities.
Research Institute of Science.
Social Science Institute.
Institute for Labour and Management.
Institute for Theological Research.

SOOKMYUNG WOMEN'S UNIVERSITY

53-12 CHUNGPA-DONG 2-KA, YONGSAN-KU, SEOUL

Founded 1938, university status 1955; private control.

President: RAK HOON CHA.
Dean of Academic Affairs: DONG-HOUN HA.
Dean of Student Affairs: KYU-JA WHANG.
Dean of General Affairs: CHANG-KYU WHANG.
Dean of Graduate School: NEUNG-WOO LEE.
Librarian: EUN-SOO PARK.

Library of *c.* 150,000 vols.

Number of teachers: *c.* 350.

Number of students: *c.* 4,179.

Colleges of Liberal Arts, Industrial Arts, Science, Political Science and Economics, Music, Pharmacy, Home Economics; Graduate School.

Research Centre for Asian Women; Pharmacy Research Institute; Research Institute of Political Affairs and Economy; Institute of Life Sciences; Research Institute of Language and Literature; Educational Problem Research Institute; Institute for Child Study.

SOONG JUN UNIVERSITY

1-1 SANG-DO 1 DONG, SEOUL 151

Founded 1897; private control.

President: BUM SOE KOH.
Registrar: KYUNG YOL KIM.

Library of 100,000 vols.

Number of teachers: *c.* 150.

Number of students: 5,651.

Colleges of liberal arts and sciences, law and economics, engineering, graduate school, evening college (Taejon: liberal arts and sciences, graduate school and evening college).

SUNG KYUN KWAN UNIVERSITY*

53, 3-KA, MYUNGRYUN-DONG, CHONGRO-KU, SEOUL

Telephone: 72-2721-9.

Founded 1895, university status 1946; private control.

Chairman of the Board of Trustees: BYUNG-CHUL LEE, A.M.
President: HUNG SEUNG-JONG.
Library: CH'ON HYE BONG.

Number of books in library: 400,000; additional college libraries.

Number of teachers: *c.* 140 full-time.

Number of students: *c.* 5,000.

Publications: *Sung Kyun Kwan Journals* (annually), *Sung Kyun Newspaper* (weekly, in Korean), *Sung Kyun Times* (monthly, in English).

DEANS:

Academic Affairs: MYUNG-KU LEE.
Student Affairs: KYUNG-KU LEE, LL.M.
General Affairs: TAI-CHANG LEE, A.B.
Planning: KI-CHONG CHOI, COMM.M.
Faculty of General Education: WOO-TACK KIM, A.M.
College of Liberal Arts: BYUNG-CHO CHUNG, A.M.
College of Confucian Studies: BYUNG-CHO CHUNG, A.M.
College of Law and Political Science: KI-SUN KIM, LL.M.
College of Economics and Commerce: DO-YUNG CHUNG, COM.M.
College of Science and Engineering: YUNG-CHAN KIM, S.M., SC.D.
College of Pharmacy: JONG-IN CHOI, S.M., PHAR.D.
College of Home Economics: MYUNG-KU YI, A.M.
Graduate School: HONG YUL YOO.
Graduate School of Foreign Trade: SANG-KOO LEE, ECON.D.
Graduate School of Economic Development: RAI-HOON CHO, A.M.

* No reply received to our questionnaire this year.

WON KWANG UNIVERSITY

344-2 SIN-YONG-NI, IRI, CHUN-PUK

Telephone: 2-6041-47.

Founded 1946.

Private control; Academic year: March to July, August to December.

President: PARK KIL-CHIN.
Registrar: LEE SUNG-TACK.
Librarian: CHUNG KAP-WON.

Number of teachers: 202.

Number of students: 7,640.

Publications†: *Theses Collection*, departmental studies, etc.

DEANS:

Graduate School: PAL KHN CHON.
College of Won Buddhism Training: CHUN EUN SONG.
College of Liberal Arts and Sciences: YOO JE-YUNG.
College of Teacher Training: SIN KIL-SOO.
College of Law and Economics: MYUNG HYUNG-SIK.
College of Agriculture: KIM JIN-SOO.
College of Pharmacy: AN MOON-KYU.
College of Oriental Medicine and Acupuncture: KANG SOON-SOO.
College of Engineering: KIM KWANG-SHU.

HEADS OF DEPARTMENTS:

Won Buddhism Training: SHU KYUNG-JUN.
Korean Language and Literature: KANG JIN-SIK.
Chemistry: SONG HAE-YUNG.
Mathematics: RHEE SHNG-WOO.
Clothing and Textiles: SHU CHUNG-HEE.
Applied Arts: HAN BONG-LIM.
Household Management: LEE CHA-SOOK.
Food and Nutrition: MOON BUM-SOO.
Craft Science: O YOON-KYUNG.
Dentistry: LEE WON-KOO.
History: AN CHOON-BAE.
Ethics: LEE TONG-YUP.
English Language and Literature: OM JUNG-OK.
German Language and Literature: KIM YOON-SUP.
Law: PARK KYU-HA.
Administration: KIM YONG-WUK.
Business Administration: YOO BOONG-SIK.
International Trade: PARK BYUNG-HONG.
Accountancy: EUN JA-KEE.
Economics: IM IK-TOO.
Pharmacy: KOH KUN-IL.
Home Economics Education: IM JUNG-JA.
Physical Education: IM IN-SOO.
Dancing Education: NAM HENG-WOONG.
English Education: LEE SANG-OH.
Japanese Language Education: SON TAE-JOON.
Fine Arts Education: CHUNG SHNG-SHUP.
Music Education: SONG EUN.
Korean History Education: CHUNG MYUNG-HO.
Korean Language Education: PARK CHONG-HEE.
Education Training: LEE KUN-IN.
Physics: PARK TAE-YUNG.
Biology: KIL BONG-SUP.
Mathematics Education: LEE TONG-MYUNG.
Commerce Education: KIM MYUNG-HEE.
Horticulture: YOO SUNG-OH.
Agriculture: CHOI SUNG-SIK.
Agriculture and Chemistry: KIM SUNG-CHO.
Forestry: OH JUNG-SOO.
Oriental Medicine: IM CHONG-KOOK.
Architecture Technology: YOON HONG-TAK.
Engineering: AN SONG-YUP.
Electricity: YOON YANG-WOONG.
Electronics: KIM HWAN-YONG.
City Construction Planning: CHUNG SA-HOI.
Ceramics: LEE BONG-KOO.

YEUNGNAM UNIVERSITY

GYONGSAN 632

Telephone: Taegu 8-2321.

Founded 1967 by the amalgamation of Taegu College and Chunggu College.

Private control; Academic year: March to February (two semesters).

President: KYOUNG HEE CHO (acting).
Dean of Administration: WON-DAL LEE.
Dean of Faculty: BOCKIE KIM.
Dean of Students: KAP DUK CHANG.
Director of Library: SU GEON LEE.

Library of 303,234 vols.

Number of teachers: 307 (full-time).

Number of students: 14,213.

Publications: *Yeungnam University Theses Collection*†, *Library Guide*, *Yeungdae Munhwa*† (Yeungnam University Culture), *Student Guide*† (annually) and various faculty and institutional publs.

DEANS:

College of Liberal Arts and Sciences: YUNG-KYU KWON.
College of Engineering: JUNG-YUEP KIM.
College of Law and Political Sciences: HYUK KI KWON.
College of Commerce and Economics: BYONG TAK KWON.
College of Medicine: JAE KYU CHUNG.
College of Pharmacy: BO-SHIK HAN.
College of Agriculture and Animal Sciences: KWANG-YUN LEE.
College of Home Economics: KYUNG JU CHOI.
College of Education: TAIK-KYU KIM.
Evening College: JAE SOO SONG.
Graduate School: BOK SU KANG.
Graduate School of Business Administration: JUN HEON KIM.
Graduate School of Environmental Studies: KAP-DUCK JIN.

ATTACHED RESEARCH CENTRES:

National Unification Research Center: Dir. Prof. CHANG WOO RHEE.

Korea-Japan Relations Research Center: Dir. Prof. SOON CHANG HONG.

Institute for Silla-Kaya Culture: Dir. Prof. JAE-WAN SHIM.

Oriental Studies Center: Dir. Prof. KYU SEOL CHO.

Institute of Industrial Technology: Dir. Prof. MAN HEE LEE.

Institute of Social Science: Dir. Prof. YONG-KU LEE.

Research Institute of Public Administration: Dir. Prof. SANG KI PAEK.

Institute of Economics: Dir. Prof. HO-KEUN YU.

Institute of Management Research: Dir. Prof. TAE-HWAN KIM.

Natural Products Research Institute: Dir. Prof. BYEONG-CHEON SEO.

Regional Adaptive Technology Center: Dir. Prof. JAE-OK BYUN.

Center for American Studies: Dir. Prof. KI DONG CHANG.

Institute of Food Resources Development: Dir. Prof. HAK CHEUL LEE.

Saemaul Research Institute: Dir. Prof. SANG JIN KIM.

Institute of Korean Culture: Dir. Prof. JAE WAN SHIM.

Computer Center: Dir. MU YOUNG LEE.

YONSEI UNIVERSITY

134 SHINCHON-DONG,
SEOUL 120
Telephone: 33-0131.
Founded 1885.

Private control; Language of instruction: Korean; Academic year: March to February (two semesters).

President: WOO CHOO LEE, M.D., D.M.SC., PH.D.
Vice-President for Academic Affairs: SE HEE AHN, PH.D.
Vice-President for Medical Affairs: HYO KYU KIM, M.D., D.M.SC.
Dean of the University: YOUNG SIK PARK, PH.D.

Library: *see* Libraries.

Number of teachers: 521.
Number of students: 14,643.

Publications: *Yonsei Annals*, *Yonsei Non-Chong*, *Abstracts of Faculty Research Reports*, *Journal of Humanities*, *Journal of Far Eastern Studies*, *Journal of East and West Studies*, *Social Science Review*, *Journal of Education Science*, *Engineering Review*, *Business Review*, etc.

DEANS:

Liberal Arts: WOONG SUN HONG, ED.D.
Business and Economics: IK SOON IM, D.B.A.
Science: OK JOON KIM, PH.D.
Engineering: HYUNG SIK LEE, D.ENG.
Theology: JOON SURH PARK, TH.D.
Political Science and Law: HYUN TAE KIM, LL.D.
Medicine: SA SUK HONG, M.D., D.M.SC.
Music: HEE SUK CHUNG, M.S.B.
Home Economics: KI YULL LEE, D.SC.
Dentistry: YONG KWAN KIM, D.P.H.
Nursing: SAN CHO CHUN, D.SC.

GRADUATE SCHOOL DEANS:

Graduate School (Academic): HOCHIN CHOI, D.ECON.
United Graduate School of Theology: SANG HEE MOON, TH.D.
Business Administration: BOONG RO YOO, D.ECON.
Education: KI HYOUNG OH, M.A.
Public Administration: CHUNG HYUN RO, PH.D.
Engineering: JONG SOO KIM, D.ENG.
Health Science and Management: JAI MO YANG, M.D., D.M.SC.

AFFILIATED INSTITUTE:

Institute of Korean Studies: f. 1977 to replace the Institute of Far Eastern Studies; the study of Korean culture and learning in relation to those of neighbouring nations; Dir. MINN YOUNG-GYU; publs. *Journal of Far Eastern Studies* (2 a year), *Bulletin*, *Annual Report*.

COLLEGES

Catholic Medical College: 89-4, Kyungwun-Dong, Chongno-Ku, Seoul; f. 1954; Dean K. S. CHO, M.D., DR. MED.SC.; Dean of Graduate School Y. C. KIM, M.D., DR.MED.SC.; library of 28,700 vols.; 235 professors; 850 students; publs. *Journal* (quarterly), *Sungui Hakbo* (monthly), *Korean Journal of Occupational Health*, *Mental Health*, *Sungui Herald* (quarterly), *Eui Mak* (annually), *Bulletin of Clinical Research Institute* (annually).

Cheju College: 581 Yong-Dam Dong, Cheju City; f. 1952; Pres. PYEON SHI-MIN.

Duk Sung Women's College: 114 Uni-Dong, Chongno-ku, Seoul; f. 1950; private control; courses in home economics, pre-school education, nutrition, Korean language and literature, English language and literature, applied arts, fine art, costume, business administration, secretarial, pharmaceutical manufacturing and pharmacy; 2,640 students; library of 87,700 vols.; Pres. JONG YULL YU; publs. *Duk Sung Research*†, *Woon Hyun* (annually), *Duk Sung Women's College Press* (2 a month).

Guk Min University: 861-1, Jeongmung-Dong, Sungbuk-ku, Seoul 132; f. 1946; private control; 124 teachers, 3,200 students; library of 120,000 vols.; Pres. KYU-SUK LEE; publs. *Kook-Min Times* (English, weekly), *Kook-Min University Press* (weekly), *Buk-AK* (annual), *Bulletin* (annual), *Theses* (annual).

Hyo Seong Women's College: 1155 Bongduck-Dong, Taegu: f. 1952; 91 teachers, 1,640 students; library of 120,000 vols.; Pres. CHEON SUK JAE; publs. *Research Bulletin*, *Journal of the Women's Problem Research Institute* (annually).

Korea Merchant Marine College: 1 Dong-sam-dong, Yong-do-Ku, Busan; f. 1945; courses for higher degrees in nautical science and marine engineering; 65 professors; 1,317 students; library of 25,000 vols.; Pres. HONG YEONG-PYO.

Seoul Agricultural College: 8-3 Junnong-dong, Dong-daemun-ku, Seoul; f. 1950; 420 students; Dean HI JAE LEE.

Seoul Women's College: P.O.B. 115, Chongyang-ni, Seoul 131; f. 1961; 121 teachers, 1,436 students; library of 50,580 vols.; Pres. Dr. WHANG-KYUNG KOH.

KUWAIT

Population 1,198,000

SOCIETIES AND INSTITUTES

Agricultural Experimental Station: c/o Agricultural Dept., Ministry of Public Works, Kuwait; f. 1953; research in various fields of agriculture including arid zone studies, soil conservation and irrigation, plant protection studies, animal husbandry, hydroponic culture, protected vegetable production and fisheries; small library; Dir. S. I. AL-MANNAI; publs. reports, information bulletins.

The Arab Planning Institute, Kuwait: P.O.B. 5834, Safat; f. 1966 with assistance from the UN Development Programme; trains personnel in economic and social devt. planning for the Arab countries; undertakes research and advisory work and organizes conferences and seminars; Dir. ABDULLA M. ALI.

British Council: P.O.B. 345, Al Arabi St., Al Mansouriyah, Safat; library of 12,373 vols., 62 periodicals; Rep. Dr. J. L. MUNBY.

Kuwait Institute for Scientific Research: P.O.B. 24885, Safat, Kuwait; f. 1967 to promote and conduct scientific research in the fields of arid zone agriculture, engineering (including solar energy, laser and electronics, building), marine biology, petroleum and petrochemistry, survey and techno-economic studies; scientific and technical information centre; Dir. Dr. ADNAN SHIHAB-ELDIN.

LIBRARIES

Kuwait Central Library: Kuwait City; f. 1936; 95,000 vols.; 12 brs.; Chief Librarian YOUSUE MULLA HUSEIN.

Kuwait University Libraries P.O.B. 17140; Kuwait City; f. 1966; 340,000 vols., 15,357 periodicals; Chief Librarian SULAIMAN M. KALANDER; publs. see University.

MUSEUMS

Antiquities Department: Ministry of Information, Kuwait City; Dir. IBRAHIM AL-BAGHLY.

Kuwait Museum: Kuwait City; excavation findings from Failaka Island, dating back to Babylonian times.

Science and Natural History Museum: Ministry of Education; f. 1972; lectures, exhibitions, film shows, etc.; sections on natural history, science, space, oil, health; planetarium; library of 1,000 vols.; Dir. HAMMAD M. AL-ATEEQI; publs. *Museum News*, guides.

UNIVERSITY

KUWAIT UNIVERSITY

P.O.B. 5969, KUWAIT

Telephone: 811188.

Founded 1962, inaugurated 1966.

State control; Language of instruction: Arabic, except in Faculties of Science, Engineering and Petroleum, Medicine and Department of English; Academic year: September to June (2 semesters).

Chancellor: H.E. The Minister of Education.

Rector: Dr. HASSAN AL- EBRAHEEM.

Secretary-General: SAAD AL-SAAD (acting).

Registrar: Dr. REYADH R. KHAZAL.

Library: see Libraries.

Number of teachers: *c.* 450.
Number of students: *c.* 9,300.

Publications: *Journal of Palestine Studies*† (English, quarterly), *University Library Journal* (irregular), *Bulletin of the Faculty of Commerce, Economics and Political Science*† (English, annually), *Bulletin of the Faculty of Arts and Education*† (Arabic, 2 a year), *Bulletin of the Faculty of Science*† (English, annually), *Prospectus of Kuwait University* (English and Arabic, annually), *Gulf and Arabian Studies Magazine* (Arabic, quarterly), *News Bulletin* (Arabic, irregular), etc.

DEANS:

Faculty of Science: Prof. M. W. AL-DHAHIR.

Faculty of Arts and Education: Dr. KHALDOUN AL-NAQEEB (acting).

Faculty of Law and Shari'ah: Prof. AHMAD KAMAL ABULMAJD.

Faculty of Commerce, Economics and Political Science: Prof. ALI ABDUL-RAHEEM.

Faculty of Engineering and Petroleum: Dr. SAAD AL-MULLA.

Faculty of Medicine: Prof. A. AL-ABDUL-RAZZAK.

Student Affairs: Dr. S. ABBAS.

Language Centre: Dr. Y. AL-EZABI.

Centre for Community and Continuing Education: Dr. S. S. AL-BADR (acting).

HEADS OF DEPARTMENTS:

Faculty of Science:

AL-HASSAN, J., Biochemistry
AL-KAISI, K. A., Phycology and Marine Botany (acting)
AL-SHAMLAN, A. A., Invertebrate Palaeontology (acting)
BADR, M., Genetics
EL-RAYYES, N. R., Organic Chemistry (acting)
HIGAZI, K. A., Physics (acting)
MULLA, F. SH., Pure Mathematics (acting)

Faculty of Arts and Education:

ABDEL-RAHMAN, S. M., Psychosociometrics
ALALOUSI, H. M., Islamic Philosophy
AL-GHONEIM, A. Y., Geography (acting)
AL-MEHANNA, A. A., History of Arabic Literature (acting)
AL-SAYYED, D. H., Linguistics
AL-THAKEB, F., Sociology (acting)
ISMAIL, S. J., Philosophy of Education (acting)
MOSTAFA, S., Islamic History

Faculty of Law and Shari'ah:

AL-GHANDOUR, A. N., Islamic Fikh
AL-YASIN, M. A., Public Law (acting)
EL-ADAWI, H. M., International Law
SALEM, A. B., Penal Law
WALI, F. I., Civil Law

Faculty of Commerce, Economics and Political Science:

ABDELLA, S. M., Business Administration

ALNAFISI, A. F., Political Science (acting)
HUSSEIN, A. A., Applied Statistics
SHAFE'I, I. A., Demography
SHUAIB, S. A., Accounting and Auditing (acting)

Faculty of Engineering and Petroleum:

ALREMAWI, W. H., Civil Engineering
EL-MOSLIMANY, M. A., Electrical Engineering
MAYYASI, A. M., Mechanical Engineering
MOUSA, A. N., Chemical Engineering (acting)

Faculty of Medicine:

ADAMS-SMITH, W. N., Human Morphology
AL-AWADY, H. M., Surgery (acting)
ARMSTRONG, W. G., Biochemistry
BANNA, M. R., Pharmacology (acting)
BEZJAK, V., Microbiology
HATHOUT, H., Gynaecology and Obstetrics
KURTZ, R. A., Community Medicine and Behavioural Sciences
MAHMOUD, NASR EL-DIN, Physiology
YOUSOF, A. R., Medicine

LAOS

Population 3,540,000

SOCIETIES

Lao Buddhist Fellowship: Maha Kudy, That Luang, Vientiane; f. 1964; Pres. Rev. THONG KHOUNE ANANTASUNTHONE; Vice-Pres. Rev. PHONG SAMALEUK, Rev. PRECHA SOUTHAMAKOSANE; Sec.-Gen. Rev. SIHO SIHAVONG.

Laos-China Association: National Plan Office, P.O.B. 46, Vientiane; f. 1976; Pres. MA KHAIKHAMPHI THOUNE.

Laos-Mongolia Association: 80 Setthathiraj Ave., P.O.B. 122, Vientiane; f. 1976; Pres. SISANA SISANE.

Laos-Soviet Association: Ministry of Agriculture, Forestry and Irrigation, Nongbone Rd., Vientiane; f. 1976; Pres. KHAMSOUK SAISOMPHENG; Vice-Pres. LEUAM INSISENGMAY.

Laos-Viet Nam Association: Ministry of Public Health, Fa Ngum Rd., Vientiane; f. 1976; Pres. CHAO SOUK VONGSAK.

LIBRARIES

Bibliothèque Nationale: B.P. 704, Vientiane; f. 1957; 50,000 vols. in French, Lao and English; Dir. SOMTHONG.

Dongsaphangmeuk Library: Dongdok, Vientiane; f. 1959; 3,000 vols.

MUSEUMS

Ho Phakeo: Setthathiraj Rd., Vientiane; built 1563 by King Setthathiraj, became national museum 1965.

That Luang: Saysettha District, Vientiane; built 1566 by King Saysetthathiraj, restored 1930.

Wat Sisaket: Lane Xang Ave., Vientiane; f. 1828 by King Anuvong.

UNIVERSITY

SISAVANGVONG UNIVERSITY

MINISTRY OF EDUCATION, LANE XANG AVE., VIENTIANE

Telephone: 22-13.

Founded 1958.

Languages of instruction: Lao and French; Academic year September to June.

Rector: KHAMTANH CHANTHALA.

Libraries: each institute has its own library.

Number of teachers: 149.

Number of students: 2,000.

Comprises the following institutions:

Faculty of Education: Dongsaphangmeuk, Vientiane; f. 1959; library of 2,000 vols.; 33 teachers, 190 students; Dir. SOMPHOLPHAKDY LITTANA.

Faculty of Art: Directorate of Fine Arts, P.O.B. 122, Vientiane.

Faculty of Agriculture, Forestry and Irrigation: Dept. of Agriculture, Forestry and Irrigation, Vientiane.

Technical College: P.O.B. 196, Pakpasak, Vientiane; f. 1954; library of 3,200 vols.; Dirs. HIEM PHOMMACHANH, VISORN CHANSAMORN, Mme KETSANEE.

Polytechnic: Km. 3, Thadeua Rd., Sisatthanak District, Vientiane; f. 1969.

Fa-Ngum College: Sokpaluang, Sisatthanak District, Vientiane; f. 1971; library of 800 vols., Dir. KHAMHUNGTREE.

Lycée Vientiane: Lane Xang Ave., Vientiane; library of 4,200 vols.; Dirs. BOUN LEUNGPHACHANE, KHAMPENE SILAVONG.

Pali Institute: Wat Ongtu, Vientiane; f. 1964; Buddhist institute; 34 teachers (inc. 9 monks), 234 students; library of 3,000 vols.; Dirs. Rev. KAO BUDDHAVONG, Rev. VICHIT SIHARAJ, Rev. SIHO, CHANHOM THEPKHAMVONG.

Sanskrit Institute: Wat That Luang, Vientiane; f. 1975; same staff as Pali Institute; 85 students.

Faculty of Medicine: P.O.B. 131, Samsenthai Rd., Vientiane; under Ministry of Health; library of 1,000 vols.; Dir. NHENARA CHUNRAMANY.

There are regional technical colleges in Luang Pradang, Savannaket, and Champasak.

LEBANON

Population 3,100,000

LEARNED SOCIETIES AND RESEARCH INSTITUTES

(*see* also under Universities)

Association Libanaise des Sciences Juridiques: Faculté de Droit et des Sciences politiques, Université Saint Joseph, B.P. 293, Beirut; f. 1963; represents the Lebanon in the International Association of Legal Science; Pres. Prof. PIERRE GANNAGÉ.

British Council: Beit Fawzi Azar Sharia Sidani, Ras Beirut, Beirut; library of 13,760 vols., 74 periodicals; Rep. H. F. GRANT.

Centre Culturel Hispanique (*Spanish Cultural Centre*): Rue Baalbeck, Imm. Youssef Assaf, 1er étage, B.P. 113/5344, Beirut; Dir. PRIMITIVO MARTINEZ MATEO.

Centre de Documentation Economique sur le Proche-Orient: Faculté de Sciences Economiques et de Gestion des Entreprises, Université Saint Joseph, B.P. 293, Beirut; f. 1971; selection and study of documents and publications on the economy of Middle Eastern Arab countries and oil economy; Dir. KATIA SALAME.

Conseil National de la Recherche Scientifique: Bir Hassan, Beirut; Pres. JOSEPH NAJJAR.

Goethe-Institut Beirut: 11 rue Bliss, B.P. 113-5139, Beirut; f. 1954; Dir. HINRICH R. REINSTROM; br. at Tripoli.

Institut de Géographie du Proche et Moyen Orient: Avenue de Damas, B.P. 2691, Beirut; f. 1946; Dir. M. LE LANNOU.

Institut de Gestion des Entreprises (*Institute of Business Management*): Faculté de Droit et des Sciences Economiques, Université Saint Joseph, B.P. 293, Beirut; f. 1957; Dir. ROLAND PRINGUEY.

Institut de Recherches d'Economie Appliquée: Faculté de Sciences Economiques et de Gestion des entreprises, Université Saint Joseph, B.P. 293, Beirut; f. 1963; economic studies of the Lebanon and other Middle Eastern countries; Pres. Prof. ALEXANDRE CHAIBAN; publ. *Proche-Orient, études économiques* (quarterly).

Institut Français d'Archéologie: rue du Proche-Orient, P.O.B. 11. 1424, Beirut; f. 1946; Dir. ERNEST WILL; library of 26,000 vols.; publs. *Syria, Revue d'Art et d'Archéologie*, and *Bibliothèque Archéologique et Historique*.

Institute for Palestine Studies: P.O.B. 11-7164, Beirut; f. 1963; independent non-profit Arab research organization; to promote a better understanding of the Palestine problem; library of 22,000 vols. (Arabic, Hebrew, English, French, German, Spanish and Russian); microfilm collection, private papers and archives; Chair. CONSTANTINE ZURAYK; Exec. Sec. WALID KHALIDI; publs. monographs, research papers (English, Arabic, French, Spanish), documentary material including *International Documents on Palestine* (in English), *Palestinian Arabic Documents* (annually, in Arabic), reprints of major works on Palestine (in English), *Bulletin* (Arabic, quarterly), *Journal of Palestine Studies* (English, quarterly), *Palestine Yearbook* (Arabic), *Knesset Debates* (annually, Arabic).

Istituto Italiano di Cultura: rue de Rome-1 mm. Najjar, P.O.B. 4128, Beirut; f. 1951; library of 6,900 vols.; Dir. Prof. ALDO PENASA.

John F. Kennedy American Center: Abdul Aziz St., Beirut.

The Lebanese Library Association: c/o National Library, Place de l'Etoile, Beirut; f. 1960; Pres. M. RAFEH; Sec. L. HASSAN.

Unesco Regional Office for Education in the Arab Countries (*Bureau Régional de l'Unesco pour l'Education dans les Pays Arabes*): P.O.B. 5244, Cité Sportive Avenue, Bir Hassan, Beirut; f. 1973; carries out Unesco activities in the Arab region in the field of education; training of personnel, advisory services to Arab countries, studies and research, information and documentation; Dir. CHIKH BEKRI; publs. *Review Education* (quarterly), *Bulletin de Liaison*.

LIBRARIES

Bibliothèque de l'Ecole Supérieure des Lettres: rue de Damas, Beirut; Librarian FADL KASSEM; 22,000 vols.

Bibliothèque Nationale du Liban: Place de l'Etoile, Beirut; f. 1921; Dir. ABDALLAH TABBAE; copyright library, depository for UN documents; 100,000 vols. and 2,500 MSS.

Bibliothèque Orientale: rue de l'Université St. Joseph, P.O.B. 293, Beirut; f. 1881; 174,058 vols., 2,800 MSS., 700 periodicals; Dir. Rev. MARTIN MCDERMOTT, S.J.

Libraries of the St. Joseph University:

Library of the Faculties of Law and Political Science, Economics and Business Administration: Université Saint Joseph, B.P. 293, Beirut; f. 1913; Librarian NADA CORBAN; 40,000 vols., 251 periodicals.

Library of Medical Sciences: Université Saint Joseph, B.P. 115076, Beirut; f. 1893; 10,369 vols., 70 periodicals; Librarian Dr. IGNACE AOUAD.

Library of the Faculty of Engineering: Université Saint Joseph, P.O.B. 1514, Beirut; f. 1931; 2,914 vols., 300 periodicals; Dir. Rev. HENRI KETTERER.

Library of the Faculty of Arts and Human Sciences: Université St. Joseph, B.P. 293, Beirut; f. 1977; 6,000 vols., 50 periodicals; Dir. LUCIENNE KHOURY.

Librairie du Liban: P.O.B. 945, Imm. Esseily, Place Riad Solh, Beirut; f. 1944; includes dictionaries, scholars' and reference works in Arabic, English and French; Mans. SOUHAIL A. BERJAOUI, ANTOINE J. DARGAM.

Library of the American University: Beirut; f. 1866; 407,000 vols.; 2,200 MSS.; 4,950 current periodicals; Librarian YUSUF K. KHOURY, PH.D., M.L.S.; publ. *Arab Political Documents*† (annual, in Arabic).

Library of the Monastery of Saint-Saviour (*Basilian Missionary Order of Saint-Saviour*): Saïda; f. 1711; 28,500 vols. and 2,550 MSS.; Librarian GABRIEL HADDAD; publs. *Ar-Riçalat* (monthly), *Al-Wahdat*† (quarterly), *L'Ordo Grec-Catholique*.

Library of the Near East School of Theology: P.O.B. 7424, Beirut; f. 1932; ATLA; 33,000 vols.; collection of MSS., collection of The American Press; 135 religious periodicals; Librarian J. C. MCCULLOUGH, PH.D.; publ. *Theological Review*.

Library of the St. John Monastery (*Basilian Shweiriet Order*): Khonchara; f. 1696; 12,000 vols., 372 MSS.; the Order preserves the first printing press in the Middle East with Arabic and Greek letters (first book 1734); Abbot-General Rt. Rev. Mgr. ATHANASE HAGE.

Library of the Syrian Patriarchal Seminary: Seminary of Charfet, Daroon-Harissa; f. 1786; number of volumes: 30,500 and 3,000 Syriac and Arabic MSS.; publ. *Trait d'Union*.

Library of Beirut Arab University: P.O.B. 5020, Beirut; important collections on Lebanese, Arabic and Islamic studies; Chief Librarian MAHMOUD KOSPAR; 200,000 vols. and 3,500 periodicals.

MUSEUMS

American University Museum: Ras Beirut; f. 1868; Stone Age flint implements; bronze tools and implements from Early Bronze Age to Byzantine Period; pottery and other artefacts from the Bronze and Iron Ages, Classical, Hellenistic, Roman and Byzantine Periods; Arabic pottery from the 8th–16th centuries; Phoenician glassware; Egyptian artefacts from Neolithic to Dynastic Periods; pottery from the Neolithic Period of Mesopotamia and cylinder seals and cuneiform tablets from Sumer and Akkad; numismatics of the countries in the eastern basin of the Mediterranean; Dir. Dr. LEILA BADRE.

Daheshite Museum and Library: P.O.B. 202, Beirut; contains aquarelles, gouaches, original paintings, engravings, sculptures in marble, bronze, ivory and wood carvings; library of 30,000 vols. (20,000 Arabic, 10,000 English and French), on arts, philosophy, history, literature, religions, etc.; Dir. Dr. A. S. M. DAHESH.

Musée des Beaux-Arts: P.O.B. 3939, Beirut; Dir. Dr. DAHESH.

Musée Khalil Gibran: Besharre; dedicated to the life and works of the author.

Musée National (*National Museum of Lebanon*): rue de Damas, Beirut; f. 1920; Dir.-Gen. Emir MAURICE CHÉHAB; exhibits: royal jewellery, arms and statues of the Phoenician epoch; sarcophagus of King Ahiram (13th century B.C.), with first known alphabetical inscriptions; the collection of Dr. G. Ford of 25 sarcophagi of the Greek and Hellenistic epoch; large collection of terracotta statuettes of the Hellenistic period; Roman and Byzantine mosaics; Arabic woods and ceramics; publs. *Bulletin* and monographs.

Sursock Museum: Beirut.

UNIVERSITIES

AMERICAN UNIVERSITY OF BEIRUT

BEIRUT

Telephone: 340740.

Telex: 20801 AMUNOB LE.

Founded 1866.

Private control; Language of instruction: English; Academic year: October to June.

President: HAROLD E. HOELSCHER, PH.D.

Vice-President for Academic Affairs: SAMIR K. THABET, PH.D.

Vice-President for Administration: DAVID S. DODGE, M.A.

Registrar: F. HADDAD, PH.D.

Librarian: YOUSUF K. KHOURY, PH.D., M.L.S.

Comptroller: EINAR LARSEN.

Director of Information: R. A. MAWLAWI, M.SC.

Number of teachers: *c.* 400.

Number of students: 4,700.

Publications: *Berytus Archaeological Studies* (English annual), *Al-Abhath* (Arab Studies, English and Arabic, quarterly), *Arab Political Documents* (Arabic annual), *Annual Research Report, University Catalogue*.

DEANS:

Faculty of Arts and Science: ELIE A. SALEM, PH.D.

Faculty of Health Sciences: Dr. EUGENE GANGAROSA.

Faculty of Engineering and Architecture: KANAAN KANO, D.ENG.

Faculty of Agricultural and Food Sciences: JOHN L. FISCHER, PH.D.

Faculty of Medicine: Dr. RAJA KHOURI.

PROFESSORS:

Faculty of Arts and Sciences:

ABBAS, I., PH.D., Arabic
ABOU CHAAR, C., PH.D., Biology
ARNITA, S., M.I.C.C.S., Philosophy
BABIKIAN, L. G., PH.D., Biology
BATATU, J., PH.D., Political Studies and Public Administration
BENT, F., PH.D., Business and Management
BEYDOUN, Z., D.PHIL., Geology
BITAR, K., PH.D., Physics
BRUIN, F., PH.D., Physics
BUSHRUI, S., PH.D., English
CROW, R., PH.D., Political Studies and Public Administration
DIAB, L., PH.D., Social and Behavioural Sciences
FAKHRY, M., PH.D., Philosophy
HADDADIN, MAKHLUF, PH.D., Chemistry
HANANIA, G. I., PH.D., Chemistry
HANNA, AZMI, PH.D., Mathematics
HAWI, K., PH.D., Arabic
HEINEKEN, F., PH.D., Physics
HOELSCHER, HAROLD, PH.D., Business Administration
IBISH, Y., PH.D., Political Studies and Public Administration
ISSIDORIDES, C., PH.D., Chemistry
KHALAF, S., PH.D., Social and Behavioural Sciences
KHALIDI, W., B.LITT. Political Studies and Public Administration
KHURI, F., PH.D., Social and Behavioural Sciences
MAKINSON, D., D.PHIL., Philosophy
MAUROMATIS, H., PH.D., Physics
MUNRO, J., PH.D., English
MUWAFI, A., PH.D., Mathematics
NAJM, M. Y., PH.D., Arabic
PROTHRO, E. T., PH.D., Social and Behavioural Sciences
SALEM, E., PH.D., Political Studies and Public Administration
SALIBI, K. S., PH.D., History and Archaeology
TARAZI, F., PH.D., Arabic
TAYIM, H., PH.D., Chemistry
THABET, S. K., PH.D., Chemistry
WARD, W., PH.D., History and Archaeology
YFF, P., PH.D., Mathematics
ZAYID, M., PH.D., History and Archaeology

Faculties of Medical Sciences:
School of Medicine:
ABU FEISAL, K., M.D., Respiratory Medicine
ABU HAYDAR, N., M.D., Endocrinology
AFIFI, A., M.D., M.S., Human Morphology, Neurology
ALAMI, S., PH.D., M.D., Laboratory Medicine
AZAR, J., M.D., Infectious Diseases
AZOURI, B., M.D., D.M.SC., Surgery, Clinical Urology
AZOURI, R., M.D., Obstetrics and Gynaecology, Pathology
BARAKA, A., M.B., B.CH., D.A., D.M., M.D., Anaesthesiology
BERGMAN, R. A., PH.D., Human Morphology
BIRBARI, A., M.D., Nephrology
COE, E., PH.D., Biochemistry
DAGHER, I., M.D., Surgery
DURR, I., PH.D., Biochemistry
FAWAZ, G. A., PH.D., M.D., Pharmacology and Therapeutics
FULEIHAN, F., J.D., M.D., Respiratory Medicine
HADDAD, F. S., M.D., F.R.C.S.(C.), Neurosurgery
HAJJ, S., M.D., Obstetrics and Gynaecology
JABBUR, S., M.D., PH.D., Physiology
AL-KHALIDI, U., PH.D., Biochemistry
KHURI, R., M.D., Physiology, Nephrology
KURBAN, A., M.D., Dermatology
MATOSSIAN, R., M.D., Microbiology
MELHEM, R., M.D., Radiology
MROUEH, A., M.D., Obstetrics and Gynaecology
MUALLEM, M., M.D., Anaesthesiology
NAJJAR, S., M.D., Paediatrics
NASSIF, R. E., M.D., Laboratory Medicine
NSOULI, A., M.D., Orthopaedic Surgery
RIZK, G., M.D., Radiology
SABRA, F., M.D., Neurology
SHAMMAA, M., M.D., Gastroenterology
SHEHADEH, S., M.D., Plastic Surgery
SHWAYRI, E. I., M.D., Nephrology
SIMAAN, J., M.D., Pharmacology and Therapeutics
SLIM, M., M.D., Paediatrics
TABBARA, R. A., M.D., Cardiology

Faculty of Health Sciences:
AZAR, J. E., M.D., Infectious Diseases and Epidemiology
DAJANI, R., PH.D., Environmental Toxicology
GANGAROSA, E. J., M.D., Public Health
NELSON, A. P., M.P.H., Nursing

Faculty of Engineering and Architecture:
HANANIA, J. I., M.I.E.E., Electrical Engineering
HOELSCHER, H., PH.D., Engineering
ILIYA, R. A., PH.D., Civil Engineering
KANO, K. A., PH.D., Electrical Engineering
MALOUF, K., PH.D., Civil Engineering
SABAH, N., PH.D., Electrical Engineering
SAKKAL, F. M., PH.D., M.I.MECH.E., Mechanical Engineering

Faculty of Agricultural and Food Sciences:
DAGHIR, N., PH.D., Poultry Science
FISCHER, J. L., PH.D., Agricultural Economics and Rural Development
AL-HAJ, F., PH.D., Extension Education
HALLAB, A. H., PH.D., Food Technology and Nutrition
HENDERSON, H. D., PH.D., Agricultural Engineering
KAWAR, N. S., PH.D., Entomology
MACKSOUD, S. W., D.ENG., Irrigation
SAAD, A., PH.D., Plant Pathology
SAGHIR, A. R., PH.D., Weed Science
TANNOUS, R. I., SC.D., Food Technology and Nutrition

Division of Education and Extension Programmes:
BASHSHUR, M., PH.D., Education
ZA'ROUR, G., PH.D., Education and Science and Mathematics Education Centre

BEIRUT ARAB UNIVERSITY

TARIK EL-JADIDÉ,
P.O.B. 5020, BEIRUT
Telephone: 300110.
Founded 1960.

Private control, established by the Muslim Welfare Society; academically associated with the University of Alexandria.

Language of instruction: Arabic (Faculty of Architecture: Arabic and English, Faculty of Electrical Engineering and Faculty of Science: English); Academic year: October to June.

Rector: Dr. MOHSEN KHALIL KAMEL.
Secretary General: JAMIL KIBBI.
Registrar: MUSTAFA MUSA.
Chief Librarian: MAHMOUD KOSPAR.

Library: *see* Libraries.
Number of teachers: 217.
Number of students: 27,000 (internal and external).

DEANS:

Faculty of Arts: Dr. M. Z. ESHMAOUI.
Faculty of Law: Dr. A. ABOU-EL-WAFA.
Faculty of Commerce: Dr. A. E.-A. AJAMIYA.
Faculty of Architecture: Dr. M. ZAHRAN.
Faculty of Engineering: Dr. M. EL-KAYAR.
Faculty of Science: Dr. MOHAMED SALEH.

PROFESSORS:

Faculty of Arts:
ABDALLA, N., French Literature
ABOU-EL-ENEIN, H., Physical Geography
ASFOUR, M. A. M., Egyptology
ESHMAOUI, M. Z., Arabic Literature
FINDI, M. T., Philosophy of Science
GOUDA, G. H., Geomorphology
KANDIL, S. D., Education
KOT, A. K. H., Arabic Literature
MARZOUK, H. A., Arabic Literature
NASR, M. A. M., Political Philosophy
RAGIHI, A., Arabic Linguistics
SAATY, H., Sociology
SHERIF, N., English Literature
WAHIBA, A. F. M., Human Geography
YAHIA, L. A. W., Ancient History
ZAIDAN, M. F., Modern Philosophy

Faculty of Law:
ABOU-EL-WAFA, A. A. L., Law
SADDA, A. M. F., Civil Law
SADEK, H. S. A., International Law
SHALABI, M. M., Islamic Law
SULTAN, A. S., Civil Law

Faculty of Commerce:
AJAMIYA, M. A. A., Economics
DEIF, A. K., Accountancy
DRAZ, H., Public Finance
GANAYEM, A., Business Administration
HAYKAL, A. A. F., Statistics

Faculty of Architecture:
ZAHRAN, M. M., Architecture

Faculty of Engineering:
ABD-EL-GHANI, S. D., Electrical Machinery
ABOU-SOUOUD, A. K., Electronics
BARAKAT, M. A., Soil Mechanics
BAYOUMI, A., Mechanical Engineering
DIWAN, A. F. S., Construction Engineering
GOUDA, M. A. H., Construction Engineering
HAKIM, Y. A., Computer Science
HAMEDA, H. M., Civil Engineering
ISMAIL, M. K. M., Electrical Machinery
EL-KAYAR, A. M. I., Hydraulics
MOUSTAFA, A. S., Electronics
SABBAGH, H. H., Communications

Faculty of Science:
AHMED, M. Z., Physics
SHERIF, I. I., Physics

UNIVERSITÉ LIBANAISE
(Lebanese University)

PLACE MUSÉE, BEIRUT
Telephone: 386817, 386818.

State control; Languages of instruction: Arabic, French and English.

Rector: Dr. GEORGES TOHMÉ.
Secretary: Dr. ABBAS ALAMEDDINE.

Number of teachers: 534.
Number of students: 39,000.

DEANS:

Faculty of Literature and Humanities: Dr. AHMAD MAKKI.
Faculty of Sciences: Dr. RAJI ABOU CHACRA.
Faculty of Law, Political and Administrative Sciences: Dr. RAYMOND FARHAT.
Faculty of Pedagogy: Dr. KHALIL EL JOR.
Faculty of Business Administration: Dr. SAMI NESSAYRI.
Faculty of Information: Dr. HASSAN SAAB.
Faculty of Engineering: Dr. JACQUES NASR.
Faculty of Agriculture: OMAR ADADA.

ATTACHED INSTITUTES:

Institute of Social Sciences: Dr. HACHEM HAIDAR.
Institute of Fine Arts: Dr. SANAA ABED EL SAMAD.

UNIVERSITÉ SAINT-ESPRIT DE KASLIK

JOUNIEH
Telephone: 930124, 932124.
Telex: USEK 22225 LE.
Founded 1950.

Private control (Lebanese Maronite Order); Languages of instruction: French and Arabic; Academic year: October to June.

Chancellor: Fr. CHARBEL KASSIS.
Rector: Fr. PIERRE AZZI.
Vice-Rector: Fr. JEAN TABET.
Secretary-General: Fr. ANTOINE KHALIFE.

Library of 115,000 vols.

Number of teachers: 295.
Number of students: 2,200.

Publications: *Parole de l'Orient*† (2 a year), *Bibliothèque de l'Université Saint-Esprit, Les Conférences de l'Université Saint-Esprit.*

DEANS:

Faculty of Theology: Fr. ELIE KHALIFE.
Faculty of Philosophy and Humanities: Fr. THOMAS MOUHANNA.
Faculty of Commercial Sciences: Fr. BASILE HACHEM.
Faculty of Arts: Fr. PAUL NAMAAN.
Faculty of Fine and Applied Arts: Fr. JOSEPH MOUANESS.

DIRECTORS:

Institute of Musicology: Fr. LOUIS HAGE.
Institute of Liturgy: Fr. JEAN TABET.
Institute of History: Fr. PAUL NAAMAN.
Institute of Languages: Fr. THOMAS MOUHANNA.

UNIVERSITÉ SAINT JOSEPH

RUE HUVELIN, B.P. 293, BEIRUT
Telephone: 326-636.
Founded 1881.

Private control (Roman Catholic): Languages of instruction: French and Arabic; Academic year: October to June.

Rector: Rev. Fr. JEAN DUCRUET, S.J.
Vice-Rector: Prof. ZAKARIA NSOULI.

Library: *see* Libraries.

Number of teachers: 479.
Number of students: 5,663.

Publications: *Mélanges de l'Université Saint Joseph* (annually), *Travaux et Jours* (quarterly), *Proche-Orient, Etudes Juridiques, Proche-Orient, Etudes Economiques* (2 a year).

DEANS:

Faculty of Theology: Rev. Fr. AUGUSTIN DUPRÉ LA TOUR.
Faculty of Medicine: Dr. NAJIB TALEB.
Faculty of Pharmacy: Dr. FAWAZ FAWAZ.
Faculty of Dentistry: Dr. ELIE ARAMOUNI.
Faculty of Engineering: SÉLIM CATAFAGO.
Faculty of Law and Political Science: PIERRE GANNAGE.
Faculty of Economics and Business Administration: ALEXANDRE CHAIBAN.
Faculty of Arts and Humanities: Fr. SÉLIM ABOU.

COLLEGES

BEIRUT UNIVERSITY COLLEGE

P.O.B. 11-4080, BEIRUT
Telephone: 252590.

Founded 1924 by the United Presbyterian Church, U.S.A.; now an independent non-profit corporation.

President: ALBERT BADRE, PH.D.
Dean: RIYAD NASSAR, PH.D.

Library of 66,000 vols., 350 English and Arab periodicals.

Number of teachers: 74 (full-time).
Number of students: 1,560 (full-time).

Offers liberal and specialized education.

CENTRE D'ÉTUDES ET DE RECHERCHES MATHÉMATIQUES ET PHYSIQUES

RUE DE DAMAS, B.P. 3855, BEIRUT
Founded 1945.

Director of Mathematics Department: M. FLAMANT.
Director of Physics Department: P. QUEDEC.

Number of students: 425.

ÉCOLE SUPÉRIEURE DES LETTRES DE BEYROUTH

B.P. 1931, BEIRUT
Founded 1944.

Director: MICHEL CORVIN.
Secretary-General: E. WAKIM.

Number of teachers: 60, including 16 professors.
Number of students: 802.
Publication: *Cahiers* (irregular).

HAIGAZIAN COLLEGE

P.O.B. 1748, BEIRUT
Founded 1955.

Languages of instruction: Arabic, Armenian and English; Private control; Academic year: October to June.

President: JOHN J. MARKARIAN, PH.D.
Dean: (vacant).
Librarian: JIRAIR TANIELIAN.

Libraries (Armenian and English) of 35,500 vols.

Number of teachers: 35.
Number of students: 315.

CHAIRMEN OF DIVISIONS:

Armenian Center: YERVANT KASSOUNY, PH.D.
Humanities: INGRID SEMAAN, PH.D.
Sciences: BISHARA LIBBUS.
Social Sciences: (vacant).
Business Administration and Economics: HRATCH HADJETIAN, PH.D.

MIDDLE EAST COLLEGE

Private control; Language of instruction: English, Academic year: September to June (three terms), and six-week summer session.

President: J. I. ESTEPHAN, PH.D.
Academic Dean: D. EICHNER, PH.D.
Registrar and Secretary for Admissions: J. MANASSIAN, M.A.
Dean of Men: J. MANASSIAN, M.A.
Dean of Women: Mrs. A. ESTEPHAN, A.A.
Librarian: (vacant).

Library of 20,000 vols.

Offers B.A. degrees in business administration, education (primary), and religion.

NEAR EAST SCHOOL OF THEOLOGY

P.O.B. 7424, BEIRUT
Founded 1932.

An ecumenical institution of higher learning. It offers theological education and pastoral training to qualified candidates for church ministries, as well as to lay candidates regardless of church affiliation, sex, race or nationality.

President: Rev. V. H. FLETCHER, PH.D.
Academic Dean: J. C. MCCULLOUGH, PH.D.

Library of 30,000 vols.
Number of teachers: 8.
Number of students: 30.

Publication: *NEST Theological Review.*

LESOTHO

Population 1,216,000

LEARNED SOCIETY AND RESEARCH INSTITUTES

British Council: P.O.B. 429, Hobson's Square, Maseru 100; library (*see* below); Rep. M. G. HOLCROFT.

Ministry of Agriculture, Co-operatives and Marketing: P.O.B. 24, Maseru; research station at Maseru and field experimental stations.

Geological Survey Department: Dept. of Mines and Geology, P.O.B. 750, Maseru 100; Commr. M. M. MOFOLO.

LIBRARIES AND ARCHIVES

British Council Library: P.O.B. 429, Maseru 100; f. 1965; 15,510 vols., 55 periodicals; Librarian Mrs. M. LEVY.

Lesotho Government Archives: P.O.B. 47, Maseru; f. 1958; undertakes research; records date from 1869; Archivist M. L. MANYELI.

UNIVERSITY AND COLLEGE

NATIONAL UNIVERSITY OF LESOTHO

P.O. ROMA

Telephone: Roma 201.

Founded 1966 as University of Botswana, Lesotho and Swaziland. In 1975 the Lesotho Government unilaterally declared the Roma campus the National University of Lesotho.

Language of instruction: English; Academic year: August to May.

Chancellor: H.M. King MOSHOESHOE II.
Vice-Chancellor: M. T. MASHOLOGU.
Registrar: B. A. TLELASE.
Librarian: Mrs. M. N. TAU.

Number of teachers: 92.
Number of students: 727 full-time, 300 part-time.

DEANS:

Faculty of Science: Prof. A. BROCK.
Faculty of Humanities: Rev. D. FAHY.
Faculty of Social Sciences: M. SEFALI.
Faculty of Education: V. M. BAM.
Institute of Extra-Mural Studies: A. M. SETSABI.

PROFESSORS:

Faculty of Science:
BROCK, A., Physics
HOFSOMMER, D. J., Mathematics
HUTCHEON, A. T., Chemistry
MENZIES, J. I., Biology
SCHMITZ, G., Geography

Faculty of Social Sciences:
BIRMINGHAM, W., Economics
MILLN, J. C., Accounting and Commerce
PADMANABHA, G. J., English
POULTER, S. M., Law

Faculty of Humanities:
RUCH, E. A., Philosophy

Faculty of Education:
MOHAPELOA, J. M., Education

LESOTHO AGRICULTURAL COLLEGE

P.O.B. 829, MASERU

Telephone: 22484

Founded 1955.

State control; Language of instruction: English; Academic year: September to July (three semesters).

Principal: K. A. J. YOUNGER.
Registrar: K. A. LEPHOLISA.

LIBERIA

Population 1,715,000

LEARNED SOCIETIES AND RESEARCH INSTITUTES

American Cultural Center: Ashmun St., Monrovia; administered by International Communication Agency; library of 5,000 vols.; 120 periodicals.

Central Agriculture Experimental Station: Suakoko; f. 1946; under Ministry of Agriculture; research on crops, animal husbandry, horticulture, soil, and inland fisheries; bilateral and international agencies; service centre for supply of improved seeds, plant material and animals; Dir. Dr. H. O. JARRETT.

Geological, Mining and Metallurgical Society of Liberia: P.O.B. 9024, Monrovia; f. 1964; 78 mems.; Pres. A. MOMOLU MASSAQUOI; Sec. M. W. GODA BAKER; publ. *Bulletin*† (2 a year).

Kendeja National Cultural Centre: Kendeja; f. 1963; traditional arts and crafts; the national dance troupe is based here.

Liberia Arts and Crafts Association: P.O.B. 885, Monrovia; f. 1964; 14 mems.; aims to encourage artists and craftsmen through exhibitions, sales, workshops; Pres. B. M. N'JAI; Sec. KONA KHASU.

The Liberian Institute of the American Foundation for Tropical Medicine, Inc.: P.O.B. 64, Harbel; f. 1952; research into the tropical diseases of man; the diseases of domestic animals which can be a source of food in tropical countries; and the improvement and development of crops which can be grown in the tropics as food for man and domestic animals; Dir. E. W. REBER.

Nimba Research Laboratory: c/o Lamco J. V. Operating Co., Grassland, Nimba, Robertsfield; f. 1962; under supervision of Nimba Research Committee of International Union for Conservation of Nature and Natural Resources in co-operation with UNESCO; biological and ecological exploration and field work in the Mount Nimba region and conservation; library of 100 vols. and access to LAMCO library, Yekepa; Chair. KAI CURRY-LINDAHL, Bruce House, Standard St., Nairobi.

Society of Liberian Authors: P.O.B. 2468, Monrovia; f. 1959; aims to stimulate general interest in writing and encourage literature in local vernacular; Pres. A. DORIS BANKS-HENRIES; publ. *Kaafa* (2 a year).

United States Educational and Cultural Foundation in Liberia: Bank of Liberia Bldg., Monrovia; administers exchange of persons programme; bi-national Board of Directors.

LIBRARIES

Government Public Library: Ashmun St., Monrovia; f. 1959; 15,000 vols.

Liberian Information Service Library: Monrovia; reference.

UNESCO Mission Library: Dept. of Education, Monrovia.

University of Liberia Libraries: University of Liberia, P.O.B. 9020, Monrovia; f. 1862; 100,000 vols., 1,600 periodicals; Dir. C. WESLEY ARMSTRONG.

MUSEUMS

Africana Museum: Cuttington University College, c/o Episcopal Church Office, P.O.B. 277, Monrovia; f. 1960; 2,500 items from Liberia and neighbouring countries; traditional arts and crafts, ethnographical material; 2 traditional houses representing Kpelle and Grebo architecture; depository for archaeological collections; serves as a teaching collection for the College and as a research facility for visiting scholars; specialized research library of *c.* 200 vols. in the museum research centre, in addition to the research library in the College; Dir. OLULU N'GELE.

National Museum: Monrovia.

Tubman Centre of African Culture: Robertsport, Grand Cape Mount County; f. 1964; library of 1,500 vols.; General Chair. Senator CHARLES D. SHERMAN; Dir. EDWIN O. FAHNBULLEH.

UNIVERSITY AND COLLEGES

UNIVERSITY OF LIBERIA

P.O.B. 9020, MONROVIA

Telephone: 221537, 222515.

Founded as Liberia College 1862; University 1951.

Language of instruction: English; Academic year: February to December (two semesters).

The University incorporates the following colleges and institutes: Liberia College (College of Social Sciences and Humanities), William V. S. Tubman Teachers College, Louis Arthur Grimes School of Law, College of Agriculture and Forestry, College of Business and Public Administration, A. M. Dogliotti College of Medicine, T. J. R. Faulkner College of Science and Technology, Institute of African Studies and the extra-mural division.

President: Dr. MARY ANTOINETTE BROWN SHERMAN.
Vice-President for Administration: Dr. C. E. ZAMBA LIBERTY.
Vice-President for Academic Affairs: Dr. J. TEAH TARPEH.
Registrar: WILLIAM S. HOFF.
Director of Libraries: Dr. C. WESLEY ARMSTRONG.

Library: *see* Libraries.

Number of teachers: *c.* 278.

Number of students: 3,247.

Publications: *The University of Liberia Catalogue and Announcements, The University of Liberia Journal, This Week on Campus, Liberian Economic and Management Review, Liberian Law Journal, UL Science Magazine, University Spokesman.*

DEANS:

Liberia College: Prof. WEDE S. JONES.
Teachers College: Prof. THEODORE WARD JACKSON.
School of Law: TOYE C. BARNARD.
College of Agriculture and Forestry: Dr. MCKINLEY A. DESHIELD, Jr.
College of Business and Public Administration: Dr. FLOMO Y. STEVENS.
College of Medicine: Dr. FESTUS M. HALAY.

College of Science and Technology: Prof. AGNES COOPER DENNIS.

PROFESSORS:

BARNARD, C., Law
BREWER, R., Pathology
BROWN SHERMAN, A., Education
BRUMSKINE, W., Surgery
BRYANT, M., Biology
COOPER, H. N., Surgery
COOPER DENNIS, A., Biology
DESHIELD, A., Agriculture
DIGGS, J., Radiology
HANNA, M., Medicine
HASSELMAN, Geography
JAMES, L. A., Political Science
JONES, S. W., English
PREVOST, M., Surgery
RAO, S. P. V., Mathematics
ROSTRON, C., Civil Engineering
SAMUEL, R., Physics
SIO, F. K., Forestry
SRINIVASAN, K., Chemistry
SRIVASTAVA, M., Demography
STEVENS, F. Y., Management
THEBAUD, E., Psychiatry
TOGBA, J. N., Public Health
TOPOR, W., Philosophy
WARD, V., Chemistry
YAIDOO, H. W., Economics

ATTACHED INSTITUTES:

Institute of African Studies: Dir. S. JABARU CARLON.

Extra-mural Division: Dir. JOHN S. VARFLEY, Jr.

BOOKER WASHINGTON INSTITUTE

KAKATA

Owned and operated by the Government of Liberia through the Ministry of Education and a Board of Governors. Agricultural and industrial courses.

Principal: F. AMADU SIRLEAF.

CUTTINGTON UNIVERSITY COLLEGE

c/o EPISCOPAL CHURCH OFFICE BUILDING,
P.O.B. 277, MONROVIA
Telephone: Monrovia 221065.

Founded 1889 (closed 1929 and reopened 1949).

Maintained by the Episcopal Church of America, subsidized by the Government, receives donated service from the United Lutheran Church and the Fulbright Program.

Language of instruction: English; Academic year: March to November.

Chairman of the Board of Trustees: Bishop GEORGE D. BROWNE, M.TH., D.D.

President: Rev. Canon EMMANUEL W. JOHNSON, M.A., LL.D.

Registrar and Director of Admissions: CHARLOTTE CASHER, M.SC.

Dean of Administration: HENRY G. KWEKWE, ED.D.

Dean of Students: BENGALY KAMARA, B.S.

Dean of Academic Affairs: STEPHEN M. YEKESON, PH.D.

Librarian: EMMANUEL R. C. NYAMADI, M.L.S.

The library contains *c.* 92,000 vols., 250 periodicals.

Number of teachers: 50.

Number of students: 524.

Publications: *Cuttington University College Catalogue, Phebe Nursing Brochure, Que Circa.*

HEADS OF DIVISIONS:

Education: EVELYN WHITE-FREEMAN, ED.D.

Science: MATHEW PANICKER, M.SC.

Humanities: WILLIAM MOMOLU, M.SC.

Social Science: PATRICK PIEH, PH.D.

Nursing: VIRGINIA BORTAS, M.SC.

Theology: The Ven. E. BOLLING ROBERTSON, M.SC.

ATTACHED INSTITUTES:

Rural Development Institute: Dir. EDWARD A. HOLMES, PH.D.

Africana Museum: (*see* under Museums).

WILLIAM V. S. TUBMAN COLLEGE OF TECHNOLOGY

P.O.B. 3570, MONROVIA

Founded 1970, opened 1978.

State control; Language of instruction: English; Academic year: March to December.

President: J. NOGNWOLU KOLLEH.

Dean: E. GILATE.

Number of teachers: 10.

Number of students: 100.

Three-year associate degree course in engineering technology.

LIBYA

Population 3,014,000

LEARNED SOCIETIES

Centre Culturel Français: 15–17 rue Karachi, P.O.B. 683, Tripoli; f. 1955; instruction in French and Arabic languages, conferences, concerts, seminars and theatre; library of 7,000 vols.; Dir. ALAIN CRESPO.

Intellectual Society of Libya: 136 Shar'a Baladia, P.O.B. 1017, Tripoli; f. 1959; Pres. Dr. A. N. ANEIZI.

Istituto Italiano di Cultura: Italian Embassy in Libya, c/o Ministry of Foreign Affairs, Rome; library of 7,000 vols.

LIBRARIES AND ARCHIVES

Awqaf Public Library: 3 Awqaf St., Tripoli; f. 1898; *c.* 6,000 vols.; Man. MOHAMMED ALGAFAERY.

Egyptian Cultural Centre Library: 310 Shar'a 'Umar al-Mukhtar, Tripoli; f. 1955; 26,000 vols.; Librarian MUHAMMAD ABDULMAGHAM DI'AB.

Government Library: 14 Shar'a al-Jazair, Tripoli; f. 1917 35,500 vols.; Librarian BASHIR AL-BADRI.

General People's Committee for Information Libraries: c/o Maidan ash-Shuhada, Tripoli.

Tripoli: f. 1961; 7,000 vols.; Librarian 'UMAR MUHAMMAD FARJANI.

Benghazi: f. 1963; 4,100 vols.; Librarian 'ABDULLATIF AL-FITURI.

National Archives: Castello, Tripoli; f. 1928; controlled by Department of Antiquities, General People's Committee for Education, Tripoli; extensive collection of documents relating to the history of Tripolitania, mostly in Turkish from the Ottoman period; Curator ABDULAALI OWN.

Public Library: Shar'a 'Umar al-Mukhtar, Benghazi; f. 1955; 11,000 vols.; Librarian AHMAD GALLAL.

Qurinna Library: Mukhtar St., Benghazi; Arab, French and English books.

Supreme Court Library: Shar'a ash-Shatt, Tripoli; f. 1953; 1,700 vols.; Librarian MUHAMMAD AL-AJAILI AZ-ZAHRA.

University of Garyounis Library: P.O.B. 1308, Benghazi; f. 1955; 294,844 vols.; 2,170 periodicals; 7 depts., including 2,360 MSS., 70,000 documents, 10,000 microfilms and rare books; Chief Librarian AHMED GALLAL; publs. available for exchange.

MUSEUMS

Department of Antiquities: Assarai al-Hamra, Tripoli; responsible for all museums and archaeological sites in Libya; Pres. Dr. SALAHEDDIN HASSAN.

Archaeological, Natural History, Epigraphy, Prehistory and Ethnography Museums: Assarai al-Hamra, Tripoli.

Leptis Magna Museum: Leptis Magna.

Sabratha Museum of Antiquities: Sabratha.

Islamic Museum: Tripoli.

Kaicab Museum: Gaigab (near Cyrene).

Cyrene Museum: Cyrene (Shahat).

Ptolemais Museum: Tolmeitha.

Tauchira Museum: Tokra.

Apollonia Museum: Marsa Soussa.

Germa Museum: Germa (Fezean).

Benghazi Museum: Benghazi.

Zanzur Museum: Zanzur (Tripoli).

Department of Antiquities, Eastern Region: Beida; responsible for archaeological sites throughout the former Cyrenaica, including Ptolemais (Tolmeitha), Apollonia (Susa) and the mosaics at Qasr Libia; Controller BRAYEK ATTIYA.

Department of Antiquities, Fezzan: Sebha; f. 1961; a museum exhibits the important finds from Jerma (Jarma) and the Ubari-Ghat track; Dir. Dr. AYUB; Asst. Dir. M. BOUBAKR.

UNIVERSITIES

ALFATEH UNIVERSITY

P.O.B. 13040, TRIPOLI

Telephone: 604000.

Founded 1973 from existing faculties of the University of Libya; present name 1976.

Languages of instruction: Arabic, English, French.

Chancellor: IBRAHEIM EL-MUNTASER.
Vice-Chancellor: AMIN SHEGLILA.
Registrar: TAHER ISSA.
Librarian: DAU ELMUZUGHI TEEBAR.

Number of teachers: 450.
Number of students: 7,500.

Publications: *Libyan Journal of Sciences*†, *Libyan Journal of Agriculture*†, *Bulletin of the Faculty of Education*†, *Bulletin of the Faculty of Engineering*† (all annually).

DEANS:

Faculty of Science: Dr. YOUSIF MUHARIQ.
Faculty of Engineering: Dr. SALEH M. BU-GREIS.
Faculty of Agriculture: Dr. MUSTAFA BEN HAUM.
Faculty of Education: Dr. SALEM EL-HAJJAJI.
Faculty of Petroleum: Dr. AMIN SHIGLILA.
Faculty of Medicine: Dr. ABDUL RAZZAK ZWAWIE.
Faculty of Pharmacy: Dr. SIDDIK SHAKSHOOKI.

UNIVERSITY OF GARYOUNIS

P.O.B. 1308,
BENGHAZI

Telephone: 87462.

Founded 1955 as University of Libya, re-named 1973, present name 1976; campuses at Benghazi and Beida.

State control; Languages of instruction: Arabic and English.

Chancellor: Dr. YOUSIF HAMED ELSHEIN.
Vice-Chancellor: SALEM SHEBANI.
Vice-Chancellor for Postgraduate Studies: Dr. ASHOUR ELZOKI.
Registrar: OMAR ELBARGHTI.

Library: *see* Libraries.
Number of teachers: 510.
Number of students: 9,410.

Publications: various faculty bulletins.

DEANS:

Faculty of Arts and Education: Dr. SOBHI GUNOS.
Faculty of Economics: Dr. FARAHAT SHERANA.
Faculty of Law: Dr. EL-MADANE BO TEWRAT.
Faculty of Medicine: Dr. MURAD LENGHI.
Faculty of Education: Dr. SHWEB EL MANSOURI.
Faculty of Science: Dr. SAAD BEN HAMIED.
Faculty of Engineering: Dr. DWEB EL-AKDAR.
Faculty of Dentistry: Dr. OTHMAN SHALADI.
Faculty of Agriculture: Dr. ABDULLA LAIRG.

COLLEGES

Arts and Crafts School: Shar'a 24 December, Tripoli; Principal Mr. SALIM ZEGALLAI.

Higher Institute of Electronics: P.O.B. 12041, Tripoli; B.Sc. degree course.

Higher Institute of Technology: P.O.B. 12024, Tripoli; f. 1976; depts. of general sciences, medical technology, food technology and environmental sciences; library of 10,000 vols.; 50 teachers, 500 students; Dean AMAR GLEZA.

Posts and Telecommunications Institute: P.O.B. 2428; Tripoli; f. 1963; library of 510 vols.; Dir. K. MARABUTACI.

LUXEMBOURG

Population 357,000

ACADEMY AND LEARNED SOCIETIES

Académie Scientifique Internationale pour la Protection de la Vie, l'Environnement et la Biopolitique: Pres. Prof. JOSUÉ DE CASTRO; includes:

Société Internationale pour la Recherche sur les Maladies de Civilisation et les Substances Vitales: *see* International section.

Collège Médical: 57 blvd. de la Pétrusse, Luxembourg; f. 1818; governmental consultative body; 11 mems.; Pres. Dr. GEORGES ARNOLD; Sec. PAUL HOFFMANN.

Commission d'Instruction: rue du Saint Esprit, Luxembourg; special collections: psychology, pedagogy; 400 vols. in library; Pres. Prof. ALBERT NOTHUMB.

Institut Grand-Ducal: includes six sections: (*a*) Historical (Pres. JOS GOEDERT; Sec. PAUL SPANG), (*b*) Medical (Pres. HENRI METZ; Sec. JEAN NEUEN), (*c*) Scientific (Pres. PAUL METZ; Sec. RENÉ WEISS), (*d*) Linguistic and Folklore (Pres. CORNEL MEDER; Sec. HENRI KLEES), (*e*) Arts and Literature (Pres. PAUL HENKES; Sec. HENRI BLAISE), (*f*) Moral and Political Sciences (Pres. ALPHONSE HUSS; Sec. CARLOS HEMMER).

Société des Naturalistes Luxembourgeois: B.P. 327, L-2013 Luxembourg; f. 1872; 480 mems.; Pres. JOSEPH LAHR; Secs. MANON BINTZ, TH. THOLL, A. HARY; Librarian H. VAN WERSCH; publ. *Bulletin*† (annual).

LIBRARIES AND ARCHIVES

Archives de l'Etat: Plateau du Saint-Esprit, B.P. 6, Luxembourg 2; Dir. PAUL SPANG.

Bibliothèque de la Ville: rue Emile Mayrisch 26, Esch-sur-Alzette; f. 1919; German, French, English and Italian literature; popular science books; 55,000 vols.; special collection of Luxembourgensia; Record Library; Chief Librarian FERNAND ROELTGEN.

Bibliothèque Nationale: 37 blvd. F. D.-Roosevelt, Luxembourg; f. 1798, re-organized 1897, 1945, 1958 and 1973; 550,000 vols., 502 MSS., 132 incunabula; special collection of 42,000 Luxembourgensia; Dir. Prof. Dr. GILBERT TRAUSCH; publs. *Bibliographie Luxembourgeoise*†, *Bibliographie d'histoire luxembourgeoise*† (annually), special bibliographies.

MUSEUM

Musées de l'Etat (*State Museums*): Marché-aux-Poissons, Luxembourg; f. 1845; archaeology, fine arts, industrial and popular arts, history of Luxembourg, planetarium and natural sciences; library of 20,000 vols.; Dir. GÉRARD THILL; publs. *P.S.H.*, *Hémech*† (reports and studies).

UNIVERSITY

CENTRE UNIVERSITAIRE DE LUXEMBOURG

162A AV. DE LA FAIENCERIE,
LUXEMBOURG

Telephone: 216-21.

Founded 1969.

State control; Languages of instruction: German, English, French; Academic year: October to June.

President: PAUL MARGUE.

Director: EDMOND REUTER.

Administrative Officer: Mme COLETTE KNEPPER-POOS.

Librarian: CARLO HURY.

Library of 110,000 vols.

Number of teachers: 140.
Number of students: 500.

DIRECTORS:

Letters and Human Sciences: MARIE-THÉRÈSE SCHROEDER-HARTMANN.

Law and Economics: PAUL MARGUE.

Sciences: RENÉ WEISS.

Teacher Training: EDMOND WAGNER.

Legal Training: LÉON LIESCH.

CONSTITUENT INSTITUTE:

Institut Universitaire International de Luxembourg: f. 1974; post-graduate summer courses.

President: NORBERT KUNITZKI.

Number of teachers: 12.
Number of students: 70.

DEPARTMENTS:

Centre international d'études juridiques et de droit comparé: Sec. NICOLAS DECKER.

Centre international d'économie politique: Sec. MARC MULLER.

Centre international d'études et de recherches européennes: Sec. JEAN MISCHO.

COLLEGES

Conservatoire de Musique d'Esch-sur-Alzette: 10 rue de l'Eglise, B.P. 145, Esch-sur-Alzette; f. 1969 (formerly Ecole Municipale de Musique f. 1926.

Principal: FRED HARLES.

Secretary: MIREILLE BUSCH.

Number of teaching staff: 33.
Number of students: 800

Publication: *Annuaire* (Year Book).

Conservatoire de Musique de la Ville de Luxembourg: 16 rue du Saint Esprit, Luxembourg; f. 1906.

Director: JOSY HAMER.

Secretary: PIERRE BERG.

Librarian: HENRI JEITZ.

Number of teaching staff: 69 professors.

Ecole des Arts et Métiers: rue Guillaume Schneider 19, Luxembourg; f. 1958, formerly Ecole d'Artisans de l'Etat; f. 1896.

Classes in electronics, mechanics, building (four-year course), fine arts and decorative arts (four-year course).

Director: CAMILLE LEBEAU.

Ecole Professionnelle et Ménagère: 101 rue de Luxembourg, Esch-sur-Alzette; Dir. M. MARIA-HILF.

Institut d'Hygiène et de Santé Publique: 42 rue du Laboratoire, Luxembourg.

Director: Dr. ARSÈNE BETZ.

Institut Supérieur de Technologie: Kirchberg-Luxembourg; mechanical, electrical and civil engineering; 50 teachers, 550 students.

Director: PAUL N. FEIDERT.

Lycée Technique agricole: Avenue Salentiny 72, Ettelbruck; f. 1883; 27 teachers, 220 students.

Director: E. JACQUÉ.

Lycée Technique d'Esch-sur-Alzette: place Victor Hugo, Esch-sur-Alzette; f. 1914; 171 teachers, 2,248 students.

Director: ALOYSE REIFFERS.

MADAGASCAR

(MALAGASY REPUBLIC)

Population 9,112,000

LEARNED SOCIETIES AND RESEARCH INSTITUTES

Académie Malgache: Tsimbazaza, Antananarivo; f. 1902; studies in human and natural sciences; monthly meetings; 150 mems.; Pres. Dr. C. RABENORO; publs. *Bulletin, Mémoires.*

American Cultural Center: 4 Làlana Dr. Razafindratandra, Ambohidahy, Antananarivo; library of 6,000 vols.; Dir. F. G. MASON, Jr.

Bureau de Recherches Géologiques et Minières: B.P. 458, Antananarivo; Dir. G. BOURNAT. (*See* main entry under France.)

Centre National de Recherche Appliquée au Développement Rural (CENRADERU): B.P. 1690, Antananarivo; f. 1974; research into agriculture, forestry and fisheries, zoology, veterinary studies and rural economy; Pres. P. A. ANDRIANARISON.

CENRADERU—IRCT: B. P. 227, Mahajanga; research on cotton and other fibres; main research station at Toliary; regional station at Tanandava; sisal research at Mandrare.

Centre Technique Forestier Tropical: B.P. 904, Antananarivo; f. 1961; Dir. C. BAILLY. (*See* main entry under France).

Cercle Germano-Malagasy: B.P. 1200, Antananarivo; f. 1969; 260 mems.; Pres. M. S. RAJAONA.

Institut de Recherches Agronomiques de la République Malgache: B.P. 1444, Antananarivo; stations at Alaotra, Antalaha, Betioky-sud, Ivoloina, Anseranana, Mahajanga, Fianarantsoa and Toliary; Dir. J. VELLY.

Institut d'Elevage et de Médecine Vétérinaire des Pays Tropicaux: Antananarivo; central laboratory, research stations at Kianjasoa and Miadana. (*See* also main entry under France.)

Institut Malgache des Arts Dramatiques et Folkloriques—Imadefolk: Centre Culturel Albert Camus, Ave. de l'Indépendance, Antananarivo; f. 1964; traditional songs and dances; Dir. O. RAKOTO.

Institut National de Géodésie et Cartographie: 3 Làlana Ravelomanantsoa, B.P. 323, Antananarivo; f. 1945; re-organized 1974; Dir. S. ANDRIAMIHAJA.

Institut Pasteur: B.P. 1274, Antananarivo; f. 1898; biological research; library of 3,000 vols.; Dir. P. COULANGES; publ. *Archives de l'Institut Pasteur de Madagascar* (2 a year).

Mission I.R.A.T. à Madagascar: B.P. 438, Bamako; agricultural research; Dir. M. ARRAUDEAU. (*See* main entry under France.)

Observatoire d'Antananarivo: Université de Madagascar, Faculté des Sciences, B.P. 3843, Antananarivo; f. 1889, affiliated to the University 1967; study of climatology, terrestrial magnetism, seismology, VLF Waves propagation and the ionosphere; Dir. M. RAKOTONDRAINIBE; publs. *Mesures Magnétiques* (annual), *Bulletin* (monthly), *Bulletin Météorologique.*

Office de la Recherche Scientifique et Technique Outre-Mer: Mission ORSTOM, B.P. 434, Antananarivo; hydrology; Head D. BAUDUIN. (*See* also main entry under France).

Service Géologique: B.P. 280, Antananarivo; f. 1926; library of 42,919 vols.; Dir. A. RAZAFINI PARANY; publs. *Rapport annuel, Travaux du Bureau Géologique, Annales géologiques, Documentation du Service Géologique, Atlas des fossiles caractéristiques de Madagascar.*

LIBRARIES

Archives Nationales: B.P. 3384, Antananarivo; f. 1958; *c.* 3,000 vols.; Dir. Mme RAZOHARINORO-RANDRIAMBOAVONJY.

Bibliothèque du Centre Culturel "Albert Camus": 11 avenue Grandidier, Isoraka, Antananarivo; f. 1962; 13,630 vols.

Bibliothèque Municipale: Antsirabé; Librarian JEANNE RABODOMALALA.

Bibliothèque Municipale: avenue du 18 juin, Antananarivo; f. 1961; 22,600 vols.

Bibliothèque Nationale: Antaninarenina, B.P. 257, Antananarivo; f. 1961; 150,000 vols.; special collections: History, Literature, the Arts, Applied Sciences, Information on Madagascar; Dir. L. RALAISAHOLIMANANA; publs. *Bibliographie de Madagascar* (annually), *Ny Boky no loharanom-pandrosoana* (quarterly).

Bibliothèque Universitaire: Campus Universitaire, Ambohitsaina, B.P. 908, Antananarivo; f. 1960; 120,000 vols.; Dir. M. RANIVO; publ. *Bibliographie Annuelle de Madagascar*†.

MUSEUMS

Musée d'Art et d'Archéologie de l'Université de Madagascar: B.P. 564, Antananarivo; f. 1970; research work, archaeological digs and camps; exhibitions, conferences; library of 1,500 vols.; Dir. J.-A. RAKOTOARISOA; publs. *Taloha*† (annual), *Travaux et Documents*† (2 a year).

Musée Historique: Palais de la Reine, Antananarivo.

UNIVERSITY

UNIVERSITÉ DE MADAGASCAR

CAMPUS UNIVERSITAIRE AMBOHITSAINA,
B.P. 566, ANTANANARIVO

Telephone: 260-00.

Founded 1961.

Rector: FRANÇOIS RAJAOSON.

Administrative Director: GUY RAKOTOVAO.

Library: *see* **Libraries.**

Number of teachers: 280.
Number of students: 21,000 (inc. regional centres).

REGIONAL CENTRES:

Antananarivo Regional Centre:

Department of Law, Economics, Business Studies, Sociology: Dir. P. ANDRIANOMANANA.

Department of Sciences: Dir. J. RABESIAKA.

Department of Letters: Dir. Mme J. RAMBELOSON.

Polytechnic Department: Dir. E. RAKOTOMARIA.

Department of Agriculture: Dir. G. RAVELOJAONA.

Department of Health Sciences: Dir. M. ANDRIANJATOVO

Antsiranana Regional Centre: Sec.-Gen. M. RADOFILAO.

Fianarantsoa Regional Centre: Sec.-Gen. M. RAVELONANOSY.

Mahajanga Regional Centre: Sec.-Gen. Mme. ANDRIANJATOVO.

Toamasina Regional Centre: Sec.-Gen. N. RANDRIAMIARISOA.

Toliary Regional Centre: Sec.-Gen. F. FANONY.

COLLEGE

Collège Rural d'Ambatobe: B.P. 1629, Antananarivo; Dir. M. ROGER RAJOELISOLO.

MALAWI

Population 5,561,000

LEARNED SOCIETIES AND RESEARCH INSTITUTES

British Council: P.O.B. 30222, Lilongwe 3; Rep. J. MULHOLLAND, O.B.E.; library (*see* below).

Geological Survey of Malawi: P.O.B. 27, Liwonde Rd., Zomba; f. 1921; geological mapping and surveys; mineral investigation, engineering, geology, geophysics, drilling, etc.; library of 5,000 vols.; Chief Geologist Dr. R. L. JOHNSON; publs. *Bulletins, Records, Memoirs.*

Malawi Library Association: P.O.B. 62, Zomba; f. 1976; *c.* 100 mems.; Chair. JOSEPH J. UTA; Sec. DICK D. NAJIRA; publ. *Bulletin.*

Ministry of Agriculture and Natural Resources: P.O.B. 30134, Capital City, Lilongwe 3; controls the following stations directly:

Chitedze Agricultural Research Station: P.O.B. 158, Lilongwe; f. 1948; conducts applied research into cereals, grain legumes, oil seeds, pasture and the general agronomy of the Central Region and into livestock improvement, especially of local Zebu cattle.

Bvumbwe Agricultural Research Station: P.O.B. 5748, Limbe; f. 1950 to conduct applied research into tree and horticultural crops, especially tung, macadamia, cashew and coffee, and the general agronomy of the Southern uplands.

Makhanga Agricultural Research Station: P.O.B. 20, Chiromo; f. 1953 to conduct applied research into the general agronomy of the Shire Valley, specializing in cotton and irrigated crops.

Lunyangwa Agricultural Research Station: P.O.B. 59, Mzuzu; f. 1968 to conduct applied research into the general agronomy of the Northern Region, specializing in rice, coffee, tea, cassava and pasture work.

Mbawa Agricultural Research Station: P.O.B. 8, Embangweni; f. 1953; applied research on the general agronomy of the S. Rukuru Valley.

Baka Agricultural Research Station: P.O.B. 43, Karonga; f. 1974; applied research on the general agronomy of the Karenga and Chitipa regions.

Shire Valley Research Programme: P.M.B. Ngabu; f. 1972; applied research on the general agronomy of the Shire Valley.

Fisheries Research Unit: P.O.B. 27, Monkey Bay; f. 1954; researches into fisheries of Lake Malawi.

Mikolongwe Livestock Improvement Centre: P.O.B. 5193, Limbe; f. 1955 to improve productive capacity of local Zebu cattle and fat tailed sheep; the station also contains the Poultry Improvement Unit and the Veterinary Staff training school.

Central Veterinary Laboratory: P.O.B. 517, Lilongwe; f. 1974; research into endemic diseases.

Veterinary Research Laboratory: P.O.B. 55, Blantyre; diagnostic laboratory.

Veterinary Research Laboratory: P.O.B. 8, Mzuzu; diagnostic laboratory.

Chitala Agricultural Research Station: Private Bag 13, Salima; f. 1978; part of Lakeshore Rural Development Programme.

Kasinthula Agricultural Research Station: P.O.B. 28, Chikwawa; f. 1976; irrigation research.

Lifuwu Agricultural Research Station: P.O.B. 102, Salima; f. 1973; rice research.

Forest Research Institute of Malawi: P.O.B. 270, Zomba; research into silviculture, tree breeding, pathology, entomology, soils, mycorrhizae and wood products.

The Ministry is also indirectly responsible for research work at the following stations:

Tea Research Foundation of Central Africa: P.O.B. 51, Mulanje; f. 1966 to promote research into tea production in Central and Southern Africa, and other tea producing regions; Dir. R. T. ELLIS.

Mwimba Tobacco Research Station: P.O.B. 224, Kasungu; f. 1979; applied research on improvement and production of flue cured, burley, fire cured, air and oriental tobaccos in Malawi.

Society of Malawi (*Historical and Scientific*): P.O.B. 125, Blantyre; f. 1948; study and records of history and natural sciences; 360 mems., including 100 overseas institutes; library of 1,000 vols.; Chair. G. D. HAYES, M.B.E.; Sec. Mrs. B. C. LAMPORT-STOKES; publ. *Journal* (2 a year).

LIBRARIES AND ARCHIVES

British Council Libraries: P.O.B. 30222, Lilongwe 3; f. 1963; 8,000 vols., 19 periodicals; Librarian (vacant); P.O.B. 456, Blantyre; f. 1951; 24,281 vols., 80 periodicals; Librarian H. T. ZIDYANI.

Malawi National Library Service: P.O.B. 30314, Lilongwe 3; f. 1968; 130,000 general and reference works; nationwide loan service; Dir. R. S. MABOMBA, A.L.A.; publs. *Annual Report*†, *Bulletin*†.

National Archives of Malawi: P.O.B. 62, Zomba; f. 1947, as branch of Central African Archives; became National Archives of Malawi 1964; public archives, records management, historical manuscripts, legal deposit library, films, microfilms, gramophone records, postage stamps, tapes and maps; 28,100 vols., 230 periodicals; Archivist S. S. MWIYERIWA, F.L.A.; publ. *Malawi National Bibliography*† (annual).

University of Malawi Library: P.O.B. 280, Zomba; f. 1965; 170,000 vols.; Librarian S. A. PATCHETT; publs. *Accessions List*† (quarterly), *Report to Senate*† (annually).

U.S. Information Service Library: St. Andrew's St., Blantyre, P.O.B. 589; 4,000 vols.

MUSEUM

Museums of Malawi, The: P.O.B. 30360, Blantyre 3; f. 1959; Curator N. G. M. MKANDAWIRE.

UNIVERSITY

UNIVERSITY OF MALAWI

P.O.B. 278, ZOMBA
Telephone: Zomba 2394.
Founded 1964.

Language of instruction: English; Private control; Academic year: September to July.

Chancellor: H.E. Dr. H. KAMUZU BANDA, M.D., F.R.C.S.
Vice-Chancellor: Prof. DAVID KIMBLE, O.B.E., PH.D.
Registrar: R. B. MBAYA, B.A., D.P.A.
Librarian: S. A. PATCHETT, M.LIB.SC.

Number of teachers: 163.
Number of students: 1,523.

Publications: *Biannual University Calendar*†, *Umodzi, University Magazine, Register of Graduates and Diplomates*†, *Research Report to Senate, Bunda College Research Bulletin, Journal of Social Science.*

CONSTITUENT INSTITUTES:

Bunda College of Agriculture: P.O.B. 219, Lilongwe.
Principal: N. F. LUNGU, PH.D.
Registrar: W. E. MVALO, B.A.

The library contains: 22,000 vols.
Number of teachers: 31.
Number of students: 373.

DEAN:

School of Agriculture: Dr. N. F. LUNGU.

PROFESSORS:

BOSHOF, W. H., PH.D., Agricultural Engineering
BUTTERWORTH, M. H., PH.D., Livestock Production
LAWSON, E. C., M.SC., PH.D., Agricultural Engineering
MUGHOGHO, L. K., PH.D., Crop Production

Chancellor College: P.O.B. 278, Zomba.
Principal: B. B. CHIMPHAMBA, M.SC., PH.D., F.L.S.
Registrar: H. H. LONGWE, B.A.

The library contains 124,444 vols.
Number of teachers: 88.
Number of students: 692.

DEANS:

School of Arts: (vacant).
School of Science: J. P. G. EWER.
School of Education: E. D. KADZOMBE.
School of Law and Public Administration: (vacant).
School of Social Science: Dr. Z. D. KADZAMIRA.

PROFESSORS:

BONE, R. C., M.A., Education
LEISTEN, J. A., PH.D., F.R.I.C., Chemistry
MAZUMDAR, H. K., M.A., M.S.S., D.SC., Economics
MCCRACKEN, J., History
ROSCOE, A. A., M.A., PH.D., English
SOM, A. K., M.SC., PH.D., F.I.P., Physics

Malawi Polytechnic: P.B. 303, Chichiri, Blantyre 3.
Principal: A. V. KAMBALAMETORE, M.SC.
Registrar: J. E. CHIPETA, B.A.

The library contains 36,618 vols.
Number of teachers: 31.
Number of students: 323.

DEANS:

School of Business and Liberal Studies: J. R. NESBITT.
School of Technology: D. A. BROAD.

PROFESSOR:

JOHNS, W. D. A., B.ENG., F.I.C.E., Engineering

Kamuzu College of Nursing: P.B. 1, Lilongwe.
Principal: Mrs. G. S. MPUTENI, S.R.N. (acting).
Registrar: E. T. CHIBWEYA, B.A (acting).

The library contains 6,000 vols.
Number of teachers: 13.
Number of students: 135.

MALAYSIA

Population 12,700,000

LEARNED SOCIETIES AND RESEARCH INSTITUTES

Alliance Française: 15 Lorong Gurney, Kuala Lumpur 15-01; French cultural association and school of French language; library of 4,500 vols.; brs. in Petaling-Jaya and Ipoh; Pres. TUNKU NAQUIYUDDIN; Dir. STÉPHAN CHARRAS.

Asia Foundation: 197-7 Jalan Ampang, Kuala Lumpur 16-03; f. 1954 as one of 12 branches of the main organization in the U.S.A. (*q.v.*); to assist local institutions and organizations concerned with educational and socio-economic development; Rep. LAWRENCE T. FORMAN.

British Council: P.O.B. 539, Jalan Bukit Aman, Kuala Lumpur 10-01; library (*see* Libraries); Rep. E. T. J. PHILLIPS; P.O.B. 746, Kota Kinabalu, Sabah; Regional Rep. J. L. DOBSON; P.O.B. 615, Kuching, Sarawak; Regional Rep. M. D. SARGENT.

Dewan Bahasa dan Pustaka (*Language and Literary Agency of the Ministry of Education*): P.O.B. 803, Kuala Lumpur 08–08; f. 1956 to develop and enrich the Malay language and literature, to standardize spelling and terminology, including technical terms, etc. in Malay, to print and publish books, dictionaries, magazines, etc. in Malay and other languages; library of 51,394 vols.; Chair. of Board Tan Sri Haji Sh. HAMDAN BIN TAHIR; Dir.-Gen. Datuk Haji HASSAN AHMAD; publs. *Dewan Bahasa, Dewan Masyarakat, Dewan Sastera, Dewan Budaya, Dewan Siswa, Dewan Pelajar* (each monthly), *Tenggara* (2 a year).

Division of Agriculture: Ministry of Agriculture, Kuala Lumpur; f. 1906; undertakes all aspects of research and extension for improvement of agricultural crops and disseminates information among the farming community; library of *c.* 60,000 vols.; Dir. MOHAMAD BIN JAMIL, J.M.N.; publs. *Malaysian Agricultural Journal, Technical Bulletins, Leaflets in Vernacular and English, Statistical Digest.*

Forest Research Institute: Kepong, Selangor; f. 1929; consists of 1,480 acres of experimental plantations, an arboretum of over 250 different species, a small coniferetum, a nursery, a museum, a herbarium of nearly 95,000 sheets of tree species, a large bark collection, a wood collection of nearly 8,000 specimens, and a library of 12,000 vols.; branches in Silviculture, Forest Mensuration, Forest Botany and Ecology, Timber Research, Entomology, Chemistry and Wood Identification, Plant Pathology, Statistics, Soil Science; Dir. Forestry and Wood Products Research Encik ISMAIL BIN HAJI JOHARI; publs. *The Malayan Forester, The Malayan Forest Records, Malayan Forest Research Pamphlets.* Attached to the Institute is a Forest School training 90 Malay forest subordinates each year; courses in timber identification held annually, also a newly established Forest College to train 30 sub-professional Forest Officers by a three-year course.

Freshwater Fisheries Research Station: Batu Berendam, Malacca; f. 1957; research on freshwater fish and ponds, water chemistry, fish nutrition and fish reproductive physiology; crustacean biology with special emphasis on *Macrobrachium rosenbergii*; library of 3,000 vols.; Head AHMAD TAJUDDIN BIN ZAINUDDIN.

Geological Survey of Malaysia: Scrivenor Rd., Ipoh, Perak; f. 1903; 619 mems.; basic geological information on East and West Malaysia with special emphasis on mineral resources; library of 13,000 vols. (East Malaysia), 19,500 vols. (West Malaysia); Dir. S. K. CHUNG, Deputy Dir. D. SANTOKH SINGH; publs. *Annual Reports, Regional Memoirs, Reports* and *Bulletins* (East), *Map Bulletins, Economic Bulletins, District Memoirs, Annual Reports* and *Professional Papers* (West).

Geological Survey of Malaysia: Kuching, Sarawak; f. 1949; 69 mems.; geological mapping, mineral investigations, engineering geology, hydrogeology; library of 13,000 vols.; Principal Geologist C. H. KHO; publs. *Annual Report*†, *Bulletin, Geological Papers, Memoirs, Reports.*

Geological Survey of Malaysia: Kota Kinabalu, Sabah; f. 1949; 32 mems.; geological mapping, mineral investigations, engineering geology, hydrogeology; library of 2,500 vols.; Principal Geologist D. T. C. LEE; publs. *Annual Report*†, *Bulletin, Geological Papers, Memoirs, Reports.*

Goethe-Institut (*German Cultural Centre*): 1 Jalan Langgak Golf, P.O.B. 178, Kuala Lumpur; f. 1958; library of 8,000 vols.; Dir. Dr. RUDOLF EPPEL.

Institute for Medical Research (IMR): Jalan Pahang, Kuala Lumpur 02-14; f. 1900; now research branch of Ministry of Health; undergraduate and postgraduate training; WHO Centre for Research and Training in Tropical Diseases and Nutrition for the West Pacific Region; National Centre for Tropical Medicine, SEAMEO; library of 18,350 vols.; 591 teachers; Dir. Dr. G. F. DE WITT, PH.D., C.CHEM., F.R.S.C., F.M.I.C., A.M.; publs. *Bulletin, Study, Annual Report.*

Malayan Nature Society: P.O.B. 750, Kuala Lumpur; f. 1940; an independent society to promote an interest in natural history in Malaya and the surrounding region; *c.* 1,100 mems.; small library; Pres. Dr. SALLEH MOHD. NOR; Vice-Pres. Dr. P. N. AVADHANI; Hon. Sec. Dr. F. S. P. NG; publ. *The Malayan Nature Journal* (quarterly).

Malaysian Agricultural Research and Development Institute (MARDI): Bag Berkunci 202, Pejabat Pos U.P.M., Serdang, Selangor, West Malaysia; f. 1969; an autonomous organization which conducts scientific, technical, economic and sociological research in Malaysia with respect to the production, utilization and processing of all crops (except rubber), livestock and fresh-water fisheries; Dir.-Gen. Dato' MOHD. TAMIN b. YEOP; publs. *MARDI Research Bulletin*†, *MARDI Reports*†, *Annual Reports*†.

Malaysian Biochemical Society: c/o Biochemistry Dept., University of Malaya, Kuala Lumpur; f. 1973; talks and seminars, annual conference; 110 mems.; Pres. Dr. OO KHAIK CHEANG; Sec. Dr. WANG CHEE WOON; publ. *Proceedings of Annual Conference*†.

Malaysian Branch of the Royal Asiatic Society: Arkib Negara Malaysia, Jl. Sultan, Petaling Jaya; f. 1877 for the increase and diffusion of knowledge of the territories of Malaysia, Singapore, and Brunei; 954 mems.;

Pres. Tun MOHAMED SUFFIAN BIN HASHIM; Hon. Sec. Tan Sri Datuk MUBIN SHEPPARD; publs. *Journal* (2 a year), monographs, reprints.

Malaysian Historical Society: 958 Jl. Hose, Kuala Lumpur; f. 1953; activities include restoration and preservation of historical sites; 160 indiv. and institutional mems.; Pres. Dato HUSSEIN ONN; publs. *Malaysia in History, Malaysia Dari Segi Sejarah* (every 2 years).

Malaysian Institute of Architects: 4–6 Jl. Tangsi, P.O.B. 855, Kuala Lumpur; f. 1948; 648 mems.; Pres. K. C. CHEANG; publs. *Berita Akitek*† (monthly), *Majallah Akitek*† (quarterly), *Panduan Akitek*† (annually).

Malaysian Library Association: Peti Surat 2545, Kuala Lumpur; f. 1959; Pres. Mrs. RAGAYAH Dato' Hj. MOHD. EUSOFF; Sec. Miss NOOR AINI OSMAN.

Malaysian Rubber Research and Development Board: 150 Jl. Ampang, P.O.B. 508, Kuala Lumpur 04–06; f. 1959 to plan and determine policies and programmes for natural rubber research, technical development and promotion nationally and worldwide; to collate and interpret information pertaining to the rubber industry; to co-ordinate all research, development and publicity financed by the Board; dependent units are the Rubber Research Institute of Malaysia (*see* below), the Malaysian Rubber Producers' Research Association, U.K., and 15 Malaysian Rubber Bureaux located in 11 major rubber consuming areas; Controller of Rubber Research and Chair. Tan Sri Dr. B. C. SEKHAR; publs. *Annual Report, Malaysian Rubber Review* (irregular), *Natural Rubber News* (monthly), *Getah Asli* (quarterly), *Rubber Developments* (quarterly), *Rubber Products Bulletin* (quarterly), *Natural Rubber Technology* (quarterly).

Malaysian Scientific Association: P.O.B. 911, Kuala Lumpur; f. 1954; 170 mems., engaged in scientific and technological work; Pres. Tan Sri Dr. B. C. SEKHAR; Hon. Sec. Prof. Dr. J. I. FURTADO.

Malaysian Zoological Society: 301 Lee Yan Lian Bldg., Jalan Tun Perak, Kuala Lumpur; Pres. Y. B. Encik MOHD. KHIR JOHARI; Chair. Y. B. Tan Sri Dato V. M. HUTSON; Sec.-Treas. YUEN TANG & Co.

Rubber Research Institute of Malaysia: P.O.B. 150, Kuala Lumpur 01-02; est. 1925, operates under the Rubber Research Institute of Malaysia (R.R.I.M.) Extension and Amendment Bill, 1972; consists of a Directorate, 13 Divisions, 3 sections, research laboratories, 2 experimental stations of over 6,000 acres; engaged in research, extension services, technical advisory service and information on all aspects of rubber production; library of *c.* 70,000 vols. (including bound periodicals); number of senior staff 212.

Director: Haji ANI BIN AROPE, J.M.N., K.M.N., M.SC.

Deputy Director (Research): NG ENG KOK, J.S.M., PH.D.

Deputy Director (Administration): ABDUL WAHAB BIN ABDULLAH, K.M.N., J.M.N., B.A.

HEADS OF DIVISIONS:

Analytical Chemistry: M. M. SINGH, J.S.M., PH.D., F.R.I.C., F.M.I.C., F.M.S.A.

Applied Chemistry and Development: CHEONG SAI FAH, M.SC., P.R.I., A.P.R.I., A.N.C.R.T.

Applied Economics: ABDULLAH BIN SEPIEN, M.SC.AGR.

Advisory Services: ARIFFIN BIN MOHD. NOR, M.B.A., D.SC.

Crop Protection and Microbiology: ABDUL AZIZ BIN SHEIKH ABDUL KADIR, PH.D.

RRIM Station, Kota Tinggi: CHEN KIM KOY, A.I.S.P., A.M.B.I.M.

Experimental Station, Sungei Buloh: MOHD. SHARIF BIN KUDIN, M.SC.

Plant Science: YOON POOI KONG, PH.D.

Polymer Chemistry and Physics: A. SUBRAMANIAM, PH.D.

Publications, Library and Information Division: J. S. SOOSAI, B.SC., F.L.A., A.I.INF.SC.

Soils and Crop Management: E. PUSHPARAJAH, D.SC., M.I.BIOL., F.M.S.A.

Specifications and Quality Control: AMLIR BIN AZIZ, M.SC., A.N.C.R.T., A.P.R.I.

Smallholders Project Research: P. D. ABRAHAM, J.S.M., PH.D., F.I.BIOL., F.M.S.A.

Statistics: G. CHIDAMBARA IYER, M.SC.

Technology: SEKARAN NAIR, J.S.M., PH.D., F.P.R.I., F.M.S.A., A.R.I.C., A.I.K.M.

Training, Personnel and Staff Development: SAMSUDIN BIN TUGIMAN, PH.D.

Publs. *Journal of the R.R.I.M.* (3 a year), *Jurnal Sains* (Malay, 2 a year), *Planters' Bulletin* (quarterly), *Chung Tze Jen Chee Ken* (Mandarin, quarterly), *Siaran Pekebun* (Malay, quarterly), *Annual Report, Planting Manual, Divisional Reports*. Also books, monographs, pamphlets, etc., on specific topics in three languages.

Standards and Industrial Research Institute of Malaysia (SIRIM): P.O.B. 35, Shah Alam, Selangor; f. 1975 by merger of National Institute of Scientific and Industrial Research and the Standards Institution of Malaysia; facilitates industrial development through research into existing and future problems relating to engineering and production of processed and fabricated industrial products; provides a range of technical services that include quality assurance, metrology, industry testing, technology modification and improvement, consultancy, industrial information and extension services; undertakes applied research and prototype production to adapt or modify known processes and technologies; finds new uses for locally available raw materials and by-products, and develops new products and processes based on indigenous raw materials; the drafting and publications of Malaysian standards and standards testing; library of 7,000 vols., 150,000 standard specifications, 400 periodicals; Controller ABDULLAH BIN MOHD. YUSOF; Dirs. Dr. ABDUL RAHIM BIN BIDIN (Research), LIM HO PHENG (Standards), MOHAMAD BIN ANAS (Admin.); publs. *News Bulletin*†, *Annual Report*†, *Malaysian Standards*.

Tamil Language Society: c/o Department of Indian Studies, University of Malaya, Kuala Lumpur; f. 1957; 350 mems.; aims at the promotion and propagation of the Tamil language and Indian culture; Pres. M. JAYAKUMAR; Hon. Sec. L. KRISHNAN; publs. *Tamil Oli*† (Tamil, English and Bahasa Malaysia, annual).

U.S. International Communication Agency: AIA Bldg., Jl. Ampang, Kuala Lumpur; branch: Lincoln Cultural Center, 181 Jl. Ampang, Kuala Lumpur; lending library of 10,000 vols.; reference and current awareness service; Chief Librarian CH'NG KIM SEE; publs. *Bibliography, Portfolio* (irregular).

LIBRARIES

British Council Libraries: P.O.B. 539, Jalan Bukit Aman, Kuala Lumpur 01-02; f. 1952; 33,182 vols., 219 periodicals; Librarian N. WILKINSON, F.L.A.; brs. in Penang (P.O.B. 595), f. 1971; 4,929 vols., 77 periodicals; Librarian Miss LOI GEN YOK; Kota Kinabalu (P.O.B. 746), f. 1961; 7,534 vols., 68 periodicals; Librarian Miss N. T. GOMES.

Carnegie Free Library: Jalan Doktor, Kota Bharu, Kelantan; f. 1938; 1,936 vols.; Librarian The Chief Education Officer, Kelantan.

Kuala Lumpur Public Library: Sam Mansion, Jalan Tuba, Kuala Lumpur; f. 1966; 45,000 vols.; Librarian SOONG WAN YOONG.

Malacca Public Library Corporation: First Floor, Hang Tuah Hall, Hang Tuah Rd., Malacca; f. 1977; 16,000 vols.; Librarian RIHANUN BTE MD. SAMIN.

Ministry of Agriculture and Rural Development Library: Swettenham Rd., Kuala Lumpur 10-02; 60,000 vols.; publs. *Bulletin*† (irregular), *Malaysian Agricultural Journal*† (4 issues in 2 years).

National Archives and Library of Malaysia: f. 1971; comprising the National Archives of Malaysia and National Library of Malaysia; Dir.-Gen. Mrs. ZAKIAH HANUM (acting).

National Archives of Malaysia: Federal Government Building, Jalan Sultan, Petaling Jaya; f. 1957; public records, archives, audio-visual records, private and business records; Prime Minister's archives, Tun Abdul Razak Memorial Library; reference library of 2,000 vols.; Deputy Dir. Mrs. ZAKIAH HANUM NOR; publs. *Annual Report, Accessions list 1957–1967, Hervey Papers, National Archives of Malaysia, Swettenham Papers, Records management manual.*

National Library of Malaysia: 7th Floor, U.M.B.C. Bldg., Jalan Sultan Sulaiman, Kuala Lumpur 01-33; f. 1971; under provisions of the National Library Act, 1972, it is responsible for making available information resources and services, co-ordinating the library resources of the nation and promoting a nationwide system of public libraries; provides reference, information and bibliographical services, operates Preservation of Books Act, 1966, legal depository for Malaysian, UNESCO and ASEAN publications; library of 43,500 vols.; Deputy Dir. D. E. K. WIJASURIYA; Asst. Dir. Miss PHILOMENA NG SOO CHING; publs. *Annual Report, Malaysian National Bibliography* (quarterly), *Malaysian Periodicals Index* (annual), *Standard Headings for Malaysian Statutory Bodies.*

Penang Public Library: Dewan Sri Pinang 2nd Floor, Penang; f. 1817, reorganized 1973; 37,000 vols.; Chair. YANG BERHORMAT ENCHE KHALID AHMAD BIN SULAIMAN; Librarian Miss G. S. KHOO (acting).

Perpustakaan Sultan Ismail: Jalan Dato Onn, Johore Bahru; f. 1964; administered by the Town Council; 10,100 mems.; 40,600 vols. in Chinese, English, Malay and Tamil; Librarian (vacant); publ. *Lapuran Tahunan (Annual Report)*†.

Rubber Research Institute of Malaysia Library: P.O.B. 150, Kuala Lumpur; est. 1925; 75,000 vols., including a multilingual coverage of publications on the Agricultural, Chemical and Technological, Statistical and Economical aspects of Natural Rubber; Librarian J. S. SOOSAI, B.SC., F.L.A., A.I.INF.SC.; publs. *Bibliographies, Recent Additions to the Library, List of RRIM Translations.*

Sabah State Libraries (Perpustakaan Negeri Sabah): P.O.B. 1136, Kota Kinabalu, Sabah; f. 1953; now a state department within the Ministry of Culture, Youth and Sports (Sabah); public reference and lending library of 221,600 vols., mainly in Bahasa Malaysia, English and Chinese; special local history collection on Borneo; comprises 16 brs. (in addition to main library) and 3 mobile libraries for rural areas; Dir. ADELINE LEONG.

Sarawak State Library: Jalan Jawa, Kuching; f. 1950; administered by the Ministry of Local Government; 150,000 vols. in Bahassa Malaysia, English, Iban and Chinese; Librarian JOHNNY K. S. KUEH.

Selangor Public Library: 21 Jalan Raja, Kuala Lumpur; f. 1971; 317,000 vols.; 6 brs. and 10 mobile units; Chief Librarian Mrs. SHAHANEEM MUSTAFA; publs. *Annual Report*†, *Accession List*†.

Tun Abdul Razak Library: Mara Institute of Technology, Shah Alam, Selangor; f. 1960; 150,000 vols.; collections of maps, prints, films, slides, cassettes and microfilms; Librarian Mrs. RUGAYAH ABDUL RASHID.

Tun Razak Library: Jl. Club, Ipoh, Perak; f. 1931; special collections on Malaysia and Singapore; UNESCO depository; special language section; 143,466 vols. in English, Chinese, Malay and Tamil; Librarian CHANG SINN NEAN, A.L.A.; publs. *Annual Reports, Malaysiana Collection*, quarterly accession lists.

University of Malaya Library: Pantai Valley, Kuala Lumpur; f. 1957; 683,316 vols., of which 633,905 are in Western languages; Librarian (vacant).

MUSEUMS

National Museum of Malaysia (Muzium Negara): Jalan Damansara, Kuala Lumpur; f. 1963; houses collections of ethnographical, archaeological and zoological materials; comprehensive reference library on Malaysia and many Asian subjects, reference collections of archaeology, zoology and ethnography are also preserved in the Perak Museum, Taiping; Dir.-Gen. SHAHRUM BIN YUB, B.A., A.M.A.; publ. *Federation Museums Journal.*

Penang Museum and Art Gallery: Farquhar St., Penang; f. 1963; Chair., Penang State Museum Board, Capt. Dato Haji MOHAMED NOOR BIN MOHAMED, D.S.P.N., J.S.M., P.J.K., E.D., J.P.; Curator Encik KHOO BOO CHIA; publ. *Annual Report*†.

Perak Museum: Taiping, Perak; f. 1883; antiquities, Perak archives, ethnography, zoology and a library; Dir.-Gen. SHAHRUM BIN YUB, B.A., A.M.A.

Sabah Museum: Kota Kinabalu; f. 1886, destroyed in Second World War, reopened 1965; anthropological, archaeological and natural history and historical collections; Curator DAVID W. MCCREDIE, B.SC., F.R.G.S.

Sarawak Museum: Jl. Tun Hj. Openg, Kuching; f. 1886; anthropological and ethnological collections; reference library; State archives; Curator and Government Ethnologist BENEDICT SANDIN; publ. *Sarawak Museum Journal.*

UNIVERSITIES

UNIVERSITI KEBANGSAAN MALAYSIA
(National University of Malaysia)

BANGI, SELANGOR

Telephone: 03-331500, 03-331211, 03-331099.

Founded 1970.

Languages of instruction: Malay and English; Academic year: from June.

Chancellor: Tuanku JAAFAR Ibni AL-MARHUM Tuanku ABDUL RAHMAN.
Vice-Chancellor: Prof. Datuk Dr. AWANG HAD BIN SALLEH.
Deputy Vice-Chancellors: Prof. Datuk MOHD. GHAZALI BIN HAJI ABDUL RAHMAN, Dr. MOHD. YUSOF BIN MOHD. NOR.
Registrar: SYED ARABI IDID.
Librarian: ZAINAL AZMAN BIN RAJUDIN (acting).

Library of 258,499 vols.
Number of teachers: 860.
Number of students: 5,745.

Publs. *University Calendar* (annually), *Journal of Education* (annually), *Jernal Akademika, Jernal Sains Malaysiana, Jernal Ekonomi, Jernal Perubatan, Jernal Ilmu Alam, Jernal Islamia*† (2 a year).

DEANS:

Faculty of Economics: Dr. MOHD. SHEFFIE BIN ABU BAKAR.
Faculty of Islamic Studies: Dr. ISMAIL BIN HAJI IBRAHIM.
Faculty of Medicine: Prof. Datuk Dr. ABDUL HAMID BIN ABDUL RAHMAN.
Faculty of Science: Dr. MOHD. ZAWAWI BIN HAJI ISMAIL.
Faculty of Social Sciences and Humanities: Dr. ABDUL HALIM BIN OTHMAN (acting).
Faculty of Business Management: Dr. NIK ABDUL RASHID BIN ISMAIL.
Faculty of Science and Natural Resources: Dr. MOHD. YUSOF BIN ABDUL HAMID.

PROFESSORS:

ABDUL HAMID BIN ABDUL RAHMAN, Anaesthesiology
ISMAIL BIN SAAD, Radiology
MOHD. GHAZALI BIN HAJI ABDUL RAHMAN, Biochemistry
MUHAMMAD BIN HAJI SALLEH, Literature
NORAMLY BIN MUSLIM, Chemistry
QUAZI M. IQBAL, Orthopaedics
SYED MOHD. NAGUIB AL-ATTAS, Institute of Malay Language, Literature and Culture
TJIA HONG DJIN, Geology
TIN OHN, Medicine
ZAINAL ABIDIN BIN ABDUL WAHID, History

UNIVERSITI TEKNOLOGI MALAYSIA

(Technological University of Malaysia)

JALAN GURNEY, KUALA LUMPUR 15-01

Telephone: 929033.

Telex: 30090.

Founded 1954 as a Technical College; University status 1972.

State control; Language of instruction: Bahasa Malaysia; Academic year: June to March.

Chancellor: DYMM Sultan ISMAIL IBNI AL-MARHUM SULTAN IBRAHIM.

Vice-Chancellor: Tan Sri AINUDDIN BIN ABDUL WAHID.

Deputy Vice-Chancellor (Student Affairs): Encik ABDUL HAMID BIN MOHD. TAHIR.

Deputy Vice-Chancellor (Administration): YB Prof. Madya Dato ABDUL AZIZ BIN DIN.

Registrar: AZMIL BIN MOHD. DAUD.

Bursar: Mrs. AZIZAH BINTI ZAHARI.

Librarian: PUAN HAJJAH CHE SHAM BTE HAJI MOHD. DARUS.

The library contains 52,000 vols.

Number of teachers: 410.
Number of students: 3,582.

Publications: *Annual Report, University Bulletin, Calendar, Guidance Book* (annually), *UTM in Brief* (irregularly).

DEANS:

Faculty of Civil Engineering: ISHAK ABDUL RAHMAN.

Faculty of Mechanical Engineering: Encik ABU BAKAR BIN HAMID.

Faculty of Electrical Engineering: ISHAK BIN ISMAIL.

Faculty of Built Environment: PARID WARDI BIN SUDIN.

Faculty of Surveying: Encik ABDUL WAHID BIN HAJI IDRIS.

Centre for Science Studies: YB Tan Sri Dato Haji AINUDDIN BIN ABDUL WAHID (Chair.).

Centre for Humanities Studies: Encik ABDUL HAMID BIN AWANG (Chair.).

HEADS OF DEPARTMENTS:

Faculty of Civil Engineering:
Soil Mechanics and Geology: Encik MOHD. ZAIN BIN HAJI YUSOFF.
Environmental Engineering: Encik MOHD. KHANAFIAH BIN HAMIDON.
Structures and Materials: Encik ZAINAI BIN MOHAMED.
Hydraulics and Hydrology: (vacant).

Faculty of Electrical Engineering:
Electrical Power: Encik ZAINAL ARIPIN BIN ZAKARIAH.
Electrical Control: SHAHAMI BIN HAJI SHAFIEE.
Electrical Communication: Dr. MOHD. ARIF BIN NUN.

Faculty of Mechanical Engineering:
Thermofluids: Ir. AZLIR BIN DARISUN.
Mechanical Design: Encik ABDUL GHANI BIN MOHD.
Petroleum: Encik MOHD. SHARIFUDDIN BIN MOHYIDDIN.

Faculty of Built Environment:
Architecture: Encik SHARUDDIN BIN MD. YUNUS.
Urban and Regional Planning: Encik AMIRUDDIN BIN ABU BAKAR.
Quantity Surveying: Encik MAHMUD BIN ABD. HAMID.

Faculty of Surveying:
Property Management and Valuation: Encik MOHD AZMI BIN ARIFFIN.
Photogrammetry and Cartography: Encik MOHD. IBRAHIM BIN SEENI MOHD.
Geodesy and Astronomy: Encik AYOB BIN SHARIFF.
Engineering and Cadastral Surveying: Encik ROSLI BIN AHMAD.

Centre for Science Studies:
Chemistry: Encik MOHD. HUSSAIN IBRAHIM.
Physics: Encik SABIRIN BIN HAJI IKHSAN.
Mathematics: Encik M. JOGARAJAN.

Centre for Humanities Studies:
Social Sciences: Tuan Haji NASSERI BIN HAJI TAIB.
Education: Encik ABU BAKAR BIN HAJI HASHIM.

UNIVERSITI PERTANIAN MALAYSIA

(University of Agriculture)

SERDANG, SELANGOR

Telephone: (03) 356304, 355426-9.

Founded 1973.

Languages of instruction: English and Malay; Academic year: June to April (two terms).

Chancellor: The SULTAN OF SELANGOR.

Vice-Chancellor: Prof. Tan Sri Datuk MOHD. RASHDAN BIN HAJI BABA, PH.D.

Registrar: SHAHDAN BIN ASRI, B.A., M.P.A.

Librarian: SYED SALIM AGHA, B.SC., A.L.A.

Director of Sarawak Branch Campus: IBRAHIM BIN MOHD. YUSOF, PH.D.

Total staff: 272.
Number of students: 3,100.

Publications: *Universiti Pertanian Handbook, Universiti Pertanian Calendar, Faculty Handbook, Newsletter.*

DEANS:

Faculty of Agriculture: Prof. MOHAMAD ZAIN BIN HJ. ABDUL KARIM, M.AGR.SC., PH.D.

Faculty of Forestry: YUSOF HADI, M.F.S.

Faculty of Veterinary Medicine and Animal Science: Prof. OMAR BIN ABDUL RAHMAN, PH.D., M.R.L.V.S.

Faculty of Educational Services: Prof. ATAN BIN LONG, PH.D.

Centre for Extension and Continuing Education: NAYAN BIN ARIFFIN, PH.D.

Faculty of Science and Environmental Studies: Dr. ARIFFIN BIN SUHAIMI, PH.D.

Faculty of Agricultural Engineering: CHOA SWEE LIN, M.S.
Faculty of Resource Economics and Agribusiness: Dr. RADZUAN BIN ABDUL RAHMAN, PH.D.

UNIVERSITI MALAYA
(University of Malaya)

LEMBAH PANTAI, KUALA LUMPUR 22-11

Telephone: 560022.

Founded 1962.

Languages of instruction: Bahasa Malaysia and English; State control; Academic year: June to February (three terms).

Chancellor: Duli Yang Maha Mulia Tuanku Hajjah BAHIYAH BINTI ALMARHUM TUANKU ABDUL RAHMAN, D.K., D.K.H., D.M.N.

Pro-Chancellor: YANG AMAT ARIF KETUA HAKIM NEGARA Tun MOHAMED SUFFIAN BIN HASHIM, S.S.M., P.S.M., J.M.N., S.M.B., P.J.K., M.A., LL.B., BAR.-AT-LAW.

Vice-Chancellor: Prof. UNGKU ABDUL AZIZ, D.ECONS.

Deputy Vice-Chancellors: Prof. AHMAD NAWAWI BIN HJ. AYOB, PH.D., L. J. FREDERICKS, M.B.A., AGR.DR., ZAINAL KLING, PH.D.

Registrar: LIM CHUNG TAT, K.M.N., B.A.

Librarian: (vacant).

Number of teachers: 1,157.

Number of students: 8,644 full-time, 319 part-time.

Publications: *University of Malaya Calendar*†, *Annual Report*†, *University of Malaya Gazette*† (all annual).

DEANS:

Faculty of Arts and Social Sciences: Prof. MOHD. TAIB BIN OSMAN, M.A., PH.D., J.S.M.
Faculty of Dentistry: Prof. IBRAHIM BIN HAJI MOHAMMED YASSIN, J.S.M., P.J.K., L.D.S., D.P.D.
Faculty of Economics and Administration: ABDUL GHANI BIN HJ. OTHMAN, M.POL.ECON.
Faculty of Education: Prof. ISAHAK BIN HARON, M.ED., PH.D.
Faculty of Engineering: Dr. TENGKU MOHD. AZZMAN SHARIFFADEEN BIN TENGKU IBRAHIM, M.SC., PH.D.
Faculty of Law: Prof. AHMAD BIN MOHAMMED IBRAHIM, J.M.N., M.A., BAR.-AT-LAW.
Faculty of Medicine: Prof. K. SOMASUNDARAM, M.B.B.S., F.R.C.S.ED., F.R.C.S.
Faculty of Science: Prof. HO COY CHOKE, PH.D.
Institute of Advanced Studies: Prof. V. NAVARATNARAJAH, M.ENG.SC., M.I.C.E., M.I.E.(M).

PROFESSORS:

ABDUL KAHAR BADOR, PH.D., Sociology
ABDUL MAJEED MOHAMED MACKEEN, PH.D., Islamic Studies
ABU BAKAR BIN ABDUL HAMID, M.A., Creative and Descriptive Writing
AHMAD BIN MOHAMMED IBRAHIM, M.A., Malaysian Law
AHMAD NAWAWI, PH.D., Botany
ASMAH HAJI OMAR, PH.D., Malay Linguistics
AWANG HAD BIN SALLEH, PH.D., D.S.D.K., J.M.N., Social Psychology
BALASUBRANAMIAM, P., M.B.B.S., F.R.C.S., Orthopaedic Surgery
CHAI HON CHAN, M.A., ED.D., Sociology
CHAN KAI CHEONG, F.R.I.C., M.SC., PH.D., Organic Chemistry
CHANDRAN, J. M., M.A., PH.D., Asian History
CHANG CHONG SING, P., PH.D., Pharmacology
CHEN CHIEH YEE, P., M.P.H., S.M.HYG., M.B.B.S., Social and Preventive Medicine
CHENG MEE CHOOI, PH.D., Applied Mathematics
CHONG KONG MING, M.SC., PH.D., Pure Mathematics
DELIKAN, A. E., F.F.A.R.C.S., M.B.B.S., Anaesthesiology
DHALIWAL, S. S., M.SC., PH.D., Genetics and Cellular Biology
FATIMAH HAMID-DON, M.A., PH.D., Curriculum Development
FRANKE, W., DR.PHIL., Chinese Studies
FURTADO, J. I. D. R., PH.D., Zoology
GILLINGS, B. R. D., PH.D., M.S., F.R.A.C.D.S., Dental Prosthetics
HO COY CHOKE, PH.D., Microbiology
HUTCHISON, C. S., PH.D., F.G.S., Applied Geology
IBRAHIM BIN HAJI MOHD. YASSIN, J.S.M., F.J.K., L.D.S., D.P.D., Preventive Dentistry
ISAHAK BIN HARON, M.ED., PH.D., Pedagogical Studies
ISMAIL BIN HUSSEIN, Drs., M.A., Malay Literature
JAIN, M. P., LL.M., J.S.D., Public Law
JOSEPH, K. T., M.AGR.SC., PH.D., Land Use Study
KARIM, M. A., PH D., Anatomy
KHOO KAY KIM, M.A., PH.D., Malaysian History
KUMAR DAS, V. G., PH.D., Inorganic Chemistry
LAM KHUAN LENG, D.C.H., M.R.C.P., M.B.B.S., Paediatrics
LEE POH AUN, PH.D., Statistical Mathematics
LEE SENG GUAN, Datuk, P.S.D., L.D.S., F.D.S.R.C.S., Conservative Dentistry
LOH THIAM GHEE, M.B.B.S., M.R.C.P., M.R.C.P.(GLAS.), M.R.C.P.(E.), Medicine
LOKE KWONG HUNG, M.SC., PH.D., F.R.S.C., Biochemistry
MOHAMMED TAIB BIN OSMAN, M.A., PH.D., Malay Studies
MOKHTAR BIN TAMIN, M.SC., PH.D., Rural Development
NAVARATNARAJAH, V., B.SC.(ENG.), M.I.C.E., M.I.E.(CEYL.), M.I.E.(M.), M.ENG.EC., Civil Engineering
NG SOON, M.S., PH.D., Physical Chemistry
PRATHAP, K., M.D., M.R.C.PATH., Pathology
RAMAN, A., M.B.B.S., M.D., PH.D., Physiology
SINNATHURAY, T. A., M.B.B.S., M.D., F.I.C.S., F.R.C.S.ED., F.R.C.S., F.R.C.O.G., Obstetrics and Gynaecology
SOEPADMO, E., PH.D., Ecology
SOMASUNDRAM, K., M.B.B.S., F.R.C.S.ED., F.R.C.S., Surgery
STAUFFER, P. H., M.SC., PH.D., Geology
SYED ABID HUSSAIN, M.SC., PH.D., Applied Physics
TAN BENG CHEOK, PH.D., Basic Physics
TAN HONG SIANG, M.SC., PH.D., Electrical Engineering
THONG TIN SIN, G., M.B.A., PH.D., Business Administration
TUNKU SHAMSUL BAHRIN, M.A., South-East Asian Geography
YIP YAT HOONG, M.A., PH.D., Applied Economics

UNIVERSITI SAINS MALAYSIA
(University of Science, Malaysia)

MINDEN, PENANG

Telephone: 883822.

Founded 1969.

Federal control; Languages of instruction: Bahasa Malaysia and English; Academic year: from June.

Chancellor: H.R.H. Tuanku Syed PUTRA IBNI AL-MARHUM SYED HASSAN JAMALULLAIL, D.K., D.K. (M), D.N.M., S.M.N., S.P.M.P., S.P.D.K.

Pro-Chancellors: Hon. Mr. Justice Tan Sri RAJA AZLAN SHAH IBNI AL-MARHUM SULTAN YUSOF IZZUDDIN SHAH, D.K., P.S.M., S.P.M.P.; LIM HUCK AIK, J.M.N., D.J.N., M.A.

Vice-Chancellor: Hon. Tan Sri Datuk HAJI HAMDAN SHEIKH TAHIR, P.S.M., D.M.P.M., K.M.N., B.A., F.R.G.S.

Deputy Vice-Chancellors: Assoc. Prof. SHAROM AMAT, J.M.N., M.A., PH.D., Assoc. Prof. AMIR AWANG, M.ED., PH.D.

Registrar: N. A. OGLE, J.S.M., P.K.T., B.A.

Librarian: EDWARD LIM HUCK TEE, B.A., F.L.A.

Library of 250,000 vols.

Number of teachers: 412.

Number of students: 3,132 full-time, 796 off-campus and 91 higher degree candidates.

Publications: *Annual Report, Schools' Handbooks, Calendar, Library Handbook. University Gazette, Students' Handbook* (all annually), *MIDAS* (monthly industrial and scientific information).

DEANS:

School of Applied Sciences: Prof. J. I. CUNNEEN, PH.D., D.SC., C.CHEM., F.R.I.C., F.P.R.I.
School of Biological Sciences: ISHAK TAMBI KECHIK, PH.D.

School of Chemical Sciences: Prof. A. ONG SOON HOCK, M.SC., PH.D., C.CHEM., F.R.I.C., F.M.I.C.

School of Comparative Social Sciences: KAMAL MAT SALIH M.A., PH.D.

School of Housing, Building and Planning: FAWIZAH LUCAS, R.I.B.A.

School of Humanities: Tuan Haji SHAHNON AHMAD, K.M.N.M.A.

School of Mathematical Sciences: TAN WANG SENG, M.MATHS., PH.D.

School of Medicine: MOND. ROSLANI BIN ABDUL MAJID, M.B.B.S., D.T.M.H., D.PATH., D.C.P.

School of Physics: R. RATNALINGAM, M.SC., D.PHIL., M.INST.P.

School of Pharmaceutical Sciences: GAN EE KIANG, PH.D.

DIRECTOR:

Centre for Policy Research: Prof. K. J. RATNAM, J.M.N., M.A., PH.D.

PROFESSORS:

CHATAR SINGH, M.SC., PH.D., F.INST.P., X-ray Crystallography
CUNNEEN, J. I., PH.D., D.SC., F.R.I.C., F.I.R.I., Polymer Science and Technology
KELLY, F. H. C., D.SC., Applied Sciences
MORSINGH, F., M.SC., D.PHILL., F.M.I.C., Organic Chemistry
NAIR, N. K., M.SC., PH.D., Physical Chemistry
ONG SOON HOCK, A., M.SC., PH.D., F.R.I.C., F.M.I.C., Organic Chemistry
RAMACHANDRAN, C. P., M.SC., D.SC., F.I.BIOL., Parasitology
RATNAM, K. J., M.A., PH.D., F.R.S.E., F.R.I.C., M.I.CHEM.E., F.P.I., Political Science
SHAROM BIN AHMAT, M.A., PH.D., History
SHEN, R. T. H., M.SC., Building Science

COLLEGES

CO-OPERATIVE COLLEGE OF MALAYSIA

P.O.B. 60, PETALING JAYA, SELANGOR

Founded 1956.

Provides in-service and pre-service training; specialized and diploma courses: book-keeping, retailing, auditing, management and salesmanship.

Principal: AHMAD GHAZI HAMID, M.A.(ECON.).

Library of 13,500 vols.

Number of students: 1,400.

THE LANGUAGE INSTITUTE
(Maktab Perguruan Bahasa)

LEMBAH PANTAI, KUALA LUMPUR

Founded 1958.

Number of students: *c.* 350.

The College offers a three-month in-service course to trained teachers in the Malay language and in English as a second language; students are selected by the Ministry of Education.

MARA INSTITUTE OF TECHNOLOGY

SHAH ALAM, SELANGOR

The Institute is under the Ministry of Education. It offers training in 73 different courses and at three levels: sub-professional, professional and degree standard.

Director: Prof. Dato' AWANG HAD SALLEH, D.S.D.K., J.M.N.

Number of teachers: 639.

Number of students: 7,747.

MUSLIM COLLEGE
(Jalan University)

PETALING JAYA, SELANGOR

Principal: Dr. ABD. JALIL HASSAN.

Registrar: MOHD. ZAIN ABD. MAJEED.

Librarian: ALI HAJI AHMAD.

UNGKU OMAR POLYTECHNIC

DAIRY ROAD, IPOH, PERAK

Founded 1969 with Unesco aid.

Principal: MOHD. NAWAWI BIN MOHD. ZAIN.

Registrar: MOHD. HASHIM (acting).

Librarian: LISA BEDNAR.

Library of 50,000 vols., 150 periodicals.

Number of teachers: 105.

Number of students: 1,800.

HEADS OF DEPARTMENTS:

Mechanical Engineering: CHEONG SEE LEONG.

Civil Engineering: MOHD. HASHIM.

Electrical Engineering: HEE TIENG FOK.

Commerce: AḤMAD BIN ABD. RAHMAN.

Language: KAMARUZAMAN YUNUS.

MALI

Population 6,308,000

RESEARCH INSTITUTES

Centre National de Recherches Fruitières: B.P. 30, Bamako; f. 1962; Mission in Mali of the Institut Français de Recherches Fruitières Outre-Mer (IFAC); controls experimental plantations, phytopathological laboratory, technological laboratory and pilot schemes; Dir. P. JEANTEUR.

Centre National de Recherches Zootechniques: B.P. 262, Bamako; f. 1927; experimental farm with sections on genetics (bovine, swine, poultry), nutrition and biochemistry, pasture, veterinary medicine; library of 1,000 vols.; Dir. Dr. FERNAND TRAORE.

Centres de Recherche Rizicole: Two rice research centres, at Kankan and at Ibetemi.

Institut de Recherches Agronomiques Tropicales et des Cultures Vivrières (I.R.A.T.): B.P. 438, Bamako; f. 1962; controls stations at Bamako, Koulikoro, Kogoni par Nioro, Ibetemi (Mopti), and sub-stations at Kita and Koporokenie-Pe; general agronomy, land amelioration, cultivation techniques, fertilization needs, plant breeding (sorghum, pennisetum, short and floating rices, maize, wheat, groundnuts and formerly sugar cane); Dir. M. THIBOUT. (*See* main entry under France.)

Institut de Recherche Scientifique du Mali: Bamako; Koulouba; Dir. ABDOULAYE FINIGARÉ.

Institut d'Ophtalmologie Tropicale de l'Afrique de l'Ouest Francophone: B.P. 248, Bamako; f. 1953; specializes in trachoma research; Dir. Dr. E. LOREAL.

Institut de Recherches sur la Lèpre: B.P. 251, Bamako; f. 1935; medical research, teaching, treatment and epidemiology, specializing in leprosy; Dir. Prof. P. ST.-ANDRÉ.

Mission I.R.C.T. à Mali: B.P. 114, Bamako; cotton research centre at N'Tarla-M'Pesoba. (*See* main entry under France.)

Office de la Recherche Scientifique et Technique Outre-Mer: B.P. 726, Bamako; hydrology, geophysics, archaeology; Dir. J. P. LAMAGAT. (*See* main entry under France.)

Office du Niger: B.P. 1660, Ségou; f. 1932, taken over by Mali govt. 1958; research stations at Bougomi and Sahel (cotton), Kayo (rice), Soninkoura (fruit).

Service Météorologique: B.P. 237, Bamako; Dir. N. KEITA.

SONAREM (Service de Documentation): B.P. 2, Kati; f. 1961; geology, mining (gold mining in Kalana, phosphates in Bourem), hydrogeology; 5 staff; library of 5,000 vols.; Dir. DAOUDA DIAKITE.

LIBRARIES AND ARCHIVES

Bibliothèque Nationale, Institut des Sciences Humaines: Koulouba, Bamako; f. 1913; 6,000 vols., 215 current periodicals; Librarian CHEICK DUMAR DRAME.

Archives Nationales du Mali, Institut des Sciences Humaines: Koulouba, Bamako; f. 1913; Archivist MOUSSA NIAKATÉ.

Bibliothèque Municipale: Bamako.

Centre de Documentation et de Recherches Historiques "Ahmed Baba" (CEDRAB): B.P. 14, Timbuktu; f. 1970; to preserve the historical heritage of the region; collects and conserves Arabic MSS.; *c.* 5,000 archives; Sec. BABA MAHMOUDOU HASSÈYE.

Centre Français de Documentation: Ambassade de France, B.P. 1547, Bamako; f. 1962; 13,000 vols.; public library.

U.S. International Communication Agency Library: B.P. 34, Bamako.

COLLEGES

Ecole des Hautes Etudes Pratiques: B.P. 242, Bamako; f. 1974, present name 1979; diploma courses in accountancy, business studies; 35 teachers, 471 students; Dir. ABDOULAYE HAIDARA.

Ecole Nationale d'Administration: B.P. 276, Bamako.

Ecole Nationale d'Ingénieurs: B.P. 242, Bamako.

Ecole de Médecine et de Dentisterie: Point G, Bamako; f. 1968.

Ecole Normale Supérieure: B.P. 241, Bamako; 1962; 462 students.

Centre Pédagogique Supérieur: f. 1970; postgraduate studies; 35 students.

Institut Polytechnique Rural de Katibougou: B.P. 6, Koulikoro; f. 1965; teaching and research in agronomy, agricultural economics, stockbreeding, forestry, veterinary science, rural technology; *c.* 300 teachers; *c.* 12,000 students; Dir. M. SANOGO.

MALTA

Population 311,000

LEARNED SOCIETIES

Agrarian Society: Palazzo de la Salle, Valletta; f. 1844; 200 mems.; Pres. Judge W. HARDING, C.B.E., K.M., B.LITT., LL.D.; Hon. Sec. Dr. JOSEPH A. MIACLLEF, LL.D.

Chamber of Architects and Civil Engineers: 1 Wilga St., Paceville, St. Julians.

Cultural Institute: 5/3 Sceberras Square, Floriana; f. 1949; concerts, drama; 800 mems.; Dir. Prof. GASTON TONNA BARTHET, M.B.E.; publ. *Bulletin*† (monthly).

Ghaqda Bibljotekarji/Library Association (Valletta): Din-1-Art Helwa, 133 Britannia St., Valletta; f. 1969; professional association to safeguard the interests of librarians and promote legislation concerning libraries; holds courses and examinations in librarianship; Chair. ANTHONY SAPIENZA, S.J.; Sec. MARGARET R. PSAILA; publs. *Year Book*†, *Newsletter*†.

Malta Society of Arts, Manufactures & Commerce: 219 Kingsway, Valletta.

LIBRARIES AND MUSEUMS

Gozo Public Library: Vajrinaa Street, Victoria, Gozo; f. 1853, amalgamated with the Royal Malta (now National) Library 1948; copyright deposit library; 45,000 vols.; Librarian PAUL M. CASSAR.

National Library of Malta: Valletta; f. 1555; part of Public Libraries Dept.; Librarian VINCENT A. DEPASQUALE B.A., LL.D.

University of Malta Library: Msida; f. 1769; 210,000 vols.; Librarian Dr. P. XUEREB, B.A., LL.D.; publs. *Library Annual Report, Monthly Library Accessions Lists*†.

Museums Department: Valletta: f. 1903; Dir. F. S. MALLIA; Curator Fine Arts Fr. MARIUS J. ZERAFA; Curator Archaeology T. C. GOUDER; Asst. Curator Natural History G. Z. MAEMPEL, PH.C., M.D., F.G.S.

UNIVERSITY

(Under a new Education Act, 1980, the Royal University has been abolished and all higher education is undertaken at the New University, now University of Malta.)

UNIVERSITY OF MALTA*

MSIDA

Founded 1961 as College of Arts, Science and Technology, university status 1978.

Principal: V. W. CLACK, D.I.C., C.ENG., F.I.MECH.E., F.I.PROD.E., F.I.W., A.M.B.I.M.

Registrar: F. DALMAS.

Library: *see* Libraries.

Number of teachers: *c.* 120.

Number of students: *c.* 2,000.

* No reply received to our questionnaire this year.

MAURITANIA

Population 1,407,000

RESEARCH INSTITUTES

Direction des Mines et de l'Industrie: B.P. 199, Nouakchott; f. 1962; 28 mems.; library of 2,000 vols.; Dir. C. CAMARA.

Institut de Recherches sur les Fruits et Agrumes (I.R.F.A.): B.P. 87, Nouakchott; stations at Kaédi (pedology), Kankossa (dates); Dir. M. REY. (*See* main entry under France.)

LIBRARIES

Arab Library: Boutilimit; library of the late Grand Marabout, Abd Allah Ould Cheikh Sidya.

Arab Library: Chinguetti; several private religious libraries; totalling 3,229 vols., including pre-Islamic MSS.; Librarian MOHAMED ABDALLAHI OULD FALL.

Arab Library: Kaédi; ancient religious texts.

Arab Library: Oualata.

Arab Library: Tidjikja; Librarian AHMEDOU OULD MOHAMED MAHMOUD.

Archives Nationales: B.P. 77, Nouakchott; f. 1955; library of 3,000 vols., 1,000 periodicals; documentation centre; Dir. MOHAMMED OULD GAOUAD.

Bibliothèque Nationale: B.P. 20, Nouakchott; dependent on Ministry of Cultural Affairs; f. 1965; depository for all the country's publications; documentation centre for western Africa; 10,000 vols., collection of over 4,000 old MSS.; 8 mems.; Head Librarian OUMAR DIOUWARA; Historian Prof. MOKTAR OULD HAMIDOU.

Bibliothèque Publique Centrale: B.P. 77, Nouakchott.

Centre de Documentation Pédagogique: B.P. 171, Nouakchott; f. 1962; 1,000 vols., 58 periodicals; educational and general works; Librarian MOHAMMED SAID.

COLLEGES

Ecole Nationale d'Administration: B.P. 252, Nouakchott; f. 1966; a documentation and research centre for the study of administration and politics in Mauritania; Dir. Mme TURKIA DADDAH; 30 teachers, 300 students; publs. *Annales, Futurs Cadres* (3 a year).

Institut national des hautes études islamiques: Boutilimit; f. 1961; 300 students.

MAURITIUS

Population 896,000

LEARNED SOCIETIES AND RESEARCH INSTITUTES

Académie Mauricienne de Langue et de Littérature: Curepipe; 16 life members; Sec. C. DE RAUVILLE; publ. *Oeuvres et Chroniques de l'Océan Indien*.

Mauritius Institute: P.O.B. 54, Port Louis; f. 1880; a branch of the Ministry of Education; research centre for the study of the local fauna and flora; a public library and three museums are attached (*see* below); Dir. C. MICHEL, A.M.A.; publs. *Annual Reports, Bulletin*.

Royal Society of Arts and Sciences of Mauritius: Mauritius Institute, Port Louis; f. 1829; Royal title 1847; 5 honorary, 107 ordinary mems.; Pres. F. STAUB; Hon. Sec. C. MICHEL; publ. *Proceedings*.

Société de l'Histoire de l'Ile Maurice: 13 Sir W. Newton St., Port Louis; f. 1938; 350 ordinary mems.; Hon. Sec. G. RAMET; publs. *Bulletin, Dictionary of Mauritian Biography*.

Société de Technologie Agricole et Sucrière de l'Ile Maurice: Mauritius Sugar Industry Research Institute, Réduit; f. 1910; 363 mems.; Pres. J. D. DE R. DE ST. ANTOINE; Hon. Sec. CLAUDE FIGON; publ. *Revue Agricole et Sucrière de Maurice*.

Sugar Industry Research Institute: Réduit; f. 1953; research on cane breeding, agriculture, soils, diseases, pests, weeds, botany, sugar manufacture, by-products, also on food crops cultivated between rows of sugar-cane and between cane cycles; library; *see* Libraries; 30 senior research workers; Dir. J. R. DE R. DE ST. ANTOINE, B.S.; publs. *Annual Report*†, *Weed Flora*†, *Occasional Papers*†, *Cultures Vivrières*.

LIBRARIES

British Council Library: Royal Rd., Rose Hill; f. 1949; 15,478 vols., 103 periodicals; Librarian Mrs. M. SMITH.

Carnegie Library: Queen Elizabeth II Ave., Curepipe; f. 1920; important collection of Mauritania; *c.* 55,000 vols.; Librarian MADELEINE PHILIPPE.

City Library: City Hall, P.O.B. 422, Port Louis; f. 1851; 60,000 vols.; important collections on Mauritius; music scores; Librarian G. M. BENOIT, F.L.A.; publs. *Annual Report*†, *Newspapers Index*† (2 a year), *Subject Bibliography on Mauritius*† (annually).

Mauritius Archives: Sunray Hotel, Coromandel, Beau-Bassin; f. 1815; contains records of the French Administration (1721–1815) and the British Administration (1810 to Independence); comprises Divisions of MS. Records, Printed Records, Notarial Registry, Land Registry and Maps and Plans, and a Photographic Service; Chief Archivist Dr. P. H. SOOPRAYEN; publs. *Annual Reports*†, *Memorandum of Books Printed in Mauritius*† (quarterly), *Bulletin*.

Mauritius Institute Public Library: P.O.B. 54, Port Louis; f. 1902; legal deposit library; 51,000 vols., including an extensive collection of books, articles and reports on Mauritius; Librarian S. JEAN-FRANÇOIS, A.L.A.

Sugar Industry Research Institute Library: Réduit; 18,365 vols.; representative collection on all aspects of sugar cane cultivation and sugar manufacture, and expanding collection on food crops; wide coverage of technical periodical literature; collection of prints and drawings and early publications on sugar cane; botanical and agricultural archives; collection of *Mauritiana* on the natural sciences; Librarian MADELEINE LY-TIO-FANE, PH.D.

University of Mauritius Library: Réduit; f. 1965; important collections in fields of administration, agriculture, technology and Mauritiana; partial depository for UN publications and Canadian Government publications; 60,000 vols.; Librarian B. R. GOORDYAL.

MUSEUMS

Historical Museum: Mahebourg; f. 1950; a branch of the Mauritius Institute; comprises collection of old maps, engravings, water-colours and naval relics of local interest, exhibited in an 18th-century French house.

Mauritius Herbarium: Sugar Industry Research Institute, Réduit; f. 1960; public herbarium for education and research; specializes in flora of Mascarene Islands; Curator H. R. JULIEN, PH.D.

Port Louis Museum: Mauritius Institute, Port Louis; f. 1880; comprises a Natural History Museum, collections of fauna, flora and geology of Mauritius and of the other islands of the Mascarene region; Dir. C. MICHEL, A.M.A.

UNIVERSITY AND COLLEGES

UNIVERSITY OF MAURITIUS

REDUIT

Telephone: 54-1041.

Founded 1965.

Language of instruction: English; Academic year: September to August.

The primary aim of the University is the greater development of the Island. Teaching programmes and research projects concentrate particularly on those areas where needs are greatest: Economics and Public Administration, Engineering Technology, Agriculture and Natural Resources and Education.

Chancellor: H.R.H. Princess ALEXANDRA.

Pro-Chancellor and Chairman of the Council: (vacant).

Vice-Chancellor: Prof. J. MANRAKHAN, M.SC.

Registrar: B. K. SEEBALUCK, B.A.

Library: *see* Libraries.

Number of teachers: 74.

Number of students: 306 full-time, 340 part-time.

Publications: *Vice-Chancellor's Report*†, *Calendar*† (annually), *University of Mauritius Journal* (quarterly).

HEADS OF SCHOOLS:

School of Administration: Prof. D. AH-CHUEN, M.B.A., F.C.A., M.B.I.M., A.I.P.M.

School of Agriculture: Prof. A. S. KASENALLY, PH.D., F.R.I.C.

School of Industrial Technology: Prof. G. T. G. MOHAMEDBHAI, PH.D.

Mahatma Gandhi Institute: Moka; f. 1973; 30 teachers, 325 students; Pres. Rt. Hon. Sir SEEWOOSAGUR RAMGOOLAM; Dir. Dr. K. HAZAREESINGH, O.B.E.

Mauritius College of the Air: Moka; f. 1972; multi-media institution using distance-teaching techniques for further education and in secondary schools; Dir. KENNETH NOYAU.

MEXICO

Population 66,940,000

ACADEMIES

Academia Mexicana de la Lengua (*Mexican Academy of Languages*): Donceles 66, México 1, D.F.; 3rd in order of foundation in Spanish America; correspondent of the Real Academia Española, Madrid.
Director: Lic. AGUSTÍN YÁÑEZ.
Secretaries: JOSÉ IGNACIO DÁVILA GARIBI, JOSÉ ROJAS GARCIDUEÑAS (acting)
Librarian: ANDRÉS HENESTROSA.

MEMBERS:

FRANCISCO MONTERDE.	ALÍ CHUMACERO.
ANTONIO CASTRO LEAL.	ANTONIO ACEVEDO ESCOBEDO.
ANTONIO GÓMEZ ROBLEDO.	ERNESTO DE LA TORRE VILLAR.
JESÚS GUISA Y AZEVEDO.	EDMUNDO O'GORMAN.
JESÚS SILVA HERZOG.	ALFONSO NORIEGA CANTÚ.
MAURICIO MAGDALENO.	IGNACIO BERNAL.
JOSÉ LUIS MARTÍNEZ.	MARÍA DEL CARMEN MILLÁN.
FRANCISCO FERNÁNDEZ DEL CASTILLO.	JOSÉ MARTÍNEZ SOTOMAYOR.
MANUEL ALCALÁ.	PORFIRIO MARTÍNEZ PEÑALOZA.
MIGUEL LEÓN-PORTILLA.	JUAN RULFO.
RUBÉN BONIFAZ NUÑO.	SALVADOR ELIZONDO.
SALVADOR AZUELA.	MANUEL PONCE ZAVALA.
	JOSÉ G. MORENO DE ALBA.

Academia Mexicana de la Historia, correspondiente de la Real de Madrid (*Mexican Academy of History*): Plaza de Carlos Pacheco 21, México 1, D.F.; f. 1940; library of 9,300 vols.; Dir. Dr. EDMUNDO O'GORMAN; publ. *Memoria de la Academia* (quarterly, since 1942).

Academia Nacional de Ciencias (formerly Sociedad Científica "Antonio Alzate") (*National Academy of Science*): Apdo. M-77-98, México 1, D.F.; f. 1884; library of 260,000 vols.; 60 mems.; Pres. Ing. RICARDO CICERO Y GARITA; Perm. Sec. Dr. ANTONIO POMPA Y POMPA; publs. *Revista, Memorias*.

Academia Nacional de Historia y Geografía (*National Academy of History and Geography*): Londres 60, Mexico 6, D.F.; f. 1925; 179 mems.; Dir. ANTONIO FERNÁNDEZ DEL CASTILLO; publ. *Revista*.

Academia Nacional de Medicina de México (*Mexican National Academy of Medicine*): Apdo. M 8075, Bloque "B" 3er piso de la Unidad de Congresos del Centro Médico Nacional, Av. Cuauhtémoc 330, Mexico 7, D.F.; f. 1864; 50 sections; 302 mems. (28 hon., 199 ord., 49 tit., 25 corresp.); library of 13,000 vols.; Pres. Dr. FELIPE MENDOZA; Sec.-Gen. JORGE CORVERA; publ. *Gaceta Médica de México*.

El Colegio Nacional: Luis González Obregón 23, Mexico 1, D.F.; f. 1943 by the Government for the dissemination of national culture; library of 15,000 vols.; publ. *Memoria* (annually).

MEMBERS:

ADEM, Dr. JOSÉ, Mathematics
ADEM, Dr. JULIÁN, Geophysics
BERNAL, Dr. IGNACIO, Archaeology
BONIFAZ NUÑO, Dr. RUBÉN, Poetry and Literature
CARRILLO FLORES, Dr. ANTONIO, Law
CASAS CAMPILLO, Dr. CARLOS, Microbiology
CASTRO LEAL, Dr. ANTONIO, Literature
CHÁVEZ, Dr. IGNACIO, Medicine
DE LA FUENTE MUÑIZ, Dr. RAMÓN, Psychiatry
FIX-ZAMUDIO, Dr. HÉCTOR, Constitutional and Procedural Law
FUENTES, CARLOS, Literature
GARCÍA-COLÍN SCHERER, Dr. LEOPOLDO, Physics and Chemistry
GARCÍA MAYNEZ, Dr. EDUARDO, Philosophy
GARCÍA ROBLES, Dr. ALFONSO, International Law
GARCÍA TERRÉS, JAIME, Literature
GÓMEZ ROBLEDO, ANTONIO, Law and Philosophy
GONZÁLEZ Y GONZÁLEZ, LUIS, History
HARO, Dr. GUILLERMO, Astronomy
KUMATE RODRÍGUEZ, Dr. JESÚS, Medicine and Immunology
LEÓN-PORTILLA, Dr. MIGUEL, History of Mexico
MARTÍNEZ BÁEZ, Dr. MANUEL, Preventive Medicine
MOSHINSKY, Dr. MARCOS, Theoretical Physics
PAZ, OCTAVIO, Literature and Poetry
ROSENBLUETH, Dr. EMILIO, Engineering
SALMERÓN, Dr. FERNANDO, Philosophy
SEPÚLVEDA, BERNARDO, Gastroenterology
SILVA HERZOG, Dr. JESÚS, Economics
SOLÍS, LEOPOLDO, Economics
VILLAGRAN GARCIA, Arq. JOSÉ, Architecture
VILLORO TORANZO, LUIS, Philosophy
XIRAU, Dr. RAMÓN, Philosophy
YÁÑEZ, Lic. AGUSTIN, Literature
ZAVALA, Dr. SILVIO, History

LEARNED SOCIETIES

AGRICULTURE AND VETERINARY SCIENCE

Sociedad Agronómica Mexicana (*Mexican Agricultural Society*): López No. 23, Mexico, D.F.

Sociedad Forestal Mexicana (*Mexican Forestry Society*): Calle de Jesús Terán 11, Mexico 1, D.F.; f. 1921; 225 mems.; Exec. Pres. Ing. RIGOBERTO VÁSQUEZ DE LA PARRA; Sec.-Gen. Lic. ADOLFO AGUILAR Y QUEVEDO; publ. *México Forestal* (bi-monthly).

ARCHITECTURE AND TOWN PLANNING

Asociación de Ingenieros y Arquitectos de México (*Association of Mexican Engineers and Architects*): 3A Calle del Puente de Alvarado 58, Mexico, D.F.; f. 1868; 560 mems.; library of 7,565 vols.; Pres. Ing. FEDERICO DOVALI RAMOS; Sec. Ing. JOSÉ ACOSTA SÁNCHEZ; publ. *Revista Mexicana de Ingeniería y Arquitectura*† (quarterly).

THE ARTS

Asociación Musical Manuel M. Ponce, A.C.: Bucareli No. 12, Desp. 411, Mexico 1, D.F.; f. 1948 to promote traditional and modern Mexican music; a yearly programme of about 20 concerts; 50 mems. as well as corporate membership; library of musical scores, tapes, records and books; Pres. LUIS HERRERA DE LA FUENTE; Vice-Pres. JESÚS ALVARADO ORTÍZ; Co-ordinator MARÍA DE LOS ANGELES CALCÁNEO; Secs. EDELMIRA ZUÑIGA, Prof. VÍCTOR URBAN; publs. *Diarios Excelsior, Universal y Novedades*.

Ateneo Veracruzano (*Veracruz Athenaeum*): Edif. del Museo de la Ciudad, Zaragoza y E. Morales, Vera Cruz; f. 1933; 68 mems. (18 corres.); Pres. C. P. T. FRANCISCO BROISSIN A.; Sec. Prof. ANTONIO SALAZAR PÁEZ; publ. *Boletín* (monthly).

Instituto Nacional de Bellas Artes (*National Institute of Fine Arts*): Palacio de Bellas Artes, Mexico 1, D.F.; f. 1947; consists of depts. of music, plastic arts, drama, literature, dance, theatrical production, architecture, artistic education and administration; Dir. JUAN JOSÉ BREMER MARTINO; publ. *La Semana de Bellas Artes* (quarterly).

Centro Nacional de Conservación de Obras Artísticas: Tolsá 6, Mexico 1, D.F.; f. 1963; restoration of works of art; Dir. TOMÁS ZURIÁN UGARTE.

BIBLIOGRAPHY AND LIBRARY SCIENCE

Asociación Mexicana de Bibliotecarios, A.C. (*Mexican Library Assn.*): c/o Biblioteca Nacional, República del Salvador 70, México, D.F.; f. 1924; 250 mems.; Pres. GUADALUPE CARRION R.; Sec. GILBERTO DÍAZ S.; publ. *Noticiero de la AMBAC* (quarterly).

Centro de Información Científica y Humanística: Universidad Nacional Autónoma de México, Ciudad Universitaria, Apdo. 70-392, Mexico 20, D.F.; f. 1971; documentation service, current awareness service, retrospective bibliographical service; maintains a specialized information and reference library; 10,000 periodicals received; Dir. Dr. ARMANDO M. SANDOVAL; publs. *CLASE* (quarterly index of Latin American sociological and humanistic periodicals), *AL DIA* (weekly information bulletin), *PERIODICA* (quarterly index of Latin American scientific and technical periodicals).

Sociedad Mexicana de Bibliografía (*Mexican Bibliographical Society*): Hemeroteca Nacional, Carmen y San Ildefonso, Mexico, D.F.; f. 1945; 91 mems., 39 corresponding mems.; Dir. Dr. AGUSTÍN MILLARES CARLO; Sec. FRANCISCO GAMONEDA; publ. *Boletín* (quarterly).

ECONOMICS, LAW AND POLITICS

Barra Mexicana-Colegio de Abogados (*Mexican Bar Association—College of Advocates*): Varsovia No. 1, Esq. P. de la Reforma, México 6, D.F.; f. 1922; 1,040 mems.; library of 5,260 vols.; Pres. Lic. ALVARO ESPINOSA BARRIOS; Sec. MIGUEL I. ESTRADA SAMANO; publ. *El Foro* (quarterly review).

Dirección General de Estadística (*Statistics Office of the Secretaría de Programación y Presupuesto*): Avda. Balderas No. 71, Agencia de Correos 245, Mexico 1, D.F.; f. 1922.

EDUCATION

Asociación Nacional de Universidades e Institutos de Enseñanza Superior (ANUIES): Avda. Insurgentes Sur 2133, 3°, México 20, D.F.; f. 1950; co-ordinates and represents institutes of higher education, studies academic and administrative problems of the national higher education system; promotes exchange of personnel, information and services between the affiliated institutions; 78 affiliated universities and colleges; library of 6,050 vols.; Gen. Exec. Sec. Dr. RAFAEL VELASCO FERNÁNDEZ; publs. *Revista de la Educación Superior*† (quarterly), *Boletín Informativo* (monthly), statistical yearbooks, reports, studies and academic support material, directories of higher education institutes (every 2 years) and catalogues of studies.

Centro Nacional de Documentación e Información Pedagógica y Museo Pedagógico Nacional: Calle Presidente Masaryk 526, Mexico 5, D.F.; f. 1971; library of 10,000 vols.; Dir. Prof. MARIANO CRUZ PÉREZ; publs. *Sep-Forjadores*† (monthly), *Documentación e Información*† (monthly), *Lista de Canje*† (2 a year).

Dirección General de Relaciones Educativas, Científicas y Culturales (*Board of Educational, Scientific and Cultural Relations*): Secretaría de Educación Pública, Brasil 31, piso 2, Mexico 1, D.F.; f. 1960; comprises Sections of Technical Assistance, International Relations in the fields of Education, Science and Culture and Exchange; serves as co-ordinating agency between the UN, UNESCO, the OAS and the Mexican Govt.; Dir. Dr. ENRIQUE G. LEÓN LÓPEZ.

Sociedad de Educación (*Educational Society*): Sección Educacional, Edif. del Banco de Londres y México, Desp. 7/8, Mexico, D.F.

HISTORY, GEOGRAPHY AND ARCHAEOLOGY

Academia de Ciencias Históricas de Monterrey (*Academy of Historical Sciences of Monterrey*): Apdo. 389, Nuevo León, Monterrey; f. 1947; Pres. CARLOS PÉREZ-MALDONADO; Sec. JOSÉ P. SALDAÑA; publ. *Memorias.*

Departamento de Antropología e Historia de Nayarit: Avda. Mexico 91, Tepic, Nayarit; f. 1946; Dir. EVERARDO PEÑA NAVARRO; Sec. MARÍA E. GONZÁLEZ A.

Dirección General del Servicio Meteorológico Nacional (*National Meteorological Dept.*): Av. Observatorio 192, Tacubaya; f. 1915; library of 12,243 vols., 80,796 pamphlets; Dir.-Gen. SILVINO AGUILAR ANGUIANO; the Department is divided as follows: **Oficina de Estudios Especiales:** Dir. Ing. ALFONSO MARIO MEDINA RAMÍREZ, O.S.C.; publs. climatological and meteorological pamphlets; **Oficina de Previsión del Tiempo:** Dir. MARIO LIZAOLA REYNA; publs. *Boletín Mensual de Temperaturas y Lluvias* (monthly), daily weather map, *Boletín anual de observaciones meteorológicas*; **Oficina de Estadística Climatológica:** Dir. ARMANDO MAÑÓN BELMONT.

Sociedad Mexicana de Geografía y Estadística (*Mexican Society of Geography and Statistics*): Calle de Justo Sierra 19, Apdo. 10739, Mexico, D.F.; f. 1833; 525 active mems.; 450 corresponding mems.; library of 95,000 vols.; Dir. CONCEPCIÓN SAAVEDRA; publs. *Boletín* (twice yearly), and special works.

Sociedad Mexicana de Historia de la Ciencia y la Tecnologia (*Mexican Society for History of Science and Technology*): Avda. Dr. Vertiz 724, Mexico 12, D.F.

Sociedad Nuevoleonesa de Historia, Geografía y Estadística (*Historical, Geographical and Statistical Society of Nuevo León*): Biblioteca Universitaria "Alfonso Reyes", Apartado Postal 1575, Monterrey; f. 1942; 80 mems.; Pres. TIMOTEO L. HERNÁNDEZ; various publs.

INTERNATIONAL CULTURAL INSTITUTES

British Council: Apdo. 30–588, Calle M. Antonio Caso 127, Col. San Rafael, Mexico 4, D.F.; Rep. Dr. R. T. TAYLOR.

Deutsch-Mexikanisches Kultur-Institut Alexander von Humboldt: Tehuantepec 255-4, Mexico 7; f. 1934; 398 mems.; library of 5,492 vols.; Pres. Dr. ANTONIO MARTÍNEZ BÁEZ; Sec. and Man. Lic. DORA ZURHELLEN NOLLAU; publ. *El México Antiguo* (every 3 or 4 years).

Federación de Alianzas Francesas de México, A.C./ Fédération des Alliances Françaises du Mexique, A.C.: Sócrates 156, 4° piso, Colonia Polanco, México 5, D.F.; f. 1966 to promote French language and culture; 32 brs. and 12 affiliated teaching centres; libraries of 38,593 vols. in Mexico City; Pres. AGUSTÍN LEGORRETA; Sec.-Gen. RENÉ GOUEDIC; publ. *Journal* (monthly).

Instituto Anglo-Mexicano de Cultura (*Anglo-Mexican Cultural Institute*): Calle M. Antonio Caso 127, Mexico 4, D.F.; f. 1943; 1,500 mems.; library of 24,139 vols., 61 periodicals.

Instituto Francés de América Latina: Nazas 43, Mexico 5, D.F.; f. 1944; films, records, slides, selective bibliographies; French language courses; pedagogy; research in the field of American studies; library of 26,000 vols.; Dir. JEAN GALARD; Sec.-Gen. MICHELLE SIENNE.

Instituto Mexicano-Norteamericano de Relaciones Culturales (*Mexican-N. American Institute of Cultural Relations*): Hamburgo 115, Mexico 6, D.F.; f. 1944; library of 2,800 vols.; Spanish and English teaching; art gallery; auditorium; brs. in 14 towns.

Istituto Italiano di Cultura: Avda. Francisco Sosa 77, Coyoacán, México 21, D.F.; f. 1952; library of 10,000 vols.; 90 mems.; Dir. Prof. LUCIANO RAIMONDI; publs. *Italia-México* (6 a year), *Bollettino* (monthly).

Language and Literature

Centro Mexicano de Escritores (*Mexican Authors' Centre*): San Francisco No. 12, Mexico 12, D.F.; f. 1951 to promote Mexican literature and encourage and support young authors; 185 mems.; small library; Pres. Plácido García Reynoso; Sec. of Exec. Cttee. Felipe García Beraza.

Medicine

Academia Mexicana de Cirugía (*Mexican Academy of Surgery*): Brasil y Venezuela, Mexico 1, D.F.; f. 1933; Pres. Dr. Manuel Mateos Fournier; publ. *Revista* (monthly).

Academia Mexicana de Dermatología: c/o Academia Nacional de Medicina, Av. Cuauhtémoc 330, Mexico, D.F.; f. 1952; publ. *Boletín Dermatológico* (twice yearly).

Asociación de Médicas Mexicanas, A.C. (*Mexican Association of Women Doctors*): Oklahoma 151, Mexico 18, D.F.; f. 1923; 3,000 mems.; represents members' interests as doctors, citizens and women; Pres. Dra. Irene Talamas V.; publ. *Revista*.

Asociación Médica Franco-Mexicana (*Franco-Mexican Medical Association*): Dr. Balmis 148, México 7, D.F.; f. 1928; 600 mems.; library of 3,500 vols.; Pres. Dr. Jorge Espino Vela; Vice-Pres. Dr. Jesús Kumate; Sec. Dr. Emilio Stoopen; Librarian Dr. Serge Brachet; publ. *Pasteur* (quarterly).

Asociación Mexicana de Facultades y Escuelas de Medicina: Av. V. Carranza No. 870, Desp. 15, Apdo. 836, San Luis de Potosí; f. 1957; mems. 30 medical schools; Pres. Dr. Ramón Arrizabalaga; Sec.-Gen. Dr. Miguel R. Barrios; publ. *Boletín*.

Asociación Mexicana de Ginecología y Obstetricia: Avda. Baja California No. 311, Mexico 11, D.F.; f. 1945; 350 mems.; Pres. Dr. Carlos Fernández del Castillo; Sec. Dr. Roberto Ahued Ahued; publ. *Ginecología y Obstetricia de México* (monthly).

Sociedad Mexicana de Cardiología: Calle de Juan Badiano 1, Tlalpan, México 22, D.F.; f. 1935; 400 mems.; Pres. Dr. Eduardo Salazar; Sec. Dr. Simón Horwitz; publ. *Arch. Inst. de Cardiología de México* (bi-monthly).

Sociedad Mexicana de Eugenesia (*Mexican Society of Eugenics*): 3A Acapulco 44, Mexico, D.F.; f. 1931; 150 mems.; library of 2,800 vols.; Pres. Dr. Eugenio Echeverría Arnaux; Sec. Dr. Alfredo M. Saavedra.

Sociedad Mexicana de Historia y Filosofía de la Medicina: Plaza Jorge Washington 9–4, México 6, D.F.; f. 1957; 180 mems; library of 1,500 vols; Pres. Juan Somolinos Palencia.

Sociedad Mexicana de Nutrición y Endocrinología, A.C.: Viaducto Tlalpan y Avda. San Fernando, México 22, D.F.; f. 1960; 245 mems.; Pres. Dr. Héctor Bourges R.; Sec. Dr. Fernando Bolaños G.

Sociedad Mexicana de Parasitología, A.C.: Nicolás de San Juan 1015, Apdo. 12813, Mexico 12, D.F.; f. 1960; 20 active mems. and 31 hon. mems. from 14 countries; Dir. Luis Flores Barroeta.

Sociedad Latinoamericana de Alergología: Calle Dr. Márquez 162, Mexico, D.F.; f. 1964; 485 mems.; Pres. Dr. Luis Gómez-Orazco; Sec. Dr. Luis Villanueva; publ. *Allergia* (monthly).

Sociedad Mexicana de Pediatría (*Mexican Paediatrics Society*): Centro Materno-Infantil "Gral. M. Avila Camacho", Calzada de Madereros 240, Mexico, D.F.; f. 1954; 257 mems.; Pres. Dr. Ignacio Avila Cisneros; Dir. Dr. Rogelio H. Valenzuela; publ. *Revista* (monthly).

Sociedad Mexicana de Salud Pública (*Mexican Public Health Society*): Leibnitz 32, 1er. piso, Mexico 5, D.F.; f. 1944; 750 mems.; small library; Pres. Dr. Ramón Alvarez Gutiérrez; Sec.-Gen. Dr. José Carrillo Coromina.

Natural Sciences

General

Ateneo de Ciencias y Artes de Chiapas: 3/a, Oriente 28, Tuxtla Gutiérrez; f. 1942; 76 mems.; Pres. Lic. Alberto Marín Barreiro.

Ateneo Nacional de Ciencias y Artes de México (*National Athenaeum of Sciences and Arts*): Bucareli 12, Mexico, D.F.; f. 1920 as Ateneo Estudiantil de Ciencias y Artes, then Ateneo de Ciencias y Artes de México 1926, present name 1934; comprises Sections of Architecture, Astronomy and Mathematics, Biology, Broadcasting, Cinematography, Criminology and Penal Law, Engineering, Eugenics, Geography, History, Hygiene, Law (Civil, Industrial, and International), Literature, Medicine, Military Studies, Music, Pedagogics, Political Economy, Natural Science, Statistics; 7 corresp. centres: Monterrey, Mérida, Veracruz, Chiapas, Tijuana, Oaxaca, Tlaxcala; over 1,000 mems., including hon. and corresponding; library of 10,000 vols.; Hon. Pres. Dr. Alfonso Pruneda; Pres. Emilio Portes Gil; Vice-Pres. Luis Garrido and Arq. Edmundo Zamudio; Sec.-Gen. José L. Cossio; publs. *Boletín*, pamphlets.

Centro Científico y Técnico Francés en México (*French Scientific and Technical Centre in Mexico*): Liverpool 67, México 6, D.F.; f. 1960; a dependency of the French Embassy in Mexico; undertakes scientific and technical co-operation between France and Mexico in the field of culture; service of French scientific documentation and film library; teaching of French and Spanish by audiovisual methods; Dir. Jacques Aknin.

Biological Sciences

Asociación Mexicana de Microbiología, A.C.: Ciprés 176, Mexico 4, D.F.; f. 1949; Pres. Armando Bayona; publ. *Revista Latinoamericana de Microbiología y Parasitología*.

Sociedad Botánica de México, A.C. (*Mexican Botanical Society*): Apdo. 70-385, México 20, D.F.; f. 1941; promotes the study, teaching and technology of botany; organizes 12 meetings a year, and the National Botany Congress every 3 years; 700 mems.; Pres. Antonio Lot; Exec. Sec. Victoria Sosa; publs. *Boletín* (annually), *Macpalxochitl, boletín informativo* (monthly), *Guías Botánicas de Excursiones en México*.

Sociedad de Estudios Biológicos (*Society for Biological Studies*): Balderas 94, Mexico, D.F.; Sec. Prof. Aurelio del Rio.

Sociedad Mexicana de Biología (*Mexican Biological Society*): Avenida de Brasil, Mexico, D.F.; f. 1921; Pres. Fernando Ocaranz; publ. *Revista Mexicana de Biología*.

Sociedad Mexicana de Entomología (*Mexican Entomological Society*): Apdo. 31-312, Mexico 7, D.F.; f. 1952; *c.* 450 mems.; Pres. Dr José Luis Carrillo; publ. *Folia Entomológica Mexicana*†.

Sociedad Mexicana de Historia Natural (*Mexican Natural History Society*): Avda. Dr. Vertiz 724, Mexico 12, D.F.; f. 1868, refounded 1938; 400 mems.; library of 5,000 vols.; Sec. Dr. Ambrosio González Cortés; publ. *Revista de la Sociedad Mexicana de Historia Natural*.

Sociedad Mexicana de Fitogenética (*Mexican Society of Plant Genetics*): Centro Nacional de Enseñanza, Investigación y Extensión Agrícola, Apdo. 21, Chapingo, Mexico; f. 1965; 200 mems.; Pres. Dr. Joaquín Ortíz Cereceres; Sec. Ing. Efraím Hernández X.; publ. *Plant Genetics Journal* (weekly).

Sociedad Mexicana de Fitopatología, A.C. (*Mexican Society of Phytopathology*): Centro de Fitopatología, Colegio de Postgraduados, Chapingo; f. 1958; 325 mems.; holds 6 meetings per year and one national meeting every 2 years; Pres. Dr. DANIEL TÉLIZ; Sec. Dr. NAHUM MARBÁN; publ. *El Vector*.

Sociedad Mexicana de Micología (*Mexican Society of Mycology*): Apdo. 26-378, México 16, D.F.; f. 1965; 300 mems.; Pres. Ing. ERNESTO OCAMPO ALVAREZ; publ. *Boletín* (annually).

Mathematical Sciences

Centro Nacional de Cálculo: Unidad Profesional Zacatenco-IPN-Lindavista, Mexico 14, D.F.; f. 1963; Dir. Ing. ALEJANDRO VÁZQUEZ GUTIÉRREZ; publ. *Revista*.

Sociedad Matemática Mexicana (*Mexican Mathematical Society*): Facultad de Ciencias, UNAM, Apdo. 70-450, Mexico 20, D.F.; f. 1943; 500 mems., 5 hon.; sponsors National Congresses and Regional Assemblies of mathematicians; Pres. Dra. ZENAIDA E. RAMOS ZUÑIGA; publs. *Boletín* (2 a year), *Matemáticas y Enseñanza, Miscelánea Matemática, Carta informativa* (quarterly).

Physical Sciences

Asociación Mexicana de Geólogos Petroleros (*Mexican Association of Petroleum Geologists*): Ciprés 176, Mexico 4, D.F.; f. 1949; 600 mems.; Pres. ING. JAVIER MENESES GYVES; Sec. ISRAEL HERNÁNDEZ ESTEVEZ; publ. *Boletín* (quarterly).

Sociedad Astronómica de México (*Mexican Astronomical Society*): Jardín Felipe Xicotencatl, Colonia Alamos, Mexico 13, D.F.; f. 1902; library of 6,500 vols.; Pres. JORGE GABRIEL PÉREZ; Sec.-Gen. ANTONIO LAMADRID; publ. *El Universo*† (quarterly).

Sociedad Geológica Mexicana (*Mexican Geological Society*): Ciprés No. 176, Mexico, D.F.; f. 1904; 350 mems.; library of 1,250 vols.; Pres. Ing. DIEGO A. CÓRDOBA; Vice-Pres. Ing. JERJES PANTOJA-ALOR; Sec. Ing. JORGE GARCÍA-CALDERÓN; publ. *Boletín*.

Sociedad Química de México (*Mexican Chemical Society*), Ciprés 176, Apdo. Postal 4-875, Mexico, 4 D.F.; f. 1956; 2,300 mems.; Pres. Dr. JAVIER PADILLA OLIVARES; Sec. Dr. FEDERICO GARCÍA JIMÉNEZ; publ. *Revista de la S.Q.M.* (every 2 months).

PHILOSOPHY AND PSYCHOLOGY

Sociedad Mexicana de Estudios Psico-Pedagógicos (*Mexican Society for Psycho-Pedagogical Studies*): Nayarit 86, Mexico, D.F.

RELIGION, SOCIOLOGY AND ANTHROPOLOGY

Sociedad Mexicana de Antropología (*Mexican Anthropological Society*): Apdo. Postal 660, México 1, D.F.; f. 1937; 208 mems.; Secs. Arq. NOEMI CASTILLO and Ling. LEONARDO MANRIQUE C.; publ. *Revista Mexicana de Estudios Antropológicos* (3 a year).

TECHNOLOGY

Asociación Franco-Mexicana de Ingenieros y Técnicos, A.C. (*Franco-Mexican Association of Engineers and Technicians*): Liverpool 67, Mexico 6, D.F.; association for the development of relations between Mexican and French engineers living in Mexico.

Sociedad Mexicana de Ingeniería Sísmica: Apdo. 70-257: Mexico 20, D.F.; f. 1962; 300 mems.; Pres. Ing. ENRIQUE DEL VALLE; publ. *Revista Ingeniería Sísmica*.

RESEARCH INSTITUTES

(*see* also under Universities).

AGRICULTURE AND VETERINARY SCIENCE

Campo Agrícola Experimental Rio Bravo: Apdo. 172, Rio Bravo, Tamps.; f. 1965; research into regional problems and diversification; Dir. Ing. Agr. MANUEL CARNERO HERNÁNDEZ.

Centro Internacional de Mejoramiento de Maiz y Trigo (*International Maize and Wheat Improvement Center*): Apdo. Postal 6-641, Londres 40, Mexico 6, D.F.; f. 1966; supported by Rockefeller Foundation, Mexican Ministry of Agriculture, and various international agencies; aims to improve world-wide cereal yields; operates breeding programmes, provides specialized training for scientists and technicians; 8 experimental stations in Mexico; staff stationed in various countries providing full-time assistance; library of 3,000 vols, 700 periodicals; Dir.-Gen. ROBERT HAVENER; publs. *Annual Report*, bulletins, etc.

Instituto Mexicano del Café: Km. 4 Carretera Xalapa-Veracruz, Xalapa, Ver.; Dir.-Gen. Lic. FAUSTO CANTÚ PEÑA.

Instituto Nacional de Investigaciones Agrícolas: Apdo. 6-882, Mexico 6, D.F.; f. 1960; conducts research in all aspects of agricultural development and production, specializing in developing new crop varieties; five research centres with laboratories of soil science, entomology and phytopathology; Dir. Dr. EDUARDO ALVÁREZ LUNA; publs. *Novedades Horticolas* (quarterly), *Agricultura técnica en México* (twice yearly).

Instituto Nacional de Investigaciones Forestales: Av. Progreso No. 5, Mexico 21, D.F.; f. 1958; silviculture, forest botany, soils, products and pathology, photogrammetry, national forestry conservation; library of 9,985 vols. and periodicals; Dir.-Gen. Ing. OSCAR CEDEÑO SÁNCHEZ; publs. information and technical bulletins.

Instituto Nacional de Investigaciones Pecuarias (*National Institute of Livestock Research*): Km. 15.5, Carretera México-Toluca, Palo Alto, D.F.; f. 1941, reorganized 1968; stock breeding, veterinary science; 150 mems.; library of 7,000 vols.; Dir. Dr. CARLOS ARELLANO SOTA; publ. *Técnica Pecuaria en México* (quarterly).

BIBLIOGRAPHY

Instituto de Investigaciones Bibliográficas: c/o Biblioteca Nacional de México, República de El Salvador 70, Mexico 1, D.F. and Hemeroteca Nacional de México, Carmen 31, Mexico 1, D.F.; f. 1899, re-opened 1959; compiles the national bibliographies and books on bibliographical subjects; Dir. Mtra. MARÍA DEL CARMEN RUIZ CASTAÑEDA.

ECONOMICS, LAW AND POLITICS

Centro de Relaciones Internacionales: Ciudad Universitaria, UNAM, Mexico, D.F.; attached to the Faculty of Political and Social Sciences of the Universidad Nacional Autónoma de México; f. 1970; co-ordinates and promotes research in all aspects of international relations and Mexico's foreign policy, as well as the training of researchers in different fields: Disciplinary construction problems, Co-operation and International Law, Developing nations, Actual problems in world society; 30 full mems.; Dir. Dr. LEOPOLDO GONZÁLEZ AGUAYO; publs. *Relaciones Internacionales*† (quarterly), *Cuadernos*†.

EDUCATION

Centro de Estudios Educativos, A.C.: Av. Revolución 1291, Mexico 20, D.F.; f. 1963; scientific research into the problems of education in Mexico and Latin America; 22 researchers; library of *c.* 15,200 vols. and 267 periodicals; Pres. JOSÉ T. MATA; Dir.-Gen. ENRIQUE GONZÁLEZ; publ. *Revista* (quarterly).

Centro Regional de Educación de Adultos y Alfabetización Funcional para América Latina (*Latin American*

Centre for Functional Literacy in Rural Areas): Quinta Eréndira, Pátzcuaro, Mich.; f. 1951 by UNESCO and OAS, now administered nationally; specialist training, research; 68 staff; library of 56,000 vols.; Dir. Dr. ADALBERTO A. VELÁZQUEZ SALAZAR; publs. *Boletín Informativo* (every 2 months), *Revista Educación y Adultos* (quarterly), *Cuadernos del CREFAL*.

MEDICINE

Centro de Higiene y Estación de Adiestramiento en Enfermedades Tropicales (*Hygiene Centre and Training Station for Tropical Diseases*): Av. Veracruz, Boca del Río, Ver.; f. 1946; Dir. Dr. ARNOLDO LÓPEZ RICO.

Instituto de Salubridad y Enfermedades Tropicales (*Institute of Public Health and Tropical Diseases*): Calle de Carpio 470, México 17, D.F.; f. 1938; carries out laboratory research into the main problems of public health in Mexico and into the diagnosis and classification of infectious diseases; acts as a training centre; library of 3,930 vols., 603 journals and 150 current periodicals; Dir. Dr. DIEGO FERNÁNDEZ DE CASTRO.

Instituto Miles de Terapéutica Experimental: Calzada Xochimilco 77, Apdo .22026, Mexico 22, D. F.; f. 1962; conducts basic and applied research in pharmacology; Dir. Dr. HORACIO VIDRIO.

Instituto Nacional de Cardiología (*National Cardiological Institute*): Juan Badiano 1, Tlalpan, México 22, D.F.; f. 1944; 205 medical mems.; library of 6,071 medical vols. and 651 titles of medical journals; Dir. Dr. IGNACIO CHÁVEZ SÁNCHEZ; Head of Medical Division Dr. FELIPE MENDOZA; Head of Research Division Dr. RAFAEL MÉNDEZ; Head of Medical Education Division Dr. IGNACIO CHÁVEZ-RIVERA; Head of Planning Division Dr. JORGE SONÍ; Superintendent Dr. CARLOS MARTÍNEZ; Library Dir. Dr. ANTONIO ESTANDÍA CANO; publ. *Archivos*† (6 nos., 1 vol. per year).

Instituto Nacional de Higiene (*National Institute of Hygiene*): Czda. Mariano Escobedo 20, Mexico 17, D.F.; f. 1904; 153 mems.; library of 10,000 vols.; Dir. JORGE FERNÁNDEZ DE CASTRO PEREDO.

Instituto Nacional de Neumología: Tlalpán, Mexico 22, D.F.; small library; publs. *Anales*, *Boletín* (quarterly).

MUSEOLOGY

Centro Latinoamericano de Estudios para la Conservación y Restauración de Bienes Culturales (*Latin American Centre for the Study of the Conservation and Restoration of Cultural Property*): Antiguo Convento de Churubusco, Mexico 21, D.F.; f. 1967 by the Mexican Government and UNESCO to train specialists in museography, techniques of restoration and conservation, and formulation of policies for the preservation of cultural property; fellowships offered by the Mexican Government, UNESCO, and OAS for the nine-month course; staff of 60; library and documentation centre of 3,000 vols., specialized periodicals, photographic archives; Dir. Prof. CARLOS CHANFÓN OLMOS; publ. *Boletín Informativo* (quarterly).

NATURAL SCIENCES

General

Academia de la Investigación Científica (*Academy of Scientific Research*): Avda. Revolución 1909, 8° piso, México, D.F.; f. 1959; general scientific research; 310 mems.; Pres. Dr. AGUSTÍN AYALA-CASTANARES; Sec. Dr. ENRIQUE MARTÍN DEL CAMPO; publ. *Boletín*.

Centro de Investigación y de Estudios Avanzados del Instituto Politécnico Nacional: Apdo. 14-740, Mexico 14, D.F.; f. 1961; postgraduate research and training centre in sciences; the Centre integrates the work of the Depts. of Biochemistry, Physics, Physiology and Biophysics, Electrical Engineering, Mathematics, Genetics, Cellular Biology, Molecular Biology, Chemistry, Biotechnology, Bio-engineering, Neuroscience, Pharmacology, Bio-electronics, Educational Mathematics, Toxicology and Educational Research; library of 41,161 vols.; Dir. Dr. MANUEL V. ORTEGA ORTEGA.

Instituto Mexicano de Recursos Renovables, A.C. (*Institute for the Conservation of Natural Resources*): Dr. Vertiz 724, Mexico 12, D.F.; f. 1953; library of 7,000 vols. and 200 regular periodicals; Dir. Dr. ENRIQUE BELTRÁN.

Biological Sciences

Centro Nacional de Ciencias y Tecnologías Marinas: Instituto Tecnológico Regional de Veracruz, Apdo. 512, Veracruz; f. 1957 as Estación de Biología Marina, name changed 1967; 23 mems.; Dir. T. P. RAÚL MÁRQUEZ CANEPPA.

Instituto de Ecología, A.C.: Apdo. 18-845, Mexico 18, D.F.; f. 1974; animal ecology and taxonomy, biogeography, dynamics and structure of eco-systems and biotic resources conservation; 65 researchers; Dir. Dr. GONZALO HALFFTER.

Instituto Nacional de Investigaciones sobre Recursos Bióticos (*National Institute for Research on Biotic Resources*): Apdo. postal 63, Xalapa, Veracruz; f. 1975; scientific and technological research in the fields of biology and ecology, in order to evaluate the effect of development programmes on renewable natural resources; participates in the training of technicians and professionals in this area; 39 research staff; library of 5,700 vols.; Dir.-Gen. Dr. ARTURO GÓMEZ-POMPA; publs. *Biotica*, *Flora de Veracruz*, *Cuadernos de Divulgación*.

Instituto Nacional de Pesca (*National Fishery Institute*): Avda. Cuauhtemoc 80, Mexico 7, D.F.; f. 1962; research in marine biology; library of 3,000 vols.; Dir. LUIS KASUGA OSAKA; publs. *Serie científica*, *Serie Técnica*, *Serie Informativa*, *Serie Divulgación*.

Mathematics

Instituto de Matemáticas (*Institute of Mathematics*): Area de la Investigación Científica Circuito Exterior, Ciudad Universitaria, México 20, D.F.; f. 1949; 37 mems.; research in mathematics; library of 9,432 vols.; Dir. Dr. HUMBERTO CÁRDENAS TRIGOS; publs. *Anales*†, *Monografías*†, *Publicaciones Preliminares*.

Physical Sciences

Centro de Preclasificación Oceánica de México: c/o Centro de Ciencias del Mar y Limnología, Apdo. 70-305, Mexico 20, D.F.; f. 1972; under the auspices of CONACYT (*q.v.*), the National University of Mexico, and UNESCO; part of the *Colaboración de México a las Investigaciones Cooperativas del Caribe y Regiones Adyacentes* (*CICAR*); Dir. M. en C. CÉSAR FLORES COTO.

Instituto de Astronomía (*Institute of Astronomy*): Apdo. Postal 70-264, Mexico 20, D.F.; f. 1878; an Institute of the National Autonomous University of Mexico; research in astronomy and astrophysics; 54 mems.; library of 31,000 vols.; Dir. Dr. ARCADIO POVEDA; publ. *Revista Mexicana de Astronomía y Astrofísica*† (2 or 3 a year).

Instituto Nacional de Astrofísica, Optica y Electrónica: Apdos. Postales 216 y 51, (Tonantzintla), Puebla, Pue.; f. 1971; formerly Observatorio Nacional de Astrofísica, f. 1942; 20 research mems.; library of 3,000 vols., 138 journals; Gen. Dir. Dr. GUILLERMO HARO; Technical Dir. ALEJANDRO CORNEJO; publ. *Boletín del Instituto de Tonantzintla*†.

Instituto Nacional de Investigaciones Nucleares (*National Institute of Nuclear Research*): Apdo. postal 27-190, México 18, D.F.: f. 1979 (previously part of *Instituto Nacional de Energía Nuclear*, f. 1955); planning, research and development of nuclear technology, including peaceful use of nuclear energy; library of 29,879 vols., 20,000 vols. of periodicals and 280,870 scientific reports; Gen. Dir. DALMAU COSTA ALONSO.

RELIGION, SOCIOLOGY AND ANTHROPOLOGY

Instituto Indigenista Interamericano: Avda. Insurgentes Sur 1690, México 20, D.F.; f. 1940; supplies technical assistance to member governments for the Indian population of the continent; library of 30,000 vols.; Dir. Dr. OSCAR ARZE QUINTANILLA; Sec.-Gen. SERGIO A. DELGADO; publs. *América Indígena*† (quarterly), *Serie Ediciones Especiales*†, *Serie Antropología Social*†, *Boletín Indigenista*†.

Instituto Nacional de Antropología e Historia (*National Institute of Anthropology and History*): Córdoba 45, Mexico 7, D.F.; f. 1939; consists of the following departments: *Monumentos Prehispánicos* for research and conservation of archaeological monuments; *Monumentos Coloniales* for conservation and restoration of historical monuments; *Prehistoria* for research into Mexican Pre-history and allied subjects, small specialized library; *Investigaciones Antropológicas* for research in physical and social anthropology and ethnography; *Investigaciones Históricas:* Museo Nacional de Historia (*q.v.*). The Institute also controls the following institutions (*see* under respective sections): Museo Nacional de Antropología, Museo Nacional de Virreinato, Museo de las Culturas, and numerous regional museums; Archivo y Laboratorio Fotográfico, Archivos Históricos y Bibliotecas, Escuela Nacional de Antropología e Historia; Dir.-Gen. Dr. GUILLERMO BONFIL BATALLA; publs. *Anales*†, *Boletín*†.

Instituto Nacional Indigenista: Avenida Revolución No. 1279, Mexico 20, D.F.; f. 1948; the integration of Indian communities into national life; 1,891 mems.; in addition to the central office there are 84 Co-ordinating Centres in the interior; specialized library of 5,000 vols.; Dir. Lic. IGNACIO OVALLE FERNÁNDEZ; publs. *México Indígena* (monthly), *Antropología Social*, *Clásicos de la Antropología Mexicana*.

TECHNOLOGY

Consejo Nacional de Ciencia y Tecnología—CONACYT (*National Council for Science and Technology*): Insurgentes Sur 1677, Mexico 20, D.F.; f. 1970; co-ordinates scientific research and development and formulates policy; Dir.-Gen. Dr. EDMUNDO FLORES.

Instituto Mexicano de Investigaciones Tecnológicas, A.C. (IMIT) (*Institute of Technical Research*): Calzada Legaria 694, Mexico 10, D.F.; f. 1950; applied research on natural resources and development of industrial processes; pre-investment reports and pre-engineering studies; specialized library in chemical technology of 6,700 vols.; Gen. Dir. I. DESCHAMPS.

Instituto Mexicano del Petróleo (*Mexican Petroleum Institute*): Avda. 100 Metros 152, P.O.B. 14-805, México 14, D.F.; research on petroleum products and equipment, petroleum and petrochemical industries, economic studies, exploration, refining; training and specialist courses; 3,000 mems.; Gen. Dir. AGUSTÍN STRAFFON ARTEAGA; publ. *Revista*.

LIBRARIES AND ARCHIVES

Mexico City

Archivos Históricos y Bibliotecas: Calzada M. Gandhi y Paseo de la Reforma, Mexico 5, D.F.; attached to the Instituto Nacional de Antropología e Historia; Mexican history and anthropology; 300,000 vols. and documents; Dir. Prof. A. POMPA Y POMPA.

Biblioteca Benjamin Franklin/U.S. International Communication Agency: Londres 16, México 6, D.F.; f. 1942; 35,000 vols.; Dir. JESSE T. REINBURG.

Biblioteca Nacional de México (*National Library*): Republica del Salvador 70; f. 1833; now one of the Institutes of the National University of Mexico; 1,000,000 vols., 150,000 printed documents relating to the political, social, artistic, literary and historical development of Mexico, 80,787 MSS., microfilms, Braille coll., tapes, gramophone records; Dir. Mtra. MARIA DEL CARMEN RUIZ CASTAÑEDA; publs. *Bibliografía Mexicana*, *Anuario Bibliográfico*, *Boletín del Instituto de Investigaciones Bibliográficas*.

Archivo General de la Nación (*National Archives*): Tacuba 8, 2° piso, México 1, D.F.; f. 1823; documents relating to the vice-regal administration of New Spain, the Inquisition, the years of independence 1821–40, the 19th century, the Mexican Revolution 1910, and the years up to 1976 (151,000 vols.); 45,000 books; 1,050 prehispanic paintings; newspaper collection of 1,272,000 copies; microfilm service and library; Dir. Dra. ALEJANDRA MORENO TOSCANO; publs. *Boletín* (quarterly), guides, calatogues and inventories.

Government Libraries:

Biblioteca de Derecho y Legislación de la Secretaría de Hacienda (*Law Library, Finance Ministry*): Correo Mayor 31; f. 1925, present form 1928; 13,000 vols.; specialized library relating to ancient and existing federal laws, tax laws from 1831, foreign and international laws; Librarian SOFÍA SILVA.

Biblioteca de Historia de la Secretaría de Hacienda (*Historical Library, Finance Ministry*): Palacio Nacional; f. 1939 with the collections of the old library of the Finance Ministry and those of Genaro Estrada acquired by the Government; 8,750 vols., 14,000 pamphlets relating to Mexico.

Biblioteca de la Secretaría de Comunicaciones y Transportes (*Library of the Ministry of Communications and Transport*): Tacuba y Xicotecatl; f. 1891; 10,000 vols.; Dir. RENATO MOLINE ENRÍQUEZ.

Biblioteca de la Secretaría de Gobernación (*Library of the Ministry of the Interior*): Bucareli 99; f. 1917; 45,000 vols.

Biblioteca de la Secretaría de Industria y Comercio: Av. Cuauhtemoc y Dr. Liceaga, Mexico 7, D.F.; f. 1918; economic material, statistical annuals, census returns for population, livestock, etc.; trade statistics; 42,250 vols.; Librarian Lic. MARÍA TERESA HERNÁNDEZ G.

Biblioteca de la Secretaría de Relaciones Exteriores (*Library of the Ministry of Foreign Affairs*): R. Flores Magón 1, México 3, D.F.; f. 1922; 40,000 vols.; specializes in history and social sciences; Dir. CARLOS FERRER.

Biblioteca de la Secretaría de Salubridad y Asistencia y de la Escuela de Salud Pública (*Library of the Ministry of Public Health and Welfare and the School of Public Health*): Dr. Francisco de P. Miranda 177, 4° piso, Plateros, Mixcoac, Mexico 19, D.F.; f. 1884; specialized collections in medical administration, hygiene, preventive medicine, epidemiology, statistics, mental hygiene, nutrition, rehabilitation, occupational safety, industrial hygiene and water, air, noise and waste pollution engineering; 20,000 vols., 750 periodical titles; Dir. LIC. MARTHA MERCADER DE LEÓN.

Biblioteca del Congreso de la Unión (*Congress Library*): Edificio del ex-Convento de Santa Clara, Tacuba 29; f. 1936 with the collections of the old library of the Chamber of Deputies; 116,000 vols.; Dir. Ing. ALBERTO NEGRETE FRÍAS.

Biblioteca "Miguel Lerdo de Tejada" de la Secretaría de Hacienda y Crédito Público (*General Library, Finance Ministry*): Av. República de El Salvador 49, Mexico 1, D.F.; f. 1928; 250,000 vols.; Dir. ROMÁN BELTRÁN MARTÍNEZ.

Departamento de Bibliotecas y Publicaciones (*Department of Libraries and Publications*): Av. Cuauhtemoc y Dr. Liceaga; f. 1929; 34,159 vols.; 10,000 periodicals; Dir. Lic. MARÍA TERESA HERNÁNDEZ GONZÁLEZ; publs. include *Revista de Estadística, Gaceta de Patentes y Marcas, Boletín de Minas y Petróleo* (monthly), *Barómetros Económicos* (quarterly), *Compendio Estadístico* (annual), *Anuario Estadístico, Anuario de Comercio Exterior*, etc.

Biblioteca Central de la Universidad Nacional Autónoma de México: Ciudad Universitaria; f. 1924; 300,000 vols.; *c.* 10,000 periodicals; Dir. Q.F.B. MARGARITA ALMADA DE ASCENCIO.

Biblioteca de México: Plaza de la Ciudadela 6, Mexico 1, D.F.; f. 1946; 122,482 vols., 2,500 children's books, 258 periodicals, 15 daily newspapers, special collections; Dir. CARMEN E. DE GARCÍA MORENO.

Biblioteca Ibero-Americana y de Bellas Artes (*Spanish-American and Fine Arts Library*): Palacio de Bellas Artes; f. 1923; over 20,000 vols.; also mobile library; Dir. GUSTAVO SAINZ.

Biblioteca "Miguel de Cervantes Saavedra": Héroes y Esmeralda; f. 1924; 27,200 vols.; Dir. ESTHER ELENA JIMÉNEZ.

Biblioteca Nacional de Antropologia e Historia "Dr. Eusebio Davalos Hurtado" (*National Library of Anthropology and History*): Paseo de la Reforma y Calzada Gandhi; f. 1880 as Library of the Instituto Nacional de Antropología e Historia de México (*see* under Research Institutes); specializes in archaeology, linguistics, history, ethnography and anthropology; 500,000 vols.; 11,000 periodicals; Dir. Mtra. YOLANDA MERCADER MARTÍNEZ; publs. *Serie Archivo Histórico, Serie Bibliografía, Serie Códices, Serie Investigación, Serie Microfilm, Serie Procesos Técnicos, Información al día en antropología y ciencias sociales* (every 2 months), *Boletín Bibliográfico*† (every 2 months).

Hemeroteca Nacional de México (*National Library of Periodicals*): Ciudad Universitaria, México 20, D.F.; f. 1912; 300,000 vols. of newspapers and periodicals; Mexican Gazette of 18th century; Dir.-Librarian Maestra MARÍA DEL CARMEN RUIZ CASTAÑEDA; Gen. Co-ordinator JESÚS MÁRQUEZ.

Provinces

(Listed alphabetically by Town)

Biblioteca Central: Universidad Autónoma Chapingo, Chapingo; f. *c.* 1870, reorganized 1978; agriculture, animal breeding, rural sociology, agricultural economics, genetics, plant pathology, botany, hydraulic engineering; 46,893 vols., 1,200 periodicals; Dir. MARTHA VEGA VELASCO; publs. *Agrociencia* (quarterly), *Chapingo* (quarterly).

Biblioteca Pública del Estado de Jalisco: 16 de Septiembre 849, Ciudad de Guadalajara; f. 1861; 452,303 vols.; Dir. HELEN L. DE GUEVARA COX.

Biblioteca del Instituto Tecnológico y de Estudios Superiores de Monterrey: Sucursal de Correos "J", Monterrey (Nuevo León); f. 1943; 120,000 vols., 2,000 periodicals; Dir. Lic. ARTEMIO BENAVIDES H.

Biblioteca de la Universidad de las Américas: P.O.B. 100, Santa Catarina Mártir, Puebla, Pue.; f. 1940; humanities, science and technology; 130,000 vols., 1,750 periodicals; Dir. TOM JAKE WATTS.

Biblioteca del Instituto Panamericano de Geografía e Historia (*Library of the Pan-American Institute of Geography and History*): Tacubaya; f. 1928; approx. 60,000 vols.; 54,000 periodicals and 24,000 maps.

Biblioteca Pública del Estado de México: Plaza Hidalgo, Altos, Toluca (Estado de México); f. 1898; 35,577 vols., 125 periodicals; Dir. GONZALO PÉREZ GÓMEZ.

Biblioteca Pública Central del Estado de Chiapas: Ciudad de Tuxtla Gutiérrez (Chiapas); f. 1906; 45,000 vols.; Dir. JOSÉ MARIO GARCÍA.

Biblioteca Pública del Estado "Elias Amador": Zacatecas (Zacatecas); f. 1832; 22,000 vols.

MUSEUMS AND ART GALLERIES

Mexico City

Museo de Arte Moderno (*Museum of Modern Art*): Chapultepec, México 5, D.F.; f. 1964; attached to the National Institute of Fine Arts; Mexican and international permanent collection and exhibitions of modern art; Dir. FERNANDO GAMBOA; publ. *Artes Visuales* (quarterly).

Museo de las Culturas: Calle de Moneda 13, Mexico 1, D.F.; attached to the Instituto Nacional de Antropología e Historia; f. 1965; collections of archaeology and ethnology from all over the world; public lectures, special courses for teachers, training in plastic arts; library of 11,000 vols.; Dir. Arq. JORGE CANSECO VINCOURT.

Museo de Pintura y Escultura de San Carlos (*Gallery of Painting and Sculpture of San Carlos*): Puente de Alvarado 50, México 1, D.F.; f. 1968; exhibition of 14th-19th-century European paintings and 19th-century Mexican sculpture; library of 500 vols.; Dir. Sra. GRACIELA REYES RETANA; publ. *Bulletin* (every 2 months).

Museo Don Benito Juárez (*Juárez Museum*): Palacio Nacional; f. 1957; historic relics related to the life and death of Benito Juárez; specialized library of 1,700 vols. on history of reform in Mexico; Dir. DANIEL MUÑOZ Y PÉREZ; Librarian MARÍA ENRIQUETA ROJAS GUTIÉRREZ.

Museo Etnográfico de Esculturas de Cera (*Wax Sculpture Ethnographical Museum*): Seminario No. 4 esquina con Guatemala; f. 1964; sculptures of indigenous dancers, idols and figures from temples; Dir. CARMEN DE ANTÚNEZ.

Museo Nacional de Antropologia (*National Museum of Anthropology*): Paseo de la Reforma y Gandhi, México 5, D.F.; f. 1825; attached to the Instituto Nacional de Antropología e Historia; anthropological, ethnological, and archaeological subjects relating to Mexico; 600,000 exhibits; library of 300,000 vols.; Dir. ARTURO ROMANO PACHECO; publs. *Cuadernos, Guides*, etc.

Museo Nacional de Artes e Industrias Populares: Ave. Juárez 44; f. 1951; examples of popular Mexican art of all periods, conservation and encouragement of traditional handicrafts; Dir. MARÍA TERESA POMAR.

Museo Nacional de Historia (*National Historical Museum*): Castillo de Chapultepec; f. 1825, moved to Chapultepec Castle 1941, opened 1944, attached to the Instituto Nacional de Antropología e Historia; history of Mexico from the Conquest in the 16th century to the Constitution of 1917; over 150,000 objects (historical paintings, flags, weapons, documents, jewellery, clothing and other objects of social and cultural history); Dir. Arq. FELIPE LACOUTURE F.; publ. *Série Científica*.

Pinacoteca Nacional de San Diego (*San Diego National Art Gallery*): Dr. Mora 7, Mexico 1, D.F.; under auspices of Instituto Nacional de Bellas Artes; collection of paintings of the colonial era in Mexico; cultural programmes, recitals, etc.; Dir. CARMEN M. DE ANDRADE.

Actopán, Hidalgo

Museo Regional de Actopán: f. 1933; collections relating to the Otomie Indians housed in the former convent of Actopán.

Campeche, Camp.

Museo Arqueológico, Etnográfico e Histórico del Estado: Calle 8; Dir.-Gen. of Museums, State of Campeche, Arq. RAUL PAVÓN ABREU.

Guadalajara, Jalisco

Museo del Estado de Jalisco: f. 1700; collections of early Mexican objects; folk art and costumes; archaeological discoveries.

Museo Regional de Antropología e Historia: f. 1918; special collections of pre-Spanish and Colonial period art and paintings; Curator JOSÉ G. ZUNO.

Museo-Taller José Clemente Orozco: Calle Aurelio Aceves 27; became a museum after the artist's death in 1949; paintings and sketches; Dir. BERTA VALDIVIA.

Guanajuato, Guan.

Museos de la Universidad de Guanajuato (*University Museums*): Lascurain de Retana 5; f. 1870; comprise. Natural History, Geology, Mineralogy, and include the natural history collection of Alfredo Duges with many rare specimens; Dir. QF. LUZ-MARÍA PRADO SOTO.

Jalapa, Veracruz

Museo de Antropología de la Universidad Veracruzana: Av. 20 de Noviembre Norte s/n; special regional archaeological collections of the Olmec, Totonac and Huastec cultures of ancient Mexico; 20 research staff; library of 5,000 vols.; Dir. ALFONSO MEDELLÍN ZENIL.

Madero, Tamaulipas

Museo de la Cultura Huasteca (*Museum of Huastec Culture*): Av. 1° de Mayo, Cd. Madero, Tam.; f. 1960; attached to the Instituto Nacional de Antropología e Historia; library of 400 vols.; Dir. Sra. ALICIA VÁZQUEZ DE VALERO.

Mérida, Yucatán

Museo de Arqueología de Yucatán: c/o Instituto Nacional de Antropología e Historia, Córdoba 45, México 7, D.F.; f. 1920, reorganized 1959; attached to the Instituto Nacional de Antropología e Historia; collections of Pre-hispanic, Mayan and Olmec cultures, precious stones, ceramics, objects in copper and gold; Curator Profra. LETICIA ROZO KRAUSS.

Monterrey, Nuevo León

Museo Regional de Nuevo León: Cerro del Obispado, Apdo. Postal 566 Suc. C; regional and Mexican history, archaeology and painting; Dir. Prof. FELIPE J. GARCÍA CAMPUZANO.

Morelia, Michoacán

Museo Michoacano (*Michoacan Museum*): Calle de Allende 305; f. 1886; archaeological, ethnographical and prehistoric collections of the district; Dir. Arq. JOSÉ CORONA NÚÑEZ; publ. *Anales*.

Nayarit, Jalisco

Museo Regional de Nayarit: Av. México 91 Norte; regional and Mexican history and archaeology; Dir. JORGE HERNÁNDEZ MORENO.

Oaxaca, Oax.

Museo Regional de Oaxaca: Ex-Convento de Santo Domingo 33; f. 1933; anthropology, archaeology, ethnography and religious art; contains the famous archaeological treasures found in Tomb No. 7, Monte Albán, jewellery, etc.; Curator WANDA TOMMASI DE MAGRELLI.

Patzcuaro, Michoacán

Museo Regional de Artes Populares (*Regional Museum of Arts and Crafts*): Enseñanza y Alcantarilla s/n; f. 1935; ancient and modern ethnographical exhibits relating to the Tarascan Indians of Michoacán; colonial and contemporary native art; Dir. MARÍA TERESA DÁVALOS DE L.

Puebla, Pue.

Museo de Arte "José Luis Bello y González": Avda. 3 Poniente 302; f. 1938, opened to the public 1944; contains: ivories, porcelain, wrought iron, furniture, clocks, watches, musical instruments, etc., Mexican, Chinese and European paintings, sculptures, pottery, vestments, tapestries, ceramics, miniatures, etc.; Dir. ALICIA TORRES DE ARAUJO.

Museo Regional del Estado de Puebla: Casa del Alfeñique, 4 Oriente No. 416; f. 1931; notable historical collections; Dir. JUAN ARMENTA CAMACHO.

Museo Regional de Santa Mónica: Avda. Poniente 103; f. 1940; religious art; comprises the collections of various disbanded convents and now housed in that of Santa Mónica.

Querétaro, Qro.

Museo Regional de Querétaro (*Querétaro Historical Museum*): Calle Corregidora 3 Sur; f. 1936; local history and art; Dir. Prof. EDUARDO LOARCA CASTILLO.

Teotihuacán, México Estado

Museo Arqueológico de Teotihuacán: Pirámides; f. 1922; archaeological, ethnographical, anthropological and historical collections from the Teotihuacán Valley; Dir. MANUEL CASTAÑEDA.

Tepotzotlán, México Estado

Museo Nacional del Virreinato (*National Museum of the Vice-Royalty*): f. 1922, refounded 1964; attached to the Instituto Nacional de Antropología e Historia; collections on the art and culture of the Colonial period; library of *c.* 4,000 vols. dating from 16th to 19th centuries; Dir. Lic. MA. DEL CONSUELO MAQUÍVAR M. (acting).

Toluca, México Estado

Museo de Arte Popular (*Museum of Folk Art*): Morelos y Hidalgo; Dir. Lic. CARMON B. DE CALDERÓN.

Museo de Ciencias Naturales (*Museum of Natural Sciences*): Parque Matlatzincas; natural science dioramas, astronomy, wild life, ecology, etc.; Dir. Dr. LAWRENCE CASTAÑEDA.

Museo de las Bellas Artes (*Museum of Fine Arts*): Calle de Santos Degollado 102; paintings, sculptures, Mexican colonial art; exhibitions, theatre, lectures, art courses; Dir. Prof. JOSÉ M. CABALLERO-BARNARD.

Tuxtla Gutiérrez, Chiapas

Museo Regional de Antropología e Historia: Casa de la Cultura; f. 1939; archaeological, colonial and anthropological collections; Dir. ARMANDO DUVALIER.

Tzintzuntzan, Michoacán

Museo Etnográfico y Arqueológico: f. 1944; ethnographical and archaeological collections relating to the Tzintzuntzan and Tarascan zones of Lake Pátzcuaro.

UNIVERSITIES

UNIVERSIDAD NACIONAL AUTÓNOMA DE MÉXICO (National Autonomous University of Mexico)

CIUDAD UNIVERSITARIA, VILLA OBREGÓN, MEXICO 20, D.F.
Telephone: 5-48-65-00.

Founded 1551; classes commenced 1553.

Language of instruction: Spanish.

Rector: Dr. GUILLERMO SOBERÓN ACEVEDO.
Secretary-General: Dr. FERNANDO PÉREZ CORREA.
Admissions and Records Co-ordinator: Ing. GUILLERMO AGUILAR CAMPUZANO.

In addition to the National Library and Central Library (*see* under Libraries), there are 92 specialized libraries attached to the faculties, schools and research institutes.

Number of teachers: 19,977.
Number of students: 271,266 (not including postgraduates).

Publications†: *Anales del Instituto de Geofísica, Universidades, Investigación Económica, Estudios de Cultura Náhuatl, Estudios de Cultura Maya, Revista Hispanoamericana de Filosofía, Revista Meyibó, Estudios de Historia Moderna y Contemporánea de México, Anales de Antropología, Veterinaria, Tablas de Predicción de Mareas, Anales del Instituto de Matemáticas, Punto de Partida, Revista Mexicana de Ciencia Política, Problemas del Desarrollo, Revista de la Facultad de Derecho, Anuario Jurídico, Boletín del Instituto de Investigaciones Bibliográficas, Boletín de Estudios Médicos y Biológicos, Anales Serie Botánica, Anales Serie Zoología, Biología Experimental, Anales Centro de Ciencias de Mar y Limnología, Datos Geofísicos, Serie A-Oceanografía, Revista Mexicana de Sociología, Boletín Mexicano de Derecho Comparado, Crítica, Repertorio Anual de Legislación, Anuario de Letras, Anuario de Bibliotecología, Estudios de Historia Novohispana, Anuario del Observatorio Astronómico Nacional, Anales del Instituto de Investigaciones Estéticas, Relaciones Internacionales, Indice General de la Revista Mexicana de Ciencias Políticas y Sociales, Estudios Políticos, Anuario del Centro de Estudios Latinoamericanos, Anuario de Historia, Anuario de Asia, Anuario de Geografía, Anuario Ciencia Veterinaria, Legislación y Jurisprudencia.*

DIRECTORS OF FACULTIES AND SCHOOLS:

Faculty of Accounting and Business Administration: C.P. MANUEL RESA GARCÍA.
Faculty of Chemistry: Dr. JAVIER PADILLA OLIVARES.
Faculty of Dentistry: Dr. MANUEL REY GARCÍA.
Faculty of Economics: Mta. MARÍA ELENA SANDOVAL.
Faculty of Engineering: Ing. JAVIER JIMÉNEZ ESPRIÚ.
Faculty of Law: Dr. PEDRO ASTUDILLO URSÚA.
Faculty of Medicine: Dr. OCTAVIO RIVERO SERRANO.
Faculty of Philosophy and Letters: Dr. ABELARDO VILLEGAS.
Faculty of Political and Social Sciences: Lic. JULIO DEL RÍO REYNAGA.
Faculty of Psychology: Dra. ELVIA G. RODRÍGUEZ DE ARIZMENDI.
Faculty of Sciences: Dra. ANA MARÍA CETTO DE LA PEÑA.
Faculty of Veterinary Medicine and Zoology: M.V.Z. JUAN GARZA RAMOS.

National Schools:

Architecture: Arqto. JESÚS AGUIRRE CÁRDENAS.
Music: Prof. FRANCISCO MARTÍNEZ GALNARES.
Nursing and Obstetrics: Profa. MARINA GUZMÁN V. DE CISNEROS.
Plastic Arts: Mto. ANTONIO RAMÍREZ ANDRADE.
Preparatory: Lic. ENRIQUE ESPINOSA SUÑER.
Social Work: Dr. MANUEL SÁNCHEZ ROSADO.
College of Sciences and Humanities: Lic. JORGE SÁNCHEZ AZCONA.
Courses for Foreign Students: Lic. ELSA BIELER.

ATTACHED RESEARCH INSTITUTES AND CENTRES:

Sciences:

Astronomical Institute (*Instituto de Astronomía*): *see* Research Institutes.

Institute of Applied Mathematics and Systems Research (*Instituto de Investigación en Matemáticas Aplicadas y en Sistemas*): Dir. Dr. TOMÁS GARZA HERNÁNDEZ.

Institute of Biology (*Instituto de Biología*): Dir. Dr. CARLOS MÁRQUEZ MAYAUDON.

Institute of Biomedical Research (*Instituto de Investigaciones Biomédicas*): Dir. Dr. JAIME MARTUSCELLI.

Institute of Chemistry (*Instituto de Química*): Dir. Dr. RAÚL CETINA ROSADO.

Institute of Engineering (*Instituto de Ingeniería*): Dir. Ing. DANIEL RESÉNDIZ NÚÑEZ.

Institute of Geography (*Instituto de Geografía*): Lic. RUBÉN LÓPEZ RESÉNDIZ.

Institute of Geology (*Instituto de Geología*): Dir. Ing. DIEGO A. CÓRDOBA MÉNDEZ.

Institute of Geophysics (*Instituto de Geofísica*): Dir. Dr. IGNACIO GALNIDO ESTRADA.

Institute of Mathematics (*Instituto de Matemáticas*): Dir. Dr. HUMBERTO CÁRDENAS TRIGOS.

Institute of Physics (*Instituto de Física*): Dir. Dr. JORGE A. FLORES VALDÉS.

Centre of Atmospherical Sciences: Dir. Ing. PEDRO A. MOCIÑO ALEMÁN.

Computing Services Centre (*Centro de Servicios de Cómputo*): Dir. Ing. FRANCISCO MARTÍNEZ PALOMO.

Instruments Centre (*Centro de Instrumentos*): Dir. HÉCTOR DEL CASTILLO.

Centre of Marine Sciences and Limnology (*Centro de Ciencias del Mar y Limnología*): Dir. Dr. ALFREDO LAGUARDIA.

Centre of Materials Research (*Centro de Investigación de Materiales*): Dir. Dr. JORGE RICKARDS CAMPBELL.

Centre of Nuclear Studies (*Centro de Estudios Nucleares*): Dir. Dr. MARCOS ROSENBAUM PITLUCK.

Centre of Scientific and Humanities Research (*Centro de Investigaciones Científicas y Artes*): Dir. Dr. ARMANDO SANDOVAL.

Humanities:

Institute of Anthropological Research (*Instituto de Investigaciones Antropológicas*): Dir. Dr. JAIME LITWAK KING.

Institute of Aesthetics Research (*Instituto de Investigaciones Estéticas*): Dir. Dr. JORGE ALBERTO MANRIQUE.

Institute of Bibliographical Research (*Instituto de Investigaciones Bibliográficas*): Dir. Mtra. MARÍA DEL CARMEN RUIZ CASTAÑEDA.

Institute of Economics Research (*Instituto de Investigaciones Económicas*): Dir. Lic. ARTURO BONILLA SÁNCHEZ.

Institute of Historical Research (*Instituto de Investigaciones Históricas*): Dir. Dr. JORGE GURRIA LACROIX.

Institute of Juridical Research (*Instituto de Investigaciones Jurídicas*): Dir. Lic. HÉCTOR FIX ZAMUDIO.

Institute of Philological Research (*Instituto de Investigaciones Filólogicas*): Dir. Dr. RUBÉN BONIFAZ NUÑO.

Institute of Philosophical Research (*Instituto de Investigaciones Filosóficas*): Dir. Dr. HUGO MARGAIN CHARLES.

Institute of Social Research (*Instituto de Investigaciones Sociales*): Dir. Lic. JULIO LABASTIDA MARTÍN DEL CAMPO.

EDUCATIONAL CENTRES:

Centre for Foreign Languages Teaching (*Centro de Enseñanza de Lenguas Extranjeras*): Dir. Lic. RAÚL ORTÍZ Y ORTÍZ.

Centre for Nuclear Studies (*Centro de Estudios Nucleares*): Dir. Mto. en C. MANUEL NAVARRETE TEJERO.

University Centre for Cinematic Studies (*Centro Universitario de Estudios Cinematográficos*): Dir. Prof. MANUEL GONZÁLEZ CASANOVA.

UNIVERSIDAD AUTÓNOMA DEL ESTADO DE MÉXICO

(Autonomous University of the State of Mexico)

CONSTITUYENTES 100 ORIENTE, TOLUCA, EDO. DE MÉXICO

Telephone: 5-45-04.

Founded 1956.

Private control; Language of instruction: Spanish.

Rector: Dr. JESÚS BARRERA LEGORRETA.

Secretary-General: Lic. JORGE O. ALVAREZ HERRERA.

Librarian: L. A. E. ELVIA ESTRADA LARA.

Library of 6,000 vols.

Number of teachers: 2,000.

Number of students: 20,000.

Institutes of Medicine, Civil Engineering, Economics, Commerce and Administration. Schools of Philosophy and Letters, Architecture, Nursing, and Tourism.

UNIVERSIDAD FEMENINA DE MÉXICO

AVDA. CONSTITUYENTES 151, MÉXICO 18, D.F.

Telephone: 515-13-11, 515-24-74.

Founded 1943.

Private control; Language of instruction: Spanish; Academic year: August to June.

Rector: Dra. ELISA MARGAONA.

Vice-Rectors: Lic. DINORAH ELBA RENDÓN ALATORRE (*Administrative*), Ing. CARLOS BÉCKER PERDOMO (*Academic*).

Librarian: Lic. ARMANDO GONZÁLEZ FLORES.

Library of 12,000 vols.

Number of teachers: 170.

Number of students: 1,100.

Publications: *Catálogo General Anual*†, *Periódico Bimestral*.

DEANS:

School of Law: Lic. JESUS CARRASZO Y CHÁVEZ.

School of Education: Profra. CELIA GARDUÑO.

School of Pharmacobiological Chemistry: Q.F.B. ENRIQUE CALDERÓN GARCÍA.

School of Interior Decoration: Arq. CARLOS CANTÚ BOLLAND.

School of Pedagogy: Maestra ISOLINA MA. MAURI PÉREZ DE MILLOR.

School of Social Work: T. S. ROSA CARMINA RIVERA LUNA.

School of Psychology: Lic. LUZ ANTONIETA POLANCO DE GARZÓN.

School of Tourist Business Administration: Lic. ARMANDO GONZÁLEZ FLORES.

School of Journalism and Communication: Lic. MA. DE LA LUZ CHÁVEZ AVILÉS.

School of International Relations: Lic. EVERARDO CABRERA.

School of Clinical Laboratories: Q.B.P. VÍCTOR MANUEL SÁNCHEZ HIDALGO.

Secretarial School: C.P. ROBERTO E. AMPUDIA LEGASPI.

UNIVERSIDAD AUTÓNOMA DE AGUASCALIENTES

JARDÍN DEL ESTUDIANTE 1, AGUASCALIENTES, AGS.

Telephone: 5-43-91.

Founded 1973.

Private control; Language of instruction: Spanish; Academic year starts September.

Rector: Dr. ALFONSO PÉREZ ROMO.

Secretary-General: Lic. JESÚS EDUARDO MARTÍN JAUREGI.

Registrar: Sra. VERÓNICA I. LOZANO DE LA LUNA.

Librarian: L.A.E. SAUL GALLEGOS LÓPEZ.

Number of teachers: 423.

Number of students: 2,229.

Publications: *Voz Universitaria, Correo Universitario.*

DEANS:

Biomedical Centre: Dr. CARLOS MARTÍN GAYTAN G.

Agriculture Centre: Dr. JAIME DELGADO HERRERA.

Centre for Arts and Humanities: Lic. GUILLERMO BALLESTEROS GUERRA.

Centre for Secondary Education: Lic. RIGOBERTO BERNAL DE LA ROSA.

Centre for Economics and Administration: C.P. EDUARDO GUERRA ESTÉBAÑEZ.

Technological Centre: Arq. MARIO GARCÍA NAVARRO.

Centre for Basic Sciences: JUAN JOSÉ MARTÍNEZ GUERRA.

UNIVERSIDAD DE LAS AMÉRICAS

(University of the Americas)

APDO. POSTAL 100, SANTA CATARINA MÁRTIR, PUEBLA

Telephone: 47-00-00.

Founded 1940 as Mexico City College; became Universidad de las Américas in 1963.

Private control; Languages of instruction: English and Spanish; Academic year: August to May.

Rector: Dr. FERNANDO MACÍAS RENDÓN.

Academic Vice-Rector: Dr. LUIS ERNESTO DERBEZ.

Administrative Vice-Rector: Dr. HAROLD L. KIRKPATRICK.

Vice-Rector for Planning: Dr. JESÚS ORTEGA ZAMORA.

Registrar: Lic. JOSÉ DEL TORO.

Librarian: JAKE WATTS.

Number of teachers: 242.

Number of students: 3,500.

Publications: *Meso-American Notes, Boletín de Estudios Oaxaqueños, Universitas Perspectivas, Americas Alumnas, The Mexico Quarterly Review.*

DEANS:

Faculty of Social Sciences and Humanities: Dr. PEDRO HERNÁNDEZ.

Faculty of Economics and Administrative Sciences: Prof. PAUL YANDRE (acting).

Faculty of Technology: Ing. BERNARDO REYES G.

Faculty of Adult and Continuing Education (Mexico City): Dr. JACQUELINE LOU HODGSON.

Office for Continuing Education (Puebla): Lic. RICARDO OREA.

Graduate Division: Dr. EDWARD SIMMEN.

PROFESSORS:

DERBEZ, LUIS ERNESTO
HODGSON, JACQUELINE L., Economics
KIRKPATRICK, HAROLD L., History and International Relations
MACÍAS RENDÓN, FERNANDO, Chemical Engineering
NUÑEZ, RAFAEL, Psychology
PADDOCK, JOHN, Anthropology
SIMMEN, EDWARD, Modern Literature

ATTACHED INSTITUTES:

Institute for Oaxacan Studies: Apdo. Postal 464, Oaxaca, Oax.; Dir. Dr. JOHN PADDOCK.

Center for University Studies: 250 Hamburgo, México, D.F.; Dir. Dr. JACQUELINE L. HODGSON.

UNIVERSIDAD ANÁHUAC

APDO. POSTAL 10-844, LOMAS ANÁHUAC, MÉXICO 10, D.F.

Telephone: 589-22-00.

Founded 1963.

Private control; Academic year: September to June (two terms).

Rector: Dr. FAUSTINO PARDO VILLA.

Secretary-General: Lic. GREGORIO LÓPEZ.

General Academic Director: Lic. THOMAS WHITE.

Librarian: Lic. ALEJANDRO RAMÍREZ E.

Library of 50,000 vols.

Number of teachers: 429.

Number of students: 3,500.

DEANS:

School of Actuarial Sciences: Act. JAVIER MEDINA MORA.

School of Architecture and Design: Arq. ERNESTO RÍOS.

School of Commerce and Business Administration: Lic. SAMUEL CORRAL.

School of Economics: Dr. SALVADOR KALIFA.

School of Engineering: Ing. JORGE PÉREZ Y BOURAS.

School of Psychology: Dra. ROSA MARÍA VALLE DE MARTÍNEZ PALOMO.

School of Social Communication: Dr. ANGEL SAEZ SAÍZ.

School of Education: Dr. CARLOS BRAVO.

School of Law: Lic. PATROCINIO GONZÁLEZ BLANCO.

School of Medicine: Dr. VÍCTOR ESPINOSA DE LOS REYES.

UNIVERSIDAD AUTÓNOMA DE BAJA CALIFORNIA

APDO. POSTAL 459, RIO CONCHOS Y PASEO DEL VALLE, MEXICALI, BAJA CALIFORNIA

Telephone: 8-20-77.

Founded 1957.

Private control; Language of instruction: Spanish.

Rector: RIGOBERTO CÁRDENAS V.

Vice-Rector: Lic. OSCAR VALENZUELA AVILA.

Registrar: Lic. RAÚL CUEVAS.

Librarian: Lic. JAVIER RUIZ CARRILLO.

Number of teachers: 1,200.
Number of students: 17,000.

Publication: *CALAFIA*.

DIRECTORS:

School of Accountancy and Administration: C. P. ERNESTO VIDAL WILHELMY.

School of Agricultural Training: Ing. LUIS F. NUÑEZ.

School of Agronomy: Ing. RICARDO OLVERA OCAMPO.

School of Architecture: Arq. RUBEN CASTRO BOJORQUEZ.

School of Dentistry: JORGE OCHOA CERVANTES.

School of Education: Prof. MARIO LUNA BOJORQUEZ.

School of Engineering: Ing. JORGE CONTRERAS LIÑAN.

School of Law: Lic. HECTOR MANUEL GALLEGO GARCIA.

School of Medicine: Dr. HUMBERTO TORRES SANGINES.

School of Nursing: Dr. ALFREDO SANTAELLA GROSS.

School of Social Sciences and Politics. Lic. ENRIQUE PRIEGO MENDOZA.

There are branches in Ensenada and Tijuana.

UNIVERSIDAD AUTÓNOMA CHAPINGO

DOMICILIO CONOCIDO, CHAPINGO, EDO. DE MEXICO

Telephone: 585-45-55.

Founded 1854 as Escuela Nacional de Agricultura; name changed 1978.

Private control; Academic year: August to June.

Rector: Ing. ROGELIO POSADAS DEL R.

Technical Secretary: Dr. FELIPE ROMERO.

Administrative Secretary: Ing. RAFAEL CAMPOS.

Agricultural Economics, Agricultural Industries, Irrigation, Parasitology, Phytotechnics, Forestry, Stock-breeding, Soil Science, Rural Sociology.

The library contains 100,000 vols. and 939 periodical titles.

Number of teachers: 350.
Number of students: 2,550.

Postgraduate College: f. 1959.

Director: Dr. EDUARDO CASAS DÍAZ.

Genetics, Entomology, Botany, Statistics, Phytopathology, Soil Science, Agricultural Economics, Agricultural Extension, Irrigation and Drainage.

Number of teachers: 125.

Publication: *Agrociencia*†.

UNIVERSIDAD AUTÓNOMA DE CHIAPAS

2A PONIENTE SUR 118, 5° PISO, APDO. POSTAL 343, TUXTLA GUTIERREZ, CHIAPAS

Telephone: 2-53-55.

Founded 1975.

Private control; Academic year: September to July (two semesters).

Rector: C.P. FEDERICO SALAZAR NARVAEZ.

Secretary-General: Lic. JORGE L. ARIAS ZEBADUA.

Librarian: ALBERTO SANCHEZ MERCHANT.

Number of teachers: 294.
Number of students: 2,746.

Publications: *Criterio Universitario, Vida Universitaria.*

DIRECTORS:

Administration and Accountancy: C. P. EMILIO E. SALAZAR NARVAEZ.

Physics and Mathematics: Ing. CARLOS SERRATO ALVARADO.

Human Medicine: Dr. JOSE CARLOS LOPEZ REYES.

Veterinary Medicine and Animal Husbandry: Dr. ABRAHAM MORALES MESSNER.

Law: Lic. FRANCISCO AGUILAR LOPEZ.

Social Sciences: Lic. ARTURO RIVERA TREJO.

Administration: C.P. VÍCTOR M. PIMENTEL GONZÁLEZ.

Chemistry: Ing. ERAY HERNÁNDEZ GÓMEZ.

Agriculture: L.A.E. JOSE RAQUEL HERNÁNDEZ GONZÁLEZ.

Humanities: Profra. ANNABELLA MUÑOA RINCON.

UNIVERSIDAD AUTÓNOMA DE CHIHUAHUA*

CIUDAD UNIVERSITARIA, CHIHUAHUA, CHIH.

Telephone: 2-57-08.

Founded 1954.

Rector: Lic. JOSÉ R. MILLER H.

Secretary-General: Lic. JESÚS RODRÍGUEZ GUTIÉRREZ.

Number of students: *c.* 5,000.

Publications: *Lecturas Jurídicas, Boletín Bibliográfico-Escuela de Derecho.*

Courses in sciences, engineering, law, philosophy and letters, medicine, agriculture. Branch in Ciudad Juarez (public administration and political science).

* No reply received to our questionnaire this year.

UNIVERSIDAD AUTÓNOMA DE COAHUILA

BLVD. VENUSTIANO CARRANZA Y DURANGO, APDO. POSTAL 308, SALTILLO, COAHUILA

Telephone: 2-01-55.

Founded 1867, refounded 1957.

State control; Language of instruction: Spanish; Academic year: August to June (two terms).

Rector: L. Ab. OSCAR VILLEGAS RICO.

Secretary-General: L. Ab. L. ALBERTO L. SALAZAR RODRÍGUEZ.

Librarian: ANTONIO MALACARA.

Number of teachers: *c.* 900.
Number of students: 13,923.

DIRECTORS:

Faculty of Education: M. C. MA. ESTHER FLORES R.

Faculty of Law: L.Ab.Fco. LUIS YAÑEZ A.

School of Chemistry: L.C.Q. EUGENIO RAMÍREZ I.

School of Economics: L.Ec. VICTOR M. SILVA R.

School of Civil Engineering: Lic. ROBERTO MARTÍNEZ C.

School of Architecture: L.Ar. HÉCTOR DE J. LAREDO R.

School of Psychology: L.Ps. MARTHA A. FLORES PRIDA.

"Dr. Santiago Valdes Galindo" School of Nursing and Obstetrics: L.Md.C. JOSÉ FALLAD BADILLO.

School of Social Work: T.T.S. DOMINGO RITO M.

"*Ruben Herrera*" *School of Plastic Arts:* Prof. ELOY CERECERO S.
School of Medicine: L.Md.C. HEXIQUIO GOMEZ A.
Open University Institute: ALEJANDRO DÁVILA FLORES.

Torreon Section
School of Medicine: L.Md.C. JOAQUIN DEL VALLE S.
School of Dentistry; L.C.D. ROLANDO GUERRERO S.
School of Commerce and Administration: L.C.P. MANUEL AGUILERA C.
School of Political Science and Political Administration: L.C.P. FERMÍN CUÉLLAR GONZÁLEZ.
School of Law and Social Sciences: L. Ab. DAVID ORTIZ RAMÍREZ.
School of Economics: L.Ec. JORGE H. PÉREZ H.
School of Nursing: L.Md.C. MANUEL ESTRADA QUEZADA.
Open University Institute: MARÍA DE LA LUZ AVILA RIVAS.

Norte Section
School of Mechanical and Electrical Engineering: L.I.M.E. JOSÉ JUAN LARA SAUCEDO.
School of Mining and Metallurgy: L.I.Mt. JUAN JOSÉ GONZÁLEZ R.

UNIVERSIDAD DE COLIMA

AVDA. UNIVERSIDAD 333,
COLIMA, COL.
Telephone: 2-01-07, 2-25-33.

Founded 1867 as Universidad Popular de Colima, reorganized 1962.

Private control; Academic year: August to July.

Chancellor: J. HUMBERTO SILVA OCHOA.
Rector: ALBERTO HERRERA CARRILLO.
Secretary-General: C.P. RAÚL CÁRDENAS JIMÉNEZ.
Librarian: **ARAÓN VÁZQUEZ REQUENA.**

Number of teachers: 632.
Number of students: 7,822.

Faculties of law and social sciences, public administration, accounting, management, medicine, civil engineering, topography and geodesy, agronomy, education.

UNIVERSIDAD JUÁREZ DEL ESTADO DE DURANGO

CONSTITUCIÓN 404, SUR,
DURANGO, DURANGO
Telephone: 2-00-44.

Founded as a Civil College 1856, became University 1957.

Private control; Language of instruction: Spanish; Academic year: February to June, August to December.

Rector: Lic. JOSÉ HUGO MARTÍNEZ ORTIZ.
Secretary-General: Lic. MARIO R. VALERO SALAS.
Chief Administrative Officer: L.A.E. JUAN JOSÉ REYES VALENZUELA.
Librarian: A.B. JOSÉ LINO HERNÁNDEZ CAMPOS.

Number of teachers: 740.
Number of students: 7,931.

DEANS:
School of Commerce and Administration: C. P. RUBÉN VARGAS QUIÑONES.
School of Law: Lic. CAMERINO CASTRO GONZÁLEZ.
School of Medicine: Dr. ALEJANDRO PESCHARD FERNÁNDEZ.
School of Veterinary Medicine and Zootechnics: M.V.Z. RAÚL RANGEL ROMERO.
School of Dentistry: C.D. GUILLERMO PESCHARD DELGADO.
School of Agriculture and Zootechnics: Ing. JOSÉ ALBERTO CENICEROS V.

ATTACHED INSTITUTIONS:
Instituto de Investigación Científica (*Institute of Scientific Research*): Dir. Dr. ROBERTO RIVERA DAMM.
Instituto de Ciencias Sociales (*Institute of Social Sciences*): Dir. Lic. RAÚL RÍOS GÜERECA.

UNIVERSIDAD DE GUADALAJARA

AVDA. JUÁREZ No. 975,
GUADALAJARA, JAL.
Telephone: 25-22-42.

Founded 1792.

Controlled by General Universities Council of the Government of Mexico; Academic year: September to August.

Rector: Arq. JORGE ENRIQUE ZAMBRANO VILLA.
Secretary-General: Lic. ENRIQUE JAVIER ALFARO ANGUIANO.
Chief Administrative Officer: Prof. MARÍA LUZ LÓPEZ RUBALCAVA.
Librarian: HELEN LADRON DE GUEVARA COX.

The library contains *c.* 450,000 vols.
Number of teachers: 6,207.
Number of students: 156,621.

Publications: *Revista de la Universidad de Guadalajara* (quarterly), and various faculty and departmental publs.

DEANS AND DIRECTORS:
Faculty of Administration: Lic. JUAN OCHOA LUNA.
Faculty of Architecture: Arq. VICENTE PÉREZ CARÁBIAS.
Faculty of Chemical Sciences: Q.F.B. ARMANDO MÁXIMO VENEGAS ALARCÓN.
Faculty of Commerce and Administration: C.P. AURELIO RODRÍGUEZ SANTANA.
Faculty of Law: Lic. JOSÉ MORA LUNA.
Faculty of Economics: Lic. ANDRÉS LÓPEZ DÍAZ.
Faculty of Philosophy and Letters: Dr. PEDRO QUEVEDO CASTAÑEDA.
Faculty of Engineering: Ing. IGNACIO RAFAEL MONTOYA FLORES.
Faculty of Medicine: Dr. GUILLERMO ESQUIVIAS LEAÑO.
Faculty of Veterinary Medicine and Animal Husbandry: M.V.Z. ABEL BUENROSTRO SILVA.
Faculty of Dentistry: Dr. MARIO CAMPERO OJANGUREN.
Faculty of Design: Arq. PABLO ROBLES GÓMEZ.
School of Vocational Training: Lic. CARLOS MORA LÓPEZ.
School of Plastic Arts: Lic. JORGE SEIMANDI RAMÍREZ.
School of Nursing: Dr. J. FELIPE TORRES PLANK.
Graduate School: Dr. AMADO RUIZ SÁNCHEZ.
School of Music: Prof. MIGUEL VILLASEÑOR GARCÍA.
Polytechnic School: Ing. IGNACIO MORA LUNA.
School of Agriculture: Ing. ANTONIO ALVAREZ GONZÁLEZ.
School of Psychology: Dr. WENCESLAO OROZCOY SEVILLA.
School of Social Work: Dra. IRENE ROBLEDO GARCÍA.
School of Tourism: Lic. PEDRO ORTIZ DECENAS.
Institute of Medico-biological Sciences: PEDRO RODRÍGUEZ MOSQUEDA.
Institute of Librarianship: Maestra HELEN LADRÓN DE GUEVARA COX.
Institute of Botany: Dr. ENRIQUE ESTRADA FAUDÓN.
Institute of Geography and Statistics: JOSÉ MANUEL VELASCO GUDINA.
Institute of Experimental Pathology: Dr. AMADO RUIZ SÁNCHEZ.
Institute of Social Studies: Lic. MANUEL RODRÍGUEZ LAPUENTE.
Institute of Social Sciences and Humanities: Prof. FELIPE ZEPEDA FIGUEROA.
Technological Institute: Lic. JAIME OROZCO MONTES.
Institute of Wood, Pulp and Paper: Ing. KARL AUGUSTÍN GRELLMANN.

There are also 10 Preparatory Schools, 1 Regional Nursing School and 4 Vocational Training Centres.

UNIVERSIDAD AUTÓNOMA DE GUADALAJARA

APDO. POSTAL 1-440,
GUADALAJARA, JAL.
Telephone: 41-50-51.

Founded 1935.

Private control; Language of instruction: Spanish; Academic year: August to May.

Rector: Dr. LUIS GARIBAY GUTIÉRREZ.
Vice-Rector: Lic. ANTONIO LEAÑO ALVAREZ DEL CASTILLO.
Registrar: Ing. LUIS ONTIVEROS HERNÁNDEZ.
Librarian: Profa. TERESITA CASTILLO DE SÁINZ.

The library contains 80,285 vols., 2,729 maps, 2,000 periodicals.

Number of teachers: 1,430.
Number of students: 19,002.

Publications: *Docencia* (2 a month), *Alma Mater* (monthly), *Antorcha* (weekly), *Ocho Columnas* (daily).

DEANS AND DIRECTORS:

Humanities and Social Sciences: Dir. of Academic Affairs Lic. HUMBERTO LÓPEZ DELGADILLO.
Institute of Humanities and Social Sciences: Lic. ALFONSO RIVAS SALMÓN.
School of Anthropology: Lic. ANDRÉS LÓPEZ DE NAVA.
Institute of Design: Arq. JOSÉ MORALES GONZÁLEZ, M.SC.
School of Architecture: Arq. RAÚL MENDOZA RIVERA, M.SC.
School of Plastic Arts: Arq. GUILLERMO DE LA TORRE RIZO.
School of Law and Social Work: Lic. GUILLERMO HERNÁNDEZ ORNELAS.
School of Administration, Accountancy, Economics and Tourism: C.P. TOMÁS SANTANA ROMÁN.
School of Linguistics: Profa. CARMEN CORONA BRONDO.
School of Communication Sciences: Dr. SILVIANO HERNÁNDEZ GONZÁLEZ.
School of Psychology: Dr. JUAN IGNACIO ACEVES MUÑOZ.
School of Philosophy and Letters: Lic. SALVADOR RIVAS SALMÓN.
School of Pedagogy: Lic. JOSÉ MA. ANGEL RODRÍGUEZ.

Bio-Medicine: Dir. of Academic Affairs Dr. NÉSTOR VELASCO PÉREZ.
Institute of Biological Sciences: Dr. JESÚS FLORES SÁNCHEZ.
School of Nursing: MARÍA G. GAXIOLA DE AVALOS.
School of Medicine: Dr. NÉSTOR VELASCO PÉREZ.
Clinics: Dr. ANGEL OROZCO BRAVO.
School of Dentistry: Dr. LUIS FERNANDO VELÁZQUEZ PÉREZ.
Community Medicine: Lic. HÉCTOR J. SALCEDO S.
University Hospital Ramón Garibay: Dr. RAÚL SAAVEDRA.
University Hospital Angel Leaño: Dr. JUAN MANUEL LEPE V.
Health Education Office: Dr. IGNACIO MONCAYO.
Audio Visual Education Office: Dr. EUSTOLIO VÁLDEZ FLORES.

Science and Technology: Dir. of Academic Affairs Ing. RAMÓN ESCOBAR TABERA CARRILLO.
Institute of Exact and Earth Sciences: Ing. ALFREDO DÁVILA CAMACHO.
School of Chemistry: Ing. JUAN J. TRUJILLO DEL RÍO.
School of Engineering: Ing. LUIS JORGE AGUILERA CASILLAS.
School of Mathematics: Ing. EDUARDO MANUEL OJEDA PEÑA.
School of Information Science: Ing. JOSÉ YAROSLAW OLEYNICK FIGUEROA.
School of Biology: Biol. JOSÉ DE JESÚS VIZCARRA TIRADO.

UNIVERSIDAD DE GUANAJUATO

LASCURÁIN DE RETANA No. 5, GUANAJUATO
Telephone: 2-03-04.

Founded 1732 as Colegio de la Purísima Concepción; changed in 1928 to Colegio del Estado; present name 1945.

Rector: NESTOR RAUL LUNA HERNÁNDEZ.
Secretary: C.P. MARCO ANTONIO VERGARA LARIOS.
Librarian: Mtra. SUSANA FRANCO VILLASEÑOR.

Library of 19,200 vols.
Number of teachers: 1,153.
Number of students: 7,179.

Publication: *Colmena Universitaria* (monthly).

DEANS:

School of Law: Lic. JUAN JORGE ZAMORA FONSECA.
School of Accountancy and Administration: C.P. MA. ELENA MORALES SÁNCHEZ.
School of Architecture: Arq. JOSÉ LUIS MARTÍNEZ COSSIO.
School of Mining Engineering: Ing. ANTONIO NIETO ANTUNEZ.
School of Civil Engineering: Ing. ERNESTO VAZQUEZ HERRERA.
School of Topography and Hydraulics: Ing. VICTOR ADRIAN MANRIQUE DIAZ.
School of Philosophy and Letters: Mtro. LUIS PALACIOS HERNÁNDEZ.
School of Nursing: Enfra. ELIA LONA DE LARA.
School of Chemistry: Ing. DAVID GUERRA CARRILLO.
School of Medicine (León): Dr. JAIME FUENTES SANTOYO.

ATTACHED INSTITUTES:

Instituto de Investigaciones Cientificas (*Institute of Scientific Research*): Dir. Ing. ARMANDO LÓPEZ M. DEL CAMPO.

Instituto de Investigaciones Tecnológicas (*Institute of Technological Research*): Dir. Ing. WENCESLAO X. LÓPEZ.

Instituto de Investigaciones Psicopedagógicas (*Institute of Psycho-Educational Research*): Dir. Lic. CARMEN CARRASCO.

UNIVERSIDAD AUTÓNOMA DE GUERRERO

AVDA. JUÁREZ 13, CHILPANCINGO, GUERRERO

Founded 1867.

Rector: Q.B.P. ARQUÍMEDES MORALES CARRANZA.
General Secretary: Ing. Quím. JOSÉ LUIS PARRA MIJANGOS.
Librarian: Lic. FELIPE DE JESÚS RENDÓN HERNÁNDEZ.

DIRECTORS:

Faculty of Law and Social Sciences: Lic. MANUEL LEÓN ROMÁN.
School of Pedagogy: Lic. ILDEGUNDA SANTOS DE ARCOS.
School of Sciences: Quim. ARQUÍMEDES MORALES CARRANZA.
School of Engineering: Ing. ADALBERTO GARCIA PÉREZ.
School of Agronomy and Zootechnics: Ing. FÉLIX DE LA O MENA.
School of Nursing and Obstetrics: Dr. CÉSAR PIÑA CÁMARA.
School of Humanities: Lic. JORGE RENDÓN ALARCÓN.
School of Commerce and Administration: C.P. JOSÉ MANUEL AVILA GÓMEZ.

UNIVERSIDAD AUTÓNOMA DE HIDALGO*

ABASOLO No. 600, PACHUCA, HIDALGO
Telephone: 2-65-34.

Founded 1869 as the Instituto Científico y Literario, present status 1961.

Rector: Ing. CARLOS HERRERA ORDÓÑEZ.
Secretary: Lic. RAFAEL ARRIAGA PAZ.

Number of teachers: 680.
Number of students: 8,293.

Publications: Occasional scientific or commemorative publications.

Courses in social sciences, public administration and accounting, sciences, medicine, dentistry, social work.

UNIVERSIDAD IBEROAMERICANA

AV. CERRO DE LAS TORRES 395, MEXICO 21, D.F.
Telephone: 549-35-00.

Founded 1943.

Languages of instruction: Spanish and English (Summer School only); Private control; Academic year: August to May (two semesters).

Rector: Lic. ENRIQUE PORTILLA O.
Registrar: JOSEFINA REYES.
General Director of Undergraduate Studies: Dr. ARMANDO SALCEDO.
General Director of Graduate Studies: Dr. ERNESTO DOMINGUEZ.
Director of Academic Services: Fis. GABRIEL ANAYA.
General Director of Public Relations: JORGE VÉRTIZ.
General Director of Promotion and Development: Lic. JOSE J. VELASCO.
General Director of General Services: ARMANDO LEÑERO.
General Director of Finance: C.P. HUMBERTO ROJAS.
Director of Centers: Mtro. RUBEN MURILLO.
Librarian: Arq. JUAN ANAYA DUARTE.

Library of *c.* 110,000 vols.
Number of teachers: 1,200.
Number of students: 6,900.

Publications: *Catálogo General*† (annually), *Boletín* (monthly), *Comunidad*† (every 2 months), *Didac* (every 2 months), *Jurídica* (annually), *Anuario de Humanidades* (annually), *Catálogo de Planes de Estudio* (annuallv), *Catálogo de Posgrado* (annually).

DIRECTORS OF INSTITUTES:

Social Sciences: Dr. ANGEL PALERM.
Humanities: Dr. HÉCTOR GONZÁLEZ-URIBE.

DIRECTORS OF DEPARTMENTS:

Accounting: C.P. VÍCTOR AGUILAR.
Architecture and Urban Design: Arq. JOSÉ NAVA.
Anthropology: Dra. CARMEN VIQUEIRA.
Art: Mtro. FAUSTO RAMIREZ-ROJAS.
Business Administration: Mtro. NEY VILLAMIL.
Civil Engineering: Ing. GUILLERMO CELIS COLIN.
Communication: Lic. JAVIER MARTÍNEZ RIVERA.
Economics: Lic. AGUSTIN ROZADA.
Engineering and Chemical Sciences: Ing. ARMANDO RUGARCIA.
History: Mtra. BEATRIZ RUIZ GAYTÁN.
Industrial and Graphic Design: D. I. MANUEL ALVAREZ FUENTES.
Industrial Relations: Lic. AMADO AGUIRRE.
International Affairs: Mtra. CARMELA ALONSO DE BERNAL.
Law: Lic. JORGE DÍAZ.
Literature: Dr. LUIS-FERNANDO BREHM.
Mathematics: Ing. ALFONSO MORALES.
Mechanical and Electrical Engineering: Ing. GUILLERMO MARTÍNEZ DEL CAMPO.
Nutrition: Dra. ELBA DURAN DE FLORES.
Philosophy: Mtro. MIGUEL ANGEL ZARCO.
Psychology: Dra. TERE LARTIGUE BECERRA.
Physics: Fis. JUAN ANTONIO FLORES LIRA.
Sociology and Political Science: Mtro. JESÚS LUIS GARCÍA GARZA.
Theology: Mtro. XAVIER CACHO VÁZQUEZ.

UNIVERSIDAD INTERCONTINENTAL

INSURGENTES SUR 4135,
MÉXICO 22, D.F.

Telephone: 573-85-44.

Founded 1976.

Rector: Dr. AGUSTÍN G. LEMUS TALAVERA.
General Secretary: Lic. J. AMBROSIO RUIZ MERCADO.
Administrative Officer: Lic. JUAN JOSÉ CORONA LÓPEZ.
Librarian: Lic. ANTONIO LARA GONZÁLEZ.

Number of teachers: 209.
Number of students: 967.

Publication: *Ediciones de la Rectoría.*

Departments of administration, architecture, communications, computer science, law, philosophy, dentistry, education, psychology, theology.

UNIVERSIDAD AUTÓNOMA DE CIUDAD JUÁREZ

APDO. POSTAL 1594-D,
AV. LÓPEZ MATEOS 20,
CIRCUITO PRONAF,
CIUDAD JUÁREZ, CHIHUAHUA

Telephone: 3-12-22, 3-08-88.

Founded 1973.

Languages of instruction: Spanish and English.

Rector: Dr. RENE FRANCO BARRENO.
Vice-Rector: Lic. ENRIQUE VILLARREAL MACÍAS.
Chief Administrative Officer: C.P. EDUARDO LEÓN MEDINA.
Librarian: Lic. ENRIQUE VILLARREAL MACÍAS.

Number of teachers: 380.
Number of students: 4,000.

Publications: *Tribuna Universitaria, Educación, Radio Universidad, Imágenes.*

DEANS:

Institute of Biomedical Science: Dr. ROBERTO MORENO RAZO.
Institute of Engineering and Town Planning: Ing. JOSÉ LOZANO FRANCO.
Institute of Social Sciences and Administration: Lic. ENRIQUE VILLAREAL MACÍAS.

UNIVERSIDAD DEL VALLE DE MÉXICO

SADI CARNOT No. 57,
COLONIA SAN RAFAEL,
MEXICO 4, D.F.

Telephone: 566-97-33.

Founded 1960.

Private control.

Rector: Lic. RAFAEL J. HERNÁNDEZ.
General Secretary: DAVID HERNÁNDEZ AGÍS.

Number of teachers: 250.
Number of students: 4,200.

Schools of Accounting, Industrial Relations, Administration, Preparatory Studies.

UNIVERSIDAD LA SALLE DE MÉXICO

BENJAMIN FRANKLIN 47,
MEXICO 18, D.F.

Telephone: 516-99-60.

Founded 1962.

Private control; Language of instruction: Spanish; Academic year: September to June.

Rector: Dr. FRANCISCO LEONEL DE CERVANTES LECHUGA.
Registrar: GONZALO ZAVALA ONTIVEROS.
Academic Vice-Rector: Mtro. CESAR RANGEL BARRERA.
Administrative Vice-Rector: C. P. ROGELIO BARRÓN RODRÍGUEZ.
Librarian: Lic. MARÍA TERESA CORNEJO DE GUERRERO.

Number of teachers: 840.
Number of students: 8,010.

Publications: *Gaceta*†, *Indicador, Diez dias*†, *Boletín de Preparatoria, Boletín de Biblioteca, Nomos*†, *Ezeta*†, *M.A.S.*†, *Logos*†.

DIRECTORS:

School of Preparatory Studies: Lic. SALVADOR GONZÁLEZ RODRÍGUEZ.
School of Accountancy and Management: L.A. ÁNGEL ELIZONDO LÓPEZ.
School of Architecture: Arq. JOSÉ MANUEL ECHAVARRI OLVERA.
School of Chemistry: Dra. ARACELI SÁNCHEZ DE CORRAL.
School of Law: Dr. JAIME DE LA PEÑA.
School of Medicine: LAURO M. LORIA.
School of Philosophy: Lic. JORGE MUÑOZ BATIZTA.
Centre of Mathematics, Computing and Systems Analysis: Ing. JAIME PALACIOS CASTAÑÓN.
School of Engineering: Ing. SERGIO BARRERO COVARRUBIAS.
Institute of Religious Sciences: Mtro. ADALBERTO ARANDA RAMÍREZ.

UNIVERSIDAD AUTÓNOMA METROPOLITANA

APDO. POSTAL 325,
MEXICO 1, D.F.

Telephone: 576-79-00.

Founded 1973.

Rector-General: Dr. FERNANDO SALMERÓN.
Chief Administration Officer: Lic. ROLANDO GUZMÁN F.
Librarian: KAMILA KNAP ROUBAL.

Number of teachers: 1,627.
Number of students: 20,170.

Publication: *Organo Informativo*† (weekly), *Casa del Tiempo*† (monthly), *Boletín de Tablas de Contenido* (quarterly), *Reportes de Investigación* (irregular).

Azcapotzalco Campus

Rector: Ing. JORGE HANEL DEL VALLE.
Secretary: Lic. JORGE RUIZ DUEÑAS.
Librarian: ROSA MARÍA FERNÁNDEZ DE ZAMORA.

DIRECTORS:

Basic Sciences and Engineering: Dr. OSCAR M. GONZÁLEZ CUEVAS.
Social Sciences and Humanities: Lic. FRANCISCO JOSÉ PAOLI BOLIO.
Art and Design: Arq. MANUEL SÁNCHEZ DE CARMONA.

Iztapalapa Campus

Rector: Dr. ADOLFO ROSADO GARCÍA.
Secretary: Mtro. JAVIER HERNÁNDEZ GALINDO.
Librarian: Lic. ALEJANDRO RAMÍREZ ESCÁRCEGA.

DIRECTORS:

Basic Sciences and Engineering: Dr. EDUARDO PIÑA GARZA.
Biological and Health Sciences: Dr. FERNANDO ANTON-TAY.
Social Sciences and Humanities: Mtro. JORGE MARTÍNEZ CONTRERAS.

Xochimilco Campus

Rector: Dr. LUIS FELIPE BOJALIL JABER.
Secretary: Dr. WALTERIO GARCÍA.
Librarian: Lic. FRANCISCO FIERRO ALVAREZ.

DIRECTORS:

Biological and Health Sciences: Dr. MIGUEL ARENAS VARGAS.
Social Sciences and Humanities: Dr. RAÚL LIVAS VERA.
Art and Design: Ing. OSCAR A. CHAVARRI PAVÓN.

UNIVERSIDAD MICHOACANA DE SAN NICOLÁS DE HIDALGO

SANTIAGO TAPIA 403,
MORELIA, MICHOACÁN

Telephone: 2-05-69, 2-04-91.

Founded 1540, University in 1917.

Private control; Language of instruction: Spanish; Academic year: September to May.

Rector: Dr. JAIME GENOVEVO FIGUEROA ZAMUDIO.
Secretary-General: Lic. FERNANDO JUÁREZ ARANDA.
Registrar: Ing. CARLOS AVILA FIGUEROA.
Director of Library: Prof. JAVIER ARREOLA CORTÉS.

Library of 25,000 vols.
Number of teachers: 1,282.
Number of students: 29,167.

Publications: *El Universitario* (weekly), *Actividad* (fortnightly), *Boletines Informativos de Cada Dependencia Universitaria.*

UNIVERSIDAD DE MONTEMORELOS

APDO. 16, MONTEMORELOS,
NUEVO LEÓN

Telephone: 3-32-33.
Founded 1973.

Rector: Lic. JAIME CASTREJÓN SÁNCHEZ.
Vice-Rector: C.P. DANIEL MARTÍNEZ CRUZ.
Administrative Officer: Ing. ALVARO SAUZA.
Librarian: DAVID W. RÍOS.

Number of teachers: *c.* 100.
Number of students: 1,531.

Courses in medicine, education, business administration, nursing, music.

UNIVERSIDAD DE MONTERREY

AVDA. GONZALITOS 300 SUR,
APDO. 4442, SUC. J,
MONTERREY, NUEVO LEÓN

Telephone: 46-89-70, 46-89-71.
Founded 1969.

Private control; Language of instruction: Spanish.

Chancellor: Ing. DON CAMILO G. SADA.
Rector: J. ROLANDO ESPINOSA RAMÍREZ, C.P.
Registrar: Ing. RUTILO DE LA MORA.
Librarian: Lic. IMELDA RODRÍGUEZ.

Number of teachers: 379.
Number of students: 3,335.

Publication: *FORO* (Rector's Information Bulletin).

Institutes of Humanities and Social Sciences, Natural and Exact Sciences, Economic and Administrative Sciences, Health, Education, Law, and the Arts. Postgraduate School and University Extension.

UNIVERSIDAD AUTÓNOMA DEL ESTADO DE MORELOS

CUERNAVACA, MORELOS

Telephone: 3-10-90.
Founded 1939.

Private control; Language of instruction: Spanish.

Rector: Quim. Ind. SERGIO FIGUEROA CAMPOS.
Registrar: Ing. FAUSTO GUTIÉRREZ ARAGÓN.
Librarian: Prof. GUALBERTO CASTAÑEDA LINARES.

Number of teachers: 598.
Number of students: 11,337.

Publication: *University Gazette* (monthly).

DEANS AND DIRECTORS:

School of Biological Sciences: Dr. FÉLIX FRÍAS SÁNCHEZ.
School of Chemical Sciences: Q.I. ROBERTO BARRERA URBE.
School of Commerce and Administration: C.P. RAÚL TRUJILLO.
School of Law and Social Sciences: Lic. JOAQUÍN MAGDALENO G.
School of Medicine: Dr. ENRIQUE DÍAZ SANTANA.
School of Psychology: Psic. HUBERTO FABRE P.
School of Architecture: Arq. JESÚS SOTELO ORTEGA.
Teacher Training School for Men: Prof. JOSÉ CONCHA REYES.
Teacher Training School for Women: Profra. ALMA CELIA SOTELO A.
School of Nursing and Obstetrics: Enf. CONCEPCIÓN FLORES ORTIZ.

There are also 19 Preparatory Schools and 3 Teacher Training Schools.

UNIVERSIDAD MOTOLINIA A.C.

CERRADO DE AMEYALCO 227,
MEXICO 12, D.F.

Telephone: 523-48-13.
Founded 1918.

Private control; Language of instruction: Spanish; Academic year: August to July.

Principal: LUZ MARÍA PORTILLO ARROYO.
Chief Administrative Officer: MARÍA DEL REFUGIO HERRERA FLORES.
Librarian: JUANA MARÍA CAMARGO MUÑOZ.

Number of teachers: 35.
Number of students: 90.

There is also a campus at Pedregal.

UNIVERSIDAD AUTÓNOMA DE NAYARIT

CIUDAD DE LA CULTURA
AMADO NERVO, TEPIC,
NAYARIT

Founded 1930 as Instituto de Ciencias y Letras de Nayarit, refounded as university 1969.

Rector: Lic. RUBÉN HERNÁNDEZ DE LA TORRE.
Secretary-General: Lic. FERMÍN FLETES A.

Number of teachers: *c.* 230.
Number of students: *c.* 2,480.

Schools of Agriculture, Dentistry, Nursing, Commerce and Administration, Law, Economics, Chemical Engineering, Medicine, Zoology, Veterinary Medicine.

UNIVERSIDAD AUTÓNOMA DEL NORESTE

MONCLOVA 1430, 2° PISO,
COL. REPÚBLICA,
SALTILLO, COAHUILA

Telephone: 2-44-22, 3-66-46.
Founded 1974.

Rector: Prof. HIGINIO GONZALEZ CALDERON.
Secretary-General: Lic. MAURICIO DIAZ GARCIA.
Administrative Officer: Ing. ENRIQUE SANTOS COY DE LA FUENTE.
Librarian: Lic. GERARDO CASTILLO.

Number of teachers: 365.
Number of students: 2,973.

Courses in business administration, accountancy, education and psychology, sociology, biology. Branches in Monclova, Torreón, Piedras Negras, Sabinas.

UNIVERSIDAD DEL NORTE

CUAUHTÉMOC SUR 985,
MONTERREY, NUEVO LEÓN

Telephone: 40-16-04.
Founded 1973.

Rector: C.P. JOSÉ G. RODRÍGUEZ GARZA.
Vice-Rector: C.P. ANTONIO J. GONZÁLEZ VILLARREAL.
Administrative Officer: C.P. CARLOS RODRÍGUEZ GONZÁLEZ.
Librarian: Ing. SALIM GIACOMAN M.

Number of teachers: 58.
Number of students: 681.

Courses in engineering, business administration.

UNIVERSIDAD AUTÓNOMA DE NUEVO LEÓN

TORRE DE LA RECTORÍA, 8° PISO,
CIUDAD UNIVERSITARIA, MONTERREY, NUEVO LEÓN

Telephone: 52-55-81, 52-33-22.
Founded 1933.

Private control; Language of instruction: Spanish.

Rector: Dr. LUIS EUGENIO TODD PÉREZ.
Secretary-General: JESÚS LOZANO DÍAZ.
Academic and Library Director: Ing. OREL DARÍO GARCÍA RODRÍGUEZ.

Number of teachers: *c.* 1,400.
Number of students: 80,000.

Publications: *Armas y Letras* (quarterly), *Interfolia-Biblioteca Universitaria "Alfonso Reyes"* (monthly), *Humanitas* (annually) and *Universidad* (fortnightly).

DIRECTORS:

Faculty of Agronomy: Ing. FERMIN MONTES.
Faculty of Architecture: Arq. ANTONIO FUENTES ESPINOSA.
Faculty of Biological Science: Biol. JOSÉ CASTILLO TOVAR.
Faculty of Chemistry: I.Q. SERGIO SANTOS BERMEJO.
Faculty of Civil Engineering: Ing. ELIEZAR GRACIA LEAL.
Faculty of Commerce and Business Administration: C.P. JOSÉ CÁRDENAS CAVAZOS.
Faculty of Dentistry: Dr. MIGUEL GARCIA.
Faculty of Economics: Lic. FRANCISCO MAYDÓN GARZA.
Faculty of Law and Social Sciences: Lic. NEFTALI GARZA CONTRERAS.
Faculty of Mathematics and Physics: Lic. JOSÉ LUIS COMPARÁN.
Faculty of Mechanical and Electrical Engineering: Ing. JORGE M. URENCIO ABREGO.
Faculty of Medicine: Dr. FERNANDO OVALLE BERUMEN.
Faculty of Nursing: Lic. ESTHER GALLEGOS.
Faculty of Philosophy and Letters: Lic. TOMÁS GONZÁLEZ DE LUNA.
Faculty of Physical Education: Ing. CAYETANO GARZA GARZA.
Faculty of Psychology: Lic. CIRILO GARCÍA.
Faculty of Social Work: Lic. PEDRO CASTELLANOS.
Faculty of Veterinary Medicine and Zootechnics: Dr. ARIEL ORTIZ.
School of Public Health: Dr. RODRIGO GONZÁLEZ PÉREZ.

UNIVERSIDAD AUTÓNOMA "BENITO JUÁREZ" DE OAXACA

APDO. 76, ESQ. AVDA. INDEPENDENCIA Y MACEDONIO ALCALÁ, OAXACA, OAX.

Telephone: 6-38-70, 6-46-86.
Founded 1827, university status 1955.

Private control; Academic year: September to July.

Rector: Lic. ILDEFONSO ZORRILLA CUEVAS.
General Secretary: Q.F.B. MANUEL MATA RAMÍREZ.
Librarian: JOSÉ LUIS BONECHI.

Library of 77,237 vols.
Number of teachers: 690.
Number of students: 10,000.
Publication: *Planeación.*

DEANS:

Faculty of Architecture: Arq. JORGE QUINTANAR CASTILLO.
Faculty of Jurisprudence: Lic. FERNANDO BARRITO LÓPEZ.
Faculty of Medicine: Dr. CARLOS ORTÍZ ESCORCIA.
Faculty of Commerce and Administration: LAE. LEOBARDO LAUARIEGA BERNABÉ.
Faculty of Chemistry: Q.F.B. MANUEL MATA RAMÍREZ.
Faculty of Nursing and Obstetrics: Enf. TERESA SÁNCHEZ CALDERÓN.
Faculty of Fine Arts: Prof. SALVADOR MELO FARRERA.
Faculty of Odontology: Dr. ENRIQUE PÉREZ MATOS.
Faculty of Veterinary Studies: Dr. CARLOS ORTÍZ ESCORCIA.
Language Centre: Prof. ERICK O'CONNEL.

UNIVERSIDAD AUTÓNOMA DE PUEBLA*

4 SUR NO. 104, PUEBLA, PUE.

Telephone: 1-32-69.
Founded 1937.

Private control; Academic year: February to September.

Rector: Ing. LUIS RIVERA TERRAZAS.
Secretary-General: Lic. VICENTE VILLEGAS GUZMÁN.

Library of 36,000 vols.
Number of teachers: *c.* 1,000.
Number of students: *c.* 10,500.

DIRECTORS:

***School of Business Administration:* Lic. MANUEL RODRÍGUEZ CONCHA.**
***School of Architecture:* Arq. VÍCTOR E. TERÁN BONILLA.**
***School of Economic Sciences:* RAFAEL MORENO VALLE.**
***School of Physics and Mathematics:* Ing. LUIS RIVERA TERRAZAS.**
***School of Chemical Sciences:* Quím. ISAAC WOLFSON O.**
***School of Civil Engineering:* Lic. ANTONIO OSORIO GARCÍA.**
***School of Chemical Engineering:* GUADENCIO CASTAÑEDA GUTIÉRREZ.**
***School of Economics:* Lic. FRANCISCO ADAME DÍAZ.**
***School of Nursing and Obstetrics:* Dr. ROLANDO REVILLA IBARRA.**
***School of Philosophy and Letters:* JOAQUÍN SÁNCHEZ MACGREGOR.**
School of Medicine: Dr. GUILLERMO CABRERA CANDIA.
***School of Dentistry:* Dr. ROBERTO PLIEGO PASTOR.**
***School of Law and Social Sciences:* Lic. AMADO CAMARILLO SÁNCHEZ.**

* No reply received to our questionnaire this year.

UNIVERSIDAD POPULAR AUTÓNOMA DEL ESTADO DE PUEBLA

9 PONIENTE 1508, PUEBLA, PUE.

Telephone: 46-57-22.
Founded 1973.

President: L.A. MARIO IGLESIAS GARCÍA TERUEL.
Registrar: Ing. VICENTE PACHECO CEBALLOS.
Librarian: Prof. MARIO URQUIAGA.

Number of teachers: 500.
Number of students: 3,580.
Publication: *Revista Universidad.*
Departments of humanities, technology, health sciences.

UNIVERSIDAD AUTÓNOMA DE QUERÉTARO

APDO. POSTAL 184, CENTRO UNIVERSITARIO, CERRO DE LAS CAMPANAS, QUERÉTARO, QRO.

Telephone: 2-54-68, 2-67-69.
Founded 1618.

Private control; Language of instruction: Spanish; Academic year: September to June.

Rector: Dr. ENRIQUE RABELL FERNANDEZ.

Secretary-General: Lic. MARIANO AMAYA SERRANO.

Chief Administrative Officer: Lic. BRAULIO GUERRA MALO.

Librarian: L.A.E. ARTURO HERNANDEZ SIERRA.

Number of staff: 300 (95 full-time).
Number of students: 6,000.

Publications: *Universidad, Dialogo Universitario, Nuestra Verdad.*

DIRECTORS:

School of Engineering: Ing. JUAN JOSÉ VAZQUEZ PEÑA.
School of Chemical Sciences: JOSÉ LUIS MUÑOZ LICEA.
School of Law: Lic. JORGE GARCIA RAMIREZ.
School of Accountancy and Administration: MANUEL MEZA SEPULVEDA.
School of Psychology: Lic. FERNANDO TAPIA RIVERA.
School of Nursing: ROSA MA. DE LA VEGA.
Graduate School: Ing. AGUSTIN PACHECO CARDENAS.
Language Institute: Prof. MIGUEL CERVANTES ADKINS.
Institute of Fine Arts: FELIPE DE LAS CASAS.

UNIVERSIDAD REGIOMONTANA

VILLAGRÁN 238 SUR, APDO. POSTAL 243, MONTERREY, N.L.

Telephone: 42-52-94, 42-01-51

Founded 1957.

Private control; Languages of instruction. Spanish and English; Academic year: September to August.

Rector: Prof. Dr. AGUSTÍN BASAVE FERNÁNDEZ DEL VALLE.

Chief Administrative Officer: Prof. C.P. JAIME ARROYO VILLARREAL, M.B.A.

Registrar: Prof. HÉCTOR VALDÉS TREVIÑO.

Librarian: Prof. Lic. GEORGINA ARTEAGA CARLEBACH, M.L.S.

Library of 6,500 vols.
Number of teachers: 509.
Number of students: 7,200.

Publication: *URBI*†.

DEANS:

Division of Engineering, Architecture and Exact Science: Prof. Dr. GABRIEL GÓJON ZORRILLA, PH.D.
Division of Humanities and Social Sciences: Prof. Lic. BAUDELIO CASTILLO FLORES.
Division of Information Science: Prof. Lic. GUILLERMO SÁNCHEZ GARAY.
Graduate Division: Prof. Lic. MANUEL BARRAGÁN CODINA.
Preparatory Division: Prof. RICARDO TORRES MARTÍNEZ.
Research Division: Prof. Dr. GIORGIO BERNI.
Training Division: Prof. Q. I. JOSÉ RANGEL LEÓN.

UNIVERSIDAD AUTÓNOMA DE SAN LUIS POTOSÍ

ALVARO OBREGÓN 64, SAN LUIS POTOSÍ

Founded 1826 as Instituto Científico y Literario.

Rector: Lic. GUILLERMO DELGADO ROBLES.

Secretary-General: MARÍA LUISA LÓPEZ ACOSTA.

The library contains 65,000 vols.
Number of teachers: *c.* 670.
Number of students: *c.* 7,800.

DEANS:

Faculty of Medicine: Dr. LUIS F. RANGEL FRANCO.
Faculty of Law: **Lic. CARLOS MEDINA DE LOS SANTOS.**
Faculty of Chemical Sciences: **Ing. JOSÉ DE JESÚS GONZÁLEZ ARELLANO.**
Faculty of Engineering: **Ing. GUILLERMO LABARTHE HERNÁNDEZ.**
Faculty of Physics: **Fís. JUAN FERNANDO CÁRDENAS.**
Faculty of Nursing: **NICOLAS LEYVA TORRES.**
Faculty of Commerce and Administration: **JOSÉ E. HERNÁN DEL GARZA.**
Faculty of Economics: **Lic. MARIO DELGADO CORTÉS.**

AFFILIATED INSTITUTE:

Instituto de Investigación de Zonas Desérticas: Apdo. postal 458, San Luis Potosí; f. 1954; 24 research staff; work on the renewable natural resources of the arid zones of San Luis Potosí; library of 4,283 vols.; Dir. FERNANDO MEDELLÍN-LEAL; publs. *Acta Científica Potosina, Contribuciones.*

UNIVERSIDAD AUTÓNOMA DE SINALOA

APDO. POSTAL 1919, CALLE ANGEL FLORES S/N, CULIACÁN, SINALOA

Founded 1873.

Rector: Lic. ARTURO CAMPOS ROMÁN.

Secretary-General: Lic. ARTURO ZAMA ESCALANTE.

Registrar: Lic. J. B. GAXIOLA COTA.

Number of teachers: 403.
Number of students: 6,470.

DIRECTORS:

School of Law and Social Science: Lic. RAÚL VALENZUELA LUGO.
School of Chemistry: Ing. ABELARDO REYNOSA VEGA.
School of Physics and Mathematics: Ing. SERGIO MOYA NÚÑEZ.
School of Accountancy and Administration: RAMIRO CERVANTES CASTRO.
School of Economics: Lic. OCTAVIO GUERRERO BERNAL.
School of Nursing: MARÍA LUISA GARCÍA G.
School of Agriculture: Ing. LEONARDO HERNÁNDEZ ARAGÓN.
School of Social Work: Dr. JESÚS RODOLFO ACEDO CÁRDENAS.

UNIVERSIDAD DE SONORA

APDO. POSTAL 336 Y 106, HERMOSILLO, SONORA

Telephone: 2-10-46.

Charter granted 1938; opened and officially inaugurated 1942.

Private control; Language of instruction: Spanish; Academic year: September to June.

Rector: Lic. ALFONSO CASTELLANOS IDIÁQUEZ.

Secretary-General: Lic. RAÚL VELDERRAIN OTERO.

Librarian: Profra. ARTEMIZA L. DE QUIJADA.

Library of 45,000 vols.
Number of teachers: 421.
Number of students: 8,372.

Publications: *Revista de la Universidad* (quarterly), *Gaceta Uni-Son.*

CO-ORDINATORS:

School of Social Work: T.S. ROSA CECILIA ESQUER MORENO.
School of Nursing: Enf. Inst. EMMA CORELLA FONTES.
School of Advanced Studies: Ing. IGNACIO AYALA ZAZUETA.
School of Law and Social Sciences: Lic. FRANCISCO ROSS GÓMEZ.
School of Chemical Sciences: Q.B.P. JORGE VILLAREAL GARZA.
School of Engineering: Ing. GABRIEL IBARRA FÉLIX.
School of Accountancy and Administration: C.P. HERIBERTO AJA CARRANZA.
School of Economics: Lic. MARIO CAMBEROS CASTRO.
School of Agriculture and Animal Husbandry: Biol. PEDRO AVILA SALAZAR.
School of Farm Administration: Ing. FRANCISCO DENOGEAN B.

UNIVERSIDAD DEL SUDESTE

APDO. POSTAL 204, **CIUDAD UNIVERSITARIA, CAMPECHE, CAMP.**

Telephone: 6-55-03, 6-22-44.

Founded 1756, refounded 1965.

Rector: Lic. ERMILO SANDOVAL CAMPOS.

Secretary-General: Licda. MILDRED ACUÑA DE SANDOVAL.

Treasurer: C. José C. Bolívar Galeano.
Librarian: Dr. Juan José Casanova I.

Number of teachers: 178.
Number of students: 1,959.

Deans:

Faculty of Law: Lic. Wilbert Ortíz Pazos.
School of Commerce: Luis F. Guerrero Ramos.
School of Engineering: Ing. Humberto Lanz Cárdenas.
School of Dentistry: Dr. Jorge González Francis.
School of Medicine: Dr. Manuel Gracián Barrera.
School of Nursing: Dr. Alvaro Vidal Vera.

UNIVERSIDAD AUTÓNOMA JUAREZ DE TABASCO*

ZONA DE LA CULTURA,
VILLAHERMOSA, TABASCO
Telephone: 2-16-37.
Founded 1958.

Rector: Dr. Juan José Beauregard Cruz.
Secretary-General: L.A.E. Jorge Rico Meza.

Library of 23,000 vols.
Number of teachers: 171.
Number of students: 2,070.

Schools of Accountancy and Administration, Civil Engineering, Law, Medicine, Veterinary Science and Zoology, Nursing, Dentistry.

* No reply received to our questionnaire this year.

UNIVERSIDAD AUTÓNOMA DE TAMAULIPAS

APDO. POSTAL 186,
CIUDAD VICTORIA, TAMAULIPAS
Telephone: 2-07-89.
Founded 1950/51.

Private control; Language of instruction: Spanish; Academic year: August to December, February to June.

Rector: Lic. Jesús Lavín Flores.
Secretary-General: Lic. José Manuel Adame Mier.
Librarian: Lic. Leoncio Arreola Montes.

Library of 11,055 vols.
Number of teachers: 1,033.
Number of students: 14,243.

Publication: *Boletín de Investigaciones* (monthly).

Directors:

Tampico:
Faculty of Medicine: Dr. Juan Vela Trujillo.
Faculty of Dentistry: Dr. Eduardo Deutsch Balleza.
Faculty of Law and Social Sciences: Lic. José Reyes Gómez.
Faculty of Engineering: Ing. Alberto Bolaños Hernández.
Faculty of Architecture: Arq. Armando Hidalgo Guerrero.
Faculty of Commerce and Administration: C.P. Fernando R. Chung Hernández.
Faculty of Nursing: Enf. Olga Vázquez de Arias.
Faculty of Music: Prof. Manuel Barroso.

Victoria:
Faculty of Veterinary Medicine: M.V.Z. Héctor Gojón de la Garza.
Faculty of Agriculture: Ing. Humberto Filizola Haces.
Faculty of Commerce and Administration: L.A.E. Andrés Valle González.
Faculty of Education: Ing. Fernando Garza Díaz.
Faculty of Law and Social Sciences: Lic. Felipe Flores García.
Faculty of Social Work: T.S. Yoliria Joch González.
School of Nursing: José González Caballero.

Mante:
Faculty of Agriculture: Ing. Ignacio Morales Vázquez.

Matamoros:
Faculty of Human Medicine: Dr. Octavio Longoria Cervantes.
School of Nursing: Enf. Irma Sanjuana López de Ramos.

Reynosa:
Faculty of Chemical Sciences: Q. Miguel Garza Castillo.

Nuevo Laredo:
Faculty of Commerce and Administration: C.P. Reynol González Cantu.
School of Nursing: Dr. José Espinoza García.

UNIVERSIDAD VERACRUZANA

ZONA UNIVERSITARIA,
LOMAS DEL ESTADIO,
XALAPA, VER.
Founded 1944.

Academic year: August to June.

Rector: Lic. Roberto Bravo Garzón.
Secretary-General: Lic. Emilio Gidi Villarreal.
Librarian: Enrique Cruz Huerta.

Number of teachers: 2,520.
Number of students: 40,414.

Publications: *La Palabra y el Hombre* (quarterly), *Colección Pedagógica Universitaria, Dualismo, Tramoya* (quarterly), *Anuario de Historia, Estudios Juridicos, Cosmos, Zeta,* etc.

Xalapa Campus

Administrative Delegate: C.P. Octavio Gil García.

Heads of Divisions:

Humanities: Lic. Aureliano Hernández Palacios.
Medical and Biological Studies: Dr. Antonio Pérez Díaz.
Technology: Arq. Mario Fernández de la Garza.
Economics and Administration: C.P. Timoteo Aldana Carreón.
Arts: (vacant).

Directors:

Faculty of Architecture: Arq. Hugo Mario Dizfinck.
Faculty of Law: Lic. Francisco Loyo Ramos.
Faculty of Economics: Lic. Javier Juárez Sánchez.
Faculty of Psychology: Psic. Misael Hernández Ventura.
Faculty of Plastic Arts: Mtro. Carlos Jurado Delmar.
Faculty of Dance: Mtra. Guadalupe Conteras Aguilera.
Faculty of Music: Mtro. Ernesto Tarragó.
Faculty of Theatre: Mtro. Raúl Zermeño Saucedo.
Commerce and Administration Unit: C.P. Hector López Martinez.
Basic Sciences Multidisciplinary Unit: Mat. Iván Sáenz Tejeda Tajonares.
Humanities Interdisciplinary Unit: Mtro. Jesús Morales Fernández.
Health Sciences Interdisciplinary Unit: Dr. Pedro Carreto Velázquez.

Veracruz Campus

Administrative Delegate: Lic. Fernando A. Montiel Hernández.

Directors:

Faculty of Communications Science: Lic. Ignacio Oropeza López.
Faculty of Medicine: (vacant).
Faculty of Dentistry: Dr. Isaias Lara Bello.
Faculty of Nutrition: Nutric. Luz María Mayorade Holguin.
Faculty of Veterinary Medicine and Animal Husbandry: Dr. Augusto Mansicidor Ahuja.
School of Nursing and Obstetrics: Dr. Carlos Gasteasoro Argumedo.
School of Physical Education: Prof. Alfonso García Montáñez.
Engineering and Chemical Sciences Interdisciplinary Unit: Ing. Marvin A. Gutiérrez M.

Cordoba-Orizaba Campus

Administrative Delegate: C.P. Juan Alberto Santana Montero.

Directors:

Faculty of Chemical Sciences: M. en C. Francisco Lara Ochoa.
School of Nursing: Enf. Alicia Romero Virueta.
Faculty of Medicine: Dr. Joel Romero Ramírez.
Faculty of Commerce: C.P. Sadot Núñez Balmori.

Poza Rica-Tuxpam Campus

Administrative Delegate: Lic. RAUL DE LA HUERTA VALDEZ.

DIRECTORS:

Faculty of Social Work: Lic. en T.S. PIEDAD MARGARITA HERNÁNDEZ LÓPEZ.
Health Sciences Unit: Dr. RICARDO DE LA FUENTE.
Engineering and Chemical Sciences Unit: Ing. SERGIO ROBERTO AYALA NIETO.

Coatzacoalcos-Minatitlan Campus

Administrative Delegate: C.P. EUBERTO ENRÍQUEZ ARJONA.

DIRECTORS:

Faculty of Engineering and Chemical Sciences: Quim. SOCORRO SÁNCHEZ DE MARTÍNEZ.
Faculty of Commerce and Administration: Quim. SOCORRO SÁNCHEZ DE MARTÍNEZ.
School of Nursing and Obstetrics: Enf. SILVIA ANAYA CASTILLO.
Faculty of Medicine: Dr. MARIO VELÁSQUEZ LUNA.

UNIVERSIDAD DE YUCATÁN

APDO. 415, CALLES 57 POR 60, MÉRIDA, YUCATÁN

Telephone: 1-35-05, 1-35-53.

Founded 1624, refounded 1922.

Rector: **Dr. ALBERTO ROSADO G. CANTÓN.**
Secretary-General: Lic. AUGUSTO PÉREZ ALPUCHE.
Librarian: **Dr. RODOLFO RUZ MENÉNDEZ.**

The Central Library has 35,453 vols. and 10,146 periodicals, reviews, etc. Specialized libraries are attached to the Faculties of Medicine, Jurisprudence, Engineering, Chemistry, Business and Administration, Dentistry, Anthropology and Architecture.

Number of teachers: 680.
Number of students: 8,054.

Publication: *Revista de la Universidad de Yucatán*†.

DIRECTORS:

Faculty of Medicine: Dr. RENÁN ALZINA LIZAMA.
A School of Nursing is affiliated to the Faculty; Dir. AMADA HERNÁNDEZ CHÁVEZ.
Faculty of Jurisprudence: **Dr. JOSÉ ALFONSO LÓPEZ MANZANO.**
Faculty of Chemistry: **Quim. Farm.** F. ESCALANTE RUZ.
Faculty of Dentistry: Dr. VICTOR MANUEL BORGES LIZAMA.
Faculty of Engineering: Ing. ALVARO MIMENZA CUEVAS.
School of Business and Administration Studies: C.P. JOSÉ FELIPE CEPETILLO CESARES.
School of Economics: Ing. JUAN DUEH GARY.
School of Veterinary Studies: M. VZ. JORGE LEÓN DOUSSET.
School of Architecture: Arq. AERCEL ESPADAS MEDÍNA.
School of Anthropology: Lic. SALVADOR RODRÍGUEZ LOSA.
School of Psychology: Mtro. VÍCTOR M. CASTILLO VALES.
Preparatory School: Dr. GUILLERMO REPETTO MILÁN.

UNIVERSIDAD AUTÓNOMA DE ZACATECAS

GALEANA No. 1
ZACATECAS, ZAC.

Telephone: 2-01-60.

Founded 1836.

Rector: Lic. JESÚS MANUEL DÍAZ CASAS.
Secretary-General: Dr. TAZAKI KUSULAS TEJADA.
Chief Administrative Officer: C.P. SALVADOR SANTILLAN HERNÁNDEZ.
Librarian: JUAN BOSCO HUERTA RUELAS.

Library of 20,000 vols.
Number of teachers: 640.
Number of students: 8,200.

DIRECTORS:

School of Law: Lic. MAGDALENO VARELA LUJÁN.
School of Engineering: Ing. RUBÉN A. PREZZA ROBLES.
School of Chemistry: **Ing. ANTONIO LÓPEZ ARAIZA.**
School of Nursing: **Dr. ROQUE MARTÍNEZ LUGO.**
School of Accounting and Administration: C.P. JOSÉ ANTONIO DE LA TORRE DUEÑAS.
School of Economics: Lic. JESÚS PÉREZ CUEVAS.
School of Animal Breeding and Veterinary Medicine: M.V.Z. GILBERTO A. FLORES SANDOVAL.
School of Dentistry: **Dr. JOSÉ D. HUERTA P.**
School of Medicine: Dr. ROBERTO D. MACDONALD.

TECHNICAL UNIVERSITIES

INSTITUTO POLITÉCNICO NACIONAL*
(National Polytechnic Institute)

UNIDAD PROFESIONAL ZACATENCO, MEXICO 14, D.F.

Telephone: 5-86-21-22.

Founded 1936.

State control; Academic year: September to July.

Director-General: Dr. JOSÉ GERSTL VALENZUELA.
Secretary-General: Dr. IGNACIO BARRAGÁN SÁNCHEZ.

Number of teachers: 11,000.
Number of students: 110,000.

Publications: *Gaceta Politécnica, Acta Politécnica, Acta Médica, Anales de la Escuela Nacional de Ciencias Biológicas, Acta Mexicana de Ciencia y* *Tecnología, Economía Política.*

Constituent schools of biology, business administration, economics, physics and mathematics, architecture, electrical and chemical engineering, textiles, medicine, paediatrics and obstetrics, specialist technology.

ATTACHED INSTITUTION:

Centro de Investigación y de Estudios Avanzados: *see* under Research Institutes.

* No reply received to our questionnaire this year.

INSTITUTO TECNOLÓGICO Y DE ESTUDIOS SUPERIORES DE MONTERREY
(Institute of Technology and Higher Education)

SUCURSAL DE CORREOS "J" MONTERREY, NUEVO LEÓN

Telephone: 58-20-00.

Founded 1943.

Private control; Academic year: August to May.

President: Ing. FERNANDO GARCÍA ROEL.
Academic Vice-President: Ing. SANTIAGO E. CHUCK.
Administrative Vice-President: C.P. FRANCISCO ABEL TREVIÑO.
Vocational Vice-President: Lic. ALFONSO RUBIO Y RUBIO.
Development Vice-President: Lic. ALFONSO GONZÁLEZ SEGOVIA.
Student Affairs Vice-President: Ing. RICARDO TREVIÑO GARZA.
Vice-Presidents for Out-of-State Campuses: Dr. CÉSAR MORALES (Central and North Zones); Dr. RAFAEL RANGEL (Bajío Zone).
Registrar: **Ing. FERNANDO ESQUIVEL.**
Librarian: **Lic. ARTEMIO BENAVIDES.**

The library contains 110,000 vols. and 21,000 periodicals.

Number of teachers: 740.
Number of students: 17,000.

Publications: ***Boletín de Agronomía*** (twice monthly), ***Revista de la Escuela*** *de Contabilidad,* ***Economía y Administración*** **(quarterly),** ***Anuario de la*** *Escuela de Agricultura.*

DIRECTORS OF ACADEMIC DIVISIONS:

Division of Administration and Social Sciences: **C.P. ROLANDO ESPINOSA.**
Division of Agricultural and Marine Sciences: **Ing. LEONEL ROBLES.**
Divison of Sciences and Humanities: **Dr. JOSÉ TREVIÑO ABREGO.**

Division of Engineering and Architecture: Ing. RAMÓN DE LA PEÑA.
Division of International Programmes: Ing. SATURNINO CAMPOY.

DIRECTORS OF ACADEMIC DEPARTMENTS:

Agricultural Management: Ing. JORGE ELIZONDO.
Agronomy: Dr. PEDRO REYES CASTAÑEDA.
Biology: Dr. HOMERO GAONA.
Soils: Ing. DANIEL MORALES.
Zootechnics: Ing. CANDELARIO CARRERA.
Physics: Ing. ABELARDO TRUJILLO.
Humanities: Lic. ROSAURA BARAHONA.
Mathematics: Ing. ROBERTO ALANÍS.
Systems: Ing. ANTONIO DONADÍO MEDAGLIA.
Chemistry: Dr. XORGE A. DOMÍNGUEZ.
Architecture: Arq. J. LUIS ORTIZ.
Civil Engineering: Ing. CARLOS CRESPO.
Electrical Engineering: Dr. TEÓFILO RAMOS.
Industrial Engineering: Ing. JORGE GONZÁLEZ.
Mechanical Engineering: Ing. OCTAVIO HERRERA.
Chemical Engineering: Dr. HÉCTOR MOREIRA.
Thermodynamics: Dr. JOSÉ A. MANRIQUE.
Financial Accountancy: C.P. DAVID NOEL RAMÍREZ.
Finance: C.P. MARÍA DEL CARMEN DE LA GARZA.
Marketing: Lic. CARLOS RUY MARTÍNEZ.
Organization: Ing. YOLANDA M. DE HERNÁNDEZ.
Human Resources: Dr. CARLOS H. GARCÍA.
Communication: Lic. JORGE GARCÍA MURILLO.
Economics: Dr. LUIS DERBEZ.

COLLEGES

CENTRO DE ENSEÑANZA TÉCNICA Y SUPERIOR

APDO. POSTAL 797,
MEXICALI, BAJA CALIFORNIA

Founded 1961.

Rector: Dr. FÉLIX CASTILLO JIMÉNEZ.
Librarian: Lic. GILBERTO GARCIA MENDEZ.

Library of 11,000 vols.
Number of students: 1,300.

Publications: *Catálogo, Revista* (quarterly).

DIRECTORS:

Promotion: Ing. J. ALFONSO MARÍN JIMÉNEZ.
Studies: Lic. ELENA PEREZ DE PADILLA.
Planning and Statistics: Ing. SERGIO THOMAS SAYAVEDRA DOMINGUEZ.
Graduate School: Ing. JOSÉ GALINDO GALVÁN.
Engineering: Ing. JOAQUIN DÍAZ MARTINEZ.
Accountancy and Management: OSCAR LICONA NIETO.
Bachillerato: Ing. ANGEL MONTAÑEZ AGUILAR.
Tijuana Campus: Lic. HÉCTOR VELARDE GRIEGO.
Ensenada Campus: Ing. JOAQUIN DIAZ HERMOSILLO.

COLEGIO DE MÉXICO, EL

CAMINO AL AJUSCO 20,
MÉXICO 20, D.F.

Telephone: 568-60-33.

Founded 1940.

President: VÍCTOR L. URQUIDI.
Secretary: Lic. CARLOS ARRIOLA.
Library Director: ARIO GARZA M.

Library: 200,000 vols.
Number of teachers: 102.
Number of students: 250.

Publications: *Nueva Revista de Filología Hispánico*† (2 a year), *Historia Mexicana*† (quarterly), *Foro Internacional* (quarterly), *Estudios de Asia y Africa del Norte*† (quarterly), *Demografía y Economía*† (3 a year), *Diálogos*† (6 a year).

DIRECTORS:

Centre of Historical Studies: Dr. JOSEFINA VÁZQUEZ.
Centre of Sociological Studies: Dr. JOSÉ LUIS REYNA.
Centre of International Studies: Dr. LORENZO MEYER.
Centre of Economic and Demographic Studies: Lic. LUIS UNIKEL.
Centre of Asian and North African Studies: Lic. MANUEL RUIZ.
Centre of Hispanic Linguistics and Hispanic Literary Studies: Dra. BEATRIZ GARZA.

ESCUELA MILITAR DE INGENIEROS
(Military School of Engineers)

BATALLA DE CELAYA No. 202,
MEXICO 10, D.F.

Founded 1822.

The school is dependent on the Secretaría de la Defensa Nacional.

Director: Coronel I. C. JACOBO WITTMAN ROJANO.

Library of 10,000 vols.
Number of students: 142.

Publications: *Apuntes, Conferencias.*

ESCUELA NACIONAL DE ANTROPOLOGÍA E HISTORIA
(National School of Anthropology and History)

CALZADA M. GANDHI Y
PASEO DE LA REFORMA,
MEXICO 5, D.F.

Founded 1937.

Director: JAVIER ROMERO MOLINA.
Librarian: ANTONIO POMPA Y POMPA.

Library of 250,000 vols.

Number of teachers: *c.* 85.
Number of students: *c.* 1,675.

Publications: *Acta Antropológica, Tlatoani, Anuario,* Theses.

DEPARTMENT HEADS:

ABASCAL, R., Archaeology
BOEGE, E., Social Anthropology
MANRIQUE, L., Linguistics
MARIN, C. M., Ethnohistory
SERRANO, C., Physical Anthropology
TERAN, S., Ethnology

ESCUELA NACIONAL DE BIBLIOTECONOMÍA Y ARCHIVONOMÍA
(National School of Librarianship and Archives)

VIADUCTO MIGUEL ALEMAN 155,
MEXICO 13, D.F.

Founded 1945.

Director: Mtro. EDUARDO SALAS.
Associate Director: Mtro. GILBERTO DÍAZ SANTANA.
Secretary: Prof. GUILLERMO OROPEZA.

Library of 5,000 vols.
Number of teachers: 72.
Number of students: 420.

Publication: *Bibliotecas y Archivos*†.

INSTITUTO DE ESTUDIOS IBEROAMERICANOS
(Institute of Spanish American Studies)

GUERRERO 312, APDO. 358,
SALTILLO, COAHUILA

Telephone: 3-89-99.

Private control; Languages of instruction: Spanish and English; Academic year: September to June (two terms of 18 weeks).

Director: DAVID SIMMONS, M.A., LL.D., F.I.I.
Academic Dean: Prof. J. DE LA ROSA.
Dean of Students: ROBERT HANCOCK, PH.D.
Librarian: ELIZABETH FOSTER, M.L.S.

Library of 7,000 vols.

Provides courses for U.S. B.A. and M.A. degrees, as well as specializing in summer school courses in all aspects of Latin American civilization. There are Divisions of Spanish Language and Literature, Latin American Studies and Arts and Crafts.

INSTITUTO DE FILOLOGÍA HISPÁNICA

HIDALGO SUR 468, APDO. 144,
SALTILLO, COAHUILA

Telephone: 2-15-11.

Founded 1968.

Private control; Academic year: autumn and winter terms with extra sessions in January and summer.

Director: RODOLFO VALDÉS.

Academic Dean and Librarian: MARÍA BOEHM DE VALDÉS.

Dean of Students and Registrar: PATRICIA AXLINE DE SÁNCHEZ.

Secretary: JOVITA MALTOS.

Courses in language, literature, history, sociology, folklore, art and native music.

INSTITUTO PANAMERICANO DE ALTA DIRECCIÓN DE EMPRESA

FLORESTA 20, MEXICO 16, D.F.

Founded 1967.

Private control.

Director: CARLOS ACEDO VALENZUELA.

Librarian: Mrs. MARTHA E. S. DE GUILLÉN.

Director of External Scientific Activities: FRANCISCO J. LARIS.

Library of 6,500 vols.
Number of teachers: 25.
Number of students: 250.

INSTITUTO TECNOLÓGICO AUTÓNOMO DE MÉXICO

MARINA NACIONAL No. 350, MÉXICO 17, D.F.

Telephone: 531-70-00.

Founded 1946.

President: ALBERTO BAILLERES.

Rector: JAVIER BERISTAIN ITURBIDE.

Academic Director: JORGE ARREOLA LOPERENA.

Library of 40,000 vols.
Number of students: 1,400.

Publication: *Revista del ITAM*† (quarterly).

Courses in Business Administration, Economics, Accounting, Mathematics and Social Sciences.

INSTITUTO TECNOLÓGICO Y DE ESTUDIOS SUPERIORES DE OCCIDENTE

AVE. NIÑOS HÉROES 1342-8, GUADALAJARA, JAL.

Founded 1957.

Rector: Lic. CARLOS VIGIL AVALOS.

Secretary-General: Lic. HUMBERTO OCHOA GRANADOS.

Director of Studies: Ing. MIGUEL BAZDRESCH PARADA.

Library of 50–60,000 vols.
Number of teachers: 300.
Number of students: 1,900.

Publications: *Boletín Informativo ITESO*, *Inter-Com* (monthly), *Catálogo*† (annually).

Courses in architecture, business administration, communication, public accountancy, civil, industrial and electronic engineering, chemical processing and administration, mathematics, computer systems, psychology, industrial relations, human development, farming, marketing, education and computation.

INSTITUTO TECNOLÓGICO REGIONAL DE CELAYA

INSURGENTES E IRRIGACIÓN, APDO. POSTAL 57, CELAYA, GTO.

Telephone: 2-20-23.

Founded 1958.

Director: Ing. MANUEL RESENDIZ PONCE.

Vice-Director: Ing. BULARMO FUENTES LEMUS.

Administrative Director: Ing. JAIME RODRÍGUEZ RUÍZ.

Library of 8,261 vols.

Number of students: 2,530.

Publication: *Boletín.*

Degree courses in Industrial Engineering, Mechanics, Chemistry and Biochemistry, Production and Business Administration; Technical courses in Mechanics, Electricity, Chemistry, Accounting, Marketing and Personnel Management.

INSTITUTO TECNOLÓGICO REGIONAL DE CHIHUAHUA

APDO. POSTAL 119, CHIHUAHUA, CHIH.

Founded 1948.

Director: Ing. FRANCISCO AGUAYO LEÓN.

Vice-Director: Ing. MANUEL CAMPOS CAMPOS.

Library of 13,800 vols.

Number of teachers: 44 full-time, 115 part-time.

Number of students: 2,600.

Courses in industrial engineering (electrical, mechanical, chemical, electronic, production).

INSTITUTO TECNOLÓGICO REGIONAL DE DURANGO

BLVD. F. PESCADOR 1830 OTE., APDO. POSTAL 465, DURANGO

Founded 1948.

Dependent on the Dirección General de Institutos Tecnológicos Regionales, S.E.P.

Director: Ing. VICTOR DE LA BARRERA.

Library of *c.* 13,000 vols.

First degree courses in engineering, and postgraduate course in industrial planning.

INSTITUTO TECNOLÓGICO REGIONAL DE CIUDAD JUÁREZ

AV. TECNOLÓGICO S/N, CIUDAD JUÁREZ, CHIHUAHUA

Telephone: 3-23-40 and 3-15-53.

Founded 1964.

Director: Ing. JOSÉ CARLOS RIOJAS BERNAL.

Vice-Director: Ing. JOSÉ ROLANDO LICÓN BAEZA.

Library of 5,000 vols.

Number of teachers: 115.

Number of students: 1,200.

INSTITUTO TECNOLÓGICO REGIONAL DE CIUDAD MADERO

APDO. POSTAL 20, CD. MADERO, TAM.

Telephone: 5-21-53, 5-60-51.

Founded 1954.

Director: Ing. MIGUEL ZEPEDA SÁNCHEZ.

Library of 15,000 vols.

Number of students: 4,000.

INSTITUTO TECNOLÓGICO REGIONAL DE MÉRIDA

APDO. POSTAL 561 MÉRIDA, YUCATÁN

Founded 1961.

Director: Ing. ALBERTO J. GUTIÉRREZ ALCALÁ.

Library of 14,276 vols.

Number of students: 3,423.

Publications: *Imagenes*† (every 2 months), *Directorio de Recursos Humanos* (every term), *Lo que dice la prensa . . .* (monthly).

Courses in Industrial, Biochemical and Civil Engineering, Industrial Technology, Management and Tourism.

INSTITUTO TECNOLÓGICO REGIONAL DE MORELIA

CARRETERA MORELIA SALVATIERRA, APDO. POSTAL 750, MORELIA, MICHOACÁN

Founded 1965.

Director: Ing. HEBER SOTO FIERRO.

Library of 9,000 vols.
Number of students: 3,000.

Courses in Industrial Engineering and Technology.

INSTITUTO TECNOLÓGICO REGIONAL DE OAXACA

CALZ. TECNOLÓGICO Y WILFRIDO-MASSIEU S/N, OAXACA, OAX.

Telephone: 6-17-22, 6-44-13, 6-52-48.

Founded 1968.

Director: Ing. ARMANDO D. PALACIOS GARCÍA.

Number of teachers: 280.
Number of students: 3,000.
Publication: *Itrosíntesis.*

Courses in mechanical, electrical, chemical and civil engineering, business management and industrial planning.

INSTITUTO TECNOLÓGICO REGIONAL DE ORIZABA

AVDA. INSTITUTO TECNOLÓGICO S/N, APDO. POSTAL 324, ORIZABA, VER.

Founded 1957.

Director: Ing. PASCUAL ROBLES.

Technical Assistant Director: Ing. DELFINO CASTAÑEDA.

Administrative Assistant Director: Ing. ROSALINO CARRERA.

Number of teachers: 297.
Number of students: 2,479.

Courses in Industrial Engineering and Technology.

INSTITUTO TECNOLÓGICO REGIONAL DE QUERÉTARO

APDO. POSTAL 124, AVDA. TECNOLÓGICO Y GRAL MARIANO ESCOBEDO, QUERÉTARO, QRO.

Telephone: 2-22-81, 2-02-44.

Founded 1967.

Director: Ing. J. AGUSTÍN CHACÓN ESTRADA.

Vice-Director: Ing. GUSTAVO VÁZQUEZ MARTÍNEZ.

Library of 12,000 vols.
Number of teachers: 200.
Number of students: 1,800.

Courses in industrial engineering and technology.

INSTITUTO TECNOLÓGICO REGIONAL DE SALTILLO

APDO. POSTAL 600, ENTRONQUE CARRETERAS MONTERREY Y PIEDRAS NEGRAS, SALTILLO, COAHUILA

Founded 1951.

Director: Ing. LUIS ROSALES CELIS.

Library of *c.* 8,750 vols.

Number of students: 3,000.

Publications: *Boletín de Seguridad Industrial, Boletín de Fundición, Boletín de Microenseñanza* and various faculty bulletins.

Courses in industrial and metallurgical engineering and technology.

INSTITUTO TECNOLÓGICO DE SONORA

AVDA. RODOLFO ELÍAS CALLES Y CHIHUAHUA, CIUDAD OBREGÓN, SON.

Founded 1955.

Rector: Dr. OSCAR RUSSO VOGEL.

Vice-Rector for Academic Affairs: Lic. FRANCISCO RUBIO FÉLIX.

Vice-Rector for Administrative Affairs: C. P. HÉCTOR LÓPEZ LIMÓN.

Library of 10,000 vols.

Number of teachers: 180.
Number of students: 3,000.

Courses in industrial, civil and chemical engineering, agricultural technology, administration, business and accounting, psychology.

INSTITUTO TECNOLÓGICO REGIONAL DE VERACRUZ

CIRCUNVALACIÓN NORTE E ICAZO, VERACRUZ, VER.

Founded 1957.

Dependent on the Dirección General de Enseñanzas Tecnológicas (Ministry of Education).

Director: Ing. JOSÉ LÓPEZ MEDINA.

SCHOOL OF MUSIC

Conservatorio Nacional de Música (*National Conservatoire*): Avenida Presidente Masaryk 582, México 5, D.F.; f. 1866; 208 teachers; Dir. Maestro ARMANDO MONTIEL OLVERA; library of 48,900 vols.; publs. *Boletín del Conservatorio, Gaceta de la Biblioteca.*

MONACO

Population 25,000

LEARNED SOCIETIES AND RESEARCH INSTITUTES

Association de Préhistoire et de Spéléologie: Musée d'Anthropologie, blvd. du Jardin Exotique; f. 1950; 100 mems.; Pres. LOUIS BARRAL; publ. *Bulletin.*

Centre Scientifique de Monaco: Villa Girasole, 16 Boulevard de Suisse, Monte-Carlo; f. 1960; research in marine radioactivity, radiocarbon, meteorology, seismology, marine microbiology, marine pollution, molecular neurobiology; Laboratories in Musée Océanographique de Monaco; 25 mems.; Pres. C. C. SOLAMITO.

LIBRARIES AND ARCHIVES

Archives et Bibliothèque du Palais de Monaco: private archives of the princes of Monaco including documents from the 13th century; collection of money minted in Monaco since 1640; Librarian FRANCK BIANCHERI.

Bibliothèque de Monaco: 8 rue de la Poste; f. 1909; 128,000 vols.

MUSEUMS

Musée d'Anthropologie Préhistorique: blvd. du Jardin Exotique; Curator SUZANNE SIMONE.

Musée National: 11 ave. Princess Grace, Monte Carlo; Dir. G. OLLIVIER.

Musée Océanographique de Monaco: ave. Saint-Martin; inaugurated 1910 by Prince Albert I of Monaco; as well as a museum, there is an aquarium, 30 laboratories and 2 ships for research; library of 50,000 vols.; Dir. JACQUES-YVES COUSTEAU (associated with the Institut Océanographique in Paris); publs. *Bulletin de l'Institut Océanographique, Mémoires de l'Institut Océanographique.*

COLLEGE

Académie de Musique Prince Rainier III de Monaco: 17 Rue Princesse Florestine; f. 1934; 30 professors, 560 students; Dir. JACQUES MOSCATO.

MONGOLIAN PEOPLE'S REPUBLIC

Population 1,641,000

LEARNED SOCIETIES AND RESEARCH INSTITUTES

Academy of Sciences: Ulan Bator; f. 1921 as the Committee of Sciences, reorganized as the Academy in 1961; directs all practical research in economics, geography, geology, natural history, and in the history, language and literature of the Mongolian people; Pres. Academician BADZARYN SHIRENDEV; Learned Sec. PUNTSAGYN LUVSANDORJ.

Institute of Botany: Dir. D. BANDRAGCH.

Institute of Chemistry: Dir. T. BALDAN.

Institute of Communal Economy and Services: Dir. N. BANDZRAGCH.

Institute of Economics: Dir. H. DASHDONDOV.

Institute of General and Experimental Biology: Dir. O. SHAGDARSÜREN.

Institute of Geography and Permafrost Studies: Dir. SH. TSEGMED.

Institute of Geology: Dir. B. LUVSANDANDZAN.

Institute of History: Dir. SH. NATSAGDORJ.

Institute of Language and Literature: Dir. A. LUVSANDENDEV.

Institute of Mathematics: Dir. H. NAMSRAY.

Institute of Natural Compounds: Dir. TS. HAYDAV.

Institute of Pedagogical Sciences: Dir. D. SHAGDAR

Institute of Philosophy, Sociology and Public Law: Dir. S. NOROVSAMBUU.

Institute of Physics and Applied Physics: Dir. B. CHADRAA.

Institute of Oriental Studies: Dir. SH. BIRA.

Department of Scientific Information: Dir. G. RINCHEN.

Institute of Animal Husbandry and Veterinary Science: Dir. DONDOGDORJIYN MOYOOBUU.

Institute of Architecture: Dir. D. SAYN-ER.

Institute of Health Studies, Infectious Diseases and Bacteriology: Dir. J. KUPUL.

Institute of Hydrology and Meteorology: Dir. R. MIJIDDORJ.

Institute of Pasture and Fodder: Dir. L. TOVUU.

Institute of Plants and Crops: Dir. A. HÜCHIT.

Research Institute of Biological Preparations and Blood: Dir. A. DANDIY.

Research Institute of Material and Technical Supply.

Research Institute of the Ministry of Light and Food Industry: Dir. SHIRNEN.

Research and Design Institute of the Fuel and Power Industry: Dir. D. TSEDENDAMBA.

Research Institute of Prices and Standards: Dir. T. DÖRBYETHAN.

Research Institute for Protection of Mothers and Newborn Children: Dir. E. LUVSANDAGVA.

Research Institute of Water Resources: Dir. TS. BALDANDORJ.

Research Institute (of the State Planning Commission and Academy of Sciences) of Development and Location of Productivity Forces: Dir. T. NAMJIM.

Research Institute (of State Procurator's Office) of Causes of Crime: Deputy Dir. L. RINCHIN.

Production and Research Institute of the Ministry of Communications: Dir. G. BALDANDORJ.

Production and Research Institute of the Ministry of Geology and Mining Industry: Dir. CH. EEBUM.

Production and Research Institute of Forestry and Hunting.

Production and Research Institute of Trade and Catering: Deputy Dir. O. NYANGAR.

LIBRARIES

State Archives: Ulan Bator; Dir. G. NOROVSAMBUU.

State Public Library: Ulan Bator; f. 1921; 3,000,000 vols. in Mongolian, Manchurian, Chinese, Tibetan, Russian, English, German, French, and other languages; rare editions including "Kanjur" and "Tanjur", Buddhist Encyclopaedia of 335 vols.; ancient Mongolian books; exchange system with libraries in Asia, Europe and America; Dir. DZ. TSENDRAGCHAA; publ. *Bibliographies.*

MUSEUMS

State Central Museum: Ulan Bator; natural history, history, art, and archaeology collections; Gobi desert dinosaur eggs and skeletons.

Museum of Religion: Ulan Bator; housed in Choyjin Lamyn Hüree, a former lamasery; collection includes many Lamaic relics.

Revolutionary Museum: Altanbulag; f. 1971 at the seat of the provisional revolutionary government in 1921.

Friendship Museum: Darhan; describes Soviet-Mongolian co-operation in the founding and development of Mongolia's newest industrial city.

Central Museum of the Revolutionary Movement: Ulan Bator; the collection illustrates the history and achievement of Mongolia since 1921.

Sühbaatar and Choybalsan Museum: Ulan Bator; the museum is devoted to the lives of the two revolutionary leaders after whom it is named.

Ulan Bator Museum: Ulan Bator; devoted to the history of the town and its reconstruction.

Palace Museum: Ulan Bator; the palace of the former Bogd Gegeen, Head of the Buddhist Church in Mongolia and Head of State 1911–24, and neighbouring lamasery.

Fine Arts Museum: Ulan Bator; paintings and sculpture.

Natsagdorj Museum: Ulan Bator; devoted to the life and works of the author and poet Dashdorjiyn Natsagdorj (1906–37).

V. I. Lenin Museum: Ulan Bator; devoted to the life and works of the founder of the Soviet Union.

G. K. Zhukov Museum: Ulan Bator; illustrates the career of the famous Soviet Marshal who, as a young officer, fought with the Mongolian and Soviet armies against Japan at Halhyn Gol (Nomonhan) in 1939.

UNIVERSITY

MONGOLIAN STATE UNIVERSITY

(Mongol Ulsyn Ih Surguul')

P.O.B. 377,
ULAN BATOR
Telephone: 20668.

Founded 1942.

Rector: Prof. N. SODNOM.
Pro-Rectors: B. BATSUUR', B. LUVSANTSEREN, D. SANJAYJAV.

Library of 350,000 vols.

Number of students: 8,000.

Publications: *Proceedings*, Scientific Reports.

FACULTIES AND DEANS:

Physics and Mathematics, with department of physics mathematics and meteorology.
Dean: A. MEKEY.

Chemistry and Biology, with departments of chemistry and biology.
Dean: M. YUNDEN.

Social Sciences, with department of law.
Dean: D. LUVSANTSEREN.

Economics, with departments of finance, loans, book-keeping, statistics and commerce.
Dean: M. NAMJAA.

Philology, with departments of Mongolian and Russian languages.
Dean: O. SÜH.

Higher Russian Language School: Rector S. GALSAN.

Higher Polytechnic Institute: Rector CH. AVDAY.

Number of teachers: 240.
Number of students: 3,000.

FACULTIES AND DEANS:

Engineering and Economics, with departments of industrial economy and building economy.
Dean: L. GÜRJAV.

Geology/Mining, with departments of geology, geography and mining.
Dean: J. BOLD.

Power/Energy, with departments of electrical, heat, and communications engineering.
Dean: N. MIJIDDORJ.

Building Engineering, with departments of civil engineering, architecture, machine-mechanics, technology of materials and hydraulics.
Dean: B. DAMBIYNYAM.

Mechanical/Technological and Auto-engineering with departments of mechanics, auto-engineering.
Dean: B. BAT-OCHIR.

Postgraduate.

Evening and Correspondence Faculty, with departments of industry, book-keeping, planning, law, journalism, commerce and statistics.
Dean: B. NARANTSATSRAL.

Refresher Faculty.
Dean: D. BYAMBADORJ.

STATE HIGHER SCHOOLS

Agricultural School: Ulan Bator; Zoology, Veterinary Medicine, Agronomy, Forestry, Agricultural Engineering, Fodder, Accounting; correspondence courses; Rector R. INDRA.

D. Sühbaatar Higher Party School: Ulan Bator; four-year courses for graduate party functionaries and executives in agriculture, industry and government organizations; Rector G. MIYEEGOMBO.

Medical School: Ulan Bator; all branches of study; Rector: Prof. D. BALDANDORJ.

D. Sühbaatar Military School: Ulan Bator; Military Affairs, Social Science, Communications, Motor Transport; four-year courses; Commandant Maj.-Gen. JAMSRANGIYN YONDON.

VOCATIONAL SCHOOLS

Agricultural Schools: Altanbulag, Choybalsan, Hovd, Mandalgov'.

Communications School: Ulan Bator; telephone and radio equipment.

Construction School: Ulan Bator; building methods, electricity, technical drawing, plumbing; Dir. JUMDAAN.

Construction School: Darhan.

Finance and Economics School: Ulan Bator; industry, transport, planning, accountancy, statistics.

Forestry School: Hyalganat, near Erdenet.

Health Schools: Altay, Saynshand, Darhan.

Law School: Ulan Bator.

Light and Food Industry School: Ulan Bator.

Medical School: Ulan Bator; medicine, midwifery, nursing, X-ray, dentistry, pharmacy, hygiene; Dir. GÜNTEV.

Polytechnic: Darhan; electrical engineering, heating, geophysics, geological surveying, hydrogeology, mining, food industry technology, wool production.

Railway Engineering School: Ulan Bator; railway construction and operation; Dir. D. SAMBUU.

Trade School: Ulan Bator; Dir. D. CHOYSÜREN.

Trade School: Uliastay.

Water Supply School: Sharyngol; hydrotechnology and meteorology.

There are Teacher Training Schools in Ulan Bator, Hovd, and Tsetserleg, and a School of Physical Culture in Ulan Bator.

TECHNICAL SCHOOLS

Agriculture: Tsetserleg, Ulaangom, Öndörhaan, Dzaamar, Dalandzadgad, Altay, Choybalsan, Bayanchandman, Tsagaantolgoy, Shaamar, Ugtaal, Sharga.

Water Supply: Arvayheer.

Building: Ölgiy, Choybalsan, Bayanhongor, Ulan Bator, Darhan, Mandalgov, Uliastay.

Industrial: Sühbaatar and Mörön (forestry), Ulan Bator (light industry, food industry), Nalayh (geology and mining), Erdenet (mining).

Trade: Ulan Bator, Dzavhan.

Communal Economy and Services: Ulan Bator.

Transport: Ulan Bator.

Railways: Ulan Bator.

Communications: Ulan Bator.

MOROCCO

Population 18,900,000

LEARNED SOCIETIES

Alliance Française du Maroc: 8 rue Benzerte, Rabat; f. 1946; French language and culture; 540 mems. inc. 285 adult students attending language courses; library of 2,000 vols.; Pres. AHMED SEFRIOUI; Sec. Gen. AZIZ SEGHROUCHNI.

American Cultural Center: 43 ave. Allal Ben Abdallah, Rabat; also in Casablanca (10 place Bel Air, Quartier Gauthier).

Association des Amateurs de la Musique Andalouse: 26 rue de Strasbourg, Casablanca; f. 1956 to preserve and catalogue traditional Moroccan (Andalusian) music; maintains a School of Andalusian music at Casablanca, directed and subsidized by the Ministry of Education and Fine Arts; Dir. Hadj DRISS BENJELLOUN.

British Council: 22 ave. Moulay Youssef, B.P. 427, Rabat; library (*see* Libraries); Rep. A. J.-J. DUNN, M.B.E.

Centre d'Etudes de Documentations et d'Informations Economiques et Sociales (C.E.D.I.E.S.): 23 blvd. Mohamed Abdouh, Casablanca.

Centro Cultural Español: 5 rue Mohamed Al Fatih, Rabat; f. 1969; courses in Spanish, concerts, films, conferences and lectures; brs. at Fez, Casablanca, Tangier and Agadir; 1,500 mems.; libraries of 10,000 vols.; Dir. RODOLFO GIL.

Goethe-Institut (Casablanca): Place du 16 novembre; f. 1961; cultural activities, German language courses; library of 10,000 vols.; Dir. Dr. R. KLATT.

Goethe-Institut (Rabat): 10 rue Djebli; Dir. Dr. NOBBE.

Mission Universitaire et Culturelle Française au Maroc (*French University and Cultural Mission in Morocco*): rue Gandhi, Rabat; f. 1957; examination courses, cultural and artistic visits and exhibitions, lectures; other centres with libraries in Rabat, Casablanca, Fez, Marrakesh, Tangier and Tetouan; Dir. M. GIQUEL.

Société de Géographie du Maroc (*Université Mohamed V*): Faculté des Lettres et des Sciences Humaines, Rabat; f. 1916; 500 mems.; Pres. ABDELMAJID HAKAM; publ. *Revue de Géographie du Maroc* (twice yearly).

Société de Préhistoire du Maroc: Syndicat d'Initiative, blvd. de la Gare, Casablanca; f. 1926; Pres. M. BOUDY; Sec.-Gen. M. ANTOINE; publ. *Bulletin* (twice yearly).

Société des Sciences Naturelles et Physiques du Maroc: Institut Scientifique Chérifien, ave. Moulay Chérif, Rabat; f. 1920; 420 mems.; Pres. H. FARAJ; Sec.-Gen. A. SASSON; publs. *Bulletin, Comptes-rendus, Travaux de la Section de Pédologie, Atabéa, Bulletin de la Section des Naturalistes enseignants.*

Société d'Etudes Economiques, Sociales et Statistiques du Maroc: B.P. 535, Rabat—Chellah; f. 1930; 12 mems.; Dir. NACER EL FASSI; publ. *Bulletin Economique et Social du Maroc*† (irregular).

Société d'Horticulture et d'Acclimatation du Maroc: P.O.B. 854, Casablanca; f. 1914; 300 mems.; Pres. JEAN BOROT; Sec. MARCEL MÉNARD.

RESEARCH INSTITUTES

(*see* also under Universities)

Bureau de Recherches et de Participations Minières (B.R.P.M.): 5–7 Charii Moulay Hassan, B.P. 99, Rabat; f. 1928; state agency for oil and mines; Gen. Man. MOHAMED CHAHID; publ. *Rapport d'Activité* (annually).

Comité National de Géographie du Maroc: Institut Universitaire de la Recherche Scientifique, Rabat; f. 1959; Pres. The MINISTER OF EDUCATION; Sec.-Gen. A. LAOUINA; publs. *Atlas du Maroc,* maps.

Direction de la Géologie: c/o Ministry of Energy and Mines, Rabat; f. 1921; National Geological Survey; library of *c.* 25,000 vols.; Dir. EL ARBI HILALI; publs. *Notes et Mémoires du Service Géologique du Maroc*†, *Mines, Géologie et Energie*†.

Direction de la Recherche Agronomique: B.P. 415, Rabat; f. 1924; undertakes research in ecology, pedology, climatology, horticulture, phytopathology, etc.; library of 11,400 vols.; Dir. M. FARAJ; publs. *Al Awamia, Cahier de la Recherche Agronomique, Collection technique.*

Direction des Services Techniques: Ministère de la Santé, Rabat; applied research in epidemiology and hygiene.

Division de l'inventaire du patrimoine culturel: c/o Ministry of State for Cultural Affairs, Rabat; Dir. DRISS DKHISSI.

Division du Théâtre, de la Musique et du Folklore: c/o Ministère d'Etat aux Affaires Culturelles, Rabat; undertakes research into all aspects of Moroccan folk art and ethnography.

Institut National d'Hygiène: ave. Ibn Batuta, Rabat; f. 1930; departments of bacteriology, parasitology, physics and chemistry, toxicology; library of 3,000 vols.; Dir. Prof. A. ALAOUI.

Institut Pasteur: Place Charles Nicolles, Casablanca.

Institut Pasteur: B.P. 415, Tangier; f. 1912; Dir. Dr. M. MAILLOUX.

Institut Scientifique: ave. Ibn Batota, B.P. 703, Rabat; f. 1920, reorganized 1975; fundamental research on nature; departments of entomology, geography, geology, seismology, geomagnetism, zoology, etc.; 25 researchers; Dir. H. MSOUGAR; publs. *Travaux*†, *Bulletin*†.

Instituto Muley El Hassan: P.B. 84, Tetuan; research on Hispano-Muslim works; library of 5,500 vols.; Dirs. MOHAMMED BEN TAUFT, MARIANO ARRIBAS PALAU.

Laboratoire Public d'Essais et d'Etudes: 25 rue d'Azilal, Casablanca; study of soil, materials and methods of construction.

Mission Pédologique: Ministère de la Réforme Agraire, B.P. 432, Rabat; pedology; Dir. J. L. GEOFFROY.

Centre d'Expérimentations d'Hydraulique Agricole: f. 1953; Dir. E. DAGNELIES.

Institut Scientifique des Pêches Maritimes: rue de Tiznit, Casablanca; affiliated to the Office National des Pêches; f. 1948; oceanography and applied oceanography, marine biology, evaluation of resources, processing of marine products; staff of 10 scientists; Dir. MOHAMMED AZZOU; publ. *Bulletin.*

Office de la Recherche Scientifique et Technique Outre-Mer: 12 rue d'Armagnac, Rabat Agdal; hydrology; Dir. F. MONIOD. (*See* main entry under France).

Service de Physique du Globe: Faculté des Sciences, Ave. Moulay Chérif, Rabat; f. 1933; research on terrestrial magnetism, surge, seismology, gravimetry, etc.

LIBRARIES AND ARCHIVES

Casablanca

Bibliothèque de la Communauté Urbaine de Casablanca: 142 ave. des Forces Armées Royales; f. 1917; law, political economy, sciences, philosophy, history, literature, the arts, geography, medicine, sport, travel, fiction; 55,000 vols. in Arab section, 230,000 vols. in foreign section; 96 periodicals, several foreign daily newspapers; Dir. HAJ MOHAMED BOUZID.

Fez

Bibliothèque de l'Université Quaraouyine: place des Seffarines; 22,071 vols., 5,157 MSS, 38 archives.

Marrakesh

Bibliothèque Ben Youssef: Dar Glaoui, rue Rmila; 10,128 vols., 24,000 MSS; Dir. SEDDIK BELLARBI.

Rabat

Bibliothèque de l'Institut Scientifique Chérifien: ave. Moulay Chérif; f. 1921; 28,122 vols., 1,510 periodicals; Librarian A. GHANDOUR.

Bibliothèque Générale et Archives: ave. Moulay Chérif; f. 1920; over 230,000 vols., 30,000 MSS and over 1 million archives; Dir. ABDERRAHMANE EL FASSI; 6 periodical publs. including *Bibliographie Nationale Marocaine* (monthly), *Bibliographie Nationale Marocaine: Dépôt Légal* (annual), *Hesperis*†, *Bulletin Economique et Social*†.

British Council Library: B.P. 427; f. 1960; 16,976 vols., 48 periodicals; Librarian Mrs. MIR.

Centre National de Documentation: B.P. 826; f. 1968; documentation on the economic and social development of the country; library of 3,440 vols. and 60,000 microfilms; Dir. AHMED FASSI-FIHRI; publs. *Index rétrospectifs Specialisés*† (every 2 months), *Index de la documentation économique, scientifique et technique*† (quarterly).

Tangier

Biblioteca Pública Española: 9 rue Belgique; f. 1941; the library is divided into Arabic and European Sections; 38,711 vols.; Dir. and Librarian DORA BACAICOA ARNAIZ.

Tetouan

Bibliothèque Générale et Archives: B.P. 41; f. 1939; 37,771 vols., 1,735 MSS and 20,659 archives; Dir. M. DELLERO.

MUSEUMS

Division des Musées, des Sites, de l'Archéologie et des Monuments Historiques: Ministère d'Etat chargé des Affaires Culturelles, rue Gandhi, Rabat; Dir. AHMED SEFRIOUI; Chief of Archaeological Service Mme J. HASSAR-BENSLIMANE; Chief of Museum Service BELHADI BELHAJ; administers the following museums:

Musée des Oudaïa: Rabat; f. 1915; Moroccan art; Curator Mme DEMNATI BEN MOUSSA NADIA.

Musée des Antiquités: 23 rue el Brihi, Rabat; f. 1917; Curator Mme J. HASSAR-BENSLIMANE.

Musée de Dar Batha: Fez; history of art; Curator AMAHAN ALI.

Musée d'Armes de Borj Nord: Fez; Curator AMAHAN ALI.

Musée de la Kasbah: Tangier; archaeology and folklore; Curator Mme TOUJANI LATIFA.

Musée de Dar Jamaï: Meknès; Moroccan art; Curator Mme HIMEUR.

Musée de Dar si Saïd: rue de la bahia riad Zitoun Kdim (palais Dar si Saïd); Dir. BELARBI HASSAN.

Musée des Arts Traditionnels: Tetouan; Curator BENNOUNA MALEK.

Musée Archéologique: 2 rue Boukçein, Tetouan; Curator AMINE AL YOUSSI.

Musée des Antiquités: Volubilis (Moulay Driss Zerhoun); Curator ABDELOUAHED BEN TALHA.

UNIVERSITIES

UNIVERSITÉ HASSAN II

CASABLANCA

Founded 1976: in process of formation.

Number of teachers: 256.
Number of students: 11,582.

Faculties of Economics, Law, Medicine, Social Sciences.

UNIVERSITÉ MOHAMMED BEN ABDELLAH

B.P. 42, DHAR MEHRAZ, FEZ

Telephone: 413-91.

Founded 1973.

Dean: ABDELOUAHAB TAZI SAOUD.
Secretary-General: ABDELKRIM RAISS.
Librarian: MOHAMED BEN BRAHIM.

Library of 60,000 vols.
Number of teachers: 309.
Number of students: 9,877.

HEADS OF DEPARTMENTS:

English: MOHAMED OUAKRIME.
French: HASSAN ES-SMILI.
Spanish: Dr. MOHAMED MELEHI.
Arabic: Dr. EL-HARRAS.
Philosophy: MOHAMED SABILA.
History: MOHAMED TAZI-SAOUD.

UNIVERSITÉ MOHAMMED V

CAMPUS UNIVERSITAIRE, SOUISSI, AGDAL, RABAT

Founded 1957.

Academic year: October to June.

Rector: Dr. BEN ABDELLATIF BEN ABDELJALIL.

Number of teachers: 1,188.
Number of students: 30,294.

CONSTITUENT INSTITUTES:

Faculty of Letters: 3 ave. Ibn Batouta; 214 teachers, 7,984 students.

Faculty of Law: B.P. 721, Ave. Nations Unies; 175 teachers, 11,353 students.

Faculty of Sciences: Ave. Ibn Batouta; 287 teachers, 5,618 students.

Faculty of Medicine: 230 teachers, 4,440 students.

Mohammadia School of Engineering: B.P. 775, Ave. Ibn Sina; 199 teachers, 535 students; Dir. Dr. H. Kettani.

Teacher Training College: Haut Agdal; 83 teachers, 364 students.

UNIVERSITÉ QUARAOUYINE

B.P. 60, FEZ

Founded A.D. 859, enlarged in 11th century.

Academic year: November to June.

Number of teachers: 90.

Number of students: 1,647.

Constituent Institutes:

Faculty of Sharia (Law): Dhar El Mahraz, Fez; 32 teachers, 707 students.

Faculty of Arabic Language: Ave. Fatima Zahra, Marrakesh; 21 teachers, 411 students.

Faculty of Theology and Philosophy: 2 blvd. d'Alger, Tetuan; 22 teachers, 425 students.

School of Languages: 2 rue Dahomey, Rabat; 15 teachers, 104 students.

COLLEGES

Conservatoire de musique: Rue Souk, Hay Essenaï, Agadir; Dir. Nafil Bouzkarn.

Conservatoire de musique: Chefchaouen; Dir. Al Hachmi Essafyani.

Conservatoire de musique: Dar Adaîl, Fez; Dir. Abdelkarim Raïss.

Conservatoire de musique: Kasr El Kebir; Dir. Bahmed Abdelghani.

Conservatoire de musique: Dar Al Makhzen, Larache; Dir. Driss Charradi.

Conservatoire de musique: Jenan El Harti, Marrakesh; Dir. Al Montasser Hassan.

Conservatoire de musique: Av. Al Konsolia Al Faransia, Dar El Bacha Alkadima, Safi; Dir. Najih Mohammed.

Conservatoire de musique: Av. Zighi ibn atia, Taza; Dir. Abdellah Kharraz.

Conservatoire de musique: Tetouan; Dir. Med Larbi Temsamani.

Conservatoire National de Musique, de Danse et d'Art Dramatique: Rabat; trains students in European, Moroccan and Eastern music. The Conservatoire has three orchestras: a classical symphony orchestra; an orchestra for traditional Andalusian music; an orchestra for Eastern music; Dir. Awatef Ahmed.

Conservatoire de Tanger: Av. Belgique, Tangier; Dir. Raîssi Mohamed.

Ecole des Métiers d'Art (*School of Native Arts and Crafts*): Bab Okla, B.P. 89, Tetouan; f. 1921; textiles, carpets, rugs, ceramics, engraving, plaster inlays, woodwork, precious metal work, leather and Arabic woodcarving; 350 mems.; Dir. Fekhar Abdellah.

Ecole Nationale d'Administration Publique: B.P. 165, 1 ave. de la Victoire, Rabat; f. 1948; library of 5,463 vols. in Arabic, 6,329 vols. in French; 80 teachers, 590 students; Dir. Mohamed Birouk.

Ecole Nationale des Beaux-Arts: Ave. Mohamed V, Cité Scolaire B.P. 89, Tetouan; f. 1946; drawing, painting, sculpture, decorative arts; Dir. Mohammed M. Serghini.

Ecole Nationale de musique: 133 Av. Ziraoui, Casablanca; Dir. Oulhadj Brahim.

Ecole Nationale de musique: 22 rue Marrakchia, Kaa Ouarda, Meknès; Dir. Abdelaziz Benabdeljalil.

Ecole des Sciences de l'Information: B.P. 762, Rabat-Agdal; f. 1975; 2- and 3-year diploma courses for archivists, librarians, documentalists; library of 1,500 vols., 160 periodicals; 37 teachers, 207 students; Dir. Mohamed Benjelloun.

Institut Agronomique et Vétérinaire Hassan II: B.P. 704, Rabat-Agdal; f. 1966; library of 15,000 documents, 670 periodicals; Dir. M. Abdellah Bekkali; Sec. Gen. M. Larbi Firdawcy; publ. *Hommes, Terre et Eaux: Revue Marocaine des Sciences Agronomiques et vétérinaires* (quarterly).

Institut National de musique et de danse: Ave. Mohamed V, (derrière la 2° arrondissement), Kénitra; Dir. Abbès Alkhayyati.

Institut National de Statistique et d'Economie Appliquée: B.P. 406, Rabat; f. 1961; library of 3,700 vols.; Dir. C. Benazzou.

Instituto Español de Tánger (*Spanish Institute in Tangier*): Plaza Kuwait 1, Tangier; f. 1949; 500 students; library of 6,335 vols.; Dir. Don Octavio Nieto Taladriz; publ. *Revista Casban* (monthly).

MOZAMBIQUE

Population 9,444,000

LEARNED SOCIETIES AND RESEARCH INSTITUTES

Direcção dos Serviços de Geologia e Minas: Caixa Postal 217, Maputo; f. 1930; 157 mems.; geological studies and mining research; 15,000 books in library; Dir. J. R. F. REBOLO; publs. *Boletim dos Serviços de Geologia e Minas de Moçambique, Carta Geológica de Moçambique.*

Instituto de Algodão de Moçambique (*Cotton Research Institute*): Caixa Postal 806, Maputo; f. 1962; departments of agronomy, botany, soils, economics, genetical cytology, entomology and phytopathology; 4 experimental stations; library of 2,500 vols., 210 journals and reviews; Dir. Eng. Agr. MARIO DE CARVALHO; publ. *Memórias e Trabalhos.*

Instituto de Investigação Cientifica Moçambique (*Mozambique Institute of Scientific Research*): Caixa Postai 1780, Maputo; f. 1955; centres of ecology, communication studies, and appropriate technology; library and scientific documentation centre, Museu de História Natural (*see* below); Dir. PEDRO J. C. ALCÂNTARA; publs. occasional papers.

Instituto de Saúde Publica de Moçambique (*Mozambique Public Health Institute*): Avenida Fernandes Tomáz 179, Caixa Postal 1572, Maputo; f. 1955; departments of Epidemiology (Malacology, Demography and Statistics), Microbiology (Protozoology, Helminthology, Bacteriology), Clinical Pathology (Therapeutics, Biochemistry, Haematology, Pathology), Documentation and Scientific Information; Dir. L. T. DE ALMEIDA FRANCO.

Observatório Astronómico e Meteorológico Campos Rodrigues (*Campos Rodrigues Astronomical and Meteorological Observatory*): Serviço Meteorológico de Moçambique, Caixa Postal 256, Maputo; f. 1907; Dir. JOSÉ F. GOMES PEPE; publs. *Anuario de Observações* (2 vols.), I *Observações Meteorológicas de Superficie*†, II *Observações Meteorológicas de Altitude*†, *Boletim Séismique*†, *Informações de Caracter Astronómico, Boletim Geomagnético Preliminar*†, *Boletim Meteorológico para a Agricultura, Publicações Eventuais.*

LIBRARIES

Arquivo Histórico de Moçambique: C.P. 2033, Maputo; f. 1934; 7,468 vols.; Dir. MARIA INÊS GONÇALVES.

Biblioteca e Centro de Documentação e Informação: C.P. 1406, Maputo; f. 1977; part of Ministry of Education; library of 2,000 vols.; in process of reorganization.

Biblioteca Municipal: Maputo; 7,951 vols.

Biblioteca Nacional de Moçambique (*National Library of Mozambique*): C.P. 141, Maputo; f. 1961; 110,000 vols.; Dir. ANTÓNIO M. B. COSTA E SILVA.

MUSEUMS

Museu de História Natural: C.P. 1780, Maputo; f. 1911; Natural History Museum and Ethnographic Gallery; attached to the University; Dir. JAIME AUGUSTO TRAVASSOS SANTOS DIAS.

Museu Freire de Andrade: Department of Geology and Mines, Maputo; f. 1940; Dir. Eng. JOSÉ DOS REIS FERNANDES REBOLO.

UNIVERSITY

UNIVERSIDADE EDUARDO MONDLANE

C.P. 257, MAPUTO

Telephone: 27851.

Founded 1962.

State control; Language of instruction: Portuguese; Academic year: February to December.

Rector: Prof. FERNANDO DOS REIS GANHÂO.

Administration Officer: CÉLIA MARIA RODRIGUES DINIZ.

Academic Director: JOÃO CARLOS MONTEIRO RAPOSO BEIRÃO.

Documentation Information Service: WANDA DE AMARAL.

Number of teachers: *c.* 260.
Number of students: 746.

DEANS:

Faculty of Agricultural Sciences: JOSÉ RODRIGUES PEREIRA.

Faculty of Biology: MARIA MADALENA S. A. BAETA.

Faculty of Law: DETLEF JOSEPH.

Faculty of Economics: FERNANDO JORGE CARDOSO.

Faculty of Civil Engineering: CARLOS A. V. QUADROS.

Faculty of Electrical Engineering: JORGE M. P. RODRIGUES.

Faculty of Mechanics and Chemistry: ANTÓNIO SARAIVA DE SOUSA.

NAMIBIA
(SOUTH WEST AFRICA)

Population 888,000

LEARNED SOCIETIES AND RESEARCH INSTITUTES

Desert Ecological Research Unit of the Council for Scientific and Industrial Research: Namib Desert Research Station, P.O.B. 953, Walvis Bay, 9190; f. 1963; carries out exploration and research in Namib Desert, emphasising basic research in the dune ecosystem and applied research on desert conditions in general and on nature conservation in the desert; library of 600 vols.; Dir. M. K. SEELY; publ. *Madoqua* (Scientific papers).

Institute of South West African Architects: P.O.B. 1478, Windhoek 9100; f. 1952; 36 mems.; Pres. K. S. MCNAMARA.

South West African Association of Arts: Windhoek.

S.W.A. Scientific Society: P.O.B. 67, Windhoek 9000; f. 1925; ornithology, spelaeology, botany, archaeology, herpetology, astronomy, ethnology; 815 mems. and 200 exchange mems.; library of 5,473 vols.; Pres. H. FINKELDEY; Sec. W. SYDOW; publs. *Mitteilungen/Newsletter/Nuusbrief, Mitteilungen der Ornithologischen Arbeitsgruppe, Botanische Mitteilungen* (monthly), *Journal* (annually), and others irregularly.

LIBRARY AND ARCHIVES

Government Archives: Private Bag 13250, Windhoek 9000; f. 1939; houses government records, private collections, maps, photographs, and *c.* 3,000 publications; Chief S. A. HARPER.

Windhoek Public Library: P.O.B. 3180, Windhoek 9000; f. 1924; 61,236 vols.; Librarian Miss M. M. VILJOEN.

MUSEUMS

Lüderitz Museum: P.O.B. 512, Lüderitz 9045; f. 1966; incorporates finds of Friedrich Eberlanz of archaeological, herpetological, botanical and mineralogical interest, incl. Bushman Stone Age tools; Supervisor Mrs. A. DYCK.

State Museum: P.O.B. 1203, Windhoek; f. 1958; natural history, cultural history; library of 3,000 vols. and 300 journal titles; Dir. C. G. COETZEE, M.SC., H.E.D.; publs. *Cimbebasia*†, *Memoirs*.

Swakopmund Museum: P.O.B. 56, Strand Street, Swakopmund; f. 1951; natural history, mineralogy, marine life, history; Chair. Dr. A. M. WEBER; publs. *Nachrichten* (quarterly), *Namib und Meer* (annually).

NEPAL

Population 13,421,000

ACADEMY

Royal Nepal Academy: Kalamandi, Kathmandu; f. 1957; 178 mems.; Chancellor LAIN SINGH BANGDEL.

LEARNED SOCIETIES

American Cultural Center and Library: New Rd., Kathmandu.

British Council: Kantipath, P.O.B. 640, Kathmandu; f. 1959; Rep. N. M. Ross.

French Cultural Centre: Bag Bazar, Kathmandu; f. 1969; teaching, cinema, exhibitions; 600 mems.; 400 students; library of 3,000 vols.; Dir. J.-PH. GELEY.

LIBRARIES

Bir Library: Ranipolhari, Kathmandu; f. 14th century; *c.* 15,000 MSS.

British Council Library: Kanti Path, Kathmandu; f. 1959; 11,003 vols., 64 periodicals; Librarian Miss S. MANANDHAR, B.A., B.L.SC.

National Library: Kathmandu; Chair. NARAYAN P. SHARMA.

Nepal-Bharat Sanskritik Kendra Pustakalay: Ganga Path, Kathmandu; f. 1952; 13,000 vols.; Librarian B. N. SARKAR.

Singh Darbar: Secretariat Library, Kathmandu.

Tribhuvan University Library: Kirtipur; f. 1959; 67,000 vols.; Librarian Mrs. SHANTI MISHRA; publs. *Journal of Tribhuvan University*†, *Education Quarterly*†.

MUSEUM

National Museum of Nepal: Museum Rd., Chhauni, Kathmandu; f. 1938; art, history, culture, ethnology, natural history; a conservation laboratory is being set up with Unesco aid; reference library; art gallery; Mahendra Memorial Museum illustrates the life of H.M. King Mahendra; Dir. PASHUPATI KUMAR DWIVEDI.

UNIVERSITY

TRIBHUVAN UNIVERSITY

TRIPURESWAR, KATHMANDU

Telephone: 15313.

Founded 1959.

Autonomous control; Languages of instruction: Nepali and English; Academic year: July to August.

Chancellor: H.M. King BIRENDRA BIR BIKRAM SHAH DEV.
Vice-Chancellor: JAGAT MOHAN ADHIKARI.
Rector: Dr. KAMAL PRAKASH MALLA.
Registrar: GOPAL DHOJ SHRESTHA.

Library: *see* Libraries.

Number of teachers: 2,311.

Number of students: 31,522.

Publications: *T.U. Bulletin*† (monthly), *University Journal*† (2 a year), *Contribution to Nepalese Studies*† (2 a year), *Research Bulletin*† (quarterly), *CEDA News*† (quarterly, Centre for Economic Development and Administration), *Education Quarterly*†, *Journal of Forestry*† (annually), *Journal of Institute of Science*† (2 a year), *Banijya Sansar*†, *Public Administration Journal*†, *Journal of Economics*†, *Voice of History*†, *Journal of Geography*† (annually).

DEANS:

Institute of Humanities and Social Science: Dr. PARTHIBESWAR PRASAD TIMILSINA.
Institute of Science: DWIJA RAJ UPRETY.
Institute of Business Administration, Commerce and Public Administration: UPENDRA BAHADUR PRADHANANG.
Institute of Education: Dr. KEDAR NATH SHRESTHA.
Institute of Sanskrit: AMBIKA PRASAD ADHIKARI.
Institute of Engineering: GAURI NATH RIMAL.
Institute of Medicine: Dr. HEMANG DIXIT.
Institute of Agriculture and Animal Science: NETRA BAHADUR BASNET.
Institute of Law: CHANDRA DHAR UPRETY (acting).
Institute of Forestry: MAZRUL HAQ.

DIRECTORS:

Research Centre for Applied Science and Technology: Dr. AMIR BAHADUR SHRESTHA.
Centre for Economic Development and Administration: SANTA BAHADUR GURUNG (acting).
Research Centre for Nepal and Asian Studies: DOR BAHADUR BISTA.

PROFESSORS:

Institute of Humanities and Social Science:
BARAL, L. R., Political Science
BISTA, D. B., Anthropology
CHOUDHARY, T. P., Economics
JHA, H. N., Culture
MALLA, K. P., English
MALLA, U. M., Geography
MISHRA, H. D., Sanskrit
PANDEY, M. R., History
POKHAREL, B. K., Nepali
SHARMA, K. P., Economics
TRIPATHI, B. D., Nepali

Institute of Science:
AMATYA, D. M. S., Chemistry
BAJRACHARYA, D. N., Botany
DHOUBHADEL, S. P., Chemistry
GAJUREL, C. L., Chemistry
JOSHI, B. R., Physics
MAJUPURIA, T. C., Zoology
PRADHAN, S. P., Physics
SHRESTHA, K. L., Physics
SINGH, S. S., Zoology

Institute of Business Administration, Commerce and Public Administration:
RAJBAHAK, R. P., Commerce

Institute of Education:
KASAJU, P. K., Education
PRADHAN, P. L., Psychology

Centre for Economic Development and Administration:
AGRAWAL, G. R., Business Administration
PRADHAN, P. P., Public Administration
RANA, R. S., Geography
SAINJU, M. M., Economics

Research Centre for Applied Science and Technology:
SUWAL, P. N., Industrial Chemistry

Research Centre for Nepal and Asian Studies:
SHARMA, P. R., Culture

THE NETHERLANDS

Population 13,985,000

ACADEMY

Koninklijke Nederlandse Akademie van Wetenschappen (*Royal Netherlands Academy of Arts and Sciences*): Amsterdam, Kloveniersburgwal 29 (Trippenhuis); f. 1808; reorganized in 1851; re-formed as above 1855; publs. *Jaarboek, Proceedings of the Section of Sciences Series A, B and C, Indagationes Mathematicae, Verslag van de Gewone Vergaderingen der Afdeling Natuurkunde, Verhandelingen Eerste en Tweede Reeks der Afdeling Natuurkunde, Mededelingen der Afdeling Letterkunde, Verhandelingen der Afdeling Letterkunde.*

President: Mr. S. Dresden.

Secretary-General: Prof. Dr. F. A. Stafleu.

Section for Mathematics and Natural Sciences:

President: Prof. Dr. J. Lever.

Secretary: Prof. Dr. F. A. Stafleu.

Section for Philology, Literature, History and Philosophy:

President: Prof. Dr. J. van der Hoeven.

Secretary: Prof. Dr. G. Nuchelmans.

Director: Mr. J. Th. A. Klarenbeek.

Director of the Library: Drs. J. A. W. Brak.

Section for Mathematics and Natural Sciences:

Ordinary Members:

	Elected		*Elected*
H. C. van de Hulst	1956	J. H. van der Waals	1971
N. G. de Bruijn	1957	C. T. de Wit	1971
P. M. Endt	1957	G. Bras	1972
G. P. Baerends	1958	J. H. van Lint	1972
S. R. de Groot	1958	W. G. Zijlstra	1972
W. T. Koiter	1959	D. W. van Bekkum	1973
A. van Wijngaarden	1959	M. A. Bouman	1973
J. F. Arens	1960	L. L. M. van Deenen	1973
C. J. Bouwkamp	1960	D. A. van Dorp	1973
A. C. Zaanen	1960	J. Drenth	1973
D. Durrer	1962	W. T. van Est	1973
A. Blaauw	1963	R. T. Hegnauer	1973
J. Boldingh	1964	H. E. Henkes	1973
E. C. Slater	1964	N. G. van Kampen	1973
T. A. Springer	1964	F. A. Stafleu	1973
J. de Wilde	1964	H. J. Zwart	1973
J. J. Van Loghem	1965	J. M. L. Janssen	1974
W. P. De Roever	1965	A. H. Stouthamer	1974
G. A. van Arkel	1967	N. J. Trappeniers	1974
E. den Tex	1967	V. Westoff	1974
E. L. Mackor	1968	J. A. Battjes	1975
C. W. Drooger	1969	Th. J. de Boer	1975
C. de Jager	1969	J. Korevaar	1975
E. J. Ariëns	1970	H. Kramers	1975
J. Lever	1970	H. Postma	1975
P. Mazur	1970	C. Haas	1976
W. Baarda	1971	A. S. Troelstra	1976
L. N. M. Duysens	1971	D. De Wied	1976
E. W. Dykstra	1971	H. van Genderen	1977
F. K. Ligtenberg	1971	J. W. Kuiper	1977
J. P. Murre	1971	K. Teer	1977
W. L. van der Poel	1971	J. J. M. Beenakker	1978
Th. Quené	1971	J. Borgman	1978
L. M. J. U. van Straaten	1971	P. Borst	1978
		L. Bosch	1978
L. H. van der Tweel	1971	H. F. Linskens	1978
J. D. van Manen	1978	F. H. Sobels	1979
D. Polder	1978	H. de Waard	1979
A. R. Ritsema	1978	P. M. de Wolf	1979
J. J. van Rood	1978	A. Zwaveling	1979
H. J. Vink	1978	W. R. van Zwet	1979
J. Th. Wiebes	1978	H. H. Cohen	1980
A. van der Avoird	1979	J. Kistemaker	1980
H. J. C. Berendsen	1979	H. Kuijpers	1980
R. Brouwer	1979	D. G. H. Latzko	1980
C. F. A. Bruijning	1979	M. Veltmann	1980
H. M. Buck	1979	H. K. A. Visser	1980
P. W. Kasteleyn	1979	A. Vos	1980
H. van der Laan	1979	W. H. Zagwijn	1980
E. Mandema	1979	P. Zandbergen	1980
W. M. H. Sachtler	1979		

Section for Philology, Literature, History and Philosophy:

Ordinary Members:

	Elected		*Elected*
A. M. Donner	1955	D. J. van de Kaa	1976
S. Dresden	1955	A. C. F. Koch	1976
L. de Jong	1963	J. G. Sauveplanne	1976
C. W. Dubbink	1967	P. Gerbenzon	1977
E. M. Uhlenbeck	1967	L. M. de Rijk	1977
A. D. Leeman	1968	I. Schöffer	1977
W. den Boer	1969	E. M. Barth	1978
J. A. A. van Doorn	1969	A. Th. van Deursen	1978
W. C. L. van der Grinten	1969	W. A. van Es	1978
		Ch. P. A. Geppaart	1978
C. W. Mönnich	1969	W. P. Gerritsen	1978
A. G. H. Bachrach	1970	C. Goedhart	1978
H. Tj. Waterbolk	1970	F. J. van Ingen	1978
Mia I. Gerhardt	1971	T. Koopmans	1978
A. H. Kuipers	1971	W. J. M. Levelt	1978
C. J. Ruijgh	1971	R. A. de Moor	1978
A. Teeuw	1971	F. R. Noske	1978
G. J. D. Aalders	1972	E. Te Nijenhuis	1978
J. Pen	1972	S. L. Radt	1978
C. Reedijk	1972	H. Daudt	1979
R. Feenstra	1973	C. L. Ebeling	1979
I. Gadourek	1973	N. H. Frijda	1979
A. D. de Groot	1973	P. de Haan	1979
E. H. Kossmann	1973	R. B. C. Huygens	1979
J. Zijlstra	1973	P. W. Klein	1979
H. Drion	1974	C. J. Lammers	1979
		R. Meischke	1979
R. A. V. Baron van Haersolte	1974	H. W. Pleket	1979
		J. Remmelink	1979
P. E. de Josselin de Jong	1974	W. Snijders	1979
J. W. Salomonson	1974	W. H. Somermeijer	1979
		J. de Vries	1979
P. Vertoren van Themaat	1974	J. C. Boogman	1980
A. S. van der Woude	1974	J. A. Bornewasser	1980
J. van der Hoeven	1975	P. J. Drenth	1980
C. van de Kieft	1975	P. J. G. Kapteyn	1980
A. J. F. Köbben	1975	E. P. Meijering	1980
		C. J. A. Peeters	1980
G. R. F. M. Nuchelmans	1975	F. de Roos	1980
D. B. J. Schouten	1975	A. L. Sotemann	1980
E. Zürcher	1975	P. J. Sijpesteijn	1980
J. L. Bouma	1976	H. J. Witteveen	1980
J. Bruyn	1976		

Each section has some Members abroad, a number of Emeriti, 50 Foreign Members and 50 and 40 corresponding members respectively.

LEARNED SOCIETIES

General

Hollandsche Maatchappij der Wetenschappen (*Dutch Society of Sciences*): Spaarne 17, Haarlem; f. 1752; furthering contact between scientists and laymen by arranging lectures on scientific subjects and awarding annual prizes and subsidies for research and publication of scientific work; 400 mems.; Pres. Dr. L. de Gou; Sec. Prof. Dr. A. Quispel.

Agriculture and Veterinary Science

Hollandsche Maatschappij van Landbouw (*Dutch Agricultural Society*): Anna Paulownastraat 20-22, The Hague; Sec. Ir. D. S. Tuynman.

Koninklijk Genootschap voor Landbouwwetenschap (*Royal Netherlands Society of Agricultural Science*): P.O.B. 79, 6700 AB Wageningen; f. 1886; 2,400 mems.; Pres. Dr. Ir. P. Gaastra; First Sec. Dr. Ir. F. J. Breteler; Second Sec. Ir. H. J. van 't Klooster; Admin. P. C. Kuijpers; publs. *Landbouwkundig Tijdschrift* (monthly), *Netherlands Journal of Agricultural Science* (English, quarterly).

Koninklijke Maatschappij Tuinbouw en Plantkunde (*Royal Horticultural Society*): Kwekerijweg 2, 2597 JK The Hague; f. 1872; 45,000 mems.; Pres. N. C. Hofman; Sec.-Gen. J. C. M. Wassenaar; publ. *Groei en Bloei*† (monthly).

Koninklijke Nederlandse Bosbouw Vereniging (*Royal Netherlands Forestry Society*): Lovinklaan 1, Arnhem; f. 1910; 325 mems.; Chair. Ir. A. J. v. d. Poel; Sec. Ir. J. L. Volmuller; publ. *Nederlands Bosbouwtijdschrift* (monthly).

Nederlandse Tuinbouwraad (*Netherlands Horticultural Council*): Schiefbaanstraat 29, 2596 RC The Hague; Sec. Ir. A. Groot.

Stichting Nederlands Agronomisch-Historisch Instituut (*Netherlands Agronomic-Historical Foundation*): Vismarkt 40, Groningen; f. 1949; library of 10,000 vols.; Pres. R. J. Clevering; Dir. (vacant); Sec. A. F. Stroink; publ. *Historia Agriculturae.*

Architecture and Town Planning

Architektenraad (*Architects' Registration Council*): Keizersgracht 321, 1016 EE, P.O.B. 19611, 1000 GP Amsterdam; f. 1946 to maintain Register of Architects and supervise observance of Code of Conduct; 12 mems.; Chair. Th. Limperg; Sec. Ms. J. Höweler.

Bond Heemschut (*Society for the Preservation of Architectural Beauty in the Netherlands*): Amsterdam-C., "Korenmetershuis", N. Z. Kolk 28; f. 1911; mems.: *c.* 10,000 societies and individuals; Chair. G. K. J. M. Hamm, Sec. J. G. Oost Lievense; 11 Provincial subcttees.; publ. *Heemschut* (illustrated monthly).

Genootschap Architectura et Amicitia (A. et A.): Amsterdam, Waterlooplein 67; f. 1855; 300 mems.; Chair. Arch. J. P. H. Ch. Girod; Sec. Ir. K. Rijnboutt; publ. *Forum* (monthly).

Koninklijke Maatschappij tot Bevordering der Bouwkunst Bond van Nederlandse Architekten (B.N.A.) (*Royal Institute of Dutch Architects*): P.O.B. 19606, Keizersgracht 321, 1000 GP Amsterdam; f. 1842; 1,830 mems.; publ. *Plan.*

Monumentenraad (*Council for Monuments*): Zeist, Broederplein 41; f. 1961; 40 mems.; Pres. (vacant); Sec. Drs. F. J. L. van Dulm; publs. *Geillustreerde beschrijving der Nederlandse monumenten van Geschiedenis en Kunst, Kunstreisboek voor Nederland*, Annual Report.

Rijksdienst voor de Monumentenzorg (*Government Dept. for the Preservation of Historical Monuments*): Broederplein 41, Zeist; f. 1918; re-formed 1946; library of 29,000 vols.; Head Dir J. Jessurun; publ. Annual Report.

Stichting Centrale Raad voor de Academies van Bouwkunst (*Central Council of the Academies of Architecture*): Keizersgracht 321, 1016 EE Amsterdam; Chair. (vacant).

The Arts

De Nederlandse Kunststichting (*The Netherlands Art Foundation*): Oostelijke Handelskade 29, Postbus 1258, Amsterdam; f. 1951; organizes exhibitions of contemporary art in the Netherlands; Dir. H. Visser.

Koninklijke Nederlandse Toonkunstenaars-vereniging (*Royal Netherlands Asscn. of Musicians*): Amsterdam, Van Miereveldstraat 13; f. 1875; 2,000 mems.; Chair. Peter Jense; Sec. Theo van Eijk; publ. *Muziek en Dans* (10 a year).

Maatschappij "Arti et Amicitiae": Amsterdam, Rokin 112; f. 1839; a national society of painters, sculptors and graphic artists; 1,100 mems.; library of 6,000 vols.; gallery for members' works; Pres. Willem Gorter; Sec. Gen. Rik van der Mey.

Maatschappij tot Bevordering der Toonkunst (*Society for Advancement of Music*): Amsterdam, 1e Jac. Van Campenstraat 59; f. 1829; 6,000 mems.; library contains 18,000 vols; Chair. Prof. J. E. Spruit; Sec. Wouter Paap; publ. *Toonkunst-Nieuws.*

Nederlands Theater Instituut (*Netherlands Theatre Institute*): Herengracht 166-168, Amsterdam; f. 1978; theatre museum; library of 40,000 vols. and sound and film archives of the Dutch theatre; Netherlands centre of the International Theatre Institute; Co-ordinator E. Alexander; publ. *Amphitheater* (10 a year).

Nederlandse Toonkunstenaarsraad (*Council of Organisations of Musicians in the Netherlands*): Amsterdam, Valeriusplein 20; f. 1948 to protect professional interests; 3,000 mems.; Chair. Dr. N. J. C. M. Kappeyne van de Coppello; Man. Dir. Ir. R. C. Broek; publ. *A Musical Guide for Holland* (biennial).

Rijksbureau voor Kunsthistorische Documentatie (*Netherlands Institute for Art History*): The Hague, 7 Korte Vijverberg; f. 1932; library of 260,000 vols., periodicals and catalogues; press-cuttings, archives, 1,000,000 photos and reproductions; Dir. J. Nieuwstraten, m.a.; publs. *Annual Report, Bibliography of Dutch and Flemish Art*†, *Iconographic Index, Exhibitions Calendar, Oud-Holland.*

Stichting Verenigd Nederlands Filminstituut (*Netherlands Film and TV Institute*): P.O.B. 515, Hilversum, Steynlaan 8; f. 1948; lecture and information service, and a Film Distribution Service; Man. Dir. Dr. J. A. Hes.

Vereniging "Sint Lucas" (*St. Luke Asscn.*): Amsterdam, Zomerdijk-straat 20; f. 1880; Chair. Bart Peizel; Sec. Theo Swagemakers.

Wagnervereeniging (*Wagner Society*): Gabriël Metsustr. 32, Amsterdam; f. 1883; Chair. Mr. W. Th. Doyer; Sec. Evert Cornelis.

Bibliography, Library Science and Museology

FOBID—Federatie van Organisaties van Bibliotheek-, Informatie-, Dokumentatiewezen (*Federation of Library, Information and Documentation Organizations*): P.O.B. 93166, 2509 AD The Hague, Taco Scheltemastraat 5; f. 1975; promotion of co-operation and integration among public, research and special libraries in the Netherlands; mem.: Nederlandse Vereniging van Bibliothekarissen and Nederlands Bibliotheek en Lektuur Centrum (*see* below); Chair. P. J. Th. Schoots.

Nederlands Bibliotheek en Lektuur Centrum (*Dutch Centre for Public Libraries and Literature*): P.O.B. 93054, 2509 AB The Hague, Taco Scheltemastraat 5, 2597 CP; f. 1972 through amalgamation of the former library societies of Centrale Vereniging voor Openbare Bibliotheken, Christelijk Lektuur Centrum, Katholiek Bibliotheek en Lektuur Centrum, Lektuurvoorlichting van de Maatschappij tot Nut van't Algemeen, Stichting C.J.V. Lektuurvoorlichting; Dir. D. REUMER; publ. *Bibliotheek en Samenleving*†.

De Nederlandse Museumvereniging (*The Dutch Museums Association*): c/o Wierdijk 18, Enkhuizen; f. 1926; 500 mems.; Chair. D. H. COUVEE; Sec. A. A. E. VELS HEIJN; publ. *Museumvisie* (quarterly).

Nederlandse Vereniging van Bibliothecarissen, Documentalisten en Literatuur Onderzoekers (*Netherlands Society of Librarians, Documentalists and Literary Researchers*): p/a Mw. H. J. Krikke-Scholten, Nolweg 13D, 4209 AW Schelluinen; f. 1912; 1,300 mems.; maintenance of lawful regulation of library system, arrangement of meetings and international co-operation, professional education; Pres. J. R. DE GROOT; Sec. D. R. F. VAN BREMEN; publ. *Open*.

Economics, Law and Politics

Hague Academy of International Law (*Académie de droit international de la Haye*): Carnegieplein 2, 2562 RK The Hague; f. 1923 as a centre of higher studies in international law (public and private) and cognate sciences, in order to facilitate a thorough and impartial examination of questions bearing on international juridical relations; Admin. Council: The Directors of the Carnegie Foundation, The Hague; Curatorium: Pres. Prof. R. AGO (Italy); Vice-Pres. M. LACHS (Poland); Sec.-Gen. Prof. R. J. DUPUY (France); mems. H. C. BATIFFOL, Prof. A TRUYOL Y SERRA, F. JIMÉNEZ DE ARÉCHAGA, M. LACHS, H. E. T. O. ELIAS, P. RUEGGER, S. TSUROKA, G. TUNKIN, Prof. W. REESE, P. DE VISSCHER, MUSTAFA KAMIL YASSEEN, W. MOSLER, W. RIPHAGEN, M. SØRENSEN, Sir HUMPHREY WALDOCK.

Internationaal Juridisch Instituut (*International Juridical Institute*): Oranjestraat 6, The Hague; Pres. W. L. HAARDT; Dir. C. D. VAN BOESCHOTEN; Sec. J. VAN RIJN VAN ALKEMADE.

Nederlands Economisch Instituut (*Netherlands Economic Institute*): Burg. Oudlaan 50, Rotterdam 3016.

Nederlandse Vereniging van het Nederlandse Stichting voor Statistiek (*Netherlands Statistics Association*): Bankaplein 1A, The Hague; market, sociological and statistical research; Dirs. Drs. P. H. VAN WESTENDORP, Drs. V. F. W. OPHOFF, TJ. H. VELDMAN, A. DE VOS, C. H. DE RUIJG.

Nederlandse Vereniging voor Internationaal Recht (*Netherlands Branch of International Law Asscn.*): f. 1910; 320 mems.; Pres. M. H. VAN HOOGSTRATEN; Hon. Sec. Mr. A. Bos, Koninginnegracht 27, The Hague; publ. *Mededelingen*.

Vereniging voor Agrarisch Recht (*Agrarian Law Society*): "de Leeuwenborch" Hollandseweg, Wageningen; Sec. Dr. Ir. P. DE VISSER.

Vereniging voor Arbeidsrecht (*Labour Law Society*): Zeestraat 73, 2518 AA The Hague; f. 1946; 450 mems.; Sec. Mr. E. G. H. VERVIERS; publ. monographs.

Vereniging voor de Staathuishoudkunde (*Dutch Economy Society*): Achterom 98, Delft; Sec. Drs. E. D. J. KRUIJTBOSCH.

Volkenrechtelijk Instituut (*International Law Institute*): Utrecht University, Janskerkhof 16; f. 1955; library of 6,000 vols.; publ. *Nova et Vetera Iuris Gentium*.

Education

Centrum voor de Studie van het Onderwijs in Ontwikkelingslanden (*Centre for the Study of Education in Developing Countries—CESO*): Badhuisweg 251, 2509 LS The Hague; f. 1963; undertakes study and research on education in developing countries; performs and coordinates evaluation studies; advises universities and ministries on development projects; organizes lectures at home and abroad; 13 mems.; library of 5,000 vols., 1,400 reports and 150 periodicals; Dir. Prof. J. H. KRAAK; publs. *Verhandelingen*†, acquisition lists.

Nederlandse Vereniging van Opvoedkundigen (*Dutch Society of Educationalists*): De Hoghe Weijdt 69, 1851 EC Heiloo; f. 1962.

Stichting der Nederlandse Universiteiten en Hogescholen voor Internationale Samenwerking (*Netherlands Universities Foundation for International Co-operation—NUFFIC*): P.O.B. 90734, 2509 LS The Hague, Badhuisweg 251; f. 1952 by the Netherlands universities to promote international co-operation in the academic and scientific field; organizes summer courses and postgraduate international courses; mediates educational and scientific help to developing countries; Dir. A. J. VAN DULST; publ. *Higher Education and Research in the Netherlands*† (quarterly, English, Spanish edns.).

History, Geography and Archaeology

Centraal Bureau voor Genealogie (*Central Bureau of Genealogy*): Prins Willem Alexanderhof 22, P.O.B. 11755, 2502 AT The Hague; f. 1945; large genealogical and heraldic collection; library of *c.* 100,000 vols.; Dir. T. N. SCHELHAAS; Curators C. W. DELFORTERIE, N. PLOMP.

Fries Genootschap van Geschied-, Oudheid- en Taalkunde (*Society of Frisian Archaeology, History and Philology*): Leeuwarden, Fries Museum, Turfmarkt 24; f. 1827; 1,842 mems.; Pres. Dr. K. J. VAN DOUWEN; Sec. W. DOLK; publs. *De Vrije Fries* (annual), *Verslag Fries Genootschap* (annual).

Historisch Genootschap "de Maze" (*Historical Association "de Maze"*): f. 1931; 86 mems.; Chair. J. W. D'HANE; Sec. A. M. VAN DER WOEL, Gemeente-archief, Mathenesserlaan 315, 3021 HL Rotterdam.

Internationaal Instituut voor Sociale Geschiedenis (*International Institute of Social History*): Amsterdam, Herengracht 262-266; f. 1935; library of 500,000 vols., archives, especially on the labour movement, 60,000 periodicals; Dir. Drs. J. R. VAN DER LEEUW; Librarian Drs. G. J. A. RIESTHUIS; Archivist Drs. ELLY KOEN; publs. include *Quellen und Untersuchungen zur Geschichte der deutschen und österreichischen Arbeiterbewegung, Publications on Social History, Archives Bakounine, Russian Series on Social History, Sociaal-Historische Studiën, International Review of Social History, De Nederlandse Arbeidersbeweging, International Institute of Social History, History and Activities* (1968), *Annual Report* (in English).

Koninklijk Nederlands Aardrijkskundig Genootschap (*Royal Dutch Geographical Society*): Amsterdam, Mauritskade 63; f. 1873; 3,000 mems.; library of 13,000 vols., 600 periodicals, 30,000 maps and charts; Pres. Drs. TH. HADDERINGH; Sec. Drs. J. A. KOETSIER; publs. *Geografisch Tijdschrift* (5 a year), *Tijdschrift voor Economische en Sociale Geographie* (6 a year), *De Nieuwe Geografenkrant* (10 a year).

Koninklijk Oudheidkundig Genootschap (*Royal Antiquarian Society*): Amsterdam, Rijksmuseum; f. 1858; possesses a collection of applied art (furniture, silver, sculpture, etc.), paintings, objects of historical value, prints and drawings concerning the topography of Amsterdam, manners and customs of the Netherlands; coins, medals, books; 500 mems.; 5,000 vols.; Pres.

L. H. VAN DER TWEEL; Secs. Mrs. D. DE HOOP SCHEFFER, B. BAKKER; publ. *Jaarverslagen* (illustrated annual reports).

Nederlands Historisch Genootschap (*Historical Assn.*): Lange Voorhout 34, The Hague; f. 1845; 1,700 mems.; Pres. Prof. Dr. E. H. KOSSMANN; Sec. Drs. G. VAN HERWIJNEN; publs. *Bijdragen en Mededelingen betreffende de Geschiedenis der Nederlanden, The Low Countries History Yearbook, Werken NHG, Nederlandse Historische Bronnen.*

Vereniging Gelre: Arnhem, Markt 1; f. 1899; historical society of the province of Gelderland; publs. *Bijdragen en Mededelingen, Werken.*

Vereniging "Het Nederlandsch Economisch-Historisch Archief" (*The Netherlands Economic-Historic Archives Society*): 220 Herengracht, Amsterdam; f. 1914; specializes in economic history and business studies; library of 70,000 vols. on economic history; Librarian Drs. C. GRAVESTEYN; Sec.-Dir. Prof. Dr. J. H. VAN STUYVENBERG; publ. *Economisch- en Sociaal Historisch Jaarboek* (annual).

INTERNATIONAL CULTURAL INSTITUTES

British Council: Keizersgracht 343, Amsterdam C; library (*see* Libraries); Rep. W. E. MOSS, O.B.E.

Goethe Institut Amsterdam: Herengracht 470, Amsterdam; provides concerts, lectures, film shows, language courses, etc.; lending library of 10,000 vols.; Dir. Dr. U. MARTIN.

Institut Français: Maison Descartes, Vijzelgracht 2A, 1017 HR Amsterdam; f. 1933; brs. in The Hague, Rotterdam; library of 32,000 vols.; Asst. Dir. J.-P. DAULNY.

Istituto Italiano di Cultura per i Paesi Bassi: Keizersgracht 564, Amsterdam; Dir. Prof. MARIO SINTICH.

Nederlands-Zuidafrikaanse Vereniging (*Netherlands South African Society*): Van Riebeeckhuis, Keizersgracht 141, 1015 CK Amsterdam; f. 1881; cultural relations between the Netherlands and South Africa; approx. 1,000 mems.; library of 15,000 vols.; Chair. Prof. Dr. F. DE WAARD; Sec. Mrs. M. C. MOUWEN-SWILDENS; publ. *Zuid-Afrika*†.

Stichting "Het Spaans, Portugees en Ibero-Amerikaans Instituut" (*Spanish, Portuguese and Ibero-American Institute Society*): Drift 29-31, Utrecht; f. 1951; Promotion of study of Spanish and Portuguese literature and culture at the University of Utrecht; public library of 43,000 vols.; Dir. G. A. VAN WOERKOM; Sec. Dr. J. O. LUURS.

U.S. Information Service: Lange Voorhout 102, The Hague.

LANGUAGE AND LITERATURE

Maatschappij der Nederlandse Letterkunde (*Society of Netherlands Literature*): c/o Universiteitsbibliotheek, Rapenburg 70-74, Leiden; f. 1766; 950 mems.; Chair. Dr. M. A. SCHENKEVELD-VAN DER DUSSEN; Sec. R. BREUGELMANS; publs. *Tijdschrift voor Nederlandse Taal- en Letterkunde*†, *Jaarboek der Maatschappij* (annual).

Netherlands Centre of the International PEN: Schrijvershuis, Huddestraat 7, 1018 HB Amsterdam; f. 1923; 305 mems.; Pres. GERRIT BORGERS; Sec. DIRK KROON (home affairs), MINEKE SCHIPPER (external affairs); publ. *PEN-Kwartaal* (quarterly).

Nederlandsche Vereniging voor Druk- en Boekkunst (*Netherlands Society for the Art of Printing and Bookproduction*): 2014 AL Haarlem, Bestevaerstr. 10; f. 1938; 300 mems.; Chair. Dr. G. W. OVINK; Sec. F. MAYER; publs. *Mededelingen* (irregular) and books.

MEDICINE

Algemene Nederlandse Vereniging voor Sociale Geneeskunde (*General Netherlands Society for Social Medicine and Public Health*): c/o Institute for Public Health and Social Medicine, P.O.B. 1738, Rotterdam; f. 1930, approx. 2,500 mems.; Sec. GASPARD A. DE JONG; M.P.H.; publ. *Tijdschrift voor Sociale Geneeskunde.*

Genootschap ter bevordering van Natuur- Genees- en Heelkunde (*Assn. for Advancement of Natural, Medical and Surgical Sciences*): Plantage Muidergracht 12, Amsterdam; f. 1790; Pres. Dr. P. J. KLOPPER; Sec. Dr. K. VAN DAM.

Koninklijke Nederlandse Maatschappij ter Bevordering der Pharmacie (*Royal Netherlands Assn. for Advancement of Pharmacy*): The Hague, Alexanderstraat 11; f. 1842; approx. 2,000 mems.; Pres. Dr. J. L. M. NIEUWENHUIS; Sec. M. F. VAN LUNEN; publ. *Pharmaceutisch Weekblad.*

Koninklijke Nederlandsche Maatschappij tot Bevordering der Geneeskunst (*Royal Netherlands Assn. for Advancement of Medicine*): Lomanlaan 103, Utrecht; f. 1849; 18,000 mems.; Pres. Dr. H. W. A. SANDERS; Sec. J. DIEPERSLOOT, M.D.; publ. *Medisch Contact* (weekly).

Nederlands Medisch Nautisch Genootschap (*Netherlands Medical Nautical Society*): f. 1961; 60 mems.; Chair. Dr. F. E. J. BOURICIUS; Hon. Sec. Dr. S. ODERKERK, Amsteldijk 75h, Amsterdam.

Nederlandse Vereniging van Specialisten in de Dento-Maxillaire Orthopaedie: Weezenhof 14-16, Nijmegen; f. 1963; Pres. Prof. Dr. H. S. DUTERLOO; Sec. Dr. TH. P. M. VAN BLADEREN.

Nederlandse Vereniging voor Heelkunde (*Dutch Assn. of Surgeons*): P.O.B. 20061, Lomanlaan 103, 3502 LB Utrecht; f. 1902; 1,200 mems.; Sec.-Gen. Dr. J. BOEVÉ; publ. *Archivum Chirurgicum Neerlandicum*† (quarterly, in English).

Nederlandse Vereniging voor Orthodontische Studie (*Netherlands Orthodontics Society*): 51 Wildernislaan, Apeldoorn; Sec. J. M. BEEK.

Nederlandse Vereniging voor Microbiologie (*Netherlands Society of Microbiology*): p/a R.I.V., Postbus 1, Bilthoven; f. 1911; 930 mems.; Pres. Prof. Dr. J. B. WILTERDINK; Sec. Dr. F. A. J. DE VRIES; publ. *Antonie van Leeuwenhoek Journal of Microbiology and Serology.*

Nederlandse Vereniging voor Neurologie: P.O.B. 20062, 3502 LB, Utrecht; f. 1871, reorganized 1974; 650 mems.; Pres. R. LE COULTRE; Sec. Dr. J. J. JANSEN; publ. *Clinical Neurology and Neurosurgery.*

Nederlandse Vereniging voor Psychiatrie (*Netherlands Assn. for Psychiatry*): P.O.B. 20062, 3502 LB, Utrecht; f. 1871, reorganized 1974; 1,175 mems.; Pres. Prof. Dr. F. H. L. BEYAERT; First Sec. Dr. H. SMITS; Second Sec. J. HOFMAN; publ. *Tijdschrift voor Psychiatrie.*

Nederlandse Vereniging voor Tropische Geneeskunde (*Netherlands Society of Tropical Medicine*): f. 1907; 800 mems.; Chair. Prof. Dr. J. J. LAARMAN; Sec. Dr. A. S. MULLER, Royal Tropical Institute, Mauritskade 63, 1092 AD Amsterdam.

NATURAL SCIENCES

General

Koninklijke Nederlandse Natuurhistorische Vereniging (*Royal Netherlands Natural History Society*): Griend 31, 3331 GE Zwijndrecht; f. 1901; 10,000 mems.; Chair. F. H. FOCKENS; publ. *Natura*† (monthly).

Stichting Natuur en Milieu (*Foundation for Nature and Environment*): Schaep en Burgh, Noordereinde 60, 's-Graveland; Dir. P. NIJHOFF; publs. *Natuur en milieu* (monthly).

Thijmgenootschap (*Christian Association for Scholars in the Netherlands*): Huygensweg 14, Nijmegen; f. 1904; Pres. Prof. Dr. D. A. A. Mossel; Sec. Dr. G. A. M. Beekelaar; publ. *Annalen* (quarterly).

Vereniging tot Behoud van Natuurmonumenten in Nederland (*Society for the Promotion of Nature Reserves in the Netherlands*): Schaep en Burgh, Noordereinde 60, 's-Graveland; f. 1906; 250,000 mems.; the society controls over 135 nature reserves; Pres. J. G. ten Houten; Dirs. F. J. Kroesen, P. van Herwerden, E. P. L. Hessels; publ. *Natuurbehoud* (quarterly).

Biological Sciences

Koninklijke Nederlandse Botanische Vereniging (*Royal Dutch Botanical Society*): Amsterdam; f. 1845; 880 mems.; Pres. Prof. Dr. C. Kalkman; 1st Sec. Dr. Ir. G. W. M. Barendse, Botanisch Laboratorium, Katholieke Universiteit, Toernooiveld, 6525 ED Nijmegen; publs. *Acta Botanica Neerlandica, Flora Neerlandica.*

Nederlandse Dierkundige Vereniging (*Netherlands Zoological Society*): Dept. of Chemical Animal Physiology, Utrecht; f. 1872; 782 mems.; Pres. Prof. Dr. A. M. Th. Beenakkers; Sec. Dr. J. A. M. van den Biggelaar; publs. *Netherlands Journal of Zoology*†, *Netherlands Journal of Sea Research*†.

Nederlandse Entomologische Vereniging (*Netherlands Entomological Society*): Plantage Middenlaan 64, 1018 DH Amsterdam; f. 1845; library of 20,000 vols.; approx. 650 mems.; Pres. R. H. Cobben; Sec. Dr. R. de Jong; publs. *Tijdschrift voor Entomologie*†, *Entomologische Berichten*†, *Entomologia Experimentalis et Applicata*†, *Monographieën*†.

Nederlandse Mycologische Vereniging (*Netherlands Mycological Society*): f. 1908; 400 mems.; study of fungi; Pres. F. Benjaminsen; Sec. Dr. H. A. van der Aa, Eemnesserweg 90, 3741 GC Baarn; publ. *Coolia*† (quarterly).

Nederlandse Ornithologische Unie (*Netherlands Ornithological Union*): J. M. Coenenstraat 31-II, 1071 WE Amsterdam; 1,000 mems.; Pres. Dr. R. H. Drent; publs. *Ardea*† (2 a year) and *Limosa*† (quarterly).

Nederlandse Vereniging voor Parasitologie (*Netherlands Society for Parasitology*): c/o National Institute of Public Health, P.O.B. 1, 3720 BA Bilthoven; f. 1962; 124 mems.; Pres. H. J. van der Kaay; Sec. Dr. F. van Knapen.

Nederlandse Zoötechnische Vereniging (*Netherlands Association for Animal Production*): Kerkstraat 22, 3972 EL Driebergen; f. 1930; 700 mems.; Pres. Prof. Ir. S. Boer Iwema; Sec. Dr. Ir. E. W. Brascamp.

Stichting Koninklijk Zoölogisch Genootschap "Natura Artis Magistra" (*Royal Zoological Society*): Amsterdam, Plantage Kerklaan 40; f. 1838; Dir. Dr. B. M. Lensink; publs. *Bijdragen tot de Dierkunde* (bi-annual), *Artis* (bi-monthly).

Mathematics

Vereniging voor Statistiek (*Netherlands Society for Statistics and Operations Research*): Weena 700, P.O.B. 299, 3000 AG Rotterdam; f. 1945; *c.* 1,200 mems.; Pres. Prof. Dr. J. Th. Runnenburg; Sec. W. M. Kalmijn; publs. *Statistica Neerlandica* (quarterly), *VVS-Bulletin* (monthly).

Wiskundig Genootschap (*Mathematical Society*): Singel 421, 1012 WP Amsterdam; f. 1778; *c.* 1,250 mems.; library of *c.* 16,000 vols. and journals of physics and mathematics; Pres. Prof. Dr. P. C. Baayen; Sec. Dr. H. Bavinck; publ. *Nieuw Archief voor Wiskunde*† (3 a year).

Physical Sciences

Koninklijk Nederlands Meteorologisch Instituut (*Royal Netherlands Meteorological Institute*): Wilhelminalaan 10, P.O.B. 201, 3730 AE De Bilt; f. 1854; meteorology, climatology, oceanography, geophysics (seismology, geomagnetism); Dir.-in-Chief Dr. H. C. Bijvoet; publs. *Jaarboek A. Meteorologie, Jaarboek B. Geomagnetism*, seismic records, upper-air data, marine climatological summaries, *Mededelingen en Verhandelingen*, and many papers on the above-mentioned subjects.

Branch offices for issuing meteorological information to civil aviation are situated at aerodromes: Amsterdam (Schiphol), Rotterdam (Zestienhoven), etc.

Koninklijke Nederlandse Chemische Vereniging (*Royal Netherlands Chemical Society*): The Hague, Burnierstraat 1; f. 1903; 8,400 mems.; Division: Netherlands Organization for Chemical Information; Pres. Prof. Dr. G. Dijkstra; Sec. Dr. D. P. Den Os; publs. *Chemisch Weekblad* (weekly), *Recueil, Journal of the Royal Netherlands Chemical Society* (monthly), *Chemisch Jaarboek* (bi-annually).

Koninklijk Nederlands Geologisch Mijnbouwkundig Genootschap (*Royal Geological and Mining Society of the Netherlands*): The Hague, Postbus 190; f. 1912; 1,400 mems.; Pres. Prof. H. N. A. Priem; Hon. Sec. L. J. Fick; publs. *Geologie en Mijnbouw* (quarterly), *Verhandelingen* (Transactions), *Nieuwsbrief* (10 a year).

Nederlandse Natuurkundige Vereniging (*Netherlands Physical Society*): Fysisch Laboratorium, Princetonplein 5, Utrecht; f. 1921 to improve the study of physics in every way and safeguard the interests of physicists; 2,578 mems.; Chair. Prof. Dr. P. R. Wyder; Sec. Dr. G. van Middelkoop; publ. *Nederlands Tijdschrift voor Natuurkunde* (2 a month).

Nederlandse Vereniging voor Microscopie (*Netherlands Microscopy Society*): Oostplein 43, Rotterdam 16; Sec. F. Noteboom.

Nederlandse Vereniging voor Weer- en Sterrenkunde (*Netherlands Society for Meteorology and Astronomy*): Stichting De Koepel, Nachtegaalstr. 82-bis, 3581 AN Utrecht; f. 1901; *c.* 7,000 mems.; publs. *Zenit* (monthly), *De Sterrengids* (annually).

Philosophy and Psychology

Algemene Nederlandse Vereniging voor Wijsbegeerte (*General Netherlands Philosophical Society*): Lorentzplein 4, 2012 HG Haarlem; f. 1933; 150 mems.; Pres. Prof. Dr. J. Plat; Sec. Drs. F. W. J. den Ottolander; publ. *Algemeen Nederlands Tijdschrift voor Wijsbegeerte.*

Genootschap voor Wetenschappelijke Filosofie: Frederik Hendriklaan 5AII, The Hague; Pres. Drs. M. Jager.

Wijsgerige Vereniging Het Spinozahuis: Pascalstraat 6, Amsterdam; Sec. G. van Suchtelen.

Nederlandse Vereniging voor Logica en Wijsbegeerte der Exacte Wetenschappen: In de Wolken 47, Amstelveen; Sec. Drs. H. C. Doets.

Stichting Internationale School voor Wijsbegeerte: Dodeweg 8, Leusden (U.) bij Amersfoort.

Vereniging voor Calvinistische Wijsbegeerte: Centrale Interfaculteit V.U., De Boelelaan 1105, Amsterdam; Sec. B. Kee.

Vereniging voor Filosofie-Onderwijs: Sec. Drs. C. Schavemaker; César Franckrode 10, Zoetermeer.

Vereniging voor Wijsbegeerte te 's-Gravenhage: Mariastraat 56, The Hague; Sec. Drs. P. P. Leewens.

Vereniging voor Wijsbegeerte des Rechts: Rostocklaan 15, Bussum; Sec. Prof. Dr. H. J. van Eikema Hommes.

Wijsgerige Vereniging "Thomas van Aquino": Dominicuskerk, Spuistraat 12, Amsterdam 1001; Sec. Drs N. Versluis.

Bataafsch Genootschap der Proefondervindelijke Wijsbegeerte (*Experimental Natural Philosophy Society*): Rotterdam, P.O.B. 597; f. 1769; Pres. P. SLIJKHUIS; Sec. H. R. S. TIJSSENS.

Nederlands Psychoanalytisch Genootschap (*Netherlands Psychoanalytical Association*): Maliestraat 1, Utrecht; Sec. Dr. P. J. G. METTROP.

RELIGION, SOCIOLOGY AND ANTHROPOLOGY

Koninklijk Instituut voor Taal-, Land- en Volkenkunde (*Royal Institute of Linguistics and Anthropology*): 2300 RA Leiden, Stationsplein 10, P.O.B. 9507; f. 1851; 1,248 mems.; Pres. Dr. A. J. PIEKAAR; Gen. Sec. Dr. J. NOORDUYN; publs. *Bijdragen* (quarterly), *Verhandelingen, Werken, Bibliotheca Indonesica*†, translation series, bibliographical series.

Stichting Wonen (*Foundation for Information on Man-made Environment*): Amsterdam, Leidsestraat 5; f. 1946; Dir. R. L. BROUWERS; publ. *Wonen TA/BK* (twice a month).

TECHNOLOGY

Koninklijk Instituut van Ingenieurs (*Royal Inst. of Engineers in the Netherlands*): Prinsessegracht 23, 2514 AP The Hague; f. 1847; 15,000 mems.; Pres. Ir. A. G. PENNING; publs. *De Ingenieur* (weekly paper), *Yearbook, Journal A* (quarterly), various reports.

Stichting Economisch Instituut voor de Bouwnijverheid (*Economic Institute for the Building Industry*): Cronenburg 150, 1081 GN Amsterdam; f. 1956; Dir. Drs. A. P. BUUR.

RESEARCH INSTITUTES

(*see* also under Universities)

AGRICULTURE AND VETERINARY SCIENCE

Centrum voor Agrobiologisch Onderzoek (*Centre for Agrobiological Research*): Wageningen, Bornsesteeg 65; f. 1976; Dir. Dr. Ir. P. GAASTRA.

Instituut voor de Veredeling van Tuinbouwgewassen (*Institute for Horticultural Plant Breeding*): 6700 AA Wageningen, P.O.B. 16, Mansholtlaan 15; f. 1943; 123 mems.; library of 12,500 vols.; Dir. Ir. C. DORSMAN; publs. *Yearbook*†, *Mededelingen*† (irregular).

International Institute for Land Reclamation and Improvement (ILRI): Staring Bldg., Marijkeweg 11, P.O.B. 45, 6700 AA Wageningen; f. 1955; collects and disseminates information on land reclamation and improvement and undertakes supplementary research work; 30 mems.; Dir. F. E. SCHULZE; publs. series: *Publications, Bulletins, Bibliographies, Annual Report.*

Koninklijk Instituut voor de Tropen (*Royal Tropical Institute*): Mauritskade 63, 1092 AD Amsterdam; f. 1910; 700 mems.; research, education and training, association with development projects, information; 3 depts.: Agricultural Research, Tropical Hygiene, Social Research; library: *see* Libraries; Tropical Museum: *see* Museums and Art Galleries; Chair. Mr. C. T. C. HEYNING; Pres. Ir. F. DEELEMAN; publs. *Jaarverslag*† (annual report), *Abstracts on Tropical Agriculture*† (monthly), series *Landendocumentatie* (information on tropical countries), *Tropical Man, Tropical and Geographical Medicine.*

Landbouw-Economisch Instituut (*Agricultural Economics Research Institute*): 175 Conradkade, 2517 CL The Hague; f. 1940 to further the knowledge of business and social economics and related problems concerning Dutch agriculture and fisheries in the widest sense; Dir. Prof. Dr. A. MARIS.

Nederlands Agronomisch-Historisch Instituut (*Institute of Agricultural History*): Groningen, Vismarkt 40; f. 1949; to advance the study of and to facilitate scientific research in agricultural history by maintaining an Institute at Groningen University and an international library of 10,000 vols.; Dir. (vacant); publ. *Historia Agriculturae*† (records and bibliographical surveys, every one or two years).

Plantenziektenkundige Dienst (*Plant Protection Service*): Geertjesweg 15, P.O.B. 9102, 6700 HC Wageningen; f. 1899; activities include phytosanitary inspection of plants, issue of plant health certificates and design of laws for disease and pest prevention and control, diagnostics of diseases and pests, testing of pesticides; District Offices; Dir. Dr. N. VAN TIEL; Deputy Dir. Ir. H. J. DE BRUIN; Asst. Dir. K. F. SCHOLTEN; publ. *Verslagen en Mededelingen Plantenziektenkundige Dienst* (Reports and Communications Plant Protection Service, Separate Series).

Proefstation voor de Rundveehouderij (*Research and Advisory Institute for Cattle Husbandry*): Lelystad, Runderweg 6; f. 1970; grassland management, fodder harvesting and conservation, livestock improvement, livestock feed, calf-rearing, milk and beef production, animal health, training advisory officers, etc.; 70 mems.; library of 20,000 vols.; Dir. Ir. L. H. HUISMAN; Deputy Dir. Ir. M. P. DE JONG; publs. *Rapporten*† (10 a year), *Publikaties*† (4 a year), *Jaarverslag*† (annually).

Rijksinstituut voor Natuurbeheer (*Research Institute for Nature Management*): Kemperbergerweg 67, 6816 RM, Arnhem and Kasteel Broekhuizen, 3956 NS Leersum; f. 1969; supplies scientific information for formulation of government policy, and on technical aspects of nature management; Gen. Dir. Prof. Dr. A. J. WIGGERS; Dirs. Dr. Ir. P. GRUYS (Arnhem), Dr. G. J. SAALTINK (Leersum); numerous publs.

Rijksinstituut voor het Rassenonderzoek van Cultuurgewassen (*Government Institute for Research on Varieties of Cultivated Plants*): P.O.B. 32, 6700 AA Wageningen; f. 1942; Dir. Ir. M. J. HIJINK; publ. *Descriptive List of Varieties of Field Crops, Descriptive List of Varieties of Vegetable Crops* (annual).

Rijksinstituut voor Visserijonderzoek (*Netherlands Institute for Fishery Investigations*): P.O.B. 68, 1970 AB IJmuiden; f. 1912; biological, chemical, hydrographical and technical fishery investigations; annexe of the Shellfish Department at Yerseke; Dir. K. H. POSTUMA.

Rijksproefstation voor Zaadcontrole (*Government Seed-Testing Station*): 6709 PD Wageningen, Binnenhave 1; Dir. Ir. M. HEUVER.

Stichting voor Plantenveredeling (SVP) (*Foundation for Agricultural Plant Breeding*): P.O.B. 117, 6700 AC Wageningen; Dir. Dr. Ir. H. LAMBERTS.

ECONOMICS, LAW AND POLITICS

Centraal Bureau voor de Statistiek (*Central Bureau of Statistics*): Prinses Beatrixlaan 428, P.O.B. 959, 2270 AZ Voorburg; (and Kloosterweg 1, P.O.B. 4481, 6401 CZ Heerlen); f. 1899; Dir.-Gen. Prof. Dr. W. BEGEER; publs. *Maandschrift*† (Monthly Bulletin),

Statistical Yearbook of the Netherlands†, *Statistisch zakboek*† (Pocket Yearbook), *Tachtig jaren statistiek in tijdreeksen*† (Statistical Studies, Historical Series of the Netherlands) and others.

Institute of Social Studies: *see* under Colleges.

Nederlands Genootschap voor Internationale Zaken (*Netherlands Institute of International Affairs*): 2 Alexanderstraat, 2514 JL The Hague; f. 1945; 800 mems.; research on international issues; lectures; 2 post-graduate courses of 4 months; library of 8,000 books and 200 periodicals; Sec.-Gen. J. L. HELDRING; publs. *Internationale Spectator* (monthly), *Wereldwijzer* (daily).

Polemological Institute of the University of Groningen: Rijksstraatweg 76, P.O.B. 121, 9750 AC Haren (Gron.); f. 1961; peace research institute for multidisciplinary research on war and conflict, and university teaching; 12 staff, 15 students; library of 9,000 vols., 120 periodicals; Dir. Dr. H. W. TROMP; publs. Studies in peace research (mostly in Dutch), Institute's Papers (in Dutch), *Transaktie* (journal for peace and conflict studies).

INFORMATION AND LIBRARY SCIENCE

Nederlands Orgaan voor de Bevordering van de Informatieverzorging—NOBIN (*Netherlands Organization for Information Policy*): Burg. Van Karnebeeklaan 19, The Hague; f. 1971; co-ordinates and promotes information handling and contributes to a national policy for the organization of scientific and technical information; Sec. A. VAN DER LAAN.

MEDICINE

Nederlands Instituut voor Hersenonderzoek (*Netherlands Institute for Brain Research*): IJdijk 28, P.O.B. 41850, 1009 DB Amsterdam; f. 1909; research into maturation and adaptation of the nervous system; 60 mems.; library of 5,000 vols.; Dir. Prof. D. F. SWAAB; publ. *Yearly Progress Report* with list of publications†.

Nederlands Instituut voor Praeventieve Gezondheidszorg TNO (*Netherlands Institute for Preventive Health Care*): Wassenaarseweg 56, P.O.B. 124, Leiden; f. 1929; scientific research in the fields of occupational medicine, child development, environmental management and health services research; post-graduate courses in public health; library of 10,000 vols.; Dir. Dr. M. J. HARTGERINK; publ. *Annual Report*.

Vereniging Het Nederlands Kankerinstituut (*Netherlands Cancer Institute*): Plesmanlaan 121, 1066 CX Amsterdam; f. 1913; Patron H.R.H. JULIANA, Princess of the Netherlands; Pres. Prof. Dr. E. H. VAN DER BEUGEL; Sec. Mr. J. P. WILLEUMIER; publ. *Annual Report*.

NATURAL SCIENCES

General

Nederlandsche Centrale Organisatie TNO (*Central Organization for Applied Scientific Research in the Netherlands TNO*): P.O.B. 297, 2501 BD The Hague (Juliana van Stolberglaan 148, 2595 CL The Hague); f. 1930 to ensure that applied scientific research is put at the service of the community in the most efficient manner possible; four branch organizations have been established (*see below*); the Central Organization acts as a co-ordinating body and executes work in fields where no specialized organization exists; the Board is appointed by the Crown from nominations submitted, half by the Royal Academy of Sciences and half by the Social and Economic Council; total staff approx. 4,920; library of *c.* 16,000 publs.; Pres. Ir. W. A. DE JONG; Gen. Sec. J. JONKER; Librarian Head Office Mrs. T. J. WAGEMAKERS; publs. *TNO-Project*† (monthly, in Dutch), *Report*† (annually, in Dutch).

The Central Organization TNO groups 21 research institutes, departments and committees, including:

Nationale Raad voor Landbouwkundig Onderzoek TNO (*National Council for Agricultural Research TNO*): P.O.B. 297, 2501 BD The Hague; f. 1957; Pres. Ir. A. DE ZEEUW; Sec. Ir. G. WANSINK; groups 28 research committees and units.

Raad voor Gezondheidsresearch TNO (*Council for Health Research TNO*): P.O.B. 297, 2501 BD The Hague; f. 1970; Pres. Dr. P. SIDERIUS; Sec. Dr. R. J. VAN ZONNEVELD.

The four branch organizations are:

Nijverheidsorganisatie TNO (*Organization for Industrial Research TNO*): P.O.B. 297, 2501 BD The Hague; f. 1934; groups 22 institutes and research departments; Pres. Ir. M. J. SPANRAFT; Sec. H. R. WEGERIF.

Voedingsorganisatie TNO (*Organization for Nutrition and Food Research TNO*): P.O.B. 297, 2501 BD The Hague; f. 1940; Pres. Dr. G. KLEIN; Sec. E. J. MEIS; groups 5 research institutes and 1 research unit.

Rijksverdedigingsorganisatie TNO (*National Defence Research Organization TNO*): P.O.B. 208, 2501 CE The Hague; f. 1946; groups 4 laboratories and 1 research institute; Pres. Prof. Dr. Ir. H. J. DIRKSEN; Sec. J. L. JANSEN.

Gezondheidsorganisatie TNO (*Organization for Health Research TNO*): P.O.B. 297, 2501 BD The Hague; f. 1949; includes 8 research institutes, 7 research units, and 2 committees; Pres. Prof. Dr. Ir. A. RÖRSCH; Sec. Mrs. M. W. H. SLAG.

Nederlandse Organisatie voor Zuiver-Wetenschappelijk Onderzoek (Z.W.O.) (*Netherlands Organization for the Advancement of Pure Research*): 2509 AC The Hague, P.O.B. 93138, Juliana van Stolberglaan 148; f. 1950; advancement of pure scientific research particularly by awarding grants; advancement of applied scientific research in the field of humanities and social sciences; Pres. Prof. Mr. W. F. DE GANY FORTMAN; Dir. Prof. Dr. R. VAN LIESHOUT; publs. *Jaarboek* (Yearbook), *Current research in the Netherlands*.

Stichting voor Wetenschappelijk Onderzoek van de Tropen (WOTRO) (*Netherlands Foundation for the Advancement of Tropical Research*): 2509 AC The Hague, P.O.B. 93138, Juliana van Stolberglaan 148; f. 1964; advancement of tropical research both pure and applied by awarding grants; Pres. Prof. Dr. J. W. SCHOORL; Sec. Prof. Dr. R. VAN LIESHOUT; publ. *Annual Report*.

Biological Sciences

Biologisch Centrum: P.O.B. 14, 9750 AA Haren (Gn.); plant physiology; Dir. Prof. Dr. Ir. P. J. C. KUIPER.

Hortus Botanicus: De Wolf, P.O.B. 14, 9750 AA Haren (Gr.); f. 1642, renewed 1929; 10,000 species; Dir. Dr. B. M. MOELIONO; Botanist Dr. J. VAN BORSSUM WAALKES; Horticulturist O. BARENDSEN.

Hubrecht Laboratory: (*see* under International Section—Science: Society of Developmental Biologists).

Instituut voor Plantenziektenkundig Onderzoek I.P.O. (*Research Institute for Plant Protection*): Wageningen, Binnenhaven 12; f. 1949; 130 mems.; library of 24,000 vols.; Dir. Ir. G. S. ROOSJE; publ. *Mededelingen Instituut voor Plantenziektenkundig Onderzoek*† (irregular).

Rijksherbarium (*National Herbarium*): Leiden, Schelpenkade 6; f. 1829; investigation of the flora (taxonomy, geography), particularly of the Netherlands and tropical Asia; library contains 18,200 vols., over 1,000 periodicals; 24 scientific staff; Dir. Prof. Dr. C. KALK-

MAN; publs. *Blumea*† (general), *Persoonia*† (Mycology), *Gorteria*† (Netherl. flora), *Flora Malesiana* (Phanerog., ferns), *Flora Malesiana Bulletin*†.

Mathematics

Mathematisch Centrum (*Foundation Mathematical Centre*): Kruislaan 413, 1098 SJ Amsterdam; f. 1946; 150 mems.; six sections: (1) Pure Mathematics (Prof. Dr. P. C. BAAYEN); (2) Applied Mathematics/Mathematical Physics (Prof. Dr. H. A. LAUWERIER); (3) Mathematical Statistics (Prof. Dr. J. HEMELRIJK); (4) Computer Science (Prof. Dr. J. W. DE BAKKER); (5) Numerical Mathematics (Prof. Dr. P. J. VAN DER HOUWEN); (6) Operations Research (Prof. Dr. G. DE LEVE); Dir. Prof. Dr. Ir. A. VAN WIJNGAARDEN; publs. *Report* series† (irregular), *M.C. Tracts*†, *M.C. Syllabus*†, *Jaarverslagen*† (annual reports); library (*see* Libraries).

Nederlands Interuniversitair Demografisch Instituut (*Netherlands Interuniversity Demographic Institute*): P.O.B. 955, 2270 AZ Voorburg; f. 1970; research, training, information and documentation in the field of population studies; library of 2,500 vols., 2,500 reprints, 15,000 articles, etc.; Dir. Dr. D. J. VAN DE KAA; publs. *Bevolking en Gezin* (Population and Family, 3 a year), *Demografie* (6 a year), working papers, monographs.

Physical Sciences

Biometeorological Research Centre: Aviemonenweg 9, 2241 XH Wassenaar; f. 1955; to study the influence of weather and climate on man and its clinical applications; Dir. Dr. S. W. TROMP; publs. Monographs and Report Series.

FOM-Instituut voor Atoom- en Molecuulfysica (*FOM Institute of Atomic and Molecular Physics*): Amsterdam/Watergraafsmeer, Kruislaan 407; f. 1953; 150 mems.; facilities include Mass-spectrometers, Spectrographs, Molecular Beam apparatuses, Microwave interferometers, Laser equipment, Beam Plasma Experiments, and a PDP 11 computer; library of 2,200 vols.; Gen. Dir. Prof. Dr. J. KISTEMAKER; Sec. Mrs. LOUISE ROOS; publs. *Annual Report* and Articles, Lectures, etc.

FOM-Instituut voor Plasma-Fysica (*Institute of Plasma-physics*): Rijnhuizen, Rond het Ford 22, Nieuwegein; f. 1959; research in plasmaphysics, plasmacontainment, heating; 120 mems.; library of 7,000 vols., 13,000 reports; Dir. Prof. Dr. C. M. BRAAMS.

FOM—Stichting voor Fundamenteel Onderzoek der Materie (*Foundation for Fundamental Research on Matter*): Van Vollenhovenlaan 659-663, 3527 JP Utrecht; f. 1946; carries out physics research through 75 university teams and in its own 4 laboratories; Man. Dir. Dr. A. A. BOUMANS.

Instituut voor Kernphysisch Onderzoek (*Institute for Nuclear Physics Research*): Oosterringdijk 18, Amsterdam-O;building a 500 MeV linear electron accelerator for high duty cycle and with the necessary auxiliary instrumentation for fundamental nuclear research; Gen. Scientific Dir. Prof. Dr. A. H. WAPSTRA; Man. Dir. Dr. J. SCHUTTEN.

Laboratorium voor Ruimteonderzoek (*Space Research Laboratory of the Astronomical Institute*): Beneluxlaan 21, 3527 HS Utrecht; f. 1961; high energy astrophysics; 100 mems.; Dir. Prof. C. DE JAGER; publ. *Reprints of the Utrecht Astronomical Institute*†.

Nederlands Instituut voor Onderzoek der Zee (*Netherlands Institute for Sea Research*): 't Horntje, Postbus 59, Texel; f. 1876; purely scientific marine research; ships, aquarium; Dirs. Prof. Dr. H. POSTMA, Dr. J. J. ZIJLSTRA; publ. *Netherlands Journal of Sea Research* (quarterly).

Rijks Geologische Dienst (*Geological Survey of the Netherlands*): P.O.B. 157, 2000 AD Haarlem; f. 1903; combines the Bureau, listed below, and district offices; 205 mems.; Dir. Ir. B. P. HAGEMAN; publs. Annual Reports†, Geological Maps† and Memoirs†.

Geologisch Bureau (*Geological Bureau*): P.O.B. 126, 6400 AC Heerlen; f. 1924.

Sterrekundig Instituut te Utrecht (*Astronomical Institute at Utrecht*): Observatory, Sonnenborgh University of Utrecht, Zonnenburg 2, 3512 NL Utrecht; f. 1642; studies in solar physics, stellar atmospheres, plasma-astrophysics, space research, high energy astrophysics; 40 staff mems.; library of 30,000 vols.; Scientific Dirs. Prof. C. DE JAGER, Prof. M. KUPERUS, Prof. C. ZWAAN; publs. reprints (*Utrechtse Sterrekundige Overdrukken*)†.

Stichting voor Bodemkartering (*Soil Survey Institute*): Staringbuilding Wageningen, Marijkeweg 11, P.O.B. 98, 6700 AB Wageningen; f. 1945; soil survey and interpretations, soil and landscape investigations; 143 mems.; library of 25,000 vols., 15,000 reprints; Dir. Ir. R. P. H. P. VAN DER SCHANS; publs. *Soil Survey of the Netherlands* (irregular) and maps.

Sociology

Instituut voor Maatschappij Wetenschappelijk Onderzoek in Ontwikkelingslanden (IMWOO) (*Institute for Social Science Research in Developing Countries*): Badhuisweg 251, P.O.B. 90734, 2509 LS The Hague; f. 1972; promotes and co-ordinates social science research in developing countries; Dir. Drs. J. W. VAN NIEUWENHUIJSEN; publ. *IMWOO-Bulletin* (in Dutch, quarterly).

Stichting Interuniversitair Instituut voor Sociaal-Wetenschappelijk Onderzoek (*Netherlands Universities' Joint Social Research Centre*): P.O.B. 19079, 1000 GB Amsterdam; f. 1960 to foster social science research in the Dutch universities; financed almost entirely by Ministry of Education and Sciences; 33 scientific staff work in 8 divisions: town and country planning and social geography; sociology of housing; labour, organization and occupation; educational research; well-being and the quality of life; public administration; science research; methodology; organizes work-groups for specialists in these areas; library; Chair. Prof. Dr. M. DE SMIDT; Dir. Dr. J. G. M. STERK; publ. *Berichten over Onderzoek*† (Research News, 6 a year).

Technology

Instituut voor Bewaring en Verwerking van Landbouwprodukten (*Institute for Storage and Processing of Agricultural Produce*): 6700 AA Wageningen, Bornsesteeg 59, P.O.B. 18; f. 1956; 85 mems.; Dir. Ir. P. WIERTSEMA.

Instituut voor Mechanisatie, Arbeid en Gebouwen (*Institute of Agricultural Engineering*): Wageningen, Mansholtlaan 10-12; f. 1974; 240 mems.; Dir. Ir. F. COOLMAN; publs. Reports on Research Projects, test bulletins.

Nationaal Lucht- en Ruimtevaartlaboratorium (*National Aerospace Laboratory, N.L.R.*): Anthony Fokkerweg 2, 1059 CM Amsterdam; f. 1919; library of 5,000 vols., 250,000 reports; Chair. of Board Prof. Dr. Ir. O. H. GERLACH; Dir. Ir. J. A. VAN DER BLIEK; publs. technical reports† and miscellaneous†.

Netherlands Energy Research Foundation—ECN: Scheveningseweg 112, The Hague; research centre: 3 Westerduinweg, Petten (N.H.); P.O.B. 1, 1755 ZG Petten (N.H.); f. 1955 as *Reactor Centrum Nederland—RCN*;

name changed 1976, and scope broadened from research in the whole field of energy supply; 840 staff; Chair. Dr. Ir. H. Hoog; Dirs. Dr. R. W. R. Dee, Ir. J. Pelser, Prof. Dr. J. A. Goedkoop; publs. reports†, *Energiespectrum*† (monthly).

Sprenger Instituut (*Institute for Research on Storage and Processing of Horticultural Produce*): Wageningen, Haagsteeg 6, Postbus 17; f. 1936; 20 mems.; library of 3,000 vols.; Dir. Drs. G. J. H. Rijkenbarg; publ. *Annual Report.*

ARCHIVES

Algemeen Rijksarchief te 'sGravenhage (*General State Archives*): Prins Willem Alexanderhof 20, The Hague; f. 1802; 65 kilometres of archives; library of 65,000 vols.; Dir. A. E. M. Ribberink; Archivists H. M. Brokken, G. W. van der Meiden, E. van Laar; Librarian J. J. H. de Vries.

Archief der Gemeente Leeuwarden en Stedelijke Bibliotheek (*Archives of the City of Leeuwarden, Municipal Library and Art Collection*): Groote Kerkstraat 29, 8911 DZ Leeuwarden; f. 1838; works (incl. MSS. and incunabula) about Leeuwarden and the Province of Friesland; art collection, mainly historical; library of *c.* 15,000 vols.; Archivist and Librarian R. Kunst; publs. *Catalogue, The Hague 1932, Verslag over het Archief, de boekerij en de Kunstverzameling.*

Gemeente-Archief (*Municipal Record Office*): Alkmaar, Oude Gracht 247; municipal archives, books about Alkmaar and North Holland, etc.; also regional archives for the area; pictures, prints, maps, relating to Alkmaar and surroundings; number of vols. 30,000; Municipal Archivist W. A. Fasel; publs. *Annual Report, Inventories of Archives.*

Gemeente-Archief (*Record Office*): 7411 NH Deventer, 3 Klooster; f. 1853; municipal archives 1241–1930, judicial archives 1423–1811, archives of chapter 1123–1791, church registers 1542–1811, notarial archives 1811–95; Archivist Drs. B. Woelderink.

Gemeente-Archief (*Record Office*): 3311 XS Dordrecht, Stek 13; f. 1885; archives of the City of Dordrecht; books and prints of Dordrecht and its environs; number of vols. 35,000; Archivist Dr. Th. W. Jensma; publ. *Kwartaal en Teken van Dordrecht*† (quarterly).

Gemeente-Archief (*Record Office*): Kampen; archives of the town 1251–1945; Archivist Drs. D. van der Vlis; publ. *De Archieven der gemeente Kampen, I, II* and *III.*

Gemeentelijke Archiefdienst (*Municipal Record Office*): Rotterdam, Mathenesserlaan 315; f. 1857; city archives, church records, notarial archives, Chamber of Commerce records, family archives, topographical collection, sound archives, historical library; Archivist R. A. D. Renting; publs. *Annual Report*†, *Rotterdams Jaarboekje.*

Gemeentelijke Archiefdienst Maastricht (*Municipal Record Office of Maastricht*): Grote Looiersstraat 17; f. 1849; municipal and family archives, church records, MSS., topographical collections relating to Maastricht and the Province of Limburg; Archivist Drs. A. H. Jenniskens.

Rijksarchief in Drenthe te Assen (*State Archives of Drenthe*): Brink 4, 9401 HS Assen; f. 1879; public records of the Province of Drenthe; archives of private persons, institutions and enterprises; library of 7,500 vols.; Dir. Dr. F. Keverling Buisman (acting).

Rijksarchief in Friesland te Leeuwarden (*State Archives of Friesland*): Leeuwarden, Boterhoek 3; Dir. J. Rinzema.

Rijksarchief in Gelderland: Arnhem, Markt 1; f. 1878; contains the archives of the Dukes of Guelders and of other authorities in that area; Archivist G. J. Mentink; publs. *Jaarverslag van de Rijksarchiefdienst, Publicaties* (Publications), *Inventarissen* (Inventories of Archives).

Rijksarchief in Groningen (*State Archives of Groningen*): 9712 JN Groningen, St. Jansstraat 2; f. 1824; Archivist J. H. de Vey Mestdagh, ll.d.

Rijksarchief in Limburg te Maastricht (*State Archives of Limburg*): Maastricht, St. Pieterstraat 7; Archivist Drs. J. H. M. Wieland; publs. *Jaarverslag van de Rijksarchiefdienst, G. W. A. Panhuysen, Overzicht van de inhoud van het Rijksarchief in Limburg te Maastricht.*

Rijksarchief in Noord-Holland te Haarlem (*State Archives of North Holland*): Haarlem, Ceciliasteeg 12; Dir. Drs. F. J. M. Otten.

Rijksarchief in Overijssel (*State Archives of Overijssel*): Zwolle, Eikenstraat 20; f. 1838; provincial archives 1528–1948, judicial archives 1333–1877, notarial archives 1811–95, old church registers and civil registers 1592–1902, archives of monasteries 1225–1811, etc.; historical library of 17,000 vols.; length of archives 7,000 yds., number of vols. 50,000; Archivist E. D. Eijken.

Rijksarchief in de Provincie Noord-Brabant (*State Archives of North Brabant*): 'sHertogenbosch, Waterstraat 20; f. 1860; records from 13th–20th centuries; approx. 102,500 vols. in Record Office, 21,530 vols. in library, 6,000 charters; Archivist Dr. L. P. L. Pirenne; publ. *Jaarverslag* (annual report), *Inventarisreeks.*

Rijksarchief in de Provincie Utrecht (*State Archives of Utrecht*): Utrecht, Alexander Numankade 201; f. 1843; records of the Province of Utrecht; Archivist Dr. C. Dekker; publ. *Verslagen omtrent 'sRijks Oude Archieven.*

Rijksarchief in Zeeland (*Zeeland State Archives*): Middelburg, St. Pieterstraat 38; f. 1843; Archivist Drs. R. L. Koops.

Rijksinstituut voor Oorlogsdocumentatie (*Netherlands State Institute for War Documentation*): Amsterdam, Herengracht 474; f. 1945; extensive collections on the history of World War II; Dir. Drs. A. H. Paape.

LIBRARIES

Amersfoort

Bibliotheek van het Oud Katholiek Seminarie (*Library of the Old Catholic Seminary*): Koningin Wilhelminalaan 3; f. 1725; 20,000 vols.; Rector E. Wijker.

Openbare Leeszaal en Bibliotheek (*Public Library*): Muurhuizen 9; f. 1913; Librarian H. Brouwer; *c.* 30,000 vols.

Amsterdam

Administratieve Bibliotheek (*Administrative Library*): Stadhuis Amsterdam, kamer 121, O.Z. Voorburgwal 199; f. 1892; 25,000 vols. on law and administration; Librarian E. G. Roos.

Bibliotheek der Koninklijke Nederlandse Akademie van Wetenschappen (*Library of Royal Netherlands Academy* *of Arts and Sciences*): Kloveniersburgwal 29; f. 1808; 450,000 vols., 17,000 periodicals, mostly on natural sciences, particularly biology, chemistry, physics, pharmacy and medicine; clearing house for INIS International Nuclear Information System) and *Excerpta Medica*; SDI and retrospective information services available; Dir. Drs. J. A. W. BRAK.

Bibliotheek der Rijksakademie van Beeldende Kunsten (*Library of State Academy of Fine Arts*): Stadhouderskade 60, Amsterdam-Z; 20,000 vols.

Bibliotheek der Vrije Universiteit (*Library of the Free Reformed University*): De Boelelaan 1105, P.O.B. 7161; f. 1880; 510,000 vols. on sciences, humanities and reformed theology; Librarian Dr. Ir. J. STELLINGWERFF.

Bibliotheek Katholieke Theologische Hogeschool (*Catholic Theological and Philosophical Library*): Keizersgracht 105; f. 1967; 50,000 vols.; Librarian Drs. J. TH. WIJNHOVEN.

Bibliotheek Mathematisch Centrum (*Mathematical Centre Library*): Kruislaan 413, 1098 SJ Amsterdam; f. 1946; special scientific library on non-elementary mathematics and its applications and computer sciences; 25,500 vols., 893 current periodicals, 25,000 microfiches; Chief Librarian Dr. A. B. A. SCHIPPERS; publs. *Aanwinstenlijst* (list of acquisitions), *Indagationes Mathematicae*† (quarterly), Report Series†.

British Council Library: Keizergracht 343; f. 1946; 8,550 vols., 87 periodicals; Librarian Mrs. ANIA LENZ.

Centrale Bibliotheek van het Koninklijk Instituut voor de Tropen (*Central Library of the Royal Tropical Institute*): Mauritskade 63; f. 1910; 95,000 vols., 10,000 periodicals, 20,000 maps; Librarian Drs. A. VAN DER WAL; publ. *Aanwinstenlijst* (List of acquisitions) (monthly).

Nederlands Documentatiecentrum voor Ontwikkelingslanden (*Netherlands Documentation Centre for Developing Countries*): f. 1974 to make accessible Dutch books, reports, articles, etc. on social and economic development in the Third World; publ. *Nedo-Abstracts* (quarterly).

Economisch-Historische Bibliotheek Amsterdam: Herengracht 218–220; f. 1932; a dept. of Netherlands Economic-Historical Archives Society; special collection of 16–18th century books on commerce and book-keeping; approx. 70,000 vols.; Librarian C. GRAVESTEYN.

Netherlands – America Institute Library: Prinsengracht 919, Amsterdam-C; 8,000 vols.; Librarian YVONNE BAKKER; publ. *Accessions lists*†, *Bibliographies*†.

Universiteitsbibliotheek van Amsterdam (*University Library*): Singel 421-425; f. 1578; 2,100,000 vols., 45,000 maps, *c.* 5,000 MSS, 40,000 letters; includes Bibliotheca Rosenthaliana (f. 1880, *c.* 100,000 vols., *c.* 600 MSS), Réveil-Archives, Albert Verwey Archives, Provo Archives and underground collections; Tetterode Library; Vondel Museum; Frederik van Eeden Museum and Dortmond Museum of Scripts and Handwriting; libraries of Dutch Booksellers Asscn., Royal Geographical Soc., Royal Netherlands Soc. of Medicine, etc.; Chief Librarian Dr. E. BRACHES; publs. lists of new acquisitions (monthly), special catalogues series.

Arnhem

Stichting Arnhemse Openbare en Gelderse Wetenschappelijke Bibliotheek (*Arnhem Public and Learned Library*): Koningstraat 26, 6811 DG, P.O.B. 1168, 6801 ML; f. 1856; 400,000 vols., 130 MSS.; Librarian Drs. A. GROENEWEG.

De Bilt

Bibliotheek van het Koninklijk Nederlands Meteorologisch Instituut (*Library of the Royal Netherlands Meteorological Institute*): Wilhelminalaan 10, 3732 GK; f. 1854; vols. on meteorology, climatology, oceanography and geophysics.

Delft

Bibliotheek der Technische Hogeschool (*Library of the Delft University of Technology*): Doelenstraat 101, 2611 NS; f. 1842; 595,000 vols., 8,600 current periodicals; Dir. Dr. J. ZANDVLIET.

Bibliotheek Gemeentelijke Archiefdienst (*Library of Archives*): Oude Delft 169; 30,000 vols. mainly on history, genealogy and heraldry; special collections: Naundorff, House of Orange; Librarian J. G. P. C. VAN TIGGELEN.

Deventer

Stads- of Athenaeumbibliotheek (*Municipal Library*): P.O.B. 351, Klooster 12; f. 1560; 150,000 vols., 550 MSS., 300 incunabula, 400 post-incunabula; Librarian Dr. A. C. F. KOCH.

Echt

Bibliotheca Tilboschensis (*Tilbosch Library*): f. 1885; 20,000 vols.; Librarian P. U. STRIJBOSCH.

Eindhoven

Bibliotheek der Technische Hogeschool (*Library of the University of Technology*): P.O.B. 513; f. 1956; 280,000 vols., 3,600 current periodicals; Dir. Drs. P. J. C. A. PINXTER.

Gemeenschappelijke Openbare Bibliotheek (*Common Public Library*): Eindhoven, Begijnenhof 7-9; f. 1916; 680,000 vols.; Librarian M. VERKUIJL.

Enschede

Bibliotheek der Technische Hogeschool Twente: P.O.B. 217, 7500 AE Enschede; 120,000 vols., 2,500 periodicals; Dir. G. A. HAMEL.

Groningen

Bibliotheek der Rijksuniversiteit te Groningen (*Library of the State University*): Oude Kijk in't Jatstraat 5; f. 1615; 1,000,000 vols., 1,000 MSS., 210 incunabula; Librarian W. R. H. KOOPS.

Haarlem

Bibliotheek van Teyler's Stichting (*Teyler Endowment Library*): Damstraat 21; f. 1778; 100,000 vols.; Librarian J. G. DE BRUYN; publs. *Verhandelingen Teylers Godgeleerd Genootschap*†, *Verhandelingen Teylers Tweede Genootschap*†, *Haarlemse Voordrachten*†, *Netherlands Journal of Zoology*†, *Grondboor en Hamer*†.

Stadsbibliotheek en Leeszaal (*Municipal and Public Library*): Doelenplein 1; f. 1596; 470,000 vols., 150 MSS., 174 incunabula; Dir. C. VAN DYK.

The Hague

Bibliotheek- en Documentatiecentrum van de Economische Voorlichtingsdienst (*Library and Documentation Centre of the Economic Information Service*): Bezuidenhoutseweg 151; f. 1936; under Ministry of Economic Affairs; 90,000 vols., 2,000 current periodicals, 1,800 directories (mainly trade); centre of economic documentation and information; Head Drs. J. L. E. M. SCHULTZ; publs. abstract journals, e.g. *Key to Economic Science*, *Economic Titles/Abstracts* (2 a month, tapes available); information bulletins on small business and various branches of industry (6 a year).

Bibliotheek en Documentatiedienst van de Tweede Kamer der Staten-Generaal (*Library and Documentation Service of the Second Chamber of the States-General*): Binnenhof 1A; f. 1815; Librarian Miss A. G. KUNST; 114,000 vols.

Bibliotheek van het Centraal Bureau voor de Statistiek (*Library of the Netherlands Central Bureau of Statistics*): Prinses Beatrixlaan 428, P.O.B. 959, 2270 AZ Voorburg; f. 1899; 163,000 vols.; Librarian B. M. VAN DER HARST.

Bibliotheek van het Vredespaleis (*Library of the Peace Palace*): f. 1913; international and foreign law, diplomatic history, international relations; Grotius Collection; 450,000 vols.; Dir. and Chief Librarian Drs. J. B. VAN HALL; publs. catalogue 1916–1952, selective bibliographies†.

Koninklijke Bibliotheek (*Royal Library*): Lange Voorhout 34, P.O.B. 30469, 2500 GL The Hague; f. 1798; National Library, central to the organization of Dutch libraries; depository for Dutch publications; Union Catalogue of Books in over 80 libraries and of Periodicals in about 250 libraries; 1,500,000 vols., 7,000 MSS., humanities, including social sciences; special collections: 2,000 incunabula, 4,000 post-incunabula, 300 illuminated Western MSS., pamphlets, newspapers, Dutch song books, collections on Spinoza, Joan of Arc, Dante, falconry, modern French belles-lettres, chess (Bibliotheca Van der Linde-Niemeijeriana); Librarian Dr. C. REEDIJK; publs. *Jaarverslag, Bibliografie van in Nederland verschenen officiele uitgaven bij Rijksoverheid en provinciale besturen, Bibliografie van in Nederland verschenen kaarten, Centrale Catalogus van Periodieken en Seriewerken in Nederlandse Bibliotheken*, etc.

Openbare Bibliotheek (*Public Library*): Bilderdijkstraat 1-3; f. 1906; 1,005,000 vols., 321,300 children's books, music library of 45,500 vols. and 44,700 records; 17 branch libraries, 2 mobile libraries; Dir. Dr. P. J. VAN SWIGCHEM.

's-Hertogenbosch

Bibliotheek van het Provinciaal Genootschap van Kunsten en Wetenschappen in Noord-Brabant (*Library of North Brabant Provincial Association for Art and Science*): St. Josephstraat 1, P.O.B. 1388; f. 1837; 75,000 vols.; *c.* 15,000 topographical, historical and folkloristic engravings and drawings, etc.; specialization: Brabantica; Librarian Drs. G. G. A. M. KEUKENS.

Openbare Bibliotheek 's-Hertogenbosch: Hinthamerstraat 72; f. 1915; 128,000 vols.; Librarian Mrs. P. F. M. SORMANI.

Hilversum

Openbare Bibliotheek (*Public Library*): 's-Gravelandseweg 55; f. 1909; 90,000 vols.; Librarian B. WINEKE.

Leeuwarden

Buma Bibliotheek (*Buma Library*): Boterhoek 1; f. 1876; books on Greek and Roman antiquities; 45,000 vols.: Librarian Dr. S. DOUMA.

Provinciale Bibliotheek van Friesland (*Frisian Provincial Library*): P.O.B. 464, Boterhoek 1; f. 1852; 350,000 vols.; Librarian Drs. J. J. M. VAN GENT.

Leiden

Bibliotheek der Rijksuniversiteit Leiden (*Library of the State University*): Rapenburg 70-74, P.O.B. 9501; f. 1575; 2,200,000 vols., 19,000 MSS., 40,000 maps; Librarian J. R. DE GROOT.

Bibliotheek van de Maatschappij der Nederlandse Letterkunde (*Library of the Society of Netherlands Literature*): Rapenburg 70-74, P.O.B. 58; f. 1766; 107,000 vols., 2.100 MSS.; Librarian J. R. DE GROOT.

Maastricht

Stadsbibliotheek Maastricht (*Municipal Library*): Nieuwenhofstraat 1; f. 1662; 300,000 vols., including 90 incunabula, 225 post-incunabula, special collections and documentation relating to the Province of Limburg; Librarian A. H. SCHE-YVEN; publ. *Publicaties*.

Middelburg

Provinciale Bibliotheek van Zeeland (*Zeeland Provincial Library*): Abdijplein 9 (Abdijgebouwen); f. 1859; 300,000 vols., 3,000 MSS.; Librarian W. D. DE BRUINE (*see* also Technische Bibliotheek Zeeland below).

Documentatiecentrum Zeeuws Deltagebied (*Documentation Centre of Zeeland Delta territory*): Abdijplein 9 (Abdijgebouwen); f. 1961; cuttings, slides, photographs, films, tape- and video-recordings; Dir. M. P. DE BRUIN.

Nijmegen

Bibliotheek Katholieke Universiteit (*Library of the Catholic University*): Erasmuslaan 36; f. 1923; 600,000 vols.; Librarian G. G. A. M. PIJNENBORG.

Rotterdam

Bibliotheek en Leeszalen der Gemeente (*Municipal Library*): Nieuwe Markt 1; f. 1604; 1,095,000 vols., 200 MSS., Erasmus collection 2,400 vols.; Chief Librarian P. J. TH. SCHOOTS.

Rotterdamsch Leeskabinet (*Rotterdam Library*): Burg. Oudlaan 50 (P.O.B. 1738, 3000 DR Rotterdam); f. 1859; philosophy, theology, social sciences, literature, history, art; 170,000 vols.; Librarian Drs. J. W. DE JONG; publs. *Kwartaalbericht, Jaarverslag*.

Universiteitsbibliotheek Erasmus Universiteit Rotterdam (*Library of the Erasmus University of Rotterdam*): Burgemeester Oudlaan 50; f. 1913; 300,000 vols.; Librarian Drs. P. W. VAN MILAAN.

Tilburg

Bibliotheek der Hogeschool te Tilburg (*Library of Tilburg University*): Hogeschoollaan 225; f. 1927; 250,000 vols.; Librarian Dr. J. WIEERS.

Bibliotheek der Katholieke Leergangen: Tivolistraat 3; f. 1912; 60,000 vols.; Dutch, German, French and English grammar and literature, education, history, theology; Librarian A.-M. CLAASEN-BERGER.

Centrale Bibliotheek Fraters: Gasthuisring 54; f. 1845; scientific and educational; 145,000 vols.; Librarian H. G. SIEBELT.

Utrecht

Bibliotheek der Rijksuniversiteit (*Library of the State University*): Wittevrouwenstraat 9-11; f. 1581; 1,700,000 vols., 2,500 MSS.; Librarian Drs. J. VAN HEIJST.

Stichting Utrechtse Openbare Bibliotheken (*Public Libraries*): Oudegracht 167; f. 1892; 670,000 vols., 10 brs., music library; Chief Librarian W. VAN HALL.

Vlissingen

Technische Bibliotheek Zeeland: Edisonweg 4, 4382 NW Vlissingen; f. 1968; 32,000 vols., 700 periodicals on science and technology; maritime collection; Librarian Ing. J. T. H. C. SCHEPMAN.

Wageningen

Bibliotheek der Landbouwhogeschool (*Library of the Agricultural University*): Gen. Foulkesweg 1a, P.O.B. 9100, 6700 HA Wageningen; f. 1873; 760,000 vols., 15,000 current periodicals; Librarian Drs. G. G. VAN WIJK; publs. *Mededelingen Landbouwhogeschool*†, miscellaneous papers†, Theses†.

MUSEUMS AND ART GALLERIES

Alkmaar

Stedelijk Museum te Alkmaar: Nieuwe Doelen, Doelenstraat; f. *c.* 1550; municipal museum; antiquarian and art collection from Alkmaar and its environs, paintings by van Heemskerck, van de Velde the Elder, Allart and Caesar B. van Everdingen, Honthorst, Saenredam; objects include old silver, glass, pottery, porcelain, tiles and modern art; collection of antique toys and dolls; Dir. Mr. K. J. Kriek.

Amsterdam

Amstelkring Museum: Oudezijds Voorburgwal 40; f. 1887; merchant's house of 1661 with a clandestine church in the attic; exhibits of 17th–18th-century ecclesiastical art; baroque concerts; Pres. A. B. van Dun.

Amsterdams Historisch Museum (*Amsterdam Historical Museum*): Kalverstraat 92 (postal address: Nieuwezijds Voorburgwal 359, 1012 RM Amsterdam); f. 1926, reorganized and moved into former Civic Orphanage in 1975, the 700th anniversary of the founding of Amsterdam; exhibits of the city's history over 700 years including archaeological finds, artefacts, paintings and models; Dir. B. Haak.

Rembrandt-Huis Museum: Jodenbreestr. 4; f. 1907; Rembrandt etchings and drawings; the artist lived here 1639–60; Curator Eva Ornstein; publs. Catalogues, *Bulletin*† (2 a year).

Rijksmuseum (*State Museum*): Stadhouderskade 42; f. 1808; painting, sculpture, drawings, history, porcelain, glass, costumes, silver, furniture, Asiatic art; library of 50,000 vols.; Dir.-Gen. Dr. S. H. Levie; Curators: Paintings, Dr. P. J. J. van Thiel; Sculpture and Applied Art, A. L. den Blaauwen; National Historical Collection, W. H. Vroom; Print Room, Dr. J. W. Niemeijer; Asiatic Art, K. W. Lim; Librarian Mrs. E. v. d. Vossen; Educational Dept. G. J. van der Hoek; publs. *Bulletin* (quarterly), annual reports, pocket guides and catalogues.

Rijksmuseum "Nederlands Scheepvaart Museum" (*Netherlands Maritime Museum*): Kattenburgerplein 1, 1018 KK Amsterdam; f. 1916; paintings, models, charts, globes, technical drawings, navigational instruments, arms and relics; library of 53,000 vols.; Dir. H. Hazelhoff Roelfzema; Curator Drs. C. F. L. Paul.

Rijksmuseum Vincent van Gogh (*Vincent van Gogh National Museum*): Paulus Potterstraat 7, 1071 CX; P.O.B. 5366, 1007 AJ; f. 1973 to house collections of the Vincent van Gogh Foundation; 200 paintings and 100 drawings by his contemporaries; his correspondence (*c.* 600 letters), his own collections, including English and French prints and Japanese wood-cuts; documentary material, library on Van Gogh, reading room, lecture hall; Gen. Dir. Dr. S. H. Levie; Dir. J. van der Wolk.

Stedelijk Museum: Paulus Potterstraat 13; f. 1895; modern paintings and sculpture, especially American and European trends since 1950; graphics and drawings; applied art and industrial design; temporary exhibitions on contemporary art; library of 15,000 vols., 70,000 catalogues; Dir. E. L. L. de Wilde; publs. *Museumjournaal* (English summaries, bi-monthly), Catalogues†.

Tropenmuseum (*Museum of the Royal Tropical Institute*): Linnaeusstraat 2; f. 1910; presents a picture of life and work in the tropics and sub-tropics; children's museum; library of 15,000 vols.; publs. *Yearbook*, occasional papers.

Apeldoorn

Oranje-Nassau Museum: c/o Rijksmuseum Paleis Het Loo; collection of pictures, prints, coins, etc., relating to the Netherlands royal family, the House of Orange-Nassau; Dir. Dr. A. W. Vliegenthart.

Arnhem

Gemeentemuseum Arnhem: Utrechtseweg 87; f. 1856; archaeology, history, and history of art of Arnhem and Gelderland, art of the lower Rhine area, Dutch painting, Delftware, Arnhem Delft, china, glass and old silver, topographic collection of Gelderland, temporary exhibitions of art; Dir. P. L. A. Janssen.

Rijksmuseum voor Volkskunde "Het Nederlands Openluchtmuseum" (*The Netherlands Open Air Museum*): Schelmseweg 89; f. 1912; history of daily life; information retrieval; library of 31,000 vols.; Dir. J. H. Jager Gerlings; publs. *Annual Report*†, *Biblioskoop*† (information bulletin), *Bijdragen en Mededelingen*†, monographs, buildings and handicrafts series, and guide books.

Delft

Rijksmuseum "Huis Lambert van Meerten" te Delft: Oude Delft 199; f. 1909; Dutch tiles, old furniture, paintings, Delftware; Dir. R. A. Leeuw.

Stedelijk Museum "Het Prinsenhof": St. Agathaplein 1; contains historical collection, paintings of the Delft School, tapestries, silver, Delft pottery; Dir. R. A. Leeuw.

Art Gallery "De Volle Maan": Oude Delft 185; modern art exhibitions; Dir. R. A. Leeuw.

Deventer

Gemeentemusea van Deventer (*Municipal Museums of Deventer*): Brink 56, Deventer; f. 1915; Dir. O. Verhagen.

Museum de Waag: local history.

Museum de Drie Haringen: history of toys.

Museum voor Mechanisch Speelgoed: mechanical toys, trains.

Eindhoven

Municipal van Abbemuseum in Eindhoven: Bilderdijklaan 10; f. 1936; large collection of modern and contemporary art including Lissitzky collection; library of 35,000 vols.; Dir. R. H. Fuchs; Curators J. Bremer, Miss M. Suren, J. Debbaut; publs. exhibition catalogues† (20 a year).

Enschede

Rijksmuseum Twenthe te Enschede: Lasondersingel 129; f. 1930; prehistorical finds of eastern Netherlands, local history and paintings, collection of art from Middle Ages to *c.* 1930; library of 24,000 vols.; Dir. Drs. A. L. Hulshoff.

Gouda

Stedelijk Museum "de Moriaan" (*"The Blackamoor" Municipal Museum*): 29 Westhaven; Dutch Merchants' house containing old tobacco shop; collection of Dutch pipes, pottery, Gouda tiles and pictures; Dir. Drs. J. E. de Bruyn Kops.

Stedelijk Museum "Het Catharina Gasthuis" (*St. Catherine Hospital, Municipal Museum*): 10 Oosthaven; 17th-century town dispensary; antique toys, surgeons' Guild Room, period-rooms of 17th, 18th and 19th centuries, Gasthuis kitchen, important collection of 15th- to 20th-century art; Dir. Drs. J. E. de Bruyn Kops.

Groningen

Groninger Museum voor Stad en Lande: Praediniussingel 59; f. 1890; prehistory and history; paintings of local school; Dutch and Flemish of 16th and 17th centuries: Fabritius, Jordaens, Rubens, Sweerts, Teniers; drawings: Rembrandt, Averkamp, Van Goyen, Cuyp,

Lievens; 19th- and 20th-century painting; extensive collection of Far-Eastern ceramics; collection of applied art; Dir. F. HAKS.

Haarlem

Frans Halsmuseum: Groot Heiligland 62; f. 1862; pictures by Frans Hals and Haarlem school, antique furniture, collection of modern art; Dir. D. H. COUVÉE.

Teylers Museum: Damstraat 21; f. 1778; pictures, drawings, palaeontology, geology, mineralogy, natural history, physics, numismatics; library of 100,000 vols.; Curators J. H. VAN BORSSUM BUISMAN (art collection), Prof. Dr. J. KISTEMAKER (physics), Dr. J. H. C. WALENKAMP (palaeontology and mineralogy), Prof. Dr. H. E. VAN GELDER (numismatics), J. G. DE BRUIJN (library); publs. *Verhandelingen van Teyler's Godgeleerd Genootschap*†, *Verhandelingen van Teyler's 2e Genootschap*†.

The Hague

Gemeentemuseum: Stadhouderslaan 41; f. 1862; collections: modern arts from 1800 onwards (paintings including Mondriaan collection, sculptures, watercolours, prints, decorative art from 1890 onward); ancient decorative art (Near and Far East, Europe from early Greek to 1800); ceramics, glass, metal, furniture, textiles, period-rooms, musical instruments and music library; history of The Hague; Dir. Drs. T. VAN VELZEN.

Koninklijk Kabinet van Schilderijen (Mauritshuis) (*Royal Picture Gallery*): Korte Vijverberg 8; opened to public as museum 1820; 15th, 16th and 17th century Dutch masters (Rembrandt, Vermeer, Hals, Rubens, Van Dyck, Holbein, R. v.d. Weyden, G. David, Matsys, etc.); Dir. H. R. HOETINK; publs. catalogues, illustrated guide books, etc. and Annual Report.

Koninklijk Penningkabinet (Koninklijk Kabinet van Munten, Penningen en Gesneden Stenen) (*Royal Coin Cabinet*): Zeestraat 71b; f. 1816; coins and medals from Greek and Roman times to the present day, engraved gems; library of 10,000 vols. on numismatics and glyptics; Dir. Drs. H. W. JACOBI; Curators Drs. G. VAN DER MEER, Drs. J. P. A. VAN DER VIN; publs. *Jaarboek voor Munt- en Penningkunde*†, *De Beeldenaar*† (every 2 months).

Museum Bredius: Prinsegracht 6, 2512 GA The Hague; f. 1923; 17th-century Dutch art including paintings and drawings by Rembrandt, van Ruysdael, Jan Steen, Adriaen van Ostade; Dir. Drs. T. VAN VELZEN.

Nederlands Kostuummuseum (*Netherlands Costume Museum*): Lange Vijverberg 14/15, 2513 AC The Hague; European fashion from *c.* 1750 to the present day; Dir. Drs. T. VAN VELZEN; Curator Miss M. C. DE JONG.

Nederlands Postmuseum (*Netherlands Postal Museum*): 82 Zeestraat; f. 1929; objects and documents, etc., concerning the history and working of the services of posts, telegraphs and telephones in the Netherlands; international stamp gallery; library of 14,000 vols.; Dir. Drs. H. J. RONDAY; publs. annual reports, illustrated guide.

Rijksmuseum Hendrik Willem Mesdag te 'sGravenhage: Laan van Meerdervoort 7F; f. 1903; Dutch pictures 1860-1900; French pictures of the Barbizon school; Oriental objects; Dir. H. R. HOETINK; Administrator F. J. M. JEHEE; publs. *Annual Report, Museum Mesdag Nederlandse 19e eeuwse Schilderijen.*

Rijksmuseum Meermanno-Westreenianum en Museum van het Boek: Prinsessegracht 30, 2514 AP The Hague; Egyptian, Greek and Roman antiquities, medieval manuscripts, incunabula; modern typography, book plates; Dir. Dr. C. REEDIJK; Keeper Drs. R. E. O. EKKART.

Heerlen

Thermae Museum Heerlen: Coriovallumstraat 9; f. 1977; collection includes Roman bath excavated in 1940-41 and other objects from Roman period; Dir. Drs. J. T. J. JAMAR; publ. *Het Land van Herle.*

Den Helder

Helders Marinemuseum: Havenplein 3; f. 1962; history of the Royal Netherlands Navy from 1813 to the present day, collections of models, paintings and photographs; small specialized library; Curator Cdr. W. M. G. H. CANISIUS.

'sHertogenbosch

Noordbrabants Museum: Bethaniestr. 4; f. 1837; North Brabant prehistorical, historical and folklore collections, paintings, prints, coins, etc.; Dir. Drs. M. M. A. VAN BOVEN.

Hoorn

Westfries Museum: "Huis Verloren", Kerkstraat 10; the baroque building dates from 1632, museum f. 1879; 17th- and 18th-century painting, prints, oak panelling, glass, pottery, silver, furniture, costumes, interiors, objects of trade, navigation and business, folk art, historical objects from Hoorn and West Friesland, West Friesland naive painting, prehistoric finds; Dir. W. A. BRAASEM; publs. annual reports.

Leerdam

Stichting Nationaal Glasmuseum (*National Glass Museum*): Lingedijk 28; f. 1953; art glass, industrial glass and bottles, contemporary Dutch collection and works from other European countries and America; small library; Supervisor F. MEYDAM.

Leeuwarden

Fries Museum: Turfmarkt 24; f. 1827; painting, local history, archaeology, decorative arts; Dir. C. BOSCHMA; publs. *Fries Zilver* (catalogue), *Visitor's Guide* (English and German), exhibition catalogues.

Franeker (Fr.) Fries munt- en penningkabinet: f. 1972; coin collections; publ. *Gids.*

Kerkmuseum Janum: f. 1947; medieval art; publ. *Gids.*

Veenklooster (Fr.) Fogelsangh State Museum: f. 1963; country-house museum; publ. *Gids.*

Gemeentelijk Museum het Princessehof: Grote Kerkstraat 9-15; f. 1917, reopened after enlargement 1973; now a general ceramics study centre, specializing in Chinese, Japanese and Vietnamese pottery and porcelain, wall and floor tiles (from Europe and the Middle East), modern pottery and contemporary ceramics; library of 20,000 vols. on ceramics and applied arts; Dir. B. HARRISSON; publs. *Annual Report*†, catalogues†.

Leiden

Koninklijk Nederlands Leger- en Wapenmuseum "Generaal Hoefer" (*Royal Netherlands "General Hoefer" Army and Arms Museum*): 7 Pesthuislaan; f. 1913; weapons from pre-history to the present day, uniforms, equipment, medals, paintings; library of 50,000 vols. and collection of early prints; Dir. W. HELDER; publs. *Annual Report, Armamentaria* (annually).

Rijksmuseum van Geologie en Mineralogie (*National Museum of Geology and Mineralogy*): Hooglandse Kerkgracht 17; f. 1820 as part of the Rijksmuseum van Natuurlijke Historie, became separate institution 1878; exhibitions and extensive reference and research, including mechanical data processing of pollen descriptions and geological collections; fossils, rocks and minerals mainly from S.E. Asia, Europe and West Indies; Dir. Prof. Dr. P. C. ZWAAN (acting); publs.

Sammlungen des Geologischen Reichsmuseums in Leiden (1881–1923), Leidse Geologische Mededelingen (1925–1971), Scripta Geologica (1971–) (300–400 pages annually).

Rijksmuseum van Natuurlijke Historie (*National Museum of Natural History*): Raamsteeg 2, P.O.B. 9517, 2300 RA Leiden; f. 1820; systematic zoology, including entomology and biological oceanography; library of 65,000 vols., 3,000 periodicals, 115,000 reprints; Dir. W. Vervoort; publs. *Zoologische Mededelingen*†, *Zoologische Verhandelingen*†, *Zoologische Bijdragen*†, *Verslag van de directeur*† (Annual Report), *Zoologische Monographieën*.

Rijksmuseum van Oudheden (*National Museum of Antiquities*): Rapenburg 28, 2311 EW; f. 1818; Netherlands prehistory, Roman period, Middle Ages, Egyptian, Mesopotamian, Greco-Roman and ancient European collections; Dir. Dr. H. D. Schneider; publs. *Oudheidkundige Mededelingen, Collections*.

Rijksmuseum voor de Geschiedenis van de Natuurwetenschappen en van de Geneeskunde "Museum Boerhaave" (*National Museum of History of Science*): Steenstraat 1A; f. 1928; historical scientific instruments and documents, anatomical preparations, portraits; library of 16,000 vols., MSS.; Dir. A. J. F. Gogelein; publ. *Communications Series* (irregular).

Rijksmuseum voor Volkenkunde (*National Museum of Ethnology*): Steenstraat 1, Postbus 212; f. 1837; collections from Africa, the Middle East, the Islamitic and Indian cultural areas, the Far East, Pacific, South-east Asia and the Americas; Dir. Dr. P. H. Pott; publs. *Mededelingen*†, *Verre Naasten Naderbij*† (3 a year), *Annual Report*.

Stedelijk Museum "de Lakenhal" Leiden: Oude Singel 28; f. 1872; pictures of Leiden school; memorial table (triptych) and altar pieces by Lucas van Leyden and C. Engebrechtsz; Rembrandt, Jan Steen, Jan van Goyen, van Mieris, Dou, modern Leiden school: Verster, Kamerlingh Onnes; furniture, silver, glass, tapestry, etc.; period rooms; history of the town; Dir. M. L. Wurfbain; publs. various†.

Maastricht

Bonnefantenmuseum (Stichting Limburgs Museum voor Kunst en Oudheden) (*Provincial Museum of Art and Antiquities*): Dominikanerplein 5; f. 1863, refounded 1968; prehistory, Roman archaeology, ecclesiastical art, furniture, applied arts, ancient, modern and contemporary painting and sculpture, collection of video art; temporary exhibitions and free exhibitions for contemporary artists; library of 4,000 vols.; Dir. I. L. Szénássy.

Natuurhistorisch Museum te Maastricht (*Natural History Museum*): Bosquetplein 7; f. 1912; flora, fauna and soils of the Limburg area; 30,000 vols. in library; Dir. Dr. D. G. Montagne; publs. *Natuurhistorisch Maandblad* (monthly), *Publicaties Natuurhistorisch Genootschap*† (irregular).

Muiden

Muiderslot Rijksmuseum (*State Museum*): f. 1871; 13th-century castle furnished in early 17th-century style: paintings, tapestries, furniture and armoury; Dir. S. P. Baron Bentinck; publs. *Annual Report, Guides, Het Muiderslot, Dat was te Muiden*.

Naarden

Comenius Museum: Turfpoorstraat 27; f. 1924; also a mausoleum given to the Czechoslovakians on a long lease in 1933, and a monument, given to the town of Naarden in 1957; library of 2,500 vols.

Nijmegen

Nijmeegs Museum "Commanderie van St. Jan": Franseplaats 3, 6511 VS; f. 1974; collections from the Middle Ages to the present, mainly related to the history and art of Nijmegen; exhibitions of modern art; Dir. Drs. G. Th. M. Lemmens.

Rijksmuseum G. M. Kam te Nijmegen: Museum Kamstraat 45; f. 1922; contains Roman antiquities (pottery, glass, bronze, etc.) found in Nijmegen and surroundings; also some prehistoric and Frankish antiquities; collections include those of the town of Nijmegen and of the St. Canisius College; Dir. Drs. A. V. M. Hubrecht; Curator Drs. Antoinette M. Gerhartl-Witteveen; publs. *Annual Report*† (in Dutch), *Bronze Vessels*† (catalogue in English), *Figural Bronzes*† (catalogue in English).

Otterlo

Rijksmuseum "Kroller-Muller": Nationale Park de Hoge Veluwe; f. 1938; large collection of paintings by Van Gogh, paintings of the 19th and 20th centuries, old masters, open-air sculpture collection, ceramics, drawings, graphic art; library of *c.* 5,000; Dir. Dr. R. Oxenaar; publ. *Museum Journaal* (6 a year).

Tegelmuseum "It noflik sté" (*Museum of Tiles*): Eikenzoom 10, 6731 BH; extensive collection of Netherlands tiles, dating from 1300 to the present day; Curator P. B. M. Bolwerk.

Roermond

Gemeentelijk Museum (*Municipal Museum*): Andersonweg 8; f. 1932; paintings, etchings, drawings, objects illustrating history of Roermond; Curator J. G. F. M. G. Baron van Hövell tot Westerflier.

Rotterdam

Historisch Museum der Stad Rotterdam: Korte Hoogstraat 31; f. 1861; objects referring to the history of Rotterdam, ceramics, maps, sculptures, period rooms 18th-19th century, pictures, silver, 17th-century inn; Dir. A. M. Meyerman. (Temporarily closed for restoration; c/o Eendrachtsweg 23.)

"De Dubbelde Palmboom": Voorhaven 12; f. 1975; objects referring to the history of Rotterdam, ceramics, maps, sculpture, archaeology, toys, silver, glass, etc.; Dir. A. M. Meyerman.

"Zakkendragershuisje": Voorstraat 13-15; pewter museum with demonstrations in pewter casting.

Maritiem Museum "Prins Hendrik": c/o Scheepmakershaven 48; f. 1873; models of ships dating back to 15th century, globes, atlases, *c.* 10,000 books, etc.; Dir. P. van Empelen; Curators Mrs. E. Bos-Rietdyk, L. M. Akveld; publ. *Jaarverslag*.

Museum Boymans-van Beuningen: Mathenesserlaan 18; f. 1847; Dutch School including paintings by Van Eyck, Bosch, Pieter Brueghel, Hals, Rembrandt, van Ruysdael, Hobbema, Jan Steen; Baroque School, French School, Impressionists; old, modern and contemporary paintings and sculpture; drawings from Dutch, Flemish, French, German, Italian and Spanish schools from the XV-XX centuries; old and modern prints; glass, Dutch silver, old pewter, laces and ceramics, among which an important collection of Persian, Spanish, Italian and Dutch pottery and tiles, furniture; Dir. Drs. W. Beeren; publs. catalogues†.

Museumship "Buffel": Leuvehaven 1; iron-clad turret-ram of the Dutch Royal Navy restored to its original state (1868); displays on maritime subjects; Dir. P. van Empelen.

Museum voor Land- en Volkenkunde (*Museum of Ethnology*): Willemskade 25; f. 1883; ethnological and archaeological collections from Indonesia, realm of Islam, Asia, Africa, America, New Guinea and Oceania; numismatic collection; library of 20,000 vols.; Dir. J. A. van Gorkom, LL.D.; publs. *Jaarverslag, Trois problèmes d'Ethnologie Maritime, Esquisse d'une Ethnographie Navale des Peuples Annamites, Une Collection ethnographique des Ababdes et des Bicharins dans le Museum voor Land- en Volkenkunde, Les Jonques chinoises I-X, Tibet: Buddhisme, Firozkohi (Afghanistan), Batik op Java, IJzerwerk van Centraal-Afrika.*

Utrecht

Centraal Museum der Gemeente Utrecht: Agnietenstraat 1 (15th-century building); used as museum since 1921; comprises two museums:

Centraal Museum: Department of pre-1850 art: Agnietenstraat 1; paintings and sculpture of Utrecht School, folklore, local history, costumes, period rooms, doll's house, 8th-century Utrecht ship, furniture, coins and medals; Department of post-1850 art: Maliebaan 42; paintings, sculpture, graphic art, furniture, ceramics; Dir. Drs. A. M. Janssens; publs. exhibition and collection catalogues.

Museum van het Provinciaal Utrechts Genootschap voor Kunsten en Wetenschappen (*Museum of the Utrecht Province Soc. of Arts and Sciences*): Agnietenstraat 1; pre-Roman, Roman and early mediaeval antiquities; Curator Dr. C. Isings; publs. *Annual Report, Guide.*

Veere

Museum "De Schotse Huizen": Kade 25-27; Chinese and Japanese ceramics; prints, national costumes, furniture, ships' models.

Oudheidskamer (*Cabinet of Antiquities*): Markt 5; f. 1881; old standards and flags; pictures; golden cup of Maximilian from Burgundy (1546).

Venlo

Goltziusmuseum: Goltziusstraat 21; f. 1967; prehistory, Roman collection, town history, applied art, period rooms, coins, prints; library; Dir. and Curator W. Th. M. Hendriks.

Vlissingen, Flushing

Stedelijk Museum te Vlissingen: Bellamypark 19; f. 1890; souvenirs of Admiral de Ruyter; coins, medals, paintings, ceramics, wood-carvings, topography, tiles, etc.; Curator (vacant).

Wageningen

Nederlands Landbouw Museum (*Netherlands Agricultural Museum*): c/o Gen. Foulkesweg 90; f. 1935; Dir. Dr. J. M. G. van der Poel.

Zwolle

Provinciaal Overijssels Museum: Melkmarkt 41; f. 1884; 16th–20th-century interiors; library of 3,000 vols.; Dir. J. W. M. de Jong.

UNIVERSITIES

UNIVERSITEIT VAN AMSTERDAM
(University of Amsterdam)

SPUI 21, AMSTERDAM
Telephone: 020-5259111.
Founded 1877.

Academic year: September to July.

Chairman of the Board: G. J. P. Cammelbeeck.
Chairman of the University Council: Drs. A. Grewel.
Rector Magnificus: Prof. Dr. J. Bruyn.
Secretary: Dr. A. J. I. van Dam.
Librarian: Dr. E. Braches.

Library: *see* Libraries.
Number of professors: 220.
Number of students: 25,000.
Publications: ***Studiegidsen der Universiteit van Amsterdam.***

Deans:

Faculty of Theology: Prof. S. de Boer.
Faculty of Law: Prof. Dr. A. G. Lubbers.
Faculty of Medicine: Prof. Dr. J. Th. F. Boeles.
Faculty of Mathematical and Natural Sciences: H. E. Rondeel.
Faculty of Arts: Prof. Dr. J. W. Smit.
Faculty of Economics: Prof. Dr. P. E. Venekamp.
Faculty of Social Sciences: Prof. Dr. Fr. de Jong Edz.
Central Inter-Faculty: Prof. Dr. Th. van Velthoven.
Inter-Faculty Geography and Prehistory: Prof. Dr. P. D. Jungerius.
Inter-Faculty Actuarial Sciences and Econometrics: Prof. Dr. J. S. Cramer.
Faculty of Philosophy: Prof Dr. van der Hoeven.

VRIJE UNIVERSITEIT, AMSTERDAM
(Free University)

DE BOELELAAN 1105,
P.B. 7161,
1007 MC AMSTERDAM
Telephone: 548 91 11.
Founded 1880.

Rector Magnificus: Prof. Dr. H. Verheul.
Co-Rector: Prof. Dr. D. C. Mulder.

Number of teachers: *c.* 650.
Number of students: *c.* 12,903.

Deans:

Faculty of Sciences: Prof. Dr. P. Mullender.
Faculty of Law: Prof. Mr. I. A. Diepenhorst.
Faculty of Theology: Prof. Dr. J. Veenhof.
Faculty of Arts: Prof. Dr. D. M. Bakker.
Faculty of Medicine: Prof. Dr. Chr. L. Rümke.
Faculty of Economics: Prof. Dr. H. Linnemann.
Faculty of Social Sciences: Prof. Dr. J. de Wit.

RIJKSUNIVERSITEIT TE GRONINGEN
(State University at Groningen)

BROERSTRAAT 5, 9700 AB
GRONINGEN, P.O.B. 72
Telephone: 050-119111.
Founded 1614.

President: B. ter Borch.
Secretary: Drs. H. A. Kurvers.
Rector Magnificus: Prof. Dr. J. Borgman.
Librarian: Mr. W. R. H. Koops.

Number of teachers: 415, including 257 professors.
Number of students: 16,500.
Publications: *Jaarboek, Gids, Universiteitskrant.*

Deans:

Faculty of Theology: Prof. Dr. A. F. J. Klijn.
Faculty of Law: Prof. Mr. C. J. H. Brunner.
Faculty of Medicine: Prof. Dr. W. Lammers.
Faculty of Science: Dr. F. van der Woude.
Faculty of Arts: Prof. Dr. J. Ensink.
Faculty of Economics: Prof. Dr. H. J. Wagener.
Faculty of Social Sciences: Prof. Dr. P. E. Boeke.

Professors:

Faculty of Theology:

Baaren, T. P. van, History of Religions
Drijvers, H. J. W., Hellenism and the Roman Empire
Geense, A., Dogmatics and Ecclesiastical Law
Hubbeling, H. G., Philosophy of Theology
Klijn, A. F. J., Old Christian Literature and the New Testament
Knetsch, F. R. J., History of the Dutch Church
Nijenhuis, W., History of Christianity
Roldanus, J., History of Early Western and Eastern Christianity
Roscam Abbing, P. J., Biblical and Practical Theology
Woude, A. S. van der, Old Testament

Faculty of Law:

Bakels, H. L., Law of Economic Planning
Brunner, C. J. H., Civil Law
Cohen Henriquez, E., Notarial Law
Doedens, H. J., Fiscal Law
Donner, A. M., Constitutional Law
Gerbenzon, P., Old Canonic Law and Old Frisian Law
Goudsmit, W., Psychiatry
Griffiths, J., Sociology of Law
Jongman, R. W., Juvenile Criminology
Lokin, J. H. A., Roman Law and its History
Meuwissen, D. H., Dutch Constitutional Law
Mok, M. R., Economic Law
Pen, J., Economics
Scheltema, M., Administrative Law
Schilfgaarde, P. van, Commercial Law
Teunissen, P. J., International Law
Timmermans, C. W. A., European Law
Uniken Venema, C., Anglo-American Law
Valkenburgh, P., Political Science
Veen, Th. W. van, Criminal Law
Weitenberg, J., Public Finance
Wiarda, J., Civil Law, Commercial Law and International Law

Faculty of Medicine:

Anders, G. J. P. A., Anthropology
Arends, A., Pathological Anatomy
Arends, J., Materia Technica
Beks, J. W. F., Neuro-Surgery
Berg, Jw. van den, Medical Physics
Blécourt, J. J. de, Rheumatology
Blickman, J. R., Roentgenology
Boeke, P. E. Clinical Psychology
Boer, P. W., Urology
Boering, G., Dentistry
Bossina, K. K., Child Cardiology
Bouman, P. R., Experimental Endocrinology
Deen, K. J. van, Social Hygiene
Dijk, W. K. van, Psychiatry
Doorenbos, H., Clinical Endocrinology
Dorlas, J. C., Anaesthesiology
Duterloo, H. S., Orthodontics
Fernandes, J., Paediatrics
Giel, R., Social Psychiatry
Goudsmit, W., Psychiatry
Hadders, H. N., Pathological Anatomy
Herxheimer, A., Clinical Pharmacology
Hoedemaeker, Ph., Pathological Anatomy
Hoeksema, P. E., Oto-Rhino-Laryngology
Hogerzeil, H. H. W., Social Medicine
Homan van der Heide, J. N., Thoracic Surgery
Huffstadt, A. J. C., Plastic Surgery
Huisjes, H. J., Gynaecology
Janssens, J., Gynaecology
Keuning, F. J., Histology
Klokke, A. H., Dermatology
Kroon, A. M., Physiological Chemistry
Kuijjer, P. J., Surgery
Lamberts, H. B., Radiopathology
Lammers, W., Pharmacology
Langrehr, D., Anaesthesiology
Loomeijer, F. J., Physiological Chemistry
Mandema, E., Internal Medicine
Minderhoud, J. M., Neurology
Molenaar, I., Submicroscopic Cytology
Nielsen, H. K. L., Orthopaedics
Nieveen, J., Heart and Coronary Diseases
Nieweg, H. O., Haematology
Oldhoff, J., General Surgery
Orie N. G. M., Pulmonary Diseases
Penning, L., Neuro-Radiology
Poel, A. C. M. van der, Prosthodontics
Prechtl, H. F. R., Neurology
Rashbass, C., Physiology
Ritsma, R. J., Audiology
Schweitzer, N. M. J., Ophthalmology
Slikke, L. B. van der, Introduction to Internal Medicine
Sluiter, H. J., Pulmonary Infections
Veldkamp, D. F., Dentistry
Vermeij, J., Radiotherapy
Waaij, D. van der, Medical Microbiology
Wilde, A. G. de, Anatomy and Embryology
Wilterdink, J. B., Virology
Woldring, M. G., Clinical Chemical Analysis
Zylstra, W. G., Physiology

Faculty of Science:

Atkinson, D., Theoretical Physics
Baerends, G. P., Zoology
Berendsen, H. J. C., Physical Chemistry
Boers, A. L., Technical Physics
Borgman, J., Techniques of Astronomical Observation
Braaksma, B. L. J., Mathematics
Brinkman, H., Experimental Physics
Bruggen, E. F. J., van, Biochemistry
Challa, G., Chemistry and Technology of Polymers
Dekker, A. J., Physics of Solids
Doornbos, D. A., Pharmaceutical-chemical Analysis
Drenth, J., Structural Chemistry
Engberts, J. B. F. N., Organic Chemistry
Faber, J. S., Pharmacy
Feenstra, W. J., Genetics
Francken, J. C., Technical Physics
Gerritsen, D. J., Applied Chemistry
Gruber, M., Biochemistry
Haas, C., Inorganic and Analytical Chemistry
Hoek, C. van den, Plant Taxonomy
Hogeveen, H., Organic Chemistry
Hugenholtz, N. M., Theoretical Physics
Huizinga, T., Pharmacotherapy
Iachello, F., Nuclear Physics
Janssen, M. J., Organic Chemistry
Jellinek, F., Inorganic Chemistry
Kellogg, R. M., Organic Chemistry
Kommandeur, J., Physical Chemistry
Kruijt, J. P., Zoology
Kuiper, J. W., Biophysics
Kuiper, P. J. C., Physiology of Plants
Lammers, W., Pharmacology
Lerk, C. F., Pharmaceutical Technology
Nieuwpoort, W. C., Structural Chemistry
North, J. D., History of Philosophy
Perdok, W. G., Mineralogy
Plaut, L., Astronomy
Ponstein, J., Operational Research
Postma, H., Oceanography
Pottasch, S. R., Astrophysics
Put, M. van der, Mathematics
Ruiter, L. de, Comparative Physiology
Schaafsma, W., Mathematical Statistics
Siemssen, R. H., Experimental Nuclear Physics
Smith, Ph. B., Experimental Physics
Sparenberg, J. A., Technical Mechanics
Stam, A. J., Applied Mathematics
Stemerding, S., Physical Technology of Applied Chemistry
Straaten, L. M. J. U. van, Marine Geology and Petrology
Takens, F., Theory of Mathematics
Thomas, G. E., Theory of Mathematics
Tolhoek, H. A., Theoretical Physics
Veldkamp, H., Microbiology
Verweij, J. F., Technical Physics
Vooren, A. I. van de, Applied Mathematics
Vos, Mrs. A., Structural Chemistry
Waard, H. de, Experimental Physics
Wegener Sleeswijk, A., Technical Physics
Wessels, J. G. H., Botany
Whitfield, H., Computers
Wijnberg, H., Organic Chemistry
Willems, J. C., Applied Mathematics

Faculty of Arts:

Abraham, W., German Language and Literature
Århammar, N. R., Frisian Language and Literature
Baaren, T. P. van, Egyptian Language and Literature
Bakker, R., Philosophy
Barth, Mrs. E. M., Analytical Philosophy
Baudet, H., Economic and Social History
Berg, G. J. van den, Planology and Demography
Blok, W., Dutch Literature
Bremen, W. J. van den, Economic and Social Geography
Briosi, A. R. T., Italian Language and Literature
Delfgaauw, B. Philosophy
Drijvers, H. J. W., Semitic Language and Literature and Archaeology of the Near East
Engels, L. J., Medieval Latin
Ensink, J., Sanskrit
Entjes, H., German Language and Literature
Gerritsen, J., English Linguistics and English Literature of the Middle Ages
Heny, F. W., Linguistics and Philosophy in Language
Holk, A. G. F. van, Slavonic Languages
Holz, H. H., History of Philosophy
Hospers, J. H., Semitic Language and Literature and Eastern Archaeology
Jongkees, A. G., Medieval History
Kossmann, E. H., History after the Middle Ages
Kylstra, A. D., German Language
Lipschitz, I., Modern History
Lukkes, P., Economics and Social Geography
Lulofs, F., Dutch Language and Literature
Maaskant-Kleibrink, Mrs. M., Classical Archaeology
Marken, Mrs. A. van, Scandinavian Languages and Literature
Mooij, J. J. A., Analytical Philosophy
Noomen, W., French Literature
North, J. D., History of Science
Oostendorp, H. T., Spanish Language and Literature
Os, H. W. van, History of Art
Radt, S. L., Greek
Sassen, A., Dutch Language
Schrijvers, P. H., Latin
Schulte Nordholt, H., History of Art

STEFFEN, H., German Language
STUART, D. G., Experimental Phonetics
TAMSMA, R., Economic and Social Geography
TANS, J. A. G., Modern French Language and Literature
WATERBOLK, E. H., History after the Middle Ages
WATERBOLK, H. TJ., Archaeology
WES, M. A., Ancient History
WILKINSON, D. R. M., English and American Literature after the Middle Ages

Faculty of Economics:
BAUDET, H., Economic and Social History
BOSMAN, A., Business Administration
BOUMA, J. L., Business Administration
BREMEN, J. W. VAN DEN, Economic and Social Geography
DAEMS, H. P. C., Business Management
DEGENKAMP, J. TH., Introduction to Law
DOEDENS, H. J., Fiscal Law
GADOUREK, I., Sociology
GALAN, C. DE, Economy of Labour
HAAN, H. DE, Economics
HARTOG, F., Economics
KLOOSTER, A. J. VAN 'T, Business Organization
KOOYMAN, M. A., Statistics and Econometry
KUIPERS, S. K., General Economics
LEEUW, A. C. J. DE, Operational Research
LUKKES, P., Economics and Social Geography
MADDISON, A., Economic Sociology
PEN, J., Political Economy
PIKKEMAAT, G. F. W. M., Mathematics
PONSTEIN, J., Operational Research
RIJKEN V. OLST, H., Statistics and Econometry
TAMSMA, R., Economic and Social Geography
WAL, J. D. VAN DER, Accountancy
WATTEL, A., Operational Research
WEITENBERG, J., Public Finance

Faculty of Social Science:
BAERENDS, G. P., Zoology
BAKKER, R., Philosophy
BAUDET, H., Social and Economic History
BERG, G. J. VAN DEN, Planology and Demography
BEUGEN, M. VAN, Andragology
BOEKE, P. E., Clinical Psychology
BRANDENBURG, W. J., Didactics
DIJK, W. K. VAN, Psychiatry
ELLEMERS, J. E., Empirical Sociology
GADOUREK, I., Sociology
GALAN, C. DE, Labour Economics
GELDER, L. VAN, Pedagogy
GILS, M. R. VAN, Operational Research
HARMSEN, G., East European Philosophy
HOFSTEE, W. K. B., Psychology
KEMENADE, J. A. VAN, Educational Research
KLIP, E. C., Psychology
MICHON, J. A., Interdisciplinary Aspects of Traffic
MOLENAAR, W., Statistical Analysis
MULDER, L. H., Didactics
NAUTA, L. W., Philosophy
PRINS, A. H. J., Cultural Anthropology
RISPENS, J., Orthopedagogics
SNIJDERS, J. TH., Psychology
STOKMAN, F. N., Methods and Techniques
STRIEN, P. J. VAN, Psychology of Work
VALKENBURGH, P., Political Science
VEEN, P., Social Psychology
WERFF, J. J. VAN DER, Psychology
WILKE, H. A. M., Experimental Social Psychology

RIJKSUNIVERSITEIT TE LEIDEN
(Leiden State University)

STATIONSWEG 46, 2313 AV LEIDEN
Telephone: 071-148333.
Founded 1575.

Language of instruction: Dutch; Academic year: September to July.

President: K. J. CATH.
Secretary: D. P. DEN OS.
Rector: A. A. H. KASSENAAR.
Librarian: J. R. DE GROOT.

Number of teachers: 1,678 full-time, including 237 professors.

Number of students: 16,000.

Publications: *Studiegids, Mare, Na het eindexamen naar Leiden?, Almanak, Vademecum, Admission to Leiden University.*

DEANS:

Faculty of Theology: J. VAN DEN BERG.
Faculty of Law: A. VAN BRAAM.
Faculty of Medicine: G. J. TAMMELING.
Faculty of Science: J. C. LEYTE.
Faculty of Arts: H. STEIMMETZ.
Faculty of Social Science: J. D. SPECKMANN.
Central Interfaculty of Philosophy: R. A. V. Baron VAN HÆRSOLTE.
Interfaculty of Geography and Prehistory: P. J. R. MODDERMAN.

PROFESSORS:

Faculty of Theology:
ADRIAANSE, H. J., Religion, Philosophy
BERG, J. VAN DEN, Ecclesiastical History
BERKHOF, H., Dogmatics, Biblical Theology
BOLKESTEIN, M. H., Practical Theology
HARTMANN, B., Ancient Religions
JONGE, M. DE, New Testament
MULDER, M. J., Old Testament
POSTHUMUS MEYJES, G. H. M., History of Christianity
SPINDLER, M. R., Ecumenics and Missiology

Faculty of Law:
BLOEMBERGEN, A. R., Civil Law
BLOK, N., English Private Law
BRAAM, A. VAN, Public Administration
BUIKHUISEN, W., Criminology and Penology
CRAMER, N., History of State Institutions and Parliamentary History
DAALDER, H., Political Science
EIZENGA, W., Economics and Statistics
FEENSTRA, R., Roman Law and its History
FELDBRUGGE, F. J. M., East European Law
FRANKEN, H., Introduction to the Principles of Law
FROENTJES, W., Criminalistics
GIELE, J. F. M., Taxation Law
GOEDE, B. J. DE, Constitutional and Administrative Law
GRAPPERHAUS, F. H. M., Taxation Law
GUNSTEREN, H. R. VAN, Political Theories and their History
HAERSOLTE, Baron R. A. V. VAN, Philosophy of Law
HALBERSTADT, V., Doctrine of Public Finances
KLEYN, W. M., Civil Law, Notarial Law
KOOIJMANS, P. H., Law of Nations
KRAAL, A., Business Economics
LIJPHART, A., International Relations
MELAI, A. L., Criminal Law, Criminal Procedure
MOURIK, M. J. A. VAN, Notarial Law
OVEN, A. VAN, Commercial Law
PESTMAN, P. W., Comparative History of Ancient Law
PRAAG, B. M. S. VAN, Western Economics
ROOD, M. G., Labour Law
SCHELTENS, J. P., Taxation Law
SCHERMERS, H. G., Law of International Organizations
SMIDT, J. TH. DE, Dutch Historical Law
STERK, T. A. W., Civil Procedure
VERBURG, J., Taxation Law
VERHEUL, J. P., International Private Law
VINKE, P., Sociology of Law
WASSENBERGH, H. A., Aviation Law
WOUW, J. A. C. J. VAN DER, Canon Law
ZEEGERS, M., Forensic Psychiatry

Faculty of Medicine:
ARNTZENIUS, A. C., Cardiology
BAKKER, A. R., Biomedical Informatics
BASTIAANS, J., Psychiatry
BENNEBROEK GRAVENHORST, J., Obstetrics and Gynaecology
BROM, A. G., Thoracic Surgery
BRUYN, G. W., Medical Neurology
BRUYNING, C. F. A., Parasitology
CATS, A., Rheumatology
COHEN, E. M., Biological Toxicology
DAEMS, W. TH., Submicroscopic Cytology
DOELEMAN, F., Social Medicine
DONKER, P. J., Urology
DOOREN, L. J., Paediatrics
DUYFJES, F., Orthopaedics
DUYN, P. VAN, Histochemistry
DIJKHUIS, H. J. P. M., General Medical Practice
DYKMAN, J. H., Pulmonary Diseases
FURTH, R. VAN, Infectious Diseases
GELDEREN, H. H. VAN, Paediatrics
GRAEFF, JHR. J. DE, Nephritic Diseases
HAEX, A. J. CH., Gastroenterology
HALL, E. V. VAN, Obstetrics and Gynaecology
HEMKER, H. C., Cardiobiochemistry
HUSON, A., Anatomy and Embryology
HUYSMANS, H. A., Thoracic Surgery
KASSENAAR, A. A. H., Pathological Chemistry
LAIRD, J. D., Physiological Physics
LANDSMEER, J. M. F., Anatomy and Embryology
LOELIGER, E. A., Haematomorphology
LUYENDYK, W., Neurosurgery
MOUTON, R. P., Microbiology and Bacteriology
MULDER, J. D., Radiodiagnostics
NOACH, E. L., Pharmacology
OOSTERHUIS, J. A., Ophthalmology
QUERIDO, A., Endocrinology
RIJSSEL, TH. G. VAN, Pathology
ROOD, J. J. VAN, Immuno-Haematology
ROOYMANS, H. G. M., Clinical Psychiatry
RÖRSCH, A., Molecular Genetics
ROTHCHILD, I., Pharmacology
SCHABERG, A., Pathology
SCHMIDT, P. H., Oto-Rhino-Laryngology
SMEENK, D., Endocrinology
SOBELS, F. H., Radiation Genetics
SPIERDYK, J., Anaesthesiology
SUURMOND, D., Dermatology and Venereology
TAMMELING, G. J., Physiology

TERPSTRA, J. L., Vascular and Transplantation Surgery
THOMAS, P., Radiotherapy
THUNG, P. J., Relations between Science and Medicine
VERLINDE, J. D., Microbiology
VERVEEN, A. A., Physiology
VINK, M., Surgery
VOORTHUISEN, A. E. VAN, Radiodiagnostics
WERFF TEN BOSCH, J. J. VAN DER, Experimental Endocrinology
ZWAVELING, A., Clinical Oncological Surgery

Faculty of Science:
ADDINK, A. D. F., Animal Physiology
BAKKER, K., Animal Ecology
BEENAKKER, J. J. M., Experimental Physics
BLAAUW, A., Astronomy
BOOM, J. H. VAN, Organic Chemistry
BOSCH, L., Biochemistry
BÖTTCHER, C. J. F., Physical Chemistry
BREIMER, D. D., Pharmacology
BRONGERSMA, H. H., Application of Bundel Methods in Chemistry
BROUWER, A., Stratigraphy and Palaeontology
BRUYN OUBOTER, R. DE, Experimental Physics
BRUYNING, C. F. A., Parasitology
COX, J. A. M., Theoretical Physics
DULLEMEIJER, P., Animal Morphology
DUYSENS, L. N. M., Biophysics
FABIUS, J., Calculus of Probability
GERRITSMA, K. W., Pharmaceutical Chemistry
GREENBERG, J. M., Astrophysics in the Laboratory
GROOT, B. DE, Development Genetics
HARTMAN, P., Crystallography
HEGNAUER, R., Experimental Systematic Botany
HORDIJK, A., Operations Research
HUISKAMP, W. J., Experimental Physics
HULST, H. C. VAN DE, Theoretical Astronomy
HUMMEL, A., Radiation Chemistry
IERSEL, J. J. A. VAN, Experimental Zoology
JEUKEN, M., Philosophy of Biology
JONG, H. J. DE, Pharmaceutical Analysis
KALKMAN, C., Special Botany
KASTELEIJN, P. W., Theoretical Physics
KLOOSTERZIEL, H., Organic Chemistry
KNAAP, H. F. P., Experimental Physics
KONIJN, T. M., Cellular Biology and Morphology
LAAN, H. VAN DER, Radio-astronomy
LEYTE, J. C., Physical Chemistry
LIBBENGA, K. R., General Botany
MANDEL, M., Physical Chemistry
MAZUR, P., Theoretical Physics
MURRE, J. P., Algebraic Geometry
PELETIER, L. A., Analysis and Applied Mathematics
POLDERMAN, J., Pharmaceutical Technology
POULIS, N. J., Experimental Physics
QUISPEL, A., Experimental Botany
ROMERS, C., Roentgen and Electron Defraction in Chemistry
RÖRSCH, A., Biochemistry
SCHOONEVELD, C. VAN, Signal Processing for Observation Systems
SPIJKER, M. N., Numerical Mathematics
STAVERMAN, A. J., Physical Chemistry
STEENBRINK, J. H. M., Geometry
SVENDSEN, A. BAERHEIM, Pharmacognosy
TACONIS, K. W., Experimental Physics
TEX, E. DEN, Petrology, Mineralogy and Crystallography
TIJDEMAN, R., Analysis and Theory of Numbers
UBBINK, J. B., Philosophy of Science
VEN, A. J. H. M. VAN DE, Topology
VERRIJN STUART, A. A., Informatics
VERVOORT, W., Systematic Zoology
WAALS, J. H. VAN DER, Experimental Physics
WIEBES, J. TH., Systematic Zoology and Evolution Biology
ZAANEN, A. C., Mathematical Analysis
ZWART, H. J., Structural Geology
ZWET, W. R. VAN, Mathematical Statistics

Faculty of Arts:
ANCEAUX, J. C., Austronesian Languages
ARKEL, D. VAN, Social History
BACHRACH, A. G. H., English Literature
BALJON, J. M. S., Islamology
BOER, W. DEN, Ancient History
BOSCHLOO, A. W. A., History of Art
BRUGMAN, J., Arabic Language and Cultural History
CASPARIS, J. G. DE, Archaeology and Ancient History of South and South-east Asia
DRESDEN, S., Theory of Literature
DREWES, A. J., South-Semitic Language and Literature
FLEMMING, B., Turkish Language and Literature
GEERTMAN, H. A. A. P., Ancient Archaeology
GOMPERTS, H. A., Modern Dutch Literature
HEESTERMAN, J. C., Languages and Cultural History of South Asia
HENNEPHOF, H., Byzantinology, Modern Greek Language and Literature
HIJMANS-TROMP, I., Italian Language and Literature
HOFTIJZER, J., Hebrew, Israeli Antiquities and Ugaritic
HUYGENS, R. B. C., Medieval Latin
IDEMA, W. L., Chinese Language and Literature
JANSEN, H. P. H., History of the Middle Ages
JANSSEN, J. J., Egyptology
KOOIJ, J. G., Dutch Linguistics
KORTLANDT, F. H., Balto-Slavonic Languages
KRAUS, F. R., Languages and History of Babylonia and Assyria
KUIPERS, A. H., Descriptive Linguistics and Caucasian Languages
LANGE, K. P., German Language
LECHNER, J., Spanish Language and Literature
LUNSINGH SCHEURLEER, TH. H., History of Art
MODDERMAN, P. J. R., Pre-history
MOK, Q. I. M., French Language and Literature
NUCHELMANS, G. R. M. F., Philosophy
OSSELTON, N. E., English Linguistics
PEURSEN, C. A. VAN, Philosophy
PLEKET, H. W., Greek and Latin Epigraphy
POTT, P. H., Museology
REVE, K. VAN HET, Slavonic Literature
RIJK, L. M. DE, Classical and Medieval Philosophy
ROORDA, D. J., Modern History
SCHÖFFER, I., History of the Netherlands
SCHRIJVERS, P. H., Latin Language and Literature
SCHULTE NORDHOLT, J. W., History and Culture of North America
SICKING, C. M. J., Greek Language and Literature
STARRE, E. VAN DER, French Literature
STEINMETZ, H., German Literature
STEWARD, J. M., Comparative African Linguistics
TEEUW, A., Bahasa Indonesia and Malay
TERWEN, J. J., History of Architecture
UHLENBECK, E. M., General Linguistics and Javanese
VEEN, J. VAN DER, History of Music
VETTER, T. E., Buddhism, Indian Philosophy and Tibetan
VOORHOEVE, J., African Linguistics
VOS, F., Japanese and Korean Language and Literature
WESSELING, H. L., Contemporary History
ZÜRCHER, E., History of the Far East

Faculty of Social Science:
ALLEGRO, J. T., Labour and Organization Psychology
BERG, J. H. VAN DEN, Psychological Phenomenology, Conflict Psychology and Pastoral Psychology
BERTELS, C. P., Philosophy of Sociology
BRAAM, A. VAN, Public Administration
BRAND, W., Economics of Non-Western **Areas**
BROEK, P. VAN DEN, Educational Psychology and School Teaching
CHORUS, A. M. J., Psychology
DAALDER, H., Political Science
DIJKHUIS, J. J., Clinical Psychology and Psychotherapy
FLORES D'ARCAIS, G. B., Psychological Functions Science
GALJART, B. F., General Sociology of Non-Western Peoples
GEER, J. P. VAN DE, Data Theory
GENT, B. VAN, Andragology
GERBRANDS, A. A., Cultural Anthropology and Ethnography
HAERSOLTE, R. A. V., Baron VAN, Philosophy of Law
HORST, W. TER, Clinical Education, Ortho-Education
JOSSELIN DE JONG, P. E. DE, Cultural Anthropology of South Asia and the Pacific
KIEVIET, F. K., Applied Education, Dialectics
KLERK, L. DE, Education
KOHNSTAMM, G. A., Development Psychology
KUPER, A. J., Sociology and Culture of Africa South of the Sahara
LAMMERS, C. J., Sociology of Organization
LAYENDECKER, L., General Sociology
LIER, R. A. J. VAN, Sociology and Culture of Middle and South America and Developing Countries
LOENEN, J. H. M. M., Philosophy
MARX, E. C. H., Organization
RIETVELD, W. J., Physiological Psychology
ROEST, P., Theory and Practice of Teaching Methods
SPECKMANN, J. D., Empirical Sociology of non-Western Peoples
TULDER, J. J. M. VAN, Statistical Sociological Methods
VALL, M. VAN DER, Sociological Methods
VLIST, R. VAN DER, Social Psychology

(The 3 inter-faculties are staffed by professors attached to the faculties above.)

RIJKSUNIVERSITEIT LIMBURG
(State University of Limburg)

P.O.B. 616, 6200 MD MAASTRICHT
Telephone: (043) 88-88-88.

Founded 1975.

State control; Language of instruction: Dutch; Academic year: September to June.

Chairman of Board of Trustees: R. B. VAN DEN BIGGELAAR, LL.B.

Rector: Prof. Dr. W. H. F. W. WIJNEN.
Chairman of the University Board: R. STARMANS.
Librarian: Dr. J. VAN DIJK.

Number of teachers: 250.
Number of students: 525.

DEANS:

Faculty of Medicine: Prof. Dr. J. M. GREEP.
General Faculty: Prof. Dr. H. PHILIPSEN.

PROFESSORS:

BOVEN, C. P. A. VAN, Medical Microbiology
BONKE, F. I. M., Physiology
BREDA VRIESMAN, P. J. C. VAN, Pathology and Immunology
BREMER, J. J. C. B., Medical Psychology
BROUWER, W., General Practice
DRUKKER, J., Anatomy/Embryology
GREEP, J. M., General Surgery
GREVE, L. H., Pulmonology
GROOT, L. M. J., Health Economics
HAAN, J. DE, Gynaecology and Obstetrics
HEMKER, H. C., Biochemistry
HULSMANS, H. A. M., Internal Medicine
LAMERS, W. P. M. A., Ophthalmology
LELKENS, J. P. M., Anaesthesiology
LEMMENS, H. A. J., General Surgery
LINDEN, A. J. VAN DER, Orthopaedics
LUGT, P. J. M. VAN DER, Neurology
MOL, J. M. F., Clinical Neurophysiology
PHILIPSEN, H., Medical Sociology
RAHN, K. H., Pharmacology
RENEMAN, R. S., Physiology
RICHARTZ, M. M. W., Social Psychiatry
ROMME, M. A. J., Social Psychiatry
SPORKEN, P., Medical Ethics
SWAEN, G. J. V., Pathology and Immunology
WELLENS, H. J. J., Cardiology
WIJNEN, W. H. F., Development and Research of Higher Education
ZWAAL, R. F. A., Biochemistry

KATHOLIEKE UNIVERSITEIT NIJMEGEN

(Catholic University Nijmegen)

COMENIUSLAAN 4, NIJMEGEN
Telephone: 51-93-33.
Telex: 8211 KUNM NL.
Founded 1923.

Languages of instruction: Dutch, English; Private control; Academic year: September to June.

Governing Body: Stichting Katholieke Universiteit.
Chairman of the Board of Curators: Ir. W. C. M. VAN LIESHOUT.
Secretary of the Board of Curators: Mr. J. M. HAGEMAN.
Rector Magnificus: Prof. Dr. P. G. A. B. WIJDEVELD.
Librarian: Mr. G. G. A. M. PIJNENBORG.

Number of teachers: 1,014.
Number of students: *c.* 15,000.
Publication: *K. U. Nieuws* (weekly).

DEANS:

Faculty of Theology: Prof. Dr. M. B. F. VAN JERSEL.
Faculty of Arts: Prof. A. KRAAK.
Faculty of Law: Prof. Mr. W. C. L. VAN DER GRINTEN.
Faculty of Medicine: Prof. Dr. H. J. LAMMERS.
Faculty of Sciences: Prof. Dr. A. G. M. JANNER.
Faculty of Social Sciences: Prof. Dr. J. H. J. G. GIESBERS.
Central Inter-Faculty: Dr. W. DUPRÉ.
Inter-faculty of Geography and Prehistory: Prof. P. J. W. KOUWE.

ATTACHED INSTITUTES:

Dr. Veeger Institute: Verlengde Groenestraat 75, Nijmegen; research in social medicine; Dir. Prof. Dr. P. HEYENDAEL.

Gemeenschappelijk instituut voor toegepaste psychologie: Berg en Dalseweg 127, Nijmegen; application of psychological theory; Dirs. Prof. Dr. J. J. A. VOLLEBERGH, Drs. W. H. SNIJDERS, Drs. M. M. OTTO.

Instituut voor toegepaste sociologie: Graafseweg 274, Nijmegen; application of sociological theory; Dir. Dr. J. M. VAN WESTERLAAK.

Hoogveld-institute: Stikke Hezelstraat 1, Nijmegen; educational research; Dir. Dr. V. J. WELTEN.

Titus Brandsma institute: Heyendaalseweg 121A, Nijmegen; bibliography and documentation of the study of religious experience and spiritual life; Dir. Dr. Prof. G. M. O. STEGGINK.

Katholiek Documentatiecentrum: Erasmuslaan 36, Nijmegen: documentation of Dutch catholicism; Dir. Dr. J. H. ROES.

Reinier de Graafstichting: evolutionary studies.

Instituut voor Onderzoek van het Wetenschappelijk Onderwijs: Bisschop Hamerhuis, Verlengde Groenestraat 75, Nijmegen; institute for scientific education research; Dir. Drs. J. F. M. J. VAN HOUT.

ERASMUS UNIVERSITEIT ROTTERDAM

(Erasmus University of Rotterdam)

BURGEMEESTER OUDLAAN 50, P.B. 1738, 3000 DR ROTTERDAM
Telephone: 010-145511.

Founded 1973 by amalgamation of the Nederlandse Economische Hogeschool and the Medische Faculteit Rotterdam.

Academic year: September to July.

President of Board of Governors: J. VAN OS VAN DEN ABEELEN.
Rector: Prof. Dr. J. SPERNA WEILAND.
Secretary: O. A. THISSEN, LL.M.
Librarian: Dr. R. L. SCHUURSMA.

Number of students: 8,500.
Publications: *Calendar, Annual Report, Quod Novum* (weekly).

DEANS:

Faculty of Economics: Prof. Mr. W. J. SLAGTER.
Faculty of Law: Prof. Mr. W. G. VERKRUISEN.
Faculty of Medicine: Prof. Dr. H. J. VAN DER MOLEN.
Faculty of Philosophy: Prof. Dr. H. KIMMERLE.
Sub-Faculty of Social—Cultural Sciences: Prof. Dr. W. P. BLOCKMANS.
Sub-Faculty of Social History: Prof. Dr. P. W. KLEIN.

RIJKSUNIVERSITEIT TE UTRECHT

(State University of Utrecht)

UTRECHT,
KROMME NIEUWE GRACHT 29
Telephone: 030/33-57-22.
Founded 1636.

Academic year: September to July.

President: (vacant).
Rector Magnificus: Prof. Dr. A. VERHOEFF.
President of the University Council: Prof. Dr. P. G. DE HAAN.
University Librarian: Drs. J. VAN HEIJST.

Number of teachers: 276 professors.
Number of students: *c.* 21,000.
Publications: *Jaarverslag, Gids.*

DEANS:

Faculty of Theology: Prof. Dr. O. J. DE JONG.
Faculty of Law: Dr. W. KOERS.
Faculty of Medicine: Prof. Dr. R. GISPEN.
Faculty of Science: Prof. Dr. G. BLASSE.
Faculty of Arts: Prof. Dr. H. L. W. NELSON.
Faculty of Veterinary Medicine: Dr. G. J. W. VAN DER MEIJ.
Faculty of Social Sciences: Dr. H. J. HEEREN.
Central Interfaculty: Prof. Dr. K. J. SCHUHMANN.
Interfaculty of Geography and Prehistory: Prof. Dr. M. DE SMIDT.

PROFESSORS:

Faculty of Theology:

BRONKHORST, A. J., 20th Century Church History
BRÜMMER, V., Philosophy of Religion
EYSINK, A. H., Canon Law
GRIJS, F. J. A. DE, Systematic Theology
GRAAFLAND, C., Calvinistic Dogmatics
HASSELAAR, J. M., Dogmatics, Church History, Ethics
HOENS, D. J., Religious History
HEEGER, F. R., Ethics including Philosophical Ethics and Encyclopaedic Theology
JONG, O. J. DE, History of the Christian Religion
JONKER, H., Biblical and Practical Theology, Apostolate
KOK, J. A. DE, Church History
KRUIJF, TH. C. DE, New Testament Exegesis

LEEUWEN, C. VAN, Old Testament and History of Jewish Religion
LINDE, J. M. VAN DER, Church History
QUISPEL, G., Early Church History
REILING, J., History and Dogmatics of Baptism
TROMP, N. J., Old Testament Exegesis
VERMASEREN, M. J., Religious History of Hellenism
VISSER, J., Structure of the Early Catholic Church
WEGMAN, H. A. J., Dogmatics and Liturgy
WEIPPERT, M. H. E., Hebrew Language and Literature, Jewish Archaeology and Accadian
ZANDEE, J., History of Ancient Religions, Egyptian

Faculty of Law:

ALGRA, N. E., Introduction to Theory of Law
BERGH, G. C. J. J. VAN DEN, Historical Development of Dutch Law
BEYAERT, F. H. L., Psychiatric Aspects of Law, Forensic Psychiatry
BOS, M., International Law
BURKENS, M. C. B., Constitutional and Administrative Law
CRINCE LE ROY, R., Administrative Law
DIJK, P. VAN, Law of International Organizations
HELLEMA, A. W., Civil Law
HESS, H., Criminology
MEERING, A., Tax Law
NIEUWENBURG, C. K. F., Political Economy
NIEUWENHOVEN HELBACH, E. A. VAN, Intellectual Property Law
PETERS, A. A. G., Penal Law, Criminal Procedure, Criminology
RANG, J. F., Labour Law
ROOD-DE BOER, Mrs. M., Juvenile Law
SAUVEPLANNE, J. G., International Private Law
SLOT, R., Political Economy
SOONS, A. L. M., Civil Law
SPRUIT, J. E., History of Dutch Law
STEENBEEK, J. G., Constitutional and Administrative Law
VERBURGH, M. J. P., Civil Law
VERLOREN VAN THEMAAT, P., Social Economic Law
VERPAALEN, O. A. C., Civil Procedure Law
VISSER 'T HOOFT, H. P., Philosophy and Methodology of Law
VREE, J. K. DE, International and Political Relations
WACHTER, B., Commercial Law

Faculty of Medicine:

AKEN, J. VAN, Dental Radiology
BACKER DIRKS, O., Preventive Dentistry
BALLIEUX, R. E. P. A., Clinical Immunology
BIERSTEKER, P. A., Physiology
BOUMAN, M. A., Medical Physics
BRANDE, J. V. L. VAN DEN, Paediatrics
BRAS, G., Pathology
BRENKMAN, C. F., Social Medicine
DEENSTRA, H., Pulmonary Diseases
DENIER VAN DER GON, J. J., Human Physics
DERKSEN, A. A. D., Methodology of Dental Instruction, Gnatology
DOORENMAALEN, W. J. VAN, Anatomy and Embryology
EGYEDI, P., Orthodontics and Oral Surgery
EPHRAÏM, K. H., Application of Radioactive Isotopes in Medicine
ES, J. C. VAN, General Practice
FLÖGEL, G. E., Prosthetic Dentistry
HASPELS, A. A., Obstetrics and Gynaecology
HATTINGA VERSCHURE, J. C. M., Hospital Management
HEYST, A. N. P. VAN, Reanimation and Clinical Toxicology
HOLLANDER, C. F., Medical Gerontology
HONIG, C. A., Plastic Surgery
HUIZINGA, J., Physical Anthropology
HULST-STEYN-PARVÉ, E. P., Physiological Chemistry
JANSEN, M. T., Histology and Microscopic Anatomy
JANSZ, H. S., Physiological Chemistry
KAMP, L. N. J., Child Psychiatry
KEMP, A., Neurology
KLINKHAMER, A. C., Roentgenology
KREMER, J., General Obstetrics and Gynaecology
MAES, R. A. A., Toxicology
MEIJLER, F. L., Cardiovascular diseases
MUSTAPH, H., Medical Sexology
PEPERZEEL, Mrs. H. A. VAN, Radiotherapy
PRAAG, H. M. VAN, Psychiatry
PUYLAERT, C. B. A. J., Roentgenology
SCHWARZ, F., Clinical Endocrinology
SEDEE, G. A., Oto-rhino-laryngology
SIXMA, J. J., Haematology
SLUYS VEER, J. VAN DER, Clinical Medicine
SMALHOUT, B., Anaesthesiology
SMEETS, H. J. L., Orthodontics
STOOP, J. W., Paediatrics
STRUYVENBERG, A., Clinical Medicine
SYBRANDY, S., Orthopaedics
TIDDENS, H. A. W. M., Teaching Methods in Medicine, Paediatrics
UNNIK, J. A. M. VAN, Pathological Anatomy
WAARD, F. DE, Social Medicine
WIED, D. DE, Pharmacology
WINKELMAN, J. E., Ophthalmology
WITTEBOL, P., Surgery

Faculty of Science:

ALKEMADE, C. TH. J., Experimental Physics
ARENS, J. F., Organic Chemistry
ARKEL, G. A. VAN, Genetics
BARKMAN, J. J., Vegetation Science and Plant Ecology
BEENAKKERS, A. M. TH., Experimental Zoology
BLAEIJ, C. J. DE, Biopharmacy
BLASSE, G., Solid State Chemistry
BLIJ, F. VAN DER, Pure Mathematics, Analysis and Theory of Numbers
BOER, D. H. W. DEN, Theoretical Organic Chemistry
BOUMAN, M. A., Human Physics
BRAAMS, C. M., Plasmaphysics
BRAAMS, R., Biophysics
BROUWER, R., Botany
BRUYN, PH. L. DE, Basic Chemistry
BUEREN, H. G. VAN, Astronomy
COHEN, J. W., Operational analyses
DEENEN, L. L. M. VAN, Biochemistry
DENIER VAN DER GON, J. J., Human Physics
DIE, J. VAN, Botany
DIJKSTRA, A., Analytical Chemistry
DIJKSTRA, G., Spectrochemical Analysis
DORRESTEIN, R., Physical Oceanography
DRENTH, W., Physical Organic Chemistry
DROOGER, C. W., Stratigraphy and Palaeontology
DUISTERMAAT, J. J., Pure and Applied Mathematics
ECKHAUS, W., Mathematics
ENDT, P. M., Experimental Physics
ENGELMANN, F. A. O., Theoretical Physics
GENDEREN, H. VAN, Biological Toxicology
GEURTS, J. P. M., Philosophy
GOOL, W. VAN, Inorganic Chemistry
GROENEWEGE, M. P., Chemistry
HAAN, P. G. DE, Microbiology
HAAS, G. DE, Biophysics
HARTMAN, P., Crystallography
HEIJST, A. N. P. VAN, Clinical Toxicology
HELBIG, K., Exploration Geophysics
HOOFT, G. 'T., Theoretical Physics
HOOGENBOOM, A. M., Experimental Physics
JAGER, C. DE, Space Research
KAMER, J. C. VAN DE, Zoology
KAMPEN, N. G. VAN, Theoretical Physics
KERK, G. J. M. VAN DER, Technical Organic Chemistry
KLUIVER, H. DE, Plasmaphysics
KUPERUS, M., Astrophysics
LEPPINK, G. J., Mathematical Statistics
LEVINE, Y. K., Biophysics
LINDENMAYER, A., Philosophy of Biology
MAES, R. A. A., Toxicology
MOORMANN, F. R., Geology
MOSTERT, P. J., Electrical Engineering
NELEMANS, F. A., Pharmacotherapy
NIEHAUS, A., Experimental Physics
NIEUWKOOP, P. D., Experimental Embryology
NIJBOER, B. R. A., Theoretical Physics
NOORDWIJK, K. J. VAN, Pharmacology
OORDT, P. G. W. J. VAN, Comparative Endocrinology
OORT, F., Pure Mathematics
OVERBEEK, J. TH. G., Physical Chemistry
PEERDEMAN, A. F., General Chemistry
PRIEM, H. N. A., Geo-chronology and Isotope Geology
RUYGROK, TH. W., Theoretical Physics and Mechanics
SALEMINK, C. A., Organic Chemistry
SCHARLOO, W., Genetics
SCHUILING, R. D., Geochemistry
SCHUURMANS, C. J. E., Meteorology
SENS, J. C., Experimental Physics
SIMONS, TH. J., Meteorology
SLUIS, A. VAN DER, Numerical Mathematics
SNELDERS, H. A. M., History of Science
SOONS, J. B. J., Clinical Chemistry
SPRINGER, T. A., Mathematics
STAFLEU, F. A., Systematic Botany
STOFFERS, A. L., Botany
STUMPERS, F. L. H. M., Digital Signal-processing
TEX, E. DEN, Petrology, Mineralogy and Crystallography
TJON JOE GIN, J. A., Theoretical Physics
UBBINK, J. B., Philosophy of Science
VELDKAMP, F. D., Pure Mathematics
VELTMAN, M. J. G., Theoretical Physics
VERDONK, N. H., General Veterinary Medicine
VERHEYEN, F. J., Comparative Physiology
VERHOEFF, K., Plant Pathology
VLAAR, N. J., Geophysics
VOLGER, J., Physical Measurement
VOORMA, H. O., Molecular Biology
VRIJ, A., Physical Chemistry
WIJN, H. W. DE, Solid State Physics
ZANDEE, D. I., Chemical Physiology of the Animal
ZONNEVELD, J. I. S., Physical Geography
ZWART, H. J., Structural Geology

Faculty of Arts:

ALINEI, M. L., Italian
ALVAREZ PÉREZ, G. E., Spanish Language and Literature
BETSKY, S., American Literature
BODEWITZ, H. W., Sanskrit and Indo-European
BOOGMAN, J. C., Modern History
COHEN, A., English Language

DITTRICH, Z. R., History of Eastern Europe
DUNK, H. W. VON DER, 20th Century History
ELDERS, W. I. M., History of Music
FLOTHUIS, M. H., Musicology
GERRITSEN, W. P., Dutch Medieval Literature
HERRLITZ, W., German Literature
HOFMAN, H. F., Turkish
HUGENHOLTZ, F. W. N., Medieval History
HUISMAN, J. A., Comparative German Philology
JONGH, E. S. DE, History of Art, Iconology
KOHLBRUGGE, Miss D. J., Persian Language
KÜPPER, P. M. PH., Modern German Literature
LEEUWE, H. J. J. DE, Theatre Science
MAATJE, F. C., Literature
MEYER, J. M., Russian
MIEDEMA, H. T. J., Frisian
NELSON, H. L. W., Latin
OVERSTEEGEN, J. J., Theory of Literature
PLESSEN, J. J. M., French Literature
REININK, A. W., History of Architectural Art
REZNICEK, E. K. J., History of Art after 1200
RIJK, L. M. DE, History of Philosophy
SALOMONSON, J. W., Archaeology
SCHULTINK, H., Linguistics
SÖTEMANN, A. L., Modern Dutch Literature
SPITS, F. C., Military History
TIJN, TH. VAN, Economic and Social History
VERWERS, G. J., Prehistory
VERHOEFF, A., English Literature
WAALS, J.-D. VAN DER, Cultural Prehistory
WALLINGA, H. T., Ancient History
ZWANENBURG, W., French

Faculty of Veterinary Medicine:

BEKKUM, J. G. VAN, Virology
BERGH, S. G. VAN DEN, Veterinary Biochemistry
BOIS, C. H. W. DE, Gynaecology and Obstetrics
BOUW, J., Zootechnics
BRAND, A., Herd Health Department
FRIK, J. F., Veterinary Bacteriology
GENDEREN, H. VAN, Veterinary Pharmacology and Biological Toxicology
HORZINEK, M. C., Virology
HUISMAN, G. H., Veterinary Physiology
HOETINK, H., Cultural Anthropology
KLOOSTER, A. TH. VAN'T, Animal Nutrition
KROL, B., Meat and Dairy Technology
LOGTESTIJN, J. G. VAN, Nutrition of animal origin
MOSSEL, D. A. A., Nutrition of animal origin
MOUWEN, J. M. V. M., Animal Pathology
NUMANS, S. R., Veterinary Surgery
RIJNBERK, A., Medicine of Small Domestic Animals
SWIERSTRA, D., Parasitology
VOOGD VAN DER STRAATEN, W. A. DE, Cytology, Histology and Microscopical Anatomy
WAGENAAR, G., Clinical Veterinary Medicine
WENSING, C. J. G., Veterinary Anatomy and Embryology
WENSVOORT, P., Veterinary Pathology
ZWART, P., Tropical Diseases

Faculty of Social Sciences:

BECKER, H. A., Sociology
BONARIUS, J. C. J., Differential Psychology
BRENNER, Y. S., Economics
DENGERINK, J. D., Reformation Theology
DIJKHUIS, J. H., Clinical Psychology
GROENMAN, SJ., Sociology of Building and Environment
HAZEWINKEL, A., Applied Social Psychology
HESSEN, J. S. VAN, Sociology
HINDERINK, J., Social Geography of Developing Countries
HOMMES, E. W., Sociology
JOHNSON, M. U., Parapsychology
KOEMAN, C., Cartography
KOK, J. F. W., Psychology
LUBBERS, R., Pedagogics
MANSFELD, J., History of Ancient Philosophy
MEIDEN, A. VAN DER, Theory of Public Relations
MOSSEL, R. S., Didactics
PARREREN, C. F. VAN, Psychology
PRAAG, H. VAN, Parapsychology
RABBIE, J. M., Social Psychology
SCHUHMANN, K. J., History of Modern Philosophy
SIXMA, J., Education
SMIDT, M. DE, Social Geography of Industrial Urbanization
THODEN VAN VELZEN, H. U. E., Cultural Anthropology
THOENES, P., Sociology
WIPPLER, R., Theoretical Sociology
WIT, O. C., Social Pedagogics

LANDBOUWHOGESCHOOL
(Agricultural University)

SALVERDAPLEIN 10,
P.B. 9101,
6700 HB WAGENINGEN
Telephone: 08370-89111.
Telex: 45105.

Founded 1918.

President: Ir. P. VAN DER SCHANS.
Rector Magnificus: Prof. Dr. H. C. VAN DER PLAS.
Dean of the Faculty of Agriculture: Prof. Dr. Ir. J. SCHENK.
Secretary of the University: Ir. R. MARIS.
Librarian: Drs. G. G. VAN WIJK.

Number of teachers: 600, including 113 professors.
Number of students: 6,000.
Publications: *Mededelingen, Gids.*

PROFESSORS:

ADEMA, A. H., Air Pollution
ADRICHEM, P. W. M. VAN, General and Farm Animal Physiology
BAKKER, H., Animal Husbandry
BAN, A. W. VAN DEN, Extension Education
BENNEMA, J., Tropical Soil Science
BERGEIJK, J. VAN, Pedagogics and General Didactics
BIERHUIZEN, J. F., Horticulture
BIERSTEKER, K., General, Social and Tropical Hygiene
BOER IWEMA, S., Animal Nutrition
BOL, M. M. G. R., Forest Technique
BOLT, G. H., Soil Chemistry and Physics
BRUIN, S., Food Processing Engineering
BRUINSMA, J., Physiology of Plants
BRUIJN, P. J., Physics
BULDER, C. J. E. A., Industrial Microbiology
BURINGH, P., Tropical Pedology
BIJSTERBOSCH, B. H., Physical and Colloid Chemistry
COBBEN, R. H., Entomology
CONSTANDSE, A. K., Sociological Principles of Town Planning
CORSTEN, L. C. A., Mathematical Statistics
DEFARES, P. B., Social Psychology
DEKKER, J., Phytopathology
DIEST, A. VAN, Soil Fertility
DIRVEN, J. G. P., Grassland Husbandry
DOORENBOS, J., Horticulture
DUIN, R. H. VAN, Land Drainage and Land Development
DUSSELDORP, D. B. W. M. VAN, Development Planning
ELZAS, M. S., Computer Science
FERWERDA, J. D., Tropical Agriculture
FINDENEGG, G. R., Soil Fertility and Plant Nutrition
FLACH, M., Tropical Crops
FOHR, P. G., Water Purification
FRANKE, A., Agricultural Economics of the Tropics
GROOT, Æ. DE, Organic Chemistry
HAAN, F. A. M. DE, Soil Pollution
HARTOG, C. DE, Hydrobiology
HAUTVAST, J. G. A. J., Nutrition
HELLINGA, F., Drainage and Improvement of the Soil
HERMSEN, J. G. TH., Plant Breeding
HOOGH, J. DE, Agricultural Economics
HORST, L., Irrigation
HUISMAN, E. A., Pisciculture and Fishery
JANSEN, F. P., Agricultural Economics of the Tropics and Sub-Tropics
JONG, J. D. DE, Geology
JONGE, N. M. DE, Landscape Architecture
KAMMEN, A. VAN, Molecular Biology
KAMPELMACHER, E. H., Food Microbiology and Food Hygiene
KAMPFRAATH, A. A., Industrial Economics and Management
KETELAARS, E. H., Poultry Husbandry
KLOMP, H., Animal Ecology
KOEMAN, J. H., Toxicology
KOOY, G. A., Family Sociology
KRAIJENHOFF VAN DE LEUR, D. A., Hydraulics, Catchment Hydrology and Soil Mechanics
KUIPERS, H., Tillage and Soil Dynamics
KUPERS, L. J. P., Arable Crop Cultivation
LAAN, P. VAN DER, Mathematical Statistics
LEEUWEN, H. VAN, Ecology of Habitat
LEGRO, R. A. H., Plant Taxonomy and Geography of Temperate Regions
LIER, H. N. VAN, Land and Water Use
LYKLEMA, J., Physical and Colloid Chemistry
MAAREN, A. VAN, Forest Economics
MEIJER, A. M. TH., Philosophy
MEIJER, E. R., Art History
MEULENBERG, M. T. G., Marketing and Market Research
MOENS, A., Agricultural Production Engineering
MOLEN, W. H. VAN DER, Agro-Hydrology
MULDER, E. G., General and Soil and Water Microbiology
MÜLLER, F., Biochemistry
NOORT, P. C. VAN DEN, Agricultural Economics
NOOIJ, A. TH. J., Methodology of Social Research
OLDEMAN, R. A. A., Forestry
OOSTERLEE, C. C., Animal Husbandry
OPPENOORTH, F. J., Mechanism of Action of Insecticides and Resistance
OSSE, J. W., General Zoology

PIERIK, R. L. M., Horticulture
PILNIK, W., Food Technology
PLAS, H. C. VAN DER, Organic Chemistry
PLAS, L. VAN DER, Geology
POEL, J. M. G. VAN DER, History of Agriculture
POLITIEK, R. D., Animal Husbandry
PONS, L. J., Regional Soil Science
PRESVELOU, Mrs. C., Home Economics
PRINS, A., Dairying
RIEMSDIJK, J. F. VAN, Farm Management and Organization
ROOTSELAAR, B. VAN, Mathematics
SCHAAFSMA, T. J., Molecular Physics
SCHENK, J., Physics, Meteorology and Climatology
SCHOONHOVEN, L. M., General and Comparative Animal Physiology
SNEEP, J., Plant Breeding
SNELDERS, H. A. M., History of Sciences
STAMHUIS, E., Civil Engineering
STORTENBEKER, C. W., Nature Conservation
STURMANS, F., Epidemiology
SYBENGA, J., Genetics
THOMAS-LYCKEMA À NIJEHOLT, Mrs. G., Social Mainstreams: Emancipation
THURLINGS, T. L. M., Economics
TIMMERMANS, Mrs. L. P. M., General Zoology
VEEGER, C., Biochemistry
VEEN, J. H. VAN DER, Genetics
VERVELDE, G. J., Arable Crops
VREDENBERG, W. J., Plant Physiology
VROOM, M. J., Landscape Architecture
WALSTRA, P., Dairying
WANT, J. P. H. VAN DER, Virology
WARTENA, L., Biometeorology
WELY, G. A. VAN, Surveying
WENT, J. L. VAN, Botany
WIEPKEMA, P. R., Ethology
WILDE, J. DE, Entomology
WILLEMSE, M. T. M., Botany
WIT, C. T. DE, Theoretical Crop Husbandry
WOUDE, A. M. VAN DER, Rural History
ZADOKS, J. C., Phytopathology
ZONDERWIJK, P., Weed Science

TECHNICAL UNIVERSITIES

TECHNISCHE HOGESCHOOL TE DELFT
(Delft University of Technology)

134 JULIANALAAN,
P.O.B. 5, DELFT
Telephone: 015-789111.

Founded 1842.

State control; Language of instruction: Dutch; Academic year: September to July.

Chairman of the University Council: Ir. K. M. VAN DER LAAN.

Chairman of the Executive Board: Drs. C. DE HART.

Rector Magnificus: Prof. Dr. Ir. F. J. KIEVITS.

Secretary: Drs. P. A. VUURENS.

Librarian: Dr. J. ZANDVLIET.

Library of *c.* 550,000 vols.

Number of teachers: 160 full-time professors.

Number of students: 10,000.

Publications: *Studiegids, Jaarboek* (annual report), *THD-Nieuws* (fortnightly magazine), *Quarterly Progress Report.*

CHAIRMEN OF DEPARTMENTS:

Department of General Science: Prof. Ir. D. H. WOLBERS.
Subdepartment of Philosophy and Humanities: Dr. A. H. C. M. WALRAVENS.
Subdepartment of Mathematics: Prof. Ir. D. H. WOLBERS.
Department of Civil Engineering: Ir. P. HAKKESTEEGT.
Department of Geodesy: Prof. Dr. Ir. M. J. M. BOGAERTS.
Department of Architecture: Dr. Ir. H. PRIEMUS.
Department of Mechanical Engineering: Prof. Ir. A. L. STOLK.
Department of Electrical Engineering: Prof. Dr. Ir. S. MIDDELHOEK.
Department of Chemical Engineering and Chemistry: Prof. Dr. Ir. N. W. F. KOSSEN.
Department of Mining Engineering: Ir. M. G. ATJAK.
Department of Applied Physics: Prof. Dr. Ir. J. J. J. KOKKEDEE.
Interdisciplinary Department of Industrial Design: Prof. Ir. B. M. SCHIERBEEK.
Department of Naval Architecture, Shipbuilding and Marine Engineering: Prof. Dr. Ir. R. WERELDSMA.
Department of Aeronautical and Aerospace Engineering: Ir. J. A. GHESEL GROTHE.
Interdisciplinary Department of Metals Science and Technology: Prof. Dr. Ir. B. M. KOREVAAR.

PROFESSORS:

Department of General Science:
AARTS, J. M., Mathematics
BOS, G. G. J., Economics
DEKKER, L., Computer Science Hybrid Systems
DOORMAN, S. J., Philosophy
DUPARC, H. J. A., Mathematics
DIJKMAN, J. G., Mathematics
GRAAF, M. H. K. VAN DER, Industrial Psychology
HERSCHBERG, I. S., Computer Science
LOMBAERS, H. J. M., Industrial Dynamics
LOONSTRA, F., Mathematics
LOOTSMA, F. A., Operational Analysis
MALOTAUX, P. CH. A., Industrial Organization
MEIJER, H. G., Mathematics
PELETIER, L. A., Mathematical Physics
POEL, W. L. VAN DER, Computer Science
POLL, E. H. VAN DE, Transportation Engineering
SCHEFFER, C. L., Probability Theory
SIEBEN, J. W., Statistics
SIKKEMA, P. C., Mathematics
WESSELING, P., Numerical Analysis
WOLBERS, J. H., Computer Science

Department of Civil Engineering:
AGEMA, J. F., Hydraulic Engineering
BIJKER, E. W., Coastal Engineering
BOUMA, A. L., Engineering Mechanics
BRUGGELING, A. S. G., Concrete Structures
DAM, J. C. VAN, Hydrology
DOUWEN, A. A. VAN, Steel Structures
HAFERLAND, F., Structural Engineering
HUISMAN, L., Environmental Engineering
JOSSELIN DE JONG, G. DE, Soil Mechanics and Engineering Mechanics
LOHUIZEN H. P. S. VAN, Civil Engineering
POLL, E. H. VAN DE, Traffic Engineering
PÖPEL, H. H., Enviromental Engineering
SCHOEMAKER, H. J., Irrigation
SCHÖNFELD, J. CH., Pure and Applied Mechanics
VELDE, P. A. VAN DE, Hydraulic Engineering
VERHOEVEN, A. C., Civil Engineering Constructions
VERRUIJT, A., Mechanics
VOLMULLER, J., Traffic Science and Engineering
VRIES, M. DE, Fluid Mechanics
WAGENMAKER, H. J., Building Construction Management
WIGGERTS, H., Physical Planning
WITTMAN, F. H., Materials Science

Department of Geodetics:
BAARDA, W., Geodetics
BOGAERTS, M. J. M., Land Information Systems

Department of Architecture:
BOLLEREY, F., History of Urbanization
DICKE, D., Strength of materials
DREWE, P., Urban Design
FALUDI, A., Urban Planning Theory
GOUT, M., Building Methodology and Construction
HEIMANS, A., Urban Design
KRANENDONK, A. VAN, Architectural Design
KRUYT, C. S., Sociology
MAAS, F. M., Landscape Architecture
MOOS, S. VON, History of Art and Architecture
OOSTERHOFF, J., Structural Engineering
PENNINK, P. K. A., Architectural Design
PRAK, N. L., Basic Design
PRIEMUS, H., Public Housing
RANDEN, A. VAN, Building Methodology and Construction
STERENBERG, J. J., Architectural Design
TEMMINCK GROLL, C. L., Architectural Design and Restoration
WEEBER, C. J. M., Architectural Design
WESSEL, J., Public Administration

Department of Mechanical Engineering:
BESSELING, J. F., Engineering Mechanics
BLOK, H., Machine Elements
BOEKE, A. W., Air conditioning
BOITEN, R. G., Measurements and Control Engineering
BOSCH, H., Production Engineering and Management
BURGT, G. J. VAN DER, Automobile Engineering
CLERQ, H. LE, Mechanical Engineering

Eldik Thieme, H. C. A. van, Vehicle Engineering
Harten, K. van, Fibre Engineering
Imbach, H. E., Turbo Machines
In 't Veld, J., Industrial Organization
Jong, D. de, Precision Engineering
Jong, E. J. de, Chemical Engineering Equipment
Koning, J. de, Earth-moving Equipment
Latzko, D. G. H., Mechanical Engineering (nuclear power)
Lekkerkerke, J. G., Engineering Mechanics
Lier, J. J. C. van, Steam-power Engineering
Meeuse, G. C., Transportation Systems Engineering
Merk, H. J., Aero and Hydrodynamics
Meyers, P., Engineering Mechanics
Ooms, G., Aero- and Hydrodynamics
Pater, A. D. de, Engineering Mechanics
Pekelharing, A. J., Workshop Technology
Prins, G., Mechanical Handling Equipment
Ranckers, H., Industrial Production Mechanics
Reyers, L. N., Numerical Controlled Machine Tools
Stassen, H. G., Man-Machine Systems
Stolk, A. L., Refrigeration Engineering
Stuart Mitchell, R. W., Gas Turbines and Combustion Engineering
Zuiderweg, F. J., Chemical Engineering

Department of Electrical Engineering:
Boerema, H. B., Electrical Power Supply
Bordewijk, J. L., Transmission of Information
Boxma, Y., Information and Communication Theory
Burg, F. A. W. van den, Dynamic of Electrical Machines
Davidse, J., Electronics
Deleroi, W., Network Theory
Dewilde, P. M., Network Theory
Goor, A. J. van der, Switching Theory and Design of Information Processing Machines
Heijn, F. A., High Voltage Engineering
Hoop, A. T. de, Electromagnetic Theory
Kroes, J. L. de, Automatic Traffic Systems
Krul, L., Microwave Technology
Middelhoek, S., Solid State Physics
Nauta Lemke, H. R. van, Control Engineering
Poorter, T., Electronics
Schwarz, F. C., Power Electronics

Department of Chemistry and Chemical Engineering:
Bekkum, H., van, Organic Chemistry
Berends, W., Biochemistry
Berg, P. J. van den, Chemical Engineering
Beijerman, H. C., Organic Chemistry
Diepen, G. A. M., General and Inorganic Chemistry
Hende, J. H. van den, Automation of Instrumental Chemical Analysis
Houtman, J. P. W., Chemical Aspects of Nuclear Reactors
Jong, W. A. de, Chemical Engineering
Kossen, N. W. F., Chemical Technology
Meijering, J. L., Inorganic Chemistry
Radelaar, S., Thermo-dynamics and Solid State Physics
Reijen, L. L. van, Physical Chemistry
Schenck, P. A., General Chemistry
Smith, J. M., Physical Transport Phenomena
Wepster, B. M., Theoretical Organic Chemistry

Department of Mining Engineering:
Koefoed, O., Geophysics
Roorda, H. J., Mineral Dressing
Uytenbogaardt, W., Geology
Velzeboer, P. Th., Mining Engineering

Department of Applied Physics:
Berkhout, A. J., Applied Acoustics
Frankena, H. J., Optics
Hoogendoorn, C. J., Heat Transport Phenomena
Kokkedee, J. J. J., Theoretical Physics
Le Poole, J. B., Electron Optics
Leeuwen, J. M. J. van, Theoretical Physics
Loef, J. J. van, Radiation Physics
Postma, H., Low Temperature Physics
Smidt, J., Nuclear and Magnetic Resonance
Smith, J. M., Physical Transport Phenomena
Veltman, B. P. Th., Theoretical Physics, Signal Processing
Verhagen, C. J. D. M., Systems Engineering—Measuring and Pattern Recognition
Westerdijk, J. B., Infra-red Techniques
Wolff, P. M. de, Crystal Physics

Department of Naval Architecture, Shipbuilding and Marine Engineering:
Gallin, C., Ship Design
Gerritsma, J., Ship Hydrodynamics
Wereldsma, R., Strength of Ship Constructions

Department of Aeronautical and Aerospace Engineering:
Arbocz, I., Aircraft Construction
Erdmann, S. F. A. H. P., Aerodynamics
Gerlach, O. H., Flight Mechanics, Stability and Control
Ingen, J. L. van, Aerodynamics
Schijve, J., Aircraft Construction and Materials
Spies, G. J., Aircraft Design
Steketee, J. A., Aerodynamics
Wittenberg, H., Aircraft Design and Flight Mechanics

Interdisciplinary Department of Metals Science and Technology:
Geerlings, H. G., Welding Technology
Jongenburger, P., Materials Science
Kievits, F. J., Applied Metallurgy
Korevaar, B. M., Metallurgy
Penning, P., Solid State Physics

Interdisciplinary Department of Industrial Design:
Dirken, J. M., Industrial Design
Schierbeek, B. B., Industrial Design
Truijen, E. A. H., Industrial Design

TECHNISCHE HOGESCHOOL EINDHOVEN
(Eindhoven University of Technology)

DEN DOLECH 2,
POSTBUS 513, 5600 MB
EINDHOVEN

Telephone: 040-47-91-11.

Founded 1956.

State control; Language of instruction: Dutch; Academic year: September to August.

Chairman of the Board of Governors: Drs. H. J. ter Heege.
Secretary: Drs. P. J. Krens.
Rector Magnificus: Ir. J. Erkelens.
Chairman of the University Council: Mr. P.J. G. J. Notermans.
Information Officer: J. F. M. van Dongen.
Librarian: Drs. P. J. C. A. Pinxter.

Number of teachers: 125 professors.
Number of students: 4,500.

Publications: *Wetenschappelijk verslag, Jaarverslag, Gids, T.H.-Berichten.*

Deans:

Department of General Science: Prof. Dr. J. Wemelsfelder.
Department of Mathematics: Prof. Dr. S. T. M. Ackermans.
Department of Industrial Engineering: Prof. Ir. W. M. J. Geraerds.
Department of Physics: Prof. Dr. O. J. Poppema.
Department of Mechanical Engineering: Prof. Ir. W. L. Esmeijer.
Department of Electrical Engineering: Prof. Dr. H. Groendijk.
Department of Chemical Engineering: Prof. Dr. G. D. Rieck.
Department of Architecture, Housing and Building Construction: Prof. Dr. Ir. M. F. Th. Bax.

Professors:

Department of General Science:
Bakker, J. J. M., Applied Philology
Groen, M., Pedagogy, Adolescent Psychology and General Education
Houten, B. C. van, Sociology
Kwee, S. L., Philosophy
Meuwese, W. A. T., Social Psychology
Steenkamp, P. A. J. M., Social History
Wemelsfelder, J., Economics

Department of Mathematics:
Ackermans, S. T. M., Mathematics
Alblas, J. B., Mechanics
Benders, J. F., Mathematics
Boersma, J., Mathematics
Bruijn, N. G. de, Mathematics
Cijsouw, P. L., Mathematics
Doornbos, R., Mathematics
Graaf, J. de, Mathematics
Hautus, M. L. J., Mathematics
Lint, J. H. van, Mathematics
Lunbeck, R. J., Computer Science
Meiden, W. van der, Mathematics
Peremans, W., Mathematics
Rem, M., Mathematics
Schurer, F., Mathematics
Seidel, J. J., Mathematics
Simons, F. H., Mathematics
Steutel, F. W. Accounting and Statistics
Veltkamp, G. W., Mathematics
Wessels, J., Mathematics

Department of Technical Physics:
Broer, L. J F., Theoretical Physics
Gijsman, H. M., Physics
Hagedoorn, H. L., Applied Nuclear Physics
Jonge, W. J. M. de, Solid State Physics
Maesen, F. van der, Physics
Poppema, O. J., Physics and Nuclear Physics
Poulis, J. A., Physics: Analysis of Physical Measurements
Rademaker, O., Process Control
Schram, D. C., Technical Physics
Schram, P. P. J. M., Physical Transport Phenomena
Sluijter, F. W., Theoretical Physics
Steenland, M. J., Physics

Steller, J. Ph., Technical Education in Physics
Verhaar, B. J., Theoretical Physics
Vossers, G., Hydro- and Aerodynamics
Vries, D. A. de, General Physics and Heat Transfer

Industrial Engineering Department:

Bagchus, P. M., Organizational Social Psychology
Beer, C. de, Industrial and Mechanical Engineering
Bemelmans, Th. M. A., Control Information Systems and Automation
Botter, C. H. V. A., Industrial Engineering
Daniëls, M. J. M., Industrial Engineering, Psychology and its Application in Industry
Enden, C. van der, Management Accounting
Feitsma, H., Organization Theory and History
Geraerds, W. M. J., Production Planning and Management
Monhemius, W., Operational Research in Industrial Engineering
Mulder, F. A., Production Organization
Sanders, P. G., Statistics
Sitter, L. U. de, Comparative Analysis of Production Systems
Tilanus, C. B., Quantitative Economic Methods

Mechanical Engineering Department:

Balkestein, J. G., Mechanical Engineering Design and Technical Management
Erkelens, J., Industrial Mechanization
Esmeijer, W. L., Engineering Mechanics
Janssen, J. D., Engineering Mechanics
Klostermann, J. A., Materials Science
Koning, J., Measurement
Koppen, C. W. J. van, Heat Technology
Koumans, W. A., Transport Research
Mooren, A. L., van der, General Engineering Mechanics
Nieuwenhuizen, J. K., Plant and Equipment for the Process Industry
Schlösser, W. M. J., Mechanical Design
Schouten, M. J. W., Mechanical Engineering
Veenstra, P. C., Production Engineering
Vollenhoven, J. van, Internal Combustion Engines
Wolf, A. C. H. van der, Production Engineering
Zaat, J. H., Physical Metallurgy

Electrical Engineering Department:

Arnback, J., Telecommunications
Beneken, J. E. W., Measurement and Control
Butterweck, H. J., Theoretical Electrical Engineering
Eykhoff, P., Measurement and Control
Groendijk, H., Electronics
Heetman, A., Telecommunications—Data Processing Techniques
Heuvel, W. M. C. van den, Electrotechnics
Hooge, F. N., Electrical Material Science
Jess, J., Electronics
Kleinpenning, T. G. M., Materials Science
Kooy, C., Theoretical Electrotechnics
Kylstra, F. J., Measurement and Control
Laan, P. T. van der, Apparatus and Systems for Electrical Energy Supply
Niesten, J. G., Electronics
Plaats, J. van der, Telecommunications
Rietjens, L. H. T., Direct Energy Conversion
Schalkwijk, J. P. M., Telecommunications
Schot, J. A., Electrical Mechanics
Weenink, M. P. H., Theoretical Electrical Engineering

Chemical Engineering Department:

Baan, H. S. van der, Chemical Technology
Barendrecht, E., Electrochemistry
Buck, H. M., Physical Organic Chemistry
Cramers, C. A. M. G., Instrumental Analysis
Everaerts, F. M., Analytical Methods
German, A. L., Substance Technology
Godefroi, E. F., Organic Chemistry
Heikens, D., Chemical Technology
Hooff, J. H. C. van, Inorganic Chemistry
Metselaar, R., Physical Chemistry
Prins, R., Inorganic Chemistry
Rieck, G. D., Physical Chemistry
Stein, H. N., General Chemistry
Tels, M., Physical Technology
Thoenes, D., Physical Technology

Department of Architecture, Housing and Building:

Bax, M. F. Th., Architectural Design
Fassbinder-Hörr, H., Urban Renovation
Goudappel, H. M., Urban Planning and Design
Huisman, W., Structural Design
Kamerling, J. W., Structural Design
Kreijger, P. C., Building Materials
Lange, P. A. de, Building Construction
Neste, J. A. van, Structural Design
Schmid, P., Building Construction
Sikkel, L. P., Building Operations
Slebos, D., Architectural Design
Slothouber, G. J., Geometry
Vlugt, B. W. van der, Structural Design
Vorenkamp, J., Physical Engineering in Relation to Building Design

TECHNISCHE HOGESCHOOL TWENTE
(Twente University of Technology)

ENSCHEDE, P.O.B. 217
Telephone: 899111.
Founded 1961.

Rector: Prof. Dr. H. van den Kroonenberg.

Board of Governors: Drs. E. Bolle, Dr. W. S. Hulscher, J. Thomas, Prof. H. van den Kroonenberg, Mr. C. van Lookeren Campagne.

Registrar: J. C. N. Schrijver.

Librarian: Mr. G. A. Hamel.

Number of students: 2,750.

Chairmen of Departments:

Mechanical Engineering: Prof. Ir. W. Drayer.

Electrical Engineering: Prof. Ir. D. Bosman.

Chemical Technology: Prof. Dr. J. Schuyer.

Technical Physics: Prof. Dr. L. C. van der Marel.

Applied Mathematics: Prof. Dr. H. Kwakernaak.

Social Sciences and Philosophy: Dr. P. Boskma.

Business Administration: Dr. H. C. J. G. Janssen.

Public Administration: D. W. P. Ruiter.

Professors:

Bakker, Dr. Ir. W., Production Organization
Bantjes, Dr. A., Macromolecular Materials Technology
Berg, Ir. C. van den, Process Equipment
Blaauw, Dr. G. A., Digital Techniques
Bosma, Ir. R., Tribology
Bosman, Ir. D., Measurement and Instrumentation
Braam, Dr. G. P. O., General Sociology
Breedveld, Ir. M. P., Electronics
Burggraaf, Dr. Ir. A. J., Science and Technology of Inorganic Materials
Caspers, Dr. W. J., Theoretical Physics
Dahmen, Dr. Ir. E. A. M. F., Analytical Chemistry
Draijer, Ir. W., Industrial Heat Science
Duijvestijn, Dr. Ir. A. J. W., Pure and Applied Mathematics
Feil, Dr. D., Chemical Physics
Gellings, Dr. P. J., Inorganic Chemistry and Science of Materials
Gröneveld, Ir. E. W., Information and Communication Theory
Groot Wassink, Ir. J., Process Engineering
Halbertsma, Ir. K. T. A., Project Organization and Management
Hanken, A. T. G., System Theory
Hasselt, Ir. R. van, Production Engineering
Herrmann, Dr. Ing. D. E., Network Theory
Hessel, Dr. W., Economics
Hoesel, Dr. A. F. G. van, Industrial Psychology
Hoogerwerf, Dr. A., Management Processes in Public Administration
Hulshof, Drs. A. H., Organization Theory
Ingen Housz, Ir. J. F., Metal Forming Plastics Technology
Janssen, Ir. J. M. L., Operational Methods in Management
Jonker, Dr. G. H., Science of Materials
Jonkers, Ir. C. O., Materials Handling Engineering
Kals, Dr. Ir. H. J. J., Production Engineering
Kok, A., Communications
Kreiken, Dr. J., Business Administration and Management Economics
Kroonenberg, Dr. Ir. H. H. van den, Design and Construction
Kwakernaak, Dr. Ir. H., Stochastic Mathematical Physics
Marel, L. C. van der, Technical Physics
Memelink, Ir. O. W., Solid State Electronics
Muller, Ir. C. A., Microwave Technology
Nawijn, Dr. Ir. A., Light Engineering
Noordenbos, Ir. P. K., Mechanization and Automation
Nottrot, Dr. R., Mathematical Physics
Offereins, Ir. R. P. Cybernetics
Pater, Ir. C. de, Mechanical Technology
Pool, Dr. J. A. van der, Industrial Systems
Reinhoudt, Dr. Ir. D. N., Organic Chemistry
Rijken, Ir. A., Industiral Plant Techniques

RIJNSDORP, Ir. J. E., Process Dynamics
RODENBURG, Ir. C., Electronics
RUITER, Dr. D. W. P., Industrial Law
SCHRAMEL, I. J., Communications
SCHUIJER, Dr. J., Macromolecular Chemistry and Technology
SMOLDERS, Dr. C. A., Chemistry
SPARNAAIJ, Dr. M. J., Solid State Physics
SPIEGEL, Dr. I. W. VAN, Pure and Applied Mathematics
SWAAIJ, W. P. M. VAN, Chemical Reaction Engineering
TERPSTRA, Dr. T. J., Pure and Applied Mathematics
VELDE, Dr. E. VAN DER, General Philosophy
VERBEEK, Dr. L. A. M., Information Technology
VERBRAAK, Dr. Ir. C. A., Science of Materials
WALLEN MIJNLIEFF, Dr. P. VAN DER, Transport Phenomena
WARRIES, E., General and Comparative Education
WESTERTERP, Dr. Ir. K. R., Industrial Processes
WETTERLING, Dr. W., Mathematics
WIJNGAARDEN, Dr. Ir. L. VAN, Fluid Mechanics and Heat Transfer
WINTER, Ir. H. G. DE, Technical Physics
WITTEMAN, Dr. Ir. W. J., Quantum-Optics
ZANDBERGEN, Dr. Ir. P. J., Mathematics
ZUTHEM, Dr. H. J. VAN, Industrial Sociology

COLLEGES OF UNIVERSITY STANDING

INSTITUTE OF SOCIAL STUDIES

2597 JR THE HAGUE,
BADHUISWEG 251

Telephone: 70-572201.

Telex: 31491.

Founded 1952.

Language of instruction: English.

Rector: Prof. L. EMMERIJ.
Secretary: A. G. HEYNING.
Director: F. KOOPMAN.

Library of *c.* 22,000 vols.
Number of teachers: 56.
Number of students: *c.* 200.

Publications: *Development and Change* (quarterly), *Research Reports*†, *Occasional Papers*† (irregular).

Master's degree in development studies (courses structured so as to offer a wide choice and variety of specializations), and diploma programmes in development planning techniques, international relations and development, rural and agricultural project planning, state enterprise in economic development, international law and development.

HOGESCHOOL TE TILBURG
(Tilburg University)

HOGESCHOOLLAAN 225,
P.O.B. 90153, 5000 LE TILBURG

Telephone: 013-669111.

Founded 1927.

State control; Academic year: September to August.

Chancellor: Drs. J. B. L. VERSTER.
Rector: Prof. J. E. A. M. VAN DYCK.
Administrative Officer: Drs. H. J. M. HOPMAN.
Librarian: Dr. J. WIEERS.

Number of teachers: 85.
Number of students: 4,000.

Publication: *Tilburgs Hogeschoolblad* (weekly).

DEANS:

Faculty of Economics: Prof. Dr. R. BANNINK.
Faculty of Econometrics: Prof. Dr. B. B. VAN DER GENUGTEN.
Faculty of Social Science: Prof. Dr. J. H. G. SEGERS.
Faculty of Law: Prof. J. P. A. COOPMANS.
Faculty of Psychology: Prof. Dr. J. M. VAN MEEL.
Faculty of Theology: Prof. Dr. A. H. SMITS.

PROFESSORS:

Faculty of Economics:

ALTING VON GEUSAU, Dr. F. A. M., International Law
BANNINK, R., Managerial Economics
BELKUM, Dr. J. W. VAN, Accountancy
BOSMAN, H. W. J., Banking and Finance
DALMULDER, J. J. J., Econometrics, Statistics
DIJCK, J. E. A. M. VAN, Fiscal Law
GENUGTEN, B. B. VAN DER, Econometrics
GOLDSCHMIDT, H. O., Managerial Economics
JANSSEN, L. H., Underdeveloped Areas
JONG, S. E. DE, Managerial Economics
KLUNDERT, TH. C. M. J. VAN DE, Economics
KOLNAAR, A. H. J., Economics
KRIENS, J., Econometrics
MOLENAAR, F., Civil Law and Commercial Law
NIELEN, G. C., Informatics
PLATTEL, M. G., Social Philosophy
REYNAERTS, W. H. J., Industrial Relations
SCHOUTEN, D. B. J., Economics
STEVERS, TH. A., Public Finance
STORM, C. M., Management Economics
TIEMSTRA, N., Managerial Economics
VEEN, P. VAN, Economics
VERHEYEN, P. A., Econometrics
VRIES, J. DE, Economic History

Faculty of Social Science

ARNTZ, J., Philosophy
BERTHOLET, C., Sociology of Underdeveloped Areas
DIJCK, J. J. J. VAN, Industrial Sociology
EERENBEEMT, H. F. J. M. VAN DEN, History
GRUNFELD, F., Town and Country Planning
MOOR, R. A. DE, Sociology of Education
SEGERS, J., Methods of Sociological Research
STALPERS, J. A., Social Studies
ZIJDERVELD, A. C., Sociology

Faculty of Law:

BURG, F. H. VAN DER, Constitutional Administrative Law
COOPMANS, J. P. A., General Introduction to Law
DEELEN, J. E. J. TH., Private International, Comparative, Civil and Commercial Law
FRENKEL, B. S., Labour Law
GEPPAART, CH. P. A., Tax Law
JEUKENS, H. J. M., Constitutional Law
NIEBOER, W., Criminal Law and Law of Criminal Procedure
LÖWENSTEYN, F. W. J., Civil and Commercial Law
OLDE KALTER, A. L., History of Roman Law
SCHOORDIJK, H. C. F., Civil, Commercial and Private International Law
SMULDERS, A. A. J., Economics
WIELAND, J. H., Philosophy and Philosophy of Law

Faculty of Psychology:

BRUNIA, C. H. M., Physiology and Physiological Psychology
DOOREN, F. J. P. VAN, Social Psychology, Organizational Psychology
HETTEMA, P. J., Personalities and Psycho-Diagnostics
KLERK, L. F. W. DE, Instructional Psychology
MEEL, J. M. VAN, Developmental Psychology
MOOR, W. DE, Clinical Psychology and Psychotherapy
PEETERS, H. F. M., Historical Psychology
STOUTHARD, PH. C., Statistics
VELDHOVEN, G. M. VAN, Economic Psychology
WILLEMS, P. J., Experimental Psychology and Human Engineering

Faculty of Theology:

BERGER, H. H., Philosophy
BORNEWASSER, J. A., Church History
BOUWMAN, G., New Testament Exegesis
GODDIJN, W., Sociology of Religion
LESCRAUWAET, J. F., Dogmatic Theology
LUIJPEN, W. A. M., Philosophy of Culture
POULSSEN, N. R. M., Old Testament
RIJEN, A. C. VAN, Moral Theology
SMITS, A. H., Dogmatic Theology

ATTACHED INSTITUTES:

Economic Institute Tilburg: Dir. Prof. Dr. R. BANNINK.

Fiscal Institute Tilburg: Dir. Prof. Dr. TH. A. STEVERS.

Institute for Social Research: Dir. Dr. I. SNELLEN.

Institute for Public Health: Dir. Dr. I. SNELLEN.

Development Research Institute: Dir. Drs. B. H. EVERS.

John F. Kennedy Institute: Dir. Prof. Jhr. Dr. F. A. M. ALTING VON GEUSAU.

STICHTING NIJENRODE INSTITUUT VOOR BEDRIJFSKUNDE (Netherlands School of Business)

STRAATWEG 25,
3621 BG BREUKELEN
Telephone: 03462-1944.
Founded 1946.

Government-maintained.

Rector: Dr. E. B. J. POSTMA.

Director of Administration: J. P. C. BEERMAN.

Director of Studies: Dr. C. M. A. VAN DEN OUDENRIJN.

Dean of Students: Drs. A. A. MOLIER.

Librarian: Drs. J. S. MACKENZIE OWEN.

Number of teachers: 39.
Number of students: 400.

Publications: *Informatiebladen, Gids*†.

HEADS OF DEPARTMENTS:

Economics: Dr. H. W. DE JONG.

Liberal Sciences: Dr. J. A. KOLKHUIS TANKE.

Modern Languages: J. M. NOIRET.

Physical Education: Dr. E. H. TAN.

THEOLOGISCHE HOGESCHOOL VAN DE GEREFORMEERDE KERKEN (Theological College of the Reformed Churches)

BROEDERWEG 15, KAMPEN
Telephone: 05202-12878.
Founded 1854.

President of Curators: Rev. H. BOUMA.

Rector: Prof. Dr. C. TRIMP.

Secretary of the Senate: Prof. Drs. D. DEDDENS.

Librarian: Prof. Drs. J. P. LETTINGA.

PROFESSORS:

BRUGGEN, Dr. J. VAN, New Testament Exegesis

DEDDENS, D., Church History and Polity

DOUMA, Dr. J., Ethics, Encyclopaedia of Theology

KAMPHUIS, J., Dogmatics, History of Dogma

LETTINGA, Drs. J. P., Semitic Languages

SCHILDER, Drs. H. J., Old Testament Exegesis

TRIMP, Dr. C., Pastoral Theology

SCHOOLS OF ART AND MUSIC

Academie van Beeldende Kunsten Rotterdam (*Rotterdam Academy of Art*): G. J. de Jonghweg 4, Rotterdam 3002; f. 1773 to develop talent in art and design; 80 mems.; library of 3,500 vols.; Pres. J. VAN OLDENBORGH; Principal N. BARENDREGT.

Academie van Bouwkunst Rotterdam (*Rotterdam Academy of Architecture*): Bospolderplein 16, Rotterdam; f. 1965; library of 5,200 vols.; 170 students; Dir. Ir. F. J. SMITS; Sec. G. VAN KRUISTUM.

Academie voor Beeldende Kunsten St. Joost (*St. Joost Academy of Art and Design*): St. Janstraat 18, Breda; f. 1945; Dir. J. PEETERS.

Akademie van Bouwkunst (*Academy of Architecture*): Waterlooplein 67, 1011 PB Amsterdam; f. 1908; Pres. Arch. J. VERSTER; Sec. Arch. H. W. HUBERS; Dir. Drs. U. F. HYLKEMA.

Akademie van Bouwkunst: Sonsbeekweg 22, 6814 BC Arnhem; Dir. Ir. A. VOS DE WAEL.

Akademie van Bouwkunst: Hoge der A 12, 9712 AC Groningen; f. 1966; Pres. Mr. J. VAN BODEGOM; Sec. Mr. Ir. P. BÜGEL.

Akademie van Bouwkunst: Capucijnenstraat 98, Maastricht.

Akademie van Bouwkunst: Voltstraat 60, 5021 SE Tilburg.

Akademie voor Beeldende Kunsten (*Academy of Art*): Onderlangs 9, Arnhem; Dir. J. SCHROFER.

Akademie voor Beeldende Kunsten "Akademie Minerva" (*Minerva Academy of Fine Arts*): Schoolholm 23, Groningen; f. 1798; courses in fine, commercial and decorative arts, fashion, pedagogics; 65 teachers, 460 students; Dir. Drs. A. VAN HIJUM; Secs. P. G. J. LEYDEKKERS, A. W. VEEN, P. KNOOPS.

Akademie voor Beeldende Kunst Enschede (*Academy of Fine Arts, Architecture and Design*): Enschede, 155 Roessinghsbleekweg; f. 1949; 46 teachers; Chair. Prof. W. DRAIJER; Sec. Dr. O. TER KUILE; Dir. Prof. J. L. M. HARDY.

Akademie Industriële Vormgeving Eindhoven (*Eindhoven Academy of Industrial Design*): Elzentlaan 20, P.B. 2125, 5600 CC Eindhoven; f. 1950; 50 teachers, 200 students; Dir. C. F. W. HOUTMAN.

Conservatorium Maastricht-Holland: Bonnefantenstraat 15, Maastricht; f. 1957; 125 teachers, 580 students; library of *c.* 16,000 vols.; Dir. W. HIJSTEK.

Koninklijk Conservatorium voor Muziek en Dans (*Royal Conservatory of Music and Dance*): The Hague, 7 Korte Beestenmarkt; f. 1826; 170 teachers, 735 students; library of 13,000 vols.; Dir. JAN VAN VLIJMEN; Co-Dirs. CHRISTIAAN TIMM and RENÉ VINCENT (Dance Department).

Koninklijke Academie van Beeldende Kunsten (*Royal Academy of Fine and Applied Arts*): The Hague, 4 Prinsessegracht; f. 1682; departments of painting, sculpture, monumental and environmental design, graphic and typographic design, textile design, interior decoration; Dir. J. J. BELJON.

Koninklijke Akademie voor Kunst en Vormgeving (*Royal Academy of Art and Design*): Pettelaarseweg 2, 's Hertogenbosch; f. 1812; courses in painting, sculpture, graphic art, ceramics, decorative art, fashion and publicity; 70 teachers, 400 students; Dir. A. C. P. VAN DEN BERG.

Rijksakademie van Beeldende Kunsten (*State Academy of Fine Arts*): P.O.B. 5508, 1007 AM Amsterdam; five-year courses; Dir. Prof. Dr. J. VAN RIEMSDIJK.

Rotterdams Conservatorium: Pieter de Hoochweg 122, Rotterdam; f. 1971; 130 teachers, 620 students; Dir. KEES STOLWIJK.

Stichting Sweelinck Conservatorium Amsterdam: Postbus 7168, 1007 JD Amsterdam; f. 1975; 200 teachers, 900 students; library of 30,000 vols.; Dir. JAN DE MAN; Pres. Drs. A. G. F. BOERSMA; Sec. Drs. G. W. K. VAN DER VALK BOUMAN.

Utrechts Conservatorium: Utrecht, Mariaplaats 28; f. 1947; 100 teachers, 415 students; library of 14,000 vols.; Dir. TON HARTSUIKER; Pres. Ir. L. C. VIËTOR; Sec. Ir. E. J. G. SCHEFFER.

NETHERLANDS ANTILLES

Population 246,000

LEARNED SOCIETIES AND RESEARCH INSTITUTES

Caraibisch Marien-Biologisch Instituut: Piscadera Baai, Curaçao; f. 1956; Pres. Dr. R. A. RÖMER; Dir. Dr. INGVAR KRISTENSEN; library of 3,000 vols.

Meteorologische Dienst van de Nederlandse Antillen (*Meteorological Service of the Netherlands Antilles*): Seru Mahuma z/n, Curaçao; f. 1950; Dir. C. F. REUDINK; publ. *Statistics of Meteorological Observations in Netherlands Antilles* (annual).

Veeartsenijkundige Dienst en Warenkeuring (*Veterinary Service and Food Inspection*): Post Box 85, Curaçao; administered by the Department of Public Health.

LIBRARIES

Openbare Leeszaal en Bibliotheek: Johan van Walbeeckplein 13, Willemstad, Curaçao; f. 1922; *c.* 100,000 vols.; local and Caribbean collection; public, children's, mobile and schools' library services, 2 branch libraries; Librarian Miss R. M. DE PAULA.

Openbare Leeszaal en Boekerij: Eilandgebied, Aruba; f. 1949; operates two public libraries, hospital and prison libraries and two bookmobiles on the island of Aruba; 75,000 vols.; library services, inter-library loans; Dir. Mrs. ALICE VAN ROMONDT.

Stichting Wetenschappelijke Bibliotheek (*Scientific Library Foundation*): Drukkerijstraat 4, Willemstad, Curaçao; f. 1950; all fields of pure and applied science; union catalogue of all non-fiction books in the Netherlands Antilles; Chief Librarian Miss MARITZA F. EUSTATIA; publ. *Annual Report, Curaçao Folklore, Curaçao Music, Nansi Stories.*

MUSEUM

Curaçao Museum: Otrabanda, Curaçao; housed in an old Dutch quarantine station, built 1853; paintings and historical exhibits.

UNIVERSITIES

UNIVERSIDAT DI ARUBA

ARUBA

Telephone: 2811.

Founded 1970.

President: Dr. CARLIN I. BROWNE.
Librarian: ANITA WALFENZAO.

Library contains 3,000 vols.

Number of teachers: 15.
Number of students: 150.

DEANS:

College of Liberal Arts and Sciences: Dr. J. MANSUR.
College of Business Administration: Dr. WILLY ACHEBE.
College of Languages: Dr. C. BROWNE.
College of Pre-profession Sciences: Dr. HOWARD B. HORNE.
College of Education: Dr. EDWARD BRYANT.

UNIVERSITY OF THE NETHERLANDS ANTILLES

P.O.B. 682, WILLEMSTAD, CURAÇAO

Founded 1970 at Institute of Higher Studies, university status 1979.

President: P. T. M. SPROCKEL.

Library of 70,000 vols.
Number of teachers: 62.
Number of students: 500.

Faculties of law, technical sciences, social and economic sciences.

MUSIC SCHOOLS

Aruba Public School of Music: Aruba; Government support.

Curaçao Public School of Music: Scharlooweg 5, Willemstad; Curaçao; f. 1960; *c.* 450 students; Dir. B. SMITS.

NEW ZEALAND

Population 3,095,000

LEARNED SOCIETIES

THE ROYAL SOCIETY OF NEW ZEALAND
BOX 12249, WELLINGTON
Founded 1867.

The Royal Society is the senior scientific institution of New Zealand. It has 43 branches and member bodies.

President: Dr. R. K. DELL, B.A., D.SC., F.M.A.N.Z., F.R.S.N.Z.

Executive Officer: A. W. F. THYNNE.

Publications: *Journal of the Royal Society of New Zealand*†, *Bulletins*.

Branches at Auckland, Canterbury, Hawke's Bay, Manawatu, Nelson, Otago, Rotorua and Wellington.

MEMBER BODIES:

Auckland Institute and Museum: (*see* under Museums).

New Zealand Ecological Society (Inc.): P.O.B. 31007, Christchurch; 494 mems.; Sec. J. P. PARKES.

New Zealand Society of Soil Science (Inc.): c/o Soil Bureau, Private Bag, Lower Hutt; 493 mems.; Sec. R. LEE.

Geological Society of New Zealand (Inc.): New Zealand Geology Survey, Univ. of Canterbury, Private Bag, Christchurch; 569 mems,; Hon. Sec. D. SMALE.

New Zealand Institute of Chemistry: P.O.B. 1926, Christchurch; 1,405 mems.; Sec. Mrs. E. WIGNALL.

New Zealand Institute of Agricultural Sciences (Inc.): Box 11175, Wellington; Sec. Mrs. C. L. MADDEN.

Institute of Physics in N.Z.: Physics Dept., University of Canterbury, P.B. Christchurch; 165 mems.; Sec. Dr. G. FRASER.

New Zealand Hydrological Society: P.O.B. 12300, Wellington; Sec. Mrs. J. LAWRENCE.

New Zealand Archaeological Association (Inc.): c/o Anthropology Dept., Auckland University P.B. Auckland; 416 mems.; Sec. B. TROTTER.

New Zealand Microbiological Society: Department of Microbiology and Genetics, Massey University, Palmerston North; 347 mems.; Sec. Dr. B. D. W. JARVIS.

Institute of Energy (*New Zealand Section*): 7 Ngahere St., Stokes Valley, Wellington; 96 mems.; Sec. Dr. E. R. PALMER.

Nutrition Society of New Zealand: 854 Manukau Rd., Royal Oak, Auckland 6; 301 mems.; Sec. Miss P. KING.

Entomological Society of New Zealand (Inc.): 8 Maymorn Rd., Te Marua, Upper Hutt; 301 mems.; Sec. Mrs. S. MILLER.

Ornithological Society of New Zealand (Inc.): 31 Wyndham Rd., Pinehaven, Hutt; 1,320 mems.; Sec. R. SLACK.

New Zealand Psychological Society (Inc.): c/o Psychological Dept., Sunnyside Hospital, Christchurch; 456 mems.; Sec. Mrs. M. BEEKHUIS.

New Zealand Marine Sciences Society: c/o Fisheries Research Division, Ministry of Agriculture and Fisheries, P.O.B. 10962, Wellington; 225 mems.; Sec. Dr. A. J. BASS.

Royal Aeronautical Society (*New Zealand Division*): c/o Shell Oil Co. NZ Ltd., P.O.B. 2091, Wellington; 1,149 mems.; Sec. M. E. MURRAY.

New Zealand Institute of Dairy Science and Technology (Inc.): Dairy Research Institute, Private Bag, Palmerston North; Sec. E. ROSTERN.

New Zealand Institute of Food Science and Technology: c/o Kellax Foods Ltd., 16a Industry Rd., Penrose, Auckland 6; Sec. T. ATKINSON.

New Zealand Veterinary Association (Inc.): c/o McCulloch, Butler and Spence, P.O.B. 524, Wellington; 726 mems.; Sec. R. A. HENRY.

New Zealand Geographical Society (Inc.): *see* below.

Royal Astronomical Society of New Zealand (Inc.): *see* below.

Operational Research Society of New Zealand (Inc.): 4 Ranfurly St., Upper Hutt; 250 mems.; Sec. J. COLLINS.

New Zealand Computer Society (Inc.): P.O.B. 30606, Lower Hutt; 1,583 mems.; Sec. Cdr. W. R. WILLIAMS.

The Clean Air Society of Australia and New Zealand (N.Z. Branch): P.O.B. 27116, Wellington; Sec. R. C. PILGRIM.

New Zealand Society for Parasitology: c/o Plant Diseases Division, D.S.I.R., Private Bag, Auckland; 73 mems.; Sec. Dr. W. M. WOUTS.

New Zealand Statistical Association (Inc.): c/o Biometrics Section, M.A.F. P.O.B. 2298, Wellington; 311 mems.; Sec. J. JOWETT.

Physiological Society of New Zealand (Inc.): Dept. of Physiology, University of Otago, Box 913, Dunedin; 140 mems.; Sec. J. I. HUBBARD.

New Zealand Dietetic Association (Inc.): Box 5065, Wellington; 347 mems.; Sec. Mrs. A. FISHER.

New Zealand Mathematical Society: Mathematics Dept., University of Waikato, Private Bag, Hamilton; 193 mems.; Sec. Dr. M. SCHRODER.

New Zealand Institute of Foresters (Inc.): P.O.B. 3, Darfield; 723 mems.; Sec. W. P. STUDHOLME.

New Zealand Cartographic Society (Inc.): P.O.B. 9331, Wellington; 260 mems.; Sec. D. MCCORMACK.

New Zealand Association of Clinical Biochemists (Inc.): Wallace Laboratory, Auckland Hospital, Auckland; 181 mems.; Sec. Mrs. P. E. WADE.

New Zealand Biochemical Society: Dept. of Biochemistry, University of Auckland, Private Bag, Auckland; Sec. Dr. A. M. ROBERTON.

New Zealand Society of Animal Production (Inc.): Ruakura Animal Research Station, Private Bag, Hamilton; Sec. Dr. J. F. SMITH.

The Society of Automotive Engineers—Australasia (Inc.): *see* under Australia.

Art Galleries and Museums Association of New Zealand (Inc.): P.O.B. 57016, Owairaka, Auckland; f. 1947 to promote and improve galleries and museums; 300 mems.; Pres. K. GORBEY; Sec. Capt. J. H. MALCOLM; publ. *AGMANZ News* (quarterly).

Bibliographical Society of Australia and New Zealand: *See* under Australia.

British Council: c/o British High Commission, P.O.B. 1812, Wellington; Rep. P. J. C. DART.

New Zealand Academy of Fine Arts: National Museum, Buckle St., Wellington 1; f. 1882, changed to present name 1889; promotes the study, practice and cultivation of the fine arts; exhibitions and assemblies throughout the year; *c.* 1,683 mems.; Pres. BRIAN S. CARMODY; Dir. GUY NGAN; Sec. JOAN PASCOE.

New Zealand Association of Scientists: Box 1874, Wellington; f. 1940; Pres. K. J. ALDOUS; publs. *New Zealand Science Review* (6 a year), *Directory of New Zealand Science* (every 3–4 years).

New Zealand Atomic Energy Committee: c/o D.S.I.R., Private Bag, Lower Hutt; f. 1966; advises the Minister of Science on research development or application of nuclear science; Chair. C. K. STONE; Sec. W. M. MACQUARRIE.

New Zealand Geographical Society: Department of Geography, University of Canterbury, Christchurch; f. 1944 to promote and stimulate the study of geography; brs. in Auckland, Christchurch, Dunedin, Hamilton, Palmerston North and Wellington; 1,300 mems. in New Zealand, 630 overseas mems.; Pres. A. E. MCQUEEN; Sec. R. G. CANT, M.A., PH.D.; publs. *New Zealand Geographer*† (twice yearly), *New Zealand Journal of Geography*† (twice yearly), *Proceedings of the New Zealand Geography Conference* (irregular).

New Zealand Institute of Architects: 3rd floor, Maritime Bldg., 2–10 Customhouse Quay, Wellington; P.O.B. 438; f. 1905; Pres. E. J. MCCOY; Chief Exec. A. K. PURDIE; publ. *New Zealand Architect* (every 2 months).

New Zealand Institute of International Affairs: P.O.B. 19-102, Aro St., Wellington 2; f. 1934; small specialized library; Pres. G. R. LAKING, C.M.G.; Dir. Dr. C. C. AIKMAN; publs. pamphlets, *New Zealand International Review* (every 2 months).

New Zealand Institution of Engineers: P.O.B. 12241, 101 Molesworth St., Wellington; f. 1914; 5,200 mems.; 16 brs.; Pres. A. M. KENNEDY; Sec. A. J. BARTLETT; publ. *New Zealand Engineering* (monthly).

New Zealand Law Society: 26 Waring Taylor St., Wellington; f. 1869; 3,871 mems.; Sec.-Gen. W. M. RODGERS.

New Zealand Library Association, Inc.: 10 Park St., P.O.B. 12-212, Wellington 1; f. 1910; 1,900 mems.; Pres. J. E. TRAUE; Exec. Officer H. STEPHEN-SMITH; publs. *New Zealand Libraries* (quarterly), *Fiction List* (monthly), *Library Life* (monthly, except January).

New Zealand National Research Advisory Council: P.O.B. 12240, Wellington; f. 1964 by N.Z. Government to advise the Minister of Science and Technology on the promotion and development of scientific research in New Zealand and on the planning and co-ordination of scientific research and services; 12 mems.; Chair. A. W. MACKNEY; Exec. Dir. H. J. WAKELIN; publs. *Annual Report, Senior and Post-doctoral Research Fellowships.*

New Zealand National Society for Earthquake Engineering: P.O.B. 243, Wellington; f. 1968; membership open to engineers, architects, scientists and others concerned with earthquake phenomena; Pres. Prof. T. PAULAY; publ. *Bulletin* (quarterly).

P.E.N. International New Zealand Centre: P.O.B. 2283, Wellington 5; f. 1934; has achieved governmental recognition of Public Lending Right, is associated with Unesco, and co-operates with the N.Z. Book Council and the N.Z. Literary Fund Advisory Cttee.; awards 2 annual prizes; 250 mems.; Pres. MICHAEL KING; Sec. ALAN LONEY; publ. *P.E.N. Gazette* (quarterly).

Polynesian Society: f. 1892 to promote studies and publications of the Polynesians and related peoples; library; 1,300 mems.; Pres. Prof. B. BIGGS; Sec. P. RANBY, Anthropology Dept., Univ. of Auckland, Private Bag, Auckland 1; publs. *Memoirs, Journal* (quarterly), *Maori Monographs, Maori Texts.*

Queen Elizabeth II Arts Council of New Zealand: P.O.B. 6040, Te Aro, Wellington; f. 1963; a statutory body formed to foster, encourage and promote the practice and appreciation of the arts; subsidizes a wide variety of artistic organizations involved with all areas of the arts including a National Drama School and a National School of Ballet; makes yearly grants and awards to New Zealanders for study at home and abroad; 13 mems.; Chair. HAMISH KEITH; Dir. MICHAEL VOLKERLING; various publs. and exhibition catalogues.

Royal Agricultural Society of New Zealand: P.O.B. 669, Blenheim; f. 1924; Livestock Breed Co-ordination for N.Z.; library of 1,000 vols.; Pres. J. L. HERRICK; Sec. J. G. HUMM; publs. *Gazette* (annually), and other agricultural papers.

Royal Astronomical Society of New Zealand (Inc.): P.O.B. 3181, Wellington; f. 1920; 290 mems.; Pres. A. C. GILMORE; Exec. Sec. J. K. PARKER; publs. *Southern Stars* (quarterly), *Newsletter* (monthly).

Sociological Association of Australia and New Zealand: *see under* Australia.

University Grants Committee: P.O.B. 12-348, Wellington; f. 1961 to advise the N.Z. Government on all matters relating to university education and research; 8 mems.; Chair. Dr. A. T. JOHNS; Sec. J. R. CALDWELL; publ. *Annual Report.*

Waikato Geological Society (Inc.): P.O.B. 62, Hamilton; f. 1966; Pres. G. W. URQUHART; publ. *Earth Science Journal* (bi-annual).

RESEARCH INSTITUTES

(*see* also under Universities)

Astronomical Observatory: Mount John, Lake Tekapo, South Canterbury; f. 1965; operated by University of Canterbury, Christchurch; research especially into variable stars and stellar spectroscopy; four telescopes.

Auckland Medical Research Foundation: P.O.B. 7151, Auckland; f. 1956; financed by public subscription to sponsor and encourage medical research; Pres. Sir HARCOURT CAUGHEY; Sec. GERALD WAKELY; publ. *Annual Report*†.

Canterbury Medical Research Foundation: Christchurch Group of Hospitals; promotion and support of all aspects of medical research; privately financed; Sec. A. W. MANN.

Carter Observatory: P.O.B. 2909, Wellington; f. 1939; main instrument is 407 mm. f/13.5 Cassegrain reflector; astronomical research in photographic photometry, high-speed photometry and photo-electric timing of occultations; theoretical studies of galactic structure and formation; co-operation with schools, colleges and universities for education in astronomy; national centre for distribution of astronomical information; library of 1,000 vols., 30 journals; Dir. B. M. LEWIS; publ. *Astronomical Bulletin*† (2 a year).

Cawthron Institute: P.O.B. 175, Nelson, N.Z.; f. 1919; chemical and biological testing, microbial processes in relation to resource utilization and conservation, environmental assessment, feasibility studies; 40 mems.; library of 3,500 vols.; Dir. Dr. R. THORNTON; publ. *Cawthron Lectures*.

Christchurch Industrial Development Division, Department of Scientific and Industrial Research: 244 St. Asaph St., P.O.B. 1152, Christchurch; research for industry and government departments in New Zealand; sections: materials science including metallurgy, electronics and acoustics, instrumentation, power engineering, standards testing and product development, industrial engineering, industrial liaison; Dir. T. H. SCOTT, B.E., C.ENG., M.I.E.E., M.N.Z.I.E.

Department of Scientific and Industrial Research (N.Z.): Private Bag, Wellington 1; f. 1926; Dir.-Gen. Dr. E. I. ROBERTSON.

DIVISIONS:

Antarctic Division: Supt. R. B. THOMSON.
Applied Biochemistry Division: Dir. Dr. R. W. BAILEY.
Applied Mathematics Division: Dir. Dr. H. R. THOMPSON.
Auckland Industrial Development Division: Dir. W. R. BEASLEY.
Botany Division: Dir. H. E. CONNOR.
Chemistry Division: Dir. I. R. C. McDONALD.
Christchurch Industrial Development Division: Dir. T. H. SCOTT.
Crop Research Division: Dir. Dr. H. C. SMITH.
Ecology Division: Dir. Dr. J. A. GIBB.
Entomology Division: Dir. J. F. LONGWORTH.
Geological Survey: Dir. Dr. R. P. SUGGATE.
Geophysics Division: Dir. Dr. T. HATHERTON.
Grasslands Division: Dir. Dr. R. W. BROUGHAM.
Horticulture and Processing: Dir. Dr. R. L. BIELESKI.
Institute of Nuclear Sciences: Dir. Dr. B. J. O'BRIEN.
Oceanographic Institute: Dir. Dr. D. E. HURLEY.
Physics and Engineering Laboratory: Dir. M. A. COLLINS.
Plant Diseases Division: Dir. Dr. P. J. BROOK.
Plant Physiology Division: Dir. Dr. J. P. KERR.
Riwaka Research Station: Dir. A. A. FROST.
Science Information Division: Supt. J. G. GREGORY.
Soil Bureau: Dir. Dr. R. B. MILLER.
Wheat Research Institute: Dir. R. W. CAWLEY.
Minister (Scientific) London: R. W. FOSTER.

Publs. *New Zealand Journal of Agricultural Research* (quarterly), *New Zealand Journal of Botany* (quarterly), *New Zealand Journal of Geology and Geophysics* (quarterly), *New Zealand Journal of Marine and Freshwater Research* (quarterly), *New Zealand Journal of Experimental Agriculture* (quarterly), *New Zealand Journal of Zoology* (quarterly), *New Zealand Journal of Science* (quarterly), *DSIR Research* (annual), *Annual Report, Bulletins, Information Series, Geological Bulletins and maps, Palaeontological Bulletins, Seismological Bulletins, Soil Bulletins and maps, Geophysical Memoirs and maps, Oceanographic, Coastal and Lake Charts, Oceanographic Memoirs, Publications List* (irregular), and Divisional Publications. All are available for exchange for others of equal standing.

GRANT-AIDED RESEARCH ASSOCIATIONS:

Building Research Association of New Zealand (Inc.): Dir. Dr. P. K. FOSTER.
Coal Research Association of New Zealand (Inc.): Dir. P. A. TOYNBEE.
New Zealand Concrete Research Association: Dir. Dr. J. E. F. FIELD.
New Zealand Dairy Research Institute: Dir. Dr. W. A. McGILLIVRAY (*see* below).
New Zealand Fertilizer Manufacturers' Research Association (Inc.): Dir. D. J. HIGGINS.
New Zealand Heavy Engineering Research Association (Inc.): Dir. Dr. R. SHEPHERD.
Research Institute of Textile Services (Inc.): Dir. L. P. J. CHAPMAN.
New Zealand Leather and Shoe Research Association (Inc.): Dir. Dr. G. W. VIVIAN.
New Zealand Logging Industry Research Association (Inc.): Dir. J. J. K. SPIERS.
Meat Industry Research Institute of New Zealand (Inc.): Dir. Dr. C. L. DAVEY.
New Zealand Pottery and Ceramics Research Association (Inc.): Dir. Dr. H. J. PERCIVAL.
Wool Research Organization of New Zealand (Inc.): Dir. Dr. W. S. SIMPSON.

Forest Research Institute: Private Bag, Rotorua; f. 1947; co-ordinates and supervises all research carried out by the New Zealand Forest Service; 139 research scientists; library of over 70,000 vols. (incl. monographs and periodicals); Dir. of Research C. BASSETT, DIP.FOR., PH.D.; publ. *Journal of Forestry Science* (quarterly).

Hawke's Bay Medical Research Foundation (Inc.): P.O.B. 596, Napier.

Maori Education Foundation: P.O.B. 3745, Wellington; f. 1961; government subsidized to assist in the education of Maoris; Chair. J. M. BENNETT; publ. *Annual Report*.

Medical Research Council of New Zealand: P.O.B. 5541, Wellesley St., Auckland; f. 1950; initiates, fosters and supports medical research; furnishes information, advice and assistance to persons and organizations concerned with medical research; collects and disseminates scientific information; 13 mems.; Chair. J. C. FAIR; Dir. Dr. J. V. HODGE; Sec. R. J. SKINNER; publs. Reports, *Research Review* (annually).

Ministry of Agriculture and Fisheries: P.O.B. 2298, Wellington; directs the following research stations and centres:

AGRICULTURAL RESEARCH DIVISION:

Ruakura Agricultural Research Centre: Regional Dir. Dr. J. P. JOYCE.
Ruakura Animal Research Station: Dir. K. E. JURY.
Ruakura Soil and Field Research Organisation: Dir. N. A. CULLEN.
Wairakei Research Station: Technical Officer-in-Charge L. F. C. BRUNSWICK.
Whatawhata Hill Country Research Station: Dir. (vacant).
Manutuke Research Station: Senior Technical Officer: D. P. SINCLAIR.
Te Kauwhata Viticultural Research Station: Technical Officer J. G. WHITTLES.

Wallaceville Animal Research Centre: Dir. Dr. W. A. TE PUNGA.
Taieri Hydatid Unit: Scientist-in-Charge M. A. GEMMELL.

Winchmore Irrigation Research Station: Dir. D. S. RICKARD (acting).
Templeton Research Station: Scientist-in-Charge K. G. GEENTY.

Invermay Agricultural Research Centre: Regional Dir. Dr. A. J. ALLISON.

Tara Hills High Country Research Station: Scientist-in-Charge D. J. MUSGRAVE.

Woodlands Research Station: Scientist-in-Charge K. F. THOMPSON.

Levin Horticultural Research Centre: Dir. W. R. BOYCE.

Pukehohe Horticultural Research Station: Scientist-in-Charge G. J. WILSON.

Hastings Horticultural Research Station: Technical Officer-in-Charge J. L. BURGMANS.

Publications: *Agricultural Research in the New Zealand Ministry of Agriculture* (annually), *Ruakura Farmers' Conference Proceedings* (annually).

ADVISORY SERVICES DIVISION:

Flock House Farm Training Institute: Principal J. J. STEWART.

Telford Farm Training Institute: Principal (vacant).

Plant Health Diagnostic Stations:

Auckland: Officer-in-Charge P. S. DALE.

Levin: Officer-in-Charge Dr. A. F. RAINBOW.

Lincoln: Officer-in-Charge Dr. J. HEDLEY.

Seed Testing Station: Officer-in-Charge D. J. SCOTT.

ANIMAL HEALTH DIVISION LABORATORIES:

Whangarei: Supt. D. MARTINOVICH.

Ruakura: Supt. J. W. MOXHAM.

Palmerston North: Supt. Dr. B. H. SIMPSON.

Lincoln: Supt. C. M. ALLAN.

Invermay: Supt. G. SHIRLEY.

Animal Health Reference Laboratory: Supt. Dr. P. O'HARA.

Central Brucellosis Laboratory: Supt. (vacant).

FISHERIES RESEARCH DIVISION:
Dir. G. D. WAUGH.

Publications: *Fisheries Research Bulletins*† (irregular), *Occasional Publications Series* (irregular), *Information Leaflets* (irregular), *Fisheries Research Reprints*† (irregular).

FISHERIES MANAGEMENT DIVISION:
Dir. B. T. CUNNINGHAM.

Publications: *Fisheries Technical Reports, Reprints.*

New Plymouth Astronomical Society Observatory: P.O.B. 818, New Plymouth; f. 1920; 65 mems.; Dir. J. WALMSLEY.

New Zealand Council for Educational Research: P.O.B. 3237, Wellington; f. 1933; research into educational problems; develops achievement tests for N.Z., and acts as clearing-house for research and information on educational matters; 700 mems.; Chair. Prof. R. S. ADAMS; Dir. J. E. WATSON; publs. *Annual Report*†, *Newsletter*† (twice yearly), *New Zealand Journal of Educational Studies*†, and others.

New Zealand Dairy Research Institute: Private Bag, Palmerston North; established 1927 as a unit of the D.S.I.R., inc. 1947; central research organization within New Zealand dairy industry; concerned with fundamental and applied research and development work related to the composition and manufacture of dairy products; Dir. P. S. ROBERTSON; publs. *N.Z. Journal of Dairy Science and Technology* (3 a year), *Research Review* (every 2 years).

New Zealand Institute of Economic Research: P.O.B 3479, Wellington; f. 1958; research into New Zealand economic development; quarterly analysis and forecast of economic conditions; quarterly survey of business opinions; economic investigations on contract basis; Dir. T. K. McDONALD; Chair. J. MOWBRAY; Sec. Mrs. S. M. USHER.

Palmerston North Medical Research Foundation: c/o P.O.B. 607, Palmerston North; f. 1959; privately financed; general medical research; Sec. JOHN FORSYTHE; publ. *Annual Report.*

PEL Geophysical Observatory: St. Elmo Courts, Hereford St., P.O.B. 2111, Christchurch; f. 1901 as Magnetic Survey, present name 1946; operates ionosondes at Christchurch, Rarotonga (Cook Islands), Campbell Island, Scott Base (Antarctica); operates magnetic observatories at Apia (West Samoa), Eyrewell (near Christchurch), Lauder (near Dunedin), Campbell Island and Scott Base; conducts magnetic surveys throughout New Zealand and its dependencies; preparation of magnetic charts of New Zealand and South West Pacific; research in ionospheric physics with emphasis on effects of winds, magnetic storms and internal gravity waves; research on auroral phenomena, particularly radio aurora; VLF/ELF studies of the earth/ionosphere waveguide; Officer-in-Charge R. S. UNWIN; publs. *Ionospheric Data*† (hourly values, monthly), *Magnetic Results*† (hourly values, etc., annually).

Ross Dependency Research Committee: Department of Scientific and Industrial Research, Private Bag, Wellington 1; responsible to the Minister of Science for co-ordinating all New Zealand activity in the Ross Dependency; Chair. J. H. MILLER; Sec. N. SIMPSON.

Veterinary Services Council: P.O.B. 417, Wellington; f. 1946; veterinary administration.

Wellington Medical Research Foundation: c/o The Secretary, P.O.B. 766, Wellington; privately financed.

Wheat Research Institute: 197 Hereford St., Christchurch; f. by Act of Parliament 1928; the Institute is part of the Department of Scientific and Industrial Research; functions are research, advice and teaching with the object of improving wheat, flour and bread; Dir. R. W. CAWLEY, M.SC., F.N.Z.I.C.; Sec. D. F. McINNES; publ. *New Zealand Wheat Review*† (three-yearly).

LIBRARIES AND ARCHIVES

National Library of New Zealand: Private Bag, Wellington 1; f. 1966 by amalgamation of several state libraries; 477,000 vols., 91,000 periodicals, 431,000 microfiche, not including the figures below for special collections; National Librarian MARY A. RONNIE, M.A., F.N.Z.L.A.

Alexander Turnbull Library: P.O.B. 12,349, Wellington; f. 1919; 177,000 vols., including 13,000 rare books, chiefly in English literature; special collections include New Zealand and Oceania, Milton, Katherine Mansfield; 1,647 linear metres of MSS.; 35,000 pictures and prints; 379,000 photographic negatives and prints; 19,000 maps; compiles *New Zealand National Bibliography*†, current and retrospective; Chief Librarian J. E. TRAUE, M.A., F.N.Z.L.A.; publs. *Turnbull Library Record*†, *Monograph Series*†, print reproductions.

Extension Service: f. 1938; 973,000 vols.; provides services to public libraries, hospitals, prisons; Dir. J. S. GULLY; publ. *Books to Buy.*

General Assembly Library: f. 1858; 264,000 vols., 160,000 periodicals and 23,000 maps; exchange repository; special collections: New Zealand literature and largest New Zealand newspaper and periodical collection in country; Chief Librarian D. I. MATHESON.

General Services: provides ordering and cataloguing services for National Library and for government departments; maintains National Union Catalogue; services New Zealand Library Resources Committee; Dir. A. L. OLSSON, M.A., B.COM., F.N.Z.L.A.; publs. *Index to New Zealand Periodicals, Union List of Serials in New Zealand Libraries, Expensive Materials Bulletin.*

User Services: provides national information and request service; acts as clearing-house for inter-library lending; co-ordinates Scientific and Technical Information Service (SATIS); Dir. AILEEN J. CLARIDGE, B.A., A.N.Z.L.A.

School Library Service: f. 1942; services to primary and secondary schools; 2,826,000 vols.; Dir. PHYLLIS L. McDONALD; publs. *Children's Books to Buy, For the Primary School Library, School Library Review.*

Auckland Public Library: P.O.B. 4138, Lorne St., Auckland 1; f. 1880; 12 branch libraries, 2 mobile libraries, reference library; 914,009 vols.; special collections: Grey and Shaw Collections of MSS. and incunabula, Grey Maori Collection, Lewis Eady Music Collection, Reed Dumas Collection; 21,726 music scores; Librarian R. DUTHIE, O.B.E., B.A., DIP.N.Z.L.S., F.N.Z.L.A.

Auckland University Library: Private Bag, Auckland; f. 1884; 900,000 vols., 12,000 periodicals; Librarian P. B. DUREY, B.A., F.L.A., A.L.A.A.; publ. *Bibliographical Bulletin*†.

Canterbury Public Library: P.O.B. 1466, 109 Cambridge Terrace, Christchurch; f. 1859; 360,000 vols.; Lending, Children's and Reference Divisions; New Zealand and Pacific Room 20,000 vols.; 16 suburban libraries served; City Librarian J. E. D. STRINGLEMAN, CERT.N.Z.L.S., F.N.Z.L.A.; publ. *Journal.*

Canterbury University Library: Christchurch; f. 1873; *c.* 500,000 vols.; Librarian R. W. HLAVAC, B.A., M.A., A.N.Z.L.A.

Department of Scientific and Industrial Research Central Library: P.O.B. 9741, Wellington; f. 1947; a centralized processing and servicing unit for 17 divisional and campus libraries; maintains a union catalogue of departmental holdings; provides consulting and training services in science information; Chief Librarian P. SZENTIRMAY.

Dunedin Public Library: P.O.B. 906, Dunedin; f. 1908; 328,000 vols.; collection of illuminated MSS., McNab New Zealand collection 36,100 vols., Reed Bible/Dickens/Johnson/Farjeon/Bolitho collection 3,700 vols.; Librarian MICHAEL WOOLISCROFT, B.A., A.N.Z.L.A.

Lyes Institute Branch, Auckland Public Libraries: 20 St. Mary's Rd., Ponsonby; f. 1905; early New Zealand history; general literature, basic vocabulary collection for children and adults with literacy difficulties; Librarian Miss N. FOSTER.

Library of the Otago District Law Society: Stuart St., Dunedin; f. 1859; 13,500 vols.; Librarian Miss K. C. DOLBY.

Lincoln College Library: George Forbes Memorial Library, Lincoln College, University College of Agriculture, Canterbury; f. 1960; 68,000 vols.; specializes in agricultural and horticultural science, including engineering, economics, resource management, rural sociology, valuation, recreation and landscape architecture; responsible for exchange distribution of all publications of Lincoln College and associated research institutes; Librarian JOHN A. FRAMPTON, B.A., DIP.N.Z.L.S., A.N.Z.L.A.

National Archives: Air Centre Bldg., 129–141 Vivian St., Wellington (P.O.B. 6162, Te Aro); f. 1926; Chief Archivist Miss J. S. HORNABROOK, M.A.; publs. Inventories† and annual summaries of work†.

National Museum Library: Buckle St., Wellington; f. 1865; 120,000 vols.; Librarian ROGER G. CHAPMAN, B.A.

Otago University Library: P.O.B. 56, Dunedin; f. 1870; 750,000 vols.; Librarian W. J. McELDOWNEY, M.A., F.N.Z.L.A.; incorporates:

Hocken Library: P.O.B. 56, Dunedin; f. 1910; history and ethnology of New Zealand and the Pacific; 124,000 vols., many MSS., maps and pictures; Librarian M. G. HITCHINGS, B.A., F.N.Z.L.A.

Medical Library: Great King St., Dunedin; includes Historical Library, containing Monro's collection of books and MSS.; 77,000 vols.; Librarian D. G. JAMIESON, M.A., A.N.Z.L.A.

Science Library: P.O.B. 56, Dunedin; 126,000 vols.; Librarian P. R. KIDD, M.A., A.N.Z.L.A.

Palmerston North Public Library: P.O.B. 1948, Palmerston North; f. 1876; 190,000 vols.; lending, reference, children's sections; one branch; one mobile library; Librarian I. W. MALCOLM, B.A., A.N.Z.L.A., A.N.Z.I.M., DIP.N.Z.L.S.

Victoria University Library: Private Bag, Wellington, f. 1897; 467,000 vols.; Librarian J. P. SAGE, M.A.; DIP.N.Z.L.S., F.N.Z.L.A.

Wellington Public Library: P.O.B. 1992, Wellington, f. 1893; 431,000 vols.; City Librarian B. K. McKEON; B.A., DIP.N.Z.L.S., F.N.Z.L.A.; 10 br. libraries and mobile suburban service.

MUSEUMS AND ART GALLERIES

Algantighe Art Gallery: 49 Wai-iti Rd., Timaru; New Zealand and British painters; Dir. AINSLIE G. MANSON.

Anderson Park Art Gallery: P.O.B. 755, Invercargill; incorporates Invercargill Public Art Gallery; mainly New Zealand works; Pres. K. BALLINGER.

Auckland City Art Gallery: P.O.B. 5449, Auckland 1; f. 1888; 12th to 20th century European paintings, sculpture, prints and drawings, Frances Hodgkins collection, Fuseli drawings, 19th and 20th century New Zealand painting, sculpture and prints; photographs, artists' books and records, audio- and video-tapes; library of 15,000 vols.; Dir. ANDREW BOGLE; publs. *Art Gallery Yearbook*†, *Annual Report*, exhibition catalogues.

Auckland Institute and Museum: Private Bag, Auckland 1; f. 1852 (Museum), 1867 (Institute), united 1869; natural history, ethnology, applied arts and armed services; *c.* 57,000 vols.; Dir. G. S. PARK, M.A., A.M.A.; Librarian IAN G. THWAITES, B.A., DIP.N.Z.L.S., A.N.Z.L.A.; publs. *Annual Report*†, *Records*† (annual), *Bulletin*† (as required), handbooks and educational leaflets.

Canterbury Museum: Rolleston Ave., Christchurch 1; f. 1867; ethnology of New Zealand and Pacific Basin; archaeology of N.Z. and Chatham Islands; natural history (notably entomology, geology and ornithology) of N.Z.; applied arts of China and Japan, and pre-Victorian Britain; relics of colonial settlement; national centre on natural history and exploration of Antarctic Continent; official repository for Canterbury archives, incl. photographs, paintings, sketches and maps; Dir. JOHN C. WILSON, M.A.; publs. *Records* (annual), *Popular Guide, Bulletin* (occasional), pamphlets.

Dunedin Public Art Gallery: Logan Park, Dunedin; f. 1884; maintains a conservation laboratory and arranges tours of gallery collections; holdings include: New Zealand paintings, prints and sculptures; Australian paintings and prints; British portraits, landscapes and genre paintings; Smythe Collection of 18-19th-century British watercolours; European painting; ancillary collections of furniture, ceramics, glass, silver, historic costume, oriental rugs; Dir. F. H. DICKINSON; Pres. Dr. J. NG; publs. *Annual Report*†, *Gallery Newsletter*†, exhibition catalogues†.

Gisborne Museum and Arts Centre: P.O.B. 716, Gisborne; f. 1953; Dir. WARNER HALDANE.

Hawke's Bay Art Gallery and Museum: P.O.B. 429, Herschel St., Napier; Maori and Polynesian artefacts, N.Z. painting, pottery and sculpture, early home and farm equipment; local archives, historical reference library.

Melanesian Mission Museum: Mission Bay, Auckland 5; f. 1928; Melanesian arts and crafts; Curator E. C. HIGGINS.

Museum of Transport and Technology of New Zealand Inc. (MOTAT): Western Springs, Auckland; f. 1960; vehicles, aircraft, machinery and equipment of historical and technical interest; includes Picneer Village; operates electric tramway and steam locomotives; library of 11,000 vols.; includes Walsh Memorial Historical Aviation Library; Dir. M. M. JAMESON.

National Art Gallery: Buckle St., Wellington; f. 1936; British, European, Australian and New Zealand paintings and sculpture; collections and bequests include the Sir Harold Beauchamp (early English watercolours), the Sir John Ilott, the Nan Kivell, the Harold Wright and the Bishop Monrad (British and European prints), the National Collection of New Zealand drawings and watercolours and a small collection of Old Master drawings; library of over 2,000 vols.; archival section; Dir. LUIT BIERINGA.

National Museum: Buckle St., Wellington; f. 1865; ethnology, natural history, fine arts; library: *see* Libraries; Dir. J. C. YALDWYN, PH.D., F.M.A.N.Z.; publs. *Records*†, *Bulletin*†, *Miscellaneous Series*†.

Nelson Provincial Museum: Isel Park, Stoke, Nelson; f. 1963; incorporating the Nelson Institute Museum (f. 1841) and Nelson Historical Society; Maori prehistory, colonial history, and natural history of the province; Dir. A. S. BAGLEY.

New Zealand Geological Survey: State Fire Building, Andrews Ave., P.O.B. 30368, Lower Hutt; f. 1865; collections of rocks, minerals and fossils of New Zealand and other countries; Suter collection of New Zealand Mollusca; responsible for national geological mapping and all applied geology; Dir. R. P. SUGGATE, M.A., D.SC., F.R.S.N.Z.; 20,000 books in library; publs. *Bulletin*†, *n.s., Palaeontological Bulletin*†, *N.Z. Volcanological Record*† (annual), Geological Maps† (all irregular).

Otago Museum: Great King St., Dunedin; f. 1868; natural sciences, N.Z. and Pacific anthropology, classical archaeology, European and Asian ceramics; Dir. R. R. FORSTER; publs. *Annual Report, Handbooks to the Collections, Records, Bulletins* (occasional).

Robert McDougall Art Gallery: Botanic Gardens, Rolleston Ave., Christchurch; f. 1932; New Zealand, British, European, Australian and Japanese works; Dir. T. L. RODNEY WILSON; publ. *Bulletin*† (every 2 months), *Educational Programme*† (monthly), exhibition catalogues.

Sarjeant Gallery: Queen's Park, P.O.B. 637, Wanganui; f. 1919; 18th-, 19th- and 20th-century European and English watercolours, representative New Zealand collection, Gilfillan collection, Barraud collection, drawings by Bernadoin Poccetti, collection of First World War cartoons.

Southland Museum and Art Gallery: Victoria Ave., Invercargill; natural history, Maori and Polynesian section, "Victoriana", art gallery, astronomical observatory; Dir. RUSSELL J. BECK.

Suter Art Gallery: Queen's Gardens, Nelson; f. 1895, rebuilt 1978; includes works of F. Brangwyn, M. Chagall, John Gully, Francis Hodgkins, Ivor Hitchins, F. Leger, J. Lurcat, J. Piper, J. C. Richmond, G. Rouault, M. Rothenstein, M. Stoddard, J. Webber; Dir. AUSTIN DAVIES.

Theomin Gallery, Dunedin: "Olveston", 42 Royal Terrace, Dunedin; built 1904–6; Jacobean-style house designed by British architect Sir Ernest George for David Edward Theomin, bequeathed to the city by his daughter, Dorothy, 1966, opened to the public 1967; antique furniture, ceramics, crystal, bronzes, Persian rugs, silver, early English, European and N.Z. oils and watercolours; Sec./Man. D. R. BRICKELL.

Waitangi Treaty House: Waitangi National Reserve, Paihia, Bay of Islands; site of Treaty of Waitangi; carved Maori meeting house and war canoe; exhibits of New Zealand historical interest up to 1840.

Wanganui Regional Museum: P.O.B. 352, Wanganui; f. 1895; ethnology, natural history and colonial history; Curator D. W. CIMINO, M.N.Z.H.I.

West Coast Historical Museum: Tancred St., Hokitika; historical record, wild life and mineral collections; gold mining exhibition and pioneer settlement; Dir. J. R. EYLES.

UNIVERSITIES

UNIVERSITY OF AUCKLAND

PRIVATE BAG, AUCKLAND 1

Telephone: 792-300.

Founded 1882 as Auckland University College; university status 1958.

Visitor: H.E. The Governor-General of New Zealand.
Chancellor: The Hon. Mr. Justice G. D. SPEIGHT, LL.B.N.Z.
Pro-Chancellor: M. J. A. BROWN, LL.B.
Vice-Chancellor: C. J. MAIDEN, M.E., D.PHIL.
Registrar: (vacant).
Librarian: P. B. DUREY, B.A., F.L.A., A.L.A.A.

Library: *see* Libraries.

Number of teachers: 750 (full-time).
Number of internal students: 12,500.
Publications: *University Calendar, News.*

DEANS:

Faculty of Arts: P. N. TARLING, M.A., PH.D., LITT.D., F.R.A.S., F.R.HIST.S.
Faculty of Science: A. C. KIBBLEWHITE, M.SC., PH.D., F.INST.P., D.I.C.
Faculty of Commerce: G. L. D. MORRIS, B.COM., B.C.A.
Faculty of Law: J. F. NORTHEY, LL.M., D.JUR., LL.D.
Faculty of Music: P. D. H. GODFREY, M.A., MUS.B., F.R.C.O., A.R.C.M.
Faculty of Architecture and Town Planning: A. A. WILD, B.ARCH., F.N.Z.I.A., R.I.B.A.
Faculty of Engineering: R. F. MEYER, PH.D., F.C.A.S.I., M.A.I.A.A., F.N.Z.I.E.
Faculty of Fine Arts: J. D. SAUNDERS, M.S.I.A., F.N.Z.S.I.D., F.R.S.A.
Faculty of Medicine: D. S. COLE, B.MED.SC., M.B.CH.B., F.R.C.S., F.R.A.C.S.

PROFESSORS:

ALEXANDER, C. J., M.B.CH.B., M.D., F.R.A.C.R., Radiology
ASHER, J. A., M.A., DR.PHIL., German Language and Literature
BALLANTINE, W. J., M.A., PH.D., Dir., Leigh Laboratory
BARTLETT, P. J., PH.D., R.I.B.A., A.N.Z.I.A., Architectural Design

Beadle, P. J., m.n.z.s.i.d., m.n.z.s.s.p., m.f.i.m., f.r.s.a., Fine Arts
Bergquist, P. L., m.sc., ph.d., f.r.s.n.z., Cell Biology
Biggs, B. G., m.a., ph.d., f.r.s.n.z., Anthropology
Blyth, C. A., m.a., ph.d., Economics
Boileau, I. E., m.a., ph.d., f.r.t.p.i., m.n.z.p.i., f.r.a.p.i., Town Planning
Bonham, D. G., o.b.e., m.a., m.b., b.chir., f.r.c.s., f.r.a.c.s., f.r.c.o.g., Obstetrics and Gynaecology
Braae, G. P., m.com., d.phil., Economics
Brothers, R. N., m.sc., ph.d., d.i.c., f.g.s., f.m.s.am., f.r.s.n.z., Geology
Bulmer, R. N. H., m.a., ph.d., Anthropology
Butcher, J. C., m.sc., ph.d., d.sc., f.i.m.a., Computer Science
Cambie, R. C., m.sc., ph.d., d.phil., d.sc., f.n.z.i.c., f.r.s.n.z., Chemistry
Carman, J. B., b.med.sc., m.b., ch.b., d.phil., Anatomy
Catt, A. J. L., m.com., Economics
Chapman, R. M., m.a., Political Studies
Clay, Marie, m.a., ph.d., f.n.z.ps.s., Education
Cole, D. S., b.med.sc., m.b., ch.b., f.r.c.s., f.r.a.c.s., Surgery
Collins, E. R., o.b.e., m.sc., ph.d., f.inst.p., f.r.s.n.z., Physics
Coote, B., ll.m., ph.d., Law
Corballis, M. C., b.a., m.sc., ph.d., m.a., Psychology
Court, R. H., m.a., ph.d., Economics
Davis, B. R., ph.d., d.phil., d.s.c., f.n.z.i.c., Chemistry
de la Mare, P. B. D., m.sc., ph.d., d.sc., f.n.z.i.c., f.r.s.c., f.r.s.n.z., Chemistry
Dower, J. C., a.b., m.d., Paediatrics
Elliot, R. B., m.d., f.r.a.c.p., Paediatrics
Gavin, J. B., ph.d., d.d.s., Experimental Pathology
Godfrey, P. D. H., m.b.e., m.a., mus.b., f.r.c.o., a.r.c.m., Music
Gray, D. H., m.med.sc., ch.m., f.r.a.c.s., Orthopaedic Surgery
Green, A. S. G., m.a., **ph.d.**, f.r.s.a., a.n.z.s.s.p., Art History
Green, R. C., ph.d., f.r.s.n.z., Anthropology
Hall, D., m.sc., d.sc., ph.d., f.n.z.i.c., f.r.s.n.z., Chemistry
Henshall, B. D., ph.d., d.sc., c.eng., f.r.a.e.s., Management Studies
Herdson, P. B., b.med.sc., m.b., ch.b., ph.d., f.r.c.p.a., Pathology
Hill, G. L., m.b.ch.m., f.r.a.c.s., f.r.c.s., Surgery
Hinde, G. W., ll.m., Law
Hochstein, M. P., dr.rer.nat., Dir., Geothermal Institute
Hollyman, K. J., m.a., d.u., French
Hooton, D. J., m.sc., ph.d., f.inst.p., Physics
Ibbertson, H. K., m.b., ch.b., f.r.c.p., f.r.a.c.p., Endocrinology
Irwin, R. J., m.a., ph.d., f.n.z.ps.s., Psychology
Kalman, J. A., m.a., a.m., ph.d., Mathematics
Kibblewhite, A. C., m.sc., ph.d., f.inst.p., d.i.c., f.a.s.a., Geophysics
Lacey, W. K., m.a., Classics
Lancashire, D., m.a., b.d., Asian Languages and Literature
Liggins, G. C., m.b., ch.b., ph.d., f.r.c.s.ed., f.r.a.c.s., f.r.c.o.g., f.r.s., f.r.s.n.z., Obstetrics and Gynaecological Endocrinology
Liley, Sir William, k.c.m.g., b.med.sc., m.b.ch.b., ph.d., f.r.s.n.z., f.r.c.o.g., Perinatal Physiology
Lovell, P. H., ph.d., Botany
McNaughton, A. H., m.a., ph.d., dip.ed., Education
Malone, M. A., Dir., Centre for Continuing Education
Mantell, C. D., b.med.sc., m.b.ch.b., m.r.c.o.g., Obstetrics and Gynaecology
Marshall, A. H., ph.d., r.i.b.a., f.n.z.i.a., m.a.s.a., Architecture
Matthews, R. E. F., f.r.s., m.sc., ph.d., sc.d., f.n.z.i.c., f.r.s.n.z., Cell Biology
Meyer, R. F., b.e., ph.d., m.a.i.a.a., f.c.a.s.i., f.n.z.i.e., Mechanical Engineering
Morton, J. E., m.sc., ph.d., d.sc., f.r.s.n.z., Zoology
Newhook, F. J., m.sc., ph.d., d.i.c., f.r.s.a., Plant Pathology
North, J. D. K., m.b., ch.b., d.phil., f.r.c.p., f.r.a.c.p., Medicine
Northey, J. F., d.jur., ll.m., ll.d., Public Law
Odell, A. L., m.sc., ph.d., d.sc., f.n.z.i.c., Chemistry
Paton, D. M., m.b., ch.b., m.d., f.i.biol., f.r.c.p.can., Pharmacology and Clinical Pharmacology
Percy, J. H., ph.d., f.n.z.i.e., Mechanical Engineering
Poletti, A. R., m.sc., d.phil., f.inst.p., f.a.p.s., f.r.s.n.z., Physics
Ralph, R. K., m.sc., ph.d., d.sc., m.n.z.i.c., Cell Biology
Raudkivi, A. J., ph.d., c.eng., f.i.c.e., v.d.i., f.n.z.i.e., Civil Engineering
Renwick, A. G. C., m.a., m.d., ph.d., m.r.c. path., f.r.s.c., Biochemistry
Sampson, H., m.a., ph.d., f.n.z.ps.s., Psychology
Saunders, J. D., m.s.i.a., n.d.d., f.n.z.s.i.d., f.r.s.a., Fine Arts
Scott, A. J., m.sc., ph.d., Mathematics
Scott, F. S., m.a., m.litt., English Language
Scott, P. J., m.b., ch.b., m.d., f.r.c.p., f.r.a.c.p., Medicine
Seber, G. A. F., m.sc., ph.d., Mathematics
Segerberg, K., ph.d., Philosophy
Sinclair, J. D., m.d., ch.b., b.med.sc., f.r.a.c.p., Physiology
Sinclair, K., m.a., ph.d., litt.d., History
Smith, D. I. B., m.a., d.phil., English
Sorrenson, M. P. K., m.a., d.phil., History
Stead, C. K., m.a., ph.d., English
Stoffel, H. P., dr.phil., Russian
Tabb, J. B., m.com., ph.d., a.c.a., Accountancy
Tarling, P. N., ph.d., litt.d., f.r.a.s., f.r.hist.s., History
Taylor, P. W., ph.d., c.eng., f.i.c.e., f.n.z.i.e., f.a.s.c.e., Civil Engineering
Titchener, A. L., b.sc., b.e., sc.d., a.o.s.m., m.i.mech.e., f.n.z.i.e., m.a.i.m.e., f.i.m., Chemical and Materials Engineering
Veale, A. M. O., m.b., ch.b., ph.d., f.r.a.c.p., Community Health
Waters, T. N. M., m.sc., ph.d., d.sc., f.n.z.i.c., Chemistry
Webb, P. R. H., m.a., ll.b., ll.d., Law
Werry, J. S., m.d., f.r.c.p., m.r.a.n.z.c., Psychiatry
Whale, H. A., m.sc., ph.d., f.inst.p., s.m.i.e.e.e., Radio Research Centre
White, J. C. B., m.sc., ph.d., Director, Computer Centre
Wild, A. A., b.arch., f.n.z.i.a., r.i.b.a., f.r.s.a., Architecture
Williams, P. W., m.a., ph.d., Geography
Woodward, J. L., m.a.sc., f.i.e.e., f.i.e.aust., m.n.z.i.e.
Young, E. C., m.sc., ph.d., d.i.c., Zoology

UNIVERSITY OF CANTERBURY

CHRISTCHURCH, 1

Telephone: 488-489.

Founded 1873.

Academic year: February to November.

Chancellor: Jean M. Herbison, c.m.g., m.a., a.i.e.

Vice-Chancellor: A. D. Brownlie, m.com.

Registrar: W. Hansen, j.p., b.com., a.c.a.

***Librarian:* R. W. Hlavac, m.a., a.n.z.l.a.**

Library: ***see*** **Libraries.**

Number of teachers: 426, including 60 professors.

Number of students: 7,441.

Publications; *University Calendar*†, *Student Handbook, Chronicle.*

Deans:

Faculty of Arts: C. E. Manning, m.a.
Faculty of Commerce: G. M. McNally, m.com.
Faculty of Engineering: D. G. Elms, m.s.e., ph.d., f.n.z.i.e.
Faculty of Forestry: P. J. McKelvey, b.sc.
Faculty of Law: J. F. Burrows, ll.m., ph.d.
Faculty of Music and Fine Arts: D. F. Sell, m.mus., l.r.s.m., l.mus., t.c.l.
Faculty of Science: D. F. Robinson, ph.d., a.k.c.

Professors:

Arnold, B. C., m.sc., Botany
Arrillaga, J., m.sc., ph.d., Electrical Engineering
Bancroft, L. D., ph.d., French
Bargh, J. K., m.e., ph.d., Electrical Engineering
Bates, R. H. T., d.sc., Electrical Engineering
Burrows, J. F., ll.m., ph.d., Law
Caldwell, R. A., m.a., Law
Carter, T. E., b.a., German
Clark, W. C., ph.d., d.i.c., Zoology
Clarke, B. J., ph.d., m.com., Accountancy
Conway, A. A., m.a., ph.d., American History
Crawford, A. R., m.sc., ph.d., Geology
Davy, D., b.a., English
Deely, J. J., m.s., ph.d., Mathematics
Devonport, F., m.com., Accountancy
Ellis, E. L., m.s., ph.d., Wood Science
Elms, D. G., m.s.e., ph.d., Civil Engineering
Erasmus, L. A., ph.d., Mechanical Engineering
Hartshorn, M. P., d.phil., Chemistry
Jackson, W. K., ph.d., Political Science
Johnston, W. B., m.a., Geography
Jones, W. L., ph.d., Physics
Kay, L., ph.d., Electrical Engineering
Keey, R. B., ph.d., Chemical Engineering
Kennedy, A. M., ph.d., Chemical Engineering
Kerr, R. P., m.sc., ph.d., Mathematics
King, B., ph.d., English

KNOX, G. A., M.SC., Zoology
LANGE, R. A., M.A., PH.D., Asian Languages
LEE, K. H., PH.D., Classics
LOVIS, J. D., B.SC., PH.D., Botany
LU, F. P. S., B.SC., Business Administration
MCCALLION, H., PH.D., D.SC., Production Technology
MCINTYRE, W. D., M.A., PH.D., History
MCKELVEY, P. J., B.SC., Forestry
MCLELLAN, A. G., M.SC., PH.D., Physics
MANNING, R., PH.D., Economics
NUTHALL, G. A., M.A., PH.D., Education
PARK, R., M.E., PH.D., Civil Engineering
PAULAY, T., PH.D., Civil Engineering
PENFOLD, B. R., M.SC., PH.D., Chemistry
PENNY, J. P., M.SC., PH.D., Computer Science
PETERSEN, G. M., M.A., PH.D., D.SC., Mathematics
PHILLIPS, L. F., M.SC., PH.D., D.SC., Chemistry
PILGRIM, R. L. C., M.SC., PH.D., Zoology
RAYNER, A. C., B.COM., M.SOC.SC., M.A., Economics
RITCHIE, J. A., MUS.B., L.MUS., T.C.L., L.T.C.L., Music
SIMPSON, H. J., A.T.D., Fine Arts
SOONS, JANE M., PH.D., Geography
STEVENSON, D. C., M.SC., PH.D., Mechanical Engineering
STOOTHOFF, R. H., B.A., B.PHIL., Philosophy and Religious Studies
STRONGMAN, K. T., PH.D., Psychology
VAUGHAN, J., M.SC., Chemistry
WILKINS, C. J., M.SC. PH.D., Chemistry
WILLIAMSON, A. G., M.SC., PH.D., Chemical Engineering
WILLMOTT, W. E., M.A., PH.D., Sociology
WOOD, I. R., M.E., PH.D., Civil Engineering
WOODS, B. A., B.E., Mathematics
WOODWARD, G. W. O., M.A., PH.D., History
WYBOURNE, B. G., M.SC., PH.D., Physics

LINCOLN COLLEGE

CANTERBURY

Telephone: Christchurch 228029.

Founded 1878; formerly the Canterbury Agricultural College; a constituent college of the University of Canterbury from 1961 with a separate governing body, academic body and financial status, its degrees being the degrees of the University of Canterbury; Academic year: March to October.

Chair. of Council: D. W. BAIN, C.M.G., M.B.E.

Principal: J. D. STEWART, M.A., PH.D.

Vice-Principal: R. H. M. LANGER, PH.D., F.R.S.N.Z.

Registrar: G. A. HAY, J.P., LL.B.

Librarian: J. A. FRAMPTON, B.A., DIP.N.Z.L.S., A.N.Z.L.A.

Library: *see* Libraries.

Number of teachers: 171, including 13 professors.

Number of students: 2,275 including short-course students.

Publications: *College Calendar, Technical Publications* (irregular), *Research Publications* (irregular).

PROFESSORS:

DENT, J. B., M.AGR.SC., PH.D., Farm Management
HENDERSON .A. E., PH.D., Wool Science
HOWARD, B. H., PH.D., Biochemistry
IRVINE, C. H. G., D.SC., Veterinary Science
LANGER, R. H. M., PH.D., Plant Science
MULCOCK, A. P., M.SC., PH.D., Agricultural Microbiology
O'CONNOR, K. F., PH.D., Range Management
ROSS, B. J., M.AGR.SC., Agricultural Economics and Marketing
ROWE, R. N., PH.D., Horticulture
SWIFT, R. S., PH.D., Soil Science
SYKES, A. R., PH.D., Animal Science
WARD, G. T., PH.D., Agricultural Engineering
WILLIAMS, G. R., PH.D., Entomology

ATTACHED RESEARCH INSTITUTES:

Agricultural Economics Research Unit: Dir. Prof. J. B. DENT, M.AGR.SC., PH.D.

New Zealand Agricultural Engineering Institute: Dir. E. M. WATSON, B.SC.(ENG.).

Tussock Grasslands and Mountain Lands Institute: Dir. Prof. K. F. O'CONNOR, PH.D.

MASSEY UNIVERSITY

P.O. PALMERSTON NORTH

Telephone: 69-099 Palmerston North.

Founded 1926 as Massey Agricultural College and merged with the Palmerston North Branch of the Victoria University of Wellington 1963.

Academic year: February to November.

Chancellor: Sir ARTHUR WARD, K.B.E., A.C.A., F.N.Z.I.A.S.

Vice-Chancellor: A. STEWART, C.B.E., M.AGR.SC., D.PHIL., F.N.Z.I.A.S.

Registrar: A. J. WEIR, J.P., B.SC., F.C.A.N.Z.

Librarian: D. L. JENKINS, A.O.S.M., B.SC., DIP.N.Z.L.S., A.L.A.A.

Number of teachers: 510.

Number of students: 12,966.

Publications: *Dairy Farming Annual*†, *Sheep Farming Annual*†, *Calendar*†.

DEANS:

Faculty of Agricultural and Horticultural Science: A. R. FRAMPTON, M.AGR.SC., PH.D.

Faculty of Food Science and Biotechnology: R. L. EARLE, B.E., B.SC., PH.D.

Faculty of Veterinary Science: E. D. FIELDEN, B.AGR.SC., B.V.SC.

Faculty of Science: R. D. BATT, M.SC., M.A., PH.D., D.PHIL.

Faculty of Humanities: J. DUNMORE, M.A., PH.D.

Faculty of Social Sciences: K. W. THOMSON, M.A., PH.D.

Faculty of Business Studies: G. H. HINES, M.B.A.

Faculty of Education: R. S. ADAMS, M.A., PH.D.

PROFESSORS:

ADAMS, R. S., M.A., PH.D., Education
ANDERSON, R. D., M.AGR.SC., PH.D., Sheep Husbandry
BACON, D. F., M.SC., PH.D., Microbiology
BATT, R. D., M.SC., PH.D., M.A., D.PHIL., F.N.Z.I.C., Chemistry and Biochemistry
BLACKMORE, D. K., PH.D., F.R.C.V.S., Veterinary Public Health and Meat Hygiene
BRUERE, A. N., PH.D., Veterinary Clinical Sciences
CARTWRIGHT, R. W., PH.D., Marketing
DUNMORE, J., PH.D., French
EARLE, R. L., PH.D., Biotechnology
FIELDEN, E. D., B.AGR.SC., B.V.SC., Veterinary Clinical Science
FLUX, D. S., M.AGR.SC., PH.D., Dairy Husbandry
FRAMPTON, A. R., M.AGR.SC., PH.D., Agricultural Economics and Farm Management
FRASER, G. S., M.A., PH.D., Sociology
FREAN, R. G., M.A., A.M., PH.D., English
HAYMAN, B. I., M.SC., M.A., PH.D., Mathematics
HINES, G. H., M.B.A., Business Studies
HODGES, R., M.SC., PH.D., Chemistry
KAWHARU, I. H., M.A., B.LITT., D.PHIL., Social Anthropology
MALCOLM, G. N., M.SC., PH.D., F.N.Z.I.C., Physical Chemistry
MANKTELOW, B. W., PH.D., Veterinary Pathology
MCFARQUHAR, M.A., PH.D., Economics
MILNE, K., M.AGR.SC., PH.D., Horticulture and Plant Health
MUNFORD, R. E., M.AGR.SC., PH.D., Physiology and Anatomy
OLIVER, W. H., M.A., D.PHIL., History
RAE, A. L., M.AGR.SC., PH.D., Sheep Husbandry and Wool Science
RICHARDS, E. L., M.SC., PH.D., Food Technology
ROBINSON, R. G., M.A., PH.D., Philosophy
SCOTT, J. K., B.E. (HONS.), Industrial Technology
SHOUKSMITH, G., M.A., PH.D., Psychology
SYERS, J. K., PH.D., Soil Science
TATE, G., M.SC., Computer Science
THOMAS, R. G., PH.D., Botany
THOMPSON, K. W., M.A., PH.D., Geography
TOWNSLEY, R. J., PH.D., M.AGR.SC., Agricultural Economics and Farm Management
VEALE, J. A., M.SC., PH.D., D.I.C., F.R.I.H., M.I.B., Horticulture
WATKIN, B. R., M.AGR.SC., PH.D., Agronomy

UNIVERSITY OF OTAGO

P.O.B. 56, DUNEDIN

Telephone: 771-640.

Founded 1869.

Academic year: March to November.

Chancellor: Very Rev. J. S. SOMERVILLE, C.M.G., M.C., M.A.

Pro-Chancellor: M. JOEL, Q.S.O., E.D., LL.B.

Vice-Chancellor: R. O. H. IRVINE, M.D., F.R.C.P., F.R.A.C.P.

Registrar: D. W. GIRVAN, M.A., LL.B., W.S.

Librarian: W. J. MCELDOWNEY, M.A., F.N.Z.L.A.

Library: *see* Libraries.

Number of teachers (full-time): 479.
Number of students: 7,110.

Publication: *University Calendar*.

DEANS:

Faculty of Arts and Music: A. E. MUSGRAVE, PH.D.
Faculty of Science: A. D. CAMPBELL, M.SC., PH.D., F.N.Z.I.C.
Faculty of Law: P. B. A. SIM, LL.M.
Faculty of Medicine: G. L. BRINKMAN, M.D., D.C.H., F.R.C.P.(E.), F.R.A.C.P., F.A.C.P.
Clinical School (Christchurch): (vacant).
Clinical School (Wellington): R. H. JOHNSON, M.A., D.M., D.PHIL., M.D., D.SC., F.R.C.P.(GLAS.), F.R.S.E.
Faculty of Dentistry: M. R. KEAN, M.D.S., F.R.A.C.D.S.
Faculty of Home Science: PATRICIA D. COLEMAN, DIP.H.SC., M.S.
Faculty of Commerce: R. TURNER, M.TECH., D.M.S., A.N.Z.I.M.
Faculty of Theology: (vacant).

PROFESSORS:

AICKIN, D. R., M.B., CH.B., M.D., D.OBST., F.R.C.S.(E.), F.R.A.C.S., F.R.C.O.G., Obstetrics and Gynaecology
ALLDRED, A. J., M.B., CH.B., F.R.C.S., F.R.A.C.S., Orthopaedic Surgery
BAKER, A. B., M.B., B.S., D.PHIL., F.F.A.R.A.C.S., F.F.A.R.C.S., Anaesthetics
BANNISTER, P., PH.D., Botany
BARSBY, J. A., M.A., Classics
BEAVEN, D. W., M.B., CH.B., F.R.C.P., F.R.C.P.(E.), F.R.A.C.P., Medicine
BECK, D. J., M.SC., D.D.S., F.R.A.C.D.S., Community Dental Health
BIRKBECK, J. A., M.B., CH.B., F.R.C.P.(C.), Nutrition
BLENNERHASSETT, J. B., M.B., CH.B., F.R.A.C.P., F.R.C.P.A., F.R.C.P. (Canada), Pathology
BRINKMAN, G. L., M.D., D.C.H., F.R.C.P.ED., F.R.A.C.P., F.A.C.P., Medicine
BUCKINGHAM, D. A., M.SC., PH.D., F.N.Z.I.C., F.R.A.C.I., F.R.S.N.Z., Chemistry
CALVERT, BARBARA, M.A., M.H.SC., Education
CAMPBELL, A. D., M.SC., PH.D., F.N.Z.I.C., Chemistry
CARRELL, R. W., M.B., CH.B., PH.D., F.R.A.C.P., F.R.S.N.Z., Pathology
CLARKE, A. M., CH.M., F.R.A.C.S., Surgery
COLEMAN, PATRICIA D., DIP.H.SC., M.S., Home Science
COOMBS, D. S., PH.D., M.SC., F.R.S.N.Z., F.G.S., Geology
COOPER, M. H., B.A., Economics
CORBETT, R. E., PH.D., M.SC., F.N.Z.I.C., F.R.S.N.Z., Chemistry
COWAN, T. K., M.COM., F.C.A., C.M.A., M.N.Z.C.S., Accountancy
COX, B. G., M.SC., PH.D., F.B.C.S., F.N.Z.C.S., M.A.C.M., Computer Science
DAVIDSON, W., PH.D., D.SC., F.R.A.S., F.I.M.A., F.R.S.N.Z., Applied Mathematics
DODD, J. N., PH.D., M.SC., F.INST.P., F.R.S.N.Z., Physics
DOWDEN, R. L., PH.D., D.SC., F.INST.P., Physics
DRUMMOND, J. D., PH.D., Music
ESPINER, E. A., M.B., CH.B., M.D., F.R.A.C.P., Medicine
FLYNN, J. R., M.A., PH.D., Political Studies
FREEMAN, R. F. H., B.SC., M.A., Zoology
GIBSON, C. A., M.A., PH.D., English
GRANT, P. K., M.SC., PH.D., F.N.Z.I.C., Chemistry
HEAP, S. W., M.B., B.S., D.M.R.D., F.R.C.R., M.R.A.C.R., Radiology
HERD, E. W., M.A., German
HIGHAM, C. F. W., M.A., PH.D., Anthropology
HORSMAN, E. A., M.A., English
HOWIE, J. B., M.D., D.PHIL., F.R.C.PATH., F.R.A.C.P., F.R.C.P.A., Pathology
HUBBARD, J. I., M.A., D.M., PH.D., F.R.A.C.P., F.R.S.N.Z., Physiology
ISBISTER, W. H., M.D., F.R.C.S.(E.), F.R.A.C.S., Surgery
JAMES, B., B.SC., M.B., B.CH., F.R.A.N.Z.C.P., D.P.M., F.R.A.C.P., M.R.C.PSYCH., Psychological Medicine
JOHNSON, R. H., M.A., D.M., D.PHIL., M.D., D.SC., F.R.C.P.(GLAS.), F.R.S.E., Medicine
JOHNSTON, J. W., E.D., D.D.S., Prosthetic Dentistry
JONES, B. M., M.SC.SUR., PH.D., M.N.Z.I.S., Surveying
KEAN, M. R., M.D.S., F.R.A.C.D.S., Orthodontics
KIRK, E. E. J., M.D.S., F.D.S.R.C.S., F.R.A.C.D.S., Conservative Dentistry
LAVERTY, R., V.R.D., M.SC., PH.D., F.N.Z.I.C., Pharmacology
LISTER, R. G., B.A., F.R.G.S., Geography
LOUTIT, J. S., PH.D., Microbiology
MACALISTER, A. D., E.D., D.D.S., F.R.A.C.D.S., F.D.S.R.C.S., F.I.C.D., Oral Medicine and Surgery
MACBETH, W. A. A. G., M.B., B.S., F.R.C.S., F.R.C.S.(E.), F.R.A.C.S., Surgery
MCGIVEN, A. R., M.D., PH.D., F.R.C.P.A., Pathology
MCKELLAR, T. P. H., M.A., PH.D., F.B.PS.S., F.N.Z.P.S., Psychology
MCKERRACHER, D. W., M.A., M.ED., PH.D., Education
MACKNIGHT, A. D. C., PH.D., M.D., Physiology
MCLEOD, W. H., M.A., PH.D., History
MCQUEEN, E. G., V.R.D., M.B., PH.D., F.R.C.P., F.R.A.C.P., Clinical Pharmacology
MANDEL, S. P. H., M.SC., PH.D., Mathematical Statistics
MARK, A. F., M.SC., PH.D., F.R.S.N.Z., Botany
MOESEKE, P. VAN, M.E., M.S., M.A., PH.D., Economics
MOLLOY, P. J., M.B., CH.B., F.R.C.S., F.R.A.C.S., Cardiac Surgery
MORTIMER, J. G., M.B., CH.B., D.C.H., F.R.A.C.P., Paediatrics and Child Health
MUELLER-HEUMANN, G., DR.RER.POL., M.A.M.A., M.S.M.E.I., Marketing
MUSGRAVE, A. E., B.A., PH.D., Philosophy
NEWELL, K. W., M.B., CH.B., D.P.H., M.D., Community Health
O'DONNELL, T. V., M.D., F.R.C.P.(E.), F.R.A.C.P., Medicine
OMER-COOPER, J. D., M.A., History
PARR, J. C., M.B., CH.B., F.R.C.S., F.R.A.C.S., D.O.M.S., Ophthalmology
PETERSEN, G. B., M.SC., M.A., D.PHIL., F.N.Z.I.C., Biochemistry
ROBINSON, R. G., G.M., M.B., B.S., CH.M., F.R.C.S., F.R.A.C.S., Neurosurgery
ROLLESTON, G. L., M.B., CH.B., F.R.A.C.R., D.M.R.D., Radiology
ROSSELL, P. E., M.A., F.N.Z.I.M., Management
SATCHELL, G. H., PH.D., F.R.S.N.Z., F.A.A.A.S., Zoology
SAWYER, D. B., M.A., Pure Mathematics
SEDDON, R. J., M.B., CH.B., F.R.C.O.G., Obstetrics and Gynaecology
SHANNON, F. T., M.B., CH.B., F.R.C.P., F.R.A.C.P., Paediatrics
SIM, P. B. A., LL.M., Law
SIMPSON, F. O., M.B., CH.B., F.R.C.P.ED., F.R.A.C.P., Medicine
SKEGG, D. C. G., B.MED.SC., M.B., CH.B., D.PHIL., Preventive Medicine
SMILLIE, A. C., M.D.S., PH.D., Oral Biology
SNEYD, J. G. T., B.MED.SC., M.B.CH.B., PH.D., F.R.A.C.P., Clinical Biochemistry
STEHBENS, W. E., M.D., D.PHIL., F.R.C.PATH., F.R.C.P.A., Pathology
STEWART, R. D. H., M.B., CH.B., M.D., F.R.C.P., F.R.A.C.P., Medicine
STONE, R. G., M.A., D.U., French
SUTTON, R. J., B.A., LL.M., Law
TAYLOR, D. W., M.D., Physiology
TAYLOR, H., PH.D., F.P.S., Pharmacy
TROTTER, W. D., M.B., CH.B., D.PHIL., Anatomy
WESTON, H. J., M.B., CH.B., F.R.C.P., F.R.A.C.P., D.C.H., Paediatrics and Child Health
WILSON, P. J., M.A., PH.D., Anthropology

ATTACHED RESEARCH INSTITUTE:

Wellcome Research Institute: under the administrative control of the Department of Medicine in the Medical School.

VICTORIA UNIVERSITY OF WELLINGTON

PRIVATE BAG, WELLINGTON
Telephone: 721-000.

Founded 1897.

Language of instruction: English.

Academic year: March to October (two semesters).

Chancellor: K. B. O'BRIEN, M.COM.
Pro-Chancellor: The Rt. Hon. Mr. Justice RICHARDSON, S.J.D.
Vice-Chancellor: D. B. C. TAYLOR, M.SC., PH.D., F.M.I.MECH.E.
Deputy Vice-Chancellor: J. W. TOMLINSON, PH.D., D.I.C., F.R.S.C., F.N.Z.I.C.
Pro-Vice-Chancellor: W. E. DASENT, M.SC., F.N.Z.I.C.
Academic Pro-Vice-Chancellor: S. F. W. JOHNSTON, M.A.
Registrar: W. E. HARVEY, M.SC., PH.D., F.N.Z.I.C.
Librarian: **J. P. SAGE, M.A., DIP.N.Z.L.S.**

Library: *see* **Libraries.**

Number of full-time teachers: 422, including 67 professors.

Number of students: 7,269.

Publications: *Victoria University of Wellington Calendar, Vice-Chancellor's Report, News Vuw.*

DEANS:

Faculty of Architecture: H. TIPPETT, M.B.A., F.R.A.I.A.
Faculty of Arts: T. H. BEAGLEHOLE, M.A., PH.D.
Faculty of Commerce and Administration: G. FOGELBERG, M.COM., M.B.A., PH.D.

Faculty of Languages and Literature: C. W. DEARDEN, PH.D.
Faculty of Law: K. J. KEITH, LL.M.
Faculty of Science: R. L. W. AVERILL, M.AGR.SC., PH.D., G. R. BURNS, M.SC., PH.D.

PROFESSORS:

ARNOLD, R. D., M.A., PH.D., Education
AVERILL, R. L. W., M.AGR.SC., PH.D., Physiology
BEAGLEHOLE, D., M.SC., PH.D., Physical Electronics
BLOCK, G., M.ARCH., PH.D., Architecture
CAVE, R., M.A., PH.D., F.L.A., Librarianship
CHAPMAN, N. G., M.SC., PH.D., Nuclear Physics
CHOWNING, A., M.A., PH.D., Anthropology
CLARK, M., M.A., PH.D., Political Science
CLARK, R. H., M.SC., PH.D., F.G.S., Geology
CLIFT, J. C., M.SC., University Teaching and Research
CRESSWELL, M. J., M.A., PH.D., LITT.D., Philosophy
CULLWICK, T. D. C., M.TECH., PH.D., Marketing
CURTIS, N. F., M.SC., PH.D., F.R.S.N.Z., Chemistry
DEARDEN, C. W., PH.D., Classics
DUNCAN, J. F., M.A., M.SC., D.SC., PH.D., F.R.S.N.Z., Theoretical Chemistry
EGGLETON, I. R. C., M.B.A., B.COM., B.C.A., Accountancy
EVISON, F. F., M.A., PH.D., D.I.C., F.R.S.N.Z., Solid Earth Geophysics
FARQUHAR, D. A., M.A., MUS.B., Music
FERRIER, R. J., PH.D., F.R.S.N.Z., F.N.Z.I.C., Organic Chemistry
FIRTH, M. A., M.PHIL., M.SC., PH.D., Accountancy
FOGELBERG, G., M.B.A., M.COM., PH.D., Business Administration
FORBES, A. R., M.A., PH.D., Psychology
FRANKLIN, S. H., M.A., LITT.D., Geography
GARRICK, J. A. F., M.SC., PH.D., Zoology
GEERING, L. G., M.A., B.D., Religious Studies
GOULD, J. D., M.A., Economic History
HAMER, D. A., D.PHIL., F.R.HIST.S., History
HAWKE, G. R., D.PHIL., Economic History
HEYES, J. K., M.SC., PH.D., Botany
HILL, M., PH.D., Sociology
HUGHES, G. E., M.A., Philosophy
JACKSON, L. F., M.A., Econometrics
JANAKI, K., M.A., PH.D., International Relations
KEITH, K. J., LL.M., Jurisprudence and Constitutional Law
KOOZNETZOFF, C., DR.PHIL., German
LANG, H. G., C.M.G., B.A., B.COM., Economics
MCCREARY, J. R., M.A., Social Administration
MCKAY, L., LL.M., English and New Zealand Law
MCKENZIE, D. F., M.A., PH.D., English
MALCOLM, W. G., M.A., PH.D., Pure Mathematics
MARSH, R. W., M.A., PH.D., Education
MATHIESON, D. L., PH.D., Law
MEAD, S. H., M.A., PH.D., Maori
MUNZ, P., M.A., PH.D., History
NICULESCU, B. M., M.A., PH.D., Economics
NONWEILER, T., PH.D., Applied Mathematics
NORRISH, P. J., M.A., PH.D., French
ORR, G. S., LL.M., Law
PHILPOTT, B. P., M.COM., M.A., Economics
PRIDE, J. B., M.A., English Language
QUENTIN-BAXTER, R. Q., B.A., LL.B., Jurisprudence
ROBB, J. H., M.A., PH.D., Sociology
ROBERTS, J. L., LL.B., D.P.A., Public Administration
ROBINSON, R. D., M.A., PH.D., English
SHEPPARD, D., M.A., PH.D., Money and Finance
SMITH, J. N., PH.D., D.SC., F.R.S.N.Z., Biochemistry
TAYLOR, A. J. W., M.A., PH.D., F.B.PS.S., Clinical Psychology
TIPPETT, H., B.ARCH., M.B.A., F.R.A.I.A., Architecture
TOMLINSON, J. W., PH.D., F.N.Z.I.C., Physical Chemistry
TROW, D. G., B.COM., Accountancy
VERE-JONES, D., M.SC., D.PHIL., Mathematics
VIGNAUX, G. A., PH.D., D.I.C., Information Science
WADDINGTON, P. H., M.A., PH.D., Russian
WELLS, J. B. J., PH.D., Zoology
WINIATA, W., M.B.A., PH.D., Accountancy
YOUNG, F. J. L., M.A., Industrial Relations

ATTACHED RESEARCH INSTITUTES:

Antarctic Research Centre: Dir. P. J. BARRETT, M.SC., PH.D.

English Language Institute: Dir. H. V. GEORGE, M.A.

Industrial Relations Centre: Dir. F. J. L. YOUNG, M.A.

Institute of Criminology: Dir. W. YOUNG, PH.D.

Institute of Geophysics: Dir. F. F. EVISON, M.A., PH.D.

Institute of Statistics and Operations Research: Chair. D. VERE-JONES, M.SC., D.PHIL.

UNIVERSITY OF WAIKATO

HAMILTON

Telephone: 62889.

Founded 1964.

Academic year: February to November (three terms).

Chancellor: C. D. ARCUS, LL.B.
Vice-Chancellor: D. R. LLEWELLYN, D.PHIL., D.SC., F.N.Z.I.C., F.R.I.C., F.R.S.A.
Registrar: I. T. SNOWDON, M.A.
Librarian: JEANETTE KING, B.A., B.SC., DIP.N.Z.L.S., A.N.Z.L.A.

Number of teachers: 196.

Number of students: 3,381.

Publication: *University of Waikato Calendar.*

DEANS:

School of Humanities: R. ZIEDINS.
School of Management Studies: G. J. SCHMITT.
School of Social Sciences: J. E. RITCHIE.
School of Science: J. D. MCCRAW.
Waikato College of Teacher Education: I. A. MCLAREN.

PROFESSORS:

ARTHUR, C. M., LL.M., A.C.A., A.C.I.S., Management Studies
BETTISON, D. G., M.A., PH.D., Sociology
DUNCAN, C., M.A., PH.D., Geography
FREYBERG, P. S., M.A., PH.D., Education
HOSKING, R. J., PH.D., Mathematics
JENSEN, J. H., M.A., PH.D., History
LILEY, B. S., M.SC., PH.D., Physics
MACKAY, K. M., PH.D., F.R.S.C., F.N.Z.I.C., Chemistry
MARSHALL A., B.A., Management Studies
MARSHALL, F. W., M.A., D.U., French
MCCRAW, J. D., M.SC., D.SC., Earth Sciences
MCLAREN, I. A., M.A., PH.D., Education
NIESCHMIDT, H. W., DR.PHIL., German
OED, G. V., B.COM., F.C.A., C.M.A., Management Studies
PETERSON, R., B.COM., M.A., F.C.A., A.A.S.A.(S.), A.A.U.Q., Management Studies
POOL, D. I., M.A., PH.D., Sociology
PRENDERGAST, J. G., M.SC., PH.D., D.I.C., F.R.E.S., Biological Sciences
RITCHIE, J. E., M.A., PH.D., F.B.PS.S., Psychology
ROY, W. T., M.A., Politics
SCHMITT, G. J., M.A., B.COM., D.P.A., F.C.A., C.M.A., Management Studies
SELBY, M. T., M.A., D.PHIL., Earth Sciences
SILVESTER, W. B., M.SC., PH.D., Biological Sciences
THOMAS, D. R., PH.D., Psychology
WALKER, G. M., PH.D., English
WALLS, D. F., PH.D., F.INST.P., Physics
WARD, J. T., M.LITT., PH.D., Economics
ZIEDINS, R., M.A., PH.D., Philosophy
ZULAUF, A., DR.RER.NAT., PH.D., Mathematics

TECHNICAL INSTITUTES

Auckland Technical Institute: Wellesley St. East, Private Bag, C.P.O., Auckland 1; f. 1964; courses in trades, technical, professional and commercial subjects; 275 full-time and 454 part-time teachers, 1,276 full-time and 14,340 part-time students; library of 33,951 vols.; Principal I. M. MOSES, B.A., B.COM.; Registrar R. E. KORN, A.C.I.S.

Christchurch Polytechnic: P.O.B. 22-095, Christchurch 1; f. 1965; courses at trade technician and professional level; 180 full-time and 512 part-time teachers, 14,000 students; library of 30,000 vols.; Dir. J. D. A. HERCUS, M.SC.

Manukau Technical Institute: P.O.B. 61066, Otara, Auckland; f. 1970; courses in trades, technical and professional subjects; 150 teachers, 9,500 students; Principal R. J. WILLYAMS, M.A., A.C.A., A.N.Z.I.M.; Registrar F. R. MASON, A.C.A.; Librarian Mrs. A. M. M. HUANG, M.A., A.N.Z.L.A.

New Zealand Technical Correspondence Institute: Private Bag 30-335, Lower Hutt; **f. 1946; courses by correspondence in trades, technical, agricultural and commercial subjects; 408 full-time teachers, 35,000 students; Principal Hon. A. E. KINSELLA, M.A.**

Otago Polytechnic: Private Bag, Dunedin; f. 1966; courses in commercial, technical and professional subjects; 110 teachers, 5,500 students; library of 10,000 vols.; Principal E. C. AITCHISON, B.COM., A.C.A.

Petone Technical Institute: P.O.B. 38-177, Buick St., Petone, nr. Wellington; f. 1976; courses in trades, commercial and technical subjects; staff of 147, 6,300 students; library of 6,000 vols.; Principal R. C. SMITH, B.SC.

Waikato Technical Institute: P.O.B. 982, Hamilton; f. 1968; courses in trades, commercial and technical subjects, nursing; small library; 160 teachers, 9,000 students: Principal J. C. WILSON, M.A.; Registrar Mrs. J. TILL.

Wellington Polytechnic: Private Bag, Wellington; f. 1962; courses in commercial, technical and professional subjects; 200 teachers, 8,000 students; library of 20,000 vols.; Principal D. S. ABBOTT, A.A.DIPL., F.N.Z.I.A., A.R.I.B.A.; Registrar F. A. BELL, F.C.A.

SCHOOLS OF ART AND MUSIC

School of Fine Arts: Faculty of Fine Arts, University of Auckland, Whitaker Place, Auckland; f. 1949; library of 17,000 vols.; Dean Prof. JOLYON D. SAUNDERS, M.S.I.A., F.N.Z.S.I.D., F.R.S.A.; publs. *Prospectus, Library Bulletin.*

School of Fine Arts: Faculty of Music and Fine Arts, University of Canterbury, Christchurch; f. 1882; degree course in History of Art; diploma and honours courses in engraving, painting, sculpture, graphic design, film, photography; studies in art education; Head Prof. H. J. SIMPSON, A.T.D.

NICARAGUA

Population 2,324,000

ACADEMIES

Academia Nicaragüense de la Lengua (*Nicaraguan Academy of Languages*): Apdo. 2711, Managua; f. 1928; 16th in order of foundation in Latin America; correspondent of the Real Academia Española, Madrid; archives and library destroyed by fire 1972.
Director: PABLO ANTONIO CUADRA.
Secretary: JULIO YCAZA TIGERINO.
Librarian: EDUARDO ZEPEDA-HENRÍQUEZ.

Academia de Geografía e Historia de Nicaragua: Managua; f. 1934; Pres. ROSENDO ARGÜELLO; Sec. MODESTO ARMIJO; publ. *Revista.*

Academia Nacional de Filosofía (*National Academy of Philosophy*): Managua; f. 1964.
President: EDUARDO ZEPEDA HENRÍQUEZ.
Secretary: CARLOS JIMÉNEZ CAJINA.

LEARNED SOCIETIES AND RESEARCH INSTITUTES

(*see* also under Universities)

Agrarian Institute of Nicaragua: Managua; f. 1964; Dir. Dr. RODOLFO MEJILLA UBILLA; publ. *Agrarian News* (monthly).

Servicio Geológico Nacional (*National Geological Survey*): Apdo. postal 13-47, Managua; f. 1956; research into country's mineral resources and general scientific research; offers grants; specialized library; Dir. R. SOLÓRZANO MARÍN; publ. *Boletín* (annually).

Sociedad de Oftalmología Nicaragüense: Clínica Especializada, Managua; f. 1949; Pres. R. LACAYO G.

Sociedad Nicaragüense de Psiquiatría y Psicología: Centro Médico, Managua; f. 1962; Pres. Dr. R. GUTIÉRREZ.

LIBRARIES

Archivo General de la Nación: 6a Calle No. 402, Apdo. 101, Managua; f. 1882; 40,356 vols.; Dir. LUIS CUADRA CEA.

Biblioteca Central de la Universidad Nacional de Nicaragua: León; f. 1816; 34,000 vols.; Dir. Prof. WALTERIO LÓPEZ ADAROS.

Biblioteca del Instituto Centroamericano de Administración de Empresas: Apdo. 2485, Managua; specialized library of 20,000 vols. on business administration, economic development and central American social and economic conditions; Dir. Lic. THOMAS BLOCH.

Biblioteca Económica y Financiera (*Economic and Financial Library*): Managua.

Biblioteca "Eduardo Montealegre": Chinandega.

Biblioteca "El Ateneo": Masaya; f. 1941; 35 mems.; Dir. Dr. SANTIAGO FAJARDO F.; publ. *Revista* (yearly).

Biblioteca "Morazan": Matagalpa.

Biblioteca Municipal: Nagarote, León.

Biblioteca Municipal: Bluefields, Zelaya.

Biblioteca Nacional: Calle del Triunfo No. 302, Apdo. 101, Managua; f. 1882; 70,000 vols.; Dir. CARLOS A. BRAVO.

Biblioteca "Rubén Darío": Calle Candelaria 308, Managua; f. 1942; 11,000 vols.

Biblioteca "Segovia": Ocotal, Nueva Segovia.

MUSEUMS

Museo Nacional de Nicaragua: Apdo. 416, Colonia Dambach, Managua; f. 1896; archaeology, ceramics, zoology, botany and geology; library of *c.* 500 vols.; Dir. LEONOR MARTÍNEZ DE ROCHA.

Museo "Tenderi": Masaya.

UNIVERSITIES

UNIVERSIDAD NACIONAL AUTÓNOMA DE NICARAGUA

LEÓN, NICARAGUA, C.A.
Telephone: 26-12, 26-13, 26-14.
Founded 1812.

Academic year: June to March.

The Universidad Nacional is the result of the union of the Universidad de Oriente y Mediodía with the Universidad de Occidente y Septentrión, respectively founded in 1804 and 1806.

Rector: Dr. MARIANO FIALLOS OYANGUREN.
Administrative Vice-Rector: Lic. JULIÁN CORRALES MUNGUÍA.
Vice-Rector (*Managua*): Lic. JULIÁN CORRALES MUNGUÍA.
Secretary-General: Dr. DENIS MARTÍNEZ CABEZAS.

Library of 36,000 vols.
Number of teachers: 756.
Number of students: 14,889.
Publications: *Gaceta Universitaria, Cuadernos Universitarios.*

DEANS:

Faculty of Medicine: Dr. JOAQUÍN SOLÍS PIURA.
Faculty of Dentistry: Dr. NÉSTOR ARÁUZ GODOY.
Faculty of Humanities (*Managua*): Dr. MARIO PALMA IBARRA.
Faculty of Economics (*Managua*): Lic. JULIO CÉSAR VEGA RAMÍREZ.
Faculty of Juridical and Social Sciences: Dr. JESÚS ALVAREZ ALVARADO.
Faculty of Chemistry: Dra. MARÍA ELENA BERRÍOS DE OROZCO.
Faculty of Physical-Mathematical Sciences (*Managua*): Dr. OTONIEL ARGÜELLO HERRERA.
Faculty of Sciences and Letters: Dr. MOISÉS HASSAN MORALES.

ATTACHED INSTITUTES:

Instituto de Investigaciones del Desarrollo (*Development Research Institute*): Faculty of Economics; Dir. FRANCISCO LÁINEZ.

Instituto de Capacitación Sindical (*Institute of Trade Union Training*): Faculty of Law; Dir. Dr. LUSI FELIPE PÉREZ CALDERA.

UNIVERSIDAD CENTRO-AMERICANA (Sección de Nicaragua)

APARTADO 69, MANAGUA
Telephone: 80351, 80352.
Founded 1961.

Private control; Roman Catholic; Academic year: January to December.
President: Ing. ALBERTO CHAMORRO B.
Rector: Dr. JUAN B. ARRÍEN, S.J.
Vice-Rector: Dr. INDALECIO RODRÍGUEZ A.
Registrar: Lic. MÁXIMO GARCÍA S.
Librarian: Lic. MAYRA MIRANDA DE PEÑA.

Number of teachers: 230.
Number of students: 4,137.
Publication: *Revista Encuentro*†.

DEANS:
Faculty of Engineering: Dr. JAIME DOWNING URTECHO.
Faculty of Law: Dr. RODOLFO SANDINO.
Faculty of Business Administration: Lic. JAIME ARGÜELLO DOWNING.
Faculty of Business Administration: Dr. JULIO LINARES.
Faculty of Humanities and Sciences: Dr. JAIME INCER BARQUERO.
Faculty of Veterinary Medicine and Zootechnics: Dr. INDALECIO RODRÍGUEZ ALANIZ.

ATTACHED INSTITUTES:
Instituto de Investigación Social "Juan XXIII".
Instituto Histórico Centroamericano.

UNIVERSIDAD POLITÉCNICA DE NICARAGUA

APARTADO 3595, MANAGUA
Telephone: 40-8-24.

Founded 1968 as institute, university status 1976.

Private control; Academic year: August to May.

Rector: Lic. SERGIO DENIS GARCÍA VELÁSQUEZ.
Vice-Rector: Dr. RAMIRO CRUZ URBINA.
Registrar: Lic. ALEYDA AVILÉS ROJAS.
Librarian: AURA CELA DE OCÓN.

Number of teachers: 70.
Number of students: 600.

DEANS AND DIRECTORS:
School of Nursing: LOIDA GARCÍA DE MARTÍNEZ.
School of Industrial Technology: ALEJANDRO MARTÍNEZ.
Department of Commerce and Business: JAIME BACA CASTELLÓN.
Department of Decorative Arts: MIRIAM DE ANZOÁTEGUI.

PROFESSORS:
ACEVEDO, REYNALDO, Soldering
ANZOÁTEGUI, MIRIAM DE, Decoration
AUXILIADORA HERNANDEZ, MARIA, Gynaecology
CANTÓN, ROBERTO, General Insurance
CISNEROS L., NENA DE, Works Organization and Administration
DÁVILA, SERGIO, Structural Drawing
DÍAZ, EDUARDO, Soldering Workshop
FLORES, ALEYDA, Decorative Arts
FLORES, ROLANDO, Soldering
GARCÍA, GLORIA MARÍA, English
GUTIÉRREZ, RUTH, Resistance of Materials
JUNCADELLA, SANTIAGO, Organization in Physical Education and Sport
LÓPEZ, ÁNGEL, Swimming
MADRIZ, THELMA, Food and Nutrition
MARTÍNEZ, FULVIO, Industrial Safety
MARTÍNEZ, ROSA, Nursing
MENDIETA, PEDRO, Public Relations and Publicity
MENDOZA, EVENOR, Publicity Administration, Design Control and Management
MORALES, RAFAELA, Nursing
MORENO, NERY DE, Decorative Arts
OLIVAS, HUMBERTO, Baseball
PADILLA, LUISA, Psychiatric Nursing
PINEDA, ALICE, Nursing
RAYO, ISAURA, Dressmaking, Industrial Arts
RIVAS NAVAS, GUILLERMO, Drawing
RODRÍGUEZ, AMPARO DE, Nursing
ROMÁN, LUIS, Practical Teaching for Physical Education
QUINO DE CORDONERO, NINFA, Nursing

COLLEGES

Colegio de Médicos y Cirujanos de Nicaragua: Apartado Postal 1867, Managua; f. 1965; Pres. Dr. JOSÉ ANTONIO CANTÓN; Dir. Dr. JORGE GARCÍA ESQUIVEL; publ. *Voz Médica Informativa.*

Escuela Nacional de Agricultura y Ganadería: Apdo. Postal 453, Kilómetro 12, Carretera Norte, Managua; f. 1929; attached to Instituto Nicaraguense de Tecnología Agropecuaria (INTA); library of 12,000 vols.; Dir. FRANK SEQUEIRA BUSTAMANTE.

Instituto Centroamericano de Administración de Empresas (INCAE): Apdo. 2485, Managua; f. 1964 with technical assistance from Harvard Univ.; two-year master's programme in business administration; executive training programmes; management research and consulting; library: *see* Libraries; Rector Dr. ERNESTO CRUZ.

Instituto Nicaraguense de Cine: Apdo. postal 4660, Managua; f. 1979; attached to the Ministry of Culture; centre for artistic creation and training for all aspects of cinematography: production, distribution, exhibition, mobile cinema, film criticism, national film library; Dir. CARLOS VICENTE IBARRA.

NIGER

Population 4,994,000

RESEARCH INSTITUTES

Bureau de Recherches Géologiques et Minières: B.P. 458, Niamey; Dir. M. GREIGERT. (*See* main entry under France).

Centre Culturel Américain: B.P. 11201, Niamey.

Centre Régional de Recherche et de Documentation pour la Tradition Orale: B.P. 369, Niamey; f. 1968 by agreement with UNESCO; 23 mems.; library of 5,000 tape recordings of songs, tales, fables and historical records in the following languages: Fulfuldé, Hausa, Zerma, Songhay, Tamasheq, Kanuri; aims to collect, transcribe, translate and publish all works of the oral tradition from West Africa, Cameroon and Chad; Pres. HAMA BOUBOU; Exec. Sec. ISSAKA DANKOUSSOU; publ. *Bulletin périodique de liaison et d'information*.

Compagnie Française pour le Développement des Fibres Textiles—CFDT: B.P. 10189, Niamey; Dir. D. SALVY.

Institut de Recherches en Sciences Humaines—IRSH: B.P. 318, Université de Niamey, Niamey; f. 1976 as successor to *Centre Nigérien de Recherches en Sciences Humaines*; library of 8,000 vols.; 5 sections: archaeology, history, sociology, linguistics, audio-visual; Dir. D. HAMANI; Sec. A. ALZOUMA; publs. *Etudes Nigériennes, Mu kaara Sani* (3 a year).

Institut de Recherches sur les Fruits et Agrumes (IRFA): B.P. 886, Niamey; Dir. M. HAURY. (*See* main entry under France.)

Institut National de recherches agronomiques au Niger (INRAN): B.P. 150, Niamey; soil science; stations at Tarna and Kolo; Dir. J. NABOS.

INRAN—Département des Recherches Forestières: B.P. 225, Niamey; f. 1975; silviculture, soil improvement and conservation; Dir. M. BARBIER.

Laboratoire vétérinaire de Niamey: Niamey.

Office de la Recherche Scientifique et Technique Outre-Mer: B.P. 11416, Niamey; hydrology, archaeology, geophysics; Dir. M. HOEPFFNER. (*See* main entry under France.)

Office National de l'Energie Solaire: B.P. 621, Niamey.

Station Avicole et Centre d'Elevage Caprin: Maradi; f. 1961; Dir. HASSANE BAZA; publ. *Report* (annual).

Station Sahélienne Expérimentale de Toukounous: Service d'Elevage du Niger, Toukounous/Filingué; f. 1931; selection and breeding of Zebu Azaouak cattle and distribution of selected bulls to improve the local heterogeneous breed; Dir. Dr. MANFRED LINDAU; publs. *Berlin Münchner Tierärztliche Wochenschrift*, Annual Report.

LIBRARY AND ARCHIVES

Archives de la République du Niger: Niamey; f. 1913; documents to the end of the 19th century.

Centre de Documentation: Commissariat Général au Développement, Présidence de la République, Niamey; f. 1965; Librarian ALOU MOUMOUNI.

MUSEUM

Musée National du Niger: B.P. 248, Niamey; f. 1959; representative collection of tribal costumes, crafts, tribal houses; includes park and zoo, ethnographic museum, palaeontology and pre-history museums; also Handicrafts Centre and Cultural Activities Centre; Curator ALBERT FERRAL.

UNIVERSITY

UNIVERSITÉ DE NIAMEY

B.P. 237, NIAMEY

Telephone: 73-27-13/14/15.

Founded 1971; University status 1973.

Rector: ABDOU MOUMOUNI.

Secretary-General: CHRISTIAN GARRAUD.

Number of teachers: 200.

Number of students: 850.

CONSTITUENT INSTITUTES:

Ecole des Sciences: Dir. Prof. P. FOULANI.

Ecole des Lettres: Dir. Dr. A. HAMANI.

Ecole de Pédagogie: Dir. ANDRÉ SALIFOU.

Institut de Recherche pour l'Enseignement des Mathématiques: Dir. Dr. A. TRAORE.

Ecole Supérieure d'Agronomie: Dir. Dr. H. BAZA.

Ecole des Sciences de la Santé: Dir. Dr. H. SÉKOU.

Institut de Recherches en Sciences Humaines: see under Research Institutes.

A new university, Université Islamique d'Afrique de l'Ouest, is under construction at Say. The first stage will incorporate a faculty of Islamic studies and a polytechnic.

COLLEGE

Ecole Nationale d'Administration du Niger: B.P. 542, Niamey; f. 1963 to train civil servants and other officials; library of 18,000 vols.; number of teachers: 44 full-time, 22 part-time; number of students: 580; Dir. M. DAN-BOUZOUA.

NIGERIA

Population 72,217,000

ACADEMY

Nigerian Academy of Science: Secretariat: Dept. of Physics, University of Ibadan, Ibadan; f. 1977; 45 Foundation Fellows.

COUNCIL

President: Prof. C. A. ONWUMECHILI.

Vice-President: Prof. C. I. O. OLANIYAN.

Secretary (Physical and Mathematical Sciences): Prof. AWELE MADUEMEZIA.

Secretary (Biological Sciences): Prof. J. B. E. AWACHIE.

Treasurer: Prof. O. AWE.

MEMBERS:

Mathematical and Physical Sciences:
ADEGOKE, O. S.
EMOVON, E. U.
EZEILO, J. O. C.
OLADAPO, I. O.
OYAWOYE, M. O.

Biological Sciences:
ADEGBOLA, A. A.
BASSIR, O.
FABIYI, A.
OSENI, A. M.
UDEKWU, F. A. O.

LEARNED SOCIETIES

Association for Teacher Education in Africa: University of Lagos Faculty of Education, Lagos; f. 1968; annual conferences, workshops, teacher exchange programme, award of Fellowships for higher degrees; 33 mem. institutions, which are University Colleges, Departments and Institutions of Education in Africa (31), U.K. (1) and U.S.A. (1); Pres. Prof. NEWMAN SMART (Sierra Leone); Exec. Secs. Dr. J. C. B. BIGALA (Kenya), Prof. S. N. NWOSU (acting) (Nigeria); publs. *Reports of Conferences* (annual), *ATEA Newsletter* (twice a year), *ATEA Brochure* (every two years).

British Council: P.O.B. 3702, Western House, Broad St., Lagos; Rep. G. R. TRIBE, O.B.E.; also at: P.O.B. 330, Enugu; Dir. G. MELLORS; P.M.B. 3003, Kofar Nasarawa, Kano City; Dir. R. G. LOGAN REID; P.O.B. 81, Kaduna; Dir. A. A. NORRIS; libraries (*see* Libraries).

Ecological Society of Nigeria: c/o Dept. of Biology, University of Ife, Ile-Ife, Oyo State; f. 1973; 100 mems.; Pres. Prof. C. I. O. OLANIYAN; Sec. Prof. A. M. A. IMEVBORE.

Entomological Society of Nigeria: c/o Dept. of Agricultural Biology, University of Ibadan, Ibadan, Oyo State; f. 1965 to further the study of insects in Nigeria; 170 mems.; Pres. Prof. ANTHONY YOUDEOWEI; Sec. Dr. BAYO ODEBIYI; publ. *Nigerian Journal of Entomology* (2 a year).

Fisheries Society of Nigeria: P.M.B. 12529, Lagos; f. 1976; 200 mems.; Pres. E. O. BAYAGBONA; Hon. Sec. B. F. DADA; publs. *Nigerian Journal of Fisheries and Hydrobiology, Proceedings, Fishery Bulletin, Advisory Notes.*

Forestry Association of Nigeria: P.O.B. 4185, Ibadan, Oyo State; f. 1969 to further interest in forests and forest resources management and utilization; 355 personal mems., 13 corporate mems.; Pres. A. M. OSENI; Sec. P. R. O. KIO; publs. *Nigerian Journal of Forestry* (irregular), *Proceedings of Annual Conferences.*

Genetics Society of Nigeria: c/o International Institute of Tropical Agriculture, Oyo Rd., P.M.B. 5320, Ibadan, Oyo State; f. 1972 to further interest in genetics for the benefit of mankind and in the various areas of crops, livestock and medicine; 75 mems.; Pres. Dr. O. A. OJOMO; Sec. Dr. A. O. ABIFARIN; publ. *Proceedings.*

Geological Survey of Nigeria: P.M.B. 2007, Kaduna South; f. 1919; geological mapping; survey of Nigeria's mineral resources; geophysical surveys and consultation on geological problems; library of 26,000 vols.; Chief Officer C. N. OKEZIE; publs. *Annual Report, Bulletins*†, *Occasional Papers*†, *Records*†, geological maps†.

German Cultural Institute (Goethe-Institut): 174 Broad St., P.O.B. 957, Lagos; f. 1961; teaching of German language; cultural activities; library of 5,300 vols.; Dir. Dr. R. RUPRECHT.

Historical Society of Nigeria: c/o Dept. of History, University of Lagos, Lagos; f. 1955 to encourage interest and work in connection with the study of history, especially Nigerian history; Pres. Prof. J. F. A. AJAYI; Sec. Prof. A. I. ASIWAJU; publs. *Journal, Tarikh* (2 a year), *Bulletin of News* (quarterly).

Istituto Italiano di Cultura: 77 Brickfield Road, Lagos; Dir. Prof. UMBERTO COMI.

Nigerian Bar Association: 25 Odion Rd., P.O.B. 403, Warri; f. 1962; Nat. Pres. Dr. MUDIAGA ODJE; Chair. Chief V. O. ESAN; Gen. Sec. DEBO AKANDE.

Nigerian Economic Society: Department of Economics, University of Ibadan, Ibadan; f. 1958; to advance social and economic knowledge particularly about Nigeria; 600 mems.; Pres. Prof. O. TERIBA; Sec. S. TOMORI; publ. *Nigerian Journal of Ecomomic and Social Studies* (3 a year, Editor Dr. M. O. KAYODE).

Nigerian Geographical Association: c/o Dept. of Geography, University of Ibadan, Ibadan; f. 1955; to further interest in geography and its methods of teaching with special reference to Nigeria; 500 mems.; Pres. Prof. R. K. UDO; Sec. Dr. I. ADALEMO; publ. *Nigerian Geographical Journal.*

Nigerian Institute of International Affairs: Kofo Abayomi Rd., Victoria Island, P.O.B. 1727, Lagos; f. 1963 to provide a non-political forum for the study of international affairs; library of 100,000 vols.; Dir.-Gen. Dr. A. BOLAJI AKINYEMI.

Nigerian Institute of Management: 145 Broad St., P.O.B. 2557, Lagos; f. 1961; a professional body for managers and administrators and a training institution for practising managers; from both private and public sectors (trains more than 1,800 annually); 4,000 mems.; library of *c.* 4,000 vols.; Dir.-Gen. Chief O. I. A. AKINYEMI; publ. *Management in Nigeria.*

Nigerian Library Association: c/o The Library, Kwara College of Technology, P.M.B. 1375, Ilorin, Kwara State; f. 1962; 900 mems.; Pres. Mallam ABDULLAHI NINGI; Sec. FRANCIS OLATUNJI; publs. *Nigerian Libraries* (3 a year), *N.L.A. Newsletter* (monthly), occasional papers; a bulletin is published by each of the State Divisions.

Nigerian Society for Microbiology: c/o Dept. of Medical Microbiology, University College Hospital, Ibadan,

Oyo State; f. 1973 to promote the advancement of medical veterinary and industrial microbiology; holds annual conferences in the Nigerian universities; 80 mems.; Pres. Prof. O. OGUNBI; Sec. Dr. A. O. OSOBA; publ. *Journal* (2 a year).

Nigerian Veterinary Medical Association: c/o Faculty of Veterinary Medicine, Ahmadu Bello University, Samaru, P.M.B. 1044, Zaria, Kaduna State; f. 1963 to advance the science and art of veterinary medicine, including its relationship to public health and agriculture; 500 mems.; Pres. Dr. I. ALHAJI; Sec. Dr. D. S. ADEGBOYE; publ. *Nigerian Veterinary Journal* (2 a year).

Nutrition Society of Nigeria: c/o Dept. of Food Science and Technology, University of Ife, Ile-Ife, Oyo State; f. 1966; 350 mems.; Pres. Prof. OLUMBE BASSIR; Sec. Dr. J. B. FASHAKIN; publ. *Nigerian Nutrition Newsletter.*

U.S. International Communication Agency (fmrly. U.S. Information Service): Cocoa House, Bank Rd., Ibadan; brs. in Lagos, Kaduna, Kano.

West African Association of Agricultural Economists: c/o Dept. of Agricultural Economics, University of Ibadan, Ibadan, Oyo State; f. 1972; 170 mems. from Benin Republic, Cameroon, Ghana, Ivory Coast, Liberia, Mali, Nigeria, Senegal, Sierra Leone, Togo and Upper Volta; Pres. Prof. RUFUS O. ADEGBOYE; Sec. Dr. ANTHONY E. IKPI; publ. *West African Journal of Agricultural Economics.*

RESEARCH INSTITUTES

(*see* also under Universities)

National Science and Technology Development Agency: 8 Strachan St., P.M.B. 12695, Lagos; f. 1977; executive responsibility for promotion and development of science and technology including initiation of policy; prepares periodic master plans for development, advises on the financial requirements for their implementation, prepares annual budgets for scientific research development and receives grants for allocation to research institutions and special research projects conducted by the universities under the aegis of the Agency; supervises and co-ordinates activities of research institutes, allocates special research projects to universities; publishes or sponsors publication of scientific research journals; library: see Libraries; Exec. Sec. Dr. V. O. S. OLUNLOYO; publs. *Index of Post Graduate Dissertations in Science and Technology Accepted by Nigerian Universities 1948–78*†, *Union Catalogue of Scientific and Technical Periodicals held in the Libraries of the NSTDA, its Research Institutes and the IITA*†.

Cocoa Research Institute of Nigeria: Onigambari, P.M.B. 5244, Ibadan, Oyo State; f. 1938; research into cocoa, cola, coffee, cashew and tea; research aspects include entomology, plant-breeding, plant pathology, soil chemistry and bio-chemistry; library of 10,000 vols.; Dir. S. T. OLATOYE, PH.D.; publs. *CRIN News, Annual Report, Memoranda*, advisory leaflets, research report papers.

Forestry Research Institute of Nigeria: P.M.B. 5054, Ibadan; f. 1954; conducts intensive research into all aspects of forestry and forest products utilization; 2 Forestry Schools at Ibadan and Jos; library of 30,000 vols.; Dir. O. A. ATANDA, PH.D.; publs. *Annual Report, Index of Research, Technical Notes* (irregular), *Research Papers* (Series).

Kainji Lake Research Institute: P.M.B. 666, New Bussa, Kwara State; f. 1965; research into the limnological behaviour and characteristics of the Kainji and other man-made lakes and their effects on the fish and other aquatic life; the abundance, distribution and other biological characteristics of species of fish and practical methods of their exploitation; the behaviour and characteristics of wildlife and its conservation; range ecology; the development of irrigated crops; public health problems, and the socio-economic effects of the construction of the Kainji and other man-made lakes on rural populations; Asst. Dir. H. M. YESUFU, PH.D.; publs. *Newsletter, Annual Report.*

Lake Chad Research Institute: Malamfatori, P.O.B. 227, Maiduguri, Borno State; f. 1975; research into the hydrological behaviour and characteristics of Lake Chad and the limnology of the associated surface and ground waters; the abundance, distribution and other biological characteristics of species of fish and other aquatic life in the lake and practical methods of their exploitation; the behaviour and characteristics of the wildlife associated with the lake and its conservation; ecology and methods of control of crop pests and diseases of economic importance; improvement of the methods of control of dry farming and livestock husbandry in the severe environmental condition around the lake; improvement of cultivation of wheat, barley, and other crops by irrigation; the socio-economic and public health effects of the introduction of large-scale irrigation schemes and improved methods of animal husbandry and fishing on the rural populations around the lake; Dir. E. O. BAYAGBONA, B.SC.

Leather Research Institute of Nigeria: Samaru, P.M.B. 1052, Zaria, Kaduna State; f. 1964; trains Hides and Skins Improvement Officers, leather craftsmen, boot and shoe technologists; research into indigenous tanning materials and techniques; serves as the Nigerian Standards Organisation's centre for leather and leather goods; Dir. A. S. MSHLBWALA; publs. *Monthly Newsletter, Journals*; three sub-centres at Sokoto, Maiduguri and Oji River for extension services.

National Cereals Research Institute: Moor Plantation, P.M.B. 5042, Ibadan, Oyo State; f. 1910, formerly Federal Department of Agricultural Research; research into the production and products of rice, maize and grain legumes of economic importance for improving the genetic potential of the crops; improving agronomic and husbandry practices; mechanization and improvement of methods of cultivating, harvesting, processing and storage of crops; improving the utilization of by-products; ecology of crop pests and diseases and improved methods of their control; integration of crop cultivation into farming systems in different ecological zones and its socio-economic effects on the rural population; library of 8,000 vols.; includes a Plant Quarantine Training Centre; Dir. C. O. OBASOLA, B.SC.; publs. *Annual Report, Memoranda, Research Bulletins, Information Papers.*

National Horticultural Research Institute: Idi-Ishin, Jericho Reservation Area, P.M.B. 5432, Ibadan, Oyo State; two sub-stations at Mbato, near Okigwe, Imo State and at Bagauda, near Tiga, Kano State; f. 1975; research into fruit and vegetable production and consumption; in particular improvement of the genetic potentials of the cultivated, semicultivated and wild crops; improvement of agronomic and husbandry practices; mechanization and improvement of methods of cultivating, harvesting, processing and storage; improvement of the utilization of by-products; ecology of crop pests and diseases and improved methods of their control; integration of crop cultivation into farming systems in different ecological zones and its socio-economic effects on the rural populations; Dir. S. A. O. ADEYEMI, M.SC.

National Root Crops Research Institute: Umudike, P.M.B. 1006, Umuahia, Imo State; f. 1955; federal status 1972; experimental farms; research on yams, cocoyams, cassava, sweet potato and Irish potato; library of 4,000 vols.; Dir. O. O. Ojehomon, ph.d.; publs. *Annual Report, Programmes of Work, Advisory Bulletins.*

National Veterinary Research Institute: Vom, near Jos, Plateau State; f. 1924; intensive research into all aspects of animal diseases and their treatment and control; all aspects of animal nutrition; production of vaccine and sera; introduction of exotic stock to improve meat, milk and egg production; standardization and quality control of manufactured animal feeds; training livestock superintendents, laboratory technicians and technologists; library of 12,000 vols., 4,000 reports, etc.; Asst. Dir. Abubakar Lamorde, ph.d.; publs. *Index of Veterinary research, Annual Report, Research Papers* (irregular), *Quarterly Newsletter.*

Nigerian Institute for Oceanography and Marine Research: Victoria Beach, P.M.B. 12529, Lagos; f. 1975; research into the resources and physical characteristics of the Nigerian territorial waters and the high seas beyond; Dir. E. O. Bayagbona, b.sc.; publs. *Newsletter, Annual Report.*

Nigerian Institute for Oil Palm Research: P.M.B. 1030, Benin City, Bendel State; f. 1939; research into the production and products of oil palm and other palms of economic importance and recommendation of improved methods; Dir. B. E. Onochie, ph.d.; publs. *Journal, Annual Report.*

Nigerian Institute for Trypanosomiasis Research: P.M.B. 2077, Kaduna, Kaduna State; f. 1951; research into trypanosomiasis and onchocerciasis generally; the pathology, immunology and methods of treatment of the diseases; the ecology and life-cycle of the vectors and the mode of transmission of the disease; chemical, biological and other methods of vector control, the socio-economic effects of the disease on the rural populations; library of 1,000 vols.; Dir. K. A. O. Sansi, ph.d.; publ. *Annual Report.*

Nigerian Stored Products Research Institute: P.M.B. 12543, Lagos; f. 1960; research, advisory work, training and analytical services for stored agricultural commodities; Dir. S. D. Agboola, m.sc.; publ. *Annual Report.*

Rubber Research Institute of Nigeria: Iyanomo, P.M.B. 1049, Benin City, Bendel State; f. 1961; research on natural rubber (*Hevea brasiliensis*) production; Dir. E. K. Okaisabor, ph.d., m.i.biol.; publs. *Annual Report, Advisory Circular Letters.*

Institute of Agricultural Research and Training: University of Ife, Moor Plantation, P.M.B. 5029, Ibadan, Oyo State; f. 1954, university institute 1970; Research Unit works on improvement of food crops, control of diseases, soils and livestock; Services Unit works on production of improved seeds for Ministries of Agriculture, soil survey and land use development for government, private and other agro-based agencies; Training Unit provides training for middle and junior manpower in the agricultural sector; library of 50,000 vols.; experimental stations at Ikenne, Ilora, Fashola, Eruwa; Dir. T. A. Ajibola Taylor, ph.d., f.r.e.s.; publs. *Annual Reports, Research Bulletins, Farmers' Guides, Agricultural News.*

Institute for Agricultural Research: Ahmadu Bello University, P.M.B. 1044, Samaru, Zaria; f. 1924; research staff of 206; improvement of production of sorghum, millet, wheat, groundnuts, cotton and fibres, cowpea, sesame, soyabean and vegetables; maintenance of soil fertility; land resources assessment; crop environment; cropping systems and intercropping; mechanization; soil and water management; socio-economic studies of small farm management, marketing, credit, supply systems and extension; Dir. Ango Abudullai, ph.d.; publs. *Samaru Research Bulletins, Samaru Miscellaneous Papers, Samaru Agricultural Newsletter* (every 2 months), *Samaru Conference Papers, Soil Survey Reports, Annual Report.*

National Animal Production Research Institute (NAPRI): Ahmadu Bello University, Shika, P.O.B. 116, Zaria; f. 1927; research staff of 25; research on dairy, beef and sheep production with emphasis on nutrition, management and breeding, range and pasture research and improvement, livestock economics and rural sociology of pastoral nomads; library of 13,000 vols.; Dir. Saka Nuru, ph.d., m.r.c.v.s., m.p.v.m.; publs. (jointly with I.A.R. above).

Agricultural Extension and Research Liaison Services: Ahmadu Bello University, P.M.B. 1044, Zaria; f. 1963; staff of 22; a link between Research and Extension; interpretation and dissemination of research findings and practices of long standing to State extension field staff and identification and feedback to research institutes of field problems; in-service training for States extension staff; advisory services in pest and disease control, organization of agricultural shows and establishment of agricultural audio visual units; consultancy services; preparation of audio visual materials; applied research: testing recommendations, conducting surveys and extension methods. Programme areas are: crop production, including mechanization and irrigation; animal production, including poultry and veterinary service; home economics; farm management, including co-operatives; and rural youth organization; Dir. M. B. Ajakaiye, ph.d. (acting); publs. *Extension Bulletins, Guides, Recommended Practices, Conference and Seminar Proceedings, Extension Newsletter* (monthly), *Annual Reports.*

International Institute of Tropical Agriculture: Oyo Rd., P.M.B. 5320, Ibadan; f. 1968; funds provided by the Ford Foundation, Rockefeller Foundation, World Bank (IBRD), Canada, U.S., Iran, Netherlands, Nigeria, U.K., Belgium, Federal Germany, UNEP; four main research programmes: farming systems, grain legume improvement, cereal improvement, and root and tuber improvement; training programme for researchers in tropical agriculture; library of 15,000 vols.; Dir.-Gen. William K. Gamble; publs. *Annual Report, IITA Letter* (3 a year), *Technical Bulletins*†, *IITA Reprints*†.

Federal Institute of Industrial Research: Oshodi, P.B.M. 1023, Murtala Muhammed Airport, Ikeja, Lagos; f. 1955; helps set up new industries based on Nigerian raw material; investigates the suitability of Nigeria's raw material for use in proved industrial processes and modifies these to suit local conditions; gives technical assistance to existing industries by provision of laboratory products, and seeks solutions to their basic technical problems; free advice to government or private companies; Dir. Dr. O. A. Koleoso (acting); publs. *Annual Report,* brochure†.

Projects Development Institutes: 3 Independence Layout, P.O.B. 609, Enugu; f. 1977; Dir. Prof. Ezenrkwe.

National Institute for Medical Research: Edmund Crescent, P.M.B. 2013, Yaba, Lagos; f. 1974; to identify the major health problems of the country and their determinants; research into environmental hazards and their effect on the population's health; Dir. (vacant).

Nigerian Institute of Road and Building Construction: c/o Federal Ministry of Works, Lagos; Dir. Dr. A. O. MADEDOR.

Nigeria Educational Research Council: P.O.B. 8058, Lagos; f. 1965; curriculum development and general educational research; 26 mems.; library of 10,000 vols.; Chair. Chief B. SOMADE; Sec./Dir. J. M. AKINTOLA; publs. conference and workshop reports.

Nigerian Institute of Social and Economic Research: P.M.B. 5, University of Ibadan, Ibadan; f. 1950 as W.A. Institute of Social and Economic Research, present name 1956; government-financed; applied research on problems of immediate relevance to Nigerian development plans: economic planning and development, agricultural and industrial development, foreign and international trade, public finance and social planning and development; training for staff of planning organizations; Dir. Prof. H. M. A. ONITIRI, M.A., PH.D.

LIBRARIES

British Council Libraries: P.M.B. 3003, Kano; f. 1950; 12,004 vols., 67 periodicals; Librarian (vacant); P.O.B. 81, Kaduna; f. 1960; 16,344 vols., 64 periodicals; Librarian L. A. IROKA; P.O.B. 330, Enugu; f. 1947; 7,534 vols., 78 periodicals; Librarian L. C. NELSON.

Central Medical Library: Federal Ministry of Health, Yaba, Lagos; f. 1945; serves the entire country; 14,027 vols.; Librarian C. A. OLALEYE.

Anambra State Library Board: Private Mail Bag 1026, Enugu; f. 1970, renamed 1976; Dir. of Library Services K. C. OKORIE, O.O.N., M.B.E., F.L.A.

State Central Library: Market Road, Enugu; f. 1956; lending and reference library activities; legal deposit and regional centre for bibliographical information and research; 65,500 volumes, Nigeriana collection, and a mobile library unit. The Board now has two divisional libraries in operation at Umuahia and Onitsha; the third divisional library is being built at Owerri; two further divisional libraries are being planned, while a model branch library is being developed; publ. *Annual Report.*

Kano State Library: P.M.B. 3094, Kano; f. 1968; 46,000 vols.; Librarian M. ABDULLAHI H. NINGI.

Lagos City Libraries: P.M.B. 2025, Lagos; f. 1950; 229,150 vols.; Librarian Mrs. B. B. OGUNLANA, A.L.A., A.M.B.I.M.; publ. *Annual Report.*

Bendel State Library Board: P.M.B. 1127, Benin City; f. 1970; 50,000 vols.; Central Reference Library with emphasis on the needs of the State Government; School Library Division; Public Library Division; Mobile Services to remote areas; Dir. WINIFRED ONYEONWU, B.A., M.L.S.; publs. *Newsletter*† (monthly), *Recent Accessions List*† (monthly), *Annual Reports.*

National Archives: P.M.B. 4, University of Ibadan Post Office, Ibadan; f. 1951, legally recognized 1957; charged with collection, rehabilitation, reproduction and preservation of all public records including private papers; library of 6,000 vols.; branch offices at Enugu and Kaduna; Dir. S. O. SOWOOLU; publs. *Annual Report, Special Lists,* etc.

National Library of Nigeria: 4 Wesley St., P.M.B. 12626, Lagos; f. 1962; branches at Enugu and Jos; 140,000 vols. in main library, 18,000 at branches; special collections of Nigerian and U.K. government publications, UN documents, Rhodes House Library Collection (private papers of past colonial civil servants); depository for UN and OAU publs.; Chair. Prof. O. C. NWANA; Dir. S. B. AJE; publs. *Annual Report, National Bibliography* (monthly), etc.

National Science and Technology Development Agency, Library and Documentation Centre: Moor Plantation, P.M.B. 5382, Ibadan, Oyo State; f. 1973; 2,000 vols., 600 current periodicals, 22 microfiches, 350 reprints; newspaper clippings; the Liaison Office in Nigeria for both AGRIS (International Information System for Agricultural Sciences and Technology) and CARIS (Current Agricultural Research Information Service); Librarian J. O. ODUMOSU, A.L.A., A.M.N.I.M.; publs. *Library Accessions List* (quarterly), *List of Serials* (annually).

Kaduna State Library Board: P.M.B. 2061, Kaduna; f. 1953, renamed 1976; 150,000 vols.; Dir. INUWA DIKO; publs. *Annual Report, List of Items received under the Copyright Law,* Bibliographies, Readers' Guides.

Ondo State Library: Ministry of Education, P.M.B. 719, Akure; f. 1976; 15,769 vols.; Librarian R. A. AREJE.

University of Ibadan Library: Ibadan; f. 1948; 300,000 vols., 5,400 periodicals; depository for OAU and UN specialized agencies publs.; special collection of Africana; Librarian T. OLABISI ODEINDE, B.SC., A.L.A.; publs. *Annual Report, Library Record, Ibadan University Library Bibliographical series.*

University of Ife Library: Ile-Ife; f. 1961; 216,000 vols., 4,592 periodicals; entitled to two copies of all works published in the Oyo, Ondo and Ogun States of Nigeria; depository for publications of UN, WHO, GATT, OAU, I.A.E.A., World Fertility Survey and the Economic Commission for Africa; Librarian J. O. DIPEOLU, B.A., A.L.A.; publs. notes and news (quarterly).

University of Lagos Library: Lagos; f. 1962; 250,000 vols., 4,500 periodicals; legal depository for Lagos State; depository for all publications of ECA, GATT, ICJ and ILO; collections on UNESCO, WHO and FAO; Librarian E. B. BANKOLE, A.B., M.S.L.S., A.L.A.; publs. *Annual Report*†, *Unilag: Quarterly News Bulletin*†, *Reader's Guide, Library Notes.*

University of Nigeria Libraries: Nsukka, Anambra State; f. 1960; total of 200,000 vols. at Nsukka, Enugu and the Economic Development Institute; Librarian S. C. NWOYE, B.A., A.L.A., DIP.LIB.

MUSEUMS

Federal Department of Antiquities: Nigerian Museum, Onikan Rd., Lagos; Dir. Prof. EKPO EYO. Controls the following museums:

Benin Museum: Benin; Benin antiquities, bronzes.

Esie Museum: via Ilorin, Kwara State; stone antiquities (*c.* 1,000 half life size human figures).

Gidan Makama Museum: Kano; f. 1959; local art work.

Ife Museum: Ife; f. 1954; bronze, terracotta and stone antiquities of Ife.

Jos Museum: Jos, Plateau State; f. 1952; ethnography and archaeology of Nigeria; terracotta Nok figurines, modern and traditional Nigerian pottery; zoological and botanical gardens; museum of traditional architecture; transport museum; UNESCO School for Museum Technicians; pottery workshop; national monuments section; library of 6,200 vols. and 1,600 Arabic MSS; Dir. Dr. E. O. EYO; Curators Dr. O. O. NJOKU, O. P. DAMOLA.

National Museum: P.M.B. 2127, Kaduna; f. 1975; archaeology and ethnography; houses the "Craft Village" where traditional hair-plaiting, weaving, pottery, calabash decoration, wood carving, brass casting and smithery are done; library of 600 vols.; Curators M. AKANBIEMU, A. U. AKPAN; publ. *Tambari*.

Nigerian Museum: Onikan Rd., Lagos; f. 1957; ethnography, archaeology and traditional art; Dir. EKPO EYO.

Oron Museum: Oron; f. 1959; ancestral carvings of the Oron area.

Owo Museum: Federal Dept. of Antiquities, P.O.B. 84, Owo, Ondo State; f. 1959; arts and crafts; some ethnographic relics mainly from the Eastern part of the Yoruba region; Curator E. OLA ABEJIDE.

UNIVERSITIES

AHMADU BELLO UNIVERSITY
ZARIA

Telephone: Zaria 2581, 2585.

Founded 1962.

Federal control; Language of instruction: English.

Vice-Chancellor: Dr. A. ABDULLAHI, PH.D.

Registrar: Y. D. ALIYU, B.A., A.M.N.I.M.

Librarian: K. MAHMUD, M.A.

Number of teachers: 1,176, including 47 professors.

Number of students: 15,731, including 178 foreign students.

Publications: *University Calendar, University Prospectus, Vice-Chancellor's Annual Report, University Bulletin, University Research Report, University Public Lectures, Student Handbook, University Gazette,* annual reports of directors of attached institutes.

DEANS:

Faculty of Administration: P. C. A. DAUDU, M.P.A.

Faculty of Agriculture: L. B. OLUGBEMI, PH.D.

Faculty of Arts and Social Sciences: A. D. YAHAYA, PH.D..

Faculty of Education: A. MOHAMMED, M.S.L.A., C.A.S., PH.D.

Faculty of Engineering: S. Y. AKU, M.SC., PH.D.

Faculty of Environmental Design: Prof. E. A. ADEYEMI, PH.D., M.N.I.A., ASSOC.A.I.P.

Faculty of Law: B. M. SHANNI, LL.M.

Faculty of Medicine: A. B. BANDIPO, M.P.H., D.I.P., F.M.C.P.H., F.W.A.C.P.

Faculty of Pharmaceutical Sciences: Prof. G. OSUIDE, PH.D., F.S.A.N.

Faculty of Science: U. D. GOMWALK, PH.D.

Faculty of Veterinary Medicine: I. ALHAJI, D.V.M., M.SC., PH.D.

PROFESSORS:

Faculty of Administration:
PANDYA, B. B., B.SC., B.A., A.C.A., Accounting
TYAGI, A. R., PH.D., Public Administration.

Faculty of Agriculture:
FEWSTER, J. A., PH.D., Plant Science
MOOLANI, M. K., M.SC., M.S., PH.D., Agronomy
SINGH, A., M.SC., PH.D., Soil Science

Faculty of Arts and Social Sciences:
BHAMBRI, R. S., B.A., B.SC., Economics
SMIT, A., M.A., History
TEMU, A. J., PH.D., History

Faculty of Education:
BAIKIE, D. A., ED.D.
BENGE, R. C., M.A., F.L.A., Library Science
DHESI, MRS. J. K., PH.D.
REEDS, J. A., PH.D., Education

Faculty of Engineering:
DIAMANT, B. Z., M.PH., F.I.C.E., F.I.P.H.E., F.R.S.H., M.A.S.C.E.
GILL, M. A., D.I.C., PH.D.
KAUL, R. N., PH.D., Agricultural Engineering
OGUNROMBI, J. A., PH.D., M.N.S.E., M.W.P.C., F.M.A.S.C.E.
OLESZKIEWICZ, M., PH.D., D.SC., M.P.S.C.E., Building

Faculty of Environmental Design:
ADEYEMI, E. A., M.SC., PH.D., M.N.I.A., Architecture

Faculty of Law:
HASSAN, M. S., LL.M., J.S.D., Private Law

Faculty of Medicine:
ATTAH, ED'B, M.S., M.R.C., F.N.M., F.W.A.C.P., F.R.C.P., Pathology
BUNNING, P. S. C., O.B.E., M.B.B.S., Human Anatomy
EGLER, L. J., M.D., Microbiology
FLEMING, A. F., M.A., M.D., M.R.C.PATH., F.R.C.PATH., Haematology
HARRISON, H. A., M.D., Obstetrics and Gynaecology
JAKUBOWSKI, A. W., DR.M., Radiology
PATHAK, U., M.B.B.S., F.R.C.O.G., Obstetrics and Gynaecology
SINGH, A., M.SC., PH.D., M.V.SC., Human Physiology
VERMA, O. P., M.B.B.S., D.P.H., F.I.P.H.A., Community Medicine

Faculty of Science:
AJAKAIYE, Mrs. D. E., PH.D., Physics
CHOUDHURI, H. C., PH.D., Biology
EMEJUAIWE, S. O., PH.D., Radioisotope Technology, Microbiology
EWUSIE, J. Y., PH.D., Biological Sciences
GOMWALK, U. D., PH.D., Chemistry
HARRIS, B. J., PH.D., F.L.S., Biological Sciences
KOGBE, C. A., D.SC., Geology
RAHMAN, M. M., PH.D., Biochemistry
RASHID, M. A., PH.D., D.I.C., Mathematics.
STANSFIELD, F., PH.D., A.R.I.C., Organic Chemistry

Faculty of Veterinary Medicine:
BIDA, S. A., PH.D., Pathology and Microbiology
MOHAMMED, A. N., D.A.P. & E., PH.D., Parasitology and Entomology
NJOKU, C. O., D.V.M., PH.D., F.R.U.C., Pathology and Microbiology

ATTACHED INSTITUTES:

Institute of Administration: P.M.B. 1013, Zaria; f. 1954 and attached to the University in 1962; Dir. Dr. S. KOMO.

Institute for Agricultural Research: *see* under Research Institutes.

Institute of Education: Main Campus, Samaru, Zaria; f. 1965; Dir. J. O. NDAGI, PH.D.

OTHER ATTACHED UNITS:

Division of Agricultural and Livestock Services Training: P.M.B. 1044, Zaria; f. 1971; incorporates schools of agriculture in Kabba and Samaru; Dir. O. C. ONAZI, M.SC., PH.D., D.I.C., F.R.E.S.; Sec. A. A. BUKAR, M.SC.

Adult Education and Extension Services Centre: Main Campus, Zaria; Dir. G. BELLO, M.PHIL. (acting).

National Animal Products Research Institute: *see* under Research Institutes.

School of Basic Studies: Main Campus, Samaru, Zaria; f. 1970; Principal U. A. ANGULU, PH.D.

Centre for Nigerian Cultural Studies: Dir. M. ADAMU, M.A., PH.D.; Sec. U. LADAN, M.A.

Educational Technology Centre: Dir. F. E. OKE, ED.D.

Centre for Islamic Legal Studies: P.M.B. 1013, Zaria; Dir. M. I. SHANI, LL.B. (acting).

BAYERO UNIVERSITY
P.M.B. 3011, KANO

Telephone: 2018.

Founded 1975; previously Abdullahi Bayero College of Ahmadu Bello University.

Chancellor: H. H. OFALA OKAGBUE, Obi of Onitsha.

Vice-Chancellor: Dr. I. H. UMAR.

Registrar: Mal. Y. A. IBRAHIM, M.A.

Librarian: H. I. SAID, PH.D., M.L.S.

Library of 63,000 vols., 1,400 periodicals.

Number of teachers: 232.

Number of students: 2,128.

DEANS:

Faculty of Arts and Islamic Studies: Dr. M. K. M. GALADANCI.

Faculty of Education: M. MAQSUD.

Faculty of Law: Dr. ATA AL-SID.

Faculty of Science: Prof. G. G. PARFITT.

Faculty of Social and Management Sciences: Dr. MUSA ABDULLAHI.

Faculty of Technology: Prof. B. W. YOUNG.

PROFESSORS:

ABDUL RAHIM, M., Political Science
LAST, D. M., History

MORETIMORE, M., Geography
PARFITT, G. G., Physics
RAYAN, K., English
SALTER-DUKE, B. J., Chemistry
SELDEN, J., Mathematics
SHOTTER, R. A., Biological Sciences
WATTS, R. K., Accounting
YOUNG, B. W., Civil Engineering

UNIVERSITY OF BENIN

P.M.B. 1154, EKENWAN RD., BENIN CITY
Telephone: 343.
Founded 1970.

Federal control; Language of instruction: English; Academic year: October to June.

Chancellor: Hon. Mr. Justice H. U. KAINE, B.A., B.L.
Vice-Chancellor: Prof. D. A. BAIKIE, PH.D.
Registrar: B. O. AKWUKWUMA.
Librarian: O. O. OGUNDIPE, M.A., A.L.A., F.L.A.

Library of 6,264 vols.
Number of teachers: 81.
Number of students: 2,000.

DEANS:

Faculty of Arts and Social Sciences: Prof. P. O. SADA, M.A., PH.D.
Faculty of Engineering: E. K. OBIAKOR, PH.D. (acting).
Faculty of Education: N. A. NWAGWU, ED.D. (acting).
School of Medicine: Prof. K. DIETE-KOKI, PH.D., L.R.C.P., M.F.C.S.
School of Pharmacy: Prof. L. I. L. NDIKA, PH.D., M.P.S.
School of Dentistry: Prof. A. O. EJIDE, M.B., B.S., B.D.S., F.R.C.S.
Faculty of Science: Prof. S. A. OLAITAN, PH.D.
Provost, College of Medical Sciences: Prof. M. T. OGBEIDE, M.B., B.S., M.R.C.P., F.R.C.P., F.M.C.PAED.

PROFESSORS:

ALLI, A. F., Pathology
BHAT, G. N., Petroleum/Chemical Engineering
DIETE-KOKI, K., Physiology
EJIDE, A. O., Dentistry
EMOVON, E. U., Chemistry
ENE, J. C., Biology
GHOSH, B. P., Biochemistry
IGBAFE, P. A., History
IYAHEN, S. O., Mathematics
NDIKA, L. I. L., Pharmacy
OGBEIDE, M. I., Child Health
OGBUEHI, P. O., Physics
OLAITAN, S. A., Biochemistry
OPPENHEIM, Sir A., Mathematics
OSAMO, N. O., Pathology
SADA, P. O., Social Studies
SMITH, N. R., Mechanical Engineering
SOFOLUWE, G. O., Community Health

UNIVERSITY OF CALABAR

P.M.B. 1115, CALABAR, CROSS RIVER STATE
Telephone: 222695.

Founded 1975; previously a campus of the University of Nigeria.

Federal control; Language of instruction: English; Academic year: September to June.

Chancellor: H.H. ALHAJI HARUNA, Emir of Gwandu.
Vice-Chancellor: Prof. E. A. AYANDELE.
Registrar: O. A. UFOT.
Librarian: N. O. ITA.

Number of teachers: 235.
Number of students: 1,675.

DEANS:

Faculty of Arts: Prof. O. E. UYA, PH.D.
Faculty of Medicine: Prof. O. A. WILLIAMS, M.B., B.CH., B.A., F.R.C.P., F.M.C.
Faculty of Science: Prof. M. S. TAMBIAH, PH.D.
Faculty of Social Science: Prof. S. M. ESSANG, PH.D.
Faculty of Education: Prof. O. E. UYA, PH.D. (acting).

PROFESSORS:

EKA, O. U., Biochemistry
ENYENIHI, U. K., Zoology and Parasitology
ESSANG, S. M., Economics
ETTA, K. M., Physiology
FLOYD, B. N., Geography
GEORGE, O. D., Applied Mathematics
IYER, G. Y., Biochemistry
MONSURATE, E. J., Anatomy
SULLIVAN, Physics
TAMBIAH, M. S., Botany
UYA, O. E., History
WILLIAMS, O. A., Pathology

UNIVERSITY OF IBADAN

IBADAN
Telephone: Ibadan 62550.

Founded 1962. Previously established as University College, Ibadan, 1948.

Federal control; Language of instruction: English; Academic year: September to July.

Visitor: H.E. Gen. OLUSEGUN OBASANJO.
Chancellor: H.H. Alhaji ADO BAYERO.
Pro-Chancellor and Chairman of Council: Alhaji ABDURRAHMAN OKENE.
Vice-Chancellor: Prof. S. O. OLAYIDE, M.SC., PH.D.
Registrar: S. J. OKUDU, J.P., B.A.
Librarian: T. OLABISI ODEINDE, B.SC., A.L.A.

Library: *see* Libraries.

Number of teaching staff: 787.
Number of students: 8,865.

Publications: *Calendar*†, *Annual Report, Research Bulletin of the Centre for Arabic Documentation* (bi-annual), *The Gazette, Vice-Chancellor's Bulletin.*

DEANS:

Faculty of Arts: Prof. L. A. BANJO, M.A., PH.D.
Faculty of Science: Prof. S. O. ALASOADURA, PH.D.
Faculty of Medicine: Prof. E. O. AKANDE, M.B., B.S., D.PHIL., M.R.C.O.G., F.M.C.O.G., F.I.C.S.
Faculty of Agriculture and Forestry: Prof. N. O. ADEDIPE, PH.D., M.I.BIOL.
Faculty of Social Sciences: Prof. E. C. EDOZIEN, M.A., PH.D.
Faculty of Education: Prof. F. ADETOWUN OGUNSHEYE, M.A., M.L.S.
Faculty of Veterinary Medicine: Prof. G. O. ESURUOSO, M.SC., PH.D., M.R.C.V.S.
Faculty of Technology: F. O. ABOABA, M.SC., PH.D., F.I.AGR.E., M.A.S.A.E.
Postgraduate School: Prof. M. J. C. ECHERUO, M.A., PH.D.

PROFESSORS:

Faculty of Arts:

ADEDEJI, J. A., M.A., PH.D., Theatre Arts
AJAYI, J. F. A., PH.D., History
AYANDELE, E. A., PH.D., History
BAMGBOSE, T. A., B.A., DIP.LING., PH.D., Linguistics and Nigerian Languages
BANJO, L. A., M.A., PH.D., English
ECHERUO, M. J. C., M.A., PH.D., English
EL-GARH, PH.D., Arabic and Islamic Studies
EVANS, H. G. J., PH.D., Modern Languages
HOFFMANN, C. F., D.PHIL., Linguistics and Nigerian Languages
IKIME, O., PH.D., History
IRELE, F. A., D.U., Modern Languages
KUJORE, O., PH.D., Classics
TAMUNO, T. N., B.A., PH.D., History
THOMPSON, L. A., M.A., Classics
UNOH, S. O., M.A., M.ED., PH.D., Language Arts
WILLIAMSON, K. R. M., M.A., PH.D. Linguistics and Nigerian Languages

Faculty of Science:

AFONJA, B., M.S., PH.D., Statistics
ALASOADURA, S. O., PH.D., Botany
AWE, O. PH.D., Physics
BAMKOLE, T. O., Chemistry
EKONG, D. E. U., B.SC., DIP.CHEM., DR.RER.NAT., Chemistry
ETTE, A. I. I., PH.D., Physics
FAYOSE, E. A., M.SC., PH.D., Geology
HIGASINAKA, H., DR.SC., Geology
HIRST, J., PH.D., Chemistry
LONGE, O., M.S., PH.D., Computer Science
MADUEMEZIA, A., PH.D., Physics
OKOGUN, J. I., Chemistry
OLUBUMMO, A., M.A., PH.D., Mathematics
TEJUMOLA, H. O., PH.D., Mathematics
TOYE, S. A. PH.D., Zoology
UKOLI, F. M. A., PH.D., Zoology

Faculty of Medicine:

ABIOYE, A. A., L.R.C.P., L.M., PH.D., Pathology
ADELOYE, A., M.B., M.S., M.R.C.P., F.R.C.S., F.I.C.S., F.M.C.S., F.W.A.C.S., Surgery
ADETUYIBI, PH.D., M.R.C.P., Medicine
AIMAKHU, V. E., M.B., B.S., M.R.C.O.G., F.I.C.S., F.M.C.O.G., Obstetrics and Gynaecology
AJAYI, O. O. A., M.B., B.S., F.R.C.S., F.I.C.S., F.M.C.S., F.W.A.C.S., Surgery
AKANDE, E. O., M.B., B.S., D.PHIL., M.R.C.O.G., F.M.C.O.G., F.I.C.S., Obstetrics and Gynaecology
AMURE, B. O., M.D., D.T.M. & H., M.R.C.P., Physiology

ANTIA, A. U., M.D., D.C.H., D.T.M. & H., Paediatrics
ASUNI, T., M.A., M.D., D.P.M., F.R.C.PSYCH., F.M.C.P., F.W.A.C.P., Psychiatry
BASSIR, O., B.SC., PH.D., F.R.I.C., M.I.NUC.ENG., Biochemistry
BOSZORMENYI, Z., M.SC., PH.D., Biochemistry
DARITY, W. A., B.S., M.S.P.H., PH.D., Preventive and Social Medicine
DAVID-WEST, T. S., M.SC., PH.D., F.R.S.H., M.R.C.PATH., Virus Research Laboratory
DESALU, A. B. O., M.B., CH.B., M.S., PH.D., Anatomy
ESAN, G. J. F., M.B., B.S., PH.D., M.R.C.P., F.M.C.PATH., Haematology
ESSIEN, E. M., M.D., D.PATH., F.M.C.PATH., Haematology
FABIYI, A., M.SC., PH.D., F.A.A.M., F.S.A.N., F.A.S., Virus Research Laboratory
FAMILUSI, J. B., M.B., B.S., F.R.C.P., F.M.C., Paediatrics
FRANCIS, T. I., M.B., B.S., F.R.C.P., D.T.M. & H., F.M.C.P., F.W.A.C.P., F.A.S., Medicine
JAMES, D. M., M.PHARM., PH.D., Pharmacology
KOLAWOLE, T. M., M.B., B.S., D.M.R.D., F.R.C.R., Radiology
LAGUNDOYE, S. B., M.B., B.S., D.M.R.D., F.M.C.R., Radiology
MAGBAGBEOLA, J. A., O. M.B., CH.B., D.A., R.C.S.C.P., F.F.A.R.C.S.I., Anaesthesia
MARTINSON, F. D., M.B., CH.B., F.R.C.S., F.A.C.S., Oto-Rhino-Laryngology
MONTEFIORE, D. G., M.D., DIP.BACT., F.R.C.PATH., F.M.C.PATH., Medical Microbiology
NYLANDER, P. P. S., M.D., M.R.C.P., F.R.C.O.G., F.M.C.O.G., Obstetrics and Gynaecology
ODUNTAN, S. A., M.B., B.S., D.A., R.C.S. & P., F.F.A.R.C.S.I., Anaesthesia
OGUNLESI, T. O., L.M.S., L.R.C.P., M.R.C.S., M.R.C.P., F.R.F.P.ED., Medicine
OJO, O. A., M.A., M.D., M.A.O., F.R.C.O.G., F.M.C.O.G., Obstetrics and Gynaecology
OKPAKO, D. T., PH.D., M.I.BIOL., Pharmacology and Therapeutics
OLATAWURA, M. O., M.B., B.S., M.SC., D.P.M., F.M.C.PSYCH., F.W.A.C.P., Psychiatry
OLATUNBOSUN, D. A., M.B., B.S., M.D., F.M.C.PATH., F.S.A.N., F.W.A.C.P., Chemical Pathology
OLURIN, E. O., M.B., CH.B., F.R.C.S., F.M.C.S., F.W.A.C.S., Surgery
OLURIN, O., CH.M., D.O., F.M.C.S.(OPHTH.), Ophthalmology
OLUWASANMI, J. O., M.B., M.S., F.R.C.S., F.I.C.S., F.W.A.C.S., F.M.C.S., Surgery
OMOLOLU, A., D.P.H., D.C.H., F.R.C.P.I., F.M.C.P.H., Human Nutrition
OSOBA, A. O., B.A., M.B., B.CH., B.A.O., M.A., F.M.C.PATH., M.D., Medical Microbiology
OSUNKOYA, B. O., M.B., B.S., PH.D., F.M.C.PATH., F.S.A.N., F.W.A.C.P., Immunology
OSUNTOKUN, B. O., D.SC., M.D., PH.D., F.R.C.P., F.W.A.C.P., F.A.S., Medicine
OYEDIRAN, A., M.D., M.R.C.P., D.T.M. & H., F.M.C.P.H., F.W.A.C.P., Preventive and Social Medicine
SALAKO, L. A., M.B.B.S., PH.D., M.R.C.P., F.M.C.P., Pharmacology and Therapeutics
SCHATZ, L., M.S., PH.D., Anatomy
SOFOWORA, E. O., M.B., B.S., F.R.C.P., D.T.C.D., M.R.C.S., F.M.C.P., Medicine
SOLANKE, T. F., M.B., CH.B., F.R.C.S., F.I.C.S., F.M.C.S., F.W.A.C.S., Surgery
SOYANNWO, M. A. O., M.B., B.S., PH.D., M.D., F.R.C.P.I., M.R.C.P., F.M.C.P., Medicine
WILLIAMS, A. O., M.A., M.B., B.CH., M.D., F.R.C.P.I., M.R.C.P., M.R.C.PATH., F.M.C.PATH., Pathology

Faculty of Agriculture and Forestry:
ADEGBOYE, R. A., M.SC., PH.D., Resource Economics
ADENIJI, M. O., BS.C., PH.D., Phytopathology
ADEPIPE, N. O., PH.D., M.I.BIOL., Crop Physiology
ADEYOJU, S. K., PH.D., Forest Resources Management
ANTHONIO, Q. B. O., M.SC., PH.D., Marketing and Agricultural Development and Policy
BABATUNDE, G. M., M.SC., PH.D., Animal Science
CHHEDA, H. R., M.SC., PH.D., Agronomy
ESURUOSO, O. F., PH.D., D.I.C., Phytopathology
FAYEMI, A. A., M.SC., PH.D., F.L.S., Agronomy
FETUGA, B. L., PH.D., Animal Science
MBA, A. U., PH.D., Animal Science
ODU, C. T. I., PH.D., Agronomy
OKALI, D. U. U., M.A., PH.D., Forestry
OYENUGA, V. A., PH.D., F.R.I.C., F.S.A.N., F.A.S., D.SC., Animal Science
PATEL, A. U., M.SC., PH.D., Agricultural Extension Services
WILLIAMS, S. K. T., M.A., M.SC., PH.D., Agricultural Extension Services
YOUDEOWEI, A., PH.D., F.R.E.S., Entomology

Faculty of Social Sciences:
ABOYADE, O., PH.D., Economics
DUDLEY, B. J., PH.D., M.A., Political Science
EDOZIEN, E. C., M.A., PH.D., Economics
ESSIEN-UDOM, E. U., M.A., PH.D., Political Science
IMOAGENE, S. O., M.SC., PH.D., Sociology
MABOGUNJE, A. L., PH.D., Geography
OGUNTOYINBO, J. S., M.SC., PH.D., F.R.MET.SOC., Geography
PHILLIPS, A. O., M.A., PH.D., Economics
TERIBA, O., M.A., PH.D., Economics
UDO, R. K., B.SC., PH.D., Geography

Faculty of Education:
BAKARE, C. G. M., A.D.E., PH.D., Guidance and Counselling
MAJASAN, J. A., PH.D., DIP.ED., F.R.G.S., Teacher Education
OGUNSHEYE, F. A., M.A., M.L.S., DIP.ED., Library Studies
OKUNROTIFA, P. O., M.A., PH.D., Teacher Education
TOMORI, S. H. O., M.A., DIP.ED., PH.D., Adult Education
YOLOYE, E. A., B.SC., DIP.ED., PH.D., Education

Faculty of Veterinary Medicine:
ESURUOSO, G. O., M.SC., PH.D., M.R.C.V.S., Veterinary Public Health and Preventive Medicine
HILL, D. H., O.B.E., D.V.M., M.R.C.V.S., Veterinary Medicine and Surgery
ISOUN, T. T., D.V.M., PH.D., Veterinary Pathology
OJO, M. O., M.R.C.V.S., PH.D., Veterinary Microbiology and Parasitology

Faculty of Technology:
ABOABA, F. O., M.SC., PH.D., N.D.AGR.E., F.I.AGR.E., M.A.S.A.E., Agricultural and Forestry Engineering
HARRIS, J., PH.D., C.ENG., M.I.MECH.E., M.INST.M.C., Design and Production Engineering
SRINIVASAN, C., M.A., PH.D., Petroleum Engineering

ATTACHED INSTITUTES:

Institute of African Studies: Dir. Prof. S. O. BIOBAKU, C.M.G., M.A., PH.D.

Institute of Education: Dir. Prof. E. A. YOLOYE, PH.D.

Institute of Child Health: Dir. O. SERIKI, M.B., CH.B., D.CH., D.T.M. & H., F.R.C.P.

UNIVERSITY OF IFE

ILE-IFE

(Ibadan Branch, Ibadan)

Telephone: Ife 2291, Ibadan 412861.

Founded 1961.

Federal control; Language of instruction: English; Academic year: September to July.

Chancellor: EREJUWA II, The Olu of Warri.
Vice-Chancellor: C. A. ONWUMECHILI, PH.D.
Registrar: E. O. ADETUNJI, PH.D.
Librarian: **J. O. DIPEOLU, B.A., A.L.A.**
Bursar: S. O. OWALABI, A.C.I.S., B.SC.

Number of teachers: 891.
Number of students: 8,712.

Publications: *Odu, A Journal of West African Studies* (twice-yearly), *Quarterly Journal of Administration, University Bulletin, Handbook*†, *Gazette, Calendar*†, *Second Order* (2 a year).

DEANS:

Faculty of Agriculture: A. O. ADENUGA.
Faculty of Arts: OYIN OGUNBA.
Faculty of Social Sciences: O. ADEJUYIGBE.
Faculty of Law: A. O. OKUNNIGA.
Faculty of Science: A. ABODERIN.
Faculty of Education: A. FAJANA.
Faculty of Pharmacy: V. O. MARQUIS.
Faculty of Technology: A. SANNI.
Faculty of Health Sciences: T. A. I. GRILLO.
Faculty of Administration: O. O. ADAMOLEKUN.

PROFESSORS:

Faculty of Agriculture:
ADENUGA, A. O., PH.D., Plant Science
ADEMOSUN, A. A., PH.D., Animal Science
ALAO, J. A., PH.D., Extension Education and Rural Sociology
ASHAYE, I. I., PH.D., Soil Science
TAYLOR, T. A., PH.D., Plant Science

Faculty of Arts:
ABIMBOLA, W., M.A., PH.D., African Languages and Literature
AFOLAYAN, A., PH.D., English Language
AKINJOGBIN, I. A., PH.D., History
GRUBER, J. S., PH.D., Linguistics
OGUNBA, O., PH.D., Literature in English
OLORUNTIMEHIN, B. O., PH.D., History
PUNTO, R. M., D.EN.L., Portuguese
SODIPO, J. O., PH.D., Philosophy
SOYINKA, W., B.A., Dramatic Arts
TAYLOR, R. D., PH.D., Literature in English

Faculty of Education:
ADERALEGBE, A., M.A., PH.D., Educational Administration and Planning
AWOKOYA, S. O., B.SC., Educational Administration and Planning
FAJANA, A., PH.D., Continuing Education

Faculty of Health Sciences:
ADENIYI-JONES, A., M.P.H., D.PH., M.R.C.S., Community Health (Family) and Nutrition
ADETUGBO, H. K., PH.D., Chemical Pathology, Haematology and Immunology
BANKOLE, M. A., M.B., B.S., Paediatrics and Surgery
BAXTER-GRILLO, D. L., PH.D., Anatomy and Cell Biology
BRUNSON, J. G., M.D., Morbid Anatomy and Medical Microbiology
DARAMOLA, T., Community Health (Family) and Nutrition
FLICK, J. A., M.D., Morbid Anatomy and Medical Microbiology
GRILLO, S. A., Physiological Sciences
GRILLO, T. A. I., M.A., PH.D., SC.D., Anatomy and Cell Biology
MONEKOSSO, G. L., M.D., D.T.M., Medicine and Mental Health.
NWOSU, U. C., M.D., Obstetrics, Gynaecology and Perinatology

Faculty of Law:
IJALAYE, D. A., LL.M., J.S.D., International Law
ODUNMUSU, O. I., LL.M., PH.D., Public Law
OLAWOYIN, G. A., Business Law

Faculty of Pharmacy:
GRUDZINSKI, S. K., PH.D., D.SC., Pharmaceutical Chemistry
MARQUIS, V. O., PH.D., Pharmacology
OGUNLANA, E. O., M.SC., PH.D., M.P.S., Pharmaceutics
SOFOWORA, E. A., PH.D., Pharmacognosy

Faculty of Science:
ABIODUN, R. F. A., PH.D., Mathematics
ABODERIN, A., Biochemistry
ADEGOKE, O. S., PH.D., Geology
ALADEKOMO, J. B., PH.D., Physics
BALOGUN, R. A., M.SC., PH.D., F.R.E.S., Zoology
DASH, B. P., M.SC., D.I.C., PH.D., Geology
IMEVBORE, A. M. A., PH.D., Zoology
KAYODE, A. A., M.S., PH.D., Geology
OGUNKOYA, L. O., PH.D., Chemistry
OKE, O. L., PH. D., Chemistry
OLUWOLE, A. F., PH.D., Physics
SANFORD, W. W., M.A., Botany
SEGUN, A. O., PH.D., Zoology
SHARMA, B. L., M.A., PH.D., Mathematics

Faculty of Social Sciences:
ADEJUWON, J. O., M.SC., PH.D., Geography
ADEJUYIGBE, O., PH.D., Geography
AKIWOWO, A. A., PH.D., Sociology and Anthropology
EKUNDARE, R. O., M.A., B.C.L., Economics
IGUN, A. A., PH.D., Demography and Social Statistics
OJO, G. J. A., PH.D., Geography

Faculty of Technology:
MAKANJUOLA, G. A., PH.D., Agricultural Engineering
NGODDY, P. O., PH.D., Food Science and Technology
SANNI, S. A. PH.D., Chemical Engineering
WILLIAMS, V. A., PH.D., Electronic and Electrical Engineering

Faculty of Administration:
ADAMOLEKUN, O. O., D.PHIL., Public Administration
ALUKO, I. O., PH.D., International Relations
WEINRICH, J. E., PH.D., General and Quantitative Management

AFFILIATED INSTITUTES:

Institute of Agricultural Research and Training: *see* under Research Institutes.

Institute of Education: f. 1962; sponsored by the University, the West State Ministry of Education and the Association of Principals of Teacher Training Colleges and Secondary Schools in the State; a mobile library equipped with books, audio-visual aids and film aids demonstration among colleges and secondary schools; Dir. A. A. TAIWO, PH.D. (acting); Sec. A. G. A. TORIOLA, B.SC.SOC.; publ. *News Bulletin* (quarterly).

Institute of Physical Education: f. 1970; Dir. J. A. OYEWUSI, M.A.; trains physical education specialist teachers, runs academic programmes in physical education in collaboration with the Faculties of Art and Education and caters for recreational interests of all students.

UNIVERSITY OF ILORIN

P.M.B. 1515, ILORIN
Telephone: 0352, 2525.
Telex: UNILON 33144 NG.
Founded 1976.

State control; Language of instruction: English; Academic year: September to February, March to July.

Chancellor: Alhaji UMAR SELEIMAN, Emir of Bedde.
Pro-Chancellor and Chairman of Council: Hon. Justice AMBROSE A. ALLAGOA, LL.B., B.L., K.S.G., C.O.N.
Vice-Chancellor: Prof. AKIN O. ADESOLA, M.D., M.CH., F.R.C.S., F.A.C.S., F.W.A.C.S., F.M.C.S.
Registrar: OLU DARAMOLA, M.A.
Librarian: B. A. ONI-ORISAN, B.A.

Library of 20,616 vols.
Number of teachers: 224.
Number of students: 2,000

DEANS:

Faculty of Arts and Social Sciences: Prof. DELE AWOBULUYI, M.A., PH.D.
Faculty of Science: Prof. M. O. OLOFINBOBA, PH.D.
Faculty of Education: Prof. J. O. O. ABIRI, M.ED., PH.D.
Faculty of Health Sciences: Prof. A. ADENIYI, M.D., B.S., D.C.H., F.M.C. (PAED.), F.INT.C.P.
Faculty of Engineering and Technology: Prof. V. O. S. OLUNLOYO, PH.D.

HEADS OF DEPARTMENT AND PROFESSORS:

Faculty of Arts and Social Sciences:
AWOBULUYI, O., M.A., PH.D., Linguistics and Nigerian Languages
BALOGUN, I. A. B., PH.D., Religions
COOK, D., M.A., Modern European Languages

Faculty of Science:
ARO, T. O., D.PHIL., M.INST.P., Physics
FAWOLE, M. O., PH.D., Biology
OLOFINBOBA, M. O., PH.D., Biology
OYINLOYE, J. O., PH.D., Physics
TIKKIWAL, B. D., PH.D., Statistics
YOLOYE, V. L. A., PH.D., Biology

Faculty of Education:
ABIRI, J. O. O., PH.D., Teacher Education
ADESINA, S., ED.D., Educational Guidance and Management
OGUNSOLA, A. F., PH.D., Continuing Education and Extension

Faculty of Health Sciences:
ADENIYI, A., M.D., D.C.H., Child Health
ALAUSA, O. K., M.D., M.P.H., Community Health and Epidemiology
HAMILTON, J. D., M.B., F.R.C.P., F.R.C.P.(C.), Medicine
OGUNREMI, O. O., M.D., D.P.M., F.N.M.C., F.W.A.C.P., Behavioural Sciences
SAMUEL, I., M.D., M.R.C.PATH., Pathology
SOGBANMU, M. O., M.B.CH.B., M.R.C.O.G., M.R.H., Obstetrics and Gynaecology

Faculty of Engineering and Technology:
OLUNLOYO, V. O. S., PH.D., A.S.M.E., A.I.A.A., M.N.S.E., Mechanical Engineering
OWOLABI, I. E., PH.D., M.INST.P., C.ENG., M.I.E.E., M.N.S.E., Electrical Engineering

UNIVERSITY OF JOS

P.M.B. 2084, JOS, PLATEAU STATE
Telephone: 3174/3311.

Founded 1975; previously a campus of the University of Ibadan.

Federal control; Language of instruction: English.

Chancellor: Chief DOUGLAS JAJA.
Pro-Chancellor: Justice OYEMADE.
Vice-Chancellor: Prof. E. U. EMOVON, PH.D.
Registrar: Dr. C. S. ABASHIYA, PH.D. (acting).
Librarian: B. U. NWAFOR.

Number of teachers: 180.
Number of students: 1,337.
Publication: *University Calendar* (annually).

DEANS AND DIRECTORS:

Faculty of Arts: Prof. G. O. M. TASIE.
Faculty of Education: Prof. J. M. COOPER.
Faculty of Medical Sciences: Prof. A. C. IKEME.
Faculty of Natural Sciences: Prof. H. I. AJAEGBU.
Faculty of Social Sciences: Prof. S. M. H. ZAIDI.
Centre for Development Studies: Prof. E. B. E. NDEM.
Division of Continuing Education: G. SALAMA.

PROFESSORS:

Faculty of Arts:
ISICHEI, E., History

TASIE, G. O. M., Religious Studies
WESOLOWSKI, J., Theatre Arts

Faculty of Education:
COOPER, J. M.

Faculty of Medical Sciences:
IKEME, A. C., Medicine
KRAUSE, M., Physiology
OLISA, E. G., Pathology
WEBER, W. V., Physiology
WTCHRZYCKA, E. Y., Pathology

Faculty of Natural Sciences:
AJAEGBU, H. I., Geography
BERRIE, G. K., Botany
MESSIHA, S. A. S., Mathematics
UMINSKI, T., Physics

Faculty of Social Sciences:
TSEAYO, J. I., Sociology
ZAIDI, S. M. H., Psychology

Centre for Development Studies:
NDEM, E. B. E.

Faculty of Environmental Studies:
SERAFIN, B., Building
RADWANOWSKI, I. J., Architecture

UNIVERSITY OF LAGOS

P.M.B. 12003, LAGOS

Telephone: 41360-9.

Founded 1962.

Federal control; Language of instruction: English; Academic year: September to June.

Visitor: Lt.-Gen. OLUSEGUN OBASANJO.
Chancellor: Sir KASHIM IBRAHIM, K.C.M.G., M.B.E.
Pro-Chancellor: Mallam NUHU BAYERO.
Vice-Chancellor: Prof. B. K. ADADEVOH.
Deputy Vice-Chancellor: Prof. I. O. OLADAPO.
Registrar: M. O. EPEROKUN.
Librarian: E. B. BANKOLE.

Library: *see* Libraries.

Number of teachers: 513.
Number of students: *c.* 8,000.

Publications: *Gazette* (2 a year), *Calendar, Annual Report, Newsletter* (fortnightly), *Notes on the University, Diary* (annually).

DEANS:

Faculty of Social Sciences: Prof. P. O. OLUSANYA.
Faculty of Law: Prof. M. I. JEGEDE.
Faculty of Engineering: Prof. C. O. ORANGUN.
Faculty of Arts: Prof. N. O. ALAO.
Faculty of Science: Prof. C. I. O. OLANIYAN.
Faculty of Business Administration: Prof. M. A. ADEYEMO.
Faculty of Environmental Design: Prof. R. SEMKA (acting).
Faculty of Education: Prof. L. J. BOWN.

PROFESSORS:

ACHOLONU, A. D., Microbiology
ADALEMO, I. A., Geography
ADEPEGBA, D., Civil Engineering
ADEKOLA, A. O., Civil Engineering
ADERIBIGBE, A. B., History
ADEYEMO, M. A., Business Administration
AHMED, I., Paediatrics
AKINLA, O., Obstetrics and Gynaecology
AKINOSI, J. O., Oral Surgery
AKINRIMISI, E. O., Biochemistry
ANUMONYE, A., Psychiatry
ALAO, N. O., Geography
AMAKU, E. O., Surgery
ANA, J. R., Preventive Dentistry
ASIWAJU, A. I., History
ATIYA, F. S., Electrical Engineering
AWOJOBI, A. O., Mechanical Engineering
BABALOLA, A., African Studies
BAMGBOSE, S. A., Pharmacology
BOWN, L. J., Adult Education
BOYO, A. E., Pathology
CLARK, J. P., English
DIEJOMAOH, V. P., Economics
DITTMANN, E., Environmental Design
DOSEKUN, F. O., Physiology
DUROJAIYE, M. O. A., Educational Psychology
EKUNDAYO, J. A., Biology (Microbiology)
EKWUEME, L. E. N., Music
EL ARABATY, A. M., Electrical Engineering
ELEBUTE, E. A., Surgery
ELEBUTE, O., Physiology
ENAHORO, H. E., Mechanical Engineering
EUBA, A., Music/Cultural Studies
FASAN, P. O., Community Health
FEMI-PEARSE, D., Medicine
FFOULKES-CRABBE, D. J. O., Anaesthesia
FREGENE, A. O., Radiotherapy
HENSHAW, N. E., Restorative Dentistry
HERBERT, A., French
HUNPONU-WUSU, O., Community Health
JAJA, M. O. A., Surgery
JEGEDE, M. I., Law
JOHNSON, T. O., Medicine
LANDOR, S. R., Chemistry
LASI, G. N., Anatomy
LAWSON, G. W., Botany
MABAYOJE, J. O., Medicine
MUNDY-CASTLE, A. C., Psychology
NAMBUDIRI, C. N. S., Business Administration
NASSIF, M., Mathematics
NWANKWO, G. O., Finance
OBENSON, G., Surveying
ODUNJO, O., Morbid Anatomy
OGUNBI, O., Microbiology
OGUNYE, A. F., Chemical Engineering
OJO, G. O., Physiology
OKEDIJI, O. O., Sociology
OLADAPO, I. O., Civil Engineering
OLANIYAN, C. I. O., Zoology
OLAWOYE, C. O., Law
OLOKO, O., Sociology
OLASUNYA, P. O., Sociology
OLUSANYA, G. O., History
OMO-DARE, P., Surgery
OPUBOR, A. E., Mass Communication
ORANGUN, C. O., Civil Engineering
RANSOME-KUTI, O., Paediatrics
SODIPO, J. O., Anaesthesia
WILLIAMS, G. A., Education

College of Medicine

IDI-ARABA, SURULERE,
P.M.B. 12003, LAGOS

Language of instruction: English; State control.

Chairman of the Court of Governors: (vacant).
Provost: E. A. ELEBUTE, M.A., M.D., F.R.C.S., F.M.C.S.
Secretary: Z. A. ALABI, D.P.A.

Number of teachers: 156.
Number of students: *c.* 1,000.
Publication: *Prospectus*.

ATTACHED INSTITUTES:

Comparative Education Study and Adaptation Centre.
Director: O. OZORO.

Continuing Education Centre.
Director: Dr. J. O. OGUNLADE.

Institute of Child Health.
Director: Prof. O. RANSOME-KUTI.

Centre for Cultural Studies.
Director: Prof. AKIN EUBA.

Institute of Education.
Director: Prof. G. A. WILLIAMS.

UNIVERSITY OF MAIDUGURI

P.M.B. 1069, MAIDUGURI

Telephone: 232607.

Founded 1975.

Chancellor: H. H. The Ewi of Ado-Ekiti, OBA ALADESANMI II.
Vice-Chancellor: Prof. J. M. AMINU.
Registrar: Mallam DAHIRU BOBBO.
Librarian: Dr. S. E. IFIDON.

Number of teachers: 146.

Publications: *Information Bulletin, Annual Report.*

DEANS:

Faculty of Agriculture: F. A. ADENIJI (acting).
Faculty of Arts: S. A. KAMALI.
Faculty of Education: C. C. AGUOLU.
Faculty of Law: N. TOBI (acting).
Faculty of Science: N. M. GADZAMA.
Faculty of Social and Management Studies: G. G. R. THAMBYAHPILLAY.
College of Medical Science: G. M. EDINGTON.

PROFESSORS:

ABDEL-MALEK, A., Zoology
AHMAD, K., Pharmacology
BRANN, C. M. B., Languages and Linguistics
EDINGTON, G. M., Medicine
SENGUPTA, J. K., Physiology
THAMBYAHPILLAY, G. G. R., Geography

UNIVERSITY OF NIGERIA

NSUKKA,
ANAMBRA STATE

Telephone: Nsukka 6251/5.

Founded 1960.

Federal control; Language of instruction: English; Academic year: September to June.

Visitor: Lt.-Gen. OLUSEGUN OBASANJO.
Chancellor: Rt. Hon. Sir ADETOKUNBO ADEMOLA, K.B.E., C.F.R., M.A.
Pro-Chancellor: Dr. C. E. ABEBE.
Vice-Chancellor: Prof. F. N. NDILI, PH.D.
Registrar: A. E. ORADUBANYA, B.A.
Librarian: S. C. NWOYE, B.A., DIP.LIB., A.L.A.

Library: *see* Libraries.
Number of teachers: 641.
Number of students: 7,099.

Publications: *University of Nigeria Calendar*† (annual), *Undergraduate Prospectus, Postgraduate Prospectus* (annual), *University Gazette*† (quarterly), *The Record*† (weekly), *Information Bulletin*† (fortnightly), *Academic Regulations* (annually), *Annual Report*†.

DEANS:

Faculty of Agriculture and Veterinary Medicine: Prof. M. M. IKEME.
Faculty of Arts: Prof. A. E. AFIGBO.
Faculty of Biological and Pharmaceutical Sciences: Prof. S. N. C. OKONKWO.
Faculty of Business Administration: Dr. W. O. UZOAGA.
Faculty of Education: Prof. O. C. NWANA.
Faculty of Engineering: Prof. O. J. UZOMAKA.
Faculty of Environmental Studies: Prof. G. E. K. OFOMATA.
Faculty of Law: Prof. C. O. OKONKWO.
Faculty of Medicine: Prof. F. A. NWAKO.
Faculty of Physical Sciences: Prof. J. N. ADICHIE.
Faculty of the Social Sciences: Prof. S. KODJO.

PROFESSORS:

ACHEBE, C. A., B.A., English
ACHUFUSI, M., PH.D., History
ADICHIE, J. N., PH.D., Statistics
AFIGBO, A. E., PH.D., History
AKUBUE, P. I., PH.D., Pharmacy
AMAZIGO, J. C., PH.D., Mathematics
AMOBI, C. C., PH.D., Botany
ANIKWE, R. M., M.D., CH.M., Surgery
ANIMALU, A. O. E., M.A., PH.D., Physics
ANUMONYE, A., M.D., M.SC., Psychological Medicine
ANYA, A. O., PH.D., Zoology
ANYANWU, E. A., M.A., D. PHIL., Economics
AWA, E. O., PH.D., Political Science
AWACHIE, J. B. E., PH.D., Zoology
BHATTATHIRY, E. P. M., PH.D., Medical Biochemistry
CHIJIOKE, M. O., PH.D., Electrical and Electronics Engineering
CHUKE, P. O., M.B.B.S., Medicine
DATTA, K. L., G.D.ARCH., Architecture
EKPECHI, O. L. V., PH.D., D.T.M. & H., Medicine
EKPETE, D. M., PH.D., Soil Science
EKWUEME, O., M.D., Surgery
ENWONWU, C. O., D.SC., Medical Biochemistry
EZEDINMA, F. O. C., PH.D., Crop Science
EZEILO, G. C., M.SC., D.T.M. & H., Physiology
EZEILO, J. O. C., M.D., PH.D., Mathematics
EZEJIOFOR, G., PH.D., Commercial and Property Law
EZEKWE, G. O., PH.D., Mechanical Engineering
FUBARA, D. M. J., PH.D., Surveying, Geodesy and Photogrammetry
GUGNANI, H. C., PH.D., Microbiology
HARTLE, D. D., PH.D., Archaeology
HEERAN, M. P., PH.D., Physics
HEGDE, K. S., M.S., PH.D., Veterinary Pathology
HEGDE, V. R., G.M.V.C., Veterinary Anatomy and Physiology
HOQUE, M., PH.D., Geology
IBRAHIM, A. A., PH.D., Agricultural Engineering
IGBOELI, G., PH.D., Animal Science
IJERE, M. O., M.A., PH.D., Agricultural Economics and Extension
IKEME, M. M., PH.D., Veterinary Pathology
KODJO, S., DR.RER.POL., DR.HABIL., Economics
MADU, R. M., PH.D., Civil Engineering
MADUEWESI, J. N. G., PH.D., Botany
MAJOROSSY, K., M.D., PH.D., Anatomy
MALLY, K. V., M.SC., Veterinary Medicine and Surgery
MITAL, H. C., M.PHARM., PH.D., Pharmacy
NJOKU-OBI, A. N. U., M.SC., PH.D., Microbiology
NWABARA, S. N., M.A., PH.D., African Studies
NWAKO, F. A., M.CHIR., B.A.O., Surgery
NWANA, O. C., M.ED., PH.D., Education
NWOGA, D. I., PH.D., English
NWOGUGU, E. I., PH.D., International Law and Jurisprudence
NWOKOLO, C., Medicine
NZIMIRO, I., D.PHIL., PH.D., Sociology and Anthropology
OBIECHINA, E. N., PH.D., English
ODOKARA, E. O., PH.D., Extra-Mural Studies
OFAMATA, G. E. K., B.A., DR. 3E. CYCLE, Geography
OGAN, A. U., PH.D., Biochemistry
OGAN, O. K., Obstetrics and Gynaecology
OKAFOR, C. O., PH.D., Chemistry
OKAFOR, N., PH.D., Microbiology
OKEKE, U., Fine and Applied Arts
OKONKWO, C. O., LL.M., Public and Private Law
OKONKWO, S. N. C., PH.D., Botany
OKONJO, C., B.SC., DR.RER.NAT., Economics
OKORO, A. N., M.B., CH.B., Medicine
OKOYE, S. E., PH.D., Physics
OKPALA, I., M.SC., Zoology
ONUAGULUCHI, G. O., PH.D., Pharmacology and Therapeutics
ONUIGBO, W. I. B., PH.D., Morbid Anatomy
OSISIOGU, I. U. W., PH.D., Pharmacy
PAWLIKOWASKI, M., D.SC., D.HABIL., Architecture
SHEHU, U., M.B.B.S., Community Medicine
UDEKWU, F. A. O., M.A., M.D., Surgery
UKEJE, B. O., M.A., ED.D., Education
UKPABI, S. C., M.A., PH.D., History
UMEH, J. A., M.SC., Estate Management
UMERAH, B. C., M.B., B.CH., B.A.O., Radiation Medicine
UZOAMAKA, O. J., PH.D., Civil Engineering

ATTACHED INSTITUTES:

Curriculum Development and Instructional Materials Centre: Dir. Prof. O. C. NWANA.

Economic Development Institute: University of Nigeria, Enugu Campus, Enugu, Anambra State; Dir. E. J. NWOSU (acting).

Institute of African Studies: Dir. Prof. S. N. NWABARA.

Institute of Education: Dir. Dr. A. F. NDUBISI (acting).

UNIVERSITY OF PORT HARCOURT

P.M.B. 5323, PORT HARCOURT, RIVERS STATE
Telephone: 2118, 21085.
Founded 1975.

Vice-Chancellor: Prof. D. E. U. EKONG.
Registrar: M. E. AKPE.
Librarian: G. B. AFFIA.

Library of 3,000 vols.
Number of teachers: 73.
Number of students: 400.

DEANS:

School of Humanities: Prof. E. J. ALAGOA.
School of Biological Sciences: Prof. F. A. ONOFEGHARA.
School of Physical Sciences: Prof. G. ZELMER (acting).
School of Social Sciences: Prof. C. AKE.
School of Basic Studies: Dr. T. H. ANDERSON.
School of Chemical Sciences: Prof. F. A. ONOFEGHARA.
School of Education: Prof. E. J. ALAGOA (acting).

UNIVERSITY OF SOKOTO

P.M.B. 2346, SOKOTO
Telephone: 232058.
Founded 1975; first student intake September 1977.

Vice-Chancellor: Dr. S. A. S. GALADANCI, M.LITT., PH.D.
Registrar: H. B. AFOLABI, B.A., M.P.A.
Librarian: (vacant).

Number of students: *c.* 1,200.

DEANS:

Faculty of Arts and Islamic Studies: A. A. GWANDU.
Faculty of Science: Prof. S. H. Z. NAQUI.
Faculty of Social Sciences and Administration: K. SWINDELL.
Faculty of Education: B. RAJU.
Faculty of Law: (vacant).

COLLEGES

FEDERAL POLYTECHNIC, AKURE

P.M.B. 758, AKURE
Telephone: 230727.
Founded 1978.

Rector: Prof. E. K. OBIAKOR.
Registrar: Dr. B. I. C. IJOMAH.
Librarian: Y. A. IZEVBEKHAI.

Library of 2,100 vols.
Number of teachers: 86.
Number of Students: 652.

HEADS OF SCHOOLS:

Engineering: G. O. S. ADEJINMI.
Technology: Dr. S. R. V. RIZVI.
Business and General Studies: C. I. NWOSU.

FEDERAL POLYTECHNIC, BIDA

P.M.B. 55, BIDA
Founded 1977.

Rector: Engr. Dr. G. A. ADEBIYI.

Registrar: 'BANJI OLATONA.
Librarian: S. KASIMU.

Library of 8,000 vols.
Number of teachers: 75.
Number of students: 600.

HEADS OF DEPARTMENTS:

Business Studies: Dr. I. A. AKANBI.
Chemical Engineering: S. O. OKONGWU.
Civil Engineering: OYE OGUNNUSI.
Electrical Engineering and Electronics: I. B. OLADIMEJI.
Mechanical Engineering: Dr. M. ADEYEMI.
Science and Liberal Arts: Dr. H. JACKSON-BELLO.
Secretarial Studies: P. I. AWE.

COLLEGE OF TECHNOLOGY

P.M.B. 1110, CALABAR,
CROSS RIVER STATE
Telephone: 222418, 222303.
Founded 1973.

Principal: LAWRENCE I. EBONG.
Registrar: CLAY I. ONAH.
Librarian: (vacant).

Library of 16,000 vols.
Number of teachers: 114
Number of students: 833.

Nigerian National Diploma (NND) courses in: Group A: architecture, civil engineering, electrical/electronic engineering, mechanical engineering, science laboratory technology, wood and paper technology, National Technical Teachers' Certificate, Nigerian Certificate in Education (Technical); Group B: accountancy, business administration, estate management, secretarial studies, town and regional planning; National Technical Teachers' Certificate, Nigerian Certificate in Education (Business).

INSTITUTE OF MANAGEMENT AND TECHNOLOGY

P.M.B. 1079, ENUGU
Telephone: 252335.
Founded 1973.

Rector: Prof. R. M. MADU, PH.D., F.I.H.E., M.I.C.E., M.N.S.E., C.ENG.
Dean of Studies: C. I. OSUOJI, M.A., PH.D.
Registrar: B. O. MBA, M.A.
Librarian: (vacant).

Library of 47,904 vols.
Number of teachers: 170.
Number of students: 3,806.

Publications: *Calendar*†, *Information Booklet*†, *Bulletin*† (monthly), *MANTECH* (quarterly).

DIRECTORS OF SCHOOLS:

Business and Administration: N. G. NWOKOYE, PH.D.
Technology: J. K. NWUDE, B.SC., M.S., D.E.
Engineering: E. I. E. OFODILE, M.S., PH.D.
Technical Teacher Education: R. O. UNEGBU, M.A., PH.D.
General Studies: G. E. EMEMBOLU, M.SC., M.A., PH.D.
Continuing Education: P. A. C. AMECHI, M.SC.

THE POLYTECHNIC

P.M.B. 5063, IBADAN
Telephone: 410255, 414551.

Founded 1961, Polytechnic status 1970.

Rector: A. O. AJAYI, M.SC., M.A., ED.D.
Vice-Rector: O. R. OLADJIRE.
Registrar: N. O. SOTOYINBO, B.A., M.SC.
Librarian: A. ALADEJANA, B.A., DIP. LIB.

Library of 35,108 vols.
Number of teachers: 222.
Number of students: 2,428.

Publication: *Calendar/Prospectus* (annually).

FEDERAL POLYTECHNIC, IDAH

P.M.B. 1037, IDAH, BENUE STATE
Telephone: Idah 40, 36.

Rector: Dr. S. E. CHUKWUJEKWU.
Registrar: Mallam YAKUBU IBRAHIM (acting).
Librarian: J. A. ACHEMA.

Library of 3,000 vols.
Number of teachers: 72.
Number of students: 750.

DEANS:

School of Business Studies: Mrs. O. A. OYEDELE.
School of Engineering: A. C. OKONWEZE.
School of Food Technology and Catering: M. L. GROVER.

KADUNA POLYTECHNIC

P.M.B. 2021, KADUNA
Telephone: 22551, 211582, 211673, 211744, 211835.
Founded 1968.

Rector: Eng. H. A. TUKUR.
Secretary: I. A. OLAREWAJU.
Librarians: A. OJENIKE, E. A. OLALERE, S. OLABODE.

Library on three campuses of 6,000 vols.
Number of teachers: 500.
Number of students: 8,000.

Four-year courses in Science and Technology, Mining and Geology, Environmental Studies.

KANO STATE INSTITUTE FOR HIGHER EDUCATION

P.M.B. 3401, KANO

Director: Alhaji SHEHU ABDULWAHAB.
Registrar: Alhaji TIJJANI INUWA.

Number of teachers: 137.
Number of students: 2,351.

PRINCIPALS:

School of Social and Rural Development: Alhaji BILYA ABDULLAHI.
Gumel Advanced Teachers' College: ADO GWARAM.
School of Preliminary Studies: TIJJANI IBRAHIM.
School of Islamic Legal Studies: ADAMU GWARAM.
School of Management Studies: IBRAHIM HASSAN.
School of Technology: Dr. A. T. SULEIMAN.
Audo Bako School of Agriculture: Alhaji MUSA RINGIM.

KATSINA COLLEGE OF ARTS, SCIENCE AND TECHNOLOGY

P.M.B. 1061, ZARIA
Telephone: 3206 2841.

Founded 1974; pre-degree courses at Zaria Campus and Advanced Certificate courses at Katsina Campus.

Rector: M. D. ABDULLAHI.
Deputy Rectors: A. UMAR (Zaria Campus); A. ALIYU (Katsina Campus).
Registrar: SALISU HALIDU.
Librarian: M. S. ONYE (acting).

Libraries of 15,633 vols. (Zaria Campus) and 1,050 vols. (Katsina Campus).
Number of teachers: 72 (Zaria Campus), 16 (Katsina Campus).
Number of students: 1,220 (Zaria Campus), 350 (Katsina Campus).

HEADS OF DEPARTMENTS:

Arts and Social Science: G. O. OYESOLA.
Science: A. B. RASEKOALA.
Languages: N. S. DAURA.
Administrative and Business Studies: T. LYNN.

KWARA STATE COLLEGE OF TECHNOLOGY

P.M.B. 1375, ILORIN
Telephone: 2440, 2459, 2687.
Founded 1972.

Principal: Dr. J. O. AMODE, M.S.M.E., PH.D.
Registrar: S. O. OGUNTEBI, B.SC.
Librarian: S. O. ALIMI, B.A.

Library of 20,155 vols.
Number of teachers: *c.* 350.
Number of students: 4,200.

Publications: *Calendar*†, *Prospectuses*† (annually), *Library Bulletin*† (3 a year), *Kwaratech News*† (quarterly).

DIRECTORS:

School of Basic Studies: O. AJOLORE.

School of Management and Vocation: A. E. BAKARE.
School of Mines: T. ADEGBOHUNGBE (acting).
School of Technology: G. A. ADEBIYI.

LAGOS STATE COLLEGE OF SCIENCE AND TECHNOLOGY

P.M.B. 21606, IKEJA, ISOLO RD., ISOLO, LAGOS

Founded 1977.

Principal: Dr. H. O. OSENI.
Registrar: G. G. AGBENOHEVI.
Librarian: E. O. SOYINKA.

Library of 19,000 vols.
Number of teachers: 110.
Number of students: 1,350.

HEADS OF DEPARTMENTS:

Mathematics: T. O. ONABANJO.
Science: Dr. G. E. NWANKPELE.
Crop and Animal Production and Horticulture: Mrs. H. O. ANJORIN.
Secretarial Studies: Mrs. D. D. ADERIYE.
Social Studies: P. K. WIREDU (acting).
Business Administration: Mrs. L. O. ONAFOWORA (acting).
Architecture: Mrs. O. A. EJIWUNMI (acting).

MURTALA POLYTECHNIC

P.M.B. 2084, MAKURDI, BENUE STATE

Founded 1976.

Rector: Dr. S. ANANDE-KUR (acting).
Librarian: V. N. OZOWA (acting).

Library of 7,415 vols.
Number of teachers: 55.
Number of students: 1,200.

HEADS OF DEPARTMENTS:

Business and Administrative Studies: Dr. J. O. OBIKOYA.
Agriculture: Dr. C. T. BELLONWU.
Fine and Applied Art: S. SOLOMON AKIGA.
Science and Technology: Y. AWODI.
General Studies: I. ACHINEKU.
Engineering: (vacant).

COLLEGE OF TECHNOLOGY, OWERRI

P.M.B. 1036, OWERRI

Founded 1977.

Principal: Prof. O. J. E. UZAMAKA.
Registrar: S. E. OGBONNA (acting).
Librarian: M. OJI.

Library of 4,000 vols.
Number of teachers: 60.
Number of students: 821.

DIRECTORS:

School of Basic and Industrial Sciences: Dr. M. O. OLEKA (acting).
School of Business and Public Administration: H. I. ONYEWUCHI.
School of Engineering Technology: Dr. O. B. EPELLE.
School of Environmental Design: Dr. O. B. EPELLE.

UNIVERSITY OF SCIENCE AND TECHNOLOGY

P.M.B. 5080, PORT HARCOURT, RIVERS STATE

Founded 1971, university status 1980.

Vice-Chancellor: Prof. T. T. ISOUN, D.V.M., PH.D.
Registrar: M. B. MIEYEBO, B.SC.
Librarian: J. A. OMBU, M.L.S.

Library of 36,000 vols.
Number of teachers: 220.
Number of students: 1,800.

DIRECTORS:

School of Business: G. R. K. NAIR, M.COM., F.C.A.
School of Engineering: J. C. CHINWAH, M.SC., PH.D.
School of Science: T. M. ADERIRAN, PH.D.
School of Agriculture: U. W. U. AYONOADU, M.SC., PH.D.

PETROLEUM TRAINING INSTITUTE

P.M.B. 1116, WARRI, BENDEL STATE

Founded 1972.

Principal: L. E. FOLIVI.
Registrar: J. A. POPO.
Librarian: T. OMOERHA.

Library of 25,000 vols.
Number of teachers: 73.
Number of students: 455.

HEADS OF DEPARTMENTS:

Petroleum Processing Technology: D. O. EGBUNA.
Electrical Engineering: M. R. VARMA.
Mechanical Engineering: D. O. OGUNLADE.
Petroleum Engineering: H. O. ONIPEDE.
Science and General Studies: C. I. NWANKWO.
School of Welding: M. C. EDDOH.

YABA COLLEGE OF TECHNOLOGY

P.M.B. 2011, YABA, LAGOS

Founded 1948.

Principal: G. M. OKUFI, F.C.C.A., A.C.A.
Registrar: S. O. ADEYEYE, M.A., PH.D.
Librarian: S. O. ISHOLA, A.L.A.

Library of 35,000 vols.
Number of teaching staff: 135.
Number of students: 1,996 full-time, 864 part-time.

Publications: *Prospectus, Newsletter.*

Federal School of Dental Hygiene: 1 Broad St., P.M.B. 12562, Lagos; f. 1957; Principal Dr. S. JOHNSON, B.D.S., D.D.O.

School of Agriculture: P.M.B. 623, Akure, Ondo State; f. 1957; 500 students; library of 2,100 vols.; Principal S. A. OYENEYE, M.SC.; publ. *The Tractor.*

School of Agriculture: P.M.B. 5029, Moor Plantation, Ibadan; f. 1921; 180 students; Principal G. S. OSITELU.

School of Forestry: Forestry Research Institute of Nigeria, P.M.B. 5054, Ibadan; f. 1941; technical forestry training, ordinary and higher diploma courses; library of over 2,000 vols; 10 teachers, 250 students; Principal A. O. ADEOLA.

NORWAY

Population 4,066,000

ACADEMY

Det Norske Videnskaps-Akademi (*The Norwegian Academy of Science and Letters*): Drammensveien 78, Oslo 2; f. 1857; publs. *Skrifter*†, *Avhandlinger*†, *Årbok*†.

Hon. President: H.M. THE KING.
President: Prof. Dr. JOHS. ANDENAES.
Vice-President: Prof. Dr. JUL LÅG.
Secretary-General: Prof. Dr. A. SEMB-JOHANSSON.
Executive Secretary: KJELL K. HERLOFSEN, B.A.

MEMBERS:

Honorary Members:

H.R.H. Crown Prince HARALD.
H.R.H. Crown Princess SONJA.
H.E. President KRISTJÁN ELDJÁRN (Iceland).
JAHRE, ANDERS.

Mathematics and Natural Sciences:

ÅLVIK, GUNNAR (Botany).
AAS, KNUT A. (Medicine).
AASER, CARL S. (Veterinary Medicine).
ALFSEN, ERIK M. (Mathematics).
ANDERSEN, PER (Medicine).
ARNESEN, KRISTEN (Medicine).
AUBERT, KARL EGIL (Mathematics).
BASTIANSEN, OTTO (Chemistry).
BERG, KÅRE (Medicine).
BERG, ROLF YNGVAR (Botany).
BERGE. SAMSON (Agriculture).
BERNER, ENDRE Q. (Chemistry).
BRAARUD, TRYGVE (Biology).
BRAATHE, PEDER (Forestry).
BRATTSTRÖM, HANS (Marine Biology).
BREIREM, KNUT (Agriculture).
BRINKMANN, AUGUST (Zoology).
BROCH, EINAR (Physics).
BROCH, OLE J., (Medicine).
BRODAL, ALF (Medicine).
BRUSTAD, TOR (Biophysics).
BUGGE, JENS A. W. (Geology).
CHRISTOPHERSEN, ERLING (Botany).
DAHL, EILIF (Botany).
DAHL, HELMER H. (Engineering).
DAHL, ODD (Engineering).
DALE, JOHANNES (Chemistry).
DALE, TORLEIF (Medicine).
DANBOLT, NIELS (Medicine).
DEVIK, FINN (Medicine).
DEVIK, OLAF M. (Physics).
EEG-LARSEN, NICOLAY (Odontology).
EFSKIND, LEIF (Medicine).
EITINGER, LEO (Medicine).
ELDJARN, LORENTZ (Medicine).
ELIASSEN, ARNT (Geophysics).
ENDER, FREDRIK C. W. (Biochemistry).
FÆGRI, KNUT (Botany).
FENSTAD, JENS E. (Mathematics).
FINHOLT, PER E. (Pharmacy).
FJELDSTAD, JONAS EKMAN (Oceanography).
FJØRTOFT, RAGNAR (Meteorology).
FLOOD, HÅKON (Chemistry).
FØRLAND, TORMOD (Chemistry).
FOSS, OLAV (Chemistry).
FØYN, BJØRN (Zoology).
FRIMANN-DAHL, JOHAN (Medicine).
FURBERG, SVEN (Chemistry).
GARM, OTTO N. (Veterinary Medicine).
GJÆREVOLL, OLAV (Botany).
GJELSVIK, TORE (Geology).
GJESSING, JUST F. R. (Geography).
GJONE, EGIL (Medicine).
GOKSØYR, JOSTEIN (Microbiology).
GRJOTHEIM, KAI G. (Chemistry).
HAFSTEN, ULF (Botany).
HAGEM, OSCAR M. (Botany).
HAGEN, YNGVAR (Zoology).
HAGERUP-LARSSEN, GEORG (Engineering).
HALLDAL, PER (Botany).
HARALDSEN, HAAKON (Chemistry).
HARBOE, MORTEN (Medicine).
HASLE, GRETHE R. (Marine Botany).
HASSEL, ODD (Physics and Chemistry).
HAUGE, T. DANNEVIG (Engineering).
HEIDE, OLA M. (Botany).
HEIER, KNUT S. (Geochemistry).
HELVIG, MAGNE (Geography).
HEMMER, PER CHR. (Physics).
HENNINGSMOEN, GUNNAR (Palaeontology).
HENRIKSEN, SVERRE (Medicine).
HJORT, PETER F. (Medicine).
HOLGERSEN, HOLGER (Zoology).
HOLTE, JOHAN B. (Chemistry).
HOLTEDAHL, HANS (Geology).
HOMB, THOR (Agriculture).
HVIDSTEN, HARALD J. (Agriculture).
HØEG, OVE ARBO (Botany).
HÖEGH-KROHN, RAPHAEL (Mathematics).
HØGÅSEN, TORMOD H., (Physics).
HYGEN, GEORG (Botany).
IHLEN, ALF (Engineering).
IVERSEN, OLAV HILMAR (Medicine).
JANSEN, JAN (Medicine).
JANSEN, JAN K. S. (Medicine).
JENSEN, EBERHART (Astronomy).
JOHANSEN, KJELL (Zoology).
JOHANSSON, INGEBRIGT (Mathematics).
JYSSUM, KAARE (Medicine).
KAADA, BIRGER (Medicine).
KIIL, FREDRIK (Medicine).
KOFSTAD, PER K. (Chemistry).
KOLSRUD, MARIUS (Physics).
KREYBERG, LEIV (Medicine).
KRISTIANSEN, KRISTIAN (Medicine).
KROG, JOHN (Zoology).
KULLERUD, GUNNAR (Geology).
KVALE, ANDERS (Geology).
KVIFTE, GOTFRED (Geophysics).
KÅSS, ERIK (Medicine).
LÅG, JUL (Agriculture).
LALAND, SØREN (Biochemistry).
LANDMARK, BJØRN (Physics).
LANGFELDT, GABRIEL (Medicine).
LANGSÆTER, ALF (Forestry).
LARSEN, GERHARD (Medicine).
LARSEN, HELGE (Biochemistry).
LIED, FINN (Physics and Electronics).
LOTHE, JENS (Physics).
LØVLIE, ARNE (Zoology).
LUNDBY, ARNE (Physics).
LUNDEN, AKSEL P. (Agriculture).
LUNDEVALL, JON (Medicine).
LYCHE, RALPH TAMBS (Mathematics).
MALLING, BIRGER (Medicine).
MALTBY, PER (Astrophysics).
MANUM, SVEIN B. (Geology).
MORK, MARTIN (Geophysics).
MOSBY, HÅKON (Oceanography).
MYKLEBOST, HALLSTEIN (Geography).
MÜLLER, CARL (Medicine).

NATVIG, JACOB B., (Medicine).
NEUMANN, HENRICH (Mineralogy).
NICOLAYSEN, RAGNAR (Medicine).
NORDAL, ARNOLD (Pharmacy).
NORMAN, NICOLAI (Physics).
OEDING, PER (Medicine).
OFTEDAHL, CHRISTOFFER (Geology).
OFTEDAL, PER (Genetics).
OLSEN, HAAKON A. (Physics).
OMHOLT, ANDERS (Physics).
OPHEIM, ODD (Medicine).
ORVIN, ANDERS (Geology).
OUREN, TORE (Geography).
OWREN, PAUL (Medicine).
PALM, ENOK (Mechanics).
PAPPAS, ALEXIS (Chemistry).
PIHL, ALEXANDER (Medicine).
POPPE, ERIK (Medicine).
RAEDER, M. G. (Chemistry).
RANDERS, GUNNAR (Astronomy).
REFSUM, SIGVALD (Medicine).
REICHBORN-KJENNERUD, I. (Odontology).
RETTERSTØL, NILS (Medicine).
ROBAK, HÅKON (Botany).
ROSENQVIST, IVAN (Geology).
ROSSELAND, SVEIN (Astronomy).
SAMSET, IVAR (Forestry).
SANDVIK, OLAV (Microbiology).
SCHJØTT-RIVERS, ERNST (Medicine).
SELBERG, ATLE (Mathematics).
SELBERG, HENRIK (Mathematics).
SELBERG, SIGMUND (Mathematics).
SELMER, ERNST S. (Mathematics).
SEMB-JOHANSSON, ARNE (Zoology).
SIVERTSEN, ERLING (Zoology).
SKJERVOLD, HARALD (Veterinary Medicine).
SOLBERG, PETER (Agriculture).
SORTEBERG, ASBJØRN (Agriculture).
SØMME, AXEL (Geography).
SØRENSEN, N. A. (Chemistry).
SØRENSEN, SVEN OLUF (Physics).
STORSTEIN, OLE (Medicine).
STØRMER, ERLING (Mathematics).
STØRMER, PER (Botany).
STUBBAN, JOHN OLAV (Mathematics).
SVENKERUD, ROLF R. (Pathology).
SÆLEN, ODD H. (Oceanography).
TANGEN, ROALD (Physics).
THOMASSEN, THORE LIE (Medicine).
TJØTTA, SIGVE (Mathematics).
TORVIK, ANSGAR (Medicine).
TSCHUDI, AADEL BRUN (Geography).
USTVEDT, HANS JACOB (Medicine).
VELLE, WEIERT (Veterinary Medicine).
WAALER, BJARNE A. (Medicine).
WAALER, ERIK (Medicine).
WAALER, GEORG (Medicine).
WALAAS, OTTO (Medicine).
WALBERG, FRED (Medicine).
WALLØE, LARS (Information Cybernetics).
WERGELAND, HARALD (Physics).
WESTIN, SVERRE (Physics).
WIBORG, KRISTIAN F. (Marine Biology).
WIDERØE, ROLF (Engineering).
ØDEGÅRD, ØRNULV (Medicine).
ØDELIEN, MIKKEL (Agriculture).

There are also 80 Foreign Members.

Historical and Philosophical Sciences:
AALL, LILY WEISER (Folklore).
AARBAKKE, MAGNUS (Law).
AMUNDSEN, LEIV (Classical Philology).
ANDENAES, JOHANNES (Law).
ANDERSEN, KRISTEN (Law).
ANKER, ØYVIND (Literature).
ASHEIM, IVAR (Theology).
AUBERT, J. VILHELM (Sociology).
BARTH, FREDRIK (Social Anthropology).
BEITO, OLAV (Philology).
BENESTAD, FINN (Music).
BERG, KNUT (Art History).
BERGSLAND, KNUT (Philosophy).
BEYER, EDVARD (Literature).
BIRKELAND, BJARTE (Literature).
BIRKELI, FRIDTJOV (Theology).

BLOCH-HOELL, NILS EGEDE (Theology).
BORGSTRØM, CARL (Philology).
BØ, OLAV (Folklore).
BRÆKHUS, SJUR (Law).
BRATHOLM, ANDERS (Law).
BULL, EDVARD (History).
CHRISTIE, HÅKON (Art History).
CHRISTIE, NILS (Criminology).
DAHL, HELGE (Pedagogy).
DAHL, NILS ALSTRUP (Theology).
DAHL, OTTAR (History).
DAHL, OTTO C. (Philology).
DAL, INGERID (Philology).
DANIELSEN, ROLF CHR. (History).
ECKHOFF, TORSTEIN (Law).
EINARSEN, JOHAN (Economics).
FAEHN, HELGE (Theology).
FALKANGER, THOR (Law).
FALKENBERG, JOHS. (Ethnography).
FLYDAL, LEIV (Philology).
FRAENKL, PAVEL (Literature).
FØLLESDAL, DAGFINN (Philosophy).
GALLIS, ARNE (Philology).
GALTUNG, JOHAN (Development).
GRØTVEDT, PER N. (Philology).
GULLVÅG, INGEMUND (Philosophy).
HAAKONSEN, DANIEL (Literature).
HAAVELMO, TRYGVE (Economics and Statistics).
HAGEN, ANDERS (Archaeology).
HALVORSEN, EYVIND FJELD (Philology).
HAMRE, LARS (History).
HANSSEN, **JENS S. TH. (Philology).**
HAUGE, INGARD (Literature).
HAUGLID, ROAR (Art History).
HELLE, KNUT (History).
HENNE, HENRY (Linguistics).
HEYERDAHL, GERD H. (Philology).
HEYERDAHL, THOR (Ethnology).
HOFF, INGEBORG (Philology).
HOFFMANN, MARTA (Folklore).
HOLM, SVERRE (Sociology).
HOLM-OLSEN, LUDVIG (Philology).
HOLMBOE, A. C. STUB (Law).
HOLMSEN, ANDREAS (History).
HOLTER, ÅGE (Theology).
HOLTER, HARRIET (Sociology).
HOVDA, PER (Philology).
HOVDHAUGEN, SVEN (Linguistics).
HYGEN, JOHAN B. (Theology).
HØDNEBØ, FINN (Linguistics).
JACOBSEN, KNUT DAHL (Administration).
JANSEN, H. LUDIN (Theology).
JERVELL, JACOB (Theology).
JOHANSEN, ARNE B. (Archaeology).
JOHANSEN, ERLING (Archaeology).
JOHANSEN, LEIF (Economics).
JOHNSEN, ARNE ODD (History).
KAARTVEDT, ALF (History).
KAPELRUD, ARVID (Theology).
KLEVE, KNUT (Philology).
KOLSRUD, KNUT (Folklore).
KRAG, ERIK (Literature).
KRAGERUD, ALV (Theology).
KRAGGERUD, EGIL (Classical Philology).
KVAERNE, PER (Classical Philology).
LANGHOLM, SIVERT (History).
LEIVESTAD, RAGNAR (Theology).
LIE, HALLVARD (Philology).
LINDEMAN, FREDRIK, OTTO (Linguistics).
L'ORANGE, H. P. (Archaeology).
LUNDEBY, EINAR (Philosophy).
LUNDEN, SIRI SVERDRUP (Philology).
LØDRUP, PETER (Law).
LØNNING, PER (Theology).
MAGERØY, HALLVARD (Philology).
MANNSÅKER, DAGFINN (History).
MARSTRANDER, SVERRE (Archaeology).
MAEHLE, LEIF (Literature).
MATHIASSEN, TERJE (Linguistics).
MIDBØE, HANS L. (Literature).
MUNTHE, PREBEN (Economics).
MØRLAND, HENNING (Philology).
MYKLAND, KNUT (History).
NAESS, ARNE (Philosophy).
NESHEIM, ASBJØRN (Philology).

NETTUM, ROLF N. (Literature).
NOME, JOHN (Theology).
NORDHAGEN, PER JONAS (Art History).
NORDHAL, HELGE (Linguistics).
NORENG, HARALD (Literature).
OFTEDAL, MAGNE (Celtic Philology).
OPSAHL, TORKEL (Law).
PETERSEN, ERLING (Economics).
POLAK, ADA B. (Art History).
RAND, PER J. (Pedagogy).
REIERSØL, OLAV (Statistics).
REINTON, LARS (History).
ROBBERSTAD, KNUT (Law).
ROMMETVEIT, RAGNAR (Psychology).
RØSTVIG, MAREN-SOFIE (Literature).
SALTVEIT, LAURITS (Pedagogy).
SANDVEN, JOHANNES (Psychology).
SANDVIK, GUDMUND (History).
SEJERSTED, FRANCIS (History).
SEIP, JENS A. (History).
SELMER, KNUT S. (Law).
SELVIG, ERLING (Law).
SEMMINGSEN, INGRID (History).
SEYERSTED, PER (Philosophy).
SJØVOLD, THORLEIF (Archaeology).
SKAARE, KOLBJORN (Numismatics).
SKARD, SIGMUND (Literature).
SKODVIN, MAGNE (History).
SLETSJØE, LEIF (Philology).
SMEDSLUND, JAN (Psychology).
SMIDT, KRISTIAN (Literature).
SMITH, CARSTEN (Law).
STEEN, ELLISIV (Literature).
STEEN, SVERRE (History).
SVENDSEN, PAULUS (Literary History).
SVERDRUP, ERLING (Statistics).
THONSTAD, TORE (Economics/Statistics).
TRANØY, KNUT ERIK (Philosophy).
TØNNESSEN, JOHAN NICOLAY (History).
TØNNESSON, KÅRE D. (History).
TORP, HJALMAR (Art History).
TSCHUDI-MADSEN, STEPHAN (Art History).
VENÅS, KJELL (Philology).
VOGT, HANS (Philology).
VOGT, JOHAN (Economics).
WILLOCH, SIGURD (Art History).
ØSTBY, LEIF (Art History).

There are also 71 Foreign Members.

PRIZE FOUNDATION

The Norwegian Nobel Committee (Nobel Peace Prize) and the Norwegian Nobel Institute
19 Drammensveien, Oslo.

The Peace Prize is distributed on the anniversary of the death of Dr. Nobel, December 10th. The award may, however, be made known before that date. On December 10th the prize winner (or winners) receives the amount of the Prize together with a diploma designed by the Norwegian artist ÖRNULF RANHEIMSÆTER, and a gold medal made by the Norwegian sculptor, GUSTAV VIGELAND. The first award of the Nobel Peace Prize was in 1901.

Nobel Committee: f. 1897 in pursuance of the will of Dr. ALFRED NOBEL. (*See* also Sweden chapter.)

General Secretary: JAKOB SVERDRUP.

Members: J. SANNESS (Chair.), E. AARVIK (Deputy Chair.), T. HAUGELAND, S. LINDEBRÆKKE, E. GERMETEN.

Peace Prizewinners since 1973:

1973 HENRY A. KISSINGER (American).
1973 LE DUC THO (North Vietnamese) (refused to receive the prize).
1974 EISAKU SATO (Japanese).
1974 SÉAN MACBRIDE (Irish).
1975 ANDREI D. SAKHAROV (Russian).
1976 MAIREAD CORRIGAN and BETTY WILLIAMS (Northern Ireland).
1977 Amnesty International.
1978 ANWAR SADAT (Egypt) and MENACHEM BEGIN (Israel).
1979 MOTHER TERESA OF CALCUTTA.

Norwegian Nobel Institute: f. 1903 to follow the development of international relations, especially the work for the pacific settlement of them, and thereby to advise the Committee with regard to the distribution of the Prize.

Director: JAKOB SVERDRUP.
Library of 100,000 vols.
Publications: *Publications de l'Institut Nobel Norvégien* (scientific treatises).

To the Institute are attached *Advisers* on international law, modern history and economics, appointed for a period of three years. Those serving at present are: AUGUST SCHOU and HELGE PHARO (history) and PREBEN MUNTHE (economics). The Advisers, in collaboration with the Director of the Institute, deliver to the Nobel Committee confidential reports on the candidates for the Peace Prize.

LEARNED SOCIETIES

Architecture and Town Planning

Norske Architekters Landsforbund (*Norwegian Architects' League*): Josefinesgt. 34, Oslo 3; f. 1911; 1,985 mems.; Pres. Architect M.N.A.L. Ragnvald Bing Lorentzen; publs. *Byggekunst, Arkitektnytt, Norske Arkitektkonkurranser.*

The Arts

Billedkunstfaglig Sentralorganisasjon (*Art Assn.*): Wergelandsveien 17, Oslo 1; f. 1979; 11 mems. elected by some 1,600 painters, sculptors and artists; Pres. Ingolf Holme; Sec. Chr. Roscher-Nielsen.

Filharmonisk Selskap (*Philharmonic Society*): Oslo Concert Hall, Munkedamsveien 14, Oslo 1; f. 1919; Man. Alv Rasmussen; publ. *Konsert-Nytt* (8 a year).

Musikselskabet "Harmonien": Grieghallen, Lars Hilles gt. 3A, N-5000 Bergen; f. 1765; 70 musicians, 1,200 mems.; specialized music library of 3,500 vols.; Pres. Njaal Sæveraas; Music Dir. and Perm. Conductor Karsten Andersen; Man. Dir. Laila Kismul.

Norges Kunstnerråd (*Norwegian Artists' Council*): Kirkegaten 34, Oslo 1; f. 1940; Pres. Knut M. Hansson; Sec. Kari Forsberg.

Norsk Musikk-informasjon (*Norwegian Music Information Centre*): Tordenskioldsgate 6B, Oslo 1; f. 1978; objects: to promote and offer information on Norwegian music and composers, music institutions, performing groups and soloists; to build up a representative collection of contemporary Norwegian music; to stimulate community interest in Norwegian music; Man. Diane Hanisch; publs. catalogues of Norwegian music.

Norwegian Cultural Council: Rosenkrantz gt. 11, Oslo; f. 1965 in connection with the Cultural Fund to stimulate artistic life and cultural activities in Norway and to distribute the resources of the Fund in grants and subsidies; nine mems. appointed by the Government and four by the Storting (Parliament) all for a period of four years; Chair. Edvard Beyer; Deputy Chair. Anne Breivik; Man. Dir. Aasmund Oftedal; publ. *The Norwegian Cultural Fund.*

Bibliography, Library Science and Museology

Norske Kunst- og Kulturhistoriske Museer (*Association of Museums of Art and Cultural History*): Pilestredet 15-6°, Oslo 1; f. 1918; 331 mems.; library of 1,000 vols.; Pres. Halvard Björkvik; Sec. Frida Gjerdrum; publ. *Museumsnytt* (Museum News).

Norsk senter for informatikk (*Norwegian Centre for Informatics*): Forskningsveien 1, Oslo 3; f. 1944 as Studieselskapet for Norsk Industri; projects in information science and techniques, information services for public administration and industry; information staff acts on contract with Royal Norwegian Council for Scientific and Industrial Research; I.D.E. service (retrospective data base searches), technology transfer, I.R. software programmes, E.D.P. services; Norwegian node in SCANNET E.D.P. network computer (NORD 10/S) and data base centre; organizes international trade fairs; 320 mems. from industry and organizations; library of 20,000 vols., 1,200 periodicals; Man. Dir. Hans K. Krog; publs. *Artikkel-Indeks* (polytechnical abstract journal and tape recording, SDI service), *Ajour-Forskning og Teknikk*† (technical digest journal).

Economics, Law and Politics

Norsk Forening for Internasjonal Rett (*Norwegian Society for International Law*): Kongensgt. 6, Oslo; f. 1925; 102 mems.; Pres. Finn Seyersted; Sec. E. Rygh.

Statsøkonomisk Forening (*Economic Association of Norway*): Dronningensgt. 16, Oslo; f. 1883; approx. 450 mems.; Pres. Gunnar Bramness; Sec. Bjørn Stenseth; publ. *Statsøkonomisk Tidsskrift* (2 a year).

History, Geography and Archaeology

Foreningen til norske Fortidsminnesmerkers Bevaring (*Society for the Preservation of Ancient Monuments in Norway*): Dronningensgt. 11, Oslo 1; f. 1844; *c.* 4,500 mems.; Chair. Unnleiv Bergsgard; Sec. Mari Kollandsrud; publ. *Ärbok for Foreningen til norske Fortidsminnesmerkers Bevaring* (annual), *Fortidsvern* (quarterly).

Kirkehistorisk Samfunn (*Church History Society*): Box 116, Voksenlia, Oslo 3; f. 1956; 49 mems.; Pres. Prof. Dr. Theol. Nils Egede Bloch-Hoell; Sec. c.ph. Johannes Elgvin; publs. *Norvegia Sacra* (incl. *Bibliotheca Norvegiae Sacrae*).

Landslaget for Bygde- og Byhistorie: Universitetet i Oslo, Institutt for Folkeminnevitenskap, Postboks 1014, Blindern, Oslo 3; f. 1920; local history; co-ordinates the work of 150-200 local organizations; library of 3,000 vols.; Pres. Olav Bø; publ. *Heimen* (quarterly).

Norsk Arkeologisk Selskap (*Norwegian Archaeological Society*): Frederiks gt. 2, Oslo 1; f. 1936; 1,100 mems.; Pres. Arne I. Hoem; Sec.-Gen. Prof. Dr. Sverre Marstrander; publ. *Viking.*

Norsk Historisk Forening (*Norwegian Historical Society*): Historisk institutt, Postboks 23, 5014 Bergen-Universitetet; f. 1869; Pres. Prof. Knut Helle; publ. *Historisk Tidsskrift* (quarterly).

Norsk Lokalhistorisk Institutt: Folke Bernadottes v. 21, Oslo 8; f. 1955; guidance for local historians, research in local history including publication of sources, etc., valuable for research; Dir. Dr.philos. Rolf Fladby.

Norsk Slektshistorisk Forening (*Norwegian Genealogical Society*): P.O.B. 9562, Egertorvet, Oslo 1; f. 1926; about 1,400 mems.; Pres. Per Seland; publ. *Norsk Slektshistorisk Tidsskrift.*

International Cultural Institutes

British Council: Fridtjof Nansensplass 5, Oslo 1; Rep. Miss M. Wane, O.B.E.

Goethe-Institut: Uranienborg terrasse 6, Oslo 3; f. 1958; language instruction, cultural programme; library of *c.* 13,000 vols.; br. at Bergen; Dir. Karl-Heinz Kemmner.

Indo-Iransk Institutt (*Indo-Iranian Institute of the University of Oslo*): Niels Treschows Hus, P.O.B. 1035, Blindern, Oslo; f. 1920; the study of Indian and Iranian languages, culture, history, etc.; library of 30,000 vols.; Pres. Knut Kristiansen.

Istituto Italiano di Cultura: Meltzersgate 5, Oslo 2; Dir. Dott. Achille Ribechi.

Norway-America Association: Drammensvn. 20C, Oslo 2; f. 1919; approx. 700 mems.; a non-profit organization to further cultural ties between the U.S., Canada and Norway primarily through student and trainee exchanges and scholarships; Chair. of the Board Dr. Gunnar Randers; Dir. Miss Ragnhild Galtung; publ. *Yearbook*†.

U.S. International Communication Agency: Drammensveien 18, Oslo 2; Reference Centre: *see* Libraries.

Language and Literature

Norske Akademi for Sprog og Litteratur (*Norwegian Academy for Language and Literature*): Stortinget, Oslo; f. 1953; protects and authorizes dictionaries of the traditional "Riksmaal"; Pres. Prof. ASBRJØN AARNES; Sec. L. R. LANGSLET.

Norske Forfatterforening, Den (*The Norwegian Authors' Society*): Rådhusgata 7, Oslo 1; f. 1893; 400 mems.; Pres. CAMILLA CARLSON; Sec. TORDIS OLSEN.

Norske PEN-Klubb, Den (*Norwegian Centre of International PEN*): f. 1922; contact of Norwegian writers with rest of writing world; Pres. Prof. JOHAN VOGT (Faculty of Social Science, Oslo University, Oslo 3).

MEDICINE

Medicinske Selskap i Bergen, Det (*Medical Society of Bergen*): Med. dpt. B, Haukeland Hospital, N-5016 Bergen; f. 1831; 220 mems.; Chair. Dr. LEIF UTNE; Sec. Dr. A. SCHREINER; publ. *Medicinsk Revue* (section of *Nordisk Medisin*, weekly).

Norsk Farmaceutisk Selskap (*Norwegian Pharmaceutical Society*): f. 1924; to further the scientific and practical development of pharmacy; 450 mems.; Chair. cand. pharm. INGSE RESBERG OLSEN; Sec. cand. pharm. HOLGER MOE TØRISEN (Sørligt. 8, Oslo 5); publ. *Meddelelser fra Norsk Farmaceutisk Selskap*†

Norsk Kirurgisk Forening (*Norwegian College of Surgeons*): Norwegian Medical Association, Inkognitogt. 26, Oslo 2; 500 mems.; Chair. HANS ROSTAD; publ. *Vitenskapelige forhandlinger* (annually).

Norske Medicinske Selskab, Det (*Medical Society*): Drammensvn. 44, Oslo 2; f. 1833; 600 mems.; Chair. Prof. NILS HELSINGEN; Sec. Dr. T. TEIGE.

Norske Laegeforening, Den (*Norwegian Medical Asscn.*): Inkognitogt. 26, Oslo; f. 1886; 8,300 mems.; Pres. Dr. HARALD HAUGE; Sec. Dr. HARRY MARTIN SVABÖ; publ. *Tiddsskrift for den norske lægeforening* (thrice monthly).

Norske Tannlaegeforening, Den (*The Norwegian Dental Association*): Kronprinsens gt. 9, Oslo 2; f. 1886; 3,866 mems.; Pres. ARNLJOT GAARE; Sec.-Gen. ARNE SOLLUND; publ. *Den norske tannlaegeforenings Tidende* (monthly).

NATURAL SCIENCE

General

Chr. Michelsens Institutt for Videnskap og Aandsfrihet (*Institute of Science and Intellectual Freedom*): 5036 Fantoft, Bergen; f. 1929; occupied with scientific research as well as cultural work; library of *c.* 15,000 vols.; Chair. L. HOLBAEK-HANSSEN; Dir. A. JOHNSEN; Dirs. of Research: Dept. of Science and Technology Dr. FRODE L. GALTUNG; Dept. of Social Sciences and Development JUST FAALAND; publ. *Beretninger*† (Reports).

Kongelige Norske Videnskabers Selskab, Det (*Royal Norwegian Society of Sciences*): Trondheim; f. 1760; reorganized 1926; 140 Norwegian, 30 foreign mems.; Pres. Prof. Dr. SIGMUND SELBERG; Sec.-Gen. Prof. Dr. OLAF I. RØNNING; publs. *Skrifter*†, *Forhandlinger*† (both annually).

Polytekniske Forening, Den (*The Polytechnical Society*): Rosenkrantzgt. 7, Oslo; f. 1852; 10,000 mems.; Sec. TOR KJØRREFJORD; publ. *Teknisk Ukeblad*.

Selskapet til Vitenskapenes Fremme (*The Society for the Advancement of Science*): Fysisk Institutt, Universitetet i Bergen, Allegt. 55, 5014 Bergen-Univ.; f. 1927; 446 mems.; objects: to promote and stimulate intellectual activities generally by regular series of lectures, excursions; Pres. Prof. LEIF REIN NJAA; Gen. Sec. Prof. ARVID ERDAL.

Biological Sciences

Norsk Botanisk Forening (*Norwegian Botanical Association*): Botanisk Museum, Oslo 5; f. 1935; 1,000 mems.; Pres. Curator SIGMUND SIVERTSEN; publ. *Blyttia* (quarterly).

Physical Sciences

Norsk Geologisk Forening (*Norwegian Geological Society*): Geologisk Museum, Sarsgate 1, Oslo 5; f. 1905; 650 mems.; Chair. BJØRN NEUMAN; Gen. Sec. SIGURD HUSEBY; publ. *Norsk Geologisk Tidsskrift* (quarterly).

Norsk Kjemisk Selskap (*Norwegian Chemical Society*): P.O.B. 1107-Blindern, Oslo 3; f. 1893; 1,400 mems.; Gen. Sec. Dr. ASTRI ROGSTAD; Pres. Prof. SVEN G. TERJESEN; publs. *Kjemi, Acta Chemica Scandinavica, Year Book*.

TECHNOLOGY

Norges Tekniske Vitenskapsakademi (*Norwegian Academy for Technical Sciences*): Trondheim; f. 1955; 246 mems.; Pres. Prof. ARNE SELBERG; Vice-Pres. Prof. ANDREAS TONNING; Sec.-Gen. Prof. A. HAGEMANN.

Norske Sivilingeniørers Forening (*Norwegian Society of Chartered Engineers*): Ingeniørenes Hus, Kronprinsens gate 17, Oslo 2; f. 1874; professional society; promotes research and development; represents engineering profession in its relations with other organizations and countries; 13,600 mems.; Pres. JON C. WALTER; Sec.-Gen. BJØRN SLUNGAARD; publ. *Teknisk Ukeblad* (weekly), *Elektro* (2 a month), *Plan og Bygg, Kjemi, Maskin, Norsk oljerevy, Våre veier* (10 a year).

RESEARCH INSTITUTES

(*see* also under Universities)

GENERAL

Hovedkomiteen for Norsk Forskning (*Central Committee for Norwegian Research*): Huitfeldtsgt. 47, Oslo 1; f. 1965; 15 mems.; advisory board to the Government on all problems concerning research and handles separate cases independently; Chair. KNUT DAHL JACOBSEN; Sec.-Gen. E. FJELLBIRKELAND.

Research Councils:

Norges Almenvitenskapelige Forskningsråd (*Norwegian Council for Science and the Humanities*): Munthesgt. 29, Oslo 2; f. 1949; 94 mems.; attached to Ministry of Education, semi-independent; comprises four divisional councils, Humanities, Social Sciences, Medicine, Natural Sciences, and a sub-council for research in social planning; awards research grants and fellowships; edits and finances the greater part of Norwegian scientific periodicals; Chair. GERHARD STOLTZ; Dir. ANDERS OMHOLT.

Norges Fiskeriforskningsråd (*Norwegian Council for Fisheries Research*): Håkon Magnussons gt. 1B, Trondheim; f. 1971; 27 mems.; attached to Ministry of Fisheries; awards research grants and fellowships, runs a research institute; Chair. JOHANNES MOE; Dir. NELVIN FARSTAD.

Norges Landbruksvitenskapelige Forskningsråd (*The Agricultural Research Council of Norway*): Wergelandsveien 15, Oslo 1; f. 1949; 28 mems.; attached to Ministry of Agriculture; awards research grants and Fellowships; Chair. ERIK KJØS; Dir. O. JAMT.

Norges Teknisk-Naturvitenskapelige Forskningsråd (NTNF) (*Royal Norwegian Council for Scientific and Industrial Research*): Gaustadalleen 30, Oslo 3; f. 1946; 36 mems.; attached to Ministry of Industry; awards research grants and fellowships and runs its own research establishments (*see* below); Chair. HAAKON SANDVOLD; Dir. R. MAJOR.

ECONOMICS, LAW AND POLITICS

Norsk Utenrikpolitisk Institutt (*Norwegian Institute of International Affairs*): P.O.B. 8159, Dep., Oslo 1; f. 1959; research and specialized information, sections for security policy, resources, international economy, third world and development studies, decision-making problems in foreign policy; Pres. EILIF DAHL; Dir. DANIEL HERADSTVEIT; Dir. of Administration HARALD NJØS; publs. *International Politikk*† (quarterly), *NUPI Notat, NUPI Rapport* (Research reports), *Forum for utviklingsstudier, Hvor Hender Det?, Norsk Utenrikspolitisk Årbok, Norwegian Foreign Policy Studies.*

NATURAL SCIENCE

Biological Sciences

Fiskeridirektoratets Havforskningsinstitutt (*Marine Research Institute of the Directorate of Fisheries*): P.O.B. 1870-72, N-5011 Bergen; f. 1900; part of the Ministry of Fisheries; applied research related to fisheries; six main divisions: physical-chemical oceanography, biological oceanography, demersal fish, pelagic fish north, pelagic fish south, aquaculture; 55 scientific staff; library of 54,400 vols.; Dir. GUNNAR SAETERSDAL; publs. research reports, *Årsmelding*† (annual report).

Nordisk Kollegium for Marinbiologi (*Nordic Council for Marine Biology*): Institute of Marine Biology, Espegrend, N-5065 Blomsterdalen; f. 1956; financed by Scandinavian governments to co-ordinate research and education at the marine biological institutions in Denmark, Finland, Norway and Sweden; 23 mems.; Gen. Sec. Cand. real. TORGEIR BAKKE; publ. *Nordmar*† (annually).

Mathematics

Statistisk Sentralbyrå (*Central Bureau of Statistics*): P.O.B. 8131, Dep, Dronningensgt. 16, Oslo 1; f. 1876; library of 142,000 vols,; Dir. PETTER JAKOB BJERVE; Librarian RANDI GRAN; publs. *Serien: Norges offisielle statistikk* (Series: Norway's Official Statistics) (irregular), *Statistik månedshefte* (Monthly Bulletin of Statistics), *Månedsstatistikk over utenrikshandelen* (Monthly Bulletin of External Trade), *Statistisk ukehefte* (Weekly Bulletin of Statistics), *Samfunnsokonomiske studier* (Social Economic Studies), *Artikler fra Statistisk Sentralbyrå* (Articles from the Central Bureau of Statistics).

Physical Sciences

Geofysiske Kommisjon, Den (*Geophysical Commission*): Det Norske Meteorologiske Institutt, Blindern, Oslo 3; f. 1917; 5 mems.; Pres. Dr. R. FJØRTOFT; Vice-Pres. Dr. M. MORK; Sec. J. HAUGEN; publ. *Geofysiske Publikasjoner* (publ. by Det Norske Videnskaps-Akademi in Oslo, *q.v.*).

Norges Geologiske Undersokelse (*Geological Survey of Norway*): Leiv Erikssons Vei 39, Trondheim; Man. Dir. KNUT S. HEIER; library of 70,000 vols. and 850 periodicals; publs. *Bulletin, Skrifter.*

Norsk Polarinstitutt (*Norwegian Polar Institute*): Rolfstangveien 12, 1330 Oslo Lufthavn; f. 1948 as a continuation and expansion of Norges Svalbard- og Ishavs-undersøkelser (*Norwegian Explorations in Svalbard and the Polar Seas*); f. 1928; objects: preparation and publication of maps and charts of Norwegian territories in the polar regions; scientific investigations in the fields of geology, geophysics and biology; establishment and maintenance of aids to navigation, administration and maintenance of an all-year scientific station Ny-Ålesund, Svalbard; library of 20,000 vols. and 12,000 pamphlets and authors' MSS.; Dir. TORE GJELSVIK, PH.D., geologist; publs. *Skrifter*†, *Meddelelser*†, *Årbok*†, and *Norwegian-British-Swedish Antarctic Expedition 1949–52, Scientific Results.*

Norske Meteorologiske Institutt, Det (*Norwegian Meteorological Institute*): Blindern, Oslo 3; f. 1866; library of 30,000 vols.; Dir. Dr. K. LANGLO; Vice-Dir. P. M. BREISTEIN; Librarian Miss GRETE KROGVOLD; publs. *Norsk Meteorologiskr Årbok*† (annually), *Nedbøriakttagelser i Norge*† (annually), *Årbseretning for de Meteorologiske Instutusjoner i Norge*† (annual report), *Meteorologiske Annaler*† (irregular), *Klimatologisk månedsoversikt* (monthly), *Technical Report* (irregular).

RELIGION AND SOCIOLOGY

Instituttet for sammenlignende kulturforskning (*Institute for Comparative Research in Human Culture*): Drammensveien 78, Oslo 2; f. 1922; concerned mainly with comparative study of languages, religions, folklore, law, ethnology, archaeology, and sociology, sponsoring research programmes, arranging lectures and publishing; Pres. H. HENNE; Vice-Chair. K. KOLSRUD; Sec. K. HERLOFSEN; publs. *Lectures, Writings, Reports.*

TECHNOLOGY

Institutes affiliated with NTNF (see above):

Elektrisitetsforsyningens forskningsinstitutt (*Norwegian Research Institute of Electricity Supply*): 7034 Trondheim-NTH; f. 1952; Dir. OLAV S. JOHANSEN.

Institutt for energiteknikk (*Institute for Energy Technology*): P.O.B. 40, 2007 Kjeller; f. 1948; national energy research establishment; the main research centre is located at Kjeller, where, among other facilities, one research reactor, JEEP II, is in operation; the Institute's boiling water reactor at Halden is the subject of a joint international research project under the auspices of OECD; the Institute's main activities are: general energy technology, including nuclear power, reactor fuel technology, chemical separation processes, isotope production and applications, irradiation technology, general chemical analyses, solid state physics and materials technology; Man. Dir. V. O. ERIKSEN.

Institutt for fjellsprengningsteknikk (*Rock Blasting Institute*): Forskningsveien 3B, P.B. 341, Blindern, Oslo 3; f. 1961; to identify the most economical methods of rock-blasting, and see that the results of research are applied in practice; Dir. A. M. HELTZEN; publ. *Abstract service* (irregular).

Norges byggforskningsinstitutt (*Norwegian Building Research Institute*): Forskningsveien 3B, Oslo 3; f. 1953; library of 31,000 vols., 370 periodicals; Dir. SVEN ERIK LUNDBY; publs. *Rapporter* (Reports, irregular), *Håndbøker* (Handbooks, English summary), *Byggdetaljblad* (Data sheets), *Saertrykk* (reprints), technical briefs.

Norges geotekniske institutt (*Norwegian Geotechnical Institute*): Sognsveien 72, P.B. 40, Tasen, Oslo 8; f. 1953; 130 mems; soil, rock and snow mechanics, foundation engineering, instrumentation; library of 21,500 vols., 267 periodicals; Dir. KAARE HØEG, D.SC.; publs. *Publications* (irregular, series of monographs and reprints), *Technical Report* (irregular).

Norges skipsforskningsinstitutt (*Ship Research Institute of Norway*): P.O.B. 4125, Valentinlyst, N7001 Trondheim; f. 1951; research, development and commission work related to technical, organizational, social and economic problems of design, construction and operation of ships and offshore constructions, hydrodynamic testing facilities; library of 10,000 vols., 300 periodicals; Man. Dir. ARNOLD HANSEN; publs. *Meddelelser* (Notes), *Reports* (irregular, in Norwegian and English), *Ships Abstracts* (monthly, in English), *NSFI-Nytt* (News).

NORSAR—Norwegian Seismic Array: P.B. 51, 2007 Kjeller; f. 1968/69; research on problems in distinguishing between subterranean nuclear explosions and earthquakes; applied seismology research; Dirs. F. RINGDAL (projects), E. S. HUSEBYE (research).

Norsk institutt for by- og regionforskning (*Norwegian Institute for Urban and Regional Research*): Nycoveien 1, Oslo 4; f. 1965; 72 mems.; library of 13,000 vols., 160 periodicals; Dir. EGIL TOMBRE; publs. *Reports*†, *PLANDATA* (Information series), *NIBR notater*† (NIBR notes).

Norsk institutt for Luftforskning (*Norwegian Institute for Air Research*): P.B. 130, 2001 Lillestrøm; f. 1969; national and international research and consultation in air pollution, atmospheric dispersion and measurements; library of 3,300 vols., 100 periodicals; Dir. Dr. BRYNJULF OTTAR; publ. Annual Report†.

Norsk institutt for vannforskning (*Norwegian Institute for Water Research*): P.O.B. 333, Blindern, Oslo 3; f. 1958; research and contract projects on technical, economical and sanitary problems in connection with water supply, waste water and pollution in rivers and lakes/fjords; library of 21,000 vols., 600 periodicals; Dir. KJELL BAALSRUD; publs. *Reports*.

Norsk Regnesentral (*Norwegian Computing Centre*): Forskningsveien 1B, Oslo 3; f. 1952; contributes to the utilization of quantitative methods and computers, carries out own and contract research, disseminates information; library of 3,500 vols., 120 periodicals; Dir. DRUDE BERNTSEN; publ. *Simula newsletter* (quarterly).

Norsk senter for informatikk (*Norwegian Centre for Informatics*): Forskningsveien 1, Oslo 3; f. 1944; carries out information services for industry, administration and research; carries out certain staff functions for NTNF; library of 25,000 vols., 1,200 periodicals; Dir. A. DISCH; publs. *Artikkel-Indeks* (monthly index of technical literature), *Ajour—T.I.* (monthly technical digest), *FoU-Indeks* (R & D Report Index), *Olje-Indeks* (Oil-Index).

Selskapet for industriell og teknisk forskning ved Norges tekniske høgskole (SINTEF) (*Scientific and Industrial Research Foundation at the University of Trondheim*): 7034 Trondheim-NTH; f. 1950; chemistry, metallurgy, machine design, production engineering, automation, data processing electronics, acoustics, physics, civil engineering, hydrodynamics, social and hospital research; 6 affiliated institutes; Man. Dir. J. MOE; publs. *Reports*.

Sentralinstitutt for industriell forskning (*Central Institute for Industrial Research*): Forskningsveien 1, Oslo 3; f. 1950; on contract with industry and others, carries out research in science and technology for the benefit of industry; library of 25,000 vols., 1,200 periodicals (in co-operation with NSI, *see* above); Man. Dir. T. K. RODERBURG.

Transportøkonomisk institutt (*Institute of Transport Economics*): Grensevn 86, Oslo 6; f. 1964; library of 10,500 vols., 240 periodicals; Dir. DAG BJØRNLAND; publ. *Samferdsel* (Communication, 10 a year).

Papirindustriens Forskningsinstitutt (*The Norwegian Pulp and Paper Research Institute*): Postboks 250, Vinderen, Oslo 3; f. 1923; 60 mems.; library of 16,000 vols.; Head E. BØHMER; publs. *Litteraturutdrag* (Literature abstracts).

Skipsfartsøkonomisk Institutt (*Institute for Shipping Research*): Norwegian School of Economics and Business Administration, Breiviken 2, N-5000 Bergen; f. 1958; research and publication of results, aims to provide a centre for research fellows in sea transport and shipping economics from Norway and abroad, to promote co-operation with similar institutions, and post-graduate education in shipping economics; library of *c.* 3,000 vols., 1,450 periodicals, reports, etc.; Dirs Prof. ARNLJOT STRØMME SVENDSEN, Prof. TOR WERGELAND; Sec. TORA CHRISTENSEN.

LIBRARIES AND ARCHIVES

Arendal og Hisøy Bibliotek (*Municipal Library*): f. 1832; 1972 incorporated *Aust-Agder Fylkesbibliotek* (County Library); 90,000 vols.; Head Libr. CLARA TUNOLD.

Bergen offentlige Bibliotek (*Municipal and County Library*): f. 1874; 548,000 vols.; Grieg collection of 100 MSS. and 5,000 letters; City Librarian JAHN STORUM.

Deichmanske Bibliotek (*City Library of Oslo*): Henrik Ibsens gt. 1, Oslo 1; f. 1785; 1,232,000 vols.; Chief Librarian HANS FLØGSTAD.

Drammen Folkebibliotek (*Public Library of Drammen*): Gamle Kirkepl. 7, Box 1136, 3001 Drammen; f. 1916; public library of Drammen and central library for the county of Buskerud; 216,224 vols.; Pres. EINAR G. NYHUUS; Chief Librarian MAGNE HAUGE.

Fredrikstad Bibliotek (*Municipal Library and Central Library of Ostfold Fylke*): Fredrikstad; f. 1926; 123,218 vols.; Chief Librarian ARNE KR. SOLLID.

Kongelige Norske Videnskabers Selskabs Bibliotek: see Universitetsbiblioteket Avd. B, Trondheim.

Kristiansands Folkebibliotek (*Municipal Library*): Kristiansand S.; f. 1909; since 1938 also central library for Vestagder; 208,600 vols.; Chief Librarian HELGE TERLAND.

Norges Landbrukshøgskoles Bibliotek (*Library of the Agricultural University of Norway*): 1432 Ås-NLH; f. 1859; literature concerning all branches of agricultural science and forestry, chemistry, general biology, botany, etc.; 395,000 vols.; Head Librarian JON HJELTNES; publ. *Meldinger fra Norges Landbrukshøgskole*† (Scientific Reports of the Agricultural University of Norway).

Norges Tekniske Høgskole, Biblioteket (*Library of the Norwegian Institute of Technology, affiliated to the University of Trondheim*): N-7034 Trondheim-NTH; f. 1910 aim: to serve and promote scientific and industria research through providing and preparing for use the literature necessary for these purposes; maintains a science information service, SDI and on-line information retrieval services and has a documentary film and xerox department; since 1957 is also the *Central Technical Library of Norway*; 800,000 vols., with special collections of patents, reports and industrial trade literature; Librarian KNUT THALBERG; publs. *Meldinger og Boklister*†, *Litteraturlister I*† (Bibliographies), *Facsimilia Scientifica et Technica Norvegica*†, *Rapport*†, *Cumulative Supplement to periodicals* (annually).

Riksantikvaren (*Central Office of Historic Monuments*): Bygning 18, Akershus Festning, Oslo 1; f. 1912; inspectorate for national monuments, medieval buildings, protected buildings, churches over 90 years old; archives: *c.* 500,000 photos; library of 25,000 vols.; Dir. STEPHAN TSCHUDI-MADSEN.

Riksarkivet (*National Archives of Norway*): Folke Bernadottes vei 21, Oslo 8; f. 1817; takes charge of the archives of the ministries and other branches of the central administration; library of 50,000 vols.; Dir. DAGFINN MANNSÅKER.

Rjukan Bibliotek (*Public Library of Rjukan*): Rjukan; f. 1914; 83,922 vols. (6 branches); Chief Librarian INGEBORG BOTNEN.

Statens Bibliotektilsyn (*Directorate for Public and School Libraries*): Munkedamsveien 62, P.O.B. 8145-dep., Oslo 1; Dir. ELSE GRANHEIM; publ. *Bok og Bibliotek*† (8 a year), *Bokbladet*† (quarterly).

Statistisk Sentralbyrås Bibliotek (*Library of the Central Bureau of Statistics*): Dronningensgt. 16, Oslo; postal address: P.B. 8131, Dep. Oslo 1; f. 1876, reorganized 1917–24; 142,000 vols. mainly economic, demographic and statistical literature (official and international statistics included); open to the public; Chief Librarian RANDI GRAN; publ. *Biblioteksnytt* (monthly).

Statsarkivet i Hamar (*Regional State Archives*): Strandgata 71, N-2300 Hamar; f. 1917; public record office, archives; public reading-room open on weekdays; library of 12,500 vols.; Chief Archivist JAN H. OLSTAD.

Stavanger Bibliotek (*Stavanger Library*): Stavanger; f. 1885; municipal library for the town of Stavanger, central library for the county of Rogaland; 270,000 vols.; music and picture collection; Librarian ARNT OSELAND.

Stortingsbiblioteket (*Library of the Norwegian Parliament*): Stortinget., Oslo 1; f. 1871; political literature; 128,000 vols.; open to the public on application; Chair. HALDIS HAURØY; Head Librarian OLAF CHR. TORP; publs. *Årsberetning*† (Annual Report), *Nytt fra Stortingsbiblioteket*† (monthly).

Styret for det Industrielle Rettsvern. Bibliotek (*Library of the Norwegian Patent Office*): Middelthunsgt. 15b, Oslo, Postboks 8160 Oslo-Dep. Oslo 1; f. 1888; 46,000 vols. scientific and technical books and periodicals of reference for patent research; 17,000,000 patent specifications; Chief Librarian KJELL A. HANSEN; publs. *Norske Patentskrifter*†, *Norsk Tidende for det Industrielle Rettsvern*†, *Norske Utlegningsskrifter*†.

Universitetsbiblioteket avd. B, Trondheim (*University Library of Trondheim, Section B*): Erling Skakkesgt. 47c, 7000 Trondheim; consists of the library of the *Kongelige Norske Videnskabers Selskab* (f. 1760) and the library of *Norges Lærerhøgskole* (f. 1922); 700,000 vols.; special collections of MSS, maps, prints, music and drama; since 1939 receives deposit copies of all Norwegian books desired; Librarian STEN F. VEDI; publs. *Det Kongelige Norske Videnskabers Selskab, Skrifter*†, *Forhandlinger*†, *Det Kongelige Norske Videnskabers Selskab, Museet, Rapport*†, *Miscellanea/Gunneria*†.

Universitetsbiblioteket i Oslo (*University Library, Oslo*): Drammensveien 42, Oslo; f. 1811; 1,950,000 vols., of which 46,900 are bound vols. of newspapers (3 million vols., including institute libraries); special collections of manuscripts, maps, prints and drawings, music, drama, incunabula, papyri and orientalia; the University Library receives by law copies of all Norwegian books, and edits the official Norwegian book catalogue; Librarian JOHN BRANDRUD; publs. *Norsk Bokfortegnelse*† (The National Bibliography), *Bibliografi over Norges offentlige publikasjoner*† (Bibliography of Norwegian Government publications), *Universitetsbiblioteket i Oslo*†, *Utenlandske Avdelings Tilvekst av Faglitteratur. D.1-3*† (bi-monthly accession lists of foreign non-fiction literature), *Utenlandske periodika i Norge*† (Union Catalogue of foreign periodicals in Norwegian libraries).

Universitetsbiblioteket i Bergen (*The University Library of Bergen*): f. 1825 as Bergens Museums Bibliotek; 900,000 vols.; special divisions for newspapers, manuscripts, pictures and maps; Norwegian depository library; Dir. Dr. MATTIAS TVEITANE; publs. *Sarsia*† (Marine Biology), *Norwegian Archaeological Review*.

United States Reference Center: American Embassy, Drammensveien 18, Oslo 2; f. 1945; 5,000 vols. (including government publs.); part of the International Communication Agency; supplies information about the U.S. by means of its documentation and research.

Utenriksdepartementets Bibliotek (*Library of the Ministry of Foreign Affairs*): 7. Juni-Plassen 1, Oslo; f. 1901, reorganized 1919–22; objects: foreign affairs, international law and international relations—political, social, economic and commercial; library is a reference library for Govt. Depts.; is also open to the public; 120,000 vols., including periodicals and pamphlets, 5,000 maps; Head Librarian GERD BIRKELUND KRAG; publ. *Tilvekst Utenriksdepartementets Bibliotek* (bi-monthly).

MUSEUMS AND ART GALLERIES

Bergen

Botanisk Museum, Universitetet i Bergen: P.O.B. 12, N-5014 Bergen; f. 1886; exhibits of Norwegian flora; research and teaching; Curator DAGFINN MOE.

Geologisk Museum, Universitetet i Bergen: 5014 Bergen-Universitetet; f. 1825; part of Geological Institute of the University; large public exhibition and research collection of rocks, minerals and fossils; Dir. (vacant).

Historisk Museum, Universitetet i Bergen: P.B. 25, N-5014 Bergen; f. 1825, part of University 1848; depts. of Archaeology, Middle Ages, Post-Medieval Social History, Church Art, Ethnography; library of 10,000 vols.; Dir. KJELL FALCK; publs. *Arkeo*†, *Arkeologiske Skrifter*†.

Vestlandske Kunstindustrimuseum (*Western Norway Museum of Applied Art*): Bergen, Nordahl Brunsgate 9; f. 1887; 300 mems.; *c.* 20,000 objects including Norwegian and European furniture, glass, porcelain, silver and textiles from the renaissance to modern times; Gen. Munthe's collection of Chinese art; Anna and William H. Singer's collection of antiquities; specialized library of fine and applied arts contains 15,000 vols.; Dir. PETER M. ANKER; Curator THALE RIISØEN; Librarian MARIT KOLLTVEIT; publ. *Vestlandske Kunstindustrimuseums Årbok*†.

Zoologisk Museum, Universitetet i Bergen: Muséplass 3, N-5014 Bergen; f. 1825; public exhibition of Norwegian and foreign animals; closed collection available to research workers and scientists; main activity is as institute of the University: teaching in all fields of zoology, research in ecology, morphology and systematics; library of 3,500 vols. and 2,000 vols. of periodicals; Dir. ROALD LARSEN.

Bodø

Nordland Fylkesmuseum: Prinsens gt. 116, 8000 Bodø; f. 1888; covers all aspects of life in the county of Nordland; 4,000 items, specialities: fisheries, boats, etc.; library of 6,000 vols.; Dir. EIVIND THORSVIK; Curator OLA SAETHER; publ. *Annual Report*.

Drammen

Drammens Museum: Fylkesmuseum for Buskerud: Konerudgaten 7, 3000 Drammen; f. 1908; local history, folk art, and open air museum; library of 13,625 vols.; Dir. HENNING ALSVIK, M.A.; publ. *Årbok*†.

Fredrikstad

Fredrikstad Museum: Torvgaten 60, P.O.B. 1144, 1601 Fredrikstad; f. 1903; cultural history of the town and district; Curator FREDRIK GAUSTAD; publ. *Yearbook*.

Hamar

Hedmarksmuseet og Domkirkeodden: Box 1053, 2301 Hamar; f. 1902; open-air museum and medieval collection; ruins of the medieval cathedral, bishop's palace (now housing a modern exhibition), and other medieval ruins; excavations in progress; farm buildings depicting local history and domestic life; also includes Norwegian emigration museum; cabins from North Dakota and Minnesota, and collections from all over the world; library of 14,000 vols.; Dir. RAGNAR PEDERSEN; Curator REIDAR BAKKEN; publ. *Årbok*†.

Lillehammer

Lillehammer Bys Malerisamling (*Lillehammer Municipal Art Gallery*): Kirkegaten 69, Lillehammer; f. 1921; contains collections of Norwegian paintings, sculpture and graphic art; Dir. OLE RØNNING JOHANNESEN; publ. *Lillehammer Bys Malerisamling Årbok*† (Year Book).

Sandvigske Samlinger, De (*Sandvig Collection*): Maihaugen, Lillehammer; f. 1887 as private collection; now owned by the Selskapet De Sandvigske Samlinger; 100 old houses of historical interest and 60 old workshops in a new exhibition hall; Dir. Dr. FARTEIN VALEN-SENDSTAD; publs. *Guides, Maihaugen, De Sandvigske Samlingers Skrifter.*

Oslo

Botanisk Hage og Museum (*Botanical Garden and Museum of the University*): Trondheimsveien 23B, Oslo 5; f. 1863; library of 38,000 vols.; Dir. (vacant); Curators ELMAR MARKER, HILDUR KROG; publ. *Norwegian Journal of Botany*† (quarterly).

Forsvarsmuseet (*Defence Museum*): Oslo mil/Akershus, Oslo 1; f. 1860; library of 10,000 vols.; Dir. Major E. EYVANG; publ. *Haermuseets Årbok.*

Kunstindustrimuseet i Oslo (*The Oslo Museum of Applied Art*): St. Olavsgate 1, Oslo; f. 1876; illustrates the applied arts mainly from *c.* 1200 until today; classified Norwegian, European and modern collections; comprises ceramics, glass, furniture, textiles (especially Norwegian tapestries and costumes), metal-work and book production; library of fine and applied arts containing 30,000 vols.; workshop for preservation and repair of old textiles; Dir. LAURITZ OPSTAD; publ. *Kunstindustrimuseets Årbok*† (Year Book).

Nasjonalgalleriet: Universitetsgaten 13, Oslo 1; f. 1837; the principal art gallery in Norway, containing collections of Norwegian paintings and sculpture, old European paintings, icon collection, examples especially of modern French, Danish and Swedish art, a collection of prints and drawings, and a small collection of Greek and Roman sculpture; also a collection of casts; *c.* 25,000 vols. in library; Dir. KNUT BERG; Keepers OSCAR THUE (Sculpture), MAGNE MALMANGER (Paintings), SIDSEL HELLIESEN (Prints and Drawings); Librarian ANNE LISE RABBEN.

Norsk Folkemuseum (*Norwegian Folk Museum*): Bygdøy, Oslo 2; f. 1894; consists of indoor and open-air sections comprising more than 160,000 objects; special exhibits in the indoor section include: rural culture (including display of weaving), church history, Henrik Ibsen's study, Lapp collection; open-air museum consists of: 170 old buildings (including 13th-century Gol stave church), examples of different farms ("Landsbygda" section), relics from all over Norway arranged as an old town quarter ("Gamlebyen" section); library of 33,000 vols.; Dir. HALVARD BJØRKVIK; publs. *By og Bygd*† (yearbook), *Guides* (in English, German, French and Norwegian).

Norsk Sjøfartsmuseum (*Norwegian Maritime Museum*): Bygdøynesvn. 37, Oslo 2; f. 1914; museum opened 1974; illustrates Norwegian maritime history; collection of portraits, models, instruments, historic ships (Amundsen's "Fram", 'Heyerdahl's "Kon-Tiki" and "Ra II"); library of 20,000 vols., archives of photographs, MSS., maps; lectures, excavations, expeditions for young people; Dir. SVEIN MOLAUG; Curator BÅRD KOLLTVEIT; publ. *Norsk Sjøfartsmuseums årsberetning*† (annual).

Norsk Teknisk Museum (*Norwegian Museum of Science and Industry*): Fyrstikkalléen 1, Oslo 6; f. 1914; library of 40,000 vols.; Dir. T. LINDTVEIT; publ. *Yearbook.*

Oslo Kommunes Kunstsamlinger: P.O.B. 2812, Toyengaten 53, Oslo 5; Dir. ALF BØE. The collections comprise the art galleries and museums of Oslo as follows:

Munch-museet: f. 1963; contains works of Edvard Munch; 1,100 paintings, 2,600 drawings and watercolours, 17,000 graphic works, 8 sculptures, 6,000 books, letters and other documents; Curator ARNE EGGUM.

Vigelands-museet: f. 1947; contains works of Gustav Vigeland; 1,650 sculptures, 3,700 graphic works, 11,000 drawings; Curator TONE WIKBORG.

Vigeland-parken: 192 sculptures.

Amaldus Nilsen malerisamling: 292 paintings, 101 drawings.

Ludwig Ravensberg Donation: 126 works of art.

Rolf E. Stenersens Donation: 939 works of art.

Universitetets Etnografiske Museum (*Ethnographical Museum, University of Oslo*): Frederiksgate 2, Oslo; f. 1857; approx. 40,000 exhibits, including Roald Amundsen collections in the Arctic section, Carl Lumholtz's Borneo collections in the Indonesian section; library of *c.* 25,000 vols.; Dir. Dr. H. BEYER BROCH; publs. *Bulletins.*

Universitetets Mineralogisk Geologiske Museum: Sarsgate 1, Oslo 5; f. 1915; collections of rocks and minerals; research laboratories in mineralogy, petrology, geochemistry; library together with Universitetets Paleontologiske Museum (*q.v.*) of 75,000 vols.; Dir. JOHANNES A. DONS.

Universitetets Paleontologiske Museum: Sars gate 1, Oslo 5; f. 1916; main collections consist of Cambrian-Devonian, Permian and Pleistocene fossils from Norway and Cambrian-Pleistocene fossils from Arctic regions, especially Svalbard; library together with Universitetets Mineralogisk Geologiske Museum (*q.v.*) of 75,000 vols.; Dir. Prof. GUNNAR HENNINGSMOEN.

Universitetets Samling av Nordiske Oldsaker (*University Museum of National Antiquities*): Frederiksgate 2, Oslo 1; f. 1829; rich collection of exhibits from prehistoric and Viking times, including Viking ships (at Bygdøy), and the Middle Ages; approx. 70,000 exhibits; library of 30,000 vols.; Dir. Prof. SVERRE MARSTRANDER; publs. *Universitetets Oldsaksamlings Årbok*† (annual), *Universitetets Oldsaksamlings Skrifter*†, *Norske Oldfunn*†, *Guides*† (in English, French, German, Italian, Spanish and Norwegian for the Viking Ship Museum).

Zoologisk Museum (*Zoological Museum*): Sarsgate 1, Oslo 5; f. *circa* 1813 (present building 1904–08); Norwegian vertebrates and invertebrates, Arctic, Antarctic and exotic, particularly Australian, collections; library of approx. 21,000 vols., 52,000 pamphlets; Dir. Prof. Dr. ROLF VIK; Vertebrate Section HJALMAR MUNTHE-KAAS LUND, JORGEN PEDERSEN and PER PETHON; Invertebrate Section MARIT E. CHRISTIANSEN and TOR A. BAKKE; Entomological Section ALBERT LILLEHAMMER; publs. *Contributions, Nytt fra Universitetets Zoologiske Museum, Oslo, Rhizocrinus, Ferskvannsbiologisk Informasjon.*

Sandefjord

Kommandør Chr. Christensens Hvalfangstmuseum (*Commdr. Chr. Christensen's Whaling Museum*): Rådlingsgaten 2A, 3200 Sandefjord; f. 1917; shows the development of whaling from primitive to modern times; geography, ethnology, zoology, maritime history, etc.; library of 4,000 vols.; Curator EINAR WEXELSEN.

Skien

Fylkesmuseet for Telemark og Grenland (*Telemark Historical Museum*): Övregt. 41, 3700 Skien; f. 1909; conservation and research on items of historical interest from the Telemark region; situated in Brekkeparken, with open air museum (log houses dating from the Middle Ages) and a manor house furnished in 17th-, 18th- and 19th-century styles; collections on folk art, handicrafts, navigation, church art, Ibsen Collection and Ibsen's childhood home, Venstøp Farm; library of *c.* 6,000 vols.; Dir. TOR GARDÅSEN.

Stavanger

Arkeologisk Museum i Stavanger (*Archaeological Museum in Stavanger*): Storgt. 27, 4000 Stavanger; exhibitions shared with Stavanger Museum (*q.v.*); own library; research, administration of Law of Antiquities in Rogaland, Conservation Laboratories, education and public relations work; Dir. ODMUND MØLLEROP; publs. *AmS-skrifter*†, *AmS-varia*†, *AmS-Småtrykk*, *Frå haug ok heidni* (quarterly).

Stavanger Museum: 4000 Stavanger; f. 1877; urban and rural culture, zoology, ornithology; a maritime museum and the mansions of Ledaal and Breidablikk are in the museum's care; library of 30,000 vols.; Dir. Dr. A. BANG-ANDERSEN; publs. *Årbok*† (yearbook), *Skrifter*† (irregular), *Sterna*† (irregular).

Tromsø

Tromsø Museum (Universitetet i Tromsø: Institutt for museumsvirksomhet): 9000 Tromsø; f. 1872; has seven depts.: Botany, Geology, Zoology, Marine Biology, Archaeology, Folk Culture, Lapp Ethnography; library of 130,000 vols.; Dir. of Board HARALD MEHUS; Man. Dir. BEN SCHEI; publs. *Acta Borealia*† (*A* and *B*), *Skrifter*†, *Astarte*,† *Årsberetninger*† (annual report), *Ottar*†, *Antikvariske registreringer i Nord-Norge*†, *Tromura* (scientific reports).

Trondheim

Kongelige Norske Videnskabers Selskab, Museet (*The Royal Norwegian Society of Sciences and Letters, The Museum*): Erling Skakkesgate 47, 7000 Trondheim; f. 1760; attached to University of Trondheim; library: *see* Libraries; zoological, botanical, mineralogical, numismatics and archaeological departments; marine station; schools service; Pres. REIDAR BREKKE; Dir. Prof. Dr. Philos. OLAV GJÆREVOLL; publ. *Gunneria*.

Nordenfjeldske Kunstindustrimuseum (*Museum of Applied Art*): Munkegaten 5, 7000 Trondheim; f. 1893; approx. 12,000 exhibits; depts. of furniture, textiles, glass, ceramics, metalwork from the Renaissance period to modern times; Dir. (vacant).

UNIVERSITIES

UNIVERSITETET I BERGEN
(University of Bergen)

5014 BERGEN UNIVERSITETET

Telephone: (05)-210040.

Founded 1948.

State control; Academic year: September to June.

Rector: Prof. Ø. ØYEN, PH.D.
Vice-Rector: Prof. Dr. A. GRAUE.
Director: M. LERHEIM.
Librarian: Dr. philos. M. TVEITANE.

Library: *see* Libraries.

Number of teachers: 785, including 161 professors.

Number of students: 8,000.

Publications: *Årbok* (Year Book), *Naturen*† (a popular scientific review), *Skrifter*, *Småskrifter*, *Sarsia*†.

DEANS:

Faculty of Humanities: Prof. O. ØVERLAND.
Faculty of Natural Sciences: Prof. Dr. A. GRAUE.
Faculty of Medicine: Prof. Dr. J. CHR. GIERTSEN.
Faculty of Social Sciences: Asst. Prof. J.-P. BLOM.
Faculty of Dentistry: Prof. Dr. K. SELVIG.
Faculty of Law: Prof. Dr. M. S. NYGARD.
Faculty of Psychology: Prof. H. KLØVE.

PROFESSORS:

Faculty of Humanities:
BIRKELAND, B., Scandinavian Literature
BOHLIN, T., Christianity
DANIELSEN, R., History
ERBE, B., Theater
FASTING, S., Russian Language and Literature
GJÆRDER, P., History of Art
GRUNDT, L. D., French Language
HAGEN, A., Archaeology
HARTVEIT, L., English Literature
HELLE, K., History
HENRICHSEN, A.-J., French Philology
HOLM-OLSEN, L., Old Norse Philology
HÄGG, T., Classical Philology
KOLLER, W., German Language
KAARTVEDT, A., History
KITTANG, A., General Literature
KRAGERUD, A., History of Religion
MJELDHEIM, L., History
MYKLAND, K., History
PETTERSEN, E., Scandinavian Philology
PIERCE, R. M., Egyptology
RESTAN, P., Russian Language
RISTE, O., History
ROPPEN, G., English Literature
SANDBERG, H.-J., German Literature
SKIRBEKK, G., Philosophy
SKÅNLAND, V., Latin
SUNDBY, B., English Philology
ULVESTAD, B., German Philology
ØVERLAND, O., American Literature
AARAAS, H. T., French Literature

Faculty of Natural Sciences:
AKSNES, G., Chemistry
ANDERSEN, B. G., Quaternary Geology
BATHURST, R. G. C., Petroleum Geology
BENGTSON, S. A., Zoology (Ecology)
BJØRLYKKE, K., Petroleum Geology
BRINKMANN, A., Zoology
BRÆKKAN, O., Nutrition Sciences
BRUN, T., Chemistry
DRAGESUND, O., Fisheries Biology
DUNDAS, I. E. D., Marine Microbiology
FOSS, O., Chemistry
GADE, H. G., Physical Oceanography
GOKSØYR, J., Microbiology
GRAMMELTVEDT, A., Theoretical Meteorology
GRAUE, A., Physics
HOLTEDAHL, H., Marine Geology
JARLSKOG, C., Physics
JOHNSEN, K., Physics
KNUTSEN, G.H., Botany
MAALØE, S. B., Geology
MANNE, R. E., Chemistry
MATTHEWS, J. B. L., Marine Biology
MORK, M., Oceanography
NISSEN, P., Botany
OLSEN, S., Fisheries Biology
OVERHOLT, K. J., Information Science and Numerical Analysis
SELLEVOLD, M., Seismology
SELMER, E. S., Mathematics
SKAVLEM, S., Physics
SKJEGGESTAD, O., Physics
STORETVEDT, K., Geomagnetism
STURT, B. A., Geology
SÆLEN, O. H., Physical Oceanography
SÆTHER, O. A., Zoology
SÆTHERSDAL, G., Fisheries Biology
TJØSTHEIM, D., Statistics
TJØTTA, J. N., Applied Mathematics
TJØTTA, S., Applied Mathematics
TREFALL, H., Physics
TVERBERG, H. A., Mathematics
UTAAKER, K., Meteorology
WIBORG, K. F., Marine Biology
WIIK, B., Physics

Faculty of Medicine:
ALHO, A., Surgery
ARNESJØ, B., Surgery
AUKLAND, K., Physiology
BERGSJØ, P., Gynaecology and Obstetrics
BERTELSEN, T. I., Ophthalmology
BJELKE, E., Hygiene
BURHOL, P., Gastroenterology
D'ELIA, G., Psychiatry
FARSTAD, M. N., Clinical Biochemistry
FLATMARK, T., Biochemistry
GOGSTAD, A. C., Social Medicine
GIERTSEN, J. C., Medicine of Law
GØTHLIN, J., Radiology
HARKMARK, W., Anatomy
HARTVEIT, F., Pathology
HAUKENES, G., Virology
HUMERFELT, S., General Medicine

KLEPPE, K., Biochemistry
KROGH, H. K., Dermatology
LUND-JOHANSEN, P., Clinical Medicine
LÆRUM, O. D., Experimental Pathology and Oncology
OEDING, P., Bacteriology
OFSTAD, J., Internal Medicine
QVARNSTRØM, U., Nursing
ROSENGREN, B., Roentgenology
SCHELINE, R. R., Biochemical Pharmacology
SIRNES, T. B., Pharmacology
SOLBERG, C. O., Infectious Diseases
STEEN, E. J., Oto-Rhino-Laryngology
STØA, K. F., Hormonal Research
SÆTERSDAL, T., Anatomy
THUNOLD, S., Pathology
TØNDER, O., Immunology
AARLI, J. A., Neurology
AARSKOG, D., Paediatrics

Faculty of Dentistry:
BANG, G., Pathology
BIRKELAND, J. M., Cariology
FOSSE, G., Oral Anatomy
GILHUUS-MOE, O. T., Operative Dentistry
HASUND, A., Orthodontics
HAUGEJORDEN, O., Social Odontology
HEGDAHL, T., Technology
KRISTOFFERSEN, T., Paedodontics
MØRCH, T., Paedodontics
RYGH, P., Dentistry
SELVIG, K. A., Dentistry
SILNES, J., Prosthetics
TRONSTAD, L., Endodontics

Faculty of Social Sciences:
BALDERSHEIM, H., Public Administration and Organization
GRØNHAUG, R., Social Anthropology
HANSEN, J. C., Geography
HELVIG, M., Geography
HERNES, G., Sociology
HØYER, R., Information Science
JACOBSEN, K. D., Public Administration and Organization
KNUDSEN, K., Sociology
NORDBOTTEN, S., Information Science
OLSEN, J. P., Public Administration and Organization
RØDSETH, T., Political Economy
ØYEN, E., Social Politics and Social Administration
ØYEN, Ø., Sociology

Faculty of Law:
ANDENÆS, M., Law
BERNT, J. F., Law
FRIHAGEN, A., Law
GRAHL-MADSEN, A., Law
HOV, J., Law
HÆREM, A., Law
KRÜGER, K., Law
NYGARD, M. S., Law
NYGAARD, N., Law
SANDVIK, T., Law
STAVANG, P., Law

Faculty of Psychology:
CHRISTIANSEN, B., Psychology
EIKELAND, H. M., Psychology
GJESSING, H. J., Psychology
KILE, S., Psychology
KLØVE, H., Psychology
MAREK, J., Psychology
OLWEUS, D., Psychology
RAAHEIM, K., Psychology
URSIN, H., Psychology
ØHMAN, A., Psychology

ATTACHED INSTITUTES:

Biological Station: University of Bergen; open to research workers from all countries; research vessels *Fridtjof Nansen* and *August Brinkman*.

EDB-avdeling (*EDP Department*): Dir. Siv. ing. CARL ERIK ELLINGSEN.

Medisinsk-historiske samlinger (*Bergen Collections on the History of Medicine*): Dir. Dr. LORENTZ M. IRGENS.

Milde Arboretum: 5067 Milde; f. 1971; plant research, laboratory for students; open to the public; Dir. Lic. agro. POUL SØNDERGAARD.

Pedagogiske seminar (*Department of Education*): Rector Cand. psychol. JAN FR. WAAGE.

See also under Museums.

UNIVERSITETET I OSLO
(University of Oslo)

BOX 1071, BLINDERN, OSLO 3
Telephone: 466800.
Founded 1811.

Rector: Prof. Dr. BJARNE A. WAALER.
Vice-Rector: Prof. Dr. JACOB JERVELL.
Director: O. M. TROVIK.
Vice-Director: J. LÖFSGAARD.
Treasurer: R. BERGMANN.
Librarian: JOHN BRANDRUD.

Library: *see* Libraries.

Number of teachers: 1,538, including 286 professors.

Number of students: 19,200.

DEANS:

Faculty of Theology: Prof. Dr. INGE LØNNING.
Faculty of Law: Prof. Dr. PETER LØDRUP.
Faculty of Medicine: Asst. Prof. Dr. IVAR HØRUEN.
Faculty of History and Philosophy: KJELL BJØRNSKAU.
Faculty of Mathematics and Natural Sciences: Prof. Dr. TORE OLSEN.
Faculty of Dentistry: Prof. Dr. KJELL KARLSEN.
Faculty of Social Sciences: Prof. Dr. IVAR LIE.

PROFESSORS:

Faculty of Theology:
BLOCH-HOELL, N. E., Oecumenics
FÆHN, H., History of the Norwegian Church
JERVELL, J., Theology
KAPELRUD, A. S., Theology
LEIVESTAD, R. S., Theology
LÖNNING, I., Theology
MONTGOMERY, I., History of the Church

Faculty of Law:
ANDENÆS, J., Law
BRATHOLM, A., Law
BRÆKHUS, S., Law
CHRISTIE, N., Criminology
ECKHOFF, T., Law
FALKANGER, T., Law
FLEISCHER, C.A., Law
KJØNSTAD, A., Law
LÖDRUP, P., Law
MATHIESEN, THS., Sociology of Law
OPSAHL, T., Law
SANDVIK, G., History of Law
SELMER, K., Actuarial Science
SELVIG, E. C. Ö., Law
SEYERSTED, F., Law
SMITH, C., Law
AARBAKKE, M., Law

Faculty of Medicine:
AMUNDSEN, E., Surgery
ANDERSEN, P. O., Neurophysiology
ANSETH, ARVID, Ophthalmology
ARNESEN, K., Pathology
AUNE, S., Surgery
BERG, K. I., Genetics
BERGAN, F., Surgery
BJERKEDAL, T., Hygiene
BJERKELUND, CHR., Medicine
BJØRO, K. J., Obstetrics and Gynaecology
BLACKSTAD, TH. W., Anatomy
BORCHGREVINK, CHR., General Medicine
BREMER, J., Medicine, Biochemistry
BØVRE, K., Microbiology
EITINGER, L., Psychiatry
ELGJO, K. M., Pathology
ENGE, J. P., Medicine
ENGER, E., Medicine
EVENSEN, A. K., Diagnostic Radiology
FLATMARK, A. L., Surgery
FREY, H. M. M., Medicine
GJONE, E., Medicine
HALL, J. G., Oto-Rhino-Laryngology
HALL, K. V., Surgery
HALVORSEN, S., Paediatrics
HARBOE, M., Immunology
HAUGE, M. F., Orthopaedic Surgery
HELLEM, A. J., Medicine
HELSINGEN, N. N., Surgery
HÖST, H., Radiation and Medical Cancer Therapeutics
IVERSEN, O. H., General and Experimental Pathology
JANSEN, J. K. S., Physiology
JYSSUM, K., Microbiology
KIIL, F., Experimental Medicine
KOLSTAD, P., Gynaecology
KRINGLEN, E., Medical Behavioural Research
KUAMME, E., Neurochemistry
KÅSS, E., Medicine
LAAKE, H., Medicine
LUNDEVALL, J., Forensic Medicine
MALM, O. J., Pathophysiological Surgery
MYHRE, E., Medicine
MYHRE, E. K., Pathology
MYREN, J. A., Medicine
MÜLLER, J. C., Medicine
NESBAKKEN, R., Neuro-surgery
NORUM, K. R., Nutrition Research
NYBERG-HANSEN, R., Neurology
PIHL, A. A., Cancer, Biochemistry
PRYDZ, H., Medicine
RAJKA, G., Dermatology
RETTERSTØL, N., Psychiatry
RINVIK, E., Anatomy
SEIP, M., Paediatrics
STOKKE, O., Medicine
STOVNER, J., Medicine
STRØMME, J. H., Clinical Chemistry
STØREN, G., Surgery
SUND, A., Psychiatry
SUNDBY, P., Social Medicine
TEISBERG, P., Medicine
THUNE, P. O., Dermatology
TORVIK, A., Neuropathology
VASLI, S., Surgery
WAALER, B. A., Physiology
WALAAS, O., Physiology
WALBERG, F., Anatomy
WESSEL-AAS, T., Pulmonary Diseases
WINTHER, F. Ö., Oto-Rhino-Laryngology
YTTEBORG, J., Ophthalmology
ZWETNOW, N., Neurosurgery
ØYE, I., Pharmacology

Aakhus, T., Radiology
Aas, K., Medicine

Faculty of History and Philosophy:
Benestad, F., Music
Benum, E., History
Bergsland, K., Finno-Ugrian Languages
Beyer, E., Nordic Literature
Bö, O., Norwegian Folklore
Dahl, O., History
Fløistad, G., History of Ideas
Føllesdal, D., Philosophy
Haakonsen, D., Nordic Literature
Halvorsen, E. F., Nordic Philology
Hamre, L., History
Hannevik, A., Literature
Hauge, I., Nordic Literature
Heltveit, T., English Philology
Henne, H., Chinese and Japanese
Heyerdahl, G. H., Germanic Philology
Hovdhaugen, E., General Linguistics
Kjetsaa, G., Russian Literature
Kleve, K., Classical Philology
Knudsen, E. E., Semitic Languages
Kolsrud, K., Ethnology
Koppang, O., German Literature
Kraggerud, E., Classical Philology
Kvaerne, P., History of Religions
Langholm, S., History
Langvik-Johannessen, K., Dutch
Lindeman, F. O., Linguistics
Lundeby, E. J., Nordic Languages
Lunden, K., History
Lunden, S. S., Slavonic Languages
Mageröy, H., Icelandic
Marstrander, S., Nordic Archaeology
Maehle, L., Norwegian Language and Literature
Mykllebost, H., Geography
Mønnesland, S., Slavonic Languages
Nordahl, H., Romance Philology
Oftedal, M., Celtic
Palme, P. O., History of Fine Arts
Ropeid, A., Ethnology
Røstvig, Maren-Sofie, English Literature
Saltveit, L., Germanic Philology
Sandved, A. O., English Language
Sanness, J., History
Schjelderup-Ebbe, D., Music
Seeberg, A., Classical Archaeology and Fine Art History
Sejersted, F., Economic and Social History
Seyersted, P. E., American Literature
Simson, G. V., Indian Language and Literature
Sjøvold, T., Nordic Archaeology
Skodvin, M., History
Smidt, K., English Literature
Stigen, A., Philosophy
Torp, H., Classical Archaeology and Fine Art History
Tranøy, K. E., Philosophy
Tönnesson, K. D., History
Ulleland, M. G., Romance Philology
Venås, K., Nordic Languages
Vinje, F. E., Modern Nordic Language
Worren, A., Romance Literature
Wyller, E. A., Ancient History
Aarnes, A., French Literature

Faculty of Mathematics and Natural Sciences:
Abdullah, M. I., Chemical Oceanography
Alfsen, E. M., Mathematics
Aubert, K. E., Mathematics
Bastiansen, O., Chemistry
Berg, R., Botany
Bernatek, E. R., Pharmaceutical Chemistry
Briseid, K., Pharmaco-dynamics
Bugge, J. A. W., Geology
Clausen, O. G., Microbiology
Dahl, O.-J., Numerical Mathematics
Dale, J., Organic Chemistry
Eckblad, F.-E., Botany
Egeland, A., Geophysics
Eliassen, A., Geophysics
Enger, P. S., Zoophysiology
Feder, J. G., Physics
Fenstad, J. E., Mathematical Logic
Finholt, P., Pharmacy
Fjørtoft, R., Meteorology
Furberg, S. V., Chemistry
Gjessing, J., Geography
Gjevik, B., Hydrodynamics
Gray, J. S., Marine Zoology
Griffin, W. L., Geochemistry
Grjotheim, K., Chemistry
Halldal, P. H. H., Botany
Hasle, G. R., Marine Botany
Henningsmoen, G., Paleontology
Husebye, E. S., Seismology
Jacobsen, E., Chemistry
Jensen, E., Astronomy
Kjekshus, A., Chemistry
Kjensmo, J., Limnology
Kofstad, P., Chemistry
Kolsrud, M., Theoretical Physics
Krog, J. O., Zoophysiology
Laland, S., Bio-chemistry
Lofthus, A., Physics
Lothe, J., Physics
Lundby, A., Nuclear Physics
Lundh, Y. G., Informatics
Løvlie, A. M., Zoology
Neumann, H., Geology
Norman, N., Physics
Nygaard, K., Informatics
Oftedal, P., General Genetics
Olsen, T., Electronics
Palm, E., Applied Mathematics
Pappas, A., Radio-Isotope Chemistry
Pedersen, B., Chemistry
Peskine, Chr., Mathematics
Paasche, E. K. M., Marine Biology
Ramberg, I. B., Geology
Ravndal, F., Theoretical Physics
Reenskaug, T. M. H., Cybernetics
Rekstad, J. B., Physics
Riste, T., Physics
Rosenqvist, I. Th., Mineralogy and Geology
Seip, H. M., Chemistry
Semb-Johansson, A., Zoology
Skattebøl, L., Chemistry
Spurkland, S., Informatics
Størmer, E., Mathematics
Sverdrup, E., Insurance Mathematics and Mathematical Statistics
Sørensen, S. O., Physics
Thiede, J., History of Geology
Torgersen, E. N., Statistics
Vik, R., Zoology
Weber, J. E., Geophysics
Wingård, B., Geophysics
Wold, J. K., Pharmacognosy
Aanderaa, S. O., Mathematics

Faculty of Dentistry:
Dahl, E., General and Oral Anatomy
Eeg-Larsen, N., Physiology
Fehr, F. R., von der, Dentistry
Heløe, L. A., Social Dentistry
Johansen, J. R., Dentistry
Jonsen, J., Microbiology
Karlsen, K., Dentistry
Rølla, G., Dentistry
Slagsvold, O. K., Dentistry
Stokke, T., Pathology
Aas, E., Dental Surgery

Faculty of Social Sciences:
Aubert, V., Sociology
Barth, T. F. W., Ethnography
Bråten, S. L., Sociology
Burns, T. R., Sociology
Dahl, H., Pedagogy
Holter, H., Psychology
Johansen, L., Economics and Statistics
Klausen, A. M., Ethnography
Lie, I. R., Psychology
Lysgaard, S., Sociology
Lysne, A., Pedagogy
Meinich, P., Economics and Statistics
Midgaard, K. O., Political Science
Munthe, P., Distribution Economy
Odner, K., Ethnography
Ramsøy, N. R., Sociology
Ramsøy, O., Sociology
Rand, P., Pedagogy
Rommetveit, R., Psychology
Saugstad, P., Psychology
Serck-Hanssen, J., Economics
Smedslund, J. F., Psychology
Soelberg, P., Administrative Science
Stensaasen, S., Pedagogy
Stigum, B. P., Economics and Statistics
Sørensen, Aa. B., Sociology
Thonstad, T., Economics and Statistics
Thorsrud, E., Psychology
Torgersen, U., Political Science
Valen, H., Political Science
Wyller, T. Chr., Political Science

UNIVERSITETET I TROMSØ
(University of Tromsø)

POSTBOKS 635, 9001 TROMSØ
Telephone: 083-86560.
Founded 1968.

State control; Academic year: August to June.

Rector: Prof. Yngvar Løchen.
University Director: Harald Overvaag.
Director of Studies: Bjørnar Lund.
Librarian: Ole Brønmo.

Number of teachers: 268.
Number of students: 1,741.

Deans:

Institute of Biology and Geology: Jens Petter Taasen.
Institute of Mathematical and Physical Sciences: Odd Gropen
School of Medicine: Kristian Hannestad.
Institute of Social Sciences: Trond Thuen.
Institute of Languages and Literature: Erik Egeberg.
Institute of Museology: Harald Mehus.
Institute of Fisheries: Arne R. Strom.

UNIVERSITETET I TRONDHEIM
(University of Trondheim)

TRONDHEIM
Founded 1968.

Constituent institutions: Det Kongelige Norske Videnskabers Selskab, Museet (*see* Museums); Norges lærerhøgskole; Norges tekniske høgskole; Faculty of Medicine.

President of the Provisional Board: Prof. Inge Johansen.
Secretariat of the Provisional Board: The University Planning and Development Secretariat, Håkon Magnussonsgt. 1B, 7000 Trondheim.
Secretariat Director: Nils A. Selseth.

CONSTITUENT COLLEGES:

NORGES LÆRERHØGSKOLE
(College of Arts and Science)
UNIVERSITY CENTRE,
7055 DRAGVOLL,
TRONDHEIM
Telephone: (47-75) 96-500.
Founded 1922.

Rector: Prof. EVA SIVERTSEN.
Pro-Rector: Prof. OLAF RØNNING.
Head of Administration: PETER LYKKE.
Librarian: WILHELM K. STØREN.

Number of teachers: 214, including 54 professors.
Number of students: 3,540.

DEANS:

Faculty of Philology: Prof. JØRN SANDNES.
Faculty of Mathematics and Natural Sciences: KJELL MORK.
Faculty of Social Sciences: IVAR ARNLJOT BJØRGEN.

PROFESSORS:

Faculty of Philology:
BLOM, G. A., History
BØCKMANN, P. W., Religion
BORGEN, P., Religion
BRØGGER, J., Social Anthropology
BULL, E., History
CLAYBOROUGH, A., English Literature
DAHL, W. M., Nordic Literature
DJUPEDAL, R., Nordic Languages
FINTOFT, K., Phonetics
FRETHEIM, T., Applied Linguistics
FUGLUM, P., History
GULLVÅG, I., Philosophy
HAGNELL, V., Drama
HALVORSEN, A., French Language
HANNAY, R. A., Philosophy
HULDT-NYSTRØM, H., Music
INGRAM, E., Applied Linguistics
JAKOBSEN, A., Old Norse
LINDBERG, C., English Language
PÜTZ, H., German Language
SANDNES, J., History
SIVERTSEN, EVA, English Language

Faculty of Mathematics and Natural Sciences:
ESPMARK, Y., Zoology
GJAEREVOLL, O., Botany
HAFSTEN, U., Botany
HAFTORN, S., Zoology
IVERSEN, T.-H., Botany
JOHNSSON, A. C. G., Physics
OLSEN, H., Physics
REITE, O. B., Zoology
RØNNING, O., Environmental Studies
SUNDNES, G., Zoology
TRATTEBERG, M., Chemistry
WAADELAND, H., Mathematics
AARNES, J. F., Mathematics

Faculty of Social Sciences:
BJØRGEN, I. A., Psychology
HARBO, T., Education
LINDBEKK, T., Sociology
MARTINUSSEN, W. M., Sociology
MYHRE, R., Education
AASE, A., Geography

NORGES TEKNISKE HØGSKOLE
(Norwegian Institute of Technology)
7034 TRONDHEIM-NTH
Telephone (47-75) 94-000.
Founded 1900.

President: Prof. INGE JOHANSEN.
Vice-President: Prof. ÅGE Ø. WALØEN.
Secretary of the Board and of the Council: IDA-MARIE WOLD (acting).
Administrator for Business Affairs: ASLE RUDJORD (acting).
Administrator for Educational Affairs: KJELL CARLSEN.
Chief Librarian: **KNUT THALBERG.**

Number of teachers: 649 full-time.
Number of students: 4,450.

DEANS:

Department of Architecture: L. NORDGÅRD.
Department of Mining and Metallurgy: S. OLSEN.
Department of Civil Engineering: R. SAGEN.
Department of Electrical Engineering: O. A. SOLHEIM.
Department of Chemical Engineering: T. HELLE.
Department of Mechanical Engineering: A. BAGGERUD.
Department of General Science: E. H. HAUGE.
Department of Naval Architecture and Marine Engineering: D. KAVLIE.

PROFESSORS:

Department of Architecture:
ESDAILE, R. J., Architecture II
GRANUM, H., Architectural Engineering
KRAG, H., Architecture III
MOEN, L. O., Architecture IV
RØE, B., Town and Regional Planning
SINDING-LARSEN, S., History of Architecture

Department of Mining and Metallurgy:
BERGE, I., Mining Engineering
DIGRE, M., Mineral Dressing
HOSPERS, J., Applied Geophysics
OFTEDAHL, CHR., Mineralogy and Geology
ROSENQVIST, T., Metallurgy
RYUM, N., Metallurgy
SELMER-OLSEN, R., Mineralogy and Geology
VOKES, F. M., Mineralogy and Geology
WYSZINSKY, Z. S., Petroleum Engineering

Department of Civil Engineering:
HÅDEM, J., Photogrammetry
HEGGSTAD, R., Hydraulic Construction
HOLAND, I., Structural Mechanics
HOLSEN, J., Geodesy
HUGSTED, R., Constructional Engineering
JANBU, N., Soil Mechanics and Foundation Engineering
LENSCHOW, R., Concrete Structures
NORDAL, R. S., Road and Railway Construction
SAGEN, R., Transportation Engineering
SIMENSEN, T. H., Hydraulic Construction
SVENDSEN, S. D., Building Technology

Department of Electrical Engineering:
BALCHEN, J. G., Automatic Control
FAANES, H. H., Power Systems Engineering
GRØNLIE, L. Ø., Electrotechnical Laboratory Telecommunications
HAGFORS, T., Telecommunication Theory
JOHANSEN, I., High Voltage Systems
KROKSTAD, A., Acoustics
LANDSVERK, O., Automatic Control
SOLHEIM, O. A., Systems Engineering
SØRBYE, H., Telephone Switching Systems
STETTE, G. R., Electrotechnical Laboratory, Telecommunications
TODNEM, O., Power Systems Engineering and Electroheat
TONNING, A., Electromagnetic Theory
WESSEL-BERG, T., Applied Electronics
WESTGAARD, E., Electrical Machinery

Department of Chemical Engineering:
CYVIN, S. J., Physical Chemistry
ERGA, O., Chemical Engineering
FØRLAND, T., Physical Chemistry
GIERTZ, H. W., Cellulose Technology
HOLTAN, H., Industrial Electrochemistry
JENSEN, S. L., Organic Chemistry
LARSEN, H., Applied Biochemistry
LYDERSEN, A., Chemical Engineering
MOTZFELDT, K., Silicate and High Temperature Chemistry
PARKER, V. D., Organic Chemistry
UGELSTAD, J., Industrial Chemistry
ØYE, H. A., Inorganic Chemistry

Department of Mechanical Engineering:
ALMAR-NÆSS, A., Physical Metallurgy and Working Processes
ALMING, K., Water Power Laboratory
BJØRKE, Ø., Applied Thermodynamics
FANNELØP, T., Aero and Gas Dynamics
GRIMSRUD, L., Applied Thermodynamics
IVERSEN, G., Machine Elements
LORENTZEN, G., Refrigeration Engineering
RØDAHL, E., Heating, Ventilation and Sanitary Engineering
SØNJU, O. K., Applied Thermodynamics and Combustion
WALØEN, Å., Machine Elements

Department of General Sciences:
BAAS, N. A., Mathematics
BØE, G., Economics
EIK-NES, K., Biophysics
HARLEM, G., Science of Working Life
HAUGE, E. H., Theoretical Physics
HÅVIE, T., Mathematics
HELLAN, K., Applied Mechanics
HEMMER, P. C., Theoretical Physics
HOLE, N., General Physics
HOLT, K., Industrial Organisation and Management
HØYLAND, A., Mathematical Statistics
JENSSEN, O., Applied Mechanics
KREYBERG, H. J., Economics
MARTENS, H. H., Mathematics
NJÅSTAD, O., Mathematics
PERSEN L. N., Applied Mechanics
SIKKELAND, T., Experimental Physics
SØLVBERG, A., Division of Computing Science
SØRUM, H., X-Ray Physics

Department of Naval Architecture and Marine Engineering:
ENGJA, S., Ship Machinery
ERICHSEN, S., Ship Design
FALTINSEN, O., Naval Architecture and Shipbuilding
HAMMER, A., Nautical Studies
KAVLIE, D., Ship Structures
MOAN, T., Ship Structures
SARSTEN, A., Internal Combustion Engineering
WALDERHAUG, H. AA., Naval Architecture and Shipbuilding

FACULTY OF MEDICINE
EIRIK JARLS Gt. 4,
TRONDHEIM
Telephone: (47-75) 25535.

Dean: Prof. HANS CATO GULDBERG, PH.D.

PROFESSORS:

ANSETH, A., Ophthalmology
BAHBETEIG, L. S., Epidemiology
BENTSEN, B. G., Community Medicine
BERG, K. J., Nephrology
BLOMHOFF, J. P., Gastroenterology
CHRISTOPHERSEN, B., Clinical Chemistry
DALEN, A., Microbiology
DALGARD, O. S., Psychiatry
EDVARDSEN, P., Orthopaedic Surgery
GOTESTAM, K. G., Psychiatry
GULDBERG, H. C., Pharmacology
GUNDERSEN, T., Oto-rhino-laryngology
HAUGEN, O. A., Pathology
HELLGREN, L., Dermatology and Venereology
LAMVIK, J., Immunology
MAELAND, J., Microbiology
MOE, J. P., Paediatrics
PETERSEN, H., Gastroenterology
ROKSETH, R., Cardiology
SANDERUD, A., Surgery
SJAASTAD, O. Neurology
TVETER, K., Surgery

COLLEGES OF UNIVERSITY STANDING

Arkitekthøgskolen i Oslo (*The Oslo School of Architecture*): Postboks 6768, St. Olavs Plass, Oslo 1; Telephone: 208316; f. 1945; State control; Academic year: September to June.

President: Prof. ARE VESTERLID.
Registrar: HELGE HAALAND.
Librarian: ANNE FROYDIS FRIVOLL.

The library contains *c.* 20,000 vols.
Number of teachers: 33.
Number of students: 211.

PROFESSORS:

APELAND, K., Building Technology
FEHN, S., Architectural Design III
LORANGE, E., Planning I
NORBERG-SCHULZ, C., Architectural Theory and History
NORDIN, E., Planning
VESTERLID, A., Architectural Design II

Norges Handelshøyskole (*The Norwegian School of Economics and Business Administration*): Helleveien 30, 5000 Bergen; Telephone: (05) 256500; f. 1936; State control; Academic year: September to June.

Rector: GERHARD STOLTZ.
Vice-Rector: ARNLJOT STRØMME SVENDSEN.
Director: SIGISMUND KOESTER.
Librarian: JOHN EGILL STEEN.

The library contains *c.* 160,000 vols.
Number of teachers: 123, including 27 professors.
Number of students: *c.* 1,370.
Publications: exchange list sent on request.

DEANS:

Department of Economics: LEIF B. METHLIE.
Department of General Studies: TRYGVE SOLHAUG.

PROFESSORS:

ARNDT, J., Business Administration
BORCH, K. H., Insurance
CHRISTENSEN, C., German
GERHARDSEN, G. M., Fishery Economics
GUNDERSEN, F. F., Law
HAGEN, K. P., Economics
HANSEN, T., Business Administration
HOLBAEK-HANSSEN, L., Marketing
JENSEN, O., H., Business Administration
KARLSEN, R., English
KAUFMAN, G., Organizational Psychology and Personnel Administration
LANGHOLM, O., Business Administration
METHLIE, L. B., Data Processing
MOSSIN, J., Business Administration
MYRVOLL, O., Economics
NORMAN, V. D., Economics
OUREN, T., Economic Geography
PETERSSOHN, E., Business Administration
RAFTO, T. Economic History
SANDMO, A., Economics
SOLHAUG, T., Economics History
STOLTZ, G., Economics
STRØMME SVENDSEN, A., Shipping Economics
VERBRAEKEN, R., French
WEDERVANG, F., Economics

ATTACHED INSTITUTES:

Extension Division: Dir. ARNE FOSTVEDT.

Administrative Research Foundation.

Det Teologiske Menighetsfakultet (*Free Faculty of Theology, Church of Norway*): Gydas Vei 4, Oslo 3; f. 1907; State and Private control; Academic year: September to June.

Principal Dean: LUDVIG MUNTHE.
Secretary: ERLING SERVAN.
Librarian: HELENE HVEEM.

Number of teachers: 35, including 10 professors.
Number of students: 950.
Publications: ***Tidsskrift for Teologi og Kirke***†, *Lys og Liv, Mellom Sösken, Ung Teologi,*

PROFESSORS:

ASHEIM, I., Philosophy of Christian Education and Ethics
AUSTAD, T., Dogmatics and Moral Theology
BJØRNDALEN, A. J., Old Testament Exegesis
DALE, AA., Church Education and Catechetics
ELLINGSEN, I., Practical Theology
HOLTER, Å., Church History
LARSSON, E., New Testament Exegesis
MODALSLI, O., Dogmatics and New Testament Exegesis
MUNTHE, L.; History of Missions
SÆBØ, M., Old Testament Exegesis

Norges Veterinarhøgskole (*Veterinary College of Norway*): P.O.B. 8146 dep, Oslo 1; Tel. 02 693690; f. 1935; Academic year: August to December January to June.

Rector: WEIERT VELLE.
Director: ARVID SILJAN.
Registrar: DAG MATHIESEN.
***Librarian:* ANNE SAKSHAUG.**

The library contains 45,000 vols.
Number of teachers: 79, including 15 professors.
Number of students: 240.

PROFESSORS:

BERG, O. A., Internal Medicine (Small Animals)
DAHLE, HANS K., Chemical Food Hygiene
FOSSUM, K., Microbiology and Immunology
GJESDAL, F., Forensic Medicine
HAUGE, J. G., Biochemistry
KROGH, N. M., Internal Medicine (Large Animals)
NICANDER, L., Anatomy
ONSTAD, O., Physiology and Pathology of Reproduction
SKJERVEN, O., Obstetrics
SKULBERG, A., Food Hygiene
SØGNEN, E., Pharmacology and Toxicology
STRANDE, A., Surgery
SVENKERUD, R., Pathology
UNDERDAL, B., Food Hygiene
VELLE, W. M., Physiology

ATTACHED INSTITUTES:

Dal Research Farm for Fur-Bearing Animals: Dir. O. MØLLER, D.V.M.

Kjeller Research Farm for Animal Husbandry: Dir. S. TOLLERSRÜD, D.V.M.

Norges landbrukshøgskole (*Agricultural University of Norway*): 1432 Ås-NLH; Tel. (02) 940060; f. 1859 as State College.

Rector: Prof. Dr. O. M. HEIDE.
Vice-Rector: Prof. G. SYRRIST.
Director: G. ØYGARD.
Secretary: A. SKIPENES.
Librarian: J. HJELTNES.

Number of teachers: 120, including 58 full and associate professors.
Number of students: 970, plus 100 post-graduates.
Publications: *Meldinger fra Norges landbrukshøgskole*† (Scientific Reports of the Agricultural University of Norway).

SCHOOLS OF ART AND MUSIC

A/S Bergens Musikkonservatorium: Olav Kyrresgt. 59, Bergen; f. 1905; Dir. ROLF DAVIDSON.

Norges Musikkhøgskole (*Norwegian State Academy of Music*): Nordahl Brunsgt. 8, Oslo 1; f. 1973 (formerly Musik-Konservatoriet, f. 1883); 120 teachers, 300 students; library of 37,000 vols. (includes sheet music), 3,000 records; Principal HARALD HERRESTHAL.

Statens Kunstakademi (*National Academy of Fine Arts*): Uranienborgveien 2, Oslo 2; f. 1909; training in painting, sculpture and graphics at university level; 12 teachers, 130 students; library of 3,296 vols.; Rector LUDVIG EIKAAS; Administrator AINA HELGESEN.

Statens Håndverks- og Kunstindustriskole (*National College of Art and Design*): Ullevålsvn. 5, Oslo; f. 1818; includes departments of commercial art, book illustration, ceramics, fashion design, interior decorating, metal design, painting and textile design; library of 34,000 vols.; 63 teachers, 334 students; Principal FR. WILDHAGEN.

OMAN

Population 750,000

British Council: P.O.B. 1090, Mutrah; f. 1973; recruits and administers British staff in schools and ministries; arranges training in Britain for Omani nationals; administers scholarship schemes; provides advice and assistance on educational matters; runs English language classes; library of 9,077 vols., 34 periodicals; Rep. C. G. HOUSDEN; Librarian Mrs. B. R. HOOPER.

Directorate of the Omani Heritage: Ministry of National Heritage and Culture, P.O.B. 668, Muscat; f. 1973; collects MSS., documents, archives, etc., relevant to Oman's historical past; Dir.-Gen. MOHAMMED SAID AL-WOHAIBI.

Historical Association of Oman: P.O.B. 612, Muscat; f. 1971; study of history and monuments of Oman; organizes lectures and field trips to places of interest, film-shows, etc., and provides help to official expeditions and museums; 145 mems.; Vice-Pres. KAMAL ABDULREDA SULTAN; publ. *Bulletin* (*c.* 6 a year).

Oman Museum: Ministry of National Heritage and Culture, Qurm (P.O.B. 600); f. 1974; National Museum of archaeology and ethnology.

COLLEGE

Vocational Training Centre: P.O.B. 3123, Ruwi; f. 1968; attached to the Ministry of Social Affairs and Labour; technical and commercial diploma courses; 39 staff, 350 full-time, 300 part-time students; Dir. SAMIR KUMAR GUPTA.

PAKISTAN

Population 76,770,000

ACADEMIES

Pakistan Academy of Letters: 36 48th St., F8/4, Islamabad; f. 1979; promotion of literary works; determination of research priorities in literature; evaluation of the performance of literary bodies; setting up of Bureau of Translation; introduction of Pakistani literature to foreign readers; organizes seminars on literary and academic issues; advises the Government on international literary gatherings; nominates recipients for various literary awards and distinctions; provides financial assistance to scholars; Dir. M. A. SIDDIQUI.

Pakistan Academy of Sciences: Constitution Ave., Islamabad; f. 1953; to promote research in pure and applied sciences, establish and maintain libraries; awards grants and fellowships and gold medals; 45 mems.; Pres. Dr. M. A. KAZI; Sec. Dr. M. RAZIUDDIN SIDDIQI; publs. *Proceedings*† (2 a year), *Proceedings of Symposia* (irregular).

Quaid-i-Azam Academy: 297 M.A. Jinnah Rd., P.O.B. 894, Karachi; f. 1976; research on Quaid-i-Azam Mohammad Ali Jinnah, on the historical background (including cultural, religious, literary, linguistic, social, economic and political aspects) of the Pakistan Movement, and on various aspects of Pakistan; gives scholarships and professorships; awards prizes for scholarly work; publs. source materials and research papers on its area of study; Dir. SHARIF AL MUJAHID; publs. bibliographies, research studies and monographs.

LEARNED SOCIETIES

ARCHITECTURE

Pakistan Institute of Architects: 25 Main Gulberg, Lahore; Pres. ZAHEERUDDIN KHAN.

ARTS

The Arts Council of Pakistan: M. R. Kayani Rd., Karachi; f. 1956 to foster the development of fine arts and crafts, drama, dance, music, and to promote the study and appreciation thereof by sponsoring exhibitions, lectures, etc.; 361 mems.; Pres. PERVEZ AHMED BUTT; Dir. IRFAN HUSAN; Sec. H. NASEEM.

Music Foundation of Pakistan: Buch Terrace, Preedy St., Karachi 3; f. 1964 to serve the cause of classical music through academic instruction, promote it by means of concerts, and foster an international exchange of ideas; Dir. F. BUCHOME, B.A., L.R.S.M.

National Institute of Folk Heritage: 61 4th St., F/7, Islamabad; museum, library on Pakistan, especially folk heritage; publications on folk heritage; Dir. UXI MUFTI.

BIBLIOGRAPHY AND LIBRARY SCIENCE

National Book Council of Pakistan: Theosophical Hall, Jinnah Rd., Karachi; an autonomous organization sponsored by the Government; f. 1962; regional office at Lahore f. 1965; aims to promote reading habit; organizes book festivals and exhibitions; provides technical advice and training in modern techniques of book production and distribution through manuals, workshops, seminars and training courses; Dir.-Gen. S. H. R. RIZVI; publs. *Kitab* (Urdu, monthly), trade directories, manuals, bibliographies.

Pakistan Library Association: c/o Pakistan Institute of Development Economics, P.O.B. 1091, Islamabad; to advance the cause of the library movement throughout Pakistan; 112 mems.; Pres Dr. Z. A. HASHMI; Sec. AKHTAR A. SIDDIQUI; publs. *Journal* (quarterly), *Newsletter* (monthly), *Proceedings* (annual).

Sind Library Association: P.O.B. 126, Hyderabad; f. 1966 to enhance the cause of the library profession through symposia, seminars, etc.; 50 student librarians; Pres. Miss RAFIA SULTANA KADIR, M.L.S.; Sec. I. A. S. BOKHARI, M.A.; publ. *Newsletter*.

Unesco Regional Office for Culture and Book Development in Asia: 44/J/6, Razi Rd., P.E.C.H.S., Karachi 2904; f. 1958; assists Asian member states in their book development and book promotion programmes; provides information and advisory services; organizes meetings, seminars and in-service professional training; research and studies on publishing and distribution; acts as Field Office in Asia for the Int. Copyright Information Centre; reference library of 5,500 vols.; Dir. Mrs. MAENMAS CHAVALIT; publ. *Newsletter*† (quarterly, in English).

ECONOMICS, LAW AND POLITICS

Institute of Cost and Management Accountants of Pakistan: Soldier Bazaar, P.O.B. 7284, Karachi 3; f. 1951; 200 Fellows, 500 Assoc. Mems.; library of 30,000 vols.; Exec. Dir. A. M. ANSARI; publs. *Students Handbook* (annual), *Industrial Accountant* (quarterly).

Pakistan Institute of International Affairs: Aiwan-e-Sadar Rd., Karachi 1; f. 1947 to study international affairs and to promote the scientific study of international politics, economics and jurisprudence; library of 20,000 vols., 650 mems.; Pres. The Minister of Foreign Affairs; Sec. QADEERUDDIN AHMED; publs. *Pakistan Horizon*† (quarterly), books and monographs†.

EDUCATION

All-Pakistan Educational Conference: Saeeda Manzil, Nazimabad, Karachi 18; f. 1951; promotes education at all levels; has established Sir Syed Girls' (degree) College, a public library, reading-room and a museum; publishes books on education and culture; library; 118 mems.; Pres. Major SHAMSUDDIN MOHD.; Sec. SYED ALTAF ALI BRELVI; publ. *Al-Ilm* (quarterly).

Punjab Bureau of Education: Lahore; f. 1958; clearing house for information on education of all aspects and levels, at home and abroad; Documentation Section, Statistical Section, Publication Section and Research Section; Dir. Dr. ABDUR RAUF; publs. statistical bulletins, bibliographies, directories and educational research journals.

HISTORY

Pakistan Historical Society: 30 New Karachi Co-operative Housing Society, Karachi 5; f. 1951; historical studies and research, particularly history of Islam and the Sub-continent; library of 7,709 vols.; Pres. HAKIM MOHAMMED SAID; Gen. Sec. Dr. S. MOINUI HAQ; publs. *Journal* (quarterly), Monographs, Research Studies.

INTERNATIONAL CULTURAL INSTITUTIONS

American Center: Collector's Lane, Karachi 4; also in Lahore, Hyderabad, Peshawar, Rawalpindi; library of 10,000 vols.; Dir. MICHAEL A. BETCHER.

Asia Foundation, The: P.O.B. 1165, Islamabad; one of 12 branches of the main organization in the U.S.A. (*q.v.*); Representative Dr. John O. Sutter.

British Council: P.O.B. 1135, 23 87th St., Sector G 6/3, Islamabad; libraries: *see* Libraries; Rep. D. A. Latter; Regional Offices:

P.O.B. 146, 20 Bleak House Rd., Karachi 0409; Regional Rep. T. L. G. Mullen;

P.O.B. 88, 32 Mozang Rd., Lahore; Regional Dir. A. B. Davidson.

Goethe Institut: 256 Sarwar Shaheed Rd., Karachi 0105; f. 1964; library of 7,500 vols.

Goethe Institut (*Pakistan-German Cultural Centre*): 92-E-1, Gulberg III, P.O.B. 339, Lahore; f. 1958; library of 5,000 vols., 70 periodicals; Dir. Dr. H.-D. Handrack.

Iran Cultural Centre: 14 Seafield Rd., Karachi 4; f. 1954; brs. in Hyderabad, Lahore, Multan, Peshawar, Quetta, Rawalpindi; reference library of 4,500 vols., mostly in Persian; Dir. Ahmad Mir Alai; publ. monthly bulletin.

Pakistan Arab Cultural Association: P.O.B. 5257, Karachi 2; Pres. Dr. Yasin Zuberi; Gen. Sec. A. R. Siddiqi.

Language and Literature

Anjuman Taraqqi-e-Urdu Pakistan: Baba-e-Urdu Rd., Karachi 1; f. 1903 in pre-partition India, 1948 in Pakistan; promotion of the Urdu language and literature; preparing a 6-volume bibliography of Urdu books, in collaboration with Unesco; general library of 12,000 vols., research library of 50,000 vols. and MSS.; Pres. Akhtar Husain, c.s.p.; Sec. Jamiluddin A'Ali; publs. *Urdu* (quarterly), *Qaumi Zaban* (monthly).

Baluchi Academy: Patel Rd., Quetta, Baluchistan; f. 1960 to promote Baluchi language and literature; publishes books on Baluchi history, poetry, culture, folk stories, and a Baluchi/Urdu dictionary; 25 mems.; Chair. Sardar Khan Baluch; Gen. Sec. Aziz Mohammad Bugti.

Central Urdu Development Board: 1-A, Gulberg 11, Lahore; f. 1962; aims to promote Urdu as the common language of Pakistan, to remove deficiencies in Urdu in technologies, natural and social sciences, and to co-ordinate the work of the other organizations engaged in similar work; library of 7,022 vols.; Chair. Q. U. Shahab; Dir. Ishfaq Ahmed Khan.

Idarah-i-Yadgar-i-Ghalib: P.O.B. 2268, Nazimabad 2, Karachi 18; f. 1968; holds literary meetings; helps with research and university studies; library of 15,000 vols., 50,000 periodicals in Urdu; Pres. Faiz Ahmed Faiz; Sec. Mirza Zafarul Hassan; publ. *Ghalib*.

Institute of Islamic Culture: Club Rd., Lahore 3; f. 1950; publications on Islamic subjects in English and Urdu; Dir. Prof. M. Saeed Sheikh; Sec. M. Ashraf Darr; publ. *Al-Ma'arif*† (monthly).

Iqbal Academy: 116 McLeod Rd., Lahore; f. 1951; publishes books and pamphlets and maintains an Iqbal museum, special Iqbal research library; Pres. Federal Minister of Education; Dir. Dr. M. Moizuddin; publ. *Iqbal Review* (quarterly).

Pakistan Writers Guild: B-16 Sindhi Muslim Housing Society, Karachi; f. 1959; 4 regional offices; promotes authorship, dispenses literary prizes, sees to welfare of writers; Sec.-Gen. Mahbub Jamal Zahedi; publ. *Ham Qalam* (monthly).

Pashto Academy: University of Peshawar, Peshawar; f. 1955; research into Pashto language and literature, history, art and culture; research library; Dir. Prof. Mohd. Nawaz Tair; publ. *Puhktoon* (Pashto, monthly).

Punjabi Adabi Academy: 12-G, Model Town, Lahore 14; f. 1957; publishes literary, historical and scientific works concerned with Punjab; 18,000 vols.; Chair. Prof. Dr. Muhammed Baqir.

Shah Waliullah Academy: Hyderabad; f. 1963; to propagate the philosophy of Shah Waliullah; library of his works; publ. *Al-Rahim* (monthly in Sindhi, Alwali and Urdu).

Sindhi Adabi Board: P.O.B. 12, Hyderabad, Sind; f. 1951; autonomous literary and cultural institution set up by the government to foster the language, literature and culture of the Sind region; publishes books in English, Sindhi, Urdu, Persian and Arabic; library of 4,743 vols. in these 5 languages, and 324 rare MSS.; Chair. Allama Ghulam Mustafa Qasmi; Sec. Ghulam Rabbani A. Agro; publs. *Mehran* (quarterly in Sindhi), *Gul Phul* (children's monthly in Sindhi).

Urdu Academy: Bahawalpur; f. 1959 to develop Urdu literature and language; publishes books in English and Urdu; publ. *Az-Zubair* (Urdu, quarterly).

Urdu Development Board: 41D Block B, N. Nazimabad, Karachi 33; f. 1959 by Government of Pakistan; projects include an Urdu dictionary on the historic principles; classics and rare MSS.; Chair. Hadi Husain; Hon. Sec. Abul Lais Siddiqui; publ. *Urdu Nameh*.

Medicine

All-Pakistan Homoeopathic Association: Pakistan Chowk, Karachi; f. 1949; 5,780 mems.; Sec. Dr. S. Akhtar; publs. *Pakistan Homoeopathic Journal* (monthly), *Homoeopathic Light*.

College of Physicians and Surgeons, Pakistan: 7th Central St., Defence Housing Society, Karachi 46; f. 1962 by government ordinance; aims to promote specialist practice of medicine, surgery and gynaecology and allied disciplines by means of improvement in hospital teaching and methods; arranges postgraduate medical, surgical and other specialist training; provides for medical research and organizes scientific conferences for Pakistani medical experts; 528 Members (M.C.P.S.), 150 Fellows (F.C.P.S.); library of *c.* 10,000 vols., 50 foreign specialist journals; Pres. Lt. Gen. W. A. Burki; Sec. Col. M. A. Subhan Khan.

Pakistan Medical Association: P.M.A. House, Garden Rd., P.O.B. 7267, Karachi 3; Pres. Prof. Abdul Aziz; Sec.-Gen. Dr. Mir Rehman Ali Hashmi.

Museology

Pakistan Museum Association: c/o National Museum, Burns Garden, Karachi; f. 1949; objects: to advance and improve the work of museums in Pakistan; establish close contact with universities, educational and services institutions; open new museums in important towns in Pakistan; provide facilities for the training of curators; establish an archaeological laboratory; and to popularize museum movement in the country by the following means: (1) sending circulating exhibitions, (2) guided tours, (3) delivering popular lectures and publishing literature on Pakistan museums; Pres. Mumtaz Hassan; Gen. Sec. (vacant); publs. *Museums Journal of Pakistan* (2 a year), *Museum Studies*.

Natural Sciences

Pakistan Association for the Advancement of Science: 14 Shah Jamal Scheme, P.O. Ichhra, Lahore-12; f. 1947 for the promotion of science in all its branches, including its application to practical problems and research; organizes national and international conferences; 1,500 mems.; Pres. M. I. D. Chughtai, d.sc., ph.d.; publs. *Pakistan Journal of Science*, *Pakistan Journal of Scientific Research*, Monographs, Bibliographies, Proceedings, Annual Reports.

Scientific Society of Pakistan: University Campus, University of Karachi, Karachi 32; f. 1954 to promote and popularise science through the national language (Urdu); 3,000 mems.; Pres. Dr. Aslam Khan; Secs. Atfab Hassan, Dr. S. H. Mahmood; publs. *Jadeed Science*† (every 2 months), *Science Bachchon Key Liye*† (monthly), *Science Nama* (fortnightly), *Proceedings of Annual Science Conferences* (all in Urdu).

Philosophy and Psychology

Pakistan Philosophical Congress: Club Rd., Lahore 3; f. 1954 for the promotion of philosophical studies; Pres. Dr. C. A. Qadir, Sec. Dr. Kazi A. Kadir; publs. *Annual Proceedings, Pakistan Philosophical Journal* (2 a year).

Religion, Sociology and Anthropology

Hamdard National Foundation: Hamdard Centre, Nazimabad, Karachi 18; f. 1953; conferences, seminars on religion (Islam), medicine, etc.; library of 50,000 vols.; Pres. Hakim Mohammed Said; publs. *Akhbar-ut-Tib* (fortnightly), *Hamdard-i-Sehat, Hamdard Naunehal* (monthly), *Hamdard Islamicus, Hamdard Medicus* (quarterly).

Jamiyatul Falah: Akbar Rd., Saddar, P.O.B. 7141, Karachi; to encourage the study of the Koran and to set up and maintain Islamic missions; reading room, library (5,000 vols.), Seerat Academy, Falah Research Centre; Pres. Hussain Imam; Sec. Prof. Syed Lutful-lah; publ. *Voice of Islam* (English, monthly).

Karachi Theosophical Society: Jamshed Memorial Hall, M. A. Jinnah Rd., Karachi 1; f. 1896; 100 mems.; activities include study of comparative religion, philosophy and science; investigation of unexplained laws of nature; library of 20,000 vols. and reading room; Pres. Dara F. Mirza; Sec. A. A. Hoodbhoy; publ. *Theosophy in Karachi* (monthly).

Technology

Institute of Engineers (Pakistan): Gulberg, Lahore.

Institution of Electrical Engineers (Pakistan): 4 Lawrence Rd., Lahore; f. 1969; lectures, seminars and publications on electrical and electronic engineering; 800 corporate mems., 225 individual mems.; library of 200 vols.; Pres. Maj. Gen. (retd.) Abdul Qayoom; publs. *Quarterly Journal*†, *Monthly Newsletter.*

Pakistan Concrete Institute: 11 Bambino Chambers, Karachi; Pres. B. A. Chaudhri; Sec. Rehman Akhtar.

RESEARCH INSTITUTES

(*See* also under Universities)

Agriculture and Veterinary Science

Pakistan Agricultural Research Council: P.O.B. 1031, Islamabad; f. 1964 (charter revised 1978); organizes, co-ordinates and promotes scientific research in agriculture and allied fileds; 4 full-time, 25 part-time staff; Chair. Dr. Amir Muhammed; publs. *Pakistan Journal of Agricultural Research*† (quarterly), *Progressive Farming*† (every 2 months), *Annual Report*†, monographs, bulletins.

Pakistan Animal Husbandry Research Institute: Veterinary Research Inst., G.P.O., Peshawar Cantt., Pakistan; f. 1949; Officer-in-Charge M. Y. Ansari, g.b.v.c., p.g.

Pakistan Forest Institute: Peshawar, N.W.F.P.; f. 1947; library of 25,000 vols.; Forestry Museum; two training courses leading to B.Sc. and M.Sc. in Forestry; Dir.-Gen. Dr. G. M. Khattak, ph.d.; publ. *Pakistan Journal of Forestry.*

Punjab Veterinary Research Institute: Lahore 13; f. 1958; objects: to promote and improve the development of the livestock industry and control diseases; production of vaccines, research on animal health problems; disease diagnosis and investigation; development of improved laboratory techniques; publs. *Pakistan Journal of Animal Sciences* (quarterly), *The Livestock News* (monthly).

Rice Research Institute: Dokri.

Economics, Law and Politics

Applied Economics Research Centre: University of Karachi, Karachi 32; f. 1974; policy-orientated quantitative research on problems in applied economics; 23 mems.; library of 2,500 vols.; publs. *Discussion Paper Series, Research Report Series.*

Central Statistical Office: 17 Muslimabad, Karachi; f. 1950; studies prices, foreign trade, national income, industrial and labour statistics; library of 1,198 vols.

Centre for South Asian Studies: University of the Punjab, Lahore; f. 1973; interdisciplinary centre for research and advanced study of the contemporary societies, South Asian states, and big powers in their relations with South Asian countries; study programmes leading to M.Phil. and Ph.D.; research library; publishes books; Dir. Dr. Rafiq Ahmad; publs. *Monograph, South Asia Paper* (monthly).

Institute of Strategic Studies: P.O.B. 1173, Islamabad; f. 1973; promotes a broad-based and informed public understanding of vital strategic and allied issues affecting Pakistan, the world of Islam, and the south Asian region; library of *c.* 6,000 vols. and *c.* 50 foreign periodicals; Dir. Noor A. Hussain; publs. *Strategic Studies*† (quarterly), *Islamabad Papers*† (research papers).

National Institute of Public Administration: University Rd., Karachi 47; f. 1962; research in government administration; in-service training courses; Dir. I. A. Khan; publ. *Pakistan Journal of Public Administration* (2 a year).

National Institute of Public Administration: 78 Shahrah-i-Quaid-i-Azam, Lahore; f. 1962; administrative training for management in public and private sectors; research on government administration; publ. *Public Administration Review* (quarterly).

Pakistan Economic Research Institute (P.E.R.I.): 9 Jan Mohammad Rd., Anarkali, Lahore, Pakistan; f. 1955 to undertake socio-economic investigations and co-ordinate research in economic problems of Pakistan; to collect, compile and interpret statistical data; to publish the results and findings of investigations; Dir. Aziz A. Anwar; Sec. Rashid A. Arshad; publs. *Economics and Commerce* (fortnightly), Research Papers.

Pakistan Institute of Development Economics: P.O.B. 1091, Islamabad; f. 1957 to carry out basic research on the economic problems of development in Pakistan and other Asian countries, and to train postgraduate scholars in methods of economic research, planning and administration; library of 15,100 vols., 310 current periodicals; Dir . Dr. Syed Nawab Haider Naqvi; Deputy Sec. M. A. Hafeez; publ. *Pakistan Development Review* (quarterly).

History

Research Society of Pakistan: University of the Punjab, 2 Narsingdas Garden, Club Rd., Lahore; est. 1963 to organize research in national affairs, particularly in the national struggle that led to the establishment of Pakistan; research on cultural, political, literary, linguistic, economic, historical, topographical and archaeological features of Pakistan; reference library; publishes research results; Dir. Dr. Abdul Hamid; publ. *Journal of the Research Society of Pakistan* (quarterly).

Medicine

Cancer Research Institute: Dept. and Institute of Radiotherapy, Jinnah Post-graduate Medical Centre, Karachi 35; f. 1954.

Medical Social Research Project: G.P.O. Box 349, Lahore; f. 1961; investigates the factors which influence the health of mothers and babies; library; Dir. A. Rasheed Ghazi.

Pakistan Medical Research Council: Jinnah Postgraduate Medical Centre, Karachi; f. 1953; reconstituted 1962; aims to promote research in fields of medicine and public health, to disseminate and arrange for utilization of this research, and to establish liaison with national and international organizations; 21 mems.; Chair. Lt.-Gen. (Rtd.) MOHAMMAD AYUB KHAN; Dir. Dr. JAVID A. HASHMI; publ. *Pakistan Journal of Medical Research* (quarterly).

SCIENCES

General

Fazi-i-Omar Research Institute: Rabwah, District Jhang; f. 1946; objects: to promote the study of science and the development of industries in the country; library of 5,000 vols.; Dir. MURBARAK MUSLEM-UD-DIN AHMAD.

National Science Council of Pakistan: 63 School Rd., Shalimar 7/4, Islamabad; f. 1961; aims to formulate the National Science Policy, co-ordinates and evaluates the activities of the various Research Councils in the country; advises various organizations on the utilization of the results of research and acts as the highest advisory body to the Government of Pakistan on all matters of scientific and technological research; library of 700 vols.; Chair. Dr. Z. A. HASHMI; Sec. Dr. M. N. AZAM; publ. *Science News* (quarterly).

Pakistan Council of Scientific and Industrial Research: Press Centre, Shahrah-e-Kemal Ataturk, Karachi 1; f. 1953; promotes scientific research and its applications to the development of the national industries and the utilization of the natural resources of the country; Chair. Dr. M. A. KHAN; Sec. ASHFAQ KAZI; publs. *Pakistan Journal of Scientific and Industrial Research* (every 2 months), *Technology Digest* (monthly), *Science Chronicle* (quarterly), *Karawan-e-Science* (Urdu, quarterly).

P.C.S.I.R. Laboratories: Karachi 39; physical, chemical, biochemical, pharmaceuticals and pest infestation, engineering research divisions; 8,000 vols., 12,000 journals and periodicals; Dir. M. ASLAM.

P.C.S.I.R. Laboratories: Peshawar; indigenous drugs, fruit and vegetable technology, mineralogical and wool research divisions; Dir. Dr. R. A. SHAH.

P.C.S.I.R. Laboratories: Lahore 16; metallurgical, industrial fermentation, oils and fats, glass, ceramics and food technology research divisions; Dir. YUSUF AHMAD.

Fuel and Leather Research Centre: D/102/S.I.T.E., Karachi 16; fuel, leather and pilot-plant studies; Head of Division A. H. CHOTANI, M.SC.

Pak-Swiss Precision Mechanics and Instrumentation Training Centre: Karachi 39; training in electronics, instrumentation, instrument repair, official instruments, precision and analytical balances; Principal A. WAHAB SIDDIQUI.

Biological Sciences

Department of Plant Protection: Jinnah Ave., Malir Halt, Karachi; f. 1947; library of 3,000 vols., 50 current periodicals; to control insect pests and locusts and to undertake research work in mycology, plant pathology and physiology; Dir. FARIDUDDIN AHMED.

Institute of Marine Biology: University of Karachi, Karachi 32; f. 1973; 20 mems.; library of 2,000 vols., 30 periodicals; Dir. Dr. S. M. HAQ; publ. *Bulletin* (2 a year).

Zoological Survey Department: Hotel Nazli Bldg., Nishtar Rd., Karachi 3; f. 1948 to promote research in taxonomy, marine biology, oceanography, and wild life of Pakistan; library of 15,000 vols., 115 periodicals; Dir. MOHAMMAD FAROOQ, M.SC., F.Z.S.

Physical Sciences

Astronomical Observatory of the University of the Punjab: Punjab University Observatory, Cust Rd., Lahore; f. 1920; University's Dept. of Astronomy located within the Observatory; undergraduate courses; Dir. MUHAMMAD ANWAR BHATTI, M.SC.

Pakistan Atomic Energy Commission: P.O.B. No. 1114, Islamabad; f. 1956; the Commission is directly responsible for peaceful uses of atomic energy in the field of power generation, industry, agriculture and medicine; Chair. MUNIR AHMAD KHAN; publ. *The Nucleus* (quarterly).

Establishments under its control:

Karachi Nuclear Power Plant (KANUPP): Karachi.

Pakistan Institute of Nuclear Science and Technology (PINSTECH): P.O. Nilore, Islamabad; houses a 5-MW research reactor of swimming-pool type.

Atomic Energy Minerals Centre: Lahore; prospection, exploration and mining of indigenous nuclear minerals resources.

Atomic Energy Agricultural Research Centre: Tandojam; application of isotopes and radiation in the field of plant physiology, soil science, entomology and plant genetics (mutation breeding).

Nuclear Institute for Agriculture and Biology (NIAB): Faisalabad; application of radio-isotopes and radiation in plant and molecular genetics.

Atomic Energy Agricultural Research Centre: Tarnab.

Atomic Energy Medical Centres: Karachi, Jamshoro, Larkana, Multan and Lahore; to promote the use of radio-isotopes in diagnosis and therapy.

Institute of Radiotherapy and Nuclear Medicine (IRNUM): Peshawar.

Chashma Nuclear Power Project (Chasnupp): a proposed 600-MW nuclear power station.

Pakistan Meteorological Department: 37-X, Block 6, P.O.B. 8017, P.E.C.H.S., Karachi 29; f. 1947; Dir. Gen. MUHAMMED RAHMATULLAH, M.SC., F.R.MET.S.; publs. bulletins on geophysics and meteorology. Directorate of Forecasting and Climatology: 34-J, Block 6, P.E.-C.H.S., Karachi 29; Dir. S. AKHLAQ HUSSAIN, M.SC.; Regional Directorates at: Karachi Airport; f. 1945; Dir. H. U. QIDWAI, M.SC.; 46 Gulberg Rd., Lahore; f. 1945; Dir. S. A. A. KAZMI, M.SC.; Geophysical Centre, Quetta; Dir. (vacant).

RELIGION, SOCIOLOGY AND ANTHROPOLOGY

Institute of Sindhology: University of Sind, Jamshoro, Sind; f. 1963 as Sindhi Academy, name changed 1964; aims to interpret Sind and its contribution to history and civilization, encourage translation and original work in the fields of social and natural sciences; to project Sind on an international level by publishing relevant research material in foreign languages, to develop working tools (dictionaries, historical surveys, etc.) for scholars, to advance research in history, culture, literature and fine arts; includes a bureau of production, publication and translation, a documentation, information and research cell, a research library, a dept. of preservation of documents and rare material, Sind Art Gallery and Museum, a dept. of performing arts, sound and film; library of 40,717 rare books, MSS, periodicals, magazines and reports, etc.; Dir. Dr. GHULAM ALI ALLANA.

Islamic Research Institute: P.O.B. 1035, Islamabad; f. 1960; to conduct and co-ordinate research in Islamic studies; library of 30,000 vols., 419 microfilms, 96 MSS.; Dir. RASHID JALLUNDHARI; publs. *Islamic Studies* (English, quarterly), *Al-Dirasat al-Islamiyya* (Arabic, quarterly), *Fikr-o-Nazar* (Urdu, monthly).

TECHNOLOGY

Hydrocarbon Development Institute of Pakistan: 1 School Rd., Shalimar 6/1, P.O.B. 1308, Islamabad; f. 1975; research, development and training in petroleum geology and geochemistry, reservoir engineering, crude oils, fuels and lubricants, pilot plants, engines and automobiles, oil and gas appliances, petroleum conservation and economics, specifications and standards, products quality control; 150 mems.; library of *c.* 1,000 vols., 150 periodicals; Chair. Prof. Dr. M. SHAFQUAT HUSAIN SIDDIQUI; Operations Man. (Karachi) A. H. CHOTANI, (Islamabad) HILAL A. RAZA; publ. *Hydrocarbon Digest*† (every 2 months).

Irrigation, Drainage and Flood Control Research Council: 84-D, Satellite Town, Rawalpindi; f. 1964; aims to promote research in the fields of hydraulics, irrigation, drainage, reclamation, tubewells and flood control; Chair. Prof. Dr. NISAR AHMAD; Sec. S. B. HASAN; publ. *Bulletin* (2 a year).

Irrigation Research Institute: The Mall, Lahore; f. 1925; deals with irrigation and allied engineering problems in Pakistan; a field model station, three sub-stations and two subsidiary laboratories for soils, foundation engineering, tube well experiments, etc.; library of 15,000 vols.; Administrator A. RASHID KAZI; Dir. Dr. MUSHTAQ AHMAD; publ. Reports, Records, Memoirs.

Pakistan Institute of Cotton Research and Technology: New Queens Rd., Karachi; f. 1951; to carry out research work on cotton production, fibres, textiles and marketing; library of 25,000 vols., 225 periodicals; Dir. I. AFZAL; Sec. M. AHMED; publ. *The Pakistan Cotton Quarterly*.

Pakistan Institute of Management: Shahrah Iran, Clifton, Karachi 6; f. 1954; 199 institutional and 85 individual mems.; dedicated to the management development programme in Pakistan; the Institute offers *c.* 100 short courses in functional and integrated aspects of management each year; library of *c.* 3,839 vols., 128 films, 68 periodicals; Principal IRSHAD H. KHAN; publ. *Pakistan Management Review*† (quarterly).

Pakistan Standards Institution: 39 Garden Rd., Saddar, Karachi 3; f. 1951; member of the International Organization for Standardization (ISO) and International Electrotechnical Commission (IEC); objects: to recommend national standards for the measurement of length, weight, volume and energy, to prepare and promote general adoption of standards on national and international basis relating to materials and commodities, and to promote standardization, quality control and simplification in industry and commerce, enforcement of standards, etc., Dir. SYED MUHAMMAD SHAHID; publs. *PSI Yearbook*, *PSI Annual Report*, *Pakistan Standards Specification*, *Test Methods and Code of Practice*.

Small Industries Institute: 3-A Gulberg Rd., Lahore; f. 1963; research on the industrial potential of Pakistan; feasibility studies, public and private projects in small industries; library.

LIBRARIES AND ARCHIVES

National Library of Pakistan: postal adress: c/o Dept. of Libraries, Stadium Rd., Karachi 5; new building to be constructed in Islamabad; depository library for all publications; 20,000 vols.; Project Dir. A. H. AKHTAR.

Archaeological Library: Taxila Museum, Taxila; f. 1960; 1,450 vols. on history and arts, especially the ancient history and archaeology of Pakistan; Custodian A. A. FAROOQ.

Atomic Energy Minerals Centre Library: P.O.B. 658, Lahore; f. 1961; nuclear minerals; Librarian M. SALEEM.

British Council Libraries: Chartered Bank Building, Shahaah-e-Quaid-i-Azam, P.O.B. 88, Lahore; f. 1950; 32,489 vols., 240 periodicals; Librarian I. J. GOODACRE, A.L.A.; 14 Civic Centre, Ramna 6, Islamabad; f. 1969; 11,314 vols., 85 periodicals; Librarian M. Y. JAN; 20 Bleak House Rd., Karachi 0409; f. 1950; 37,865 vols., 117 periodicals; Librarian M. A. SIDDIQUI, F.L.A., C.L.SC.; 35 The Mall, Peshawar; f. 1959; 20,331 vols., 82 periodicals; Librarian F. H. QUERESHI.

Central Medical Library: Directorate General of Health, Government of Pakistan, Islamabad.

Central Secretariat Library: Government of Pakistan, No. B-10, Block 7 & 8, Central Union Commercial Area, Shaheed-i-Millat Rd., Karachi; f. 1951; specializes in Central and Provincial Government publications; 21,700 vols., excluding public documents; Dir. A. H. AKHTAR.

Dr. Alidina Memorial Library and Ismaili Archives: 178 Britto Rd., Garden East, Karachi; f. 1964; 5,000 vols.; Pres. SHERALI ALIDINA; Sec. SHIRAZ.

Dr. Mahmud Hussain Library, University of Karachi: Karachi 32; f. 1952; 228,000 vols., 5,000 microfilms, 400 current periodicals, 10,000 vols. in seminar libraries; Librarian ADIL USMANI.

Dyal Singh College Library: Lahore; f. 1910; 43,618 vols.; Librarian ALTAF HUSSAIN.

Ewing Memorial Library: Forman Christian College, Lahore 11; f. 1866; 54,085 vols.; Librarian ETHEL A. MELLORS.

Government College Library: Lahore; f. 1864; 31,449 vols.; Librarian M. SIDDIQUE, B.A., LIB.DIP.

International Book Exchange Centre: c/o Central Secretariat Library, Government of Pakistan, Bldg. B-10-Block 7-8, Karachi Central Commercial Area, Shaheed-e-Millat Rd., Karachi; f. 1958; 29,100 public documents; Dir. A. H. AKHTAR.

Islamia College Library: Civil Lines, Lahore; f. 1958 after split of Old Islamia College; 37,163 vols., 37 current periodicals; Librarian MUNIZ AHMAD NALENS; publ. *Faran* (annually).

Khalikdina Hall Library Association: M. A. Jinnah Rd., Karachi; f. 1856; reading room, library (6,000 vols.), language classes, social and cultural events; Pres. S. M. Y. RIZVI.

Liaquat Hall Library: Bagh-e-Jinnah, Victoria Road, Karachi 4; f. 1852 as Frere Hall Library; 23,000 vols.; Librarian NEMATULLAH BEGG.

Liaquat Memorial Library: Stadium Rd., Karachi 5; f. 1950; depository for all Pakistani publications; 100,000 vols. (50,000 English and European languages, 30,000 Oriental languages, plus MSS and serials, etc.); Dir. A. H. AKHTAR.

Ministry of Agriculture and Works Library: Ministry of Agriculture, Food and Under-developed Areas, Library, Government of Pakistan, Islamabad; f. 1947; 26,000 vols.; 159 periodicals; Librarian S. S. FATIMI, D.L.SC.; publs. *Economic Survey of the Muslim Countries*†, *Food and Forestry*†.

National Archives of Pakistan: Secretariat Block-D, Islamabad; f. 1948; Dir. ATIQUE ZAFAR SHEIKH.

National Assembly Library: Islamabad; f. 1947; approx. 20,000 vols., 35 current periodicals; United Nations publications; Librarian S. HABIB AKHTAR HASAN.

National Bank of Pakistan—Head Office Library: I. I. Chundrigar Rd., Karachi 2; f. 1965; *c.* 40,000 vols. (30,000 English, 10,000 Oriental); 1,600 old coins of world currencies; 100 MSS. in Urdu, Arabic and Persian; central and provincial government publs.; 125 current periodicals; UN publs.; Librarian Mrs. JAMEELUNISA AHMED; publs. *Index of Economic Literature* (monthly), *List of Acquisitions* (quarterly).

Pakistan National Centre Library and Culture Centre: Hyderabad, Sind; 13,000 vols.; Dir. JAUHER HUSAIN, M.A., LL.B.

Pakistan Scientific and Technological Information Centre (Pastic): P-13, Al-markaz, Sector F-7/2 Islamabad; f. 1956 as PANSDOC under Pakistan Council of Scientific and Industrial Research, reorganized 1974 under the Pakistan Science Foundation; sub-centres at Karachi, Lahore, Peshawar and Quetta; facilities include National Science Reference Library, Documentation Services, Scientific and Technical Information Services, Scientific Publications and Compilation of Scientific Statistics; Project Dir. Dr. A. R. MOHAJIR, PH.D.; publs. *Pakistan Science Abstracts* (quarterly), *Translation Index* (2 a year), *Pakistan Current Contenst* (monthly), *Subject List of Foreign Patents, List of Bibliographies* (annually), *Union Catalogue of Scientific Periodicals* (annually).

Punjab Public Library: Lahore; f. 1884; 200,000 vols., 1,100 MSS., 90 European language and 90 Oriental language periodicals; Bait-ul-Quran Section with MSS., rare material on the Quran and audio-visual units; Librarian MUHAMMAD RIAZ, M.A.

Punjab University Library: Lahore; f. 1882; *c.* 290,000 vols., 20,000 MSS, 700 journals; Librarian M. ANWAR-UL-HAQUE.

Talim-ul-Islam College Library: Rabwah, Pakistan; f. 1944; 14,000 vols.; Librarian MAHFUZ-UR-RAHMAN, M.A., LIB.DIP.

Sind Government Library: Hyderabad; f. 1951; reference and general; 25,000 vols.; Librarian KHAIR MUHAMMED MUGHAL.

Sind University Central Library: Sind University New Campus, Jamshoro, Sind; f. 1947; 118,800 vols.; Librarian MOINUDDIN KHAN.

MUSEUMS

National Museum of Pakistan: Burns Garden, Karachi; f. 1950; collections comprise palaeolithic implements from the Soan Valley, antiquities from Amri, Serai Khola, Kot-Diji, Mohenjodaro, Harappa, Chanhudaro, and Jhukar (2,500–1,500 B.C.), Gandhara (1st century A.D.–6th century A.D.), Buddhist and Hindu sculptures; collection of coins from 6th century B.C. to date; handicrafts, miniature painting, calligraphic and other MSS. of the Muslim period, ethnological material from various regions of Pakistan; Supt. TASWIR HUSAIN HAMIDI, M.A.; publs. *Pakistan Archaeology, Museum Journal.*

Archaeological Museum: Harappa, Dist. Montgomery, Pakistan; Assistant Custodian MOHD. ABDUL HALIM, M.A.

Archaeological Museum: Moenjodaro, Larkana, Sind; f. 1924; a variety of antiquities unearthed from the 5,000-year-old prehistoric site—Moenjodaro; Curator I. H. NADIEM.

Archaeological Museum: Taxila, Rawalpindi; f. 1928; Gandhara sculptures in stone and stucco; gold and silver ornaments; household utensils, pottery; antiquities of every description from the sites of Taxila and monastic area, covering the years from 6th century B.C. to 5th century A.D.; library: *see* Libraries; Custodian A. A. FAROOQ.

Archival Museum: Central Record Office (Government of Pakistan), Peshawar; f. 1950; Archives Dir. Prof. S. M. JAFFAR.

Forest Museum: Pakistan Forest Institute, Peshawar University; f. 1952; Forestry and Allied Subjects; Curator ABBAS KHAN KHATTAK.

Industrial and Commercial Museum: Poonch House, Multan Rd. Lahore, Pakistan; permanent up-to-date collection of the raw material resources, handicrafts, art-ware and manufactured products of Pakistan; industrial library, reading-room and auditorium attached; provides free economic intelligence to trade and industry; Curator MUSHTAQ AHMAD, B.SC.

Lahore Fort Museum: Lahore; Mughal Gallery: Mughal paintings, coins, calligraphy, MSS., faience, carving; Sikh Gallery: arms and armour, paintings and art of Sikh period; Sikh Painting Gallery: oil paintings from the Princess Bamba Collection; Supt. of Archaeology AHMAD NABI KHAN.

Lahore Museum: Lahore; f. 1864; collection of Graeco-Buddhist sculpture, Indo-Pakistan coins and miniature paintings of the Mughal, Rajput, Kangar and Pahari schools; Hindu, Buddhist and Jaina sculpture, local arts, Chinese porcelain, armoury, fabrics, Pakistan postage stamps; library of 25,000 vols.; Dir. Dr. SAIFUR RAHMAN DAR; Chair. B. A. KURESHI, S.PK., S.Q.A., C.S.P.; publs. *Guide Book, Catalogue of Coins, Catalogue of Miniatures, Catalogue of Manuscripts, Kharoshti Premier.*

Peshawar Museum: Peshawar; f. 1906; the collections of this museum are devoted mainly to the sculptures of the Gandhara School; they comprise an unrivalled collection of images of Buddha, the Bodhisattvas, Buddhist deities, reliefs illustrating the life of the Buddha and Jataka stories, architectural pieces and minor antiquities excavated at Charsadda, Sahri-Bahlol, Shahji-ki-Dheri, Takht-i-Bahi and Jamal Garhi; a Muslim gallery of Koranic MSS and other Muslim exhibits, and a Hall of Tribes; Dir. Prof. FIDAULLAH SEHRAI.

Punjab Government Central Record Office and Archival Museum: Lahore; valuable library collection; museum contains precious documents, lithographs and prints; Keeper N. A. CHAUDRY.

Quaid-i-Azam Birthplace, Reading Room, Museum and Library: Karachi 2; f. 1953; historic; Librarian and Custodian-in-Charge CH. HAJI MUHAMMAD, M.A.

Zoological Museum: Lahore; Curator M. IKRAMULLAH KHAN.

UNIVERSITIES

UNIVERSITY OF AGRICULTURE

FAISALABAD

Telephone: 25911-16.

Founded 1909 as Panjab Agricultural College, present name 1973.

Language of instruction: English.

Chancellor: THE GOVERNOR OF THE PUNJAB.

Vice-Chancellor: Dr. GHULAM RASUL CHAUDHRY.

Registrar: RIAZ-UR-REHMAN, M.SC.

Librarian: NAJAF ALI KHAN, M.SC.

Number of teachers: 370.
Number of students: 3,660.

Publications: *Calendar, Journal of Agricultural Sciences* (quarterly), *Research Studies*, and various other publications.

DEANS:

Faculty of Agriculture: Dr. MANZOOR AHMAD KHAN.
Faculty of Veterinary Science: Dr. M. IRFAN.
Faculty of Animal Husbandry: Dr. HAJI MOHAMMAD CHAUDHRY.
Faculty of Agricultural Economics and Rural Sociology: Dr. AGHA SAJJAD-HAIDER.
Faculty of Agricultural Engineering and Technology: ADBUL HAMID KHAN.
Faculty of Science: Dr. A. N. SHERI.

DIRECTORS:

Advanced Studies: Dr. MOHAMMAD ASLAM.
Research: Dr. MOHAMMAD SHAFIQ CHAUDHRY.
Education and Extension: Dr. TANWEER AHMAD KHAN LODHI.

PROFESSORS:

AHMAD, M., Animal Reproduction
AHMAD, W., Animal Reproduction
AJMAL, M., Microbiology
ASLAM, M., Plant Breeding and Genetics
CHOUDHRY, A. M., Farm Management
CHOUDHRY, H. M., Nutrition
HAIDER, A. S., Agricultural Economics
IRFAN, M., Veterinary Pathology
KAUSAR, A. G., Plant Pathology
KHAN, A. G., Plant Pathology
KHAN, A. S., Fibre Technology
KHAN, D. A., Horticulture
KHAN, M. A., Plant Breeding and Genetics
KHAN, M. R., Entomology
KHAN, S. R. A., Agronomy
LODHI, T. A. K., Agricultural Education
MAJID, M. A., Anatomy
MOHAMMAD, S., Soil Science
QAYYUM, H. A., Entomology
QURESHI, M. J., Livestock Management
REHMAN, A., Plant Breeding and Genetics
SHEIKH, G. S., Basic Engineering
YUSAF, M., Plant Breeding and Genetics

CONSTITUENT COLLEGE:

College of Veterinary Science: Lahore; Principal M. T. KHAN.

ALLAMA IQBAL OPEN UNIVERSITY

SECTOR H-8, ISLAMABAD

Telephone: 43591/5.

Founded 1974 as People's Open University; correspondence and audio-visual courses in general education, functional education, teachers' education, adult education. Languages of instruction: Urdu and English.

Vice-Chancellor: Dr. S. M. ZAMAN, M.A., PH.D.

Registrar: Mrs. MUZAFFARI QURAISHI, M.A., B.ED.

Librarian: MAHMUD UL-HASSAN, M.A.

Library of 22,079 vols.

Number of teachers: 53.
Number of students: *c.* 57,000.

Publications: *Magazine* (annually), *University Bulletin* (monthly).

DIRECTORS:

Institute of Arabic and Islamic Studies: M. KHALIL-UR-REHMAN, M.A. (acting).
Institute of Education: Dr. SHAUKAT ALI SIDDIQUI, PH.D.
Department of Social Sciences: A. H. RATHORE, M.A.
Department of Basic Sciences: Mrs. NADIRA KHAN, M.SC.
Department of Urdu: M. S. K. SHIBLI, PH.D.
Department of English: Prof. RIAZ HASSAN, M.LIT.
Department of Industrial Education: ASLAM ASGHAR, PH.D.
Department of Agriculture: Dr. HIDAYATULLAH, PH.D.
Department of Home Economics: (vacant).
Department of Iqbaliat: (vacant).
Institute of Educational Technology: A. J. KAZI, M.A.

BAHAUDDIN ZAKARIYA UNIVERSITY

UNIVERSITY CAMPUS, BOSAN RD., MULTAN

Telephone: 74523, 76565.

Founded 1975 as University of Multan.

Languages of instruction: Urdu and English; Academic year: May to April.

Chancellor: THE GOVERNOR OF PUNJAB.

Vice-Chancellor: Prof. M. ALTAF ALI QURESHI.

Registrar: I. R. ARSH SIDDIQUI.

Librarian: (vacant).

Library of 27,642 vols.

Number of teachers: 90.
Number of students: 1,327.

Publications: *Iqbal and Quaid-i-Azam, Semester*, workshop proceedings.

DEANS:

Faculty of Arts and Social Science: M. ISHAQ AKHTAR.
Faculty of Commerce, Law and Business Administration: MUHAMMAD SAIYID-UZ-ZAFAR.
Faculty of Islamic Studies and Languages: M. ISHAQ AKHTAR.
Faculty of Medicine, Dentistry and Pharmacy: MUHAMMAD HAYAT ZAFAR.
Faculty of Science, Engineering and Agriculture: AEJAZ AHMAD MALIK.

CONSTITUENT COLLEGE:

University Law College: f. 1971; Multan; Principal INAM BARI QURESHI.

There are 24 affiliated colleges.

UNIVERSITY OF BALUCHISTAN

SARIAB RD., QUETTA

Telephone: 70431.

Founded 1970.

Language of instruction: English; Academic year: March to December.

Chancellor: THE GOVERNOR OF BALUCHISTAN.

Vice-Chancellor: AGHA AKBAR SHAH.

Registrar: M. ANWAR KHETRAN.

Librarian: M. A. KAZMI.

Library of 34,629 vols.

Number of teachers: 127.
Number of students: 826.

DEANS:

Faculty of Science: Dr. S. B. HASSAN ABIDI.
Faculty of Arts: Prof. SHUKRULLAH KHAN.

DIRECTORS:

Centre of Excellence in Mineralogy: NASIR ALI DURRANI.
Pakistan Study Centre: ABDULLAH JAN JAMALDINI.
University Law College: MUHAMMAD KHAN RAISANI.

PROFESSORS:

ABIDI, S. B. HASSAN, Physics
HUSSAIN, MUJTABA, Urdu
KHAN, SAEED AHMED, Physical Chemistry
KHAN, SHUKRULLAH, Economics

There are 12 affiliated colleges.

GOMAL UNIVERSITY

D. I. KHAN, N.W.F.P.

Telephone: 3697.

Founded 1974.

State control; Language of instruction: English; Academic year: September to June.

Chancellor: THE GOVERNOR OF N.W.F.P.

Vice-Chancellor: Prof. ABDUL ALI KHAN.

Registrar: SHER ZAMAN KHAN GANDAPUR.

Librarian: MURID KAZIM.

Library of 44,529 vols.

Number of teachers: 118.
Number of students: 945.

Publication: *The Journalist* (fortnightly).

DEANS:

Faculty of Sciences: Dr. MOHAMMAD YAR KHAN.

Faculty of Arts: Dr. D. M. MALIK.

PROFESSORS:

KHAN, MOHAMMAD SHARIF, Law
KHAN, M. YAR, Physics
MIANA, G. A., Pharmacy

ATTACHED INSTITUTE:

Institute of Education and Research: f. 1974; Dir. Dr. D. M. MALIK.

There are nine affiliated colleges.

ISLAMIA UNIVERSITY

BAHAWALPUR

Telephone: 2476, 2228.

Founded 1975.

Languages of instruction: Urdu and English.

Vice-Chancellor: Prof. ABDUL QAYYUM QURESHI.

Registrar: MOHAMMAD AFZAL KHAN.

Librarian: MUHAMMAD FAZIL.

Library of 43,000 vols.
Number of teachers: 73.
Number of students: 768.

DEANS:

Faculty of Islamic Learning: Prof. Dr. SAGHIR HASAN MASUMI.

Faculty of Science: Prof. MUHAMMAD SHAFIQ KHAN.

Faculty of Arts: Dr. IFTIKHAR AHMED SIDDIQUI.

HEADS OF DEPARTMENTS:

Physics: SOHAIL AZIZ KHAN.
Chemistry: Prof. MUHAMMAD SHAFIQ KHAN.
Statistics: MUNIR AKHTAR.
Mathematics: HAFIZ ALI MUHAMMAD.
Economics: ZUBAIR AHMED QURESHI.
History: MUHAMMAD SALEEM AHMAD.
Islamic Studies: Prof. Dr. M. SAGHIR HASAN MASOOMI.
Political Science: ABDUL HAMEED KHAN.
Arabic: ELAHI BAKHSH JARULLAH.
English: SYED MAZHAR SAEED QAZMI.
Urdu: Dr. IFTIKHAR AHMED SIDDIQUI.
Law: MUHAMMAD NAEEM BUTT.

There are 10 affiliated colleges (including one medical college).

UNIVERSITY OF KARACHI

UNIVERSITY CAMPUS, KARACHI 32

Telephone: 419291.

Founded 1951.

State control; Languages of instruction: English and Urdu; Academic year: October to July.

See also under University of Sind.

Chancellor: THE GOVERNOR OF SIND.

Vice-Chancellor: Dr. MASUM ALI TIRMIZI.

Pro-Vice-Chancellor: Dr. S. SABIR ALI.

Registrar: Dr. ISMAIL SAAD.

Librarian: M. ADIL USMANI, M.L.S.

Number of teachers: 440.
Number of students: 7,323.

Publications: *Jareeda* (Journal of the Bureau of Composition, Compilation and Translation, annually), *Science* (quarterly), *Pakistan Journal of Psychology* (quarterly), *Pakistan Journal of Botany* (2 a year), *Karachi University Gazette* (monthly), *University Code, Prospectus* (annually), *Courses of Studies.*

DEANS:

Faculty of Arts: Dr. M. AHMED.
Faculty of Business Administration: Prof. S. A. HASHMI.
Faculty of Pharmacy: Dr. MOHAMMAD SABIR.
Faculty of Science: Dr. RAFIQ AHMAD.
Faculty of Medicine: Prof. A. WAHID, F.I.C.S.
Faculty of Islamic Studies: Dr. SHARAFAT HASMI.
Faculty of Law: Prof. MOHAMMAD KHALILULLAH.
Faculty of Education: Mrs. B. KHAN.
Faculty of Engineering: A. A. QURESHI.

ATTACHED INSTITUTES:

Central and West Asian Institute: f. 1970; Pres. Dr. I. H. QURESHI.

Institute of Business Administration and Commerce: f. 1959; Dir. Dr. MATIN AHMAD KHAN.

Institute of Marine Biology: (*see* Research Institutes).

Institute of European Studies: Dir. SHAMIM AKHTAR.

Husein Ibrahim Jamal Postgraduate Institute of Chemistry: Dir. Dr. SALIMUZZAMAN SIDDIQI, F.R.S.

There are 56 affiliated colleges.

MEHRAN UNIVERSITY OF ENGINEERING AND TECHNOLOGY

NAWABSHAH

Telephone: 23797.

Founded 1963 as constituent college of University of Sind; present status 1977.

Language of instruction: English; Academic year: October to August.

Chancellor: THE GOVERNOR OF SIND.

Vice-Chancellor: S. M. QURESHI, M.ENG., PH.D.

Registrar: MOULA BUX QURESHI, B.E.

Librarian: MAHTAB AHMED ZUBAIRI, M.A., M.L.S.

Library of 30,000 vols.
Number of teachers: 123.
Number of students: 1,459.

Publication: *Mehran Varsity News* (monthly).

DEANS:

Faculty of Engineering: A. A. ABRO, M.SC., PH.D.
Faculty of Technology: A. A. JUNEJO, PH.D.
Postgraduate Studies and Research: MUMTAZ-UL-IMAM, PH.D.

PROFESSORS:

ABRO, A. A., Civil Engineering
JUNEJO, A. A., Mechanical Engineering
MEMON, H. M., Civil Engineering
MUMTAZUL-IMAM, Mathematics and Computer Science
QURESHI, M. A., Civil Engineering
QURESHI, S. M., Civil Engineering

There are three affiliated colleges.

NED UNIVERSITY OF ENGINEERING AND TECHNOLOGY

UNIVERSITY RD., KARACHI 32

Telephones: 419315/9, 419053/5.

Founded 1922 as NED Government Engineering College, university status 1977.

Language of instruction: English.

Chancellor: THE GOVERNOR OF SIND.

Vice-Chancellor: A. M. AKHOOND.

Registrar: INAYAT HUSAIN.

Librarian: SYED HABIB ALI.

Library of 36,178 vols.
Number of teachers: *c.* 100.
Number of students: 1,828.

Publications: *Prospectus* (annually), *The Young Engineer* (annually).

PROFESSORS:

AHMED, A., Mechanical Engineering
ALI, S. F., Mechanical Engineering
ALVI, A. Q., Civil Engineering
GANATRA, S. A. G., Civil Engineering
KHALIQUE, M. A., Mechanical Engineering
KHAN, A. T., Dean, Faculty of Engineering
KHAN, J. A., Mechanical Engineering
MIRZA, N. T., Humanities
QAZI, A. Q., Electrical Engineering
QUIDWAI, M. A., Mathematics and Sciences

AFFILIATED COLLEGES:

National College of Engineering and Technology: Muslimabad, Karachi; Principal Dr. M. I. HUSSAIN.

Pakistan Air Force College of Aeronautical Engineering: Korangi Creek, Karachi; Principal Air Cdre. KAMAL MASUD HASAN.

Pakistan Naval Engineering College: PNS Karsaz, Karachi; Principal Capt. M. RAZI MIRZA.

Government College of Technology: S.I.T.E., Karachi; Principal S. Q. H. NAQVI.

UNIVERSITY OF ENGINEERING AND TECHNOLOGY

GRAND TRUNK RD., LAHORE 31

Telephone: 331875, 339205, 332160.

Founded 1961.

Language of instruction: English.

Chancellor: THE GOVERNOR OF THE PUNJAB.

Vice-Chancellor: A. H. QURESHI, M.SC., PH.D., C.ENG., F.I.MECH.E., M.I.PROD.E.

Registrar: MIAN MOHD. TUFAIL, M.A.

Librarian: MOHAMMAD RAMZAN, M.A., M.L.S.

Library of 60,000 vols.

Number of teachers: 207.

Number of students: 3,070 (Lahore Campus), 620 (Taxila Campus).

Publications: *ECHO* (annually), *Annual Report, Calendar, University Prospectus, Research Bulletin, Varsity News* (fortnightly).

DEANS:

Faculty of Architecture and Planning: NAZIR AHMAD CH.

Faculty of Engineering: Z. M. KHILJI.

PROFESSORS:

AKHTAR, M. Y., PH.D., C.ENG., M.I.E.E., Electrical Engineering
AWAN, N. M., PH.D., M.I.E., Civil Engineering
BANDEY, A. H., M.S., F.I.CH.E., Chemical Engineering
DAR, I. H., PH.D., M.A.I.M.E., M.I.M.E., Mining Engineering
DURRANI, K. E., PH.D., Electrical Engineering
HAQUE, S. M., PH.D., F.I.E., Electrical Engineering
IKRAM KHAN, M., PH.D., F.I.E., C.ENG., M.I.MECH.E., Mechanical Engineering
IKRAMULLAH, M., PH.D., M.I.E., M.A.S.C.E., Civil Engineering
INAMUL HAQ, M., PH.D., Mathematics
IQBAL, M. Z., M.SC., A.E.E., Electrical Engineering
KHAN, Q. U. A., PH.D., M.I.E.E.E., Electrical Engineering
MAHMOOD, K., PH.D., M.I.E., M.A.C.I., Civil Engineering
RASHID, S. A., M.A., M.SC., Mathematics
SAEEDUDDIN, K., M.E., PH.D., F.I.E., Civil Engineering
SALEEM, M. I., M.SC., M.A.S.E.E., Mechanical Engineering
SHEIKH, A., PH.D., F.I.E., University Workshops
TARIQ, M. N., PH.D., F.P.S.P.H.E., F.I.E., Public Health Engineering

UNIVERSITY OF PESHAWAR

PESHAWAR, N.W.F.P.

Telephone: 8200, 8251.

Founded 1950.

Languages of instruction: Urdu, Pushto and English; Academic year: September to June, three terms.

Chancellor: THE GOVERNOR OF THE NORTH WEST FRONTIER PROVINCE.

Vice-Chancellor: Prof. MOHAMMAD ZUBAIR SAHIBZADA.

Registrar: ABDUS SADIQ.

Librarian: A. U. KHAN.

Library: 106,000 vols., 691 MSS. and 441 current periodicals.

Number of teachers: 483.

Number of students: 8,494.

Publications: *Zamaka, Tartara, Khiaban, Ancient Pakistan* (annuals), *Annual Report, Journal of Science and Technology, Journal of Humanities and Social Sciences, Journal of Languages.*

DEANS:

Faculty of Arts: Dr. S. M. MOGHNI.

Faculty of Science: Dr. S. MARGHOOB ALI.

Faculty of Agriculture: S. BASIT ALI SHAH.

Faculty of Engineering: S. IQBAL HUSSAIN SHAH.

PROFESSORS:

Faculty of Arts:

ASHRAF, MAULANA M., Arabic
DURRANI, FARZAND ALI, Archaeology
KHAN, Dr. Mrs. A. SALIM, Political Science
KHAN, Dr. MUNAWAR, History
MUGHNI, Dr. S. M., Psychology
NASIM, Dr. K. B., Persian
NAZIR, Dr. MIAN M., Economics
QAYUM, ABDUL, Philosophy
REHMAN, Dr. QAZI MUJIBUR, Islamic Studies
SIDDIQUI, Dr. MOHAMMAD SHAMSUDDIN, Urdu

Faculty of Sciences:

ALI, Dr. S. MARGHOOB, Botany
FARIDI, Dr. M. A., Botany
KAZMI, H. A., Botany
KHALI, Dr. A. R. KHAN TAHIR, Geology
KHAN, Dr. M. NAZIR, Mathematics
KHAN, MOHAMMAD JAN, Physics
KHATTAK, MOHAMMAD ALI, Physics
NOWSHERVI, Dr. A. R., Chemistry
SIDDIQI, NASIM, Zoology

Faculty of Agriculture:

KHAN, Dr. M. ATTAULLAH
KAHN, MOHAMMAD HUSSAIN
LODHI, Dr. A. F.
SHAH, S. BASIT ALI
SIDDIQUI, Dr. AL JAMIL

Faculty of Engineering:

ABDULLAH, Dr. M., Electrical Engineering
KHAN, Dr. JAMAL, Mechanical Engineering
KHAN, Dr. M. ATTAULLAH, Civil Engineering
SHAH, S. IQBAL HUSSAIN, Mechanical Engineering

CONSTITUENT COLLEGES:

Islamia College: Peshawar; f. 1913; Principal ABDUS SATTAR.

Jinnah College for Women: Peshawar; f. 1954; Principal Mrs. R. Y. HIDAYATULLAH (acting); publ. *Hearth* (annually).

College of Home Economics: University of Peshawar; f. 1954; Principal Miss AKHTAR MOHYUDDIN, M.SC.

Quaid-e-Azam College of Commerce: f. 1962; Principal ABDUL MALIK HASHMI, B.COM., LL.B., M.B.A.

College of Education: f. 1950; Principal Dr. MOHAMMAD JAMSHED KHAN.

Law College: f. 1950; Principal ABDUL GHAFOUR, LL.M.

Basic Sciences and Humanities Division: Dir. S. A. H. RIZVI.

There are 40 affiliated colleges.

UNIVERSITY OF THE PUNJAB

1 SHAHRAH-E-AL-BERUNI, LAHORE 2

Telephone: 54428.

Founded 1882.

State control; Languages of instruction: Urdu, English; Academic year begins September.

Chancellor: THE GOVERNOR OF THE PUNJAB.

Vice-Chancellor: Prof. KHAIRAT MUHAMMAD IBN-E-RASA.

Registrar: M. ABDUL QADIR QURESHI.

Librarian: ANWAR-UL-HAQ.

Library of 296,465 vols.

Number of teachers: 386.

Number of students: 7,794.

Publications: various faculty and institute bulletins.

DEANS:

Faculty of Arts: Prof. RIFAT RASHID.

Faculty of Science and Engineering: Prof. MUHAMMAD NAZIR ROMANI.

Faculty of Islamic and Oriental Learning: Prof. Dr. ABDUL WAHEED QURAISHI.

Faculty of Law: Prof. Sh. IMTIAZ ALI.

Faculty of Pharmacy: Prof. MUHAMMAD AMIN.

PROFESSORS:

Faculty of Arts:

AHMAD, R., M.A., D.PHIL., Economics
CHUGHTAI, M. U. D., Political Science
KHAN, Y. M., PH.D., History
KHAWAJA, G. S., M.A., Philosophy
RASHID, R., M.A., ED.D., Social Work
SAEED, K. A., M.COM., C.A., M.B.A., Business Administration

Faculty of Islamic and Oriental Learning:

BRELVI, E., M.A., PH.D., Urdu
MALIK, Z. A., M.A., PH.D., Arabic
QURAISHI, W., M.A., PH.D., D.LITT., Urdu

Faculty of Law:

ALI, S. I., LL.M.
MOKAL, S. M. I. K., LL.B.

Faculty of Pharmacy:

AMIN, M., D.SC., A.R.I.S.
ASHRAF, M., PH.D.

Faculty of Science and Engineering:

AHMAD, M., M.SC. PH.D., Zoology
ELAHI, M. K., PH.D., Geography
HASAN, R., PH.D., Applied Psychology
HIRAI, A. S., M.A., M.SC., Statistics
HUSSAIN, F., M.SC., PH.D., Physical Chemistry
KHALID, H. S., PH.D., Botany
KHAN, D., Zoology
KHAN, I. H., Chemical Engineering and Technology
KURESHY, K. U., M.A., PH.D., Geography
REHMAN, R., PH.D., General and Inorganic Chemistry
SALEEM, M., PH.D., Physics
SHAMS, F. A., M.SC., M.A., PH.D., Geology
SHAUKAT, M. A., M.SC., PH.D., Physics
SHAUKAT, N., PH.D., Education
ZAHUR, M. S., PH.D., Botany

ATTACHED INSTITUTES AND CONSTITUENT COLLEGES:

Institute of Chemistry: f. 1923; Dir. Prof. M. Z. IQBAL.

Institute of Chemical Engineering and Technology: f. 1917; Dir. Prof. M. N. ROMANI.

Institute of Statistics: f. 1950; Dir. KHUDA DAD KHAN.

University Law College: f. 1868; Principal Prof. SH. IMTIAZ ALI.

Hailey College of Commerce: f. 1927; Principal A. A. SIDDIQUI.

Institute of Education: f. 1959; Principal Prof. K. U. KURESHY.

Centre for Solid State Physics: f. 1973; Dir. Dr. M. A. SHAH.

QUAID-I-AZAM UNIVERSITY

P.O.B. 1090, ISLAMABAD

Telephone: 24801, 29603/09/002.

Founded 1965; incorporated 1967; name changed 1977.

State control; Language of instruction: English; Academic year January to December (2 semesters).

Chancellor: THE PRESIDENT OF THE ISLAMIC REPUBLIC OF PAKISTAN.

Vice-Chancellor: Prof. AHMED MOHIYUDDIN, PH.D., F.P.A.S.

Registrar: ASLAM FAROOQ BUTT (acting).

Librarian: Z. H. NAQVI.

Library of 87,000 vols.

Number of teachers: 149.
Number of students: 1,475.

Publications: *Prospectus*†, *Scrutiny*† (2 a year), *Journal of Mathematics and Sciences*† (2 a year).

DEANS:

Faculty of Natural Sciences: Prof. M. H. QAZI.

Faculty of Social Sciences: Prof. S. H. HASHMI.

PROFESSORS:

AFZAL, M., M.SC., PH.D., Physical Chemistry
AHMAD, AFZAL, M.SC., PH.D., Organic Chemistry
ARSALAN, M., M.SC., PH.D., Physiology
DANI, A. H., PH.D., History
FAYYAZUDDIN, M.SC., PH.D., Physics
GHORI, Q. K., M.A., PH.D., Mathematics
HASHMI, S. H., M.A., PH.D., Administrative Sciences
HASSAN, Mrs. M., M.SC., PH.D., Organic Chemistry
HUSSAIN, M., M.SC., PH.D., Experimental Physics
HUSSAIN MALICK, M. A., M.A., PH.D., Economics
KHAN, M. A., M.SC., PH.D., Physical Chemistry
MURTAZA, G., M.SC., PH.D., Elementary Particle Physics
NASEEM, S. M., M.SC., PH.D., Economics
QAZI, M. H., PH.D., Biology
RAUF, M. A., M.A., PH.D., Social Anthropology
RAZMI, M. S. K., M.SC., PH.D., Elementary Particle Physics
RIAZUDDIN, M.SC., PH.D., Theoretical Physics
WAHIDUZZAMAN, M.A., PH.D., History
YOUSUF, S. M., PH.D., Mathematics

ATTACHED INSTITUTES:

Centre for Area Study of North America, Latin America and Africa: f. 1979; Dir. Dr. RAIS AHMAD KHAN.

Institute of Historical and Cultural Research: f. 1973; Dir. N. A. BALOCH.

National Institute of Pakistan Studies: Dir. FETAH MOHAMMED MALIK.

National Institute of Modern Languages: Dir. LAEEQ AHMED BABRI.

Army Medical College.

National Defence College.

National Institute of Psychology.

UNIVERSITY OF SIND

JAMSHORO, DISTRICT DADU

Telephone: 25981.

Founded in 1947 in Karachi, and transferred to Hyderabad, Sind, in 1951, when it was decided to found a separate Karachi University. There are central teaching departments but the university also functions as an affiliating and examining body.

Languages of instruction: Urdu, Sindhi and English.

Chancellor: THE GOVERNOR OF SIND.

Vice-Chancellor: MOHD. ILYAS ABRO.

Registrar: DUR MOHAMMAD NAREJO.

Librarian: M. A. KAZI, M.A., PH.D.

Library of 124,514 vols.

Number of teachers: 406.
Number of students: 2,838.

Publications: *Sind University Research Journal*, Arts series, Humanities and social science series, *Sind University (Science) Research Journal*.

DEANS:

Faculty of Arts: Dr. M. A. A. BEG.
Faculty of Education: Dr. A. A. ARAIN.
Faculty of Science: Dr. I. ARAIN.

DIRECTORS:

Centre of Excellence in Analytical Chemistry: Dr. G. H. KAZI.
Far East and South East Asia Study Centre: Dr. D. H. SHAH.
Institute of Chemistry: Dr. I. ARAIN.
Institute of Education and Research: Dr. A. A. ARAIN.
Institute of Languages: Dr. M. A. QADRI.
Institute of Sindhology: Dr. G. A. ALLANA.
Pakistan Study Centre: Dr. H. KHUHRO.

PROFESSORS:

Faculty of Arts:
ALLANA, G. A., Sindhi
BAIG, M. A. A., Economics
DAUDPOTA, N. B., Commerce
FAROOQUI, W. A., Philosophy
HUSSAINY, A. S., Persian
KHAMISANI, A., English
KHUHRO, H., General History
MUGHAL, N. A., Political Science
QADRI, M. A., Arabic

Faculty of Education:
ARAIN, A. A.

Faculty of Science:
AHMED, K. S., Geography
AHMED, M. R., Biology
AKHTAR, M. I., Chemistry
ARBANI, S. N., Biology
ARAIN, I., Chemistry
KHAN, K. M., Botany
SALAHUDDIN, M., Chemistry
SHAH, A. H., Physics
SHAH, A. Q. Chemistry
SHAIKH, D. M., Physiology

There are 70 affiliated colleges.

Sind University, Shah Abdul Latif Campus

KHAIRPUR, SIND

Telephone: 2472.

Founded 1975.

Chancellor: Gen. S. M. ABASSI.

Vice-Chancellor: Prof. MUHAMMAD ILYAS ABRO.

Pro-Vice-Chancellor: Dr. S. M. I. SHAH BUKHARI.

Registrar: Dr. SHAH NAWAZ ARBANI.

Librarian: MUHAMMED SALEH BHATTI.

Library of 4,800 vols.

Number of teachers: 40.
Number of students: 371.

HEADS OF DEPARTMENTS:

Microbiology: Dr. A. R. MALIK.
Chemistry: VINOD KUMAR.
Commerce: RASOOL BUX SHAIKH.
Economics: MUHAMMAD NAWAZ CHAND.
Archaeology: MUHAMMAD MUKHTIAR KAZI.
International Relations: ABDUL LATIF ALVI.

SIND AGRICULTURE UNIVERSITY

TANDOJAM, DISTRICT HYDERABAD, SIND

Telephone: 26881.

Founded 1977.

Language of instruction: English.

Chancellor: THE GOVERNOR OF SIND.

Vice-Chancellor: Dr. ABDUL QADIR ANSARI.

Registrar: GHULAM KADIR ISANI.

Librarian: MUHAMMAD IDREES KHOKHAR.

Number of teachers: 186.
Number of students: 1,574.

PROFESSORS:

AGHA, K. H., Agronomy
ANSARI, N. N., Botany and Plant Breeding
KHAN, B., Horticulture
MALIK, M. M. S., Plant Pathology
SOOMRO, A. H., Entomology
TAGAR, S., Chemistry

COLLEGES

Jinnah Postgraduate Medical Centre: Government of Pakistan, Karachi 35; f. 1958; provides postgraduate training and education leading to M.Phil. and Ph.D. in the basic medical subjects, and Fellowship and Membership of the College of Physicians and Surgeons (F.C.P.S., M.C.P.S.) of Pakistan; also degrees in medical technology, occupational therapy and physiotherapy, postgraduate nursing diploma; library of 16,500 vols., periodicals; Dir. Dr. B. A. QUREISHI.

Dawood College of Engineering and Technology: M. A. Jinnah Rd., Karachi 5, f. 1964; library of 18,741 vols.; 63 teachers, 1,350 students; Principal Engr. Dr. M. I. HUSSAIN.

HEADS OF DEPARTMENTS:

Architecture: MOHAMMAD AMIN SHAIKH.

Chemical Engineering: Dr. HAROON JANGDA.

Electronics: S. MAJID ALI.

Metallurgical Engineering: (vacant).

Basic Sciences, Mathematics and Humanities: Dr. MOHAMMAD KAMIL.

Pakistan Administrative Staff College: Shahrah-i-Quaid-i-Azam, Lahore; f. 1960; research and training in administration and advanced management; library of 27,539 vols.; publ. *Journal* (2 a year).

Rawalpindi Government College of Technology: Shahrah-e-Shershah, Rawalpindi; f. 1958; three-year diploma courses in various subjects, degree courses in electrical power technology, electronics and communication technology; 1,700 students; library of 22,000 vols.; Principal Col. MUHAMMAD AFSAR; publ. *Technician* (annual).

Swedish Pakistani Institute of Technology: Government of Pakistan, Landhi, G.P.O. Box 186, Karachi 22; f. 1958; training in electrical and mechanical technology, woodworking, welding and clothing technology; 29 teachers; library of 20,000 vols.; Dir. M. AFZAL, T.Q.A.

PANAMA

Population 1,919,000

ACADEMIES

Panama City

Academia Panameña de la Lengua (*Panama Academy*): 12th in order of foundation in Spanish America; correspondent of the Real Academia Española, Madrid; publ. *Boletín*.

Honorary Director: RICARDO J. ALFARO.
Director: BALTASAR ISAZA CALDERÓN.
Secretary: MIGUEL MEJÍA DUTARY.

MEMBERS:

DUNCAN, JEPTHA B.
FÁBREGA, JOSÉ ISAAC
GUARDIA NAVARRO, ERNESTO DE LA
ROUX, RAÚL DE

Elected:

DOMÍNGUEZ ALBA, BERNARDO
FÁBREGA, OCTAVIO
GOYTÍA, VÍCTOR FLORENCIO
MIRÓ, RODRIGO
OBALDÍA, MARÍA OLIMPIA DE
OZORES, RENATO
RITTER AISLÁN, EDUARDO
ROSA, DIÓGENES DE LA

Academia Nacional de Ciencias de Panamá (*National Academy of Sciences of Panama*): Apdo. 4570; f. 1942 by Dr. GUILLERMO PATTERSON, Jr.; 24 mems.; research on scientific, including industrial and health, problems; the Academy advises the National Government.

President: Dr. GUILLERMO DE PAREDES, M.D., M.P.H., DR.P.H.
First Vice-President: FRANCISCO J. MORALES, B.S., C.E.
Second Vice-President: Dr. ALFREDO MELHADO, CH.E., M.D.
Third Vice-President: ALFONSO TEJEIRA, B.S.A.
Publications: *Boletín, Lecturas Científicas.*

Academia Panameña de la Historia (*Panama Academy of History*): Apdo. 973, Zona 1; f. 1921; Pres. MIGUEL A. MARTÍN; Sec. SAMUEL A. GUTIÉRREZ; publ. *Boletín.*

LEARNED SOCIETIES AND RESEARCH INSTITUTES

(*see* also under Universities)

Centro Cultural Panameño-Norte-Americano: Avda. Perú 66, Panama City.

Centro para el Desarrollo de la Capacidad Nacional de Investigación (*National Research Centre*): Estafeta Universitaria, Universidad de Panamá; f. 1976; co-ordinates all scientific and technical research; Dir. Dr. ALFREDO SOLER B.

Comisión Nacional de Arqueología y Monumentos Históricos: Apdo. 662, Panamá 1; f. 1946; Pres. REINA TORRES DE ARAÚZ; Sec. DEMETRIO TORAL.

Gorgas Memorial Laboratory of Tropical and Preventive Medicine: Avda. Justo Arosemena 35-30; Apdo. 6991, Panamá 5 or P.O.B. 935, APO Miami, Fl. 34002, U.S.A.; f. 1928; medical research in tropical medicine; 29 staff mems. and 125 supporting personnel; library: *see* Libraries; Dir. Dr. ABRAM S. BENENSON; Admin. Lic. JAIME MORALES; publs. *Annual Report*†, *Bibliography of the Gorgas Memorial Laboratory Publications*†.

Instituto Nacional de Cultura: Apdo. 662, Panamá 1; Dir. ARISTIDES MARTÍNEZ ORTEGA.

Instituto Nacional de Música: Apdo. 1414, Panamá 1; f. 1941; Dir. DAMIAN CARLES P.

Smithsonian Tropical Research Institute: P.O.B. 2072, Balboa; f. 1946; administered by the Smithsonian Institution (*see* under U.S.A., Learned Societies); for the research and promotion of tropical biology, education and conservation; staff of 90; library of 16,000 vols.; Dir. IRA RUBINOFF, M.A., PH.D.

LIBRARIES

Panama City

Archivo Nacional: Apdo. 6618; f. 1912; Dir. LUIS CARLOS NORIEGA HURTADO.

Biblioteca de la Dirección de Estadística y Censo: Apdo. 5213, Panamá 5; f. 1949; specializes in statistics; 47,500 vols.; Librarian IRIS V. DE ESPINOSA; publs. *Panamá en Cifras*† (annual), *Series de Estadística Panameña*†, *Volúmenes de los Censos Nacionales de 1970*†, *Suplemento de Estadística Panameña* (irregular).

Biblioteca Nacional (*National Library*): Apdo. 2444; f. 1892 as Biblioteca Colón, reorganized as Biblioteca Nacional 1942; a branch of the Ministry of Education's Public Libraries system, its special function is to provide a Government information service; 200,000 vols. (including bound reviews and periodicals); Dir. Prof. ALGIS BORRERO E.

Biblioteca de la Universidad de Panamá (*University Library*): Estafeta Universitaria; f. 1935; 206,436 vols., including 77,755 vols. in medical library; maintains interchange with 200 institutions; Dir. NURIA F. DE GONZÁLEZ.

Biblioteca Bio-Médica del Laboratorio Conmemorativo Gorgas (*Gorgas Memorial Laboratory Bio-Medical Library*): Avda. Justo Arosemena No. 35-30, Apdo. 6991, Panamá 5, or P.O.B. 935, APO Miami, Fl. 340002, U.S.A.; f. 1929; 10,000 vols., mainly in tropical medicine and related fields, 503 current biomedical periodicals; 3 librarians; Dir. Prof. MANUEL VÍCTOR DE LAS CASAS, Medical Librarian.

Biblioteca Amador-Washington (*U.S. International Communication Agency Library*): Avda. Federico Boyd, Panama City; f. 1964; 10,000 vols.; Acting Librarian HOODMY EYNAR SAMUDIO V.

Biblioteca de la Oficina de Estudios del Canal Interocéanico: Apdo. 9650, Zona 4; 1,000 vols.; Dir. SIMÓN QUIROS GUARDIA.

MUSEUMS

Dirección Nacional del Patrimonio Histórico: Apdo. 662, Panamá 1; library of 8,000 vols.; Dir. Dra. REINA TORRES DE ARAÚZ.

Canal Zone Library-Museum: Balboa Heights; f. 1914; 264,000 books, 56,000 additional items including photographs, periodicals, documents, MSS., microfilm, etc.; English and Spanish sections; Panama Collection, covering the Panama Railroad and the Panama Canal; Dir. BEVERLY C. WILLIAMS.

Museo de Arte Religioso Colonial: Apdo. postal 662, Panamá 1; f. 1974; located in restored 17th-century Dominican chapel; varied collection of objects of religious art of the Colonial period; cultural programmes, lectures, etc.; Dir. JORGE HORNA.

Museo de Ciencias Naturales: Avda. Cuba Calle 29 y 30, Apdo. 662; f. 1925; natural history; fauna of Panama and other countries; library of 270 vols.; Dir. Lic. NURIA ESQUIVEL DE BARILLAS.

Museo de Historia de Panamá: Palacio Municipal, Apdo. 662, Panamá 1; f. 1977; Dirs. Prof. OSCAR A. VELARDE B., Lic. JULIETA DE LA GUARDIA DE ARANGO; publs. guide books.

Museo del Hombre Panameño: Plaza 5 de Mayo, Apdo. 662, Panamá 1; f. 1976; archaeology and ethnography; Dir. Prof. MARCELA CAMARGO DE COOKE.

UNIVERSITIES

UNIVERSIDAD DE PANAMÁ

ESTAFETA UNIVERSITARIA, PANAMA CITY
Telephone: 23-0210.
Founded 1935.

State control; Language of instruction: Spanish; Academic year: May to September, September to February.

Rector: Dr. DIÓGENES CEDEÑO CENCI.
Vice-Rector (Academic Affairs): Dr. CEFERINO SÁNCHEZ.
Vice-Rector (Administration): Prof. PEDRO A. SALAZAR CH.
General Secretary: Prof. DIOMEDES CONCEPCIÓN.
Librarian: Lic. NURIA F. DE.GONZÁLEZ.

Number of teachers: 2,300.
Number of students: 33,833 (including part-time).

Publications†: *Boletín, Estadísticas Universitarias, Dialogo Universitario, Ecos de la Colina, Gaceta Universitaria, Boletín Informativo, Manual de Matrícula, Conciencia.*

DEANS:

Faculty of Agriculture: Ing. EZEQUIEL ESPINOZA (acting).
Faculty of Architecture: Prof. RAUL RODRÍGUEZ PORCELL.
Polytechnic Institute: Dr. VÍCTOR LEVI.
Faculty of Law and Political Sciences: Dr. ROGERIO DE MA. CARRILLO (acting).
Faculty of Medicine: Dr. GASPAR GARCÍA DE PAREDES.
Faculty of Natural Science and Pharmacy: Dr. FRANKLIN VERGARA (acting).
Faculty of Dentistry: Dr. SILIO GALO ORTÍZ.
Faculty of Public Administration and Commerce: Prof. AMELIA DE PÉREZ.
Faculty of Philosophy, Letters and Education: Dra. SUSANA R. DE TORRIJOS.

ATTACHED INSTITUTES:

Centro de Investigaciones Agropecuarias: Tocumen, Faculty of Agriculture.

Instituto de Criminología: Faculty of Law and Political Sciences.

Centro de Investigaciones Antropológicas: Faculty of Philosophy, Letters and Education.

Instituto Centroamericano de Administración y Supervisión de la Educación: Faculty of Philosophy, Letters and Education.

Centro de Investigacionès Jurídicas: Faculty of Law and Political Science.

Centro Experimental de Ingeniería: Polytechnic Institute.

UNIVERSIDAD SANTA MARÍA LA ANTIGUA

APARTADO 6-1696, PANAMA 6
Telephone: 60-6311.
Founded 1965.

Private control; Language of instruction: Spanish; Academic Year: April to December.

Chancellor: Mgr. MARCOS GREGORIO MCGRATH.
Rector: Rev. CARLOS M. ARIZ, C.M.F.
Vice-Rector: RODOLFO FERRAZZUOLO.
Secretary-General: GASPAR ESTRIBÍ G.
Librarian: ANA MARÍA JAÉN.

Number of teachers: 178.
Number of students: 1,916.

Publication: *Boletín Informativo.*

HEADS OF DEPARTMENTS:

Law and Political Science: BONIFACIO DÍEZ.
Administrative Sciences: YOLANDA PORTILLO.
Technology and Natural Science: LUCIANO ANGELONI.
Humanities and Religious Studies: ANGEL REVILLA.
Social Sciences: JOSÉ VICENTE ROMEU.

OTHER INSTITUTES

Escuela Nacional de Música: Apdo. 1414, Panama 1; affiliated to Instituto Nacional de Cultura (*q.v.*); f. 1941; 41 teachers, 396 students; Dir. Mo. JORGE LEDEZMA BRADLEY.

Escuela Nacional de Artes Plásticas: Apdo. 1004, Panama 1; f. 1913; affiliated to Instituto Nacional de Cultura (*q.v.*); 10 teachers, 128 students; Dir. Prof. ADRIANO HERRERABARRÍA; publs. *La Estrella de Panamá, El Matutino, El Panamá American.*

Escuela Nacional de Danzas: Apdo. 662, Panama 1; affiliated to Instituto Nacional de Cultura (*q.v.*).

Escuela Nacional de Teatro: Apdo. 662, Panama 1; f. 1974; attached to Instituto Nacional de Cultura (*q.v.*); 10 teachers, 40 students; Dir. Prof. IVÁN R. GARCÍA.

Escuela Naútica de Panamá: Apdo. 5936, Zona 2, Panamá; f. 1959 for secondary studies, higher studies 1972; courses in nautical engineering, specializing in naval machinery and maritime navigation and transport; offers professional training and qualification; library of 4,500 vols., 1,200 periodicals; 28 higher level teachers; 175 higher level students; Pres. Capt. PABLO DURÁN; Dir. Capt. ANTONIO MOTTA D.; Sec. Gen. DEYANIRA H. DE LÓPEZ; publs. *Boletín Informativo, El Cadete.*

PAPUA NEW GUINEA

Population 3,078,000

LEARNED SOCIETIES

Papua New Guinea Scientific Society: c/o National Museum, P.O.B. 5560, Boroko; f. 1949 to promote the sciences, exchange scientific information, preserve scientific collections and establish museums; 203 mems.; Pres. H. SAKULAS; publ. *Proceedings*.

Papua New Guinea Library Association: P.O.B. 5368, Boroko; f. 1973; 80 mems.; Pres. REBECCA GURUMA; Sec. STEPHEN R. WRIGHT; publs. *Toktok bilong haus buk* (Journal, quarterly), *Directory of Libraries in Papua New Guinea*.

RESEARCH INSTITUTES

Institute of Applied Social and Economic Research: P.O.B. 5854, Boroko; f. 1976; promotion of research into Papua New Guinea society and economy; consultancy services for Government; practical research opportunities for trainee research workers; library of 5,000 vols.; Dir. J. D. CONROY, PH.D.; publs. *Monograph*† (quarterly), *Discussion*†, *Luksave*†, *Bibliography*†, *Post Courier Index*†, (series, occasional).

Institute of National Affairs: P.O.B. 3530, Port Moresby: f. 1979; aims to foster the development of the national economy by contributing data on issues which are important to enterprises and the development of Papua New Guinea; undertakes research in matters of interest to management, the findings of which are communicated to interested bodies; organizes seminars, public meetings, etc., on matters of importance to economic development; Pres. W. MCLELLAN; Treas./Sec. J. MILLETT; Dir. of Research TERRY J. PITT; publs. discussion papers, speech series.

Institute of Papua New Guinea Studies: Box 1432, Boroko; f. 1973; study and documentation of Papua New Guinea cultures; field research in music, art, folklore, oral history, creative literature, dance; music archive (*c.* 300 items), folklore archive (*c.* 1,500 stories), photo archive; film section; Dir. Dr. J. KOLIA; publ. *Bikmaus* (quarterly).

Papua New Guinea Institute of Medical Research: P.O.B. 60, Goroka; f. 1968; medical, human biological, nutritional and sociological research, all matters relating to research into human health and disease within Papua New Guinea; 60 staff; library of 2,000 vols.; Dir. Dr. M. ALPERS; publs. monographs (irregularly), *Annual Report*†.

LIBRARY

National Library Service: P.O.B. 5770, Boroko; f. 1978; division of the Dept. of Education; the building and contents were an independence gift from the Australian Government; national reference library; legal deposit library; lending and educational services, responsibility for National Archives and Public Records Services; important holdings of New Guineana, particularly Government publications; 25,000 vols.; National Librarian Sir JOHN YOCKLUNN.

MUSEUM

Papua New Guinea National Museum and Art Gallery: P.O.B. 5560, Boroko; f. 1954; field research in cultural anthropology, ethno-aesthetics, natural history; tours, lectures, broadcasts, etc.; aims to implement the National Cultural Property (Preservation) Act to protect Papua New Guinea's cultural heritage; library of 1,000 vols.; Dir. GEOFFREY MOSUWADOGA; publs. *Records*†, *Annual Report*†.

UNIVERSITIES AND COLLEGE

UNIVERSITY OF PAPUA NEW GUINEA

BOX 4820, UNIVERSITY POST OFFICE, PORT MORESBY

Telephone: 253900.

Founded 1965.

Language of instruction: English; State control; Academic year: February to November (two semesters).

Chancellor: ALKAN TOLOLO, O.B.E.

Pro-Chancellor: Miss ROSE KEKEDO, M.B.E., B.A.

Vice-Chancellor: RENAGI R. LOHIA, M.A.

Secretary: DAMIEN P. S. SARWABE, B.A.

Academic Registrar: D. P. P. SAMARASEKERA, B.A.

Librarian: A. C. BUTLER, B.A.

Number of teachers: 238.

Number of students: 1,682.

Publications: *Calendar*, *U.P.N.G. News* (quarterly), *Research Report*, *Handbook of Courses*, *Melanesian Law Journal*, *Yagl-Ambu*, *Science in New Guinea*, *Research in Melanesia*, *The University This Week*, departmental occasional papers.

DEANS:

Faculty o Agriculture: Prof. R. STEPHEN, PH.D.

Faculty of Arts: Prof. R. J. JACKSON, M.A., PH.D.

Faculty of Science: J. L. MUNRO, PH.D.

Faculty of Law: B. BRUNTON, LL.B.

Faculty of Education: J. M. WILSON, M.A.

Faculty of Medicine: P. PANGKATANA, D.M. & S., D.P.H.

PROFESSORS:

BIDDULPH, R. A. J., M.B., B.S., D.T.M. & H., M.R.C.P., Clinical Science
BROGAN, B., B.COM., Economics
BURACZEWSKI, A., PH.D.
COOK, G. C., M.D., D.SC., F.R.C.P., Clinical Science
DENOON, D. J. N., PH.D., History
DEUBERT, L. W., M.D.S., Dentistry
DROVER, D. P., PH.D., Chemistry
JACKSON, R. T., M.A., PH.D., Geography
LYNCH, J. D., PH.D., Language
O'COLLINS, E. M., D.S.W., Anthropology and Sociology
ROGERS, C. A., M.A., PH.D., Education
STEPHEN, R. C., PH.D., Agriculture
SWIFT, M. J., M.A., PH.D., Biology

PAPUA NEW GUINEA UNIVERSITY OF TECHNOLOGY

P.O.B. 793, LAE

Telephone: 42 4999.

Telex: UTECH NE 42428.

Founded 1965.

Language of instruction: English; State control; Academic year: February to November (two semesters).

Chancellor: A. TOLOLO, O.B.E.

Vice-Chancellor: A. P. MEAD, O.B.E., PH.D.

Deputy Vice-Chancellor: M. MORAMORO, B.TECH.(ACCOUNT.), B.COM.

Registrar: I. IRVING GASS, B.A.

Librarian: W. J. PLUMBE, F.L.A.

Library of 40,000 vols.

Number of teachers: 145.
Number of students: 1,200.

Publications: *Calendar*, *Reporter*, *Research Report*, *Handbook*.

HEADS OF DEPARTMENTS:

ANANTHAN, C. S., D.SC., Fisheries Technology
BALASUBRAMANIAM, E., PH.D., Applied Physics
BEALL, J., M.A.,PH.D., Accountancy and Business Studies
FUSSEY, D. E., PH.D., Mechanical Engineering
GREENWOOD, P., M.SC, Electrical and Communication Engineering
LYONS, K. J., PH.D., Surveying
JONES, P. L., PH.D., Mathematics
MORLEY, D. A., M.SC., PH.D., Civil Engineering
RICHARDSON, D., PH.D., Forestry
SMITHIES, M., M.A., Language and Social Science
STEWART, D. F., PH.D., Chemical Technology

Papua New Guinea Institute of Administration: P.O.B. 1216, Boroko; f. 1963; 190 staff, *c.* 700 students; library of 75,000 vols.; diploma and certificate studies in public and land administration, public finance and accountancy, local government, management, law, social development, library studies; short courses in law, communication skills, secretarial skills, public service procedures, auditing, human relations, financial management, project planning and control, clerical skills; courses are run at 4 centres; Principal SIMON KENEHE; publ. *Administration for Development*† (2 a year).

PARAGUAY

Population 2,887,000

ACADEMIES

Asunción

Academia Paraguaya (*Paraguayan Academy*): 14th in order of foundation in Spanish America; correspondent of the Real Academia Española, Madrid; publ. *Anales*.
Honorary President: JUAN E. O'LEARY.
President: LUIS DE GÁSPERI.
Vice-President: ANSELMO JOVER PERALTA.
Secretaries: LUIS A. LEZCANO, ROQUE GAONA.

Academia de la Lengua y Cultura Guarani: Calle España y Mompox; f. 1975; Pres. Dr. RUFINO AREVALO PARIS; Sec. ANTONIO E. GONZÁLEZ; publ. *Revista*.

LEARNED SOCIETIES AND RESEARCH INSTITUTES

Asunción

Asociación Indigenista del Paraguay: Calle España y Mompox, Casilla 1838; f. 1942; anthropology, development of indigenous communities; 130 mems.; library of 1,450 vols.; Pres. Gen. RAMÓN CÉSAR BEJARANO; Exec. Sec. BALBINO VARGAS ZÁRATE.

Centro Cultural Paraguayo-Americano: Avda. España 352; f. 1942; 8,139 vols. in library; Librarian MARÍA DEL CARMEN PÉREZ.

Centro de Estudios Antropológicos de la Universidad Católica: Casilla de Correo 1718; f. 1950, affiliated to Universidad Católica 1971; 25 mems.; Dir. ADRIANO IRALA BURGOS; Sec. FELICIANO PEÑA PÁEZ; publs. *Suplemento Antropológico, Universidad Católica*† (biannual).

Centro de Investigaciones de la Universidad Católica: Casilla de Correo 1718; f. 1974; Pres. JUAN OSCAR USHER.

Centro Paraguayo de Estudios de Desarrollo Económico y Social: Casilla 1189.

Centro Paraguayo de Ingenieros: Avda. España 959, Casilla 336; 609 mems.; Pres. Ing. RAMÓN BENITEZ CIOTTI; Sec. Ing. GUILLERMO F. SÁNCHEZ R.

Deutsch-Paraguayisches Kulturinstitut (*German-Paraguayan Culture Institute*): Rio Paraguay e/España y Juan de Zalazar; f. 1958; 200 mems.; library of 6,000 vols.

Instituto Geográfico Militar: Avda. Perú y Artigas; Dir. Gral. Brig. RUBEN ORTIZ P.; Sec. E. LOPEZ MOREIRA.

Instituto Nacional de Investigaciones Cientificas (*National Institute of Scientific Research*): P.O.B. 1141; physics, chemistry, mathematics, psychology and education.

Instituto Nacional de Parasitologia (*National Institute of Parasitology*): Instituto de Microbiología, Facultad de Medicina, Casilla Correo 1102; f. 1963; 5 mems.; library; Dir. Dr. ARQUIMEDES CANESE; publ. *Revista Paraguaya de Microbiología*† (annual).

Instituto de Numismática y Antigüedades del Paraguay: Calle 25 de Mayo 802 esquina Tacuarí; f. 1943; Pres. JUAN BAUTISTA GILL AGUÍNAGA; Vice-Pres. CARLOS ALBERTO PUSINERI SCALA.

Jardin Botánico y Museo de Historia Natural (*Botanical Gardens and Natural History Museum*): Residencia López, Trinidad; f. 1914; Dir. Ing. GILDO INSFRÁN GUERROS; herbarium, zoological garden and museum, bacteriological laboratory, agricultural experimental station; publ. *Revista*.

Servicio Técnico Interamericano de Co-operación Agricola: Casilla de Correo 819; f. 1943; 10,000 vols.; Librarian LUCILA M. I. CARDUS.

Sociedad Cientifica del Paraguay (*Paraguayan Scientific Society*): Avenida España 505; f. 1921; Pres. Dr. ANDRÉS BARBERO; Sec. G. TELL BERTONI; 80 mems.; publs. *Revista*, pamphlets.

Sociedad de Pediatria y Puericultura del Paraguay (*Paediatrics and Child Welfare Society*): 25 de Mayo y Tacuaí; f. 1928; 28 mems.; Pres. Dr. GUIDO RODRÍGUEZ ALCALÁ; Sec. Dr. GUSTAVO A. RIART; publ. *Revista Médica del Paraguay*.

Unión Sudamericana de Asociaciones de Ingenieros (USAI) (*South American Union of Engineers' Associations*): Head Office: Casilla de Correos, 336, Asunción; f. 1935; mem. countries: Argentina, Bolivia, Brazil, Chile, Colombia, Ecuador, Paraguay, Peru, Uruguay and Venezuela; Dir. and Pres. Ing. CARLOS ESPINOZA MACIEL; Sec. Ing. HERMANN BAUMANN.

LIBRARIES AND ARCHIVES

Asunción

Biblioteca y Archivo Nacionales: Mariscal Estigarriba 95; f. 1869; 44,000 vols.; Dir. Dr. H. SÁNCHEZ QUELL.

Government Libraries:

Biblioteca Pública del Ministerio de Defensa Nacional (*Public Library of Ministry of Defence*): Av. Mariscal López 1040; Dir. Col. MANUEL W. CHAVES.

Biblioteca y Archivo del Ministerio de Relaciones Exteriores (*Library of the Ministry of Foreign Affairs*).

Biblioteca Americana (*American Library*): Mariscal Estigarribia e Iturbe; attached to the Museo Nacional de Bellas Artes (*q.v.*).

Biblioteca de la Sociedad Cientifica del Paraguay (*Library of Paraguayan Scientific Society*): Avda. España 505; f. 1921; 29,300 vols. on science; publ. *Flora brasiliensis* by Martins, first edition.

MUSEUMS

Asunción

Casa de la Independencia: 14 de Mayo y Pte. Franco; f. 1965; historical museum of colonial period; Pres. Dr. FABIO RIVAS; Dir. CARLOS ALBERTO PUSINERI SCALA.

Colección Carlos Alberto Pusineri Scala: Hernandarias 1313; f. 1950; collections of Guaraní archacology, trophies of Paraguyan wars, colonial objects; small library of Paraguayan history, numismatics and anthropology; Dir. CARLOS ALBERTO PUSINERI SCALA.

Colección "Gill Aguinaga": Juan E. O'Leary 285; private collection of Juan Bautista Gill Aguínaga; numismatics, arms, archives, maps, photographs, periodicals.

Museo Nacional de Bellas Artes: Mariscal Estigarribia e Iturbe; f. 1887; the paintings and sculpture of Juan Silvano Godoy form the basis of the collection; Dir. JOSÉ LATERZA PARODI.

Museo de Cerámica y Bellas Artes "Julián de la Herreria": Estados Unidos 1120; f. 1938; ceramics by Herreria; other modern works by Paraguayan artists; Paraguayan folk art; library of 5,000 vols., 1,000 of which concerned with the arts, particularly ceramics; Founder and Dir. JOSEFINA PLÁ.

Museo Etnográfico "Andres Barbero": España 395; archaeology, ethnography, archives, manuscripts, books; Dir. BRANKA J. SUSNIK.

Museo Histórico Militar (*Museum of Military History*): Avda. Mariscal López 140; recent war collections; Dir. MANUEL WENCESLAO CHAVES.

Yaguarón

Museo Doctor Francia: f. 1968; relics of Paraguay's first dictator, "El Supremo"; Pres. Dr. FABIO RIVAS; Dir. Dr. JULIO CÉSAR CHAVES.

UNIVERSITIES AND COLLEGES

UNIVERSIDAD CATÓLICA "NUESTRA SEÑORA DE LA ASUNCIÓN"

INDEPENDENCIA NACIONAL Y COMUNEROS, ASUNCIÓN

Telephone: 41-044, 47-173 and 45-114.

Private control; Language of instruction: Spanish; Academic year: March to December.

Founded 1960.

Chancellor: Most Rev. Mgr. ISMAEL ROLÓN, Archbishop of Asunción.
Rector: Dr. JUAN OSCAR USHER.
Vice-Rector: Dr. RAMÓN JUSTE, S.J.
Secretary-General: Dr. ELIXENO AYALA.
Librarian: Lcda. MARGARITA KALLSEN.

Number of teachers: 434.
Number of students: 7,186.

Publications: *Suplemento Antropológico*†, *Estudios Paraguayos*†.

DEANS:

Faculty of Philosophy and Human Sciences: Lcda. VITALINA PÁEZ.

Faculty of Business Administration and Accounting: Lcdo. ALEJANDRO LEÓN NOÉ.

Faculty of Law ana Diplomatic Science: Dr. JERÓNIMO IRALA BURGOS.

Higher Institute of Theology and Religion: Dr. RAMÓN JUSTE, S.J.

PROVINCIAL FACULTIES:

Villa Rica

Faculty of Arts and Sciences: Ing. JOSÉ FÉLIX GONZÁLEZ.

Concepción

Faculty of Arts and Sciences: Lcdo. JOSÉ NEMESIO BOBADILLA.

Encarnación

Faculty of Arts and Sciences: R.P. Lcdo. PEDRO PABLO ROTTER.

Pedro Juan Caballero

Business Administration and Accounting: R.P. Lcdo. PEDRO SANABRIA.

UNIVERSIDAD NACIONAL DE ASUNCIÓN*

COLÓN 73, ASUNCIÓN

Telephone: 4056.

Founded 1890.

Rector: Prof. Dr. D. G. TORRES.
Secretary-General: Prof. Dr. G. B. BARRIENTOS.

Number of teachers: *c.* 500.
Number of students: *c.* 8,000.

DEANS:

Business Administration and Accounting: R.P. Lcdo. PEDRO SANABRIA.
Faculty of Medicine: Prof. Dr. R. F. OLMEDO.
Faculty of Physics and Mathematics: Prof. Ing. L. A. PALEARI.
Faculty of Economics: Prof. Dr. HERMÓGENES GONZÁLEZ MAYA.
Faculty of Odontology: Prof. Dr. EDUARDO RUIZ PERALTA.
Faculty of Chemistry and Pharmacy: Prof. Dr. JOSÉ DANILO PECCI.
Faculty of Philosophy: Prof. Dr. GLADYS S. LÓPEZ.
Faculty of Agriculture and Veterinary Medicine: Prof. Dr. E. RUIZ ALMADA.
Faculty of Architecture: Prof. E. NAPOUT.

* No reply received to our questionnaire this year.

Escuela Nacional de Agricultura "Mariscal Estigarriba": Ruta A, San Lorenzo, Asunción.

Escuela Superior de Filosofía, Ciencias y Educación: Calle Eligio Ayala 128, Asunción; f. 1944.

PERU

Population 16,820,000

ACADEMIES

Lima

Academia Peruana (*Peruvian Academy*): c/o Instituto Nacional de Cultura, P.O.B. 5247, Lima; the Peruvian Academy is 7th in order of foundation in Spanish America; correspondent of the Real Academia Española, Madrid; publ. *Revista*.

Director: (vacant).

Secretary: JOSÉ JIMÉNEZ BORJA.

Academia Nacional de Ciencias Exactas, Físicas y Naturales de Lima (*Lima Academy of Exact, Physical and Natural Sciences*): Casilla 1979; f. 1939; Pres. Dr. GODOFREDO GARCÍA; publ. *Actas*.

Academia Nacional de Medicina (*National Academy of Medicine*): Apdo. 987; f. 1884; 40 mems., 60 hon. mems., 6 corresp. mems.; Pres. Dr. OSWALDO HERCELLES; Perm. Sec. Dr. JORGE VOTO BERNALES; (for publ. *see* Sociedad Peruana de Historia de la Medicina).

Academia de Estomatología del Perú (*Peruvian Academy of Stomatology*): Apdo. 2467; f. 1929; Pres. Dr. HUGO ZEGARRA MANRIQUE; Sec. Dr. RAMÓN CASTILLO MERCADO; publ. *Revista* (monthly).

Academia Peruana de Cirugía: Camaná 773, Lima; f. 1940; activities relate to the development of surgery in Peru; national and foreign membership; 100 titular mems. and unlimited number of associates; Pres. Dr. VÍCTOR BARACCO; publ. *Revista de la Academia Peruana de Cirugía*.

LEARNED SOCIETIES

AGRICULTURE

Sociedad Nacional Agraria (*National Agricultural Society*): A. Miró Quesada 327-341, Lima, Apdo. 350; f. 1824; Pres. ALBERTO SACIO LEÓN; First Vice-Pres. PERCY BARCLAY; Second Vice-Pres. IGNACIO MASÍAS; Treas. CÉSAR TRAVERSO; Man. CARLOS DERTEANO U.; 50 Dirs., 14 Perm. Cttees. and 1 Arbitration Tribunal; cotton, sugar, grapes and wine, rice, seeds, potato products, other crops, stock farming, economics, coffee, plants; 107 Local Cttees., 9,258 mems.; publs. *Informativo Quincenal*, *La Hoja Agrícola* (bi-monthly), *Memoria Anual*.

ARCHITECTURE AND TOWN PLANNING

Colegio de Arquitectos del Perú: Avda. San Felipe 999, Jesús María, Lima; f. 1963; 486 mems.; Dir. HILDE SCHEUCH DE RODA; Sec. JOSÉ MATUTE PROAÑO.

ARTS

Asociación de Artistas Aficionados: Ica 323, Lima; f. 1938; Pres. ANTONIO TARNAWIECKI; 254 mems.; presentation of plays, classical ballet and varied music programmes.

Instituto de Arte Peruano (*Institute of Peruvian Art*): Alfonso Ugarte 650, Lima; under the control of Museo Nacional de la Cultura Peruana; Dir. ROSALÍA AVALOS DE MATOS.

Instituto Nacional de Cultura: Casilla 5247, Lima; f. 1965; official cultural institute; 14 brs.; Dir.-Gen. MARTHA HILDEBRANDT; publs. *Fénix*†, *Revista de Historia y Cultura*†, *Runa*†.

Instituto Peruano de Cultura Hispánica (*Peruvian Institute of Hispanic Culture*): Calle de la Riva 426, Lima; f. 1947; 280 mems.; Dir. PEDRO BENVENUTTO MURRIETA; publ. *Boletín*.

Instituto Peruana para la Promoción de la Cultura: Parque León García no. 163, Pueblo Libre, Lima 21; Pres. Dr. HANS ILLMANN LA ROSA.

BIBLIOGRAPHY AND LIBRARY SCIENCE

Asociación Peruana de Archiveros (*Peruvian Association of Archivists*): Archivo General de la Nación, Calle Manuel Cuadros s/n., Palacio de Justicia, Apdo. 3124, Lima.

Asociación Peruana de Bibliotecarios (*Peruvian Association of Librarians*): Apdo. 3760, Lima.

ECONOMICS, LAW AND POLITICS

Instituto de Investigaciones Económicas y Sociales: Pasaje San Luis no. 181, Oficina 303, Lince, Lima 14; Pres. ANDRÉS CHONG GENG.

Sociedad Peruana de Derecho Internacional: Jirón Lampa 879, Oficina 307, Lima.

EDUCATION

Consejo Nacional de la Universidad Peruana (*National Peruvian University Council*): Apdo. 4664, Calle Aldabas 3era, cdra. s/n, Surco, Lima 33; f. 1969; 33 mems.; library of 30,000 vols.; Pres. Dr. JUAN DE DIOS GUEVARA; Exec. Dir. Arq. SANTIAGO AGURTO CALVO; publ. *Cuadernos* (quarterly).

HISTORY, GEOGRAPHY AND ARCHAEOLOGY

Centro de Estudios Histórico-Militares del Perú (*Centre of Historico-Military Studies of Peru*): Paseo Colón 190, Lima 1; Dir. Dr. ALFONSO SOLÓRZANO ROJAS.

Centro de Investigación y Restauración de Bienes Monumentales del Instituto Nacional de Cultura: Jr. Ancash no. 769, Lima.

Instituto Geográfico Militar (*Military Geographical Institute*): Apdo. 2038, Lima; f. 1921; 259 mems.; library of 2,850 vols.; Dir.-Gen. JORGE LUNA SALINAS; publs. topographical, physical and political maps of Peru, *Boletín Informativo*.

Instituto Vizcardo de Estudios Históricos (*Vizcardan Institute of Historical Studies*): Porta 540, Miraflores, Lima; f. 1954; study of revolutionary movements for Spanish-American independence (1781-1820); Dir. CÉSAR GARCÍA ROSELL; publ. *Revista*.

Sociedad Geográfica de Lima (*Lima Geographical Society*): Jirón Puno 456, Apdo. 1176, Lima; f. 1888; library of 10,000 vols., also archives and museum; 500 mems., including corresp. and hon.; Dir. Dr. EMILIO ROMERO; publs. *Boletín, Anuario Geográfico del Perú, Bibliografía Geográfica y Oceanográfica del Perú, Bibliografía Amazonica, Enseñanza de Geografia del Perú, Diccionario Geográfico del Perú.*

INTERNATIONAL CULTURAL INSTITUTES

Alianza Francesa: Avda. Inca Garcilaso de la Vega 1550, Lima; 7 branches.

Asociación Cultural Peruano-Alemana (*Peruvian-German Cultural Association*): Jirón-Ica 426, Lima; Dir. G. HOCK.

Asociación Cultural Peruano-Británica (*Peruvian-British Cultural Association*): Camaná 787, Apdo. 1608, Lima; f. 1936; library (*see* Libraries); 550 mems.; Pres. Dr. ANTONIO PINILLA; Dir. J. LEIGH, M.A. The Association is a Peruvian organization established to strengthen cultural and educational links between Peru and Britain; over 11,000 students attend English classes and there is a regular cultural programme; publ. *Bulletin* (monthly).

British Council: Apdo. 11114, Edificio Pacífico-Washington Piso 11, Natalio Sanchez 125, Avda. Arequipa (Sexta cuadra), Lima; Rep. T. F. HIBBETT.

Instituto Cultural Peruano-Norteamericano (*Peruvian-North American Cultural Institute*): Jirón Cuzco 446, Apdo. 304, Lima; f. 1938; library of 12,000 vols.; 200 mems.; 7,000 students; publ. *Boletín.*

Instuto Italiano di Cultura (*Italian Cultural Institute*): Av. Arequipa 1075, Lima; f. 1934; library of 6,100 vols.; Dir. Dr. DONATO RIVIELLO.

LANGUAGE AND LITERATURE

Asociación Nacional de Escritores y Artistas (ANEA) (*Association of Writers and Artists*): Puno 421, Lima 1; f. 1938; 954 mems.; library of 7,461 vols.; Pres. Dr. ALBERTO TAURO.

International PEN Centre (*Centro del PEN Internacional*): Apdo. 1161, Lima; f. 1940; 25 mems.; Pres. Dr. JOSÉ GÁLVEZ; Sec. FERNANDO ROMERO.

MEDICINE

Asociación Médica Peruana "Daniel A. Carrión" (*Peruvian Medical Association*): Jirón Ucayali 218, Lima; f. 1920; 1,499 mems.; Dir. Dr. MAX ARNILLAS ARANA; Sec. Dr. MANUEL PAREDES MANRIQUE; publ. *Revista Médica Peruana.*

Comité Nacional de la Federación Dental Internacional (F.D.I.): Edificio Dall Orso, Plaza de San Martín 917, Lima; Sec. PEDRO AYLLÓN.

Consejo Peruano de la Federación Odontológica Latino-Americana (F.O.L.A.) (*Peruvian Council of Federation of Latin-American Dentists*): Edificio Dall Orso, Of. 208, Plaza de San Martín 917, Lima; Pres. Dr. PEDRO AYLLÓN.

Federación Médica Peruana (*Peruvian Medical Association*): Apdo. 4439, Lima; f. 1942; 1,230 mems.; Pres. Dr. VICENTE UBILLÚS; Sec. Dr. ENRIQUE FERNÁNDEZ V.; publ. *Boletín de la Federación Médica Peruana.*

Sociedad Peruana de Historia de la Medicina (*Peruvian Society of History of Medicine*): Apdo. 987, Lima; f. 1939; library and museum, primarily Peruvian collections; lectures and exhibitions of public interest; 80 mems., 30 hon. mems.; Pres. Dr. CARLOS E. PAZ SOLDÁN; Sec. Dr. J. B. LASTRES; publ. *Anales.*

Sociedad Peruana de Tisiología y Enfermedades Respiratorias (*Peruvian Phthisiological Society*): Domingo Casanova 116, Lince, Lima; f. 1935; 280 mems.; Pres. CARLOS MENDOZA EUWING; Sec. RUBEN PAZ ANSSUINI; publ. *Revista Peruana de Tuberculosis y Enfermedades Respiratorias*† (2 a year).

NATURAL SCIENCES

Biological Sciences

Sociedad Entomológica del Perú: Apdo. No. 4796, Lima; f. 1956; 600 mems.; library of *c.* 2,500 vols.; Pres. JUAN HERRERA A.; Sec. PEDRO G. AGUILAR F.; publs. *Revista Peruana de Entomología*† (annual).

Mathematics and Statistics

Oficina Nacional de Estadística (*National Institute of Statistics*): P.O.B. 2095, Av. 28 de Julio 1056, Lima; f. 1975; involved in population, housing, economic and agricultural censuses; plans statistical policy of country; library of 7,000 vols.; Dir. RAÚL GARCIA BELGRANO; publs. *Indice de precios al consumidor*† (monthly), *Indice de precios al por mayor*† (quarterly), *Cuentas Nacionales*† (annually), censuses, etc.

Physical Sciences

Asociación Peruana de Astronomía: Jirón Inclán no. 200, La Magdalena, Lima; f. 1946; Dir. Ing. VÍCTOR ESTREMADOYRO ROBLES.

Sociedad Geológica del Perú (*Peruvian Geological Society*): Apdo. 2559, Lima; f. 1924; library of 16,000 vols.; 600 mems.; Pres. Dr. FERNANDO ZÚÑIGA Y RIVERO; Librarian Ing. HUGO VALDIVIA; publ. *Boletín* (3 a year).

Sociedad Nacional de Minería: Plaza San Martín 917, Lima.

Sociedad Peruana de Espeleología (*Peruvian Speleological Society*): Porta 540, Miraflores, Lima; f. 1965; Pres. CÉSAR GARCÍA ROSELL; publ. *Cavernas Peruanas.*

Sociedad Química del Perú (*Peruvian Chemistry Society*): Apdo. 891, Lima; f. 1933; 600 mems.; library of 5,000 vols.; Pres. Dr. JUAN DE DIOS GUEVARA R.; Vice-Pres. Ing. MANUEL NIETO VELEZ; Sec.-Gen. LEONIDAS UNZUETA ROMERO; publ. *Boletín* (quarterly).

RELIGION, SOCIOLOGY AND ANTHROPOLOGY

Instituto de Estudios Etnológicos (*Institute of Ethnological Studies*)· Alfonso Ugarte 650, Lima; under auspices of Museo Nacional de la Cultura Peruana; Dir. ROSALÍA AVALOS DE MATOS.

Instituto de Estudios Islámicos: Calle Rey de Bahamonde 121, Vista Alegre, Surco, Lima 33; f. 1959; sound archives, numismatic collection, etc.; interests include economics, sociology and politics of contemporary Muslim world, the Palestinian problem and the diffusion of Islamic religious values in South America; special interest in Islamic-America relations in 16th and 17th centuries and nowadays; Pres. Dr. RAFAEL GUEVARA BAZÁN; Chief Officers Prof. ELVA ZEGARRA TORREBLANCA, Dr. ANTOLÍN BEDOYA VILLACORTA.

Instituto Indigenista Peruano (*Peruvian Institute of Indian Affairs*): Avenida Salaverry, 4° piso, Lima; f. 1947; Dir.-Gen. Dr. PELEGRÍN ROMÁN UNZVETA; Sec.-Gen. Dr. MANUEL D. VELASCO NUÑEZ; publs. *Perú-Indígena* (yearly), series of monographs (irregular).

TECHNOLOGY

Asociación de Ingenieros Civiles del Perú: Nicolás de Piérola No. 788, 4to Piso, Lima.

Asociación Electrotécnica Peruana: Avda. República de Chile No. 284, Oficina 201, Lima; f. 1943; Pres. Ing. JUAN ORELLANA ZÚNIGA.

Instituto Peruano de Ingenieros Mecánicos: Avda. República de Chile, No. 284, Of. 201, Lima; Dir. ROBERTO HEREDIA ZAVADA.

Sociedad de Ingenieros del Perú (*Society of Peruvian Engineers*): Av. N. de Piérola 788, Casilla 1314, Lima; library of 15,000 vols.; Sec. Ing. ADOLFO BUSTAMANTE T.; publ. *Ingeneria* (3 a year).

RESEARCH INSTITUTES

(*See* also under Universities)

Dirección General de Meteorología del Perú (*National Meteorological Service*): Avda. Arequipa 5200, Apdo. 1308, Miraflores, Lima; f. 1928; 79 primary stations; Dir.-Gen. Maj.-Gen. FAP ROLANDO GERVASI B.; National Co-ordinator Maj. FAP JACOB DEL MAR CORREA; Head of Forecasting Maj. FAP JUAN LUMBRERAS C.; Head of Operations Capt. FAP JACOB DEL MAR C.; Head of Climatology Capt. FAP HUGO GONZÁLEZ P.; publ. *Boletín* (annual).

Estación Experimental Agropecuaria de Tulumayo (*Tulumayo Agricultural Research Station*): Apdo. 78, Tingo María, Huánuco; f. 1942; under Dirección General de Investigaciones Agropecuarias, Ministerio de Agricultura y Alimentación; library of 400 vols.; technical staff of 6; Dir. Ing. MARCO A. NUREÑA SANGUINETTI; publs. *Informe Anual, Boletín Técnico, Boletín Extensión.*

Estación Altoandina de Biología y Reserva Zoo-Botánica de Checayani (*High Andean Biological Station and Zoo-Botanical Reserve of Checayani*): Checayani, Azángaro (Puno); f. 1953; owned and operated by the Macedo Ruiz family; biological research on the Higher Andes, especially Titicaca Basin and surrounding areas; animal and plant reserve of 5,000 hectares of land and a lake of 800 hectares; Dir. HERNANDO DE MACEDO; Sec. Mrs. GLORIA PINELO DE MACEDO; publ. *Folia Biológica Andina.*

Estación Experimental Agrícola del Norte (*Northern Agricultural Experimental Station*): Atahualpa No. 211, Lambayeque; f. 1927, reorganized 1941; Pres. POMPEY CONTRERAS MONTENEGRO.

Instituto Birchner-Benner: Schell 598, Miraflores, Lima; f. 1979; research into diet, especially of meat-substitutes and high-nutrition and low-cost food mixtures; library of 500 vols. and periodicals; film and sound archives; Pres. CÉSAR MORALES GARCÍA; Sec. NORMA VILLEGAS COZ.

Instituto de Biología Andina (*Institute of Andean Biology*): Apartado 5073, Lima; f. 1930; affiliated to the Faculty of Medicine, San Marcos Univ.; laboratories in Lima, Morococha and Puno; mobile laboratory research on physiology of inhabitants of the Andes and their resistance to high altitudes, acclimatization and fertility of animals taken to high altitudes with a view to industrial use, methods of hygiene, adaptive faculties of men at great heights, chronic mountain sickness and remedies, ecology and sociological problems; Dir. Dr. TULIO VELÁSQUEZ; publ. *Archivos de Biología Andina*† (quarterly).

Instituto de Ciencias de la Comunicación (*Institute of Communication Sciences*): Las Moreras 220, Urbanización Camacho, Ate, Lima 3; research into development of means of communication, especially in Latin America; problems of freedom of expression; improvements in national journalism; exchanges between journalists of different countries; library of 15,000 vols.; Pres. Ing. MARIO PAREDES CUEVA; Sec. Sta. PERPETUA CUEVA.

Instituto de Investigaciones Alérgicas (*Allergy Research Institute*): Avda. La Marina 2501, Maranga, San Miguel.

Instituto Experimental de Educación Primaria No. 1: Barranco Av. Miraflores No. 200, Lima; f. 1940; to study systems and methods for the development of learning and the means to evaluate and control the results; library of scholastic texts; Dir. Prof. NARCISO GONZÁLEZ CH.; publ. *Boletín.*

Instituto de Zoonosis e Investigación Pecuaria: Apdo. 1128, Lima; f. 1911; research into diseases transmissible from animals to man; 104 mems.; library of 6,542 vols.; Dir. Dr. CÉSAR LORA O.; publ. *Revista del Instituto de Zoonosis e Investigación Pecuaria.*

Instituto Geofísico del Perú (*Geophysical Institute*): Apdo. 3747, Lima; f. 1919 as Huancayo Magnetic Observatory of the Carnegie Institution of Washington, transferred to the Peruvian Government 1947; Education Sector within National Institute of Higher Learning; observatories in Huancayo, Jicamarca, Ancón, Talara, Lima; basic and mission-oriented research; international programmes especially in relation to the magnetic equator; Dir.-Gen. ALBERTO A. GIESECKE M.; publs. magnetic, ionospheric and meteorological data, seismological bulletin, miscellaneous geophysical reports, including cosmic-ray and sunspot work.

Instituto Geológico Minero y Metalurgico (*Institute of Geology, Mining and Metallurgy*): Apdo. 889, Pablo Bermudez 211, Lima; f. 1978 as result of merging Instituto Científico Tecnológico Minero and Instituto de Geología y Minería; 452 staff; carries out and co-ordinates research and evaluates mineral resources; library of 10,000 vols.; Dir. BENJAMIN MORALES ARNAO; publs. *Revistas, Boletín.*

Instituto del Mar del Perú (*Peruvian Marine Institute*): Esq. Gral. Valle y Gamarra, Callao, Apdo. 22; f. 1964; library of 65,000 vols.; Tech. Dir. FELIPE ANCIETA CALDERÓN; publs. *Informe*†, *Boletín*†, *Memoria Anual.*

Instituto Nacional de Investigación Agraria (*National Agricultural Research Institute*): Sinchi Roca 2728, Oficina 802, Lima 14; f. 1927; library of 40,000 vols.; Exec. Dir. Dr. JAVIER GAZZO FERNÁNDEZ DÁVILA; Technical staff 250; publs. *Revista de Investigación, Avances en Investigación, Serie de Boletín Técnico, Informes Especiales, Divulgaciones, Boletín de la Biblioteca.*

Instituto Nacional de Salud (*National Health Institute*): Capac Yupanqui 1400, Apdo. 451, Lima 1; f. 1955; Dir. Dr. O. MIRÓ-QUESADA CANTUARIAS.

Instituto Peruano de Energía Nuclear (*Peruvian Nuclear Energy Institute*): Av. Canadá 1470, Urb. Santa Catalina, Apdo. 1687, Lima; f. 1955; research into peaceful uses of nuclear energy in medicine, biology, agriculture and industry, and prospecting for radioactive materials; Pres. Brig. Gen. JUAN BARREDA DELGADO; Exec. Dir. Col. JOSÉ MALDONADO; delegates from Armed Forces, Ministries of Finance, Energy, Mines, Agriculture, Public Health and Peruvian Universities; library of 3,000 vols.; publ. *Boletín de Informaciones* (quarterly).

Instituto Peruano de Investigaciones Genealógicas (*Institute for Genealogical Research*): Santa Luisa 205, San Isidro, Lima; f. 1945; 45 mems.; Pres. JORGE FERNÁNDEZ STOLL; Sec.-Gen. and Treas. EMILIO OLIVARES VALLE-RIESTRA; publ. *Revista.*

Instituto Peruano para la Investigación de la Estadística: Calle Porta-170-Miraflores, Lima (18); Pres. Prof. ALFONSO SOLÓRZANO ROJAS.

Mission ORSTOM au Pérou—Coopération auprès du Ministerio de Energía y Minas: La Mariscala 115, San Isidro, Lima 27; f. 1967; geological research; 6 staff; library of 200 vols.; Dir. R. MAROCCO. (*See* main entry under France.)

LIBRARIES AND ARCHIVES

Lima

Archivo General de la Nación (*National Archives*): Palacio de Justicia, Calle Manuel Cuadros s/n., Apdo. 3124; f. 1861; three sections, Notarial-Judicial, Administrative and Historical; Dir. Dr. GUILLERMO DURAND FLOREZ; publs. *Revista del Archivo General de la Nación*† (2 a year), *Catálogo*†.

Biblioteca Nacional (*National Library*): Avda. Abancay, Apdo. 2335; f. 1821 by José de San Martín; possesses copies of the first printed works in Peru and the Americas; 661,232 vols., 171,381 MSS., 11,643 maps, 7,512 music scores, 7,564 photographs, 1,585,609 vols. of reviews and newspapers; Dir. MARÍA C. BONILLA DE GAVIRIA; publs. *Fénix*†, *Anuario Bibliográfico Peruano*†, *Boletín de la Biblioteca Nacional*†, *Gaceta Bibliotecaria del Perú*.

Biblioteca Central de la Pontificia Universidad Católica del Peru: Ciudad Universitaria-Final de la Av. Bolívar, s/n Fundo Pando, Apdos. 1761-5729; f. 1917; 130,000 vols.; Dir. CARMEN VILLANUEVA.

Biblioteca Central de la Universidad Nacional Mayor de San Marcos (*San Marcos National University General Library*): Apdo. 454; f. 16th century; the collection corresponding to the colonial period was incorporated in the *Biblioteca Pública*—now the *Biblioteca Nacional*—when the latter was founded in 1821; the Peruvian Section has valuable material on history, law, and literature; Dir. Dr. FRANCISCO VELASCO GALLO; 450,000 vols.; publ. *Boletín Bibliográfico* (annual).

Biblioteca Central del Ministerio de Educación Pública (*Central Library of the Ministry of Education*): f. 1957; 11,000 vols.; Librarian LUISA VERGARA.

Biblioteca de la Asociación Cultural Peruano-Británica: Av. Arequipa 3495, San Isidro; f. 1936; 14,000 vols.; Librarian CARMEN DE CASTRO.

Biblioteca de los Escritores del Perú (*Peruvian Writers' Library*): ANEA, Puno 421, Lima 1. f. 1938; 5,255 vols., 2,206 periodicals.

Biblioteca del Club Arequipa (*Arequipa Club Library*): Ejercicios 105-105A, Casilla 16; f. 1871; Dir. MIGUEL ANGEL CORNEJO CHÁVEZ; 7,500 vols.

Biblioteca del Ministerio de Relaciones Exteriores (*Library of the Ministry of Foreign Affairs*): Palacio Torre-Tagle; f. 1921; 12,351 vols.; Dir. MANUEL G. GALDO; publ. *Maris Aestus*.

Biblioteca de la Universidad Nacional de Ingeniería: Apdo. 1301; 29,000 vols.; Librarian JUANA PAREJA MARMANILLO.

Biblioteca Municipal de Lima: Apdo. 1232; f. 1935; 16,000 vols.; Librarian LUIS F. MÁLAGA.

Arequipa

Biblioteca de la Universidad Nacional de San Agustín: Apdo. 23; f. 1900; 33,247 vols., 1,204 pamphlets and 535 periodicals; in addition the University has 12 specialized libraries with a total of 93,761 vols.; Dir. Dr. ENRIQUE AZÁLGARA BALLÓN; publ. *Revista de Investigación de la Universidad*†.

Biblioteca Pública Municipal de Arequipa: Ejercicios No. 310, Apdo. 435; f. 1879; 28,000 vols.; Librarian ENRIQUE ALZÁGARA BALLÓN; also houses **Casa de la Cultura.**

Callao

Biblioteca de la Escuela Naval del Perú (*Naval School Library*): La Punta; f. 1914; Librarian ABEL ULLOA FERNÁNDEZ-PRADA; specialized library of 6,500 vols.

Biblioteca Pública Municipal Piloto: Esq. Ruiz y Colón; f. 1936, reorganized 1957; 48,312 vols.; 42 mems.; Dir. ROSA SÁNCHEZ DE WU.

MUSEUMS

Lima

Museo Arqueológico "Rafael Larco Herrera" (*Archaeological Museum*): Avenida Bolívar 1515, Pueblo Libre; f. 1926; library of 10,000 vols.; 37,000 exhibits of ceramics, 50,000 of gold, silver, copper, lead, wood, and stone objects, textiles, etc.; largest collection of Peruvian antiques in the world.

Museo de Arte (*Museum of Art*): Paseo Colón 125; inaugurated in its present form in 1961; 10,000 exhibits of Peruvian art from its origins to the present day; Pre-Colombian Department: ceramics, carvings, Paracas woven material dating from 400 B.C.; Colonial Department: furniture, sculpture, paintings, religious art; Modern Department: furniture and paintings from the 19th century to the present day; Conservation Laboratory for microchemical analysis and treatment of works of art; Dir. Dr. ALBERTO SANTIBAÑEZ SALCEDO.

Museo de Arte Italiano: Casilla 5247; f. 1921; a section of the Instituto Nacional de Cultura; statues, paintings; Curator ELIDA ROMÁN.

Museo de Historia Natural "Javier Prado" (*"Javier Prado" Natural History Museum*): Universidad Nacional Mayor de San Marcos, Av. Arenales 1256, Apdo. 1109; f. 1918; includes Herbario San Marcos, with 250,000 specimens largely of Peruvian Flora and departments of Zoology, Botany, and Geology; library of 5,000 vols.; Dir. Dr. RAMÓN FERREYRA H.; publs. *Serie "A" Zoología, Serie "B" Botánica, Serie "C" Geología, Memorias*.

Museo de la República (*Historical Museum*): Plaza Bolívar, Pueblo Libre, Lima 21; f. 1921; library of 4,500 vols.; Dir. MARÍA ROSTWOROWSKI DE DÍEZ CANSECO; publ. *Historia y Cultura*† (annually).

Museo del Virreinato (*Museum of the Viceroys*): Quinta de Presa; f. 1935; sited in an 18th-century mansion; exhibits relating to the period of the Spanish Viceroys; Dir. JOSÉ FLORES ARAOS; publ. *Revista*.

Museo Geológico de la Universidad Nacional de Ingeniería del Perú (*Geological Museum of the National University of Engineering*): Av. Tupac Amaru; f. 1891 as Museo de Yacimentos Minerales y Metalíferos de la Escuela Nacional de Ingenieros, name changed 1955; incorporates the Raymondi collections; Chief of Dept. of Geology JULIO DAVILA V.; publs. catalogues.

Museo Nacional de Antropología y Arqueología (*Anthropological and Archaeological Museum*): Plaza Bolívar s/n, Pueblo Libre; f. 1822; library of 20,000 vols.; collection contains pre-Inca and Inca remains; Dir. Dr. FEDERICO KAUFFMANN DOIG; publs. *Boletín del Museo Nacional de Antropología y Arqueología, Arqueológicas*.

Museo Nacional de la Cultura Peruana: Avda. Alfonso Ugarte 650, Apdo. 3048; f. 1946; responsible for Instituto de Estudios Etnológicos and the Instituto de Arte Peruano; also has an ethno-historical library and a photographic workshop; Dir. Dr. ROSALÍA AVALOS DE MATOS; publ. *Revista del Museo Nacional*.

Museo Postal y Filatélico Correo Central de Lima (*Postal and Philatelic Museum*): Conde Superunda no. 170; Dir. MARIA CONSUELO TICONA R.

Ancash

Museo Arqueológico de Ancash (*Archaeological Museum*): f. 1936; 3,100 exhibits including 400 stone carvings and megalithic statues from Huarás; Dir. Dr. AUGUSTO SORIANO INFANTE; publ. *Memoria*.

Arequipa

Museo Arqueológico (*Archaeological Museum*): Universidad San Agustín; ceramics, mummies; Dir. Dr. E. LINARES.

Ayacucho

Museo Histórico Regional de Ayacucho (*Regional Historical Museum of Ayacucho*): Jirón 28 de Julio no. 106; f. 1954; archaeology, anthropology, history and popular crafts; library of 4,724 vols. (including bound periodicals, etc.); Dir. CÉSAR O. PRADO; Curator TOBÍAS HUAMANCUSI GAMBOA; publ. *Anuario*.

Callao

Museo Histórico Militar del Peru (*Military History Museum*): Castillo del Real Felipe; fortress built under the Viceroys, unique in South America; museum f. 1946; collections date from 1730; Dir. OSCAR DIEZ VALDEZ.

Museo Naval del Peru "C. de N. Julio J. Elias M." (*Naval History Museum*): Av. Jorge Chávaz 126, Plaza Grau; f. 1958; specialist library of 4,598 vols.; Dir. JOSÉ C. COSIO; publ. *Fuentes para la Historia Naval*.

Cuzco

Museo Arqueológico: Calle Tigre 165; Dir. Dr. LUIS A. PARDO.

Museo Histórico Regional de Cuzco: Calle Heladeros, Casa Garcilaso de la Vega; f. 1946; Peruvian colonial art, Cuzco school; Dir. TEÓFILO BENAVENTE VELARDE; publ. *Revista del Museo Histórico Regional*.

Huancayo, Junín

Museo Arqueológico "Federico Gálvez Durand" de la Gran Unidad Escolar "Santa Isabel": Pichcus s/n; f. 1952; 1,654 archaeological specimens from Nazca and other Peruvian cultures; examples of weaving, gold and bronze ornaments, fossils.

Huánuco

Museo-Biblioteca "Leoncio Prado": 2 de Mayo y Tarapacá; f. 1945; Curator RICARDO E. FLORES.

Ica

Museo Histórico Regional de Ica (*Regional Museum*): Plaza de Armas; f. 1946; Dir. Dr. JAVIER CABRERA.

Lambayeque

Museo Regional Arqueológico "Bruning" de Lambayeque (*"Bruning" Archaeological Museum*): Calle 2 de Mayo 48; f. 1924; nearly 8,000 exhibits, of which 1,366 gold, 110 silver; textile, ceramic, wooden and stone pieces; two unique blue and black granite mortars incised with mythological figures in "Chavin" style; Dir. OSCAR FERNÁNDEZ DE CÓRDOVA.

Trujillo, La Libertad

Museo de Arqueología de la Universidad de Trujillo: Apdo. 299; f. 1946; Calle Bolívar 446; Dir. Dr. JORGE ZEVALLOS QUIÑONES; publ. *Chimor*.

UNIVERSITIES

UNIVERSIDAD NACIONAL AGRARIA

APDO. 456, LA MOLINA, LIMA

Telephone: 352035 and 352123.

Founded 1902; formerly Escuela Nacional de Agricultura.

Rector: Ing. MARIO ZAPATA TEJERINA.
Vice-Rector: Ing. GUILLERMO PARODI VERA.
Secretary-General: Dr. JOSÉ PAZ GARAY.
Head of Public Relations and Information: Prof. CLARA VERA LA ROSA.
Librarian: Ing. JUAN HERRERA ARANGUENA.

Number of teachers: 388.
Number of students: 3,510.

Publications: *Boletín Informativo* (weekly), *Anales Científicos*.

DIRECTORS OF ACADEMIC PROGRAMMES:

Agriculture: Dr. SVEN VILLAGARCÍA H.
Sciences: Dr. ALBERTO FUJIMORI.
Graduates: Dr. FAUSTO CISNEROS VERA.
Agricultural Engineering: Ing. CÉSAR BELLIDO PERALTA.
Food Science: Ing. JUAN HERRERA ROBLEDO.
Fisheries: Ing. JULIA ARAKAKI DE SHIRASAKA.
Zootechnics: Ing. ARTURO CARRASCO G.
Forestry: Ing. JORGE BUENO ZÁRATE.
Economics and Planning: Ing. WALTER FEGAN ESCOBAR.

UNIVERSIDAD NACIONAL AGRARIA DE LA SELVA

APDO. 156, TINGO MARÍA, HUÁNUCO

Telephone: 2341.

Founded 1964.

State control; Language of instruction: Spanish; Academic year: April to December.

Rector: Med. Vet. JUAN DE DIOS ZUÑIGA.
Vice-Rector: OSCAR CÉSARE GUERRA.
Administrative Officer: Ing. Agr. LUIS VÁSQUEZ QUIROZ.
Librarian: LUCY CHARBONNEAU DE GARCIA.

Number of teachers: 46.
Number of students: 650.

Publications: *Revista UNAS*†, *Divulgaciones Agropecuarias*†.

DIRECTORS OF ACADEMIC PROGRAMMES:

Agriculture: Ing. Agr. JOSÉ LOAYZA TORRES.
Animal Breeding: Ing. PEDRO CORDOVA ALVA.
Food Industries: Q. F. MANUEL LEÓN ORTEGA.

UNIVERSIDAD FEMENINA DEL SAGRADO CORAZÓN

AV. LOS FRUTALES S/N, MONTERRICO, APDO. 3604, LIMA

Telephone: 364641.

Founded 1962.

Private control; Language of instruction: Spanish; Academic year: April to December (two semesters).

Rector: R.M. Dra. RAQUEL CORRALES GÄTJENS.
Vice-Rector: Dr. JOSÉ ANTONIO BRAVO AMÉZAGA.
Administrative Director: Dra. DORA RAMÍREZ FEBRES.
Librarian: Sra. MARÍA LA SERNA DE MAS.

Library of 22,000 vols.

Number of teachers: 180.
Number of students: 1,050.

Publications: *La Unifé Informa*, *Cuaderno de Psicología*.

DIRECTORS OF ACADEMIC PROGRAMMES:

Architecture: Arq. CÉSAR DÍAZ GONSÁLEZ.
Education: Dra. MARGARITA GUERRA MARTINIERE.
Nursery Education: Dra. OTILIA LOAYZA ATHÓ.

Teacher Training: Dra. LUZ MARÍA ALVAREZ CALDERÓN.
Psychology: Dr. JOSÉ CUNY SALAZAR.
Sociology: Dr. EDUARDO ZARAUZ VELÁSQUEZ.
Translation and Interpretation: Dra. AÍDA JIMÉNEZ DE HORACEK.
Specialization in Mental Retardation: Dra. FRIEDDA FERNÁNDEZ BRAVO.
General Studies: Dr. ADRÍCO VÍA ORTEGA.

UNIVERSIDAD "INCA GARCILASO DE LA VEGA"*

AVDA. AREQUIPA 3610, LIMA
Telephone: 220924.
Founded 1964.
Private control.

Rector: Dr. AMPARO SALINAS RODRÍGUEZ.
Registrar: ALFREDO TEJADA LAPOINT.
Librarian: NANCY HARMAN DE ALVARADO.

Number of teachers: *c.* 240.
Number of students: *c.* 7,000.
Publication: *Garcilaso.*

DIRECTORS:

Academic Programme of General Studies: MARGARITA ARNAO DE MACGREGOR.
Academic Programme of Education: VICENTE GONZALEZ MONTOLIVO.
Academic Programme of Economics and Accountancy: EMILIO ROMERO PADILLA.
Academic Programme of Administration: GUILLERMO HASEMBANK ARMAS.
Academic Programme of Social Science: ARNALDO CANO JAUREGUI.

* No reply received to our questionnaire this year.

UNIVERSIDAD DE LIMA

PROLONGACIÓN JAVIER PRADO S/N. MONTERRICO, APDO. 852, LIMA
Telephone: 350677.
Founded 1963.
Private control.

Rector: Dra. ILSE WISOTZKI LOLI.
Vice-Rector: R.P. HAROLD GRIFFITHS ESCARDÓ.
Secretary-General: Dr. ANTONINO ESPINOSA LAÑA.
Librarian: NANCY LIZÁRRAGA CANO.

Number of teachers: 334.
Number of students: 6,500.

DIRECTORS OF ACADEMIC PROGRAMMES:

Educational Administration: Dra. AMELIA PACHECO VÁSQUEZ.
Communication Sciences: Dr. DESIDERIO BLANCO LÓPEZ.
Administration: Lic. CARLOS FREUNDT CRUZ.
Accountancy: C.P.C. CARLOS ALVAREZ RAMÍREZ.
Economics: Dr. JOSÉ A. ENCINAS DEL PANDO.
General Studies: Dr. FERNANDO S. SANTISTEBAN BERNAL.
Industrial Engineering: Ing. JUAN J. IBARRA PANIZO.
Systems Engineering: Dr. ENRIQUE ANDERSON ROSAS.
Metallurgical Engineering: Ing. ENRIQUE MONGE GORDILLO.

UNIVERSIDAD NACIONAL DE LA AMAZONÍA PERUANA

APDO. 496, IQUITOS
Telephone: 235351.
Founded 1962.

State control; Language of instruction: Spanish; Academic year: April to February (two terms).

Rector: Ing. GUILLERMO CETRARO DE SOUZA (acting).
Librarian: JOSEFINA RODRÍGUEZ BARTET.

Number of teachers: 164.
Number of students: 3,274.
Publication: *Conocimiento.*

DIRECTORS:

Department of Education and Humanities: Dra. NELLY MERCAU LÓPEZ.
Department of Sciences: Ing. SEGUNDO PASCUAL CAMACHO.
Department of Agronomy: Ing. WALTER A. VÁSQUEZ RIBEYRO.
Department of Forestry: Ing. CÉSAR ZALAZAR NOVOA.
Department of Chemistry: ANA MARÍA LY SÁNCHEZ.

UNIVERSIDAD NACIONAL DEL CENTRO DEL PERÚ

CALLE REAL 160, APDO. 138, HUANCAYO
Telephone: 233032.
Founded 1962.

State control; Language of instruction: Spanish; Academic year: April to December (two terms).

Rector: Ing. CARLOS CARVO BALTAZAR.
Vice-Rector: Dr. JOAQUÍN CHIVÍLCHEZ CHÁVEZ.
Librarian: PEDRO VILLANUEVA LIZÁRRAGA.

Number of teachers: 279.
Number of students: 6,161.

Publications: *Boletín Informativo*† (monthly), *Proceso*† (irregular), *Anales Científicos*†, *Cuadernos Científicos* (irregular).

DIRECTORS OF ACADEMIC PROGRAMMES:

Agronomy: Ing. RAÚL BERRIOS MORATILLO.
Forestry: Ing. FABIO GUTARRA MORENO.
Zootechnics: Ing. ROBERTO BERROSPI MÉNDEZ.
Economic and Administrative Sciences: Lic. JESÚS FIGUEROA BARDALES.
Social Sciences: Lic. JUAN RONDÁN SÁNCHEZ.
Nursing and Social Services: Enf. SHERIN KREDERDT ARAUJO.
Architecture: GUSTAVO RAMÍREZ PIZÁ.
Electronics and Mechanics: Ing. MANUEL REYES CORTEZ.
Chemistry, Metallurgy and Mining: Ing. GUSTAVO ROMERO GÁLVEZ.
Education: Prof. JUAN PIZARRO CÓRDOVA.

UNIVERSIDAD NACIONAL "DANIEL ALCIDES CARRIÓN"*

CALLE LIMA 323, APARTADO 77, CERRO DE PASCO
Telephone: 120.
Founded 1965.

Rector: Ing. ANÍBAL CAMPOS SUELDO.

Number of teachers: *c.* 90.
Number of students: *c.* 1,000.

Faculties of economics, education, mining and metallurgy.

* No reply received to our questionnaire this year.

UNIVERSIDAD NACIONAL DE EDUCACIÓN "ENRIQUE GUZMAN Y VALLE"

LA CANTUTA S/N, CHOSICA, LIMA
Telephone: 910052.
Founded 1967.

State control; Language of instruction: Spanish.

Rector: Ing. HUGO PACHECO GARMENDIA.
Vice-Rector: CARLOS SANTANDER GARCÍA.
General Secretary: Dr. JAIME ROSADO BEJARANO.
Registrar: Dra. CLOTILDE ALBARRACÍN DE NOVOA.
Librarian: Dr. ENRIQUE ADOLFO MOYA SAAVEDRA.

Library of 15,076 vols.
Number of teachers: 58.
Number of students: 4,200.
Publication: *Cantuta.*

UNIVERSIDAD NACIONAL DE HUÁNUCO "HERMILIO VALDIZÁN"

JR. DOS DE MAYO 680, APARTADO 278, HUÁNUCO
Telephone: 2340, 2341.
Founded 1964.

State control; Language of instruction: Spanish; Academic year: May to February (2 semesters).

Rector: Ing. Agr. MIRKO CUCULIZA TORRE.
Vice-Rector: Prof. JOSÉ LIZÁRRAGA VELASCO.
Head of Administration: HONORATA GÓMEZ DE CAVERO.
Librarian: ILEANA RÍOS EGOÁVIL.

Library of 6,521 vols.
Number of teachers: 135.
Number of students: 5,545.

Publications: *Cuadernos de Investigación*†, *Boletines Informativos*, *Visita de la Provincia de León de Huánuco en 1562—Iñigo Ortiz de Zúñiga, visitador—Vols. I and II*†.

DEANS:

Economic and Commercial Sciences: ENCARNACIÓN FLORES PÉREZ.
Agronomy: Ing. Agr. LUIS A. GODOY LA ROSA.
Education: Prof. TEODORICO AMPUDIA ZARZOSA.
Nursing and Obstetrics: Enf. MAFALDA DÍAZ JAVE.
Civil Engineering: Ing. V. BESADA FERNÁNDEZ.
Industrial Engineering: Ing. GUILLERMO GARNICA TOHALINO.

UNIVERSIDAD NACIONAL "FEDERICO VILLARREAL"

AVDA. NICOLÁS PIÉROLA 412, APDO. 1518, 6049, LIMA
Telephone: 287882-320806.
Founded 1963.

State control; Language of instruction: Spanish.

Rector: JUSTO ENRIQUE DEBARBIERI RIOJAS.
Vice-Rector: Dr. ORESTES RODRÍGUEZ CAMPOS.
General Secretary: Dr. VÍCTOR TANTALEÁN VANINI.
Librarian: Dr. PERCY MURILLO GARAYCOCHEA.

Number of teachers: 1,386.
Number of students: 22,000.

Publications: *La Memoria Anual del Rector*, *Revista Villarreal*, *Boletines Informativos*.

DIRECTORS OF PROGRAMMES:

Education and Humanities: Dr. EUGENIO CHANG CRUZ.
Law and Political Sciences: Dr. LUIS ALARCÓN QUINTANA.
Social Sciences: Lic. JOSÉ PÉREZ DEL AGUILA.
Administrative Sciences: Lic. JUAN ARCE FERNÁNDEZ.
Economics: Econ. ALBERTO LINA CÁMERO.
Accountancy: C. P. C. ENRIQUE HERMOZA ZEVALLOS.
Architecture and Town Planning: Arq. MANUEL UNGARO ZEVALLOS.
Odontology: Dr. JORGE FERNÁNDEZ ÑIQUE.
Oceanography and Fisheries: Ing. HUMBERTO ALFARO HERNÁNDEZ.
Human Medicine: Dr. CARLOS G. MORALES STIGLICH.
Medical Technology: Dr. SANTIAGO CARRANZA VARAS.
Geographical Engineering: Dr. EFRAÍN ORBEGOZO RODRÍGUEZ.
Co-operativism: Dr. JUAN CASTILLO MORALES.
Psychology: Dr. JAVIER SOTOMAYOR URQUIZO.
Civil Engineering: Ing. CARLOS LARREA CROVETTO.
Industrial Engineering: Ing. RODOLFO VELARDE PALOMINO.
Graduate Programme: Dr. PEDRO ALMORA CAMPOS.

UNIVERSIDAD NACIONAL DE INGENIERÍA (National University of Engineering)

CASILLA 1301, LIMA
Telephone: 811035-811070.

Founded 1896 as Escuela Nacional de Ingenieros del Perú, present name 1955.

State control; Language of instruction: Spanish; Academic year: April to December.

Rector: Ing. JORGE CABRERA TAPIA.
Vice-Rector (Academic): ALEJANDRO SÁNCHEZ OLANO.
Vice-Rector (Administration): ANTONIO MORENO ESPINOZA.
Secretary-General: Dr. LUIS REYES CARRASCO.

Library: *see* Libraries.
Number of teachers: 800.
Number of students: 10,431.

Publications: *Boletín "Quilca"*, *Revista Técnico "Tecnia"*, *Revista Artes y Ciencias "Amaru"*.

DIRECTORS OF ACADEMIC PROGRAMMES:

Architecture, Town Planning and Fine Arts: Arq. VÍCTOR SMIRNOFF BRACAMONTE.
Science: Dr. GERARDO RAMOS CABREDO.
Economics: Dr. HUGO RIVERA LÓPEZ.
Civil Engineering: Ing. ALEJANDRO SÁNCHEZ OLANO.
Geological, Mining and Metallurgical Engineering: Ing. FERNANDO WADSWORTH M.
Industrial and Systems Engineering: Ing. JUAN NUÑEZ RONDÓN.
Petroleum and Petrochemical Engineering: Ing. JUAN RODRÍGUEZ DEL CASTILLO.
Chemical and Manufacturing Engineering: Ing. LUIS MACCHIAVELLO FERRERO.
Sanitary Engineering: Ing. ENRIQUE JIMENO BLASCO.

UNIVERSIDAD NACIONAL "JOSÉ FAUSTINO SÁNCHEZ CARRIÓN"

AV. GRAU 592, OF. 301, APDO. 81, HUACHO
Telephone: 2437.
Founded 1968.

President: BALDOMERO CACERES SANTA MARIA.
Chief Administrator: OSCAR VACCARI HORGOUT.
Librarian: JULIA DEL PRADO MORALES.

Library of 5,000 vols.
Number of teachers: 97.
Number of students: 2,675.

DIRECTORS:

Fisheries: CECILIO E. ALVINO ROSSEL.
Administration and Accountancy: JORGE I. CASTILLO MONTERO.
Industrial Engineering: ROGER CENTENO ROBLES.
Nutrition: DANIEL VALENZUELA SAN MARTIN.
Sociology: CIRO SOLIS ESPINOZA.

UNIVERSIDAD NACIONAL PEDRO RUIZ GALLO

8 DE OCTUBRE 637, APDO. 48, LAMBAYEQUE
Telephone: 2134 and 2080.
Founded 1970.

State control; Language of instruction: Spanish.

President: DEMETRIO CARRANZA LAVADO, I.A., M.SC.
Vice-President: AUGUSTO DELGADO VÉLEZ, I.A.
Librarian: Dr. GUILLERMO BACA AGUINAGA.

Number of teachers: 261.
Number of students: 5,460.

DIRECTORS OF ACADEMIC PROGRAMMES:

Agriculture: Ing. MANUEL ECHEANDIA NAVARRO.
Biology: LEOPOLDO VÁSQUEZ NUÑEZ.
Accounting: Ing. MANUEL CARBAJAL CHUMIOQUE.
Law: Dr. JORGE ANGULO IBERICO.
Nursing: ALICIA I. DE VEGA.
Agricultural Engineering: Ing. ERIC LÓPEZ ÑAÑEZ.
Civil Engineering: Ing. HUMBERTO OLORTE VILLAREAL.
Veterinary Medicine: Dr. JULIO RAMOS BARRENECHEA.
Sociology: Prof. AMÉRICO HERRERA CALDERÓN.
Zootechnics: Ing. JOSÉ MORALES ABANTO.

UNIVERSIDAD NACIONAL MAYOR DE SAN MARCOS DE LIMA

CIUDAD UNIVERSITARIA, LA PUNTA, CALLAO
Telephone: 314629, 313271, 316700.
Founded 1551.

Rector: Dr. JUAN DE DIOS GUEVARA ROMERO.
General Secretary: Dr. JOSÉ TARAZONA CAMACHO.
Librarian: Dr. FRANCISCO VELASCO GALLO.

Number of teachers: 2,394.
Number of students: 22,260.

Publications: *Boletín Informativo, Boletín Bibliográfico, Revista de San Marcos*, etc.

Directors of Academic Programmes:

Mathematics and Physics: Dr. José Ampuero Aguayo.
Chemistry and Chemical Engineering: Dr. César A. Díaz Tassara.
Geology and Geography: Ing. Guillermo Morales Serrano.
Biology: Dr. Fortunato Blancas Sánchez.
Pharmacy and Biochemistry: Dr. Jack Harrison Thiel.
Veterinary Science: Dr. Quiterio Núñez Miranda.
Medicine: Dr. Aurelio Díaz Ufano.
Dentistry: Dr. Jorge Díaz Cuadros.
Social Science: Dr. Aníbal Ismodes C.
Law and Political Science: Dr. René-boggio Amat y León.
Philosophy, Psychology and Art: Dr. José Russo Delgado.
Linguistics, Literature and Philology: Dr. Washington Delgado Tresierra.
Education: Dr. José Flores Barboza.
Administrative Science and Accountancy: Dr. Justo Franco Falcón.
Economics: Dr. Raúl García Lara.
Engineering: Dr. Emilio Isla Cruzado.
Metallurgy: Dra. Gladys Yong Olazábal de Banchero.
Physical Education: Dr. Juan Petrlick Atoche.
Perfection: Dr. Meilach Burstein Pait.

Attached Institutes:

IVITA: Carretera Panamericana Sur, Km. 5½, San Luis, Lima.

Instituto de Biología Andina: Hospital Loayaza, Lima.

Instituto de Medicina Tropical: Ciudad Universitaria, Lima.

Centro de Investigación de Recursos Naturales: Jirón Puno 1002, Lima.

Instituto de Patología: Hospital Loayza, Lima.

Instituto de Zootécnica: Carretera Panamericana Sur, Km. 5½, Lima.

Instituto de Bioquímica y Nutrición: Jirón Puno 1002, Lima.

Instituto de Derecho de Trabajo y de la Seguridad Social: Ciudad Universitaria, Lima.

UNIVERSIDAD NACIONAL DE SAN AGUSTÍN*

SIGLO XX 227,
APDO. 23, AREQUIPA
Telephone: 9864.
Founded 1828.

State control; Language of instruction: Spanish.

Rector: Dr. Manuel Zevallos Vera.
Vice-Rector: Dr. Félix Náquira Vildoso.
Secretary: Dr. Manuel Zevallos Vera.
Librarian: Dr. Enrique Azálgara Ballón.

Library of *c.* 127,000 vols.
Number of teachers: *c.* 480.
Number of students: *c.* 10,900.

Publications: *Humanitas, Revista de la Facultad de Derecho, Revista de la Facultad de Ciencias Económicas, Revista de la Facultad de Educación, Boletín del Instituto Geofísico de Characato* (all annual).

Directors:

Academic Programme of Law: Dr. Jesus Rodríguez González.
Academic Programme of Humanities: Jorge Cornejo Polar.
Academic Programme of Biology: José Calienes Rodríguez.
Academic Programme of Education: Dr. Gerardo Peralta Narrea.
Academic Programme of Social Sciences: Dr. Mario Sotillo Humire.
Academic Programme of Medicine: Dr. José Gutiérrez Correa.
Academic Programme of Geology: Dr. Rómulo Cerdeña Aguirre.
Academic Programme of Chemistry: Elizalde Ortiz Torrello.
Academic Programme of Economics and Accountancy: Dr. Pedro S. Delgado.
Academic Programme of Architecture: René Uría Arrisueño.
Academic Programme of General Studies: Dr. Eduardo Gómez Becerra.

* No reply received to our questionnaire this year.

UNIVERSIDAD NACIONAL DE SAN ANTONIO ABAD

AVDA. DE LA CULTURA S/N.,
APDO. 367, CUZCO
Telephone: 2440-41.
Founded 1962; reorganized 1969.

Rector: Dr. Hugo Pacheco Garmendia.
Secretary-General: Dr. Arturo Félix P.
Librarian: Dr. Arturo Félix Pimentel.

Number of professors: 425.
Number of students: 15,000.

Publication: *Revista Universitaria* (annually).

Directors:

Academic Programme of Law: Dr. Enrique Holgado Valer.
Academic Programme of Letters: Dr Carlos E. Bárcena Cruz.
Academic Programme of Biology: Ing. Horacio Zamalloa Díaz.
Academic Programme of Physics and Mathematics: Ing. Hugo Macedo Díaz.
Academic Programme of Education: Dr. Segundo Villasante Ortíz.
Academic Programme of Economics and Accountancy: Jorge Aguirre Villalobos.
Academic Programme of Chemistry: Ing. Orestes Villafuerte Romero.
Academic Programme of Civil Engineering and Architecture: Ing. Carlos Gómez Palza.
Academic Programme of Agronomy: Ing. Carlos Chacón Galindo.
Academic Programme of Anthropology: Dr. Flores Ochoa.

UNIVERSIDAD NACIONAL DE SAN CRISTÓBAL DE HUAMANGA

APDO. 220, AYACUCHO
Telephone: 2522.
Founded 1677; reopened 1959.

State control; Language of instruction: Spanish; Academic year: 10 months.

Rector: Ing. Enrique Moya Bendezu.
Vice-Rector: Dr. Victor Díaz León.
Secretary-General: Dr. Enrique Bustamante Cristobal.
Librarian: Herminia Flores Paitán.

Number of professors: 416.
Number of students: 7,209.

Publications: *Boletín de Estadistica* (yearly), *Universidad* (monthly).

Directors of Academic Programmes:

Education: Zenón Naveda Almonacid (acting).
Biology: Prof. Luis Oblitas Quispe.
Nursing and Obstetrics: Esperanza Ruiz Florian.
Agronomy: Ing. César Ruiz Canales.
Mining: Ing. Guillermo Munar Calderón.
Chemical Engineering: Ing. César Granados Rafael.
Social Sciences: Prof. Jaime Rivera Palomino.
Economics and Administration: Ing. Antonio Díaz Martínez.
Law and Political Sciences: Dr. Oscar Vidal García.

Heads of Departments:

Agriculture and Zootechnics: Ing. Edgardo Ramirez Gonzalez.
Biology: Orlando Escalante Riva.
Historical and Social Sciences: Dr. Lorenzo Huertas Vallejos.
Engineering: Ing. Vidal Fernández Sulca.
Education and Humanities: Prof. Zenon Naveda Almonacid.
Languages and Literature: Prof. Víctor Tenorio García.
Medicine: Prof. Alejandro Gonzáles.
Mathematics and Physics: Ing. Gerardo Valeriano Povis.
Economics, Accountancy and Administration: Prof. Winston Villene Peñares.
Law: Dr. Carlos Velarde Alvarez.

UNIVERSIDAD NACIONAL "SAN LUIS GONZAGA"*

APDO. 106, BOLÍVAR 232, ICA

Telephone: 2437 and 2868.

Founded 1961.

Rector: Dr. MANASÉS OCAMPO RÍOS.
Secretary-General: Dr. MIGUEL CALDERÓN REINA.

Number of teachers: 459.
Number of students: 6,295.

Academic Programmes in Agronomy, Economic and Social Sciences, Law, Arts and Education, Pharmacy and Biochemistry, Dentistry, Civil Engineering, Mechanical Engineering and Electricity, Medicine, Veterinary Medicine, Fisheries and Biological Sciences.

Publications: *Letras y Educación, Educación Dental.*

*No reply received to our questionnaire this year.

UNIVERSIDAD NACIONAL DE TRUJILLO

DIEGO DE ALMAGRO 396, APDO. 315, TRUJILLO

Telephone: 24-3721, 23-2961

Founded 1824 by Simón Bolívar.

State control; Language of instruction: Spanish; Academic year: April to December.

Rector: Ing. HÉCTOR LUJÁN PERALTA.
Vice-Rector: Dr. RAMÓN BOCANEGRA CARRASCO.
Librarian: SEGUNDO HELÍ ALVA VIGO.

Library of 23,806 volumes, 36,001 periodicals and pamphlets.

Number of teachers: 553.
Number of students: 8,721.

Publications: *Memoria Rectoral*†, *Boletín del Servicio de Información*†, *Revista de Derecho*†, *Lenguaje y Ciencia*†, *Libri-UNT*†.

UNIVERSITY DIRECTORS:

Planning: Dr. GUILLERMO GUERRA CRUZ.
Research: Dr. ANTENOR GUERRA MARTÍNEZ.
Community Projection: Dra. ELIA ALVAREZ DEL VILLAR.
Academic Services: Dr. ORLANDO HERNÁNDEZ DÍAZ.
Economic and Administrative Services: Dr. JUAN CÁCERES OLÓRTEGUI.
Student Welfare: Dr. JULIO VÁSQUEZ VARGAS.
Personnel: Dr. FLORENCIO MIXAN MASS.

DIRECTORS OF ACADEMIC PROGRAMMES:

Law and Political Sciences: Dr. EFRAÍN ZEGARRA SÁNCHEZ.
Educational Sciences: Dr. EDUARDO GALLARDO GARCÍA.
Economic and Commercial Sciences: Prof. CÉSAR LIZA ORTÍZ.
Medical Sciences: Dr. JORGE CÁRDENAS ARÉVALO.
Engineering: Ing. LUIS SÁNCHEZ VASQUEZ.
Biological Sciences: Dr. ALFONSO VILLANUEVA VÁSQUEZ.
Physical and Mathematical Sciences: Prof. JUAN GARCÍA CRIBILLEROS.
Pharmacy and Biochemistry: Dr. ROBERTO TANTALEÁN RAMELLA.
Social Sciences: Dr. VÍCTOR RODRÍGUEZ SUY-SUY.

UNIVERSIDAD NACIONAL TÉCNICA DE CAJAMARCA

APDO. 289, CAJAMARCA

Telephone: 2559.

Founded 1962.

State control; Academic year: March to December (two semesters).

Rector: Ing. MARIANO CARRANZA ZAVALETA.
Vice-Rector: Ing. ORALIO CÓRDOVA QUIROGA.
General Secretary: NICOLÁS ROBLES ESPICHÁN.
Librarian: Prof. LUIS RONCAL ALCÁNTARA.

Number of teachers: 90.
Number of students: 1,561.

Publications: *Gaceta Universitaria, Revista de la U.N.T.C.*

DIRECTORS:

Education: Dr. CARLOS AVILA ALZAMORA.
Agronomy: Ing. LUIS DUARTE BLASHKA.
Civil Engineering: Ing. JAIME DÍAZ ALIAGA.
Nursing: Dr. JORGE SÁNCHEZ SILVA.
Veterinary Medicine: Dr. ELIO DELGADO.

UNIVERSIDAD NACIONAL TÉCNICA DEL ALTIPLANO

CALLE PUNO 415, CASILLA 291, PUNO

Telephone: 324.

Founded 1865, Reopened 1961

State control; Language of instruction: Spanish; Academic year: April to December (two semesters).

Rector: Dr. JULIO BUSTINZA MENÉNDEZ.
Vice-Rector: Dr. VÍCTOR SOTOMAYOR PEREZ.
Administrative Director: Dr. AUGUSTO MATUSITA RIOS.
Librarian: Dr. ANARCO VALENCIA.

Number of teachers: 250.
Number of students: 6,500.

Publications: *Revista de la Universidad* (annually), *Boletines Técnicos.*

UNIVERSIDAD DEL PACÍFICO

AVDA. SALAVERRY 2020, JESÚS MARÍA, LIMA 11, APARTADO 4683

Telephone: 71-2277.

Founded 1962.

Private control; Academic year: April to March.

Rector: J ESTUARDO MARROU LOAYZA.
Secretary: JOSÉ JAVIER PÉREZ RODRÍGUEZ.
Librarian: RICARDO ARBULÚ VARGAS.

Number of professors: 90.

Number of students: 1,100 full-time, 700 part-time.

Publications: *Apuntes*†, *Estudios Andinos*†.

DIRECTORS:

Academic Programme of Accounting and Business: ALEJANDRO LAVALLE.
Academic Programme of Economics: JÜRGEN SCHULDT.
Graduate Academic Programme of Business Administration: RAIMUNDO VILLAGRASA NOVOA.

HEADS OF DEPARTMENTS:

Accounting and Business: GREGORIO LEONG.
Economics: JOSÉ QUIÑONES.
Mathematics: FERNANDO BONIFAZ.
Humanities: CÉSAR PACHECO.
Social Sciences: BRUNO PODESTÁ.
Research Institute: Dir. LUIS BUSTAMANTE.

UNIVERSIDAD NACIONAL DE PIURA

CALLE APURÍMAC 461, APDO. 295, PIURA

Telephone: 32-3091.

Founded 1962.

State control; Language of instruction: Spanish.

Rector: Dr. BENJAMÍN FERNÁNDEZ DÁVILA OLIVERA.
Vice-Rector: Dr. VÍCTOR AGUILAR RONCAL.
Secretary-General: JORGE F. MONROY GÁLVEZ.
Librarian: Ing. HUMBERTO LAM PASTOR.

Number of teachers: 244.
Number of students: 5,414.

Publications: *Boletín de la DUPS*† (monthly), *La Gaceta*† (fortnightly), *Boletín Informativo.*

DIRECTORS:

Accountancy and Business Administration: LUIS GINOCCHIO ZAPATA.
Agronomy and Animal Husbandry: Ing. NORVIL MERA RAFAEL.
Economics: LUIS GUEVARA SAAVEDRA.
Fisheries Engineering: FREDDY ZÚÑIGA VARILLAS.

Industrial and Mining Engineering: Ing. HERBERT ECHENIQUE BALCÁZAR.

PROFESSORS:

Faculty of Accounting and Business Administration:
AGUILAR, V. R., Business Administration in the Agricultural Sector
CASTRO, J. P., Auditing and Management Accountancy
CUEVA, A. Q., Banking Accountancy
GALLARDO, W. L., Accounting Systems and Methodology, Accountancy in the Fishing and Livestock Industries
GINOCCHIO, L. Z., Company Accounts, Budget Preparation
HUIMAN, V. S., Professional Accounting Practices
LAVALLE, R. C., Analysis and Interpretation of Statements of Account, Mining Accounting, Financial Administration
LI WONG, P., Cost Accounting
PASTOR, A. P., Business Organization and Administration, Marketing

Faculty of Agronomy and Phytology:
MONTESINOS, A. V., Olericulture
NIEVES, R. C., Phytology, Cotton Cultivation
RAMOS, R. P., Cultivation of Tropical Fruits

Faculty of Biological Sciences:
CARDOZA, M. H., Biology, Biochemistry
DIAZ DE JUAREZ, M., Microbiology
MORALES, A. A., Plant Physiology, Botany
PEREYRA, C. C., Genetics
ZÚÑIGA, F. V., Ecology

Faculty of Chemistry and Mines:
CASTRO, V. C., Chemistry
FARIAS, F. A., Chemistry
SAMANUD, P. A., Unitary Operations

Faculty of Crop Maintenance:
DELGADO, M. J., Phytopathology
MASIAS, O. Y., Disease Control
VIÑAS, L. V., Insect Breeding and Evaluation

Faculty of Economics:
AGURTO, H. P., Economic Analysis, Econometrics
CASAVERDE, G. Z., Microeconomics, Demography
CHUECAS, E. V., Economics, Economic Analysis
DAVIES, A. G., International Trade
GUEVARA, L. S., General Accountancy
JUAREZ, F. T., Agricultural and Livestock Economics
TAFUR, H. B., Fiscal Policy, Preparation and Assessment of Estimates

Faculty of Fisheries Engineering:
MOGOLLON, M. L., Fisheries Infrastructure and Fish Processing
NAÑEZ, E. A., Fishing Methods and Equipment
TIMOTEO, S. C., Physical Geography and Marine Geology

Faculty of General and Physical Engineering:
BARRANTES, O. C., Geometry, Technical Drawing
BARRON, G. F., Mechanics
CARDENAS, C. B., Technical Drawing
CASTILLO, R. G., Materials Resistance, Rural Construction
CORONADO, H. N., Geometry, Technical Drawing
JOO CHANG, A., Meteorology and Climatology
LAM, H. P., Principles of Irrigation
SADOWSKY, M. S., Electrical Engineering

Faculty of Mathematics:
CARRASCO, R. S., Advanced Mathematics
CESPEDES, S. L., Linear Algebra, Mathematical Analysis
HUAMANCHUMO, J. M., Mathematical Analysis
PAUCAR, J. V., Mathematics, Mathematical Analysis

Faculty of Statistics and Computing:
BENITES, V. C., Experimental Design, Heat Measurement
CHUNGA, P. P., Applied Statistics, Linear Models
YENGLE, C. R., Practical Research, Computer Programming

UNIVERSIDAD PARTICULAR "SAN MARTÍN DE PORRES"

JR. CAMANÁ 168, LIMA

Telephone: 237821.

Founded 1965.

Rector: Dr. LUIS A. MELGAR VASQUEZ.

Number of teachers: 256.
Number of students: 9,850.

UNIVERSIDAD PARTICULAR PERUANA "CAYETANO HEREDIA"*

CALLE HONORIO DELGADO 932, KM. 3.5, PANAMERICANA NORTE, CARRETERA ANCÓN, APDO. 5045, LIMA

Telephone: 815772-815401.

Founded 1961.

Rector: Dr. A. CAZORLA-TALLERI.
Vice-Rector: Dr. OSCAR SOTO.
Director of Academic Programme of Medicine: Dr. ALBERTADO HURTADO.
Secretary-General: Dr. EDUARDO PÉREZ ARANÍBAR.

Number of teachers: 636.
Number of students: 803.

The university comprises a Premedical School, Medical School, High Altitude Research Institute and Postgraduate School and is particularly interested in promoting research into national medical problems.

* No reply received to our questionnaire this year.

UNIVERSIDAD PARTICULAR "VICTOR ANDRES BELAUNDE"

JR. 28 DE JULIO 106A, APDO. 48, AYACUCHO

Telephone: 251.

Founded 1967.

President: Dr. MARINO MONTENEGRO CASTRO.
Librarian: RANULFO PEÑA MONGE.

Library of 4,000 vols.
Number of teachers: 61.
Number of students: 1,600.

DEANS:

Academic Programme of Law: Dr. ORLANDO PÉREZ CORONADO.
Academic Programme of Education: Prof. ALFREDO PRADO PRADO.
Academic Programme of Economic Sciences: Prof. CARLOS RAFFO TOLEDO.

PONTIFICIA UNIVERSIDAD CATÓLICA DEL PERÚ

FUNDO PANDO, APDO. POSTAL 1761 Y 5729, LIMA 100

Telephone: 62-25-40.

Founded 1917.

Private control; Language of instruction: Spanish; Academic year: March to January (two terms).

Rector: Dr. JOSÉ TOLA PASQUEL.
Secretary-General: Dr. ALBERTO VARILLAS MONTENEGRO.
Registrar: ANGELITA BASSO.
Librarian: CARMEN VILLANUEVA.

Library of 140,000 vols.
Number of teachers: 700.
Number of students: 7,300.

Publications: *Revista* (2 a year), *Histórica, Lexis, Medios, Boletín del Departamento de Ciencias, Debates, Derecho* (annual), *Boletín del Instituto Riva-Aguero* (annual).

DIRECTORS:

Academic Programme of Science and Engineering: Ing. FERNANDO GIUFFRA.
Academic Programme of Law: Dr. FERNANDO DE TRAZEGNIES.
Academic Programme of Administrative Sciences: JOSÉ CABRERA.
Academic Programme of Social Sciences: Dr. ROLANDO AMES C.
Academic Programme of Letters and Humanities: Dr. JOSÉ ANTONIO DEL BUSTO D.
Academic Programme of Social Work: CLEMENCIA SARMIENTO.
Academic Programme of General Studies:
Sciences: Dra. LIUDMILA CHAINSKAIA.
Letters: Dr. PEDRO RODRÍGUEZ.
Graduate School: Ing. MÁXIMO VEGA CENTENO B.
School of Fine Arts: Prof. ADOLFO WINTERNITZ.
School of Social Work in Trujillo: Dr. SEGUNDO CARBAJAL.
Languages Centre: Dra. IRMA ALCÁZAR.
Tele-education Centre: Prof. OSCAR MAVILA M.

ATTACHED RESEARCH INSTITUTES:

Instituto Riva-Agüero: Dir. Dr. JOSÉ A. DE LA PUENTE.

Instituto de Investigaciones Jurídicas: Dir. Dr. HÉCTOR CORNEJO CHÁVEZ.

UNIVERSIDAD PARTICULAR RICARDO PALMA*

AVENIDA ARMENDARIZ 349, MIRAFLORES, LIMA

Telephone: 459035.

Founded 1969.

Private control.

Rector: Dr. EDMUNDO GUILLÉN GUILLÉN.

Number of teachers: 228.
Number of students: 6,996.

* No reply received to our questionnaire this year.

UNIVERSIDAD CATÓLICA DE SANTA MARIA

AVDA. SANTA CATALINA 410, CASILLA 1350, AREQUIPA

Telephone: 9474.

Founded 1961.

President: Dr. FRANCISCO CHIRINOS SOTO.
Vice-President: Dr. EUSEBIO CARDEÑA RIVERA.
Secretary-General: Dr. RAMIRO VALDIVIA CANO.

Number of teachers: 264.
Number of students: 5,572.

DIRECTORS OF ACADEMIC PROGRAMMES:

Social Communications: Dr. JORGE LLERENA VALDIVIA.
Accounting: Dr. LEÓN GUILLÉN CALDERÓN.
Law: Dr. ALBERTO HEREDIA MÁRQUEZ.
Education: Dr. AMADOR ROJAS SARMIENTO.
Economics and Business Management: Dr. OSCAR LANCHIPA QUINTANILLA.
Nursing: Sra. DOMINGA VARGAS DE FLORES.
Dentistry: Dr. DILLMAN GALLEGOS CÁRDENAS.
Social Service: Sra. SILVIA MATUK DE LA TORRE.

UNIVERSIDAD NACIONAL TÉCNICA DEL CALLAO

APDO. 138, CALLAO

Telephone: 296607-295921.

Founded 1966.

State control; Language of instruction: Spanish; Academic year: January to December (two terms).

Rector: Ing. JORGE ARROYO PRADO.
Vice-Rector: MÁXIMO DA FIENO VELIT.
Registrar: ISAÍAS CARRASCO MOLINA.
Librarian: ROSALÍA QUIROZ PAPA.

Number of teachers: 252.
Number of students: 6,600.

Publications: *Memoria Anual del Rector, Planes Actuales de Funcionamiento, Boletines Informativos, Suplementos.*

DEANS:

Academic Programme of Chemical Engineering: Ing. ALFONSO QUISPE CÓRDOVA.
Academic Programme of Economics: JESÚS COLLAZOS CERRÓN.
Academic Programme of Electrical Engineering: Ing. NICANOR NINAHUAMÁN MUCHA.
Academic Programme of Fisheries Engineering: SISINIO MORALES ZAPATA.
Academic Programme of Mechanical Engineering: Ing. ALBERTO HEREDIA ZAVALA.

UNIVERSIDAD NACIONAL TECNICA DE PIURA*

CALLE TACNA 620, PIURA

Telephone: 2129-3859.

Founded 1962.

Rector: Ing. MAXIMO URBINA GUTIERREZ.

Schools of Agronomy and Economics.

Number of teachers: 101.
Number of students: 902.

* No reply received to our questionnaire this year.

COLLEGES

ESCUELA DE ADMINISTRACIÓN DE NEGOCIOS PARA GRADUADOS (Graduate School of Business)

APDO. 1846, LIMA 100

Telephone: 351760.

Founded 1963, as a joint venture between the Peruvian Government and the U.S. Department of State Agency for International Development.

Academic Director: KONRAD FISCHER ROSSI.
Dean: LANDER PACORA COUPEN.

Library of 28,000 vols.
Number of teachers: 25.
Number of students: 2,500.

Publications: *Bibliography and Publications of the Documentation Center;* working papers of the Research Department.

Escuela Nacional de Bibliotecarios (*National School of Librarianship*): Av. Abancay 4A Cuadra, Apdo. 2335, Lima; f. 1943; 40 teachers; 70 students; library of 1,609 vols.; Dir. MARÍA BONILLA DE GAVIRIA; Dir. of Studies TERESA SILVA SANTISTEBAN.

Instituto Superior de Administración y Tecnología: Av. Arequipa 173, Lima; f. 1905; 65 teachers, 976 students; library of 4,800 vols.; Dir. ARISTIDES VEGA N.; Registrar Prof. ALBERTO LÓPEZ; publ. *ISAT en Marcha.*

SCHOOLS OF ART AND MUSIC

Conservatorio Nacional de Música (*National Academy of Music*): Emancipación 180, Apdo. 2957, Lima; f. 1908 as Academia Nacional de Música "Alcedo", present name 1946, autonomous since 1966; 715 students; specialized library *c.* 8,000 vols., and record library; choir and orchestra; Dir. CARLOS SÁNCHEZ MÁLAGA; Sec. ROBERTO CARPIO VALDÉS.

AFFILIATED INSTITUTES:

Escuela Regional de Música de Arequipa: Dir. AURELIO DÍAZ.

Escuela Regional de Música de Ayacucho: Dir. CÉSAR BEDOYA.

Escuela Regional de Música del Cuzco: Dir. JORGE DELGADO.

Escuela Regional de Música de Huanuco: Dir. JAIME DÍAZ.

Escuela Regional de Música de Piura: Dir. ERNESTO LÓPEZ MINDREAU.

Escuela Regional de Música de Trujillo: Dir. ULISES CALDERÓN.

Escuela de Artes Plásticas de la Universidad Católica: Apdo. 1761, Lima; f. 1939; Dir. ADOLFO WINTERNITZ.

Escuela Nacional Superior de Bellas Artes (*National School of Fine Arts*): Ancash 681, Lima; f. 1918; to train artists and teachers; Library of over 4,500 vols. on art; Dir. JUAN MANUEL UGARTE ELÉSPUPU; publ. *Anuario Académico.*

Escuela Regional de Bellas Artes: Puente Bolognesi 104, Arequipa.

Escuela Regional de Bellas Artes: "Diego Quispe Tito": Cuzco.

REPUBLIC OF THE PHILIPPINES

Population 46,351,000

ACADEMY

Academia Filipina (*Philippine Academy*): Apdo. Postal 1522, Manila; the Philippine Academy is 11th in order of foundation of the corresponding academies of the Real Academia Española, Madrid. *President:* EMETERIO BARCELÓN Y BARCELÓ-SORIANO; *Secretary:* ENRIQUE FERNANDEZ LUMBA.

MEMBERS:

JOSÉ MARIA DELGADO (*Vice-President*)
MANUEL I. ABELLA
FERNANDO DE LA CONCEPCIÓN
Rev. ANGEL HIDALGO
MIGUEL CUENCO
SABINO PADILLA (*Librarian*)
BENITO VALDÉS VACCANI (*Treasurer*)
FRANCISCO ZARAGOZA (*Censor*)
GLORIA ZÓBEL DE PADILLA
Rev. FIDEL VILLAROEL

LEARNED SOCIETIES

AGRICULTURE AND VETERINARY SCIENCE

Crop Science Society of the Philippines: Agronomy Dept., UPLB, College, Laguna; f. 1970; *c.* 300 mems.; Pres. JORGE G. DAVIDE; Vice-Pres. TEODORICO R. ESCOBER.

Philippine Association of Agriculturists: 692 San Andres, Malate, Manila; f. 1946; 178 mems.; Pres. ANTONIO S. DIMALANTA; Vice-Pres. JESÚS M. BONDOC; Sec. PATERNO N. ALCUDAI.

Philippine Veterinary Medical Association: c/o College of Veterinary Medicine, University of the Philippines, Diliman, Quezon City; f. 1914; 1,200 mems.; Pres. Dr. ROLENDIO A. RODEROS; Sec. Dr. ZENAIDA G. CRUZ.

Society for the Advancement of Research: University of the Philippines, Los Baños College, Laguna; f. 1930; 157 life mems., 192 full mems., 168 assoc. mems.; Pres. VICENTE G. MOMONGAN; Sec. DELFINA M. TORRETA.

Society for the Advancement of the Vegetable Industry (SAVI): University of the Philippines at Los Baños College, Laguna; f. 1967; Pres. ERNESTO C. OLIFERNES; Exec. Sec. EMMA S. DATA; publ. *Proceedings of Annual Meeting*†.

ARCHITECTURE

Philippine Institute of Architects: P.O.B. 350, Manila; f. 1933; 405 mems.; Pres. MANUEL T. MAÑOSA, Jr.; Vice-Pres. G. A. DE LEON; Sec. M. P. ANGELES, Jr.

THE ARTS

Art Association of the Philippines: National Museum, Old Legislative Bldg., Manila; f. 1948; Pres. ALLAN V. COSIO; Sec. EDGAR FERNANDEZ.

BIBLIOGRAPHY AND LIBRARY SCIENCE

Association of Special Libraries in the Philippines (ASLP): College of Public Administration Library, University of the Philippines, P.O.B. 474, Manila D-406; f. 1954; 300 mems.; Pres. FILOMENA C. MERCADO; Sec. EDNA P. ORTIZ; publs. *ASLP Bulletin* (quarterly), *Directory of Special Library Resources and Facilities*, *ASLP Newsletter* (irregular).

Philippine Library Association Inc.: c/o San Beda College Library, Mendiola St., Manila 2804; f. 1923; 1,009 mems.; Pres. CANDIDA C. AGCAOILI; Sec. HERMOGENA LL. CARPIO.

ECONOMICS

Philippine Economic Society: P.O.B. 1764, Manila; f. 1961; 350 mems.; Pres. MAHAR K. MANGAHAS; Sec.-Treas. CESAR P. MACUJA; publ. *Philippine Economic Journal* (quarterly).

EDUCATION

Institute of Philippine Culture: Ateneo de Manila University, Loyola Heights, Quezon City, P.O.B. 154, Manila; f. 1960 as a university research organization to study aspects of rural and urban poverty, social change and socio-economic development, women's status and research methodology; 40–100 mems. depending on projects; library of 1,339 books, 1,869 reprints and vertical file, data bank; Dir. Dr. RICARDO G. ABAD; publs. *IPC Papers*† (irregular), *IPC Monograph Series*†, *IPC Reprints*†, *IPC Final Reports*.

HISTORY, GEOGRAPHY AND ARCHAEOLOGY

Institute of History: c/o University of Santo Tomás, España St., Manila.

Philippine Historical Association: c/o University of the East, Sampaloc, Manila; f. 1955; 500 mems.; Pres. Prof. DIOSDADO G. CAPINO; Exec. Dir. Prof. JORGE L. REVILLA; publ. *PHA Bulletin*† (quarterly).

Philippine Numismatic and Antiquarian Society: 1340 España Blvd., Manila; f. 1929; 102 mems.; Pres. M. MANAHAN; Sec. C. CIRIACO; publ. *Monographs*.

INTERNATIONAL CULTURAL INSTITUTES

Asia Foundation, The: P.O.B. 3588, Manila; one of 10 branches of the main organization in the U.S.A. (*q.v.*); Rep. EDITH S. COLIVER.

British Council: 7 3rd St., New Manila, Quezon City; Rep. I. R. JOHNSON.

Goethe Institut: 687 Aurora Blvd., Metro Manila, P.O.B. 2883, Manila; f. 1961; library of 5,900 vols.; Dir. Dr. G. BRETZLER; publ. *Monthly Calendar of Events*.

International Communication Agency: Thomas Jefferson Cultural Center, 12 Gregorio Araneta Blvd., Manila; f. 1946; 25,000 mems.; library of 20,000 vols. and 300 American periodicals; also at SSS Bldg., Cebu City, Cebu; f. 1947; 20,000 mems.; library of 8,000 vols. and 50 periodicals; Claro M. Recto Ave., Davao City, Mindanao; f. 1966; 5,000 mems.; library of 3,500 vols. and 25 periodicals.

MEDICINE

Colegio Médico-Farmacéutico de Filipinas, Inc.: c/o Food and Drug Administration, Dept. of Health, Quezon City; f. 1899, incorporated 1911; Pres. Dr. P. TANINGCO; Sec.-Treas. Prof. E. D. ESPINOSA.

Manila Medical Society: 1201 Florida St., Manila; f. 1902; 1,249 mems.; Pres. Dr. EDGARDO T. CAMPARAS; Sec.-Treas. Dr. ERLINDA T. NOVALES.

Medical Research Foundation of the Philippines, Inc.: Singian Memorial Hospital, 998 Gral. Selano, San

Miguel, Manila; f. 1963; promotes and subsidizes research in medical and natural sciences; Chair. DON MANOLO ELIZALDE; Vice-Chair. and Pres. Dr. A. P. CAÑIZA.

Philippine Association of Nutrition, Inc.: c/o Food and Nutrition Research Institute, Pedro Gil St., Ermita, Manila; f. 1947; 500 professional, 600 assoc. mems.; Pres. Dr. TRINIDAD A. GOMEZ; publ. *Philippine Journal of Nutrition* (quarterly).

Philippine Medical Association: P.M.A. House, North Ave., Diliman, Quezon City; f. 1903; 90 component societies, 49 affiliated speciality societies; Pres. Dr. JAIME F. LAYA; Sec. Dr. VICENTE J. A. ROSALES; publs. *Journal*, *PMA News*.

Philippine Paediatric Society, Inc.: P.O.B. 3527, Manila; f. 1947; 620 mems.; Pres. EUSTACIA M. RIGOR, M.D.; Sec. MIGUEL NOCHE, Jr., M.D.; publ. *Philippine Journal of Paediatrics* (bi-monthly).

Philippine Pharmaceutical Association: 10th Floor, Cardinal Bldg., corner Herran and F. Agoncillo Streets, Ermita, Manila; f. and incorporated 1920; 47 brs.; 4,300 mems.; Pres. Mrs. LOURDES TALAG ECHAUZ, Sr.; Sec. Dr. ELVIRA F. SILVA; Treas. Mrs. PURIFICACIÓN SUACO; publ. *Journal*.

Philippine Society of Parasitology: Institute of Public Health, University of the Philippines, 625 Pedro Gil, Ermita, Manila; f. 1930; 416 mems.; Pres. ANGELINA A. LATONIO; Sec.-Treas. FRANCISCO S. SY.

NATURAL SCIENCES

Los Baños Biological Club: College, Laguna; f. 1923; Pres. EDGARDO C. QUISUMBING; Sec. IRINEO DOMINGO.

Philippine Council of Chemists: 1572-F San Marcelino St., Paco, P.O.B. 1202, Manila; f. 1958; 500 mems.; Nat. Pres. MIGUEL G. AMPIL; Gen. Sec. and Treas. SHIRLEY E. NESSIA; publ. *Bulletin*.

PHILOSOPHY

Philosophical Association of the Philippines: P.O.B. 3797, Manila; f. 1973; 150 mems.; Pres. Dr. RAMON REYES; Exec. Dir. Prof. JORBE L. REVILLA; publ. *Philippine Journal of Philosophy* (annual).

TECHNOLOGY

Philippine Association of Mechanical and Electrical Engineers (PAMEE): P.O.B. 416, Manila; f. 1930; 879 mems.; Pres. PETE MA. CARINO; Sec. DAMASO C. TRIA.

Philippine Society of Civil Engineers: c/o Bureau of Public Works, Bonifacio Drive, Manila; f. 1918; assumed present title 1933; Pres. FLORENCIO MORENO; Sec.-Treas. TOMAS DE GUZMÁN; publ. *The Philippine Engineering Record* (quarterly).

Philippine Society of Mining, Metallurgical, and Geological Engineers: P.O.B. 1595, Manila; f. 1940; 117 mems.; Pres. JONES R. CASTRO; Sec.-Treas. LEOPOLDO F. ABAD.

RESEARCH INSTITUTES

(*see* also under Universities)

National Research Council of the Philippines: University of the Philippines, Diliman, Quezon City; f. 1934.

Chairman and Member-at-Large: Dr. JUAN SALCEDO, Jr.

Vice-Chairman and Member-at-Large: Eng. MANUEL I. FELIZARDO.

Executive Secretary and Senior Director: Dr. PATROCINIO VALENZUELA.

Assistant Executive Secretary: Dr. ALFREDO C. SANTOS.

Treasurer: Prof. ARTURO ALCARAZ.

National Science Development Board: P.O.B. 3596, Manila; government agency; board consists of Ministers of Education and Culture, National Economic and Development Authority, Industry, Energy, the President of the University of the Philippines, and 2 mems. from the private sector representing the fields of agriculture, industry, technology, education and community development; Chair. Minister MELECIO S. MAGNO; Exec. Dir. Hon. SEGUNDO V. ROXAS; Sec. Atty. AMALIA F. DY; publs. *NSDB Technology Journal*, *Philippine Science Journal*, *Philippine Abstracts*, *Philippine Science Index*.

AFFILIATED GOVERNMENT INSTITUTES:

National Institute of Science and Technology

Philippine Inventors Commission

Forest Products Research and Industries Development Commission

Philippine Textile Research Institute

Commission on Volcanology

Food and Nutrition Research Institute

ATTACHED AGENCIES:

Philippine Science High School

Science Foundation of the Philippines

National Research Council of the Philippines

Philippine Council for Agriculture and Resources Research

National Academy of Science and Technology

National Institute of Science and Technology: 727 Pedro Gil St. (P.O.B. 774), Manila; Commissioner Dr. VEDASTO R. JOSÉ.

Biological Research Center: Dr. QUINTIN L. KINTANAR.

Microbiological Research Department: Prof. ROMEO V. ALICBUSAN.

Medical Research Department: FELICIDAD E. ANZALDO.

Agricultural Research Department: CRESENCIO MOLINYAWE.

Industrial Research Center: Dr. NOEL BALITACTAC.

Ceramics Research Department: GUILLERMINA C. MAÑALAC.

Chemical Research Department: VIOLETA P. ARIDA.

Engineering Research Department: RODULFO P. GARCES.

Food Technology Research Department: OLYMPIA N. GONZALES.

Tests and Standards Division: JOSE P. PLANAS.

Scientific Instrumentation Division: EDGARDO JUAN.

Division of Information and Documentation: ROSARIO B. DE CASTRO.

Planning and Programming Division: ALBERTO S. PESIGAN.

Administrative Division: PRIMO M. GATPANDAN.

Bureau of Mines and Geosciences: P.O.B. 1595, Taft, Pedro Gil St., Manila; f. 1936; administers the utilization of the country's mineral wealth; conducts geological and mineral surveys, and evaluates mineral deposits; geological and metallurgical research; library of 10,000 vols.; Dir. JUANITO C. FERNÁNDEZ.

Bureau of Plant Industry: Ministry of Agriculture, Manila; f. 1930; research, regulation and crop protection; library of 10,000 vols.; Dir. DOMINGO F. PANGANIBAN; publ. *Philippine Journal of Plant Industry*†.

Forest Products Research and Industries Development Commission (FORPRIDECOM): College, Laguna; f. 1957 to investigate wood properties, improve processes, and to develop wood uses and lengthen useful life of wood products; Commissioner FRANCISCO N. TAMOLANG; library of 4,000 vols.; publs. *Forpride Digest* (quarterly), *FORPRIDECOM Technical Note* (monthly series).

Philippine Atomic Energy Commission: Don Mariano Marcos Ave., Diliman, Quezon City; f. 1958; library of 3,535 vols.; Commissioner LIBRADO D. IBE; publs. *Philippines Nuclear Journal* (2 a year), *Atomedia* (annually), *Philippine Atomic Bulletin* (every 2 months).

Philippine Atomic Research Center: Dir. ZOILO M. BARTOLOME.

Southeast Asian Ministers of Education Organization (SEAMEO) Regional Center for Educational Innovation and Technology (INNOTECH): 3rd Floor, College of Education Bldg., University of the Philippines, Diliman, Quezon City; f. 1970; identifies basic educational problems common to the Southeast Asian region and assists the SEAMEO member countries in the solution of these problems; conducts training and research programmes; 13 professional staff; library of 3,674 vols.; Dir. Dr. LICERIA BRILLANTES SORIANO; publs. *INNOTECH Newsletter*† (every 2 months), *INNOTECH Journal*† (2 a year).

LIBRARIES

Ateneo de Manila University Libraries: P.O.B. 154, Manila; libraries at Loyola Heights Campus and Makati Campus; 148,335 vols. collegiate and graduate levels and law; assoc. libraries: geo- and solar physics 12,550 vols., philosophy and theology 50,000 vols.; Dir. Rev. R. J. SUCHAN, S.J.

Far Eastern University Library: Quezon Blvd., Manila; 143,851 vols.; Dir. CELEDONIO O. RESURRECCIÓN.

Loyola House of Studies Library: P.O.B. 4082, Manila; 55,000 vols. collegiate and graduate philosophy and theology; Librarian Rev. RALPH GEHRING, S.J.

Manila City Library: Kamaynilaan Bldg., Arroceros St., Manila 10401; Superintendent EDUARDO MALONES.

National Library: T. M. Kalaw, Ermita, Manila; f. 1900; 1,296,809 vols.; Dir. Dr. SERAFIN QUIASON; publs. *Philippine National Bibliography*, *TNL News* (both quarterly).

Philippine Women's University Library: Taft Ave., Manila 2801; six branch libraries for fine arts, graduate school, science, social work, music and high school; 82,500 vols.; Librarian Mrs. ESPERANZA A. SANTA CRUZ.

Scientific Library and Documentation Division, National Science Development Board (formerly *Division of Documentation, National Institute of Science and Technology*): Bicutan, Tagig, Metro Manila, P.O.B. 3596; f. 1902; 26,120 bound vols. and 6,985 periodical titles; Chief Dr. IRENE D. AMORES; publs. *Philippine Abstracts*† (quarterly), *Philippine Science Index*† (every 2 months), *SEA Abstracts* (2 a month).

Silliman University Library: Dumaguete City 6501; f. 1906; 125,000 vols.; Librarian GORGONIO D. SIEGA.

University of Manila Central Library: 546 Dr. M. V. de los Santos St., Sampaloc, Manila; f. 1913; 28,600 vols.; other libraries 23,000 vols.; Chief Librarian TEÓFILO A. PAGARIGAN.

University of San Carlos Library: P. del Rosario St., Cebu City 6401; f. 1947; 181,879 vols.; 13,175 vols. of Filipiniana; research in fields of anthropology, natural sciences, psychology, folklore, linguistics, demography, hydrology, marine biology and Cebuano literature; Dir. of Libraries Mrs. MARILOU P. TADLIP.

Cebuano Studies Center: P. del Rosario St., Cebu City 6401; f. 1975; special library and research center; 2,411 vols., 416 periodicals, 411 theses; musical compositions, maps, MSS., photographs, tape, microfiche and microfilm collections; research and grants in Cebuano studies in the humanities and social sciences; Dir. RESIL B. MOJARES.

University of Santo Tomás Library: España St., Manila; *c.* 260,000 vols.; collections of Filipiniana and rare and ancient books; special libraries of Ecclesiastical Faculties, Medicine, Music, Engineering, Fine Arts and Commerce; High School and Elementary School libraries; microfilms and slides; Prefect of Libraries Fr. X. ARRAZOLA, O.P.; Chief Librarian Miss JUANA L. ABELLO.

University of the East Library: Claro M. Recto Ave., Manila ZC 2806; 180,175 vols.; Librarian Miss NARCISA F. TIOCO.

University of the Philippines Library: Diliman, Quezon City; 722,185 vols.; 36 brs.; Librarian MARINA G. DAYRIT.

MUSEUMS

Jose P. Laurel Memorial Museum and Library: Tanauan, Batangas; documents and personal possessions of the late Dr. J. P. Laurel (1890-1960).

Lopez Memorial Museum and Library: 10 Lancaster Ave., Pasay, Metro Manila; f. 1960; paintings of the Filipino painters, Juan Luna and Felix Resureccion Hidalgo; letters and MSS. of José Rizal; library of 14,000 vols., including rare Filipiniana; Dir. CELSO G. CABRERA.

National Museum of the Philippines: P.O.B. 2659, Old Legislative Bldg., Padre Burgos St., Rizal Park, Manila; f. 1901; Divisions of Anthropology, Botany, Geology-Palaeontology, Zoology, Museum Education, Restoration, Arts, Cultural Properties, Planetarium; library of 5,000 vols.; Dir. GODOFREDO L. ALCASID; publs. monographs†, serials†, guide books†, etc.

Santo Tomás Museum: Main Building, University of Santo Tomás, España St., Manila; f. before 1682, reorganized 1865; Divisions of Natural History, Ethnology (mainly of the Philippines), History (including Numismatics), Archaeology (including Chinese Ceramics), and an Art Gallery containing especially the popular religious art of the Philippines; Dir. Rev. Fr. JESÚS M. MERINO ANTOLÍNEZ, O.P.

UNIVERSITIES

ADAMSON UNIVERSITY

900 SAN MARCELINO ST.,
ERMITA, MANILA 2801
Telephone: 50-20-11.

Founded 1932.

Language of instruction: English; Private (Roman Catholic) control; Academic year: June to March.

President: Rev. LEANDRO MONTAÑANA, C.M.
Vice-President for Financial Affairs: Rev. MAXIMINO TEMPRADO, C.M.
Vice-President for Academic and Student Affairs: Dean MARCOS HERRAS.
Registrar: Dr. JOSE DE OCAMPO.
Librarian: Mrs. HILARIA VILLANUEVA.

Number of teachers: 488.
Number of students: 19,492.

DEANS:

College of Law: MARCOS HERRAS.
Graduate School: JOSEFA ESTRADA.
Liberal Arts and Sciences: Rev. ROLANDO DELA GOZA, C.M.
College of Engineering: PABLO P. GABRIEL.
College of Education: JOSE M. DE OCAMPO.
College of Commerce and Business Administration: LOURDES L. SANVICTORES.
School of Architecture: GODUARDO SANTOS.
College of Pharmacy: ELADIO TINIO.

HEADS OF DEPARTMENTS:

Graduate Studies in Chemistry: LYDIA CRISOSTOMO.
Industrial Research and Undergraduate Chemistry: RECAREDO A. SANTOS.
English: EDWARD KUINISALA.
Spanish: GUILLERMO GOMEZ.
Mathematics: Dr. ACHILLES DEL CALLAR.
Chemical Engineering: ANTONIO VILLEGAS.
Civil Engineering: PETER URETA.
Mechanical Engineering: EMMANUEL NIÑO.
Electrical Engineering: MELCHOR SALVADOR.
Industrial and Ceramic Engineering: AMADOR A. MAÑALAC.
Geology and Mining Engineering: EDGARDO VILLAVICENCIO.
Social Sciences: Sr. MARIA YONSON, D.C.
Theology: Sr. ELIODORA SALECINA.
Physics: PABLO TORRECAMPO.
Accounting: MANUEL ALBAY.
Banking and Finance: RICARDO SORIANO.
Biological Science: NORMA PESAYCO.
Commercial Law: Atty. AUGUSTO REYES.
Economics: ELPIDIO BALANQUE.
Secretarial Studies: MONSERRAT BETSAYDA.
Pilipino: JANET FLORES.

ANGELES UNIVERSITY FOUNDATION

ANGELES CITY
Telephone: 29-58.

Founded 1962.

Private control; Languages of Instruction: English, Pilipino; Academic year: June to March.

President: Dr. EMMANUEL Y. ANGELES.
Vice-President for Academic Affairs: Dr. RICARDO C. GALLANG.
Chief Administrative Officer: JOSÉ V. ARCEBIDO, Jr.
Registrar: ANTERO S. ANAYAN.
Librarian: TERESITA M. MANARANG.

Library of 42,075 vols.
Number of teachers: 181.
Number of students: 6,159.
Publications: *AUF Journal*†, *The Pioneer*†.

DEANS:

Graduate School: Dr. RICARDO C. GALANG.
College of Arts and Sciences and Education: Mrs. MILAGROS M. LAXAMANA.
College of Commerce: Miss TERESITA B. IRENEO.
College of Engineering: Engr. FILOMENO M. BONIFACIO, Jr.
College of Nursing: Mrs. MARIETTA H. GADDI.
Polytechnic School: SANCHO B. CUYUGAN.

AQUINAS UNIVERSITY

LEGAZPI CITY 4901
Telephone: 22-27.

Founded 1948; University 1968.

Private (Roman Catholic) control.

President: Very Rev. Fr. MANUEL T. PINON, O.P.
Registrar: CEFERINO MAGDAONG.
Librarian: Mrs. CONCEPCION C. SURATOS.

Library of 49,150 vols.
Number of teachers: 158.
Number of students: 4,500.

DEANS:

Faculty of Law: Prof. VICENTE A. PERALTA.
Faculty of Engineering: Engr. FRANCISCO N. NIDEA.
Faculty of Arts and Sciences: Miss SENECA NEBRES.
Faculty of Business Administration: Mrs. OFELIA S. VEGA.
Faculty of Education: LOURDES M. SABATER.
Faculty of Nursing Education: Sr. VISITACION ALECTO, O.P.
Graduate Studies and Research: (vacant).

ARELLANO UNIVERSITY

2600 LEGARDA STREET,
SAMPALOC, MANILA
Telephone: 60-74-41.

Founded 1938.

Language of instruction: English; Private control.

President: JOSE T. ENRIQUEZ.
Executive Vice-President: PAULINO F. CAYCO.
Registrar: Mrs. JOSEFA V. LEBRON.
Librarian: Mrs. SOLITA S. TAMAYO.

Number of teachers: 277.
Number of students: 8,592.

Publications: *Arellano Standard* (temporarily suspended), *Philippine Education Quarterly*.

DEANS:

Graduate School: Dr. RUFINO ALEJANDRO.
Arellano Law College: Atty. RODOLFO D. ROBLES.
College of Arts and Sciences: Dr. RUFINO ALEJANDRO.
College of Education and Normal College: Dra. AMPARO S. LARDIZABAL.
College of Commerce: FRANCISCO P. CAYCO.
College of Nursing: Mrs. TRINIDAD L. VERANO.

ATENEO DE MANILA UNIVERSITY

P.O.B. 154, MANILA
Telephone: 99-87-21.

Founded 1859; University 1959.

Language of instruction: English; Private control; Academic year: June to March (two terms).

President: Rev. JOSE A. CRUZ, S.J.
Executive Vice-President: Rev. ANTONIO S. SAMSON, S.J.
Vice-President and Treasurer: Rev. THOMAS R. FITZPATRICK, S.J.
University Registrar: Dr. CARMEN-DIAZ TAÑEDO.
Librarian: Rev. R. SUCHAN, S.J., M.S.L.S.

Number of teachers: 552.
Number of students: 9,617.

Publications: *Philippine Studies*†, *Guidon*, *Alumni Guidon*† (all quarterly), *Loyola School of Theology Monographs*†, *IPC Reports*.

DEANS:

School of Arts and Sciences: Rev. BIENVENIDO F. NEBRES, S.J.
Graduate School of Business: Rev. THOMAS R. FITZPATRICK, S.J. (acting).
College of Law: JESÚS R. DE VEYRA.

UNIVERSITY OF BAGUIO

BAGUIO CITY 0220

Founded 1948 as a Technical College.

Private control; Languages of instruction: English and Pilipino; Academic year: June to March.

President: REINALDO C. BAUTISTA.
Vice-President for Administration: CANUTO H. MABALOT.
Vice-President for Academic Affairs: WILFREDO A. WI.
Associate Vice-President for Supervision of Instruction: PIO TADAOAN.
Associate Vice-President for Research, Planning and Development: FELIPE L. DE GUZMAN.
Treasurer: LEONIDES C. BAUTISTA.
Registrar: Mrs. APOLONIA D. ACADEMIA.
Librarian: BRIGITT SAGALLA.

Library of 52,643 vols.
Number of teachers: 235.
Number of students: 8,770.
Publications: *University of Baguio Journal*† (2 a year), *The U.B. Bulletin* (monthly).

DEANS:

College of Arts and Sciences: WILFREDO WI.
College of Commerce: ISABELO V. DACONES.
College of Education: Mrs. ILUMINADA C. BOADO.
Graduate School: TIMOTEO S. TELLEZ.
College of Engineering: SALVADOR NAVARETTE.
Technical School: JAMES M. MALAYA (Director).

BICOL UNIVERSITY*

REGAN BARRACKS, LEGAZPI CITY

Telephone: 1010.

Founded 1969.

State control; Languages of instruction: English, Filipino.

President: **Dr. RICARDO A. ARCILLA.**
Registrar: **RENATO A. MAGISTRADO.**
Librarian: **ARACELI ANTE.**

Library of 17,347 vols.
Number of teachers: 400.
Number of students: 12,522.

DEANS:

Graduate School: **LAZARA JULIANDA.**
Agriculture: **LEONCIO MENESES.**
Fisheries: **GERONIMO LAVILLA.**
Engineering: **VICENTE O. NAVARRO.**
Education: **PATRIA G. LORENZO.**
Nursing: **MAURO S. NIEVA.**
Arts and Sciences: **JUSTITA LOLA.**

* No reply received to our questionnaire this year.

CENTRAL LUZON STATE UNIVERSITY

MUÑOZ, NUEVA ECIJA

Founded 1907, attained university status 1964.

State control; Languages of instruction: English and Pilipino; Academic year: June to March.

President: Dr. AMADO C. CAMPOS.
Vice-President: Dr. PEDRO A. ABELLA.
Registrar: RICARDO M. FERMIN.
Administrative Officer: Atty. RICARDO BERNARDO.
Librarian: Prof. CELIA D. DE LA CRUZ.

Number of teachers: 340.
Number of students: 5,000.

Publications: *CLSU Collegian* (2 a semester), *CLSU Newsletter* (2 a month), *CLSU Scientific Journal*† (2 a year).

DEANS:

College of Agriculture: MARCELO M. ROGUEL.
College of Home Science and Industry: Prof. ANA B. ALONZO.
College of Education: NATHANIEL LAPITAN.
Graduate School: FERMINA T. RIVERA.
College of Engineering: GAUDENCIO VILLAROMAN.
College of Arts and Sciences: ADORACION M. HALILI.
College of Inland Fisheries: RAFAEL GUERRERO III.
College of Veterinary Science and Medicine: Dr. FAUSTINO S. MENSALVAS.

HEADS OF DEPARTMENTS:

College of Agriculture:
Agri-Management: JIMMY RAMIREZ.
Animal Science: Prof. DIONISIO O. ORDEN.
Crop Protection: Mrs. EPIFANIA P. CASTRO.
Crop Science: Dr. JOSUE A. IRABAGON.
Soil Science: Dr. JULIANA B. DACAYO.

College of Arts and Sciences:
Humanities and Languages: Prof. LUCILA SD. LASAM.
Physical Sciences: Mrs. EVELYN C. MAGPALE.
Behavioural Sciences: FLOR AMOR MONTA.
Biological Sciences: Prof. LINDA P. ALONZO.

College of Engineering:
Agricultural Engineering: Dr. HONORATO ANGELES.
Agricultural Mechanics: AVELINO REYES.
Agricultural Science: Prof. ISAAC M. VERA CRUZ.

College of Inland Fisheries:
Aquatic Biology: Prof. LUZVIMINDA GUERRERO.
Aquaculture: Dr. EMMANUEL M. CRUZ.
Inland Fisheries Management: Dr. CATALINO R. DE LA CRUZ.

College of Education:
Agricultural Education: DEOGRACIAS PONCE.
Agricultural Extension: Dr. JOSE C. ALONZO.

College of Home Science and Industry:
Garment Technology: Prof. CEFERINA AGNES.
Food Technology: Prof. ROSARIO E. EUSEBIO.
Home Economics Education and Extension: Prof. LOURDES F. SAN JUAN.

AFFILIATED INSTITUTES:

Central Luzon Agricultural Research Center, CLSU: Dir. Dr. FILOMENA F. CAMPOS.

Freshwater Aquaculture Center, CLSU: Dir. Dr. CATALINO R. DE LA CRUZ.

CENTRAL MINDANAO UNIVERSITY

UNIVERSITY TOWN, MUSUAN, BUKIDNON

Founded 1952 as the Mindanao Agricultural College; University 1965.

State control.

Languages of instruction: English and Pilipino; Academic year: June to April (two semesters and a summer school).

President: Dr. ISABELO S. ALCORDO.
Assistants to the President: OSEAS M. RESUS (Administration), ESTHER M. CABOTAJE (Academic Affairs), TEOFILO H. MONTEMAYOR (External Affairs), IRENEO B. MENDOZA (Research and Extension), RAYMUNDO E. FONOLLERA (Planning and Resources Development).
Registrar: RICARDO C. ESTRELLA, M.A.
Librarian: Dr. ZENAIDA CAINTIC.

Library of 20,222 vols.
Number of teachers: 298.
Number of students: 5,544.
Publications: *CMU Journal of Food and Agriculture* (quarterly).

DEANS:

College of Arts and Sciences: MARCELINO N. MACEDA, PH.D.
College of Agriculture: LAMBERTO B. BOLORON.
College of Education: ISOLINO A. BOLIVIA.
College of Engineering: RIZALINO P. GREGORIO.
College of Home Economics: NORMA R. MONTEMAYOR.
College of Forestry: EDGARDO G. CUETO.
College of Veterinary Medicine: WILFREDO E. TAMIN.
Graduate School: ALFONSO T. PAINAGAN.
Elementary Laboratory School: HEIDI V. ALCORDO.
High School: SALVACIÓN U. LIMBO.

DIRECTORS:

CMU Central Experiment Station: JOSÉ D. ESCARLOS, PH.D.
Extension: VICTORICO T. CRUZADO, PH.D.
Tropical Ranch Management and Research Institute: PRUDENCIO B. MAGADAN, M.S.

Agribusiness Management Training Projects: ALFREDO M. AGUILAR, Jr., M.B.A.

CENTRAL PHILIPPINE UNIVERSITY

P.O.B. 231, ILOILO CITY
Telephone: 7-34-73/4/5.
Founded 1905.

Language of instruction: English; Private control; Academic year: June to March (two terms).

President: AGUSTIN A. PULIDO, PH.D.
Assistant to the President: LEDA G. ALBA, M.A.
Treasurer: REUEL F. NUÑEZ, B.S.C.
Vice-President for Administration: JORGE Y. TAMAYO, M.S.C.E.
Registrar: CRISPIN D. DRILON, B.S.E., LL.B.
Librarian: NORMA P. JAYME, M.S.

Number of teachers: 249.
Number of students: 8,461.

Publications: *The Central Echo* (student paper), *Centralite* (student annual), *Link* (Alumni organ), *Southeast Asia Journal*†.

DEANS:

College of Agriculture: ENRIQUE S. ALTIS.
College of Arts and Sciences: ELIZA U. GRIÑO.
College of Commerce: MILAGROS DIGNADICE.
College of Education: JOSEFINA ARANDELA.
College of Engineering: WALDEN S. RIO.
College of Law: PANFILO B. ENOJAS.
College of Nursing: NATIVIDAD C. CAIPANG.
College of Theology: JOHNNY V. GUMBAN.
School of Graduate Studies: ELMA S. HERRADURA.

CENTRO ESCOLAR UNIVERSITY

9 MENDIOLA ST., SAN MIGUEL, MANILA
Telephone: 47-26-28.
Founded 1907.

Language of instruction: English; Private control; Academic year: June to March.

President: DIONISIO C. TIONGCO.
Senior Vice-President, Vice-President for Administrative Affairs: BERNARDO C. TIONGCO.
Executive Vice-President, Vice-President for Academic Affairs: MINERVA G. LAUDICO.
Vice-Presidents: NATIVIDAD L. AMPIL (Special Services), PAZ P. MENDEZ (Research and Development), MARIA L. AYUYAO (Business Affairs), JUAN J. CARLOS (Technological Services).
Registrar: FRANCISCA V. CABRIETO.
Librarian: MARINA G. DAYRIT.

Number of teachers: 353.
Number of students: 11,404.

Publications: *Faculty and Graduate Studies, Scholar, Rose and Leaf, Rosebud, Clarion.*

DEANS:

College of Arts and Sciences: Dr. FELICIANA A. REYES.
College of Chemistry: Prof. PURIFICACIÓN SUACO.
College of Commerce and Secretarial Administration: Prof. CLEOTILDE PROTOMARTIR.
College of Dentistry: Dr. FELIPE D. GALVAN.
College of Education: Dr. EMILIA R. VILLACERÁN.
College of Nutrition and Home Economics: Prof. JULIETA TADLE.
College of Medical Technology: Dr. VELIA TRINIDAD.
Conservatory of Music: Prof. ALFREDO BUENAVENTURA.
College of Nursing: Prof. IDA KIMSENG.
College of Optometry: Dr. AVELINO REYES.
College of Pharmacy: Dr. DIOSCORA S. PADILLA.
College of Social Work: Prof. LEONORA S. DE GUZMAN.
Graduate School: Dr. PAZ POLICARPIO MÉNDEZ.

HEADS OF DEPARTMENTS:

ADANZA, ESTELA, Mathematics
AMPIL, MATILDE, Social Arts
DAYRIT, MARINA, Library Science
DIAZ, LOURDES, Reading
ESPINA, FELICIDAD, English
GONZALES, DELFINA, Spanish
HALLIDEN, Rev. DONAL, Religion
PLANA, EPIFANIA B., Biological Science
REYES, BELEN S., Audio-Visual Education
REYES, LINDA, Social Sciences
SANTILLAN, PERLA, Home Economics
SIOZON, FLORDELIZA, Physical Education
SOLIVEN, AIDA, Psychology and Philosophy
SUACO, PURIFICACION, Physical Sciences
VALMONTE, CECILIA, Filipino

DE LA SALLE UNIVERSITY

2401 TAFT AVE., D-406 MANILA
Telephone: 50-46-11.
Founded 1911.

Languages of instruction: English and Pilipino; Academic year: June to March.

Chairman of Board: VICENTE R. JAYME.
President: Bro. ANDREW A. GONZALEZ.
Academic Vice-President: Dr. PAULINO Y. TAN.
Vice-Presidents: Bro. DANIEL ORTIZ (Administration), Bro. J. BENEDICT (Planning and Development).
Registrar: LUCILA D. OCAMPO.
Librarian: NARCISA MUÑASQUE.

Number of teachers: 397.
Number of students: 6,643.

Publications: *Green and White Yearbook, The Lasallian, DLSU Newsletter, DLSU Biocircle, De La Salle Catalogue,* etc.

DEANS:

Graduate School of Education: Dr. EMERITA QUITO.
Graduate School of Business: Atty. VICENTE DAKAY.
College of Arts and Sciences: EXALTACION C. RAMOS.
College of Engineering: EDUARDO GUTIERREZ.
College of Commerce: WELLINGTON YU.

ATTACHED INSTITUTES:

Industrial Development Centre: Dir. CATALINO JAVELLANA III.

Centre for Urban Studies: Dir. EXALTACION C. RAMOS.

Educational Management Centre: Dir. Bro. MARTIN SIMPSON, F.S.C.

Programme Materials Development Centre: Dir. ROSEMARIE AQUINO.

DIVINE WORD UNIVERSITY OF TACLOBAN

IMELDA AVE., TACLOBAN CITY, LEYTE
Telephone: 2307, 2310.

Founded 1929, University status 1966.

Private control; Language of instruction: English; Academic year: June to March.

President: Rev. LEONARDO N. MERCADO, S.V.D., PH.D.
Vice-President (Finance and Administration): Rev. SAMUEL J. YAP, S.V.D., M.B.M.
Vice-President (Academic): Rev. ERNESTO LAGURA, S.V.D., M.A.
Registrar: ALBERTO G. GONZALO, B.S.E.
Librarian: GEMINA Q. AURILLO, M.S.L.S.

Number of teachers: 347.
Number of students: 10,717.

Publications: *Leyte-Samar Studies*†, *Power* (2 a year), *DWU Bulletin* (monthly), *Pulong* (every 2 months).

DEANS:

Graduate School: Rev. REMEGIO MOLLANEDA, S.V.D., PH.D.
Nursing: Sr. MARIA VERONICA L. ORIGENES, O.S.B., M.A.
Engineering: Eng. OTILIO M. CRISOSTOMO, B.SC.(ENG.).
Law: Atty. GIL STA. MARIA, LL.B.
Arts and Sciences: CLARITA FILIPINAS, M.A.
Commerce: CONRITA T. TUDTUD, M.S.
Teachers College: LEATRIZ N. MAZO, M.A.

UNIVERSITY OF THE EAST

CLARO M. RECTO AVE., MANILA
Telephone: 20-30-81 to 85.

Founded 1946 as the Philippine College of Commerce and Business Administration; University of the East 1951.

Private control.

Chief Executive Officer: JOVINO S. LORENZO.
President: Dr. C. P. AQUINO.
Executive Vice-President: BENJAMIN S. BLANCO.
Vice-President for Student Affairs: **J. ESPIRITU.**
Registrar: TEOFILO T. SALCEDO.
Chief Librarian: **NARCISA F. TIOCO.**
Library: *see* Libraries.

Number of teachers: Main Campus 1,600, Medical Center 215, Caloocan City Campus 120.

Number of students: 64,500.

Publications: *Dawn, Panorama, U.E. Today, U.E. Bulletin, U.E. Law Journal, C.A.S. Horizon, Dimensions, Engineering Journal, Secretarial Journal.*

DEANS:

Graduate School of Business: CONRADO P. AQUINO (acting).
Graduate School of Education and College of Education: ALICIA S. BUSTOS.
College of Liberal Arts and Sciences: **S. C. ESPIRITU.**
College of Secretarial Education: AMPARO E. SANTOS.
College of Law: **R. PALMA.**
College of Dentistry: **FRANCISCO M HERBOSA.**
College of Business Administration: JESUS CASIÑO.
College of Medicine: JOSE M. CUYEGKENG.
College of Nursing: **EVANGELINA M. DUMLAO.**
UERM Hospital: ROMULO B. GUEVARA, Jr. (Director).
College of Engineering and Vocational Technical Institute: OSCAR C. LIMLANGAN.
School for Music and Arts: **ANTONINO BUENAVENTURA.**
University High School and Secondary Training Department: ROSALINDA A. SAN MATEO (Principal).
Elementary Training Department: ROMULA D. MALLILLIN (Principal).
Caloocan Branch of the University: GONZALO A. LAVARIA (Director).
Centre for Language Education Research: **C. ESTACIO (Director).**
Physical Education Department: **VIRGILIO A. DALUPAN (Director).**

UNIVERSITY OF EASTERN PHILIPPINES

UNIVERSITY TOWN, NORTHERN SAMAR

Founded 1964.

State control.

President: Dr. AURORA B. MERIDA.
Business Executive, Budget and Financial Director: **P. B. MERIDA.**
Secretary of the University: LEAH M. MANGADA.
Director of Administrative Services: EDUARDO R. SORRENA.

DEANS:

College of Agriculture: Prof. NESTOR L. RUBENENCIA.
College of Arts and Sciences: Atty. TOMAS V. GUIANG.
College of Business Administration: Dr. GERARDO C. DELORINO.
College of Education: Prof. LEONOR A. ONG SOTTO.
College of Engineering: Engr. JULIAN ESQUILLO, Jr.
College of Veterinary Medicine: Dr. VICTOR PARIAL.
Graduate School: Prof. PEDRO A. BASILOY.
Student Affairs: Prof. ROMEO A. LAVIN.

FAR EASTERN UNIVERSITY

P.O.B. 609, MANILA 2806
Telephone: 21-98-31, 20-30-61.

Founded 1928 as Institute of Accountancy, incorporated in 1934 as Far Eastern University.

Language of instruction: English; Private control.

President: NICANOR M. REYES, Jr., PH.D.
Vice-President for Academic Affairs: AMADO C. DIZON, PH.D.
Vice-President for Administrative Affairs: ALFREDO M. REYES.
Registrar: ANTONIO ORENDAIN II, PH.D.
Chief Librarian: CELEDONIO O. RESURRECCION.

Library: *see* Libraries.

Number of teachers: 1,150.
Number of students: 40,321.

Publications: *FEU Gazette* (monthly), *Far Eastern University Journal*† (quarterly), *Gintong Pamana* (annually), *Far Eastern Law Review*† (half-yearly), *Graduate Journal*† (half-yearly), *FEU Medical Journal*† (quarterly).

DEANS:

Institute of Accounts, Business and Finance: TOMAS G. MAPA.
Institute of Architecture and Fine Arts: JESUS M. BONDOC.
Institute of Arts and Sciences: JOSEPHINE COJUANGCO-REYES.
Institute of Education: LOURDES P. GUTANG (acting).
Institute of Graduate Studies: AMADO C. DIZON, PH.D. (acting).
Institute of Law: TOMAS P. MATIC, Jr., LL.M.
Institute of Medicine: SERAFIN J. JULIANO, M.D., M.P.H.
Institute of Nursing: FELICIDAD D. ELEGADO, M.N.
Institute of Technology: GILBERTO G. MERCADO, M.S.

FEATI UNIVERSITY*

HELIOS ST., SANTA CRUZ, MANILA

Telephone: 48-59-51.

Founded 1946.

Private control; Academic year: May to March (two semesters).

President: **Dr. VICTORIA L. DE ARANETA, D.B.A.**
Vice-President: **JOSE M. SEGOVIA, B.S.E.E., B.S.M.E., M.E.E.**
Executive Vice-President: R. MASLOG, B.S.C.E.
Academic Vice-President: DANIEL M. SALCEDO, M.A., D.ED.
Vice-President for Internal Affairs: AURELIO S. UGALDE, B.S.C.E., M.S. (AERO.).
Registrar: ALBERTO ABIS, M.A.
Librarian: REGINA DE VERA, B.S.E.

The library has over 30,000 vols.

Number of teachers: 850.
Number of students: 30,000.

DEANS:

Graduate School: D. M. SALCEDO, M.A., S.S.D., D.ED.
Institute of Engineering: J. M. SEGOVIA, B.S.M.E., M.E.E.
Institute of Architecture and Fine Arts: ALEJANDRO ARELLANO, B.S.ARCH.
Institute of Arts and Education: MARIA LOURDES RUIZ, B.S.E., LIC., PH.D.
Institute of Business Administration: RIZALINO R. PABLO, LL.M., M.B.A.
Institute of Vocational and Technical Education: J. M. SEGOVIA, B.S.M.E., M.E.E.

* No reply received to our questionnaire this year.

FOUNDATION UNIVERSITY

DUMAGUETE CITY 6501
Telephone: 3389-2930.

Founded 1949.

Language of instruction: English; Private control; Academic year: June to March (two semesters).

President: MARCELINO C. MAXINO.
Director of Academic Affairs: OFELIA S. GECONCILLO.
University Secretary and Business Director: EDMUNDO G. SINCO.
Registrar: POMPIO L. ALMERO.
Director of Public Relations: LUCIANO C. MAXINO.
Director of Student Affairs: BALDOMERO MARTINEZ.
Librarian: PABLITA P. MUNAR.

Library of 40,815 vols.
Number of teachers: 144.
Number of students: 4,681.

Periodicals: *Horizons Unlimited, Foundation Law Review, Bloom* (all quarterly), *Foundation Time* (monthly), *Eklectika* (yearly).

DEANS:

Graduate School: TIMOTEO ORACION.
School of Arts and Science: ESTER V. TAN.
School of Education: OFELIA S. GECONCILLO.
School of Business and Economics: EDGAR L. GRIÑO.

School of Agricultural and Industrial Technology: EMMANUEL T. GERVACIO.

School of Law and Jurisprudence: LUCIANO C. MAXINO.

GREGORIO ARANETA UNIVERSITY FOUNDATION

ARANETA UNIVERSITY POST OFFICE, MALABON, METRO MANILA 3104

Telephone: 35-75-51 to 54, 34-70-31 to 33.

Founded 1946; reorganized as a foundation 1965.

Languages of instruction: English and Pilipino; Private foundation; Academic year: June to March.

President: VITALIANO BERNARDINO.

Vice-Presidents: PRIMO L. TONGKO (Academic Affairs), THOMAS P. G. NEILL (Administration and Finance).

Registrar: JOSÉ B. LALOY.

Librarian: Mrs. FELISA W. DADOR.

Number of teachers: 577.

Number of students: 16,589.

Publications: *Araneta Research Journal*† (quarterly), *The Molave*† (every 2 months), *Tinig*† (monthly), *Harvest* (annually).

DEANS:

Institute of Agriculture: Prof. PEDRO L. REYES.

Institute of Forestry: Prof. JULIAN MEIMBAN, Jr.

Institute of Veterinary Mediicne: Dr. FRANCISCA A. CHING.

Institute of Animal Science: Prof. SERVILLANO R. BOTON.

Institute of Arts and Sciences: Prof. CORAZON D. VICARIO.

Institute of Education and Extension: Dr. JOSÉ C. SADDUL, Sr.

Institute of Business and Agricultural Administration: Prof. CLARITA C. LANTION.

Institute of Language: Prof. GONSALO DEL ROSARIO.

Institute of Agricultural and Mechanical Engineering: JOSE A. ACOSTA.

Institute of Physical Education and Sports Development: Prof. NORMA S. BLANCAFOR.

Graduate School: Dr. TOMAS G. BRUAL.

UNIVERSITY OF ILOILO

COR. MAPA RIZAL, RIZAL

Founded 1968.

Schools of arts, science, commerce, civil and mechanical engineering, education and law.

LUZONIAN UNIVERSITY FOUNDATION

LUCENA CITY

Telephone: 43-61.

Founded 1947.

Private control; Languages of instruction: English and Pilipino.

President: RODOLFO B. ABADILLA.

Vice-President: MARTIN ILAGAN.

Registrar: MAXIMO O. ECHEVARRIA.

Librarian: NORA R. BARDELOSA.

Library of 29,000 vols.

Number of teachers: 132.

Number of students: 3,341.

Publ. *Luzonian Quarterly.*

DEANS:

Faculty of Technology: Eng. EDGARDO TALAGA.

Faculty of Arts and Science: JAIME BUZAR.

Faculty of Law: Atty. JOVITO TALABONG.

Faculty of Agriculture: RUPERTO ALCANTARA, Jr.

Faculty of Education and Graduate School: Dr. CESAR A. VILLARIBA.

Faculty of Business Administration: MARTIN ILAGAN.

THE UNIVERSITY OF MANILA

546 Dr. M. V. DE LOS SANTOS ST., MANILA 2806

Telephone: 27-25-57.

Founded 1913.

Private, Non-Sectarian Institution; Language of instruction: English; Academic year: June to May (three terms).

President: HELEN D. SANTOS.

Executive Vice-President: VIRGILIO DE LOS SANTOS.

Registrar: ALFONSO B. MILLENA, Jr.

Chief Librarian: TEÓFILO A. PAGARIGAN.

Number of teachers: 349.

Number of students: 10,000.

Publications: *The Campus Leader, The University of Manila Journal of East Asiatic Studies, The UM Law Gazette.*

DEANS:

College of Law: GONZALO T. SANTOS, Jr.

College of Education: MARCIANO R. RAQUEL.

College of Liberal Arts: CARMELO J. JAMIAS.

College of Business Administration: ARTURO G. ROA.

College of Engineering: ERNESTO F. RAMOS.

School of Foreign Service: FLORENCIO M. CASTILLO.

College of Criminology and Police Administration: RAMON O. NOLASCO.

Graduate Studies in Law: JOSÉ M. ARUEGO.

Graduate Studies in Arts and Sciences: MARCIANO R. RAQUEL.

MANILA CENTRAL UNIVERSITY

ZURBARAN COR. OROQUIETA, MANILA

Telephone: 26-45-86, 26-45-87.

Founded 1904.

Private control; Language of instruction: English; Academic year: June to March.

President: Mrs. P. G. TANCHOCO.

Vice-Presidents: Dr. BIENVENIDO B. MANUEL (Academic Affairs), Mrs. LUALHATI T. GONZALEZ (Administrative Affairs), Mrs. LUNINGNING T. ESTANISLAO (Foundation Affairs).

Registrar: BRAULIA MUSÑGI (acting).

Librarian: Mrs. ADALGESA MASANGKAY.

Number of teachers: 243.

Number of students: 7,261.

Publication: *MCU Gazette.*

DEANS:

College of Medicine: VICTOR C. VALENZUELA.

College of Pharmacy and Medical Technology: Mrs. AMELIA S. DE JUAN.

College of Dentistry: Dr. RUBEN C. NAVIA.

College of Arts and Sciences: Mrs. NORA AUSEJO.

College of Business Administration: Atty. LORENZO LAZARO (acting).

College of Nursing: PATRIA P. PADERNA.

College of Optometry: Dr. BERNARDITA MENCIAS.

School of Midwifery: PATRIA P. PADERNA.

Elementary and High School: Mrs. SOCORRO CRUZ (Principal).

Graduate School of Education: Dr. BIENVENIDO B. MANUEL.

PAMANTASAN NG LUNGSOD NG MAYNILA

(University of the City of Manila)

INTRAMUROS, MANILA

Telephone: 40-76-21.

Founded 1967; University status 1976.

City government control; Language of instruction: English; Academic year: June to March (2 semesters).

President: RAMON D. BAGATSING (acting).

Executive Vice-President: JOSE D. VILLANUEVA.

Vice-President for Academic Affairs: Dr. BENJAMIN G. TAYABAS (acting).

University Secretary: Atty. EDELITA F. REYES.

Registrar: BONIFACIO M. DONATO (acting).

Librarian: Mrs. REMEDIOS F. MALLARI.

Library of 20,000 vols.

Number of teachers: 109 (and 96 part-time lecturers).

Number of students: 3,720.

Publication: *PLM Review.*

Colleges of business administration, arts and sciences, engineering and technology, nursing, education, graduate school.

MINDANAO STATE UNIVERSITY

MARAWI CITY M-206

Telephone: 222-A.

Founded 1961.

Language of instruction: English.

President: (vacant).
Vice-President for Academic Affairs: RUFINO IGNACIO (acting).
Director for Administrative Services: MUSOR B. GURO.
Dean of Research: DIOSCORO RABOR (acting).
Registrar: DISOMANGCOP O. MOTI.
Librarian: ROBERTO J. RABO (acting).

Number of teachers: *c.* 320.
Number of students: *c.* 5,800.

Publications: *Mindanao Varsitarian, MSU Observer, Darangan, Kalayaan.*

DEANS:
College of Agriculture: ZACARIAS V. VALDEZ.
College of Business Administration: FELICITAS U. EVANGELISTA.
College of Community Development and Public Administration: MANUEL VILLANUEVA.
College of Education: RUFINO DE LOS SANTOS.
College of Engineering: RUFINO IGNACIO.
College of Fisheries: ROMAN ROSAGARON.
College of Forestry: SEGUNDO P. FERNANDEZ.
College of Liberal Arts: EMILY MAROHOMBSAR.
Centre for Hotel and Restaurant Management: CARMEN VILLANUEVA.
King Faisal Institute of Islamic and Arabic Studies: SALIPADA TAMANO.

UNIVERSITY OF MINDANAO

BOLTON ST., DAVAO CITY, MINDANAO

Telephone: 7-54-56 (PLDT), 38-11 (DCTS).

Founded 1946.

Private control; Language of instruction: English; Academic year: June to March.

President: Atty. GUILLERMO E. TORRES.
Senior Vice-President: Dra. CONCEPCIÓN B. DE ASIS.
Vice-President for Educational Services: Mrs. EFIGENIA C. OCCEÑA.
Vice-President for Management Services: Eng. PEDRO E. TORRES.
Vice-President for External Affairs: FLORENDO R. MANGAOIL.
Vice-President for Finance: FLORENCIO T. FACUNDO.
Registrar: ADELA M. CUEVAS.

Number of teachers: 304.
Number of students: 17,538.

Publications: *U.M. Faculty Journal Weekly Supplement.*

DEANS:
Graduate Studies: Dr. J. RODRIGUEZ.
College of Engineering and Architecture: Eng. ULDARICO D. DUMDUM.
College of Commerce: ABRAHAM DE GRACIA.
College of Liberal Arts: DELIA D. DANGO.
College of Law: Atty. JOSÉ M. KIMPO.
Teachers' College: Mrs. PAQUITA D. GAVINO.
College of Forestry and Agriculture: ALFREDO O. BAYUDAN.
College of Criminology: LEO CARRILLO.
School of Music: CARMEN HERNANDEZ.

NATIONAL UNIVERSITY

551 MARIANO F. JHOCSON ST., SAMPALOC, MANILA

Telephone: 61-34-31.

Founded 1900.

Language of instruction: English; Private control; Academic year: June to March.

President: DOMINGO L. JHOCSON, M.A., C.P.A.
Vice-President: JESUS M. JHOCSON, M.A.
Registrar: LETICIA J. PAGUIA, B.SC., C.P.A.
Head of Graduate Studies: JESUS M. JHOCSON, M.A. (acting).

DEANS:
College of Commerce: DOMINGO L. JHOCSON, M.S., C.P.A. (acting).
College of Dentistry: Dr. FEDERICO A. EUGENIO.
College of Pharmacy: EMILIA E. DE JESUS, B.S.PHARM., LL.B.
College of Education: LETICIA J. PAGUIA (acting).
College of Liberal Arts: ZENAIDA N. MAGIBA, M.A.
College of Electrical, Industrial and Mechanical Engineering: CARLO T. MAGNO, Sr., B.S.E.E., B.S.M.E.
College of Civil, Chemical and Sanitary Engineering: JESUS M. JHOCSON (acting).
College of Architecture: FERNANDO ABAD, B.S.ARCH.

UNIVERSITY OF NEGROS OCCIDENTAL-RECOLETOS

P.O.B. 214, K-501, BACOLOD CITY

Telephone: 2-50-36.

Founded 1941.

Private control; Language of instruction: English; Academic year: June to March.

President: Rev. Fr. MELQUIADES MODEQUILLO.
Vice-President: Rev. Fr. MAURO AMBUBUYOG.
Comptroller: Rev. Fr. WALTHRODE CONDE.
Registrar: ROGELIO G. GIGANAN.
Librarian: Mrs. AREBELLA M. ANANORIA.

Number of teachers: 344.
Number of students: 11,037.

Publications: *The Tolentine Star* (2 a semester), *UNO-R Gazette, OAR Quarterly*, etc.

DEANS:
Graduate School: FILOMENA BUSTAMANTE.
Arts and Sciences: EVANGELINE T. ELMA.
Law: ARTURO H. VILLANUEVA, LL.B.
Teachers' College: LETICIA DE LA RAMA, B.S.E., M.A.
Engineering: JESUS REPARADO.
College of Criminology: CIRILO TRADIO.
College of Commerce: RAFAEL P. ACENA (acting).
High School Department: Rev. Fr. JOSE ANTONIO RODRIGALVAREZ, O.A.R., B.S.E.
Elementary Department: NELINDA M. VIVA.
Research Institute: BI CHIN UY.

UNIVERSITY OF NORTHERN PHILIPPINES

VIGAN, ILOCOS SUR

Telephone: 693, 828.

Founded 1965.

State control: Languages of instruction: English and Pilipino; Academic year of two semesters.

President: ROMUALDO B. TADENA, PH.D.
Executive Vice-President: EDUARDO MA. GUIRNALDA.
Vice-President for Academic Affairs: Dr. DOROTEA C. FILART.
Vice-President for External Affairs: Mrs. CARMELING P. CRISOLOGO.
University Secretary: BERNARD RAMIREZ.
Director of Admissions: Miss ELEUTERIA REMUCAL.
Director of Planning and Budgeting: LEO OANDASAN.
Director of Research: Dr. SALVADOR EDER.

Administrative Officer: BONIFACIO A. ROSALES.

Librarian: Mrs. PEROMA L. PACIS.

Library of 14,242 vols.

Number of teachers: 164.
Number of students: 3,963.

Publications: *Tandem* (every 2 months), *New Vision* (quarterly).

DEANS AND DEPARTMENT HEADS:

College of Arts and Sciences: Dr. PACITA B. ANTIPORDA.
College of Business Administration: Mrs. CARMELING P. CRISOLOGO.
College of Criminology: Dr. FRANCISCO MACANAS.
College of Engineering: Engr. JUAN ARCE.
College of Fine Arts and Architecture: ARTHUR RABARA.
College of Nursing: Mrs. CECILIA BAYENG.
College of Teacher Education: Mrs. MARIA SUMABAT.
Institute of Social Work: DANIEL COLCOL.
Institute of Library Science: Mrs. PEROMA PACIS.

NOTRE DAME UNIVERSITY

NOTRE DAME AVE.,
COTABATO CITY

Founded 1948; University status 1969.

Private (Roman Catholic) control; Language of instruction: English; Academic year: June to March.

President: Fr. JOSE R. ARONG, O.M.I.
Vice-President for Academic Affairs: Fr. ALFONSO CARIÑO, O.M.I.
Vice-President for Student Affairs: Fr. REHNEE DOROMAL, O.M.I.
Registrar: SAMUEL CABILES.
Librarian: LEONARDO NINTE.

Library of 50,441 vols.

Number of teachers: 163.
Number of students: 4,302.

Publications: *Notre Damer, Notre Dame Journal.*

DEANS:

Graduate School: TEODORO CARRASCO.
College of Engineering: J. RODRIGUEZ.
College of Arts and Sciences: Mrs. OFELIA DURANTE.
College of Commerce: Mrs. MYRNA B. LIM.
College of Law: Atty. RAMON CARAG.
Teachers College: Mrs. AURORA CARAG.
College of Nursing: Mrs. GRACE BARRANCO.

UNIVERSITY OF NUEVA CACERES

NAGA CITY 4723
Telephone: 9287.
Founded 1948.

Private control; Language of instruction: English; Academic year: June to March (two semesters).

President Emeritus: Dr. JAIME HERNÁNDEZ.
Executive Vice-President: PERFECTO O. PALMA.
Vice-President for Administration: JAIME HERNÁNDEZ, Jr.
Registrar: Dr. ELISEO A. PALAROAN, Jr.
Librarian: Mrs. PERPETUA S. PORCALLA.

Number of teachers: 260.
Number of students: 7,276.

Publications: *Nueva Caceres Bulletin* (bi-monthly), *Red and Gray* (annual), *The Trailblazer* (monthly), *The UNCSCA* (fortnightly), *The Syndrome* (quarterly), *Journal of Graduate Studies and Research.*

DEANS:

College of Arts and Sciences: JANET B. SOLER.
College of Engineering: MAXIMINO O. PANELO, Jr.
College of Commerce: PERFECTO O. PALMA.
College of Education: JANET B. SOLER.
College of Law: P. O. PALMA.
School of Nursing: Mrs. FLORIA T. SILVA.
Graduate School: (vacant).

UNIVERSITY OF PANGASINAN

ARELLANO ST., DAGUPAN CITY
Telephone: 24-96.

Founded 1925; University status 1968.

President: Dr. BLAS F. ROYAS.
Registrar: TEOFILO ROYAS.
Librarian: MARCELINO C. RUIZ.

Library of 45,238 vols.

Number of teachers: 333.
Number of students: 10,986.

DEANS:

School of Graduate Studies: Dr. ALFONSO G. GARCIA.
College of Education: Mrs. JULITA R. PAMINTUAN.
College of Commerce: MANUEL R. POCO.
College of Liberal Arts: TOMAS Z. LIMBOS.
College of Engineering: Engr. DIONISIO M. PARAYNO.
College of Law: PORFIRIO V. SISON.
College of Architecture: Engr. ELEUTERIO A. FERNANDEZ.
School of Industrial Education: RICARTE V. HIDALGO (acting).
School of Nursing: Miss ASUNCION O. IBAY.
School of Secretarial Administration: CANDIDO Z. PARAGAS.
University High School: EULOGIO V. JIMENEZ (Principal).
University Elementary Laboratory School: Mrs. TERESITA R. VISTRO.

THE PHILIPPINE WOMEN'S UNIVERSITY

TAFT AVE., MANILA 2801
Telephone: 58-55-59, 59-25-15.
Founded 1919.

Private control; Language of instruction: English; Academic year: June to March.

Chairman of the Board of Trustees: Hon. FILEMON C. RODRIGUEZ.
Vice-Chairman: Hon. HELENA Z. BENITEZ.
President: ROSA SANTOS MUNDA (acting).
Vice-President for Fiscal Affairs: CORAZON B. TULIO
Treasurer: SALUD C. GOQUIOLAY.
Registrar: Mrs. ANGELINA S. VILLARICA.
Alumnae Relations Director: Dr. NATIVIDAD O. AGUINALDO.
Librarian: ESPERANZA A. STA. CRUZ.

Library of 66,525 vols.

Number of teachers: 588.
Number of students: 12,418.

Publications: *The Philwomenian, The Maroon and White, Graduate School Research Abstract, The Alumna Link.*

GENERAL EDUCATION PROGRAM CHAIRMEN:

Social Sciences: Mrs. M. B. GONZALEZ.
Natural and Physical Sciences: Dr. J. A. MANALO.
Humanities: J. C. NAPAL.
Education, Liberal Arts and Home Economics: T. LISING.
Nursing: Dr. ROSARIO S. DIAMANTE.
Pharmacy and Medical Technology: MILAGROS P. OCAMPO.
Graduate School: Dr. J. V. CALIXTO.

DIRECTORS OF AFFILIATED SCHOOLS:

University Extension, Quezon City: Mrs. SALUD OLIVEROS LUSTRE.
Conrado Benitez Institute for Business Education: Atty. JOSÉ O. CASAS.
College of Music and Fine Arts: CORAZON S. MACEDA.
Philippine Institute of Nutrition, Food Science and Technology: Dr. IGNACIO S. PABLO.
Philippine School of Social Work: Mrs. ERLINDA A. CORDERO.

UNIVERSITY OF THE PHILIPPINES

DILIMAN, QUEZON CITY
Telephone: 976061, 976081.
Founded 1908.

Language of instruction: English; State control; Academic year: June to March (three terms).

President: EMANUEL V. SORIANO.
Chancellor of U.P. at Los Baños: EMIL Q. JAVIER.
Chancellor of U.P. Health Sciences Center: FLORENTINO HERRERA, Jr.

Chancellor of U.P. in the Visayas: EMANUEL V. SORIANO (acting).
Vice-President for Academic Affairs: OSCAR M. ALFONSO.
Vice-President for Administration: RAMON C. PORTUGAL.
Secretary: GEMINO H. ABAD.
Dean of Students: OSCAR L. EVANGELISTA.
Dean of Admissions: M. P. BENDAÑA.
Registrar: MANUEL P. BENDAÑA.
Librarian: Miss MARINA DAYRIT.

Library: *see* Libraries.

Number of teachers: 2,950.
Number of students: 34,200.

Publications: *Acta Medica Philippina* (quarterly), *UP Annual Report*, *UP Carillon*† (quarterly), *The Diliman Review*† (quarterly), *Education Quarterly*†, *General Education Journal*† (irregular), *Graduate Seminar Journal* (every 2 months), *Index to Philippine Periodicals* (bi-annual), *Lipunan Journal* (irregular), *Natural & Applied Science Bulletin*† (quarterly), *Philippine Agriculturist* (irregular), *Philippine Collegian*† (weekly), *Philippine Journal of Public Administration* (quarterly), *Philippine Law Journal* (quarterly), *Philippine Planning Journal* (bi-annual), *Philippine Social Science and Humanities Review*† (quarterly), *Small Industry Journal* (quarterly), *UP Faculty Conference—Proceedings* (annually), *UP Gazette*† (quarterly), *UP General Catalogue*† (irregular), *UP Perspectives* (monthly), *Veterinary Medicine Bulletin* (every 2 months).

DEANS AND DIRECTORS OF ACADEMIC DEGREE GRANTING UNITS:

College of Architecture: AURELIO T. JUGUILON.
College of Arts and Sciences: FRANCISCO NEMENZO, Jr.
Natural Science Research Center: GERMELINO F. ABITO (Director).
Asian Center: JOSEFA M. SANIEL.
Asian Institute of Tourism: JOSE P. MANANZAN.
Asian Labor Education Center: MANUEL A. DIA.
College of Business Administration: MAGDALENO B. ALBARRACIN.
School of Economics: JOSÉ ENCARNACIÓN, Jr.
Institute of Economic Development and Research: ERNESTO PERNIA (Director).
College of Education: PAZ G. RAMOS.
Institute for Language Teaching: NELIA G. CASAMBRE (Director).
Reading Center: BASILIA J. MANHIT (Officer-in-Charge).
College of Engineering: MARINO M. MENA.
National Engineering Center: LEOPOLDO V. ABIS (Director).
National Hydraulic Research Center: ANGEL A. ALEJANDRINO (Director).
Industrial Research Center: JOSE A. AZARCON, Jr. (Director).
Training Center for Applied Geodesy and Photogrammetry: CRISTY R. HERNANDEZ (Director).
Transport Training Center: SALVADOR F. REYES (Director).
Building Research Service: ERNESTO G. TABUJARA (Director).
Institute of Environmental Planning: LEANDRO A. VILORIA.
College of Fine Arts: NAPOLEON V. ABUEVA.
Graduate School: EMERENCIANA Y. ARCELLANA (Officer-in-Charge).
College of Home Economics: AURORA G. CORPUZ.
Institute of Islamic Studies: ABDULRAFIH H. SAYEDY.
College of Law: FROILAN M. BACUNGAN.
Law Center: FLERIDA RUTH P. ROMERO (Director).
Institute of Library Science: URSULA G. PICACHE.
U.P. College in Manila: NESTOR N. PILAR.
Institute of Mass Communication: GLORIA D. FELICIANO.
College of Music: RAMON P. SANTOS.
Philippine Music Documentation Center: CORAZON C. DIOQUINO (Director).
Population Institute: MERCEDES B. CONCEPCION.
College of Public Administration: RAUL P. DE GUZMAN.
Administrative Development Center: RAMON M. GARCIA (Director).
Local Government Center: FELIPE V. OAMAR (Director).
Policy Studies Program: ROMEO B. OCAMPO (Director).
Institute of Social Work and Community Development: SYLVIA M. GUERRERO.
Institute of Sports, Physical Education and Recreation: CYNTHIA V. ABAD SANTOS (acting).
Statistical Center: CRISTINA P. PAREL.
College of Veterinary Medicine: SALVADOR H. ESCUDERO III.
Equine Research Center: DALMACIO TIBAY (Officer-in-Charge).
Veterinary Hospital: MAURO F. MANUEL (Officer-in-Charge).

U.P. at Los Baños:
College of Agriculture: CLEDUALDO B. PEREZ, Jr.
College of Arts and Sciences: EDELWINA C. LEGASPI.
Institute of Agricultural Engineering and Technology: REYNALDO M. LANTIN.
College of Development Economics and Management: PEDRO R. SANDOVAL.
College of Forestry: CELSO B. LANTICAN.
Graduate School: DOLORES A. RAMIREZ.
Institute of Human Ecology: GIL F. SAGUIGUIT.
ASEAN Postharvest Horticulture Training and Research Center: ERNESTO R. PANTASTICO (Director).
Center for Policy and Development Studies: RAMON L. NASOL (Director).
Dairy Training and Research Institute: LEOPOLDO S. CASTILLO (Director).
Museum of Natural History: JUAN V. PANCHO (Director).
National Training Center for Rural Development: FLORENTINO C. LIBRERO (Director).
U.P. Health Sciences Center:
School of Allied Medical Professions: GUILLERMO R. DAMIAN.
College of Dentistry: AVELINO A. MACASAET.
College of Medicine: GLORIA T. ARAGON.
College of Nursing: TEODORA A. IGNACIO.
College of Pharmacy: NATIVIDAD F. DE CASTRO.
Institute of Public Health: BENJAMIN D. CABRERA.
Comprehensive Training Center for the Health Program: SERGIO S. GASMEN (Director).
Institute of Ophthalmology: SALVADOR R. SALCEDA (Director).
National Teacher Training Center for the Health Professions: CORAZON P. GONZALES (Director).
Philippine General Hospital: GLORIA T. ARAGON (Director).
University of the Philippines in the Visayas:
College of Arts and Sciences: ELAYDA E. MABUNAY.
College of Fisheries: ROGELIO O. JULIANO.
Regional Units of the University:
U.P. College Baguio: SOPHIE M. CATBAGAN.
U.P. College Cebu: AURORA A. MIÑOZA (acting).
U.P. College Clark: GUILLERMO R. LAZARO (Officer-in-Charge).
U.P. College Tacloban: BENJAMIN M. CATANE.
Other Institutes:
Creative Writing Center: FRANCISCO ARCELLANA, Sr.
Film Center: VIRGINIA R. MORENO.
Marine Sciences Center: EDGARDO D. GOMEZ.
Philippine Executive Academy: CARLOS P. RAMOS.
Science Education Center: DOLORES F. HERNANDEZ.
Institute for Small-Scale Industries: EDUARDO M. TAYLOR.

MANUEL L. QUEZON UNIVERSITY

916 R. HIDALGO, QUIAPO, MANILA

Telephone: 47-05-41-44.

Founded 1947.

President: LEONCIO B. MONZÓN.

Vice-President: AMADO C. DIZON.
Executive Officer, Regent: **MANUEL O. CHAN.**
Registrar: Prof. VICENTE C. JORNALES.
Treasurer, Regent: **CARMELINO G. ALVENDIA.**
Director of Library and Research Center: Prof. JOSEFA V. MANAHAN.
Librarian: Prof. FLORDELIZA M. TORRES.

Number of teachers: 650.
Number of students: 22,806.

Publications: *Quezonian, Junior Quezonian, MLQU Graduate Journal.*

DEANS:

Faculty of Law: LORENZO F. MIRAVITE (acting).
Faculty of Arts and Science: FELISA C. SANTIAGO.
Faculty of Commerce: LOURDES V. ENRIQUEZ.
Faculty of Education: FRANCISCA B. ROXAS-TRINIDAD.
Faculty of Graduate Studies: ERLINDA A. CUIZON.
Faculty of Engineering: ERNESTO A. ELERIA (acting).
Faculty of Architecture: CARLOS B. BANAAG.
Faculty of Criminology: LORENZO A. SUNICO.

SAINT LOUIS UNIVERSITY

BAGUIO CITY 0216
Telephone: 30-43, 27-93.
Founded: 1911.

Language of instruction: English; Private control; Academic year: June to May (three terms).

President: Rev. GHISLEEN DE VOS, C.I.C.M.
Assistant to the President: Dr. GUADALUPE CARBONELL.
Registrar: DANIEL MILO.
Treasurer: PABLO FERNANDEZ.
Chief Librarian: EMETERIO MANANTAN.

Library of 196,772 vols.
Number of teachers: 479.
Number of students: 17,980.

Publications: *Saint Louis Chronicle* (monthly), *Saint Louis University Research Journal*† (quarterly), *Builder of Progress, General Bulletin* (both annually).

DEANS:

College of Engineering and Architecture: RICARDO TUAZON.
College of Commerce: GABINO GAROY, C.P.A.
College of Human Sciences: Miss LUISA GARCIA.
College of Education: RESTITUTO AYSON.
College of Law: FRANCISCO S. REYES.
College of Natural Sciences: Dr. GERARD BRAECKMAN, C.I.C.M.
College of Medicine: HECTOR LOPEZ.
College of Nursing: JESUSA LARA.
Graduate School of Arts and Sciences: Dr. GUADALUPE CARBONELL.
Dean of Student Affairs: MACARIO FRONDA.

DIRECTORS:

Saint Louis University Institute for Small-scale Industries: Miss ERLINDA MANOPOL.
Saint Louis University Regional Science Teaching Center and Regional Staff Development Center: GREGORIO RIMAS.
Institute of Religious Education: Rev. JAMES DESMET, C.I.C.M.
SLU Computer Center: Engr. CONRADO CABURIAN.

UNIVERSITY OF SAN AGUSTÍN

GENERAL LUNA STREET, ILOILO CITY
Telephone: 7-48-41.

Founded 1904, University status 1953.

Language of instruction: English; Private control.

Rector: Rev. Fr. EDUARDO G. PEREZ, O.S.A., M.A.
Vice-Rector: Rev. Fr. ANGEL DULANTO, O.S.A., B.S.C.
Registrar: Atty. IRENEO P. PEDROSO, LL.B.
Librarian: Rev. Fr. REGINO DIEZ, O.S.A., M.S.L.S.

Number of teachers: 401.
Number of students: 10,827.

Publications: *The Augustinian Yearbook, The Augustinian Newspaper, The Augustinian Mirror, Views.*

DEANS:

Graduate School: Dr. M. LEDA R. BAUTISTA, PH.D.
School of Law: Dr. CESAR T. TIROL, LL.D.
College of Pharmacy/Medical Technology: Mrs. FLORA S. SALAS, M.S.
College of Technology: Eng. FRANCIS L. PADILLA, B.S.C.E.
College of Commerce: Atty. PEDRO T. MACAVINTA, LL.B., C.P.A.
Teachers College: Dr. JOSEFA C. CASTRO, PH.D.
College of Nursing: Miss REMEGELIA BACOTOC, M.A.
Conservatory of Music: Rev. Fr. SANTIAGO EZCURRA, O.S.A., M.A.
College of Liberal Arts: Dr. TERESITA O. APORTADERA, PH.D.

UNIVERSITY OF SAN CARLOS

P.O.B. 182, CEBU CITY 6401
Telephone: 7-24-10, 7-24-19.

Founded 1595, University status 1948.

Language of instruction: English; Private control; Academic year: June to March (two terms).

President: GREGORIO I. PIZARRO.
Vice-President for Administration: Fr. RODERICK C. SALAZAR.
Vice-President for Academic Affairs: Fr. QUINTIN C. TERRENAL, S.V.D.
Vice-President for Finance: Fr. CECILIO P. JAYME, S.V.D.
Registrar: ROBERTO V. IRATAGOTIA.
Director of Libraries: MARILOU P. TADLIP.

Number of teachers: 444.
Number of students: 11,176.

Publications: *The University Bulletin* (fortnightly), *Semper Fidelis* (annually), *Philippine Scientist* (annually), *Philippine Quarterly of Culture and Society* (quarterly).

DEANS:

Graduate School: Dr. ALICIA J. TAN.
College of Law: FULVIO C. PELÁEZ, LL.B.
College of Liberal Arts and Sciences: Fr. BENJAMIN B. RABOY, S.V.D.
Teachers' College: CLARA T. LUCERO, M.ED.
College of Commerce: VICTORIA A. SATORRE.
College of Engineering and Architecture: PEDRO YAP, B.S.C.E.
College of Pharmacy: LETICIA G. CABRERA, PH.D.
College of Nursing: MARIETTA S. LAO.

PROFESSORS:

ANG, GERTRUDES, English
FLIEGER, WILHELM, S.V.D., Sociology
KOLK, RAYMOND, S.V.D., Education
SCHOENIG, ENRIQUE, S.V.D., Biology
TERRENAL, QUINTIN, Philosophy
VAN ENGELEN, HERMAN, S.V.D., Physics
VERSTRAELEN, EUGENE, S.V.D., Linguistics

UNIVERSITY OF SANTO TOMAS

ESPAÑA STREET, MANILA
Telephone: 47-22-31.
Founded 1611.

Private (Roman Catholic) control.

Grand Chancellor: Very Rev. Fr. VINCENT DE COUESNONGLE, O.P.
Vice-Chancellor: Very Rev. Fr. PEDRO SANSEGUNDO.
Rector: Very Rev. FREDERIK FERMIN, O.P.
Secretary-General: Fr. MAXIMO MARINA.
Registrar: Dr. NORBERTO DE RAMOS.
Librarians: Fr. FIDEL VILLARROEL, JUANA ABELLO.

Number of teachers: 1,650.
Number of students: 42,825.

Publications: *Thomasian, Varsitarian, Journal of Medicine, Law Review, Veritas, The Aquinian, Unitas, Boletín Eclesiástico, Commerce Journal*, etc.

DEANS:

Faculty of Sacred Theology: Fr. FAUSTO GOMEZ.
Faculty of Canon Law: Rev. Fr. EXCELSO GARCIA, O.P.
Faculty of Philosophy (Eccl.): Fr. DIONISIO CABEZON.

Faculty of Civil Law: Hon. ROBERTO CONCEPCION, LL.D.
Faculty of Medicine and Surgery: Dr. MANUEL BORJA.
Faculty of Pharmacy: JOSÉ DAYCO, PH.D. (acting).
Faculty of Arts and Letters: Prof. MAGDALENA VILLABA-CUE.
Faculty of Engineering: Prof. FRANCISCO G. REYES, B.S.CH.E.
College of Education: LOURDES J. CUSTODIO, PH.D.
College of Science: MARIANO PANGAN, PH.D.
College of Commerce and Business Administration: Prof. MANUEL REYES, PH.D.
College of Architecture and Fine Arts: Prof. AUGUSTO CONCIO, M.E.P.
College of Nursing: Prof. CONCHITA T. MACEDA, M.A.
Graduate School: CARMEN KANAPI, PH.D.
Religion: Fr. PAULINO GONZALEZ.

SILLIMAN UNIVERSITY

DUMAGUETE CITY 6501

Founded 1901.

Private control; Language of instruction: English; Academic year: June to March.

President: Dr. QUINTIN S. DOROMAL.
Vice-President for Academic Affairs: Dr. PROCESO U. UDARBE.
Vice-President for Research, Extension and Development: Dr. ANGEL C. ALCALA.
Comptroller: CLEONICO Y. FONTELO.
Registrar: RAYMUNDO R. DATO.
Librarian: GORGONIO D. SIEGA.

Library: *see* Libraries.

Number of teachers: 357, including 18 professors.

Number of students: 5,177.

Publications: *The Silliman Journal* (quarterly), *Sillimanian Magazine* (2 a year), *The Weekly Sillimanian, Sands and Corals* (annual literary magazine), *Portal* (yearbook), *Weekly Calendar*.

DEANS:

College of Arts and Sciences: LUZ U. AUSEJO.
College of Education: PROCESO U. UDARBE (acting).
College of Law: EDUARDO S. FLORES, LL.B.
College of Engineering: TEOGENES V. MAGDAMO.
Divinity School: PATROCINIO A. APURA.
College of Nursing: MARÍA CONCEPCIÓN M. ROBLE, M.A.
Graduate School: ANGEL C. ALCALA.
College of Business Administration: QUINTIN S. DOROMAL (acting).
School of Communication: CRISPIN C. MASLOG, PH.D.
School of Music and Fine Arts: Mrs. RUTH I. PFEIFFER, M.A. (Director).
School of Agriculture: CHRISTOPHER A. ABLAN, D.V.M. (Director).

PROFESSORS:

ALCALA, ANGEL C., Biology
AUSEJO, LUZ U., History
CORTES, TEODORO V., Law and Political Science
FAUROT, ALBERT L., Music and Fine Arts
FLORES, EDUARDO S., Law
GONZALES, RODOLFO B., Biology
KAPILI, PASCUAL H., Biology
MAQUISO, ELENA G., Religious Education
MARTINEZ, SALVADOR T., Philosophy and Religious Studies
MASLOG, CRISPIN C., Communication
ORACION, TIMOTEO S., Anthropology-Sociology
PFEIFFER, RUTH I., Music
REYNOLDS, HARRIET R., Anthropology
REYNOLDS, HUBERT I., Social Work
ROBLE, MARÍA CONCEPCIÓN M., Nursing
SITOY, VALENTINO T., Church History
TIEMPO, EDILBERTO K., English
TIEMPO, EDITH L., English
UDARBE, P. U., Theology

UNIVERSITY OF SOUTHERN PHILIPPINES

MABINI STREET, CEBU CITY

Telephone: 7-23-31, 7-29-26.

Founded 1927, University status 1949.

President: OSCAR JEREZA.
Registrar: ERLINDA M. CAMPOS (acting).

Number of teachers: 185.
Number of students: 1,536.

DEANS:

College of Arts and Sciences: IRENE ORDOÑA.
Graduate School of Law: RONALD DUTERTE.
College of Engineering: CIRIACO MIRASOL.
College of Commerce: GERONIMO S. ANA.
College of Education: GREGORIA ALCOSEBA.
Graduate School: Dr. RUPERTA MARTINEZ.
School of Social Work: EMMA PARAS.

SOUTHWESTERN UNIVERSITY

VILLA AZNAR, CEBU CITY

Telephone: 9-66-90.

Private control; Language of instruction: English.

Founded 1946.

President: MATIAS B. AZNAR III.
Vice-President (Finance): JOSE LARDIZABAL.
Vice-President (Student Affairs): Dr. MANOLO FORNOLLES.
Vice-President (Academic Affairs): CAROLINA PAÑARES.
Registrar: Dr. SEGUNDINO TORREFRANCA.
Librarian: ZOEY VASQUEZ.

Number of teachers: 450.
Number of students: 14,272.

DEANS:

Graduate School: Dr. GREGORIO URIARTE.
Faculty of Law: Atty. MANUEL QUIJANO.
Faculty of Arts and Sciences: Dr. FRANCES LUMAIN.
Faculty of Dentistry: Dr. FELICITO PASCUAL.
Faculty of Optometry: Dr. GRACE R. ALOTA.
Faculty of Commerce: JOSE LARDIZABAL.
Faculty of Pharmacy: ROSARIO BARCENILLA.
Faculty of Engineering: GREGORIO SEGURA.
Faculty of Medical Technology: ALMA HOLOPAINEN.
Faculty of Agriculture: Dr. NARCISO PEPITO.
Faculty of Veterinary Medicine: Dr. NESTOR ALONSO III.
College of Medicine: Dr. FLORANTE ALBANO.
School of Nursing: CARMEN NERI SAN LORENZO.
Teachers' College: Atty. RICARDO GABUYA.
High School: DULZURA CADAVEZ.
Elementary School: PROSERFINA DE GUZMAN.

TECHNOLOGICAL UNIVERSITY OF THE PHILIPPINES

P.O.B. 3171, AYALA BLVD.-SAN MARCELINO ST., METRO MANILA

Telephone: 58-63-55, 50-93-66

Founded 1901.

President: JOSÉ R. VERGARA.
Vice-President (Academic Affairs): GALICANO J. DATU.
Vice-President (Administration and Development): BAYANI I. GUTIERREZ.
Registrar: BASILISA O. PALMIANO.
Librarian: ESTHER T. GUTIERREZ.

Library of 23,779 vols.
Number of teachers: 201.
Number of students: 6,490.

DEANS:

College of Arts and Trades: BERNARDO F. ADIVISO.
Graduate School: ILUMINADA G. ESPINO.

First and second degree courses in industrial sciences and engineering, doctoral degree in industrial education management.

UNIVERSITY OF THE VISAYAS*

CEBU CITY

Telephone: 60-42, 68-41.

Founded 1919.

Private control.

President: JOSEPHINA RWERA GULLAS.
Executive Vice-President: EDUARDO R. GULLAS.
Vice-President for Financial Affairs: JOSE R. GULLAS.

Executive Secretary: FELISA P. ORO.
Registrar: CLARO L. MENDOZA.
Director of Public Relations: FERMIN YAP.
Librarian: SEVERINA CALLEDO.

Number of teachers: *c.* 500.
Number of students: *c.* 20,000.

Publications: *The Visayanian, The V-Spirit, U.V. Journal.*

DEANS:

Teachers' College: NEMESIO GAMBITO.
College of Law: CECILIO GILLAMAL.
College of Liberal Arts: GREGORIO URIARTE.
College of Pharmacy: YOLANDA OPORTO.
College of Criminology: EMMANUEL PEPITO.
College of Commerce: DIONISIO GONZALES.
Graduate School: CONCESA M. BADUEL.
Student Affairs: ANDREA C. TECSON.

* No reply received to our questionnaire this year.

XAVIER UNIVERSITY

ATENEO DE CAGAYAN,
CAGAYAN DE ORO CITY 8401
Telephone: 37-42.
Founded 1933.

Language of instruction: English; Private control; Academic year: June to March (two terms).

President: Rev. ERNESTO O. JAVIER.
Academic Vice-President: TERESITA T. TUMAPON.
Registrar: MODESTO L. MAGTIBAY.
Librarian: EVA BRILLO.

Number of teachers: 238.
Number of students: 4,635.

Publications: *Pag-Asa, Kinaadman*† (Wisdom), *Journal of the Southern Philippines.*

DEANS:

Faculty of Law: Judge FLORENTINO DUMLAO.
Faculty of Arts and Science: Rev. RENATO L. PUENTEVELLA.
Faculty of Education: Mrs. RUSTICA T. RACINES.
Faculty of Commerce and Business Administration: RUDOLFO D. PIMENTEL.
Faculty of Agriculture: Rev. WILLIAM F. MASTERSON, S.J.
Graduate School: Dr. AGUSTIN A. CABRERA.

ATTACHED INSTITUTES:

Research Institute for Mindanao Culture: f. 1957 to study and assist the development of north Mindanao and its peoples; Dir. FRANCIS C. MADIGAN, PH.D.; publs. *Xavier University Studies* (irregular), *Bulletin of APRIAS—Asian Population and Information Society* (quarterly).

Southeast Asian Rural Social Leadership Institute: f. 1964 for the formation of Asian rural workers for the social uplift of rural peoples; Dir. Rev. WILLIAM F. MASTERSON, S.J.

Institute of Market Analysis: f. 1967 for the determination of market trends for the information and guidance of producers, particularly farmers; Dir. Dr. ISMAEL P. GETUBIG, Jr.

Institute for the Development of Educational Administrators: a Ford Foundation—FAPE project aimed at producing professionally trained administrators for Philippine schools; Dir. Rev. ERNESTO O. JAVIER, S.J.

COLLEGES

AGRICULTURE

Don Severino Agricultural College: Indang, Cavite 2712; f. 1906; 230 staff, 1,920 students; library of 11,000 vols.; Pres. VICENTE T. PINAZO; publ. *The Cultivator.*

Northern Luzon State College of Agriculture: Piat, Cagayan; f. 1955; 400 students, 70 teachers; library of 7,034 vols.; Pres. LUIS T. CATABIAN; publ. *Citadel.*

Palawan National Agricultural College: Aborlan, Palawan; f. 1963; Pres. MIGUEL P. PALAO.

HUMANITIES

College of the Holy Spirit: 163 Mendiola St., San Miguel, Manila, P.O.B. 1817; f. 1913; private control; departments of Science and Mathematics, Fine Arts, Commerce, Foods and Nutrition, Education, Liberal Arts; library of 31,326 vols.; Pres. Sister PILAR A. GONZALEZ, S.SP.S.; Registrar Miss HONORATA M. MUYOT; publs. *Veritas*† (monthly), *Action*† (quarterly).

San Beda College: Mendiola St., Manila; f. 1901; private control; constituent grade and high schools and colleges of Law, Arts and Sciences; 208 staff, 6,856 students; libraries total 76,293 vols.; Rector Rev. BERNARDO MA. PEREZ, O.S.B.; Librarian Rev. PAUL DE VERA, O.S.B.

St. Paul College of Manila: 680 Pedro Gil St., Malate, Manila, P.O.B. 2061; f. 1912; private control; Constituent colleges of Liberal Arts, Education, Commerce, Home Economics, Nursing, Music, Foods and Nutrition; 130 staff, 2,448 students; library of 32,278 vols.; Pres. Sister MARY CYRIL CORPUS, S.P.C.

St. Scholastica's College: 2560 Leon Guinto Sr. St., Malate, Manila, P.O.B. 3153; f. 1906; private control; Schools of Liberal Arts, Commerce, Education, Music; Pres. Sister M. SOLEDAD HILADO, O.S.B.; Registrar Miss IMELDA DAVID.

EDUCATION

Philippine Normal College: Taft Ave., Manila; f. 1901; graduate and post-graduate courses in Education, Linguistics; operates Language Study Centre for Philippine languages, Health Education Centre, Child Study Centre, Reading Centre, and Special Education Centre; library of 85,390 vols.; 229 teachers, 3,274 students; Pres. Dr. BONIFACIO P. SIBAYAN.

TECHNOLOGY

Cagayan Valley Institute of Technology: Cabagan, Isabela; f. 1961; courses in agriculture, forestry, home economics, teaching; library of 3,168 vols.; Chief Officer TEOFILO H. MONTEMAYOR; publs. *Research and Extension Journal*† (2 a year), *The Technologist*† (quarterly).

Central Luzon Polytechnic College: Cabanatuan City; f. 1964; library of 5,416 vols.; Pres. ALBERTO B. GARCIA; Sec. RUBEN S. YAMBOT; publ. *Polytechnic Journal.*

Leyte Institute of Technology: Tacloban City; f. 1965; courses in engineering, science, industrial technology, education and vocational training; post-graduate courses; 309 staff; library of 12,109 vols.; Pres. G. H. TENEFRANCIA; Registrar DOMINADOR A. ESPINOSA; publs. *Annual Report, Graduate School Bulletin, Engineering Department Bulletin, School Bulletin.*

Lyceum of the Philippines: Real and Muralla Streets, Intramuros, P.O.B. 1264, Manila; f. 1952; private control; Faculties of Law, Graduate Studies, Journalism, Humanities and Sciences, Foreign Service, Economic and Business Administration, Education, Office Management, Technical Vocational, Secretarial Science, High School; Pres. Dr. SOTERO H. LAUREL; Registrar A. DE LOS SANTOS; Librarian JOSEFINA P. LAUREL; 148 teachers, 3,657 students; library of 19,686 vols.

Mapua Institute of Technology: Muralla St., Intramuros, Manila; f. 1925; private control; Faculties of Architecture and Planning, Industrial Design, Management and Industrial Engineering, Mining and Metallurgical Engineering, Civil Engineering, Electrical Engineering, Electronics and Communications Engineering, Mechanical Engineering, Geology, Environmental and Sanitary Engineering, Chemical Engineering and Chemistry; Pres. OSCAR B. MAPUA; Vice-Pres. and Treas. Mrs. GLORIA MAPUA-LIM; Registrar NIEVES M. LIM.

Mindanao Institute of Technology: Kabacan, North Cotabato; f. 1954;

departments of Agriculture, Agricultural Education, Agricultural Engineering, Trade and Industrial Education, Home Economics, Pedagogy; Officer-in-charge Atty. A. O. AUSTRIA; 6,000 students.

Namei Polytechnic Institute: 123 A. Mabini, Mandaluyong, Rizal; f. 1947; private control; courses in Naval Architecture, Mechanical, Electrical, Civil, Chemical, and Marine Engineering; Pres. FELIX PADILLA; Dir. CONRADO N. CRUZ; Registrar LEOPOLDO Z. SO.

Naval Institute of Technology: Naval, Biliran Sub-Province 6908; f. 1977; library of 5,000 vols.; 58 teachers, 1,527 students; Pres. ALFREDO C. JOSEP; Registrar SOCORRO MOCORRO; Librarian ANA B. LEONES.

Pablo Borbon Memorial Institute of Technology: Rizal Ave., Batangas City; f. 1903; library of 9,467 vols.; 85 teachers, 1,917 students; Pres. ROSAURO DE LEON; Registrar ISABELO R. EVANGELIO.

Palompon Institute of Technology: Palompon, Leyte; f. 1972; library of 4,789 vols.; 64 instructors, 1,900 students; courses in marine engineering, naval architecture, nautical science, radio communication, domestic science, trade technical education, customs administration, shipping management and accountancy; Pres. Dr. PAULINO I. VILLAGONZALO; Registrar CELSO C. RAYMUNDO.

Tarlac College of Technology: Tarlac; f. 1965; courses in technical subjects, teacher-training and business administration; Pres. JACK SMITH; Registrar Prof. AURORA A. CASTAÑEDA (acting).

POLAND

Population 35,314,000

POLISH ACADEMY OF SCIENCES

PALACE OF CULTURE AND SCIENCE, WARSAW
Founded 1952

President: Prof. Witold Nowacki.
Vice-Presidents: Prof. Jerzy Litwiniszyn, Prof. Szczepan Pieniążek, Prof. Jan Szczepański, Prof. Andrzej Trautman.
Scientific Secretary: Prof. Jan Kaczmarek.
Deputy Scientific Secretaries: Prof. Jerzy Kołodziejczak, Prof. Tadeusz Orłowski.
Secretaries of Sections:
Secretary of Section I: Prof. Wladyslaw Markiewicz.
Secretary of Section II: Prof. Adam Urbanek.
Secretary of Section III: Prof. Jan Rychlewski.
Secretary of Section IV: Prof. Maciej Nalecz.
Secretary of Section V: Prof. Zbigniew Gertych.
Secretary of Section VI: Prof. Jan Kostrzewski.
Secretary of Section VII: Prof. Zdizslaw Kaczmarek.

Members of Praesidium:

Bielański, Adam.
Chołaj, Henryk.
Dobrzánski, Bohdan.
Gibiński, Kornel.
Groszkowski, Janusz.
Hueckel, Stanisław.
Jeżowska-Trzebiatowska, Bogusława.
Kielan-Jaworowska, Zofia.
Krzymowski, Tadeusz.
Labuda, Gerard.
Leszczycki, Stanisław.
Malecki, Ignacy.
Mantueffel, Ryszard.
Melich, Alojzy.
Michajłow, Włodzimierz.
Michalski, Jan.
Michałowski, Kazimierz.
Mięsowicz, Marian.
Mossakowski, Mirosław.
Nawrocki, Stanisław.
Olech, Czesław.
Ostrowski, Włodzimierz.
Secomski, Kazimierz.
Smoleński, Dionizy.
Suchodolski, Bogdan.
Ślopek, Stefan.
Trzebiatowski, Włodzimierz.
Urbanik, Kazimierz.
Węgrzyn, Stefan.
Wiewiórowski, Maciej.

Central publs. *Bulletin de L'Académie Polonaise des Sciences:* Series of *Biological Sciences* (monthly), Series of *Mathematical Sciences* (monthly), Series of *Physical and Astronomical Sciences* (quarterly), Series of *Chemical Sciences* (monthly), Series of *Sciences of the Earth* (quarterly), Series of *Technical Sciences* (monthly), *Nauka Polska* (monthly), *The Review of the Polish Academy of Sciences* (quarterly), *Żurnal Polskoi Akademii Nauk* (quarterly, Russian version).

Section I—*Social Sciences* (*Philosophy, History, Philology, Literature, Art, Economics, Law*).

Members:

Barycz, Henryk.
Brahmer, Mieczysław.
Czachórski, Witold.
Dobrowolski, Kazimierz.
Gieysztor, Aleksander.
Górski, Konrad.
Hensel, Witold.
Jabłoński, Henryk.
Kieniewicz, Stefan.
Kotarbiński, Tadeusz.
Kuraszkiewicz, Władysław
Labuda, Gerard.
Lachs, Manfred.
Lipiński, Edward.
Lorentz, Stanisław.
Łowmiański, Henryk.
Majewski, Kazimierz.
Markiewicz, Henryk.
Markiewicz, Władysław.
Michałowski, Kazimierz.
Rosset, Edward.
Safarewicz, Jan.
Schaff, Adam.
Secomski, Kazimierz.
Skwarczyńska, Stefania.
Sławski, Franciszek.
Steffen, Wiktor.
Stieber, Zdzisław.
Suchodolski, Bogdan.
Szablowski, Jerzy.
Szczepański, Jan.
Szubert, Wacław.
Topolski, Jerzy.
Wolter, Władysław.
Żółkiewski, Stefan.

Corresponding Members:

Białostocki, Jan.
Cholaj, Henryk.
Fritzhand, Marek.
Klimowicz, Mieczysław.
Kłoskowska, Antonina.
Kula, Witold.
Kupisiewicz, Czesław.
Leśnodorski, Bogusław.
Madajczyk, Czesław.
Melich, Alojzy.
Nowakowski, Stefan.
Okoń, Wincenty.
Opałek, Kazimierz.
Pajestka, Józef.
Rostworowski, Emanuel.
Sadowski, Wiesław.
Schlauch, Margaret.
Zawadzki, Sylwester.

Section II—*Biological Sciences.*

Members:

Baranowski, Tadeusz.
Białobok, Stefan.
Chmielewska, Irena.
Ewy, Zygmunt.
Gajewski, Wacław.
Górski, Franciszek.
Grodziński, Zygmunt.
Kielan-Jaworowska, Zofia.
Kunicki-Goldfinger, Władysław.
Michajłow, Włodzimierz.
Niemierko, Włodzimierz.
Pawełkiewicz, Jerzy.
Petrusewicz, Kazimierz.
Starmach, Karol.
Szarski, Henryk.
Środoń, Andrzej.
Zabłocki, Bernard.
Zurzycki, Jan.

Corresponding Members:

Klekowski, Romuald.
Kornaś, Jan.
Kowalski, Kazimierz.
Kuźnicki, Leszek.
Lorkiewicz, Zbigniew.
Michniewicz, Marian.
Ostrowski, Włodzimierz.
Szafrański, Przemysław.
Szweykowski, Jerzy.
Tarkowski, Andrzej K.
Urbanek, Adam.
Wierzchowski, Kazimierz L.
Wojtczak, Lech.
Zarzycki, Kazimierz.
Zieliński, Kazimierz.

Section III—*Mathematical, Physical and Chemical Sciences.*

Members:

Achmatowicz, Osman.
Basiński, Antoni.
Bielański, Adam.
Bobrownicki, Włodzimierz.
Borsuk, Karol.
Danysz, Marian.
Hrynkiewicz, Andrzej.
Iwanowska, Wilhelmina.
Jabłoński, Aleksander.
Jedliński, Zbigniew.
Jezowska-Trzebiatowska, Bogusława.
Kemula, Wiktor.
Kołos, Włodzimierz.
Królikowski, Wojciech.
Łojasiewicz, Stanisław.
Malinowski, Stanisław.
Mazur, Stanisław.
Michalski, Jan.
Mięsowicz, Marian.
Mikusiński, Jan.
Orlicz, Władysław.
Piekara, Arkadiusz.
Piotrowski, Stefan.
Pniewski, Jerzy.
Ryll-Nardzewski, Czesław.
Rzewuski, Jan.
Sikorski, Roman.
Sosnowski, Leonard.
Staliński, Bohdan.
Śmiałowski, Michał.
Trautman, Andrzej.
Trzebiatowski, Włodzimierz.
Urbanik Kazimierz.
Urbański, Tadeusz.
Werle, Józef.
Wiewiórowski, Maciej.
Wróbel, Jerzy.

Corresponding Members:

Baranowski, Bogdan.
Bessaga, Czesław.
Białas, Andrzej.
Białynicki-Birula, Iwo.
Bojarski, Bogdan.
Ciesielski, Zbigniew.
Czyż, Wiesław.
Haber, Jerzy.
Janik, Jerzy.
Kołodziejczak, Jerzy.
Kroh, Jerzy.
Kryszewski, Marian.
Kuczyński, Henryk.
Lasocki, Zygmunt.
Łopuszański, Jan.
Łoś, Jerzy.
Łukaszewicz, Kazimierz.
Minczewski, Jerzy.
Mrowéc, Stanisław.
Olech, Czesław.
Paczyński, Bohdan.
Pasynkiewicz, Stanisław.
Pełczyński, Aleksander.
Pliś, Andrzej.
Ratajczak, Henryk.
Rychlewski, Jan.
Schinzel, Andrzej.
Sobczyk, Lucjan.
Sosnowski, Ryszard.
Stankowski, Jan.
Szymański, Zdzisław.
Wróblewski, Andrzej.
Zielenkiewicz, Wojciech.

Section IV—*Technical Sciences.*

Members:

Ciborowski, Janusz.
Cholewicki, Tadeusz.
Dubicki, Bolesław.
Filipczyński, Leszek.
Fiszdon, Władysław.
Groszkowski, Janusz.
Grzymek, Jerzy.
Hueckel, Stanisław.
Jakubowski, Janusz Lech.
Kaczmarek, Jan.
Kanafojski, Czesław.
Kisiel, Igor.
Kulikowski, Roman.
Malecki, Ignacy.
Misztal, Franciszek.
Nałęcz, Maciej.
Nowacki, Witold.
Olszak, Wacław.
Paszkowski, Bohdan.
Pełczyński, Tadeusz.
Pełczewski, Władysław.
Skowroński, Jerzy Ignacy.
Smoleński, Dionizy.
Smoliński, Adam.
Staniszewski, Bogumił.
Szewalski, Robert.
Szulkin, Paweł.
Szymanowski, Witold.
Truszkowski, Wojciech.
Węgrzyn, Stefan.
Zachwatowicz, Jan.
Zagajewski, Tadeusz.
Zaremba, Piotr.
Ziemba, Stefan.

Corresponding Members:

Badian, Ludwik.
Baran, Marceli.
Bojarski, Zbigniew.
Brzoska, Zbigniew.
Ciesielski, Roman.
Ciszewski, Bohdan.
Findeisen, Władysław
Gierek, Adam.
Gutkowski, Witold.
Kobyliński, Lech.
Kroszczynski, Jan.
Łubinski, Mieczysław.
Łukaszewicz, Leon.
Madejski, Jan.
Malkiewicz, Tadeusz.
Marciniak, Zdzisław.
Prosnak, Włodzimierz.
Ptak, Władysław.
Rosiński, Witold.
Sakwa, Wacław.
Sawczuk, Antoni.
Seidler, Jerzy.
Szargut, Jan.
Szczepiński, Wojciech.
Szklarski, Ludger.
Śliwiński, Tadeusz.
Świt, Alfred.
Wejchert, Kazimierz.
Więckowski, Józef.
Życzkowski, Michał.

Section V—*Agricultural and Forestry Sciences.*

Members:

Alexandrowicz, Stefan.
Bielański, Władysław.
Boratyński, Kazimierz.
Brill, Juliusz.
Dembiński, Felicjan.
Dobrzański, Bohdan.
Haman, Janusz.
Kielanowski, Jan.
Kochman, Józef.
Lekczyńska, Jadwiga.
Listowski, Anatol.
Lityński, Tadeusz.
Mańka, Karol.
Manteuffel, Ryszard.
Niewiadomski, Witold.
Nunberg, Marian.
Pieniążek, Szczepan.
Ruebenbauer, Tadeusz.
Stryszak, Abdon.
Tołpa, Stanisław.
Węgorek, Władysław.

Corresponding Members:

Brzoza, Anatol.
Domański, Eugeniusz.
Duniec, Henryk.
Gertych, Zbigniew.
Grochowski, Wiesław.
Krzymowski, Tadeusz.
Nawrocki, Stanisław.
Nowacki, Tadeusz.
Poznański, Stefan.
Rutkowski, Antoni.
Starzycki, Stanisław.
Truszczyński, Marian.
Wojtaszek, Tadeusz.
Zawadzki, Saturnin.

Section VI—*Medical Sciences.*

Members:

Albert, Zygmunt.
Aleksandrow, Dymitr.
Bobrański, Bogusław.
Dega, Wiktor.
Gibiński, Kornel.
Gruca, Adam.
Hano, Józef.
Heller, Józef.
Horst, Antoni.
Jasiński, Władysław.
Korzybski, Tadeusz.
Kostrzewski, Jan Karol.
Kowarzyk, Hugon.
Krwawicz, Tadeusz.
Kunicki, Adam.
Kuryłowicz, Włodzimierz.
Orłowski, Tadeusz.
Oszacki, Jan.
Rowiński, Ksawery.
Ślopek, Stefan.

Corresponding Members:

Bross, Wiktor.
Chorąży, Mieczysław.
Dux, Kazimierz.
Gryglewski, Ryszard.
Halikowski, Bogusław.
Kopeć, Maria.
Maj, Jerzy.
Michałkiewicz, Witold.
Mossakowski, Mirosław.
Nielubowicz, Jan.
Nikonorow, Maksym.
Nowosławski, Adam.
Ostrowski, Kazimierz.
Rudowski, Witold.

Section VII—*Earth and Mining Sciences.*

Members:

Bolewski, Andrzej.
Cebertowicz, Romuald.
Czetwertyński, Edward.
Dziewoński, Kazimierz.
Galon, Rajmund.
Kaczmarek, Zdzisław.
Klimaszewski, Mieczysław.
Książkiewicz, Marian.
Leszczycki, Stanisław.
Litwiniszyn, Jerzy.
Passendorfer, Edward.
Pawłowski, Stanisław.
Pożaryski, Władysław.
Różycki, Stefan Zbigniew
Smulikowski, Kazimierz.
Teisseyre, Roman.

Corresponding Members:

Bystroń, Henryk.
Druet, Czesław.
Dżułyński, Stanisław.
Jahn, Alfred.
Kleczkowski, Antoni S.
Knothe, Stanisław.
Kordas, Bolesław.
Kostrowicki, Jerzy.
Kowalczyk, Zygmunt.
Nawrocki, Jerzy.
Ney, Roman.
Smolarski, Andrzej Z.
Znosko, Jerzy.

Foreign Members:

Aleksandrov, Anatoly P., U.S.S.R.
Aleksandrov, Pavel Sergeyevich, U.S.S.R.
Backvis, Claude, Belgium.
Balevski, Angel T., Bulgaria.
Bandurski, Robert S., U.S.A.
Barlow, Harold Everald Monteagle, Great Britain.
Basov, Nikolai G., U.S.S.R.
Bastien, Paul, France.
Batchelor, George, Great Britain.
Bayev, Aleksandr A., U.S.S.R.
Bielov, Nikolai V., U.S.S.R.
Bing, R. H., U.S.A.
Blanquet, Josias Braun, France.
Blascovic, Dionizy, Czechoslovakia.
Blokhin, Nikolai Nikolayevich, U.S.S.R.
Bognár, Geza, Hungary.
Bogolubov, Nikolai Nikolayevich, U.S.S.R.
Bohr, Aage, Denmark.
Bonfante, Giuliano, Italy.
Branca, Vittore, Italy.
Braudel, Fernand, France.
Brekhovskikh, Leonid M., U.S.S.R.
Campus, Ferdinand, Belgium.
Caspersson, Torbjörn Oscar, Sweden.
Chang, Chien wei, China.
Charvat, Josef, Czechoslovakia.
Chavez, Ignacio, Mexico.
Cloud, Preston, U.S.A.
Cramer, Friedrich, German Fed. Repub.
Dalitz, Richard H., Great Britain.
Danowski, Tadeusz S., U.S.A.
Daskalov, Khristo Stefan, Bulgaria.
Dresch, Jean, France.
Drucker, Daniel C., U.S.A.
Dubinin, Nikolaj P., U.S.S.R.
Durand-Delga, Michel, France.
Emanuel, Nikolai M., U.S.S.R.
Engelhardt, Władimir A., U.S.S.R
Escande, Leopold, France.
Fiedosiejew, Piotr N., U.S.S.R.
Garin, Eugenio, Italy.
Gaudemet, Jean, France.
Gauze, Georgii Francevich, U.S.S.R.

GERMAIN, PAUL, France.
GLUSHKOV, VIKTOR M., U.S.S.R.
GRAVESON, RONALD H., Great Britain.
GRIVET, PIERRE AUGUSTE, France.
HAMBURGER, JEAN, France.
HORN, ARTUR, Hungary.
HUSEN, TORSTEN, Sweden.
ILEŠIČ, SVETOZAR, Yugoslavia.
ISHLINSKY, ALEKSANDR Y., U.S.S.R.
JAKOBSON, ROMAN, U.S.A.
KAPITSA, PYOTR LEONIDOVICH, U.S.S.R.
KASTLER, ALFRED, France.
KHACHATUROV, TIGRAN S., U.S.S.R.
KLARE, HERMAN, German Dem. Repub.
KOLMOGOROV, ANDREI N., U.S.S.R.
KON, STANISŁAW KAZIMIERZ, Great Britain.
KOTIELNIKOW, WŁADIMIR A., U.S.S.R.
KOŽEŠNÍK, JAROSLAV, Czechoslovakia.
KURSANOV, ANDREI LVOVICH, U.S.S.R.
LASKOWSKI, MICHAŁ, U.S.A.
LAVRENTEV, MIKHAIL A., U.S.S.R.
LEIBUNDGUT, HANS, Switzerland.
LEONARD, NELSON J., U.S.A.
LERAY, JEAN, France.
LOBANOV, PAVEL P., U.S.S.R.
LUKIĆ, RADOMIR, Yugoslavia.
MANN, TADEUSZ, Great Britain.
MASSALSKI, TADEUSZ B., U.S.A.
MASSONET, CHARLES E., Belgium.
MAYRHOFER, MANFRED, Austria.
MILCU, STEFAN, Romania.
MILLIKAN, DANIEL F., U.S.A.
MOORE, FRANCIS D., U.S.A.
NÉEL, LOUIS E. F., France.
NESMEYANOV, ALEKSANDER N., U.S.S.R.
NIKOLSKIJ, SIERGIEJ M., U.S.S.R.
OCHOA, SEVERO, U.S.A.
ODQUIST, FOLKE K. G., Sweden.
OLESCH, REINHOLD, German Fed. Repub.
PARKUS, HEINZ, Austria.
PAULING, LINUS CARL, U.S.A.
PIETROW, BORYS N., U.S.S.R.
PIETROWSKI, BORYS W., U.S.S.R.
REFSUM, SIGVALD, Norway.
ROBERT, LOUIS, France.
ROSICKÝ, BOHUMIR, Czechoslovakia.
ROTBLAT, JÓZEF, Great Britain.
RYBAKOV, BORIS A., U.S.S.R.
SÖVE-SÖDERBERGH, TORGNY, Sweden.
SCHEEL, HEINRICH, German Dem. Repub.
SEABORG, GLENN T., U.S.A.
SEVERIN, SERGEI E., U.S.S.R.
SHABAD, LEW M., U.S.S.R.
SHATILOV, IVAN S., U.S.S.R.
SHAW, MILTON C., U.S.A.
SIEMIONOV, NIKOŁAJ N., U.S.S.R.
SNEDDON, IAN N., Great Britain.
ŠORM, FRANTIŠEK, Czechoslovakia.
SPICYN, WIKTOR I., U.S.S.R.
SPŁAWA-NEYMAN, JERZY, U.S.A.
STRAUB, FERENC BRUNO, Hungary.
STOETZEL, JEAN, France.
STROGOVICH, MIKHAIL S., U.S.S.R.
STUBBE, HANS, German Democratic Republic.
SZABÓ, IMRE, Hungary.
SZENTÁGOTHAI, JANOS, Hungary.
SZIRENDYB, BAZARYN, Mongolia.
TAKHTADZHJAN, ARMEN L., U.S.S.R.
TARCZY-HORNOCH, ANTAL, Hungary.
THEORELL, HUGO, Sweden.
THIBAULT, CHARLES GEORGES, France.
TODD, ALEXANDER R., Great Britain.
ULRICH, ROGER, France.
VANE, JOHN ROBERT, Great Britain.
VONSOVSKY, SERGEI V., U.S.S.R.
WAWIŁOW, PIOTR P., U.S.S.R.
WILLIAMS, ALWYN, Great Britain.
YAGI, KUNIO, Japan.
ZHAVORONKOV, NIKOLAI M., U.S.S.R.
ZYGMUND, ANTONI, U.S.A.

ACADEMY OF SCIENCES—SCIENTIFIC ASSOCIATIONS

Gdańskie Towarzystwo Naukowe (*Gdańsk Scientific Society*): Gdańsk, ul. Grodzka 12; f. 1922 as Gdańsk Society of Friends of Science and Art; 477 mems.; Pres. Prof. Dr. ROMAN WAPIŃSKI; Sec. Dr. ANDRZEJ ZBIERSKI.

Sections:

Social Sciences and Humanities: Chair. Doc. Dr. STANISŁAW MIELCZARSKI; publs. *Rocznik Gdański, Gdańsk Wczesnośredniowieczny, Pomorze Gdańskie, Pomorskie Monografie Toponomastyczne, Gdańskie Studia Językoznawcze, Seria źródel, Seria monografii.*

Biological and Medical Sciences: Chair. Prof. Dr. FELIKS PIOTROWSKI; publs. *Monografie Wydziału II, Acta Biologica Societatis Scientiarum Gedanensis.*

Mathematical, Physical and Chemical Sciences: Chair. Prof. Dr. MARIAN KWAPISZ; publ. *Monografie Wydziału III.*

Technical Sciences: Chair. Doc. Dr. KAZIMIERZ IWANOWSKI; publ. *Acta Technica Gedanensia.*

Earth Sciences: Chair. Prof. Dr. BOLESŁAW AUGUSTOWSKI; publ. *Monografie Wydziału V.*

Łódzkie Towarzystwo Naukowe (*Łódź Scientific Society*): 90-114 Łódź, Sienkiewicza 29; f. 1936; Pres. BERNARD ZABŁOCKI; Sec. JÓZEF MATUSZEWSKI; publs. *Rozprawy Komisji Językowej*†, *Biuletyn Peryglacjalny*†, *Bulletin de la Sociéte des Sciences et des Lettres de Łódź*†, *Sprawozdania z Czynności i Posiedzeń Łódzkiego Towarzystwa Naukowego, Przegląd Socjologiczny, Zagadnienia Rodzajów Literackich*†, *Prace Polonistyczne*†, *Acta Archæologica Lodziensia*†, *Acta Geographica Lodziensia*†, *Studia Prawno-Ekonomiczne*† and others.

Opolskie Towarzystwo Przyjaciół Nauk (*Opole Society of Friends of Science*): 45-016 Opole, ul. Zamkowa 2; f. 1955; 310 mems.; library of 8,600 vols.; Pres. Dr. hab. EDWARD MENDEL; publs. *Kwartalnik Opolski* (quarterly), *Sprawozdania* (3 series, yearly), *Zeszyty Przyrodnicze* (yearly).

Polskie Towarzystwo Anatomiczne (*Polish Anatomical Society*): Warsaw, Chałubińskiego 5; f. 1923; Pres. Prof. OLGIERD NARKIEWICZ; Sec. Dr. HENRYK KOBRYŃ; publ. *Folia Morphologica.*

Polskie Towarzystwo Antropologiczne (*Polish Anthropological Society*): Warsaw, ul. Marymoncka 34; f. 1925; 500 mems.; library of *c.* 10,000 vols.; Pres. Prof. Dr. TADEUSZ DZIERŻYKRAY-ROGALSKI; Sec. Ph.D. JANUSZ CHARZEWSKI; publs. *Przegląd Antropologiczny, Człowiek w Czasie i Przestrzeni.*

Polskie Towarzystwo Archeologiczne i Numizmatyczne (*Polish Archaeological and Numismatic Society*): Warsaw, Jezuicka 6; f. 1920; Pres. Prof. Dr. RYSZARD KIERSNOWSKI; Sec. IRENA GÓRSKA; publs. *Z Otchłani Wieków, Wiadomości Numizmatyczne, Biblioteka Archeologiczna, Popularnonaukowa Biblioteka Archeologiczna, Biuletyn Numizmatyczny.*

Polskie Towarzystwo Astronautyczne (*Polish Astronautical Society*): Pałac Kultury i Nauki, pok. 2322, 00-901 Warsaw; f. 1954; 890 mems.; scientific, educational, and popular astronautics, planetology, bio-astronautics, space physics, CETI, and space law; brs. in Warsaw, Cracow, Katowice, Wrocław, Łódź, Olsztyn, Poznań, Wloclawek and Grudziądz; Pres. Prof. Dr. hab. S. BARANSKI; Exec. Sec. Dr. med. M. WOJTKOWIAK; publs. *Astronautyka*† (bi-monthly), *Postępy Astronautyki*† (Progress in Astronautics, quarterly).

Polskie Towarzystwo Astronomiczne (*Polish Astronomical*

Society): ul. Bartycka 18, 00716 Warsaw; f. 1923; 232 mems.; Pres. Dr. J. S. STODOŁKIEWICZ; Sec. Dr. M. SROCZYŃSKA-KOŻUCHOWSKA; publ. *Postępy Astronomii* (Progress in Astronomy).

Polskie Towarzystwo Biochemiczne (*Polish Biochemical Society*): 00-227 Warsaw, ul. Freta 17; f. 1958; 1,135 mems.; Pres. Prof. Dr. hab. L. WOJTCZAK, Sec. Doc. Dr. EWA SIKORSKA; publ. *Postępy Biochemii* (Advances in Biochemistry—I, quarterly).

Polskie Towarzystwo Botaniczne (*Polish Botanical Society*): Warsaw, ul. Rakowiecka 26/30; f. 1922; 935 mems.; library of 17,377 vols.; Pres. Prof. Dr. T. WODZICKI; Secs. Prof. Dr. B. RODKIEWICZ, Dr. Z. STARCK; publs. include *Acta Societatis Botanicorum Poloniae, Acta Agrobotanica, Monographiae Botanicae, Rocznik Sekcji Dendrologicznej Pol. Tow. Bot., Wiadomości Botaniczne, Acta Mycologica.*

Polskie Towarzystwo Chemiczne (*Polish Chemical Society*): ul. Freta 16, 00-227 Warsaw; f. 1919; 2,860 mems.; library of 1,100 vols.; Pres. Prof. Dr. B. BARANOWSKI; publs. *Wiadomości Chemiczne* (Chemical News), Polish Journal of Chemistry.

Polskie Towarzystwo Ekonomiczne (*Polish Economic Society*): Warsaw, Nowy Świat 49; f. 1918; 58,248 mems.; Pres. Prof. Dr. JÓZEF PAJESTKA; Gen. Sec. BOGDAN MIŁACZEWSKI; publs. *Ekonomista, Przegląd Statystyczny* (Statistical Review).

Polskie Towarzystwo Endokrynologiczne (*Polish Endocrinological Society*): 02-015 Warsaw, Starynkiewicza 3; f. 1951; 502 mems.; Pres. Prof. Dr. MAREK PAWLIKOWSKI; publ. bi-monthly Journal with English and Russian summaries.

Polskie Towarzystwo Entomologiczne (*Polish Entomological Society*): 00-330 Warsaw, Nowy Świat 72; f. 1920; theoretical and applied entomology; 800 mems.; library of 6,000 vols.; publs. *Polskie Pismo Entomologiczne-Bulletin Entomologique de Pologne*†, *Klucze do oznaczania owadów Polski*† (Keys to Identification of Polish Insects), *Wiadomości Entomologiczne*† (Entomological News).

Polskie Towarzystwo Farmaceutyczne (*Polish Pharmaceutical Society*): ul. Długa 16, 00-238 Warsaw; f. 1947; 6,500 mems.; Pres. Prof. Dr. L. KROWCZYNSKI; Gen. Sec. Dr. hab. H. CHWIALKOWSKI; publs. *Farmacja Polska* (monthly), *Acta Poloniae Pharmaceutica*† (bi-monthly), *Bromatologia i Chemia Toksykologiczna* (quarterly).

Polskie Towarzystwo Filologiczne (*Polish Philological Society*): Warsaw University, Krakowskie Przedmieście 26/28; f. 1893; aims to promote classical studies; 500 mems.; Pres. MARIA CYTOWSKA; Sec. HELENA CICHOCKA; publ. *Eos* (annual).

Polskie Towarzystwo Filozoficzne (*Polish Philosophical Society*): 00-901 Warsaw, Pałac Kultury i Nauki 1921; f. 1904; Pres. Prof. Dr. KLEMENS SZANIAWSKI; bpul. *Ruch Filozoficzny* (Philosophical Movement, quarterly).

Polskie Towarzystwo Fizjologiczne (*Polish Physiological Society*): 20-090 Lublin, Jaczewskiego 8; f. 1936 to promote scientific activity in all fields of physiology; 669 mems.; Pres. JAROSŁAW BILLEWICZ-STANKIEWICZ; Sec. DIONIZY GÓRNY; publ. *Acta Physiologica Polonica.*

Polskie Towarzystwo Fizyczne (*Polish Physical Society*): 00681 Warsaw, Hoza 69; f. 1921; *c.* 2,000 mems.; library of 1,300 vols.; Chair. Prof. Dr. Z. WILHELMI; Sec. Doc. Dr. P. DECOWSKI; publs. *Postępy Fizyki* (Advances in Physics—in Polish, bi-monthly), *Acta Physica Polonica A* and *B* (*A* monthly, *B* bi-monthly, in English, French, German and Russian), *Reports on Mathematical Physics* (bi-monthly, in English), *Delta* (monthly, in Polish).

Polskie Towarzystwo Geofizyczne (*Polish Geophysical Society*): Warsaw, Smoleńskiego 16; f. 1947; development of geophysical sciences and their popularization; 500 mems.; library of 4,000 vols.; Pres. Prof. Dr. MARIAN MOLGA; Sec.-Gen. Dr. JERZY JAWORSKI; publ. *Przegląd Geofizyczny* (Geophysical Review, quarterly).

Polskie Towarzystwo Geograficzne (*Polish Geographical Society*): Warsaw, Krakowskie Przedmieście 30; f. 1918; 3,000 mems.; Pres. Prof. Dr. STANISŁAW BEREZOWSKI; Vice-Pres. Prof. Dr. JERZY KONDRACKI; Sec. Miss IRENA BERNE; publs. *Czasopismo Geograficzne*† (quarterly), *Poznaj Świat*† (monthly), *Polski Przegląd Kartograficzny*† (quarterly).

Polskie Towarzystwo Geologiczne (*Polish Geological Society*): 30-063 Cracow, Oleandry 2a; f. 1921; 1,482 mems.; library of 22,348 vols.; Pres. Prof. Dr. hab. inż. ZBIGNIEW WILK; Sec. Doc. hab. ANDRZEJ SLĄCZKA; publ. *Rocznik Polskiego Towarzystwa Geologicznego*† (Annals of the Polish Geological Society, quarterly).

Polskie Towarzystwo Gleboznawcze (*Polish Soil Science Society*): 02-520 Warsaw, ul. Wiśniowa 61; f. 1937; 1,050 mems.; Pres. Prof. Dr. LUCJAN KRÓLIKOWSKI; Sec. Prof. Dr. Hab. ALINA KABATA-PENDIAS; publs. *Roczniki Gleboznawcze*† (quarterly), *Przegląd Naukowej Literatury Rolniczej i Lesnej* (4 a year), *Prace Komisji Naukowych* (irregular).

Polskie Towarzystwo Higieny Psychicznej (*Polish Mental Hygiene Society*): Warsaw, Łowicka 7/15; f. 1958; Pres. Prof. Dr. KAZIMIERZ DABROWSKI; publ. *Kwartalnik Zdrowia Psychicznego* (quarterly).

Polskie Towarzystwo Historii Medycyny (*Polish Medical History Society*): Warsaw, ul. Chocimska 22; f. 1957; 314 mems.; Pres. Prof. Dr. STANISŁAW KONOPKA; Sec. Dr. TEODOR KIKTA; publ. *Archiwum Historii Medycyny* (quarterly).

Polskie Towarzystwo Historyczne (*Polish Historical Society*): Warsaw, Rynek Starego Miasta 29/31; f. 1886; 3,075 mems.; Pres. Prof. Dr. MARIAN BISKUP; 41 local branches, 3 research centres; publs. *Przegląd Historyczny*† (quarterly), *Sobótka-Śląski Kwartalnik Historyczny*† (quarterly), *Studia i Materiały do dziejów Wielkopolski i Pomorza*† (series), *Komunikaty Mazursko-Warmińskie*† (quarterly), and several annuals.

Polskie Towarzystwo Immunologiczne (*Polish Immunological Society*): 53-114 Wrocław, ul. Czerska 12; f. 1969; 481 mems.; Pres. Prof. Dr. JÓZEF LISOWSKI; Sec.-Gen. Dr. ZBIGNIEW WIECZOREK; publ. *Immunologia Polska* (quarterly, in Polish and English).

Polskie Towarzystwo Językoznawcze (*Polish Linguistic Society*): Cracow, ul. Krupnicza 35; f. 1925; 650 mems.; Pres. MIECZYSŁAW SZYMCZAK; Sec. WIESŁAW BORYŚ; publs. *Biuletyn Polskiego Towarzystwa Językoznawczego.*

Polskie Towarzystwo Leśne (*Polish Forestry Society*): 02-362 Warsaw, ul. Wery Kostrzewy 3; f. 1882; 2,149 mems.; library of 1,297 vols.; Pres. Prof. Dr. h.c. FRANCISZEK KRZYSIK; Sec. Dr. ANDRZEJ GORZELAK; publ. *Sylwan*†.

Polskie Towarzystwo Ludoznawcze (*Polish Ethnographical Society*): Wrocław, Szewska 36; f. 1895; 970 mems.; 50,000 vols.; Pres. F. WOKROJ; Sec. B. BAZIELICH; publs. *Lud*† (annually), *Atlas Polskich Strojów Ludowych*†, *Prace i Materiały Etnograficzne*†, *Prace Etnologiczne*†, *Literatura Ludowa*† (every 2 months), *Archiwum Etnograficzne*†, *Biblioteka Popularna*†, *Dzieła Wszystkie O Kolberga, Łódzkie Studia Etnograficzne*† (annually).

Polskie Towarzystwo Matematyczne (*Polish Mathematical Society*): Warsaw, ul. Śniadeckich 8; f. 1919; 2,548 mems.; Pres. Prof. Dr. WŁADISŁAW ORLICZ; publs. *Annales Societatis Mathematicae Polonae: Series I Commentationes Mathematicae, Series II Wiadomości Matematyczne* (Mathematical News), *Series III Matematyka Stosowara* (Applied Mathematics), *Series IV Fundamenta Informaticae, Popularny Miesiecznik*

Matematyczno-Fizyczny DELTA (Mathematical and Physical popular monthly).

Polskie Towarzystwo Mechaniki Teoretycznej i Stosowanej (*Polish Society for Theoretical and Applied Mechanics*): Warsaw, Pałac Kultury i Nauki; f. 1958; brs. in Bydgoszcz, Częstochowa, Gdańsk, Gliwice, Cracow, Łódź, Poznań, Rzeszów, Szczecin, Warsaw, Wrocław; 713 mems.; Pres. Prof. Dr. ZBIGNIEW KĄCZKOWSKI; Gen. Sec. Prof. Dr. JAN SZMELTER; publs. *Mechanika Teoretyczna i Stosowana* (Theoretical and Applied Mechanics, quarterly).

Polskie Towarzystwo Mikrobiologów (*Polish Society of Microbiologists*): 00-791 Warsaw, ul. Chocimska 24; f. 1927; 936 mems.; Pres. Prof. JÓZEF FELIKS KUBICA; Sec. Dr. MIROSŁAW LUCZAK; publs. *Acta Microbiologica Polonica* (English, quarterly), *Medycyna Doświadczalna i Mikrobiologia* (Experimental Medicine and Microbiology, Polish, quarterly).

Polskie Towarzystwo Miłośników Astronomii (*Polish Amateur Astronomical Society*): 31-027 Cracow, ul. Ludwika Solskiego 30; f. 1921; 2,600 mems.; amateur observations, instrument-making, popularization of astronomy; Pres. M. MAZUR; Sec. M.Eng. S. LUBERTOWICZ; publs. *Urania* (monthly) and annual reports.

Polskie Towarzystwo Mineralogiczne (*Mineralogical Society of Poland*): Cracow, Al. Mickiewicza 30; f. 1969; 145 mems.; Pres. Prof. Dr. ANDRZEJ BOLEWSKI; Sec. Doc. Dr. WIESŁAW HEFLIK; publ. *Mineralogia Polonica.*

Polskie Towarzystwo Nauk Weterynaryjnych (*Polish Veterinary Sciences Society*): 03-849 Warsaw, ul. Grochowska 272; f. 1952; 1,428 mems.; library of 2,294 vols.; Pres. EDMUND PROST; Vice-Pres. STEFAN KOSSAKOWSKI; publ. *Medycyna Weterynaryjna*†.

Polskie Towarzystwo Orientalistyczne (*Polish Oriental Society*): 00-656 Warsaw, ul. Sniadeckich 8; f. 1922; Pres. TADEUSZ LEWICKI, STANISŁAW KAŁUŻYŃSKI, MIKOŁAJ MELANOWICZ, ALEKSANDER DUBIŃSKI; Sec. MACIEJ POPKO; publ. *Przegląd Orientalistyczny* (quarterly).

Polskie Towarzystwo Parazytologiczne (*Polish Parasitological Society*): 50-375 Wrocław, C. Norwida 29; f. 1948; 437 mems.; Pres. Doc. Dr. KATARZYNA NIEWIADOMSKA; publs. *Wiadomości Parazytologiczne*†, *Monografie Parazytologiczne.*

Polskie Towarzystwo Patologów (*Polish Society of Pathologists*): 02-004, Warsaw, Chałubińskiego 5; f. 1958; 600 mems.; Pres. Prof. Dr. hab. STEFAN KRUŚ; Sec. Dr. med. KRYSTYNA SZYMAŃSKA; publ. *Patologia Polska* (quarterly).

Polskie Towarzystwo Przyrodników im. Kopernika (*Polish "Copernicus" Society of Naturalists*): Warsaw, Pałac Kultury i Nauki; f. 1875; Pres. KAZIMIERZ MAŚLANKIEWICZ; Sec. ANDRZEJ FAGASIŃSKI; publs. *Wszechświat, Kosmos A.*

Polskie Towarzystwo Psychologiczne (*Polish Psychological Association*): Warsaw, Stawki 5/7; f. 1948; 1,361 mems.; Pres. Doc. Dr. IDA KURCZ; Sec. Mag. JANINA BIERZWIŃSKA; publs. *Przegląd Psychologiczny* (Psychological Review, quarterly).

Polskie Towarzystwo Semiotyczne (*Polish Society of Semiotics*): 00-901 Warsaw, Pałac Kultury i Nauki 1921; f. 1968; Pres. Prof. Dr. STEFAN ŻÓŁKIEWSKI; publ. *Studia Semiotyczne* (annually).

Polskie Towarzystwo Socjologiczne (*Polish Sociological Society*): Warsaw, Nowy Świat 72; f. 1957; Pres. Prof. STEFAN NOWAK; Sec. Prof. ANDRZEJ TYMOWSKI; publ. *Polish Sociological Bulletin*† (quarterly).

Polskie Towarzystwo Zoologiczne (*Polish Zoological Society*): 50-335 Wrocław, Sienkiewicza 21; f. 1935; 958 mems.; Pres. ANDRZEJ WIKTOR; Sec. JADWIGA NOWAK; publs. *Zoologica Poloniae, Przegląd Zoologiczny, The Ring* (quarterlies), *Notatki Ornitologiczne.*

Polskie Towarzystwo Zootechniczne (*Polish Animal Production Society*): 02-316 Warsaw, Kaliska 9; f. 1922; 1,350 mems.; library of 2,100 vols.; Pres. ZBIGNIEW ŻEBROWSKI; Dir. MIECZYSŁAWA SUSKA; publs. *Przegląd Naukowej Literatury Zootechnicznej*† (Reviews and abstracts of research in the animal sciences, quarterly), *Proceedings of Scientific Sessions*† (annually).

Poznańskie Towarzystwo Przyjaciół Nauk (*Poznań Society of Friends of Arts and Sciences*): 61-725 Poznań, ul. Sew. Mielżyńskiego 27/29; f. 1857; 923 mems.; library of 260,000 vols.; Pres. Prof. Dr. ZDZISŁAW KACZMARCZYK; Sec.-Gen. Prof. Dr. TADEUSZ PUCHAŁKA; publs. scientific, historical, social, legal, philological and philosophical works, including *Roczniki Historyczne, Roczniki Dziejów Społecznych i Gospodarczych, Poznańskie Roczniki Ekonomiczne, Lingua Posnaniensis, Slavia Occidentalis, Bulletin de la Société des Amis des Sciences et des Lettres de Poznań*—Série D: *Sciences Biologiques; Badania Fizjograficzne nad Polską Zachodnią,* Series A (Geography), Series B (Botany), Series C (Zoology), *Sprawozdania Poznańskiego Towarzystwa Przyjaciół Nauk.*

Szczecińskie Towarzystwo Naukowe (*Szczecin Scientific Society*): Sczceciń, Wielkopolska 19; f. 1956; Pres. Prof. Dr. LEON BABINSKI; Sec.-Gen. Prof. Dr. STEFAN KOWNAS; Sections (A) Social Sciences, (B) Agriculture and Natural Sciences, (C) Medicine, (D) Technical Sciences and Mathematics; publs. in each section *Series A, B, C, D.*

Towarzystwo Internistów Polskich (*Polish Society of Internal Medicine*): Wrocław, ul. Pasteura 4, Klinika Kardiologiczna; f. 1909; Pres. Prof. Dr. SEWERYN ŁUKASIK; Sec. Doc. Dr. KRZYSZTOF WRABEC; publ. *Polskie Archiwum Medycyny Wewnętrznej* (monthly).

Towarzystwo Literackie im. Adama Mickiewicza (*The Mickiewicz Literary Society*): 00330 Warsaw, Nowy Świat 72; f. 1886; 1,500 mems.; arranges lectures on literature mainly in the provinces; Pres. Prof. Dr. MIECZYSŁAW KLIMOWICZ; publ. *Rocznik* (Yearbook).

Towarzystwo Miłośników Historii i Zabytków Krakowa (*Society of Friends of the History and Monuments of Cracow*): Cracow, Sw. Jana 12; f. 1896; 980 mems.; Pres. Doc. Dr. WIESŁAW BIEŃKOWSKI; Sec. Dr. MICHAŁ ROZEK; publs. *Rocznik Krakowski, Biblioteka Krakowska, Kraków Dawniej i Dzis.*

Towarzystwo Miłośników Języka Polskiego (*Society of Friends of the Polish Language*): Cracow, Straszewskiego 27; Pres. Dr. JAN SAFAREWICZ; Sec. Dr. FRANCISZEK SŁAWSKI; publs. *Język Polski*†, *Słownik etymologiczny języka Polskiego*†.

Towarzystwo Naukowe Organizacji i Kierownictwa (*Society of Scientific Organization and Management*): Warsaw, Koszykowa 6, Box C; f. 1919; 12,000 individual mems., 3,500 collective mems.; library of 7,500 vols.; Pres. Doc. Dr. BRONISŁAW OSTAPCZUK; Dir. Mgr. WOJCIECH ZDZIENICKI; publs. *Przegląd Organizacji* (monthly), *Problemy Organizacji* (quarterly), *Organizacja i Kierownictwa* (monthly bulletin).

Towarzystwo Naukowe Płockie (*Płock Scientific Society*): 09-402 Płock, plac Narutowicza 8; f. 1820; 604 mems.; library of 170,000 vols.; Pres. JAKUB CHOJNACKI; Sec.-Gen. FRANCISZEK DOROBEK; publs. *Notatki Płockie*† (quarterly), *Sprawozdanie z działalności*† (Yearbook).

Towarzystwo Naukowe w Toruniu (*Scientific Society of Toruń*): Toruń, ul. Wysoka 16; f. 1875; 530 mems.; concerned with historical, legal and social studies, philology and philosophy, mathematics, astronomy and natural sciences; library of 57,829 vols.; Pres. Prof. Dr. KONRAD GÓRSKI; Gen. Sec. Prof. Dr. MARIAN BISKUP; publs. include *Roczniki*† (annual), *Fontes*† (irregular),

Zapiski Historyczne† (quarterly, concerned chiefly with the Pomeranian problems), *Prace Wydziału Filologiczno-Filozoficznego*†, *Sprawozdania*†, *Studia Iuridica*†, *Studia Societatis Scientiarum Torunensis*†, *Prace Popularnonaukowe*†, *Prace Archeologiczne*.

Towarzystwo Przyjaciół Nauk w Przemyślu (*Society of Science and Letters of Przemyśl*): 1. 37-700 Przemyśl, ul. Orzechowskiego 2; f. 1909; 288 mems.; library of 27,000 vols.; Pres. Mgr. Mieczysław Mazurek; Sec.-Gen. Mgr. Zygmunt Felczyński; publs. include *Rocznik Przemyśki, Biblioteka Przemyśka, Rocznik Nauk Medycznych*.

Wrocławskie Towarzystwo Naukowe (*Wrocław Scientific Society*): 51-616 Wrocław, Rosenbergów 13; f. 1946 to study social and exact sciences; 520 mems.; Pres. Hugon Kowarzyk; Sec. Jan Trzynadlowski; publs. include *Prace Wrocławskiego Towarzystwa Naukowego* (Series A: Humanistic Sciences, Series B: Exact Sciences), *Śląskie Prace Bibliologiczne i Bibliotekoznawcze, Rozprawy Komisji Historii Sztuki, Rozprawy Komisji Językowej, Sprawozdania* (series A and B), *Annales Silesiae, Litteraria*.

Zwiazek Pisarzy Polskich (*Union of Polish Writers*): 00-179 Warsaw, Krakowskie Prezedmiéscie 87; Chair. (vacant).

Żydowski Instytut Historyczny w Polsce (*Jewish Historical Institute in Poland*): 00-090 Warsaw, Al. Świerczewskiego 79; f. 1944; 83 mems.; includes a museum of Jewish art and martyrology, archives; library of 60,000 vols., 1,000 MSS.; Dir. Prof. Dr. Maurycy Horn; publs. *Biuletyn*† (quarterly, summary in Yiddish and English), *Bleter far geszichte*† (annually in Yiddish, summary in Polish and English).

Learned Societies Collaborating with the Polish Academy of Sciences

Bydgoskie Towarzystwo Naukowe (*Bydgoszcz Scientific Society*): 85-102 Bydgoszcz, ul. Jezuicka 4; f. 1959; 372 mems.; library of 14,000 vols.; Pres. Doc. Dr. hab. Henryk Bednarski; Sec.-Gen. Doc. Dr. Krystyna Kwasniewska; publs. *Bydgostiana*† (annual), *Prace Wydziału Nauk Humanistycznych*†, *Prace Wydziału Nauk Przyrodniczych*†, *Prace Wydziału Nauk Technicznych*†, *Źródła do dziejów Bydgoszczy*†, etc. (all occasional).

Kieleckie Towarzystwo Naukowe (*Kielce Scientific Society*): Kielce, ul. Ściegiennego 6; f. 1958; 140 mems.; regional scientific research in history, philology, medicine, geology, geography and nature conservation; library of 1,500 vols.; Pres. Doc. Dr. habil. Zenon Guldon; Sec. Mgr. Mieczysław Markowski; publs. *Rocznik Świetokrzyski* (Yearbook).

Lubelskie Towarzystwo Naukowe (*Lublin Scientific Society*): Lublin, Pl. Litewski 2; 1958; 335 mems.; Pres. Prof. Dr. Tadeusz Krwawicz; Sec. Doc. Dr. Kazimierz Zagórski; publ. *Folia Societatis Scientiarum Lublinensis*† (annually).

Towarzystwo Przyjaciół Nauki i Sztuki w Rzeszowie (*Rzeszów Society of Friends of Science and Art*): Rzeszów, 3 Maja 19; Pres. Mgr. Władysław Kunisz; publ. *Rocznik Województwa Rzeszowskiego* (annually).

Other Cultural Societies

British Council: 00-697 Warsaw, 59 Al. Jerozolimskie; f. 1946; library :*see* Libraries; Rep. Dr. J. Barrott.

Österreichisches Kulturinstitut: Ul. Prozna 8, Warsaw 1; f. 1965; cultural performances, Austrian library, German language courses, information service; library of 10,000 vols.; Dir. Dr. Fritz Cocron.

Polski Klub Literacki P.E.N. (*Polish P.E.N. Centre*): Pałac Kultury i Nauki, 00-901 Warsaw; f. 1925; 270 mems.; library of 5,500 vols.; Pres. Juliusz Żuławski; Vice-Pres. Jerzy Zagórski, Artur Międzyrzecki; Sec. Władysław Bartoszewski.

Stowarzyszenie Architektów Polskich (*Polish Architects' Association*): Warsaw, ul. Foksal 2; f. 1934; 6,200 mems.; library of 3,000 vols.; Sec.-Gen. Ewa Krasińska; publ. *Bulletin* (monthly).

Stowarzyszenie Bibliotekarzy Polskich (*Polish Librarians Association*): Konopczyńskiego 5/7, 00-953 Warsaw; f. 1917; 13,820 mems.; Pres. Witold Stankiewicz; Sec.-Gen. Leon Łoś; publs. *Bibliotekarz* (every 2 months), *Poradnik Bibliotekarza* (monthly), *Przeglad Biblioteczny* (quarterly).

Towarzystwo im. Fryderyka Chopina (*Frederic Chopin Society*): Warsaw, Ostrogski Palais, Okólnik 1; f. 1934; permanent Secretariat of the International Chopin Piano Competitions; central Chopin museum, archives and library for study of Chopin's life and preparation of complete edition of his works; organization of concerts; patronage of Chopin's birth-place in Zelazowa Wola; Gen. Dir. Wiktor Weinbaum.

ACADEMY OF SCIENCES—RESEARCH INSTITUTES

Section I—*Social Sciences.*

Instytut Sztuki (*Institute of Art*): 00-950 Warsaw, ul. Długa 28, P.O.B. 994; f. 1949; fine arts, music, theatre, film; photographic archive of about 250,000 negatives; 165 mems.; library of about 113,000 vols., phonograph archive of *c.* 4,000 tapes; Dir. Prof. Dr. Stanisław Mossakowski; Joint Dir. Doc. Dr. Aleksander Kumor; publs. *Biuletyn Historii Sztuki Polska Sztuka Ludowa, Pàmiętnik Teatralny, Muzyka, Polish Art Studies.*

Instytut Historii (*Institute of History*): 00-272 Warsaw, Rynek Starego Miasta 29-31; Dir. C. Madajczyk; publs.† *Kwartalnik Historyczny* (quarterly), *Dzieje najnowsze* (quarterly), *Odrodzenie i Reformacja w Polsce* (annual), *Studia Zródloznawcze* (annual), *Acta Poloniae Historica* (half-yearly in foreign languages), *Czasopismo Prawno-Historyczne* (half-yearly), *Studia z Dziejów ZSRR i Europy Srodkowej* (annual).

Instytut Historii Kultury Materialnej (*Institute of the History of Material Culture*): 00-140 Warsaw, ul. Świerczewskiego 105; f. 1953; prehistoric, classical, early medieval and industrial archaeology, ethnography; 229 mems.; library of 32,000 vols.; Dir. Prof. Witold Hensel; publs.† *Archaeologia Polona, Archaeology of Poland, Archaeology, Polish Archaeological Researches, Archaeological Reports, Archaeological Review, Inventaria Archaeologica, Archaeologia Urbium, Polish Archaeological Abstracts, Ethnologia Polona, Bibliotheca Antiqua, Quarterly Journal of the History of Material Culture, Studies and Materials of the History of Material Culture, A Catalogue of the Monuments of Industrial Building in Poland, Library of Polish Ethnography, Polish Ethnographic Atlas, Polish Ethnography, Culture of Early Medieval Europe.*

Instytut Państwa i Prawa (*Institute of State and Law*): 00-330 Warsaw, Nowy Świat 72 (Pałac Staszica); f. 1953; legal research; 94 mems.; library of 35,075 vols.; Dir. Prof. Dr. Adam Łopatka; periodical publs. *Państwo i Prawo*† (monthly), *Droit Polonais Contemporain*† (in French), *Sowriemiennoje Polskoje Prawo*† (in Russian), *Studia Prawnicze*†, *Problemy Rad Narodowych*†, *Orzecznictwo sadów polskich i komisji arbitrazowych*† (monthly), *Polish Yearbook of International Law, Archiwum Kryminologii*† (yearly), *Funkcjonowanie administracji w świetle orzecznictwa*† (every 2 years).

Instytut Badań Literackich (*Institute of Literary Research*): Nowy Świat 72, Pałac Staszica, 00-330 Warsaw; f. 1948; 17 scientific departments, and sections in Cracow, Poznań, Toruń and Wrocław; research in the theory of literature, history of Polish literature, and sociology of literature; 241 mems.: library of 172,600 vols.; Acting Dirs. Prof. MIECZYSŁAW KLIMOWICZ, Doc. STEFAN TREUGUTT, Doc. RYSZARD GÓRSKI; publs. *Pamiętnik Literacki* (Literary Journal, quarterly), *Teksty* (Texts, fortnightly), *Biuletyn Polonistyczny* (Bulletin of Polish Literary Scholarship, quarterly), *Kwartalnik Historii Prasy Polskiej* (Quarterly of the History of the Polish Press).

Instytut Baltycki (*Baltic Institute*): Instytut Badawczo-Naukowy, Gdańsk, Tkacka 11/13; f. 1925; research into the modern history of Polish-German and Polish-Scandinavian relations; 68 mems.; Dir. Dr. STANISŁAW POTOCKI; Pres. Prof. Dr. REMIGIUSZ ZAORSKI; publs. *Komunikaty Instytutu Bałtyckiego*† (half-yearly), *Gdańskie Zeszyty Humanistyczne*† (annual).

Instytut Filozofii i Socjologii (*Institute of Philosophy and Sociology*): 00-330 Warsaw, Pałac Staszica, Nowy Świat 72: f. 1956; 198 mems.; library of 103,574 vols.; Dir. Prof. T. M. JAROSZEWSKI; publs. *Studia Logica, Archiwum Historii Filozofii i Myśli Społecznej, Studia Filozoficzne, Studia Mediewistyczne, Studia Socjologiczne, Mediaevalia Philosophica Polonorum, Materiały do Historii Filozofii Średniowiecznej w Polsce, Biblioteka Pisarzy Reformacyjnych, Studia Religioznawcze, Studia Estetyczne, Roczniki Socjologii Wsi, Etyka.*

Instytut Historii Nauki, Oświaty i Techniki (*Institute of the History of Science, Education and Technology*): Warsaw, Pałac Staszica, Nowy Świat 72; Dir. Prof. Dr. JÓZEF MIĄSO; publs. *Kwartalnik Historii Nauki i Techniki* (quarterly), *Studia i Materiały z dziejów nauki polskiej* (5 series), *Monografie z dziejów nauki i techniki, Zrodła do dziejów nauki i techniki, Organon* (annual in French, English and Russian), *Monografie z Dziejów Oświaty, Rozprawy z Dziejów Oświaty, Archiwum Dziejów Oświaty.*

Instytut Rozwoju Wsi i Rolnictwa (*Institute of Development of Rural Areas and Agriculture*): Warsaw, Pałac Staszica, Nowy Świat 72; Dir. DZYMA GAŁAJ.

Instytut Śląski (*Silesian Institute*): Opole, Luboszycka 3; f. 1957; departments: History, Humanities, Economic and Social Sciences, Agriculture, International Affairs, Education, Sociology and Demography, Affairs of the Oder River; Pres. Prof. Dr. ALOJZY MELICH; Dir. Prof. Dr. JÓZEF KOKOT; publs. *Studia Śląskie*† (2 a year), *Przegląd Słosunków Międzynarodowych* (bi-monthly), *Studia Społeczno-Ekonomiczne* (yearbook), *Klasa Robotnicza na Śląsku* (yearbook), Komunikaty-Series: *Zwykła, Monograficzna, Niemcoznawcza, Literacka, Rolnicza, Ekonomiczna.*

Instytut Zachodni (*Western Institute*): Poznań, Stary Rynek 78/79; f. 1945; for the study of Polish-German relations up to the acquisition of Polish western territories, and of Western European economic, political, social and cultural matters; Dir. Prof. Dr. ANTONI CZUBÍNSKI; publs. *Przegląd Zachodni* (six times a year), *Polish-Western Affairs, La Pologne et les Affaires Occidentales* (bi-annuals).

Zaklad Archeologii Śródziemnomorskiej (*Research Centre for Mediterranean Archaeology*): Warsaw, Pałac Kultury i Nauki, Room 1909; f. 1956; documentation and publication of results of Polish excavations in the Middle East; publication of antique objects in Polish Museums; Nubian Studies; Dirs. Prof. Dr. KAZIMIERZ MICHAŁOWSKI; Prof. Dr. TADEUSZ DZIERŻYKRAY-ROGALSKI; publs. *Fouilles polonaises à Palmyre*†, *Fouilles polonaises à Faras*†, *Corpus Signorum Imperii Romani-Pologne*†, *Corpus Vasorum Antiquorum*†, *Deir el Bahari*†, *Travaux du Centre d'Archéologie Méditerranéenne*†, *Alexandrie*†, *Nea Paphos*†, etc.

Instytut Słowianoznawsta (*Slavonic Institute*): 00-901 Warsaw, Pałac Kultury i Nauki; f. 1945; Dir. Prof. Dr. JANUS SIATKOWSKI.

Section II—*Biological Sciences.*

Botanical Institute: 31-512 Cracow, Lubicz 46; f. 1954; 60,310 vols.; Dir. Prof. Dr. ADAM JASIEWICZ; publs. *Flora Polska*†, *Atlas Flory Polskiej*†, *Fragmenta Floristica et Geobotanica*†, *Acta Palaeobotanica*†, *Flora słodkowodna Polski, Mała Flora Grzybów*†.

Institute of Anthropology: 50-951 Wrocław, ul. Kuźnicza 35; f. 1952; Dir. TADEUSZ BIELICKI; publs. *Materiały i Prace Antropologiczne*†, *Studies in Physical Anthropology*†.

Institute of Biochemistry and Biophysics: 02-532 Warsaw, ul. Rakowiecka 36; f. 1954; research work in the fields of nucleic acids (structure, function, metabolism), protein biosynthesis, regulation of gene function and the structure of genes and chromosomes; library of 8,000 vols. and 7,000 periodicals; Dir. Prof. Dr. KAZIMIERZ L. WIERZCHOWSKI; publ. *Acta Biochim Polon*†.

Institute of Ecology: 05-150 Łomianki, Dziekanów Lesny; f. 1952; population and biocenotic studies in the field of productivity of ecosystems and applied ecology; library of 60,000 vols.; Dir. Prof. Dr. ROMUALD KLEKOWSKI; Scientific Sec. Z. FISCHER MALANOWSKA; publs. *Ekologia Polska*† (original articles on congress languages, quarterly), *Wiadomości Ekologiczne*† (articles in Polish with English summaries, quarterly), *International Studies on Sparrows, Polish Ecological Studies* (original articles in English, quarterly), *Polish Ecological Bibliography, Polskie Archivum Hydrobiologii* (original articles in English, quarterly).

Institute of Systematic and Experimental Zoology: 31-016 Cracow, ul. Sławkowska 17; f. 1865; library of 56,950 vols.; Dir. Prof. Dr. JERZY PAWŁOWSKI; publs. *Folia Biologica*† (quarterly), *Acta Zoologica Cracoviensia*† (annually), *Monografie Fauny Polski*† (irregular).

Institute of Zoology: 00-679 Warsaw, ul. Wilcza 64; f. 1818; research in all fields of zoology; ornithological station at Górki Wschodnie near Gdańsk and field station at Łomna near Warsaw; archives and documents; library of some 185,000 vols., 1,500 current periodicals; Dir. Prof. Dr. HENRYK SZELĘGIEWICZ; publs. *Annales Zoologici*†, *Fragmenta Faunistica*†, *Acta Ornithologica*†, *Memorabilia Zoologica*†, *Catalogus Faunae Poloniae*†, *Fauna Poloniae*†, *Keys for the Identification of Polish Invertebrates*†.

Instytut Dendrologii PAN (*Institute of Dendrology*): Kórnik, nr. Poznań; f. 1952; Dir. Prof. Dr. WŁADYSŁAW BUGAŁA; publs. *Arboretum Kórnickie* (annual), *Atlas of Distribution of Trees and Shrubs in Poland* (annual), *Monographs on Forest Trees* (irregular).

Laboratory of Water Biology: 31-016 Cracow, ul. Sławkowska 17; f. 1952; study of the plant and animal communities in ponds, rivers and dam reservoirs and productivity of these ecosystems, hydrochemistry; hydrobiological station at Goczałkowice; experimental station (fish farm) at Gołysz-Zaborze; library of 33,150 vols. and 1,245 periodicals; Dir. Prof. Dr. KAZIMIERZ MATUSIAK; publ. *Acta Hydrobiologica*†.

Mammals Research Institute: 17-230 Białowieża, woj. Białystok; f. 1954; Dir. Prof. ZDZISŁAW PUCEK; publ. *Acta Theriologica.*

M. Nencki Institute of Experimental Biology: 02-093 Warsaw, Pasteura 3; f. 1918; scientific research work in the fields of biochemistry, cell biology, neurophysiology and experimental psychology; library of 65,000 vols.; Dir. Prof. KAZIMIERZ ZIELIŃSKI; publs. *Acta Neuro-*

biologiae Experimentalis† (every 2 months), *Acta Protozoologica*† (quarterly), *Zwierzęta Laboratoryjne*† (Laboratory Animals, continuous).

Institute of Parasitology: 00-473 Warsaw, ul. Pasteura 3; f. 1952; scientific research work in parasitology, including animal parasitism, its origin, prevalence, manifestations and effects in natural and experimental parasite-host systems; sections of phylogeny and ontogeny, physiology, protozoology, immunology, environmental parasitology, parasitic zoonoses; 75 scientific and technical staff; documentation centre and library of 24,050 vols.; Dir. Prof. Dr. MARIAN ŚWIETLIKOWSKI; publ. *Acta Parasitologica Polonica*† (quarterly), *Polska Bibliografia Parazytologiczna*† (Polish Bibliography of Parasitology, annual).

Zakład Ochrony Przyrody (*Research Centre for Nature Protection*): 31-512 Cracow, ul. Lubicz 46; f. 1920; research work on all problems relating to nature conservancy; library of 32,329 vols. and 1,468 periodicals; Dir. Prof. Dr. ROMAN NEY; publs. *Ochrona Przyrody*† (Protection of Nature, annual), *Studia Naturae*†, Series A and B, *Chrońmy Przyrodę Ojczystą*† (Let Us Protect the Nature of our Homeland, bimonthly).

Zakład Paleobiologii (*Institute of Paleobiology*): Warsaw 02-089, Żwirki i Wigury 93; f. 1952; Dir. Prof. ZOFIA KIELAN-JAWOROWSKA; publs. *Palaeontologia Polonica*†. *Acta Palaeontologica Polonica*†.

Section III—*Mathematical, Physical and Chemical Sciences.*

Copernicus Astronomical Centre: 00-716 Warsaw, ul. Bartycka 18; f. 1957; Dir. Prof. JÓZEF SMAK.

Department of Astronomical Dynamics: Warsaw; Dir. Dr. JAN PIOTR LASOTA.

Department of Astrophysics I: Toruń; Dir. ANTONI STAWIKOWSKI; research in spectroscopy, stellar astronomy and radio-astronomy.

Department of Astrophysics II: Warsaw; Dir. Prof. BOHDAN PACZYŃSKI; research in polarization of light from stars, evolution of stars, interstellar magnetic fields.

Institute of Mathematics: 00-950 Warsaw, ul. Śniadeckich 8, P.O.B. 137; f. 1948; promotion of mathematical knowledge and application; local branches in Cracow, Gdańsk, Katowice, Łódź, Poznań, Toruń and Wrocław; approx. 120 mems.; library of 80,000 vols.; Dir. CZESŁAW OLECH; publs. *Colloquium Mathematicum, Acta Arithmetica, Fundamenta Mathematicae, Studia Mathematica, Annales Polonici Mathematici, Monografie Matematyczne, Dissertationes Mathematicae, Applicationes Mathematicae*†.

Stefan Banach International Mathematical Center: 00-950 Warsaw, ul. Mokotowska 25, P.O.B. 137; branch of the Institute of Mathematics; f. 1972 by an agreement of Academies of Bulgaria, Czechoslovakia, G.D.R., Hungary, Poland, Romania, U.S.S.R. and Viet-Nam; promotion of international co-operation in mathematics through organizing research-and-training semesters in different fields of maths.; no permanent staff, *c.* 100 visitors per semester; publ. *Banach Center Publications*†.

Institute of Physical Chemistry: 01-224 Warsaw, Kasprzaka 44/52; f. 1955; research work in physico-chemical fundamentals including chemical engineering and chemical technology as follows: physical chemistry of metal-hydrogen systems including surfaces and catalysis, analytical physical chemistry and instrumentation, experimental thermodynamics on organic mixtures, spectroscopy, including special-purpose apparatus, calorimetry including special-purpose apparatus and instrumentation, electrochemistry and corrosion, fuel cells, molten salts, process kinetics, statistical mechanics and thermodynamics of irreversible phenomena; library of 62,000 vols.; Dir. Prof. Dr. WOJCIECH ZIELENKIEWICZ.

Institute of Polymer Chemistry: P.O.B. 49, 34 Marie Curie-Skłodowska St., 41800 Zabrze; f. 1969; divisions of polymer chemistry (4 laboratories) and polymer physical chemistry (3 laboratories); library of 7,500 vols.; Dir. Prof. ZBIGNIEW JEDLIŃSKI.

Instytut Chemii Organicznej (*Institute of Organic Chemistry*): 00-961 Warsaw, Kasprzaka 44; f. 1954 as Research Centre for Organic Synthesis; became Institute 1965; research in synthetic organic chemistry and natural products chemistry; library of 15,400 vols.; Dir. Prof. Dr. MIECZYSŁAW MĄKOSZA.

Instytut Fizyki (*Institute of Physics*): 02-668 Warsaw, Al. Lotników 32; f. 1953; research in theoretical physics, semiconductors, magnetics, radiospectroscopy, microwaves, x-ray crystallography, optics; library of 25,000 vols.; Dir. Prof. Dr. JERZY KOŁODZIEJCZAK; publs. *Acta Physica Polonica* (monthly in two parts), *Prace Instytutu Fizyki* (reports).

Instytut Maszyn Matematycznych (*Institute of Mathematical Machines*): 02-078 Warsaw, Krzywickiego 34; f. 1957; computer science and technology, computer-aided design and manufacturing; library of 25,000 vols.; Dir. HENRYK ORŁOWSKI; publs. *Prace naukowo-badawcze Instytutu Maszyn Matematycznych*† (irregular), *Biuletyn Informacyjny—Obiektowe Systemy Komputerowe*† (technical journal, every 2 months), *Informacja Ekspresowa—Obiektowe Systemy Komputerowe*† (monthly bibliography), *Przegląd Dokumentacyjny—Obiektowe Systemy Komputerowe*† (every 2 months).

Section IV—*Technical Sciences.*

Institute of Electron Technology (*The Scientific and Production Centre of Semiconductors*): 02-668 Warsaw, Al. Lotników 32/46; f. 1966; electron technology of solid state (semiconductors, microwaves, microelectronics, optoelectronics); library of 17,000 vols.; Dir. Prof. Dr. ANDRZEJ AMBROZIAK; publs. *Electron Technology*† (quarterly), *Biblioteka Elektroniki*†, *Prace ITE* (irregular).

Instytut Maszyn Przepływowych (*Institute of Fluid Flow Machinery*): 80-952 Gdańsk-Wrzeszcz, ul. Gen. J. Fiszera 14; f. 1956; library of 19,800 vols.; Dir. Prof. Dr. h. JERZY KRZYZANOWSKI; publs. *Prace*† (Transactions), *Zeszyty Naukowe Instytutu Maszyn Przepływowych*† (Reports, in series).

Instytut Organizacji i Kierowania (*Institute of Organization, Management and Control Sciences*): Warsaw, Kraj. Rady Narod. 55; f. 1974; research and post-doctoral education in management, control sciences, praxeology, cybernetics, information systems for management, sociology and psychology of organization; library of 28,800 vols.; Dir. Prof. ANDRZEJ STRASZAK; publs. *Control and Cybernetics*† (quarterly), *Prakseologia*† (quarterly), *Humanizacja pracy*† (quarterly), *Prace Instytutu Organizacji i Kierowanie*† (quarterly).

Instytut Podstawowych Problemów Techniki (*Institute of Fundamental Technological Research*): Warsaw, Świętokrzyska 21; f. 1953; applied mechanics, vibrations, acoustics, electromagnetic fields, mechanical systems; library of 68,000 vols.; Dir. Prof. Dr. IGNACY MALECKI; publs. *Archives of Mechanics*† (every 2 months), *Rozprawy Inżynierskie*† (Engineering Transactions, quarterly), *Journal of Technical Physics*† (quarterly), *Nonlinear Vibration Problems*† (annual), *Biblioteka Mechaniki Stosowanej*† (Applied Mechanics Series), *Monografie Elektrotechniki Teoretycznej*† (Monographs on Electrical Engineering Theory), *Prace IPPT* (IFTR Reports), *Fluid Dynamics Transactions*† (irregular),

Scientific Activities of the IFTR† (annual), *Polska Bibliografia Analityczna Mechaniki*† (Polish Scientific Abstracts on Mechanics, quarterly), *Uspechi Mechaniki*† (Advances in Mechanics, quarterly), *Biblioteka Akustyki i Ultradźwięków*† (Acoustics and Ultrasonics Series).

Institute of Heat Engineering: 00-665 Warsaw, ul. Nowowiejska 25; f. 1953; Dir. Prof. Dr. Bogumił Staniszewski; Research Dir. Dr. Stanisław Wójcicki.

Instytut Budownictwa Wodnego (*Institute of Hydroengineering*): 80-953 Gdańsk-Oliwa, ul. Cystersów, Pałac Opatów; f. 1953; 200 mems.; library of 29,000 vols.; Dir. Prof. Dr. hab. Piotr Wilde; publs. *Archiwum Hydrotechniki*† (quarterly), *Rozprawy Hydrotechniczne*†.

Research Centre of Chemical Engineering and of Chemical Apparatus Construction: Gliwice, Baltycka 5; f. 1958; 74 mems.; library of 3,545 vols.; Dir. Prof. Dr. hab. inż. Andrzej Burghardt; publ. *Inżynieria Chemiczna*.

Section V—*Agricultural and Forestry Sciences.*

Centre for Forestry Research: Cracow, Ojcowska 1; f. 1956; Dir. Dr. Tadeusz Gieruszyński.

Department of Plant Physiology: 31-016 Cracow, Sławkowska 17; f. 1956; laboratories: plant growth and development, photosynthesis, cryptogamic plants, myxomycetes, cytophysiology, virology; Dir. Prof. Dr. Włodzimierz Starzecki.

Institute of Animal Physiology and Nutrition: 05-110 Jablonna, near Warsaw; f. 1955; study of nutrition of ruminants, pigs and poultry, neuroendocrinology, endocrinology, environmental physiology; staff of 84 graduates; Dir. Prof. Dr. Stanisław Buraczewski; Asst. Dir. Dr. Bernard Barcikowski.

Institute of Genetics and Animal Breeding: Jastrzębiec, 05-551 Mroków, woj. Warszawa; f. 1955; research work in animal genetics with special reference to farm animals; 138 mems.; library of 4,305 vols., 3,513 journals; Dir. Prof. Dr. Maciej Żurkowski.

Institute of Plant Genetics: 60-479 Poznań, ul. Strzeszyńska 30-36; f. 1954; Dir. Prof. Dr. hab. Ignacy Wiatroszak; publs. *Genetica Polonica*† (quarterly), *Przegląd zagranicznej literatury naukowej z zakresu genetyki i hodowli roślin* (bi-annual).

Instytut Rozwoju Wsi i Rolnictwa PAN (*Institute for Rural and Agricultural Development*): 00-330 Warsaw, Nowy Świat 72; f. 1971; research into the process of developing agriculture and rural society to socialist forms; 90 mems.; library of 3,500 vols.; Dir. Prof. Dyzma Gałaj; publ. *Countryside and Agriculture*† (quarterly in Polish, summaries in English and Russian).

Instytut Ziemniaka (*Institute for Potato Research*): Bonin, 75-016 Koszalin; f. 1966; study of the breeding, genetics, physiology, biochemistry, control, virology, production and storage of potatoes; 11 departments, 5 research stations; library of 12,000 vols.; Dir. Doc. Dr. E. Kapsa; publs. *Ziemniak*†, *Biuletyn Instytutu Ziemniaka*†.

Research Centre for Genetics: Skierniewice, Osada Pałacowa; f. 1952; Dir. Prof. Dr. Edmund Malinowski.

Zakład Higieny Weterynaryjnej (*Laboratory of Veterinary Hygiene*): 02-156 Warsaw, ul. Lechicka 21; bacteriology, virology, immunology, anatomo- and histo-pathology, biochemistry, toxicology, and parasitology (diagnosis and research work); Dir. Doc. Dr. Stefan Samól.

Section VI—*Medical Sciences.*

Laboratory of Physiology: Warsaw 36, Chełmska 27/37; f. 1957; Dir. Prof. Dr. Franciszek Czubalski.

L. Hirszfeld Institute of Immunology and Experimental Therapy: 53-114 Wrocław, ul. Czerska 12; f. 1952; research work in the field of immunology, experimental therapy; documentation and information centre; library of *c.* 16,000 vols.; Dir. Prof. Dr. Stefan Ślopek; publs. *Archivum Immunologiae et Therapiae Experimentalis*† (English, every 2 months), *Postępy Higieny i Medycyny Doświadczalnej*† (Polish, every 2 months).

Medical Research Centre: 00-784 Warsaw, Dworkowa 3; f. 1967; consisting of Departments of Neurosurgery, Surgical Research and Transplantation, Mental Health, Neurophysiology, Neuropathology, Neurochemistry, Applied Physiology, Comparative Neurology, Research Group of School Psychohygiene; Laboratories: Cardiovascular, Developmental Neuropathology, Ultrastructure of the Nervous System, Experimental Surgery, Scientific Instruments—MEDIPAN; library of 23,247 vols.; Dir. Dr. M. J. Mossakowski; Scientific Dir. Dr. W. A. Karczewski; publ. *Annual Report of Scientific Activities*.

Institute of Pharmacology: 31-343 Cracow, ul. Smętna 12; f. 1954; pharmacology, neuropsychopharmacology, behavioural, biochemical, electrophysiological and histochemical research, synthesis of new drugs, pharmacology of steroid hormones, immunobiology, acclimatization of medicinal plants, their phytochemical and pharmacological investigation; 66 mems.; library of 9,496 vols., 8,808 periodicals, 472 scientific journals; Dir. Prof. Jerzy Maj, ph.d.; publ. *Polish Journal of Pharmacology and Pharmacy*†.

Department of Biogenic Amines: 90-136 Łódz, Narutowicza 60; f. 1958; research into metabolic and allergic diseases; metabolism of histamine and its physiological role; 2 professors; 20 assistants; library of over 3,000 vols.; Dir. Prof. Dr. Czesław Maśliński.

Section VII—*Earth and Mining Sciences.*

Instytut Geografii i Przestrzennego Zagospodarowania (*Institute of Geography and Spatial Organization*): 00-927 Warsaw, Krakowskie Przedmieście 30; f. 1952; library of 100,000 vols., 40,000 vols. of periodicals, 3,000 atlases, 86,000 maps; includes the library of the Faculty of Geography and Regional Studies of Warsaw University; Dir. Prof. Dr. Jerzy Kostrowicki; publs. *Przegląd Geograficzny*† (quarterly), *Prace Geograficzne*†, *Bibliografia Geografii Polskiej*†, *Dokumentacja Geograficzna*†, *Przegląd Zagranicznej Literatury Geograficznej*†, *Geographia Polonica*.

Institute of Geological Sciences: 02-089 Warsaw, Żwirki i Wigury 93; f. 1956; stratigraphy, micropalaeontology, sedimentology, tectonics, petrography, mineralogy and geochemistry, quaternary geology, photogrammetric geology, hydrogeology; library of 22,360 books, 32,540 periodicals and 2,800 maps; Dir. Prof. Dr. J. Znosko; publs. *Studia Geologica Polonica* (irregular), *Geologia Sudetica* (2 a year).

Institute of Geophysics: 02-093 Warsaw, Pasteura 3; f. 1953; seismology and physics of the Earth's interior, geomagnetism, physics of the atmosphere and polar research; library of 25,000 vols.; Dir. Prof. Dr. Jerzy Jankowski; publs. *Acta Geophysica Polonica*, *Publications*.

Instytut Mechaniki Górotworu (*Strata Mechanics Research Institute*): 30-059 Cracow, ul. Reymonta 27; f. 1954; mechanics of granular media, rock deformation, low-speed flow of fluids, dynamics of air flow, flow through porous media, micromeritics; library of *c.* 11,000 vols.; Dir. Prof. Dr. Jerzy Litwiniszyn; publ. *Archiwum Górnictwa*† (quarterly).

INDEPENDENT RESEARCH INSTITUTES

Astronomical Observatory of Warsaw University: 00-478 Warsaw, ul. Ujazdowskie 4; f. 1825; library of 16,500 vols.; Dir. S. PIOTROWSKI.

Balneoclimatological Institute: 60-569 Poznań, ul. Szamarzewskiego 84; f. 1951; balneology, climatology and physical medicine; Chair. Doc. Dr. habil. GERARD STRABURZYŃSKI; publ. *Balneologia Polska* (quarterly).

Central Institute for Labour Protection: 00-950 Warsaw, ul. Tamka 1; f. 1950; Dir. STANISŁAW DĄBROWSKI; research into industrial safety; 260 mems.; library of 15,000 vols.; publs. *Prace*† (Transactions, quarterly), *Bezpieczeństwo Pracy*† (monthly), *Materiały do Studiów i Badań* (irregular), *Katalog-informator Sprzętu Ochron Osobistych*.

Główny Instytut Górnictwa (*Central Mining Institute*): 40-951 Katowice, Plac Gwarków 1; f. 1945; research work in rock mechanics: mining systems, blasting technique, gas, dust, water and rock burst hazards, explosion-proof electrical equipment, carbochemistry, utilization and recovery of waste water, material engineering, noise and vibration control; 1,800 mems.; library of 100,000 vols.; Gen. Dir. Dr. Eng. JÓZEF PAZDZIORA; publs. *Prace Głównego Instytutu Górnictwa* (Transactions of the Central Mining Institute, irregular, about 40 papers a year), *Annual Report of the Central Mining Institute* (in English and Russian).

Institute for Educational Research: 01-180 Warsaw, Górczewska 8; f. 1950; library of 80,000 vols.; depts. of theory of education, didactics, psychology, methodology, school organization, school economics, comparative education documentation and information; 130 mems.; Dir. Prof. Dr. habil. MAKSYMILIAN MACIASZEK; publs. *Badania Oświatowe* (quarterly).

Institute of Chemical Fibres: Łódź, ul. Skłodowskiej-Curie 19-27; f. 1952; Dir. H. PSTROCKI; publs. *Bieżąca Informacja Chemiczna, Seria: Włókna Chemiczne* (Current Chemical Information, series: Chemical Fibres, monthly), *Włókna Chemiczne* (Chemical Fibres, quarterly).

Institute of the Fat and Oil Industry: Warsaw, ul. Rakowiecka 36; f. 1949; chemical and technological research on edible oils and fats, laboratories in Warsaw and Gdańsk; Dir. Doc. Dr. A. JAKUBOWSKI; publ. *Tłuszcze Jadalne* (bi-monthly).

Institute of the Fermentation Industry: 02-532 Warsaw, ul. Rakowiecka 36; f. 1954; technology of fruit and vegetable products, wine, malt, beer, yeasts, enzymic preparations, protein products and instrumental analysis; library of 25,000 vols.; Dir. Prof. TADEUSZ GOŁĘBIEWSKI, SC.D.; publ. *Prace Instytutów i Laboratoriów Badawczych Przemysłu Spożywczego*†.

Institute of Forensic Research: Cracow, ul. Westerplatte 9; f. 1929; departments of biology, criminology, toxicology, forensic psychology; 25 mems.; library of 6,239 vols.; Dir. Doc. Dr. JAN MARKIEWICZ; publ. *Z Zagadnień Kryminalistyki*† (annual).

Institute of Industrial Chemistry: 01-793 Warsaw, ul. Rydygiera 8; f. 1922; 1,500 mems.; library of 101,300 vols., 1,067 periodicals; Dir. (vacant); publs. *Polimery Tworzywa Wielkocząsteczkowe*† (monthly), *Bieżąca Informacja Chemiczna—Seria Tworzywa Sztuczne i Kauczuki Syntetyczne, Seria Przetwórstwo Tworzyw Sztucznych*† (monthly).

Institute of Meteorology and Water Management: 01-698 Warsaw, Podleśna 61; f. 1973 from former State Institute of Hydrology and Meteorology and the Institute of Water Management; collections of data from 61 meteorological stations, 303 climatological posts, 1,219 hydrological posts, 2,205 pluviometric posts, 1,972 groundwater posts; library of 81,500 vols.; Dir. Prof. Dr. Eng. ZDZISŁAW KACZMAREK; publs. *Wiadomości*† (Proceedings), *Materiały Badawcze* (Research Papers) series: *Meteorologia, Hydrologia i Oceanologia, Gospodarka Wodna i Ochrona Wód* (Water Management and Water Protection), *Inżynieria Środowiska* (Environmental Engineering), *Inżynieria Wodna Bibliografia Meteorologii*†, *Bibliografia Hydrologii i Oceanologii*†, *Bibliografia gospodarki i inżynierii wodnej*† (Bibliography of water management and engineering), *Rocznik Meteorologiczny*† (annually), *Promieniowanie Słoneczne* (Solar radiation), *Rocznik Hydrograficzny Morza Bałtyckiego* (Baltic Yearbook).

Institute of Oncology: 00-973 Warsaw, Wawelska 15; f. 1932; brs. at Cracow and Gliwice; fundamental cancer research, clinical research, epidemiology; Dir. Prof. T. KOSZAROWSKI, M.D.; publs. *Nowotwory* (quarterly), *Polish Oncological Abstracts*† (quarterly).

Institute of Organic Industrial Chemistry: 03-236 Warsaw, ul. Annopol 6; f. 1952; research on all problems relating to auxiliaries and pesticides and chemical security; library of 26,000 vols., 450 periodicals; Dir. Dr. W. MOSZCZYŃSKI; publ. *Organika—Prace naukowe Instytutu Przemysłu Organicznego*† (annual).

Institute of Petroleum Processing: Cracow, ul. Lukasiewicza 1; f. 1958; petroleum refining and petro-chemistry; 560 mems.; library of 11,700 vols.; Dir. T. KAPCIA, M.SC.

Institute of Genetics and Breeding, Warsaw Agriculture Academy: 02-766 Warsaw, ul. Nowoursynowska 166; f. 1970; genetics and breeding, including mutations and molecular aspects of horticultural and agricultural plants; 35 scientists; library of 4,000 vols.; Dir. Prof. B. KUBICKI.

Institute of the Sugar Industry: 02-532 Warsaw, ul. Rakowiecka 36; f. 1898; research into all branches of the Sugar Industry; Raw Product, Sugar Beet, Technological, Analytical, Mechanical and Economic Research Depts.; 109 mems.; 14,570 vols. in library; Dir. Dr. Ing. WIKTOR FORNALEK; publ. *Prace Instytutów; Laboratoriów Badawczych Przemysłu Spożywczego* (quarterly), *Gazeta Cukrownicza*† (monthly).

Institute of Zootechnics: Cracow, Sarego 2; f. 1950; 26 Scientific Depts., 13 Experimental Stations; library 75,000 vols.; Dir. Dr. S. WAWRZYŃCZAK; publs. *Information Bulletin* (every 2 months), *Journal of Animal Science* (2 a year), *Research Information* (series), *Pig Progeny Test Station Reports, Cattle Progeny Test Station Reports, Sheep Progeny Test Station Reports, Poultry Test Station Reports, Monographs and Dissertations*† (irregular).

Instytut Badań Jądrowych (*Institute of Nuclear Research*): Świerk, 05-400 Otwock; f. 1955; library of 55,000 vols.; Dir. Prof. JERZY MINCZEWSKI; Chair. of Scientific Council Prof. JAN RYCHLEWSKI; publs. *Reports of the Institute of Nuclear Research*; two main research centres.

Nuclear Research Centre—Świerk: Świerk, 05-400 Otwock; low, medium and high energy physics, radiation effects in solids, liquids and gases, reactor physics, engineering and electronics, physics and technology of low- and high-temperature plasma, reactor fuels and materials technology, production of radioisotopes and their application, nuclear electronics, radiation protection.

Nuclear Research Centre—Żerań: ul. Dorodna 16, 03-195 Warsaw; radiochemistry, radiation chemistry, analytical chemistry and activation analysis, radiobiology.

Instytut Badawczy Leśnictwa (*Forestry Research Institute*): 00-973 Warsaw, Wery Kostrzewy 3; f. 1930; comprises 20 scientific sections covering all aspects of forestry, especially factors of environment, silviculture and selection, poplar cultivation and tree-planting, forest economics, management, protection, forest plant pathology, game management, water economy, logging, mechanization and transport; main documentation and information centre of forestry; library of 58,000 vols.; Dir. Dr. Ing. ZYGMUNT PATALAS; publs. *Prace Instytutu Badawczego Lesnictwa* (Transactions of the Forestry Research Institute, irregular), *Biuletyn Instytutu Badawczego Leśnictwa*, (published in *Prace Instytutu Badawczego Leśnictwa*, irregular), *Przegląd Dokumentacyjny Leśnictwa* (bi-monthly Review of Forestry Literature published in *Sylwan*); brs. at Cracow, Białowieza, Gdańsk, Katowice, Puczniew, Krzystkowice, Sękocin near Warsaw, Niedźwiady.

Instytut Chemii Nieorganicznej (*Institute of Inorganic Chemistry*): Gliwice, ul. Sowińskiego 11; f. 1946; library of 9,000 vols.; Chief Manager Prof. Dr. E. BUNTNER; publs. *Biuletyn Informacyjny Instytutu Chemii Nieorganicznej* (Information Bulletin, bi-monthly), *Bibliografia Wybrana* (Bibliography selected from current papers, monthly).

Instytut Ciężkiej Syntezy Organicznej Blachownia (*Blachownia Organic Synthesis Research Institute*): 47-225 Kędzierzyn-Koźle 5, ul. Energetykow 8; f. 1958; 610 mems.; library of 36,500 vols.; Dir. Dr. Prof. WŁODZIMIERZ KOTOWSKI.

Instytut Ekonomiki Rolnej (*Institute of Agricultural Economics*): 00-564 Warsaw, ul. Koszykowa 6; 321 mems.; library of 29,322 vols.; Dir. Prof. Dr. hab. AUGUSTYN WOS; publs. *Zagadnienia Ekonomiki Rolnej*† (Problems of Agricultural Economics, every 2 months), *Ekonomika Porównawcza Rolnictwa* (Comparative Economics of Agriculture, 2–4 a year), *Studia i Monografie* (4–5 a year).

Instytut Fizyki Jądrowej (*Institute of Nuclear Physics*): 31-342 Cracow, ul. Radzikowskiego 152; f. 1955; library of 17,000 vols. and 7,500 periodicals; Dir. Prof. Dr. ZBIGNIEW BOCHNACKI; publs. Reports (irregular).

Instytut Geologiczny (*Geological Institute*): 00-975 Warsaw, ul. Rakowiecka 4; f. 1919; geological, geophysical and hydrogeological research; five stations; library of 240,000 vols.; 423 research scientific workers; Dir. Prof. JAN MALINOWSKI; publs. *Biuletyny*† (irregular), *Prace*† (irregular), *Bibliografia Geologiczna Polski*† (annually), *Kwartalnik Geologiczny*† (quarterly), *Biuletyn Informacyjny*† (quarterly), maps and atlases, occasional books and monographs.

Instytut Górnictwa Naftowego i Gazownicta (*Institute of Petroleum and Gas*): 30-960 Cracow, ul. Lubicz 25a; f. 1944; library of over 56,000 vols.; Dir. Prof. JÓZEF RACZKOWSKI; publs. *Prace Instytutu Górnictwa Naftowego i Gazownictwa*† (Transactions of the Institute of Petroleum and Gas), *Nafta*† (monthly).

Instytut Hodowli i Aklimatyzacji Roślin (*Plant Breeding and Acclimatization Institute*): Radzików, 05-870 Błonie; f. 1951; 18 departments, 8 laboratories, 12 experimental stations for plant breeding; Dir. Prof. Dr. S. STARZYCKI; library of 12,000 vols.; publs. *Hodowla Roślin Aklimatyzacja i Nasiennictwo, Biuletyn I.H.A.R., Index Seminum, Delectus Seminum, Index Fungorum.*

Instytut Morski (*Maritime Institute*): Gdańsk, Długi Targ 41/42; f. 1950; economic and technical research in shipping, harbour and coastal engineering, corrosion, maritime law; library of 72,000 vols.; Dir. Prof. T. JEDNORAŁ; Scientific Dir. Prof. M. KRZYŻANOWSKI; publs. *Prace Instytutu Morskiego, Materiały, Serwis Bibliograficzny Instytutu Morskiego, Biuletyn Instytutu Morskiego.*

Instytut Nawozów Sztucznych (*Institute of Fertilizers*): 24-110 Puławy; f. 1959; technology of production, handling and application of chemical fertilizers; 30 scientists; library of 26,650 vols.; Dir. BOLESŁAW SKOWROŃSKI; publ. *Bieżąca Informacja Chemiczna: ser.: Nawozy Mineralne* (monthly).

Instytut Przemysłu Farmaceutycznego (*Institute of the Pharmaceutical Industry*): 01-793 Warsaw, ul. Rydygiera 8; microbiology, biochemistry, chemistry, analytical chemistry, pharmacology, technology of antibiotics and biosynthetic products; information, statistical and extension services; library of 12,500 vols.; Dir. Doc. Dr. KAZIMIERZ SAMUŁA; publ. *Biuletyn Informacyjny* (monthly).

Instytut Przemysłu Gumowego (*Institute of the Rubber Industry*): 05-820 Piastów, Harcerska 30; f. 1953; research in all brs. of rubber technology and of its development; 400 mems.; library of 7,250 vols.; Dir. A. ZIMOWSKI; publs. *Polimery*† (monthly with Institute of Plastics), *Biuletyn Informacyjny Inst. Przem. Gumowego*† (Rubber Technology Bulletin, monthly), *Przegląd Dokumentacyjny Inst. Przem. Gumowego*† (Rubber Technology Abstracts, monthly), *News Service*† (monthly).

Instytut Przemysłu Tworzyw i Farb (*Plastics and Paint Research Institute*): 44-101 Gliwice, ul. Chorzowska 50; f. 1953; research, developmental, technological and designing activities in the field of paint and varnish products and plastics processing; 57 scientific workers; library of 13,000 vols.; Dir. EUGENIUSZ TYRKA; publs. *Express Information* (monthly), *Information Bulletin* (quarterly).

Instytut Sadownictwa i Kwiaciarstwa (*Institute of Pomology and Floriculture*): 96-100 Skierniewice, ul. Pomologiczna 18; f. 1951; eleven departments including ornamental plants, small fruit, fruit and ornamental plant breeding, soil cultivation, orchard mechanization, pest and disease plant protection, orchard economics, fruit storage and transport, industrial application of fruit, bee-keeping; four control laboratories: chemical, botanical, biochemical physiological; isotope research; experimental greenhouse; phytotron, cold storage building; 13 field experiment stations; 400 scientific and technical staff; library of 17,500 vols.; Dir. Prof. S. A. PIENIĄZEK; publs. *Prace Instytutu Sadownictwa—Seria B—Prace doświadczalne z zakresu roślin ozdobynch* (Proceedings of the Institute of Pomology, Series B: Experimental Work with Ornamental Plants), Fruit Science Reports, *Pszczelnicze Zeszyty Naukowe*† (Bee Research Bulletin).

Instytut Techniki Budowlanej (*Building Research Institute*): Warsaw, ul. Filtrowa 1; f. 1945; research into the use of building materials and methods of construction; library of 62,000 vols.; Dir. MARIAN WĘGLARZ; publs. *Prace Instytutu Techniki Budowlanej* (quarterly), reports, monographs, papers.

Instytut Technologii Drewna (*Institute of Wood Technology*): 60-654 Poznań, ul. Winiarska 1; f. 1952; 24 scientific divisions; library of 40,000 vols., 32,000 special exhibits; Dir. Prof. R. BABICKI; publ. *Prace*† (quarterly).

Instytut Wzornictwa Przemysłowego (*Institute of Industrial Design*): Warsaw, ul. Swiętojerska 5/7; f. 1950; research into practical and aesthetic aspects of design based on social needs; ergonomic research and data selection; standardization; technical information service; organization of national and foreign exhibitions; training of industrial designers; collaboration with the building and engineering industries; library of 34,000 vols., 430 titles of periodicals, collection of special editions, etc.; Dir. Dr. JAN CZARNOCKI; publs. *Studies and Materials, Documentary Review of Industrial Design, Wiadomości* (News).

Morski Instytut Rybacki (*Marine Fisheries Institute*): Gdynia, Aleja Zjednoczenia 1; f. 1923; departments of ichthyology, oceanography, fishing technique, technology of fish processing, sea-fishery economics, sea professions psychology, scientific information; two branches at Kołobrzeg and Swinoujście. Dir. Dr. RYSZARD MAJ; publs. *Prace, Studia i Materialy*.

Mother and Child Research Institute: Warsaw, Kasprzaka 17; Dir. Prof. F. GROER, M.D.

Państwowy Zakład Higieny (*National Institute of Hygiene*): Warsaw, ul. Chocimska 24; f. 1918; 14 departments covering all aspects of epidemiology, bacteriology, virology, parasitology, vaccines and sera control, medical statistics, radiologic control and radiobiology, immunopathology, hygiene, foodstuffs, sanitary toxicology and education; library of 55,000 vols.; Dir.-Gen. W. KURYŁOWICZ; publs. *Roczniki Państwowego Zakładu Higieny*† (bi-monthly), *Medycyna Doświadczalna i Mikrobiologia*† (quarterly), *Przegląd Epidemiologiczny*† (quarterly).

Polish Dermatological Society: Warsaw, ul. Koszykowa 82a, Klinika Dermatologiczna A.M.; f. 1922; research and post-graduate education in dermatology and venereology; 1,200 mems.; Pres. Prof. Dr. STEFANIA JABŁOŃSKA; Sec. Doc. Dr. KAZIMIERZ JAKUBOWICZ; publ. *Przegląd Dermatologiczny* (every 2 months).

Polish Institute of International Affairs: 00-950 Warsaw, Warecka 1a; f. 1947; library of 110,000 vols.; Dir. Prof. JANUSZY SYMONIDES; publs. *Sprawy Międzynarodowe* (monthly), *Zbiór Dokumentów* (monthly, in Polish, English and French), *Polish Perspectives* (monthly, in English, French and German), *Studies in the Developing Countries* (in English), *Studies in International Relations* (in English).

Przemysłowy Instytut Telekomunikacji (*Telecommunications Research Institute*): 00-991 Warsaw, ul. Poligonowa 30; f. 1934; radar, radio links, microwave measuring instruments, mobile radio communication; library of 20,000 vols.; Dir. JERZY FIETT; Scientific Dir. JAN KROSZCZYŃSKI; publ. *Prace Przemysłowego Instytutu Telekomunikacji* †(quarterly).

Śląski Instytut Naukowy w Katowicach (*Silesian Scientific Institute*): 40-956 Katowice, ul. Graniczna 32; f. 1957; Dir. Prof. Dr. hab. BOHDAN JAŁOWIECKI; publs. *Zaranie Śląskie*† (quarterly), *Zeszyty Naukowe*† (series), *Studia i Materiały z dziejów Polski Ludowej*† (series), *Studia nad ekonomiką regionu*† (series), *Górnośląskie Studia Socjologiczne*† (series), *Bibliografia Śląska*† (series).

Tuberculosis Research Institute: Warsaw, ul. Płocka 26; f. 1948; medical library of 26,000 vols. and 295 periodicals; Dir. JERZY LEOWSKI, M.D.; publ. *Pneumonologia Polska*.

Veterinary Research Institute: Puławy; f. 1945; veterinary microbiology, immunology, parasitology, toxicology, etc.; 21 scientific departments including those at Warsaw, Bydgoszcz, Zduńska Wola, Poznań and Gdańsk, and 9 specialized laboratories; 195 scientists, including 31 professors; library of 11,733 vols.; Dir. Prof. Dr. MARIAN TRUSZCZYŃSKI; publ. *Bulletin of the Veterinary Institute in Puławy*†.

CENTRAL ARCHIVES, LIBRARIES AND INFORMATION CENTRES

CENTRAL ARCHIVES

Archiwum Akt Nowych (*Archive for Recent Documents*): 02-554 Warsaw, Al. Niepodległości 162; f. 1919.

Archiwum Dokumentacji Mechaniccnej (*Mechanical Documentation Archives*): Warsaw, Długa 7.

Archiwum Główne Akt Dawnych (*Central Archives for Historical Documents*): Warsaw, Długa 7; f. 1808; 319,744 vols.; Dir. Dr. M. MOTAS.

Archiwum Polskiej Akademii Nauk (*Archives of the Polish Academy of Sciences*): 00-330 Warsaw, Nowy Świat 72; f. 1953; 10,000 vols.; brs. in Cracow, Poznań, Zabrze; Dir. Prof. Dr. ZYGMUNT KOLANKOWSKI; publ. *Biuletyn* (annually).

Centralne Archiwum Wojskowe (*Central Military Archives*): Warsaw, ul. Czarnieckiego 51.

Naczelna Dyrekcja Archiwów Państwowych (*Main Directorate of the Polish State Archives*): Warsaw, Długa 6; f. 1945; library of 15,339,471 units; Dir.-Gen. Prof. Dr. TADEUSZ WALICHNOWSKI; publ. *Archeion*† (every 6 months).

LIBRARIES

Biblioteka Akademii Sztuk Pięknych (*Library of the Fine Arts Academy*): 00-068 Warsaw, Krakowskie Przedmieście 5; f. 1922; 17,404 vols., 4,912 periodicals; Dir. MARTA KRASSOWSKA.

Biblioteka Gdańska PAN (*Gdańsk Library of the Polish Academy of Sciences*): 80-858 Gdańsk, Wałowa 15; former City Library; f. 1596; collection: humanities, social sciences, maritime, Pomeranian and Gdańsk affairs; 590,195 vols., incl. 54,333 old books, 785 incunabula, 50,150 periodicals, 4,269 MSS., 6,182 maps, etc.; Dir. Doc. Dr. EDMUND KOTARSKI; publ *Rocznik Gdański* (2 a year).

Biblioteka Główna Akademii Górniczo-Hutniczej im. Stanisława Staszica w Krakowie (*Central Library of the Stanislas Staszic University of Mining and Metallurgy*): Cracow, Al. Mickiewicza 30; f. 1919; collection: mining, metallurgy, geodetics, electrical engineering, foundry engineering, mathematics, physics, chemistry; 845,000 vols.; Dir. MARIAN GÓRKIEWICZ.

Biblioteka Główna Akademii Sztuk Pięknych (*Central Library of the Academy of Fine Arts*): Cracow, ul. Smolensk 9; f. 1868; 112,300 units, incl. special collection, 42,730 graphics, posters, etc.; Dir. Mgr. ANNA PANKOWICZ; publs. *Plakat do roku 1939 ze zbiorów Biblioteki Glównej Akademii Sztuk Pięknych w Krakowie*†, *The Journal of Scientific Research of the Academy of Fine Arts*† (in Polish, with résumé).

Biblioteka Główna Politechniki Częstochowskiej (*Library of the Częstochowa Technical University*): Częstochowa, Al. Zawadzkiego 36; f. 1950; mechanical engineering, metallurgy, foundry, electrical engineering, building and civil engineering; 422,433 vols., incl. 94,900 books, 42,580 periodicals, 284,953 standards, patents, etc.; Dir. Mgr. ZBIGNIEW MROWIŃSKI; publs. *Wykaz Nabytków Zagranicznych*† (List of Foreign Acquisitions, monthly), *Bibliografia Pracowników Publikacji Politechniki Częstochowskiej*† (Bibliography of Publications of Workers at the University, irregular), *Wykaz Zbiorów Czasopism i Innych Wydawnictw Ciagłych*† (Collection of Periodicals and Serials, irregular).

Biblioteka Główna Politechniki Gdańskiej (*Library of Gdańsk Technical University*): Ul. Majakowskiego 11, Gdańsk-Wrzeszcz; 712,226 vols.; Librarian Mag. MIROSŁAW KOMENDECKI.

Biblioteka Główna Politechniki Krakowskiej (*Library of the Cracow Technical University*): 30-960 Cracow, ul. Warszawska 24, skr, poczt. 36; f. 1945; 580,308 vols.

incl. 227,020 books, 58,878 periodicals, 294,410 standards, patents, etc.; works on architecture, arts, town planning, civil engineering, hydraulic engineering, chemical technology, transport, mechanical technology, scientific information, bibliography, arts, communications, computer science, chemistry, higher technical education and library science; Dir. Dr. JÓZEF CZERNI; publs. *Biuletyn Ważniejszych Nabytków Zagranicznych* (Selected List of Recent Foreign Acquisitions, quarterly), *Bibliografia Publikacji Pracowników Politechniki Krakowskiej*† (The Bibliography of the Publications of the Workers of the Technical University of Cracow, annual).

Biblioteka Glówna Politechniki Łódzkiej (*Library of the Technical University of Łódź*): Żeromskiego 116, Łódź; f. 1945; architecture, automation, chemistry, economics, civil, electrical and mechanical engineering, energetics, metallurgy, physics, textiles, etc.; 160,571 vols., 66,360 periodicals, 265,014 patents, standards, etc.; Librarian Dr. JADWIGA PRZYGOCKA; publ. *Bibliografia*† (annually).

Biblioteka Główna Politechniki Poznańskiej (*Library of the Poznań Technical University*): 60-965 Poznań, Pl. Skłodowskiej Curie 5; f. 1918; 201,130 vols., 25,700 standards; Librarian Dr. STANISŁAW BADOŃ; publs. *Zeszyty Naukowe Politechniki Poznańskiej, Bibliografia*, etc.

Biblioteka Główna Politechniki Śląskiej (*Library of Silesian Technical University*): Gliwice, Ul. Wincentego Pstrowskiego 2; f. 1945; collection: architecture, automation, chemistry, civil engineering, communication, economics, electrical engineering, energetics, mining, sanitary engineering, mathematics, mechanical engineering, metallurgy, organization of work and production, physics and transportation; 906,493 vols.; Dir. HALINA BAŁUKA.

Biblioteka Główna Politechniki Szczecińskiej (*Library of the Technical University of Szczecin*). 70-322 Szczecin, Ul. Pułaskiego 19; 292,925 books, 2,980 current periodicals, 79,949 standards, technical catalogues, etc.; works on architecture, physical planning, civil engineering, chemical technology, electrical, electronic and mechanical engineering, economics, transport, automatics, mathematics, physics, desalination of seawater, economics of transport, data processing, information and library science; Dir. TERESA JASIŃSKA; publs. *Wykaz Nowych Nabytków* (List of Foreign Acquisitions, fortnightly), *Bibliografia Publikacji Pracowników Politechniki Szczecińskiej*† (irregular), *Wykaz Wydawnictw Ciągłych*† (list of periodicals, every 2 years).

Biblioteka Główna Politechniki Warszawskiej (*Library of the Technical University of Warsaw*): Plac Jedności Robotniczej 1, 00-661 Warsaw; f. 1915; architecture, automation, chemistry, chemical engineering, civil and electrical engineering, mechanical and sanitary engineering, energetics, geodesy and cartography, materials technology, typography, transport; 339,267 vols. in Central Library, 559,116 vols. in Department Libraries; Dir. Mgr. E. DOMAŃSKI; publs. *Wykaz Nabytków Zagranicznych* (List of Foreign Aquisitions, annual), *Spis Tytułów Czasopim i Innych Wydawncytw Ciagłych* (List of Titles, Collection of Periodicals and Serials, annually), *Bibliografia Adnotowana Prac Doktorsich i Habilitacyjnych* (Annotated Bibliography of Doctors' and Professors' Theses), *Bibliografia Publikacji Pracowników Politechniki Warszawskiej* (Bibliography of Publications of Workers at the Technical University of Warsaw, irregular).

Biblioteka Główna i Ośrodek Informacji Naukowo-Technicznej Politechniki Wrocławskiej (*Library and Scientific Information Centre of the Technical University of Wrocław*): 50-370 Wrocław, Wybrzeże Wyspiańskiego 27; f. 1946; 550,000 vols.; Dir. Doc. Dr. C. DANIŁOWICZ; publs. *Prace Naukowe* (irregular), *Wykaz Nabytków Wydawnictw Zagranicznych*† (New Acquisitions of Foreign Literature, every 2 months), *Prace Bibliograficzne* (annually).

Biblioteka Główna Śląskiej Akademii Medycznej im. L. Waryńskiego (*L. Waryński Library of the Silesian Medical Academy*): 40-952 Katowice, ul. Poniatowskiego 15; f. 1948; 211,000 vols.; Dir. Dr. ALFRED PUZIO; publ. *Biuletyn*† (annually).

Biblioteka Główna Szkoły Głównej Gospodarstwa Wiejskiego Akademii Rolniczej w Warszawie (*Library of the Warsaw Agricultural University*): Warsaw, ul. Rakowiecka 26/30; f. 1911; collection: agriculture, horticulture, forestry, zootechnics, veterinary science, wood technology, land improvement, agricultural economics, food processing technology and human nutrition; 247,799 vols., incl. 131 old vols., 74,863 periodicals, 306 maps, 16,200 MSS., 460 microfilms and 8,608 standards, etc.; Dir. Dr. M. TEMPCZYK; publs. *Zeszyty Naukowe*† (Scientific Papers of the Warsaw Agricultural University).

Biblioteka Główna Uniwersytetu im. Adama Mickiewicza (*Library of Adam Mickiewicz University*): 61-816 Poznań, ul. Ratajczaka 38/40; f. 1919; 1,845,026 vols. in central library, incl. 78,693 old vols., 3,113 MSS., 19,997 maps and atlases, 25,766 musical scores; 1,006,675 vols. in departmental libraries; Dir. Prof. Dr. hab. STANISŁAW KUBIAK.

Biblioteka Jagiellońska (*Jagiellonian Library*): 30-059 Cracow, ul. Mickiewicza 22; f. 1364; collection: general scientific, Polish affairs, humanities, Polish writing of the 15th–18th centuries; 995,625 vols., 310,562 periodicals, 95,324 old books, 14,952 MSS., 9,404 maps and atlases, and also notes, drawings, documents and microfilms; Dir. Asst. Prof. WŁADYSŁAW A. SERCZYK; publ. *Bulletin of the Jagiellonian Library* (bi-annual), *Foreign Acquisitions of the Jagiellonian Library* (quarterly).

Biblioteka Katolickiego Uniwersytetu Lubelskiego w Lublinie (*Library of the Catholic University of Lublin*): Lublin, ul. Chopina 27; f. 1918; general collection, with emphasis on theology, philosophy and humanities; 1,029,228 vols. (including department libraries) of which 39,854 old vols., 196,044 periodicals, 866 MSS., 4,161 maps and atlases, 4,161 vols. of music; Dir. ANDRZEJ PALUCHOWSKI; publs. *Archiwa, Biblioteki i Muzea Kościelne*† (2 a year).

Biblioteka Kornicka PAN (*Library of the Polish Academy of Sciences, Kornik*): Kornik, near Poznań; f. 1826; collection: History, History of Polish Literature, Mathematics and Natural Sciences; 260,226 vols., incl. 29,069 old prints, 54,342 periodicals, 13,183 MSS., 2,564 maps, 26,388 graphics; museum with 8,018 exhibits; Dir. Doc. Dr. MARCELI KOSMAN; publ. *Pamiętnik Biblioteki Kornickiej*†.

Biblioteka Narodowa (*National Library*): Ulica Hankiewicza 1, Warsaw 00-973; f. 1928; State central library; collection of writings in Polish and relating to Poland; basic foreign publications in the social sciences and humanities; library science literature; 3,160,245 vols., including periodicals, MSS., old books, maps and atlases, drawings, photographs, illustrations, leaflets and posters, music and phonographic materials; The National Library houses the Bibliographical Institute, Institute of Books and Public Reading, Microfilm Service Unit; Dir. Doc. Dr. hab. WITOLD STANKIEWICZ; publs. *The National Library Year Book*† (scientific library science periodical, in Polish with English summaries), *Bibliographical Guide*† (weekly), *Bibliography of Bibliographies*† (annually), *Bibliography of the Contents of Periodicals*† (monthly), *Polish Publishing in Figures*† (annually), etc.

Biblioteka PAN w Krakowie (*Library of the Polish Academy of Sciences in Cracow*): 31-016 Cracow, ul. Sławkowska 17; f. 1856; 515,242 vols.; 272,600 annual vols. of periodicals relating to the social and biological sciences, 110,110 MSS., old prints, cartography, graphic arts; Dir. ZBIGNIEW JABŁOŃSKI; publ. *Rocznik Biblioteki PAN w Krakowie*† (Yearbook).

Biblioteka PAN w Warszawie (*Library of the Polish Academy of Sciences in Warsaw*): Warsaw, Pałac Kultury i Nauki 6 p; f. 1908; collection: science of science, history of science and technology, prognosis, praxiology, library and information science, bibliography, reference works; 187,236 vols.; Dir. Dr. LEON ŁOŚ; publs. *Polska Bibliografia Naukoznawstwa i Technoznawstwa*† (Polish Bibliography of the Science of Science and of Technology, annual), *Przegląd Biblioteczny*† (Library Review, quarterly, with the Polish Librarians' Asscn.), *Wykaz Nabytków z Zakresu Naukoznawstwa i Historii Nauki* (Books on the Science of Science and the History of Science: New Acquisitions, quarterly), *Prognostyka: Nowe Publikacje* (fortnightly).

Biblioteka Poznańskiego Towarzystwa Przyjaciół Nauk (*Library of the Poznań Society of Friends of Science*): 61-725 Poznań, Sew. Mielżyńskiego 27-29; f. 1857; collection: scientific humanities; 260,000 vols., incl. 20,000 old vols., 1,500 MSS., 1,400 autographs, 4,000 photographs, 1,600 maps and atlases, 73,000 periodicals, 650 microfilms; Dir. Dr. RYSZARD MARCINIAK.

Biblioteka Publiczna m. st. Warszawy (*Public Library*): Warsaw; f. 1907; 182 brs.; general collection; 3,448,049 vols., incl. 12,123 old vols., 157,053 periodicals, 3,211 MSS., 9,487 maps and atlases, 35,982 standards, 3,501 drawings, 1,846 records; Dir. STEFAN DURMAJ; publ. *Bibliotekarz*† (The Librarian, monthly).

Biblioteka Sejmowa (*Library of the Polish Parliament*): Warsaw, ul. Wiejska 4; f. 1919; collection: legislation, official matter, economic, social, legal and political problems; 205,134 vols., incl. 431 old vols., 59,062 periodicals and international publs., 32,309 parliamentary and official publs., 559 maps and atlases; Dir. TADEUSZ KOZANECKI; publs. *Wykaz ważniejszych nabytków* (quarterly); *Zagadnienia parlamentarne w czasopismach zagranicznych* (irregular).

Biblioteka Śląska (*Silesian Library*): 40-956 Katowice ul. Francuska 12; f. 1922/23; collection: social science, economics, literature relating to Silesia; 938,568 vols., inc. 26,167 old vols., 95,174 periodicals, 5,420 MSS., 7,168 maps and atlases, 6,502 drawings and illustrations, 5,177 vols. of music.

Biblioteka Szkoły Głównej Planowania i Statystyki (*Library of the Central School of Planning and Statistics*): Warsaw; f. 1906; collection: social and economic science, geography and economic history, national economy, law, labour problems and special economics; 495,692 vols., incl. 1,878 old vols., 129,193 periodicals, 1,950 maps and atlases, 28,020 MSS., 1,007 drawings and illustrations; Dir. Dr. HANNA UNIEJEWSKA.

Biblioteka Uniwersytecka w Łodzi (*Library of Łódź University*): Łódź; f. 1945; scientific collection; 1,040,245 vols., incl. 26,856 old vols., 232,653 periodicals, 591 original MSS., 9,807 maps and atlases, 29,328 vols. of music, 26,005 drawings and illustrations, and 2,310 microfilms, 756,821 vols. in departmental libraries; Dir. Doc. Dr. hab. BOLESŁAW ŚWIDERSKI.

Biblioteka Uniwersytecka w Toruniu (*Library of Toruń University*): 87-100 Toruń, Gagarina 13; f. 1945; 1,645,000 vols., inc. 59,916 old books, 2,532 MSS., 6,739 cartographic publications, 133,574 graphics, posters, etc., 79,735 musical scores, 5,346 records, special collection (incl. *Pomeranica, Copernicana, Baltica*); 413,000 vols. in departmental libraries; Dir. Dr. BOHDAN RYSZEWSKI.

Biblioteka Uniwersytecka w Warszawie (*Library of the University of Warsaw*): 00-927 Warsaw, Krakowskie Przedmieście 26-28, 32; f. 1817; collection: history, history of literature, culture, philosophy, law, art, sociology, psychology, education, prints in the Russian alphabet up to 1915; 1,915,389 vols., inc. 124,479 old vols., 494,189 periodicals, 26,045 MSS., 7,237 maps and atlases, 42,734 drawings and illustrations, 20,245 vols. of music, 7,566 microfilms; Dir. Doc. Dr. JAN BACULEWSKI; publs. *Acta Bibliothecae Universitatis Varsoviensis*† (irregular), *Wykaz Nabytków Zagranicznych Bibliotek Uniwersytetu Warszawskiego*† (28 subject series, irregular), *Wykaz Bieżących Czasopism Zagranicznych Bibliotek Uniwersytetu Warszawskiego*† (annual).

Biblioteka Uniwersytecka w Wrocławiu (*Library of the University of Wrocław*): Wrocław, Szajnochy 10; f. 1945; collection: manuscripts, old prints, music, cartography, graphic arts, Silesiaca and Lusatica; bibliography, international relations Poland-Germany-Czechoslovakia; over 1,700,000 vols.; Dir. BARTŁOMIEJ KUZAK.

Biblioteka Uniwersytetu Marii Curie-Skłodowskiej w Lublinie (*Library of the M. Curie-Skłodowska University*): Lublin, ul. Nowotki 11; f. 1944; general scientific collection of 695,496 vols., including 15,240 old books, 131,068 periodicals, 1,012 MSS., 3,447 maps and atlases, 5,307 drawings and illustrations, 6,914 vols. of music, 1,683 tapes and records, 932 microfilms, 217,500 patents; Dir. Dr. JAN GURBA; publs. *Biuletyn* (quarterly), *Sprawozdanie z Działalności Uniwersytetu Marii-Curie-Skłodowskiej* (yearbook), *Wykaz Publikacji Pracowników UMCS w Lublinie* (annual).

Biblioteka Wyższa Szkoła Pedagogiczna (*Library of the Pedagogical High School*): 30-084 Cracow, ul. Podchorążych 2; f. 1946; 383,709 vols., 23,890 periodicals; 5,464 special collections; Dir. IRENA BURKOT.

Biblioteka Zakładu Narodowego im. Ossolińskich (*Ossolineum Library*): Wrocław; f. 1817; general scientific collection; over 1 million general books, MSS., old prints, iconography and other special collections; Dir. Dr. JANUSZ ALBIN; publ. *Ze skarbca kultury* (From the Treasure-House of Culture, 2 a year).

British Council Library: 00-697 Warsaw, Al. Jerozolimskie 59; f. 1946; 37,100 vols., 131 periodicals; Librarian J. C. SALTER, B.A., DIP.LIB.

Centralna Biblioteka Rolnicza (*Central Agricultural Library*): 00-950 Warsaw, P.O.B. 360; f. 1956; branches at Puławy and Bydgoszcz; mem. of Agris-FAO and MS Agroinform; scientific collection; 363,470 vols. on agriculture and related sciences; centre for information and documentation in agriculture and for exchange with scientific institutions abroad; Gen. Dir. Dr. JERZY RASIŃSKI; publ. *Roczniki Nauk Rolniczych*† (Polish Agricultural Annual, with English and Russian summaries).

Centralna Biblioteka Statystyczna (*Central Statistical Library*): 00-925 Warsaw, Al. Niepodległości 208; f. 1918; collection: scientific and specialized (economic and social subjects, with emphasis on statistics); 300,000 vols.; Dir. A. JOPKIEWICZ.

Centrum Informacji Naukowej, Technicznej i Ekonomicznej (*National Centre for Scientific, Technical and Economic Information*): 00-950 Warsaw, Al. Niepodległośi 186, P.O.B. 355; f. 1949; reorganized 1972; international co-operation; programming and co-ordination of information services; education and training; typographic and reprographic services; Dir.-Gen. MIECZYSŁAW DERENTOWICZ; publs. *Aktualne Problemy Informacji i Dokumentacji*† (Current Problems of Information and Documentation; every 2 months; English, French and Russian summaries); *Polish Technical and Economic Abstracts*† (quarterly), *Materiały Szkoleniowe* (Instructional Materials, irregular),

Informator Nauki Polskiej (Polish Research Guide, annually), includes:

Instytut Informacji Naukowej, Technicznej i Ekonomicznej (*Institute for Scientific, Technical and Economic Information*): f. 1949; reorganized 1972; research, development activities in the field of scientific, technical and economic information; provides professional advice and other forms of methodological and organizational assistance; library of 75,000 vols.; Dir. Prof. Dr. KONRAD FIAŁKOWSKI; publs. *Przegląd Piśmiennictwa Zagadnień Informacji*† (Abstracting Information Service, monthly), *Bibliographic Bulletin of the Clearing House at IINTE*† (annually), *Prace Instytutu INTE*† (Reports of the Institute), *UKD—Zmiany i Uzupełnienia*† (Corrections and Extensions to the UDC, quarterly), *Tablice UKD*† (Schedules of UDC, irregular).

Główna Biblioteka Lekarska (*Central Medical Library*): 00-791 Warsaw, Chocimska 22; f. 1945; mainly scientific collection; 1,092,736 vols., incl. 13,367 old vols., and a collection of medical items, drawings and illustrations; Dir. Prof. Dr. med. FELIKS WIDY-WIRSKI; publs. *Biuletyn Głównej Biblioteki Lekarskiej* (monthly bulletin), *Polska Bibliografia Lekarska* (year book), *Zródla i Dokumenty do Historii Medycyny* (Sources and Documents for the History of Medicine, irregular edition), *Przegląd Piśmiennictwa Lekarskiego Polskiego* (monthly), *Spis czasopism i wydawnictw ciągłych Głównej Biblioteki Lekarskiej, bibliotek akademii medycznych i instytutów naukowych* (Yearbook), *Informacja Bieżąca* (Survey of foreign periodicals).

Książnica Miejska im. Kopernika w Toruniu (*Copernicus Municipal Library*): 87-100 Toruń, ul. Słowackiego 8; f. 1923; international exchange of information, bibliographic inquiries, archival researches, expositions of books and printed works on educational, cultural and political history of Pomerania; 603,738 vols., incl. 26,877 old vols.; Dir. ALOJZY TUJAKOWSKI, M.P.; publs. *Works of the Copernicus Municipal Library, Profiles of Distinguished Pomeranians.*

Library of the Faculty of Geography and Regional Studies of Warsaw University: 00-927 Warsaw, Krakowskie Przedmieście 30; 66,200 books and periodicals, 1,520 atlases, 77,360 maps and 25,800 slides; Dir. B. LIPSKA; publs. *Prace i Studia Geograficzne*†.

Miejska Biblioteka Publiczna w Bydgoszczy (*Bydgoszcz Public Municipal Library*): Bydgoszcz; f. 1903; 480,011 vols., including 7,609 old books, 3,920 maps and atlases, 902 MSS.

Miejska Biblioteka Publiczna w Krakowie (*Municipal Public Library*): 31-004 Cracow, ul. Franciszkánska 1; f. 1946; educational and scientific collection; 250,000 vols. in central library; 946,000 vols. in brs.; Dir. Dr. JÓZEF ZAJĄC; publs. *Biuletyn Informacyjno-Instrukcyjny* (quarterly), *Bibliografia Krakowa* (annually).

Miejska Biblioteka Publiczna im E. Raczyńskiego w Poznaniu (*E. Raczyński Municipal Public Library*): 61-739 Poznań, Plac Wolności 19; f. 1829; scientific and educational collection; 923,375 vols., 17,438 old books, 20,629 periodicals, 7,171 MSS., 6,210 maps and atlases, 3,530 ex-libris, 3,638 photos, 213 drawings and illustrations, 151 microfilms, 14,659 records, 44 tapes; Dir. ALFRED LABOGA.

Miejska Biblioteka Publiczna im Ł. Waryńskiego w Łódzi (*L. Waryński Public Municipal Library*): 90-508 Łódź, ul. Gdańska 102; f. 1917; general; special subjects socio-economic science and the arts; 403,750 vols., incl. 3,105 old vols., 64,568 periodicals, 2,529 maps and atlases, 1,468 drawings and illustrations, 10,341 in Children's Book Museum; Dir. Prof. ROMAN KACZMAREK; publs. *Studia i Materiały* (irregular), *Sprawozdania MBP* (annually), *Catalogues of Exhibitions* (series).

Ośrodek Informacji Naukowej Polskiej Akademii Nauk (*Scientific Information Centre of the Polish Academy of Sciences*): 00-330 Warsaw, Pałac Staszica, Nowy Świat 72; f. 1953; library of 17,000 vols. and microcopies of all published Polish scientific documents; Dir. Dr. BRONISŁAW ŁUGOWSKI; publs. *Przegląd Informacji o Naukoznawstwie*† (Review of Information on Science of Science, quarterly), *Zagadnienia Informacji Naukowej*† (Problems of Information Science, 2 a year), *Zagadnienia Naukoznawstwa*† (Problems of Science of Science, (quarterly).

Wojewódzka Biblioteka Publiczna im H. Łopacińskiego (*The H. Łopacińskiego District Public Library*): Lublin, ul. Narutowicza 4; f. 1907; scientific and educational collection; 470,000 vols., 17,000 old vols., 17,071 periodicals, 2,100 MSS., 1,668 maps and atlases, 4,120 drawings and illustrations, 467 microfilms; Dir. TADEUSZ JEZIORSKI; publs. *Bibliotekarz Lubelski* (quarterly), *Bibliotekzna Służba Informacyjna Województwa Lubelskiego* (quarterly).

Wojewódzka i Miejska Biblioteka Publiczna w Szczecinie (*Voivodship and City Public Library*): Stanisława Statiszica w Szczecinie, ul. Podgórna 15, 70-952 Szczecin; f. 1945; educational, scientific and editorial activities within the scope of librarianship; staff of 86; 878,841 vols. incl. 30,000 vols. of old prints, 5,456 titles of periodicals, 32,758 vols. of music; Dir. STANISŁAW KRZYWICKI; publs. *Bibliografia Pomorza Zachodniego*† (Bibliography of Western Pomerania, every two years), *Bibliotekarz Zachodniopomorski*† (The West Pomeranian Librarian, quarterly).

MUSEUMS

Warsaw

Adam Mickiewicz Museum of Literature: Rynek Starego Miasta 20; f. 1951; museum of literary history of Poland especially 19th and 20th centuries; 80,000 vols.; Dir. JANUSZ ODROWĄŻ-PIENIĄŻEK; publ. *Blok-Notes Muzeum Literatury*†.

Historical Museum: Rynek Starego Miasta 28-42; f. 1947; exhibits relating to the history of Warsaw from the X century; 28,000 vols.; Dir. Prof. Dr. JANUSZ DURKO; publs. *Bibliography of Warsaw, Studies and Materials.*

Muzeum Narodowe (*National Museum*): Al. Jerozolimskie 3; f. 1862; paintings and sculpture; prints and drawings; numismatics; decorative arts and crafts; Egyptian, Greek, Byzantine and Roman art; medieval and modern Polish art from 12th century to present day; 14th–19th-century foreign painting; also administers museums in the Warsaw palaces: Łazienki, Wilanów, Królikarnia and the Royal Castle, and outside Warsaw, the Łowicz museum and Nieborów Palace; library of 90,000 vols.; Dir. Prof. Dr. STANISŁAW LORENTZ; publs. *Rocznik Muzeum Narodowego w Warszawie*† (Yearbook), *Bulletin du Musée National de Varsovie*† (quarterly).

Muzeum Techniki w Warszawie (*Technical Museum*): 00-901 Warsaw, Pałac Kultury i Nauki; f. 1875; popularization of science and technology and their history, preservation of monuments of technology; planetarium; library of 10,800 vols.; Dir. JERZY JASIUK; local branches: Museum of Ancient Metallurgy in Nowa Słupia, Museum of the old Polish Basin in Sielpia, water-worked forges in Stara Kuźnica and Gdańsk.

Muzeum Wojska Polskiego (*Polish Army Museum*): 00-950 Warsaw, Al. Jerozolimskie 3; f. 1920; reorganized 1945; exhibition of weapons, uniforms, banners, decorations, etc., showing the history of Polish military art from the 10th to the 20th centuries; prehistoric weapons found in Poland; militaria from Asia, Africa, Australia; collection of modern paintings, sculptures and graphics; iconographic collection; conservation workshop for metal, textile and wooden exhibits; library of over 20,000 vols.; Dir. Colonel L. JAWORSKI; publ. *Muzealnictwo Wojskowe* (Military Museology).

Państwowe Muzeum Archeologiczne (*State Archaeological Museum*): Warsaw 40, ul. Długa 52; f. 1923; prehistoric and proto-historic exhibits; organizes regional and field exhibitions, and carries out archaeological excavations throughout Poland; br. at Biskupin (an Iron Age fortified settlement), archaeological stores at Rybno; library of 29,000 vols.; Dir. (vacant); publs. *Wiadomości Archeologiczne, Materialy Starożytne i Wczesnośredniowieczne*.

Państwowe Muzeum Etnograficzne w Warszawie (*State Ethnographic Museum in Warsaw*): Warsaw, ul. Kredytowa 1; f. 1888; Polish and non-European ethnographical collection; library of 17,500 vols.; Dir. Dr. KRZYSZTOF MAKULSKI; publ. *Zeszyty Państwowego Muzeum Etnograficznego w Warszawie*† (Reports, annual).

Cracow

History Museum of the City of Cracow: Krzysztofory, Rynek Główny 35; f. 1899; traditions, history and culture of the city of Cracow, arms and clocks, history of the theatre in Cracow, history and culture of the Jews in Cracow; library of 14,560 vols.; Dir. SŁAWOMIR WOJAK; publ. *Krzysztofory-Zeszyty Naukowe* (annual).

Muzeum Etnograficzne w Krakowie (*Ethnographic Museum in Cracow*): Pl. Wolnica 1; f. 1901; history, arts and culture of the Polish village; also foreign collections from Europe, Asia, Africa, S. America; library of 15,000 vols.; archives; Dir. EDWARD WALIGÓRA; publ. *Rocznik Muzeum Etnograficznego w Krakowie*† (annual).

Muzeum Narodowe w Krakowie (*National Museum in Cracow*): Ul. Manifestu Lipcowego 12; f. 1879; Dir. TADEUSZ CHRUŚCICKI; publ. *Rozprawy i Sprawozdania Muzeum Narodowego w Krakowie*† (Yearbook); the museum consists of the following departments:

Gallery of Polish Painting and Sculpture of the XVIII-XIX Centuries: Sukiennice (*Clothiers' Hall*), *Rynek* Główny.

The Emeryk Hutten-Czapski Department: ul. Manifestu Lipcowego 12; graphic and numismatic collections, old books.

Dom Jana Matejki (*Jan Matejko's House*): ul. Floriańska 41; paintings and personal relics of the eminent 19th-century Polish painter.

Gallery of Polish Painting and Sculpture of the XIV-XVIII Centuries: pl. Szczepański 9; Far Eastern art and icon collections, militaria.

The Czartoryski Collection: ul. Pijarska 6 and ul. św. Jana 19; f. 1801; national relics, Polish and foreign painting, old arms and armour, Polish and foreign crafts, ancient archaeology.

Czartoryski Library and Archives: ul. Św. Marka 17; documents, illuminated codices, incunabula, books on history, art and culture.

Gallery of Polish Painting and Sculpture of the XX Century: al. Trzeciego Maja 1; contains also collections of Polish crafts.

Karol Szymanowski Museum: Zakopane, Atma House, Kasprusie 19; exhibits relating to the life of the eminent composer (1882–1937).

Wawel State Art Collections: Cracow, Wawel 5; f. 1925; (*a*) Collections of art in the Royal Castle: Italian Renaissance furniture, King Sigismund August's 16th-century collection of Flemish tapestries, Italian and Dutch painting, Polish carpets; (*b*) Royal treasury, crown jewels, historical relics, banners, gold objects; (*c*) Armoury: Polish and West European weapons; (*d*) Oriental objects of art: Persian and Turkish weaponry and tents; oriental rugs, Chinese and Japanese pottery; (*e*) Collection relating to the history of Wawel Hill, other archaeological materials, Polish tiles from the 15th–18th centuries; (*f*) 18th-century Meissen porcelain; library of 29,648 vols.; Dir. JERZY SZABLOWSKI; publs. *Studia do dziejów Wawelu*† (Studies in the History of the Wawel) (every 2 years), *Biblioteka Wawelska*† (Library of the Wawel).

Łódź

Centralne Muzeum Włókiennictwa: ul. Piotrkowska 282; f. 1960; collection of modern Polish textiles; departments of Ancient and Modern Artistic Textiles, History of Textile Technique, History of the Textile Industry in Łódź, Folk Weaving, Conservational Laboratory; library of about 7,000 vols.; Dir. Dr. ADAM NAHLIK.

Muzeum Archeologiczne i Etnograficzne: Pl. Wolności 14; f. 1956 as amalgamation of Archaeological and Ethnographical Museums (f. 1931); archaeology, ethnography, numismatics; radio-chemical laboratory; library of 24,000 vols.; Dir. Dr. ANDRZEJ MIKOŁAJCZYK; publs. *Guides and Reports*†, *Prace i Materiały Muzeum Archeologicznego i Etnograficznego*† (archaeology, ethnography, numismatics and conservation series).

Muzeum Sztuki w Łodzi (*Art Museum*): 90-734 Łódź, Ul. Wieckowskiego 36; f. 1930; departments: Gothic art; foreign painting of the 15th–19th centuries; Polish painting of the 18th–20th centuries; international modern art; Dir. RYSZARD STANISŁAWSKI.

Poznań

Muzeum Archeologiczne: ul. Wodna 27; f. 1857; archaeology of Great Poland and the Nile basin; library of 50,000 vols.; Dir. Dr. WŁODZIMIERZ BŁASZCZYK; publs. *Fontes Archaeologici Posnanienses*† (annual), *Biblioteka Fontes Archaeologici Posnanienses*†.

Muzeum Narodowe (*National Museum*): 61-745 Poznań, Al. Marcinkowskiego 9; f. 1894; Medieval Art, European Painting XIV–XIX centuries, Polish painting XV–XX centuries, Prints and drawings, Numismatics, Modern art; library of 72,500 vols.; Dir. Doc. Dr. H. KONDZIELA; branch museums: Muzeum Kultury i Sztuki Ludowej (*Ethnography*): Grobla 25; Muzeum Historii m. Poznania (*City Historical Museum*): Town Hall; Wielkopolskie Muzeum Wojskowe (*Military Museum*): Stary Rynek 1; Muzeum Instrumentów Muzycznych (*Musical Instruments*): Stary Rynek 45: Muzeum Rzemiosł Artystycznych (*Decorative Arts*): Góra Przemysława 1; Depts.: Gołuchow (*Paintings and Decorative Arts*); Rogalin (*Paintings and Decorative Arts*); Śmiełów (*Adam Mickiewicz Museum*); publs. *Studia Muzealne* (annually), *Monographs*, catalogues, guides.

Other Towns

Centralne Muzeum Morskie (*Polish Maritime Museum*): 80-835 Gdansk, ul. Szeroka 67/68; f. 1960; depts. of ports development, history of shipbuilding, history of maritime shipping and trade, history of inland waterways shipping, marine fine arts, history of yachting, underwater archaeology, educational services; special vessel (*Wodnik*) for underwater archaeological investigations; laboratory for conservation of artefacts recovered from sea; Lighthouse Museum in Rozewie; also br. in Hel (history of Polish fishery; open-air exhibition of types of fishing boats); library of 10,000 vols., archives: plans, drawings, photos, documents; Dir. Doc. Dr. Habil. PRZEMYSŁAW SMOLAREK; publs. *Prace*† (Proceedings—monographs), *Publikacje*† (Publications).

Church Museum: Przemyśl, Pl. Czackiego 2; f. 1902; early Christian ceramics; Gobelin tapestry probably by Guido Reni; collections of religious pictures and vestments, objects of trade and of artistic and historical importance; Dir. ZBIGNIEW BIELAMOWICZ.

Frederic Chopin Museum: Zelazowa Wola, near Warsaw; f. 1932; biographical museum, birthplace of Chopin.

Gorzow Museum: Gorzow, Ul. Warszawska 35; f. 1945; human and natural history.

Łańcut Museum: Łańcut, ul. Zamkowa 1; f. 1944; historic interiors, coaches; storehouse of Orthodox Church art; 30,000 vols. in the Palace and Museum libraries; Dir. W. CZAJEWSKI; Curator J. ZIEMBIŃSKI.

Lublin District Museum: Lublin, The Castle (Zamek); f. 1906; regional archaeological, historical and ethnographic collection, Polish painting and decorative art; armoury; numismatics; conservation dept.; library of 15,000 vols.; Dir. ALFRED GAUDA; publ. *Studia i Materiały Lubelskie*†.

Museum of Architecture: 50-156 Wrocław, ul. Bernardyńska 5; f. 1965; Polish and other architecture; modern art; library of 3,500 vols.; Dir. Prof. Dr. hab. OLGIERD CZERNER; publs. catalogues.

Muzeum in. Leona Wyczółkowskiego (*L. Wyczółkowski Museum*): 85-006 Bydgoszcz, Al. 1 Maja 4; f. 1880; Polish art of 19th and 20th centuries; paintings and graphic art of Leon Wyczółkowski and gallery of contemporary Polish paintings; Archaeological and Historical brs. and Coin Room at Bydgoszcz, Grodzka 9/11; Dir. Mgr. RAJMUND KUCZMA.

Muzeum Lenina w Poroninie (*Lenin Museum in Poronin*): Poronin, woj. Nowy Sącz, ul. Lenina 160; f. 1947 by the Society of Polish-Soviet Friendship; to increase knowledge of the life and activities of Lenin during his emigration period in Poland; library of 1,532 vols.; Dir. Mgr. WIESŁAW TOKARSKI.

Muzeum Narodowe (*National Museum*): Gdańsk, ul. Toruńska 1; f. 1945; art, ethnography; library of 10,000 vols.; Dir. JAN PRZAŁA.

Muzeum Okręgowe w Przemyślu: Przemśyl, plac. Czackiego 3; f. 1909; history, ethnography, archaeology, arts; Dir. ANTONI KUNYSZ.

Muzeum Okręgowe w Rzeszowie: Rzeszow, 3-go Maja 19; f. 1936; Dir. TADEUSZ AKSAMIT.

Muzeum Okręgowe w Toruniu (*District Museum in Toruń*): 87-100 Toruń, Rynek Staromiejski 1, Ratusz; f. 1861; art (modern graphic handicrafts, Far Eastern), history (modern, Toruń), archaeology; Castle of the Teutonic Order, Copernicus Museum; Dir. ZDZISŁAW CIARA; publ. *Rocznik Muzeum w Toruniu*† (annual).

Muzeum Sztuki Medalierskiej (*Museum of Medallic Art*): Wrocław, Ryńek-Ratusz; f. 1965; medals, medallions, plaques, orders and decorations of all countries; special library; Dir. Dr. ADAM WIĘCEK; publ. *Biuletyn*†.

Muzeum Warmii i Mazur (*Museum of Varmia and Mazuria*): 10-074 Olsztyn, ul. Zamkowa 2; f. 1945; library of 38,000 vols.; Dir. WŁADYSŁAW OGRODZIŃSKI; publ. *Rocznik Olsztyński*† (annually).

Muzeum Narodowe (*National Museum*): Szczecin, ul. Staromłyńska 27; f. 1945; archaeological, maritime, ethnographical and history of art collections, sociology, numismatics; special African collection and corresponding library; 26 research workers; 46,241 vols.; Dir. WŁADYSŁAW FILIPOWIAK; publ. *Materiały Zachodniopomorskie*† (annual).

Nicholas Kopernik Museum: 14-530 Frombork, ul. Katedralna 12; f. 1948; biographical exhibits, example of Foucault's pendulum, son et lumière, and planetarium; library of 5,000 vols.; Dir. Mgr. TADEUSZ PIASKOWSKI.

Państwowe Muzeum Oświęcim-Brzezinka: 32-603 Oświęcim 5, ul. Więźniów Oświęcimia 20; f. 1947; situated in former Nazi concentration camp at Auschwitz-Birkenau, illustrating system of mass extermination; library of 14,000 vols. and archives; publs. *Zeszyty Oświęcimskie* (in Polish and German with special editions in Polish and German), *From the History of K. L. Auschwitz* (in English and French).

Muzeum Narodowe: 50-153 Wrocław, Pl. Powstańców Warszawy 5; f. 1948; collection of medieval art, Polish painting of the 18th, 19th and 20th centuries, European painting, decorative arts, prints, ethnography and history relating to Silesia; numismatics; library of 55,000 vols.; Dir. LESZEK ITMAN; publs. *Roczniki Sztuki Śląskiej*, *Roczniki Etnografii Śląskiej* (both annual).

Muzeum Narodowe: 25-303 Kielce, Pl. Partyzantów 3-5; f. 1908; State Museum illustrating the history and culture of the Kielce province; Polish baroque interiors; Polish painting from the 17th to the 20th century; Dir. ALOJZY OBORNY; publ. *Rocznik Museum Swiętokrzyskiego*† (annual) from vol. 10 *Rocznik Muzeum Narodowego w Kielcach*†.

Tatra Museum: 34-500 Zakopane, ul. Krupówki 10; f. 1888; regional flora, fauna, history and ethnography; Dir. Mgr. TADEUSZ SZCZEPANEK.

Upper Silesian Museum: 41-902 Bytom, Pl. Thaelmanna 2; f. 1927 in Katowice, transferred in 1945; culture of Silesia: art, archaeology, history, ethnography and natural history; library of 33,391 vols.; Dir. JÓZEF KOWALEWSKI; publs. *Rocznik Muzeum Górnośląskiego w Bytomiu, Series: Archaeologia*†, *Historia*†, *Sztuka*†, *Etnografia*†, *Przyroda*† (annually).

UNIVERSITIES

UNIWERSYTET GDAŃSKI*
(University of Gdańsk)

GDAŃSK, UL. SOBIESKIEGO 18

Telephone: 52-12-71.

Founded 1970.

State control; Academic year: October to June.

Rector: Prof. Dr. hab. JANUSZ SOKOŁOWSKI.

Vice-Rectors: Prof. Dr. hab. MIROSŁAW KRZYSZTOFIAK, Prof. Dr. hab. ROMAN WAPIŃSKI, Doc. Dr. hab. EDWARD KĄTOWSKI, Doc. Dr. hab. KAZIMIERZ KURPIS, Mgr. Inz. HENRYK WEYNA.

Registrar: Mgr. Inz. BOLESŁAW PASZKOWSKI.

Librarian: Doc. Dr. ZBIGNIEW BINEROWSKI.

Number of teachers: 1,703.
Number of students: 12,512.

Publication: *Zeszyty Naukowe*†.

DEANS:

Faculty of Biology and Earth Sciences: Doc. Dr. hab. BOGUSŁAW ROSA.
Faculty of Production Economics: Prof. Dr. hab. WŁADYSŁAW NOWACZEK.
Faculty of Transport Economics: Prof. Dr. hab. BRONISŁAW RUDOWICZ.
Faculty of Humanities: Doc. Dr. hab. BOGUSŁAW CYGLER.
Faculty of Mathematics, Physics and Chemistry: Prof. Dr. hab. GOTFRYD KUPRYSZEWSKI.
Faculty of Law and Administration: Prof. Dr. hab. DONALD STEYER.

ATTACHED INSTITUTES:

Biological Station: 83-010 Gdansk-Gorki Wschodnie; Dir. Dr. KONSTANTY TUROBOYOSKI.

Limnological Station: Borucino, powial Kartuzy, wojewodztwo gdanskie; Dir. Dr. EUZEBIUSZ OKULANIS.

* No reply received to our questionnaire this year.

UNIWERSYTET JAGIELLOŃSKI
(Jagiellonian University)

GOŁEBIA 24, 31-007 CRACOW

Telephone: 210-33.

Founded 1364.

Academic year: October to June.

Rector: Prof. Dr. hab. MIECZYSŁAW HESS.

Administrator: Mgr. ZYGMUNT ZIĘCINA.

Librarian: Prof. Dr. hab. STANISŁAW GRZESZCZUK.

Number of teachers: *c.* 1,700.
Number of students: 10,000.

Publications: *Zeszyt Naukowe Uniwersytetu Jagiellońskiego* (annually).

DEANS:

Faculty of Law and Administration: Prof. Dr. hab. STANISŁAW GRODZISKI.
Faculty of Philosophy and History: Prof. Dr. hab. MARIUSZ KULCZYKOWSKI.
Faculty of Philology: Doc. Dr. hab. STANISŁAW JAWORSKI.
Faculty of Mathematics and Physics: Prof. Dr. hab. DANUTA KUNISZ.
Faculty of Biology and Earth Sciences: Prof. Dr. hab. JÓZEF SUROWIAK.

DIRECTORS OF INSTITUTES:

Institute of Administration and Management: Prof. Dr. habil JÓZEF FILIPEK.
Institute of Political Sciences: Prof. Dr. WITOLD ZAKRZEWSKI.
Institute of Economics: Prof. Dr. BRONISŁAW OYRZANOWSKI.
Institute of History and Law: Doc. Dr. WIESŁAW LITEWSKI.
Institute of Civil Law: Prof. Dr. habil. WŁADYSŁAW SIEDLECKI.
Institute of Penal Law: Prof. Dr. habil. KAZIMIERZ BUCHAŁA.
Institute of International Public Law: Prof. Dr. STANISŁAW NAHLIK.
Institute of History: Prof. Dr. JÓZEF BUSZKO.
Institute of History of Art: Doc. Dr. habil. ADAM MAŁKIEWICZ.
Institute of Pedagogics: Doc. Dr. habil. WOJCIECH KOJS.
Institute of Psychology: Prof. Dr. habil. WŁODZIMIERZ SZEWCZUK.
Institute of Sociology: Doc. Dr. habil. PIOTR SZTOMPKA.
Institute of Philosophy: Prof. Dr. habil. ZBIGNIEW KUDEROWICZ.
Institute of Study of Religions: (vacant).
Institute of Archaeology: Prof. Dr. habil. KAZIMIERZ GODŁOWSKI.
Chair of History and Music Theory: Doc. Dr. habil. ZYGMUNT SZWEYKOWSKI.
Institute of Slavonic Ethnography: Prof. Dr. JADWIGA KLIMASZEWSKA.
Institute of Polish Philology: Prof. Dr. habil. HENRYK MARKIEWICZ.
Institute of Russian Philology: Doc. Dr. habil. WŁADYSŁAW PIOTROWSKI.
Institute of Romance Philology: Doc. Dr. STANISŁAW WIDŁAK.
Institute of English Philology: Prof. Dr. habil. PRZEMYSŁAW MROCZKOWSKI.
Institute of German Philology: Prof. Dr. habil. ALEKSANDER SZULC.
Institute of Oriental Philology: Doc. Dr. habil. ANDRZEJ CZAPKIEWICZ.
Institute of Slavonic Philology: Prof. Dr. habil. FRANCISZEK SŁAWSKI.
Institute of Classical Philology: Prof. Dr. habil. ROMUALD TURASIEWICZ.
Institute of General Linguistics: Prof. Dr. habil. ADAM HEINZ.
Institute of Mathematics: Prof. Dr. habil. JÓZEF SICIAK.
Institute of Physics: Prof. Dr. habil. ADAM STRZAŁKOWSKI.
Institute of Chemistry: Prof. Dr. habil. ZDZISŁAW WOJTASZEK.
Institute of Informatics: Prof. Dr. FRANCISZEK STUDNICKI.
Astronomical Observatory: Doc. Dr. habil. JÓZEF MASŁOWSKI.
Institute of Geography: Prof. Dr. habil. MIECZYSŁAW HESS.
Institute of Botany: Prof. Dr. habil. EUGENIA POGAN.
Institute of Molecular Biology: Prof. Dr. habil. ALEKSANDER KOJ.
Institute of Zoology: Prof. Dr. habil. CZESŁAW JURA.
Institute of Geological Sciences: Doc. Dr. habil. RAFAŁ UNRUG.
Institute of Environmental Biology: Doc. Dr. habil. WŁADYSŁAW GRODZIŃSKI.
K. Estreicher Department of 19th-century Bibliography: Dr. ANDRZEJ BOROWSKI.
Polonia Research Institute: Prof. Dr. habil. HIERONIM KUBIAK.
Practical Study of Foreign Languages: Doc. Dr. MARIAN RADŁOWSKI.
Intercollegiate Institute of Inventiveness and Protection of Intellectual Property: Doc. Dr. habil. JANUSZ SZWAJA.

UNIWERSYTET ŁÓDZKI
(University of Łódź)

NARUTOWICZA 65, 90-131 ŁÓDŹ

Telephone: 858-12.

Founded 1945.

State control; Language of instruction: Polish; Academic year: October to September.

Rector: Prof. Dr. hab. R. SKOWROŃSKI.

Pro-Rectors: Prof. Dr. hab. H. MORTIMER-SZYMCZAK, Prof. Dr. hab. J. TYLMAN, Doc. Dr. hab. T. KRZEMIŃSKI, Doc. Dr. B. BOŃCZAK.

Librarian: Doc. Dr. hab. B. ŚWIDERSKI.

Library: *see* Libraries.

Number of professors: 202.
Number of students: 16,100.

Publications: *Acta Universitatis Lodziensis, Zeszyty Naukowe Uniwersytetu Łódzkiego* (Research Bulletin in three series, annual).

DEANS:

Faculty of Philology: Prof. Dr. hab. W. CYRAN.
Faculty of Philosophy and History: Doc. Dr. W. MICHOWICZ.
Faculty of Mathematics, Physics and Chemistry: Doc. Dr. hab. Z. JAKUBOWSKI.
Faculty of Biology and Earth Sciences: Prof. Dr. hab. A. ROMANIUK.
Faculty of Law and Administration: Prof. Dr. hab. N. GAJL.
Faculty of Economics and Sociology: Prof. Dr. hab. J. CHECHLIŃSKI.

PROFESSORS:

Faculty of Philology:

BAJOR, K., Russian Philology
CIEŚLIKOWSKA, T., Theory of Literature
CYRAN, W., Polish and Slavonic Languages
DEJNA, K., Slavonic and Polish Languages
GRAVIL, J. R., English Literature
HRYŃCZUK, J., German Philology
JANICKA-SWIDERSKA, I., English Philology
KAMIŃSKA, M., Polish and Slavonic Languages
KASZYŃSKI, S., Theory of Theatre
KOMORNICKA, A., Classical Philology
KRZESZOWSKI, T., Linguistics
KUPISZ, K., French Philology
OSTROWSKI, W., English Philology
POKLEWSKA, K., Polish Literature
RYTER, Z., Russian Philology
SKWARCZYŃSKI, ZDZISŁAW, Polish Literature
ŚMIECH, W., Polish Language
STARNAWSKI, J., Old-Polish Literature
STROKOWSKA, A., Polish Language
STYCZYŃSKA, A., American Literature
ŚWIDERSKI, B., Library and Information Science
SZLESIŃSKI, I., Polish Language
WERT, P., Theory of Film
WIŚNIEWSKI, B., Classical Philology

Faculty of Philosophy and History:

BANASIAK, S., Recent Polish History
BARANOWSKI, B., Modern Polish History
BARSZCZEWSKA-KRUPA, A., Modern Polish History
BORTNOWSKI, W., Modern World History
BRODOWSKA-KUBICZ, H., History of 19th and 20th Century Poland, Rural History
CZERNIAWSKA, O., Social Pedagogy
FUDALI, J., Didactics
GERSTMANN, S., Psychology
GREGOROWICZ, J., Logic with Scientific Methodology
KMIECIŃSKI, J., Archaeology
KOPCZYŃSKA-JAWORSKA, B., Ethnography
KRAKOWSKI, S., Medieval Polish History
KUCHARSKA, J., Ethnography
KUCHOWICZ, Z., History of Polish Culture
LEPALCZYK, I., Social Pedagogy
LIBISZOWSKA, Z., Polish and World History of the 17th and 18th Centuries
MICHOWICZ, W., History of International Relations
PANASIUK, R., History of 19th Century Philosophy
PAWŁOWSKA, IJA, Ethics and Scientific Methodology
PAWŁOWSKI, TADEUSZ, Logic and Scientific Methodology
PODGÓRSKA, E., History of Education
POLNY, R., Didactics
ROSIN, R., Medieval Polish History and Auxiliary Studies
ŚMIAŁOWSKI, J., Modern Polish History
ŚRENIOWSKA, M. K., History of Historiography and Methodology of History
SPORNY, K., Pedagogy
STANKIEWICZ, Z., Modern Polish History
SZCZYGIELSKI, W., Modern Polish History
WACHOWSKA, B., Recent Polish History
WŁODARCZYK, J., History

Faculty of Mathematics, Physics and Chemistry:

BARTNIK, R., Organic Chemistry
BOŃCZAK, B., Nuclear Physics
CHARZYŃSKI, Z., Analytical Functions
EPSZTAJN, J., Organic Chemistry
FILIPCZAK, M., Algebra
GRABOWSKI, M., Crystallography
HAHN, W., Organic Chemistry
IGNACZAK, M., Inorganic Chemistry
JAJTE, R., Probability Theory
JAKUBOWSKI, Z., Analytical Functions
JANIKOWSKI, J., Analytical Functions
JĘDRZEJEWSKI, W. W., Analytical Chemistry
KOTKOWSKA-MACHNIK, Z., Organic Chemistry
KOZŁOWSKI, Z., Electrochemistry
MAŁECKI, H., Nuclear Physics
MICHALAK, S., Solid State Physics
MIKOŁAJCZYK, L., Analytical Functions
PRZYTUŁA, M., Low Energy Nuclear Physics
SCHOLL, H., Physical Chemistry
SKOWROŃSKI, R., Organic Chemistry
TANIEWSKA-OSIŃSKA, S., Physical Chemistry
TIETZ, T., Theoretical Physics
TOMASZEWSKI, A., Nuclear Physics
TUROWSKA, M., Inorganic Chemistry
TYBOR, W., Theoretical Physics
WALCZAK, S., Analytical Functions
WILCZYŃSKI, W., Geometry
WŁODARSKI, L., Functional Analysis
WOJTCZAK, L., Solid State Physics
WROŃSKI, M., Chemical Technology
ZAHORSKA, H., Theoretical Physics

Faculty of Biology and Earth Sciences:

BATOROWICZ, Z., Economic Geography
CZARNECKA, I., Economic Geography
DYLIK, A., Physical Geography, Geomorphology
GABARA, B., Cytology and Cytochemistry
GONDKO, R., Biochemistry, Biophysics
GROMSKA, W., Microbiology
JAŻDŻEWSKI, K., Zoology
KADŁUBOWSKA, J., Algaeology
KAPICA, Z., Theory of Evolution
KLAJNERT, Z., Physical Geography
KLATKA, HALINA, Geomorphology
KLATKA, TADEUSZ, Geology and Geomorphology
KŁYSZEJKO-STEFANOWICZ, L., Biochemistry
KNYPL, S. J., Plant Physiology and Biochemistry
KOTEŁKO, K., Microbiology, Immunochemistry of Micro-organisms
KOTER, M., Economic Geography
KRAJEWSKI, T., Biochemistry
KRZEMIŃSKI, T., Physical Geography, Geomophology
KUKULSKA-GOŚCICKA, T., Immunology
KULAMOWICZ, A., Zoology and Ichthyology
KWIATKOWSKA, M., Plant Cytology and Cytochemistry
LEWIŃSKA, M., Animal Physiology and Neurophysiology
LEYKO, W., Biochemistry and Biophysics
LISZEWSKI, S., Economic Geography
MACIEJEWSKA-POTAPCZYK, W., Plant Physiology and Biochemistry
MIKULSKA, E., Plant Cytology and Cytochemistry
OLACZEK, R. S., Plant Systems and Geography
OLSZEWSKA, MARIA, Plant Cytology and Cytochemistry
PENCZAK, T., Zoology, Fish Ecology
ROMANISZYN, W., Entomology and Ecology
ROMANIUK, A., Animal Physiology and Neurophysiology
SEDLACZEK, L., Metabolism of Micro-organisms
SOWA, R., Plant Systems and Geography
STRASZEWICZ, L., Economic Geography
SUSŁOWSKA, W., Zoology, Fish Anatomy
TOMASZEWSKI, C., Zoology
URBANEK, H., Biochemistry
URBANOWICZ, K., Zoology, Comparative Anatomy of Ichthyoids
WALTER, Z., Biochemistry
WOJTAS, F., Zoology and Hydrobiology
WOLSKA, M., Protozoology

Faculty of Law and Administration:

BORKOWSKI, J., Administrative Law
BORTKIEWICZ, F., History of State and Law
BRONIEWICZ, W., Civil Procedure
CZUBIŃSKI, L., Penal Law
GAJL, N., Financial Law
GRACZYK, B., Administrative Law
HOŁYST, B., Criminology
KODRĘBSKI, J., Roman Law
KOSIKOWSKI, C., Financial Law
KUNDEREWICZ, C., Roman Law
LELENTAL, S., Penal Law
LEWANDOWSKI, H., Labour Law
LEWASZKIEWICZ-PETRYKOWSKA, B., Civil Law
LOGA, J., Labour Law
MATUSZEWSKI, J., History of State and Law
OLSZEWSKI, M., Criminal Procedure
REMBIELIŃSKI, A., Civil Law
ROWIŃSKI, T., Civil Procedure
RYMASZEWSKI, Z., History of State and the Law
SEWERYŃSKI, M., Labour Law
SMOKTUNOWICZ, E., Administrative Law
SZPUNAR, A., Civil Law
SZUBERT, W., Labour Law
SZYMCZAK, T., Constitutional Law
TYLMAN, J., Penal Procedure
WASZCZYŃSKI, J., Penal Law
WRÓBLEWSKI, J., Theory of State and Law

Faculty of Economics and Sociology:

BIELSKI, M., Organization and Management
BIENIEK, M., Home Trade Economics
BOKSZAŃSKI, Z., Cultural Sociology
BORKOWSKA, S., Business Administration
BOROWSKA-KWASIK, Z., Economic Theory
CABAN, W., Economic Theory
CHECHLIŃSKI, J., Finance
DIETL, J., Commercial Economics
DZIĘCIELSKA-MACHNIKOWSKA, S., Labour Sociology
GÓRSKI, J., Political Economy of Capitalism and History of Economic Theory
IWIŃSKA, I., Science of Comestibles
JARUGA, A., Cost Accounting Management Accountancy
JÓZEFIAK, C., Political Economy of Socialism
KORTAN, J., Economics and Organization of Enterprises
KULPIŃSKA, J., Industrial Sociology
LEGATOWICZ, A., Economics of Foreign Trade
LEJMAN, W., Political Economy of Capitalism
LIWOWSKI, B., Business Administration
LUTYŃSKI, J., Methodology of Social Research
MARSZAŁEK, A. G., Political Economy of Socialism
MIASTKOWSKI, L., Political Economy of Socialism
MICHALEWSKI, A., Economic Theory
MICHAŁKIEWICZ, Z., Economic Statistics
MIKOŁAJCZYK, Z., Theory of Organization and Management
MORTIMER-SZYMCZAK, H., Planning and Economic Policy
OLSZEWSKI, T., Economic Geography
PIASKOWSKI, W., Economic Analysis

Piątkowski, W., History of Economic Theory
Piotrowski, Wacław, Urban and Rural Sociology
Piotrowski, Władysław, Industrial Economics
Prochowski, Z., Investment Economics
Regulski, J., Economic Production
Szczakowski, Z., International Economic Relations
Szczepaniak, J., Organization of Data Processing
Trzeciakowski, W., Economics of Foreign Trade
Welfe, W., Econometrics and Statistics
Witkowski, J., Marketing
Woskowski, J., Sociology and Educational Sociology
Wysocki, Z., Regional Geography
Zabielski, K., Economics of Foreign Trade

Institute of Political Science:
Górbiel, A., Law
Grzelak, Z., Planning and Economic Policy
Janowski, W., Theory of Organization and Management
Surowik, C., Social Policy
Wojtkowiak, S., History

Institute of Light Industry Economics:
Gościński, J., Econometrics and Cybernetics
Janusz, T., Industrial Economics

Polish Language Tuition Centre for Foreign Students:
Wędrychowicz, A., Sociology

KATOLICKI UNIWERSYTET LUBELSKI
(Catholic University of Lublin)

20-950 LUBLIN,
AL. RACŁAWICKIE 14

Telephone: 304–26

Founded 1918.

Private control.

Rector: Rev. Prof. Dr. M. A. Krąpiec.

Vice-Rector: Prof. Dr. Stefan Sawicki.

Librarian: Dr. Andrzej Paluchowski.

Library: *see* Libraries.

Number of professors: 264.
Number of students: 2,500.

Publications: *Zeszyty Naukowe KUL*, ***Roczniki Teologiczno-Kanoniczne, Roczniki Filozoficzne, Roczniki Humanistyczne, Biuletyn Informacyjny***, etc.

Deans:

Faculty of Theology: Rev. Prof. Edward Kopeć.

Faculty of Canon Law: Rev. Prof. Dr. Józef Krukowski.

Faculty of Philosophy: Rev. Doc. Dr. hab. Zdzisław Chlewiński.

Faculty of Humanities: Prof. Zygmunt Sułowski.

UNIWERSYTET MARII CURIE-SKŁODOWSKIEJ
(Marie Curie-Skłodowska University)

PLAC MARII CURIE-SKŁODOWSKIEJ 5, 20-031 LUBLIN

Telephone: 330-30.

Founded 1944.

***Rector:* Prof. Dr. W. Skrzydło.**

Pro-Rectors: Prof. Dr. R. Orłowski, Doc. Dr. Z. Ilczuk, Doc. Dr. K. Sykut, Prof. Dr. W. Ćwik.

Chief Administrative Officer: L. Roup-pert.

Librarian: Dr. Z. Kowalski.

Library: *see* Libraries.

Number of teachers: 1,347.
Number of students: 16,468, including 8,715 extra-mural students.

Publication: *Annales Universitatis Mariae Curie-Skłodowska.*

Deans:

Faculty of Law and Administration: Prof. Dr. J. Malarczyk.

Faculty of Humanities: Doc. Dr. T. Łoposzko.

Faculty of Mathematics, Physics and Chemistry: Doc. Dr. E. Złotkiewicz.

Faculty of Biology and Geography: Prof. Dr. Z. Kawecki.

Faculty of Economics: Doc. Dr. S. Kozłowski.

Faculty of Psychology and Pedagogy: Doc. Dr. K. Poznański.

Professors:

Faculty of Law and Administration:
Antonowicz, L., International Public Law
Bałaban, A., Administrative Law
Burda, A., Constitutional Law
Chwistek, J., Public Law
Ćwik, W., History of State and Law and of Political and Law Doctrines
Gofroń, C., Penal Law and Criminology
Groszyk, H., Theory of State and Law
Hasiec, M., Labour Law
Ignatowicz, J., Civil Law and Civil Procedure
Korobowicz, A., Theory of State and Law
Kunicki, A., Civil Law and Civil Procedure
Kuryłowicz, M., Roman Law
Łętowski, J., Administrative Law
Malarczyk, J., History of State and Law and of Political and Law Doctrines
Opas, T., History of Law
Pieniążek, A., Theory of State and Law
Policzkiewicz-Zawadzka, Z., Civil Law and Civil Procedure
Poźniak-Niedzielska, M., Economic Law
Reniger, H., Financial Law
Sand, K., Administrative Law and Administrative Science
Sawczuk, M., Civil Law and Civil Procedure
Seidler, G., Theory of State and Law
Skrzydło, W., Constitutional Law
Sobolewski, Z., Penal Procedure and Criminology
Szreniawski, J., Administrative Law and Administrative Science
Tokarczyk, R., History of Political Thought
Wąsek, A., Penal Law and Criminology
Ziembiński, J., Constitutional Law
Żołnierczuk, M., Roman Law

Faculty of Economics:
Grzybowski, W., Political Economy and Economic Planning
Hoff, T., Political Economy and Economic Planning
Kozłowski, S., Political Economy
Kurek, W., Industrial Economy and Organization of Industries
Kurnal, J., Organization and Administration
Lewandowski, Z., Mathematics Applied to Economics
Mitura, Z., Industrial Economy and Organization of Industries
Orłowski, R., Economic History and Economic Thought
Pomorska, A., Finances
Przeciszewski, R., Planning and Social Policy
Siejak, L., Industrial Economy
Szeloch, Z., Industrial Economy and Organization of Industries
Tomaszewski, W., Statistics
Wich, U., Urban Planning
Zalewa, J., Agricultural Economics

Faculty of Humanities:
Aleksandrowicz, A., Theory and History of Polish Literature
Bartmiński, J., Linguistics
Borsukiewicz, I., Russian Philology
Brzeziński, J., German Philosophy
Falicki, J., Romance Philology
Gerlecka, Regina, Literature
Gurba, J., Archaeology
Gussmann, E., Linguistics
Kaczmarek, L., Logopedics
Kaczyński, M., Romance Philology
Kamienik, R., Ancient History and Archaeology
Kersten, A., Mediaeval History
Koprukowniak, A., Modern History
Kowalczyk, J., Polish Archaeology
Łesiów, M., Russian Philology
Lewicki, A., Polish Language
Łoch, E., Polish Literature
Łoposzko, T., Ancient History
Ludorowski, L., Theory of Literature
Mańkowski, Z., Recent Polish History
Mencel, T., Modern History
Myśliński, K., Mediaeval History
Orłowski, J., Russian Philology
Rott-Żebrowski, T., Russian Philology
Skubalanka, Teresa, Polish Language
Śladkowski, W., Modern History
Święch, J., Polish Literature
Świeczkowski, W., English Philology
Szala, Alina, English Philology
Szymański, J., History of Library Science
Warchoł, S., Slavonic Philology
Wiśniewska, J., Polish Linguistics
Zakrzewska-Dubasowa, Mirosława, History of U.S.S.R. and Peoples' Democracies
Zins, H., History of Anglo-Saxon Countries

Faculty of Biology and Geography:
Baszyński, T., Plant Physiology
Bednara, J., Anatomy and Plant Cytology
Buraczyński, J., Physical Geography
Bystrek, J., Plant Systematics
Cmoluch, Z., Zoology
Drożański, W., Microbiology
Ernst, J., Economic Geography
Fijałkowski, D., Systematics and Plant Geography
Gąsior, E., Molecular Biology
Górski, M., Embryology
Henkiel, A., Geomorphology
Hubicka, Józefa, Zoology
Ilczuk, Z., Applied Microbiology
Izdebski, K., Ecology and Preservation of Nature
Kałkowska, K., Animal Physiology
Karczmarz, K., Plant Systems and Geography

KAWECKI, Z., Applied Microbiology
KOBUS, J., Molecular Biology
KOWALSKI, M., Microbiology
KUBIK, I., Comparative Anatomy
KUBIK, J., Comparative Anatomy and Anthropology
LEONOWICZ, A., Biochemistry
LORKIEWICZ, Z., Microbiology
MARUSZCZAK, H., Physical Geography
MICHNA, E., Meteorology and Climatology
MODRZEJEWSKI, E., Animal Physiology
MORAWSKI, J., Geology
NAKONIECZNY, S., Physical Geography
POMIAN, J., Geochemical Laboratory
RIABININ, S., Ecology and Preservation of Nature
RODKIEWICZ, B., Anatomy and Plant Cytology
SAŁATA, B., General Botany
SURDACKI, S., Physical Geography
TROJANOWSKI, J., Biochemistry
UZIAK, S., Soil Science
WARAKOMSKI, W., Meteorology and Climatology
WILGAT, T., Hydrography
WOJTANOWICZ, J., Physical Geography

Faculty of Mathematics, Physics and Chemistry:
ADAMCZYK, B., Experimental Physics
BARCICKA, ANNA, Laboratory of Crystallography
BARCICKI, J., Chemical Technology
BIELECKI, A., Differential Equations
BRZYSKA, W., General and Inorganic Chemistry
DĄBKOWSKA, MICHALINA, General Inorganic Chemistry
GOEBEL, K., Differential Equations
GOWOREK, T., Nuclear Physics
JANCZEWSKI, M., Organic Chemistry
KADEJ, F., Central Laboratory
KRZYŻ, BARBARA, Differential Equations
KRZYŻ, J., Mathematical Functions
LEŻAŃSKI, T., Algebra and Functional Analysis
MATYSIK, J., Analytical Chemistry and Instrumental Analysis
NASUTO, R., Physical Chemistry
OŚCIK, J., Physical Chemistry
PIŁAT, M., Theoretical Physics
PODKOŚCIELNY, W., Organic Synthesis
POMORSKI, K., Theoretical Physics
PYTLARZ, J., Organic Synthesis
RADZISZEWSKI, K., Geometry
RÓŻYŁO, J., Physical Chemistry
RUDZIŃSKI, W., Physical Chemistry
STACHÓRSKA, DANUTA, General Physics
SUBOTOWICZ, M., Experimental Physics
SUPRYNOWICZ, Z., Physical Chemistry
SYKUT, K., Analytical Chemistry and Instrumental Analysis
SZCZYPA, J., Radioisotopic Laboratory
SZPIKOWSKI, S., Theoretical Physics
SZYBIAK, A., Geometry
SZYNAL, D., Mathematical Functions
WAKSMUNDZKI, A., Physical Chemistry
WYSOCKA-LISEK, JANINA, General and Inorganic Chemistry
ZĄBEK, S., Numerical Methods
ZŁOTKIEWICZ, E., Mathematical Functions
ŻUK, W., Nuclear Physics

Faculty of Psychology and Pedagogy:
CACKOWSKA, MARIA, Pedagogics
CZERNIŃSKA, J., Teaching of Conducting
DOBRZYŃSKI, K., Theory of Music
GALKOWSKI, T., Pedagogics
KLIMKOWSKI, M., Psychology
KOŁWZAN-NOWICKA, D., Fine Arts
KOMOROWSKI, B., Psychology
KULIGOWSKA, K., Didactics
ŁOBOCKI, M., Theory of Education
MARCZUK, M., Pedagogics
MIELESZKO, S., Teaching of Sculpture
POPEK, S., Psychology
NATANEK, A., Music Teaching
POZNAŃSKI, K., Pedagogics
REUTT, NATALIA, Psychology
SĘKOWSKA, ZOFIA, Pedagogics
STELMASIK, M., Teaching of Painting
WINIARSKI, R., Teaching of Painting

Inter-University Institute of Philosophy and Sociology:
CACKOWSKI, Z., Marxist Philosophy
CZARNECKI, Z., History of Sociology
DZIEMIDOK, Z., Ethics and Aesthetics
JEDYNAK, S., Ethics
KOJ, L., Logic and Methodology of Science
MARGUL, T., Eastern Religions and Philosophy
MIROWSKI, W., Sociology
NOWICKI, A., Philosophy of Culture

Inter-University Institute of Political Science:
KOPRUKOWNIAK, A.
KOŚCIAŃSKI, T.
KUCHARSKI, W.
OLSZEWSKI, E., Modern History
PIETRAŚ, J. Z., International Public Law

UNIWERSYTET IM ADAMA MICKIEWICZA W POZNANIU (Adam Mickiewicz University in Poznań)

STALINGRADZKA 1,
61-712 POZNAN
Telephone: 699-251, 564-25.
Founded 1919.

Rector: Prof. Dr. BENON MISKIEWICZ.
Pro-Rectors: Prof. Dr. K. GOLANKIEWICZ, Prof. Dr. ST. KOZARSKI, Prof. Dr. ZB. LEOŃSKI, Prof. Dr. L. OBUCHOWICZ.
Registrar: Mgr. BOLESŁAW JÓZEFOWICZ.
Librarian: Prof. Dr. S. KUBIAK.

Library: *see* Libraries.
Number of teachers: 1,577.
Number of students: 15,407.

Publications: *Zeszyty Naukowe, Skrypty, Monografie.*

DEANS:

Faculty of Law: Prof. Dr. W. ŁĄCZKOWSKI.
Faculty of History: Doc. Dr. hab. J. KRZYŻANIAKOWA.
Faculty of Philology: Doc. Dr. hab. E. PIEŚCIKOWSKI.
Faculty of Mathematics, Physics and Chemistry: Prof. Dr. Z. PAJĄK.
Faculty of Biology and Geosciences: Doc. Dr. hab. K. ROTNICKI.
Faculty of Social Sciences: Prof. Dr. S. DZIAMSKI.

UNIWERSYTET MIKOŁAJA KOPERNIKA W TORUNIU (Nicholas Copernicus University of Toruń)

UL. GAGARINA 11, 87-100 TORUŃ
Telephone: 22694.
Founded 1945.

State control; Language of instruction: Polish; Academic year: October to August (two terms).

Rector: Prof. Dr. hab. RYSZARD BOHR
Vice-Rectors: Prof. Dr. hab. WIESŁAW DOMASŁOWSKI, Prof. Dr. hab. JERZY TOMALA, Prof. Dr. hab. JAN WINIARZ.
Registrar: Mgr. T. KONARSKI.
Librarian: Dr. B. RYSZEWSKI.

Number of teachers: 883.
Number of students: 8,500.

Publication: *Acta Universitatis Nicolai Copernici.*

DEANS:

Faculty of Humanities: Prof. Dr. hab. ANTONI CZACHAROWSKI.
Faculty of Mathematics, Physics and Chemistry: Doc. Dr. KAROL KARPIŃSKI.
Faculty of Biology and Earth Sciences: Prof. Dr. hab. EDMUND STRZELCZYK.
Faculty of Law and Administration: Prof. Dr. hab. ANDRZEJ MAREK.
Faculty of Fine Arts: Doc. RYSZARD KRZYWKA.
Faculty of Economics: Prof. Dr. hab. STANISŁAW SUDOŁ.

PROFESSORS:

Faculty of Humanities:
CZACHAROWSKI, A., Medieval History
DANIELEWICZ, J., Polish History and General 19th- and 20th-Century History
GRUDZIŃSKI, T., Polish Medieval History
GRÜNBERG, K., Polish History and General 19th- and 20th-Century History
GUMAŃSKI, L., Philosophy and Logic
HUTNIKIEWICZ, A., Polish Literature
JASIŃSKI, K., Medieval History
JACZYNOWSKA, M., Ancient History
TOMCZAK, A., Polish Modern History, Archival Studies
WOJTOWICZ, J., Polish History and General 18th-Century History

Faculty of Mathematics, Physics and Chemistry:
ANTONOWICZ, K., Electronics
BAUER, R., Photoluminescence of Solutions
BĄCZYŃSKI, A., Experimental Physics
BOROWIECKI, L., Organic Chemistry
CZERWIŃSKI, Z., Physical Chemistry
DEMBIŃSKI, S., Theoretical Physics
GORGOLEWSKI, ST., Astronomy
GRONOWSKA, J., Organic Chemistry
INGARDEN, R., Thermodynamics, Radiation Theory
JEŚMANOWICZ, L., Mathematics
KONECZNY, H., Chemical Technology
KOSSAKOWSKI, A., Theoretical Physics
LESIAK, T., Heterocyclic Compounds and Isocyanides
ŁĘGOWSKI, S., Experimental Physics
ŁÓDZIŃSKA, A., Co-ordination Chemistry
NARĘBSKA, A., Physical Chemistry
SIEDLEWSKI, J., Absorption and Catalysis
SŁOMIŃSKI, J., Mathematics
SWINARSKI, A., Inorganic Chemistry
TOMASZEWSKI, J., Inorganic Chemistry-Technology
WOLNIEWICZ, L., Theoretical Physics
WOŹNICKI, W., Theoretical Physics and Chemistry
UZAREWICZ, A., Organic Chemistry

Faculty of Biology and Earth Science:
BOHR, R., Plant Systematics and Ecology
CZOPEK, J., Histology and Embryology
GROMADSKA, M., Animal Ecology
JANISZEWSKI, L., Animal Physiology
KĘPCZYŃSKI, K., Botany
MASŁOWSKI, P., Biochemistry
MICHNIEWICZ, M., Plant Physiology
NIEWIAROWSKI, W., Geomorphology
NARĘBSKI, J., Neurophysiology
PRUSINKIEWICZ, ZB., Soil Science
STRZELCZYK, E., Microbiology

Faculty of Law and Administration:
GILAS, J., International Public Law
GŁUCHOWSKI, J., Taxation Law
LANG, W., Theory of State and Law
ŁOPUSKI, J., Maritime Law and Insurance Law
MAREK, A., Criminal Law
OCHENDOWSKI, E., Administrative Law
STECKI, L., Civil Law
WINIARZ, J., Civil and Commercial Law
ZDRÓJKOWSKI, Z., History of Law

Faculty of Fine Arts:
DOMASŁOWSKI, W., Preservation and Conservation of Works of Art
PIOTROWICZ, E., Graphics

Faculty of Economics:
LICZKOWSKI, J., Agricultural Economics
SUDOŁ, S., Industrial Economics
TOMALA, J., Political Economy and Economic Policy

UNIWERSYTET SLĄSKI
(Silesian University)

40-007 KATOWICE,
BANKOWA 12

Telephone: 587-231.

Founded 1968.

Academic year: October to June.

Rector: Prof. Dr. HENRYK RECHOWICZ.

Pro-Rectors: Prof. Dr. inż. ZBIGNIEW BOJARSKI, Prof. Dr. SĘDZIMIR MACIEJ KLIMASZEWSKI, Prof. Dr. JAN KANTYKA, Prof. Dr. JÓZEF CHLEBOWCZYK, Doc. Dr. hab. ANDRZEJ WÓJTOWICZ.

Registrar: Dr. R. CICHOŃ.

Librarian: Dr. ANTONI MOLENDA.

Number of teachers: 1,310.

Number of students: 14,924.

Publication: *Zeszyty Naukowe Wydziałów*†.

DEANS:

Faculty of Philology: Doc. Dr. hab. A. WILKÓN.
Faculty of Mathematics, Physics and Chemistry: Doc. Dr. hab. F. BUHL.
Faculty of Law and Administration: Doc. Dr. hab. M. PAZDAN.
Faculty of Technical Education: Doc. Dr. J. DUDEK.
Faculty of Biology and Natural Sciences: Doc. Dr. hab. M. MAŁUSZYŃSKI.
Faculty of Geology and Geography: Prof. Dr. inż A. JACHOWICZ.
Faculty of Social Science: Doc. Dr. hab. J. PRZEWŁOCKI.
Faculty of Psychology and Education: Doc. Dr. H. GĄSIOR.
Faculty of Radio and Television: Doc. Dr. E. ZAJIČEK.
Faculty of Artistic Pedagogy: Doc. Dr. H. DANEL-BOBRZYK.

PROFESSORS:

Faculty of Mathematics, Physics and Chemistry:
BOJARSKI, Z., Chemistry
BŁAŻ, J., Mathematics
BUHL, F., Chemistry
CHABROWSKI, J., Mathematics
CHEŁKOWSKI, A., Physics
CZUCHAJOWSKI, L., Chemistry
DŁOTKO, T., Mathematics
DUBIKAJTIS, Z., Mathematics
DZIĘGIELEWSKI, J., Chemistry
GER, R., Mathematics
GÓRSKI, J., Mathematics
HAŃDEREK, J., Physics
KINEL, J., Physics
KLUK, E., Physics
KOZARZEWSKI, B., Physics
KUCZMA, M., Mathematics
LANGNER, M., Chemistry
LASOTA, A., Mathematics
MIODUSZEWSKI, J., Mathematics
MORAWIEC, H., Chemistry
MOROŃ, J., Physics
NOWAKOWSKI, J., Chemistry
PAWLIKOWSKI, A., Physics
POGORZELSKI, W., Mathematics
RATAJCZAK, A., Chemistry
SIWEK, E., Mathematics
SZYMICZEK, K., Mathematics
ŚLIWIOK, J., Chemistry
TOKARZEWSKI, L., Chemistry
WARCZEWSKI, J., Physics
ZIOŁO, J., Physics

Faculty of Biology and Natural Sciences:
BADURA, L., Natural Sciences
CELIŃSKI, F., Natural Sciences
CZECHOWICZ, K., Zoology
CHMIELOWSKI, J., Natural Sciences
DZIUBA, S., Zoology
HEJNOWICZ, Z., Biophysics
KLIMASZEWSKI, S., Biology
KUCHARCZYK, W., Biology
MAŁUSZYŃSKI, M., Biology
PRZYBYLSKI, T., Botany
PYTASZ, M., Biology
ROSTAŃSKI, K., Botany
ROSTKOWSKA, J., Zoology
SCHNAIDER, Z., Zoology
SERAFIŃSKI, W., Biology
STOLAREK, J., Botany
WOJCIECHOWSKA, B., Botany

Faculty of Law and Administration:
AGOPSZOWICZ, A.
GANDOR, K.
GÓRNIOK, O.
JASICA, R.
KORZAN, K.
LITYŃSKI, A.
MARSZAŁ, K.
NOWACKI, J.
PAZDAN, M.
PAŃKO, W.
PODGÓRSKI, K.
SOŚNIAK, M.
STASZKÓW, M.
TYSZKIEWICZ, L.
WIDACKI, J.
ZIELIŃSKI, T.
ZWIERZCHOWSKI, E.

Faculty of Geology and Geography:
BUKOWY, S., Geology
JACHOWICZ, A., Natural Sciences
JERSAK, J., Geography
KOZŁOWSKI, K., Geology
MARCZAK, M., Geochemistry
PULINA, M., Geography
RACINOWSKI, R., Physical Geography
TREMBACZEWSKI, J., Geography
WIĘCKOWSKI, R., Geology
ZUBEREK, W., Geophysics

Faculty of Psychology and Education:
BIŃCZYCKA-FELUŚ, J., Education
BOBROWSKA-NOWAK, W., Education
BOLECHOWSKA, M., Psychology
CZARNECKI, K., Psychology
GĄSIOR, H., Education
GORISZOWSKI, G., Education
HESZEN-KLEMENS, J., Psychology
KORABIOWSKA-NOWACKA, K., Education
MOROZ, H., Education
POPLUCZ, J., Education
RATAJCZAK, Z., Psychology
WOSIŃSKA, W., Psychology
WOSIŃSKI, M., Psychology
ŻECHOWSKA, B., Education

Faculty of Social Science:
BAŃKA, J., Philosophy
DŁUGOBORSKI, W., History
DOBROWOLSKI, P., History
FRĄCKIEWICZ, L., Political Science
GŁOMBIK, C., Philosophy
GLIŃSKA, A., Philosophy
HREBENDA, A., Political Science
JACHER, W., Sociology
JAROS, J., History
KANTYKA, J., History
KNOBELSDORF, W., Economics
KOCÓJ, H., History
KOMASZYŃSKI, M., History
KUNISZ, A., History
MICHALKIEWICZ, S., History
MOLENDA, A., History
MROZEK, W., Sociology
PRZEWŁOCKI, J., History
RADZISZEWSKA, J., History
RECHOWICZ, H., History
SALAMON, M., History
SERAFIN, F., History
SYREK, M., Economics
SZYDŁOWSKI, J., History
TOPOL, A., History
WERBLAN, A., History
WÓDZ, J., Sociology
WÓJTOWICZ, A., Political Science
ŻECHOWSKI, Z., Sociology

Faculty of Philology:
ABŁAMOWICZ, A., French Philology
ARABSKI, J., English Philology
BAJEROWA, J., Philology
BLICHARSKI, M., Russian Philology
BUJNICKI, T., Polish Philology
CHOJECKA, E., Polish Philology
JAROSZ, A., Polish Philology
KAKIETEK, English Philology
KAROLAK, S., Linguistics
KOCZY, K., German Philology
KOWALSKA, A., Philology
ŁOBZOWSKA, M., English Philology
LUBAŚ, W., Polish Philology
NOWAK, Z., Polish Philology
NAWROCKI, W., Polish Philology
OPACKI, I., Polish Philology
PASZEK, J., Polish Philology
PAZUCHIN, R., Spanish Philology
PIANKA, W., Slavonic Philology
POLAŃSKI, E., Polish Philology
POLAŃSKI, K., Philology
PORĘBA, G., Russian Philology
PORĘBA, S., Russian Philology
UDALSKA, E., Philology
WILKOŃ, A., Philology
WÓJCIK, W., Polish Philology
WRÓBEL, H., Polish Philology

Faculty of Technical Education:
DUDEK, J., Physics
GÓRNY, A., Electronics
PIECHA, J., Automatization
SUROWIAK, Z., Physics

SZEMA, J., Mechanical Engineering
WOŁEK, M., Mechanical Engineering

Faculty of Radio and Television:
BOGUSŁAWSKI, M., Film Directing
DUDEK, W., Political Science
HELMAN, A., Philology
PAWLICKI, M., Film Directing
PETRY-PAWLICKA, Z., Film Directing
ZAJIČEK, E., Economics

Faculty of Artistic Pedagogy:
CHLEBOWCZYK, J., History
DANEL-BOBRZYK, H., Musical Training
GABRYŚ, R., Theory of Music and Composition
GŁADYSZ, A., Polish Philology
JAŚLAR, B., Psychology
LIS, Z., Graphics
MYRDACZ, T., Piano
RYGIEL, B., Musical Training
WROŃSKI, J., Painting

UNIWERSYTET WARSZAWSKI
(University of Warsaw)
KRAKOWSKIE PRZEDMIEŚCIE 26-28, 00-325 WARSAW
Telephone: 200-381.
Founded 1818.

Academic year: October to June.

Rector: Prof. Dr. ZYGMUNT RYBICKI.
Pro-Rectors: Prof. Dr. KAZIMIERZ DOBROWOLSKI, Prof. Dr. STANISLAW ORŁOWSKI, Doc. Dr. hab. MARIA JEŻOWA, Prof. Dr. JULIUSZ ŁUKASIEWICZ (affiliated branch).
Administrative Director: Mgr. STEFAN WIĘCEK.
Librarian: Doc. Dr. JERZY SENKOWSKI.

Number of professors: 650.
Number of students: 35,000.

Publications: *Acta Philologica, American Studies, Biuletyn Geologiczny, Biuletyn Instytutu Języka i Kultury Polskiej dla Cudzoziemców, Ekonomia, Fasciculi Historici, Phytocoenosis, Prace Filologiczne, Quaestiones Medii Aevi, Roczniki Uniwersytetu Warszawskiego, Studia i Materiały Instytutu Archeologii, Studia Palmyreńskie, Światowit, Zeszyty Naukowe Instytutu Nauk Politycznych* (irregular), *Aniliza i Synteza Informacji, Africana Bulletin, Przegląd Informacji o Afryce.*

DEANS:

Faculty of Biology: Prof. Dr. KAZIMIERZ DOBROWOLSKI.
Faculty of Chemistry: Prof. Dr. JERZY WRÓBEL.
Faculty of Journalism and Political Science: Prof. Dr. BARTŁOMIEJ GOLKA.
Faculty of Physics: Prof. Dr. JERZY PNIEWSKI.
Faculty of Geography and Regional Studies: Prof. Dr. ZDZISŁAW MIKULSKI.
Faculty of Geology: Prof. Dr. WITOLD C. KOWALSKI.
Faculty of History: Prof. Dr. WALDEMAR CHMIELEWSKI.
Faculty of Mathematics, Informatics and Mechanics: Prof. Dr. ANDRZEJ BIAŁYNICKI-BIRULA.
Faculty of Economic Science: Prof. Dr. ANDRZEJ JEZIERSKI.
Faculty of Social Science: Prof. Dr. JERZY WIATR.
Faculty of Neo-Philologies: Prof. Dr. WIESŁAW KOTAŃSKI.
Faculty of Polish Philology: (vacant).
Faculty of Law and Administration: Prof. Dr. ZBIGNIEW RESICH.
Faculty of Psychology and Pedagogy: Prof. Dr. CZESŁAW KUPISIEWICZ.
Faculty of Russian and Slavonic Philologies: Doc. Dr. hab. ALBERT BARTOSZEWICZ.
Faculty of Management: Prof. Dr. KAROL SOBCZAK.
Institute of Social Prevention and Resocialization: Doc. Dr. han. ADAM KRUKOWSKI.

AFFILIATED COLLEGE IN BIAŁYSTOK:
Faculty of Administration and Economy: Prof. Dr. ANDRZEJ STELMACHOWSKI.
Faculty of Letters and Humanities: Doc. Dr. hab. EWA WIPSZYCKA-BRAVO.
Faculty of Pedagogy and Psychology: Doc. Dr. hab. JERZY NIEMIEC.
Faculty of Mathematics and Natural Sciences: Doc. Dr. hab. ALINA MYRCHA.

PROFESSORS:

Faculty of Biology:
BATKO, A., Botany
BEZUBIK, B., Microbiology
BRYŁA, J., Biochemistry—Metabolism
CYMBOROWSKI, B., Physiology
DOBROWOLSKI, K., Zoology
DOBRZAŃSKA-KACZANOWSKA, J., Zoology
DOROSZEWSKA, ALINA, Botany
FALIŃSKI, J., Botany
GAJEWSKI, W., Plant Geography
GILL, J., Physiology
GLIWICZ, M., Zoology
IZDEBSKA-SZYMONA, K., Microbiology
KACPERSKA-PALACZ, A., Botany
KANIUGA, Z., Biochemistry
KASPRZYK, Z., Biochemistry
KUNICKI-GOLDFINGER, W., Microbiology
KWIATKOWSKI, Z., Microbiology
LEWAK, S., Plant Physiology
MALESZEWSKI, S., Botany
MATUSIAK, K., Microbiology
MATUSZEWSKI, B., Cytology
MATUSZKIEWICZ, W., Plant Ecology
MYCIELSKI, R., Microbiology
PIECZYNSKA, E., Zoology
PIEKCAROWICZ, A., Microbiology
PODBIELKOWSKI, Z., Botany
POSUTA, J., Plant Physiology
SKIRGIEŁŁO, A., Plant Geography
STANKIEWICZ, M., Immunology
TARKOWSKI, A., Embryology
TOCZKO, K., Biochemistry
WĘGLEŃSKI, P., Botany
WOJCIECHOWSKI, Z., Biochemistry

Faculty of Chemistry:
BRAJTER, K., Analytical Chemistry
DRABAREK, S., Organic Chemistry
GALUS, Z., Mineral Chemistry
HULANICKI, A., Mineral Chemistry
JANASZEWSKI, B., Physical Chemistry
JANOWSKI, A., Chemistry
JASTRZĘBSKA, J., Chemistry
KALINOWSKI, M., Physical Chemistry
KĘCKI, Z., Physical Chemistry
KOCZOROWSKI, Z., Electrochemistry
KOŁOS, W., Theoretical Chemistry
KRUPKOWSKI, T., Molecular Physics
KRYGOWSKI, T., Physical Chemistry
KUBLIK, Z., Mineral Chemistry
KUROWSKI, S., Physical Chemistry
MIERZECKI, R., Physical Chemistry
MINC, S., Electro Physical and Atomic Chemistry
ORSZAGH, A., Chemical Technology
OSZCZAPOWICZ, J., Organic Chemistry
PIELA, L., Theoretical Chemistry
POLACZEK, A., Physics
RODEWALD, W., Organic Chemistry
RUBEL, S., Physical Chemistry
SAMOCHOCKA, K., Radiochemistry
SOBKOWSKI, J., Physical Chemistry
SZYMAŃSKI, A., Physical Chemistry
WERBLAN, L., Physical Chemistry
WRÓBEL, J., Organic Chemistry

Faculty of Geography and Regional Studies:
BOGACKI, M., Geomorphology
DOBRSKA, Z., Economic Geography
DUMANOWSKI, B., Regional Geography
KOMOROWSKI, S., Economic Geography
KOMOROWSKI, Z., Sociology of Africa
KUKLIŃSKI, A., Economic Geography
MIKULSKI, Hydrogeography
OTOK, S., Economic Geography
PIÓRO, Z., Regional Planning
RADŁOWSKA, C., Geomorphology
RATAJSKI, L., Cartography
RICHLING, A., Physical Geography
RYCHŁOWSKI, B., Geography
SOCZYNSKA, U., Hydrology
STOPA-BORYCZKA, M., Climatics
TOBJASZ, J., Economic Geography
WINID, B., World Regional Geography

Faculty of Social Science:
AUGUSTYNEK, Z., Philosophy
CIUPAK, E., Sociology
DOBROSIELSKI, M., Philosophy
FRITZHAND, M., Ethics
JANKOWSKI, H., Sociology
JASINSKA-KANIA, A., Sociology
KŁOSKOWSKA, A., Sociology
KRAJEWSKI, W., Philosophy
KRASZEWSKI, Z., Philosophy
KUCZYŃSKA, A., Philosophy
KUCZYŃSKI, J., Philosophy
MAJEWSKI, Z., Logic
MALANOWSKI, J., Sociology
MORAWSKI, W., Sociology
MORTIMER, H., Philosophy
NOWAK, S., Sociology
NOWAKOWSKI, S., Sociology
PELC, J., Logic
PODGÓRECKI, A., Ethics
POHOSKI, M., Sociology
PRZEŁĘCKI, M., Logic
SIEMEK, M. J., Philosophy
SIEMIENSKA-ZOCHOWSKA, R., Sociology
SIKORA, A., Philosophy
STONERT, H., Philosophy
SZACKA, B., Sociology
SZACKI, J., History of Social Thought
SZANIAWSKI, K., Sociology
WESOŁOWSKI, W., Sociology
WIATR, J., Sociology
WIŚNIEWSKI, W., Sociology
WOJNAR-SUJECKA, J., Sociology
WOLNIEWICZ, B., Philosophy
ZIEMBA, Z., Philosophy

Faculty of Journalism and Political Science:
BASZKIEWICZ, J., Political Science
BIERZANEK, R., Political Science
BŁUSZKOWSKI, J., Political Science
BODNAR, A., Political Science
CZAJKA, S., Political Science
DANECKI, J., Political Economy
DOBRZYCKI, W., Law and International Relations

FILIPIAK, T., Political Science
FRANK, M., Social Policy
GEBETHNER, S., Political Science
GOŁĘBIOWSKI, B., Political Science
GOŁĘBIOWSKI, J., Political Science
GOLKA, B., Journalism
HEMMERLING, Z., Political Science
KĄDZIELSKI, J., Journalism
KĄKOL, K., Journalism
KOWALAK, T., International Relations
KUKUŁKA, J., Political Science
KUPIS, T., Journalism
LATO, S., Journalism
MICHALSKI, B., Journalism
MROZEK, A. B., Political Science
NIECIUŃSKI, W., Social Politics
OSTROWSKI, K. P., Political Science
PAWLAK, S., International Relations
RAJKIEWICZ, A., Social Politics
ROWNY, K., Law and International Relations
ŚLISZ, A., Journalism
SŁOMKOWSKA, A., Journalism
SZULCZEWSKI, M., Journalism
TEMPSKI, Z., Journalism
TOMASZEWSKI, J., Political Science
WAJDA, A., Political Science
ZAND, H., Political Science
ZIELIŃSKI, E., Political Science

Faculty of Polish Philology:
AXER, J., Classical Philology
BARTNICKA, B., Polish Philology
BUTTLER, D., Polish Philology
CIENKOWSKI, W., Polish Philology
CYTOWSKA, M., Classical Philology
CZAPLEJEWICZ, E., Polish Literature
FRYBES, S., Polish Literature
GRZEGORCZYKOWA, R., Polish Philology
JUDYCKA, I., Polish Philology
JUREWICZ, O., Classical Philology
KANIOWSKA-LEWANSKA, I., Polish Literature
KULCZYCKA-SALONI, J., Polish Literature
KULICZKOWSKA, K., Polish Literature
KUMANIECKI, K., Classical Philology
KUPISZEWSKI, W. M., Polish Philology
KURKOWSKA, H., Polish Language
LAM, A., Polish Philology
LIBIN-LIBERA, Z., Polish Literature
MACIEJEWSKA, I., Polish Literature
MACISZEWSKI, J., Polish Culture and History
MAKOWSKI, S., Polish Literature
PUZYNA, J., Polish Philology
ROHOZIŃSKI, J., Polish Literature
RYBICKA-NOWACKA, H., Polish Philology
RYTEL, J., Polish Literature
SAMBOR, J., Linguistics
SIEKIERSKI, S., Polish Culture
STRASZEWSKA, M., Polish Literature
SZELEST, ANNA, Classical Philology
SZLIFERSZTEIN, SALOMEA, Polish Language
SZYMCZAK, M., Polish Language
TABORSKI, R., Polish Literature
WEINSBERG-WAYDA, A., Polish Language
ZALEWSKA-WARZENICA, E., Polish Philology
ZWOLIŃSKI, P., Ukrainian Philology

Faculty of Russian and Slavonic Philologies:
BARTOSZEWICZ, A., Russian Philology
CSÁPLÁROS, I., Hungarian Philology
CZAJKA, H., Bulgarian Philology
CZOCHARA, S., Linguistics
DABEK-WIRGOWA, T., Bulgarian Philology
GRUCZA, F., Linguistics
JEŻOWA, M., Slavonic Philology
KOŁAKOWSKI, T., Russian Philology
MAGNUSZEWSKI, J., Slavonic Philology
MILEJKOWSKA, H., Russian Slavonic Philology
NIEUWAŻNY, F., Russian Philology
ORZECHOWSKA-ŻIELICZ, H., South Slavonic Linguistics
PIERNIKARSKA, C., Linguistics
SEMCZUK, A., Russian Philology
SIATKOWSKA, E., Slavonic Philology
SIEROSZEWSKI, A., Hungarian Philology
ŚLIWOWSKI, R., Russian Philology
SMUŁEK, E., Ukrainian Philology
SZYSZKO, T., Russian Philology
URBAŃSKA-ŚLISZ, J., Russian Philology
WIERZBICKI, J., Slavonic Literature
WIERZCHOWSKA, B., Experimental Phonetics
WROCŁAWSKI, K., Slavonic Philology

Faculty of Neo-Philologies:
BIELAWSKI, J., Turkish Studies
BOGACKI, B. K., Italian Philology
BOGUSŁAWSKI, A., Russian Philology
BRAUN, J., Oriental Philology
BYRSKI, M. K., Oriental Philology
CHMIELEWSKI, J., Sinology
CZOCHRALSKI, J., German Philology
DĄBROWSKI, L., Oriental Philology
DOBRZYCKA, I., English Philology
KAŁUZYŃSKI, S., Oriental Philology
KASPRZYK, K., French Philology
KIENIEWICZ, J., Iberian Philology
KLAWE, J., Iberian Philology
KOTAŃSKI, J., Japanology
KRAJEWSKA, W., English Philology
KUMOR-SKRODZKA, S., English Philology
KÜNSTLER, M., Sinology
ŁYCZKOWSKA, K., Oriental Philology
MEISSNER, L., German Philology
MELANOWICZ, M., Oriental Philology
MENTAL-NIECKO, J., Ethiopian Philology
NAMOWICZ, I. T., German Philology
PARVI, J., French Philology
POPKO, M., Oriental Philology
RZADKOWSKA, E., French Philology
SAUERLAND, K. K., German Philology
SKŁADANEK, B., Iranian Philology
SŁAWIŃSKI, R., Oriental Philology
SŁUPSKI, Z., Oriental Philology
SUWAŁA, H., Italian Philology
TUBIELEWICZ, J., Oriental Philology
TYLOCH, W., Oriental Philology
WOJTASIEWICZ, O., Sinology
ŻABOKLICKI, K., French Philology
ŻUROWSKI, **M., Romance Philology**

Faculty of Geology:
ANSILEWSKI, J., Petrography
BAŁUK, A. W., Geology
BARCZYK, W., Geology
CHLEBOWSKI, R., Petrography
DEMBOWSKI, Z., Geology
FALKOWSKI, E., Hydrogeology
GLAZER, Z., Engineering Geology
GÓRKA, H., Geology
GRABOWSKA-OLSZEWSKA, B., Engineering Geology
JAROSZEWSKI, W., Geology
KOWALSKI, W., Engineering Geology
KRAJEWSKA-PINIŃSKA, J., Hydrogeology
KRAJEWSKI, S., Hydrogeology
KUTEK, J., Geology
LINDER, L., Geology
ŁOZIŃSKA-STEPIEN, H., Hydrogeology
ŁYDKA, K., Petrography
MACIOSZCZYK, T., Hydrogeology
MAKOWSKI, H., Historical Geology
MYŚLIŃSKA, E., Engineering Geology
NOWAKOWSKI, A., Petrography
ORŁOWSKI, S., Geology
PENKALA, T., Mineralogy
POLAŃSKI A., Mineralogy
RADWAŃSKI, A., Geology
RONIEWICZ, P., Geology
STUPNICKA, E., Geology
SZPILA, K., Mineralogy
SZULCZEWSKI, M., Geology
URBANEK, A., Palæontology
WALEŃCZAK, Z., Petrography
WUTTKE, K., Hydrogeology
WYRWICKI, R., Geology
WYSOKIŃSKI, L., Engineering Geology
ZIMNOCH, E., Geology

Faculty of History:
BACULEWSKI, J., Library Science
BARTNICKI, A., Modern History
BAZYLOW, L., History of U.S.S.R.
BIAŁOSTOCKI, J., History of Modern Art
BIEŃKOWSKA, B., Library Science
BIEŻUŃSKA-MAŁOWIST, I., Ancient History
CHAMERSKA, H., Science Information
CHMIELEWSKI, W., Archaeology
CHODKOWSKI, A., Musicology
CZEKAJEWSKA-JĘDRUSIK, A., Library Science
CZEKANOWSKA-KUKLINSKA, A., Musicology
GARLICKI, A., History
GASSOWSKI, J., Archaeology
GAWLIKOWSKI, M., Archaeology
GIEYSZTOR, A., Medieval History
HENSEL, W., Slav Archaeology
HOLZER, J., History
IHNATOWICZ, I., History
JABŁOŃSKI, H., 19th and 20th Century Polish History
JAKIMOWICZ, History of Art
JAROSZEWSKI, T. S., History of Art
KARPOWICZ, M., History of Art
KEMPISTY, A., Archaeology
KOLENDO, J., Archaeology
KOWALCZYK, J., History of Art
KOZŁOWSKI, S., Archeology
KUBIŃSKA, J., Archaeology
KUTRZEBA-POJNAROWA, A., Ethnography
ŁUKASIEWICZ, J., History
MACISZEWSKI, J., History
MAŁOWIST, M., Medieval History
MĄCZAK, A., Modern History
MATERNICKI, J., History
MICHAŁOWSKI, K., Archaeology
MIŁOBEDSKI, J. A., History of Art
MROCZKO, T., History of Art
OKULICZ-KOZARYN, J., Archaeology
PERZ, M., Musicology
PIEKARCZYK, S., Pre-18th Century Polish History
POPPE, A., Medieval History
PRESS, L., Archaeology
SADURSKA, ANNA, Mediterranean Archaeology
SAMSONOWICZ, H., Medieval History
SKOWRONEK, J., 19th-Century History
SKUBISZEWSKI, P., Medieval History of Art
SOKOLEWICZ, ZOFIA, Ethnography
STARZYŃSKI, J., History of Modern Art
SWIDEREK, A., Papyrology
SZAFLIK, J., History
SZTETYŁŁO, Z., Mediterranean Archaeology
TANTY, M., History of Slavonic Countries
WASILEWSKI, T., Medieval History
WAWRYKOWA, M., Modern History
WIERCIŃSKI, A. Archaeology
WOJCIECHOWSKI, M., Modern History
WYROBISZ, A., Medieval History
ZAHORSKI, A., Modern History
ŻARNOWSKA, A., Modern Polish History
ZIENTARA, D., **Medieval History**

Faculty of Mathematics, Informatics and Mechanics:
BAŁABAN, T., Mathematics
BESSAGA, C., Mathematical Analysis
BIAŁYNICKI-BIRULA, A., Mathematics
BOJARSKI, B., Mathematical Analysis
BOLC, L., Informatics

Browkin, J., Mathematics
Burnat, M., Mathematics
Dryja, M., Informatics
Engelking, R., Mathematics
Fiszdon, W., Mechanics
Kielbasinski, A., Mathematics
Kisyński, J., Mathematics
Kreczmar, A., Informatics
Krzyżewski, K., Mathematics
Kubik, L., Mathematics
Kwapień, S., Mathematics
Marek, W., Mathematics
Moszyńska, M., Mathematics
Nowacki, W., Theory of Elasticity
Olesiak, Z., Mechanics
Patkowska, H., Mathematics
Piskorek, A., Mathematics
Rasiowa, Helena, Algebra
Rauszer, C., Mathematics
Salwicki, A., Informatics
Siekłucki, K., Mathematics
Sikorski, R., Theory of Functions
Suliński, A., Algebra
Szczerba, L., Mathematics
Szmydt, Ż., Mathematics
Tatarkiewicz, K., Mathematics
Turski, S., General Mathematics
Turski, W., Informatics
Waligórski, S., Informatics
Woźniak, C., Theory of Elasticity
Woźniakowski, H., Informatics
Zawadowski, W., Mathematics

Faculty of Physics:

Baranowski, J., Experimental Physics
Białkowski, G., Atomic Theory
Białynicki-Birula, I., Optics and Mechanics
Czochralska, B., Biophysics
Decowski, P., Experimental Physics
Demiański, M., Theoretical Physics
Ginter, J., Experimental Physics
Grzedzielski, S., Astronomy
Grynberg, M., Solid Body Physics
Haman ,K., Geophysics
Hofmokl, T., Experimental Physics
Kijowski, J., Theoretical Physics
Krasiński, J., Optics
Królikowski, W., Atomic Physics
Kruszewski, A., Astronomy
Kuszell, A., Astronomy
Maurin, K., Mathematical Analysis
Mielnik, B., Theoretical Physics
Mycielski, J., Solid Body Physics
Namysłowski, J., Theoretical Physics
Napiórkowski, K., Mathematical Methods in Physics
Nazarewicz, W., Experimental Physics
Piasecki, J., Theoretical Physics
Piotrowski, S., Astrophysics
Plebański, J., Mathematical Methods in Physics
Pniewski, J., High Energy Physics
Pokorski, S., Theoretical Physics
Ruciński, S., Astronomy
Skrzypczak, E., High Energy Physics
Sosnowska, I., Experimental Physics
Sosnowski, L., Physics
Stepień, K., Astronomy
Szymacha, A., Atomic Physics
Teisseyre, R., Geophysics
Trautman, A., Electrodynamics and Theory of Relativity
Turski, Ł., Theoretical Physics
Werle, J., Thermodynamics
Wilhelmi, Z., Atomic Physics
Woronowicz, S., Mathematical Methods in Physics
Wróblewski, A., Experimental Physics
Zakrzewski, J., High Energy Physics
Żylicz, J., Experimental Physics

Faculty of Psychology and Pedagogy:

Gurycka. A., Psychology
Izdebska, H., Pedagogy
Jurkowski, A., Pedagogy
Kozielecki, J., Psychology
Kruszewski, K., Pedagogy
Kupisiewicz, C., Didactics
Kurcz-Piesowicz, I., Psychology
Lewowicki, T., Adult Pedagogy
Miaso, J., History of Pedagogy
Mika, S., Psychology
Mońka-Stanikowa, A., Pedagogy
Nowak, J., Adult Pedagogy
Okoń, W., Didactics
Pilkiewicz, M., Educational Psychology
Połturzycki, J., Pedagogics
Reykowski, J., General Psychology
Sadkowska-Przeclawska, A., Pedagogy
Slomkiewicz, S., Didactics
Strelau, J., Psychology
Swida-Ziemba, H., Pedagogy
Tomaszewski, T., General Psychology
Walczyna, Jadwiga, Pedagogy
Włodarski, Z., Educational Psychology
Wojnar, L., General Pedagogy
Wołoszyn, S., General Pedagogy
Wołoszynowa, L., Educational Psychology
Zaczynski, W., Didactics

Faculty of Law and Administration:

Andrejew, I., Penal Law
Bafia, J., Penal Law
Bałtruszajtys, G., History of Law
Bardach, J., History of Polish Law
Czachórski, W., Civil Law
Czeczot, Z., Civil Law
Dybowski, T., Civil Law
Góralczyk, W., International Law
Goronowski, W., Administrative Law
Gubiński, A., Penal Law
Gwiżdż, A., State Law
Harasimowicz, J., Financial Law
Izdebski, H., History of Law
Jakubowski, J., International Law
Jarosz, Z., Civil Law
Jastrzębski, L., Administrative Law
Jędrzejewska, M., Civil Law
Kaftal, A., Penal Law
Kalinowski, S., Penal Law
Kowalski, J., Theory of Law
Kupiszewski, H., Roman Law
Lachs, M., International Law
Lang, J., Administrative Law
La Pierre, J., Civil Law
Leśnodorski, B., History of Polish Law
Łustacz, L., State Law
Madey, M., Civil Law
Malinowski, A., State Law
Malinowski, R., Administrative Law
Murzynowski, A., Penal Law
Okolski, J., Civil Law
Pietrzak, M., History of Law
Rajski, J., Civil Law
Rejman, G., Penal Law
Resich, Z., Civil Law
Russocki, S., History of Law
Salwa, Z., Labour Law
Senkowski, J., History of Law
Służewski, J., Administrative Law
Sobociński, W., Slavonic Law
Sójka-Zielińska, K., History of Law
Stelmachowski, A., Agricultural Law
Stembrowicz, J., Constitutional Law
Suchecki, W., History of Political Theory
Turska, A., State Law
Weralski, M., Financial Law
Wierabowski, M., Administrative Law
Wołodkiewicz, W., Roman Law
Zawadzki, S., State Law
Zieliński, A., Civil Law

Faculty of Economic Sciences:

Baka, W., Political Economy
Bartel, Z., Political Economy
Chrupek, Z., Political Economy
Daniluk, M., Industry and Defence Economy
Dobroczyński, M., Political Economy
Fiejka, Z., Economic Planning
Fiszel, H., Political Economy
Gmytrasiewicz, M., Economics of Teaching
Grabowski, Z., Political Economy
Jezierski, A., Economic History
Kasprzak, T., Political Economy
Kisielnicki, J., Industrial Economy and Informatics
Kluczyński, J., Political Economy
Krencik, W., Political Economy
Kudła, W., Political Economy
Kudliński, R., Political Economy
Kula, W., Economic History
Lewandowski, J., Political Economy
Łukaszewicz, A., Political Economy
Maciejewski, W., Economic Cybernetics
Morecka, Z., Political Economy
Pajestka, J., Political Economy
Polaczek, S., International Economic Relations
Runowicz, A., Political Economy
Rutkowski, J., Political Economy
Sadowski, Z., Political Economy
Siwiński, W., Political Economy
Szeworski, A., Political Economy
Sztyber, W., Political Economy
Timofiejuk, L., Statistics

Faculty of Management:

Buczowski, L., Techniques of Management
Dobrzyński, M., Sociology and Psychology of Organization
Głowacki, R., Marketing
Jaroszyński, A., Administrative Law
Koźmiński, A., Systems Analysis
Kyzyżewski, R., Social Economics
Matuszewicz, J., Management
Muszalski, L., Employment
Ostapczuk, B., Management
Radzikowski, W., Techniques of Management
Rybicki, Z., Administrative Law
Ryć, K., Economic Theory
Śliwa, J., Planning
Sobczak, K., Administrative Law
Trusiewicz, J., Management
Więckowski, J., Statistics
Zawiślak, A., Theory of Management

Institute of Social Prevention and Resocialization:

Czapów, C., Pedagogy
Frączek, A., Pedagogy
Frankowski, S., Penal Law
Hulek, A., Pedagogy
Jankowski, K., Psychiatry
Krukowski, A., Criminology
Pilch, T., Social Pedagogy
Przecławski, K., Sociology
Walczak, S., Theory of Law
Ziemska, M., Social Psychology

Affiliated Branch in Białystok:

Aleksandrowicz, S., History
Ambrosiewicz, J. Mathematics
Barwijuk, A., Economics
Belowska, L., Mathematics
Czerepko, K., Chemistry
Falińska, K., Biology
Gnatowski, M., History
Hirsz, Z., History
Januszek, F., History
Jurkowski, M., History
Kaczyńska, E., Economics
Konieczny, M., Penal Law
Kupiec, L., Economy
Makowiecki, A., Polish Literature
Marciszewski, W., Logic
Monasterski, T., History
Myrcha, A., Biology
Mytnik, P., Mathematics
Niemiec, J., Pedagogy
Noniewicz, C., Economics
Panek, W., Psychology

Puzanowska-Tarasiewicz, H., Chemistry
Saloni, Z., Law
Sokołowska, A., Psychology
Tarasiewicz, M., Chemistry
Wipszycka-Bravo, E., History
Wrzosek, M., History

UNIWERSYTET WROCŁAWSKI IM. BOLESŁAWA BIERUTA

(Wroclaw B. Bierut University)

PLAC UNIWERSYTECKI 1,
50-137 WROCLAW

Telephone: 368-47, 402-212.
Telex: 0712791.

Founded 1702, rebuilt 1945.

State control; Language of instruction: Polish; Academic year: October to June (two terms).

Rector: Prof. Dr. Kazimierz Urbanik.

Vice-Rectors: Prof. Dr. Lucjan Sobczyk (Academic Affairs and Foreign Relations), Doc. Dr. Marek Mazurkiewicz (University Development), Doc. Dr. hab. Hanna Wałkówska (Education), Doc. Dr. hab. Karol Fiedor (Student Affairs).

Administrative Officer: Mgr. Tadeusz Mróz.

Librarian: Dr. Bartłomiej Kuzak.

Library: *see* Libraries.

Number of teachers: 1,464.

Number of students: 13,734.

Publications: *Acta Universitatis Wratislaviensis,* and departmental publications.

DEANS:

Faculty of Philology: Prof. Dr. Franciszek Sielicki.

Faculty of Philosophy and History: Doc. Dr. Czesław Buczek.

Faculty of Mathematics, Physics and Chemistry: Prof. Dr. Stanisław Wajda.

Faculty of Law and Administration: Doc. Dr. Aleksander Patrzałek.

Faculty of Natural Sciences: Prof. Dr. Anna Jerzmańska.

PROFESSORS:

Barański, Z., Russian Literature
Galasiewicz, Z., Particle Physics, Theoretical Physics
Hernas, C., History of Polish Literature
Jahn, A., Geomorphology, Physical Geography
Jakóbiec, M., Russian and Slavic Literature
Jendrośka, J., Administrative Law
Jończyk, J., Labour Law
Klimowicz, M., History of Polish Literature
Konik, E., Ancient History
Kosik, J., Civil and Private International Law
Kubiński, T., Logic
Lachowicz, T., Microbiology, Genetics of Microbes
Lipczyńska, M., Penal Procedures, Logic
Ładosz, J., Philosophy
Lopuszański, J., Mathematical Methods in Physics
Mejbaum-Katzenellenbogen, W., Biochemistry, Clinical Biochemistry
Oberc, J., Geology
Opolski, A., Observational Astrophysics
Orzechowski, K., History of the State and Polish Law
Orzechowski, M., Political Sciences
Pajdowski, L., Inorganic Chemistry and Co-ordination Chemistry
Ryll-Nardzewski, C., Mathematic Analysis
Rzewuski, J., Field Theory
Sobczyk, L., Physical Chemistry
Szczepankiewicz, S., Physical Geography
Szyrocki, M., German Literature
Trzynadlowski, J., Theory of Literature
Urbanik, K., Probability Theory
Wajda, S., Inorganic and Nuclear Chemistry
Walczak, W., Regional Geography
Wrońska, M., Chemical Kinetics
Zakrzewski, B., History of Polish Literature
Zamkowski, W., Theory of State and Law
Zielinski, H., Polish and General History

TECHNICAL UNIVERSITIES

AKADEMIA GÓRNICZO-HUTNICZA IM. STANISŁAWA STASZICA W KRAKOWIE

(Stanisław Staszic University of Mining and Metallurgy)

AL. MICKIEWICZA 30,
30-059 CRACOW

Telephone 376-00; 381-00; 391-00.
Telex: 0322203 pl.
Founded 1919.

Rector: Prof. Dr. hab. Inż. Roman Ney.

Pro-Rectors: Prof. Dr. hab. Inż. Aleksander Długosz, Prof. Dr. hab. Inż. Zygmunt Drzymała, Prof. Dr. hab. Inż. Jan Janowski.

Administrative Director: Mgr. Tytus Mróz.

Librarian: Dr. Marian Górkiewicz.

Library: *see* Libraries.

Number of teachers: 1,762.

Number of students: 12,384.

Publications: *Zeszyty Naukowe*† (Scientific Bulletins, series on Automatics, Electrification and Mechanization in Mining and Metallurgy, Geodesy, Geology, Mining, Ceramics, Mathematics - Physics - Chemistry, Metallurgy and Foundry Practice, Sociology and Sociotechnics, Technical and Economic Problems, Social and Political Problems).

DEANS:

Faculty of Mining: Prof. Dr. hab. Inż. Józef Wacławik.

Faculty of Drilling and Petroleum Engineering: Doc. Dr. Inż. Stanisław Karlic.

Faculty of Mining Geodesy: Prof. Dr. Inż. Michał Fuksa.

Faculty of Geology and Geophysical and Geological Prospecting: Doc. Dr. Inż. Zdzisław Śmietański.

Faculty of Materials Science and Ceramics: Doc. Dr. Inż. Anna Derdacka-Grzymek.

Faculty of Metallurgy: Prof. Dr. hab. Inż. Ryszard Benesch.

Faculty of Non-Ferrous Metals: Prof. Dr. hab. Inż. Zygmunt Kolenda.

Faculty of Technology and Mechanization of Foundry Engineering: Prof. Dr. hab. Inż. Władysław Longa.

Faculty of Electrical Engineering, Automatics and Electronics: Doc. Dr. Inż. Zdzisław Klonowicz.

Faculty of Mechanical Engineering in Mining and Metallurgy: Prof. Dr. hab. Inż. Józef Giergiel.

DIRECTORS:

Interdepartmental Unit Institute of Nuclear Physics and Technology: Prof. Dr. hab. Inż. Kazimierz Przewłocki.

Institute of Mining Chemistry and Physical Chemistry of Solvents: Prof. Dr. Mieczysław Lasoń.

Institute of Organization and Management of Industrial Production: Doc. Dr. Inż. Ferdynand Szwagrzyk.

Institute of Mathematics: Prof. Dr. hab. Bogdan Choczewski.

Institute of Social Sciences: Prof. Dr. hab. Anna Jankowska-Kłapkowska.

Institute of Opencast Mining: Doc. Dr. hab. Inż. Ryszard Uberman.

Institute of Underground Mining and Work Safety: Doc. Dr. hab. Inż. Ryszard Stecko.

Institute of Rock Mechanics: Prof. Dr. hab. Inż. Henryk Filcek.

Institute of Design and Construction of Mines: Prof. Dr. hab. Inż. Zbigniew Strzelecki.

Institute of Mineral Dressing and Exploitation: Prof. Dr. hab. Inż. Kazimierz Sztaba.

Institute of Drilling and Petroleum Engineering: Doc. Dr. Inż. Stanisław Karlic.

Institute of Mining and Industrial Geodesy: Doc. Dr. hab. Inż. Jan Gocał.

Institute of Environment Forming and Protection: Doc. Dr. Inż. Czesław Zuławski.

Institute of Applied Geophysics and Oil Geology: Prof. Dr. hab. Inż. Stanisław Małoszewski.

Institute of Geology and Mineral Deposits: Prof. Dr. Inż. Marian Banaś.

Institute of Hydrogeology and Engineering Geology: Prof. Dr. hab. Inż. ANTONI KLECZKOWSKI.
Institute of Building and Refractory Materials: Prof. Dr. Inż. JERZY GRZYMEK.
Institute of Materials Science: Prof. Dr. hab. STANISŁAW MROWEC.
Institute of Metallurgy: Prof. Dr. hab. Inż. RYSZARD BENESCH.
Institute of Non-Ferrous Metals: Prof. Dr. hab. Inż. TADEUSZ KARWAN.
Institute of Plastic Deformation and Physical Metallurgy: Prof. Dr. Inż. JERZY BAZAN.
Institute of Technology and Mechanization of Foundry Engineering: Prof. Dr. hab. Inż. WŁADYSŁAW LONGA.
Institute of Automation of Drives and Industrial Machinery: Prof. JAN MANITIUS.
Institute of Electrical Machines and Control of Electropower Systems: Doc. Dr. Inż. ZDZISŁAW KLONOWICZ.
Institute of Computer Science and Automatic Control: Prof. Dr. Inż. HENRYK GÓRECKI.
Institute of Electronics: Doc. Dr. hab. Inż. ZBIGNIEW WĄSOWICZ.
Institute of New Conversions of Energy: Prof. Dr. Inż. ZBIGNIEW JASICKI.
Institute of Basic Problems of Machine Construction: Doc. Dr. Inż. ADAM SIEMIENIEC.
Institute of Mining and Dressing Machines and Automatic Control: Prof. Dr. hab. Inż. ZYGMUNT KAWECKI.
Institute of Metallurgical Machines and Automatic Control: Prof. Dr. hab. Inż. ZYGMUNT DRZYMAŁA.
Institute of Mechanics and Vibroacoustics: Prof. Dr. hab. Inż. ZBIGNIEW ENGEL.

POLITECHNIKA CZĘSTOCHOWSKA
(Częstochowa Technical University)

UL. DEGLERA 35, CZESTOCHOWA

Telephone: 552-11.

Founded 1949.

Rector: Prof. Dr. Inż. J. A. LEDWOŃ.
Pro-Rectors: Prof. Dr. Inż. L. JEZIORSKI, Doc. Dr. Inż. T. WARCHALA, Doc. Dr. M. STAŃCZYK.
Chief Administrative Officer: Mgr. H. KOŹMIŃSKI.
Librarian: Mgr. Z. MROWIŃSKI.

Number of teachers: 466.
Number of students: 3,512.

Publications†: *Zeszyty Naukowe Politechniki Częstochowskiej* (Scientific Papers of Częstochowa Technical University); Series: *Nauki podstawowe* (Basic Sciences), *Nauki Techniczne: Elektrotechnika, Hutnictwo, Mechanika* (Engineering: Electrotechnics, Metallurgy, Mechanics), *Nauki Społeczno-ekonomiczne* (Social and Economic Sciences), *Skład Osobowy* (Personnel List).

DEANS:

Faculty of Mechanical Engineering: Prof. Dr. Inż. M. GIERZYŃSKA-DOLNA.
Faculty of Metallurgy: Dr. Inż. J. BRASZCZYŃSKI.
Faculty of Electricity: Prof. Dr. Inż. I. DOBRZAŃSKA.
Faculty of Civil Engineering: Doc. Dr. Inż. S. OCHOŃSKI.

PROFESSORS:

Faculty of Mechanical Engineering:

BACHMACZ, W., Mechanics and Strength of Materials
CZARNECKI, R., Plastic Working Machines and Technology
DRABEK, S., Machine Building Technology
DURLIK, J., Welding
ELSNER, J., Heat Machines
GAJEWSKI, W., Thermodynamics
GIERZYŃSKA, M., Plastic Working Machines and Technology
JANICZEK, R., Foundations of Machine Design
KLEJA, K., Heat Machines
KOSZKUL, J., Machine Building Technology
LECHOWSKI, T., Machine Building Technology
LEWANDOWSKI, S., Foundations of Machine Design
MAZANEK, E., Foundations of Machine Design
OLSZEWSKI, E., Foundations of Machine Design
PARKITNY, R., Foundations of Machine Design
PASTUCHA, L., Thermodynamics
SŁUŻALEC, A., Welding
TOMSKI, L., Foundations of Machine Design
TUBIELEWICZ, K., Machine Building Technology
WACZYŃSKI, S., Machine Building Technology
WOLAŃSKI, R., Thermodynamics

Faculty of Metallurgy:

BRASZCZYŃSKI, J., Foundry Technology
ISKIERKA, S., Physical Metallurgy
JANAS, M., Pig Iron and Steel Metallurgy
JEZIORSKI, L., Physical Metallurgy
KLIMECKI, W., Physical Chemistry of Metals
KNAP, F., Plastic Working of Metals
MOREL, S., Heat Engineering
MOSZORO, K., Heat Engineering
PACZUŁA, B., Pig Iron and Steel Metallurgy
PIŁKOWSKI, Z., Foundry Technology
PRZEWŁOCKA, H., General Chemistry
RYSZKA, E., Industrial Furnaces
STACHURA, S., Physical Metallurgy
STEC, R., Pig Iron and Steel Metallurgy
SZKODA, F., Physical Metallurgy
SZYMURA, S., Physics
UJMA, J., Physical Chemistry of Metals
WACHELKO, T., Foundry Technology
WARCHALA, T., Foundry Technology
WIERZBICKA, B., Foundry Technology
WYSŁOCKI, B., Physics

Faculty of Electricity:

BIFLAŃSKI, K., Electrical Measurements
BIERNACKI, Z., Electrical Measurements
BRANICKI, R., Machines and Electrical Drive
DANCEWICZ, J., Industrial Automation
DOBRZAŃSKA, I., Electrical Power Engineering
HORAK, J., Electrical Power Engineering
JANICZEK, S., Electrification of Industrial Plant
LUBELSKI, K., Theoretical Electrotechnics
PAPUŻYŃSKI, W., High Voltage
ROLICZ, P., Theoretical Electrotechnics

Faculty of Civil Engineering:

BATKIEWICZ, W., Industrial and General Building
LEDWOŃ, J., Protection of Buildings in Mining Areas
OCHOŃSKI, S., Industrial and General Building
PIECUCH, T., Sewage Technology and Waste Utilization
STOJANOWSKI, J., Theory of Constructions
ZIELIŃSKI, A., Theory of Constructions

Institute of Mathematics:

CZARNOTA, A., Mathematics
KAPCIA, A., Mathematics

Institute of Economic and Social Sciences:

BAKOWSKI, E., Political Sciences
GRABARA, A., Industrial Economics and Organization
ROTAUB, A., Industrial Economics and Organization
STAŃCZYK, M., Political Economy
SZTUMSKI, W., Philosophy

Interdepartmental Study for Education of Teachers of Technical Subjects:

WILK, S., Technical Education

Computing Machinery Centre:

KITA, Z., Computing Machinery

POLITECHNIKA GDAŃSKA
(Gdańsk Technical University)

GDAŃSK 6,
UL. MAJAKOWSKIEGO 11/12

Telephone: 41-57-91.
Telex: 0512302 plg pl.

Founded 1945.

Rector: Prof. MARIAN CICHY.
Vice-Rectors: Dr. W. WEŁNICKI, Dr. W. ZWIERZYKOWSKI, Dr. Cz. TARASKIEWICZ, Dr. E. WASILENKO.
Chief Administrative Officer: Ing. W. WÓJCIAK.
Librarian: Mgr. M. KOMENDECKI.

Library: *see* Libraries.

Number of teachers: 1,272.
Number of students: 8,467.

Publications: *Zeszyty Naukowe Politechniki Gdańskiej* (Scientific Papers of the Technical University of Gdańsk—irregular), *Wykazy Nowych Nabytków Biblioteki* (Library Acquisitions Lists—quarterly).

DEANS:

Faculty of Civil Engineering: J. SZCZYGIEL.
Faculty of Mechanical Engineering: Z. WIERZCHOWSKI.
Faculty of Chemistry: Z. SIKORSKI.
Faculty of Electrical Engineering: T. LIPSKI.
Faculty of Electronics: M. BIAŁKO.
Faculty of Mechanical Technology: M. MYŚLIWIEC.

Institute of Architecture and Town Planning: M. KOCHANOWSKI.
Institute of Hydrotechnics: A. TEJCHMAN.
Institute of Shipbuilding: J. WIĘCKOWSKI.
Institute of Physics: J. KALINOWSKI.
Institute of Mathematics: J. RYTERSKI.
Institute of Social Sciences: H. RÓŻAŃSKA.

PROFESSORS:

Faculty of Mechanical Engineering:

BROSCH, J., Hydraulic Turbines and Pumps
BURACZEWSKI, C., Thermodynamics
CANTEK, L., Piston Steam Engines
CHŁOPECKI, A., Refrigeration Engineering
CICHY, M., Piston Steam Engines
DĄBROWSKI, S., Hydraulic Turbines and Pumps
DABROWSKI, T., Food Technology
DUTKIEWICZ, D., Food Technology
GŁAŻEWSKI, Z., Strength of Materials
IWANOWSKI, K., Machines Construction
JASIŃSKI, W., Thermodynamics
JUR, J., Mechanical Handling Equipment
KRUSZEWSKI, J., Strength of Materials
KRZYŻANOWSKI, W., Hydraulic Turbines and Pumps
MACIAKOWSKI, R., Machines Construction
NIESPODZIŃSKI, S., Thermodynamics
NOWAKOWSKI, W., Motor Vehicles
OLSZEWSKI, O., Machine Construction
OSIECKI, A., Hydrostatic Transmission
PIOTROWSKI, W., Steam Generators
PUDLIK, W., Thermodynamics
SPUS, H., Strength of Materials
WASILUK, W., Machines Measurement
WECLAWSKI, J., Piston Steam Engines
WIERZCHOWSKI, Z., Mechanical Handling Equipment
WOJCIECHOWSKI, S., Piston Steam Engines

Faculty of Chemistry:

BIAŁOZÓR, S., Electrochemistry
BIERNAT, J., General Chemistry
BOROWSKI, E., Biochemistry
CHIMIAK, A., Organic Chemistry
DOBROWOLSKI, J., General Chemistry
DOMAŃSKI, J., Building Materials Technology
DROZDOWSKI, B., Fat Technology
FALKOWSKI, L., Drugs Technology and Biochemistry
GRYLICKI, M., Inorganic Building Materials
JUCHNIEWICZ, R., Corrosion Protection Technology
KAPCZYŃSKI, J., Chemical Technology of Inorganic Compounds
KONOPA, J., Organic Chemistry
KOWALCZYK, J., Analytical Chemistry
KOZŁOWSKI, E., Analytical Chemistry
KRUPNIK, T., Chemical Engineering
KWIATKOWSKI, A., Polymer Chemistry and Technology
LEDÓCHEWSKI, A., Drugs Chemistry and Technology
LIBUŚ, W., Physical Chemistry
LIBUŚ, Z., Physical Chemistry
POMPOWSKI, T., Chemical Technology of Inorganic Compounds
SIKORSKI, Z., Food and Fish Technology
SOKOŁOWSKA, T., Organic Chemistry
STANKIEWICZ, W., Chemical Engineering
STASZEWSKI, R., Analytical Technology
SZLEMIŃSKI, B., Chemical Engineering
URUSKA, I., Physical Chemistry
WASIELEWSKI, C., Organic Chemistry
WOJNOWSKI, W., Inorganic Chemistry
ZWIERZYKOWSKI, W., Fat Technology

Faculty of Electrical Engineering:

BARELKOWSKI, J., Electrical Power Engineering
BITEL, H., Machine and Electrical Drive
DZIEDZIC, J., Industrial Automation
FIGWER, J., Marine Electrical Engineering
GAWĘCKI, L., Marine Electrical Engineering
GRINBERG, Z., Marine Electrical Engineering
GRUDZIECKI, S., Electrical Apparatus and Traction
HELLMANN, W., Electrical Power Engineering
HRYŃCZUK, J., Principles of Electrical Engineering and High Voltage
IWICKI, M., Industrial Electrical Engineering
JACZEWSKI, J., Industrial Electrical Engineering
KOLKA, J., Electrical Machines and Drive
LIPSKI, T., Electrical Apparatus and Traction
MANITIUS, Z., Machines and Electrical Drive
MARECKI, J., Electrical Power Engineering
MILKIEWICZ, F., Industrial Automation
PAZDRO, P., Electrical Apparatus and Traction
PRZEŹDZIECKI, F., Electrical Machines and Drive
PRZYBYLSKI, T., Electrical Power Engineering
REFEROWSKI, L., Electrical Measurement
ROSZCZYK, S., Electrical Machines and Drive
SAWICKI, J., Electrical Measurement
SPICHALSKI. A., Electrical Measurement
SZCZERBA, Z., Electrical Power Engineering
WASILENKO, E., Principles of Electrical Engineering and High Voltage
WINIARSKI, W., Electrical Apparatus and Traction
WOYNAROWSKI, Z., Electrotechnology

Faculty of Electronics:

BARTKOWSKI, T., Principles of Telecommunications
BIAŁKO, M., Radio Receiving Elements Technology
BOGUŚ, Z., Principles of Telecommunications
BUDZYŃSKI, G., Hydroacoustics
GRABOWSKI, K., Microwave Technique
GUZIŃSKI, A., Principles of Telecommunications
JAGODZIŃSKI, Z., Hydroacoustics
JANKOWSKI, A., Cybernetics
KNOCH, L., Transmitter Technics
LENKOWSKI, J., Radio Receiving Equipment
MATUSEWICZ, A., Radio Receiving Elements Technology
MOSTOWSKI, W., Transmitter Technology
NIEDŹWIECKI, M., Radio Receiving Equipment
NOWAKOWSKI, J., Electronic Equipment Technology
POLOWCZYK, M., Telecommunications Technology
PORĘBSKI, W., Automation
RACZYŃSKI, ST., Electronic Equipment Technology
RUTKOWSKI, D., Principles of Telecommunications
SAŁACIŃSKI, J., Electronic Equipment Technology
SANKIEWICZ, M., Hydroacoustics
SOBCZAK, W., Cybernetics
WALASEK, S., Telecommunications Technology
WIERZBA, H., Electronic Equipment Technology
WILAMOWSKI, B., Telecommunications Technology
ZIELONKO, R., Electronic Equipment Technology
ZIENTALSKI, M., Electronic Equipment Technology

Faculty of Mechanical Technology:

BUJNIEWICZ, Z., Machine Technology
BURKIEWICZ, T., Polymers Technology
BUTNICKI, S., Metalworking
CZUCHNOWSKI, A., Machines Technology and Industry Organization
DMOWSKI, M., Machines Technology and Industry Organization
DOWDA, W., Metalworking
DZIEWANOWSKI, R., Wood and Polymer Working Machines
FELD, M., Machine Technology
GRELAK, K., Machines Technology and Industry Organization
HORISZNY, S., Machine Tools for Metals
JAKUBIEC, M., Welding
KLIMKIEWICZ, W., Wood and Polymer Working Machines
KOLMAN, R., Machine Tools for Metals
KRÓLIKOWSKI, Z., Metals Technology
LESIŃSKI, K., Welding
MYŚLIWIEC, M., Welding
SIEMIŃSKI, R., Wood and Polymer Working Machines
SZYDLIK, W., Welding
WALCZAK, W., Welding
ZIMNIAK, A., Metalworking

Institute of Architecture and Town Planning:

ANDERS, W., Town Planning
ARKUSZEWSKI, W., Ship Architecture
BRODOWICZ, Z., Painting
BUCZKOWSKI, W., Buildings Technology
CHMIEL, J., Public Buildings
CZEKANOWSKI, Z., Naval Architecture
FISZER, A., Painting
GRUSZKOWSKI, W., Town Planning
HABELA, J., History of Architecture
KOCHANOWSKI, M., Town Planning
KOHNKE, A., Health Service Architecture
KOŁODZIEJSKI, J., Regional Planning
LESZCZYŃSKA, M., Painting
MASSALSKI, R., History of Architecture
PIASECKI, D., Town Planning
SOWIŃSKI, S., Municipal Architecture
STANKIEWICZ, J., History of Architecture
SWĘDRZYŃSKI, C., Town Planning
SZTAFROWSKI, M., Office Building Architecture
ZALESKI, L., Ship Architecture

Institute of Civil Engineering:

BASRIAN, S., General Building
BIELEWICZ, E., Theory of Structures
BORKOWSKI, H., Communication
BRAUN, K., Reinforced Concrete Buildings
CYWIŃSKI, Z., Structural Mechanics
DABROWSKI, R., Structural Mechanics
KASZUBA, C., General Buildings
KAZIMIERCZAK, R., Structural Mechanics
KOZAKOW, Z., Bridges
LEWANDOWSKI, M., Economics and Organization of Building
ŁEMPICKI, J., Reinforced Concrete Buildings
MITKOWSKI, W., Communications
NIEDZIELSKI, A., Steel Structures
RATAJ, J., General Building
SZAMIN, T., General Building
SZCZYGIEŁ, J., Bridges

SZULCZYŃSKI, T., Reinforced Concrete Buildings
TARASZKIEWICZ, C., Municipal Architecture
WIELOCH, R., Reinforced Concrete Buildings
WIZMUR, M., Structural Mechanics
WYSIATYCKI, K., Bridges
ZIÓŁKO, J., Steel Structure

Institute of Hydrotechnics:
BACHANEK, S., Hydraulic Engineering
BEDNARCZYK, S., Hydraulic Construction
BIERNACKI, T., Hydraulic Construction
DEMBICKI, E., Foundation
KOWALIK, P., Geodesy
KOZERSKI, B., Hydraulic Engineering
MACKIEWICZ, S., Hydraulic Construction
MAZURKIEWICZ, B., Foundation
ODROBINSKI, W., Ground Mechanics and Foundation
ONOSZKO, J., Hydraulic Construction
PIOTROWICZ, W., Hydraulic Engineering
PIWECKI, T., Hydromechanics
PRZEWŁÓCKI, Z., Ground Mechanics
PUZYREWSKI, R., Hydraulic Engineering
SIELSKI, J., Hydromechanics
SIERADZKI, M., Geodesy
SIUZDAK, J., Communal Engineering
SUBOTOWICZ, W., Ground Mechanics
TEJCHMAN, A., Ground Mechanics
WĘDZIŃSKI, W., Geodesy
ZURAWSKI, A., Geodesy

Institute of Shipbuilding:
AGOPSOWICZ, T., Ship Designing
BUCZKOWSKI, L., Ship Designing
BURZYŃSKI, J., Auxiliary Ship Equipment
DOERFFER, J., Technology of Ships
FRĄCKOWIAK, M., Theory of Shipbuilding
GERLACH, T., Auxiliary Ship Equipment
KOBYLIŃSKI, L., Theory of Shipbuilding
KOLAGO, M., Technology of Ships
KOZŁOWSKI, J. P., Technology of Ships
KRĘŻELEWSKI, M., Theory of Shipbuilding
KUBERA, S., Technology of Ships
KURSKI, W., Mechanics of Ship Structures
PACZEŚNIAK, J., Ship Designing
PALASIK, L., Technology of Ships
PERYCZ, S., Steam and Gas Turbines
PUHACZEWSKI, Z., Steam and Gas Turbines
SOBKOWSKI, S., Steam and Gas Turbines
STALIŃSKI, J., Ship Power Plants
STASZEWSKI, J., Ship Designing
URBAŃSKI, P., Ship Power Installations
WEŁNICKI, W., Theory of Shipbuilding
WEWIÓRSKI, S., Ship Designing
WIĘCKOWSKI, J., Mechanics of Ship Structures
WIŚNIEWSKI, J., Ship Designing
WITUSZYŃSKI, K., Mechanics of Ship Structures
ZBOROWSKI, A., Hydromechanics of Ship Structures

Institute of Physics:
BERNASIK, S., Physics
BOJARSKI, C., Physics
CHOMKA, W., Physics
CHYBICKI, M., Physics
FIUTAK, J., Physics
GAZDA, E., Physics
GZOWSKI, O., Physics
JACHYM, B., Physics
JANUSZAJTIS, A., Physics
KALINOWSKI, J., Physics
POLACKI, Z., Physics
UMIŃSKI, T., Physics

Institute of Mathematics:
BESALA, P., Mathematics
DZIĘGIELEWSKI, Z., Descriptive Geometry
PALCZEWSKI, B., Mathematics
RYTERSKI, J., Mathematics

Institute of Social Sciences:
ACHMEDOW, S., Philosophy
RÓŻAŃSKA, H., Political Economy
SIKORA, Z., Political Economy
SKRZYPEK, A., Political Economy
SYNOWIECKI, A., Philosophy

POLITECHNIKA KRAKOWSKA
(Cracow Technical University)
WARSZAWSKA 24,
31-155 CRACOW
Telephone: 303-00.
Founded 1945.

Language of instruction: Polish; Academic year: September to June (two semesters).

Rector: Prof. Dr. hab. Inż. B. KORDAS.

Pro-Rectors: Doc. Dr. Inż. K. SZEWCZYK, Prof. Dr. hab. Inż. S. PIECHNIK, Prof. Dr. hab. Inż. T. ŚRODULSKI, Doc. Dr. Inż. B. OSUCH.

Chief Administrative Officer: Mgr. Inż. B. KSIAŻEK.

Librarian: Dr. J. CZERNI.

Library: *see* Libraries.

Teaching staff: 1,052.

Number of students: 10,000.

Publications: *Czasopismo Techniczne*† (Technical Bulletin—quarterly), *Zeszyty Naukowe Politechniki Krakowskiej*† (Scientific Sheets, series on Architecture, Civil Engineering, Hydraulic and Sanitary Engineering, Mechanics, Transport, Economics, Chemistry, Basic Technical Sciences and Monographs).

DEANS:

Faculty of Architecture: Prof. Dr. Inż. A. SKOCZEK.

Faculty of Civil Engineering: Prof. Dr. Inż W. MUSZYŃSKI.

Faculty of Sanitary and Hydraulic Engineering: Doc. Dr. hab. Inż. A. WIECZYSTY.

Faculty of Industrial Chemistry: Prof. Dr. hab. Inż. J. WĘGIEL.

Faculty of Mechanical Engineering: Prof. Dr. hab. Inż. S. RUDNIK.

Faculty of Transport: Prof. Dr. hab. Inż. Z. LISOWSKI.

PROFESSORS:

ALBIŃSKI, K., Milling
ARCT, Z., Industrial Architecture and Industrialization of Building
BARAŃSKI, F., Mathematics
BŁOCHOWIAK, Z., Economics and Organization of Building Technology
BOCHENEK, J., Differential Equations
BOGDANOWSKI, J., Regional Planning and Landscape Architecture
BROŚ, J., Rail-car Technology
CĘCKIEWICZ, W., Town Planning and Architectural Design
CHOWANIEC, M., Rural Architecture
CIESIELSKI, R., Theory of Structures
CYUNEL, B., Economics and Organization of Building Construction
FRAZIK, J. T., History of Architecture, Historical Monuments Preservation
GÓRSKI, L., Analytical Chemistry, Nuclear Chemistry
HARASYMOWICZ, J., Machine Tools, Instruments and Metal Cutting
KOCWA, E., Microbiology of Water and Waste Water
KORDAS, B., Applied Hydrodynamics
KORDECKI, Z., Theory of Structures
KORDZIŃSKI, C., Theory, Design and Testing of Internal Combustion Engines
KORECKI, J., Theory of Mechanisms and Machines
KORSKI, W., Architectural Design
KRZYŚ, W., Mechanics, Machine Design
LISOWSKI, B., Theory of Architecture and Industrial Architecture
LISOWSKI, Z., Wear and Reliability of Railcars
MAŃKOWSKI, T., Architectural Design
MENDERA, Z., Steel Structures
MILBERT, S., Geodesy
MŁYNARSKI, F., Energetic Machines and Mechanisms
MOJ, E., Architectural Construction
MURZEWSKI, J., Applied Mathematics and Structural Mechanics
MUSZYŃSKI, W., Technology of Concrete
NOWAK, Z., Fluid Mechanics
OBERC, A., Petrography and Geology
OLESZKIEWICZ, S., Concrete Structures
PALASIŃSKI, Z., Descriptive Geometry
PAŁKA, J., Soil Mechanics and Foundations
PERYKASZA, E., Railways
PIECHNIK, S., Theory of Elasticity, Plasticity and Creeping
PIENIAŻEK, Z., Physics of Buildings (Heat and Humidity Problems)
PIWOWARSKI, K., Concrete Structures
RUDNIK, S., Metallurgy
SKOCZEK, A., Sport and Recreation Architecture
ŚRODULSKI, T., Internal Combustion Engines
SZAFER, T. P., History and Theory of Architecture and City Planning
SZEFER, G., Theoretical and Applied Mechanics
WASZCZYSZYN, Z., Structural Mechanics
WĘGIEL, J., Chemical Technology of Carbon
WIECZYSTY, A., Water Supply and Waste Water Disposal Problems
ZABLOCKI, M., Internal Combustion Engines
ZIN, W., History of Polish Architecture
ŻYCZKOWSKI, M., Technical Mechanics

ATTACHED INSTITUTES:

Institute of Social and Economic Science: Dir. Doc. Dr. hab. S. LASKOWSKI.

Institute of Mathematics: Dir. Prof. Dr. hab. F. BARAŃSKI.

Institute of Physics: Dir. Doc. Dr. Inż. J. NIZIOŁ.

Computer Centre: Dir. Dr. hab. Inż. J. BIERNACKI.

POLITECHNIKA ŁÓDZKA
(Technical University of Łódź)
ZWIRKI 36, 90-924 ŁÓDZ
Telephone: 655-22.
Founded 1945.

Academic year: October to June (2 semesters).

Rector: Prof. Dr. hab. EDWARD GALAS.

Pro-Rectors: Prof. Dr. hab. Z. KEMBŁOWSKI, Prof. Dr. hab. M. SUCHAR, Doc. Dr. K. HAUSMAN, Doc. Dr. H. GRALAK, Doc. Dr. hab. J. SZADKOWSKI.

Director: WITOLD LENCZEWSKI.

Librarian: Dr. JADWIGA PRZYGOCKA.

Library: *see* Libraries.

Number of teachers: 1,455.
Number of students: 13,050.

Publication: *Zeszyty Naukowe Politechniki Łódzkiej.*

DEANS:

Faculty of Mechanical Engineering: Doc. Dr. H. BANASIAK.
Faculty of Electrical Engineering: Doc. Dr. hab. Z. SZCZEPAŃSKI.
Faculty of Applied Chemistry: Doc. Dr. hab. T. PARYJCZAK.
Faculty of Textile Technology: Prof. Dr. hab. G. URBAŃCZYK.
Faculty of Food Chemistry: Doc. Dr. P. MOSZCZYŃSKI.
Faculty of Civil Engineering and Architecture: Doc. Dr. T. PRZEDECKI.
Faculty of Chemical Engineering: Prof. Dr. M. SERWIŃSKI.
Faculty of Technical Physics and Applied Mathematics: Doc. Dr. J. KARNIEWICZ.

PROFESSORS:

Faculty of Mechanical Engineering:
GUNDLACH, W., Thermal Flow Machines
HAŚ, Z., Materials Technology
JĘDRZEJOWSKI, J., Car Engines
KUCZEWSKI, S., Pumps and Hydraulic Turbines
LANZENDOERFER, J., Automobile Engineering
LEYKO, J., Strength of Materials
NIEZGODZIŃSKI, M. E., Strength of Materials
ORZECHOWSKI, Z., Fluid Mechanics
PARSZEWSKI, Z., Theory of Machines
PIĄTKIEWICZ, A., Cranes and Conveyors Design
PIOTROWSKI, W., Metallurgy
SZRENIAWSKI, J., Technology of Metals

Faculty of Electrical Engineering:
BOLANOWSKI, B., Electrical Apparatus
DZIERZBICKI, S., Electrical Apparatus
JABŁOŃSKI, M., Electric Machines and Transformers
KOTER, T., Electric Machines and Transformers
PEŁCZEWSKI, W., Electric Drive
POMYKALSKI, Z., Car Electronics
PRZANOWSKI, K., Electric Energetics
SOCHOR, B., Electric Heating
TUROWSKI, J., Electric Machines and Transformers

Faculty of Applied Chemistry:
CZAKIS-SULIKOWSKA, D., Co-ordination Chemistry
KROH, J., Radiation Chemistry
KRYSEWSKI, M., Polymer Physics
LASOCKI, Z., Polymer Chemistry
LEPLAWY, M., Organic Chemistry
MICHALSKI, J., Organic Chemistry
PARYJCZAK, T., Chemical Catalysis
RUCIŃSKI, J., Polymer Technology
ZWIERZAK, A., Organic Synthesis

Faculty of Textile Technology:
KLIMEK, M., The Industrial Arrangement of Textile Institutions
MALINOWSKI, M., Spinning Technology
RACHWALSKI, J., Economics and Organization of Production
SKWARSKI, T., Synthetic Fibres Technology
SZAŁKOWSKI, Z., Bast Fibres Technology
SZOSLAND, J., Weaving Technology
URBAŃCZYK, G., Fibre Science and Fibre Physics
ZAKRZEWSKI, J., Textile Machinery Construction
ŻUREK, W., Textile Materials

Faculty of Food Chemistry:
BACHMAN, B., Spirits and Yeast Technology
MASIOR, S., Technology of Fermentation
OBERMAN, H., Microbiology
SROCZYŃSKI, A., Technology and Chemistry

Faculty of Civil Engineering and Architecture:
GODYCKI-CWIRKO, T., Reinforced and Prestressed Concrete Structures
SUCHAR, M., Theory of Building Structures and Applied Mechanics
SUŁOCKI, J., Theory of Building Structures and Applied Mechanics

Faculty of Chemical Engineering:
BŁASIŃSKI, H., Chemical Apparatus
KEMBŁOWSKI, Z., Non-Newtonian Fluid Mechanics
PUSTELNIK, C., Unit Operations
SERWIŃSKI, M., Mass Transfer
STRUMIŁŁO, C., Simultaneous Heat and Mass Transfer

Faculty of Technical Physics and Applied Mathematics:
DZIUBIŃSKI, I., Theory of Analytical Functions
KĄCKI, E., Computer Science
KRAKOWSKI, M., Theory of Electricity
SIEWIERSKI, L., Theory of Analytical Functions

Institute of Paper Making and Paper Machines:
SUREWICZ, W., Pulp and Paper Technology
SZARCSZTAJN, E., Pulp and Paper Technology

Intercollegiate Institute of Political Sciences:
POLANOWSKI, L., Economics of Domestic Trade

Branch College in Bielsko-Biala:
WAJAND, J., Automobile Engineering

POLITECHNIKA POZNAŃSKA
(Poznań Technical University)

PL. CURIE SKŁODOWSKIEJ 5, 60-965 POZNAŃ

Telephone: 33-25-81.

Founded 1918.

Rector: Prof. Dr. hab. inż. BOLESŁAW WOJCIECHOWICZ.

Pro-Rectors: Prof. Dr. hab. inż. CZESŁAW KRÓLIKOWSKI, Doc. Dr. inż. Z. RATAJCZAK, Doc. Dr. hab. inż. JÓZEF PIENTKA, Prof. Dr. hab. inż. K. WRZEŚNIOWSKI.

Chief Administrative Officer: Mgr. inż. ALEKSANDER GORZANIAK.

Librarian: Dr. S. BADÓN.

Library: *see* Libraries.

Number of teachers: 1,068.
Number of students: 8,305.

Publications: *Zeszyty Naukowe Politechniki Poznańskiej* (Faculty Bulletins).

DEANS:

Chemical Engineering: Prof. Dr. hab. inż. STEFAN GOSZCZYŃSKI.
Civil Engineering: Prof. Dr. hab. inż. ANRZEJ RYŻYŃSKI.
Electrical Engineering: Prof. Dr. hab. inż. ALEKSANDER KORDUS.
Mechanical Technological Engineering: Doc. Dr. inż. ZENON KOŃCZAK.
Working Machinery and Vehicles Engineering: Doc. Dr. inż. ZDZISŁAW KOŚMICKI.

POLITECHNIKA RZESZOWSKA
(Technical University of Rzeszów)

RZESZÓW, UL. W. POLA 2

Telephone: 432-81.

Founded 1963 as School of Engineering; University status 1974.

Academic year: October to September.

Rector: Prof. KAZIMIERZ OCZOŚ.

Vice-Rectors: ANDRZEJ BYLICA, JAN GRUSZECKI, ZDZISŁAW HIPPE.

Administrative Director: FRANCISZEK SWIDER.

Library Director: EWA BIENIASZ.

Library of 85,000 vols.

Number of teachers: 370.
Number of students: 5,100.

Publication: *Rozprawy.*

DEANS:

Faculty of Civil and Environmental Engineering: STANISŁAW POLAŃSKI.
Faculty of Electrical Engineering: JERZY LEWICKI.
Faculty of Mechanical Engineering: ADAM BATSCH.
Faculty of Chemical Technology: MIECZYSLAW KUCHARSKI.

DIRECTORS:

Institute of Machine Construction: EUGENIUSZ KOŚCIELNY.
Institute of Aviation: HENRYK KOPECKI.
Institute of Mathematics and Physics: JAN WOŹNIACKI.

POLITECHNIKA ŚLĄSKA IM. W. PSTROWSKIEGO
(Silesia Technical University)

GLIWICE, UL. PSTROWSKIEGO 7

Telephone: 31-23-49.

Founded 1945.

Rector: Prof. Dr. hab. Inż. J. NAWROCKI.

Pro-Rectors: Prof. Dr. hab. Inż. M. STARCZEWSKI (Assistant to the Rector), Doc. Dr. Inż. W. SITKO (Gliwice branch), Prof. Dr. hab. Inż. A. MACIEJNY (Katowice branch).

Chief Administrative Officer: Inż. R. WARECKI.

Library: *see* Libraries.

Number of teachers: 1,980.
Number of students: 20,100.

Publications: *Zeszyty Naukowe Politechniki Śląskiej* (Research Review—various titles).

DEANS:

Faculty of Architecture: Prof. Dr. hab. Inż. T. GAWŁOWSKI.
Faculty of Automation and Computer Theory: Doc. Dr. Inż. J. KOPKA.
Faculty of Civil Engineering: Doc. Dr. Inż. S. LESSAER.
Faculty of Chemical Technology and Engineering: Doc. Dr. hab. Inż. K. MACHEJ.
Faculty of Electrical Engineering: Doc. Dr. Inż. B. SZATKOWSKI.
Faculty of Sanitary Engineering: Prof. Dr. hab. Inż. M. ZDYBIEWSKA.
Faculty of Mining: Prof. Dr. hab. H. GIL.
Faculty of Mechanical Technology: Doc. Dr. Inż. JULIAN ZIELINSKI.
Faculty of Energy Engineering: Doc. Dr. hab. Inż. T. CHMIELNIAK.
Faculty of Mathematics and Physics. Doc. Dr. hab. Inż. B. MOCHNACKI.
Institute of Chemistry of Coke: Prof. Dr. hab. Inż. P. WASILEWSKI.

Katowice Branch:

Faculty of Metallurgy: Prof. Dr. Inż. T. LAMBER.
Faculty of Production Organization: Doc. Dr. Inż. Z. POGODA.
Faculty of Transport: Doc. Dr. Inż. H. PRZYBYLSKI.
Faculty of Metallurgical Technology: Doc. Dr. Inż. J. GUBALA.

POLITECHNIKA SZCZECIŃSKA
(Technical University of Szczecin)

AL. PIASTÓW 17, 70310 SZCZECIŃ

Telephone: 470-91.

Founded 1946.

Rector: Dr. hab. ZYGMUNT ZIELIŃSKI.
Pro-Rectors: Doc. Dr. Inż. H. PRIEBE, Doc. Dr. T. WAŚNIEWSKI, Prof. Dr. hab. Inż. A. ŻUCHOWSKI, Prof. Dr. Inż. STANISŁAW BURSA.
Registrar: Mgr. JANUSZ SOSNOWSKI.
Librarian: TERESA JASIŃSKA, M.A.

Library: *see* Libraries.

Teaching staff: 817, including 111 professors.

Number of students: 6,250.

Publication: *Prace Naukowe Politechniki Szczecińskiej* (Scientific Papers of the Technical University of Szczecin—a series for each faculty and also a monographic series and a Town and Country Planning Research series).

DEANS:

Faculty of Civil Engineering: Doc. Dr. Inż. JERZY BOCZAR.
Faculty of Mechanical Engineering and Shipbuilding: Prof. Dr. hab. Inż. W. NOWAK.
Faculty of Chemical Technology: Doc. Dr. T. WASĄG.
Faculty of Electrical Engineering: Prof. Dr. hab. Inż. S. SKOCZOWSKI.
Faculty of Transport Economics: Prof. Dr. hab. T. MADEJ.

PROFESSORS:

Faculty of Civil Engineering and Architecture:
DĄBROWSKI, L., Town Planning
MATYSZEWSKI, T., Construction Materials
MIELCZAREK, Z., General Building
RADZIKOWSKI, A., Soil Mechanics
ZAREMBA, P., Town and Regional Planning

Faculty of Mechanical Engineering and Shipbuilding:
CHUDZIKIEWICZ, R., Foundry Engineering
DZIEWANOWSKI, H., Marine Engineering
MATCHELEK, K., Machining Processes
NOWAK, W., Thermodynamics
OLSZAK, W., Machining Processes
PROWANS, S., Science of Materials

Faculty of Chemical Technology:
BURSA, S., Physical Chemistry
GLABISZ, U., Inorganic Technology
KĘPIŃSKI, J., Chemical Technology
PALUCH, K., Organic Chemistry
STREK, F., Chemical Engineering
ZIELIŃSKI, A., Organic Chemical Technology

Faculty of Electrical Engineering:
SIKORA, R., Theoretical Electrotechnics
SKOCZOWSKI, S., Automatics
ŻUCHOWSKI, A., Automatics

Faculty of Transport Engineering and Economics:
ŁASKI, Z., Economics of Industrial Enterprises
MADEJ, T., Industrial Economics
RUTKOWSKA, J., International Economic Relations
RUTKOWSKI, J., Political Economy
SAWICKI, K., Accountancy
SWATLER, L., Finance
WIERZBICKI, T., Organization of Data Processing
ZIELIŃSKI, Z., Econometrics

Interfaculty Institutes:

Transport Economics:
GÓRSKI, W., Law
GRONOWSKI, F., Economics of Sea Transport
GRZYWACZ, W., Transport Economics

Mathematics:
JAKUBOWICZ, A., Differential Geometry
WOLSZCZAN, J., Transport Economics

POLITECHNIKA WARSZAWSKA
(Technical University of Warsaw)

PLAC JEDNÓSCI ROBOTNICZEJ 1, 00-661 WARSAW

Telephone: 210070.

Founded 1826.

Rector: STANISŁAW PASYNKIEWICZ.
Pro-Rectors: Z. ADAMCZEWSKI, A. BUKOWSKI, J. RUSZKIEWICZ, J. RŻYSKO, A. ŚWIT.
Registrar: A. NOWAK.
Librarian: E. DOMAŃSKI.

Library: *see* Libraries.

Number of teachers: 2,600.

Number of students: 22,000.

Publication: *Zeszyty Naukowe* (Faculty Journals).

DEANS:

Faculty of Architecture: S. BIEŃKUŃSKI.
Faculty of Civil Engineering: H. CZUDEK.
Faculty of Chemistry: A. GÓRSKI.
Faculty of Electrical Engineering: H. TUNIA.
Faculty of Geodesy and Cartography: H. LEŚNIOK.
Faculty of Sanitary and Hydraulic Engineering: H. WALDEN.
Faculty of Electronics: J. OSIOWSKI.
Faculty of Power and Aeronautical Engineering: J. MARYNIAK.
Faculty of Machine Construction Technology: Z. ZBICHORSKI.
Faculty of Fine Mechanics: W. OLEKSIUK.
Faculty of Automobile and Heavy Machine Engineering: M. GOŻDZIECKI.
Faculty of Physics and Mathematics: W. ŻAKOWSKI.
Institute of Chemical Engineering: J. CIBOROWSKI.
Institute of Material Science: S. WOJCIECHOWSKI.
Institute of Transport: W. BAJON.
Branch College in Płock: A. BUKOWSKI.

PROFESSORS:

Faculty of Architecture:
ADAMCZEWSKA-WEJCHERT, H., Town and Country Planning
BIEŃKUNSKI, S., Housing Design
BOGUSŁAWSKI, J., Public Utilities
CIBOROWSKI, A., Architectural Planning
GOLDZAMT, E., Architectural Planning
KARŁOWICZ, R., Architecture, Town Planning
KRASSOWSKI, C. W., History of Polish Architecture
PAŁASZEWSKI, T., Economic Organization of Building
PINIŃSKI, L., Architecture of Industrial Plants
SKIBNIEWSKA, H., Housing Design
TOBOLCZYK, S., Public Utilities
TOMASZEWSKI, A., History of Polish Architecture, Conservation of Historical Monuments
TWORKOWSKI, S., Country Architecture
WEJCHERT, K., Town and Country Planning

Faculty of Chemistry:
BUCHOWSKI, H., Physical Chemistry
DAHLIG, W., Plastic Materials Technology
ECKSTEIN, Z., Chemistry and Technology of Pesticides
GÓRSKI, A., Inorganic Chemistry
MALINOWSKI, S., Organic Technology Catalysis
MARCZENKO, Z., Analytical Chemistry
PASYNKIEWICZ, S., Organometallic Chemistry
POREJKO, S., Chemistry and Technology of Plastics
PRZYŁUSKI, J., Solid State Technology
SERAFIN, B., Organic and Medicinal Chemistry
WEYCHERT, S., Chemical Engineering

Faculty of Civil Engineering:
ABRAMOWICZ, M., Reinforced Concrete Structures
BADOWSKA, H., Synthetic Materials
CIESZYNSKI, K., Technology and Organization of the Production of Prefabricated Materials
CZUDEK, H., Construction of Bridges
CZERSKI, Z., Precast and Prestressed Structures
CZULAK, J., Strength of Materials

DĄBROWSKI, K., Concrete Construction
EYMAN, H. K., Concrete Technology
GRABOWSKI, Z. T., Soil Mechanics and Foundation Engineering
KĄCZKOWSKI, Z., Structural Mechanics
KIETLINSKA, Z., Applied Geodesy
KUCZYNSKI, W., Reinforced Concrete Structures
KWIECINSKI, M., Theory of Elasticity and Plasticity
LENKIEWICZ, W. J., Technology of Building
LEŚNAK, Z., Optimization of Constructions
ŁOPATEK, Z., Civil Engineering
ŁUBINSKI, M., Civil Engineering
NEJMAN, T., Building Construction
MAZURKIEWICZ, Z., Structural Mechanics
PANCEWICZ, Z., Metal Construction
RAKOWSKI, G., Structural Mechanics
STACHURSKI, W., Building Construction
SZYMANSKI, E., Technology of Building Materials
ZIELINSKI, J. L., Reinforced Concrete

Faculty of Electrical Engineering:
BEŁDOWSKI, T., Power Stations
BERNAS, S., Power Systems
CIOK, Z., High Voltage Technology
GRUNWALD, Z., Electrical Drives
JAKUBOWSKI, J. L., High-Voltage Technology
KACZOREK, T., Control Systems Theory
KOZIÉJ, E., Design, Calculation and Thermic Phenomena in Electrical Machines
KOŻUCHOWSKI, J., Power Systems
KUJSZCZYK, S., Power System
KWIATKOWSKI, W., Electrical Metrology
LATEK, W., Electrical Machines
LIPIŃSKI, E., Power Systems, Computer Science
MAKSYMIUK, J., Electrical Drives
MATLA, R., Power Systems
OWCZAREK, J., Electrical Machines for Automatic Control
ROGUSKI, A. T., High Voltage Technology, Electrical Apparatus and Systems
SKRZYPEK, T., Electrothermics
TUNIA, H. J., Power Electronics and Electric Drives
WASILUK, W., Industrial Power System
ŻYDANOWICZ, J., Power Systems Protection

Faculty of Electronics:
FELICKI, J., Automatic Control, Organization of Research
FILIPKOWSKI, A., Analogue Integrated Circuits
FINDEISEN, W., Automatic Control
GOLDE, W., Electronic Circuits
GOSIEWSKI, A., Control Theory
HAHN, S. L., Radio Electronics
HENNEL, J., Vacuum Electronics
KOWALCZYK, E., Telecommunications
KUDREWIĆZ, J., Theory of Electronic Systems
ŁADZIŃSKI, R., Theory of Dynamic Systems
MAJEWSKI, W., Digital Telecommunications
MALECKI, J., Electroacoustics
MORAWSKI, T., Microwave Technology
OSIĄWSKI, J., Circuit Theory
PIOTKOWSKI, A., Nuclear Electronics
PUŁTORAK, J., Semiconductor Electronics
SŁAWINSKI, S., Radiolocation
SMOLINSKI, A. K., Electronic Circuits
STOLARSKI, E., Semiconductor Electronics
ŚWIT, A., Semiconductors Devices Theory Measurements and Technology
SZPINGLER, Z., Teletransmission
WIERZBICKI, A., Theory of Control and Optimization
WOLIŃSKI, W., Quantum Electronics
ZIELINSKI, A., Telecommunications

Faculty of Fine Mechanics:
LESKIEWICZ, H. J., Automatic Control
LIPKA, J., Mechanics of Fine Mechanisms
MAJCHER, J., Industrial Electronics

Faculty of Geodesy and Cartography:
ADAMCZEWSKI, Z., Geodetic Computer Science
KAMELA, C., Geodesy
LESNIOK, H., Surveying
ZOBEK, L., Higher Geodesy, Dynamic Geodesy, Geodetical Geophysics

Faculty of Machine Construction Technology:
CHODKIEWICZ, L., Mechanical Construction
DMOCHOWSKI, J., Production Engineering
GÓRSKI, E., Production Engineering
JAWORSKI, Z., Machine Technology
LIS, S., Organization and Management in Machine Industry
MARCINIAK, Z., Metal Forming
KUNSTETTER, S., Cutting Process and Tools
PĄCZKOWSKI, Z. E., Applied Mechanics
PIWOWAR, S., Welding Technology
PUFF, T., Production Engineering
RŻYSKO, J., Technical Mechanics
WROTNY, L. T., Fundamentals of Machine Tool Design
ZBICHORSKI, Z., Industrial Management

Faculty of Physics and Mathematics:
KLARNER, B., Electrophotographic Technology
KOCIŃSKI, J., Ferromagnetism
MĄCZYŃSKI, M., Mathematics
MUSZYŃSKI, J., Mathematics
PASZKOWSKI, B., Electronics
STRUGALSKI, Z., Nuclear Physics
SUKIENNICKI, A., Physics of Magnetism
TRACZYK, T., Mathematics
WOLSKA-BOCHENEK, J., Mathematics
ZAKOWSKI, W., Mathematics

Faculty of Power and Aeronautical Engineering:
BRODOWICZ, K., Chemical Engineering
BRZOSKA, Z. S., Strength of Materials and Structures
DIETRICH, M., Mechanical Engineering
GUTOWSKI, R., Theoretical Mechanics and Applied Mathematics
JUNGOWSKI, W., Experimental Dynamics of Gases
ŁUKASIEWICZ, S., Theory of Elasticity and Strength of Construction
MARYNIAK, J., Dynamics of Mobile Gases
MORECKI, A., Theory of Machines and Biomechanics
OLĘDZKI, A., Theory of Machines and Mechanisms, Machine Dynamics
PROSNAK, W. J., Fluid Mechanics
RUTKOWSKI, J., Transport Phenomena and Hydroelectromagnetics
STANISZEWSKI, B., Thermodynamics and Heat Transfer
WÒJCICKI, S., Combustion, Jet Propulsion

Faculty of Sanitary and Hydraulic Engineering:
BIERNACKI, T., Water Management
BORETTI, Z., Hydrotechnics
FANTI, K., Water Engineering, Water Power Plants
JASIEWICZ, R., Dynamics of Flow, River Regulation and Waterways
JUDA, J., Environment Protection
KOŁODZIEJCZYK, L., Heat Technology
OZGA-ZIELINSKA, M., Hydrology
ROMAN, M., Water Supply and Sewage Systems
WALDEN, H., Fluid Mechanics
WASILEWSKI, W., Heating and Ventilating
WŁODEK, S., Sanitary Biology
ZABOWSKI, J., Sanitary Chemistry

Faculty of Automobile and Heavy Machine Engineering:
LOTH, E., Building of Machines
OSINSKI, Z., Applied Mechanics
OZIEMSKI, S., Heavy Machine Engineering
SZYMANSKI, K., Heavy Machine Engineering

Institute of Chemical Engineering:
CIBOROWSKI, J. W., Chemical Engineering
KAWECKI, W. W., Chemical Reaction Engineering
MARCINKOWSKI, R., Process Dynamics
MŁODZINSKI, B., Chemical Engineering Equipment
POHORECKI, R., Process Thermodynamics
SELECKI, A., Chemical Engineering
WRONSKI, S., Process Kinetics and Thermodynamics

Institute of Material Science:
CHODOROWSKI, J., Science of Materials and Technology
GRABSKI, M., Physics of Plastic Strain, Processes in Metal Alloys
MATYJA, H., Materials Science
PONIEWIERSKI, Z. M., Physical Metallurgy
WOJCIECHOWSKI, S., Materials Science and Technology

Institute of Transport:
BAJON, W., Dynamics of Machines
DABROWA-BAJON, M., Traffic Control
SMIGIELSKI, H., Telecommunication in Transport

Interfaculty Institute of Social and Economic Studies:
GODLEWSKI, M., Education
MARCINIAK, Ś., Economics
OLSZEWSKI, E., History of Science and Technology
SZEFLER, S., Political Economy

POLITECHNIKA WROCŁAWSKA
(Wroclaw Technical University)

WYBRZEŻE WYSPIAŃSKIEGO 27,
50-370 WROCŁAW
Telephone: 22-7336.
Founded 1945.

Language of instruction: Polish; Duration of academic year: October to June; Branches in Legnica, Kłodzko, Wałbrzych, Świdnica, Jelenia Góra.

Rector: Prof. Dr. hab. Inż. TADEUSZ PORĘBSKI.

Pro-Rectors: Prof. Dr. hab. Inż. WACŁAW KASPRZAK, Doc. Dr. Inż. ALFRED DZIENDZIEL, Prof. Dr. Inż. LESZEK KRZYŻANOWSKI.

Administrative Director: Inż. STANISŁAW RUDNICKI.

Librarian: Doc. Dr. Inż. CZESŁAW DANIŁOWICZ.

Library: *see* Libraries.

Number of teachers: 1,979 including 105 professors.

Number of students: 10,580.

Publications: *Prace Naukowe*† (Scientific Papers, irregular), *Acta Polytechnicae Wratislaviensis*† (2 a year), *Environment Protection Engineering*† (2 a year), *Materials Science*† (2 a year), *Optica Applicata*† (quarterly), *Prace Naukoznawcze i Prognostyczne*† (papers on forecasting, 2 a year), *Studia Geotechnica*† (2 a year), *Systems Science*† (quarterly).

DEANS.

Faculty of Architecture: Doc. Dr. Inż. Arch. STANISŁAW SOŁOWIJ.
Faculty of Basic Problems of Technology: Doc. Dr. hab. KAZIMIERA FULIŃSKA.
Faculty of Building and Civil Engineering: Prof. Dr. hab. Inż. K. BIERNATOWSKI.
Faculty of Chemistry: Prof. Dr. Inż. W. MARKOCKI.
Faculty of Computer Science and Management: Prof. Dr. Inż. JERZY BROMIRSKI.
Faculty of Electronics: Prof. Dr. hab. JERZY JARON.
Faculty of Electrical Engineering: Prof. Dr. hab. Inż. KONSTANTY WOŁKOWIŃSKI.
Faculty of Mechanical Engineering: Prof. Dr. hab. Inż. WŁADYSŁAW KACZMAR.
Faculty of Mechanical and Power Engineering: Prof. Dr. hab. Inż. RYSZARD WYSZYŃSKI.
Faculty of Mining Engineering: Prof. Dr. hab. Inż. TADEUSZ ŻUR.
Faculty of Sanitary Engineering: Doc. Mgr. Inż. F. JANKOWSKI.

DIRECTORS OF INSTITUTES:

Institute of Architecture and Town Planning: Doc. Dr. Inż. Arch. JÓZEF GIERCZAK.
Institute of Building Engineering: Doc. Dr. Inż. ZDZISŁAW BODARSKI.
Institute of Chemistry and Technology of Petroleum and Coal: Prof. Dr. hab. Inż. JERZY GRZECHOWIAK.
Institute of Physical and Organic Chemistry: Prof. Dr. hab. JÓZEF ROHLEDER.
Institute of Inorganic Chemistry and Metallurgy of Rare Elements: Prof. Dr. hab. WALTER WOJCIECHOWSKI.
Institute of Technical Cybernetics: Prof. Dr. hab. Inż. TADEUSZ BATYCKI.
Institute of Electrical Engineering: Prof. Dr. hab. Inż. LUDWIK BADIAN.
Institute of Power Engineering: Prof. Mgr. Inż. JAN TROJAK.
Institute of Physics: Prof. Dr. hab. JERZY CZERWONKO.
Institute of Geotechnics: Prof. Dr. hab. ZDZISŁAW GERGOWICZ.
Institute of Mining Engineering: Prof. Dr. hab. Inż. JAN SAJKIEWICZ.
Institute of the History of Architecture, Art and Technology: Prof. Dr. hab. Inż. Arch. JERZY ROZPĘDOWSKI.
Institute of Chemical Engineering and Heat Installations: Prof. Dr. hab. Inż. ROMAN KOCH.
Institute of Civil Engineering: Prof. Dr. hab. Inż. JAN KMITA.
Institute of Environment Protection Engineering: Prof. Dr. hab. Inż. TOMASZ WINNICKI.
Institute of Machine Construction and Operation: Prof. Dr. hab. Inż. HENRYK HAWRYLAK.
Institute of Mathematics: Prof. Dr. hab. STANISŁAW GŁADYSZ.
Institute of Science of Materials and Technical Mechanics: Doc. Dr. hab. Inż. ZDZISŁAW GABRYSZEWSKI.
Institute of Thermal Techniques and Fluid Mechanics: Doc. Dr. Inż. BOHDAN CHOROWSKI.
Institute of Electric Metrology: Prof. Dr. hab. Inż. ZDZISŁAW KARKOWSKI.
Institute of Social Sciences: Doc. Dr. hab. KAROL BŁAHUT.
Institute of Organization and Management Systems: Prof. Dr. MIECZYSŁAW NAPIERAŁA.
Institute of Machine Building Technology: Prof. Dr. Inż. HILARY GUMIENNY.
Institute of Electronic Technology: Doc. Dr. Inż. ANDRZEJ HAŁAS.
Institute of Inorganic Technology and Chemical Fertilizers: Prof. Mgr. Inż. JERZY SCHROEDER.
Institute of Organic and Polymer Technology: Doc. Dr. Inż. STANISŁAW WITEK.
Institute of Telecommunications and Acoustics: Prof. Dr. hab. Inż. DANIEL BEM.
Institute of Electro-Machine Systems: Doc. Dr. Inż. ZBIGNIEW SZMORLIŃSKI.

HIGHER INSTITUTES

AGRICULTURE

SZKOŁA GŁOWNA GOSPODARSTWA WIEJSKIEGO—AKADEMIA ROLNICZA W WARSZAWIE
(The Agricultural University of Warsaw)

UL. RAKOWIECKA 26/30,
02-528 WARSAW

Telephone: 44-22-51.

Founded 1816, 1906.

Academic year: October to June.

Rector: Prof. Dr. H. JASIOROWSKI.
Pro-Rectors: Prof. Dr. S. LIWSKI, Prof. Dr. ANDRZEJ SZUJECKI, Prof. Dr. TOMAS WODZICKI, Prof. Dr. WOJCIECH WOLSKI.
Chief Administration Officer: GUSTAW LANG.
Librarians: Dr. MARIAN TEMPCZYK, ZOFIA SLIWCZYŃSKA.

Library: *see* **Libraries.**

Teaching staff: 1,021.
Number of students: 9,307.

Publication: *Zeszyty Naukowe SGGW-AR w Warsawie* (Scientific Paper of the Warsaw Agricultural University—irregular).

DEANS:

Faculty of Agriculture: Doc. Dr. IGNACY ŁAKOMIEC.
Faculty of Veterinary Medicine: Prof. Dr. MARCIN SZULC.
Faculty of Forestry; Prof. Dr. EDWARD KAMIŃSKI.
Faculty of Horticulture: Doc. Dr. ANDRZEJ SADOWSKI.
Faculty of Land Reclamation: Doc. Dr. JAN SKIBINSKI.
Faculty of Wood Technology: Prof. Dr. JERZY WAŻNY.
Faculty of Animal Husbandry: Prof. Dr. EWA POTEMKOWSKA.
Faculty of Agricultural Economics: Doc. Dr. JANUSZ KOSICKI.
Faculty of Agriculture and Forestry Engineering: Prof. Dr. JANUSZ HAMAN.
Faculty of Human Nutrition and Rural Home Economics: Prof. Dr. STANISŁAW BERGER.
Faculty of Food Technology: T. JAKUBCZYK.

PROFESSORS:

Faculty of Agriculture:
DOBRZÁNSKI, B., Soil Science

Faculty of Veterinary Medicine:
PREIBISCH, J., Patho-anatomy
SANDNER, E., Entomology
STRYSZAK, A., Veterinary Epidemiology

Faculty of Forestry:
DOMINIK, J., Forest and Wood Protection
KAMIŃSKI, E., Forest Utilization and Engineering
MARSZAŁEK, T., Forest Management and Economics

Faculty of Horticulture:
KRUSZE, N., Economic and Agricultural Organization
REJMAN, A., Orchard Technology

Faculty of Animal Husbandry:
JASIOROWSKI, H., Animal Science
POTEMSKOWA, E., Animal Science
RADOMSKA, M., Animal Science
WITCZAK, F., Animal Nutrition
WOYKE, J., Apiculture

Faculty of Agricultural Economics:
RYCHLIK, T., Economics
STRUŻEK, B., Agrarian Policy

Faculty of Food Technology:
IMBS, B., Economics
RUTKOWSKI, A., Food Technology

Faculty of Agriculture and Forestry Engineering:
FĄFARA, R.
HAMAN, J.
NOWACKI, T.
ZAREMBA, W.
Faculty of Human Nutrition and Rural Home Economics:
BERGER, S., Food Industry and Human Nutrition
Faculty of Land Reclamation:
SOCHOŃ, Z., Water and Soil Engineering
Faculty of Wood Technology:
KRACH, H., Organic Chemistry
WAZNY, J., Wood Protection
Institute of Plant Biology:
ŻELAWSKI, W., Plant Physiology
Institute of Basic and Agricultural Chemistry:
KUSZELEWSKI, L., Agricultural Chemistry
Institute of Plant Protection:
BOCZEK, J.
BORECKI, Z.

Akademia Rolnicza im. Hugona Kołłataja (*Hugo Kołłataj Academy of Agriculture*): Cracow, Al. Mickiewicza 21; f. 1890; faculties of agriculture and food technology, animal husbandry, water reclamation and land taxonomy, forestry, horticulture, agricultural engineering; faculty of agricultural economics and agriculture in Rzeszów; institutes of social and political science, tropical and sub-tropical agriculture and forestry; 750 teachers, inc. 128 professors, 8,229 students; library of 355,000 vols.; Rector Prof. Dr. T. WOJTASZEK; publs. *Zeszyty Naukowe Akademii Rolniczej w Krakowie* (Scientific Paper-series), *Reports of the Academy of Agriculture in Cracow, Studies and Materials* (The Institute of Tropical and Sub-tropical Agriculture and Forestry.)

Akademia Rolnicza (*Academy of Agriculture*): Lublin, ul. Akademicka 13; f. 1955; faculties of veterinary science, agriculture, zootechnics, agricultural engineering, horticulture; Rector Prof. Dr. hab. J. WELENTO; 550 staff, 5,480 students; library of 212,314 vols.

Akademia Rolniczo-Techniczna (*Academy of Agriculture and Technology*): Kortowo, 10-957 Olsztyn; f. 1950; faculties of agriculture, animal husbandry, food technology, veterinary science, geodetics, mechanics, building engineering, water conservation and inland fisheries; Rector Prof. Dr. hab. TEOFIL MAZUR; 9,300 students; library of 333,000 vols., 2,300 current periodicals; publ. *Zeszyty Naukowe*† (irregular, in Polish, with Russian and English summaries).

Akademia Rolnicza w Poznaniu (*Academy of Agriculture in Poznan*): ul. Wojska Polskiego 28, Poznań; f. 1951; faculties of horticulture, agriculture, zootechnics, silviculture, wood technology, food technology, land reclamation; Rector Prof. Dr. J. ZWOLIŃSKI; 174 staff, 4,146 students; library of 336,213 vols.; publs. *Annals*† and other irregular works.

Akademia Rolnicza (*Academy of Agriculture*): Szczecin, ul. Janosika 8; faculties of agriculture, zootechnics and seafishery; 364 staff, 3,000 students; library of 140,000 vols.; Rector Doc. Dr. hab. IDZI DRZYCIMSKI.

Akademia Rolnicza (*Academy of Agriculture*): Wrocław, Norwida 25; f. 1951; faculties of agriculture, veterinary science, animal husbandry, land reclamation and improvement, food technology; divisions of agricultural mechanization, agricultural building, land surveying; Rector Prof. Dr. R. BADURA; 711 staff, 4,500 resident students, 2,000 non-resident; library of 130,000 vols.; publ. *Zeszyty Naukowe Akademii Rolniczej we Wrocławiu.*

ECONOMICS, SOCIAL SCIENCES

Akademia Ekonomiczna w Krakowie (*Academy of Economics*): Cracow, Rakowicka 27; f. 1925; faculty of economics of production with the subdivisions of studies in industrial economics, organization and management and finance; faculty of economics of trade with the subdivisions of studies in commerce, statistics and knowledge of commodities; library of 195,000 vols.; 350 staff, 4,707 students; Rector Prof. Dr. hab. A. FAJFEREK; publ. *Zeszyty Naukowe* (Scientific Papers).

Akademia Ekonomiczna (*Academy of Economics*): Katowice, 1 Maja 50, Bogucicka 3; f. 1937; faculties of industrial economics, commerce and nutrition economics; Rector Prof. Dr. Z. MESSNER; 350 staff, 5,400 students; library of 182,000 vols.; publ. *Zeszyty Naukowe AE* (quarterly).

Akademia Ekonomiczna (*Academy of Economics*): 60-967 Poznań, Marchlewskiego 146/150; f. 1926; faculties of planning and management, economics of production and commerce and commodities science; Rector Prof. Dr. hab. J. PIASNY; 367 staff, of which 57 are professors, 5,050 students; library of 270,000 vols.; publs. *Zeszyty Naukowe*†, *Roczniki Akademii Ekonomicznej w Poznaniu*†, *Skrypty Uczelniane, Quarterly Review: Ruch Prawniczy, Ekonomiczny i Socjologiczny*†.

Akademia Ekonomiczna im Oskara Langego (*O. Lange Academy of Economics*): 53-345 Wrocław, Komandorska 118/120; f. 1947; faculties: industrial engineering and economics, national economy, computer sciences and management; 550 staff, 4,000 full-time students, 3,000 external and postgraduate students; library of 300,000 vols.; Rector Prof. J. KALETA; publ. *Prace Naukowe Akademii Ekonomicznej im O. Langego we Wrocławiu.*

Szkoła Główna Planowania i Statystyki (*Central School of Planning and Statistics*): 02-554 Warsaw, Al. Niepodległości 162; f. 1906; faculties of finance and statistics, home trade, foreign trade, economics of production, social economics; 800 staff, 12,000 (internal and external) students; Rector Prof. STANISŁAW NOWACKI.

Wyższa Szkoła Nauk Społecznych przy KC PZPR (*Higher School of Social Sciences of the Central Cttee. of the Polish United Workers' Party*): 00-585 Warsaw, ul. Bagatela 2; f. 1958; education of party activists and cadres; research into problems of theory and practice in building a socialist society, agrarian policy, Polish history and history of international workers' movement, problems of controlling scientific and technical progress, political sciences, sociology, political economy, economics; postgraduate studies in diplomatic service training, food and agricultural policy, aesthetics, managerial sciences; 162 staff; library of 200,000 vols.; Rector Prof. Dr. WŁADYSŁAW ZASTAWNY; publs. *Z Pola Walki* (From the Battlefield, quarterly), *Zeszyty Naukowe* (Scientific Notebooks).

MEDICINE

Akademia Medyczna (*Medical Academy*): Białystok, Kilińskiego 1; f. 1950; medical faculty and division of stomatology; faculty of pharmacy f. 1977; 416 staff, 1,820 students; library of 260,529 vols.; Rector Prof. Dr. KONSTANTY WIŚNIEWSKI; Dean Prof. Dr. ANTONI GABRYELEWICZ; publ. *Roczniki Akademii Medycznej im. J. Marchlewskiego w Białymstoku* (Annals with summaries in Russian and English).

Akademia Medyczna im Mikołaja Kopernika (*Nicholas Copernicus Medical Academy*): Cracow, ul. Św. Anny 12; f. 1950 from medical faculty of the Jagellonian University; faculties of medicine (with stomatological branch) and pharmacy; Rector Prof. Dr. T. POPIELA; 730 staff, 2,804 students; library of 206,239 vols.; publs. *Annales Academiae Medicae Cracoviensis*† (annually), *The Methodical Review*† (annually).

Akademia Medyczna (*Medical Academy*): 80-210 Gdańsk, ul. Marii Curie-Skłodowskiej 3a; f. 1945; faculties of medicine, stomatology and pharmacology; 1,122 staff, 2,860 students; library of 396,939 vols.; Rector Prof. Dr. ZDZISŁAW BRZOZOWSKI.

Akademia Medyczna (*Medical Academy*): 90-419 Łódź, Al. Kościuszki 4; f. 1950; faculties of medicine and pharmacy; there are 2 sub-faculties of stomatology and medical analytics, f. 1977; library of 253,058 vols.; Rector Prof. Dr. ANTONI KOTEŁKO; 107 staff, 3,448 students; publ. *Annales Academiae Medicae Lodzensis*† (quarterly).

Akademia Medyczna (*Medical Academy*): Lublin; f. 1950; Rector Prof. Dr. J. BILLEWICZ-STANKIEWICZ; 69 staff, 1,978 students.

Akademia Medyczna (*Medical Academy*): Poznań, ul. Fredry 10; f. as University faculty 1920, as Academy 1950; faculties of medicine, stomatology, pharmacy, nursing; medical analysis section; library of *c.* 250,000 vols.; Rector Prof. Dr. ROMAN GÓRAL; 1,617 staff, 3,225 students; publs. *Annuals* (with supplements).

Akademia Medyczna (*Medical Academy*): Warsaw, Filtrowa 30; f. 1950; faculties of medicine and pharmacy; library of 300,000 vols.; Rector Prof. Dr. hab. med. JERZY SZCZERBAŃ; Head of affiliated College of Stomatology Doc. L. KRYST; publ. *Quarterly*.

Akademia Medyczna (*Medical Academy*): 50-367 Wrocław, ul. Pasteura 1; f. 1950; faculties of medicine, dentistry, nursing and pharmacy; 741 staff, 4,000 students; library of 170,000 vols.; Rector Prof. Dr. hab. EUGENIUSZ ROGALSKI; publ. *Prace Naukowe Akademii Medycznej we Wrocławiu* (quarterly).

Centrum Medyczne Kształcenia Podyplomowego (*Postgraduate Medical Centre*): Warsaw, ul. Marymoncka 99; f. 1970; faculties of basic sciences, clinical and social medicine, stomatology, pharmacy; teaching hospital; Dir. Prof. Dr. BOHDAN LEWARTOWSKI; 875 staff, 4,500 students; library of 39,100 vols.; publs. *Medyczne Studia Podyplomowe, Materia Medica Polona* (quarterly in English and French).

Pomorska Akademia Medyczna (*Pomeranian Medical Academy*): Szczecin; f. 1948; 427 staff, 1,650 students; Rector Prof. Dr. ERWIN MOZOLEWSKI; publ. *Annals of the Pomeranian Medical Academy*.

Śląska Akademia Medyczna im. L. Waryńskiego (*L. Waryński Silesian Medical Academy*): 40-952 Katowice, ul. Poniatowskiego 15; f. 1948; medical, dental, pharmaceutical and nursing faculties; research in clinical medicine and particularly problems of industrial medicine; 2,149 staff, 5,527 students; library : *see* Libraries; Rector Prof. Dr. J. JONEK; publs. *Annales*† (quarterly), *Annales Societatis Doctrinae Studentium*† (irregular).

TECHNOLOGY AND ENGINEERING

Wyższa Szkoła Inżynierska (*School of Engineering*): 45-233 Opole, ul. Oleska 114; f. 1966; faculties of civil, electrical, mechanical and agricultural engineering; Rector Prof. Dr. OSWALD MATEJA; publ. *Zeszyty Naukowe*.

Wyższa Szkoła Inżynierska im. Jurija Gagarina (*Yuri Gagarin School of Engineering*): 65-246 Zielona Góra, ul. Podgórna 50; f. 1965; building, mechanical and electrical departments; 3,000 students and 250 scientific workers; library of 124,524 vols.; Rector Prof. Dr. hab. T. BILIŃSKI; publ. *Zeszyty Naukowe*.

THEOLOGY

Akademia Teologii Katolickiej (*Catholic Theological Academy*): Warsaw 01-653, ul. Dewajtis 3; f. 1954; 270 staff, 1,633 students; library of 113,000 vols.; Rector Prof. Dr. J. STĘPIEŃ; Dean of Theology Doc. Dr. H. JUROS, of Christian Philosophy Prof. Dr. T. ŚLIPKO, of Canon Law Prof. Dr. T. PAWLUK; publs. *Studia Philosophiae Christianae*† (half-yearly), *Prawo Kanoniczne*† (quarterly), *Collectanea Theologica*† (quarterly), *Bulletin d'information*† (bi-monthly).

Chrześcijańska Akademia Teologiczna (*Christian Theological Academy*): Warsaw, ul. Miodowa 21; f. 1954; 45 staff, 148 students; library of 26,000 vols.; Rector Rev. Prof. W. GASTPARY; publ. *Rocznik Teologiczny*†.

SCHOOLS OF ART AND MUSIC

Akademia Muzyczna (*Academy of Music*): Katowice; f. 1945; faculties of composition, theory, instrumental and vocal technique, music teaching, teacher training, choir conducting and light music study; 64 teaching staff, 425 students; library of 80,000 vols.; Rector L. MARKIEWICZ.

Akademia Sztuk Pięknych (*Academy of Fine Arts*): 31-157 Cracow, pl. Matejki 13; f. 1818; faculties of painting, sculpture, conservation of works of art, general studies, graphic arts (branch in Katowice), industrial design, interior design; special studies in scenography and textile design; library: *see* Libraries; 226 teachers, 730 students; Rector Prof. MARIAN KONIECZNY; publ. *Zeszyty Naukowe ASP*†.

Akademia Sztuk Pięknych (*Academy of Fine Arts*): Warsaw; f. 1908 as Warszawska Szkoła Sztuk Pięknych (Warsaw School of Fine Arts), renamed 1927; faculties of painting and graphic art, sculpture, interior design; special studies: scene painting, textile design, conservation of works of art, industrial design teaching.

Państwowa Wyższa Szkoła Muzyczna (*School of Music*): 00-368 Warsaw, ul. Okólnik 2; f. 1810; 5 faculties: composition, theory, conducting; instrumental performance; vocal performance; musical education; sound recording; 205 staff, including 64 professors; library of 70,000 books and scores, 7,500 records; Rector Prof. BOGUSŁAW MADEY; publs. professional and occasional papers.

Państwowa Wyższa Szkoła Muzyczna w Krakowie (*State Higher School of Music, Cracow*): Cracow, ul. Bohaterów Stalingradu 3; f. 1945; faculties of composition, theory and conducting; instrumental performance; vocal technique; teacher training and choir conducting; also postgraduate studies; library of 35,000 vols.; Principal Prof. KRZYSZTOF PENDERECKI.

Państwowa Wyższa Skola Muzyczna (*State Academy of Music*): 80-847 Gdańsk, ul. Lagiewniki 3; f. 1947; faculties of composition and theory, instrumentation, vocal technique, institute of music theory; 145 teachers, 460 students; library of 54,720 vols.; Rector A. POSZOWSKI; publs. *Rocznik Informacyjny*†, *Zeszyty Naukowe*†, *Prace Specjalne*†.

Wyższa Skoła Muzyczna (*Higher School of Music*): Łódź, Gdańska 32; f. 1945; faculties of composition, theory, instrumental and vocal technique, music teaching; 162 teachers, 350 students; library of 39,000 vols.; Rector Prof. Z. PŁOSZAJ.

Wyższa Szkoła Muzyczna (*School of Music*): Poznań, ul. Armii Czerwonej 87; f. 1920; faculties of composition, theory, conducting, instrumental technique, vocal technique, music teaching.

Państwowa Wyżcza Szkola Muzyczna (*State College of Music*): 53-140 Wrocław, ul. Powstańców Śląskich 204; f. 1948; departments of composition and music theory (with music therapy section), instrumental music, vocal and theatrical training and music education; 105 teachers, 403 students; library of 45,000 vols.; Rector Prof. J. ZABŁOCKI; publs. *Zeszyty Naukowe* (papers, 2 or 3 a year).

Wyższa Szkoła Sztuk Plastycznych (*School of Fine Arts*): Gdańsk,

Targ Węglowy 1; f. 1945; faculties of painting, architecture, sculpture and industrial design; 100 teachers, 607 students; library of 8,520 vols.; Rector Prof. WŁADYSŁAW JACKIEWICZ.

Wyższa Szkoła Sztuk Plastycznych (*School of Applied Arts*): 91-726 Łódź, 121 Wojska Polskiego St.; f. 1945; faculties of industrial design, textile and dress design, graphic arts, painting and sculpture; 117 teachers, 330 students; library of 16,000 vols.; Rector Doc. WIESŁAW GARBOLIŃSKI; Librarian CECYLIA DUNIN, PH.D.

Wyższa Szkoła Sztuk Plastycznych (*School of Applied Arts*): Poznań, Al. Marcinkowskiego 29; f. 1919, state-controlled from 1921; faculties of painting, graphics, sculpture, tapestry, industrial design and interior design; 102 teachers; library of 13,000 books; Rector Doc. ANTONI ZYDROŃ.

Państwowa Wyższa Szkoła Sztuk Plastycznych (*State Higher School of Fine Arts*): 50-156 Wrocław, Plac Polski 3/4; f. 1946; faculties of painting, sculpture, graphic arts, glass and ceramics design, interior architecture, industrial design; library of 10,500 vols.; Rector T. FOROWICZ.

Państwowa Wyższa Szkoła Filmowa Telewizyjna i Teatralna im. Leona Schillera (*School of Cinema, Television and Theatre*): Łódź, Targowa 61/63; f. 1948; faculties of film and TV direction, film and TV camera work, acting, production and stage management; library of *c.* 30,000 vols.; Rector Doc. S. KUSZEWSKI.

Państwowa Wyższa Szkoła Teatralna (*State Theatre Academy*): Cracow; f. 1945; faculties of acting (Wrocław) and stage craft; puppet theatre section (Wrocław); Rector JERZY KRASOWSKI.

Wyższa Szkoła Teatralna im. Al. Zelwerowicza (*Al. Zelwerowicz State Theatre School*): Warsaw; f. 1946; faculties of acting and production, puppet acting and theatre studies; Rector Prof. T. ŁOMNICKI.

PORTUGAL

Population 9,819,000

ACADEMIES

Lisbon

Academia das Ciências de Lisboa (*Lisbon Academy of Sciences*): Rua da Academia das Ciências 19, Lisbon 2; f. 1779; publs. *Anuario Académico, Boletim, Bibliographia Portuguesa, Memórias, Ciências e Letras, Biblioteca de Altos Estudos*, etc.

President: PEDRO G. PITTA.

Vice-President: H. AMORIM FERREIRA.

Secretary-General: DAMIÃO A. PERES.

Treasurer: VICTOR M. FONTES.

Library: *see* Libraries.

AFFILIATION:

Instituto de Altos Estudos (*Institute of Higher Research*): f. 1931.

Academia Portuguesa da História (*Portuguese Academy of History*): Palácio da Rosa, Largo da Rosa 5; f. 1720 as Academia Real da História Portuguesa, closed middle 18th century, re-established 1936 with present name; library of 45,000 vols.; members: 30 Portuguese, 10 Brazilian; corresponding mems: 30 Portuguese, 10 Brazilian, 20 other nationalities; publs. *Anais, Boletim, Documentos Medievais Portugueses, Subsídios para a História Portuguesa, Fontes Narrativas da História Portuguesa.*

Honorary President: Gen. ANTÓNIO DOS SANTOS RAMALHO EANES.

President: Prof. JOAQUIM VERÍSSIMO SERRÃO.

First Vice-President: Prof. D. FERNANDO DE ALMEIDA.

Second Vice-President: Prof. FERNANDO CASTELO-BRANCO.

Secretary-General: LUÍS DE BIVAR GUERRA.

Academia Nacional de Belas Artes (*National Academy of Fine Arts*): Largo da Biblioteca Pública; f. 1932; library of 20,000 vols., including some 16th-century works; 20 mems.; Pres. Prof. Dr. JOSÉ-AUGUSTO FRANÇA; Sec. Dr. FERNANDO CASTELO BRANCO; publs. *Boletim, Inventário Artistico de Portugal, Belas Artes (Revista-Boletim).*

LEARNED SOCIETIES

AGRICULTURE AND VETERINARY SCIENCE

Sociedade Portuguesa de Ciências Veterinárias (*Portuguese Society of Veterinary Science*): Rua de D. Dinis 2-A, Lisbon; f. 1902; 660 mems.; library of 2,000 vols. and 30,000 periodicals; Pres. Dr. MANUEL ELIAS TRIGO PEREIRA; Gen. Sec. Dr. EDUARDO SOUSA RAMOS DA COSTA; publ. *Revista Portuguesa de Ciências Veterinárias* (quarterly).

Affiliated Societies:

Sociedade Portuguesa de Especialistas de Pequenos Animais (*Portuguese Society of Specialists in Small Animals*): Pres. Dr. ANTÓNIO MARQUES DE ALMEIDA.

Sociedade Portuguesa de Higiene Alimentar (*Portuguese Society of Food Hygiene*): Pres. Prof. ANTÓNIO MARTINS MENDES.

Sociedade Portuguesa Veterinária de Estudos Sociológicos (*Portuguese Society of Sociological Veterinary Studies*): Pres. Prof. PAULO MARQUES.

Sociedade Portuguesa de Nutrição e Alimentação Animal (*Portuguese Society of Animal Nutrition and Foodstuffs*): Pres. Dr. JOAQUIM PORTUGAL.

Sociedade Portuguesa Veterinária de Anatomia Comparativa (*Portuguese Veterinary Society of Comparative Anatomy*): Laboratório de Anatomia Comparada, Escola Superior de Medicina Veterinária, Rua Gomes Freire, Lisbon 1; f. 1974; Pres. Prof. Dr. PAULO MARQUES.

THE ARTS

Centro de Estudos de Arte e Museologia (*Centre for Art and Museum Studies*): Museu de Arte Antiga, rua das Janelas Verdes, Lisbon; f. 1942; Dir. MARIA ALICE BEAUMONT.

Instituto Gregoriano de Lisboa (*Lisbon Institute of Gregorian Studies*): Av. 5 de Outubro 258, 1600 Lisbon; f. 1953; Dir. D. JULIA D'ALMENDRA; publ. *Canto Gregoriano.*

Sociedade Nacional de Belas Artes (*National Society of Fine Arts*): Palacio das Belas Artes, Rua Barata Salgueiro 36, Lisbon; f. 1901; organizes courses in design and visual education; library of 5,000 vols.; 800 associates; Pres. Arq. NUNO DE SAN-PAYO.

BIBLIOGRAPHY AND LIBRARY SCIENCE

Associação Portuguesa de Bibliotecários, Arquivistas e Documentalistas (*Portuguese Association of Librarians, Archivists and Documentalists*): Edif. da Biblioteca Nacional, Campo Grande 83, Lisbon 5; f. 1973; 331 mems.; Pres. LUIS FILIPE DE ABREU NUNES; Sec. MARIA PAULA DE BORJA STUBBS DE LACERDA.

EDUCATION

Instituto Açoriano de Cultura (*Azorean Institute of Culture*): Apdo. 67, 9701 Angra do Heroismo-Codex, Terceira, The Azores; f. 1956; Pres. Rev. Dr. AUGUSTO CABRAL; Sec. Rev. Dr. ARTUR DA CUNHA OLIVEIRA; publs. *Atlantida* (bi-monthly), *Colecçao Insula* (annual).

Instituto de Cultura e Lingua Portuguesa (*Institute of Portuguese Culture and Language*): Praça do Príncipe Real 14-1°, Lisbon 1200; f. 1929 as Junta de Educação Nacional, present name 1980; attached to the Ministry of Education and Culture; awards grants to foreign students in Portugal; publs. works on Portuguese culture; promotes teaching of Portuguese culture and language abroad; Pres. JOSÉ B. BLANC DE PORTUGAL (acting); Sec. ADELINO P. SILVA (acting).

Instituto de Coimbra (*Coimbra Institute*): Rua da Ilha, Coimbra; f. 1851; 150 mems., 13 hon., 156 correspondents in Portugal, 280 foreign corresponding; library of 21,000 vols.; Pres. Prof. LUIS GUILHERMS MENDONÇA de Albuquerque; Sec. Armando Carneida Silva; publ. *O Instituto* (scientific and literary).

Educational Foundation

Fundação Calouste Gulbenkian (*Calouste Gulbenkian Foundation*): Parque Calouste Gulbenkian, Avenida de Berna, Lisbon; non-profit making organization which awards grants in the fields of education, art, science and charity; Chair. Dr. José de Azeredo Perdigão; (*see* also Museums and Libraries).

History, Geography and Archaeology

Associação dos Arqueólogos Portugueses (*Association of Portuguese Archaeologists*): Largo do Carmo, Lisbon; f. 1863; library of 8,750 vols.; 574 mems.; Pres. Dr. Eduardo da Cunha Serrao; Sec.-Gen. Dr. Francisco Santana; publ. *Arqueologia e História* (annually).

Centro de Estudos Históricos Ultramarinos: Rua de Junqueira 86, 1300 Lisbon; f. 1955; history of Portuguese expansion overseas; library of 7,500 vols.; 90 mems.; Sec. Dr. Eduardo dos Santos; publ. *Studia* (2 a year).

Instituto Histórico da Ilha Terceira (*Terceira Historical Institute*): Edifício de São Francisco, Angra do Heroísmo, The Azores; f. 1942; 20 mems.; Pres. Dr. Baptista de Lima; Vice-Pres. João Afonso; publ. *Boletim do Instituto Histórico* (yearly).

Instituto Histórico do Minho (*Minho Historical Institute*): Rua da Bandeira 110, Viana do Castelo; f. 1916; Dir. Júlio de Lemos.

Instituto Português de Arqueologia, História e Etnografia (*Portuguese Archaeological, Historical and Ethnographical Institute*): Edificio dos Jerónimos, Praça do Imperio, Belém, Lisbon; Pres. (vacant); Sec. Dr. João L. Saavedra Machado; publ. *Ethnos*.

Sociedade de Geográfia de Lisboa (*Lisbon Geographical Society*): Rua das Portas de Santo Antão 100, 1100 Lisbon; f. 1875; library of 200,000 vols., 6,000 maps; 1,200 mems.; Pres. Vice-Admiral José Barahona Fernandes; Perm. Sec. Prof. Dr. António de Almeida; Sec.-Gen. Colonel António José Caria; publs. *Relatório, Boletim* (scientific and literary monthly).

International Cultural Institutes

Alliance Française: Rua Braamcamp 13, 1°, 1297 Lisbon Codex; f. 1945; 4,500 mems.; library of 1,800 vols.; Pres. António Maria Godinho; Dir. Jean-Paul Bouton.

Associação Luso-Britanica do Porto: Instituto Britanico, Rua do Breyner 155, Oporto; 2,500 students; library of 11,486 vols., 51 periodicals; Dir. of Studies F. Underwood (acting).

British Council: Rua Luís Fernandes 3, 1294 Lisbon Codex; f. 1938; Rep. A. J. Herbert; c/o Associação Luso-Britanica do Porto (see above); Reg. Dir. P. S. McKay.

British Institute: Rua Alexandre Hercolano 34, Coimbra; 1,000 students; Dir. I. Lister.

Centro Cultural Americano: Av. Duque de Loule 39, P.O.B. 2301, Lisbon.

Deutsches Institut (*German Institute*): Campo dos Mártires da Pátria 36-37, Lisbon 1; f. 1962; a branch of the Goethe-Institut for the promotion of German language and culture abroad; Dir. Dr. Egon Olessak.

Institut Français de Lisbonne (*French Institute*): Rua Santos-o-Velho 11, Lisbon-2; f. 1928; cultural centre of the French Government; library of 20,000 vols.; Dir. Robert Perroud; publs. *Bulletin des Etudes Portugaises* (yearly), *Collection des Etudes Portugaises*.

Institut Français de Porto: Praça da República 75, Oporto; f. 1938; organizes cultural studies, lectures, conferences, etc.; Dir. Francis Uteza.

Instituto Alemão (*German Institute/Goethe-Institut*): Rua do Campo Alegre 298-1°, Oporto; f. 1962; Dir. Dr. A. Himmel.

Instituto Alemão de Coimbra (Casa Alemã): Rua Alexandre Herculano 21B, Coimbra; f. 1962; Dir. Dr. Karl Heinz Delille.

Instituto de España en Lisboa (*Institute of Spain in Lisbon*): Actor Tasso 27, Lisbon; f. 1932; library of 5,000 vols.; Dir. Eduardo del Arco Alvárez.

Istituto Italiano di Cultura (*Italian Cultural Institute*): rua do Salitre 146, Lisbon 2; f. 1945; library of 12,000 vols.; Dir. Prof. Riccardo Averini; publ. *Estudos Italianos em Portugal*† (irregular).

Language and Literature

Associação Portuguesa de Escritores: Rua do Loreto 13-2°, Lisbon 2; f. 1973; protects the interests of Portuguese writers, promotes Portuguese literature abroad, supports cultural activities, conferences, debates, etc.; over 500 mems.; library of 7,500 vols.; Pres. Urbano Tavares Rodrigues; Vice-Pres. Casimiro de Brito.

Sociedade de Lingua Portuguesa (*Portuguese Language Society*): f. 1949; 8,000 mems.; Dir. Col. Hermes de Araújo Oliveira; publ. *A Bem de Lingua Portuguesa*.

Sociedade Martins Sarmento (*Martins Sarmento Society*): Rua de Paio Galvão, Guimarães; f. 1882; library of over 60,000 vols.; first edition (1572) *Os Lusiadas* by Camões; has absorbed the Municipal Library; 425 mems.; Dir. Gomes Alves; Librarian Dra. Elvira Jordão; publ. *Revista de Guimarães*.

Sociedade Portuguesa de Autores: Avda. Duque de Loulé 31, 1098 Lisbon Codex; f. 1925; copyright protection and authors' rights; cultural activities; 320 full, 3,000 assoc. mems.; library of 5,000 vols.; Pres. Dr. Luiz Francisco Rebello; publ. *Autores* (quarterly).

Medicine

Ordem dos Médicos (*Medical Association*): Avenida da Liberdade 65, 1°, 1298 Lisbon Codex; f. 1938; 16,200 mems.; Pres. Antonio Gentil Martins; publ. *Boletim da Ordem dos Médicos* (monthly).

Sociedade Anatómica Portuguesa (*Portuguese Anatomical Society*): Instituto de Histologia e Embriologia da Faculdade de Medicina do Porto, 4200 Oporto; f. 1930; 226 mems.; Pres. Prof. Dr. António Coimbra; Sec. Prof. Dr. Joaquim Pinto Machado.

Sociedade Anatómica Luso-Hispano-Americana (*Portuguese-Spanish-Latin American Anatomical Society*): Instituto de Anatomia Humana Normal, Faculdade de Medicina de Lisbon, Av. Egas Moniz, Lisbon 4; f. 1935; Pres. Prof. Dr. Armando dos Santos Ferreira (acting); publ. *Arquivo de Anatomia e Antropologia*†.

Sociedade Farmacêutica Lusitana (*Portuguese Pharmaceutical Society*): Rua Sociedade Farmacêutica 18, Lisbon; f. 1835; 3,600 mems.; library of 4,800 vols. on botany, medicine, natural history, pharmacy, etc.; famous collection of Portuguese pharmacopoeias; unique MS. *Historia Pharmaceutica das Plantas Exóticas* by Frei João de Jesus Maria, with permit to print from the Holy Office; Pres. Prof. Dr. Alberto Ralha; publs. *Revista Portuguesa de Farmacia*; affiliated to Fédération Internationale Pharmaceutique; mem. of Associação Portuguesa para o Progresso das Ciencias.

Natural Sciences

General

Associaçao Portuguesa para o Progresso das Ciências: Praça do Príncipe Real 14, Lisbon; publ. *Actas dos Congressos Luso-Espanhóis* (10 vols.).

Centro de Documentação Científica e Técnica (*Centre of Scientific and Technical Documentation*): Av. Prof. Gama Pinto 2, 1699 Lisbon Codex; f. 1936; national centre of scientific and technical information; 2,000 Portuguese and 2,000 foreign books; Dir. Carlos Pulido.

Biological Sciences

Sociedade Broteriana (*Botanical Society*): Instituto Botânico, Coimbra Univ., 3049 Coimbra; f. 1880; 300 mems.; Chair. Prof. Abílio Fernandes; publs. *Anuário*†, *Boletim*†, *Memórias*†.

Sociedade Portuguesa de Ciências Naturais (*Portuguese Natural Science Society*): Faculdade de Ciências, Rua da Escola Politécnica, 1294 Lisbon Codex; f. 1907; 720 mems., 1 hon.; library destroyed by fire 1978; publs. *Boletim*, *Naturalia*, *Natura*.

Mathematics

Instituto Nacional de Estatística (*National Statistical Institute*): Ministério do Plano e Coordenação Económica, Av. Dr. A. J. de Almeida, Lisbon; f. 1935; library of 12,000 vols., 1,197 periodicals; publs.† numerous statistical works, including *Estatísticas Demográficas*, *Anuário Estatístico: Continente e Ilhas Adjacentes*, *Boletim Mensal de Estatística*, *Comércio Externo* (annually), *Folha Mensal do Estado das Culturas e Previsão de Colheitas*, *Estatísticas Agrícolas*, *Estatísticas Industriais*, *Estatísticas Monetárias e Financeiras*, *Estatísticas da Educação*, etc.

Physical Sciences

Junta de Energia Nuclear (*Committee for Nuclear Energy*): R. de S. Pedro de Alcântara 79, Lisbon; f. 1954; Pres. Gen. Kaúlza Oliveira de Arriaga; library of 15,920 vols.; publs. *Technical Reports*†.

Sociedade Geológica de Portugal (*Geological Soc.*): Faculty of Science, Lisbon Univ.; f. 1940; 350 mems.; library destroyed by fire in 1978; Pres. Prof. Fernando Real; Secs. Prof. Rogério Rocha, Dra. Filomena Diniz; publ. *Boletim*†.

Sociedade Portuguesa de Química (*Portuguese Chemical Society*): Av. da Republica 37-4°, Lisbon; 700 mems.; Pres. Maria Alzira Almoster Ferreira; publ. *Revista Portuguesa de Química*† (quarterly), *Boletim*†.

Religion, Sociology and Anthropology

Sociedade Portuguesa de Antropologia e Etnologia (*Portuguese Anthropological and Ethnological Soc.*): Faculty of Science, The University of Oporto, Oporto; f. 1918; Pres. Prof. Joaquim Rodrigues dos Santos-Junior; Sec. Dr. Agostinho Isidoro; publ. *Trabalhos* (21 vols.).

Technology

Ordem dos Engenheiros (*Association of Engineers*): Av. de António Augusto de Aguiar 3-D, 1097 Lisbon Codex; f. 1936; Pres. Eng. João Avelino da Rocha Cunha Serra; Sec. Eng. Fernando Pessoa; publ. *Boletim* (monthly).

Sociedade de Estudos Técnicos SARL-SETEC: Rua Joaquin António de Aguiar 73, Lisbon 1; 10,000 mems.; Pres. Eng. Armando Lencastre; Sec. Eng. Jorge Ramiro; publ. *Boletim Informativo Nacional*† (monthly).

RESEARCH INSTITUTES

(*see* also under Universities)

General

Junta de Investigações Científicas (*Scientific Research Council*): Ministério da Educação e Ciência; f. 1936; publs. *Anais*, *Memórias*, *Estudos*, *Ensaios e Documentos*, *Garcia de Orta*, *Estudos de Ciências Políticas e Sociais*, *Bibliografia Científica*; geographical maps and plans of the former overseas provinces.

Departments:

Arquivo Histórico Ultramarino—AHU (*Overseas History Office*): Calçada da Boa-Hora 30, 1300 Lisbon; f. 1931.

Centro de Botânica—CB (*Botanical Centre*): Trav. Conde da Ribeira 7–9, 1300 Lisbon; f. 1948.

Centro de Documentação e Informação (*Documentation and Information Centre*): Rua Jau 47, Lisbon; f. 1957.

Centro de Documentação Técnico-Económica—CDTE (*Technological and Economic Documentation Centre*): Rua Jau 47, 1300 Lisbon; f. 1959.

Centro de Estudos de Antropobiologia—CEA (*Research Centre for Anthropobiology*): Avenida de Óscar Monteiro Torres 34, 1° Esq., 100 Lisbon 1; Archaeology and Pre-history Section: Trav. Conde da Ribeira 7–9, 1300 Lisbon; f. 1954.

Centro de Estudos de Antropologia Cultural—CEAC (*Cultural Anthropology Research Centre*): Av. Ilha da Madeira, a norte do Restelo, 1400 Lisbon; f. 1962.

Centro de Estudos de Cartografia Antiga—CECA (*Study Centre for Early Cartography*): Lisbon Section: Rua Jau 54, 1300 Lisbon; Coimbra Section: Instituto de Matemática, Universidade de Coimbra; f. 1961.

Centro de Estudos de Defesa Fitossanitária dos Produtos Ultramarinos—CEDFPU (*Study Centre for Pest Infestation Control of Tropical Stored Products*): Trav. Conde da Ribeira 7–9, 1300 Lisbon; f. 1955.

Centro de Estudos Históricos Ultramarinos—CEHU (*Overseas History Research Centre*): Rua da Junqueira 86, 1300 Lisbon; f. 1955.

Centro de Estudos de Pedologia Tropical—CEPT (*Tropical Pedology Research Centre*): Tapada da Ajuda, 1399 Lisbon; f. 1960.

Centro de Geografia do Ultramar—CGU (*Overseas Geography Centre*): Trav. Conde da Ribeira 7–9, 1300 Lisbon; f. 1946.

Centro de Investigação das Ferrugens do Cafeeiro—CIFC (*Coffee Rust Research Centre*): Estação Agronómica Nacional, 2780 Oeiras; f. 1955.

Centro de Zoologia—CZ (*Zoological Centre*): Rua da Junqueira 14, 1300 Lisbon; f. 1948.

Jardim e Museu Agrícola do Ultramar—JMAU (*Overseas Botanical Garden*): Calçada do Galvão, 1300 Lisbon; f. 1906.

Laboratório de Estudos Petrológicos e Paleontológicos do Ultramar—LEPPU (*Overseas Petrological and Paleontological Research Laboratory*): Alameda D. Afonso Henriques 41, 1° Dt°., 1000 Lisbon; f. 1958.

Laboratório de Histologia e Tecnologia de Madeiras—LHTM (*Laboratory for Wood Anatomy and Technology*): Instituto Superior de Agronomia, Calçada do Tapada, 1300 Lisbon; f. 1948.

Laboratório de Técnicas Físico-Químicas Aplicadas à Mineralogia e Petrologia—LTF-QMP (*Laboratory of Physical and Chemical Techniques applied to Miner-*

alogy and Petrology): Al. Afonso Henriques 41, 4°, Dt°, 1000 Lisbon; f. 1957.

Missão de Estudos Agronómicos do Ultramar—MEAU (*Portuguese Overseas Organization for Agricultural Research*): Sitio do Carrascal, Calçada da Tapada, 1300 Lisbon; f. 1960.

Missão Geográfica de Angola—MGA (*Angola Geographical Mission*): Rua da Junqueira 534, 1300 Lisbon; f. 1941.

Missão Geográfica de Moçambique—MGM (*Mozambique Geographical Mission*): Praça João do Rio 2, 5°., 1000 Lisbon; f. 1932.

Missão Geográfica de Timor—MGT (*Timor Geographical Mission*): Praça João do Rio 2, 5°, Lisbon; f. 1937.

Missão de Recolha e Processamento de Dados sobre a Investigação Científica e Tecnológica—MRPDICT (*Mission for Collecting and Processing Data on Scientific and Technological Research*): Rua João de Barros 27, 1300 Lisbon; f. 1967.

Agriculture and Veterinary Science

Centro de Investigações Florestais (*Forestry Research Centre*): Av. Joao Crisóstomo 28, Lisbon; f. 1919; research department of the Direcção-Geral dos Serviços Florestais e Aqüícolas; 5 research departments; library of 14,000 vols.; Dir.-Gen. Gabriel Gonçalves; publs. *Publicações Florestais, Estudos e Informação.*

Estação Agronómica Nacional (*National Agronomical Research Station*): Oeiras; f. 1937; comprises Departments of Systematic Botany and Plant Sociology, Plant Breeding, Plant Physiology, Pedology, Zoning, Genetics, Phytopathology, Microbiology, Entomology, Pomology, Chemistry, Agricultural Statistics; library of 129,215 vols.; 170 research staff; Dir. Dr. J. V. Carvalho Cardoso; Librarian Quitéria Pinto da Silva; publs. *De Flora Lusitana Comentarii*†, *Agronomia Lusitana*†, *Index Seminum*†.

Language and Literature

Instituto de Linguistica (*Institute of Linguistics*): Av. 5 de Outubro, 85, 5/6, Lisbon 1; f. 1932; library of 23,000 vols.; Pres. Dr. L. F. Lindley Cintra; publs. *Boletim de Filologia, Publicações do C.E.F.* (new series).

Instituto Português da Sociedade Cientifica de Goerres (*Portuguese Institute of the Goerres Research Society*) Rua Visconde de Seabra 2-3, 1700 Lisbon; f. 1962; research in the language and literature of the 16th and 17th centuries; library of 8,000 vols.; Dirs. Prof. Dr. Hans Flasche, Prof. Dr. José Bacelar e Oliveira; Sec. Dr. Helga Bauer; publ. *Portugiesische Forschungen.*

Medicine

Instituto "António Aurélio da Costa Ferreira" (*Institute of Medical Orthopedagogics, Psychology and Special Education*): Geral 15, Travessa das Terras de Sant' Ana 15, Lisbon 2; f. 1941; 15 mems.; library of 5,500 vols.; Dir. Dr. Maria Irene Leite da Costa; publs. *A Criança Portuguesa* (annually), *Monografias* (irregularly).

Instituto de Malariologia (*Malaria Institute*): Aguas de Moura; f. 1938; library of 3,400 vols.; Dir. (vacant).

Instituto Pasteur de Lisboa: Lt. 9 Avda. Mar. Gomes Costa, Lisbon 6.

Laboratório de Isótopos Abílio Lopes do Rego, do Instituto Português de Oncologia de Francisco Gentil (*Isotopes Laboratory of the Francisco Gentil Portuguese Institute of Oncology*): Palhavã, Lisbon; f. 1953, reorganized 1966; research centre on nuclear medicine of the Instituto de Alta Cultura; Dir. Prof. António Manuel Baptista.

Natural Sciences

General

Instituto de Investigação Cientifica "Bento da Rocha Cabral" (*Institute of Scientific Research*): Calçada de Bento da Rocha Cabral 14; f. 1922; biochemical research, pathology, bacteriology, animal and plant histology, tissue culture and physiology; Dir. J. Mirabeau Cruz; publs. *Travaux de Laboratoire, Actualidades Biológicas, Relatórios.*

Sociedade de Estudos Açoreanos "Afonso Chaves" (*Society for Research on the Azores*): Ponta Delgada, The Azores; f. 1932; 20 Fellows, 100 mems.; main interests of the Society are ethnography, natural history and geology; Pres. Col. J. Agostinho, o.b.e.; Sec. Dr. A. Cortes-Rodrigues; publ. *Açoreana* (annually).

Biological Sciences

Instituto Biológico Português: S.R.F., 20-F Av. Consuela Fernando Sousa, Lisbon 1.

Instituto de Biologia Marítima (*Marine Biological Institute*): Aquario Vasco da Gama, Dafundo, Lisbon; f. 1919; name changed 1951; a centre for the study of aquaculture, natural resources, stock assessment and marine pollution; 12 mems.; library of 1,000 vols. and 2,000 periodical publs.; Dir. Dr. Rui Monteiro; publs. *Notas e Estudos do Instituto de Biologia Marítima*†, *Boletim Informativo do Instituto de Biologia Marítima*†, *Relatorios de Actividades do Instituto de Biologia Marítima*†.

Museu, Laboratório e Jardim Botânico (*Museum, Laboratory and Botanical Gardens*): Rua da Escola Politécnica, 1294 Lisbon Codex; f. 1878; attached to Faculty of Science, University of Lisbon; systematics (fungi, musci, phanerogamy); library of 16,748 vols.; Dir. Prof. J. Pinto-Lopes; publs. *Portugaliae Acta Biologica Series A and B*†, *Delectus Sporarum et Seminum*†, *Revista de Biologia*†.

Physical Sciences

Instituto Nacional de Meteorologia e Geofisica (*National Institute of Meteorology and Geophysics*): Rua C do Aeroporto, 1700 Lisbon; f. 1946; library of 25,000 vols.; Dir. Prof. Dr. Luís Mendes Victor; publs. *Anuário Climatológico de Portugal, Anuário Sismológico de Portugal* (annually), *Boletim Meteorológico para a Agricultura, Bulletin séismique des Iles Açores* (three monthly), *Revista do Instituto Nacional de Meteorologia e Geofisica* (quarterly), *Resumos Meteorológicos para a Aeronáutica, Boletim Actinométrico de Portugal, Boletim Geoeléctrico, Boletim Mensal das Observações Meteorológicas no Arquipélago da Madeira, Boletim Geomagnético Preliminar* (monthly), *Boletim Informativo* (monthly), *Boletim Meteorológico* (daily).

Observatório Astronómico da Universidade de Coimbra (*Coimbra Univ. Astronomical Observatory*): Santa Clara, Apdo. 147, 3002 Coimbra; f. 1772; 22 mems.; library of 15,000 vols.; Dir. Dr. J. M. Reis Abreu; publs. *Anais do Observatório*† (annual), *Efemérides Astronómicas*† (annual), *Comunicações*†, *Seminários de Astronomia*†.

Observatório Astronómico da Faculdade de Ciências de Lisboa (*Astronomical Observatory of Faculty of Sciences*): Cidade Universitaria, Lisbon; f. 1875 by Escola Politécnica; Repsold meridian, etc.; Dir. Prof. Dr. Antonio Gião.

Observatório Astronómico de Lisboa (*Lisbon Astronomical Observatory*): Tapada da Ajuda; f. 1861; astrometry, meridian astronomy, time and latitude; Dir. Ezequiel Cabrita; publs. *Boletim*†, *Dados Astronómicos*†.

Serviços Geológicos de Portugal (*Portuguese Geological Survey*): Rua da Academia das Ciências 19, 2°, Lisbon-2; f. 1857; library of 74,577 vols.; Dir. Delfim de Carvalho; publs. *Comunicações*†, *Memórias*†, *Noticias*†, geological maps.

Religion, Sociology and Anthropology

Instituto de Antropologia (*Anthropological Institute*): Bairro Sousa Pinto, 3000 Coimbra; f. 1885; library of 17,000 vols.; publs. *Contribuições para o Estudo da Antropologia Portuguesa, Questões de Método.*

Technology

Direcção-Geral de Geologia e Minas (*Office of Mines and Geology*): Ministério da Industria e Energia, Rua António Enes, 7, 1097 Lisbon; f. 1918; mines, quarries, mineral waters, geology, archaeology; Dir. Dr. Alcides Rodrigues Pereira; publs. *Boletim de Minas*† (quarterly), *Arquivos*†, *Comunicações dos Serviços Geológicos de Portugal*†, *Memórias dos Serviços Geológicos de Portugal*†, *Estudos, Notas e Trabalhos do Serviço de Fomento Mineiro*† (quarterly), maps.

Estação Aqüicola (*Water Research Station*): Villa do Conde; f. 1886; Dir. Joaquim Antonio Soares Soeiro.

Instituto Hidrográfico (*Hydrographic Institute*): Rua das Trinas 49, Lisbon; hydrographic surveys, nautical charts, sailing directions, tide tables, physical oceanography, magnetic compass adjustments, laboratory; library of 10,000 vols.; Dir.-Gen. Alm. Portugal Ribeiro.

Laboratório Nacional de Engenharia Civil, Ministério das Obras Públicas (*National Civil Engineering Laboratory, Ministry of Public Works*): Av. do Brasil, Lisbon 5; f. 1947; library of 78,000 vols.; Dir. J. Ferry Borges; publs. *Memórias* (technical papers), *Especificações* (standards), etc.

Serviço de Fomento Mineiro: Rua da Ameira, S. Mamede de Infesta, Oporto; f. 1939; mining prospecting and research; 400 members; library of 50,000 vols.; Dir. Eng. Norberto Afonso Múrias de Queiros; publs. *Bibliografia Mineira de Portugal, Estudos*†, *Notas e Trabalhos, Relatórios.*

LIBRARIES AND ARCHIVES

Lisbon

Arquivo Nacional da Torre do Tombo (*National Archives of Torre do Tombo*): Palácio de S. Bento; f. 1352-1388; collection dates from ninth century; library of 13,217 vols. and 20,000 m. shelves of MSS.; Dir. Dr. José Pereira da Costa; publ. *Inventários das Portarias do Reino e das Moradias da Casa Real.*

Arquivo Histórico Militar (*Military Historical Archives*): 1196 Lisbon Codex; f. 1921; Dir. Coronel Nuno Bessa de Almeida Frazão; publ. *Boletim*; associated with:

- **Comissão de História Militar** (*Military History Commission*): Largo dos Caminhos de Ferro-Lisbon 2; f. 1923; 12 mems.; publs. biographical and historical works.
- **Museu Militar** (*Military Museum*): *see* Museums.

Arquivo Histórico do Ministério das Finanças (*Historical Archives of Ministry of Finance*): Rua de Santa Marta 61.

Biblioteca Central de Marinha (*Naval Library*): Rua do Arsenal, Ministério da Marinha, 1188 Lisbon Codex; f. 1835; valuable editions; 25,500 vols.; Dir. C/Alm. Domingos Diogo Afonso.

Biblioteca da Academia das Ciências de Lisboa (*Library of the Academy of Sciences*): Rua da Academia das Ciências 19, Lisbon 2; f. 1779; 400,000 vols., 3,000 MSS., 63 incunabula.

Biblioteca da Ajuda (*Ajuda Library*): Palácio da Ajuda, Lisbon 3; f. 1756; 100,000 vols., 30,000 MSS., 5,000 music MSS.; 213 incunabula; Dir. Dr. Mariana Amélia Machado Santos.

Biblioteca do Exército (*Army Library*): Rua Artilharia 1, Lisbon 2; f. 1837; 100,000 vols.; Dir. Col. Francisco Dias Costa.

Biblioteca e Arquivo da Assembléia Nacional (*Library of the National Assembly*): f. 1836; 37,000 vols.; Dir. Costa Brochada; publs. *Diário das Sessões, Anais da Assembléia Nacional, Sinopse da Assembléia Nacional.*

Biblioteca e Arquivo Histórico do Ministerio da Habitação e Obras Públicas (*Library and Historical Archives of the Ministry of Housing and Public Works*): Praça do Comércio, Ala Norte, 1100 Lisbon; f. 1852; 7,000 vols., documents dating from the 16th century; 200,000 textual documents on industry, agriculture, forestry, trade, public works, etc.; Dir. Dr. Mário Alberto Nunes Costa.

Biblioteca Geral da Fundação Gulbenkian: Avenida de Berna; 92,000 vols.

Biblioteca Municipal Central (*Central Municipal Library*): Palácio Galveias, Largo do Campo Pequeno; f. 1931; 128,110 vols.; Dir. Jaime Lopes Dias.

Biblioteca, Museu e Arquivo dos Hospitais Civis de Lisboa (*Library, Museum and Archives of Lisbon Civic Hospitals*): Rua José António Serrano; f. 1937; 18,533 vols.; 896 periodicals; Dir. Octávio de Brito Pinto; publ. *Boletim Clínico dos Hospitais Civis de Lisboa.*

Biblioteca Nacional (*National Library*): Campo Grande 83, 1751 Lisbon Codex; f. 1796; 1,000,000 vols., 12,000 MSS.; Dir. Dra. Maria Manuela Cruzeiro; publs. *Boletim de Bibliografia Portuguesa, Repertorio das Publicações Periodicas Portuguesas, Folha Informativa do Gabinete de Biblioteconomia.*

Biblioteca Popular de Lisboa: Rua Ivens 35, and Rua de Academia das Ciências 19; f. 1918; 97,774 vols., 835 periodicals; Librarian Durval Pires de Lima; Principal Officers Carlos Alberto de Mesquita, Maria Teresa Pires de Lima, José Paulo Ribeiro.

British Council Libraries: Rua Luis Fernandes 3, Lisbon 2; f. 1938; 21,072 vols., 139 periodicals; Librarian Miss H. K. Gilmour, B.A.; British Institute, Rua A. Herculano 34, Coimbra; 5,610 vols., 49 periodicals; Librarian Dr. A. de Lima Gouveia; library also at Associação Luso-Britanica (*q.v.*).

Repartição do Arquivo e Biblioteca do Ministério dos Negócios Estrangeiros (*Archives and Library of Ministry of Foreign Affairs*): Palácio das Necessidades; f. 1736; 25,625 vols.; Dir. Alvaro Ferrand de Almeida Fernandes.

Bragança

Arquivo Distrital, Biblioteca e Museu Regional Abade de Baçal (*District Archives, Library and Museum of Baçal Abbey*).

Coimbra

Arquivo e Museu de Arte da Universidade de Coimbra (*Archives and Art Museum of Coimbra Univ.*): The University; f. Archives 1290, Museum 1911; religious paintings; Dir. Dr. Mário Brandão.

Biblioteca Municipal (*Municipal Library*): f. 1922; 84,101 vols.; Dir. Pinto Loureiro; Librarian J. Branquinho de Carvalho; publ. *Arquivo Coimbrão.*

Universidade de Coimbra: Bibliotecas: Coimbra.

- Central Library: f. 1716; 1,000,000 vols.; Dir. Dr. Luís de Albuquerque.
- Faculty of Letters: f. 1911; 191,000 vols.; Librarian M. Armanda Almeida e Sousa.

Faculty of Medicine: f. 1853; 33,000 vols.; Librarian José António Matos Godinho.

Faculty of Law: f. 1911; 180,000 vols.; Librarian Mário Faria.

Faculty of Pharmacy: f. 1904; 13,000 vols.; Librarian Lucília Paiva.

Faculty of Science and Technology: f. 1911; 220,000 vols.; Librarian Júlia Motta de Sousa.

Évora

Biblioteca Pública e Arquivo Distrital de Évora (*Public Library and District Archives*): f. 1811; 408,472 vols.; Dir. António Leandro Alves.

Leiria

Biblioteca Erudita e Arquivo Distrital (*Public Library and District Archives*): Largo da Caixa Geral de Depósitos; f. 1916; library 60,000 vols.; archives approx. 25,000; Dir. Gentil Ferreira e Sousa.

Madeira

Arquivo Distrital do Funchal (*Funchal District Archives*): Palácio de São Pedro, Rua da Mouraria; f. 1931; 300,000 MSS.; specialized history library of 8,100 vols.; Dir. Dr António Aragão Mendes Correia; publ. *Arquivo Histórico da Madeira.*

Biblioteca Municipal do Funchal (*Municipal Library*) Palácio de São Pedro, Rua da Mouraria; f. 1838; 35,318 vols.; Librarian Rui de Ornelas Gonçalves.

Mafra

Biblioteca do Palácio Nacional de Mafra (*Mafra National Palace Library*): Terreiro de D. João V.; f. 18th century; 36,000 vols.; notable collection of rare books; Dir. Guilherme José Ferreira de Assunção.

Oporto

Arquivo Distrital do Porto (*District Archives*): Praça da República 38; f. 1931; 90,000 vols.; Dir. Artur de Magalhães Basto.

Biblioteca Pública Municipal do Porto (*Municipal Library*): Jardim de São Lázaro, 4099 Porto Codex; f. 1833; 1,325,000 vols., 2,500 MSS., 273 incunabula; Dir. Dra. Maria Fernanda de Brito; publ. *Bibliotheca Portucalensis.*

Santarem

Biblioteca Municipal Camões (*Camões Municipal Library*): f. 1880; 45,323 vols., 5,500 pamphlets; Librarian Bertino Coelho Martins.

Tôrres Novas

Biblioteca Gustavo Pinto Lopes: f. 1937; 31,200 vols.; Dir. Dr. João Robalo Pombo.

Vila Real

Biblioteca Pública (*Public Library*): f. 1834; 11,000 vols.; Dir. Agostinho Celestino da Silva.

Vizeu

Arquivo Distrital (*District Archives*): Largo Alves Martins; f. 1932; 400,000 documents; Dir. Dr. Fernando Russell Cordez.

The Azores

Biblioteca Municipal da Horta (*Town Library*): Rua D. Pedro IV 26, Horta; f. 1886; 10,000 vols.; Librarian José R. Morais Guerra.

Biblioteca Pública de Ponta Delgada (*Public Library*): f. 1845; 125,000 vols.; Dir. João de Suñas.

Biblioteca Pública e Arquivo Distrital de Angra do Heroismo (*Public Library and District Archives*): Palácio Bettencourt, Rua Conselheiro Jacinto Candido, Angra do Heroísmo; f. 1948; 60,000 vols.; 1,000,000 MSS.; Dir. Dr. Manuel C. Baptista de Lima; publ. *Boletim da Biblioteca Pública, Arquivo Distrital de Angra do Heroismo.*

MUSEUMS

Lisbon

Museu Etnográfico da Sociedade de Geografia de Lisboa (*Ethnographical Museum*): Rua das Portas de Santo Antão 100, 1100 Lisbon; f. 1875; native arts, arms, clothing, musical instruments, statues of navigators and historians, relics of voyages of discovery, scientific instruments; Dir. Prof. Dr. António de Almeida.

Museu Nacional de Arqueologia e Etnologia (Museu Etnológico Dr. Leite de Vasconcelos) (*National Museum of Archaeology and Ethnology*): Praça do Império, 1400 Lisbon; f. 1893; attached to Secretaria de Estado da Cultura; Dir. Dr. Justino M. Almeida; publ. *O Arquéologo Português*†.

Museu Nacional de Arte Antiga (*National Museum of Ancient Art*): Rua das Janelas Verdes; f. 1884; Portuguese and foreign plastic and ornamental art from the 12th to the 19th centuries; library of 16,500 vols.; Dir. Dra. Maria Alice Beaumont; publ. *Boletim do Museu Nacional de Arte Antiga.*

Museu Nacional de Arte Contemporânea (*National Museum of Contemporary Art*): Rua Serpa Pinto; f. 1911; contemporary painting and sculpture; Dir. Maria de Lourdes Bártholo.

Museu Nacional de História Natural (*National Museum of Natural History*): Faculdade de Ciências, Rua de Escola Politécnica; f. 1859; library of 27,000 vols.; Dirs. Prof. C. Torre d'Assunçao (Mineralogy and Geology), Prof. C. N. Tavares (Botany), Prof. G. F. Sacarrão (Zoology and Anthropology); publs. *Arquivos do Museu Bocage, Portugaliae Acta Biologica, Boletim.*

Museu Nacional dos Côches (*National Coach Museum*): Praça de Afonso Albuquerque, Belém; f. 1905 by Queen Amélia in the Riding School of the Royal Palace; National Museum 1908, enlarged 1944; comprehensive collection of carriages and coaches many by famous craftsmen, dating from 1619 and including those of the Portuguese ex-Royal Family; sedan chairs, harness and equipment, royal liveries, etc., silver trumpets; section of portraits, paintings and engravings; Dir. Dra. Maria Madalena de Cagigal e Silva; publs. catalogues.

Museu Arqueológico (*Archaeological Museum*): Largo do Carmo; f. 1866; directed by Associação dos Arqueólogos Portugueses; prehistoric and Stone Age collections from tumuli; Hispano-Arabic, Portuguese and Dutch tiles; coats of armour; Curator Dr. Cunha Serrão.

Museu Calouste Gulbenkian: Avenida de Berna; f. 1969; Gulbenkian art collection covering the period 2800 B.C. to 20th century; antique classical and oriental art, Egyptian, Assyrian, Greek, Roman, Islamic and Far Eastern art; European painting, sculpture, illuminated MSS, tapestries and fabrics, furniture, gold and silver, jewellery, glass, medals; Dir. Dr. Maria Teresa Gomes Ferreira.

Museu de Arte Popular (*Museum of Popular Art*): Avda.

Brasília, Belém; f. 1948; ethnology; Curator MARIA HELENA MEIRA DIAS COIMBRA.

Museu de São Roque: Largo Trinidade Coelho; f. 1905; collections of religious paintings, Church vessels in precious metals, embroidered vestments by Italian artists of the 18th century; works from the chapel of St. John the Baptist in the adjacent 16th century Church of St. Roque; Curator Dr. MARIA J. MADEIRA RODRIQUES.

Museu da Cidade (*City Museum*): Palácio Pimenta, Campo Grande 245; f. 1942; history of development of Lisbon shown by archaeological, historical, artistic and ethnological documents and exhibits; Dir. IRISALVA MOITA.

Museu-Escola de Artes Decorativas (*Museum School of Decorative Arts*): Largo das Portas do Sol 2; f. 1953; includes Ricardo do Espírito Santo Silva's private collection of Portuguese furniture, silver, china, paintings, rugs, tapestries etc., and 23 workshops in which craftsmen are trained in all aspects of interior arts including bookbinding, interior decorating, carpet and furniture restoration.

Museu e Laboratório Mineralógico e Geológico (*Museum and Laboratory of Mineralogy and Geology*): Faculdade de Ciências, Rua da Escola Politécnica, Lisbon; f. 1837; attached to the Universidade de Lisboa; geology, petrology, mineralogy, palaeontology and museology; Curators Dr. FILOMENA DINIZ, Dr. A. N. JOAQUIM; publ. *Boletim*†.

Museu e Laboratório Zoológico e Antropológico (Museu Bocage) (*Zoological and Anthropological Museum and Laboratory*): Rua da Escola Politécnica, Lisbon 2; attached to the Universidade de Lisboa; Dir. (vacant).

Museu Instrumental da Escola Superior de Música de Lisboa (*Instruments Museum*): Palacio Pimenta, Campo Grande; f. 1941; European string, wind, key and percussion instruments of the 16th to 19th centuries, also instruments from Portugal and a collection of instruments from former Portuguese colonies.

Museu Militar (*Military Museum*): Largo do Museu de Artilharia; f. 1851; exhibits of Portuguese military history, paintings from the 18th to 20th centuries; Dir. Brig. ALBERTO ARÁNJOE SILVA.

Museu Numismático Português (*Portuguese Numismatic Museum*): Imprensa Nacional-Casa da Moeda, Av. Dr. A. J. de Almeida; f. 1933; important collections of Portuguese and Colonial, Iberian, Roman and Visigothic coins; Curator Dr. CARLOS MANUEL ALMEIDA DO AMARAL.

Museu Rafael Bordalo Pinheiro: Campo Grande 382; f. 1916 as Museu Biográfico; originals and reproductions of famous caricatures, ceramics, satirical documents; Dir. IRISALVA MOITA.

Alenquer

Museu "Hipolito Cabaço" (*Municipal Museum*): Cámara Municipal; f. 1945; archaeological, historical, ethnographical, natural history, religious art; 17,000 exhibits; Dir. JOÃO JOSÉ FERNANDES GOMES; publ. *Boletim Informativo*† (monthly).

Bragança

Museu Regional Abade de Baçal (*Baçal Abbey Museum*): Dir. Dr. MARIA DE LOURDES BARTHOLO.

Cascais

Museu-Biblioteca "Conde de Castro Guimarães" (*Museum and Library*): f. 1930; 23,940 vols.; *Cronica* about Afonso Henriques, 16th-century illuminated *Codex* on parchment, 17th-century Indo-Portuguese counting frames, prehistoric ceramics; furniture, pictures, silverware; Curator J. A. SÁ PESSOA; publ. *Boletim*.

Castelo Branco

Museu de Francisco Tavares Proença Júnior (*Regional Museum*): f. 1910; archaeological, ethnographical, numismatics, art gallery (16th-century Portuguese school), tapestries; important collections of objects found in tombs at Beira Baixa; Bronze-Age weapons and ornaments from a complete workshop found at Castelo Novo; illustrations of rupestral art in the Tagus valley; 1,500 coins; four aquatints by Turner; four tapestries from Brussels dating from late 16th century; Dir. Dr. ANTÓNIO FORTE SALVADO.

Coimbra

Museu de História Natural (*Natural History Museum*): Coimbra University; f. 1772; Dept. of Mineralogy and Geology: Dir. Dr. JOÃO M. COTELO NEIVA; Dept. of Botany: Dir. Dr. ABILIO FERNANDES; Dept. of Zoology: Dir. Dr. ARSELIO PATO DE CARVALHO.

Museu e Laboratorio Zoológico de Coimbra (*Zoological Museum and Laboratory*): Coimbra Univ., Largo do Marquès de Pombal; f. 1772; library of 16,000 vols.; valuable collections of Portuguese, European and overseas fauna, studies in taxonomy, biochemical systematics, ecology, physiological genetics, cell physiology, molecular biology and biochemistry; Dir. Dr. ARSELIO PATO DE CARVALHO; publ. *Ciência Biologica*†.

Museu Nacional de "Machado de Castro" (*Machado de Castro Museum*): Largo Dr. José Rodrigues, 3000 Coimbra; f. 1911; established in the old Bishop's Palace built over Roman galleries, renewed in the 16th century and recently adapted; antiquities, sculpture, paintings, silver-work, priests' vestments, tapestries, ceramics, glass, furniture; Dir. MATILDE PESSOA DE FIGUEIREDO.

Évora

Museu de Évora: Largo do Conde de Vila Flor; f. 1915; paintings: large collections of 16th-century Flemish and Portuguese works; 17th-century works; local prehistoric tools and Roman art and archaeology; sculpture from middle ages to the 19th century; 18th-century Portuguese furniture and silver; Dir. MARIA ALICE L. TAVARES CHICÓ.

Faro

Museu Arqueológico Infante D. Henrique (*Infante D. Henrique Archaeological Museum*): Convento de N.S. da Assuncão, Praça Afonso III; f. 1894; historical, archaeological, ethnographical; Dir. Prof. PINHEIRO E ROSA.

Museu Maritimo "Almirante Ramalho Ortigão" (*Maritime Museum*): Capitania do Porto de Faro; f. 1931; formerly Museu Industrial Marítimo; f. 1889; regional methods of fishing, instruments, models of ships and equipment, paintings of marine fauna, sailors' handicrafts; Curator Com. CARLOS PACHECO PINTO.

Museu S. Antonio (*Museum of St. Anthony*): Ermida de Santo António do Alto; f. 1933; collections relating to the cult of St. Anthony of Lisbon; Founder Dr. MARIO LYSTER FRANCO; Dir. Prof. PINHEIRO E ROSA.

Figueira da Foz

Museu Municipal "Dr. Santos Rocha" (*Municipal Museum*): Rua Fernandes Tomás; f. 1894, reopened 1945; general, archaeology, ethnology and anthropology; Man. FRANCISCO ROSADO GUERRA.

Guimarães

Museu de Martins Sarmento (*Martins Sarmento Museum*): Rua de Paio Galvão; f. 1885; archaeological; numerous exhibits relating to Portuguese Celtic, Roman and Visigothic periods; Dir. GOMES ALVES.

Museu de Alberto Sampaio: Rua Alfredo Guimarães; f. 1928; architecture, paintings, sculpture (painted wood), ceramics, enamels, antiques (examples of early Christian art dating from the 8th century), embroidery; Dir. MANUEL RODRIGUES GONÇALVES.

Lamego

Museu de Lamego: f. 1917; important collection of 16th-century Brussels tapestries, Portuguese painting of 16th and 18th centuries, sculpture, religious ornaments; Dir. Dr. ABEL MONTENEGRO FLÓRIDO.

Madeira

Museu de Arte Sacra (*Museum of Sacred Art*): Rua do Bispo 21; diocesan museum.

Museu da Quinta das Cruzes: decorative arts; Dir. A. M. ABREU SOUSA.

Museu Municipal do Funchal (*Funchal Municipal Museum*): Funchal; f. 1929; Natural History Museum and Marine Aquarium; large collection of marine animals, especially deep-sea fish and crustaceans; library on marine biology; Curator G. E. MAUL; publs. *Boletim*†, *Bocagiana*†.

Oporto

Museu Nacional de Soares dos Reis (*National Museum*): Palacio dos Carrancas, Rua D. Manuel II; f. 1833; paintings, sculpture, jewellery, antiques, pottery, glass; Dir. Dr. MARIA EMÍLIA AMARAL TEIXEIRA.

Museu de Etnografia e História do Porto: Palacio de S. João Novo, 4000 Porto; ethnography, archaeology and history; Dir. Arq. FERNANDO LANHAS.

Tôrres Novas

Museu Carlos Reis: f. 1937; archaeological, historical, fine arts, ethnographical, religious art, numismatics; Dir. Dr. JOÃO ROBALO POMBO.

Vila Viçosa

Museu-Biblioteca da Casa de Bragança (*Museum and Library of House of Braganza*): Paço Ducal; f. 1933; rare 16th-century printed books, Italian 16th-century majolica, and 17th- and 18th-century musical archives; 76,000 vols.; Curator MARIA ALICE CHICÓ; Librarian MANUEL PESTANA.

Viseu

Museu de "Grão Vasco" (*National Museum*): Paco dos Tres Escalões; f. 1913; furniture, tapestry, plate, ceramics and glassware, Flemish and Portuguese paintings; Dir. Dr. F. RUSSELL CORTÊZ; publ. *Viriatis*† (annually).

The Azores

Museu de Angra do Heroismo (*Regional Museum*): Edifício de São Francisco, 9700 Angra do Heroismo; f. 1949; paintings, ceramics, furniture, sculpture, ethnography, arms, guns, carriages, etc.; Dir. Dr. BAPTISTA DE LIMA; Curator Dr. MENDES PEREIRA.

UNIVERSITIES

INSTITUTO UNIVERSITÁRIO DOS AÇORES

RUA DA MÃE DE DEUS,
9502 PONTA DELGADA
(AÇORES) CODEX

Telephone: 26318, 26319.

Founded 1976.

Rector: Prof. Dr. JOSÉ ENES.
Director of Academic Services: Dr. RICARDO FERREIRA.
Director of Documentation Services: Dra. MARIA DA GRAÇA ALMEIDA LIMA.

Library of 30,387 vols.

Number of teachers: 100.
Number of students: 438.

DIRECTORS:

Department of Agriculture: Dr. YOUNG DO AMARAL.
Department of Ecology: Prof. Dr. VASCO GARCIA.
Department of Economics and Business: Dr. FERNANDO PIEDADE.
Department of Education: Dr. IVO NUNES.
Department of Earth Sciences: Prof. Dr. AVILA MARTINS.
Department of History and Social Sciences: Dr. ARTHUR TEODORO DE MATOS.
Department of Literature and Modern Languages: Dr. ANTÓNIO MACHADO PIRES.
Department of Oceanography and Fisheries: Prof. Dr. FREDERICO MACHADO.

UNIVERSIDADE DE AVEIRO

3800 AVEIRO

Telephone: 28391/2.

Founded 1973.

State control; Academic year: September to July.

Rector: Prof. Dr. JOSÉ ERNESTO DE MESQUITA RODRIGUES.
Chief Administrative Officer: Eng. RUI HENRIQUES GALIANO BARATA PINTO.
Librarian: Dr. ADELINO AMÁLIO DE ALMEIDA CALADO.

Number of teachers: 177.
Number of students: 915.

Publications: *Revista*, *Boletim Informativo* (irregular), *Documentação corrente—boletim bibliográfico* (monthly), *Documentação corrente—Suplemento de índices de periódicos* (fortnightly), *Lista de Aquisições* (weekly).

UNIVERSIDADE DE COIMBRA*

PAÇO DAS ESCOLAS,
COIMBRA

Telephone: 22812, 26088.

Telegraphic Address: Universidade de Coimbra.

Founded 1290 (in Lisbon).

State control; Language of instruction: Prtouguese; Academic year: October to July.

Rector: Dr. ANTÓNIO DE ARRUDA FERRER CORREIA.

Library: *see* Libraries.

Number of teachers: 814, including 55 professors.

Number of students: 11,895.

Publications: *Revista da Universidade*†, *Anuário da Universidade*†, *Biblos*†, *Revista Portuguesa de História*†, *Brasilia*†, *Humanitas*†, *Revista Portuguesa de Filologia*†, *Acta Universitatis Conimbrigensis*†, *Boletim da Faculdade de Direito*†, *Revista de História Literária de Portugal*, *Boletim do Centro de Estudos Geográficos*, *Conimbriga*, *Boletim do Laboratório de Fonética Experimental*, *Revista Portuguesa de Pedagogia*, *Boletim de Ciências-Economicas*.

DEANS:

Faculty of Arts: Dra. ANDREA JEANNE FRANÇOISE CRABBÉ ROCHA.
Faculty of Law: Dr. EDUARDO HENRIQUES DA SILVA CORREIA.
Faculty of Medicine: Dr. FERNANDO ALBERTO SERRA DE OLIVEIRA.
Faculty of Science: Dr. LUÍS GUILHERME MENDONÇA DE ALBUQUERQUE.
Faculty of Pharmacy: Dr. ANTÓNIO PINHO DE BROJO.
Faculty of Economics: Dr. JOSÉ VEIGA MEIRA TORRES.

ATTACHED INSTITUTES:

Department of Psychology and Educational Science: Dean Dr. JOAQUIM FERREIRA GOMES.

Instituto Astronómico (*Astronomic Institute*): f. 1772; library of 20,000 vols.; publs. *Efemeridas Astronómicas* (annually), *Anais de Observatório Astronómico—fenómenos solares, Communicações do Observatório Astronómico da Universidade de Coimbra.*

Instituto Botânico "Dr. Júlio Henriques" (*Botanical Institute*): f. 1772; library of 91,338 vols.; Dir. Prof. ABÍLIO FERNANDES; publs. *Index Seminum, Boletim, Memórias* and *Anuário* of Sociedade Broteriana.

Instituto de Climatologia e Hidrologia (*Climatological and Hydrological Institute*): f. 1930; Pres. Dr. ANTÓNIO DE ARRUDA FERRER CORREIA; publ. *Publicações do Instituto de Climatologia e Hidrologia.*

Instituto Geofísico (*Geophysical Institute*): f. 1864; library of 1,590,000 vols.; meteorological, magnetic and seismological observatory; Dir. Prof. F. PINTO COELHO; publs. *Observações Meteorológicas, Magnéticas e Sismológicas* (annually).

* No reply received to our questionnaire this year.

INSTITUTO UNIVERSITÁRIO DE ÉVORA

LARGO DOS COLEGIAIS 2,
APARTADO 94,
7001 ÉVORA CODEX
Telephone: (069) 25572/3/4.
Telex: 18 771.
Founded 1973.

State control; Language of instruction: Portuguese; Academic year: September to September, including summer courses.

Rector: ÁRIO LOBO AZEVEDO.
Director of Administration: ANTÓNIO MARCOS PEREIRA MARTINS.

Number of teachers: 89.
Number of students: 460.

PROFESSORS:

ALBUQUERQUE, J. C. DARGENT, Farm Mechanization
ARAÚJO, J. Q. RIBEIRO, Entomology
AZEVEDO, A. LOBO, General Agronomy
CAEIRO, V. M. PAIS, Parasitology
DA SILVA, A., Sociology
DE CARVALHO, E. A. CRUZ, Ecology
DE MIRANDA, C. FERREIRA, Chemistry
DOS SANTOS, A. GONÇALVES, Jr., Hydraulics
FEIO, M. J. D'OLIVEIRA, Geography
FERNANDES, R. M. ROSADO, Classical Languages
GUERREIRO, M. GOMES, Ecology
LESSA, ALMERINDO, Human Ecology
MARTINS, J. L. RODRIGUES, Physics
MORAL, A. S. DO CARMO, Mathematics
NAZARETH, J. M. PANTOJA, Demography
PEREIRA, G. E. BRAZ, Animal Husbandry
PINHEIRO, A. C. AFONSO, Management Sciences
PORTAS, C. A. MARTINS, Horticulture
PORTUGAL, L. A. M. SIMÃO, Economy
RIBEIRO, A. M., Meat Technology
SIDARUS, ADEL, Arabic Studies
TELLES, G. RIBEIRO, Landscape Architecture

UNIVERSIDADE CATÓLICA PORTUGUESA

PALMA DE CIMA, 1600 LISBON
Telephone: 78 31 00, 78 28 44.
Founded 1968.

Private control; Language of instruction: Portuguese; Academic year: October to February, February to July.

Chancellor: Cardinal RIBEIRO ANTÓNIO.
Rector: Prof. J. BACELAR E OLIVEIRA.
Librarian: ANTÓNIO LEITE DE CASTRO.

Number of teachers: 170.
Number of students: 3,000.

Publications: *Revista Portuguesa de Filosofia*† (quarterly), *Didaskalia*† (2 a year), *Theologica*† (quarterly), *Cenáculo, Economia*† (3 a year).

DEANS:

Faculty of Philosophy: Prof. JÚLIO FRAGATA, S.J.
Faculty of Theology: Prof. JOSÉ POLICARPO.
Faculty of Social Sciences: Prof. J. ANTUNES VARELA.

PROFESSORS AND HEADS OF DEPARTMENTS:

Faculty of Philosophy:
Classical Languages: ANTÓNIO FREIRE.
Ontology: JÚLIO FRAGATA.
Philosophy of Knowledge: MANUEL GOMES MORAES, ROQUE DE AGUIAR CABRAL.
General Epistemology: JOSÉ DO PATROCÍNIO BACELAR E OLIVEIRA, LÚCIO CRAVEIRO DA SILVA.

Faculty of Theology:
Biblical Theology: JOAQUIM CARREIRA MARCELINO DAS NEVES.
Historical Theology: ANTÓNIO MONTES MOREIRA.
Systematic Theology: ANTÓNIO PEREIRA DA SILVA.
Practical Theology: JOAQUIM DE OLIVEIRA BRAGANÇA.
Philosophy: MANUEL BARBOSA DA COSTA FREITAS.

ATTACHED INSTITUTES:

Degree Course in Law: Rua do Paraíso à Foz 86, 4100 Oporto; Dir. FRANCISCO CARVALHO GUERRA.
Instituto Superior de Teologia de Braga: Seminário Conciliar, Rua de Santa Margarida, 4719 Braga; Dir. JORGE PEIXOTO COUTINHO.

UNIVERSIDADE DE LISBOA*

CIDADE UNIVERSITÁRIA,
LISBON
Telephone: 767624.
Founded 1290, restored 1911.

Rector: Prof. RAOUL MIGUEL ROSADO FERNANDEZ.
Secretary: Lic. NUNO MARIA SAMPAIO DE LEMOS.
Librarian: MARIA JOSÉ SABINO MOURA.

Number of teachers: 664, including 75 professors.

Number of students: 18,820.

Publications: *Arquivos, Anuário, Boletim Trimestral*, etc.

DIRECTORS:

Faculty of Letters: (vacant).
Faculty of Law: (vacant).
Faculty of Medicine: Prof. JOÃO CÂNDIDO DA SILVA OLIVEIRA.
Faculty of Science: (vacant).
School of Pharmacy: Prof. JOSÉ AVELAR DE ALMEIDA RIBEIRO.

ATTACHED INSTITUTES:

Centro de Estudos Geográficos (*Centre for Geographical Studies*): f. 1943; library of 8,000 vols. and 8,000 different maps; Dir. Prof. Dr. ORLANDO RIBEIRO; publs. *Finisterra* (twice-yearly), *Chorographia.*

Instituto Bacteriológico de Câmara Pestana: Campo de Santana, Lisbon 1; Dir. Prof. Dr. JOÃO CANDIDO DA SILVA OLIVEIRA.

Instituto de Oftalmologia Dr. Gama Pinto: Travessa Larga 2, Lisbon 2; Dir. Prof. Dr. JOÃO MANUEL RUAS RIBEIRO DA SILVA.

Instituto de Medicina Legal: Campo de Santana, Lisbon 1; Dir. Dr. MÁRIO MOURA BRÁS ARSÉNIO NUNES.

Instituto Português de Oncologia de Francisco Gentil: Rua Prof. Lima Basto, Palhavã, Lisbon 4; Dir. (vacant)

Instituto Geofísico do Infante D. Luís: Rua da Escola Politécnica, Lisbon 2; Dir. Prof. Dr. JOSÉ PINTO PEIXOTO.

Laboratorio Maritimo da Guia-Cascais (*Marine Laboratory of Guia-Cascais*): Guia-Cascais; Dir. (vacant).

Instituto de Orientação Profissional "Maria Luisa Barbosa de Carvalho": Largo Trindade Coelho 20, Lisbon 1; Dir. Lic. MANUEL PEGA BREDA DE MELO SIMÕES.

See also under Museums and Research Institutes.

* No reply received to our questionnaire this year.

UNIVERSIDADE DO MINHO

LARGO DO PAÇO, BRAGA
Telephone: 27021/2/3.
Founded 1973.

State control; Language of instruction: Portuguese; Academic year: October to July.

Rector: (vacant).
Vice-Rectors: JOAQUIM J. BARBOSA ROMERO, LÚCIO CRAVEIRO DA SILVA.
Chief Administrative Officer: Lic. JOÃO ANTÓNIO DOS CANTOS CABRAL.
Registrar: Eng. JOSÉ FREDERICO AGUILAR F. MONTEIRO.
Librarian: (vacant).

Number of teachers: 179.
Number of students: 1,275.

UNIVERSIDADE NOVA DE LISBOA
(New University of Lisbon)

PRAÇA DO PRÍNCIPE REAL
26 R/C, 1200 LISBON
Telephone: 367972.

Founded 1973; State control; Academic year: October to July.

Rector: Prof. Dr. ALFREDO DE SOUSA.
Chief Administrative Officer: MA. LOURDES FIGUEIREDO GIRÃO MARQUES.
Librarian: Dr. ANTÓNIO CORREIA.

Number of teachers: 455.
Number of students: 3,260.

Publication: *Anuário.*

DEANS:

Faculty of Sciences and Technology: Prof. Dr. CARLOS LLOYD BRAGA.
Faculty of Social and Human Sciences: Prof. Dr. ANTÓNIO HENRIQUE OLIVEIRA MARQUES.
Faculty of Economics: Prof. Dr. ALFREDO DE SOUSA.
Faculty of Medical Sciences: Prof. Dr. JOSÉ ANTÓNIO REBOCHO ESPERANÇA PINA.

HEADS OF DEPARTMENT:

Faculty of Sciences and Technology:
Mathematics: FERNANDO ROLDÃO DIAS AGUDO.
Physics: MANUEL FERNANDES LARANJEIRA.
Chemistry: LÍCIO SILVEIRA GODINHO.
Biology and Bioengineering: ANTÓNIO AUGUSTO VASCONCELOS XAVIER.
Environment Sciences: MANUEL GOMES GUERREIRO.
Geology and Geotechnics: MIGUEL CARLOS TELES ANTUNES.
Production and Project Engineering: JORGE NEVES DA SILVA.
Materials Sciences: LEOPOLDO JOSÉ MARTINHO GUIMARÃES.
Energy and Control: HERMÍNIO DUARTE RAMOS.
Informatics: ALEXANDRE GOMES CERVEIRA.
Social Applied Sciences: JOSÉ MANUEL BAPTISTA.

Faculty of Social and Human Sciences:
History: ANTÓNIO HENRIQUE OLIVEIRA MARQUES.
Modern Languages and Literatures: MARIA TERESA RITA LOPES.
Anthropology: MARIA RAQUEL V. SOEIRO DE BRITO.
Sociology: VITORINO MAGALHÃES GODINHO.
Philosophy: JOSE SEBASTIÃO DA SILVA DIAS.
Social Communication: ADRIANO DUARTE RODRIGUES.
Education Sciences: MARIA TERESA ESTRELA.

Faculty of Medical Sciences:
Anatomy: JOSE ANTÓNIO R. ESPERANÇA PINA.
Pathological Anatomy: VIEGAS MENDONÇA.
Biochemistry: JÚDICE HALPERN.
Surgery I: PINTO TEIXEIRA.
Surgery II: RUI DE LIMA.
Surgery III: ROLANDO MOISÃO.
Surgery IV: TEIXEIRA PINTO.
Dermatology and Venereology: CRUZ SOBRAL.
Infectious and Parasitical Diseases: CORDEIRO FERREIRA.
Pharmacology: SILVA E SOUSA.
Physiology: MÁRIO GENTIL QUINA.
Genetics: LOPES DO ROSÁRIO.
Gynaecology: CATARINO TAVARES.
Histology and Embryology: NASCIMENTO FERREIRA.
Immunology: MACHADO CAETANO.
Medicine I: SALLES LUÍS.
Medicine II: ADOLFO COELHO.
Medicine III: MÁRIO GENTIL QUINA.
Medicine IV: CARRILHO RIBEIRO.
Laboratory Medicine: MARIA JULIETA ESPERANÇA PINA.
Neurology: MONTEIRO LACERDA.
Obstetrics: AURÉLIO FAUSTINO.
Ophthalmology: FERRAZ DE OLIVEIRA.
Orthopaedics: PAIVA CHAVES.
Oto-rhino-laryngology: BRANCO CORREIA.
Paediatrics: CORDEIRO FERREIRA.
Pneumophthisiology: GALVÃO LUCAS.
Medical Psychology: CAMILO DIAS CARDOSO.
Psychiatry and Mental Health: EDUARDO CORTESÃO.
Radiology: AIRES DE SOUSA.
Public Health: GONÇALVES FERREIRA.
Urology: MATOS FERREIRA.
Biophysics: GOMES DA SILVA.
Biomathematics: MORAIS SARMENTO.
Electronic Microscopy: XAVIER MORATO.

ATTACHED INSTITUTES:

Institute of Art History: Av. de Berna 24, 1000 Lisbon; attached to Faculty of Social and Human Sciences; Dir. Prof. Dr. AUGUSTO R. FRANÇA.
Institute of Hygiene and Tropical Medicine: Rua da Junqueira 96/100, 1300 Lisbon.

UNIVERSIDADE DO PORTO

R. D. MANUEL II,
4003 OPORTO CODEX
Telephone: 315851, 314737.
Founded 1911.

Rector: Prof. ARMANDO CAMPOS E MATOS.
Secretary: Lic. JORGE ROCHA PEREIRA.

Faculties of Science, Medicine, Engineering, Pharmacy, Economics and Letters.

Number of teachers: 1,200.
Number of students: 16,000.

ATTACHED INSTITUTES:

Instituto de Botânica Dr. Gonçalo Sampaio: Rua do Campo Alegre 1191; Dir. Prof. ROBERTO SALEMA M. RIBEIRO.

Instituto de Climatologia e Hidrologia.

Instituto de Zoologia e Estação de Zoologia Maritima "Dr. Augusto Nobre" (*Zoological Institute and Maritime Zoological Station*): f. 1921; library of 13,600 vols.; Dir. Prof. Dr. AMÍLCAR MATEUS; publs. numerous scientific works, *Publicações.* (*See* also Museu de História Natural, Oporto.)

Instituto Geofisico (Observatório da Serra do Pilar) (*Geophysical Institute and Meteorological Observatory*): V. N. de Gaia; f. 1885; Dir. Lica. MARIA ANTÓNIA PONCE DE LEÃO FREI RAMOS; publs. *Boletims Mensais, Anais, Boletim Sísmico.*

Instituto de Antropologia "Dr. Mendes Corrêa" (*Anthropological Institute*): f. 1923; library of 6,616 vols.; Dir. Prof. Dr. JOÃO MARIA MACHADO CRUZ; publ. *Trabalhos.*

UNIVERSIDADE TÉCNICA DE LISBOA

RUA GONÇALVES CRESPO 20–5°,
1100 LISBON CODEX
Founded 1931.

Rector: Prof. Eng. EDUARDO R. DE ARANTES E OLIVEIRA.
Secretary: Lic. FERNANDO MANUEL ANTUNES DURÃO.

Number of professors: 170.
Number of students: 15,000.

DIRECTORS:

School of Higher Veterinary Medicine: Prof. Dr. MÁRIO BAPTISTA BRÁS.
Higher Institute of Agronomy: Prof. Eng. ZÓZIMO DE CASTRO REGO.
Higher Institute of Economics: Prof. Dr. EDUARDO SOUSA FERREIRA.
Higher Technical Institute: Prof. Eng. JOÃO POÑE FIGANIER.
Higher Institute of Social Science and Politics: (vacant).
Higher Physical Education Institute: Dr. JOSÉ ANTÓNIO R. ESPERANÇA PINA.

COLLEGES

Instituto de Higiene e Medicina Tropical (*Institute of Hygiene and Tropical Medicine*): Rua da Junqueira 96, 1300 Lisbon; f. 1902, reorganized 1967 and 1972; attached to the Ministry of Social Affairs (Secretariat of State of Health); library of 29,148 vols.; publ. *Anais* (annual).

Chair. of Council: Prof. C. M. DOS SANTOS REIS.

Number of teachers: 38.

Number of students: 103.

DIRECTORS:

Department of Public Health: Prof. C. M. DOS SANTOS REIS.

Department of Parasitology: Prof. RUI DA COSTA PINHÃO.

Department of Microbiology: MARIA WANDA CANAS FERREIRA.

Department of Clinical Tropical Medicine: Prof. F. M. M. DA CRUZ SOBRAL.

Department of Epidemiology: Prof. G. JORGE JANZ.

Instituto de Estudos Sociais: Campo Grande 185, Lisbon 5; f. 1963; social policy in the fields of labour, corporative organization and welfare; 26 teachers, 420 students; Dir. Dr. FRANCISCO NETO DE CARVALHO.

Instituto Superior de Linguas e Administração: Rua do Sacramento à Lapa 14-16, Lisbon 3; f. 1962; business management and communication, languages, tourism; 2,000 students; Dir. Prof. Dr. F. DE MELLO MOSER (acting).

SCHOOLS OF ART AND MUSIC

Conservatório Nacional (*National Academy of Music*): Rua dos Caetanos 29, Lisbon; f. 1835.

Director: (vacant).

Secretary: MANUEL DE ASCENÇÃO ANTUNES.

Escola Superior de Belas Artes (*School of Fine Arts*): Largo da Biblioteca Pública, Lisbon; f. 1836; Dir. JOAQUIM CORREIA.

Escola Superior de Belas Artes (*Higher School of Fine Arts*): Av. Rodrigues de Freitas, Oporto; f. 1836; Dir. Arch. CARLOS RAMOS.

SPECIAL TERRITORY

MACAU

Circulo de Cultura Musical (*Circle of Musical Culture*): Largo do Sto. Agostinho 3-2°; f. 1952; 68 mems.; library of 876 vols.; Artistic Dir. FRANCISCO XAVIER FREIRE GARCIA.

Biblioteca Nacional de Macau (*National Library of Macau*): Edifício do Leal Senado; Librarian: Dr. HENRIQUE RODRIGUES DE SENNA FERNANDES.

Biblioteca Sir Robert Ho Tung (*Sir Robert Ho Tung's Chinese Library*): Largo do Sto. Agostinho; Librarian: Dr. HENRIQUE RODRIGUES DE SENNA FERNANDES.

Museu Luís de Camões (*Luis de Camões Museum*): Praça Luís de Camões; Curator LINO SILVEIRA DO AMARAL; publ. *Catalogue of Chinese Paintings*† (in English and Chinese).

UNIVERSITY OF MACAU

Founded 1979; in process of formation (first student intake planned for October 1981). Language of instruction: English.

Degree courses in Arts and Letters (incl. Portuguese Studies), Social Sciences, Business Administration and Management.

PUERTO RICO

Population 3,357,000

ACADEMY

ACADEMIA PUERTORRIQUEÑA DE LA LENGUA ESPAÑOLA

APDO. 4008, SAN JUAN 00936

Corresponding with the Real Academia Española

Founded 1955.

Director: Salvador Tío.

Secretary: Segundo Cardona.

Publication: *Boletín*† (quarterly).

Members:

Manuel Alvarez Nazario.
Angel J. Casares.
Rafael Arrillaga Torrens.
José A. Balseiro.
Edna Coll.
Lidio Cruz Monclova.
Eugenio Fernández Mendez.
Ernesto Juan Fonfrías.
Humberto López Morales.
Francisco Lluch Mora.
Washington Lloréns.
Francisco Matos Paoli.
Concha Meléndez.
Luis Rechani Agrait.
Pablo Ruiz Orozco.
Aurelio Tió.
José Trías Monge.
María Teresa Babín.
Segundo Cardona.
Luis Hernández Aquino.

Elected:

Ricardo Alegría.
Jaime Benítez.
Luis Días Soler.
Jorge Font Saldaña.
Arturo Morales Carrión.
Antonio Pacheco Padrò.
Ismael Rodríguez Bou.

LEARNED SOCIETIES

San Juan

Ateneo Puertorriqueño: Edif. Ateneo, Ponce de León Ave.; f. 1876; literature, arts and sciences; library, art gallery; Pres. Lic. Eladio Rodríguez Otero.

Comisión Asesora de Teatro: c/o Instituto de Cultura Puertorriqueña; Pres. Piri Fernández de Lewis.

Festival Casals: G.P.O. 2350, San Juan, P.R. 00936; f. 1957; library of 14,000 items (9,112 musical scores, records, books, catalogues, ephemera); Pres. Mario Martínez Camacho (acting).

Instituto de Cultura Puertorriqueña: Apdo. 4184; f. 1955; studies and preserves Puerto Rican historical and cultural patrimony and promotes study of Puerto Rican culture; Dir. Luis M. Rodríguez Morales.

Centro de Investigaciones y Ediciones Musicales.

Instituto de Lexicografía Hispanoamericana Augusto Malaret: Apdo. 3828; f. 1969; study and conservation of indigenous languages, of native toponymy and of the lexicon of fauna and flora; study of the influence of the African languages in America, and of the origin of proverbs; determination of the appropriate use of technical terms; Dir. Lic. Ernesto Juan Fonfrías.

P.E.N. Club de Puerto Rico: Apdo. 2229, San Juan 00903; f. 1966; 40 mems.; Sec. Ernesto Juan Fonfrías.

Sociedad Puertorriqueña de Autores, Compositores y Editores Musicales (S.P.A.C.E.M.): 1105 Ponce de León.

Sociedad Puertorriqueña de Escritores (*Puerto Rican Society of Writers*): Apdo. 4692; f. 1937; 81 mems.; Pres. Ernesto Juan Fonfrías.

Mayaguez

Sociedad Mayaguezana Pro Bellas Artes: P.O.B. 5004, Mayaguez 00708; ballet, opera, concerts, symphonies, art and sculpture exhibitions; Pres. Dr. Luis E. Bacó Rodríguez.

Ponce

Ateneo de Ponce: Apdo. de Correos 1923; f. 1956; Pres. Ramón Zapata Acosta; Sec. Vicente Ruiz.

Rio Piedras

Sociedad de Bibliotecarios de Puerto Rico: Apdo. 22898, Universidad de Puerto Rico; f. 1961; 268 mems.; Pres. Carmen H. de León; Sec. Belsie Cappas de Piñero; publs. *Boletín*, *Cuadernos Bibliográficos*, *Cuadernos Bibliotecológicos*, *Informa*.

Santurce

Academia Puertorriqueña de la Historia: Avda. Wilson 1308, Santurce; f. 1932; 40 mems.; Pres. Aurelio Tió.

RESEARCH INSTITUTES

Arecibo Observatory: P.O.B. 995 Arecibo, PR 00612; f. 1960; world's largest radio/radar telescope; 1,000-ft. diameter fixed spherical reflector with movable feeds; for use in the study of planets and the properties of the earth's upper atmosphere and reception of natural radio emissions from celestial objects including pulsars and quasars; reflector surface upgraded to work at higher frequencies; library of 2,000 vols.; operated by National Astronomy and Ionosphere Centre, Cornell University, under contract to National Science Foundation; Dir. of Operations Dr. Harold Craft, Jr.

Institute of Tropical Forestry: U.S.D.A. Forest Service, P.O.B. AQ, Rio Piedras, 00928; f. 1939; research in timber management and ecosystem management; administration of National Forest, co-operative assistance to State and private forest landowners, timber processors; trains foreign forestry students in co-operation with FAO and USAID; 30 mems.; library of 14,000 vols.; Dir. Dr. Ariel E. Lugo.

Puerto Rico Nuclear Center: Bio-Medical Building, Caparra Heights Station, San Juan; f. 1957; operated by the University of Puerto Rico for the U.S. Atomic Energy Commission; graduate-level research and training centre primarily for Latin Americans; in Mayaguez the Center has available an oceanographic research ship, operates a pool-type 2-megawatt research reactor with pulsing capacity up to 2,000 Megawatts(t), an L-77 homogeneous training reactor, and a sub-critical assembly; educational programmes at graduate level are offered in nuclear engineering, nuclear science and technology, health physics, chemistry, agriculture, and marine biology; in Río Piedras the Center gives advanced training in radiation therapy, radiological physics, clinical uses of radioisotopes, terrestrial ecology, radiobiology and virology, radiation chemistry. Acting Dir. Dr. Lawrence S. Ritchie.

LIBRARIES AND ARCHIVES

San Juan

Archivo General de Puerto Rico: Instituto de Cultura Puertorriqueña, Apto. 4184; f. 1955; 35,000 cubic ft. of records; Dir. MIGUEL ANGEL NIEVES RODRÍGUEZ.

Caribbean Regional Library: P.O.B. 21927, University Station, San Juan, P.R. 00931; f. 1946; moved to Puerto Rico 1961; 116,000 vols.; publ. *Current Caribbean Bibliography*† (annual).

Carnegie Public Library: Ponce de León Ave., Stop. 2, San Juan 00901; f. 1916; 35,000 vols.; Dir. ANGELINA R. SALVA.

Commonwealth of Puerto Rico, Department of Justice Library: 50 Fortaleza St., San Juan, P.R. 00902; f. 1950; law library of 62,000 vols.; Librarian ANTONIO NADAL; publs. *Opiniones del Secretario de Justicia de Puerto Rico*†, *Informe Anual del Secretario de Justicia de Puerto Rico, Anuario Estadístico.*

Supreme Court of Puerto Rico Library: f. 1953; 71,776 vols.; Librarian MADELINE COLÓN DE LOCK.

Hato Rey

Department of Education Library: Librarian ROSA C. ARRUFAT.

Humaçao

"Antonio A. Roig" Public Library: P.O.B. 846; Librarian PEDRO MARTINEZ REILOVA.

Mayaguez

University of Puerto Rico, General Library: Mayaguez Campus; f. 1911; 360,013 vols.; Dir. MIGUEL ANGEL ORTIZ-GUERRA; publs. *Conoce Tu Biblioteca* (annual), *Lista de Tesis y Tesinas* (annual), *Lista de libros catalogados* (monthly), *List of Publications on Agriculture and Related Sciences* (monthly), *Serials Holdings in the Mayaguez Library* (every 2 years).

Ponce

Law Library (Catholic University of Puerto Rico): Ave. Las Américas, Ponce 00731; f. 1961; 80,000 vols.; Librarian NOELIA PADUA DE ROSARIO; publ. *Revista de Derecho Puertorriqueño* (quarterly).

Ponce Public Library: f. 1942; 20,000 vols.; Librarian ANA MARÍA ZAYAS.

Catholic University of Puerto Rico Library: f. 1948; 145,044 vols.; Dir. ANTONIO MATOS; publ. *Horizontes* (2 a year).

Rio Piedras

Agricultural Experiment Station Library (University of Puerto Rico): Box H, Río Piedras, P.R. 00928; f. 1912; agriculture and related sciences; 31,533 vols. and 273,740 documents; Dir. of Station RAÚL ABRAMS; Librarian JOAN P. HAYES.

College of Social Science Reserve Collection (University of Puerto Rico): Librarian Mrs. LUISA SANTIAGO DE DÁVILA.

Law Library (University of Puerto Rico): Box L, University Station, San Juan, P.R. 00931; f. 1913; 130,000 vols.; Librarian CARMELO DELGADO CINTRÓN.

University of Puerto Rico José M. Lázaro General Library: f 1903; 1,483,212 vols.; Librarian RAFAEL DELGADO CARRIÓN.

Santurce

Biblioteca Madre María Teresa Guevara (Universidad del Sagrado Corazón): Apdo. 12383, Correo Calle Loiza, Santurce 00914; f. 1935; 146,810 vols.; Librarian MARÍA A. MORALES DE GARIN, M.L.S.

Economic Development Administration Library: Librarian ISABEL C. LLORENS.

Puerto Rico Planning Board Library: Librarian ARLINE VIRELLA COFFEY.

MUSEUMS

San Juan

La Casa del Libro: Calle del Cristo 255; f. 1955; library-museum devoted to the art of the book; library of 5,000 vols.; Dir. DAVID JACKSON MCWILLIAMS.

Museo de Arte Religioso: Iglesia de Porta Coeli, San Germán; c/o Instituto de Cultura Puertorriqueña; 17th century church of Porta Coeli, constructed as a chapel for convent of Dominican Friars in San Germán; restored and converted into museum of religious art.

Museo de Bellas Artes: 253 Cristo St., Old San Juan; f. 1967 by the Institute of Culture; exhibition of paintings and sculptures by Puerto Rican artists from 18th century; Dir. LUIS M. RODRÍGUEZ MORALES.

Museo de Historia Militar y Naval: Fuerte San Jerónimo, Avda. Ponce de Leon, Stop 8; historical castle converted into museum of military history.

Parque Histórico en las Ruinas de Caparra: Highway No. 2, Km. 6.4, Guaynabo; site of first nucleus of Christian population in Puerto Rico, founded by Juan Ponce de León in 1508; public park and exhibition room; Dir. LUIS M. RODRÍGUEZ MORALES.

Ponce

Museo de Arte: c/o The Luis A. Ferré Foundation, Inc., Apdo. 1492, Ponce 00731; f. 1956; European and American paintings and sculpture; library of 4,000 vols.; Dir. RENÉ TAYLOR; publs. exhibition catalogues†.

UNIVERSITIES

UNIVERSIDAD DE PUERTO RICO
(University of Puerto Rico)

RIO PIEDRAS, P.R. 00931

President: ISMAEL ALMODÓVAR, PH.D.
Director, Academic Affairs: LUIS A. SOJO, D.D.S.
Director, Planning and Development: JUAN SÁNCHEZ-LASSISE, PH.D.
Director, Budget: CRUZ A. RODRÍGUEZ.
Director, Finance and Administration: ANDRÉS MEDINA-PEÑA, J.D.
Chancellor for Regional Colleges: CARLOS E. REOYO, B.S.M.E., M.S.N.E.

Number of teachers: 2,722.
Number of students: 50,492.

Publications: *La Torre* (quarterly), various faculty reviews, *Caribbean Monthly Bulletin*, etc.

Rio Piedras Campus

RIO PIEDRAS, P.R. 00931

Founded 1903.

Chancellor: ANTONIO MIRÓ MONTILLA, M.ARCH.
Dean of Studies: Dr. VERNON ESTEVES.
Dean of Administration: FRANCISCO GIRONA, M.A.
Dean of Students: Dra. ALICIA CARLO DE NET.
Director of Admissions: EVA ENID SANTIAGO, M.P.A.
Director of Planning and Development: Dra. AMALIA LLABRÉS DE CHARNECO.
Registrar: DAMIÁNI ROMÁN, M.A.
Librarian: RAFAEL R. DELGADO.

Number of teachers: 1,206.
Number of students: 23,846.

DEANS:

Business Administration: MANUEL COLÓN LEBRÓN, M.B.A.
Humanities: ELADIO RIVERA-QUIÑONES, M.A.
Law: Dr. ALEJO DE CERVERA.
Education: LYDIA GRANA, PH.D.
Natural Sciences: MANUEL GOMEZ-RODRÍGUEZ, PH.D.
Architecture: Arch. EFRER MORALES.
Social Sciences: ANTONIO J. GONZALEZ, PH.D.
Director, School of Planning: GERARDO NAVAS, PH.D.
Director, School of Public Communications: Dra. CONSUELO RIVERA DE OTERO.
Director, School of Library Science: ARTURO FERNÁNDEZ, M.L.S. (acting).
Director, School of Public Administration: Lic. LUIS BAERGA DUPREY.
Director, Division of Extension and Continuing Education: Dra. HILDA SEGARRA ORTIZ.

Mayaguez Campus

MAYAGUEZ, P.R. 00708

Founded 1911.

Chancellor: SALVADOR E. ALEMAÑY, M.S.
Dean of Studies: Dra. ENEIDA RIVERY.
Dean of Administration: RAFAEL A. PIRAZZI.
Dean of Students: JENARO R. NEGRON, M.S.
Director of Admissions: PEDRO MONTALVO, B.A.
Director of Finance: GUILLERMO SOTOMAYOR.
Registrar: FREDDIE HERNÁNDEZ-SOTO.
Librarian: MIGUEL A. ORTIZ, M.L.S.

Number of teachers: 707.
Number of students: 8,767.

DEANS:

Arts and Sciences: PABLO RODRIGUEZ-ROSADO, M.S. (acting).
Agricultural Sciences: LUIS A. MEJIA-MATTEI, PH.D.
Business Administration: OMAR RUIZ, M.B.A.
Engineering: FLAVIO ACARON, PH.D.

DIRECTORS:

Academic Extension Division: JULIO CÉSAR PÉREZ (acting).
Agricultural Extension Service: ROBERTO VÁZQUEZ-ROMERO, PH.D.
Agricultural Experimental Station: RAÚL ABRAMS, PH.D.

Medical Sciences Campus

G.P.O. BOX 5067, SAN JUAN, P.R. 00905

Founded 1950.

Chancellor: NORMAN MALDONADO, M.D.
Dean of Administration: RUBÉN ELÍ MATOS, M.A.
Registrar: GLADYS ROSARIO, B.B.A.
Librarian: LILLIAN CASAS, M.L.S.

Number of teachers: 411.
Number of students: 2,835.

DEANS:

School of Medicine: PEDRO SANTIAGO BORRERO, M.D.
School of Dentistry: RAFAEL AGUIAR, D.D.S.
School of Public Health and Preventive Medicine: GILBERTO CARDONA, M.D.
School of Pharmacy: HÉCTOR LOZADA, PH.D.
College of Bio-Medical Sciences: SVEN EVVESON, M.D.

Cayey University College

CAYEY, P.R. 00633

Founded 1967.

Director: HERMINIO LUGO-LUGO.

Number of teachers: 113.
Number of students: 2,601.

Humacao Regional College

HUMACAO, P.R. 00661

Founded 1962.

Director: HILDA SOLTERO HARRINGTON, PH.D.
Registrar: MYRIAM RIVERA-DELGADO.

Number of teachers: 202.
Number of students: 3,343.

Arecibo Regional College

ARECIBO, P.R. 00612

Founded 1968.

Director: MARCOS A. MORELL.
Registrar: JUANA M. NIEVES, B.S.

Number of teachers: 124.
Number of students: 2,359.

Ponce Regional College

PONCE, P.R. 00731

Founded 1970.

Director: RUTH FORTUÑO DE CALZADA.
Registrar: RAMÓN E. MIRANDA.

Number of teachers: 95.
Number of students: 1,622.

Bayamon Regional College

BAYAMON, P.R. 00619

Founded 1971.

Director: FELIX L. ORTIZ, M.S.
Registrar: RAMON MERCADO SORRENTINI, B.A.

Number of teachers: 136.
Number of students: 2,879.

Aguadilla Regional College

AGUADILLA, P.R. 00603

Founded 1972.

Director: MIGUEL A. JIMÉNEZ-MÉNDEZ.
Registrar: ROBERTO ORTIZ, B.A.

Number of teachers: 62.
Number of students: 1,036.

Carolina Regional College

CAROLINA, P.R. 00630

Founded 1974.

Director: EMILIO DÍAZ GONZÁLEZ, J.D.
Registrar: VICTOR CABRERA, B.A.

Number of teachers: 77.
Number of students: 1,204.

UNIVERSIDAD CATÓLICA DE PUERTO RICO

(Catholic University of Puerto Rico)

PONCE, P.R. 00731

Telephone: 844-4150.

Founded 1948.

Languages of Instruction: Spanish and English; Private control; Academic year: August to May (two semesters). Campuses at Arecibo, Guayama and Mayaguez.

Chancellor: Most Rev. FREMIOT TORRES OLIVER.
Vice-Chancellor: Most Rev. RICARDO SURIÑACH.
President: FRANCISCO J. CARRERAS, PH.D.
Vice-Presidents: Rev. Fr. TOSELLO GIANGIACOMO (Academic Affairs); Mgr. MARCOS PANCORBO (Finance); CARLOS NEGRÓN (Student Affairs).

Registrar: JUDITH LORENZO, B.A.
Librarian: ANTONIO MATOS.

Number of teachers: 583.
Number of students: 11,698.

Publications: *Horizontes, Revista de Derecho Puertorriqueño.*

DEANS:

College of Arts and Humanities: Mgr. Father FEDERICO ABAD.
College of Science: JULIO RIVERA, M.S.
School of Law: CHARLES CUPRILL.
College of Education: Sister VIRGINIA CHASAS.
College of Business Administration: CARMEN S. BOSCIO, B.A.

PROFESSORS AND HEADS OF DEPARTMENTS:

College of Arts and Humanities:
ALVAREZ, Fr. POMPILIO, History and Fine Arts
CARUNCHO, LAURA, English Language
DÍAZ MÁRQUEZ, R. L., Hispanic Studies
ECHEVARRÍA, AGUSTÍN, Political Sciences and Sociology
KOVAC, Sr. GABRIELA, Social Work
ZAPATA, RAMÓN, Hispanic Studies

College of Business Administration:
CONSTAS, K. J., Graduate Studies in Business Administration
GONZÁLEZ, O. C. DE, Secretarial Sciences
MARTÍNEZ, FREDYZ, Accounting, Economics and Finance
ROJAS, R. R., Management, Marketing and General Business

College of Education:
ORTIZ DE TORRES, G., Elementary Education
ORTIZ TORRES, H. G., Secondary Education
TORO, RAMÓN ANTONIO, Elementary Education

College of Sciences:
BLANCO, S. M., Home Economics
CARRASQUILLO, A., Chemistry
ECKERT, R. R., Physics
FERNÁNDEZ, FÉLIX, Physics
QUESADA, ANTONIO, Mathematics
RIVERA DE MARTÍNEZ, C. I., Psychology
SANTIAGO, MARCELINA, Chemistry
VILARÓ DE DESCARTES, M., Nursing

School of Law:
MARTÍNEZ IRIZARRY, D.

BAYAMÓN CENTRAL UNIVERSITY

P.O.B. 1725, BAYAMÓN, P.R. 00619
Telephone: 786-3030.

Founded 1961, independent 1970.

Private control; Language of instruction: Spanish; Academic year: August to May.

President: Rev. VINCENT A. M. VAN ROOIJ, O.P.
Vice-President: MARÍA I. MOLINERO, M.B.A., M.A.ED.
Rector: LUIS ROBERTO PIÑERO, M.A., J.D.
Academic Dean: DELFINA FERNÁNDEZ-PASCUA, M.A.
Registrar: VICTOR COLÓN-RODRÍGUEZ, M.A.

Library of 43,000 vols.
Number of teachers: 90.
Number of students: 2,000.

DEANS:

College of Business Administration: ERNESTO FERNÁNDEZ, C.P.A.
College of Natural Sciences: Dr. LUZ A. LAFUENTE.
College of Education: NÉLIDA MELÉNDEZ, M.A.ED.
College of Arts and Humanities: Dr. FRANCISCO DOMINGO.

INTER-AMERICAN UNIVERSITY OF PUERTO RICO

G.P.O. BOX 3255, SAN JUAN, P.R. 00936
Telephone: (809) 763-9622.
Founded 1912.

Private control; Languages of instruction: Spanish and English.

President: Dr. RAMÓN A. CRUZ.
Executive Assistant to the President: ELIAS RIVERA CIDRAZ.
Vice-President for Academic Affairs: DONALD KAUFFMAN (acting).
Vice-President for Financial Affairs: RAFAEL ZAPATA.
Vice-President for Planning: JUAN GONZALEZ RAMOS.
Vice-President for Administrative Affairs: FÉLIX ENRIQUE OCASIO.

Number of teachers: 1,125.
Number of students: 28,725.

Publications: *Polygraph-IAU News* (quarterly), *The President's Letter* (quarterly).

San Germán Campus

SAN GERMÁN, P.R. 00753
Telephone: (809) 892-1095.

Chancellor: Dr. FEDERICO MATHEU.
Dean of Academic Affairs: FRANCISCO JAVIER FLORES.
Registrar: C. J. CARMONA.
Librarian: MARIA MATOS.

CHAIRMEN OF DEPARTMENTS:

Languages: MARK FINCH.
Natural Sciences: CARLOS ARCELAY.
Economics and Business Administration: JULIO RAMÍREZ.
Education: DAMIÁN VELEZ.
Religion and Philosophy: EUGENIO ILLIDGE.
Social Sciences: IVONNE RAMÍREZ DE SERNA.
Fine Arts: ROBERT FITZMAURICE.

San Juan Campus

P.O.B. 1293, HATO REY, P.R. 00919
Telephone: (809) 753-8008.

Chancellor: Dr. RAFAEL CARTAGENA.
Dean of Academic Affairs: RAM. S. LAMBA (acting).
Registrar: ANA OLIVER QUILINCHINI.
Librarian: MARÍA ELENA ARGUELLO DE CARDONA.

CHAIRMEN OF DEPARTMENTS:

Humanities: MARÍA ALONSO SOTO.
Natural Sciences: GERMÁN VILLANUEVA.
Economics and Business Administration: CARMEN IRIS ROQUE.
Education: ALFONSO LÓPEZ YUSTOS.
English: DAGMAR ACUÑA.
Social Sciences: EDWARD RICHARDSON.

Regional Colleges

G.P.O.B. 4927, SAN JUAN, P.R. 00936
Telephone: (809) 763-9622.

Chancellor: FÉLIX TORRES LEÓN.
Dean of Academic Affairs: JOSÉ LEMA MOTA.

Directors, Regional Colleges:
Aguadilla: JUAN COLÓN.
Arecibo: OLGA SUÁREZ.
Barranquitas: JESUSA APONTE RUBERO.
Fajardo: JOSÉ MARTÍNEZ.
Guayama: MARÍA DE LOS ANGELES ORTIZ DE LEON.
Ponce: KENNETH KALANTAR.

School of Law

P.O.B. 8897, FERNANDEZ JUNCOS STATION,
SANTURCE, P.R. 00924
Telephone: (809) 727-1930.

Dean: ALBERTO FERRER.

UNIVERSITY OF THE SACRED HEART

P.O.B. 12383, LOIZA STATION,
SANTURCE, P.R. 00914
Telephone: 809-727-7800.
Founded 1935.
Private control; Language of instruction: Spanish.

President: Dr. PEDRO GONZÁLEZ-RAMOS.
Dean of Academic Affairs: Dra. CÁNDIDA R. T. ACOSTA.
Dean of Students: Prof. CARLOS MORALES.
Dean of Administration: ANGEL L. DE JESÚS.
Registrar: Mrs. CONSUELO RIVERA.
Librarian: MARÍA MORALES DE GARÍN, M.L.S.

Number of teachers: 100 (full-time), 180 (part-time).
Number of students: 6,425.

Publications: *Pórtico*, *Ecos* (weekly).

DIRECTORS:

Department of Business Administration: Prof. ALICE AMADOR.
Department of Education: Prof. ROBERTO ESTRELLA.
Department of Humanities: CARMEN COMELLA.
Department of Natural Sciences: Dr. JUSTO HERNÁNDEZ-MORA.
Department of Social Sciences: Prof. FRANCISCA LIMARDO.
Extension Division: Prof. CEFERINO LUGO.
Junior College Division: Prof. ORLANDO R. O'NEILL.

QATAR

Population 250,000

SOCIETY AND INSTITUTE

British Council: P.O.B. 2992, Doha; f. 1973; library of 10,260 vols., 56 periodicals; Rep. D. MUNRO.

Soil Research Station: Rodet al-Farassa.

LIBRARY

Qatar National Library: P.O.B. 205, Doha; f. 1963 as a merger of two existing libraries; 56,521 vols. in Arabic, 9,396 vols. in English, 1,300 vols. Arabic and Persian MSS., 129 current periodicals; bibliographic services on subjects of local interest; Dir. M. H. AL NASSR.

MUSEUM

National Museum: Doha; opened 1975; sited in 10 old houses restored to traditional style, and two new galleries; large collection of ethnographical, archaeological, ecological and historical material; includes a man-made lagoon on which are exhibited six Gulf sailing craft; also Museum of the Sea and aquarium.

UNIVERSITY AND COLLEGE

UNIVERSITY OF QATAR

P.O.B. 2713, DOHA

Founded 1973.

Language of instruction: Arabic; Academic year: September to June.

Vice-Chancellor: IBRAHIM KHAZEM.

Number of students: *c.* 2,000.

Faculties of Education, Science, Humanities, Social Sciences and Islamic Studies are already functioning. Faculties of Administration and Economics, Engineering, and Communication and Information are planned for the future.

Regional Training Centre: P.O.B. 1300, Doha; f. 1970 with UNDP technical aid; 450 students.

There is an INDEX OF INSTITUTIONS

at the end of Volume II